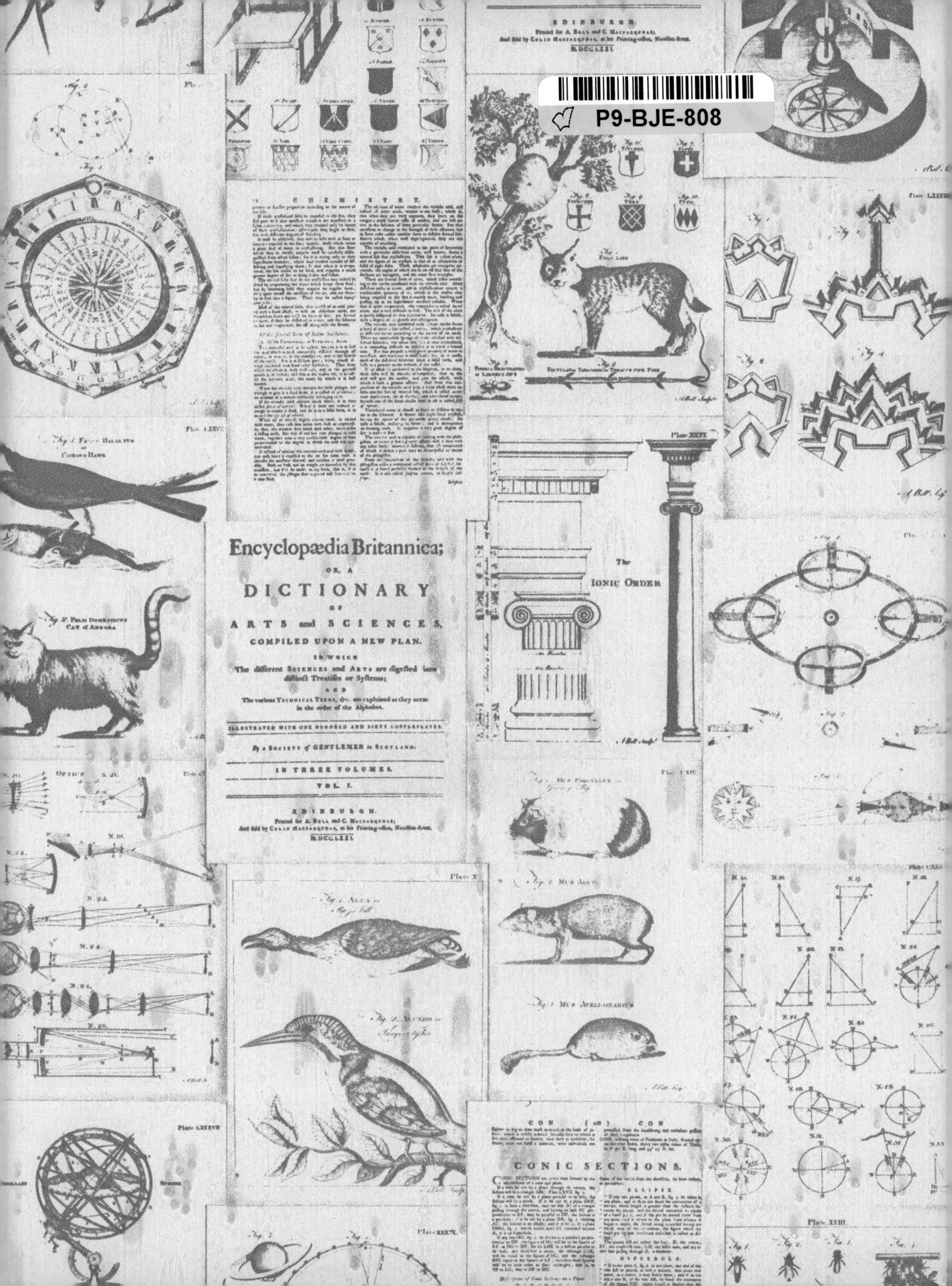
P9-BJE-808
CHEMISTRY
Encyclopædia Britannica;
OR, A
DICTIONARY
OF
ARTS and SCIENCES,
COMPILED UPON A NEW PLAN.
IN WHICH
The different Sciences and Arts are digested into distinct Treatises or Systems;
AND
The various Technical Terms, &c. are explained as they occur in the order of the Alphabet.
ILLUSTRATED WITH ONE HUNDRED AND SIXTY COPPERPLATES.
By a Society of Gentlemen in Scotland.
IN THREE VOLUMES.
VOL. I.
EDINBURGH:
Printed for A. Bell and C. Macfarquhar;
And sold by Colin Macfarquhar, at his Printing-office, Nicolson-Street.
M.DCC.LXXI.
The Ionic Order
CONIC SECTIONS.

# ENCYCLOPÆDIA
# BRITANNICA

THE UNIVERSITY OF CHICAGO

*The Encyclopædia Britannica*
*is published with the editorial advice of the faculties*
*of the University of Chicago; a committee*
*of members of the faculties of Oxford, Cambridge, London, and*
*Edinburgh universities; a committee at the University of Toronto;*
*and a committee drawn from members of the faculty*
*of the University of Tokyo*

*

"LET KNOWLEDGE GROW FROM MORE TO MORE
AND THUS BE HUMAN LIFE ENRICHED"

# ENCYCLOPÆDIA BRITANNICA

VOLUME
21

*First Published in 1768*
*by A Society of Gentlemen in Scotland*

ENCYCLOPÆDIA BRITANNICA, INC.

William Benton, Publisher

*CHICAGO · LONDON · TORONTO · GENEVA · SYDNEY · TOKYO · MANILA*

PRINTED IN THE U. S. A.

Library of Congress Catalog Card Number: 70-115815
International Standard Book Number: 0-85229-151-5

# ENCYCLOPÆDIA BRITANNICA

## Volume 21

## SPELMAN *TO* TIMMINS

**SPELMAN, SIR HENRY** (*c.* 1564–1641), English antiquary and historian whose *Concilia, Decreta, Leges, Constitutiones, in re Ecclesiarum orbis Britannici* was the first systematic compilation of church documents, was born about 1564 at Congham, Norfolk. Educated at Trinity College, Cambridge, and Lincoln's Inn, London, he was M.P. for Castle Rising in 1593 and 1597, sheriff of Norfolk in 1604, M.P. for Worcester in 1625, and served on several royal commissions. A student of antiquity, he belonged, with William Camden and Sir Robert Cotton, to the Society of Antiquaries, which he attempted to revive in 1614, and he endowed a lectureship in Anglo-Saxon at Cambridge. He died in London in 1641.

Spelman was the author of ecclesiastical and legal histories, most of which were published posthumously. His first religious work, *De non temerandis ecclesiis; a Tracte Of the Rights and Respect Due Unto Churches* (1613), was the foundation of his well-known *History and Fate of Sacrilege* (1698); but his chief work was his history of the church, *Concilia, Decreta, Leges, Constitutiones, in re Ecclesiarum orbis Britannici* (vol. 1, 1639; vol. 2, ed. by C. Spelman, 1664). Among his polemical writings were *De Sepultura* (1641) and *Tithes Too Hot to be Touched* (1646), and he also made a glossary of ancient legal terms, *Archaeologus* (part 1, 1626; part 2, ed. by W. Dugdale, 1664). (RD. C. G.)

**SPEMANN, HANS** (1869–1941), German embryologist and Nobel laureate, was born at Stuttgart on June 27, 1869. In 1891 he began the study of medicine and attended the universities of Heidelberg, Munich, and Würzburg but finally graduated in zoology, botany, and physics. From 1894 to 1908 he worked at the Zoological Institute of Würzburg and was then appointed professor of zoology and comparative anatomy at Rostock. In 1914 he became director of the Kaiser Wilhelm Institute for Biology in Berlin, and from 1919 until his retirement in 1935 he held the chair of zoology at Freiburg im Breisgau.

Spemann was awarded the Nobel Prize for physiology and medicine in 1935 for the discovery of what is known as the "organizer effect" in embryonic development (*see* EMBRYOLOGY AND DEVELOPMENT, ANIMAL: *Experimental Embryology*). He stated, "the beginnings of a human individual do not differ essentially from those of an echinoderm." His concept of organizers was based upon a lifetime of research into the early development of the common newt. Much of his success was due to his intense concentration on this seemingly narrow field; but apart from this he had the controlled imagination of the true scientist and was a master of the techniques of microsurgery. Spemann's experiments showed that, in the earliest stages, the fate of the embryonic parts has not been determined; thus, if a piece of presumptive skin tissue is excised and transplanted into an area of presumptive nervous tissue, it will form nervous tissue, not skin. These researches threw new light not only on the normal processes of development and growth but also on the genesis of various congenital abnormalities of the human body. He gave a masterly summary of his researches in his Croonian lecture before the Royal Society (1927) and in his Silliman lectures at Yale (1935). He died at Freiburg im Breisgau on Sept. 12, 1941. (W. J. BP.)

**SPENBOROUGH,** an urban district in the West Riding of Yorkshire, Eng., 6 mi. SE of Bradford. Pop. (1961) 36,417. Area 12.9 sq.mi. It is a manufacturing district in the Spen valley. The textile industry is the chief one, including carpets, rayon and woolen materials. The manufacture of machinery and sheet-metal goods is important. The urban district was formed in 1915 and combined the three former urban districts of Cleckheaton, Gomersal, and Liversedge. In 1937 its area was enlarged by the addition of the urban districts of Birkenshaw and Hunsworth and the rural district of Hartshead and part of Clifton. Brighouse and Spenborough were formed into a parliamentary borough in 1948, returning one member.

**SPENCER, HERBERT** (1820–1903), English philosopher, achieved an influential synthesis of knowledge, advocating the preeminence of the individual over society and of science over religion. He was born in Derby on April 27, 1820. His father, William George Spencer, was a schoolmaster, and his parents' dissenting religious convictions inspired Herbert with that spirit of nonconformity which continued active in him after he had abandoned the Christian faith. He declined an offer from his uncle, the Rev. Thomas Spencer, to send him to Cambridge, and his higher education was largely the result of his own reading, which was chiefly in the natural sciences. After a few months as a schoolteacher he became a railway engineer in 1837 and worked on the Birmingham and Gloucester railway until its completion in 1841.

In 1842 he contributed some letters (republished as a

pamphlet, *The Proper Sphere of Government,* 1843) to the *Nonconformist,* in which he argued that it is the business of governments to uphold natural rights and that they do more harm than good when they go beyond this. After some association with progressive journalism through such papers as the *Zoist* (devoted to mesmerism and phrenology) and the *Pilot* (the organ of the Complete Suffrage union), Spencer became in 1848 a subeditor of the *Economist.* In 1851 he published *Social Statics* (reissued with preface by F. Neilson, 1955), which contains in embryo most of his later views. He here argues in favour of an extreme form of economic and social *laissez faire* and describes progress as "not an accident but a necessity." About 1850 Spencer made the acquaintance of G. H. Lewes and Marian Evans (George Eliot). His philosophical conversations with the latter led some of their friends to expect that they would marry; but in his *Autobiography* (1904) Spencer says that there was never any such desire on his part, much as he admired Miss Evans' intellectual powers. Other friends were T. H. Huxley and J. S. Mill. In 1853 Spencer received a legacy from his uncle and, relying on this, resigned his position with the *Economist.*

Having published the first part of *The Principles of Psychology* in 1855, Spencer in 1860 issued a prospectus and obtained promises of subscriptions for a comprehensive work, *The Synthetic Philosophy,* which was to include, besides the already published *Principles of Psychology,* volumes on first principles and on biology, sociology and morality. *First Principles* was published in 1862, and between then and 1896, when the third volume of the *Principles of Sociology* appeared, the task was completed. In order to prepare the ground for *The Principles of Sociology,* Spencer, in collaboration with David Duncan and others, started in 1873 a series of works called *Descriptive Sociology,* in which information was provided about the social institutions of various societies, both primitive and civilized. The series was interrupted in 1881 because of lack of public support. Spencer was a close friend of Richard Potter, chairman of the Great Western Railway company, and thus became a friend and adviser of his children, one of whom was Beatrice Potter (who later became Beatrice Webb). She frequently visited Spencer during his last illness and left a sympathetic but sad record of his last years in *My Apprenticeship* (1926). Spencer died on Dec. 8, 1903, at Brighton, leaving a will by which trustees were set up to complete the publication of the *Descriptive Sociology.* Further volumes were written by such authorities as Sir W. Flinders Petrie and J. P. Mahaffy; the series eventually amounted to 19 parts (1873–1934).

Spencer was one of the most argumentative and most discussed English thinkers of the late Victorian period. He vigorously advocated the scientific or naturalistic view of the world against supernaturalism. He was, too, the prophet of evolution and of progress. As a liberal, he upheld the doctrine of *laissez faire* in a most uncompromising form. As a student of society, he urged the importance of examining social phenomena in a scientific way and endeavoured to do this himself. All these aspects of his thought were believed by him to form a coherent and closely ordered system. Science and philosophy, he held, gave support to individualism and progress. It is natural to cite him, therefore, as the great exponent of Victorian optimism, but it should also be noticed that he was by no means unaffected by the pessimism which from time to time clouded the Victorian confidence. Evolution, he taught, would be followed by dissolution, and individualism would come into its own only after an era of socialism and war.

**The Synthetic Philosophy in Outline.**—According to Spencer, philosophy is a synthesis of the fundamental principles of the special sciences, a sort of scientific *summa* to replace the theological systems of the middle ages. "Science is *partially-unified* knowledge; philosophy is *completely-unified* knowledge" (*First Principles,* 37). Spencer thought of unification in terms of development, and his whole scheme was suggested to him by the evolution of biological species. In an article entitled "The Development Hypothesis" (1852–54) he rejected the notion of special creation, and in "Progress: its Law and Cause" (1857) he applied the idea, borrowed from K. E. von Baer, that biological development in the individual is from the homogeneous to the heterogeneous to the evolution of the solar system, of animal species, of human society and of industry, art, language and science. It should be noticed that Spencer published his idea of the evolution of biological species before the views of Charles Darwin and Alfred Russel Wallace were known; but Spencer thought at that time that this evolution was caused by the inheritance of acquired abilities whereas Darwin and Wallace attributed it to natural selection. Spencer later accepted the theory that natural selection was one of the causes of biological evolution and himself coined the phrase "survival of the fittest" (*Principles of Biology* [1864], vol. i, p. 444). But he continued to hold that alterations caused in the organism of a particular animal by forces external to it may be passed on by it to its descendants (pp. 269–270). Furthermore, he did not think that the inheritance of acquired characteristics or the survival of the fittest were ultimate principles of evolution. In his view the principle of change from homogeneity to heterogeneity was more important than either and was itself a consequence of principles still more fundamental. In *First Principles* his argument is that there is a fundamental law of matter, which he calls the law of the persistence of force, from which it follows that nothing homogeneous can remain as such if it is acted on, because any external force must affect some part of it differently from how it affects other parts and hence cause difference and variety to arise. From this it follows that any force that continues to act on what is homogeneous must bring about an increasing variety. This law of the multiplication of effects is, in Spencer's view, the clue to the understanding of all development, cosmic as well as biological. He holds that an unknown and unknowable absolute force is continuously operating on the material world and producing variety, coherence, integration, specialization and individuation. Gases concentrate to form planets; the earth becomes more variegated and gives birth to such simple animals as the amoeba; man evolves from less complex species and at first lives in undifferentiated hordes; various social functions are developed so that there are priests, kings, scholars, workers, etc.; poetry splits off from music and painting from drama so that a diversity of arts arises; and knowledge itself is differentiated into the various sciences. But when the final stage of integration has been reached, Spencer holds, dissolution must necessarily ensue, so that the variety and coherence of the world will lapse into quiescence once more. "And have we thus to contemplate," he asks, "as the outcome of things, a boundless space holding here and there extinct suns, fated to remain for ever without further change?" (*First Principles,* 1862). His answer is that this may be, but that perhaps a new form of integration will then commence which, after reaching an equilibrium, will itself decay and be followed by new evolutions and dissolutions in an infinite alternation.

**Sociology and Social Philosophy.**—Spencer applies his general evolutionary scheme to human society. Indeed, it was from reflection on human society that he conceived it, as can be seen in *Social Statics,* where social evolution is held to be a process of increasing "individuation." Human societies, then, evolve from undifferentiated hordes, by means of increasing division of labour, into complex civilizations. Spencer believed that primitive men were smaller, less intelligent and more emotional than civilized men; that light was thrown on their mentality by study of children in civilized societies; that their religion arose from belief in ghost souls seen in dreams, so that worship was originally directed toward the spirits of dead ancestors; that civilized religions were all more or less elaborate variations on this primitive theme; and that the fundamental sociological classification was between military societies, in which co-operation was secured by force, and industrial societies, in which co-operation was voluntary and spontaneous. The word "industrial" is used here not in the sense of "technologically developed"—for Spencer gives instances of extremely simple societies such as the Todas to illustrate his meaning—but to designate societies chiefly concerned with producing for their members' needs by peaceful and voluntary co-operation. Military societies are ruled by warlike chiefs who maintain themselves in power by arms and superstition; in them women are depressed in status and often forced to do the most burdensome work; and there is an hierarchical organization in which each individual is expected to know and to keep his place. Industrial societies are the reverse of all this, although, if they become involved in war, they have to adopt the military, hierarchical organization.

Evolution is not the only biological conception that Spencer applies in his sociological theories. He also made a detailed comparison between animal organisms and human societies. In both there is a regulative system (the central nervous system in the one, government in the other), a sustaining system (alimentation in the one case, industry in the other) and a distributing system (veins and arteries in the animal body; roads, telegraphs, etc., in the social organism). The great difference, however, between an animal and a social organism is that whereas in the former there is one consciousness relating to the whole, in the latter consciousness exists in each member only and there is no consciousness relating to the whole. Society as a whole has no mind. At this point Spencer abandons description and theory in order to conclude that society exists for the benefit of its members, and not they for its benefit.

This individualism is the key to all of Spencer's work. His contrast between military and industrial societies is a contrast between types of order which he considered bad and those which he considered good. In industrial society coercion and regimentation are at a minimum, and the order achieved, although—indeed because—not planned by anyone, is delicately adjusted to the needs of all parties. In *The Man versus the State* (1884) Spencer says that the Tories support a military and Liberals an industrial social order, but he thought that the Liberals of the latter half of the 19th century were, with their legislation on hours of work, liquor licensing, sanitation, education, etc., developing a "New Toryism" and preparing the way for a "coming slavery." "The function of Liberalism in the past was that of putting a limit to the powers of kings. The function of true Liberalism in the future will be that of putting a limit to the powers of Parliaments."

In his emphasis on variety and differentiation Spencer was unwittingly repeating, in a 19th-century idiom, the metaphysics of liberalism which Spinoza and Leibniz had adumbrated in the 17th century. Spinoza had maintained that "God or Nature" has an infinity of attributes in which every possibility is actualized; and Leibniz had argued that the perfection of God is exhibited in the infinite variety of the universe. Neither of these philosophers believed that time was an ultimate feature of reality. Spencer, however, combined a belief in the reality of time with a belief in the eventual actualization of every possible variety of being. He thus gave metaphysical support to the liberal principle of variety according to which a differentiated and developing society is preferable to a monotonous and static one.

Spencer's attempt to synthesize the sciences showed a sublime audacity which was not repeated because the intellectual specialization which he welcomed and predicted increased beyond his expectations. His sociology, although it gave an impetus to the study of society, was superseded as a result of the development of social anthropology since his day and was much more concerned with providing a rationale for his social ideals than he himself appreciated. Primitive men, for example, are not the childlike emotional creatures that he thought them to be, nor is religion to be explained only in terms of the souls of ancestors. When T. H. Huxley said that Spencer's idea of a tragedy was of "a deduction killed by a fact," he called attention to the system-building feature of Spencer's work which led him to look for what confirmed his theories and to ignore or to reinterpret what conflicted with them.

Spencer's *Synthetic Philosophy* finally comprised the following books: *First Principles* (1862), rev. ed. (1900); *The Principles of Biology,* 2 vol. (1864–67), rev. ed. (1898–99); *Principles of Psychology,* 2 vol. (1855, 1872), 4th ed. (1899); *The Principles of Sociology,* 3 vol. (1876–96); and *The Principles of Ethics,* 2 vol. (1892–93). Other important books are: *Essays: Scientific, Political and Speculative,* 3 series (1857–74), final ed. 3 vol. (1891); *Education: Intellectual, Moral, Physical* (1861); *The Study of Sociology* (1873; 1961); *The Nature and Reality of Religion* (1885), withdrawn from publication; *Facts and Comments* (1902). His *Autobiography* (2 vol.) was published posthumously in 1904. *First Principles* (6th ed.) was reissued in 1937.

*See* also references under "Spencer, Herbert" in the Index.

BIBLIOGRAPHY.—Hugh Elliot, *Herbert Spencer,* with bibliography (1917); David Duncan, *The Life and Letters of Herbert Spencer* (1908); J. Rumney, *Herbert Spencer's Sociology: a Study in the History of Social Theory* (1934); E. Diaconide, *Étude critique sur la sociologie de Herbert Spencer* (1938); for a discussion of Spencer's ethical theory, G. E. Moore, *Principia Ethica,* sec. 31–35 (1903). (H. B. A.)

**SPENCER, JOHN CHARLES SPENCER,** 3RD EARL (1782–1845), English statesman, better known as VISCOUNT ALTHORP, played a major part in securing passage of the Reform Act of 1832. The eldest son of George John, who succeeded as 2nd earl in 1783, he was born at Spencer House, London, on May 30, 1782, and was educated at Harrow and at Trinity College, Cambridge. He represented Okehampton (1804–06), St. Albans (1806), Northamptonshire (1806–32), and Northamptonshire South (1833–34). When Earl Grey's administration was formed in November 1830, Lord Althorp became chancellor of the exchequer and leader of the House of Commons. His first budget (February 1831) was a failure, but this was soon forgotten in the struggles over the Reform Bill, which he and Lord John Russell twice piloted successfully through the Commons. "Althorp carried the bill," said a leading opponent, Sir Henry Hardinge, "his fine temper did it."

Althorp was neither eloquent nor nimble witted; he owed his ascendancy over the Commons to his courage, integrity, and judgment. He was able to gauge feeling among the squires who predominated in the House of his day, for he shared their tastes and habits of mind. In Sir Robert Peel, then leading the opposition, he faced a redoubtable parliamentarian, and his own following of Whigs, Radicals, and Irish was ill mixed and hard to manage; yet his success as leader was complete. "He became," wrote the diarist Charles Greville, a severe contemporary judge, "the very best leader of the . . . Commons that any party ever had . . . . The whole House liked him, his own party followed him with devoted attachment."

Lord Althorp retired from politics when called to the House of Lords in November 1834 on his father's death. His removal from the Commons was the occasion of William IV's dismissal of Viscount Melbourne's ministry. He was the first president of the Royal Agricultural Society (founded 1838) and a notable shorthorn cattle breeder. He died at Wiseton Hall, Nottinghamshire, on Oct. 1, 1845.

BIBLIOGRAPHY.—Sir D. Le Marchant, *Memoir* (1876); E. J. Myers, *Lord Althorp* (1890); Earl Spencer, "John Charles, Viscount Althorp," *The Quarterly Review,* vol. 283 (Oct. 1945). For contemporary opinions *see* C. C. F. Greville, *Memoirs,* 1st series, vol. iii (1875) and 2nd series, vol. ii (1885); A. Aspinall (ed.), *Three Early Nineteenth Century Diaries* (1952). (M. G. B.; X.)

**SPENCER, SIR STANLEY** (1891–1959), English painter of religious subjects, landscapes, portraits, and social satires, was born at Cookham, Berkshire, on June 30, 1891, son of W. Spencer, organist. He studied at the Slade School of Art and began to exhibit at the New English Art Club. During World War I he served in the Royal Army Medical Corps in Macedonia and painted "Travoys Arriving with Wounded" for the Imperial War Museum. In 1932 he completed "Resurrection of the Soldiers" and scenes from army life in the chapel at Burghclere, Hampshire. "Christ Carrying the Cross" (1920), "Resurrection" (1927), representing the dead rising from their tombs in Cookham churchyard, and a later "Resurrection" (1950) are at Tate Gallery, London. He also painted highly finished landscapes and humorous comments on the absurdity of human behaviour. He was elected a royal academician in 1950 and knighted in 1959. He died at Taplow, Buckinghamshire, on Dec. 14, 1959.

BIBLIOGRAPHY.—*Stanley Spencer Retrospective Exhibition Catalogue,* Tate Gallery (1955); Gilbert Spencer, *Stanley Spencer* (1961); M. Collis, *Stanley Spencer* (1962); George Behrend, *Stanley Spencer at Burghclere* (1965). (M. CH.)

**SPENER, PHILIPP JAKOB** (1635–1705), German theologian and one of the leading figures in German Pietism (*q.v.*), was born on Jan. 23 (new style; 13, old style), 1635, at Rappoltsweiler in Upper Alsace. His father's position at the Court of Rappoltstein and the fact that his godmother was the countess Agathe von Rappoltstein brought Spener into early contact with the higher aristocracy, a relationship that proved important in the later development of Pietism. His youth was influenced by the devotional literature of English Puritanism, and his later studies at the theological faculty of Strasbourg (1651–59) determined his lifelong interest in reform of Lutheran orthodoxy. At the age of 31 he was made president of the Lutheran Church at Frankfurt am Main. There he started his *collegia pietatis,* devotional gatherings intended to encourage personal piety and private Bible study.

In 1675 Spener published his *Pia desideria* (English translation, 1964), a concentrated expression of the reform strivings that had existed for almost 100 years within Lutheranism. His reputation spread throughout Germany in consequence of this work, which contained the basic program of Pietism and was the stimulus to its promulgation in the Lutheran Church. His appointment as first court chaplain at Dresden in 1686 brought him into the most valued position in German Lutheranism. His work, however, was hindered by bitter conflict with the elector John George III, when Spener criticized the moral life of the Saxon court. The spread of Pietism aroused so vigorous an opposition from orthodox Lutherans at Leipzig University that in 1691 Spener moved to Berlin to become provost of St. Nicholas' Church. The support of the Brandenburg-Prussian Court enabled Spener to carry out many reforms, and in 1694 Halle University was founded on a Pietist basis, with Spener's disciples A. H. Francke (*q.v.*) and Christian Thomasius holding leading professorships. By the time of Spener's death in Berlin on Feb. 5, 1705, Pietism was well established. During the last years of his life Spener had retired from polemical discussions. He left over 300 writings, among which, besides *Pia desideria,* are *Das geistliche Priestertum* ("Spiritual Priesthood"; 1677) and *Die allgemeine Gottesgelehrtheit* ("General Theology"; 1680).

BIBLIOGRAPHY.—P. Grünberg, *P. J. Spener,* 3 vol. (1893–1906); A. Ritschl, *Geschichte des Pietismus* (1884); K. Aland, *Spener-Studien* (1943). (K. A.)

**SPENGLER, OSWALD** (1880–1936), German philosopher, was born at Blankenburg am Harz on May 29, 1880. Mathematics and natural science were the main subjects of his university education, but he wrote a thesis on Heraclitus for his doctorate, taken at Halle in 1904. Spengler earned his living as a schoolmaster until 1911, when he went to live in Munich on a small inheritance. It was about this time that he began to work on *Der Untergang des Abendlandes* (Eng. trans., *The Decline of the West,* 1926–28), of which he had completed a draft by the outbreak of World War I. The first volume of this powerful book was published in Munich in July 1918, a few months before the final collapse of the German forces. It won its author immediate acclaim from the general public, if not from professional historians and philosophers. The second volume followed in 1922, and a revised version of the first a year later. Spengler tried from 1919 onward to turn his reputation to account by assuming the role of political commentator, but he met with little success in this field. He became increasingly isolated, and his difficulties were multiplied by criticism of his work by the National Socialists, despite a certain affinity between his political ideas and theirs. (*See* NATIONAL SOCIALISM.) He died in Munich of a heart attack on May 8, 1936.

THE GRANGER COLLECTION

OSWALD SPENGLER, PHOTOGRAPHED ABOUT 1930

Spengler's reputation rests entirely on *Der Untergang des Abendlandes,* which is in effect a study in the philosophy of history or in historical "morphology." Beginning, as G. Vico had done before him and as Arnold Toynbee was to do a few years later, by comparing modern Western civilization with the civilization of the Greco-Roman world, Spengler claimed to be able to discern the outline of a life cycle through which, he believed, all such civilizations must pass. Possession of this key idea, he argued, would enable us both to reconstruct the past and, more significantly, to predict "the spiritual form, duration, rhythm, meaning and product of the still unaccomplished stages of our western history." Spengler's own view of the prospects of Western civilization was a gloomy one. Since the West, he believed, had already passed through the creative stage of "culture" into the stage of reflection and material comfort (which constituted "civilization" proper in his special terminology), the future could only be a period of decline; nor was there any prospect of reversing the process, for civilizations blossomed and decayed like natural organisms, and true rejuvenation was as impossible in the one case as in the other.

Spengler's book won scant approval from professional scholars, who were scandalized by his unorthodox methods and contemptuous of his errors of fact. There could, however, be no denying his moments of genuine historical insight (as in his imaginative treatment of Greek mathematics) or the merits of his work as a contribution to social theory.

Other works by Spengler include *Preussentum und Sozialismus* (1920), *Politische Pflichten der deutschen Jugend* (1924), *Neubau des deutschen Reiches* (1924), *Der Mensch und die Technik* (1931; Eng. trans., *Man and Technics,* 1932), and *Jahre der Entscheidung* (1933; Eng. trans., *Years of Decision,* 1934). Some of his miscellaneous writings are collected in *Politische Schriften* (1932) and *Reden und Aufsätze* (1937).

BIBLIOGRAPHY.—R. G. Collingwood, "Oswald Spengler and the Theory of Historical Cycles," *Antiquity* (1927); M. Schroeter, *Metaphysik des Untergangs* (1949); P. A. Sorokin, *Social Philosophies of an Age of Crisis* (1950); H. Stuart Hughes, *Oswald Spengler: a Critical Estimate* (1952). (W. H. W.)

**SPENSER, EDMUND** (*c.* 1552–1599), the author of *The Faerie Queene,* one of the great long poems in the English language, is described on his monument in Westminster Abbey, London, as "the Prince of Poets in his tyme." The original monument, which was erected by Anne, countess of Dorset, in 1620, and replaced in 1778, gave his year of birth as "1510," probably for 1550 by a calligraphic confusion then frequent. Eighteenth-century biographers conjectured that he was born in 1553, but 1552 has been preferred since G. L. Craik, in 1845, deduced it from Spenser's own reference to his age in his sonnet sequence *Amoretti* (no. 60); however, the sonnet (itself of doubtful date) is unlikely to be exact in its use of the word "fourty." According to an early tradition, he was born in East Smithfield, London. In his *Prothalamion,* besides calling London his "most kyndly Nurse," he refers to his kinsfolk the wealthy Spencers of Wormleighton, Warwickshire, and Althorpe, Northamptonshire—to three of whom, the Ladies Carey, Compton, and Strange, he had dedicated poems—as "an house of auncient fame."

Though the Scottish historian Robert Johnston (in his *Historia rerum Britannicarum,* 1655) describes him as *in tenui re natum* ("born in mean circumstances"), Spenser's education does not suggest poverty. On Feb. 6, 1569, he received a gown and a shilling from Robert Nowell's charitable bequest, with 30 other "pore schollers"; but this was a conventional label for schoolboys, and the occasion was Nowell's funeral, at which Spenser with five others represented Merchant Taylors' School. He had entered Merchant Taylors' School when it opened in 1561 under the headmastership of Richard Mulcaster, one of the most advanced educationists of the day. He left for Cambridge in April 1569; matriculated as a sizar of Pembroke Hall on May 20; and proceeded B.A. in 1573 and M.A. in 1576. In his first months at Cambridge he contributed anonymously to the apocalyptic and anti-Catholic *Theatre for Worldlings*—a translation of a prose tract by the Dutch Protestant refugee Jan Van der Noodt—22 rhymed and unrhymed translations of "Visions" by Petrarch (through Clément Marot's French version) and Du Bellay. Some of these epigrams and sonnets he revised for the later *Complaints* volume.

In *The Faerie Queene* (Book IV, canto 11) he affectionately remembers his "mother Cambridge" and the gentle Muses and learned wits who adorned her. Among these, Gabriel Harvey (*q.v.*) became Spenser's "most special freende," encouraged in him a disciplined interest in the arts of language, and tried to share his enthusiasm for the modern literatures of Spain, Italy, and France. Spenser became "perfect in the Greek tongue," and, though Platonism and militant idealism were probably both deeply rooted in his nature, his sojourn in the Platonist university, and in a strongly Protestant college, helped to shape and direct these impulses.

Spenser seems to have remained at Cambridge at least until 1574–75; then there is a gap in our knowledge of his life. Nothing can now be made of the deliberately mystifying hint (in the *Shepheardes Calender,* June gloss) of a stay in "the Northpartes," round which conjecture has played persistently. We catch an early glimpse of him in his prose dialogue *Veue of the Present State of Ireland,* where the execution of the rebel Murrogh O'Brien at Limerick on July 1, 1577, is described with eyewitness detail. Edward Phillips' statement (in his *Theatrum Poetarum Anglicanorum,* 1675) that he was secretary to Sir Henry Sidney, lord deputy of Ireland, is inherently probable from his later career; and Milton (Phillips' uncle) seems to have had contacts with Spenser's family. In 1578 Spenser became secretary to John Young, who had been master of Pembroke when he was an undergraduate, and had been made bishop of Rochester early in the year; he is the beloved "Roffy" (from Roffensis, the name he took as bishop) of the September eclogue of the *Shepheardes Calender.* Since the whole of this work was finished by April 10, 1579, it was presumably written in the bishop's "goodly Kentish garden" at Bromley, and its setting, in so far as it is not conventionally pastoral but particularized by references to Kent, is consistent with this.

The *Shepheardes Calender,* a group of pastoral eclogues, one for each month, was entered in the Stationers' Register on Dec. 5 and published soon after under the pseudonym "Immerito." The delay in publishing it was caused by discussion with Harvey as to the best strategy for the "new poet's" first public appearance, and the elaborate critical apparatus of learned introductions and editorial glosses by "E. K." with which it was published was part of this strategy. "E. K." was perhaps Edward Kirke, a sizar at Pembroke in 1571 and probably son of a "Mystresse Kerke" mentioned in one of Spenser's letters; Edward Knight, a Puritan tract-writer of 1579, has also been suggested. Since Spenser's day readers of the *Calender* have yielded to the temptation to speculate on the identity of "Colin Clout's" (*i.e.,* Spenser's) cruel mistress Rosalind and to solve the anagram afforded (according to one of "E. K.'s" notes) by her name. The lady, however, is a fiction demanded both by the pastoral genre and by the poem's theme of love and greed: *caritas* and *cupiditas;* and the poem is not to be interpreted as an autobiographical allegory. However, on Oct. 27, 1579, Spenser married the 19-year-old Machabyas Chylde at St. Margaret's, Westminster, and the sestina added as an afterthought to the August eclogue and recording Rosalind's (*i.e.,* Love's) return to Colin may refer to Spenser's bride. The names of two children of the marriage are known: Sylvanus and Catherine.

From "E. K.," and from five letters exchanged by Harvey and Spenser between Oct. 5, 1579, and April 23, 1580, and published in July 1580, we learn of a dozen works planned or finished not now extant: *Dreames* (ready for press), *Legendes, Courte of Cupid* (which may have become the description of the Masque of Cupid, *The Faerie Queene,* Book III, cantos 11–12; Book IV, canto 10), *Pageaunts, My Slomber, Dying Pellicane* (mentioned again in 1591), a translation of Moschus' *Idyll of Wandering Love,* a critical essay called *The English Poet,* and *Epithalamion Thamesis* (an experiment in English hexameters, rewritten as *The Faerie Queene,* Book IV, canto 11). The *"Nine Comoedies"* named after the nine Muses, and also referred to by Harvey, were probably never written. Harvey, in the letter referring to them, urges his friend to pursue his emulation of Ariosto with these, rather than with *The Faerie Queene* (of which he had been sent some "parcels" on April 6, 1580). His objection to the *"Elvish Queene"* was a classical and reasonable one: antipathy to the matter of romance and fairy tale as barbarous and trivial superstition and not fit subject for a serious poem. In the same letter, he warmly welcomes the news that Spenser, with Philip Sidney and Edward Dyer (*qq.v.*), is practising English quantitative metre, or "refourmed versifying." Spenser's interest in the art was short lived and was part of a larger concern he shared with Sidney in achieving greater rhythmical subtleties and in counterpointing the movement of English words against various metrical frameworks, of which the prosodic variety of the *Shepheardes Calender* is a result.

With his entry into the Sidney circle early in 1579, Spenser had reached the centre of the cultural life of his time, the group that by patronage, criticism, taste, and encouragement became the chief begetter of the great flowering of Elizabethan literature. Patriotic and Puritan, its aim was to enrich England, as Italy and France had already been enriched, with a body of poetry comparable in artistry and range of forms with that of Greece and Rome—but a poetry Christian and morally serious. Spenser's first poem focused these aspirations. He became the "New Poet," "the rightest English Poet that ever I read" (according to William Webbe's *Discourse of English Poetrie,* 1586).

Politically, Sidney's uncle the earl of Leicester led the movement. By October 1579 Spenser was in his employ as a secretary and was looking forward to going to France on a mission: confusion in the printed dates of the Spenser-Harvey letters makes it uncertain whether this took place. To this period belong the lost Latin *Stemmata Dudleiana,* celebrating his patron's lineage, and, it is thought, an early version of *Mother Hubberds Tale.* In this poem the machinery of the beast fable is used (in allusion to Queen Elizabeth's own fondness for animal nicknames) to express the bitter opposition of Leicester's party to a match between the queen and the duc d'Anjou (Alençon)—a recurrent threat that had become acute since the arrival in England of the duke's agent Jehan de Simier (called by the queen her "monkey," and in Spenser's poem, the Ape) in January and the duke's own visit in August 1579, with the backing of Burghley (in *Mother Hubberds Tale,* the Fox). Sidney lost favour at court by writing a strong letter of protest. E. Greenlaw, in an article published in 1910, deduced from *Virgils Gnat* (Spenser's translation of the pseudo-Virgilian *Culex*) and the tone of its dedication to Leicester an estrangement between them, resulting from the poet's officious zeal at this time, and leading to his departure for Ireland under a cloud. This is in itself improbable, and the warm gratitude to, and respect for, Leicester (now dead) expressed in *The Teares of the Muses* make it more so. A mock-heroic poem like *Virgils Gnat* would fit only some trifling and private difference; it is a half-amusing exercise. Above all, Spenser's appointment from July 1580 as one of the two secretaries to the new lord deputy of Ireland, Leicester's friend Lord Grey de Wilton, was clearly no punishment but rather the effort of a patron himself now in disgrace and therefore with no advancement to offer, to settle his protégé. Ireland was certainly no exile to Spenser. He became deeply attached to the country and its people; landscapes, castles, place-names, poor peasantry—all became part of the imaginative life that created *The Faerie Queene.* All his writing reveals how distasteful to his quiet-loving spirit a prolonged stay at court would have been.

The rest of Spenser's life was spent in official posts in Ireland, with two visits to London to supervise the publication of poems. About 60 documents in his hand from this period prove that he journeyed with Grey throughout the country; *e.g.,* in the actions against Baltinglas at Glenmalure in August 1580 and against the Spanish and Italian supporters of the Munster rebels at Smerwick from Oct. 5 to Nov. 10. This latter victory, in what to the Puritan Grey was a crusade against anti-Christ, became, as Artegall's defeat of Grantorto, the high point of *The Faerie Queene,* Book V.

Various leases of houses by the poet are recorded from December 1581 onward, in Wexford, Dublin, and Kildare; and on Aug. 24, 1582, he took the splendid New Abbey, County Kildare (already temporarily leased to him on July 15, 1580), near the Bog of Allen. He used it intermittently till 1590. On Aug. 31,

1582, Grey was recalled to England by a government out of sympathy with his firm repressive methods. But by then Spenser had become, in March 1581, clerk for faculties (licences and dispensations) in the Dublin court of chancery—a post he held till June 22, 1588; in 1583–84, commissioner of musters in County Kildare; and, in November 1583, or at latest by the following April, deputy to Lodowick Bryskett in the clerkship to the Council of Munster.

In this post (which he sold in 1593) he saw a great deal more of the troubled country as he traveled with the successive presidents of the council, Sir John Norreys and (1585–89) his brother Sir Thomas, and another action against the Spaniards, in Connaught and Ulster, in the winter of 1588–89. In December 1586 he is mentioned, inexplicably, as being prebendary of Effin, County Limerick. From September 1586 to October 1589 his main concern was the surveys and claims for the government's plantation of Munster. He himself was granted in September 1588 Kilcolman Castle, a forfeited estate, and neighbouring Ballingerragh. There, just south of the Ballyhoura Hills (called by Spenser in his poems, "Old Father Mole") and between his beloved Awbeg ("Mulla") and Bregog streams, he lived for the next ten years—involved periodically from October 1589 in litigation over boundaries with his Anglo-Irish neighbour Lord Roche.

Bryskett, who had Italian family connections and literary interests, kept Spenser in touch with modern poetry. Tasso's *Gerusalemme Liberata* (1581) came as fresh stimulation. To this period belongs some such incident as that recounted by Bryskett in his *Discourse of Civill Life* (published in 1606 but written before 1589) when he describes, with some literary embellishment, a meeting of friends near Dublin at which Spenser refused to talk on moral philosophy, as he had "already well entered into" a poem on this subject in "heroical verse." Bryskett may have taken a manuscript of *The Faerie Queene,* Books I–III, to London in 1587, for it apparently began to circulate in the countess of Pembroke's circle at about that time. When Sir Walter Ralegh, who owned an estate southeast of Kilcolman, visited Spenser in the summer of 1589, he heard enough of the poem to make him persuade the poet to return with him to London and interest the queen in it. The whole of this episode Spenser made into the charming poem *Colin Clouts Come Home Againe,* written when he returned to Kilcolman in December 1591 and sent with a letter to Ralegh.

The first installment of *The Faerie Queene* (Books I–III) was entered in the Stationers' Register on Dec. 1, 1589; and a letter to Ralegh "expounding [the author's] whole intention in the course of this worke" was written on Jan. 23, 1590. Two issues of the poem appeared by early April, and it was immediately successful. After a short time in Ireland in May–June, Spenser returned to London to write *Daphnaïda* (published in January 1591), an elegy on Douglas Howard, the wife of the poet Arthur Gorges, who died on Aug. 13, 1590, and to prepare for publication early in 1591 the nine poems new and old collected as *Complaints.* The publisher of this, William Ponsonby, explains in his prefatory address to the reader that the volume is due to the "favourable passage" his edition of *The Faerie Queene* has found among readers, and regrets that he has not recovered more of the author's dispersed works, lost during his stay overseas: notably a group of biblical and religious poems (named by Ponsonby as *Ecclesiastes, Canticum canticorum translated,* the seven penitential psalms, *The Howers of the Lord,* and *The Sacrifice of a Sinner*). The titles show that Spenser shared the taste for "divine poems" inspired mainly by Du Bartas' *Uranie* (1574) as translated by James VI of Scotland in 1584. The motive expressed in Ponsonby's preface may account also for C. Burbie's publication in 1592 of a translation (as by "Edw. Spenser") of the pseudo-Platonic dialogue *Axiochus* "concerning the shortnesse and vncertainty of this life, with the contrary ends of the good and wicked"—a truly Spenserian theme. The translation was probably made in 1579–80. The unique copy of Spenser's 28-page version was found in 1931 bound up with a copy of the 1679 folio edition of Spenser's *Works.* Some attribute it to Anthony Munday.

On Feb. 25, 1591, Spenser's worth as a national poet was recognized by the award of a pension of £50; this was paid regularly till his death. He himself expresses gratitude to the queen, *e.g.,* in *Colin Clout* and in *Amoretti,* no. 74; but as early as 1602 a story is told by a John Manningham, in his diary, of how Burghley, always suspicious of poets, had whittled down the queen's original offer of £100. The same story appears independently in Thomas Fuller's *Worthies* (published 1662) and became a favourite with later biographers. From 1592 onward there are persistent reports that Burghley had the unsold copies of *Complaints* recalled because of the attack on him in *Mother Hubberds Tale.*

Less is known of Spenser's official work during his last seven years. He was twice justice for County Cork in 1594. On June 11 of that year (which was, at that period, Midsummer Day), he married Elizabeth Boyle and commemorated the event in *Epithalamion,* as he had recorded the courtship from late 1592 onward in the 89 *Amoretti* (or love sonnets). These were published together in 1595. His second wife was the daughter of Stephen and Joan Boyle of Bradden, Northamptonshire, and a kinswoman of the Spencers of Althorpe. They may have met through her family connection with Sir Richard Boyle, later earl of Cork. They had one son, Peregrine.

The year of Spenser's second visit to London, 1595–96, was, as to new publications, the most crowded of his career. Besides *Amoretti,* he issued in 1595 a volume containing *Colin Clouts Come Home Againe,* and a collection of verse tributes to Sidney's memory, of which the first two, *Astrophel* and the *Doleful Lay of Clorinda* (put into the mouth of the countess of Pembroke), were his own. Most important was the second installment of *The Faerie Queene.* Books IV–VI were entered in the Stationers' Register (Jan. 20, 1596), and they, with the second edition of Books I–III, must have appeared well before November 1596, when James VI of Scotland complained to the English ambassador in Edinburgh of the treatment of his mother Mary, queen of Scots, whose trial is described as the trial of Duessa, in Book V, canto 9. During this year also the *Veue of the Present State of Ireland* was written for presentation to those responsible for policy there. It was entered in the Stationers' Register on April 14, 1598, to await "further aucthoritee" but was first printed only in 1633 by Sir James Ware in his *Historie of Ireland.* The *Fowre Hymnes* appeared in about September of the same year; and the *Prothalamion, or a Spousall Verse* was occasioned by the double marriage at Essex House on Nov. 8 of the earl of Worcester's eldest daughters Elizabeth and Katherine. Spenser used the opportunity to praise the earl of Essex, on whom he now placed his hopes for his country, and to pay a graceful compliment on his capture of Cádiz in August.

He returned at the end of 1596 to an Ireland increasingly shadowed by the impending rebellion of Tyrone. From its outbreak in June 1598 it rapidly spread till in October Kilcolman Castle was sacked, and the Council of Munster, with many English refugees, withdrew to Cork. Spenser had, on Sept. 30, been made sheriff of Cork on the warm recommendation of the Privy Council to the lords justices, to whom he was already known "for his good and commendable parts," his learning, and his experience in the wars. But his only remaining official duty was to carry to the Privy Council and to Cecil at Whitehall urgent letters (of Dec. 9 and 13) from Sir Thomas Norreys on the desperate state of affairs. To these he added three memoranda of his own, preserved in the Public Record Office as "A breife note of Ireland," and including a report addressed to the queen, "Out of the ashes of disolacon and wastnes of this your wretched Realme of Ireland." He arrived in London on Sunday, Dec. 24, and on Dec. 30 Cecil paid him £8 for his mission. On Saturday, Jan. 13, 1599, he died in Westminster, in King Street, according to Ben Jonson. He was buried at Essex' expense in Westminster Abbey close to Chaucer, and William Camden (writing in 1615) relates that many poets threw into his open grave their elegies and the pens that wrote them. An attempt in 1938 to recover these relics was foiled by ignorance of the position of the grave, the monument having been moved.

The story that Spenser died "for lack of bread" (as Ben Jonson told William Drummond of Hawthornden, in 1618) is, in view of his official status and patrons, incredible. There is no hint of it in John Chamberlain's letter reporting the death of "our principal poet" four days after the event; it is first suggested in Joseph Hall's lines to Camden in 1600, and in the Cambridge play *The Returne from Parnassus,* part 2 (late 1601). Thus early began the romanticizing of "mild Spenser, called from Faeryland/To struggle through dark ways." This phrase of Wordsworth's enshrines a deeply misleading antithesis between the poem and the poet's life, since an active and strenuous career was indispensable to the writing of *The Faerie Queene.* More important is the tradition, recorded as early as 1607, that manuscripts of later parts of *The Faerie Queene* were lost in the destruction of Kilcolman. The first folio edition (1609) of the whole of *The Faerie Queene* prints, as well as the six completed books, two cantos, plus two stanzas *Of Mutabilitie* from a seventh book, a "Legend of Constancie." Intensive search in Ireland and England in the mid-17th century unearthed no more of what Spenser must have written during the last 4½ years of his life.

## THE WORKS

**Pastorals.**—Since Spenser's work is conceived in terms of the 16th-century aesthetic theory of the literary "kinds," each with its own decorum of style and conventions, understanding of it begins with recognition of the genres he felt himself to be making. "E. K." is at pains to underline in his introduction to the *Shepheardes Calender* that the new poet is beginning, like Virgil, with pastorals, and the "October" eclogue looks forward to the epic he will write in the future just as the Proem of Book I of *The Faerie Queene* looks back to the "lowly Shepheards weeds." But *The Shepheardes Calender,* unlike earlier pastorals by Mantuan, Sannazaro, and Spenser's favourite, Clément Marot, is a single poem, not a haphazard series of 12 eclogues. Its unifying "calendar" framework was suggested by the popular French devotional manual *Le Compost et Kalendrier des Bergiers,* which was well known in translation. Spenser's translation of the whole pagan pastoral world into Christian terms is signaled by his opening the year in January instead of in March, so counterpointing (as the General Argument to the poem explains) nature's winter death against the birth of the Redeemer, who renews "the state of the decayed world." The poem opposes the good shepherd, the "shepheard great, that bought his flocks so deare" (*i.e.,* Christ), to various bad and mercenary shepherds. Akin to the *cupiditas* (greed) of the hirelings is the crippling love of the shepherd Colin Clout for the faithless Rosalind, which has brought his flock to wretchedness, makes him break his pipes in despair, and turns him from the *caritas* (loving-kindness) of Hobbinol's (Harvey's) friendship. The theme of the two loves, to be developed so fruitfully in *The Faerie Queene,* is already shaping in Spenser's imagination. "April" offers, in the song to Eliza (Elizabeth I), an exquisite example of the poetry that Colin was once capable of; and the bleak end he faces in "December" is heightened by the death of Dido so nobly mourned and robbed of its sting in "November" —*La mort ny mord* ("Death bites not there") since "one that dyed for al."

Attention has been distracted from the poetic greatness of *The Shepheardes Calender* by its many other importances: its inauguration of English pastoral (*see* PASTORAL); its program for embellishing English, as the Pléiade poets in practice and precept had embellished French, by recovering ancient and dialect words (a motive that guided Spenser to the end), and by judicious coinages and borrowings; the rhetorical and syntactical art so admired by "E. K." in the glosses; the variety of forms—fable, satire, complaint, paean, dirge, sestina, roundelay; and the references to contemporaries, of which only a few are certain and none to be rigorously pressed.

The pastoral machinery that in *The Shepheardes Calender* marvelously holds together the roles of God-inspired poet-priest-ruler, so achieving the timelessness claimed by the "December" gloss, is transposed in *Colin Clouts Come Home Againe* into charming autobiographical anecdote: the visit with the Shepherd of the Ocean (Ralegh) to Cynthia's court, and the ladies and poets there. There is the traditional praise of country life as against courtly corruption; the Hobbinol and Rosalind themes are resumed in a happier key. The pastoral elegy *Astrophel* fittingly laments Sidney as himself a pastoral poet—author of *Arcadia* and *Astrophel and Stella. Daphnaïda* inserts into a pastoral framework an allegorical lyric modeled on the grief of the Knight in Black in Chaucer's *Book of the Duchess.* Its obvious derivativeness, highly patterned rhetoric, and sevenfold repetitions dramatize the stubbornness of Alcyon's refusal to be comforted (Alcyon being the pastoral name given to Arthur Gorges, Douglas Howard's husband), over against moments of intensely realized love and loss.

**Complaints.**—The title suggests the medieval marriage of elegiac and satiric tones. Of these "sundrie small Poemes of the Worlds Vanitie," *Muiopotmos, or the Fate of the Butterflie,* the only one entirely new in 1591, is the finest. The butterfly Clarion, destroyed by the spider Aragnoll, is in fact the victim of the ancient "dolorous debate" between Pallas and Arachne, which Spenser characteristically interweaves with his own version of the jealousy of Venus against Astery and Psyche. The whole, an impeccably tactful re-creation of the myth of "the drerie stownd . . . That of all happines hath vs depriued," of Satanic evil, temptation, and fall, is Spenser's miniature epic in answer to the mock epic *Culex,* which he had rendered as *Virgils Gnat.* So also to his versions of Petrarch's *Visions* and Du Bellay's *Songe* and *Antiquitez de Rome* (*Ruines of Rome*) he added his own specimens in the same kind: *Visions of the Worlds Vanitie,* and the vision pageants that close *The Ruines of Time*—an elegy on Leicester, Sidney, and Walsingham that turns the popular medieval theme of "Falls of Great Men" into a lament for the world's lost glories and a claim that only the immortality conferred by poetry survives the universal vicissitude. This last is the subject of *The Teares of the Muses* (the title taken from a Latin poem by Harvey), the clarification of a genre that can be seen emerging in earlier 16th-century complaints of the neglect of the arts by a barbarous age. Theseus, in Shakespeare's *A Midsummer Night's Dream* (Act V, scene i, li. 54), dismisses this poem as "some satire, keen and critical.". But the only purely satirical poem by Spenser is *Prosopopoia, or Mother Hubberds Tale.* Though formally this is in the great late medieval tradition of *Reynard the Fox* (*q.v.*), the resources of animal symbolism are little exploited, and the style and method—attack on the several estates of the realm—align the poem with William Langland's *Piers Plowman* and the work of John Skelton and Sir David Lyndsay (*qq.v.*), and with contemporary prose tracts on the ills and abuses stemming from the immense social and economic changes of the time.

**Sonnets; Spousals; Hymnes.**—Except in the three Petrarch and Du Bellay "Complaints," Spenser preferred the sonnet with linked quatrains developed from native metres by the poets of the Scottish court (*see* SONNET). Two sonnets to Harvey and Leicester (*c.* 1586) are in this form. The *Amoretti,* like other sonnet sequences of the time, have a narrative basis, hinted by the passing seasons (New Year, Easter) and the vicissitudes of the poet's love. But this courtship is, uniquely, crowned with marriage. The timeworn conceits of courtly wooing heighten the paradox of the Christian consummation celebrated in *Epithalamion.* This last, the most perfect of Spenser's poems, is a manifold symbol of fulfillment based (in 24 stanzas) on the circle of day and night, reinforced with myth and biblical echo and the movement from pains and death to joys, birth, and immortality with the saints, and dramatizing in its images of time the victory over time that its last line prays the poem itself will be. These images also mark the three great phases of the day centred in the marriage service. The marriage ode of Catullus and the French Pléiade poets has here been radically remade.

*Prothalamion* is, as its refrain says, a betrothal song, a rare genre for which Spenser invented the title. The joyous occasion is framed by the medieval device of the allegorical swan procession watched by the traditional world-weary poet, and hopes for the young couples merge with hopes for England (whose annual "Brydale day"—Nov. 17, Accession Day—is at hand: stanza 9) and a rebirth in the earl of Essex of the fallen nobility Spenser has personal reason to mourn in the fall of the earl of Leicester.

Spenser's pretended "retraction" of the first two of his *Fowre Hymnes* of love and beauty, composed "in the greener times of my youth," is no doubt only a device for pointing the contrast between the halves of his diptych, the "naturall" and the "celestiall," figuring under Platonic colouring stages like those in medieval Christian devotion. The last two hymns celebrate divine creativity, and Sapience (Old Testament "Wisdom," identified with the Word) enthroned with God.

**A Veue of the Present State of Ireland.**—If the modern reader can restrain his anachronistic horror at the ruthlessly repressive policy advocated for Ireland, he may watch unfolding in firm dramatic prose a mind equipped by firsthand observation; furious at injustices, abuses, and double-dealing; informed in political and historical theory, *e.g.*, of Jean Bodin (*q.v.*); and with a firm grasp of the civil and military needs in that "sweete countrie."

**The Faerie Queene.**—The debate of the 18th-century commentators on Spenser about the epic status of *The Faerie Queene* may be resolved if (with E. M W. Tillyard) we define epic as the embodiment in a fiction of the whole ethos and ideals of a "heroic age." Spenser was himself inspired by the critical battle fought over the Italian romances from 1548 onward, and reaching a compromise in the 1580s in the theory and practice of Torquato Tasso (*q.v.*): romantic variety in epic unity, the Christian supernatural as the "epic marvellous," war and love as the matter. His letter to Ralegh affirms his position by citing Homer and Virgil along with Ariosto and Tasso as models, by insisting on the overall unity the poem completed is to have, and by pointing to his use of the epic device of thrusting into the heart of the narrative in Book I. That the annual Feast of Gloriana, the source of the 12 tasks that are the poem's action, is to be presented last (so that in fact it was never written) sets up that sense of striving toward a goal, of outgoing and return, so central to the world of the poem; and the goal is kept before us in Arthur's dream-inspired search for Gloriana through the world. This framework is Spenser's invention, based on visions of fairy mistresses in the much read *Arthur of Little Britain* and Chaucer's *Sir Thopas,* and on the Accession Day festivities.

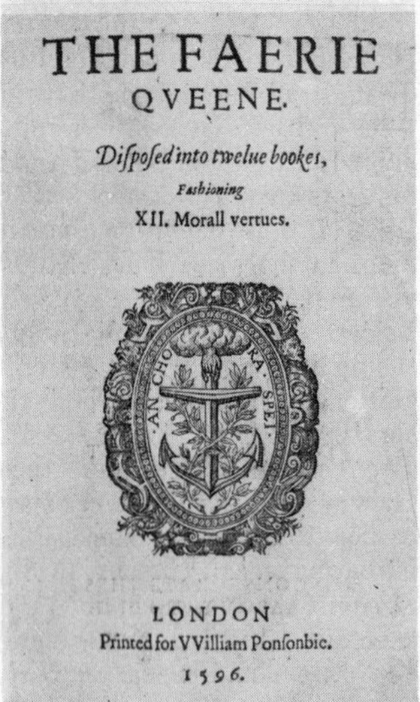
THE FAERIE QVEENE.
Dispofed into twelue bookes,
Fashioning
XII. Morall vertues.
LONDON
Printed for VVilliam Ponfonbie.
1596.

BY COURTESY OF THE TRUSTEES OF THE BRITISH MUSEUM; PHOTO, J. R. FREEMAN AND CO.

**GENERAL TITLE PAGE OF THE 1596 EDITION OF EDMUND SPENSER'S "THE FAERIE QUEENE"**

The poem as we have it (which consists of only 6 books and a fragment of the seventh, instead of the 12 intended) ends with the poet's own prayer for sight of a farther goal, the sabbath of the God of Sabaoth. But formally the poem owes its whole being to the Italian *romanzi,* as the Italianate names of its characters acknowledge. From them comes the inventive energy of *entrelacement*—continually bifurcating and infolded narrative; from Boiardo come the book and canto division (the first English use of the "canto"), the verse argument of each canto, the moralized opening and promissory ending of cantos; from Trissino, the name Acrasia and hints for Duessa; from Tasso, with little change, such episodes as the Idle Lake and the Bower of Bliss—for Tasso is closest to Spenser in gravity of spirit. The debt to Ariosto in story and motif is by far the greatest.

Spenser "overgoes" his models (as he hoped) simply by taking seriously the capacities of the romance form, by exploiting romance as a paradigm of human experience: the moral life as quest, pilgrimage, aspiration, as eternal war with an Enemy still to be known, as encounter, crisis, the moment of illumination—ethics with the dimensions of mystery, terror, love, and victory added, and all the generous virtues exalted. As setting Spenser invents the "antique image" of Faerie, a land of true fame; its capital Cleopolis, city of repute; its queen Glory, which for the Platonists was a third region besides Nature and Grace. His general aim is to change the reader, "to *fashion* a gentleman or noble person in vertuous and gentle discipline" (as he says in his letter to Ralegh)—the shaping aim of art, perfecting nature. His method is the "continued Allegory or darke conceit," polysemous like Dante's. The mode of its operation is clearly established in Book I: (*a*) Every chivalric romance (as G. K. Chesterton observed) has three characters, dragon, maiden (Una), and knight (Red Cross); to these add wicked magician (Archimago), witch and siren (Duessa doubling these roles), and dwarf; "Salvage Man"; estrangement and reunion, and rescue from danger by the bravest knight in the world (Arthur); and marriage. (*b*) The Red Cross knight's temptations and mistakes are Everyman's instruction as he journeys through life. (*c*) His device, "a bloudie Crosse. . . . The deare remembrance of his dying Lord," and the introductory letter's reference to the armour of the Christian warrior firmly place the dragon who keeps the parents of Una (who personifies Truth) out of their kingdom of Eden and who is vanquished in a three-day combat; add the rich imagery from the book of Revelation (commended to Spenser by Harvey as a poetic model in 1580), the Christian ethics taught in the House of Holiness, and the divine gracelike function of Prince Arthur. (*d*) The hero is the patron saint of England (Book I, canto 10, stanza 61), and the traditional pageantry of the cult of St. George is the source of Una's lamb, her arming of the Red Cross knight, and his twice-repeated revival during the fight. Arthur, the "Briton Knight," chief of the Nine Worthies, focuses this aspect of the poem, recalling the 16th-century myth of his reincarnation in the Tudor dynasty and the yearly impersonation in London of his company of knights. Modern impatience with the patriotic topicalities, ecclesiastical and political, throughout the poem, including its inspiration by the queen as by a muse, is a failure to recognize the apocalyptic light in which Spenser's countrymen saw the great conflict of their time between Protestant England and Catholic Spain. To him, as later to Milton, the war of Good and Evil was here and now.

Between the mid-17th century and Edward Dowden's 1882 essay (in *Transcripts and Studies,* 1888), the sage and serious poet whom Ben Jonson (like all his contemporaries) would have "read for his matter" was little regarded, and *The Faerie Queene,* his most important work, was misunderstood. Hazlitt assured the reader that if he doesn't meddle with the allegory the whole is as plain as a pikestaff. Lamb, however, sanest of Spenserian critics, saw that in the inner laws of Fairyland "we are at home and upon acquainted ground." Misunderstanding of the titles of the books is partly to blame for the chill some readers feel. Book I, called "Holiness," in fact tells the fable of sanctification and reenacts man's Fall and Redemption; Book II—Temperance—is the defense (under the guidance of a Palmer) of God's highest handiwork, man's body, which he hath tempered together like an artist and of which the harmonious architecture of the House of Alma is a gracious metaphor and the tinsel of the Bower of Bliss a travesty; the Legends of Chastity and Friendship (Books III and IV, the poem's core) are a single intricate exploration of love, lawful in Britomart, sterile and terrifying in Busirane's House, and fulfilled in the great images of Concord in Book IV, cantos 10–12—the Temple of Venus and the marriages of Thames and Medway and Florimel and Marinell; Concord, or hierarchy, is the basis of the Book of Justice (Book V); and Calidore's vision (Book VI, canto 10) of the Graces dancing to Colin's piping bodies forth that Heavenly Harmony of which Courtesy or "civilitie" (humble reverence for our diverse relations with others) is the earthly type. In the final fragment—the "mutability" cantos of Book VII, *The Legend of Constancy*—the Venuslike Christlike figure of Nature triumphs over change and decay by showing them to be part of the world's stability—"eterne in Mutabilitie."

Spenser deserves the often misunderstood title of "poet's poet" by being master of an art perfectly adapted and directed to its end: picture, music, metre, story, all indefeasibly one with their *significacio,* a moral heraldry of colours, emblems, legends, folklore, mythical allusion, all evoking deep instinctive responses. To enjoy the sensuous surface, to spell it out aright, is at once to take the "message,"or rather, not to accept a doctrine but to undergo an experience, an ascent in vision with the protagonists. The allegory is untranslatable. It is significant that the "Aristotelian" scheme of the "xii. private morall vertues" that the poem's 12 books were intended to expound (the epic number, by happy chance) lay ready to Spenser's hand in the many derivatives from Aquinas that dealt with princely and knightly instruction; and, on the other hand, the landmarks of his poem—castle, great house, forest, fountain, lake, hill—had been drenched in meaning by their use in pageant and interlude. Even the stanza he created aligns the poem with a long tradition; it is the finest of many 15th–17th century variants of Chaucer's "meetre heroicall," as George Puttenham called rime royal in 1589, by far the commonest measure between Chaucer and Sir Thomas Wyat, and used by Spenser himself in the *Ruines of Time* and the *Fowre Hymnes*.

To his contemporaries Spenser was "our only living Homer," "the Virgil of England," "our second Chaucer." He is in truth the English Dante.

Bibliography.—*Editions:* The Variorum edition of the Works, ed. by E. Greenlaw *et al.*, 9 vol. (1932–49; Index 1957) contains a summary of Spenserian scholarship and criticism. Other editions include the *Poetical Works*, ed. by J. C. Smith and E. de Selincourt, 3 vol. with textual notes (1909–10; 1 vol., with abridged notes, the Spenser-Harvey letters, and introduction, 1912); the *Works*, ed. by W. L. Renwick, 4 vol. (1928–34), omitting the *Faerie Queene* but including the *View of the State of Ireland;* the Cambridge edition, by R. E. N. Dodge (1908); and the Globe edition, by R. Morris and J. W. Hales (1869), which includes the *View*. . . .

*Spenserian Studies:* A. C. Judson, *The Life of Spenser* (1945), is included in the Variorum edition. Aids to Spenser studies include C. G. Osgood, *A Concordance to the Poems of Spenser* (1915); C. H. Whitman, *A Subject Index to the Poems of Edmund Spenser* (1918); F. I. Carpenter, *A Reference Guide to Edmund Spenser* (1923), supplement by D. F. Atkinson (1937); F. R. Johnson, *A Critical Bibliography of the Works of Spenser Printed Before 1700* (1933); H. S. V. Jones, *A Spenser Handbook* (1930); W. F. McNeir and F. Provost, *Annotated Bibliography of Edmund Spenser, 1937–1960* (1962). Critical studies include C. S. Lewis, *The Allegory of Love* (1936); A. C. Hamilton, *The Structure of Allegory in the Faerie Queene* (1961); E. Greenlaw, *Studies in Spenser's Historical Allegory* (1932); W. L. Renwick, *Spenser* (1925); J. W. Bennett, *The Evolution of the Faerie Queene* (1942); D. C. Allen and W. R. Mueller (eds.), *That Soueraine Light: Essays in Honor of Edmund Spenser, 1552–1952* (1952); R. Ellrodt, *Neoplatonism in the Poetry of Spenser* (1960); M. P. Parker, *The Allegory of the Faerie Queene* (1960); W. B. C. Watkins, *Shakespeare and Spenser* (1950); V. K. Whitaker, *The Religious Basis of Spenser's Thought* (1950); A. K. Hieatt, *Short Time's Endless Monument* (1960); W. R. Mueller (ed.), *Spenser's Critics* (1959); J. Wurtsbaugh, *Two Centuries of Spenserian Scholarship, 1609–1805* (1936); E. M. W. Tillyard, *The English Epic and Its Background* (1954); G. Hough, *A Preface to the Faerie Queene* (1962); T. P. Roche, *The Kindly Flame* (1964); A. Fowler, *Spenser and the Numbers of Time* (1964); W. Nelson, *The Poetry of Edmund Spenser* (1963), and (ed.), *Form and Convention in the Poetry of Edmund Spenser* (1961); H. Berger, *The Allegorical Temper* (1957); P. E. McLane, *Spenser's Shepheardes Calender* (1961).

(Jo. C. B.)

**SPENSERIAN STANZA,** a verse form so called from its invention by Edmund Spenser for his *Faerie Queene* (1590–1609). Its origin is disputed; Jakob Schipper derives it from the Old French ballade (*q.v.*), others from the Italian ottava rima (*q.v.*). Probably, however, its origin is Chaucer's eight-line *Monk's Tale* stanza, to which Spenser added a ninth line with an extra foot (alexandrine), thus making eight iambic pentameter lines and a ninth of six iambic feet. The rhyme scheme is *ababbcbcc*. Spenser's sonnet scheme is similar (*see* Sonnet).

The Spenserian stanza was seldom used in the 17th century though Giles and Phineas Fletcher made adaptations of it. In the 18th century it was revived by Mark Akenside in "The Virtuoso," William Shenstone in "The Schoolmistress," James Thomson in *The Castle of Indolence,* James Beattie in *The Minstrel,* and Burns in "The Cotter's Saturday Night." In the 19th century the Spenserian stanza was revived again by English poets of the Romantic movement—Byron in *Childe Harold's Pilgrimage,* Keats in "The Eve of St. Agnes," Shelley in *Adonais* and "The Revolt of Islam"—and by Tennyson in "The Lotus-Eaters." Oliver Wendell Holmes aptly described the Spenserian stanza in these verses:

> The sweet Spenserian, gathering as it flows,
> Sweeps gently onward to its dying close,
> Where waves on waves in long succession pour,
> Till the ninth billow melts along the shore; . . .

(G. W. A.)

**SPERANSKI, MIKHAIL MIKHAILOVICH,** Count (1772–1839), Russian statesman who renovated the structure of administration under the emperor Alexander I, was born at Cherkutino in the Vladimir region on Jan. 12 (new style; Jan. 1, old style), 1772, the son of the village priest. After rising to be professor of mathematics and physics in the ecclesiastical seminary in St. Petersburg, he entered the government service in 1797 and quickly attracted the attention of the tsarevitch Alexander. When the latter had become emperor as Alexander I (*q.v.*), Speranski was appointed secretary of state (1801) and put to work in the ministry of the interior, where he remained until 1807. In 1808 he accompanied Alexander to Erfurt for the conference with Napoleon, who described him as "the only clear head in Russia."

From 1809 to 1812 Speranski was all-powerful in Russia; he replaced the earlier favourites at court and was practically sole minister. Intelligent, honest, hardworking and blessed with a lucid style of writing, he started many projects (including one of a constitution, 1809) and gave concrete administrative shape to Alexander's early visionary ideals. Speranski's strength lay in his mastery of bureaucratic operation, in his genius for organization and administration. He streamlined procedure and clarified objectives already adopted; he put final touches on the organization of the ministries, the council of state and the Siberian administration. Yet at the same time he gave a direction to planning and furthering the development of a systematic national policy. Liberal in that he desired spiritual, moral and economic progress, Speranski willingly supported enlightened bureaucratic absolutism as the means of effecting the necessary reforms. An introvert who bridled the expression of his own opinions, he was thwarted in many of his projects as Alexander's liberalism faded.

Speranski's absorption in work and his social isolation left him exposed to the intrigues of enemies at court. On the eve of Napoleon's invasion of Russia, the grand duchess Catherine, N. M. Karamzin, F. V. Rostopchin and G. M. Armfelt involved him in a charge of treason. Although Alexander did not credit the charge, he had begun to fear that Speranski's realization of some of the measures that he himself had conceived might undermine his autocratic authority, and on March 29 (N.S.; 17, O.S.), 1812, he dismissed Speranski and exiled him (first to Nizhni Novgorod, then to Perm). In 1816, however, Speranski was reinstated in the public service as governor of Penza, and in 1819 he was appointed governor general of Siberia, for which he drew up a new scheme of government. In 1821 he was recalled to St. Petersburg and entered the council of state. The major productions of his last years were the complete *Collection of the Laws of the Russian Empire,* 45 vol. (1830), and the systematically co-ordinated *Digest of Laws,* 15 vol. (1832–39). Created count by the emperor Nicholas I in Jan. 1839, Speranski died a few weeks later, on Feb. 23 (N.S.; 11, O.S.), in St. Petersburg.

*See* Marc Raeff, *Michael Speransky, Statesman of Imperial Russia, 1772–1839* (1957) and *Siberia and the Reforms of 1822* (1956).

(G. A. Ln.)

**SPERMATOPHYTA** (Spermophyta), the name often used in botany to denote the seed plants, including the true flowering plants or angiosperms (*q.v.*) and the conifers and their allies or gymnosperms (*q.v.*).

**SPERRY, ELMER AMBROSE** (1860–1930), U.S. inventor, whose gyroscopic compasses and stabilizers greatly contributed to the safety and comfort of sea and air navigation, was born at Cortland, N.Y., on Oct. 12, 1860, and studied at Cornell University, Ithaca, N.Y. He began early to experiment with electric arc lights and in 1880 established a factory in Chicago to manufacture an improved model that was highly successful. He then invented the electric rotary and chain undercutting mining machines and other mining apparatus and established another factory to manufacture this machinery. He next designed an electric industrial locomotive and motor transmission machinery for streetcars. After 1900 he established a research laboratory in electrochemistry at Washington, D.C., where he invented the chlorine detinning process and a process for producing white lead from impure lead. In 1915 he produced his high-intensity arc searchlight.

Chief of Sperry's inventions related to the gyroscope (*q.v.*) is the gyrocompass (*q.v.*), first installed on the battleship "Delaware" in 1911. This compass, unaffected by iron and steel, entirely superseded the magnetic compass on submarines and battleships and was placed likewise on merchant ships. Sperry also designed and manufactured electrically sustained gyros for torpedoes. During World War I he developed aerial torpedoes with automatic gyrocontrol which proved effective at a range of 35 mi. Further experiments yielded the gyropilot for the steering of ships, the automatic gyropilot for stabilizing airplanes, the gyroscopic roll and pitch recorder for the testing of ships, and, finally, a gyroscopic ship stabilizer that was installed on a number of ships in the U.S., British, Italian, and Japanese navies. Sperry died at Brooklyn, June 16, 1930.

*See* "The Engineering and Scientific Achievements of Elmer A. Sperry," *Mech. Engng, N.Y.*, vol. xlix (1927). (S. C. Hr.)

**SPEUSIPPUS** (d. 339/338 B.C.), the successor of Plato as head of the Greek Academy (*see* Academy, Greek), was a nephew of Plato and had played a great part in his uncle's relations with Dionysius II of Syracuse and with Dion (*see* Plato). An extant letter from Speusippus to Philip of Macedon, in which he violently attacks Isocrates (his rival for Philip's favour), is further evidence of his political interests.

Of Speusippus' philosophical writings very little more than the titles survives, so that for knowledge of his doctrines we have to rely on reports and scanty fragments, the longest being from a work *On Pythagorean Numbers* (explaining such matters as the "perfections" of the number ten). He followed the lines of what Aristotle presented as Plato's doctrines; viz., the timeless derivation of all reality, intelligible and sensible, from two opposite principles, often called "the One" and "the indeterminate dyad" (the modern terms "constant" and "variable" perhaps convey somewhat similar notions), which were assumed to explain the presence of both unity and multiplicity in the universe. To this doctrine Speusippus gave a peculiar turn. Whereas other Academics assumed that "the One" and "the dyad" would also be principles of good and evil respectively and be so by being themselves good and evil, Speusippus denied that "the One" was good or "the dyad" evil; in the same context he also denied the identification of "the One" with the divine mind. Specifically, good and even being itself would appear only in the later stages of the derivative process mentioned above, so that "the One" would be no more than the germ of the good and of being and thus less than either. Such a doctrine would make Speusippus a kind of evolutionist (with the good as an end product). Yet the reports of Aristotle on which such an interpretation is based are perhaps ambiguous and misleading. There is indeed some evidence that what Speusippus meant was that "the One" is non-being in the same sense in which the Plotinian "One" is non-being; viz., by being the source of all being and thus superior to it. Another aspect of the same doctrine is the derivation of successive spheres of reality—with numbers (which exist independently from sensibles and which in Speusippus' doctrine take the place of Plato's ideas) and geometrical magnitudes as the first sphere or spheres and with sensibles as the last. "The One" and "the dyad" appear in each sphere in an appropriately different form, which Aristotle criticized as making the spheres mutually independent, so that Speusippus' universe looks like an incoherent tragedy consisting of episodes and lacking dramatic unity. According to Aristotle, between the spheres of mathematicals and of the sensible (body) Speusippus inserted the sphere of the soul. Iamblichus, however, reports that Speusippus defined the (world?-) soul as the idea (in the sense of "form") of what extends in all dimensions, which makes the soul a mathematical entity (geometrical form). In any case Speusippus in some way seems to have intimately connected the soul with mathematicals—as did Plato in the *Timaeus* and Xenocrates in defining the soul as self-changing number. As to individual souls, Speusippus asserted the immortality of the whole soul, not only of its reasonable parts.

On the whole, Aristotle is highly critical of Speusippus. Nevertheless, Speusippus' *Similitudes,* a kind of comparative anatomy or physiology of plants and animals, are comparable to Aristotle's *History of Animals*. Whether the *Similitudes* were ultimately empirical or logico-ontological is dubious; if the latter interpretation is the right one, the *Similitudes,* together with his classification of names into synonyms, homonyms, etc., may somehow have been connected with Speusippus' doctrine that no single thing can be defined unless all have been, since classification and definition are closely related.

In introducing the concept of "knowledgelike sensation," a concept related to problems in Plato's *Theaetetus,* Speusippus perhaps tried to soften the strict ontologico-epistemological dualism of Plato. (*See* Knowledge, Theory of: *Plato*.) Many scholars see in Speusippus the representative of strict antihedonism, discussed in Plato's *Philebus*. His definition of happiness as the perfection of one's natural condition tends to derive the norm of conduct from nature.

Bibliography.—For fragments and testimonies *see* P. Lang, *De Speusippi academici scriptis* (1911); E. Bickermann and J. Sykutris, "Brief an König Philipp," *Sächsische Akademie der Wissenschaften, Verhandlungen, philologisch-historische Klasse,* 80 (1927); Proclus' commentary on Plato's *Parmenides* as ed. by R. Klibansky and C. Labowsky (*Plato latinus*, iii, 1953). *See* further D. S. Margoliouth, *"Book of the Apple . . . ," Journal of the Royal Asiatic Society* (1892); E. Hambruch, *Logische Regeln der platonischen Schule . . .* (1904); E. Frank, *Plato und die sogenannten Pythagoreer* (1923); J. Stenzel, "Speusippos," Pauly-Wissowa, *Realencyclopädie der classischen Altertumswissenschaft,* 2nd series, iii, part 2 (1929); P. Merlan, *From Platonism to Neoplatonism,* 2nd ed. (1960), and "Zur Biographie des Speusippos," *Philologus,* 103 (1959); H. J. Krämer, *Der Ursprung der Geistmetaphysik* (1964). (Pp. M.)

**SPEY,** a river in Scotland, flows for 107 mi. (172 km.) in a mostly straight course northeast across the Highlands, north of the Grampians, and enters the Moray Firth between Buckie and Lossiemouth. It rises at about 1,150 ft. (350 m.) in the Corrieyairack Forest, 1 mi. W of the small Loch Spey and a few hundred yards from the west-flowing Roy-Spean-Lochy drainage. It is reputed to be one of the most rapid rivers in Scotland and is well known for salmon fishing. It flows mainly through an upland corridor between highland blocks, taking tributaries from the Monadhliath Hills, the Grampians, and the Cairngorms and draining much of southeast Inverness County, east Moray, and central and southern Banff County. The river swings between great sweeps of terraces it has cut among the hummocky glacial deposits, amid which are small lakes (Lochs Insh, Alvie, Garten, etc.) or drained lakes. The shingle spit across the shifting river mouth has been cut four times within a hundred years, and plans to make a fifth cut were approved in 1961. There are residues of the Scots pine-juniper forests; *e.g.,* in Rothiemurchus. Strathspey, the lower valley, was the home county of the Grants, with their slogan of "Stand fast Craigellachie" (a defensible hill bordering their part of the strath). (A. T. A. L.)

**SPEYER** (Spires), a town of West Germany in the *Land* (state) of Rhineland-Palatinate, Federal Republic of Germany, on the left bank of the Rhine, 16 mi. (26 km.) S of Ludwigshafen. Pop. (1961) 38,485. Remains include the Altpörtel (old gate) with a late Romanesque gate tower (13th century); the Jews' Bath with subterranean vaulting (*c.* 1100); parts of the 13th-century town walls; and the 18th-century Baroque Church of the Trinity. The Palatinate historical museum houses a unique wine museum. The Romanesque cathedral was founded in 1030 by the emperor Conrad II. Notable are the crypt and the imperial vault where eight German emperors and kings, three empresses, and a princess lie buried. The cathedral was gutted in 1689 and reconstructed from 1772 to 1784. It was again restored after World War II and reconsecrated in 1961.

The medieval city is surrounded by new industrial and residential areas. There is a college of administrative studies, the only one of its kind in the Federal Republic. A modern open-air swimming pool lies on the Rhine. Speyer is at the junction of the roads from Bonn to Karlsruhe and from Kaiserslautern to Heidelberg. The rebuilding (1956) of the Rhine bridge, destroyed in 1945, restored an important route across the Rhine. There is an electrotechnical industry, an oil refinery, metal and wood processing, printing, cotton spinning, and chemical and shoe manufactures. There are also stone, glass, and brick works, breweries, sparkling wine (*sekt*) cellars, and aircraft factories.

In 400 B.C. Speyer, known as Noviomagus, was the main Celtic settlement in the Palatinate. Under the Romans a castle was built on this site and a flourishing trading town grew up, only to be destroyed during the barbarian invasions. In the 13th century Speyer became a free imperial city, and 50 imperial diets were held there. The town was destroyed by French troops (1689) in the War of the Grand Alliance. In 1797 Speyer was incorporated into the French Republic. From 1816 to 1945 it was the capital of the Bavarian Palatinate. (Fz. S.; G. Gr.)

**SPEZIA, LA,** a city and seaport of Liguria, Italy, and headquarters of La Spezia Province, lies 70 mi. (113 km.) SE of Genoa (Genova) by road. Pop. (1961) 121,893 (commune). It is one of Italy's major naval bases and stands at the head of a gulf that provides good protection for ships. Most of the town's industries are connected with the sea; the shipbuilding yards are among the most important in Italy, and there are foundries and refineries. The naval arsenal was destroyed during World War II and has been rebuilt. Near it is a naval museum. Much of the city is modern, and there is a public park. The archaeological museum has a collection of menhirs cut in the form of human figures, and Roman remains from the ancient city of Luna. La Spezia is on the main railway and road from Genoa to Rome.

La Spezia was inhabited in Roman times, but little is known of its history before 1276, when it was sold to Genoa by the Fieschi. It became a maritime prefecture in the French Empire and then part of the Duchy of Genoa in the kingdom of Sardinia. After the transfer of the military fleet from Genoa in 1857, it became a naval headquarters.

La Spezia Province (area 341 sq.mi. [882 sq.km.]; pop. [1961] 237,808), formed in 1923, centres on the valley of the Vara River, which is surrounded by mountains of the Ligurian Apennines (Mt. Gottero, 5,380 ft. [1,640 m.]), and borders the provinces of Parma (north) and Massa-Carrara (east). The towns of Portovenere and Lerici, famous for their association with Byron and Shelley, stand on opposite sides of the Gulf of La Spezia, and the coast has holiday resorts. There is much forest; cultivation is mainly along the lower Magra River; and there is fishing. (C. Ti.)

**SPHALERITE** (Blende or Zincblende), a sulfide of zinc, is the chief ore of that metal. (For production and uses *see* Zinc.) Sphalerite, the commonest zinc mineral, and galena, the most abundant ore of lead, are intimately associated in most of the important deposits of these metals. The name derives from a Greek word for "treacherous," in allusion to the ease with which the dark-coloured, opaque varieties are mistaken for galena. The synonyms blende and zincblende, from the German word for "blind," similarly allude to the fact that it does not yield lead. Associates, in addition to galena, include chalcopyrite and pyrite among metallic minerals, and quartz, barite, dolomite, calcite and siderite as gangue minerals.

In the United States the most important deposits of sphalerite are found in the Mississippi valley region. There it occurs chiefly with chalcopyrite, galena, marcasite and dolomite in solution cavities and brecciated zones in limestone and chert. Similar deposits occur elsewhere—in the region of Silesia in Poland, the Moresnet district in Belgium and north Africa. Sphalerite also has world-wide distribution as an ore mineral in hydrothermal vein deposits, in contact metamorphic zones and in high-temperature replacement deposits. Crystals of outstanding beauty and perfection are found in cavities in a dolomite rock in the Binnenthal, Switz., and a transparent variety of a golden colour occurs at Picos de Europa, Santander, Spain. Fine specimens also come from Cornwall, Derbyshire and Cumberland in England, and from Bottino in Tuscany, Italy.

The crystal structure of sphalerite is based on a tetrahedral, four-co-ordinated framework of zinc and sulfur atoms in which the bonding is essentially covalent. The structure is similar to that of diamond, and may be imagined as derived therefrom by the alternate substitution of zinc and sulfur atoms for carbon. The unit cell dimension is 5.40 Å. The common crystal forms are the tetrahedron and the dodecahedron. The crystals frequently occur as simple or multiple contact twins, or as complicated lamellar intergrowths, in which the twin axis is [111]. Sphalerite ordinarily occurs in massive granular form, less commonly as fibrous aggregates with a layered structure or as dense microcrystalline masses. It has a well-developed dodecahedral cleavage, and the fracture is conchoidal. The hardness is 3.5 to 4, and the specific gravity of pure material is 4.0. The colour varies widely. Generally it is a shade of brown, but some sphalerite is green, yellow or, in crystals of high purity, almost colourless. Material containing iron is brownish-black or black. Sphalerite may fluoresce when irradiated with ultraviolet light or X-rays, and some specimens emit light when scratched with a sharp point (triboluminescence). According to the formula, ZnS, sphalerite contains 67.1% Zn and 32.9% S. Usually, however, it contains iron in solid solution up to a limit of about 26%, and both manganese and cadmium may be present in small amounts. (Cl. F.)

**SPHENE** (Titanite) is a titanium-bearing mineral consisting of calcium titanosilicate. Sphene crystals vary considerably in habit, but are generally thin and wedge shaped; hence the name, from a Greek word for "a wedge." The colour is green, yellow, brown or black, and the lustre resinous to adamantine. Crystals, which are monoclinic, are transparent to opaque. The composition is $CaTiSiO_5$; hardness is 5.5; specific gravity 3.5. Sphene is cut as a gem stone, though it is too soft to stand much wear; because of its high dispersive power it gives brilliant flashes of prismatic colours. As small crystals, it is found in igneous rocks (granite, syenite, trachyte, phonolite, etc.) and in gneiss, schist, crystalline limestone and pegmatite.

**SPHENOPSIDA,** a class (or subphylum) of early spore-bearing vascular plants whose sole living genus, *Equisetum,* composes the horsetails. The group flourished as trees, *e.g., Calamites* species, during the Carboniferous Period but appeared as early as the Lower Devonian. In its fossil history it is believed to have constituted a larger portion of the flora of the earth than at the present time. Other fossil genera were possibly shrublike (*Calamophyton*) or vinelike (*Sphenophyllum*).

Horsetails are worldwide in distribution except for certain parts of Australia. The majority of the 30 living species occur in the Northern Hemisphere and are generally found in wet or damp habitats, although some species have become adapted to drier conditions. Some botanists recognize six different orders in the class; others restrict the class to four orders. There is only one order, Equisetales, that has both living and extinct species; all others comprise extinct sphenopsids. Sphenopsids, fossil and living, characteristically have whorled leaves and conspicuously jointed stems. In certain orders the stems show longitudinal ribs. When branches do occur, they develop in alternating radii with the leaves. This arrangement is known in no other group of living plants, for elsewhere buds usually arise in the axils of leaves.

The horsetails, like other vascular plants, have an alternation

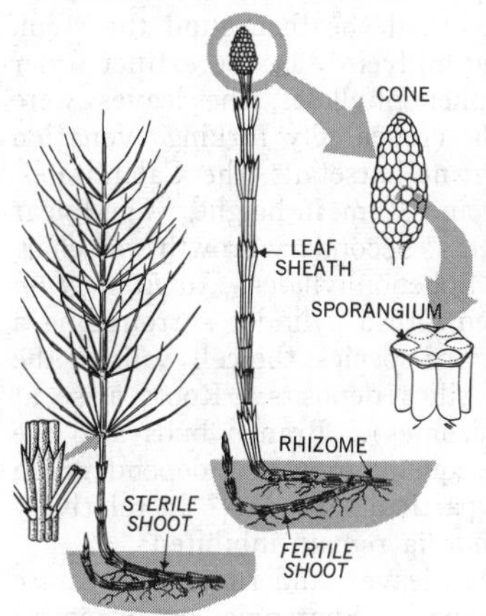


(ABOVE) FROM A. CRONQUIST, "INTRODUCTORY BOTANY"; HARPER & BROS.; (RIGHT) ROCHE

A COMMON HORSETAIL (EQUISETUM ARVENSE) WITH CONE-SHAPED REPRODUCTIVE AND BRANCHED VEGETATIVE SHOOTS

of generations: an asexual phase, represented by a sporophyte (the horsetail plant, as commonly known), and a sexual phase, the gametophyte, or prothallus, an inconspicuous, delicate, green plant. Each year thousands of prothallia are probably initiated from spores, but very few survive in nature because they are killed by direct exposure to sunlight. In the United States they have been found on the shaded side of deep-cut streams or in abandoned quarries. Horsetails apparently survived as a small group of very ancient plants mainly by vegetative reproduction rather than by a regular dependence on an alternation of sexual and asexual generations. It is assumed that fossil members had an alternation of generations, although only sporophytes have been described for them.

Generally, horsetails are 30 in. or less in height. In the tropics, however, taller species are known. Accounts are given of specimens of *Equisetum giganteum* of the American tropics that attain heights of 10–12 yd. but that have a diameter of less than an inch. By contrast, a Mexican species 2 yd. in height may have a diameter of up to 4 in. The internodes are ridged and grooved. In certain living species (*E. arvense, E. telmateia,* etc.) the whorled leaves are arranged in a toothed sheath but are without chlorophyll; photosynthesis is accomplished in the green stems.

The horsetails have had little economic importance. In years past they have been used for scouring dishes and utensils of diverse kinds; their cleaning value is attributed to the silica in the walls of the epidermal cells. Undoubtedly, the scouring rushes, as certain species were known, were beneficial in removing tarnish and dust from metallic surfaces, but the silica is equally hard on the metal itself.

In reproduction, some horsetails have terminal, conelike strobili on aerial branches that later become vegetative. Other species, however, have separate, upright, aerial branches for vegetative and for reproductive shoots. In the latter, the strobilate branches appear first, and after the spores are shed, the green, vegetative shoots develop. Fertile appendages are whorled; each consists of a stalk bearing a flattened disk at its apex, on the inner side of which is found a cycle of sporangia, each opening and shedding spores by a longitudinal slit on its inner side. (The Carboniferous, treelike horsetails and their sphenopsid allies are believed to have possessed the most elaborate reproductive strobili known among the vascular plants.) The delicate spores, under low light intensity, grow into small (up to 3 cm. in diameter), flattened, green bisexual prothallia with upright lobes. The outer spore wall regularly breaks into four bands, which are hygroscopic and so coil and uncoil with moisture changes. Entangled by bands, the spores are frequently shed in clusters.

The slender, herbaceous stems of *Equisetum* have hollow internodes; the whorled leaves are greatly reduced and are united laterally at each node to form a toothed sheath around the stem. Each leaf has a single unbranched midvein. In the extinct order of climbing sphenopsids, the Sphenophyllales, the leaves were wedge shaped with a dichotomous (repeatedly forking) venation system. Species of the extinct giant horsetails, the Calamitales, were trees up to 1 m. in diameter and 30 m. in height. The linear leaves were whorled in arrangement. Secondary growth was characteristic of the Calamitales and Sphenophyllales. In *Equisetum* the vascular strands are organized into a cylinder surrounding a large pith cavity. In the majority of species, the cell walls of the epidermis are thick and contain silica deposits. Roots arise at nodes of underground stems (rhizomes). Branch buds also are initiated at nodes, but their subsequent growth is dependent on the growth characteristics of the particular species. In relatively unbranched species, the bud primordia remain inhibited.

The sporophyte consists of stem, leaves, and roots; spores are produced in spore cases, or sporangia. Sporangia are borne on special stalked structures termed sporangiophores. The latter are organized into strobili associated with sterile bracts (Sphenophyllales, Calamitales) or without them (Hyeniales, Equisetales). Each sporangium in *Equisetum* has five to ten recurved sporangia. The entire sporangiophore appears to be a condensed dichotomous branch system, each sporangium occupying the end of a branch but lying parallel to the stalk of the sporangiophore. Eggs are produced in archegonia, at the bases of the upright lobes on the small gametophytes, and sperm are produced in antheridia, present on the lobes. The egg is fertilized in the archegonium by a multiflagellate sperm; then the zygote, by continued divisions, forms an embryo within the archegonium. The embryo (young sporophyte) is nourished by the gametophyte until it develops its own shoot and roots. One gametophyte may support two or more young sporophytes before it ultimately dies and decays.

The report of a chromosome number of about 216 for a horsetail sporophyte gives some support to the contention that the genus *Equisetum* is the end of a long line of specialization and possibly represents the oldest living genus of vascular plants.

*See* also PALEOBOTANY; TRACHEOPHYTA. (E. M. GI.)

**SPHERE,** in Greek geometry, the solid generated by the revolution of a semicircle about its diameter as an axis. In modern elementary geometry it is more generally considered as the spherical surface so generated, or as the locus of points at a constant distance from a fixed point called the centre. The constant distance is called a radius, and any line segment through the centre and limited at both ends by the sphere is called a diameter. Any section made by a plane cutting a sphere is a circle, called a great circle if the plane passes through the centre, and otherwise a small circle. The solid cut off by the plane of a great circle is a hemisphere; that cut off by the plane of a small circle, a segment. In analytic geometry the equation of a sphere in rectangular Cartesian coordinates with centre at the origin is $x^2 + y^2 + z^2 = a^2$, where $a$ is the radius, and in polar coordinates it is $r = a$. If the centre is $(\alpha, \beta, \gamma)$, the Cartesian equation becomes

$$(x - \alpha)^2 + (y - \beta)^2 + (z - \gamma)^2 = a^2$$

The surface area of a sphere is $4\pi r^2$, and the volume is $\frac{4}{3}\pi r^3$. *See* ANALYTIC GEOMETRY; CIRCLE; SOLIDS, GEOMETRIC; SURFACES; TRIGONOMETRY.

**SPHERE OF INFLUENCE,** a diplomatic term that signifies a claim by a state to exclusive control within a foreign territory. This control can be economic, military, or political, or it may concern the overall government of the territory. The territory that is made the object of a sphere of influence may be either politically unorganized, as were some of the African territories that were transformed into spheres of influence toward the end of the 19th century, or it may be under the sovereignty of a weak government, as were, for instance, Morocco, Ethiopia, and Persia when they were divided into spheres of influence at the beginning of the 20th century. The term may refer to a political claim to exclusive control, which other nations may or may not recognize as a matter of fact, or it may refer to a legal agreement by which another state or states pledge themselves to refrain from interference within the sphere of influence.

It is in the latter, legal significance that the term first gained currency in the 1880s when the colonial expansion of the European powers in Africa and Asia was nearing its completion. The last stage of that expansion was characterized by the endeavour of all major colonial powers to carry on the mutual competition for colonies peacefully through agreed-upon procedures. Agreements on spheres of influence served this purpose. Thus, the agreement between Great Britain and Germany in May 1885, the first to make use of the term, provided for "a separation and definition of their respective spheres of influence in the territories on the Gulf of Guinea." In it "Great Britain engages not to make acquisitions of territory, accept Protectorates, or interfere with the extension of German influence in that part of the coast and interior of Guinea which lies east of" a defined line. "Germany engages not to make acquisitions, accept Protectorates, or interfere with the extension of British influence in that part of the coast and interior of Guinea which lies between the line as above described . . . and the British Colony of Lagos. Both Powers agree to withdraw all Protectorates which they have already established within the limits hereafter assigned to the other party . . . Germany declares herself ready . . . to refrain from making acquisitions of territory or establishing Protectorates on the coast between the Colony of Natal and Delagoa Bay."

This agreement was followed by many of a similar nature, of

which article vii of the agreement between Great Britain and Germany of July 1, 1890, concerning East Africa may be regarded as typical. Its text is as follows: "The two Powers engage that neither will interfere with any sphere of influence assigned to the other by Articles I to IV. One Power will not in the sphere of the other make acquisitions, conclude Treaties, accept sovereign rights or Protectorates, nor hinder the extension of influence of the other. It is understood that no Companies nor individuals subject to one Power can exercise sovereign rights in a sphere assigned to the other, except with the assent of the latter."

Agreements of this type concerned territories politically unorganized and therefore subject to occupation by whatever nation complied with the rules of international law relative to the acquisition of unoccupied territory. Agreements of another type, often called spheres of interest, refer to territories that are already politically organized and are to be transformed into a sphere of influence of one of the contracting parties. This type is exemplified by article ii of the Anglo-French agreement of April 8, 1904, concerning Morocco. It provided: "The Government of the French Republic declare that they have no intention of altering the political status of Morocco. His Britannic Majesty's Government, for their part, recognize that it appertains to France, more particularly as a Power whose dominions are conterminous for a great distance with those of Morocco, to preserve order in that country, and to provide assistance for the purpose of all administrative, economic, financial, and military reforms which it may require. They declare that they will not obstruct the action taken by France for this purpose. . . ."

Of the legal effects of such agreements, three are worthy of note. First, agreements establishing spheres of influence create rights and obligations between the contracting parties only. States that are not parties to the agreement are legally free to acquire within the sphere of influence whatever rights they can; they have, however, for political reasons generally refrained from interference and acted as though they, too, were bound by the agreement. Second, such agreements do not affect by themselves the actual control over the territories concerned. So long as the state in whose favour a sphere of influence has been established chooses not to exercise its exclusive rights within that sphere, the actual control over it remains in the hands of those who exercised it when the agreement was concluded. Third, once the state in whose favour a sphere of influence has been established makes use of its rights within that sphere, all states, whether or not they are parties to the agreement, are excluded from the territory to the extent that the former state exercises actual control.

When colonial expansion came to a close with World War I, spheres of influence in the legal sense lost much of their importance. From then on, the term was used more for the unilateral political claims of great powers to a predominant position in the territories of other nations, especially those adjacent to their own. Thus, it can be said that the Monroe Doctrine, especially in its application since the presidency of Theodore Roosevelt, established the Western Hemisphere as a sphere of influence for the United States. In the aftermath of World War II, the Soviet Union created a sphere of influence as a political fact in the territories of the nations of eastern Europe and of the Balkans, with the exception of Greece (and later Yugoslavia). The political division of the Balkans into spheres of influence in the political sense was foreshadowed in the agreements concluded between Great Britain and the Soviet Union in 1944 and on the face of it was intended only to facilitate military operations and not to outlast the war. These agreements were opposed by U.S. Secretary of State Cordell Hull, who was not "a believer in the idea of balance of power or spheres of influence as a means of keeping the peace" (from Cordell Hull, *The Memoirs of Cordell Hull*, vol. ii, p. 1452, copyright 1948 by Cordell Hull, the Macmillan Company, 1948). The intervention of the United States in Santo Domingo in 1965 was justified by some observers on the ground that the island lay within the U.S. sphere of influence. Regardless of one's evaluation, it seems that spheres of influence in the political sense are an inevitable concomitant of the struggle for power among sovereign nations. *See* INTERNATIONAL LAW, PUBLIC; MONROE DOCTRINE.

*See* Frederick L. Schuman, "Regionalism and Spheres of Influence," in Hans J. Morgenthau (ed.), *Peace, Security and the United Nations* (1946). (H. J. MU.)

**SPHERICAL HARMONICS** are special mathematical functions that find application in mathematical physics to theories of gravitation, electricity and magnetism, fluid motion, and other fields; in geometry to the theory of surfaces; and in mathematical analysis to some classes of partial differential equations. They were named spherical harmonics by Lord Kelvin.

The gravitational potential in a portion of space free of masses, the electrostatic potential in a portion of space free of electric charges, and many other physical variables $R$ satisfy Laplace's equation

$$\Delta R = \frac{\partial^2 R}{\partial x^2} + \frac{\partial^2 R}{\partial y^2} + \frac{\partial^2 R}{\partial z^2} = 0 \qquad (1)$$

Solutions of equation (1) are known as harmonic functions (*see* DIFFERENTIAL EQUATIONS, PARTIAL; FUNCTION: *Analytic Functions of a Complex Variable*). A (solid) spherical harmonic (of degree $n$) is a homogeneous harmonic function of the Cartesian coordinates $x$, $y$, $z$. If the spherical coordinates $r$, $\theta$, $\phi$ are introduced by

$$x = r \sin\theta \cos\phi,\ y = r \sin\theta \sin\phi,\ z = r \cos\theta$$

a spherical harmonic $R_n$ of degree $n$ can be expressed in the form $R_n\,(x, y, z) = r^n S_n\,(\theta, \phi)$, where $S_n$ satisfies the partial differential equation

$$\frac{\partial^2 S}{\partial \theta^2} + \cot\theta \frac{\partial S}{\partial \theta} + \csc^2\theta \frac{\partial^2 S}{\partial \phi^2} + n(n+1)\,S = 0 \qquad (2)$$

and is known as a spherical surface harmonic of degree $n$. All spherical surface harmonics are homogeneous functions of degree zero of the Cartesian coordinates $x$, $y$, $z$.

If $R_n(x,y,z)$ is a spherical harmonic of degree $n$, then $(x^2 + y^2 + z^2)^{-n-\frac{1}{2}}\,R_n(x,y,z)$ is a spherical harmonic of degree $-n-1$. Solid spherical harmonics are closely related to Laplace's equation; spherical surface harmonics arise in connection with a variety of partial differential equations. They arise in connection with Laplace's equation not only in spherical but also in spheroidal and confocal coordinates (spheroidal harmonics and ellipsoidal surface harmonics, respectively). In the latter case their occurrence is due to the circumstance that the natural affine mapping of an ellipsoid onto a sphere carries the partial differential equation of ellipsoidal surface harmonics into equation (2). In spherical coordinates, spherical surface harmonics arise not only in connection with equation (1) but also in connection with: Poisson's equation $\Delta V = f\,(x,y,z)$, where $f$ is a given function; the equation $\Delta V + f(r)V = 0$, where $f$ is a given function depending only on $r$, and where special solutions of the partial differential equation have the form $F(r)S_n(\theta,\phi)$, with $F$ satisfying the ordinary differential equation

$$\frac{d^2F}{dr^2} + \frac{2}{r}\frac{dF}{dr} + \left[f(r) - \frac{n(n+1)}{r^2}\right]F = 0$$

while $S_n$ satisfies equation (2); the wave equation

$$c^2 \Delta V = \frac{\partial^2 V}{\partial t^2}$$

governing wave motion in many physical theories; the diffusion equation

$$k\Delta V = \frac{\partial V}{\partial t}$$

governing conduction of heat as well as many other diffusion processes; Schrödinger's equation in quantum mechanics (*q.v.*); and other partial differential equations.

There are spherical harmonics in spaces of several dimensions, but this discussion will be restricted to the most important class of spherical harmonics: those for which $n$ is a nonnegative integer and $R_n(x,y,z)$ is a homogeneous polynomial (of degree $n$). In this case, the corresponding spherical surface harmonic $S_n(\theta,\phi)$ is a polynomial (*q.v.*) in $\cos\theta$, $\sin\theta$, $\cos\phi$, and $\sin\phi$.

**Properties of Spherical Harmonics.**—The integral

$$\int_{-\pi}^{\pi} g(x \cos u + y \sin u + iz, u)\, du$$

represents a general solution of Laplace's equation (E. T. Whittaker, 1902). In particular, with an integrable function $f(u)$,

$$\int_{-\pi}^{\pi} (x \cos u + y \sin u + iz)^n f(u)\, du \tag{3}$$

represents a polynomial spherical harmonic of degree $n$, and every such spherical harmonic can be represented in the form of integral (3). The representation is not unique.

Let $c_n$ be a constant, let $h_1, h_2, \ldots, h_n$ be $n$ directions in space (not necessarily distinct), and let $\frac{\partial}{\partial h}$ denote directional differentiation in the direction $h$. Then

$$c_n r^{2n+1} \frac{\partial^n}{\partial h_1 \partial h_2 \ldots \partial h_n} \frac{1}{r} \tag{4}$$

represents a polynomial spherical harmonic of degree $n$, and every such spherical harmonic can be represented in this form. The representation is essentially unique. A curve on the unit sphere at the points of which a spherical harmonic (or the corresponding surface harmonic) vanishes is known as a nodal line of that spherical harmonic (surface harmonic). If the $n$ directions in spherical harmonic (4) coincide, the system of nodal lines consists of $n$ circles of latitude that divide the unit sphere into zones; this is a zonal spherical harmonic. If the $n$ directions are situated in a plane at angles of $\pi/n$, there are $n$ nodal circles of longitude that divide the sphere into sectors, and the corresponding spherical harmonics are known as sectorial spherical harmonics.

Lastly, if $n - m$ directions coincide in a direction that is known as the axis, and the remaining $m$ directions are situated in the plane that is perpendicular to the axis and are at angles $\pi/m$, then there are $m$ nodal circles of longitude and $n - m$ nodal circles of latitude that divide the sphere into spherical rectangles, and the corresponding harmonics are known as tesseral spherical harmonics.

Any linear combination of spherical harmonics of a fixed degree $n$ is again a spherical harmonic of that degree. There are $2n + 1$ linearly independent (polynomial) spherical harmonics of degree $n$. One set of $2n + 1$ linearly independent spherical harmonics whose axis is the $z$ axis is given by

$$R_n^{\pm m}(x,y,z) = r^n S_n^{\pm m}(\theta,\phi) = \frac{(-1)^{n-m}}{(n-m)!} r^{2n+1} \frac{\partial^{n-m}}{\partial z^{n-m}} \left(\frac{\partial}{\partial x} \pm i \frac{\partial}{\partial y}\right)^m \frac{1}{r} \tag{5}$$

where $m = 0, 1, \ldots, n$ and either upper or lower signs must be taken throughout equation (5). $R_n^m \pm R_n^{-m}$ is a zonal, sectorial, or tesseral harmonic according as $m = 0$, $m = n$, or $1 \leqq m \leqq n - 1$. Any polynomial spherical harmonic of degree $n$ can be represented uniquely as a linear combination of the $2n + 1$ functions of equation (5).

Any solution of equation (1) that is twice continuously differentiable inside a sphere around the origin can be expanded (inside that sphere) in an infinite series $\sum_{n=0}^{\infty} r^n S_n(\theta,\phi)$. Any solution of equation (1) that is twice continuously differentiable outside a sphere about the origin and that vanishes at infinity can be expanded (outside that sphere) in an infinite series $\sum_{n=0}^{\infty} r^{-n-1} S_n(\theta,\phi)$. In both cases, the expansions are unique.

The spherical coordinates $\theta,\phi$ determine a point on the unit sphere. For two functions $f$ and $g$ on the unit sphere there can be defined a scalar product

$$(f,g) = \int_0^{\pi} \int_{-\pi}^{\pi} f(\theta,\phi) \bar{g}(\theta,\phi) \sin \theta\, d\theta\, d\phi$$

where $\bar{g}$ is the complex conjugate of $g$. These two functions are said to be orthogonal if $(f,g) = 0$. Spherical surface harmonics are functions on the unit sphere. Any two spherical surface harmonics of different degrees are orthogonal. The spherical surface harmonics $S_n^m(\theta,\phi)$; $m = -n, -n + 1, \ldots, n$; $n = 0, 1, 2, \ldots$, defined by equation (5) form an orthogonal system (*see* FOURIER SERIES: *Orthogonal Series*) in the sense that $(S_n^m, S_{n'}^{m'}) = 0$ unless $m = m'$ and $n = n'$. This orthogonal system is complete in the sense that a continuous function (on the unit sphere) that is orthogonal to all the $S_n^m$ vanishes identically. With any integrable function $f$ on the unit sphere is associated the Laplace expansion

$$\sum_{n=0}^{\infty} \sum_{m=-n}^{n} C_{mn} S_n^m(\theta,\phi) \text{ where } C_{mn} = \frac{(f, S_n^m)}{(S_n^m, S_n^m)}$$

Under suitable conditions (for instance, if $f$ is continuous and continuously differentiable on the unit sphere), the Laplace expansion will converge to $f$.

Let

$$\cos \gamma = \cos \theta \cos \theta_0 + \sin \theta \sin \theta_0 \cos (\phi - \phi_0) \tag{6}$$

be the spherical distance of the two points $(\theta,\phi)$ and $(\theta_0,\phi_0)$ on the unit sphere, and let $K(w)$ be a fixed function that is continuous for $-1 \leqq w \leqq 1$. Then every spherical surface harmonic satisfies

$$\int_0^{\pi} \int_{-\pi}^{\pi} K(\cos \gamma)\, S_n(\theta,\phi) \sin \theta\, d\theta\, d\phi = \lambda_n S_n(\theta_0,\phi_0)$$

where $n$ is the degree of $S_n$,

$$\lambda_n = 2\pi \int_{-1}^{1} K(w) P_n(w)\, dw$$

and $P_n(w)$ is the Legendre polynomial of degree $n$ (*see* below).

**Legendre Polynomials.**—The reciprocal distance of the two points $(x,y,z)$ and $(0,0,1)$ is a solution of equation (1) that is infinitely differentiable inside the unit sphere; it therefore has an expansion in spherical harmonics that is convergent inside the sphere. In terms of the spherical coordinates $r,\theta,\phi$ of the point $(x,y,z)$ the expansion clearly does not contain $\phi$ and hence is of the form

$$\frac{1}{\sqrt{1 - 2r \cos \theta + r^2}} = \sum_{n=0}^{\infty} r^n P_n(\cos \theta), \text{ where } r < 1 \tag{7}$$

It turns out that $P_n(\cos \theta)$ is a zonal spherical surface harmonic that is a polynomial of degree $n$ in $\cos \theta$. $P_n(\cos \theta)$ is called the Legendre polynomial of degree $n$. Substituting equation (7) in equation (1), it is seen that $P_n(w)$ satisfies Legendre's equation

$$(1 - w^2) \frac{d^2P}{dw^2} - 2w \frac{dP}{dw} + n(n + 1)P = 0 \tag{8}$$

and indeed can be characterized as that solution of equation (8) that is equal to unity when $w = 1$. An explicit representation of the Legendre polynomial is furnished either by Rodrigues' formula

$$P_n(w) = \frac{1}{2^n n!} \frac{d^n}{dw^n} (w^2 - 1)^n$$

or by Laplace's integral

$$P_n(\cos \theta) = \frac{1}{2\pi} \int_{-\pi}^{\pi} (\cos \theta + i \sin \theta \sin u)^n du$$

There are also numerous explicit representations in terms of hypergeometric series (*see* FUNCTIONS, SPECIAL).

All $n$ zeroes of $P_n(w)$ are simple, real, and between $-1$ and 1. The Legendre polynomials form an orthogonal system on the interval $(-1, 1)$,

$$\int_{-1}^{1} P_n(w)\, P_{n'}(w)\, dw = \begin{cases} 0 & \text{if } n \neq n' \\ \dfrac{1}{n + \frac{1}{2}} & \text{if } n = n' \end{cases}$$

This orthogonal system is complete, and with every integrable function $f(w)$, $-1 \leqq w \leqq 1$, there is associated a Legendre series

$$\sum_{n=0}^{\infty} c_n P_n(w) \text{ where } c_n = (n + \tfrac{1}{2}) \int_{-1}^{1} f(t)\, P_n(t)\, dt$$

The series converges to $f(w)$ under suitable conditions.

$P_n(w)$ is an even or odd function of $w$ according as $n$ is even or odd. Legendre polynomials of different degrees are connected by numerous functional relations, including

$$(2n+1)\,w\,P_n(w) = (n+1)\,P_{n+1}(w) + nP_{n-1}(w)$$

$$(w^2-1)\,\frac{dP_n(w)}{dw} = (n+1)\,P_{n+1}(w) - (n+1)\,wP_n(w)$$

$$= nw\,P_n(w) - nP_{n-1}(w)$$

The complete solution of Legendre's equation is $aP_n(w) + bQ_n(w)$, where $a$ and $b$ are constants, and

$$Q_n(w) = P_n(w)\int_w^\infty \frac{1}{t^2-1}\,\frac{1}{[P_n(t)]^2}\,dt$$

is the Legendre function of the second kind.

**Associated Legendre Functions.**—It can be shown that the spherical surface harmonics defined in equation (5) are of the form

$$S_n^{\pm m}(\theta,\phi) = P_n^m(\cos\theta)\,e^{\pm im\phi} \qquad (9)$$

where $P_n^m(\cos\theta)$ is $\sin^m\theta$ multiplied by a polynomial in $\cos\theta$ of degree $n-m$ and is called an associated Legendre function of degree $n$ and order $m$. Substituting equation (9) in equation (2), it is seen that $P_n^m(w)$ satisfies the associated Legendre equation

$$(1-w^2)\frac{d^2P}{dw^2} - 2w\frac{dP}{dw} + \left[n(n+1) - \frac{m^2}{1-w^2}\right]P = 0$$

Associated Legendre functions can be expressed in terms of Legendre polynomials in the form

$$P_n^m(w) = (-1)^m\,(1-w^2)^{m/2}\,\frac{d^mP_n(w)}{dw^m} \qquad (10)$$

and in particular, $P_n^0(w) = P_n(w)$.

Explicit representations and many properties of associated Legendre functions follow readily from corresponding properties of Legendre polynomials by means of equation (10). In particular, the only zeros of $P_n^m(w)$ are $n-m$ real simple zeros between $-1$ and 1; furthermore, $w = \pm 1$ if $m \geqq 1$. For fixed $m$, associated Legendre functions form an orthogonal system and

$$\int_{-1}^{1} P_n^m(w)\,P_{n'}^m(w)\,dw = \begin{cases} 0 & \text{if } n \neq n' \\ \dfrac{1}{n+\frac{1}{2}}\,\dfrac{(n+m)!}{(n-m)!} & \text{if } n = n' \end{cases}$$

Associated Legendre functions arise also in the addition theorem of Legendre polynomials,

$$P_n(\cos\gamma) = P_n(\cos\theta)\,P_n(\cos\theta_0) + \sum_{m=1}^{n}\frac{(n-m)!}{(n+m)!}\,P_n^m(\cos\theta)\,P_n^m(\cos\theta_0)\cos m(\phi-\phi_0)$$

where $\cos\gamma$ is given by equation (6).

A general solution of the associated Legendre equation can be given as $aP_n^m(w) + bQ_n^m(w)$, where

$$Q_n^m(w) = (1-w^2)^{\frac{1}{2}m}\,\frac{d^mQ_n(w)}{dw^m}$$

is the associated Legendre function of the second kind.

Legendre functions and associated Legendre functions exist also for general (not necessarily integral) values of $n$ and $m$; these are connected with nonpolynomial spherical harmonics and will not be discussed here.

**Rotations.**—A rotation of three-dimensional space can be characterized by three angles called the Euler angles; $R(\alpha, \beta, \gamma)$ denotes the rotation characterized by the angles $\alpha$, $\beta$, $\gamma$. All rotations of three-dimensional space form a group $R(3)$ (*see* GROUPS). For each natural number $n = 1, 2, 3, \ldots$, $R(3)$ has exactly one irreducible representation of dimension $n$. (A representation of a group is a mapping of the group onto a group of matrices so that multiplication is preserved in the mapping. Such a representation is reduced if the matrices can be partitioned in such a manner that the block in the upper right-hand corner is the zero matrix; and the representation is irreducible if it cannot be transformed into a set of reduced matrices by a [fixed] similarity transformation. The number of rows in each of the matrices involved in the representation is called the dimension of the representation.) The irreducible representation $\Gamma_j$ of dimension $2j+1$, $j = 0, 1/2, 1, 3/2, \ldots$ maps the rotation $R(\alpha, \beta, \gamma)$ into the matrix whose element in the $m$th row and $m'$th column is

$$D^j_{mm'}(\alpha,\beta,\gamma) = \left[\frac{(j+m)!\,(j-m)!}{(j+m')!\,(j-m')!}\right]^{\frac{1}{2}} e^{i(m\alpha+m'\gamma)} \times (\cos\tfrac{1}{2}\beta)^{m+m'}\,(\sin\tfrac{1}{2}\beta)^{m-m'}\,P^{(m-m',\,m+m')}_{j-m}(\cos\beta)$$

Here $m,m' = j, j-1, j-2, \ldots, -j$, and

$$P^{(a,b)}_n(x) = \frac{(-1)^n}{2^n n!}(1-x)^{-a}(1+x)^{-b}\frac{d^n}{dx^n}[(1-x)^{a+n}(1+x)^{b+n}]$$

is Jacobi's polynomial. These matrix elements can be shown to be four-dimensional spherical surface harmonics.

The representations of odd dimensions $2n+1$, $n = 0, 1, 2, \ldots$ are generated by the normalized spherical surface harmonics

$$Y_n^m(\theta,\phi) = (-1)^m\left[\frac{2n+1}{4\pi}\,\frac{(n-m)!}{(n+m)!}\right]^{\frac{1}{2}} S_n^m(\theta,\phi)$$

$$m = 0,1,2,\ldots$$

$$Y_n^m(\theta,\phi) = \left[\frac{2n+1}{4\pi}\,\frac{(n+m)!}{(n-m)!}\right]^{\frac{1}{2}} S_n^m(\theta,\phi)$$

$$m = -1, -2, \ldots$$

in the sense that

$$Y_n^m(\theta',\phi') = \sum_{m'=-n}^{n} D^n_{mm'}(\alpha,\beta,\gamma)\,Y_n^{m'}(\theta,\phi)$$

if the rotation $R(\alpha, \beta, \gamma)$ carries the point $(\theta',\phi')$ on the unit sphere into the point $(\theta,\phi)$.

Define the direct sum of two matrices, $A = [a_{kl}]$ of order $M$ and $B = [b_{rs}]$ of order $N$, as the partitioned matrix

$$\begin{bmatrix} A & 0 \\ 0 & B \end{bmatrix}$$

of order $M+N$, and the Kronecker product $A \times B$ (*see* ALGEBRAS, [LINEAR]) as that matrix of order $MN$ whose element in the row labeled $kr$ and the column labeled $ls$ is $a_{kl}b_{rs}$. This underlies the Clebsch-Gordan expansion, stating that the direct product of the irreducible representations of dimensions $n$ and $n'$ is similar to the direct sum of all the irreducible representations whose dimensions $n''$ satisfy $|n-n'| \leqq n'' \leqq n+n'$. The elements of the similarity transformation involved here are the Clebsch-Gordan coefficients.

BIBLIOGRAPHY.—P. Appell and J. Kampé de Fériet, *Fonctions hypergéometriques et hypersphériques* (1926); A. Erdélyi (ed.), *Higher Transcendental Functions*, 3 vol. (1953–55); E. W. Hobson, *The Theory of Spherical and Ellipsoidal Harmonics* (1955); J. Lense, *Kugelfunktionen* (1950); T. M. MacRobert, *Spherical Harmonics*, 2nd rev. ed. (1948); Ganesh Prasad, *A Treatise on Spherical Harmonics and the Functions of Bessel and Lamé*, 2 vol. (1930–32); L. Robin, *Fonctions sphériques de Legendre et fonctions sphéroïdales*, 3 vol. (1957–59); E. T. Whittaker and G. N. Watson, *Course of Modern Analysis*, 4th ed. (1928); M. Abramowitz and I. A. Stegun (eds.), *Handbook of Mathematical Functions* (1964). (A. ER.)

**SPHEROID,** literally a spherelike body. In geometry the term is applied to figures generated by an ellipse (*q.v.*) revolving about either its minor axis (giving an oblate spheroid) or its major axis (giving a prolate spheroid). If the equation of the generating ellipse is $b^2x^2 + a^2y^2 = a^2b^2$, and the ellipse revolves about the major axis (the $x$ axis), the volume is $\frac{4}{3}\pi ab^2$; if about the minor axis, it is $\frac{4}{3}\pi a^2b$. The equation of the prolate spheroid is $b^2x^2 + a^2(y^2+z^2) = a^2b^2$; that of the oblate spheroid is $b^2(x^2+z^2) + a^2y^2 = a^2b^2$. *See* ELLIPSOID.

**SPHERULITE,** in petrology, is a small rounded body which commonly occurs in vitreous igneous rocks. Spherulites are often visible in specimens of obsidian, pitchstone and rhyolite as globules about the size of millet seed, with a duller lustre than the surrounding glassy base of the rock, and when they are examined with a lens they prove to have a radiate fibrous structure.

Spherulites are commonest in acid glassy rocks but occur also in basic glasses such as tachylyte. Sometimes they compose the whole mass; more usually they are surrounded by a glassy or felsitic base. Occasionally spherulites have zones of different colours, and while most frequently spherical they may be irregular in outline. In some New Zealand rhyolites the spherulites send branching "cervicorn" processes (like stag horns) outward through the surrounding glass of the rock. Long, elliptical or bandlike spherulites are called axiolites.

Large cavernous spherulites have been called lithophysae; they are found in obsidians at Lipari, Italy, Yellowstone National park, etc. The characteristic radiate fibrous structure is usually conspicuous, but the fibres are interrupted by cavities which are often so arranged as to give the spherulite a resemblance to a rosebud with folded petals separated by arching interspaces. Some of these lithophysae are one inch or more in diameter. Spherulites with typical radiate fibrous structure may be produced in artificial glasses, salt solutions and melts of organic substances. Their study reveals the existence of an equatorial constriction perpendicular to a line along which the growth of the original sheaf of fibres began. New fibres grow at an angle to previous fibres so that the sheaf opens up at both ends, and fibres finally meet along the equator. A cavity is left, shaped like a flattened doughnut, but it is filled by later crystallizations. (J. D. H. D.)

**SPHINX,** a composite creature with lion's body and human head. The name is Greek and the sphinx is famous in Greek legend. According to Apollodorus she was a winged, human-headed lion, offspring of two giants, who lived in the vicinity of Boeotian Thebes. She terrorized the people by demanding the answer to a riddle taught her by the Muses—what is it that has one voice and yet becomes four-footed and two-footed and three-footed?—and devouring a man each time the riddle was answered incorrectly. Eventually Oedipus gave the proper answer: man, who crawls on all fours in infancy, walks on two feet when grown and leans on a staff in old age; the sphinx thereupon killed herself. From this tale apparently grew the legend that the sphinx was omniscient, and even today the wisdom of the sphinx is proverbial. The word *sphinx* was derived by Greek grammarians from the verb *sphingein* (to bind or squeeze), but the etymology is not related to the legend and therefore dubious. The earliest form was apparently *phix,* for which no etymology has been suggested; probably the word was not originally Greek.

In ancient near eastern art the monster is well known. The earliest example is one of the most famous monuments of all antiquity, the colossal recumbent sphinx at Giza, in Egypt, dating from the reign of King Khafre (Chephren) of the 4th dynasty, *c.* 2550 B.C. This is known to be a portrait statue of the king, and the sphinx continues as a royal portrait type through most of Egyptian history, symbolizing both the mighty strength and the protective power of Egypt's ruler. Through Egyptian influence the sphinx became known in Asia, especially in the Levant in the 2nd millennium B.C., where it became a popular subject on cylinder seals and other forms of decorative art. Its meaning in Asia is uncertain; it is no longer a royal portrait but may share with its Egyptian counterpart a certain protective aspect. Asian art always showed a fondness for monstrous beings, and the Egyptian sphinx may have been added to the repertory merely as another kind of monster. Although Mesopotamia was the place of origin of many monsters, the sphinx does not occur there until around 1500 B.C., when it was clearly imported from the Levant. In appearance the Asian sphinx differs from its Egyptian model most noticeably in the addition of wings to the leonine body, a feature that continues through its subsequent history in Asia and the Greek world. Another innovation is the female sphinx, which appears in the 14th century B.C. A few are found in Egypt in the 18th dynasty but it is common in the Levant, which is probably its homeland. What meaning the change of sex may have had is uncertain, but both males and females are found in similar poses and seem to play the same role in art. On seals, ivories and metalwork they sit on their haunches, often with one paw raised, and are frequently paired with a lion, a griffin or another sphinx.

Around 1600 B.C. the sphinx first appeared in the Greek world. Seal impressions and other objects from Crete at the end of the Middle Minoan period and from the shaft graves at Mycenae at the beginning of the Late Helladic Age show the sphinx, characteristically winged, and in the later part of the Late Helladic Age (14th and 13th centuries) the creature appears frequently on ivories, metal plaques and painted pottery. Although clearly derived from the Asian sphinx, the Greek examples are not identical in appearance; they customarily wear a flat cap with a flamelike projection on top. Nothing in their context connects them with the later legend and their meaning at this time is unknown.

HIRMER FOTOARCHIV MÜNCHEN

GREEK SPHINX OF THE ARCHAIC PERIOD, FROM DELPHI. IN THE DELPHI MUSEUM, GREECE

Around 1200 B.C. came the cataclysm in both Greek and Asian lands that marks the division between the Bronze and Iron Ages; it is traditionally known in Greece as the Dorian invasion and in Asia as the invasion of the Sea Peoples. For about 400 years no sphinxes appeared in Greece, but in Asia they continued in forms and poses similar to those of the Bronze Age. By the end of the 8th century the sphinx reappeared in Greek art and was common through the orientalizing and Archaic periods (down to the end of the 6th century). It is often associated with griffins, lions and other oriental motifs and is clearly derived from the same source; from its appearance it cannot be a direct descendant of the Bronze Age Greek sphinx. The new Greek sphinx is almost always female and usually wears the long-tiered wig known on contemporary sculptures of the Daedalic style; the body becomes graceful and elegant in line and the wings develop a beautiful curving form unknown in Asia. Sphinxes decorate vases, ivories, and metal works and in the late Archaic period occur as ornaments on temples. As in the Bronze Age, the context is usually insufficient to enable their meaning to be judged, but their appearance on temples (especially the large terra-cotta acroteria on a 6th-century Artemis temple at Calydon) suggests a protective function. The handsome stone sphinx atop a votive column set up by the Naxians in the Apollo precinct at Delphi corroborates a sacred meaning of some sort, as does the use of the sphinx on sepulchral monuments. By the 5th century clear illustrations of the Oedipus legend appear on vase paintings, usually with the sphinx perched on a column (*e.g.,* the red-figured Nolan amphora in Boston), but other monuments of classical age show Oedipus in armed combat with the sphinx and suggest an earlier stage of the legend in which the contest is physical instead of mental. Of such a stage the literature gives no hint, but battles of men and monsters are common in Asian art from prehistoric times down to the Achaemenid Persians, and Greek art may have adopted from the near east a pictorial theme that Greek literature did not share.

BIBLIOGRAPHY.—Pauly-Wissowa, *Real-Encyclopädie der classischen Altertumswissenschaft,* vol. ii (6) (1929); W. Roscher, *Ausführliches Lexikon der griechischen und römischen Mythologie,* vol. iv (1909–15); A. Dessenne, *Le Sphinx, Étude iconographique* (1957). (A. Ps.)

**SPHRANTZES, GEORGE** (1401–end of the 15th century), Byzantine historian and diplomat, wrote a chronicle covering the years 1413–77. He rose to high office in the service of Manuel II and the later Palaeologan rulers, both in Constantinople and in the Peloponnese. In 1451 Sphrantzes was great logothete (chancellor) in Constantinople and on its capture by the Ottomans he fled to Mistra and then had to retreat to Corfu, where he and his wife finally entered monastic life (1468). His chronicle is probably what is known as the *Chronicon Minus* and not the *Chronicon Maius.* The *Chronicon Maius,* considered by some to be Sphrantzes' expansion of the *Minus,* was probably compiled later by Macarius Melissenus. The chronicle was written for the Corfiotes and deals with the last years of the Palaeologi in Constantinople and the Peloponnese, and it shows marked aversion to the Ottomans and the Latins.

The *Chronicon* was edited by I. Bekker in *Corpus scriptorum historiae Byzantinae,* xxiii (1838), and in J. P. Migne, *Patrologia Graeca,* vol. 156 (1866). A critical edition of books i–ii was made by J. B. Papadopoulos (1935).

*See* G. Moravcsik, *Byzantinoturcica,* vol. i, 2nd ed., pp. 282–288 (1958); G. Ostrogorsky, *History of the Byzantine State,* pp. 416–418 (1956). (J. M. Hy.)

**SPIDER,** an invertebrate animal, the best known of the arachnids, is an eight-legged relative of the insects. Spiders form the order Araneae of the class Arachnida (*q.v.*). They attract attention by the webs they spin: and though they all spin silk, not all of them live a sedentary existence on a web. Superstitions surround them. Spider folklore includes admiration for their skill, wisdom, and cunning; fear of their sinister appearance, habits, and venomous qualities; and belief in their ability to influence the weather and in their medicinal value. The taxonomic scheme followed in this article differs from that given in the article Arachnida, where more suborders are proposed for the group here known as Araneomorphae.

## GENERAL FEATURES

**Diversity and Habits.**—Spiders are ancient animals, some of which seem little changed from their ancestral fossil forms. They are now found around the world—from the polar regions to the tropics—in a great variety of habitats: on the ground, ballooning high in the air, in caves, on mountains, and even in water.

The bird spiders and allies (suborder Mygalomorphae) are more generalized than the true spiders (suborder Araneomorphae), and have become specialists in unusual ways of living. The burrowing trap-door spiders and the purseweb spiders are mygalomorphs that live in specially constructed lairs. The true spiders are a highly varied, abundant, and conspicuous group. The diurnal jumping spiders actively pursue their prey, whereas the orb weavers spin a complex web in which they remain quietly until their prey becomes ensnared.

While most spiders are encountered out-of-doors, many dwell within human habitations, where, despite their insectivorous habits, they are not always welcome. Other species live on or near the ground (family Gnaphosidae) and may make tunnels or hide in natural cavities. The trap-door spider lines his excavation with silk and has a silk-hinged door covering it. Some forms live among the dead leaves and litter of the forest floor. Others are found in tall grass, on bushes and trees. While some, like the ground spiders and the wolf spiders (Lycosidae), may be found running over the ground, actively pursuing prey, others, like the orb weavers (Argiopidae) and funnel-web spiders (Agelenidae), are encountered lying in wait in or near their webs.

While it is not unusual for spiders to resemble their background, there are forms that resemble insects, pieces of bird dung, bud scales, pieces of grass or straw, or plant galls. Some species mimic ants, not only in appearance but also in behaviour.

(LEFT) WALTER DAWN FROM NATIONAL AUDUBON SOCIETY; (RIGHT) JACK DERMID FROM NATIONAL AUDUBON SOCIETY

**(LEFT) AN ORB-WEAVING GARDEN SPIDER** (ARGIOPE ARGENTATA); **(RIGHT) GREEN LYNX SPIDER** (PEUCETIA VIRIDANS)

The variation in colour is wide, from the sombre dark grays and browns of ground spiders to the bright flower-miming colours displayed by the sedentary crab spiders (Thomisidae) and the zebra-striping of the jumping spiders (Salticidae).

The largest species known are certain hairy bird spiders (family Theraphosidae), popularly called tarantulas in America; in tropical American jungles these spiders may be more than 3 in. in body length and have a leg span of more than 10 in. While their bites are painful and their appearance fearsome, they are not dangerous to man. Among the smallest spiders are species of *Microlinypheus,* whose members are under $\frac{1}{25}$ in. long. Most spiders, however, have bodies that range in length between $\frac{1}{8}$ and 1 in.

**Economic Importance.**—It is difficult to assess the value of the predation done by spiders in any biotic community. However, they are often present in such enormous numbers that their overall effect must be significant. Various estimates place the number of spiders in a given area as follows: about 264,000 spiders per acre of forest floor in Barro Colorado Island, Panama Canal Zone; 2,265,000 per acre in undisturbed meadow in England; and 14,000 per acre on herbs and shrubs of woodland in Illinois.

## STRUCTURE AND FUNCTION

Like most arachnids, spiders are distinguished from insects by the subdivision of the body into two portions: the cephalothorax and the abdomen. The cephalothorax is a result of the fusion of the head with the thorax. This fusion is so nearly complete that the outlines of the head may be recognized only from the shallow depression (cervical groove) that separates its dorsal surface from that of the thorax. The abdomen is attached to the cephalothorax by a very slender waist, the pedicel.

**External Features.**—The body wall of spiders, like that of other arachnids, is an exoskeleton formed of chitin. Movements are possible because of the membranous character of the joints. The exoskeleton is important both for protection and attachment of muscles. Within the body are chitinous skeletal elements that also serve as points of attachment for muscles. The most important of these is the endosternite found within the cephalothorax.

The cephalothoracic shield, or carapace, is quite uniform in appearance. Above, it is usually a smooth, convex surface, but more often there is a slight cervical groove. Behind the cervical groove, many species have another conspicuous depression or pigmented line, the dorsal, or thoracic, furrow or groove. There may be three pairs of less conspicuous radial furrows behind the cervical groove. The underside of the cephalothorax is formed of two unequal chitinous plates, the sternum and the labium, or lip, the latter being one of the mouthparts.

The eyes, present at the anterior portion of the carapace, are simple ocelli like those of insects. Most spiders have four pairs, though some families have only six eyes. There are a few species in which the eyes are completely lacking. In most families, the eyes are arranged in two rows, enclosing a space called the eye area, or ocular quadrangle. Between the anterior row of eyes and the edge of the carapace is the area termed the clypeus. The relative size and placement of the eyes, and the width and inclination of the clypeus, are often important features for classifying spiders.

Below and in front of the clypeus are the paired chelicerae, used for seizing and holding prey. Each of these consists of a heavy basal section, the paturon, and a smaller distal segment, the fang. The paturon often bears a small nipplelike tubercle, and its outer surface many have a series of ridges forming a stridulating organ. The fang, usually sickle shaped, is formed of very hard chitin. The concave edge is grooved, and the lower or posterior edge is usually toothed. Near the tip of the fang is the opening of the poison gland. The opening is in a protected position and is thus prevented from being closed as the spider drives its fangs into its prey.

The second pair of appendages are the palpi (or pedipalpi), which serve different functions. Among the young and females they act as sensory organs, while in the mature male the femur

WALTER DAWN FROM NATIONAL AUDUBON SOCIETY

ANTERIOR VIEW OF WOLF SPIDER: NOTE SIX SIMPLE EYES AND THE TWO PAIRS OF APPENDAGES NEAR THE MOUTH—THE BROAD CHELICERAE UNDER THE EYES AND THE LEGLIKE PEDIPALPI BEHIND THE CHELICERAE

may be used in stridulation and the tarsus is an accessory to the reproductive system. Each palpus has six segments: the coxa, trochanter, femur, patella, tibia, and tarsus. The basal segment, the coxa, is expanded in most spiders to form the maxillary mouth-parts. Between the two maxillae is the labium. The maxilla, separated by a membrane from the coxa of the limb, is used to compress food particles and squeeze their liquid contents into the pharynx.

The tarsal segment of the male palpus serves as a sexual intromittent organ. The male palpal tibia also is different from that of the female. It is relatively shorter, and frequently has a short process on its outer side. In its simplest form, the palpal organ is situated near the tip of the tarsus in a cavity, the alveolus. The palpal organ is formed of a coiled tube with three recognizable parts: the proximal swollen bulb, an intermediate reservoir, or fundus, and a dark, elongated ejaculatory duct. From this simple condition more complex palpi have developed. In one type, the genital bulb is on the lower side of the palpus.

The palpal organ is divisible externally into basal, middle, and apical divisions. In the most complex type, the apical division (or embolus) of the genital bulb is divided into two parts. One of these, the duct through which the sperm passes, is considered the embolus proper. The other division is the conductor that functions to protect the embolus when it is in position in the alveolus.

There are always four pairs of legs, each consisting of seven segments: coxa, trochanter, femur, patella, tibia, metatarsus, and tarsus. Each segment is a chitinous cylinder united by a membrane to the adjoining one, and each, except the femur, is straight. The coxa is nearest the body. The femur is curved in some species. There are at least two claws at the end of each tarsus, and in some there is an unpaired, median ventral third claw. Usually the legs are covered with hairs; in addition there may be spines, bristles, and even scales. Among some species, one or more pairs of tarsi or metatarsi are provided with a dense brush of stiff hairs, the scopula. The spider often uses its legs for purposes other than walking. For example, the first leg, usually the longest, is an important organ of touch. Among some male spiders, it is quite elaborate and is used for display before the female during courtship.

The abdomen of spiders is very diverse. In some species it may bear colourful patterns or designs. Usually the male is more colourful than the female. The shape of the abdomen may vary considerably, with forms like the spiny-bodied spiders of the genus *Micrathena* having a bizarre appearance. The undersurface of the abdomen, near the pedicel, is more convex and is termed the epigastrium. It is separated from the rest of the abdomen by the epigastric furrow. The openings of the book lungs lie on either side of the epigastric region, and the reproductive organs open between them. The single opening of the united sperm ducts (paired interiorly) of the male spiders is small and difficult to discern. The paired oviducts of the female, however, have large apertures closely associated with the single or paired openings of the seminal receptacles, which receive and store the sperm of the male. The area surrounding the seminal receptacles, the epigynum, is quite diverse in its form and appearance.

Also present on the abdomen are the spinnerets, modified appendages of the fourth and fifth abdominal embryonic segments that are supplied with silk-producing glands. These glands open at the end of specially modified hairs, the so-called spinning tubes situated on the spinnerets. In some species, the total number of spinning tubes has been estimated to be as high as 1,000, in others it is less than 100. The cribellate spiders have a flat spinning organ, the cribellum, a sievelike plate in front of the anterior spinnerets. Associated with the cribellum is another structure, an accessory comb of hairs, the calamistrum, found on the metatarsi of the hind legs.

**Sense Organs.**—The body and legs, pedipalpi, chelicerae, and even the spinnerets are covered with numerous hairs of various kinds, some stiff and stout, others slender and pliable, some smooth, others provided with serrations. Some are sensory in function, each tactile hair having its own nerve fibre that conveys impulses to the central nervous system. Especially fine, erect hairs arising from the centre of little drumlike membranes are sensitive to slow currents of air. These hairs formerly were suspected of detecting sound vibrations. While some spiders have sound-producing organs, no organs of hearing have been found among spiders.

The anterior median eyes of the spider have a direct retina; the other eyes have an inverted retina and are often supplied with a tapetum of pigment cells, reflecting light and giving the eyes a pearly appearance. The disposition of the eyes is characteristic of whole families and is responsible for the diverging directions of the axes of the eyes. Convergent eyes do not occur in spiders. The respective fields of vision are determined by the shape and curvature of the lens; the acuity of vision is determined by the diameter and size of the image, and the distance at which the image of two points falls on a single rod. Each pair of eyes forms images of a size different from that formed by the other eyes and the fields of vision are mostly quite different. The best spider eyes have lenses with spherical surfaces, but the acuity of vision with even the best eyes is far below that of human eyes.

The olfactory sense is very poorly developed and apparently restricted to what one may call sexual odours. The males of some species are able to follow the scent left by a female on a smooth surface, such as a sheet of paper. Other scents apparently are not perceived unless the substance is of a highly irritating nature.

**Feeding and Digestion.**—Spiders are solitary predators that subsist on the juices of the prey. After subduing its prey, the spider injects it with digestive juices and then sucks the liquefied product into the mouth, which lies directly above the labium and in close contact with a flattened cone of tissue, the rostrum. The lower surface of the rostrum is covered with a chitinous plate, the epipharynx. A corresponding plate, the hypopharynx, is found on the upper surface of the labium.

The alimentary system of the spider is quite complex and consists of three main portions: the foregut, midgut, and hindgut. Only the midgut is lined with epithelium and is absorptive.

The foregut consists of the pharynx, esophagus, and gizzard, all lined with chitin, the same as that of the body wall with which they are continuous. The pharynx arises almost vertically between the epipharynx and the hypopharynx. It acts both as a pump and strainer, preventing coarse particles from passing into the esophagus. The hypopharynx is merely a tube connecting the pharynx with the gizzard, which is also a pump. The pharyngeal gland, a small oval mass of secretory cells located in a space resulting from the curvature of the epipharynx, has a duct leading to the end of the pharynx, near its junction with the esophagus.

The midgut has two functions: to produce enzymes for the digestion of foods, and to absorb the digested foods. The absorptive surface is increased in the cephalothorax by several branched sacs, or diverticula. After the digestive tube passes through the pedicel, and shortly before entering the abdomen, it curves upward and widens. The upper surface of this wider portion usually has four openings, which lead into the complex series of branched tubules known as the abdominal gland. This gland occupies the greater portion of the spider's abdomen and is penetrated by the excretory tubules. It appears to act as a digestive gland and also as a reservoir, permitting the spider to ingest large amounts of food at one time. This food is stored and gradually absorbed by the abdominal gland. The midgut also forms a large pouch, the stercoral pouch, in which wastes are stored before being excreted. The midgut passes into the hindgut, with little or no change in size. The rectum is a straight tube opening at the anus, which lies at the end of a small tubercle.

**Respiration.**—For respiratory exchange, spiders have book lungs and tracheae, occurring either separately or together. Most spiders, however, have a pair of book lungs and either a single or a paired tracheal opening. The book lungs can be seen as pale patches in the epigastric region. Actually each is a large hollow space that opens to the outside by means of a small pore. Within the space there are from 15 to 20 "leaves," each actually a fold of the body wall; therefore, each is double and the two halves are separated by many vertical supports. The top surface of the upper lamella of each fold has vertical knobbed spikes that separate the leaves and allow air to circulate freely. The blood sinuses of the abdomen communicate with the hollows within the leaves. The tracheal spiracle opens just in front of the spinnerets. The tracheae diverge in bunches at intervals from a main tube. Air diffuses directly from the lumens of the tracheae into the tissues adjoining them.

**Blood and Associated Tissues.**—The space between the alimentary canal and the body wall is almost entirely filled with blood and is known as the hemocoel. Within this cavity lie the organ systems of the spider. A true body cavity, such as that of the vertebrates, is confined to small spaces in the gonads and in the excretory glands.

The blood of the spider contains clear, rounded corpuscles, or leucocytes, floating in plasma that contains the respiratory pigment hemocyanin, similar to hemoglobin but bearing copper rather than iron. When the spider's blood is deprived of oxygen, it is colourless; oxygenated blood has a pale but pronounced blue tinge due to oxyhemocyanin.

The spider possesses a circulatory system in which the blood is in the blood vessels only during a portion of its course through the body. The heart, a straight tube lying in the dorsal portion of the abdomen, is surrounded by a thin-walled sac, the pericardium. The space between the heart and the sac, the pericardial space, is filled with blood, which enters the heart through three or four pairs of openings or ostia. The ostia have valves that prevent the blood from returning to the pericardium from the heart. Leading forward from the heart, the aorta dips down and passes through the pedicel into the cephalothorax and gives off the posterior dorsal vessels that supply the muscles of the anterior region. Behind the stomach, the aorta divides into two branches that lie between the sides of the stomach and the cephalothoracic diverticula. Other blood vessels arise from the aortic vessel and supply the organs of the cephalothorax. A series of lateral arteries arising from the heart supply the organs of the abdomen. Posteriorly, the heart continues as the caudal artery. The blood is collected in channels, then delivered to sinuses, of which there are six, three in each major portion of the body. The sinuses conduct the blood to the book lungs where it is oxygenated. The blood then flows back to the pericardium by means of the pulmonary veins.

**Excretion.**—Malpighian tubules and coxal glands are the main organs for the excretion of nitrogenous waste products. The tubules are a pair of fine branches opening into the intestine near the stercoral pouch. The uric acid secreted by these tubules appears to be in the form of sodium urate. The coxal glands, found near the first and third legs, discharge their products into a convoluted tube whose many coils occupy the area from the first to fourth coxae. The convoluted tube is lined with excretory epithelium, but does not excrete solid material. From its posterior end, a straight tube runs forward, giving off short exit tubes to the outside behind the first and third coxae.

The degree of development of this excretory system varies greatly in the different families. It is generally believed that the coxal glands represent modified nephridia (primitive excretory organs) and that various silk and poison glands have developed from similar glands in other parts of the animal.

**Nervous System.**—The nervous system is concentrated in the cephalothorax. During early development, a pair of ganglia is present in each segment of the body, but later the ganglia consolidate into a single mass surrounding the esophagus. The supraesophageal portion of the nervous system, above the esophagus, is considered the brain. The optic nerves and the nerves of the chelicerae arise from it. Below the esophagus is the subesophageal ganglion, broadly joined with the supraesophageal ganglia to form a nerve collar around the esophagus. From the subesophageal ganglion arise nerves extending to the pedipalpi and legs. The visceral nervous system consists of an unpaired nerve running along the esophagus and stomach. It is connected with the brain by paired nerves. Ganglia associated with the ventral nerve cord have also been considered as being part of the visceral nervous system.

**Reproduction.**—The tubular testes of the male are in the abdomen, just below the alimentary tract. Anteriorly, the testes are continued into the much coiled sperm ducts. These latter unite eventually to form the short seminal vesicle, which leads to the single median opening located in the epigastric furrow. The ovaries are located in a position similar to that of the testes, but they are much larger. Superficially they resemble a diminutive bunch of grapes because of the ovarian follicles projecting from their surfaces. The eggs pass through the neck of the follicle into a space within the ovary. From this space they travel into the oviducts, straight tubes that unite to form the uterus and the vagina. The chitin-lined vagina leads directly to the epigynum. Two narrow ducts lead laterally from the vagina to the seminal receptacles. In some spiders there are separate receptacular openings also found on the epigynum.

## LIFE CYCLE

**Eggs and Their Care.**—The female prepares a silken sheet upon which the eggs are laid. As she passes the eggs one by one from her genital opening, sperms, stored in a syrupy fluid in the seminal receptacles, are spread over them. Since the eggs have a very soft covering, they are easily penetrated by the sperm at any point. The number of eggs laid varies greatly: some tiny species lay only a very few eggs at a time, others up to 300; the average number is about 100. After the eggs are laid, the female covers them with a silken sheet and molds them into the egg sac characteristic of her species. Many of these sacs are beautifully designed, and the care given them by the female varies. Wolf spiders drag the sac behind them, then later carry the young on their backs; some spiders divide the risk of losing their eggs by placing them in a series of sacs that are hung in the centre of their snare or are left singly in different places.

**Development.**—The development of the spider within the egg is similar to that of other arachnids. The spiderling gradually takes form on the outer surface of the egg. In the area that becomes the cephalothorax, little buds appear. These gradually differentiate into chelicerae, palpi, and legs. Similar buds appear on the abdominal portion of the embryo with a rather definite division into 8 to 12 segments. All buds behind the sixth true segment disappear. The buds of the fourth and fifth segments develop into the spinnerets, those on the second and third segments form the book lungs. When the embryo finally encircles the outside of the egg and the ventral surface is outside, a process called reversion occurs. This reverses the position of the embryo and frees the cephalothoracic region. At about this same time, the expanding embryo presses against the chorion and by the use of its egg tooth (at the base of the palpi) ruptures the egg cover. The resulting minute spiderlike creature, the deutovum, is still surrounded by embryonal membranes. While still in the egg sac it grows rapidly and toward the end of this stage becomes visible. The first true molt takes place in the sac, after which the animal is known as a spiderling. The spiderling is able to feed, though it still uses the yolk in the abdomen, and it can spin. In favourable weather, the spiderlings escape from the sac, usually by tearing it open, and disperse. They may remain in the egg sac throughout the winter, then disperse in the spring when the weather is favourable.

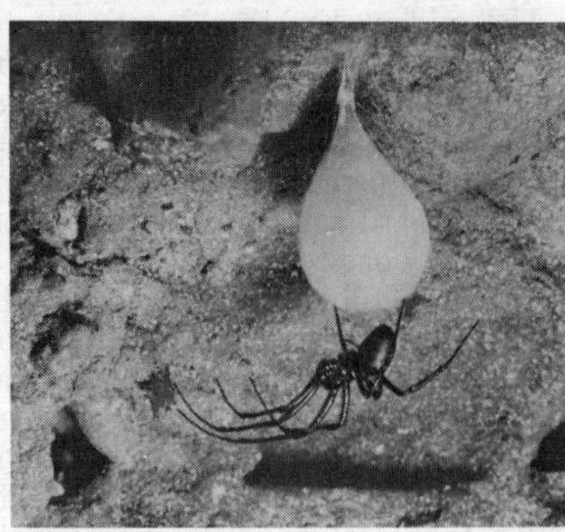

EGGS OF SPIDERS ARE ENCLOSED IN SILKEN SACS: (ABOVE) CAVE SPIDER WITH EGG SAC SUSPENDED FROM CEILING; (LEFT) FEMALE WOLF SPIDER DEFENDS HER PORTABLE EGG SAC

(LEFT) ROBERT C. HERMES FROM NATIONAL AUDUBON SOCIETY; (RIGHT) CESCO CIAPANNA FROM NATIONAL AUDUBON SOCIETY

**Growth.**—From time to time during its growth, the spider must molt. The American tarantulas spin a sheet of silk upon which they lie during the whole process. The true spiders often hang in their webs or in retreats. The freshly molted spider, very pale and soft, hardens and darkens gradually. All growth occurs during this short instar period. The number of molts necessary to attain maturity varies from species to species. Small species molt only a few times, while large ones molt several times. Large bird spiders may molt more than 20 times. The males of the black widow spider (*Latrodectus mactans*) become adult between the fourth and seventh molts; the females are adult after the seventh to ninth molt.

**Life Span.**—The spiders of the temperate zones usually live only one year. There are actually two groups, one of which is represented by over-wintered or recently matured males that become abundant in early spring and are on hand for the maturing females. In the late summer and early fall, another group of spiders mature and become conspicuous. The eggs they lay have substantial sacs and are more heavily insulated than those of the spring spiders. Their young either spend the winter in the cocoon or under debris.

In general, the male spider does not live so long as the female. In the northern United States, a wolf spider may live several years. It appears that many of the mygalomorph spiders live for several years. The males of the bird spiders mature in 8 or 9 years, but usually die a few months later, while females in captivity have been known to live for more than 20 years.

**Behaviour.**—Spiders have attained a prominent position in the world without benefit of intelligence. Their behaviour, while amazingly complex, is wholly instinctual. They perform their tasks like automatons.

*Spinning and Webs.*—The spider is an inveterate spinner throughout its life. Its silk, used for many different purposes, is a scleroprotein produced as a liquid. When drawn out of the spinnerets, it ordinarily hardens to form the threads. The mechanical stretching of the silk during the drawing of the lines, not exposure to the air, is responsible for the hardening. Spider silk is both strong and elastic, its tensile strength being second to that of fused quartz. If the threads are drawn out rapidly, they are stronger, for the fibroin chains then attain a maximum orientation. There are several types of spider silk that vary in strength and elasticity.

While spider threads may appear to be single fibres, they actually are not. The finest single fibre is about one-millionth of an inch in diameter. Much thicker threads, however, do occur. Most spider threads are formed of strands from several glands.

Whenever the spider moves about, it spins a silken line behind it. This is the dragline, which may be anchored at intervals much in the way that a mountain climber lets out a rope as he moves down a precipitous slope. An anchor is made by pressing the spinnerets against an object. The dragline is the fundamental thread of most spinning. The spider can use the dragline to "balloon" for great distances. The spiderling shortly after hatching climbs upward on tall grass or other upright object and turns toward the direction of the wind. It then extends its legs and tilts the abdomen upward. The threads from the spinnerets are drawn out by the air currents, and when the pull on the threads is strong enough, the spiderling lets go and is pulled into the air. Apparently, spiders are capable of traveling great distances in this manner, for they have been reported as landing on ships up to 200 mi. from land. While ballooning occurs all during the year, it seems to be most conspicuous in the fall.

Silk is also used for spinning egg cocoons, sperm webs, molting sheets, gossamer threads, attachment discs with cables, linings of burrows, hinges for trap doors, and for web snares of various types.

Most complex of these spinning products are the webs, of several types, more or less characteristic of spider families: sheet webs, funnel webs, tube webs, reticular webs, geometric orb webs, etc. The most complex snares are those of the geometric orb weavers (family Argiopidae). A finished web consists usually of three or four outer foundation lines, several inner foundation lines, many radial lines, a central hub, an intermediate zone, and a viscid spiral. Many species build a tent of silk or of a leaf rolled up and held together by threads of silk. In this tent, the spider hides during the day, holding in its claws the guy line connected with the centre of the web by which means the spider can detect vibrations caused by entangled insects. Species of *Argiope* weave additional X-shaped bands called stabilimentum, although they have nothing to do with stabilizing the web. Some weave a disc of lacework in the middle of the orb. *Cyclosa conica,* a little orb weaver common in both Europe and America, suspends in the diameter of its web a series of silk pellets to camouflage the egg cocoon, which occupies a place in the same row.

Many spiders build tents that are used as retreats or hiding places in which they find shelter from rain, cold, light, and enemies, or from which they can pounce upon unsuspecting victims. The Eurasian aquatic spider (*Argyroneta aquatica*) builds its tent under water in the shape of a bell and fills it with air. Special tents are often used for molting. Some females make complete envelopes of tough silk for themselves and their brood and stay inside until all the spiderlings are able to take care of themselves. Some species winter in special tents made for that purpose under the bark of trees.

Egg cocoons also show a great variety of structure. Some are circular or oval and perfectly flat; others are globular and smooth. Most cocoons are made with at least two walls. First the spider spins a sheet, deposits the eggs in it, covers them with another sheet and binds the two together, neatly clipping the edge. Then the outer sheet is made, often of a much tougher silk.

Silk is used for enswathing insects captured in a snare. This makes their escape impossible and serves to store them as food for use at a later time. In case the insect is a dangerous adversary, such as a wasp or hornet, silk may be squirted as far as an inch from the spinnerets, a distance sufficient to make the combat safe.

WEB BUILDING INVOLVES THE SECRETION (ABOVE) OF SILK FROM SPINNERETS AND THE WEAVING OF STRANDS INTO (RIGHT) GEOMETRIC TRAPS LIKE THE ORB OF THE LACE SPIDER

(LEFT) LYNWOOD H. CHACE FROM NATIONAL AUDUBON SOCIETY; (RIGHT) R. B. HOIT—PHOTO RESEARCHERS, INC.

In their methods of capturing prey, spiders show great diversity. The sheet-web weavers (family Dipluridae) utilize a maze of threads extending in all directions and tied to adjacent vegetation. At the centre is a domelike sheet. Flying insects strike the high threads, then drop upon the dome, where the spider trusses them up. One typical orb weaver, *Mastophora*, is known as the boleadora, for it uses miniature bolas weighted with a quantity of viscid silk to capture its prey. One South African spider constructs a snare about the size of a postage stamp. The corners are held by the spider's long legs, and when an insect approaches, the web is stretched and hurled over the prey.

*Courtship.*—Courtship and mating habits of spiders are remarkable. The male is smaller than the female and approaches her with caution, for he may be perceived by her as a choice edible object. Recognition and acceptance are, therefore, very important preliminaries to courtship. Spiders with good vision make use of visual signs, while shortsighted and nocturnal species use contact stimuli. Before the male can mate, he charges his modified palp with semen. To do this, he weaves a small pad of silk, deposits a drop of semen upon it, and sucks it up with the palpus. The charged palpus is inserted into the seminal receptacle of the female during copulation. Each species has a palpus with a distinctive shape, and the correspondence of the epigynum with the palpal structure is such that pairing is probably possible only between males and females of the same species or closely related ones. The small male, if he escapes safely, may pair again after recharging his palpus.

*Regeneration.*—A spider can easily discard an appendage if it is injured. This process is termed autotomy. The limb can then be replaced by regeneration (*q.v.*).

**Poisonous Qualities.**—Poison glands, found in nearly all spiders, are associated with the chelicerae. Each chelicera has two segments, the stout basal segment and the movable fang. The poison gland may be entirely contained in the basal segment, but more often, it extends farther back into the head region. The poison flows from the gland and is released from a tiny opening near the end of the fang. When the spider bites, the fangs are forced into the victim's body. Two separate punctures are made, and, at the same time, muscles squeeze the glands and force the poison into the wound. The venom usually is a colourless liquid, and the amount injected at any one time is variable. Spider venom is very complex chemically and appears to contain both neurotoxins and hematoxins.

Fortunately, the venom of most spiders is feeble and its effects upon humans transitory. A few spiders, however, produce poisons that can cause severe local or general reactions in man. Members of the genus *Latrodectus* are generally regarded as being dangerous. In the United States the black widow spider (*Latrodectus mactans*) is notorious. Its bite often causes intense pain, followed by nausea, vomiting, faintness, tremors, and shock. Although the illness may seem grave, death is rare. The very young and older persons may be more seriously affected.

The bite of the brown recluse spider (*Loxosceles reclusus*) causes rather severe local reactions that may be followed by some general disturbance. This species lives in the midwest and south-central United States. Another member of this genus (*L. laeta*) is regarded as dangerous in portions of South America.

**Enemies.**—Many lizards, toads, and some birds feed upon spiders. Some solitary wasps, in particular, depend entirely upon spiders as food provision for their larvae. Some Hymenoptera and Diptera spend their larval life as external parasites of spiders. Nematodes are commonly found as internal parasites. While the spider is molting, it is completely helpless and subject to attack by animals such as crickets, sowbugs, and mealworms, which at other times normally do not attack spiders.

## CLASSIFICATION

The two principal suborders of living spiders are the Mygalomorphae (bird spiders and allies) and the Araneomorphae (the so-called true spiders).

The mygalomorph spiders are more generalized in structure than the araneomorphs, and all live more than a single year. In general, they are quite large, averaging more than an inch in length. Their conspicuous chelicerae move in a vertical plane, a feature that distinguishes them from the true spiders. Two groups are recognized in this suborder. The first of these, the typical "tarantulas," includes the sheet-web spiders (Dipluridae) and the true trap-door spiders (Ctenizidae). They are most successful living underground. Very few are accomplished runners, jumpers, or climbers, and they do not rely on silk to capture prey as do the true spiders. The second group, the atypical "tarantulas," includes the purseweb spiders. These latter are very generalized and resemble fossil remains dating from the late Paleozoic.

The true spiders, members of the suborder Araneomorphae, are an enormous assemblage of highly varied forms, probably numbering about 40,000 species. In general, they are much smaller than the mygalomorphs, and their chelicerae move in a horizontal plane. The Araneomorphae is divided into seven main groups, each being further divided into families. These groups are the Hypochiloidea, the four-lunged true spiders; the Filistatoidea, the filistatids; the Dictynoidea, the typical cribellate spiders; the Plectruroidea, the primitive hunters and weavers; the Argiopoidea, the aerial web spinners; the Lycosoidea, the hunting spiders; and the Clubionoidea, the running spiders.

*See* also references under "Spider" in the Index.

BIBLIOGRAPHY.—W. J. Baerg, *The Tarantula* (1958); W. S. Bristowe, *The Comity of Spiders*, 2 vol. (1939–41); E. E. Buckley and N. Porges (eds.), *Venoms* (1956); J. L. Cloudsley-Thompson, *Spiders, Scorpions, Centipedes, and Mites* (1958); J. H. Comstock, *The Spider Book*, rev. by W. J. Gertsch (1940); W. J. Gertsch, *American Spiders* (1949); B. J. Kaston, *How to Know the Spiders* (1953); E. Nielsen, *The Biology of Spiders*, 2 vol. (1932); T. H. Savory, *The Biology of Spiders* (1928).

(C. J. Go.; M. L. G.)

**SPILITE,** a fine-grained or dense igneous rock, usually free of visible crystals and commonly greenish or grayish-green in colour. Spilites are commonly vesicular (blistered) or variolitic (pocked) and show wonderfully preserved pillow structure, a feature in most cases indicative of a submarine origin of the lavas from which they were formed.

The individual pillows are filled with concentric zones of vesicles filled with chlorite and calcite. The formation of pillow structure in volcanic rocks was directly observed by the English volcanologist Tempest Anderson, joint author of the "Report to the Royal Society on West Indian Eruptions, 1902 and 1907," in the case of the lava poured into the sea from the volcano Matavanu in Samoa.

On the surface of the lava, buds form and expand, giving rise to "pillows" with a glassy crust. The interspaces between the pillows are frequently filled with sediment representing the soft ooze of the sea floor. Not all pillow lavas are spilitic.

The spilites are of basaltic character, but possessing in place of the normal labradorite, a feldspar of the composition of albite. The ferromagnesian mineral is an augite of pale brown colour; spilites are, however, usually very completely decomposed, augite being represented by chlorite and calcite.

Some spilites showing pillow structure are not strictly lavas but shallow intrusions into unconsolidated submarine ooze. Excellent examples of such intrusive spilites are provided by the Devonian spilites of Nundle, New South Wales. Though the term spilite was first used by Alexandre Brongniart (1770–1847) for altered basic lavas free from phenocrysts and possessing well-marked vesicular textures, early in the 20th century a new significance was given to the term by British geologists Dewey and Flett, who urged that a special group of rocks—the spilitic suite—should be recognized.

According to these authors, a large suite of igneous rocks is genetically associated with the spilites. Their composition varies widely, but they all have some characters in common. They possess a high percentage of soda and are usually extensively altered. These rocks are albite-dolerites, minverites, picrites, keratophyres, soda-felsites, and soda-granites. The spilitic suite was originally given a status comparable with that of the alkaline and calc-alkaline suites. The spilitic series is regarded as peculiar to districts that have undergone a long continued and gentle subsidence with few or slight upward movements and no important faulting.

The lavas are poured out on the margins of geosynclines while their common sedimentary associates are black shales, limestones, and radiolarian cherts. As geosynclines are the centres of subsequent fold movements many ancient spilites have become extensively folded and metamorphosed with production of new minerals, including albite of metamorphic origin. Eruptions having the spilitic facies have occurred repeatedly over a wide area and on a large scale. (C. E. T.; X.)

**SPINA,** an ancient Etruscan port on the Adriatic coast of Italy, now about 6 mi. (10 km.) inland. It was situated on what were at the time of its foundation the coastal dunes at the mouth of a southern branch (the classical Sagis) of the Po River about 4½ mi. (7 km.) W of modern Comacchio. Spina was founded as a result of the Etruscan advance into north Italy in the closing years of the 6th century B.C., and throughout the 5th century it and Adria were the main ports of entry for the rich Greek commerce with northern Etruria. Soon after 400 B.C. Spina was sacked by the Gauls, and with the collapse of its market and the ruin of its port by the advance of the delta, it rapidly lapsed into obscurity.

The principal remains are the contents of the cemeteries of Valle Trebba and of Valle Pega (excavated at intervals since 1922 in the course of land-reclamation schemes), now in the Museo Archeologico Nazionale, Ferrara. Nearly 2,000 graves have been recovered, yielding many fine bronzes and an unrivaled collection of Greek pottery, mainly red-figured vessels of Attic origin. The sites of the canal port and of the wharves and habitations alongside it have been revealed in great detail by air photography. (J. B. W.-P.)

**SPINACH,** a hardy, leafy annual, *Spinacia oleracea,* of the family Chenopodiaceae, used as a vegetable. The large, edible leaves are arranged in a rosette, from which a seed stalk subsequently emerges. The leaves are somewhat triangular and may be flat or puckered.

The species is basically dioecious, with male flowers on one plant and female flowers on another, but monoecious plants occur with varying proportions of male and female (and sometimes perfect, or bisexual) flowers. There is some correlation between the sex expression and the leaf shape, the female forms tending to be associated with the broader-leaved and more commercially desirable types. Further, the more male types tend to bolt (produce a flower stalk) more easily than the female; hence, breeding work aimed at producing a large leaf crop combined with slow bolting has resulted in varieties with a predominance of female types. The plant is wind pollinated, and the pollen is extremely small, so that elaborate precautions are needed by breeders to prevent unwanted cross-pollination.

Spinach requires cool weather, deep rich well-limed, well-watered soil to give quick growth and maximum leaf area and to discourage bolting. Seed can be sown every two weeks from early spring to late summer, in rows 12 in. apart, the plantlets being thinned to 6–8 in. in the row. The last sowings will produce young plants that yield a crop in the autumn and stand over the winter, providing leaves in early spring, or even through the winter if the weather should be not too severe. It is essential to have enough plants to permit picking only the largest leaves from each plant. If too many leaves are removed, bolting will be encouraged; picking little and often should be the rule.

Spinach, widely grown in the United States, Holland, and the Scandinavian countries, is marketed fresh, canned, or frozen. It received much publicity in the 1920s when attention was called to its relatively high content of iron and vitamins A and C. (The comic strip "Popeye" helped to overcome, particularly among children, a resistance to spinach based largely on its unusual flavour.) Although spinach is rich in calcium, it is also rich in oxalic acid, which combines with calcium. This makes the calcium nutritionally unavailable.

Spinach beet, or perpetual spinach (*Beta vulgaris cicla*), is one of the perennial leaf beets, with leaves larger and more fleshy than those of spinach and considered by many people to be more palatable. It stands hot weather much better than true spinach and should be treated in the same way as the garden beet, but it needs a rich soil in order to encourage the development of large foliage. Of less popularity are New Zealand spinach (*Tetragonia expansa*) and mountain spinach, or orach (*Atriplex hortensis*), coarse annual herbs whose tender young leaves produce greens similar to spinach when cooked. (J. C. Ha.)

**SPINAL CORD** in man is the elongated cylindrical portion of the central nervous system located in the upper two-thirds of the vertebral canal of the vertebral column.

The reader who makes a close study of this article may be helped occasionally by consulting the related articles Brain; Nerve: *Spinal Nerves;* Nerve Conduction; Nervous System.

### ANATOMY

The spinal cord is about 45 cm. (18 in.) long. It extends from just above the first cervical vertebra (atlas) at the base of the skull to the level of the first lumbar vertebra, where it is known as the conus medullaris. Small groups of nerve fibres that are attached to the spinal cord unite to form the segmental series of dorsal roots and ventral roots (fig. 1 and 2). One dorsal root and one ventral root combine in the region of an opening, the intervertebral foramen, between the two vertebrae to form one of the 31 pairs of spinal nerves. The dorsal roots contain the nerve fibres that transmit sensory impulses from the body to the spinal cord, while the ventral roots are composed of the motor fibres that transmit nerve impulses from the cord to the muscles and glands.

The spinal cord does not occupy the entire length of the vertebral canal because the vertebral column continues to grow after the cord has reached its full length. Since the column is longer than the cord, the nerve filaments of each dorsal root leave the cord above the site where the root enters the intervertebral foramen (fig. 1).

Each thoracic, lumbar, sacral, and coccygeal spinal nerve is named from the vertebra that is just above its exit from the vertebral column. As there are 12 thoracic vertebrae, 5 lumbar vertebrae, 5 fused sacral vertebrae, and 1 (to 3) vestigial coccygeal vertebra, there are 12 thoracic, 5 lumbar, 5 sacral, and 1 coccygeal spinal nerves (fig. 1).

There are eight cervical nerves, although only seven cervical vertebrae, because in addition to a nerve passing below each cervical vertebra one exists above the first cervical vertebra. The long roots of the lower third of the vertebral canal below the conus medullaris form a structure called the cauda equina ("horse's tail").

**Meninges.**—The cord is enveloped by three coverings, the

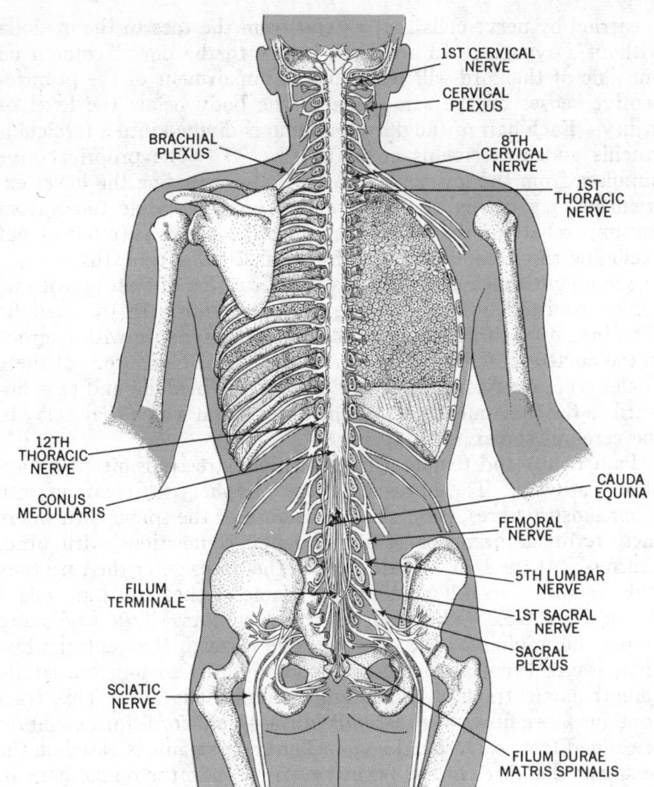


BY COURTESY OF CIBA CLINICAL SYMPOSIA, VOL. 1, NO. 6, AND THE CIBA COLLECTION OF MEDICAL ILLUSTRATIONS

FIG. 1.—THE SPINAL CORD

meninges (figs. 1 and 2). From within outward they are the pia mater, arachnoid mater, and dura mater. These meninges are continuous with comparable layers surrounding the brain. The pia mater is closely attached to the spinal cord and contains the many blood vessels that supply the cord. The pia mater continues as a strand in the middle of the cauda equina known as the filum terminale, which extends to the coccyx (fig. 1).

The second meninx is the arachnoid layer, which is connected to the pia mater by delicate strands. The region between the two layers is the subarachnoid space, which is filled with the cerebrospinal fluid. Formed mainly in the brain, the fluid cushions the spinal cord. In the region caudal to (that is, below) the conus medullaris the arachnoid forms a cul-de-sac (fig. 1)—containing the cauda equina and cerebrospinal fluid—into which lumbar puncture needles are inserted to withdraw cerebrospinal fluid for diagnostic examination and to inject spinal anesthetics. This procedure avoids damage to the spinal cord, while injury to the spinal roots is minor.

The outer layer is the dura mater, a tough fibrous tissue surrounding the cord and continuous with the sheaths of the spinal roots and spinal nerves. It extends caudally to the lower sacral region where it is reduced to a strand, the filum durae matris spinalis, attached to the coccyx (fig. 1). A thin subdural space is located between the dura mater and the arachnoid. Between the dura mater and the vertebral column is the epidural space, which contains many blood vessels, especially veins, and fat. A hypodermic needle may be inserted into this space in the lower sacral region for the injection of certain anesthetics (caudal anesthesia).

*See* also MENINGES AND CEREBROSPINAL FLUID.

**Cervical and Lumbosacral Enlargements.**—The spinal cord has two enlargements: the cervical enlargement and the lumbosacral enlargement. These regions are large because these segments are involved in the innervation of the upper and lower extremities respectively. The fifth through eighth cervical segments and the first thoracic segment comprise the cervical enlargement. The spinal nerves arising from the cervical enlargement form the brachial plexus (fig. 1).

**Cross Section.**—In cross section the spinal cord consists of an H-shaped gray matter surrounded by white matter (fig. 2 and 3). The gray matter is made up of cell bodies of nerve cells (the part of the cell containing the nucleus and other constituents) and nerve fibres oriented in the cross-sectional plane because the fibres enter and leave the gray matter from the white matter and spinal roots. The white matter consists of nerve fibres that are oriented parallel to the long axis of the spinal cord. These fibres are ascending to and descending from the brain and other levels of the spinal cord. The whiteness is due to the fatty sheath (myelin sheath) that surrounds many of the fibres. Some nonneural cells, called neuroglia, are scattered in both the gray matter and the white matter. The arms of the H that extend dorsally (that is, toward the back of the body) are called dorsal (sensory) horns, while the ventrally (toward the front) directed arms are called ventral (motor) horns. The crossbar of the H is the gray commissure and the intermediate gray. The gray matter is largest in the regions of the cervical and lumbosacral enlargements because of their relation to the innervation of the limbs. In the middle of the gray commissure is the small central canal, which is continuous with the ventricles of the brain. The white matter is subdivided into four columns: the dorsal column, between the dorsal horns; the ventral column, between the ventral horns; and the lateral columns, at the sides of the gray matter.

**Anatomical and Functional Organization of the Spinal Cord.**—This may be visualized by describing the orientation of the nerve cells of the spinal reflex arcs (*see* below, *Physiology*). For example, the withdrawal of the hand upon touching a hot stove before it is felt is a spinal reflex. The heat stimulates the terminal endings of the thermal neurons in the hand. The resulting impulses are transmitted by the fibres of these neurons through the peripheral nerves and dorsal roots into the dorsal horn. Each sensory nerve cell has its cell body in a dorsal root ganglion. Thus each nerve cell is a unit structure extending from its peripheral ending in the hand to its termination in the gray matter of the spinal cord.

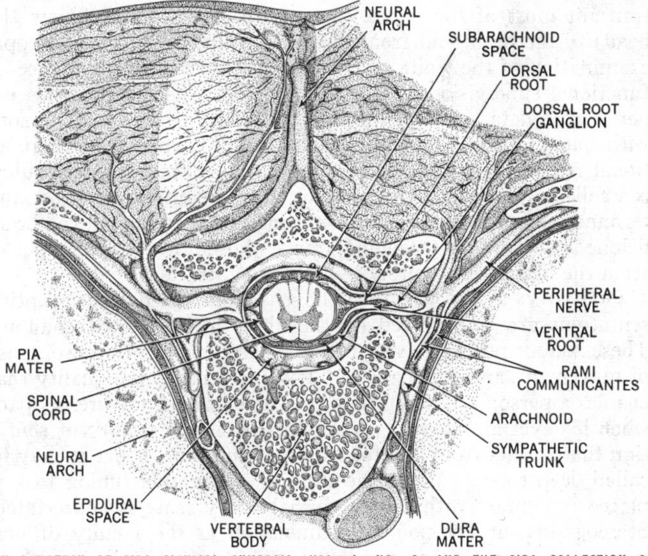


BY COURTESY OF CIBA CLINICAL SYMPOSIA, VOL. 1, NO. 6, AND THE CIBA COLLECTION OF MEDICAL ILLUSTRATIONS

FIG. 2.—CROSS SECTION THROUGH THORACIC VERTEBRA ILLUSTRATING THE SPINAL CORD, VERTEBRA, MENINGES, AND ASSOCIATED STRUCTURES

In the dorsal horn the nerve fibres have synapses (junctions) with one or more other neurons. The second nerve cells in the arc are called internuncial, or intercalated, neurons; each has a cell body in the gray matter (fig. 3). Some internuncial neurons send axons into the ventral horn and synapse with the motor cells whose cell bodies are in this horn. The axons of the motor cells reach the voluntary muscles via the ventral roots and peripheral nerves. In short, the stimulus transmitted by a nerve goes to the spinal cord via a dorsal root into the gray matter, then to an internuncial cell, and finally to the motor cell and the voluntary muscle

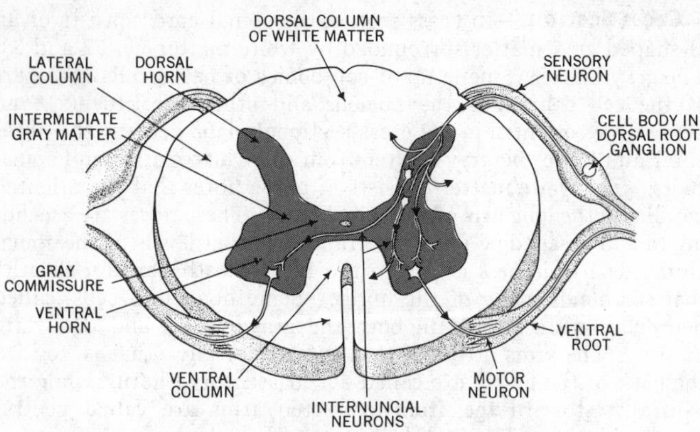


FIG. 3.—DIAGRAM OF CROSS SECTION OF THE SPINAL CORD ILLUSTRATING THE RELATIONSHIP OF THE SENSORY NEURON, INTERNUNCIAL NEURONS, AND THE MOTOR NEURON (ARROWS ON THE NEURONS INDICATE THE DIRECTION IN WHICH IMPULSES TRAVEL)

via the ventral root and the peripheral nerve. Since a series of three cells is involved, this is known as a three-neuron reflex. If the internuncial neuron is not involved, only two cells are in the series (two-neuron reflex).

In the knee-jerk reflex the sensory cells synapse directly with the motor neurons in the gray matter; it is, therefore, a two-neuron reflex. The internuncial neuron may cross over from the dorsal horn of one side to the ventral horn of the opposite side and synapse with motor cells. This is one means of coordinating one side with the other. An intersegmental reflex is a mechanism relaying impulses to higher and lower spinal cord levels to coordinate large areas of the body. The fibres of such internuncial neurons leave the gray matter and go up, down, or both (fibres may divide into two or more branches) to other spinal levels in that part of the white matter called the fasciculus proprius and comma tract (fig. 4) and reenter the gray matter to synapse with motor cells.

The white matter of the spinal cord contains nerve fibres that transmit most of the nerve impulses from the body (below the head) to the brain and from the brain to the body. Microscopic examination of the white matter does not give visible evidence of functional subdivisions. However, on the basis of numerous experimental data and examinations of spinal cords from persons with spinal injuries, the white matter can be partitioned into functional regions called tracts or pathways. A tract, or fasciculus, is a collection of nerve fibres having the same origin, function, and termination. Those fibres transmitting impulses toward the brain belong to sensory, or ascending, tracts; those transmitting impulses from the brain form motor, or descending, tracts.

**Pathways of Sensation.**—The sensations called proprioceptive sensations are transmitted by the fibres in the dorsal columns. These include position sense, pressure sense, vibratory sense, sense of movement, and stereognosis. Position sense is the quality that enables a person to know where the parts of his body are in space when his eyes are closed. Pressure sense is the quality of sensation that results from a deformation of the skin; hence it may be called deep touch. When the stem of a vibrating tuning fork is placed in contact with a bone the vibratory sense is appreciated. Stereognosis, or two-point discrimination, is the faculty of perceiving the weight, form, and shape of objects and of distinguishing the distance between two touch stimuli.

These senses are transmitted by fibres that pass from the peripheral nerves and dorsal roots into the dorsal horn of the spinal cord. These fibres with their cell bodies in the dorsal root ganglia have several branches in the gray matter. The shorter branches (collateral fibres) are utilized in the spinal reflex arcs. The main axon continues into the dorsal column to ascend in the column to the lower medulla of the brain. Two points of note are: (1) a fibre in the dorsal column is a part of the same neuron that was stimulated in the body, and (2) this fibre ascends on the same side of the spinal cord as it enters (does not cross the midline of the cord).

As a consequence, the sense of position of the toes, for example, is carried by nerve cells that extend from the toes to the medulla without a synapse. In addition, injury to the dorsal column on one side of the cord will result in the impairment of the proprioceptive senses on the same side of the body below the level of injury. Each half of the dorsal column is divided into a fasciculus gracilis and a fasciculus cuneatus (fig. 4). The proprioceptive impulses from the lower half of the body, including the lower extremities, are carried in the fasciculus gracilis, while those from the upper half of the body, including the upper extremities but excluding the head, are carried in the fasciculus cuneatus.

Some light touch sensations (gentle brushing of skin by cotton) are transmitted by fibres in the dorsal column. In the medulla the fibres of each half of the dorsal column synapse with neurons in the nucleus gracilis and nucleus cuneatus. The neurons of these nuclei cross over to the opposite side of the medulla and pass upward to the thalamus (*q.v.*) of the brain, from which they relay to the cerebral cortex.

Pain (*q.v.*) and temperature sensations are transmitted by another pathway. The fibres from the periphery, in common with other sensory fibres, enter the dorsal horn of the spinal cord where their terminal branches establish reflex connections with other neurons. At the spinal level at which the fibres enter the cord they synapse with dorsal horn neurons. Some of these cells are relays in the reflex arcs. Other neurons from the dorsal horn send axons across the midline to the opposite side through the ventral white commissure (ventral to the gray commissure) to join the lateral spinothalamic tract in the lateral columns (fig. 4). This tract contains more fibres as it ascends in the spinal cord, for new fibres are added from each spinal level. The tract's name is based on the fact that the fibres of the pathway originate in the dorsal horn of the spinal cord and terminate in the thalamus on the opposite side of the brain. Crude pain and awareness of touch may be brought to consciousness in the thalamus. Impulses from the thalamus are relayed to the cerebral cortex.

In addition to the light-touch fibres of the dorsal column, noted above, some light-touch impulses take a different pathway. After entering the dorsal horn the axons transmitting light touch synapse with neurons whose axons cross the midline to join the ventral spinothalamic tract in the ventral column (fig. 4).

The symptoms resulting from injury to the spinal cord are a consequence of the course of these pathways. For example, if the right half of the spinal cord is cut at a midthoracic level, conscious proprioception would be lost on the right side of the body below the level of the lesion (right abdomen and the right lower extremity). Pain and temperature sensations would be lost on the left side of the body below the level of the lesion. Because of the dual course of their fibres, light touch would be diminished, but not necessarily lost, below the level of the lesion. Perception of sensations from regions above the cut would be unimpaired.

Some unconscious proprioceptive impulses relay from the gray

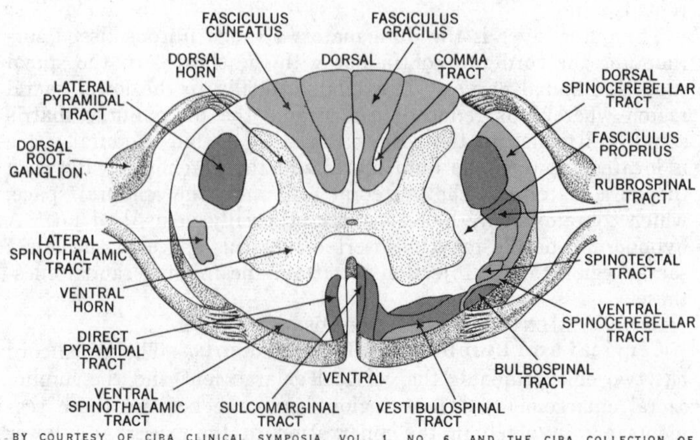


BY COURTESY OF CIBA CLINICAL SYMPOSIA, VOL. 1, NO. 6, AND THE CIBA COLLECTION OF MEDICAL ILLUSTRATIONS

FIG. 4.—SCHEMATIC SECTION THROUGH THE SPINAL CORD SHOWING THE LOCATION OF IMPORTANT TRACTS (DARK SHADED AREAS INDICATE TRACTS FROM BRAIN TO CORD; LIGHTER AREAS, FROM CORD TO BRAIN; DORSAL AND VENTRAL HORNS CONSTITUTE GRAY MATTER)

matter of the cord via the spinocerebellar tracts of the same and opposite sides and terminate in the cerebellum (fig. 4). This part of the brain is known as an unconscious proprioceptive organ.

The precise course of the pathways for sensations from the viscera (heart, intestinal tract, kidney, and so forth) through the white matter of the cord is not known.

**Motor Pathways.**—In the ventral horn of the gray matter are large motor cells whose axons pass through the ventral roots to the spinal nerves. These neurons, which innervate the voluntary muscles, are called lower motor neurons. If these cells become nonfunctional, as in poliomyelitis, the muscles are deprived of their nervous stimulation and do not contract. These muscles waste away (atrophy) and do not respond to stimulation (areflexia). This paralytic condition is known as a lower motor neuron paralysis.

The lower motor neuron cells are innervated by neurons of the spinal reflex arcs and by the descending motor tracts of the white matter. These descending tracts from the brain may synapse directly with the motor cells, but usually intercalated neurons of the gray matter are interposed between the descending tracts and the lower motor neurons. Collectively the motor tracts of the white matter are known as upper motor neurons. Their cell bodies are in the brain. Two major subdivisions of these motor tracts are recognized: the pyramidal tracts, which are phylogenetically new, and the extrapyramidal tracts, which are phylogenetically old.

The lateral pyramidal tract, or lateral corticospinal tract (fig. 4), arises in the cerebral cortex of the opposite side and crosses over just as its fibres enter the spinal cord. The direct pyramidal tract, or ventral corticospinal tract, originates in the cerebral cortex and crosses over in the spinal cord. The extrapyramidal tracts include the motor tracts that arise in regions of the brain other than the cerebral cortex. However, these tracts do receive nerve impulses from the cerebral cortex as well as other parts of the brain.

The extrapyramidal tracts include: (1) the vestibulospinal tract, which transmits impulses from the vestibular (balance) mechanisms of the inner ear; (2) the bulbospinal tract, which arises from the medulla or bulb of the lower brain stem; (3) the sulcomarginal tract, a collection of fibres from several regions of the brain stem; (4) the rubrospinal tract (minor in man) from the red nucleus in the midbrain; and (5) the reticulospinal tract (in local association with the rubrospinal tract) from the reticular formation of the brain stem.

When a number of these motor tracts are damaged, an upper neuron paralysis may result. This contrasts with the lower motor neuron paralysis previously mentioned. The reflexes are exaggerated; there is loss of voluntary motion, and the extremities become spastic. The condition, called spastic paralysis, results because the muscles are under control of a spinal cord that still mediates spinal reflex arcs but is deprived of its normal innervation from the brain. Spastic paralysis resulting from an injury of the spinal cord is observed on the same side of the body as the lesion.

The complexity of the nervous system is illustrated, for example, by spinal reflex arcs innervating the voluntary muscles. The motor pathways of the central nervous system discharge on small motor cells in the ventral horn of the spinal cord (fig. 4). These nerve cells whose axonal processes leave the spinal cord through the ventral roots stimulate small muscle fibres in certain sensory endings (neuromuscular spindles) to contract. These activated spindles in the voluntary muscles send impulses via sensory fibres through the dorsal root back to the spinal cord to synapse with the motor cells of the ventral horn. These motor cells stimulate the voluntary muscles to contract. When the voluntary muscles contract sufficiently the sensory endings in the tendons are stimulated to send impulses via sensory fibres through the dorsal root back to the spinal cord to inhibit the motor cells of the ventral horn. In brief, the sensory endings in the muscle and tendon have a critical role in muscle activity.

**Autonomic Nervous System.**—The autonomic nervous system, which is concerned with the motor innervation of glands, blood vessels, and the viscera, has neurons in the gray matter. The nerve cells of the sympathetic division of this system have their cell bodies in the lateral part of the intermediate gray, known as the intermediolateral cell column, of the thoracic and upper lumbar levels. Their axons leave the spinal cord through the ventral roots. The nerve cells of the spinal part of the parasympathetic division of this system have their cell bodies scattered in the gray matter of the midsacral levels. Their axons leave the spinal cord through the ventral roots. The sympathetic nervous system assists the body in meeting emergencies and stress. This includes increasing the rate and force of the heartbeat, the dilatation of the bronchial tubes of the lungs, and the inhibition of the motility and the secretory activity of the digestive system. The parasympathetic system contributes to the conservation of bodily energy. This includes decreasing the rate and force of the heartbeat, the constriction of the bronchial tubes, and the stimulation of the motility and secretory activity of the digestive system.

## EMBRYOLOGY

The nervous system is one of the first organ systems to develop. It differentiates as a long narrow strip of cells, the neural plate, on the dorsal surface of the early embryo. Each side of the plate grows rapidly, folds over, and fuses with its counterpart of the other side at the midline to form the neural tube with a cavity, the central canal.

During this process the cord sinks below the surface to become covered by embryonic skin. The cells lining the central canal (ependymal cells) differentiate into the nerve cells of the spinal cord and of the ganglia of the peripheral nervous system and, in addition, some neuroglia cells. In fetal life, the gray matter and the white matter are recognizable. If by some chance the fusion of the neural plate to form the neural tube is incomplete, the malformation known as spina bifida may occur.

## COMPARATIVE ANATOMY

In all the vertebrates the spinal cord is a tube with a central canal. In the jawless fishes (cyclostomes) the cord is flattened and the neurons are arranged as a pair of thin wings surrounded by unmyelinated fibres. In the sharks (elasmobranchs) the nerve fibres are myelinated, and hence the distinction between white matter and gray matter exists as in the higher vertebrates. In the amphibians the amount of gray matter increases to form the H configuration present in reptiles and mammals. In the reptiles and mammals the increase in the number of cells in the gray matter and of fibres in the white matter is significant. The basic patterns and topographical relations of the gray matter and white matter are similar in these forms. The quantitative increase is related to the complexity of the neural integrative mechanisms in the higher vertebrates.

As compared with the brain, the spinal cord is a conservative structure in vertebrate evolution.

*See* also NEUROLOGY, COMPARATIVE.

## PHYSIOLOGY

The spinal cord is only a part of the nervous organ that throughout the length of the body forms the meeting place of the nerve paths arriving from and issuing to all regions with which nerve fibres communicate.

To gain a true point of view for understanding the working of the spinal cord it is necessary to refer to the general function of the nervous system in the bodily economy.

**Relation to General Nervous System.**—An animal of microscopic size may continue throughout its life to be constituted entirely by one single cell. Animals of larger bulk, although each begins its existence as a single cell, attain their development by the multiplication of the original single cell, so that from it there comes to be formed a coherent mass of cells very many millions in number. In these multicellular animals each of the constituent cells is a minute organism, individually born, leading its own life (yet influencing other cells in countless subtle ways), and destined for individual death. The corporate power of the complex animal is the sum of the powers of those manifold individual existences, its cells, as they respond integrally to the organizational principle of the whole being.

Of the agencies which integrate the complex animal, one of the most potent is nervous action. A certain number of the unit cells composing the animal are specially differentiated from the rest to bind the whole together by nervous action. These specially differentiated cells are the nerve cells, or neurons. They constitute living threads along which waves of physicochemical disturbance are transmitted to act as releasing forces for the energy in distant cells.

It is characteristic of this nervous system, the system of neurons, that, although ramifying far and wide through the body, it is a continuum from end to end. The peripheral nerves are formed of bundles of neurons lying side by side, but these, although packed close together, are strictly isolated from one another as conductors and remain isolated throughout the whole length of the nerve.

The points of functional nexus of the neurons with one another are confined to one region only of the whole system. All their conductive connections with one another take place solely in the central nervous mass which constitutes the so-called central nervous system, a nervous organ extending axially along the length of the body midway between the body's lateral halves. Thither the neurons converge in vast numbers, those of each body segment converging to that fraction of the central organ which belongs to their body segment. The central nervous organ thus receiving these neurons is called, where it lies in the head, the brain; the rest of it is called in vertebrates the spinal cord, in worms and arthropods the nerve cord. The central organ not only receives neurons that converge to it from outside, but many of its own neurons thrust out their conductive arms from it as nerve fibres carrying nervous influence outward to regulate the activity of glands and muscles.

In the vertebrates the ingoing (afferent) neurons for each segment, and similarly the outgoing (efferent) neuron fibres, are collected into a segmental nerve. These are each attached to the spinal cord by two roots, one dorsal, consisting of the afferent fibres, the other ventral, consisting of the efferent fibres.

**The Reflex.**—The simplest complete reaction of the system is a reflex. There are many reflexes which are extremely complex, being built up of a number of simpler reflexes combined. A reflex is a reaction started by the environment acting as a stimulus upon some nerve which communicates the excitement to other nerves by connections with them in the central nervous organ. The excitement so generated and transmitted finally travels outward from the central organ by one or more of the efferent nerves and through these reaches muscles or glands, producing in them its final effect. The muscles and glands are from this point of view termed effector organs. The reaction is therefore "reflected" from the central organ. The nerve structures which include its trajectory are spoken of as a nervous arc.

The whole purpose of the central nervous organ is to bring afferent neurons into touch with efferent neurons. The whole purpose of reflex arcs is to bind one part of the organism to another part in such a way that what the environment is doing to the organism at one place may appropriately call forth or restrain movement or secretion in the muscles or glands wherever situated in the organism.

**Receptor Cells.**—There is one condition for the due performance of these reactions which is not provided by the nervous system itself. The afferent neurons are not in most cases so constituted as to be excitable themselves directly by the environment—for instance, they cannot be stimulated by light. Their amenability to the environment, their sensitization to environmental agencies, is effected by special cells adjunct to their peripheral ends. These cells form organs called receptors. They are delicately adapted to be stimulated by this or that particular agent and are classifiable into various species, so that each species is easily excited by a particular agent which is "adequate" for it, and is inexcitable or excitable only with difficulty by agencies of other kinds. Thus in the skin some receptors are adapted for mechanical stimuli (touch) and not for thermal stimuli, while others (cold spots, warm spots) are adapted for thermal stimuli and not for mechanical. As far as it is known, each afferent neuron is connected with receptors of one species only. The receptors thus confer upon the reflex arcs selective excitability. Each arc is thus tuned to respond to certain stimuli, while other arcs not having that kind of receptor do not respond. The receptors, therefore, while increasing the responsiveness of the organism to the environment, prevent confusion of reactions (in-coordination) by limiting to particular stimuli a particular reaction.

**Proprioceptors.**—The system of neurons is thus made accessible to the play of the external world acting on the body. And in addition to those receptors, which are stimulated directly by the external world, there are others lying within the mass of the organism itself, which are excitable by actions occurring in the organism. These are called proprioceptors. They are distributed preponderantly in the muscles and structures functionally adjunct to muscle, such as joints, ligaments, fasciae, etc. The reactions, both passive and active, induced in such motor structures reflexly by environmental stimuli tend therefore secondarily to be followed and accompanied by reflex reactions initiated from proprioceptors.

**Conduction.**—The process by which the excitement generated in the afferent neuron travels along the reflex arc is known as conduction. Conduction along afferent and efferent nerves differs in some important respects from that obtaining in the nerve centre; *i.e.,* in the piece of the central nervous system connecting the afferent nerve with the efferent nerve. In a nerve trunk the excited state set up in it by a stimulus travels along its fibres as a wavelike disturbance, called an impulse, at a speed of about 100 m. (325 ft.) per second. An impulse does not alter in intensity or speed as it travels. A nerve trunk when excited at some point along its length transmits the impulse in both directions (*i.e.,* both up and down each fibre) from the point stimulated. This is true whether the fibre is afferent or efferent. The speed of travel of the nervous impulse along the nerve trunk is the same whether the nervous impulse is weak or intense. The nerve trunk shows practically no delay in its response to an effective, even though weak, stimulus, and its response ceases practically at once on cessation of the exciting stimulus. When excited by repeated brief stimuli the rhythm of the response corresponds closely with that of the stimuli, even when the frequency of the latter is as high as 500 per second. Finally, nerve-trunk conduction is singularly resistant to fatigue, to impoverished blood supply, and to many drugs that powerfully affect reflex actions.

Through the central nervous organ the travel of the impulse exhibits departure from these features. Its intensity is liable to be altered in transit. Its time of transit is much longer than for a similar length of nerve trunk. Its direction of transmission becomes polarized; that is, confined to one direction along the nervous path. To a strong stimulus the central reaction, instead of being as brief as an impulse, may endure for a whole second or more. A stimulus not capable of evoking a response from a centre when applied once may by simple repetition become effective (temporal summation).

It is in the gray matter that conduction differs in these respects from conduction in nerve trunks. In the gray matter each afferent fibre breaks up into branching threadlets which ramify in various directions and terminate in close apposition with other neurons. The point of nexus of one neuron with another is termed the synapse. The distance between two neurons at the synapse is about 200 Å (angstrom units; 1 Å = $\frac{1}{10,000,000}$ mm., or about $\frac{1}{250,000,000}$ in.). The absence of cytoplasmic continuity between the neurons is the anatomical basis that accounts for the slight delay in the speed of the impulse at the synapse and for the polarization of the direction of the impulse.

**Reflex Reactions.**—When the spinal cord is severed at any point the reflex arcs of the portion of the body behind the transection are quite cut off from the rest of the nervous system in front, including the brain. The reflex reactions elicited from the thus isolated region cannot therefore be modified by the action of the higher nervous centres. In the head the local centres are overlaid by higher centres which cannot by any simple severance be separated from them. By studying, therefore, the powers of the cord behind a complete spinal transection, information can be obtained as to the powers of the purely local or segmental reflex mechanisms.

The so-called flexion reflex of the limb is one of the most accessible of the local reflex reactions which can thus be studied with an isolated portion of the spinal cord as its centre. Let it be supposed that the limb observed is the hind limb. The three main joints of the limb are the hip, the knee, and the ankle. Each of these joints is provided with muscles which flex (bend) it, and others which extend (straighten) it. It is found that the reflex throws into contraction the flexor muscles of each of these joints. It matters little which of all the various afferent nerves of the limb is stimulated; whichever of these the afferent nerve may be, the centrifugal discharge goes to practically the same muscles, namely, always to the flexors of the joints.

Not only does the reflex action not discharge motor impulses into the nerves of the extensor muscles, but if the spinal cord happens to be discharging impulses into these nerves when the reflex is evoked this discharge is suppressed or diminished (inhibited). In this way the latter muscles are prevented from impeding the action of the contracting flexors. This inhibition prevents other reflexes from upsetting for the time being the due action of the flexion reflex, for it renders the muscles opposing that reflex less accessible to motor discharge through the spinal cord, whatever the quarter from which incitation to that discharge may come.

A feature of this reflex is its graded intensity. A weak stimulus evokes in the flexor muscles a contraction which is weak and in the extensor muscles a relaxation which is slight. In the case of the muscle fibre, any strength of stimulus, if sufficient to excite it at all, excites the fibre totally and evokes its full contraction, and this latter remains the same in amount so long as the mechanical and nutritive conditions of the fibre remain constant. With each muscle fibre reacting on this "all-or-none" principle and each nerve fibre similarly responding (*see* ALL-OR-NONE LAW), different amounts of contraction yielded by the muscle under different strengths of stimulation of its nerve signify differences simply in the number of muscle fibres the stimulus excites. In other words the weaker stimuli excite fewer of the nerve fibres innervating the muscle.

When the tension developed by the muscle (*e.g.*, against a stiff spring) reaches the maximum obtainable from it, that fact tells us that all the muscle fibres are then in contraction; when the tension development is less than maximal, some of the muscle fibres are not in action. A stimulus to the nerve which evokes maximal tension from the muscle is one which succeeds in exciting all the nerve fibres innervating the muscle, and any stimulus which evokes less than maximal tension is leaving some of the nerve fibres idle.

The tension developed by a muscle under reflex excitation falls short of its maximal tension, even when the afferent nerve is stimulated maximally. The reflex activates a proportion only of the total aggregate of the muscle's fibres, and therefore a proportion only of the spinal motor neurons innervating the muscle. But within the range of the limit imposed by the maximal number of muscle fibres which it can activate, the grading of the number activated in accordance with the grading of the strength of stimulation of the afferent nerve is very delicate, much more so than in the case of the motor nerve itself. The actual fractional proportion of the muscle's total aggregate of motor units which an afferent nerve, maximally stimulated, can activate differs from one afferent nerve to another, and for the same afferent nerve in different experiments; *e.g.*, a subconvulsive dose of strychnine raises the size of the fraction. The threshold value of stimulus for the reflex is usually higher than for the contraction of the muscle from the motor nerve.

Spinal reflex action no more regards "muscles" than does a motor centre of the cerebral cortex. Both ignore muscles as entities and have in view movements purely. A weak flexion reflex activates a few fibres of each of the several flexor muscles of the limb. The reflex treats a complex composed from some (*i.e.*, those of similar threshold for the particular afferent nerve) motor units of hip flexor, of knee flexor, and of ankle flexor as functionally more homogeneous than is the total group of fibres composing any one of these muscles alone.

Reflex inhibition has its seat in the gray matter of the spinal centre. It acts at some point in the reflex arc upstream from the all-or-none motor unit (motor nerve fibre with its group of muscle fibres). The inhibitory reflex is, like the excitatory, capable of very delicate grading; its effect in diminishing or precluding this or that amount of an excitatory reflex is effected entirely by regulating the number of the motor units thrown out of action or kept out of action. Intensity of contraction or of relaxation is thus in both cases a question simply of number of motor units reacting. The reflex centre continues discharging impulses for a certain time after its exciting stimulus has ceased. This after-discharge succeeding a strong stimulus may persist even for several seconds.

**Refractory Phase.**—Besides characters common to all or many spinal reflexes certain spinal reflexes have features peculiar to themselves or exhibited by them in degrees not obvious in other reflexes. One of these features is refractory phase. The scratch reflex exemplifies this. In the dog, cat, and many other animals the hind limb often performs a rapid scratching movement, the foot being applied to the skin of the shoulder or neck as if to groom the hairy coat in that region. This movement is in the intact animal under control of the brain, and can be executed or desisted from at will. When certain of the higher centres in the brain have been destroyed, this scratching action occurs very readily and in an uncontrolled way. When the spinal cord has been severed in the neck this scratching movement of the hind limb can be elicited with regularity as a spinal reflex by merely rubbing the skin of the side of the neck or shoulder, or applying there a weak electric current to the skin.

In this reflex the stimulus excites afferent nerves connected with the hairs in the skin, and these convey impulses to the spinal centres in the neck or shoulder segments; these in turn discharge impulses into nerve fibres entirely intraspinal, passing backward along the cord to reach motor centres in the hind limb region. These motor centres in turn discharge centrifugal impulses into the muscles of the hind limb of the same side of the body as the shoulder that is the seat of irritation. The motor discharge is peculiar in that it causes the muscles of the hind limb to contract rhythmically at a rate of about four contractions per second, and the discharge is peculiar further in that it excites the flexor and extensor muscles of the joints alternately so that at the hip, for instance, the limb is alternately flexed and extended, each single phase of the movement lasting about an eighth of a second.

Now this rhythmic discharge remains the same in rate whether the exciting stimulus applied to the skin is continuous or one of many various rates of repetition. Evidently at some point in the reflex arc there is a mechanism that, after reacting to the impulses reaching it, remains for a certain brief part of a second unresponsive, and then becomes once more for a brief period responsive, and so on. This phasic alternation of excitability and inexcitability repeats itself throughout the continuance of the reflex. The phase of inexcitability is termed the refractory phase. Its seat lies in the spinal centre. A similar element almost certainly forms part of the coordinating mechanism for many other cyclic reflexes, including those of the stepping of the limbs, the movement of the jaw in mastication, the action of the eyelids in blinking, and perhaps the respiratory movements of the chest and larynx.

**Fatigue.**—Nerve trunks do not easily tire out under even the most prolonged stimulation. Reflex actions on the other hand relatively soon tire. Some are more resistant, however, than are others. The flexion reflex may be continued for ten minutes at a time. As a reflex tires, the muscular contraction which it causes tends to become less intense and less steady. The relatively rapid onset of fatigue in reflexes is counterbalanced by speedy recovery in repose. A long flexion reflex, when from fatigue it has become weak, tremulous, and irregular, will recommence after 30 seconds' repose with almost the same vigour and steadiness as if it had not recently been tired out.

The natural movements to which the artificially provoked reflexes seem to correspond do not demand prolonged motor activity or, when they do, demand it in rhythmic repetition with intervening pauses which allow repose.

**Reflex Postures.**—But there are certain reflexes which do persist for long periods at a time. These are reflex postures. The hind limbs of the spinal frog (one in which the spinal cord has been surgically isolated from the brain) assume an attitude which is reflex, for it ceases on severance of the afferent spinal roots. This attitude is one of flexion at hip, knee, and ankle, resembling the well-known natural posture of the frog as it squats when quiet in the tank. Similarly in the decerebrate dog or cat certain muscles (*e.g.,* the limb extensors) exhibit a persistent contraction. These tonic reflexes are related to attitudes. In the dog and cat they are exhibited by those muscles whose action antagonizes gravity in postures which are usual in the animal; thus the extensors of the knee and hip and shoulder and elbow are in tonic contraction during standing. The postural contraction is accompanied by electrical "action currents" like those of other contractions, though weak and indicative of self-smothering from the rhythms being asynchronous in the contributory fibre groups. The postural contraction of the extensor muscles in the maintenance of the erect posture is traceable to a reflex, called the stretch reflex. A stretch (*e.g.,* by a pull upon the tendon) lengthening the muscle by even so little as 0.5% excites reflex contraction of some of its fibres. The passive stretch is a mechanical stimulus to some of the proprioceptive organs (perhaps the muscle spindles) in the muscle. The reflex is therefore unobtainable when the afferent nerve fibres of the muscle itself have been severed. The essential centre for the stretch reflex is spinal, but midbrain and cerebellar centres much reinforce it. In the erect posture the head, neck, tail, and jaw would droop and the limbs fold up under their own weight and that of superincumbent parts, were not the "antigravity" muscles checked from yielding by the stretch reflex which their own passive yield induces in themselves. Hence the reflexly maintained standing posture is a multiple stretch reflex. Considerable latitude of actual pose is allowed to the individual parts because each muscle involved acts for itself and develops and regulates its own stretch reflex.

Characteristic of reflex postural contraction is its continuance for long spells at a time without obvious fatigue. Attempts to reproduce this feature by electrical stimulation of afferent nerves or of the muscle's motor nerve are uniformly unsuccessful. The suggestion has therefore been made that the postural contraction of muscle is due to a different process in the muscle fibre from that of the ordinary contraction executing movements and so easily and often studied under electrical stimulation in the laboratory. A. Forbes, however, offered the satisfactory explanation that the postural contraction, while the same process as that of ordinary reflex and other contraction, involves usually relatively few motor units at a time and these, as they fatigue, are replaced by others. The stretch which is the essential stimulus is automatically shifted to fresh motor units as soon as those already in operation begin to yield and give out.

The eyeballs are eminently organs which, the gaze being a posture, employ active postures throughout the waking day. The proprioception of the neck muscles excites from the cervical spinal cord reflex influences acting on the nerves of the eyeball muscles. An instance is: turning of the neck toward one side excites turning of the eyeballs toward the opposite side. Or again, a clockwise partial rotation of the neck round its long axis excites from the neck proprioceptor a compensatory counterclockwise shifting of the eyeballs. These reflex postures of the eyeballs are sometimes called compensatory, because they tend to keep the gaze level despite displacements of the head by the movements of the neck.

When the cord or the medulla and cord of an animal (cat) is surgically isolated from the brain, the animal's composite stretch reflex enables it when placed in the erect posture to maintain that attitude, even for hours at a time; but it is incapable of assuming that posture when laid, for instance, on its side. But when the midbrain is retained in addition to hindbrain and cord, the animal has that power of righting itself. These righting reflexes are likewise postural and largely evoked by the otolith organs. Although not truly spinal reflexes, their field of nervous operation overruns into the spinal cord.

**Interaction Between Reflexes.**—At the commencement of every reflex arc is a receptive neuron extending from the receptive surface to the central nervous organ. This neuron forms the sole avenue which impulses generated at its receptive point can use, whatever their destination may be. This neuron is therefore a path exclusive to the impulses generated at its own receptive point, and other receptive points than its own cannot employ it. A single receptive point may play reflexly upon a considerable number of different effector organs. It may be connected through its reflex path with many muscles and glands in many different regions. Yet all its reflex arcs spring from the one single shank or stem; *i.e.,* from the one afferent neuron that conducts from the receptive point at the periphery into the central nervous organ.

But at the termination of every reflex arc is found a final neuron, the ultimate conductive link to an effector organ (muscle or gland). This last link in the chain (*e.g.,* the motor neuron) differs obviously in one important respect from the first link of the chain. It does not subserve exclusively impulses generated at one single receptive source, but receives impulses from many receptive sources situated in many and various regions of the body. It is the sole path which all impulses, no matter whence they come, must travel if they are to act on the muscle fibres to which it leads.

Therefore, while the receptive neuron forms a private path exclusively serving impulses of one source only, the final or efferent neuron is, so to say, a public path common to impulses arising at any of many sources of reception. A receptive field (*e.g.,* an area of skin) is analyzable into receptive points. One and the same effector organ stands in reflex connection not only with many individual points, but even with many various receptive fields. Reflexes generated in manifold sense organs can pour their influence into one and the same muscle. Thus a limb muscle is the terminus of many reflex arcs arising in various parts of the body. Its motor nerve is a path common to all the reflex arcs which reach that muscle.

Reflex arcs show, therefore, the general features that the initial neuron of each is a private path belonging exclusively to a single receptive point (or small group of points); and that finally the arcs discharge into a path leading to an effector organ; and that their final path is common to all receptive points wherever they may lie in the body, so long as they have connection with the effector organ in question. Before finally converging upon the motor neuron the arcs converge to some degree. Their private paths join internuncial paths common in various degrees to groups of private paths. The terminal path may, to distinguish it from internuncial common paths, be called the final common path. The motor nerve to a muscle is a collection of final common paths.

Certain consequences result from this arrangement. One of these is the preclusion of essential qualitative difference between nerve impulses arising in different afferent nerves. If two conductors have a tract in common, there can hardly be essential qualitative difference between their modes of conduction.

A second consequence is that, each receptor being dependent for final communication with its effector organ upon a path not exclusively its own but common to it with certain other receptors, such nexus necessitates successive and not simultaneous use of the common path by various receptors using it to different or opposed effect.

In the simultaneous correlation of reflexes some reflexes combine harmoniously, being reactions that mutually reinforce. These may be termed allied reflexes, and the neutral arcs which they employ may be termed allied arcs. On the other hand, some reflexes, as mentioned above, are antagonistic one to another and incompatible. These do not mutually reinforce; instead, one of them inhibits the other.

**Allied Reflexes.**—What happens when trains of impulses, traveling by convergent afferent arcs, meet at the same common path? With convergent reflexes that are allied in the above sense, this case must be one of extremely frequent occurrence and the management of the interaction between the convergent streams of impulses must be a fundamental factor in nervous coordination. The afferent path A discharges into the intraspinal motor neurons of the knee flexor and can activate 75% of them. The afferent path B also discharges into the motor neurons of the same muscle and can activate 75% of them. When the muscle is reflexly contracting to A with a tension 75% of that of the muscle's maximal contraction, stimulation of B is added. The contraction tension in result rises to 85% of the maximal. The inference is that for 65% of the total motor units of the muscle the excitation from A acts upon the same motor units as would that from B. In other words 65% of the total aggregate of the motor units of the muscle are common to A and to B. The stream of impulses arriving at these common motor units from B when A's stream is already activating them leaves their activity unchanged, failing either to increase or to diminish it. A's stream, which is engaging them, precludes B's stream from engaging them. This is termed occlusion.

The final common path under the competition of allied arcs is comparable with a telephone line already busy for one subscriber and for that time engaged and unavailable to other subscribers. The action of the principle of the final common path may be instanced in regard to allied arcs in the scratch reflex as follows. If, while the scratch reflex is being elicited from a skin point at the shoulder, a second point 1 cm. ($\frac{2}{5}$ in.) from the first point, but also in the receptive field of skin, is stimulated, the stimulation at this second point favours the reaction from the first point. This is well seen when the stimulus at each point is of subminimal intensity. The two stimuli, though each unable separately to invoke the reflex, yet do so when applied both at the same time. The receptive field of a reflex is really the common area of commencement of a number of allied arcs.

**Antagonistic Reflexes.**—But not all reflexes connected to one and the same common final path stand to one another in the relation of allied reflexes. Suppose during the scratch reflex a stimulus is applied to the foot not of the scratching side but of the opposite side. The left leg, which is executing the scratch reflex in response to stimulation of the left shoulder skin, is cut short in its movement by the stimulation of the right foot, although the stimulus at the shoulder to provoke the scratch movement is maintained unaltered all the time. The stimulus to the right foot will temporarily interrupt a scratch reflex, or will cut it short or will delay its onset; which of these occurs depends on the time relations of the stimuli. The inhibition of the scratch reflex occurs sometimes when the contraction of the muscles innervated by the reflex conflicting with it is very slight. There is interference between the two reflexes and the one is inhibited by the other.

The reflex from the right foot evokes at the opposite (left) knee extension; in doing this it causes steady excitation of extensor neurons of that knee and steadily inhibits the flexor neurons. But the scratch reflex causes rhythmic excitation of the flexor neurons. In this conflict the flexor neurons, as a final common path, therefore lie under the influence of two antagonistic reflexes, one of which would excite them to rhythmical discharge four times a second, while the other would continually repress all discharge in them.

In all these forms of interference there is a competition, as it were, between the excitatory stimulus used for the one reflex and the excitatory stimulus for the other. Both stimuli are in progress together, and the one in taking effect precludes the other's taking effect as far as the final common path is concerned.

Again, if, while stimulation of the skin of the shoulder is evoking the scratch reflex, the skin of the hind foot of the same side is stimulated, the scratching may be arrested. Stimulation of the skin of the hind foot in a way that has the character of threatening the part with damage (nociceptive stimulus) causes the leg to be flexed, drawing the foot up by steady maintained contraction of the flexors of the ankle, knee, and hip. Here, therefore, there is an arc that discharges into a final path, common to it and to the scratch reflex arc; both these arcs employ the same effector organ, namely, the knee flexor, and employ it by the common medium of the final pathway. But though the channels for both reflexes discharge into the same final common path, the excitatory flexor effect specific to each differs strikingly in the two cases. In the scratch reflex the flexor effect is an intermittent effect; in the nociceptive flexion reflex the flexor effect is steady and maintained. The scratch reflex is set aside by that of the nociceptive arc from the homonymous foot. (The term homonymous is used here and below to indicate a common locus or other intimate experimental relationship.)

The stimulation which previously sufficed to provoke the scratch reflex is no longer effective, though it is continued all the time. But when the stimulation of the foot is discontinued the scratch reflex returns. In that respect, although there is no enforced inactivity, there is an interference that is tantamount to, if not the same thing as, inhibition. Though there is no cessation of activity in the motor neuron, one form of activity that was being impressed upon it is cut short and another takes its place. A stimulation of the foot too weak to cause more than a minimal reflex often will suffice completely to interrupt, cut short, or prevent onset of the scratch reflex.

The kernel of the interference between the homonymous flexion reflex and the scratch reflex is that both employ the same final common pathway to different effect—just as in the interference between the crossed extension reflex and the scratch reflex. Evidently, the homonymous flexion reflex and the crossed extension reflex both use the same final common pathway. And they use it to different effect. The motor neuron to the flexor of the knee being taken as a representative of the final common path, the homonymous flexion reflex inhibits it from discharging. Hence if, while the direct flexion reflex is in progress, the crossed foot is stimulated, the reflex of the knee flexor is inhibited. The crossed extension reflex therefore inhibits not only the scratch reflex but also the homonymous flexion reflex.

Further, in all these interferences between reflexes the direction taken by the inhibition is reversible. Thus the scratch reflex is not only liable to be inhibited by, but is itself able to inhibit, either the homonymous flexion reflex or the crossed extension reflex; the homonymous flexion reflex is not only capable of being inhibited by the crossed extension reflex, but conversely in its turn can inhibit the crossed extension reflex. These interferences are therefore reversible in direction. Certain conditions determine which reflex among two or more competing ones shall obtain mastery over the final common path and thus obtain expression.

As to the intimate nature of the mechanism which thus, by summation or by interference, gives coordination where neurons converge upon a common path, it is difficult to surmise. In the central nervous system of vertebrates, afferent neurons A and B in their convergence toward and impingement upon another neuron Z, toward which they conduct, do not make any lateral connection directly with one another—at least, there is no clear evidence that they do. It seems, then, that the only structural link between A and B is neuron Z itself. Z itself should therefore be the field of coalition of A and B if they transmit allied reflexes.

**Factors Determining the Sequence.**—The formation of a common path from tributary converging afferent arcs is important because it gives a coordinate mechanism. There the dominant action of one afferent arc or of a set of allied arcs in condominium is subject to supersession by another afferent arc or set of allied arcs, and the supersession normally occurs without intercurrent confusion.

Whatever may be the nature of the physiological process occurring between the competing reflexes for dominance over the common path, the issue of their competition, namely, the determination of which one of the competing arcs shall for the time being reign over the common path, is largely conditioned by four factors. These are spinal induction, relative fatigue, relative intensity of stimulus, and the functional species of the reflex.

*Spinal Induction.*—This refers to the ability of one spinal reflex to lower the threshold of another. Induction occurs in two forms: immediate and successive. In immediate induction the stimulus that excites a reflex tends by central spread to facilitate and lower the threshold for reflexes allied to that which it particularly excites. Thus there tends to be formed a constellation of reflexes that reinforce each other, so that a reflex figure results. If the stimulus shifts, allied arcs are by the induction particularly prepared to be responsive to it or to a similar stimulus.

Immediate induction occurs only between allied reflexes. Its tendency in the competition between afferent arcs is to fortify the reflex just established, or, if transition occurs, to favour transition to an allied reflex. Immediate induction seems to obtain with highest intensity at the outset of a reflex, or at least near its commencement.

Successive induction is in several ways the reverse of the preceding. If the crossed-extension reflex of the limb of the spinal dog (one whose spinal cord has been severed from the brain) is elicited at regular intervals, say once a minute, by an electrical stimulus of defined duration and intensity, the resulting reflex movements are repeated each time with much constancy of character, amplitude, and duration. If in one of the intervals a strong prolonged (*e.g.*, 30 seconds) flexion reflex is reduced from the limb yielding the extensor reflex movement, the latter reflex is found intensified after the intercurrent flexion reflex. The intercalated flexion reflex lowers the threshold for the aftercoming extension reflexes, and especially increases their after-discharge. This effect may endure, progressively diminishing, through four or five minutes, as tested by the extensor reflexes at successive intervals. Now, during the flexion reflex the extensor arcs were inhibited; after the flexion reflex these arcs are in this case evidently in a phase of exalted excitability. The phenomenon presents obvious analogy to visual contrast. The exaltation aftereffect may ensue with such intensity that simple discontinuance of the stimulus maintaining one reflex is immediately followed by spontaneous appearance of the antagonistic reflex.

The so-called mark-time reflex of the spinal dog is an alternating stepping movement of the hind limbs that occurs on holding the animal up so that its limbs dangle. The reflex can be inhibited by stimulating the skin of the tail. On cessation of that stimulus the stepping movement sets in more vigorously and at a quicker rate than before. This afterincrease might be explicable in either of two ways. It might be due to the mere repose of the reflex centre, the repose so recruiting the centre as to strengthen its subsequent action. But a similar period of repose obtained by simply supporting one limb—which causes cessation of the reflex in both limbs, the stimulus being stretch of the hip flexors under gravity—is not followed by afterincrease of the reflex. Or the afterincrease might result from the inhibition being followed by a rebound to superactivity. This latter seems to be the case. The afterincrease occurs even when both hind limbs are passively lifted from below during the whole duration of the inhibitory stimulus applied to the tail. And the reflex inhibition of the knee extensor by stimulation of the central end of its own nerve is followed by marked rebound to superactivity of the extensor itself. Again, the knee jerk, after being inhibited by stimulation of the hamstring nerve, is more brisk than before the inhibition.

By virtue of this spinal contrast, therefore, the extension reflex predisposes to and may actually induce a flexion reflex, and conversely the flexion reflex predisposes to and may actually induce an extension reflex. This process is qualified to play a part in linking reflexes together in alternating sequence.

A reflex movement must generate in its progress a number of further stimuli and throw up a shower of centripetal impulses from the moving muscles and joints into the spinal cord. Squeezing of muscles and stimulation of their afferent nerves and those of joints, etc., elicit reflexes. The primary reflex movement might be expected, therefore, of itself to initiate further reflex movement, and that secondarily to initiate further still, and so on. Yet on cessation of the external stimulus to the foot in the flexion reflex, the whole reflex comes to an end, usually at once. The scratch reflex, even when violently provoked, ceases usually within two seconds of the discontinuance of the external stimulus that provoked it. There is as yet no satisfactory explanation of this.

*Relative Fatigue.*—Another condition influencing the issue of competition between reflexes of different sources for possession of one and the same final common path is fatigue. A spinal reflex under continuous excitation or frequent repetition becomes weaker, and may cease altogether. This decline is progressive, and takes place earlier in some kinds of reflexes than it does in others. In the spinal dog the scratch reflex under ordinary circumstances tires much more rapidly than does the flexion reflex.

A reflex as it tires shows other changes besides decline in amplitude of contraction. Thus in the flexion reflex, the original steadiness of the contraction decreases; it becomes tremulous, and the tremor becomes progressively more marked and more irregular. Finally, an irregular phasic tremor of the muscles is all that remains. It is not the flexor muscles themselves which tire out, for these, when under fatigue of the flexion reflex, contract no longer for that reflex but do contract in response to the scratch reflex which also employs them.

Similar results are furnished by the scratch reflex, with certain differences in accord with the peculiar character of its individual charge. One of these latter is the feature that the individual beats of the scratch reflex usually become slower and follow each other at slower frequency. Also the beats, instead of remaining fairly regular in amplitude and frequency, tend to succeed in somewhat regular groups. The beats may disappear altogether for a short time, and then for a short time reappear.

When the scratch reflex elicited from a spot of skin is fatigued, the fatigue holds for that spot, but does not implicate the reflex as obtained from the surrounding skin. The reflex is, when tired out to stimuli at that spot, easily obtainable by stimulation 2 cm. ($\frac{4}{5}$ in.) or more away.

Recovery from the local fatigue of a spinal reflex seems to occur with remarkable speed. A few seconds' remission of the stimulus suffices for marked though incomplete restoration of the reaction. Fatigue seems a process elaborated and preserved in the selective evolution of the neural machinery. One obvious use attaching to it is the prevention of the too-prolonged continuous use of a common path by any one receptor. It precludes one receptor from occupying for long periods an effector organ to the exclusion of all other receptors. It prevents long continuous possession of a common path by any one reflex of considerable intensity. It favours the receptors taking turnabout. It helps to ensure serial variety of reaction. The organism, to be successful in a million-sided environment, must in its reaction be many sided. Were it not for such so-called fatigue, an organism might, in regard to its receptivity, develop an eye, or an ear, or a mouth, or a hand or leg, but it would hardly develop the marvelous congeries of all those various sense organs which it is actually found to possess.

The final efferent-root neuron forms the instrument for many different reflex arcs and acts. It is responsive to them in various rhythms and in various grades of intensity. In accordance with this, it seems from experimental evidence to be relatively indefatigable.

*Relative Intensity of Stimulus.*—In the transition from one reflex to another a final common path changes hands and passes from one master to another. A fresh set of afferent arcs becomes dominant on the supersession of one reflex by the next. Of all the conditions determining which one of competing reflexes shall for the time being reign over a final common path, the intensity of reaction of the afferent arc itself relatively to that of its rivals is probably the most powerful. Other things being equal, an afferent arc that strongly stimulates is more likely to capture the common path than is one excited feebly. A stimulus can establish its reflex and inhibit an opposed one only if it has intensity. This explains why, in order to produce examples of spinal inhibition, recourse has so frequently been made in past times to strong stimuli. A strong stimulus will inhibit a reflex in progress although a weak one will fail. Thus in inhibition of micturition in the spinal dog a forcible squeeze of the tail will do it, but not a weak squeeze. So, likewise, any condition that raises the excitability and responsiveness of a nervous arc will give it power to inhibit other reflexes, just as it would if it were excited by a strong stimulus.

Crossed reflexes are usually less easy to provoke, less reliable of obtainment, and less intense than are direct reflexes. Consequently, crossed reflexes usually are more easily inhibited and replaced by direct reflexes than are the latter by the former. Thus the crossed stepping reflex is easily replaced by the scratch reflex, though its stimulus may be continued all the time and though the scratch reflex itself is not a very potent reflex. But the reverse can occur with suitably adjusted intensity of stimuli.

Again, the flexion reflex of the dog's leg, when fully developed, is accompanied by extension in the opposite leg. This crossed extensor movement, though often very vigorous, may be considered as an accessory and weaker part of the whole reflex, of which the prominent part is flexion of the homonymous limb. When the flexion reflex is poorly elicitable—as, for instance, in spinal shock or under fatigue or weak excitation—the crossed extension does not appear. But, where the flexion reflex is well developed, if not merely one foot but both are stimulated simultaneously with stimuli of fairly equal intensity, steady flexion at knee, hip, and ankle results in both limbs, and extension occurs in neither limb. The part of each reflex that affects the opposite side is inhibited by the flexion on its own side. In other words, the more intense part of each reflex obtains possession of the final common paths at the expense of the less intense portion of the reflex. But if the intensity of the stimuli applied to the right and left feet is not balanced closely enough, the crossed extension of the reflex excited by the stronger stimulus is found to exclude even the homonymous flexion that the weaker stimulus should and would otherwise evoke from the leg to which it is applied.

It was pointed out above that in a number of cases the transference of control of the final common pathway from one afferent arc to another is reversible. Other things being equal, the direction of the transference can be easily governed by making the stimulation of this receptor or that receptor the more intense. A factor largely determining whether a reflex will succeed another or not is therefore intensity of stimulus.

*Functional Species of Reflex.*—The fourth main determinant for the issue of the conflict between rival reflexes is the functional species of the reflexes. Reflexes initiated from a species of receptor apparatus that may be termed nociceptive appear to dominate particularly the majority of the final common paths issuing from the spinal cord. In the simpler sensations experienced from various kinds of stimuli applied to the skin there can be distinguished those of touch, of cold, of warmth, and of pain. The pain (nociceptive) ending may be regarded as adapted to a whole group of excitants which have, in relation to the organism, one feature in common, a nocuous (injurious) character.

Considering the organism's liability to various kinds of mechanical and other damage, in a world beset with dangers amid which the individual and species have to win their way in the struggle for existence, nocuous stimuli may be regarded as part of a normal state of affairs. The skin has evolved a specific sense of its own injuries. As psychical adjunct to the reactions of that apparatus, a strong displeasurable effective quality is found in the sensations they evoke. This may be a means for branding upon memory, of however rudimentary a kind, a feeling from past events that have been perilously critical for the existence of the individuals of the species. In other words, if it is admitted that damage to such an exposed sentient organ as the skin must in the evolutionary history of animal life have been sufficiently frequent in relation to its importance, then the existence of a specific set of nerves for skin pain seems to offer no genetic difficulty, any more than does the clotting of blood or innate immunity to certain diseases. That these nerve endings constitute a distinct species is argued by their all evoking not only the same species of sensation, but the same species of reflex movement as regards purpose, intensity, resistance to shock, etc. And their evolution may well have been unaccompanied by evolution of any specialized end organ, since the naked free nerve endings would better suit the wide and peculiar range of stimuli to which reaction is in this case required. A low threshold was not required because the stimuli were all intense, intensity constituting their harmfulness; but response to a wide range of stimuli of different kinds was required, because harm might come in various forms. That responsive range is supplied by the naked nerve itself, and would be cramped by the specialization of an end organ. Hence these nerve endings remained free.

In the spinal animal—where pain is of course nonexistent—the prepotent (dominant) reflexes are excited by stimulation of areas in which pain can be excited most intensely in intact animals, and likewise by stimuli that are most fitted to excite pain in intact animals. The nervous arcs of pain nerves, broadly speaking, dominate the spinal centres in peculiar degree. Pain is thus the psychical adjunct of an imperative protective reflex. It is preferable, however, to avoid the term pain nerves, since into the merely spinal and reflex aspect of the reaction of these nerves no sensation of any kind can be shown to enter. Remembering that the feature common to all this group of stimuli is that they threaten or actually commit damage to the tissue to which they are applied, a convenient term for application to them is nocuous. In that case what from the point of view of sense are cutaneous pain nerves are from the point of view of reflex action conveniently termed nociceptive nerves.

In the competition between reflexes the nociceptive as a rule dominate with peculiar certainty and facility. This explains why such stimuli have been so much used to evoke reflexes in the spinal frog, and why, judging from them, such importance for the fate of the organism belongs to spinal reflexes.

One and the same skin surface will evoke in the hind limb of the spinal dog one or other of two diametrically different reflexes depending on whether the mechanical stimulus is a harmful or a harmless touch. A needle prick to the sole of the foot causes invariably the drawing up of the limb: the flexion reflex. A harmless smooth contact, on the other hand, causes extension: the extensor thrust described above. This flexion is therefore a nociceptive reflex. But the scratch reflex—which is so readily evoked by simple light irritation of the skin of the shoulder—is relatively mildly nociceptive. When the scratch reflex and the flexion reflex are in competition for the final neuron common to them, the flexion reflex more easily dispossesses the scratch reflex from the final neuron than does the scratch reflex the flexion reflex. If both reflexes are fresh, and the stimuli used are such that, when employed separately, they evoke their respective reflexes with some intensity, it is the flexion reflex that is usually prepotent. Yet if a strong stimulus suitable for producing the scratch reflex is applied while the flexion reflex is being moderately evoked, the steady flexion is replaced by the rhythmic scratch reflex, and this occurs even though the stimulus for the flexion reflex is maintained unaltered. When the stimulus producing the scratch reflex is discontinued the flexion reflex reappears as before.

In a decerebrate animal, where a tonic reflex (one that relaxes only very gradually) is maintaining contraction in the extensor muscles of the knee, stimulation of the nociceptive arcs of the limb easily breaks down that reflex; *i.e.,* the nociceptive reflex dominates the motor neuron previously held in activity by the postural reflex. And nociceptive reflexes are relatively little depressed by spinal shock.

Besides those receptors that react to direct nocuous stimuli the skin has others concerned with functions of vital importance to the species and bound up with sensations of similarly intense affective quality; *e.g.,* those concerned with sexual functions. In the male frog the sexual clasp is a spinal reflex. The cord may be divided both in front and behind the brachial (forelimb) region without interrupting the reflex. Experiment shows that from the spinal male at the breeding season, and also at other times, this reflex is elicited by any object that stimulates the skin of the breast. In the intact animal, on the contrary, objects other than the female are, when applied to that region, at once rejected, even though they be wrapped in the fresh skin of the female frog and in other ways made to resemble the female.

It would seem to be a general rule that reflexes arising in species of receptors which, considered as sense organs, provoke strongly affective sensation prevail (other things being equal) over reflexes of other species when in competition with them for the use of the final common path.

Of all reflexes it is those of ordinary posture that are the most easily interrupted by other reflexes. Even a weak stimulation of the nociceptive arcs arising in the foot often suffices to lower or abolish the knee jerk or the reflex extensor tonus (continuous contraction) of the elbow or knee. If various species of reflex are arranged, therefore, in their order of potency in regard to power to interrupt one another, the reflexes initiated in receptors which, considered as sense organs, excite sensations of strong affective quality are found to lie at the upper end of the scale, and the reflexes that are answerable for the postural tonus of skeletal muscles lie at the lower end of the scale.

One great function of the tonic reflexes is to maintain habitual attitudes and postures. They form, therefore, a nervous background of active equilibrium. It is obviously advantageous that this equilibrium should be easily upset, so that the animal may respond agilely to the passing events.

**Results.**—Intensity of stimulation, fatigue and freshness, spinal induction, functional species of reflex—all these physiological factors influence the result of the interaction of reflex arcs at a common path. All resolve themselves ultimately into intensity of reaction. Thus intensity of stimulus means, as a rule, intensity of reaction. Those species of reflex which are habitually prepotent in interaction with others are those which are habitually intense, and those specially impotent in competition are those habitually feeble; *e.g.*, the tonic reflexes of skeletal muscle. The tonic reflexes of attitude are thus easily interfered with and temporarily suppressed by intercurrent reflexes (those set up by passing events), which have the higher intensity.

The high variability of reflex reactions from one experiment or observation to another is often attributed to general conditions of nutrition, local blood supply, etc. However, variability seems far more often due to changes produced in the central nervous organ by its own functional conductive activity apart from fatigue. This activity itself causes from moment to moment the temporary opening of some connections and the closure of others. The chains of neurons, the conductive lines, have been richly revealed by the microscope. Anatomical tracing of nerve fibres may be likened to tracing the distribution of blood vessels after Harvey's discovery had given them meaning, but before the vasomotor mechanism was discovered. (The blood vessels of an organ may be turgid at one time, constricted almost to obliteration at another.) With the conductive network of the nervous system the temporal variations are even greater, for they extend to absolute withdrawal of nervous influence. Under reflex inhibition a skeletal muscle is relaxed to its postmortem length; *i.e.*, there may then be no longer evidence of even a tonic influence on it by its motor neuron.

The final common path is handed from some group of a plus class of afferent arcs to some group of a minus class or of a rhythmic class, and then back once more to one of the previous groups, and so on. The conductive web changes its functional pattern to and fro within certain limits. It changes its pattern at the entrances to common paths. The changes in its pattern occur there in virtue of interaction between rival reflexes: occlusion, substitution by equivalence, inhibition, immediate induction, successive induction, and fatigue are factors. A new stimulus striking the receptive surfaces causes in the central organ a shift of functional pattern of the linkage. The central organ is a vast network whose lines of conduction follow a certain scheme or pattern, but within that pattern the details of connection are, at the entrance to each common path, mutable. The gray matter may be compared with a telephone exchange, where, from moment to moment, though the end points of the system are fixed, the connections between starting points and terminal points are changed to suit passing requirements. To comprehend the exchange at work, one must add to its purely spatial plan the temporal datum that within certain limits the connections of the lines shift to and fro from minute to minute. An example is the reciprocal innervation of antagonistic muscles: when one muscle of the antagonistic pair is thrown into action, the other is thrown out of action.

Reciprocal innervation is a widespread case of the general rule that antagonistic reflexes interfere where they discharge into the same final common paths. And that rule is part of the general principle of the mutual interaction of reflexes that impinge upon the same common path: unlike reflexes have successive but not simultaneous use of the common path; like reflexes mutually reinforce each other on their common path. The principle may be expressed teleologically: the common path, although economically subservient for many and various purposes, is adapted to serve but one purpose at a time; hence it is a coordinating mechanism and prevents confusion by restricting the use of the organ, its minister, to but one action at a time.

In the case of simple antagonistic muscles, and in the instances of simple spinal reflexes, the shifts of conductive pattern due to interaction at the mouths of common paths are of but small extent. The coordination covers, for instance, one limb or a pair of limbs. But the same principle extended to the reaction of the great arcs arising in the proficient receptor organs of the head, *e.g.*, the eye, which deal with wide tracts of musculature as a whole, operates with more multiplex shift and wider ambit. Releasing forces acting on the brain from moment to moment shut out from activity whole regions of the nervous system, as they conversely call vast other regions into play. The resultant singleness of action from moment to moment is a keystone in the construction of the individual, whose unity it is the specific office of the nervous system to perfect. The interference of unlike reflexes and the alliance of like reflexes in their action upon their common paths seem to lie at the very root of the great psychical process of attention.

The spinal cord not only accommodates reflexes centring wholly within the cord itself; it also supplies conducting paths for nervous reactions initiated by impulses derived from afferent spinal nerves, but involving mechanisms situated altogether headward of the cord, in the brain. Many of these reactions affect consciousness, occasioning sensations of various kinds.

Besides the paths followed by headward-running impulses, the spinal cord contains paths for impulses passing along it backward from the brain. These paths lie in the lateral and ventrolateral columns of the cord. The fibres of which they are composed cross but little in the cord. Their sources are various; some of them come from the hindbrain and some from the midbrain, and in the higher mammalia, especially in man and in the anthropoid apes, a large tract of fibres in the lateral column (the crossed pyramidal tract) comes from the cortex of the neopallium of the forebrain. This last tract is the main medium by which impulses initiated by electrical stimulation of the motor cortex reach the motor neurons of the cord and through them influence the activity of the skeletal muscles.

Of the function of the other tracts descending from the brain into the cord little is known except that mediately or immediately they excite or inhibit the spinal motor neurons by various levels. How they harmonize one with another in their action or what their purpose in normal life may be is at present little more than conjecture. Such terms, therefore, as "paths for volition," etc., are too schematic in their bases to warrant their discussion here.

*See* also references under "Spinal Cord" in the Index.

(C. S. S.; C. R. Nk.)

Bibliography.—S. Brock (ed.), *Injuries of the Brain and Spinal Cord and Their Coverings,* 4th ed. (1960); Charles H. Best and Norman B. Taylor, *The Physiological Basis of Medical Practice,* 7th ed. (1961); L. M. Davidoff and E. H. Feiring, *Practical Neurology* (1955); Francis M. Foster, *Medical Progress 1956* (1956); H. Houston Merritt and Daniel Sciarra in T. R. Harrison and others (ed.), *Principles of Internal Medicine,* 4th ed. (1962); W. R. Brain, *Diseases of the Nervous System,* 6th ed. (1962); Roy R. Grinker and Paul C. Bucy, *Neurology,* 5th ed. rev. (1959); D. Munro, *Treatment of Injuries to the Nervous System* (1952).

**SPINAL CORD, DISEASES OF:** *see* Nervous System, Diseases of.

**SPINE, DISEASES AND DISABILITIES OF.** The spine can be affected by more than 60 different conditions. The commonest are birth malformations, acquired growth deformities, sprains, fractures and dislocations from injuries, infections, arthritis, herniation of the intervertebral discs and cancer. All may produce pain, limited back movement, muscle spasm and deformity. The pain may radiate into the arms and legs when nerves are irritated. Prolonged pressure may cause paralysis of an extremity. The diagnosis of a given condition is established by suitable examination and laboratory survey, including X rays.

**Backache.**—The usual seat of backache is the lumbar or lumbosacral region (between or just above the hips). Chronic backache may reflect a structural inadequacy or disease.

**Lumbago.**—This condition, marked by acute pain in the lower back, is caused by a sprain: overstretching of tissues, hemorrhage into muscles and tearing of ligaments. Lumbago commonly results from lifting efforts, unexpected jarring, sudden twisting movements or a blow to the spine. Treatment includes bed rest, application of heat and massage with local analgesics.

**"Whiplash" Injury.**—The "whiplash" injury to the neck, received in automobile accidents when the occupant's head is thrown backward and then forward, is actually a sprain, characterized by pain, muscle spasm and limited motion. Treatment consists of sedation, protective support for neck or back and, occasionally, weights attached to the head or legs to stretch the injured tissues and relieve pressure on nerves. Recovery occurs in several weeks but may be prolonged.

**Arthritis.**—Rheumatoid arthritis affects spines of young adults, producing progressive destructive changes in small joints leading to fusion and permanent stiffening. In other cases, the large ligaments about the vertebrae ossify and transform the spine into one piece. Pain is outstanding and is minimized by braces, X-ray therapy and cortisone. Symptoms disappear as the spine becomes rigid and the process inactive.

Degenerative arthritis is manifested by narrowing of disc spaces, sclerosis of adjacent vertebrae and formation of spurs at their margins. Other cases show changes in the facets and the joints become painful. Mild symptoms are alleviated by braces and corsets. Severe pain may necessitate bed rest, leg traction and physical therapy, followed with a back support. (*See* ARTHRITIS.)

**Infection.**—Infections producing pus in the spine are rare, but when present cause severe symptoms. The patient is usually acutely ill. Isolation of the offending bacteria and utilization of the specific antibiotic drug, together with good nursing care, is essential. Drainage of abscesses facilitates recovery.

Chronic infections, such as tuberculosis, may produce destruction of the vertebrae and adjacent discs. Pus and destroyed tissue accumulate in front of and behind the vertebrae. Pressure on the spinal cord may result in paralysis of the body below the level of infection. Treatment with modern drugs, supplemented by surgery in which the involved segment of the back is made solid, hastens recovery.

**Disc Disorders.**—The intervertebral discs serve as shock absorbers between adjacent vertebrae. The rubbery central nucleus sometimes undergoes degeneration and allows the contiguous vertebrae to rub on each other. The resultant arthritis produces local pain or radiating pain down an extremity. The nucleus, in other cases, escapes through the back wall of the disc causing spinal cord pressure. This is a protruded or herniated disc, and causes neuritic arm or leg pain, depending upon the location of the spinal lesion.

Treatment consists of traction, supports and physical therapy during the initial attack or in mild recurrent episodes. Severe, unremitting pain necessitates surgery to remove extruded nuclear material and relieve pressure on nerves. Spinal fusion is often performed simultaneously to prevent further collapse of the disc and subsequent pain.

**Cancer.**—Cancer arises in the spine from cells that normally produce bone and cartilage, from cells in the bone marrow and from covering elements of the vertebrae. The diagnosis is established by characteristic X-ray changes and from tissue obtained by needle biopsy or surgery. Cancer originating from the thyroid gland, gastrointestinal tract, kidneys and prostate gland has a tendency to spread to the spine. The prognosis is poor, but symptomatic treatment minimizes suffering.

Noncancerous growths of the spine, on the other hand, carry a good prognosis.

*See* also FRACTURES AND DISLOCATIONS. (S. W. BA.)

**SPINEL,** a group of minerals, the typical member of which is a magnesium aluminate, to which the name was originally restricted. The group includes chromite, franklinite and magnetite, important ores of chromium, zinc and iron, respectively. The magnesia spinel, sometimes known as ruby spinel, is one of the 16 minerals that have achieved importance as a gem, both natural and synthetic (*see* GEM: *Synthetic Gems*). The name is from the French *spinelle,* derived from the Latin *spina* ("thorn"), perhaps in allusion to the sharp, needlelike angles of the crystals. Spinels have the general composition $R''O \cdot R_2'''O_3$, where $R'' =$ Mg, Fe, Mn, Zn, and $R''' =$ Al, Fe''', Cr'''.

All spinels crystallize in the cubic system, typically in octahedra. Twinning is common, the octahedral face being the twin plane, giving a characteristic form known as the spinel twin.

The group of spinel minerals includes the following members:

| | | | |
|---|---|---|---|
| Magnesia spinel | $MgAl_2O_4$ | Magnesioferrite | $MgFe_2O_4$ |
| Pleonaste | $(Mg,Fe)Al_2O_4$ | Magnetite | $FeFe_2O_4$ |
| Hercynite | $FeAl_2O_4$ | Gahnite | $ZnAl_2O_4$ |
| Picotite | $(Mg,Fe)(Al,Cr)_2O_4$ | Franklinite | $(Zn,Mn)Fe_2O_4$ |
| Chromite | $FeCr_2O_4$ | | |

Cleavage is typically absent in these minerals with the exception of the zinc spinel (cleavage on 111), but an octahedral parting is observable in magnetite and franklinite. The hardness is variable; in ordinary spinel it is 7.5–8, the gem varieties being 8, but magnetite is 6 and chromite is 5.5. The specific gravity varies with the composition, from 3.6 (magnesia spinel) to 5.2 (magnetite). The light refraction shows a range from 1.718 (pure magnesia spinel), hercynite 1.80, to picotite 2.05, chromite 2.10 and magnetite 2.42.

Spinels vary much in colour. Natural magnesia spinels are pink, red and blue. The pure magnesia spinel is colourless, hercynite is dark green in thin slices and picotite and chromite are brown in the thinnest sections. Spinels are readily produced in all colours artificially. Magnesia spinel melts at 2,135° C. and between this compound and $FeAl_2O_4$ (hercynite) there is complete miscibility as revealed in spinel analyses, but solid solution between (Mg,Fe) $Al_2O_4$ (pleonaste) and magnetite is very limited. The natural spinels which are used in jewelry are found mostly in gem gravels, the chief localities being Ceylon, Thailand (Siam) and upper Burma.

Spinels occur both in igneous and metamorphic rocks. The home of the magnesia spinel is in thermally altered dolomites where it arises by reaction of alumina with dolomite. There it is usually accompanied by calcite and forsterite. The iron-rich member of the group, pleonaste, is common both in ultrabasic rocks such as dunites and in quartzless argillaceous hornfelses and gneisses. In these latter it is almost universally accompanied by cordierite and frequently by sillimanite, andalusite or corundum. Hercynite is characteristic of the granulites of Saxony in association with garnet, sillimanite, etc.

The chromiferous spinel, picotite, is relegated to the ultrabasic rocks, as dunite, lherzolite and the serpentines derived from them. Gahnite, the zinc spinel, occurs in schists associated with zinc ores and in pegmatites in Finland and at Broken Hill, New South Wales, Austr., while franklinite is associated with zinc and manganese minerals in limestone at Franklin Furnace, N.J.

*See* also CHROMITE; FRANKLINITE; MAGNETITE.

(C. E. T.; X.)

**SPINELLO ARETINO** (LUCA SPINELLO) (*c.* 1346–1410), prolific late Gothic Italian painter, was born at Arezzo in or soon after 1346. Trained in a local workshop, he seems rapidly to have come under the influence of Orcagna and Nardo di Cione, whose style is reflected in his first major work, a fresco cycle in S. Francesco at Arezzo. A facile artist, Spinello's reputation soon spread beyond his native town. In 1384–85 he painted a polyptych for Monteoliveto Maggiore (panels in the Pinacoteca at Siena, the Fogg museum at Cambridge, Mass., and Budapest), and about 1387 executed a fresco cycle in the small church at Antella, near Florence. A cycle of scenes from the life of St. Benedict in the sacristy of S. Miniato al Monte, Florence, dates from the same time.

To the year 1391 belongs a triptych commissioned for S. Andrea at Lucca, now in the Accademia, Florence, which was painted in conjunction with Lorenzo di Niccolò. In the same year he began work on some frescoes in the Campo Santo at Pisa. Further commissions at Arezzo followed, and between 1404 and his death on March 14, 1410, he seems to have divided his time between Arezzo and Siena, where he undertook work for the cathedral (lost) and executed (1407–10) a cycle of fresco scenes from the life of Pope Alexander III in the Sala di Balia of the Palazzo Pubblico. These and the Pisa frescoes constitute his most important works. Spinello was at best a minor artist with a vigorous sense of narrative, and his interest is due in the main to the transitional character of his late style, which anticipates the realistic painting of the early 15th century. (J. W. P.-H.)

**SPINET,** a small, compact form of the harpsichord. It is wing shaped, with only one set of strings placed at an oblique angle to the keyboard. The spinet appeared about 1660 and became popular as a substitute for the larger harpsichord, suitable for small rooms. Large numbers were made during the late 17th and 18th centuries, particularly in England. *See* HARPSICHORD. (G. F. OL.)

**SPINNING** is the forming of continuous thread by twisting together several overlapping fibres or filaments. (The word also refers to the extrusion of viscous materials to form long filaments of chemical origin; *see* FIBRE.) Two or more of the spun threads may again be twisted together to obtain a stronger thread or cord. These continuous threads are necessary for the production of woven fabrics and also as cordage and rope for various purposes. Before the fibre is spun it is cleaned and straightened; preliminary processes include carding and, for the finer yarns, combing (*q.v.*).

The first spinning no doubt consisted of twisting a few fibres together with the fingers to make short cords for fastenings or bindings. When longer threads were made, the finished length was wound onto a stick, and this in time developed into the spindle, the first spinning tool. An improvement took place by adding to the end of the stick a blob of clay or a round piece of wood, known as the "whorl," which enabled the stick (hanging free, vertically) to continue to twist for a time and thus to insert the turns of twist into the thread. The size and weight of the stick and whorl varied with the fineness of the yarn that was to be produced, and very fine yarns were spun by suitable choice of these weights. For thousands of years this simple device remained the only means of spinning fibres into thread. Three basic motions were performed in rotation: the fibres were drawn out, then they were twisted together, and finally the finished length of thread was wound onto the spindle. A useful but not essential accessory was the distaff, a stick, sometimes straight and sometimes forked or carved, to which the fibres were bound in a position from which they could be drawn out to the required degree of fineness. The distaff was held in the left hand or under the spinner's arm.

The first stage in the mechanization of spinning was to mount the spindle horizontally in bearings and to rotate it by a cord encircling a large hand-driven wheel. The distaff, with the fibrous material, was held in the left hand and the wheel was turned with the right hand. At the start a few turns of yarn were wound on the spindle and attached to the raw material. By drawing the raw material at an angle to the line of the spindle while it was being rotated, the thread was attenuated to the desired fineness and twist was inserted at the same time. (The thread attached to the spindle slipped over the end of the spindle and was held in place by a groove or notch.) As the twist ran more readily into the thin places in the yarn it bound up the fibres in these places so much that they resisted further attenuation, and subsequent stretching made only the thick places finer. This differential attenuation made for greater regularity in the yarn and was a great advance over the earlier method of spinning by which all the attenuation was carried out between the two hands, only twist being inserted by the twirling stick. When the length of yarn became too great for convenience, the spindle rotation was reversed and the yarn was wound on the spindle, leaving a few inches still attached to the loose material, so that another length could be spun.

This system was used in India in very early times, but was not introduced into Europe until the 14th century. It continued to be used in Europe for spinning cotton and wool until the beginning of the 19th century, and in America it survived in isolated districts until the end of the century.

The next stage of development was the Saxony wheel, introduced in Europe at the beginning of the 16th century. It incorporated a bobbin within a flyer and was an important development, for whereas the earlier spindle method was an intermittent one, first producing a length of yarn and then winding it on a stick, the Saxony wheel produced yarn and wound it on the bobbin continuously. The distaff was in this case a stationary vertical rod. Attenuation of the mass took place between the spinner's hands; the flyer, driven from the large wheel actuated by a foot treadle, inserted the twist; and the twisted yarn then passed onto the bobbin. This method could be used only for coarse-yarn production from wool or cotton; fine yarns, which were too weak to be wound onto a bobbin in this way, continued to be made by the method described above. These two systems are the basis of all modern spinning machinery.

BY COURTESY OF THE NEW YORK STATE HISTORICAL ASSOCIATION, COOPERSTOWN

EARLY AMERICAN FOOT-PEDAL SPINNING WHEEL

In the 18th century a number of developments led to the rapid industrialization of all textile manufacture (*see* INDUSTRIAL REVOLUTION: *Textile Industry*). Spinning was up to this time a household enterprise, done mostly by women (hence "spinsters," in modern usage applied to all unmarried women, and "distaff" as used for woman's domain in general); three to five spinners were required to supply one loom. John Kay's invention of the flying shuttle, which greatly increased the output of the loom, led to a shortage of yarn which in turn stimulated the search for faster spinning methods, and three different machines were invented in the space of a few years.

The first was the spinning jenny, invented about 1764 by James Hargreaves (patented 1770). This machine was virtually derived from the spinning stick method, having the same basic action in that cotton material was attenuated, twisted, and then wound on a spindle before another length was spun. It had a number of spindles side by side, operable by one person, and therefore the output per operative was increased markedly. The yarn produced was very full, and was suitable only for the coarser cloths. (This type of spinning machine is still in use in some coarse-yarn mills operating on both cotton and wool.)

The second machine was that of Richard Arkwright, invented about 1767 (patented 1769). It incorporated attenuating or drafting rollers, which had been invented independently in 1738 by Lewis Paul, followed by the spindle and bobbin arrangement of the Saxony wheel, so that yarns could be produced continuously. Again, many spindles could be built into one machine, and could be looked after by a single operator. The yarn made on this machine was stronger than that from Hargreaves' jenny, and was more suitable for the longitudinal threads, or warp, in weaving.

The third machine, which became known as the "mule," was invented by Samuel Crompton about 1779, and was more successful than either of the other two. It made use of Paul's drafting rollers for attenuation and spindles similar to those of the spinning stick, but there were numerous spindles side by side on one machine (over 1,000 in many instances) and operative productivity was high. It could spin any type of yarn, from the finest to very coarse. For well over a century this was the principal spinning machine in English factories.

Concurrently, the preparatory processes were also being mechanized. After the opening and cleaning processes, the fibres must be separated from one another by a "carding" process, originally done by hand and eventually by machine. Following the carding, the fibres in the slivers (rope-like strands delivered by the cards) must be made parallel; this was a function of Paul's draw frame, which was improved by Arkwright later in the century. The slivers had next to be made finer, by a speed frame process, first attenuating the draw frame slivers by passing them through drafting rollers, then twisting them slightly by flyers, and finally winding them onto bobbins. Two or three successive speed frame processes were commonly used to make the slivers fine enough for spinning; these fine slivers were called rovings. All these preparatory machines were bulky and heavy, and because special buildings were needed to accommodate them, they accelerated the establishment of the factory system.

The next significant development was the introduction of two other spinning machines, both invented in the United States about 1828. One was the cap spinning machine of Charles Danforth, and the other the ring spinning machine invented by John Thorp. Both had attenuating systems similar to the Paul mechanism, and while the Danforth machine had a steel cap on the spindle in place of the usual flyer, the edge of the cap guiding the yarn onto the driven bobbin enclosed by the cap, the Thorp machine had a steel ring surrounding the spindle and bobbin, and on a flange of the steel ring was clipped a steel C-shaped "traveler" through which the yarn passed on its way to the bobbin; the traveler revolved on the ring to insert twist into the yarn. Both these machines were immediately popular in the U.S. and eventually found their way into English mills. The Danforth machine was fairly popular in woolen mills, and is still used to a limited extent. The Thorp machine was not widely adopted in English cotton mills for some time, but it has now almost entirely replaced the mule on account of its greater productivity and simplicity.

Mule spinning was done almost entirely by men, but the Danforth and Thorp machines, which were simpler in operation, were looked after by women, who still constitute the majority of employees in spinning mills. At one time it was customary to work only one shift, but modern practice is to run the mills for two or three shifts daily; this practice, together with a great increase in the speed of the spindle on modern machines, has led to a considerable reduction in the number of operating mills.

*See* also COTTON MANUFACTURE; LINEN MANUFACTURE; SILK; WOOL. (V. P. P.; F. CH.)

**SPINOLA, AMBROGIO DI,** 1ST MARQUÉS DE LOS BALBASES (1569–1630), Italian soldier whose campaigns in the Netherlands in the service of Spain made him one of the outstanding generals of his time, was born at Genoa of a family of great antiquity, wealth, and power. At that time the Genoa Republic was politically a satellite of Spain. To advance the fortunes of his house, Spinola entered into a contract with the Spanish government for service in Flanders and in 1602 marched there with a force of 9,000 men raised at his own expense. On Sept. 29, 1603, he took over command of the siege of Ostend, and his capture of the city on Sept. 22, 1604, won him a high reputation. He then visited the Spanish court at Valladolid and was appointed commander in chief in Flanders, awarded the Order of the Golden Fleece, and appointed superintendent of the *hacienda* (exchequer). The war between Spain and the Dutch in the Netherlands consisted almost wholly of sieges, and Spinola became renowned for the number of towns he took in spite of the efforts of Maurice of Nassau to defend them. On Spinola's second visit to Spain in 1606 he pledged the fortune of his house to secure funds to continue the war in Flanders. He retained his command after the Twelve Years' Truce was signed in 1609.

On the outbreak of the Thirty Years' War in 1618 Spinola conducted a vigorous campaign in the Lower Palatinate and was made captain general. Following the renewal of the Dutch war in 1621, he gained his most famous victory by the capture of Breda after a long siege (Aug. 28, 1624–June 5, 1625). This success was the subject of Velázquez's great painting, the "Surrender of Breda." Breda was the culmination of Spinola's career, for lack of funds and the enmity of Philip IV's favourite, the conde-duque de Olivares, aggravated after Spinola's third visit to Spain in 1628, paralyzed his efforts. He went to Italy in September 1629 as plenipotentiary and general in the war over the succession to the duchy of Mantua (1628–31) but died at Castelnuovo Scrivia on Sept. 25, 1630, after having captured the town of Casale Monferrato.

*See* A. Rodríguez Villa, *Ambrosio Spínola* (1904). (J. RE.)

**SPINOZA, BENEDICTUS DE** (1632–1677), author of one of the greatest metaphysical systems in the history of philosophy, was born of Jewish parents in Amsterdam, Holland, on Nov. 24, 1632. The family surname occurs in various forms: Espinoza, d'Espinoza, Despinoza, de Spinoza and simply Spinoza. The philosopher's Hebrew name was Baruch (meaning "blessed"), which, in accordance with the custom of the time, was rendered into its Latin equivalent, Benedictus.

Spinoza's grandfather and father were Portuguese crypto-Jews (that is, descendants of Jews whom the Spanish Inquisition had compelled to embrace Christianity but who remained Jews at heart) who, with many others of their persuasion, had sought refuge in Holland after the successful revolt of the Netherlands against Spain and the granting of religious freedom by the union of Utrecht. His mother, who also came from Portugal, died in 1638, when Spinoza was barely six years old.

The Spinozas were prosperous merchants and respected members of the Jewish community in Amsterdam, and it may be assumed that Spinoza attended the school for Jewish boys founded there about 1638. The curriculum of this school comprised all the Hebrew subjects: the Old Testament, the Talmud, the Hebrew codes and the works of Ibn Ezra, Maimonides, Crescas and others. Outside school hours the boys had private lessons in secular subjects. Spinoza naturally learned Portuguese and Spanish from his parents and Dutch from his environment (Spanish was also the language of the Jewish school); he was taught Latin by a German scholar, Jeremiah Felbinger, who may also have taught him German; and he also knew some French and Italian. When he learned mathematics and physics is not known, but there were plenty of Hebrew books dealing with these sciences, and the Jewish school had a good lending library.

In March 1654 Spinoza's father died. There was some litigation over the estate, as Spinoza's only surviving stepsister claimed it all. Spinoza won the lawsuit, but allowed her to retain nearly everything. Henceforth he had to fend for himself.

His studies so far had been mainly Jewish, but he was an independent thinker and had found more than enough in his Jewish studies to wean him from orthodox theology. Ibn Ezra, Maimonides and Gersonides, centuries earlier, had been, to a greater or lesser extent, critical of the orthodox interpretation of Scripture; moreover, the tendency to revolt against mere tradition and authority was very much in the air in the 17th century. But the Jewish religious leaders in Amsterdam were not inclined to tolerance: they were particularly afraid that heresies which were no less anti-Christian than anti-Jewish might give offense in a country of which the Jews were not yet regarded as citizens; and they retained, furthermore, some of the intolerant spirit of the Inquisition, whose victims they had been.

Spinoza soon incurred the disapproval of the synagogue authorities. In conversations with other students he maintained that there is nothing in the Bible to support the views that God has no body, that there really are angels (as distinguished from mere imaginative visions of them) or that the soul is immortal; and he also expressed his belief that the author of the Pentateuch was no wiser in matters pertaining to physics or even theology than they were. These views were reported to the Jewish authorities who, after trying vainly to silence him with bribes and threats, excommunicated him in July 1656. The fact of his excommunication was formally reported to the civil authorities (a gesture intended to absolve the Jewish community from all responsibility for Spinoza's heresies); and Spinoza was banished from Amsterdam for a short period. After his excommunication he spent a short time at Ouwerkerk, a village near Amsterdam, and then returned to his native city. There is no evidence that he had really wanted to break away from the Jewish community, and indeed the scanty knowledge available would suggest the opposite: on Dec. 5, 1655, he had attended the synagogue and made an offering which, in view of his poverty, must have been a rare event for him; and about the time of his excommunication he had addressed a defense of his views to the synagogue. Apparently he was not entirely indifferent to the authorities' opinion of him.

PORTRAIT BY AN ANONYMOUS PAINTER, ABOUT 1670; BY COURTESY OF THE HERZOG AUGUST BIBLIOTHEK, WOLFENBÜTTEL

BENEDICTUS DE SPINOZA

Already before his estrangement from the synagogue Spinoza had become acquainted with a number of Christians. Among these was Francis van den Enden, a former Jesuit, an ardent classical scholar and something of a poet and dramatist, who had opened a school in Amsterdam in 1652. For a time Spinoza stayed with Van den Enden, helping with the teaching of the schoolchildren and receiving help in his own further education. In this way he improved his knowledge of Latin, learned some Greek and was introduced to the neoscholastic philosophy of such writers as Franco Burgersdijck (d. 1632) and Adrianus Heereboord (d. 1659). It may have also been through Van den Enden's school that Spinoza became acquainted with the "new philosophy" of René Descartes; but in any case Spinoza's other Christian acquaintances were mostly Collegiants who were especially interested in Cartesianism.

At the same time he was learning the science and art of making lenses, in which he became a great expert; and he supported himself partly by grinding and polishing lenses for spectacles, telescopes and microscopes and partly by helping various people with their private studies. One of his friends at this period was Simon Joosten de Vries, whose admiration for Spinoza was so great that he at one time pressed him to accept a gift of 2,000 florins and at another wanted to make him his sole heir. This Spinoza refused and, when left an annuity of 500 florins in his friend's will, would only accept 300. A kind of reading and discussion circle for the study of religious and philosophical problems came into being under the guidance of Spinoza, whose ideas at this period were gradually becoming formed. In order to collect his thoughts and reduce them to a system, he withdrew in 1660 to Rijnsburg, a quiet village on the Rhine, near Leiden.

Rijnsburg was the headquarters of the Collegiants, and Spinoza lodged there with a surgeon named Hermann Homan. In Homan's cottage Spinoza wrote the *Korte Verhandeling van God, de Mensch und deszelbs Welstand* (*i.e., Short Treatise on God, Man and His Well-being*), the *De intellectus emendatione* (*On the Improvement of the Understanding*), the greater part of his geometric version of Descartes's *Principia philosophiae* (with the appendix of metaphysical thoughts) and the first book of his *Ethica*. Part of the *Korte Verhandeling* consisted of notes that he had prepared in connection with the study circle in Amsterdam, which continued to meet after Spinoza's departure and to which he periodically sent the various parts of the *Tractatus* and other works for study and discussion. Both the *Korte Verhandeling* and the *De intellectus emendatione,* which were originally intended to form one work, were ready in or before April 1662. Already in these writings Spinoza's attitude shows his reaction to Cartesianism.

It was in 1661, during his stay at Rijnsburg, that Spinoza met Heinrich Oldenburg. This man, who was already a member of the Royal society in London and was to be appointed one of its two first secretaries in 1663, is of particular interest here because the most important part of Spinoza's correspondence was with him.

While giving instruction in the philosophy of Descartes, Spinoza made a geometrical version of the second part of Descartes's *Principia,* and this he showed to his Cartesian friends when on a visit to Amsterdam in 1663. They then persuaded him to do the same with the first part, which he did in a fortnight. These two parts, together with an appendix called *Cogitata metaphysica* (*i.e., Metaphysical Thoughts*), were accordingly published by his friends under the title *Renati des Cartes principiorum philosophiae pars I et II, more geometrico demonstratae per Benedictum de Spinoza* (Amsterdam, 1663), with an introduction by Lodewijk Meyer explaining that Spinoza did not share the views expressed in the book. This was the only book published in Spinoza's lifetime with his name on the title page. A Dutch translation by Pieter Balling was published in 1664.

By the early part of 1662 Spinoza had drafted an exposition of his own philosophy in a single work that was to combine the matter of the *Korte Verhandeling* with that of the *De intellectus emendatione;* but he was dissatisfied with the dialogue form employed in this draft and so turned to the geometrical method in the manner of Euclid's *Elements.* Thus originated his major work, the *Ethica ordine geometrico demonstrata,* the first part of which, "De Deo," was finished and in the hands of his friends early in 1663. The title of the whole work was at first intended to be "On God, the Rational Soul, and the Highest Happiness of Man"; and the work was planned in three parts instead of the five into which it eventually developed. The publication of his version of Descartes's *Principia* had been intended to prepare the way for the publication of his own philosophy, for he had both to secure the patronage of influential men as a shield against the hostility of the Calvinists and to show the more philosophically minded people that his rejection of Cartesianism was not due to ignorance.

In June 1663 Spinoza moved from Rijnsburg to Voorburg, near The Hague; and by June 1665 it appears that he was nearing the completion of the *Ethica.* During the next few years, however, he was at work on his *Tractatus theologico-politicus,* which was published anonymously at Amsterdam in 1670. This was "to show that not only is perfect liberty to philosophize compatible with devout piety and with the peace of the state, but that to take away such liberty is to destroy the public peace and even piety itself." Spinoza also told Oldenburg that he wanted to clear himself of the charge of atheism which had been brought against him. It would appear that, with the completion of the *Ethica* in sight, Spinoza was considering the question of its publication, but found it impracticable in view of the contemporary state of public opinion; he therefore set himself to show that the Bible, properly understood, gives no support to ecclesiastical intolerance or to clerical interference in civil and political affairs.

In May 1670 Spinoza moved to The Hague, where he remained until his death. He began to compose a Hebrew grammar, *Compendium grammatices linguae hebraeae,* but did not finish it; instead he returned to the *Ethica,* although the prospect of its publication became increasingly remote. His *Tractatus theologico-politicus* had aroused great interest and was to go through five editions in as many years, but there were many denunciations of it as an instrument "forged in hell by a renegade Jew and the devil, and issued with the knowledge of Mr. Johan de Witt." Johan de Witt, it should be said, was among those of the civil authorities of the United Provinces who showed sympathy for Spinoza; and his murder in 1672 provoked the philosopher to attempt a demonstration of protest that might have cost him his life had he not been prevented from making it public. Further, Spinoza's political situation in The Hague was compromised in 1673, when, lured by disingenuous invitations from the French army, he went in May to Utrecht (then under French occupation; *see* DUTCH WARS) with a view to possible negotiations for peace. He was badly received by the suspicious populace of The Hague on his return several weeks later. When the *Ethica* was finally completed in 1675, Spinoza had to abandon the idea of publishing it, although manuscript copies were circulated among his intimate friends. Spinoza then concentrated his attention on political problems and began his *Tractatus politicus,* which he did not live to finish.

In 1675 the scientist E. W. von Tschirnhaus visited Spinoza and brought about a resumption of his correspondence with Oldenburg, which had been interrupted for about ten years for reasons largely connected with Oldenburg's situation in England. In 1676 Spinoza was visited by Leibniz who, having heard of Spinoza as an authority on optics, had sent him an optical tract as early as 1671 and had subsequently received from Spinoza a copy of the *Tractatus theologico-politicus,* which deeply interested him. According to Leibniz' own account, he "conversed with him often and at great length." Spinoza, however, was now in an advanced stage of a pulmonary disease contracted by inhaling the glass dust from the lenses. On Sunday, Feb. 20, 1677, he died, at about 3 o'clock in the afternoon. Four days later he was buried in the New church on the Spui.

In accordance with his previous instructions, Spinoza's manuscripts were sent to the publisher Jan Rieuwertsz in Amsterdam, and his friends Jarig Jelles, Lodewijk Meyer and G. H. Schuller prepared them secretly for the press. *B.D.S. Opera posthuma* (of which there appeared also a Dutch version, *De Nagelate Schriften*), published in Amsterdam before the end of 1677, comprised the *Ethica,* the *Tractatus politicus* and the *De intellectus emendatione* as well as letters and the Hebrew grammar. A treatise on the rainbow and a treatise on the calculation of chances (*Stelkon-*

*stige reeckening van den regenboog* and *Reeckening van kanssen*) were printed together at The Hague in 1687 but thereafter long forgotten. The *Korte Verhandeling* was lost to the world until E. Boehmer's publication of it, with a Latin translation, as *Tractatus de Deo, de homine ejusque felicitate* (Halle, 1852), after which it was re-edited, together with the treatise on the rainbow, by J. van Vloten (Amsterdam, 1862).

A word must be said here of the attractiveness of Spinoza's personal character. It is discernible in all the records of his life and is recognized even by those who find themselves forced to reject his philosophical system.

## PHILOSOPHY

The philosophy of Spinoza may be regarded as a development from, and reaction to, that of Descartes. Although Spinoza was also much influenced by medieval, especially Jewish medieval, philosophy, he seems to have been much more conscious of the Cartesian influence, and his most striking doctrines are most easily understood as solutions of Cartesian difficulties. As has been said above, he had studied Descartes in detail and written an account of his philosophy in geometrical form. He accepted Descartes's physics in general, although he expressed some dissatisfaction with it toward the end of his life (*see* letter lxxxiii in A. Wolf's edition of the *Correspondence*), but he found three very unsatisfactory features in Cartesian metaphysics, namely the transcendence of God, the substantial dualism of mind and body and the ascription of free will as *liberum arbitrium* both to God and to human beings. In Spinoza's eyes, these doctrines made the world unintelligible. It was impossible to explain the relation between God and the world or between mind and body or to account for those events which are occasioned by free will.

Spinoza assumes without question that it is possible to construct a system of metaphysics, *i.e.*, an account of the world as a whole, which will render it completely intelligible. It is therefore possible in his view to present metaphysics deductively, that is, as a series of theorems derived by necessary steps from self-evident premisses expressed in terms which are either self-explanatory or defined with unquestionable correctness. His chief work, the *Ethica,* is set out in this manner (*ordine geometrico demonstrata*). The desire to secure impersonality was probably his chief motive for adopting this method of presentation. He appreciates, of course, that the use of the method guarantees true conclusions only on condition that the axioms are true and the definitions correct. Spinoza, like his contemporaries, holds that definitions are not arbitrary, but that there is a sense in which they may be correct or incorrect.

The question is discussed at length in his unfinished work, *De intellectus emendatione.* A sound definition, he holds, should make clear the possibility of the existence of the object defined, or, in the case of a necessary existent, the necessity of its existence. The *Ethica* begins with the definition of substance, the necessary existent. Since the concept of substance (*q.v.*) is among the most disputed in metaphysics, it is clear that the system could be rejected by anyone disputing the definition, however cogent the subsequent reasoning. In fact, however, as Leibniz pointed out, the demonstrations do not proceed with mathematical rigour. The system is closely knit, but not mathematically demonstrated, and the method of presentation creates some difficulties for the reader, who will at first find it easier to follow Spinoza in the prefaces to the different books and in the extended scholia where he drops the strict geometrical method. It seems in fact that, since the basic concepts, substance, attribute and mode, are in dispute and cannot, like those of geometry, be given intuitive content, metaphysics is not most suitably treated step by step, in the geometric way. The system must be accepted or rejected as a whole. If the conclusions are found to be sound, this lends support to the initial axioms and definitions.

From Spinoza's point of view a satisfactory metaphysical system would have to fulfill the following requirements: it must be intelligible in the sense explained above; it must be consistent with Cartesian or some similar physics; it must explain the main facts of human life, especially the occurrence of true and false thinking and of moral experience; and it must provide a worthy object of worship. This last point was undoubtedly of great importance for Spinoza: a deep religious feeling was one of the main motives in the construction of his system.

**God or Substance.**—Spinoza begins with the idea of substance as that which can be conceived as existing in complete independence (*Ethica,* i, definition 3). Since its existence is to be intelligible and it cannot be caused or explained by anything else, it must be its own cause (definition 1); *i.e.,* necessarily existent. There can be only one such substance, and this is quickly identified with God, the traditional necessary existent, and with the whole of Nature. Rejecting the idea of a transcendent God as unintelligible, but still accepting the traditional concept of a necessary being, Spinoza finds this being in the whole of the universe, which must contain all reality. He is able to accept this as a worthy object of worship and thus arrives at the position of pantheism (*q.v.*). Spinoza's account of the nature of God was the most shocking feature of his philosophy to his orthodox contemporaries and successors, both Christian and Jewish. With the transcendence of God, he denies also God's personality in the ordinary sense and God's providence. Spinoza undoubtedly thought that these doctrines were inseparably connected with a crude anthropomorphism. God is a conscious and, indeed, an omniscient being, but has no free will as ordinarily understood and no purposes: He acts according to the necessity of His own nature, which is to act freely in Spinoza's sense (*Ethica,* i, appendix). God cannot, therefore, have any special providential care for man; and the good man, although he loves God, will not expect God to love him in return (*Ethica,* v, 19).

**The Attributes.**—Substance has, or is constituted by, an infinite number of attributes (*Ethica,* i, definition 6); but only those two attributes of substance which enter into his own nature are known to man; viz., thought and extension. To say that these are attributes of substance is to say that the universe is a spatial whole which is conscious throughout. Spinoza accepts this conclusion and thus arrives at a panpsychist position: "All things . . . ," he says, ". . . are alive" (*Ethica,* ii, 13, scholium). The theory that there are infinite attributes is very difficult and seems to lead to inconsistencies in the development of the system. For, since all attributes qualify substance throughout, it seems to follow that there should be some entity under each attribute which corresponds to the human mind in the same way that the body corresponds to it. We should therefore expect that all the attributes would be known to man. When pressed on this point, Spinoza replies that the modes under thought which correspond to modes under attributes other than extension are not human minds, but minds of a different kind (letter lxvi in Wolf's edition). This solution, however, is inconsistent with complete parallelism, for it gives the attribute of thought a unique position, in that it corresponds to all the attributes in a way in which they do not correspond to each other.

This difficulty has led some commentators to adopt a subjectivist interpretation of the attributes; *i.e.,* to say that the attributes are simply the infinitely many possible ways in which substance could be conceived. This interpretation receives some support from the extremely obscure definition of attribute given by Spinoza: "By attribute I understand that which the intellect perceives of substance as constituting its essence." It seems clear, however, from the letter quoted that Spinoza thinks of the attributes as objective. Probably the doctrine of infinite attributes is a relic of traditionalism in Spinoza which cannot be satisfactorily interpreted in detail.

**The Modes.**—Besides consisting of infinite attributes, substance is diversified into infinite modes. The interpretation of the word "mode" has been much disputed, but it is best understood as "part" as long as it is borne in mind that such a part cannot be separated from the whole of which it is a part. Human beings and other common-sense objects, which are typically modes, are parts of nature, and Spinoza once refers to the human mind as part of the infinite intellect of God. There is a one-to-one correspondence between modes under the several attributes, and necessarily so, since every attribute must qualify the whole of substance.

This is the doctrine of the parallelism of the attributes. So far we have spoken of finite modes only, but Spinoza speaks also of infinite modes, which are, of course, not parts of substance but coextensive with it.

There are both immediate and mediate infinite modes. This part of the theory is difficult to understand, especially as Spinoza does not illustrate it very fully. The immediate infinite mode under the attribute extension is motion and rest. This is probably to be interpreted as the sum total of motion in the universe, so that this part of the theory is an attempt to incorporate the Cartesian doctrine of the conservation of motion. Similarly, the absolutely infinite understanding, which is the immediate infinite mode under thought, would be the sum total of consciousness or knowledge. The universe as a system of attributes is called *natura naturans,* as a system of modes *natura naturata.*

**Causality and Determinism.**—The whole scheme is completely deterministic: since the nature of God cannot be other than it is, the whole system of modes, which follows from or expresses the nature of God, must necessarily be as it is. This is a corollary of Spinoza's demand for intelligibility; for only on this condition can we conceive that every modal event has a cause or explanation which lies in another modal event. By "cause" Spinoza means roughly what we should mean by "explanation," and he shares with Descartes the general rationalist view that a cause must have properties in common with its effect.

It follows that a mode under one attribute cannot be caused or explained by a mode under another attribute, for they have no property in common. Any modal happening under one attribute has its explanation entirely in terms of modal happenings under that same attribute. Since the modes are infinite in number, the complete explanation of any event in concrete terms would be infinitely complex and so cannot be attained by human beings. It is possible for us, however, to explain a particular modal event to some extent by referring to the general laws which govern the occurrence of modal events under the appropriate attribute; *e.g.,* by referring to the laws of physics in the case of material events and to those of psychology in the case of mental events.

**Application of the Metaphysical Scheme to Human Beings.**—The abstract scheme gains meaning as it is applied to human beings. Spinoza develops this application in the *Ethica,* parts ii–v. A man is a mode under the two attributes, extension and thought. His body is a mode under extension and is not a single thing but a complex mode, owing its unity to the maintenance of a constant pattern of relations between changing parts (*see* the axioms, etc., following *Ethica,* ii, 13). The human mind is what corresponds under the attribute thought to the human body. It is therefore likewise a system maintaining the same pattern of relation through change of parts. Spinoza, however, does not develop his theory of the unity of the mind in the same detail as his theory of bodily unity. The mind is called the "idea of the body." Spinoza sometimes speaks of two modes, the human mind and the human body, while at other times he asserts that they are one and the same thing, conceived now under thought and now under extension. These are simply alternative expressions. A human mind is that part of God's mind which is the knowledge or awareness of a given human body. The relation between a mind and its body is, therefore, intrinsic to it; and Spinoza does not require, as Descartes and Leibniz did, to invoke the miraculous intervention of God to explain the connection between a given human mind and its body.

From the general position it follows immediately that, while there is no causal connection between mind and body, there is a mental correlate for every physical event and a physical correlate for every mental event. If "mental correlate for" is here understood as "knowledge of," we reach the paradoxical result that all events in a given human body are known to the corresponding human mind and that no other events are known to that mind. At one point Spinoza appears to accept this result: "The object of the idea which constitutes the human mind is the body or a certain mode of extension actually existing and nothing else" (*Ethica,* ii, 13). The paradox is softened, however, when we realize that the word "idea" and the closely related term "knowledge" (*cognitio*) are used by Spinoza to signify not only a state of clear and accurate knowledge but any state of consciousness whatsoever, however dim and vague. All states of consciousness must have objects, but the objects need not be in the full sense known. Interpreted in this way, the paradoxical statement resolves itself into the following two propositions: (1) every change in the human body is associated with some change of awareness, however dim and vague, in the human mind (*Ethica,* ii, 12); and (2) a human being can know external physical objects only insofar as they affect his own body (*Ethica,* ii, 26).

**Theory of Knowledge.**—Spinoza distinguishes three grades or kinds of human knowledge (*Ethica,* ii, 40, scholium 2). He distinguishes states of awareness as adequate or inadequate rather than as true or false; and the argument of *Ethica,* ii, 19–31, is directed to show that we cannot adequately know particular things, either our own bodies or their parts, or external objects. We are aware of things only in interrelation and cannot know them as they are in themselves. Thus all sense experience which is the mental correlate of the action of external things on our own bodies and all unscientific generalization from sense experience is inadequate. We cannot state the truth about a given object in itself, because it cannot be isolated from the rest of nature; and we cannot state the whole truth about it, since this would involve the whole of nature. Knowledge of this kind is called by Spinoza opinion or imagination. If, however, the consciousness is directed solely toward those properties which all objects, including the human body, have in common, there is no distortion such as occurs when objects with different properties interact. In such cases we have the second kind of knowledge or reason (*ratio*). In this way Spinoza accounts for the possibility of clear a priori knowledge in geometry, general physics and general psychology.

The third kind of knowledge, intuition (*scientia intuitiva*), seems to be the adequate knowledge of individual objects. It is difficult to see how this is possible on Spinoza's presuppositions. For the proof of the possibility he relies on the fact that it is possible to state of any individual thing that it depends on God as its complete, immanent cause (*Ethica,* ii, 47), but it is difficult to see how this general statement could be held to constitute adequate knowledge of the individual thing. It is possible that by the term "intuition" Spinoza refers to mystical experience, the insight—accompanied by strong emotion—into the dependence of all things, including the human being himself, on the whole of nature.

There are other difficulties in Spinoza's theory of knowledge, for it is hard to see how, if the theory be true, we could either be mistaken about the general properties of things (*i.e.,* have a faulty geometry or physics) or be completely right about some particular thing. The distinction between truth and falsehood about particular things occasions Spinoza great difficulty. According to his general account, the difference must be one of degree only, falsity being a matter of greater confusion or less adequacy. His account of the matter is to be found in *Ethica,* ii, 35, and there is also a long discussion of falsity in the *De intellectus emendatione.* What is clear is that our understanding of an individual thing or event will be adequate in proportion as we can explain its features in terms of the general laws, which are the concern of reason; *i.e.,* insofar as we can make correct causal statements about it. The position has important consequences for Spinoza's psychology of the emotions and for his ethics.

**Psychology of the Will and the Emotions.**—Spinoza followed Descartes in the attempt to construct a rational psychology. This is possible, according to his general theory, because there corresponds to every corporeal mode not only an idea but also an idea of that idea (*Ethica,* ii, 20). Thus introspective or reflective knowledge is possible. This seems to occasion another break in the strict parallelism of the attributes, giving again a certain primacy to the attribute of thought.

Spinoza rejects the concept of will as ordinarily understood. He does not, of course, deny that voluntary action or deliberately chosen action occurs, but this does not involve free will in the ordinary sense (*Ethica,* ii, 48) and is to be understood in the following way. Willing is primarily thinking of the course of action to be followed: "The will and the understanding are one and the same thing" (*Ethica,* ii, 49, corollarium). This mental state is the correlate of a physical state whose normal outcome is the realization of the action contemplated. When there are no hindering factors, the action in question inevitably follows (*Ethica,* iii, 2, scholium). The illusion of undetermined choice arises from our ignorance of the preceding causes of thought and action. Since Spinoza's ethics are, however, largely concerned with the distinction between bondage (*servitus*) and freedom (*libertas*), it is clear that he must provide some alternative account of freedom which does not involve free will as ordinarily understood. This is to be found in the distinction between the active and the passive emotions, which is closely bound up with his metaphysical theory.

The denial of human free will is another feature of Spinoza's system which has been found highly shocking, as involving the denial of moral responsibility and of the appropriateness of blame or punishment. It is true that Spinoza, anticipating later criminology, pleads for an objective and dispassionate treatment of undesirable human behaviour, but he by no means denies the sociological and political necessity of punishment, holding that most men must be governed by fear.

Every individual thing or mode obeys the fundamental law of nature that it should strive to preserve itself and continue in existence. This *conatus quo in suo esse perseverare conatur* ("endeavour to persist in its own being") is the essence of the individual thing. All finite modes, on account of their limited power, in the end perish. Only substance has the power of unlimited self-maintenance. In human beings *conatus* is on the physical side appetite and on the mental side desire (*cupiditas*), one of the primary emotions. The only other primary emotions are joy (*laetitia*) and grief (*tristitia*). Joy is the psychic accompaniment or consciousness of the transition to a greater degree of power, while grief is the consciousness of a transition to a lesser degree of power. The other emotions, love, hate, etc., are defined in terms of these and their different possible objects. Spinoza's analytical psychology, which has often been justly admired, is partly based on Descartes's *Les Passions de l'âme,* but without the interactionist presuppositions of that work. Insofar as human beings are able to understand themselves and their environment, they can control events rather than be controlled by them. The striving for, and transition to, a greater understanding is accompanied by desire and joy in their active forms. A man is free insofar as his emotions are active rather than passive. Freedom, for Spinoza, is then a relative notion: human beings are free in proportion as they are able to think clearly, to control their environment and to preserve themselves for the maximum time in an active state. In part iv of the *Ethica* ("Of Human Bondage"), Spinoza stresses the extreme difficulty of attaining any degree of freedom on account of the strength of the passive emotions. In part v, however, he shows that liberty may be attained and the passive emotions mastered through understanding their causes. He is the first to emphasize that the complete understanding of emotions and of their causation deprives them of their overmastering quality. In this he may be said to have anticipated psychoanalysis. He also anticipates a later attitude in his insistence on the completely objective study of the emotions, their causes and effects, "as if it were a question of lines, planes and solids" (*Ethica,* iii, preface).

**Moral Philosophy.**—Spinoza is content with an apparently subjective definition of "good": "The good is that which we know certainly to be useful to us" (*Ethica,* iii, definition 1). He also accepts the fact that the good for different species (*e.g.,* for man and for horse) is different. For God the distinction between good and evil would be meaningless, as it is essentially relative to the purposes of finite creatures; and the human being, insofar as he understands nature scientifically, makes no moral judgments (*Ethica,* i, appendix). But human beings have enough in common for the philosopher to be able to pronounce on what is really good for them—however different their views may be because of the inadequacy and confusion of their ideas. Thus "good" may be said to have an objective significance for human beings. The characteristically human good is the increase in understanding which leads to the longest possible preservation of the individual in physical and mental health. This is summed up in the phrase "knowledge of God" (*Ethica,* iv, 28). In his actual rules Spinoza may seem to overemphasize the importance of intellectual pursuits, but he is not an ascetic; for, according to his parallelistic doctrine, everything that increases physical well-being will also promote mental health.

Since the consciousness of a transition to a state of increased power or health is joy, while sadness in all its forms is the accompaniment of diminishing power, Spinoza condemns such emotions as remorse and humility as harmful and morbid in themselves, while admitting that they may have useful effects (*Ethica,* iv, 53–54).

Spinoza's ethics are essentially egoistic, but the conduct that he commends is that which would be commended by an altruistic utilitarian. Love may be at times an active emotion, but hatred never (*Ethica,* iv, 45); and Spinoza tries to prove that hatred may be overcome by love (iv, 46). His ideal man is in many respects comparable to the Stoic sage, for his aim is the maximum self-sufficiency, but Spinoza gives a more balanced picture in that he has a stronger realization of the essential interdependence of men. Co-operation and friendship between rational men is not only a means to, but an essential part of, the individual's true good (*Ethica,* iv, 60). The preservation of civil society and of peace is a necessary means to individual well-being. This is the basis of Spinoza's political philosophy, which will be considered below.

It is first necessary, however, to touch upon a difficult feature of Spinoza's individual psychology and ethics, the doctrine of the eternity of the mind. This is contained in the latter half of book v of the *Ethica,* a section which has been especially puzzling to commentators. Any theory of survival in the ordinary sense seems plainly inconsistent with Spinoza's parallelistic doctrine. He nevertheless declares that the human mind cannot be absolutely destroyed with the body, but that something remains of it which is eternal (*Ethica,* v, 23). This doctrine has never been satisfactorily explained. Spinoza connects the eternity of the mind with the third kind of knowledge, intuition, which consists essentially in understanding individuals in relation to God, and with the characteristic accompanying emotion, the intellectual love of God, which is the highest degree of acquiescence. This should be compared with the dictum of the *De intellectus emendatione* that blessedness is the knowledge which the mind has of its union with the whole of nature. Spinoza perhaps means that since men must necessarily fall short of complete activity, their highest state is the understanding of, and acquiescence in, their own necessary degree of passivity. Insofar as this is real understanding, it is shared with God and is, in that sense, eternal. But such a doctrine carries no implication of individual survival.

**Political Philosophy.**—In *Ethica,* iii and iv, Spinoza stresses not only the desirability but also the extreme difficulty of cooperation between men. This is made especially clear by the fact that the good at which human beings aim, insofar as they are affected by passive desires, is necessarily competitive; *i.e.,* if men conceive that their survival and welfare are dependent on the possession of external goods, they will necessarily be in conflict with each other (*Ethica,* iv, 32–34). The true good of human nature, the knowledge of God, is, however, noncompetitive, so that men cannot come into conflict insofar as they are affected by the active emotion of desire for this good. If this emotion were predominant in men, that is, if men were mostly rational, there would be no need for political organization, since free and rational men naturally wish to co-operate. Most men, however, are under the control of their passive emotions for the greater part of their lives and will necessarily strive for their own aggrandizement to the detriment of others. Like Thomas Hobbes, Spinoza finds the only remedy for this situation in absolute government. He maintains that it is only under government that the distinction between right and wrong, in a strict sense, arises: whereas in the state of nature "right" means "power" and man has the "right" to do whatever he thinks necessary to his own preservation, in civil society the rational man must yield full obedience to the government as the necessary bulwark against anarchy, so that what is commanded by the government is right. In relation to each other, sovereign states are in a state of nature and are bound only by the law of self-preservation; *e.g.,* treaties need not be kept when they are no longer advantageous. A wise government, however, like a rational man, will see that the surest way to self-preservation is the maintenance of peace.

Similarly it will recognize that the surest way to secure the adherence of its subjects is just government with the maximum freedom possible. Spinoza, therefore, unlike most absolutists, lays great stress on the desirability of freedom of thought and speech in matters of religion. He argues that it is impossible to coerce thought and that a man will be a more loyal citizen if he is allowed to speak his mind freely. The state has a right, however, to control the outward expression of religion. What Spinoza most fears is ecclesiastical tyranny and sectarian strife, and he regards the control of religion by the state as a much lesser evil. Among possible forms of government he prefers democracy as potentially the most stable. These views are expressed not only in the unfinished *Tractatus politicus,* but also in the *Tractatus theologico-politicus.* In this work, in which he anticipates modern biblical criticism, he bases a plea for freedom of thought and speech in religious matters on a careful examination of biblical doctrine and its relation to philosophy.

**Biblical Criticism.**—Spinoza is far ahead of his time in advocating the application of the historical method to the interpretation of the biblical narrative. He argues that it is only in respect of their moral and practical doctrine that the prophets of the Old Testament were inspired. Their factual beliefs were those appropriate to their time and must not be regarded as philosophically significant. Complete freedom of scientific and metaphysical speculation is therefore consistent with all that is important in the Bible. The miracles of the Old Testament are explained as natural events misinterpreted by the prophets and stressed for their moral effect.

**The Influence of Spinozism.**—Spinoza has an assured place in the intellectual history of the western world, both as the author of one of the most complete metaphysical systems ever conceived and as an early advocate of freedom of thought. His direct influence on technical philosophy has not, however, been great at any time. Throughout the 18th century he was almost universally decried as an atheist (sometimes, perhaps, by writers whose primary intention was to commend atheism by giving it the prestige of his name, while protecting themselves from condemnation by their formal disparagement of the very ideas that they were presenting with detailed care under cover of mere historical narration). The tone had been set by Pierre Bayle, in whose *Dictionnaire* Spinozism is described as "the most monstrous hypothesis imaginable, the most absurd and the most diametrically opposed to our minds' most evident notions"; and even David Hume felt obliged to speak of the "hideous hypothesis" of Spinoza. Throughout this period he was probably, as Voltaire says, "less read than famous," partly because an exaggerated respect for his geometrical method led to the view that his conclusions were inescapable once his premisses were accepted. He was rendered intellectually respectable by the efforts of literary critics, especially Lessing, Goethe and Coleridge, who admired the man and found an austere excitement in his works. The attraction of his work is due largely to the fact that he expresses an intensely religious attitude entirely divorced from dogma, and it has been felt less by technical philosophers than by poets, such as Goethe and Wordsworth, and by scientists of wide intellectual sympathies, like, for example, Einstein. He has nevertheless been much studied by professional philosophers since the beginning of the 19th century. Both absolute idealists and Marxists have read their own doctrines into his work, and positivists and empiricists, while rejecting his metaphysical approach, have developed fruitfully certain detailed suggestions of his theory of knowledge and psychology.

*See* also references under "Spinoza, Benedictus de" in the Index.

BIBLIOGRAPHY.—The best critical edition of Spinoza's works is by C. Gebhardt, 4 vol. (1924); there is also a good edition of the text by J. van Vloten and J. P. N. Land, 3rd ed., 4 vol. (1914). For English versions see *Spinoza's Chief Works,* ed. by R. H. Elwes, 2 vol. (1883–84); *Ethics,* trans. by Hale White and A. H. Stirling, 3rd ed. (1899); *A Short Treatise on God, Man and His Well-Being,* trans. by A. Wolf (1910); and *The Correspondence of Spinoza,* trans. by A. Wolf (1928).

For general works *see* K. Fischer, *Spinozas Leben, Werke und Lehre,* 6th ed. (1946); F. Pollock, *Spinoza: His Life and Philosophy,* 3rd ed. (1912); J. Freudenthal, *Spinoza: Leben und Lehre,* ed. by C. Gebhardt, 2 parts (1927). For biography *see* J. Freudenthal, *Die Lebensgeschichte Spinozas in Quellenschriften* (1899); E. Dunin-Borkowski, *Der Junge de Spinoza* (1910); L. Brunschvicg, *Spinoza et ses contemporains* (1923); and A. Wolf (ed. and trans.), *The Oldest Biography of Spinoza* (1927); also A. Wolf, *Spinoza: His Life and Treatise on God and Man* (1910). For studies of his philosophy *see* the bibliography given by J. A. Gunn, *Benedict Spinoza* (1925); also L. Roth, *Spinoza, Descartes, Maimonides* (1924), *Spinoza* (1929); R. McKeon, *The Philosophy of Spinoza* (1928); L. Robinson, *Kommentar zu Spinozas Ethik* (1928); H. A. Wolfson, *The Philosophy of Spinoza* (1934); H. H. Joachim, *Commentary on the Tractatus de Intellectus emendatione* (1940); S. Hampshire, *Spinoza* (1956). *See* further the periodicals *Chronicon Spinozanum* (1921 *et seq.*) and *Bibliotheca Spinozana* (1922 *et seq.*).

(M. KE.)

**SPIRAEA,** a much cultivated genus of shrubs (the common term is spirea) of the rose family (Rosaceae; *q.v.*), comprising about 80 species and scores of horticultural varieties, natives mostly of the Northern Hemisphere. They are slender shrubs, two to eight feet high, usually with simple leaves and small white, pink, or red flowers arranged in dense showy clusters. *Spiraea douglasi* (western meadowsweet) occurs on the Pacific coast. Among the best-known cultivated forms are *S. prunifolia* and the popular hybrid *S. vanhouttei,* both commonly called bridal wreath. *S. salicifolia* (queen of the meadow) occurs in England and Scotland. *S. latifolia* and *S. alba* (both known as meadowsweet) and *S. tomentosa* (hardhack; *q.v.*) are representative species of eastern North America.

The cultivated spireas are divided into generally white-flowered, spring-blooming kinds typified by the true bridal wreath (*S. prunifolia*) and its relatives, and the summer-blooming, prevailingly red or pinkish-flowered species allied to *S. billiardi.* Among these showy, summer-blooming species are *S. japonica* and *S. bumalda,* a particularly fine variety of which is Anthony Waterer. Spireas thrive in most garden soils, are relatively immune to pests, and are easily propagated by seeds or cuttings of green wood. Some bushes arch over, the stems rooting at the tips.

A few of the so-called spireas belong to several other genera, as *Astilbe, Aruncus, Filipendula,* and *Caryopteris.* (N. TR.)

**SPIRE,** in architecture, a steeply pointed termination to a tower (*q.v.*). Towers built in diminishing stages are sometimes called "spires," but in error; strictly speaking, those are steeples. Spires are in essence a kind of pointed roof, originating in the simple, four-sided pyramidal roof capping church towers in the early middle ages. In their mature Gothic development, however, only reminiscences of a roof remained, and spires became independent architectural elements, with both aesthetic and symbolic significance. (*See* also PINNACLE.)

From their first appearance to the 12th century, spires were generally abrupt and stunted in form; their history is a development toward slimmer, higher forms and a more organic relationship with the tower below. A late 11th-century tower at Le Puy en Velay shows the nature of early experiments in this direction; the successive stages of the tower recede and are broken up by projecting bays on the sides. Furthermore, the pyramidal roof itself is decorated with corner finials and small, round-headed dormers. In Germany the form was varied by ending each face of the square tower in a gable, the plane determined by adjacent gable slopes establishing the slope of the pyramid, as in the square tower of the abbey church of Laach (*c.* 1156). The pleasanter effect of the octagonal spires over octagonal towers, like another of the towers at Laach or the older of the two towers at Mainz (late 12th century), led to attempts to combine an octagonal spire with a square tower. This was accomplished in various ways, one of the simplest being the so-called broach spire, in which small, triangular planes of a less steep pitch than that of the spire proper occur at the bottom of the corner spire faces, with their lower points coinciding with the corners of the towers, as seen in the 12th-century church of St. Columba at Cologne.

A more developed form of broach spire lies in the substitution of a small pyramid at the bottom of the corner faces, instead of the triangular plane. This is a type which became common in English Gothic spires. It may be described geometrically as the inter-

(LEFT, TOP CENTRE) BILDARCHIV FOTO MARBURG; (SECOND FROM LEFT, BOTTOM CENTRE, RIGHT) A. F. KERSTING

(Above) Square tower (centre of picture) of Abbey Church at Laach, Ger., about 1156; (right) facade of Chartres Cathedral, France, showing southwest spire at right, late 12th-century, and the more elaborate 16th-century northern spire at left; (top centre) spires of St. Elizabeth, Marburg, Ger., built in the 14th century from 13th-century designs; (bottom centre) spire of St. Martin's-in-the-Fields, London, designed by James Gibbs, 1721–26; (right) spire of Salisbury Cathedral, England, 1250

section of a four-sided pyramid of low slope by an eight-sided pyramid of steep slope, as in the 14th-century spire of St. Mary's at Stamford. A more elaborate method of softening the junction between square and octagon was to carry the corner faces down unbroken to the top of the tower and fill the triangular corners thus left with decorative finials. An early example is the crossing tower of the church of St. Ours, at Loches, France (12th century).

In the southwest tower of Chartres cathedral (end of the 12th century) a further advance is made in connecting tower and spire, by adding high, gabled dormers on the faces of the spire, over the centres of the tower faces, as well as richly developing the corner pinnacles. In the spire at Senlis cathedral (13th century) a vertical, octagonal stage, or lantern, is placed between the square tower and the octagonal spire. The corners of the square tower are occupied by pinnacles and eight slim dormers surround the spire base. The edges of the Chartres and Senlis spires are decorated with projecting roll moldings, and those at Senlis are further enriched by crockets which form an admirable fretting of the silhouette. It is probable that similar crocketed spires were almost universally intended over the great towers of most of the French cathedrals. The towers at Laon, for instance, were once so crowned and spires at Reims and Amiens were begun.

**Gothic Climax.**—It was in Normandy, England and Germany that Gothic spire design reached its climax. Particularly famous are the spires of St. Sauveur at Caen (14th-century church destroyed in World War II) and the magnificent group of spires at Coutances cathedral (13th century), in which the spire dormers and the corner pinnacles are treated with the utmost richness and the sense of height and slimness emphasized in every possible manner. The customary lavishness of the French Flamboyant style is magnificently illustrated in its pierced and intricately traceried spires. The two most remarkable examples are the northern spire of Chartres cathedral (1506–13), by Jehan Texier, and the so-called Tour de Beurre (*c.* 1520) of the cathedral at Rouen.

Spires of a simple type crown many of the Italian campaniles, and during the 13th, 14th and 15th centuries, spires and lanterns were frequently added to earlier towers. In neither Italy nor Spain, however, was the highly developed spire a native form, and Italian spires were simple, slate, tile or metal covered, pyramidal or conical roofs of timber. Burgos cathedral is unique in Spain in possessing two western spires of intricate openwork masonry, which date from the 15th century. These, however, are known to have been designed by a German architect.

German luxuriance, which had already appeared in the numerous varieties of timber spires used on the Rhenish Romanesque churches, found equally congenial expression in the stone spires of the Gothic period. The early, simple type is seen in the solid spires of St. Elizabeth at Marburg (not completed until the middle of the 14th century but probably from a 13th-century design). The cathedral at Freiburg has a spire (1270–88) which is of a new and infinitely richer type. The low, square tower carries a high, octagonal lantern, each side of which is capped by a slim gable and filled with delicate tracery. The corners of the square are filled with rich, triangular pinnacles, one of which is continued up as an open, spiral staircase, giving access to the upper portion. The spire rises above the lantern, a mere cage of openwork tracery, with crocketed edges, amazingly light and delicate in effect. Somewhat similar, although even more intricate in their pierced stonework are the western spires of Regensburg cathedral (late 15th century), by Roritzer. These openwork spires became the rule in Germany, as illustrated in the intricate cage of Strasbourg cathedral (spire, 1435); the west towers of Cologne cathedral, built in the 19th century from medieval drawings; the over-complicated lacework of the cathedral at Vienna (1433) and the spire at Ulm, over 500 ft. high, built in the last years of the 19th century, from 15th-century drawings.

The spire of Oxford cathedral (1220) is a perfect example of the Early English spire type; it is octagonal, has a marked entasis or convex curve, and is decorated with dormers on each face and corner pinnacles. The great spire of Salisbury cathedral (1250), 406 ft. high, shows the tremendous aesthetic advantage of the greater steepness there present, which became the rule in the later English spires. During the Decorated period it became customary to finish the top of the tower with a parapet, either battlemented or of pierced tracery, and to set back the base of the spire behind the face of the wall. With this change the use of broaches disappeared and tall, corner pinnacles, sometimes supported on corner buttresses, filled the tower corners, as seen in the two western spires of Lichfield cathedral. In other examples a little flying buttress connects the corner pinnacles with the face of the spire, as in the exquisite Perpendicular spire of Louth church, Lincolnshire. Many Perpendicular spires are often ornamented with crockets up the angles. (*See* also GOTHIC ART AND ARCHITECTURE.)

**Renaissance.**—The spire was a form never thoroughly absorbed by the Renaissance which preferred domed lanterns crowning towers. Nevertheless, during the 17th century in Germany, most effective, fantastic, spirelike forms were developed. These, based partly on Italian baroque prototypes, usually had profiles of broken concave and convex lines, crowned at the top with a sort of onion dome, the whole rising to a considerable height, and, in imaginative quality, far surpassing any of the Italian examples. It is such fantastic spires crowning the simple towers of village churches which give much of their character to the little towns of south Germany and Austria. At the same time, in England, the spire idea was receiving a much simpler and more straightforward, and equally effective, Renaissance expression, through the efforts of Sir Christopher Wren and his followers, particularly in the churches built after the Great Fire of London in 1666, such as St. Martin's, Ludgate hill, St. Mary-le-Bow and St. Bride's, Fleet street (spire and steeple only remain), all by Wren. St. Mary-le-Strand (early 18th century) and St. Martin's-in-the-Fields (1721–26), both by James Gibbs, which simplified and refined upon their Wren prototypes, are very successful.

Even more effective are many colonial spires, which, although originally based upon the work of Wren and Gibbs, achieved a fresh beauty through still further simplification. Particularly noteworthy is the type in which a small, octagonal, arcaded lantern crowns a simple, square tower and carries, usually above an attic, a simple, slim, white spire, as in the Old South meetinghouse, Boston (1729), and the extremely delicate, white, wooden steeple of the church at Farmington, Conn. (*c.* middle 18th century). Such steeples as that of St. Paul's chapel, New York (*c.* 1767), Christ church, Philadelphia (1754), and St. Michael's, Charleston, S.C. (1742, occasionally attributed to James Gibbs himself), although more monumental in treatment and more English in effect, still retain the characteristic American delicacy. This trend toward the more slender and attenuated proportions reached its climax in the exquisitely light spire of Park Street church, Boston (1819), by Peter Banner.

The 19th-century architects made extravagant use of spires for their picturesquely irregular outlines and visually exciting shapes; Anglican Gothic Revival architects of the late 1840s, '50s and '60s used them with particular effectiveness to culminate dramatically massed compositions. Perhaps because spires were so closely associated with picturesque eclecticism, 20th-century architects have tended to limit them to rather elementary geometric shapes.

(T. F. H.; AN. G.)

**SPIRES:** *see* SPEYER.

**SPIRITS:** *see* ALCOHOLIC BEVERAGES, DISTILLED.

**SPIRITUALISM.** The word spiritualism has been used with two meanings: first, for a metaphysical theory that asserts the reality of a nonmaterial spiritual world, which is a view common to religions; second, for a system of beliefs and practices having the object of communicating with the asserted spirits of those who have died, and for the social institutions of those who hold these beliefs and carry out these practices. It is in this second sense that the word is to be understood in the present article. To avoid confusion with the more general metaphysical meaning of spiritualism, the word spiritism has been suggested as more appropriate for the beliefs and practices connected with communication after death, but this use has not generally been adopted.

Spiritualist practices commonly take place in the presence of a person (the medium) who is regarded as a human intermediary with the spirit world. Although mediums are most commonly women, some highly gifted mediums have been men, as, for example, the famed D. D. Home. The séance at which mediumistic phenomena occur may be in complete darkness, in reduced light, or, more rarely, in full daylight. The medium is sometimes in a state of trance, speaking and behaving without subsequent memory of what has been said or done, but some mediums work in a state of normal consciousness.

The main activities of spiritualism are: (1) the phenomena of mental mediumship; (2) the production of materializations and other phenomena of physical mediumship; (3) spirit photography; and (4) spirit healing (*see* also SHAMANISM).

The phenomena of mental mediumship include ostensible messages from spirits of the departed. They may be messages to their own friends and relatives present at the séance, or the communicators may claim to be describing the conditions of life beyond the grave. In some séances, long books of history or fiction have been produced. Usually the messages come through a spirit control who appears to communicate directly with the sitters; more rarely the communicators appear to communicate by direct voice.

Phenomena of physical mediumship include the playing of musical instruments, transportation of physical objects (apports), levitation of the medium or nearby objects, raps, and so on. These have sometimes been considered to be too reminiscent of horseplay to be appropriate activities of discarnate spirits. They are, however, generally explained as of value only as providing evidence for the possibility of spiritual activity. The most important physical phenomenon is the appearance of a filmy substance (ectoplasm), which is generally supposed to be a quasi-material substance derived from the body of the medium, which may take the form of a face, hand, or complete body. Such materializations have been photographed, but there have also been photographs of what purported to be ectoplasm in which the structure suggests some such material as cheesecloth. Materializations and other physical phenomena occur in darkness or in dim red light, as the exposure of ectoplasm to strong visible light is said to be injurious to the medium. Spirit photographs also have been obtained by some operators on films that may not have been exposed in a camera. It is obvious that such films could be produced fraudulently, as, for example, by the use of radioactive material, but they are also stated to have been produced under satisfactory test conditions.

An important later development of spiritualism has been in the direction of spirit healing. Unorthodox healings have in the past been associated with sacred places and religious rites, and medical science is inclined to attribute all such healings to the normal process of suggestion working under favourable conditions. But it is also claimed that there is a genuine power of paranormal healing found in certain persons, and from the spiritualist point of view these healers are regarded as mediums who act as agents of spirit doctors. Healings are claimed for a variety of conditions, some of which are regarded as incurable by orthodox medicine.

**History.**—The attempt to communicate with discarnate spirits seems to be one of the forms that religion may take in human societies and to be widely distributed in space and time. Practices very like those of a modern spiritualistic séance have been reported in various parts of the world, as, for example, Haiti and among the North American Indians, and there is no reason for supposing that these are of recent origin. The record of a materialization séance of long ago is preserved in the account in the Old Testament of Saul's visit to the witch (or medium) of Endor, in the course of which a materialization appeared that was regarded by the king as the prophet Samuel (I Sam. 28:7–19). Certain mediumistic phenomena are reported in the witch trials of the Middle Ages, particularly the appearance of spirits in quasi-material form and the obtaining of knowledge through spirits. It may be supposed that many of those persecuted for the practice of witchcraft were what would now be called mediums, although their mediumship was coloured by the fact that it was organized in a forbidden cult and the spirits with which communication was established were regarded as devils. Some mediumistic phenomena were also found among those regarded in the Middle Ages as possessed by devils; *e.g.,* speaking in languages unknown to the speaker and levitation or partial levitation (*see* Devil: *Diabolism Within the Church*).

Although spiritualistic practices seem to be widespread in space and time, they were virtually unknown in modern civilized society until March 1848, when odd happenings were reported at the house of a farmer named Fox at a small town in New York State. Previous occupants of the house had been disturbed by unexplained raps at night. After a severe disturbance by raps during Mr. Fox's tenancy, his youngest daughter, Kate, was said to have successfully challenged the supposed spirit to repeat the number of times she flipped her fingers. Once communication had apparently been established a code was agreed upon by which the raps given could answer questions, and the spirit was said to have identified himself as a man who had been murdered in the house.

The practice of having sittings for communication with spirits spread rapidly from that time. Kate Fox (afterward Mrs. Fox-Jencken) and one of her sisters gave much of their later lives to acting as mediums in the United States and in England. Many other mediums gave similar sittings, and the movement became widespread. The attempt to communicate with spirits by table turning became a popular pastime in Victorian drawing rooms.

Much of this activity was motivated by mere curiosity and the fascination of the supernatural, but it also had a more serious intention. Many inquirers wished to convince themselves as to human survival of bodily death; others suffered from the loss of loved relatives and friends and found consolation in the belief that they were able to communicate with them; others wanted information about the future life. To promote these serious ends, spiritualist associations or churches were formed.

The rise of this new cult was not allowed to take place without opposition. There was not only verbal condemnation with accusations of fraud but also mob violence. This was, no doubt, partly a popular reaction to a novel system of ideas and practices that were suspected of being based either on fraud or evil. The suspicion of evil was perhaps strengthened by a conjectured relationship to the discarded system of witchcraft. Although individual spiritualists were often members (or even ministers) of Christian churches, the general tendency of the established religious bodies was to suspect the movement and its claim to a new revelation that would either supplement or replace the Christian revelation. The spiritualist practices seemed also to some religious bodies to be a part of the forbidden activity of necromancy. A decree of the Holy Office of the Roman Catholic Church in 1898 condemned spiritistic practices, although permitting legitimate scientific investigation of mediumistic phenomena.

If there was strong and often irrational opposition to spiritualism from the early days of the movement, there was also enthusiastic and often somewhat uncritical acceptance. For those who had lost their faith in traditional Christianity, there was offered a new religion based not on an ancient tradition but on facts that could be observed by anyone. For those to whom materialistic ways of thinking had closed the possibility of a life after death, there was offered a new hope of immortality. To those suffering from grief after the death of their loved ones, there was offered the possibility of communicating with them. There were strong emotional involvements in both the rejection and the acceptance of spiritualism that have made difficult an impartial appraisal of the evidence.

**Assessment.**—From the earliest days, one of the charges against spiritualist mediums was that of fraud—*i.e.,* that they produced their results by the conscious exercise of guessing and trickery—but there does not seem to be any good reason for supposing that this holds for all mediums or for any large number of them. It is, however, clear that the conditions of mediumship are such that it is possible for fraudulent mediumship to be both easy and profitable. Those who attend séances for comfort and reassurance are liable to be uncritical of the evidence offered to them; and a medium using a mixture of guesswork, inference, and items of information such as are likely to apply to most people may mislead the credulous into thinking that they have received information that could have come only from the departed. A confederate with luminous paint, masks, and cheesecloth may put up a counterfeit series of physical manifestations that also may be accepted by the credulous. Judgment as to the genuineness of phenomena is made difficult by the possibility that a commercial medium may produce a mixture of genuine and counterfeit phenomena. If some mediums are able to produce ectoplasm and ectoplasmic forms, this ability may nevertheless be too sporadic for reliable use, and the medium dependent for his livelihood on the production of spirit forms may use cheesecloth as a supplementary method of satisfying sitters. If a mental medium can transmit genuine spirit messages, these too may be sporadic and supplemented by skilful guessing. This supplementation may indeed not be conscious fraud, since the medium may not be aware of whether he is transmitting a spirit message or using his own powers of intelligent guessing.

It is generally agreed that, when fraud is eliminated, there remains a considerable residuum of phenomena ostensibly spiritualistic, whatever may be their explanation. It does not necessarily follow that the spiritualist explanation must be accepted. Some investigators (*e.g.,* C. Richet) have been strongly convinced of the reality of both mental and physical paranormal phenomena but have considered that they are to be explained without reference to discarnate spirits by scientific principles not yet understood. Richet admitted, however, that what was observed suggested on the surface an explanation in terms of surviving spirits.

Two lines of evidence may be followed to test this type of explanation: first, there is evidence by *recognition,* when the sitter claims that he has an overwhelming impression of the personality of the communicator (his character, tricks of speech, etc.) as vivid as if he were in his living presence; second, there is evidence by *information* in which the communicator gives some piece of information that should have been known only to the deceased. The first of these may be convincing to the sitter himself but can be of no value in persuading anyone else. The confirmed skeptic may also be unconvinced by evidence from information since he may accept some normal or paranormal explanation of how the information was obtained which does not involve spirits. (*See* further Parapsychology.)

In principle, all evidence by information can be explained by postulating sufficient paranormal cognitive capacity in the medium, but to explain all of the evidence for survival in this way would require this kind of explanation to be stretched very far. At least it may be considered that there is a strong prima facie case for some communication from human spirits that have survived death. If, however, there is a genuine element of communication from the departed in some mediumistic utterances, there is also much evidence that such communications can be diluted to an unknown extent, with error supplied by the medium himself or derived from the sitters. To many of those who have thought that they were really in touch with spirits, it has seemed as if they were in touch with them imperfectly and indirectly, as if one were receiving a telephone message, not directly, but dictated through an operator who understood it imperfectly and added his own glosses as well as transmitting elements of wrong messages. It is possible to hold that mediumistic communications may be of value in providing evidence of life after death without considering that such communications provide reliable information either on the nature of that life or on any other subject. *See* also Psychical Research.

Bibliography.—F. W. H. Myers, *Human Personality and Its Survival of Bodily Death,* 2 vol. (1920); A. Conan Doyle, *History of Spiritualism* (1926); F. A. P. W. Schrenk-Notzing, *Phenomena of Materialisation* (1920); K. H. Porter, *Through a Glass Darkly* (1958); P. D. Payne and L. J. Bendit, *Psychic Sense* (1961); N. Blunsdon, *A Popular Dictionary of Spiritualism* (1962); F. Podmore, *Modern Spiritualism* (1902), reprinted as *Mediums of the 19th Century,* 2 vol. (1962); E. W. Fornell, *The Unhappy Medium* (1964). (R. H. T.)

**SPITALFIELDS,** a district of Stepney in the borough of Tower Hamlets, London, Eng. The land belonged to the rest house or "spital" of St. Mary's Priory (1197), Bishopsgate. Spitalfields Market ($6\frac{1}{2}$ ac. [3 ha.], vegetables, fruit, and flowers) was established in 1682. Footwear and furniture are made, and until about 1900 silk weaving, established by Huguenots after 1685, was important. The Eastertide Spital sermon was given at the pulpit cross in the hospital churchyard until the 17th century.

**SPITHEAD,** an extensive anchorage between the Isle of Wight and the mainland of England, the Spit bank forming the western side of the channel leading to Portsmouth harbour. This anchorage was much used by the Channel fleet in the wars of the 18th century, and is specially suitable for the great naval reviews of modern times. Queen Victoria reviewed the British fleet there in 1853 just before the Crimean War and led the fleet to sea. There was another great naval gathering at Spithead for her funeral in 1901, when her body was conveyed from the Isle of Wight to London. The review by Queen Elizabeth II on her coronation (June 1953) was attended not only by ships of war of many nations, but by every branch of Britain's seafaring industry. (R. N. BA.)

**SPITSBERGEN:** *see* SVALBARD.

**SPITTA, (JULIUS AUGUST) PHILIPP** (1841–1894), German musician, one of the principal figures in 19th-century musicology. Born at Wechold, Hanover, on Dec. 7, 1841, he studied at Göttingen and later formed a friendship with Brahms. In 1874 he helped found the Bachverein in Leipzig, and the following year he became professor of musical history at the University of Berlin. His *Johann Sebastian Bach* (2 vol., 1873–80; Eng. trans. by C. Bell and J. A. Fuller-Maitland, 3 vol., 1884–85), dealing with Bach's life and religious and technical aspects of his work, was the first comprehensive work on this composer. His editions of the works of Heinrich Schütz and Dietrich Buxtehude established a high standard of scholarship. With Brahms, K. F. F. Chrysander, and others he was one of the chief founders, in 1892, of the great edition of the works of German composers, *Denkmäler deutscher Tonkunst.* He died at Berlin on April 13, 1894.

**SPITTELER, CARL** (1845–1924), Swiss poet of visionary imagination, and author of pessimistic yet heroic verse.

Spitteler was born in Liestal, April 24, 1845. He studied theology in Basel and in Heidelberg and was private tutor for eight years in Russia and Finland. In 1881–82, after his return, his first great work, the mythical epic *Prometheus und Epimetheus* (Eng. trans., 1931), appeared shortly before Nietzsche's *Zarathustra,* a work similar in outlook and in its elevated, quasi-biblical, rhythmical prose style. Alien to the time and strange, it was met with misunderstanding and Spitteler determined "to come down to earth." During the next few years, when he had to make his living by teaching and journalism, he began to express himself in a wide range of literary forms. In 1892 a legacy enabled him to settle in Lucerne and devote himself to creative work. He died there on Dec. 29, 1924.

Spitteler's second great work (which won him the Nobel Prize in 1919) was the poetic epic *Der Olympische Frühling* (1900–05; rev. 1910), in which he found full scope for bold invention and vividly expressive power. The last years of his life were given up to rewriting of his first work. Tauter in composition than the early version and, like *Der Olympische Frühling,* in rhyming couplets, it appeared in 1924 under the title *Prometheus der Dulder.*

The widely varied peripheral works belong to Spitteler's middle period. He produced, in verse, *Extramundana* (1883), seven cosmic myths of his own invention; *Balladen* (1896); *Literarische Gleichnisse* (1892); and two cycles of lyrics, *Schmetterlinge* (1889) and *Gras- und Glockenlieder* (1906). He also wrote two masterly stories—*Die Mädchenfeinde* (1907; Eng. trans., *Two Little Misogynists,* 1922), a childhood idyll derived from his own experience, and *Conrad der Leutnant* (1898), a dramatically finished *Novelle* in which he approached the naturalism he otherwise hated. His novel *Imago* (1906) so sharply reflected his inner conflict between a visionary creative gift and middle-class values that it influenced the development of psychoanalysis. He published a volume of stimulating essays, *Lachende Wahrheiten* (1898; Eng. trans., *Laughing Truths,* 1927), and some biographical works of charm, including *Meine frühesten Erlebnisse* (1914). In 1914 he published a politically influential tract, *Unser Schweizer Standpunkt,* directed against a one-sided pro-German view of the war. An English translation of *Selected Poems* appeared in 1928.

BIBLIOGRAPHY.—*Gesammelte Werke,* 11 vol., ed. by G. Bohnenblust, W. Altwegg and R. Faesi (1945–58); *Briefwechsel mit Adolph Frey* (1933). R. Faesi, *Spitteler's Weg und Werk* (1933) and W. Stauffacher, *C. Spittelers Lyrik* (1950) contain full bibliographical information. *See* also *C. Spitteler in der Erinnerung seiner Freunde,* ed. by L. Beriger (1947).

(R. FA.)

**SPLEEN,** a soft, oblong, purplish organ in the abdomen, is an integral part of the lymphatic and blood vascular systems. Its specially designed lymphatic tissue has the major functions of (1) removing from the blood stream foreign material, including disease-producing organisms and worn-out blood cells; (2) producing lymphocytes and other blood cells; (3) producing antibodies; (4) storing iron and, in some diseases, lipids; and (5) maintaining constant volume of circulating blood. In higher vertebrates the spleen is located in the upper left quadrant of the abdomen just below the diaphragm. It varies in size in different species. Thus, in man, dogs, rats, and mice it approximates 0.25% of the total body weight; in cats and rabbits, 0.05%.

**Microscopic Anatomy.**—The spleen is covered by a contractile capsule composed of dense connective tissue and a few smooth muscle cells. The trabeculae (connective-tissue structures that penetrate the organ) are continuous with the capsule and form a coarse interior scaffolding (*see* diagram) supporting a finer framework (reticulum) of fixed reticular cells and reticular fibres. The two types of lymphatic tissue, white pulp and red pulp, differ chiefly in the relative number of cell types occurring within the reticulum. White pulp, or dense lymphatic tissue, forms a sheath of varying thickness around the arteries and is reticulum closely packed with lymphocytes. (For detailed descriptions of lymphocytes and other blood and lymph cells mentioned in this article, *see* BLOOD; LYMPH AND LYMPHATIC SYSTEM.) In the red pulp, or loose lymphatic tissue, the reticulum is pierced in all directions by venous sinuses (*see* diagram). The reticulum forms the splenic, or Billroth, cords between the sinuses and is filled with lymphocytes, free macrophages (many of which were previously fixed reticular cells), and all circulating blood cells. The venous sinuses contain the same cells but fewer large lymphoid cells and macrophages. The sinuses are lined with flattened reticular cells (littoral cells) and not with true endothelial cells, which line ordinary blood vessels. Arterial blood leaving the smallest branches (arterioles) of the trabecular arteries passes through the cords of the red pulp on its way to the sinuses and out through the trabecular veins. Whether the blood has permanent channels throughout the cords (closed circulation) or simply percolates through temporary passages (open circulation) in the reticulum is not definitely known. Both types of circulation are shown in the diagram.

**Functions.**—As the blood circulates in the spleen, it comes in contact with phagocytes—cells that ingest and destroy other cells, microorganisms, or foreign particles. The most active phagocytes are the fixed reticular cells and free macrophages of the cords; active to a lesser extent are the reticular cells lining the sinuses and free macrophages in the sinuses.

The macrophages of the spleen in the normal animal remove

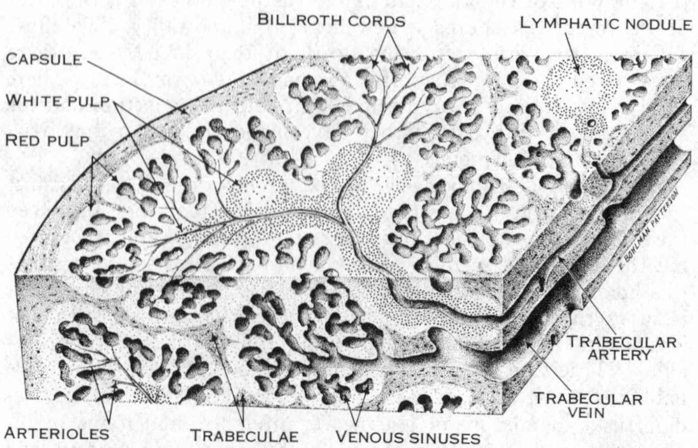


DIAGRAM OF OUTER PORTION (SECTIONED) OF THE SPLEEN. NOTE THE RELATIONSHIPS OF ARTERY AND VEIN TO THE WHITE AND RED PULP worn-out or fragmented blood cells and digest them. During this process the iron-containing component of the hemoglobin in the red cells is separated and reutilized by the body. This phagocytic activity may be so great in some blood diseases and infections as to produce anemia. The macrophages also remove foreign matter from the blood, including invading parasites. When the foreign substance is an invading organism or a vaccine containing antigens, the spleen forms antibodies against it. Such antibodies make the bacteria or other particulate antigenic material more readily ingestible by the macrophages. (For a discussion of the mechanism of immunity, *see* IMMUNITY AND IMMUNIZATION.)

Virulent infections at first generally kill many splenic cells, such as macrophages and especially lymphocytes. Death of lymphocytes results in shrinkage of the white pulp. If the animal survives, lymphocytes and, to a lesser extent, reticular cells proliferate by mitotic division. Some of the new lymphocytes replace those previously lost, and others develop into monocytes and macrophages and probably into antibody-producing cells. Some investigators believe that most of the new macrophages are thus formed from lymphocytes and monocytes and that only a small part arise by the proliferation of reticular cells. The proliferative and developmental processes frequently result in the formation of more splenic tissue, an above-normal number of cells (hyperplasia), and enlargement of the spleen (splenomegaly), which is at times very marked. The extra macrophages in such a spleen are of great functional significance, especially during early stages of infection before antibodies appear.

The spleen is not the only so-called filter organ of the blood. Others are the liver and bone marrow and, to a lesser extent, the adrenal and pituitary glands. The spleen contains the most active macrophages, but the liver, because of its size, can remove as much as 70 times more material. The spleen produces antibodies first in response to antigens in the blood. Its output then falls off, and various nonsplenic sources take over and in time surpass it. The spleen and bone marrow are, among the filter organs, the most important antibody-formers. The liver forms very few antibodies although it is the source of most of the other serum proteins. The spleen, in its blood-cell-forming capacity, produces chiefly lymphocytes, monocytes, and macrophages. The same is true of the lymph nodes and other lymphatic tissue and the bone marrow.

The spleen contains a sizable fraction of the total blood and acts as one of the reservoirs to maintain a constant volume in the general circulation under various conditions.

**Comparative Anatomy and Physiology.**—Knowledge of the physiology of the spleen of the lower vertebrates is largely limited to its role in blood-cell formation. H. E. Jordan believes that the spleen is the fundamental blood-cell-forming organ and that it appeared during the evolution of the vertebrates at about the time of hemoglobin-containing red cells. In the hagfish, among the primitive fish, it is a diffuse tissue; in the lamprey it is a more localized mass of tissue projecting into the dorsal wall of the intestine. In the lungfish it is a discrete organ but is embedded in the stomach. In all the rest of the true fishes and higher vertebrates it is a separate organ located in the dorsal mesentery. In its most primitive form it is the chief site of the formation of red cells, granular leukocytes, and lymphoid cells, but among most higher fishes it has largely lost its ability to produce granular leukocytes and shares the other functions with other tissues. The function of red-blood-cell formation is largely taken over by the red bone marrow in some reptiles and in all higher vertebrates. Although the spleen retains its function of forming lymphocytes, it shares this function with the bone marrow in the reptiles and birds and with bone marrow and lymph nodes in the mammals. It exhibits many of the foregoing capacities, however, in embryonic development or in disease. For example, it forms red cells during a considerable part of human embryonic development. The normal spleen in adult man never forms red cells, but the red pulp in such a disease as myeloid leukemia produces a large number of them, as well as other bone marrow elements. The normal spleen in some animals (*e.g.*, chickens, rats, and mice) probably always forms a few red cells and may produce enormous numbers of them in certain infections, such as malaria.

BIBLIOGRAPHY.—H. E. Jordan, "Comparative Hematology," in Hal Downey (ed.), *Handbook of Hematology,* vol. ii (1938); Aleksandr A. Maksimov and William Bloom, *A Textbook of Histology,* 7th ed. (1957); William H. Taliaferro, "Functions of the Spleen in Immunity," *Am. J. Trop. Med.*. 3:391–410 (1956). (W. H. T.; X.)

**SPLEEN, DISEASES OF.** The diseases of the spleen (*q.v.*), which are numerous, depend in large measure upon the peculiarities of that organ. The spleen has no outstanding function, yet it has many rather subtle functions. It may be removed with impunity, yet it contributes to the development of immune responses. It is ordinarily useful, yet it may become harmful to the body, particularly when enlarged. In some ways the spleen is a sponge or reservoir containing excess blood; in other respects it is like a large lymph gland situated within the abdominal (portal) circulation; it has many phagocytic cells designed to capture particles and debris.

The spleen may become enlarged (splenomegaly) for a variety of reasons: reaction to certain infections or to immune processes; congestion with excess blood as in polycythemia or in cirrhosis of the liver; stuffing with abnormal cells, as in Gaucher's disease, leukemia or a related disease called myeloid metaplasia. Certain tumours begin in the spleen (lymphosarcoma); peculiarly, ordinary cancers are usually unable to gain a foothold in that organ.

The spleen, being part of the lymphoid apparatus, becomes enlarged in diseases involving this system, as in lymphocytic leukemia and infectious mononucleosis. As part of the reticulo-endothelial system, it becomes enlarged when this phagocytic system is overactive as in tuberculosis, rheumatoid arthritis and histoplasmosis. The spleen is easily distensible, so that when the portal circulation is filled with stagnant blood under great pressure due to inability of blood to go through the liver, it takes up extra blood and becomes congested.

In many cases, enlargement of the spleen is accompanied by a reduction in the cells of the blood; thus either the red cells may be affected (anemia), or the white cells (leukopenia) or the platelets (thrombocytopenia). Involvement of all three blood elements is called pancytopenia, and this occurs fairly commonly in hypersplenism, the term given to reductions in blood elements associated with enlargement of the spleen. Sometimes the hypersplenic state is so striking and the blood counts so low that it is desirable to remove the spleen. The spleen also may be removed in certain cases of blood destruction (hemolytic anemia) and blood platelet reduction (thrombocytopenic purpura); however, in these cases all other avenues of treatment, notably the use of cortisone preparations, should be explored first. In one condition, hereditary spherocytosis or congenital hemolytic jaundice, removal of the spleen results in complete cure of the anemia. Here the spleen itself is normal, but the bone marrow produces spherocytes which are actually trapped by the spleen. Removing the spleen removes the trap and cures the condition. In certain tumours and cysts of the spleen it is best to remove the organ, especially since modern surgery allows removal without much reaction. Certain cases of leukemia with large spleens are treated with various chemicals, others by high-voltage X-rays.

(W. DK.)

**SPLIT** (Italian SPALATO), a city and seaport of the Socialist Republic of Croatia, Yugos., has the finest harbour on the Adriatic coast, with a broad bay affording deep, safe anchorage. This, combined with its central position on the coast and its good communications with northern parts of Yugoslavia by rail, has made it of great commercial importance, with an extensive trade in cement, timber, and marble. The projected direct rail communication with Bosnia will further increase the value of Split as a port. Pop. (1961) 99,462, almost entirely Croatian.

The old town is built within the palace of Diocletian, who renounced the imperial crown in A.D. 305 and lived there till his death (probably 313). The palace was built from 295 to 305, with the walls 7 ft. (2 m.) thick and 72 ft. (22 m.) high on its seaward side and 60 ft. (18 m.) high on the northern side. It has 16 towers and 4 gates: Porta Aurea (north), Porta Argentea (east), Porta Ferrea (west), and Porta Aenea (south). The Avars damaged this palace, but when their incursion was over (639), the inhabitants of the ruined city of Salona (Salonae) nearby took refuge there and built their homes within the 9½ ac. (4 ha.) covered by the palace, incorporating its walls and pillars. Its ground plan is like a Roman camp; *i.e.,* rectangular with 4 streets meeting in the middle. The streets are lined with massive arcades. The mausoleum of Diocletian has since the 7th century been a cathedral and is noteworthy for its finely carved choir stalls. The Temple of Jupiter, or Asclepius, has been long transformed into a baptistery, a beautiful Romanesque campanile having been added in the 14th and 15th centuries. In the old part of the town are the palaces Cindro, Ivello, and Papalić, and the house in which was born the medieval Slav poet Marko Marulić. Near the Porta Aurea is the huge and notable statue of Bishop Gregory of Nin by the Croatian sculptor Ivan Mestrović.

From 812 Split was under Byzantine rule, and in 1069 it fell to Croatia. After 1075 it passed under a series of masters, the Normans, Venice, Byzantium again, Hungarian-Croat kings, Bosnian rulers, and then, from 1420 till 1797, Venice. The Austrians ruled from 1797 till 1918 when Yugoslavia was formed. In 1941 Italian forces occupied the city. In September 1943 the First Partisan Brigade together with Dalmatian brigades liberated Split, but under heavy pressure from German forces the Partisans withdrew. From 1945 Split again became part of Yugoslavia.

Excavations have been carried on intermittently at the ruins of Salona, 4 mi. (6 km.) NE of Split, since 1818, and many interesting architectural remains have been discovered, together with many smaller relics now housed in the Split museum. These include prehistoric objects. Salona was made a Roman colony in 78 B.C. and was one of the chief ports of the Adriatic. Soon after 313 the city became an episcopal see, with St. Doimo as its first bishop. The palace was transformed into an imperial cloth factory. The town was captured several times by the Goths and Huns and in 639 was destroyed by the Avars, but it was not entirely deserted until the end of the 12th century. (V. DE.)

**SPLÜGEN PASS,** a pass (6,932 ft. [2,113 m.]) across the east-west range of the Ticino Alps on the Swiss-Italian frontier. The Splügen route runs south from Thusis in the Hinterrhein Valley through the defile of the Via Mala, crossed by medieval bridges at two levels until a new road was completed through a rock tunnel at a higher level. It then crosses the Schams Basin and continues west via the Rofna Gorge, past the recent Stufers barrage, to Splügen village. The road to the pass (completed 1822) leaves the San Bernardino Pass road, turning south to cross the Splügen Pass (Passo dello Spluga), then continues past the modern lake reservoir of Montespluga down the steep descent into Italy. The new road avoids the old track along the avalanche-prone Cardinello Gorge above Pianazzo, where many men of Alexandre Macdonald's army perished in 1800. Continuing south through Campodolcino, the road joins that from the Upper Engadine and the Maloja Pass at Chiavenna (railhead of the Mera Valley) and then continues south along Lake Como to Como. (A. F. A. M.)

**SPODUMENE,** a variety of pyroxene (*q.v.*) consisting of lithium aluminum silicate, is an important ore of lithium and source of ceramic materials. It was named in 1800 from the Greek word meaning "ash coloured," and soon afterward termed by the crystallographer R. J. Haüy, triphane ("appearing threefold") because it exhibited certain characteristics equally in three directions. The hardness is 6.5 to 7 and though generally a dull mineral, some varieties are so highly coloured and transparent as to be valued as gem stones, *e.g.,* the emerald-green hiddenite and the lilac-coloured kunzite, while a yellow or yellowish-green spodumene found as pebbles in Minas Gerais, Braz., resembles, when cut, some kinds of chrysoberyl. The largest natural crystals are found in pegmatite dikes in the United States in Massachusetts, Connecticut, and the Black Hills of South Dakota. Canada is an important primary producer of spodumene ore and concentrates. Chloride volatilization, alkaline leaching, and acid leaching are used to extract lithium from the ore prior to the manufacture of purified lithium chemicals. (For production and uses of compounds and the metal, *see* LITHIUM.)

Spodumene, $LiAl(SiO_3)_2$ or $Li_2O \cdot Al_2O_3 \cdot 4SiO_2$, exists in nature as a dense (specific gravity 3.2) $\alpha$ form and changes on heating at 1,000° C to a much less dense (specific gravity 2.4) $\beta$ form with a different crystal structure than the natural mineral. The large specific gravity change is used in the beneficiation procedure known as the "decrepitation" process since the rocklike mineral shatters to small particles when it is heated rapidly to temperatures above 1,000° C, facilitating the separation of accessory mineral impurities. This high temperature form has an extremely low thermal expansion, making it a very important thermal shock-resisting ceramic material. In minor amounts, spodumene is used in glass, enamels, and glazes. (F. A. HL.)

**SPOHR, LOUIS** (1784–1859), German composer, conductor, and violinist, who had great influence as a violin teacher and whose compositions illustrate the beginning of the Romantic period in German music. Born at Brunswick on April 5, 1784, he was largely self taught, acquiring his knowledge of composition from study of the scores of Mozart. At Brunswick he took violin lessons from the leader of the Brunswick orchestra and was appointed chamber musician there in 1799. In 1802 he studied with a pupil of J. W. A. Stamitz, Franz Eck, who took him on a tour to Russia. He made the first of his tours in Germany as a violinist and composer in 1804, and two years later he married the harp virtuoso Dorette Scheidler (1787–1834), with whom he toured during the following three years. While he was *Kapellmeister* in Vienna, at the Theater an der Wien (1812–15), he came under the influence of the French violinist Pierre Rode, a pupil of G. B. Viotti. Later he toured Italy with Paganini and in 1817 was appointed conductor at Frankfurt am Main. In 1820 he made the first of his six tours of England. The following year Weber recommended him to the court at Kassel, where he was appointed conductor in 1822. In 1836, after the death of his first wife, he married the pianist Marianne Pfeiffer (1807–92). In his later years Spohr suffered from the despotism of his patron, the elector of Hesse-Kassel, who pensioned him in 1857. Shortly afterward he broke his left arm and was no longer able to play the violin. He died at Kassel on Oct. 22, 1859.

As a teacher of the violin, Spohr carried into the 19th century the traditions of Stamitz and Viotti. His method was set out in his *Violinschule* (1831). Though opposed to the forward-looking composers of his time—he failed to appreciate the works of Weber and those of Beethoven's last period—he nonetheless conducted 2 works of Wagner, *The Flying Dutchman* and *Tannhäuser,* at Kassel, despite great opposition. He was a prolific composer, the style of his works, predominantly in the minor key, having some kinship with that of Schubert and Mendelssohn. Of his 10 operas, *Faust* (Prague, 1816), together with E. T. A. Hoffmann's *Undine,* was the first of the German romantic operas; his *Jessonda* (Kassel, 1823) held the stage throughout the 19th century. Of his 9 symphonies, the fourth, *Die Weihe der Töne* ("The Consecration of Sound"), was the most successful and was revived in the 20th century. The best known of his 15 violin concertos is the eighth, in A minor, written for his Italian tour. His chamber works include 34 string quartets, 4 double string quartets, and the well-known nonet. A selection of his works was published from 1949 onward at Kassel, where in 1954 the Spohr-Gesellschaft was founded.

BIBLIOGRAPHY.—*Louis Spohr's Autobiography,* 2 vol., Eng. trans. (1865); F. Goethel, *Das Violinspiel L. Spohrs* (1935); E. E. L. H. Salburg-Falkenstein, *Ludwig Spohr* (1936).

**SPOIL FIVE,** once known as the national card game of Ireland, is akin to the British napoleon, the American euchre and the French écarté (*qq.v.*). Spoil five and its variant, forty-five, were carried to the United States and Canada, while the variant auction forty-fives, introduced into Newfoundland in 1912, became the principal club game there. Spoil five is much like loo (*q.v.*). A pool is formed by equal antes. Each player receives five cards and the next card is turned up for trump. Anyone who wins three tricks must take the pool or jink it (play for all five tricks for the pool plus an extra chip from each player). The hand is spoiled if no one wins the pool, which then is added to the next pool.

The ace of hearts is always the third-best trump, whatever the trump suit. Above it are the five and jack (knave) of trumps; below it, the ace, king, queen. In the red suits the lower cards rank normally: 10 (high), 9, 8 . . . and so on, but in the black suits the rank is reversed: 2 (high), 3, 4 . . . 10 (low). When not trump the spade and club aces rank below the jack, and the diamond ace ranks below the 2.

**Forty-Five.**—This is a variant in which there is no pool; four or six play, in partnerships of two or three to a side. A side winning three tricks scores 5 points; all five tricks, 10 points. As some play, winning four tricks scores 15 points and all five tricks 25 points. The first side to reach 45 points wins.

In auction forty-fives trump and contract are determined by bidding. Each trick counts 5 and the highest trump an additional 5; game is 120. (G. Mh.)

**SPOILS SYSTEM,** the practice, also known as the patronage system, under which, in the United States, the political party winning an election rewards its campaign workers and other active supporters by appointment to public office. It involves political activity by public employees in support of their party and removal from office if their party loses the election. A change in party control of government necessarily brings new officials to high positions carrying political responsibility, but the spoils system extends personnel turnover down to routine or subordinate governmental positions. In the most extreme form of the spoils system the primary test for appointment is excellence of party service, with almost complete disregard of capacity to perform the duties of the public office concerned. The term apparently originated with a speech made in 1832 by Sen. W. L. Marcy in which he asserted that, "to the victor belong the spoils of the enemy."

The term is often applied loosely to the great variety of means by which money may be transferred more or less indirectly from the public treasury to the party coffers, as well as to other abuses of governmental power for partisan advantage. So used, the term includes abuses in the management of public expenditures, irregularities in the granting of franchises and other privileges, partisan favouritism in the administration of criminal law, discrimination in the levy of taxes, and other corrupt uses of public power. The term will be limited here to its earlier and narrower usage.

Although patronage existed in colonial times, the spoils system came to full bloom in the period 1800–29. When Jefferson became president in 1801, he found the public offices filled with persons generally hostile to him and to his party. Without espousing the principle of rotation in office, he replaced enough Federalists with Republicans (as Jefferson's followers were then called) to assure a more even distribution between the two parties in the civil service. Yet in both appointments and removals partisan considerations were not the sole criterion; it remained for President Jackson to introduce the principle of the spoils system in the national government, yet even Jackson did not make wholesale removals on political grounds. Spoils practices had been instituted earlier in the governments of states and cities. The system first became firmly rooted in New York; it was established almost as soon in Pennsylvania. By 1828 in all the states of the north and west the system existed or strong groups desired to introduce it.

In his annual message in 1829 Jackson presented a reasoned philosophy of the spoils system. "There are," he said, "perhaps few men who can for any great length of time enjoy office without being more or less under the influence of feelings unfavourable to the faithful discharge of their public duties. Their integrity may be proof against improper considerations immediately addressed to themselves, but they are apt to acquire a habit of looking with indifference upon the public interests and of tolerating conduct from which an unpracticed man would revolt." Rotation in office, then, was not an evil but a positive good. "The duties of all public offices are," he declared, "or at least admit of being made, so plain and simple that men of intelligence may readily qualify themselves for their performance; and I cannot but believe that more is lost by the long continuance of men in office than is generally to be gained by their experience."

The common explanation of the rise of the spoils system is that ways had to be found to support the activities of political parties. With the broadening of the suffrage, the use of elections to choose large numbers of officials, and other tendencies toward democratization, political parties had to assume heavy burdens in the conduct of campaigns and leadership of debate on public issues. As no class existed with the time or inclination to assume these responsibilities, parties had to be maintained by patronage. Practical considerations of party finance were reinforced by a democratic dislike of the idea of public office as private property and a hostility toward the rise of an officeholding class.

The spoils system is often said to be peculiar to the United States, but similar practices have existed elsewhere from time to time. In fact, the distribution of public offices to strengthen a regime is an ancient practice of statecraft. At the time of the founding of the United States government, the tests for appointment to the civil service were probity, ability, and loyalty to the Constitution. The test of loyalty aided in buttressing a new government emerging from controversy. The installation of Fascist dictatorships in Germany and Italy in the first half of the 20th century was accompanied by considerable partisan dilution of the permanent civil service. If the nature of a government changes radically, a degree of turnover in the civil service is likely to occur. The introduction of the spoils system into the national government of the United States coincided with a veritable revolution as new classes came to power in national affairs. Even systems for the selection of public employees on the basis of merit may, in fact, reserve the higher positions for members of the dominant groups within the community.

The spoils system flourished unchallenged in the United States until after the Civil War. Bills to reform the civil service were introduced in Congress in the 1860s, but they attracted little attention and less support. In 1871 Congress empowered the president to prescribe regulations to govern the selection of civil servants and to employ persons to aid him in determining the fitness of applicants. President Grant appointed a Civil Service Commission, but it was dissolved in 1875 after Congress had failed in 1873 and 1874 to provide funds for its support.

The National Civil Service Reform League, established in 1881, led a reform movement that succeeded gradually in restricting the spoils system by the introduction of the merit system for the selection of civil servants. The movement gained impetus from the assassination of President Garfield by a disappointed office seeker, and in 1883, the Pendleton Act, largely drafted by leaders of the Reform League, was adopted by Congress. It provided for the creation of the United States Civil Service Commission and for the merit system in the recruitment of some federal civil servants. In the same year New York adopted a civil service law requiring the selection of civil employees through competitive examination. After 1939, all states were compelled to institute merit systems for employees engaged in programs aided by federal subsidies.

In the second half of the 20th century about 75% of the U.S. cities had established some type of formal merit system. However, only 25% of the cities covered all employees, and almost half of those reporting cities with a population of less than 25,000 had established no formal civil service system. As the merit system encroached on the spoils system in state and local governments, its application was broadened in the national government by actions of various presidents. A setback to the merit principle occurred after World Wars I and II in the extension to war veterans of preference in appointments.

The coverage of civil service legislation, however, does not indicate accurately the extent to which the spoils system has been superseded. In jurisdictions with civil service laws, spoils practices may prevail. In those lacking formal merit systems, ability may govern selection of employees, and their tenure may be permanent. *See* Civil Service. (V. O. K.; X.)

**SPOKANE,** a city of eastern Washington, U.S., the county seat of Spokane county, is situated on the high river plain of the Spokane river about 50 mi. from its juncture with the Columbia, at an altitude of 1,898 ft. To the north and east lie the Selkirk and Rocky mountains, generally shielding the valley from the rigours of northeast winds which on occasion cause spells of extreme cold. The population of the city in 1960 was 181,608 and of its standard metropolitan statistical area (Spokane county), 278,333. For comparative population figures *see* table in WASHINGTON: *Population.*

Only five years after the notable Lewis and Clark expedition of 1804–06, the first white habitation of the Pacific northwest, Spokane House, a North-West Fur company post, was built on the Little Spokane river. Ft. Spokane, an Astor establishment, was built across the river from its competitor. When the Hudson's Bay company, successor to the North-West company, moved its operation to Ft. Colville in 1826, that settlement eclipsed the Spokane country. During the missionary period, the Indian disturbances and the early mining boom, Walla Walla held the stage. It was not until 1872 that a settlement was established at Spokane Falls. A village by that name was incorporated in 1881 and the following year it was chartered and also replaced Cheney as the county seat.

In 1880 the town's population was only 350. With the advent of the Northern Pacific railroad in 1883, however, it mushroomed, and by 1890 it had outstripped Walla Walla and enjoyed third rank in the state. With a revival of mining in the 1880s, this time of the more stable lode-mining type, Spokane became the region's financial and mercantile focal point. In 1886 it had an electric-light plant and a horse streetcar line. An electric trolley system in operation by 1891 served the city until 1935. Additional rail facilities, particularly the Union Pacific (1889) and the Great Northern (1892), and a number of branch feeder lines contributed to Spokane's ultimately becoming the largest railroad centre west of Omaha. From the holocaust of Aug. 4–6, 1889, when 30 blocks in the middle of the city were destroyed by fire, there emerged a more modern city.

The word "Falls" was dropped from the name in 1890. The word Spokane, said to mean "children of the sun," was the name of an Indian tribe which had formerly occupied the valley. It is pronounced to rhyme with "man."

There are three private institutions of collegiate rank: Gonzaga, a coeducational Roman Catholic university founded in 1887; Whitworth, a Presbyterian coeducational college established in 1890; and Fort Wright College of the Holy Names, a Roman Catholic college for women, incorporated in 1907.

The Fox theatre, the Spokane coliseum and the municipal stadium have been the settings for a great variety of entertainment. The city has a symphony and a junior symphony orchestra.

Diversity is the keynote of the city's economy, to which agriculture, mining, lumbering, processing of primary metals, general manufacturing and distribution contribute. An abundance of cheap hydroelectric power has been a major stimulus and was particularly instrumental in the establishment during World War II of the aluminum reduction mill at Mead and the aluminum rolling mill at Trentwood. In 1954 two large oil pipelines reached the city and natural gas was made available in 1956.

The city owns Geiger field serving commercial airlines and Felts field, which serves principally private planes. (H. J. DE.)

**SPOLETO** (ancient SPOLETIUM), a town and archiepiscopal see of the province of Perugia, Italy, 18 mi. (29 km.) NNE of Terni and 88 mi. (142 km.) N of Rome by rail. Pop. (1961) 38,569 (commune). Finely situated on a detached spur at the southern extremity of the central Umbrian Plain, it commands the passes southward toward Terni and eastward toward Norcia and the upper valley of the Nera. The old town clusters picturesquely on the hillside; modern development is largely confined to the plain below.

The most conspicuous remains of the ancient town are the walls of polygonal masonry, partly of the pre-Roman city and partly of the Roman *colonia.* The Piazza del Mercato occupies the site of the Roman Forum, with an arch of Drusus and Germanicus (A.D. 23), and beside it the remains of a temple. Other surviving Roman monuments are a theatre, an amphitheatre, a house with mosaics, and a three-arched bridge. From a circular tumulus found in 1902 at Monteleone di Spoleto comes the famous biga (two-horse chariot), a remarkable example of 6th-century B.C. bronze work, now in the Metropolitan Museum, New York.

The medieval town is dominated by the massive Rocca, built by Matteo Gattapone for Cardinal Albornoz in 1364 on the site of the ancient citadel. Just below stands the cathedral, which was consecrated in 1198 and extensively remodeled in 1634. Above the graceful Early Renaissance vestibule the facade, with its eight rose windows, and central mosaic by Solsternus (1207), is that of the 12th-century building. The interior is dominated by a magnificent fresco of the Coronation of the Virgin by Fra Filippo Lippi and pupils; Lippi's tomb, erected by Lorenzo de' Medici, is in the south transept.

The many other fine churches include Sta. Eufemia (10th century); S. Pietro (about 1200), with a richly sculptured facade; SS. Giovanni e Paolo, the paintings of which include early representations of St. Francis and of the martyrdom of St. Thomas Becket; and S. Domenico and S. Niccolò, characteristic examples of late Italian Gothic. The church of S. Salvatore is an elaborately decorated, classicizing monument, usually assigned to the 5th century but possibly dating from the late 8th century. The city is supplied with water by an aqueduct that crosses the ravine upon a bridge of ten arches built in 1364. A garrison town and the centre of a large agricultural district (predominantly olive culture), Spoleto has also developed a certain number of light industries (cotton goods, phosphorus products, printing). Since 1958 it has had an annual drama and music festival.

The site of an Umbrian township from at least the 7th to 6th centuries B.C., Spoletium became a Latin colony in 241. In 217 B.C. it successfully repulsed Hannibal, fresh from his victory on Lago Trasimeno. Strategically situated on the Via Flaminia, its importance increased in late antiquity. It became an episcopal see not later than the early 4th century, and it played an important part in the Gothic wars of Belisarius and Narses. With the foundation of the Lombard duchy about 570, it became for several centuries one of the principal cities of Italy, for a time sharing with Benevento the rule of much of the peninsula. After the middle of the 8th century, however, the duchy lost much of its autonomy, and under Gregory IX (pope 1227–41) it passed to the church. During the absence of the papal court in Avignon, it was a prey to struggles between Guelphs and Ghibellines, until in 1354 Cardinal Albornoz reestablished the authority of the church, under which it remained, except for brief intervals, until captured by the Italian troops in 1860. (J. B. W.-P.)

**SPONGE,** an aquatic animal characterized by a unique organization. Sponges, which constitute the phylum Porifera, number approximately 5,000 described species and inhabit all seas, where they occur attached to surfaces from the intertidal zone to depths of 8,500 m. or more. Only one family, the Spongillidae, is found in fresh water.

Early naturalists regarded the sponges as plants because of their frequent branching form and their lack of obvious movement. Ellis first clearly described the animal nature of sponges in 1755, and in 1765 reported his observations of their water currents and the movement of their openings. Although many zoologists regard the sponges as occupying an isolated position in the animal king-

RALPH BUCHSBAUM

FIG. 1.—LIVING BATH SPONGE PULLED FROM ITS ATTACHMENT ON THE SEA BOTTOM AND SLICED IN HALF dom and classify them in the subkingdom Parazoa, or Enantiozoa, others present arguments for relating them rather closely to the coelenterates.

## GENERAL FEATURES

**Importance.**—The bath sponge in its living state is a mass of cells and fibres. Its interior is permeated by an intricate system of canals that open out as holes of various sizes through the tough dark-brown or black skin. The skin may be hairy from the fibre endings that pierce it. Only when it is completely cleaned of its millions of living cells does the bath sponge look like the sponge of commerce, the spongin skeletal framework that serves a variety of uses. These soft elastic sponges, derived from certain species of Demospongiae (*Spongia* and *Hippospongia*), have been known since ancient times. They were familiar household items in ancient Greece and Rome, where they were used for applying paint, as mops, and by soldiers as substitutes for drinking vessels. During the Middle Ages, burnt sponge was reputed to have therapeutic value in the treatment of various diseases.

In the present day, synthetic plastic sponges have largely replaced natural ones for household use, but there is still a demand for natural sponges by various artisans and for surgical use. Commercially valuable sponges are harvested in the eastern Mediterranean, off the west coast of Florida and the Florida Keys, in the West Indies, off Mexico and British Honduras, and, to a limited extent, off the Philippines. The most valuable sponges are found in the eastern Mediterranean.

Commercial sponges are gathered from tidal level to a depth of about 200 ft. In shallow waters they are harvested by hooking or harpooning from a boat. Skin divers exploit cave populations in the Aegean Sea and along the Libyan coast and in the Philippines. Deepwater fishing in Florida, Greece, and North Africa is accomplished with the aid of diving suits. Dredging, a wasteful method, has been used in Libya but is prohibited in the Western Hemisphere. Preparation of sponges, done aboard the boat or along the shore, consists of rotting away and expressing the soft tissues, rinsing in seawater, and air drying. Certain grades of sponges are bleached before marketing.

D. P. WILSON

FIG. 2.—A CLUSTER OF SPONGES COMMON IN TEMPERATE SHALLOW SEAS

*Sycon*, the fingerlike projections at left, and *Leucosolenia*, the many-branched mass at right, are calcareous; *Halichondria*, the lump surrounding the stalk at top, is siliceous

**Form and Colour.**—Sponges vary considerably in external appearance, colour, and size. The main growth patterns are irregularly massive, branching, and encrusting, but symmetrical shapes, as spherical and lenticular, also occur. In size, sponges range from urns only a fraction of an inch long to upright vases, tubes, and branching types up to eight feet tall and broad rounded masses several feet in diameter.

Sponges, especially those growing in shallow tropical waters, are characterized by more or less irregular shapes and bright colours. They may be various shades of blue, violet, magenta, red, orange, yellow, green, brown, tan, gray, black, and white. Deep-sea species tend to be more regular in shape and more sombre in hue, usually some shade of brown, tan, cream, gray, or white. Not infrequently the same species occurs in several forms and colour phases. Freshwater sponges are irregular masses, chiefly gray, brown, tan, or white, but at least one species is bright yellow. Many freshwater sponges and some shallow-water marine species have algae or bacteria living in their cells; these organisms impart their colour to the sponges.

## STRUCTURE AND FUNCTION

A sponge is a filter-feeding animal that propels water through a system of channels in its body and feeds upon the minute organisms and particles carried in with the currents. Sponges are covered by an outer dermal membrane perforated with pores that allow water to enter. The motile power for the water currents within the sponge is provided by the coordinated whipping action of flagella on collar cells (choanocytes) grouped in the interior of the sponge. Between the dermal membrane and the choanocytes are mesenchyme cells of several sorts, some of which secrete supporting fibres of protein or spicules of calcium carbonate or silicon dioxide.

**Grades of Construction.**—Three basic grades of construction of increasing complexity may be recognized among sponges: ascon, sycon, and leucon. The simplest, or ascon, type is exemplified by the calcareous sponge genus *Leucosolenia,* which consists of colonies of upright hollow tubules. Each tubule has an external dermal membrane perforated at intervals by pores, actually openings through cells, called porocytes. The hollow interior is lined with choanocytes, the beating of the flagella of which draws water through the pores and forces it out a single large opening (oscule) at the apex of the tubule. Between the dermal membrane and the choanocytes lies a layer of mesogloea, a colloidal gel, in which lie mesenchymal cells and spicules.

A somewhat more complicated construction is the sycon type, as seen in the calcareous sponge genus *Sycon.* Here the wall of the sponge is pushed out into fingerlike projections, called radial canals, each provided with a lining of choanocytes. Water enters the radial canals directly through pores, makes its way into the central cavity or spongocoel, and leaves by way of a terminal oscule. In some Calcarea a cortex consisting of the dermal membrane and mesenchymal cells covers the outer ends of the radial canals, and water entering through dermal pores courses through incurrent channels in the cortex before reaching the radial canals.

All adult Demospongiae and many Calcarea are of the complicated leucon structure. In the Calcarea this grade of construction has evolved through a subdivision of the radial canals into numerous small flagellated chambers in which the choanocytes are localized. These chambers communicate with the dermal pores by way of incurrent canals and with the spongocoel by way of excurrent canals. In some Calcarea the leuconoid stage has apparently resulted from the union of asconoid tubules.

**Cell Types.**—The cells of sponges exhibit considerable diversity and functional specialization. The various sorts are defined with regard to their size, nuclear characteristics, cytoplasmic inclusions, and the nature of the pseudopodia, if present. It is often difficult to relate the cell types from one species of sponge to another, and the literature on sponges is somewhat confusing because of the variety of names used by different authors for what are apparently homologous cells. In the adult sponge the cells can be divided into nucleolate and anucleolate sorts. The former include unspecialized archaeocytes, amoebocytes of several types, scleroblasts, or spicule cells, and presumptive egg cells; the latter

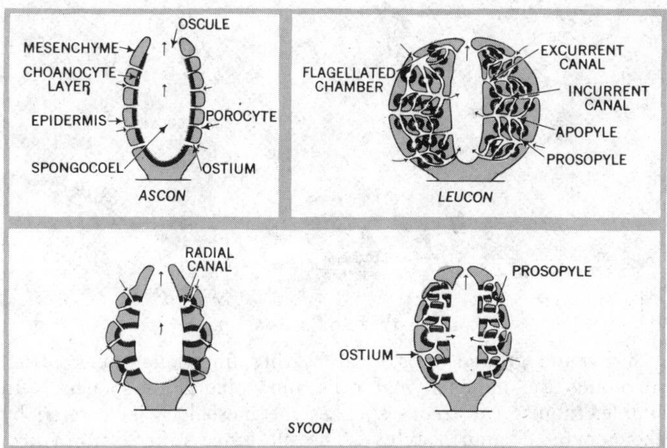


FROM JOHNSON AND SNOOK, "SEASHORE ANIMALS OF THE PACIFIC COAST"; THE MACMILLAN CO., 1927

FIG. 3.—DIAGRAM OF VARIOUS TYPES OF SPONGE ORGANIZATION (CHOANOCYTE LAYER IS BLACK; MESENCHYME LAYER IS GRAY; SMALL ARROWS INDICATE DIRECTION OF WATER FLOW)

include pinacocytes, collencytes, and choanocytes.

The archaeocytes found in the adult sponge tend to be ovoid in shape and have nucleoli and a small number of cytoplasmic inclusions. In the adult sponge they continue to give rise to scleroblasts and germ cells, but whether they can transform into all other types of cells throughout the life of the sponge, as is sometimes held, is still unsettled. The amoebocytes, which possess lobose pseudopodia, can perform a variety of functions, according to which they are often given special names: chromocytes, if they bear pigment granules or symbiotic algae; thesocytes or spherular cells, if they are filled with food reserves; or trophocytes, if they are acting as nutritive cells for developing eggs. Amoebocytes are probably also the source of mucus-secreting gland cells that occur commonly in sponges.

Pinacocytes are flattened polygonal cells that make up the external epithelium of sponges and also line the excurrent canals. Those on the exterior (exopinacocytes) lack nucleoli, whereas those lining the canals (endopinacocytes) are nucleolate. Pinacocytes may be differentiated into myocytes, spindle-shaped contractile cells that occur in circlets under the epithelium around incurrent and excurrent openings. Collencytes have been described as "internal pinacocytes"; they are star shaped, with long, thin processes that insinuate throughout the incurrent canals of the sponge. Certain collencytes, called desmacytes, or fibre cells, are found in abundance in the cortex of some species of sponges. Star-shaped collencytes with a vesicular or vacuolate structure are called cystencytes.

Choanocytes, the most highly differentiated cells in the sponge body, are also the smallest cells, exclusive of sperm. The cell body is provided with a single flagellum surrounded by a collar made up of a circlet of cytoplasmic tentacles. The flagellum of the choanocyte is consistent in basic structure with the flagella and cilia of other animals, being composed of two centrally placed fibres surrounded by a circlet of nine double fibres continuous with the basal body.

There is cytological evidence for the existence of bipolar and multipolar nerve cells in a wide variety of Calcarea and Demospongiae. Unequivocal proof that these cells do indeed have a nervous function can be supplied only by physiological techniques, however. Peculiar cells called lophocytes, which bear tufts of fibrillae, have been described in freshwater sponges and in certain marine Demospongiae. In spongillids they occur between a double layer of pinacocytes on the surface of the sponge, and in marine sponges they occur in tracts of mesenchyme near the surface. Lophocytes have been interpreted either as nervous elements or, more probably, as cells that secrete fibrils characteristic of the cortical mesenchyme of sponges.

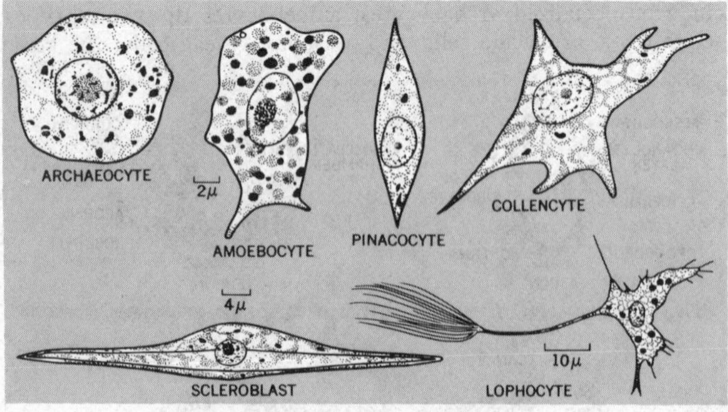


FIG. 4.—TYPES OF SPONGE CELLS

A hyaline ground substance, bearing fine collagenous fibres, surrounds the mesenchymal cells and spicules of sponges. In simple, tubular calcareous sponges the mesogloea is secreted by choanocytes or amoebocytes. The substance stiffens into a firm colloidal gel around the spicules and is capable of supporting the oscular tube after dissolution of the spicules.

**Water Current System.**—Spongillids consist of two discrete canal systems, an incurrent and an excurrent system, joined by way of numerous flagellated chambers. The external, or dermal, membrane of the sponge, composed of pinacocytes, is perforated by ostia through which water enters the incurrent canal system, usually by way of large subdermal cavities. Pinacocytes also line the excurrent canals. The incurrent canals are not so lined but instead are filled with a network of free cells, including collencytes, archaeocytes, and amoebocytes.

The choanocytes are localized in hemispherical chambers with a diameter of 40 to 60 μ. These chambers lie between the incurrent and excurrent canal systems, and water must pass through them in flowing from the incurrent canals into the excurrent canals. Two or three openings, called prosopyles, which are apparently simply spaces between choanocytes, lead into each flagellated chamber. A single larger opening, the apopyle, permits water in the chamber to flow into an excurrent canal. The excurrent canals converge on one or more openings to the outside, the oscules, surrounded by contractile myocytes that regulate the size of the opening.

The uncoordinated beating of the flagella of the choanocytes creates the flow of water through the sponge. With the collar expanded, four to six undulations can be seen in the flagellum as it beats. The rotating movement of numerous adjacent flagella in the chamber probably creates eddy currents that help to direct food particles against the collar. When the collar is contracted, as is true when choanocytes are isolated, the flagellum beats backward and forward in a manner and frequency analogous to the beating of a cilium of *Paramecium*.

In living cultures the collars of the choanocytes lining a flagellated chamber are oriented so that each directs the current created by the flagellum toward the apopyle. This opening is ten times larger than the diameters of all of the prosopyles leading into any one chamber, so that water enters a chamber with a velocity ten times greater than it leaves. The sudden slowing of the velocity of the current in the chamber probably facilitates food gathering. As a result of the fall in pressure in the chambers, the prosopyles exert a suction effect on the water in the incurrent canals and subdermal cavities, and water carrying food particles is drawn forcibly through the ostia from the external medium. The network of cells filling the incurrent canals exerts a frictional drag on the water, but this slowing effect is counterbalanced by the tendency for water to flow more rapidly through spaces of smaller diameter. The velocity of current flow is twice as great in the incurrent canals as in the excurrent canals, which have a smooth lining of pinacocytes but are also larger in diameter. The pumping action of the flagellated chambers combined with the changing size of the oscular orifice leads to an excess pressure in the excurrent canals and thus water, free of food, low in oxygen, and carrying excretory products, flows some distance from the sponge and is unlikely to reenter through the incurrent openings.

Some data exist on the amount and velocity of water filtered by marine sponges. In a tubular calcareous sponge, *Leuconia*, with a height of 9 cm. and a diameter of 1 cm., the combined activity of all flagella in the sponge was found to be sufficient to force a jet of water, moving at a rate of 8.5 cm. per sec., a distance of 23 cm. beyond the osculum at a pumping rate of 22.7 litres per day. A single tubular branch of *Callyspongia vaginalis*, 10 cm. high and 4 cm. in diameter, can discharge 78 litres of water per day through its oscule. A young spongillid with a volume of 0.2 $mm^3$ can discharge 4.5 $cm^3$ of water per day, each flagellated chamber pumping 1,200 times its volume of water per day.

In the marine siliceous sponge *Hymeniacidon heliophila*, the oscules close in quiet seawater, when exposed to air, on injury to adjacent parts, and in deoxygenated seawater. Partial closing occurs in dilute seawater and at temperatures between 35° and 45° C. The oscules remain open in currents of seawater and are apparently unaffected by low temperatures and light. The ostia close on injury to adjacent parts but remain open in quiet seawater, upon exposure to air, in deoxygenated seawater, and in seawater at 35° C. Partial closing occurs in dilute seawater, and ostia are unaffected by low temperatures and light. Closing of both oscules and ostia is brought about by the contraction of myocytes arranged as sphincters around the openings. Myocytes serve to regulate the rate of flow of water, helping the sponge to main-

An angelfish hovers above a yellow vase sponge (*Verongia fistularis*)

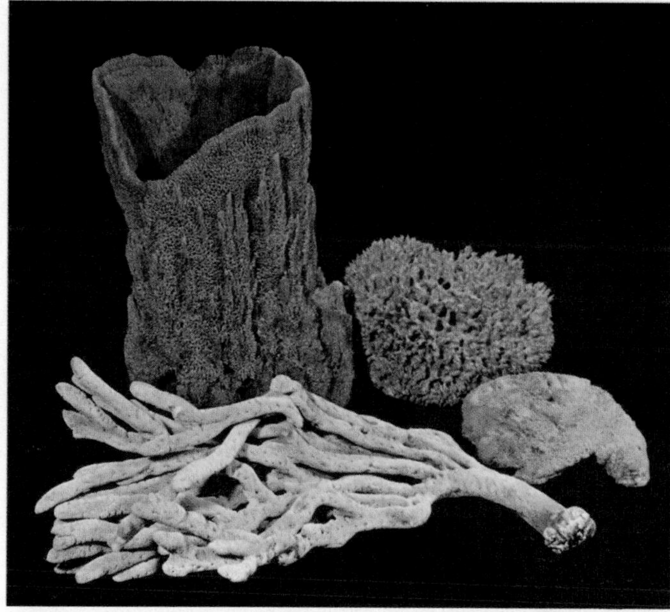

Skeletons of several Demospongiae: three bath sponges in the back row and a branching sponge with both siliceous spicules and spongin in the foreground

A commensal sponge (*Suberites*) overgrows shell of crab

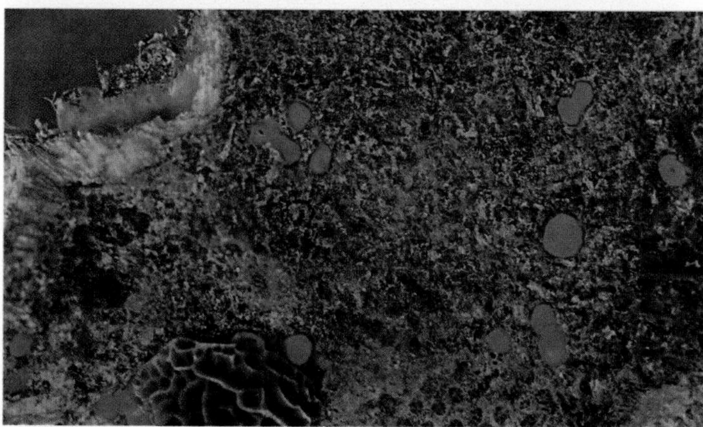

A red clionid sponge (*Cliona*) bores into rock coral and protrudes above the coral's surface; coral is broken (upper left) to reveal sponge within

Several common British sponges. Left to right, yellowish *Axinella*, *Raspailia* (with attached grayish *Sycon* "urns") and an irregularly spherical orange *Polymastia*

## A VARIETY OF SPONGES

PHOTOGRAPHS, (TOP LEFT) RUSS KINNE—PHOTO RESEARCHERS, INC., (BOTTOM LEFT) W. D. HARTMAN, (TOP RIGHT, CENTRE RIGHT) RALPH BUCHSBAUM, (BOTTOM RIGHT) DOUGLAS P. WILSON. F.R.P.S.

# SPONGE

Calcareous purse sponge (*Grantia compressa*) encrusts a rock on the Devon coast, England

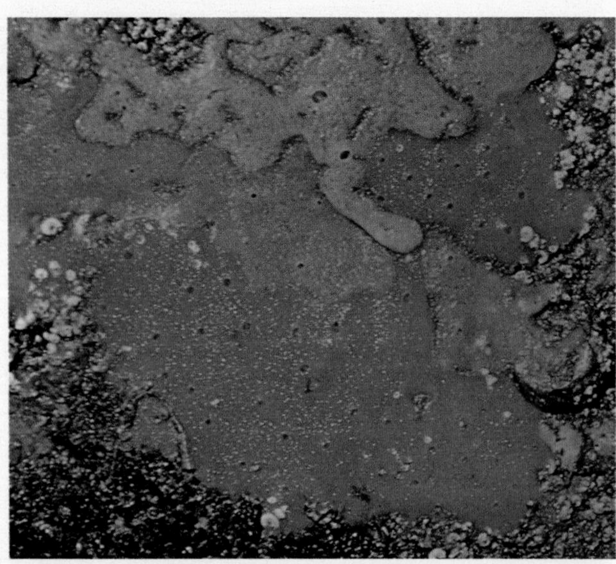

Underside of stone from shallow water reveals orange *Ophlitaspongia seriata,* brown *Adocia cinerea* and yellow *Halichondria bowerbanki*

Breadcrumb sponge (*Halichondria panicea*) encrusts an overhanging sea-shore rock. The excurrent openings (oscula) point downward

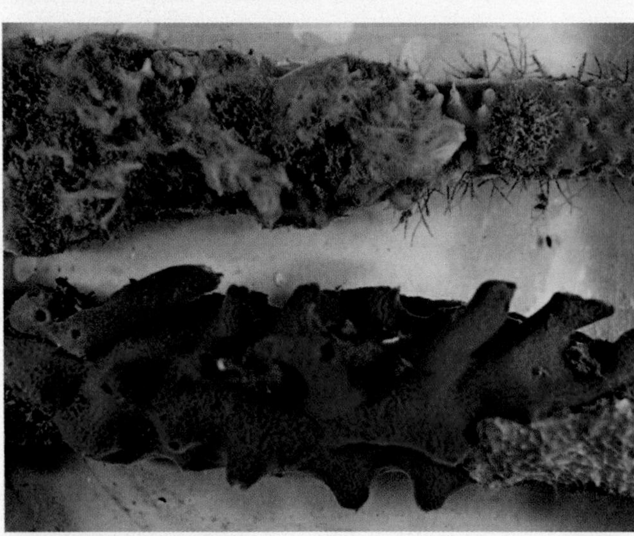

Several *Haliclona* species (blue, turquoise and lavender) grow on mangrove roots; brown area is a *Halichondria* species; in lower right is *Dysidea etheria*

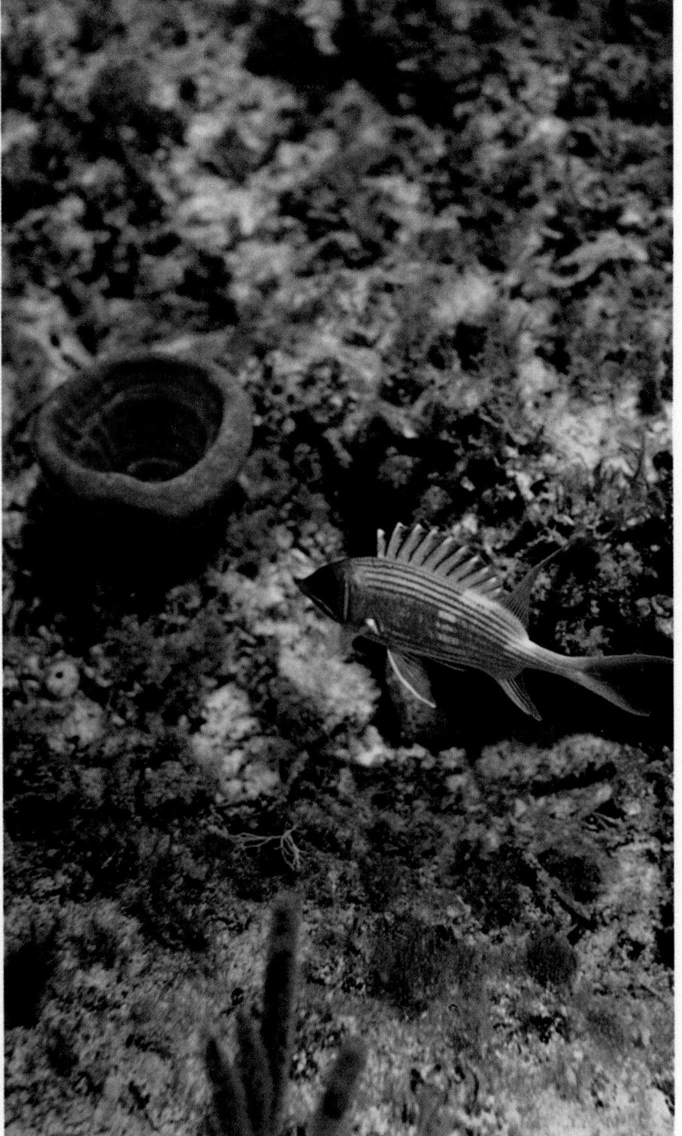

Squirrelfish and basket sponge in Jamaican waters

## SOME INSHORE SPONGES

PHOTOGRAPHS, (TOP LEFT, TOP RIGHT, CENTRE LEFT) DOUGLAS P. WILSON, F.R.P.S., (BOTTOM LEFT) W. D. HARTMAN, (BOTTOM RIGHT) RUSS KINNE—PHOTO RESEARCHERS, INC.

tain a constant jet within limits under different flagellar pressures brought about by varying environmental conditions. Thus partial closure of the oscules at moderately high temperatures increases the velocity of outflow to compensate for the fall in pressure associated with decreased flagellar activity and assures that water laden with waste products is carried out of range of the incurrent pores.

**Feeding and Digestion.**—Feeding and digestive activities are best known in freshwater sponges. A set of sieves of decreasing mesh size filters the water as it passes through the dermal membrane and the incurrent canals into the flagellated chambers. The dermal pores measure 50 $\mu$ in diameter, the prosopyles measure 5 $\mu$ in diameter, and the spaces between the cytoplasmic tentacles of the collars vary from 0.10 to 0.15 $\mu$. Only the smallest particles can enter the flagellated chambers where, coming in contact with the outside surface of the choanocyte collars, they are passed to the cell body of the choanocytes and ingested. Larger particles that pass through the dermal pores are ingested by the archaeocytes and collencytes, which form a reticulum in the incurrent canals or by the bases of the choanocytes. Particles, such as diatoms, too large to pass through the dermal pores may be ingested by the pinacocytes. Scattered observations recorded in the literature suggest that unicellular algae, flagellates, bacteria, and perhaps suspended organic detritus make up the food of sponges in nature. The finding of torulene, a red carotenoid occurring in the yeast *Torula rubra*, in several marine sponges suggests that some species feed commonly on red yeasts. Since digestion is intracellular, the size of the sponge cells involved places a limit on the size of the organisms ingested. In general, protozoans and rotifers are too large to be captured. It has been suggested that sponges feed solely by taking in dissolved organic substances; that this contention may be true in part has been neither confirmed nor disproved.

The archaeocytes appear to be the chief site of the digestive processes. Pinacocytes and collencytes also contribute to this function. In experiments powdered albumen is taken up by cells in the incurrent canals and by the choanocytes; this process is followed by ever increasing concentrations of the food in the archaeocytes, all of which are filled with vacuoles six hours later. Choanocytes, on the other hand, gradually lose the food particles that they have ingested and in ten hours are almost completely free of food. Transfer of particles from choanocytes to archaeocytes has been observed, but it is uncertain whether or not cell fusion occurs during this process. In the cells of a marine siliceous sponge, *Halichondria panicea,* the choanocytes have a higher concentration of proteolytic, lipolytic, and carbohydrate-decomposing enzymes than the archaeocytes. It appears likely, therefore, that in this species digestion is accomplished chiefly by the choanocytes. In calcareous sponges carmine particles and starch grains will concentrate chiefly in the choanocytes and will seldom appear in other cell types, although particles are apparently transferred by the choanocytes to egg cells.

In freshwater sponges, indigestible material is voided from blisterlike vacuoles in the archaeocytes, pinacocytes, and collencytes. The archaeocytes tend to migrate to the excurrent canals or the dermal membrane during later stages of digestion and there discharge indigestible particles.

**Reactions of Sponges.**—The slow rate of transmission of stimuli generally observed in sponges strongly suggests that transmission in these animals resides in the muscle cells, or myocytes. In studies on the freshwater sponge *Ephydatia fluviatilis,* the oscules remained open in both quiet and swiftly running water, but the oscular tube shortened in the latter case. Gentle mechanical stimuli and cutting into the flesh of the sponge had no effect on the oscules, but rubbing a needle around the edge of the mouth of the oscule caused the opening to contract immediately, and a wave of contraction traveled down the oscular tube at a rate of 0.25 mm. per sec.

The activity of *Ephydatia fluviatilis* was not affected by light, but this sponge was more sensitive to temperature extremes than was a marine species, *Hymeniacidon heliophila.* The freshwater sponge showed no activity, and oscules were contracted at 7° C or below; exposure to temperatures of 40° C was lethal. Electrical stimulation of the oscular tip caused the opening to close, followed by a wave of contraction down the entire length of the tube at a rate of 0.38 mm. per sec.

Evidence of the transmission of stimuli from one part of the sponge body to another was scant; electrical stimulation of the surface of the sponge at distances of 2 to 4 mm. from an oscule, however, caused an increase in the rate of flow of water from the oscules. It is possible that the choanocyte flagella had been stimulated to greater activity, suggesting that the stimulus had been transmitted from the surface to the flagellated chambers. Nervelike cells run from the pinacocytes of some sponges to the choanocytes. The observations recorded above may be interpreted as providing indirect physiological evidence of conduction along such a pathway, although it is extraordinarily slow.

**Skeleton.**—All but a few species of sponges possess a skeleton made up of spicules or organic fibres or both. The skeleton is embedded in mesogloea, probably an important auxiliary supporting element in all sponges except the Hexactinellida, which lack it.

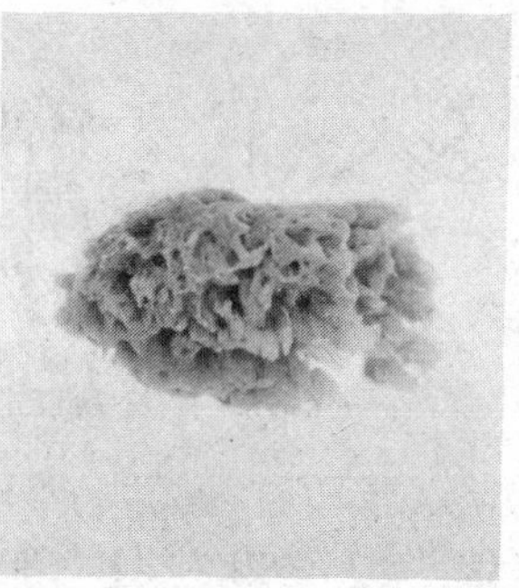

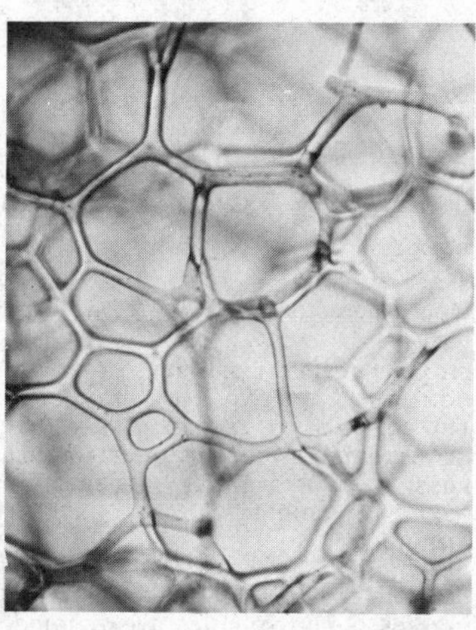

(ABOVE) JAMES R. LARSEN; (RIGHT) RALPH BUCHSBAUM

FIG. 5.—(ABOVE) SMALL PIECE OF A HORNY SPONGE SKELETON; (RIGHT) PHOTOMICROGRAPH OF SPONGIN FIBRES

Among calcareous sponges, the spicules are composed of calcium carbonate with an admixture of 4 to 14% magnesium carbonate; they are laid down as crystalline calcite. The spicules of Demospongiae and Hexactinellida are composed of hydrated silicon dioxide laid down in an amorphous form resembling opal. Organic fibres are the sole intrinsic skeletal elements in the bath sponges and their relatives. These fibres, which occur along with siliceous spicules in other Demospongiae, are composed of spongin, a collagenlike protein containing iodinated and brominated tyrosine among its component amino acids.

Sponge spicules vary greatly in form and are important in the identification of species. An elaborate nomenclature has been set up for the various types. An initial breakdown is made on the basis of size. Megascleres, the larger spicule types (usually 100 $\mu$ to several millimetres in length), are the chief supporting elements in the sponge; in the Demospongiae they are often joined together by spongin fibres. Microscleres (usually 5 to 50 $\mu$ in length), when present, are scattered in the mesogloea, where they presumably provide added support. A further subdivision of spicule types is based on the number of axes or rays present; in naming them an appropriate numerical prefix is added to the endings, *-axon,* when referring to the number of axes, or *-actine,* when referring to the number of rays or points.

Spicules are laid down as intracellular secretions of scleroblasts. In the Demospongiae each monaxonid (one axis) spicule is laid down in an individual cell by continuous deposition of hydrated silicon dioxide (opal) around an organic axial fibre. Tetraxonid spicules are also formed in single scleroblasts as far as is known. Microscleres are formed individually in special scleroblasts.

In the Calcarea, monaxonid spicules are secreted by binucleate scleroblasts. The mineral constituents of the spicule are deposited in crystalline form around an organic axial fibre. Each ray of triradiate and quadriradiate spicules is formed in a separate cell, the three or four rays eventually fusing basally to form the characteristic pattern.

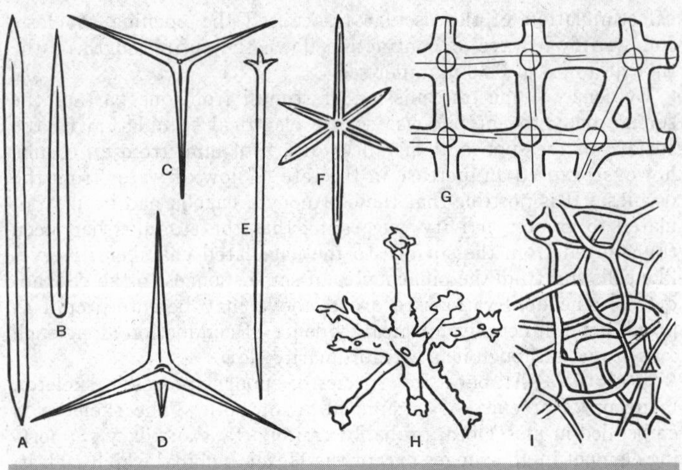


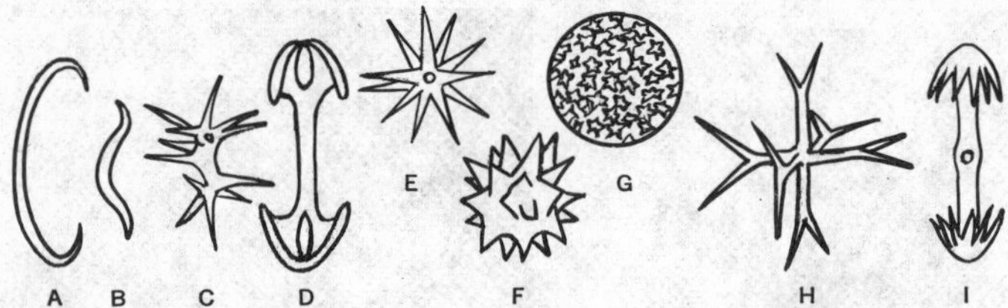


FROM L. H. HYMAN, "THE INVERTEBRATES: PROTOZOA THROUGH CTENOPHORA"; MCGRAW-HILL, 1940

FIG. 6.—SKELETAL SPICULES; (ABOVE) MEGASCLERE TYPES: (A) DIACTINAL MONAXONID (OXEA); (B) MONACTINAL MONAXONID; (C) TRIRADIATE; (D) EQUIRADIATE TETRAXONID; (E) TRIAENE; (F) HEXACTINE; (G) SILICEOUS LATTICEWORK OF A HEXACTINELLID; (H) DESMA; (I) SPONGIN FIBRES OF BATH SPONGE; (BELOW) MICROSCLERE TYPES: (A) SIGMA; (B) TOXA; (C) SPIRASTER; (D) CHELA; (E–G) ASTERS; (H) HEXASTER; (I) AMPHIDISC

Hexactinellid spicules are laid down in syncytial scleroblast masses. The spicules are formed of hydrated silicon dioxide deposited around a central organic fibre in concentric layers separated by thin films of organic matter.

Spongin fibres are secreted by mesenchymal cells called spongioblasts. In *Haliclona elegans,* spongin rods are formed in cells that line up in rows. Successive rods then fuse to form a fibre that is freed following the degeneration of the spongioblasts. In *Haliclona simulans,* each cell forms a fibre several times its own length, and these fuse secondarily.

**Reproduction and Development.**—*Sexual reproduction* is of regular occurrence in all groups of sponges except the order Choristida of the class Demospongiae, where it is known in only a few species. Egg cells have been reported by various authors to originate from the flagellated cells of the larva, from choanocytes, or from archaeocytes. It is probable that eggs always develop from choanocytes that leave the flagellated chambers, lose their collars and flagella, and become amoeboid. (The lack of agreement on this point may result from various authors reporting different stages of the process.) Sperm cells apparently arise from choanocytes. In freshwater sponges, certain choanocytes lose their flagella, become amoeboid, leave the flagellated chambers, and transform into spermatogonia. In the bath sponge *Hippospongia communis,* all the choanocytes in a chamber transform simultaneously into spermatogonia and then develop into sperm.

In the Calcarea and several species of Demospongiae, fertilization is accomplished by way of a carrier cell that transfers the sperm to the egg. This process is probably of general occurrence in these two classes of sponges but is not yet known in the Hexactinellida. In both Calcarea and Demospongiae, sperm cells enter choanocytes; the latter then lose their collars and flagella and migrate to a position adjacent to the egg. The sperm, which has lost its tail and has enlarged, then enters the egg cell (presumably following fusion of the carrier cell and egg). Subsequent development of the embryo follows one of several courses characteristic of the different groups.

In the development of calcareous sponges of the subclass Calcaronea (including the genera *Leucosolenia, Sycon,* and *Grantia*), the fertilized egg cleaves in the meridional plane three times followed by an equatorial cleavage giving rise to a 16-celled embryo, which always lies just beneath the maternal choanocyte layer. At the 16-celled stage, the tier of eight cells lying in contact with the maternal tissue is destined to give rise to pinacocytes, collencytes, and scleroblasts in the adult sponge; the other eight cells are future choanocytes and amoebocytes. The latter eight cells continue to divide and develop flagella, and the embryo develops into a hollow blastula, called a stomoblastula. The stomoblastula has an opening in the group of eight cells that lie adjacent to the maternal choanocyte layer and that have undergone no further division up to this time. The embryo now turns inside out, the flagellated cells pushing out through the opening mentioned. The flagella are now external and in a position to propel the larva when it becomes free swimming. The hollow larva, now called an amphiblastula, consists of a layer of flagellated cells at one pole and nonflagellated cells at the opposite pole. Some of the flagellated cells have passed into the interior, lost their flagella, and will give rise to amoebocytes. Near the junction of the flagellated and nonflagellated cells lies a circle of four "cross cells" that are apparently light sensitive and help to orient the larva.

Following a short free-swimming life, the amphiblastula settles on a suitable substrate by its anterior end, and gastrulation occurs by invagination of the flagellated hemisphere or by downgrowth of the nonflagellated cells. The larva metamorphoses into a small tubular asconoid sponge (olynthus) and may retain this grade of construction or differentiate to a syconoid or leuconoid structure according to the species.

Among calcareous sponges of the subclass Calcinea (such as *Clathrina*), cleavage results in a hollow blastula consisting of a single layer of flagellated cells. The posterior pole is marked in some species by the presence of one to several nonflagellated cells. During the free-swimming period of the larva, some of the flagellated cells lose their flagella and wander into the interior of the embryo from all points except the anterior pole, or at the posterior pole only. The resulting solid larva, with internal ectomesenchyme, is known as a parenchymella and soon fixes to the substrate by its anterior end and flattens out. Metamorphosis involves a change in the relative positions and functions of the larval cells. The peripheral flagellated cells migrate through the central mass of nonflagellated cells and form the lining of the spongocoel as choanocytes. An olynthus is thus formed that will develop into the adult sponge.

Among the Demospongiae, most species develop by way of parenchymella larvae, but a few forms, presumed primitive, have amphiblastula larvae. In the skeletonless genus *Oscarella,* for example, representing the basal stock of the subclass Tetractinomorpha, cleavage results in a solid embryo, or morula, that later hollows out by disintegration (cytolysis) of the interior cells, rich in food reserves. The free-swimming larva is an amphiblastula composed of a single layer of flagellated cells. Near the posterior pole is a circle of cells bearing refractive rods; these cells are presumably light sensitive and help to orient the larva. The larva soon settles on its anterior end and flattens out. Gastrulation occurs as the anterior half of the larva invaginates. After the blastopore closes, the internal layer of cells is thrown into folds that are pinched off to form cavities, the future flagellated chambers. A depression in the ectoderm forms at the posterior pole and deepens, giving off branches that push their way among the flagellated chambers and finally open into them. This constitutes the excurrent canal system. The incurrent system forms as a series of surface depressions that enlarge and unite with the flagellated chambers. This type of development and metamorphosis occurs only in the family Plakinidae among Demospongiae.

*Halisarca,* a skeletonless genus of sponges belonging to the subclass Ceractinomorpha of the class Demospongiae, has parenchymella larvae, as do most members of this class. As in the Calcarea, these larvae have an outer layer of flagellated cells and an inner mass of cells that will give rise to the dermal membrane and mesenchyme cells. After the larva has settled, the flagellated cells lose their flagella, migrate into the interior, and differentiate into choanocytes. A single internal cavity develops within the young sponge, now called a rhagon, and an oscular opening breaks through at the apex. In most Demospongiae the newly settled sponge or rhagon has a simple leuconoid canal system in which the flagellated chambers become isolated between the incurrent and excurrent canals.

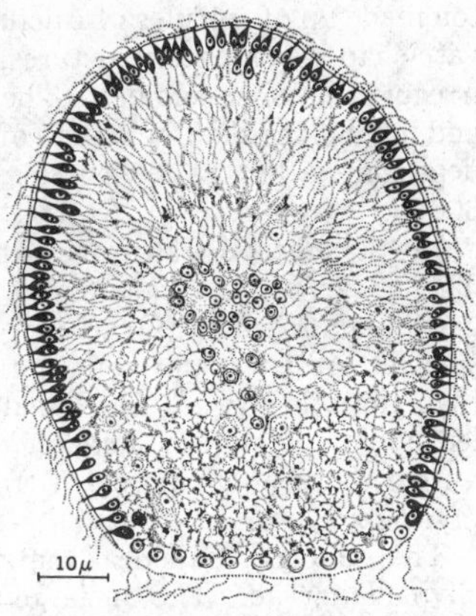

FIG. 7.—PARENCHYMELLA LARVA OF HALISARCA

*Farrea,* a hexactinellid sponge, has cleavage that results in a solid blastula. At a later stage an outer layer of closely packed cells surrounds a transparent jellylike material in which amoeboid cells wander. Tetractinal spicules and choanocytes (at first without collars and flagella) develop before the larva is set free from the parent sponge. Upon settling, the larva metamorphoses into a small tubular sponge with a terminal osculum, and pentactinal and hexactinal spicules soon develop.

*Asexual Reproduction.*—The formation of asexual reproductive bodies, called gemmules, is characteristic of almost all freshwater sponges and of many marine species. Gemmules are made up of masses of archaeocytes laden with food reserves in the form of lipids and proteins. In freshwater sponges, the inner mass of archaeocytes is surrounded by a layer of columnar cells that secrete a double layer of spongin around the archaeocytes, as well as by a protective layer of spicules that vary in shape according to the species and are useful in classification. The gemmules of marine sponges are also made up of food-laden archaeocytes, which are, in some cases, enclosed in a spongin coat that may be provided with spicules.

Freshwater sponge gemmules and those of a few marine species carry the species over periods of unfavourable conditions, such as drought or high or low temperatures, during which times the adult sponges degenerate. Germination of the gemmules follows the return of favourable conditions. In many marine sponges gemmules may be found at all seasons, and the adults show no seasonal degeneration. Intertidal marine sponges in temperate regions often remain alive during the winter season, but in some species the internal cellular structure transforms into a uniform mass of amoebocytes. The normal adult structure redifferentiates upon return of favourable conditions.

Asexually produced gemmules that develop into free-swimming flagellated larvae similar in structure to sexually produced larvae have been reported in several species of marine Demospongiae and Hexactinellida.

Budding, another type of asexual reproduction found commonly in sponges, is of especially frequent occurrence among tetractinomorph Demospongiae. In *Tethya,* for example, buds form from groups of archaeocytes that migrate to the tips of projecting spicule bundles. The buds eventually fall off and develop into new individuals.

**Regeneration.**—Sponges have remarkable powers of regeneration; any piece cut or broken from an adult sponge is very likely to attach to a suitable substrate and reform a functional individual. Suspensions of sponge cells prepared by squeezing fragments of adults through fine bolting silk will reorganize to form numerous small, functional individuals. According to most authors, the reconstitution of a new individual from dissociated cells results from the sorting out and migration of the various cell types to the positions that they characteristically occupy in the adult, but some observers report that choanocytes dedifferentiate, are phagocytized, or die, and later regenerate from other cell types.

After dissociation, masses of cells form as a result of the random movement of archaeocytes, amoebocytes, and other cells, including choanocytes that can put forth pseudopodia, as well as move by means of their flagella. There is some evidence to indicate that the adherence of cells as they come into contact with one another is a result of antigen-antibodylike forces.

If the cells of two species of sponges of different colours are mixed in suspension, they eventually sort out to form aggregates composed of cells of one species or the other.

**Biochemistry.**—Ten different sterols have been isolated from sponges, including several so far unknown in any other organisms. Twenty or more different fatty acid components of sterols occur in each of two marine sponges, including a predominance of acids with 26 or 28 carbon atoms (unsaturated fatty acids with more than 24 carbon atoms are of rare occurrence among animals). Also of interest is the fact that sterols, which are most diverse in sponges, have been reduced in number during the course of animal evolution: in man only cholesterol and a few sex hormones are synthesized.

Sponges contain deoxyribonucleic acid (DNA) and ribonucleic acid (RNA), characteristic of all animal groups. A methyl ether, anethole, and related substances (previously known only as components of plant oils) were isolated from a marine sponge and may be responsible for the odour of certain sponges. The spongin fibres characteristic of most Demospongiae have a structure similar to that of vertebrate collagens.

Chemical analyses of sponge pigments reveal that a majority of them are carotenoids, the most widely distributed animal biochromes. Carotenes have been found more commonly than xanthophylls, however, contrary to the situation in most marine plants and animals. Also present are chromolipoids, a porphyrin, and melanins.

**Organisms Associated with Sponges.**—Predators of sponges include chitons, snails, nudibranch slugs, and fish. Larvae of the neuropteran insect family Sisyridae (spongilla flies) live in, and feed upon, freshwater sponges. Many types of animals take up their abode in the natural cavities of marine sponges or form burrows of their own, but the exact nature of these relationships is little known. Hydroids, sea anemones, zoanthids, nematodes, polychaetes, octopuses, copepods, barnacles, isopods, amphipods, shrimps, brittle stars, and fishes are among the animals that dwell in temporary or permanent association with sponges. Pairs of shrimps (*Spongicola*) often inhabit the spongocoel of Venus's-flower-basket (*Euplectella*), a deep-sea hexactinellid. The shrimps are presumably imprisoned for life in the rigid siliceous reticular skeleton. *Suberites domunculus* (class Demospongiae) habitually lives on snail shells occupied by hermit crabs. Decorator crabs often choose pieces of sponge to plant or hold on their backs, presumably as a form of camouflage. Hydroids, bryozoans, ascidians, and other encrusting competitors of sponges for substrate may overgrow sponge colonies or be overgrown by them.

Many freshwater and shallow-water marine sponges harbour unicellular green algae in their amoebocytes. The sponges probably obtain some nutriment from the algae in the form of sugars, since the algal cells fail to synthesize starch when growing in sponges, and dying algal cells may be consumed as well. Apparently both the algae and the sponges can survive independently. Young sponges are reinfected with algae from free-swimming algal zoospores in the water. Unicellular and filamentous blue-green and green algae, as well as coralline algae, often grow in sponge colonies, and it is reported that bacteria living in the cells of some species of sponges impart colour to the animals. The significance of these relationships is unknown.

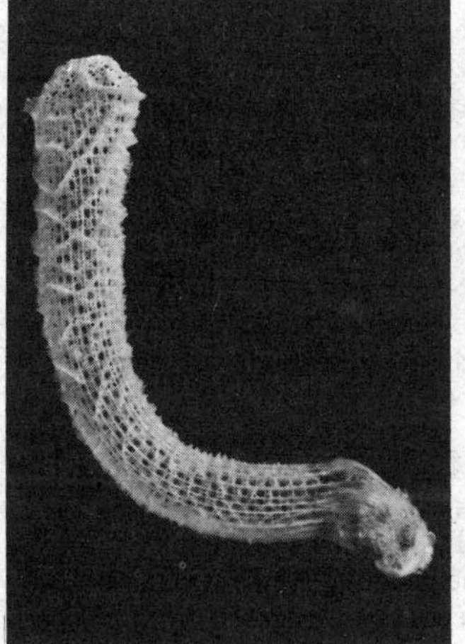
RALPH BUCHSBAUM
FIG. 8.—GLASSLIKE SKELETON OF VENUS'S-FLOWER-BASKET (EUPLECTELLA)

**Boring Sponges.**—Sponges of the family Clionidae (class Demospongiae) live in galleries that they excavate in mollusk shells, corals, limestone, and other calcareous materials. Consequently, these sponges are economically significant as weakeners of limestone breakwaters and oyster shells, rendering the latter difficult to process in canning factories.

The boring activities of clionids are accomplished by the excavation of numerous small chips of calcium carbonate. Pseudopodia and cytoplasmic films put out by sponge cells in contact with a calcareous substrate apparently insinuate themselves into the calcium carbonate, possibly by the localized secretion of an acid, and thus remove particles of relatively uniform size. The cells can also bore through conchiolin, a proteinaceous substance that separates successive layers of calcareous matter in mollusk shells, but they accomplish this less readily than they excavate the calcareous layers.

Clionids have monactinal megascleres with terminal knobs and may also have microscleres in the form of spiny diactinal spicules or spirasters or both. The sponges are not parasitic but feed on phytoplankton and detritus carried in the water currents maintained through their bodies as in other sponges. Dermal pores and oscules are localized on contractile tubules that protrude through holes in the calcareous substrate.

## CLASSIFICATION AND RELATIONSHIPS

The subdivision of the phylum Porifera into three classes—Calcarea, Hexactinellida, and Demospongiae—is based on the chemical composition of the skeletal elements. The Calcarea includes species with one- to four-rayed spicules made of calcium carbonate. Members of the Hexactinellida have siliceous spicules that are basically six rayed. Finally, the Demospongiae includes species with siliceous spicules that are usually one to four rayed, and never six rayed. Collagenlike fibres are often present as component supporting structures along with siliceous spicules in the Demospongiae, and in some species, including the bath sponges of commerce, such fibres make up the sole intrinsic skeletal elements.

**Hexactinellida.**—This class comprises sponges with skeletons made up basically of hexactinal siliceous spicules and lacking in spongin. They are exclusively marine and occur in the deeper waters of all seas from depths of about 25 m. to 8,500 m. The skeletal framework is made up of three systems of spicules: dermal, lying just beneath the dermal membrane; gastral, lying beneath the membrane bounding the spongocoel; and parenchymal, lying between the other two systems. The parenchymal megascleres of many species become fused to their neighbours to form a rigid latticework. The soft parts stretch across cavities between the skeletal systems and have the form of cobweblike or filmy trabeculae. Five regions may be distinguished in the body wall passing from the outside layer to the spongocoel: the dermal membrane, perforated by pores; the subdermal trabecular network in the midst of which subdermal cavities and incurrent canals may be identified; the thimble-shaped flagellated chambers (made up of choanocytes with fused cell bases), arranged side by side in a single layer, usually inside the parenchymal megascleres; the subspongocoelic trabecular network into which the flagellated chambers open and in which excurrent canals may be present; the perforated membrane lining the spongocoel or central cavity. From the spongocoel, water passes out of the terminal oscule, which in some species is covered by a sieve plate reinforced by a spicular network.

In the subclass Hexasterophora the parenchymal microscleres are typically hexasters (small, six-rayed spicules that often have branched ends). The sponges are commonly fixed firmly by the base to a hard substrate, but some species anchor themselves in soft bottom sediments by means of a basal spicule tuft or mat. The parenchymal megascleres are often fused into a rigid framework. Examples: *Hexactinella, Aphrocallistes, Farrea, Dactylocalyx, Euplectella, Rhabdocalyptus.*

Members of the subclass Amphidiscophora have parenchymal microscleres called amphidiscs (the distal ends of the rays bear an umbrellalike expansion). The parenchymal megascleres are always free and never fuse to form a rigid network. The sponges anchor themselves in the bottom sediments by basal tufts of spicules. Examples: *Pheronema, Hyalonema.*

**Calcarea.**—This class is characterized by sponges with a skeleton made up of spicules of calcium carbonate. The species may be vase-shaped compact structures, a loose network of thin tubes, or irregular massive colonies. The Calcarea are mostly small in size and inhabit the shallow waters of all seas, from intertidal regions to depths of 200 m.; a few species extend down to depths of at least 800 m.

In the subclass Calcaronea amphiblastula larvae are produced. The nuclei of the choanocytes are apical in position, with the flagellum in each case arising directly from the nucleus. The spicules are triradiate and characteristically have one ray longer than the other two. The canal system is asconoid, syconoid, or leuconoid. Examples: *Leucosolenia, Sycon, Grantia, Lelapia* (with a rigid skeleton composed of tracts or bundles of modified three-rayed spicules).

The subclass Calcinea contains species that produce parenchymella larvae. The nuclei of choanocytes are basal in position, with the flagellum in each case arising independent of the nucleus. At least some of the triradiate spicules in most species have equal rays and equal angles between the rays. The canal system is asconoid, radiate, or leuconoid. Tentatively included among the Calcinea are the pharetronid Calcarea, which have a rigid skeleton composed of fused spicules or of a calcareous network. Examples: *Clathrina, Leucetta, Petrobiona* (a pharetronid).

**Demospongiae.**—This class comprises sponges with a skeleton of one- to four-rayed siliceous spicules or of spongin fibres or both. A skeleton is lacking in several genera regarded as primitive. The Demospongiae are the most abundant and widely distributed sponges, occurring from intertidal regions down to depths of at least 5,500 m. in the sea. The Spongillidae is the only freshwater family. The species vary greatly in form and size, ranging from thin encrustations several centimetres in diameter to huge cake-shaped species measuring up to 2 m. in diameter.

Included among the Demospongiae are many species with desmas as spicules. These develop as a result of secondary deposits of silica around ordinary monaxonid or tetraxonid spicules. Often adjacent desmas articulate or interlock to form a stony skeleton. Such sponges are often called "lithistids," but they seem to have evolved independently among the several orders of Demospongiae and do not constitute a natural group of their own.

In the subclass Tetractinomorpha the skeleton is variously composed of scattered equirayed tetraxonid spicules and their derivatives, or of tetraxonid (usually triaenes) and monaxonid spicules arranged in a radiate pattern, or of monaxonid spicules alone arranged in radiating or plumose tracts. Spongin is scarce except among the axinellids. Microscleres are chiefly asters, streptasters, sigmas, and small monactinal or diactinal forms often provided with spines. Most of the species of this subclass, for which reproductive processes are known, are oviparous. The larvae of the primitive family Plakinidae are amphiblastulae, but parenchymellae occur in most species where sexual reproduction is known

BY COURTESY OF THE AMERICAN MUSEUM OF NATURAL HISTORY

FIG. 9.—FRESHWATER SPONGE (SPONGILLA), ENCRUSTED ON TWIGS

to occur. Tetractinomorph sponges vary greatly in shape, from encrustations and spherical forms to massive and branching colonies. They occur in all seas from tidal waters down to depths of at least 5,500 m. Examples: *Oscarella* (lacking a skeleton), *Plakina, Geodia, Cinachyra, Tethya, Suberites, Cliona, Axinella.*

Members of the subclass Ceractinomorpha are Demospongiae with a skeleton of monaxonid spicules joined together by more or less spongin or of spongin fibres alone. Microscleres of many varieties may occur, but asters are never present. Members of this subclass are viviparous and have parenchymella larvae. Examples: *Halisarca* (lacking a skeleton), *Aplysilla, Spongia, Haliclona, Spongilla* (freshwater), *Microciona, Halichondria.*

**Origin and Relationships.**—The origin of sponges and their relationship to other multicellular animal groups are still unsettled questions. As to their origin it seems most likely that they have descended from a group of flagellates. The structure of the choanocytes of sponges is almost identical to that of the component cells of choanoflagellate colonies, and it is these zooflagellates that are generally cited as the most probable sponge ancestors. The collar of both types of cells is now known to be composed of cytoplasmic filaments as a result of the electron microscope studies of Kilian and Rasmont. Choanoflagellates are holozoic and capture food by means of the collar. Among existing protistans, the choanoflagellates thus appear to be nearest to the ancestral line of sponges.

Fossil sponges are known from Cambrian and succeeding strata. Scattered records of sponge spicules in Precambrian rocks are in need of confirmation. The best-preserved fossil sponges belong to those groups that have skeletons of articulated or fused spicules, namely, many families of hexasterophoran Hexactinellida, lithistid families among the Demospongiae, and the pharetronid Calcarea. Only isolated spicules of other sponge groups tend to be preserved except under unusually favourable conditions.

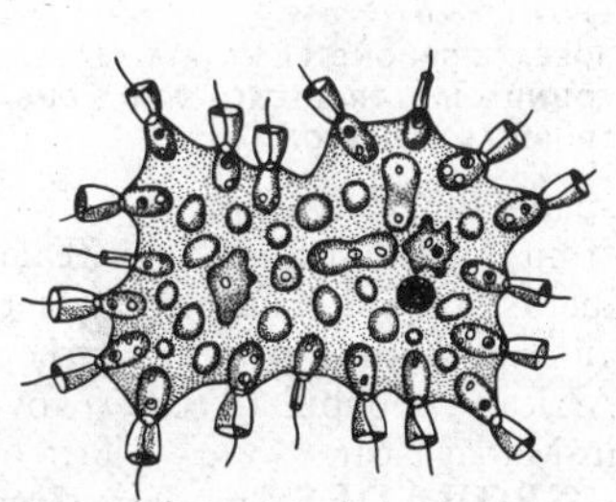

FROM L. H. HYMAN, "THE INVERTEBRATES: PROTOZOA THROUGH CTENOPHORA"; MCGRAW-HILL, 1940

FIG. 10.—PROTEROSPONGIA, A COLONIAL CHOANOFLAGELLATE CONSIDERED AS A PROBABLE LINK BETWEEN THE PROTOZOANS AND SPONGES

Undoubted fossil hexactinellids are first recorded in the Lower Cambrian. The group is exceptionally well represented in Devonian strata, in the Lower Carboniferous, in the Lower Jurassic, and in the Cretaceous. Species of the class Demospongiae are also found in Cambrian strata and upward; they reach a peak of abundance as lithistids in Cretaceous beds. Calcareous sponges have been reported from Cambrian strata, but the first certain fossil remains occur in the Devonian Period. Pharetronids are well represented from Permian and successive strata.

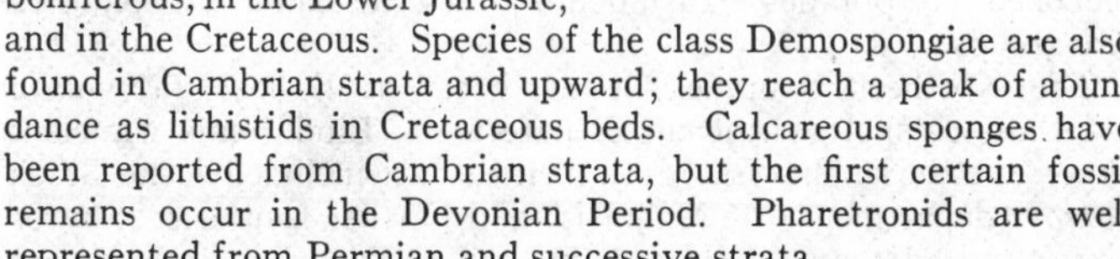

The question now arises as to what relationship sponges bear to other multicellular animals. According to some authors, the sponges represent a distinct subkingdom of animals that has arisen independently of all other metazoan groups. The uniqueness of the sponge body plan and peculiarities of fertilization and development are cited in support of this hypothesis. Special importance is given to the fact that in both amphiblastula and parenchymella larvae the flagellated cells that give rise to the choanocytes occupy the anterior hemisphere, while the nonflagellated ectomesenchymal cells are posterior in position. Such an arrangement is opposite that occurring in all other multicellular animals, in which the presumptive endoderm occupies a posterior position in the embryo and the ectoderm is anterior. Whether the germ layers of sponges are reversed in comparison with other animals or whether the choanocytes of sponges cannot be homologized with the endoderm of other Metazoa, this fact supports the wide separation of sponges from all other multicellular forms. The subkingdom Parazoa or Enantiozoa has been set up for the sponges by proponents of this theory.

Other authors have argued in favour of the basic similarity of the development of sponges and other Metazoa. The supposed inversion of the germ layers in sponge embryos is explained as a consequence of the inversion of the surfaces of the amphiblastula as described above for the Calcaronea. Sponges have been regarded as an offshoot from the evolutionary line that gave rise to the coelenterates. It is of interest to point out that collar processes have been observed to surround the flagella of coral epithelial cells. In *Mussa angulosa* the processes give rise to between 9 and 12 microvilli, giving the cell a structure strikingly similar to a sponge choanocyte with its collar of cytoplasmic filaments. Minute microvilli are apparently also characteristic of the ciliated epithelia of mollusks and vertebrates. (Wi. D. H.)

### ARTIFICIAL SPONGES

Artificial sponges are produced by the chemical expansion of natural crude rubber, such synthetic rubbers as neoprene, and certain plastics, of which polyvinyl chloride is a type.

In processing, the treatment of neoprene may be taken as typical of the sponge rubbers. Basically, neoprene sponge is compounded of sulfur-modified neoprene, magnesia, zinc oxide, an antioxidant, a mineral filler, such as channel carbon black or whiting, and an expanding or "blowing agent," which may be sodium bicarbonate. The stock may be treated further with other chemical agents as special needs indicate. A lubricant is used to keep the cells from sticking together. The stock is softened on mill rolls and then mixed. The chemicals are added when the neoprene becomes elastic and before it reaches its granular phase. Mixing continues until the stock is plastic. The rate of the subsequent curing process is carefully controlled to ensure a desired degree of "blow."

Sponge rubber can be processed in sheets on a machine called a calender. They can be produced also in slabs, die-cut shapes, and molded forms. They have many uses, of which gasketing, insulation, cushioning, shock absorption, and vibration damping are examples.

Similar to sponge rubbers are expanded rubbers and expanded plastics having a closed-cell structure, which possess a superior insulating quality and greater buoyancy. Closed-cell polyvinyl chloride is widely used for floats, whereas the open-cell form is useful as cushioning.

Foam rubber, used in bedding, upholstery, and cushioning, is made from rubber latex chemically foamed to produce a soft structure of interconnecting cells.

*See* also references under "Sponges" in the Index. (E. L. Y.)

Bibliography.—An excellent general account of the sponges is given by L. H. Hyman in *The Invertebrates,* vol. i, *Protozoa Through Ctenophora,* pp. 284–364 (1940); more recent literature is reviewed by L. H. Hyman in *The Invertebrates,* vol. v, *Smaller Coelomate Groups,* pp. 715–718 (1959); E. J. Cresswell, *Sponges* (1930), an account of commercial sponges; novel phylogenetic speculations may be found in E. N. Willmer, *Cytology and Evolution* (1960). (Wi. D. H.)

**SPONTANEOUS GENERATION,** in biology, is the theory, now disproved, that living organisms at present arise from nonliving matter. It is sometimes referred to as abiogenesis, as opposed to biogenesis, the now-established fact that living organisms arise only from the reproduction of previously existing organisms.

*See* Biology: *History: Biogenesis Versus Abiogenesis;* Life.

**SPONTINI, GASPARO LUIGI PACIFICO** (1774–1851), Italian opera composer, whose early Paris operas, based on heroic historical themes, are representative of the spirit of the Napoleonic era, and whose German operas had some influence on the early works of Wagner. He was born at Majolati, Ancona, on Nov. 14, 1774, of humble parents. In 1793 he studied singing and composition at Naples, and his first opera, *I Puntigli delle donne,* was produced in Rome in 1796, followed by others given at Venice, Florence, Naples, and Palermo. In 1803 he went to Paris, where, after writing unsuccessful works in the light French style, he collaborated with the writer Étienne de Jouy in dramatic operas, producing *Milton* (1804) and his masterpiece, *La Vestale* (1807). The success of the latter, which had been given at the Opéra under the patronage of the empress Josephine, led to the award of a prize to Spontini from Napoleon. *Fernand Cortez* (1809), the subject of which appealed to Napoleon in view of his plans for a Spanish war, was similarly successful, and the following year Spontini was appointed director of the Italian Opera in Paris.

As a conductor Spontini introduced to Paris works of Haydn and Mozart. In 1814 he was appointed court composer by Louis XVIII and wrote various stage works in glorification of the Restoration, among them *Pélage, ou le roi de la paix* (1814). Later he held a similar appointment at the court of Frederick William III in Berlin, where, between 1821 and 1829, he produced *Olympia* (earlier given in Paris as *Olympie;* the libretto, which was based on Voltaire, was translated into German by E. T. W. Hoffmann); *Nurmahal* (based on Thomas Moore's *Lalla Rookh*); *Alcidor;* and *Agnes von Hohenstaufen.*

Spontini spent his later years in France and Germany and eventually returned to his birthplace, Majolati, where he died on Jan. 24, 1851.

BIBLIOGRAPHY.—G. Abraham, "The Best of Spontini" in *Music and Letters* (April, 1942); A. Ghislanzoni, *G. Spontini* (1951); A. Belardinelli, *Documenti spontiniani inediti,* 2 vol. (1955).

**SPOON,** an implement consisting of a bowl-shaped receptacle supported by a stem or handle. The word originally meant a piece of some such substance as wood or horn carved from a larger section. (The Greeks and Romans adopted more permanent materials, such as bronze and sometimes silver.) Although it is the tablespoon that has largely engaged the interest of collectors and writers, it was not the only kind in antiquity; some of the most interesting and beautiful ancient spoons had ceremonial or toilet use, such as the long incense spoons depicted in Egyptian art and the cosmetic spoons, often engagingly carved with anthropomorphic or zoomorphic handles, that have survived from Egyptian burials.

The history of tablespoons belongs to that of western culture. Spoons made of silver were among the first pieces of plate that a successful medieval citizen strove to acquire; they were sufficiently esteemed to be bequeathed singly. Long, pointed bowls characterize the few early medieval spoons excavated in the British Isles. The English coronation spoon used for the anointing of the sovereign belongs to this type and period (*see* CROWN AND REGALIA). The shape of bowl and stem evolved according to table manners in the course of the centuries. The fig-shaped bowl prevailed from the later Middle Ages, the stem culminating either in a conventional pattern of knop or in one especially ordered by the customer.

BY COURTESY OF VICTORIA AND ALBERT MUSEUM

SILVER APOSTLE SPOONS, MADE IN ENGLAND, 15TH CENTURY

In general favour were "Maidenhead" knops, representing a female bust, traditionally that of the Virgin, and "Apostle" knops. Entire sets of these apostle spoons, 12 in number (or 13 when Jesus Christ was included), rarely survive, because it was common to present single spoons as christening gifts.

Matching sets of spoons and forks were common by the mid-18th century in various standard patterns; the modern form of tablespoon, with the stem ending in a rounded curve turned downward, was adopted about 1760. For the manufacture of spoons, *see* FLATWARE.

*See* G. E. P. and J. P. How, *English and Scottish Silver Spoons,* 3 vol. (1952–57); C. C. Oman, *English Domestic Silver,* 4th ed. (1959).
(J. F. H.)

**SPOONBILL,** any one of six species of moderately large wading birds constituting the subfamily Plataleinae and, with the ibises (*q.v.*), the family Threskiornithidae (order Ciconiiformes). The head is partly or entirely bare, the plumage white (except in the roseate spoonbill), often with a rosy tinge, some with a nuptial crest or foreneck plumes. They differ from ibises in having a long nearly straight bill, narrow in the middle and broad and flat at the end, which they immerse in feeding, swinging it from side to side and sifting small animals from the mud and water of estuaries, salt-water bayous and lakes. In flight they flap steadily, usually without sailing. They breed in colonies, often with ibises and herons, build a good nest of sticks, sometimes lined with leaves or bark, among reeds or in a low bush or tree about ten feet up, and lay three to five white eggs blotched with reddish-brown.

The beautiful roseate spoonbill (*Ajaia ajaja*), 32 in. long, head and throat bare, legs red, is deep pink with neck and upper back white, wing coverts and tail coverts deep carmine and tail and sides of breast tawny-buff. It ranges from the Gulf coast of Texas (and a very few in Florida), the West Indies and central Mexico to Argentina and Chile. In many places it was exterminated by plume hunters. The yellow-legged spoonbill (*Platibis flavipes*) of Australia is white with straw-coloured foreneck and a yellow forehead, upper throat and bill. The white spoonbill (*Platalea leucorodia*), about 34 in. long, breeds sparsely in the Netherlands and Spain and somewhat more commonly from southeastern Europe and the Sudan to India and China; the black-billed spoonbill (*P. regia*), white with black wing tips and black legs, from Australia and New Zealand to New Guinea, Celebes, Moluccas and Solomons; the lesser spoonbill (*P. minor*), from Korea and southern Japan to southern China and the Philippines; the African spoonbill (*P. alba*), over Africa south of the Sahara and in Madagascar.
(G. F. Ss.)

ALLAN D. CRUICKSHANK FROM THE NATIONAL AUDUBON SOCIETY

ROSEATE SPOONBILL (AJAIA AJAJA), FOUND IN TROPICAL AND SUBTROPICAL AMERICA

**SPORADES** (modern Greek SPORÁDHES), the "scattered islands" of the Aegean Sea, as distinct from the Cyclades (*q.v.*) grouped around Delos, and, usually, not including any of the coastal islands of Greece or Asia Minor. Both ancient and modern writers differ as to the list. Some or all of the islands in the south of the Cyclades—Melos (Mílos), Pholegandros (Folégandros), Síkinos, Thera (Thíra), and Anaphe (Anáfi)—were sometimes reckoned as Sporades. In modern times the name is applied to two groups.

The Northern Sporades lie northeast of Euboea (Évvoia): Skíathos, Skópelos (ancient Peparethos), Iliodhrómia (ancient Ikos), and the smaller islands to their east are included in the Greek *nomos* (department) of Magnisía, and, farther southeast, Skyros (*q.v.*) and adjacent islands are in that of Euboea. Both Skyros and the beautifully wooded Skíathos have excellent harbours. There has been little archaeological exploration conducted on the islands, but there are classical remains on Skyros and a notable find of Mycenaean goldwork from Skópelos (1936). Almost every householder in the islands is the owner, joint owner, or skipper of a sailing ship.

The Southern Sporades, lying off the southwest of Asia Minor in a roughly northwest-southeast band, are from north to south, as follows: Ikaría, Pátmos (*q.v.*), Léros, Calymnos (Kálimnos), Astypalaea (Astipálaia), Cos (*q.v.*), Nisyros (Nísiros), Telos (Tílos), Symé (Sími), Khálki, Rhodes (*q.v.*), and many smaller islands. All but the first named formed part of the Dodecanese (*q.v.*). The Dodecanese were occupied by the Italians from 1912 to 1947.

*See* A. Philippson, *Die Griechischen Landschaften,* vol. iv (1959).
(J. Bo.)

**SPOROZOA,** a subphylum of Protozoa incorporating several problematic groups of microscopic parasites, among them *Plasmodium,* the causative agent of malaria. Their reproductive processes and life cycles are complex; spores are formed in some but not all members. *See* PROTOZOA.

**SPORTING RECORD.** The following lists include the world records and championships of all major sports that are international in character, and also records of some minor sports of unusual or particular interest; some professional and amateur sports that attract huge national followings (as baseball and football in the U.S., cricket in the Test Match countries); and some exceptions (as golf, tennis, and rowing) in which national events may overshadow international competition.

The main sports—from Archery to Yachting—are covered by separate articles, and there are many supplementary articles on individual events. For a survey of *Encyclopædia Britannica*'s coverage *see* SPORTS (ARTICLES ON). For any particular sport or event, refer to the Index.

In many sports the international competition provided by the Olympic Games every four years constitutes the world championships; those conducting inter-Olympic championships are included in the listings below. For the complete table of Olympic competition since 1896 *see* the article OLYMPIC GAMES.

This article contains records of the following sports:

Air Records
Angling: *see* Fishing
Archery
Association Football: *see* Football
Athletics: *see* Track and Field Sports
Automobile Racing
Badminton
Baseball
Basketball
Bicycle Racing: *see* Cycling
Billiards
Bobsledding
Bowling
Bowls
Boxing
Bridge
Canoeing
Casting: *see* Fishing
Chess
Cricket
Curling
Cycling
Dog (Greyhound) Racing
Drag Racing: *see* Automobile Racing
Equestrianism: *see* Show Jumping
Fencing
Fishing
Football
Gliding: *see* Air Records
Golf
Gymnastics
Harness Racing: *see* Horse Racing
Highland Games
Hockey: *see* Ice Hockey
Hockey, Field
Horse Racing
Hunting
Ice Hockey
Ice Skating
Judo
Lawn Tennis: *see* Tennis
Luge: *see* Tobogganing
Modern Pentathlon
Motorboating
Motorcycling
Motor Racing: *see* Automobile Racing
Parachute Jumping
Pigeon Racing
Ping-Pong: *see* Table Tennis
Polo
Pool: *see* Billiards
Roller Skating
Rowing
Rugby League and Rugby Union: *see* Football
Sailing: *see* Yachting
Shooting
Show Jumping
Skiing
Sky Diving: *see* Parachute Jumping
Snooker: *see* Billiards
Soaring: *see* Air Records
Squash Rackets
Swimming
Table Tennis
Tennis
Tobogganing
Track and Field Sports
Trampoline: *see* Gymnastics
Volleyball
Water Skiing
Weight Lifting
Wrestling
Yachting

U.P.I. COMPIX

JACQUELINE COCHRAN (U.S.), WHO SET THE WOMEN'S AIR-SPEED RECORD OF 1,429.2 MPH IN AN F-104G SUPER STAR JET ON MAY 18, 1964, SHOWN WITH HER SEVERSKY PURSUIT PLANE AFTER WINNING THE BENDIX TROPHY IN 1938

CAPT. J. P. COONEY, MAJ. W. F. DANIEL, MAJ. N. T. WARNER, COL. D. ANDRÉ (COPILOT), AND COL. R. L. STEPHENS (PILOT), U.S., SET AIR-SPEED RECORD OF 2,070.102 MPH IN LOCKHEED YF-12A AT EDWARDS AIR FORCE BASE, CALIF., MAY 1, 1965

BY COURTESY OF NATIONAL AERONAUTIC ASSOCIATION

## AIR RECORDS

| World Airplane Records* | Name; Country | Craft | Record | Place | Date |
|---|---|---|---|---|---|
| Speed | R. L. Stephens and D. André; U.S. | Lockheed YF-12A | 2,070.102 mph | Edwards AFB, Calif., U.S. | May 1, 1965 |
| Speed over closed circuit | M. Komarov; U.S.S.R. | E-266 Jet | 1,850.61 mph | U.S.S.R. | Oct. 5, 1967 |
| Distance over closed circuit | W. Stevenson; U.S. | Boeing B-52H | 11,336.92 mi. | Seymour Johnson AFB, N.C., U.S. | June 6–7, 1962 |
| Distance over straight course | C. P. Evely; U.S. | Boeing B-52H | 12,532.28 mi. | Kadena, Okinawa, to Madrid, Spain | Jan. 10–11, 1962 |
| Altitude (rocket powered) | J. A. Walker; U.S. | North American X-15A-2 | 354,200 ft. | Edwards AFB, Calif., U.S. | Aug. 22, 1963 |
| Altitude (jet powered) | G. Mossolov; U.S.S.R. | Mikoyan E-66A | 113,892 ft. | U.S.S.R. | April 28, 1961 |
| **Women's Records** | | | | | |
| Speed | J. Cochran; U.S. | F-104G Super Star | 1,429.2 mph | Edwards AFB, Calif., U.S. | May 18, 1964 |
| Altitude | N. Prokhanova; U.S.S.R. | E-33 Jet | 79,842 ft. | U.S.S.R. | May 22, 1965 |
| **Lighter-Than-Air Craft (balloons)** | | | | | |
| Altitude | M. Ross and V. Prather; U.S. | | 113,739 ft. | Gulf of Mexico | May 4, 1961 |
| Distance | H. Berliner; Ger. | | 1,896.9 mi. | Bitterfeld, Ger., to Kirgishan, U.S.S.R. | Feb. 8–10, 1914 |
| **Soaring (Gliding, Sailplaning)** | | | | | |
| Speed—100-km. triangle | H. M. Linke; W. Ger. | Libelle | 85.93 mph | El Mirage, Calif., U.S. | July 30, 1967 |
| Distance to declared goal and return | K. Striedieck; U.S. | KA-8b | 472.2 mi. | Inglefield, Pa. U.S. | Mar. 3, 1968 |
| Absolute altitude | P. F. Bikle, Jr.; U.S. | Schweizer SGS1-23E | 46,267 ft. | Mojave Desert, Calif., U.S. | Feb. 25, 1961 |
| Gain of height | P. F. Bikle, Jr.; U.S. | Schweizer SGS1-23E | 42,304 ft. (released from 3,963 ft.) | Mojave Desert, Calif., U.S. | Feb. 25, 1961 |

*International Aeronautical Federation categories.

## ARCHERY*

### World Championship Records

| Event | Name; Country | Score | Year |
|---|---|---|---|
| Individual men | H. Ward; U.S. | 2,423 | 1969 |
| Team (3 men) | U.S. | 7,194 | 1969 |
| Individual women | D. Lidstone; Can. | 2,361 | 1969 |
| Team (3 women) | U.S.S.R. | 6,897 | 1969 |

BY COURTESY OF MRS. VICTORIA COOK

WOMEN'S INDIVIDUAL ARCHERY RECORD HOLDER IN 1963, MRS. VICTORIA COOK, U.S.

### World Championships

#### Men's Individual

| Year | Winner; Country | Place | Points | Team † Winner; points |
|---|---|---|---|---|
| 1957 | O. K. Smathers; U.S. | Prague, Czech. | 2,231 | U.S.; 6,591 |
| 1958 | S. Thyssen; Swed. | Brussels, Belg. | 2,101 | Finland; 5,936 |
| 1959 | J. Caspers; U.S. | Stockholm, Swed. | 2,247 | U.S.; 6,634 |
| 1961 | J. Thornton; U.S. | Oslo, Nor. | 2,310 | U.S.; 6,601 |
| 1963 | C. Sandlin; U.S. | Helsinki, Fin. | 2,332 | U.S.; 6,887 |
| 1965 | M. Haikonen; Fin. | Västeras, Swed. | 2,313 | U.S.; 6,792 |
| 1967 | R. Rogers; U.S. | Amersfoort, Neth. | 2,298 | U.S.; 6,816 |
| 1969 | H. Ward; U.S. | Valley Forge, U.S. | 2,423 | U.S.; 7,194 |

#### Women's Individual

| Year | Winner; Country | Place | Points | Team † |
|---|---|---|---|---|
| 1957 | C. Meinhart; U.S. | Prague, Czech. | 2,120 | U.S.; 6,187 |
| 1958 | S. Johansson; Swed. | Brussels, Belg. | 2,053 | U.S.; 6,058 |
| 1959 | A. Weber Corby; U.S. | Stockholm, Swed. | 2,023 | U.S.; 5,847 |
| 1961 | N. Vonderheide; U.S. | Oslo, Nor. | 2,173 | U.S.; 6,376 |
| 1963 | V. Cook; U.S. | Helsinki, Fin. | 2,253 | U.S.; 6,508 |
| 1965 | M. Lindholm; Fin. | Västeras, Swed. | 2,214 | U.S.; 6,358 |
| 1967 | M. Maczynska; Pol. | Amersfoort, Neth. | 2,240 | Pol.; 6,686 |
| 1969 | D. Lidstone; Can. | Valley Forge, U.S. | 2,361 | U.S.S.R.; 6,897 |

*Double Fédération Internationale de Tir à l'Arc Rounds (see the article ARCHERY: Tournaments) adopted 1957.

†Team champions prior to 1957: MEN: 1931, France; 1932, Poland; 1933, Belgium; 1934, Sweden; 1935, Belgium; 1936, Czechoslovakia; 1937, Poland; 1938, Czechoslovakia; 1939, France; 1946, Denmark; 1947, Czechoslovakia; 1948, Sweden; 1949, Czechoslovakia; 1950, Sweden; 1952, Sweden; 1953, Sweden; 1955, Sweden. WOMEN: 1933, Poland; 1934, Poland; 1935, U.K.; 1936, Poland; 1937, U.K.; 1938, Poland; 1939, Poland; 1946, U.K.; 1947, Denmark; 1948, Czechoslovakia; 1949, U.K.; 1950, Finland; 1952, U.S.; 1953, Finland; 1955, U.K.

## AUTOMOBILE RACING

**World Land-speed Records** Official and unofficial progressive highest land speeds by mechanically propelled wheeled vehicles (one run only over 1 km., 1 mi., or the distance between). All tests were at Bonneville Salt Flats, Utah, U.S.

| Name; Country | Car | Record mph | Date |
|---|---|---|---|
| J. R. Cobb; U.K. | Railton Mobil Special (2,500 bhp) | 375.325* | Sept. 14, 1947 |
| J. R. Cobb; U.K. | Railton Mobil Special (2,500 bhp) | 403.135† | Sept. 16, 1947 |
| M. Thompson; U.S. | "Challenger I" (2,600 bhp) | 406.6 | Sept. 9, 1960 |
| C. Breedlove; U.S. | "Spirit of America" (5,240-lb. thrust) | 436.600‡ | Aug. 5, 1963 |
| A. Arfons; U.S. | "Green Monster" (17,000-lb. thrust) | 491.903§ | Oct. 5, 1964 |
| C. Breedlove; U.S. | "Spirit of America" (5,750-lb. thrust) | 507.470§ | Oct. 13, 1964 |
| C. Breedlove; U.S. | "Spirit of America" (5,750-lb. thrust) | 519.493§ | Oct. 15, 1964 |
| C. Breedlove; U.S. | "Spirit of America" (5,750-lb. thrust) | 547.415§ | Oct. 15, 1964 |
| A. Arfons; U.S. | "Green Monster" (17,000-lb. thrust) | 571.376§ | Oct. 27, 1964 |
| A. Arfons; U.S. | "Green Monster" (17,000-lb. thrust) | 575.724§ | Nov. 7, 1965 |
| A. Arfons; U.S. | "Green Monster" (17,000-lb. thrust) | 577.386§ | Nov. 7, 1965 |
| C. Breedlove; U.S. | "Spirit of America—Sonic I" (15,000-lb. thrust) | 597.152§ | Nov. 15, 1965 |
| C. Breedlove; U.S. | "Spirit of America—Sonic I" (15,000-lb. thrust) | 604.740§ | Nov. 15, 1965 |
| C. Breedlove; U.S. | "Spirit of America—Sonic I" (15,000-lb. thrust) | 608.211§ | Nov. 15, 1965 |
| C. Breedlove; U.S. | "Spirit of America—Sonic I" (15,000-lb. thrust) | 613.995§ | Nov. 15, 1965 |

* One run only over 1 km. (5.96 sec.). A second run considered too dangerous.
† Peak speed reportedly 415 mph.
‡ Three-wheeled jet, sanctioned by Fédération Internationale Motocycliste.
§ Jet propelled. No direct wheel drive.

### World Drivers' Championship

| Year | Winner; Country | Car |
|---|---|---|
| 1950 | G. Farina; It. | Alfa Romeo |
| 1951 | J. Fangio; Arg. | Alfa Romeo |
| 1952 | A. Ascari; It. | Ferrari |
| 1953 | A. Ascari; It. | Ferrari |
| 1954 | J. Fangio; Arg. | Mercedes & Maserati |
| 1955 | J. Fangio; Arg. | Mercedes |
| 1956 | J. Fangio; Arg. | Ferrari |
| 1957 | J. Fangio; Arg. | Maserati |
| 1958 | M. Hawthorn; U.K. | Ferrari |
| 1959 | J. Brabham; Austr. | Cooper-Climax |
| 1960 | J. Brabham; Austr. | Cooper-Climax |
| 1961 | P. Hill; U.S. | Ferrari |
| 1962 | G. Hill; U.K. | BRM |
| 1963 | J. Clark; U.K. | Lotus-Climax |
| 1964 | J. Surtees; U.K. | Ferrari |
| 1965 | J. Clark; U.K. | Lotus-Climax |
| 1966 | J. Brabham; Austr. | Repco-Brabham |
| 1967 | D. Hulme; N.Z. | Repco-Brabham |
| 1968 | G. Hill; U.K. | Lotus-Ford |
| 1969 | J. Stewart; U.K. | Matra-Ford |

### International Automobile Federation (FIA)

Formula One Constructors' Championship

| Year | Car | Year | Car |
|---|---|---|---|
| 1955 | Mercedes | 1963 | Lotus-Climax |
| 1956 | Ferrari | 1964 | Ferrari |
| 1957 | Maserati | 1965 | Lotus-Climax |
| 1958 | Ferrari | 1966 | Repco-Brabham |
| 1959 | Cooper-Climax | 1967 | Repco-Brabham |
| 1960 | Cooper-Climax | 1968 | Lotus-Ford |
| 1961 | Ferrari | 1969 | Matra-Ford |
| 1962 | BRM | | |

WORLD DRIVERS' CHAMPIONS (RIGHT) GRAHAM HILL (U.K.), 1962, '68, AND (BELOW) JACK BRABHAM (AUSTR.), 1959, '60, '66

(RIGHT) WIL BLANCHE FOR "SPORTS ILLUSTRATED," © TIME INC., (BELOW) PICTORIAL PARADE INC.

**Drag Racing** Speed is measured at the end of a ¼-mi. course and races are from a standing start.

| Event | Record | Car | Place | Date |
|---|---|---|---|---|
| Speed | 229.59 mph | Beebe-Mulligan AA/F Chrysler | Irvine, Calif. | Sept. 14, 1968 |
| Elapsed time | 6.88 sec. | Lee-Westmoreland AA/F Chrysler | York, Penn. | Aug. 12, 1967 |

Source: National Hot Rod Association.

## Principal Grand Prix

**UNITED STATES (instituted 1959)**

| Year | Winner | Car | Average speed mph | Place |
|---|---|---|---|---|
| 1959 | B. McLaren | Cooper-Climax | 98.87 | Sebring, Fla. |
| 1960 | S. Moss | Lotus-Climax | 99.00 | Riverside, Calif. |
| 1961 | I. Ireland | Lotus | 103.22 | Watkins Glen, N.Y. |
| 1962 | J. Clark | Lotus | 108.61 | Watkins Glen, N.Y. |
| 1963 | G. Hill | BRM | 109.91 | Watkins Glen, N.Y. |
| 1964 | G. Hill | BRM | 111.10 | Watkins Glen, N.Y. |
| 1965 | G. Hill | BRM | 107.98 | Watkins Glen, N.Y. |
| 1966 | J. Clark | Lotus-BRM | 114.94 | Watkins Glen, N.Y. |
| 1967 | J. Clark | Lotus-Ford | 120.95 | Watkins Glen, N.Y. |
| 1968 | J. Stewart | Matra-Ford | 124.89 | Watkins Glen, N.Y. |
| 1969 | J. Rindt | Lotus-Ford | 126.36 | Watkins Glen, N.Y. |

**FRENCH**

| Year | Winner | Car | Average speed mph | Place |
|---|---|---|---|---|
| 1956 | P. Collins | Lancia-Ferrari | 122.29 | Reims |
| 1957 | J. Fangio | Maserati | 100.02 | Rouen |
| 1958 | M. Hawthorn | Ferrari | 125.46 | Reims |
| 1959 | T. Brooks | Ferrari | 127.44 | Reims |
| 1960 | J. Brabham | Cooper | 132.19 | Reims |
| 1961 | G. Baghetti | Ferrari | 119.84 | Reims |
| 1962 | D. Gurney | Porsche | 101.89 | Rouen |
| 1963 | J. Clark | Lotus | 125.31 | Reims |
| 1964 | D. Gurney | Brabham | 109.00 | Rouen |
| 1965 | J. Clark | Lotus | 89.20 | Clermont-Ferrand |
| 1966 | J. Brabham | Repco-Brabham | 136.70 | Reims |
| 1967 | J. Brabham | Repco-Brabham | 98.90 | Le Mans |
| 1968 | J. Ickx | Ferrari | 100.40 | Rouen |
| 1969 | J. Stewart | Matra-Ford | 97.70 | Clermont-Ferrand |

**GERMAN** (at Nürburg except 1959, Avus)

| Year | Winner | Car | Average speed mph |
|---|---|---|---|
| 1956 | J. Fangio | Lancia-Ferrari | 85.57 |
| 1957 | J. Fangio | Maserati | 88.79 |
| 1958 | T. Brooks | Vanwall | 90.35 |
| 1959 | T. Brooks | Ferrari | 143.60 |
| 1960 | J. Bonnier | Porsche | 80.28 |
| 1961 | S. Moss | Lotus | 92.34 |
| 1962 | G. Hill | BRM | 80.28 |
| 1963 | J. Surtees | Ferrari | 95.83 |
| 1964 | J. Surtees | Ferrari | 96.50 |
| 1965 | J. Clark | Lotus | 99.79 |
| 1966 | J. Brabham | Repco-Brabham | 86.70 |
| 1967 | D. Hulme | Repco-Brabham | 101.40 |
| 1968 | J. Stewart | Matra-Ford | 86.82 |
| 1969 | J. Ickx | Brabham-Ford | 108.43 |

**ITALIAN** (all races at Monza)

| Year | Winner | Car | Average speed mph |
|---|---|---|---|
| 1956 | S. Moss | Maserati | 129.75 |
| 1957 | S. Moss | Vanwall | 120.30 |
| 1958 | T. Brooks | Vanwall | 121.17 |
| 1959 | S. Moss | Cooper-Climax | 124.40 |
| 1960 | P. Hill | Ferrari | 132.06 |
| 1961 | P. Hill | Ferrari | 130.08 |
| 1962 | G. Hill | BRM | 123.62 |
| 1963 | J. Clark | Lotus | 127.74 |
| 1964 | J. Surtees | Ferrari | 127.69 |
| 1965 | J. Stewart | BRM | 130.46 |
| 1966 | L. Scarfiotti | Ferrari | 135.90 |
| 1967 | J. Surtees | Honda | 140.50 |
| 1968 | D. Hulme | McLaren-Ford | 145.50 |
| 1969 | J. Stewart | Matra-Ford | 146.50 |

## Monte Carlo Rally

Rally-driving became established early in 1907. The classic event is the Monte Carlo Rally now started in various European cities with Monaco as its terminal point.

| Year | Winner | Car |
|---|---|---|
| 1911 | H. Rougier | Turcat Mery |
| 1912 | J. Bütler | Berliet |
| 1924 | Ledure | Bignan |
| 1925 | F. Repusseau | Renault |
| 1926 | V. Bruce | A.C. |
| 1927 | Lefebvre, Despeaux | Amilcar |
| 1928 | J. Bignan | Fiat |
| 1929 | S. van Eijk | Graham Paige |
| 1930 | H. Petit | Licorne |
| 1931 | D. Healey | Invicta |
| 1932 | M. Vasselle | Hotchkiss |
| 1933 | M. Vasselle | Hotchkiss |
| 1934 | Gas, Trevoux | Hotchkiss |
| 1935 | Lahaye, Quatresous | Renault |
| 1936 | Zamfirescu, Cristea | Ford |
| 1937 | Le Begue, Quinlin | Delahaye |
| 1938 | Schut, Ton | Ford |
| 1939 | Trevoux, Lesurque | Hotchkiss |
| | Paul, Contet | Delahaye |
| 1949 | Trevoux, Lesurque | Hotchkiss |
| 1950 | Becquart, Secret | Hotchkiss |
| 1951 | Trevoux, Crovetto | Delahaye |
| 1952 | Allard, Warburton | Allard |
| 1953 | Gatsonides, Worledge | Ford Zephyr |
| 1954 | Chiron, Basadonna | Lancia Aurelia |
| 1955 | Malling, Fadum | Sunbeam-Talbot |
| 1956 | Adams, Bigger | Jaguar |
| 1958 | Monraisse, Feret | Renault |
| 1959 | Coltelloni, Alexandre | Citroen |
| 1960 | Schock, Moll | Mercedes |
| 1961 | Martin, Bateau | Panhard |
| 1962 | Carlsson, Häggbom | *Saab |
| 1963 | Carlsson, Palm | Saab |
| 1964 | Hopkirk, Liddon | Mini-Cooper |
| 1965 | Makinen, Easter | Mini-Cooper |
| 1966 | Toivonen, Mikander | Citroen |
| 1967 | Aaltonen, Liddon | Mini-Cooper |
| 1968 | Elford, Stone | Porsche |
| 1969 | Waldegaard, Helmer | Porsche |
| 1970 | Waldegaard, Helmer | Porsche |

Not held in 1913-23, 1940-48, and 1957. *Smallest ever winner at 841 cc.

## Le Mans 24-hour Grand Prix d'Endurance

Held on the 8.86-mile Sarthe circuit, Le Mans, Fr.

| Year | Winner | Car |
|---|---|---|
| 1923 | Legache, Leonard | Chenard-Walcker |
| 1924 | Duff, Clement | Bentley |
| 1925 | Courcelles, Rossignol | Lorraine-Dietrich |
| 1926 | Block, Rossignol | Lorraine-Dietrich |
| 1927 | Benjafield, Davis | Bentley |
| 1928 | Barnato, Rubin | Bentley |
| 1929 | Barnato, Birkin | Bentley |
| 1930 | Barnato, Kidston | Bentley |
| 1931 | Howe, Birkin | Alfa Romeo |
| 1932 | Sommer, Chinetti | Alfa Romeo |
| 1933 | Sommer, Nuvolari | Alfa Romeo |
| 1934 | Chinetti, Etancelin | Alfa Romeo |
| 1935 | Hindmarsh, Fontes | Lagonda |
| 1937 | Wimille, Benoist | Bugatti |
| 1938 | Chauboud, Tremoulet | Delahaye |
| 1939 | Wimille, Veyron | Bugatti |
| 1949 | Chinetti, Selsdon | Ferrari |
| 1950 | Rosier, Rosier | Talbot |
| 1951 | Walker, Whitehead | Jaguar |
| 1952 | Lang, Riess | Mercedes-Benz |
| 1953 | Hamilton, Rolt | Jaguar |
| 1954 | Gonzalez, Trintignant | Ferrari |
| 1955 | Hawthorn, Bueb | Jaguar |
| 1956 | Flockhart, Sanderson | Jaguar |
| 1957 | Flockhart, Bueb | Jaguar |
| 1958 | Gendebien, Hill | Ferrari |
| 1959 | Salvadori, Shelby | Aston Martin |
| 1960 | Frere, Gendebien | Ferrari |
| 1961 | Hill, Gendebien | Ferrari |
| 1962 | Hill, Gendebien | Ferrari |
| 1963 | Scarfiotti, Bandini | Ferrari |
| 1964 | Guichet, Vaccarella | Ferrari |
| 1965 | Gregory, Rindt | Ferrari |
| 1966 | McLaren, Amon | Ford Mk II |
| 1967 | Gurney, Foyt | Ford Mk IV* |
| 1968 | Rodriguez, Bianchi | Ford G.T. 40 |
| 1969 | Ickx, Oliver | Ford G.T. 40 |

*Record 3,251.57 mi. (average 135.48 mph).

## Indianapolis 500-mile Event

| Year | Winner | Average speed mph |
|---|---|---|
| 1911 | R. Harroun | 74.59 |
| 1912 | J. Dawson | 78.72 |
| 1913 | J. Goux | 75.93 |
| 1914 | R. Thomas | 82.47 |
| 1915 | R. DePalma | 89.84 |
| 1916* | D. Resta | 84.00 |
| 1919† | H. Wilcox | 88.06 |
| 1920 | G. Chevrolet | 88.62 |
| 1921 | T. Milton | 89.62 |
| 1922 | J. Murphy | 94.48 |
| 1923 | T. Milton | 90.95 |
| 1924 | L. L. Corum<br>J. Boyer | 98.23 |
| 1925 | P. DePaolo | 101.13 |
| 1926‡ | F. Lockhart | 95.88 |
| 1927 | G. Souders | 97.54 |
| 1928 | L. Meyer | 99.48 |
| 1929 | R. Keech | 97.58 |
| 1930 | W. Arnold | 100.45 |
| 1931 | L. Schneider | 96.62 |
| 1932 | F. Frame | 104.14 |
| 1933 | L. Meyer | 104.16 |
| 1934 | W. Cummings | 104.86 |
| 1935 | K. Petillo | 106.24 |
| 1936 | L. Meyer | 109.07 |
| 1937 | W. Shaw | 113.58 |
| 1938 | F. Roberts | 117.20 |
| 1939 | W. Shaw | 115.03 |
| 1940 | W. Shaw | 114.28 |
| 1941 | F. Davis, M. Rose | 115.12 |
| 1946† | G. Robson | 114.80 |
| 1947 | M. Rose | 116.33 |
| 1948 | M. Rose | 119.81 |
| 1949 | W. Holland | 121.33 |
| 1950§ | J. Parsons | 124.00 |
| 1951 | L. Wallard | 126.24 |
| 1952 | T. Ruttman | 128.92 |
| 1953 | W. Vukovich | 128.74 |
| 1954 | W. Vukovich | 130.84 |
| 1955 | R. Sweikert | 128.21 |
| 1956 | P. Flaherty | 128.49 |
| 1957 | S. Hanks | 135.60 |
| 1958 | J. Bryan | 133.79 |
| 1959 | R. Ward | 135.86 |
| 1960 | J. Rathmann | 138.77 |
| 1961 | A. J. Foyt | 139.13 |
| 1962 | R. Ward | 140.29 |
| 1963 | P. Jones | 143.14 |
| 1964 | A. J. Foyt | 147.35 |
| 1965 | J. Clark | 150.68 |
| 1966 | G. Hill | 144.32 |
| 1967 | A. J. Foyt | 151.20 |
| 1968 | R. Unser | 152.88 |
| 1969 | M. Andretti | 156.87 |
| 1970 | A. Unser | 155.75 |

*300-mi. race. †No races during wartime years, 1917-18 and 1942-45. ‡Race called at 400 mi. (rain). §Race called at 345 mi. (rain).

## BADMINTON

### Men's International Champions (Thomas Cup)

| Year | Winner |
|---|---|
| 1948–49 | Malaya |
| 1951–52 | Malaya |
| 1954–55 | Malaya |
| 1957–58 | Indonesia |
| 1960–61 | Indonesia |
| 1963–64 | Indonesia |
| 1966–67 | Malaysia (by default) |
| 1969–70 | Indonesia |

### Ladies' International Champions (Uber Cup)

| Year | Winner |
|---|---|
| 1956–57 | U.S. |
| 1959–60 | U.S. |
| 1962–63 | U.S. |
| 1965–66 | Japan |
| 1968–69 | Japan |

BY COURTESY OF AMERICAN BADMINTON ASSOCIATION

CHAMPION BADMINTON PLAYER JUDITH HASHMAN, U.S. UBER CUP TEAM MEMBER AND RECORD WINNER OF ALL-ENGLAND AND U.S. OPEN SINGLES AND DOUBLES CHAMPIONSHIPS

WIDE WORLD

HOME RUN BY FRANK ROBINSON WON THE FOURTH GAME OF THE 1966 WORLD SERIES (BALTIMORE 1, LOS ANGELES 0); THE ORIOLES WON FOUR GAMES IN A ROW TO SWEEP THE SERIES

## BASEBALL

### BASEBALL'S HALL OF FAME

| Year elected | Members |
|---|---|
| 1936 | Ty Cobb, Honus Wagner, Babe Ruth, Christy Mathewson, Walter Johnson |
| 1937 | Nap Lajoie, Tris Speaker, Cy Young, George Wright, Morgan Bulkeley, Byron Bancroft Johnson, John McGraw, Connie Mack |
| 1938 | Grover Cleveland Alexander, Henry Chadwick, Alexander Cartwright |
| 1939 | George Sisler, Eddie Collins, Willie Keeler, Lou Gehrig, Albert Spalding, Cap Anson, Charles Comiskey, Buck Ewing, Charles Radbourn, William Cummings |
| 1942 | Rogers Hornsby |
| 1944 | Judge Kenesaw M. Landis |
| 1945 | Hugh Duffy, Jimmy Collins, Hugh Jennings, Ed Delahanty, Fred Clarke, Mike Kelly, Wilbert Robinson, Jim O'Rourke, Dan Brouthers, Roger Bresnahan |
| 1946 | Jesse Burkett, Frank Chance, Jack Chesbro, Johnny Evers, Clark Griffith, Tom McCarthy, Joe McGinnity, Eddie Plank, Joe Tinker, Rube Waddell, Ed Walsh |
| 1947 | Carl Hubbell, Frank Frisch, Mickey Cochrane, Lefty Grove |
| 1948 | Herb Pennock, Pie Traynor |
| 1949 | Charles Gehringer, Charles Nichols, Mordecai Brown |
| 1951 | Mel Ott, Jimmie Foxx |
| 1952 | Harry Heilmann, Paul Waner |
| 1953 | Dizzy Dean, Al Simmons, Chief Bender, Bobby Wallace, William Klem, Tom Connolly, Ed Barrow, Harry Wright |
| 1954 | Rabbit Maranville, Bill Dickey, Bill Terry |
| 1955 | Joe DiMaggio, Ted Lyons, Dazzy Vance, Gabby Hartnett, Ray Schalk, Frank (Home Run) Baker |
| 1956 | Hank Greenberg, Joe Cronin |
| 1957 | Joe McCarthy, Sam Crawford |
| 1959 | Zack Wheat |
| 1961 | Max Carey, William Hamilton |
| 1962 | Bob Feller, Jackie Robinson, Bill McKechnie, Edd Roush |
| 1963 | Eppa Rixey, Sam Rice, Elmer Flick, John Clarkson |
| 1964 | Luke Appling, Urban Faber, Burleigh Grimes, Tim Keefe, Heine Manush, Miller Huggins, John Montgomery Ward |
| 1965 | Pud Galvin |
| 1966 | Ted Williams, Casey Stengel |
| 1967 | Lloyd Waner, Branch Rickey, Charles Ruffing |
| 1968 | Kiki Cuyler, Goose Goslin, Ducky Medwick |
| 1969 | Stan Musial, Roy Campanella, Waite Hoyt, Stan Coveleski |
| 1970 | Lou Boudreau, Ford Frick, Earle Combs, Jesse Haines |

Source: "The Sporting News."

### MODERN MAJOR LEAGUE RECORDS*

| Individual | Single season | Lifetime |
|---|---|---|
| Games played | 165—Maury Wills, 1962 | 3,033—Ty Cobb, 1905–28 |
| Batting average | .424—Rogers Hornsby, 1924 | .367—Ty Cobb, 1905–28 |
| Hits | 257—George Sisler, 1920 | 4,191—Ty Cobb, 1905–28 |
| Home runs | 61—Roger Maris, 1961 | 714—Babe Ruth, 1914–35 |
| Runs batted in | 190—Hack Wilson, 1930 | 2,209—Babe Ruth, 1914–35 |
| Runs scored | 177—Babe Ruth, 1921 | 2,244—Ty Cobb, 1905–28 |
| Stolen bases | 104—Maury Wills, 1962 | 892—Ty Cobb, 1905–28 |
| Games won by pitcher | 41—Jack Chesbro, 1904 | 511—Cy Young, 1890–1911 |
| Best won and lost average | .947—El Roy Face, 1959 | No record |
| Strikeouts | 382—Sandy Koufax, 1965 | 3,508—Walter Johnson, 1907–27 |
| Earned-run average | 1.14—Walter Johnson, 1913 | 2.56—Grover Alexander, 1911–30 |
| **Team** | | |
| Batting average | .319—New York Giants, 1930 | |
| Fielding average | .985—Baltimore Orioles, 1964 | |
| Home runs | 240—New York Yankees, 1961 | |
| Runs scored | 1,067—New York Yankees, 1931 | |
| Games won | 116—Chicago Cubs, 1906 | |

*Modern major league records date back to 1900, before which it is felt differences in the rules and the play of the game make comparisons unrealistic. See also the article BASEBALL.

Source: "The Sporting News."

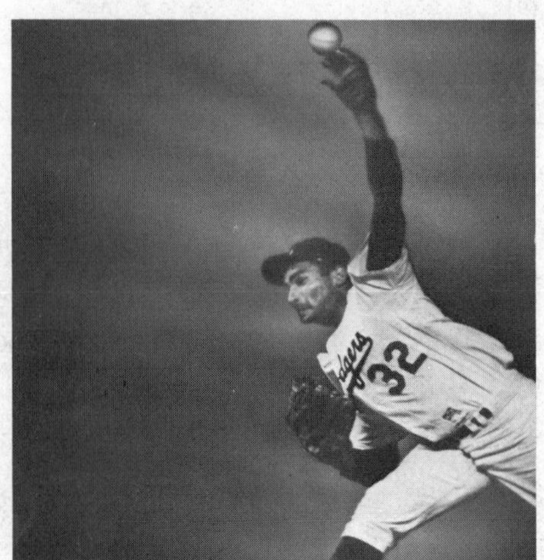

BILL BRIDGES

SANDY KOUFAX IN 1965 SET A SEASON'S RECORD OF 382 STRIKEOUTS

## RECORD OF WORLD SERIES COMPETITION*

| Year | Winning team and games won | | Losing team and games won | | Year | Winning team and games won | | Losing team and games won | |
|---|---|---|---|---|---|---|---|---|---|
| 1903 | Boston (A.L.) | 5 | Pittsburgh (N.L.) | 3 | 1937 | New York (A.L.) | 4 | New York (N.L.) | 1 |
| 1904 | No series | | | | 1938 | New York (A.L.) | 4 | Chicago (N.L.) | 0 |
| 1905 | New York (N.L.) | 4 | Philadelphia (A.L.) | 1 | 1939 | New York (A.L.) | 4 | Cincinnati (N.L.) | 0 |
| 1906 | Chicago (A.L.) | 4 | Chicago (N.L.) | 2 | 1940 | Cincinnati (N.L.) | 4 | Detroit (A.L.) | 3 |
| 1907† | Chicago (N.L.) | 4 | Detroit (A.L.) | 0 | 1941 | New York (A.L.) | 4 | Brooklyn (N.L.) | 1 |
| 1908 | Chicago (N.L.) | 4 | Detroit (A.L.) | 1 | 1942 | St. Louis (N.L.) | 4 | New York (A.L.) | 1 |
| 1909 | Pittsburgh (N.L.) | 4 | Detroit (A.L.) | 3 | 1943 | New York (A.L.) | 4 | St. Louis (N.L.) | 1 |
| 1910 | Philadelphia (A.L.) | 4 | Chicago (N.L.) | 1 | 1944 | St. Louis (N.L.) | 4 | St. Louis (A.L.) | 2 |
| 1911 | Philadelphia (A.L.) | 4 | New York (N.L.) | 2 | 1945 | Detroit (A.L.) | 4 | Chicago (N.L.) | 3 |
| 1912† | Boston (A.L.) | 4 | New York (N.L.) | 3 | 1946 | St. Louis (N.L.) | 4 | Boston (A.L.) | 3 |
| 1913 | Philadelphia (A.L.) | 4 | New York (N.L.) | 1 | 1947 | New York (A.L.) | 4 | Brooklyn (N.L.) | 3 |
| 1914 | Boston (N.L.) | 4 | Philadelphia (A.L.) | 0 | 1948 | Cleveland (A.L.) | 4 | Boston (N.L.) | 2 |
| 1915 | Boston (A.L.) | 4 | Philadelphia (N.L.) | 1 | 1949 | New York (A.L.) | 4 | Brooklyn (N.L.) | 1 |
| 1916 | Boston (A.L.) | 4 | Brooklyn (N.L.) | 1 | 1950 | New York (A.L.) | 4 | Philadelphia (N.L.) | 0 |
| 1917 | Chicago (A.L.) | 4 | New York (N.L.) | 2 | 1951 | New York (A.L.) | 4 | New York (N.L.) | 2 |
| 1918 | Boston (A.L.) | 4 | Chicago (N.L.) | 2 | 1952 | New York (A.L.) | 4 | Brooklyn (N.L.) | 3 |
| 1919 | Cincinnati (N.L.) | 5 | Chicago (A.L.) | 3 | 1953 | New York (A.L.) | 4 | Brooklyn (N.L.) | 2 |
| 1920 | Cleveland (A.L.) | 5 | Brooklyn (N.L.) | 2 | 1954 | New York (N.L.) | 4 | Cleveland (A.L.) | 0 |
| 1921 | New York (N.L.) | 5 | New York (A.L.) | 3 | 1955 | Brooklyn (N.L.) | 4 | New York (A.L.) | 3 |
| 1922† | New York (N.L.) | 4 | New York (A.L.) | 0 | 1956 | New York (A.L.) | 4 | Brooklyn (N.L.) | 3 |
| 1923 | New York (A.L.) | 4 | New York (N.L.) | 2 | 1957 | Milwaukee (N.L.) | 4 | New York (A.L.) | 3 |
| 1924 | Washington (A.L.) | 4 | New York (N.L.) | 3 | 1958 | New York (A.L.) | 4 | Milwaukee (N.L.) | 3 |
| 1925 | Pittsburgh (N.L.) | 4 | Washington (A.L.) | 3 | 1959 | Los Angeles (N.L.) | 4 | Chicago (A.L.) | 2 |
| 1926 | St. Louis (N.L.) | 4 | New York (A.L.) | 3 | 1960 | Pittsburgh (N.L.) | 4 | New York (A.L.) | 3 |
| 1927 | New York (A.L.) | 4 | Pittsburgh (N.L.) | 0 | 1961 | New York (A.L.) | 4 | Cincinnati (N.L.) | 1 |
| 1928 | New York (A.L.) | 4 | St. Louis (N.L.) | 0 | 1962 | New York (A.L.) | 4 | San Francisco (N.L.) | 3 |
| 1929 | Philadelphia (A.L.) | 4 | Chicago (N.L.) | 1 | 1963 | Los Angeles (N.L.) | 4 | New York (A.L.) | 0 |
| 1930 | Philadelphia (A.L.) | 4 | St. Louis (N.L.) | 2 | 1964 | St. Louis (N.L.) | 4 | New York (A.L.) | 3 |
| 1931 | St. Louis (N.L.) | 4 | Philadelphia (A.L.) | 3 | 1965 | Los Angeles (N.L.) | 4 | Minnesota (A.L.) | 3 |
| 1932 | New York (A.L.) | 4 | Chicago (N.L.) | 0 | 1966 | Baltimore (A.L.) | 4 | Los Angeles (N.L.) | 0 |
| 1933 | New York (N.L.) | 4 | Washington (A.L.) | 1 | 1967 | St. Louis (N.L.) | 4 | Boston (A.L.) | 3 |
| 1934 | St. Louis (N.L.) | 4 | Detroit (A.L.) | 3 | 1968 | Detroit (A.L.) | 4 | St. Louis (N.L.) | 3 |
| 1935 | Detroit (A.L.) | 4 | Chicago (N.L.) | 2 | 1969 | New York (N.L.) | 4 | Baltimore (A.L.) | 1 |
| 1936 | New York (A.L.) | 4 | New York (N.L.) | 2 | 1970 | Baltimore (A.L.) | 4 | Cincinnati (N.L.) | 1 |

*A.L.—American League; N.L.—National League. †One tied game.

**BASKETBALL.** Basketball originated in the United States (*see* the article BASKETBALL) where it is a major collegiate, amateur, and professional sport. In Olympic years since 1936 world amateur championships have been decided at the games (for table of champions *see* the article OLYMPIC GAMES); inter-Olympic world amateur championships are held under the auspices of the International Amateur Basketball Federation.

BOB COUSY, STAR OF THE BOSTON CELTICS, DRIVING PAST FRANK SELVY OF THE LOS ANGELES LAKERS IN THE FINAL GAME OF THE 1962 NBA CHAMPIONSHIP

WIDE WORLD

### World Amateur Championships

| Year | Winning Team | Place |
|---|---|---|
| 1951 | Argentina | Buenos Aires, Arg. |
| 1954 | U.S. (Central Peoria Cats) | Rio de Janeiro, Braz. |
| 1959 | Brazil | Santiago, Chile |
| 1963 | Brazil | Rio de Janeiro, Braz. |
| 1967 | U.S.S.R. | Montevideo, Urug. |
| 1970 | Italy | Ljubljana, Yugos. |

### Women's World Amateur Championships

| Year | Winning Team | Place |
|---|---|---|
| 1953 | U.S. | Santiago, Chile |
| 1957 | U.S. | Rio de Janeiro, Braz. |
| 1959 | U.S.S.R. | Moscow, U.S.S.R. |
| 1964 | U.S.S.R. | Lima, Peru |
| 1967 | U.S.S.R. | Prague, Czech. |

### Professional Champions National Basketball Association (NBA)

| Season | Champion |
|---|---|
| 1946–47 | Philadelphia Warriors |
| 1947–48 | Baltimore Bullets |
| 1948–49 | Minneapolis Lakers |
| 1949–50 | Minneapolis Lakers |
| 1950–51 | Rochester Royals |
| 1951–52 | Minneapolis Lakers |
| 1952–53 | Minneapolis Lakers |
| 1953–54 | Minneapolis Lakers |
| 1954–55 | Syracuse Nationals |
| 1955–56 | Philadelphia Warriors |
| 1956–57 | Boston Celtics |
| 1957–58 | St. Louis Hawks |
| 1958–59 | Boston Celtics |
| 1959–60 | Boston Celtics |
| 1960–61 | Boston Celtics |
| 1961–62 | Boston Celtics |
| 1962–63 | Boston Celtics |
| 1963–64 | Boston Celtics |
| 1964–65 | Boston Celtics |
| 1965–66 | Boston Celtics |
| 1966–67 | Philadelphia 76ers |
| 1967–68 | Boston Celtics |
| 1968–69 | Boston Celtics |
| 1969–70 | New York Knickerbockers |

### Amateur Athletic Union of the United States (AAU)

| Year | Champion |
|---|---|
| 1897 | 23d St. YMCA, New York |
| 1899–1900 | Knickerbocker A.C., New York |
| 1901 | Ravenswood YMCA, Chicago |
| 1904 | Buffalo (N.Y.) YMCA |
| 1910 | Portage, Wis., National Guard |
| 1913–14 | Cornell (Armour Playground), Chicago |
| 1915 | San Francisco Olympic Club |
| 1916 | University of Utah |
| 1917 | Illinois A.C. |
| 1919 | Los Angeles A.C. |
| 1920 | New York University |
| 1921 | Kansas City A.C. |
| 1922 | Lowe and Campbell, Kansas City |
| 1923 | Kansas City A.C. |
| 1924 | Butler University |
| 1925 | Washburn College |
| 1926–27 | Hillyards, St. Joseph, Mo. |
| 1928–29 | Cook Paint Co., Kansas City |
| 1930–32 | Henry Clothiers, Wichita, Kan. |
| 1933–34 | Diamond DX Oilers, Tulsa, Okla. |
| 1935 | So. Kansas Stage Lines, Kansas City |
| 1936 | Globe Refiners, McPherson, Kan. |
| 1937 | Denver (Colo.) Safeways |
| 1938 | Healey Motors, Kansas City |
| 1939 | Denver (Colo.) Nuggets |
| 1940 | Phillips Oilers |
| 1941 | 20th-Century Fox, Hollywood, Calif. |
| 1942 | American Legion, Denver, Colo. |
| 1943–48 | Phillips Oilers |
| 1949 | Oakland (Calif.) Bittners |
| 1950 | Phillips Oilers |
| 1951 | Stewart Chevrolets, San Francisco |
| 1952–54 | Peoria (Ill.) Cats |
| 1955 | Phillips Oilers |
| 1956 | Buchan Bakers, Seattle |

**Basketball (continued)**

| | |
|---|---|
| 1957 | U.S. Air Force |
| 1958 | Peoria (Ill.) Cats |
| 1959 | Wichita (Kan.) Vickers |
| 1960 | Peoria (Ill.) Cats |
| 1961 | Cleveland Pipers |
| 1962–63 | Phillips 66ers |
| 1964 | Goodyear Wingfoots |
| 1965 | Armed Forces All-Stars |
| 1966 | Ford Mustangs |
| 1967 | Akron Goodyears |
| 1968–70 | Armed Forces All-Stars |

### National Collegiate Athletic Association (NCAA)

**UNIVERSITY DIVISION**

| | |
|---|---|
| 1939 | Oregon |
| 1940 | Indiana |
| 1941 | Wisconsin |
| 1942 | Stanford |
| 1943 | Wyoming |
| 1944 | Utah |
| 1945–46 | Oklahoma A&M |
| 1947 | Holy Cross |
| 1948–49 | Kentucky |
| 1950 | CCNY |
| 1951 | Kentucky |
| 1952 | Kansas |
| 1953 | Indiana |
| 1954 | La Salle |
| 1955–56 | San Francisco |
| 1957 | North Carolina |
| 1958 | Kentucky |
| 1959 | California |
| 1960 | Ohio State |
| 1961–62 | Cincinnati |
| 1963 | Loyola (Ill.) |
| 1964–65 | UCLA |
| 1966 | Texas Western |
| 1967–70 | UCLA |

**COLLEGE DIVISION**

| | |
|---|---|
| 1957 | Wheaton |
| 1958 | South Dakota |
| 1959–60 | Evansville |
| 1961 | Wittenberg |
| 1962 | Mount St. Mary's |
| 1963 | South Dakota State |
| 1964–65 | Evansville |
| 1966 | Kentucky Wesleyan |
| 1967 | Winston-Salem |
| 1968–69 | Kentucky Wesleyan |
| 1970 | Kentucky State |

### National Invitation Tournament (NIT)

| | |
|---|---|
| 1938 | Temple |
| 1939 | Long Island U. |
| 1940 | Colorado |
| 1941 | Long Island U. |
| 1942 | West Virginia |
| 1943–44 | St. John's (Bklyn.) |
| 1945 | DePaul |
| 1946 | Kentucky |
| 1947 | Utah |
| 1948 | St. Louis |
| 1949 | San Francisco |
| 1950 | CCNY |
| 1951 | Brigham Young |
| 1952 | La Salle |
| 1953 | Seton Hall |
| 1954 | Holy Cross |
| 1955 | Duquesne |
| 1956 | Louisville |
| 1957 | Bradley |
| 1958 | Xavier (Cincinnati) |
| 1959 | St. John's (Bklyn.) |
| 1960 | Bradley |
| 1961 | Providence |
| 1962 | Dayton |
| 1963 | Providence |
| 1964 | Bradley |
| 1965 | St. John's (Bklyn.) |
| 1966 | Brigham Young |
| 1967 | Southern Illinois |
| 1968 | Dayton |
| 1969 | Temple |
| 1970 | Marquette |

## BILLIARDS.

**BILLIARDS.** World professional billiards competition, constituted in 1870, had largely died out by 1932 (*see* the article BILLIARDS); world three-cushion championships were discontinued after 1953; and snooker was so dominated by Joe Davis, 1927–46, that professional championships fell into abeyance. New world amateur championships were instituted in 1951; pocket billiards competition has continued from 1878.

### World Amateur Champions

| | |
|---|---|
| 1951 | R. Marshall; Austr. |
| 1952 | A. L. Driffield; U.K. |
| 1954 | T. Cleary; Austr. |
| 1958 | W. Jones; India |
| 1960 | J. H. Beetham; U.K. |
| 1962 | R. Marshall; Austr. |
| 1964 | W. Jones; India |
| 1967 | A. L. Driffield; U.K. |
| 1969 | J. Karnehm; U.K. |

**Records:**

Amateur record break: 702
R. Marshall; Austr., 1953
Professional record break: 4,137
W. Lindrum; Austr., 1932

### World Pocket Billiards Champions (since 1918)

| | |
|---|---|
| 1919–24 | R. Greenleaf |
| 1925 | F. Taberski |
| 1926 | R. Greenleaf |
| 1926 | E. Rudolph |
| 1926 | T. Hueston |
| 1927 | F. Taberski |
| 1927–28 | R. Greenleaf |
| 1928 | F. Taberski |
| 1929 | R. Greenleaf |
| 1929 | F. Taberski |
| 1930 | E. Rudolph |
| 1930–32 | R. Greenleaf |
| 1933–34 | E. Rudolph |
| 1935 | A. Ponzi |
| 1936 | J. Caras |
| 1937 | R. Greenleaf |
| 1938–39 | J. Caras |
| 1940 | A. Ponzi |
| 1941 | W. Mosconi |
| 1941 | E. Rudolph |
| 1942 | I. Crane |
| 1942 | W. Mosconi |
| 1943 | A. Ponzi |
| 1944–46 | W. Mosconi |
| 1946 | I. Crane |
| 1947–48 | W. Mosconi |
| 1949 | J. Caras |
| 1950–53 | W. Mosconi |
| 1955 | I. Crane |
| 1955* | W. Mosconi |
| 1963–64 | L. Lassiter |
| 1964 | A. Cranfield |
| 1965 | J. Balsis |
| 1966–67 | L. Lassiter |
| 1968 | I. Crane |
| 1969 | L. Lassiter |
| 1970 | I. Crane |

*No tournament 1956–62.

### Snooker

Record break (professional): 147
(maximum possible)
Joe Davis; U.K., 1955
Rex Williams; U.K., 1965
Record break (amateur): 122
R. Badar; India, 1964
Most match centuries (lifetime): 687
Joe Davis (retired 1965)

DAVID GAHR

JOSEPH BALSIS BEATING LUTHER LASSITER IN THE WORLD POCKET BILLIARDS CHAMPIONSHIP, NEW YORK CITY, 1965

## BOBSLEDDING

### World Champions Two-man Bobsleds

| Year | Team; Country | Time min.:sec. | Place |
|---|---|---|---|
| 1931 | H. Kilian, S. Huber; Ger. | 7:34.20 | Oberhof, Ger. |
| 1932* | J. H. Stevens, C. Stevens; U.S. | 8:14.74 | Lake Placid, U.S. |
| 1933 | A. Papana, D. Hubert; Rum. | 5:50.14 | Schreiberhau, Ger. |
| 1934 | A. Frim, V. Dimitriescu; Rum. | 9:31.30 | Engelberg, Switz. |
| 1935 | R. Capadrutt, E. Diener; Switz. | 3:31.72 | Igls, Aus. |
| 1936* | I. E. Brown, A. M. Washbond; U.S. | 5:29.29 | Garmisch-Partenkirchen, Ger. |
| 1937 | F. McEvoy, B. H. Black; U.K. | 6:09.53 | Cortina d'Ampezzo, It. |
| 1938 | I. Fischer, R. Thielecke; Ger. | 5:34.0 | St. Moritz, Switz. |
| 1939 | Baron Lunden, J. Kuffer; Belg. | 5:29.20 | St. Moritz, Switz. |
| 1947 | F. Feierabend, S. Wasser; Switz. | 5:27.10 | St. Moritz, Switz. |
| 1948* | F. Endrich, F. Waller; Switz. | 5:29.20 | St. Moritz, Switz. |
| 1949 | F. Endrich, F. Waller; Switz. | 5:18.52 | Lake Placid, U.S. |
| 1950 | F. Feierabend, S. Wasser; Switz. | 5:57.73 | Cortina d'Ampezzo, It. |
| 1951 | A. Ostler, L. Nieberl; Ger. | 5:11.94 | L'Alpe d'Huez, Fr. |
| 1952* | A. Ostler, L. Nieberl; Ger. | 5:25.54 | Oslo, Nor. |
| 1953 | F. Endrich, F. Stockli; Switz. | 5:01.90 | Garmisch-Partenkirchen, Ger. |
| 1954 | G. Scheibmeier, A. Zambelli; It. | 5:47.08 | Cortina d'Ampezzo, It. |
| 1955 | F. Feierabend, H. Warbourton; Switz. | 5:33.28 | St. Moritz, Switz. |
| 1956* | L. D. Costa, G. Conti; It. | 5:30.14 | Cortina d'Ampezzo, It. |
| 1957 | E. Monti, R. Alverá; It. | 5:17.94 | St. Moritz, Switz. |
| 1958 | E. Monti, R. Alverá; It. | 5:05.78 | Garmisch-Partenkirchen, Ger. |
| 1959 | E. Monti, R. Alverá; It. | 5:23.86 | St. Moritz, Switz. |
| 1960 | E. Monti, R. Alverá; It. | 5:17.54 | Cortina d'Ampezzo, It. |
| 1961 | E. Monti, S. Siorpaes; It. | 4:42.67 | Lake Placid, U.S. |
| 1962 | R. Ruatti, E. de Lorenzo; It. | 5:03.73 | Garmisch-Partenkirchen, Ger. |
| 1963 | E. Monti, S. Zardini; It. | 4:27.04 | Innsbruck, Aus. |
| 1964* | A. Nash, R. Dixon; U.K. | 4:21.90 | Innsbruck, Aus. |
| 1965 | A. Nash, R. Dixon; U.K. | 5:11.30 | St. Moritz, Switz. |
| 1966 | E. Monti, S. Siorpaes; It. | 5:07.52 | Cortina d'Ampezzo, It. |
| 1967 | E. Thaler, R. Durnthaler; Aus. | 1:55.54† | L'Alpe d'Huez, Fr. |
| 1968* | E. Monti, L. de Paolis; It. | 4:41.54 | L'Alpe d'Huez, Fr. |
| 1969 | N. De Zordo, A. Frassinelli; It. | 4:31.73 | Lake Placid, U.S. |
| 1970 | H. Floth, J. Bader; W. Ger. | 5:05.39 | St. Moritz, Switz. |

*Olympic champions recognized as world champions. †Curtailed: two heats.

## World Champions Four-man Bobsleds

| Year | Country; Team | Time min.:sec. | Place |
|---|---|---|---|
| 1924 | Switzerland (E. Scherrer, A. Neveu, A. Schlaeppi, H. Schlaeppi) | 5:45.54 | Chamonix, Fr. |
| 1927 | U.K. (N. C. Martineau, P. E. Diggle, N. A. Milles, P. Reid, E. R. Hall)† | 6:09.30 | St. Moritz, Switz. |
| 1928* | United States (W. Fiske, N. Taker, C. Mason, C. Gray, P. Parke)† | 3:20.50 | St. Moritz, Switz. |
| 1930 | Italy (F. Zanietta, G. Giasini, A. Dorini, G. Rossi) | 11:29.95 | Caux, Switz. |
| 1931 | Germany (W. Zahn, R. Schmidt, F. Bock, E. Hinderfeld) | 5:15.50 | St. Moritz, Switz. |
| 1932* | United States (W. Fiske, E. Eagan, C. Gray, J. O'Brien) | 7:53.68 | Lake Placid, U.S. |
| 1934 | Germany (H. Kilian, F. Schwarz, H. Valta, S. Huber) | 5:32.75 | Garmisch-Partenkirchen, Ger. |
| 1935 | Germany (H. Kilian, A. Gruber, H. Valta, F. Schwarz) | 5:33 | St. Moritz, Switz. |
| 1936* | Switzerland (P. Musy, A. Gartmann, C. Bouvier, J. Beerli) | 5:19.85 | Garmisch-Partenkirchen, Ger. |
| 1937 | United Kingdom (F. McEvoy, D. S. Looker, C. P. Green, B. H. Black) | 5:08.50 | St. Moritz, Switz. |
| 1938 | United Kingdom (F. McEvoy, D. S. Looker, C. P. Green, C. E. W. C. Macintosh) | 5:40.32 | Garmisch-Partenkirchen, Ger. |
| 1939 | Switzerland (F. Feierabend, H. Cattani, A. Hoerning, J. Beerli) | 5:30.37 | Cortina d'Ampezzo, It. |
| 1947 | Switzerland (F. Feierabend, F. Waller, F. Endrich, S. Wasser) | 5:16.20 | St. Moritz, Switz. |
| 1948* | United States (F. Tyler, P. Martin, E. Rimkus, W. D'Amico) | 5:20.10 | St. Moritz, Switz. |
| 1949 | United States (S. Benham, P. Martin, W. Casey, W. D'Amico) | 4:56.29 | Lake Placid, U.S. |
| 1950 | United States (S. Benham, P. Martin, J. Atkinson, W. D'Amico) | 5:28.72 | Cortina d'Ampezzo, It. |
| 1951 | Germany (A. Ostler, L. Nieberl, X. Leitl, M. Possinger) | 2:24.98 | L'Alpe d'Huez, Fr. |
| 1952* | Germany (A. Ostler, L. Nieberl, F. Kuhn, F. Kemser) | 5:07.84 | Oslo, Nor. |
| 1953 | United States (L. Johnson, P. Biesiadecki, H. Miller, J. Smith) | 2:28.79 | Garmisch-Partenkirchen, Ger. |
| 1954 | Switzerland (F. Feierabend, G. Diener, H. Warbourton, H. Angst) | 5:15.94 | Cortina d'Ampezzo, It. |
| 1955 | Switzerland (F. Kapus, G. Diener, R. Alt, H. Angst) | 5:10.52 | St. Moritz, Switz. |
| 1956* | Switzerland (F. Kapus, G. Diener, R. Alt, H. Angst) | 5:10.44 | Cortina d'Ampezzo, It. |
| 1957 | Switzerland (H. Zoller, H. Theier, R. Küderli, H. Lev) | 5:11.45 | St. Moritz, Switz. |
| 1958 | Germany (H. Roesch, A. Hammer, W. Haller, T. Bauer) | 4:49.33 | Garmisch-Partenkirchen, Ger. |
| 1959 | United States (A. Tyler, G. Sheffield, P. Vooris, T. Butler) | 5:10.82 | St. Moritz, Switz. |
| 1960 | Italy (E. Monti, R. Nordi, B. Regoni, S. Siorpaes) | 5:04.75 | Cortina d'Ampezzo, It. |
| 1961 | Italy (E. Monti, R. Nordi, B. Regoni, S. Siorpaes) | 2:18.40 | Lake Placid, U.S. |
| 1962 | Germany (F. Schelle, O. Goebl, S. Sterff, L. Siebert) | 2:33.66 | Garmisch-Partenkirchen, Ger. |
| 1963 | Italy (S. Zardini, R. Bonagura, F. D. Torre, R. Mocellini) | 4:19.34 | Innsbruck, Aus. |
| 1964* | Canada (V. Emery, P. Kirby, D. Anakin, J. Emery) | 4:14.46 | Innsbruck, Aus. |
| 1965 | Canada (V. Emery, P. Kirby, G. Presley, M. Young) | 5:17.78 | St. Moritz, Switz. |
| 1966 | Cancelled owing to fatal accident | — | Cortina d'Ampezzo, It. |
| 1967 | Abandoned owing to poor state of the track | — | L'Alpe d'Huez, Fr. |
| 1968* | Italy (E. Monti, R. Zandonella, M. Armano, L. de Paolis) | 2:17.39 | L'Alpe d'Huez, Fr. |
| 1969 | W. Germany (W. Zimmerer, S. Geisreiter, W. Steinbauer, P. Utzschneider) | 4:20.75 | Lake Placid, U.S. |
| 1970 | Italy (N. de Zordo, R. Zandonella, M. Armano, L. de Paolis) | 4:55.44 | St. Moritz, Switz. |

*Olympic champions recognized as world champions. †5-man team. Note: Olympic bobsled events were not staged in 1960.

U.S. SLED DRIVEN BY STANLEY BENHAM WINNING WORLD FOUR-MAN BOB-SLED CHAMPIONSHIP, LAKE PLACID, N.Y., 1949

U.P.I. COMPIX

**BOWLING** (Tenpins). The modern game of tenpins became regularized with the formation of the American Bowling Congress (ABC) in 1895. The ABC Championships were instituted in 1901 and currently represent the highest and most competitive standards in the world.

## All-time Records for League and Tournament Play

| Event | Holder | Record | Year |
|---|---|---|---|
| Individual total | A. Brandt | 886 | 1939 |
| All-events score | F. Benkovic | 2,259 | 1932 |
| Doubles total | L. Celestino, J. Troyano | 1,609 | 1963 |
| Team total | Budweiser Beer, St. Louis | 3,858 | 1958 |
| Most sanctioned 300 games | E. Mesger | 22 | 1969 |

## World Championships

| Year | Place | Event | Winner; Country |
|---|---|---|---|
| 1967 | Malmö, Swed. | Men's singles | D. Pond; U.K. |
| | | Men's doubles | D. Pond, J. Morley; U.K. |
| | | Men's fives | Finland |
| | | Men's eights | United States |
| | | Women's singles | H. Weston; U.S. |
| | | Women's doubles | T. Orozco, A. Sarabia; Mex. |
| | | Women's fours | Finland |
| | | Women's fives | Finland |

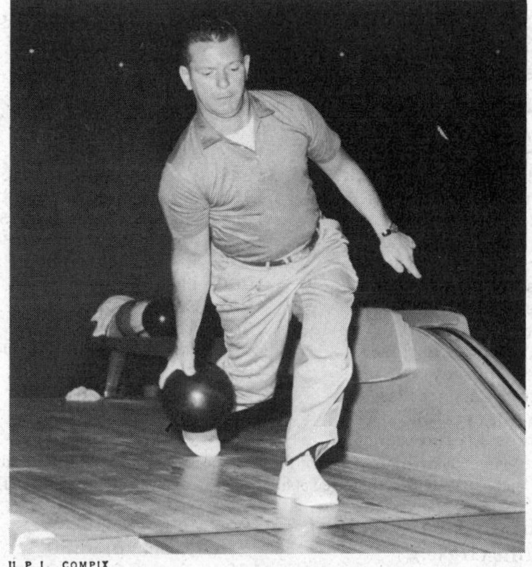

U.P.I. COMPIX

EDWARD LUBANSKI, ALL-EVENTS AND SINGLES BOWLING CHAMPION OF 1959

| All-events Champions (regular division) | | | Singles Champions (regular division) | |
|---|---|---|---|---|
| Year | Holder | Record | Holder | Record |
| 1946 | J. Wilman | 2,054 | L. Rollick | 737 |
| 1947 | J. McMahon | 1,965 | J. McMahon | 740 |
| 1948 | N. Day | 1,979 | L. Protich | 721 |
| 1949 | J. Small | 1,941 | B. Rusche | 716 |
| 1950 | F. Santore | 1,981 | E. Leins | 757 |
| 1951 | T. Lindemann | 2,005 | L. Jouglard | 775* |
| 1952 | S. Nagy | 2,065 | A. Sharkey | 758 |
| 1953 | F. Santore | 1,994 | F. Santore | 749 |
| 1954 | B. Lewis | 1,985 | T. Sparando | 723 |
| 1955 | F. Bujack | 1,993 | E. Gerzine | 738 |
| 1956 | B. Lillard | 2,018 | G. Wade | 744 |
| 1957 | J. Spalding | 2,088 | B. Allen | 729 |
| 1958 | A. Faragalli | 2,043 | E. Shay | 733 |
| 1959 | E. Lubanski | 2,116 | E. Lubanski | 764 |
| 1960 | V. Lucci | 1,985 | P. Kulbaga | 726 |
| 1961 | L. Karan | 1,960 | L. Spooner | 726 |
| 1962 | B. Young | 2,015 | A. Renaldy | 720 |
| 1963 | B. Oswalt | 2,055 | F. Delello | 744 |
| 1964 | L. Zikes | 2,001 | J. Stefanich | 726 |
| 1965 | T. Hathaway | 1,922 | K. Roeth | 700 |
| 1966 | J. Wilcox, Jr. | 2,004 | D. Chapman | 761 |
| 1967 | G. Lewis | 2,010 | F. Perry | 723 |
| 1968 | V. Mazzanti | 1,971 | W. Kowalski | 738 |
| 1969 | E. Jackson | 1,988 | G. Campbell | 751 |

*ABC Tournament Record.

**BOWLS** (Lawn Bowls). Bowls (lawn bowls or bowling on the green) is an organized sport in the United Kingdom, Australia, New Zealand, South Africa, Canada, and the United States, and accredited teams from these countries have exchanged visits intermittently (*see* the article Bowls). The Inaugural World Championships were staged at Sydney, Austr., in 1966.

### World Championships

| Year | Place | Event | Winner; Country |
|---|---|---|---|
| 1966 | Sydney, Austr. | Singles | D. Bryant; U.K. |
| | | Pairs | G. Kelly, A. Palm; Austr. |
| | | Triples | Australia (J. Dobbie, D. Collins, A. Johnson) |
| | | Fours | New Zealand |
| | | Team (Leonard Trophy) | Australia |

SPORT AND GENERAL FROM PICTORIAL PARADE INC.

DAVID BRYANT, UNITED KINGDOM, WINNER OF THE INAUGURAL BOWLS SINGLES CHAMPIONSHIP, 1966

**BOXING.** There is no world governing body in professional boxing, therefore the status of "world champions" has varied from those globally recognized down to those recognized in one continent or even in a minority of U.S. states. In the compilation below claimants with a disputed status have been italicized. Nationalities relate to the country of birth.

### World Heavyweight Champions

| Year | Champion |
|---|---|
| 1892 | James J. Corbett*; U.S. |
| 1897 | Bob Fitzsimmons; U.K. |
| 1899 | James J. Jeffries; U.S. |
| 1905 | Marvin Hart; U.S. |
| 1906 | Tommy Burns; Can. |
| 1908 | Jack Johnson; U.S. |
| 1915 | Jess Willard; U.S. |
| 1919 | Jack Dempsey; U.S. |
| 1926 | Gene Tunney; U.S. |
| 1930 | Max Schmeling; Ger. |
| 1932 | Jack Sharkey; U.S. |
| 1933 | Primo Carnera; It. |
| 1934 | Max Baer; U.S. |
| 1935 | James J. Braddock; U.S. |
| 1937 | Joe Louis; U.S. |
| 1949 | Ezzard Charles; U.S. |
| 1951 | Jersey Joe Walcott; U.S. |
| 1952 | Rocky Marciano; U.S. |
| 1956 | Floyd Patterson; U.S. |
| 1959 | Ingemar Johansson; Swed. |
| 1960 | Floyd Patterson; U.S. |
| 1962 | Sonny Liston; U.S. |
| 1964 | Cassius Clay (Muhammad Ali)†; U.S. |
| 1965 | *Ernie Terrell*‡; U.S. |
| 1968 | *Joe Frazier;* U.S. |
| 1968 | *Jimmy Ellis;* U.S. |
| 1970 | Joe Frazier; U.S. |

*Knocked out John L. Sullivan (U.S.), last of the bare-knuckle champions, in 21 rounds at New Orleans, La., on Sept. 7, 1892. †Deprived of title in 1967. ‡Defeated by Clay on Feb. 6, 1967.

### World Light-Heavyweight Champions (175 lb.)

| Year | Champion |
|---|---|
| 1903 | Jack Root; Aus. |
| 1903 | George Gardner; Ire. |
| 1903 | Bob Fitzsimmons; U.K. |
| 1905 | "Philadelphia" Jack O'Brien; U.S. |
| 1907 | *Tommy Burns;* Can. |
| 1914 | Jack Dillon; U.S. |
| 1916 | Battling Levinsky; U.S. |
| 1920 | Georges Carpentier; Fr. |
| 1922 | Battling Siki; Sen. |
| 1923 | Mike McTigue; Ire. |
| 1925 | Paul Berlenback; U.S. |
| 1926 | Jack Delaney; Can. |
| 1927 | Tommy Loughran; U.S. |
| 1930 | Jimmy Slattery; U.S. |
| 1930 | Maxie Rosenbloom; U.S. |
| 1934 | Bob Olin; U.S. |
| 1935 | John Henry Lewis; U.S. |
| 1939 | *Melino Bettina*; U.S. |
| 1939 | *Len Harvey;* U.K. |
| 1939 | *Billy Conn;* U.S. |
| 1941 | *Anton Christoforidis;* Gr. |
| 1941 | *Gus Lesnevich;* U.S. |
| 1942 | *Freddie Mills;* U.K. |
| 1946 | Gus Lesnevich; U.S. |
| 1948 | Freddie Mills; U.K. |
| 1950 | Joey Maxim; U.S. |
| 1952 | Archie Moore; U.S. |
| 1962 | Harold Johnson; U.S. |
| 1963 | Willie Pastrano; U.S. |
| 1965 | José Torres; P.R. |
| 1966 | Dick Tiger; Nig. |
| 1968 | Bob Foster; U.S. |

### World Middleweight Champions

(158 lb. until raised to 160 lb. in 1915)

| Year | Champion |
|---|---|
| 1884 | Jack Dempsey (The Nonpareil); Ire. |
| 1891 | Bob Fitzsimmons; U.K. |
| 1898 | Tommy Ryan; U.S. |
| 1907 | *Stanley Ketchel;* U.S. |
| 1908 | Stanley Ketchel; U.S. |
| 1908 | Billy Papke; U.S. |
| 1908 | Stanley Ketchel; U.S. |
| 1911 | *Bily Papke;* U.S. |
| 1913 | *Fralnk Klaus;* U.S. |
| 1913 | *George Chip;* U.S. |
| 1914 | *Al McCoy;* U.S. |
| 1917 | *Mike O'Dowd;* U.S. |
| 1920 | *Johnny Wilson;* U.S. |
| 1921 | Johnny Wilson; U.S. |
| 1923 | Harry G reb; U.S. |
| 1926 | Tiger Flowers; U.S. |
| 1926 | Mickey Walker; U.S. |
| 1931 | *Gorilla Jones;* U.S. |
| 1932 | *Marcel Thil;* Fr. |
| 1932 | *Ben Jeby;* U.S. |
| 1933 | *Lou Brouillard;* Can. |
| 1933 | *Vince Dundee;* It. |
| 1934 | *Teddy Yarosz;* U.S. |
| 1935 | *Babe Risko;* U.S. |
| 1936 | *Freddy Skeele;* U.S. |
| 1937 | *Fred Apostoli;* U.S. |
| 1938 | *Al Hostak;* U.S. |
| 1938 | *Solly Krieger;* U.S. |
| 1939 | *Al Hostak;* U.S. |
| 1939 | *Ceferino Garcia;* Phil. |
| 1940 | *Tony Zale;* U.S. |
| 1940 | *Ken Overlin;* U.S. |
| 1941 | *Billy Soose;* U.S. |
| 1941 | Tony Zale; U.S. |
| 1947 | Rocky Graziano; U.S. |
| 1948 | Tony Zale; U.S. |

VICENTE SALDIVAR (LEFT) RETAINED THE WORLD FEATHERWEIGHT BOXING CHAMPIONSHIP BY DEFEATING JAPAN'S MITSUNORI SEKI, 1966
WIDE WORLD

"SUGAR" RAY ROBINSON AFTER KNOCKOUT OF CARL "BOBO" OLSON TO REGAIN WORLD MIDDLE-WEIGHT BOXING CHAMPIONSHIP, 1955
U.P.I. COMPIX

1948 Marcel Cerdan; Alg.
1949 Jake La Motta; U.S.
1951 Ray Robinson; U.S.
1951 Randy Turpin; U.K.
1951 Ray Robinson; U.S.
1953 *Carl Olson;* U.S.
1955 Ray Robinson; U.S.
1957 Gene Fullmer; U.S.
1957 Ray Robinson; U.S.
1957 Carmen Basilio; U.S.
1958 Ray Robinson; U.S.
1959 Gene Fullmer; U.S.
1960 *Paul Pender;* U.S.
1961 *Terry Downes;* U.K.
1962 *Paul Pender;* U.S.
1962 Dick Tiger; Nig.
1963 Joey Giardello; U.S.
1965 Dick Tiger; Nig.
1966 Emile Griffith; U.S.
1967 Nino Benvenuti; It.
1967 Emile Griffith; U.S.
1968 Nino Benvenuti; It.

### World Welterweight Champions
(147 lb. but 145 lb. in the early years)

1892 "Mysterious" Billy Smith; U.S.
1894 Tommy Ryan; U.S.
1896 Kid McKoy; U.S.
1897 "Mysterious" Billy Smith; U.S.
1900 Rube Ferns; U.S.
1900 Matty Matthews; U.S.
1901 Rube Ferns; U.S.
1901 Joe Walcott; Barbados
1904 Dixie Kid; U.S.
1904 *Joe Walcott;* Barbados
1906 Honey Mellody; U.S.
1907 Mike Twin Sullivan; U.S.
1910–15 Title vacant
1915 Ted Kid Lewis; U.K.
1919 Jack Britton; U.S.
1922 Mickey Walker; U.S.
1926 Pete Latzo; U.S.
1927 Joe Dundee; It.
1928 *Young Jack Thompson;* U.S.
1929 Jackie Fields; U.S.
1930 Young Jack Thompson; U.S.
1930 Tommy Freeman; U.S.
1931 Young Jack Thompson; U.S.
1931 Lou Brouillard; Can.
1932 Jackie Fields; U.S.
1933 Young Corbett III; It.
1933 Jimmy McLarnin; U.K.
1934 Jimmy McLarnin; U.K.
1934 Barney Ross; U.S.
1935 Barney Ross; U.S.
1938 Henry Armstrong; U.S.
1940 Fritzie Zivic; U.S.
1941 Freddie Cochrane; U.S.
1946 Marty Servo; U.S.
1946 Ray Robinson; U.S.
1951 *Johnny Bratton;* U.S.
1951 Kid Gavilan; Cuba
1954 Johnny Saxton; U.S.
1955 Tony DeMarco; U.S.
1955 Carmen Basilio; U.S.
1956 Johnny Saxton; U.S.
1956 Carmen Basilio; U.S.
1958 Virgil Akins; U.S.
1958 Don Jordan; U.S.
1960 Benny Paret; Cuba
1961 Emile Griffith; U.S.
1961 Benny Paret; Cuba
1962 Emile Griffith; U.S.
1963 Luis Rodriguez; Cuba
1963 Emile Griffith; U.S.
1966 Curtis Cokes; U.S.
1969 José Napoles; Mex.

### World Lightweight Champions
(135 lb. but 133 lb. in the early years)

1896 George (Kid) Lavigne; U.S.
1899 Frank Erne; Switz.
1902 Joe Gans; U.S.
1908 Battling Nelson; Den.
1910 Ad Wolgast; U.S.
1912 Willie Ritchie; U.S.
1914 Freddie Welsh; U.K.
1917 Benny Leonard; U.S.
1925 Jimmy Goodrich; U.S.
1925 Rocky Kansas; U.S.
1926 Sammy Mandell; U.S.
1930 Al Singer; U.S.
1930 Tony Canzoneri; U.S.
1933 Barney Ross; U.S.
1935 Tony Canzoneri; U.S.
1936 Lou Ambers; U.S.
1938 Henry Armstrong; U.S.
1939 Lou Ambers; U.S.
1940 Lew Jenkins; U.S.
1941 Sammy Angott; U.S.
1942 *Beau Jack;* U.S.
1943 *Bob Montgomery;* U.S.
1943 *Beau Jack;* U.S.
1944 *Bob Montgomery;* U.S.
1944 *Juan Zurita;* Mex.
1945 *Ike Williams;* U.S.
1947 Ike Williams; U.S.
1951 Jimmy Carter; U.S.
1952 Lauro Salas; Mex.
1952 Jimmy Carter; U.S.
1954 Paddy DeMarco; U.S.
1954 Jimmy Carter; U.S.
1955 Wallace Bud Smith; U.S.
1956 Joe Brown; U.S.
1962 Carlos Ortiz; P.R.
1965 Ismael Laguna; Pan.
1965 Carlos Ortiz; P.R.
1968 Carlos Cruz; Dom. Rep.
1969 Mando Ramos; U.S.

### World Featherweight Champions
(126 lb. but 118 lb. and 122 lb. in the early years)

1892 George Dixon; Can.
1896 Frank Erne (122 lb.); Switz.
1897 George Dixon (122 lb.); Can.
1897 Solly Smith (120 lb.); U.S.
1900 Terry McGovern (118 lb.); U.S.
1901 Young Corbett II (126 lb.); U.S.
1904 *Abe Attell* (122 lb.); U.S.
1904 *Tommy Sullivan* (122 lb.); U.S.
1908 *Abe Attell;* U.S.
1912 Johnny Kilbane; U.S.
1923 Eugene Criqui; Fr.
1923 Johnny Dundee; It.
1925 Louis (Kid) Kaplan; Russia
1927 *Benny Bass;* Russia
1928 Tony Canzoneri; U.S.
1928 Andre Routis; Fr.
1929 Battling Battalino; U.S.
1932 *Tommy Paul;* U.S.
1932 *Kid Chocolate;* Cuba
1933 *Freddie Miller;* U.S.
1936 *Petey Sarron;* U.S.
1937 *Henry Armstrong;* U.S.
1938 *Joey Archibald;* U.S.
1940 *Harry Jeffra;* U.S.
1941 *Joey Archibald;* U.S.
1941 *Chalky Wright;* Mex.
1942 *Willie Pep;* U.S.
1946 Willie Pep; U.S.
1948 Sandy Saddler; U.S.
1949 Willie Pep; U.S.
1950 Sandy Saddler; U.S.
1957 Hogan Bassey; Nig.
1959 Davey Moore; U.S.
1963 Sugar Ramos; Cuba
1964 Vicente Saldivar; Mex.
1968 *Howard Winstone;* U.K.
1968 *Raul Rojas;* U.S.
1968 *José Legra;* Sp.
1968 *Sho Saijyo;* Jap.
1969 Johnny Famechon; Austr.

### World Bantamweight Champions
(118 lb. but 105, 112, and 116 lb. in the early years)

1890 George Dixon; Can.
1892 *Billy Plimmer;* U.K.
1894 *Jimmy Barry* (112 lb.); U.S.
1895 *Pedlar Palmar;* U.K.
1899 Terry McGovern; U.S.
1901 *Harry Forbes;* U.S.
1903 Frankie Neil; U.S.
1904 Joe Bowker; U.K.
1904 *Digger Stanley;* U.K.
1905 Jimmy Walsh; U.S.
1907 Title vacant
1908 Johnny Coulon; Can.
1914 Kid Williams; Den.
1915 *Johnny Ertle;* Aus.
1917 Pete Herman; U.S.
1920 Joe Lynch; U.S.
1921 Pete Herman; U.S.
1921 Johnny Buff; U.S.
1922 Joe Lynch; U.S.
1924 Abe Goldstein; U.S.
1924 Eddie Martin; U.S.
1925 Charlie Rosenberg; U.S.
1927 *Bud Taylor;* U.S.
1929 *Al Brown;* Pan.
1932 Al Brown; Pan.
1934 *Sixto Escobar;* P.R.
1935 *Baltasar Sangchili;* Sp.
1935 *Lou Salica;* U.S.
1935 *Sixto Escobar;* P.R.
1937 *Harry Jeffra;* U.S.
1938 *Sixto Escobar;* P.R.
1941 Lou Salica; U.S.
1942 Manuel Ortiz; Mex.
1947 Harold Dade; U.S.
1947 Manuel Ortiz; Mex
1950 Vic Toweel; S.Af.
1952 Jimmy Carruthers; Austr.
1954 Robert Cohen; Alg.
1956 Mario d'Agata; It.
1957 Alphonse Halimi; Alg.
1959 Jose Becerra; Mex.
1960 *Alphonse Halimi;* Alg.
1960 *Eder Jofre;* Braz.
1961 Eder Jofre; Braz.
1965 Fighting Harada; Jap.
1968 Lionel Rose; Austr.
1969 Ruben Olivares; Mex.

### World Flyweight Champions
(112 lb.)

1913 Sid Smith; U.K.
1913 Bill Ladbury; U.K.
1914 Percy Jones; U.K.
1914 Joe Symonds; U.K.
1916 Jimmy Wilde; U.K.
1923 Pancho Villa; Phil.
1925 Fidel la Barba; U.S.
1927 Izzy Schwartz; U.S.
1930 Midget Wolgast; U.S.
1930 Frankie Genaro; U.S.
1931 Young Perez; Tun.
1932 Jackie Brown; U.K.
1935 Benny Lynch; U.K.
1938 Peter Kane; U.K.
1943 Jackie Paterson; U.K.
1947 Rinty Monaghan; U.K.
1950 Terry Allen; U.K.
1950 Dado Marino; Hawaii
1952 Yoshio Shirai; Jap.
1954 Pascual Perez; Arg.
1960 Pone Kingpetch; Thai.
1962 Fighting Harada; Jap.
1963 Pone Kingpetch; Thai.
1963 Hiroyuki Ebihara; Jap.
1964 Pone Kingpetch; Thai.
1965 Salvatore Burruni; It.
1966 Walter McGowan; U.K.
1966 *Chartchai Chionoi;* Thai.
1969 Efren Torres; Mex.
1969 Hiroyuki Ebihara; Jap.
1969 Bernabe Villacampo; Phil.

## BRIDGE

### World Team Championship (The Bermuda Bowl)

| Years | Winner | Place |
|---|---|---|
| 1950 | U.S. | Bermuda |
| 1951 | U.S. | Naples, It. |
| 1953 | U.S. | New York, U.S. |
| 1954 | U.S. | Monte Carlo, Monaco |
| 1955 | Great Britain | New York, U.S. |
| 1956 | France | Paris, Fr. |
| 1957 | Italy | New York, U.S. |
| 1958 | Italy | Como, It. |
| 1959 | Italy | New York, U.S. |
| 1961 | Italy | Buenos Aires, Arg. |
| 1962 | Italy | New York, U.S. |
| 1963 | Italy | St. Vincent, It. |
| 1965 | Italy | Buenos Aires, Arg. |
| 1966 | Italy | St. Vincent, It. |
| 1967 | Italy | Miami Beach, U.S. |
| 1969 | Italy | Rio de Janeiro, Braz. |

### World Bridge Olympiad

| Years | Winner | Place |
|---|---|---|
| 1960 | France | Turin, It. |
| 1964 | Italy | New York, U.S. |
| 1968 | Italy | Deauville, Fr. |

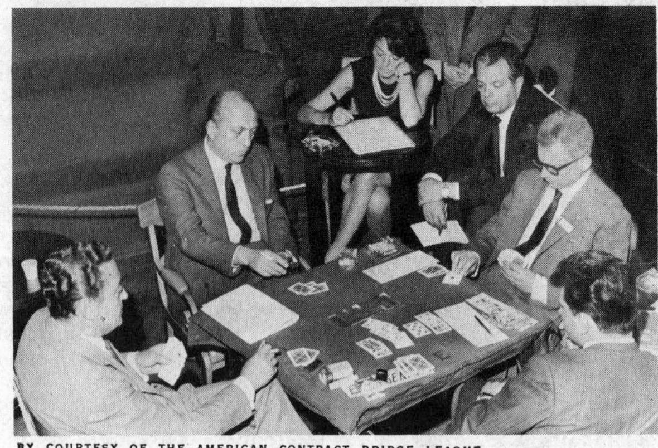

BY COURTESY OF THE AMERICAN CONTRACT BRIDGE LEAGUE

WORLD BRIDGE TEAM CHAMPIONSHIP AT BUENOS AIRES, 1965, BETWEEN THE WINNING ITALIAN TEAM AND THE ARGENTINE TEAM

**CANOEING.** The Olympic canoeing events from 1936 are regarded by the International Canoe Federation (ICF) as world championships. World championships in non-Olympic years are listed below. The events were held in Vaxholm, Swed., 1938; Copenhagen, Den., 1950; Mâcon, Fr., 1954; Prague, Czech., 1958; Jajce, Yugos., 1963; East Berlin, Ger., 1966; Moscow, U.S.S.R., 1969.

**Kayak Singles (K. 1) 500 m.**
1950 F. Kobberup; Den.
1954 G. Fredriksson; Swed.
1958 S. Kaplaniak; Pol.
1963 A. Vernescu; Rum.
1966 A. Vernescu; Rum.
1969 A. Tichenko; U.S.S.R.

**Kayak Singles (K. 1) 1,000 m.**
1938 Widmark; Swed.
1950 G. Fredriksson; Swed.
1954 G. Fredriksson; Swed.
1958 F. Briel; W. Ger.
1963 E. Hansen; Den.
1966 A. Schaparenko; U.S.S.R.
1969 A. Schaparenko; U.S.S.R.

**Kayak Singles (K. 1) 10,000 m.**
1938 Widmark; Swed.
1950 T. Strömberg; Fin.
1954 Hutlacsky; Hung.
1958 T. Strömberg; Fin.
1963 F. Briel; W. Ger.
1966 M. Hesz; Hung.
1969 V. Tsarev; U.S.S.R.

**Kayak Pairs (K. 2) 500 m.**
1950 Glasser, Hedberg; Swed.
1954 Steinhauer, Miltenberger; W. Ger.
1958 Kaplaniak, Zielinski; Pol.
1963 Nicoara, Ivanov; Rum.
1966 Vernescu, Sciotnic; Rum.
1969 Vernescu, Sciotnic; Rum.

**Kayak Pairs (K. 2) 1,000 m.**
1938 Triebe, Eberle; Ger.
1950 Glasser, Hedberg; Swed.
1954 Meszaros, Meszaros; Hung.
1958 van der Moere, Verbrugghe; Belg.
1963 Nicoara, Ivanov; Rum.
1966 Schaparenko, Stezenko; U.S.S.R.
1969 Schaparenko, Morozov; U.S.S.R.

**Kayak Pairs (K. 2) 10,000 m.**
1938 Johansson, Berndtsson; Swed.
1950 Akerlund, Wetterström; Swed.
1954 Raub, Wiedermann; Aus.
1958 Uranyi, Fabian; Hung.
1963 Fabian, Timar; Hung.
1966 Szoelloesi, Fabian; Hung.
1969 Szaba, Timar; Hung.

**Kayak Fours (K. 4) 1,000 m.**
1938 Kube, Bruggeman, Gebrüder, Strahtman; Ger.
1950 Pihl, Eriksson, Pettersson, Haeppling; Swed.
1954 Vagyosky, Kovacs, Nagy, Szigetti; Hung.
1958 Scheuer, Lietz, Schmidt, Kleine; W. Ger.
1963 Perleberg, Krause, Rossberg, Lange; E. Ger.
1966 Sciotnic, Turcas, Ivanov, Calenic; Rum.
1969 Will, Augustin, Ebeling, Mattern; E. Ger.

**Kayak Fours (K. 4) 10,000 m.**
1950 Andersson, Gustavsson, Johansson, Andersson; Swed.
1954 Pihl, Frick, Heurlin, Andersson; Swed.
1958 Scheuer, Lietz, Schmidt, Kleine; W. Ger.
1963 Fabian, Timar, Koltai, Novotny; Hung.
1966 Shchushchikov, Grishchin, Morozov, Ionov; U.S.S.R.
1969 Norway

**Singles Relay 4 x 500 m.**
1950 Sweden
1954 Sweden
1958 West Germany
1963 Rumania
1966 U.S.S.R.
1969 U.S.S.R.

**Canadian Singles (C. 1) 1,000 m.**
1938 Newmuller; Ger.
1950 Holecek; Czech.
1954 Parti; Hung.
1958 G. Bukharin; U.S.S.R.
1963 Ismailkius; Rum.
1966 D. Lewe; W. Ger.
1969 T. Vichman; Hung.

**Canadian Singles (C. 1) 10,000 m.**
1950 Boutigny; Fr.
1954 Vokner; Czech.
1958 G. Bukharin; U.S.S.R.
1963 M. Zamotin; U.S.S.R.
1966 A. Hajba; Hung.
1969 T. Vichman; Hung.

**Canadian Pairs (C. 2) 1,000 m.**
1938 Proissl, Weinstabl; Ger.
1950 Bvzak, Kudrna; Czech.
1954 Liebhart, Lulla; Aus.
1958 Ismailkius, Alexe; Rum.
1963 Jakovici, Sidorov; Rum.
1966 Calabiciov, Covaliov; Rum.
1969 Patzaichin, Covaliov; Rum.

**Canadian Pairs (C. 2) 10,000 m.**
1938 Karlik, Brzak; Czech.
1950 Bvzak, Kudrna; Czech.
1954 Wieland, Halmai; Hung.
1958 Oschenkov, Silaev; U.S.S.R.
1963 Geister, Makarenko; U.S.S.R.
1966 Maxim, Simionov; Rum.
1969 Szerna, Hingl; Hung.

**Kayak Singles (K. 1) Women 500 m.**
1938 Kalka; Fin.
1950 Saimo; Fin.
1954 Zenz; Ger.
1958 Kislova; U.S.S.R.
1963 Zhubina; U.S.S.R.
1966 Pinayeva; U.S.S.R.
1969 Schimanaskaya; U.S.S.R.

**Kayak Pairs (K. 2) Women 500 m.**
1938 Paulisova, Zuolankova; Czech.
1950 Saimo, Gronholm; Fin.
1954 Punter, Banfalvi; Hung.
1958 Shubina, Gruzintseva; U.S.S.R.
1963 Zimmerman, Esser; E. Ger.
1966 Kobuss, Ulze; E. Ger.
1969 Schimanaskaya, Lyaushko; U.S.S.R.

EASTFOTO

A. VERNESCU (RUMANIA), WINNER OF THE WORLD KAYAK SINGLES 500-M. CHAMPIONSHIP AT BERLIN, 1966

# CHESS*

## World Champions

| | |
|---|---|
| 1866 | W. Steinitz; Aus. |
| 1894 | E. Lasker; Ger. |
| 1921 | J. R. Capablanca; Cuba |
| 1927 | A. Alekhine; Fr. |
| 1935 | M. Euwe; Neth. |
| 1937 | A. Alekhine; Fr. |
| 1948 | M. Botvinnik;† U.S.S.R. |
| 1957 | V. Smyslov; U.S.S.R. |
| 1958 | M. Botvinnik; U.S.S.R. |
| 1960 | M. Tal; U.S.S.R. |
| 1961 | M. Botvinnik; U.S.S.R. |
| 1963 | T. Petrosian; U.S.S.R. |
| 1966 | T. Petrosian; U.S.S.R. |
| 1969 | B. Spassky; U.S.S.R. |

## World Women's Champions

| | |
|---|---|
| 1950–53 | L. Rudenko; U.S.S.R. |
| 1953–56 | E. Bykova; U.S.S.R. |
| 1956–58 | O. Rubtsova; U.S.S.R. |
| 1958–62 | E. Bykova; U.S.S.R. |
| 1962– | N. Gaprindashvili; U.S.S.R. |

## World Team Championships

| Year | Winner | Place |
|---|---|---|
| 1927 | Hungary | London, U.K. |
| 1928 | Hungary | The Hague, Neth. |
| 1930 | Poland | Hamburg, Ger. |
| 1931 | United States | Prague, Czech. |
| 1933 | United States | Folkestone, U.K. |
| 1935 | United States | Warsaw, Pol. |
| 1937 | United States | Stockholm, Swed. |
| 1939 | Germany | Buenos Aires, Arg. |
| 1950 | Yugoslavia | Dubrovnik, Yugos. |
| 1952 | U.S.S.R. | Helsinki, Fin. |
| 1954 | U.S.S.R. | Amsterdam, Neth. |
| 1956 | U.S.S.R. | Moscow, U.S.S.R. |
| 1958 | U.S.S.R. | Munich, W. Ger. |
| 1960 | U.S.S.R. | Leipzig, E. Ger. |
| 1962 | U.S.S.R. | Varna, Bulg. |
| 1964 | U.S.S.R. | Tel Aviv, Isr. |
| 1966 | U.S.S.R. | Havana, Cuba |
| 1968 | U.S.S.R. | Lugano, Switz. |

*For historical details, including pre-1866 champions, see the article CHESS: *History*, especially *The World Championship* and *Fédération Internationale des Echecs*.

†Winner of World Chess Federation (FIDE) tournament; title had been vacant since the death of Alekhine in 1946.

MILLER SERVICES LTD.

FAST BOWLER FREDDIE TRUEMAN (U.K.) TOOK HIS 300TH TEST WICKET WHEN NEIL HAWKE (AUSTR.) WAS CAUGHT OUT BY COLIN COWDREY IN THE OVAL IN 1964; TRUEMAN HOLDS THE RECORD AT 307 (1952–65)

# CRICKET

## Major Records in First Class Cricket

| BATTING | Holder; Country | Place | Record | Date |
|---|---|---|---|---|
| Highest individual innings | H. Muhammad; Pak. | Karachi, Pak. | 499 runs | Jan. 8–11, 1959 |
| Longest innings | H. Muhammad: Pak. | Bridgetown, Barb. | 16 hr. 39 min. | Jan. 20–23, 1958 |
| Career record for batting | J. Hobbs; U.K. | | 61,237 runs | 1905–1934 |
| Test match record aggregate | W. Hammond; U.K. | | 7,247 runs | 1927–1947 |
| Season record for batting | D. Compton; U.K. | | 3,816 runs | 1947 |
| Most centuries (career) | J. Hobbs; U.K. | | 197 | 1905–34 |
| Most centuries (season) | D. Compton; U.K. | | 18 | 1947 |
| Most centuries (tests) | D. Bradman; Austr. | | 29 | 1928–48 |
| Highest career batting average | D. Bradman; Austr. | | 28,067 runs in 338 innings (95.14 av.) | 1927–49 |
| **BOWLING** | | | | |
| Most wickets taken (career) | W. Rhodes; U.K. | | 4,187 | 1898–1930 |
| Most wickets taken (tests) | F. Trueman; U.K. | | 307 | 1952–65 |
| Most wickets taken (season) | A. P. Freeman; U.K. | | 304 | 1928 |
| Lowest average (season) | A. Shaw; U.K. | | 177 wickets for 1,525 runs (8.61 av.) | 1880 |
| **FIELDING** | | | | |
| Most catches (career) | F. Woolley; U.K. | | 913 | 1906–38 |
| Most catches (season) | W. Hammond; U.K. | | 78 | 1928 |
| Most catches (match) | W. Hammond; U.K. | | 10 | 1928 |
| Most catches at wicket (match) | A. Long; U.K. | | 11 | July 18–21, 1964 |

## Test Cricket, 1877–1969. All-time standings*

| | England | Australia | South Africa | West Indies | New Zealand | India | Pakistan |
|---|---|---|---|---|---|---|---|
| England | — | 66/57 | 46/38 | 20/22 | 19/21 | 18/16 | 8/9 |
| Australia | 80/57 | — | 29/13 | 17/7† | 1/0 | 16/6 | 2/3 |
| South Africa | 18/38 | 7/13 | — | No matches | 9/6 | No matches | No matches |
| West Indies | 16/22 | 7/7† | No matches | — | 5/2 | 12/11 | 4/1 |
| New Zealand | 0/20 | 0/0 | 2/6 | 2/2 | — | 2/7 | 1/7 |
| India | 3/16 | 3/6 | No matches | 0/11 | 7/7 | — | 2/12 |
| Pakistan | 1/9 | 1/3 | No matches | 3/1 | 4/7 | 1/12 | — |

*Reading across, the first figure is the all-time number of wins and the second the number of drawn matches against a given opponent. The number of losses to any opponent can be ascertained by reading downward.
†Including one tie.

# CURLING

## World Championship (Scotch Cup; instituted 1959)*

| Year | Place | Winner |
|---|---|---|
| 1959 | Scotland (various) | Canada |
| 1960 | Scotland (various) | Canada |
| 1961 | Scotland (various) | Canada |
| 1962 | Scotland (various) | Canada |
| 1963 | Scotland (various) | Canada |
| 1964 | Calgary, Can. | Canada |
| 1965 | Perth, Scot. | U.S. |
| 1966 | Vancouver, Can. | Canada |
| 1967 | Perth, Scot. | Scotland |
| 1968 | Montreal, Can. | Canada |
| 1969 | Perth, Scot. | Canada |
| 1970 | Utica, N.Y. | Canada |

*Nations participating: Canada, Scotland, U.S. (beginning 1961), Sweden (1962), Norway and Switzerland (1963), France (1966), and West Germany (1968).

# CYCLING

## World's Unpaced One-Hour Progressive Records (*indicates amateur)

| Holder | Track | Record mi. | Record yd. | Year |
|---|---|---|---|---|
| H. Desgrange; Fr.* | Paris-Buffalo, Fr. | 21 | 1,674 | 1893 |
| J. Dubois; Fr. | Paris-Buffalo, Fr. | 23 | 1,320 | 1894 |
| M. van den Eynde; Belg. | Paris-Municipale, Fr. | 24 | 676 | 1897 |
| W. W. Hamilton; U.S. | Denver, U.S. | 25 | 600 | 1898 |
| Petit-Breton; Fr. | Paris-Buffalo, Fr. | 25 | 961 | 1905 |
| M. Berthet; Fr.* | Paris-Buffalo, Fr. | 25 | 1,410 | 1907 |
| O. Egg; Switz. | Paris-Buffalo, Fr. | 26 | 308 | 1912 |
| R. Weise; Ger. | Berlin-Zehl, Ger. | 26 | 509 | 1913 |
| M. Berthet; Fr. | Paris-Buffalo, Fr. | 26 | 984 | 1913 |
| O. Egg; Switz. | Paris-Buffalo, Fr. | 27 | 81 | 1913 |
| M. Berthet; Fr. | Paris-Buffalo, Fr. | 27 | 356 | 1913 |
| O. Egg; Switz. | Paris-Buffalo, Fr. | 27 | 871 | 1914 |
| M. Richard; Fr. | Saint-Trond, Fr. | 27 | 1,450 | 1933 |
| G. Olmo; It. | Vel Vigorelli, Milan, It. | 28 | 33 | 1935 |
| M. Richard; Fr. | Vel Vigorelli, Milan, It. | 28 | 368 | 1936 |
| F. Slaats; Neth. | Vel Vigorelli, Milan, It. | 28 | 545 | 1937 |
| M. Archambaud; Fr. | Vel Vigorelli, Milan, It. | 28 | 851 | 1937 |
| F. Coppi; It. | Vel Vigorelli, Milan, It. | 28 | 885 | 1942 |
| J. Anquetil; Fr. | Vel Vigorelli, Milan, It. | 28 | 1,201 | 1956 |
| E. Baldini; It.* | Vel Vigorelli, Milan, It. | 28 | 1,458 | 1956 |
| R. Rivière; Fr. | Vel Vigorelli, Milan, It. | 29 | 276 | 1957 |
| R. Rivière; Fr. | Vel Vigorelli, Milan, It. | 29 | 739 | 1958 |
| F. Bracke; Belg. | Rome, It. | 29 | 1,555 | 1967 |
| O. Ritter; Den. | Mexico City, Mex. | 30 | 396 | 1968 |

## World Track Championships

| Year and Place | Amateur Sprint | Professional Sprint | Amateur Pursuit | Professional Pursuit |
|---|---|---|---|---|
| 1893 Chicago, U.S. | (1 mi.) A. Zimmerman; U.S. | | | |
| 1893 Chicago, U.S. | (10 mi.) A. Zimmerman; U.S. | | | |
| 1894 Antwerp, Belg. | (1 mi.) A. Lehr; Ger. | | | |
| 1894 Antwerp, Belg. | (10 km.) J. Eden; Neth. | | | |
| 1895 Cologne, Ger. | J. Eden; Neth. | R. T. C. Protin; Belg. | | |
| 1896 Copenhagen, Den. | H. Reynolds; U.K. | P. Bourrilon; Fr. | | |
| 1897 Glasgow, U.K. | E. Schrader; Den. | W. Arend; Ger. | | |
| 1898 Vienna, Aus. | P. Albert; Ger. | G. A. Banker; U.S. | | |
| 1899 Montreal, Can. | T. Summergill; U.K. | Major Taylor; U.S. | | |
| 1900 Paris, Fr. | Didier-Nauts; Belg. | E. Jacquelin; Fr. | | |
| 1901 Berlin, Ger. | E. Maitrot; Fr. | T. Ellegaard; Den. | | |
| 1902 Rome, It. | C. Piard; Fr. | T. Ellegaard; Den. | | |
| 1903 Copenhagen, Den. | A. L. Reed; U.K. | T. Ellegaard; Den. | | |
| 1904 London, U.K. | M. Hurley; U.S. | I. Lawson; U.S. | | |
| 1905 Antwerp, Belg. | J. S. Benyon; U.K. | G. Poulain; Fr. | | |
| 1906 Geneva, Switz. | F. Verri; It. | T. Ellegaard; Den. | | |
| 1907 Paris, Fr. | J. Devoissoux; Fr. | E. Friol; Fr. | | |
| 1908 Berlin, Ger. | V. L. Johnson; U.K. | T. Ellegaard; Den. | | |
| 1909 Copenhagen, Den. | W. J. Bailey; U.K. | V. Dupre; Fr. | | |
| 1910 Brussels, Belg. | W. J. Bailey; U.K. | E. Friol; Fr. | | |
| 1911 Rome, It. | W. J. Bailey; U.K. | T. Ellegaard; Den. | | |
| 1912 Newark, U.S. | D. MacDougall; U.S. | F. L. Kramer; U.S. | | |
| 1913 Berlin, Ger. | W. J. Bailey; U.K. | W. Rutt; Ger. | | |
| 1920 Antwerp, Belg. | M. Peeters; Neth. | R. Spears; Austr. | | |
| 1921 Copenhagen, Den. | M. Andersen; Den. | P. Moeskops; Neth. | | |
| 1922 Paris, Fr. | H. T. Johnson; U.K. | P. Moeskops; Neth. | | |
| 1923 Zürich, Switz. | L. Michard; Fr. | P. Moeskops; Neth. | | |
| 1924 Paris, Fr. | L. Michard; Fr. | P. Moeskops; Neth. | | |
| 1925 Amsterdam, Neth. | J. Meyer; Neth. | E. Kauffman; Switz. | | |
| 1926 Milan, It. | A. Martinetti; It. | P. Moeskops; Neth. | | |
| 1927 Cologne, Ger. | M. Engel; Ger. | L. Michard; Fr. | | |
| 1928 Budapest, Hung. | W. Falck Hansen; Den. | L. Michard; Fr. | | |
| 1929 Zürich, Switz. | A. Mazairac; Neth. | L. Michard; Fr. | | |
| 1930 Brussels, Belg. | L. Gerardin; Fr. | L. Michard; Fr. | | |
| 1931 Copenhagen, Den. | H. Harder; Den. | W. Falck Hansen; Den. | | |
| 1932 Rome, It. | A. Richter; Ger. | J. Scherens; Belg. | | |
| 1933 Paris, Fr. | J. van Egmond; Neth. | J. Scherens; Belg. | | |
| 1934 Leipzig, Ger. | B. Pola; It. | J. Scherens; Belg. | | |
| 1935 Brussels, Belg. | T. Merkens; Ger. | J. Scherens; Belg. | | |
| 1936 Zürich, Switz. | A. van Vliet; Neth. | J. Scherens; Belg. | | |
| 1937 Copenhagen, Den. | J. van de Wyver; Neth. | J. Scherens; Belg. | | |
| 1938 Amsterdam, Neth. | J. van de Wyver; Neth. | A. van Vliet; Neth. | | |
| 1939 Milan, It. | J. Derksen; Neth. | | | |
| 1946 Zürich, Switz. | O. Plattner; Switz. | J. Derksen; Neth. | R. Rioland; Fr. | G. Peters; Neth. |
| 1947 Paris, Fr. | R. Harris; U.K. | J. Scherens; Belg. | G. Messina; It. | F. Coppi; It. |
| 1948 Amsterdam, Neth. | M. Ghella; It. | A. van Vliet; Neth. | G. Messina; It. | G. Schulte; Neth. |
| 1949 Copenhagen, Den. | S. Patterson; Austr. | R. Harris; U.K. | K. E. Anderson; Den. | F. Coppi; It. |
| 1950 Liège, Belg. | M. Verdeun; Fr. | R. Harris; U.K. | S. Patterson; Austr. | A. Bevilacqua; It. |
| 1951 Milan, It. | E. Sacchi; It. | R. Harris; U.K. | N. de Rossi; It. | A. Bevilacqua; It. |
| 1952 Paris, Fr. | E. Sacchi; It. | O. Plattner; Switz. | P. van Heudsen; Neth. | S. Patterson; Austr. |
| 1953 Zürich, Switz. | M. Morettini; It. | A. van Vliet; Neth. | G. Messina; It. | S. Patterson; Austr. |
| 1954 Cologne, W. Ger. | C. Peacock; U.K. | R. Harris; U.K. | L. Faggin; It. | G. Messina; It. |
| 1955 Milan, It. | G. Ogna; It. | A. Maspes; It. | N. Sheil; U.K. | G. Messina; It. |
| 1956 Copenhagen, Den. | M. Rousseau; Fr. | A. Maspes; It. | E. Baldini; It. | G. Messina; It. |
| 1957 Liège, Belg. | M. Rousseau; Fr. | J. Derksen; Neth. | C. Simonigh; It. | R. Rivière; Fr. |
| 1958 Paris, Fr. | V. Gasparella; It. | M. Rousseau; Fr. | N. Sheil; U.K. | R. Rivière; Fr. |
| 1959 Amsterdam, Neth. | V. Gasparella; It. | A. Maspes; It. | R. Altig; W. Ger. | R. Rivière; Fr. |
| 1960 Leipzig, E. Ger. | S. Gaiardoni; It. | A. Maspes; It. | M. Delattre; Fr. | R. Altig; W. Ger. |
| 1961 Zürich, Switz. | S. Bianchetto; It. | A. Maspes; It. | H. Nydam; Neth. | R. Altig; W. Ger. |
| 1962 Milan, It. | S. Bianchetto; It. | A. Maspes; It. | K. Jensen; Den. | H. Nydam; Neth. |
| 1963 Liège, Belg. | P. Sercu; Belg. | S. Gaiardoni; It. | J. Walschaerts; Belg. | L. Faggin; It. |
| 1964 Paris, Fr. | P. Trentin; Fr. | A. Maspes; It. | T. Groen; Neth. | F. Bracke; Belg. |
| 1965 San Sebastian, Sp. | O. Phakadze; U.S.S.R. | G. Beghetto; It. | T. Groen; Neth. | L. Faggin; It. |
| 1966 Frankfurt, W. Ger. | D. Morelon; Fr. | G. Beghetto; It. | T. Groen; Neth. | L. Faggin; It. |
| 1967 Amsterdam, Neth. | D. Morelon; Fr. | P. Sercu; Belg. | G. Bongers; Neth. | T. Groen; Neth. |
| 1968 * | L. Borghetti; It. | G. Beghetto; It. | M. Frey-Jensen; Den. | H. Porter; U.K. |
| 1969 † | D. Morelon; Fr. | P. Sercu; Belg. | X. Kurmann; Switz. | F. Bracke; Belg. |

*Amateur at Montevideo, Urug.; professional at Rome. †Amateur at Brno, Czech.; professional at Antwerp, Belg.

## Tour de France—Postwar Champions.

The Tour was inaugurated in 1903 over courses of varying length and severity—the longest being 3,567 mi. for the race of June 20–July 18, 1926. The closest winning margin was 38 sec. in 1968 when Jan Janssen beat Hermann Van Springel (Belg.) in 133 hr. 49 min. 42 sec.

| Year | Winner; Country | Miles | Year | Winner; Country | Miles |
|---|---|---|---|---|---|
| 1947 | J. Robic; Fr. | 2,883 | 1960 | G. Nencini; It. | 2,654 |
| 1948 | G. Bartali; It. | 3,058 | 1961 | J. Anquetil; Fr. | 2,730 |
| 1949 | F. Coppi; It. | 2,967 | 1962 | J. Anquetil; Fr. | 2,654 |
| 1950 | F. Kubler; Switz. | 2,987 | 1963 | J. Anquetil; Fr. | 2,572 |
| 1951 | H. Koblet; Switz. | 2,918 | 1964 | J. Anquetil; Fr. | 2,799 |
| 1952 | F. Coppi; It. | 2,987 | 1965 | F. Gimondi; It. | 2,595 |
| 1953 | L. Bobet; Fr. | 2,684 | 1966 | L. Aimar; Fr. | 2,674 |
| 1954 | L. Bobet; Fr. | 3,016 | 1967 | R. Pingeon; Fr. | 2,936 |
| 1955 | L. Bobet; Fr. | 2,793 | 1968 | J. Janssen; Neth. | 2,937 |
| 1956 | R. Walkowiak; Fr. | 2,813 | 1969 | E. Merckx; Belg. | 2,556 |
| 1957 | J. Anquetil; Fr. | 2,911 | | | |
| 1958 | C. Gaul; Luxem. | 2,684 | | | |
| 1959 | F. Bahamontes; Sp. | 2,709 | | | |

ROGER RIVIÈRE (FRANCE), WORLD CYCLING PROFESSIONAL PURSUIT CHAMPION OF 1957–59
KEYSTONE

## World Road Race Champions

| Year | Place | Amateur | Professional |
|---|---|---|---|
| 1921 | Copenhagen, Den. | G. Skold; Swed. | |
| 1922 | Liverpool, U.K. | D. Marsh; U.K. | |
| 1923 | Zürich, Switz. | L. Ferrario; It. | |
| 1924 | Paris, Fr. | A. Leducq; Fr. | |
| 1925 | Amsterdam, Neth. | H. Hoevanaers; Belg. | |
| 1926 | Turin, It. | O. Dayen; Fr. | |
| 1927 | Adenau, Ger. | J. Aerts; Belg. | A. Binda; It. |
| 1928 | Budapest, Hung. | Grandi; It. | G. Ronsse; Belg. |
| 1929 | Zürich, Switz. | P. Bertolazzi; It. | G. Ronsse; Belg. |
| 1930 | Liège, Belg. | G. Martano; It. | A. Binda; It. |
| 1931 | Copenhagen, Den. | H. Hansen; Den. | L. Guerra; It. |
| 1932 | Rome, It. | G. Martano; It. | A. Binda; It. |
| 1933 | Paris, Fr. | P. Egli; Switz. | G. Speicher; Fr. |
| 1934 | Leipzig, Ger. | K. Pellenaars; Neth. | K. Kaers; Belg. |

**World Road Race Champions (continued)**

| Year | Place | Amateur | Professional |
|---|---|---|---|
| 1935 | Floreffe, Belg. | I. Mancini; It. | J. Aerts; Belg. |
| 1936 | Bern, Switz. | E. Buchwalder; Switz. | A. Magne; Fr. |
| 1937 | Copenhagen, Den. | A. Leoni; It. | E. Meulenberg; Belg. |
| 1938 | Valkenburg, Neth. | H. Knecht; Switz. | M. Kint; Belg. |
| 1946 | Zürich, Switz. | H. Aubry; Fr. | H. Knecht; Switz. |
| 1947 | Reims, Fr. | A. Ferrari; It. | T. Middelkamp; Neth. |
| 1948 | Valkenburg, Neth. | H. Snell; Swed. | A. Schotte; Belg. |
| 1949 | Copenhagen, Den. | H. J. Faanhof; Neth. | H. van Steenbergen; Belg. |
| 1950 | Moorslede, U.K. | J. Houbin; Austr. | A. Schotte; Belg. |
| 1951 | Varese, It. | G. Ghidini; It. | F. Kubler; Switz. |
| 1952 | Luxembourg, Lux. | L. Ciancolo; It. | H. Müller; W. Ger. |
| 1953 | Schweiz, Switz. | R. Filippi; It. | F. Coppi; It. |
| 1954 | Solingen, W. Ger. | E. van Cautier; Belg. | L. Bobet; Fr. |
| 1955 | Rome, It. | S. Ranucci; It. | S. Ockers; Belg. |
| 1956 | Ballerup, Den. | F. Mahn; Neth. | R. van Steenbergen; Belg. |
| 1957 | Waregem, Belg. | L. Proost; Belg. | R. van Steenbergen; Belg. |
| 1958 | Reims, Fr. | G. Schur; E. Ger. | E. Baldini; It. |
| 1959 | Zandvoort, Neth. | G. Schur; E. Ger. | A. Darrigade; Fr. |
| 1960 | Sachsenring, E. Ger. | B. Eckstein; E. Ger. | R. van Looy; Belg. |
| 1961 | Bern, Switz. | J. Jourden; Fr. | R. van Looy; Belg. |
| 1962 | Salo, Fin. | R. Bongioni; It. | J. Stablenski; Fr. |
| 1963 | Renaix, Belg. | F. Vicentini; It. | B. Beheyt; Belg. |
| 1964 | Sallanches, Fr. | E. Merckx; Belg. | J. Janssen; Neth. |
| 1965 | San Sebastian, Sp. | J. Botherell; Fr. | T. Simpson; U.K. |
| 1966 | Nurburgring, W. Ger. | E. Dolman; Neth. | R. Altig; W. Ger. |
| 1967 | Heerlen, Neth. | G. Webb; U.K. | E. Merckx; Belg. |
| 1968 | * | V. Marcelli; It. | V. Adorni; It. |
| 1969 | † | L. Mortensen; Den. | H. Ottenbros; Neth. |

*Amateur at Montevideo, Urug.; professional at Imola, It. †Amateur at Brno, Czech.; professional at Zolder, Neth.

EDDY MERCKX (CENTRE) OF BELGIUM WINNING THE WORLD PROFESSIONAL ROAD RACE CHAMPIONSHIP IN 1967. HE WON THE AMATEUR TITLE IN 1964

U.P.I. COMPIX

GIUSEPPE BEGHETTO (ITALY) WINNING THE 1966 WORLD PROFESSIONAL CYCLING SPRINT CHAMPIONSHIP

PICTORIAL PARADE INC.

**DOG (GREYHOUND) RACING.** The sport of greyhound racing, which originated in the U.S., has gained its greatest popularity in the U.K. (*See* the article DOG RACING.)

**Record speeds**

| Event | Winner |
|---|---|
| 500 yd. (straightaway) | Beef Cutlet in 26.13 sec. (39.13 mph) Blackpool, U.K.; May 1933 |
| 525 yd. (499-yd. circuit) | Yellow Printer in 28.30 sec. (37.94 mph) White City, London, U.K.; June 3, 1968 |
| 525 yd. and 4 flights of hurdles (British Grand National; instituted 1927) | Barrowside in 29.43 sec. White City, London, U.K.; May 1955 |
| 700 yd. (562-yd. circuit) | Don't Divulge in 38.72 sec. (36.98 mph) West Ham, London, U.K.; May 1959 |

**Greyhound Derby.** The premier greyhound event in the world is the Greyhound Derby (instituted in 1927) run at the White City Stadium, London. The course is 525 yd.

| Year | Name | Time/sec. | Year | Name | Time/sec. |
|---|---|---|---|---|---|
| 1945 | Ballyhennessy Seal | 29.56 | 1958 | Pigalle Wonder | 28.65 |
| 1946 | Monday News | 29.24 | 1959 | Mile Bush Pride | 28.76 |
| 1947 | Trev's Perfection | 28.95 | 1960 | Duleek Dandy | 29.15 |
| 1948 | Priceless Border | 28.78 | 1961 | Palm's Printer | 28.84 |
| 1949 | Narrogar Ann | 28.95 | 1962 | The Grand Canal | 29.09 |
| 1950 | Ballymac Ball | 28.72 | 1963 | Lucky Boy Boy | 29.00 |
| 1951 | Ballylanigan Tanist | 28.62 | 1964 | Hack Up Chieftain | 28.92 |
| 1952 | Endless Gossip | 28.50 | 1965 | Chittering Clapton | 28.82 |
| 1953 | Daw's Dancer | 29.20 | 1966 | Faithful Hope | 28.52 |
| 1954 | Pauls Fun | 28.84 | 1967 | Tric-Trac | 29.00 |
| 1955 | Ruston Mack | 28.97 | 1968 | Camera Flash | 28.89 |
| 1956 | Dunmore King | 29.22 | 1969 | Sand Star | 28.76 |
| 1957 | Ford Spartan | 28.84 | | | |

**American Greyhound Derby.** The American Greyhound Derby was instituted in 1949 at Taunton, Mass. The distance was 525 yd. in 1949; 675 yd. 1950–61; $\frac{3}{8}$ mi. since 1962.

| Year | Winner | Owner | Time sec. |
|---|---|---|---|
| 1949 | Oklahoman | E. L. Williams | 30.2 |
| 1950 | Real Huntsman | Randle Brothers | 38.4 |
| 1951 | Real Huntsman | Randle Brothers | 38.2 |
| 1952 | On The Line | Chappel Kennel | 38.2 |
| 1953 | However | C. H. Lovely | 38.3 |
| 1954 | Mellojean | J. Prevatt | 38.2 |
| 1955 | Koliga | R. L. Block | 39.1 |
| 1956 | Go Rock | Deep Rock Kennels | 38.2 |
| 1957 | Clydesdale | O. Moses | 38.2 |
| 1958 | Feldcrest | O. Moses | 38.3 |
| 1959 | Go Super | O. Block | 38.4 |
| 1960 | Serape | O. Moses | 38.5 |
| 1961 | Velvet Sis | H. E. Heaton | 39.0 |
| 1962 | Cactus Noel | A. R. Gouveia | 37.6 |
| 1963 | Thermel | M. Viveiros | 38.5 |
| 1964 | Canadian Hi There | F. Trevillion | 38.3 |
| 1965 | Nitrana | O. Moses | 38.5 |
| 1966 | Golden In | L. Nave | 37.84 |
| 1967 | Xandra | J. E. Alderson | 38.10 |
| 1968 | L. G.'s Ada | L. Clager | 38.03 |
| 1969 | Lucky Bannon | R. E. Thomas | 37.82 |

## FENCING

### World Championships

| | | INDIVIDUAL | | | | TEAM | | | |
|---|---|---|---|---|---|---|---|---|---|
| Year | Place | Men's Foil | Épée | Sabre | Women's Foil | Men's Foil | Épée | Sabre | Women's Foil* |
| 1937 | Paris, Fr. | G. Marzi; It. | B. Schmetz; Fr. | P. Kovacs; Hung. | H. Mayer; Ger. | Italy | Italy | Hungary | Hungary |
| 1938 | Piestany, Czech. | G. Guaragna; It. | M. Pécheux; Fr. | A. Montano; It. | M. Sediva; Czech. | Italy | France | Italy | Not contested |
| 1947 | Lisbon, Port. | C. d'Oriola; Fr. | E. Artigas; Fr. | A. Montano; It. | E. Müller-Preiss; Aus. | France | France | Italy | Denmark |
| 1949 | Cairo, Egy. | C. d'Oriola; Fr. | D. Mangiarotti; It. | G. Daré; It. | E. Müller-Preiss; Aus. | Italy | Italy | Italy | Not contested |
| 1950 | Monte Carlo, Mon. | R. Nostini; It. | M. Luchow; Den. | J. Levavasseur; Fr. | R. Garilhe; Fr., and E. Müller-Preiss; Aus., tied | Italy | Italy | Italy | France |
| 1951 | Stockholm, Swed. | M. di Rosa; It. | E. Mangiarotti; It. | A. Gerevich; Hung. | I. Elek; Hung. | France | France | Hungary | France |
| 1953 | Brussels, Belg. | C. d'Oriola; Fr. | J. Sakovits; Hung. | P. Kovacs; Hung. | I. Camber; It. | France | Italy | Hungary | Hungary |
| 1954 | Luxembourg, Luxem. | C. d'Oriola; Fr. | E. Mangiarotti; It. | R. Karpati; Hung. | K. Lachman; Den. | Italy | Italy | Hungary | Hungary |
| 1955 | Rome, It. | J. Gyuricza; Hung. | G. Anglesio; It. | A. Gerevich; Hung. | L. Domolki; Hung. | Italy | Italy | Hungary | Hungary |
| 1957 | Paris, Fr. | M. Fulop; Hung. | A. Movyal; Fr. | J. Pawlowski; Pol. | A. Zabelina; U.S.S.R. | Hungary | Italy | Hungary | Italy |
| 1958 | Philadelphia, U.S. | G. C. Bergamini; It. | H. W. F. Hoskyns; U.K. | Y. Rylskiy; U.S.S.R. | V. Kisseleva; U.S.S.R. | France | Italy | Hungary | U.S.S.R. |
| 1959 | Budapest, Hung. | A. Jay; U.K. | B. Khabarov; U.S.S.R. | R. Karpati; Hung. | E. Efimova; U.S.S.R. | U.S.S.R. | Hungary | Poland | Hungary |
| 1961 | Turin, It. | R. Parulski; Pol. | J. Guittet; Fr. | Y. Rylskiy; U.S.S.R. | H. Schmid; W. Ger. | U.S.S.R. | U.S.S.R. | Poland | U.S.S.R. |
| 1962 | Buenos Aires, Arg. | G. Sveshnikov; U.S.S.R. | I. Kausz; Hung. | Z. Horvath; Hung. | O. Orban-Szabo; Rum. | U.S.S.R. | France | Poland | Hungary |
| 1963 | Gdansk, Pol. | J. C. Magnan; Fr. | R. Losert; Aus. | Y. Rylskiy; U.S.S.R. | I. Rejto; Hung. | U.S.S.R. | Poland | Poland | U.S.S.R. |
| 1965 | Paris, Fr. | J. C. Magnan; Fr. | Z. Nemere; Hung. | J. Pawlowski; Pol. | G. Gorokhova; U.S.S.R. | U.S.S.R. | France | U.S.S.R. | U.S.S.R. |
| 1966 | Moscow, U.S.S.R. | G. Sveshnikov; U.S.S.R. | A. Nikanchikov; U.S.S.R. | J. Pawlowski; Pol. | T. Samusenko; U.S.S.R. | U.S.S.R. | France | Hungary | U.S.S.R. |
| 1967 | Montreal, Can. | V. Putyatin; U.S.S.R. | A. Nikanchikov; U.S.S.R. | M. Rakita; U.S.S.R. | A. Zabelina; U S.S.R. | Rumania | U.S.S.R. | U.S.S.R. | Hungary |
| 1969 | Havana, Cuba | F. Wessel; W. Ger. | B. Andrejevski; Pol. | V. Sidiak; U.S.S.R. | E. Novikova; U.S.S.R. | U.S.S.R. | U.S.S.R. | U.S.S.R. | Rumania |

Olympic titles are regarded as world championships (*see* table in OLYMPIC GAMES). European championships, started in 1921, were styled "World Championship" from 1937.

*The championship, not being part of the Olympic Games until 1960, was also held: 1948 at The Hague, winner Denmark; 1952 at Copenhagen, winner Hungary; 1956 at London, winner U.S.S.R.

WORLD FENCING CHAMPION JEAN CLAUDE MAGNAN (FRANCE) SCORES AGAINST L. CARPANEDA (ITALY) TO RETAIN THE MEN'S FOIL FENCING TITLE AT PARIS IN 1965

U.P.I. COMPIX

WORLD ÉPÉE CHAMPIONSHIP BOUT IN WHICH A. NIKANCHIKOV (U.S.S.R.), RIGHT, DEFEATED C. BOURQUARD (FRANCE) TO WIN THE WORLD TITLE AT MOSCOW IN 1966

SOVFOTO

## FISHING

### World Freshwater Rod and Reel Records

| Fish | Weight | Length | Girth | Place | Date | Angler | Caught by Any Method: Lb. Oz. | Caught by Any Method: Place |
|---|---|---|---|---|---|---|---|---|
| Black Bass, Largemouth | 22 lb. 4 oz. | 32½″ | 28½″ | Montgomery Lake, Ga. | June 2, 1932 | G. W. Perry | Same | |
| Black Bass, Smallmouth | 11 lb. 15 oz. | 27″ | 21⅔″ | Dale Hollow L., Ky.-Tenn. | July 9, 1955 | D. L. Hayes | Same | |
| Bass, Redeye | 6 lb. ½ oz. | 20½″ | 15⅘″ | Hallawakee Cr., Ala. | Mar. 24, 1967 | T. L. Sharpe | Same | |
| Bass, Spotted | 8 lb. 8 oz. | 25″ | 17¾″ | Smith Lake, Ala. | May 23, 1968 | W. James | Same | |
| Bass, White | 5 lb. 4 oz. | 17″ | 15½″ | Toronto, Kans. | May 4, 1966 | H. A. Baker | Same | |
| Bluegill Sunfish | 4 lb. 12 oz. | 15″ | 18¼″ | Ketona Lake, Ala. | Apr. 9, 1950 | T. S. Hudson | Same | |
| Bullhead, Black | 8 lb. | 24″ | 17¾″ | Lake Waccabuc, N.Y. | Aug. 1, 1951 | K. Evans | Same | |
| Carp | 55 lb. 5 oz. | 42″ | 31″ | Clearwater Lake, Minn. | July 10, 1952 | F. J. Ledwein | 83-8 | Pretoria, S. Af. |
| Catfish, Blue | 97 lb. | 57″ | 37″ | Missouri River, S.D. | Sept. 16, 1959 | E. B. Elliott | 117 | Osage R., Mo. |
| Catfish, Channel | 58 lb. | 47¼″ | 29⅛″ | Santee-Cooper Res., S.C. | July 7, 1964 | W. B. Whaley | Same | |
| Char, Arctic | 27 lb. 4 oz. | 40¼″ | 26¼″ | Tree River, N.W.T. | Sept. 2, 1963 | W. Murphy | Same | |
| Crappie, Black | 5 lb. | 19¼″ | 18⅝″ | Santee-Cooper Res., S.C. | Mar. 15, 1957 | P. E. Foust | Same | |
| Crappie, White | 5 lb. 3 oz. | 21″ | 19″ | Enid Dam, Miss. | July 31, 1957 | F. L. Bright | Same | |
| Gar, Alligator | 279 lb. | 93″ | | Rio Grande, Tex. | Dec. 2, 1951 | W. Valverde | Same | |
| Gar, Longnose | 50 lb. 5 oz. | 72¼″ | 22¼″ | Trinity River, Tex. | July 30, 1954 | T. Miller | Same | |
| Grayling, Arctic | 5 lb. 15 oz. | 29⅞″ | 15⅛″ | Katseyedie R., N.W.T. | Aug. 16, 1967 | J. P. Branson | Same | |
| Muskellunge | 69 lb. 15 oz. | 64½″ | 31¾″ | St. Lawrence R., N.Y. | Sept. 22, 1957 | A. Lawton | 102 | Minocqua Lake, Wis |
| Perch, White | 4 lb. 12 oz. | 19½″ | 13″ | Messalonskee Lake, Me. | June 4, 1949 | E. Small | Same | |
| Perch, Yellow | 4 lb. 3½ oz. | | | Bordentown, N.J. | May 1865 | C. C. Abbot | Same | |
| Pickerel, Eastern Chain | 9 lb. 6 oz. | 31″ | 14″ | Homerville, Ga. | Feb. 17, 1961 | B. McQuaig, Jr. | Same | |
| Pike, Northern | 46 lb. 2 oz. | 52½″ | 25″ | Sacandaga Res., N.Y. | Sept. 15, 1940 | P. Dubuc | Same | |
| Pike, Walleyed | 25 lb. | 41″ | 29″ | Old Hickory L., Tenn. | Aug. 1, 1960 | M. Harper | Same | |
| Salmon, Atlantic | 79 lb. 2 oz. | | | Tana River, Nor. | 1928 | H. Henriksen | 103-2 | River Devon, Scot. |
| Salmon, Chinook | 92 lb. | 58½″ | 36″ | Skeena River, B.C. | July 19, 1959 | H. Wichmann | 126-8 | Petersburg, Alaska |
| Salmon, Landlocked | 22 lb. 8 oz. | 36″ | | Sebago Lake, Me. | Aug. 1, 1907 | E. Blakely | 35 | Crooked River, Me. |
| Salmon, Silver | 31 lb. | | | Cowichan Bay, B.C. | Oct. 11, 1947 | P. Hallberg | Same | |
| Sauger | 8 lb. 5 oz. | 28″ | | Niobrara, Nebr. | Oct. 22, 1961 | B. Tepner | Same | |
| Sturgeon, White | 360 lb. | 111″ | 86″ | Snake River, Ida. | Apr. 24, 1956 | W. Cravens | Same | |
| Sunfish, Redear | 2 lb. 15 oz. | 14″ | 15¾″ | Ponte Vedra Beach, Fla. | Mar. 6, 1965 | R. D. Gray, Jr. | 4-4 | Gordon, Ala. |
| Trout, Brook | 14 lb. 8 oz. | 31½″ | 11½″ | Nipigon River, Ont. | July 1916 | W. J. Cook | Same | |
| Trout, Brown | 39 lb. 8 oz. | | | Loch Awe, Scot. | 1866 | W. Muir | 40 | Great L., Tasmania |
| Trout, Cut-throat | 41 lb. | 39″ | | Pyramid Lake, Nev. | Dec. 1925 | J. Skimmerhorn | Same | |
| Trout, Dolly Varden | 32 lb. | 40½″ | 29¾″ | L. Pend Oreille, Ida. | Oct. 27, 1949 | N. L. Higgins | Same | |
| Trout, Golden | 11 lb. | 28″ | 16″ | Cook's Lake, Wyo. | Aug. 5, 1948 | C. S. Reed | Same | |
| Trout, Lake | 63 lb. 2 oz. | 51½″ | 32¾″ | Lake Superior | May 25, 1952 | H. Hammers | 102 | L. Athabasca, Sask. |
| Trout, Rainbow | 37 lb. | 40½″ | 28″ | L. Pend Oreille, Ida. | Nov. 25, 1947 | W. Hamlet | 42 | Corbett, Oreg. |
| Trout, Sunapee | 11 lb. 8 oz. | 33″ | 17¼″ | Lake Sunapee, N.H. | Aug. 1, 1954 | E. Theoharis | Same | |
| Warmouth | 1 lb. 2 oz. | 10″ | 10″ | Cooper River, S.C. | May 18, 1968 | R. L. Joyner | Same | |
| Whitefish, Mountain | 5 lb. | 19″ | 14″ | Athabasca R., Alberta | June 3, 1963 | O. Welch | Same | |

Source: "Field & Stream."

BY COURTESY OF THE TENNESSEE DEPARTMENT OF CONSERVATION

WORLD RECORD SMALLMOUTH BLACK BASS CAUGHT BY DAVID L. HAYES AT DALE HOLLOW LAKE, KY.-TENN., ON JULY 9, 1955. THE FISH WEIGHED 11 LB. 15 OZ.

BY COURTESY OF RONALD D. GRAY, JR.

WORLD RECORD REDEAR SUNFISH, WEIGHING 2 LB. 15 OZ., CAUGHT BY RONALD D. GRAY, JR., AT PONTE VEDRA BEACH, FLA., ON MARCH 6, 1965

## World Marine All Tackle Records

| Fish | Weight | Length | Girth | Place | Date | Angler | Line Weight (lb.) |
|---|---|---|---|---|---|---|---|
| Albacore | 69 lb. 2 oz.<br>69 lb. 1 oz.<br>69 lb. | 3′10″<br>4′ ¼″<br>3′ 6″ | 32″<br>33¼″<br>32½″ | Montauk, N.Y.<br>Hudson Canyon, N.J.<br>St. Helena, Atlantic O. | Aug. 21, 1964<br>Oct. 8, 1961<br>Apr. 7, 1956 | L. R. Kranz<br>W. C. Timm<br>P. Allen | 80<br>50<br>130 |
| Amberjack | 149 lb. | 5′11″ | 41¾″ | Bermuda | June 21, 1964 | P. Simons | 30 |
| Barracuda | 103 lb. 4 oz. | 5′ 6″ | 31¼″ | West End, Bahama Is. | Aug. 11, 1932 | C. E. Benet* | 80 |
| Bass, Giant Sea† | 563 lb. 8 oz. | 7′ 5″ | 72″ | Anacapa Island, Calif. | Aug. 20, 1968 | J. D. McAdam, Jr. | 80 |
| Bass, California White Sea | 83 lb. 12 oz. | 5′ 5½″ | 34″ | San Felipe, Mex. | Mar. 31, 1953 | L. C. Baumgardner | 30 |
| Bass, Channel | 83 lb. | 4′ 4″ | 29″ | Cape Charles, Va. | Aug. 5, 1949 | Z. Waters, Jr. | 50 |
| Bass, Black Sea | 8 lb. | 1′10″ | 19″ | Nantucket Sound, Mass. | May 13, 1951 | H. R. Rider | 50 |
| Bass, Striped | 73 lb. | 5′ | 30½″ | Vineyard Sound, Mass. | Aug. 17, 1913 | C. B. Church* | 50 |
| Blackfish (or Tautog) | 21 lb. 6 oz. | 2′ 7½″ | 23½″ | Cape May, N.J. | June 12, 1954 | R. N. Sheafer | 30 |
| Bluefish | 24 lb. 3 oz. | 3′ 5″ | 22″ | San Miguel, Azores | Aug. 27, 1953 | M. A. da Silva Veloso | 12 |
| Bonefish | 19 lb. | 3′ 3⅝″ | 17″ | Zululand, S. Af. | May 26, 1962 | B. W. Batchelor | 30 |
| Bonito, Oceanic | 39 lb. 15 oz. | 3′ 3″ | 28″ | Walker Cay, Bahama Is. | Jan. 21, 1952 | F. Drowley | 50 |
| Cobia | 102 lb. | 5′10″ | 34″ | Cape Charles, Va. | July 3, 1938 | J. E. Stansbury* | 130 |
| Cod | 98 lb. 12 oz. | 5′ 3″ | 41″ | Isle of Shoals, Mass. | June 8, 1969 | A. J. Bielevich | 20 |
| Dolphin | 85 lb. | 5′ 9″ | 37½″ | Spanish Wells, Bahamas | May 29, 1968 | R. Seymour | 50 |
| Drum, Black | 98 lb. 8 oz. | 4′ 5″ | 40″ | Willis Wharf, Va. | June 12, 1967 | G. H. Kelley | 50 |
| Flounder | 22 lb. 1 oz. | 3′ 1″ | 35″ | Caleta Horcon, Chile | Dec. 8, 1965 | F. I. Aguirrezabal | 30 |
| Jewfish‡ | 680 lb. | 7′ 1½″ | 66″ | Fernandina Beach, Fla. | May 20, 1961 | L. Joyner | 80 |
| Kingfish | 78 lb. | 5′ 6½″ | 28½″ | Guayanilla, P.R. | May 25, 1963 | R. M. Coon | 50 |
| Marlin, Black | 1,560 lb. | 14′ 6″ | 81″ | Cabo Blanco, Peru | Aug. 4, 1953 | A. C. Glassell, Jr. | 130 |
| Marlin, Blue | 845 lb. | 13′ 1″ | 71″ | St. Thomas, Virgin Is. | July 4, 1968 | E. J. Fishman | 80 |
| Marlin, Pacific Blue | 1,153 lb. | 14′ 8″ | 73″ | Ritidian Point, Guam | Aug. 21, 1969 | G. D. Perez | 180 |
| Marlin, Striped | 465 lb. | 10′ 6″ | 65″ | Mayor Island, N.Z. | Feb. 27, 1948 | J. Black | 130 |
| Marlin, White | 161 lb. | 8′ 8″ | 33″ | Miami Beach, Fla. | Mar. 20, 1938 | L. F. Hooper | 80 |
| Permit | 50 lb. | 3′ 7″ | 34½″ | Miami, Fla. | Mar. 27, 1965 | R. F. Miller | 12 |
| Pollack | 43 lb. | 4′ | 29″ | Brielle, N.J. | Oct. 21, 1964 | P. Barlow | 50 |
| Roosterfish | 114 lb. | 5′ 4″ | 33″ | La Paz, Mex. | June 1, 1960 | A. Sackheim | 30 |
| Runner, Rainbow | 30 lb. 15 oz. | 3′11″ | 22″ | Kauai, Hawaii | Apr. 27, 1963 | H. Goodale | 130 |
| Sailfish, Atlantic | 141 lb. 1 oz. | 8′ 5″ | | Ivory Coast, Af. | Jan. 26, 1961 | A. Burnand | 130 |
| Sailfish, Pacific | 221 lb. | 10′ 9″ | | Santa Cruz I., Galápagos Is. | Feb. 12, 1947 | C. W. Stewart | 130 |
| Shark, Blue | 410 lb.<br>410 lb. | 11′ 6″<br>11′ 2″ | 52″<br>52½″ | Rockport, Mass.<br>Rockport, Mass. | Sept. 1, 1960<br>Aug. 17, 1967 | R. C. Webster<br>M. C. Webster | 80<br>80 |
| Shark, Mako | 1,000 lb. | 12′ | | Mayor Island, N.Z. | Mar. 14, 1943 | B. D. H. Ross* | 130 |
| Shark, Man-Eater (or White) | 2,664 lb. | 16′10″ | 114″ | Ceduna, S. Austr. | Apr. 21, 1959 | A. Dean | 130 |
| Shark, Porbeagle | 430 lb. | 8′ | 63″ | Channel Islands, Eng. | June 29, 1969 | D. Bougourd | 80 |
| Shark, Thresher | 922 lb. | | | Bay of Islands, N.Z. | Mar. 21, 1937 | W. W. Dowding* | 130 |
| Shark, Tiger | 1,780 lb. | 13′10½″ | 103″ | Cherry Grove, S.C. | June 14, 1964 | W. Maxwell | 130 |
| Snook (or Robalo) | 52 lb. 6 oz. | 4′ 1½″ | 26″ | La Paz, Mex. | Jan. 9, 1963 | J. Haywood | 30 |
| Swordfish | 1,182 lb. | 14′11¼″ | 78″ | Iquique, Chile | May 7, 1953 | L. Marron | 130 |
| Tanguigue | 81 lb. | 5′11½″ | 29¼″ | Karachi, Pak. | Aug. 27, 1960 | G. E. Rusinak | 80 |
| Tarpon | 283 lb. | 7′ 2⅗″ | | Lake Maracaibo, Venez. | Mar. 19, 1956 | M. Salazar | 30 |
| Tuna, Allison (or Yellowfin) | 269 lb. 8 oz. | 6′ 9″ | 53″ | Hanalei, Hawaii | May 30, 1962 | H. Nishikawa | 180 |
| Tuna, Atlantic Big-Eyed | 295 lb. | 6′ 6½″ | 40″ | San Miguel, Azores | July 8, 1960 | A. Cordeiro | 130 |
| Tuna, Pacific Big-Eyed | 435 lb. | 7′ 9″ | 63½″ | Cabo Blanco, Peru | Apr. 17, 1957 | R. V. A. Lee | 130 |
| Tuna, Blackfin | 36 lb. 4 oz.<br>36 lb. | 3′ 1½″<br>3′ ¼″ | 28⅛″<br>28⅞″ | Challenger Bank, Bermuda<br>Bermuda | Aug. 6, 1966<br>July 14, 1963 | R. C. McPherson<br>J. E. Baptiste, Jr. | 30<br>50 |
| Tuna, Bluefin | 977 lb. | 9′ 8″ | 94½″ | St. Ann's Bay, Nova Scotia | Sept. 4, 1950 | D. McI. Hodgson | 130 |
| Wahoo | 149 lb. | 6′ 7¾″ | 37½″ | Cat Cay, Bahamas | June 15, 1962 | J. Pirovano | 130 |
| Weakfish | 19 lb. 8 oz. | 3′ 1″ | 23¾″ | Trinidad, W. Indies | Apr. 13, 1962 | D. B. Hall | 80 |
| Weakfish, Spotted | 15 lb. 3 oz. | 2′10½″ | 20½″ | Ft. Pierce, Fla. | Jan. 13, 1949 | C. W. Hubbard | 50 |
| Yellowtail | 111 lb. | 5′ 2″ | 38″ | Bay of Islands, N.Z. | June 11, 1961 | A. F. Plim | 50 |

*Line not tested. †Sometimes also called California Black Sea Bass. ‡Sometimes also called Giant Sea Bass.
Source: International Game Fish Association.

**CASTING.** World records are recognized by the International Casting Federation. The World Championship is awarded to the competitor having the most points upon conclusion of the ten official accuracy and distance events in bait casting, fly casting, and spin casting. The first world championships under International Casting Federation Rules were held in Kiel, Ger., in 1957.

### World Records

| Official Event | Record Holders | Record | Year |
|---|---|---|---|
| No. 1. Skish fly accuracy | G. Schop, Nor.; A. Kolseth, Nor.; S. Scheen, Nor.; J. Daubry, Fr.; J. Tarantino, U.S.; U. Janson, Swed.; T. Kristensen, Nor.; O. Söderblom, Swed.; V. Thölstedt, Ger. | 100 points | (Years not available) |
| No. 2. Fly distance and accuracy | O. Söderblom, Swed.<br>S. Aleshi, U.S.<br>A. J. Schultz, Nor.<br>O. Söderblom, Swed. | 92.13 points<br>41 accuracy<br>52.09 m. average<br>54.00 m. long cast | 1967<br>1960<br>1963<br>1967 |
| No. 3. Fly distance single handed | W. Stubbe, Ger.<br>W. Stubbe, Ger. | 57.72 m. average<br>61.21 m. long cast | 1968<br>1968 |
| No. 4. Fly distance two handed | S. Scheen, Nor.<br>S. Scheen, Nor. | 72.33 m. average<br>78.38 m. long cast | 1968<br>1968 |
| No. 5. Skish bait accuracy, revolving spool, ⅝ oz. | U. Janson, Swed. | 96 points | 1964 |
| No. 6. Skish bait accuracy, spinning, ⅜ oz. | U. Janson, Swed. | 90 points | 1964 |
| No. 7. Bait distance, revolving spool, ⅝ oz. | N. Oinert, Swed.<br>K. Rosengren, Swed. | 103.36 m. average<br>105.75 m. long cast | 1968<br>1968 |
| No. 8. Bait distance, spinning, ⅜ oz. | K. Rosenstrom, Den.<br>W. Kummerow, Ger. | 91.91 m. average<br>96.20 m. long cast | 1968<br>1968 |
| No. 9. Bait distance, revolving spool, single handed, ⅝ oz. | N. Oinert, Swed.<br>N. Oinert, Swed. | 144.23 m. average<br>146.70 m. long cast | 1968<br>1968 |
| No. 10. Bait distance, spinning, 30 g., two handed | W. Kummerow, Ger.<br>W. Kummerow, Ger. | 168.37 m. average<br>175.01 m. long cast | 1968<br>1968 |

### Casting World Champions

| Champion; Country | Place | Year |
|---|---|---|
| J. Tarantino; San Francisco, U.S. | Kiel, Ger. | 1957 |
| J. Tarantino; San Francisco, U.S. | Brussels, Belg. | 1958 |
| J. Tarantino; San Francisco, U.S. | Scarborough, U.K. | 1959 |
| J. Tarantino; San Francisco, U.S. | Zürich, Switz. | 1960 |
| J. Tarantino; San Francisco, U.S. | Oslo, Nor. | 1961 |
| J. Tarantino; San Francisco, U.S. | Rotterdam, Neth. | 1962 |
| J. Tarantino; San Francisco, U.S. | Nürnberg, Ger. | 1963 |
| R. Fredrickson; Göteborg, Swed. | Stockholm, Swed. | 1964 |
| W. Kummerow; Lübeck, Ger. | Spa, Belg. | 1965 |
| C. Rigamer; New Orleans, U.S. | Scarborough, U.K. | 1966 |
| W. Kummerow; Lübeck, Ger. | Oslo, Nor. | 1967 |
| W. Kummerow; Lübeck, Ger. | Lenzerheide, Switz. | 1968 |

(RIGHT) REAL MADRID DEFEATED EINTRACHT FRANKFURT 7–3 AT GLASGOW, SCOT., IN 1960 TO WIN ITS FIFTH CONSECUTIVE EUROPEAN SOCCER CUP. (BELOW) ENGLAND WINNING THE 1966 WORLD CUP BY DEFEATING WEST GERMANY 4–2

(RIGHT) LONDON DAILY EXPRESS, (BELOW) CENTRAL PRESS, BOTH FROM PICTORIAL PARADE INC.

## FOOTBALL

### ASSOCIATION FOOTBALL (Soccer)

### World Cup (Jules Rimet Trophy) Competition

| Year | Place | Result | |
|---|---|---|---|
| 1930 | Montevideo, Urug. | Uruguay 4 | Argentina 2 |
| 1934 | Rome, It. | Italy 2 | Czechoslovakia 1 |
| 1938 | Paris, Fr. | Italy 4 | Hungary 2 |
| 1950 | Rio de Janeiro, Braz. | Uruguay 2 | Brazil 1 |
| 1954 | Bern, Switz. | West Germany 3 | Hungary 2 |
| 1958 | Stockholm, Swed. | Brazil 5 | Sweden 2 |
| 1962 | Santiago, Chile | Brazil 3 | Czechoslovakia 1 |
| 1966 | London, U.K. | England 4 | West Germany 2 |
| 1970 | Mexico City, Mex. | Brazil 4 | Italy 1 |

The World Cup record for goal scoring is 13 by Just Fontaine, Fr., in 1958. The record for a World Cup final is 3 goals by Geoffrey Hurst, Eng., in 1966. The world record for receipts at any match is £204,805 ($573,454) at Wembley Stadium, North London, U.K., at the final on July 30, 1966.

### European Cup (for National League champions)

| | | | |
|---|---|---|---|
| 1955–56 | Paris, Fr. | Real Madrid 4 | Reims 3 |
| 1956–57 | Madrid, Spain | Real Madrid 2 | Fiorentina 0 |
| 1957–58 | Brussels, Belg. | Real Madrid 3 | Milano 2 |
| 1958–59 | Stuttgart, W. Ger. | Real Madrid 2 | Stade de Reims 0 |
| 1959–60 | Glasgow, U.K. | Real Madrid 7 | Eintracht Frankfurt 3 |
| 1960–61 | Bern, Switz. | Benfica 3 | Barcelona 2 |
| 1961–62 | Amsterdam, Neth. | Benfica 5 | Real Madrid 3 |
| 1962–63 | London, U.K. | Milano 2 | Benfica 1 |
| 1963–64 | Vienna, Aus. | Inter-Milan 3 | Real Madrid 1 |
| 1964–65 | Milan, It. | Inter-Milan 1 | Benfica 0 |
| 1965–66 | Brussels, Belg. | Real Madrid 2 | Partizan Belgrade 1 |
| 1966–67 | Lisbon, Port. | Glasgow Celtic 2 | Inter-Milan 1 |
| 1967–68 | London, U.K. | Manchester United 4 | Benfica 1 |
| 1968–69 | Madrid, Spain | A.C. Milan 4 | Ajax Amsterdam 1 |

## European-Cup Winners' Cup

| Year | Place | Result | |
|---|---|---|---|
| 1960–61 | Glasgow, U.K., and Florence, It. | Fiorentina 4 | Glasgow Rangers 1 |
| 1961–62 | Glasgow, U.K., and Stuttgart, W. Ger. | Atletico Madrid 3 | Fiorentina 0 |
| 1962–63 | Rotterdam, Neth. | Tottenham Hotspur 5 | Atletico Madrid 1 |
| 1963–64 | Antwerp, Belg. | Sporting Lisbon 1 | MTK Budapest 0 |
| 1964–65 | London, U.K. | West Ham United 2 | TSV Munich 0 |
| 1965–66 | Glasgow, U.K. | Borussia (Dortmund) 2 | Liverpool 1 |
| 1966–67 | Nürnberg, W. Ger. | Bayern Munich 1 | Glasgow Rangers 0 |
| 1967–68 | Rotterdam, Neth. | AC Milan 2 | SV Hamburg 0 |
| 1968–69 | Basel, Switz. | Slovan Bratislava 3 | FC Barcelona 2 |

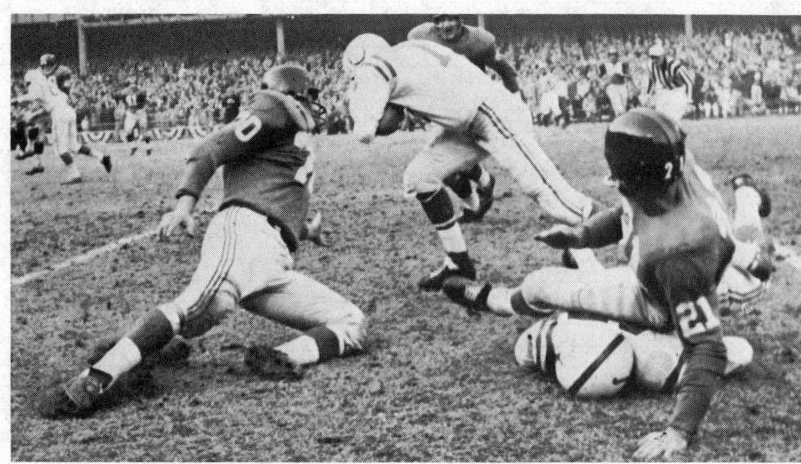

BALTIMORE COLTS WINNING THE 1958 NATIONAL FOOTBALL LEAGUE TITLE, DEFEATING THE NEW YORK GIANTS, 23–17, IN AN OVERTIME GAME
U.P.I. COMPIX

## U.S. PROFESSIONAL FOOTBALL

### National Football League Champions

| Year | Place | Result | |
|---|---|---|---|
| 1933 | Chicago | Chicago Bears 23 | New York 21 |
| 1934 | New York | New York 30 | Chicago Bears 13 |
| 1935 | Detroit | Detroit 26 | New York 7 |
| 1936 | New York | Green Bay 21 | Boston 6 |
| 1937 | Chicago | Washington 28 | Chicago Bears 21 |
| 1938 | New York | New York 23 | Green Bay 17 |
| 1939 | Milwaukee | Green Bay 27 | New York 0 |
| 1940 | Washington | Chicago Bears 73 | Washington 0 |
| 1941 | Chicago | Chicago Bears 37 | New York 9 |
| 1942 | Washington | Washington 14 | Chicago Bears 6 |
| 1943 | Chicago | Chicago Bears 41 | Washington 21 |
| 1944 | New York | Green Bay 14 | New York 7 |
| 1945 | Cleveland | Cleveland 15 | Washington 14 |
| 1946 | New York | Chicago Bears 24 | New York 14 |
| 1947 | Chicago | Chicago Cardinals 28 | Philadelphia 21 |
| 1948 | Philadelphia | Philadelphia 7 | Chicago Cardinals 0 |
| 1949 | Los Angeles | Philadelphia 14 | Los Angeles 0 |
| 1950* | Cleveland | Cleveland 30 | Los Angeles 28 |
| 1951* | Los Angeles | Los Angeles 24 | Cleveland 17 |
| 1952* | Cleveland | Detroit 17 | Cleveland 7 |
| 1953 | Detroit | Detroit 17 | Cleveland 16 |
| 1954 | Cleveland | Cleveland 56 | Detroit 10 |
| 1955 | Los Angeles | Cleveland 38 | Los Angeles 14 |
| 1956 | New York | New York 47 | Chicago Bears 7 |
| 1957 | Detroit | Detroit 59 | Cleveland 14 |
| 1958 | New York | Baltimore 23 | New York 17† |
| 1959 | Baltimore | Baltimore 31 | New York 16 |
| 1960 | Philadelphia | Philadelphia 17 | Green Bay 13 |
| 1961 | Green Bay | Green Bay 37 | New York 0 |
| 1962 | New York | Green Bay 16 | New York 7 |
| 1963 | Chicago | Chicago 14 | New York 10 |
| 1964 | Cleveland | Cleveland 27 | Baltimore 0 |
| 1965 | Green Bay | Green Bay 23 | Cleveland 12 |
| 1966 | Dallas | Green Bay 34 | Dallas 27 |
| 1967 | Green Bay | Green Bay 21 | Dallas 17 |
| 1968 | Cleveland | Baltimore 34 | Cleveland 0 |
| 1969 | Bloomington, Minn. | Minnesota 27 | Cleveland 7 |

*League was divided into American and National Conferences 1950–52.
†Won at 8:15 of sudden-death overtime period.

GREEN BAY TACKLER THROWS DALLAS QUARTERBACK FOR LOSS AS PACKERS DEFEAT COWBOYS 34–27 TO WIN THEIR SEVENTH NATIONAL FOOTBALL LEAGUE CHAMPIONSHIP, AT DALLAS, IN 1966
WIDE WORLD

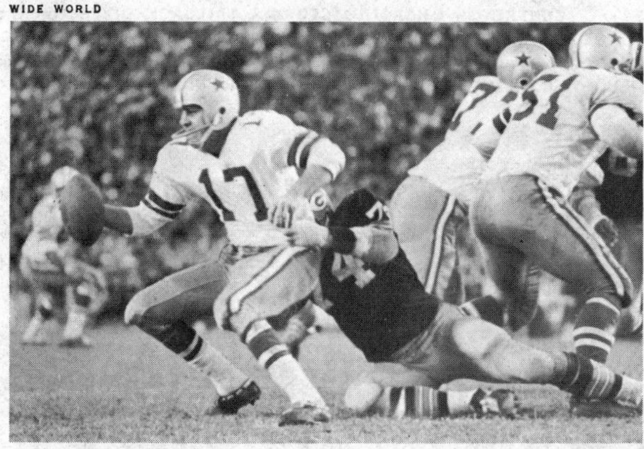

### American Football League Champions

| Year | Place | Result | |
|---|---|---|---|
| 1960 | Houston | Houston 24 | Los Angeles 16 |
| 1961 | San Diego | Houston 10 | San Diego 3 |
| 1962 | Houston | Dallas 20 | Houston 17* |
| 1963 | San Diego | San Diego 51 | Boston 10 |
| 1964 | Buffalo | Buffalo 20 | San Diego 7 |
| 1965 | San Diego | Buffalo 23 | San Diego 0 |
| 1966 | Buffalo | Kansas City 31 | Buffalo 7 |
| 1967 | Oakland | Oakland 40 | Houston 7 |
| 1968 | New York | New York 27 | Oakland 23 |
| 1969 | Oakland | Kansas City 17 | Oakland 7 |

*Won at 2:45 of second sudden-death overtime period.

### NFL-AFL Championship

| Year | Place | Result | |
|---|---|---|---|
| 1966–67 | Los Angeles | Green Bay 35 | Kansas City 10 |
| 1967–68 | Miami | Green Bay 33 | Oakland 14 |
| 1968–69 | Miami | New York 16 | Baltimore 7 |
| 1969–70 | New Orleans | Kansas City 23 | Minnesota 7 |

## U.S. COLLEGE FOOTBALL

### Major Statistical Records

Official records for the principal offensive and defensive categories, reported annually since 1941 (except for Scoring Defense for 1942).

| Year | Total offense | Yd. per game | Rushing offense | Yd. per game | Passing offense | Yd. per game | Scoring (pts. scored per game) |
|---|---|---|---|---|---|---|---|
| 1941 | Duke | 372.2 | Missouri | 307.7 | Arizona | 177.7 | Duke 34.5 |
| 1942 | Georgia | 429.5 | Hardin-Simmons | 307.4 | Tulsa | 233.9 | Tulsa 42.7 |
| 1943 | Notre Dame | 418.0 | Iowa Navy | 324.4 | Brown | 133.1 | Notre Dame 37.7 |
| 1944 | Tulsa | 434.7 | Army | 298.6 | Tulsa | 206.3 | Army 56.0 |
| 1945 | Army | 462.7 | Army | 359.3 | St. Mary's | 161.3 | Army 45.8 |
| 1946 | Notre Dame | 441.3 | Notre Dame | 340.1 | Nevada | 198.1 | Georgia 37.2 |
| 1947 | Michigan | 412.7 | Detroit | 319.7 | Michigan | 173.9 | Notre Dame 75.3 |
| 1948 | Nevada | 487.0 | Texas Mines | 378.3 | Nevada | 255.0 | Nevada 44.4 |
| 1949 | Notre Dame | 434.8 | Texas Western | 333.2 | Fordham | 183.4 | Wyoming 37.5 |
| 1950 | Arizona State | 470.4 | Arizona State | 347.0 | S. Methodist | 214.6 | Princeton 38.8 |
| 1951 | Tulsa | 480.1 | Arizona State | 334.8 | Loyola (Calif.) | 210.6 | Maryland 39.2 |
| 1952 | Tulsa | 466.6 | Tulsa | 321.5 | Fordham | 225.8 | Oklahoma 40.7 |
| 1953 | Cincinnati | 409.5 | Oklahoma | 306.9 | Stanford | 179.5 | Texas Tech. 38.9 |
| 1954 | Army | 448.7 | Army | 322.0 | Purdue | 177.3 | UCLA 40.8 |
| 1955 | Oklahoma | 410.7 | Oklahoma | 328.9 | Navy | 185.1 | Oklahoma 36.5 |
| 1956 | Oklahoma | 481.7 | Oklahoma | 391.0 | Washington State | 206.8 | Oklahoma 46.6 |
| 1957 | Arizona State | 444.9 | Colorado | 322.4 | Utah | 195.2 | Arizona St. 39.7 |
| 1958 | Iowa | 405.9 | Colorado Pacific | 259.6 | Army | 172.2 | Rutgers 33.4 |
| 1959 | Syracuse | 451.5 | Syracuse | 313.6 | Stanford | 227.8 | Syracuse 39.0 |
| 1960 | New Mexico State | 419.6 | Utah State | 312.0 | Washington State | 185.5 | New Mex. State 37.4 |
| 1961 | Mississippi | 418.7 | New Mexico State | 299.1 | Wisconsin | 188.4 | Utah State 38.7 |
| 1962 | Arizona State | 384.4 | Ohio State | 278.9 | Tulsa | 199.3 | Wisconsin 31.7 |
| 1963 | Utah State | 395.3 | Nebraska | 262.6 | Tulsa | 244.8 | Utah 31.7 |
| 1964 | Tulsa | 461.8 | Syracuse | 251.0 | Tulsa | 317.9 | Tulsa 38.4 |
| 1965 | Tulsa | 427.8 | Nebraska | 290.0 | Tulsa | 346.4 | Arkansas 32.4 |
| 1966 | Houston | 437.2 | Harvard | 269.0 | Tulsa | 272.0 | Notre Dame 36.2 |
| 1967 | Houston | 427.9 | Houston | 270.9 | Texas (El Paso) | 301.1 | Texas (El Paso) 35.9 |
| 1968 | Houston | 562.0 | Houston | 361.7 | Cincinnati | 335.8 | Houston 42.5 |
| 1969 | San Diego State | 532.2 | Texas | 363.0 | San Diego State | 374.2 | San Diego State 46.4 |

| Year | Total defense | Yd. allowed per game | Rushing defense | Yd. allowed per game | Passing defense | Yd. allowed per game | Scoring defense (pts. allowed per game) |
|---|---|---|---|---|---|---|---|
| 1941 | Duquesne | 110.6 | Duquesne | 56.0 | Purdue | 27.1 | Duquesne 2.8 |
| 1942 | Texas | 117.3 | Boston College | 48.9 | Harvard | 45.4 | — |
| 1943 | Duke | 121.7 | Duke | 39.4 | N. Carolina | 36.5 | Duke 4.2 |
| 1944 | Virginia | 96.8 | Randolph Field | 29.6 | Michigan State | 26.7 | Army 3.8 |
| 1945 | Alabama | 109.9 | Alabama | 33.9 | Holy Cross | 37.7 | St. Mary's 4.6 |
| 1946 | Notre Dame | 141.7 | Oklahoma | 58.0 | Holy Cross | 53.7 | Notre Dame 2.6 |
| 1947 | Penn State | 76.8 | Penn State | 17.0 | N.C. State | 39.3 | Penn State 3.0 |
| 1948 | Georgia Tech. | 151.3 | Georgia Tech. | 74.9 | Northwestern | 54.1 | Michigan 4.8 |
| 1949 | Kentucky | 153.8 | Oklahoma | 55.6 | Miami (Fla.) | 54.7 | Kentucky 4.8 |
| 1950 | Wake Forest | 163.2 | Ohio State | 64.0 | Tennessee | 67.5 | Army 4.4 |
| 1951 | Wisconsin | 154.8 | San Francisco | 51.6 | Washington & Lee | 67.9 | Wisconsin 5.9 |
| 1952 | Tennessee | 166.7 | Michigan State | 83.9 | Virginia | 50.3 | S. California 4.7 |
| 1953 | Cincinnati | 184.3 | Maryland | 83.9 | Richmond | 40.3 | Maryland 3.1 |
| 1954 | Mississippi | 172.3 | UCLA | 73.2 | Alabama | 45.8 | UCLA 4.4 |
| 1955 | Army | 160.7 | Maryland | 75.9 | Florida | 42.0 | Georgia Tech. 4.6 |
| 1956 | Miami (Fla.) | 189.4 | Miami (Fla.) | 106.9 | Villanova | 43.8 | Georgia Tech. 3.3 |
| 1957 | Auburn | 133.0 | Auburn | 67.4 | Georgia Tech. | 33.4 | Auburn 2.8 |
| 1958 | Auburn | 157.5 | Auburn | 79.6 | Iowa State | 39.0 | Oklahoma 4.9 |
| 1959 | Syracuse | 96.2 | Syracuse | 19.3 | Alabama | 45.7 | Mississippi 2.1 |
| 1960 | Wyoming | 149.6 | Wyoming | 82.4 | Iowa State | 30.2 | LSU 5.0 |
| 1961 | Alabama | 132.6 | Utah State | 50.8 | Pennsylvania | 56.9 | Alabama 2.2 |
| 1962 | Mississippi | 142.2 | Minnesota | 52.2 | New Mexico | 56.8 | LSU 3.4 |
| 1963 | S. Mississippi | 131.2 | Mississippi | 77.3 | Texas Western | 43.8 | Mississippi 3.7 |
| 1964 | Auburn | 164.7 | Washington | 61.3 | Kent State | 53.6 | Arkansas 5.7 |
| 1965 | S. Mississippi | 161.1 | Michigan State | 45.6 | Toledo | 69.8 | Michigan State 6.2 |
| 1966 | S. Mississippi | 163 | Wyoming | 38.5 | Toledo | 87.3 | Alabama 3.7 |
| 1967 | Nebraska | 157.6 | Wyoming | 42.3 | Nebraska | 90.1 | Oklahoma 6.8 |
| 1968 | Wyoming | 206.8 | Arizona State | 57.0 | Kent State | 107.6 | Georgia 9.8 |
| 1969 | Toledo | 209.1 | Louisiana State | 38.9 | Dayton | 90.0 | Arkansas 7.6 |

(LEFT) A PASS INTERCEPTION WITH STANFORD LEADING 7–6 WAS A KEY PLAY IN ILLINOIS'S 40–7 VICTORY OVER STANFORD (ROSE BOWL, 1952). (CENTRE) A CHARGING GEORGIA TAILBACK DIVES OVER SOUTHERN METHODIST UNIVERSITY DEFENSIVE LINEMEN TO GAIN FOUR YARDS. SUCH STEADY GAINS GAVE GEORGIA A 24–9 WIN (COTTON BOWL, 1966). (RIGHT) A GOAL LINE FUMBLE MOMENTARILY DISRUPTS THE GEORGIA TECH OFFENSE BUT TECH RECOVERED TO BEAT MISSISSIPPI 24–7 (SUGAR BOWL, 1953)

U.P.I. COMPIX

**U.S. College Football Unofficial National Champions.** The team selected each year by the Associated Press poll of sports writers and the United Press International poll of football coaches is popularly accepted as the unofficial national champion. The AP poll began in 1936 and the UPI poll in 1950; where the polls designated different teams, both are listed. Prior to the polls, from 1924 to 1936, the Rissman and Knute Rockne trophies symbolized the championship.

| Year | Team | Year | Team |
|---|---|---|---|
| 1924 | Notre Dame | 1947 | Notre Dame |
| 1925 | Dartmouth | 1948 | Michigan |
| 1926 | Stanford | 1949 | Notre Dame |
| 1927 | Illinois | 1950 | Oklahoma |
| 1928 | S. California | 1951 | Tennessee |
| 1929 | Notre Dame | 1952 | Michigan State |
| 1930 | Notre Dame | 1953 | Maryland |
| 1931 | S. California | 1954 | Ohio State, UCLA |
| 1932 | Michigan | 1955 | Oklahoma |
| 1933 | Michigan | 1956 | Oklahoma |
| 1934 | Minnesota | 1957 | Auburn, Ohio State |
| 1935 | SMU | 1958 | LSU |
| 1936 | Minnesota | 1959 | Syracuse |
| 1937 | Pittsburgh | 1960 | Minnesota |
| 1938 | TCU | 1961 | Alabama |
| 1939 | Texas A & M | 1962 | S. California |
| 1940 | Minnesota | 1963 | Texas |
| 1941 | Minnesota | 1964 | Alabama |
| 1942 | Ohio State | 1965 | Alabama, Michigan State |
| 1943 | Notre Dame | 1966 | Notre Dame |
| 1944 | Army | 1967 | S. California |
| 1945 | Army | 1968 | Ohio State |
| 1946 | Notre Dame | 1969 | Texas |

**U.S. College National Ratings.** The most successful major teams since 1936, according to the ratings produced by the press association polls, have been Notre Dame and Oklahoma. Counting 10 points for each season-end first-place rating, 9 for second, and so on, the Irish have accumulated 143 points, the Sooners 103, with the rest far behind:

| Team | Points | Team | Points |
|---|---|---|---|
| 1. Notre Dame* | 143 | 9. S. California | 67 |
| 2. Oklahoma | 103 | 10. Army | 61 |
| 3. Ohio State | 85 | 11. Minnesota | 57 |
| 4. Alabama | 84 | 12. LSU | 53 |
| 5. Texas | 80 | 13. Mississippi | 53 |
| 6. Tennessee* | 79 | 14. UCLA | 52 |
| 7. Michigan | 76 | 15. Navy | 50 |
| 8. Michigan State | 72 | 16. Georgia Tech. | 39 |

*Per Associated Press only.

HAMILTON TIGER-CATS WINNING OVER THE BRITISH COLUMBIA LIONS IN THE 1963 GREY CUP COMPETITION

U.P.I. COMPIX

U.P.I. COMPIX

FULLBACK NEIL WORDEN OF TOP-RANKED NOTRE DAME SCORED A RECORD FOUR TOUCHDOWNS IN 48–6 DEFEAT OF INDIANA IN 1951

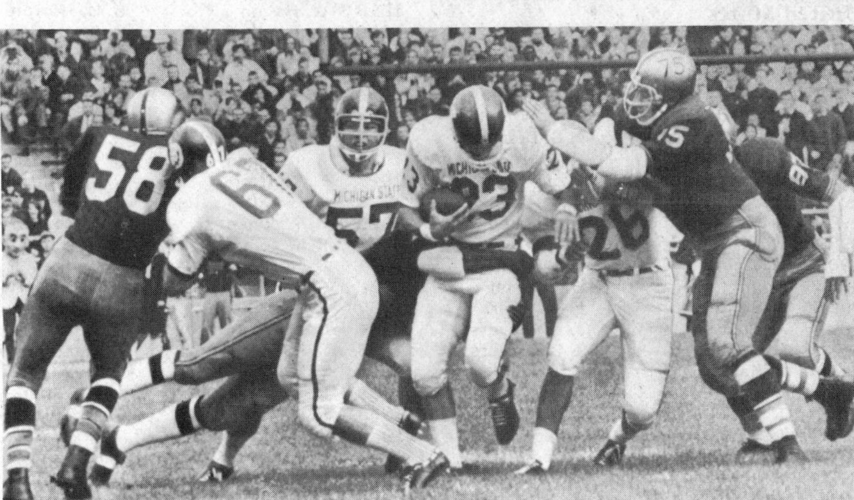

WIDE WORLD

HELD HERE FOR NO GAIN, MICHIGAN STATE FINALLY DEFEATED PURDUE 14–10 AND WENT ON TO SHARE THE 1965 TITLE WITH ALABAMA

## CANADIAN FOOTBALL

### Grey Cup Competition

| Year | Team |
|---|---|
| 1909–11 | U. of Toronto |
| 1912 | Hamilton Alerts |
| 1913 | Hamilton Tigers |
| 1914 | Toronto Argos |
| 1915* | Hamilton Tigers |
| 1920 | U. of Toronto |
| 1921 | Toronto Argos |
| 1922–24 | Queens University |
| 1925–26 | Ottawa Rough Riders |
| 1927 | Toronto Balmy Beach |
| 1928–29 | Hamilton Tigers |
| 1930 | Toronto Balmy Beach |
| 1931 | Montreal AAA |
| 1932 | Hamilton Tigers |
| 1933 | Toronto Argonauts |
| 1934 | Sarnia Imperials |
| 1935 | Winnipeg Blue Bombers |
| 1936 | Sarnia Imperials |
| 1937–38 | Toronto Argonauts |
| 1939 | Winnipeg Blue Bombers |
| 1940 | Ottawa Rough Riders |
| 1941 | Winnipeg Blue Bombers |
| 1942 | Toronto RCAF Hurricanes |
| 1943 | Hamilton Wildcats |
| 1944 | St. Hyacinthe-Donnaconna |
| 1945–47 | Toronto Argonauts |
| 1948 | Calgary Stampeders |
| 1949 | Montreal Alouettes |
| 1950 | Toronto Argonauts |
| 1951 | Ottawa Rough Riders |
| 1952 | Toronto Argonauts |
| 1953 | Hamilton Tiger-Cats |
| 1954–56 | Edmonton Eskimos |
| 1957 | Hamilton Tiger-Cats |
| 1958–59 | Winnipeg Blue Bombers |
| 1960 | Ottawa Rough Riders |
| 1961–62 | Winnipeg Blue Bombers |
| 1963 | Hamilton Tiger-Cats |
| 1964 | British Columbia Lions |
| 1965 | Hamilton Tiger-Cats |
| 1966 | Saskatchewan Roughriders |
| 1967 | Hamilton Tiger-Cats |
| 1968–69 | Ottawa Rough Riders |

*No games 1916–19. East-West Playoff began in 1921.

**RUGBY UNION FOOTBALL.** The game, for amateurs only, is organized internationally by the International Rugby Union Football Board, which has seven members: England, Ireland, Scotland, Wales, Australia, New Zealand, and South Africa.

The game is organized in Europe by the International Amateur Rugby Federation (FIRA), which has ten members including France. France also plays international matches against the seven International Board countries.

**Record of International (or Test) Matches* 1871 to Dec. 1969**

| | England | Scotland | Ireland | Wales | British Isles | South Africa | New Zealand | Australia | France |
|---|---|---|---|---|---|---|---|---|---|
| **England** | — | 41/14 | 47/8 | 32/11 | — | 1/1 | 1/0 | 1/0 | 28/4 |
| **Scotland** | 29/14 | — | 41/3 | 32/2 | — | 3/0 | 0/1 | 3/0 | 21/2 |
| **Ireland** | 26/8 | 36/3 | — | 25/4 | — | 1/0 | 0/0 | 4/0 | 20/2 |
| **Wales** | 31/11 | 39/2 | 43/4 | — | — | 0/0 | 3/0 | 4/0 | 28/2 |
| **British Isles†** | — | — | — | — | — | 10/3 | 2/2 | 2/0 | — |
| **South Africa** | 4/1 | 5/0 | 6/0 | 6/0 | 17/3 | — | 13/2 | 18/0 | 5/2 |
| **New Zealand** | 7/0 | 4/1 | 5/0 | 5/0 | 16/2 | 11/2 | — | 40/3 | 10/0 |
| **Australia** | 4/0 | 1/0 | 1/0 | 2/0 | 2/0 | 7/0 | 13/3 | — | 0/0 |
| **France** | 12/4 | 16/2 | 19/2 | 12/2 | — | 5/3 | 1/0 | 4/0 | — |

*Reading across, the first figure is the all-time number of wins and the second the number of drawn matches against a given opponent. The number of losses to any opponent can be ascertained by reading downward. †The British Isles ("British Lions") is a combined team from the four "Home Unions" (England, Ireland, Scotland, and Wales).

**RUGBY LEAGUE FOOTBALL.** The game, established in 1895, was first played by professionals in 1898. The number of players has been 13 per side since 1906 and the title Rugby League was adopted in 1922.

**World Cup Competition**

| Year | Place | Result | |
|---|---|---|---|
| 1954 | Paris, Fr. | England 16 | France 12 |
| 1957 | Sydney, Austr. | New Zealand 29 | England 21 |
| 1960 | England | England 66 | Australia 37 |
| 1968 | Australia | Australia 20 | France 2 |

**Test Matches**

The three principal Test-match series stand as follows:

England versus Australia (instituted 1909)
Played 80: England 45, Australia 31, 4 draws

England versus New Zealand (instituted 1908)
Played 48: England 32, New Zealand 15, 1 draw

England versus France (instituted 1957)
Played 26: England 15, France 8, 3 draws

**GOLF.** The most important championships in golf have been The Open and Amateur (British) and the U.S. Open, Amateur, Professional (PGA), and Masters. International two-man team competition by professionals for the Canada Cup was inaugurated in 1953; and the World's Amateur Golf Council Eisenhower Cup tournament was inaugurated in 1958. Competition between teams representing the United States and the United Kingdom for the Walker Cup (amateur) began in 1922, and for the Ryder Cup (professional) in 1927. The premier events in women's golf are the U.S. Women's Open and Women's Amateur and the British Women's Amateur. International team competition for women includes the Curtis Cup for U.S. and British amateurs since 1932, and the World Women's Amateur Team Championships instituted in 1964. For historic and other details *see* the article GOLF.

**OPEN AND AMATEUR CHAMPIONS**
**United States**

| Year | Open | Amateur |
|---|---|---|
| 1895 | H. Rawlins | C. B. Macdonald |
| 1896 | J. Faulis | H. J. Whigham |
| 1897 | J. Lloyd | H. J. Whigham |
| 1898 | F. Herd | F. S. Douglas |
| 1899 | W. Smith | H. M. Harriman |
| 1900 | H. Vardon (U.K.) | W. J. Travis |
| 1901 | W. Anderson | W. J. Travis |
| 1902 | L. Auchterlonie | L. N. James |
| 1903 | W. Anderson | W. J. Travis |
| 1904 | W. Anderson | H. C. Egan |
| 1905 | W. Anderson | H. C. Egan |
| 1906 | A. Smith | E. M. Byers |
| 1907 | A. Ross | J. D. Travers |
| 1908 | F. McLoed | J. D. Travers |
| 1909 | G. Sargent | R. Gardner |
| 1910 | A. Smith | W. C. Fownes, Jr. |
| 1911 | J. J. McDermott | H. H. Hilton |
| 1912 | J. J. McDermott | J. D. Travers |
| 1913 | F. Ouimet | J. D. Travers |
| 1914 | W. Hagen | F. Ouimet |
| 1915 | J. D. Travers | R. A. Gardner |
| 1916* | C. Evans | C. Evans |
| 1919 | W. Hagen | S. D. Herron |
| 1920 | E. Ray (U.K.) | C. Evans |
| 1921 | J. Barnes | J. Guildford |
| 1922 | G. Sarazen | J. Sweetser |
| 1923 | R. T. Jones, Jr. | M. Marston |
| 1924 | G. Walker | R. T. Jones, Jr. |
| 1925 | W. MacFarlane, Jr. | R. T. Jones, Jr. |
| 1926 | R. T. Jones, Jr. | G. von Elm |
| 1927 | T. D. Armour | R. T. Jones, Jr. |
| 1928 | J. Farrell | R. T. Jones, Jr. |
| 1929 | R. T. Jones, Jr. | H. R. Johnston |
| 1930 | R. T. Jones, Jr. | R. T. Jones, Jr. |
| 1931 | B. Burke | F. Ouimet |
| 1932 | G. Sarazen | C. R. Somerville |
| 1933 | J. Goodman | G. T. Dunlap |
| 1934 | O. Dutra | W. L. Little, Jr. |
| 1935 | S. Parks | W. L. Little, Jr. |
| 1936 | T. Manero | J. Fischer |
| 1937 | R. Guldahl | J. Goodman |
| 1938 | R. Guldahl | W. P. Turnesa |
| 1939 | B. Nelson | M. H. Ward |
| 1940 | W. L. Little, Jr. | R. D. Chapman |
| 1941* | C. Wood | M. H. Ward |
| 1946 | L. Mangrum | S. E. Bishop |
| 1947 | L. Worsham | R. H. Riegel |
| 1948 | B. Hogan | W. P. Turnesa |
| 1949 | C. Middlecoff | C. R. Coe |
| 1950 | B. Hogan | S. Urzetta |
| 1951 | B. Hogan | W. J. Maxwell |
| 1952 | J. Boros | J. Westland |
| 1953 | B. Hogan | G. Littler |
| 1954 | E. Furgol | A. Palmer |
| 1955 | J. Fleck | J. H. Ward |
| 1956 | C. Middlecoff | J. H. Ward |
| 1957 | D. Mayer | H. Robbins |
| 1958 | T. Bolt | C. R. Coe |
| 1959 | W. Casper | J. Nicklaus |
| 1960 | A. Palmer | D. R. Beman |
| 1961 | G. Littler | J. Nicklaus |
| 1962 | J. Nicklaus | L. E. Harris, Jr. |
| 1963 | J. Boros | D. R. Beman |
| 1964 | K. Venturi | W. Campbell |
| 1965 | G. J. Player (S.Af.) | R. Murphy |
| 1966 | W. Casper | G. Cowan (Can.) |
| 1967 | J. Nicklaus† | B. Dickson |
| 1968 | L. Trevino | B. Fleisher |
| 1969 | O. Moody | S. Melnyk |

*No competition 1917–18; 1942–45.
†Scored record 275.

JAMES DRAKE FOR "SPORTS ILLUSTRATED," © TIME INC.
ARNOLD PALMER, JUBILANT AT WINNING THE MASTERS GOLF TOURNAMENT FOR AN UNPRECEDENTED FOURTH TIME, AT AUGUSTA, GA., IN 1964

U.P.I. COMPIX
MARVIN WARD, TWICE U.S. AMATEUR GOLF CHAMPION, TEEING OFF IN THE 1939 TOURNAMENT FINALS. WARD ALSO WON THE TITLE IN 1941

## OPEN AND AMATEUR CHAMPIONS

### United Kingdom

U.P.I. COMPIX

T. H. COTTON, THRICE WINNER OF THE BRITISH OPEN GOLF TOURNAMENT, PLAYING IN THE 1937 RYDER CUP COMPETITION AT AINSDALE, SOUTHPORT, ENG.

| Year | Open | Amateur |
|---|---|---|
| 1860 | W. Park | |
| 1861 | T. Morris, Sr. | |
| 1862 | T. Morris, Sr. | |
| 1863 | W. Park | |
| 1864 | T. Morris, Sr. | |
| 1865 | A. Strath | |
| 1866 | W. Park | |
| 1867 | T. Morris, Sr. | |
| 1868 | T. Morris, Jr. | |
| 1869 | T. Morris, Jr. | |
| 1870* | T. Morris, Jr. | |
| 1872 | T. Morris, Jr. | |
| 1873 | T. Kidd | |
| 1874 | M. Park | |
| 1875 | W. Park | |
| 1876 | B. Martin | |
| 1877 | J. Anderson | |
| 1878 | J. Anderson | |
| 1879 | J. Anderson | |
| 1880 | B. Ferguson | |
| 1881 | B. Ferguson | |
| 1882 | B. Ferguson | |
| 1883 | W. Fernie | |
| 1884 | J. Simpson | |
| 1885 | B. Martin | A. F. Macfie |
| 1886 | D. Brown | H. G. Hutchinson |
| 1887 | W. Park, Jr. | H. G. Hutchinson |
| 1888 | J. Burns | J. Ball |
| 1889 | W. Park, Jr. | J. E. Laidlay |
| 1890 | J. Ball | J. Ball |
| 1891 | H. Kirkaldy | J. E. Laidlay |
| 1892 | H. H. Hilton | J. Ball |
| 1893 | W. Auchterlonie | P. Anderson |
| 1894 | J. H. Taylor | J. Ball |
| 1895 | J. H. Taylor | J. M. Melville |
| 1896 | H. Vardon | F. G. Tait |
| 1897 | H. H. Hilton | A. J. T. Allan |
| 1898 | H. Vardon | F. G. Tait |
| 1899 | H. Vardon | J. Ball |
| 1900 | J. H. Taylor | H. H. Hilton |
| 1901 | J. Braid | H. H. Hilton |
| 1902 | A. Herd | C. Hutchings |
| 1903 | H. Vardon | R. Maxwell |
| 1904 | J. White | W. J. Travis (U.S.) |
| 1905 | J. Braid | A. G. Barry |
| 1906 | J. Braid | J. Robb |
| 1907 | A. Massy (Fr.) | J. Ball |
| 1908 | J. Braid | E. A. Lassen |
| 1909 | J. H. Taylor | R. Maxwell |
| 1910 | J. Braid | J. Ball |
| 1911 | H. Vardon | H. H. Hilton |
| 1912 | E. Ray | J. Ball |
| 1913 | J. H. Taylor | H. H. Hilton |
| 1914* | H. Vardon | J. L. C. Jenkins |
| 1920 | G. Duncan | C. J. H. Tolley |
| 1921 | J. Hutchison (U.S.) | W. I. Hunter |
| 1922 | W. Hagen (U.S.) | E. W. E. Holderness |
| 1923 | A. G. Havers | R. H. Wethered |
| 1924 | W. Hagen (U.S.) | E. W. E. Holderness |
| 1925 | J. Barnes (U.S.) | R. Harris |
| 1926 | R. T. Jones (U.S.) | J. Sweetser (U.S.) |
| 1927 | R. T. Jones (U.S.) | W. Tweddell |
| 1928 | W. Hagen (U.S.) | T. P. Perkins |
| 1929 | W. Hagen (U.S.) | C. J. H. Tolley |
| 1930 | R. T. Jones (U.S.) | R. T. Jones (U.S.) |
| 1931 | T. D. Armour (U.S.) | E. Martin Smith |
| 1932 | G. Sarazen (U.S.) | J. de Forest |
| 1933 | D. Shute (U.S.) | M. Scott |
| 1934 | T. H. Cotton | W. Little (U.S.) |
| 1935 | A. Perry | W. Little (U.S.) |
| 1936 | A. H. Padgham | H. Thomson |
| 1937 | T. H. Cotton | R. Sweeny, Jr. (U.S.) |
| 1938 | R. A. Whitcombe | C. R. Yates (U.S.) |
| 1939* | R. Burton | A. T. Kyle |
| 1946 | S. Snead (U.S.) | J. Bruen |
| 1947 | F. Daly | W. P. Turnesa (U.S.) |
| 1948 | T. H. Cotton | F. R. Stranahan (U.S.) |
| 1949 | A. D. Locke (S.Af.) | S. M. M'Cready |
| 1950 | A. D. Locke (S.Af.) | F. R. Stranahan (U.S.) |
| 1951 | M. Faulkner | R. D. Chapman (U.S.) |
| 1952 | A. D. Locke (S.Af.) | E. H. Ward (U.S.) |
| 1953 | B. Hogan (U.S.) | J. B. Carr (Ire.) |
| 1954 | P. W. Thomson (Austr.) | D. W. Bachli |
| 1955 | P. W. Thomson (Austr.) | J. W. Conrad (U.S.) |
| 1956 | P. W. Thomson (Austr.) | J. C. Beharrell |
| 1957 | A. D. Locke (S.Af.) | R. Reid Jack |
| 1958 | P. W. Thomson (Austr.) | J. B. Carr (Ire.) |
| 1959 | G. J. Player (S.Af.) | D. Beman (U.S.) |
| 1960 | K. D. G. Nagle (Austr.) | J. B. Carr (Ire.) |
| 1961 | A. Palmer (U.S.) | M. F. Bonallack |
| 1962 | A. Palmer (U.S.) | R. D. Davies (U.S.) |
| 1963 | R. J. Charles (N.Z.) | M. S. R. Lunt |
| 1964 | T. Lema (U.S.) | G. J. Clark |
| 1965 | P. W. Thomson (Austr.) | M. F. Bonallack |
| 1966 | J. Nicklaus (U.S.) | R. Cole (S.Af.) |
| 1967 | R. de Vicenzo (Arg.) | B. Dickson (U.S.) |
| 1968 | G. J. Player (S.Af.) | M. F. Bonallack |
| 1969 | A. Jacklin | M. F. Bonallack |
| 1970 | J. Nicklaus (U.S.) | M. F. Bonallack |

*No competition 1871; 1915–19; 1940–45.

## U.S. PROFESSIONAL GOLFERS' ASSOCIATION (PGA) CHAMPIONS

| | | | |
|---|---|---|---|
| 1916 | J. Barnes | 1945 | B. Nelson |
| 1919 | J. Barnes | 1946 | B. Hogan |
| 1920 | J. Hutchison | 1947 | J. Ferrier |
| 1921 | W. Hagen | 1948 | B. Hogan |
| 1922 | G. Sarazen | 1949 | S. Snead |
| 1923 | G. Sarazen | 1950 | C. Harper |
| 1924 | W. Hagen | 1951 | S. Snead |
| 1925 | W. Hagen | 1952 | J. Turnesa |
| 1926 | W. Hagen | 1953 | W. Burkemo |
| 1927 | W. Hagen | 1954 | C. Harbert |
| 1928 | L. Diegel | 1955 | D. Ford |
| 1929 | L. Diegel | 1956 | J. Burke, Jr. |
| 1930 | T. Armour | 1957 | L. Hebert |
| 1931 | T. Creavy | 1958 | D. Finsterwald |
| 1932 | O. Dutra | 1959 | R. Rosburg |
| 1933 | G. Sarazen | 1960 | J. Hebert |
| 1934 | P. Runyan | 1961 | J. Barber |
| 1935 | J. Revolta | 1962 | G. J. Player (S.Af.) |
| 1936 | D. Shute | 1963 | J. Nicklaus |
| 1937 | D. Shute | 1964 | B. Nichols |
| 1938 | R. Runyan | 1965 | D. Marr |
| 1939 | H. Picard | 1966 | A. Geiberger |
| 1940 | B. Nelson | 1967 | D. January |
| 1941 | V. Ghezzi | 1968 | J. Boros |
| 1942 | S. Snead | 1969 | R. Floyd |
| 1944 | B. Hamilton | | |

## MASTERS TOURNAMENT

Augusta National Golf Course, Augusta, Ga.

| Year | Winner | Score | Year | Winner | Score |
|---|---|---|---|---|---|
| 1934 | H. Smith | 284 | 1954 | S. Snead | 289 |
| 1935 | G. Sarazen | 282 | 1955 | C. Middlecoff | 279 |
| 1936 | H. Smith | 285 | 1956 | J. Burke | 289 |
| 1937 | B. Nelson | 283 | 1957 | D. Ford | 283 |
| 1938 | H. Picard | 285 | 1958 | A. Palmer | 284 |
| 1939 | R. Guldahl | 279 | 1959 | A. Wall | 284 |
| 1940 | J. Demaret | 280 | 1960 | A. Palmer | 282 |
| 1941 | C. Wood | 280 | 1961 | G. J. Player (S.Af.) | 280 |
| 1942 | B. Nelson | 280 | 1962 | A. Palmer | 280 |
| 1946 | H. Keiser | 282 | 1963 | J. Nicklaus | 286 |
| 1947 | J. Demaret | 281 | 1964 | A. Palmer | 276 |
| 1948 | C. Harmon | 279 | 1965 | J. Nicklaus | 271 |
| 1949 | S. Snead | 282 | 1966 | J. Nicklaus | 288 |
| 1950 | J. Demaret | 283 | 1967 | G. Brewer | 280 |
| 1951 | B. Hogan | 280 | 1968 | R. Goalby | 277* |
| 1952 | S. Snead | 286 | 1969 | G. Archer | 281 |
| 1953 | B. Hogan | 274 | 1970 | W. Casper | 279 |

*R. de Vicenzo (Arg.) also scored 277 but was disqualified for a playoff when he signed an incorrect scorecard, making his score officially 278.

## PGA LEADING OFFICIAL MONEY WINNERS

| Year | Player | Total |
|---|---|---|
| 1941 | B. Hogan | $ 18,358 |
| 1942 | B. Hogan | 13,143 |
| 1943* | | |
| 1944 | B. Nelson | 37,967† |
| 1945 | B. Nelson | 63,335† |
| 1946 | B. Hogan | 42,556 |
| 1947 | J. Demaret | 27,936 |
| 1948 | B. Hogan | 32,112 |
| 1949 | S. Snead | 31,593 |
| 1950 | S. Snead | 35,758 |
| 1951 | L. Mangrum | 26,088 |
| 1952 | J. Boros | 37,032 |
| 1953 | L. Worsham | 34,002 |
| 1954 | B. Toski | 65,819 |
| 1955 | J. Boros | 63,121 |
| 1956 | T. Kroll | 72,835 |
| 1957 | D. Mayer | 65,835 |
| 1958 | A. Palmer | 42,607 |
| 1959 | A. Wall, Jr. | 53,167 |
| 1960 | A. Palmer | 75,262 |
| 1961 | G. J. Player | 64,540 |
| 1962 | A. Palmer | 81,448 |
| 1963 | A. Palmer | 128,230 |
| 1964 | J. Nicklaus | 113,284 |
| 1965 | J. Nicklaus | 140,752 |
| 1966 | W. Casper | 121,944 |
| 1967 | J. Nicklaus | 211,566 |
| 1968 | W. Casper | 205,168 |
| 1969 | F. Beard | 175,223 |

*No records kept.
†In government bonds.
Source: The Professional Golfers' Association of America.

## INTERNATIONAL TEAM MATCHES

### WALKER CUP (U.S. v. Great Britain—amateurs)

| Year | Result |
|---|---|
| 1922 | United States 8, Great Britain 4; at National Links, Long Island, N.Y. |
| 1923 | United States 6, Great Britain 5, 1 halved; at St. Andrews, Scot. |
| 1924 | United States 9, Great Britain 3; at Garden City, N.Y. |
| 1926 | United States 6, Great Britain 5, 1 halved; at St. Andrews, Scot. |
| 1928 | United States 11, Great Britain 1; at Chicago Golf Club, Wheaton, Ill. |
| 1930 | United States 10, Great Britain 2; at Royal St. George's, Sandwich, Eng. |
| 1932 | United States 8, Great Britain 1, 3 halved; at Brookline, Mass. |
| 1934 | United States 9, Great Britain 2, 1 halved; at St. Andrews, Scot. |
| 1936 | United States 9, Great Britain 0, 3 halved; at Pine Valley, N.J. |
| 1938 | Great Britain 7, United States 4, 1 halved; at St. Andrews, Scot. |
| 1947 | United States 8, Great Britain 4; at St. Andrews, Scot. |
| 1949 | United States 10, Great Britain 2; at Winged Foot, N.Y. |
| 1951 | United States 6, Great Britain 3, 3 halved; at Birkdale, Lancs., Eng. |
| 1953 | United States 9, Great Britain 3; at Marion, Mass. |
| 1955 | United States 10, Great Britain 2; at St. Andrews, Scot. |
| 1957 | United States 8, Great Britain 3, 1 halved; at Minikahda, Minn. |
| 1959 | United States 9, Great Britain 3; at Muirfield, Scot. |
| 1961 | United States 11, Great Britain 1; at Seattle, Wash. |
| 1963 | United States 12, Great Britain 8, 4 halved; at Turnberry, Scot. |
| 1965 | United States 11, Great Britain 11, 2 halved; at Baltimore, Md. |
| 1967 | United States 13, Great Britain 7, 4 halved; at Sandwich, Eng. |
| 1969 | United States 10, Great Britain 8, 6 halved; at Milwaukee, Wis. |

### RYDER CUP (U.S. v. Great Britain—professionals)

| Year | Result |
|---|---|
| 1927 | United States 9, Great Britain 2, 1 halved; at Worcester, Mass. |
| 1929 | Great Britain 6, United States 4, 2 halved; at Moortown, Leeds, Eng. |
| 1931 | United States 9, Great Britain 3; at Scioto, Columbus, O. |
| 1933 | Great Britain 6, United States 5, 1 halved; at Southport and Ainsdale Course, Southport, Eng. |
| 1935 | United States 8, Great Britain 2, 2 halved; at Ridgewood, N.J. |
| 1937 | United States 7, Great Britain 3, 2 halved; at Southport, Eng. |
| 1947 | United States 11, Great Britain 1; at Portland, Ore. |
| 1949 | United States 7, Great Britain 5; at Ganton, Scarborough, Eng. |
| 1951 | United States 9, Great Britain 2, 1 halved; at Pinehurst, N.C. |
| 1953 | United States 6, Great Britain 5, 1 halved; at Wentworth, Surrey, Eng. |
| 1955 | United States 8, Great Britain 4; at Palm Springs, Calif. |
| 1957 | Great Britain 7, United States 4, 1 halved; at Lindrick, Sheffield, Eng. |
| 1959 | United States 7, Great Britain 2, 3 halved; at Palm Desert, Calif. |
| 1961 | United States 13, Great Britain 8, 3 halved; at Royal Lytham & St. Annes, Eng. |
| 1963 | United States 20, Great Britain 6, 6 halved; at Atlanta, Ga. |
| 1965 | United States 18, Great Britain 11, 3 halved; at Royal Birkdale, Eng. |
| 1967 | United States 21, Great Britain 6, 5 halved; at Houston, Tex. |
| 1969 | United States 13, Great Britain 13, 6 halved; at Royal Birkdale, Eng. |

JACK NICKLAUS, LEADING PROFESSIONAL-GOLF MONEY WINNER IN 1964, 1965, AND 1967, CHIPPING TOWARD GREEN IN 1963 WORLD SERIES OF GOLF AT AKRON, O.

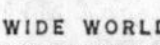

WIDE WORLD

WIDE WORLD

BILLY CASPER, LEADING MONEY WINNER IN 1966 AND 1968, WAVES HIS PUTTER IN ACKNOWLEDGMENT OF THE CHEERS OF THE GALLERY AS HE TAKES THE LEAD IN THE PLAYOFF WITH ARNOLD PALMER FOR THE 1966 U.S. OPEN CHAMPIONSHIP

## WORLD CUP (formerly CANADA CUP)
## (Two-man teams, professionals)

| Year | Winner | Place |
|---|---|---|
| 1953 | Argentina (A. Cerda and R. de Vicenzo) | Toronto, Ont. |
| 1954 | Australia (P. Thomson and K. Nagle) | Laval-sur-le-Lac, Que. |
| 1955 | United States (C. Harbert and E. Furgol) | Washington, D.C. |
| 1956 | United States (B. Hogan and S. Snead) | Wentworth, Eng. |
| 1957 | Japan (T. Nakamura and K. Ono) | Tokyo, Jap. |
| 1958 | Ireland (H. Bradshaw and C. O'Connor) | Mexico City, Mex. |
| 1959 | Australia (P. W. Thomson and K. Nagle) | Melbourne, Austr. |
| 1960 | United States (S. Snead and A. Palmer) | Portmarnock, Ire. |
| 1961 | United States (S. Snead and J. Demaret) | Dorado Beach, P.R. |
| 1962 | United States (S. Snead and A. Palmer) | Buenos Aires, Arg. |
| 1963 | United States (A. Palmer and J. Nicklaus) | St. Nom-La-Breteche, Fr. |
| 1964 | United States (A. Palmer and J. Nicklaus) | Maui, Hawaii |
| 1965 | South Africa (G. Player and H. R. Henning) | Madrid, Sp. |
| 1966 | United States (A. Palmer and J. Nicklaus) | Tokyo, Jap. |
| 1967 | United States (A. Palmer and J. Nicklaus) | Mexico City, Mex. |
| 1968 | Canada (A. Balding and G. Knudson) | Rome, Italy |
| 1969 | United States (O. Moody and L. Trevino) | Singapore |

## EISENHOWER TROPHY
## (Four-man teams, amateurs)

| Year | Winner | Place |
|---|---|---|
| 1958 | Australia (B. Devlin, P. Toogood, R. F. Stevens, D. Bachli) | St. Andrews, Scot. |
| 1960 | United States (D. R. Beman, R. W. Gardner, W. Hyndman, J. Nicklaus) | Ardmore, U.S. |
| 1962 | United States (D. R. Beman, W. J. Patton, R. Silkes, L. Harris) | Kawana, Jap. |
| 1964 | United Kingdom (J. Carr, non-playing captain, R. Shade, M. Lunt, R. Foster, M. Bonallack) | Olgiata, Rome, It. |
| 1966 | Australia (H. Berwick, P. Billings, K. Donohue, K. Hartley) | Mexico City, Mex. |
| 1968 | United States (R. Siderowf, J. Lewis, Jr., M. Giles, B. Fleisher) | Melbourne, Austr. |

MICKEY WRIGHT DISPLAYING HER FOURTH U.S. WOMEN'S OPEN GOLF CHAMPIONSHIP CUP AFTER SHE WON THE TITLE IN 1964
WIDE WORLD

BABE DIDRIKSON ZAHARIAS, THE FIRST AMERICAN TO WIN THE BRITISH WOMEN'S AMATEUR GOLF CHAMPIONSHIP, 1947
U.P.I. COMPIX

## U.S. WOMEN'S OPEN CHAMPIONS

| Year | Champion | Year | Champion |
|---|---|---|---|
| 1946 | P. Berg | 1959 | M. Wright |
| 1947 | B. Jameson | 1960 | B. Rawls |
| 1948 | M. D. Zaharias | 1961 | M. Wright |
| 1949 | L. Suggs | 1962 | M. Lindstrom |
| 1950 | M. D. Zaharias | 1963 | M. Mills |
| 1951 | B. Rawls | 1964 | M. Wright |
| 1952 | L. Suggs | 1965 | C. Mann |
| 1953 | B. Rawls | 1966 | S. Spuzich |
| 1954 | M. D. Zaharias | 1967 | C. Lacoste (Fr.)* |
| 1955 | F. Crocker | 1968 | S. Berning |
| 1956 | K. Cornelius | 1969 | D. Caponi |
| 1957 | B. Rawls | 1970 | D. Caponi |
| 1958 | M. Wright | | |

*Amateur.

## U.S. WOMEN'S AMATEUR CHAMPIONS

| Year | Champion | Year | Champion | Year | Champion | Year | Champion |
|---|---|---|---|---|---|---|---|
| 1895 | C. S. Brown | 1913 | G. Ravenscroft | 1932 | V. van Wie | 1953 | M. L. Faulk |
| 1896 | B. Hoyt | 1914 | K. Jackson | 1933 | V. van Wie | 1954 | B. Romack |
| 1897 | B. Hoyt | 1915 | C. H. Vanderbeck | 1934 | V. van Wie | 1955 | P. Lesser |
| 1898 | B. Hoyt | 1916 | A. Stirling | 1935 | G. Collett Vare | 1956 | M. Stewart (Can.) |
| 1899 | R. Underhill | 1917–18* | | 1936 | P. Barton (U.K.) | 1957 | J. Gunderson |
| 1900 | F. C. Griscom | 1919 | A. Stirling | 1937 | E. L. Page | 1958 | A. Quast |
| 1901 | G. Hecker | 1920 | A. Stirling | 1938 | P. Berg | 1959 | B. McIntire |
| 1902 | G. Hecker | 1921 | M. Hollins | 1939 | B. Jameson | 1960 | J. Gunderson |
| 1903 | B. Anthony | 1922 | G. Collett | 1940 | B. Jameson | 1961 | A. Quast Decker |
| 1904 | G. M. Bishop | 1923 | E. Cummings | 1941 | B. H. Newell | 1962 | J. Gunderson |
| 1905 | P. Mackay | 1924 | D. C. Hurd | 1942–45* | | 1963 | A. Quast Welts |
| 1906 | H. S. Curtis | 1925 | G. Collett | 1946 | M. D. Zaharias | 1964 | B. McIntire |
| 1907 | M. Curtis | 1926 | H. B. Stetson | 1947 | L. Suggs | 1965 | J. Ashley |
| 1908 | K. C. Harley | 1927 | M. B. Horn | 1948 | G. Lenczyk | 1966 | J. Gunderson Carner |
| 1909 | D. I. Campbell | 1928 | G. Collett | 1949 | D. G. Porter | 1967 | L. Dill |
| 1910 | D. I. Campbell | 1929 | G. Collett | 1950 | B. Hanson | 1968 | J. Gunderson Carner |
| 1911 | M. Curtis | 1930 | G. Collett | 1951 | D. Kirby | 1969 | C. Lacoste (Fr.) |
| 1912 | M. Curtis | 1931 | H. Hicks | 1952 | J. Pung | | |

## BRITISH WOMEN'S AMATEUR CHAMPIONS

| Year | Champion | Year | Champion | Year | Champion | Year | Champion |
|---|---|---|---|---|---|---|---|
| 1893 | M. Scott | 1910 | G. Suttie | 1931 | E. Wilson | 1953 | M. Stewart (Can.) |
| 1894 | M. Scott | 1911 | D. Campbell | 1932 | E. Wilson | 1954 | F. Stephens |
| 1895 | M. Scott | 1912 | G. Ravenscroft | 1933 | E. Wilson | 1955 | J. Valentine |
| 1896 | A. B. Pascoe | 1913 | M. Dodd | 1934 | A. M. Holm | 1956 | M. Smith (U.S.) |
| 1897 | E. C. Orr | 1914 | C. Leitch | 1935 | W. Morgan | 1957 | P. Garvey |
| 1898 | L. Thomson | 1915–19* | | 1936 | P. Barton | 1958 | J. Valentine |
| 1899 | M. Hezlet | 1920 | C. Leitch | 1937 | J. Anderson | 1959 | E. Price |
| 1900 | R. K. Adair | 1921 | C. Leitch | 1938 | A. M. Holm | 1960 | B. McIntire (U.S.) |
| 1901 | M. A. Graham | 1922 | J. Wethered | 1939 | P. Barton | 1961 | A. D. Spearman |
| 1902 | M. Hezlet | 1923 | D. Chambers | 1940–45* | | 1962 | A. D. Spearman |
| 1903 | R. K. Adair | 1924 | J. Wethered | 1946 | J. Hetherington | 1963 | B. Varangot (Fr.) |
| 1904 | L. Dod | 1925 | J. Wethered | 1947 | M. D. Zaharias (U.S.) | 1964 | C. Sorenson (U.S.) |
| 1905 | B. Thompson | 1926 | C. Leitch | 1948 | L. Suggs (U.S.) | 1965 | B. Varangot (Fr.) |
| 1906 | L. Kennion | 1927 | T. de la Chaume (Fr.) | 1949 | F. Stephens | 1966 | E. Chadwick |
| 1907 | M. Hezlet | 1928 | N. le Blan (Fr.) | 1950 | Viscomtesse de Saint Sauveur (Fr.) | 1967 | E. Chadwick |
| 1908 | M. Titterton | 1929 | J. Wethered | 1951 | P. G. MacCann | 1968 | B. Varangot (Fr.) |
| 1909 | D. Campbell | 1930 | D. Fishwick | 1952 | M. Paterson | 1969 | C. Lacoste (Fr.) |

*No competition.

**CURTIS CUP (United States v. British Isles—women amateurs)**

| Year | Players | Place | Year | Players | Place |
|---|---|---|---|---|---|
| 1932 | United States 5½, British Isles 3½ | Wentworth, Eng. | 1956 | British Isles 5, United States 4 | Sandwich, Eng. |
| 1934 | United States 6½, British Isles 2½ | Chevy Chase, Md. | 1958 | British Isles* 4½, United States 4½ | West Newton, Mass. |
| 1936 | United States* 4½, British Isles 4½ | Gleneagles, Scot. | 1960 | United States 6½, British Isles 2½ | Lindrick, Eng. |
| 1938 | United States 5½, British Isles 3½ | Manchester, Mass. | 1962 | United States 8, British Isles 1 | Broadmoor C.C., Colorado Springs, Col. |
| 1948 | United States 6½, British Isles 2½ | Southport, Eng. | 1964 | United States 10½, British Isles 7½ | Porthcawl, Wales |
| 1950 | United States 7½, British Isles 1½ | Buffalo, N.Y. | 1966 | United States 13, British Isles 5 | Hot Springs, Va. |
| 1952 | British Isles 5, United States 4 | Muirfield, Scot. | 1968 | United States 10½, British Isles 7½ | Newcastle, N. Ire. |
| 1954 | United States 6, British Isles 3 | Ardmore, Pa. | | | |

An informal match in 1930 at Sunningdale, Eng., was won by the British Isles 8 to 6.

*In case of tie the defenders retain the cup.

**WORLD WOMEN'S AMATEUR TEAM CHAMPIONSHIPS**

**Espirito Santos Trophy** (instituted 1964)

| Year | Winner | Place |
|---|---|---|
| 1964 | France | St. Germain, Fr. |
| 1966 | United States | Mexico City, Mex. |
| 1968 | United States | Melbourne, Austr. |

## GYMNASTICS*

### World Championships—Men

| Year | Place | Team | Points | Combined Exercises | Points | Horizontal Bar | Points | Parallel Bars | Points |
|---|---|---|---|---|---|---|---|---|---|
| 1950 | Basle, Switz. | Switzerland | 852.25 | W. Lehmann; Switz. | 143.30 | P. Aaltonen; Fin. | 19.45 | H. Eugster; Switz. | 19.85 |
| 1954 | Rome, It. | U.S.S.R. | 689.90 | V. Mouratov; U.S.S.R. | 115.45 | V. Mouratov; U.S.S.R. | 19.70 | V. Tchoukarin; U.S.S.R. | 19.60 |
| 1958 | Moscow, U.S.S.R. | U.S.S.R. | 575.45 | B. Chakhlin; U.S.S.R. | 116.05 | B. Chakhlin; U.S.S.R. | 19.575 | B. Chakhlin; U.S.S.R. | 19.65 |
| 1962 | Prague, Czech. | Japan | 574.65 | Y. Titov; U.S.S.R. | 115.65 | T. Ono; Jap. | 19.675 | M. Cerar; Yugos. | 19.625 |
| 1966 | Dortmund, W. Ger. | Japan | 575.10 | M. Voronin; U.S.S.R. | 116.15 | A. Nakayama; Jap. | 19.675 | S. Diamidov; U.S.S.R. | 19.55 |

| Year | Pommeled Horse | Points | Rings | Points | Long Horse | Points | Floor Exercise | Points |
|---|---|---|---|---|---|---|---|---|
| 1950 | J. Stalder; Switz. | 19.70 | W. Lehmann; Switz. | 19.60 | E. Gebendinger; Switz. | 19.45 | J. Stalder; Switz. | 19.25 |
| 1954 | G. Chaguinvane; U.S.S.R. | 19.30 | A. Azarian; U.S.S.R. | 19.75 | L. Sotornik; Czech. | 19.25 | V. Mouratov; U.S.S.R. | 19.25 |
| 1958 | B. Chakhlin; U.S.S.R. | 19.55 | A. Azarian; U.S.S.R. | 19.875 | Y. Titov; U.S.S.R. | 19.35 | M. Takemoto; Jap. | 19.55 |
| 1962 | M. Cerar; Yugos. | 19.750 | Y. Titov; U.S.S.R. | 19.550 | P. Krbec; Czech. | 19.550 | N. Aihara; Jap. | 19.500 |
| 1966 | M. Cerar; Yugos. | 19.525 | M. Voronin; U.S.S.R. | 19.750 | H. Matsuda; Jap. | 19.425 | A. Nakayama; Jap. | 19.400 |

### World Championships—Women

| Year | Place | Team | Points | Combined Exercises | Points | Beam | Points |
|---|---|---|---|---|---|---|---|
| 1950 | Basle, Switz. | Sweden | 607.016 | H. Rakoczy; Pol. | 94.016 | H. Rakoczy; Pol. | 23.433 |
| 1954 | Rome, It. | U.S.S.R. | 524.31 | G. Roudiko; U.S.S.R. | 75.68 | K. Tanaka; Jap. | 18.89 |
| 1958 | Moscow, U.S.S.R. | U.S.S.R. | 381.620 | L. Latynina; U.S.S.R. | 77.464 | L. Latynina; U.S.S.R. | 19.399 |
| 1962 | Prague, Czech. | U.S.S.R. | 384.988 | L. Latynina; U.S.S.R. | 78.030 | E. Bosakova; Czech. | 19.499 |
| 1966 | Dortmund, W. Ger. | Czechoslovakia | 383.625 | V. Caslavska; Czech. | 78.298 | N. Kuchinskaya; U.S.S.R. | 19.650 |

| Year | Parallel Bars | Points | Long Horse | Points | Floor Exercise | Points |
|---|---|---|---|---|---|---|
| 1950 | T. Kolar; Aus. | 24.00 | H. Rakoczy; Pol. | 23.556 | H. Rakoczy; Pol. | 23.166 |
| 1954 | A. Keleti; Hung. | 19.46 | T. Manina; U.S.S.R. | 18.96 | T. Manina; U.S.S.R. | 19.39 |
| 1958 | L. Latynina; U.S.S.R. | 19.499 | L. Latynina; U.S.S.R. | 19.233 | E. Bosakova; Czech. | 19.400 |
| 1962 | I. Pervuschina; U.S.S.R. | 19.566 | V. Caslavska; Czech. | 19.649 | L. Latynina; U.S.S.R. | 19.716 |
| 1966 | N. Kuchinskaya; U.S.S.R. | 19.616 | V. Caslavska; Czech. | 19.583 | N. Kuchinskaya; U.S.S.R. | 19.733 |

*For Olympic years *see* the article OLYMPIC GAMES; for events *see* the article GYMNASTICS

WORLD CHAMPION GYMNAST NATASHA KUCHINSKAYA (U.S.S.R.) WORKING ON THE BEAM. SHE WON WORLD TITLES ON THE BEAM, ON PARALLEL BARS, AND IN FLOOR EXERCISE AT DORTMUND, W. GER., IN 1966

SOVFOTO

## TRAMPOLINE

### World Championships (instituted in 1964)

| Men's title | Women's title |
|---|---|
| 1964 D. Millman; U.S. | J. Wills; U.S. |
| 1965 G. Erwin; U.S. | J. Wills; U.S. |
| 1966 W. Miller; U.S. | J. Wills; U.S. |
| 1967 D. Jacobs; U.S. | J. Wills; U.S. |
| 1968 D. Jacobs; U.S. | J. Wills; U.S. |

WORLD CHAMPION GYMNAST MIKHAIL VORONIN (U.S.S.R.) WINNING A TITLE ON THE RINGS AT DORTMUND, W. GER., IN 1966. VORONIN ALSO HOLDS THE WORLD CHAMPIONSHIP FOR COMBINED EXERCISES

EASTFOTO

**HIGHLAND GAMES** became sporting events in 1848 when Queen Victoria took up residence in the Highlands of Scotland. The present program usually embraces track and field athletics (amateur or professional), highland dancing, tug of war, piping contests, wrestling, and sometimes cycling events and sheep trials. A feature event is throwing the caber (earliest mention 1862). The great Braemar Caber (which reached the maximum dimensions: 21 ft. long and 230 lb.) defied all comers until tossed in September 1951 by George Clark (Scotland). *See* further the article HIGHLAND GAMES.

**HOCKEY, FIELD.** The only world championships are in the Olympic Games (*see* the article OLYMPIC GAMES).

GEORGE CLARK TOSSING THE GREAT BRAEMAR CABER AT THE 1951 HIGHLAND GAMES

ABERDEEN JOURNALS LTD.

KELSO SETTING A RECORD AS WORLD'S FASTEST HORSE AT 1½ MILES BY OUTRUNNING GUN BOW AT LAUREL, MD., 1964

WIDE WORLD

## HORSE RACING

### World's Fastest Performances—Thoroughbreds

| Furlongs | Mi. | Time | Horse | Place | Date |
|---|---|---|---|---|---|
| 2 | ¼ | 20.8 sec. | Big Racket | Mexico City, Mex. | Feb. 5, 1945 |
| 3 | ⅜ | 33.5 sec. | Atoka | Butte, U.S. | Sept. 7, 1906 |
| 4 | ½ | 45 sec. | Gloaming | Trentham, N.Z.* | Jan. 12, 1921 |
| | | 45 sec. | Beau Madison | Phoenix, U.S. | March 30, 1957 |
| | | 45 sec. | Another Nell | Cicero, U.S. | May 8, 1967 |
| 5 | ⅝ | 55.4 sec. | Zip Pocket | Phoenix, U.S. | April 22, 1967 |
| 6 | ¾ | 1 min. 6.2 sec. | Gelding by Blink-Broken Tendril | Brighton, U.K.† | Aug. 6, 1929 |
| | | 1 min. 7.4 sec. | Zip Pocket | Phoenix, U.S. | Dec. 4, 1966 |
| 7 | ⅞ | 1 min. 20 sec. | El Drag | Inglewood, U.S. | May 21, 1955 |
| | | 1 min. 20 sec. | Native Diver | Inglewood, U.S. | May 22, 1965 |
| 8 | 1 | 1 min. 31.8 sec. | Soueida | Brighton, U.K.† | Sept. 19, 1963 |
| | | 1 min. 31.8 sec. | Loose Cover | Brighton, U.K.† | June 9, 1966 |
| | | 1 min. 32.2 sec. | Dr. Fager | Arlington Heights, U.S. | Aug. 24, 1968 |
| 9 | 1⅛ | 1 min. 46.4 sec. | Bug Brush | Arcadia, U.S. | Feb. 14, 1959 |
| | | 1 min. 46.4 sec. | Colorado King | Inglewood, U.S. | July 4, 1964 |
| | | 1 min. 46.4 sec. | Quicken Tree | Del Mar, U.S. | Sept. 2, 1968 |
| | | 1 min. 46.4 sec. | Ole Bob Bowers | San Mateo, U.S. | Oct. 12, 1968 |
| 10 | 1¼ | 1 min. 58.2 sec. | Noor | Albany, U.S. | June 24, 1950 |
| 11 | 1⅜ | 2 min. 13.8 sec. | Winifreux | Doomben, Austr. | July 9, 1966 |
| 12 | 1½ | 2 min. 23.8 sec. | Kelso | Laurel, U.S. | Nov. 11, 1964 |
| 13 | 1⅝ | 2 min. 38.2 sec. | Swaps | Inglewood, U.S. | July 25, 1956 |
| 14 | 1¾ | 2 min. 50.8 sec. | Swartz Pete | Auckland, N.Z. | Jan.1, 1966 |
| 15 | 1⅞ | 3 min. 13.8 sec. | Pharawell | Hallandale, U.S. | April 8, 1947 |
| 16 | 2 | 3 min. 15 sec. | Polazel | Salisbury, U.K. | July 8, 1924 |
| 24 | 3 | 5 min. 15 sec. | Farraquet | Agua Caliente, Mex. | March 9, 1941 |

*Straight course. †Course downhill for 5 furlongs.

### World's Fastest Performances—Trotting

| Furlongs/Mi. | Time | Horse | Place | Date |
|---|---|---|---|---|
| 1 mi. (1 mi. track) | 1 min. 54.8 sec. | Nevele Pride | Indianapolis, U.S. | Aug. 31, 1969 |
| (½ mi. track) | 1 min. 56.8 sec. | Nevele Pride | Saratoga Springs, U.S. | Sept. 6, 1969 |
| 8½ furlongs | 2 min. 5.6 sec. | Senator Frost | Inglewood, U.S. | Oct. 17, 1959 |
| | 2 min. 5.6 sec. | Dartmouth | Westbury, U.S. | Sept. 26, 1964 |
| 9½ furlongs | 2 min. 22.8 sec. | Scotch Victor | Inglewood, U.S. | Nov. 6, 1954 |
| 10 furlongs | 2 min. 30.6 sec. | Pronto Don | Inglewood, U.S. | Nov. 24, 1951 |
| 12 furlongs | 3 min. 2.5 sec. | Greyhound | Indianapolis, U.S. | Sept. 14, 1937 |
| 2 mi. | 4 min. 6 sec. | Greyhound | Indianapolis, U.S. | Sept. 19, 1939 |

### World's Fastest Performances—Pacing

| Furlongs/Mi. | Time | Horse | Place | Date |
|---|---|---|---|---|
| 1 mi. (1 mi. track) | 1 min. 53.6 sec. | Bret Hanover | Lexington, U.S. | Oct. 7, 1966 |
| (½ mi. track) | 1 min. 55.6 sec. | Adios Butler | Delaware, U.S. | Sept. 21, 1961 |
| 8½ furlongs | 2 min. 3.2 sec. | Adios Vic | Inglewood, U.S. | Oct. 23, 1965 |
| 9 furlongs | 2 min. 11.2 sec. | Adios Butler | Inglewood, U.S. | Nov. 4, 1961 |
| | 2 min. 11.2 sec. | Irvin Paul | Inglewood, U.S. | Oct. 27, 1962 |
| 12 furlongs (½ mi. track) | 3 min. 2.6 sec. | Overcall | Yonkers, U.S. | June 5, 1969 |
| 2 mi. (½ mi. track) | 4 min. 8.8 sec. | Irvin Paul | Yonkers, U.S. | June 28, 1962 |

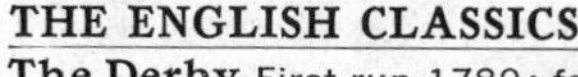

MILLER SERVICES LTD.
ROUNDING TATTENHAM CORNER IN THE 1965 ENGLISH DERBY WON BY SEA BIRD II, AT EPSOM DOWNS, ENG.

## THE ENGLISH CLASSICS

**The Derby** First run 1780; for 3-year-old colts and fillies (geldings excluded since 1904); over 1½ mi.; at Epsom Downs, Surrey.

| Year | Winner | Owner | Trainer | Jockey |
|---|---|---|---|---|
| 1946 | Airborne | J. Ferguson | R. Perryman | T. Lowrey |
| 1947 | Pearl Diver | Baron de Waldner | C. Halsey | G. Bridgland |
| 1948 | My Love | Aga Khan III | R. Carver | W. R. Johnstone |
| 1949 | Nimbus | Mrs. M. Glenister | G. Colling | C. Elliott |
| 1950 | Galcador | M. Boussac | C. Semblat | W. R. Johnstone |
| 1951 | Arctic Prince | J. McGrath | W. Stephenson | C. Spares |
| 1952 | Tulyar | Aga Khan III | M. Marsh | C. Smirke |
| 1953 | Pinza | Sir V. Sassoon | N. Bertie | G. Richards |
| 1954 | Never Say Die | R. Clark | J. Lawson | L. Piggott |
| 1955 | Phil Drake | Mme L. Volterra | F. Mathet | F. Palmer |
| 1956 | Lavandin | P. Wertheimer | A. Head | W. R. Johnstone |
| 1957 | Crepello | Sir V. Sassoon | N. Murless | L. Piggott |
| 1958 | Hard Ridden | Sir V. Sassoon | J. Rogers | C. Smirke |
| 1959 | Parthia | Sir H. de Trafford | C. Boyd-Rochfort | W. Carr |
| 1960 | St. Paddy | Sir V. Sassoon | N. Murless | L. Piggott |
| 1961 | Psidium | Mrs. A. Plesch | H. Wragg | R. Poincelet |
| 1962 | Larkspur | R. Guest | V. O'Brien | N. Sellwood |
| 1963 | Relko | F. Dupré | F. Mathet | Y. Saint-Martin |
| 1964 | Santa Claus | J. Ismay | J. Rogers | A. Breasley |
| 1965 | Sea Bird II | J. Ternynck | E. Pollet | T. P. Glennon |
| 1966 | Charlottown | Lady Zia Wernher | G. Smyth | A. Breasley |
| 1967 | Royal Palace | H. Joel | N. Murless | G. Moore |
| 1968 | Sir Ivor | R. Guest | M. V. O'Brien | L. Piggott |
| 1969 | Blakeney | A. Budgett | A. Budgett | E. Johnson |

Record time—2 min. 33⅘ sec. (average 35.06 mph) by Mahmoud in 1936.

**The Oaks** First run 1779; for 3-year-old fillies, over 1½ mi.; at Epsom Downs, Surrey.

| Year | Winner | Owner | Trainer | Jockey |
|---|---|---|---|---|
| 1946 | Steady Aim | Sir A. Butt | F. Butters | H. Wragg |
| 1947 | Imprudence | Mme P. Corbiere | J. Lieux | W. R. Johnstone |
| 1948 | Masaka | Aga Khan III | F. Butters | W. Nevett |
| 1949 | Musidora | N. Donaldson | C. Elsey | E. Britt |
| 1950 | Asmena | M. Boussac | C. Semblat | W. R. Johnstone |
| 1951 | Neasham Belle | L. Holliday | G. Brooke | S. Clayton |
| 1952 | Frieze | A. Keith | C. Elsey | E. Britt |
| 1953 | Ambiguity | Lord Astor | J. Colling | J. Mercer |
| 1954 | Sun Cap | Mme R. Forget | R. Carver | W. R. Johnstone |
| 1955 | Meld | Lady Zia Wernher | C. Boyd-Rochfort | W. Carr |
| 1956 | Sicarelle | Mme L. Volterra | F. Mathet | F. Palmer |
| 1957 | Carrozza | Queen Elizabeth II | N. Murless | L. Piggott |
| 1958 | Bella Paola | F. Dupré | F. Mathet | M. Garcia |
| 1959 | Petite Etoile | Aly Khan | N. Murless | L. Piggott |
| 1960 | Never Too Late II | Mrs. H. Jackson | E. Pollet | R. Poincelet |
| 1961 | Sweet Solera | Mrs. S. Castello | R. Day | W. Rickaby |
| 1962 | Monade | G. Goulandris | J. Lieux | Y. Saint-Martin |
| 1963 | Noblesse | Mrs. J. Olin | P. Prendergast | G. Bougoure |
| 1964 | Homeward Bound | Sir F. Robinson | J. Oxley | G. Starkey |
| 1965 | Long Look | J. C. Brady | V. O'Brien | J. Purtell |
| 1966 | Valoris | C. Clore | V. O'Brien | L. Piggott |
| 1967 | Pia | Countess M. Batthyany | W. Elsey | E. Hide |
| 1968 | LaLagune | H. Berlin | F. Boutin | G. Thiboeuf |
| 1969 | Sleeping Partner | Lord Rosebery | D. Smith | J. Gorton |

Record time—2 min. 34⅗ sec. by Beam in 1927.

VALORIS CROSSING THE FINISH LINE IN THE 188TH OAK STAKES AT EPSOM DOWNS, ENG., 1966
WIDE WORLD

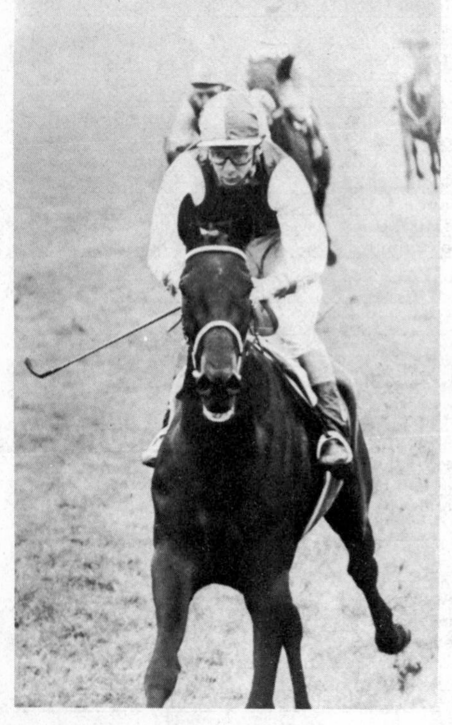

**The St. Leger** First run 1776; for 3-year-old colts 126 lb. and fillies 123 lb., over 1 mi. 6 furlongs 123 yd.; at Doncaster, West Riding, Yorkshire.

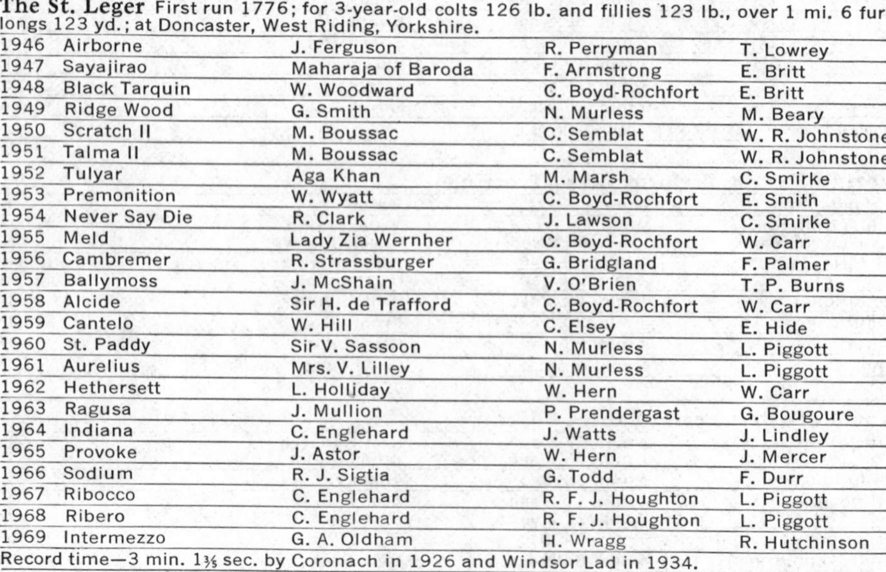

| Year | Winner | Owner | Trainer | Jockey |
|---|---|---|---|---|
| 1946 | Airborne | J. Ferguson | R. Perryman | T. Lowrey |
| 1947 | Sayajirao | Maharaja of Baroda | F. Armstrong | E. Britt |
| 1948 | Black Tarquin | W. Woodward | C. Boyd-Rochfort | E. Britt |
| 1949 | Ridge Wood | G. Smith | N. Murless | M. Beary |
| 1950 | Scratch II | M. Boussac | C. Semblat | W. R. Johnstone |
| 1951 | Talma II | M. Boussac | C. Semblat | W. R. Johnstone |
| 1952 | Tulyar | Aga Khan | M. Marsh | C. Smirke |
| 1953 | Premonition | W. Wyatt | C. Boyd-Rochfort | E. Smith |
| 1954 | Never Say Die | R. Clark | J. Lawson | C. Smirke |
| 1955 | Meld | Lady Zia Wernher | C. Boyd-Rochfort | W. Carr |
| 1956 | Cambremer | R. Strassburger | G. Bridgland | F. Palmer |
| 1957 | Ballymoss | J. McShain | V. O'Brien | T. P. Burns |
| 1958 | Alcide | Sir H. de Trafford | C. Boyd-Rochfort | W. Carr |
| 1959 | Cantelo | W. Hill | C. Elsey | E. Hide |
| 1960 | St. Paddy | Sir V. Sassoon | N. Murless | L. Piggott |
| 1961 | Aurelius | Mrs. V. Lilley | N. Murless | L. Piggott |
| 1962 | Hethersett | L. Holliday | W. Hern | W. Carr |
| 1963 | Ragusa | J. Mullion | P. Prendergast | G. Bougoure |
| 1964 | Indiana | C. Englehard | J. Watts | J. Lindley |
| 1965 | Provoke | J. Astor | W. Hern | J. Mercer |
| 1966 | Sodium | R. J. Sigtia | G. Todd | F. Durr |
| 1967 | Ribocco | C. Englehard | R. F. J. Houghton | L. Piggott |
| 1968 | Ribero | C. Englehard | R. F. J. Houghton | L. Piggott |
| 1969 | Intermezzo | G. A. Oldham | H. Wragg | R. Hutchinson |

Record time—3 min. 1⅗ sec. by Coronach in 1926 and Windsor Lad in 1934.

WIDE WORLD
KASHMIR II BEATING GREAT NEPHEW IN THE 1966 TWO THOUSAND GUINEAS RACE AT NEWMARKET

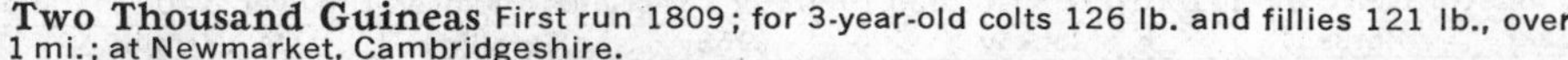

**Two Thousand Guineas** First run 1809; for 3-year-old colts 126 lb. and fillies 121 lb., over 1 mi.; at Newmarket, Cambridgeshire.

| Year | Winner | Owner | Trainer | Jockey |
|---|---|---|---|---|
| 1946 | Happy Knight | Sir W. Cooke | H. Jelliss | T. Weston |
| 1947 | Tudor Minstrel | J. Dewar | F. Darling | G. Richards |
| 1948 | My Babu | Maharaja of Baroda | F. Armstrong | C. Smirke |
| 1949 | Nimbus | Mrs. M. Glenister | G. Colling | C. Elliott |
| 1950 | Palestine | Aga Khan III | M. Marsh | C. Smirke |
| 1951 | Ki Ming | Ley On | M. Beary | A. Breasley |
| 1952 | Thunderhead II | E. Constant | E. Pollet | R. Poincelet |
| 1953 | Nearula | W. Humble | C. Elsey | E. Britt |
| 1954 | Darius | Sir P. Loraine | H. Wragg | E. Mercer |
| 1955 | Our Babu | D. Robinson | G. Brooke | D. Smith |
| 1956 | Gilles de Retz | A. Samuels | C. Jerdein | F. Barlow |
| 1957 | Crepello | Sir V. Sassoon | N. Murless | L. Piggott |
| 1958 | Pall Mall | Queen Elizabeth II | C. Boyd-Rochfort | D. Smith |
| 1959 | Taboun | Aly Khan | A. Head | G. Moore |
| 1960 | Martial | R. Webster | P. Prendergast | R. Hutchinson |
| 1961 | Rockavon | T. Yuill | G. Boyd | N. Stirk |
| 1962 | Privy Councillor | G. Glover | T. Waugh | W. Rickaby |
| 1963 | Only for Life | Miss M. Sheriffe | J. Tree | J. Lindley |
| 1964 | Baldric II | Mrs. H. Jackson | E. Fellows | W. Pyers |
| 1965 | Niksar | W. Harvey | W. Nightingall | D. Keith |
| 1966 | Kashmir II | P. Butler | C. Bartholomew | J. Lindley |
| 1967 | Royal Palace | H. Joel | N. Murless | G. Moore |
| 1968 | Sir Ivor | R. Guest | M. V. O'Brien | L. Piggott |
| 1969 | Right Tack | J. R. Brown | J. Sutcliffe | G. Lewis |

Record time—1 min. 35 4/5 sec. by My Babu in 1948.

**One Thousand Guineas** First run 1814; for 3-year-old fillies, over 1 mi.; at Newmarket, Cambridgeshire.

| Year | Winner | Owner | Trainer | Jockey |
|---|---|---|---|---|
| 1946 | Hypericum | King George VI | C. Boyd-Rochfort | D. Smith |
| 1947 | Imprudence | Mme P. Corbiere | J. Lieux | W. R. Johnstone |
| 1948 | Queenpot | Sir P. Loraine | N. Murless | G. Richards |
| 1949 | Musidora | N. Donaldson | C. Elsey | E. Britt |
| 1950 | Camaree | J. Ternynck | A. Liseux | W. R. Johnstone |
| 1951 | Belle of All | H. Tufton | N. Bertie | G. Richards |
| 1952 | Zabara | Sir M. McAlpine | V. Smyth | K. Gethin |
| 1953 | Happy Laughter | H. Wills | J. Jarvis | E. Mercer |
| 1954 | Festoon | J. Dewar | N. Cannon | A. Breasley |
| 1955 | Meld | Lady Zia Wernher | C. Boyd-Rochfort | W. Carr |
| 1956 | Honeylight | Sir V. Sassoon | C. Elsey | E. Britt |
| 1957 | Rose Royale II | Aga Khan III | A. Head | C. Smirke |
| 1958 | Bella Paola | F. Dupré | F. Mathet | S. Boullenger |
| 1959 | Petite Etoile | Aly Khan | N. Murless | D. Smith |
| 1960 | Never Too Late II | Mrs. H. Jackson | E. Pollet | R. Poincelet |
| 1961 | Sweet Solera | Mrs. S. Castello | R. Day | W. Rickaby |
| 1962 | Abermaid | R. More O'Ferrall | H. Wragg | W. Williamson |
| 1963 | Hula Dancer | Mrs. P. Widener | E. Pollet | R. Poincelet |
| 1964 | Pourparler | Lady Granard | P. Prendergast | G. Bougoure |
| 1965 | Night Off | L. Holiday | W. Wharton | W. Williamson |
| 1966 | Glad Rags | Mrs. J. P. Mills | V. O'Brien | P. Cook |
| 1967 | Fleet | R. Boucher | N. Murless | G. Moore |
| 1968 | Caergwrle | Mrs. N. Murless | N. Murless | A. Barclay |
| 1969 | Full Dress II | R. B. Moller | H. Wragg | R. Hutchinson |

Record time—1 min. 37 sec. by Camaree in 1950.

KEYSTONE
RELIANCE II WINNING THE 1965 PRIX DU JOCKEY CLUB (FRENCH DERBY) AT CHANTILLY, FRANCE

## FRANCE

**Prix du Jockey Club** (French Derby). First run 1836; for 3-year-old colts and fillies, over 2,400 m. (about 1½ mi.); at Chantilly.

| Year | Horse | Jockey | Year | Horse | Jockey | Year | Horse | Jockey |
|---|---|---|---|---|---|---|---|---|
| 1945* | Coaraze | J. Doyasbère | 1954 | Le Petit Prince | R. Bertiglia | 1963 | Sanctus | M. Larraun |
| 1946* | Prince Chevalier | C. Bouillon | 1955 | Rapace | F. Palmer | 1964 | Le Fabuleux | J. Massard |
| 1947* | Sandjar | R. Poincelet | 1956 | Philius | S. Boullenger | 1965 | Reliance II | Y. Saint-Martin |
| 1948 | Bey | W. R. Johnstone | 1957 | Amber | M. Garcia | 1966 | Nelcius | Y. Saint-Martin |
| 1949 | Good Luck | P. Blanc | 1958 | Tamanar | J. Deforge | 1967 | Astec | A. Jezequel |
| 1950 | Scratch | W. R. Johnstone | 1959 | Herbager | G. Chancelier | 1968 | Tapalque | Y. Saint-Martin |
| 1951 | Sicambre | P. Blanc | 1960 | Charlottesville | G. Moore | 1969 | Goodly | F. Head |
| 1952 | Auriban | W. R. Johnstone | 1961 | Right Royal V | R. Poincelet | | | |
| 1953 | Chamant | M. Garcia | 1962 | Val de Loir | F. Palmer | | | |

*Run at Longchamp.

**Grand Prix de Paris** Instituted 1863; for 3-year-olds, over 3,100 m. (about 1⅞ mi.); at Longchamp.

| Year | Horse | Jockey | Year | Horse | Jockey | Year | Horse | Jockey |
|---|---|---|---|---|---|---|---|---|
| 1945 | Caracalla | A. Rabbe | 1954 | Popof | F. Palmer | 1963 | Sanctus | R. Poincelet |
| 1946 | Souverain | M. Lollierou | 1955 | Phil Drake | F. Palmer | 1964 | White Label | L. Heurteur |
| 1947 | Avenger | C. Smirke | 1956 | Vattel | M. Garcia | 1965 | Reliance II | Y. Saint-Martin |
| 1948 | My Love | W. R. Johnstone | 1957 | Altipan | R. Poincelet | 1966 | Danseur | Y. Saint-Martin |
| 1949 | Bagheera | C. Bouillon | 1958 | San Roman | R. Poincelet | 1967 | Phaéton | L. Flavien |
| 1950 | Vieux Manoir | F. Palmer | 1959 | Birum | L. Flavien | 1968 | Dhaudevi | F. Head |
| 1951 | Sicambre | P. Blanc | 1960 | Charlottesville | G. Moore | 1969 | Chaparral | F. Head |
| 1952 | Orféo | F. Palmer | 1961 | Balto | M. Garcia | | | |
| 1953 | Northern Light | G. Lequeux | 1962 | Armistice | J. Deforge | | | |

**Prix de l'Arc de Triomphe** Instituted 1920; for 3-year-olds and over, run over 2,400 m. (about 1½ mi. or 12 furlongs); at Longchamp.

| Year | Horse | Jockey |
|---|---|---|
| 1945 | Nikellora | W. R. Johnstone |
| 1946 | Caracalla | E. C. Elliott |
| 1947 | Le Paillon | F. Rochetti |
| 1948 | Migoli | C. Smirke |
| 1949 | Coronation VI | R. Poincelet |
| 1950 | Tantième | J. Doyasbère |
| 1951 | Tantième | J. Doyasbère |
| 1952 | Nuccio | R. Poincelet |
| 1953 | La Sorellina | M. Larraun |
| 1954 | Sica Boy | W. R. Johnstone |
| 1955 | Ribot | E. Camici |
| 1956 | Ribot | E. Camici |
| 1957 | Oroso | S. Boullenger |
| 1958 | Ballymoss | A. Breasley |
| 1959 | Saint Crespin | G. Moore |
| 1960 | Puissant Chef | M. Garcia |
| 1961 | Molvedo | E. Camici |
| 1962 | Soltikoff | M. Depalmas |
| 1963 | Exbury | J. Deforge |
| 1964 | Prince Royal II | R. Poincelet |
| 1965 | Sea Bird II | T. P. Glennon |
| 1966 | Bon Mot III | F. Head |
| 1967 | Topyo | W. Pyers |
| 1968 | Vaguely Noble | W. Williamson |
| 1969 | Levmoss | W. Williamson |

## UNITED STATES

**The Triple Crown** The following horses have won the "Triple Crown" (the Kentucky Derby, the Preakness Stakes, and the Belmont Stakes):

| Year | Horse |
|---|---|
| 1919 | Sir Barton |
| 1930 | Gallant Fox |
| 1935 | Omaha |
| 1937 | War Admiral |
| 1941 | Whirlaway |
| 1943 | Count Fleet |
| 1946 | Assault |
| 1948 | Citation |

**The Kentucky Derby** Instituted 1875; at Churchill Downs, Louisville, Ky.; now over 1¼ mi. (10 furlongs), at 121 lb. for fillies, 126 lb. for colts, at 3 years.

| Year | Winner | min.:sec. | Jockey | Owner |
|---|---|---|---|---|
| 1945 | Hoop, Jr. | 2:07 | E. Arcaro | F. W. Hooper |
| 1946 | Assault | 2:06⅗ | W. Mehrtens | King Ranch |
| 1947 | Jet Pilot | 2:06⅘ | E. Guerin | Mrs. E. Graham |
| 1948 | Citation | 2:05⅖ | E. Arcaro | Calumet Farm |
| 1949 | Ponder | 2:04⅕ | S. Brooks | Calumet Farm |
| 1950 | Middleground | 2:01⅗ | W. Boland | King Ranch |
| 1951 | Count Turf | 2:02⅗ | C. McCreary | J. J. Amiel |
| 1952 | Hill Gail | 2:01⅗ | E. Arcaro | Calumet Farm |
| 1953 | Dark Star | 2:02 | H. Moreno | H. F. Guggenheim |
| 1954 | Determine | 2:03 | R. York | A. J. Crevolin |
| 1955 | Swaps | 2:01⅘ | W. Shoemaker | R. C. Ellsworth |
| 1956 | Needles | 2:03⅖ | D. Erb | D. & H. Stable |
| 1957 | Iron Liege | 2:02⅕ | W. Hartack | Calumet Farm |
| 1958 | Tim Tam | 2:05 | I. Valenzuela | Calumet Farm |
| 1959 | Tomy Lee | 2:02⅕ | W. Shoemaker | F. Turner |
| 1960 | Venetian Way | 2:02⅖ | W. Hartack | I. Blumberg |
| 1961 | Carry Back | 2:04 | J. Sellers | Mrs. K. Price |
| 1962 | Decidedly | 2:00⅖ | W. Hartack | G. A. Pope, Jr. |
| 1963 | Chateaugay | 2:01⅘ | B. Baeza | J. W. Galbreath |
| 1964 | Northern Dancer | 2:00* | W. Hartack | E. P. Taylor |
| 1965 | Lucky Debonair | 2:01⅕ | W. Shoemaker | Mrs. A. L. Rice |
| 1966 | Kauai King | 2:02 | D. Brumfield | M. J. Ford |
| 1967 | Proud Clarion | 2:00⅗ | R. Ussery | J. W. Galbreath |
| 1968 | Dancer's Image | 2:02⅕ | R. Ussery | P. Fuller† |
| 1969 | Majestic Prince | 2:01⅘ | W. Hartack | F. McMahon |
| 1970 | Dust Commander | 2:03⅖ | M. Manganello | R. E. Lehmann |

*Fastest time. †Second place finisher Forward Pass awarded first place purse.

**The Preakness Stakes** Instituted 1873; now at Pimlico, Md.; over 1³⁄₁₆ mi. (9½ furlongs), at 121 lb. for fillies, 126 lb. for colts, at 3 years.

| Year | Winner | min.:sec. | Jockey | Owner |
|---|---|---|---|---|
| 1945 | Polynesian | 1:58⅘ | W. D. Wright | Mrs. P. A. B. Widener |
| 1946 | Assault | 2:01⅖ | W. Mehrtens | King Ranch |
| 1947 | Faultless | 1:59 | D. Dodson | Calumet Farm |
| 1948 | Citation | 2:02⅖ | E. Arcaro | Calumet Farm |
| 1949 | Capot | 1:56 | T. Atkinson | Greentree Stable |
| 1950 | Hill Prince | 1:59⅕ | E. Arcaro | C. T. Chenery |
| 1951 | Bold | 1:56⅖ | E. Arcaro | Mrs. I. D. Sloane |
| 1952 | Blue Man | 1:57⅖ | C. McCreary | White Oak Stable |
| 1953 | Native Dancer | 1:57⅘ | E. Guerin | A. G. Vanderbilt |
| 1954 | Hasty Road | 1:57⅖ | E. Arcaro | Hasty House Farm |
| 1955 | Nashua | 1:54⅗* | W. Hartack | Belair Stud |
| 1956 | Fabius | 1:58⅖ | E. Arcaro | Calumet Farm |
| 1957 | Bold Ruler | 1:56⅕ | I. Valenzuela | Mrs. H. C. Phipps |
| 1958 | Tim Tam | 1:57⅕ | J. Adams | Calumet Farm |
| 1959 | Royal Orbit | 1:57 | W. Harmatz | Estate of J. Braunstein |
| 1960 | Bally Ache | 1:57⅗ | R. Ussery | Turfland |
| 1961 | Carry Back | 1:57⅗ | J. Sellers | Mrs. K. Price |
| 1962 | Greek Money | 1:56⅕ | J. L. Rotz | Brandywine Stable |
| 1963 | Candy Spots | 1:56⅕ | W. Shoemaker | R. C. Ellsworth |
| 1964 | Northern Dancer | 1:56⅘ | W. Hartack | E. P. Taylor |
| 1965 | Tom Rolfe | 1:56⅕ | R. Turcotte | R. Guest |
| 1966 | Kauai King | 1:55⅖ | D. Brumfield | M. J. Ford |
| 1967 | Damascus | 1:55⅕ | W. Shoemaker | Mrs. E. W. Bancroft |
| 1968 | Forward Pass | 1:56⅖ | I. Valenzuela | Calumet Farm |
| 1969 | Majestic Prince | 1:55⅗ | W. Hartack | F. McMahon |
| 1970 | Personality | 1:56⅕ | E. Belmonte | Mrs. E. D. Jacobs |

*Fastest time.

**The Belmont Stakes** Instituted 1867; since 1962 at Aqueduct, New York City; over 1½ mi. (12 furlongs), at 126 lb. for colts, at 3 years.

| Year | Winner | min.:sec. | Jockey | Owner |
|---|---|---|---|---|
| 1945 | Pavot | 2:30⅕ | E. Arcaro | W. M. Jeffords |
| 1946 | Assault | 2:30⅘ | W. Mehrtens | King Ranch |
| 1947 | Phalanx | 2:29⅖ | R. Donoso | C. V. Whitney |
| 1948 | Citation | 2:28⅕ | E. Arcaro | Calumet Farm |
| 1949 | Capot | 2:30⅕ | T. Atkinson | Greentree Stable |
| 1950 | Middleground | 2:28⅗ | W. Boland | King Ranch |
| 1951 | Counterpoint | 2:29 | D. Gorman | C. V. Whitney |
| 1952 | One Count | 2:30⅕ | E. Arcaro | Mrs. W. M. Jeffords |
| 1953 | Native Dancer | 2:28⅗ | E. Guerin | A. G. Vanderbilt |
| 1954 | High Gun | 2:30⅘ | E. Guerin | King Ranch |
| 1955 | Nashua | 2:29 | E. Arcaro | Belair Stud |
| 1956 | Needles | 2:29⅘ | D. Erb | D. & H. Stable |
| 1957 | Gallant Man | 2:26⅗* | W. Shoemaker | R. Lowe |
| 1958 | Cavan | 2:30⅕ | P. Anderson | J. E. O'Connell |
| 1959 | Sword Dancer | 2:28⅖ | W. Shoemaker | Brookmeade Stable |
| 1960 | Celtic Ash | 2:29⅗ | W. Hartack | J. E. O'Connell |
| 1961 | Sherluck | 2:29⅕ | B. Baeza | J. Sher |
| 1962 | Jaipur | 2:28⅘ | W. Shoemaker | G. D. Widener |
| 1963 | Chateaugay | 2:30⅕ | B. Baeza | J. W. Galbreath |
| 1964 | Quadrangle | 2:28⅖ | M. Ycaza | P. Mellon |
| 1965 | Hail to All | 2:28⅖ | J. Sellers | Mrs. B. Cohen |
| 1966 | Amberoid | 2:29⅗ | W. Boland | R. M. Webster |
| 1967 | Damascus | 2:28⅘ | W. Shoemaker | Mrs. E. W. Bancroft |
| 1968 | Stage Door Johnny | 2:27⅕ | H. Gustines | Greentree Stables |
| 1969 | Arts and Letters | 2:28⅘ | B. Baeza | P. Mellon |
| 1970 | High Echelon | 2:34 | J. Rotz | Mrs. E. D. Jacobs |

*Fastest time.

**The Washington D.C. International** Instituted 1952; at Laurel, Md.; over about 1½ mi. (12 furlongs), for 3-year-olds and over.

| Year | Winner | Jockey | Owner; Country |
|---|---|---|---|
| 1952 | Wilwyn | E. Mercer | R. Boucher; U.K. |
| 1953 | Worden II | C. Smirke | R. Strassburger; Fr. |
| 1954 | Fisherman | E. Arcaro | C. V. Whitney; U.S. |
| 1955 | El Chama | R. Bustamente | C. Rincones; Venez. |
| 1956 | Master Boing | G. Chancelier | A. Lombard; Fr. |
| 1957 | Mahan | S. Boulmetis | Hasty House Farms; U.S. |
| 1958 | Sailor's Guide | H. Grant | A. C. Dibb; Austr. |
| 1959 | Bald Eagle | M. Ycaza | Cain Hoy Stable; U.S. |
| 1960 | Bald Eagle | M. Ycaza | Cain Hoy Stable; U.S. |
| 1961 | T.V. Lark | J. Longden | P. Madden; U.S. |
| 1962 | Match II | Y. Saint-Martin | F. Dupré; Fr. |
| 1963 | Mongo | W. Chambers | Mrs. M. du Pont Scott; U.S. |
| 1964 | Kelso | I. Valenzuela | Mrs. R. du Pont; U.S. |
| 1965 | Diatome | J. Deforge | Baron de Rothschild; Fr. |
| 1966 | Behistoun | J. Deforge | A. Weisweiller; Fr. |
| 1967 | Fort Marcy | M. Ycaza | P. Mellon; U.S. |
| 1968 | Sir Ivor | L. Piggott | R. Guest; U.S. |
| 1969 | Karabas | L. Piggott | Earl of Iveagh; Ire. |

## HUNTING

**Big Game, North American.** Records of North American Big Game trophies are maintained by the Boone and Crockett Club. Records as of the end of 1963 were published in *Records of North American Big Game,* edited by Milford Baker, the Boone and Crockett Club (1964). Six new world records were established in subsequent competitions (1964–65; 1966–67).

| World Records* | Score | Length R. | Length L. | Inside spread | Circumference R. | Circumference L. | Points R. | Points L. | Locality | Year | Hunter or owner |
|---|---|---|---|---|---|---|---|---|---|---|---|
| Whitetail deer† (typical antlers) | 206 5/8 | 30 | 30 | 20 1/8 | 6 2/8 | 6 1/8 | 5 | 5 | near Sandstone, Minn. | unknown | R. Ludwig |
| Whitetail deer (non-typical) | 286 | 23 1/8 | 18 7/8 | 15 6/8 | 4 2/8 | 4 2/8 | 23 | 26 | Brady, Tex. | 1892 | J. Benson |
| Mule deer (typical) | 217 | 28 4/8 | 28 2/8 | 26 6/8 | 5 5/8 | 5 6/8 | 6 | 6 | Hoback Canyon, Wyo. | unknown | W. C. Lawrence |
| Mule deer (non-typical) | 355 2/8 | 26 2/8 | 26 1/8 | 22 1/8 | 5 | 4 7/8 | 22 | 21 | Chip Lake, Ala. | 1926 | E. Broder |
| Blacktail deer† | 170 1/8 | 23 | 22 6/8 | 19 5/8 | 5 | 4 6/8 | 5 | 5 | Tally Creek, Ore. | 1963 | W. W. Gibbs |
| Coues deer (typical) | 143 | 20 2/8 | 20 5/8 | 15 3/8 | .5 4/8 | 5 6/8 | 5 | 6 | Pima Co., Ariz. | 1953 | E. Stockwell |
| Coues deer ‖(non-typical) | 151 4/8 | 18 4/8 | 18 5/8 | 15 6/8 | 5 4/8 | 5 4/8 | 9 | 8 | Cochise Co., Ariz. | 1929 | C. C. Mabry |
| Wapiti | 442 3/8 | 55 5/8 | 59 5/8 | 45 4/8 | 12 1/8 | 11 2/8 | 8 | 7 | Dark Canyon, Colo. | 1915 | J. Plute |
| Mountain caribou‡ | 462 | 49 7/8 | 52 | 57 3/8 | 8 2/8 | 7 2/8 | 24 | 26 | Cassiar, B.C. | 1923 | G. L. Pop |
| Woodland caribou‡ | 419 5/8 | 50 1/8 | 47 3/8 | 43 2/8 | 6 1/8 | 6 5/8 | 19 | 18 | Newfoundland | before 1910 | National Collection |
| Barren ground caribou‡ | 474 6/8 | 60 4/8 | 61 1/8 | 58 2/8 | 6 4/8 | 6 1/8 | 22 | 30 | Nain, Lab. | 1931 | Z. Elbow |
| Canada moose‡ | 238 5/8 | 49 6/8 | 43 1/8 | 66 5/8§ | 7 5/8 | 7 7/8 | 18 | 19 | Bear Lake, Que. | 1914 | S. H. Witherbee |
| Alaska-Yukon moose‡ | 251 | 46 3/8 | 51 | 77 4/8§ | 7 7/8 | 8 1/8 | 18 | 17 | Mt. Susitna, Alsk. | 1961 | B. Klineburger |
| Wyoming moose‡ | 205 4/8 | 38 6/8 | 38 5/8 | 53§ | 6 7/8 | 6 7/8 | 15 | 15 | Green River Lake, Wyo. | 1952 | J. M. Oakley |
| Bighorn sheep† | 208 1/8 | 44 7/8 | 45 | 23 1/8§ | 16 5/8 | 16 5/8 | | | Blind Canyon, Alberta | 1911 | F. Weiller |
| Desert sheep | 205 1/8 | 43 5/8 | 43 6/8 | 25 5/8§ | 16 6/8 | 17 | | | Lower Calif., Mex. | 1940 | C. K. Scrivens |
| White sheep | 189 6/8 | 48 5/8 | 47 7/8 | 34 3/8§ | 14 5/8 | 14 6/8 | | | Wrangell Mts., Alsk. | 1961 | H. L. Swank, Jr. |
| Stone sheep | 196 6/8 | 50 1/8 | 51 5/8 | 31§ | 14 6/8 | 14 6/8 | | | Muskwa River, B.C. | 1936 | L. S. Chadwick |
| Mountain goat‡ | 56 6/8 | 12 | 12 | 9 2/8§ | 6 4/8 | 6 4/8 | | | Babine Mts., B.C. | 1949 | E. C. Haase |
| Pronghorn‡ | 101 6/8 | 19 4/8 | 19 4/8 | 14 7/8§ | 7 6/8 | 7 4/8 | | | Antelope Valley, Ariz. | 1878 | Academy of National Sciences |
| Barren ground muskox | 113 2/8 | 28 | 29 | 28 5/8§ | 4 7/8 | 4 7/8 | | | Barren Grounds, N.W.T. | unknown | National Collection |
| Greenland muskox | 115 2/8 | 26 | 27 | 27§ | 5 4/8 | 5 4/8 | | | Ellesmere Land, Can. | 1900 | I. S. Wombath |
| Bison | 136 4/8 | 21 2/8 | 23 2/8 | 35 3/8§ | 16 | 15 | | | Yellowstone Nat. Pk., Wyo. | 1925 | S. Woodring |
| | | **Length of skull** | | **Width of skull** | | | | | | | |
| Alaskan brown bear | 30 12/16 | 17 15/16 | | 12 13/16 | | | | | Kodiak Is., Alsk. | 1952 | R. Lindsley |
| Grizzly bear | 26 10/16 | 16 10/16 | | 10 | | | | | Rivers Inlet, B.C. | 1954 | F. Nygaard |
| Black bear | 21 15/16 | 13 3/16 | | 8 12/16 | | | | | Land o'Lakes, Wis. | 1953 | E. Strobel |
| Polar bear | 29 15/16 | 18 8/16 | | 11 7/16 | | | | | Kotzebue, Alsk. | 1963 | S. Longoria |
| Mountain lion (puma, cougar)† | 16 | 9 4/16 | | 6 12/16 | | | | | Wayne Co., Utah | 1964 | G. Roberts |
| Jaguar† | 18 7/16 | 10 4/16 | | 6 14/16 | | | | | Cienega, Sinaloa, Mex. | 1965 | C. J. McElroy |
| | | **Tusk** | | **Circumference** | | | | | | | |
| Atlantic walrus | 118 6/8 | 30 5/8 | 30 3/8 | 8 3/8 | 8 4/8 | | | | Greenland | before 1954 | National Collection |
| Pacific walrus | 145 6/8 | 32 2/8 | 32 1/8 | 12 2/8 | 13 | | | | Point Hope, Alsk. | 1957 | Jonas Bros. of Seattle |

*Measurements are in inches. †New record, 1964-65. ‡Additional measurements included in scores. §Greatest spread. ‖New record, 1966-67.

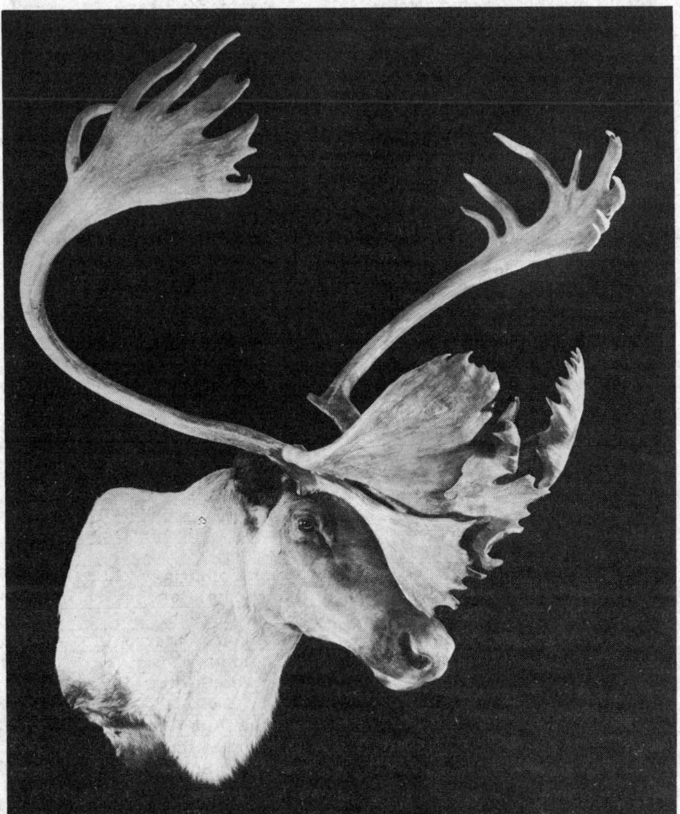

WORLD RECORD BARREN GROUND CARIBOU, TAKEN BY ZACK ELBOW NEAR NAIN, LABRADOR, 1931

BY COURTESY OF BOONE AND CROCKETT CLUB, "RECORDS OF NORTH AMERICAN BIG GAME," 1964 EDITION; PHOTOGRAPH BY GRANCEL FITZ

WORLD RECORD STONE SHEEP, SHOT BY L. S. CHADWICK, MUSKWA RIVER, BRITISH COLUMBIA, 1936

BY COURTESY OF BOONE AND CROCKETT CLUB, "RECORDS OF NORTH AMERICAN BIG GAME," 1964 EDITION; PHOTOGRAPH BY GRANCEL FITZ

## ICE HOCKEY

**The Stanley Cup** (instituted 1894). This cup, given the Canadian or U.S. winner of the National Hockey League playoffs since 1917, is tantamount to world professional championship.

| | | | | | |
|---|---|---|---|---|---|
| 1917 | Seattle Metropolitans | 1934 | Chicago Black Hawks | 1950 | Detroit Red Wings |
| 1918* | Toronto Arenas | 1935 | Montreal Maroons | 1951 | Toronto Maple Leafs |
| 1920 | Ottawa Senators | 1936 | Detroit Red Wings | 1952 | Detroit Red Wings |
| 1921 | Ottawa Senators | 1937 | Detroit Red Wings | 1953 | Montreal Canadiens |
| 1922 | Toronto St. Patricks | 1938 | Chicago Black Hawks | 1954 | Detroit Red Wings |
| 1923 | Ottawa Senators | 1939 | Boston Bruins | 1955 | Detroit Red Wings |
| 1924 | Montreal Canadiens | 1940 | New York Rangers | 1956 | Montreal Canadiens |
| 1925 | Victoria Cougars | 1941 | Boston Bruins | 1957 | Montreal Canadiens |
| 1926 | Montreal Maroons | 1942 | Toronto Maple Leafs | 1958 | Montreal Canadiens |
| 1927 | Ottawa Senators | 1943 | Detroit Red Wings | 1959 | Montreal Canadiens |
| 1928 | New York Rangers | 1944 | Montreal Canadiens | 1960 | Montreal Canadiens |
| 1929 | Boston Bruins | 1945 | Toronto Maple Leafs | 1961 | Chicago Black Hawks |
| 1930 | Montreal Canadiens | 1946 | Montreal Canadiens | 1962 | Toronto Maple Leafs |
| 1931 | Montreal Canadiens | 1947 | Toronto Maple Leafs | 1963 | Toronto Maple Leafs |
| 1932 | Toronto Maple Leafs | 1948 | Toronto Maple Leafs | 1964 | Toronto Maple Leafs |
| 1933 | New York Rangers | 1949 | Toronto Maple Leafs | 1965 | Montreal Canadiens |
| | | | | 1966 | Montreal Canadiens |
| | | | | 1967 | Toronto Maple Leafs |
| | | | | 1968 | Montreal Canadiens |
| | | | | 1969 | Montreal Canadiens |
| | | | | 1970 | Boston Bruins |

*The 1919 series was suspended after 5 games because of an influenza epidemic.

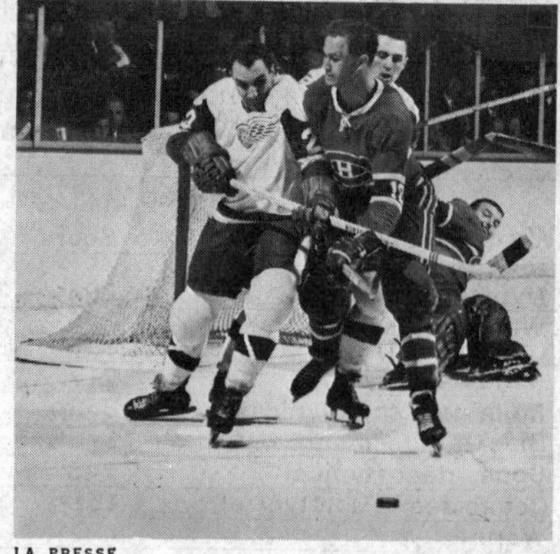

LA PRESSE

MONTREAL (DARK JERSEYS) AND DETROIT BATTLE FOR THE PUCK IN THE 1966 STANLEY CUP PLAYOFFS. THE MONTREAL CANADIENS WON THE BEST OF SEVEN SERIES

**World Amateur Championships***

| Year | Winner | Place |
|---|---|---|
| 1930 | Canada | Chamonix, Fr. |
| 1931 | Canada | Krynica, Pol. |
| 1933 | United States | Prague, Czech. |
| 1934 | Canada | Milan, It. |
| 1935 | Canada | Davos, Switz. |
| 1937 | Canada | London, U.K. |
| 1938 | Canada | Prague, Czech. |
| 1939 | Canada | Zürich, Switz. |
| 1947 | Czechoslovakia | Prague, Czech. |
| 1949 | Czechoslovakia | Stockholm, Swed. |
| 1950 | Canada | London, U.K. |
| 1951 | Canada | Paris, Fr. |
| 1953 | Sweden | Zürich, Switz. |
| 1954 | U.S.S.R. | Stockholm, Swed. |
| 1955 | Canada | Düsseldorf, Ger. |
| 1957 | Sweden | Moscow, U.S.S.R. |
| 1958 | Canada | Oslo, Nor. |
| 1959 | Canada | Prague, Czech. |
| 1961 | Canada | Geneva, Switz. |
| 1962 | Sweden | Colorado Springs, U.S. |
| 1963 | U.S.S.R. | Stockholm, Swed. |
| 1965 | U.S.S.R. | Tampere, Fin. |
| 1966 | U.S.S.R. | Zagreb, Yugos. |
| 1967 | U.S.S.R. | Vienna, Aus. |
| 1969 | U.S.S.R. | Stockholm, Swed. |
| 1970 | U.S.S.R. | Stockholm, Swed. |

*In Olympic years the championships are Olympic events (*see* OLYMPIC GAMES).

## ICE SKATING

### SPEED SKATING

**World Record Holders—Men**

| Distance | Name; Country | Time | Year |
|---|---|---|---|
| 500 m. | A. Lepeshkin; U.S.S.R. | 38.8 sec. | 1969 |
| 1,000 m. | I. Eriksen; Nor. | 1 min. 19.5 sec. | 1969 |
| 1,500 m. | C. Verkerk; Neth. | 2 min. 02.0 sec. | 1969 |
| 3,000 m. | D. Fornaess; Nor. | 4 min. 17.4 sec. | 1969 |
| 5,000 m. | C. Verkerk; Neth. | 7 min. 13.2 sec. | 1969 |
| 10,000 m. | C. Verkerk; Neth. | 15 min. 03.6 sec. | 1969 |

**World Record Holders—Women**

| Distance | Name; Country | Time | Year |
|---|---|---|---|
| 500 m. | T. Sidorova; U.S.S.R. | 43.3. sec. | 1970 |
| 1,000 m. | L. Titova; U.S.S.R. | 1 min. 29.5 sec. | 1970 |
| 1,500 m. | J. Schut; Neth. | 2 min. 18.5 sec. | 1969 |
| 3,000 m. | J. Schut; Neth. | 4 min. 50.3 sec. | 1969 |
| 5,000 m. | R. Zhukova; U.S.S.R. | 9 min. 01.6 sec. | 1953 |

### FIGURE SKATING

**World Champions—Men**

| Year | Winner; Country | Place |
|---|---|---|
| 1890* | L. Rubenstein; Can. | St. Petersburg, Russia |
| 1896 | G. Fuchs; Ger. | St. Petersburg, Russia |
| 1897 | G. Hügel; Aus. | Stockholm, Swed. |
| 1898 | H. Grenander; Swed. | London, U.K. |
| 1899 | G. Hügel; Aus. | Davos, Switz. |
| 1900 | G. Hügel; Aus. | Davos, Switz. |
| 1901 | U. Salchow; Swed. | Stockholm, Swed. |
| 1902 | U. Salchow; Swed. | London, U.K. |
| 1903 | U. Salchow; Swed. | St. Petersburg, Russia |
| 1904 | U. Salchow; Swed. | Berlin, Ger. |
| 1905 | U. Salchow; Swed. | Stockholm, Swed. |
| 1906 | G. Fuchs; Ger. | Munich, Ger. |
| 1907 | U. Salchow; Swed. | Vienna, Aus. |
| 1908 | U. Salchow; Swed. | Troppau, Czech. |
| 1909 | U. Salchow; Swed. | Stockholm, Swed. |
| 1910 | U. Salchow; Swed. | Davos, Switz. |
| 1911 | U. Salchow; Swed. | Berlin, Ger. |
| 1912 | F. Kachler; Aus. | Manchester, U.K. |
| 1913 | F. Kachler; Aus. | Vienna, Aus. |
| 1914 | G. Sandahl; Swed. | Helsingfors, Fin. |
| 1922 | G. Grafström; Swed. | Stockholm, Swed. |
| 1923 | F. Kachler; Aus. | Vienna, Aus. |
| 1924 | G. Grafström; Swed. | Manchester, U.K. |
| 1925 | W. Böckl; Aus. | Vienna, Aus. |
| 1926 | W. Böckl; Aus. | Berlin, Ger. |
| 1927 | W. Böckl; Aus. | Davos, Switz. |
| 1928 | W. Böckl; Aus. | Berlin, Ger. |
| 1929 | G. Grafström; Swed. | London, U.K. |
| 1930 | K. Schäfer; Aus. | New York, U.S. |
| 1931 | K. Schäfer; Aus. | Berlin, Ger. |
| 1932 | K. Schäfer; Aus. | Montreal, Can. |
| 1933 | K. Schäfer; Aus. | Zürich, Switz. |
| 1934 | K. Schäfer; Aus. | Stockholm, Swed. |
| 1935 | K. Schäfer; Aus. | Budapest, Hung. |
| 1936 | K. Schäfer; Aus. | Paris, Fr. |
| 1937 | F. Kaspar; Aus. | Vienna, Aus. |
| 1938 | F. Kaspar; Aus. | Berlin, Ger. |
| 1939 | G. Sharp; U.K. | Budapest, Hung. |
| 1947 | H. Gerschwiler; Switz. | Stockholm, Swed. |
| 1948 | R. Button; U.S. | Davos, Switz. |
| 1949 | R. Button; U.S. | Paris, Fr. |
| 1950 | R. Button; U.S. | London, U.K. |
| 1951 | R. Button; U.S. | Milan, It. |
| 1952 | R. Button; U.S. | Paris, Fr. |
| 1953 | H. Jenkins; U.S. | Davos, Switz. |
| 1954 | H. Jenkins; U.S. | Oslo, Nor. |
| 1955 | H. Jenkins; U.S. | Vienna, Aus. |
| 1956 | H. Jenkins; U.S. | Garmisch-Partenkirchen, Ger. |
| 1957 | D. Jenkins; U.S. | Colorado Springs, U.S. |
| 1958 | D. Jenkins; U.S. | Paris, Fr. |
| 1959 | D. Jenkins; U.S. | Colorado Springs, U.S. |
| 1960 | A. Giletti; Fr. | Vancouver, Can. |
| 1962 | D. Jackson; Can. | Prague, Czech. |
| 1963 | D. McPherson; Can. | Cortina d'Ampezzo, It. |
| 1964 | M. Schnelldorfer; W. Ger. | Dortmund, W. Ger. |
| 1965 | A. Calmat; Fr. | Colorado Springs, U.S. |
| 1966 | E. Danzer; Aus. | Davos, Switz. |
| 1967 | E. Danzer; Aus. | Vienna, Aus. |
| 1968 | E. Danzer; Aus. | Geneva, Switz. |
| 1969 | T. Wood; U.S. | Colorado Springs, U.S. |
| 1970 | T. Wood; U.S. | Ljubljana, Yugos. |

*Unofficial title but beat all comers.

# FIGURE SKATING

## World Champions—Women

| Year | Winner; Country | Place | Year | Winner; Country | Place |
|---|---|---|---|---|---|
| 1906 | M. Syers; U.K. | Davos, Switz. | 1938 | M. Taylor; U.K. | Stockholm, Swed. |
| 1907 | M. Syers; U.K. | Vienna, Aus. | 1939 | M. Taylor; U.K. | Prague, Czech. |
| 1908 | L. Kronberger; Hung. | Troppau, Czech. | 1947 | B. Scott; Can. | Stockholm, Swed. |
| 1909 | L. Kronberger; Hung. | Budapest, Hung. | 1948 | B. Scott; Can. | Davos, Switz. |
| 1910 | L. Kronberger; Hung. | Berlin, Ger. | 1949 | A. Vrzanova; Czech. | Paris, Fr. |
| 1911 | L. Kronberger; Hung. | Vienna, Aus. | 1950 | A. Vrzanova; Czech. | London, U.K. |
| 1912 | M. Horvath; Hung. | Davos, Switz. | 1951 | J. Altwegg; U.K. | Milan, It. |
| 1913 | M. Horvath; Hung. | Stockholm, Swed. | 1952 | J. du Bief; Fr. | Paris, Fr. |
| 1914 | M. Horvath; Hung. | St. Moritz, Switz. | 1953 | T. Albright; U.S. | Davos, Switz. |
| 1922 | M. Plank; Aus. | Stockholm, Swed. | 1954 | G. Busch; Ger. | Oslo, Nor. |
| 1923 | M. Plank; Aus. | Vienna, Aus. | 1955 | T. Albright; U.S. | Vienna, Aus. |
| 1924 | M. Plank; Aus. | Christiania, Nor. | 1956 | C. Heiss; U.S. | Garmisch-Partenkirchen, Ger. |
| 1925 | M. Plank; Aus. | Davos, Switz. | 1957 | C. Heiss; U.S. | Colorado Springs, U.S. |
| 1926 | M. Plank; Aus. | Stockholm, Swed. | 1958 | C. Heiss; U.S. | Paris, Fr. |
| 1927 | S. Henie; Nor. | Oslo, Nor. | 1959 | C. Heiss; U.S. | Colorado Springs, U.S. |
| 1928 | S. Henie; Nor. | London, U.K. | 1960 | C. Heiss; U.S. | Vancouver, Can. |
| 1929 | S. Henie; Nor. | Budapest, Hung. | 1962 | S. Dijkstra; Neth. | Prague, Czech. |
| 1930 | S. Henie; Nor. | New York, U.S. | 1963 | S. Dijkstra; Neth. | Cortina d'Ampezzo, It. |
| 1931 | S. Henie; Nor. | Berlin, Ger. | 1964 | S. Dijkstra; Neth. | Dortmund, W. Ger. |
| 1932 | S. Henie; Nor. | Montreal, Can. | 1965 | P. Burka; Can. | Colorado Springs, U.S. |
| 1933 | S. Henie; Nor. | Stockholm, Swed. | 1966 | P. Fleming; U.S. | Davos, Switz. |
| 1934 | S. Henie; Nor. | Oslo, Nor. | 1967 | P. Fleming; U.S. | Vienna, Aus. |
| 1935 | S. Henie; Nor. | Vienna, Aus. | 1968 | P. Fleming; U.S. | Geneva, Switz. |
| 1936 | S. Henie; Nor. | Paris, Fr. | 1969 | G. Seyfert; E. Ger. | Colorado Springs, U.S. |
| 1937 | C. Colledge; U.K. | London, U.K. | 1970 | G. Seyfert; E. Ger. | Ljubljana, Yugos. |

## World Champions—Pairs

| Year | Winners; Country | Place | Year | Winners; Country | Place |
|---|---|---|---|---|---|
| 1908 | H. Burger, A. Hübler; Ger. | St. Petersburg, Russia | 1947 | P. Baugniet, M. Lannoy; Belg. | Stockholm, Swed. |
| 1909 | J. Johnson, J. Johnson; U.K. | Stockholm, Swed. | 1948 | P. Baugniet, M. Lannoy; Belg. | Davos, Switz. |
| 1910 | H. Burger, A. Hübler; Ger. | Berlin, Ger. | 1949 | E. Kiraly, A. Kekessy; Hung. | Paris, Fr. |
| 1911 | W. Jakobsson, L. Eilers; Fin. | Vienna, Aus. | 1950 | M. Kennedy, K. Kennedy; U.S. | London, U.K. |
| 1912 | J. Johnson, J. Johnson; U.K. | Manchester, U.K. | 1951 | P. Falk, R. Baran; W. Ger. | Milan, It. |
| 1913 | K. Mejstrik, N. Engelmann; Aus. | Stockholm, Swed. | 1952 | P. Falk, R. Falk; W. Ger. | Paris, Fr. |
| 1914 | W. Jakobsson, W. Jakobsson; Fin. | St. Moritz, Switz. | 1953 | J. Nicks, J. Nicks; U.K. | Davos, Switz. |
| 1922 | H. Berger, N. Engelmann; Aus. | Manchester, U.K. | 1954 | N. Bowden, F. Dafoe; Can. | Oslo, Nor. |
| 1923 | W. Jakobsson, W. Jakobsson; Fin. | Davos, Switz. | 1955 | N. Bowden, F. Dafoe; Can. | Vienna, Aus. |
| 1924 | H. Berger, N. Engelmann; Aus. | Christiania, Nor. | 1956 | K. Oppelt, S. Schwarz; Aus. | Garmisch-Partenkirchen, Ger. |
| 1925 | L. Wrede, J. Szabo; Aus. | Vienna, Aus. | | | |
| 1926 | P. Brunet, A. Joly; Fr. | Berlin, Ger. | 1957 | R. Paul, B. Wagner; Can. | Colorado Springs, U.S. |
| 1927 | L. Wrede, J. Szabo; Aus. | Vienna, Aus. | 1958 | R. Paul, B. Wagner; Can. | Paris, Fr. |
| 1928 | P. Brunet, A. Joly; Fr. | London, U.K. | 1959 | R. Paul, B. Wagner; Can. | Colorado Springs, U.S. |
| 1929 | O. Kaiser, L. Scholz; Aus. | Budapest, Hung. | 1960 | R. Paul, B. Wagner; Can. | Vancouver, Can. |
| 1930 | P. Brunet, A. Brunet; Fr. | New York, U.S. | 1962 | O. Jelinek, M. Jelinek; Can. | Prague, Czech. |
| 1931 | L. Szollas, B. Rotter; Hung. | Berlin, Ger. | 1963 | H. Bäumler, M. Kilius; W. Ger. | Cortina d'Ampezzo, It. |
| 1932 | P. Brunet, A. Brunet; Fr. | Montreal, Can. | 1964 | H. Bäumler, M. Kilius; W. Ger. | Dortmund, W. Ger. |
| 1933 | L. Szollas, B. Rotter; Hung. | Stockholm, Swed. | 1965 | O. Protopopov, L. Belousova; U.S.S.R. | Colorado Springs, U.S. |
| 1934 | L. Szollas, B. Rotter; Hung. | Helsingfors, Fin. | 1966 | O. Protopopov, L. Belousova; U.S.S.R. | Davos, Switz. |
| 1935 | L. Szollas, B. Rotter; Hung. | Budapest, Hung. | 1967 | O. Protopopov, L. Belousova; U.S.S.R. | Vienna, Aus. |
| 1936 | E. Baier, M. Herber; Ger. | Paris, Fr. | 1968 | O. Protopopov, L. Belousova; U.S.S.R. | Geneva, Switz. |
| 1937 | E. Baier, M. Herber; Ger. | London, U.K. | 1969 | I. Rodnina, A. Ulanov; U.S.S.R. | Colorado Springs, U.S. |
| 1938 | E. Baier, M. Herber; Ger. | Berlin, Ger. | 1970 | I. Rodnina, A. Ulanov; U.S.S.R. | Ljubljana, Yugos. |
| 1939 | E. Baier, M. Herber; Ger. | Budapest, Hung. | | | |

OLEG PROTOPOPOV AND LUDMILA BELOUSOVA (U.S.S.R.), WORLD CHAMPION ICE SKATING PAIR, 1965–68, PERFORMING IN MOSCOW'S SPORTS PALACE, MARCH 1968

TASS FROM SOVFOTO

## ICE DANCE (World Champions)

| Year | Winners; Country | Place |
|---|---|---|
| 1950 | M. McGean, L. Waring; U.S. | London, U.K. |
| 1951 | L. Demmy, J. Westwood; U.K. | Milan, It. |
| 1952 | L. Demmy, J. Westwood; U.K. | Paris, Fr. |
| 1953 | L. Demmy, J. Westwood; U.K. | Davos, Switz. |
| 1954 | L. Demmy, J. Westwood; U.K. | Oslo, Nor. |
| 1955 | L. Demmy, J. Westwood; U.K. | Vienna, Aus. |
| 1956 | P. Thomas, P. Weight; U.K. | Garmisch-Partenkirchen, Ger. |
| 1957 | C. Jones, J. Markham; U.K. | Colorado Springs, U.S. |
| 1958 | C. Jones, J. Markham; U.K. | Paris, Fr. |
| 1959 | C. Jones, D. Denny; U.K. | Colorado Springs, U.S. |
| 1960 | C. Jones, D. Denny; U.K. | Vancouver, Can. |
| 1962 | P. Roman, E. Romanova; Czech. | Prague, Czech. |
| 1963 | P. Roman, E. Romanova; Czech. | Cortina d'Ampezzo, It. |
| 1964 | P. Roman, E. Romanova; Czech. | Dortmund, W. Ger. |
| 1965 | P. Roman, E. Romanova; Czech. | Colorado Springs, U.S. |
| 1966 | B. Ford, D. Towler; U.K. | Davos, Switz. |
| 1967 | B. Ford, D. Towler; U.K. | Vienna, Aus. |
| 1968 | B. Ford, D. Towler; U.K. | Geneva, Switz. |
| 1969 | B. Ford, D. Towler; U.K. | Colorado Springs, U.S. |
| 1970 | L. Pakhomova, A. Gorshkov; U.S.S.R. | Ljubljana, Yugos. |

## JUDO

### World Champions*

| Year | Class | Winner; Country | Place |
|---|---|---|---|
| 1956 | Open | Natsui; Jap. | Tokyo, Jap. |
| 1958 | Open | Sone; Jap. | Tokyo, Jap. |
| 1961 | Open | Geesink; Neth. | Paris, Fr. |
| 1965 | Open | Inokuma; Jap. | Rio de Janeiro, Braz. |
| 1967 | Open | Matsunaga; Jap. | Salt Lake City, U.S. |
| 1969 | Open | Shinomaki; Jap. | Mexico City, Mex. |

*The Olympic Judo championship of 1964 is regarded also as a world title event (see the article OLYMPIC GAMES).

ANTON GEESINK (NETH.), WINNER OF THE OPEN JUDO CHAMPIONSHIP IN 1961, PINNING AKIO KAMINAGA (JAP.) TO WIN THE 1964 OLYMPIC TITLE AT TOKYO

WIDE WORLD

SOVFOTO

IGOR NOVIKOV (U.S.S.R.), MODERN PENTATHLON WORLD CHAMPION FROM 1957 TO 1961, DURING A CROSS-COUNTRY RACE, MOSCOW, 1959

## MODERN PENTATHLON

### World Champions*

| Year | Winner; Country | Winning team | Place |
|---|---|---|---|
| 1949 | Bjurefelt; Swed. | Sweden | Stockholm, Swed. |
| 1950 | L. Hall; Swed. | Sweden | Bern, Switz. |
| 1951 | L. Hall; Swed. | Sweden | Halsingsborg, Swed. |
| 1953 | G. Benedek; Hung. | Sweden | Santiago, Chile |
| 1954 | B. Thofelt; Swed. | Hungary | Budapest, Hung. |
| 1955 | S. Konstantin; U.S.S.R. | Hungary | Bern, Switz. |
| 1957 | I. Novikov; U.S.S.R. | U.S.S.R. | Stockholm, Swed. |
| 1958 | I. Novikov; U.S.S.R. | U.S.S.R. | Aldershot, U.K. |
| 1959 | I. Novikov; U.S.S.R. | U.S.S.R. | Harrisburg, U.S. |
| 1961 | I. Novikov; U.S.S.R. | U.S.S.R. | Moscow, U.S.S.R. |
| 1962 | S. Dobnikov; U.S.S.R. | U.S.S.R. | Mexico City, Mex. |
| 1963 | A. Balczo; Hung. | Hungary | Bern, Switz. |
| 1965 | A. Balczo; Hung. | Hungary | Leipzig, E. Ger. |
| 1966 | A. Balczo; Hung. | Hungary | Melbourne, Austr. |
| 1967 | A. Balczo; Hung. | Hungary | Jönköping, Swed. |
| 1969 | A. Balczo; Hung. | U.S.S.R. | Budapest, Hung. |

The highest individual scores in World Championship competitions have been:

| Event | Score (pt.) | Name; Country | Place | Date |
|---|---|---|---|---|
| Riding | 1,237† | S. Escobedo; Mex. | Rome, It. | Aug. 26, 1960 |
| Fencing (Epée) | 1,140 | I. Novikov; U.S.S.R. | Stockholm, Swed. | Oct. 25, 1957 |
| Shooting | 1,066 | P. Macken, Austr.; and R. Phelps, U.K. | Leipzig, E. Ger. | Sept. 21, 1965 |
| Swimming | 1,144 | K-H. Kutsche; E. Ger. | Jönköping, Swed. | Sept. 1967 |
| Cross country | 1,312 | A. Balczo; Hung. | Bern, Switz. | Sept. 26, 1963 |
| Overall | 5,515 | A. Balczo; Hung. | Budapest, Hung. | Aug. 19–26, 1969 |

*In the Olympic years since 1912 the world championships have been Olympic events. See table in the article OLYMPIC GAMES.
†Currently limited to a maximum of 1,100 points.

## MOTORBOATING

### World Speed Records

| Class | Driver; Country | Boat | Place | Record | Date |
|---|---|---|---|---|---|
| Unlimited jet | L. Taylor; U.S. | "Hustler" | Guntersville, U.S. | 285.21 mph | June 30, 1967 |
| Unlimited inboard (propeller) | R. Duby; U.S. | "Miss U.S. I" | Guntersville, U.S. | 200.42 mph | April 17, 1962 |
| Class OX outboard (propeller) | B. Ross; U.S. | Jones/Mercury | Lake Washington, U.S. | 115.54 mph | May 4, 1960 |
| Diesel propulsion | D. Aronow; U.S. | "Maltese Magnum" | Miami, U.S. | 64.47 mph | 1967 |

**The Gold Cup** Instituted in 1903, the cup has been contested annually, except in 1928 and the war years 1942–45. The lap and race records are:

| | | | | | |
|---|---|---|---|---|---|
| Lap (3 mi.) | B. Brow; U.S. | "Miss Exide" | Seattle, U.S. | 120.356 mph | Aug. 4, 1965 |
| Race (60 mi.) | R. Musson; U.S. | "Miss Bardahl" | Detroit, U.S. | 105.119 mph | July 7, 1963 |

(LEFT) LEE TAYLOR (U.S.) SETTING WORLD MOTORBOATING (UNLIMITED-JET CLASS) SPEED RECORD OF 285.21 MPH IN 1967 AT GUNTERSVILLE, U.S. DRIVING THE "HUSTLER," TAYLOR SURPASSED THE RECORD SET BY DONALD CAMPBELL IN 1964. (RIGHT) RON MUSSON (U.S.) WINNING THE GOLD CUP RACE IN RECORD TIME, AT DETROIT, IN 1963

(LEFT) WIDE WORLD, (RIGHT) NEIL LEIFER FOR "SPORTS ILLUSTRATED," © TIME INC.

## MOTORCYCLING

### Progressive Speed Records*

| Year | mph | Rider; Country | Machine | Place |
|---|---|---|---|---|
| 1920 | 103.5 | F. Walker; U.S. | 994 Indian | Daytona Beach, U.S. |
| 1923 | 108.48 | C. F. Temple; U.K. | 996 British Anzani | Brooklands, U.K. |
| 1924 | 119 | H. le Vack; U.K. | 867 Brough Superior JAP | Arpajon, Fr. |
| 1926 | 121.4 | C. F. Temple; U.K. | 996 OEC Temple | Arpajon, Fr. |
| 1928 | 124.62 | O. M. Baldwin; U.K. | 996 Zenith JAP | Arpajon, Fr. |
| 1929 | 129.06 | H. le Vack; U.K. | 995 Brough Superior | Arpajon, Fr. |
| 1929 | 134.68 | E. Henne; Ger. | 740 BMW | Munich, Ger. |
| 1930 | 137.32 | J. S. Wright; U.K. | 994 OEC Temple JAP | Arpajon, Fr. |
| 1930 | 137.66 | E. Henne; Ger. | 735 BMW | Munich, Ger. |
| 1930 | 150.70 | J. S. Wright; U.K. | 995 OEC Temple JAP | Cork, Ire. |
| 1932 | 151.86 | E. Henne; Ger. | 735 BMW | Tat, Hung. |
| 1934 | 153 | E. Henne; Ger. | 735 BMW | Gyon, Hung. |
| 1935 | 159.1 | E. Henne; Ger. | 735 BMW | Frankfurt am Main, Ger. |
| 1936 | 169.01 | E. Henne; Ger. | 495 BMW | Frankfurt am Main, Ger. |
| 1937 | 169.78 | E. C. Fernihough; U.K. | 995 Brough Superior JAP | Gyon, Hung. |
| 1937 | 170.37 | P. Taruffi; It. | 493 Gilera | Brescia, It. |
| 1937 | 173.67 | E. Henne; Ger. | 493 BMW | Frankfurt am Main, Ger. |
| 1951 | 180.1 | W. Hertz; Ger. | 499 NSU | Munich, W. Ger. |
| 1955 | 185.15 | R. Wright; N.Z. | 998 Vincent HRD | Christchurch, N.Z. |
| 1956 | 211.04 | W. Hertz; Ger. | 499 NSU | Bonneville, U.S. |
| 1962† | 224.57 | W. A. Johnson; U.S. | 667 Triumph T120 | Bonneville, U.S. |

*FIM (Fédération Internationale Motocycliste).

†Johnson reached 232.258 mph in an unrecognized mile run 12 days earlier on Aug. 24.

*Note:* On Aug. 25, 1966, B. Leppan (U.S.) recorded 247.763 mph on a run on Bonneville Salt Flats, Utah, that was unobserved by the FIM. The FIM now recognizes three-wheel jet-powered vehicles as Class D motorcycles. The record in this category is 535.332 mph over a flying kilometre by Craig Breedlove (U.S.) in his "Spirit of America" (General Electric J47-15 5,700 lb. jet) at Bonneville, Utah, on Oct. 15, 1964.

**FIM Road Racing World Championships.** These championships, established in 1949, are staged for machines of engine capacity of 125, 250, 350, and 500 cc. and also for a sidecar event. The champions for the 500-cc. class are listed below.

| Year | Champion; Country | Machine |
|---|---|---|
| 1949 | W. A. Lomas; U.K. | Norton |
| 1950 | V. Masetti; It. | Norton |
| 1951 | G. E. Duke; U.K. | Norton |
| 1952 | V. Masetti; It. | Gilera |
| 1953 | G. E. Duke; U.K. | Gilera |
| 1954 | G. E. Duke; U.K. | Gilera |
| 1955 | G. E. Duke; U.K. | Gilera |
| 1956 | J. Surtees; U.K. | M.V. |
| 1957 | L. Liberati; It. | Gilera |
| 1958 | J. Surtees; U.K. | M.V. |
| 1959 | J. Surtees; U.K. | M.V. |
| 1960 | J. Surtees; U.K. | M.V. |
| 1961 | G. Hocking; Rhod. | M.V. |
| 1962 | S. M. B. Hailwood; U.K. | M.V. |
| 1963 | S. M. B. Hailwood; U.K. | M.V. |
| 1964 | S. M. B. Hailwood; U.K. | M.V. |
| 1965 | S. M. B. Hailwood; U.K. | M.V. |
| 1966 | G. Agostini; It. | M.V. |
| 1967 | G. Agostini; It. | M.V. |
| 1968 | G. Agostini; It. | M.V. |
| 1969 | G. Agostini; It. | M.V. |

MILLER SERVICES LTD.

S. M. B. HAILWOOD (U.K.), SIX-TIME WINNER OF THE TOURIST TROPHY (INTERNATIONAL SENIOR EVENT), SHOWN CORNERING IN THE 1965 RACE ON THE ISLE OF MAN, U.K.

**Tourist Trophy.** The world's leading and oldest series of races is the Auto-Cycle Union Tourist Trophy event, known as the TT races, staged annually on the Isle of Man, U.K. The Senior TT has been staged since 1911 over the "Mountain" circuit of 37.73 mi. with 264 curves and corners and is now run over 6 laps. Results of the International Senior event since World War II are listed below.

| Year | Rider; Country | Machine | mph |
|---|---|---|---|
| 1947 | H. L. Daniell; U.K. | Norton | 82.813 |
| 1948 | A. J. Bell; U.K. | Norton | 84.969 |
| 1949 | H. L. Daniell; U.K. | Norton | 86.93 |
| 1950 | G. E. Duke; U.K. | Norton | 92.27 |
| 1951 | G. E. Duke; U.K. | Norton | 93.83 |
| 1952 | H. R. Armstrong; U.K. | Norton | 92.97 |
| 1953 | W. R. Amm; Rhod. | Norton | 93.85 |
| 1954 | W. R. Amm; Rhod. | Norton | 88.12 |
| 1955 | G. E. Duke; U.K. | Gilera | 97.93 |
| 1956 | J. Surtees; U.K. | M.V. | 96.57 |
| 1957 | R. McIntyre; U.K. | Gilera | 98.99 |
| 1958 | J. Surtees; U.K. | M.V. | 98.63 |
| 1959 | J. Surtees; U.K. | M.V. | 89.94 |
| 1960 | J. Surtees; U.K. | M.V. | 102.44 |
| 1961 | S. M. B. Hailwood; U.K. | Norton | 100.60 |
| 1962 | G. Hocking; Rhod. | M.V. | 103.51 |
| 1963 | S. M. B. Hailwood; U.K. | M.V. | 104.64 |
| 1964 | S. M. B. Hailwood; U.K. | M.V. | 100.95 |
| 1965 | S. M. B. Hailwood; U.K. | M.V. | 91.69 |
| 1966 | S. M. B. Hailwood; U.K. | Honda | 103.11 |
| 1967 | S. M. B. Hailwood; U.K. | Honda | 105.62 |
| 1968 | G. Agostini; It. | M.V. | 101.63 |
| 1969 | G. Agostini; It. | M.V. | 104.75 |

**Speedway.** The sport, usually limited to 4 starters, is run over 4 laps on cinder or dirt circuits. Speedway originated in Australia in 1927 and was introduced into Europe in 1928.

| World Champions | |
|---|---|
| 1936 | L. van Praag; Austr. |
| 1937 | J. Milne; U.S. |
| 1938 | B. Wilkinson; Austr. |
| 1939* | |
| 1949 | T. Price; U.K. |
| 1950 | F. Williams; U.K. |
| 1951 | J. Young; Austr. |
| 1952 | J. Young; Austr. |
| 1953 | F. Williams; U.K. |
| 1954 | R. Moore; N.Z. |
| 1955 | P. Craven; U.K. |
| 1956 | O. Fundin; Swed. |
| 1957 | B. Briggs; N.Z. |
| 1958 | B. Briggs; N.Z. |
| 1959 | R. Moore; N.Z. |
| 1960 | O. Fundin; Swed. |
| 1961 | O. Fundin; Swed. |
| 1962 | P. Craven; U.K. |
| 1963 | O. Fundin; Swed. |
| 1964 | B. Briggs; N.Z. |
| 1965 | B. Knutsson; Swed. |
| 1966 | B. Briggs; N.Z. |
| 1967 | O. Fundin; Swed. |
| 1968 | I. Mauger; N.Z. |
| 1969 | I. Mauger; N.Z. |

*Not completed.

## PARACHUTE JUMPING

**World Record:** 4 turns (720° in horizontal plane) plus 2 back loops (vertical plane)

| | | | | |
|---|---|---|---|---|
| **Men** | 7.4 sec. | V. Krestyanikov; U.S.S.R. | Leipzig, E. Ger. | Aug. 2, 1966 |
| **Women** | 9.1 sec. | T. Voinova; U.S.S.R. | Leipzig, E. Ger. | Aug. 1, 1966 |

### World Championships

| Year | Place | Individual Champions Men | Women | Team Men | Women |
|---|---|---|---|---|---|
| 1951 | Lesce-Bled, Yugos. | P. Lard; Fr. | — | — | — |
| 1954 | Saint-Yan, Fr. | I. Sedtshchishchin; U.S.S.R. | — | U.S.S.R. | — |
| 1956 | Moscow, U.S.S.R. | G. Koubek; Czech. | J. Maxoua; Czech. | Czechoslovakia | U.S.S.R. |
| 1958 | Bratislava, Czech. | P. Ostrovskiy; U.S.S.R. | N. Priachina; U.S.S.R. | U.S.S.R. | U.S.S.R. |
| 1960 | Sofia, Bulg. | Z. Kapalan; Czech. | B. Rejzlova; Czech. | U.S.S.R. | Czechoslovakia |
| 1962 | Orange, Mass., U.S. | J. Arender; U.S. | M. Simbro; U.S. | Czechoslovakia | United States |
| 1964 | Leutkirch, W. Ger. | R. Fortenberry; U.S. | T. Taylor; U.S. | Czechoslovakia | United States |
| 1966 | Leipzig, E. Ger. | V. Krestyanikov; U.S.S.R. | L. Yeremina; U.S.S.R. | U.S.S.R. | U.S.S.R. |
| 1968 | Graz, Aus. | T. Tkachenko; U.S.S.R. | T. Voinova; U.S.S.R. | U.S. | U.S.S.R. |

**PIGEON RACING.** The invention of the electric telegraph in the 1840s resulted in the disposal of many lofts of trained homing or racing pigeons (the rock dove *Columba livia*) and the start of pigeon racing as sport (*see* also the article PIGEON FLYING).

### RECORDS

#### Distance

Homing Flights, about 7,000 mi.
Ichabo Islands, W. Af., to Nine Elms, London, U.K., 55 days: April 8–June 1, 1845 (bird owned by the 1st duke of Wellington)

#### Race Speed

97.4 mph
Beattie Bros.' winner of the Dungarvan race, Republic of Ireland, 1961

#### 24-hour Record

751 mi. (flying time 15 hr. 52 min.)
Edfelt and Wahistrom's winner of the Lulea-Ystrad, Swed., race, 1951

A CHAMPIONSHIP RACING PIGEON, FLYING DUTCHMAN, 1961 WINNER OF THE SPAIN INTERNATIONAL AND THE DUTCH INTERNATIONAL RACES, EACH 746 MI., OWNED BY FRANK GEORGE, WELLINGBOROUGH, ENG.

BY COURTESY OF GEORGE TWOMBLY

## POLO

### All-time roster of 10-goal handicap players

| U.S. (10-goal handicap instituted 1891) | | U.K. (10-goal handicap instituted 1910) | | Argentina (10-goal handicap instituted 1910) | |
|---|---|---|---|---|---|
| F. Keene | 1891–1920 | H. Lloyd | 1911–14 | L. Lacey (previously for U.K.) | 1928–34 |
| T. Hitchcock, Sr. | 1894–1901 | R. G. Ritson | 1913 | J. Cavanagh | 1950–58 |
| J. E. Cowdin | 1894–95 | L. Cheape | 1911–14 | R. Cavanagh | early 1960s |
| R. L. Agassiz | 1894 | L. Lacey (subsequently for Arg.) | 1924 | C. Menditeguy | 1960–65 |
| L. Waterbury | 1900–20 | V. Lockett | 1911–21 | S. Dorignac | mid-1960s |
| J. M. Waterbury | 1902–18 | P. C. Roarke | 1922–35 | J. C. Harriott | mid-1960s |
| D. Milburn | 1917–28 | G. Balding | 1934–39 | | |
| H. P. Whitney | 1917–21 | R. Skene (Austr. citizen) | 1951–65 | | |
| L. E. Stoddard | 1922–23 | | | | |
| J. W. Webb | 1922–25 | | | | |
| T. Hitchcock, Jr. | 1922–40 | | | | |
| J. M. Stevenson | 1925–28 | | | | |
| E. Boeseke, Jr. | 1934 | | | | |
| C. Smith | 1934–62 | | | | |
| S. B. Inglehart | 1937–60 | | | | |
| M. G. Phipps | 1939–47 | | | | |

CECIL SMITH (U.S.), CENTRE, 10-GOAL HANDICAP PLAYER, IN ACTION DURING AN INTERNATIONAL POLO MATCH BETWEEN THE U.S. AND MEXICO, 1946

WIDE WORLD

BY COURTESY OF THE FÉDERATION INTERNATIONALE DE ROLLER SKATING

P. L. FAGGIOLI (IT.), WORLD RECORD ROLLER SKATER AT 1,000 M., 1,500 M., AND 1 MI.

## ROLLER SKATING

### World Records (Road Records)

#### Men

| Distance | Name; Country | Record | Year |
|---|---|---|---|
| 440 yd. | G. Cantarella; It. | 34.9 sec. | 1963 |
| 500 m. | G. Cantarella; It. | 43.7 sec. | 1963 |
| 880 yd. | G. Cantarella; It. | 1 min. 13.5 sec. | 1963 |
| 1,000 m. | P. L. Faggioli; It. | 1 min. 30.0 sec. | 1957 |
| 1,500 m. | P. L. Faggioli; It. | 2 min. 12.4 sec. | 1957 |
| 1 mi. | P. L. Faggioli; It. | 2 min. 22.5 sec. | 1957 |

#### Women

| Distance | Name; Country | Record | Year |
|---|---|---|---|
| 440 yd. | A. Vianello; It. | 40.6 sec. | 1955 |
| 500 m. | A. Vianello; It. | 49.6 sec. | 1955 |
| 880 yd. | A. Vianello; It. | 1 min. 23.4 sec. | 1955 |
| 1,000 m. | A. Vianello; It. | 1 min. 42.7 sec. | 1955 |
| 1,500 m. | A. Vianello; It. | 2 min. 38.3 sec. | 1955 |
| 1 mi. | A. Vianello; It. | 2 min. 50.1 sec. | 1955 |

## ROWING

**World Titles.** The Olympic Games have served as world championships from 1896. Additional world championships were staged between Olympic regattas for the first time in 1962 at Lucerne, Switz., and again in 1966 at Bled, Yugos.

| Year | Single sculls | Min.: sec. | Double sculls | Min.: sec. | Coxed pairs | Min.: sec. |
|---|---|---|---|---|---|---|
| 1962 | V. Ivanov; U.S.S.R. | 7:07.9 | R. Duhamel-B. Monnereau; Fr. | 6:33.9 | Jordan-Neuss; W. Ger. | 6:29.12 |
| 1966 | D. M. Spero; U.S. | 7:05.92 | M. Buergin-M. Studach; Switz. | 6:34.89 | H. van Nes-J. van de Graaf; Neth. | 7:12.83 |

| Year | Coxless pairs | Min.: sec. | Coxed fours | Min.: sec. | Coxless fours | Min.: sec. | Eights | Min.: sec. |
|---|---|---|---|---|---|---|---|---|
| 1962 | Bender-Z. Keller; Ger. | 6:54.62 | W. Germany | 6:29.12 | W. Germany | 6:19.24 | W. Germany | 5:50.83 |
| 1966 | P. Kremtz-A. Goehler; E. Ger. | 6:53.96 | E. Germany | 6:29.54 | E. Germany | 6:18.41 | W. Germany | 5:56.28 |

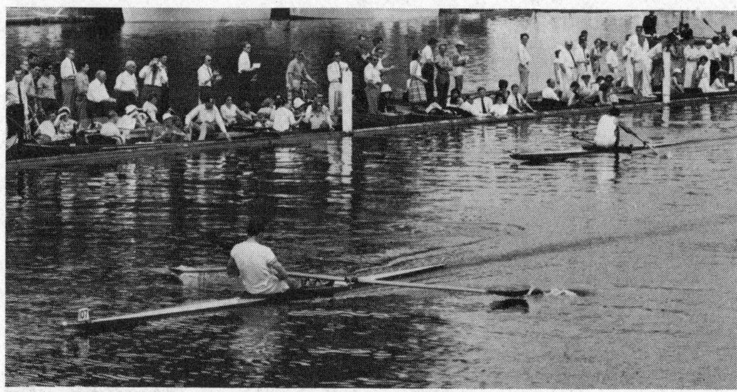

MILLER SERVICES LTD.
S. A. MACKENZIE (AUSTR.), WINNER OF THE DIAMOND CHALLENGE SCULLS AT HENLEY-ON-THAMES, ENG., 1957–62, CROSSING THE FINISH LINE IN 1962

**University Boat Race.** The University Boat Race between Eights from Oxford and Cambridge universities was instituted on June 10, 1829. The record time for the course of 4 mi. 374 yd. from Putney to Mortlake on the River Thames is 17 min. 50.0 sec. by Cambridge in 1948. The results up to the 115th race in 1969 have been Cambridge 63 wins, Oxford 51 wins, and one dead heat (in 1877).

CENTRAL PRESS FROM PICTORIAL PARADE INC.
THE OXFORD UNIVERSITY CREW LEADING CAMBRIDGE IN THE 112TH ANNUAL UNIVERSITY BOAT RACE ON THE THAMES IN LONDON, 1966, WON BY OXFORD

**The Diamond Challenge Sculls.** The annual single sculls event in the regatta at Henley-on-Thames, Oxfordshire, Eng., instituted 1844, is open to the world. The course is 1 mi. 550 yd.

| Year | Winner | Min.: sec. | Year | Winner | Min.: sec. |
|---|---|---|---|---|---|
| 1920 | J. Beresford, Jr. (Thames R.C.) | 8:57 | 1948 | M. T. Wood (New South Wales Police R.C., Austr.) | 8:24 |
| 1921 | F. E. Eyken (Delft Univ. B.C., Neth.) | 8:26 | 1949 | J. B. Kelly (Univ. of Pennsylvania, U.S.) | 8:12 |
| 1922 | W. M. Hoover (Duluth B.C., Minnesota, U.S.) | 9:32 | 1950 | A. D. Rowe (Leander Club) | 9:11 |
| 1923 | M. K. Morris (London R.C.) | 8:23 | 1951 | T. A. Fox (Pembroke Coll., Cam.) | 8:59 |
| 1924 | J. Beresford, Jr. (Thames R.C.) | 10:32 | 1952 | M. T. Wood (Sydney R.C., Austr.) | 8:12 |
| 1925 | J. Beresford, Jr. (Thames R.C.) | 8:26 | 1953 | T. A. Fox (London R.C.) | 8:12 |
| 1926 | J. Beresford, Jr. (Thames R.C.) | 8:45 | 1954 | P. Vlasic (Mornar Club, Yugos.) | 8:42 |
| 1927 | R. T. Lee (Worcester Coll., Oxf.) | 9:06 | 1955 | T. Kocerka (A.Z.S. Bydgoszcz, Pol.) | 8:33 |
| 1928 | J. Wright, Jr. (Argonaut R.C., Can.) | 8:24 | 1956 | T. Kocerka (A.Z.S. Bydgoszcz, Pol.) | 8:37 |
| 1929 | L. H. F. Gunther (Roei-Zeilvereening de Amstel, Neth.) | 8:42 | 1957 | S. A. Mackenzie (Sydney R.C., Austr.) | 8:25 |
| 1930 | J. S. Guest (Don R.C., Can.) | 8:29 | 1958 | S. A. Mackenzie (Sydney R.C., Austr.) | 8:06 |
| 1931 | R. Pearce (Leander B.C., Hamilton, Can.) | 10:03 | 1959 | S. A. Mackenzie (Sydney R.C., Austr.) | 8:29 |
| 1932 | H. Buhtz (Berliner R.C., Ger.) | 9:15 | 1960 | S. A. Mackenzie (Leander Club) | 8:03 |
| 1933 | T. G. Askwith (Peterhouse, Cam.) | 9:07 | 1961 | S. A. Mackenzie (Mosman R.C., Austr.) | 8:34 |
| 1934 | H. Buhtz (Berliner R.C., Ger.) | 8:10 | 1962 | S. A. Mackenzie (Leander Club) | 8:38 |
| 1935 | E. Rufli (F.C. Zürich R.C., Switz.) | 8:15 | 1963 | G. Kottmann (Belvoir R.C., Switz.) | 8:09 |
| 1936 | E. Rufli (F.C. Zürich R.C., Switz.) | 9:22 | 1964 | S. Cromwell (Nonpareil R.C., U.S.) | 8:06 |
| 1937 | J. Hasenohrl (Ruderverein Ellida, Aus.) | 9:12 | 1965 | D. M. Spero (U.S.) | 7:42* |
| 1938 | J. W. Burk (Penn Athletic Club, U.S.) | 8:02 | 1966 | A. Kile (E. Ger.) | 8:15 |
| 1939 | J. W. Burk (Penn Athletic Club, U.S.) | 9:13 | 1967 | M. Studach (Switz.) | 8:27 |
| 1946 | J. Séphériadés (Société Nautique de la Basse Seine, Fr.) | 8:21 | 1968 | H. Wardell-Yerburgh (U.K.) | 10:25 |
| 1947 | J. B. Kelly (Univ. of Pennsylvania, U.S.) | 8:49 | 1969 | H. J. Bohmer (S.C. Dynamo, Berlin) | 8:06 |

*Record.

**The Grand Challenge Cup.** The annual event for Eights in the regatta at Henley-on-Thames, Oxfordshire, Eng., instituted 1839, is open to the world. The course is 1 mi. 550 yd.

| Year | Winner | Min.: sec. | Year | Winner | Min.: sec. |
|---|---|---|---|---|---|
| 1920 | Magdalen Coll., Oxford | 7:24 | 1948 | Thames R.C. | 7:02 |
| 1921 | Magdalen Coll., Oxford | 6:54 | 1949 | Leander Club | 6:54 |
| 1922 | Leander Club | 7:36 | 1950 | Harvard Univ., U.S. | 7:23 |
| 1923 | Thames R.C. | 6:45 | 1951 | Lady Margaret B.C., Cambridge | 7:16 |
| 1924 | Leander Club | 8:03 | 1952 | Leander Club | 6:38 |
| 1925 | Leander Club | 6:53 | 1953 | Leander Club | 6:49 |
| 1926 | Leander Club | 6:56 | 1954 | Club Krylia Sovetov, U.S.S.R. | 7:16 |
| 1927 | Thames R.C. | 7:16 | 1955 | Univ. of Pennsylvania, U.S. | 6:56 |
| 1928 | Thames R.C. | 6:56 | 1956 | Centre Sportif des Forces de l'Armée Francaise | 7:06 |
| 1929 | Leander Club | 7:00 | 1957 | Cornell Univ., U.S. | 6:53 |
| 1930 | London R.C. | 6:59 | 1958 | Trud Club, Leningrad, U.S.S.R. | 6:40 |
| 1931 | London R.C. | 7:33 | 1959 | Harvard Univ., U.S. | 6:57 |
| 1932 | Leander Club | 7:19 | 1960 | Molesey B.C. | 6:35 |
| 1933 | London R.C. | 7:36 | 1961 | Central Sports Club of U.S.S.R. Navy | 6:43 |
| 1934 | Leander Club | 6:45 | 1962 | Central Sports Club of U.S.S.R. Navy | 6:40 |
| 1935 | Pembroke Coll., Cambridge | 6:52 | 1963 | University of London | 6:38 |
| 1936 | F. C. Zürich R.C., Switz. | 7:25 | 1964 | Club Zjalghris Viljnjus, U.S.S.R. | 6:25 |
| 1937 | R. Wiking, Ger. | 7:33 | 1965 | Ratzeburger, W. Ger. | 6:16* |
| 1938 | London R.C. | 6:58 | 1966 | Turn und Sports Club (Berlin) | 6:35 |
| 1939 | Harvard Univ., U.S. | 7:40 | 1967 | S. C. Wissenschaft, E. Ger. | 6:46 |
| 1946 | Leander Club | 7:01 | 1968 | University of London | 7:56 |
| 1947 | Jesus Coll., Cambridge | 7:14 | 1969 | S.C. Einheit, E. Ger. | 6:28 |

*Record.

## SHOOTING

### Official World Records

| Event | Name; Country | Score | Place | Year |
|---|---|---|---|---|
| Free rifle 300 m. 3 × 40 shots | G. L. Anderson; U.S. | 1,157 | Mexico City, Mex. | 1968 |
| Small-bore rifle 50 m. 3 × 40 shots | L. W. Wigger, Jr.; U.S.<br>G. L. Anderson; U.S. | 1,164<br>1,164 | Tokyo, Jap.<br>Johannesburg, S.Af. | 1964<br>1969 |
| Service rifle 300 m. 3 × 20 shots | A. Tilik; U.S.S.R. | 555 | Moscow, U.S.S.R. | 1958 |
| Free pistol 50 m. 60 shots | A. Jegrishchin; U.S.S.R. | 570 | Lahti, Fin. | 1968 |
| Rapid free pistol 25 m. 60 shots | V. Antanasiu; Rum. | 596 | Wiesbaden, W. Ger. | 1966 |
| Centre-fire pistol 25 m. | T. D. Smith III; U.S. | 597 | São Paulo, Braz. | 1963 |
| Skeet (200 possible) | N. Durnev; U.S.S.R. | 200 | Cairo, U.A.R. | 1962 |

The (British) National Rifle Association (instituted 1860) annual Queen's (or King's) prize shoot has a possible top score of 300. The record score is 292 by Capt. C. H. Vernon on July 15–16, 1927.

JERRY COOKE FOR "SPORTS ILLUSTRATED," © TIME INC.
JEAN CLAUDE KILLY (FRANCE) WINNING THE WORLD DOWNHILL TITLE AT PORTILLO, CHILE, 1966

**SHOW JUMPING.** The Olympic Games (since 1900, except 1908) provide the only world championships. For results *see* the article OLYMPIC GAMES.

### World Records

| Event | Horse | Rider; Country | Record | Place | Date |
|---|---|---|---|---|---|
| High jump | Huaso | A. L. Morales; Chile | 8 ft. 1¼ in.* | Santiago, Chile | Feb. 5, 1949 |
| Long jump (over water) | Amado Mio | L. del Hierro; Sp. | 27 ft. 2¾ in. | Barcelona, Sp. | Nov. 12, 1951 |
| Best unofficial high jump—Men | Golden Meade | J. Martin; Austr. | 8 ft. 6 in. | Cairns, Austr. | July 25, 1946 |
| Best unofficial high jump—Women | Plain Bill | B. Perry; Austr. | 7 ft. 5½ in. | Cairns, Austr. | 1940 |

*Official Fédération Équestre Internationale record.

## SKIING

**SKI JUMPING: Progressive World Records.** Records are strictly comparable only for a specific hill.

| Year | Distance ft. | Name; Country | Place | Year | Distance ft. | Name; Country | Place |
|---|---|---|---|---|---|---|---|
| 1912 | 154.2 | G. Anderson; Nor. | Gustad, Nor. | 1938 | 351.0 | S. Bradl; Aus. | Planica, Yugos. |
| 1913 | 157.5 | T. Knudsen; Nor. | Davos, Switz. | 1941 | 387.1 | R. Gehring; Ger. | Planica, Yugos. |
| 1913 | 169 | R. Omtuedt; Nor. | Ironwood, U.S. | 1948 | 393.7 | F. Tshannen; Switz. | Planica, Yugos. |
| 1915 | 177.2 | R. A. Ommundsen; Nor. | Vikoll, Nor. | 1950 | 406.8 | W. Gantschnigg; Aus. | Oberstdorf, W. Ger. |
| 1916 | 190 | R. Omtuedt; Nor. | Steamboat Springs, U.S. | 1950 | 416.7 | S. Weiler; W. Ger. | Oberstdorf, W. Ger. |
| 1917 | 202 | A. Haugen; Nor. | Steamboat Springs, U.S. | 1950 | 442.9 | D. Netzell; Swed. | Oberstdorf, W. Ger. |
| 1917 | 203 | H. Hall; U.S. | Steamboat Springs, U.S. | 1951 | 456.0 | T. Luiro; Fin. | Oberstdorf, W. Ger. |
| 1919 | 213 | A. Haugen; Nor. | Dillon, U.S. | 1961 | 462.6 | J. Slibar; Yugos. | Oberstdorf, W. Ger. |
| 1921 | 230 | H. Hall; U.S. | Revelstoke, Can. | 1962 | 462.6 | P. Lesser; E. Ger. | Mitterndorf/Külm, Aus. |
| 1924 | 239.5 | N. Nelson; U.S. | Revelstoke, Can. | 1964 | 465.9 | D. Motejlek; Czech. | Oberstdorf, W. Ger. |
| 1930 | 246.1 | R. Badrutt; Switz. | Bernina, It. | 1964 | 472.4 | N. Zandanel; It. | Oberstdorf, W. Ger. |
| 1931 | 251.0 | B. Ruud; Nor. | Oddnes, Nor. | 1965 | 475.7 | P. Lesser; E. Ger. | Mitterndorf/Külm, Aus. |
| 1931 | 267.5 | S. Ruud; Nor. | Davos, Switz. | 1966 | 479.0 | B. Wirkola; Nor. | Vikersund, Nor. |
| 1932 | 270.5 | R. Lymburne; Can. | Revelstoke, Can. | 1967 | 482.0 | L. Grini; Nor. | Oberstdorf, W. Ger. |
| 1933 | 275.6 | S. Ruud; Nor. | Villars, Switz. | 1967 | 485.0 | K. Sjoeberg; Swed. | Oberstdorf, W. Ger. |
| 1933 | 282.2 | S. Ruud; Nor. | Villars, Switz. | 1967 | 492.0 | L. Grini; Nor. | Oberstdorf, W. Ger. |
| 1933 | 285.4 | H. Rüchet; Switz. | Villars, Switz. | 1967 | 505.2 | R. Bachler; Aus. | Vikersund, Nor. |
| 1934 | 301.8 | B. Ruud; Nor. | Planica, Yugos. | 1969 | 512 | B. Wirkola; Nor. | Planica, Yugos. |
| 1935 | 305.1 | R. Andersen; Nor. | Planica, Yugos. | 1969 | 512 | J. Raska; Czech. | Planica, Yugos. |
| 1935 | 318.2 | S. Marusarz; Pol. | Planica, Yugos. | 1969 | 525 | B. Wirkola; Nor. | Planica, Yugos. |
| 1935 | 324.8 | R. Andersen; Nor. | Planica, Yugos. | 1969 | 538 | J. Raska; Czech. | Planica, Yugos. |
| 1935 | 326.4 | F. Kainersdorfer; Switz. | Ponte di Legno, It. | 1969 | 541.3 | M. Wolf; E. Ger. | Planica, Yugos. |
| 1936 | 331.4 | S. Bradl; Aus. | Planica, Yugos. | | | | |

**WORLD CHAMPIONSHIPS: Nordic and Alpine.** From 1925 until 1937 the major titles were called Fédération Internationale de Ski (FIS) Championships. The Olympic champions since 1924 are regarded as world champions (*see* the article OLYMPIC GAMES).

| Event | 1925 | 1926 | 1927 | 1929 | 1930 |
|---|---|---|---|---|---|
| **Nordic** | **Johannesbad, Czech.** | **Lahti, Fin.** | **Cortina d'Ampezzo, It.** | **Zakopane, Pol.** | **Oslo, Nor.** |
| 50-km. cross-country | Donth; Ger. | Raivio; Fin. | S. H. Lindgren; Swed. | A. Knuttila; Fin. | S. Utterström; Swed. |
| 18-km. cross-country | Nemecky; Czech. | J. Grøttumsbraaten; Nor. | S. H. Lindgren; Swed. | V. Saarinen; Fin. | A. Rustadstuen; Nor. |
| Jump | Dick; Ger. | T. Thams; Nor. | T. Edman; Swed. | S. Ruud; Nor. | G. Andersen; Nor. |
| Combined | Nemecky; Czech. | J. Grøttumsbraaten; Nor. | R. Purkert; Czech. | H. Vinjarengen; Nor. | H. Vinjarengen; Nor. |
| Military relay | — | — | — | — | Norway |

| Event | 1931 | 1933 | 1934 | 1935 |
|---|---|---|---|---|
| **Nordic** | **Oberhof, Ger.** | **Innsbruck, Aus.** | **Sollefteau, Swed.** | **Štrbské Pleso, Czech.** |
| 50-km. cross-country | O. Stenen; Nor. | V. Saarinen; Fin. | E. Viklund; Swed. | N. Englund; Swed. |
| 18-km. cross-country | J. Grøttumsbraaten; Nor. | N. Englund; Fin. | S. Nurmela; Fin. | K. Karppinen; Fin. |
| Jump | B. Ruud; Nor. | M. Reynolds; Switz. | K. Johansen; Nor. | B. Ruud; Nor. |
| Combined | J. Grøttumsbraaten; Nor. | S. Eriksson; Swed. | O. Hagen; Nor. | O. Hagen; Nor. |
| Military relay | — | Sweden | Finland | Finland |
| **Alpine** | **Mürren, Switz.** | **Innsbruck, Aus.** | **St. Moritz, Switz.** | **Mürren, Switz.** |
| Men's downhill | W. Prager; Switz. | W. Prager; Switz. | D. Zozz; Switz. | F. Zingerle; Aus. |
| Special men's downhill | — | H. Hauser; Aus. | — | — |
| Men's slalom | D. Zogg; Switz. | A. Seelos; Aus. | F. Pfnur; Ger. | A. Seelos; Aus. |
| Men's combined downhill slalom | — | A. Seelos; Aus. | D. Zozz; Switz. | A. Seelos; Aus. |
| Women's downhill | E. Mackinnon; U.K. | I. Wersin-Lantschner; Aus. | A. Ruegg; Switz. | C. Cranz; Ger. |
| Women's slalom | E. Mackinnon; U.K. | I. Wersin-Lantschner; Aus. | C. Cranz; Ger. | A. Ruegg; Switz. |
| Women's combined | — | I. Wersin-Lantschner; Aus. | C. Cranz; Ger. | C. Cranz; Ger. |

| Event | 1937 | 1938 | 1939 | 1950 |
|---|---|---|---|---|
| **Nordic** | **Chamonix, Fr.** | **Lahti, Fin.** | **Zakopane, Pol.** | **Lake Placid and Rumford, U.S.** |
| 50-km. cross-country | P. Niemi; Fin. | K. Jalkanen; Fin. | L. Bergendahl; Nor. | G. Ericksson; Swed. |
| 18-km. cross-country | L. Bergendahl; Nor. | P. Pitkainen; Fin. | J. Kurikkala; Fin. | K. E. Aastrom; Swed. |
| Jump | B. Ruud; Nor. | A. Ruud; Nor. | J. Bradl; Aus. | H. Bjornstad; Nor. |
| Combined | S. Roen; Nor. | O. Hoffsbakken; Nor. | H. Beraur; Czech. | H. Hasu; Fin. |
| Military relay | Norway | Finland | Finland | — |
| 40-km. relay | — | — | — | Sweden |
| **Alpine** | **Chamonix, Fr.** | **Engelberg, Switz.** | **Zakopane, Pol.** | **Aspen, U.S.** |
| Men's downhill | E. Allais; Fr. | J. Couttet; Fr. | H. Lantschner; Ger. | Z. Colo; It. |
| Men's slalom | E. Allais; Fr. | R. Rominger; Switz. | R. Rominger; Switz. | G. Schneider; Switz. |
| Men's giant slalom | — | — | — | Z. Colo; It. |
| Men's combined | E. Allais; Fr. | E. Allais; Fr. | J. Jennewein; Ger. | — |
| Women's downhill | C. Cranz; Ger. | L. Resch, Ger. | C. Cranz; Ger. | T. Beiser-Jochum; Aus. |
| Women's slalom | C. Cranz; Ger. | C. Cranz; Ger. | C. Cranz; Ger. | D. Rom; Aus. |
| Women's giant slalom | — | — | — | D. Rom; Aus. |
| Women's combined | C. Cranz; Ger. | C. Cranz; Ger. | C. Cranz; Ger. | — |

| Event | 1954 | 1958* | 1962† | 1966 |
|---|---|---|---|---|
| **Nordic** | **Falun, Swed.** | **Lahti, Fin.** | **Zakopane, Pol.** | **Oslo, Nor.** |
| 50-km. cross-country | V. Kusin; U.S.S.R. | S. Jernberg; Swed. | S. Jernberg; Swed. | G. Eggen; Nor. |
| 30-km. cross-country | V. Kusin; U.S.S.R. | K. Haemaelaeinen; Fin. | E. Mäntyranta; Fin. | E. Mäntyranta; Fin. |
| 15-km. cross-country | V. Hakulinen; Fin. | V. Hakulinen; Fin. | A. Rönnlund; Swed. | G. Eggen; Nor. |
| Jump | M. Pietikainen; Fin. | M. Maatela; Fin. | T. Engen; Nor.‡ | B. Wirkola; Nor.§ |
| Special jump | — | J. Karkinen; Fin. | H. Rechnagel; E. Ger.‖ | B. Wirkola; Nor.‖ |
| Combined | S. Stenerson; Nor. | P. Korhonen; Fin. | A. Larsen; Nor. | G. Thoma; W. Ger. |
| 40-km. relay | Finland | Sweden | Sweden | Norway |
| Women's 10-km. cross-country | L. Kosyreva; U.S.S.R. | A. Koltchina; U.S.S.R. | A. Koltchina; U.S.S.R. | C. Boyarskikh; U.S.S.R. |
| Women's 5-km. cross-country | — | — | A. Koltchina; U.S.S.R. | A. Koltchina; U.S.S.R. |
| Women's 15-km. relay | U.S.S.R. | U.S.S.R. | U.S.S.R. | U.S.S.R. |
| **Alpine** | **Are, Swed.** | **Bad Gastein, Aus.** | **Chamonix, Fr.** | **Portillo, Chile** |
| Men's downhill | C. Pravda; Aus. | A. Sailer; Aus. | K. Schranz; Aus. | J. C. Killy; Fr. |
| Men's slalom | S. Eriksen; Nor. | J. Rieder; Aus. | C. Bozon; Fr.¶ | C. Senoner; It.¶ |
| Men's giant slalom | S. Eriksen; Nor. | A. Sailer; Aus. | E. Zimmerman; Aus. | G. Perillat; Fr. |
| Men's combined | S. Eriksen; Nor. | A. Sailer; Aus. | K. Schranz; Aus. | J. C. Killy; Fr. |
| Women's downhill | I. Schopfer; Switz. | L. Wheeler; Can. | C. Hass; Aus. | E. Schinegger; Aus. |
| Women's slalom | T. Klecker; Aus. | I. Bjornbakken; Nor. | M. Jahn; Aus.¶ | A. Famose; Fr.¶ |
| Women's giant slalom | L. Schmith-Couttet; Fr. | L. Wheeler; Can. | M. Jahn; Aus. | M. Goitschel; Fr. |
| Women's combined | I. Schopfer; Switz. | F. Danzer; Switz. | M. Goitschel; Fr. | M. Goitschel; Fr. |

* Included Men's Nordic team (unofficial)—Finland; and Men's Alpine team (unofficial)—Austria.
† Included combined jump (60-m. hill)—Y. Rto; Jap.
‡ 65-m. hill. § 70-m. hill. ‖ 90-m. hill. ¶ Special slalom.

**World Cup.** Aggregate best performance at downhill, slalom, and giant slalom over a series of major events; inaugurated 1967.

| Year | Men | Women |
|---|---|---|
| 1967 | J. C. Killy; Fr. | N. Greene; Can. |
| 1968 | J. C. Killy; Fr. | N. Greene; Can. |
| 1969 | K. Schranz; Aus. | G. Gabl; Aus. |
| 1970 | K. Schranz; Aus. | M. Jacot, Fr. |

### World Biathlon Champions

| Year | Individual title | Team title |
|---|---|---|
| 1958 | A. Wiklund; Swed. | Sweden |
| 1959 | V. Melanin; U.S.S.R. | U.S.S.R. |
| 1961 | K. Huuskonen; Fin. | Finland |
| 1962 | V. Melanin; U.S.S.R. | U.S.S.R. |
| 1963 | V. Melanin; U.S.S.R. | U.S.S.R. |
| 1965 | O. Jordet; Nor. | Norway |
| 1966 | J. Istad; Nor. | Norway |
| 1967 | V. Mamatov; U.S.S.R. | Norway |
| 1969 | A. Tikhonov; U.S.S.R. | U.S.S.R. |

KEYSTONE

BJORN WIRKOLA (NORWAY), SKI JUMP CHAMPION IN 1966, THE YEAR IN WHICH HE SET A WORLD RECORD AT VIKERSUND, NOR., AND WON THE 70-M. AND 90-M. HILL JUMPS AT OSLO, NOR.

NANCY GREENE (CAN.), WINNER OF THE WOMEN'S WORLD CUP TITLE FOR 1967 AND 1968, EXECUTING THE SLALOM AT CHAMROUSSE, FRANCE, FEB. 13, 1968

WIDE WORLD

## SQUASH RACKETS

**World Amateur Championships** (instituted 1967).*

| Year | Place | Individual | Team |
|---|---|---|---|
| 1967 | Sydney, Austr. | G. B. Hunt; Austr. | Australia |
| 1968 | London, U.K. | G. B. Hunt; Austr. | Australia |

**Open Championships** (instituted 1930).

| | | | |
|---|---|---|---|
| 1930 | C. R. Read†; U.K. | 1955 | H. Khan; Pak. |
| 1930 | D. G. Butcher; U.K. | 1956 | R. Khan; Pak. |
| 1931 | D. G. Butcher; U.K. | 1957 | H. Khan; Pak. |
| 1932 | F. D. Amr Bey; Egy. | 1958 | A. Khan; Pak. |
| 1934 | F. D. Amr Bey; Egy. | 1959 | A. Khan; Pak. |
| 1935 | F. D. Amr Bey; Egy. | 1960 | A. Khan; Pak. |
| 1936 | F. D. Amr Bey; Egy. | 1961 | A. Khan; Pak. |
| 1937 | F. D. Amr Bey; Egy. | 1962 | M. Khan; Pak. |
| 1938 | J. Dear; U.K. | 1963 | A. F. A. Taleb; U.A.R. |
| 1946 | M. A. Karim; Ind. | 1964 | A. F. A. Taleb; U.A.R. |
| 1947 | M. A. Karim; Pak. | 1965 | A. F. A. Taleb; U.A.R. |
| 1948 | M. A. Karim; Pak. | 1966 | J. Barrington; U.K. |
| 1949 | M. A. Karim; Pak. | 1967 | J. Barrington; U.K. |
| 1950 | H. Khan; Pak. | 1968 | G. B. Hunt; Austr. |
| 1951 | H. Khan; Pak. | 1969 | J. Barrington; U.K. |
| 1952 | H. Khan; Pak. | | |
| 1953 | H. Khan; Pak. | | |
| 1954 | H. Khan; Pak. | | |

*All years listed indicate first half of season.
†Designated inaugural champion.

**Amateur Championships** (instituted 1922), staged annually in London, open to all the world amateurs.*

| | | | |
|---|---|---|---|
| 1922 | T. O. Jameson; U.K. | 1950 | N. F. Borrett; U.K. |
| 1923 | T. O. Jameson; U.K. | 1951 | G. Hildick-Smith; S. Af. |
| 1924 | W. D. Macpherson; U.K. | 1952 | A. Fairbairn; U.K. |
| 1925 | V. A. Cazalet; U.K. | 1953 | A. Fairbairn; U.K. |
| 1926 | J. E. Palmer-Tomkinson; U.K. | 1954 | R. B. R. Wilson; U.K. |
| | | 1955 | I. Amin; Egy. |
| 1927 | V. A. Cazalet; U.K. | 1956 | R. B. R. Wilson; U.K. |
| 1928 | W. D. Macpherson; U.K. | 1957 | N. H. R. A. Broomfield; U.K. |
| 1929 | V. A. Cazalet; U.K. | 1958 | N. H. R. A. Broomfield; U.K. |
| 1930 | V. A. Cazalet; U.K. | 1959 | I. Amin; U.A.R. |
| 1931 | F. D. Amr Bey; Egy. | 1960 | M. A. Oddy; U.K. |
| 1932 | F. D. Amr Bey; Egy. | 1961 | M. A. Oddy; U.K. |
| 1933 | F. D. Amr Bey; Egy. | 1962 | K. Hiscoe; Austr. |
| 1934 | F. D. Amr Bey; Egy. | 1963 | A. A. Jawaid; Pak. |
| 1935 | F. D. Amr Bey; Egy. | 1964 | A. A. Jawaid; Pak. |
| 1936 | F. D. Amr Bey; Egy. | 1965 | A. A. Jawaid; Pak. |
| 1937 | F. D. Amr Bey; Egy. | 1966 | J. Barrington; U.K. |
| 1938 | K. C. Gander-Dower; U.K. | 1967 | J. Barrington; U.K. |
| 1946 | N. F. Borrett; U.K. | 1968 | J. Barrington; U.K. |
| 1947 | N. F. Borrett; U.K. | 1969 | G. B. Hunt; Austr. |
| 1948 | N. F. Borrett; U.K. | | |
| 1949 | N. F. Borrett; U.K. | | |

*All years listed indicate first half of season.

## SWIMMING

**WORLD RECORDS**—Records as of Jan. 1, 1970, at distances recognized by the International Amateur Swimming Federation (Fédération Internationale de Natation Amateur). Only performances set at metric distances are recognized as world records; records set at yard-measured distances are no longer officially recognized.

### Men

| Distance | Min.:sec. | Name; Country | Place | Date |
|---|---|---|---|---|
| **FREESTYLE** | | | | |
| 100 m. | 52.2 | M. Wenden; Austr. | Mexico City, Mex. | Oct. 19, 1968 |
| 200 m. | 1:54.3 | D. A. Schollander; U.S. | Long Beach, U.S. | Aug. 30, 1968 |
| | 1:54.3 | M. Spitz; U.S. | Santa Clara, U.S. | July 12, 1969 |
| 400 m. | 4:04.0 | H. Fassnacht; W. Ger. | Louisville, U.S. | Aug. 14, 1969 |
| 800 m. | 8:28.8 | M. Burton; U.S. | Louisville, U.S. | Aug. 17, 1969 |
| 1,500 m. | 16:04.5 | M. Burton; U.S. | Louisville, U.S. | Aug. 17, 1969 |
| **BREASTSTROKE** | | | | |
| 100 m. | 1:05.8 | N. Pankin; U.S.S.R. | Magdeburg, E. Ger. | Apr. 20, 1969 |
| 200 m. | 2:25.4 | N. Pankin; U.S.S.R. | Magdeburg, E. Ger. | Apr. 19, 1969 |
| **BUTTERFLY STROKE** | | | | |
| 100 m. | 55.6 | M. Spitz; U.S. | Long Beach, U.S. | Aug. 30, 1968 |
| | 55.6 | M. Spitz; U.S. | Santa Clara, U.S. | July 11, 1969 |
| 200 m. | 2:05.7 | M. Spitz; U.S. | W. Berlin, Ger. | Oct. 8, 1967 |
| **BACKSTROKE** | | | | |
| 100 m. | 57.8 | R. Matthes; E. Ger. | Würzburg, W. Ger. | Aug. 23, 1969 |
| 200 m. | 2:06.4 | R. Matthes; E. Ger. | E. Berlin, Ger. | Aug. 29, 1969 |
| **INDIVIDUAL MEDLEY** | | | | |
| 200 m. | 2:09.6 | G. Hall; U.S. | Louisville, U.S. | Aug. 17, 1969 |
| 400 m. | 4:33.9 | G. Hall; U.S. | Louisville, U.S. | Aug. 15, 1969 |
| **FREESTYLE RELAYS** | | | | |
| 4 x 100 m. | 3:31.7 | United States national team (Z. Zorn, S. Rerych, M. Spitz, K. Walsh) | Mexico City, Mex. | Oct. 17, 1968 |
| 4 x 200 m. | 7:52.1 | United States national team (S. E. Clark, R. A. Saari, G. S. Ilman, D. A. Schollander) | Tokyo, Jap. | Oct. 18, 1964 |
| | 7:52.1 | Santa Clara Swim Club, U.S. (D. A. Schollander, M. Spitz, G. S. Ilman, M. Wall) | Oak Park, U.S. | Aug. 12, 1967 |
| **MEDLEY RELAYS (backstroke, breaststroke, butterfly stroke, freestyle)** | | | | |
| 4 x 100 m. | 3:54.9 | United States national team (C. Hickcox, D. McKenzie, D. Russell, K. Walsh) | Mexico City, Mex. | Oct. 26, 1968 |

ARTHUR RICKERBY, "LIFE," © 1964, TIME INC.
DON SCHOLLANDER (U.S.), OLYMPIC GOLD MEDALIST AND WORLD CHAMPION FREESTYLE SWIMMER

EASTFOTO
ROLAND MATTHES (E. GER.) SET WORLD RECORDS IN THE 100-M. AND 200-M. BACKSTROKE

UPI—COMPIX
MIKE BURTON (U.S.) IN 1969 BROKE HIS OWN 1968 WORLD RECORDS IN THE 800-M. AND 1,500-M. FREESTYLE

SWIMMING WORLD PUBLICATIONS
DEBBIE MEYER (U.S.), WHO HELD SEVERAL FREESTYLE RECORDS IN 1969

## Women

### FREESTYLE

| Distance | Min.:sec. | Name; Country | Place | Date |
|---|---|---|---|---|
| 100 m. | 58.9 | D. Fraser; Austr. | N. Sydney, Austr.† | Feb. 29, 1964 |
| 200 m. | 2:06.7 | D. Meyer; U.S. | Los Angeles, U.S. | Aug. 24, 1968 |
| 400 m. | 4:24.5 | D. Meyer; U.S. | Los Angeles, U.S. | Aug. 25, 1968 |
| 800 m. | 9:10.4 | D. Meyer; U.S. | Los Angeles, U.S. | Aug. 28, 1968 |
| 1,500 m. | 17:19.9 | D. Meyer; U.S. | Louisville, U.S. | Aug. 17, 1969 |
| **BREASTSTROKE** | | | | |
| 100 m. | 1:14.2 | C. Ball; U.S. | Los Angeles, U.S. | Aug. 25, 1968 |
| 200 m. | 2:38.5 | C. Ball; U.S. | Los Angeles, U.S. | Aug. 26, 1968 |
| **BUTTERFLY STROKE** | | | | |
| 100 m. | 1:04.5 | A. Kok; Neth. | Budapest, Hung. | Aug. 14, 1965 |
| 200 m. | 2:21.0 | A. Kok; Neth. | Blackpool, U.K.* | Aug. 25, 1967 |
| **BACKSTROKE** | | | | |
| 100 m. | 1:05.6 | K. Y. Muir; S. Af. | Utrecht, Neth. | July 6, 1969 |
| 200 m. | 2:21.5 | S. Atwood; U.S | Louisville, U.S. | Aug. 14, 1969 |
| **INDIVIDUAL MEDLEY** | | | | |
| 200 m. | 2:23.5 | C. A. Kolb; U.S. | Los Angeles, U.S. | Aug. 25, 1968 |
| 400 m. | 5:04.7 | C. A. Kolb; U.S. | Los Angeles, U.S. | Aug. 24, 1968 |
| **FREESTYLE RELAYS** | | | | |
| 4 x 100 m. | 4:01.0 | Santa Clara Swim Club; U.S. (L. Gustavson, L. D. Watson, P. Carpinelli, J. Henne) | Santa Clara, U.S. | July 6, 1968 |
| **MEDLEY RELAYS (backstroke, breaststroke, butterfly stroke, freestyle)** | | | | |
| 4 x 100 m. | 4:28.1 | United States national team (K. Hall, C. Ball, E. Daniel, S. Pedersen) | Colorado Springs, U.S. | Sept. 14, 1968 |

*Salt water. †Fresh and salt water mixed.

SWIMMING WORLD PUBLICATIONS
ADA KOK (NETH.), HOLDER OF THE 100-M. AND 200-M. BUTTERFLY STROKE RECORDS

SWIMMING WORLD PUBLICATIONS
KAREN MUIR (SOUTH AFRICA), HOLDER OF THE 100-M. BACKSTROKE RECORD

WIDE WORLD
CATIE BALL (U.S.) SET A WORLD RECORD OF 2:38.5 IN THE 200-M. BREASTSTROKE, AUG. 26, 1968

WIDE WORLD
CLAUDIA KOLB (U.S.) SETTING WORLD RECORD IN INDIVIDUAL MEDLEY, AT 5:04.7, LOS ANGELES, CALIF., 1968

SWIMMING WORLD PUBLICATIONS
CHARLES HICKCOX (U.S.), A MEMBER OF THE WINNING MEDLEY RELAYS TEAM IN 1968

GARY HALL (U.S.), HOLDER OF WORLD RECORDS IN 200-M. AND 400-M. INDIVIDUAL MEDLEY, AUGUST 1969
WIDE WORLD

DOUG RUSSELL (U.S.), BUTTERFLY SWIMMER, HELPED WIN 400-M. MEDLEY RELAY AT MEXICO CITY, OCT. 26, 1968
WIDE WORLD

**SWIMMING PROGRESSIVE WORLD RECORDS. 100-m. Freestyle.**
Records subsequent to May 1, 1957, have been accepted only if set in 50-m. pools.

| Men | | | | Women | | | |
|---|---|---|---|---|---|---|---|
| Year | Time min.: sec. | Name; Country | Place | Year | Time min.: sec. | Name; Country | Place |
| 1905 | 1:05.8 | Z. Halmay; Hung. | Vienna, Aus. | 1908 | 1:35.0 | M. Gerstung; Ger. | Magdeburg, Ger. |
| 1910 | 1:02.8 | C. Daniels; U.S. | New York, U.S. | 1910 | 1:26.6 | C. Guttenstein; Belg. | Schaerbeck, Belg. |
| 1912 | 1:02.4 | K. Bretting; Ger. | Brussels, Belg. | 1912 | 1:20.6 | D. Curwen; U.K. | Birkenhead, U.K. |
| 1912 | 1:02.4 | D. Kahanamoku; Hawaii | Stockholm, Swed. | 1915 | 1:16.2 | F. Durack; Austr. | Sydney, Austr. |
| 1920 | 1:00.4 | D. Kahanamoku; Hawaii | Antwerp, Belg. | 1920 | 1:13.6 | E. Bleibtrey; U.S. | Antwerp, Belg. |
| 1924 | 59.0 | J. Weissmuller; U.S. | Paris, Fr. | 1923 | 1:12.8 | G. Ederle; U.S. | Newark, U.S. |
| 1924 | 57.4 | J. Weissmuller; U.S. | Miami, U.S. | 1924 | 1:12.2 | M. Wehselau; U.S. | Paris, Fr. |
| 1936 | 56.4 | P. Fick; U.S. | New Haven, U.S. | 1926 | 1:10.0 | E. Lackie; U.S. | Toledo, U.S. |
| 1947 | 55.8 | A. Jany; Fr. | Menton, Fr. | 1929 | 1:09.8 | E. Garatti; U.S. | Honolulu, Hawaii |
| 1948 | 55.4 | A. Ford; U.S. | New Haven, U.S. | 1929 | 1:09.4 | A. Osipowich; U.S. | San Francisco, U.S. |
| 1954 | 54.8 | D. Cleveland; U.S. | New Haven, U.S. | 1932 | 1:06.8 | H. Madison; U.S. | Los Angeles, U.S. |
| 1956 | 55.4 | J. Henricks; Austr. | Melbourne, Austr. | 1933 | 1:06.6 | H. Madison; U.S. | Boston, U.S. |
| 1957 | 55.2 | J. Devitt; Austr. | Sydney, Austr.* | 1936 | 1:04.6 | W. den Ouden; Neth. | Amsterdam, Neth. |
| 1957 | 54.6 | J. Devitt; Austr. | Brisbane, Austr. | 1956 | 1:04.5† | D. Fraser; Austr. | Sydney, Austr. |
| 1961 | 53.6 | M. dos Santos; Braz. | Rio de Janeiro, Braz.* | 1956 | 1:04.0 | C. Gastelaars; Neth. | Scheidam, Neth. |
| 1964 | 52.9 | A. Gottvalles; Fr. | Budapest, Hung. | 1956 | 1:02.4 | L. Crapp; Austr. | Melbourne, Austr. |
| 1964 | 52.9 | S. Clark; U.S. | Tokyo, Jap. | 1956 | 1:02.0 | D. Fraser; Austr. | Melbourne, Austr. |
| 1967 | 52.6 | K. Walsh; U.S. | Winnipeg, Can. | 1958 | 1:01.5† | D. Fraser; Austr. | Melbourne, Austr. |
| 1968 | 52.2 | M. Wenden; Austr. | Mexico City, Mex. | 1958 | 1:01.4† | D. Fraser; Austr. | Cardiff, U.K. |
| | | | | 1958 | 1:01.2 | D. Fraser; Austr. | Schiedam, Neth. |
| | | | | 1960 | 1:00.2† | D. Fraser; Austr. | Sydney, Austr.* |
| | | | | 1962 | 1:00.0† | D. Fraser; Austr. | Melbourne, Austr. |
| | | | | 1962 | 59.9† | D. Fraser; Austr. | Melbourne, Austr. |
| | | | | 1962 | 59.5† | D. Fraser; Austr. | Perth, Austr. |
| | | | | 1964 | 58.9 | D. Fraser; Austr. | N. Sydney, Austr.* |

*Salt or mixed salt-and-fresh water pool. †Record timed at 110-yd. mark (100.58 m.).

STEVE CLARK (U.S.) SWAM THE OPENING LEG OF THE WORLD RECORD 4 X 200 M. RELAY IN 1964

N. R. FARBMAN, "LIFE," © 1964, TIME INC.

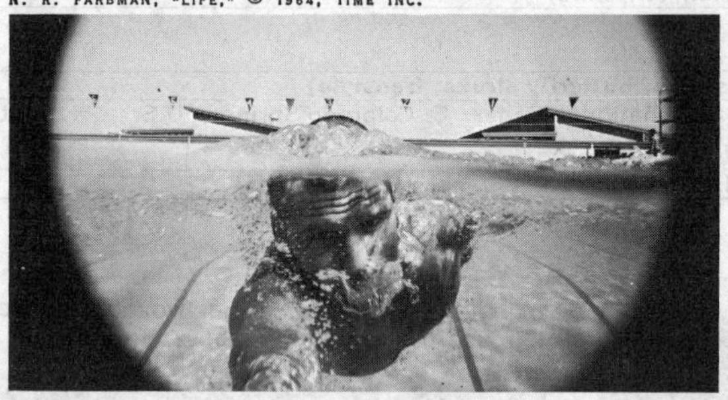

DAWN FRASER (AUSTR.), WINNER OF NINE CONSECUTIVE PROGRESSIVE WORLD RECORDS IN THE 100-M. FREESTYLE

WIDE WORLD

## TABLE TENNIS

### World Championships (biennial since 1957)

| Year | Place | Men's Singles | Men's Doubles | Women's Singles |
|---|---|---|---|---|
| 1927 | London, U.K. | R. Jacobi; Hung. | R. Jacobi, R. Pecsi; Hung. | M. Mednyanszky; Hung. |
| 1928 | Stockholm, Swed. | Z. Mechlovits; Hung. | A. Liebster, R. Thum; Aus. | M. Mednyanszky; Hung. |
| 1929 | Budapest, Hung. | F. J. Perry; U.K. | G. V. Barna, M. Szabados; Hung. | M. Mednyanszky; Hung. |
| 1930 | Berlin, Ger. | G. V. Barna; Hung. | G. V. Barna, M. Szabados; Hung. | M. Mednyanszky; Hung. |
| 1931 | Budapest, Hung. | M. Szabados; Hung. | G. V. Barna, M. Szabados; Hung. | M. Mednyanszky; Hung. |
| 1932 | Prague, Czech. | G. V. Barna; Hung. | G. V. Barna, M. Szabados; Hung. | A. Sipos; Hung. |
| 1933 | Baden, Aus. | G. V. Barna; Hung. | G. V. Barna, S. Glancz; Hung. | A. Sipos; Hung. |
| 1934 | Paris, Fr. | G. V. Barna; Hung. | G. V. Barna, M. Szabados; Hung. | M. Kettnerova; Czech. |
| 1935 | London, U.K. | G. V. Barna; Hung. | G. V. Barna, M. Szabados; Hung. | M. Kettnerova; Czech. |
| 1936 | Prague, Czech. | S. Kolar; Czech. | R. G. Blattner, J. H. McClure; U.S. | R. H. Aarons; U.S. |
| 1937 | Baden, Aus. | R. Bergmann; Aus. | R. G. Blattner, J. H. McClure; U.S. | Title vacant |
| 1938 | London, U.K. | B. Vana; Czech. | J. H. McClure, S. Schiff; U.S. | T. Pritzi; Aus. |
| 1939 | Cairo, Egy. | R. Bergmann; Aus. | R. Bergmann; Aus.—G. V. Barna; Hung. | V. Depetrisova; Czech. |
| 1940–46 | No competition. | | | |
| 1947 | Paris, Fr. | V. Vana; Czech. | B. Vana, A. Slar; Czech. | G. Farkas; Hung. |
| 1948 | London, U.K. | R. Bergmann; U.K. | B. Vana, L. Stipek; Czech. | G. Farkas; Hung. |
| 1949 | Stockholm, Swed. | J. Leach; U.K. | F. Tokar, I. Andreadis; Czech. | G. Farkas; Hung. |
| 1950 | Budapest, Hung. | R. Bergmann; U.K. | F. Sido, F. Soos; Hung. | A. Roseanu; Rum. |
| 1951 | Vienna, Aus. | J. Leach; U.K. | B. Vana, I. Andreadis; Czech. | A. Roseanu; Rum. |
| 1952 | Bombay, India | H. Satoh; Jap. | N. Fujii, T. Hayashi; Jap. | A. Roseanu; Rum. |
| 1953 | Bucharest, Rum. | F. Sido; Hung. | F. Sido, J. Koczian; Hung. | A. Roseanu; Rum. |
| 1954 | London, U.K. | I. Ogimura; Jap. | V. Harangozo, Z. Dolimar; Yugos. | A. Roseanu; Rum. |
| 1955 | Utrecht, Neth. | T. Tanaka; Jap. | I. Andreadis, L. Stipek; Czech. | A. Roseanu; Rum. |
| 1956 | Tokyo, Jap. | I. Ogimura; Jap. | I. Ogimura, Y. Tomita; Jap. | T. Okawa; Jap. |
| 1957 | Stockholm, Swed. | T. Tanaka; Jap. | I. Andreadis, L. Stipek; Czech. | F. Eguchi; Jap. |
| 1959 | Dortmund, W. Ger. | Kuo-tuan Jung; China | I. Ogimura, T. Murakami; Jap. | K. Matsuzaki; Jap. |
| 1961 | Peking, China | Chuang Tse-tung; China | N. Hoshino, K. Kimura; Jap. | Chiu Chung-hui; China |
| 1963 | Prague, Czech. | Chuang Tse-tung; China | Chiang Shih-lin, Wang Chih-liang; China | K. Matsuzaki; Jap. |
| 1965 | Ljubljana, Yugos. | Chuang Tse-tung; China | Chuang Tse-tung, Hsu Yin-sheng; China | N. Fakazu; Jap. |
| 1967 | Stockholm, Swed. | N. Hasegawa; Jap. | K. Johansson, H. Asler; Swed. | S. Morisawa; Jap. |
| 1969 | Munich, W. Ger. | S. Ito; Jap. | K. Johansson, H. Asler; Swed. | T. Kowada; Jap. |

**Table Tennis World Championships (continued)**

| Year | Place | Women's Doubles | Mixed Doubles (man's name first) |
|---|---|---|---|
| 1927 | London, U.K. | M. Mednyanszky; Hung.—F. Flamm; Aus. | Z. Mechlovits, M. Mednyanszky; Hung. |
| 1928 | Stockholm, Swed. | E. Metzger, E. Ruester; Ger. | Z. Mechlovits, M. Mednyanszky; Hung. |
| 1929 | Budapest, Hung. | M. Mednyanszky, A. Sipos; Hung. | I. Kelen, A. Sipos; Hung. |
| 1930 | Berlin, Ger. | M. Mednyanszky, A. Sipos; Hung. | M. Szabados, M. Mednyanszky; Hung. |
| 1931 | Budapest, Hung. | M. Mednyanszky, A. Sipos; Hung. | M. Szabados, M. Mednyanszky; Hung. |
| 1932 | Prague, Czech. | M. Mednyanszky, A. Sipos; Hung. | G. V. Barna, A. Sipos; Hung. |
| 1933 | Baden, Aus. | M. Mednyanszky, A. Sipos; Hung. | I. Kelen, M. Mednyanszky; Hung. |
| 1934 | Paris, Fr. | M. Mednyanszky, A. Sipos; Hung. | M. Szabados, M. Mednyanszky; Hung. |
| 1935 | London, U.K. | M. Kettnerova, M. Smidova; Czech. | G. V. Barna, A. Sipos; Hung. |
| 1936 | Prague, Czech. | V. Depetrisova, V. Votrubcova; Czech. | M. Hamr, G. Kleinova; Czech. |
| 1937 | Baden, Aus. | V. Depetrisova, V. Votrubcova; Czech. | B. Vana, V. Votrubcova; Czech. |
| 1938 | London, U.K. | T. Pritzi, D. Bussnann; Aus. | L. Bellak; Hung.—W. Woodhead; U.K. |
| 1939 | Cairo, Egy. | * | B. Vana, V. Votrubcova; Czech. |
| 1940–46* | | | |
| 1947 | Paris, Fr. | T. Pritzi; Aus.—G. Farkas; Hung. | F. Soos, G. Farkas; Hung. |
| 1948 | London, U.K. | V. Thomas, P. Franks; U.K. | R. Miles, T. Thall; U.S. |
| 1949 | Stockholm, Swed. | H. Elliot; U.K.—G. Farkas; Hung. | F. Sido, G. Farkas; Hung. |
| 1950 | Budapest, Hung. | D. Beregi, H. Elliot; U.K. | F. Sido, G. Farkas; Hung. |
| 1951 | Vienna, Aus. | D. Rowe, R. Rowe; U.K. | B. Vana; Czech.—A. Roseanu; Rum. |
| 1952 | Bombay, India | T. Nashimura, S. Narahara; Jap. | F. Sido; Hung.—A. Roseanu; Rum. |
| 1953 | Bucharest, Rum. | A. Roseanu; Rum.—G. Farkas; Hung. | F. Sido; Hung.—A. Roseanu; Rum. |
| 1954 | London, U.K. | D. Rowe, R. Rowe; U.K. | I. Andreadis; Czech.—G. Farkas; Hung. |
| 1955 | Utrecht, Neth. | A. Roseanu, E. Zeller; Rum. | K. Szepesi, E. Koczian; Hung. |
| 1956 | Tokyo, Jap. | A. Roseanu, E. Zeller; Rum. | E. Klein, L. T. Neuberger; U.S. |
| 1957 | Stockholm, Swed. | L. Mosoczy, A. Simon; Hung. | I. Ogimura, F. Eguchi; Jap. |
| 1959 | Dortmund, W. Ger. | T. Namba, K. Yamaizumi; Jap. | I. Ogimura, F. Eguchi; Jap. |
| 1961 | Peking, China | M. Alexandru, G. Pitica; Rum. | I. Ogimura, K. Matsuzaki; Jap. |
| 1963 | Prague, Czech. | K. Matsuzaki, M. Seki; Jap. | K. Kimura, K. Ito; Jap. |
| 1965 | Ljubljana, Yugos. | Liu Hui-ching, Cheng Min-chin; China | K. Kimura, M. Seki; Jap. |
| 1967 | Stockholm, Swed. | S. Morisawa, S. Hirota; Jap. | N. Hasegawa, N. Yamanaka; Jap. |
| 1969 | Munich, W. Ger. | Z. Rudnova, S. Grinberg; U.S.S.R. | N. Hasegawa, Y. Konno; Jap. |

*No competition.

U.P.I. COMPIX

MARY KETTNEROVA (CZECH.), WORLD'S TABLE TENNIS WOMEN'S SINGLES CHAMPION IN 1934, 1935, HELPS VERA VOTRUBCOVA (CZECH.) ADJUST NET. MISS VOTRUBCOVA WAS A MEMBER OF THE WOMEN'S DOUBLES TITLE WINNING TEAM IN 1936, 1937, AND THE MIXED DOUBLES TEAM IN 1937 AND 1939

RICHARD BERGMANN (U.K.), WINNER OF THE WORLD'S TABLE TENNIS SINGLES CHAMPIONSHIP IN 1937, 1939, 1948, AND 1950

U.P.I. COMPIX

**Team Championships**

| Year | Place | Men* | Women† |
|---|---|---|---|
| 1927 | London, U.K. | Hungary | — |
| 1928 | Stockholm, Swed. | Hungary | — |
| 1929 | Budapest, Hung. | Hungary | — |
| 1930 | Berlin, Ger. | Hungary | — |
| 1931 | Budapest, Hung. | Hungary | — |
| 1932 | Prague, Czech. | Czechoslovakia | — |
| 1933 | Baden, Aus. | Hungary | — |
| 1934 | Paris, Fr. | Hungary | Germany |
| 1935 | London, U.K. | Hungary | Czechoslovakia |
| 1936 | Prague, Czech. | Austria | Czechoslovakia |
| 1937 | Baden, Aus. | United States | United States |
| 1938 | London, U.K. | Hungary | Czechoslovakia |
| 1939 | Cairo, Egy. | Czechoslovakia | Germany |
| 1940–46‡ | | | |
| 1947 | Paris, Fr. | Czechoslovakia | United Kingdom |
| 1948 | London, U.K. | Czechoslovakia | United Kingdom |
| 1949 | Stockholm, Swed. | Hungary | United States |
| 1950 | Budapest, Hung. | Czechoslovakia | Albania |
| 1951 | Vienna, Aus. | Czechoslovakia | Albania |
| 1952 | Bombay, India | Hungary | Japan |
| 1953 | Bucharest, Rum. | United Kingdom | Rumania |
| 1954 | London, U.K. | Japan | Japan |
| 1955 | Utrecht, Neth. | Japan | Rumania |
| 1956 | Tokyo, Jap. | Japan | Rumania |
| 1957 | Stockholm, Swed. | Japan | Japan |
| 1959 | Dortmund, W. Ger. | Japan | Japan |
| 1961 | Peking, China | China | Japan |
| 1963 | Prague, Czech. | China | Japan |
| 1965 | Ljubljana, Yugos. | China | China |
| 1967 | Stockholm, Swed. | Japan | Japan |
| 1969 | Munich, W. Ger. | Japan | U.S.S.R. |

*Swaythling Cup. †Corbillon Cup. ‡No competition.

**TENNIS.** The Davis Cup for international competition was inaugurated in 1900 (*see* the article TENNIS: *Lawn Tennis*). The four major national championships are the All England (Wimbledon), U.S., French, and Australian. In March 1968 the International Lawn Tennis Association voted to sanction open tennis with professionals allowed to compete against amateurs in a limited number of tournaments to be approved by the federation.

## THE DAVIS CUP

| Year | Winner |
|---|---|
| 1900 | United States |
| 1902 | United States |
| 1903 | British Isles* |
| 1904 | British Isles |
| 1905 | British Isles |
| 1906 | British Isles |
| 1907 | Australasia† |
| 1908 | Australasia |
| 1909 | Australasia |
| 1911 | Australasia |
| 1912 | British Isles |
| 1913 | United States |
| 1914 | Australasia |
| 1919 | Australasia |
| 1920 | United States |
| 1921 | United States |
| 1922 | United States |
| 1923 | United States |
| 1924 | United States |
| 1925 | United States |
| 1926 | United States |
| 1927 | France |
| 1928 | France |
| 1929 | France |
| 1930 | France |
| 1931 | France |
| 1932 | France |
| 1933 | United Kingdom |
| 1934 | United Kingdom |
| 1935 | United Kingdom |
| 1936 | United Kingdom |
| 1937 | United States |
| 1938 | United States |
| 1939 | Australia |
| 1946 | United States |
| 1947 | United States |
| 1948 | United States |
| 1949 | United States |
| 1950 | Australia |
| 1951 | Australia |
| 1952 | Australia |
| 1953 | Australia |
| 1954 | United States |
| 1955 | Australia |
| 1956 | Australia |
| 1957 | Australia |
| 1958 | United States |
| 1959 | Australia |
| 1960 | Australia |
| 1961 | Australia |
| 1962 | Australia |
| 1963 | United States |
| 1964 | Australia |
| 1965 | Australia |
| 1966 | Australia |
| 1967 | Australia |
| 1968 | United States |
| 1969 | United States |

*Included Ireland up to 1922. †Included New Zealand up to 1923.

## WIMBLEDON*

### Men's Singles

| Year | Winner |
|---|---|
| 1877 | S. W. Gore |
| 1878 | P. F. Hadow |
| 1879 | J. T. Hartley |
| 1880 | J. T. Hartley |
| 1881 | W. Renshaw |
| 1882 | W. Renshaw |
| 1883 | W. Renshaw |
| 1884 | W. Renshaw |
| 1885 | W. Renshaw |
| 1886 | W. Renshaw |
| 1887 | H. F. Lawford |
| 1888 | E. Renshaw |
| 1889 | W. Renshaw |
| 1890 | W. J. Hamilton |
| 1891 | W. Baddeley |
| 1892 | W. Baddeley |
| 1893 | J. L. Pim |
| 1894 | J. L. Pim |
| 1895 | W. Baddeley |
| 1896 | H. S. Mahony |
| 1897 | R. F. Doherty |
| 1898 | R. F. Doherty |
| 1899 | R. F. Doherty |
| 1900 | R. F. Doherty |
| 1901 | A. W. Gore |
| 1902 | H. L. Doherty |
| 1903 | H. L. Doherty |
| 1904 | H. L. Doherty |
| 1905 | H. L. Doherty |
| 1906 | H. L. Doherty |
| 1907 | N. E. Brookes; Austr. |
| 1908 | A. W. Gore |
| 1909 | A. W. Gore |
| 1910 | A. F. Wilding; N.Z. |
| 1911 | A. F. Wilding; N.Z. |
| 1912 | A. F. Wilding; N.Z. |
| 1913 | A. F. Wilding; N.Z. |
| 1914† | N. E. Brookes: Austr. |
| 1919 | G. L. Patterson; Austr. |
| 1920 | W. T. Tilden; U.S. |
| 1921 | W. T. Tilden; U.S. |
| 1922 | G. L. Patterson; Austr. |
| 1923 | W. M. Johnston; U.S. |
| 1924 | J. Borotra; Fr. |
| 1925 | R. Lacoste; Fr. |
| 1926 | J. Borotra; Fr. |
| 1927 | H. Cochet; Fr. |
| 1928 | R. Lacoste; Fr. |
| 1929 | H. Cochet; Fr. |
| 1930 | W. T. Tilden; U.S. |
| 1931 | S. B. Wood; U.S. |
| 1932 | H. E. Vines; U.S. |
| 1933 | J. H. Crawford; Austr. |
| 1934 | F. J. Perry |
| 1935 | F. J. Perry |
| 1936 | F. J. Perry |
| 1937 | J. D. Budge; U.S. |
| 1938 | J. D. Budge; U.S. |
| 1939† | R. L. Riggs, U.S. |
| 1946 | Y. Petra; Fr. |
| 1947 | J. A. Kramer; U.S. |
| 1948 | R. Falkenburg; U.S. |
| 1949 | F. R. Schroeder; U.S. |
| 1950 | J. E. Patty; U.S. |
| 1951 | R. Savitt; U.S. |
| 1952 | F. A. Sedgman; Austr. |
| 1953 | E. V. Seixas; U.S. |
| 1954 | J. Drobny; Czech. |
| 1955 | M. A. Trabert; U.S. |
| 1956 | L. A. Hoad; Austr. |
| 1957 | L. A. Hoad; Austr. |
| 1958 | A. J. Cooper; Austr. |
| 1959 | A. Olmedo; Peru |
| 1960 | N. A. Fraser; Austr. |
| 1961 | R. G. Laver; Austr. |
| 1962 | R. G. Laver; Austr. |
| 1963 | C. R. McKinley; U.S. |
| 1964 | R. Emerson; Austr. |
| 1965 | R. Emerson; Austr. |
| 1966 | M. Santana; Sp. |
| 1967 | J. Newcombe; Austr. |
| 1968† | R. G. Laver; Austr. |
| 1969† | R. G. Laver; Austr. |
| 1970† | J. Newcombe; Austr. |

MILLER SERVICES LTD.

ROY EMERSON (AUSTR.) PLAYING IN HIS FIRST MATCH OF THE 1965 WIMBLEDON TENNIS CHAMPIONSHIP. HE WON HIS SECOND CONSECUTIVE WIMBLEDON TITLE

### Women's Singles

| Year | Winner |
|---|---|
| 1884 | M. E. A. Watson |
| 1885 | M. E. A. Watson |
| 1886 | B. Bingley |
| 1887 | C. Dod |
| 1888 | C. Dod |
| 1889 | B. Bingley Hillyard |
| 1890 | L. Rice |
| 1891 | C. Dod |
| 1892 | C. Dod |
| 1893 | C. Dod |
| 1894 | B. Bingley Hillyard |
| 1895 | C. Cooper |
| 1896 | C. Cooper |
| 1897 | B. Bingley Hillyard |
| 1898 | C. Cooper |
| 1899 | B. Bingley Hillyard |
| 1900 | B. Bingley Hillyard |
| 1901 | C. Cooper Sterry |
| 1902 | M. E. Robb |
| 1903 | D. K. Douglass |
| 1904 | D. K. Douglass |
| 1905 | M. G. Sutton; U.S. |
| 1906 | D. K. Douglass |
| 1907 | M. G. Sutton; U.S. |
| 1908 | C. Cooper Sterry |
| 1909 | D. P. Boothby |
| 1910 | D. Douglass Chambers |
| 1911 | D. Douglass Chambers |
| 1912 | E. W. Larcombe |
| 1913 | D. Douglass Chambers |
| 1914 | D. Douglass Chambers |
| 1919 | S. Lenglen; Fr. |
| 1920 | S. Lenglen; Fr. |
| 1921 | S. Lenglen; Fr. |
| 1922 | S. Lenglen; Fr. |
| 1923 | S. Lenglen; Fr. |
| 1924 | K. McKane |
| 1925 | S. Lenglen; Fr. |
| 1926 | K. McKane Godfree |
| 1927 | H. N. Wills; U.S. |
| 1928 | H. N. Wills; U.S. |
| 1929 | H. N. Wills; U.S. |
| 1930 | H. Wills Moody; U.S. |
| 1931 | C. Aussem; Ger. |
| 1932 | H. Wills Moody; U.S. |
| 1933 | H. Wills Moody; U.S. |
| 1934 | D. E. Round |
| 1935 | H. Wills Moody; U.S. |
| 1936 | H. Hull Jacobs; U.S. |
| 1937 | D. E. Round |
| 1938 | H. Wills Moody; U.S. |
| 1939 | A. Marble; U.S. |
| 1946 | P. M. Betz; U.S. |
| 1947 | M. E. Osborne; U.S. |
| 1948 | A. L. Brough; U.S. |
| 1949 | A. L. Brough; U.S. |
| 1950 | A. L. Brough; U.S. |
| 1951 | D. J. Hart; U.S. |
| 1952 | M. C. Connolly; U.S. |
| 1953 | M. C. Connolly; U.S. |
| 1954 | M. C. Connolly; U.S. |
| 1955 | A. L. Brough; U.S. |
| 1956 | S. J. Fry; U.S. |
| 1957 | A. Gibson; U.S. |
| 1958 | A. Gibson; U.S. |
| 1959 | M. E. Bueno; Braz. |
| 1960 | M. E. Bueno; Braz. |
| 1961 | A. Mortimer |
| 1962 | J. R. Susman; U.S. |
| 1963 | M. Smith; Austr. |
| 1964 | M. E. Bueno; Braz. |
| 1965 | M. Smith; Austr. |
| 1966 | B.-J. Moffitt King; U.S. |
| 1967 | B.-J. Moffitt King; U.S. |
| 1968† | B.-J. Moffitt King; U.S. |
| 1969† | A. Jones |
| 1970† | M. Smith Court; Austr. |

*Won by nationals except as indicated.
†Open championship.

## U.S. CHAMPIONS*

### Men's Singles

| Year | Winner |
|---|---|
| 1881 | R. D. Sears |
| 1882 | R. D. Sears |
| 1883 | R. D. Sears |
| 1884 | R. D. Sears |
| 1885 | R. D. Sears |
| 1886 | R. D. Sears |
| 1887 | R. D. Sears |
| 1888 | W. Slocum, Jr. |
| 1889 | W. Slocum, Jr. |
| 1890 | O. S. Campbell |
| 1891 | O. S. Campbell |
| 1892 | O. S. Campbell |
| 1893 | R. D. Wrenn |
| 1894 | R. D. Wrenn |
| 1895 | F. H. Hovey |
| 1896 | R. D. Wrenn |
| 1897 | R. D. Wrenn |
| 1898 | M. D. Whitman |
| 1899 | M. D. Whitman |
| 1900 | M. D. Whitman |
| 1901 | W. A. Larned |
| 1902 | W. A. Larned |
| 1903 | H. L. Doherty; U.K. |
| 1904 | H. Ward |
| 1905 | B. C. Wright |
| 1906 | W. J. Clothier |
| 1907 | W. A. Larned |
| 1908 | W. A. Larned |
| 1909 | W. A. Larned |
| 1910 | W. A. Larned |
| 1911 | W. A. Larned |
| 1912 | M. E. McLoughlin |
| 1913 | M. E. McLoughlin |
| 1914 | R. N. Williams |
| 1915 | W. M. Johnston |
| 1916 | R. N. Williams |
| 1917† | R. L. Murray |
| 1918 | R. L. Murray |
| 1919 | W. M. Johnston |
| 1920 | W. T. Tilden |
| 1921 | W. T. Tilden |
| 1922 | W. T. Tilden |
| 1923 | W. T. Tilden |
| 1924 | W. T. Tilden |
| 1925 | W. T. Tilden |
| 1926 | R. Lacoste; Fr. |
| 1927 | R. Lacoste; Fr. |
| 1928 | H. Cochet; Fr. |
| 1929 | W. T. Tilden |
| 1930 | J. H. Doeg |
| 1931 | H. E. Vines, Jr. |
| 1932 | H. E. Vines, Jr. |
| 1933 | F. J. Perry; U.K. |
| 1934 | F. J. Perry; U.K. |
| 1935 | W. L. Allison |
| 1936 | F. J. Perry; U.K. |
| 1937 | J. D. Budge |
| 1938 | J. D. Budge |
| 1939 | R. L. Riggs |
| 1940 | W. D. McNeill |
| 1941 | R. L. Riggs |
| 1942 | F. R. Schroeder, Jr. |
| 1943 | J. R. Hunt |
| 1944 | F. A. Parker |
| 1945 | F. A. Parker |
| 1946 | J. A. Kramer |
| 1947 | J. A. Kramer |
| 1948 | R. A. Gonzales |
| 1949 | R. A. Gonzales |
| 1950 | A. Larsen |
| 1951 | F. Sedgman; Austr. |
| 1952 | F. Sedgman; Austr. |
| 1953 | M. A. Trabert |
| 1954 | E. V. Seixas, Jr. |
| 1955 | M. A. Trabert |
| 1956 | K. R. Rosewall; Austr. |
| 1957 | M. Anderson; Austr. |
| 1958 | A. J. Cooper; Austr. |
| 1959 | N. A. Fraser; Austr. |
| 1960 | N. A. Fraser; Austr. |
| 1961 | R. Emerson; Austr. |
| 1962 | R. G. Laver; Austr. |
| 1963 | R. H. Osuna; Mex. |
| 1964 | R. Emerson; Austr. |
| 1965 | M. Santana; Sp. |
| 1966 | F. S. Stolle; Austr. |
| 1967 | J. Newcombe; Austr. |
| 1968‡ | A. Ashe |
| 1969‡ | R. G. Laver; Austr. |

*Won by nationals except as indicated.
†The 1917 event was a "Patriotic Tournament." ‡Open championship.

## U.S. CHAMPIONS*
### Women's Singles

1887 E. F. Hansell
1888 B. L. Townsend
1889 B. L. Townsend
1890 E. C. Roosevelt
1891 M. E. Cahill
1892 M. E. Cahill
1893 A. M. Terry
1894 H. R. Helwig
1895 J. P. Atkinson
1896 E. H. Moore
1897 J. P. Atkinson
1898 J. P. Atkinson
1899 M. Jones
1900 M. McAteer
1901 E. H. Moore
1902 M. Jones
1903 E. H. Moore
1904 M. G. Sutton
1905 E. H. Moore
1906 H. Homans
1907 E. Sears
1908 M. Bargar-Wallach
1909 H. V. Hotchkiss
1910 H. V. Hotchkiss
1911 H. V. Hotchkiss
1912 M. K. Browne
1913 M. K. Browne
1914 M. K. Browne
1915 M. Bjurstedt; Nor.
1916 M. Bjurstedt; Nor.
1917† M. Bjurstedt; Nor.
1918 M. Bjurstedt; Nor.
1919 H. Hotchkiss Wightman
1920 M. Bjurstedt Mallory
1921 M. Bjurstedt Mallory
1922 M. Bjurstedt Mallory
1923 H. N. Wills
1924 H. N. Wills
1925 H. N. Wills
1926 M. Bjurstedt Mallory
1927 H. N. Wills
1928 H. N. Wills
1929 H. N. Wills
1930 B. Nuthall; U.K.
1931 H. Wills Moody
1932 H. Hull Jacobs
1933 H. Hull Jacobs
1934 H. Hull Jacobs
1935 H. Hull Jacobs
1936 A. Marble
1937 A. Lizana; Chile
1938 A. Marble
1939 A. Marble
1940 A. Marble
1941 S. Palfrey Cooke
1942 P. M. Betz
1943 P. M. Betz
1944 P. M. Betz
1945 S. Palfrey Cooke
1946 P. M. Betz
1947 A. L. Brough
1948 M. Osborne du Pont
1949 M. Osborne du Pont
1950 M. Osborne du Pont
1951 M. C. Connolly
1952 M. C. Connolly
1953 M. C. Connolly
1954 D. J. Hart
1955 D. J. Hart
1956 S. J. Fry
1957 A. Gibson
1958 A. Gibson
1959 M. E. Bueno; Braz.
1960 D. R. Hard
1961 D. R. Hard
1962 M. Smith; Austr.
1963 M. E. Bueno; Braz.
1964 M. E. Bueno; Braz.
1965 M. Smith; Austr.
1966 M. E. Bueno; Braz.
1967 B.-J. Moffitt King
1968‡ V. Wade; U.K.
1969‡ M. Smith Court; Austr.

*Won by nationals except as indicated. †The 1917 event was a "Patriotic Tournament." ‡Open championship.

MILLER SERVICES LTD.
MARGARET SMITH (AUSTR.), WINNER OF WOMEN'S SINGLES TENNIS TITLES IN AUSTRALIA, UNITED STATES, ENGLAND, AND FRANCE, PLAYING IN THE 1964 SEMIFINALS AT WIMBLEDON

## FRENCH (HARD COURT) CHAMPIONS*

This event was instituted in 1891 but was not open to the world until 1925.

### Men's Singles

1925 R. Lacoste
1926 H. Cochet
1927 R. Lacoste
1928 H. Cochet
1929 R. Lacoste
1930 H. Cochet
1931 J. Borotra
1932 H. Cochet
1933 J. H. Crawford; Austr.
1934 G. von Cramm; Ger.
1935 F. J. Perry; U.K.
1936 G. von Cramm; Ger.
1937 H. Henkel; Ger.
1938 J. D. Budge; U.S.
1939 W. D. McNeill; U.S.
1946 M. Bernard
1947 J. Asboth; Hung.
1948 F. A. Parker; U.S.
1949 F. A. Parker; U.S.
1950 J. E. Patty; U.S.
1951 J. Drobny; Czech.
1952 J. Drobny; Czech.
1953 K. R. Rosewall; Austr.
1954 M. A. Trabert; U.S.
1955 M. A. Trabert; U.S.
1956 L. A. Hoad; Austr.
1957 S. Davidson; Swed.
1958 M. G. Rose; Austr.
1959 N. Pietrangeli; It.
1960 N. Pietrangeli; It.
1961 M. Santana; Sp.
1962 R. G. Laver; Austr.
1963 R. Emerson; Austr.
1964 M. Santana; Sp.
1965 F. S. Stolle; Austr.
1966 F. Roche; Austr.
1967 R. Emerson; Austr.
1968 K.R.Rosewall; Austr.
1969 R. G. Laver; Austr.

### Women's Singles

1925 S. Lenglen
1926 S. Lenglen
1927 K. Bouman; Neth.
1928 H. N. Wills; U.S.
1929 H. N. Wills; U.S.
1930 H. Wills Moody; U.S.
1931 C. Aussem; Ger.
1932 H. Wills Moody; U.S.
1933 M. C. Scriven; U.K.
1934 M. C. Scriven; U.K.
1935 H. K. Sperling; Den.
1936 H. K. Sperling; Den.
1937 H. K. Sperling; Den.
1938 S. Mathieu
1939 S. Mathieu
1946 M. E. Osborne; U.S.
1947 P. C. Todd; U.S.
1948 N. Landry; Belg.
1949 M. Osborne du Pont; U.S.
1950 D. J. Hart; U.S.
1951 S. J. Fry; U.S.
1952 D. J. Hart; U.S.
1953 M. C. Connolly; U.S.
1954 M. C. Connolly; U.S.
1955 A. Mortimer; U.K.
1956 A. Gibson; U.S.
1957 S. J. Bloomer; U.K.
1958 S. Kormorczi; Hung.
1959 C. C. Truman; U.K.
1960 D. R. Hard; U.S.
1961 A. S. Haydon; U.K.
1962 M. Smith; Austr.
1963 L. R. Turner; Austr.
1964 M. Smith; Austr.
1965 L. R. Turner; Austr.
1966 A. Haydon Jones; U.K.
1967 F. Durr
1968 N. Richey; U.S.
1969 M. Smith Court; Austr.

*Won by nationals except as indicated.

## AUSTRALIAN CHAMPIONS*

### Men's Singles

1905 R. W. Heath
1906 A. F. Wilding; N.Z.
1907 H. M. Rice
1908 F. B. Alexander; U.S.
1909 A. F. Wilding; N.Z.
1910 R. W. Heath
1911 N. E. Brookes
1912 J. Cecil Parke; U.K.
1913 E. F. Parker
1914 P. O'Hara Wood
1915 F. Gordon Lowe; U.K.
1920 A. R. F. Kingscote; U.K.
1921 R. H. Gemmell
1922 J. O. Anderson
1923 P. O'Hara Wood
1924 J. O. Anderson
1925 J. O. Anderson
1926 J. B. Hawkes
1927 G. L. Patterson
1928 J. Borotra; Fr.
1929 J. C. Gregory; U.K.
1930 E. F. Moon
1931 J. H. Crawford
1932 J. H. Crawford
1933 J. H. Crawford
1934 F. J. Perry; U.K.
1935 J. H. Crawford
1936 A. K. Quist
1937 V. B. McGrath
1938 J. D. Budge; U.S.
1939 J. E. Bromwich
1940 A. K. Quist
1946 J. E. Bromwich
1947 D. Pails
1948 A. K. Quist
1949 F. A. Sedgman
1950 F. A. Sedgman
1951 R. Savitt; U.S.
1952 K. McGregor
1953 K. R. Rosewall
1954 M. G. Rose
1955 K. R. Rosewall
1956 L. A. Hoad
1957 A. J. Cooper
1958 A. J. Cooper
1959 A. Olmedo; Peru
1960 R. G. Laver
1961 R. Emerson
1962 R. G. Laver
1963 R. Emerson
1964 R. Emerson
1965 R. Emerson
1966 R. Emerson
1967 R. Emerson
1968 W. Bowrey
1969 R. G. Laver
1970 A. Ashe; U.S.

### Women's Singles

1922 B. H. Molesworth
1923 B. H. Molesworth
1924 S. Lance
1925 D. Akhurst
1926 D. Akhurst
1927 E. Boyd
1928 D. Akhurst
1929 D. Akhurst
1930 D. Akhurst
1931 C. Buttsworth
1932 C. Buttsworth
1933 J. Hartigan
1934 J. Hartigan
1935 D. E. Round; U.K.
1936 J. Hartigan
1937 N. Wynne
1938 D. M. Bundy; U.S.
1939 V. Wetscott
1940 N. Wynne
1946 N. W. Bolton
1947 N. W. Bolton
1948 N. W. Bolton
1949 D. J. Hart; U.S.
1950 A. L. Brough; U.S.
1951 N. W. Bolton
1952 T. D. Long
1953 M. C. Connolly; U.S.
1954 T. D. Long
1955 B. Penrose
1956 M. Carter
1957 S. J. Fry; U.S.
1958 A. Mortimer; U.K.
1959 M. Carter Reitano
1960 M. Smith
1961 M. Smith
1962 M. Smith
1963 M. Smith
1964 M. Smith
1965 M. Smith
1966 M. Smith
1967 N. Richey; U.S.
1968 B.-J. Moffitt King; U.S.
1969 M. Smith Court

*Won by nationals except as indicated.

## TOBOGGANING (Luge)

### World Champions

| Year | Place | Men | Women | Two-Seater |
|---|---|---|---|---|
| 1955 | Oslo, Nor. | A. Salvesen; Nor. | K. Kienzl; Aus. | H. Krausner, J. Thaler; Aus. |
| 1957 | Davos, Switz. | H. Schaller; W. Ger. | M. Isser; Aus. | J. Strillinger, F. Nachmann; W. Ger. |
| 1958 | Krynica, Pol. | J. Wojnar; Pol. | M. Semczyszak; Pol. | J. Strillinger, F. Nachmann; W. Ger. |
| 1959 | Villard, Fr. | H. Thaler; Aus. | E. Lieber; Aus. | — |
| 1960 | Garmisch, W. Ger. | H. Berndt; W. Ger. | M. Isser; Aus. | R. Frosch, E. Walch; Aus. |
| 1961 | Girenbad, Switz. | J. Wojnar; Pol. | E. Naegele; Switz. | G. Pichler, E. Prinot; It. |
| 1962 | Krynica, Pol. | T. Köhler; E. Ger. | I. Geisler; E. Ger. | J. Graber, G. Ambrosi; It. |
| 1963 | Imst, Aus. | F. Nachmann; W. Ger. | I. Geisler; E. Ger. | R. Pedrak, L. Kudzia; Pol. |
| 1965 | Davos, Switz. | H. Plenk; W. Ger. | O. Enderlein; E. Ger. | W. Scheidel, M. Köhler; E. Ger. |
| 1966 | Friedrichrode, E. Ger. | T. Köhler; E. Ger. | O. Enderlein; E. Ger. | J. Feistmantl, M. Stengl; Aus. |
| 1967 | Hammarstrand, Swed. | T. Köhler; E. Ger. | O. Enderlein; E. Ger. | T. Köhler, K. Bonsack; E. Ger. |
| 1968 | Königssee, W. Ger. | J. Feistmantl; Aus. | P. Tierlich; W. Ger. | I. Schmid, E. Walsh; Aus. |

## TRACK AND FIELD SPORTS

**WORLD RECORDS (Outdoor) Men.** World Records for men's track and field events recognized by the International Amateur Athletic Federation, as of Jan. 1, 1970. For Olympic records and world records set in the Olympics *see* the article OLYMPIC GAMES.

### Running

| Event | Min.: sec. | Name; Country | Place | Date |
|---|---|---|---|---|
| 100 yd. | 9.1 | R. L. Hayes; U.S. | St. Louis, U.S. | June 21, 1963 |
| | 9.1 | H. W. Jerome; Can. | Edmonton, Can. | July 15, 1966 |
| | 9.1 | J. R. Hines; U.S. | Houston, U.S. | May 13, 1967 |
| | 9.1 | C. E. Greene; U.S. | Provo, U.S. | June 15, 1967 |
| | 9.1 | J. Carlos; U.S. | Fresno, U.S. | May 10, 1969 |
| 100 m. | 9.9 | J. R. Hines; U.S. | Mexico City, Mex. | Oct. 14, 1968 |
| | 9.9 | J. R. Hines; U.S. | Sacramento, U.S. | June 20, 1968 |
| | 9.9 | R. R. Smith; U.S. | Sacramento, U.S. | June 20, 1968 |
| | 9.9 | C. E. Greene; U.S. | Sacramento, U.S. | June 20, 1968 |
| 200 m. straight | 19.5 | T. Smith; U.S. | San Jose, U.S. | May 7, 1966 |
| 200 m. turn | 19.8 | T. Smith; U.S. | Mexico City, Mex. | Oct. 16, 1968 |
| 220 yd. straight | 19.5 | T. Smith; U.S. | San Jose, U.S. | May 7, 1966 |
| 220 yd. turn | 20.0 | T. Smith; U.S. | Sacramento, U.S. | June 11, 1966 |
| 400 m. | 43.8 | L. Evans; U.S. | Mexico City, Mex. | Oct. 18, 1968 |
| 440 yd. | 44.7 | C. Mills; U.S. | Knoxville, U.S. | June 21, 1969 |
| 800 m. | 1:44.3 | P. G. Snell; N.Z. | Christchurch, N.Z. | Feb. 3, 1962 |
| | 1:44.3 | R. Doubell; Austr. | Mexico City, Mex. | Oct. 15, 1968 |
| 880 yd. | 1:44.9 | J. R. Ryun; U.S. | Terre Haute, U.S. | June 10, 1966 |
| 1,000 m. | 2:16.2 | J. May; E. Ger. | Erfurt, E. Ger. | July 20, 1965 |
| | 2:16.2 | F. J. Kemper; W. Ger. | Hanover, W. Ger. | Sept. 21, 1966 |
| 1,500 m. | 3:33.1 | J. R. Ryun; U.S. | Los Angeles, U.S. | July 8, 1967 |
| 1 mi. | 3:51.1 | J. R. Ryun; U.S. | Bakersfield, U.S. | June 23, 1967 |
| 2,000 m. | 4:56.2 | M. Jazy; Fr. | Saint-Maur, Fr. | Oct. 12, 1966 |
| 3,000 m. | 7:39.6 | K. Keino; Kenya | Hälsingborg, Swed. | Aug. 27, 1965 |
| 2 mi. | 8:19.6 | R. W. Clarke; Austr. | London, U.K. | Aug. 24, 1968 |
| 3 mi. | 12:50.4 | R. W. Clarke; Austr. | Stockholm, Swed. | July 5, 1966 |
| 5,000 m. | 13:16.6 | R. W. Clarke; Austr. | Stockholm, Swed. | July 5, 1966 |
| 6 mi. | 26:47.0 | R. W. Clarke; Austr. | Oslo, Nor. | July 14, 1965 |
| 10,000 m. | 27:39.4 | R. W. Clarke; Austr. | Oslo, Nor. | July 14, 1965 |
| 10 mi. | 46:44.0 | R. Hill; U.K. | Leicester, U.K. | Nov. 9, 1968 |
| 20,000 m. | 58:06.2 | G. Roelants; Belg. | Louvain, Belg. | Oct. 28, 1966 |
| 15 mi. | 1 hr. 12:48.2 | R. Hill; U.K. | Bolton, U.K. | July 21, 1965 |
| 25,000 m. | 1 hr. 15:22.6 | R. Hill; U.K. | Bolton, U.K. | July 21, 1965 |
| 30,000 m. | 1 hr. 32:25.4 | J. J. Hogan; U.K. | Walton-on-Thames, U.K. | Nov. 12, 1966 |
| 1 hr. | 12 mi. 1,478 yd. 1 ft. 3 in. (20,664 m.) | G. Roelants; Belg. | Louvain, Belg. | Oct. 28, 1966 |

SHEEDY AND LONG FOR "SPORTS ILLUSTRATED," © TIME INC.

J. R. RYUN (U.S.) SETTING HIS FIRST MILE RECORD IN 3:51.3 AT BERKELEY, CALIF., JULY 17, 1966. HE LOWERED THE RECORD TO 3:51.1 AT BAKERSFIELD, CALIF., JUNE 23, 1967

SETTING TWO WORLD RECORDS, R. W. CLARKE (AUSTR.) FINISHED THE 5,000-M. RACE IN 13:16.6 AT STOCKHOLM, SWED., JULY 5, 1966; IN THE SAME RACE HE WAS TIMED FOR THE 3 MI. IN 12:50.4

WIDE WORLD

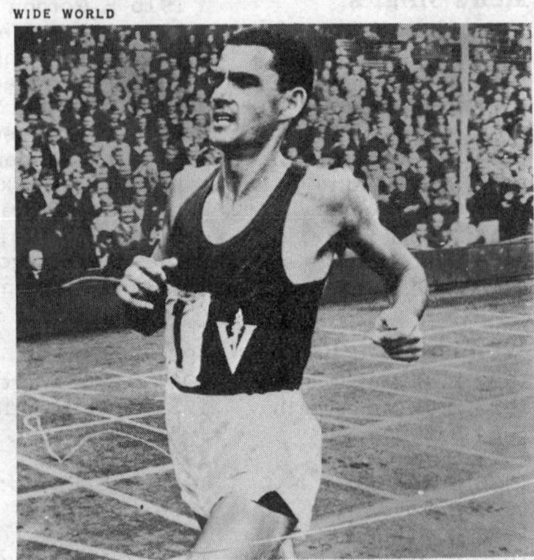

THE FIRST FOUR-MINUTE MILERS, ROGER BANNISTER (ENG.), LEFT, AND JOHN LANDY (AUSTR.), RACING IN THE BRITISH EMPIRE GAMES AT VANCOUVER, B.C., AUGUST 1954, FINISHED IN TIMES OF 3:58.8 (BANNISTER) AND 3:59.6 (LANDY)

MARK KAUFFMAN FOR "SPORTS ILLUSTRATED," © TIME INC.

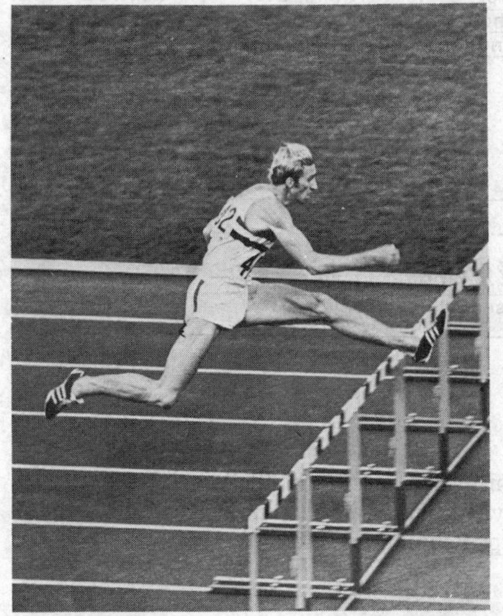

MARK SHEARMAN

DAVID HEMERY (U.K.) SETS WORLD RECORD OF 48.1 SEC. IN THE 400-M. HURDLES, AT MEXICO CITY, MEX., 1968

**Hurdling**

| Event | Min.:sec. | Name; Country | Place | Date |
|---|---|---|---|---|
| 120 yd. (3'6" hurdles) | 13.2 | K. M. Lauer; W. Ger. | Zürich, Switz. | July 7, 1959 |
| | 13.2 | L. Q. Calhoun; U.S. | Bern, Switz. | Aug. 21, 1960 |
| | 13.2 | E. McCullouch; U.S. | Minneapolis, U.S. | July 16, 1967 |
| 110 m. (3'6") | 13.2 | K. M. Lauer; W. Ger. | Zürich, Switz. | July 7, 1959 |
| | 13.2 | L. Q. Calhoun; U.S. | Bern, Switz. | Aug. 21, 1960 |
| | 13.2 | E. McCullouch; U.S. | Minneapolis, U.S. | July 16, 1967 |
| 200 m. (2'6") straight | 21.9 | D. A. Styron; U.S. | Baton Rouge, U.S. | April 2, 1960 |
| 200 m. (2'6") turn | 22.5 | K. M. Lauer; W. Ger. | Zürich, Switz. | July 7, 1959 |
| | 22.5 | G. A. Davis; U.S. | Bern, Switz. | Aug. 20, 1960 |
| 220 yd. (2'6") straight | 21.9 | D. A. Styron; U.S. | Baton Rouge, U.S. | April 2, 1960 |
| 220 yd. (2'6") turn | 22.7 | C. E. Tidwell; U.S. | Bakersfield, U.S. | June 14, 1958 |
| | 22.7 | C. E. Tidwell; U.S. | Norman, U.S. | May 16, 1959 |
| 400 m. (3'0") | 48.1 | D. P. Hemery: U.K. | Mexico City, Mex. | Oct. 14, 1968 |
| 440 yd. (3'0") | 49.3 | G. C. Potgieter; S.Af. | Bloemfontein, S.Af. | April 16, 1960 |
| 3,000 m. steeplechase | 8:22.2 | V. Dudkin; U.S.S.R. | Kiev, U.S.S.R. | Aug. 19, 1969 |

**Relays**

| Event | Min.: sec. | Team | Place | Date |
|---|---|---|---|---|
| 4 x 100 m. (two turns) | 38.2 | U.S. national team (C. Greene, M. Pender, R. R. Smith, J. R. Hines) | Mexico City, Mex. | Oct. 20, 1968 |
| 4 x 110 yd. (two turns) | 38.6 | U. of Southern California, U.S. (E. McCullouch, F. Kuller, O. J. Simpson, L. Miller) | Provo, U.S. | June 17, 1967 |
| 4 x 200 m. and 4 x 220 yd. | 1:22.1 | San Jose State College, U.S. (K. Shackleford, R. Talmadge, L. E. Evans, T. Smith) | Fresno, U.S. | May 13, 1967 |
| 4 x 400 m. | 2:56.1 | U.S. national team (V. Matthews, R. Freeman, L. James, L. E. Evans) | Mexico City, Mex. | Oct. 20, 1968 |
| 4 x 440 yd. | 3:02.8 | Trinidad and Tobago (L. Yearwood, K. Bernard, E. Roberts, W. Mottley) | Kingston, Jam. | Aug. 13, 1966 |
| 4 x 800 m. | 7:08.6 | West German "A" team (M. Kinder, W. Adams, D. Bogatzki, F.-J. Kemper) | Wiesbaden, W. Ger. | Aug. 13, 1966 |
| 4 x 880 yd.* | 7:14.6 | West German national team (B. Tümmler, H. Norpoth, W. Adams, F.-J. Kemper) | Fulda, W. Ger. | June 13, 1968 |
| 4 x 1,500 m. | 14:49.0 | French "A" team (G. Vervoort, C. Nicolas, M. Jazy, J. Wadoux) | Saint-Maur, Fr. | June 25, 1965 |
| 4 x 1 mi. | 16:05.0 | U. of Oregon; U.S. (R. Divine, C. W. Bell, A. Kvalheim [Norway] D. Wilborn) | Eugene, U.S. | May 30, 1968 |

*A United Kingdom national team (G. D. Grant, G. P. M. Varah, C.S. Carter, and J. P. Boulter) also recorded 7:14.6 at the Crystal Palace, London, on June 22, 1966, but lap times were illegally communicated to the runners.

THE TRINIDAD AND TOBAGO RELAY TEAM (L. YEARWOOD, K. BERNARD, E. ROBERTS, W. MOTTLEY) AT THE ANNOUNCEMENT OF THE WORLD'S RECORD THEY SET IN KINGSTON, JAMAICA. THEY RAN THE 4 X 440 YD. IN 3:02.8 ON AUG. 13, 1966

BIPPA

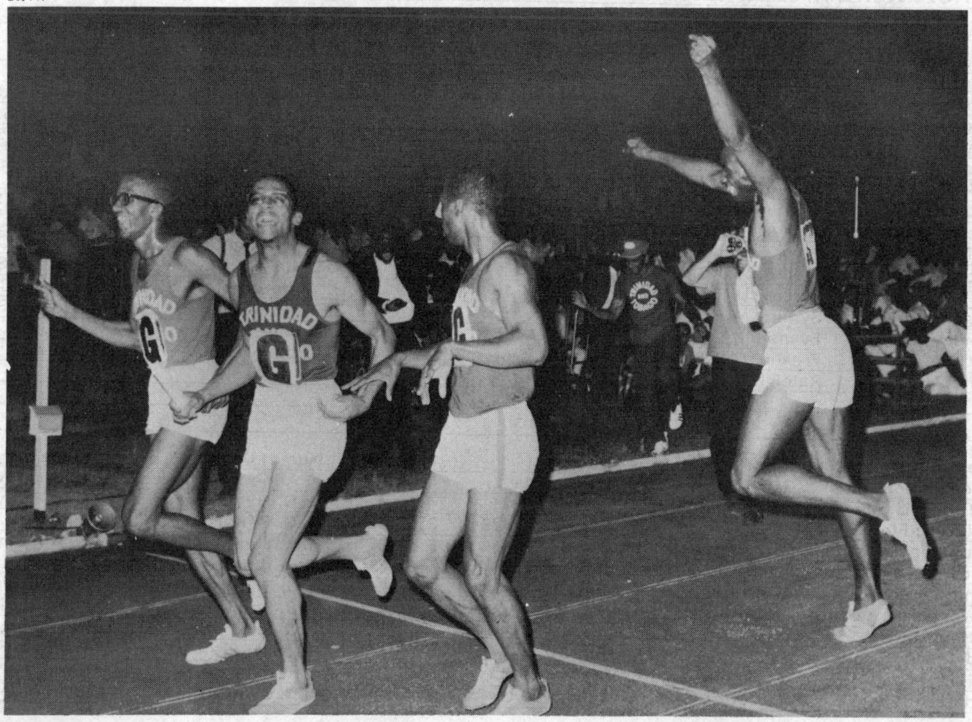

### Field Events

| Event | Ft. | in. | Metres | Name; Country | Place | Date |
|---|---|---|---|---|---|---|
| High jump | 7 | 5¾ | 2.28 | V. N. Brumel; U.S.S.R. | Moscow, U.S.S.R. | July 21, 1963 |
| Pole vault | 17 | 10¼ | 5.44 | J. T. Pennel; U.S. | Sacramento, U.S. | June 21, 1969 |
| Long jump | 29 | 2⅜ | 8.90 | R. Beamon; U.S. | Mexico City, Mex. | Oct. 18, 1968 |
| Triple jump | 57 | 0⅝ | 17.39 | V. Saneev; U.S.S.R. | Mexico City, Mex. | Oct. 17, 1968 |
| Shot put | 71 | 5½ | 21.78 | J. R. Matson; U.S. | College Station, U.S. | April 22, 1967 |
| Discus throw | 224 | 5 | 68.40 | L. J. Silvester; U.S. | Reno, U.S. | Sept. 18, 1968 |
| Hammer throw | 247 | 7½ | 75.48 | A. Bondarchuk; U.S.S.R. | Rovno, U.S.S.R. | Oct. 11, 1969 |
| Javelin throw | 304 | 1 | 92.70 | J. V. P. Kinnunen; Fin. | Tampere, Fin. | June 18, 1969 |

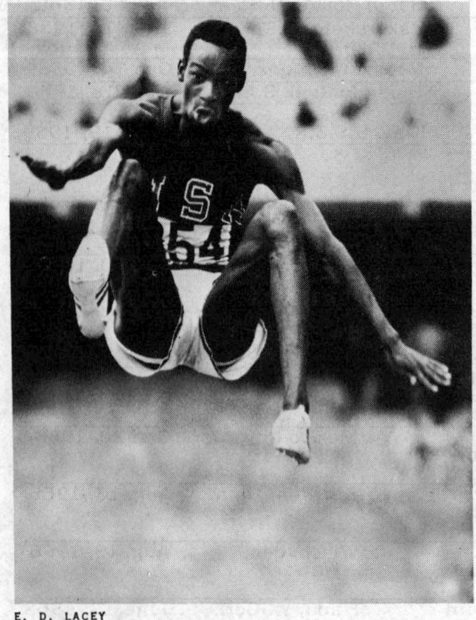

E. D. LACEY

BOB BEAMON (U.S.) LEAPS 29 FT. 2⅜ IN. TO SET OLYMPIC AND WORLD RECORDS IN THE LONG JUMP, AT MEXICO CITY, MEX., 1968

### Decathlon (1964 Scoring Tables)

| | | | |
|---|---|---|---|
| 8,417 points | W. Toomey; U.S.<br>1st day: 100 m. 10.3 sec., long jump 25′ 5½″, shot put 47′ 2¼″, high jump 6′ 4″, 400 m. 47.1 sec.<br>2nd day: 110 m. hurdles 14.8 sec., discus 152′ 6″, pole vault 14′ 0¼″, javelin 215′ 8″, 1,500 m. 4:39.4 | Los Angeles, U.S. | Dec. 10–11, 1969 |

**The Marathon.** There is no official Marathon record because of the varying severity of the courses. The best time over 26 mi. 385 yd. (standardized in 1924) is 2 hr. 8 min. 33.6 sec. by D. Clayton (Australia) at Antwerp, Belgium, on May 30, 1969.

**Cross-Country.** Like the Marathon, there is no official record for Cross-Country running because of the varying severity of the courses. Cross-Country was an Olympic event from 1912 to 1924 (*see* table in the article OLYMPIC GAMES). For history of the sport *see* the article RUNNING.

| Year | Individual winner; Country | Team winner |
|---|---|---|
| 1965 | J. Fayolle; France | England |
| 1966 | B. El Ghazi; Morocco | England |
| 1967 | G. Roelants; Belgium | England |
| 1968 | M. Gammoudi; Tunisia | England |
| 1969 | G. Roelants; Belgium | England |

## PROGRESSIVE OFFICIAL WORLD RECORDS

### 100 Yards

| Time sec. | Name; Country | Place | Date |
|---|---|---|---|
| 9.6 | D. J. Kelly; U.S. | Spokane, U.S. | June 23, 1906 |
| | H. P. Drew; U.S. | Berkeley, U.S. | March 28, 1914 |
| | C. W. Paddock; U.S. | Berkeley, U.S. | March 26, 1919 |
| | C. H. Coaffee; Can. | Hamilton, Can. | Aug. 12, 1922 |
| 9.5 | T. E. Tolan; U.S. | Evanston, U.S. | May 25, 1929 |
| 9.4 | F. C. Wykoff; U.S. | Los Angeles, U.S. | May 10, 1930 |
| | D. J. Joubert; S.Af. | Grahamstown, S. Af. | May 16, 1931 |
| | J. C. Owens; U.S. | Ann Arbor, U.S. | May 25, 1934 |
| | C. H. Jeffrey; U.S. | Long Beach, U.S. | May 16, 1940 |
| | M. E. Patton; U.S. | Modesto, U.S. | May 24, 1947 |
| 9.3 | M. E. Patton; U.S. | Fresno, U.S. | May 15, 1948 |
| | H. D. Hogan; Austr. | Sydney, Austr. | March 13, 1954 |
| | J. J. Golliday; U.S. | Evanston, U.S. | May 14, 1955 |
| | L. King; U.S. | Fresno, U.S. | May 12, 1956 |
| | D. W. Sime; U.S. | Raleigh, U.S. | May 19, 1956 |
| 9.3 | B. J. Morrow; U.S. | Austin, U.S. | June 14, 1957 |
| | O. R. Norton; U.S. | San Jose, U.S. | April 12, 1958 |
| | W. Woodhouse; U.S. | Abilene, U.S. | May 5, 1959 |
| | R. Cook; U.S. | Modesto, U.S. | May 30, 1959 |
| | D. Johnson; Jamaica | San Jose, U.S. | March 11, 1961 |
| | F. J. Budd; U.S. | Villanova, U.S. | May 5, 1961 |
| | H. W. Jerome; Can. | Corvallis, U.S. | May 20, 1961 |
| 9.2 | F. J. Budd; U.S. | New York, U.S. | June 24, 1961 |
| | H. W. Jerome; Can. | Vancouver, Can. | Aug. 25, 1962 |
| 9.1 | R. L. Hayes; U.S. | St. Louis, U.S. | June 21, 1963 |
| | H. W. Jerome; Can. | Edmonton, Can. | July 15, 1966 |
| | J. R. Hines; U.S. | Houston, U.S. | May 13, 1967 |
| | C. Greene; U.S. | Provo, U.S. | June 15, 1967 |
| | J. Carlos; U.S. | Fresno, U.S. | May 10, 1969 |

### 1 Mile

| Time min.: sec. | Name; Country | Place | Date |
|---|---|---|---|
| 4:14.4 | J. P. Jones; U.S. | Cambridge, U.S. | May 31, 1913 |
| 4:12.6 | N. S. Taber; U.S. | Cambridge, U.S. | July 16, 1915 |
| 4:10.4 | P. J. Nurmi; Fin. | Stockholm, Swed. | Aug. 23, 1923 |
| 4:09.2 | J. Ladoumègue; Fr. | Paris, Fr. | Oct. 4, 1931 |
| 4:07.6 | J. E. Lovelock; N.Z. | Princeton, U.S. | July 15, 1933 |
| 4:06.8 | G. Cunningham; U.S. | Princeton, U.S. | June 16, 1934 |
| 4:06.4 | S. C. Wooderson; U.K. | Motspur Pk., U.K. | Aug. 28, 1937 |
| 4:06.2 | O. G. Hägg; Swed. | Göteborg, Swed. | July 1, 1942 |
| | A. Andersson; Swed. | Stockholm, Swed. | July 10, 1942 |
| 4:04.6 | O. G. Hägg; Swed. | Stockholm, Swed. | Sept. 4, 1942 |
| 4:02.6 | A. Andersson; Swed. | Göteborg, Swed. | July 1, 1943 |
| 4:01.6 | A. Andersson; Swed. | Malmö, Swed. | July 18, 1944 |
| 4:01.4 | O. G. Hägg; Swed. | Malmö, Swed. | July 17, 1945 |
| 3:59.4 | R. G. Bannister; U.K. | Oxford, U.K. | May 6, 1954 |
| 3:58.0 | J. M. Landy; Austr. | Turku, Fin. | June 21, 1954 |
| 3:57.2 | G. D. Ibbotson; U.K. | London, U.K. | July 19, 1957 |
| 3:54.5 | H. J. Elliott; Austr. | Dublin, Ire. | Aug. 6, 1958 |
| 3:54.4 | P. G. Snell; N.Z. | Wanganui, N.Z. | Jan. 27, 1962 |
| 3:54.1 | P. G. Snell; N.Z. | Auckland, N.Z. | Nov. 17, 1964 |
| 3:53.6 | M. Jazy; Fr. | Rennes, Fr. | June 9, 1965 |
| 3:51.3 | J. R. Ryun; U.S. | Berkeley, U.S. | July 17, 1966 |
| 3:51.1 | J. R. Ryun; U.S. | Bakersfield, U.S. | June 23, 1967 |

WIDE WORLD
JOHN PENNEL (U.S.) POLE VAULTING TO A WORLD RECORD 17 FT. 10¼ IN. AT SACRAMENTO, CALIF., JUNE 21, 1969

### High Jump

| Height Ft. in. | Name; Country | Place | Date |
|---|---|---|---|
| 6 7 | G. L. Horine; U.S. | Stanford, U.S. | May 18, 1912 |
| 6 7¼ | E. Beeson; U.S. | Berkeley, U.S. | May 2, 1914 |
| 6 8¼ | H. M. Osborn; U.S. | Urbana, U.S. | May 27, 1924 |
| 6 8⅝ | W. Marty; U.S. | Fresno, U.S. | May 13, 1933 |
| 6 9⅛ | W. Marty; U.S. | Palo Alto, U.S. | April 28, 1934 |
| 6 9¾ | C. C. Johnson; U.S.<br>D. D. Albritton; U.S. | New York, U.S.<br>New York, U.S. | July 12, 1936<br>July 12, 1936 |
| 6 10⅜ | M. Walker; U.S. | Malmö, Swed. | Aug. 12, 1937 |
| 6 11 | L. Steers; U.S. | Los Angeles, U.S. | June 17, 1941 |
| 6 11½ | W. F. Davis; U.S. | Dayton, U.S. | June 27, 1953 |
| 7 0½ | C. E. Dumas; U.S. | Los Angeles, U.S. | June 29, 1956 |
| 7 1 | Y. N. Stepanov; U.S.S.R.* | Leningrad, U.S.S.R. | July 13, 1957 |
| 7 1½ | J. C. Thomas; U.S. | Philadelphia, U.S. | April 30, 1960 |
| 7 1¾ | J. C. Thomas; U.S. | Cambridge, U.S. | May 21, 1960 |
| 7 2 | J. C. Thomas; U.S. | Bakersfield, U.S. | June 24, 1960 |
| 7 3¾ | J. C. Thomas; U.S. | Palo Alto, U.S. | July 1, 1960 |
| 7 4 | V. N. Brumel; U.S.S.R. | Moscow, U.S.S.R. | June 18, 1961 |
| 7 4⅜ | V. N. Brumel; U.S.S.R. | Moscow, U.S.S.R. | July 16, 1961 |
| 7 4⅝ | V. N. Brumel; U.S.S.R. | Sofia, Bulg. | Aug. 31, 1961 |
| 7 5 | V. N. Brumel; U.S.S.R. | Palo Alto, U.S. | July 22, 1962 |
| 7 5⅜ | V. N. Brumel; U.S.S.R. | Moscow, U.S.S.R. | Sept. 29, 1962 |
| 7 5¾ | V. N. Brumel; U.S.S.R. | Moscow, U.S.S.R. | July 21, 1963 |

*Official record achieved with built-up shoes which were subsequently banned by the IAAF.

PETER SNELL (N.Z.) RUNNING THE MILE IN 3:54.4, THE WORLD RECORD IN 1962, AT WANGANUI, N.Z.
WIDE WORLD

## WORLD RECORDS (Outdoor) Women

World Records for women's track and field events recognized by the International Amateur Athletic Federation, as of Jan. 1, 1970.

### Running

| Event | Min.: sec. | Name; Country | Place | Date |
|---|---|---|---|---|
| 60 m. | 7.2<br>7.2 | B. Cuthbert; Austr.<br>I. R. Bochkaryova; U.S.S.R. | Sydney, Austr.<br>Moscow, U.S.S.R. | Feb. 21, 1960<br>Aug. 28, 1961 |
| 100 yd. | 10.3<br>10.3<br>10.3 | M. J. Willard; Austr.<br>W. Tyus; U.S.<br>W. Tyus; U.S. | Sydney, Austr.<br>Kingston, Jam.<br>Dayton, U.S. | Mar. 20, 1958<br>July 17, 1965<br>June 8, 1968 |
| 100 m. | 11.0 | W. Tyus; U.S. | Mexico City, Mex. | Oct. 15, 1968 |
| 200 m. (turn) | 22.5 | I. Kirszenstein-Szewinska; Pol. | Mexico City, Mex. | Oct. 17, 1968 |
| 220 yd. (turn) | 22.9 | M. A. Burvill; Austr. | Perth, Austr. | Feb. 22, 1964 |
| 400 m.* | 51.7<br>51.7 | N. Duclos; Fr.<br>C. Besson; Fr. | Athens, Gr.<br>Athens, Gr. | Sept. 18, 1969<br>Sept. 18, 1969 |
| 440 yd. | 52.4 | J. F. Pollock; Austr. | Perth, Austr. | Feb. 27, 1965 |
| 800 m.* | 2:00.5 | V. Nikolic; Yugos. | London, U.K. | July 20, 1968 |
| 880 yd. | 2:02.0<br>2:02.0 | D. I. Willis; Austr.<br>J. F. Pollock; Austr. | Perth, Austr.<br>Stockholm, Swed. | Mar. 3, 1962<br>July 5, 1967 |
| 1,500 m. | 4:10.7 | J. Jehlickova; Czech. | Athens, Gr. | Sept. 20, 1969 |
| 1 mi. | 4:36.8 | M. F. P. Gommers; Neth. | Leicester, U.K. | June 16, 1969 |

*Shin Geum Dan (N. Kor.) has also achieved the following performances: 400 m. 51.4 sec. at Jakarta, Indon., on Nov. 13, 1963, and 51.2 sec. at P'yongyang, N. Kor., on Oct. 21, 1964; 800 m. 1:59.1 at Jakarta on Nov. 12, 1963, and 1.58.0 at P'yongyang on Sept. 5, 1964; but the meeting in Indonesia, the Games of the New Emerging Forces (GANEFO), was not recognized by the IAAF, and she was under suspension by the IAAF at the time of the other performances.

### Hurdling

| Event | Min.: sec. | Name; Country | Place | Date |
|---|---|---|---|---|
| 100 m. | 12.9 | K. Balzer; E. Ger. | E. Berlin, Ger. | Sept. 5, 1969 |
| 200 m. | 25.8 | P. Kilborn; Austr. | Melbourne, Austr. | Dec. 17, 1969 |

VERA NIKOLIC (YUGOS.) AFTER COVERING 800 M. IN 2 MIN. 00.5 SEC. FOR A WOMEN'S WORLD RECORD AT LONDON, JULY 20, 1968
CENTRAL PRESS PHOTOS

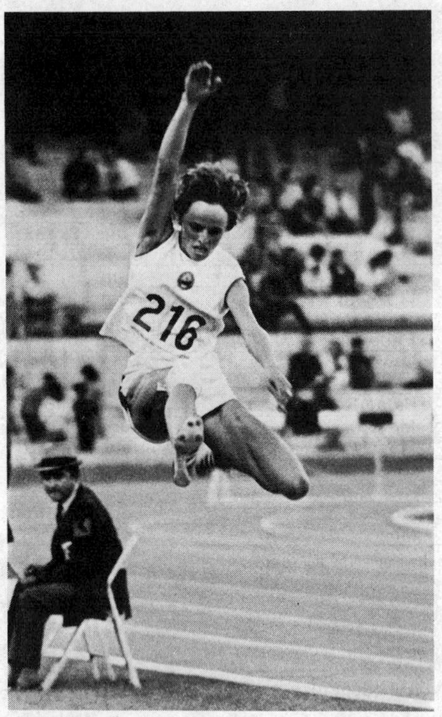


MARK SHEARMAN

VIORICA VISCOPOLEANU (RUM.) SETTING WOMEN'S WORLD RECORD OF 22 FT. 4½ IN. IN THE LONG JUMP, AT MEXICO CITY, 1968

### Relays

| Event | Min:sec. | Team | Place | Date |
|---|---|---|---|---|
| 4 x 100 m. | 42.8 | U.S. national team (B. Ferrell, M. Bailes, M. Netter, W. Tyus) | Mexico City, Mex. | Oct. 20, 1968 |
| 4 x 110 yd. | 45.0 | U.K. national team (A. Neil, J. M. Simpson, M.D. Tranter, L.B. Board) | Portsmouth, U.K. | Sept. 14, 1968 |
| 4 x 200 m. | 1:33.8 | U.K. national team (M. D. Tranter, D. P. James, J. M. Simpson, V. Peat) | London, U.K. | Aug. 24, 1968 |
| 4 x 400 m. | 3:30.8 | U.K. national team (R. O. Stirling, P. J. Lowe, J. M. Simpson, L. B. Board) | Athens, Gr. | Sept. 20, 1969 |
| | 3:30.8 | French national team (B. Martin, N. Duclos, E. Jacq, C. Besson) | Athens, Gr. | Sept. 20, 1969 |
| 4 x 220 yd. | 1:36.0 | E. Germany (H. Sadau, G. I. Birkemeyer, B. Mayer, C. Stubnick) | Leipzig, E. Ger. | July 26, 1958 |
| 3 x 800 m. | 6:15.5 | Netherlands national team (I. Keizer, M. C. van der Made, M. F. P. Gommers) | Sittard, Neth. | Aug. 20, 1968 |
| 3 x 880 yd. | 6:25.2 | U.K. national team (R. O. Stirling, P. B. Lowe, P. J. Piercy) | Budapest, Hung. | July 30, 1967 |

### Field Events

| Event | Ft. | in. | M. | Name; Country | Place | Date |
|---|---|---|---|---|---|---|
| High jump | 6 | 3¼ | 1.91 | I. Balas-Söter; Rum. | Sofia, Bulg. | July 16, 1961 |
| Long (broad) jump | 22 | 4½ | 6.82 | V. Viscopoleanu; Rum. | Mexico City, Mex. | Oct. 14, 1968 |
| Shot put | 67 | 0¼ | 20.43 | N. Chizhova; U.S.S.R. | Athens, Gr. | Sept. 16, 1969 |
| Discus throw | 205 | 2½ | 62.54 | L. Westermann; W.Ger. | Werdohl, W. Ger. | July 24, 1968 |
| Javelin throw | 204 | 8½ | 62.40 | Y. Y. Gorchakova; U.S.S.R. | Tokyo, Jap. | Oct. 16, 1964 |

### Pentathlon

| Points | Name | Place | Date |
|---|---|---|---|
| 5,352 points | L. Prokop, Austria<br>100-m. hurdles 13.5 sec.; shot put 49 ft. ½ in.; high jump 5 ft. 8¾ in.; long jump 21 ft. 8¾ in.; 200 m. 24.6 sec. | Vienna, Aus. | Oct. 4–5, 1969 |

SPORT & GENERAL PRESS AGENCY, LONDON

L. B. BOARD (RIGHT) RUNS WITH BATON PASSED BY J. M. SIMPSON (LEFT) DURING WORLD RECORD 4 X 110 YD. RELAY AT PORTSMOUTH, U.K., SEPT. 14, 1968. WINNING TIME 45 SEC.

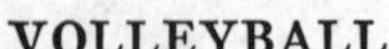

## VOLLEYBALL

### World Championships

| Year | Place | Men | Women |
|---|---|---|---|
| 1949 | Prague, Czech. | U.S.S.R. | — |
| 1952 | Moscow, U.S.S.R. | U.S.S.R. | U.S.S.R. |
| 1956 | Paris, Fr. | Czechoslovakia | U.S.S.R. |
| 1960 | São Paulo, Braz. | U.S.S.R. | U.S.S.R. |
| 1962 | Moscow, U.S.S.R. | U.S.S.R. | Japan |
| 1964* | Tokyo, Jap. | U.S.S.R. | Japan |
| 1966 | Prague, Czech. | Czechoslovakia | Japan |
| 1967 | Tokyo, Jap. | Not held | Japan |
| 1968* | Mexico City, Mex. | U.S.S.R. | U.S.S.R. |

*Olympic Games tournament.

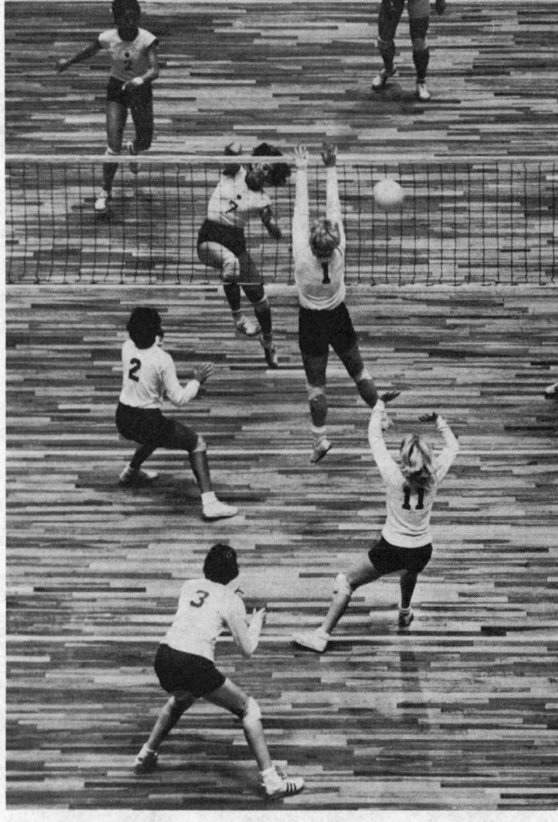

JAPAN'S WOMEN'S VOLLEYBALL TEAM (BACKCOURT) DEFEATED THE UNITED STATES TEAM IN THREE STRAIGHT SETS TO WIN THE WORLD CHAMPIONSHIP AT TOKYO, 1964

KEYSTONE

# WATER SKIING

## WORLD CHAMPIONS—Men

| Date | Place | Overall | Slalom | Figures or Tricks | Jumping |
|---|---|---|---|---|---|
| 1949 | Juan les Pins, Fr. | C. Jourdan; Fr. G. de Clercq; Belg. | C. Jourdan; Fr. | P. Gouin; Fr. | G. de Clercq; Belg. |
| 1950 | Cypress Gardens, U.S. | R. Pope, Jr.; U.S. | R. Pope, Jr.; U.S. | J. Andresen; U.S. | G. de Clercq; Belg. |
| 1953 | Toronto, Can. | A. Mendoza; U.S. | C. Blackwell; Can. | W. Witherell; U.S. | A. Mendoza; U.S. |
| 1955 | Beirut, Leb. | A. Mendoza; U.S. | A. Mendoza; U.S. | S. Scott; U.S. | A. Mendoza; U.S. |
| 1957 | Cypress Gardens, U.S. | J. Cash; U.S. | J. Cash; U.S. | M. Amsbry; U.S. | J. Mueller; U.S. |
| 1959 | Milan, It. | C. Stearns; U.S. | C. Stearns; U.S. | P. Logut; Fr. | B. MacCalla; U.S. |
| 1961 | Long Beach, U.S. | B. Zaccardi; It. | J. Jackson, U.S. | J. Muller; Fr. | L. Penacho; U.S. |
| 1963 | Vichy, Fr. | W. Spencer; U.S. | W. Spencer; U.S. | W. Spencer; U.S. | J. Jackson; U.S. |
| 1965 | Surfers' Paradise, Austr. | R. Hillier; U.S. | R. Hillier; U.S. | K. White; U.S. | L. Penacho; U.S. |
| 1967 | Sherbrooke, Can. | M. Suyderhoud; U.S. | T. Antunano; Mex. | A. Kempton; U.S. | A. Kempton; U.S. |
| 1969 | Copenhagen, Den. | M. Suyderhoud; U.S. | V. Palomo; Sp. | B. Cockburn; Austr. | W. Grimditch; U.S. |

U.P.I. COMPIX

NANCIE RIDEOUT (U.S.), WOMEN'S WORLD CHAMPION WATER SKI JUMPER IN 1957 AND 1959, COMPETING AT CYPRESS GARDENS, FLA., IN 1957

## WORLD CHAMPIONS—Women

| Date | Place | Overall | Slalom | Figures or Tricks | Jumping |
|---|---|---|---|---|---|
| 1949 | Juan les Pins, Fr. | W. Worthington; U.S. | W. Worthington; U.S. | M. Bouteiller; Fr. | W. Worthington; U.S. |
| 1950 | Cypress Gardens, U.S. | W. McGuire; U.S. | E. Wofford; U.S. | W. McGuire; U.S. | J. Kirkpatrick; U.S. |
| 1953 | Toronto, Can. | L. Rawls; U.S. | E. Wofford; U.S. | L. Rawls; U.S. | S. Swaney; U.S. |
| 1955 | Beirut, Leb. | W. McGuire; U.S. | W. McGuire; U.S. | M. Doria; Switz. | W. McGuire; U.S. |
| 1957 | Cypress Gardens, U.S. | M. Doria; Switz. | M. Doria; Switz. | M. Doria; Switz. | N. Rideout; U.S. |
| 1959 | Milan, It. | V. van Hook; U.S. | V. van Hook; U.S. | P. Castlevetri; It. | N. Rideout; U.S. |
| 1961 | Long Beach, U.S. | S. Hulsemann; Luxem. | J. Kirtley; U.S. | S. Hulsemann; Luxem. | R. Hansluwska; Aus. |
| 1963 | Vichy, Fr. | J. Brown; U.S. | J. Brown; U.S. | G. Dalle; Fr. | R. Hansluwska; Aus. |
| 1965 | Surfers' Paradise, Austr. | E. Allan; U.S. | B. Cooper-Clack; U.S. | D. Duflot; Fr. | E. Allan; U.S.* |
| 1967 | Sherbrooke, Can. | J. Stewart-Wood; U.K. | E. Allan; U.S. | D. Duflot; Fr. | J. Stewart-Wood; U.K. |
| 1969 | Copenhagen, Den. | E. Allan; U.S. | E. Allan; U.S. | E. Allan; U.S. | E. Allan; U.S. |

*Women's world record: E. Allan, 110 ft., 1968 (Callaway Gardens, Ga.).

U.P.I. COMPIX

BY COURTESY OF CYPRESS GARDENS

(LEFT) BRUNO ZACCARDI (ITALY), OVERALL WATER SKIING CHAMPION IN 1961, COMPETING IN A SLALOM EVENT AT VEREENIGING, S. AF., 1966. (RIGHT) ROLAND HILLIER (U.S.), WORLD CHAMPION IN THE OVERALL AND SLALOM WATER SKIING EVENTS IN 1965 AT SURFERS' PARADISE, AUSTR.

## PROGRESSIVE RECORDS—Men

All records (American Water Ski Association) were set by U.S. jumpers unless indicated.

| Year | Distance (ft.) | Jumper | Place |
|---|---|---|---|
| 1947 | 49 | C. R. Sligh, Jr. | Cypress Gardens, Fla. |
| | 61 | B. Boyle; T. Pickett (tie) | Holland, Mich. |
| 1948 | 68 | B. Boyle | Cypress Gardens, Fla. |
| 1949 | 72 | B. Boyle | Cypress Gardens, Fla. |
| 1950 | 75 | B. Boyle | Cypress Gardens, Fla. |
| | 80 | J. McGuire | Seattle, Wash. |
| | 84 | J. McGuire; R. Pope, Jr. (tie) | Cypress Gardens, Fla. |
| 1951 | 85 | R. Pope, Jr. | Cypress Gardens, Fla. |
| 1952 | 87 | R. Cozzens | Cypress Gardens, Fla. |
| 1953 | 90 | R. Nathey | Lakeland, Fla. |
| | 91 | A. Mendoza | Cypress Gardens, Fla. |
| | 96 | W. Witherell | Lake George, N.Y. |
| | 97 | A. Mendoza | Long Beach, Calif. |
| 1954 | 98 | B. Rosenberg | Cypress Gardens, Fla. |
| | 99 | A. Mendoza | Cypress Gardens, Fla. |
| | 102 | B. Rosenberg; R. Binette (tie) | Laconia, N.H. |
| | 106 | W. Witherell | Spofford Lake, N.H. |
| 1955 | 116 | A. Mendoza | Cypress Gardens, Fla. |
| | 125 | B. Rosenberg | Lakeland, Fla. |
| 1957 | 126 | A. Bromberg | Fort Myers, Fla. |
| | 126 | J. Cash | San Diego, Calif. |
| 1959 | 142 | J. Cash; M. Osborn (tie) | Fort Myers, Fla. |
| 1960 | 150 | P. Baker | Austin, Tex. |
| 1962 | 155 | L. Penacho | Seattle, Wash. |
| 1964 | 158 | D. Rahlves | Denver, Colo. |
| | 150* | J. Jackson | Callaway Gardens, Ga. |
| 1966 | 152* | J. Jackson | Callaway Gardens, Ga. |
| 1967 | 160* | J. J. Pottier; Fr. | Gerona, Spain |
| 1968 | 155* | M. Suyderhoud | Callaway Gardens, Ga. |
| | 157* | L. Penacho | Canton, Ohio |
| | 160 | M. Suyderhoud | Berkeley, Calif. |
| 1969 | 162 | M. Suyderhoud | Callaway Gardens, Ga. |

*World Water Ski Union records.

## WEIGHT LIFTING

### OFFICIAL WORLD RECORDS

| Class | Lift | Name; Country | Record lb. | Place | Date |
|---|---|---|---|---|---|
| Flyweight (under 56 kg./123.46 lb.) | Press | V. Krishishin; U.S.S.R. | 250 | Lvov, U.S.S.R. | Dec. 16, 1969 |
| | Snatch | K. Miki; Jap. | 220¼ | Yufuin, Jap. | Aug. 19, 1966 |
| | Jerk | V. Krishishin; U.S.S.R. | 283¼ | Lvov, U.S.S.R. | Dec. 16, 1969 |
| | Total | V. Krishishin; U.S.S.R. | 743¾ | Warsaw, Pol. | Sept. 20, 1969 |
| Bantamweight (56 kg./123.46 lb.) | Press | I. Födli; Hung. | 275½ | Budapest, Hung. | June 21, 1969 |
| | Snatch | K. Miki; Jap. | 250 | Osaka, Jap. | Nov. 15, 1968 |
| | Jerk | M. Nassiri; Iran | 330½ | Mexico City, Mex. | Oct. 13, 1968 |
| | Total | I. Födli; Hung. | 815¼ | Budapest, Hung. | Nov. 30, 1969 |
| Featherweight (60 kg./132.28 lb.) | Press | M. Kuchev; Bulg. | 288¾ | Sofia, Bulg. | July 13, 1969 |
| | Snatch | Y. Miyake; Jap. | 276½ | Matsuura, Jap. | Oct. 28, 1969 |
| | Jerk | Y. Miyake; Jap. | 337¼ | Matsuura, Jap. | Oct. 28, 1969 |
| | Total | Y. Miyake; Jap. | 881½ | Matsuura, Jap. | Oct. 28, 1969 |
| Lightweight (67.5 kg./148.81 lb.) | Press | Y. Katsura; U.S.S.R. | 320¾ | Ordzhonikidze, U.S.S.R. | July 28, 1966 |
| | Snatch | W. Baszanowski; Pol. | 299¾ | Warsaw, Pol. | Sept. 23, 1969 |
| | Jerk | W. Baszanowski; Pol. | 375¾ | Warsaw, Pol. | Sept. 23, 1969 |
| | Total | W. Baszanowski; Pol. | 980¾ | Warsaw, Pol. | Sept. 23, 1969 |
| Middleweight (75 kg./165.35 lb.) | Press | V. Kurentsov; U.S.S.R. | 356 | Rostov, U.S.S.R. | May 16, 1969 |
| | Snatch | M. Ohuchi; Jap. | 319½ | Yufuin, Jap. | June 18, 1967 |
| | Jerk | V. Kurentsov; U.S.S.R. | 413¼ | Mexico City, Mex. | Oct. 16, 1968 |
| | Total | V. Kurentsov; U.S.S.R. | 1,063¼ | Dubno, U.S.S.R. | Aug. 31, 1968 |
| Light heavyweight (82.5 kg./181.88 lb.) | Press | H. Bettembourg; Swed. | 380¼ | Kil, Swed. | Dec. 7, 1969 |
| | Snatch | M. Ohuchi; Jap. | 336 | Warsaw, Pol. | Sept. 29, 1969 |
| | Jerk | G. Ivanchenko; U.S.S.R. | 422 | Lvov, U.S.S.R. | Dec. 18, 1969 |
| | Total | G. Ivanchenko; U.S.S.R. | 1,102 | Vilnius, U.S.S.R. | April 24, 1970 |
| Middle heavyweight (90 kg./198.42 lb.) | Press | K. Pumpurinsh; U.S.S.R. | 399 | Lvov, U.S.S.R. | Dec. 19, 1969 |
| | Snatch | K. Kangasniemi; Fin. | 354¾ | Kiruna, Swed. | Nov. 15, 1969 |
| | Jerk | F. Capsoaras; U.S. | 440 | New York, U.S. | Apr. 19, 1969 |
| | Total | K. Kangasniemi; Fin. | 1,168 | Lahti, Fin. | Oct. 26, 1969 |
| Heavyweight (110 kg./242.51 lb.) | Press | V. Szarostenko; U.S.S.R. | 427½ | Lvov, U.S.S.R. | Dec. 19, 1969 |
| | Snatch | M. Lindroos; Fin. | 353¾ | Kotka, Fin. | Dec. 21, 1969 |
| | Jerk | Y. Talts; U.S.S.R. | 468¼ | Warsaw, Pol. | Sept. 27, 1969 |
| | Total | R. Bednarski; U.S. | 1,210 | Chicago, U.S. | June 15, 1969 |
| Super heavyweight (above 110 kg.) | Press | V. Alexeyev; U.S.S.R. | 483¾ | Szombathely, Hung. | June 28, 1970 |
| | Snatch | L. Zhabotinsky; U.S.S.R. | 388 | Leningrad, U.S.S.R. | June 25, 1968 |
| | Jerk | V. Alexeyev; U.S.S.R. | 497 | Szombathely, Hung. | June 28, 1970 |
| | Total | V. Alexeyev; U.S.S.R. | 1,350¼ | Szombathely, Hung. | June 28, 1970 |

### PROGRESSIVE WORLD RECORDS Clean and Jerk, Heavyweight

| Year | Name; Country | Record kg. | lb. |
|---|---|---|---|
| 1924 | C. Rigoulot; Fr. | 147.5 | 325 |
| | C. Rigoulot; Fr. | 152.5 | 336 |
| 1925 | C. Rigoulot; Fr. | 157 | 346 |
| | C. Rigoulot; Fr. | 160.5 | 353¾ |
| | C. Rigoulot; Fr. | 161.5 | 356 |
| 1931 | E. S. Nosseir; Egy. | 167 | 368 |
| 1937 | A. Luhäär; Est. | 167.5 | 369¼ |
| 1945 | M. Gaissa; Egy. | 170.5 | 375¾ |
| 1946 | Y. Kutsenko; U.S.S.R. | 171 | 376¾ |
| 1947 | Y. Kutsenko; U.S.S.R. | 173 | 381¼ |
| | Y. Kutsenko; U.S.S.R. | 174 | 383½ |
| | J. Davis; U.S. | 174.5 | 384½ |
| 1948 | J. Davis; U.S. | 177.5 | 391¼ |
| 1951 | J. Davis; U.S. | 180 | 396¾ |
| | J. Davis; U.S. | 182 | 401¼ |
| 1953 | N. Schemansky; U.S. | 187.5 | 413¼ |
| 1954 | N. Schemansky; U.S. | 188.5 | 415½ |
| 1954 | N. Schemansky; U.S. | 192.5 | 424¼ |
| 1955 | P. Anderson; U.S. | 196.5 | 433 |
| 1959 | Y. Vlasov; U.S.S.R. | 197.5 | 435¼ |
| 1960 | Y. Vlasov; U.S.S.R. | 202 | 445¼ |
| 1961 | Y. Vlasov; U.S.S.R. | 205 | 451¾ |
| | Y. Vlasov; U.S.S.R. | 206 | 454 |
| | Y. Vlasov; U.S.S.R. | 208 | 458½ |
| | Y. Vlasov; U.S.S.R. | 210.5 | 464 |
| 1962 | Y. Vlasov; U.S.S.R. | 211 | 465 |
| 1963 | Y. Vlasov; U.S.S.R. | 212.5 | 468¼ |
| 1964 | L. Zhabotinskiy; U.S.S.R. | 213 | 469½ |
| | Y. Vlasov; U.S.S.R. | 215.5 | 475 |
| | L. Zhabotinskiy; U.S.S.R. | 217.5 | 479½ |
| 1966 | L. Zhabotinskiy; U.S.S.R. | 218 | 480½ |
| 1967 | L. Zhabotinskiy; U.S.S.R. | 218.5 | 481½ |
| | L. Zhabotinskiy; U.S.S.R. | 219 | 482¾ |
| 1968 | R. Bednarski; U.S | 220.9 | 486 |
| 1970 | V. Alexeyev; U.S.S.R. | 225.6 | 497 |

YURIY VLASOV (U.S.S.R.), WORLD HEAVYWEIGHT RECORD HOLDER, CLEAN-AND-JERK EVENT, 1959–64

SOVFOTO

LEONID ZHABOTINSKIY (U.S.S.R.), WORLD HEAVYWEIGHT CLEAN-AND-JERK RECORD HOLDER, 1964 AND 1966–67

WIDE WORLD

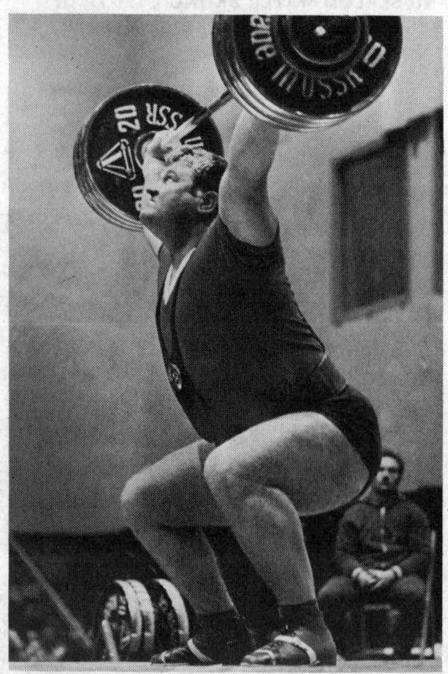

## WRESTLING

### World Champions—Greco-Roman Style

| Event | 1958 Budapest, Hung. | 1961 Yokohama, Jap. | 1962 Toledo, U.S. | 1963 Helsingborg, Swed. |
|---|---|---|---|---|
| Flyweight | B. Gurevitch; U.S.S.R. | A. Saydov; U.S.S.R. | S. Rybalko; U.S.S.R. | B. Vukov; Yugos. |
| Bantamweight | O. Karavaev; U.S.S.R. | O. Karavaev; U.S.S.R. | M. Ichiguchi; Jap. | J. Varga; Hung. |
| Featherweight | I. Polyak; Hung. | H. Mostafia; U.A.R. | I. Polyak; Hung. | G. Sapunov; U.S.S.R. |
| Lightweight | R. Dogan; Turk. | A. Koridge; U.S.S.R. | K. Ayvaz; Turk. | S. Horvat; Yugos. |
| Welterweight | K. Ayvaz; Turk. | V. Bularca; Rum. | A. Kolesov; U.S.S.R. | A. Kolesov; U.S.S.R. |
| Middleweight | G. Kartozia; U.S.S.R. | V. Zenin; U.S.S.R. | T. Kis; Turk. | T. Kis; Turk. |
| Light heavyweight | R. Abashidze; U.S.S.R. | I. Gooris; Hung. | R. Abashidze; U.S.S.R. | R. Abashidze; U.S.S.R. |
| Heavyweight | I. Bozdane; U.S.S.R. | I. Bogdan; U.S.S.R. | I. Kozma; Hung. | A. Roschin; U.S.S.R. |

| Event | 1965 Tampere, Fin. | 1966 Toledo, U.S. | 1967 Bucharest, Rum. | 1969 Mar del Plata, Arg. |
|---|---|---|---|---|
| Flyweight | S. Rybalko; U.S.S.R. | A. Keresov; Bulg. | V. Bakulin; U.S.S.R. | F. Aluzadeh; Iran |
| Bantamweight | I. Chernya; Rum. | F. Stange; W. Ger. | I. Baciu; Rum. | R. Kasakov; U.S.S.R. |
| Featherweight | Y. Grigorie; U.S.S.R. | R. Rurua; U.S.S.R. | R. Rurua; U.S.S.R. | R. Rurua; U.S.S.R. |
| Lightweight | G. Sapunov; U.S.S.R. | S. Horvat; Yugos. | E. Tapio; Fin. | S. Popescu; Rum. |
| Welterweight | A. Kolesov; U.S.S.R. | V. Igumenov; U.S.S.R. | V. Igumenov; U.S.S.R. | V. Igumenov; U.S.S.R. |
| Middleweight | R. Bogdanas; U.S.S.R. | V. Olenik; U.S.S.R. | L. Sillai; Hung. | P. Kroumov; Bulg. |
| Light heavyweight | J. Anisimov; U.S.S.R. | B. Radev; Bulg. | N. Iakovenko; U.S.S.R. | A. Yurkevich; U.S.S.R. |
| Heavyweight | N. Shmakov; U.S.S.R. | I. Kozma; Hung. | I. Kozma; Hung. | N. Iakovenko; U.S.S.R. |

### World Champions—Freestyle

| Event | 1954 Tokyo, Jap. | 1957 Istanbul, Turk. | 1959 Teheran, Iran | 1961 Yokohama, Jap. | 1962 Toledo, U.S. |
|---|---|---|---|---|---|
| Flyweight | H. Akbas; Turk. | M. Kartel; Turk. | A. Aliev; U.S.S.R. | A. Aliev; U.S.S.R. | A. Aliev; U.S.S.R. |
| Bantamweight | M. Dagistanli; Turk. | H. Akbas; Turk. | H. Akbas; Turk. | M. Safetoor; Iran | H. Akbas; Turk. |
| Featherweight | S. Sasahara; Jap. | M. Dagistanli; Turk. | M. Dagistanli; Turk. | V. Rubashvili; U.S.S.R. | O. Watanabe; Jap. |
| Lightweight | L. Tovfighe; Iran | A. Bestaev; U.S.S.R. | V. Siniavskii; U.S.S.R. | M. Sanatcaran; Iran | E. Valtchev; Bulg. |
| Welterweight | I. Baldoadze; U.S.S.R. | B. Wachtany; U.S.S.R. | E. Habibi; Iran | E. Habibi; Iran | E. Habibi; Iran |
| Middleweight | M. Zandi; Iran | N. Sorubi; Iran | G. Skhirtladze; U.S.S.R. | M. Mehdizadeh; Iran | M. Mehdizadeh; Iran |
| Light heavyweight | A. Inglas; U.S.S.R. | S. Petkop; Bulg. | G. Takhti; Iran | G. Takhti; Iran | A. Medved; U.S.S.R. |
| Heavyweight | A. Mekokishvili; U.S.S.R. | H. Kaplan; Turk. | L. Akhmedov; Bulg. | W. Dietrich; W. Ger. | A. Ivanitski; U.S.S.R. |

| Event | 1963 Sofia, Bulg. |
|---|---|
| Flyweight | Y. Cemal; Turk. |
| Bantamweight | A. Ibragimov; U.S.S.R. |
| Featherweight | O. Watanabe; Jap. |
| Lightweight | I. Horiuchi; Jap. |
| Welterweight | G. Sagaradze; U.S.S.R. |
| Middleweight | P. Gardjev; Bulg. |
| Light heavyweight | A. Medved; U.S.S.R. |
| Heavyweight | A. Ivanitski; U.S.S.R. |

| Event | 1965 Manchester, U.K. |
|---|---|
| Flyweight | Y. Yoshida; Jap. |
| Bantamweight | T. Furkuda; Jap. |
| Featherweight | M. Saifpour-Sodabadi; Iran |
| Lightweight | A. Movahed; Iran |
| Welterweight | G. Sagaradze; U.S.S.R. |
| Middleweight | M. Mehdizadeh; Iran |
| Light heavyweight | A. Ayik; Turk. |
| Heavyweight | A. Ivanitski; U.S.S.R. |

| Event | 1966 Toledo, U.S. |
|---|---|
| Flyweight | S. Jang Chang; S. Kor. |
| Bantamweight | A. Aliev; U.S.S.R. |
| Featherweight | A. Kaneko; Jap. |
| Lightweight | A. Movahed; Iran |
| Welterweight | A. Mahmut; Turk. |
| Middleweight | P. Gardjev; Bulg. |
| Light heavyweight | A. Medved; U.S.S.R. |
| Heavyweight | A. Ivanitski; U.S.S.R. |

| Event | 1967 New Delhi, India |
|---|---|
| Flyweight | S. Nakata; Jap. |
| Bantamweight | A. Aliev; U.S.S.R. |
| Featherweight | A. Kaneko; Jap. |
| Lightweight | A. Mohaved; Iran |
| Welterweight | D. Robin; Fr. |
| Middleweight | B. Gurevich; U.S.S.R. |
| Light heavyweight | A. Ayik; Turk. |
| Heavyweight | A. Medved; U.S.S.R. |

| Event | 1969 Mar del Plata, Arg. |
|---|---|
| Flyweight | R. Sanders; U.S. |
| Bantamweight | T. Tanaki; Jap. |
| Featherweight | S. Abdulbekov; U.S.S.R. |
| Lightweight | A. Mohaved; Iran |
| Welterweight | Z. Berishavili; U.S.S.R. |
| Middleweight | F. Fozzard; U.S. |
| Light heavyweight | B. Gurevich; U.S.S.R. |
| Heavyweight | C. Lomidze; U.S.S.R. |
| Superheavyweight | A. Medved; U.S.S.R. |

For Olympic class winners *see* table in the article OLYMPIC GAMES.

A. IVANITSKI, LEFT (U.S.S.R.), WORLD FREESTYLE HEAVYWEIGHT WRESTLING CHAMPION IN 1966, AND A. MEDVED (U.S.S.R.), WINNER OF THE SAME EVENT IN 1967, IN A PRACTICE BOUT BEFORE THE 1966 CHAMPIONSHIPS IN TOLEDO, U.S.

TASS FROM SOVFOTO

## YACHTING

**America's Cup Races.** The America's Cup, open to challenge since 1870, was originally presented by the Royal Yacht Squadron for the 1851 race around the Isle of Wight, U.K.

| Year | Winning yacht | Owner | Losing yacht | Owner |
|---|---|---|---|---|
| 1851 | "America" (U.S.) | J. C. Stevens | — | — |
| 1870 | "Magic" (U.S.) | F. Osgood | "Cambria" (U.K.) | J. Ashbury |
| 1871 | "Columbia"<br>"Sappho" (U.S.) | F. Osgood<br>W. P. Douglas | "Livonia" (U.K.) | J. Ashbury |
| 1876 | "Madeleine" (U.S.) | J. Dickerson | "Countess of Dufferin" (Can.) | G. Gifford |
| 1881 | "Mischief" (U.S.) | J. Busk | "Atalanta" (Can.) | A. Cuthbert |
| 1885 | "Puritan" (U.S.) | J. Forbes | "Genesta" (U.K.) | Sir R. Sutton |
| 1886 | "Mayflower" (U.S.) | C. J. Paine | "Galatea" (U.K.) | W. Henn |
| 1887 | "Volunteer" (U.S.) | C. J. Paine | "Thistle" (U.K.) | J. Bell |
| 1893 | "Vigilant" (U.S.) | C. Iselin and syndicate | "Valkyrie II" (U.K.) | Lord Dunraven |
| 1895 | "Defender" (U.S.) | C. Iselin and syndicate | "Valkyrie III" (U.K.) | Lord Dunraven |
| 1899 | "Columbia" (U.S.) | C. Iselin and syndicate | "Shamrock" (U.K.) | Sir T. Lipton |
| 1901 | "Columbia" (U.S.) | J. P. Morgan | "Shamrock II" (U.K.) | Sir T. Lipton |
| 1903 | "Reliance" (U.S.) | C. Iselin and syndicate | "Shamrock III" (U.K.) | Sir T. Lipton |
| 1920 | "Resolute" (U.S.) | C. Vanderbilt and syndicate | "Shamrock IV" (U.K.) | Sir T. Lipton |
| 1930 | "Enterprise"* (U.S.) | H. Vanderbilt and syndicate | "Shamrock V" (U.K.) | Sir T. Lipton |
| 1934 | "Rainbow"* (U.S.) | H. Vanderbilt and syndicate | "Endeavour" (U.K.) | T. Sopwith |
| 1937 | "Ranger"* (U.S.) | H. Vanderbilt | "Endeavour II" (U.K.) | T. Sopwith |
| 1958 | "Columbia"† (U.S.) | H. Sears and syndicate | "Sceptre"† (U.K.) | H. Goodson and syndicate |
| 1962 | "Weatherly"† (U.S.) | H. Mercer and syndicate | "Gretel"† (Austr.) | Sir F. Packer and syndicate |
| 1964 | "Constellation"† (U.S.) | NYYC syndicate | "Sovereign"† (U.K.) | J. A. Boyden |
| 1967 | "Intrepid"† (U.S.) | NYYC syndicate | "Dame Pattie"† (Austr.) | Royal Sydney Yacht Squadron |
| 1970 | "Intrepid"† (U.S.) | NYYC syndicate | "Gretel II"† (Austr.) | Royal Sydney Yacht Squadron |

*J-class yacht. †12-metre yacht.

RICHARD MEEK FOR "SPORTS ILLUSTRATED," © TIME INC.
"GRETEL" (AUSTR.), FOREGROUND, AND "WEATHERLY" (U.S.) IN 1962 RACE FOR THE AMERICA'S CUP, WON BY "WEATHERLY"

WIDE WORLD
"RANGER" (U.S.), RIGHT, ON FINAL LEG PASSES "ENDEAVOUR II" (U.K.) IN 1937 COMPETITION FOR AMERICA'S CUP

BEKEN & SON
"CLARION OF WIGHT," 1963 WINNER OF THE FASTNET CUP, SHOWN DURING THE RACE FROM PLYMOUTH, ENG., TO FASTNET ROCK AND RETURN

## OCEAN RACING

**The Bermuda Race.** This was originally, in 1906–10, an annual race between Gravesend Bay, N.Y. (Marblehead, Mass., in 1908), and Bermuda. Seven races were held 1923–34. Since 1936 it has been raced biennially from Newport, R.I., over a 635 mi. course.

| Year | Winning yacht | Owner | Type |
|---|---|---|---|
| 1936 | "Kirawan" | R. P. Baruch | 53-ft. sloop |
| 1938 | "Baruna" | H. C. Taylor | 72-ft. yawl |
| 1940–44* | | | |
| 1946 | "Gesture" | A. H. Fuller | 57-ft. sloop |
| 1948 | "Baruna" | H. C. Taylor | |
| 1950 | "Argyll" | W. T. Moore | 57-ft. yawl |
| 1952 | "Carina" | R. S. Nye | 46-ft. yawl |
| 1954 | "Malay" | D. D. Strohmeier | 39½-ft. yawl |
| 1956 | "Finisterre" | C. Mitchell | 39-ft. yawl |
| 1958 | "Finisterre" | C. Mitchell | 39-ft. yawl |
| 1960 | "Finisterre" | C. Mitchell | 39-ft. yawl |
| 1962 | "Nina" | D. C. Fales | 59-ft. schooner |
| 1964 | "Burgoo" | M. Ernstof | 38-ft. sloop |
| 1966 | "Thunderbird" | T. V. Learson | 40-ft. sloop |
| 1968 | "Robin" | T. Hood | 51½-ft. yawl |

*No competition.

**The Transpacific Race.** This race was inaugurated in 1906 over 2,225 mi. between San Pedro, Calif., and Diamond Head, Oahu, Hawaii. At first held at irregular intervals, in 1939 it was made biennial, alternating with the Bermuda race. The event was resumed after World War II with the 15th race in 1947.

| Year | Winning yacht | Owner |
|---|---|---|
| 1947* | "Dolphin" | F. Morgan |
| 1949* | "Kitten" | F. W. Lyon |
| 1951* | "Sea Witch" | A. L. McCormick |
| 1953† | "Staghound" | I. P. Fulmor |
| 1955† | "Staghound" | I. P. Fulmor |
| 1956‡ | "Jada" | W. Sturgis |
| 1957§ | "Legend" | C. Ullman |
| 1959† | "Nalu II" | P. Grant |
| 1961† | "Nam Sang" | A. B. Robbs, Jr. |
| 1963† | "Islander" | T. Corkett |
| 1965* | "Psyche" | D. Salisbury |
| 1967† | "Holiday Too" | R. Allan |
| 1969* | "Argonaut" | J. Andron |

*San Pedro, Calif., to Diamond Head Light.
†Los Angeles, Calif., to Diamond Head Light.
‡This off-year race was sailed from Los Angeles to Tahiti, 3,671 mi.
§San Francisco, Calif., to Diamond Head Light.

**The Fastnet Cup.** The premier event of the Royal Ocean Racing Club is the Fastnet Race, held annually from 1925 to 1930 and biennially from 1931, from Plymouth to Fastnet Rock off southwestern Ireland and return.

| Year | Winning yacht | Owner; Country |
|---|---|---|
| 1925 | "Jolie Brise" | E. G. Martin; U.K. |
| 1926 | "Ilex" | Royal Engineers Yacht Club; U.K. |
| 1927 | "Tally Ho!" | Lord Stalbridge; U.K. |
| 1928 | "Niña" | P. Hammond; U.S. |
| 1929 | "Jolie Brise" | R. Somerset; U.K. |
| 1930 | "Jolie Brise" | R. Somerset; U.K. |
| 1931 | "Dorade" | R. Stephens; U.S. |
| 1933 | "Dorade" | R. and O. Stephens; U.S. |
| 1935 | "Stormy Weather" | P. le Boutillier; U.S. |
| 1937 | "Zeearend" | C. Bruynzeel; Neth. |
| 1939 | "Bloodhound" | I. Bell; U.K. |
| 1941–45* | | |
| 1947 | "Myth of Malham" | J. Illingworth; U.K. |
| 1949 | "Myth of Malham" | J. Illingworth; U.K. |
| 1951 | "Yeoman" | O. A. Aisher; U.K. |
| 1953 | "Favona" | Sir M. Newton; U.K. |
| 1955 | "Carina" | R. S. Nye; U.S. |
| 1957 | "Carina" | R. S. Nye; U.S. |
| 1959 | "Anitra" | S. Hansen; Swed. |
| 1961 | "Zwerver" | W. N. H. van der Vorm; Neth. |
| 1963 | "Clarion of Wight" | D. J. Boyer and D. Miller; U.K. |
| 1965 | "Rabbit" | R. E. Carter; U.S. |
| 1967 | "Pen Duick III" | E. Tabarly; Fr. |
| 1969 | "Red Rooster" | R. Carter; U.S. |

*No competition.

For Olympic class winners *see* table in the article OLYMPIC GAMES.

**SPORTS (ARTICLES ON).** A universal form of recreation, sports are also one of the great expressions of the aspiration to excel. The victories of athletes were sung by the great poets of classical Greece. Many of *Encyclopædia Britannica's* articles on sports discuss their development in the context of social history. Among the articles in this group are BASEBALL; BOWLING; BOXING; CRICKET; FOOTBALL; GOLF; and WRESTLING.

For records of all major sports *see* SPORTING RECORD. TRACK AND FIELD SPORTS is supplemented by articles on individual events, such as DISCUS THROWING; POLE VAULTING; SHOT-PUT; etc. The history, development and present status of the major winter sports are covered in separate articles such as BOBSLEDDING; CURLING; ICE HOCKEY; and SKIING.

Some of the aquatic sports articles are BOATING; CANOE; MOTORBOAT; ROWING; SKIN DIVING; SWIMMING; WATER POLO.

Among the articles dealing with racing sports are AUTOMOBILE RACING; CYCLING; HORSE RACING AND BREEDING; MOTORCYCLING; RUNNING; and WALKING.

Among the court games to which articles are devoted are BADMINTON; DECK TENNIS; RACKETS; and TENNIS. Additional articles on games played with a ball include BASKETBALL; FIVES; HANDBALL; JAI ALAI; LACROSSE; ROUNDERS.

A general view of the sports that have been popular among or adapted to the needs of children is given in CHILDREN'S GAMES AND SPORTS.

In some sports of almost universal interest, man's strength and resourcefulness are matched against other forms of life or against forces of nature. Articles dealing with these activities include FISHING; HUNTING; and MOUNTAINEERING. TOURNAMENT deals with the great sport of medieval chivalry. Sports of antiquity that are still practised are treated in ARCHERY; FALCONRY; and FENCING.

GAMES, CLASSICAL, describes the athletic festivals that played an important part in the life of ancient Greece and Rome. Articles dealing with modern sports festivals include BRITISH COMMONWEALTH GAMES; HIGHLAND GAMES; OLYMPIC GAMES; and PAN-AMERICAN GAMES.

AMATEUR traces the ancient distinction between the amateur and professional and describes the contemporary rules governing amateur standing. GYMNASTICS discusses the evolution of the art, the types of exercises, and the skills involved. GYMNASIUM deals with types of equipment. The function of gymnastics in educational programs is discussed in PHYSICAL EDUCATION.

For articles on nonathletic games, such as cards and board games, *see* GAMES (ARTICLES ON).

**SPOTSYLVANIA,** a county in Virginia, U.S., midway between Washington, D.C., and Richmond, Va.; the scene of four major battles during the American Civil War (*q.v.*). At Fredericksburg (Dec. 13, 1862) and Chancellorsville (May 1–3, 1863) Confederate Gen. R. E. Lee inflicted severe defeats on Union armies attempting to move on Richmond. The Wilderness (May 5–6, 1864) and Spotsylvania Courthouse (May 9–20, 1864) were costly but indecisive battles in Union Gen. U. S. Grant's successful campaign of that year. (*See* also CHANCELLORSVILLE; FREDERICKSBURG.)

The population of the county in 1960 was 13,819; its area is 409 sq.mi. About half of the area is devoted to agriculture, much of it dairy farming. Manufacturing, mainly of lumber and lumber products, is the principal employer of the labour force. First settled in the late 17th century, the county was formed in 1720 and named for Alexander Spotswood, then governor of Virginia. (M. BR.)

**SPOTTED FEVER:** *see* ROCKY MOUNTAIN SPOTTED FEVER AND OTHER SPOTTED FEVERS

**SPRAYS AND DUSTS IN AGRICULTURE.** Spraying, dusting, and fumigating are the standard methods of applying pest control chemicals and other compounds that are of increasing importance in agriculture. In spraying, the chemicals to be applied are dissolved or suspended in water, or less commonly in an oil-based carrier. The mixture is then applied as a fine mist to plants, animals, soils, or products to be treated. As an alternative method, dry, finely powdered chemicals may be mixed with an inert carrier and applied with some type of blower. Dry granular materials also have been used instead of dusts or sprays where adequate coverage can be obtained. In fumigation, gases or the vapours of volatile compounds are held in contact with the materials to be treated—grain in a tight bin, for example.

The development of more and more effective sprays and dusts and their increasingly widespread use in agriculture have prompted concern among biologists and others that man may disrupt nature and endanger his food supply and his own health (*see* also POLLUTION, ENVIRONMENTAL: *Water Pollution: Pollutants: Plant Nutrients* and *Organic Pesticides*). New chemicals and new precautions have greatly reduced these dangers. At the same time experience has shown that some of the widely feared, older chemicals are essentially nontoxic to man.

Sprays and dusts are used to control insects, mites, and fungous and bacterial diseases of plants; insects, such as lice and flies, on animals; and weeds, by means of chemical weed killers or herbicides. Sprays and dusts may also be used for such special purposes as applying mineral fertilizers, increasing or decreasing fruit set, delaying the dropping of nearly mature fruits, and for defoliation or vine killing to facilitate the harvest of such plants as cotton or potatoes.

Sprays have advantages over dusts in their ability to adhere to and spread over treated surfaces. Spreading-sticking agents or surfactants are commonly added to spray mixtures to increase adhesion and wetting of waxy surfaces. These wetting agents decrease the tendency of water to collect in drops and permit the chemical solution to spread over a leaf in a very thin film, bringing the spray chemical into maximum contact with the fungi, bacteria, insects, or mites to be controlled. After about 1948 there was a rapid increase in the use of air sprayers or "wet dusting." The use of a concentrated spray distributed in the airstream from a powerful fan combines many of the advantages of both spraying and dusting.

Fumigation (*q.v.*) may be used to control insects and some diseases in stored products or to control insects such as wireworms and grubs, nematodes, and sometimes fungi and weeds in soil. The chemical may be applied as a gas or as a volatile liquid. Partial fumigation of the soil may be accomplished by applying the chemical in a spray or granular material and immediately working it into the soil. For better pest control (*q.v.*) on small areas like seedbeds the treated soil is covered with a gastight, plastic cover.

**Fungicidal Treatments.**—The practice of spraying plants to control plant diseases (*q.v.*) was discovered accidentally near Bordeaux, France, in the 19th century when a copper-lime mixture applied to grapes near a road to reduce pilfering was observed to control downy mildew, a serious disease of the grape plant. This spray, soon known as Bordeaux mixture, long remained a standard fungicide. From about 1946 organic materials largely replaced the older copper and sulfur dusts and sprays. Among the dozens of organic fungicides, some of the most useful are: captan (N-trichloromethylthio-4-cyclohexene-1,2-dicarboximide), used alone or in multipurpose mixtures, to treat seeds and bulbs and as a spray or dust on fruits, vegetables, turf, and ornamentals for control of a wide range of fungous diseases; ferbam (ferric dimethyldithiocarbamate), used in sprays and dusts on fruits and ornamentals; zineb (zinc ethylenebis-dithiocarbamate) and maneb (manganese ethylenebis-dithiocarbamate), multipurpose fungicides used alone and in mixtures to control foliage and fruit diseases of vegetables and ornamentals; and Daconil 2787 (tetrachloroisophthalonitrile), for broad-spectrum use on turf, flowers, vegetables, and certain fruits. These materials, as well as PCNB (pentachloronitrobenzene) and Dexon (p-dimethylamino benzenediazo sodium sulfonate), are also applied alone or in various combinations to soil—as dusts or soil drenches—to control seed decay and damping-off of seedling plants, and also crown and root rots of vegetables, ornamentals, turf, and fruits. In general, these compounds control more diseases under more conditions and are less toxic to treated plants than the older copper and sulfur materials. Streptomycin, an antibiotic, controls several bacterial plant diseases. Another antibiotic, Acti-dione (cycloheximide), is antifungal and controls various rusts, powdery mildews, and turf diseases.

**Insecticidal Treatments.**—Older insecticides were primarily arsenic compounds like Paris green, lead and calcium arsenates for chewing insects, nicotine for soft-bodied, sucking insects, and oil and lime-sulfur for scale insects. Tobacco powders and infusions were used in Europe before 1800 and pyrethrum powders in Asia Minor at an unknown early date. Paris green (copper acetoarsenite) was used successfully against the potato beetle in Illinois in 1868 and against major apple insects a few years later. Calcium arsenate was the chief insecticide used on cotton from 1920 to 1945.

The compound popularly known as DDT (dichlorodiphenyl-trichloroethane) was among the first of a new group of organic insecticides that includes aldrin (hexachloro-hexahydro-endo, exo-dimethanonaphthalene), lindane (gamma isomer of benzene hexachloride), methoxychlor (trichloro-methoxyphenylethane), parathion (diethylnitrophenyl phosphorothioate), carboryl (1 naphthyl-N-methylcarbamate), Naled (1,2-dibromo-2,2-dichloroethyl dimethyl phosphate), and many others. Most of these are chlorinated hydrocarbons. A wide choice of insecticides is valuable because of the ability of insects to develop resistance to many of these compounds when they are used repeatedly.

The organic phosphorus compounds, such as parathion, are among the most effective poisons, but are exceedingly dangerous to operating personnel unless strict precautions are observed. Malathion (ethoxy-carbonyl-ethyl-dimethyl phosphorodithioate) shows much of the effectiveness of parathion and is much safer to use. In addition to their high toxicity, these organic phosphorus compounds decompose quickly after use and can be applied safely to food crops a few days to a week before harvest.

As a rule, organic fungicides and insecticides are sold as wettable powders for sprays and dusts, and insecticides in emulsifiable, concentrated solutions. (*See* also ENTOMOLOGY: *Agricultural and Forest Entomology;* PEST CONTROL: *Chemical Control*).

**Herbicidal Treatments.**—Weed-killing chemicals are normally applied as sprays, or as dry, granular formulations of compounds that act through the soil. Their use is comparatively recent, although ferrous sulfate was used to control mustard in grain fields before 1900; sodium chlorate was used in increasing volume as a nonselective herbicide after 1905; and kerosene, a medium boiling point petroleum fraction, was used to control dandelions in lawns in the 1930s. The simultaneous discovery of 2,4-D (2,4-dichlorophenoxyacetic acid) in the United States and of MCPA (2-methyl-4-chlorophenoxyacetic acid) in England during World War II, however, marked the beginning of the widespread use of herbicidal chemicals. These compounds are essentially nontoxic to grains and grasses at rates that kill most broadleaved weeds. (*See* also WEED: *Control of Weeds.*)

Herbicides may be classed as selective or sterilant. Ferrous sulfate is a selective herbicide for mustard in grain because it adheres to the leaves of the mustard but not to those of the grain. The compound 2,4-D is selective because of its greater toxicity for most broadleaved plants than for grasses, including grains. Trichloroacetic acid (TCA) is selectively toxic to grasses. Sodium chlorate is a general toxin, used to eradicate noxious perennial weeds at the cost of temporary soil sterility or to control all vegetation on railway roadbeds and similar areas. Chlorate is absorbed through the roots from the soil and should be applied so that rainfall or irrigation will carry it into the root zone. Rates of application vary from one or two to ten or twelve pounds per square rod.

MCPA and 2,4-D may be translocated downward through the roots of perennial weeds. Rates, in contrast to those for chlorate, are commonly one-half to two pounds an acre, applied in a spray. The compound 2,4,5-T, 2,4-D with an extra chlorine in the 5-position, is slower in action and more effectively translocated than 2,4-D. It is preferred for controlling brush and some perennials. Great care is necessary when using most of these compounds near susceptible plants, as drifting spray or even the fumes may cause injury.

The use of a special petroleum fraction known as Stoddard solvent in weeding carrots and other members of the parsley family is a striking example of differential herbicidal action. These plants are resistant, while most others are killed by the spray. Other oils are used for various purposes. Moderately heavy oils high in aromatic compounds are useful on such surfaces as ditch banks and roadbeds.

The herbicide picture changed rapidly after the late 1950s. New chemicals were produced in numbers, and 2,4-D and MCPA were essentially the only older herbicides that remained important. These chemicals remained the general choice for controlling broad-leaved weeds in grains or grasses. Among the newer compounds, Atrazine (2-chloro-4-ethylamino-6-isopropylamino-1,3,5-triazine) is especially used for preemergence control of broadleaved and grassy weeds in corn (maize), sorghum, sugarcane, pineapple, and orchards. It persists in the soil for a year or more, and is not used the year preceding small grains, soybeans, sugar beets, tobacco, and many vegetable crops. Amiben (3-amino-2,5-dichlorobenzoic acid) replaces Atrazine as a preemergence treatment on, or the year before, a sensitive crop. Ramrod (2-chloro-N-isopropylacetanilide) is used as a preemergence treatment for grasses, nut sedge, and certain broadleaved weeds. Propanil (3-4-dichloropropionanilide) is an important postemergence spray for grasses and broadleaved weeds in rice. Picloram (Tordon) (4-amino-3,5,6-trichloropicolinic acid) is used for control of brush and perennial broadleaved weeds, particularly in range or pastures.

**Miscellaneous Treatments.**—Soluble fertilizer materials may be applied in sprays, either to the soil when accurate distribution of small quantities is required, or to the leaves of the plants. Sprays are used extensively to apply iron, zinc, or manganese to pineapple leaves and less extensively to supply nitrogen—in the form of urea—to apple trees. Various defoliant sprays and dusts are used to eliminate the leaves from cotton and some other plants before machine harvesting. A cotton defoliant must cause the leaves to drop naturally rather than kill them, since the crumbled dead leaves reduce the grade of the lint. Cyanide dusts and dilute chlorate sprays are among the more successful treatments.

Toxic compounds like sodium dinitro-*o*-cresylate and hormone-type sprays like naphthaleneacetic acid have both been used to thin fruits when excessive crops are set. Dinitro kills a percentage of the young fruit and injures the foliage more or less extensively. Hormones cause embryo abortion in young fruits and accentuate natural drop. The same hormone compound may be used later to reduce preharvest drop of nearly mature fruit. Naphthaleneacetic compounds, dilute 2,4-D, or other hormone-type materials may be used to increase fruit set in tomatoes or beans, and to prevent sprouting of potatoes, or leaf and berry drop of holly in Christmas decorations. Wax emulsions are sprayed on nursery stock to reduce water loss during shipping and after transplanting. New uses for new chemicals, applied as sprays, dusts, or fumigants, are constantly being developed.

BIBLIOGRAPHY.—Bulletins on sprays and dusts are generally available from state agricultural experiment stations and the U.S. Department of Agriculture. *See* especially the U.S. Department of Agriculture, "Insects and Diseases of Vegetables in the Home Garden," *Home and Garden Bulletin no. 46* (1955), "Controlling Nematodes in the Home Garden," *Farmers Bulletin no. 2048,* rev. (1958), "Safe Use of Agricultural and Household Pesticides," *Agricultural Handbook no. 321* (Jan. 1967). For more extensive treatments *see* M. C. Shurtleff, *How to Control Plant Diseases—in Home and Garden* (1966); L. P. Reitz, *Biological and Chemical Control of Plant and Animal Pests* (1960); C. L. Metcalf and W. P. Flint, *Destructive and Useful Insects, Their Habits and Control,* 4th ed., rev. by R. L. Metcalf (1962); H. Martin, *The Scientific Principles of Crop Protection,* 5th ed. (1965); E. G. Sharvelle, *The Nature and Uses of Modern Fungicides* (1961); Weed Society of America, *Herbicide Handbook* (1967)—a brief but thorough discussion of more than 100 of the more important herbicides; G. H. Ahlgren, G. C. Klingman, and D. E. Wolf, *Principles of Weed Control* (1952); A. S. Crafts and W. W. Robbins, *Weed Control,* 3rd ed. (1962); A. S. Crafts, *The Chemistry and Mode of Action of Herbicides* (1961). (For the means for the use of sprays and dusts, see FARM MACHINERY: *Chemical Control Methods.*) (W. E. LS.; M. C. SH.)

**SPREE,** a river of Germany about 247 mi. (398 km.) long, of which about 90 mi. are navigable, with a drainage area of 3,900 sq.mi. (10,100 sq.km.). The river rises in the mountains of upper

Lusatia, near the Czechoslovak frontier, and flows north past Bautzen, Spremberg, and Cottbus, dividing between the first two towns for a time into two arms. Below Cottbus the river splits into a network of channels, forming the marshy region known as the Spreewald as far as Lübben, then passes Fürstenwalde and Köpenick, and winds through Berlin in several branches to join the Havel (a tributary of the Elbe) at Spandau. The Spree is connected with neighbouring rivers by canals. The chief of these is the Oder-Spree Canal, which runs southeast from Berlin.

The Spreewald is a dominantly forested area, about 37 mi. (60 km.) long and up to 5 mi. (7 km.) wide; forest clearance and drainage of the bogs were encouraged by Frederick II the Great. Much of the land is now cultivated (market gardening). Many towns and villages are accessible only by boat in summer and skis in winter. This is an area of survival of Slav (Wendish) dialects, customs, and folk dress. *See* LUSATIA. (R. E. DI.)

**SPRING** is, in almost all cases, the natural overflow or point of escape from some underground reservoir of water. Its classification may be either according to the geological conditions governing the point of location or according to the chemical composition of its waters. When considerable chemical impurity is present, it is usually termed a "mineral spring."

The rocks that constitute the crust of the earth are either permeable or impermeable to water. During most seasons of the year, in temperate climates, a certain amount of rainfall soaks into any crust formed of permeable strata; the part absorbed may be the complete rainfall during winter months, when the air is saturated with moisture, or may fall to near zero during a dry summer, when all the rainfall is returned to the air as evaporation from the surface. That portion of the rainfall that soaks down below the level of plant roots goes to replenish the underground reservoir. The shape of the reservoir varies indefinitely, according to the geological structure of the area; but it is only the shape of its water surface that concerns springs. This surface, known as the water table, divides the fully saturated rocks from those that only hold moisture in their minute pores.

In an area of completely permeable rocks the springs issue at or near the valley bottoms; when, however, the district is made of alternating permeable and impermeable beds, each impermeable bed holds up water on its surface. If the strata are horizontal, small springs may be found all round the outcrops; but if they are tilted or folded, the flow of the underground water will be toward the lowest point on the base of the permeable water-bearing bed. At this point the main spring for that local reservoir will be located.

In strata that are, in the main, impermeable but somewhat brittle, the presence of joints and cracks is of prime importance in determining the direction and amount of flow in the underground waters. In jointed rocks the rainwater may sink to great depths down one set of joints and rise again along a second, issuing at the surface as a warm or thermal spring; this is the probable cause of the hot springs at Bath. When a permeable bed and an impermeable one are brought into juxtaposition through faulting, the flow of water in the permeable one is checked; but since faulting frequently shatters the rock, it affords a plane of weakness along which the water will tend to flow. If the water is flowing under pressure due to an overlying impermeable cover, it may reach the surface as an artesian spring. The water of artesian springs sometimes carries small particles of solid matter in suspension, as well as salts in solution. The solid particles are dropped at the point of exit of the spring and may be cemented by the salts deposited from solution. When this takes place, a mound is built up, from the summit of which the spring issues. Hence the "mound springs," such as are seen at their best in the great artesian basin of Australia.

Some of the largest springs issue from thick beds of massive limestone. This type of rock is usually well jointed, and, being soluble in rainwater, the joints and marked bedding planes become enlarged by solution, and the whole of the rainfall is absorbed in the mass of the rock and flows underground to issue as large springs. Frequently these springs yield a somewhat hard water of otherwise great purity.

**Mineral Springs.**—All springs containing noticeable quantities of salts in solution, other than the carbonate and sulfate of lime, are known by this name. The commonest minerals found are common salt, giving rise to "bitter springs"; and iron, sulfur, magnesia, etc., giving medicinal waters.

**Thermal Springs.**—The springs coming under this heading are derived from two sources. Firstly, meteoric waters (those derived from the atmosphere of the earth), which have penetrated down to considerable depths and rise again along well-defined fissures issuing as springs at the surface but with the temperature of the rocks from which they have come; and, secondly, volcanic waters, either in the form of geysers or hot springs (*see* VOLCANO); in these the water may be either meteoric or in part, at any rate, juvenile (water issuing at the surface for the first time). Most of these waters contain mineral substance in solution, which is deposited on cooling and forms basins and terraces of sinter, such as the famous pink and white terraces of New Zealand.

*See* also GROUND WATER. (W. B. R. K.)

**SPRINGFIELD,** the capital city of Illinois, U.S., and the seat of Sangamon county near the Sangamon river, 99 mi. N.E. of St. Louis, Mo., and 185 mi. S.W. of Chicago, Ill. In the winter of 1818–19 several adventurous settlers located in the area, although John Kelly is acknowledged to be the first to build a cabin (at the northwest corner of Second and Jefferson streets) where the city now stands. Others, generally from North Carolina, Virginia and Kentucky, built near this cabin. In 1821 Sangamon county was created and the little settlement was named temporary county seat; the following year a post office was put into operation. The village was confirmed as county seat in 1825 and incorporated in 1832, and in 1837, with a population of less than 3,000, it was selected as the capital of Illinois.

Those most responsible for the legislative transfer of the capital from Vandalia to Springfield were the Sangamon county representatives, the "long nine" (so called because their aggregate height was 54 ft.). Their leader was young Abraham Lincoln, who came to Springfield from the rude village of New Salem (25 mi. N.W. of Springfield) on April 15, 1837, and lived there until he left for Washington, D.C., on Feb. 11, 1861, to be inaugurated as president of the U.S. Lincoln and the city matured together and the many places identified with his life attract hundreds of thousands of tourists annually.

The old state capitol building (begun in 1837, completed in 1853), rebuilt in the 1960s as a state shrine, is located in the centre of the business district. There Lincoln served his last term in the legislature, 1840–41, practised before the state supreme court, delivered several of his most notable speeches, including the "House Divided" address, and maintained an office as president elect; and it was there that his body lay in state (May 4, 1865). An unpretentious house at Eighth and Jackson streets, maintained by the state of Illinois as a memorial, is the only home owned by Lincoln. He purchased it for $1,500 in 1844 and in it three of his children were born; the house has been restored and many of the original furnishings are on display.

One and a half miles northwest of the business district is the Lincoln tomb and memorial in Oak Ridge cemetery. The marble burial chamber on the ground floor holds the bodies of Lincoln, his wife Mary and three of their children, Edward Baker, William Wallace and Thomas ("Tad"); their other child, Robert Todd, is buried in Arlington National cemetery. The memorial is 117 ft. tall and is surmounted by a granite shaft. The state of Illinois owns and maintains the structure. The present tomb and memorial is the third erected on this site. The last reconstruction was completed in 1931 with a new interior but without change to the exterior. The First Presbyterian church displays the original pew rented by the Lincoln family. The Wabash railroad passenger station, although converted to freight use, is still standing; there Lincoln delivered his celebrated Farewell Address. The locations of Lincoln's three law offices, the Globe tavern, the place where the First Inaugural was written, and other spots of Lincoln interest are marked with bronze plaques.

In the centre and towering over the Illinois state buildings is the statehouse, the fifth capitol building owned by the state. Begun in 1868 and finished in 1888 at a cost of $4,500,000, this massive limestone structure is in the form of a Latin cross and measures 361 ft. in height (to the top of the flagpole, 405 ft.). Extensive interior renovation was done in 1958. The Centennial building, southeast of the statehouse, erected 1918–23 at a cost of $3,000,000, commemorates the 100th anniversary of Illinois statehood; it houses the state historical library, museum, hall of flags, state library and other state offices. In the historical library is a famous collection of Lincoln letters, documents and memorabilia as well as extensive collections concerning the history of Illinois. Immediately west is the state archives building, the third of its type in the U.S.; completed in 1938 at a cost of $820,000, its unique construction provides superior protection to the official, noncurrent records of the state. Immediately northwest of the archives is the state office building, first occupied in 1955 (cost, $11,500,000); within this modern structure is a post office, a cafeteria and the offices of more than 20 state departments. North of the capitol is the state armoury and office building; completed in 1937 and costing more than $1,000,000, it replaced an armoury destroyed by fire in 1934. The supreme court building, adjacent to the Centennial building, is occupied by the two highest Illinois courts and by the attorney general. The governor's mansion, nearby, was first occupied by Gov. Joel A. Matteson in 1855 and has since been the residence of Illinois governors.

Springfield is a large wholesale and retail centre for a rich agricultural area; the once significant soft coal industry is no longer important to the city's economy. Principal industrial products include electric meters and electronic equipment, tractors, heavy-duty boilers, castings, automotive equipment, miners' lamps, mattresses and shoes, boxes, paints, livestock feeds, soybean oil and meal, and flour and cereal products. City parks total about 1,000 ac. Around Lake Springfield, completed in 1935 to provide water, the city has developed residential and recreational areas. Pop. (1960) city, 83,271; standard metropolitan statistical area (Sangamon county), 146,539. For comparative population figures *see* table in ILLINOIS: *Population.* (C. C. W.)

**SPRINGFIELD,** a city of Massachusetts, U.S., on the east bank of the Connecticut river is the seat of Hampden county and a central city of the Springfield-Chicopee-Holyoke standard metropolitan statistical area (SMSA). This area comprises four cities (Chicopee, Holyoke, Springfield, Westfield) and ten towns (Agawam, East Longmeadow, Hampden, Longmeadow, Ludlow, Monson, Palmer, Southwick, West Springfield, Wilbraham) in Hampden county; one city (Northampton) and four towns (Easthampton, Granby, Hadley, South Hadley) in Hampshire county; one town (Warren) in Worcester county; and one town (Somers) in Tolland county, Conn. Most of these municipalities were part of Springfield when it was incorporated in 1641. Pop. (1960) Springfield, 174,463; Springfield-Chicopee-Holyoke SMSA, 493,999. (For comparative population figures *see* table in MASSACHUSETTS: *Population.*)

Springfield, the financial, commercial, and industrial centre of the area, is the third largest city in Massachusetts. Its population has grown at a fairly consistent pace, the 1960 census figure being two and a half times that of 1900. Its area provided ample room for internal population growth so that the surrounding communities did not start growing at a more rapid pace than the core city until the middle of the 20th century.

The metropolitan area covers much of the Connecticut valley lowland that stretches about 30 mi. N. from the Connecticut border and from the Berkshire foothills in Westfield to the eastern uplands in Wilbraham. The Westfield and the Chicopee rivers, two tributaries of the Connecticut, cut the area east and west.

The region was settled in 1635 by William Pynchon, one of the original patentees of the Massachusetts Bay Colony, and a group from Roxbury, Mass. The patentees moved from what is now Agawam to the east side of the Connecticut river the following year for greater safety from the Indians and they called the community Springfield after Pynchon's home in England. Their leader's autocratic rule ended in 1652 when Pynchon returned to England as a result of the furor caused by his book attacking the Calvinist doctrine of atonement. The settlement was an agricultural and trading community at first; its industrialization was hastened by the building of an arsenal which received congressional endorsement in 1777; by the development of water power, especially in Chicopee and Holyoke, in the early 19th century; and by the arrival of the railroad in 1835.

Machinery, electrical equipment and printed goods are the most important products of the highly diversified economy of Springfield. The U.S. arsenal and armoury, established in 1794, were long important. More than 800,000 of the famous Springfield muskets were made there during the Civil War. It later became the home of the famous Springfield rifle and the Garand rifle and a principal manufactory of small arms for the U.S. army. After the federal armoury was deactivated in 1968, part of it housed a newly established two-year technical institute. The Smith and Wesson revolver factory is located there. G. & C. Merriam company, publishers of Merriam-Webster dictionaries since 1843, has its headquarters in Springfield.

Springfield was incorporated as a city in 1852. Long unique in Massachusetts for its partisan municipal elections and bicameral city council, the city voted in 1959 to change to a strong-mayor, unicameral-council government with nonpartisan elections. Evidence of city planning and of an active cultural life are seen in the so-called municipal group, consisting of the city hall and the municipal auditorium that houses the city's symphony orchestra, and in a nearby quadrangle made up of art and natural history museums, a planetarium and a library. Renewed interest in planning in the 1960s resulted in a two-level mall in the central business district, an industrial park and the completion of a large urban renewal project. Springfield college, founded in 1885 by the Young Men's Christian association and now the home of the Naismith Memorial Basketball Hall of Fame, and American International college, established in Lowell in 1885 as the French-Protestant college and moved to Springfield in 1888, are the two major institutions of higher private education in the city. The city's extensive park system consists of 2,000 ac. and includes one of the largest zoos in New England. (GE. G.)

**SPRINGFIELD,** a city of southwestern Missouri, U.S., the county seat of Greene County. Kansas City, 175 mi. NW, is the nearest larger city. Until the end of World War II Springfield was commercially important chiefly as the centre of a fertile agricultural area, as a distribution point for manufactured products and as the seat of the major shops of the St. Louis-San Francisco railroad. Its rapid growth after that time is attributable mainly to the expansion westward of eastern manufacturing firms. Springfield's population in 1960 was 95,865; that of its standard metropolitan statistical area (Greene County) was 126,276. (For comparative population figures *see* table in MISSOURI: *Population.*)

Springfield was first settled in 1829 by families from Tennessee and Kentucky. The Civil War split friends and families; the merchants and professional men, largely from the southern lowlands, included many slaveowners, while the settlers with rural backgrounds, mainly from the mountain regions, sympathized with the North. Springfield became a strategic point in the war and a battle was fought at Wilson's Creek, 10 mi. from the city. In a federal cemetery Confederate and Union graves lie side by side.

There are three liberal arts colleges in the city. Drury (Congregational) was established in 1873, Southwest Missouri State began as a teachers' college in 1905 and Evangel (Assemblies of God) was established in 1953. In addition, there are two college-level religious-training institutions—Central Bible Institute (Assemblies of God) and Baptist Bible College.

Besides farm products—chiefly meat, livestock, dairy products, small fruits, eggs and poultry—Springfield produces paper cups, machine belts, portable typewriters, flooring, furniture, truck trailers and men's clothing. Institutions include a federal prison hospital and the international headquarters of the Assemblies of God. Springfield is also the seat of a Roman Catholic diocese.

Within a 50-mi. radius from Springfield are Ozarks resort areas, with stretches of scenic beauty in between, and the city is a popular stopover for tourists. It is noted for its pleasant tree-lined streets and attractive residential areas. Springfield adopted the council-manager form of government in 1953. (E. R. ST.)

**SPRINGFIELD,** a city of Ohio, U.S., 45 mi. W of Columbus and 82 mi. N of Cincinnati; the county seat of Clark county. Scattered settlements had been made in this region before James Demint built his log cabin on Lagonda (now Buck) creek in 1799. Two years later a townsite was surveyed on the river bottomlands opposite; the settlement is said to have been named Springfield because of spring water coming down the cliffs bordering the valley. The rapid influx of settlers led the Ohio legislature in 1818 to establish Clark county with Springfield as the county seat. In 1850 it was made a city, its population at that time being 5,108. The population of Springfield in 1960 was 82,723 and that of its standard metropolitan statistical area (Clark county) was 131,440; for comparative population figures *see* table in OHIO: *Population.*

The economic life of the residents rests on the processing of the products of the surrounding farms and the output of over 200 manufacturing establishments. A wide variety of industrial products ensures business stability and well-paid labour.

Educational facilities include Wittenberg University, a Lutheran institution chartered in 1845, Roman Catholic and public schools. The Warder Public library serves all of Clark county. Springfield supports a symphony orchestra. City parks cover over 600 ac.

Ten miles west of Springfield lies the Wright-Patterson air force research and development base, a national centre for defense activity. Many Springfield residents find employment there.

(B. H. P.)

**SPRINGS,** a town of the Transvaal, in South Africa, lies 28 mi. E of Johannesburg. Pop. (1960) 137,253, of whom 36,935 were European, 97,406 Bantu, 1,375 Asian, and 1,537 Coloured. The town has been a municipality since 1904 and the seat of a magistracy since 1909. Its life began with the opening of the first coal mine in 1885. In 1908 the mining of gold started at Geduld mine, and the closing in 1913 of the last colliery left gold mining as the sole industry. During the next 25 years Springs became the most highly concentrated gold-field in the world. Two of the mines also yield uranium, and an extraction plant was officially opened in 1953. Secondary industry has gradually been attracted to the town, and factories include those for the making of paper, glass, machine tools, alloy steels, electrical goods, and bicycles. Educational training facilities include a branch of the Witwatersrand Technical College and a government miners' training school. Springs has rail and road communication with other important centres, including Durban (410 mi.) and Lourenço Marques (393 mi.); Johannesburg is linked by electric railway. Jan Smuts Airport, the principal air terminal of the country, is 18 mi. from Springs by road.

**SPRINGTAIL,** any one of a group of small (minute to about $\frac{1}{5}$ in.), primitive, wingless insects of uncertain origin and relationship, so called because many species possess appendages under the abdomen which can be forced down and back, catapulting the insects into the air. They are widely distributed, ranging from the Antarctic to the Arctic, and are abundant, though often unobserved, in moist plant debris. Certain springtails known as snow fleas are active at near-freezing temperatures and may appear in large numbers on snow surfaces. Although they usually feed on decaying vegetable material or fungi, they occasionally attack living plants, and some species are predatory or feed on animal material. Young, which hatch from spherical eggs, closely resemble the adults.

The lucerne flea causes crop injury in Australia and the garden springtail attacks many cultivated plants in North America. Occasionally springtails are pests of mushrooms, and two species are nuisances in houses. Springtails belong to the order Collembola, which is separated into two suborders, one in which the body is elongate with discrete abdominal segments, the other in which the body is oval or globular, most of the abdominal segments having united with the thorax. *See* also INSECT. (H. B. M.)

**SPRUCE,** an important genus (*Picea*) of evergreen trees in the pine family (Pinaceae), including about 40 species native to the temperate and cold regions of the northern hemisphere. They are pyramidal trees with whorled branches; thin, scaly bark; linear, spirally arranged leaves, each jointed near the stem on a separate woody base; and ovoid to cylindrical pendent cones. The spruces are distinguished from the pines by solitary instead of fascicled leaves, which leave peg-like projections on the twig when they fall, and from firs in having pendent, persistent-scaled, instead of upright, deciduous-scaled cones. Spruce trees are subject to severe damage from pests and fire.

Seven species of spruce occur in the United States and Canada, 1 in Mexico, 2 in Europe, and 29 in Asia. North American spruces have light, soft, compact, straight-grained wood that is strong, easy to work, and low in resin content. The wood is resonant and used extensively for sounding boards in pianos and the bodies of violins. It is used also for construction, boats, oars, boxes, food containers, barrels and casks, and many other products requiring light, strong, elastic wood. Its chief use has been for pulpwood, 3,000,000,000 to 4,000,000,000 bd.ft. of spruce timber going into pulpwood annually, with cutting exceeding natural replacement.

The red spruce (*P. rubens*) is important from Nova Scotia to New York and through the Appalachians to Georgia. Most trees attain a height of 60 to 100 ft. and diameters to 24 in., but specimens 4 ft. in diameter and 120 ft. tall have occurred. The boles are slenderly cylindrical and rise from shallow, widely spreading root systems. Vigorous trees begin to produce seed when 30 to 40 years old, mature in about 100 years, and may live 300 to 400 years.

Black spruce (*P. mariana*) and white spruce (*P. glauca*) have almost the same range—from Labrador to New York and the Great Lakes, thence across Canada into Alaska, where they reach the arctic tree line. Both are used for pulp; white spruce produces good lumber, and black spruce is the source of spruce gum. White spruce sometimes reaches a height of 120 ft., but usually is 60 to 70 ft. tall and 18 to 24 in. in diameter. It forms extensive pure stands or is mixed with other conifers, aspen, balsam poplar, and birch. The cones of black spruce are purplish, those of white spruce brownish, just prior to maturity.

In the west, Engelmann spruce (*P. engelmanni*), the most important spruce lumber tree, attains a diameter of 18 to 30 in. (exceptionally to 6 ft.) and a height of 100 to 165 ft. It grows best on loamy soils with high moisture content, but matures slowly. Trees 400 to 600 years old have been reported. It produces large crops of seeds at three- to six-year intervals, and the small seeds (average, 135,000 per pound) have a high germination rate, often to 97%. Reproduction by seed is excellent in both humus and mineral soil. Layering sometimes occurs, but trees from such origins usually are stunted. Engelmann spruce ranges from 1,500 to 12,000 ft. in altitude, from British Columbia and western Alberta to Montana, northeastern California, and New Mexico. Living timber of Engelmann spruce has been estimated at 63,000,000,000 bd.ft., with half of this reserve in British Columbia.

The blue, or Colorado, spruce (*P. pungens*) ranges from Yellowstone National Park to Idaho, central Utah, and southern Arizona, at altitudes slightly below the Engelmann spruce belt. It is smaller than the latter tree and, although of some importance for lumber, the trees grow scattered or in small patches so logging is expensive. Because of the bluish caste of the foliage and its symmetrical growth in open situations it is used extensively as an ornamental. Its deep root system makes it remarkably windfirm and resistant to drought.

The above species have four-angled leaves, but weeping spruce (*P. breweriana*) and Sitka spruce (*P. sitchensis*) have flattened leaves. The weeping spruce, confined to the mountains of northwestern California and adjacent Oregon, has slender, pendent twigs and drooping branches that often reach the ground. The tree has little commercial value. Sitka spruce ranges along the coast from the base of the Alaska peninsula to California and to about 50 mi. inland. It is the largest of the new world representatives, trees 4 ft. in diameter and 200 ft. tall being common; a specimen 16 ft. in diameter and 300 ft. tall has been reported. Most mature trees scale 6,000 to 8,000 bd.ft., but exceptionally large ones have run to 40,000 bd.ft. of usable timber. Production of Sitka spruce lumber in Washington and Oregon alone amounted to 106,580,000 bd.ft. in 1948 but since that time has steadily declined.

The most important European spruce is the Norway spruce (*P. abies* or *P. excelsa*), native to northern Europe and used extensively in reforestation there and in North America. It approaches Sitka spruce in size, some trees attaining 170 ft. in height and a diameter of 5 to 6 ft. The branches have a tendency to droop, the lower ones often touching the ground. Its six- to seven-inch long cones are heavy seed producers and are confined to the tips of the upper branches. The species ranges from Norway to the Lena River in Russia and from latitude 68° N to the Pyrenees, the Swiss Alps, and the Altai Mountains. It furnishes lumber, poles, mining timbers, pulpwood, and limited quantities of material for making stringed instruments. It is planted widely as an ornamental. It stands the smoke of cities better than most members of the family, although aged trees sometimes are disfigured by blight and insect attack.

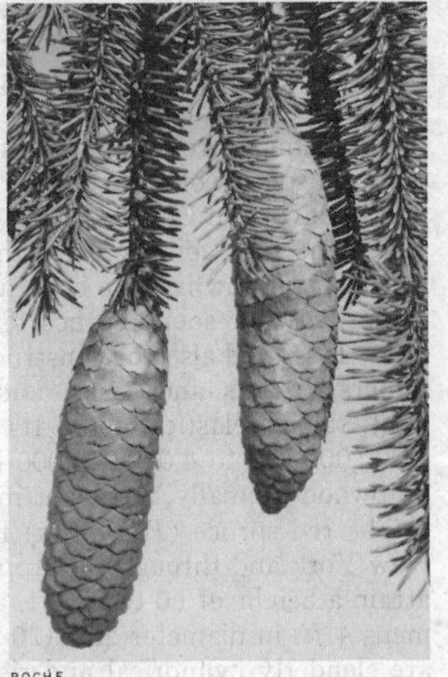

ROCHE

NORWAY SPRUCE (PICEA ABIES) BEARING CONES

Among the Old World spruces used ornamentally are the Serbian (*P. omorika*); Oriental (*P. orientalis*) of Asia Minor; Himalayan spruce (*P. smithiana*); Alcock spruce (*P. bicolor*); and the tiger's-tail spruce (*P. polita*), the last two being native to Japan.

BIBLIOGRAPHY.—L. H. Bailey, *The Cultivated Conifers in North America* (1933), *Standard Cyclopedia of Horticulture* (1943); S. J. Record and R. W. Hess, *Timbers of the New World* (1943); W. Dallimore and A. Jackson, *A Handbook of Coniferae* (1948); W. Harlow and E. Harrar, *Textbook of Dendrology* (1958). (I. L. W.)

**SPRUE** (PSILOSIS) is a deficiency disease characterized by voluminous frothy stools, gastrointestinal distention and discomfort, sore tongue (glossitis), weakness, marked loss of weight, and anemia. It occurs primarily among Caucasians residing in hot climates. Infrequently it develops in natives of the tropics and in Caucasians in cooler climates. Sprue is characteristically a disease of middle life and is more common in women than in men. It much resembles celiac disease (idiopathic steatorrhea), which occurs chiefly in children.

Sprue is associated with nutritional deficiency, resulting from (1) inadequate supply of animal proteins, whole cereals, and fresh fruits or vegetables containing certain vitamins, iron, and calcium salts, together with excessive intake of carbohydrates; (2) inability of the intestine to absorb adequate amounts of essential food elements; (3) inability of the stomach to secrete essential components of gastric juice; or (4) a combination of these factors. Previous intestinal disease or some other debilitating condition may be a precipitating or contributory cause.

Sprue is typically insidious in its onset. The patient develops an inflamed, denuded, extremely sore tongue and copious, frothy, watery stools, with associated intestinal tenderness and at times colicky pains. Examination shows that the stools contain inadequately saponified fats. The food deficiencies produce subtotal atrophy of the intestinal villi, which, in turn, is responsible for inadequate fat digestion and absorption. The patient may also have low blood pressure, and at times subnormal temperature, moderate to advanced emaciation, early loss of weight, increasing weakness, and macrocytic hyperchromic anemia; during remissions these symptoms tend to improve but return with each relapse. The clinical findings as a group distinguish sprue from the usual type of pernicious anemia, pellagra, chronic colitis, diabetes, tuberculosis, and cancer, although any one of these diseases may complicate sprue.

Prevention of sprue consists primarily in observance of an adequate, balanced diet and early correction of intestinal disorders. Treatment is based on administration of folic acid together with a low-fat, gluten-free diet rich in vitamins and protein. Corticosteroid therapy often is dramatically effective in relapsed cases.

BIBLIOGRAPHY.—G. G. Lopez *et al.*, "Folic Acid in the Rehabilitation of Persons with Sprue," *JAMA*, 132:906–911 (1946); P. Manson-Bahr, "The Riddle of Tropical Sprue," *J. Trop. Med.* (*Hyg.*), 63:49–55 (1960); T. D. Spies, "Observations on Treatment of Tropical Sprue with Folic Acid," *J. Lab. Clin. Med.*, 31:227–241 (1946); R. Rodriguez-Molina, R. Cancio, and C. F. Asenjo, "The Effect of Folic Acid on the Steatorrhea of Tropical Sprue and Other Tests for Intestinal Absorption," *Am. J. Trop. Med.*, 9:308–314 (1960). (E. C. F.)

**SPURGEON, CHARLES HADDON** (1834–1892), English Baptist minister, one of the most popular and prolific preachers in an age of great preaching, was born at Kelvedon, Essex, on June 19, 1834. His father and grandfather were Congregational ministers, but in 1850 he joined the Baptist Church and in the same year preached his first sermon. In 1852 he became minister at Waterbeach, Cambridgeshire, and in 1854 minister of New Park Street Chapel, Southwark, London. Within a year this was too small to hold the congregations who flocked to hear him; a larger new building also proved inadequate, and while the huge Metropolitan Tabernacle, Newington, was being built, Spurgeon preached to crowds of over 10,000 at the Surrey Gardens Music Hall. The Tabernacle (which held 6,000) was opened in 1861, and from then until his death (at Menton on Jan. 31, 1892) Spurgeon continued to attract vast congregations, also publishing sermons that, collected, fill more than 50 volumes. He edited a monthly magazine, founded a college for ministers (1856) and an orphanage (1867), and wrote a number of books, the best known being *John Ploughman's Talks; or, Plain Advice for Plain People* (1869). His sermons were widely translated, and their sales were astronomical.

Spurgeon was a fundamentalist, and in 1887 distrust of modern biblical criticism led him to leave the Baptist Union. His theme was personal salvation, and he combined sincerity with natural gestures, easy delivery, and skilful choice of illustration, often humorous and always homely. *See* also PREACHING.

BIBLIOGRAPHY.—*Autobiography*, compiled from his diary, sermons, records, and letters, 4 vol. (1897–1900; rev. ed. of vol. i and ii as *The Early Years*, 1962); *Letters* (1923); *see* also lives by R. Shindler (1892); W. Y. Fullerton (1920); and J. C. Carlile (1933); and W. M. Smith (ed.), *The Treasury of C. H. Spurgeon* (1956).

**SPURN HEAD,** foreland of the North Sea coast of Yorkshire, Eng., projecting across the mouth of the Humber. From Kilnsea it is 4 mi. long but seldom exceeds 300 yd. in width. Formed of sand and shingle from the rapidly denuding Holderness coast to the north, it is only a few feet above sea level.

**SPY:** *see* INTELLIGENCE, MILITARY, POLITICAL, AND INDUSTRIAL.

**SPYRI, JOHANNA** (née HEUSSER) (1827–1901), Swiss writer whose story for children, *Heidi*, is loved all over the world. Her psychological insight into the child mind, her humour, and her ability to enter into childish joys and sorrows give her books their attraction and their lasting value. She was born in Hirzel on Lake Zürich, June 12, 1827; her father was a doctor and her mother a poet. After her marriage in 1852 to Bernhard Spyri, a lawyer engaged in editorial work, she moved to Zürich. Her first book, *Ein Blatt auf Vronys Grab* (1870), was followed by many others. The best known, *Heidi* (2 vol., 1880–81), has been widely translated. Others include *Heimatlos* (1881) and *Gritli* (1882). Johanna Spyri died at Zürich, July 7, 1901. Her love of homeland, feeling for nature, unobtrusive piety, and cheerful wisdom gave both her work and her life their unique quality.

*See* M. Paur-Ulrich, *Johanna Spyri, ein Lebensbild*, 2nd ed. (1940). (M. P.-U.)

**SQUALL AND SQUALL LINE.** A squall is a strong wind that sets in suddenly, lasts for several minutes then dies away somewhat less suddenly. Any squall includes a succession of gusts, or irregular fluctuations of wind speed at intervals of a few seconds to a minute; an individual gust may be half again as strong as the average squall wind speed.

Wind speeds in squalls commonly reach 30 to 60 m.p.h. (50–100 km.p.h.), and gusts of 80 to 100 m.p.h. (130–160 km.p.h.) or more sometimes occur, although gusts of this strength are rare in most localities. Usually, squalls are straightaway winds, although some types of rotary winds are called squalls (*e.g.*, "typhoon squall," a form of waterspout several hundred yards in diameter).

It is common practice to name a squall after the weather phenomenon which accompanies it: rain, snow, hail, thunder, etc.

The most spectacular common type is the thundersquall. As a thunderstorm approaches, the wind often dies down, then blows gently toward the storm; finally, as the rain is almost at hand, a violent wind abruptly sets in, blowing outward from the storm and usually lasting for only a short time. (*See* also THUNDERSTORM.)

A squall of this kind is caused by the spreading out of cold air formed in the rain area of the thunderstorm. A thunderstorm, as a whole, is warmer than the surrounding air at a given level. In the heavy rain region, however, a certain amount of relatively dry air, drawn into the thundercloud from the outside, causes partial evaporation of the rain. This evaporation cools the air, and a cold downdraft forms because the air is then more dense than the surroundings, and sinks in the same way as a heavy liquid will sink when poured into a lighter one. As the downdraft approaches the earth's surface, it is forced to spread out horizontally; the squall occurs near the edge and for a short distance within the boundary of the spreading cold air. If the air below a thundercloud is very dry, all rain may evaporate before reaching the ground, and the squall may be dry, often with dust or sand being picked up from the surface. This is a common cause of desert sandstorms.

Local rain squalls of the same nature are very common in the oceanic doldrums, and several may be visible simultaneously from a ship. The wind squalls are often evident from whitecaps traveling over the sea surface.

A different type of squall occurs with the drainage of cold air down steep slopes. Such squalls derive their force from gravity, and depend on the descending air being colder and thus more dense than the air it replaces. The outstanding example of this type of wind is the bora, an extraordinarily fierce wind (intermittent squalls of 100 to 130 m.p.h.) observed during the winter when cold air originating in Russia spills over the mountains of Yugoslavia to the relatively warm coast of the Adriatic sea. Squally fall winds of the same nature are common on mountainous coasts in high latitudes, where cold air from glaciated highlands spills down fiords (Norway, Greenland) or deep valleys (*e.g.*, "williwaws" of Alaska). The force of the wind is increased where the air is funneled between narrow valley walls.

(*See* also WIND.)

Squalls of a less local character occur with the passage of cold fronts (*see* METEOROLOGY), where large masses of cold air replace warm air. Although the squall is likely to be most pronounced just when the front passes, high winds with gusts are likely to be sustained for several hours. Special names for this type of wind include "norther" (Great Plains, North America); "pampero" (Argentina, Uruguay); and "southerly burster" (Australia).

**Squall Line.**—A squall line (sometimes, line squall), as the name suggests, is a line along which a number of places simultaneously experience squalls. At one time, this term was used to designate the cold front of a cyclone (*q.v.*) but in modern usage applies only to a line of squalls associated more or less directly with thunderstorms. Such a squall line may be several hundred miles long, but with gaps. The line is usually irregular, consisting of several large clusters of thunderstorms, in some cases separate, but more generally connected by relatively inactive cloud masses or sheets formed from old, decadent thunderstorms.

The first sign of an approaching squall line may be layer clouds, alto-cumulus and dense cirrus types, blown out ahead of the thunderstorms by the strong winds in high levels. The squall line when near at hand may appear as a solid wall of cumulo-nimbus cloud, with low ragged clouds beneath and sometimes an arch or straight line of low cloud with an apparent rolling motion. Most generally, however, the main solid wall of cloud is obscured from a ground observer by general low cloudiness, and the only clear evidence of a squall line approaching may be the line of heavy rain, dark low ragged clouds and lightning.

Passage of a squall line is marked by a sudden onset of strong gusty winds, with a marked change in wind direction and a rapid drop in temperature (perhaps 10° or 15° in as many minutes), followed by heavy rain, thunder and lightning, and often hail. Rain amounts of one to two inches in an hour, with one-half inch in the first ten minutes, are not unusual. On the average, rain falls for about 45 minutes, with a gradual decrease in intensity after the first rain burst. Arrival of the squall is also signaled by a sudden increase in barometric pressure, often amounting to one-tenth inch mercury or more, followed after a few minutes by a more gradual fall of pressure; at the same time, the wind gradually returns to what it was before the squall line passed.

Since there are gaps between active thunderstorms in a squall line, a considerable variation in weather conditions is to be expected at different points. Thus a squall line passing two towns, 10 or 20 mi. apart, may cause only weak squall conditions at one and violent winds, heavy rain and hail at the other.

The cumulo-nimbus clouds with squall lines generally extend to heights of five to ten miles, and present a considerable hazard to aircraft because of the strong and turbulent vertical air currents within them. Increasingly accurate weather forecasting, together with pinpointing of the thunderstorms by radar and radio direction-finding (static) devices, however, enable aircraft either to circumnavigate squall lines or to fly through the inactive parts.

A squall line may be found at a cold front, but ordinarily either forms ahead of or moves out ahead of the front under the influence of strong winds in upper levels, so that on the average squall lines are found 50 to 200 mi. ahead of the cold front, on the southeast side of a cyclone. In middle latitudes, squall lines most commonly approach from the west or northwest (at a speed averaging 30–35 m.p.h.), while in low latitudes, for example in west Africa, they commonly approach from the east.

Squall lines are most frequent during the spring months, in localities occupied by moist tropical air masses but near the zone of the polar front which separates the tropical from the cooler air masses of higher latitudes. The greatest number of squall lines is observed in the Great Plains and middle western United States, a region open to frequent incursions of both tropical and polar air masses.

Phenomena of the same type are observed in eastern India-Pakistan ("nor'westers") and west Africa ("tornadoes"; not rotary storms as are American tornadoes), which are not associated with air mass fronts in the same way as in higher latitudes.

Although the strong winds occurring with squall lines are responsible for considerable damage, most of the damage reported is due to hail and rotary tornadoes occurring with the squall lines. Most tornadoes are associated with squall-line type thunderstorms, and as many as 20 to 30 or even more have been reported with a single squall line (*e.g.*, May 2 and 3, 1956, United States). Damage from one squall line may run into millions of dollars.

The cause of the squall winds with a squall line is in general the same as discussed above in connection with thundersqualls. The original formation of squall lines, as of thunderstorms in general, is most favoured when the air is unstable, having a strong decrease of temperature with height (*see* METEOROLOGY), and also when the air is very humid in the lowest few thousand feet and relatively dry higher up. These conditions are best satisfied in moist tropical air during mid-afternoon when surface temperatures are warmest, and there is a strong preference for squall lines to form at that time.

Once a squall line has formed, usually by some kind of lifting of the air near a cold front which sets off the first thunderstorms, it seems to carry with it its own self-regenerating mechanism. A mass of rain-cooled air beneath the thunderstorms spreads out and lifts the warm moist air ahead of the squall line, forming new thunderstorms which become incorporated into the squall line, and these repeat the same process. In this way, squall-line thunderstorms are able to keep going for many hours even during the night. Six to 12 hours is a common duration, but some squall lines have been observed to continue for as long as 36 hours.

Because it is blown out ahead of the cold front by the strong winds in upper levels, a squall line after 12 or 24 hours may be found several hundred miles away from a cold front near which it started, and a new squall line may have been initiated near the same cold front.

BIBLIOGRAPHY.—Interesting examples of squalls are given by Sir William Napier Shaw, *Manual of Meteorology*, vol. ii (*see* especially pp. 374–380; 429) (1942). Detailed discussions of the mechanism of thundersquall formation are to be found in *The Thunderstorm,* United States Weather Bureau (1949). For complete discussions of squall lines, *see* Sverre Petterssen, *Weather Analysis and Forecasting,* 2nd ed., vol. ii (1956), and article by J. R. Fulks, "Instability Lines," in *Compendium of Meteorology,* American Meteorological Society (1951). *See* also reports of U.S. Weather Bureau National Severe Storms Project. (C. W. N.)

**SQUARCIONE, FRANCESCO** (1397–*c.* 1468), the founder of Paduan Renaissance painting, was an artist of great historical importance, few of whose works survive. Born in Padua in 1397 and active there after 1423, he was associated in 1434 with Fra Filippo Lippi during the latter's stay in Padua. Neither of the extant panel paintings by Squarcione, an undated Madonna in the Staatliche Museen, Berlin, and a polyptych of 1449–52 in the Museo Civico at Padua, throws much light on the nature of his contribution to the early work of his most distinguished pupil, Mantegna, who was a member of Squarcione's workshop before 1448. The only record of his mature style is contained in a cycle of frescoes of scenes from the life of St. Francis on the exterior of S. Francesco at Padua, probably painted between 1452 and 1466. Such compositions as can be reconstructed confirm the traditional view of Squarcione as one of the channels through which the style of the great Florentine Renaissance painters was diffused in Padua. According to Scardeone (the prime source for knowledge of the painter's work), Squarcione had 137 pupils. Among the artists he taught or influenced were Marco Zoppo, Gregorio Schiavone, Cosimo Tura (*q.v.*), and Carlo Crivelli (*q.v.*).

*See* M. Muraro, "A Cycle of Frescoes by Squarcione in Padua," in *Burlington Magazine,* CI, 1959, pp. 89–96. (J. W. P.-H.)

**SQUARE,** in geometry, is a plane rectilinear figure with four equal sides and four right (90°) angles. Such a figure is a special kind of rectangle (equilateral) and parallelogram (equilateral and equiangular). It has four axes of symmetry, and its two finite diagonals (as in the case of any rectangle) are equal. If the side of a square is $s$, the area is $s^2$, read as "$s$ squared" and derived from this geometric relation. Hence, the algebraic square is the product arising from multiplying any algebraic expression by itself; *e.g.,* $(a+b)^2 = (a+b)(a+b) = a^2 + 2ab + b^2$ (*see* BINOMIAL THEOREM). Latin writers called the side of a square its *latus* (side), and hence the square root of a number was often called the *latus.*

The word also is applied to instruments used for drawing or testing right angles, as in the T square and the familiar carpenter's square.

*See* also GEOMETRY: *The Beginnings of Geometry: Greek Geometry.*

**SQUARE DANCE** is the term applied to the most popular and widely known type of American folk dance to distinguish it from those types classified as contra, or longways, and circle dances. Historians trace its origin to both the Kentucky running set of English derivation and to the cotillion, a stately French dance in square formation, popular at the court of Louis XV but supplanted later by the quadrille.

The americanized quadrille or square dance begins and progresses rapidly in beautifully ordered patterns within the framework of a relatively compact square, sets of four couples forming its four sides. To the traditional accompaniment of accordion, banjo, fiddle, and guitar and to prompting, patter, and singing calls, couples perform a variety of steps, all based on a smooth, "shuffling" walk. Formerly danced in five main figures, the contemporary square dance is comprised of three. *See* also QUADRILLE.

BIBLIOGRAPHY.—B. A. Botkin, *A Treasury of American Folklore* (1944); Anne Schley Duggan *et al., Folk Dance Library* (1948); Gene Gowing, *The Square Dancers' Guide* (1957); Richard Kraus, *Square Dances of Today* (1950); Grace L. Ryan, *Dances of Our Pioneers* (1939); Curt Sachs, *World History of the Dance* (1937); Lloyd Shaw, *Cowboy Dances* (1939). (A. S. D.)

**SQUASH** is the fruit of *Cucurbita maxima* and certain varieties of *C. pepo* (*see* also PUMPKIN). Summer squash is a quick-growing, small-fruited, nontrailing or bush type of *C. pepo.* The plants are upright spreading, 1½ to 2½ ft. high, and produce a remarkable diversity of fruit forms, ranging from flattened through oblong to elongate and crooked. Colours range from white through cream to yellow, also green and variegated. The fruit surfaces or contours may be scalloped, smooth, ridged, or warty. The fruits develop very rapidly and must be harvested only a few days after they form, before the seeds and rinds harden. They must be used soon after harvest. The entire fruit is usually cut into pieces, boiled, and served with butter. The bush forms are grown about two feet apart in rows three to four feet apart. To obtain early yields, seedlings are often started in pots in frames or greenhouses and transplanted into the field after three or four leaves have developed and after danger of frost is past.

J. HORACE MCFARLAND CO.

A VARIETY OF SUMMER SQUASH (CUCURBITA PEPO)

Winter varieties of squash, *C. maxima,* are long-vining, generally large-fruited, long-season kinds that can be stored many months if kept dry and well above freezing. The fruit stems are greatly enlarged next to the fruits, and the fruits show a wide range of sizes, shapes, and colours. They are higher in nutritive value than summer squash or so-called pumpkins and are commonly baked or made into pies. They are extensively grown in the United States in home gardens, market gardens, and on a large field scale for canning. Squash is native to the New World, where it was widely cultivated by the Indians long before European settlement. (V. R. B.; X.)

**SQUID,** a ten-armed cephalopod mollusk related to the cuttlefish (*q.v.*). Squids are both coastal (*Loligo, Sepioteuthis*) and oceanic (*Ommastrephes, Onychoteuthis*); they may be swift swimmers or part of the drifting life of the sea (*Cranchia*). In size they range from about 1 in. to the giant *Architeuthis,* which attains a length of more than 60 ft., including the tentacles.

The common squid of eastern North America, *Loligo pealei,* and its European counterpart, *L. vulgaris,* have an elongate tubular body, a triangular fin on each side posteriorly, and a short compact head with large covered eyes. Eight of the arms bear two rows of suckers on the inner side, the rims protected by a horny ring bearing small teeth. Two of the arms are developed into longer tentacles, slender with expanded ends that bear four rows of suckers with toothed, horny rings. The body of most squids is strengthened by a feather-shaped, internal shell (the "pen" or gladius) composed of a horny material.

The squids, or teuthoids, are divided into two groups: the Myopsida (*Pickfordiateuthis, Loligo*), in which the eye is covered by the outer skin of the head, and the sucker rings are smooth or toothed; and the Oegopsida (*Ommastrephes, Illex*), in which the eye is exposed, and the suckers may form long, slender hooks or claws (*Onychoteuthis, Abralia, Galiteuthis*). The Myopsida are a small, homogeneous, well-distinguished group, but the Oegopsida are varied in form. C. Chun divided the Oegopsida into the Libera, in which the mantle loosely articulates with the head (*Illex, Architeuthis*), and the Consuta, in which the mantle is fused at the neck and on either side of the funnel (*Cranchia, Taonius*). The Consuta are highly modified forms, often transparent, and poorly known.

Little is known of the life history of squids. *Loligo* is presumed to live only three or four years. The European *Loligo vulgaris* may lay about 40,000 eggs in large clusters attached to floating weeds or other objects. In the Pacific American squid, *Loligo opalescens,* which attaches its eggs to the bottom, the male dies after mating, and the female dies soon after spawning. In mating, the male passes the sperm containers (spermatophores) to the female, where they become cemented to special pads until spawning, when they rupture, releasing the sperm. Larger squids (*Architeuthis, Ommastrephes*) may live considerably longer. In *Loligo* the young appear somewhat similar to the adults at hatching, but in the oceanic squids (*Chiroteuthis, Ommastrephes*) the young are very dissimilar and have a planktonic larval stage.

The luminescent squids (*Lycoteuthis, Abralia, Watasenia*) are spectacular creatures bearing numerous light organs embedded in the surface of the mantle, head, arms, tentacles, on the eyeball, or within the mantle cavity. The light is produced by a luciferin-luciferase reaction, as in the firefly, and the photophore may be equipped with light source, reflector, lens, and colour screens. In *Lycoteuthis diadema,* which bears 22 light organs, there are 10 different types. The exact function of the light organs is unknown, but they may be for recognition and for attracting prey.

Squid eyes, as complex as those of man, have cornea, vitreous fluid, iris diaphragm, lens, and pigment screens. In most of the squids they are set into the sides of the head, but in *Bathothauma* and *Corynomma* they project from the head on long stalks. The eyes of a giant squid may have a diameter of 15 in. In *Histioteuthis* the head is asymmetrical, the left eye being about twice as large as the right.

Squids are numerous in the sea and afford food to a host of animals. The sperm whale feeds almost exclusively upon squid, often eating the giant *Architeuthis.* Many commercial bony fishes include squid as an important part of their diet. Squids are highly prized as food by many peoples; there are extensive fisheries in Spain and Portugal, where they are canned in olive oil for export. In Japan 600,000–700,000 tons are landed annually, most of which are dried. There is an extensive fishery in the United States, where squid are exported or sold as bait. In Newfoundland about 49,000 tons of *Illex* were landed in 1964, mostly for bait in the local cod fishery.

*See* CEPHALOPODA for features of the class to which squids, cuttlefishes, and octopuses belong. (G. L. V.)

**SQUILL,** a bulbous herb of the genus *Scilla,* belonging to the lily family (Liliaceae); several of its species are grown in gardens for their early spring bloom. Squills have narrow, basal leaves and flower stalks that bear blue, purplish, or white, nodding, bell-shaped blossoms in loose clusters. Especially desirable is the early-blooming, shade-tolerant Siberian squill (*S. siberica*), with intense blue flowers on stalks about 4–6 in. high. The later-blooming English bluebells, or wild hyacinth (*S. nonscripta*), and Spanish bluebells (*S. hispanica*) are about a foot high. Squills look best in mass plantings beneath trees or shrubs or in rock gardens. Bulbs planted at intervals in early autumn, set into the soil three times their own depth and three to four inches apart, will provide a succession of blooms in spring.

ROCHE
SIBERIAN SQUILL (SCILLA SIBERICA)

"Squill" is also applied to the sea onion (*Urginea maritima*), which in its white-bulbed variety was formerly used in medicine. The fleshy inner scales of its bulbs contain several glycosides that act as heart stimulants, expectorants, and diuretics. A red-bulbed variety constitutes the rat poison, red squill.

**SQUINCH,** in architecture, a general term for several means by which a square or polygonal room has its upper corners filled in to form a support for a dome (*q.v.*): by corbeling out the courses of masonry, each course projecting slightly beyond the one below; by building one or more arches diagonally across the corner; by building in the corner a niche with a half dome at its head; or by filling the corner with a little conical vault which has an arch on its outer diagonal face and its apex in the corner. The arched squinch seems to have been developed almost simultaneously by the Roman builders of the late imperial period and the Sassanians in Persia.

Squinches are often found both in Romanesque architecture and Islamic architecture. In Italy the form is either the conical type as in the church of S. Ambrogio at Milan or as a succession of arched rings as in the 13th-century central tower of the abbey church at Chiaravalle Milanese. More complex forms with niches and colonnettes are characteristic of the French Romanesque of Auvergne, as in the cathedral of Le Puy en Velay (late 11th and early 12th century); the allied churches of the southwest coast, such as Saint-Hilaire at Poitiers, use conical squinches of the Italian type. Islamic architecture, borrowing from the Sassanian precedent, makes great use of squinch forms, particularly in the Syrian, Egyptian, and Moorish phases; the stalactite work, which is so marked a feature of later Islamic architecture, is, in essence, merely a decorative development of a combination of niche squinch forms. In Gothic architecture squinch arches are frequently used on the insides of square towers to support octagonal spires. *See* ARCH AND VAULT; BYZANTINE ART AND ARCHITECTURE; GOTHIC ART AND ARCHITECTURE; ISLAMIC ARCHITECTURE; ROMANESQUE ART AND ARCHITECTURE.

**SQUINT** (STRABISMUS) is a turning of one eye or the other inward (convergent squint, cross-eyedness); outward (divergent squint, walleyedness); or, more rarely, upward or downward (vertical squint). A squint may always affect the same eye (monocular, unilateral squint) or it may affect one eye, then the other (alternating squint). It may arise at any time of life as a result of paralysis of one or more of the muscles of the eye (paralytic squint). Cross-eyedness, the commonest form of squint, occurring in early childhood or infancy, is generally not of paralytic origin; it tends to be familial, and often results from an undue strain of the focusing mechanism (accommodation) of the eyes required by an optical error (farsightedness). However, a squint may have many other causes, including mechanical ones and faults in the neural mechanisms that control the position of the two eyes relative to each other. It is essential for the normal functioning of the two eyes together that they be properly aligned during the early years of life. If a squint has established itself, the child will neglect the vision in one eye to avoid the double vision that results from improper alignment of the eyes and will develop other faulty visual habits, all of which may make it extremely difficult or impossible to restore adequate binocular vision in later life. Deep-seated loss of vision may occur in an eye that is allowed to be turned all the time.

Children do not outgrow a squint. To allow normal development of visual function and to prevent loss of vision, it is essential that medical advice be sought as soon as a squint is observed. No child is too young to be examined or to have some form of treatment. Such treatment may be by eyeglasses, patching of one eye, exercises, locally applied drugs or surgery, or by a combination of any of these means. *See* also EYE, HUMAN: *Diseases of the Eye and Visual Disorders: Diseases of the Extraocular Muscles, Their Nerves, and Central Control Apparatus.* (H. M. BU.)

**SQUIRES, SIR RICHARD ANDERSON** (1880–1940), Liberal prime minister of Newfoundland, was born at Harbour Grace, Nfd., on Jan. 18, 1880. He graduated in law from Dalhousie University, Halifax, N.S., and was a member of the Newfoundland House of Assembly from 1909 to 1913, of the Legislative Council from 1914 to 1919, and of the House of Assembly again from 1919 to 1924 and 1928 to 1932. He was minister of justice and attorney general (1914–17), colonial secretary (1917–18), and prime minister (1919–23, 1928–32). He was knighted in 1921.

From 1908 to 1918 Squires belonged to the People's Party, led by his law partner, Sir Edward Morris, opposing the old Liberal Party until 1917 and then cooperating with it in a war coalition. But when Morris was succeeded as prime minister in 1918 by the Liberal leader William Lloyd, Squires left the coalition, denouncing in particular William Coaker, president of the Fishermen's Protective Union (FPU), who had backed the Liberals since 1913. Yet in 1919, when Sir Michael Cashin reorganized the government in a conservative direction, dropping Coaker, Squires proclaimed himself a Liberal and formed an alliance with the FPU leader that was the key to his future success.

Sir Richard remains the most controversial of Newfoundland's prime ministers. His opportunistic political career, marked by personal abuse of his opponents, extravagance, and corruption, was ended by the depression. On the other hand, he promoted education and industrial development, and the Liberal Party that he refounded in 1919 survived him to become the predominant political force in the province after the union in 1949 with Canada. Squires died at St. John's on March 26, 1940. He was a member of the United Church of Canada. (G. O. R.)

**SQUIRREL,** any rodent of the family Sciuridae, but sometimes restricted to the familiar arboreal species. Squirrels are small or medium-sized mammals with strong hind legs and well-developed tails, which in tree-dwelling forms are long and bushy and serve as balancing organs or, wrapped about them, for warmth and protection. There are four toes on each front foot, five on each hind. Each side of the jaw has four or five cheek teeth above and four below; these teeth are rooted and their crowns have low cusps adapted for crushing food—nuts, seeds, grasses, tubers, roots and fruits. Internal cheek pouches provide space for temporary storage of large amounts of food, which may be carried elsewhere or may be stored in a cache for later use. Most squirrels are active in the daytime, the year round. Flying squirrels, however, are nocturnal. Ground squirrels may hibernate in cold climates.

Squirrels as a group are nearly cosmopolitan, occurring in all major land masses except Australia, the extreme polar regions and such islands as Madagascar, New Zealand, New Guinea, and Hawaii. They are particularly numerous in India and the tropics. More than 40 living genera and countless species are recognized; fossils are known from the Miocene of Europe and North America. Throughout their wide range, squirrels have become modified for life in many different ecological situations; they are good examples of the evolutionary process of adaptive radiation.

Most familiar are the tree squirrels of forested regions. In North America the gray squirrel (*Sciurus carolinensis*) prefers heavily forested lowlands, while the larger fox squirrel (*S. niger*) favours open forests of the uplands; but both species have adapted well to urban habitats and are familiar tamed residents in city parks. Each species stores small amounts of food, chiefly hardwood nuts and seeds, in widely scattered caches. Winter nests are carefully made weatherproof dens in holes of trees or tightly constructed twig and leaf nests high in trees; summer nests are large, flimsily made balls of leaves and twigs. Mating occurs in midwinter, and the young, usually two or three, are born about 45 days later. A second mating takes place in late spring. The smaller red squirrels, or chickarees (*Tamiasciurus*), which occupy a wide variety of woodland habitats but are especially abundant in coniferous forests, store food in one or two large reserves, usually in a damp place, and in numerous smaller units. Usually five or six young are born about 40 days after mating.

JOHN H. GERARD

GRAY SQUIRREL (SCIURUS CAROLINENSIS)

The common old world squirrel (*Sciurus vulgaris*) ranges from Norway to Japan, with numerous colour variants in different parts of its range. In Great Britain the common squirrel has been largely replaced by the gray squirrel, which was introduced from North America.

Both albinistic and melanistic individuals are common in American gray squirrels. At least three well-marked colour phases are recognized in the fox squirrels. The complex of Asiatic squirrels is an intriguing zoological puzzle. The sharp division of range between the tassel-eared Kaibab squirrels (*Sciurus kaibabensis*), confined to the Kaibab plateau on the north rim of the Grand Canyon in Arizona, and Abert's squirrel (*S. aberti*), on the south rim, is an interesting ecological problem for the zoogeographer.

The pygmy squirrel (*Myosciurus*) of west Africa and the dwarf squirrel (*Nannosciurus*) of southeastern Asia are the size of a mouse, while the black and yellow giant squirrel (*Ratufa*) of the Malay archipelago reaches the size of a house cat. The striped palm squirrels (*Funambulus*) are the commonest species in India. The oil-palm squirrels (*Protoxerus*) and the isindi (*Heliosciurus*) occur in Africa. These tree squirrels are extremely agile and adept at climbing and leaping; they not only ascend but also descend trees head first with ease.

LEONARD LEE RUE III FROM NATIONAL AUDUBON SOCIETY

THIRTEEN-LINED GROUND SQUIRREL (CITELLUS TRIDECEMLINEATUS)

A ground squirrel may be any burrowing member of the Sciuridae, but more commonly the term is restricted to the spermophiles, genus *Citellus*, or *Spermophilus*, rodents characterized by having cheek pouches, short ears, long front claws and generally a short tail. They are omnivorous, feeding upon vegetation, seeds, insects, etc. Although chiefly North American, one, known as the suslik, reaches Eastern Europe and others occur in Asia. The arctic species (*C. parryi*) is about 12 in. long, the tail 5 in.; it is yellowish brown, speckled with gray. Rock squirrels (*C. variegatus* and allies) are about the same size, with a longer tail and larger ears. The mantled ground squirrels (*C. lateralis* and *C. saturatus*) are often confused with chipmunks, having black and white lateral stripes. The thirteen-lined ground squirrel (*C. tridecemlineatus*), often called gopher (the true gopher, however, is of a different family), is pale buff, marked with brownish lines and whitish spots.

Among the other ground-dwelling sciurids are the marmots (including the American woodchuck), chipmunks, and prairie dogs (*qq.v.*).

Spiny squirrels, a group of African ground squirrels characterized by spiny fur, belong to the genera *Xerus, Euxerus, Atlantoxerus,* and *Geosciurus*. Their external ears are small or absent and their claws are long and nearly straight. Typical spiny squirrels live in clefts or holes of rocks or in burrows.

Flying squirrels are found in two very different groups of nocturnal, tree-dwelling rodents, in both of which a parachutelike expansion of the skin of the flanks enables them to take long gliding leaps. They all have large, dark-adapted eyes, and are omnivorous, berries, seeds, nuts and insects being the chief diet.

The first group comprises about 11 genera forming the sciurid subfamily Petauristinae and occurs from Scandinavia to Japan and the Malay region, and in North America from northern Canada to Honduras. The greater number of species occur in the Indian and Malayan regions, where some, *Petaurista* species, reach large size, more than a yard in total length, and may be foxy red, red spotted with white, or black in colour. The gliding membranes of these large species are more extensive than those of smaller forms; a fold connects the hind limbs with the tail. Flying squirrels glide from a position high on one tree to a lower level on another tree or log, sometimes covering 200 ft. or more in a glide. Species of the North American genus *Glaucomys* are smaller buff-coloured sciurids.

The second group, called scaly-tailed "squirrels," is African and consists of certain members of the family Anomaluridae, some of which, however, have no parachute. The flying species differ from those of the last group in that the membrane is supported by a bone at the elbow joint instead of by a cartilage at the wrist. There are two flying genera, *Anomalurus* and *Idiurus*, each containing several species. They are all similar in habits to the previous group and, like them, are very squirrellike in appearance. The term "flying squirrel" is also applied to certain marsupials, but these are more properly called flying phalangers (*see* PHALANGER; MARSUPIAL).

Squirrels sometimes damage crops and occasionally feed on eggs of desirable birds. Certain species carry diseases transmissible to man, among them the plague, rabies and tularemia. Larger squirrels are often hunted for their palatable flesh and for their pelts, which are used chiefly for trimming. In American folklore one of the ground squirrels, the ground hog or woodchuck (*q.v.*), is a weather prophet (*see* Ground-Hog Day).

*See* Rodent; *see* also references under "Squirrel" in the Index. (R. H. Ma.; J. E. Hl.; X.)

**SQUIRRELFISH** (Soldierfish), a small (less than a foot long), tropical, marine fish, numerous about coral reefs. Squirrelfishes belong to the family Holocentridae, of the order Beryciformes. They have notably large eyes, a strong backwardly directed spine at the corner of the preopercle (on the lower side of the head), a long spinous dorsal fin contiguous with a shorter one of soft rays behind it, a short anal fin with one of its initial spines notably long and strong, a forked caudal (or tail) fin, and the body covered with firm scales of moderate size. Their colours

BY COURTESY OF MIAMI SEAQUARIUM

SQUIRRELFISH (HOLOCENTRUS ASCENSIONIS) COMMON TO THE WEST INDIAN REGION

are bright—red and yellow—and lengthwise stripes on the body predominate. Squirrelfishes with larger mouths (*Flammeo*) are sometimes separated generically from those with smaller mouths (*Holocentrus*). About 12 species of squirrelfishes inhabit the waters of Indonesia; 9, some of which are the same, those of Hawaii; about 7 (of which *Holocentrus ascensionis* is the commonest), the West Indian region. (J. T. N.)

**SRIKAKULAM** (formerly Chicacole), a town in Andhra Pradesh, India, and the administrative headquarters of the district of the same name. Pop. (1961) 35,071. The town lies on the left bank of the Languliya River, which is crossed by a bridge at this point, about 35 mi. (56 km.) ENE of Vizianagram and 4 mi. (6 km.) from the sea. It contains an imposing mosque built in 1641. The town was formerly noted for its muslins. Under the Mughal emperors it was the capital of one of the Northern Circars (*see* Circar), as it was later of a British district.

Srikakulam District has an area of 3,901 sq.mi. (10,104 sq.km.). Pop. (1961) 2,340,878. It was created in 1960 by the division of Vishakhapatnam District. A notable feature of the district is the Machkund hydroelectric project, completed in 1955. (S. Gl.)

**SRINAGAR,** the capital of the Indian state of Jammu and Kashmir, lies on both banks of the Jhelum River at an altitude of 5,250 ft. (1,600 m.), about 400 mi. (640 km.) NNW of Delhi. Pop. (1961) 285,257. The river, which winds its way through the city with an average width of 240 ft. (73 m.), is spanned by nine bridges. One of these, of modern design, leads to the shopping centre and to the busy streets on the outskirts of the town. Srinagar is also traversed by a number of canals. The curious grouping of the houses, no two of which are alike, the irregular embankment of the river, and the mountains in the background form a quaint and picturesque spectacle. The town is well known for its mosques, which include the Jami Masjid, originally built at the beginning of the 15th century and reputedly the largest mosque in Kashmir; the Shah Hamadan, constructed entirely of wood; and the Hazrat-bal, with its relic of the Prophet Mohammed. Other notable features are the museum, the Shankaracharya Hill with the temple of Shiva on the summit, the Hari Parbat Hill, and the Dal Lake with its "floating" gardens, bordered by the famous Mughal Gardens. Among the industries of Srinagar are carpet and silk mills, silver, leather, and copperware manufacture, and woodcarving. Srinagar is linked by air with Delhi and Amritsar and by air and road with Jammu. The town is the seat of the University of Jammu and Kashmir (1948). (S. Gl.)

**SRIRANGAM,** a town in Tiruchchirappalli District, Madras, India, stands on an island formed by the bifurcation of the Cauvery River, about 2 mi. N of Tiruchchirappalli City. Pop. (1961) 41,949. The town is celebrated for its great 17th-century temple dedicated to Vishnu, one of the most sacred shrines of southern India. It is composed of seven rectangular enclosures, one within another, the outermost having a perimeter more than two miles in length. A remarkable feature of the temple is the so-called Hall of a Thousand Pillars with its colonnade of rearing horses. There were earlier temples on the site, and several inscriptions are preserved dating from the 10th to the 11th centuries and also from the 12th century, when the theologian Ramanuja lived at Srirangam. At Jambukesvara, near Srirangam, is an important shrine of Shiva. (F. R. A.)

**SSU-MA CH'IEN** (145/135-*c.* 90 b.c.) is the first major Chinese historian of whom there is any appreciable knowledge, and one of the greatest. His lifework, the *Shih Chi* or *Records of the Historian*, completed around 100 b.c., has been widely read not only in China but in Korea and Japan as well, and has exercised a profound influence upon the literature and historiography of those countries.

Scholars disagree on the date of Ssu-ma Ch'ien's birth, some placing it in 145 b.c., others in 135 b.c.; he appears to have died around 90 b.c. In youth he traveled widely through the Chinese empire, gaining firsthand acquaintance with the geography and historic places. Most of his life was spent at the court of Emperor Wu of the Han dynasty. He inherited the court position of grand historian (sometimes translated as "grand astrologer") from his father, Ssu-ma T'an, whom he credits with the conception of the *Shih Chi*. Late in his life, Ssu-ma Ch'ien was condemned to suffer castration for defending a disgraced general. Though it was customary under such circumstances to commit suicide, he chose to bear the disgrace in order to complete his history.

The *Shih Chi* is a monumental work in 130 chapters covering about 2,000 years of Chinese history from the earliest recorded times to the lifetime of the historian. The existing text is very nearly complete. Divided into five sections, the work begins with 12 chapters of basic annals dealing with the emperors who ruled China. These are followed by ten chronological tables listing in graph form the important events of the past with their dates, and eight treatises on such subjects as music, ritual, astronomy, and economics. Thirty chapters entitled "Hereditary Houses" treat the feudal kingdoms of early China. The work concludes with 70 chapters of biographies or memoirs relating the lives of famous men or describing the peoples of Korea, southeast Asia and central Asia with whom the Chinese had contact. Though histories in simple chronicle form existed earlier, this method of dividing material into annals, biographies, etc., was original with Ssu-ma Ch'ien and, in spite of certain disadvantages, was widely imitated in later Chinese historical works.

Ssu-ma Ch'ien's approach to history was essentially biographical. Throughout his work he was primarily concerned with the lives of the great men of the past and the moral inspiration and guidance they provide. Written in a vivid, concise style and enlivened by dramatic scenes and episodes, his history presents an invaluable picture of life in ancient China and has done much to mold the historical consciousness and literary tastes of generations of Chinese.

*See* Edouard Chavannes, *Les Mémoires historiques de Se-ma Ts'ien*, 6 vol. (1895–1905); Burton Watson, *Ssu-ma Ch'ien: Grand Historian of China* (1958). (B. D. W.)

**SSU-MA KUANG** (1019–1086), Chinese scholar-statesman, compiler, with chosen associates, of the monumental *Tzu-chih t'ung-chien*, or "Comprehensive Mirror for Aid in Government." As an emulation of the *Ch'un-ch'iu*, or "Spring and Autumn Annals," believed to have been edited by Confucius, it presented the general chronicle of Chinese history from 403 b.c. to a.d. 959, from the standpoint of Confucian moral principles and their practicalities. Its major attention to political events did not result in neglect of other important subjects, such as rites, music, astronomy, geography, and economy. Nor was the Confucian perspective permitted to interfere with Ssu-ma Kuang's rigorous scientific procedure and critical standards. One major weakness is the work's relative lack of analysis of prevailing patterns and underlying trends. Over the centuries, however, many historians were inspired to develop further this annalistic genre, as well as other related genres, such as narrative summaries. By its high level of research excellence, the work also contributed to the "School of Evidence Investigation," which rose in the 17th and 18th centuries. The great Neo-Confucian philosopher Chu Hsi (*q.v.*) compiled an outline for it, which, in turn, became most influential in Confucian indoctrination. Even in mainland China today, where Confucianism is under attack, Ssu-ma's scholarship still stands high.

Politically, Ssu-ma Kuang led the faction that opposed the reforms of Wang An-shih (*q.v.*) in 1069–85. Conservative in his interpretation of the Confucian classics, Ssu-ma argued for the cause of good government through moral leadership rather than assertive measures and through improved functioning of tested institutions rather than drastic changes. Shortly before his death, he became the leading minister to initiate the antireform policy of 1085–93, which, however, did not prove to be particularly successful. Nevertheless, he is still remembered as one of the best in the Confucian image—morally upright, learned in many ways, prominent in government. In modern children's books he still sets an example, in the familiar story of how, as a child, he wisely broke a water tank to save from drowning his playmate who had fallen into it.

BIBLIOGRAPHY.—W. G. Beasley and E. G. Pulleyblank (eds.), *Historians of China and Japan* (1961); C. S. Gardner, *Chinese Traditional Historiography* (1961); J. Meskill (ed.), *Wang An-shih, Practical Reformer?* (1963); J. T. C. Liu, *Reform in Sung China* (1959); W. T. de Bary (ed.), *Sources of Chinese Tradition* (1960). *See* also general histories of the Sung dynasty. (J. T. C. L.)

**ST. or STE.** Geographic names beginning with the abbreviation "St." or "Ste." are entered under "Saint" (English, French) or "Sainte" (French) for consistency. Local usage frequently determines whether "Saint" or "Sainte" is spelled out in full or abbreviated. "São" is used for Portuguese geographic names, and "San" and "Santa" for Spanish and Italian places.

**STABIAE,** an ancient town of Campania in Italy, destroyed by the eruption of Vesuvius in A.D. 79, on the coast at the eastern end of the Gulf of Naples (modern Castellammare di Stabia). Originally an Oscan settlement, it took part in the Social War (the war of the Italian *socii,* "allies") against Rome in 90 B.C. and was destroyed by Sulla in 89, its territory being given to Nuceria as a reward for loyalty to Rome. It was noted for the medicinal properties of its waters, and the neighbourhood became a popular locality for villas. The elder Pliny perished at Stabiae, near the villa of his friend Pomponianus, in the eruption of 79. Subsequent settlement was of minor importance.

Excavations, begun in the 18th century, were recommenced in 1949. The extent of the pre-Roman town (*oppidum*) has been assessed. The layout of the later town (89 B.C.–A.D. 79), unlike the *insula* (grid) planning of many Roman towns, appears to have been adapted to the needs of a spa. A striking feature of the later excavations has been the wall paintings, which compare very favourably with those of Pompeii and Herculaneum.

BIBLIOGRAPHY.—M. Ruggiero, *Degli scavi di Stabia dal 1749 al 1782* (1881); G. Cosenza, *Stabia* (1908); O. Elia, *Pitture di Stabia* (1957).
(H. H. SD.)

**STABILIZATION AGREEMENTS, INTERNATIONAL,** are entered into by countries that are large producers or consumers of commodities that play a major role in international trade. Stabilization agreements are made to deal with difficulties that arise with these commodities such as a persistent imbalance between production and consumption, burdensome stock accumulations, and pronounced fluctuations in prices. After the early 1930s such agreements were concluded for a number of commodities, including wheat, sugar, rubber, tea, timber, tin, coffee, and olive oil. Customarily such agreements were of five years' duration, although some covered shorter periods.

**The Interwar Period.**—The international commodity agreements introduced in the period between World Wars I and II were essentially of a restrictive type; that is, they represented an attempt on the part of producers, acting during general economic depression, to arrest downward trends in prices by restricting supplies flowing to the world market. This was usually achieved by assigning each participating country a basic quota, subject to periodic adjustment in the light of price trends and the market situation generally. Such agreements depend for their success upon an absence of close substitutes for the commodity concerned and upon participation by all the main producing countries. Some earlier attempts to regulate the market through less comprehensive agreements, such as that for rubber between Malaya and Ceylon (1922–28), failed because higher prices merely stimulated production in and exports by countries outside the agreement. The agreements concluded in the 1930s did, in fact, embrace all the major producing countries and they further extended control over supplies by measures such as the prohibition of the export of planting material from participants to nonparticipants.

It is difficult to reach any general conclusions about the effectiveness of these earlier agreements. The 1933 wheat agreement was undoubtedly a failure, its operative clauses for all practical purposes being abandoned toward the end of the first year of its operation. The scheme of export regulation broke down and difficulties arose over the implied obligations of the four principal exporting countries to reduce acreage. On the other hand, the tea agreements (1933 and 1936 [revised 1938]) and rubber agreements (1934 and 1938) regulated exports in accordance with the agreed quotas and exerted a stabilizing and strengthening influence on prices. In 1937 the League of Nations Committee for the Study of the Problem of Raw Materials reported that the regulation schemes then in operation had, generally speaking, "been an important factor in the improvement in economic conditions experienced in producing countries during the depression as well as in the development of international trade."

**World War II and After.**—With the onset of World War II and the consequent disruption of supplies and higher prices, such agreements became largely redundant. However, certain of them, including those for sugar, tea and rubber, were extended by protocol, shorn of any effective quota provisions, largely to ensure the ready availability of machinery to meet expected postwar needs. In the case of wheat the protocol of 1942, signed by Canada, the United States, Argentina, Australia and the United Kingdom, made definite provision for a postwar international wheat conference and established an International Wheat council to review the situation meanwhile. Exceptionally for coffee, the special conditions brought about by the war, particularly the loss of the important European market, themselves gave rise to the first international coffee agreement (1940). Known as the Inter-American Coffee agreement, this was essentially an export quota agreement, but it constituted the first important international commodity scheme in which a consuming country, the United States, participated and played a dominating role by providing through the quota system an organized outlet for exports from Latin America.

In the early postwar years there was no immediate resort to international commodity agreements. Although a series of wheat conferences was held, introduction of the first postwar agreement for this commodity was delayed until 1949. The International Sugar agreement of 1937 became inoperative in 1944, although the International Sugar council remained in existence, and it was not until 1953 that a new agreement was successfully negotiated. Regulation of the rubber market was not resumed after the war because of the need to rehabilitate the far eastern producing areas and because of the rapid development of the synthetic rubber industry. Tea export quotas remained nominally in force until 1955, but in the later years they were in excess of 100% of the high basic quotas established under the 1936 agreement (revised in 1938) and had no real restrictive effect.

The subject of international commodity agreements was given detailed consideration by the preparatory committee (1946–47)

*See* also *Correspondance générale,* ed. by B. W. Jasinski (1960– ); F. C. Lonchamp, *L'Oeuvre imprimé de Mme G. de Staël* (1949).

*Biography and Criticism:* The definitive biography is Lady Blennerhassett, *Frau von Staël, ihre Freunde und ihre Bedeutung in Politik und Literatur* (1887–89; Eng. trans. by J. E. G. Cumming, 1889; Fr. trans. by A. Dietrich, 1890). *See* also D. G. Larg, *Mme de Staël: la vie dans l'oeuvre, 1766–1800* (1924; Eng. trans. by V. Lucas, 1926), and *Mme de Staël: la seconde vie, 1800–1807* (1928); R. McNair Wilson, *Mme de Staël* (1931); R. L. Hawkins, *Mme de Staël and the United States* (1930); R. Escarpit, *L'Angleterre dans l'oeuvre de Mme de Staël* (1954); J. C. Herold, *Mistress to an Age: a Life of Mme de Staël* (1958); A. Lang, *Une Vie d'orages* (1958); B. d'Andlau, *Mme de Staël* (1960). (R. Es.)

**STAFF, MILITARY,** a term used to designate the officers who assist the commander of a military force. The basic meaning of the term is similar in all armies, though staff organizations and their functioning vary considerably. The staff is commonly distinguished from the "line," the purely combatant portion of the army. (For naval staff, *see* below.)

The staff assists the commander by performing the detailed duties of administration, planning, supply and co-ordination that are necessary to control and maintain his forces. It works out detailed plans in support of the commander's intentions, translates his decisions into orders and issues the orders to the troops. The staff is the commander's channel for maintaining contact with the subordinate units of his force and for receiving the information and advice he requires. A chief of staff normally heads the organization, which is divided into sections responsible for definite fields of activity, such as personnel, intelligence, plans and operations, training and supply. Staff officers have no command authority in their own right; they act always as agents of the commander, issuing orders in his name.

All modern armies, following a concept developed during the 19th century, employ some form of general staff. While the term has had various uses and often designates the staff of a general commanding any major unit of division size or greater, it most commonly denotes the staff of the central headquarters directing the nation's entire army establishment. Such a staff, usually located in the national capital, assists the officer in supreme command of the entire army in the performance of his functions. That officer is responsible to the government for all aspects of the readiness of the army for war, and usually for direction of the army's operations after hostilities have begun. Accordingly, the general staff in peacetime is concerned both with the training and administrative control of existing forces and with the preparation of plans for any war in which the nation might become involved.

## EARLY HISTORY

**Ancient and Medieval Armies.**—As warfare advanced beyond the type of tribal conflict in which a single chieftain could keep his entire force within sight and lead it with his own battle cry, the commander's need for assistants grew. The need was met in a variety of ways, but the institution of the military staff showed no consistent development prior to the Thirty Years' War (1618–48), when regularization of army organization along relatively modern lines began. Until that time, staffs were usually on an informal basis. The commander merely retained a group of officers as his personal party, calling on them for whatever service the moment required, such as reconnaissance or the delivery of orders.

Even in permanently organized formations such as the Roman legion, staff functions were not clearly defined. In the army of the Roman republic, six tribunes headed each legion. The actual command rotated among them, and the five tribunes not currently in command were available for staff duty. In the last days of the republic the legion came under the permanent command of a legate. The six tribunes remained as his assistants, but, with these positions held by men of less stature and experience than under the former system, the tribunes appear to have been little more than orderlies.

In the warfare of the feudal era, with its short campaigns and limited forces, military staff organization had no place. Staff development began when larger armies, representing the ruling dynasties of the emerging national states of Europe, took the field in the 16th and 17th centuries.

**Gustavus to Napoleon.**—By the early 1630s Gustavus Adolphus had developed the Swedish army into an exceptionally well-organized force. Composed of companies and regiments of uniform size, with a set hierarchy of officers, it had a supply system that functioned smoothly, its soldiers were regularly paid, and its activities were governed by written regulations upheld by courts-martial. While the assistants Gustavus gathered about him were still largely a group of individual officers rather than an organized staff, most of them were assigned titles and definite responsibilities, such as the provost marshal, the judge advocate and the quartermaster. The Gustavian military organization was widely copied, and, indeed, a substantial part of the Swedish king's army passed intact into the service of France a few years after his death in 1632.

Over the next century and a half in most European armies the duties of the quartermaster (*q.v.*) tended to expand until that officer took on many of the attributes of a modern chief of staff. The quartermaster's responsibility for quartering and feeding the troops centred his thought on what lay ahead—the direction and route of the next day's march, the selection, laying out and fortification of the next camp site, and the daily extension of the line of supply. In time that officer became responsible for reconnaissance, for directing marches and ultimately for drafting operational orders, in addition to his basic supply function.

In the French army developed by Richelieu and inherited by Louis XIV in the mid-17th century the emergence of a chief of staff had already begun. The army organization included several officers bearing the title *maréchal de camp,* who handled the quartermaster functions. In one of these, the *maréchal général de camp,* were centralized some of the duties of a chief of staff, serving the marshal of France who was conducting the campaign. At the same time there was a *maréchal de bataille,* who formed the army in battle array and directed its tactical movements. The latter officer soon passed from the scene, and by the end of the 17th century the chief of staff's position, now called the *maréchal général des logis,* had assumed some responsibility for operations as well as intelligence and supply.

In the Prussian army that Frederick the Great led in his campaigns of the mid-18th century, on the other hand, staff organization developed slowly in the presence of military genius. Frederick was, in effect, his own operations officer and chief of staff. He required few assistants but gave careful attention to their professional training. Recognizing a need for officers to perform reconnaissance, select and fortify camp sites and guide troops on the march, he personally chose and instructed 12 officers in these duties, adding them to his small quartermaster general's staff.

Frederick's interest in the intellectual preparation of officers for high-level duties led him in 1765 to establish an academy where young noblemen were trained in diplomacy and the military art. It was the forerunner of the *Kriegsakademie* that capped the educational system of the German general staff in the 19th century.

**Napoleon.**—By the time another military genius appeared in the person of Napoleon Bonaparte, the conditions of warfare had been altered in a way that allowed a larger place to military staff operations. The concept of the nation in arms that arose during the French Revolution produced mass armies several times larger than those commanded by Frederick a quarter of a century earlier, but there was also a striking increase in their mobility and maneuverability. Infantry, made more secure against cavalry attack by the socket bayonet and the increased firepower of the flintlock musket, combined with the first really mobile field artillery to mark the end of the rigidly indivisible army. Napoleon organized his army into autonomous corps and divisions, capable of sustaining themselves when separated by a day's march or more. Dispersion of his units not only made it easier to live off the country but permitted rapid movement by the use of parallel roads.

Command centred in the person of Napoleon himself. He required all intelligence reports to be delivered directly to him, and he sought no staff advice when devising his plans and instructions. But a staff was needed to keep track of the disposition of the corps and divisions and to translate Napoleon's decisions into written orders that would set the subordinate units into co-ordinated motion toward the accomplishment of his design. For these relatively technical staff duties Napoleon had an able practitioner in his chief of staff, Marshal Louis Alexandre Berthier.

A studious soldier and a tireless master of detail, Berthier had reduced to writing his conception of ideal staff organization and functioning as early as 1796. More influential in generating thought and study on the subject was the manual of staff doctrine and procedure published in 1800 by another French staff officer, Paul Thiébault, which was soon reproduced in English, German, Russian and Spanish. Both writers stressed the requirement for speed in staff work and for accuracy and conciseness in the writing of reports.

### DEVELOPMENT TO WORLD WAR II

**General Staff.**—Warfare had developed during the Napoleonic era into a complex activity that engaged the full efforts and resources of nations. The work of the military staff consequently rose from the level of planning the next day's march to a more comprehensive form of activity. The 19th century saw the emergence of the concept of the general staff as an organization that prepared war plans in peacetime and systematically collected information that would be useful in the future conduct of operations. In most countries the first activity of this type was topographical reconnaissance and surveying for the production of military maps, because with greater mobility and dispersion of units, generals found it necessary to conduct war on the map rather than by direct observation of the field. The information gathered soon included all that could be learned about the army and military resources of every potential enemy state. The general staff became concerned as well with the intellectual preparation of officers for command and staff duties, through historical study, war games, field maneuvers and attendance at staff colleges.

**German Staff System.**—The general staff system developed in the Prussian army was the first and for many years the most successful. Extended as the German general staff when the Prussian king became the emperor of a unified Germany, it profoundly influenced the development of modern military staffs in other armies during the years through World War I.

The Prussian general staff took form around the small quartermaster general's staff used by Frederick the Great, which had gained some additional functions under his successor and in 1796 had been directed to prepare a complete military map of Prussia. Under the influence of an energetic lieutenant quartermaster general, Col. Christian von Massenbach, the staff after 1801 passed beyond the mere gathering of geographical information and began formulating a somewhat theoretical set of plans for possible operations.

The enduring development of the general staff began with Gerhard von Scharnhorst's (*q.v.*) reorganization of the Prussian army following its defeat at Jena in 1806. In form the staff was little changed from Massenbach's day, but Scharnhorst introduced features that kept staff officers in close touch with the commanders and troops and prevented them from living in a world of theory. Under his system officers were selected from all branches of the army to serve on the general staff, and they returned periodically to regular duty with the troops. In addition to maintaining their practical proficiency as soldiers, this rotation permitted a greater number of officers to gain experience in general staff duties, qualifying them for staff assignments when war increased the size of the army.

With the final defeat of Napoleon in 1815, the main body of the Prussian general staff was concentrated in Berlin as the "great general staff," distinguished from the officers of the "general staff with troops," who served in vital staff positions in corps and division commands. In 1821 the two elements of the general staff were placed under a single chief of the general staff, who was thereafter the supreme professional military head of the Prussian army. At the same time, the Prussian king removed the general staff from the control of the war ministry and made it directly responsible to the sovereign.

Thereafter the general staff developed under the leadership of a succession of able chiefs, most of whom held the position for extended periods. Count Helmuth von Moltke (*q.v.*), serving from 1857 to 1888, was the most distinguished. The master plans for speedy mobilization and strategic deployment of the Prussian forces produced by the general staff under his direction led to the rapid victories over Austria in the Seven Weeks' War of 1866 and over France in 1870. Success owed much to Moltke's quick appreciation of the importance of railways as a new factor in warfare. Full exploitation of their potentialities allowed him to deploy the army for war under a plan whose precision and reliability rivaled that of the railroad timetable itself.

To neighbouring countries the effectiveness and efficiency of the German general staff constituted both a menace and a model. During the last half of the 19th century all major nations on the European continent instituted or matured some form of general staff to make detailed plans for war in time of peace. Italy and Austria-Hungary closely followed the German system, and its influence on Russian staff development was marked. During the same period the rising power in the far east, Japan, adopted a high command and staff system that virtually duplicated the German.

Meanwhile in the German government the general staff attained a unique position of power that lasted through World War I. Fortified by the prestige of its victories and protected from civilian control and effective parliamentary questioning by its confidential relationship to the kaiser, the general staff frequently wielded great influence in the selection of ministers and the formulation of foreign policy.

**French Staff System.**—Attempting to meet the need for a system that would be effective in the absence of a self-sufficient military genius of Napoleon's type, Marshal Gouvion Saint-Cyr as minister of war made a promising beginning toward the creation of a professional staff corps in 1818. He established the *corps d'état-major,* which was to supply officers to staff the headquarters of all units of the French army, drawing its members from the graduates of a newly founded staff college. Saint-Cyr's wise provision that at successive stages in their careers staff officers should perform regular tours of line duty with the troops was abandoned in 1833, and the staff corps became a closed service. Restricted membership, a rather narrow type of training and permanent assignment to staff duties tended to separate the staff corps from the main life of the army and even generated some distrust and disdain of its services by field commanders. Weakness in staff work and in comprehensive planning for war ranked high among the reasons for the French defeat in 1870–71.

During their remarkable period of national resurgence following the Franco-Prussian War the French soon came to emulate, if they did not directly copy, the German general staff system that had designed their defeat. By the 1880s they had replaced the former staff corps with a true general staff, headed by a chief titled the *chef d'état-major général de l'armée.* Staff candidates passed through an advanced school, the École Supérieure de Guerre, and alternated thereafter between staff assignments and regimental duty.

By 1914 France had a highly proficient general staff that was employed, like its German counterpart, in keeping a prepared file of campaign and mobilization plans up to date while overseeing all other aspects of the readiness of the army for war. Staffs at all levels in the French army were organized, under their chief, into three bureaus. The first bureau handled both supply and administrative matters such as recruitment, organization of units, casualty reports and the assignment, promotion and discipline of personnel. Enemy information was the concern of the second bureau, while the third prepared orders for military movements and operations.

The continuous combat operations of World War I, differing from the set battles of the past, brought the creation of a fourth bureau that assumed responsibility for the duties of supply, transportation and casualty evacuation formerly held by the first bureau. Thus the French system that matured during World War I displayed a distinct separation of staff functions into categories of administration, intelligence, operations and supply. It continued in this form without substantial change in later years.

**Russian Staff System.**—Imperial Russia was another country where military staff institutions took form around the expanding responsibilities of the quartermaster. Peter the Great appointed the first quartermaster general, in 1701, and the duties of that office grew steadily during the 18th century, often in imitation of the Prussian model. By 1815, when Tsar Alexander I established the "Headquarters Staff of his Imperial Majesty," the quartermaster general's section was the main staff component, responsible for most aspects of military operations. At the recommendation of Baron Antoine Henri Jomini (*q.v.*), formal education of officers for staff duties began with the founding of the Nicholas academy in 1832.

Reorganizations in which the influence of the German general staff concept was apparent followed both the Crimean War (1853–56) and the Russo-Japanese War (1904–05). The imperial Russian army entered World War I under a general staff immediately subordinate to the minister of war—a directing system that appeared to be as well appointed as any other on the continent. That there had been no proper staff training, however, became apparent when the deficiencies soon revealed in staff planning for the supply of the fighting forces contributed greatly to the disorganization and defeat that prepared the way for the Revolution of 1917 and the dissolution of the imperial army.

The Red army was brought into existence in 1918 to defend the new Bolshevik government against counterrevolutionary forces and foreign invaders. To provide their army with competent leadership the Communist masters found it necessary to enlist many former officers of the imperial army, particularly general staff officers and instructors for the military schools. As a result, staff doctrine and organization tended to remain unchanged, and most of the elements of the old general staff continued to function under the new commissariat of the army and navy. Moreover, the traditional German influence was renewed when Soviet officers began receiving training in Berlin military academies following the treaty of Rapallo in 1922.

One notable innovation was the commissar system, which placed a political officer on the staff of every Red army commander to monitor his activities and insure loyalty to the Communist regime. Since no operational order was valid until countersigned by the commissar, he was virtually the equal of the military commander. After 1934 the commissar served only as supervisor of the morale and political indoctrination of the troops, but his cocommander status was restored for a period after the great purge of the military command in 1937 and following the German invasion of June 1941. The commissar was again reduced to the role of political adviser and propagandist in Oct. 1942, and Red army units came under the single direction of their professional military officers. The Red army staff reached a high standard.

**British Staff System.**—Since Great Britain had failed to keep step with 19th-century developments on the continent, the British army entered World War I with only a decade of experience in the operation of a general staff system. In a period when military thought had centred largely on defense of the British Isles against invasion and the problems of India and other distant colonies, staff development had been slow, despite the founding of a staff college in 1858.

Interest in army reforms began to quicken following the publication in 1890 of *The Brain of an Army* by an Oxford lecturer, H. Spenser Wilkinson. His book explained the importance of the general staff in the successes of the German army and underscored the need for introduction of a similar system in Britain. Pronounced deficiencies in the British command and staff system revealed during the Boer War completed the argument. In 1904 the report of Lord Esher's committee investigating the war office demanded the formation of a general staff, "as the term is understood in all well-organized armies." The position of chief of the general staff was created in that year, the general staff itself being formally constituted in 1906. With expanded functions, the title was changed in 1909 to chief of the imperial general staff.

British staffs in all major army units during both World Wars I and II were divided into three branches. One, called the general staff, handled intelligence and the planning and conduct of operations. The adjutant general's (A) staff dealt with personnel and administration, while the quartermaster general's (Q) staff managed supply and transportation. Broadly stated, the general staff section was concerned with the use of the army while the other two branches looked after its maintenance. The chief of the general staff section co-ordinated the work of the entire staff, collaborating with the chief administrative staff officer, who supervised both the A and Q branches. Only the headquarters of the largest formations employed separate chiefs of staff to head the whole organization.

**U.S. Staff System.**—Before 1903 there was no general staff in the United States army. The term was sometimes used, but merely as a collective designation for the army's generals and the officers whose assignment to engineer, ordnance and other duties set them apart from the infantry, cavalry and artillery. An officer titled the commanding general of the army had authority over the troops but not over the quartermaster, adjutant general and chiefs of the other technical and administrative bureaus of the war department, whose activities were vital to the successful operation of his forces. Each bureau chief, supreme authority in his own field, reported only to the civilian secretary of war. How little this unco-ordinated system was geared to actual preparation for war was indicated by the statement of the commissary general that his office was functioning perfectly until the Spanish-American War disrupted and disorganized it.

The striking administrative failures of the Spanish-American War revealed the inadequacy of the bureau system and opened the way for reforms under a new secretary of war, Elihu Root. He founded the Army War college in 1902 and the following year obtained from congress authorization to create a general staff. Root's carefully reasoned explanations of the purpose of a general staff, based partly on his reading of *The Brain of an Army*, overcame the fears of some legislators that the change would result in "Prussianization" of the U.S. army. The legislation of 1903 established a chief of staff immediately under the secretary of war and the president, and gave him both the responsibilities of the former commanding general of the army and supervisory authority over the bureaus. To comprise the new general staff corps, officers were selected from the army at large for duty on the war department general staff or on the staffs of field commanders as members of "the general staff serving with troops." Since its beginning the U.S. army general staff corps has been manned by rotation rather than permanent assignment.

As leader of the American expeditionary forces in France in 1917, Gen. John J. Pershing studied British and French organization before erecting his own staff structure. Its final form closely resembled the French, including a chief of staff and five sections devoted to personnel, intelligence, operations, supply and training. When Pershing became chief of staff of the army in 1921 he reorganized the war department along the lines of his World War I headquarters, retaining the "G" system of designation borrowed from the French. The five divisions, each headed by an assistant chief of staff, were called personnel (G–1), military intelligence (G–2), operations and training (G–3), supply (G–4) and the war plans division. This establishment underwent no basic change until the United States entered World War II.

## WORLD WAR II AND AFTER

**Joint and Combined Staffs.**—World War II, truly global in scope and fought by coalitions of great and lesser powers, presented problems of co-ordination and direction that called forth new, higher levels of command and staff organization. The war of 1939–45 saw the rise of air power to full stature as a third armed force, coequal with sea and ground power. Amphibious operations, in which the efforts of all three forces were joined, proved to be a major feature. Thus a controlling organization was needed to encompass both interservice and inter-Allied co-ordination.

As the supreme military body for the strategic planning and direction of the Allied war effort in all areas except the Soviet front, the United States and Great Britain established the combined chiefs of staff early in 1942. Located in Washington, D.C., the combined chiefs of staff organization was directly responsible to the U.S. president and the British prime minister as a combined executive. The three British services were represented by the first sea lord, the chief of the imperial general staff and the chief of the air staff. Within the British government these three offices had been joined since 1923 as the chiefs of staff committee, bearing a corporate responsibility for the command and strategic direction of United Kingdom forces and for supplying military advice to the cabinet and prime minister.

To provide United States membership on the combined chiefs of staff to match this British representation, a new agency known as the joint chiefs of staff came into existence in the U.S. The title followed an agreed definition of terms whereby "combined" signified collaboration between two or more of the Allied nations while "joint" was used to designate the interservice collaboration of one nation. The original members of the U.S. joint chiefs of staff were the army chief of staff; the naval officer holding the double title of commander in chief, U.S. fleet, and chief of naval operations; and the commanding general of the army air forces. Later in 1942 an officer serving as chief of staff to the president became the fourth member.

Beneath the combined chiefs of staff was a planning organization that operated on the committee principle. Combined committees for strategic planning, logistics, intelligence, munitions assignment and other purposes were manned by army, navy and air force staff officers drawn in equal numbers from the two nations.

In March 1942 a reorganization of the U.S. war department increased the effectiveness with which the general staff supported the army chief of staff in his expanding duties at the joint and combined levels. Redesignated the operations division, the former war plans division became the agency through which the chief of staff exercised command authority over the widely deployed forces of the army. The four "G" sections of the general staff concerned themselves only with the development of broad policy, since responsibility for training, the actual operation of the supply system and such technical services as the ordnance, medical and signal branches had been decentralized to three subordinate commands: the army ground forces, the army air forces and the army service forces.

Anglo-U.S. unity in the higher direction of the war was reflected in the field, where forces of both nations were placed under the single authority of a supreme commander with a combined staff. The principle found its fullest expression in the two staffs commanded by Gen. Dwight D. Eisenhower in his Allied force headquarters (AFHQ) in Africa and his supreme headquarters, Allied expeditionary force (SHAEF), in Europe, where officers of the two nations were completely integrated.

The SHAEF staff followed U.S. doctrine in its basic organization, with assistant chiefs of staff for personnel (G–1), intelligence (G–2), operations (G–3), supply (G–4) and civil affairs (G–5). The G–1, G–3 and G–4 staff chiefs were American, while British officers headed G–2 and G–5, but each chief had a deputy of the opposite nationality. In Gen. Walter Bedell Smith the Americans provided an able chief of staff, who was supported by three British deputies. One deputy handled air matters; the responsibilities of the other two followed the usual British division between operations and intelligence functions on the one hand and the "A" and "Q" administrative functions on the other.

In contrast to the western Allies, Germany was poorly organized to deal with its relatively simpler problems of co-ordination. In theory the *Oberkommando der Wehrmacht* (OKW), or armed forces high command, corresponded to the U.S. joint chiefs of staff or the British chiefs of staff committee as the agency for strategic direction and co-ordination of the three services. In practice OKW was dominated by the army and was not a true joint staff. Its control over the armed forces was slight, since the heads of the air force and navy stood in a favoured relationship to Hitler, while the dictator himself assumed control of the army through its high command staff, the *Oberkommando des Heeres* (OKH). Rather than being the supreme military authority, OKW came to be roughly coequal with OKH, controlling German operations in the west while OKH dealt with the Russian front.

When invaded by Germany in 1941, the Soviet Union quickly redesigned its highest governing agencies for centralized control of the war effort. Stalin assumed personal direction of military operations, gathering under himself a supreme headquarters called the *stavka.* Composed of about 20 top military officers of various arms, the *stavka* developed over-all strategic plans for Stalin's approval. The chief of the general staff was a member, and his organization served directly under the *stavka,* providing information and working out detailed operational plans and orders to implement the approved strategy. Normally these operational orders were transmitted to the front commanders for execution, but the *stavka* occasionally detached a command group from its own membership to conduct a particular campaign.

**Trends After World War II.**—Continuation and elaboration of the unified command and joint staff practices initiated during World War II marked the postwar period. In the United States, the National Security act of 1947 made the air force a separate service but placed it with the army and navy under a single department of defense. The act also gave legal recognition to the wartime joint chiefs of staff (JCS), provided them with a full-time joint staff, and designated the joint chiefs of staff the principal military advisers to the president and the secretary of defense. Amendments in 1949 made them the military advisers to the National Security council as well. Composed of the army chief of staff, the chief of naval operations and the air force chief of staff, JCS after 1949 had a fourth and senior member called the chairman. In most areas where U.S. forces were stationed, JCS set up a unified command in which a single commander with a joint staff controlled units of all three services.

Great Britain also consolidated its wartime experience by making the ministry of defense a permanent office in 1946, with authority over the three services. At the beginning of 1956 the British chiefs of staff committee, like JCS, received a chairman as its fourth member.

In the Soviet Union during 1946 the wartime *stavka* was disbanded and a single ministry of the armed forces assumed control of military affairs. A division into ministries of war and navy occurred in 1950, but the services were united again in 1953 under the ministry of defense. The general staff served directly under the minister of defense, and its chief was one of his deputies. The general staff was basically the former Red army general staff, elevated to responsibility for military planning and co-ordination applicable to all the Soviet armed forces.

New circumstances brought forth new varieties of international staffs, resembling the Anglo-U.S. combined chiefs of staff of World War II. The 12 nations signatory to the North Atlantic treaty agreed in 1949 to set up regional military committees in which as many as five countries would be represented. Under the treaty an extensive international staff organization was created at the supreme headquarters, Allied powers in Europe (SHAPE).

(V. E. D.)

**Naval Staff.**—There is no general staff corps in the Royal Navy or the U.S. navy to resemble the general staff corps in various armies. Service opinion has always been strongly against such a corps, but both navies have attempted to educate officers for staff duties without designating them as specialists. The U.S. navy established the Naval War college at Newport, R.I., in 1884, the first institution of this kind. The Royal Navy has a naval war college and a naval staff college as components of the Royal Naval college, Greenwich. Through the efforts of men like Adm. Sir Herbert W. Richmond, the attempt was made to foster the scientific study of war, to develop logical and consistent habits of thought in connection with the employment of naval force in war and to emphasize that matériel alone will not win wars. Both the Royal Navy and the U.S. navy have always stressed professional competence in seamanship, but Adm. Stephen B. Luce (*q.v.*), who founded the U.S. Naval War college, Adm. Alfred Thayer Mahan (*q.v.*), who succeeded Luce as head of the War college, Admiral Richmond and other British and American officers attempted through their writing and teaching to bring naval staff work up to the high standards of seamanship which prevailed already. The officers who do the naval staff work in Whitehall, and on the staffs of British admirals, as well as those who do such work in the navy department, and on the staffs of American admirals, are assigned to the admiralty or to naval operations or to a seagoing staff for a period of not more than three years, after which they take some other assignment. Thus the staff work is done by seagoing officers fresh from a nonstaff billet who expect to return to duties which might involve responsibility for executing basic plans which they have helped to formulate while serving on the naval staff.

The first sea lord is chief of the British naval staff. He is assisted by a vice chief of staff and two deputy chiefs of staff, all flag officers. The naval staff is located in the admiralty office and is directly responsible for intelligence, planning, operations and tactical doctrine. In addition, there are staff divisions which advise on the policy concerning training in all its aspects, and on the requirements for new ships, aircraft and weapons.

In the United States the chief of naval operations is the naval member of the joint chiefs of staff organization. He heads what is, in fact, the naval staff of the U.S. navy, although it does not bear that name. The naval operations organization performs the naval staff duties, as well as day-to-day administrative functions, much the same as does the admiralty in London. (J. B. Hn.)

Bibliography.—Paul Bronsart von Schellendorf, *Duties of the General Staff*, 4th Eng. ed. (1905); Walter Goerlitz, *History of the German General Staff, 1657–1945* (1953); B. H. Liddell Hart (ed.), *The Red Army* (1956); H. Spenser Wilkinson, *The Brain of an Army*, rev. ed. (1895); W. R. Robertson, *Soldiers and Statesmen, 1914–1918* (1926); Otto L. Nelson, Jr., *National Security and the General Staff* (1946); J. D. Hittle, *The Military Staff: Its History and Development*, rev. ed. (1949); Forrest C. Pogue, *The Supreme Command* (1954); Ray S. Cline, *Washington Command Post: the Operations Division* (1951); Oliver L. Spaulding, *The United States Army in War and Peace* (1937); R. Ernest Dupuy and Trevor N. Dupuy, *Military Heritage of America* (1956); Philip C. Jessup, *Elihu Root* (1938); James G. Harbord, *The American Army in France, 1917–1919* (1936).

**STAFFA** (Norse for staff, column or pillar island), uninhabited island of the Inner Hebrides, Argyll, Scot., 33 mi. W of Oban, about 6 mi. NE and SE from the nearest points of Mull and 6 mi. N by E of Iona. It lies almost due north and south, is $\frac{3}{4}$ mi. long by about $\frac{1}{3}$ mi. wide, and its highest point is 144 ft. above sea level. In the northeast it shelves to a shore, but otherwise the coast is rugged and much indented with numerous caves. During the tourist season it is visited regularly by steamer from Oban. In section the isle has first a basement of tufa, from which rise, secondly, colonnades of basalt in hexagonal pillars forming the faces and walls of the principal caves which in turn are overlaid, thirdly, by a mass of amorphous basalt. On the southeast coast is the Clamshell, or Scallop Cave. It is about 130 ft. long, and on one side of it the ridges of basalt stand out like the ribs of a ship. Near this cave is the rock of Buachaille ("The Herdsman," from a supposed likeness to a shepherd's cap), a pile of columns, fully seen only at low water. On the southwest shore are the Boat Cave and Mackinnon's, or the Cormorant's, Cave. Fingal's Cave (*q.v.*), the most famous, situated in the southern face of the isle, is 227 ft. long. On its western side the pillars are 36 ft. high. The cave is the haunt of seals and sea birds.

**STAFFORD,** the name of a famous English family that at different times from the 13th to the 17th century held the titles of Baron Stafford, earl of Stafford, and duke of Buckingham. The family was founded in England by Robert (d. *c.* 1088), a younger son of Roger de Toeni, the standard-bearer of the duchy of Normandy. After the Norman Conquest Robert received a great fief extending into seven Midland counties and became known as Robert de Stafford from his large holdings in Staffordshire. On the death of his great-grandson Robert (d. 1193/4) the male line became extinct. This Robert's sister Millicent (d. 1225) had married one of Robert's vassals, Hervey Bagot, who succeeded in the fief in her right and assumed the name de Stafford. Their great great-grandson Edmund (1273–*c.* 1308) was summoned to Parliament as Baron Stafford in 1299. His son Ralph (1301–72) in 1346 was prominent at the defense of Aiguillon and at Crécy. He was made a knight of the Garter (*c.* 1348) and was created earl of Stafford in 1351.

His son Hugh (*c.* 1342–86), 2nd earl, was one of the 12 peers appointed during the Good Parliament (1376) to confer with the Commons on their grievances. Hugh's son Thomas (*c.* 1368–92), 3rd earl, married Anne, daughter and heiress of Thomas of Woodstock, duke of Gloucester, the youngest son of Edward III. The 3rd earl's brother William (1375–95), 4th earl, died a minor and was succeeded by another brother Edmund (1378–1403), 5th earl, who married the 3rd earl's widow, Anne. Edmund was appointed to the office of constable of England in 1403 by virtue of its hereditary descent through Anne's mother, Eleanor Bohun. His son Humphrey (1402–60), 6th earl, was created duke of Buckingham in 1444, and in 1447 was granted precedence "before all dukes who might thenceforth be created, excepting descendants of the king's body."

Henry (1455–83), 2nd duke (*see* Buckingham, Henry Stafford, 2nd Duke of), grandson of Humphrey, was beheaded and attainted for rebelling against Richard III. Henry's eldest son, Edward (1478–1521), 3rd duke, was restored to the family lands and title by act of Parliament in November 1485 after the accession of Henry VII. He was beheaded for treason (1521) against Henry VIII, and his attainder was confirmed by act of Parliament in 1523. His only son, Henry (1501–63), married (1519) Ursula, daughter of Sir Richard Pole by Margaret, daughter of George, duke of Clarence, and niece of Edward IV and Richard III. He was declared Baron Stafford in a new creation in 1547.

Henry's son Henry (*c.* 1533–66) became 2nd baron. His next brother, Thomas (*c.* 1534–57), opposed the marriage (1554) of Mary I to Philip (later Philip II) of Spain and plotted against her from France. Claiming to be heir to the throne by royal descent from both of his parents, he seized Scarborough Castle in Yorkshire (April 1557) but was captured and executed for treason. His younger brother, Edward (1536–1603), 3rd baron, was a judge at the trial of Mary Stuart in 1586. Edward's great-grandson Henry (1621–37), 5th baron, died unmarried, and the barony passed to his impoverished cousin and male heir Roger (1572/5–*c.* 1640), the only son of Richard, youngest son of the 1st baron. Roger surrendered the barony to Charles I in 1639 for £800. When he died unmarried the direct male line of the Staffords became extinct. Charles I bestowed the title in 1640 on Mary (*c.* 1619–94), sister of the 5th baron, and on her husband William Howard, fifth son of the 14th earl of Arundel, in whose descendants the barony is now vested.

**STAFFORD,** a market town, municipal borough, and the county town of Staffordshire, Eng., is situated on the River Sow in the green belt separating the industrial areas to the north and south of the county. Pop. (1968) 53,590. Public buildings include the Shire Hall (1798–99), Borough Hall (1876–77), Guildhall (1934), and the Municipal Central Library, with an art gallery and museum (1914, extended 1962). The College of Further Education, the College of Art, and the county administrative buildings are also in the borough. Chetwynd House (now the post office) was associated with Richard Brinsley Sheridan, dramatist and member of Parliament for Stafford from 1780 to 1806, and the Swan Hotel with Charles Dickens and George Borrow. The half-timbered "High House" was built in 1555, and the Martin Noel almshouses are also Elizabethan. St. Chad's Church was founded in the reign of Stephen, and St. Mary's parish church, Early English and once collegiate, adjoins the site (excavated in 1954) of the Saxon church of St. Bertelin, patron saint of Stafford. In Eastgate is the reputed birthplace of Izaak Walton, whose cottage at Shallowford, 4 mi. (6.4 km.) outside, is under the trusteeship of Stafford Borough Council.

Founded by Aethelflaed, daughter of Alfred the Great, Stafford had its own mint from the reign of Aethelstan to that of Henry II. William the Conqueror built a castle there and appointed as governor Robert de Toeni, baron de Stafford. In 1643, during the Civil War, Royalist Stafford was occupied by Parliamentarians, who demolished the town walls and castle (a building in the style of a medieval castle begun in 1810 is now in ruins). Granted its first charter in 1206 by King John, Stafford returned two members to Parliament from 1313 to 1885, and thereafter only one.

Stafford lies on the London-Birmingham-Manchester route by road (M.6) and rail. Industries include electrical engineering, reinforced concrete structures, adhesives, grinding wheels, diesel engines, salt, and shoes. (M. P. D.; X.)

**STAFFORDSHIRE,** a midland county of England, is bounded north by Cheshire and Derbyshire; east by Derbyshire, Leicestershire, and Warwickshire; south by Warwickshire and Worcestershire; and west by Shropshire and Cheshire. Its geographical area is 1,154 sq.mi. (2,989 sq.km.).

**Physical Features.**—Of the five physical regions of the county, the Pennine northeast uplands belong to highland Britain; and the Potteries coalfield, the central agricultural belt, Cannock Chase, and the South Staffordshire coalfield to lowland Britain.

The northeast uplands, between 800 and 1,500 ft. (about 240 and 460 m.), consist of folded north-south ridges of Millstone Grit and areas of Carboniferous Limestone, both of which are deeply incised to form bold scars by the Dove, Churnet, Hamps, and Manifold rivers, the headstreams of the Mersey and Trent. Much of the bleak treeless limestone area was in 1951 designated part of the Peak District National Park. To the southwest is the triangular-shaped Potteries coalfield, cut into by the River Trent and composed of sandstones, clays, and shales, with coal seams. To the west and south the coal dips below the sandstones. The central agricultural belt consists of Triassic rocks and is drained by the Trent. The undulating land of Bunter and Keuper sandstones, which adjoins the south of the Potteries coalfield and the uplands, extends along the county's western margin. It is upfaulted in a north-south ridge east of Stafford and extends to the southern boundary of the county to the east and west of the South Staffordshire coalfield. It also forms Cannock Chase; at about 600–700 ft. (180–210 m.) this barren heath was formerly part of a royal forest and today is an attractive amenity north of the Black Country communities. Apart from these sandstone areas, the centre of the county is occupied by the heavy soils and rather featureless landscape of the Keuper marls, which, reaching from north of Uttoxeter to Tamworth in the east, extend westward in a broad belt across the county. The South Staffordshire coalfield is a drift-capped plateau that forms part of the main east-west watershed in central England; drainage is by the River Stour to the Severn on the west and to the Trent on the east. The coalfield consists of ridges and low hills at about 400–500 ft. (120–150 m.), which are the sites of such towns as Wednesbury. The Rowley Hills, of igneous intrusive rock and the earlier Silurian shales and limestones, link together to form a ridge of highland from Rowley Regis to Wolverhampton.

**History.**—Traces of Neolithic man and his Bronze Age successors remain, especially in the northeast. Of the Iron Age, hilltop forts at Castle Ring on Cannock Chase and at Bury Ring near Stafford are probably the most notable. The Romans cut important roads through the forests that covered the country, notably Watling Street, running roughly east-west across what became later the southern part of Cannock Forest, and Ryknield Street, running south-southwest, which intersected Watling Street at Letocetum (Wall) near Lichfield. Farther west at Pennocrucium (near Penkridge) was another military station on Watling Street.

From the 7th to the 9th century the kingdom, and in the 10th to 11th centuries the ealdormanry, of Mercia had its centre in this area. Tamworth was the royal city of Mercia; Lichfield, soon after the region's conversion to Christianity, became its diocesan centre in 669. Between 873 and 874 the Danes ravaged the area, but evidence of permanent settlement by them is slight except on the eastern boundary where the present county adjoins what became known as Danelaw. Nevertheless, much of it then lay within the area assigned to the Danes by the treaty of about 886. From 910, when Edward the Elder defeated the Danes at Tettenhall, he and his sister Aethelflaed, "Lady of the Mercians," reconquered the area, building fortified enclosures (boroughs) at Tamworth and Stafford in 913. Renewed fighting with the Danes at the end of the 10th century caused further damage, and the first reference to Staffordshire as such tells of its being devastated in 1016.

The county as revealed by Domesday Book toward the close of the 11th century was divided into five hundreds, or subdivisions: Totmanslow, Pirehill, Offlow, Cuttlestone, and Siesdon. Much of it was sparsely populated and poor, a state of affairs to which its devastation by William the Conqueror following the rising of 1069–70 doubtless contributed. At that time the crown and the church were the dominating landholders, and, although by the late Middle Ages the Stafford dukes of Buckingham (descendants of another 11th-century Staffordshire landholder) had acquired great local and national influence, the crown retained its immediate importance in the county by the acquisition in 1399 (on the accession of Henry IV) of the property of the duchy of Lancaster. The large crown estates and the normal support given in the 15th century to the Lancastrians by the dukes of Buckingham ensured that, at any rate during the first phase of the Wars of the Roses, most Staffordshire influence supported them rather than the Yorkists. During Queen Elizabeth I's reign it became clear that many influential adherents of Catholicism remained in the county, although this did not prevent the earl of Shrewsbury, appointed custodian of Mary Stuart, from keeping her for short periods at Tutbury Castle and at his house at Chartley. It was the Roman Catholic gentry who added considerably to the support received in Staffordshire by the Royalists during the Civil War (1642–51). Nevertheless, the Parliamentarian committee at Stafford gradually established control of the whole county, in which, apart from a battle upon Hopton Heath (March 1643), the fighting was largely confined to sieges like those of Lichfield Close. Charles II's flight after the Battle of Worcester (1651) took him to hiding places at Boscobel, Moseley Old Hall, and Bentley Hall.

Staffordshire's later history is largely that of its industries, though coal and iron have been worked from at least the 13th century. The 16th century probably saw an increase in production of both industries. In coal mining this was accompanied by the use of somewhat deeper mines, while at Cannock Wood and Oakamoor blast furnaces were built instead of the older bloomsmithy. Historical documents give a vivid picture of the development of these undertakings, as well as social and industrial conditions among the blacksmiths, nailers, and spurriers in the south of the county. Other industries that developed in this and subsequent periods included glassmaking in the southwest and near Eccleshall and copper works near Cheadle. In the north of the county around Stoke-on-Trent during the 18th century, the long-established pottery industries achieved a national and then a worldwide market. The brewing industry at Burton upon Trent developed a similar reputation in the 19th century. It was potters like Josiah Wedgwood, and then other industrialists, who were the driving force behind turnpike road and canal schemes and who in the next century gave the county a network of railways.

By the 19th century the Potteries and the Black Country (*qq.v.*), with nearby Birmingham, had become major industrial areas, important for the social and economic problems they posed, for the religious and social thought to which these gave rise, as well as for the goods manufactured in these regions.

Prominent Staffordshire people have included Izaak Walton; Samuel Johnson; James Brindley, the canal builder; Hugh Bourne, the founder of Primitive Methodism; the admirals Lord Anson and Lord St. Vincent; the actor and playwright R. B. Sheridan, who was member of Parliament for Stafford; and David Garrick.

**Population and Administration.**—The area of the administrative county is 1,071 sq.mi. (2,774 sq.km.) and its population (1961) 985,113. There are 6 county boroughs, 8 noncounty boroughs, 17 urban districts, and 10 rural districts. Lichfield and Stoke-on-Trent are cities. Old market towns include Abbots Bromley, Brewood, Cheadle, and Eccleshall. The county is in the Oxford Circuit, and assizes are held at Stafford. There is one Court of Quarter Sessions and 20 petty sessional divisions. Stafford and Wednesbury have separate commissions of the peace, while Lichfield, Newcastle-under-Lyme, and the county boroughs have separate courts of quarter sessions as well. The county boroughs are Stoke-on-Trent (pop. [1961] 265,306), Wolverhampton (150,825), Walsall (118,498), Burton upon Trent (50,751), West Bromwich (96,041) (*qq.v.*), and Smethwick (68,390). The municipal boroughs are Lichfield (14,087), Newcastle-under-Lyme (75,688), Stafford, the county town (47,806), Tamworth (13,646), Wednesbury (34,511), Bilston (33,067), Rowley Regis (48,146), and Tipton (38,100) (*qq.v.*).

The moorlands are still sparsely populated, though the growth of road transport has reduced their isolation. The industrial towns, particularly of the Potteries and the Black Country, have much poor housing and ravaged land as a legacy of the 19th century, but developments since World War II have included attempts to relieve the congested population by overspill and to reclaim the large areas of desolate and derelict land for redevelopment.

In 1962 the University College of North Staffordshire, founded at Keele in 1949, became the University of Keele.

**Industries and Communications.**—William Camden in the 16th century remarked on the richness of the grazing lands, and, despite industrial development, about 75% of the land is agricultural, Staffordshire being in the main a dairying county. The rough pasture and grass of the moorlands give way to mixed general and dairy farming along the Cheshire and Shropshire borders. On the other side of Cannock Chase is the mideastern region of grassland. Arable land to the south includes market gardens round Lichfield and Tamworth, where, in contrast to the predominance of fodder crops in the rest of the county, these are outweighed by wheat, potatoes, sugar beets, and vegetables. The Forestry Commission grows timber on Cannock Chase and in 1964 owned 12,566 ac. (5,086 ha.) in the county. Chartley Moss is a national nature reserve, and in 1964 the National Trust owned 1,783 ac. (722 ha.) in Staffordshire; 1,773 ac. were protected.

Of the iron ore and coal deposits on which the Black Country's industries were founded, the iron supply has been exhausted, and coal mining is now largely confined to the northern fringe of the area and to Cannock Chase. Nevertheless, the area retains its importance for the great volume of its manufactures, both hardware and engineering products. It consists of a number of towns, most of which, whether large like Wolverhampton and Walsall, smaller like Willenhall, or villages like the Gornals, have their own industrial tradition. The Potteries, besides their earthenware and china products, share with Newcastle-under-Lyme and other smaller towns in the neighbourhood extensive coal and iron industries. Towns like Stafford have large engineering and shoe works; Stone has a shoe and glass factory; Armitage makes sanitary ware; Leek produces silk and rayon; Tamworth manufactures paper; and Burton upon Trent is famed for its beer. Gravel workings and stone quarries are widespread, especially in the moorlands near Cauldon and at Hollington.

The greater part of the railway network is operated by the Midland region of British Railways. The main line from London to Crewe runs through Tamworth, Lichfield, and Stafford, while the Birmingham line passes through Wolverhampton and joins the London-Crewe line at Stafford. The Western Region Birmingham to Shrewsbury line passes through Wolverhampton, which also has an airport. The county's canals include those in the Birmingham system; the Trent and Mersey Canal, built by James Brindley in 1766–77; and the Shropshire Union.

BIBLIOGRAPHY.—The Staffordshire Record Society (formerly the William Salt Archeological Society), *Collections for a History of Staffordshire* (1880—); *Transactions* of the North Staffordshire Field Club (1866—); Stebbing Shaw, *The History and Antiquities of Staffordshire,* 2 vol. (1798, 1801); Simeon Shaw, *History of the Staffordshire Potteries* (1829); Robert Plot, *The Natural History of Staffordshire* (1686); C. J. B. Masefield, *Staffordshire* (1930); Staffordshire County Council, *Development Plan, 1951* (1958); W. White, *Directory and Gazetteer of Staffordshire* (1851); W. H. B. Court, *The Rise of the Midland Industries, 1600–1838* (1953); J. Myers and S. H. Beaver, *Staffordshire,* "Land of Britain Series," no. 61 (1945). (FR. B. S.)

**STAGE,** in architecture, an elevated floor, particularly the various stories of a bell tower, etc. The term is also applied to the plain parts of buttresses between cap and cap where they set back, or where they are divided by horizontal strings and paneling. It is, too, the floor or platform on which plays are acted, whence the term has come to signify both the theatre and the drama (*q.v.; see* also STAGE DESIGN). From its etymological meaning of a station comes the sense of a place for rest on a journey, the distance between such places, etc. *See* also THEATRES (STRUCTURES).

**STAGE DESIGN** is the art of creating settings for theatrical performances. It takes into consideration such elements as scenery, costuming, lighting, stage machinery, and the construction of the stage itself, and also the question of theatrical style, where the sphere of the designer merges with that of the director. This article outlines the history of stage design and concludes with an account of modern practice. Familiarity with the articles ACTING, DIRECTION AND PRODUCTION; DRAMA; and THEATRE will enhance the reader's grasp of the subject, and he may wish to refer frequently to THEATRES (STRUCTURES) on matters of detail. Costuming is treated separately in the article COSTUME DESIGN, THEATRICAL. Stage lighting—a highly specialized craft belonging mainly to the modern era—is here discussed in relation to stage design as a whole; for detailed history and more technical aspects, *see* STAGE LIGHTING.

The present article contains the following sections:



## I. HISTORY

**1. Greece.**—The earliest surviving complete Greek play, Aeschylus' *The Persians* (472 B.C.), was almost certainly presented in the bare earthen orchestra of the primitive Dionysian theatre. The action was appropriately set in the deserted countryside. When a wooden building, the *skene* (from which word are derived Latin *scaena* and English "scene"), was erected opposite the circle of spectators (*c.* 465 B.C.), its front wall began to influence the settings of the tragedies and comedies that followed. Each of its three (later five) doors was given a formal use—serving, for example, to indicate arrival from a distant place; this tradition continued far into the Renaissance. Later in the 5th century B.C. the wooden *skene* was replaced by stone. In the 4th century B.C. the *skene* acquired a long, narrow platform that elevated and separated the dramatis personae from the chorus in the orchestra.

Aristotle says that scene painting was first used for Sophocles; according to the Roman architect Vitruvius, it was for Aeschylus. It seems certain that painted panels were used on the front of the *skene,* perhaps in the same conventional style as Greek vase painting. The *periaktoi,* a three-sided device on which two scenes could be changed while the third was presented to the audience, was employed for quick scene changes. Vitruvius in *De architectura* distinguishes three types of settings—for tragic, comic, and satiric plays—during the Hellenistic period. He also describes a device called a *scaena ductile,* a moving scene on wheels, drawn onto the stage from the left.

In Greek theatres a subterranean passage below the orchestra emerged in "Charon's steps." There was also a variety of stage machines. The *eccyclema,* a movable platform much used in Euripides' plays to suggest interiors, may have been pivoted through, or pushed straight through, a stage door onto the stage. The *mechane,* a crane rigged at the top of the *skene,* was employed to lower gods from Olympus; this machine, as might be expected, was a source of humour for the Greek comic writers.

Greek plays usually began at sunrise, thus offering their dramatists all the effects of natural light; in Euripides' *Iphigeneia in Aulis* the fading stars and the coming of dawn are both written into the action, which continues thereafter in full daylight.

**2. Rome.**—The *frons scaenae,* or facade of the building at the rear of the Roman stage, was gorgeously decorated with pillars, statues, and entablatures to a height of two or more stories; at the top a roof projected over the stage. A curtain hid the stage at the beginning of a performance; it was dropped into a recess under the stage and raised once more at the end of the play. In later times the curtain came into use between acts, permitting changes of scene; it is not known how the temporary settings differed from the permanent architectural facade. As on the Greek stage, the *frons scaenae* represented a street, and interior scenes could not be shown; even banquet scenes had to be brought outdoors. The evidence suggests that the so-called architectural stage was the result of some measure of choice rather than circumstance, since scenery of considerable realism was available in the 1st century B.C., at the beginning of stone theatre building in Rome. Furthermore, by the period of decadence both the ballet (not performed in the theatre) and the arena had adopted scenery of specific locales, together with elaborately contrived properties; the theatre had not.

Roman stage design, like the action of the play, proceeded conventionally. The appearance of the stage and the costumes and movements of the actors were as formalized in their way as the moves on a chessboard. Nevertheless, stage properties—spears, torches, even a chariot and horses—were real objects. It is not likely that the playwright-directors of the Greek and Roman theatre discriminated between the conventional and illusory elements they employed. Indeed, not until the advent in modern times of Naturalism and Epic Theatre were stage people much concerned over that mixture of styles.

**3. China.**—The platform of the Chinese stage was originally set up in teahouses and palaces. In its present form it is almost square. A rear wall and two lacquered red or black columns downstage (nearest the audience) support the stage roof. The wall, covered with a silk-embroidered curtain, has two curtained openings: an entrance (right) and an exit (left). Musicians sit at one side of the stage. Property men not only set the stage in full view of the audience but are in attendance on the actors at all times; they even bring them stage properties, taking away the properties when the actors have finished with them. The use of properties is, as a rule, formalized; *e.g.*, an actor may step up on and down from a chair to indicate that he has crossed a mountain. On the other hand, many of the properties are used quite literally.

For stage design in Japan (derived from Chinese practice), *see* KABUKI THEATRE; NŌ DRAMA.

**4. Middle Ages.**—In the Western world during the Middle Ages the church became the scene of the drama, revived after a long period of degeneration. Beginning in the 10th century the mystery play used the raised area of the altar to show the events of Easter and Christmas, erecting there a tomb or decorated manger. The stories of Christ's birth and passion were retold within a setting composed of religious sculpture and painting, coloured lights from stained-glass windows, music, and incense, with the addition of costume and spectacle. This liturgical "theatre" fused dramatic and scenic elements to achieve the synthesis advocated centuries later by Richard Wagner (*q.v.; see* also ART: *Concerts of Arts*).

As the size of the audiences increased, plays were transferred to the west door of the church and then outside church precincts. These plays featured a number of booths, or "mansions," each representing a locale of the story; *e.g.*, a decorated Heaven (which might be in the upper part of a two-leveled wagon), or a Hell mouth belching smoke. The booths were simultaneously available to the action, with the players making appropriate entrances and exits. This type of staging was continued for miracle and morality plays and, in England, for the guild pageants.

Nor was machinery absent during the Middle Ages. An elaborate spectacle was staged about 1400 in the Church of S. Felice in Florence for the Annunciation. A "nosegay" of singing cherubs was suspended in a copper dome in the roof of the church, from which descended a copper globe, opening to reveal the angel. The *nuvole*, moving clouds which revealed personages in the tradition of the Greek *mechane*, seem also to have originated in the church in the 15th century, the mechanisms being masked by cotton wool. Fires, fountains, thunder, fireworks, and the like were popular effects in the passion plays.

**5. Renaissance.**—At the Italian courts theatres ranked high as an index of social and political prestige. Banquets, masked balls, and other festivities were enriched by neoclassic entertainments designed by leading artists. Roman comedies were revived and a number of playhouses were built on what were supposed to be classical models after the publication of Vitruvius' *De architectura* in 1511. The best known of these is the Teatro Olimpico (completed 1583) at Vicenza. Vincenzo Scamozzi's elaborate *frons scaenae* was pierced by doorways through which were visible (as through street gates) street scenes in forced perspective. Action took place in front of this scene.

The introduction of perspective (*q.v.*) was as momentous for scene design as was that of electric lighting later. The first recorded use of perspective on stage was for Ariosto's *Cassaria* at Ferrara in 1508. Its success laid the groundwork for a facsimile imitation of nature. A few years later Baldassare Peruzzi showed how painted perspective scenes could prove as effective as those with sets of solid wooden three-dimensional wings, recommended by Sebastiano Serlio. When Serlio's *Second Book of Architecture* appeared, in 1545, it contained designs in perspective for stock scenes of comic, tragic, and satiric plays. The choice of one of three settings may seem totally inadequate to a modern audience, but this arrangement based on Vitruvius was a real advance; for whereas the classic stage used a single, permanent facade with modifications, Serlio's stock sets fitted the whole stage setting to the type of play.

During this period the rediscovered *mechane* of the Greeks came into frequent use in the form of the *gloria*, or *paradiso*, a hoisting scaffold masked by cutout, painted clouds. The Renaissance stage also had trapdoors and machines, including devices for creating thunder and lightning. There were moving suns and moons, and even conflagrations, accomplished with a liberal use of aqua vitae. There was also a beginning of an aesthetics of stage lighting. About 1550 Leone de' Somi in his *Dialoghi in materia di rappresentazioni sceniche* (*Dialogues on Stage Affairs*) considered the problems of achieving natural-looking scenes of day and moonlight and was the first to counsel lighting from one side to give a plastic effect to the scene. The intensity of lights was controlled for mood and dramatic effect; *e.g.*, comedies were well lighted, but at intimations of tragedy the lights were dimmed.

Another significant step in the direction of modern staging was the completion, in 1619, of the Teatro Farnese, at Parma—an elaborate theatre with a permanent proscenium, or decorative frame, forming an arch with a stage curtain in front of the scenery. (About 50 years earlier Francesco Salviati had introduced the proscenium frame as a temporary structure for performances at court.) The changing of scenery to suit different locales did not occur at once, however, emphasis being at first on atmosphere and spectacle. The falling of the proscenium curtain for scene changes between acts was not common in England until the mid-18th century, and until the late 19th century the convention of visible scene changing continued.

The first mode of shifting, as generally practised, was to remove the house fronts of the first scene, revealing those of a second scene behind them. As the front sets of Serlian houses were more or less three-dimensional, this offered some difficulties; the practical tendency, therefore, was to strip down the weight of these constructions, and this eventually resulted in two-dimensional wings and backdrops that could be peeled off like cards off a deck. By the beginning of the 17th century this arrangement had been completed by sky borders—hanging horizontal strips of blue cloth, six feet apart in depth, bridging the stage above the wings.

Many practical suggestions for making shifts were offered by Nicola Sabbatini in the *Pratica di fabricar scene e macchine ne' Teatri* (*Manual for Constructing Theatrical Scenes and Machines*; 1638), a complete manual on every aspect of making and operating theatre machinery, including many magical effects, such as devices for simulating waves on stage. His ideas included the use of the *periaktoi* and the running of wing flats in grooves (soaped for smoothness), used in England (though less popular on the continent) until the 19th century.

By the close of the 16th century the work of Italian scene designers was already celebrated throughout Europe. The English designer Inigo Jones visited Giulio Parigi when in Italy in 1613–14 and returned to a successful career designing court masques, his opening-and-shutting scenes and use of moving clouds being particularly admired.

In France the Hôtel de Bourgogne, a theatre that had almost a monopoly of tragedy in Paris until the mid-17th century, favoured the use of multiple settings (*décor simultané*), also derived from Italy. All the locales were on the stage together (as with the medieval mansions). The plays of Corneille, which usually observed the unities, helped replace this with a single decor. When Molière first went to the Petit-Bourbon (1658) he was obliged to adapt his plays to the type of setting used by the theatre's regular tenants, a *commedia dell'arte* troupe called the Comédie-Italienne. This setting, a permanent one that showed houses arranged around a town square, was traditional, by then, for comic action, but it was shortly to be replaced by the Baroque (*see* below).

The scenic resources of the public theatres of Madrid at the opening of the 17th century were limited; however, those of Lope de Vega's plays performed at court, the *comedias de ruido* or *de teatro,* were staged with more pomp and machinery in the Italian manner. The new theatre built in 1635 in the palace of Buen Retiro was equipped for spectacular productions, and Lope's successor Calderón was to write for the full Baroque stage.

**6. Baroque.**—The wings-and-backdrop setting characterized the Baroque, which in France continued the Italian tradition of scenic splendour but with greater mobility and ornateness. Wings were placed three or more on each side of the stage, parallel to each other and at a slight angle to the footlights, with the backdrop closing the rear; on a deep stage, with the floor raked toward the back, the whole gave a picture of a deep perspective—a street, a path through a park, a corridor in a prison, and so on. Spectacles were common. In spite of its use of perspective and of *trompe l'oeil* painting, the Baroque set was distinctly conventional. Its total effect was that of a flimsy architecture, a gracious, elaborately painted formal area; its formality was accentuated by the chandeliers that hung over the stage and shed their radiance impartially over a succession of locales that might even include a vista of a storm at sea. Action was usually carried out on the extensive forestage, since at least one-third of the audience could not see to the depth of the main stage. The actors, however, gradually retreated into the scene, the forestage shrinking until the 19th century "picture stage" was complete.

From the Teatro Novissimo of Giacomo Torelli (1608–78) in Venice came the theatre machinery used throughout Europe during the next two centuries. This machinery included the revolving stage and most of the other devices known to the modern theatre. Most famous was a method of quick scene changing: wings ascended from the basement through slits in the stage on battens or ladders called masts, the whole movement being controlled by a drum belowstage.

After the middle of the 17th century this system of machinery was gradually adopted in France. Corneille wrote *Andromède,* staged in 1650 at the Petit-Bourbon, to show off the latest Italian machinery of Torelli, brought to Paris in 1645 at the command of Louis XIV. When the Petit-Bourbon closed in 1660, Molière's troupe transferred to the Palais-Royal (built in 1641 by Richelieu), which had ample scenery space. This theatre was re-equipped in 1671 with the latest machinery for the staging of *Psyché* by Molière. By 1660 the Théâtre du Marais was beginning to specialize in so-called machinery plays. The new Comédie Française (1689), into which the amalgamated comedy troupes moved, was well equipped with machinery.

Outdoor theatres of an intimate type, with living hedges for wings, were a charming variation of 18th-century theatre. (The garden theatre at Drottningholm, Swed., is a fine example.) These were the work of landscape gardeners. The indoor Baroque settings, however, were planned by professional scenic artists who were individually famous. The most outstanding of these were the Italians, who practised their art throughout Europe. Chief among them were Bernardo Buontalenti (1536–1608), G. L. Bernini (1598–1680), Lodovico Burnacini (1636–1707), Giambattista Piranesi (1720–78), and members of the Galli da Bibiena family (three prolific generations, from the mid-17th century to nearly the close of the 18th) and of the Galliari family (throughout the 18th century). (For a detailed exemplification of the Italian influence, *see* BIBIENA, GALLI DA.) Their legacy is evident in the contemporary French theatre, which relies to a noticeable degree on painted scenery. It is seen also on most of the world's operatic stages; in ballet, where "painty" settings had a renaissance in the work of pre-Soviet Russian designers (Léon Bakst, Nicholas Roerich, Alexandre Benois, Nathalie Gontcharova, Mikhail Larionov, and Serge Soudeikine); and in backdrops by French artists of the rank of Picasso, Léger, Matisse, and Dufy. Baroque design in the theatre was so distinctive, so remarkably integrated, that the following two centuries witnessed a continuing accommodation to it along with a struggle against its authority.

**7. Popular Theatre.**—Side by side with the court theatres of the Renaissance and the Baroque there existed a popular theatre known in Italy as the *commedia dell'arte,* or professional comedy. This was a theatre of wandering actors, hardly more than gypsies in status, who performed their coarse, comic improvisations at fairs and in marketplaces. Their stage, a bare platform laid over trestles or barrels and backed by a shabby painted curtain, was the same as that used for the medieval farces known as interludes, the Hanswurst comic plays of Germany, and the student dramas of Bohemia. (The mobile popular theatre, the *carpa,* of Mexico is a living example.) Sometimes these itinerant companies were able to use enclosed innyards, where they could erect their platform at one end. Such were the pre-Elizabethan theatres of England and the very similar *corral* theatres of 16th-century Spain. The stages remained platforms but with an awning to shelter them from the weather. For the revival of the platform stage in the 20th century, see *Scene Shifting,* below.

The stage of the Globe, the theatre in which the plays of Shakespeare were performed from 1599, ran deeply into the audience. At the back was a small, curtained inner stage in which scenes could be "discovered." Above this was a balcony, and above this a musicians' gallery—an arrangement that offered a choice of acting levels. In the attic were winches by which heavy properties, such as a throne, could be lowered to the stage floor. Traps were available, along with a variety of effects, including fireworks. Tables, chairs, and other furniture were moved by stagehands, visible to the audience, or as part of stage business by actors. Onstage killings were commonplace in Elizabethan drama, and provision had to be made for removing dead bodies from the curtainless main stage by the actors, plausibly motivated. (Two well-known examples occur in *Hamlet:* the prince "lugs the guts" of Polonius into a "neighbour room" and is himself carried out, near the close of the play, on the shields of Fortinbras' troops.) As in the Japanese Nō theatre, isolated scenic elements helped to indicate locale: two or three small trees to suggest a forest; rope rigging, stretched from the balcony or gallery to the stage floor, to suggest the deck of a ship. These tokens of locale, however, remained entirely subordinate to the free use of stage space; the dramatist himself identified the environment of a scene by allusions to it in the dialogue. Stage lighting was equally naïve. Since performances began at 2 P.M. in this roofless theatre, daylight was the normal illumination and lighted candles or torches were only part of the stage business. The Shakespearean stage, however, for all its apparent naïveté, had a remarkable fluidity of movement, which explains how *Antony and Cleopatra* (1607), with its 38 scenes, could have been performed without stage waits. Much of Shakespeare's vigour and pace were lost when his plays were presented later on, with the painted drops and cumbersome interiors fashionable until the end of the 19th century.

Public performances of Shakespeare, however, must be distinguished from private and court performances where the multiple setting (as employed at the Hôtel de Bourgogne) and signboards indicating locations may have been used. Elaborately staged court masques had always been a tradition separate from drama, and an attempt to unite the two arts early in the 17th century led in England to bitterness between the playwright Ben Jonson and

Inigo Jones. Plays were not wed to the scenic tradition in England until the Restoration, with the opening of indoor public theatres.

An English amateur group, the Elizabethan Stage Society, under the direction of William Poel, between 1895 and 1905 undertook performances in the manner of the Globe Theatre. Subsequently, Shakespearean plays lent themselves to endless scenic experiment, but almost always with a dominant feeling for the movement of the actor in space.

**8. Romanticism and the 19th Century.**—In the mid-18th century Baroque formality was being challenged in the theatres of France, England, and Germany. The greatly expanded middle-class audience influenced not only the choice of plays and the manner of acting but the setting as well. By the mid-19th century this had resulted in both the elaboration of the Baroque stage and its decay. While retaining wings-and-backdrop, the Romantic stage abandoned the formalism of the Baroque. Architectural perspective was replaced by a neo-Gothic sentimentalization of nature: moonlit mountains, exotic, palm-fringed landscapes, weeping willows over riverbanks were familiar scenes. Wing scenery was pushed to the extreme sides of the stage, which was now dominated by the backdrop; the forestage practically disappeared.

With painted Romantic scenery came a growing scientific awareness, but this was often pedantic and "antiquarian." In 1823 J. R. Planché designed the costumes for Charles Kemble's production of Shakespeare's *King John* on the basis of painstaking historical research, and every Shakespearean production thereafter took academic advice on the historic accuracy of its sets and costumes.

Gas lighting, though concealed from the spectators, now revealed every detail of the elaborate settings. Leading scene designers of the period included Philippe Jacques de Loutherbourg, who took charge of the sets for David Garrick's productions; he used not only the type of cutout drops made famous by the Bibiena family but also transparent scenery for magical effects, and he introduced the act drop—a painted drop that conceals a change of set going on behind it while action continues on the narrow strip of forestage in front. He and such scenic artists as William Capon (1757–1827), who designed sets for J. P. Kemble, and Goethe's designer, Karl Friedrich Schinkel (1781–1841), bathed the whole stage in an "atmosphere" of picturesque illusion.

By the 1850s the wing system had altered: interiors showed side walls and a back wall, with doors and windows, as in the production in London of Dion Boucicault's *London Assurance* (1841)—but the doors and windows were of framed and painted canvas, as a rule, and even some of the furniture was painted on the walls in *trompe l'oeil* style. In the United States, at least, this type of shoddy painted scenery endured until the ascendancy, about 1900, of the director David Belasco (*q.v.*). Without really abolishing the Baroque form, the Romantic set had deprived it of meaning. The conventional splendour of court theatricals had become the outer dress of psychological, middle-class drama.

Reform in scene design began in the 1870s with the work of the director-designer George II, duke of Saxe-Meiningen, a small German principality. He turned away from the two-dimensional setting and the bare stage floor and required that the setting be related to the actor architectonically; he broke up the stage floor into dramatic levels and utilized stage lighting both as a realistic and a dramatic element in production. Characteristically, Meiningen did not merely design backgrounds: before going into rehearsal he drew, in pen and ink, whole scenes showing the actors in the proposed settings.

**9. Naturalism.**—The Meiningen troupe's methods had their effect upon the younger stage people of Europe and particularly upon André Antoine, a Parisian amateur director, who was also impressed by Émile Zola's statement that "the experimental and scientific spirit of the century will enter the domain of drama." Stage Naturalism can be dated to the staging of Zola's short play *Jacques Damour* in 1887 in Paris by a newly organized group of amateurs, the Théâtre Libre, under Antoine's direction. The movement toward transposing to the stage "life as it is" showed itself not only in the nature of the play but also in the setting of a back room of a shop: its furniture was imported from the dining room of Antoine's mother. For *Les Bouchers* (1886) real carcasses of beef were hung on the stage. The proscenium opening now became the imaginary fourth wall of interiors that were facsimile reproductions of real environments.

The new style took firm root at the Moscow Art Theatre (*q.v.*), founded by Konstantin Stanislavski and Vladimir Nemirovich-Danchenko in 1897. As directed by Stanislavski the plays of Chekhov, Turgenev, Tolstoi, and Gorki became masterpieces of Naturalism. Stanislavski's directorial notebook for his production of Chekhov's *The Seagull* in 1898 contains ground plans of the entire Sorin estate: the park of birch trees, the house with its veranda, the lawn, the path, the lake, the little stream with its wooden bridges—for he wished to steep himself in a complete illusion of the estate. Within a decade the so-called Free Theatre movement had conquered the Western world. Ibsen played a part in this, his *Gengangere* (*Ghosts*) being selected for the opening performance of the Freie Bühne (1889) under Otto Brahm in Berlin and the Independent Theatre (1891) in London organized by J. T. Grein; and in 1890 it was performed at the Théâtre Libre. August Strindberg, too, wrote for the Naturalistic stage, only to revolt against it in the last two decades of his life. In New York the movement was sponored by David Belasco; by the beginning of World War I, "Belascoism" had triumphed in the United States theatre.

**10. Symbolism.**—In Paris reaction against Naturalism came swiftly. In 1891 Paul Fort organized the Théâtre d'Art and urged the spectator to "abandon himself completely to the poet" and to see "visions terrible and charming, lands of deception into which none but he [the poet] can penetrate." The Symbolist opponents of Naturalism had no use for "the carcass of reality" or for "the prose theatre": they wished to capture not a facsimile of life but its essence. For their settings they had the assistance of painters like Pierre Bonnard and Odilon Redon; but it was Fritz Erler, Symbolist designer for the Munich Künstlertheater, who gave full expression, scenically, to the new point of view. His settings for *Faust* in 1908 were characterized by shafts of light, pools of shadow, light joyous or sorrowful, and colours calculated to affect the emotions.

The U.S. producer and drama critic Kenneth Macgowan in 1921 condensed the scenic program of the Symbolists into four main principles: simplification of effect and means; a proper relationship of actors to background; suggestion, as when a single candlestick served to give the whole quality of the Baroque period for *La Tosca;* and synthesis, "a complex and rhythmic fusion of setting, lights, actors, and play."

In electric lighting, which had replaced gas on the world's stages by 1900, the Symbolists found an invaluable ally. It brought out the planes and accentuations of the setting, created a cubic volume of stage space, and in conjunction with the plaster cyclorama, a curved rear wall that reflected light without shadows, gave the effect of infinite vistas. To the Swiss Adolphe Appia (*q.v.*) the modern theatre is indebted for both theory and practice in handling this new medium. Designing for Richard Wagner in Germany, he showed in sketches, models, and light plots how Wagner's idea of "the projection of music into visible scenic form" could be carried out onstage. The result was the plastic setting, a sculptured or architectonic structure shaped to the movement of the actors. It proved especially valuable for Shakespearean and other many-scened plays, in which a combination of steps, platforms, and ramps became a generalized stage on which the light played in a continuously changing pattern.

The Symbolist technique created a corps of brilliant stage designers and directors the world over. Yet Symbolism, with its search for the essence of locale, did not prove altogether satisfying to its adherents. It was more selective, more colourful, more poetic than Naturalism; but it could be criticized as being merely Naturalism purified. Just as Antoine and Stanislavski felt the need to go beyond Naturalism into Symbolist experiment, so the Symbolist designers and directors were inclined to abandon the picture stage and to return to the older, direct form of theatre. Their thinking—called, without any derogatory connotation, Theatricalism—was summed up by the U.S. designer Norman Bel

Geddes (*q.v.*) when he said, "There is no more reason or logic in asking an audience to look at a play through a proscenium arch than there would be in asking them to watch a prize fight through one."

**11. Theatricalism.**—Theatricalism attracted designers like Edward Gordon Craig (*q.v.*) in England and Robert Edmond Jones (*q.v.*), Lee Simonson, and Geddes in the U.S. It appealed to directors like Max Reinhardt (*q.v.*) and Leopold Jessner in Germany, Jacques Copeau, Louis Jouvet (*qq.v.*), A. M. Lugné-Poë, Charles Dullin, Gaston Baty, and Georges Pitoëff in France, and Vsevolod Meyerhold (*q.v.*), Aleksandr Taïrov, and Evgheny Vakhtangov in Russia. In their view, to turn one's back on Naturalism—even on the selective Naturalism of the Symbolists—was to draw inspiration from the spirit of the theatre itself. The picture-frame stage called for passivity of response in audiences and their separation from the actors, lest the spell of illusion be broken. Wagner understood this so well that when his Bayreuth opera house was opened in 1876 it contained a deep orchestra pit (a "mystic abyss") and not one but two prosceniums intervening between stage and public. The Theatricalists, on the contrary, favoured a platform projecting into the audience to put the actor in the same room as the spectator, in direct alert contact. They accepted the obvious truth that the playgoers were in a theatre and that actors were on a stage, carrying out dramatic action with the help of settings that were obviously scenic constructions illuminated by stage spotlights; and they believed, further, that the abolition of barriers between actors and audience was reestablishing full dramatic communication between them.

This dramatized the difference between the Naturalist-Symbolist technique of illusion and the method of convention, which was the immemorial usage of theatre. With the Theatricalists the contrast was unmistakable, though it was never absolute. Thus in his Symbolist settings for Shaw's *Back to Methuselah* in 1922 for the New York Theatre Guild, Simonson made use of projected backgrounds that were a palpable artifice. Another U.S. designer, Jo Mielziner, frequently pushed beyond the boundaries of Symbolism to Theatricalism, especially in his use of transparencies; *e.g.*, in his designs for Arthur Miller's *Death of a Salesman* in 1949, in which parts of a house were rendered transparent as if by X-ray.

In musical plays and ballet, partly because of the exigencies of shifting and partly because a certain extravagance of style is traditionally expected, the Theatricalist tendency was much stronger than in drama: *Oklahoma!* as designed by Lemuel Ayers in 1943, or *My Fair Lady* in the settings by Oliver Smith in 1956, were outstanding examples. Theatricalism in drama was especially evident in the many-scened play, which almost always demands an arrangement that is basically abstract, even though each component scene appears as a plausible illusion; *e.g.*, Mordecai Gorelik's designs for the New York Group Theatre's 1933 production of Sidney Kingsley's *Men in White*, where the play's seven scenes, each a room in a hospital, consisted only of furniture or screens that appeared inside an architectural frame.

Akin to Theatricalism was the technique of stylization, which took one aspect of a locale as a convention for its whole quality; *e.g.*, the use by Simonson of Japanese screens as backgrounds throughout John Masefield's *The Faithful* in 1919. For *Macbeth* in 1921 Jones used, throughout, a group of Gothic arches that seemed to advance in military formation during Macbeth's rising career, but with the tyrant's later decline in fortunes a single arch remained leaning awry. This, however, was mild compared with the more extreme forms—Expressionism, Dadaism, Surrealism—that pushed Symbolism to its farthest limits.

Expressionism, mostly a German phenomenon (though foreshadowed by Strindberg in Stockholm at the end of the 19th century) originated in 1910 at the Sturmbühne in Berlin and reached its full development during and after World War I. It took a subjective, often hysterical view of environment. For example, Max Slevogt's design for Mozart's *Don Giovanni* at Dresden in 1924 twisted the palace out of shape; Vakhtangov presented S. Ansky's *The Dybbuk* in 1922 in a quasi-Cubist style that gave additional eeriness to the tale of demoniac possession; and at the Kamerny Theatre, Moscow, Aleksandr Taïrov presented Racine's *Phèdre* in 1922 and Eugene O'Neill's *Desire Under the Elms* in 1926 in a style that was Cubist even to the makeup of the actors.

G. Apollinaire's *Les Mamelles de Tirésias*, staged in Paris in 1917, was the ancestor of an assortment of plays that challenged not only Naturalism but reality; its staging was inspired by Dadaism (*q.v.*), the more destructive precursor of Surrealism (*q.v.*). With its ideological program of the liberation of the unconscious (even at the expense of apparent disintegration) as an irrational creative force, Surrealism inspired Salvador Dalí's backdrop for the 1939 performance at Monte Carlo of the ballet *Bacchanale*, which showed a gigantic swan with a ruined pediment lodged in its neck; and his 1949 set for the scene of the dance of the seven veils in Oscar Wilde's *Salome* at Covent Garden showed a neo-Gothic pavilion under a scarred and frightening moon and with a great peacock's tail for background. Less grotesque was Pavel Tchelitchew's set for Jean Giraudoux's *Ondine* (1939), where the fisherman's hut turned transparent to reveal a structure of fishes' bones. Cryptic in such plays as Ionesco's *The Chairs* (1947), Kafka's *The Trial* (1949), and Samuel Beckett's *Waiting for Godot* (1952), Surrealism lent itself to communicable satire. For example, Christian Bérard's set for Giraudoux's *La Folle de Chaillot* (1945) included a house front with nothing behind it; the V and W Theatre's presentation in Prague of *Heaven and Earth* (1936) parodied the Baroque style; and Kjeld Abell's designs for his own play *Melodien, den blev væk* (*The Melody That Got Lost*), produced in Copenhagen in 1935, cynically pointed up with magic lantern slides the dreariness of lower-middle-class life.

A thoroughgoing Theatricalism includes a return to platform staging—or at least to its psychology, since Theatricalists often perforce had to do their work on picture stages. Beginning at Munich in 1906, Max Reinhardt proceeded to re-create, in vast spectacles, some of the platform classics of the earlier eras of theatre. For *Sumurun* (1912), *The Miracle* (1911), and *Danton's Death* (1916) action took place partly on the stage and partly in the centre of the orchestra, with the actors coming to the stage through the aisles of the theatre. The grandiose quality of these productions was fully realized, beginning in 1919, in the arena of the Grosses Schauspielhaus, a reconstructed circus building in Berlin. In his nonarena presentations, Reinhardt at times made use of a huge revolving stage that turned in full view of the audience, the actors moving at the same time from one section of the turning stage to another. For *Othello*, in 1910, five major scenes were preset as a miniature Venice complete with canals and bridges.

In Petrograd, Vsevolod Meyerhold removed the proscenium and front curtain of the Aleksandrinski Theatre and presented Molière's *Don Juan* in 1910 with little Negro servants moving properties and ringing tiny silver bells to engage the attention of the audience. Less spectacularly, Copeau, at the intimate playhouse of the Vieux-Colombier, Paris, erected a permanent scenic facade on his curtainless stage, varying its details for each of his productions.

The greater vitality of Theatricalism resulted sometimes in productions of genius, sometimes in productions that were displays of dazzling mediocrity. Having carried out its mission of smashing the atmospheric stage picture, the movement could not merely go on reiterating that theatre must be theatre.

**12. Socialist Realism.**—To the dismay of many of the older people of the theatre, a new philosophy appeared in the Soviet Union proclaiming the theatre a weapon in the class war. After 1934 the Soviet ideal in the theatre was officially declared to be Socialist Realism, by which was meant stage productions realistic in orientation and socialist in political viewpoint. Meyerhold embraced this view, "seizing his audience by its lapels" and turning direct staging into a political virtue. Condemning the picture stage as bourgeois, Meyerhold tore out not only the front curtain of the stage but its sky drop as well, exposing the stage to its back wall and gridiron. His version of Gogol's *Revizor* (*The Inspector General*) in 1926, with its semicircle of 15 polished mahogany doors and raked platforms, was his outstanding achievement. Of great technical interest is his period of Constructivism: his production of Émile Verhaeren's *Les Aubes* (*Dawns*) in 1921 used, in utter negation of facsimile, structures resembling builders' scaffolding whose purpose was not to imitate any interior or exterior but to give the actors new and dramatic ways of moving about.

Meyerhold's successors were mindful of the values of Constructivism but rejected nonrepresentational settings for recognizable locales. Among Soviet directors most indebted to Meyerhold was Nikolai Okhlopkov, who produced "in the round" at the Realistic Theatre, Moscow, from 1932 to 1936. In the era of Stalinist reaction, Okhlopkov's arena productions became less popular in the U.S.S.R., but they inspired a major trend in the noncommercial playhouses of the United States.

Besides emphasizing directness and exploring stage space, Soviet scenic art established the principles known as machine-for-theatre and environment-in-motion. For Soviet designers, as for the Naturalists, the setting represented an environment, not mere decorative background: it affected human beings and was affected by them. Technically, the settings were considered to be mechanisms serving the actors and were capable of movement. The English stage historian Huntley Carter compared Soviet settings, like those by Isaak Rabinovich for Aristophanes' *Lysistrata,* in 1923, to "a scientific toy which can be taken to pieces and put together in different forms." Designed for the Moscow Musical Theatre, a group of colonnades was used in various combinations to form the streets, citadel, and gates of Athens. For the Kamerny Theatre production of Vsevolod Vishnevsky's *The Optimistic Tragedy* in 1933, the designer Vadim F. Rindin employed a raked turntable containing a pit and working on an eccentric pivot so that, with minor changes, it served equally as a battleship, a shell crater, trenches, or a prison camp.

The political aspect of Soviet theatre is illustrated by Nikolai Akimov's production of *Hamlet* at the Vakhtangov Theatre in 1932. By surrounding Hamlet with books and scientific instruments while exaggerating the rude military architecture of Elsinore, he emphasized the contrast between the feudal court and Hamlet himself, a man of the Renaissance. This influencing of the spectator by emotional partisanship is, of course, common also to the bourgeois theatre, though the morals drawn differ.

**13. Epic Theatre.**—Problem plays staged with a medley of nonillusory ("living newspaper") techniques comprised the Epic Drama, which was almost the personal handiwork of the director Erwin Piscator and the playwright-director Bertolt Brecht (*q.v.*). Piscator inaugurated, with his staging of Alfons Paquet's *Fahnen* (*Flags*) in Berlin in 1924, the use of film sequences on stage. In 1927 in Piscator's *Die Abenteuer des braven Soldaten Schweik* (*The Good Soldier Schweik*) fragments of scenery, as well as life-size cutout cartoons, traveled across the stage on a double treadmill while an animated antiwar cartoon unfolded on a screen behind the actors. Leo Lania's *Competition* in 1928 showed oil derricks actually being erected on stage. In the same year and also in Berlin, Brecht's *Die Dreigroschenoper* (*The Threepenny Opera*) had a pipe organ outlined in electric lights as a permanent background, along with free-standing pieces of scenery that included iron-barred prison cages and a long stairway on casters. Brecht did not resort to films on stage but did use projection screens showing explanatory titles and illustrations, usually one on either side of the stage or above the actors' heads. Half-curtains strung on wires across the front of the stage screened the scene changes but otherwise left the proscenium open. Brecht's most impressive drama, *Mutter Courage und ihre Kinder* (*Mother Courage and Her Children*), as staged by Brecht and Erich Engel at the Deutsches Theater in Berlin in 1949, also had half-curtains and projected titles. The production contained no settings in the ordinary sense, only stage properties; even the two peasant huts had the quality of "props." The main feature was Mother Courage's market wagon, which rolled from country to country and from year to year, maintaining its place against the movement of a revolving stage. The many locales were indicated by means of names woven out of tree branches and let down from the flies. The lighting, otherwise completely uncoloured, changed to a golden illumination for the song numbers.

The stage methods of Brecht and Piscator aroused a lively interest in Germany before both men went into exile in the U.S. for the duration of World War II. The Berliner Ensemble, organized in East Berlin on Brecht's return and run by his wife, Helene Weigel, established a reputation as the most advanced of the world's producing companies. In part it owed this reputation to the talent of its scene designers, among them Caspar Neher, Teo Otto, and Karl von Appen.

The scenic innovations of Epic Theatre were part of a conception of staging larger than that of its contemporaries. In part its staging method was the result of inadequate playscripts: both the films and the still projections were intended to expand the material of scripts written by "psychological" dramatists who were unaccustomed to a larger scope in playwriting. Neither Brecht nor Piscator felt that his particular trademarks in production were more than the crude beginning of a new, classic technique in the theatre. Still the Epic scenic methods were already carrying out Brecht's principle of alienation (a term perhaps better translated as "distancing" or "cooling"). Brecht's purpose was to hold the dramatic story at arm's length, to "cool it off," in order to make his audiences more reflective and critical, to keep them from being swept away by an overemotional empathy. His use of lettered comment or projected titles was one means of putting a brake on audience excitement. Brecht's theory was thus directly opposed to Wagner's.

The Epic setting was so strictly functional that it could not be distinguished from an organized group of large stage properties. It was *sachlich* (finite, materialistic). It banished all scenic "atmosphere" from the stage: locales were represented in documentary form, by means of properties, by such fragments of reproduced environment as were necessary for the action, or by "reports" (*i.e.,* photo-murals or framed paintings hung behind or above the actors). Working in an "inductive" rather than "deductive" manner, the designer supplied the actors with whatever was required for their work—furniture and other properties, doors and windows (sometimes without surrounding walls), lighting to make the actors clearly visible. The lighting did not attempt to simulate natural effects but functioned obviously as stage illumination. In contrast to Wagner's principle of synthesis, Brecht called for autonomy for each of the stage elements, demanding that they be used in the precise, deliberate manner of a lecture-demonstration. At the same time this did not relieve the Epic designer of the need for making his materials and their composition as beautiful as they were functional.

Conservative Marxist critics were as dubious as many Western commentators about the merits of Epic staging. However, the postwar presentations of the Berliner Ensemble and Piscator's resumed work in Hamburg and West Berlin made a deep impression. Epic was so totally conventional that, for the first time in the history of theatre, it put an end to the dichotomy between conventional and illusionary staging. At the same time it was not unprecedented; it shared many of the tenets of Theatricalism and was strongly influenced by Oriental staging. The most striking feature of Epic Theatre was its scientific bent, which opened a whole new field of scenic invention.

## II. CONTEMPORARY STAGE DESIGN

**1. Stage Equipment.**—Since most professional theatres now in use were built before 1940, their stages continue to appear as a gilded frame enclosing an animated, lighted picture. The stage area of these playhouses has a base of 70 × 35 ft. or more in width and depth, and a height of 70 ft. or more. The proscenium opening is roughly 35–45 ft. wide and about 30 ft. high. The proscenium width can be decreased by means of tormentors (framed vertical panels on either side), and its height can be reduced to a normal working dimension of about 14 ft. by means of the lower edge of the act curtain and of a teaser, or cloth border, hung overhead. The stage set (the scenery as a whole) occupies an area approximately 40 ft. wide, 25 ft. deep, and, if the backdrop, or cyclorama, is considered, perhaps 30 ft. high. The stage floor outside the set accommodates stored scenery and properties, accessory switchboards, etc. Additional scenery is flown (hoisted) out of sight between the top of the setting and the gridiron next

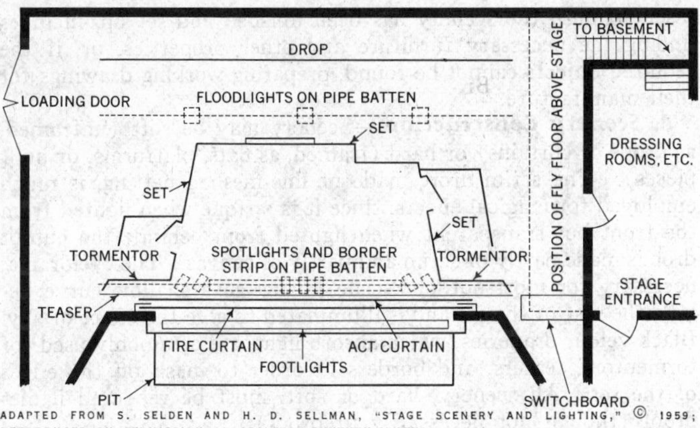


ADAPTED FROM S. SELDEN AND H. D. SELLMAN, "STAGE SCENERY AND LIGHTING," © 1959; REPRODUCED BY PERMISSION OF APPLETON-CENTURY-CROFTS

FIG. 1.—PLAN OF A TYPICAL EARLY-20TH-CENTURY STAGE, 52 FT. WIDE AND 28 FT. DEEP WITH A PROSCENIUM OPENING OF 28 FT.

to the ceiling of the stage house. In older theatres the rear wall of the stage is equipped with pulleys and scaffolding for the use of scene painters.

From the gridiron, or series of parallel steel girders, ropes descend to wooden or steel-pipe battens to which drops, or parts of built settings, can be attached. The fly gallery, or fly floor, part way up one of the side walls of the stage, has a pinrail where the lines (rigging) are tied; the gallery also provides standing room for stagehands (flymen). The stage sometimes contains, closer to the proscenium, a lower and smaller balcony where the electrician operates his main switchboard.

Normally the centre of the acting area is supplied with at least one trapdoor; often the entire stage floor is made up of trapdoors. The floor is of soft pine boards to accommodate the screws that hold down the ends of stage braces. The braces have prongs that fit into cleats in back of the scenery flats (panels of painted cloth on wooden frames), which can thus be quickly placed and then supported upright on the stage.

The lighting units have swivel joints and are clamped to the steel-pipe battens or to vertical steel pipes. A large number of these units hang on the first pipe batten just behind the proscenium and above the set. Additional projectors, spotlights, strip-lights, and floor lights flank the set on movable stands called boomerangs, or are scattered at strategic points, including several places in the auditorium. For big musicals the lighting instruments may be counted in hundreds.

A decorative house curtain, or act curtain, closes the proscenium opening; in front of it, likewise filling the opening, hangs the safety (or fire) curtain, formerly built of sheet iron but now generally woven of asbestos. The curtains, like drops, rise or descend in one piece. The stage roof above the gridiron has a large glass skylight which can be opened swiftly to allow the escape of smoke in case of fire onstage.

In theatres built after World War I there were some noticeable changes in the appearance and operation of the stage. A system of iron counterweights and steel cables began to take the place of sandbags and rope rigging; in many new theatres the counterweight system is now handled electrically. The formal, inherited arrangement of footlights combined with borderlights (strips of lights directly over the set) gave way to a more elaborate and flexible system of light sources located on every conceivable perch around the set and even in hidden crevices in the set itself. The conspicuous footlights (almost a metaphor for theatre) were sunk discreetly into the floor of the stage or removed altogether. In a number of playhouses the cloth cyclorama was replaced by a plaster dome, consisting of a concave quarter-sphere of slightly roughened plaster, which gives a much superior illusion of sky or of unlimited space. Revolving stages of the type used in Japan, where they were worked by a hand-operated windlass under the stage, became a feature of many new Western theatres. Electrically operated by remote control, they could not only turn but could be raised or lowered above or below the stage level. It even became possible to load huge operatic sets on platforms in the stage basement, sending them up, at the touch of a button, to replace one another onstage.

In more recent years there has been an accelerated movement away from picture staging and the so-called fourth wall. Instead of trying to reproduce "life itself" onstage, the tendency has been toward a straightforward acceptance that the stage is an artificial medium subject to its own laws of artistry. This has resulted in a shift of emphasis from the proscenium to the stage platform. Thus, on the "open stage" (as exemplified in the Vivian Beaumont Theatre, New York), while the proscenium may remain, it is no longer gorgeously decorated but merges into the side walls of the auditorium; it may be supplemented by smaller side stages and may be capable of moving electrically to widen or reduce the size of the main stage opening. As in the pre-19th century theatres, the forestage, or stage apron, thrusts into the audience, replacing the orchestra pit. In most theatres built since World War II, the enlarged forestage is a separate elevator unit, operated electrically. An even more radical departure from late Victorian and Edwardian tradition is the arena stage, surrounded on three (sometimes four) sides by the audience. In the United States the arena stage is often found as an experimental adjunct to the main stage in university and community theatres.

Innovations have continued in the system of stage lighting (*see* further STAGE LIGHTING). Sound effects have been electrified, and, in the form of recordings on magnetic tape, issue from sound-mixing tables, either backstage or from the electrician's booth at the back of the auditorium, being conveyed from there by means of amplifiers to various parts of the stage or of the house. An entire library of taped sound effects is available. During rehearsals the director, dance director, and scene designer communicate with backstage by "intercom." The stage manager can call actors from their dressing rooms by means of a buzzer and may even see them and the stagehands by closed-circuit television.

In addition to modern scientific devices, the stage may make use of special effects, many of them centuries old. They include shaded mirrors for the creation of phantoms; cables and harnesses to enable supernatural beings to fly through the air; breakaways of various kinds, including bottles made of wax, chairs and tables with legs sawed off and hinged back on, or stairs whose risers flatten out, forming a chute. There is lycopodium powder for sudden flames, and confetti for snow; there are plumbing and troughs for rain, fan-fluttered ribbons for torches and open fires.

Although mechanization and automation have found widespread use onstage and will in all likelihood continue to do so, their value in the service of drama is still contested in some quarters. Such gifted directors as Erwin Piscator have not hesitated to call for the installation of stages as superbly functional as modern factories. An opposing school of thought insists that the theatre was better off with less machinery and more imagination; and, that in practice, elaborate machinery, such as revolving and elevator stages, often lies neglected. The answer to this question may eventually be determined by the types of plays that are written and the demands made by dramatists on the stage technicians.

**2. Principles of Design.**—Design for the stage is a specialized art with its own laws. It is not an illustration of the locale of a playscript but is intended for the use of actors and is itself an element of the play's action. The designer must therefore be aware of the way in which the setting is related to the director's interpretation of the play. Factual documentation of history and geography, as in the Naturalistic theatre, is not enough. The designer's sets must express the underlying dramatic quality, which may differ from their ostensible appearance. This kind of analysis is called pointing up the theme; the stage director and the designer must agree about it and about the blocking (the charting of the actors' movements).

As a visual art, scene design obeys the laws of pictorial composition (the picture stage), of architecture and interior decoration (Naturalism), of sculpture (the plastic stage), and of engineering (Constructivism). At least two additional requirements are specific to scene design: the first is the law of sight lines—*i.e.,* keeping the action and at least the significant parts of the

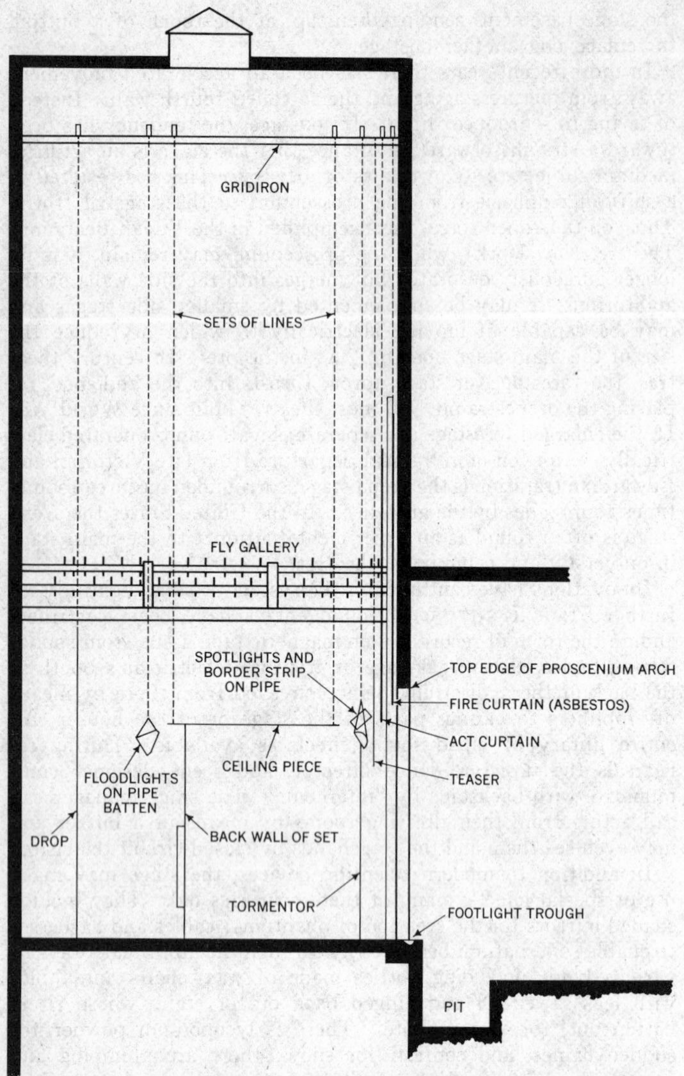


ADAPTED FROM S. SELDEN AND H. D. SELLMAN, "STAGE SCENERY AND LIGHTING," © 1959; REPRODUCED BY PERMISSION OF APPLETON-CENTURY-CROFTS

FIG. 2.—VERTICAL SECTION (SIDE VIEW) OF A TYPICAL EARLY-20TH-CENTURY STAGE

set within the audience's range of vision. Perfect viewing from all seats is rarely achieved, but the designer must do his utmost to increase visibility from all parts of the house, even at the cost of some distortion. The second specific law is economy of construction, shifting, storage, and transportation. The sets have to be put together and taken apart easily and quickly. In the United States professional scenery is not built in sections wider than 5 ft. 9 in., since a freightcar door is 6 ft. high.

**3. Working Out the Design.**—The designer and the director discuss the designer's rough sketches and ground plans. Agreement being reached, the designer makes finished sketches and a scale model (commonly $\frac{1}{2}$ in. to the foot). Ordinarily the sketches are in water colour and the models in unpainted cardboard. When every aspect of the model has been approved, the designer or his assistant begins to draft the working drawings of the show. These include a dimensioned ground plan, front elevation, section, and a hanging chart showing where drops, curtains, cloth borders, and other "flown" pieces are to be hung from the gridiron. There are also detailed drawings of the more unusual or complicated sections of scenery and of all properties that are to be constructed. These drawings go to the carpenter, who prepares his own drawings from them. The designer (or, in some cases, a lighting expert) then prepares light charts in ground plan and section, showing what lighting instruments will be used, their location, and the areas they will illuminate. Scenery completed by the carpenter goes to the scene painter, to whom the designer has sent colour samples and scaled colour sketches. Supervision by the designer, essential until the scenery has been finished and set up, includes finding the necessary furniture and other properties, or, if the required objects cannot be found, preparing working drawings for their manufacture.

**4. Scenery Construction.**—Scenery may be soft (unframed, as drops or curtains) or hard (framed, as flats, platforms, or built pieces). The scrim drop, made of fine-meshed netting, is much employed for magical effects, since it is opaque when lighted from the front but transparent when lighted from behind; the cutout drop is made partly of scrim and partly of canvas. The cyclorama, necessary for most outdoor scenes, hangs in a shallow curve behind the rest of the set and is illuminated to give the effect of sky. Black velour draperies, which absorb light, are commonly used for tormentors, teasers, and borders in order to mask off the edges of the set. All scenery, hard or soft, must be rendered flameproof (though not necessarily fireproof).

In the 20th century there has been a marked tendency toward framed construction and heavy building, and a thin, flexible veneer called profile board is often used instead of canvas. The simplest framed unit is the rectangular flat used for sections of wall, for backings behind door openings, and (in a modified form) for ceilings. The ground row is an irregularly shaped flat resting on the stage floor and used most often to mask the lights that illuminate the lower part of the cyclorama. The built piece is a solid construction such as a window, door, or stairway. The standard stage platform, which folds together when not in use, is called a parallel. Parts of a set are joined by lashing with thin rope or by the use of hinges with removable pins. For storage, all pieces of heavy construction come apart from all flat pieces.

Most scene painting on flats is done with opaque water colours on the sized surface. Large drops and cycloramas are not sized but are painted with transparent dye colours. When careful painting of ornaments, human figures, or perspectives is required, the designer's sketch is transferred (as in mural painting) by dividing the design and the drop into marked-out squares and then copying outlines, one square at a time. Modern scene painters do little *trompe l'oeil* painting, but their work is nevertheless skilled: spattering and stippling are done with the brush, spraying with an airbrush; glazing, more customary in the case of oil paint, is used especially for woodwork.

**5. Scene Shifting.**—Shifting must be considered in the stage design. In shifting by hand, scene 1 may be removed and replaced by scene 2. For a faster arrangement, scene 2 may be placed behind and around scene 1, requiring only the removal of properties and certain flats from the first scene and the introduction of the properties of scene 2. (Obviously this arrangement will not do if the first set has to be larger than the second.) Movable platforms holding entire sets (including their furniture and properties) permit much faster scene changes and save labour, although their initial cost is high. A favoured platform method is the revolving platform, or turntable, occupying most of the stage area. Two sets are erected on it, back to back; scene 3 may be loaded while scene 2 is playing, and so on. If the locales are supposed to be adjacent in space they may be merged into a single composition filling the whole turntable, as was demonstrated by Reinhardt in his staging of *Othello* and *A Midsummer Night's Dream*. Sliding platforms, freewheeling on casters or moving on metal or fibre tracks, are also available for shifting.

Sets for arena theatres present some special difficulties. If the stage is entirely surrounded by the audience, large scenery must be excluded. The presence of doors and windows is implied by gestures; corners of rooms may be indicated by means of vertical strips of tape, wood, or metal. Furniture, however, must be arranged logically. It is virtually impossible to conceal the lighting units of the arena stage, nor is it really necessary to do so, since arena production is fundamentally Theatricalist. Still, light sources should be so placed that they do not glare into the eyes of the audience. On the arena stage, scenery must often be moved through the aisles of the theatre, and if quick shifts are desired they must be made in the dark. However, an arena-stage director, within the tradition of Theatricalism, can make adroit use of the property man, after the Chinese or Elizabethan manner. When

Remains of the Greek theatre at Delphi with the valley of the Pleistus as the natural background to the stage

Scenery for the *Adelphi* by Terence from an illustration in the edition of Terence's plays published in Lyons, France, in 1483. Victoria and Albert museum

Engraving of the permanent scene for the stage of the Teatro Olimpico, Vicenza, Italy, designed by Andrea Palladio (1508–1580) in 1580 and completed by Vincenzo Scamozzi (1552–1616) in 1585. Victoria and Albert museum

Close-up of the stage and the central portion of the *frons scaenae* (façade of stage building) of the partially restored Roman theatre at Orange, France, *c.* A.D. 50

Stage design by Sabastiano Serlio (1475–1554) for a scene of a satiric play from the English edition (1611) of Serlio's book *Architettura* published in 1545. The British museum

## GREEK, ROMAN AND RENAISSANCE STAGING

BY COURTESY OF (CENTRE LEFT, BOTTOM LEFT) VICTORIA AND ALBERT MUSEUM, (BOTTOM RIGHT) THE TRUSTEES OF THE BRITISH MUSEUM; PHOTOGRAPHS, (TOP LEFT) THE MANSELL COLLECTION, (TOP RIGHT) THECLA, (BOTTOM RIGHT) JOHN R. FREEMAN & CO.

# STAGE DESIGN

Stage designed by Inigo Jones (1573–1652) in the Italian manner for a production of *Florimène* in 1635. Devonshire collection, Chatsworth, England

Setting for a performance of Molière's *Le Malade imaginaire,* shown being given at the palace of Versailles in 1674. Engraving by Le Pautre dated 1676. Victoria and Albert museum

Drawing for an interior setting by Giuseppe Galli Bibiena (1696–1757), a member of a family of Italian scenic artists whose work greatly influenced stage design throughout Europe and particularly that of the operatic stage. Victoria and Albert museum

Back cloth for a prison setting by Philippe J. de Loutherbourg (1740–1812), scenic designer for David Garrick at the Theatre Royal, Drury Lane, London. Victoria and Albert museum

A scene from *Miss Sara Sampson,* by Gotthold Lessing, designed about 1884 by George II, duke of Saxe-Meiningen (1826–1914). The Staatliche Museen, Meiningen, Germany

Detail from the sketch by Victor Simov for the scenery of Anton Chekhov's *The Seagull* staged by Konstantin Stanislavski (1863–1938) at the Moscow Art theatre in 1898

## STAGE DESIGN OF THE 17TH, 18TH AND 19TH CENTURIES

BY COURTESY OF (CENTRE LEFT AND RIGHT) VICTORIA AND ALBERT MUSEUM, (BOTTOM LEFT) THE STAATLICHE MUSEEN, MEININGEN, THÜRINGEN, GERMANY: PHOTOGRAPHS, (TOP LEFT) COPYRIGHT DEVONSHIRE COLLECTIONS, THE TRUSTEES OF THE CHATSWORTH SETTLEMENT, (TOP RIGHT) GIRAUDON, (BOTTOM RIGHT) NOVOSTI PRESS AGENCY, LONDON

Naturalistic setting by David Belasco (1853–1931) for his New York production of *Tiger Rose* in 1917

Symbolist setting by Lee Simonson for George Bernard Shaw's *Back to Methuselah,* New York Theatre Guild, 1922

Sketch by Adolphe Appia (1862–1928) for a scene in Wagner's *Die Walküre,* 1892, showing one of his plastic sets, a sculptured or architectonic structure shaped to the movement of the actor

Norman Bel Geddes (1893–1958) stage design for *Hamlet,* 1931, a non-realistic setting that combined many stage levels with special lighting to evoke the varying moods of the play

Stage design by Jo Mielziner for a scene in Arthur Miller's *Death of a Salesman,* 1949, a unit setting in which different parts of a house are visible at the same time

Design for the forum scene in Shakespeare's *Julius Caesar* by Edward Gordon Craig, 1922. Victoria and Albert museum

## 19TH- AND 20TH-CENTURY STAGE DESIGN

BY COURTESY OF (TOP LEFT AND RIGHT) THEATRE COLLECTION, NEW YORK PUBLIC LIBRARY, (CENTRE LEFT) FONDATION ADOLPHE APPIA, COLLECTION SUISSE DU THEATRE, BERNE, (CENTRE RIGHT) HOBLITZELLE THEATRE ARTS LIBRARY, UNIVERSITY OF TEXAS, (BOTTOM LEFT) JO MIELZINER, (BOTTOM RIGHT) EDWARD GORDON CRAIG, ESQ.; PHOTOGRAPHS, (BOTTOM LEFT) PETER A. JULEY & SON, (BOTTOM RIGHT) VICTORIA AND ALBERT MUSEUM

# STAGE DESIGN

A simultaneous setting by Robert Edmond Jones (1887–1954) for Eugene O'Neill's *Desire Under the Elms,* Provincetown Playhouse production, 1924

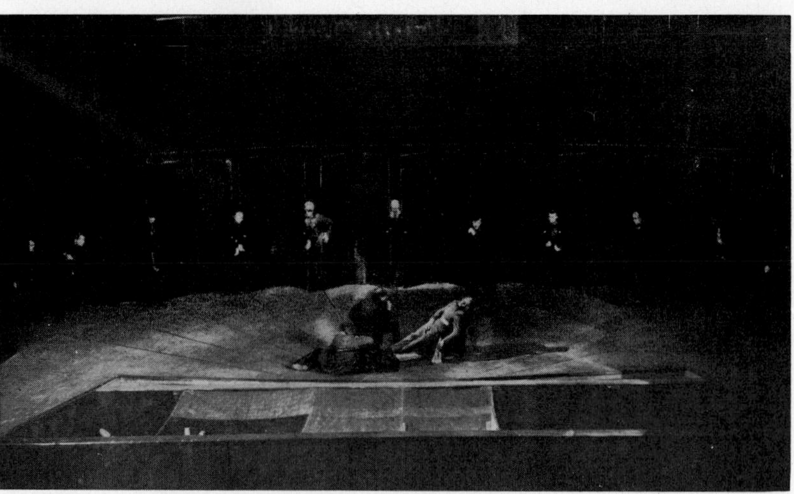

The anti-illusionist stage of Vsevolod Meyerhold (1874–1942) designed for his production of Nikolai Gogol's *Revizor* (*The Government Inspector*), Moscow, 1926, showing the mahogany doors, and movable sloped platform in the style of the Greek exostra

Set for Molière's *L'École des femmes,* Paris, 1936, directed by Louis Jouvet (1887–1951), one of many directors who rejected naturalism and symbolism in favour of artificiality in staging

Scene from Friedrich von Schiller's *Die Jungfrau von Orleans* designed by Paul Walter and directed by Hans Schüler at the National theatre, Mannheim, Ger., 1957–58

Epic setting for a scene in *Mutter Courage und ihre Kinder* staged by the author, Bertolt Brecht (1898–1956), and Erich Engel and produced by the Berliner Ensemble in 1949

Theatricalist setting by Oliver Smith for the Ascot Gavotte scene in *My Fair Lady,* a musical adaptation of Shaw's *Pygmalion* by Alan Jay Lerner and Frederick Loewe, New York, 1956

## 20TH-CENTURY STAGE DESIGN

BY COURTESY OF (TOP LEFT) THEATRE COLLECTION, NEW YORK PUBLIC LIBRARY, (TOP RIGHT) SOCIETY FOR CULTURAL RELATIONS WITH THE U.S.S.R., (CENTRE LEFT AND RIGHT, BOTTOM LEFT) MORDECAI GORELIK COLLECTION; PHOTOGRAPHS, (CENTRE LEFT) LIPNITZKI, PARIS, (CENTRE RIGHT) ADOLF FALK FOTOGRAFIE, MANNHEIM, GERMANY, (BOTTOM LEFT) THE BERLINER ENSEMBLE, (BOTTOM RIGHT) FRIEDMAN-ABELES the stage is surrounded on only three sides, the wall side may be used for full-height settings, for practical entrances and exits, or for simple scene changes.

The semipermanent set, whether in the arena or on the traditional stage, has the minimum of things to shift. A classical instance was Simonson's arrangement for Eugene O'Neill's *Marco Millions* in 1928. A decorative neutral frame occupied the back wall and sides of the stage while nine scene changes from Venice to India, Syria, Persia, and China were accomplished by changing the scenic plugs that fitted into the three openings in the frame; there were also changes of properties, draperies, backdrops, and lighting. With the "simultaneous" set there is no scene shifting. The stage is divided into compartments and the lighting moves with the action from one area to another. An example was Robert Edmond Jones's setting for O'Neill's *Desire Under the Elms* in 1924, in which the lower and upper rooms of a New England farmhouse were visible, together with the front yard and gate.

Sometimes scene changes may take place in view of the audience as a deliberate part of the performance. Examples are the turntable scenes used by Reinhardt, the mobile elements in Brecht's plays, and the treadmills of Piscator. In the American theatre, shifts of this sort are likely to be found in musicals rather than in drama, but there have been numerous exceptions, as in the scene devised by Peter Larkin for John Patrick's *The Teahouse of the August Moon* in 1953, in which an entire teahouse was put together onstage in front of the audience. Displays of this sort are fully supported by Theatricalist technique, which looks upon the setting less as an atmospheric background for the actors than as a dramatic element in its own right. This functional aspect interests particularly the scene designers of the Soviet Union, who regard the stage set as "machine for theatre."

**6. Platform Staging.**—The stage platform in its most primitive shape (*see* above, *Popular Theatre*) took a new lease on life in the 20th century, with mobile acting companies using motor trucks for conveyance and temporary platforms for stages. Plays were thus brought into the remote areas of many countries, sometimes as adventurous student productions, as in the United States, sometimes as government-sponsored cultural or propaganda media, as in the Soviet Union, Fascist Italy, or Communist China. Often the platform of the truck itself was improvised as a stage, with scraps of settings to indicate locale. The *Schwankbühne* ("farce stage"), the early German version of the *commedia* platform, also found employment: Günther Weisenborn's drama *Tyl Eulenspiegel* (1949) in West Berlin and Carl Orff's comic opera *The Clever Woman* (1948) in East Berlin both placed *commedia* platforms boldly on the stage of the proscenium theatre, making good use of the flavour and vigour of this naïvely effective method.

BIBLIOGRAPHY.—*History and Theory.*—L. Burlingame, *The Art, Life and Theories of Richard Wagner* (1875); Adolphe Appia, *Die Musik und die Inscenierung* (1899); Vitruvius, *Ten Books on Architecture* (Eng. trans. by M. H. Morgan, 1914); H. K. Moderwell, *The Theatre of To-day* (1927); E. Stern and H. Harald, *Max Reinhardt und seine Bühne* (1918); L. Moussinac, *La décoration théâtrale* (1922); *The New Movement in the Theatre,* Eng. trans. (1932); J. Gregor, *Wiener szenische Kunst* (1924–25), (ed.) *Monumenta Scenica,* 12 portfolios (1925–30); O. Fischel, *Das moderne Bühnenbild* (1923); O. M. Sayler (ed.), *Max Reinhardt and His Theatre* (1924); P. Zucker, *Die Theaterdekoration des Klassizismus* (1925); E. G. Craig, *On the Art of the Theatre,* 2nd ed. (1924); S. Cheney, *Stage Decoration* (1928); W. R. Fuerst and S. J. Hume, *Twentieth Century Stage Decoration,* 2 vol. (1929); R. Cogniat, *Décors de théâtre* (1930); L. Simonson, *The Stage Is Set* (1932), *Part of a Lifetime* (1943); D. Oenslager, *Scenery: Then and Now* (1936); Mordecai Gorelik, *New Theatres for Old* (1940); Robert Edmond Jones, *The Dramatic Imagination* (1941); P. Sonrel, *Traité de scénographie* (1943); J. Laver, *Drama: Its Costume and Décor* (1951); N. Decugis and S. Reymond, *Le décor du théâtre en France* (1953); Ralph Pendleton (ed.), *The Theatre of Robert Edmond Jones* (1958); International Theatre Institute, *Stage Design Throughout the World Since 1935,* ed. by René Hainaux (1957); R. Gilder and R. M. MacGregor, *Stages of the World* (1949); Norman Bel Geddes, *Miracle in the Evening* (1960); Orville K. Larson (ed.), *Scene Design for Stage and Screen* (1961); International Theatre Institute, *Stage Design Throughout the World Since 1950,* ed. by René Hainaux (1964).

*Technical.*—John Dolman, Jr., *The Art of Play Production* (1928); N. P. Izvekov, *Stage,* Eng. trans. (1935); S. Selden and H. D. Sellman, *Stage Scenery and Lighting* (1930); R. Southern, *Changeable Scenery* (1952); D. Zinkeisen, *Designing for the Stage* (1938); H. Burris-Meyer and E. C. Cole, *Scenery for the Theatre* (1939); John Gassner (ed.), *Producing the Play* (1941); B. W. Hewitt *et al., Play Production* (1952); J. Moyner, *Bibliothèque des Merveilles: L'Envers du Théâtre* (1873); F. Kranich, *Das Bühnentechnik der Gegenwart,* 2 vol. (1928–33); H. Heffner, S. Selden, and H. D. Sellman, *Modern Theatre Practice* (1936); S. Cornberg and E. L. Gebauer, *A Stage Crew Handbook* (1941); H. Nelms, *A Primer of Stagecraft* (1941); M. Smith, *Play Production for Little Theaters, Schools and Colleges* (1948); A. S. Gillette, *Stage Scenery: Its Construction and Rigging* (1959); International Theatre Institute, *An International Vocabulary of Technical Theatre Terms* (1960); Harold Burris-Meyer and Vincent Mallory, *Sound in the Theatre* (1964); Jo Mielziner, *Designing for the Theatre* (1965). (Mo. G.)

**STAGE DIRECTING:** *see* ACTING, DIRECTION AND PRODUCTION.

**STAGE LIGHTING** is the youngest of the arts of the theatre. Playwriting, acting, music, theatre architecture, and scene design all have centuries of tradition behind them, but it is only since the development of electric light, *i.e.,* since about 1880, that lighting has been capable of playing a major role on the stage. Lighting by open flame—torch, candle, oil lamp, or gas—provided illumination of a sort for the actors but allowed of little or no control. Electricity gave the theatre a source of light that was safe, convenient, flexible, and fully controllable.

The tendency of the 20th-century theatre toward scenic variety and flexibility, *e.g.,* in the use of platforms and ramps as acting areas, would have been impossible without controlled lighting. Stereotyped sets consisting of flat walls, backdrops, and borders are disappearing, and creative lighting with architectural forms and drapery is taking their place. The designer now uses light as one of his major tools, and with it makes clearer, cleaner stage pictures than his predecessors ever achieved with tortured detail in paint, wood, and canvas. Thus, a column and a stained-glass window make the entire stage a cathedral; a corner of a facade, when lighted, becomes an entire building; and a single shaft of light into empty space illuminates anything from the fields before Troy to the interior of a crowded nightclub.

This article is concerned mainly with the technical aspects of stage lighting. For the aesthetic role of lighting in dramatic representation, *see* STAGE DESIGN. Information on particular types of lamps mentioned may be found in the article LIGHTING.

## HISTORY

**Early Lighting.**—Torches, lanterns, or candles have been carried onto the stage at all eras to indicate darkness. The Greeks occasionally used fires when their dramas continued after sunset, or to indicate night scenes. The Roman theatres may sometimes have given evening performances lighted by torches and oil lamps. When private theatrical performances began to be given in indoor halls, after dark, the problem was to provide light on the large scale needed to illuminate the entire hall, as much as to light the stage.

The first treatise describing artificial light as an integral part of stage presentation is that of Sebastiano Serlio in his *Second Book of Architecture* (1545, Eng. trans. 1611); this was elaborated by Leone de' Somi in the *Dialoghi in materia di rappresentazioni sceniche* (*Dialogues on Stage Affairs; c.* 1550). Both describe the use of torches behind glasses of coloured water for lighting effects. Serlio adds that the light can be intensified by setting a bright basin behind the torch. These lights were on stage, for instance behind windows, and De' Somi claimed that the glasses were first used to screen the direct light from the audience's eyes. He advocated concealing the light sources as far as possible and having few lights in the auditorium set well back behind the audience so that the stage should appear bright by contrast.

Nicola Sabbatini's *Pratica di fabricar scene e macchine ne' Teatri* (*Manual for Constructing Theatrical Scenes and Machines;* 1638) describes how to make various types of lights and a fuse to light the lamps simultaneously, and illustrates a dimmer, which descended over the candles. He describes footlights behind a small parapet at the front of the stage, but he preferred side lighting and lighting behind the "heavens." Besides the drawback of smoke and smell, with footlights "one can see better the costumes of the actors and the dancers," he wrote, "but . . . their faces seem so pale and wan that they look as though they have just had a bad fever."

The earliest illustration of lighting in the English theatre is the frontispiece of Francis Kirkman's *The Wits* (1672). Six double-wick oil-float lamps and two chandeliers with eight candles each lighted the stage.

Throughout the Baroque era the stage was lighted by chandeliers that remained in view whatever the scene below. The actor-manager Tate Wilkinson in his *Memoirs* describes these on the English Restoration stage. Chandeliers over the stage appear also in pictures of a leading Parisian theatre, the Hôtel de Bourgogne, in 1688 and in a painting of the Comédie Française about 1670; the latter view also shows footlights, 34 candles along the edge of the apron stage, their glare kept from the audience by metal shades.

Though David Garrick did not introduce footlights to the English theatre—they were already in use at the Drury Lane—contemporaries were clear that the lighting reforms he brought about in 1765 with the help of his scene designer P. J. de Loutherbourg were a sensational improvement. He abolished the stage chandeliers (visible to the audience and obscuring the view from the gallery) and at the same time improved the quality of the lighting while concealing its source. Garrick relied mainly on sidelights (on the prompter's side only) mounted all the way up so-called wing ladders—an arrangement already in use but only as a subsidiary source of light. These he supplemented with concealed footlights and perhaps with concealed lights above the stage.

The introduction of the Argand burner (*q.v.*) provided a brighter light source; but before it had time to influence the technique of stage lighting, it was superseded by gas.

**Gas.**—Illuminating gas first was used regularly to light the stage in 1816, in the New Theatre, Philadelphia. The gas had to be manufactured by the theatre itself, at great expense; it also required miles of piping. Several London theatres soon adopted the new medium, but it did not come into common use until about 1850. Gas permitted for the first time control of all lights from one central location; it could be turned off and on either at the mains or with secondary valves from a "gas table" near the prompter. The original gas burners were open flames or flames in glass chimneys (superseded after 1887 by the more efficient Welsbach mantle); blazing alcohol wads on long poles were used to light the jets. Chief among the defects of this system was the danger of fire: theatre fires promptly doubled in the U.S., Great Britain, and France, and the thin costumes of dancers sometimes caught fire from the footlights. Fire regulations, therefore, were established, which fixed the position and number of burners and made the presence of guards compulsory.

Until the reforms introduced by Henry Irving at the Lyceum, which he acquired in 1878, little thought was given to the artistic potential of gas, which was accepted for its brighter illumination and its controllability. Irving experimented with realistic effects. The auditorium was darkened, and he used individual lights to achieve more plastic illumination onstage; *e.g.*, lights picked out the lovers Romeo and Juliet although the bedroom scene was set at night. He also devised an elaborate system of drawing coloured silks and screens in front of his lamps for colour mixing, and later he employed spotlights.

**Limelight.**—The calcium ("lime") light, invented by Thomas Drummond around 1820, may have been used in the theatre by 1837 and was widely used by the 1860s. A block of calcium heated to incandescence in jets of burning oxygen and hydrogen provided a soft, very brilliant light that could be directed and focused. (In England front-of-balcony lights may still be called limes.) Limelights were mounted on adjustable stands and could follow actors and dancers with localized light.

**Electric Light.**—*Arc Lamps.*—The arc lamp provided the earliest form of electrical lighting in the theatre. Invented by Sir Humphry Davy (who also contributed greatly to the development of the limelight) in 1809, it did not come into general use in the theatre until about 1870, although it had been used experimentally by M. Duboscq and Léon Foucault in 1846 in a production of the *Prophète* at the Paris Opéra. Duboscq went on to develop a lightning machine (still used), a rainbow projector, and a luminous fountain, all using arc light.

The Jablochkov candle, a light arcing between two parallel sticks of carbon, was first used theatrically in the Paris Hippodrome in 1878, and 52 were installed in a theatre at Lyons, the Bellecour, in 1879. It was, however, never widely used as it could not compete with the incandescent lamp.

*Incandescent Lamps.*—The invention of the carbon-filament incandescent lamp by Thomas A. Edison in 1879 brought a relatively high-powered, easily controlled, and comparatively safe light source to the theatre. Light could now be used as a fully plastic medium, coloured, and varied in form and intensity in ways of which earlier designers had only dreamed. The synthesis of acting, music, scene design, and light into the composite whole advocated by Richard Wagner could at last be achieved.

In 1880–81 the Paris Opéra experimented with the first theatrical installation of electricity (completed by 1886). The Savoy Theatre, home of Gilbert and Sullivan, in London and the Bijou Theatre in Boston had electricity by 1882. The Landestheater in Stuttgart, the Residenztheater in Munich, the Staatsoper in Vienna, and the Staattheater in Brünn (now Brno) were electrified by 1883; the People's Theatre on the Bowery in New York City, by 1885. Most theatres had installed electricity by about 1890 (although at first gas was retained along with the newer medium).

The early electric globes (those with carbon filaments) gave a relatively dull light, orange in colour. Improved methods of construction, however, increased efficiency and decreased size. Today 750-w. and 1,000-w. lamps only $1\frac{1}{2}$ in. in diameter are common in spotlights, and there are single globes up to 10,000 w.

New equipment was designed to make efficient use of these light sources; for example, by the American Steele MacKaye (*q.v.*) in the last quarter of the 19th century in the Madison Square and Lyceum theatres in New York. The Italian Mariano Fortuny, working in Germany, developed about 1902 the *Kuppelhorizont,* a half dome made of silk or plaster, from which light was reflected upon the whole stage; it is still the most perfect means of simulating natural sky backgrounds. Obsolete because prohibitively expensive, this has been developed into the cyclorama, a semicircular plaster or taut canvas wall surrounding the back of the stage, sometimes 90 ft. high, which can be lighted from top and bottom to give sky effects.

In the U.S., David Belasco and his electrician Louis Hartman began lighting experiments in 1879. Hartman developed the first practicable lensed spotlight, using simple plano-convex lenses to concentrate the rays. Belasco almost eliminated footlights, substituting spotlights in the auditorium and wings. His standards of realism remain a major influence in modern productions.

With the development of new lamps, lens systems other than Hartman's were possible. By using a tubular instead of a globular lamp, the extremely short-focused Fresnel lens (invented in the 1820s) could be used in the theatre; this provided a smooth, brilliant throw of light with no clearly defined edge, which was very valuable in blending illumination in acting areas (*see* fig. 1).

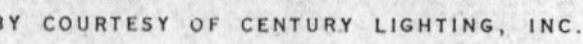

BY COURTESY OF CENTURY LIGHTING, INC.

FIG. 1.—(LEFT) 500-WATT FRESNEL SPOTLIGHT WITH MOUNTING CLAMP; (RIGHT) 750-WATT ELLIPSOIDAL FRAMING SPOTLIGHT

## MODERN STAGE LIGHTING

**Spotlights.**—The most important single instrument in stage lighting today is the ellipsoidal framing spotlight (*see* fig. 1). The light is gathered and redirected by the reflector, which passes the rays generated at one focal point of the ellipse through the other. A gate (aperture), adjustable in size and shape, is placed between the two focal points, and one or two objective lenses then project the image of the aperture onto the area to be illuminated. Fields of even intensity are produced, the beam may be shaped, hard or soft edges are possible, and efficiencies comparable to those of the Fresnel lens are obtained. With the framing spotlight, light can be masked perfectly, kept away from the orchestra, scenery, or draperies, and projected with extreme accuracy to the exact spot where it is required.

Follow spotlights have advanced greatly from the days of the limelight. The carbon arc still remains the most brilliant and smallest light source, but modern arcs operate at much lower amperages than formerly, with resultant increases in brilliance and lowered installation and operating costs. A modern 10-amp. follow spotlight will provide a very brilliant 3-ft. circle at a distance of 100 ft., or will flood a 40-ft. stage at the same distance. Such lights have selective colour controls and are balanced for smooth, easy operation. Other arc spotlights ranging from 20 to 200 amp. are used for all productions requiring a brilliant circle of light following the performers. Incandescent follow spotlights, having the same general lens and colour systems and commonly provided with 1,500- , 3,000- , or 5,000-w. lamps, are used for shorter throws.

**Floodlights.**—While spotlights are the basis of modern stage lighting, various forms of floodlights give general illumination and cover wide areas. Footlights are one form of floodlight; borderlights, standard in most theatres today, are another. Present-day foots and borders either have individual reflectors of spun aluminum or use lamps with internal reflectors. Individual colour filters are provided for each lamp.

Single floodlights have always been used for illuminating offstage areas, cycloramas, and similar large expanses where detailed light is not required or desired. The earliest floodlights were the so-called bunch lights utilizing clusters of candles, torches, or small incandescent globes. They were followed by the olivette, a square box-type reflector on a portable stand, using a single large lamp. The modern stage floodlight has a spun aluminum reflector, with a soft matte surface, and usually a 1,000- or 1,500-w. lamp. It may be placed on a stand or hung overhead. Because of their shape, such lights are usually referred to as scoops. Mounted singly or in groups, they provide smooth, featureless light over broad expanses.

**Light Control (Dimming).**—Control of illumination has always been a prime requisite for the theatre. Opaque slides and screens, blasts of air to extinguish candles, and other devices preceded the valves of the gas table and laid the foundations for the electric dimmer. The first electric dimmers were water barrels with two metal plates immersed in a weak brine solution. One plate rested at the bottom of the barrel; the other could be raised and lowered, increasing or decreasing the distance the current had to pass through the brine and thus varying the brilliance of the light. The system worked, after a fashion, but produced extremely uncertain results and much bad odour.

Resistance dimmers, consisting of a coil of resistance wire tapped at many points, with a turning contact touching the taps at successive points, provided the next type of dimmer. Resistance dimmers simply turned radiant energy from light into heat, diverting the electricity from one use to another. In spite of their large size, hotness, and comparative lack of sensitivity, they were the most widely used dimmers for 50 years and have by no means been entirely superseded today. The fact that they will control only loads near their rated capacity is a disadvantage, but they will operate with equal efficiency on either direct or alternating current.

The dimmer in commonest use at the present time is the autotransformer, which acts as a valve rather than as a diverting device, not utilizing the current when the lights are dimmed. Autotransformers are efficient from their full rated capacity down to almost zero, are cool and silent in operation, and provide extremely smooth changes in light intensity. They are manufactured in sizes ranging from 100 to 8,000 w.

Resistance and autotransformer dimmers may be operated either manually or by motors. In the average manually operated autotransformer dimmer board (*see* fig. 2), the dimmers may be selectively interlocked mechanically into banks (groups), which in turn may be interlocked into a grand master. In motor-operated dimmers, switches controlling the motors select the direction in which they travel, either dimming or brightening the lights. Because of their slow operation, motor-operated dimmers are seldom used for the stage but are common for auditorium lights.

BY COURTESY OF KLEIGL BROS. UNIVERSAL ELECTRIC STAGE LIGHTING CO.

FIG. 2.—(LEFT) MANUAL AUTOTRANSFORMER DIMMER BOARD; (RIGHT) TYPICAL PATCHING PANEL FOR A LARGE DIMMER BOARD

A more modern addition to the field of theatrical dimmers is the magnetic amplifier. A saturated coil reactor was first used at the Earls Court Theatre in London as early as 1890, but it was not perfected for stage use until the middle of the 20th century. Dimming is accomplished entirely electrically, without moving parts except in the control devices. Magnetic amplifiers are operated remotely by low-voltage circuits; therefore, the actual dimmers may be placed at any convenient location and the console located so that the operator can see the stage. Magnetic amplifiers are long lived, have low maintenance costs, and operate silently.

One of the most widely known systems of electronic dimming was invented by George C. Izenour and carries his name. This board uses a remote console and preset panel that contain all switches and various controls for selecting the intensity of each circuit. Circuits may be operated singly or combined in an endless variety of groups. As in the magnetic amplifier boards, the actual tubes are remote from the console, which can be located where the operator has a clear view of the action. The Izenour system can handle varying loads on any circuit, is highly flexible, and responds very rapidly. A certain amount of noise is generated in operation, but this is of comparatively minor importance if the tube racks are located far enough from the stage.

During the 1960s the silicon-controlled rectifier dimmer passed all other forms and became the most popular and widely used. It employs two P-N-P-N semiconductor devices connected together (*see* TRANSISTOR) and with the lamp load in such a manner that an electric signal will control the conductivity of the P-N devices and thus the brilliance of the light. Silicon-controlled rectifier dimmers (SCR) have all the advantages of other forms and in addition are smaller, lighter, and require less maintenance. Remote control is efficient at low voltages, making installation simple and inexpensive. SCR dimmers are manufactured in capacities ranging from 1,800 to 6,000 watts. Lightweight, compact, portable dimmer systems are now entirely practicable, a condition never before obtainable in satisfactory manner.

An essential part of almost all modern dimmer switchboards is a patching panel (*see* fig. 2), which makes it possible to connect any load circuit in the theatre to any dimmer. Each dimmer has a number of outlets, into which cords connected to the lights are plugged. Changes in patching make it possible to use the same dimmer for different loads during a single production. Thus, every dimmer can be utilized to its maximum, and the board is smaller and more efficient.

**Placement of Light Sources.**—Dividing the stage into pools provides a basis for focusing. The pools are usually located downstage (toward the front) left, centre, and right; then upstage (toward the back) left, centre, and right. Spotlights from the ante-proscenium beam (located in the auditorium ceiling about 50° up from the curtain line), balcony, borders, and sides are focused to cover each pool from several angles and in different colours. The director can then call for a single pool complete, or for any of its components, or for any combination of one or more pools. As it requires a minimum of change between shows, this system works well in a permanently equipped theatre where many varied productions are undertaken in quick succession. For professional productions, however, it limits both designer and director by forcing them to adapt areas set arbitrarily by the lighting.

In most cases, acting light comes from the front and above. Banks of ellipsoidal framing spotlights in the ante-proscenium beam are considered the ideal basic source. Following them for choice, or if necessary substituting for them, are lights on the balcony rail, then "boomerang" spotlights from the sides of the auditorium. A completely equipped theatre has all three sources.

Ante-proscenium beam lights overcome confusing shadows on the scenery, which are always present when balcony lights and footlights are used alone. Side lighting provides "modeling," giving the actor a third dimension of light and avoiding the flatness of straight illumination. Lighting from the auditorium with long-range units has made footlights practically obsolete, though they are occasionally used for blending and toning spotlighted areas and still illuminate backdrops and curtains.

The so-called concert border or first pipe is a bank of spotlights, usually with Fresnel lenses, suspended immediately behind the front curtain. These may be augmented with framing spotlights and borderlight sections, usually called "X-rays" when placed in this location. Trees (towers of spotlights) behind the tormentors (screens that mask the space between the front edges of the set and the proscenium arch) provide supplemental and modeling lights. Additional pipes overhead hold more spotlights and floodlights, as the production requires, either for direct lighting or for backlighting. Backlighting is particularly important in giving finish and clarity to the illumination. Floodlights for cycloramas, offstage areas, doorways and windows, and other specific areas are placed above, below, or beside each such area. Projectors, special-effects lights, and detail lights may be anywhere on the stage or in the auditorium. Follow spotlights are usually operated from the projection room or balcony but may be on or above the stage.

The growth of large outdoor productions during the 20th century has led to much experimentation in long-range lighting. Since it is usually impracticable to have a proscenium arch outdoors, the lighting units must be placed at great distances from the stage, either at the back of the seating area or at the sides on towers. Beam-projector units, commonly referred to as "sunspots," have been found most efficient for this type of installation, where throws may range up to 200 ft. Beam projectors have no lenses, depending for their brilliance on large mirrored reflectors. Detailed lighting can be provided with high-intensity arc spotlights. The sunspots are supplemented by smaller units in the footlights and concealed within the setting.

**Colour.**—*Technique.*—Obtaining satisfactory colour in stage lighting has always presented problems. Fortuny and his contemporaries used coloured silks and reflectors, but high intensity was impossible with these techniques. Lamp dips and lacquers applied directly to the glass were developed almost as soon as the electric light, but these cannot withstand high temperatures. So-called natural colour lamps, manufactured with permanent dyes in the glass, provide satisfactory colour but are quite expensive, are limited in colour range, and have a very high light loss.

Gelatin, in the form of transparent coloured sheets that are fitted in front of lighting units, is the most widely used colour medium. It is available in a wide range of colours and is flame resistant and inexpensive. After several hours' use it becomes brittle and fades. Since it absorbs water readily and then tends to melt, it is very unsatisfactory in damp localities. A newer medium is plastic. It is impervious to water, fades more slowly than gelatin, is heat resistant, and is stiff enough to be used in small lights without a reinforcing metal colour frame. The range of colours is about the same as that for gelatin, and the price is much higher. The greater expense is offset, however, by the longer life and lowered costs of making changes.

Glass is used in borderlights and footlights but has never become general in spotlights and floodlights. Permanence of colour and physical strength, its chief advantages, are offset by fragility, high initial expense, and narrow colour range. Breakage from heat is also a drawback, though asbestos mountings and expansion cracks have largely overcome this defect. Colour frames for border- and spotlights are usually so designed that glass can be used for general applications, with gelatin substituted for special productions.

Lighting with primary colours has found wide favour in Europe and to some degree in the United States. By combining spectroscopically true shades of red, green, and blue, white light can be created. While this is of unquestioned value, particularly on sky cycloramas, it is generally more efficient and economical to use a colour medium of the desired shade than to create the colour by mixing.

*Design.*—Generally speaking, it is usual to have warm colours coming from one side of the stage and cool from the other, since this is normal in natural lighting. Lighter colours are used on faces; darker, richer tones on settings. In the legitimate theatre the setting is usually lighted sufficiently by spill light from the acting areas. In more spectacular productions, such as opera and ballet, lighting on sets and backdrops is important.

For lighting faces the most widely used colours are light flesh pink, light lavender, and light scarlet, called, respectively, flesh, surprise pink, and bastard amber. These are augmented with steel blues, light straws, and occasionally deeper colours for acting areas. For backgrounds and sets a much wider range of colours is used, including several shades of blue and blue-green, magenta, green, amber, and red.

**Special Effects.**—Special effects are provided by a wide variety of electrical and lighting devices, ranging from mica slides projected by ordinary ellipsoidal spotlights to elaborate moving projections, such as rippling water, drifting clouds, and dancing flames. The effects are generally painted on mica disks that revolve in front of a spotlight, an additional objective lens being placed in front of the disk to focus the moving image. Such projection may come from the front, back, or, occasionally, sides of the stage.

So-called black-light phenomena have become highly popular special effects. Costumes, scenery, and properties are dyed or painted with pigments containing fluorescent materials; when exposed to ultraviolet light from which the visible rays have been filtered, the prepared objects show up vividly against an almost invisible background. Theatrical sources of black light are varied, the most widely used being mercury-vapour lights behind deep-purple glass filters, and black-light fluorescent tubes. Arc spotlights are also effective sources. Since little ultraviolet radiation is present in the standard incandescent lamp, ordinary spotlights and floodlights are seldom used. Combinations of black and visible light are used to produce many unusual effects.

Shadow projectors are old in principle, most present-day units being based on the apparatus developed by Adolf Linnebach and commonly known as the Linnebach projector. The unit consists of a deep box painted black inside and utilizing a concentrated-filament high-intensity lamp. One side of the box is open and contains a glass or mica slide carrying the design to be projected. Sharp projections are not possible, but silhouettes and wide outlines can be provided over wide areas. A modern light of this type contains a wide-angle lens system and provides a very clear delineation for either front or rear projection. In the latter case a drop (translucent screen) is required.

Bibliography.—P. Corry, *Lighting the Stage,* 2nd ed. (1958); T. Fuchs, *Stage Lighting* (1929), *Home-built Lighting Equipment for the Small Stage* (1939); L. Hartman, *Theatre Lighting* (1930); F. Kranich, *Bühnentechnik der Gegenwart* (1933); S. McCandless, *A Method of Lighting the Stage,* 4th ed. (1958); W. O. Parker and H. K. Smith, *Scene Design and Stage Lighting* (1963); J. E. Rubin and L. H. Watson, *Theatrical Lighting Practice* (1954); S. Selden and H. D. Sellman, *Stage Scenery and Lighting,* 3rd ed. (1959); F. M. Whiting, *An Introduction to the Theatre,* rev. ed. (1961). (W. C. To.)

**STAGG, AMOS ALONZO** (1862–1965), U.S. football coach, known as the "grand old man of football," had the longest coaching career in the history of the sport. Born on Aug. 16, 1862, in West Orange, N.J., he attended Yale University, where he played end and was chosen to the initial All-America team selected by Walter Camp (1889). He also was an outstanding baseball pitcher and rejected several offers to turn professional. Graduating with a divinity degree, he decided not to become a minister and instead entered Springfield (Mass.) College, where he coached and also played on the team. In 1892 he went to The University of Chicago as coach and head of the physical education department. He soon made the Maroons one of the great football powers of the early 1900s and was credited with more innovations than any coach of his era, some of which were the end-around play, the hidden-ball trick (since outlawed), huddle, shift, man in motion, and the practice tackling dummy. Five of his Chicago teams were undefeated, six of them won Western Conference championships. At the age of 70 he retired from Chicago (1933) with an overall record of 268 victories and 141 losses. In 1934 he became coach of the College of the Pacific at Stockton, Calif., and he was named coach of the year in 1943. In 1946 he went to Susquehanna (Pa.) College to help his son, head coach Amos Alonzo Stagg, Jr., in an advisory capacity, and he also was an adviser at Stockton (Calif.) Junior College from 1953 to 1960. Throughout his 71-year coaching career, he constantly emphasized character development, devotion to clean habits, and a healthy mind and body. Stagg was among the first to be chosen to the Football Hall of Fame (1951) and the only one to be selected as a player and a coach. Stagg died at Stockton on March 17, 1965. (D. Sr.)

**STAGNELIUS, ERIK JOHAN** (1793–1823), one of the outstanding poets of the romantic movement in Sweden. The son of a pastor who became bishop of Kalmar, he was born on the island of Öland, Oct. 14, 1793. He had no regular schooling, but received a good grounding in the classics. After studying law at Uppsala University, he became a civil servant in Stockholm in 1815. Little is known of his later life. He seems to have led a very isolated existence, and it is doubtful whether the ardent love poems to "Amanda" were actually addressed to a real person. His health was undermined by heavy drinking and he died poor and lonely at Stockholm, April 3, 1823.

In his earliest known poetry, Stagnelius adopted a neoclassical style and showed an Epicurean attitude to life. He remained consistent in his aspiration for clear, concise form; his sensuality also persisted in his choice of imagery, although after 1815 Epicureanism gradually gave way to extreme philosophical idealism. Some of the poems from his later theosophic period are difficult to interpret. He was influenced not only by F. W. J. von Schelling, but by such mystics as Jakob Böhme, L. C. de Saint-Martin and Emanuel Swedenborg. The underlying elements of his philosophy are derived from various neo-Platonic and Gnostic systems. The human soul, or Anima, has left its home in the spiritual world, Pleroma, and is subject to Demiurgos, the ruler over sensual reality. This realm is felt to be a bewitched and enchanted world, a desert or a prison, whence man, like the rest of creation, longs to return to his heavenly home.

Stagnelius' poetic inspiration is wide-ranging and he is master of an unusual variety of forms. Among his notable works are a monumental epic in hexameters on the Christianization of Russia, *Wladimir den store* (1817), and several plays which, though lacking in dramatic intensity, contain passages of brilliant rhetoric and melodious verse. Some are set against a background of early Scandinavian mythology, others (*e.g.,* the blank verse play, *Bacchanterna,* 1822) have a classical setting. But Stagnelius is, above all, a lyrical poet. Of a more metaphysical cast of mind than Keats, of whom he was an almost exact contemporary, he shared with him unusual lyrical intensity and powers of illumination.

One of the few works published in his lifetime was the collection of poems *Liljor i Saron* (1821). The critical edition by F. Böök, 5 vol. (1911–19), has an indispensable commentary.

*See* F. Böök's monograph on Stagnelius (1919; abbreviated and rev. ed., 1954). (S. B.)

**STAHL, GEORG ERNST** (1660–1734), German chemist and physician, was known chiefly for his doctrine of phlogiston (*see* Chemistry: *History of Chemistry: The Phlogiston Theory*), which held that "phlogiston" was the material of fire. He was born on Oct. 21, 1660, at Ansbach, and graduated in medicine from Jena in 1684. He became court physician to the duke of Saxe-Weimar (1687), professor of medicine at Halle (1694), and physician to the king of Prussia at Berlin (1716), where he died on May 14, 1734.

The essentials of his theory were derived from Johann J. Becher (1635–82). Stahl also propounded a view of fermentation, which, in some respects, resembles that supported by Justus von Liebig 150 years later. He was a firm believer in animism. In his youth he believed in alchemy, but later he warned against its frauds. He observed that acids are of different strengths, that the basic component of common salt differs from that of potash, and he recognized the particular nature of the earthy constituent of alum. His views of combustion were first presented in his *Zymotechnia fundamentalis* (1697). His chief medical treatise was *Theoria medica vera* (1707). His principal chemical work was *Fundamenta chymiae* (1723).

*See* C. W. Beck, "Georg Ernst Stahl . . . ," *J. Chem. Educ.,* vol. 37 (1960). (R. E. O.; X.)

**STÅHLBERG, KAARLO JUHO** (1865–1952), the architect of the Finnish constitution and the first president of independent Finland. He was born at Suomussalmi on Jan. 28, 1865. A lawyer by training, he made legality the keynote of his political thinking. Joining the Constitutionalist Party, he was elected to the Diet in 1904 and entered the government of the autonomous Grand Duchy of Finland in 1905 but resigned office in 1907. From 1908 to 1918 he was professor of administrative law at the University of Helsinki.

One of the more prudent Constitutionalists, Ståhlberg consistently gave proof of his democratic outlook: he was among the first to demand universal and equal suffrage. His draft of a republican constitution (1917) became the basis of the actual constitution of 1919, still in force in the mid-1960s. On the reshuffling of the political parties when national independence was achieved, Ståhlberg joined the National Progressive Party. Elected president of the new republic (1919), he set the pattern for his successors by making full use of his constitutional powers. He did his utmost to narrow the gap between "Reds" and "Whites" after the Civil War. At the end of his term (1925) he did not seek reelection, as he thought that the right would become reconciled to the republic sooner if he stood aside. He was a victim of personal violence during the outbreak of right-wing extremism in 1930. He was defeated by two votes in the presidential election of 1931 and by one vote in that of 1937. He died in Helsinki on Sept. 22, 1952. (*See* Finland: *History.*) (E. K. I. J.)

**STAINED GLASS.** All coloured glass is, strictly speaking, "stained" by the metallic oxide added to it in the process of manufacture, but the term is popularly, as well as technically, understood to refer to stained glass windows. In the great period covering the development of the narrative or pictorial window, with which this article is primarily concerned, the stained glass window was composed of an ensemble of pieces of glass, coloured or otherwise, held together in a framework of leading and painted to form an image or pattern design. Neither leading nor painting was an essential feature of the earlier mosaic window, nor of the continuation of this abstract tradition into Islamic architecture, where jewel-like glass is usually set in cement tracery. Contemporary stained glass, like contemporary art in general, is characterized by an experimental approach that precludes any narrow technical definition.

This article deals with the early development of stained glass, then with the techniques of assembling and painting windows, and finally with the history of stained glass windows from the 12th century to modern times.

## EARLY DEVELOPMENT

As a substance, glass itself is of considerable antiquity, and glass objects dating from the 3rd millennium B.C. have been found in both Egypt and Babylonia. The commercial application of the art of glass blowing, possibly a Syrian invention in the first place, was decisive in the development of the glass window. It was probably introduced into the Roman world in the 1st century B.C. By the 1st century A.D. improvements in manufacturing techniques had resulted in the provision of larger glass window panes and a consequent increase in the size of windows. This development was not restricted to Italy. Window glass has been discovered at almost every Romano-British dwelling site, ranging chronologically from the mid-1st century to the end of the 4th century A.D.

The writings of the Fathers of the Latin church, Lactantius, (before 330), Prudentius (before 413), and St. Jerome (before 420), mention glass windows in the early Christian basilicas, and it is recorded that Pope Leo III (795–816) provided windows of glass, of different colours, for St. Paul's church at Rome. The earliest record of glazing in an English church is found in the *Life* of St. Wilfrid (*q.v.*), Archbishop of York (*c.* 634–709). His biographer, writing shortly after the saint's death, records how Wilfrid restored the church at York, probably between the years 669 and 671, and that "by putting glass in the windows he prevented the birds or the rain from getting in." This glass was almost certainly obtained from abroad, as a few years later, about 675, Benedict Biscop, abbot of Monkwearmouth, imported glaziers from Gaul to glaze the windows of his monastic church, and the Venerable Bede in recording this observes that the craft was previously unknown in Britain. Excavations carried out in 1962 at Monkwearmouth recovered a number of pieces of window glass in various colours, green, blue, amber, and red, and the edges of several pieces were grozed (*i.e.*, cut) for fitting into a window. None of the pieces, however, were painted and there is no evidence of the overall design. This glass, which is certainly pre-9th century in date, may have been part of Biscop's foundation (*see* BENEDICT BISCOP, SAINT). In form these early windows varied considerably: the actual window openings were at first filled with thin sheets of marble, alabaster, or gypsum, or even wooden boards, which were pierced with holes, coloured glass being inserted into these holes. In addition to glass other materials were used for the same purpose, thin strips of alabaster set in a bronze frame being not infrequent. This form of window design persisted even in Western Europe into the Romanesque period, and 11th-century examples are to be found at Torcello Cathedral and in the church of San Miniato at Florence. The employment of leading to hold together the pieces of glass in a window opening was possibly used contemporaneously with the above early methods, since leading which may have been used in window glazing dating from the 4th century has been uncovered in excavations.

The use of leading was of fundamental importance in the development of the figurative window, for this strong yet pliable substance can hold together the most intricately shaped pieces of glass, thus giving the glazier considerably more freedom in imaginative design and making the narrative window possible. The earliest example of a leaded window design was a small panel at Séry-les-Mézières (Aisne, Fr., destroyed in 1918) which was probably of the 9th century. It appears certain that as at Séry-les-Mézières many of these early windows contained coloured glass arranged in comparatively simple decorative designs, with little use of the painted design, and there is no documentary evidence even to suggest the existence of pictorial windows until the 9th century, when several rather vague references testify to the appearance of figures in German and French glass. In the 10th-century history of the church of St. Remi at Reims, rebuilt by Adalbéron, Bishop of Reims (969–988), the monk Richer, writing about 995, states that the windows contained various stories.

Other early evidence regarding pictorial windows depends on fragments discovered in excavations. Those carried out in 1932 at Lorsch (Ger.) recovered the remains of what might be the earliest pictorial window extant. It was possible to reconstruct from fragments a head of Christ, which shows some stylistic affinity with Carolingian manuscript paintings and probably dates from the 9th, 10th, or 11th century. Another head excavated at Magdeburg (Ger.) might be connected with the building of the cathedral founded by Otto the Great in 955 and is possibly before the year 1000 in date. Somewhat later is the well-known head of Christ from Wissembourg, now in the Strasbourg museum, which is to be dated *c.* 1070–1100, but unfortunately its painted surface has been reworked by a modern restorer. The earliest complete pictorial windows extant are those containing five figures of prophets in Augsburg cathedral. Their date has been the subject of some dispute in the past but they are now widely accepted as belonging to the beginning of the 12th century.

The evolution of the stained glass window was a slow process. Both texts and excavation testify to the existence of stained glass windows before the 12th century, but the textual references suggest that it was a rather exceptional form of decoration, creating much admiration and no little astonishment. Also, in Carolingian and Romanesque architecture the window openings, partly for structural reasons, were small and few in number, so that polychrome decoration was naturally concentrated on the large mural areas and the vaults rather than on the windows. It was not until the developments of the 12th century that glass painting became a major art form and in Northern Europe the most important single element in church decoration.

Although the pictorial stained glass window is normally regarded as the invention of Western Europe, where its development can be followed with reasonable coherency from the beginning of the 12th century onward, there is still much that is obscure about its earlier evolution. The discovery during excavations by the Byzantine Institute in Istanbul (Dumbarton Oaks Papers 1963) of stained glass windows, apparently deriving from a tradition independent of that in the West and datable before 1136, adds to the complexity of the fragmentary evidence already cited.

## TECHNIQUE

The account provided by Theophilus (*q.v.*) in his treatise *De Diversis Artibus* ("The Various Arts,") probably written between 1110 and 1140 in northwest Germany, gives a picture of the general technique of assembling and painting a window that remains valid throughout the great period of the stained glass window from the 12th to the 15th century.

A full-size working drawing of the finished design for each panel was first made on a whitewashed board and the colours of the component parts were indicated by letter. Pieces of glass were then shaped to the outlines required by the design: first rough-cut from sheets of glass using an iron with a red-hot point which when pressed onto the glass cut with ease in any direction, and then trimmed to the exact shape using a grozing iron, a flat tool with a notch in one end. These shaped pieces were then laid over the drawing on the table so that the details of the design could be painted on the glass with a pigment of dark opaque enamel, consisting of powdered glass mixed with a metallic oxide (iron or copper) in a solution of wine or urine. Paintbrushes were made from animal furs, the tails of martens, badgers, squirrels, or cats, or even the mane of an ass. The effect of shadows and highlights could be produced on faces and draperies by varying the thickness of the brush strokes and using thin washes of a medium tone. The overall design could be further enhanced, particularly on draperies and backgrounds, by covering the glass with a thin wash of enamel and then picking out a decorative pattern or foliage design, using the end of the paintbrush or a sharpened stick. On completion of the painting the glass was placed in a pan, layers of glass alternating with whiting (ash or quicklime), and fired in a kiln to fuse the painted enamels. When the firing was over and the glass had cooled, it was rearranged on the table prior to leading. The strips of lead used for joining the pieces of glass together had an H shape in section and were cast in iron or wooden molds. When the leading, cut to the required length and shape, had been inserted between the pieces of grozed glass it was then soldered together at the points of junction, and cement or putty was forced between the leaves of lead and the glass to make the whole panel watertight. The panels were fixed in place in the window by means of leaden strips soldered to the leads on the outside surface of the glass and attached to iron saddle-bars let into the masonry. Large windows were made in smaller units and these units fitted into an iron framework or armature, which often formed a geometric pattern that was incorporated into the overall design of the window. The basic function of the armature was, however, structural: it supported and distributed the total weight of the glass, for without it a large window would collapse.

From the 12th to the 15th century variations in the technique of stained glass were confined to a few important refinements, the most important of which was the discovery in the first decade of the 14th century that glass could be stained yellow by using a derivative of sulfide of silver. This stain was invariably applied to the outer surface of the glass, forming on it a very thin transparent film which varied in tone according to the texture of the glass and the heat of the furnace. In addition to its use on white glass it could be applied to coloured glass; *e.g.,* its use on blue glass produced a brilliant green. This discovery saved the glass painter much time and labour by eliminating a certain amount of leading. For example, a yellow crown could be stained on the same piece of glass as its wearer's head. Similarly, decorative patterns and details of foliage decoration, particularly on the white quarries (or diamond-shaped panes), could be picked out in yellow stain.

Medieval coloured glass is known as "pot-metal" glass because in the primary stages of its manufacture the glass and colouring material (generally a metallic oxide) were fused together in the melting pot. An exception to this rule is ruby glass, which was so dark that to obtain sufficient translucency the glass was "flashed"; that is, clear glass while still pliant was dipped into molten coloured glass. The glass when formed into a sheet was thus coated with coloured glass on one side only. Detailed effects, unhindered by intricate leading, could then be achieved by grinding away part of one of the layers. This technique was first practised in the late 13th and early 14th century; one of the earliest extant examples at Mussy-sur-Seine (Aube, Fr.) shows a blue groundwork diapered with ruby roses with white centres, each rose being a single piece of glass. This class of work is, however, more common in the 15th and 16th centuries; as later glass was much thinner the practice of this type of refinement was technically easier to execute.

Eventually in the middle of the 16th century the technique of painting in enamel colours on glass began to be of major importance. In this method the various colouring matters made from the metallic oxides, copper for green, cobalt for blue, manganese for purple, and so on, are mixed with flux, which is soft ground glass with a melting point lower than that of the glass to be painted. After firing in the kiln, the glass is allowed to cool and the flux, which has been melted in the process, hardens and together with its colouring matter adheres closely to the glass. For some time this new technique went side by side with the old technique of pot-metal glass. The political disturbances of the mid-17th century created a scarcity of pot-metal glass and gradually the ancient methods were replaced by the new technique of painting in enamel colours.

In the Middle Ages ecclesiastical art was primarily didactic. The subjects painted in the windows played an important part in the expounding of the Scriptures and the glorification of the church and its saints, and it must be assumed that clerics supplied the master glazier with a program to which he had to conform. A 13th-century roll in the British Museum contains a series of circular drawings illustrating the life of St. Guthlac (Harley Roll Y 6). These drawings might have been intended as a model for a glazier, but the scenes could equally well have been expressed in wall paintings, sculpture, or metal work. Our knowledge is more complete for the later Middle Ages. The glazier was given written instructions from which to prepare provisional sketches that were submitted for the patron's approval before being redrawn in actual size to form the final cartoon. The provisional sketch was known as a *vidimus* (literally, "we have seen"). One example of such written instructions is extant. It is the program for a window given by Henry VII to the Grey Friars church at Greenwich (British Museum Egerton MS. 2341). A typical entry is that for St. Audry: "Seint Audry, a kynge's doughter shryned at Ely. Make her in thabbytte of a Nonne wyth an opyn Crowne crowned with a croyse in her ryght honde, a booke in her left honde." The Greenwich roll blazons the shield of arms appropriate to each figure and to prevent misunderstandings, each shield is also painted in the left hand margin of the roll. There is ample evidence to show that by the 14th century it was the practice of glaziers to have a stock of finished cartoons, executed on parchment or paper, which could be adapted for different glazing schemes. That these cartoons were used and reused over a long period can be deduced from the will of William Inglish, a York glazier who died in 1450, in which he bequeathed to his son Thomas "all the cartoons belonging to my work."

It is evident that in the later Middle Ages the master glazier's workshop was a highly organized enterprise, capable of producing various classes of designs, according to the expense his patrons were prepared to incur. John Prudde, glazier to King Henry VI, provided four main types of design at varying prices for the glazing of the parish church and college chapel at Eton between the years 1445 and 1450. He charged eightpence halfpenny a foot for figures set on a simple groundwork of quarries, while heraldic work of shields of arms set on quarries cost tenpence a foot and other glass wrought with different figures and borders was one shilling (twelve pence) a foot. Subject windows, presumably with narrative scenes, were supplied at two prices, one at one shilling and two pence a foot, the other at one shilling and fourpence.

Although the donor, cleric or layman, exercised considerable influence over the choice of subject and its manner of representation, the finished design was essentially the creation of the master glazier. The latter was often an artist in his own right, expressing in the formal language of his own technique the artistic aspirations of his time.

## HISTORY

### 12th Century

In the 12th century the production of stained glass windows, particularly in Northern Europe, was considerable, and regional schools begin to be discernible.

**France.**—A number of important regional schools of glass painting emerged, one of the earliest of which was in western France. The most important products of this group include the Ascension window at Le Mans, *c.* 1145, and the Crucifixion window in Poitiers Cathedral *c.* 1165. In Champagne appeared another quite distinct group, whose best work is found in the Redemption and St. Stephen windows at Châlons-sur-Marne, *c.* 1150–60, together with the very important later windows at Saint-Remi at Reims, *c.* 1190.

The most important workshop in the Île-de-France was connected with the rebuilding of the choir of Saint-Denis, undertaken by the Abbot Suger, 1140–44. Only fragments of these windows are left, but the three windows of the west facade at Chartres are later products of the Saint-Denis workshop, about 1150–55.

The stylistic antecedents of these schools are difficult to pinpoint. The Saint-Denis-Chartres group has certain similarities to north French manuscript paintings associated with Marchiennes, Saint-Omer, and Anchin, but the dates of the manuscripts are not precisely known, and the problem is further complicated by the Abbot Suger's recording that the glaziers employed at Saint-Denis comprised "many masters from different regions." The strongly Romanesque character of the Le Mans Ascension window, its general composition and the particular stylization of drapery forms, is similar to such earlier manuscript paintings from western France as the illustrated Life of St. Aubin of the second half of the 12th century (Paris Bibliothèque Nationale, MS. nouv. acq. Lat. 1390). The Crucifixion window at Châlons-sur-Marne, on the other hand, has precedents in general arrangement in Ottonian manuscript painting and is also closely related in style and composition to contemporary metal work of the Meuse valley. The similarities between the two are so marked that it is not impossible that the artist worked in both media.

**Germany.**—There is less 12th-century glass extant in Germany than in France. The outstanding example of German glass painting of the early years of the century is the series of five prophets at Augsburg, already referred to. These figures have the monumentality of design, rigidly frontal and schematic, characteristic of Romanesque art; they are extremely impressive but rather impersonal and remote. In the second half of the century art in Northern Europe generally, and perhaps more so in Germany, was influenced by Byzantine models. An example in glass painting is the Moses and the Burning Bush window now in the Städelsches Museum at Frankfurt am Main.

**England.**—England has only fragmentary remains of 12th-century glass. The nave clerestory windows at York Minster contain some reused panels from a series of narrative windows, one of which depicted the life of St. Benedict, *c.* 1140–60. Another panel, a single figure of a king from a Tree of Jesse, shows some affinity in style with the glass at Saint-Denis and Chartres, but is probably later in date, *c.* 1190. The outstanding survival from the end of the century is the splendid series of figures representing the descent of Christ from Adam, made for the choir clerestory windows of Canterbury Cathedral *c.* 1178–1200. Their features show a new humanism and there is a sense of movement, even tension, in their bodies and draperies, comparable to contemporary English manuscript painting.

**General Trends.**—It is possible that many of the early windows were of the single figure, monumental in character like the Augsburg and Canterbury examples or the well-known Virgin and Child known as "La Belle Verrière" at Chartres, but the most important feature of the 12th century was the development of the narrative window, consisting of a series of medallions painted with pictorial subjects. This development was, so far as we know, first used extensively at Saint-Denis under the direction of Abbot Suger, 1140–44. The exigencies of narrative exposition led to the decorative arrangement of the medallions within an armature or iron framework which was itself a subject for pattern, and very skilful and intricate designs were evolved, showing a counterplay of circles, lozenges, quatrefoils, and squares with their appropriate borders and interspaces, these latter being particularly elaborate. A secondary but significant development of the second half of the century was the use of decorative pattern diapers on the groundwork adjacent to the figures. This class of design was probably more common at first in Germany than elsewhere, and an early example is in the Jesse window, *c.* 1170–80, at Frankfurt am Main (Städelsches Museum). In France the earliest remaining examples are the incomplete series of scenes from the Legend of St. Matthew of the late 12th century now incorporated in the 13th-century south rose window of Notre Dame, Paris.

### 13th Century

An enormous amount of glass remains from this century and much of it has yet to be studied in detail.

**France.**—In France, where surviving material is most extensive, the various regional schools are mostly the natural development of their immediate predecessors. There is no radical change in style or technique during the first quarter of the century. In the West the severe Romanesque style was softened and refined, as seen in the St. Vital window at Le Mans about 1200, the Saint-Martin window at Angers *c.* 1210, and the slightly later windows of Abraham, Lot, and Joseph at Poitiers. Another distinct workshop, centred at Lyons and responsible *c.* 1215–20 for the apse windows of Lyons cathedral, is characterized by a strong Byzantine influence, particularly in iconography. An important workshop in Champagne had already in the late 12th century produced the clerestory windows of Saint-Remi at Reims that foreshadowed the mature Gothic style, while later products of this atelier can be found in the clerestory windows of Reims Cathedral, *c.* 1235, and the choir clerestory windows at Troyes. In the Île-de-France and eastern France the situation is complicated by the almost complete loss of the later 12th-century works. The north rose window of Laon Cathedral *c.* 1200–05 is stylistically related to the contemporary sculptures of the facade and to manuscript painting such as the Ingeborg Psalter (Musée Condé, Chantilly). The work of this atelier is extremely distinguished, with an elegance and purity of style and a knowledge of classical art which transcend most of its contemporaries. The rose window of Lausanne Cathedral (Switz.), which was made 1231–35 by a wandering Picard, Peter of Arras, is related in style and iconography to the Laon workshop.

The most extensive glazing program of the first half of the century was at Chartres Cathedral, where the years 1200–36 saw the completion of some 175 windows, a tremendous enterprise which brought together various workshops from different regions. The stylistic interactions between the different workshops resulted, particularly in the second quarter of the century, in a more general similarity of style between the various regional workshops. Contemporary with Chartres are the windows of the east end of Bourges Cathedral, *c.* 1214–35, while four windows at Sens Cathedral, pre-1225, are related in composition and ornament to Chartres and Bourges and also have certain stylistic affinities with the contemporary windows at Canterbury Cathedral.

Considerable activity was also centred in the Paris area during the second quarter of the century. The major monument of the period is the Sainte-Chapelle, Paris, 1243–48, which contains the most extensive narrative cycle ever produced in this medium; they represent the medallion window at the peak of its development. Stylistically, these windows are closely related to Parisian court art of the same date and their influence can be seen in the later windows at Le Mans, about 1254–60, and at Tours 1245/55–76.

**England.**—The only extensive remains of 13th-century glass in England are found at Canterbury Cathedral, where the 12 Theological windows were produced *c.* 1200 and the windows relating to St. Thomas Becket *c.* 1200–30. Lincoln Cathedral retains impressive fragments of a series of windows made between 1200 and 1220, but it is impossible fully to appreciate either of these series without making comparison with French work. There are important similarities between Canterbury and Sens, on the one hand, and probably between Lincoln and Paris on the other. The glaziers, however, were English with a close acquaintance with French models.

**Germanic Countries.**—Glass painting of this period in Germanic lands, however, was comparatively uninfluenced by French models. It is more forceful in design, with agitated draperies, expressive faces, and a complicated ornamental character, particularly in the backgrounds. There were many distinct regional schools, among which Cologne was an important centre. The full-length figures of saints and the Legend of St. Kunibert window in the church of St. Kunibert at Cologne (*c.* 1220–30) have elaborate geometrical frames around the figures and scenes that are without parallel in French art. These frames are a typical feature of German work; they occur again in later work of this school in the St. Nicholas window at Büchen (Weser), *c.* 1240–50, and elsewhere. Another workshop, which produced the Jesse window at Freiburg-im-Breisgau *c.* 1225, shows a marked affinity with the slightly earlier enamel and metalwork produced by Nicholas of Verdun and his circle, while the remains of a group of windows made for the Franciscan church at Erfurt, *c.* 1230, constitute a particular group strongly indebted to Byzantine models. It appears that after the completion of the Erfurt windows, this workshop, or at least some of its members, went to Italy and produced the three windows of the apse of the Upper Basilica at Assisi between the years 1230 and 1240. The most outstanding glass of the mid-century is a related series of windows at Naumburg Cathedral, Strasbourg, and Frankfurt. The Naumburg window of Holy Knights and Virgins can be contrasted with the delicate mannered style of Parisian court art.

**General Trends.**—A significant feature of the 13th century was the development of the grisaille window, composed largely of white glass, generally painted with foliage designs and leaded into a more or less complicated geometric pattern. This class of design was employed partly as a means of introducing a larger

Fragments of painted window glass from the Church of the Saviour Pantocrator (Zeyrek Kilise Camii), Istanbul; second quarter of the 12th century

"Virgin and Child," window known as "La Belle Verrière," in the south ambulatory of Chartres Cathedral, France; mid-12th century

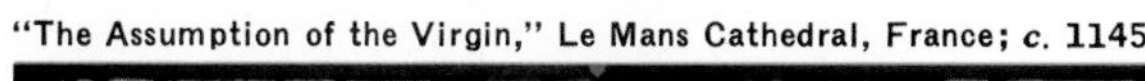

"The Assumption of the Virgin," Le Mans Cathedral, France; *c.* 1145

BYZANTINE AND FRENCH STAINED GLASS

BY COURTESY OF (TOP LEFT) THE BYZANTINE INSTITUTE, INC.; PHOTOGRAPHS, (BOTTOM LEFT, RIGHT) GIRAUDON

"The Entombment," Abbey Church, Königsfelden, Switz.; *c.* 1325-30

"St. John the Evangelist," from the chapel of Winchester College, England; *c.* 1400. In the Victoria and Albert Museum

## SWISS AND ENGLISH STAINED GLASS

"Annunciation to the Shepherds," roundel showing the use of silver stain; latter half of the 14th century. In the Victoria and Albert Museum

**ENGLISH AND ITALIAN STAINED GLASS**

"Jesus and the Centurion," by Guglielmo de Marcillat, Arezzo Cathedral, Italy; *c.* 1520

"The Incredulity of St. Thomas," King's College Chapel, Cambridge, England; 1526-31

# STAINED GLASS

The Tribe of Benjamin, one of the 12 windows of the Tribes of Israel, created by Marc Chagall for the Synagogue of the Hadassah-Hebrew University Medical Center, Jerusalem, Israel; 1961

MODERN STAINED GLASS

amount of light and partly because it was considerably cheaper than coloured glass. The combination of grisaille glass and coloured subject medallions, or figures, however, disrupted the monumental overall unity, which is a feature of a window composed entirely of coloured glass, by allowing the penetration of pure light. This change had an important effect on style; the painted design became more linear and refined, the scale more broken and delicate. Although the combination of grisaille and medallions or figures is not unknown in the early part of the century it is more common in the second half, particularly in France and England. Important examples occur in France at Troyes Cathedral about 1270, Saint-Radegund, Poitiers, about 1290, and Saint-Pierre, Chartres, about 1300, and in England at Stanton Harcourt (Oxfordshire) *c.* 1250, Checkley (Staffordshire) *c.* 1280–90, Merton College, Oxford, 1289–96, and the Chapter House of York Minster, *c.* 1290–1300.

The movement toward humanism, partly inspired by St. Francis of Assisi and his teaching, was accompanied by a related tendency toward naturalism discernible in the visual arts in the later 13th century. The conventional formalized foliage designs of the 12th and earlier 13th century gave place to more natural plant motives of oak, vine, and maple, and these break out of the formal patterns and coil with a more organic natural movement.

### 14th Century

**1300–1380: Influence of Italian Painting on Stained Glass.**—The 14th century saw the full flowering of the Gothic style side by side with the beginnings of stylistic developments that were to culminate in the Renaissance. The new movement toward the representation of volume and spatial depth, by means of modelling and linear perspective, had its origins in Italian painting, particularly in the work of Giotto at Padua, 1300–05. That the glass painter was quickly influenced by this new style is seen, for example, in the St. Anthony window in the Lower Basilica at Assisi. North of the Alps the earliest extant manifestation of this new interest in linear perspective and modeling, based on Italian models, occurs in the chancel windows of the Habsburg expiatory church at Königsfelden (Switz.) made between 1325 and 1330. The knowledge of Italian models spread quickly and extensively and can be seen in France in the windows at Saint-Ouen, Rouen, 1325–39, and at Évreux Cathedral, *c.* 1330. In the Germanic lands it influenced the transept windows at Augsburg and the east window of Vienna Cathedral, *c.* 1340, while the earliest remaining example in English glass painting is probably the nave windows of Stanford-on-Avon (Northamptonshire) *c.* 1330–35, although it occurs earlier in manuscript painting and seal design, *c.* 1325–30.

The interest in linear perspective strongly influenced the development of canopy design. The practice of representing a figure beneath an architectural canopy was an established convention of the 13th century, particularly used in clerestory windows. In the early examples the canopy plays a comparatively unimportant part in the total design, but by the end of the 13th century, although still two-dimensional, it had become more elaborate and is an important ornamental feature of the windows of Merton College, Oxford. The introduction of linear perspective, however, brought about a radical change, and the canopy became organized as a group of miniature buildings viewed in perspective. In German and Austrian glass painting in particular the canopy work is often extremely elaborate and complex in its spatial organization; typical examples are found at Vienna Cathedral, *c.* 1340, and Erfurt, *c.* 1360–70.

The art of glass painting, however, did not respond equally to these new influences emanating from Italy. It subdivides itself into two groups of which France and England together make up one, characterized by its resistance to Italian influences resulting in a modification of their general styles. The use of linear perspective was purposefully restrained, so that the essential overall surface unity of the design was not violently upset, for the use of flat patterned diaper grounds effectively counterbalanced the suggestion of spatial effect. In the first half of the century the most important work in France is found in the choir windows of Évreux Cathedral *c.* 1330 and at Saint-Ouen, Rouen, *c.* 1325–39. The English glaziers of this period were extremely prolific, with Oxford, Coventry, and York as important regional centres. The nave windows of York Minster were made during the period 1300–38 and are the largest single collection of this period in the country. It appears probable that some of the later glass at York, *c.* 1350–70, now distributed over the windows of the choir clerestory, was the work of an imported French glazier, probably from Rouen. A flourishing school in the West Country and Herefordshire, whose best work is found at Wells Cathedral and Eaton Bishop (Herefordshire), shows some familiarity with German work. The best French and English work, however, is distinguished by a lightness of colour and graphic refinement that is enhanced by an extensive use of yellow stain. After *c.* 1300 the geometric grisaille glass gave way to the simpler form of diamond-shaped quarries, painted with delicate trails of foliage, and leaded together to give the effect of trellis work.

The second group, which might be termed 'Germanic' as it embraces east Germany, Bohemia, and Austria, displays a much more plastic style; the colours are deeper and more saturated, the compositions are more complex, both on the surface and in depth, and the canopy designs particularly are often very complicated essays in perspective; the figures are shorter in proportion and their volume more accentuated. It is brusque, almost harsh, contrasting strongly with the elegance of French and English work. All these traits can be seen, for example, in the panels from Strassengel, near Graz, Aus., *c.* 1350 (Victoria and Albert Museum, London), the earlier windows at St. Maria-am-Gestade, Vienna, *c.* 1350–60, at Erfurt, *c.* 1360–70, and the window from the Herzogenkapella in Vienna Cathedral, c. 1380. A particular trait of this Germanic group, of which Erfurt is a good example, is a tendency to extend a single composition across the main lights of a window, ignoring the natural divisions of the stonework. The reason for this is partly architectural: the windows are comparatively much narrower and taller than French or English windows.

**1380–1430: The International Style.**—The arts of this period which are conveniently grouped together under the title of "The International Style" belong essentially to an era of court art inspired by the patronage of kings and the nobility and the higher orders of ecclesiastics. Surviving monuments are extensive and interactions between the various centres of patronage, complicated by family alliances and the exchange of works of art and artists, are particularly complex. The various national and regional styles can still be distinguished but there is a general tendency toward a mannered, extremely sophisticated elegance of style, sometimes verging on the precious, combined with an interest in portrait realism.

The glass painting of this period is of high quality. The most significant examples in France are the "Royal" windows at Évreux, given by Pierre de Mortain *c.* 1395, and the window of Bishop Guillaume de Cantiers. At Bourges there are tantalizing fragments from the Sainte-Chapelle built for Jean, duc de Berry, *c.* 1405, and also the windows presented to the cathedral there by the families of Trousseau and Aligret, *c.* 1414. In England the major examples of this period are the windows of the chapel of William of Wykeham's college at Winchester painted about 1393 by Master Thomas of Oxford, and the great East Window of York Minster. This was made between 1405 and 1408 by John Thornton of Coventry and must be considered as one of the outstanding works of art of the Middle Ages.

In Germany and Austria the International Style brought about a softening and refining of the "plastic style" of the earlier part of the century. In Austria an important atelier associated with the court produced the window given by Duke Albert III to the church of St. Erhard in der Breitenau *c.* 1386–95, and later the series of windows at Viktring *c.* 1400 and for the Freisingerkapella at Klosterneuburg *c.* 1410. Germany contains a large amount of work of this period. At Erfurt the window given by Johann von Tiefengruben *c.* 1400, with its lighter tones and more refined pictorial style, should be compared with the earlier windows there. The series of windows at Rothenburg, which were probably made about 1400, should be noted, together with the cycle of windows, probably painted by Lucas Moser, for the Bessererkapelle at Ulm

Minster, *c.* 1420–30. The latter show an astonishingly refined technique.

### 15th and 16th Centuries

**Decline of Stained Glass as an Independent Art Form.**—The period 1430–1550 saw not only the decline of the Gothic style and the establishment of the new Renaissance style but also the beginning of the transformation of the art of glass painting from a significant means of artistic expression into a hybrid art form: the translucent reflection of a panel or mural painting.

The International Style continued to influence glass painting during the first half of the 15th century, but to a lesser degree. Its mannered elegance and extravagant costumes can still be seen in the two rose windows at Le Mans Cathedral, *c.* 1440, although technically this work is somewhat coarse, and also the rose windows at Angers Cathedral of 1441–42. In England this aesthetic is continued in the east window of Great Malvern Priory (Worcestershire), about 1423–39, the chapel windows of All Souls College, Oxford, 1441–47, and in the windows made by John Prudde, the king's glazier, for the Beauchamp Chapel of St. Mary's, Warwick, which were commissioned in 1447. The Germanic lands provide many examples, particularly the window from St. Lambrecht, after 1424, now in the museum at Graz, Aus., and the charming St. Katherine window at Sélestat, Fr., *c.* 1425–1450.

**Influence of Flemish and Italian Realism.**—There were, however, important new influences affecting the styles of glass painting. In northern Europe during the first half of the 15th century a flourishing school of painting emerged in Flanders. Although the origin of the Flemish style is partly to be found in the International Style of 1390–1400, it developed, as can be seen in the paintings of Jan Van Eyck, a more realistic manner of representation and a detailed awareness of actuality that is almost the antithesis of the mannered sophistication and the essentially unrealistic world of the International Gothic. In Italian sculpture and painting also a new realism is found, particularly in the later works of Ghiberti (1378–1455) and Donatello (*c.* 1386–1466) and their new developments in the use of perspective to create the illusion of reality.

It was impossible for the glass painter to participate fully in the new realism. Glass is a translucent material; the passage of light through it is alone sufficient to create a feeling of unreality. Furthermore, although the panel or mural painter could use the new discoveries of perspective to heighten the sense of reality, the glass painter had to compromise with the presence of the leading line which emphasizes the surface plane. This creates a tension and a sense of ambiguity between the actual surface and the illusion of depth. Attempts were made to resolve the problems, but with little success: one result was that the leading line became partly divorced from the design instead of being an integrated part of it. The increasing use, from the mid-16th century onward, of vitreous enamel pigments hastened this process.

**Importance of Flemish Glaziers.**—The period 1450–1550 saw no decline in demand. One of the most productive and influential areas at this time was Flanders. The six windows of the church of St. Gommaire at Lier, *c.* 1475–1500, and the Virgin window at Anderlecht, *c.* 1482, although very restored, have original portions of excellent quality and close affinity with contemporary painting. The trading and political links between Flanders and England in the second half of the 15th century encouraged the influx of Flemish works of art and artists into England. A number of Flemish glaziers established themselves in Southwark, London, and some even assumed English names. The early 16th century was marked by a series of disputes between the London Guild of Glaziers and the foreigners. The latter were particularly patronized by the Court and the more wealthy merchants. The two outstanding monuments of this imported style are the windows of Fairford church (Gloucestershire), *c.* 1480, and the King's College Chapel, Cambridge, 1515–31. Many of the windows at King's were probably designed by the painter and engraver Dirck Vellert of Antwerp (working 1485–1534).

The spread of the new realism can be traced in French glass painting. The interactions with Flemish glaziers can be seen, for example, in the realism of the windows from the duke of Burgundy's chapel at Dijon, which are the work of Flemish glaziers, *c.* 1430–40, now in the Victoria and Albert Museum, London, and also the Jacques Coeur window at Bourges Cathedral, *c.* 1450, which is markedly Flemish in style. The native glaziers were extremely prolific at this time, and Normandy and particularly the city of Rouen contain an incomparable display of windows produced by a large number of distinctive workshops. The outstanding figures of the first part of the 16th century were Arnoult of Nijmegen (*c.* 1470–*c.* 1540) and the Le Prince family at Beauvais. Arnoult of Nijmegen worked in both Flanders and France. His most important works are at Tournai Cathedral, 1490–1500, and the Jesse window at Saint-Godard Church, Rouen, of 1506, which is one of the most impressive monuments of glass painting. The works by the Le Prince family are equally impressive, particularly the Tree of Jesse at Saint-Étienne, Beauvais, *c.* 1522–25.

**Germany and Italy and Spain.**—In Germany the later 15th century is dominated by the prolific activity of Peter Hemmel von Andlau and his workshop, active 1430–1500. Typical examples of his work are found in St. Wilhelm's Church, Strasbourg, *c.* 1470–80. In Italy the period is mainly associated with the name of Guglielmo de Marcillat (1467–1529), a Frenchman whose works display an outstanding mastery of technique. His finest windows are at Arezzo Cathedral and there is a very typical example from the cathedral of Cortona, dated 1516, in the Victoria and Albert Museum. The building of Milan Cathedral caused an important school of glass painting to develop there, and the work of Conrad Munch, a German from Cologne, and Nicolo da Varallo carried out during the second half of the 15th century is of particular importance. The Milan school continued in full activity during the 16th and 17th centuries. In Spain, especially at Seville, León, and Avila, there are some magnificent 16th century windows; they are in all cases the work of imported Flemish glass painters.

The full flowering of the Renaissance style in Italy and the intense interest in classical art that it stimulated resulted, *c.* 1500, in a profusion of ornamental details, borrowed from the formal language of classical art, in contemporary window designs. In addition the glaziers at this time often drew inspiration from contemporary engravings, particularly those of Albrecht Dürer (1471–1528).

### 17th and 18th Centuries

**Dominance of the Painted Technique.**—Political disturbances and the devastation of Lorraine with the destruction in 1636 of the important glass works there resulted in some scarcity of pot-metal glass, but the use of vitreous enamel colours was already dominating the technique of glass painting. In the windows at Gouda, Holland, painted by the brothers Dirk and Waiter Crabeth at the end of the 16th century, and in the works of Abraham and Bernard Van Linge, made between 1620 and 1640, the realization of the window as a translucent canvas painting is complete. Abraham Van Linge's windows painted 1630–40 for Christ Church Cathedral, Oxford, are an excellent example of the destruction of the lead line as an integral part of the design. The leading simply holds together the square sheets of glass: the effect is the same as looking at a picture set behind a rectangular grid. This type of design was continued by English artists such as Henry Gyles (1645–1709), and the Price and Peckitt families, all of York, and by artists like Francis Eginton (1737–1805) and James Pearson (d. 1805). At its best the work of these centuries has a certain charm with a delicacy of painting and often some technical expertise.

**Domestic Glass.**—The most interesting work of the period was the extensive production of small subject roundels and heraldic panels, particularly fashionable for use in domestic windows, made in vast quantities in Flanders and Switzerland.

### 19th and 20th Centuries

**Gothic Revival.**—The Gothic revival that came as an offspring of the Romantic movement of the late 18th and early 19th centuries represents the beginning of a revitalization of glass painting. The revival of interest in Gothic art stimulated an interest in both the technique and history of medieval glass painting. The pioneer figures in this field were E. Viollet-Le-Duc (1814–79) in France and Charles Winston (1814–65) in England. Winston was a lawyer and antiquarian who associated with various London glaziers and, with the technical help of Messrs. James Powell and Sons, brought about a considerable improvement in the technical quality of pot-metal glass. The experiments were continued by W. E. Chance, who first successfully produced "antique" glass in 1863.

In the first half of the 19th century the styles and methods of the early Gothic period were reconstructed, but without much aesthetic appreciation of medieval art. Much of the work was stereotyped and mass produced, particularly in Germany, and varied considerably in technical quality. The latter part of the century is dominated in England by Edward Burne-Jones (1833–98) and William Morris (1834–96). Burne-Jones provided the designs and Morris adapted them to the medium of stained glass. In windows by them the leading work is restored as an integral part of the design, as seen, for example, in the windows for Birmingham Cathedral of 1897. Although the style and sentiment of 19th-century work is not much in favour today, the period had great historical significance in the revival of the actual technique of making stained glass.

**Modern Trends.**—The advent of "modern art" created new opportunities for the art of stained glass. Contemporary achievements in structural engineering allow for the maximum use of glass as a material, and the abstract and semi-abstract styles of modern art are particularly well suited for expression in this medium. The exploration of these possibilities has interested major artists, and stained glass is being restored as a monumental art occupying a significant and complementary position within its architectural setting.

Although the bulk of this activity belongs to the period after World War II, earlier experiments in France and Germany suggested the range of possibilities that were being opened up. In France the church of Le Raincy (Seine-et-Oise), with abstract window designs of 1922 by Maurice Denis, had great technical significance for the future in its combination of glass and concrete, while in Germany the work of Jan Thorn-Prikker and Karl Schmidt-Rottluff gave to the symbols and images of Christianity an intensity and realism for which there had been no parallel in glass this side of the Renaissance.

After 1946 there was an amazing burst of activity. Technical freedom was greater than ever before, and the experimental nature of much contemporary work, as well as the differing aims of the various artists and architects involved, make it difficult to generalize. On the whole, however, there was a marked tendency to abandon leading in favour of a concrete setting, and designs were either abstract or semi-abstract. Abstract compositions, which explore the possibilities of pure light and colour, include Matisse's "Life" of 1953 at New York, and the works of Jean Bazaine at the Châteaux de la Chaux of 1954 and J. L. Perrot's window at the church of Sainte-Jeanne d'Arc at Belfort (both in France). In Ireland work of great distinction was carried out by Evie Hone, whose semi-abstract windows can also be seen in England; *e.g.*, at Eton College (1952). Traditional iconography reinterpreted in a modern idiom, with a depth of spirituality and sureness of technique that invite comparison with the greatest works of medieval art, is also to be found in Fernand Léger's window of the Marriage at Cana at Courfaivre (Switz.) of 1954 and the St. Dominic window designed by Georges Braque at Varengeville (Seine-Maritime, France). Among the outstanding achievements of the 1960s were Marc Chagall's magnificent series of windows for the synagogue of the Medical Centre at Jerusalem of 1961 and John Piper's Baptistry window at Coventry Cathedral of 1962.

BIBLIOGRAPHY.—C. Winston, *Memoirs Illustrative of the Art of Glass Painting* (1865); N. H. J. Westlake, *A History of Design in Painted Glass*, 4 vol. (1881–94); H. Oidtmann, *Die Glasmalerei, ihre Technik und Geschichte* (1893), *Geschichte der Schweizer Glasmalerei* (1905); L. F. Day, *Windows*, 3rd ed. (1909); L. Balet, *Schwäbische Glasmalerei* (1912); M. Drake, *A History of English Glass Painting* (1912); H. Schmitz, *Die Glasgemälde des Kgl. Kunstgewerbemuseums in Berlin*, 2 vol. (1913); G. Heinersdorff and K. Scheffler, *Die Glasmalerei* (1913); P. Nelson, *Ancient Painted Glass in England* (1913); J. L. Fischer, *Handbuch der Glasmalerei* (1914); H. Schmitz, *Deutsche Glasmalereien der Gothik und Renaissance (Rund- und Kabinettscheiben)* (1923); H. Lehmann, *Zur Geschichte der Glasmalerei in der Schweiz* (1926); A. Hoff, *Thorn-Prikker und die neuere Glasmalerei* (1925); J. D. Le Couteur, *English Medieval Painted Glass* (1926); H. Read, *English Stained Glass* (1926); F. Kieslinger, *Gotische Glasmalerei in Österreich bis 1450* (1927); F. Geiges, *Der Mittelalterliche Fensterschmuck des Freiburger Münsters* (1931); G. M. Rushforth, *Medieval Christian Imagery* (1936); J. Knowles, *Essays in the History of the York School of Glass-Painting* (1936); J. Lafond, *La Résurrection d'un maître d'autrefois. Le Peintreverrier Arnoult de Nimège* (1942), *Pratique de la Peinture sur Verre* (1943); B. Rackham, *The Ancient Glass of Canterbury Cathedral* (1949); C. Woodforde, *Stained Glass of New College, Oxford* (1951); J. Helbig, *Die Glasschilderkunst in België* (1951); H. Wentzel, *Meisterwerke der Glasmalerei* (1954); L. Lefrançois-Pillon and J. Lafond, *L'Art du XIVe siècle en France* (1954); C. Woodforde, *English Stained and Painted Glass* (1954), *Norwich School of Glass-Painting* (1950); E. J. Beer, *Die Glasmalereien der Schweiz vom 12. bis zum Beginn des 14. Jahrhunderts* (Corpus Vitrearum Medii Aevi: Schweiz. I. 1956); G. Marchini, *Italian Stained Glass Windows* (1957); M. Aubert *et al.*, *Le Vitrail Français* (1958); H. Wentzel, *Die Glasmalereien in Schwaben von 1200–1350* (C.V.M.A. Deutschland. Band 1. 1958); M. Aubert, L. Grodecki, J. Lafond, J. Verrier, *Les Vitraux de Notre Dame et la Sainte-Chapelle de Paris* (C.V.M.A. France I 1959); J. Helbig, *Les vitraux médiévaux conservés en Belgique, 1200–1500* (C.V.M.A. Belgique. I. 1961); E. Frodl-Kraft, *Die mittelalterlichen Glasgemälde in Wien* (C.V.M.A. Österreich. Band I. 1962); A. H. H. Megaw, "Notes on Recent Work at the Byzantine Institute in Istanbul," in *Dumbarton Oaks Papers, XVII* (1963). (P. A. N.)

**STAINES,** an urban district formerly in Middlesex, Eng., which under the London Government Act 1963 became part of Surrey on April 1, 1965 (*see* LONDON). It is on the Thames, 18 mi. (29 km.) SW of Charing Cross. Pop. (1961) 49,838. A Roman station was situated there, on the main road from London, and this Thames crossing was one of the earliest bridged. The old bridge, by George Rennie, was opened in 1832; a new one in nearby Egham (1961) carries a bypass. The London Mark Stone was placed there in 1285 to mark the western limit of the City of London's jurisdiction over the Thames. An annual fair granted in 1228 was abolished in 1895. The urban district includes Ashford, Laleham, and Stanwell; it is mainly residential, but there are engineering works and some factories.

**STAINLESS STEEL.** Stainless steel basically is an alloy of chromium and iron containing more than 10% chromium. When chromium is added to iron in such quantities, it imparts throughout the entire body of the metal remarkable resistance to corrosion and heat. Other elements may be added to the iron-chromium combination to obtain steels with special characteristics. The most important of these is nickel, which is used to produce 18–8 (that is, 18% chromium, 8% nickel, balance iron). Other useful additions are niobium, manganese, molybdenum, phosphorus, selenium, silicon, sulfur, titanium and zirconium, all of which result in modifications for special service or fabrication. As is true of many scientific discoveries no single nation can claim full credit for the development of stainless steel. Between 1903 and 1912 Harry Brearley of England, F. M. Becket of the United States and Benno Strauss and Eduard Maurer of Germany shared in its initial development.

Selected scrap which contains only those elements desired in the finished product usually makes up the bulk of the furnace charge used for producing stainless steel. If alloy scrap is not available, clean open-hearth scrap may be used, but more alloy is required to meet specifications. Pig iron containing 4% carbon, anthracite, or other carbonaceous material may be employed when a high-carbon melt is desired. Lime, silica, crushed coke, aluminum, silicon, fluorspar and iron ore are materials used for slag constituents and for controlling the composition of the metal bath. Because of the high temperatures and precise chemical control required, all stainless steel is produced in the electric furnace. Oxidizing and reducing slags may be used successively in the same heat, depending on the composition of the charge and the analysis of the product. Sulfur is removed from the metal with a reducing slag containing more than 2% calcium carbide, and silicon, phosphorus, manganese, chromium and carbon, with an oxidizing slag. However, carbon presents a problem in the presence of chromium, because of the chemical affinity chromium has for carbon. Carbon may be absorbed by the metal at the same time chromium is being oxidized and going into the slag. To oxidize carbon in a charge containing a high percentage of stainless steel scrap requires an excess of oxygen and extremely high temperatures (more than 3,200° F. [1,760° C.]). Oxygen supplied through a lance into the molten bath is used to a large extent to replace iron ore as a source of this element. Considerable chromium is oxidized along with the carbon, and the resultant slag will contain a high percentage of chromium oxide. Chromium oxide may be reduced and returned to the metal by the addition of lime and crushed ferrosilicon.

The stainless steels may be grouped according to chemical composition and response to heat treatment as follows: (1) ferritic steels, nonhardenable steels containing 15% to 30% chromium and with low carbon contents (from 0.08% to 0.20%), (2) martensitic steels, hardenable (by quenching) steels containing 10% to 18% chromium with varying carbon contents (0.08% to 1.10%), and (3) austenitic steel containing 16% to 26% chromium and 6% to 22% nickel, which is hardenable without quenching.

**Ferritic Stainless Steels** are better than the martensitic type and as good as the austenitic type in resistance to corrosion. However, because of their lower ductility they are not used to replace the austenitic type. Ferritic steels are magnetic and can be hot- and cold-worked but usually undergo excessive grain growth during prolonged exposure at elevated temperatures. They have lower high-temperature strength than the other two types and may develop brittleness after electric-arc, resistance or gas welding. Machinability is good and can be improved by adding sulfur or selenium. There is no tendency toward intergranular corrosion.

Ferritic stainless steel, American Iron and Steel Institute (A.I.S.I.) type 430, is widely used for automotive and architectural trim.

**Martensitic Stainless Steels** are magnetic; they can be cold-worked without difficulty, especially when the carbon content is low; show satisfactory resistance upon exposure to weather, water and some chemicals; can be machined satisfactorily; have toughness; and are easily forged or otherwise hot-worked. The corrosion resistance is usually increased by hardening, which is accomplished by quenching. Welds made by the electric-arc, resistance or gas methods contain some martensite after cooling in air. A.I.S.I. type 410 is the most widely used of the martensitic grades. In sheet or strip form, this grade is used extensively in the oil industry for bubble trays, bubble caps and liners.

**Austenitic Stainless Steels** are not magnetic unless severely cold-worked. They can be hot-worked, and cold-worked if proper allowance is made for their rapid work hardening. Except for surface hardening, their alloys cannot be hardened by heat treatment. They are extremely shock-resistant and difficult to machine unless they contain sulfur or selenium. These steels can be welded with difficulty, and, if the welding operation is controlled properly, the resistance to corrosion is not impaired. These steels have the best high-temperature strength and resistance to scaling of the stainless steels. However, they are subject to intergranular corrosion at temperatures between 800° and 1,600° F. (425° to 870° C.) unless the structure is stabilized to prevent the presence of carbides at or near grain boundaries which are vulnerable to corrosion. Stabilization may be done by the addition of titanium (4 to 6 times the carbon content) or niobium (8 to 10 times the carbon content), which combine with carbon and prevent the formation of chromium carbides. The corrosion resistance of the austenitic stainless steels is usually better than that of the other two groups.

A.I.S.I. type 304, a companion grade to types 301 and 302 with somewhat lower carbon (0.08% maximum), is the most widely used of austenitic grades. It is well suited to withstand severe forms of corrosion encountered in the paper and chemical industries. The austenitic grades most resistant to oxidation are types 309 and 310, which are high in nickel and chromium. These steels resist scaling up to 2,100° F. (1,150° C.) and consequently are used for furnace parts and heat exchangers.

The heat treatment of stainless steels may be carried out with any conventional type of electric, gas-fired, oil-fired, salt-bath or induction furnace. Although all stainless steels are highly resistant to oxidation, they may be expected to scale slightly at high heat-treating temperatures. The scale formed on the stainless steels is tenacious and relatively impervious and, consequently, is more difficult to remove than scale on ordinary carbon steel. Two basic methods are used: mechanical, such as sandblasting and tumbling; and chemical, such as pickling in acid solutions.

An important development in the stainless steel industry was the increased use of austenitic stainless steels containing manganese instead of nickel as a major alloying element. These were substituted for A.I.S.I. type 301 (18% Cr, 8% Ni), because of the current shortage of nickel. Manganese, like nickel, has the property of producing an austenitic structure in steel, although it takes twice as much to do it. Steel containing 15% Cr minimum, 16.5% Mn, 0.10% carbon maximum, and 1% Ni as a substitute for type 301 stainless is being used.

*See* also STEELS, ALLOY; IRON AND STEEL INDUSTRY: *Steel Metallurgy*.

BIBLIOGRAPHY.—Ernest E. Thum (ed.), *The Book of Stainless Steels* (1935); American Iron and Steel Institute, *Annual Statistical Report*, pp. 45, 726 (1952); Allegheny Ludlum Steel Corporation, *Handbook on Stainless Steel* (1946); Allegheny Ludlum Steel Corporation, *Stainless Steel Handbook* (1951); Rustless Iron and Steel Corporation, *Heat Treatment of Stainless Steels* (1944); American Society for Metals, *Metals Handbook* (1961); J. H. G. Monypenny, *Stainless Iron and Steel*, 2 vol., 3rd ed. (1951); D. K. Bullens, *Steel and Its Heat Treatment*, 5th ed. (1949); J. M. Camp and C. B. Francis, *Making, Shaping and Treating of Steel*, United States Steel Corporation, ch. 35, pp. 1313–1337 (1951); *Iron Age*, vol. 171, no. 1, pp. 135–138 (1953); U.S. Dept. of the Interior, Bureau of Mines films, *Stainless Steel*, no. 201.89, and *The Melting and Refining of Stainless Steel*, no. 240.33.

(N. B. MR.)

**STAIR, JAMES DALRYMPLE,** 1ST VISCOUNT OF (1619–1695), Scottish lawyer and statesman, president of the Court of Session from 1671 to 1681 and from 1689 to 1695, was born in May 1619 at Drummurchie, in Ayrshire. Regent of the University of Glasgow (1641–47), he was admitted to the bar in Edinburgh in February 1648. He was secretary of the commissions sent by the Scottish Parliament to treat with Charles II at The Hague (1649) and at Breda (1650), and during the latter negotiations the king decided, on learning of the failure of the marquess of Montrose's expedition in Scotland (May 1650), to accept the Covenants, whereby he could return to Scotland as king. Dalrymple met him on his landing in Moray in June. He refused in 1654 to take the oath of allegiance to the Commonwealth, but in 1657, on the recommendation of George Monck, he was appointed a commissioner of justice in Scotland.

After the restoration of Charles II in 1660, he was received with favour by the king, was knighted, and in February 1661 was made a judge in the Court of Session as Lord Stair. He refused in 1664 to take the declaration that the National Covenant and the Solemn League and Covenant were unlawful oaths and resigned, but the king allowed him to take the declaration under an implied reservation. In 1669 a family disaster took place, the exact facts of which will probably never be known. His daughter Janet, who had been betrothed to Lord Rutherford, was married to David Dunbar the Younger, of Baldoon, and some tragic event occurred on the wedding night from which she soon died. Sir Walter Scott took the plot of *The Bride of Lammermoor* from the incident.

Lord Stair was appointed president of the Court of Session in January 1671. He was member of Parliament for Wigtownshire (1672–74, 1678, 1681) and for Ayrshire (1689–90). He refused to sign a test or oath renouncing the Covenants in 1681 and was replaced as president by Sir George Gordon. He now published his great legal work, *The Institutions of the Law of Scotland* (1681), with a dedication to the king. In October 1682 he went to Holland and lived at Leiden. Whilst there he published in 1683 at Edinburgh the *Decisions of the Court of Session Between 1661 and 1671*, and in 1686 at Leiden a small treatise on natural science, *Physiologia Nova Experimentalis*. In his absence a prosecution for treason (1685) was raised against him and others of the exiles by Sir George Mackenzie, the law advocate, but the charge was dropped when his son, Sir John, the master of Stair, who had made his peace with James II and VII, was appointed lord advocate in 1687. Lord Stair returned to England with William of Orange at the Revolution in 1688. He was again made president of the Court of Session in November 1689 and was created viscount of Stair in April 1690. The massacre of the MacDonalds of Glencoe (Feb. 13, 1692), for which his son, the master of Stair, was largely responsible, naturally reflected on him. Stair died in Edinburgh in November 1695.

*See* J. M. Graham, *Annals and Correspondence of the Viscount . . . of Stair,* 2 vol. (1875); A. J. G. Mackay, *Memoir of Sir James Dalrymple* (1873). (G. S. P.)

**STAIR,** a series of steps arranged one above the other, occasionally varied by platforms known as landings. The total height of a stair is the rise, the total horizontal distance between the top and bottom steps is the run. A series of steps without a landing is called a flight. The horizontal surface of a step is called its tread, and the vertical front its riser. The projection of the tread beyond the face of the riser is termed a nosing. Staircase is a term for stairs accompanied by walls.

## HISTORY

It is uncertain what is the oldest stair in existence. On the sacred road up the mountain of T'ai Shan, in Shantung, China, there are many great flights of ancient granite steps. The earliest staircases seem to have been built with walls on both sides, as in Egyptian pylons which date from the 2nd millennium B.C. Contemporary models of houses, dating back to the middle kingdom, show a staircase leading up the side of a court to a roof terrace, with continuous wall below.

The origin of such stairs may have been earlier structures in wood, or even ladders cut out of logs. Egyptians may have used the self-supporting staircase in which each step is supported at its front by the step below and prevented from turning by having its end built solidly into a wall. The Assyrian ziggurat (*q.v.*) of the 9th or 8th century B.C. was often adorned with massive stairs; and the palace terrace at Persepolis has a double flight of steps, of great beauty, which shows the skill of the Persians in the 6th century B.C.

Farther west, stairs played an important part in the Cretan palaces, as in the palaces at Knossos and Phaistos (both *c.* 1500 B.C.). In Hellenic Greece the monumental stair was of less importance, due to the Greek love of informal and picturesque approaches. Thus in Athens the Propylaea of the Acropolis was probably entered by a winding path and the present great flight of stairs, dating from the Roman period, is not part of the original design. Interior staircases were common but unimportant; they were placed in out-of-the-way corners, and often built of wood. In the post-Alexandrian period there developed a new love of monumental grandeur, largely Asian in origin, which produced such magnificent stairs as those of the altar of Zeus at Pergamon (180 B.C.).

A similar monumental sense distinguished Roman stairs. Those of the propylaea at Baalbek (time of Hadrian), over 100 ft. wide, are typical, and again and again stairs are made essential parts of great architectural conceptions, as in the Temple of the Sun on the Quirinal hill at Rome, built by Aurelian (A.D. 273), some of the steps of which were taken, in 1348, to build the famous stairs of the Aracoeli on the Capitoline hill at Rome. Many of the apartment houses indicated on the marble plan of Rome (*c.* A.D. 205), now in the Palazzo dei Conservatori at Rome, seem to have had stair towers built in the centre of a courtyard. The Colosseum at Rome (completed A.D. 80) has elaborate and practical entrance and exit stairs, by which the crowds could be readily handled. These, in general, are supported and roofed by sloping vaults. Similar staircases were common in the theatres.

Merely inclined planes lead up within enormous buttresses at the ends of the narthex of Hagia Sophia (532) at Constantinople, so giving access to the galleries. In St. George at Salonika (late 5th century) a spiral staircase surrounds an open well. In the early Romanesque there is a growing use of the spiral staircase. To this development the great thickness of Romanesque walls and buttresses was particularly congenial, as it allowed the staircases to be built in solid masonry. Not only was the open circular well used, but the solid newel, in which each step had cut upon it a cylindrical form to act as part of the newel. This type of spiral staircase is still in use.

Although during the European middle ages stairs were used more for utilitarian than aesthetic purposes, where they were necessary they received adequate treatment, usually more direct and informal and more picturesque than those of the Roman tradition. Thus at Le Puy en Velay, in France, the 11th-century cathedral, which was built on a hilltop, is approached by a magnificent stair that provides a superb foreground to the polychrome façade. The steps that mount up to and past the apse of the 14th-century cathedral at Erfurt, in Germany, show the direct and beautiful relationship between the building itself and the stairs which is characteristic of the best Gothic usage.

The Gothic spiral staircase was cut with the utmost cleverness. Such circular staircases as those which lead up in the traceried turrets of the spire of Strasbourg cathedral in Alsace (1435) are miracles of daring design and delicate execution. The spiral staircase at the abbey church at St. Gilles, which is known as Vis St. Gilles, is of hewn stone built round a circular newel and covered with a semicircular rising vault.

The late Gothic period also produced a great number of beautiful interior staircases, like the "Stair of the Library" in Rouen cathedral (1477–79), which show that the possibilities of the staircase with straight runs were at last being realized. Of rich interior spiral staircases, the early 16th-century staircase leading to the organ in St. Maclou, in Rouen, and the contemporary staircase to the jube (*q.v.*), or rood loft, of St. Étienne du Mont in Paris (in which a certain amount of Renaissance feeling is present) are noteworthy. In the larger houses the lack of communicating passages led to many staircases. Thus in the house of Jacques Coeur at Bourges (*c.* 1450) there are eight separate spiral staircases, whose exterior treatment, in rich, traceried towers, furnishes a great deal of the picturesqueness and varied beauty of such a building.

In France the spiral staircase added by Francis I to the château at Blois (1515–24) and the double circular staircase of the château of Chambord (begun 1519) are remarkable. The early Renaissance, however, produced its most remarkable results in the richly ornamented wooden staircases of Tudor and Jacobean houses of England. The usual arrangement was to have the staircase divided into comparatively short flights, at right angles to each other, around a central open well. The heavy newels at the corners were finished with urnlike finials at the top and carved drops at the bottom; the railing consisted of a large rail supported either by miniature arcades or square balusters, whose moldings were often sloped to follow the stairs; and the whole was covered with intricate surface ornament of strapwork. The staircase at Hatfield house (1611) is typical.

The early Renaissance staircases of Spanish palaces are in most cases placed in one corner of the courtyard and run up between walls to a landing with a return flight that opens out onto the upper-floor gallery. The walls, and sometimes even the treads and risers, are often cased in brilliant faïence tiles. Even in staircases of more Italian type, with balusters, the richness of wall surface remains, as in the staircase of the hospital of Santa Cruz at Toledo (1504–14), by E. de Egas. The climax of Spanish Renaissance monumental stair design is reached in the Escalera Dorada at Burgos cathedral (1519), by D. de Siloe, with its exquisite metal railing.

The Renaissance produced a recrudescence of the tradition of Roman formality in stair design. Despite such tours de force as G. Vignola's spiral stair in the palace at Caprarola (*c.* 1550), the general practice was to have important staircases run up in a straight flight, sometimes varied by landings, and sometimes with changes in direction between walls often crowned with a slanting vault. The most perfect developments of this type were made chiefly during the baroque period. The magnificence of the huge interior flights of the Genoese palaces (*e.g.*, the University, 1623, by B. Bianco) is famous. The so-called Spanish stairs at Rome in the Piazza di Spagna (1723–26), by F. de Sanctis, those of the

BY COURTESY OF (TOP RIGHT) THE ITALIAN INSTITUTE, LONDON; PHOTOGRAPHS, (TOP LEFT) FOTO MAS, (BOTTOM LEFT) GIRAUDON, (BOTTOM RIGHT) A. F. KERSTING

(TOP LEFT) THE STAIRCASE OF THE HOSPITAL OF SANTA CRUZ (1504–14), TOLEDO, SPAIN; BY ENRIQUE DE EGAS. (TOP RIGHT) STAIRS OF THE ARACOELI (1348), ON CAPITOLINE HILL, ROME, ITALY. (BOTTOM LEFT) SPIRAL STAIRCASE LEADING TO THE JUBE, OR ROOD LOFT (*c.* 1600), IN THE CHURCH OF SAINT-ÉTIENNE DU MONT, PARIS; BY PIERRE BIARD. (BOTTOM RIGHT) THE STAIRCASE OF HATFIELD HOUSE (1611), HERTFORDSHIRE, ENG.

Campidoglio, at Rome (begun 1547), by Michelangelo, and the infinitely varied terrace stairs of the Italian villas should also be mentioned. The inspiration of these Italian baroque stairs was felt throughout Europe and is largely the foundation of stair design in modern city and garden planning. Thus the enormous stairs of the gardens of Versailles (1667–88), by A. Le Nôtre, owe much to the Italian precedent, and were themselves imitated widely all over Europe.

Classicism combined with the baroque to give a new trend to staircase design throughout Europe. In France a gorgeous series of staircases was produced, of which the Escalier des Princes of Versailles is typical. The reaction to the lightness and gaiety of the Louis XV period (*see* LOUIS STYLES) led to the development of many gracious and inviting house staircases of the type known as self-supporting, full of sweeping curves and with railings frequently of metal. In the Louis XVI period the new, popular classicism restrained the exuberance of the earlier staircases but retained their graciousness and lightness; of these, one of the loveliest is that of the Petit Trianon at Versailles (1766), by A. J. Gabriel, with a beautiful iron railing. Meanwhile, the classic trend had expressed itself in England by the substitution of open-string for closed-string stairs, that is, with the balusters coming down to the top of each tread rather than being supported on a slanting member, or string, which received the ends of the treads. This at once made for a more interesting treatment at the ends of the steps and led, eventually, to the development of the bracketed step end, in which scrolls and leafage of great richness were carved under the end of each riser. Moreover, the fact that English stairs were largely of wood inspired the design of turned balusters and newels of great variety.

During the last half of the 18th century a growing trend toward lightness and delicacy of design led to the substitution of plain, tapered shafts in place of elaborate balusters, and the use of stairs rising in continuing curves instead of straight flights and landings. The same development took place during the 18th century in the colonial work of North America.

Thus certain of the earliest houses, like the Capen house at Topsfield, Mass., 1683, have closed strings and heavy newels of Jacobean type, while the Lee mansion at Marblehead, Mass., 1768, has a magnificent open-string staircase, whose steps have paneled and scrolled ends and whose twisted balusters are as rich as any contemporary work in England. The curved staircase of the Valentine museum at Richmond, Va., 1812, is typical of the later delicacy.

During the middle and the third quarter of the 19th century staircase design reached its lowest ebb, not only in England and France, but throughout Europe, except in the case of those monumental and official buildings in Europe whose design never fell a victim to the current taste. Closed strings, balusters and newels of gargantuan proportions, and bulbous and meaningless elaboration again became the fashion. Yet one of the most gorgeous and effective staircases in the world dates from this period, that of the Paris Opéra (1861–75), by Charles Garnier.

Two elements have vastly affected modern staircase design, steel and reinforced concrete. The use of steel has led to simple plans of straight runs, and railings delicate and straightforward in design. Reinforced concrete, on the other hand, is a material so flexible that the most daring curves and fantastic sweeps become structurally sound. The masters of contemporary architecture have given new vitality to staircase design with such superb examples as the glass enclosed circular staircase of the Werkbund Exposition building at Cologne, Ger. (W. Gropius and A. Meyer), the interior stair of Frank Lloyd Wright's own house at Spring Green, Wis., and "Les Terrasses" at Garches, France, by Le Corbusier.

Contemporary architecture has largely de-emphasized the monumental stair and the monumental building. Most frequently entrances are effected at ground level. Emphasis has been placed on the small, light, open, free-standing stair (Gropius house, Lincoln, Mass., W. Gropius, 1939); on the intimate and picturesque (Wellesley college art centre, Mass., P. Rudolph, 1957); and on the short-run formalized axial solution (Architecture building, Illinois Institute of Technology, Chicago, Mies van der Rohe, 1955). There is, perhaps, some evidence that contemporary architects have given exterior stairs something less than adequate study.

In the orient the stairs leading down to the river at Benares, in India, of various dates, combine monumentality and picturesqueness; a similar skill is shown in the design of large numbers of temple and palace steps throughout the peninsula. Farther east the ruins of Angkor use wide flights of steps with magnificent effect in connecting the various levels of the terraced group. The Chinese have always been superb stair designers and builders, and there is hardly a temple or large house or palace which does not owe some of its effect to its stairs, either monumental and formal, like those of the Forbidden City or the Temple of Heaven, both in Peking, or winding and informal, as in Chinese garden design. Many of the temple stairs have, in the centre, an inclined plane running the entire height of the rise, richly carved with the symbolic dragon—the so-called spirit stairs by which the beneficent powers are supposed to enter. In Japan the tradition is much more informal, but the hilly nature of the country makes stairs an important feature of almost every temple layout.

### STRUCTURAL DESIGN

Long use has demonstrated that certain proportions of riser and tread are safe and easy. For interior stairs twice the height of the riser, plus the length of the tread, should be 23, all dimensions being in inches. A variant is that the sum of riser and tread should be between 17 and $17\frac{1}{2}$ in.; a third rule specifies that the product of riser and tread, in inches, should be not less than 70 nor more than 75. In general, English usage advocates a slightly lower rise for a given tread than U.S. usage, while in Europe the rise is frequently greater. For exterior stairs, the general usage is to keep the riser below 6 in. and the tread above 12.

**Stone and Marble Staircases.**—Modern stone and marble staircases are of two main types. In the first the actual exposed treads and risers form, themselves, the structural elements. In the other type the treads and risers are supported upon a separate structural base which may consist of a masonry vault, a steel framework or a reinforced concrete slab. In the first class, in which the steps themselves are structural, the staircase is usually built into a wall at one side. Each step rests for a small distance upon the step below and is built into the wall for a distance sufficient to make the weight of the wall above prevent it from turning. The undersides of the steps, where exposed, are frequently cut to form an inclined surface, following the slope of the stairs, and may be decorated with paneling or carving or other ornament. This type of stair can be used both for straight and curved runs, and is particularly applicable to monumental entrance halls, where the stair, in a triple run with two landings, or in a continuous, curved sweep, fills a recess opposite the door. In such staircases the railing is usually of metal with the uprights securely doweled into the ends of the steps. Stairs somewhat similar can be built with the ends of the steps built into the walls on both sides, where a monumental run rises between two walls.

**Wooden Staircases.**—These can be divided into two classes, closed- and open-string stairs. In both, the essential support is given by rough timbers called carriages, which follow the slope of the stairs and are cut roughly to the shape of the underside of the steps.

In the case of closed-string staircases both sides of the staircase are finished by a sloping, straight-sided plank, approximately an inch and a half thick, on the inner faces of which grooves are cut, whose upper and outer faces exactly fit the top and side of the tread and riser; the under- and inner sides are, however, sloped, so that wedges may be driven in to force the tread and riser boards into position and hold them with perfect rigidity. Similar wedges are driven in between the rough carriages and the undersides of treads and risers. To give additional strength, the treads and risers are themselves rebated together, so that a small, projecting strip of the tread fits into a groove in the bottom of the riser, and a similar strip on the top of the riser fits into a groove on the bottom of the tread. The projecting portion of the tread is molded and an additional small cover mold placed below to cover the joint.

In the open-string staircase the strings at the end are cut to the shape of the steps, and the vertical cuts are usually mitred at 45°, so that the ends of the risers, also mitred, may form with them an invisible joint. In the ends of the treads dovetailed sockets are left to receive the dovetailed ends of the balusters; a molding, exactly similar to the nosing, is then applied across the end of the step and covers the bottom of the balusters. At times, bracketed and carved pieces are mitred at the ends of the risers and applied over the face of the string. It is this type of staircase that was the rule during the Georgian period in England and in the developed American colonial and early republic work. Where an open-string stair is built against a wall, it is usually finished at the wall end by a closed or housed string, similar to that described, forming a baseboard for the wall.

The structural strength for a wooden staircase is usually furnished by framing a heavy member, called a header, at the top and bottom of every run; to these headers the rough carriages are spiked, and the newels, if they exist, firmly fastened. The newels themselves are designed to receive the finished stair strings, and also the finished string member that is occasionally used at the edges of a floor in the stair-well opening. In modern staircases of this type additional strength is obtained by inserting iron or steel bands into the handrail; occasional balusters may be of steel, well fastened to the string.

(TOP LEFT) GOURSAT—RAPHO, (TOP RIGHT) BRIHAT—RAPHO, (BOTTOM LEFT) TOM HOLLYMAN—PHOTO RESEARCHERS, (BOTTOM RIGHT) BONNEY

(TOP LEFT) STAIRCASE OF THE PARIS OPÉRA (1861–75); BY CHARLES GARNIER. (TOP RIGHT) EXTERIOR SPIRAL STAIRCASE OF THE UNITÉ D'HABITATION (1947–52), MARSEILLES, FRANCE; BY LE CORBUSIER. (BOTTOM LEFT) STAIRCASE OF THE NATHANIEL RUSSELL HOUSE (*c.* 1806), CHARLESTON, S.C. (BOTTOM RIGHT) CIRCULAR CONCRETE STAIRCASE OF THE MARTEL HOUSE (1926), PARIS, FRANCE; BY R. MALLET-STEVENS

**Steel Staircases.**—These have become almost universal in modern fireproof buildings of all types, except where unusual monumental effect is desired. The design of steel staircases is largely standardized. They consist of a steel string on each side, which takes the form of a plate or channel of sufficient rigidity to carry the weight.

Iron spiral staircases are usually formed of cast-iron members, each of which forms a tread and riser and has, at its inner end, a collar arranged to slip over a vertical pipe or cylindrical bar forming the central newel. Such spiral staircases are rigid independently of any wall, and are frequently used in open spaces, such as those existing in power houses, gymnasiums and the like. Reinforced concrete, sometimes finished as artificial stone, is used for stairs and permits of infinite variety of form.

**Moving Staircases.**—In many places where continuous transit between floors is necessary, as in large shops, underground railway stations and the like, moving stairs, sometimes known as escalators, are much used. (*See* ESCALATOR.)

**Legal Regulation.**—As stairs form one of the most necessary methods of exit from a building, their design has formed one of the most important portions of the building legislation of modern municipalities, especially in the case of public, commercial, industrial and educational buildings. Thus, in addition to the universal requirements for structural solidity, the attempt is generally made to furnish at least two stair exits to any large, enclosed, upper-floor area; and where fire risk and the danger of panic are unusually great, as in the case of theatres, to demand sufficient stairs to allow the building to be emptied in a very short time without disorder. Design is controlled by specifying the relationships of tread and riser, the distance apart and size of landings, whether or not curved stairs are allowed, etc., and often, because of the smoke danger, requiring exit stairs to be enclosed in a fireproof tower, with fireproof, self-closing doors at all entrances.

*See* also references under "Stair" in the Index.

BIBLIOGRAPHY.—A. Swan, *The British Architect or the Builder's Treasury of Staircases* (1775); Viollet-le-Duc, *Dictionnaire Raisonné de l'Architecture* (1854–76); P. Le Tarouilly, *Edifices de Rome Moderne* (1840–55); Byne and Stepley, *Spanish Architecture of the 16th Century* (1917); P. G. Knoblauch, *Good Practice in Construction* (1923–26); T. F. Hamlin, *Forms and Functions of Twentieth-Century Architecture*, vol. i (1952).

(T. F. H.; H. MN.)

**STALACTITES AND STALAGMITES.** Stalactites are elongated pendent forms of various minerals deposited from solution where very slow drip water may enter a void. Stalagmites are complementary forms of thicker proportions which grow up on the bottom of a cavity from the same drip-water source but whose mineral was deposited after free fall across the open space in the rock. An inclusive name for both forms is dripstone.

The dominant mineral in dripstone deposits is calcium carbonate (*see* CALCITE) and the largest displays are formed in caves in limestone and dolomite. Other minerals which may be deposited in these forms include other carbonates, opal, chalcedony, limonite and some sulfides. Icicles are stalactites of water. Ice in stalagmitic form is very rare.

Conditions which favour dripstone deposition of calcium carbonates are (1) a source rock above the cavity; (2) downward percolation of water supplied from rain; (3) tight but continuous passageways for this water which determine a very slow drip; (4) adequate air space in the void to allow either (*a*) evaporation or (*b*) escape of carbon dioxide from the water which thus loses some of its solvent ability. Minor and imperfect stalactites may hang from the underside of masonry and concrete bridges and arches, and from ceilings of concrete arched tunnels and subways. One-way traffic through such structures may produce forms that hang out of plumb, inclining in the direction taken by recurrent air currents engendered by passing vehicles. Even in some caves, an air circulation is believed to have been the cause of inclined stalactites.

Stalactites, but not stalagmites, commonly exhibit a central tube or the trace of a former tube whose diameter is that of a drop of water hanging by surface tension. Examination will show that the drop on the tip of a growing stalactite leaves a deposit only around its rim. Downward growth of the rim makes the tube. The simplest stalactite form, therefore, is a thin-walled stone straw, and these fragile forms may reach lengths of two feet or more where air currents have not seriously disturbed the growth. The more common form of a downward-tapering cone is simply a thickening of the primitive straw type by deposition from a film descending the exterior of the pendant. This also makes the concentric structure seen in broken stalactites, slight variations in colour from impurities demarking successive additions. Neither these nor the comparable rings of stalagmite structure are annual rings.

Related to stalagmites are broader, flatter cones on a cave floor which generally grade outward into a sheet of secondary lime known as cave travertine but more specifically as flowstone.

Stalactite forms may grade into very broad pendent leaves, sheets, blades and drapes, whose growth is entirely on the edges. Other variants of the conventional carrot-shaped stalactite may have a bulbous upper portion resembling the form of a radish, beet or turnip. More puzzling than this enlargement is a common ceiling attachment by a slender stem. Compound forms of much complexity may result from continued lateral enlargement of closely adjacent stalactites and stalagmites. Not every stalactite has a complementary stalagmite, and many of the latter may have no stalactite above them. Where the paired relation exists, however, continual elongation of one or both eventually results in a junction and the formation of a column. Large stalagmites and columns have a habit of developing shelves or brackets in vertical series, with depending drapes or relatively small stalactites growing down from the bottom of each.

BY COURTESY OF U.S. DEPARTMENT OF THE INTERIOR

JUNCTURE OF STALACTITES AND STALAGMITES FORMS A COLUMN OF LIMESTONE IN THE GREEN LAKE ROOM, CARLSBAD CAVERNS NATIONAL PARK, CARLSBAD, N.M.

Known as the Veiled Statue, this formation is the result of the deposition of carbonate of lime, carried in solution by descending ground water

The slow rate of growth of these calcium carbonate deposits is conditioned by a variety of variable factors. Deposition from drip water indicates saturation of the water under the existing conditions. But these conditions may change so much that deposition will cease although the drip continues. In some cases, solution of a previously growing stalagmite may occur and produce a cratered concavity where once was a projecting conical tip.

Lava caves containing lava stalactites have a wholly different genesis. The cave results from surface solidification of a lava flow during the last stages of its activity. Thus what is essentially a frozen crust may form over still mobile and actively flowing liquid rock. Dwindling of the supply may then leave long tunnels under this crust. Volcanic gases from bubbles in the lava collect under the tunnel roof. Mingled with air from vents in the roof, more intense heating from oxidation may raise the temperature of the gas sufficiently to re-fuse the ceiling rock, which then drips with the remelted lava, which may congeal in place to form rude stalactites.

*See* also CAVE and articles on various caves, such as LURAY CAVERN.

(J H. Bz.)

**STALACTITE WORK,** in architecture, one of the most general characteristics of all of the Islamic styles, consisting of a series of little niches, bracketed out one above the other, or of projecting prismatic forms in rows and tiers, connected at their upper ends by miniature arches. Its infinite varieties may be classified into three groups, the first consisting of those basically niche shaped, in which the concave curve is the most important feature; the second group includes those in which the vertical edges between the niches are the most important feature, being set at all sorts of angles and having generally prismatic forms; the last group consists of elaborately intersecting, miniature arches. The first two groups occur commonly in Syrian, Moorish and Turkish work and in their simpler forms, in Persia; the last group is typically Persian and is found also in Mogul work in India.

Stalactites are of comparatively late development in Islamic art, the earliest buildings in Syria, Egypt and north Africa showing no traces of them. They seem to appear suddenly all over the Islamic world toward the beginning of the 12th century. Thus simple forms are found in the mosque at Ani in Armenia, built between 1072 and 1110, and they are common in Algiers and Sicily during the course of the century, as in the gate at Chella (1118–84), and in the building, which is known as La Ziza at Palermo (1154).

In Egypt the stalactites appear in panels flanking the main entrance of the El Akmar mosque at Cairo (1125–50). They reached their highest development in the 14th and 15th centuries, becoming the normal decoration for the heads of door niches and the bracketing under cornices and minaret galleries. The richest examples of the prismatic type are to be found in Moorish work in Spain, especially in the intricate wood and plaster ornament of such palaces as the 14th- and 15th-century Alhambra (*q.v.*) in Granada and the 14th-century Alcázar at Seville.

In Turkey, a peculiar type of faceted crystal shape is found and the form became the most common capital decoration.

*See* ISLAMIC ARCHITECTURE.

**STALIN, JOSEPH VISSARIONOVICH** (DZHUGASHVILI) (1879–1953), leader of the Communist Party of the Soviet Union, prime minister, generalissimo, and dictator of the U.S.S.R., one of the most powerful, complex, and controversial figures in world history. He was born on Dec. 21, 1879, in the Transcaucasian town of Gori, in Georgia.

His father, Vissarion Dzhugashvili, a poor shoemaker, died when Joseph was 11 years old. His mother, Ekaterina, the daughter of a serf, was an illiterate and deeply religious washerwoman. After the death in infancy of three children, Joseph was her only son. She brought him up with much tenderness and devotion and chose for him an ecclesiastical career in the Georgian Orthodox Church.

SOVFOTO

STALIN

**The Young Revolutionary.**—Georgian folklore, native tribal traditions, fresh memories of serfdom, and Georgian patriotic (anti-Russian) sentiment were the strongest influences in Joseph's childhood. He attended the parish school at Gori, and in the autumn of 1894 he matriculated at the theological seminary of Tiflis (Tbilisi). He was a very able pupil, a voracious reader, and an ambitious debater. In 1898, while he was still at the seminary, he joined the ranks of Mesame Dasi (the Third Group), a Georgian patriotic and socialist organization; and he came under the influence of Marxism, which was rapidly spreading among the Russian and Georgian intelligentsia. In 1899, when he was about to graduate, he was expelled from the seminary because of his "disloyal" views.

The young Dzhugashvili plunged into revolutionary propaganda and agitation. At the turn of the century the revolutionary movement in Russia shed the ideas of agrarian socialism preached by the Narodniki (*q.v.*) and adopted the Marxist social-democratic program, advocated by G. V. Plekhanov and V. I. Lenin (*qq.v.*) in the journal *Iskra*. Dzhugashvili was a supporter of *Iskra*. In 1901 he was elected to the clandestine Social Democratic Committee of Tiflis. Police persecution forced him to "go underground." Arrested in April 1902, he remained in prison until the end of 1903. But while in prison he was elected to the Social Democratic Committee guiding the movement in the whole of the Caucasus. Deported to Siberia, he escaped from there and returned to Tiflis early in 1904, shortly after the Social Democratic Party had split into Bolsheviks and Mensheviks. He joined the Bolsheviks, who wielded little influence in Georgia. At this early stage he was already under the overwhelming influence of Lenin's writings; and in local clandestine sheets and periodicals he translated Lenin's ideas from the Russian into the Georgian.

In the revolution of 1905 (*see* RUSSIAN HISTORY), Dzhugashvili played no conspicuous part, but he was active in the background as an organizer of Bolshevik fighting squads and partisan groups. He had a hand in organizing raids on treasury transports, the so-called exes (expropriations), the raiders "expropriating" government funds and using them to finance the party's revolutionary activity. He first met Lenin at a party conference at Tampere (Tammerfors), in Finland, in 1905. In 1906 and 1907 he participated in party congresses held in Stockholm and London; in opposition to Lenin he advocated a policy of agrarian revolution identical with that later adopted by the Bolsheviks in 1917. After the failure of the 1905 revolution he distinguished himself as the Bolshevik leader of Baku. Many times arrested and deported, he succeeded each time in escaping from the places of exile.

In 1912 the Bolsheviks finally broke with the Mensheviks and formed a separate party. Lenin then "co-opted" Dzhugashvili as member of the new central committee. Stalin (he began to use this pseudonym, the Man of Steel, early in 1913) was the first editor of *Pravda,* which began to appear on May 5, 1912. At the end of that year he attended important Bolshevik conferences in Cracow, in Austrian Poland, and then went to Vienna to write *Marxism and the National Problem.* This important study was a theoretical argument in favour of the Bolshevik program of "self-determination" of oppressed nations. The work established his reputation as a foremost expert in this field, but he was looked upon as a man of action and an organizer, not a theoretician. On his return to St. Petersburg he was again arrested and deported to the Turukhan Province in the polar circle. He remained in exile until the outbreak of the March Revolution of 1917. (*See* RUSSIAN REVOLUTION.)

**Stalin's Role in 1917.**—Stalin's role in the events of 1917 was not prominent. This was the heyday of the brilliant revolutionary orators and agitators; and Stalin was not one of them. He was overshadowed not only by L. D. Trotski (*q.v.*), who was much more than an orator and agitator, but by G. E. Zinoviev, A. V. Lunacharski, Aleksandra Kollontai, and other less important Bolshevik leaders. After his return from Siberia in March, he became editor of *Pravda* and adopted a vaguely conciliatory attitude toward the provisional government of Prince G. E. Lvov. Soon afterward the Bolsheviks, prompted by Lenin, embarked upon a revolutionary course of action; but Stalin remained one of their chief organizers and *Pravda*'s coeditor. At the height of the anti-Bolshevik campaign in July he organized Lenin's escape from Petrograd; and in the absence of Lenin, Trotski, L. B. Kamenev, and Zinoviev, he guided the 6th Party Congress immediately after the "July Days." During the famous controversy that developed in September and October between Lenin, advocating an armed rising, and Zinoviev and Kamenev, opposing insurrectionary tactics, Stalin was among Lenin's adherents, although in *Pravda* he attempted to bridge the gulf between the two factions. He was elected member of a Bolshevik insurrectionist "centre" that was to join the Military Revolutionary Committee headed by Trotski; but he played no part at all in the insurrection itself.

**The People's Commissar.**—After the Bolshevik seizure of power Stalin was appointed commissar of nationalities, and he held this post for nearly five years. Under Lenin's guidance he set out to put into effect the party's program of "self-determination" for oppressed nationalities. One of his first official acts was to proclaim on behalf of the new Russian government the independence of Finland. He participated closely in the drafting of the first Soviet constitutions of 1918 and 1923. In 1919 he was, in addition, appointed commissar of the Workers' and Peasants' Inspectorate, an important department whose function it was to supervise all other branches of the Soviet administration.

Stalin's voice carried much weight in the inner Bolshevik councils during the civil war, although he continued to be overshadowed by Trotski, the founder and inspirer of the Red Army. As member of the Council of Defense, political commissar, and inspector of fronts, Stalin was in charge of the defense of Tsaritsyn (later Stalingrad and now Volgograd) in 1918; he organized the defense of Petrograd (Leningrad) against Gen. N. N. Yudenich's offensive in May 1919, and the Battle of Orel in October of the same year, when the Red Army halted Gen. A. I. Denikin's advance on Moscow and passed to the counteroffensive. He served as political commissar with S. M. Budenny's cavalry corps during the advance on Lwow (Lvov) in 1920; and he was in charge of the preparations for the final campaign against Gen. P. N. Wrangel's army and of the dramatic battle of the Perekop Isthmus, the last battle of the civil war. Some of these episodes, especially his role in the defense of Tsaritsyn and in the march to Poland, were the subjects of much controversy. During the civil war an intense rivalry developed between him and Trotski, the commissar of war. Not without justification, Trotski charged Stalin with surreptitiously supporting the left-wing Communists who were opposed to the employment of old army officers in the Red Army and to the army's centralized structure and discipline established by Trotski. Trotski's influence remained paramount, but even in 1919 Stalin wielded enough power to bring about the dismissal of I. I. Vatsetis, Trotski's protégé, from the post of commander in chief and his replacement by Gen. Sergei S. Kamenev. After the civil war, in February 1921, Stalin initiated the Bolshevik invasion of Georgia without the knowledge of Trotski or the commander in chief.

In April 1922, after the 11th Party Congress, the last congress attended by Lenin, Stalin was appointed secretary-general of the party and relinquished his posts in the Council of People's Commissars. This was a turning point in his career: as secretary-general he soon came to control the whole machinery of the party and through it the government.

**The Succession to Lenin.**—Lenin's illness in 1923 and his death (January 1924) coincided with a crisis of the revolutionary regime. The Bolsheviks had from the beginning denied political freedom to the old ruling classes and their parties who opposed arms in hand the "proletarian dictatorship." But the Bolsheviks had also pledged to respect and secure "Soviet democracy," that is, freedom of political expression for the working classes and their parties. The proletarian dictatorship had been conceived as a system of representative government, but instead of a parliament, the councils of workers' and peasants' deputies were to form the representative organs. Toward the end of the Lenin era, however, the regime had already developed into a single-party system. All non-Bolshevik parties had been banned, and only within Bolshevik ranks was some freedom of expression preserved. Inevitably the question arose whether the Bolsheviks themselves could enjoy the freedom they denied to others. The other critical development concerned the party's international orientation. The hope for an imminent spread of revolution abroad, which had inspired the Bolsheviks, was decisively undermined in 1923 after the defeat of Communism in Germany. Bolshevik Russia was at last recognized by most bourgeois governments, but as a Communist state it stood alone. Bolshevism was withdrawing into its national shell and was ill at ease with the revolutionary internationalism of the Lenin era. All these issues were brought to a head in the struggle over the succession to Lenin.

In 1923 Stalin, Zinoviev, and L. B. Kamenev formed a triumvirate with the purpose of debarring from power Trotski, who was generally regarded as Lenin's successor. In his last will Lenin advised his followers to remove Stalin from the general secretariat of the party on the ground that Stalin was rude and inclined to abuse power. But Stalin, supported by Zinoviev and Kamenev, retained his office. In a constant struggle against his opponents he abolished whatever freedom of expression still existed within the party and transformed the party into a "monolithic" body. In the autumn of 1924 he expounded the theory of "socialism in one country," proclaiming the self-sufficiency of the Russian Revolution. This doctrinal innovation marked a departure from Leninist internationalism, although Stalin did his utmost to present his views as orthodox Leninism.

In April 1925, having defeated Trotski, Stalin openly broke with the other members of the triumvirate and, at the 14th Party Congress, joined hands with the party's right wing led by N. I. Bukharin, A. I. Rykov, and M. P. Tomski. Zinoviev and Kamenev, on the other hand, made common cause with Trotski. They denounced the theory of "socialism in one country," advocated a policy of industrialization and a struggle against the kulaks (well-to-do farmers), and demanded the restoration of "inner party democracy." At this stage Stalin, anxious to keep in line with Bukharin's moderate group, pursued a very cautious policy: he refused to undertake a drive against the kulaks and treated the demand for rapid industrialization as unreal. But in 1928–29, after he had defeated and expelled from the party Trotski, Zinoviev, Kamenev, and their followers, Stalin turned against Bukharin, Rykov, and Tomski. He then effected a most drastic change of policy and began to industrialize the U.S.S.R. and to collectivize agriculture with a speed and ruthlessness that horrified the original advocates of these policies. In 1929 he expelled Trotski from the U.S.S.R. and forced all opposition leaders, right and left, to surrender and "recant." He had become undisputed master of the U.S.S.R.

**Industrialization and Collectivization.**—"We are 50 or 100 years behind the advanced countries. We must make good this lag in 10 years. Either we do it or they crush us." Thus Stalin explained the purpose of industrialization to a conference of industrial managers on Feb. 4, 1931. In the course of the decade the U.S.S.R. was indeed transformed from one of the most backward states into a great industrial power; this was one of the factors that was to assure Soviet victory in World War II. Stalin emphatically insisted on the need to develop primarily the heavy industries. Industrialization was consequently accompanied by an extreme scarcity of consumer goods and by widespread popular discontent. Stalin violently suppressed the discontent. With utmost determination he enforced a policy of incentive rewards to skilled workers, technicians, and administrators, which provoked much indignation among party members brought up in an egalitarian spirit. They denounced Stalin as the leader of new privileged social groups.

Industrialization on the gigantic scale envisaged in the successive five-year plans encountered many other difficulties that might have baffled and defeated a government less ruthless than Stalin's. In the 1930s alone about 25,000,000 peasants were forcibly shifted from rural areas to the industrial centres and transformed into factory workers by means of intensive training and with the help of an extremely harsh industrial discipline. Throughout the Stalin era the U.S.S.R.'s urban population grew by about 45,000,000. In order to free labour for industry and to secure food for the swelling urban population, Stalin collectivized farming. In 1929 there were about 25,000,000 primitive rural smallholdings in the U.S.S.R. In 1952 there were 100,000 large and highly mechanized collective farms. The peasantry at first bitterly resisted collectivization. Stalin broke its resistance and ordered the deportation of many kulaks into the notorious labour camps. Despite initial failures and famines, the new system of farming achieved a degree of consolidation in later years that enabled it to survive the shocks of World War II and its aftermath; but it did not attain high productivity.

**The Great Purges.**—At the height of the industrial drive, shortly after he had introduced the quasi-liberal constitution of 1936, Stalin staged the great purge trials in which most of the old Bolsheviks and some military leaders were charged with treason, terrorism, and espionage and brought to "confess" guilt. In this way Stalin exterminated the men who might have been able to overthrow him and form an alternative government during a national crisis. The purges, carried out on a mass scale, imparted to the Stalinist regime its peculiar terroristic character.

**Foreign Policy Prior to 1941.**—The national crisis that Stalin feared was approaching with World War II. After Hitler's rise to power in Germany, Stalin grappled with a dilemma: should he enter an anti-Hitler coalition with the Western Powers or an agreement with Hitler? At first his diplomacy aimed at building up the anti-Hitler coalition, but finding the West reluctant to commit itself to an alliance with the U.S.S.R., Stalin hinted at his readiness to come to terms with Hitler in a speech at the 18th Party Congress in March 1939. In August, with the agreement signed in Moscow by his foreign minister, V. M. Molotov, and the German foreign minister, J. von Ribbentrop, he struck the bargain with Hitler under which the U.S.S.R. and Germany divided their spheres of influence in Eastern Europe, and the U.S.S.R. avoided immediate involvement in the war that broke out a few days later. (*See* World Wars: *World War II.*)

The twists and turns of Stalin's foreign policy affected closely the attitude of the Communist International. After a long series of purges and expulsions Stalin succeeded in transforming the International into a "monolithic" organization, identifying the interests of world Communism with Stalin's dogmas and policies. Thus the Communist International had supported Chiang Kai-shek during the Chinese revolution of 1925–27 when Soviet diplomacy regarded the Chinese generalissimo as its ally. In 1935–39 the Communist parties organized the "popular fronts" to help the U.S.S.R. in its search for bourgeois democratic allies against Hitler. In 1939 they lent moral support to the Ribbentrop-Molotov pact.

**Generalissimo.**—The German attack on the U.S.S.R., started on June 22, 1941, caught Stalin unawares, as he himself later publicly admitted. In preparation for critical times he had assumed the premiership on May 6, but he still hoped to be able to postpone the inevitable conflict between the U.S.S.R. and Germany. After the German attack he formed the State Defense Committee, consisting of himself, V. M. Molotov, G. M. Malenkov, L. P. Beria, and K. E. Voroshilov. On July 3, 1941, he made the famous call on the Soviet people to "scorch the earth" occupied by the invader. "In occupied regions conditions must be made unbearable for the enemy and all his accomplices. They must be hounded and annihilated at every step, and all their measures frustrated."

Throughout World War II Stalin was personally responsible for the major military and diplomatic decisions of his government, although he left considerable freedom of initiative to his generals. After the initial period of confusion, his strategy, following the traditional Russian pattern of 1812, was to withdraw, to conserve strength, to gather new reserves, and to force the attacker to spend his impetus and extend his lines—only after that could the U.S.S.R. pass to the offensive. He displayed extraordinary will power, tenacity, and coolheadedness. He stayed on in the Kremlin when Hitler's armies stood at the gates of Moscow and the Soviet government was evacuated to Kuibyshev. From the Kremlin he organized a hasty yet effective evacuation from the threatened areas of industrial plants and of many millions of industrial workers. The shifting of industry from west to east enabled the U.S.S.R. to recover from the first blows and to build up a new and enormous armed power.

Stalin's political conduct of the war was characterized by strong emphasis on Russian patriotism, nationalism, and traditionalism. Evoking the memories of 1812, he described the struggle as the Great Patriotic War, and he extolled the national heroes of Mother Russia and the military traditions of Peter the Great, Suvorov, and Kutuzov. He rehabilitated the Orthodox Church and disbanded the Communist International. These moves, dictated primarily by considerations of domestic policy, were calculated to meet the needs of his foreign policy as well. He was anxious to preserve the alliance with the Western Powers, and his conduct of the war in a nationalist rather than in a revolutionary spirit helped keep the grand alliance together, despite inner contradictions and tensions.

Some of the tensions were due to the fact that the Western Allies repeatedly postponed the opening of the "second front" in Western Europe. This was the main point in Stalin's controversies with Winston Churchill in 1942–43. But as the Soviet Army broke Germany's military power in the "ten offensives" that followed the Battle of Stalingrad in 1943, this issue lost importance. The course of the war revealed a profound shift in the international balance of power, a shift due primarily to the growth of Soviet and U.S. power. Stalin bargained adroitly during the conferences at Teheran and Yalta, and his diplomacy secured for the U.S.S.R. the predominance in Eastern and Central Europe that was in any case bound to result from the success of Soviet arms. The Teheran and Yalta agreements contained, however, the seeds of the discord that was to lead to the breakdown of the grand alliance after the war. Stalin was also the presiding spirit at the Potsdam Conference of July–August 1945, at which he committed the U.S.S.R. to join the United States and Great Britain in the war against Japan, and at which he worked out together with the Western Allies a rather impracticable armistice regime for occupied Germany.

**Stalin's Last Years.**—The year 1945 marked the climax in Stalin's crowded and checkered career. As generalissimo and uncontested leader he was surrounded by an adulation and a cult that assumed its most grotesque forms toward the end of his life. Soviet scientists, writers, musicians, linguists, philosophers, and others were made to accept his judgment as final. Underlying the bizarre cult were Stalin's indubitable achievements. He was the originator of planned economy; he found Russia working with wooden plows and left it equipped with atomic reactors; and he was "father of victory." But his achievement was marred by the despotism and cruelty of his dictatorship; and the patriarchal character of his rule, suited perhaps to the mentality of an illiterate and backward people, became an anachronism in the industrialized and modernized Russia of the 1950s.

Stalin's personal role in the conduct of Soviet foreign policy from 1945 to 1953 remained enigmatic. Communists and anti-Communists alike had seen in him the architect of the revolutions in Eastern Europe and China. In the light of the documentary information available, this view appears to be ill founded. From the beginning Stalin was opposed to Tito's revolutionary policies in Yugoslavia; and he viewed without sympathy Mao Tse-tung's revolutionary strategy and tactics in China. On the other hand, he undoubtedly inspired some of the Communist revolutions in Eastern Europe; and he expected all Communist revolutions, those he had supported and those he had obstructed, to adopt the Stalin cult. During his last years a struggle developed in his entourage between the diehards of Stalinism and those who stood for domestic reform, and also between adherents of a "tough" foreign policy and advocates of conciliation. Stalin tried to keep a balance between the conflicting attitudes and to shape Soviet policy as the resultant of the conflicting trends. After his death his successors became openly divided over these issues, and also in their attitudes toward the Stalinist legacy.

Stalin died from cerebral hemorrhage in the Kremlin on March 5, 1953.

Stalin's writings include *Marxism and the National and Colonial Question* (written and first published in 1912–13; definitive ed. 1934), *Problems of Leninism* (1st collection of articles 1926; 11th ed. 1939), co-author of *History of the Communist Party of the Soviet Union* (1938; new ed. 1952), *Concerning Marxism in Linguistics* (1951), and *Economic Problems of Socialism in the U.S.S.R.* (1952). A collected edition of Stalin's works appeared in 1946–50.

Bibliography.—B. Souvarine, *Stalin: a Critical Survey of Bolshevism* (1939); L. Trotski, *Stalin: an Appraisal of the Man and His Influence* (1947); I. Deutscher, *Stalin: a Political Biography* (1949; new ed. 1967); R. Payne, *The Rise and Fall of Stalin* (1965). (I. D.)

**STALINABAD:** *see* Dushanbe.

**STALINGRAD:** *see* Volgograd.

**STALINO:** *see* Donetsk.

**STALINOGORSK:** *see* Novomoskovsk.

**STALINSK:** *see* Novokuznetsk.

**STALL,** in church architecture, is a fixed seat enclosed at the back and separated from adjacent stalls at the sides by high projecting arms. Stalls are placed in one or more rows on the north and south sides of the chancel in cathedrals, monastic churches, and large parish churches. In an English cathedral the canons and prebendaries each have a stall assigned to them. In the chapels of the various knightly orders the stalls are assigned to the members of the order, thus, in St. George's Chapel, Windsor, are the stalls of the knights of the Garter, in Henry VII's Chapel in Westminster Abbey are those of the knights of the Bath, adorned with the stall plates emblazoned with the arms of the knight occupying the stall, above which is suspended his banner. Architecturally considered, the stalls of a cathedral or church are a marked feature of the interior adornment. They are richly carved, and are frequently surmounted by canopies of tabernacle work. The seats generally can be folded back so as to allow the occupant to stand upright or kneel; beneath the seat, especially in monastic churches, is fixed a small bracket, a *miserere,* which affords a slight rest for the person while standing. Among specimens of carved stalls may be mentioned the Early Decorated stalls in Winchester Cathedral (1296); the Early Perpendicular ones in Lincoln Minster (*c.* 1370); the early 15th-century canopies in Norwich Cathedral (15th century); and the towering corner stalls with their ornate carving filled with figures in Amiens Cathedral (1508–20).

**STALYBRIDGE,** a municipal borough of Cheshire, Eng., lies 8 mi. (13 km.) E of Manchester. Pop. (1961) 21,947. It was incorporated in 1857, and its boundaries were extended in 1881 and 1936. Stalybridge is one of the oldest cotton towns (first cotton mill 1776), but its industries now include—besides cotton—engineering, cable making, and plastics. The town has two extensive parks (one jointly with Ashton-under-Lyne), and there is a pleasant residential district on the Derbyshire side. There is a municipal art gallery. Stayley Hall, the home of the family from which the town derives its name, was erected about 1343.

**STAMBOLISKI, ALEKSANDR** (1879–1923), Bulgarian statesman, the fearless opponent of King Ferdinand's pro-German policy in World War I and the formidable champion of the peasantry as head of the government from 1920 to 1923, was born at Slavovitsa on March 1, 1879. He attended the agricultural college of Halle in Germany. On returning to Bulgaria, aged 18, he took up journalism and, in 1902, became editor of the organ of the newly formed Agrarian League. Six years later he was elected to the *Narodno Sobranye* (National Assembly), where he led the Agrarian Party. He began to organize the peasant masses, who formed 80% of the population of Bulgaria, into agricultural associations. In 1911, when the *Narodno Sobranye* met at Turnovo to amend the constitution, his first conflict with King Ferdinand (*q.v.*) occurred. After the Treaty of Bucharest (1913; *see* BALKAN WARS), Stamboliski and the Agrarians were unmerciful in their criticisms of Ferdinand's policy, though deterred from extreme measures by fear of external complications. His opposition to Ferdinand came to a head in 1915 during the negotiations that preceded Bulgaria's entry into World War I. In spite of the king's anger, pressure from the government, and the growing influence of the Central Powers, Stamboliski strongly resisted the government's warlike policy. Summoned before the king, he threatened him with violence if he should fight against the Allies, reminding him that he had a crown to lose. Ferdinand ordered his arrest. Stamboliski was tried by court-martial and condemned to penal servitude for life.

In September 1918, when the resistance of the Bulgarian troops began to crumble, Ferdinand released Stamboliski, who left for the Macedonian front. He returned at the head of the insurrectionary troops, and their arrival at Sofia resulted in Ferdinand's abdication and flight. A supporter of the new ruler, King Boris, Stamboliski became a member of the Cabinet in January 1919 and prime minister in October. He then went to Paris to sign the Treaty of Neuilly. Having dissolved the *Sobranye* in February 1920, he was returned to power in the elections of March at the head of a homogeneous Agrarian majority.

The Agrarians under Stamboliski ruled Bulgaria with a rod of iron. They had Vasil Radoslavov's Cabinet, which had brought Bulgaria into World War I, condemned to death by popular vote. Stamboliski's determination to promote the interests of the peasantry against the bourgeoisie of the capital was expressed in the words: "Sofia, that Sodom, that Gomorrah, may disappear . . . I shall not weep for it." Through his influence Bulgaria loyally carried out the terms of the Treaty of Neuilly, won the esteem of the Allies, and secured a reduction of reparations. Stamboliski also made persistent efforts to improve Bulgaria's relations with Yugoslavia, with which country he concluded an agreement at Niš (1922). His ultimate ideal was probably some kind of federal South Slav state, embracing Bulgaria.

The overthrow of the government by a military conspiracy on June 9, 1923, was caused partly by dissatisfaction with Stamboliski's domestic policy and partly by the influence of the Macedonian Party. The change of regime took place in one night, the Agrarian ministers being arrested in their homes. Stamboliski, pursued by an armed detachment to his native village, fled across the mountains, hoping to reach the frontier, but was overtaken and shot on June 14. Stamboliski's demeanour was fierce and his movements ungainly; his rough-hewn face was crowned by a mass of black hair; he impressed everyone with his strength and the sincerity of his advocacy of a "Green International" to unite the peasants of all countries.

*See* N. D. Petkov, *Aleksandr Stamboliski* (1946). (N. I. M.)

**STAMBULOV, STEFAN** (1854–1895), Bulgarian statesman, a participant in the emancipation of his country from Turkish rule, an effective opponent of Russian influence, and for seven years the despotic head of a government with practically unlimited power. He was born on Jan. 31, 1854, an innkeeper's son, at Turnovo, the ancient capital of the Bulgars. He went to Russia to study for the priesthood at the Odessa seminary but was expelled for associating with Nihilists. Going to Rumania, he linked himself with Bulgarian revolutionary committees at Bucharest and at Giurgiu. Returning to Bulgaria, he led an anti-Turkish rising at Nova Zagora in 1875 and organized another at Orekhovitsa in 1876. Having fought as a volunteer in the Serbian campaign against Turkey (autumn 1876), he joined the Bulgarian irregular contingent with the Russian forces in the war of 1877–78 (*see* RUSSO-TURKISH WARS). After the Congress of Berlin (*q.v.*) he settled at Turnovo as a lawyer. Soon elected to the *Sobranye* (National Assembly), he became president of it in 1884. He was instrumental in persuading Prince Alexander (*q.v.*) to accept the union of Eastern Rumelia with Bulgaria in 1885. When the Serbo-Bulgarian War (*q.v.*) broke out in consequence, Stambulov served as a soldier in the army. (*See* also BULGARIA: *History.*)

When pro-Russian officers abducted Prince Alexander (August 1886), Stambulov set up a government loyal to him at Turnovo, issued a manifesto to the nation, nominated his brother-in-law, Gen. Sava Mutkurov, commander in chief of the army, and invited the prince to return. His measures led to the downfall of the provisional government set up by the pro-Russian faction at Sofia. On Prince Alexander's final abdication (Sept. 8) Stambulov became head of a council of regency, with Mutkurov and Petko Karavelov as his colleagues; the latter, however, soon made way for Stambulov's friend Georgi Zhivkov. Stambulov frustrated the mission of Gen. N. V. Kaulbars, the Russian emperor Alexander III's special commissioner to Bulgaria; held elections for the *Sobranye,* despite the interdict of Russia; and eventually secured the election of Prince Ferdinand (*q.v.*) of Saxe-Coburg-Gotha to the vacant throne (July 7, 1887). Under Ferdinand he became prime minister and minister of the interior.

The aim of Stambulov's foreign policy was to obtain the recognition of Prince Ferdinand and to win the support of the Triple Alliance (Austria-Hungary, Germany, and Italy) and of Great Britain against Russian interference in Bulgaria. He gained the confidence of the Turkish government and secured recognition from it for a few Bulgarian bishops in Macedonia (*see* MACEDONIAN QUESTION). With the assistance of Austria-Hungary and Great Britain he negotiated large foreign loans, which enabled him to develop the military strength of Bulgaria.

Stambulov ruthlessly stamped out recurrent plots and armed risings engineered by equally ruthless political opponents who were backed by Pan-Slavist circles in Russia. Allowing no clear distinction between party strife and sedition, he used his police, and sometimes the army, to deal with either. Maj. Konstantin Panitsa, after leading a conspiracy, was shot at Sofia in 1890; four political opponents were hanged in 1891; and Karavelov was sentenced to five years' imprisonment. Among the deadliest enemies of Stambulov's regime were the Macedonian committees, responsible for the assassination of his finance minister, Khristo Belchev, in 1891, and of his minister in Istanbul, Georgi Vlkovich, in 1892.

Stambulov's arrogance, and the growing violence of the opposition throughout the country, became unbearable to Prince Ferdinand, who wanted, moreover, an accommodation with Russia. He contrived to get his unmanageable prime minister to resign and accepted his resignation in May 1894. Stambulov was now exposed to the vengeance of his enemies. Attacked and barbarously mutilated by a band of Macedonian assassins in the streets of Sofia on July 15, 1895, he died of his injuries three days later.

(J. D. B.; N. I. M.)

**STAMFORD,** a municipal borough in the Parts of Kesteven, Lincolnshire, Eng., on the River Welland, the boundary between Lincolnshire and Northamptonshire. Pop. (1961) 11,743. It lies 11 mi. NW of Peterborough in the Rutland and Stamford parliamentary division. Stamford is a very ancient market town, built of local gray stone and once famous for its cloth. Its position on the Great North Road and on the borders of the Fens contributed to its importance. Its modern industries include general and agricultural engineering, brick and tilemaking, and the manufacture of plastics and toys. Of the old churches six remain: St. Mary's (with a Decorated spire), All Saints (with fine brasses), and St. Martin's (which contains the Burghley tombs) are the most noteworthy. There are remains of the 7th-century Benedictine priory of St. Leonard and a west gate of the Carmelite monastery (1291). Browne's Hospital is one of the almshouses known as Calises, from the wool merchants of Calais. There was a Danish fort at Stamford, which later became one of the five Danish boroughs. A charter of Edgar dated A.D. 972 mentions a market and a mint. In the reign of Edward the Confessor Stamford was a royal borough governed by 12 lawmen. The Norman castle was built before 1086. Henry III gave the town a charter in 1256 and it was incorporated in 1461–62.

Stamford was known for its wool trade, its churches, and its monastic schools, and in 1333 was chosen as the headquarters of the students who seceded from Oxford. An Early Decorated doorway (1300) remains of Brasenose Hall. The attempt to establish a regular university was prohibited by royal authority. The history of the place centred around the family of Cecil when the great Lord Burghley built Burghley House (1577–85), a fine quadrangular mansion south of the town, now the seat of the marquess of Exeter. The house contains notable art collections.

**STAMFORD,** a city of Connecticut, U.S., is 35 mi. NE of New York City, on Long Island Sound. Founded in 1641 by 29 secessionists from the Wethersfield Church, the town was under the New Haven Colony, which later merged with the Hartford Colony into what became the state of Connecticut. In 1644 one-third of the population of Stamford emigrated to Long Island, but the town continued to grow as an agricultural, lumber, leather, and shipbuilding community. By the time of the American Revolution it had approximately 5,000 residents. A city government was formed within the town in 1893, and the town and city merged in 1949. The population quadrupled in the first half of the 20th century, reaching 74,293 in the 1950 census. The population in 1960 was 92,713 for the city and 178,409 for the standard metropolitan statistical area, comprising Stamford city and Darien, Greenwich, and New Canaan towns of Fairfield County. (For comparative population figures, *see* table in CONNECTICUT: *Population.*)

The countryside still retains much of a rural New England atmosphere north of the Merritt Parkway, which bisects the city, but rapid population growth marks its emergence as a suburban industrial, commercial, and commuter centre. It is the site of major chemical research laboratories; manufactures include chemical products, postage meters, ball bearings, and die castings. In addition to arterial highway and major rail facilities, the city is connected to New York by regular helicopter service and is near the Westchester County, N.Y., airport. It is served by public and private secondary schools, a branch campus of the University of Connecticut, and a museum and nature centre. Recreational facilities include municipal beaches, a municipal golf course, private and public marinas, about 600 ac. of parkland, and numerous private clubs.

(W. L. T.)

**STAMITZ,** Czech family of musicians settled at Mannheim, in the Palatinate, where they exercised a great influence on the development of the symphony.

JOHANN WENZEL ANTON STAMITZ (1717–1757) was born at Deutschbrod (now Havlickuv Brod, Czech.) on June 19, 1717. Little is known of his early life, except that he received his first musical tuition from his father before going to a Jesuit school. He appeared as a violinist at the coronation of the emperor Charles VII in Frankfurt am Main in 1742, but it appears likely that he was already in the musical establishment of the elector palatine at Mannheim, where he was later made director of the court chamber music.

Stamitz brought the Mannheim court orchestra to a standard unrivaled both for precision and scope of expression. Although he did not invent the crescendo and diminuendo effects in orchestral playing, he developed them as a feature of his style, which was then imitated by other Mannheim and later by other European musicians. Another characteristic of his style was the use of "sighing" suspensions, especially at cadences. These became incorporated in *galante* music throughout Europe. His use of the minuet-and-trio as the third movement of a four-movement symphony was similarly adopted by classical composers. His orchestral trios, a *galante* version of the Baroque sonata, were perhaps more influential in the development of the sonata form than were his symphonies, since they were more regular in design.

It is indeed difficult to overestimate Stamitz' influence in these various fields. Although contemporary composers in Berlin, Vienna, and in Italy likewise developed some of these features, it was the first generation of Mannheimers (Stamitz and his associates, F. X. Richter, A. Filtz, I. Holzbauer, and F. Beck) who were most influential in establishing the mid-18th-century style of orchestral writing.

Stamitz' most advanced symphony was composed when Mozart was still an infant. He died at Mannheim on March 27, 1757.

CARL PHILIPP STAMITZ (1745–1801), son of the above, was a leading composer of the second Mannheim generation. Born on May 7, 1745, he wrote a large number of instrumental works, including symphonies, more extended than those of his father: concertos and concertante works for various instruments, quartets, trios, and sonatas. These were published in Paris and London. He left Mannheim with his younger brother JOHANN ANTON STAMITZ (1754–*c.* 1809), settled in Paris, and visited England and Russia. Carl Stamitz died at Jena on Nov. 9, 1801.

The works of the Stamitz family, together with thematic catalogues and biographical introductions, appear in *Denkmäler deutscher Tonkunst in Bayern,* ed. by H. Riemann, vol. iii, vii, xv, and xvi.

BIBLIOGRAPHY.—H. Ulrich, *Symphonic Music* (1952); A. Carse, *The Orchestra in the 18th Century* (1940); P. Gradenwitz, *Johann Stamitz,* 2 vol. (1936), "The Stamitz Family," in *Notes* (Dec. 1949), "The Symphonies of J. Stamitz," in *Music Review,* vol. i (1940).

(Cs. CH.)

**STAMMERING:** *see* SPEECH DISORDERS.

**STAMMLER, RUDOLF** (1856–1938), German jurist and the most influential legal philosopher of the early 20th century, especially in Germany, Spain, and Latin America, was born on Feb. 19, 1856, in Alsfeld (Hesse). He was professor of law in Marburg (1882–84), Giessen (1884), Halle (1885–1916), and Berlin (1916–23).

Stammler broke the dominance of legal positivism and historicism and directed legal philosophy toward neo-Kantian ideas by developing a modernized philosophy of natural law. By distinguishing the "concept" of law, which is a purely formal definition, from the "idea" of law, which is the realization of justice, he reintroduced into jurisprudence the search for ideals to which law ought to conform. These ideals, however, unlike the immutable law of nature of the classical period, constituted a "natural law with a changing content"; *i.e.,* they served as a broad criterion to judge the degree of social harmony attainable in a particular place and time. Stammler's work, at once philosophical and sociological, directed attention to the ideal and the concrete, the universally valid and the varying, contents of justice.

One of his important works, *Die Lehre von richtigen Recht* (new ed., 1926), was translated by I. Husik as *The Theory of Justice* (1925). Stammler died April 25, 1938, at Wernigerode.

*See* Morris Ginsberg, "Stammler's Philosophy of Law," in *Modern Theories of Law* (1933), and George H. Sabine, "Rudolph Stammler's Critical Philosophy of Law," 18 *Cornell Law Quarterly* 321 (1933). (N. S. Tr.; X.)

**STANDARD, BATTLE OF THE,** fought on Cowton Moor near Northallerton (Yorkshire) on Aug. 22, 1138, between the Scots under King David I and the English, inspired by Archbishop Thurstan of York and led by William of Aumale, later earl of York, resulted in the total defeat of the Scottish Army. King David had invaded England in support of his niece, the empress Matilda, and of his own claims to Northumberland and Cumberland. He had a vast host, but he was short of armoured troops. The English were encouraged by the timely arrival of cavalry sent by King Stephen; otherwise, their army was recruited chiefly from Yorkshire, Norman knights mingling with English peasantry, and all fighting on foot. The battle took its name from the English "standard," a mast mounted on a cart and bearing the Host and the banners of the Yorkshire saints, Peter of York, Wilfrid of Ripon, and John of Beverley. The victory was due to courage and a skilful combination of archers with mailclad knights. Complete though it was, King Stephen was too weak to exploit it, and King David retained control of the northern counties throughout his reign. (G. W. S. B.)

**STANDARD DEVIATION,** in statistics, is a measure of the variability (dispersion or spread) of any set of numerical values around their arithmetic mean (*see* MEAN). Suppose $X_1$, $X_2, \ldots, X_n$ are the $n$ values in a set; for example, $n(=5)$ students earn test scores $X$ of 80,81,82,83,84, respectively. Their arithmetic mean $M$ is the sum of these scores $\Sigma X$ divided by $n$; *i.e.,* $M = \Sigma X/n = 410/5 = 82$. Each score falls at a specific distance from $M$; this distance is called the deviation $x$ for that score, and $x = X - M$. For $X = 80$, the deviation $x = 80 - 82 = -2$, showing that the score of 80 is 2 units below the arithmetic mean of the set. In this way the five deviations for the students are $-2, -1, 0, 1, 2$, respectively.

The standard deviation $\sigma$ is defined as the square root of the arithmetic mean of the squared deviations:

$$\sigma = \sqrt{\frac{\Sigma x^2}{n}}$$

and $\sigma^2$ is called the variance of the set. In this case $\Sigma x^2 = (-2)^2 + (-1)^2 + (0)^2 + (1)^2 + (2)^2 = 10$, and $\sigma = \sqrt{10/5} = \sqrt{2}$.

If any set of values forms a normal (Gaussian) distribution (*see* ERRORS, THEORY OF), about 99.7% of all the values fall within the range $M \pm 3\sigma$, about 95% within $M \pm 2\sigma$, and about 68% within $M \pm \sigma$. The standard deviation is more commonly used than are other less reliable measures of variability, which include: the total range (the range between the high and low values); the semi-interquartile range (half the range covered by the middle 50% of the values); and the average deviation (or mean deviation, defined as the arithmetic mean of the absolute values of the deviations $x$). All are interpreted in the same general way: the larger the measure of variability, the wider the spread of values within the set.

The standard deviation, aside from being used to describe empirically collected sets of data, is also used to indicate the dispersion of probability distributions. More precisely, suppose a discrete random variable with values $X$ has probabilities $p(X_1)$, $p(X_2), \ldots, p(X_n)$. Let $\mu = X_1p(X_1) + X_2p(X_2) + \ldots + X_np(X_n)$. The variance of the random variable is defined as

$$\sigma^2 = (X_1 - \mu)^2p(X_1) + (X_2 - \mu)^2p(X_2) + \cdots + (X_n - \mu)^2p(X_n)$$

The standard deviation of the variable is simply the square root of the quantity on the right.

In the case of a continuous random variable $X$ having probability density function $f(X)$ on the interval $(a,b)$ similarly

$$\mu = \int_a^b Xf(X)dX \text{ and } \sigma^2 = \int_a^b (X-\mu)^2f(X)dX$$

*See also* PROBABILITY, MATHEMATICAL; STATISTICS. (C. CE.)

**STANDARDIZATION,** the process of developing and bringing about the utilization of standards. While standardization of some kind or degree is part of almost every human activity, normal usage of the term refers to planned and systematic industrial standardization. In the broadest sense a standard is anything used to measure; *e.g.,* a standard of conduct, a standard of value or a standard of weight or length. This discussion, however, deals mainly with the nature and importance of standardization in industry rather than the evolution of standards in social customs, language, games, music or law.

**Classifications of Standards.**—Since industrial standards may cover anything from product attributes to safety practices it is well to start by giving a definition for the word "standard" that is applicable in every context: A standard is that which has been selected as a model to which objects or actions may be compared. In every case a standard provides a criterion for judgment and its form thus depends on what is to be judged and how it is to be judged. Standards may be devices or instruments such as precision-gauge blocks, light meters or trip scales for making comparisons of size, weight, colour or other attributes. They may be physical models to which things are compared to determine whether, within agreed limits, they are identical. The term is also applied to written mathematical or symbolical descriptions, drawings or formulas setting forth the important features of objects to be produced or actions to be performed.

Company standards are those developed or adopted by a single enterprise for its own use. Industrial standards are those accepted and followed by a group of firms with similar activities and products. National standards are those promulgated by interindustrial or governmental standardizing bodies. International standards are issued by organizations such as the Universal Postal union, the International Wool Textile organization and the International Organization for Standardization. A business firm in its operations may find it useful to make reference to standards drawn from any or all of these sources.

From the standpoint of the individual company where industrial standards find their principal use, standards may be classified as: (1) technical if they deal with products, materials, methods and equipment; (2) managerial if they deal with administrative practices and procedures; (3) substantive if they deal with what is to be done; and (4) procedural if they describe how something is to be accomplished. Some standards are applicable throughout the company while others apply to only one department. From the point of view of their intended use, standards may be classified as follows:

*a.* Engineering standards applied in technical work and including properties of materials, fits and tolerances, terminology, drafting practices and the like.

*b.* Product standards intended to describe attributes and ingredients of manufactured items and embodied in drawings, formulas, material lists, descriptions or models.

*c.* Production standards for processes, methods, operations and equipment included in technical specifications, inspection and test methods, machine setup drawings and operation sheets.

*d.* Purchasing standards covering specifications for materials, parts, equipment and supplies bought by the firm.

*e.* Office and procedural standards referring to record-keeping, procedures for production and inventory control, report forms, methods of analysis, budgeting and cost accounting and other administrative practices.

*f.* Safety standards on machine operations, plant housekeeping, identification of hazards and personnel deportment.

**Importance of Standardization.**—Standards and the benefits derived from them are so much taken for granted that their importance is not appreciated until an annoyance or emergency stemming from incomplete standardization or utter lack of it is encountered. The traveler abroad finds an electrical appliance designed to operate on one cycle basis of electricity does not operate on another. The purchaser of an imported article discovers that metric sizes do not mesh with feet and inches. The homeowner learns that the replacement part manufactured for the current model of the dishwasher he owns does not fit his earlier model without costly adaptation. The housewife's food bargain does not turn out to be such a bargain when she sees that Grade A does not mean the same thing for butter that it does for canned fruit.

Modern mass production and mass marketing could not exist in anything like their present forms without comprehensive standardization. Without standards there could be no manufacture on the basis of interchangeable parts. Without standards, manufacturers could not accurately communicate about materials with scattered suppliers and would have to spend more time inspecting incoming items. Without product standards, buyers could not rely on brand names as indicators of consistent quality. The first cost of complicated production equipment would be much higher than it is now and would be much more expensive to maintain if standard equipment components were not available. Standards play a vital role at every point in the complex system of communication, transportation, production and exchange which must operate smoothly to produce and distribute large quantities of low-cost goods in an advanced economy.

**Standards as Management Tools.**—Standardization enables industry to retain and build on its experience to produce better products, for standards are one of the principal forms in which technical knowledge is recorded. By liberating effort that would otherwise have to be expended in rediscovering and reinventing, standards aid in increasing the productivity of industry on which material progress ultimately depends. The use of standards embodying the most economical available methods reduces costs and conserves resources. But while industrial standardization is responsive to consumer needs and desires, its utility for managerial purposes gives it its strongest impetus.

It is management's job to plan, organize and control company operations. Expression of plans via standards and application of systems of control in which deviations from standards cause corrective measures to be taken permit managers to delegate routine tasks and concentrate on major decisions. Extensive use of standards makes for clarity in communication and facilities coordination. It is generally accepted that standards help management find the best solutions to problems whether they concern product qualities, material properties, process characteristics or operating methods. As standards reach beyond individual companies to suppliers and users of products, further advantages appear.

Standards for products that prevent needless variation and avoid the waste of excessive quality lead in turn to production economies: cheaper materials may be made to serve, painstaking production steps eliminated, inspection requirements reduced and simpler equipment and operations employed. Reduction of product variety also brings dividends through design simplification, making the use of special equipment feasible by permitting longer production runs on fewer items, reduction of inventories and use of simpler planning and control procedures.

*Company Standards Programs.*—Every company has standards but not every company consciously pursues standardization as a means of cost reduction and improvement of operations. Many companies handle standards problems informally; they do not systematically review and codify their standards or use them as an integral part of the management process. Companies that do have formal programs for the development and administration of standards employ a variety of organizational arrangements and procedures but they usually have some things in common. Some have a separate group headed by a standards engineer devoting full time to standards work; in other companies the work may be assigned to permanent committees or to committees convened for particular standards projects. In many firms consultative or coordinative committees are established in addition to the staff groups or working committees which do the detailed work of standards preparation and distribution.

Regardless of the organizational scheme, those responsible for standards work are usually expected to advise and assist top management in the formulation of policies relating to standards and their use. They are called upon to draw up procedures for creating new standards or revising old standards, to report on standards practice and evaluate the company program, to act as coordinators and mediators as standards are being developed, to serve as company representatives to technical associations and other standardizing bodies, to provide technical assistance to standards users and to maintain standards manuals and other records.

*Other Contributors to Standardization.*—Individual firms secure significant benefits by conducting their own standardization programs but there is a point at which standardization on a wide scale becomes necessary to prevent wasteful conflict and duplication of effort among competing systems of standards. Certain fundamental standards should be developed in forms that make them universally usable, and mechanisms for coordination of intersecting standards being evolved in separate fields should be provided. The standards activities of governmental departments, trade associations, technical associations and other organizations serve in part to meet national standards needs, but the presence of a specialized standardizing organization which can coordinate the diverse standardization activities of many different types of organizations and promote general acceptance of basic standards can be a strong force for progress.

In the U.S. the American Standards association (A.S.A.), which has over 110 technical organizations and 2,300 companies as members, performs this function. The A.S.A. does not initiate or write standards but provides the means by which national standards can be developed and approved. All groups having substantial concern with a proposal under consideration in an A.S.A. project have the right to representation. The association makes no effort to enforce any standard but relies on the voluntary support of interested groups.

What the A.S.A. does nationally, the International Organization for Standardization (I.S.O.) does internationally. National and international standards are essentially the same and are developed in the same way. However, just as there are fewer industrial than company standards and fewer national than industrial standards, there are fewer international than national standards. Developing, writing and adopting an international standard is difficult because of the breadth of representation and the diversity of needs and viewpoints that must be reconciled.

To say that standardization is one of the most pervasive and crucial of industrial and scientific activities is no exaggeration. Everyone's life is touched continuously by standards directly or indirectly. Scientific research that widens basic knowledge depends on accurate standards for physical constants and properties of materials as does applied industrial research. Companies may buy and sell with clear understanding on both sides of transactions when they negotiate in standard terms. Producers can manufacture articles of uniform quality and operate more efficiently with standardized processes and products. Consumers may buy agricultural products, meat, processed foods, pharmaceuticals, textiles, clothing, house furnishings and appliances with the assurance that they are getting what they pay for and that the goods are safe to use. *See* MASS PRODUCTION. *See* also references under "Standardization" in the Index.

BIBLIOGRAPHY.—Dickson Reck (ed.), *National Standards in a Modern Economy* (1956); Benjamin Melnitsky, *Profiting from Industrial Standardization* (1953); Jack Rogers, "Industrial Standardization: Company Programs and Practices," National Industrial Conference Board, *Studies in Business Policy,* no. 85 (1957). (J. D. Rs.)

**STANDARD OF LIVING,** in popular usage, the kind and quantity of consumer goods available to an individual, family, or entire nation. Those who have a generous supply of such goods are said to have a high standard of living. But in social science the phrase is used in a different sense and there are supplementary concepts. Standard of living does not denote the goods and services actually available but the aspirations or desires of the individual or group, and is confined to wants that generate a strong desire for fulfillment. Because the terms level of living and level of consumption relate to existing conditions—what is experienced in contrast with what is considered essential—many so-called standard of living studies might more accurately be described as studies of consumption levels. They do, of course, give indirect information about standards since use tends to indicate what is most desired.

A few people undoubtedly have, at least for short periods of time, an excess of some of the things they desire, in which case their level of living is higher than their standard. The standard of others may be higher than their level. Vague, fleeting wants do not constitute a part of the standard, for, as noted above, it relates only to wants that generate a strong drive for fulfillment. Their achievement brings a marked sense of gratification and their continued lack leads to unrest and a sense of frustration.

Standards of consumption affect population growth and long-run labour supply through their effect on the age of marriage and the birth rate. They also affect the total labour supply in the short run in that people weigh the relative merits of more income against more leisure or more direct production for the family; they affect the labour supply in a given occupation insofar as more income and the additional consumer goods thus made possible may compensate for less pleasant work. The existence of the desire for more consumer goods is also important in inducing families to migrate. Standards of living also have a bearing on the business cycle. Forecasters must take into account the extent to which families will cut consumption when their income declines. To what extent will they decrease savings and draw on assets in order to maintain customary consumption? If production rises, will it find a ready market because of desires previously unmet? Or will the additional income go wholly or largely to savings? (*See* CONSUMPTION.) In the administration of a war economy or other emergency when customary levels of consumption cannot be maintained it is helpful to know where cuts will be least resented, and how best to carry on an information program in order to make clear the need for the shortages and thus minimize unrest and frustration.

The standard of living has long been a matter of major interest to population analysts. Thomas Malthus, in his *Essay on Population* (1798), argued that population growth is determined by means of subsistence. He believed that it was held in check chiefly by starvation, pestilence, and war, all of which were direct results of population pressure on means of subsistence. This view assumed a static standard of living. By the beginning of the 20th century, the decline in the rate of population growth in industrialized countries after decades of rising productivity shifted attention to the effect of a rising standard of living. Then two fears came to be expressed: (1) that families in general would come to place such a high value on material goods for themselves and their children that the birth rate would fall to a point where total population would decline; and (2) that the effect of a high standard of living on the birth rate was especially marked among families with high income; thus, the quality of the population was likely to be adversely affected. An upturn of the birth rate in some western countries after the middle 1930s, however, allayed the first fear. For example, the 1950 census of the United States reported a 53% increase since 1940 in children under 5 years of age, while the total population increased by only 15%.

Policies and programs of the United Nations during the 1960s brought to the forefront once more a consideration of the validity of the Malthusian doctrine. Among the nations of the world high birth rates occur where the level of consumption is low, and where death rates are high. The value system of these societies tends to stimulate high birth rates. Only thus can the population be maintained in the face of high death rates. Experience indicates that industrialization brings a reduction in mortality before a decline in the birth rate. To what extent is a decline in the birth rate dependent on a rising standard of living? What is the process of bringing this about? There are no clear-cut answers, in spite of the experience in western countries with falling birth rates which resulted, in part, from a rising standard of living.

Standards of living of individuals are a dominant driving force in a society. There are, in addition, social standards of living which are the basis of many types of policies. The levels of consumption provided those in prison or on relief are, for example, an expression of a society's minimum standard for its members. Social standards are implicit in minimum wages, unemployment benefits, public old age pension systems, family allowances and the provision of various goods from public funds. In addition to individual and social standards there are normative standards provided by specialists which are used as yardsticks in evaluating consumption.

*See* also COST OF LIVING.

BIBLIOGRAPHY.—C. C. Zimmerman, *Consumption and Standards of Living* (1936); F. Zweig, *Labour, Life and Poverty* (1948); Scientific Conference on Statistical Problems, *The Standard of Living: Some Problems of Analysis and International Comparison*, ed. by M. Mód (1962); James N. Morgan *et al.*, *Income and Welfare in the United States* (1962); H. E. Pipping, *Standard of Living: the Concept and Its Place in Economics* (1953). (M. G. R.)

**STANDARDS, NATIONAL BUREAU OF.** Since its founding in 1901, the National Bureau of Standards has become the chief U.S. government agency for fundamental research in physics, chemistry, metallurgy, and engineering sciences. It functions as a national physical science laboratory to improve physical measurement, determine physical constants and critical properties of materials, and render technical services to other government agencies. It is responsible for maintaining and developing the country's standards of measurement. It constructs physical standards, tests and calibrates measuring apparatus, improves measuring techniques, and promotes better state laws, industrial practices, and international agreements concerning standards. The bureau also investigates the chemical nature of materials, high- and low-temperature phenomena, radiation, atomic and molecular structure of chemical elements, electronics, radio transmission, building materials, and metallurgy. These investigations are instrumental in advancing basic science, industrial technology, merchandising, communication, public health and safety, and space exploration.

Federal responsibility for standard weights and measures dates back to the nation's founding when the U.S. Constitution gave Congress the power to fix such standards. While serving as secretary of state, both Thomas Jefferson (1790) and John Quincy Adams (1821) made elaborate reports on weights and measures. Since Congress for many decades did not legislate in this field, federal action took place primarily by executive order. Most of the early efforts to determine standards were made by the Treasury Department because it operated the customs houses and the Coast Survey, which needed accurate standards. Since the latter agency possessed the needed personnel and instruments, it assumed responsibility for weights and measures until the National Bureau of Standards was created in 1901. The first superintendents of the Coast Survey (later called the Coast and Geodetic Survey), Ferdinand Rudolph Hassler, a Swiss mathematician and engineer, and Alexander Dallas Bache, noted American educator and scientist, acted as superintendent of the Office of Weights and Measures. In the 1830s this office adopted standard weights and measures and began making copies of them for the customs houses, individual state governments, and sometimes foreign governments.

The work of this office gradually became inadequate for the growing needs of industrial technology, especially when the electrical industry developed. With the need for electrical standards, pressure mounted in the 1890s to reorganize and expand the agency. Great Britain and Germany had national physical laboratories and were ahead of the United States in developing standards. Aided by leading scientific societies, government scientists drafted a bill for an expanded standards laboratory. The organic act of March 3, 1901, that created the National Bureau of Standards made it responsible for the custody, preparation, and testing of standards, the solving of problems involving standards, and the determination of physical constants and properties of materials. It was empowered to assist other government agencies in matters of standards and, for a fee, to give such aid to scientific societies, business firms, and universities. The act placed the bureau in the Treasury Department, but in 1903 it was shifted to the new Department of Commerce and Labor. After this department was divided into a Department of Labor and a Department of Commerce, the Bureau of Standards was assigned to the

Department of Commerce along with various other scientific agencies. In 1965 the Weather Bureau, the Coast and Geodetic Survey, and the Central Radio Propagation Laboratory of the National Bureau of Standards were combined to form the Environmental Science Services Administration.

The early scientific divisions of the Bureau of Standards included electricity; weights and measures; thermometry, pyrometry, and heat measurement; optics; chemistry; and engineering instruments and materials. Divisions were soon created for metallurgy and for structural, engineering, and miscellaneous materials. When experimentation in radio communications became important, Congress in 1916 appropriated funds for a radio laboratory (*see* above). In the 1920s, under Secretary of Commerce Herbert Hoover, the bureau greatly increased its research activities that were directly beneficial to industry and fostered commercial standardization to eliminate industrial waste and promote efficiency. An aeronautical division was created, and trade associations supported research associates at the bureau for work on technical problems of industry. This practice reached significant levels in the 1950s.

Although the bureau retrenched during the depression, it mushroomed during and after World War II. It developed the proximity fuze (*see* AMMUNITION, ARTILLERY) and took part in the nuclear research that led to the development of the atomic bomb. In the early 1950s it handled extensive developmental work on military ordnance and missiles until this work was transferred to the military services. It also increased its work on standards and physical properties, especially in electronics, nuclear physics, data-processing systems, building technology, cryogenic engineering, and radio propagation. It endeavoured to develop a precise, interrelated system of highly accurate measures of length, time, and mass based on specific atomic constants. It executed research for numerous government agencies on technical problems, and prepared specifications and tests required for materials purchased by the government. Its work advanced basic science, benefited many industries, and contributed to health, safety, and national defense. It investigated scientific and technological problems of space exploration, including radiation, instrumentation, new alloys and synthetic materials, and behaviour of materials under extreme conditions of temperature, speed, and pressure.

The bureau concentrates much of its research in physics, chemistry, and engineering in Washington, D.C., where it has divisions for electricity and electronics, optics and metrology, heat, atomic and radiation physics, chemistry, mechanics, organic and fibrous materials, metallurgy, mineral products, building technology, applied mathematics, and data-processing systems. It also has technical offices of weights and measures, basic instrumentation, and technical information. The bureau's laboratory at Boulder, Colo., is a major installation with divisions for cryogenic engineering, radio propagation physics, radio propagation engineering, radio standards, and radio communication and systems. The bureau has several field stations for testing and developmental purposes, including the testing and monitoring of radio frequencies and propagation. When it took over the functions of the Office of Technical Services the bureau established a Clearinghouse for Federal Scientific and Technical Information. The bureau divided its activities into four institutes: Institute for Basic Standards, Institute for Materials Research, Institute for Applied Technology, and Central Radio Propagation Laboratory.

In addition to special reports and nonperiodical publications, the bureau publishes its research findings in three periodicals: the *Journal of Research* (issued monthly until 1959, thereafter quarterly in four separate sections—Physics and Chemistry, Mathematics and Mathematical Physics, Engineering and Instrumentation, and Radio Science) and the monthly *Technical News Bulletin* and *Central Radio Propagation Laboratory Ionospheric Predictions.*

*See* A. Hunter Dupree, *Science in the Federal Government* (1957); Gustavus A. Weber, *The Bureau of Standards* (1925). (F. G. H.)

**STANDISH, MYLES** or MILES (*c.* 1584–1656), American colonist and military leader, was born in Lancashire, Eng. He became a soldier and fought in the Netherlands, where he probably met the English religious exiles now known as the Pilgrims. He sailed with them to America in the "Mayflower" in 1620 and served as their military leader when they established Plymouth in New England. He was the first to learn the language of the local Indians and led several expeditions against hostile tribes. He went to England on business for the colony in 1625–26, and in 1627 was one of the leaders of the group in the colony that bought out the London investors (merchant adventurers). In 1628 Standish helped to break up the colony of Thomas Morton (*q.v.*) at nearby Merry Mount when it proved too unpuritanical to suit Plymouth. He also served as assistant governor and as treasurer of the colony (1644–49). He moved to Duxbury in 1632 and died there in 1656. After his wife died during the first winter at Plymouth, he married again in 1624.

A short, stocky man with red hair, referred to as "Captain Shrimp" by Morton, Standish was known for his quick temper. There is no historical evidence for the story told in Longfellow's poem, "The Courtship of Miles Standish," that he asked John Alden to propose marriage for him to Priscilla Mullins.

(B. SM.)

**STANFORD, AMASA LELAND** (1824–1893), U.S. senator from California and one of the builders of the first transcontinental railroad, was born in Watervliet, N.Y., March 9, 1824. Having prospered in the retail trade in Sacramento, Calif., in 1861 he became president of the Central Pacific Railroad, which built eastward to a junction with the Union Pacific at Promontory Point, Utah, in 1869. Stanford, a Republican, served as Civil War governor of California (1861–63) and was elected to two terms in the U.S. Senate. In memory of their only child, who died at 15, Stanford and his wife, Jane, founded Leland Stanford Jr. University (commonly known as Stanford University) in 1885, granting 9,000 ac. on the San Francisco peninsula and an endowment of $21,000,000. Stanford died June 21, 1893.

*See* George T. Clark, *Leland Stanford* (1931). (P. C. A.)

**STANFORD, SIR CHARLES VILLIERS** (1852–1924), Irish composer, conductor, and teacher who had a wide influence on the younger British composers of his time, was born in Dublin on Sept. 30, 1852. He studied the organ at Trinity College, Dublin, and from 1870 at Queen's College, Cambridge. Between 1874 and 1877 he studied with Karl Reinecke in Leipzig and with Friedrich Kiel in Berlin. In 1883 he was appointed professor of composition at the Royal College of Music, London, and in 1887 professor of music at Cambridge. Ralph Vaughan Williams, Sir Arthur Bliss, and Gustav Holst were among his pupils. Between 1885 and 1902 he was conductor of the London Bach Choir and from 1901 to 1910 of the Leeds Triennial Festival. He was knighted in 1901.

Stanford was a prolific composer in all spheres but was especially known during his lifetime for his orchestral works, his songs, and his operas. He adopted the broad features of the late-19th-century romantic style into which he introduced Irish folk song elements. His first opera, *The Veiled Prophet of Khorassan,* was given in German as *Der verschleierte Prophet* at Hanover in 1881, and this was followed by *Savonarola,* given at Hamburg in 1884. He developed his Irish manner in *Shamus O'Brien,* performed in London in 1896. *Much Ado About Nothing,* based on Shakespeare, and *The Critic,* based on Sheridan, were given in London respectively in 1901 and 1916, but *The Travelling Companion,* based on a story of Hans Andersen, was not performed until 1925, at Liverpool. Stanford's orchestral works include seven symphonies and five *Irish Rhapsodies.* Among his choral works are *Songs of the Sea* and *Songs of the Fleet,* both on poems of Henry Newbolt. His lyrical style is best seen in his songs, which include settings of Keats, Shelley, Tennyson, and Heine. His pedagogical works are *Musical Composition* (1911) and, with C. Forsyth, *A History of Music* (1916). He died in London on March 29, 1924.

*See* H. P. Greene, *Charles Villiers Stanford* (1935).

**STANFORD UNIVERSITY** is near Palo Alto, Calif., in the Santa Clara Valley. It was founded in 1885 as the Leland Stanford Jr. University by Leland Stanford (1824–93) and his wife, Jane Lathrop (1825–1905), as a memorial to their only child, Leland Stanford, Jr., who died in 1884 at the age of 15. The founder was governor of California in 1861–63 and U.S. senator from 1885 until his death. The doors were opened in 1891 to 559 students. The university campus consists of Stanford's former Palo Alto farm, comprising about 9,000 ac. The founders also established an endowment of $21,000,000.

The buildings, conceived by Frederick Law Olmsted, the creator of Central Park in New York City, are of soft buff sandstone in a style similar to the old California mission (Moorish-Romanesque) architecture, being long and low with wide colonnades, open arches, and red-tiled roofs.

Inner and outer quadrangles of buildings, centring on Stanford Memorial Church, form the original group of classrooms and offices. Buildings later erected in adjoining areas include the art gallery, the theatre, the music auditorium, main and undergraduate libraries, the Hoover Institution on War, Revolution, and Peace, the museum of art and archaeology, the medical centre, gymnasiums, laboratories of physics, chemistry, and engineering, the computer centre, Stanford University Press, alumni headquarters, the student activities centre, the student health centre, international house, and the faculty club. Laurence Frost Amphitheater seats 8,000.

The Hopkins Marine Station is maintained by the University at Pacific Grove on the Bay of Monterey. It operates the "Te Vega," a 135-ft. schooner equipped for biological oceanographic studies by scientists and graduate students.

As part of its General Studies Program, Stanford maintains branch campuses in France, Italy, Germany, Austria, and England. About half of its undergraduates study overseas for six-month periods. Advanced study centres are maintained in Japan, Formosa, and several other countries.

The departments of the university are organized into schools of law, medicine, education, engineering, business, earth sciences, and humanities and sciences. Enrollment reached 11,000 in the 1960s.

In 1921 the Food Research Institute of Stanford University was organized, with the help of the Carnegie Corporation of New York. The Hoover Institution, founded by Herbert Hoover during World War I, contains more than 1,000,000 printed and manuscript items dealing with World Wars I and II, revolutionary movements of the 20th century, and international relations.

The Stanford Linear Accelerator Center was established in 1961 when Congress appropriated $114,000,000 for construction on the campus of an accelerator 2 mi. long under contract with the Atomic Energy Commission. The Stanford Medical Center, completed on the campus in 1959, includes eight buildings, three of them the Palo Alto-Stanford Hospital of 438 beds. A 1,000-bed Veterans Administration Hospital is also on Stanford lands.

Five thousand of the university's acres were set aside for the educational campus and the remaining 4,000 ac. for residential, light industrial, commercial, and professional uses on a leasehold basis. There is an arboretum of about 300 ac.

The university campus was zoned, and space was reserved for an extension of the residence hall system for men and for women, together with the athletic fields. The large extent of the campus made it possible to develop athletic fields of considerable size and diversity, including an 18-hole golf course and a 90,000-seat stadium. Space was reserved also for experimental and ornamental purposes and as residence sites for faculty. David Starr Jordan (*q.v.*) was the first president. (R. L. W.; P. C. A.)

**STANHOPE, CHARLES STANHOPE,** 3rd Earl (1753–1816), English statesman and scientist, an eccentric with a touch of genius, who made a name for himself not only as a thoroughgoing radical but also as an experimental scientist, was born in London, Aug. 3, 1753, and educated at Eton and Geneva. As Lord Mahon, he was M.P. for Chipping Wycombe from 1780 until his succession to the peerage in 1786. He opposed the American war, but also the Fox-North coalition. In 1783 he declined office under William Pitt, whose sister he had married in 1774, but remained his supporter until the French Revolution. He sympathized with the aims of the French republicans, loved to call himself "Citizen Stanhope," and was chairman of the Revolution Society, one of the popular societies advocating the democratization of Parliament. He opposed the war with France, and deprecated interference with its internal affairs. Being "in a minority of one" in the House of Lords he seceded from Parliament for five years (1795–1800).

Stanhope's inventions included the printing press and the microscopic lens which bear his name, two calculating machines, a steam carriage, and a steamship for conveying coal from Newcastle to London, which, however, said Lord Holland, "would have consumed its cargo before it could have reached its destination." He made a new kind of cement, much more durable than ordinary mortar, and artificial slates or tiles composed of tar, chalk, and fine sand. He projected a canal to link up his Devonshire estate at Holsworthy with the Bristol Channel, and experimented with new methods of raising and lowering the barges. His writings include *Considerations on the Means of Preventing Fraudulent Practices on the Gold Coin* (1775), *Principles of Electricity* (1779), *A Letter to Burke, Containing a Short Answer to His Late Speech on the French Revolution* (1790), and pamphlets supporting Fox's libel bill (1792) and opposing the union with Ireland (1800). Lady Hester Stanhope was his eldest daughter by his first wife. He died at Chevening, on Dec. 15, 1816.

*See* G. P. Gooch, *Life of Charles, 3rd Earl Stanhope* (1914). (A. Al.)

**STANHOPE, JAMES STANHOPE,** 1st Earl (1673–1721), English soldier and statesman, was a grandson of the first earl of Chesterfield, and eldest son of Alexander Stanhope, a diplomatist, from whom he acquired both strong Whig principles and a knowledge of languages and diplomacy. He was born in Paris and was later naturalized as a British subject. In 1691 he went to Italy to study the art of war under the duke of Savoy. Subsequently he served in Flanders, Spain and Portugal under such distinguished generals as Marlborough and the duke of Ormonde. He accompanied the earl of Peterborough to Spain in 1705, supporting his plan to divert the campaign to Italy, and distinguished himself in the attack on Barcelona (*see* Spanish Succession, War of the). In 1706 as minister to the titular Charles III of Spain, he advocated an aggressive strategy, but allied dissensions led to defeat at Almanza (1707). Commander in chief in Spain in 1708, Stanhope captured Port Mahon to provide a winter anchorage for the Mediterranean fleet, and in 1710 his bold methods won victories at Almenar and Saragossa. Stanhope, however, occupied Madrid instead of excluding from Spain the French reinforcements which, under the duc de Vendôme, defeated and captured him at Brihuega (Dec. 1710). The Tory government in England did little for the release of so pronounced a Whig, and Stanhope did not return until August 1712.

Stanhope had become M.P. for Newport (Isle of Wight) in 1701, and occupied the duke of Somerset's seat at Cockermouth, 1702–13. In 1710 he was among the chief managers of the Sacheverell trial (*see* Sacheverell, Henry), and the Whigs strove furiously to get him elected in his absence for Westminster at the ensuing general election. He accepted the Utrecht treaty once it was signed, but contrived to defeat the projected Tory commercial treaty with France. Stanhope rebuffed Tory accusations of speculation in Spain, and was now so prominent in opposition that when defeated at Cockermouth in 1713, he was overwhelmed with offers of seats and chose to sit for Wendover; the opposition moreover gave him supreme charge of the secret military measures designed to secure the Hanoverian succession.

To the general surprise, Stanhope was made southern secretary on the accession of George I, sharing with Robert Walpole the leadership of the house of commons. It was in foreign policy, however, that Stanhope revealed his genius. He at once renounced the Tory policy of alliance with France which had not ended with the Austro-Spanish conflict, in favour of the Whig tradition of agreement with the emperor, and, if necessary, war against France. By prolonged negotiation Stanhope persuaded the emperor to concede a Barrier treaty to the Dutch in 1715, which foreshadowed the ending of British diplomatic isolation by the treaty of Westminster with the emperor and Dutch in 1716. He also secured a very favourable commercial treaty with Spain in May 1716. The regent, the duke of Orléans, now hoped that Britain would support his succession to the French crown should Louis XV die; Stanhope was at first very hostile to his overtures, but was won to them in 1716 by Russian threats to the German interests of Hanover, and by a projected Russo-Swedish *rapprochement* which might intensify Swedish intrigues with the English Jacobites. The Triple alliance (1717) with France and the Dutch minimized foreign support for the Jacobites, and gained for England the valuable diplomatic influence and organization of France in northern Europe. Stanhope now sought to reconcile Spain and the emperor by offering the succession to the Italian duchies to Don Carlos, the queen of Spain's son, and compensating the emperor by exchanging his island of Sardinia for Sicily, then held by Savoy. In 1718 Stanhope brought the emperor into the Quadruple alliance to impose peace on these terms, terms which Spain accepted under duress in 1720. Stanhope's peace plan was not completely fulfilled for a decade after his death, but his French alliance made Britain for 15 years the diplomatic arbiter of the west, and earned him a viscountcy in 1717 and an earldom in 1718.

In the north Stanhope was less successful, for England was at loggerheads not only with Sweden (for its attacks on English shipping and Jacobite conspiracies) and Russia (for its incursions into Germany), but also with its ally France which desired to save the German territories of Sweden, coveted by Hanover and its allies, by sacrificing to Russia Sweden's Baltic lands from which the British navy derived essential stores. The king and the Hanoverian ministers were tempted to divert the fleets (sent to the Baltic every year after 1715 to protect British shipping) to illegal Hanoverian purposes, thus provoking the resignation of the Townshend-Walpole connection from the government in 1717; Stanhope was now chief minister. On the death of Charles XII in 1718, he sought favourable terms from Sweden and offered to defend it against Russia by a coalition of the other Baltic powers. To form this coalition he himself broke the resistance of the Hanoverian ministers to an alliance with Prussia in 1719, and in the following year finally ended Hanoverian interference in English affairs. Under his direction Sweden was reconciled with all its Baltic neighbours except Russia, but in 1721, after Stanhope's death, Peter the Great was able to dictate his own terms to Sweden.

Stanhope had no fixed home in England until after he was 40, and never rivaled Walpole's grasp of domestic politics, but as secretary of state and first lord of the treasury (1717–18) he held a leading role in home affairs. He co-operated cordially with Sir Robert Walpole and Lord Townshend in suppressing the Jacobite revolt of 1715, softened Townshend's fall in the winter of 1716–17, and carried through the comprehensive financial scheme introduced by Walpole in 1717. Always the champion of religious minorities, he repealed the Occasional Conformity and Schism acts in 1718, but further concessions to Protestant dissenters and Roman Catholics were prevented by the split in the Whig party. In 1719 he unreservedly backed the earl of Sunderland's plan to reunite the Whigs by promoting the Peerage bill to fix the number of peers, state control of the universities and the repeal of the Septennial act which he himself had passed in 1716. By defeating the first of these measures, however, Walpole ensured both the abandonment of the rest, and his own return to office. The last year of Stanhope's life was darkened by the South Sea company scandal (*see* SOUTH SEA BUBBLE), and, though in no way implicated, he was about to retire from politics into Marlborough's place of captain general when in Feb. 1721 he died of a blood vessel burst in anger during a South Sea debate in the house of lords.

*See* the standard life of Stanhope, B. Williams, *Stanhope: a Study in Eighteenth-Century War and Diplomacy* (1932). (W. R. WD.)

**STANISLAVSKI, KONSTANTIN SERGEEVICH ALEKSEEV** (1863–1938), great Russian actor, producer, and theoretician of the art of acting, was born in Moscow on Jan. 17 (new style; 5, old style), 1863. His father, S. V. Alekseev, was a wealthy industrialist, and his grandmother, a French actress. He began his acting career at 15 in the Alekseev Circle, an amateur group consisting mostly of the members of his family. In December 1888 he founded the Society of Art and Literature, one of Moscow's most popular amateur theatrical companies. In June 1897 V. I. Nemirovich-Danchenko (*q.v.*), playwright and director of the drama school of the Moscow Philharmonic Society, invited him to form a new theatre. They drew up the program of the Moscow Art Theatre (*q.v.*), Nemirovich-Danchenko undertaking responsibility for literary and administrative matters and Stanislavski for staging and production. Stanislavski scored his first great success as producer with A. P. Chekhov's *The Seagull,* in December 1898, and through his genius the Moscow Art Theatre became world famous. Chekhov wrote *The Three Sisters* (1901) and *The Cherry Orchard* (1903) specially for it, and in 1923 Stanislavski toured the United States with it. Stanislavski's fame, however, rests chiefly on his theory of acting, his celebrated system or method: "What is important to me is not the truth outside myself, but the truth within myself . . . the truth of my attitude towards anything on the stage, towards my partners who represent other characters in the play and towards their thoughts and feelings." (*My Life in Art;* Theatre Arts Books, New York, 1924; renewed 1952 by Elizabeth Reynolds Hapgood.) Other writings include *An Actor Prepares* (Eng. trans. 1936) and *Building a Character* (Eng. trans. 1949). He died in Moscow on Aug. 7, 1938. *See* also ACTING, DIRECTION AND PRODUCTION: *Acting: Stanislavski.*

*See* D. Magarshack, *Stanislavsky: a Life* (1951). (D. MK.)

**STANISLAW, SAINT** (?1030–1079), bishop of Cracow from 1072, murdered by King Boleslaw II (*q.v.*), was the first Pole to be canonized (1253) and is a patron saint of Poland. He was born at Szczepanow, near Tarnow, on July 26, 1030, into a Polish noble family, and was educated at Gniezno, the Polish metropolitan see, and probably also in Paris. Elected bishop of Cracow in 1072, he was accused in 1079 of treason against his sovereign. The royal court—in which the head of the Polish Church, the metropolitan of Gniezno, participated—found Stanislaw guilty and sentenced him to the loss of his limbs. As the knights who had been ordered to execute the sentence hesitated, King Boleslaw slew the bishop himself on April 11 in the St. Michael chapel in Cracow.

This tragedy remains an unsolved mystery. Polish historians of repute believe that the bishop participated in a Bohemian-German plot designed to remove the able King Boleslaw and replace him by his indolent brother, Wladyslaw Herman. Polish Catholic writers describe the execution as a contemptible act of revenge against a saintly bishop who had excommunicated a cruel and licentious king. St. Stanislaw's feast is May 8 in Poland, May 7 elsewhere.

BIBLIOGRAPHY.—T. Wojciechowski, "Factum św. Stanisława," in *Szkice historyczne XI wieku,* 2nd ed. (1925); D. Borawska, *W sprawie genezy kultu św. Stanisława* (1950); J. Lisowski, *Kanonizacja św. Stanisława* (1953); K. Lanckorońska, "W sprawie zatargu między Bolesławem Śmiałym a św. Stanisławem," in *Teki Historyczne,* London IX (1958); *The Cambridge History of Poland,* vol. i (1950). (K. SM.)

**STANISLAW I** (STANISLAW LESZCZYŃSKI) (1677–1766), twice elected king of Poland and finally duke of Lorraine and Bar. He was born in Lvov on Oct. 20, 1677, the only son of a Poznanian magnate. His education was completed by travels in Western Europe. His first election as king of Poland (July 12, 1704) was procured by the Swedish king, Charles XII, in the first phase of the Northern War (*q.v.*), after Charles had enforced the deposition of King Augustus II (Frederick Augustus I of Saxony). After the defeat of Charles at Poltava (1709), Stanislaw left Poland and settled at Wissembourg, in Alsace, while Augustus II recovered the kingdom.

In 1725 Stanislaw's daughter Marie was married to Louis XV of France; and in 1733, after Augustus II's death, France supported his candidature to the Polish throne. Stanislaw went in disguise to Warsaw and, on Sept. 12, 1733, was elected king by an overwhelming majority of the Diet. The War of the Polish Succession (*q.v.*) then broke out, as Russian armies entered Poland to annul his election. Under Russian pressure, a small minority in the Diet accepted the Saxon elector Frederick Augustus II as king of Poland, with the style of Augustus III, on Oct. 5, 1733. Stanislaw had to take refuge in Gdansk, which his enemies then besieged. Before the capitulation of the city he escaped to Königsberg in Prussia, whence he directed the guerrilla warfare of his partisans in Poland. The preliminary peace between France and Austria (1735) and the definitive Peace of Vienna (1738) decided that Augustus III was to remain on the throne, and that Stanislaw, retaining his royal title, was to have Lorraine and Bar for life.

In Lorraine, Stanislaw proved himself a good administrator and a promoter of economic development. His court at Lunéville became famous as a cultural centre. He founded an Academy of Science at Nancy and a military college. His authorship of the "Free Voice to Make Freedom Safe," published in 1749 and outlining constitutional reforms for Poland, is controversial. He died at Lunéville on Feb. 23, 1766. There are editions of his letters to his daughter Marie (1901), to the kings of Prussia (1906), and to Jacques Hulin, his minister at Versailles (1920).

BIBLIOGRAPHY.—P. Boyé, *Stanislas Leszczynski et le troisième traité de Vienne* (1898) and *Stanislas Leszczynski et la cour d'Espagne, 1723–33* (1938); J. Feldman, *Stanisław Leszczyński* (1948); E. Rostvorowski, *Legendy i fakty XVIII W.* (1963). (A. ZA.)

**STANISLAW II** (STANISLAW AUGUST PONIATOWSKI) (1732–1798), the last king of independent Poland, was born at Wolczyn, near Brzesc (Brest), in Polesie, on Jan. 17, 1732, the sixth child of Stanislaw Poniatowski, palatine of Mazovia, and Princess Konstancja Czartoryska. After careful education he traveled in England, France, Holland, and Germany. In 1757, during the Seven Years' War (*q.v.*), he was sent by the Czartoryskis (*see* CZARTORYSKI) to St. Petersburg to obtain Russian support for their plans to reform the state and to dethrone King Augustus III (Frederick Augustus II of Saxony). At first he was officially on the staff of the British embassy, but later he was appointed Polish envoy to Russia. Without doing much for the Czartoryskis, he consolidated his personal position in St. Petersburg, becoming a favourite of the future empress Catherine II (*q.v.*).

With Catherine's support, Poniatowski was elected king of Poland on Sept. 7, 1764. He tried to strengthen the royal power, to modernize the state administration, and to improve the parliamentary system; but his reforms were opposed by a group of magnates, and Catherine II, by threatening him with dethronement (1768), forced him to drop his plans. He was then faced with the Confederation of Bar (*q.v.*), which proclaimed an interregnum, thus making the king even more dependent on Russia.

In 1772 Russia, Prussia, and Austria carried out the first partition of Poland (*see* POLAND: *History*). The Polish king in vain appealed to the Western powers. During the *Sejm* (Diet) of 1772–75 he tried to obtain the consent of the partitioning powers for constitutional reforms. Eventually his power was further limited, and he became president of the Permanent Council (a government elected every two years by the *Sejm*). Between 1776 and 1788, though he was severely handicapped by the magnates' opposition and by Russian supervision, he managed to strengthen his power to some degree. With his support the Commission of National Education was formed; and he invited artists to his court, made a famous collection of paintings, reconstructed the royal castle in Warsaw and built a fine suburban residence—Lazienki.

During the Four Years' *Sejm* (1788–92), the king took an active part in its attempt at reform. This led to the voting of the constitution of May 3, 1791. To oppose the new constitution, the Confederation of Targowica was formed, with Russian backing; and as the Russians invaded Poland the king joined the confederation. He participated in the captive *Sejm* at Grodno (1793), which had to assent to the second partition of Poland. During the Polish insurrection of 1794, Tadeusz Kosciuszko (*q.v.*) overrode all royal authority; and after the defeat of the insurrection the king abdicated, at Grodno on Nov. 25, 1795. In semicaptivity in St. Petersburg, he died on Feb. 12, 1798. His *Mémoires*, in two volumes, were published by S. M. Goryaninov (1914–24).

BIBLIOGRAPHY.—R. Nisbet Bain, *The Last King of Poland* (1909); J. P. Palewski, *Stanislas-Auguste Poniatowski* (1946); J. Fabre, *Stanislas-Auguste Poniatowski et l'Europe des lumières* (1952); S. Mackiewicz, *Stanisław August* (1953); A. Zahorski, *Stanisław August, polityk* (1959). (A. ZA.)

**STANLEY,** the name of a famous English family which has held the title of earl of Derby since 1485. It derives its name from Stanley, near Leek, in Staffordshire. The first known ancestor is ADAM DE STANLEY (fl. mid-12th century). His son WILLIAM received Stanley and half of Balterley, in Staffordshire, from his cousin Adam de Audley. William's descendant WILLIAM acquired the hereditary forestership of Wirral through his marriage in 1282 to Joan, daughter and coheir of Philip de Baumvile.

This William's great-grandson WILLIAM married Margery, daughter of William de Hooton, and was the ancestor of the Stanleys (afterward Erringtons) of Hooton, whose baronetcy, created in 1661, became extinct in 1893. His brother JOHN (d. *c.* 1414) was lord deputy in Ireland (1386–88) and the king's lieutenant in Ireland (1399–1401, 1413–14). In 1406 he was granted the Isle of Man in fee. By his marriage (*c.* 1385) to Isabel Lathom, heiress of a great estate in Lancashire, he founded his family's fortunes. John's grandson THOMAS (*c.* 1405–1459) was the king's lieutenant in Ireland (1431–37) and in 1456 was summoned to Parliament as Baron Stanley. Thomas's eldest son, also THOMAS (*c.* 1435–1504), 2nd baron, placed the crown on the head of Henry VII on the battlefield of Bosworth (Aug. 22, 1485). Created earl of Derby (October 1485), he was the ancestor of the Stanley earls of Derby (*q.v.*).

The 1st baron's second son WILLIAM (d. 1495) of Holt gave crucial support to Henry VII at Bosworth. He was implicated in the plot to put Perkin Warbeck on the throne and was beheaded, but it is probable that the king's desire for William's great wealth was responsible for his execution. JOHN, the third son of the 1st baron, married Elizabeth, daughter and heir of Sir Thomas Weever. John's grandson THOMAS (d. 1672) was made a baronet in 1660 and his descendant JOHN THOMAS (1766–1850), 7th bart., was created Baron Stanley of Alderley in 1839. His son EDWARD JOHN (1802–1869), 2nd baron, was president of the Board of Trade (1855–58) and postmaster general (1860–66). He was created Baron Eddisbury of Winnington in 1848. His third son, EDWARD LYULPH (1839–1925), 4th baron, inherited the barony of Sheffield of Roscommon in 1909 from a kinsman. This Edward's grandson, EDWARD JOHN (1907– ) is the present holder of the titles.

**STANLEY, SIR HENRY MORTON** (1841–1904), Welsh explorer of Africa, a naturalized American who later resumed his British nationality, is popularly famous for his relief of David Livingstone in 1871, but his true importance lies in his discovery and development of the Congo. He was born on Jan. 28, 1841, at Denbigh, North Wales, the illegitimate son of John Rowlands and Elizabeth Parry, and was registered as John Rowlands. His mother left him to the care of her father, Moses Parry, and he grew up partly in the charge of reluctant relatives and partly in the St. Asaph workhouse, where he suffered from the severity of the workhouse master, James Francis. He acquired a reasonable education at St. Asaph, developed a strong religious faith and learned to value order and cleanliness; but the humiliations of institutional life left deep marks on his character, as did his mother's continued neglect. At the age of 15 he ran away from the workhouse and his escape was followed by an unhappy interlude of dependence on his mother's relations which only ended when he sailed from Liverpool as a cabin boy to New Orleans, La., where he landed in 1858.

There Rowlands met Henry Morton Stanley, a benevolent merchant who took charge of him, gave him his own name and declared his intention of providing for him. Although Stanley died abroad soon afterward, leaving his protégé once more alone in the world, his kindness gave a new direction to the boy's life; henceforth young Stanley felt that at least one person had loved him and believed in him, and in his own prosperous middle age he too adopted a son.

For some years Stanley led a roving life: a soldier in the American Civil War, a seaman in merchant ships and in the federal navy, a journalist in the early days of frontier expansion—he even included a trip to Turkey. Twice he visited his mother in Wales only to encounter the same indifference she had shown since his birth.

In 1867 Stanley offered himself to James Gordon Bennett Jr. of the *New York Herald* as special correspondent on the British Abyssinian campaign, and was first with the news of the fall of Magdala in 1868. He was in Madrid covering the Spanish Civil

War for the *New York Herald* when, in 1869, Bennett summoned him to Paris and commissioned him to "find Livingstone."

**Relief of Livingstone, 1869–73.**—Little had been heard of Livingstone after he left for the interior of Africa in 1866 to explore the central African lakes and to ascertain the source of the Nile, but he was thought to be in the neighbourhood of Ujiji on Lake Tanganyika. Bennett instructed Stanley to travel to Africa by way of Egypt (for the opening of the Suez canal), Syria and Palestine, and it was not until Jan. 6, 1871, that he reached Zanzibar. Intent on a "scoop," Stanley was secretive with the Zanzibar authorities, including the British consul, Sir John Kirk, who was responsible for Livingstone's supplies. Stanley set out for the interior on March 21, and with a well-equipped caravan forced his way through a countryside disturbed by fighting and stricken with sickness. He reached Ujiji in November, where he found Livingstone, greeting him with the famous words "Dr. Livingstone, I presume." Together they explored Lake Tanganyika, proving that the Rusizi river flowed into and not out of the northern end of the lake and so could not be the Nile as had been suggested by those geographers who doubted J. H. Speke's choice of Lake Victoria as the main source. Stanley arrived back in Zanzibar in May 1872, leaving Livingstone to pursue his search for the Nile further west in the region of what, as Stanley himself was later to prove, was the Congo. Stanley was not well received in England, where it was felt that he had anticipated Livingstone's sponsors and the feeling against him was increased by the knowledge that Livingstone had been in real need of relief and that his own friends had failed where a stranger had succeeded. In the same year (1872) Stanley published his story in *How I Found Livingstone.*

Stanley did little to conciliate either Sir John Kirk or Sir Henry Rawlinson, president of the Royal Geographical society; nevertheless, the society awarded him their Patron's medal for 1873. He addressed the British association at Brighton in October, and he was received by Queen Victoria who gave him a gold snuffbox and her thanks for his services. In 1873 Stanley went to Ashanti as war correspondent for the *New York Herald* and in 1874 he published *Coomassie and Magdala: the Story of Two British Campaigns in Africa* describing his experiences there and in Abyssinia.

**Through the Dark Continent (1874–77).**—Livingstone died in 1873, and Stanley resolved to take up the exploration of Africa where he had left off. The problem of the Nile sources and of the position and size of the central African lakes had been only partly solved by Livingstone, Sir Richard Burton, Speke and Sir Samuel Baker, and Stanley secured financial backing from the *Daily Telegraph* and the *New York Herald* for an expedition to Africa. Well manned and provisioned and with three white companions, Stanley left Zanzibar on Nov. 11, 1874, and headed for Lake Victoria. His visit to King Mtesa of Buganda during 1875 paved the way for the admission of Christian missionaries in 1876 and for the eventual establishment of a British protectorate. Circumnavigating Lake Victoria in his boat, the "Lady Alice," Stanley confirmed Speke's estimate of its size and importance. Skirmishes with suspicious natives on the lake shore, and especially the fight at Bumbireh which resulted in a number of casualties, gave rise to much criticism in England of this new kind of traveler with his journalistic outlook and forceful methods. On this voyage were sown the seeds of Stanley's later unpopularity and of the rough political campaigns when he was heckled as a "man of blood." His claim to be acting in self-defense was put forward in aggressive terms which did not reassure public opinion in England.

Stanley was prevented by tribal unrest from investigating Lake Albert, and he turned south to Lake Tanganyika, which he also circumnavigated, finding no outlet to connect it with Lake Albert and the Nile system.

By the end of 1876 Stanley was ready for what he called "the grandest task of all"—the identification of the Lualaba river which Livingstone had hoped might be the Nile but thought more likely to be the Congo. In 1876 the expedition reached Nyangwe, Livingstone's furthest point north on the Lualaba, and set off down the river reinforced by Tippoo Tib, the leading Arab trader of the region.

When the Arabs turned back at the limit of their trading area, Stanley launched the "Lady Alice" and sailed down the unknown river to the lake he called Stanley pool; from there he marched overland to the sea which he reached on Aug. 12, 1877. His three white companions and half his Africans were dead, but he had traced the Congo. Stanley described this tremendous journey in *Through the Dark Continent* (1878).

**The Founding of the Congo Free State (1879–84).**—Failing to interest the British government in developing the Congo, Stanley accepted the invitation of King Leopold of the Belgians to lead an expedition there under the auspices of the Comité d'Études du Haut Congo, later merged in Leopold's International association for exploring and developing Africa. From Aug. 1879 to June 1884 Stanley was in the Congo basin where he made a road from the lower Congo up to Stanley pool, launched steamers on the upper river and built a chain of stations. His perseverance in the face of difficulties earned him from his men the nickname of Buta-Matari—the "rock breaker." The Berlin conference of 1884–85, which Stanley attended, recognized the Congo Free state under the sovereignty of King Leopold, representing the International association.

**Relief of Emin Pasha (1887–1889).**—Stanley's last expedition in Africa was for the relief of Mehmed Emin Pasha, governor of the Equatorial province of Egypt. Emin had been cut off by the Mahdi revolt of 1882 in the neighbourhood of Lake Albert. Sir William MacKinnon, chairman of the British East Africa company, launched a rescue fund and invited Stanley to lead an expedition. Stanley chose to travel by way of the Congo; he knew the route and relied on Tippoo Tib to supply porters. He left England in Jan. 1887 and, stopping to recruit men in Zanzibar, arrived at the mouth of the Congo in March. The expedition reached the navigable head of the river in June and there, at Yambuya, Stanley left a rear column under Maj. E. M. Barttelot and J. S. Jameson, with orders to await Tippoo Tib's porters and to follow on if these failed to arrive.

Stanley, with Lieut. W. G. Stairs, Capt. R. H. Nelson, Surgeon T. H. Parke and A. J. Mounteney Jephson, led the advance guard out of camp on June 28, reaching Lake Albert five months later after a grueling march through dense forest. They did not contact Emin until April 1888 when Stanley found, to his astonishment, that the pasha was unwilling and unready to evacuate his province. Leaving him to assemble his troops, Stanley then returned to look for the missing rear column. He reached Balanya, just short of Yambuya, on Aug. 17, where he found the remains of the column, depleted and demoralized. Tippoo Tib had not sent the porters, Barttelot had been murdered and Jameson died soon after from fever.

Stanley blamed Barttelot and Jameson for the disaster, and on his return to England a controversy arose about the fate of the rear guard. This was the most bitter of the many quarrels that did so much damage to Stanley's reputation.

Back at the lake in Jan. 1889, Stanley heard that Emin and Jephson had been detained by disaffected troops, but eventually the party was reunited and on April 10, 1889, some 1,500 persons set out, arriving at Bagamoyo on the east coast on Dec. 4. Stanley cleared up some geographical points on this expedition. The mist-covered Ruwenzori range which had been concealed when Baker discovered Lake Albert in 1864, and which Stanley himself had passed unnoticed in 1876 was identified as the legendary Mountains of the Moon; the size of Lake Albert was correctly estimated and its tributary the Semliki river traced south to the lake which Stanley named Albert Edward on the homeward journey. *In Darkest Africa* (1890) is Stanley's account of this arduous and unlucky expedition.

**The Last Years.**—Stanley married Dorothy Tennant on July 12, 1890, and they adopted a son, Denzil. Stanley was renaturalized a British subject in 1892, and sat in parliament as Liberal Unionist member for North Lambeth from 1895 to 1900. In 1897 he visited South Africa and wrote *Through South Africa* (1898). He was awarded a grand cross of the Bath in 1899. His last years were spent mainly at Furze Hill near Pirbright, Surrey, a small estate bought in 1898.

Stanley died in London at 2, Richmond Terrace, Whitehall, on May 10, 1904, and was buried at Pirbright after a service in Westminster abbey.

**Summary.**—From a modern viewpoint, much contemporary criticism of Stanley appears unjust. To the select band of travelers whose centre was the Royal Geographical society, dedicated to the pursuit of knowledge, Stanley appeared as an outsider, an American journalist, with huge funds at his disposal. His motives in exploring were suspect and his methods were considered to be rough. His humble origin probably mattered less than he supposed to men who came, in fact, from a variety of social backgrounds, but his uncouth and uncooperative manners and his tendencies to self-righteousness and to boastfulness, ensured him an unpopularity which injures his reputation to this day. Harsh and humourless, touchy and intolerant, Stanley antagonized many who should have been his friends, and the controversies which arose around him have tended to obscure his achievements.

THE BETTMANN ARCHIVE, INC.

STANLEY, PHOTOGRAPHED IN 1890 ON HIS RETURN FROM THE EMIN PASHA EXPEDITION

Nevertheless, to Stanley belongs the credit of having assembled the geographical discoveries and guesses of an earlier generation into the coherent whole which is the map of central Africa as it is now known. He is the bridge between the old and the new; at first the intrepid explorer, the friend of Livingstone and the discoverer of the Congo; then the pioneer who made the Congo Free State; finally, the elder statesman who lived into the age of Cecil Rhodes and of the opening up of modern Africa. *See* also references under "Stanley, Sir Henry Morton" in the Index.

BIBLIOGRAPHY.—Cadwallader Rowlands, *H. M. Stanley* (1872); A.-J. Wauters, *Stanley au secours d'Émin-Pacha* (1890); Mrs. J. S. James, *Story of the Rear Column* (1890); W. G. Barttelot, *The Life of E. M. Barttelot* (1890); Sir Harry Hamilton Johnston, *The Nile Quest* (1903); H. Brode, *Tippoo Tib, the Story of His Career in Central Africa* (1907); Dorothy Stanley (ed.), *The Autobiography of Henry Morton Stanley* (1909); Olivia Manning, *The Remarkable Expedition* (1947); Ian Anstruther, *I Presume* (1956); Brian Farwell, *The Man Who Presumed* (1957). (D. MN.)

**STANLEY, THOMAS** (1625–1678), English poet, translator and the first English historian of philosophy, was born at Cumberlow, Hertfordshire, in 1625, and educated by William Fairfax, son of the translator of Tasso. He became a good classical scholar and an enthusiastic student of French, Italian, and Spanish poetry. Stanley entered Pembroke Hall (later College), Cambridge, in 1639 and studied there and at Oxford, graduating M.A. in 1641. He traveled on the continent during the Civil War and on his return lived in the Middle Temple, London, where he devoted himself to literary work. He died in London on April 12, 1678.

Stanley was the friend of many poets and himself a prolific writer of original and translated verse. His first volume of poems appeared in 1647. Subsequent volumes included translations from Guarini, Marino, Petrarch, Ronsard, Ausonius, Oronta, Montalvan, and others. His classic renderings of the Anacreontic poems appeared in 1651, and the same collection contains his version of Pico della Mirandola's *Platonick Discourse upon Love.* His *History of Philosophy* was published in 1655–62 and his edition of Aeschylus with Latin translation and commentary in 1663. He had a graceful if tenuous gift as a lyrical poet and was a versatile and accomplished translator. His *History of Philosophy,* based largely on Diogenes Laërtius, long remained a standard work.

BIBLIOGRAPHY.—L. I. Guiney (ed.), *Original Lyrics* (1907); G. Saintsbury (ed.), *Minor Poets of the Caroline Period,* vol. iii (1921); E. G. Gardner (ed.), *A Platonick Discourse upon Love* (1914). (V. DE S. P.)

**STANLEY, WENDELL MEREDITH** (1904– ), U.S. biochemist and Nobel Prize winner, was born on Aug. 16, 1904, in Ridgeville, Ind. After receiving his Ph.D. degree from the University of Illinois, Urbana, in 1929, he became a research associate and instructor in chemistry there. In 1931 he entered the Rockefeller Institute for Medical Research, and in 1940 became a member of the institute. In 1948 he became director of the laboratory for virus research at the University of California. In research on the virus which caused the mosaic disease in tobacco plants, Stanley found that while it appeared to act like an inanimate chemical it presented evidence of being a living and growing organism. For "their preparation of enzymes and virus proteins in a pure form," Stanley and John H. Northrop divided equally one-half of the Nobel Prize in Chemistry in 1946, the other half being awarded to James B. Sumner for his discovery "that enzymes can be crystallized."

*See* E. Farber, *Nobel Prize Winners in Chemistry, 1901–1961* (1963).

**STANLEY,** an urban district of County Durham, Eng., lies 12 mi. NW of the city of Durham. Pop. (1961) 46,319. Since 1937 it has included the neighbouring urban districts of Annfield Plain and Tanfield, and the Craghead portion of the Lanchester rural district. Stanley is between 500 and 1,000 ft. (150 and 300 m.) above sea level, the highest point being Pontop Pike where stands the BBC television station for the northeast. From about A.D. 120 to 240 Stanley was the site of a Roman cattle camp for the supply of food to camps at Newcastle and South Shields. Causey Arch, built in 1727 as a wagon-way (tramroad) to a colliery, has a span of 103 ft. (31 m.). The first borings for coal to be made in England were at the now defunct White-le-Head colliery, early in the 18th century. Though principally a coal mining area, other industries include the manufacture of roller bearings and clothing (including gloves), baking, and milk processing and distribution. (J. J. SH.)

**STANLEY** (PORT STANLEY), the chief town and, since 1844, capital of the Falkland Islands, lies on the northeast coast of East Falkland Island, along the southern slope of Port William inlet. The town's fine inner and outer harbours drew the early British settlers because of the protection afforded their sailing vessels. Though Stanley served as a naval base for British cruisers during World War II, the harbours now serve mostly merchant ships.

Stanley's population (1,074 in 1962) accounts for about half the population of the Falkland Islands. As a communications centre it has a radiotelegraphy station that maintains regular schedules with London, Oslo, Montevideo, and Buenos Aires, and a radio station maintained by the British Antarctic Survey for communications with British scientific bases in the Antarctic. The town is the headquarters of the British Antarctic Meteorological Service and the site of the islands' only hospital.

Notable structures include Christ Church Cathedral (1892), Government House, a monument commemorating the British victory over a German cruiser squadron in the battle of 1914, and the Town Hall. The last provides recreational facilities, a good library, and public offices, as well as a chamber for the Town Council. In the environs of Stanley are penguin rookeries and fine white beaches.

Stanley drew worldwide attention in 1966 as the site of an abortive "invasion" by a group of 18 Argentine nationalists who planned to capture the governor and with him the Falkland Islands. However, the governor was away, and, failing to persuade the townspeople that they had been captured, the invaders surrendered and submitted to the town's hospitality.

**STANLEYVILLE** (Congo): *see* KISANGANI.

**STANOVOY RANGE** (STANOVOY KHREBET), a mountainous range in the far east of the U.S.S.R., along the boundary between Amurskaya Oblast' and the Yakut Autonomous Soviet Socialist Republic. It is orientated west-east, linking the mountain complex of Transbaikalia (Zabaykal'ye) to the Dzhugdzhur Range which fronts the Sea of Okhotsk, and is part of the watershed between the Pacific and Arctic oceans, separating the Lena Basin to the north from the Amur Basin to the south. The mountains are generally not high, although reaching 8,268 ft. (2,520 m.) at the eastern end. They are densely forested with taiga, dominated by larch, but higher summits are bare. The Aldan Highway, linking Yakutia (Yakutiya) to the Trans-Siberian Railway, crosses the range. (R. A. F.)

**STANTON, EDWIN McMASTERS** (1814–1869), U.S. lawyer, secretary of war during the Civil War, was born on Dec. 19, 1814, in Steubenville, O. He entered Kenyon College, but lack of funds compelled him to leave before graduating. After studying law, he was admitted to the bar in 1836. A sharp, incisive reasoner, he soon became a successful attorney and handled important constitutional and civil law cases. In 1847 he moved to Pittsburgh, Pa., and in 1856 to Washington, D.C., where he achieved a wide practice in the federal courts. In 1851, in his most important case, he successfully argued before the U.S. Supreme Court that a bridge over the Ohio River at Wheeling, Va. (now West Virginia), which had been authorized by Virginia law, was an obstruction to interstate commerce. In 1858, as a special U.S. counsel opposing pre-Mexican War land grants alleged to have been made by the Mexican government in California, he won a series of notable victories. During these years he remained a Jacksonian Democrat.

THE GRANGER COLLECTION

EDWIN MCMASTERS STANTON; PHOTOGRAPH BY MATHEW BRADY

In December 1860, when Pres. James Buchanan reorganized his cabinet, he appointed Stanton as attorney general; in this post Stanton opposed the abandonment of Ft. Sumter by the Union forces. Fearing the success of secessionist plotting, he secretly advised Republican leaders of the cabinet's proceedings. He became a caustic critic of the newly elected president, Abraham Lincoln, but nevertheless was made legal adviser to the secretary of war, Simon Cameron. When Cameron resigned under attack, Lincoln appointed Stanton as his successor on Jan. 13, 1862. During the remainder of the Civil War, Stanton proved to be an able, explosively energetic administrator. A nervous, asthmatic man, cranky and contradictory, he tirelessly presided over the giant Union military establishment. His sharp tongue and brusque manner provoked violent quarrels with nearly every important Union military commander. In the confusion following Lincoln's assassination, Stanton, for a few days, was a virtual dictator.

Remaining in the cabinet after Lincoln's successor, Andrew Johnson, became president, Stanton was soon at loggerheads with him over reconstruction policy. Stanton used his position to further harsher reconstruction measures than Johnson desired, and so forced Johnson to attempt his removal. Stanton refused to be dismissed, claiming that the Tenure of Office Act, passed over Johnson's veto, protected him in his official position. Because Johnson persisted, he was impeached by the House of Representatives. When the Senate refused to convict Johnson, Stanton surrendered his office on May 26, 1868, and returned to the practice of law. He died in Washington, D.C., on Dec. 24, 1869, four days after the Senate had confirmed his appointment to the U.S. Supreme Court.

*See* Fletcher Pratt, *Stanton, Lincoln's Secretary of War* (1953); B. P. Thomas and H. M. Hyman, *Stanton: the Life and Times of Lincoln's Secretary of War* (1962). (R. J. Ro.)

**STANTON, ELIZABETH CADY** (1815–1902), U.S. leader in the women's rights movement, was born in Johnstown, N.Y., on Nov. 12, 1815. The daughter of Judge Daniel Cady, she learned in his law office of the discriminatory laws under which women lived, and observed many tragic cases which determined her to win equal rights for her sex. In 1840 she married the abolitionist Henry Brewster Stanton. In 1848 she circulated petitions to secure the passage in New York of a law giving married women property rights. Also in 1848 she and Mrs. Lucretia Mott (*q.v.*) were the leaders of the first women's rights convention in the U.S. at Seneca Falls, N.Y. For it Mrs. Stanton drew up a woman's bill of rights setting forth the inferior and unjust position of women in state, church, law, and society, and resolutions demanding redress of wrongs, which were adopted. A resolution, introduced without Mrs. Mott's approval, favouring women's suffrage (*q.v.*) was the first organized demand for it in the U.S. In 1850 Mrs. Stanton became associated with Susan B. Anthony (*q.v.*), and for 40 years they worked together, Mrs. Stanton writing and Miss Anthony managing business affairs. They cooperated in editing *The Revolution* (1868–70), a women's rights newspaper, and with Matilda Gage were joint editors of the first three volumes of *The History of Woman Suffrage* (six volumes, 1881–1922). Mrs. Stanton died in New York City on Oct. 26, 1902.

*See* T. Stanton and H. S. Blatch (eds.), *Elizabeth Cady Stanton as Revealed in Her Letters, Diary and Reminiscences*, 2 vol. (1922); Alma Lutz, *Created Equal* (1940).

**STANYHURST, RICHARD** (1547–1618), English translator of Virgil, was born in Dublin. At University College, Oxford, his commentaries on Porphyry won him a reputation for precocious learning. He read for the bar and after a stay in Ireland became a Roman Catholic. Most of his subsequent life was spent in the Netherlands, where he became a priest (probably *c.* 1607) and a chaplain to Archduke Albert of Austria. He died in Brussels.

Stanyhurst wrote the *Description* and *History* of Ireland found in Holinshed's *Chronicles* (1577) and Latin works including *De rebus in Hibernia gestis* (1584). His chief work, however, was his translation of *The First Four Books of Virgil His Aeneis* (1586), which attempted to prove Gabriel Harvey's theory that classical prosody could be applied to English poetry.

Thomas Nashe said that his translation "trod a foule, lumbring, boystrous, wallowing measure." But though forced to the point of absurdity and unintelligibility, from a prosodic viewpoint his translation, with its attempt to indicate quantity by spelling, is interesting.

*See* editions of the *Aeneis* by E. Arber (1880) and D. van der Haar (1933).

**STAR,** a self-luminous object, shining by radiation derived from energy sources within itself. By contrast, planets shine by reflected light only, while gaseous and diffuse nebulae may shine either by reflected light or (essentially) by fluorescence. The universe contains billions of stars, only about 6,000 of which are visible to the naked eye. As noted below, stars are not identical to one another but vary considerably in many respects, such as brightness, colour, age, size, temperature, and chemical composition.

As far as its properties can be compared with those of other stars, the sun is a typical star. It has a mass more than 300,000 times that of the earth, $1.99 \times 10^{30}$ kg., a radius of 696,000 km. (about 432,200 mi.) and a power output of $3.8 \times 10^{23}$ kw. The masses, radii and luminosities of other stars are often expressed in terms of that of the sun.

Table I gives data pertaining to the 20 brightest stars or, more precisely, stellar systems, since some of them are double or even triple stars. Note that all of these stars are as bright or brighter than the sun; some of the companions are fainter. Stars such as Altair, $\alpha$ Centauri and Procyon are called dwarf stars; their dimensions are roughly comparable with that of the sun. Sirius and Vega are also dwarf stars; their higher temperatures give a large rate of emission per unit area. Aldebaran, Arcturus and Capella are examples of giant stars. Thus, measurements with the interferometer (which gives the angular diameter) combined with parallax measurements give diameters of 24 and 45 solar diameters for Arcturus and Aldebaran, respectively. Betelgeuse and Antares are examples of supergiants. The latter has a diameter 200 times that of the sun whereas the diameter of Betelgeuse (if we choose a distance 1,500 light-years) is 220 times. Other examples of supergiants include $\alpha$ Herculis and the variable Mira whose diameters are 580 and 460 times as great as that of the sun. Several white dwarf stars of low luminosity and high densities are listed.

Table II gives the 20 nearest known stars. Only $\alpha$ Centauri, Procyon and Sirius appear in both lists. All other stars are fainter than the sun and most of them can be seen only by the use of a telescope. The highly luminous stars can be seen at great distances; intrinsically faint stars can be seen only if they are very near the sun.

This article is divided into the following sections and subsections:



## I. DISTANCES OF THE STARS

Before any adequate discussions of stars as celestial bodies can be made, it is necessary to know their distances. Several methods have been devised, some of them of a statistical nature, which permit the distances of various types of objects to be ascertained.

**1. Trigonometric Parallaxes.**—If the position of a nearby star is measured from two points on opposite sides of the earth's orbit, a small angular displacement will be observed. Using the earth's orbit as the base line, the distance of the star can be found from the angular size of the parallax, $p$ (*see* fig. 1). If $p = 1''$, the star's distance would be 206,265 times the distance of the earth from the sun, or 3.26 light-years. This unit of distance is called the parsec; hence

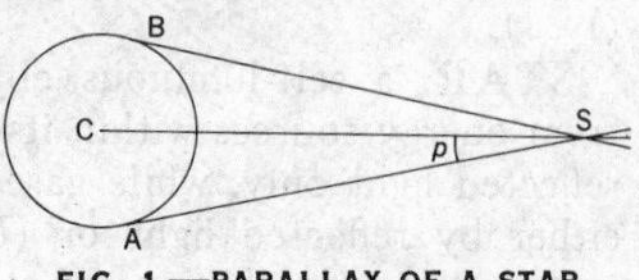

FIG. 1.—PARALLAX OF A STAR

Circle AB represents orbit of earth; angle CSA is heliocentric parallax, $p$

$$r = 1/p \quad (r \text{ in parsecs if } p \text{ is in seconds of arc}) \tag{1}$$

The nearest star (the triple-star system of $\alpha$ Centauri) has a parallax of 0."752. Its distance is 1.33 parsecs, or 4.34 light-years. Trigonometric parallaxes can be measured only for relatively close stars. The probable error of such a parallax is 0."005. This means that there is a 50–50 chance that a star whose parallax is 0."01 lies between 67 and 200 parsecs (corresponding to $p = 0.015$ and 0.005, respectively) and an equal chance that it lies outside that range.

For measuring the distance of more remote stars other methods must be used.

**2. Statistical Methods Based on Stellar Motions.**— In spite of their designation as "fixed stars," the stars are neither fixed in positions on the celestial sphere, nor in space. Edmund Halley, from a comparison of the positions of Arcturus, Aldebaran and Sirius, in the 18th century with earlier measurements showed that there was an actual motion of the stars across the line of sight (proper motion). The amount of the proper motion (in seconds of arc per year) depends on two factors, the distance of the star and its velocity in km. per second in the plane of the celestial sphere (tangential velocity)

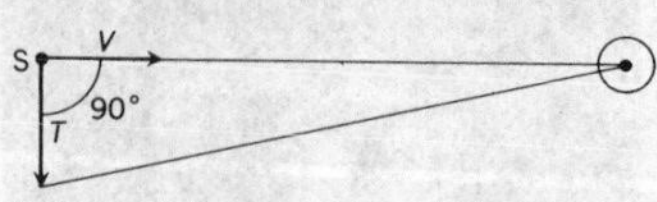

FIG. 2.—COMPONENTS OF STELLAR MOTION

$V$ represents radial velocity; $T$ is tangential velocity of the star S with respect to the sun ⊙

$$T = 4.74\,\frac{\mu \text{ sec.}}{\text{parallax}} \tag{2}$$

$$\text{or tangential velocity} = \frac{\text{annual proper motion}}{\text{parallax}} \times 4.74 \text{ km. per second.}$$

The motion in the line of sight (radial velocity) is obtained directly from spectroscopic observations (fig. 2). If $\lambda$ is the wave length of a characteristic spectrum line emitted by the star (*e.g.*, a line of iron) and $\lambda_L$ is the wave length of the same line measured in a laboratory on the earth, the difference $\Delta\lambda = \lambda - \lambda_L$ is related to the radial velocity $V$, by Doppler's principle (*see* LIGHT: *Waves and Interference*) by

$$\Delta\lambda/\lambda = V/c \tag{3}$$

where $c$ is the velocity of light. Shifts of the spectral line (positive $V$) toward red indicate recession. If the parallax is known, measurements of $\mu$ sec. and $V$ enable one to determine the space motion of the star. Radial velocities must be corrected for the motion of the earth around the sun so that they will refer to the relative line-of-sight motion of the star with respect to the sun.

The observed motion of a given star is made up of two effects, the motion of the star with respect to the average of the nearby stars (the local standard of rest) and the motion of the sun with respect to this same standard of rest. The first problem that has to be solved is the determination of the sun's motion with respect to the nearby stars, both in velocity and direction. This vector quantity is established most reliably from radial velocity data. Stars in the region of the sky toward which the sun is moving (apex of the sun's way) show a predominantly negative velocity (approach) whereas those in the opposite region of the sky show a positive velocity (recession). Stars at position 90° away from the apex or antapex show a random mixture of positive and negative radial velocities. A statistical analysis of the observed radial velocities permits the determination of the apex and the velocity of the sun $V_0$ with respect to the average of the nearby stars. From the radial velocities of 2,149 bright stars, W. W. Campbell and J. H. Moore found the position of the apex to be $\alpha = +271°$, $\delta = 29°$ (constellation

TABLE I. *The Twenty Brightest Stars*

| Name | Visual magnitude and spectrum | | | | Distance in light-years | Absolute magnitude | | Visual luminosity (⊙ = 1) | | Integrated visual magnitude |
|---|---|---|---|---|---|---|---|---|---|---|
| | A | | B | | | A | B | A | B | |
| Sirius | —1.45 | AIV | 8.60 | A5 (w.d.)* | 8.7 | 1.42 | 11.5 | 22.4 | 0.0021 | – 1.46 |
| Canopus | —0.71 | F0Ib | — | — | 240: | –5 | — | 8,700: | — | – 0.71 |
| α Centauri† | —0.01 | G2V | 1.27 | K4V | 4.3 | 4.39 | 5.75 | 1.45 | 0.44 | – 0.28 |
| Arcturus | —0.05 | K1III | — | — | 36 | –0.25 | — | 100 | — | – 0.05 |
| Vega | 0.04 | A0V | — | — | 26 | +0.53 | — | 50 | — | 0.04 |
| Capella‡ | 0.85 | G5III | 0.85 | G0III | 45 | 0.15 | 0.15 | 72 | 72 | 0.09 |
| Rigel§ | 0.10 | B8Ia | — | — | 1,500: | –8.2: | — | 150,000: | — | 0.10 |
| Procyon | 0.35 | B5IV–V | 10.7 | F (w.d.) | 11 | +2.6 | 13.0 | 7.2 | 0.0005 | 0.35 |
| Achernar | 0.49 | B5IV | — | — | 115 | –2.24 | — | 650 | — | 0.49 |
| Betelgeuse | 0.4–1.2 (Var.) | M2Ia | — | — | 1,500: | –7.9: | — | 100,000: | — | Var. |
| β Centauri | 0.62 | B1II | — | — | 425: | –4.9 | — | 8,000: | — | 0.62 |
| Altair | 0.77 | A7V | — | — | 16.5 | +2.25 | — | 10.4 | — | 0.77 |
| Aldebaran | 0.80 | K5III | 13.2 | M2 | 68 | –0.8 | — | 170 | 0.0017 | 0.80 |
| Antares | 0.92 | M11b | 5.2 | B4 | 370: | –4.3 | – 0.1 | 4,500: | 90 | 0.91 |
| Spica | 0.97 | B1V | — | — | 210 | –3.1 | — | 1,400: | — | 0.97 |
| Fomalhaut | 1.15 | A3V | — | — | 23 | +1.9 | — | 14 | — | 1.15 |
| Pollux | 1.15 | K0III | — | — | 35 | 1.00 | — | 33 | — | 1.15 |
| Deneb | 1.25 | A2Ia | — | — | 1,000: | –6.2: | — | 25,000 | — | 1.25 |
| β Crucis | 1.27 | B0III | — | — | 450: | –4.4 | — | 5,000: | — | 1.27 |
| α Crucis | 1.35 | B1IV | 1.83 | B3IV | 245 | –3.03 | – 2.5 | 1,300: | 800: | 0.82 |

*(w.d.) = white dwarf.
†α Centauri has a distant companion, Proxima Centauri, an 11th magnitude M star.
‡Peter van de Kamp lists two additional components to Capella: an M1 star, $M_v = 10.0$, and an M5 star $M_v = 13.7$ with luminosities 0.014 and 0.0005 that of the sun (*Publications of Astronomical Society of the Pacific*, 65:30, 1953).
§It is assumed that Rigel and Betelgeuse both belong to the great Orion complex, 1,500 light-years distant.
The data are quoted largely from C. W. Allen, *Astrophysical Quantities*, and from P. van de Kamp (*op. cit.*).

of Hercules not far from star $\mu$ Herculis). The space velocity of the sun was found to be 19.5 km. per second.

Once the direction of the solar motion is known, the proper motion of any star can be divided into two components, one along the great circle passing through the apex, the star, and the antapex and the other perpendicular thereto. The first mentioned component is called the upsilon component, the other is called the tau component (fig. 3). Now the upsilon component contains the effects of both the star's own peculiar motion and the reflection of the sun's motion. The backward drift caused by the sun's motion will be a maximum for stars 90° from the apex, and zero at both the apex and antapex. The tau component is unaffected by the solar motion. Let us suppose that $|\overline{V_s}|$ is the average radial velocity (without regard to sign and corrected for the solar radial velocity) of all the stars of a particular kind; *e.g.*, giant stars like Arcturus. Now $|\overline{V_s}| = |\overline{V_\tau}|$, the average tau component of velocity, if the stellar motions are at random. Hence, using equation (2)

$$\bar{p} = 4.74 \frac{|\bar{\tau}|}{|\overline{V_s}|} \qquad (4)$$

where $(\bar{\tau})$ is the average of tau components without regard to sign. Notice that what is obtained is the average parallax; the parallax cannot be obtained for any individual star, since in any particular instance $V_s$ will not be the same as $V_\tau$. Nevertheless, if attention is confined to groups of stars of the same intrinsic luminosities (and not over too great a spread in distance) the method will give good results.

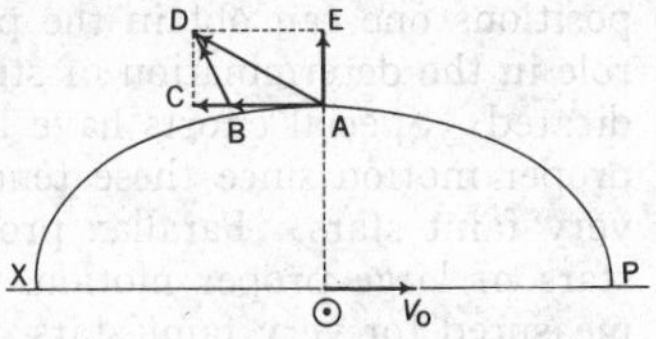

FIG. 3.—PERSPECTIVE DIAGRAM SEEN FROM ABOVE OF EFFECTS OF SOLAR MOTION

P is apex, X is antapex, A is position of a star where proper motion is observed. AE (perpendicular to lines A⊙ and AC) is tau component of star's motion; it lies perpendicular to plane of great circle, PAX, passing through apex, star and antapex. AC is upsilon component; AB, the reflection of the sun's motion $V_0$. Vectors BD and CB represent motion of star with respect to local standard of rest

It is assumed that the stars are moving at random and, strictly speaking, solar motion should be determined with respect to this particular group of stars. Statistical parallaxes fail for very remote objects and require reliable proper motions. Since the accuracy of a proper motion depends on the time interval between two epochs of observation, an increasing base line in time will serve to improve the data.

**3. Moving Cluster Methods.**—If a group of stars constitute what is called a moving cluster, their space motions are parallel to one another. Provided the cluster fills a substantial area of the sky, the place in the celestial sphere toward which the cluster appears to be moving, *i.e.*, its convergent point, can be found from a careful observation of the proper motions (*see* fig. 4). The radial velocities are also measured. The angular distance $\theta$ between the centre of the cluster and its convergent point being known, the tangential velocity $T$ can be computed in km. per second from the radial velocity $V$. Since the tangential velocity expressed in seconds of arc is the total proper motion $\mu$ sec., the parallax can be found from equation (2). This method has been applied to the Ursa Major cluster (which includes five of the seven stars of the Big Dipper) and to other groups such as the Hyades.

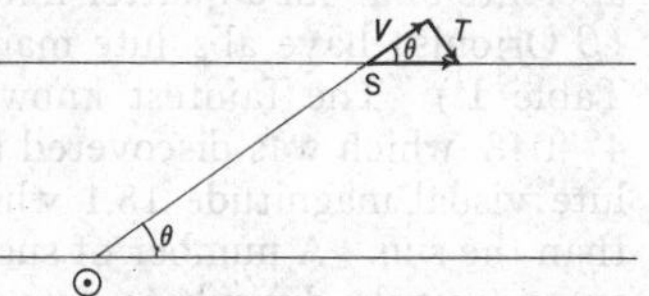

FIG. 4.—METHOD FOR DETERMINING THE DISTANCE OF A MOVING CLUSTER

S is a star in a moving cluster, $\theta$ is angle between cluster and convergent point. Tangential velocity $T = V \tan \theta$

**4. Dynamical Parallaxes.**—The distance of a double star whose orbit is known can be found from its apparent brightness provided the star follows the mass-luminosity correlation (*see* below). This method is useful for double stars in clusters (such as the Pleiades).

**5. Membership in Galactic Clusters.**—A star cluster such as the Pleiades contains stars similar in intrinsic brightnesses and colours to the sun and its neighbours. Hence if the apparent brightnesses of these stars are measured and compared with their true brightnesses, the distance of the cluster can be found from an application of the inverse-square law. If absorption of light in interstellar space between the cluster and the sun occurs, its amount has to be determined and the apparent brightnesses of the stars corrected to what they would have been for no interstellar absorption. This method is standard for establishing the distances of remote clusters.

**6. Galactic Rotation.**—The Milky Way is in slow rotation about a centre roughly 28,000 light-years distant from the sun. This rotation is like that of the planetary system in that the stars more distant from the centre travel more slowly. The general nature of the galactic rotation can be established from the gaseous component of the interstellar medium with the aid of both optical and radio-frequency observations. From the radial velocities of very remote stars their distances may be obtained with the aid of equations derived by J. H. Oort.

**7. Remote Systems.**—All of these methods fail for remote systems such as the Magellanic clouds or the Triangulum or Andromeda galaxies. For these systems other methods must be used. Certain types of objects, such as blue stars, supergiants and variable stars, are recognized in some of them. The intrinsic brightnesses of these objects being known, their apparent brightnesses in the stellar systems under investigation are measured and thus their distances are obtained. Again, corrections for space absorption must be applied if necessary.

Checks on the methods of distance determinations can sometimes be made when two or more different techniques can be applied to the same stars or system of stars. One example is provided by the Ursa Major moving cluster where R. M. Petrie and B. Moyls obtained distances in good agreement with those found from direct trigonometric parallaxes of the same stars. A second illustration is supplied by the binary Procyon. The orbit of the bright star about the centre of gravity of the system and its inclination to the plane of the sky are known. K. Strand measured the radial velocity of the star from plates secured at Mount Wilson and converted them to actual orbital velocities. With the aid of the known period, he then found the average radius (semi-major axis) of the orbit, $a$. Since $a$ is also known in seconds of arc, the parallax is found directly. Again, results in good agreement with the trigonometric measurements are found. Occasionally discrepancies are found, as in the Pleiades, but such discordances sometimes turn out to yield other dividends, such as clues to stellar evolution.

To summarize, stellar distances are accurately known for nearby objects. Stars in remoter parts of the galactic systems do not yield such satisfactory values for their distances.

Finally, it should be mentioned that the distance, or more accurately speaking the intrinsic brightness of a star whose apparent brightness can be readily measured, can sometimes be found from its spectrum. Such spectroscopic parallaxes are becoming increasingly important in astronomy, but they have to be calibrated by measuring the distances of the prototype of each spectroscopic species of stars by some method such as those described in the preceding sections.

## II. OBSERVABLE DATA FOR STARS

**1. Nomenclature.**—The earliest designations of the stars still in common use are the Arabic names. These follow no particular system, are often fanciful in character and are rarely used except by navigators and amateurs. The brighter stars in each constellation are now denoted by a system introduced in 1603 by Johann Bayer. The brightest star in the constellation is denoted as $\alpha$, the next brightest as $\beta$, etc. When stars are of comparable brightness, as in the Big Dipper, they are lettered according to their position in the constellation. Later John Flamsteed introduced a system of numbers assigned in order of right ascension.

Stars too faint to be given a Bayer letter or Flamsteed number are listed in star catalogues, the most extensive of which is the *Bonner Durchmusterung* (B.D.). The first B.D. catalogue prepared by Argelander gives the positions and rough brightnesses of more than 324,000 stars north of −2° declination. Schönfeld extended the catalogue to 23° south and added 133,000 stars while

TABLE II.—*The Twenty Nearest Stars*

| Name | Visual magnitude and spectrum | | | | Distance in light-years | Visual Luminosity (⊙ = 1) | |
|---|---|---|---|---|---|---|---|
| | A | | B | | | A | B |
| Proxima Centauri† | 10.07 | | — | | 4.28 | 0.000074 | — |
| α Centauri | −0.01 | G2V | 1.27 | K4V | 4.34 | 1.45 | 0.44 |
| Barnard's star = +4° 3561 | 9.53 | M5 | * | | 6.0 | 0.00043 | * |
| Wolf 359 | 13.66 | M6e | — | | 7.7 | 0.000016 | — |
| Lalande 21185 = BD + 36° 2147 | 7.47 | M2 | * | | 8.2 | 0.0056 | — |
| Luyten 726-8 | 12.41 | M6e | 12.95 | M6e | 8.70 | 0.000063 | 0.000042 |
| Sirius | −1.45 | AIV | 8.60 | A5(w.d.) | 8.70 | 22.4 | 0.0021 |
| Ross 154 | 10.6 | M5 | — | | 9.3 | 0.00040 | — |
| Ross 248 | 12.25 | M6e | — | | 10.3 | 0.00011 | — |
| ε Eridani | 3.74 | K2 | — | | 10.8 | 0.31 | — |
| Ross 128 | 11.13 | M5 | — | | 10.9 | 0.00033 | — |
| Luyten 789-6 | 12.58 | M6e | — | | 11.0 | 0.000087 | — |
| 61 Cygni‡ | 5.20 | K5 | 6.03 | K7 | 11.2 | 0.081 | 0.036 |
| Procyon | 0.35 | F5 | — | | 11.0 | 7.3 | 0.0005 |
| ε Indi | 4.73 | K5 | — | | 11.4 | 0.13 | — |
| Σ 2398 = BD + 59° 1915 | 8.90 | M4 | 9.69 | M5 | 11.5 | 0.0028 | 0.0014 |
| Groombridge 34 | 8.08 | M2 | 11.05 | M5 | 11.7 | 0.0062 | 0.0004 |
| τ Ceti | 3.50 | G8 | — | | 11.8 | 0.43 | — |
| Lacaille 9352 | 7.2 | M4 | — | | 11.9 | 0.013 | — |
| Luyten + 5° 1668 | 9.92 | M4 | — | | 12.4 | 0.0012 | — |

*Unseen companion is detected from gravitational effects.
†Proxima Centauri belongs to α Centauri system.
‡The faint component has a planetlike companion.
Compiled from C. W. Allen, *Astrophysical Quantities*, and Peter van de Kamp, *Publications of Astronomical Society of the Pacific*.

the rest of the southern hemisphere was covered by the *Cordoba Durchmusterung* (C.D.) and the *Cape Photographic Durchmusterung* (C.P.D.). Star charts are provided for each catalogue so that the identification of a given star is not difficult.

A somewhat less extensive catalogue but one that gives accurate positions for 33,342 stars is the Boss *General Catalogue*. The stars are listed according to their positions for 1950. A much smaller catalogue, the *Fourth Fundamental Catalogue* (1963), gives accurate positions for 1,538 stars. It is generally accepted as the basic standard reference for astrometric work. Perhaps the most frequently used catalogue is the Henry Draper Catalogue (H.D.), which gives the brightnesses, spectral classes and rough positions for 1900 for 225,000 stars (Harvard Observatory Annals, vol. 91–99). Extensions have been published for certain regions in the sky. The roughly 6,000 naked-eye stars plus many telescopic stars are included in the H.D. catalogue.

For yet fainter stars, *e.g.*, objects 100 times as faint as the dimmest star that can be seen with the unaided eye, the *Astrographic Catalogue* or *Carte du Ciel* can be used; however, it is not yet complete for all parts of the sky.

Star charts or photographs of large regions of the sky have also been published. The most extensive series of these charts is the National Geographic society–Palomar survey carried out with the 48-in. Schmidt camera. This survey covers only the part of the sky observable from Palomar mountain but includes photographs taken in both the blue spectral region and the red spectral region with an appropriate filter. Hence, strongly coloured stars and gaseous nebulae can be readily identified. More within resources of amateurs are the B.D. charts or the Skalnate Pleso charts.

**2. Stellar Positions.**—Accurate measurements of stellar position play a basic role in many problems of modern astronomy. The positions of the brighter stars in the equatorial co-ordinate system (right ascension $\alpha$ and declination $\delta$ for some given epoch) are measured with a meridian circle. The fainter stars are measured upon photographic plates with respect to these brighter stars and finally the entire group is referred to the system of extragalactic nebulae. The reason for this last step is that these external galaxies define an essentially fixed or immovable system, whereas both the bright and faint stars are affected by large-scale stellar motion connected with galactic rotation.

For problems concerned with the structure of the galaxy, the positions are often given in terms of galactic co-ordinates, galactic longitude, $l$, and galactic latitude, $b$, in which the plane of the Milky Way is the analogue of the plane of the equator.

**3. Stellar Motions.**—From accurate measurements of stellar positions one can obtain the proper motions whose fundamental role in the determination of stellar distances has already been indicated. Special efforts have been made to detect stars of large proper motion since these tend to be nearby, often intrinsically very faint stars. Parallax programs are often based on lists of stars of large proper motion. Although proper motions can be measured for very faint stars, radial velocities can be determined only for stars whose spectra can be photographed. This limits our measurements to fairly bright stars. (*See* SPECTROHELIOGRAPH.)

**4. Brightness of the Stars.**—The brightnesses of the stars are usually expressed by means of their magnitudes, a usage which has come down from classical antiquity. A star of the 1st magnitude is 2.5 times as bright as one of the 2nd magnitude, which in turn is 2.5 times as bright as one of the 3rd magnitude, etc. A star of the 1st magnitude is 100 times as bright as one of the 6th magnitude. Sirius, apparently the brightest star in the sky, is −1.5; Canopus, the second brightest, is −0.7, while the faintest star that can normally be seen without telescopic aid is of the 6th magnitude. Stars as faint as the 23rd magnitude have been measured with the Hale 200-in. telescope.

The scale of magnitudes constitutes a geometrical progression. To convert from magnitudes to light ratios the formula

$$\log \frac{l_m}{l_n} = 0.4\,(n - m) \tag{5}$$

is used where $l_n$ and $l_m$ are the brightnesses of stars of magnitudes $n$ and $m$, respectively. To the extent that brightness ratios can be regarded as power ratios we can think of one magnitude as corresponding to four decibels. Note that magnitudes are actually defined in terms of observed brightnesses and this quantity will depend on the light detecting device employed. Thus we may speak of visual magnitudes as measured with the eye, photographic magnitudes as measured with a photographic plate, and also of various types of photoelectric magnitudes.

In such a way one defines the magnitude scale; one must also give the zero point of the scale. This point is fixed arbitrarily with regard to the star catalogues of Ptolemy and Hipparchus.

The brightnesses which are actually measured give the apparent magnitudes. These cannot be converted to intrinsic brightnesses until the distances of the objects concerned are known. The absolute magnitude of a star is defined as the magnitude it would have if it were placed at the standard distance of 10 parsecs, or 32.6 light-years (2,062,650 astronomical units). The apparent visual magnitude of the sun is −26.9, that of the full moon −12.7 and the brightest star is −1.5. The absolute magnitude of the sun corresponds to a diminution in brightness by a factor $(2{,}062{,}650)^2$ and is therefore $-26.9 + 2.5 \times \log\ (2{,}062{,}650)^2 = -26.9 + 31.6 = 4.7$. The corresponding absolute magnitude of the full moon would be about +32 and would require a telescope with an aperture of about a quarter-mile. The brightest stars such as Rigel ($\beta$ Orionis) have absolute magnitudes of −8 or even −9. (*See* Table I.) The faintest known star, the companion to B.D. + 4°4048, which was discovered by G. van Biesbroeck, has an absolute visual magnitude 18.1 which makes it 200,000 times fainter than the sun. A number of such stars may exist in space, but they are extremely difficult to detect. Included among the faint stars are the white dwarflike objects that are extremely dense stars near the end of their evolution.

**5. Stellar Colours.**—Even the casual observer knows that all stars are not of the same colour. Consider the constellation of Orion, for example. Most of the naked-eye stars are blue-white in colour, but Betelgeuse ($\alpha$ Orionis) is a deep red. As seen in the telescope, Albireo ($\beta$ Cygni) consists of two stars: one blue, the other orange. Some quantitative means of measuring stellar colours is needed. One method is to compare the visual magnitude of the star with a magnitude measured with a photographic plate. The photographic plate is insensitive to yellow and red light but sensitive to blue and violet, so that hot blue stars appear bright, and yellow and red stars are faint. The scale of photographic and all other magnitudes is the same as for visual magnitudes, *i.e.*, one magnitude step corresponds to a brightness ratio of 2.5 but the zero point is adjusted so that white stars with surface temperatures of about 10,000° K. have the same visual and photographic magnitudes. A blue star with a temperature of 20,000° K. is then brighter photographically than visually by about half of a magnitude, whereas a cooler star like the sun ($T$ = 5,700° K.) is about half a magnitude fainter photographically than visually. The conventional colour index is defined as the photographic magnitude minus the visual magnitude. According to this system, the colour index of the sun is $M_p(\odot) - M_v(\odot) = +5.26 - 4.73 = 0.53$.

Later, "visual" magnitudes were determined photographically with the aid of orthochromatic or yellow-sensitive plates and yellow filters. Such magnitudes are referred to as photovisual magnitudes and differ from visual magnitudes less than visual magnitudes (as found by different observers) differ among themselves.

As a fundamental light or colour measuring device, the photographic plate has certain disadvantages. In particular, the amount of blackening of the emulsion is not proportional to the intensity of the light (or to the exposure time). The connection between blackening and intensity can be calibrated but it varies with the colour of the light, development and exposure time. Fundamental measurements of stellar magnitudes and colours are now made by photoelectric photometry although the photographic plate continues to play a vital role as an interpolation device. For example, it may be necessary to measure the magnitudes and colours of hundreds of stars in a star cluster. Such a task would be prohibitive if one had to observe each individual star with a photoelectric photometer. Instead, the observer selects a sequence of 20 or 30 stars covering the entire range of magnitude and colour in the cluster, measures them carefully with the photoelectric photometer and compares with them all the other cluster stars recorded on the photographs. (*See* PHOTOMETRY, ASTRONOMICAL: *Photoelectric Photometry;* PHOTOGRAPHY, CELESTIAL.)

The photoelectric photometer has several great advantages. First, it permits measurements to be made with an accuracy limited only by the atmosphere. Second, the relation between the number of electrons ejected from the photocathode and the light intensity is a strictly linear one. Stellar colours can be measured very quickly and conveniently by placing appropriate filters in front of the cell.

The older system of stellar magnitudes employed only photographic and photovisual (or visual) magnitudes. It encountered a number of severe difficulties. Only two of them will be mentioned here. The first grows out of the fact that most stars do not radiate like black bodies. In particular, stars with temperatures in the range 8,000° K. to 20,000° K. have a very strong drop in their energy outputs near λ3,700 Å and continuing to the ultraviolet. When the magnitudes of these stars were determined with photographic lenses, this region was cut out by the flint glass components of the achromatic objectives. But when the same stars were observed with reflecting telescopes with aluminized mirrors, radiation from the ultraviolet region was included, with the result that photographic magnitudes highly discordant with respect to previous determinations were obtained. A second difficulty is that when only one colour is observed ($M_p - M_v$), it is impossible to distinguish between the effects of reddening due to space absorption and reddening due to a low temperature. That is, if a star is measured and its colour is found to be red, it is not possible to say whether the star is red because it is cool or whether it is really a hot star whose colour has been reddened by the absorption and reddening of light in space. By measuring the magnitudes of the same stars in three colours it is possible to overcome these difficulties. W. Becker used the methods of photographic photometry to establish the amount of interstellar reddening.

J. Stebbins and A. E. Whitford used a photoelectric photometer with colour filters to measure six colours extending from the infrared to the limit of transmission of the earth's atmosphere. In many respects the most satisfactory and probably the most widely used and practical system of stellar magnitudes and colours, however, is the UBV photoelectric system of Harold Johnson and W. W. Morgan. The ultraviolet or "U" filter has a broad band pass centred near 0.35 $\mu$ (3,500 Å). It transmits the region of the spectrum beyond the big intensity drop at λ3,700 in the moderately hot stars. The blue or "B" filter has a broad maximum centred near λ4,200 with cutoffs in both the ultraviolet and green. It renders magnitudes roughly similar to (but not identical with) the old system of photographic magnitude. The visual or "V" filter transmits over a broad band pass from about 0.49 $\mu$ to 0.65 $\mu$ with a maximum near 0.55 $\mu$. It yields essentially visual magnitudes. The Johnson-Morgan system of colours and magnitudes is precisely defined in terms of stars of accurately known spectral classes and intrinsic luminosities; *i.e.*, surface temperatures and surface gravities. Furthermore, the stars cover a sufficiently wide range in colour, absolute magnitude and distribution over the sky to permit the observer to use them most effectively. In this system, the visual absolute magnitude of the sun is $M_v = 4.79$, and its corresponding blue magnitude is $M_B = +5.41$; the colour index, B − V, is +0.62.

**6. Stellar Spectra.**—Probably the largest amount of information that is attainable for a single star is obtained from its spectrum. The spectrum of a star gives at once its temperature and information about its chemical composition. Stellar spectrograms secured with a slit spectrograph on a sufficient scale reveal also whether the star is a member of a close binary system, whether it is a highly luminous supergiant, a moderately bright giant or a dwarf star like the sun.

Such spectrograms may permit a determination of the quantitative chemical composition of the star. They will also tell if the star is in rapid rotation, if it has an extended atmosphere and if it has a strong magnetic field.

(*See* SPECTROSCOPY, ASTRONOMICAL.)

The vast multitude of stars fall in a small number of spectral classes. The system of spectral classification embodied in the *Henry Draper Catalogue* embraces the following classes (ranging from the hottest to the coolest stars): O B A F G K M. (*See* fig. 5.) This group is supplemented by the R and N stars (sometimes referred to as the carbon C stars) and the S stars. The R, N and S stars differ from the others in chemical composition; they are invariably giant or supergiant stars and include no dwarfs.

The spectral sequence, O-M, represents a group of stars of essentially the same chemical composition but of differing temperatures and atmospheric pressures. This simple interpretation was put forward in the early 1920s by Meg Nad Saha and has provided the basis for all subsequent interpretations of stellar spectra. The spectral sequence is also a colour sequence; the O and B stars are intrinsically the bluest and hottest; the M, R, N and S stars are the reddest and coolest. When the effects of space reddening are eliminated and stars of a given kind, *e.g.*, dwarf stars, are considered, there is a one-to-one correspondence between colour and spectral class.

Consider first the cool stars of class M. They exhibit spectral lines of familiar metals such as iron, calcium, magnesium, etc., and also (particularly in the red and green part of the spectrum) strong bands with sharp edges on the red side caused by titanium

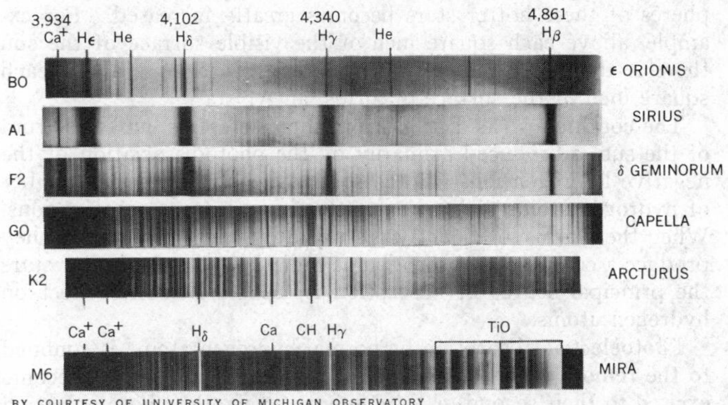


FIG. 5.—REPRESENTATIVE SPECTRAL TYPES

Principal Draper classes are represented. Note the great strength of the hydrogen lines in spectral class A1 (Sirius), the helium lines in BO (ε Orionis), the metallic lines in GO (Capella) and K2 (Arcturus) and the molecular bands in the long period variable, M6 (Mira) oxide. In the cooler stars of class M these bands become very strong and smother the continuous spectrum of the star. In spectral class K, represented in fig. 5 by Arcturus, the titanium oxide (TiO) bands disappear, and the spectrum exhibits a wealth of lines of the metals. A few especially refractory fragments of molecules such as cyanogen (CN), the hydroxyl radical (OH) and CH persist in these stars and even in G stars such as the sun. The spectra of the G stars are dominated by the metallic lines, particularly those of iron, calcium, sodium, magnesium and titanium. The λ4,227 line of calcium (produced in the flame or bunsen burner) is much weaker than in the M stars, but the λ3,968 and λ3,933 (H and K) lines of ionized calcium ($Ca^+$) are much stronger than any other feature. This behaviour of calcium illustrates the phenomenon of thermal ionization. At low temperatures a calcium atom retains all its electrons and radiates a spectrum characteristic of the neutral or normal atom. If the temperature is raised, collisions between atoms and electrons and the absorption of radiation tend to detach electrons and produce ionized $Ca^+$ atoms. At the same time ions and electrons may recombine to produce neutral calcium atoms. The situation may be expressed by the reversible reaction:

$$Ca \leftrightarrows Ca^+ + \epsilon \qquad (6)$$

If the temperature is high or the electron pressure low, or both, the atoms tend to be mostly ionized. At low temperatures and high densities the equilibrium favours the neutral state. The concentrations of ions and neutral atoms can be computed from the temperature, density and the ionization potential (the energy required to detach an electron from the atom; it is usually expressed in electron volts). In the stars of spectral class F, the lines of the neutral atoms become relatively weak in comparison with those of the ionized atoms. The hydrogen lines become stronger, attaining their maximum intensities in spectral class A, where the temperature is around 9,000° K. Thereafter they gradually fade as hydrogen becomes ionized.

Spectral lines are produced by transitions between energy levels. The yellow D lines of sodium or the H and K lines of ionized calcium are produced by jumps from the lowest energy levels of these atoms. The observable hydrogen lines, however, are produced by jumps from atoms in the second energy level, which lies far above the ground level. Only at high temperatures are sufficient numbers of atoms maintained in this level by collisions, radiations, etc., to permit an appreciable number of absorptions to occur. At the low temperatures of the M or even of the K stars there are few atoms in the second level. On the other hand, at the very high temperatures of the B and O stars, the hydrogen atoms are mostly ionized and thus cannot absorb any radiation.

Another feature to be noticed is that the lines of most ionized metals, such as iron, in the F stars never attain the strength that their neutral lines do in the K stars. This effect is partly due to the circumstance that these lines involve higher energy levels which are more sparsely populated than the lower levels. Another factor, however, is that the general fogginess or opacity of the atmospheres of these hotter stars becomes greatly increased. For example, above each square inch of the visible surface of the sun there is about 20 times as much material as there is above each square inch of the surface of Sirius, an A1 star.

The continuous (as distinct from the discrete or line) spectrum of the sun is produced primarily by the photodissociation of the negative hydrogen ion. In the solar atmosphere a small number of hydrogen atoms pick up extra electrons to form negative ions. When these are subsequently destroyed by photodissociation they produce a continuous absorption of radiation. In the hotter stars the principal source of absorption is the photoelectric effect on hydrogen atoms.

Photoelectric absorption by normal hydrogen atoms is confined to the remote ultraviolet, but if the hydrogen atoms can become excited to their second or third energy levels, the photoionization energies then required are much lower and the continuous absorptions fall in the normally observable range. Other sources of opacity exist but are relatively minor except in the coolest stars with dense band absorption.

The hotter stars of spectral class B, *e.g.*, ε Orionis, are characterized by lines of helium, singly ionized oxygen, nitrogen and neon. In the O stars, the lines of ionized helium appear. Other prominent lines include those of doubly ionized nitrogen, oxygen and carbon and trebly ionized silicon. In the hottest stars of spectral class O, the lines of hydrogen and helium are still visible.

The physical processes behind the formation of stellar spectra are well enough understood to permit determinations of temperatures, densities and quantitative chemical compositions of stellar atmospheres. The star studied in greatest detail is, of course, the sun, but other stars also have been investigated carefully.

Although the general line intensity variations of the spectral sequence can be understood in terms of a variation of temperature, these same features also depend on the densities of stellar atmospheric gases. These densities depend in turn on the surface gravities. Stars of high surface gravities (dwarfs) tend to have high densities; those of low surface gravities, giants and supergiants, have relatively low surface densities. The hydrogen lines provide an illustration in point. Normally, an undisturbed atom radiates a very narrow line. If its energy levels are disturbed by charged particles passing nearby it will no longer radiate at its characteristic frequency $\nu_o$ but at some nearby frequency $\nu_1 = \nu_o + \Delta\nu_o$. In a hot gas, charged particles will pass radiating atoms in a random fashion and at different distances, for each of which there is a corresponding value of the frequency shift $\Delta\nu$. The spectrum line radiated by the whole mass of gas accordingly will be blurred out, the amount of the blurring depending on the density of the gas in a known fashion. The dwarf stars of spectral class A such as Sirius show broad hydrogen lines with extensive "wings" whereas supergiant A stars such as Deneb (α Cygni) show relatively narrow hydrogen lines. Another example is the λ4,227 line of neutral calcium, which shows broad wings in dwarf M stars and is very narrow in supergiants. The ionization of the calcium in the supergiant is greater than in the dwarf, but the principal effect arises from density broadening. Luminosity effects in stellar spectra have to be established empirically. The procedure is (1) to observe a group of stars of different but known absolute luminosities; (2) to select among these stars spectral lines that are sensitive to luminosity but are not used for assigning the Draper class. Molecular bands (such as those of CN) as well as atomic lines are used for absolute magnitude criteria. Much effort has been expended on this problem by E. Hertzsprung, W. S. Adams and A. Kohlschütter, A. H. Joy, B. Lindblad and his associates in Sweden, and many others. In the modern system of spectral classification introduced by W. W. Morgan and P. C. Keenan, the luminosity class of the star is assigned along with the Draper class. Thus α Persei is classed as F5Ia, which means that it falls about halfway between the beginning of class F (FO) and of class G (GO). The Ia means that it is a particularly luminous supergiant with an absolute visual magnitude of the order of −7. The star π Cephei G2III is a giant falling between GO and KO but much closer to GO. The sun is classified as G2V. A star of luminosity class II falls between supergiants and giants; one of class IV is a subgiant. (*See* Table I.)

Positions, magnitudes and colours can be measured for vast numbers of stars. Spectrograms can be secured for certain of the brighter stars. If the star is close enough, its trigonometric parallax can be measured. If it is a member of a visual binary system whose orbit and parallax are known, the mass can be found. The orbit of each component must be known with respect to the centre of gravity in order to determine the individual masses. The masses of components of eclipsing binaries can also be found if both spectroscopic and photometric data are available.

**7. Stellar Diameters.**—Eclipsing binary systems provide the most extensive data on stellar dimensions. Fortunately, eclipsing systems include examples not only of dwarf stars such as the sun and Sirius but also of supergiant stars such as 31 Cygni and VV Cephei. The angular diameters of bright red giant and supergiant stars were measured in the 1920s with the Michelson stellar interferometer. The principle upon which this instrument is based goes back to the interference pattern produced by two slits when they are illuminated with light from a single narrow slit source.

In the stellar interferometer the two slits are replaced by two mirrors. The disk of the star can be regarded as being equivalent to two narrow sources placed side by side. Each source produces its own interference pattern; the observer sees the patterns superposed on one another. By varying the distance between the two movable mirrors the two interference patterns from the two sides of the star can be made to cancel one another. From the known separation of the mirrors and the effective wave length of the light, the angular diameter of the stars can be computed. Unfortunately, the instrument is sensitive to atmospheric seeing and only the largest stars can be measured by this method. R. Q. Twiss and Hanbury Brown developed another type of interferometer that depends on photon correlations. With it they have measured the angular diameters of Sirius, Vega and several bright stars in the southern hemisphere.

Finally, if the absolute magnitude of a star and its temperature are known, its size can be computed. The temperature determines the rate at which energy is emitted by each unit of area, and the total luminosity gives the total power output. Thus the surface area of the star and its diameter may be estimated. This method is actually the only one available for estimating the dimensions of white dwarf stars. The chief uncertainty is often in choosing the temperature that represents the rate of energy emission.

**8. True Stellar Luminosities; Bolometric Magnitudes.**—In theoretical studies of stellar structure and evolution the quantities that must be known are the mass, the radius, the luminosity and the chemical composition. The masses and radii of stars are found directly. The chemical compositions are found only for the surface layers and may differ from those of the interior, at least with respect to the hydrogen-helium ratio, since hydrogen is converted into helium there by thermonuclear processes.

Consider the determination of the true luminosity of the star; *i.e.,* its actual energy output. When the energy radiated by a star is observed, only that portion to which the energy detection device is sensitive and which the atmosphere transmits is obtained. The luminous efficiency for stars like the sun is very high; most of their energy is emitted in spectral regions that can be observed. An M star with a surface temperature of 3,000° K. has an energy maximum (on a wave length scale) at 10,000 Å; *i.e.,* far in the infrared. A cooler M star radiates most of its energy in the 1.5–3 $\mu$ region. Only a small portion of the actual stellar spectrum is normally observed. Bright cool stars can be observed, however, with the thermocouple. If two dissimilar metals are fastened together to form a continuous circuit and one junction is heated while the other junction remains cool, a small current will flow. The amount of the current will depend on the temperature rise and on the nature of the metals employed in a known fashion. As used at the telescope, one junction of the thermocouple is actually heated by the radiation of the star; hence the sizes of the thermoelements must be very small. Nevertheless, E. Pettit and S. B. Nicholson succeeded in measuring the energy output of certain cool, bright stars such as Betelgeuse, Antares and the long period variables $\chi$ Cygni and Mira ($o$ Ceti). Corrections for the heavy absorption by molecular bands of water vapour and other constituents of the earth's atmosphere have to be determined and applied. Magnitudes measured with a thermocouple are referred to as radiometric magnitudes.

The problem posed by the hottest stars is more difficult. Whereas there are numerous "windows" in the infrared, the transparency of the earth's atmosphere in the ultraviolet diminishes to zero at 2,900 Å (due to the extinction by ozone). A star whose surface temperature is 20,000° K. or above will radiate most of its energy in the inaccessible ultraviolet. Furthermore, the shape of the energy distribution may deviate widely from that of a black body. Continuous absorption caused by the photoionization of the hydrogen atom from its normal (lowest) level reduces the emergent energy flux to a very low value in the region beyond about 920 Å. On the redward (longward) side of this limit the atmospheric gases have a high transparency so that energy can flow outward relatively easily. The only defensible procedure for calculating this energy distribution is to construct a theoretical model of the star's atmosphere that will reproduce the features of the spectrum that can be observed, particularly the energy distribution in the observable range. If a satisfactory fit can be obtained for the observable part of the spectrum, some estimate of the energy outside the observable range can be made. Nevertheless, the uncertainties are so great that it is a matter of some urgency to obtain observations from outside the earth's atmosphere, either by rockets or by a spectrograph in an orbiting astronomical observatory.

Magnitudes that refer to the total energy radiated by the star, rather than simply the energy emitted over a narrow wave length range, are called bolometric magnitudes. The bolometric corrections required to reduce visual magnitudes to bolometric magnitudes are thus large both for very cool and for very hot stars but are relatively small for stars such as the sun.

## III. DOUBLE STARS

Binary stars are considered in three categories, depending on the mode of observation employed. Visual binaries are objects that can be seen as double stars in the telescope. True doubles, as distinguished from optical doubles, display a common space motion (as revealed by proper motions and radial velocities) and sometimes a common orbital motion as well. Spectroscopic binaries are found from radial velocity observations. A component of such a binary shows a continuously changing velocity with a fixed period; the velocity curve repeats itself exactly from one cycle to the next, and the motion can be interpreted as orbital motion in a close binary. If two stars of approximately equal brightness are observed, as in Mizar, two superposed spectra are found. The lines caused by the individual stars indicate velocity variations that can be interpreted as orbital motion. Eclipsing binaries are detected from the light variations they show when one star passes in front of the other. The best-known example is Algol ($\beta$ Persei), and good data are known for many such systems.

**1. Visual Binaries.**—The earliest observers of double stars tended to regard them as optical pairs; *i.e.,* as two independent stars seen along the same line of sight. W. Herschel measured a number of these pairs hoping to find evidence for parallactic displacements caused by the earth's orbital motion. Instead, he found displacements in several of these systems indicating a true orbital motion of the stars themselves. In the 19th century a great deal of effort was expended in discovering and cataloguing binary stars. R. G. Aitken (1927) listed 17,180 pairs north of −30°, E. Rossiter added 7,350 more, while the catalogue of Van den Bos listed 16,000 pairs south of −19°. The surveys appear to be complete to about the 9th magnitude. The *Index Catalogue of Visual Double Stars* by H. M. Jeffers and Van den Bos (1963) lists essentially all known such objects among its 64,000 systems. Most of these objects show little or no orbital motion, but a few are interesting systems. Visual binaries must be relatively near the sun in order to be detected, whereas spectroscopic binaries and particularly eclipsing binaries can be found at great distances.

The importance of visual binary systems lies in the fact that they permit the determination of stellar masses when the parallax is known. If the period, $P$, of the binary system is expressed in years and the radius of the orbit, $a$ (more accurately its semimajor axis), is expressed in astronomical units, the sum of the masses is given by Kepler's law:

$$m_1 + m_2 = \frac{a^3}{P^2} = \frac{a''^3}{p''^3 P^2} \tag{7}$$

where $p''$ is the parallax in seconds of arc and $a''$ is the semimajor axis in the same units. For example, for the well-known binary 70 Ophiuchi, $P = 87.85$ years, $p'' = 0''.199$, $a'' = 4''.55$, so that $a = 22.8$ astronomical units, and $m_1 + m_2 = 1.56$ solar masses. Furthermore, from a measurement of the motions of the two components with respect to the background stars, K. Strand and R. Spong were able to determine the orbit of each star with respect to the common centre of gravity. The mass ratio $m_2/(m_1 + m_2)$ is 0.422 and the individual masses are 0.90 and 0.66 solar masses. (*See* Orbit: *Kepler's Laws.*)

The faintest known binary for which accurate masses are available is Krüger 60. The two stars, spectral classes M4 and M6, are separated by 9.5 astronomical units, have a period of 44.5 years and have masses 0.26 and 0.16 that of the sun. The binary with the shortest known period (4.56 years) is H.D. 9,770, for which Dawson finds a mean separation of 4.7 astronomical units and a combined mass of about 5 solar masses.

A number of multiple systems are known. These consist of a close spectroscopic binary and a more distant visual companion. The Mizar-Alcor system is the classical example. Mizar and Alcor (the naked-eye pair) are so far apart that they show no orbital motion, only a common motion through space. Mizar is a visual double, but each component is itself a spectroscopic binary.

In some respects 61 Cygni is the most interesting visual binary system. It was the first star whose distance was measured and the first stellar system found to contain a planet. In the telescope it is a double star consisting of two K-type components separated by 837 astronomical units and moving about one another with a period of 720 years. One of these stars has an invisible companion with a mass $\frac{1}{60}$ that of the sun which moves about it with a period of about five years. According to all accepted criteria this companion must be regarded as a bona fide planet. Careful examination of the motions of other stars in the neighbourhood of the sun has suggested that other planetary companions may exist. For example, the single star called Ross 614, distant about 13 light-years from the sun, has an invisible companion of $\frac{1}{12}$ the sun's mass.

**2. Spectroscopic Binaries.**—J. H. Moore and F. J. Neubauer (1948) listed 480 systems for which orbital elements had been determined. Since then, about 150 new systems have been added. Unfortunately, it is not possible to find the semimajor axes or the masses for most spectroscopic binaries since the angle between the plane of the stellar orbit and the plane of the sky cannot be determined. If two spectra can be observed, mass ratios can be determined. If only one spectrum can be observed the best that can be done is to find a quantity called the mass function, which enables one to calculate a lower limit to the stellar masses. If the spectroscopic binary is also observed to be an eclipsing system, the inclination and often the masses of the individual stars can be found.

**3. Eclipsing Binaries.**—An important type of double star is the eclipsing binary, which consists of two close stars moving in an orbit so oriented in space that the light of one may be occulted or eclipsed by the other. Depending on the orientation of the orbit and the sizes of the stars, the eclipses may be total and annular or both eclipses may be partial. The best-known example of eclipsing binaries is the famous $\beta$ Persei or Algol, which has a period of 2.87 days (interval between eclipses). The brighter star (of spectral class B8) contributes about 92% of the light of the system and the eclipsed star much less than 8%. The system contains a third star that is not eclipsed.

The basic observation datum for an eclipsing binary is the light curve. It displays magnitude measurements of the system over the length of a complete light cycle. Usually the measurements are made by comparing the light of the variable star with that of a nearby comparison star of presumably fixed brightness. Consider fig. 6A. The deep or primary minimum is produced when the star of higher surface brightness is eclipsed. It represents the total eclipse and is characterized by a flat bottom. The shallower secondary eclipse occurs when the star of higher surface brightness passes in front of the other; it corresponds to an annular eclipse (or transit). In a partial eclipse (fig. 6B) neither star is ever completely hidden and the light changes continuously during an eclipse; there are no flat bottomed minima.

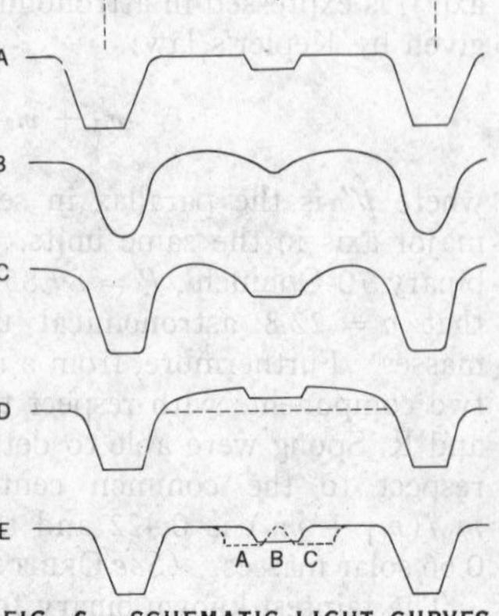

FIG. 6.—SCHEMATIC LIGHT CURVES OF ECLIPSING BINARIES

An analysis of the shape of the light curve during an eclipse, following the methods of H. N. Russell, gives the ratio of the radii of the two stars, $r_1$, $r_2$ and also $r_1$ in terms of the size of the orbit, the ratio of the luminosities $l_1$, $l_2$, and the inclination of the plane of the orbit to the plane of the sky.

If radial velocity curves are available, *i.e.*, if the system can be observed as a spectroscopic binary as well as an eclipsing binary, additional information is found. In the fortunate circumstances where both velocity curves are observable, the absolute dimensions of the orbit and the sizes, masses and densities of the stars can be found. Furthermore, if the parallax of the system can be found the temperatures of the individual stars may be estimated from their luminosities and diameters. These procedures can be carried out for the faint binary Castor C and the bright B-star $\mu$ Scorpii.

Light curves of the types as shown in figs. 6A and 6B usually occur in systems where the companions are moderately distant from one another. If the stars are close to one another, additional effects occur that cause the light to vary between eclipses. One of these effects is the tidal distortion produced by the gravitational attraction of one star upon the other. The stars become elongated along the line joining them. Hence, midway between eclipses they appear broadside to the observer and the light of the system is a maximum. (*See* fig. 6C.)

The reflection effect is exhibited in fig. 6D. Suppose that a small, high temperature star is paired with a larger object of low surface brightness. If the distance between the stars is small, the hemisphere of the cool star presented toward the hotter one will be substantially illuminated. Just before (and just after) secondary eclipse this illuminated hemisphere is pointed toward the observer, and the total light of the system is a maximum. The reflection effect may be large for two stars of greatly differing surface temperature. It vanishes if both stars are of the same surface temperature.

If a light curve is affected by reflection effects and tidal distortion as exhibited in figs. 6C and 6D, it is necessary to correct these variations before the light curve can be analyzed. Such a process is called rectification. If the stars are oblate in shape due to rapid rotation or if the surface brightness is altered as a consequence of the variation of gravity over the surface, it is necessary to allow for these effects in the interpretation of the light curve. Eclipses of oblate stars are necessarily more troublesome to handle than those of spherical stars.

If the disk of the sun is photographed with a high-speed camera, the centre is found to be brighter than the limb. The difference in brightness depends on the wave length of the light used. It is large in the violet, small in the red and almost vanishes in the infrared. This limb darkening arises from the fact that the sun gets hotter toward its core. At the centre of the disk, radiation is received from deeper and hotter layers (on the average) than from the limb. A similar situation holds for the stars; for any given colour of the spectrum the degree of limb darkening will depend on the temperature of the star. Limb darkening must be taken into account in the analysis of the light curve. If it is neglected, the calculated size of the eclipsed star will be too small.

Modern light curves obtained with the photoelectric cell are sometimes so accurate that the tiny differences produced by different degrees of limb darkening can be found and the correct law of darkening as well as the stellar sizes accurately established.

One other effect on the light curves must be mentioned. Some stars move about one another in elliptical orbits. If the major axis of the orbit is at right angles to the line drawn to the observer the stars will take a different length of time to go from primary minimum to secondary minimum than from secondary minimum to primary minimum because they move faster when close together than when far apart (more precisely, the radius vector of the orbit sweeps out equal areas in equal times). Hence the secondary minimum will not fall precisely at the midpoint between primary eclipses (fig. 6E[A]). If the system is observed at a later date the secondary minimum may be symmetrically placed, but now the two eclipses are of unequal duration (fig. 6E[B]). At this time the major axis is pointed toward the observer. One eclipse occurs when the occulting star is moving most rapidly, the other when it is moving most slowly. At a still later date the secondary minimum is displaced to the opposite side from the midpoint (fig. 6E[C]). Observation of these effects in any eclipsing system demonstrates that the major axis of the orbit is rotating and establishes the rate of rotation. What causes this rotation of the orbit? A third body might do it and possibly sometimes does, but such a body would produce other effects that could be observed; in most instances it must be concluded that only two stars are present.

Two isolated spherical stars attract one another as point masses and move about one another in elliptical orbits whose orientation remains fixed in space. If, however, the stars are distorted by their mutual tidal attractions, the elliptical orbit will slowly rotate; the speed of rotation will depend in a precisely known fashion on their separation, masses, radii and the degree of mass concentration to the centre. The orbit would turn at a maximum possible speed for stars that were homogeneous; it would not rotate at all for stars whose masses were essentially all concentrated to the centre. All theories of stellar structure predict large mass concentrations toward the centre. (For the sun the central density is about 80 times the mean density.) These predictions can be tested by the eclipsing binaries, and it turns out that in all instances the central condensations are large (as required by theory) but that in some systems the central density may be great. This latter result can be understood in terms of the more modern work on stellar structure. Thus, as Russell called it, the "royal road of eclipses" provides information on the densities, radii and masses of the stars as well as on their internal structures. It is becoming evident that eclipsing stars are going to provide many useful clues to the problem of stellar evolution.

Since the individual stars are often close to one another, extreme examples of tidal distortion, etc., are found. The commonest type of eclipsing binaries, those of the W Ursae Majoris type, are pairs of stars apparently similar to the sun in size but revolving about one another while almost touching.

Although eclipsing binary systems give much detailed data on stars, they do not necessarily give good statistics applicable to isolated single stars. Systems in which a smaller hotter star is accompanied by a larger cooler object are easier to detect than are systems that contain, for example, two main sequence stars. Furthermore, the evolutionary development of two stars near one another does not exactly parallel that of two well-separated or isolated stars.

About 17 or 18 naked-eye eclipsing binaries are known. They include combinations of a variety of stars ranging from objects smaller than the sun (Castor C) to huge supergiants (such as VV Cephei) which would engulf Jupiter and all the inner planets if placed at the position of the sun.

**4. Statistics of Stellar Systems.**—If the known data for all binaries are combined, some interesting statistics emerge. In the neighbourhood of the sun most of the stars are members of binary systems, and some of the nearest single stars are suspected of having companions.

Although some binary systems consist of stars separated by hundreds of astronomical units while others are contact binaries, the most probable binary system is built on the same scale as the solar system. The average separation between components is of the order of ten astronomical units. Studies of the relative masses of the two components show that there is a tendency for the division in mass between two components of a binary to be nearly at random. A mass ratio of about $\frac{1}{20}$ could occur about 5% of the time, and under these circumstances a solar system might form.

Thus, according to the work of G. P. Kuiper, the formation of double and multiple stars on the one hand and of solar systems on the other are different facets of the same process. A solar system could certainly not be formed by an encounter between two stars. Rather, planets may be produced by a process akin to that depicted in the nebular hypothesis of Laplace except that most of the mass and angular momentum is swept out of the system. Only a small fraction of the original material is retained as planets. Solar systems may be frequent in the earth's galaxy; perhaps 100,000,000 stars have bona fide planets.

## IV. STELLAR VARIABILITY

A fair number of the stars in the sky are intrinsically variable; that is, their total energy output fluctuates with time. Some of these stars were found by accident, but many were detected as a result of carefully planned searches. Variable stars are important in astronomy for a number of reasons. They usually appear to be stars at critical or short-lived phases of their evolution; detailed studies of their light and spectral characteristics, spatial distribution and association with other types of stars may provide important clues to the life histories of various classes of stars. Certain kinds of variable stars such as Cepheids and novae are extremely important in that they make it possible to establish the distances of remote stellar systems such as the Magellanic Clouds and some of the nearer extragalactic nebulae or external galaxies (*see* NEBULA: *The Extragalactic Distance Scale*). The principle is this: If the intrinsic luminosity of a particular kind of variable is known and this kind of variable star can be recognized in a distant stellar system, the distance of the latter can be estimated from a measurement of the apparent luminosity. If $l$ is the apparent brightness, $L$ the intrinsic brightness corresponding to the standard distance, $R$, of 10 parsecs or 32.6 light-years, $l/L = R^2/r^2$ where $r$ is the distance of the star. If the stellar brightness is expressed in magnitudes

$$y = m - M = 5 \log r - 5 \tag{8}$$

If there is absorption of light in space, the apparent magnitude, $m$, must be corrected for the amount of extinction. (*See* INTERSTELLAR MATTER.)

The most important classes of variable stars are the following:

| | |
|---|---|
| Cepheids and RR Lyrae stars | Supernovae |
| Long-period variables | R Coronae Borealis stars |
| Semiregular variables | $\beta$ Canis Majoris stars |
| Irregular red variables | T Tauri stars |
| Novae | Spectrum and magnetic variables |
| SS Cygni stars | Flare stars |

The long-period variables, the novae and the Cepheids were the types earliest recognized. The first four classes probably owe their variability to pulsation. The next three are sometimes referred to as catastrophic variables, while the remaining five types owe their variability to less dramatic but perhaps just as bizarre causes.

The spectrum and magnetic variables, spectral class A, show small amplitudes of light variation but pronounced spectroscopic changes. Their spectra are characterized by strong lines of heavy metals, particularly rare earths, which vary in intensity in a periodic fashion. H. W. Babcock discovered that these stars have strong magnetic fields, up to 30,000 gauss. Not all magnetic stars are known to be variable in light, but the variable ones seem also to possess variable magnetic fields.

The T Tauri variables are dwarf stars of spectral classes G and K. They invariably fall in regions of high obscuration; *i.e.*, dense clouds of absorbing material. Their changes in brightness are erratic; some, such as R Monocerotis, are associated with small fan-shaped nebulae. Their spectra show bright lines and washed-out absorption lines suggesting that they are rapidly spinning objects in clouds of diffuse material. Flare stars are cool dwarfs (spectral class M) that display flares apparently like those of the sun except that they fade away much more rapidly.

Various lines of evidence suggest that these stars are objects either recently formed or in the process of formation from the interstellar medium.

The $\beta$ Canis Majoris stars are high temperature (spectral class B) stars that often show complicated variations in spectral line shapes and intensities, velocity curves and light. They often have two periods of variation so similar in duration that complicated interference or "beat" phenomena are observed.

R Coronae Borealis variables are giant stars of about the sun's temperature whose atmospheres are characterized by excessive quantities of carbon. Their brightness remains constant until suddenly the star dims by several magnitudes and then slowly recovers its original brightness; the star's colour remains the same during the changes in brightness. The dimmings occur in a random fashion. L. Berman and J. A. O'Keefe have suggested that the

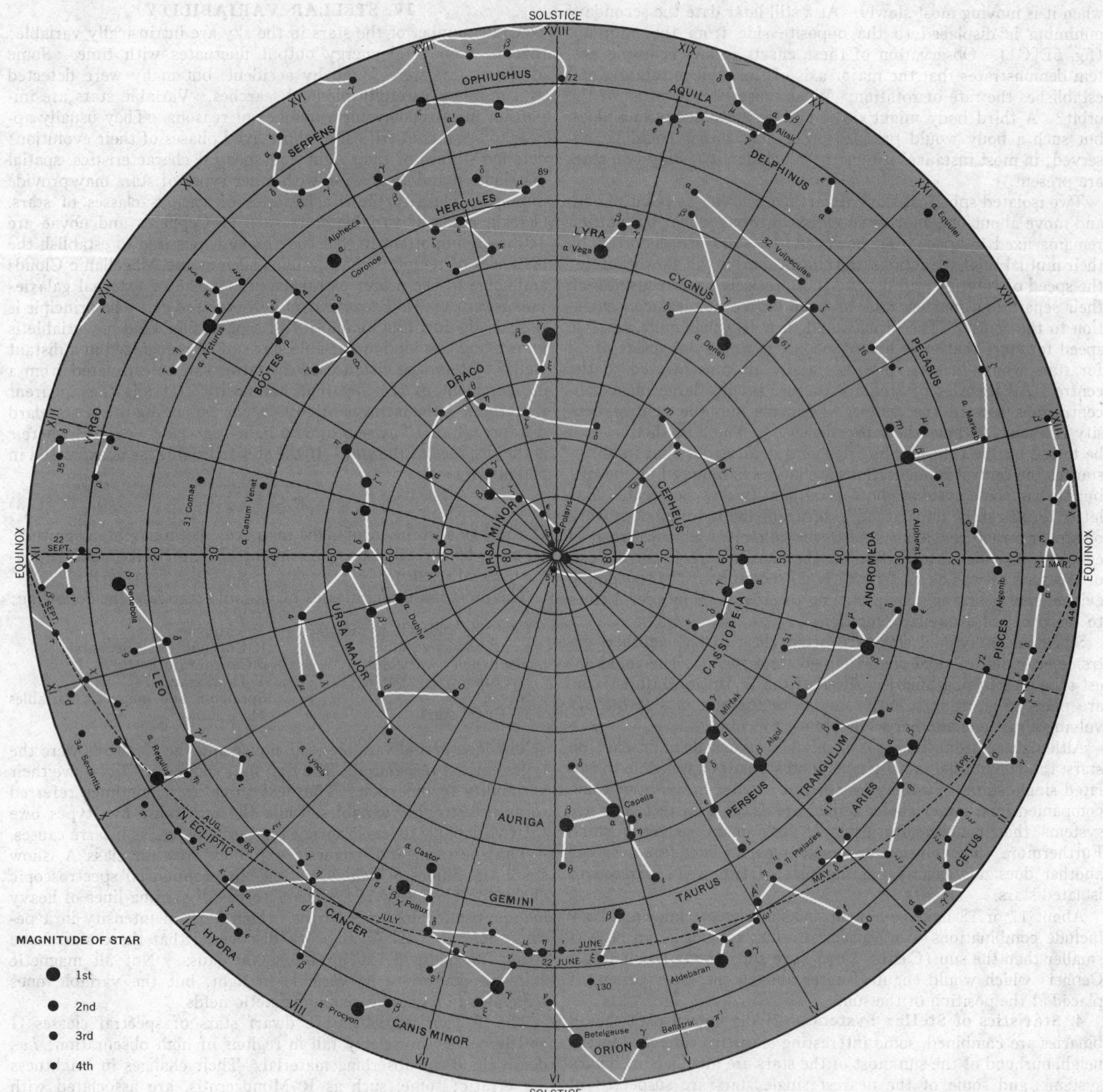


BY COURTESY OF J. C. CLANCEY, I.S.O., F.R.A.S., FROM "SIMPLIFIED STELLAR MAPS" PUBLISHED BY THE SUPERINTENDENT, GOVERNMENT PRINTING AND STATIONERY, RANGOON

**STAR CHART OF NORTH POLAR HEMISPHERE**

**Most stars visible to the naked eye and north of the celestial equator are shown in this chart. The North Star, Polaris, is shown slightly to the right of the north celestial pole. This star is not exactly true north. At the bottom of the chart is the first magnitude star Betelgeuse in the constellation of Orion. This was the first of the large stars to have its diameter measured. At the left of the north celestial pole is the "Great Bear" with its pointer stars in line with the North Star. In the upper part of the chart is the constellation Hercules toward which the entire solar system is moving at the rate of about 12 miles per second. Owing to the rotation of the earth on its axis, all stars shown in this chart appear to rotate around the north celestial pole in a counterclockwise direction**

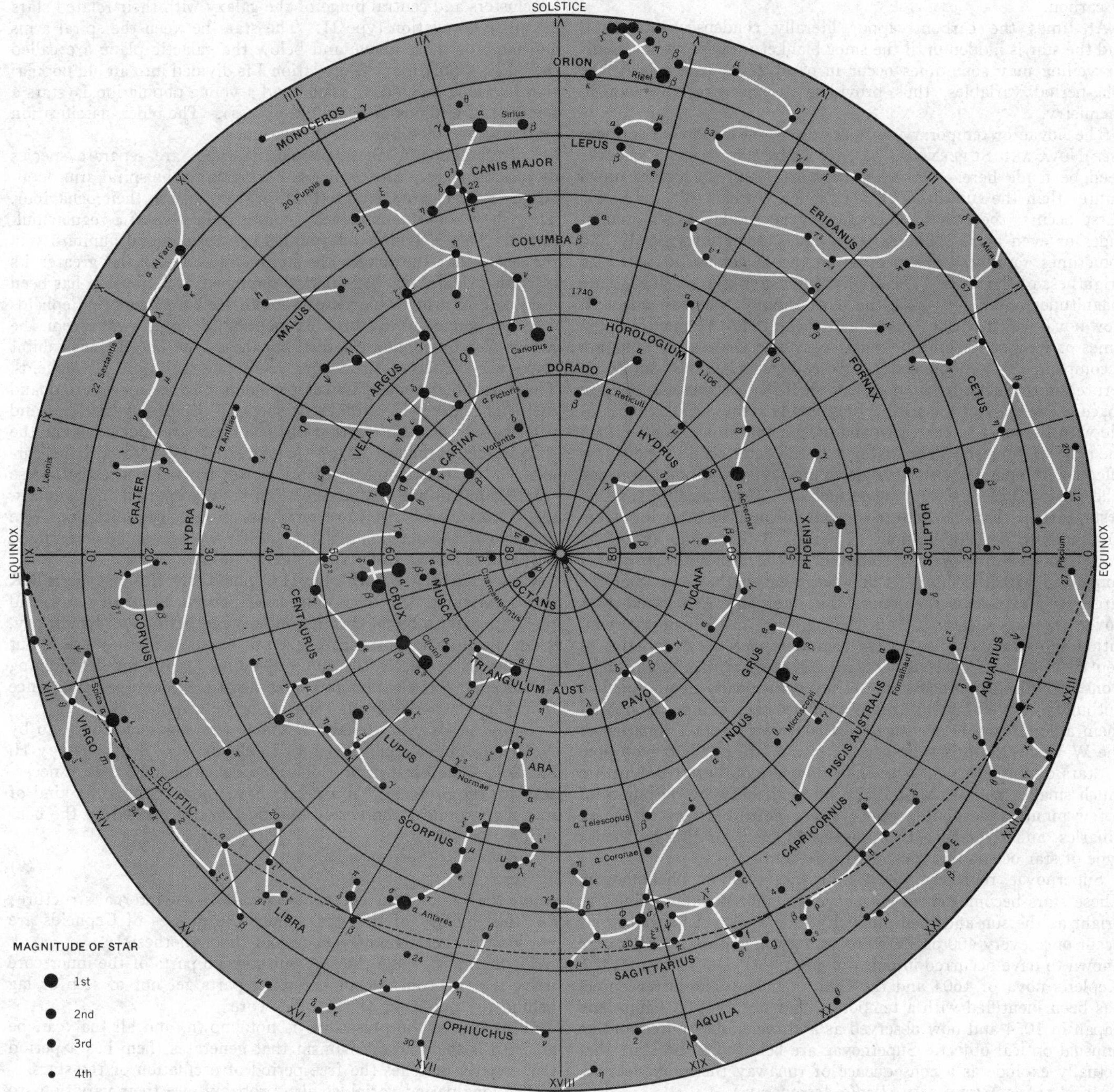


BY COURTESY OF J. C. CLANCEY, I.S.O., F.R.A.S., FROM "SIMPLIFIED STELLAR MAPS" PUBLISHED BY THE SUPERINTENDENT, GOVERNMENT PRINTING AND STATIONERY, RANGOON

## STAR CHART OF THE SOUTH POLAR HEMISPHERE

**Showing all of the principal stars visible to the naked eye found south of the celestial equator. To the left of the south celestial pole in the chart is the Southern Cross (Crux). Notice the 2 pointers, α and β Centauri, just below Crux; α Centauri is a triple star, one of whose members is the nearest star to the earth. Below the south celestial pole and slightly to the left is Scorpius which contains the supergiant red star Antares, which is one of the largest stars that has been measured up to the present time. It is visible from practically every point in the inhabited world. To the right of the south celestial pole is Fomalhaut, a first magnitude star in the constellation "The Southern Fish." Sirius, of the constellation "The Big Dog" and the brightest star in the sky, is near the top of the chart. All stars shown in chart appear to revolve around the south celestial pole in a clockwise direction due to the rotation of the earth on its axis**

clue to the variability was to be sought in the huge concentrations of carbon.

At times the carbon vapour literally condenses into soot, and the star is hidden until the smog blanket is evaporated. Similar veiling may sometimes occur in other stars, particularly the long-period variables, thus providing an engaging problem in chemistry.

The novae or temporary stars are discussed in detail elsewhere (*see* NOVA AND SUPERNOVA) so only a few summarizing remarks need be made here. Normally they are small blue stars much fainter than the sun although very much hotter. When an outburst occurs, the star may brighten very suddenly, ten magnitudes or even more. Thereafter it fades, sometimes slowly and sometimes rapidly. The rate of fading is connected with the brightness of the nova. The brightest novae, which reach absolute magnitudes about $-8$, fade the most rapidly, whereas a typical slow nova, which reaches an absolute magnitude $-5$, may take ten times as long to decline in brightness. The changes in light are accompanied by pronounced spectroscopic changes that can be interpreted as arising from an ejected shell that dissipates slowly in space. The mass of the shell is presumably rather small, comparable with the mass of the earth and presumably much smaller than the mass of Jupiter. Presumably only the outer shell of the star is affected; the main mass settles down until a new outburst appears. The existence of repeating novae such as T Coronae Borealis suggests that perhaps all novae repeat at intervals ranging from thousands to perhaps millions of years. B. Kukarkin and P. P. Parenago suggested that the amplitude of the outbursts is probably connected with the intervals between them in the sense that the larger the explosion the longer the interval. Associated with novae are stars such as Z Andromedae which in their normal condition show remarkable spectra combining the characteristics of cool M-type stars, gaseous nebulae and hot stars with bright emissions of hydrogen and helium. They occasionally show novalike outbursts. Several novae are close binary stars, and perhaps all of them are. It has been suggested that dwarf contact binaries of the W Ursae Majoris type become novae late in their evolution.

Stars of the SS Cygni type show novalike outbursts but with a much smaller amplitude and with intervals between outbursts of a few months to about a year. These novalike stars often are binaries, and it may be that the development of this particular type of star occurs in a close binary system.

Supernovae represent quite a distinct type of phenomenon. These stars become ten or even several hundred million times as bright as the sun and then gradually fade away. Such outbursts occur once every 400 or 500 years in a given galaxy, but three are known to have occurred in our own galaxy—Tycho's star of 1572, Kepler's nova of 1604 and the Crab Nebula. The latter object has been identified with a temporary star observed in China and Japan in 1054 and now observed as a strong radio source and an unusual optical object. Supernovae are believed to be stars that actually explode as a consequence of runaway thermonuclear reactions. (*See* ASTRONOMY: *Radio Astronomy.*)

Stellar pulsations are believed to account for the variability of the Cepheids, the long-period variables, the semiregular variables and even the irregular red variables. Of this group the Cepheids have been studied in greatest detail, both theoretically and by observation. These stars are regular in their behaviour; some repeat their light curves with great faithfulness from one cycle to the next.

Much confusion existed in the study of Cepheids until it was recognized that there existed two families of stars now denoted as population types I and II. Population type I is that associated with the spiral arms of this and other galaxies. It contains stars of all ages, from those in the process of formation to defunct white dwarfs. The best examples of type I populations are galactic or open clusters such as the Pleiades or the beautiful double cluster in Perseus (h and $\chi$ Persei). Population type II comprises the stars of the central bulge of our galaxy, elliptical nebulae, globular clusters and most of the stars moving between the spiral arms. These stars are all very ancient; their ages are probably more than 7,000,000,000 years.

Some writers employ a more elaborate classification. The globular clusters and central bulge of the galaxy with their related stars comprise population type II. The stars between the spiral arms and most of those above and below the galactic plane are called the "disk population." Population I is divided into an old population I (which includes the sun) and a young population I (stars a few tens of millions of years old or less). The older classification system is retained for this discussion.

Corresponding to these population types are separate species of variable stars. The Cepheids belonging to the spiral arm population (type I) are characterized by regularity in their behaviour. They show continuous velocity curves indicative of a regular pulsation. They exhibit a relation between period and luminosity in the sense that the longer the period of the star the greater its intrinsic brightness. This period-luminosity relationship has been used to establish distances of remote stellar systems. Cepheids are also found in the type II population, *e.g.,* away from the Milky Way in globular clusters, but these type II Cepheids exhibit some very different properties from classical type I Cepheids. They are bluer than classical Cepheids of the same period and their light curves have different shapes. Studies of the light and velocity curves indicate that shells of gas are ejected from the stars as discontinuous layers that later fall back toward the surface. Most disappointing of all, however, is the fact that these stars exhibit no well-defined relation between period and luminosity. Consequently, they are worthless as distance indicators. The distance of a Cepheid in a distant stellar system can be determined only if it is known to be a classical Cepheid.

Closely associated with type II Cepheids are cluster-type or RR Lyrae variables. All these stars have periods less than a day, and there appears to be no correlation between period and luminosity. Their absolute magnitudes are about $+0.6$; *i.e.,* they are about 47 times as bright as the sun. They are useful for determining distances of star clusters and some nearby external galaxies, since their short periods permit them to be detected readily.

The possibility of stellar pulsations was suggested long ago by A. Ritter; direct applications to Cepheids were made first by H. Shapley, while Sir Arthur Eddington developed the theory necessary for the problem. If all stars have roughly the same kind of internal structure, the period and density are related by the condition

$$P\sqrt{\rho} = \text{constant} \tag{9}$$

where the value of the constant depends on the internal structure; *i.e.,* the "model" of the star. Since the masses of Cepheids are not known, there is no direct test of this hypothesis.

Furthermore, while the star pulsates, all parts of the inner core move in synchronism, but the outer parts get out of step or lag behind the pulsation of the inner core.

What causes the pulsations is not known, and all that can be asserted is that the mechanism that generates them has a period that exactly matches the free period of oscillation of the stars.

The long-period variables also probably owe their variations to pulsations. Here the situation is complicated by the vast extent of their atmospheres. These stars appear to fall into two groups: (1) those with shorter periods (of the order of 200 days) tend to be associated with the type II population; (2) those of periods of the order of a year belong to the type I population. These stars are invariably red cool giant and supergiant stars of spectral classes M (normal composition), R and N (carbon rich), or S (heavy-metal rich). The range in visual brightness may be a hundredfold, but the range in total energy output is much less because at very low temperatures (1,500° K.–3,000° K.) most of the energy is radiated as heat rather than as light. A slight change in temperature can produce a huge change in the output of visible radiation. At these temperatures, compounds and probably solid particles are formed so that the light change may be profoundly affected by chemical as well as physical factors.

Red semiregular variables such as the RV Tauri stars show complicated light and spectrum changes. They do not repeat themselves from one cycle to the next; their behaviour suggests a simultaneous operation of two or more modes of oscillation.

Betelgeuse is an example of an irregular red variable. In these stars the free period of oscillation does not coincide with the periodicity of the driving mechanism.

Variable stars may provide very important clues to stellar evolution. Probably all of them represent more or less ephemeral phases in the evolution of a star. Aside from such catastrophic events as a supernova in which an entire star is torn asunder, some phases of stellar variability may be of such brief duration as to permit detectable changes during an interval of 50 or 100 years. Other stages may require many thousands of years. For example, the period of δ Cephei has not changed by a detectable amount since its variability was discovered.

## V. CORRELATIONS BETWEEN LUMINOSITY, SPECTRUM, AND MASS

Some of the most important generalizations concerning the nature and evolution of stars can be made from correlations between different observable properties and from certain statistical results. One of the most important of these correlations concerns the spectrum and luminosity.

If one plots the absolute magnitudes of the stars (or their intrinsic luminosities on a logarithmic scale) against the spectral types, as Russell was the first to do in 1913, the stars do not fall at random on the diagram but tend to congregate in certain restricted domains (*see* fig. 7). Most of the congregated stars are dwarfs belonging to what is called the main sequence. These stars range from hot blue objects 10,000 times (or more) brighter than the sun, down through white A stars such as Sirius, yellow-white F stars such as Procyon, through the sun, down to orange K stars such as ε Eridani, and finally to faint red dwarfs thousands of times fainter than the sun. The sequence is continuous, the luminosities fall off smoothly with decreasing surface temperature, the masses and radii decrease but at a much slower rate and the densities gradually increase.

The second group of stars to be recognized was the giants, objects such as Capella, Arcturus and Aldebaran, yellow, orange or red stars about 100 times as bright as the sun and with diameters of 10,000,000 or 20,000,000 mi. The supergiants include stars of all spectral classes; they show a big spread in intrinsic brightness; some even approach absolute magnitudes −7 or −8. Some red supergiants such as the variable VV Cephei exceed in size the orbit of Jupiter or even Saturn, although most of them are smaller. The short-lived supergiants are rare in space; their great luminosity enables them to be seen at great distances.

The subgiants are stars that are redder and larger than main sequence stars of the same luminosity. Most of the known examples are found in close binary systems, particularly in eclipsing systems where conditions favour the detection of doubles in which a subgiant is paired with a main sequence star.

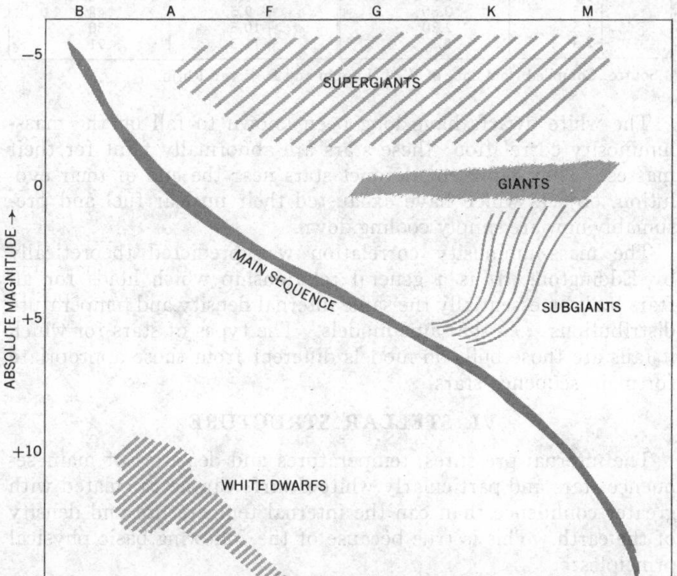


FIG. 7.—SCHEMATIC SPECTRUM LUMINOSITY CORRELATION (RUSSELL-HERTZSPRUNG DIAGRAM) AND SPIRAL ARM POPULATION (NEIGHBOURHOOD OF THE SUN)

The white dwarfs comprise a group of stars falling about ten magnitudes below the main sequence. Numerically, they exceed the representatives of any group except the main sequence. These objects are of interest for several reasons, not the least of which is that they represent the last stage in stellar evolution, the last feeble glow of a dying star. Their masses are comparable with that of the sun; their densities exceed anything that can be produced in the laboratory. The first of these remarkable objects to be recognized was the companion to Sirius, originally detected by its gravitational attraction upon the larger, brighter star and only later discovered visually as a faint object, about 10,000 times fainter than Sirius. Its mass was about equal to that of the sun. Later work showed that the colour and spectrum of this star corresponded to about spectral class A; *i.e.,* it had a surface temperature of 8,000° K. or 10,000° K. Hence the rate of emission of energy from the surface must be much greater than that of the sun. Since it was about 500 times fainter than the sun, it must have a much smaller surface area and therefore a much smaller volume. Thus the density would have to be a great deal higher than that of the sun. The average density is about 10,000 times that of water. Under these conditions the electrons are nearly all stripped off the atoms and form what is called a degenerate gas. Such material has remarkable properties. It does not obey the ordinary gas laws and is an almost perfect conductor of heat.

Notice that the spectrum luminosity diagram has numerous gaps. For example, above the white dwarfs and to the left of the main sequence there are very few stars. The main sequence and the giants are separated by a gap named after E. Hertzsprung, who was the first to clearly recognize (in 1911) the difference between main sequence and giant stars. The actual concentration of stars in different parts of the diagram changes considerably. Highly luminous stars are rare; those of low luminosity are very numerous.

One feature of fig. 7 must be emphasized. It applies to the spiral arm in the neighbourhood of the sun and represents what would be obtained if Russell-Hertzsprung diagrams were constructed for a large number of open clusters such as *h* and χ Persei, the Pleiades, Coma Berenices and the Hyades and added all together. It includes very young stars (only a few million years old) as well as very ancient (8,000,000,000 or 9,000,000,000 years old) stars. This spiral arm population is called by Walter Baade a type I population to distinguish it from the type II population associated with the globular clusters and the central bulge of the galaxy.

Fig. 8 exhibits the type of spectrum-luminosity relation characteristic of the globular clusters, the central bulge of the galaxy and the elliptical external galaxies. Since these systems are very remote from the observer, the stars are very faint and their spectra cannot be observed. Instead it is necessary to resort to measurements of their magnitudes and colours. Since the colours are closely related to the spectral classes, equivalent spectral classes may be used, but it is to be noted that stellar colours, not spectral classes, are observed in this instance.

The difference between fig. 7 and 8 is striking. In fig. 8 there are no supergiants, and instead of falling at $M_v = 0.0$ the giant branch starts around −3.5 for very red stars and forms a continuous sequence until an absolute magnitude of about −1 is reached. Then there is a band of stars, all about the same colour, proceeding downward (*i.e.,* to fainter stars) to about $M = +3$. The giant branch is then connected to the main sequence at about +3.5 by a narrow band. The main sequence extends to fainter and redder stars in much the same way as in the spiral arm population. The main sequence ends just above the sun, however, and does not extend up through the A, B and O spectral classes. Occasionally a few stars are found in the region normally occupied by the main sequence.

The horizontal branch falls near magnitude 0 and fills the Hertzsprung gap. The striped area in fig. 8 indicates the domain of the RR Lyrae stars. M. Schwarzschild found that every short-

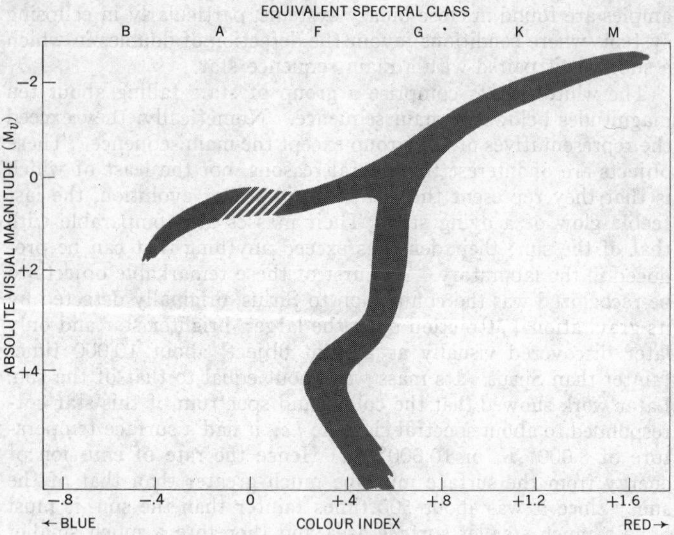


ADAPTED FROM "ASTROPHYSICAL JOURNAL"; REPRODUCED BY PERMISSION OF THE UNIVERSITY OF CHICAGO PRESS

**FIG. 8.—COLOUR-MAGNITUDE ARRAY FOR A TYPICAL TYPE II POPULATION AS REPRESENTED BY A GLOBULAR CLUSTER**

**Absolute visual magnitude is plotted against the colour index of the star in the sense C.I. $= M_v - M_p$. It is assumed that the RR Lyrae stars have an absolute magnitude of +0.6. Equivalent spectral types are plotted at top of diagram**

period cluster variable fell in this small region of the diagram. Conversely, every star in this range of magnitude and colour has been found to be a variable. The horizontal branch extends beyond the RR Lyrae stars; among these blue stars are found novae and the nuclei of planetary nebulae. Not all globular clusters show identical colour-magnitude arrays. Some clusters such as M3 have many RR Lyrae stars; others such as M13 have very few. Some have numerous giants; others have numerous blue stars on the horizontal branch. In M92 the whole giant branch is bluer than in M13.

Spectroscopic observations indicate that stars in globular clusters do not all have the same hydrogen-metal ratios. Among the extreme examples of Baade's population type II stars found in the neighbourhood of the sun are the so-called subdwarfs. The abundance of metals in these stars is perhaps $<1\%$ to $10\%$ that in the sun. Stars of a somewhat similar composition are found in certain globular clusters, particularly M92. Many globular clusters appear, however, to have compositions intermediate between that of the sun and these extreme subdwarfs.

Not all stars of Baade's population type II are confined to globular clusters and the central bulge of the galaxy. Many are found scattered throughout the galactic system; some are encountered in the neighbourhood of the sun. High velocity stars are of Baade's type II, but not all type II stars display a high velocity. Numerically the ancient type II population probably greatly exceeds the type I population in our galaxy.

Another item of great statistical interest is the relationship between the luminosities of the stars and their frequency of occurrence. The naked-eye stars are nearly all brighter than the sun. On the other hand, if a census is taken of the known stars within 20 light-years of the sun it is found that the opposite situation is true. Most of these stars are fainter than the sun (*see* Table II). The bright stars are easily seen at great distances; the faint ones can be detected only if they are close. For example, a star of absolute magnitude −4.0 would be visible to the unaided eye at a distance of 1,000 parsecs, whereas a star of magnitude +11 would be visible only if it fell closer than 1 parsec. That is, only if stars of magnitude +11 were 1,000,000,000 times more abundant in space than stars of magnitude −4 would one observe them in equal numbers, provided one observed all stars to some fixed limit of apparent brightness.

Table III gives the relation between the numbers of stars and their luminosities for stars in the neighbourhood of the sun. Thus, in a cube 100 parsecs on a side one could expect to find about 18 stars between the 4th and 5th magnitude and 80 stars between the 10th and 11th, but there would be less than one chance in a thousand of finding a star brighter than −5. The fainter end of the luminosity function is not well established. It appears to have a maximum near the 14th magnitude and to fall off to yet fainter stars in a fashion not yet established.

The luminosity function depends on the part of the galaxy under consideration. The neighbourhood of the sun includes examples of both populations type I and II. For a pure population type II the luminosity function will differ substantially from that of a pure population type I. Also, the luminosity function changes with distance from the galactic plane and, of course, with the age of the sample studied.

One of the most important correlations is that between mass and luminosity for main sequence (dwarf) stars. If one takes the visual binaries for which good parallaxes and masses are known and plots the mass of each star against its bolometric luminosity one finds that the points tend to fall on a curve which shows that the more massive stars are simultaneously the more luminous. Discussions by various astronomers show that for stars in the neighbourhood of the sun the luminosity is very nearly proportional to the fourth power of the mass, the actual relation being

$$L \cong \text{constant } M^{3.8} \tag{10}$$

where $L$ and $M$ are expressed in terms of the luminosity and mass of the sun respectively. The constant is very nearly unity; *i.e.*, the sun lies on the mass-luminosity curve defined by the nearby stars. The relationship is not a precise one, because for each mass there does not correspond a unique luminosity. In fact, a small range in luminosity exists for main sequence stars as a consequence of stellar evolution. A range also seems to exist because of chemical composition differences.

The mass-luminosity correlation is derived from visual double star systems and applies to main sequence stars. It fails for giants and supergiants and for the faint components of eclipsing binaries that usually are subgiants. Also it does not apply to any of the stars in a globular cluster brighter than absolute magnitude $M = +4.0$, or, in other words, stars other than those that fall on the main sequence.

TABLE III.—*Relation Between Numbers of Stars and Their Luminosities*

| Absolute magnitude | Numbers of stars | Absolute magnitude | Numbers of stars |
|---|---|---|---|
| −5.5 | 0.00040 | + 3.5 | 10.5 |
| −4.5 | 0.0024 | + 4.5 | 18.5 |
| −3.5 | 0.0085 | + 5.5 | 27.0 |
| −2.5 | 0.030 | + 6.5 | 36.0 |
| −1.5 | 0.093 | + 7.5 | 46.0 |
| −0.5 | 0.270 | + 8.5 | 56 |
| +0.5 | 0.80 | + 9.5 | 68 |
| +1.5 | 2.20 | +10.5 | 80 |
| +2.5 | 5.2 | +11.5 | 91 |

Source: Compiled from data of W. J. Luyten and P. J. van Rhijn.

The white dwarfs have long been known to fall off the mass-luminosity correlation; these stars are abnormally faint for their masses. They represent defunct stars near the end of their evolution, objects which have exhausted their nuclear fuel and presumably now are simply cooling down.

The mass-luminosity correlation was predicted theoretically by Eddington. It is a general relationship which holds for all stars built on essentially the same internal density and temperature distributions: *i.e.*, the same models. The types of stars for which it fails are those built on models different from those appropriate for main sequence stars.

## VI. STELLAR STRUCTURE

The internal pressures, temperatures and densities of main sequence stars and particularly white dwarfs can be calculated with greater confidence than can the internal temperature and density of the earth. This is true because of the following basic physical principles:

First, we suppose that the star is in mechanical equilibrium. That is, at each point the pressure exactly balances the weight of the overlying layers. If $g$ is the acceleration of gravity, $\rho$ is the density and $\Delta P$ the increase in pressure over a small increment in distance $\Delta r$, then

$$\Delta P = g\rho\Delta r \tag{11}$$

A second equation expresses the continuity of mass. That is, if $M_r$ is the mass of material lying in a sphere within a radius $r$, the amount of mass added when one goes a distance $\Delta r$ through a shell of volume $4\pi r^2\Delta r$ is:

$$\Delta M = 4\pi r^2\rho\Delta r \tag{12}$$

The third relation involved is what is called an equation of state; it expresses the relation between the pressure, density and temperature of the material. Throughout the body of the star the material is entirely gaseous. In most stars it obeys closely the perfect gas law:

$$P = \frac{\Re\rho T}{\mu} \tag{13}$$

Here $P$ is the pressure (usually expressed in dynes per square centimetre although it may also be given in atmospheres), $\rho$ is the density (g. per cubic centimetre) and $T$ is absolute temperature (° K.). $\Re$ is the gas constant (defined for a gram molecule of material). Finally, $\mu$ is the molecular weight: 2 for molecular hydrogen, 4 for helium and 56 for iron vapour. In the interior of a typical star, however, almost all of the material is completely ionized. Under these circumstances the hydrogen molecules are not only broken down into individual atoms but the atoms themselves are broken down (ionized) into protons and electrons. Hence, the molecular weight of ionized hydrogen is $\frac{1}{2}$, since the average mass of a proton and an electron is $\frac{1}{2}$ on the atom weight scale. On the other hand, a completely ionized helium atom contributes a mass of 4 with 2 electrons of negligible mass; hence the molecular weight is $\frac{4}{3}$. A completely ionized nickel atom contributes one nucleus of mass 58.7 plus 28 electrons; hence, its molecular weight is $\frac{58.7}{29} = 2.02$. Since stars contain a preponderance of hydrogen and helium which are completely ionized throughout the interior,

$$\mu = \frac{1}{2X + (3/4)Y + \alpha(1 - X - Y)} \tag{14}$$

where $X$ and $Y$ are the concentrations by weight of hydrogen and helium, respectively, and $\alpha$ is nearly $\frac{1}{2}$. Hence the molecular weight will depend critically on the chemical composition, particularly on the ratio of hydrogen to helium and the total content of heavier material.

If the temperature is sufficiently high, the radiation pressure, which is numerically equal to one-third of the energy density, must also be taken into account. Hence the total equation of state is

$$P = P_g + P_r = \frac{\Re\rho T}{\mu} + \frac{1}{3}aT^4 \tag{15}$$

where $a = 7.56 \times 10^{-15}$ is called the radiation density constant. Set $\mu = 2$ (upper limit), $\rho = 1.4$ g. per cubic centimetre (mean density of sun) and calculate the temperature at which the radiation pressure would equal the gas pressure. With $\Re = 8.32 \times 10^7$ the required temperature is 28,000,000°, which is much hotter than the centre of the sun, where the density is about 100 times that of water. Hence radiation pressure in the sun may be neglected, but it cannot be neglected in hotter, more massive stars. Radiation pressure may indeed set an upper limit to stellar luminosity (as Eddington suggested long ago).

Certain stars, notably the white dwarfs, do not obey the perfect gas law. Instead, the pressure is almost entirely contributed by the electrons, which obey a law called the degenerate gas law. The pressure and density are related by a law of the form

$$P = 9.9 \times 10^{12}\left(\frac{\rho}{\mu'}\right)^{\frac{5}{3}} \tag{16}$$

where $\mu'$ is the average mass per free electron of the totally ionized gas. Notice that the temperature does not enter at all. At yet higher densities the equation of state becomes more intricate, but S. Chandrasekhar showed in elegant fashion how even this complicated equation of state could be employed in the calculation of the internal structure of these white dwarf stars. There are probably better models for the white dwarfs than for most other objects.

In order to make further progress it must be known how energy is transported in the interior. Thermal conduction cannot play any significant role inasmuch as the heat conductivity of gases is very low. One mode of transport is the actual flow of radiation through the star. Starting out as X-rays the radiation is gradually "softened" as it works its way to the surface to emerge as ordinary light and heat. The rate of flow of radiation is proportional to the temperature gradient, $\Delta T/\Delta r$, the rate of change of temperature with distance. Specifically,

$$\text{Rate of energy flow} = \frac{4acT^3}{3\kappa\rho}\left(\frac{\Delta T}{\Delta r}\right) \tag{17}$$

Here $a$ is the radiation density constant, $c$ is the velocity of light, $\rho$ is the density and $\kappa$ is a measure of the opacity of the material. That is, the larger the value of $\kappa$, the smaller the transparency of the material and the steeper the temperature fall required to push the energy outward at the required rate. The opacity $\kappa$ can be calculated for any temperature, density and chemical composition. The actual computations are difficult; $\kappa$ is found to depend in a complicated way on the density and temperature.

In the outer layers of the sun and particularly in certain giant stars, transport of energy takes place by quite another mechanism: large-scale mass motions of gases or convection. Large volumes of gas deep within the star become heated, rise to higher layers and mix with their surroundings, thus releasing great quantities of energy. The extremely complicated flow patterns cannot be followed in detail, but when convection occurs there exists a relatively simple relation between pressure and density, namely

$$P = K\rho^\gamma \tag{18}$$

where $\gamma$ is $\frac{5}{3}$ for a completely ionized gas and $K$ is a constant of proportionality.

Finally, the most fundamental property of stars must be considered, namely, that they radiate energy and hence must derive their energy from sources within themselves. For normal main sequence stars such as the sun, the source of the energy lies in the conversion of hydrogen into helium. The reaction believed to occur in the sun is the proton-proton reaction proposed first by H. Bethe and R. Critchfield and later revised by C. C. Lauritsen and W. A. Fowler and independently by E. Schatzman. The reactions are:

$$\begin{aligned} {}_1H^1 + {}_1H^1 &\rightarrow {}_1H^2 + (\epsilon^+) \\ {}_1H^1 + {}_1H^2 &\rightarrow {}_2He^3 + \gamma \\ {}_2He^3 + {}_2He^3 &\rightarrow {}_2He^4 + 2H^1 \end{aligned} \tag{19}$$

Two protons collide to form a deuteron (heavy hydrogen nucleus) with the liberation of a beta ray, or positive electron (positron). This positive electron meets a negative electron and the two annihilate one another with the liberation of energy in accordance with the Einstein relation

$$E = mc^2 \tag{20}$$

where $m$ is the mass annihilated, $c$ is the velocity of light and $E$ is the energy released. Here $m$ is the mass of the two electrons. The annihilation energy amounts to 1.02 Mev. This process is one of low probability, and many proton-proton collisions occur before a positive electron is created.

Next, a proton collides with the deuteron to form the nucleus of the light helium atom of atomic weight 3. Finally, two light helium nuclei collide to form a nucleus of ordinary helium and two protons. In the course of this reaction four protons have been consumed to form one helium nucleus, and two negative electrons have perished.

The mass of four hydrogen atoms is $4 \times 1.00797 = 4.03188$; that of a helium atom is 4.0026. Hence 0.02928 atomic mass units or 0.7% of the original mass has disappeared. Some of this has disappeared in the form of the elusive neutrinos, but most of it has been converted into radiant energy. To keep shining at its present rate, the sun has to convert 674,000,000 tons of hydrogen into 670,000,000 tons of helium every second. More than 4,000,000 tons of matter literally disappear into radiation every second. The rate of energy generation according to the proton-proton reaction varies as about the fourth power of the temperature.

In hotter stars the principal source of energy is the carbon cycle, in which hydrogen is converted into helium with carbon serving as a catalyst. The reactions are as follows: First, a carbon nucleus captures a hydrogen nucleus or proton to form a nucleus of $N^{13}$, thus

$$C^{12} + H^1 \rightarrow N^{13} + \gamma \tag{21}$$

A gamma ray is emitted in the process. The light $N^{13}$ nucleus is unstable, however. It emits a positive electron which encounters a negative electron and the two annihilate one another. The resulting $C^{13}$ nucleus is stable. Eventually the $C^{13}$ nucleus captures another proton, forms $N^{14}$ and emits another gamma ray.

$$\begin{aligned} N^{13} &\rightarrow C^{13} + \epsilon^+ \\ C^{13} + H^1 &\rightarrow N^{14} + \gamma \end{aligned} \tag{22}$$

The $N^{14}$ is stable, ordinary nitrogen. When it captures a proton to form $O^{15}$, the resulting nucleus is unstable against beta decay. That is, it emits a positive electron.

$$\begin{aligned} N^{14} + H^1 &\rightarrow O^{15} + \gamma \\ O^{15} &\rightarrow N^{15} + \epsilon^+ \end{aligned} \tag{23}$$

That is, the $O^{15}$ nucleus emits a positive electron that meets a negative electron and is annihilated. Eventually the $N^{15}$ nucleus encounters a fast-moving proton and captures it. It might be supposed that at this point a nucleus of ordinary $O^{16}$ would be formed. Actually this process occurs rarely, the favoured reaction being

$$N^{15} + H^1 \rightarrow C^{12} + He^4 + \gamma \tag{24}$$

The capture of the proton causes the resultant nucleus to break down into the original $C^{12}$ nucleus and an alpha particle, or helium nucleus of mass 4. Thus, the original carbon nucleus reappears, and the four protons that have been added permit the formation of an alpha particle. The same amount of mass has disappeared although a different fraction of it may have been carried off by the neutrinos.

The physicist with his particle accelerator produces these reactions by firing protons with hundreds or even thousands of kilovolts of energy at targets of graphite or nitrogen compounds. Since both the heavy nucleus and the proton have positive charges, they repel one another by Coulomb's law. Occasionally the particles come close enough together for short-range attractive forces in the nucleus to allow the proton to stick. The higher the energy involved, the greater the probability of proton capture.

In the interior of a star the particles are moving rapidly about as a consequence of their high energies. Once in a while a proton is directed sufficiently close to a nucleus for it to be captured so that a nuclear reaction can occur. Only the protons of very highest energy (many times the average energy in a star like the sun) are capable of producing reactions. Since the energies of the protons depend very strongly on the temperature, the rate of energy production rises steeply with the temperature. The temperature dependence is much steeper for the carbon-nitrogen cycle than it is for the proton-proton reaction.

The hottest stars of the main sequence (and probably also the supergiants) shine with energy produced by the carbon cycle. The faint red dwarf stars use exclusively the proton-proton reaction, whereas the sun shines mostly by the proton-proton reaction but has some contribution from the carbon cycle.

With the aid of the aforementioned mathematical relationships including the law of energy generation it is possible to attack the problem of stellar structure. In the first approximation it is usually assumed that the stars have a uniform chemical composition throughout their interiors. This assumption simplifies the calculations greatly, but it has to be abandoned when stellar evolution is concerned. The mathematical and physical relationships involved are such that solutions expressible in algebraic form or as functions of types known to mathematicians are not obtainable. The solutions have to be carried out numerically by a step-by-step process known as mechanical integration. At the surface the pressure and density vanish; at the centre of the star the pressure, density and temperature must remain finite. A frequent procedure is to carry the calculations from the surface inward and from the centre outward, the condition being that the two solutions must fit together, giving the same pressure, density, temperature, etc., when they meet. One of the most important generalizations that can be drawn from such calculations is the famous mass-luminosity relation, discovered by Eddington. It may be written in the form

$$L = C\frac{M^a\mu^b}{R^c} \tag{25}$$

where $M$ is the mass of the star, $\mu$ the molecular weight, and $R$ the radius. $C$ is a constant that depends on the particular numerical choice of physical relationships involved, for example, on the exact value of the opacity. Here $a$, $b$ and $c$ are constants that also depend for their precise values on the exact form of the law of opacity, for example. Numerically, $a$ is of the order of 5, $b$ of 7 or 8 and $c$ about 1.5. This means that the luminosity depends steeply on the mass but even more steeply on the molecular weight and therefore on the chemical composition. A relationship of this type must exist because the greater the mass, the greater the internal pressure and, therefore, by equation (15), the greater the internal temperature. The temperature gradient likewise increases and, therefore, so does the outward flux of energy.

Still another relationship between luminosity, mass, radius and molecular weight is derived from temperature, density distribution and the known nuclear energy sources. For a star shining on the carbon cycle a relation is obtained of the form

$$L = B(1 - X - Y)\mu^d\frac{M^e}{R^f} \tag{26}$$

where $X$ and $Y$ are the proportions by weight of hydrogen and helium, respectively. Here $d$ is of the order of 20, $e$ about 22 and $f$ about 23 since the carbon cycle depends on a high power of the temperature. This equation is called the energy output relation and was used by Schwarzschild to demonstrate how, for a given model, one could obtain both the hydrogen and the helium contents.

Calculations of stellar models have occupied the attention of astronomers for a number of years. For young main sequence stars it is possible to obtain satisfactory solutions with a chemical composition that is uniform throughout the star. In the sun and fainter stars of the main sequence energy is transported throughout the outer layers by convection currents whereas in the deep interior, energy is transported by radiation. Among the hotter stars of the main sequence the reverse appears to be true. The deep interiors of stars which derive their energy primarily from the carbon cycle are in convective equilibrium whereas in the outer parts the energy is carried by radiation. It is possible to reproduce the observed masses, luminosities and radii of main sequence stars with reasonable assumptions concerning their chemical composition.

Chemically homogeneous models of giant and supergiant stars cannot be constructed. That is, if it is assumed that a yellow giant star such as Capella is built on the same model as the sun or other main sequence stars, the central temperature will turn out to be so low that no known nuclear process can possibly supply the observed energy output. Progress has been made only by assuming that these stars were once main sequence objects which, in the course of their lives, exhausted the hydrogen in their deep interiors. As a consequence these stars developed inert cores composed mostly of helium, which is the ash of the hydrogen burning processes. Since helium is impervious to nuclear reactions at the few tens of millions degrees and the densities likely to prevail in these interiors, no thermonuclear energy could be obtained from these depleted cores. Energy is assumed to be generated in a thin shell surrounding the inert core and is presumably produced by the carbon-nitrogen cycle. Such models are called shell-source models. As the star uses up more and more of its hydrogen supply, the core increases in mass but the outer envelope of the star continues to expand in size. These shell-source models appear to be capable of explaining the observed luminosities, masses and radii of giant and supergiant stars.

The depletion of hydrogen fuel is appreciable even for a dwarf star such as the sun. The sun appears to be about 5,000,000,000 years old and to have been shining at its present rate for about 1,000,000,000 years. On the assumption that the sun was initially composed of about $\frac{4}{5}$ hydrogen by weight, Schwarzschild, Howard and Härm, found that at the present time the concentration of hydrogen in the centre of the sun must be only about 30% by weight. Furthermore, most of the sun was in radiative equilibrium, leaving only about 0.33% in the outer convection zone. In order to maintain its observed luminosity, the sun's central temperature has increased noticeably since the time the solar system was formed, largely as a consequence of the depletion of the hydrogen in the interior with the accompanying increase in molecular weight and temperature. As the sun has evolved it has also become brighter. Schwarzschild, Howard and Härm concluded that over the past 5,000,000,000 years the sun brightened by about half a magnitude, and they suggest that in the early Pre-Cambrian era (about 2,000,000,000 years ago) the solar luminosity was about 20% less than now. The average temperature on the earth's surface must have been about the freezing point of water. It is possible, of course, that the earth's atmosphere might then have acted as a more efficient heat trap and permitted the surface temperature of the earth to be actually higher than this rather cool value.

Table IV, giving results of one calculation of the internal structure of the sun, takes into account both the carbon cycle and the proton-proton reaction. At the centre of the sun the temperature is about 14,600,000° and the density is about 134 times that of water. Nevertheless, in spite of its high density the material is very nearly a perfect gas. Weymann's model takes into account the depletion of hydrogen in the interior of the sun, as a consequence of its evolution.

TABLE IV.—*Internal Structure of the Sun*

| r/R | Temperature (°A.) | Density (water = 1.0) | r/R | Temperature (°A.) | Density (water = 1.0) |
|---|---|---|---|---|---|
| 0.00 | 14,600,000 | 134 | 0.60 | 2,500,000 | 0.405 |
| 0.10 | 12,650,000 | 85.5 | 0.70 | 2,270,000 | 0.124 |
| 0.20 | 9,350,000 | 36.4 | 0.80 | 1,270,000 | 0.0354 |
| 0.30 | 6,650,000 | 12.9 | 0.90 | 605,000 | 0.00945 |
| 0.40 | 4,740,000 | 4.13 | 0.96 | 226,000 | 0.00217 |
| 0.50 | 3,430,000 | 1.30 | 0.98 | 111,000 | 0.00073 |

Source: After R. Weymann.

## VII. STELLAR EVOLUTION

From what has been said it is clear that one must anticipate some evolution among the stars. The aforementioned calculations by Schwarzschild and his co-workers of Princeton university show that these evolutionary effects have not been negligible even for the sun. For a more massive star the effects must be even more spectacular since the rate of conversion of mass into energy is increased. The sun produces energy at the rate of about 2 ergs per gram per second, but a luminous main sequence star may produce energy at the rate of 2,000 ergs per gram per second. Consequently, while evolutionary effects may require billions of years to be manifest in a star such as the sun, they may occur within a few millions of years in highly luminous stars. A supergiant star such as Antares, a bright main sequence star such as one of the belt stars of Orion or even a more modest star such as Sirius cannot have endured as long as the sun. Therefore, if it has existed for as long as 5,000,000,000 years it must have spent most of its life as a nonstellar object. Alternatively, these stars may have been formed relatively recently in the history of the galaxy. Thus, one might expect to find within the galaxy (and even within the neighbourhood of the sun itself) stars that are well evolved and/or even approaching extinction, as well as occasional stars that must be very young or even in the process of formation. First, let us examine the life history of a star as it can best be envisaged on the basis of modern theories of physics and stellar evolution. Stars are presumably formed from the grains and gas in the interstellar medium. The material between the stars is not uniformly distributed in space but is spread in a patchy fashion. Occasionally a cloud will form sufficiently massive for gravitational attractions to draw it together.

As it begins to pull itself together, the internal temperature and density start to rise until finally the star breaks into incandescence with a faint red glow. At this stage the star is still shining by its gravitational contraction; *i.e.*, by the conversion of potential energy into heat. As the internal temperatures rise to a few million degrees, deuterium (heavy hydrogen) is first destroyed. Then lithium, beryllium and boron are broken down into helium as their nuclei are bombarded by protons moving at high velocities.

Detailed calculations published by E. Salpeter, by L. Henyey and his associates, and by C. Hayashi show that a star originally falls above the main sequence because it is too bright for its colour. As it contracts it moves downward and to the left toward the main sequence.

Finally, as the central temperature and density continue to rise, a state is reached where the proton-proton or carbon cycle reaction becomes active and the development of the star is stabilized. The star then reaches the main sequence, where it remains for most of its active life. The time required for the contraction phase depends on the mass of the star. A star of the sun's mass may require millions of years to reach the main sequence, while one of much greater mass may reach the main sequence in a few hundred thousand years.

By the time the star reaches the main sequence it is still chemically homogeneous. As time goes on and the hydrogen in the core is converted into helium, the temperature slowly rises to compensate for the depletion of the fuel. If the star is sufficiently massive to have a convective core, the material in this region has a chance to be thoroughly mixed, but the outer region does not mix with the core. In the sun, on the other hand, there is no convective core and the helium-hydrogen ratio is maximum at the centre and decreases outward. During the lifetime of the sun there has been a steady depletion of the hydrogen so that at the centre the concentration of hydrogen is probably only about one third of the original amount. The rest has all been converted to helium.

The rate of evolution depends strongly on the mass of the star. In the sun the effects are only slightly manifest (they could not have been found if observers had not been seeking them). A star of twice the sun's mass burns its energy at such a rate that it cannot last more than about 3,000,000,000 years, whereas a star of ten times the sun's mass has a lifetime measured in tens of millions of years.

As the composition of the star's interior becomes seriously modified it begins to move away from the main sequence, slowly at first, and then more rapidly. When about 10% of the star's mass has been converted into helium, the structure of the star changes drastically. The core becomes inert. That is, all the hydrogen has been burned out and this central region is composed almost entirely of helium with small admixtures of heavier elements. The energy production now takes place in a thin shell where hydrogen is consumed and added to the inert core. The outer portion of the star expands outward, and as the star swells up it may gradually rise in luminosity. The details of the evolution depend on the hydrogen-metal ratio, and the course of evolution will differ for stars of the two population types.

Consider first a globular cluster (fig. 8). The main sequence does not extend to stars brighter than absolute magnitude +3.5. The giant sequence begins at this point and extends on the colour magnitude diagram to the right and vertically upward for several magnitudes. Then it gradually bends over, the most luminous stars in the cluster being the red giants. This colour-magnitude diagram exhibits the effects of stellar evolution. All main sequence stars more massive than about 1.5 solar masses have evolved off the main sequence and most of them have died. The colour-magnitude array then represents an evolutionary picture of the cluster. The giant branch is not, strictly speaking, the path of evolution but rather the locus or envelope of evolutionary paths. It represents a snapshot of stars of different masses but of the same age. Presumably the stars leave the main sequence and evolve into stars of steadily increasing luminosity until they reach the peak of the diagram. Then what? Presumably later stages of evolution are connected with the horizontal branch at absolute magnitude zero where the RR Lyrae stars and other blue objects are found. The last stages of evolution are represented by the white dwarfs which are too faint to be detected in globular clusters, but they must be present there in great numbers.

F. Hoyle and Schwarzschild have calculated the evolutionary track of a star from the point where it leaves the main sequence until it reaches the top of the giant branch. When the core of the star becomes depleted of hydrogen, the energy generation is confined to a narrow shell and the outer part of the star becomes distended. That is, the star swells up and moves to the right in the colour-magnitude array. The energy is carried outward by large-scale convection currents. By the time about 20% of the total mass of hydrogen has been converted into helium, these convection currents have become so rapid that they approach the velocity of sound. Then as the star evolves upward in the diagram, the temperature in the energy-producing shell begins to rise, slowly at first, then more rapidly until near the top of the giant sequence the central temperature reaches a value of about 40,000,000° K. While this is happening the total energy output of the star rises, and the core shrinks by gravitational contraction. Eventually, it may become a degenerate gas. The compression of the core raises its temperature and density until the core reaches a temperature of about 120,000,000° K. At that temperature, the previously inert helium is quickly consumed in the production of heavier elements. Much of the energy released is expended in speeding up the core electrons and removing the degeneracy of the gas. It never escapes from the star.

If two helium nuclei are jammed together one might expect them to form a nucleus of beryllium of mass 8, thus

$$_2He^4 + {_2He^4} \rightarrow {_4Be^8} \quad (27)$$

Actually $_4Be^8$ is unstable and breaks down again quickly into two helium nuclei. If the density and temperature are high enough, however, the ephemeral $Be^8$ nucleus may capture another helium nucleus to form a nucleus of $C^{12}$, thus

$$_4Be^8 + {_2He^4} \rightarrow {_6C^{12}} \quad (28)$$

and reactions such as

$$\begin{aligned} {_6C^{12}} + {_2He^4} &\rightarrow {_8O^{16}} \\ {_8O^{16}} + {_2He^4} &\rightarrow {_{10}Ne^{20}} \\ {_{10}Ne^{20}} + {_2He^4} &\rightarrow {_{12}Mg^{24}} \end{aligned} \quad (29)$$

may also occur. The energy output of helium burning (per ton of material) is much less than for hydrogen burning. The evolution of the star beyond this "helium-flash" stage is highly uncertain. The star presumably moves quickly to the horizontal branch of the colour-magnitude diagram but its lifetime there is not long. Presumably it evolves to bluer colours and lower luminosities but certainly ends as a white dwarf. The energy output of the white dwarfs is so low that they may go on shining by radiating away their store of energy until none is left to emit. The final stage of a star is a ball not much larger than the earth, but with a density 50,000 times that of water, possibly covered with a thin layer of ice and surrounded by an atmosphere of hydrogen and helium a few feet thick.

One of the interesting results of the calculations by Hoyle, A. R. Sandage and Schwarzschild is a determination of the ages of globular clusters. The critical datum is the point in the colour magnitude diagram at which the main sequence ends. In some globular clusters it appears that this point falls below a solar mass. Such objects are presumably ten thousand million years old or older. The results are strongly influenced by observational uncertainties. Certainly, the globular clusters are very ancient

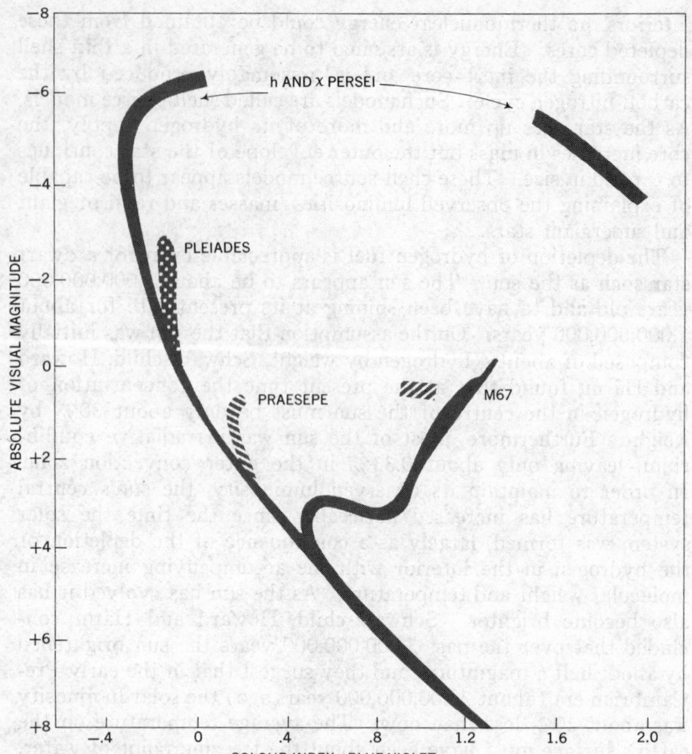


FROM "ASTROPHYSICAL JOURNAL"; REPRODUCED BY PERMISSION OF THE UNIVERSITY OF CHICAGO PRESS

**FIG. 9.—COLOUR-MAGNITUDE ARRAYS FOR FOUR GALACTIC CLUSTERS OF DIFFERENT AGES**

objects, probably among the oldest in our galactic system.

Turning to population type I a very different situation is found. If the colour-magnitude arrays for different galactic clusters are compared, the situation is that exhibited in fig. 9. In the double cluster h and $\chi$ Persei the main sequence extends to about magnitude −6 where it turns off abruptly to the right. There are also a few red supergiant stars. The Pleiades main sequence turns upward from the usual main sequence at about magnitude 0 but there are no giant stars while the Praesepe (Beehive cluster in Cancer) shows a giant sequence and a main sequence that is curved up at about +2. The cluster M67 has a colour-magnitude array that resembles superficially that of the giant branch of a globular cluster, except that there is no horizontal branch and the most luminous giants are much fainter than the globular cluster giants.

The feature distinguishing these different clusters is their different ages. The youngest cluster, the pair h and $\chi$ Persei, contains stars of a great range in luminosity. Some stars have already evolved into the supergiant stage so that the top end of the main sequence is bent over. The stars of luminosity greater than 10,000 times that of the sun have already largely depleted the hydrogen in their cores and are leaving the main sequence.

The brightest stars of the Pleiades (Alcyone, Maia, Taygeta, etc.) have started to leave the main sequence and are approaching the critical phase when they will have exhausted all the hydrogen in their cores. There are no giants in the Pleiades. Presumably the cluster contained no stars as massive as some of those found in h and $\chi$ Persei. The cluster is also older than the double cluster.

The Beehive or Praesepe cluster is still older than the Pleiades. All stars much more luminous than Procyon (+3) have started to leave the main sequence, and there are some giants. The Hyades display a similar colour-magnitude array. These clusters contain a number of white dwarfs, indicating that the initially most luminous stars have already run the full gamut of evolution. Finally, M67 must be the oldest cluster of all; the best data of stellar structure indicate that it is several thousand million years old. All the bright main sequence stars have long since disappeared.

Some estimated ages of typical galactic clusters, judged from

TABLE V.—*Estimated Ages of Typical Galactic Clusters*

| Cluster | Age (millions of years) | Cluster | Age (millions of years) |
|---|---|---|---|
| Orion association | <1 | Praesepe | 320 |
| h and χ Persei | 12 | Hyades | 700 |
| Pleiades | 50 | M67 | 5,000 |

Source: After Sandage (1958), Lohmann (1957), and Von Hoerner (1957).

the turnoff points of the main sequence, are given in Table V.

Hoyle and Schwarzschild were also able to establish that the difference between the giant branches in M67 and in the globular clusters was to be attributed to differences in chemical composition, in particular to the hydrogen-metal ratio. In the type II stars, they took the ratio of hydrogen to the metals by numbers as 135,000 (in accordance with the spectroscopic data for the subdwarfs) whereas for the type I stars they took a ratio of 10,000. The population type I giant stars, as a consequence of their larger metal contents, produced a more extended envelope and hence later spectral classes.

The giant stars of the Praesepe are comparable with the brightest stars in M67. Now the M67 giants have evolved from the main sequence near absolute magnitude +3.5, whereas the Praesepe giants must have evolved from main sequence stars of absolute magnitude about +0.5. Consequently, the Praesepe giants must have masses about twice as great as those of the M67 giants. Thus the failure of the mass-luminosity law for giant stars is easily understood. Giant stars of the same luminosity may therefore have appreciably different masses.

An example in point is provided by the components of the giant star Capella, for which K. O. Wright found masses three times that of the sun, whereas each component of the giant binary TW Cancri has a mass 1.3 times that of the sun, according to D. M. Popper. Thus Capella is presumably a relatively young star, TW Cancri an ancient one.

Several other differences between the various galactic clusters are to be noted. The M67 giant sequence is continuous with the main sequence, whereas there is an appreciable gap between the giant and main sequence stars in the Praesepe and a much wider one in h and χ Persei. One suspects that these vacant regions are connected with domains of instability in the structure of the star.

One interesting fact noted by R. Kraft and John Irwin was that several Cepheids are found in galactic clusters, and in each instance where the colour-magnitude arrays can be constructed the Cepheid appears to fall in the gap.

If some star clusters such as h and χ Persei are only a few million years old, whereas others such as the Hyades are a thousand million years old, the process of star formation in clusters must be going on at the present time, and we ought to be able to catch occasional stars or groups of stars in the process of formation. G. Herbig and G. Haro have found evidence that the T Tauri stars, variables found only in regions where there are great quantities of interstellar dust and gas, are stars in the process of formation. They probably are still contracting and have not yet started to shine by thermonuclear hydrogen burning reactions.

Some of the most striking evidence for star formation was found by Parenago in the region of the Orion nebula and by M. F. Walker in the cluster associated with S Monocerotis NGC 2264.

## VIII. FORMATION OF THE ELEMENTS IN STARS

Many years ago in an anonymous communication to a scientific journal William Prout proposed the hypothesis that all elements originated from hydrogen. Although this suggestion gathered dust for many years it has been revived in connection with the possible origin of elements within stars. Astronomers and nuclear physicists have devoted much effort to this problem.

The first investigation of the abundances of elements was undertaken by F. W. Clarke and H. S. Washington, who analyzed samples of the earth's crust. Later, V. M. Goldschmidt pointed out that a much more representative sample of the probable composition of our part of the universe could be obtained from meteorites, at least as far as nonvolatile constituents were concerned. Finally, in his pioneering analysis of the sun, Russell gave the first clear perspective of the relative abundances of the elements in our part of the universe. Subsequent work has revised and extended Russell's early results; in particular, it has demonstrated the overwhelming preponderance of hydrogen and helium, compared with which all other elements can be regarded as mere impurities. Table VI, based largely on work at the University of Michigan on the composition of the sun and early-type stars, gives the most abundant elements (by numbers) in a representative sample of our part of the universe.

Among the elements lighter than iron which have even atomic numbers, those with atomic numbers divisible by four tend to be most abundant (rule of Oddo and Harkins). Other abundance effects have been noted; the abundances of light elements tend to be greater than those of heavier elements. That is, a plot of abundance against atomic weight, *A*, shows a decline with increasing *A* to about *A* = 100. Thereafter the abundance is more nearly constant. A plot of numbers of atoms against atomic weight or number is far from smooth. Aside from the irregularities produced by the rule of Oddo and Harkins there are huge fluctuations for certain elements. Thus lithium, beryllium and boron are very rare compared with carbon, nitrogen or oxygen. There is a pronounced abundance peak at iron and less conspicuous peaks at other elements, often connected with the so-called magic number nuclei. There is also a maximum at lead, the most stable of heavy elements.

TABLE VI.—*The Most Abundant Elements* (*by Numbers*)
(Silicon = 10,000)

| Element | Abundance | Element | Abundance |
|---|---|---|---|
| H | $3.2 \times 10^8$ | P | 79 |
| He | $5.1 \times 10^7$ | S | 7,100 |
| C | 125,000 | Cl | 550 |
| N | 35,000 | Ar | 2,400 |
| O | 280,000 | K | 16 |
| F | 300 | Ca | 470 |
| Ne | 141,000 | Ti | 17 |
| Na | 89 | Cr | 52 |
| Mg | 8,000 | Mn | 30 |
| Al | 525 | Fe | 1,250 |
| Si | 10,000 | Ni | 280 |

Astronomers and physicists believe that the abundance curve of the elements provides definite clues as to their origins. The preponderance of hydrogen suggests that perhaps all nuclei were built up from protons. G. Gamow suggested that the elements were created as the consequence of the expansion of a huge mass consisting of neutrons. As the density decreased the neutrons decayed into protons and electrons. The protons then captured neutrons, one after another, underwent beta decay (ejection of electrons) and built up heavy elements. The big difficulty with this hypothesis is that atomic masses 5 and 8 are unstable and there is no way to build nuclei beyond helium. Other difficulties have been pointed out, and the Gamow hypothesis must be greatly modified or discarded.

The alternative hypothesis to the effect that heavy elements are built in stars has much to recommend it. Consider, first of all, the following observation facts. Not all stars have the same chemical composition. A long time ago R. H. Curtiss pointed out that the splitting in the spectral sequence among the cooler stars could be understood in terms of composition differences. The R and N stars contain more carbon than oxygen, whereas the S stars appear to have an enhanced content of zirconium as compared with titanium. From a more detailed spectroscopic study of the cool stars, P. W. Merrill has found evidence for differences in both the carbon-oxygen ratios and in the ratio of the zirconium group to titanium group of metals. The M stars appear to have a "normal" (*i.e.* Solar) composition with oxygen more abundant than carbon and the zirconium group of elements much less abundant than the titanium group.

Other abundance anomalies are found in the Wolf-Rayet stars where objects containing predominantly helium, carbon and oxygen are distinguished from objects containing helium and nitrogen, some carbon and small quantities of oxygen.

Significantly, all these abundance anomalies are found in stars believed to be well advanced in their evolutionary development.

No main sequence dwarf stars show such effects.

The most critical observation, however, was Merrill's detection of the unstable element technetium in the S stars. The element has been produced on the earth synthetically. The longest lived isotope $Tc^{99}_{43}$, which can be produced by neutron capture, has a half life of 200,000 years and can be formed by the following reaction:

$$Mo^{98} + n \rightarrow Mo^{99}$$
$$Mo^{99} \rightarrow Tc^{99} + \beta^- \quad (30)$$

That is, molybdenum of mass 98 captures a neutron to form molybdenum of mass 99, which decays (in about 67 hours) to form technetium of mass 99 with the ejection of a negative electron. Furthermore, the Tc in the S stars appears to be about as abundant as the neighbouring elements, ruthenium and molybdenum. The implication is that all these elements were built in the S stars and that these objects have lifetimes of about 200,000 years. How the star gets the heavy elements from the core to the surface without exploding is unknown at present.

Work by the Burbidges, F. Hoyle, W. Fowler and A. G. W. Cameron has demonstrated how elements may be built in stars by nuclear processes occurring at very high temperatures and densities. No one mechanism can account for all the elements, and several distinct processes have been proposed.

The great abundance of helium is easily understood. It is the normal "ash" of hydrogen consumption. In the dense cores of massive stars the helium itself may be consumed to form $C^{12}$, $O^{16}$, $Ne^{20}$ and $Mg^{24}$. At yet higher temperatures a host of nuclear reactions may occur to produce the elements up to iron. Heavy elements such as zirconium cannot be produced in this manner, but apparently only by the capture of neutrons.

Cameron suggested that the light isotope of carbon, $C^{13}$, could get mixed into the helium core and combine with alpha particles (helium nuclei) to produce $O^{16}$ and neutrons as follows:

$$C^{13} + He^4 \rightarrow O^{16} + n + (2.6 \text{ Mev}) \text{ energy} \quad (31)$$

These neutrons are available for capture by heavier nuclei, particularly those with large target areas, to form yet heavier elements. Thus the elements of the zirconium group, for example, could be built from lighter elements by successive neutron capture. Fowler and the Burbidges suggested other nuclear processes that could result in the production of neutrons and the subsequent formation of heavy elements. They concluded that about 40% of the iron in a mixture will be transformed into heavier elements if about 20 neutrons could be produced for every iron atom in the mixture.

After a given nucleus captures a neutron, it may find itself too heavy for its charge and decay into the nucleus of the element next to it in atomic number. Beta decay is often very slow, and if the flux of neutrons is high the nucleus may capture another neutron before it can undergo decay. Hoyle suggested that in supernovae explosions vast quantities of neutrons are produced and these result in the rapid build-up of massive elements. One interesting feature of the building up of heavy elements by neutron capture at a high rate in a supernova explosion is that nuclei much heavier than lead or uranium can be built. In particular, nuclei of the synthetic element californium 254 may be produced; these nuclei decay by spontaneous fission with a half life of 55 days.

Hoyle, the Burbidges and Fowler suggest that the vast supplies of energy liberated in supernovae outbursts may be connected with this reaction since the light curve of a supernova closely resembles the decay curve of $Cf^{254}$. In any event it is not possible to explain all the different kinds of isotopes of all the elements with their proper abundance ratios without invoking several different mechanisms. Thus helium clearly comes from hydrogen burning; carbon, oxygen, neon and magnesium come from the subsequent consumption of helium in three particle reactions.

The abundance peak at iron is presumed to be produced by an equilibrium between various types of nuclei set up at enormously high temperatures and densities—possibly in supernovae.

Some nuclei must be produced by neutron captures that proceed at a leisurely rate. Thus, whatever produces the neutrons in the cores of the S stars does so in such a way that the neutrons are captured by nuclei at such a rate that these new nuclei may undergo beta decay (ejection of positive or negative electrons) before a new neutron is captured. Other nuclei must be produced by the rapid capture of neutrons by nuclei in such a way that beta decay cannot occur before another neutron is captured.

No known nuclear process is capable of producing deuterium (heavy hydrogen), lithium, beryllium and boron in stellar interiors. They are probably produced by the breaking down of heavier elements, such as iron and magnesium, by high energy particles in stellar atmospheres or in the early stages of stellar formation. Presumably these high energy particles originate as a consequence of electromagnetic disturbances in the neighbourhood of sunspots and are probably connected with such things as flares, which may be more active in early stages of a star's gravitational contraction to form a stable body.

Finally, in certain of the magnetic stars, some elements such as the rare earths have enormously enhanced abundances. Possibly the nuclei of these elements also are produced by high energy reactions involving electromagnetic accelerations of charged particles. *See* ASTROPHYSICS; COSMOGONY; COSMOLOGY; CELESTIAL MECHANICS; *see* also references under "Star" in the Index.

BIBLIOGRAPHY.—G. O. Abell, *Exploration of the Universe* (1964); D. B. McLaughlin, *Introduction to Astronomy* (1961); L. H. Aller, *Astrophysics*, 2nd ed. (1963), *Abundance of the Elements* (1961); M. Schwarzschild, *Structure and Evolution of the Stars* (1958); G. P. Kuiper and B. Middlehurst (ed.), *Stars and Stellar Systems*, vol. 3, 5, 6, 7, 8 (1960). (L. H. A.)

**STARCH** is a plant substance that is a major constituent of man's diet. Its molecules are composed of hundreds of sugar molecules joined together chemically, and it is these sugar units, freed during digestion, that are used by humans, and other animal organisms, to produce energy that maintains life. In plants, starch serves as a reserve food supply, and during their earliest period of development, new seedlings make use of starch that is stored in the seed. In industry, starch is used as a stiffening agent and as a component of paper, textiles, adhesives, explosives, and cosmetics.

**Occurrence and General Properties.**—Starch is found in transitory form in green leaves, where its chemical synthesis from carbon dioxide, water, etc., is begun. For transfer to more permanent storage areas, the polymeric starch molecules are broken down, and the resulting sugars dissolve in the sap, pass through the cell walls, and are reconverted to starch in new locations. Cellulose, an important constituent of plant cell walls, is a similar polymer of sugar units, differing from starch chiefly in the way the sugars are joined together. Common storage areas for starch in plants are roots and tubers, such as tapioca and potato; stem piths, such as sago; and fruit and seeds, such as wheat and corn. In some seeds—corn grains, for example—starch may constitute as much as two-thirds of the total dry weight. Some tubers, *e.g.*, the white potato, contain more than 70% starch on a dry basis, but, because of the large proportion of water present, only about 11–22% on a wet basis.

Within the plant storage areas, the starch molecules are clustered together in tiny granules ranging from 2 to 150 $\mu$ in diameter. When separated from the plant, the granules show characteristic differences of shape and size depending on the source. Some types of starch have rounded granules, others have oval or polygonal ones. Potato starch grains are the largest of any commercial starch variety, and rice granules are the smallest. An experienced observer can usually identify the plant source of starch granules observed under the microscope. In plants the granules are remarkably resistant to the action of bacteria and molds.

When separated from the plant source, starch is a soft, white, shiny powder, insoluble in cold water, alcohol, and other solvents. Starch gives a strong blue colour with iodine, a reaction that is employed as a test for the presence of starch in various materials and as a technique for the quantitative determination of many substances having oxidizing properties (*see* IODINE: *Analytical Chemistry*). Starches of all types contain considerable moisture, averaging around 10–15%. When starch suspensions in water are heated above certain temperatures more or less characteristic of the type of starch, the granules swell and disintegrate to give viscous, opalescent dispersions. On cooling, the dispersions set to thick pastes.

**Early History.**—Discoveries of manufactured articles, such as papyrus from ancient Egypt (about 3500 B.C.), indicate that starch was used at a very early date as a sizing agent and an adhesive. The Greek name for starch, *amylon,* suggests that ancient peoples prepared starch "without milling"; *i.e.,* without the dry-milling procedures used to make flour from cereal grains. Instead, starch was probably made by soaking kernels of the grain, such as barley or wheat, under water until they were soft and then pounding them in a mortarlike device to produce a suspension of starch granules in water; the resulting starch milk could be drawn off, sieved through fine cloth, and allowed to settle, after which the water could be decanted and the sediment of rather pure starch spread out to dry.

Though starch is easily obtained in fairly pure form, no extensive industry was established to produce it until modern times. Even as late as the 17th and 18th centuries, starch appears to have been used principally to powder wigs, with an additional small amount employed to stiffen articles of clothing. With 19th-century developments in the Industrial Revolution, however, increasing applications for starch were found in the manufacture of textiles, paper, food, and other products. Many further uses were made possible by the discovery by G. S. C. Kirchhoff in 1811 that when starch is heated in a dilute acid solution it is broken down by hydrolysis into a sweet syrup containing the sugar dextrose, frequently called glucose.

**Manufacture.**—Modern starch manufacture uses the same wet-milling process (*see* below) invented by the ancients. Variations in technique occur with the different substrates depending on whether they are cereal grains, roots, tubers, or stem pith, and only those sources are used that can be grown economically in abundance. Of these the most important are corn (maize), tapioca (cassava, manihot, manioc, yucca), white and sweet potatoes, rice, wheat, and sago. Corn is the world's chief source of prepared starch for commercial applications. Corn starch is produced largely in the Western Hemisphere, about 5% of the U.S. corn crop being converted into starch and related products. In 1964 U.S. millers produced 2,495,000,000 lb. of corn starch. Tapioca starch is made principally in the East Indies and in South America. Some sago starch is produced in the East Indies, and arrowroot starch is made almost exclusively in the British West Indies. Europe has been the chief producer of white potato starch, whereas sweet potato and rice starches are produced in considerable volume in the Orient. Production of potato starch in the U.S. in 1961–62 reached 200,000,000 lb., but the amount varies from year to year, because production is based chiefly on potato culls. Potatoes are at a disadvantage as an industrial starch source because they cannot be stored as easily as cereal grains. Small amounts of wheat starch are made in scattered localities in both the Eastern and Western hemispheres. In the late 1960s U.S. production of wheat starch was estimated at 100,000,000 lb.

The type of starch used for a specific purpose depends on the cost and purity, on the stiffness or viscosity of the paste produced with hot water, and on the size of the granules. Potato, corn, rice, and wheat starches are chiefly used for industrial purposes. Rice, corn, arrowroot, cassava, and sago are the starches used in foodstuffs; and the small-granulated starches, rice and corn, are used extensively for laundering, since the granules are required to enter the texture of the cloth before becoming gelatinized by the hot iron.

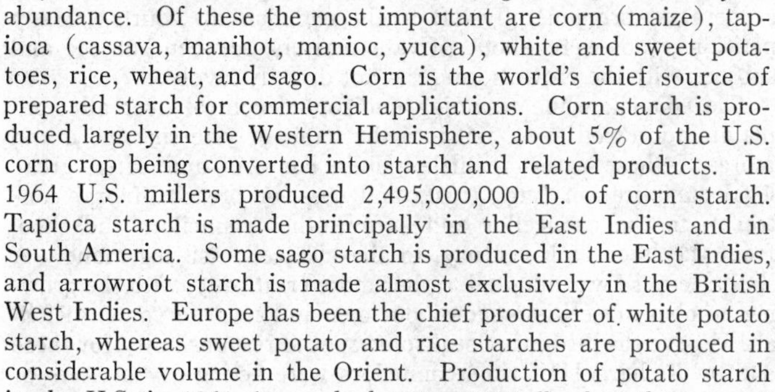

AMYLOSE

**Wet-Milling Processes.**—The methods used for obtaining starch from the various root and tuber sources are much the same throughout the world, though the procedures evolved differ somewhat in efficiency and elaboration. Cereal starches are prepared by similar methods, with; however, some important differences.

Tubers first go through washers, where earth, stones, sand, and grit are removed; they then pass to rasping machines, which completely rupture the cells. The resulting pulp is washed in a fine stream of water on fine-mesh brass sieves, which separate the starch from vegetable fibre and other solids. The resulting milky starch liquor is run into vats to eliminate sand and grit by settlement; the liquid is then passed through fine silk sieves for further purification and finally sent over long, shallow, wood troughs, where the pure starch settles out and the impurities pass off the ends with the water. Finally, the pure white starch is washed from the troughs with a jet of water and pumped to filter presses or centrifuges, which remove all but 40–45% of the water, leaving the starch in the form of a damp cake.

Cereals contain varying proportions of protein material, or gluten, associated with the starch, and special preliminary treatments are needed to remove it. The protein contained in rice is rendered soluble and removed by very weak caustic soda solutions. For corn it is also necessary to remove the corn germs, which contain large amounts of corn oil. In this case the grain is steeped in warm 2% sulfurous acid and roughly ground; the separated hulls are removed by coarse screens, and the corn germs are floated away. The gluten in wheat forms an elastic paste with water and cannot be removed by levigation (separation of coarse from fine particles in suspension), and therefore the grain is reduced to flour, made into a dough with water, divided into small pieces, and placed in a sieve, where traveling rollers press out the starch.

**Drying.**—The final drying of the starch must be carried out at very low temperatures to prevent gelatinization of the granules. This may be done either by bringing the starch in contact with a continuous current of warm air or by evaporating the excess moisture in a vacuum chamber. For producing powdered starch, the moist lumps are placed on an endless band in an enclosed chamber through which warm air is drawn, or put on trays that pass through a tunnel in contact with warm air. For food uses and other applications, the dried starch is ground and passed over silk sieves, or air classifiers, which yield a fine powder.

Prism or crystal starch, prepared from corn or rice starch for laundry purposes, is made by forming the damp starch into blocks, which are dried very slowly until they break up into the irregularly shaped prisms technically termed "crystals." To make pearl tapioca, the slightly moist starch from manioc is steam heated in copper pans with constant stirring until some of the cells become gelatinized and adhere together in small irregular masses. Granulated, or pearl, sago is prepared by drying the starch in such a way that it forms a plastic dough, in which a portion of the granules have become gelatinized, forcing this through sieves, and drying the resulting granules in the air.

**Modified Starches.**—The body and consistency of starch pastes vary greatly with the severity and intensity of the cooking and mechanical agitation to which they are subjected. These variations result from modifications in the starch due mainly to physical changes—that is, to the tearing apart of the starch granules without materially altering their chemical structure. In the presence of acids or enzymes, however, the starch molecules themselves are attacked, the products formed representing a breakdown of the original molecules. The type of starch degeneration product developed in the presence of these agents, and the extent to which the original molecules are broken down, depends on the nature of the acid or enzyme used, as well as on the temperature, concentration, and other factors. In this manner the thin-boiling, low-viscosity starches, and the dextrins, syrups, and sugars are made. Examples are the corn syrups used extensively in confectionery, and the glucose sugars used in brewing. Hydrolytic enzymes from malt are employed in brewing to convert starch into material capable of fermentation by yeast.

Dry starch heated to upward of 320° F (160° C) is transformed into dextrin, a pale yellowish powder soluble in water, known as British gum. Dextrins of lighter colour are made by spraying starch with aqueous acids and heating at lower temperatures.

In other cases, starches are chemically modified for specific use by treatment with particular chemical agents. Oxidized starches are prepared by treating a slurry of starch with an alkaline solution of sodium hypochlorite until the desired viscosity is reached. Starches containing added chemical groups, such as ethers, esters, etc., are produced by treatment with appropriate chemical agents. Unlike cellulose, starch that has been modified to only a relatively slight extent may show great changes in its physical properties. Lightly substituted starch ethers carrying positive charges on the molecules, and known as cationics, are of great importance in the paper-making industry.

**Industrial Applications.**—Vast quantities of starch are consumed by man in unpurified form in his daily diet. Starches that have been separated from their vegetable source and treated to give a relatively pure product also find use in home cooking and in the food processing industry as sweeteners and as thickening, emulsifying, and jelling agents. Corn syrups, a highly degraded starch product, also are widely used as sweeteners.

The largest commercial application of purified starch is in paper manufacturing, where, in 1962, an estimated 150,000 tons were used. Starch is employed to increase the strength of the paper and to reduce loss of inorganic fillers, cationic starch being particularly efficient in both functions. Starch also is used in large amounts for surface sizing of paper and as a binder in clay coated papers. Good quality, low-cost paper could not be produced without the use of starch at some stage in its manufacture.

The making of corrugated paperboard is possibly the second largest use of starch, particularly in the U.S., and probably the largest use of unmodified, heavy-boiling starch. In this application, adhesion is produced by the swelling of starch granules under the heat of fluting rolls.

Very large amounts of thin-boiling starch are consumed in the textile industry as warp sizing, which imparts strength to the thread during weaving (by forming a tough, but readily removable, film). Starches also are used to size-finish woven fabrics, and the use of starch to stiffen fabrics after laundering is well known.

Additional large fields of application for starch, especially thin-boiling and dextrinous types, are the manufacture of paper bags and boxes, carton sealers, tube windings, laminated paperboard, and gummed paper and tape. Starch nitrates were employed as explosives in World Wars I and II and still find such use today. Corn syrups are important in the textile, leather tanning, adhesives, pharmaceutical, paper, and tobacco industries. Starch and starch products also are source materials for the fermentation industries, conditioning agents for drilling muds for oil wells, coagulants in refining aluminum ore digests, binders in the production of printing pastes and foundry sand molds, and vehicles for dyes in printing calicoes and acetates.

**Chemical Structure.**—The polymeric carbohydrate molecules of which starch is composed are of two principal types. Both conform to the general formula $(C_6H_{10}O_5)_n$ and are polymers of glucose. One, called amylose, is a linear polymer, and the other, amylopectin, has a branched structure. Typical cornstarch consists of about 73% amylopectin and 27% amylose. Generally amylopectin has a much higher molecular weight than does amylose, but there is some uncertainty over the individual values because of the difficulties involved in carrying out molecular weight determinations on polymeric materials and because the starch polymers are partially degraded during purification.

In the amylose molecules, adjacent glucose units are joined together in their ring form, or glucopyranose, by oxygen bridges between the carbon atoms at positions 1 and 4. Amylopectin molecules have the same basic chainlike structure as the amylose molecules, but, in addition to the 1–4 links, occasional bridges between the 1 and 6 carbons also occur; these provide the branch points that give the amylopectin molecules their unique character. The 1–4 linkages in starch have the *alpha* configuration, giving the molecules a tendency to adopt a helical conformation. In cellulose these linkages have the *beta* configuration, and this is the chief difference between the starch and cellulose molecules.

*See* also CARBOHYDRATES: *Polysaccharides, Starch.*

BIBLIOGRAPHY.—R. W. Kerr (ed.), *Chemistry and Industry of Starch,* 2nd ed. (1950); J. A. Radley, *Starch and Its Derivatives,* 4th ed. (1968); Roy L. Whistler and E. F. Paschall, *Starch: Chemistry and Technology,* vol. 1 (1965), vol. 2 (1967).

**STAR CHAMBER** was the name given, because of the stars depicted on the ceiling of the main room, to a building in the king of England's palace of Westminster. It was constructed in the reign of Edward III and apparently from the first was one of the regular meeting places of the king's council. In the 16th century the name came to be applied also to the meetings there of councilors and judges sitting as a court.

This court inherited its jurisdiction from the medieval king's council (*see* PRIVY COUNCIL). The king of England, despite the evolution of the various courts of common law from the 12th century onward, had never parted with supreme jurisdiction or the right to supplement and reinforce the action of the ordinary courts. This right he exercised largely through his council, which dealt also with judicial business that fell outside the normal scope of those courts. Thus, to the council were referred, from at least the early 14th century, the petitions of suitors who sought the special intervention of the crown either because the ordinary courts had no remedy to offer in their cases or because the remedies were being frustrated by force or fraud or corruption. The council as a body did not itself deal with all these matters. Cases directly involving life or property were regarded as outside its scope and were generally left to the common-law courts. Many petitions, too, were about private matters between subject and subject, with the crown's interests not directly involved.

The council, while retaining undisputed control over all complaints addressed to it, fell into the habit of referring more and more of these cases of little public concern, and often great legal complication (*e.g.,* trusts and uses, or breach of oral contract), to the chancellor and a few other councilors and then, from the later 15th century, to the chancellor sitting alone. A similar course was adopted, rather more erratically, with the growing number of petitions from poor men and royal servants. Richard II gave the lord privy seal some special responsibility for these and by Richard III's time councilors were acting as "masters of requests"—perhaps as a "court" of requests—to deal with them.

The council as a body, however, generally retained for its own peculiar province the handling of cases involving public order, such as riot, breach of the peace, the maintenance of lawbreakers, the keeping of retainers and the corruption of officials in which the crown had a more direct interest. Here its procedures gave it considerable advantages over the ordinary courts. It was less bound by rigid forms. It did not depend upon juries either for indictment or for verdict. It could act upon the petition of an individual complainant or upon information received. It could put an accused person on oath to answer the petitioner's bill and to reply to detailed interrogatories. It had the help of the judges in reaching its decisions and its sentences were backed by the full majesty of the state and the law. On the other hand its methods lacked the safeguards which common-law procedures provided for the liberty of the subject, and parliaments in the 14th and 15th centuries, while recognizing the occasional need for and usefulness of those methods, had attempted to limit their use to causes beyond the scope or power of the ordinary courts. Thus the judicial activity of the king's council in these matters continued to be a special intervention from outside the regular course of justice.

Under the Tudors, however, this activity became so frequent and continuous that it developed into a regular part of the normal machinery for enforcing the law. Henry VII (*q.v.*), having a council fully obedient to the royal will, made great use of its jurisdiction to repress lawlessness, particularly riot, livery, maintenance, embracery and corruption of sheriffs and jurors. His famous act of 1487, later misleadingly titled *pro camera stellata,* though it did not create a court of star chamber, did reassert statutory sanction for regular employment of the council's procedures in such cases as those just mentioned. Also, using a common Tudor device, it placed upon certain councilors a special responsibility for dealing with them. Moreover, the councilors named included the lord chancellor and the two chief justices (or two other judges) of the courts of king's bench and common pleas. As these were all tied to Westminster during term time, the act confirmed the council's habit of dealing with such cases in term time at its headquarters, the star chamber. For it did not, of course, prevent other councilors, if available, from dealing with those causes, nor did it in any way limit the meetings in the star chamber to these matters or indeed to judicial business. Nevertheless, the presence of the judges helped to distinguish these meetings from others; and in general the act helped to give greater fixity of place and greater regularity of time to this aspect of the council's judicial activity.

It was during Thomas Wolsey's chancellorship (1515–29) that this activity, as well as the activity of chancery in civil equity (*see* ENGLISH LAW: *The Growth of Equity*), grew with greatest rapidity. He not only used it, with as much vigour as Henry VII, against riot, maintenance and so forth; he also used it with increased vigour against perjury, forgery, fraud, slander and any actions that could be considered as tending to breach of the peace. And he encouraged suitors to appeal to it in the first instance and not merely after failing to find an efficient remedy in the ordinary courts. Thus, with Wolsey this activity of the king's council began to take its place as a regular part of the administration of justice, as a regular "court" alongside the ordinary courts of law. At the same time, the continued growth and increasing definition of chancery's equity jurisdiction in civil suits between subject and subject; the final emergence of a distinct court of requests for poor men's causes; and such other developments as that of the high court of admiralty—all helped to define, as it were by subtraction, the function of the meetings of councilors and judges in public session in the star chamber. They became meetings, above all, for the exercise of the semicriminal jurisdiction of the king-in-council. Not exclusively so, for "all cases may be here examined and punished if the King will"; but matters of riot or tending to riot, robbery, libel, slander, perjury and offenses against royal proclamations were their primary concern.

The final stage in the evolution of this semicriminal jurisdiction of the king's council into the court of star chamber came with the emergence of a more clearly defined privy council. This was, again, the result of pressure of business, this time of executive and administrative business following upon the breach with Rome. The privy council, while retaining and frequently exercising (under the name of the council table) a "supereminent" jurisdiction, was evolved primarily to perform the advisory and executive functions of the older king's council. It attended upon the king; it met in private, all the year around, and often daily. In 1540 it began to have its records kept in a separate book by a clerk (later four clerks) of its own, distinct from the senior clerk of the council (who came to be called clerk of the star chamber). From that date its activities can thus be fairly clearly differentiated from the public sessions of councilors and judges held in the star chamber at Westminster, as a rule during term time only, and usually (at least by the time of Elizabeth I) on Wednesdays and Fridays. These meetings then gradually ceased to be thought of as meetings of the king's council and came to be regarded as sessions of a court of star chamber.

Even so, the distinction between this court and the privy council remained one of function and procedure rather than of persons. Certainly under Elizabeth I and the Stuarts membership of the court was, except for the presence of the judges, almost entirely confined to privy councilors. As a result, it retained much of the majesty, even if it lost the name, of the king's council. It also, of course, continued to use the conciliar procedures. Cases began upon petition or information. The accused, summoned by writ of subpoena, had to answer on oath and could be examined upon interrogatories framed by the prosecution. Depositions were taken from witnesses, but no jury was used. Proceedings were in English and much was done in writing. The punishments, which were arbitrary and sometimes made to fit the crime, included imprisonment, fine, the pillory, whipping, branding, mutilation, but never death.

The court did useful work in enforcing the law where other courts were subject to corruption or perversion, in providing remedies where others were inadequate, and in supplementing local justice. Its popularity in the 16th century was great—it has been estimated that about 43,000 cases may have come before it during the reign of Elizabeth I. That popularity lasted well into the Stuart period, despite the court's increasing fees and the growing number of its officials. Sir Edward Coke, for example, described it as "the most honorable court (our parliament excepted) that is in the Christian world." However, its employment to enforce unpopular policies, particularly in ecclesiastical matters, made it increasingly hated by the parliamentary and Puritan opponents of Charles I and of Archbishop Laud. As a result it was abolished by an act of the Long parliament in 1641.

(R. B. WM.)

**STAR CLUSTER.** In the astronomical sense, a star cluster is a stellar organization held together by the mutual gravitational attraction of its members, which are physically related through common origin. They move through space together like a swarm of bees. Binary and multiple stars, star clusters and star clouds are all examples of gravitational organizations of generically related stars. Star clusters are distinguished from star clouds by their subordinate size. In some instances, clusters appear as condensations or subsidiary organizations within star clouds.

On the basis of definition, there is no strict separation of multiple stars and very poor star clusters. The astronomer employs the descriptive term that is most convenient. As a working rule, a star cluster should contain enough stars to be describable statistically.

Related to star clusters are stellar associations, loose space groupings of stars of common origin without sufficient total mass in the group to remain together as an organization. In some cases, star clusters or multiple stars appear as nuclei within associations. The expansion rates of some associations have been measured. Associations are, in terms of the usual astronomical time scale, disintegrating rapidly. The stars composing them must have been formed comparatively recently. The measured rate of expansion of the $\zeta$ Persei association, for example, indicates that the stars composing the association must have been formed approximately 1,300,000 years ago.

**Classes of Star Clusters.**—In the galaxy, the huge stellar system of which the solar system is a member of insignificant size, two general classes of star clusters are found: globular clusters and galactic clusters. These two classes of objects may be briefly contrasted as follows: The globular clusters contain very large numbers—tens or hundreds of thousands—of stars. The galactic clusters typically contain rather few stars—only a few tens or hundreds. The brightest stars in a typical globular cluster are red. They are distended stars of low surface temperature. Generally, the brightest stars in a galactic star cluster are blue.

These two kinds of clusters, which differ so markedly in their physical properties, are found in characteristically different parts of the galaxy. Fig. 1 shows a schematic side view of the galaxy, with its in excess of 100,000,000,000 stars. It is primarily a flat system, roughly circular in plane view, with a diameter of the order of 100,000 light-years. Spiral arms, similar to those seen in many external galaxies, marked out by highly luminous blue stars, gas and dark, nonluminous material, exist in this plane. The galaxy is rotating around an axis perpendicular to the flat plane and passing through the centre, or nucleus, of the galaxy. At the sun's position, about 30,000 light-years from the galactic nucleus, approximately 200,000,000 years are required to complete one rotation. The galaxy does not rotate as a solid disk.

Shorter or longer rotation periods are observed for objects nearer to, or more distant from, the centre.

The galactic star clusters are found primarily in the galactic plane and there predominantly within the spiral arms. As judged by the kinds of stars they contain, as well as by their motions

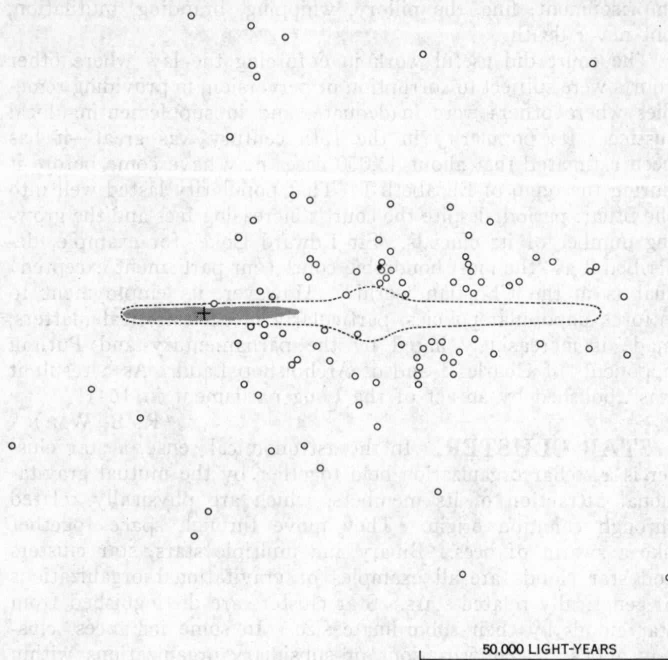


FIG. 1.—SPACE DISTRIBUTION OF GALACTIC AND GLOBULAR STAR CLUSTERS

Our stellar system as it would appear to an outside observer. Dotted line indicates probable outline of flattened lens-shaped system formed by the stars, as seen edgewise. Eccentric position of our sun is shown by cross. Known galactic star clusters are scattered among the stars in shaded region. Small circles represent globular clusters surrounding the star system like satellites

and space distribution, the galactic clusters are related to the Milky Way star clouds. They, like the star clouds and other objects associated with the spiral arms, must have originated in the highly flattened outer parts of the stellar system. They move in orbits that are approximately circles centred on the galactic nucleus and lying in planes close to and nearly parallel to the galactic plane.

The globular star clusters, of which more than a hundred are now known to be members of the galactic system, differ markedly from the galactic star clusters in their distribution in space. The globular clusters are distributed in the form of an extensive halo about the galaxy (*see* fig. 1). They have their greatest space concentration in the region of the galactic nucleus and are probably generically related to the stars in the nucleus and the galactic halo. As a system, they rotate about the axis through the galactic centre, but much more slowly than the stars forming the main body of the galaxy. Individual globular clusters move around the galactic nucleus in greatly elongated orbits that lie in planes of various orientations.

**Lists and Catalogues of Clusters.**—Many of the most outstanding examples of star clusters of both classes were discovered by the early telescopic observers of the 17th and 18th centuries. In 1874 the French astronomer Charles Messier published a catalogue of nebulae and clusters in which he tabulated 57 star clusters. A systematic search of the whole heavens undertaken by Sir William Herschel and continued by his son Sir John Herschel led to the discovery of the majority of clusters known at present. The cluster catalogue published by Alter, Ruprecht and Vanysek (1958) listed 117 globular clusters and 576 galactic clusters.

Whenever possible, a cluster is designated by its number in the *New General Catalogue of Nebulae and Clusters of Stars* (N.G.C.), or *Index Catalogues* (I.C.), compiled by John L. E. Dreyer. Less frequently, it is designated by its number in the catalogue published by Messier, or its name, such as the Pleiades, if it is a well-known cluster.

Clusters exist in external galaxies, as well as in our own. This discussion will be limited to members of our own galaxy.

## GLOBULAR STAR CLUSTERS

**Total Number in the Galaxy.**—The halolike distribution of globular clusters about the galaxy causes many of them to appear at high galactic latitudes, well away from the great masses of stars and dark clouds of obscuring material that form the body of the galaxy. The dense globular clusters are thus seen against a sparse stellar background and are readily discovered. Their great intrinsic brightness (10,000 to 1,000,000 times the sun's luminosity) makes them visible even at great distances. The list of known globular clusters that belong to the galactic system must therefore be at least 50% complete.

**Classification of Globular Clusters.**—*By Appearance.*—Globular clusters, though displaying a general similarity of appearance, differ in stellar content and the distribution of stars composing them. Cluster compactness has provided the basis of a classification scheme based on appearance and used by H. Shapley and H. B. Sawyer, who distinguished 12 classes. Class I clusters have the highest central concentration, class XII the least. The globular clusters are fairly evenly divided among all 12 classes, with some tendency for fewer clusters to occur in the extreme classes. Apparent ellipticity may be added as a second classification parameter.

*By Physical Properties.*—The integrated spectrum or, alternatively, measurements of integrated brightness at selected frequencies over a wide wave-length range provide one type of index of stellar population. The integrated spectral types estimated by N. U. Mayall extend from mid-A to mid-G type, with the average being F7.6. Published multicolour photometric results are insufficient to provide analogous colour statistics. Other physical properties of the clusters that might be utilized as classification parameters are numbers and properties of variable stars (*see* below) within the cluster, character of the magnitude-colour diagram of the cluster, etc. Much remains to be learned from such classification parameters and combinations of them.

**Stellar Content of the Globular Clusters.**—*Colour-Magnitude or Magnitude Spectral-Type Diagrams.*—The stellar content of a cluster can be determined if for large numbers of individual stars in the cluster there are established at least two properties: magnitude (or brightness) and colour, or magnitude and spectral type. Fig. 2 displays a schematic magnitude-colour diagram for a typical globular cluster. The brightest stars in the globular cluster are red, cool stars. There are no very bright blue, hot stars so characteristic of the great majority of galactic clusters. The hot, blue stars (some are exceedingly blue) in the globular clusters are intrinsically very much fainter than stars of the same colour located in the vicinity of the sun. In fact, in the globular clusters (*see* fig. 2) the bluer a star, the fainter it is. In the solar neighbourhood, the bluer a star, the brighter it is.

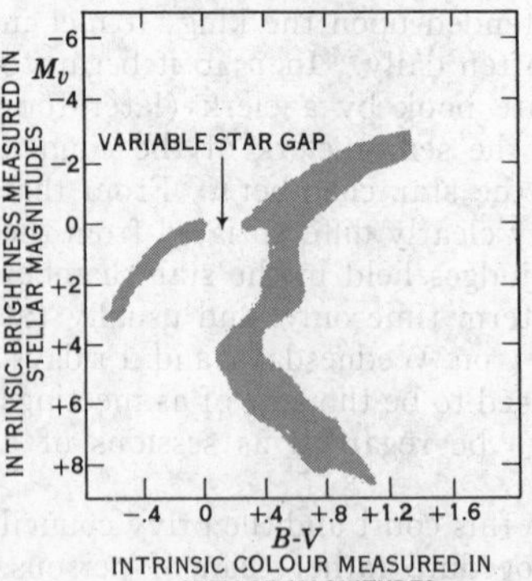


FIG. 2.—SCHEMATIC MAGNITUDE-COLOUR DIAGRAM OF GLOBULAR STAR CLUSTER

Shaded areas indicate regions of the plane occupied by globular cluster stars. Variable star gap indicates region in which cluster variables occur

The magnitude-colour diagram of a globular cluster bears little resemblance to the magnitude-colour diagram of stars found in the vicinity of the sun. It is, presumably, characteristic of the nuclear region of the galaxy.

*Variable Stars.*—The presence of great numbers of variable stars in globular clusters was demonstrated by S. I. Bailey of Harvard College observatory. The overwhelming majority of the more-than-a-thousand variables known in globular star clusters have periods of less than a day. These are the cluster type or RR Lyrae variables; they occur only in the small region of the magnitude-colour plane (fig. 2) labeled variable star gap. All stars that fall in this narrowly defined region are variable stars. The light variation of a cluster-type variable is caused by pulsation; *i.e.*, by rhythmic contraction and expansion of the star.

Globular clusters differ markedly in their variable star content. Thus, the well-known cluster ω Centauri contains in excess of 160 cluster variables, while 47 Tucanae contains almost none.

Over 100 periodic or semiregular variables with periods longer than one day are known in globular clusters; they are brighter than the cluster-type variables. Approximately half of these stars have periods between 1 and 40 days; they may be regarded as Cepheidlike variables characteristic of the globular-cluster population.

It is remarkable that in all the known globular clusters only three eclipsing variable stars have been discovered. Conditions within globular clusters, unlike conditions within galactic clusters and the neighbourhood of the sun, are apparently unfavourable for the formation of double stars.

The cluster-type variables in a cluster are all of very nearly the same brightness. Under the assumption that the brightnesses of these stars are the same from one cluster to another and, further, that they are the same as the brightnesses of the RR Lyrae stars in the solar vicinity, the astronomer possesses a powerful means of determining globular-cluster distances. He can, from the measured motions and apparent brightnesses of the RR Lyrae stars in the vicinity of the sun, calibrate or determine the brightnesses of these nearby variables. He can then measure the apparent brightnesses of the cluster-type variables in a globular cluster and from the difference in the apparent brightnesses of the variables in the cluster and the derived brightnesses of the nearby variables infer the distance of the globular cluster. The cluster distances measured in this way range from 12,000 to more than 100,000 light-years.

The determination of these enormous distances with a reasonable degree of accuracy constitutes one of the triumphs of modern astronomical investigation. A new era in the astronomer's understanding of the galaxy began when Shapley used such distances to investigate the space distribution of the globular clusters and, from that distribution, derived the direction of and distance to the galactic centre.

**Spectral Characteristics of Stars in Globular Clusters.**—The spectra of stars in globular clusters differ from those of stars in the solar neighbourhood or in galactic clusters. In globular cluster stars the spectral lines arising from the metals are very weak. This fact has caused difficulties in assigning spectral types to individual stars in clusters, especially when small dispersion spectra have been employed. The degree of line weakness appears to be consistent within any one globular cluster but to differ from one cluster to another.

The phenomenon of the weak spectral lines of the metals in stars in globular clusters may be explained in terms of an underabundance of metals (taking the local stars as normal), ranging from a factor of 20 to 200 or more in different globular clusters. Such a difference in the abundances of the elements in stars in globular clusters and in galactic clusters (and in different parts of the galaxy) must arise from differences in the composition of the primeval material from which the stars were formed. The differences constitute an important fact to be included in any theory of the formation and evolution of stars in the galaxy.

**Size and Structure of Globular Clusters.**—Specification of a precise diameter for a globular cluster is difficult. The stars simply thin out at greater and greater distances from the cluster centre. The linear diameters of different globular clusters range from 50 to 300 light-years, not counting the outermost stars. Clusters rich in stars are generally larger than those poor in stars. The space density of stars in all globular clusters is very much higher than it is in the general region of space around the sun or even in galactic star clusters.

A typical globular cluster is slightly flattened, as though the cluster were rotating. The flattening reveals itself through the elliptical form of the projected image of the cluster, a directly observable quantity. It is not possible to determine independently the true flattening of a cluster and the inclination of its equatorial plane to the line of sight. However, it is possible to say, from the results at hand, that some clusters have equatorial diameters at least 25% greater than their polar diameters.

The kinetic theory of gases has stimulated much work on the statistical laws governing the distribution of stars in globular clusters. No completely satisfactory representation of an observed distribution law has yet been found. The studies that have been made, of course, have involved only a few thousands of the brightest (and more massive) stars. The fainter objects in the globular star clusters have not been adequately considered in any of these treatments.

## GALACTIC STAR CLUSTERS

**Number of Galactic Clusters in the Galaxy.**—The galactic clusters located in the flat-disk portion of the galaxy and concentrated in the spiral arms of the galaxy are far more numerous than the globular clusters. The catalogue published by Alter, Ruprecht and Vanysek listed 576 galactic star clusters, but in contrast to the situation of the globular clusters only a very small portion of the existing galactic star clusters have been found. The reason is, of course, that the galactic star clusters are located in the part of the Milky Way in which much dark obscuring material exists; we can therefore survey only a small portion of the total volume of the Milky Way in which these clusters are located. It is estimated from statistical studies that at least 40,000 galactic clusters exist throughout the entire galaxy.

**Classification of Galactic Clusters.**—*By Appearance.*—The general purpose of any classification of clusters made on the basis of appearance is to make possible selection of homogeneous groups of objects. Among the classification schemes proposed for the galactic clusters, the one by R. J. Trumpler has been the most successful. He assigned three-symbol designations to each cluster on the basis of: (1) the degree of central concentration (consideration was given to the fact that the cluster was "detached" or involved in a dense star field); (2) the range in luminosity of the cluster stars; (3) the number of stars contained in the cluster. Further notations were employed to indicate peculiarities (elongated or unsymmetrical form, nebulosity, etc.) of a few clusters. Clusters that have the same three-symbol designation in this system appear to be quite similar in linear dimensions.

*By Physical Characteristics.*—Trumpler also devised a classification scheme based upon the nature of the magnitude-spectral-type diagrams of the clusters. Typical diagrams are exhibited in fig. 3. A two-symbol designation characterizes the cluster.

Class 1 includes those clusters that contain main sequence stars. Class 2 clusters have a small or moderate number of red giant stars in addition to main sequence stars. Class 3, of which there are few examples, is composed of clusters in which the number of giant stars is very considerable.

In each of these three classes the clusters may again be distinguished by the earliest spectral type found in the cluster. For example, 1B3 designates a cluster composed of main sequence stars, the earliest of which is B3.

Trumpler made the significant discovery that in this classification scheme not all classes are occupied. He found no class 2 objects with stars earlier than B4, for example. This classification scheme relates to the larger, more general questions of the stellar content of the clusters, which, we know now, relate directly to cluster age. Trumpler's discoveries have given impetus to studies of stellar evolution.

**Stellar Content of the Galactic Clusters.**—An outstanding characteristic of the galactic star clusters is that they are much richer in highly luminous stars than the general solar neighbourhood, even though they are found in the same region of the galaxy as the sun. Stars in clusters are often thousands of times more luminous than the sun; in fact, the clusters contain some of the most luminous stars known. The clusters are also found to be much more frequently associated with gas and dust, which appear as bright nebulosity when illuminated by the cluster stars, than would be expected on the basis of chance alone.

Recent observations of the colour-magnitude diagrams of galac-

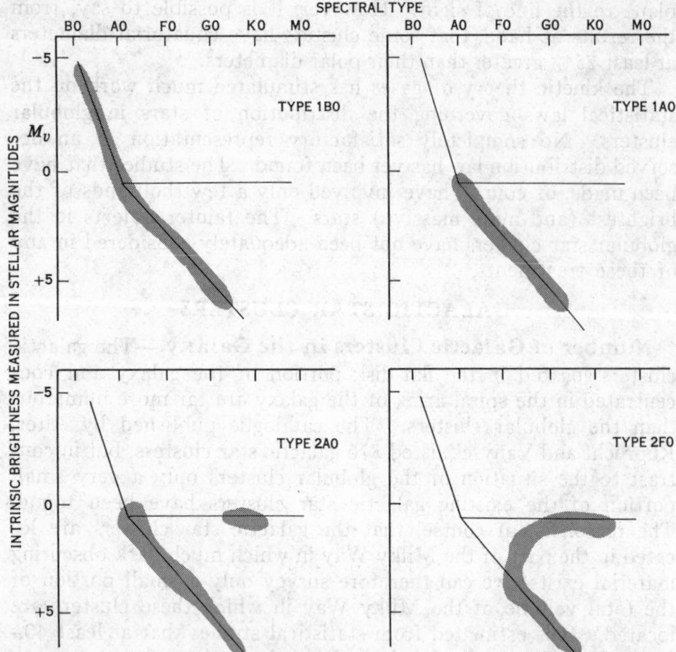


FIG. 3.—TRUMPLER'S CLASSIFICATION OF GALACTIC STAR CLUSTERS

Diagrams showing two principal classes 1 (above) and 2 (below), with two spectral types, or subclasses, for each class. Shaded areas indicate areas of the plane occupied by stars in galactic clusters

tic clusters (*see* fig. 4) indicate the kinds of stars found within the clusters and illustrate in detail Trumpler's classification scheme as well. Of particular interest is the position of the turnup of the upper portions of the main sequences of the clusters, a feature early noted by Trumpler and now known to be related to cluster age. The great majority of galactic clusters observed

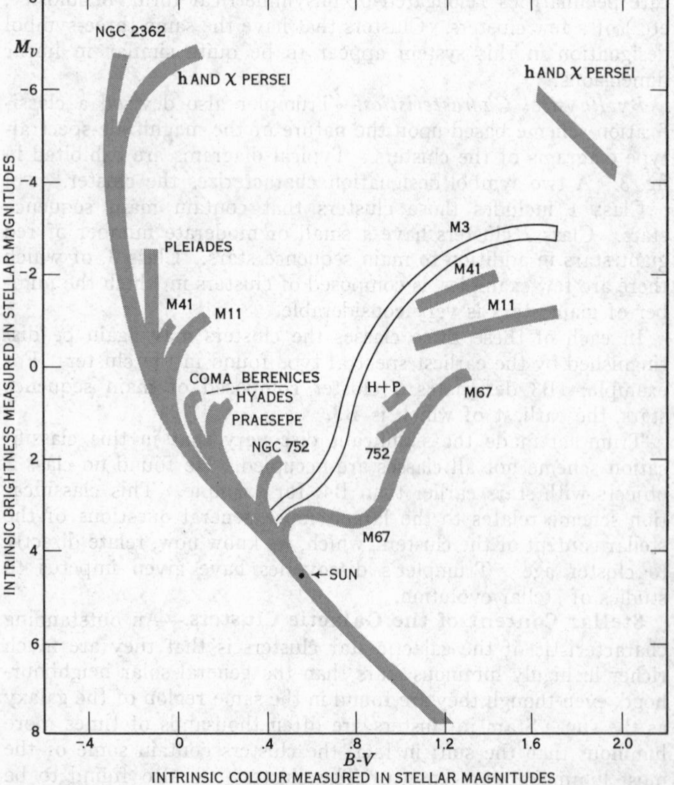


FIG. 4.—COMPOSITE MAGNITUDE-COLOUR DIAGRAM OF GALACTIC AND GLOBULAR STAR CLUSTERS. M3 IS A GLOBULAR CLUSTER; OTHERS ARE GALACTIC CLUSTERS. THE POSITION OCCUPIED BY THE SUN IS INDICATED

are far younger than the globular clusters or, presumably, than the general group of stars forming the main body of the galaxy. As a star grows old, its brightness and colour change. The forms of the main sequences of the various clusters have given us our most valuable observational evidence of the shapes of the evolutionary paths in the colour-magnitude plane followed by stars of different masses.

Investigations of the numbers of stars of different brightnesses in the galactic clusters show that, in comparison with the stellar population in the region of the sun or in the globular star clusters, there is a great deficiency in the numbers of faint stars in the galactic cluster. This phenomenon, reflecting the way in which matter breaks up into stars, must arise from differences in conditions obtaining: (1) very long ago when the globular clusters and the stars in the general body of the galaxy were formed; and (2) more recently when the majority of galactic clusters condensed out of the interstellar medium. Such evolutionary problems as these are among the central ones of modern astronomical investigation.

**Variable Stars in Galactic Clusters.**—Galactic clusters contain very few intrinsically variable stars; they do contain a significant number of double stars, which are observed as spectroscopic binary stars or eclipsing variables.

The small population of intrinsic variable stars in galactic clusters differs radically from that observed in the globular clusters. Galactic clusters contain no RR Lyrae variables, which are numerous in globular clusters. However, they do contain a few Cepheid variable stars. These galactic-cluster Cepheids appear to be identical in nature with the classical Cepheid variables found in the solar neighbourhood. The galactic clusters do not contain any counterparts of the periodic or semiregular variables that are found in the globular clusters and that have periods longer than one day.

Like the differing colour-magnitude diagrams of the galactic and globular clusters, the differing variable-star populations of these two types of clusters indicate that globular and galactic clusters are objects that are very different in stellar content and physical characteristics. Their ages and their past histories must also be quite different.

**Strange Stellar Types in Young Clusters.**—The stars in galactic clusters are generally similar to the stars in the vicinity of the sun with respect to spectral and other physical characteristics. Notable exceptions to this rule occur in some very young clusters, which characteristically contain very bright stars and are frequently associated with extensive clouds of dust and gas. They also contain strange stellar types—stars that, as judged on the basis of the common variety of nearby stars, are too red (too cool) for their brightness (roughly solar brightness or fainter). In some instances these young groups contain examples of the very interesting T Tauri variety of erratic intrinsic variable stars. The T Tauri variables have intrinsic brightnesses similar to, or fainter than, the sun; their spectral types are G or later. It is presumed that these strange stellar types represent stars less fully developed than stars of similar masses in older clusters or in the vicinity of the sun. Much remains to be learned from the study of such stars.

**Sizes and Structure of Galactic Clusters.**—The limiting diameters of galactic clusters vary between 15 and 75 light-years; the richer clusters are larger than the poor ones. Stars of different brightnesses or masses do not show the same space distribution throughout the cluster. The brighter (more massive) stars within any cluster are generally found concentrated near the centre of the cluster. The fainter (and less massive) stars are spread over a larger volume of space and indicate a larger diameter. The apparent diameter of a cluster estimated on a photograph is generally no more than one-third of the limiting cluster diameter for the faint stars. The galactic clusters are far less regular in form than the globular clusters. Diameters are therefore especially difficult to estimate.

In the central, and therefore denser, parts of galactic clusters, each star is, on the average, separated from its nearest neighbour by a distance of approximately 1½ light-years. However, in the central portion of rich clusters the space density of stars is at least a hundred times as great as the space density of stars in the solar neighbourhood. If we were to construct a model of an average galactic cluster, using pinheads for stars, we should require a few hundred pins. We should then have to scatter these throughout a sphere approximately 150 mi. in diameter. On the average, the pinheads would be some 4 or 5 mi. apart.

**Disintegration of Galactic Star Clusters.**—The stars in a cluster continuously interact gravitationally; they are in continuous motion. Chance close encounters between stars produce strong perturbations in their motions. As a result of such perturbations a star may be given sufficient velocity to escape from the gravitational field of the cluster. Through such "evaporation" of stars a cluster shrinks both in linear size and in stellar content. Very general considerations show that the stars of small mass evaporate from the cluster more rapidly than those of large mass. Even if they do not gain enough energy to evaporate from the cluster, the small-mass stars will tend to move to greater-than-average distances from the cluster centre because of perturbations; they form an extended halo about the cluster. This theoretical prediction may provide at least a partial explanation of the observation that the fainter members of a cluster occupy a larger volume of space than the brighter and more massive members.

The cluster tends to be disrupted by the differential rotation of the galaxy, as well as by the chance encounters that occur between a cluster and the complexes of dark material and stars as the cluster moves in its orbit around the galactic nucleus. The encounters between the cluster and cloud-star complexes produce more important disintegration forces than the differential galactic rotation. The smaller the diameter of the cluster and the greater the total mass of stars in the cluster the longer the time required for disruption. For a cluster like the Pleiades, the disruption time is of the order of 1,000,000,000 years.

*See* STAR; NEBULA; ASTROPHYSICS; ASTRONOMY.

BIBLIOGRAPHY.—P. Ten Bruggencate, *Sternhaufen* (1927), a monograph dealing critically with only a part of the field; Harlow Shapley, "Star Clusters," *Harv. Obs. Monogr.* (1930), a general treatise on globular and galactic star clusters, containing full bibliography prior to 1930, "Stellar Clusters," *Handbuch der Astrophysik,* vol. ii, ch. 5 (1933); R. J. Trumpler, "Preliminary Results on the Distances, Dimensions and Space Distribution of Open Star Clusters," *Lick Obs. Bull.,* vol. xiv, p. 154 (1930); Per Collinder, "On Structural Properties of Open Galactic Clusters and Their Spatial Distribution," *Ann. Lund Obs.,* no. 2 (1931); H. Mineur, "Equilibre des nuages galactiques et des amas ouverts dans la voie lactee, evolution des amas," *Ann. Astrophys.,* vol. ii, no. 1 (1939); A. J. Deutsch, "Principes fondamentaux de classification stellaire," *Colloq. int. Cent. nat. Rech. sci.* (1955); L. Spitzer, "Disruption of Galactic Clusters," *Astrophys. J.,* vol. 127, p. 17 (1958); G. Alter, J. Ruprecht and V. Vanysek, *Catalog of Star Clusters and Associations* (1958); O. Struve, "Gas and Dust in Globular Clusters," *Sky and Telescope* (June 1960) "The Structure of Galactic Clusters," *Sky and Telescope* (April 1960). (H. F. WR.)

**STARETS** (plural *startsy*), a holy man, usually a monk, commanding wide popular respect for his gift of spiritual guidance, in the Russian church of the 18th and 19th centuries. The fact that most of the *startsy* were monks meant that their influence was unconnected with priesthood. They were mainly simple people who relied on direct guidance from the Holy Spirit and were not connected with the official church hierarchy. The Church Slavonic word *starets* in the Middle Ages was simply a translation of the Greek word *geron,* which, in the Orthodox world, meant no more than "monk." However, with the advance of the hesychastic movement (*see* HESYCHASM), which aimed essentially at a reformation after the monastic ideal of the ancient eremitic settlements in the Egyptian and Palestinian-Syrian deserts, the word began to signify especially that type of aged monk whose "inward activity" (*noera ergasia*) of contemplation was so far developed that he was chosen by younger monks as a spiritual leader. The way of life of the skete (ascetic settlements grouped round a common church), arising in connection with this reforming movement, encouraged the *starets* in this special sense.

The first great *starets* on Russian soil was Nil Sorski (*q.v.*), who preached the skete manner of life to Russian monks. His disciples, the Transvolgian *startsy,* concerned with the purely ascetic, moral way of life, were defeated in a dispute with the Josephites (followers of Joseph, abbot of Volotsk), who clung to the public functions of the monasteries; *e.g.,* care of the poor and aged and the training of young men for the church hierarchy. The ideals of ascetic sanctification, however, were kept alive in the desert monasteries through the writings of Nil Sorski, and in the 18th century they produced the true Russian *starets* in the narrow sense of the word. This development was assisted by the neohesychast ideas from Mt. Athos, which the *starets* Paissy Velichkovsky (d. 1794) introduced to the Slav world through his Church Slavonic translation of the hesychast *Philokalia* (*q.v.*) of Nikodimos Hagioritis.

A further step was taken when *startsy* became not merely spiritual leaders inside the monasteries but also pastors and counselors of the laity (*see* also SERAPHIM, SAINT). People now began to make pilgrimages to the *startsy,* the most famous of whom were those of the monastery of Optina Pustynye, in central Russia: Leonid (d. 1841), Makarios (d. 1860), and Ambrosius (d. 1881). Also important for Russian spiritual life in the 19th century were the two former bishop *startsy,* Ignatius Bryanchaninov (d. 1867) and Feofan Zatvornik (Theophanes the Recluse; d. 1894), the first for his ascetic writings and letters and the second for his modern Russian edition of the *Philokalia.* A fine example of the type of spirituality produced by the *startsy* teaching is the anonymous 19th-century *Way of a Pilgrim.* Dostoevski made the *startsy* famous in world literature by his *starets* Zossima in *The Brothers Karamazov. See* also MONASTICISM: *Christian Monasticism: Eastern Monasticism.*

*See* I. Smolitsch, *Leben und Lehre der Starzen,* 2nd ed. (1952). (F. v. L.)

**STARFISH** and sea star are names given to radially symmetrical, more or less star-shaped, bottom-dwelling animals found on the margins of almost all seas. They constitute the class Asteroidea of the phylum Echinodermata. Sea stars, which range from the tide lines to depths of 19,700 ft. (6,005 m.), are particularly abundant in numbers and species along the rocky coasts of the North Pacific. In size they vary from ½ in. to 3 ft. (0.9 m.) in diameter. The commonest colours are shades of yellow, orange, pink, or red; but gray, green, blue, and purple forms are also known.

The body is more or less flattened, with the mouth located centrally on the underside. From the body project a number of radially arranged arms, usually 5, but in a few species up to 44, as in the South American genus *Heliaster,* which looks like a giant sunflower. In the tropical cushion star *Culcita* and in many cookie stars, the body is simply pentagonal, whereas in other species the arms may be long and snakelike, as in some of the deepwater forms that live on mud. Along the midline of the arm, on the underside, runs the ambulacral groove, which shelters the numerous, fluid-filled tube feet and the radial water canal from which they originate. Beneath the radial canal lies the skeleton, rows of narrow ossicles united by muscles. The sides of the arms are edged by two rows of plates, the marginals, which in the more primitive forms are large and conspicuous and give a certain rigidity to the arm. In more advanced forms, these plates are small and the arms possess a greater flexibility. The upper side of the body and arms has a skeletal cover of different types, suitable to the animal's mode of life. In forms that hide in sand, the surface is often covered by plates with bundles of spines, giving a brushlike effect; in others, imbricating scales are present; and in the most modern and quick-moving forms, the skeleton is a loose-meshed network of ossicles, with or without projecting spines. Usually conspicuous on the upper side is the madreporic plate, through which water is taken into the water vascular system by means of ciliated pores. Many sea stars possess pedicellariae, spines modified into pincers. In their simplest form they are pairs or rows of spines that can be moved against each other; in more advanced species they are stalked, of complex structure, and often present in enormous numbers, especially on the vulnerable upper side of the animal. Pedicellariae remove dirt from the surface, pass food down to the mouth, and defend the animals against enemies. In the more active forms like *Asterias* and its relatives, the body surface is increased by numerous respiratory extensions from the body cavity; in species where they are really well developed, these extensions may form a "velvet" over the upper surface. In the dry specimen their place is indicated by pores between the ossicles.

The sea stars have a large stomach, divided into a cardiac and a pyloric part. In many forms there is no intestine and no anus. In the more advanced forms, large digestive glands are present, extending into the lumen of the arms. The sex glands open by pores between the arms. In most forms, enormous numbers of eggs and sperms are set free. The free-swimming larva, the bipinnaria, is of relatively simple form, indicating that the sea stars are comparatively primitive echinoderms. After a shorter or longer period, during which it may be carried afar by the ocean currents, the larva undergoes a drastic metamorphosis and settles down as a bottom form. Many species, particularly cold-water forms and those from deep water, have large eggs that undergo direct development. Some of these "brood" their young by crouching over them. In one species the eggs are taken into the mother's stomach, where the young develop; the mother ceases to take in food during the incubation period.

The class is quite successful, with about 1,200 known species. Because of their rather fragile skeletons, sea stars do not preserve well as fossils, and are therefore rather incompletely known from earlier geological periods. Many, particularly the more primitive forms, live at great depths, often on muddy bottoms, and take most of their food in along ciliated grooves, which carry the minute, decaying particles to the mouth. In shallow water, particularly on rocky coasts, the more modern forms abound, with their flexible body, increased number of tube feet, and often eversible cardiac stomach. They are often found where there is an abundance of bivalves (oysters, clams, mussels) and are responsible for considerable damage in commercial bivalve beds.

The sea star's ability to open a bivalve by pulling the shells apart has been known for centuries. The feat is accomplished by the sea star affixing itself by its tube feet to the two shells, applying "pull" to separate the shells—a fraction of an inch is enough—and squeezing a part of its eversible stomach into the interior. The victim, adversely affected by the stomach fluid secreted by the sea star, opens its shells wider, allowing the predator to insert more of its stomach and to complete the digestion of the soft tissue.

Where commercially important bivalves occur in quantities, continuous efforts are made to prevent sea stars from entering these areas, and to remove them by dragging nets over the bottom. Their power to regenerate missing arms is spectacular, some sea stars being able to re-form completely from as little original tissue as the mouth framework (*see* REGENERATION). Where fishnets are left untended for any length of time, sea stars may move in and devour a large amount of the catch; they are also known to enter lobster pots and eat the bait. Sea stars are acceptable as food only to a few animals. For man they are utterly useless, except where large quantities are gathered and used as a lime-yielding fertilizer.

*See* also ECHINODERMATA; and references under "Starfish" in the Index. (EL. D.)

**STARK, JOHANNES** (1874–1957), German physicist who in 1919 received the Nobel Prize for Physics for his discovery that spectral lines are distorted in an electrical field—the so-called Stark effect (*q.v.*). He was born April 15, 1874, at Schickenhof, Bavaria. He studied at Munich and in 1900 became an assistant at the University of Göttingen. He went as professor in 1909 to the technical college at Aachen, in 1917 to Greifswald and in 1920 to Würzburg. He retired in 1922. Stark devoted himself principally to the study of the modern theory of radiation and the atomic theory. He discovered the Doppler effect in parallel rays, for which the Vienna Academy awarded him the Baumgartner Prize in 1909. His essays include "Prinzipien der Atomdynamik" (1910–15); "Die elektrischen Quanten, Die elektrische Strahlung, Die Elektrizität in Gasen" (1902); and "Atomstruktur und Atombindung" (1928). Stark was the founder of the *Jahrbuch für Radioaktivität und Elektronik* (1904), which he edited until 1919. A supporter of Hitler and an anti-Semitic racial theorist, he was president of the Reich Physical-Technical Institute, 1933–39. In 1947 a denazification court sentenced him to four years in a labour camp. He died at Traunstein, Bavaria, June 21, 1957.

**STARK, JOHN** (1728–1822), U.S. general during the American Revolution, was born at Londonderry, N.H., on Aug. 28, 1728. During the French and Indian War he served till 1759 in Rogers' Rangers, as a lieutenant and, later, captain. At the outbreak of the American Revolution, he was named a colonel and fought at Bunker Hill, in the invasion of Canada, and in New Jersey. In March 1777 he resigned his commission, but when English Gen. John Burgoyne invaded New York he was made brigadier general of militia and defeated two Hessian detachments near Bennington, Vt., on Aug. 16, 1777. For this victory Stark was given the rank of brigadier general in the Continental Army. He helped force the surrender of Burgoyne at Saratoga in October 1777 and for a short time was commander of the northern department. He served in Rhode Island in 1779 and at the battle of Springfield, N.J., in 1780. In September 1783 he was made a major general. He retired to his farm and died at Manchester, N.H., on May 8, 1822. (H. H. P.)

**STARK EFFECT** is the splitting of spectral lines observed when the radiating atoms, ions, or molecules are subjected to a strong electric field. Soon after P. Zeeman discovered the magnetic splitting of spectral lines the electric analogue of the Zeeman effect (*q.v.*) was sought by many physicists, but success came first to Johannes Stark (*q.v.*) in 1913. The earlier experiments failed since a strong electric field could not be maintained in conventional spectroscopic light sources (*see* SPECTROSCOPY) because of the high electrical conductivity of luminous gases or vapours. Stark observed the hydrogen spectrum emitted just behind the perforated cathode in a canal-ray tube. By placing a second charged electrode parallel and close to this cathode he was able to produce a strong electric field in a space of a few millimetres. At low gas pressure the mean free path of the atoms was much greater than the distance between the plates so that few conducting ions could be produced by collisions. In an electric field of the order of 100,000 v. per centimetre Stark observed, with a spectroscope pointing across the field, that the Balmer lines of hydrogen were split into a number of symmetrically spaced components, some of which were linearly polarized parallel to the lines of force, the remainder being polarized perpendicular to the direction of the field. This transverse Stark effect resembles in some respects the transverse Zeeman effect, except that the separations (in wave numbers per volt in the first case, per oersted in the second) are larger, the number of Stark levels increases with electron-shell number (*i.e.*, principal quantum number), and the intensity distribution among the components is different. A satisfactory explanation of the Stark effect in hydrogen, given in 1916 independently by K. Schwarzschild and by P. Epstein, was a great triumph for quantum mechanics (*q.v.*).

The Stark effect was also observed in the spectra of metals by employing special (LoSurdo) tubes containing a cathode of the metal under investigation, and viewing the light emitted near the cathode where a large potential gradient exists. In general, the electric splitting in spectra of metals is small compared with that in hydrogen, and unlike the Zeeman effect, which is symmetrical in spacing and intensity distribution of components, the Stark effect is usually only a displacement of unresolved components toward greater or smaller wavelengths. This effect does not depend in a simple way on the nature of the combining atomic energy levels and for this reason the Stark effect in comparison with the Zeeman effect has little practical value in the analysis of complex spectra or of atomic structure. (W. F. M.)

*See* H. G. Kuhn, *Atomic Spectra* (1962); H. J. Tobler *et al.*, "Distortion of Line Shapes in Stark Modulated Microwave Spectrometers," *J. Scient. Instrum.*, vol. 42 (1965).

**STARLEY, JAMES** (1830–1881), whose inventions earned him the title of "father of the cycle industry," was born at Albourne, Sussex, Eng., on April 21, 1830, and was educated in the village school. After working on the land in Kent he went in 1855 to London where he was employed in the manufacture of sewing machines, and then moved to Coventry, where he became managing foreman at the Coventry Sewing Machine Co. (later the Coventry Machinists' Co. Ltd.) and patented new models.

In the late 1860s, however, he became interested in the early forms of bicycle then appearing (through his firm's manufacture of *vélocipèdes* first for the French and later for the British market). Starley's first invention was the "C" spring and step machine, popularly known as the Coventry model. He followed this success in 1871 with the Ariel bicycle, notable for its centre pivot steering; then the Tangent; and, in 1876, the still excellent Coventry tricycle. Starley also invented the double-throw crank, the chain, and the chain wheel drive, all of which became standard parts of every bicycle.

Starley died at Coventry on June 17, 1881. *See* also BICYCLE: *The "Ordinary" Bicycle.*

**STARLING, ERNEST HENRY** (1866–1927), English physiologist, one of the foremost of his age, was born in London, April 17, 1866. Educated at King's College school, he entered Guy's hospital in 1882 and graduated M.D. in 1890. In that year he was appointed lecturer in physiology at Guy's. He was elected a fellow of the Royal society in 1899, and in 1900 became Jodrell professor of physiology at University college, London, where he worked until, in 1922, he retired from the Jodrell chair and was appointed Foulerton research professor of the Royal society.

The subjects for investigation that particularly attracted Starling were those physiological processes that seemed capable of interpretation in terms of chemistry and physics. The conditions determining transudation from the vessels and lymph flow occupied his attention for several years, and he showed that the hydrostatic and osmotic pressures within the vessels supplied the balance of force necessary to explain the previously perplexing experimental facts. His researches on the movements of the intestines, in conjunction with Sir William Bayliss (*q.v.*), demonstrated the neuromuscular mechanisms involved. Their discovery of secretin not only laid bare the way in which the secretion of the pancreas was called forth and adjusted, but also stimulated further research on the chemical integration of the body functions. By ingenious experimental methods Starling was successful in maintaining the mammalian kidney, isolated from all connection with the body, in a state of functional activity, thereby bringing to light new facts concerning renal secretion. His most important researches, however, were those dealing with the heart and circulation. He demonstrated the mechanism by which the heart is able to increase automatically the energy of each contraction in proportion to the mechanical demand made upon it and, apart from the nervous system, to adapt its work to the needs of the body.

During World War I Starling was director of research at the Royal Army Medical Corps college and engaged in devising defensive methods against poison gas. Subsequently, 1917–19, he was chairman of the Royal society's food committee, scientific adviser to the ministry of food and British scientific delegate on the Inter-Allied Food commission. He died on May 2, 1927.

**STARLING,** the name for birds of the passerine family Sturnidae, which contains about 103 species. The normal range of the family is Africa, Europe and Asia, to Australia, with most species in the tropics. Certain species have been introduced into various other parts of the world, such as Madagascar and Hawaii, and into North America, where the common starling of Europe, *Sturnus vulgaris,* is widespread.

Dark, iridescent plumage characterizes many starlings, but duller birds exist, and one species is mostly white. Bare, coloured areas of skin, or wattles, decorate the heads of some. Certain species of the tropical forest are mostly arboreal and eat fruit; those of open country walk about on the ground and eat insects. Several species are familiar birds, coming about houses and gardens, where they may cause annoyance by usurping the nesting sites of other birds.

JOHN H. GERARD

STARLING (STURNUS VULGARIS), COMMON TO EUROPE AND NORTH AMERICA (WINTER PLUMAGE)

Gregariousness is a common trait. The birds may feed or roost in large flocks, and some nest in colonies. The nest may be in a hole in a tree, bank or building or may be an oval, pensile structure. The eggs are plain or spotted.

A number of starlings are kept as cage birds, notably the talking mynas and several other southeast Asian species. The African oxpeckers, genus *Buphagus,* that eat ticks off the skin of hoofed animals are aberrant starlings. *See* also BIRD. (A. L. RD.; X.)

**STAR-SPANGLED BANNER,** the national anthem of the United States of America. It was officially adopted by an act of Congress signed by Pres. Herbert Hoover on March 3, 1931, although it had been in common use for well over a century before that date. The words were written by an American lawyer, Francis Scott Key (*q.v.*), Sept. 13–14, 1814. The music, long a subject of considerable controversy, is now generally credited to the British composer, John Stafford Smith (1750–1836). The argument that Samuel Arnold, Smith's predecessor as organist of the Chapel Royal, was the composer was effectively answered by Oscar G. Sonneck, chief of the Division of Music of the Library of Congress in a report in 1914.

The original version of the melody was written for a social club, the Anacreontic Society of London, with the title "To Anacreon in Heaven," with words by the organization's president, Ralph Tomlinson, probably about 1780. There were no less than five early publications of the words and music without credit to the composer, but in 1799 the combination appeared in Smith's *Fifth Book of Canzonets, Catches, Canons and Glees,* as "harmonized by the author," and since all the other melodies were of his own creation, there seems to be no reason for making an exception of "the Anacreontic Song."

This historic ditty naturally lauded the Greek poet Anacreon, the Society's patron saint, who wrote mostly about wine and women, as emphasized in the closing couplet of each stanza, which urged the members to "entwine the myrtle of Venus with Bacchus's vine." It is not generally realized that the Anacreontic tune was used many times, with a variety of words of political, patriotic, social, and sometimes ribald, nature. Richard Hill, a successor to Sonneck at the Library of Congress, reported the discovery of more than 80 such texts for this one melody.

The outstanding American adaptation of "To Anacreon in Heaven" (before "The Star-Spangled Banner") was a song called "Adams and Liberty," written for the presidential campaign of John Adams by a certain Thomas Paine, who called himself Robert Treat Paine, Jr., to avoid confusion with his more famous namesake. The same author used the Anacreon tune again as the musical setting of a poem entitled "Spain," and it is logical to assume that Francis Scott Key was familiar with one or both of these songs.

The story of Key's creation of his immortal lines has often been told, with some conflicting details. The significant facts are that the young lawyer, then living in Georgetown, near Washington, D.C., was asked to negotiate with the British Navy for the release of his friend, William Beanes, of Upper Marlborough, Md., a doctor who had been taken into custody as a result of his own highly irregular arrests of stragglers from the invading British army. According to Key's own account, he was taken on board one of the British ships that were then preparing for an attack on Baltimore by way of Fort McHenry (or M'Henry as it was often written). Obviously neither he nor Beanes could be released until the battle had taken place, and thus the stage was set for the all-night vigil of Sept. 13–14, which inspired the poem first called "The Defence of Fort M'Henry" and eventually "The Star-Spangled Banner."

Francis Scott Key watched the bombardment by the light of bombs (as artillery shells were then called) and rockets; at dawn he saw that the American flag was still flying over the fort, proof that the fort had not been captured. Using the back of an envelope, Key started writing his poem while on board the British ship. He continued it in the small boat that later took him and Beanes ashore and finished it at a hotel in Baltimore. He showed it to his brother-in-law, Judge J. H. Nicholson, who immediately had it printed and distributed in broadside form. "The Defence of Fort M'Henry" appeared in the *Baltimore Patriot* of Sept. 20, 1814, and the following day also in the *Baltimore American,* both papers indicating that it should be sung to the tune of "To Anacreon in Heaven." The title was soon changed to "The Star-Spangled Banner," appearing thus in the 1814 catalogue of Carr's Music Store in Baltimore and in several popular "songsters" (collections) of the same year.

An actor named Ferdinand Durang is given credit for having sung "The Star-Spangled Banner" for the first time in public, at a tavern next to the Holiday Theatre, where it soon became a regular feature of the performance. Durang claimed that he fitted the Anacreon tune to the words, but little fitting was required because Key clearly had this music in mind when he wrote the words. He had, in fact, written an earlier song, "The Warrior's Return," to the same melody.

The music of "The Star-Spangled Banner" has been criticized on the ground that it covers too great a range (an octave and a fifth) for a song meant to be sung by everyone. Difficult it undoubtedly is, but in the key of B♭, A, or A♭, it is by no means unsingable. Innumerable publications of the song through the years have shown variations in both words and music. An official arrangement was prepared by John Philip Sousa for the U.S. Army and Navy, and music educators have spent much time and effort in arriving at a practical version for American schools. The second and third stanzas are customarily omitted out of courtesy to the British. The accepted text of "The Star-Spangled Banner" is as follows:

Oh, say can you see by the dawn's early light
What so proudly we hail'd at the twilight's last gleaming,
Whose broad stripes and bright stars through the perilous fight
O'er the ramparts we watch'd were so gallantly streaming?
And the rockets' red glare, the bombs bursting in air,
Gave proof through the night that our flag was still there.
Oh, say does that star-spangled banner yet wave
O'er the land of the free and the home of the brave?

On the shore dimly seen through the mists of the deep,
Where the foe's haughty host in dread silence reposes,
What is that which the breeze, o'er the towering steep,
As it fitfully blows, half conceals, half discloses?
Now it catches the gleam of the morning's first beam,
In full glory reflected now shines in the stream.
'Tis the star-spangled banner, oh, long may it wave
O'er the land of the free and the home of the brave!

And where is that band who so vauntingly swore
That the havoc of war and the battle's confusion
A home and a country should leave us no more?
Their blood has wash'd out their foul footstep's pollution.
No refuge could save the hireling and slave
From the terror of flight or the gloom of the grave,
And the star-spangled banner in triumph doth wave
O'er the land of the free and the home of the brave.

Oh, thus be it ever when freemen shall stand
Between their lov'd home and the war's desolation!
Blest with vict'ry and peace may the heav'n-rescued land
Praise the power that hath made and preserv'd us a nation!
Then conquer we must, when our cause it is just,
And this be our motto, "In God is our Trust,"
And the star-spangled banner in triumph shall wave
O'er the land of the free and the home of the brave.

(S. Sp.)

**STARVATION** is a state of extreme malnutrition caused by the long-continued deprivation of essential nutrients. It usually results from insufficient food intake, either because food is not available or because the person is unable to eat, due to illness or other factors. Starvation may also result from disturbances in digestion, absorption or utilization of food. *See* MALNUTRITION; FAMINE.

**STASSFURT,** a *Kreisstadt* (county capital) of East Germany in the *Bezirk* (district) of Magdeburg, German Democratic Republic. Pop. (1964) 24,803. The town is 25 mi. (40 km.) S of the district capital, Magdeburg, and on the Bode River. It is a railway junction and has chemical, engineering, scientific apparatus, and radio equipment enterprises. It is chiefly known, however, for its potash mines and the exploitation of other rock salts. The chronicles note the existence of salt deposits as early as 1227. The mining of potash salts began in 1861; since then Stassfurt has been known as the cradle of the German potash mining industry. First mentioned in the chronicles in 810, it received its municipal charter in 1276, when it was transferred from the duchy of Saxony to the archbishopric of Magdeburg. From 1680 it belonged to the electorate of Brandenburg, and between 1807 and 1813 to the kingdom of Westphalia.

**STATE.** When the first studies of organized political society were made in Greece, mainly by Plato and Aristotle, in the 4th century B.C., the unit of study was the polis or city-state. The Romans, adapting Greek political ideas, applied them to a larger territorial unit, the *respublica,* which may be freely translated as public concern; or the *status rei publicae,* state of the public concern. It is this Roman application of the term that is most commonly used today. It is altogether probable that we derive the word state from the Roman *status.* In the early 16th century Machiavelli used the term "state" extensively in his works in its modern meaning.

Authorities agree on certain essential properties of a state—population, territory, a government clothed with a monopoly of force for the preservation of peace and order, and having a plenitude of authority within the state independent of external control except that of international law. Since a state cannot function under that law unless it is recognized by the members of the community of nations, such diplomatic recognition is often considered another property of the state. In addition, most political theorists emphasize purpose or end in their definition of the state; this purpose is stated as the promotion of the common good or general welfare.

Two terms are to be distinguished from the term "state," namely, society and nation. The free association of people in families and in social and cultural groupings constitutes a society; these groups lie largely outside of political control. The nation, strictly speaking, is a unit of society with a common language, tradition, and culture that may or may not coincide with state boundaries.

The states of the United States do not constitute states in the accepted meaning of the term. Nor may the term be applied to protectorates or semi-independent commonwealths, such as Puerto Rico. The term "estates-general" derives from the French *états* ("estates"), referring to the various orders or conditions of society, as the clergy, nobility, and third estate or common people, which were represented in European states-general of the medieval period.

*See* also SOVEREIGNTY.

BIBLIOGRAPHY.—W. W. Willoughby, *Fundamental Concepts of Public Law* (1924); R. M. MacIver, *The Modern State* (1926); H. J. Ford, *Natural History of the State* (1915); J. Maritain, *Man and the State* (1951).

(J. G. KN.)

**STATE, DEPARTMENT OF:** *see* GOVERNMENT DEPARTMENTS.

**STATE GOVERNMENT (U.S.).** In 1776 the 13 British colonies in America proclaimed themselves to be independent states, and in 1781, under the Articles of Confederation, they formed a "perpetual Union." The perpetuity of the union was not assured, however, for the articles which established that "firm league of friendship" provided also that each state should retain its "sovereignty, freedom and independence," and in the following years the states showed a strong disposition to exercise the sovereignty thus retained. The federal Constitution, drafted in 1787 and put into effect two years later, established a stronger national government, the "more perfect" union that was needed. The Constitution made no reference to the troublesome question of sovereignty, leaving that to be disposed of by time—to be denied to the states, as it turned out, by the Civil War.

**The Place of the States in the Federal System.**—The federal Constitution divides the powers of government between the national (commonly called federal) government and the states. The federal government has those powers that are delegated to it by the Constitution and the authority to make all laws that may be "necessary and proper" to implement the powers so delegated. The delegated powers are not numerous, but they are fundamental, including those to make war, conduct foreign relations, regulate interstate and foreign commerce, and, of course, to levy taxes. The last-named power may be exercised not only to pay and provide for the common defense but also for the general welfare. Federal power has been extended by constitutional amendments, but it has been expanded much more significantly by the liberal use that Congress has made of the "necessary and proper" clause of the Constitution and by the judicial sanction of such use.

In many areas of government responsibility, federal power and influence have been extended through a system of grants-in-aid to the states and through them to the local governments. The basic features of the plan are that Congress, acting under its authority to appropriate money for the general welfare or under some other specific authorization, makes funds available to the states for a particular purpose, on condition that the states make appropriations for the same purpose and meet a standard set by Congress for the manner in which the federal-state funds shall be expended. This aid system expanded rapidly after the middle of the 20th century, both in the number of projects supported and in the funds appropriated for them. In the late 1960s, 4 different grants were made for public welfare, 5 for highways, 18 for education (these three received the largest grants and in that order), 36 for public health, and scores of grants for eight or nine other areas. The total amount of the grants was roughly 13% of the federal tax receipts. It seemed probable that the categorical grants would be supplemented by a plan under which the federal government would return to the state and local governments a small, lump-sum share of the national revenue, thus leaving those governments independent as to the purposes for which the money may be used.

The U.S. Constitution imposes upon the states certain specific prohibitions. By far the most significant ones are those of the 14th Amendment, which stipulate that no state shall "deprive any person of life, liberty, or property without due process of law, nor deny to any person within its jurisdiction the equal protection of the laws." Since about 1930, a liberal judicial interpretation of those prohibitions has greatly enlarged civil liberties in general and the rights of racial minorities in particular.

The states have all the powers not conferred upon the federal government by the Constitution and not prohibited by it to the states. The powers of the states are thus residual. They are numerous and comprehensive, despite the steady extension of federal power. Furthermore, the national government has left much authority to the states that it might reserve to itself. For example, it permits the states to regulate interstate commerce relating to matters that are primarily of local concern. And it leaves the states in almost complete authority to police the interstate highways.

Examples of state power exist on every hand. The United States has a limited criminal code, but the great bodies of criminal law are incorporated in the state codes. The laws of contracts, torts, negotiable instruments, sales, and many others closely related to business are state laws. Property laws are within the special province of the states, and so are those respecting wills and inheritance. Marriage, divorce, and domestic relations fall within the jurisdiction of the states. The states determine who may vote, provided only that they make no discrimination on account of race, sex, or wealth (the poll tax is thus banned). Practically all of the laws relating to political parties and elections are acts of the state legislatures. Local governments are established and controlled by the states. Public education is a leading state function.

The state is close to the individual. His birth certificate and his burial permit are issued by the state; and as he progresses from the cradle to the grave, the state protects his personal rights and secures his property; carries the major part of the cost of his education; licenses him to enter a calling or a profession; ministers to his convenience in numerous ways; and penalizes his delinquencies.

**Nature of State Governments.**—Each state has a written constitution of its own design, subject only to the requirement that it shall not violate the federal Constitution. State constitutions follow the federal pattern in that they contain bills of rights and adhere to the cherished American principle of the distribution of powers among the legislative, executive, and judicial branches. Most of the state constitutions provide in considerable detail for both the organization and the functions of government and in consequence they are rather long documents, in contrast to the national Constitution. Such elaboration of detail makes frequent amendment necessary, a process that is in almost continuous operation in a number of states.

The bicameral (two-house) legislature is used in all the states except Nebraska, which instituted the unicameral system in 1937. During and for several years following the Revolutionary War, the legislatures enjoyed public confidence and practically unlimited powers in state government. Chiefly because a number of legislatures failed in their trust, the states developed the practice of placing limits on their powers to deal with revenue, appropriations, borrowing, local government, and certain other subjects. Furthermore, in the course of time, the state courts assumed a restrictive view of legislative powers. And finally, between 1898 and 1918, general dissatisfaction with legislatures led more than a third of the states to adopt the initiative and referendum. These limitations do not deprive legislative bodies of essential powers, and they may have the effect of improving their work.

In 1964 the U.S. Supreme Court, in a decision of far-reaching importance, ruled that within each state the districts from which state legislators are elected must contain, as nearly as possible, the same number of inhabitants. This decision, popularly characterized as the "one man, one vote" principle, struck at the overrepresentation of rural areas in many state legislatures and gave greater political power to residents of metropolitan areas.

In colonial America the governor exercised wide powers; during the Revolution he was stripped of much of his authority; but after about 1850, the tendency was to make him an effective force in legislation, and, since 1915, to strengthen greatly his control over administration. Although his authority over administration has often been impaired by the fact that much of the work of the state has been parceled out to boards, commissions, and other relatively independent agencies, in perhaps half the states this situation has been partially corrected by the establishment of a limited number of administrative departments and the placement of a group of related services in each of them. In such states the department heads are commonly appointed by the governor and serve under his immediate direction, thus giving him an administrative position somewhat analogous to that of the president of the United States. In the great majority of the states the governor's influence over legislation is particularly significant, and it is explained by a variety of factors, including his political position, his permanent and sometimes professional staff, his veto power, and the time limit under which a majority of the legislatures must work. The hand of the governor has been incidentally strengthened by the trend to increase the length of his term.

The system of law and justice in the states was inherited from Great Britain, but it has been modified in the states to fit their requirements. One such modification is in the matter of the selection of judges, most of the states following the elective system and limiting the term of office to four, six, or some other number of years. The courts in all the states follow the practice of judicial review; that is, they pass upon the constitutionality of statutes where such determination is necessary to decision in cases appropriately before them. Largely because of the absence of any judicial supervisory authority, the administration of justice has fallen below a desirable standard in a number of states. Several states have rectified this condition by establishing a unified court system under which the chief justice is authorized to assign judges in the lower courts where they are most needed and, with his colleagues in the supreme court, to make rules of judicial procedure for all the courts and otherwise systematize and expedite the work of the courts. (*See* COURT: *United States.*)

After 1950 the cost of state government increased about fivefold and, despite the numerous and often generous federal-aid programs, a number of the states had difficulties in financing the cost of their services. In considerable measure, however, such difficulties stemmed from the extreme reluctance of many legislators, particularly rural ones, to increase tax rates or to produce additional revenues by instituting such improvements in the existing tax structure as the abolishment of property tax exemptions enjoyed by certain interest groups and the adoption of an income tax.

A majority of the states were slow to meet the responsibilities imposed by modern developments and hardly any states dealt effectively with the great metropolitan issues and crises. The necessity for active federal participation in action on fronts that were formerly almost entirely reserved to the states became an old story. But the pervasive activities of the national government did not retard state action. On the contrary, the states greatly expanded their functions and increased their budgets, particularly for highways, education, health, and welfare. It may be maintained that after World War II the states, acting alone or in cooperation with the national government, significantly strengthened their performance as vital units of government.

*See* also LOCAL GOVERNMENT; STATES' RIGHTS; and sections on government in separate articles on each of the states; and references under "State Government (U.S.)" in the Index.

BIBLIOGRAPHY.—The Council of State Governments, *The Book of the States* (biennial); Thomas R. Dye, *Politics in States and Communities* (1969); Malcolm E. Jewell, *The State Legislature* (1962); V. O. Key, Jr., *American State Politics: an Introduction* (1956); Coleman B. Ransone, Jr., *The Office of Governor in the United States* (1956); W. Brooke Graves, *American Intergovernmental Relations: Their Origins, Historical Development and Current Status* (1964). (C. O. J.)

**STATEN ISLAND,** an island of New York, U.S., lying in New York harbour south of Manhattan between New Jersey and Brooklyn; it forms Richmond county and Richmond borough, the third largest of the five New York city boroughs. Triangular in shape, the island has about 35 mi. (56 km.) of waterfront and an area of about 60 sq.mi. (155 sq.km.). Although principally a residential suburb of the Borough of Manhattan and neighbouring New Jersey cities, Staten Island has considerable manufacturing, shipbuilding, oil refining, and metalworking. The borough is connected with Manhattan by the Staten Island ferry, which carries passengers and automobiles; with New Jersey by the Outerbridge Crossing, Goethals, and Bayonne bridges; and with Brooklyn by the Verrazano-Narrows Bridge. Opening of the latter in 1964 added considerable impetus to development of the island. Population (1960) 221,991.

When discovered by Europeans, Staten Island was inhabited by a few Aquehonga Indians, a branch of the Raritans. Beginning in 1630 and during the next three decades several settlements were attempted by such Dutch leaders as Patroon D. P. de Vries, Gov. Willem Kieft (or Kiefft) and Cornelis Melyn. These attempts at settlement proved unsuccessful because of Indian attacks which, particularly in 1655, laid waste the white settlements on the island. The first permanent settlement was made in 1661 when the Dutch West India company, having purchased the Staten Island estate of Melyn, granted land to French Waldenses and Huguenots. This settlement was established at Oude Dorp (Old Town), a few miles south of The Narrows.

The island was named during the period of Dutch control for the states-general of the Dutch Republic. Following the acquisition of New Netherland in 1664 by the duke of York, Welsh and English farmers established homes and farms on the island. During the American Revolution Staten Island was the scene of talks between the three representatives of the Continental congress—Benjamin Franklin, John Adams and Edward Rutledge—and Lord Howe in an unsuccessful attempt at reconciliation. This meeting was held at the Billopp or "Conference" house in Tottenville on the southern shore of the island on Sept. 11, 1776. The island was the residence of Giuseppe Garibaldi, the Italian patriot, in the early 1850s during his exile from Italy. After the American Civil War industrialization increased while farming and fishing waned in importance. In 1898 Staten Island became one of New York City's boroughs. (*See* also NEW YORK [CITY]; RICHMOND.)

The island has numerous points of interest which include Barrett park, containing the Staten Island zoo; the museum of the Staten Island Institute of Arts and Sciences; the Staten Island Historical museum; the Sailors' Snug Harbor (a home for retired U.S. seamen); and the Billopp or "Conference" house. There are two liberal arts colleges on the island, Wagner college, a Lutheran coeducational institution founded in 1883, and Notre Dame College of Staten Island, a four-year Roman Catholic college for women, established in 1931.

There are many historic churches and houses still standing, among which is the Voorlezer's house (1696), one of the earliest known elementary school buildings in the U.S. (D. L. D.)

**STATES OF THE CHURCH:** *see* PAPAL STATES.

**STATES' RIGHTS,** a phrase used to describe those governmental powers retained by the individual states of a federal union under the provisions of the federal constitution. In the United States, Switzerland, and Australia, these powers are those that remain after the powers of the central government are enumerated in the constitution. In Canada and the German Federal Republic, on the other hand, the powers of both the levels of government are defined by specific constitutional provisions.

In the United States the term states' rights has also been widely used for a variety of political programs. Before the Civil War it was the rallying cry of southern opponents of northern-inspired tariffs and northern proposals to abolish or restrict slavery (*see* NULLIFICATION). By the second half of the 20th century, it had become the catchword of those who opposed integration of Negroes and whites in public schools, and of those who criticized the growing power of the federal government.

The governmental authority actually remaining in the member governments varies greatly among federal systems. It is perhaps greatest in the United States and weakest in countries such as Mexico and Brazil, where most power is concentrated in the central government and the states are little more than administrative agencies. State power declined rapidly after 1900 in the United States, and somewhat similarly in Canada and Australia. The major causes of this trend in the U.S. were the increased activity of the central government through the power of Congress to control interstate commerce, federal financial subsidies to the state governments or their subdivisions, national measures for combating depression, and participation in World Wars I and II.

In general, states' rights suffer more from financial subsidies of the federal government than from the commerce clause. These subsidies sometimes involve substantial central control in fields that are not included in the federal government's enumerated powers. If the state government rejects the subsidy, it presumably damages its area financially. The result of the subsidy process in the second half of the 20th century in the United States was that the federal government exercised varying degrees of influence, ranging from considerable to determinative, in public policy involving vocational education, public housing, airport construction, sewage plant construction, state and local road construction, fish and game conservation, and other fields which a reading of the Constitution would clearly indicate were states' rights. Canadian and Australian experience in the 20th century was similar, the central governments concerned moving through subsidies into many fields of state or provincial action.

Some political scientists believe that a federal system of government (*see* FEDERAL GOVERNMENT) is merely a transitional form that will be ultimately succeeded by unified government. A quick glance at 20th-century federal systems would seem to confirm this view. However, states' rights may persist a long time. In three of the federal countries—the United States, Australia, and Canada—study commissions have concluded that it is desirable to maintain the autonomous authority of the state or provincial governments. The reasons given included the training of the citizenry in democratic processes through state and local self-government, the greater opportunity under a federal system to adapt governmental policies to the needs of particular areas, and the deconcentration of power resulting from a federal system. There was considerable evidence that for these reasons a large number of thoughtful people in the three countries wished to maintain states' rights.

BIBLIOGRAPHY.—K. C. Wheare, *Federal Government,* 4th ed. (1964); report and studies of the U.S. Commission on Intergovernmental Relations (1955); report and studies of the Royal Commission on Dominion-Provincial Relationships (1938); S. Seabury, *The New Federalism* (1950); C. J. Bloch, *States' Rights* (1958); Arthur M. Schlesinger, "The States' Rights Fetish," *New Viewpoints in American History* (1922); D. P. Currie (ed.), *Federalism in the New Nations* (1964); W. Brooke Graves, *American Intergovernmental Relations* (1964). (G. C. S. B.)

**STATIC,** in radio, a hissing or crackling noise in the receiver that interferes with the desired signal. It may be either natural or man-made, and it consists of spurious electromagnetic waves ranging in frequency from a few hundred cycles per second to many thousand kilocycles. The most common natural source of static is lightning discharges, which may be detected by sensitive AM receivers at distances of more than 1,000 mi. (1,609 km.). Man-made sources of static include automobile ignition systems, electric motors, and any improperly operating electrical equipment in which sparking occurs. Because most static signals are of an amplitude-modulated form, they are not detected by FM receivers. *See* also RADIO; RADIO RECEIVER.

**STATICS** is a branch of mechanics concerned with the conditions under which a body remains at rest. Although statics relates strictly to both solid and fluid systems, it is common to give special names to the statics of some particular types of deformable bodies. In particular, elasticity and plasticity theory concern specific types of solids, while the statics of liquids is known as hydrostatics. This article is devoted to a brief discussion of the statics of rigid bodies, a subject of critical importance in the design and construction of such objects as bridges, aircraft, buildings, dams, submarines, high-heeled shoes, automobiles, and braces for straightening teeth. The discussion to follow assumes a familiarity with the article MECHANICS.

**A Simple Problem of Rigid Statics.**—Consider the simplest type of railway bridge, consisting essentially of a metal beam supported by two masonry abutments. Suppose that it is wished to estimate the amount of the force transmitted to the stationary beam at one of the abutments. This information might be needed for a variety of reasons, although the designer of the structure would normally postulate some suitable loading of the beam when making strength calculations. This required force can be found from consideration of the statics of the beam, isolated for the purposes of analysis as in fig. 1.

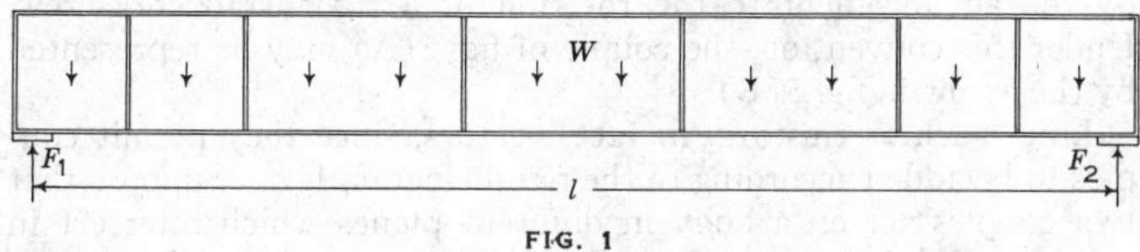


FIG. 1

This beam has forces applied to it: they are its weight $W$ (a distributed body force) and also the vertical forces $F_1$ and $F_2$ transmitted by the supports separated by distance $l$. Conditions under which this beam can be in equilibrium are: (1) the resultant force applied to it, in any direction, shall be nil; and (2) the resultant moment of all the applied forces about any fixed axis shall be nil. The beam in fig. 1 is at rest, and mathematical expression may now be given to this fact. Requirement (1) demands that

$$W - F_1 - F_2 = 0$$

The total moment (force × distance) acting about the left-hand support can be reckoned (*see* LEVER); if the centre of mass of the bridge is midway across the span, then

$$\frac{Wl}{2} - F_2 l = 0$$

From these two equations the expected result can be established that

$$F_1 = F_2 = \frac{W}{2}$$

Thus the required force is equal to half the weight of the beam in this case.

In this simple calculation, no allowance is made for the fact that the bridge is to some extent flexible. On the contrary, the bridge is assumed to be rigid inasmuch as use is made of a characteristic length $l$ which could be measured before the beam is lifted off the ground and placed on its supports. Obviously, if the bridge were made of rubber, the distance between the supports would be much less than the length of the unsupported span, so that mathematically the required length $l$ would depend upon $W$.

Since it is reasonable to assume that the variation of $l$ is too small to be of consequence, this structure is said to be statically determinate. The effect of statical determinacy is to separate the mathematical problem of equilibrium from that of compatibility (*see* ELASTICITY: *Theory of Strain*). Assumptions of this sort account largely for the great importance of the statics of rigid bodies: it is not that the bodies are really rigid but that they may be assumed so for the purposes of calculation.

**The Statics of a Rigid Body.**—The conditions under which a body, supposed rigid, can remain at rest must next be considered in more detail. Expressed algebraically, the problem is the examination of equations (21) and (22) of the article MECHANICS, when all the time derivatives are 0. That is, for any rigid body at rest it is necessary to satisfy force equations

$$\left.\begin{aligned} F_x &= \Sigma f_x = 0 \\ F_y &= \Sigma f_y = 0 \\ F_z &= \Sigma f_z = 0 \end{aligned}\right\} \qquad (1)$$

and also moment equations

$$\left.\begin{aligned} M_z &= \Sigma(xf_y - yf_x) = 0 \\ M_x &= \Sigma(yf_z - zf_y) = 0 \\ M_y &= \Sigma(zf_x - xf_z) = 0 \end{aligned}\right\} \qquad (2)$$

In words, equation (1) states that the sums of the resolved parts of the external forces in the directions of fixed orthogonal axes OX, OY, and OZ shall be 0. The quantities $M_x$, $M_y$, $M_z$ are the moments about OX, OY, and OZ of the external forces, and these also must vanish.

While equations (1) and (2) govern the forces acting on a body at rest, it is not necessarily possible to solve these equations explicitly. Statically determinate systems only are of concern here, so that this difficulty will not arise.

**Static Equivalence; Transmissibility.**—Suppose that a rigid body is under the action of forces, one of which is of magnitude $f$ and is applied to it at some point P (fig. 2).

Let the component of $f$ in the plane XOY be $r$; it is obtained by projecting the force vector parallel to ZO. Now the state of rest of the body will not be altered if two equal and opposite forces $f$ are applied at Q (as in fig. 2), Q being a point lying on the line of action of $f$. They too will have components $r$ (*see* VECTOR ANALYSIS).

The effect on the equilibrium of the outer pair of these components $r$ (dashed arrows in fig. [2B]) is nil, since they are equal and opposite and have no net moment about the axis OZ. If removed, these components leave only the one component $r$ shown.

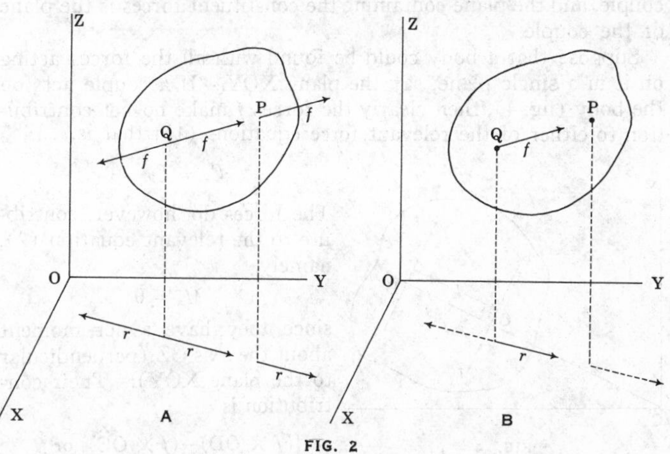


FIG. 2

Similar conclusions are reached by projecting the original forces at P and Q on to the planes YOZ and ZOX. If the three remaining components (of which $r$ in fig. 2[B] is one) are now compounded, they give the force $f$ at Q, as shown in fig. 2(B). The remaining force $f$ at Q is statically equivalent to the original force $f$ at P in that substitution of one for the other has no effect on the state of equilibrium of the body. To this extent, then, the point of application of $f$ may be transmitted along the line of action; this is known as the property of transmissibility of a force.

**Parallel Forces and Couples.**—Consider two parallel forces which act on a body; their lines of action define a plane. The addition of these forces is clearly a case which cannot be dealt with by the parallelogram law of vectors, since the lines of action do not intersect (*see* FORCE).

A simple extension of the above reasoning shows that the statical effects of a given system of forces acting on a body are unaltered by the imposition of two equal and opposite forces having the same line of action. If, therefore, $f_1$ and $f_2$ (shown in fig. 3) are two parallel forces (acting in the plane of the paper) whose resultant is required, the equal and opposite forces $P$ can be superposed as shown. The resultant of $P$ and $f_1$ is $R_1$ and that of $P$ and $f_2$ is $R_2$. Let the lines of action of $R_1$ and $R_2$ intersect at A; this point may be regarded as the point of application of $R_1$ and $R_2$ and hence of $f_1$ and $f_2$ without the forces $P$.

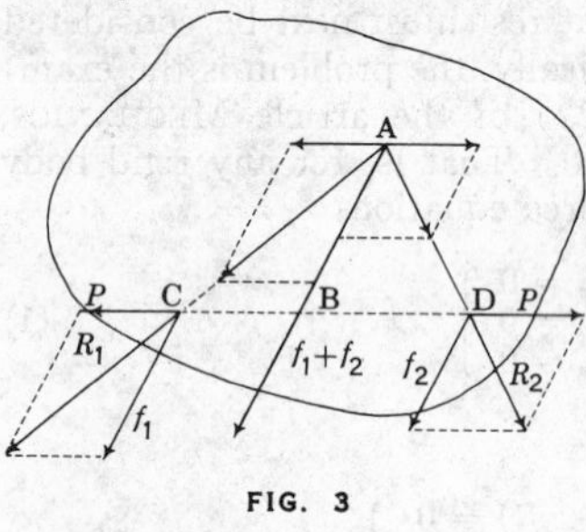

FIG. 3

The forces $R_1$ and $R_2$, supposed acting at A, may now be replaced by their components $P$-plus-$f_1$ and $P$-plus-$f_2$, respectively. Since the forces $P$ again neutralize each other, there is left the resultant force which is parallel to $f_1$ and $f_2$, is of magnitude $f_1 + f_2$ and acts through A. The position of the line of action of the resultant force may easily be deduced. For, by consideration of similar triangles (*see* SIMILAR FIGURES),

$$\frac{CB}{BA} = \frac{P}{f_1}; \frac{BD}{BA} = \frac{P}{f_2}$$

It follows that

$$\frac{CB}{BD} = \frac{f_2}{f_1}$$

If the parallel forces $f_1$ and $f_2$ act in opposite directions, their resultant can be found by similar means. It will act in the plane of $f_1$ and $f_2$ and will be found to act outside the space between the lines of $f_1$ and $f_2$. The magnitude of the resultant is then the difference between $f_1$ and $f_2$, and its direction is that of the greater of the two.

The lines of action of $R_1$ and $R_2$ (which fix the point A in fig. 3) are parallel if $f_1$ and $f_2$ are equal in magnitude and opposite in direction, so that a single resultant force cannot be found. A pair of forces of this nature is said to constitute a couple, and the plane containing the constituent forces is the plane of the couple.

Suppose that a body could be found with all the forces acting on it in a single plane, say the plane XOY. If a couple acts on the body (fig. 4), then clearly the forces $f$ make no net contribution to either of the relevant force equations (1); that is,

$$F_x = F_y = 0$$

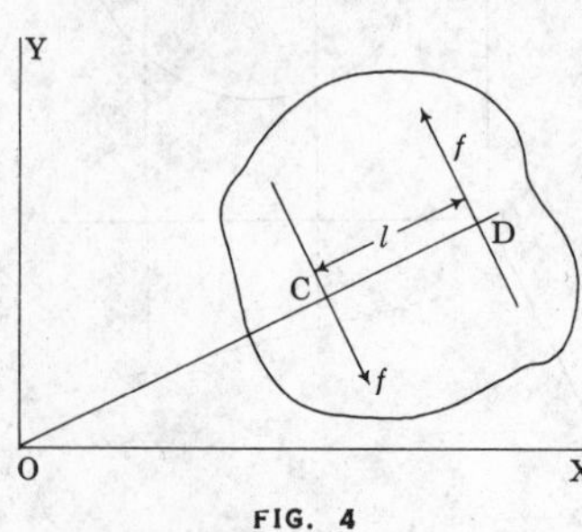

FIG. 4

The forces do, however, contribute to the relevant equation (2), namely,

$$M_z = 0$$

since they have a net moment about the axis OZ (perpendicular to the plane XOY). Their contribution is

$$[(f \times OD) - (f \times OC)] \text{ or } fl$$

where OCD is perpendicular to the lines of action of the two forces $f$, and $l$ is the distance between these lines.

The moment of the couple in this case is of magnitude $fl$. Evidently the two forces could be moved to act in the plane at any points of the body and in any direction in this plane without affecting the conditions of equilibrium. It is necessary only that the product of the magnitude of the forces and the distance between their lines of action should be kept equal to $fl$. In this problem, in which all forces act in one plane, a couple is completely defined by the magnitude and direction (clockwise or counter-clockwise) of its moment.

**Vectorial Nature of Couples.**—It has been shown that the effect of a couple on the equilibrium of a body is not altered if the couple is moved in its own plane. It is next shown that if the equilibrium exists, it is not disturbed if the plane of action of the couple is moved parallel to itself.

Let a couple of moment $fl$ act on a body in a plane A (fig. 5[A]). The equilibrium of the body will be unaffected if two pairs of equal forces $f$ are applied with their lines of action distance $l$ apart on a parallel plane B. Now the forces $f'$ may be added, giving the resultant $R'$, while the forces $f''$ give the resultant $R''$. And since $R' = R''$, these resultants neutralize each other and may therefore be removed without influencing the equilibrium. There remain only the two forces in plane B, which form a couple of moment $fl$.

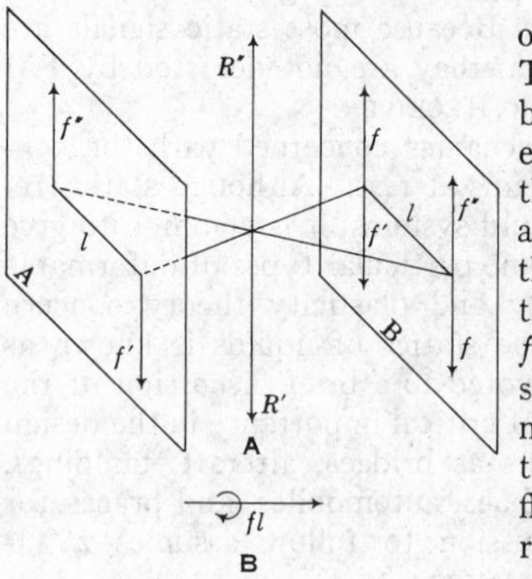

FIG. 5

The previous conclusions can now be extended to cover couples in space. It may be seen that a couple is completely defined by (1) the magnitude of its moment; (2) the orientation of the plane in which it acts; and (3) the sense in which it acts (thus the couple in fig. 5[A] acts in the clockwise sense when looking from plane A to plane B). It is evident that a couple can be represented by a line whose length represents its moment, whose direction is normal to the plane of the couple, and which points in a direction whose relation to the sense of the couple is that borne by the advancement to the rotation of a right-hand corkscrew. Under this convention, the couple of fig. 5(A) may be represented by the arrow in fig. 5(B).

Lines such as this are, in fact, vectors, since they permit couples to be added according to the parallelogram law. Suppose that two couples act on a body in different planes which intersect in a line containing two points C and D (fig. 6[A]). By movement in their own planes and movement of the type just described, the couples can be replaced by forces $f_1$ and forces $f_2$, whose lines of action are separated by the distance $l$ between

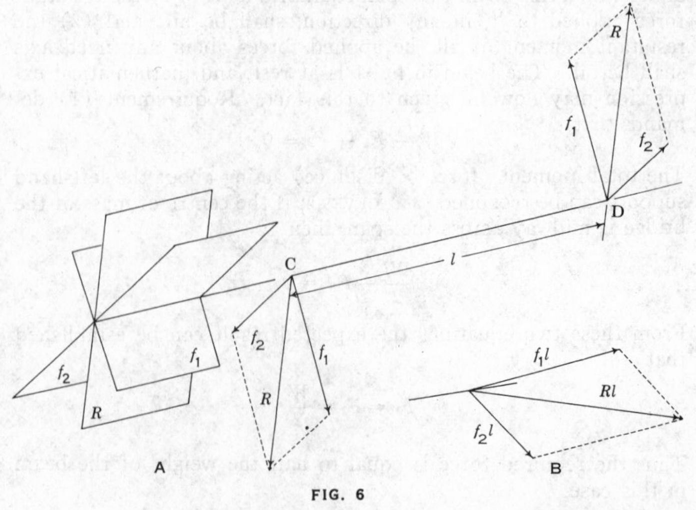

FIG. 6

C and D; it is merely necessary, when finding $f_1$ and $f_2$, that the moments of the couple be $f_1l$ and $f_2l$.

The forces at C and D can be compounded in the usual way, giving the resultant forces $R$. Thus the sum of the two original couples is a couple of magnitude $Rl$ whose plane is fixed by the vectors $R$. The planes containing the pairs of forces $f_1$ and $f_2$ and $R$ are indicated in the figure.

Now the original couples can be represented by the lines of length $f_1l$ and $f_2l$ (fig. 6[B]) in accordance with the corkscrew rule, these lines being perpendicular to the planes containing the pairs of forces $f_1$ and $f_2$, respectively. If these lines are now added by the parallelogram rule as shown, it can be seen that the construction is geometrically similar to those made before at C and D; the parallelogram is rotated through a right angle, and its sides are $l$ times as long as the previous ones. The diagonal, therefore, correctly represents the resultant couple $Rl$.

If a body is acted upon by several couples, then these may be compounded by repeated use of the parallelogram rule or, just as with the forces acting on a particle, by means of a space polygon.

If the polygon closes, there is no resultant couple acting. Further, any couple may be resolved into components by the parallelogram rule.

**Static Equilibrium of a Rigid Body.**—The analytical conditions for equilibrium of a rigid body are those of equations (1) and (2), which will now be interpreted in terms of vectors.

Suppose that a force $f$ is applied at some point A $(x,y,z)$ of a rigid body and consider its component $f_x$ (fig. 7). This component of the force enters equations (1) and (2) through: (1) its contribution to $F_x$; and (2) its contributions $-yf_x$ to $M_z$ and $zf_x$ to $M_y$. If, therefore, the component $f_x$ is replaced by a force of equal magnitude acting at O, together with the couples shown in the figure, the equilibrium of the body would not be influenced. If O lies outside the body, the force and couples may be imagined as being applied to an extension of the body which extends to the origin.

A similar argument may now be applied to the remaining components $f_y$ and $f_z$ of $f$. The force acting at A is therefore statically equivalent to a force passing through O (with components $f_x$, $f_y$, and $f_z$) and a couple whose components in the directions OX, OY, and OZ, are $(yf_z - zf_y)$, $(zf_x - xf_z)$, and $(xf_y - yf_x)$. The components of this couple are the contributions of $f$ to $M_x$, $M_y$, $M_z$.

This force $f$ may be regarded as typical of all the applied forces so that equations (1) and (2) can be regarded merely as statements that the sum of the components of these equivalent forces and couples must all be 0. In other words, there must be no resultant equivalent force acting at O and no resultant couple. The space polygons of the equivalent forces and couples must both close. Thus, except for no forces or the special case of two equal and opposite forces, the minimum number that can produce equilibrium is three forces.

Furthermore, an unbalanced couple can be balanced only by an equal couple with opposite sense.

**Centre of Gravity.**—The weight of a body is the external force exerted upon it by the gravitational attraction. It is the resultant of the contributions (to the total body force) of the separate gravity forces exerted upon the particles which may be thought of as forming the body. The force on each particle is proportional to its mass, and the forces are assumed parallel; under these circumstances it may be shown that their resultant always passes through a particular point fixed in the body.

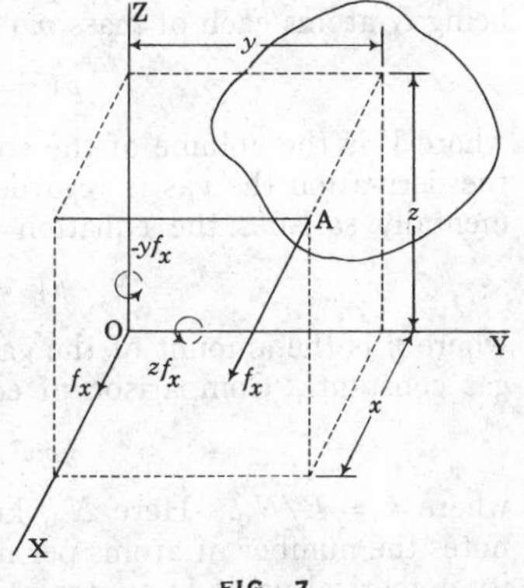

FIG. 7

Referring again to fig. 7, let $f_x$ be the component in the direction OX of the gravity force of one of the constituent particles. Now whatever the direction of the gravity forces on the various particles, their components in any direction will be proportional to the masses of the particles. Let these components be

$$(f_x)_1 = km_1 \; ; \; (f_x)_2 = km_2 \; ; \ldots$$

for the particles $m_1, m_2, \ldots$

It will now be seen by reference to fig. 7 that these various components could be replaced by a force

$$f_x = k\,\Sigma m = kM$$

directed along OX together with couples

$$\Sigma(-yf_x) = -k\,\Sigma my \text{ about OZ}$$

and

$$\Sigma zf_x = k\,\Sigma mz \text{ about OY}$$

Consider now a single force $F_x$, acting parallel to OX. Evidently it will be statically equivalent to all the components $(f_x)_1$, $(f_x)_2$, . . . etc., provided that its equivalent force and couples at O are the same as before. It is necessary that

$$F_x = kM \; ; -F_x\bar{y} = -k\,\Sigma my \; ; F_x\bar{z} = k\,\Sigma mz$$

where $\bar{y}$ and $\bar{z}$ are the distances of the line of action of $F_x$ from the planes XOZ and XOY, respectively. It follows that

$$\bar{y} = \frac{\Sigma my}{M} \; ; \bar{z} = \frac{\Sigma mz}{M}$$

In the same way the components of gravity force in the directions OY and OZ can be considered. It follows that a single force $F$ having components $F_x$, $F_y$, and $F_z$ can represent the sum of the various forces on the particles. Each component of $F$ is equal to the sum of the corresponding components of the particle forces. Further it is necessary that $F$ should act at the point $(\bar{x}, \bar{y}, \bar{z})$ of the body. This point may sometimes be referred to as the centre of mass, but it is called the centre of gravity in the present context (*see* NAVAL ARCHITECTURE: *Weight and Buoyancy*). *See* also DYNAMICS.

BIBLIOGRAPHY.—A. P. McMullen and E. W. E. Kempson, *Elementary Experimental Statics for Schools* (1936), contains a very simple introduction to the subject; A. S. Ramsey, *Statics* (1941) is an elementary textbook with a mathematical flavour; S. P. Timoshenko and D. H. Young, *Statics,* 4th ed. (1956), introduces the subject of statics and emphasizes its engineering applications; E. J. Routh, *A Treatise on Analytical Statics,* 2 vol., 2nd ed. (1896–1902), deals with more advanced problems in statics. *See* also R. H. Goff and D. E. Hardenbergh, *Introduction to Statics* (1965). (R. E. D. B.)

**STATIONERY,** a word that now covers all writing materials and implements, together with the numerous appliances of the desk and of business offices. For the principal articles and operations of the stationery trade, *see* INK; OFFICE MACHINES AND APPLIANCES; PAPER MANUFACTURE; PEN; PENCIL.

**STATISTICAL MECHANICS,** also called statistical thermodynamics, is that branch of theoretical physics in which the measurable properties of macroscopic substances (whether solids, liquids, or gases) are related to or predicted from the attributes of the microscopic systems (atoms or molecules) of which these substances are composed. Since all substances obey the laws of thermodynamics, these laws themselves must emerge as a consequence of the molecular structure of matter, and it is by the success of the theory in justifying this supposition that the alternative designation is best vindicated. On the other hand, since the theory itself is basically a combination of mechanics and probability theory, or statistics, the phrase statistical mechanics, originating (1901) from the U.S. mathematical physicist J. Willard Gibbs (1839–1903), is perhaps more accurately descriptive of the subject.

Statistical mechanics, indeed, owes to Gibbs much more than its name. Its formal, mathematical structure for computational purposes is still, apart from the inevitable but comparatively minor changes introduced by the development of quantum mechanics, essentially that presented in Gibbs's *Elementary Principles in Statistical Mechanics* (1902). But much progress has since been made both in the application of this formalism to particular physical situations and in the understanding of its justification. Satisfactory agreement with experience had to await the creation of the quantum theory about 25 years later. Moreover, Gibbs himself produced the formal structure as a statistical model which obeyed or embodied the laws of thermodynamics without fully justifying this model on the basis of molecular behaviour. Judged pragmatically, Gibbs's formalism certainly provides the correct prescription for calculating equilibrium macroscopic properties from microscopic ones, but a complete justification of the procedure from the laws of molecular dynamics presented a difficult and only partially solved problem in the 1960s. Advances in the mathematical theory of probability, however, have done much to clarify the situation. For critical discussion of the foundations of statistical mechanics reference should be made to the books by R. C. Tolman, D. ter Haar, and especially A. I. Khinchin, listed in the bibliography at the end of this article.

The history of the subject properly starts, however, not with Gibbs, who by largely abandoning the details of molecular mechanics broke with tradition, but three or four decades earlier with the contributions by James Clerk Maxwell (1831–79) and Ludwig Boltzmann (1844–1906) to the kinetic theory of gases. Kinetic theory itself dates from the 18th century, though it was not until after the work of the English chemist John Dalton and the Italian physicist Amedeo Avogadro in the early 19th century that the concepts of atoms and molecules could be entertained seriously as physical realities. The laws of thermodynamics also are 19th-century discoveries (*see* THERMODYNAMICS).

Although the atomic hypothesis played its part in the overthrow of caloric theory (*see* HEAT), the laws of thermodynamics are purely phenomenological, making no reference to the ultimate constitution of matter. These laws are phrased in terms of concepts, some of which are peculiar to thermodynamics; of these temperature is the most familiar example. Others, such as the work done on a thermodynamic system by external agencies, relate directly to mechanics or to the energetics of electromagnetic theory. It is convenient at this point to summarize these laws, using modern notation and with a minimum of discussion. The account does not pretend to logical completeness and should be regarded solely as a brief recapitulation of phenomenological heat theory.

1. One may speak of thermal equilibrium between two systems; thus if two systems are each in thermal equilibrium with a third, then they are in thermal equilibrium with each other. This permits empirical temperature scales to be defined (*see* THERMOMETRY).

2. One may speak of an adiabatically enclosed (thermally insulated) system, and then the work required to change the system from one equilibrium state to another is independent of how this work is supplied. This allows internal energy ($U$) to be defined apart from an additive constant.

3. No cyclic heat engine can simply extract internal energy from a system and convert it fully into useful mechanical work. This permits a logical introduction of the concepts entropy ($S$) and absolute temperature ($T$). $S$, like $U$, is defined apart from an additive constant, and $T$ is arbitrary to the extent of a scale factor.

Statement 1, which underlies the whole science of thermometry, has been accepted as a matter of common experience since at least the time of Galileo, but its recognition as a basic phenomenological law of thermodynamics is comparatively recent. The descriptive phrase, the zeroth law, was coined by Sir Ralph Fowler.

The second statement constitutes the so-called first law of thermodynamics. When a system is not adiabatically enclosed the extra energy, apart from the work ($\Delta W$) done on the system, required to produce the resulting change in internal energy ($\Delta U$) is known as the heat supplied ($\Delta Q$), so that

$$\Delta U = \Delta Q + \Delta W \tag{1}$$

The third statement summarizes the so-called second law of thermodynamics. Alternative statements (for example, that without compensating changes heat cannot flow from colder to hotter bodies), suitably interpreted, can be shown to be equivalent to it. For the purposes of this article, however, it suffices to confine attention to the mathematical consequence of statement 3; *i.e.*, for any small change from one equilibrium state to another the heat ($\delta Q$) absorbed by a thermodynamic system may be written

$$\delta Q \leq T dS \tag{2}$$

where the equality holds only for a reversible or quasi static process. Thus for a spontaneous adiabatic process (for which $\delta Q = 0$), $dS$ is positive; *i.e.*, the entropy of the system increases. It is important to appreciate that $S$, like $U$ or $T$, is a thermodynamic property whose value is fixed when the state of the system is given. It is for this reason that the differential notation $dS$ has been employed in equation (2).

The history of both the first and second laws of thermodynamics is complex. Suffice it to note that although the term entropy was first introduced by R. J. E. Clausius as late as 1865, the foundations for the understanding of this law had been laid by N. L. Sadi Carnot 40 years earlier. That heat is energy in transit (to use a modern phrase) was perhaps first convincingly demonstrated by J. P. Joule in the 1840s. Certainly by the 1850s both the first and second laws were fairly well established, Clausius and William Thomson, later Lord Kelvin, having played a chief part in clarifying the situation. It was Thomson who introduced the concept of absolute temperature, founding this directly on Carnot's earlier work.

It is to be emphasized, as was clearly appreciated by both Maxwell and Boltzmann, that this thermodynamic story is quite independent of any molecular picture of matter. Moreover, although energy is part of the mechanical description of things, temperature and entropy are concepts foreign to mechanics. Thus if a thermodynamic system (for example, a monatomic gas) is regarded as an assembly of enormously many atoms suffering mutual collisions (and perhaps with other forces between them, but essentially moving in accordance with the established laws of mechanics), it is proper to inquire what features of this mechanical situation are reflected or revealed in the thermodynamic concepts of temperature and entropy. Landmarks in the development of statistical mechanics are provided by Maxwell's work on the temperature problem (1859) and Boltzmann's on the entropy problem (1877). Although incomplete and partially faulty or obscure in their logic, these investigations effectively paved the way to modern statistical theory.

The link between the mechanical aspect of a system and its temperature, developed by Maxwell (and later [1868] by Boltzmann, too), is perhaps the most readily established link between mechanical and thermodynamic properties, though not the strongest. As will be seen, it did not fully withstand the transition from classical to quantum mechanics; and even had it done so its usefulness would inevitably have been somewhat limited. Nevertheless, its importance in the development of theoretical physics is immense; and where applicable it is still a useful working tool.

The connection is most simply established by considering the pressure exerted by a gas on the walls of its containing vessel. Mechanically this pressure represents the rate of dissipation, per unit area of the surface, of momentum directed at right angles to it. Clausius (1857) showed that if the atoms all had the same velocity $v$ and moved in completely random directions then (there being $N$ atoms each of mass $m$) the pressure would be given by

$$pV = \tfrac{1}{3}Nmv^2 \tag{3}$$

where $V$ is the volume of the container. Under the conditions of the derivation the gas is regarded as ideally dilute and so experimentally satisfies the equation of state

$$pV = nRT \tag{4}$$

where $n$ is the amount of the gas in moles, and $R$ is the so-called gas constant. Comparison of equations (3) and (4) yields

$$\tfrac{1}{2}mv^2 = \tfrac{3}{2}kT \tag{5}$$

where $k = R/N_0$. Here $N_0$, known as Avogadro's number, denotes the number of atoms per mole (in a monatomic substance); its numerical value is approximately $6.02 \times 10^{23}$.

That absolute temperature is thus a measure of the mean translational kinetic energy of the atoms of a gas was fully appreciated by Clausius (for the above argument barely depends on the assumption of equal velocities for all atoms); and Clausius also surmised that if the atoms or molecules were endowed with other forms of kinetic energy, *e.g.*, rotational motion, then the kinetic energy of translational motion would simply constitute a definite proportion of the total kinetic energy of the molecular systems. It was, however, Maxwell who first derived the actual distribution of velocities among the systems of a gas. It also was Maxwell (though the theory owes much to Boltzmann) who gave precision and more than plausibility to this surmise of Clausius.

On the first point concerning the distribution of velocities among the atoms of a monatomic gas (or the molecules of a molecular gas) Maxwell used probability considerations to produce his celebrated formula

$$n(v) = N\frac{4a^{\frac{3}{2}}}{\pi^{\frac{1}{2}}}v^2e^{-av^2} \tag{6}$$

where $a$ is a parameter, and $n(v)dv$ denotes the number of systems whose velocities lie in the interval $v$ to $v + dv$. The factor $4a^{\frac{3}{2}}/\pi^{\frac{1}{2}}$ ensures that all systems are taken into account; *i.e.*, that

$$\int_0^\infty n(v)dv = N$$

If this distribution law is now used to find the mean translational kinetic energy of a system, it is found that

$$\tfrac{1}{2}m\overline{v^2} = \frac{m}{2}\int_0^\infty v^2n(v)dv = 3m/(4a)$$

But by equation (5) this mean translational energy is $\frac{3}{2}kT$; thus $a = m/(2kT)$ and equation (6) may be written

$$n(v) = N\frac{4m^{\frac{3}{2}}}{\pi^{\frac{1}{2}}(2kT)^{\frac{3}{2}}}v^2e^{-mv^2/(2kT)} \tag{7}$$

Maxwell's arguments leading to equation (6) are omitted here, partly for brevity and partly because the precise extent to which the laws of classical mechanics and probability theory imply this equation were not entirely clear in the 1960s. Yet there can be no doubt that equation (6) or (7) is, in fact, truly descriptive of the molecular state of affairs in a gas. There have been direct experimental verifications of this, also many indirect verifications. For example, since all directions of molecular motion are obviously equally probable, equation (7) may be rewritten

$$n(v_1,v_2,v_3) = \frac{N}{4\pi}\frac{4m^{\frac{3}{2}}}{\pi^{\frac{1}{2}}(2kT)^{\frac{3}{2}}}e^{-m(v_1^2+v_2^2+v_3^2)/(2kT)} \tag{8}$$

where now $n(v_1, v_2, v_3)\ dv_1dv_2dv_3$ denotes the number of systems whose velocities in three mutually perpendicular directions lie respectively in the ranges $v_1$ to $v_1 + dv_1$, $v_2$ to $v_2 + dv_2$, and $v_3$ to $v_3 + dv_3$. Thus, if $n_1(v_1)dv_1$ is the number whose velocity component in a given direction lies between $v_1$ and $v_1 + dv_1$ (regardless of any motion perpendicular to this direction), it is found on integrating over all values of $v_2$ and $v_3$ that

$$n_1(v_1) = \frac{mN}{(2\pi mkT)^{\frac{1}{2}}}e^{-mv_1^2/(2kT)} \tag{9}$$

This particular consequence of equation (7) can be directly tested in several ways. One way is through the Doppler effect on the wavelength of light emitted by a moving atom. This produces broadening of the spectral line (*see* SPECTROSCOPY) and gives it a characteristic profile that can be observed experimentally and also calculated very simply from equation (9). Indeed, equation (9) is so confidently accepted that it has been used since 1954 to infer from observed Doppler broadening the temperatures obtained in magnetically confined plasmas during attempts to achieve controlled thermonuclear reactions (*see* MAGNETOHYDRODYNAMICS).

Maxwell's second chief contribution to kinetic theory lay in his attempt to deduce from the laws of mechanics (combined inevitably with always rather fragile probability arguments) just how, if alternative forms of kinetic energy were available to the systems of a gas, the total energy would be distributed among these forms. His work, and later that of Boltzmann, led to what is now known as the Maxwell-Boltzmann law of equipartition of energy. This asserts that when a system having $s$ mechanical degrees of freedom is in thermal equilibrium at temperature $T$, then the expectation value of the kinetic energy associated with each degree of freedom is $\frac{1}{2}kT$, so that the total kinetic energy averaged over many such systems is $\frac{1}{2}skT$ per system (*see* KINETIC THEORY OF MATTER).

A particularly simple illustration of this law is afforded by equation (5): a moving atom has three translational degrees of freedom. In general the number of degrees of freedom of a system is given by the number of coordinates required completely to specify its position in space and its internal configuration. For a diatomic molecule $AB$ there are necessarily three positional coordinates (those of the mass centre), two angles are required to describe the orientation in space of the line $AB$, and the distance $AB$ must also be regarded as variable. This would suggest that the internal energy of a diatomic gas is given by $U = 3NkT$, since $s$ is now 6. Consequently the specific heat at constant volume $C_v$ or $(\partial U/\partial T)_v$ should be $3R$ per mole for all diatomic gases, which is not the case. It is much closer to $\frac{5}{2}R$ at ordinary temperatures but varies with temperature and is not the same for all such gases. For monatomic gases the specific heat $C_v$ is indeed $\frac{3}{2}R$ per mole, in agreement with the equipartition law.

Two other illustrations of the practical failure of the law warrant mention. Although derived from considerations relating to thermal equilibrium among the molecules of a gas, there would seem little reason that the law should not be applied equally to calculate the specific heat of a solid. In a monatomic solid each atom is in thermal equilibrium with the rest of the substance, and each atom has three degrees of freedom (corresponding to the three coordinates needed to specify its position in space). So it would be expected that the specific heat of a monatomic crystal like copper would be $\frac{3}{2}R$ per mole. This is about half the room-temperature value. Now it is clear that in a solid the atoms do not move freely in space but vibrate about certain mean positions. They may indeed be supposed to execute simple harmonic motion about these mean positions under the influence of elastic restoring forces. In simple harmonic motion there is on the average as much potential as kinetic energy. Consequently, second thoughts demand twice as much internal energy per mole of crystal as that given by the kinetic energy alone, and a specific heat of $3R$ per mole, in good agreement with many room-temperature values for appropriate solids. But this inclusion of an equal potential-energy term when vibrational motions are involved does not help to resolve, but indeed increases, the discrepancy in the case of diatomic gases. And, just as disastrously, the specific heats of solids are found experimentally to decline to zero at very low temperatures (*see* SOLID STATE PHYSICS: *Physical Properties of Solids: Principles Determining Physical Form*).

The second illustration comes from application of the law to thermal radiation (*see* BLACK BODY). Here concern is with thermal equilibrium among all the possible electromagnetic waves that can exist within an enclosure of volume $V$. The number of mutually independent excitations with frequency between $\nu$ and $\nu + d\nu$ can be shown to equal

$$\frac{8\pi V}{c^3}\nu^2d\nu \tag{10}$$

where $c$ is the velocity of light. Since these are harmonic vibrations, each contributes $kT$ to the internal energy of the enclosure. Consequently, the total energy of black-body radiation per unit volume at temperature $T$ is

$$\frac{8\pi kT}{c^3}\int \nu^2d\nu \tag{11}$$

However, all frequencies from $\nu = 0$ to $\nu = \infty$ are possible, and the integral diverges at the upper limit (*i.e.*, at high frequencies or short wavelengths). This, the so-called ultraviolet catastrophe, cannot be dismissed on the grounds that an infinite energy might be physically unobservable, since the formula also predicts an infinite specific heat, and it certainly does not require infinite energy to change the temperature within a finite enclosed vacuum.

The earlier of these discrepancies were familiar to Maxwell and Boltzmann. The ultraviolet catastrophe, discovered by Lord Rayleigh in 1900, only dramatically emphasized the unsatisfactory state of statistical theory at that time. Nevertheless, it was not in statistical mechanics as such, but in classical mechanics itself, that the fault lay. These failures of the theory were directly instrumental in promoting the creation of quantum mechanics to replace classical mechanics in atomic situations (*see* MECHANICS; QUANTUM MECHANICS). Where classical mechanics is applicable, the law of equipartition of energy is valid. It can be used profitably, for example, to discuss the amplitude of the thermal torsional oscillations of a suspended galvanometer mirror.

Nevertheless, even were it always valid, the law of equipartition of energy could never provide a direct link between mechanics and thermodynamics; thus Boltzmann's work relating entropy to mechanical concepts will now be discussed.

The most striking property of entropy is that of increasing with time in spontaneous changes of a thermodynamic system. The clue to the mechanical interpretation of entropy was first afforded by Boltzmann's discovery (1872) of a feature of the mechanical description of a molecular assembly having a like property. For simplicity consider a monatomic gas that is not necessarily in an equilibrium state. Suppose that at a particular instant $f(x,y,z,v_1,v_2,v_3)dxdydzdv_1dv_2dv_3$ defines the number of atoms within the volume element $dx\,dy\,dz$ whose velocity components lie in the ranges $v_1$ to $v_1 + dv_1$, $v_2$ to $v_2 + dv_2$, $v_3$ to $v_3 + dv_3$. Boltzmann showed that the quantity $H$ defined by

$$H \equiv \int \ldots \int f \ln f \, dx\, dy\, dz\, dv_1\, dv_2\, dv_3 \tag{12}$$

(where ln stands for natural logarithm) never increases as the result of atomic collisions. More precisely, it remains constant if $f(x,y,z,v_1,v_2,v_3) = n(v_1,v_2,v_3)/V$, where $n(v_1,v_2,v_3)$ is given by Maxwell's velocity distribution law, equation (8); otherwise it decreases. This result, Boltzmann's celebrated $H$ theorem, was certainly not proved rigorously: statistical assumptions in the classification of collisions are certainly made, as Boltzmann came to realize; and these demand more justification than they received at that time. Nevertheless, the historical importance of Boltzmann's $H$ theorem can hardly be overestimated, and for a critical discussion of its status, reference must be made to the appropriate works already cited, and listed in the bibliography below. More generally, for nonuniform molecular gases each molecule having $s$ degrees of freedom requires $s$ coordinates $q_1, q_2, \ldots q_s$ to specify its positional state. In the language of analytical mechanics there are now $s$ momenta $p_1, p_2, \ldots p_s$ conjugate to these coordinates, and $f(q_1,q_2, \ldots q_s,p_1,p_2, \ldots p_s)\, dq_1 \ldots dq_s\, dp_1 \ldots dp_s$ may be defined as the number of systems at any instant whose coordinates lie in the ranges $q_1$ to $q_1 + dq_1$, etc., and whose momenta lie in the ranges $p_1$ to $p_1 + dp_1$, etc. In place of equation (12), the quantity which as a result of molecular collisions is nonincreasing in time is now given by

$$H = \int \ldots \int f \ln f \, dq_1 \ldots dq_s dp_1 \ldots dp_s \tag{13}$$

Boltzmann realized that $H$ so defined behaves essentially as the negative of the entropy of the gas.

Boltzmann, however, went further than this. The conceptual space in which a coordinate system is provided by the $2s$ quantities $q_1, \ldots q_s, p_1, \ldots p_s$ is known in analytical mechanics as phase space (more precisely, it is the phase space appropriate to a single molecule of the gas); and Boltzmann (1877) imagined this phase space subdivided into a number of equal cells labeled $1, 2, \ldots i, \ldots r$, each of magnitude $dq_1 \ldots dq_s dp_1 \ldots dp_s$, equal to $\tau$. If now $n_i$ denotes the number of molecules at a given instant such that their coordinates and momenta define a point within the $i$th cell in phase space then, on replacing the integral by a sum, equation (13) may be written

$$H = (\sum_i n_i \ln n_i)\tau \tag{14}$$

Because concern is only with changes in $H$, just as only changes in entropy can be determined calorimetrically, and since $\sum_i n_i = N$ is a fixed quantity, equation (14) may be modified to read

$$H = \tau[\sum_i (n_i \ln n_i - n_i) - (N \ln N - N)] \tag{15}$$

or

$$H = -\tau \ln \frac{N!}{n_1!n_2! \ldots n_r!} \tag{16}$$

In deriving equation (16) from equation (15) use is made of the approximation

$$\ln n! = n \ln n - n$$

which effectively holds mathematically for the logarithm of the factorial of a large number. It has therefore been assumed that all the distribution numbers $n_1, n_2, \ldots n_r$ are large; *i.e.*, that the cells in phase space provide only a rather crude description of the instantaneous dynamic state of the gas.

Now $N!/(n_1!n_2! \ldots n_r!)$ is simply the number of ways in which $N$ molecules can be so distributed among the cells in phase space that the $i$th cell contains $n_i$ of them; *i.e.*, $n_i$ of them are in dynamic states corresponding to points in the $i$th cell. Boltzmann called this the number of complexions $W$ pertaining to the set of distribution numbers $n_1, n_2, \ldots n_r$; and equation (16) reads

$$H = -\tau \ln W$$

If $H$ then is proportional to the negative of the entropy $S$, it follows that for a change in the state of the gas

$$S_2 - S_1 \text{ is proportional to } \ln W_2 - \ln W_1 \tag{17}$$

The more famous formula

$$S = k \ln W \tag{18}$$

is due not to Boltzmann but to Max Planck, but the constant $k$, later to be identified with the $k$ of equation (5) above, is known as Boltzmann's constant. Its numerical value is about $1.38 \times 10^{-16}$ ergs per degree. Unlike equation (17), equation (18) specifies a value for the entropy $S$ and, therefore, necessarily exceeds thermodynamic requirements. The quantity $W$ received the unfortunate name "thermodynamic probability"—it is neither a thermodynamic quantity nor a probability, being a large integer.

Boltzmann did, however, proceed to identify the state of maximum "thermodynamic probability" with the equilibrium state of the gas. It is known that for a given adiabatically enclosed system the entropy increases until an equilibrium state is reached. Consequently, the equilibrium state of the gas is expected to be describable by distribution numbers $n_1, n_2, \ldots n_r$ which make $W$ a maximum subject to the two restrictive conditions

$$\sum_i n_i = N \tag{19}$$

$$\sum_i n_i \epsilon_i = U \tag{20}$$

Here $\epsilon_i$ is the energy appropriate to the $i$th cell in phase space; the first condition prescribes a closed thermodynamic system, and the second further specifies adiabatic enclosure. The mathematical problem of maximizing $W$ subject to these restrictive conditions is straightforward, with the solution (in customary current notation)

$$n_i^* = N\lambda e^{\beta\epsilon_i} \tag{21}$$

The parameters $\lambda$ and $\beta$ are fixed by the conditions of equations (19) and (20). $\lambda$ can be eliminated easily enough by using equation (19); but $\beta$ demands a physical interpretation.

Returning to the thermodynamic equations (1) and (2) above, for two neighbouring equilibrium states of any thermodynamic system

$$TdS = dU - \delta W \tag{22}$$

and for a gas (or any homogeneous fluid) $\delta W$ can be replaced by $-pdV$. Consequently equation (22) may be written

$$dU = TdS - pdV \tag{23}$$

the basic equation of all equilibrium thermodynamics. From equation (23)

$$\left(\frac{\partial S}{\partial U}\right)_v = \frac{1}{T} \tag{24}$$

On the other hand, substituting from equation (21) into equation (18) gives

$$S = Nk \ln \sum_i e^{\beta\epsilon_i} - k\beta U \tag{25}$$

whence

$$\left(\frac{\partial S}{\partial U}\right)_v = -k\beta \tag{26}$$

even though $\beta$ itself depends implicitly on $U$ through equation (20). Comparison of equations (24) and (26) suggests that $\beta$ has the physical significance of $-1/(kT)$, so that equation (21) may be written

$$n_i^* = N\lambda\, e^{-\epsilon_i/kT} \tag{27}$$

It may also be observed that equation (25) yields

$$A = -NkT \ln \sum_i e^{-\epsilon_i/k} \tag{28}$$

where $A$ is the thermodynamic quantity known as Helmholtz energy and defined as $U - TS$, so that from equation (23)

$$dA = -SdT - pdV \tag{29}$$

The above identification of $\beta$ with $-1/kT$ is not strictly in accordance with the rules of statistical mechanics, since there has been an appeal to thermodynamic formulas which should themselves follow from statistical theory. The identification is most properly made by considering the work done in slightly changing the volume of the gas and showing that this has the form $dU + dS/k\beta$. However, the present, shorter approach is not without its interest. In any case, the identification is what would have been expected from equation (7), since for translational motion $\epsilon = \frac{1}{2}mv^2$.

Equation (27), perhaps written in the form

$$\frac{n_i^*}{n_j^*} = \frac{e^{-\epsilon_i/kT}}{e^{-\epsilon_j/kT}} \tag{30}$$

is known as Boltzmann's distribution law. Maxwell's law is a particular case of it and indeed Maxwell himself came close to this generalization of his velocity distribution formula. Equation (28) is particularly basic to further developments.

The generalizations and rather different attitude introduced by Gibbs will be described in the language of the quantum theory; but first Boltzmann's results will be recapitulated in this new language. The rather arbitrary cells in phase space have effectively the magnitude $h^s$, where $h$ is Planck's constant (about $6.62 \times 10^{-27}$ erg sec.). More importantly, summation over cells is replaced by summation over allowed energy levels, so that equations (28) and (30) become

$$A = -NkT \ln \sum_i \omega_i e^{-\epsilon_i/kT} \tag{31}$$

and

$$\frac{n_i^*}{n_j^*} = \frac{\omega_i e^{-\epsilon_i/kT}}{\omega_j e^{-\epsilon_j/kT}} \tag{32}$$

where $\omega$ is the quantum-mechanical degeneracy associated with the energy $\epsilon$; *i.e.*, the number of independent wave functions with this energy. In equation (32), the distribution numbers now refer to molecules having certain energies, rather than to certain cells in phase space. Since the energy levels themselves explicitly depend on the volume of the enclosure, it is clear that equation (31) provides an expression for $A$ as a function of $V$ and $T$ from which, by equation (29), all other equilibrium thermodynamic properties of the molecular assembly can be computed. The route from mechanical to thermodynamic properties is complete, at least for gases.

Boltzmann justified his $H$ theorem by considering in detail the effects of molecular collisions, and in so doing had necessarily particularized assumptions about molecular interactions. Gibbs wished to free statistical mechanics from any such conceivably unrealistic suppositions. And at the same time he sought a formalism equally appropriate to solids or liquids as to gases. Instead of considering a gas as a statistical assembly of many molecules, he considered a statistical ensemble of very many replicas of the molecular assembly, whether the latter be gaseous, liquid, or solid. The individual members of this ensemble might have different total energies $E_i$ and, in particular, Gibbs focused attention on a so-called canonical ensemble in which the number of assemblies with energy $E_i$ is proportional to

$$\Omega_i e^{\beta E_i}$$

Here $\beta$ is a parameter independent of $E$, and $\Omega_i$ in quantum-mechanical language is the number of independent wave functions descriptive of a molecular assembly with energy $E_i$. He then assumed that the measurable properties of an actual physical molecular assembly would be given by averages over the corresponding canonical ensemble so that in particular

$$U = \sum_i E_i\Omega_i e^{\beta E_i} / \sum_i \Omega_i e^{\beta E_i} \tag{33}$$

The different members of a Gibbsian ensemble have, of course, no physical interactions with each other; classical mechanics, or the quantum theory, is invoked only to show that a canonical ensemble will remain a canonical ensemble as time proceeds, which is essential if such averages are to yield equilibrium thermodynamic properties.

The similarity between equation (33) and the equation of the Boltzmann theory

$$U = \sum_i \epsilon_i n_i^* = N \sum_i \epsilon_i \omega_i e^{-\epsilon_i/kT} / \sum \omega_i e^{-\epsilon_i/kT} \tag{34}$$

is self-evident, and it is not surprising that Gibbs succeeded in showing that the parameter $\beta$ in a canonical distribution would reflect the physical features of reciprocal temperature. It can, of course, be identified with $-1/kT$. Gibbs showed, indeed, that quantities calculated as averages over canonical ensembles would obey all the laws of equilibrium thermodynamics, the Helmholtz energy of a molecular assembly being given by

$$A = -kT \ln \sum_i \Omega_i e^{-E_i/kT} \tag{35}$$

Applied to a gas, whose individual molecules may have energies $\epsilon_1, \epsilon_2, \ldots$, with degeneracies $\omega_1, \omega_2, \ldots$, equation (35) leads identically to equation (31) if

$$\Omega = \sum_{\text{(allowed } n\text{'s)}} W(n_1, n_2, \ldots)$$

where

$$\sum_i n_i = N, \quad \sum_i n_i\epsilon_i = E$$

and

$$W = \frac{N!}{n_1!\, n_2! \ldots} \omega_1^{n_1} \omega_2^{n_2} \ldots \tag{36}$$

And this, of course, is just the number of ways in which it would be expected that individual energies could be ascribed to the molecules of a gas whose total energy is given.

Gibbs thus brilliantly succeeded in producing a self-consistent statistical model embodying the laws of thermodynamics; at the same time providing a universal recipe for computing measurable, macroscopic, physical properties—equations of state, specific heats, and so on—from the dynamic description of any molecular assembly. This recipe or prescription certainly receives full a posteriori justification. What he does not do is properly justify, a priori, the identification of physical measurements with ensemble averages. And here, as in the Maxwell-Boltzmann theory, the gaps in the logic have to be filled in by more recent developments in statistical mechanics which are beyond the scope of this article.

Equation (35) is the basic equation of statistical mechanics for computational purposes. The quantity $\sum \Omega_i e^{-E_i/kT}$ is known as the partition function for the molecular assembly. If all the energy within the assembly may be regarded as shared among individual molecules—as in a sufficiently dilute gas, when intermolecular forces may be ignored—then, as has been shown

$$\sum_i \Omega_i e^{-E_i/kT} = (\sum \omega_i e^{-\epsilon_i/kT})^N \tag{37}$$

The quantity $\sum_i \omega_i e^{-\epsilon_i/kT}$ is then known as the partition function for a single molecule. In either case each separate term in the partition function measures the relative probability in an actual physical system at temperature $T$ of the particular mechanical state to which it refers.

Equation (37) is simply a particular case of the important factorization property of partition functions. If, for precision, the molecules of a gas can have two completely independent sources of energy (for example, translational and rotational energies $\epsilon_i'$ and $\epsilon_i''$ with degeneracies $\omega_i'$ and $\omega_i''$) then

$$\sum_i \omega_i e^{-\epsilon_i/kT} = (\sum_i \omega_i' e^{-\epsilon_i'/kT}) (\sum_i \omega_i'' e^{-\epsilon_i''/kT})$$

since $\epsilon_i = \epsilon_j' + \epsilon_k''$ and $\omega_i = \omega_j'\omega_k''$. It follows that each independent source of mechanical energy makes its own contribution to the Helmholtz energy of the assembly, and thence its own contribution to the internal energy $U$, given by $-T^2\partial(A/T)/\partial T$, and to the specific heat $C_v$.

Returning to the language of classical mechanics, the partition function $\sum_i \omega_i e^{-\epsilon_i/kT}$ has now to be replaced by the phase integral

$$\frac{1}{h^s}\int \ldots \int e^{-\epsilon(q_1, \ldots q_s, p_1, \ldots p_s)/k} \, dq_1 \ldots dq_s dp_1 \ldots dp_s$$

where the energy is now expressed as a function of position in phase space. The factor $1/h^s$, where $h$ is Planck's constant, ensures that the quantum-mechanical partition function and the classical phase integral have the same numerical value at high temperatures; *i.e.*, when $kT$ is large compared with the effective spacing between energy levels allowed by quantum mechanics.

For the translational motion of atomic or molecular systems in a gas, the statistically important energy levels are always very close together compared with $kT$, and the partition function for translational motion is given by

$$\frac{1}{h^3}\int \ldots \int e^{-[p_1^2 + p_2^2 + p_3^2]/2mkT} \, dxdydzdp_1dp_2dp_3 \tag{38}$$

*i.e.*,

$$\left(\frac{2\pi mkT}{h^2}\right)^{\frac{3}{2}} V$$

Consequently (proceeding from $A$ to $U$) the contribution to the internal energy from the translational motion is $\frac{3}{2}kT$ per molecule, in accordance with the equipartition law. Rotational motion can normally also be considered classically and, because the rotational energy is again a separable quadratic function of the relevant momenta, this motion also normally contributes the equipartition value to the internal energy of the gas. However, vibrational motion can seldom be discussed classically, the energy levels being too far apart; which accounts for the various failures of the equipartition law already instanced.

On substitution from equations (37) and (38) into equation (35) there is found for the Helmholtz free energy of a monatomic gas the expression

$$A = -\tfrac{3}{2}NkT \ln (2\pi mkT/h^2) - NkT \ln V \tag{39}$$

a result that cannot be correct. For, increasing $V$ and $N$ proportionately does not likewise increase $A$, although thermodynamically $A$ is, of course, a simple extensive property of the gas. Gibbs realized this and suggested that the trouble arose from the indistinguishability of the $N$ atoms of the gas. If only distinguishable complexions of the assembly were to be counted, then the above partition function for the gas ought to be divided by $N!$ or alternatively in place of equation (36) there should be

$$W = \frac{\omega_1^{n_1}\omega_2^{n_2} \ldots}{n_1! \, n_2! \ldots} \tag{40}$$

Equation (39) now becomes

$$A = -\tfrac{3}{2} NkT \ln (2\pi mkT/h^2) - NkT \ln V + NkT \ln N - NkT \tag{41}$$

which is dimensionally correct. This is certainly the right procedure, but the indistinguishability of the systems of the gas has more profound quantum-mechanical effects than Gibbs was in a position to appreciate.

For simplicity let it be supposed that the translational energy levels are nondegenerate. Equation (40) then becomes

$$W = \frac{1}{n_1! \, n_2! \ldots} \tag{42}$$

which, since the $n$ values are integers, can hardly describe the number of ways of assigning energies to the systems of the gas in accordance with given distribution numbers. Indeed according to quantum theory

$$W = 1 \tag{43}$$

for when the single particle energies are known the state of the system is fixed.

With particles of atomic or molecular mass, equation (42) though strictly incorrect often (indeed usually) leads to right answers such as equation (41). The systems are then said to obey Maxwell-Boltzmann statistics. But equation (43) is necessary in dealing with substantially lighter particles such as electrons or photons (which have zero rest mass).

For electrons equation (43) and the conditions imposed by the Pauli exclusion principle, $n_i = 0$ or 1, must be invoked. The systems are said to obey Fermi-Dirac statistics, Enrico Fermi and Paul Dirac having independently deduced this consequence of quantum theory in 1926. A practical result is that the conduction electrons of a metal like copper do not, except at very low temperatures, contribute appreciably to the specific heat.

For photons or for helium atoms equation (43) suffices without further conditions on the $n$ terms, a case of the use of Bose-Einstein statistics, the appropriate theory having been developed by Satyendra Nath Bose and by Albert Einstein in 1924.

The most important features of these specifically quantal statistics are summarized in the analogues of equation (21). For Fermi-Dirac statistics

$$n_i^* = \frac{\lambda e^{-\epsilon_i/kT}}{1 + \lambda e^{-\epsilon_i/kT}} \tag{44}$$

while for Bose-Einstein statistics

$$n_i^* = \frac{\lambda e^{-\epsilon_i/kT}}{1 - \lambda e^{-\epsilon_i/kT}} \tag{45}$$

The left-hand side of equation (44) or (45), as also of equation (21), must, of course, be interpreted as an average or expectation value; it is not necessarily an integer. In the particular case of photons or black-body radiation there is no restriction $\sum_i n_i = N$, since photons are not numerically conserved. This has as consequence that $\lambda = 1$ in equation (45). Since a photon of frequency $\nu$ has energy $h\nu$, equations (45), (20), and (10) combine to give

$$U = \int_0^\infty \frac{8\pi V}{c^3} \frac{h\nu e^{-h\nu/kT}}{1 - e^{-h\nu/kT}} \nu^2 d\nu = \alpha V T^4 \tag{46}$$

where $\alpha = 8\pi^5 k^4/15h^3c^3$.

Equation (46) was discovered semiempirically by Planck (1900) and historically marked the beginning of the quantum theory. Unlike equation (11), the integral in equation (46) does not diverge, and the integrand correctly reproduces the energy distribution in the frequency spectrum.

Except in the case of photons, the predictions of Fermi-Dirac and Bose-Einstein statistics coincide with those of Maxwell-Boltzmann statistics at sufficiently high temperatures; specifically whenever

$$\left(\frac{2\pi mkT}{h^2}\right)^{\frac{3}{2}} V \gg N$$

And this condition is certainly satisfied in practice for all atomic or molecular gases, with the possible exception of helium at very low temperatures.

This brief outline of the formal structure of statistical mechanics and of its historical origins could well end here. The calculation of transport coefficients, such as coefficients of viscosity or thermal conductivity, still requires detailed consideration of molecular collisions and is perhaps better regarded as part of the kinetic theory of gases than of statistical mechanics proper. However, a few more comments about the mechanistic interpretation of entropy may not be out of place.

Because the number of degrees of freedom of a macroscopic molecular aggregate is so large (of the order of $10^{23}$) it can be shown that

$$\ln \sum_i \Omega_i e^{-E_i/kT}$$

can be replaced without loss by

$$\ln (\Omega^* e^{-E^*/kT})$$

where $\Omega^* e^{-E^*/kT}$ is the greatest of the terms in the above sum; *i.e.,* in the corresponding partition function. Consequently, by equation (35)

$$S = k \ln \Omega^* \qquad (47)$$

where $E^* = U$. More properly this argument should invoke not a fixed energy but an infinitesimal energy range. Here, however, concern is not with mathematical rigour, and equation (47) must suffice. This is not precisely the same equation as Planck's equation (18), since all complexions for a given energy are now counted and not simply those corresponding to the most probable distribution numbers. Again, however, because fluctuations are macroscopically negligible, it is virtually equivalent to Planck's formula.

Now $\Omega^*$, or $\ln \Omega^*$, is a measure of what is not known about the dynamic state of an assembly if it is known only that it has total energy $U$. It is for this reason that entropy is sometimes said to measure our ignorance or uncertainty about the detailed dynamic state of the enormous number of microscopic systems (atoms or molecules) that together comprise the macroscopic systems of which there is direct physical experience.

BIBLIOGRAPHY.—L. Boltzmann, *Vorlesungen über Gastheorie,* 2 vol. (1896–98); J. W. Gibbs, *Elementary Principles in Statistical Mechanics . . .* (1902), *Collected Works,* vol. ii, part 1 (1948); R. H. Fowler, *Statistical Mechanics,* 2nd ed. (1936); R. C. Tolman, *The Principles of Statistical Mechanics* (1938); S. Chapman and T. G. Cowling, *The Mathematical Theory of Non-Uniform Gases,* 2nd ed. (1952); J. E. Mayer and M. G. Mayer, *Statistical Mechanics* (1940); A. I. Khinchin, *Mathematical Foundations of Statistical Mechanics,* Eng. trans. by G. Gamow (1949); D. ter Haar, *Elements of Statistical Mechanics* (1954); A. Münster, *Statistische Thermodynamik* (1956); E. A. Guggenheim, *Thermodynamics,* 3rd ed. (1957); L. D. Landau and E. M. Lifshitz, *Statistical Physics,* Eng. trans. by E. and R. F. Peierls (1958); K. Huang, *Statistical Mechanics* (1963); F. H. Crawford, *Heat, Thermodynamics and Statistical Physics* (1963); J. DeBoer and G. E. Uhlenbeck (eds.), *Studies in Statistical Mechanics,* 3 vol. (1962–65); F. Reif, *Fundamentals of Statistical and Thermal Physics* (1965).

At a more elementary level: E. A. Guggenheim, *Boltzmann's Distribution Law* (1955); G. S. Rushbrooke, *Introduction to Statistical Mechanics* (1949). (G. S. R.)

**STATISTICAL ORGANIZATIONS, INTERNATIONAL.** The term international statistics refers to compilations of data on economic and social characteristics of peoples and countries, drawn up in such a way as to permit intercountry comparisons. Such comparisons, to be of substantial validity, depend upon the application in each country of broadly uniform concepts, definitions and classifications to the subjects under investigation.

## EARLY HISTORY

**The International Statistical Congress.**—Efforts to develop uniform standards for international comparisons began in 1853 with the meeting in Brussels of the first International Statistical congress. The moving spirit of the first congress, and indeed of later ones, was Adolphe Quételet (1796–1874), a noted Belgian astronomer and one of the founders of scientific statistics. The congress held eight subsequent meetings between 1855 and 1876 in various European cities. The objective of the congresses was to agree upon and to seek to give effect to uniform practices for the compilation of national statistics in the interests of international comparability. Statisticians of more than 20 countries usually participated, including such distinguished persons as William Farr, Ernst Engel, Edward Jarvis and, of course, Quételet.

During this period it became clear that continuity between sessions was needed to advance the work more systematically and to avoid repetitious discussions. Various solutions were proposed, culminating in 1872 with agreement to establish a small permanent commission. In the course of the next few years the commission held four meetings and soon sought to become an authoritative institution to impose recommendations upon governments. This policy proved unacceptable; invitations to send representatives to another meeting of the commission in 1879 and to what would have been the tenth meeting of the International Statistical congress, in 1880, were refused by the German prime minister Bismarck and subsequently by the governments of several other European states. The scheduled meetings were not held, and the work of the congress and its permanent commission thereupon collapsed.

Despite the controversies that marked the end of the congress, its activities had given a strong impetus to the development of official statistics in Europe and to improvements in comparability. The congress had encouraged the compilation of internationally comparable tables, the most important of these being the publication in 1865 of *Statistique internationale de la population,* probably the first statistical publication compiled under international auspices, prepared by Quételet and Xavier Heuschling at the suggestion of the fourth congress (1860).

In addition, the congress was instrumental in encouraging the development of uniform standards. At the 1872 meeting, the congress agreed upon a list of items to be collected in population censuses. In 1853 initial work was done on what was to become the International Statistical Classification of Diseases, Injuries and Causes of Death.

**The International Statistical Institute.**—The dissolution of the congress by no means disposed of the then recognized need for international collaboration in statistics. International collaboration in a number of economic and social fields intensified the usefulness of statistical comparisons. These new developments, which led some statisticians to fear that statistics would become increasingly dispersed, together with the real need to continue the work of the International Statistical congress, led to the creation of the International Statistical institute (I.S.I.) in 1885.

The occasion was the jubilee meeting of the Statistical Society of London (since 1877 the Royal Statistical society) attended by about 40 foreign statisticians invited by the government of the United Kingdom. Unanimous agreement was reached upon proposals to create an international statistical organization that would avoid the difficulties encountered by the defunct congress. It was to be a private, scientific and unofficial body.

The I.S.I. held its first session in Rome in 1887 and met biennially until 1913 when World War I interrupted its meetings. During the period 1923 to 1938 it held ten sessions, its activities being once more interrupted by a world war. Members were elected in their personal capacities; many of them were official statisticians in their own countries.

The institute restricted its agenda to a smaller number of problems than had engaged the congress—a policy which resulted in more systematic work and in more carefully considered resolutions. The system of biennial meetings, while effective, could hardly keep pace with the rapidly expanding needs. A permanent office was established in 1913 to assist in the development of comparable methods, to assemble information from governments and to make arrangements for periodical publications. Special attention was given to demographic statistics. The first publication, in 1916, *Annuaire international de statistique,* was a compilation of the population statistics of European countries. Subsequent yearbooks covered other areas and other subjects. The *Annuaire* continued through 1921 and was superseded in 1922 by the *Aperçu de la démographie des divers pays du monde,* which appeared at intervals up to 1939, there being six issues in all.

In the meantime other international institutions were established. An international labour bureau was founded in Basel, Switz., in 1901. The International Institute of Agriculture (I.I.A.) was established in Rome in 1905, and in 1914 published the first issue of *Annuaire international de statistique agricole.* L'Office International d'Hygiène was organized in Paris in 1907, and in 1909 began to issue a monthly information bulletin, dealing, in part, with statistics on contagious diseases. An international conference on customs statistics, meeting in Brussels in 1910, laid the basis for an international convention, adopted in 1913, establishing the Bureau International de Statistique Commerciale, which was charged with compiling and publishing statistics on external trade in terms of a uniform commodity classification.

## DEVELOPMENTS UP TO WORLD WAR II

**Problems of Organization.**—The outbreak of World War I naturally resulted in restriction or suspension of many of these developing activities. The end of the war brought new developments: the establishment in 1919 of the League of Nations and the International Labour Organization (ILO). The League and the I.S.I. were charged with broad responsibilities calling implicitly for the preparation of comparable statistics. Many of the then important subjects of official statistics had been taken up by one or another specialized organization, while the I.S.I. occupied a strong position of intellectual leadership, with a program actually or potentially embracing all fields of statistics. The newly created intergovernmental organizations could hardly divest themselves of responsibilities for compiling the statistics pertinent to their operations and for making recommendations to governments concerning these statistics. At the same time, the I.S.I. was loath to relinquish the position of leadership it had acquired over so many years.

During the next few years various schemes of collaboration were proposed and rejected. The I.S.I. and the League finally agreed on a system of mixed committees that prepared technical reports for submission to sessions of the I.S.I.: recommendations on external trade and fishery statistics were approved in 1923 at Brussels, on industrial (production) censuses in 1925 at Rome and on indexes of industrial activity in 1927 at Cairo.

**The International Convention.**—The recommendations of the I.S.I. were transmitted to the economic committee of the League, and when they were submitted for government comment, it appeared that several governments wished steps to be taken to give effect to the proposed standards. Accordingly, in 1927, the council of the League authorized the convening of a conference to prepare an international convention incorporating the recommendations. The International Conference Relating to Economic Statistics, meeting in Geneva in 1928, was attended by representatives of 42 states and drew up the International Convention Relating to Economic Statistics. This marked, up to that time, the high point in the development of international comparability.

The articles of the convention set out the type and frequency of statistics to be compiled on a wide range of economic subjects. It also established the Committee of Statistical Experts, which was charged with improving and amplifying the principles of the convention and advising on other classes of statistics in the interests of international uniformity. Certain classes of statistics—on agriculture, labour, transport and finance—were excluded from consideration because they fell within other jurisdictions. The committee was composed mainly of members of the I.S.I. serving in their personal capacities; arrangements were made for representatives of the ILO and the I.I.A. to participate in the work of the committee.

The Committee of Statistical Experts held eight meetings between 1931 and 1939 and made notable contributions to the improvement of comparability and to the development of statistics generally. The main accomplishments of the committee are contained in the series *Studies and Reports on Statistical Methods,* six of which were published by the League in 1938 and 1939 and the remaining three by the United Nations in 1947. Considerable attention was devoted to external trade statistics, the result of which was, among other things, the preparation of the Minimum List of Commodities for International Trade Statistics, designed to replace the Brussels classification referred to above. Other subjects covered by the methodological studies included statistics of the gainfully occupied population (an industrial classification), timber statistics, housing statistics, indexes of industrial production and statistics relating to capital formation. The committee also studied banking and balance of payments statistics. Reports on these latter subjects, and upon national income, were completed after the committee had ceased to function as a result of World War II.

**Other Statistical Organizations.**—During the period when the I.S.I. and the League were elaborating the principles that were to be contained in the convention, the ILO was active in preparing standards for labour statistics. This work was carried on principally by the International Conference of Labour Statisticians, the first meeting, in 1923, taking up the classification of occupation and industry, and statistics of wages, hours of work and industrial accidents. Later conferences discussed cost of living index numbers, unemployment statistics and real wages (1925); methods of family budget studies and statistics of collective agreements and industrial disputes (1926); and international comparison of real wages (1931). In 1933 the ILO established a committee of statistical experts to undertake preparatory work for the international conferences of labour statisticians and to advise upon problems of international comparisons of wages and the cost of living. The fifth conference (1937) prepared an international convention on statistics of wages and hours of work, signed in June 1938. The I.I.A. continued its work, especially the publication of a monthly bulletin and the *International Yearbook of Agricultural Statistics,* usually published biennially. While some hopes for more sophisticated agricultural statistics were never realized, much useful work was done, including the elaboration of the standards for agricultural and related statistics which were contained in the 1928 convention.

While the League and the I.S.I. were working out harmonious ways of collaboration, a somewhat different situation prevailed between l'Office International d'Hygiène Publique and the Health organization of the League. Agreement was finally reached whereby l'Office retained its independence, the Health organization was put on a permanent basis and the permanent committee of l'Office became the General Advisory Health council to the League although the League had its own health committee. The Health organization, among other subjects, took a strong interest in the International Statistical Classification of Diseases, Injuries and Causes of Death, a classification initiated at the first International Statistical congress in 1853 and finally adopted by the I.S.I. in 1893.

**Statistical Publications.**—Because of the controversy in the early 1920s between the I.S.I. and intergovernmental organizations, the statistical secretariat in the League was restricted to modest proportions. Nevertheless, in July 1921 the economic and financial section of the League assumed responsibility for the publication of the *Monthly Bulletin of Statistics,* which had been initiated in 1919 by the Supreme Economic Council of the Allied and Associated Powers. By 1927 it was possible to issue the *International Statistical Year-Book,* as a companion volume to the *Bulletin,* containing more subjects and more details. Subsequently, a number of specialized periodical publications were issued, many of them representing new departures in international statistics. The most important of these were: *Memorandum on Balances of Payments and Foreign Trade Balances* (1924) (later *International Trade Statistics*); *Memorandum on Production and Trade* (1926) (later *World Production and Prices*); and *International Trade in Certain Raw Materials and Foodstuffs by Countries of Origin and Destination* (1936–38). The *Network of World Trade*, published in 1942, became something of a classic in its analysis of trade relationships.

The ILO also began the publication of an increased quantity of labour statistics. From 1923 on, special articles appeared in the *International Labour Review,* and in 1936 the *Year-Book of Labour Statistics* appeared as an independent publication. The I.I.A. continued to publish a yearbook on agricultural statistics. Demographic statistics were published in the *Aperçu*, and health statistics mainly in the *Epidemiological Report* of the League's Health organization.

### WORLD WAR II AND AFTER

International statistical collaboration was virtually suspended during World War II. In June 1946, following the preparatory conference establishing the United Nations and the report of a temporary statistical commission, the United Nations Economic and Social council (ESC) established a permanent Statistical commission of representatives of 12 (later 15) states to promote the development of national statistics and their comparability and to co-ordinate international statistical work generally. The Statistical office of the United Nations, as a central organ, was also established to collect, compile, analyze and publish statistics, to assist in statistical development and to maintain an international centre for statistics.

Two sessions of the commission were held in 1947 as it was considered necessary to organize the work as rapidly as possible. The commission met annually from 1948 to 1954, thereafter meeting biennially. The League's International convention, while remaining in force, was transferred by protocol to the ESC, which, advised by the Statistical commission, in effect replaced the Committee of Statistical Experts.

The fear, expressed by some observers, that a commission composed of governmental representatives instead of experts acting in their personal capacities would necessarily be ineffective proved groundless. With very rare exceptions, the members nominated by governments were the heads of their national statistical services and commanded international prestige. The fact that these representatives can assist directly to give effect to the recommendations of the commission in their own countries is an important advantage. The technical recommendations of the commission are not mandatory; they depend for their acceptance upon their cogency and applicability.

The problem of co-ordination also required immediate attention. The commission drew up the terms of a standard agreement covering statistical relationships between the UN and each of the specialized agencies. In general, the statistical activities appropriate to the special sphere of each agency were reserved to it.

**Secretariat Activities.**—In the meantime the normal secretariat duties of collection and publication of statistics were resumed or expanded. The Statistical office of the UN took over the publication of the *Monthly Bulletin of Statistics* with the Jan. 1947 issue, thus continuing without interruption the publication which during the latter part of the war had been published by the League both in Geneva and in Princeton, N.J. Arrangements were made to compile the *Statistical Yearbook,* which resumed publication in 1949. A new publication, the *Demographic Yearbook,* also appeared in 1949. The statistical services of other international agencies commenced publication of current and annual statistics: the International Monetary fund (IMF) initiated the monthly *International Financial Statistics* (1948) and the *Balance of Payments Yearbook* (1949). The Food and Agriculture organization (FAO) continued the *Yearbook of Food and Agricultural Statistics,* issued additional yearbooks on forest products and fisheries (1947) and began publication of the *Monthly Bulletin of Agricultural Economics and Statistics* (1948). The ILO maintained and expanded the *Year Book of Labour Statistics* and the *Statistical Supplement* of the *International Labour Review.* In accordance with the agreements, each agency compiles the statistics relevant to its field and supplies them to any other agency upon request. Thus, labour statistics contained in UN publications are provided by ILO, and the UN provides statistics on population, trade, national income and the other subjects within its sphere. In 1963 the United Nations Educational, Scientific, and Cultural Organization (UNESCO) began publication of the *UNESCO Statistical Yearbook.*

The *List of Statistical Series Collected by International Organizations,* issued from time to time by the UN Statistical office, gives the sources of the series together with the titles of the international statistical publications.

Taken together, these developments resulted in a world-wide statistical system characterized by the full exchange of statistics and information among international agencies, by extensive consultation on technical questions and by active collaboration of national statistical services upon which international agencies must depend for statistics and for advice and assistance in the formulation of statistical standards. This latter function continues to be one of the most important and takes up a major part of the time of the various statistical services and of the Statistical commission itself.

Among the standards that have been developed by the UN and the specialized agencies through international consultations are: classification of international trade, classification of economic activities, occupational classification and various classifications and definitions applicable to censuses of population, housing, agriculture and industrial production and distribution. Principles have been established for the compilation of vital statistics, index numbers of industrial production, balance of payments, statistical sampling and other important economic and social subjects.

It has long been recognized that the divergent economic, social and political institutions in different countries and regions of the world require differentiated standards, so that absolutely uniform systems are not necessarily applicable from one country to another. Nevertheless, there are many common elements that find broad application in all countries and additional elements that may be applied on a regional or a community of interest basis. This situation has led to the development of regional groups for discussion of common statistical principles. The UN has established arrangements in Europe, Asia and Africa for periodic conferences and working parties to develop standard methods that are based on international standards but that are adapted to regional conditions.

The Inter-American Statistical institute (1940), in co-operation with the UN, serves as a forum for the Americas. Other arrangements of this kind are of long standing: the Scandinavian countries met to discuss statistical matters as early as 1888, and the first conference of statisticians of the British Commonwealth and empire was held in 1920.

Complete lists of applicable international standards are issued by the Statistical office from time to time in the *Directory of International Standards for Statistics.* Standard definitions and methods for many of the important economic and social subjects have been prepared, and work continues under way in many other subjects. Existing standards must be reviewed periodically to evaluate their continued applicability; new problems and concepts constantly emerge requiring statistical treatment. For example, increasing attention has been given to input-output studies, to money-flow analysis, to conditions and levels of living and to the refinement of national accounting and price-index techniques.

Bibliography.—A. Quételet, *Congrès international de statistique* (1873); W. F. Wilcox, "The International Statistical Congress, 1853–1878," *Estadística* (June 1943); *Bulletin de l'institut international de statistique,* tome I (1886); Friedrich Zahn, *50 Années de l'institut international de statistique* (1934); League of Nations, *Report with Annexes, International Statistical Commission,* A 10 (1921); Asher Hobson, *The International Institute of Agriculture* (1931); International Labour Office, *The International Standardization of Labour Statistics Studies and Reports,* "N Series" (Statistics) no. 25 (1943); Neville Goodman, *International Health Organizations and Their Work* (1952); W. Martin Hill, *The Economic and Financial Organization of the League of Nations* (1946); H. Campion, "International Statistics," *Journal of the Royal Statistical Society,* "A Series" (General), vol. cxii, part ii (1949). (W. R. LD.)

**STATISTICS** was a term first applied to such data of importance to the political state as population, yield of taxation, value of trade, and mortality (*see* CENSUS); and to the study and interpretation of such data. As commonly understood nowadays, statistics is a mathematical discipline concerned with the study of masses of numerical data of any kind. *See* also ECONOMETRICS; INDEX NUMBERS; BIOMETRY; STATISTICAL MECHANICS.

## DESCRIPTIVE STATISTICS

**Statistical Tables.**—A simple way of arranging numerical data is to set them in tabular form. With knowledge of the amount of sugar consumed in a given country in each year of a given period, for example, a table may be drawn up as indicated by the headings below:

*Consumption of Sugar*

| (1) Year | (2) Total consumption thousand lb. | (3) Population thousands | (4) Consumption per head, lb. |
|---|---|---|---|

Tabular arrangements of statistical data are found throughout these volumes; for example, *see* OLYMPIC GAMES; DEBT, PUBLIC. A detailed discussion of tabular material is given under MATHEMATICAL TABLES.

**Graphs.**—It is frequently useful to represent tabular data graphically. A number of examples of such graphs may be found in the articles PRICES, STATISTICS OF; LIFE EXPECTANCY.

Discrete variables comprise clear-cut classes; *e.g.,* in a group of men and women, the sex variable has two distinct categories. A bar graph (separate bars drawn to different heights showing the number in each category) can represent discrete data. A continuous variable can change along a continuum (*e.g.,* weight or I.Q. in a group of men). It may be graphed by a relatively smooth curve (frequency polygon) that changes in height to reflect the number of cases at different points on the continuum.

Even though graphs fall short of numerical tables in precision, they have the advantage of allowing a large mass of figures to be grasped as a whole much more readily than is possible when those figures are presented in one or more tables (*see* GRAPH).

**Averages and Dispersion.**—An illustration of a type of statistical table known as a frequency distribution is seen in the following summary of the heights of a number of men:

| Height in inches . . . | 61 | 62 | 63 | 64 | 65 | 66 | 67 |
|---|---|---|---|---|---|---|---|
| Frequency . . . . | 2 | 10 | 11 | 38 | 57 | 73 | 106 |
| Height in inches . . . | 68 | 69 | 70 | 71 | 72 | 73 | 74 |
| Frequency . . . . | 126 | 109 | 87 | 75 | 23 | 9 | 4 |

The table indicates that 126 men were found to be between 5 ft. 7½ in. and 5 ft. 8½ in. and similarly for other heights. In tables such as this some method of dealing with cases falling exactly on the dividing line between two adjacent intervals must be laid down, and a common method is to assign half the number found on the dividing line to each of the classes of which it forms the limit. This procedure may, of course, result in frequencies in some of the intervals which are not integers. The accurate average height of the 730 men covered by the table can be ascertained only by reference to a more detailed statement showing the height of each man exactly, instead of in a number of groups. It will be observed that 297 were not taller than 5 ft. 7½ in., while 307 were 5 ft. 8½ in. or more, the distribution being not quite symmetrical on both sides of the numerically largest group. The approximate average height was about $\frac{1}{20}$ in. less than 5 ft. 8 in. (*see* MEAN).

A table of this kind indicates more than the average height of the individuals represented. Note that 191 were not more than 5 ft. 6½ in. in height and 198 were not less than 5 ft. 9½ in. in height. By calculation from the figures shown, assuming that the individual heights were distributed with approximate regularity along the intervals from inch to inch, the points representing 5 ft. 6.3 in. and 5 ft. 9.7 in. would divide the series of heights so that one-quarter of the whole number fell below the former, and one-quarter of the whole number above the latter. A similar calculation gives, as the point dividing the series into two equally numerous groups, 5 ft. 8.04 in. This last point is called the median of the series, and the two others are the lower and upper quartiles, the three points serving to divide the whole number examined into four groups of equal numbers of cases. The distance between the upper and lower quartiles, in the case in question 3.4 in., gives the range within which the middle half of the instances recorded lay. This distance (a measure of dispersion called the interquartile range) expresses much more definitely the degree of concentration of the individuals in the neighbourhood of the median height than, for example, the whole range (14 in.) within which all the measurements lie. If a more exact description of the nature of the distribution than is afforded by the specification of the median and quartiles, but of the same general character, is desired, the group may be divided into a number of parts, *e.g.,* into ten equally numerous parts, the points of division being then known as deciles. Points of division called centiles (percentiles) divide the group into 100 equal parts (*see* PERCENTAGE). For the most commonly used measure of dispersion (*i.e.,* variability or spread within a frequency distribution) *see* STANDARD DEVIATION.

In many statistical problems the form of the distribution is of a recognizably definite character. It is found that, in numerous cases, the manner in which the individual observations are distributed is in close accordance with that of events dependent on chance. Such a case is presented by the following. A number of balls, indistinguishable in size, weight, or form, are placed in a bag, half of the balls being white and half black. If one ball be drawn from the bag, its colour, whether white or black, may be noted. The ball being replaced and the bag shaken, another drawing will give a result wholly independent of the first.

If a large number of sequences of $x_r$ white (or of $x_r$ black) balls are recorded on $Y_r$ occasions, the total number $n$ of drawings will be expressed by $n = x_1Y_1 + x_2Y_2 + x_3Y_3 + \ldots + x_rY_r + \ldots$. The relative frequencies of the different series are $y_1$, $y_2$, etc., where $n \cdot y_1 = Y_1$, $n \cdot y_2 = Y_2$, etc., and, when $n$ is indefinitely increased, the relation between the $x$ and $y$ values is represented by what is known as the normal probability curve, sometimes called the Gaussian curve or normal distribution (*see* PROBABILITY, MATHEMATICAL).

In any actual series of observations (*e.g.,* of the colours of balls drawn from a bag) the observed numbers expressing the frequency of different events will be found to differ more or less from those expressed by the normal curve. Prolonged trials would give results approximating to those derived from theoretical calculations and expressed in the shape of the probability curve. Thus, in the case of the heights of 730 men, it is probable that records covering larger numbers of men, of the same race and social condition and within the same limits of age as those from which the 730 were selected, would give a distribution of heights more closely corresponding to that shown by a typical probability curve than the numbers cited. This Gaussian (normal) distribution is illustrated and discussed in greater detail under ERRORS, THEORY OF.

**Skew Distributions.**—Particular statistical problems yield distributions that are not symmetrical on either side of their mean (as compared with the symmetrical normal probability curve). These are said to be skewed: *i.e.,* grouped more closely on one side of the mean than on the other. The following distribution of weights of men shows marked skewness.

| Weight in lb. . . . . | 105 | 120 | 135 | 150 | 165 | 180 | 195 | 210 |
|---|---|---|---|---|---|---|---|---|
| Frequency . . . . | 17 | 722 | 2,175 | 1,346 | 485 | 155 | 33 | 3 |

In this case the average (or arithmetic mean) of the weights of the 4,936 men is, on the assumption of continuous distribution, approximately 141.6 lb. The median is at about 140.5 lb. In the previous illustration of heights, the median was greater than the mean, so that the skewness shown is of opposite direction in the two cases. If the mean is the greater of the two measures, the distribution is said to be positively skewed, or skewed to the right. When the median is the greater of these two measures of central tendency, the distribution is negatively skewed, or skewed to the left.

This illustration serves also to show a third measure of central tendency called the mode. The group of which 135 lb. is the central point is notably more numerous than any other. The weight 135 lb. may be called, as far as the figures furnish a ready indication, the most generally occurring weight or the modal weight. The point in the distribution thus determined is called the mode. A table like this, however, gives only a crude estimate of the most prevalent (modal) weight.

If the data in the table of weights had been less roughly grouped, the mode could be more accurately estimated. In a skew distribution the mode is related to the other two measures of central tendency as follows: it is lower than the arithmetic mean and the median in positive skewness; and is higher than these two in negative skewness.

**Three Variable Elements.**—In what precedes, the statistical material considered has consisted of series of pairs of quantities, the values of the two quantities in each pair being related; for example, where one of the quantities is the height of a man, the other the relative frequency with which men of that height were observed (*see* FUNCTION). Now consider series of three quantities, for example, where two of the quantities express the measures of different phenomena (which may be connected in some way, or may be independent) and the third expresses the relative frequency with which any combination of the other two occurs. Such a series is represented in the table given below, which shows how 1,000 marriages were distributed according to the ages of brides and bridegrooms.

| Ages of wives at date of marriage | Ages of husbands at date of marriage | | | | | | Total wives |
|---|---|---|---|---|---|---|---|
| | Under 25 | 25–34 | 35–44 | 45–54 | 55–64 | 65 and over | |
| Under 25 | 10 | 75 | 46 | 13 | 3 | .. | 147 |
| 25–34 | 20 | 175 | 167 | 65 | 17 | 3 | 447 |
| 35–44 | 5 | 54 | 104 | 79 | 29 | 7 | 278 |
| 45–54 | .. | 5 | 18 | 36 | 33 | 9 | 101 |
| 55–64 | .. | .. | 1 | 5 | 13 | 5 | 24 |
| 65 and over | .. | .. | .. | .. | 1 | 2 | 3 |
| Total husbands | 35 | 309 | 336 | 198 | 96 | 26 | 1,000 |

It is clear, from the clustering of frequencies in a band crossing the table from its upper left side toward its lower right side, that there is some association (correlation) between the ages of the wives and husbands, old women tending to marry old men, and young women tending to marry young men. (A. W. F.)

**Correlation.**—Variables that tend to change together systematically are said to be correlated. If their values tend to rise and fall together the variables are positively correlated. Thus, from the table, age of husband is positively correlated with age of wife. If the value of one variable tends to fall as the other rises, the two are negatively correlated. For example, consider a boy at one end of a balanced plank (seesaw), and a girl at the other end. As the boy rises, the girl falls; and vice versa. Thus the elevation of the boy is negatively correlated with the elevation of the girl. Variables that change together in a completely random fashion are said to exhibit zero correlation. The weights of 100 pairs of soldiers selected at random (*see* RANDOMIZATION) from an infantry regiment would be expected to show zero correlation.

If each value of one variable exactly specifies one associated value for its correlated variable, the two variables are said to be perfectly correlated. In the example of the seesaw, the two elevation variables are perfectly correlated since the position of one child always specifies that of the other. The age correlation among marital partners is less than perfect, since any group of men of the same age tend to have wives who span a range of ages. Note from the table that husbands 65 and over have wives whose ages range all the way down to the 25–34 interval. This is an example of what is called regression: extreme values on one variable $X$ tend to be associated with a range of values on the other, $Y$. The arithmetic mean of this $Y$ range tends to be less extreme (to regress, or fall toward the $Y$ average). In perfect correlation there is zero regression, since each $X$ value exactly specifies one $Y$ value; there is complete regression in zero correlation, each $X$ value being associated with a range of $Y$ values whose arithmetic mean is the same as the mean for all $Y$ values combined.

Correlation can be quantified with a number (correlation coefficient) that ranges from $+1.00$ (perfect positive), through 0.00 (completely random), to $-1.00$ (perfect negative). The algebraic sign indicates only the direction (positive or negative) of correlation. Degree of relationship is shown by the absolute size of the coefficient. Thus a correlation coefficient of $+.50$ shows the same degree of relationship as does one of $-.50$.

Suppose five people A, B, C, D, E are measured on variables $X,Y$ to yield the following:

| Individual | X Score | Y Score |
|---|---|---|
| A | 60 | 83 |
| B | 55 | 109 |
| C | 40 | 121 |
| D | 20 | 126 |
| E | 10 | 130 |

Note that these data represent a perfect negative correlation ($-1.00$), since A scored highest on $X$, lowest on $Y$; B next highest on $X$, next lowest on $Y$; and so on.

One way to express this quantitatively is to calculate a Spearman rank-order correlation coefficient $\rho_{XY}$ based on

$$\rho_{XY} = 1 - \frac{6\Sigma D^2}{N(N^2 - 1)}$$

where $D$ is the difference between each pair of scores (each score expressed in rank form), $N$ is the number of individuals (in this case 5), and $\Sigma D^2$ is the sum of squared differences. Thus, assigning rank 1 to the highest score in each array, rank 2 to the next highest, and so on, the initial calculations are

| Individual | Rank X | Rank Y | D | $D^2$ |
|---|---|---|---|---|
| A | 1 | 5 | −4 | 16 |
| B | 2 | 4 | −2 | 4 |
| C | 3 | 3 | 0 | 0 |
| D | 4 | 2 | 2 | 4 |
| E | 5 | 1 | 4 | 16 |
| | | | | $40 = \Sigma D^2$ |

Substitute appropriately in the equation and the correlation between $X$ and $Y$ is $\rho_{XY} = 1 - [6 \times 40/5(25 - 1)] = -1.00$; a perfect negative correlation as expected.

Alternately the degree of relationship may be quantitatively estimated as a Pearson product-moment correlation coefficient $r_{XY}$ calculated from

$$r_{XY} = \frac{\Sigma xy}{\sqrt{\Sigma x^2 \cdot \Sigma y^2}}$$

where $x$ is the difference between each value of $X$ and the arithmetic mean $M_X$ of all $X$ values (*i.e.*, $x = X - M_X$); and $y = Y - M_Y$. Thus $r_{XY}$ considers the actual values $X,Y$ while $\rho_{XY}$ considers only their ranks.

Both $\rho$ and $r$ can be used only with continuous variables (*e.g.*, height *v.* weight, gas pressure *v.* temperature); for such discontinuous (discrete) variables as sex (male *v.* female), marital status (married *v.* not married), employment status (employed *v.* unemployed), other methods for calculating correlation coefficients must be sought. Among these special methods (only mentioned here) are the biserial, point-biserial, tetrachoric, and phi correlation coefficients.

The Pearson $r$ will underestimate the degree of relationship when $X$ and $Y$ fail to change together in a linear (straight-line) fashion; *i.e.*, when they fail to show linear regression. This may be observed by constructing what is called a scatterplot, representing each pair of values $X,Y$ as a point in rectangular Cartesian coordinates. If the scatterplot shows a curvilinear relationship between $X$ and $Y$, the Spearman $\rho$ may be substituted. However, if the curvilinearity is so marked that the slope of the scatterplot reverses direction (tends to become parabolic), $\rho$ will also underestimate the degree of relationship, and the so-called eta coefficient (only mentioned here) should be used. Such parabolic scatter-plots are sometimes encountered in industry, where employees on simple routines tend to produce best if they are of middle-range intelligence, those who are extremely dull or bright tending to do poorly.

To interpret the meaning of correlation coefficients it is helpful to think of them as expressing the degree to which variables $X,Y$ exhibit variation in common. Such variation is usually given as the variance (*i.e.*, the square of the standard deviation) for each variable. If all assumptions underlying the accurate use of $r$ are met, then an $r_{XY}$ of either $+1.00$ or $-1.00$ means that $X$ accounts for all of the $Y$ variance; it is then said that $X$ and $Y$ show 100% variance overlap, or that $Y$ explains 100% of the $X$ variance. However, an $r$ of $\pm.90$ does not represent 90% overlap; instead, it indicates 81% common variance. In other words, variance overlap is a function of the square of the correlation coefficient: $r = \pm.80$ signifies 64% common variance; $\pm.70$ represents 49% overlap; and so on.

For example, in estimating the effectiveness (validity) of intelligence test scores in predicting academic grades, it is common to compute the correlation coefficient between test scores and grades for different samples of students (*see* PSYCHOLOGICAL TESTS AND MEASUREMENTS). A typical validity coefficient from such studies is $+.60$. In terms of overlap the test is then said to explain 36% of the variance in academic grades, 64% of the variance remaining unexplained. (C. CE.)

## STATISTICAL INFERENCE

Thus far the discussion has been concerned with descriptive statistics: methods for succinctly describing masses of numerical data. Statistical inference deals with techniques used to assess the probable characteristics of masses of data when these data are incompletely known. For example, such methods are used to infer the probable average height of a large human population (or universe) on the basis of measurements taken from a sample of people derived from the universe. An understanding of STATISTICS, MATHEMATICAL should be helpful in understanding what follows.

**Statistical Tests.**—A statistical test is a procedure for testing a given hypothesis about the distribution law of a population from which a sample is assumed to have been drawn. The hypothesis in its simplest form is whether the cumulative distribution function of the population is some specific function $F_1(x)$ alternative to a specified function $F_0(x)$. It is assumed that the sample comes from one of these populations. To test the hypothesis, a function $u(x_1, x_2, \ldots, x_n)$ of the sample $x$ values is constructed, and a range $R$ of critical values of this function is found so that the probability is a given value $\delta$ (usually .01 or .05) of $u(x_1, x_2, \ldots, x_n)$ lying in $R$ if the population cumulative distribution function is $F_0(x)$, and also such that the probability of $u(x_1, x_2, \ldots, x_n)$ falling in $R$ when the population distribution $F_1(x)$ is made as large as possible—certainly larger than $\delta$. Then the claim can be made that the sample has been drawn from the population having distribution $F_1(x)$ with a risk of probability $\delta$ of making a type-I error. By a type-I error is meant the error committed by saying that the sample is not from the population having distribution $F_0(x)$, when, in fact, it is. In other words, when the value of $u(x_1, x_2, \ldots, x_n)$ falls in $R$ there is a risk of erroneously claiming the sample not to have come from the population with distribution $F_0(x)$ when it actually does come from such a population. If the value of $u(x_1, x_2, \ldots, x_n)$ does not fall in range $R$ the test calls for the assertion that the sample comes from the population having distribution $F_0(x)$, which is considered as the only alternative to $F_1(x)$ at present. There is a risk of being in error in this assertion, too, because the sample could have come from the population with distribution $F_1(x)$. The probability $\epsilon$ of this error is obtained by finding the probability of $u(x_1, x_2, \ldots, x_n)$ not falling in range $R$, when the sample has actually been drawn from the population having distribution $F_1(x)$. This error is called a type-II error. The probability of $u(x_1, x_2, \ldots, x_n)$ falling in $R$ when the sample is from the population having distribution $F_1(x)$ is $1 - \epsilon$ and is called the power of the test based on $u(x_1, x_2, \ldots, x_n)$. When $u(x_1, x_2, \ldots, x_n)$ falls in $R$ it is often said to be statistically significant at the $\delta$ probability level. Usually, $F_1(x)$ is a member of a family of functions $F(x, \theta)$, when $\theta$ is a parameter, which would be a specific member of the family, say $F(x, \theta_0)$. In this case the power $1 - \epsilon$ for the various alternatives corresponding to all values of $\theta$ (except $\theta_0$) would depend on $\theta$ and is called the power function of the test based on $u(x_1, x_2, \ldots, x_n)$. The essential idea underlying type-I and type-II errors was originally introduced by Bell Telephone Laboratories' quality control engineers who first referred to them in their own applications as producer's risk and consumer's risk, respectively. The producer's risk is the probability that a given lot of products of satisfactory quality offered by a producer will be rejected on basis of the results of an inspected sample from the lot, whereas the consumer's risk is the probability of the consumer's accepting a lot of products of unsatisfactory quality on basis of the results of the inspected sample. J. Neyman and E. S. Pearson (1928) developed the idea that underlies these two risks into the present theory of testing statistical hypotheses. Contributions to this theory and its application to various problems are numerous. Two important examples will be briefly discussed.

A. Wald (1950) further generalized the ideas by developing a theory of statistical decision functions in which decisions regarding a statistical hypothesis may be more numerous than simply acceptance or rejection and where the risks associated with such decisions are measured.

*The Student t-Test.*—Consider a sample of $n$ items taken from a normally distributed population to test whether this population has a given mean $\mu_0$. Each measurement based on one case within the sample is signified by $x_i$. The criterion for this $t$-ratio test is

$$\frac{\sqrt{n}\,(\bar{x} - \mu_0)}{s} = t$$

where $\bar{x}$ is the sample mean, and $s^2$ is the sample variance

$$\frac{1}{n-1}\sum_{i=1}^{n}(x_i - \bar{x})^2$$

The sampling distribution of $t$ when the sample has been drawn from a normal population with mean $\mu_0$ is

$$dF(t) = \frac{\Gamma\left(\frac{n}{2}\right)}{\Gamma\left(\frac{n-1}{2}\right)\sqrt{\pi(n-1)}}\left(1 + \frac{t^2}{n-1}\right)^{-\frac{n}{2}} dt \qquad (1)$$

where $\Gamma(m)$ is the gamma function which equals $(m-1)!$, if $m$ is a positive integer and provides a good interpolation function for $(m-1)!$ if $m$ is real but not a positive integer. In either case, $\Gamma(m)$ can be expressed as a definite integral. The distribution law expressed by equation (1) is known as the Student (1908) distribution law with $n - 1$ degrees of freedom. The range $R$ of critical values of the function $t$ is taken as the set of values of $t$ outside the interval $(-t_\delta, t_\delta)$ where $t_\delta$ is given by the relation

$$\int_{-t_\delta}^{+t_\delta} dF(t) = 1 - \delta$$

This means that the probability is $1 - \delta$ that the sample will be such that

$$-t_\delta < \frac{\sqrt{n}\,(\bar{x} - \mu_0)}{s} < +t_\delta \qquad (2)$$

when the sample is actually from a normal population with mean $\mu_0$. If the sample yields values of $\bar{x}$ and $s$ so that the inequality (2) is not satisfied the hypothesis is rejected that the sample is from a normal population with mean $\mu_0$. The risk of rejecting this hypothesis falsely is measured as the type-I error $\delta$. Tabulations of values of $t_\delta$ have been presented in various statistics books for $\delta = .01$, .05, and other values and for different values of $n - 1$. There are many applications of the Student $t$-test.

*The Chi-Square Test.*—As a second example, consider an infinite population in which each element belongs to one and only one of the mutually exclusive classes $A_1, A_2, \ldots, A_k$ having probabilities $p_1, p_2, \ldots, p_k$, where

$$\sum_{i=1}^{k} p_i = 1$$

In a sample of $n$ elements from this population, the probability of getting $x_1$ $A_1$'s, $x_2$ $A_2$'s, ..., $x_k$ $A_k$'s is given by the multinomial law

$$m(x_1, x_2, \ldots, x_k) = \frac{n!}{x_1!x_2!\ldots x_k!} p_1^{x_1} p_2^{x_2} \ldots p_k^{x_k}$$

It is important in many statistical problems to test whether the observed frequencies $x_1, x_2, \ldots, x_k$ could have reasonably come from a population in which $p_1, p_2, \ldots, p_k$ have specified values $p'_1, p'_2, \ldots, p'_k$; *i.e.*, whether the $x$ values depart significantly from their expected values $np'_1, np'_2, \ldots, np'_k$ under the hypothesis that the sample came from a population with these specified $p$ values. The criterion for testing this hypothesis which was originally proposed by K. Pearson (1900) is:

$$\chi^2 = \sum_{i=1}^{k} \frac{(x_i - np'_i)^2}{np'_i} \quad (3)$$

known as the chi-square test criterion. It will be seen that it satisfies the intuitive requirement that it should somehow measure the discrepancy between each $x_i$ and its expected value. The more the $x$ values depart from their mean or expected values, the larger the value of $\chi^2$ (chi-square). Thus, the range $R$ of critical values which suggests itself consists of all values of $\chi^2$ greater than a suitable chosen value $\chi^2_\delta$. For larger values of $n$, and assuming that none of the $p$ values are very small, the sampling distribution of $\chi^2$, if the hypothesis is true that the sample came from a population in which the $p$'s have the values specified, is approximately

$$dF(\chi^2) = \frac{\left(\frac{\chi^2}{2}\right)^{\frac{k-3}{2}}}{2\Gamma\left(\frac{k-1}{2}\right)} e^{-\frac{1}{2}\chi^2} d(\chi^2) \quad (4)$$

This is an important sampling distribution, known as the chi-square distribution with $k - 1$ degrees of freedom. Values of $\chi^2_\delta$ have been tabulated for which

$$\int_{\chi^2_\delta}^{\infty} dF(\chi^2) = \delta$$

has various values from .01 to .99 and for values of $k$ from 2 to 30. There are many statistical functions having sampling distributions that are of the form given as equation (4).

As a simple example of the application of equation (3), suppose a bridge player has kept a record of the number of aces he has obtained in each of 500 bridge hands. Suppose he received no aces in 165 hands, one ace in 210 hands, and more than one ace in 125 hands. Is this distribution of aces consistent with the hypothesis of thorough shuffling and fair dealing? Under the hypothesis of thorough shuffling and fair dealing one finds by applying the theory of combinations (*see* COMBINATORIAL ANALYSIS) that the probabilities of no aces, one ace, and more than one ace are approximately 0.30, 0.44, 0.26, respectively. The expected numbers of hands containing no ace, one ace, and no aces in 500 hands are, therefore, 150, 220, 130, respectively. The value of $\chi^2$ computed from equation (3) is

$$\chi^2 = \frac{(165 - 150)^2}{150} + \frac{(210 - 220)^2}{220} + \frac{(125 - 130)^2}{130} = 2.147$$

This is not a significantly large value of $\chi^2$. For example, in a large number of sets of 500 bridge hands more than 30% of the sets would yield hands deviating more widely from the expected distribution of aces than in the present case. To have significant discrepancies at the 0.05 probability level the observed distribution of aces would have to yield a value of $\chi^2$ equal to about 6 or larger.

**Analysis of Variance.**—With the rapid development of statistical theory, an increasing amount of attention is being paid to the original design or setting up of any type of an experiment or an investigation which depends heavily upon statistical analysis of the results for interpretation. Consideration of experimental design led to the development of theory and procedures for determining what combinations of factors important to the entire experiment should be introduced to simplify statistical analysis of the data and its interpretation, and also to determine how many repetitions or replications of the experiment should be performed to detect important differences in experimental results attributable to the various factors or combinations of factors. R. A. Fisher was the leading exponent of the importance of carefully designed experiments. Fisher and his school developed experimental designs together with an appropriate statistical procedure known as analysis of variance for analyzing the data from such experiments. The principal idea in this work is to arrange the entire experiment in an orderly manner as a set of subexperiments (which may consist of as few as one trial each), these subexperiments differing from each other by varying one or more factors, so as to permit the effect of the variation of the factor (or factors) on the outcome of the experiment to assert itself in case there is such an effect. A statistical test function is designed to detect whether the outcome of the experiment is such that the differences in results from one subexperiment to another are attributable to the variation of the factors being tested, or whether they are simply chance differences; and to measure such differences if they are statistically significant (*i.e.*, unlikely to have occurred by chance).

Suppose samples are drawn from each of two populations that have normal distribution laws with equal variances. The question is this: could the two samples have reasonably come from normal populations with the same mean? If the numbers of items, means, and variances of the two samples are $n', n''$; $\bar{x}', \bar{x}''$; $s'^2, s''^2$, respectively, a suitable criterion for making the test is $\sqrt{n}(\bar{x}' - \bar{x}'')/s$ where $n = n' + n''$, and

$$s^2 = \frac{(n' - 1)s'^2 + (n'' - 1)s''^2}{n' + n'' - 2}$$

Thus, the greater the difference between the sample means in relation to $s$, the greater the value of the criterion and the more unfavourable it is to the hypothesis of equality of population means. This criterion computed from pairs of samples from normal populations having the same means has a distribution law given by equation (1) with $n' + n'' - 2$ degrees of freedom; *i.e.*, with $n - 1$ replaced by $n' + n'' - 2$. Therefore, if the absolute value of the criterion exceeds $t_\delta$, the samples' means are said to be significantly different at the $\delta$ probability level, which means that the samples are likely to have come from normal populations with the same means with a risk of probability $\delta$ of making a type-I error. This test is useful in testing whether the effects of two treatments $A$ and $B$ on a given measurable characteristic are significantly different; *e.g.*, whether two rations $A$ and $B$ are different in their effects in increasing the weight of pigs. The experiment might be set up with 30 pigs of a given age to receive ration $A$ and 30 more pigs matched with those in the first group on age and weight to receive ration $B$. Thus, there are two subexperiments. After a given time each of the 30 pigs in each sample would be weighed, and these two sets of weights would be the two samples of $x$ values to be used in the criterion.

Note that in using the two-sample criterion described above it has been assumed that the variances of the populations are equal. Actually, it may be wished to test this assumption, assuming only that the two population distributions are normal. A criterion (sometimes called an $F$-ratio; sometimes written $\mathcal{J}$-ratio) is available for making this test, namely

$$\mathcal{J} = s'^2/s''^2$$

which has the following distribution law when the hypothesis of equal population variances is true:

$$dF(\mathcal{J}) = \frac{\Gamma\left(\frac{n'+n''-2}{2}\right)}{\Gamma\left(\frac{n'-1}{2}\right)\Gamma\left(\frac{n''-1}{2}\right)}\left(\frac{n'-1}{n''-1}\right)^{\frac{n'-1}{2}} \mathcal{J}^{\frac{n'-3}{2}} \tag{5}$$

$$\cdot\left(1+\frac{n'-1}{n''-1}\mathcal{J}\right)^{-\frac{n'+n''-2}{2}} d\mathcal{J}$$

which is known as Snedecor's $\mathcal{J}$ distribution and defined on the interval $(0, \infty)$. The $\mathcal{J}$ criterion is intuitively reasonable since small or large values of it are unfavourable to the hypothesis of equal population variances. The critical range $R$ of values of $\mathcal{J}$, for a given level of significance $\delta$, is found by cutting off the lower tail of the distribution at $1/\mathcal{J}_\delta$ and the upper tail at $\mathcal{J}_\delta$ so that the probability of $\mathcal{J}$ falling between $1/\mathcal{J}_\delta$ and $\mathcal{J}_\delta$ is $1 - \delta$. Equation (5) is the basic probability law involved in making statistical tests in analysis of variance.

Next, consider a slightly more elaborate experiment. Suppose it is desired to test whether the quality of screws of a given type as measured by number of defectives per 1,000 varies significantly from machine to machine or from operator to operator. An experiment might be designed along the following lines: consider eight machines and eight operators; let each operator make 1,000 screws on each machine, and let $x_{ij}$ be the number of defectives in the 1,000 screws produced by the $i$th operator on the $j$th machine. Assume that $x_{ij}$ is made up of the sum of four parts: $m$ which is the same for all combinations of operators and machines, $r_i$ an effect attributable to the $i$th operator, $c_j$ an effect attributable to the $j$th machine, and a random error $e_i$, which is normally and independently distributed for all combinations of $i$ and $j$ with mean zero and variance $\sigma^2$. Then $x_{ij} = m + r_i + c_j + e_{ij}$. The $r_i$ and $c_j$ may be thought of as corrections to $m$, which may be positive or negative; $r_i$ a correction to be made for the $i$th operator; and $c_j$ a correction of the $j$th machine. They are such that

$$\sum_{i=1}^{8} r_i = \sum_{j=1}^{8} c_j = 0$$

The $x_{ij}$ are sample values and what is wished is to set up a criterion for testing whether the operator corrections $r_i$ are all zero (*i.e.*, no average change from operator to operator), and similarly whether the machine corrections $c_j$ are all zero. The likelihood ratio or least squares criterion for testing for no significant variation from operator to operator is

$$7 \sum_{i=1}^{8} (\bar{x}_{i\cdot} - \bar{x})^2 / \sum_{i,j=1}^{8} (x_{ij} - \bar{x}_{i\cdot} - \bar{x}_{j\cdot} + \bar{x})^2$$

where $\bar{x}_{i\cdot}$ is the average of $x_{i1}, x_{i2}, \ldots, x_{i8}$, with a similar meaning for $\bar{x}_{j\cdot}$; $\bar{x}$ is the average of all $x$ values. The denominator of this expression is rather insensitive to variations due to operators or machines although the numerator tends to be sensitive to operator variations, and the ratio tends to have large values if there is significant variation from operator to operator. The criterion has as its sampling distribution the $\mathcal{J}$ distribution of equation (5) with $n' - 1 = 7$, and $n'' - 1 = 49$ if there is no significant operator to operator variation, which provides a method of obtaining a critical value of the ratio beyond which it would be declared that operator variation is significant. A similar analysis would be made for testing significance of machine to machine variation.

*See* also references under "Statistics" in the Index.

(S. S. W.)

Bibliography.—L. G. Gotkin and L. S. Goldstein, *Descriptive Statistics*, 2 vol. (1964); C. R. Li, *Statistical Inference*, 2 vol. (1964); N. L. Johnson and F. C. Leone, *Statistics and Experimental Design in Engineering and the Physical Sciences*, 2 vol. (1964); W. C. Guenther, *Analysis of Variance* (1964); G. M. Smith, *A Simplified Guide to Statistics, for Psychology and Education*, 3rd ed. (1962); F. E. Croxton and D. J. Cowden, *Practical Business Statistics*, 3rd ed. (1960); R. A. Fisher, *Statistical Methods for Research Workers*, 13th ed. rev. (1958); H. M. Walker and J. Lev, *Elementary Statistical Methods*, rev. ed. (1958); G. U. Yule and M. G. Kendall, *An Introduction to the Theory of Statistics*, 14th rev. ed. (1958); D. A. S. Fraser, *Nonparametric Methods in Statistics* (1957).

**STATISTICS, MATHEMATICAL.** In traditional usage mathematical statistics denotes a conglomeration of mathematical discussions connected with efforts to most efficiently collect and use numerical data subject to random variation (*see* Statistics). These efforts can be classified as behaviouristic and inductive.

## BEHAVIOURISTIC APPROACH

Behaviouristically, mathematical statistics is concerned with methods people use in guiding their actions to minimize the chances of committing errors. More exactly, it may be defined as dealing with statistical decision functions (*see* below). The definition originates from the human habit (so-called inductive behaviour) of adjusting to pertinent frequency relations. For example, since accumulations of clouds are frequently followed by rain, people who see clouds when embarking on a trip may think of taking an umbrella. Vaccinated persons contract smallpox much less frequently than others; thus smallpox vaccination is almost universal. In these examples the decisions (to take an umbrella or not, to be vaccinated or not) are based on the relative frequency of specific occurrences and the possible consequences of the different decisions.

Thus mass vaccination is desirable if the vaccine frequently prevents disease and if it causes dangerous reactions only infrequently. Obviously, people prefer to speak in terms of certainty instead of in terms of relative frequency. However, either the nature of the phenomena or ignorance of their causes compel an indeterministic approach based on how frequently this or that happens.

Questions of relative frequency are the concern of the theory of probability (*see* Probability, Mathematical). It deals with so-called chance mechanisms that combine the unpredictability of a single trial with the stability of relative frequencies in a long series of trials. The probability is an idealization of the long-run relative frequency of an outcome of a chance mechanism. When the probability that a given coin will fall heads is said to equal $\frac{1}{3}$, it means that this unusual coin tends to fall heads one-third of the time in a long series of tosses.

In the theory of probability the term random variable denotes a variable quantity determined by a chance mechanism. If $X$ is a random variable and $x$ any specified number, then the relevant chance mechanism determines the probability $P[X \leqq x]$ that $X$ will assume a value not exceeding $x$. This same mechanism determines the probability $P[X = x]$ that $X$ will equal $x$. The probability $P[X \leqq x]$, considered as a function of $x$, determines the properties of the random variable $X$ and is called its distribution function, or simply its distribution.

Solution of typical probability problems consists in determining the distributions of some random variables from the given distributions of other random variables. A typical result of elementary probability theory is the distribution of the so-called binomial variable $X$ (*see* Binomial Theorem), defined as the number of successes in $n$ independent trials, where the probability of success has the same value $p$. Here $n$ is a positive integer and $p$ an arbitrary number between 0 and 1. The distribution function of $X$ so defined may be obtained from

$$P[X = x] = \frac{n!}{x!(n-x)!} p^x(1-p)^{n-x} \tag{1}$$

for $0 \leqq x \leqq n$. In particular, this formula may serve to compute the probability that in $n = 10$ independent tosses, with a coin falling heads with a long-run frequency $p$ of $\frac{1}{3}$, heads will appear not more than once, twice, and so on.

This example deals with a chance mechanism, the throw of a coin, repeated independently $n = 10$ times; that is, the outcome of any given throw is assumed to have no effect on the outcomes of the others. If the order in which heads may occur is ignored, there are $n + 1 = 11$ possible outcomes: the number $X$ of heads thrown may be $0, 1, 2, \ldots, 10$.

The unpredictably varying outcomes of scientific experiments are treated as manifestations of a chance mechanism and the quantitative characteristics of these outcomes are treated as random variables. Simplifying severely, the results of the use of a vaccine on a particular subject may be expected to vary according to his individual susceptibility to the disease, to aftereffects of vaccination, and according to the degree of his exposure to infection with the disease.

The decision for or against mass vaccination may be based on an experiment using a random selection out of a large parent population (universe) of $n$ (experimental) individuals to be vaccinated and an equal number of (control) individuals to be left untreated. Then all $2n$ individuals are exposed to infection and observed. The outcome may be described by the number $X_1$ of "good" results among the vaccinated and the number $X_2$ of such results among the controls. The two variables $X_1$ and $X_2$ have the same set of possible values: $0, 1, 2, \ldots, n$. It is assumed that $X_1$ and $X_2$ are random variables with approximate distributions represented by equation (1), with $p = p_v$ for the vaccinated group and $p = p_0$ for the nonvaccinated. The symbol $p_v$ represents the proportion of individuals in the parent population for whom the vaccine would give "good" results: $p_0$ stands for the proportion of the parent population for whom such results would be observed without vaccination. The desirability of mass vaccination depends on the values of $p_v$ and $p_0$. Unfortunately these values are unknown and the decision for or against mass vaccination must be taken on the values of the random variables $X_1$ and $X_2$ found empirically from the sample of subjects in the experiment.

In practice, the outcomes of trials with a vaccine are not classified as just "good" and "bad," and many different trials are performed. In many situations there is a set $A$ of possible actions $a_1, a_2, \ldots$ from which one must be selected. Also, the desirability of this or that action depends on the distribution $F$ of some observable random variables $X = (X_1, X_2, \ldots, X_n)$. The distribution $F$ is unknown, at least in all details, and the choice of action has to be based on the observed values $x = (x_1, x_2, \ldots, x_n)$ of the random variables $X$. Each possible combination $x$ of values of $X$ is described as a possible sample point and the set of all such combinations is the sample space.

In the vaccine example there are only two observable random variables $X_1$ and $X_2$. The sample space $W$ consists of $(n+1)^2$ different points with coordinates (0,0), (0,1), (1,0), . . . , $(n,n)$. The datum of the general problem also includes a family or set $\Omega$ of possible distributions of the observable random variables $X$, described as the set of admissible hypotheses or the set of possible states of the universe. To each distribution $F$ of the set $\Omega$ there corresponds a "preferred" action, and for each $F$ in $\Omega$ and each possible action $a$ in $A$ there is a more or less explicitly ascertainable degree of desirability. The datum of the problem may (but usually does not) give the so-called a priori probabilities of the various distributions $F$ of the set $\Omega$ (*see* PROBABILITY: *Inverse Probability*).

In the vaccine example, when the population from which subjects are selected is large, the family $\Omega$ of possible distributions of the two observable variables $X_1$ and $X_2$ is determined approximately by all combinations of two equations of type (1). If $p_0$ (the potential proportion of "good" results in the parent population without vaccination) is greater or equal to $p_v$, then the preferred action is $a_1$ (abstain from mass vaccination). On the other hand if $p_v$ is greater then the preferred action is $a_2$ (embark on mass vaccination) with the desirability of $a_2$ increasing with the difference $p_v - p_0$.

Any systematically defined rule for selecting actions can have the following form: if the observations yield $X = x'$, then take action $a(x')$; if the observations yield $X = x''$, then take action $a(x'')$, and so on, for all possible sample points. In effect a rule for making decisions must establish the action to be taken as a function of the sample point to be observed. This function $a(x)$ is called the statistical decision function. Since $X$ is a random variable, so is the degree of desirability of the action taken using a given decision function. The datum of the problem allows calculation of the probability (at least the limits within which the probability is inferred to lie) that a given decision function will lead to the adoption of a very undesirable action. Thus mathematical statistics may be defined as the mathematical discipline dealing with properties of statistical decision functions. The general problem of mathematical statistics is to determine (from the data of the given problem) the particular decision function that has specified desirable properties; *e.g.*, the decision function (if it exists) that minimizes the probability of a wrong decision.

Probabilities are involved in probability theory and in mathematical statistics; if the unknown is a probability, the problem is one of probability theory; if the unknown is a decision function, the problem belongs to mathematical statistics. The viewpoint and terminology used here are generalizations due to Abraham Wald (1902–50) of two earlier theories described below. While many mathematical statisticians would agree with this characterization of their field, others would feel it too restrictive.

**Theory of Testing Statistical Hypotheses.**—The theory of testing statistical hypotheses, developed in the 1930s by Jerzy Neyman and Egon S. Pearson, is a chapter of mathematical statistics referring to the case where the set $A$ of possible decisions contains only two elements: action $a_1$ and action $a_2$ considered as the negation of $a_1$ (*e.g.*, $a_1$ = arrange a mass vaccination campaign, and $a_2$ = do not). The terminology refers to statistical hypotheses and their rejection. A statistical hypothesis means any assumption regarding the distribution of the observable random variables. The fact that only two possible actions are contemplated implies the existence of two contradictory hypotheses $H_1$ and $H_2$ such that if $H_i$ happens to be true then the preferred action is $a_i$ for $i = 1,2$. This indicates symmetry between $H_1$ and $H_2$ that usually disappears when the consequences of selecting a wrong action are considered. There are two different situations in which a wrong action may be selected; *i.e.*, there are two different kinds of error possible in testing a hypothesis:

$(H_1,a_2)$ = the true hypothesis is $H_1$ and the action taken is $a_2$ which is reject $H_1$

$(H_2,a_1)$ = the true hypothesis is $H_2$ and the action taken is $a_1$ which is accept $H_1$.

Alternatively, $a_2$ may be described as acceptance of $H_2$, and $a_1$ as rejection of $H_2$. Usually error $(H_1,a_2)$ is qualitatively different from error $(H_2,a_1)$. According to the individual's subjective evaluation one of the errors may be judged more important to avoid than the other. The one held more important to avoid is called the error of the first kind; the other is called the error of the second kind. One of the hypotheses $H_1$ and $H_2$ is selected to be the hypothesis tested or the null hypothesis $H$ so that unjust rejection of $H$ represents the error of the first kind. Thus if $(H_1,a_2)$ is more important to avoid than $(H_2,a_1)$ the hypothesis tested is $H_1$. For two contemplated actions the definition of any statistical decision function is now equivalent to selecting a subset $w$ of the sample space $W$, called the critical region or region of rejection. Then a rule is made to reject the tested hypothesis $H$ whenever the observations determine a sample point falling within $w$, and to abstain from this action in all other cases. Thus to define a test means to select a critical region.

The general character of the problems of testing hypotheses may be illustrated in the simplest case where the set $\Omega$ of admissible hypotheses contains only two hypotheses ($H$ and its negation $\bar{H}$), each specifying the distribution of the observable variables in all details. It is assumed that there is a clear distinction in the importance of avoiding the two kinds of error.

Noting the importance of avoiding the error of the first kind, arbitrarily select a small number $\alpha$ called (somewhat inappropriately) the level of significance, and seek the critical regions $w(\alpha)$ such that their use will insure that the probability of committing an error of the first kind cannot exceed $\alpha$. Ordinarily there are many such regions $w(\alpha)$; select for use the one $w_0(\alpha)$ that insures the greatest probability of avoiding the error of the second kind. The region $w_0(\alpha)$ that satisfies these two conditions is called the most powerful critical region for testing $H$ against $\bar{H}$ at the level of significance $\alpha$. Its use insures that the probability (*i*) of rejecting $H$ when $H$ is true is no more than the preassigned level $\alpha$ and, subject to restriction (*i*), the probability (*ii*) of rejecting $H$ when $H$ is false is greatest.

After a region $w_0(\alpha)$ is found (on occasion there are many) it is appropriate to compute the probability $\beta\ [\omega_0(\alpha)]$ (termed power) that the test will reject $H$ when this hypothesis is false.

When the selected level of significance $\alpha$ is very low then the power of the test is very low too, and application of the test does not hold much promise in "detecting the falsehood of $H$." It may then be decided to take a greater risk in controlling the error of the first kind (*i.e.*, a larger $\alpha$) to increase chances of rejecting the hypothesis tested when it is false.

In summary, the basic concepts of the Neyman-Pearson theory are those of critical region, two kinds of error, and power of a test.

**Theory of Estimation.**—The problem of statistical estimation has two different forms, known as point estimation and interval estimation (more generally, estimation by a set). Both are particular cases of the general problem of mathematical statistics and refer to situations in which the set of contemplated actions contains (roughly speaking) a large number of actions, comparable with the number of distributions of the observable random variables $X$. More specifically, to each distribution $F$ of the set $\Omega$ there corresponds one particular preferred action $a(F)$ belonging to $A$. In these circumstances the decision to take a particular action $a(F)$ in a sense is equivalent to the assertion that the function $F$ represents the distribution of $X$. Such assertions based on observed values of random variables represent the process of statistical estimation.

In many cases the possible distributions of observable random variables $X$ are identified by values of one or more parameters $\theta_1, \theta_2, \ldots, \theta_s$. Thus the distributions of variables $X_1$ and $X_2$ in the vaccine example are identified by values of two parameters $p_v$ and $p_0$. In such situations the problem of estimation is reduced to that of making assertions regarding the values of all or of some of the parameters involved. Consider one particular parameter $\theta$ with possible numerical values contained in interval $(a,b)$.

It is called point estimation of the parameter $\theta$ when the statistical decision function contemplated has the following form: if the observations yield the sample point $X = x$, then $\theta$ has the value $\hat{\theta}(x)$. Here $\hat{\theta}$ stands for a function defined for all possible sample points and has its values in the interval $(a,b)$. The function $\hat{\theta}$ so used is called a point estimator of $\theta$.

It is called interval estimation of $\theta$ when the decision function contemplated depends on functions $\hat{\theta}_1$ and $\hat{\theta}_2$, both defined over the sample space $W$, both having their possible values in the interval $(a,b)$, and when for every possible sample point $\hat{\theta}_1 < \hat{\theta}_2(x)$. Then the statistical decision function is defined as follows: if the observations yield $X = x$, then assert that $\hat{\theta}_1(x) \leqq \theta \leqq \hat{\theta}_2(x)$. In other words instead of trying to predict the exact value of $\theta$, interval estimation involves an effort to predict the limits $\hat{\theta}_1(x)$ and $\hat{\theta}_2(x)$ within which this value presumably lies.

Suppose functions $\hat{\theta}_1(x)$ and $\hat{\theta}_2(x)$ are defined. Substituting random variable $X$ for its particular value $x$ produces a random interval $I(X) = [\hat{\theta}_1(X), \hat{\theta}_2(X)]$. This interval is called an interval estimator of $\theta$.

Explicit consideration of the problems of point estimation goes back at least to Galileo, but the major early figures in the development discussed here were Pierre Simon Laplace (1749–1827) and Carl Friedrich Gauss (1777–1855). Their view, adopted by A. A. Markov (1856–1922) and subsequently generalized by Wald, may be described by comparison with a game of chance in which the statistician can never win, but can lose an amount that increases with the size of the error of estimation. For every possible value $\vartheta_1$ of the estimated parameter $\theta$, and for every possible value $\vartheta_2$ of the point estimator, there is assumed a loss function $L(\vartheta_1,\vartheta_2) \geqq 0$ representing the amount to be paid by the statistician if $\theta = \vartheta_1$ and he asserts that $\theta = \vartheta_2$. The exact nature of the loss function must be specified by practical considerations; Laplace considered $L(\vartheta_1,\vartheta_2) = |\vartheta_1 - \vartheta_2|$; Gauss preferred $L(\vartheta_1,\vartheta_2) = (\vartheta_1 - \vartheta_2)^2$ and subsequently other loss functions were considered. The various aspects of point estimation are based on different limitations imposed on the estimator, on different loss functions adopted, and on different definitions of optimum properties of an estimator. Here is an example:

(a) The estimator $\hat{\theta}(X)$ shall be a linear function of the observable random variables $\hat{\theta}(X) = a_1X_1 + a_2X_2 + \ldots + a_n X_n$. This restriction ensures that the estimator will be easy to compute.

(b) The estimator $\hat{\theta}(X)$ shall be unbiased; *i.e.*, its mathematical expectation shall be equal to the parameter $\theta$.

(c) The loss function $L(\vartheta_1,\vartheta_2)$ shall be equal to the square of the error of estimation (*i.e.*, shall be Gaussian).

(d) Under conditions (*a*), (*b*), and (*c*), the estimator $\hat{\theta}(X)$ shall minimize the mathematical expectation of the loss.

This particular problem was first formulated by Gauss who made a very elegant broadly applicable solution that became known as the method of least squares (*see* LEAST SQUARES, METHOD OF). Developments in this direction include the study of estimators subject to conditions (c) and (d), but not necessarily (a) and (b); loss functions other than the Gaussian also are considered.

Although vague ideas underlying interval estimation can be traced to the end of the 18th century, the first clear statement was formulated in 1931 by Harold Hotelling. In the 1930s a comprehensive theory was developed by Neyman. The basic concept here is that of the confidence interval. It is said that the interval estimator $I(X)$ is a confidence interval for estimating $\theta$ at the confidence coefficient $\alpha$ if, whatever be the value $\vartheta$ of the estimated parameter $\theta$, the probability that the interval $I(X)$ will cover $\vartheta$ is at least equal to $\alpha$.

It is shown that (in many cases) more than one confidence interval for a given parameter can be found, all corresponding to the same confidence coefficient $\alpha$. In such cases the problem of optimality arises, an important section of the theory. A typical problem is as follows:

(a) For a given confidence coefficient $\alpha$ (say $\alpha = .99$), and whatever be the true value $\vartheta$ of the parameter $\theta$, the interval estimator $I_0(X)$ shall cover $\vartheta$ with probability equal to $\alpha$.

(b) Whatever be the true value $\vartheta_1$ of $\theta$, whatever be the false value $\vartheta_2$ of the same parameter, and whatever be the interval estimator $I(X)$ satisfying (a), the interval estimator $I_0(X)$ shall cover the false value $\vartheta_2$ less frequently (more precisely, not more frequently) than $I(X)$.

If an estimator $I_0(X)$ satisfying (a) and (b) exists, it is called the shortest confidence interval for estimating $\theta$. The systematic use of shortest confidence intervals (to estimate the same parameter or different parameters) insures the prescribed long-run frequency (*e.g.*, 99%) of correct assertions combined with the greatest precision of such assertions understood in the sense of condition (b).

**Theory of Experiments.**—Statistical considerations initiated an important scientific discipline called theory of experiments or design of experiments. The first attempt to build a unified theory was by Ronald A. Fisher (1930s) who sought ways of designing experiments to provide more relevant information than others requiring the same investment in funds and effort. Thus originated the systematic study of optimal designs.

Fisher and his school were chiefly concerned with designs of single experiments, with what might be called experimental tactics. Developments concerned with experimental strategy are due to Wald (1940s), and deal with a sequence of experiments that in principle may be continued indefinitely.

Fisher originally was concerned with agricultural experimentation. Later it was found that the same kinds of problems are encountered in almost all experimental work. One of these problems is that of biased selection of material used in experiments. To avoid such bias he introduced the principle of randomization (*see* RANDOMIZATION), an outstanding achievement.

Many experimental tactics introduced by Fisher and developed by his school are meant to diminish the effects of variability in experimental material, and include such specific designs as randomized blocks and Latin squares (*see* MAGIC SQUARE). In testing a drug on mice, the randomized blocks design consists in using $N$ litters of mice and in selecting at random from each litter; for example, three mice to be treated and another three to be left untreated. The six mice of each litter so selected constitute one randomized block. Considering substantial hereditary variation from one litter to the next, intuition and theory agree that such an experiment is less subject to random error than one based on unrestricted randomization of $6N$ mice.

Fisher was also concerned with the possibility of experiments answering several questions at once. This may be illustrated by an elegant example due to Frank Yates. Consider an effort to weigh three objects A, B, and C with a balance that has an undetermined (changeable) zero point so that at each weighing the indicator has to be read while there is no load. Let the symbol (1) denote such a reading; also let (A), (B), . . . , (BC), and (ABC) stand for readings when the scale is loaded with A alone, with B alone, . . . , with B and C combined, and with A, B, and C combined.

An estimate of weight A will be provided by the difference (A) − (1); *i.e.,* weight A differs from (A) − (1) only by an unavoidable random experimental error. One method of weighing A would be to make some (say $4n$) independent readings (1) and the same number of (A), to compute $4n$ differences (A) − (1) and to average them. Done separately for all three objects A, B, and C, the total number of readings would be $24n$. With the so-called factorial design due to Fisher, estimates of these three weights of exactly the same precision may be made from only $8n$ readings. This is done by making $n$ independent readings each of (1), (A), (B), (C), (AB), (AC), (BC), and (ABC). To estimate weight A arrange the $4n$ differences as follows:

(A) − (1)
(AB) − (B)
(AC) − (C)
(ABC) − (BC)

It may be seen that each of these differences is an independent estimate of weight A and that the average of $4n$ of them is just as precise an estimate as the average of $4n$ differences (A) − (1). The same readings provide an estimate of weight B as follows:

(B) − (1)
(AB) − (A)
(BC) − (C)
(ABC) − (AC)

A similar procedure is used for weight C. Thus one factorial experiment of $8n$ readings can yield the precision requiring three times as many readings arranged conventionally.

A limitation on factorial designs is imposed by the requirement that the treatments studied must be additive. In the example just given (assuming a robust balance is used) this condition will be satisfied so that, apart from random error, (A) − (1) is equal to (AB) − (B), and so on. However, if the phenomena studied are not weights but the effects of chemical elements in fertilizers (*e.g.,* nitrogen, potassium, and phosphorus) on the yield of wheat per acre, then the effect of nitrogen alone (N) − (1) need not (and usually does not) equal the effect of the same nitrogen in the presence of potassium (NK) − (K), and so on. Thus in such a case the use of fractional design may lead to unexpected complications.

In problems of experimental strategy concerned with sequences of tactically correct experiments, after $n$ experiments have been completed there are different ways in which the $(n + 1)$th experiment may be designed. There is also the possibility of discontinuing experimentation and reaching a so-called terminal decision. The problem of experimental strategy is to develop rules for using the results of $n$ completed experiments to decide what to do next. The statement of the general problem and some remarkable mathematical developments were published by Wald (1950). One strategic problem of experimentation has attracted considerable attention and created a substantial literature. It is known as the problem of the Robbins-Monroe procedure and consists in the following.

For every number $x$ in the interval $(a,b)$ an experiment can be made yielding a value of a random variable $Y(x)$. Only a limited amount of information is available about $Y(x)$. However, this random variable is known to have an expectation $M(x)$. The exact nature of the function $M(x)$ is not known except that it is continuous and increasing and that for some value $x_0$ of $x$ it is equal to zero. The experimental problem consists in determining the approximate value of $x_0$. The Robbins-Monroe procedure for attaining this goal begins by selecting in $(a,b)$ an arbitrary number $x_1$, perhaps the midpoint of $(a,b)$, and in observing $Y(x_1)$. Let the observed value be $y_1$. Then using the values $x_1$ and $y_1$ another choice is made of a number $x_2$ within $(a,b)$ and an experiment is made to observe $Y(x_2)$. The result of this observation is denoted by $y_2$. By continuing this procedure it is hoped to obtain a sequence of numbers $x_1, x_2, \ldots x_n, \ldots$ approaching the unknown $x_0$ as a limit. The problem of experimental strategy is to determine how best to use the observed values of $x$ and $y$ to choose $x_{n+1}$ so that the sequence of $x$ values converges rapidly to $x_0$.

The characteristic feature that identifies this as a problem of experimental strategy is the chainlike dependence of the arrangements for the $(n + 1)$th experiment on the designs and on the outcomes of the earlier experiments.

## INDUCTIVE APPROACH

A view that is sharply antagonistic to the behaviouristic approach is represented by several inductive schools of thought symbolized by the names of Fisher and Harold Jeffreys. As in the behaviouristic approach, all these schools are concerned with the best utilization of data subject to random variation. Hence their ultimate results (unavoidably) are particular statistical decision functions; that is, the conclusion is based on the observational data. However, the statistical decision functions are not considered explicitly; when a particular function is proposed, arguments in its favour are formulated not in terms of the consequences of its use but in terms of degrees of confidence in the underlying hypotheses. Essentially each inductive school begins by laying down one or more basic formulas (posterior probability of a hypothesis in some cases, likelihood and fiducial probability in others) represented as norms of human beliefs and actions. The handling of these formulas is then labeled by such terms as inductive reasoning or scientific inference. More radical inductive arguments in favour of a particular point estimator (called maximum likelihood estimator) ignore the consequences of its systematic use but refer to the fact that the estimator maximizes the likelihood described (Fisher) as "the mathematical quantity . . . appropriate for measuring our order of preference. . . ." In relatively simple problems the decision functions developed by inductive schools frequently coincide with those of behaviouristic theory. In particular, as shown by Hotelling, Joseph L. Doob, and Wald, the maximum likelihood estimators have desirable properties in a broad category of problems. However, in the 1960s these inductive systems represented major areas of controversy in mathematical statistics.

## HISTORICAL BACKGROUND

Development of the conceptual content of mathematical statistics was gradual, extending over a century and a half. As noted earlier the behaviouristic approach to problems of estimation is found in the work of Laplace and Gauss. Laplace seems one of the first to test statistical hypotheses; but at that time there was no question of mathematical statistics as an independent discipline. Laplace's criteria for testing statistical hypotheses were intuitive rather than mathematical and in no way similar to his approach to the problem of point estimators. The behaviouristic approach to estimation was soon forgotten.

Mathematical statistics as an independent discipline seems to have appeared in the latter part of the 19th century in the work of A. Quételet, G. T. Fechner, K. Pearson (*qq.v.*), E. Czuber, G. U. Yule, and V. I. Bortkevich. The then existing branches of applied mathematics, (*e.g.,* analytical mechanics) were, so to speak, individualistic. Many scientific problems required a new mathematical discipline concerned with aggregates of objects, all of which satisfy a specific definition but differ in individual characteristics. Such an aggregate (population) might be all men of military age in a country; these men differ in height. Another population would be the set of gas molecules in a container; each molecule has a unique velocity as its individual characteristic.

However, any population has its own characteristics, conditioned by those of the individual members, but essentially different. Gas pressure is a characteristic of the population of molecules conditioned by their velocities; temperature is another such characteristic. These are examples of what Fechner called *Kollektivmass.* The average height of recruits is also a *Kollektivmass,* as is the frequency with which they are found with height between 5 ft. 10 in. and 5 ft. 11 in. The set of such frequencies (the frequency distribution) is also a *Kollektivmass.*

In the late 19th and early 20th centuries mathematical statistics emphasized the *Kollektivmasslehre,* a mathematical discipline concerned with collective characteristics of populations. The term descriptive statistics was introduced to mean the use of a variety of methods (including graphical and tabular methods) for describing such characteristics of populations. An important method of descriptive statistics is to consider a family of flexible curves or surfaces (depending on a moderate number of parameters) that can be used to approximate the empirical frequency distribution. A number of such families was developed, all representing interpolation formulas. The most successful system seems to be that due to Karl Pearson.

A conceptual problem studied by Wilhelm Lexis (1837–1914) developed to deprive *Kollektivmasslehre* of its independent status. Lexis was concerned with the year-to-year fluctuation of sex ratio among children born in a city, and similar ratios arising in the study of vital statistics. The question was whether an empirical index of dispersion is consistent with the assumption that determination of sex is governed by a simple chance mechanism such as a toss of a coin. This renewed a continuing effort concerned with chance mechanisms acting on individuals to produce the observed collective characteristics.

Interest in flexible formulas specifically developed to fit empirical distributions gradually decreased, except for those that could be deduced from clearly defined chance mechanisms. In the 1920s George Pólya constructed a system of chance mechanisms that can generate almost all the distributions of Karl Pearson's system. Thus mathematical statistics shifted from *Kollektivmasslehre* to the construction of chance mechanisms or (as they are called) stochastic models of phenomena. This idea was explicitly stated by Émile Borel (1871–1956): "The basic problem of mathematical statistics is to invent a system of simple chance mechanisms, such as throws of a coin, so that the probabilities determined by this system agree with the observed relative frequencies of the various details of the phenomena studied."

Although Borel's definition was appealing, developments following its formulation indicated that it leaves mathematical statistics without a field of its own. Depending on the attitudes of given research workers, stochastic models belong to the relevant substantive fields or to the theory of probability. Thus stochastic models of hereditary phenomena are an integral part of genetics; stochastic models of epidemics are an integral part of epidemiology; and so on. However, considerable literature on stochastic processes developing in time (*e.g.,* birth and death stochastic process constructed to represent the growth of biological populations) is one of the most active sections of the theory of probability. Each problem of the theory of stochastic processes is reducible to that of determining probabilities (*e.g.,* that a biological population will eventually die out). While the field indicated in Borel's definition continued to grow in importance, it was claimed by other disciplines, leaving nothing to mathematical statistics.

While these ideas were in the process of dissolution, increasing effort was given to problems of estimation and of testing hypotheses. In connection with his system of curves, Karl Pearson developed a method of point estimation known as the method of moments; in 1900 he published his famous $\chi^2$ (chi-square) test for goodness of fit. In 1908 F. Y. Edgeworth (1845–1926) found that consistent use of the method of moments must yield an excessive frequency of large errors of estimation (a distinctly behaviouristic approach) and proposed a new method of estimation, conjectured to be much better. Fourteen years later, Fisher discussed the same ground more rigorously and intensively. He introduced the term method of maximum likelihood. Student (pseudonym of W. S. Gosset) and Fisher developed a number of tests of particular hypotheses. However, studies of this kind were not yet connected by any unifying idea, and were limited to particular decision functions. Problems of testing hypotheses and of estimation remained unrecognized as an independent field for systematic study.

Such recognition came when Fisher (1922) gave a new definition of statistics. Stating that the object of statistical methods is the reduction of bulky data, Fisher distinguished three basic problems: those of specification of the kind of population from which the data come (*i.e.,* of the *Kollektivmass*), of estimation, and of distribution (probabilistic problems connected with point estimation). This was followed by a paper concerned specifically with the theory of estimation; the ideas underlying these papers are distinct precursors of the behaviouristic approach to mathematical statistics described earlier.

*See* also GAMES, THEORY OF.

BIBLIOGRAPHY.—R. B. Braithwaite, *Scientific Explanation* (1953); W. G. Cochran and G. M. Cox, *Experimental Designs,* 2nd ed. (1957); H. Cramér, *Mathematical Methods of Statistics* (1946); R. A. Fisher, *The Design of Experiments,* 7th ed. (1960), *Statistical Methods and Scientific Inference* (1956); M. Fisz, *Probability Theory and Mathematical Statistics* (1963); H. Jeffreys, *Scientific Inference,* 2nd ed. (1957); E. L. Lehmann, *Testing Statistical Hypotheses* (1959); A. M. Mood and F. A. Graybill, *Introduction to the Theory of Statistics,* 2nd ed. (1963); J. Neyman, *First Course in Probability and Statistics* (1950), *Lectures and Conferences on Mathematical Statistics,* U.S.D.A. Graduate School (1952); L. J. Savage, *The Foundations of Statistics* (1954); A. Wald, *Sequential Analysis* (1947), *Statistical Decision Functions* (1950); S. S. Wilks, *Elementary Statistical Analysis* (1948); W. Sadowski, *The Theory of Decision-Making* (1965).

**STATIUS, PUBLIUS PAPINIUS** (*c.* A.D. 45–96), one of the principal epic and lyric poets of the silver age of Latin literature, was born in Naples. His father was also a poet, and Statius seems to have been trained as one from childhood. Little is known of his life. He lived in Rome, and was a court poet under the emperor Domitian, who awarded him a prize at the poetic festival at Alba, in A.D. 89 or 90. He was, however, unsuccessful in the Capitoline competition, probably on its third celebration in 94, and shortly afterward he returned to Naples.

The role of court poet seems to have suited Statius. His flattery is as different from the gentle propitiatory tone of Quintilian as it is from the exaggerated humility of Martial. Statius adopted without scruple the flattery that was inevitable under Domitian, exploiting it in a way which suited his own nature. He was exceptionally talented, and his poetic expression is, with all its faults, richer, as well as more buoyant and felicitous than is generally to be found in silver Latin.

Statius is at his best in his occasional verses, the *Silvae,* in five books containing 32 poems altogether, of which all but 6 are in hexameters. Five poems are devoted to flattery of the emperor and his favourites. Another group gives picturesque descriptions of the villas and gardens of the poet's friends. The *Kalendae Decembres* gives a striking description of the gifts and amusements provided by the emperor for the Roman populace at the Saturnalia. In his attempt at an epithalamium Statius is forced and unhappy, but his birthday ode in Lucan's honour has, along with the accustomed exaggeration, some good lines, and shows appreciation of earlier Latin poets. Those poems, too, which deal with family affection or personal loss are moving, and the short poem to Sleep (v, 4) is deservedly famous.

Statius also wrote two epics, the *Thebais* (in 12 books) and the *Achilleis* (in two, unfinished). The latter gives a charming and accomplished account of the early education of Achilles by Chiron the centaur, and of his being hidden in girl's clothing among the daughters of Lycomedes by his mother, Thetis, in order to save him from the Trojan war. He is discovered by Odysseus and taken off to Troy; but at this point the poem was evidently interrupted by the poet's death.

The *Thebais* is a more ambitious work, describing the struggle of the brothers Polynices and Eteocles for the throne of Thebes. It has been called an "episodic" epic; but apart from one long digression it keeps to its theme well enough. It has many features borrowed from Virgil, such as the catalogue of warriors, the games and the battle scenes. It often suffers from overstatement and exaggeration, and some of the scenes of horror are too gruesome, but many more are admirable and original, such as the fight between Tydeus and his pursuers in book ii and the martyrdom of Menoeceus in book x. The work begins and ends with two passages, the fight in a storm between the two young warriors on the threshold of the king's palace at Argos and the meeting of Polynices' mother and sister at night on the battlefield, which convey an atmosphere of dramatic tension and reveal considerable tragic power.

BIBLIOGRAPHY.—Editions in the "Teubner Series" by A. Klotz, 3 vol. (1902–07); in the Oxford classical texts by H. W. Garrod (*Thebais* and *Achilleis,* 1906) and J. S. Phillimore (*Silvae,* 2nd ed., 1918); in the "Loeb Series" with Eng. trans. by J. H. Mozley, 2 vol. (1928); *Silvae* with commentary by F. Vollmer (1898); *Thebais* i–vi with commentary by O. Müller (1870); *Achilleis* with English commentary by O. A. W. Dilke (1954). Eng. trans. of the *Silvae* by D. A. Slater (1908). (AN. K.)

**STATUE OF LIBERTY:** *see* LIBERTY, STATUE OF.

**STATUTE LAW.** A statute was defined by the famous English lawyer Sir Edward Coke (d. 1634) as "an Act of Parliament made by the King, the Lords and the Commons." The present article is restricted to this use of the term and, therefore, to statutes of the United Kingdom; for the U.S. and other countries, *see* LEGISLATION; LEGISLATURE; and the articles on the legal systems of individual countries.

Coke's definition is still apt in English law, except that in certain cases, provided for by the Parliament Act, 1911, a bill may become an act even though the House of Lords has not consented to it. The procedure for the enactment of statutes is regulated mainly by usage and the standing orders of Parliament. Church Assembly measures passed under the Church of England Assembly (Powers) Act of 1919 and presented for the royal assent after a favourable resolution of both houses of Parliament have the power and effect of acts of Parliament.

The earliest English statute is the Statute of Merton, 1235. Acts were engrossed upon the statute roll from the time (1278) of the Statute of Gloucester (6 Edw. I), but this practice has long been discontinued. Official copies of acts are now made on vellum and lodged at the Public Record Office and in the House of Lords. In the case of Church Assembly measures, a third vellum copy is printed and sent to the Church Assembly.

**Classification of Statutes.**—Acts of Parliament are classified as (1) public general acts; (2) local (or "local and personal") acts, including public acts of a local character; (3) private personal acts; (4) Church Assembly measures (*see* above).

Except for certain classes of private personal acts (such as naturalization and divorce acts), which are virtually obsolete, all acts of Parliament are printed by the queen's printer. There are two separate series of volumes, one containing the public general acts and Church Assembly measures, the other containing local and personal acts together with certain statutory orders.

For purposes of the law of evidence, however, a different classification applies, and by section 9 of the Interpretation Act, 1889, every act passed after 1850 is a public act unless the act expressly provides to the contrary. Such acts are judicially noticed and no proof of them is required. Acts stated not to be public acts are usually provable by the production of a queen's printer's copy.

Acts may also be classified according to their object by such terms as penal, beneficial, imperative, directory, enabling, disabling, taxing, codifying, consolidating, perpetual, temporary, and so forth. This last classification is important for the purposes of interpretation (*see* below).

Penal acts are those which impose a new disability; beneficial, those which confer a new favour. An imperative statute (often negative or prohibitory in its terms) makes a certain act or omission absolutely necessary and subjects a contravention of its provisions to a penalty. A directory statute (generally affirmative in its terms) recommends a certain act or omission, but imposes no penalty for contravention of its provisions. To determine whether an act is imperative or directory the act itself must be looked at, and many nice questions have arisen on the application of this rule of law to a particular case. Enabling statutes are those which enlarge the common law, while disabling statutes restrict it. Declaratory statutes, or those simply affirming the common law, once not uncommon, are now practically unknown; the Treason Act, 1351 (25 Edw. III), is an example. Statutes are sometimes passed in order to overrule specific decisions of the courts. Examples are the Territorial Waters Jurisdiction Act, 1878, the Married Women's Property Act, 1893, and the Trade Disputes Act, 1906.

Every act has a short title by which it may be cited; *e.g.,* the Transport Act, 1962.

**Interpretation of Statutes.**—The Interpretation Act, 1889, provides an authentic interpretation for numerous words and phrases of frequent occurrence in statutes. Moreover, most modern acts contain an interpretation section which explains particular expressions in that act. The main body of the law on this subject is, however, to be found in judicial decisions; *i.e.,* the common law. The main rules are as follows: (1) The meaning of an act is primarily to be sought in the act itself. (2) The words of an act are to be construed in their ordinary and natural sense, unless there is something to the contrary in the context or in the scheme of the act. (3) The act is to be construed as a whole, and acts on similar subjects are to be construed together as forming one system. (4) Contemporaneous circumstances may be taken into account where the intention of the legislature cannot otherwise be ascertained. What is known as the rule in Heydon's case (1584) (3 Coke Rep., 7a) provides that the factors to be ascertained in this connection are: (*a*) the common law before the act; (*b*) the mischief or defect for which the common law did not provide; (*c*) the remedy Parliament has provided; and (*d*) the true reason for the remedy. (5) Where words can be interpreted in two different ways the inconvenient, unjust, or absurd consequences of adopting the one way may guide the court to adopt the other. (6) The full title and the preamble but not the short title, heading, or marginal note may be used for the purpose of interpreting the act as a whole, or in order to resolve any ambiguity. (7) Acts which purport to interfere with existing rights must be clearly expressed. (8) Statutes are to be interpreted, as far as their language admits, so as not to be inconsistent with the comity of nations or with the established rules of international law. (9) Some acts are to be liberally or benevolently construed, others strictly. Instances of those which fall into the former category are acts which are remedial; amending; explanatory; for the maintenance of religion, the advancement of learning, and the relief of the poor; directory as distinguished from mandatory or imperative enactments; and those in favour of the liberty of the subject. The acts to be strictly construed include those restricting the liberty of the subject; penal acts; fiscal and revenue acts; acts creating statutory powers and duties; private acts; acts affecting the prerogative of the crown, existing private rights, or the jurisdiction of the courts. In the case of penal statutes, for instance, strict construction means that the thing charged as an offense must be within the plain meaning of the words used; the words must not be strained as if there has been a slip or an omission, or as if the thing is so clearly within the intent of the legislature that it would have been included if thought of. Great care must be taken not to extend penal laws beyond what the legislature has clearly meant and adequately expressed. Similarly, in the case of taxation statutes the court is not to be guided so much by the objects which it thinks such acts are to achieve, as by considering whether the words of the act have reached the alleged subject of taxation. There is no presumption as to a tax; nothing is to be read in; nothing is to be implied. One can only look fairly at the language used. (10) Codifying and consolidating acts give rise to an inference of intention to reproduce the existing position and not to alter the law. A codifying act is, however, in the first instance, to be looked at without reference to the previous law if it is unambiguous, whereas reference is to be made to the previous law to ascertain the intention of the legislature in the case of an amending or consolidating act. (11) In construing acts, such as taxing acts, which apply to both England and Scotland, it is well settled that a construction should, if possible, be adopted which will make the incidence of taxation the same in both countries. (12) A special act which imposes mutual obligations on several parties so that it has a contractual operation should be construed in the same way as a contract to the same effect.

**Operation of Statutes.**—The date of the "passing" of an act is the date when it becomes law, *i.e.,* the date when it receives the royal assent; this date is also, in the absence of a provision to the contrary, the time of the "commencement" of the act, *i.e.,* the time when it comes into effect.

An act of the United Kingdom Parliament is to be construed prima facie as applying to the whole of the United Kingdom and not to any place outside. The United Kingdom does not include the Channel Islands or the Isle of Man.

An "extent" or "application" clause will, however, vary the effect of this rule. Acts are extended to apply to waters adjacent to the United Kingdom and other parts of the British Commonwealth (*see* below) for certain purposes.

An act generally applies only to those within the allegiance of the crown and does not extend to foreign subjects out of the queen's dominions. An act applicable to the queen's dominions is, if the context permits, to be construed as applying to all British subjects wherever they may be.

It is a clear rule of law that the crown is not bound by an act of Parliament unless it is expressly named or clear words of implication are used. The crown here includes the great departments of state, but bodies such as nationalized industries have been held not to be its servant or agent for this purpose. The crown may, however, be held to be bound by implication if the beneficent purpose of the act would be otherwise wholly frustrated; but it is entitled to the benefit of an act although not named.

Generally speaking the courts will hold that statutes are not retrospective, if it is possible so to construe them. This fundamental rule of English law involves another to the effect that a statute is not to be construed so as to have a greater retrospective operation than its language renders necessary. Where an act is repealed the repeal does not in general affect its previous operation.

The provisions of a public act can be overridden or varied only by express enactment or clear implication. Where the common law is to be changed, and especially the common law which a statutory provision has recognized and enforced, the intention of any new enactment to abrogate it must plainly exclude a construction by which both may stand together. Similarly, existing rights are not destroyed by a statute unless there are express words or the plainest implication to that effect. The principle applies whether the rights be common-law rights, rights of action, rights of ownership, or rights arising under a contract. Again, the jurisdiction of the superior courts over matters originally cognizable by them cannot be taken away except by express words or necessary implication. On the other hand, it has long been settled that the creation of a right of appeal is an act requiring legislative authority.

Temporary acts may be made perpetual or may be continued from time to time. The latter is now achieved largely by periodic Expiring Laws Continuance acts. The Army and Air Force acts are instances of temporary acts reenacted annually.

**Enforcement of Statutes.**—Crimes created by statute are tried either summarily or by indictment, and there are some which are tried by courts, such as courts-martial, having jurisdiction over a limited class of persons. Again, a breach of a statutory command in a matter of public concern is indictable at common law, and in the absence of a special statutory remedy the performance of a public duty may be enforced by indictment or by information filed by the attorney general. An injunction against a continuance of the breach may be granted in appropriate cases. An order of mandamus (a judicial writ in the sovereign's name) lies for the enforcement of a public duty provided there is no more appropriate remedy.

In some cases a person injured by a breach of statutory duty may bring proceedings to recover his loss. This holds only where no remedy for the breach by way of penalty or otherwise is prescribed, or where it appears that the duty is imposed for the benefit of particular persons.

The operation of an act may be suspended by a subsequent statute. Many instances of this occurred during World War II by means of emergency legislation. Similarly, an act may be repealed or amended by a later act. Repeal by implication may occur where the provisions of a later enactment conflict with the earlier, but such repeal is never to be favoured. An act in its application to England cannot be repealed solely by disuse (*see* below as to Scotland). There is a presumption that, where statutory provision has been made for a specific class of cases, a subsequent general enactment is not intended to interfere with such provision. The Interpretation Act, 1889, contains many provisions relating to repeal.

**Delegated Legislation.**—Modern statutes tend increasingly to provide that a particular authority shall have power to make orders, rules, and regulations in relation to particular matters arising under the act. Power may also be conferred to make statutory orders in council. These were previously termed statutory rules and orders, but by the provisions of the Statutory Instruments Act, 1946, they were named statutory instruments, the procedure in relation to them being governed by that act. Copies of such instruments printed under the authority of Her Majesty's Stationery Office are receivable in evidence. Some hold that legislation by statutory instrument has gone too far and that Parliament itself should consider substantive legislation even if this requires the establishment of Scots and Welsh and possibly other regional legislatures in order to lighten the burden of the United Kingdom Parliament. (*See* also ORDER IN COUNCIL.)

**Scotland.**—Much of what has already been said applies to Scotland, although Scotland has its own provisions of law and its own courts whose decisions are often quite different from those of the English courts. A public general statute applies generally to Great Britain and Northern Ireland, which includes Scotland, unless otherwise stated. By the Private Legislation Procedure (Scotland) Act, 1936, which applies to Scotland only, where any public authority or persons desire a private act they may apply to the secretary of state for Scotland for a provisional order. In the absence of any opposition the secretary of state for Scotland is directed to introduce into Parliament a confirmation bill, and any resulting act is a public act of Parliament.

In the 17th and 18th centuries the Court of Session promulgated acts of sederunt (*i.e.,* of a judicial body) amounting to general legislation. In modern times these acts relate exclusively to procedure and are usually passed in virtue of a specific authority in some particular statute. In 1948 an act of sederunt approved new consolidated rules and repealed the provisions of any previous act inconsistent with them. An act of adjournal is an act passed by the High Court of Justiciary for regulating procedure in that court and in inferior criminal courts.

A statute may be impliedly repealed by falling into disuse. This rule is applicable only to Scots acts; *i.e.,* those passed before 1707. There is no analogous principle in England, and even in Scotland no statute passed after the union in 1707 has been held by the Scottish courts to have fallen into desuetude.

Scots acts, which are usually expressed briefly and without detailed provisions, have been interpreted in a very liberal spirit. In their construction it is a recognized rule that, whatever the literal meaning of the statutory words, they are to be read as interpreted by decisions pronounced shortly after the act was passed. Apart from this important difference, the rules of interpretation in Scotland are similar to those discussed above.

**Northern Ireland.**—The Parliament of Northern Ireland consists of the queen, the Senate of Northern Ireland, and the House of Commons in Northern Ireland. The Government of Ireland Act, 1920, deals with legislation in Northern Ireland and gives power to make laws for the peace, order, and good government of Northern Ireland with certain matters reserved to the United Kingdom Parliament. Parliament at Westminster does not in practice legislate for Northern Ireland in matters within the jurisdiction of the Northern Ireland Parliament although it has power to.

**British Commonwealth.**—Acts of the United Kingdom Parliament do not extend to self-governing Commonwealth countries, colonies, or dependencies unless these are specially named therein. Moreover, the United Kingdom Parliament cannot legislate for the self-governing countries without their consent. Colonies are either self-governing or crown colonies. By the Colonial Laws Validity Act, 1865, the "charter of colonial independence," any colonial law repugnant to the provisions of any act of Parliament extending to the colony is void to the extent of such repugnancy, and no colonial law is to be void by repugnancy to the law of England unless it is repugnant to such an act of Parliament. For colonies without representative legislatures the crown usually legislates. The relationship between the U.K. Parliament and the self-governing countries' legislatures is dealt with by the Statute of Westminster, 1931.

**Other Countries.**—In most other countries, with the exception of the United States, there is a code of law. The assent of two chambers and of the head of the state is generally necessary to legislation.

The term "statute" is used by international jurists to denote the whole body of the municipal law of the state. In this sense, statutes are either real, personal, or mixed. A real statute is that part of the law which deals directly with property, whether movable or immovable. A personal statute has for its object a person and deals with questions of status such as marriage, legitimacy, and infancy. A mixed statute affects both property and persons and it is said to deal with acts and obligations. Personal statutes are of universal validity; real statutes have no extraterritorial authority. *See* also PARLIAMENT. (P. E. L.)

**STAUDINGER, HERMANN** (1881–1965), German chemist, awarded the 1953 Nobel Prize for chemistry for his work on the macromolecule. He was born on March 23, 1881, in Worms. He was educated in the universities of Halle, Munich, and Darmstadt. At Halle he became doctor of philosophy in 1903. He taught in Strasbourg, in Karlsruhe as professor of organic chemistry at the Technische Hochschule, and in Zürich as professor of general chemistry (1912–26). In 1926 he was elected to the chair of chemistry in Freiburg im Breisgau, where in 1940 he became director of the chemical laboratory and research institute for macromolecular chemistry. His main contributions to chemistry have been in the field of plastics. He showed that small molecules polymerize by chemical interaction, not simply by physical aggregation, and that linear molecules could be built up synthetically in this way by a variety of processes and maintain their individuality even when subject to chemical modification.

He further showed how it is possible to build up high-polymer networks and that these expanded only to a finite extent when immersed in suitable solvents. He established the relationship between the molecular weight of a high polymer and its viscosity in solution. After leaving the research institute for macromolecular chemistry in 1956, Staudinger wrote his memoirs, *Arbeitserinnerungen* (1961). Staudinger died in Freiburg on Sept. 8, 1965.

*See* further PLASTICS; POLYMERIZATION.

*See* E. Farber, *Nobel Prize Winners in Chemistry, 1901–1961* (1963). (D. McK.)

**STAUNING, THORVALD** (1873–1942), Denmark's leading Social Democratic statesman for a quarter of a century, was born in Copenhagen on Oct. 26, 1873, the son of an artisan. A tobacco-worker and an active trade unionist, he was elected secretary of the Social Democratic League in 1898 and a member of the *folketing* in 1906, becoming chairman of his party in 1910. His organizing ability and his realism served the Social Democrats well; and in 1916 he became minister in Carl Theodor Zahle's Radical government (1913–20), subsequently carrying through a number of social reforms. He opposed antiparliamentarian tendencies within the labour movement; and despite the "Easter crisis" of 1920 (*see* DENMARK: *History*), he established good relations with the Royal House. The elections of April 1924 enabled him to form the first Social Democratic government, which was supported by the Radical Liberals till disagreement over legislation to restore the economy brought about its fall in December 1926. When the elections of April 1929 gave the Social Democrats a huge majority, Stauning formed a coalition government with the Radical Liberals. Social reforms were prepared, and during the depression the government carried through extensive legislation by concluding "crisis agreements" with the opposition. Respected for his firm and always loyal conduct, Stauning transformed his party from an essentially working-class one into one that stood for a broad social policy; and in September 1936 his government's supporters won a majority in the *landsting* also. In 1939, however, Stauning's attempt to achieve a constitutional reform failed; and his later efforts to strengthen defense could not prevent the German occupation of Denmark in 1940. He died on May 3, 1942. (F. SK.)

**STAUNTON,** a city of Virginia, U.S., 110 mi. (177 km.) NW of Richmond, near the southern end of the Shenandoah Valley, is the seat of Augusta County. This city of narrow streets and steep hills was founded by John Lewis on land granted to William Beverley by King George II in 1736 and was named for Lady Rebecca Staunton, wife of Sir William Gooch, a colonial governor. Settled by Scotch-Irish and English, the town in 1738 became the seat of the newly organized county, which then stretched to the Mississippi River. It was an important junction point for travelers. During the American Revolution the Virginia General Assembly met for a brief period in Trinity Church there. The American Civil War twice brought Federal occupation.

Staunton is the heart of a general farming area that produces sheep, cattle, and apples. The manufacture of flour, furniture, clothing, air-conditioning units, and razor blades brought in new workers from the North and East. Mary Baldwin College, a Presbyterian school for women, was established in 1842. Stuart Hall, an Episcopal preparatory school for girls, was founded in 1843, and Staunton Military Academy, a private school for boys, in 1860. The Virginia School for the Deaf and Blind and two state hospitals are in the city. Woodrow Wilson was born in the manse of the First Presbyterian Church, and in 1941 the building was made a national shrine.

Incorporated as a city in 1871, Staunton in 1908 became the first city in the U.S. to adopt the city-manager form of government. For comparative population figures, *see* table in VIRGINIA: *Population*. (G. M. BE.)

**STAUROLITE,** a mineral consisting of basic aluminum and ferrous iron silicate. Crystals are orthorhombic and have the form of six-sided prisms. Interpenetrating cruciform twinned crystals are very common and characteristic; they were early known as *pierres de croix* or *lapis crucifer,* and the name staurolite, from the Greek words for "stone" and "cross," has the same meaning. In fig. 1 the twin plane is [032] and the two prisms intercross at an angle of 91°22′; in fig. 2 the twin plane is [232] and the prisms

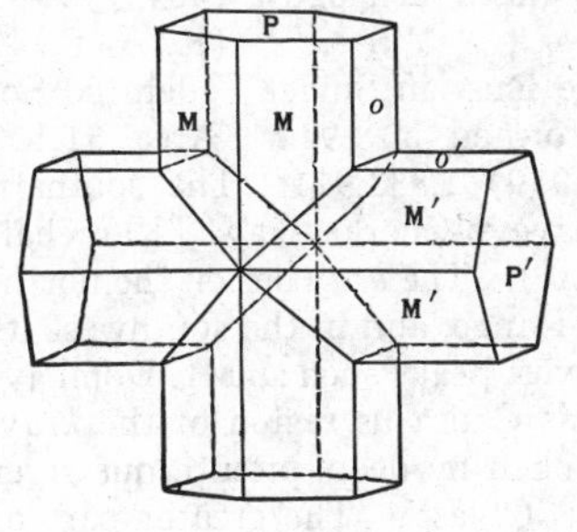


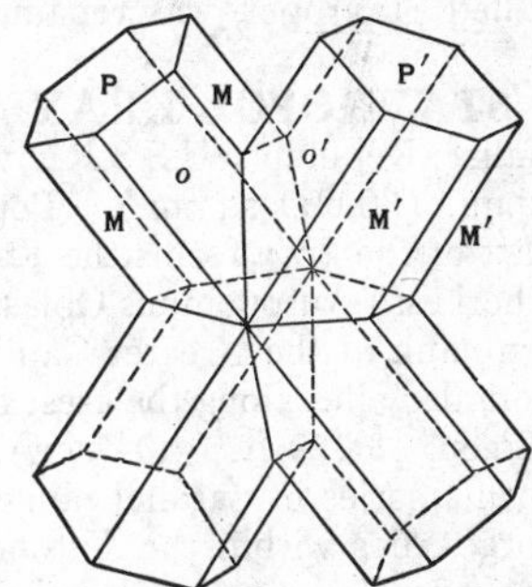


FIG. 1 AND 2.—TWIN CRYSTALS OF STAUROLITE

intercross at nearly 60°. The mineral is translucent to opaque and dark reddish-brown in colour. Waterworn pebbles of material sufficiently transparent for cutting as gem stones are occasionally found in the diamantiferous sands of Brazil. The formula is $FeAl_4(SiO_4)_2(OH)O$. The hardness is 7.5; specific gravity 3.75. Staurolite is a characteristic mineral of crystalline schists, and it is also a product of contact metamorphism. It is found at various points in Virginia, North Carolina, and Georgia embedded in schist or weathered loose in the soil, often as fine twinned crystals that are prized as good luck charms (fairy stones). Lustrous brown crystals occur with kyanite on Monte Campione, Ticino, Switz., and large twinned crystals are found in the mica schists of Brittany. (CL. F.)

**STAVANGER,** a major seaport of southwest Norway and the administrative centre of Rogaland *fylke* (county), lies at the mouth of Gandafjorden (Gannsfjord), an arm of Boknafjorden (Boknfjord), at the north of the rich agricultural and industrial district of Jæren, 200 mi. (322 km.) WSW of Oslo. Pop. (1965 est.) 78,435. Very little is known about its history before it became a bishopric (*c.* 1125), which was later removed to Kristiansand in 1682. A Lutheran bishopric was created in 1925. Parts of the town centre still have a medieval appearance with narrow streets and wooden houses, but much has been rebuilt. The cathedral of St. Swithun, founded by the first bishop, Reinald, of Winchester, Eng., has been called the most interesting stone church in Norway after Trondheim Cathedral. Other places of interest include the Kongsgård Grammar School (1824), on the site of the former episcopal palace; the Valberg Tower; several parks; an art gallery; and two museums, one of which, the town museum in the Ledaal mansion (family home of the 19th-century novelist Alexander Kielland), also serves as the king's residence when he visits the town. Stavanger is the chief centre of the Norwegian canning industry and is the location of the Norwegian Canning School and the industry's central research laboratory. Shipbuilding is the other main industry. The chief exports are brisling, kippers, and other canned products. The town has an international airport at Sola, 9 mi. (14 km.) SW, and a fine harbour with a busy coastal and foreign traffic. It is also the terminus of the railway and road from Oslo and Kristiansand. (A. B. A.)

**STAVROPOL,** a town and administrative centre of the *kray* of the same name of the Russian Soviet Federated Socialist Republic, U.S.S.R., lies on the Stavropol Upland of the Caucasian foreland, near the source of the Grachëvka River. Pop. (1959) 141,023. The town was founded by General Suvorov as a fortress in 1777. Its position on the main highway from Russia to the Caucasus led to its development as an important military, administrative, and trading centre. This significance declined after the construction of the Rostov-Baku railway, which passes south of Stavropol. A branch railway now joins the town to the trunk line at Kropotkin. The town has a range of industries processing the produce of the rich farmland of its region: flour milling, wine and fruit juice making, meat-packing, butter making, leatherworking, to name the most important ones. Machine building and the clothing industry are also important. Stavropol is an attractive town, with tree-lined streets laid out on a gridiron pattern. It has medical, agricultural, foreign language, and pedagogic institutes, and a research institute for sheep and goat rearing.

The town in Kuybyshevskaya (Kuibyshev) Oblast', formerly called Stavropol, was renamed Togliatti in August 1964.

(R. A. F.)

**STAVROPOL KRAY** of the Russian Soviet Federated Socialist Republic, U.S.S.R., was formed in 1924. Area 31,120 sq.mi. (80,600 sq.km.). Pop. (1959) 1,882,911. The southern part of the *kray* forms the Karachayevo-Cherkesskaya (Karachai-Cherkess) Autonomous Oblast' (*q.v.*). The *kray* lies on the northern flank of the Greater Caucasus Range, and in the southwest its boundary lies along the crest line, with peaks such as Mt. Dombay-Ul'gen, 13,278 ft. (4,047 m.). This Caucasus region of the *kray*, with a series of parallel ranges, broken by deep, picturesque river gorges, lies within the Autonomous Oblast'. The greater part of the *kray* is occupied by the Caucasian foreland, known as the Stavropol Upland. This reaches 2,730 ft. (832 m.) in Mt. Strizhament. The upland falls away in the east to the Caspian Lowland and in the north to the Kumo-Manych Depression, through which the Caspian was formerly linked to the Sea of Azov. The larger part of the *kray* is drained to the Caspian by the Kuma and its tributaries, the west draining by way of the Kuban to the Sea of Azov. Many of the rivers are seasonal, and lakes are often saline. The great variety of relief gives rise to considerable climatic variation, but in general the climate is continental. Divnoye in the Manych Valley has a January average temperature of −6.1° C (21° F) and a July average of 24.4° (76°). Rainfall, except in the mountains, is low, from 18 in. (457 mm.) a year in the west to 12 in. (305 mm.) or less in the east. The mountains are characterized by vertical zones of vegetation: deciduous forest, coniferous forest, alpine meadow, and rock and ice. The upland and lowlands are mostly steppe on chernozem soils, but the natural grass vegetation survives in very limited areas. In the drier east, the Nogay Steppe, conditions become increasingly semidesert, with chestnut and saline soils and sage vegetation.

Of the 1959 population, about 31% (587,369) was urban, living in 12 towns and 10 urban districts. The largest towns are the administrative centre of Stavropol (*q.v.*) (141,023) and the resorts of Kislovodsk (79,097) and Pyatigorsk (69,617). These last two places are the largest of a group of resort towns, deriving their importance from the abundant mineral springs of the Caucasus. Large deposits of natural gas, first discovered in 1910, are piped as far as Moscow. There are also several small oil deposits. Most industry in the *kray* is concerned with processing the produce of the highly developed agriculture, which dominates the economy. The chernozem soil area is up to 80% arable. Winter wheat and maize (corn) occupy the largest area, but industrial crops are very important, notably sunflowers, flax, mustard, castor beans, and potatoes. Fodder crops are widely grown in connection with the large-scale cattle and sheep rearing. Much of this is based on transhumance between the high mountain pastures in the summer and the dry Nogay Steppe in the winter.

(R. A. F.)

**STEAM,** the term commonly applied to vaporized water. In the pure state steam is an odourless, invisible gas, but when interspersed with minute droplets of water, it has a white cloudy appearance.

The generation of steam from water is one of the most important processes of our modern industrial age. Steam is used for heating many large office buildings, hotels, apartment houses, and factories. It is also widely used in industry for the manufacture of steel, aluminum, copper, nickel, and other metals; for the refining of oil; and for the production of chemicals and many other products. In the home, such items as steam irons are common appliances, and steam has long been used for cooking. In addition, it drives the huge turbogenerators that furnish the major portion of our electric power.

This article is divided into the following sections and subsections:

## I. PROPERTIES

To understand the properties of steam imagine a vertical cylinder containing one pound of water as illustrated in fig. 1A. Resting on the water is a weighted movable piston exerting a constant pressure on the contents. Imagine the water to be initially at room temperature—in this condition it is called subcooled liquid because it exists at a temperature below its boiling point. It occupies the volume indicated at point A′ in fig. 1. Next imagine heat to be slowly added to the water until it reaches the boiling-point temperature and volume represented by point B′, which is slightly greater than A′. In this condition the water is said to be in the saturated liquid state. The volume is often designated by the symbol $v_f$, meaning specific volume of the saturated fluid (liquid). If still more heat is added, boiling occurs and steam is formed underneath the piston, forcing it upward as illustrated in fig. 1C.

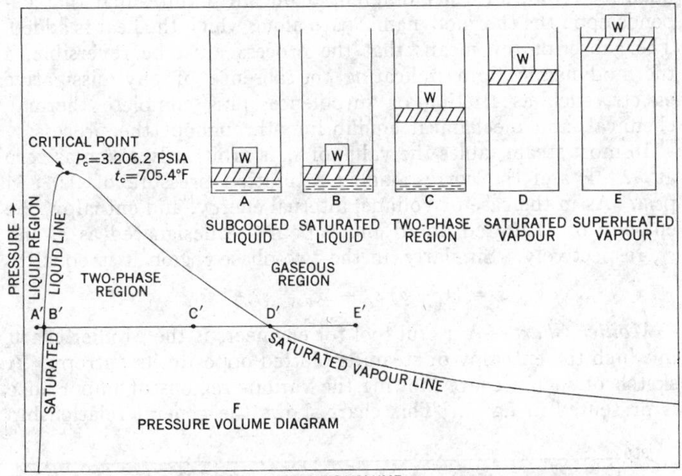


FIG. 1.—DIAGRAM ILLUSTRATING THE BEHAVIOUR OF STEAM. IN THE TWO-PHASE REGION (C) BOTH SATURATED LIQUID AND SATURATED VAPOUR ARE PRESENT

When liquid and steam coexist the contents are said to be in the two-phase region, meaning that the water exists in two physical forms, liquid and gas. As long as this condition exists, the mixture will remain at its boiling-point temperature because additional heat will merely cause more water to boil. Similarly, if heat is withdrawn, some of the steam will condense but the temperature will not change. Between points B′ and D′ in fig. 1F, therefore, the temperature is constant and will depend only on the pressure exerted by the piston. (*See* PHASE EQUILIBRIA.)

If just enough heat is added to vaporize the last droplet of liquid the entire volume will be occupied by steam. Under this condition the steam is said to be dry saturated and will be represented by the point D′. Its volume is usually designated by the symbol $v_g$, meaning specific volume of the saturated gas (vapour). If still more heat is added there will no longer be any liquid to boil, and the temperature will rise. In this condition the steam is said to be superheated, meaning that it is heated above its boiling- or condensation-point temperature. As indicated in fig. 1E, the volume of a pound of superheated steam is greater than the volume of a pound of saturated steam when both are under the same pressure. A typical point in the superheated region is that represented by E′ in fig. 1F.

The temperature at which water will boil depends on its pressure. For example, at standard atmospheric pressure of 14.7 psia (pounds per square inch absolute), the boiling-point temperature of water is 212° F (100° C). If the pressure is reduced, the boiling-point temperature is also reduced. As the pressure is increased, more molecular activity is required to effect the escape of water molecules from the liquid into the gaseous state. This greater molecular activity requires a higher temperature. If the pressure is made just high enough to make escape impossible, the water is said to be at its critical pressure. The temperature of saturated liquid at this pressure is called the critical temperature and is equal to 705.4° F (374.11° C). Since no boiling can occur under these conditions, saturated liquid and saturated vapour become identical. The point corresponding to this situation, called the critical point, is indicated in fig. 1F.

The amount of heat required to vaporize one pound of saturated liquid into one pound of saturated vapour is called the latent heat of vaporization. This latent heat varies with the pressure, being greatest at low pressures and diminishing to zero at the critical pressure.

The importance of steam for the heating of buildings, generation of power, and many other applications has resulted in a need to know its physical properties over a wide range of pressure and temperature. The most important properties of steam, described below, are its specific volume, internal energy, enthalpy, and entropy.

**1. Specific Volume.**—The specific volume is defined as the volume per unit mass. In the English system of units it is measured in cubic feet per pound. The variation of specific volume with pressure and temperature is illustrated by the pressure-volume diagram of fig. 2. The diagram presents the variation of volume with pressure along constant temperature lines, or isotherms. The diagram is divided into three regions: liquid, two-phase, and gaseous. Everything to the left of the saturated liquid line and below the critical temperature of 705.4° F is normally considered to be in the liquid region. Everything to the right of the saturated vapour line or above 705.4° F is normally considered to be in the gaseous region. At pressures above the critical this designation is quite arbitrary, since there is really no physical distinction between liquid and vapour across the critical temperature line. The two-phase region lies between the saturated liquid and saturated vapour lines. In this region lines of constant temperature are horizontal and therefore correspond to lines of constant pressure.

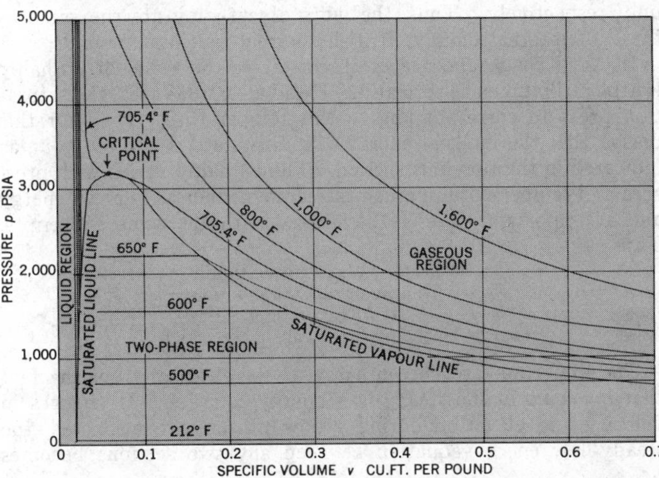


FIG. 2.—PRESSURE-VOLUME RELATIONS OF STEAM

Examination of one of the constant-temperature lines reveals that there is little change of volume with pressure in the liquid region, indicating that liquid water is almost incompressible. During boiling the specific volume increases at constant pressure and temperature until the saturated vapour line is reached, after which a reduction in pressure is required for an increase in volume at constant temperature.

Specific volumes along the saturated liquid line are designated as $v_f$, while those along the saturated vapour line are designated as $v_g$. In the two-phase region, which is sometimes called the saturated region, the fraction by weight of the mixture which is vapour is called the quality. It is usually designated by the symbol $x$. Thus, if at a given pressure 90% of the water-vapour mixture is saturated vapour and 10% saturated liquid, the steam would be said to have a quality of $x = 0.90$ or 90%. From a knowledge of the quality the specific volume of the steam can readily be computed by adding together the fraction that is liquid times its saturated liquid specific volume and the fraction that is vapour times the specific volume of saturated vapour. Since the fraction that is vapour is $x$ and that which is liquid is $(1-x)$, the specific volume in the two-phase region will be

$$v=(1-x)v_f+xv_g=v_f+x(v_g-v_f)=v_f+xv_{fg} \quad (1)$$

where $v_{fg}$ represents the change in volume from liquid to vapour $(v_g-v_f)$.

**2. Internal Energy.**—The internal energy of steam is that energy possessed by virtue of the motion and configuration of its molecules. It is usually measured above a fixed datum state in which its value is arbitrarily taken as $-0.185\ p_fv_f$, where $p_f$ and $v_f$ are the pressure and specific volume of saturated liquid at the freezing-point temperature of 32° F (0° C). The reason for this value will become clear in the following section on enthalpy. The internal energy is most frequently designated by the symbol $u$ and in the English system of units is measured in British thermal units (BTU) per pound. As in the case of volume, it also varies with pressure and temperature and is designated at important states with the same subscripts. Thus

$u_f$ = internal energy of saturated liquid
$u_g$ = internal energy of saturated vapour
$u = (1-x)u_f + xu_g = u_f + xu_{fg}$
= internal energy in the two-phase region

**3. Enthalpy.**—The enthalpy of steam is a property obtained by adding the pressure-volume product to the internal energy. Thus, in consistent units,

$$h = u + \frac{144pv}{778} = u + 0.185pv \text{ BTU per pound} \quad (2)$$

In this expression $p$ is the pressure in pounds per square inch absolute, and $v$ is the specific volume in cubic feet per pound. The numerical constants 144 and 778 are conversion factors representing the number of pounds per square inch in one pound per square foot and the number of foot pounds in a British thermal unit, respectively. Thus, the units of enthalpy are the same as those of internal energy, British thermal units per pound.

In the Keenan and Keyes steam tables the value of enthalpy is arbitrarily taken as zero at 32° F and at 0.08854 psia, the saturation pressure corresponding to this temperature. It is for this reason that the internal energy $u$ at this state is $-0.185\ p_fv_f$, as indicated in the previous section. The enthalpy varies with pressure and temperature in much the same manner as internal energy and at important states is designated with the same subscripts. Thus

$h_f$ = enthalpy of saturated liquid
$h_g$ = enthalpy of saturated vapour
$h = (1-x)\ h_f + xh_g = h_f + xh_{fg}$
= enthalpy in the two-phase region

The importance of the enthalpy of steam arises from the fact that it occurs in the steady-flow energy equation. If changes in velocity and elevation during a flow process are neglected, the steady-flow energy equation between any two sections becomes

$$h_1 \pm {}_1Q_2 \pm {}_1W_2 = h_2 \quad (3)$$

where $h_1$ and $h_2$ are the enthalpies of the steam at sections 1 and 2, respectively, and $\pm{}_1Q_2$ is the heat added or abstracted and $\pm{}_1W_2$ the work done on or by the steam between the two sections, all in British thermal units per pound of steam. If heat is added in some device such as a boiler, where no work is done, the equation becomes

$${}_1Q_2 = h_2 - h_1 \quad (4)$$

This means that the difference in enthalpy is a measure of the heat added and that to compute the amount of heat added one need only subtract the initial enthalpy from the final enthalpy. Similarly, if one considers the flow of steam through a steam turbine, where ${}_1Q_2 = 0$ and ${}_1W_2$ is positive, the equation becomes

$${}_1W_2 = h_1 - h_2 \quad (5)$$

The work done by the turbine is therefore obtained by subtracting the final enthalpy from initial enthalpy. Also, when water is vaporized into steam at constant pressure the amount of heat required (latent heat of vaporization) is equal to the difference between the final and initial enthalpies $h_g - h_f$, designated as $h_{fg}$.

**4. Entropy.**—The entropy of steam is a property defined mathematically by the equation

$$s = s_o + \int\left(\frac{\delta Q}{T}\right)_{\text{rev}} \quad (6)$$

It is one of the most useful properties of steam and is employed for evaluating that portion of heat energy that is unavailable for conversion into useful work. A complete discussion of this property cannot be undertaken in this article because it would involve an extensive excursion into thermodynamics (*q.v.*).

Equation (6) states that the entropy $s$ at a given state is equal to the entropy $s_0$ at an arbitrarily chosen initial state, plus the integral between the two states of the infinitesimal of heat added, divided by the absolute temperature at which the heat is added. The term $\delta Q$ is used instead of the usual $dQ$ to indicate that the quantity is not an exact differential but an infinitesimal that depends upon the thermodynamic path along which the heat is added. The subscript rev means that the process must be reversible, a thermodynamic term indicating the absence of any dissipative effects, such as friction or turbulence, plus complete thermal, chemical, and mechanical equilibrium throughout the process.

In most steam tables the value of $s_0$ is arbitrarily taken as zero at 32° F and the corresponding saturation pressure of 0.08854 psia. As in the case of volume, internal energy, and enthalpy, the entropy of saturated liquid and vapour are designated as $s_f$ and $s_g$, respectively. Similarly, in the two-phase region it is equal to

$$s = (1-x)\ s_f + xs_g = s_f + xs_{fg}$$

*Mollier Chart.*—A useful tool for engineers is the Mollier chart, in which the enthalpy of steam is plotted opposite its entropy. A sketch of such a chart showing the various regions of importance is presented in fig. 3. This chart shows the general relationship

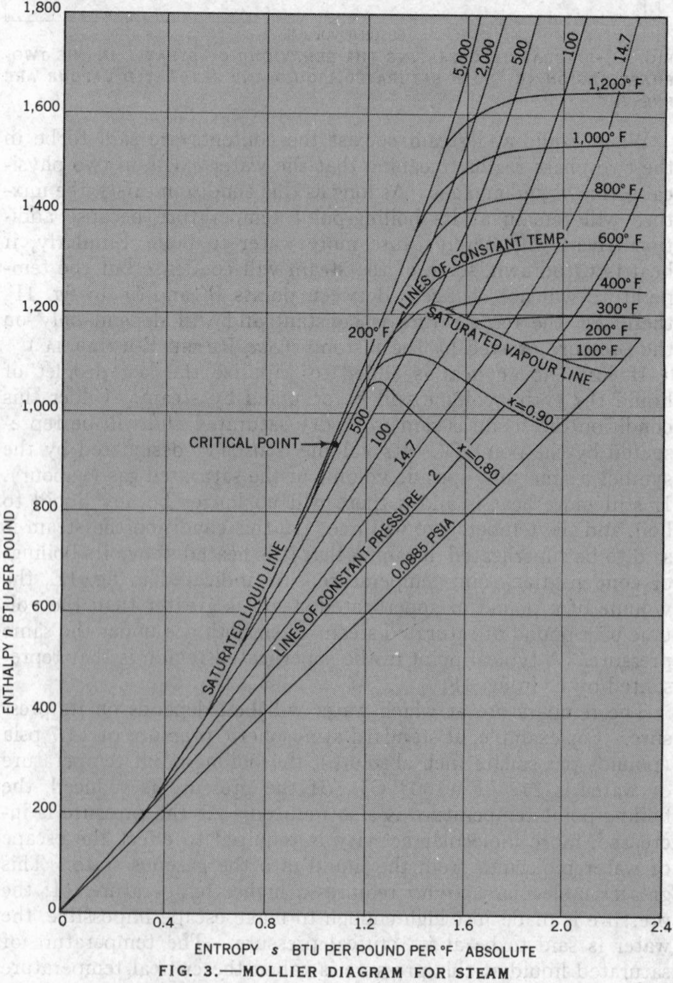

FIG. 3.—MOLLIER DIAGRAM FOR STEAM

between pressure, temperature, enthalpy, and entropy for steam. On the left is the saturated liquid line along which values of enthalpy for saturated liquid $h_f$ can be read. This region is not included in most Mollier charts since it can more accurately be covered with tables. Along the saturated vapour line, values of enthalpy of saturated vapour $h_g$ can be read. Above this line the enthalpy of superheated vapour is obtainable. In the two-phase region where liquid and vapour coexist and where the temperature depends only on the pressure, the enthalpy can be obtained as a function of pressure and steam quality, $x$.

*Tables.*—Our modern knowledge of the properties of steam is largely due to H. L. Callendar of England and, more recently, to Joseph H. Keenan and numerous other investigators. With the help of equations of state and other information, the basis of which is partly theoretical and partly empirical, Callendar and Keenan have rationalized the experimental data and compiled comprehensive tables intended for use by engineers and scientists.

Further research on the properties of steam has been under way on an international scale since 1929 under the guidance of the International Conference on the Properties of Steam. The objective is a more accurate evaluation of the thermodynamic properties of steam over a wider range of pressures and temperatures. The properties are to be formulated and published in a manner suitable for use with modern electronic computers.

(Rd. A. Br.)

## II. STEAM ENGINE

A steam engine is a heat engine in which the working substance is steam. By a heat engine is meant a machine for doing mechanical work through the agency of heat: it does this by taking in heat at comparatively high temperature, converting part of the heat into another form of energy, and rejecting the remainder of the heat at a lower temperature. The working substance is the vehicle by which heat is taken in and rejected. In a steam engine heat is added to the working substance in a separate vessel, the boiler, where it is vaporized before being admitted to the engine. In the engine the steam expands under pressure, thereby converting part of the heat energy into work. Finally, the remainder of the heat is rejected, either by allowing the steam to escape to the atmosphere, as in locomotives, or by condensing it in a separate apparatus called a condenser, at comparatively low temperature and pressure. A condenser allows for a greater expansion of the steam, thus materially increasing the quantity of work obtained.

The fraction of heat added that is converted into work by the engine is called the thermal efficiency of the engine. The addition of the condenser, while increasing the efficiency, also complicates the mechanism. It requires a supply of cooling water or some equivalent means of keeping the temperature and pressure low in the condenser by absorbing the heat that the steam rejects during condensation. It also requires a pump or other means of removing the condensed substance together with any air that may leak into the condenser from the surrounding atmosphere. In the case of large power plants, where fuel economy is important, the advantage of a condenser is so great that virtually all engines employed for this kind of service are of the condensing type.

Given the upper limit of temperature at which heat is taken in, the efficiency attained by the engine is determined by the lowness of the temperature at which heat is rejected. Similarly, when the lower limit of temperature at which heat is rejected is assigned, the engine's efficiency is increased by raising the temperature at which the working substance takes in heat. To secure high efficiency there must be a wide range through which the temperature of the working substance falls, as a consequence of expansion within the engine, from the level of temperature at which heat is received to the level at which heat is rejected. Thus in the steam engine the most efficient performance, *i.e.*, the greatest output of work in relation to the heat supplied, is secured by keeping the condenser as cold as the available cooling water will allow, and at the same time using a high boiler pressure, so that the working substance is very hot while it receives heat in the act of changing from water into steam. For this reason the tendency is always toward higher and higher boiler pressures as the mechanical difficulties of boiler construction and high pressure are overcome.

After conversion into steam the working substance may take in a supplementary supply of heat on its way from the boiler to the engine by passing through a superheater, where its temperature is raised above that of the boiler. A common form of superheater is a group of parallel pipes with their surfaces exposed to hot gases of the boiler furnace.

Steam engines are classified into two general types according to the manner in which the steam does work during its expansion. In the first, or piston-and-cylinder type, the steam, in a confined space, namely the part of the cylinder behind the piston, enlarges the volume of that space by pushing the piston forward. It does work by exerting a static pressure on the moving piston (the movement of the steam itself is of no significance). In the second class, to which belong all kinds of steam turbines, the action is less direct. The pressure of the steam is first employed to set the steam itself into motion, forming a jet or group of jets, the momentum of which causes work to be done on a moving part of the machine, either by the impulsive action of the jet or jets on revolving vanes or by the reaction on revolving guide blades during the formation of the jets, or in some instances by a combination of impulse and reaction. In any turbine the action of the steam is kinetic, in contrast with its static action in an engine of the piston type. In both types there is progressive expansion of the steam from the high pressure and relatively small volume at which it is admitted to the low pressure and relatively very great volume at which it is discharged. The principle already stated, that a large range of temperature and pressure between admission and exhaust is essential to efficiency, applies equally to both types. In practice, the turbine has several advantages over the piston-and-cylinder engine. First, it operates much more smoothly because it avoids the reciprocating motion of pistons and the complications associated with them. Secondly, it is capable of expanding the steam to a much larger volume than could otherwise be achieved, thereby greatly increasing the efficiency of operation. Lastly and most important, it can be built to produce tremendous quantities of power with a unit of relatively small size. Because of these advantages the turbine has become the universally accepted method of generating large quantities of power with steam. (*See* Turbine: *Steam Turbines.*)

### A. History

The *Pneumatica* of Hero of Alexandria (about the 1st century a.d.) described the aeolipile, a primitive steam reaction turbine, which consisted of a hollow globe pivoted so that it could turn on a pair of hollow tubes through which steam was supplied from a cauldron. The steam escaped from the globe to the outside air through two bent pipes facing tangentially in opposite directions at the ends of a diameter perpendicular to the axis. The globe revolved by reaction from the escaping steam. Hero's volume also mentioned another device which may be described as the prototype of the pressure engine. A hollow altar containing air was heated by kindling a fire on it; as the air expanded, its pressure drove some of the water in a vessel below into a hanging bucket, which then descended, opening the doors of a shrine. When the fire was extinguished, the air contracted, the bucket emptied, and the doors closed.

A treatise on pneumatics (1601) by Giovanni Battista della Porta described a somewhat similar apparatus, but with steam for the working substance. Its pressure forced water upward from a separate vessel. He also noted that the condensation of the steam could be used to produce a vacuum and thereby suck water from a lower vessel. This was the fundamental idea for the first commercially successful steam engine developed a century later by Savery.

Meanwhile Edward Somerset, 2nd marquess of Worcester, described in his *Century of Inventions* (1663) a method of raising water by the agency of steam. His description was obscure, and no drawings of the device are extant. It appears to have consisted of a pair of displacement chambers, from each of which alternately

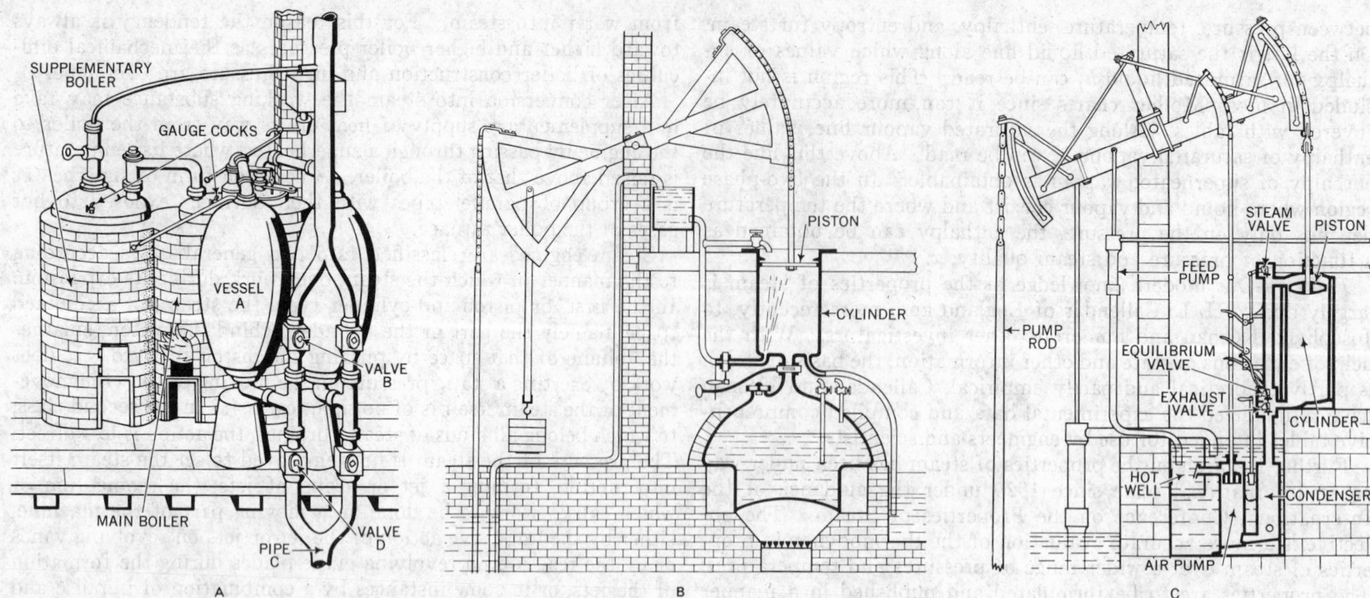


FIG. 4.—EARLY STEAM ENGINES: (A) SAVERY'S ENGINE OF 1698; (B) NEWCOMEN AND CAWLEY ENGINE OF 1705; (C) WATT'S PUMPING ENGINE, 1769

water was forced, probably by admitting steam from an independent boiler, while the other vessel was allowed to refill.

**1. Savery's Engine.**—The earliest practical steam engine was that of Thomas Savery, who, in 1698, obtained a patent for a water-raising engine (fig. 4A). Steam was admitted to one of the oval vessels A, displacing water, which it drove up through the check valve B. When the vessel A was emptied of water, the supply of steam was stopped, and the steam already there was condensed by allowing a jet of cold water from a cistern above to stream over the outer surface of the vessel. This produced a vacuum and caused water to be sucked up through the pipe C and the valve D. Meanwhile steam had been displacing water from the other vessel and was ready to be condensed there. The valves B and D opened only upward. The supplementary boiler and furnace fed water to the main boiler, both of which were supplied with gauge cocks. Another form of Savery's engine had only one displacement chamber and worked intermittently. Savery's engine marked an inventive advance in practical features as well as in the use of artificial means to condense the steam and in the application of a vacuum to raise water by suction from a level lower than that of the engine. It found considerable employment in pumping mines and in raising water to supply houses and towns, and even to drive waterwheels. Its general use in mines was curtailed by the fact that the height through which it would lift water was limited by the pressure the boiler and vessels could bear. Pressures as high as eight or ten atmospheres were employed—and that, too, without a safety valve—but Savery found it no easy matter to deal with high-pressure steam. Also, there was an enormous waste of fuel from the condensation of steam that took place on the surface of the water and on the sides of the displacement chamber during each operation. In proportion to the work done, the consumption of coal was about 20 times greater than in a modern engine.

Before Savery's engine was displaced by its successor, Newcomen's, it was improved by J. T. Desaguliers, who applied a safety valve (invented by Denis Papin) and substituted condensation by a jet of cold water within the vessel for the surface condensation used by Savery. To Savery is ascribed the first use of the term "horsepower" as a measure of performance.

In 1690 Denis Papin suggested that the condensation of steam should be employed to make a vacuum under a piston previously raised by the expansion of the steam. Papin's was the earliest cylinder-and-piston steam engine, and his plan of using steam later took practical shape in the atmospheric engine of Newcomen. But his scheme was made unworkable because he proposed only one vessel as both boiler and cylinder. A small quantity of water was placed at the bottom of a cylinder and heat was applied. When the piston had risen the fire was removed, the steam was allowed to cool, and the piston did work in its downstroke under the pressure of the atmosphere. After hearing of Savery's engine in 1705, Papin devised a modified form, with a floating diaphragm or piston on the top of the water to keep the water and steam from direct contact with one another. Papin's engine may be described as a noncondensing single-acting steam pump, with steam cylinder and pump cylinder in one.

**2. Newcomen's Atmospheric Engine.**—While Papin was thus going back from his first notion of a piston engine to Savery's cruder type, a new inventor made the piston engine a practical success by separating the boiler from the cylinder and by using (as Savery had done) artificial means to condense the steam. This was Thomas Newcomen, who in 1705, with his assistant John Cawley, gave the steam engine the form shown in fig. 4B. Steam admitted from the boiler to the cylinder by opening a valve allowed the piston to be raised by a heavy counterpoise on the other side of the beam. Then the steam valve was closed, and a jet of cold water entered the cylinder and condensed the steam. The piston was consequently forced down by the pressure of the atmosphere and did work on the pump. The next entry of steam expelled the condensed water from the cylinder through an escape valve, and the piston was kept tight by a layer of water on its upper surface. Condensation was at first effected by cooling the outside of the cylinder, but an accidental leakage of the packing water past the piston showed the advantage of condensing by a jet of injection water, and this plan took the place of surface condensation. The engine used steam whose pressure was little if at all greater than that of the atmosphere.

About 1711 Newcomen's engine began to be introduced for pumping mines. It is doubtful whether the action was originally automatic or whether it depended on the periodical turning of taps by an attendant. By 1725 the engine was in common use in collieries, and it held its place without material change for about three-quarters of a century. Near the close of its career Newcomen's engine was much improved in its mechanical details by John Smeaton, who built many large engines of this type about the year 1770.

Compared with Savery's engine, Newcomen's had (as a pumping engine) the great advantage that the intensity of pressure in the pumps was not in any way limited by the pressure of the steam. It shared with Savery's, in a scarcely less degree, the defect already pointed out, that steam was wasted by the alternate heating and cooling of the vessel into which it was led. Though obviously capable of more extended uses, it was almost exclusively employed to raise water—in some instances for the purpose of turning waterwheels to drive other machinery.

**3. Watt's Engines.**—James Watt (*q.v.*), an instrument maker in Glasgow, Scot., while engaged by the university in repairing a model of Newcomen's engine, was struck with the waste of steam to which the alternate chilling and heating of the cylinder gave rise. He saw that the remedy would lie in keeping the cylinder as hot as the steam that entered it. With this view he added to the engine a new organ—namely the "separate condenser"—an empty vessel separate from the cylinder, into which the steam should be allowed to escape from the cylinder, to be condensed there by the application of cold water either outside or as a jet. To preserve the vacuum in his condenser he added an air pump that would extract the condensed steam and water of condensation, as well as any air that might come in by leakage or by solution in the steam or the injection water. Then, as the cylinder was no longer used as a condenser, he was able to keep it hot by insulating it and providing a steam jacket—a layer of hot steam between the cylinder and an external casing. Further and still with the same object, he covered the top of the cylinder, taking the piston rod out through a steamtight gland, or stuffing box, and allowed steam instead of air to press upon the piston's upper surface. After much experiment Watt patented his improvements in 1769.

Highly important as Watt's first inventions were, they resulted for a time in nothing more than a greatly improved engine of the Newcomen type, much less wasteful of fuel and able to make faster strokes but still only suitable for pumping, still single-acting, with steam admitted during the whole stroke, the piston, as before, pulling the beam by a chain working on a circular arc. The condenser was generally worked by injection, but Watt has left a model of a surface condenser made up of small tubes, in every essential respect like the condensers now used.

Fig. 4C is an example of the Watt pumping engine of this period. Although the top of the cylinder is closed, and steam has access to the upper side of the piston, this is done only to keep the cylinder and piston warm. The engine is still single-acting; the steam on the upper side merely plays the part which was played in Newcomen's engine by the atmosphere; and only the lower end of the cylinder is put in communication with the condenser. There are three valves: the steam valve, the equilibrium valve, and the exhaust valve. At the beginning of the downstroke, the exhaust valve is opened to produce a vacuum below the piston, and the steam valve is opened to admit steam above it. At the end of the downstroke, the steam valve and the exhaust valve are shut, and the equilibrium valve is opened. This puts the two sides in equilibrium and allows the piston to be pulled up by the pump rod, which is heavy enough to serve as a counterpoise. A vacuum is maintained in the condenser by an air pump, which extracts water, steam, and air from the condenser and then discharges the contents into the hot well, from which water for the feed pump is drawn.

In a second patent (1781) Watt described the sun-and-planet wheels and other methods of making the engine give continuous revolving motion to a shaft provided with a flywheel. The crank and connecting rod—already a familiar mechanical device from its use on the treadle of a lathe—would have been the natural means of doing this, but its application to the steam engine had been made the subject of a patent by James Pickard, and Watt, rather than coming to terms with Pickard, whom he regarded as a plagiarist of his own ideas, made use of his sun-and-planet motion until the patent on Pickard's crank expired. The reciprocating motion of earlier forms had served only for pumping; by making the steam engine drive a revolving shaft, Watt opened up many other channels of usefulness. The engine was still single-acting; the connecting rod was attached to the far end of the beam; and that carried a counterpoise which served to raise the piston when steam was admitted below it.

In 1782 Watt patented two further improvements of great importance, both of which he had invented some years before. One was the use of double action; *i.e.,* the application of steam and vacuum to each side of the piston alternately. The other (invented as early as 1769) was the use of the steam's expansion. With this arrangement, which was essential to economy of fuel, admission of steam to the cylinder was stopped when the piston had made only a part of its stroke, thus allowing the rest of the stroke to be performed by the expansion of the steam already in the cylinder. To let the piston push as well as pull the end of the beam, Watt devised his so-called parallel motion, an arrangement of links connecting the piston-rod head with the beam in such a way as to guide the rod to move in a very nearly straight line. He further added a throttle valve for regulating the rate of admission of steam and a centrifugal governor, in the form of a double conical pendulum, which controlled the speed by a throttle valve.

Among other important devices associated with Watt was the indicator, by which diagrams showing the relation of the steam pressure in the cylinder to the movement of the piston are automatically drawn. Its invention seems to have been mainly due to his assistant John Southern.

In partnership with Matthew Boulton in Birmingham, Eng., Watt manufactured and sold his engines with great success and held the field against all rivals in spite of severe assaults on the validity of his patents. Notwithstanding the advantage to be gained by using steam expansion, he continued to employ only low pressures—seldom more than 7 psi (pounds per square inch) over that of the atmosphere. His boilers were fed, as Newcomen's had been, through an open pipe rising high enough to let the column of water in it balance the pressure of the steam. He gave a definite numerical significance to the term "horsepower," defining it as the rate at which work is done when 33,000 lb. are raised one foot in one minute.

Although Watt's first patent described a noncondensing engine that would have required steam of a higher pressure, he did not pursue this idea, perhaps because as early as 1725 a noncondensing engine had been described by Jacob Leupold in his *Theatrum machinarum.*

It was not until much later that the thermodynamic principles underlying the action of the steam engine came to be understood. Engineers were consequently slow to appreciate the fact that to obtain fuel economy it was advantageous to employ a high initial pressure, in combination with much expansion in the cylinder and with the separate condenser of Watt.

**4. Trevithick, Bull, and Evans.**—The introduction of the noncondensing and, at that time, relatively high-pressure engine was effected in England by Richard Trevithick about 1798 and in the U.S. by Oliver Evans about 1800. Both Evans and Trevithick applied their engines to propel carriages on roads, and both used for the boiler a cylindrical vessel with a cylindrical flue inside containing the fire—the construction now known as the Cornish boiler. In association with Edward Bull, Trevithick had previously made direct-acting pumping engines, with an inverted cylinder set over and in line with the pump rod, thus dispensing with the beam that had been a feature in all earlier forms. But in these Bull engines, as they were called, the steam was condensed by a jet of cold water in the exhaust pipe, and Boulton and Watt successfully opposed them as infringing Watt's patent. To Trevithick belongs the honour of being the first to use a steam carriage on a railway; in 1804 he built a locomotive to run on what had formerly been a horsecar route, in Wales. It may be added that as early as 1769 a steam carriage for roads had been built in France by Nicholas Joseph Cugnot, who used a pair of single-acting high-pressure cylinders to turn a driving axle by means of pawls and ratchet wheels. To the initiative of Evans may be ascribed the early general use of high-pressure steam in the United States, a feature which for many years distinguished American from English practice. (*See* RAILWAY: *Locomotives.*)

**5. Compound Engine and Cornish Engine.**—Among contemporaries of Watt the name of Jonathan Hornblower deserves special mention. In 1781 he constructed and patented what would now be called a compound engine, with two cylinders of different sizes. Steam was first admitted into the smaller cylinder and then passed over into the larger, doing work against a piston in each. The two cylinders were placed side by side, and both pistons worked on the same end of a beam overhead. This was an instance of the expansive force of steam and as such was earlier than the patent, though not earlier than the invention of expansive working by Watt. Hornblower lost a patent suit to the Birmingham firm for infringing their patent in the use of a separate condenser and air pump. However, the compound engine was revived in 1804 by Arthur Woolf, with whose name it is often associated. By using steam of fairly high pressure and cutting off the supply before the end of the stroke in the small cylinder, Woolf expanded the steam to several times its original volume. Mechanically the two-cylinder compound engine has some advantage over a one-cylinder engine with the same amount of expansion, in exerting a more uniform driving effort. But another and more important advantage lies in the fact that by dividing the whole range of expansion into two parts the cylinders in which these are separately performed are subject to a reduced range of fluctuation in their temperature. This helps to limit a source of waste present in all piston engines, namely the waste resulting from the heating and cooling of the metal by its alternate contact with hot and cooler steam. The introduction of compound expansion formed the most outstanding improvement that steam engines of the piston-and-cylinder type had undergone since the time of Watt.

Woolf introduced the compound engine about 1814 as a pumping engine in the mines of Cornwall, Eng., but it met a strong competitor in the high-pressure single-cylinder engine of Trevithick, which had the advantage of greater simplicity in construction. Woolf's engine fell into comparative disuse, and the single-cylinder type took a form which, under the name of the Cornish pumping engine, was for many years famous for its great fuel economy. In this engine the cylinder was set under one end of a beam, and from the other end hung a heavy rod that operated a pump at the foot of the shaft. Steam was admitted above the piston for a short portion of the stroke, thereby raising the pump rod, and was allowed to expand for the remainder of the stroke. An equilibrium valve connecting the space above and below the piston, as in fig. 4C, was then opened, and the pump rod descended, doing work in the pump and raising the engine piston. The large mass that had to be started and stopped at each stroke served by its inertia to counterbalance the unequal pressure of the steam, for the ascending rods stored up energy of motion in the early part of the stroke, when the steam pressure was greatest, and gave out energy in the later part, when the pressure was much lowered by expansion. The frequency of the stroke was controlled by a device called a cataract, consisting of a small plunger pump, in which the plunger, raised at each stroke by the engine, was allowed to descend more or less slowly by the escape of fluid below it through an adjustable orifice. In its descent it liberated catches that held the steam and exhaust valves from opening. A similar device controlled the equilibrium valve; it could be set to pause at the end of the piston's downstroke so that the pump cylinder might have time to become filled.

The final revival of the compound engine did not occur until about the mid-19th century, and then several agencies combined to effect it. In 1845 John M'Naught introduced a plan to improve beam engines of the original Watt type by adding a high-pressure cylinder whose piston acted on the beam between the centre and the flywheel end. Steam of higher pressure than had formerly been used, after doing work in the new cylinder, passed into the old or low-pressure cylinder, where it was further expanded. Many engines with insufficient power for the extended machinery they had to drive were "M'Naughted" in this way and after conversion were found not only to yield more power but to show a marked economy of fuel. The compound form was selected by William Pole for the pumping engines of Lambeth, Eng., and other waterworks about 1850; in 1854 John Elder began to use it in marine engines; in 1857 E. A. Cowper added a steam-jacketed intermediate reservoir for steam between the high- and low-pressure cylinders, which made it unnecessary for the stroke of the low-pressure piston to be just beginning when that of the other piston was just ending. As facilities increased for the use of high-pressure steam, compound expansion came into more general use, its advantage becoming more conspicuous with every increase in boiler pressure. In marine practice, where economy of fuel was an obviously important factor in design, the principle of compound expansion was extended by the introduction of triple- and even quadruple-expansion engines.

**6. Application to Locomotives and Steamboats.**—The adaptation of the steam engine to railways, begun by Trevithick, became a success in the hands of George Stephenson, whose engine, the "Rocket," when tried along with others in 1829, outshone its competitors. The principal features of the "Rocket" were an improved steam blast for urging the combustion of coal and a boiler (suggested by Henry Booth) in which a large heating surface was provided by the use of many small tubes through which the hot gases passed. Further, the cylinders, instead of being vertical as in earlier locomotives, were set at a slope, but later altered to a position more nearly horizontal. To these features was added later the link motion, a contrivance that enabled the engine to be easily reversed and the amount of expansion to be readily varied. In the hands of George Stephenson and his son Robert, the locomotive took a form that in the main was retained by the far heavier locomotives later in use.

The first practical steamboat was the tug "Charlotte Dundas," built by William Symington and tried in the Forth and Clyde Canal in 1802. A Watt double-acting condensing engine, placed horizontally, acted directly by a connecting rod on the crank of a shaft at the stern, which carried a revolving paddle wheel. The trial was successful, but steam towing was abandoned for fear of injuring the banks of the canal. Ten years later Henry Bell built the "Comet," with side paddle wheels, which ran as a passenger steamer on the Clyde; but an earlier inventor to follow up Symington's success was Robert Fulton of the U.S. After successful experiments on the Seine, he fitted a steamer on the Hudson River in 1807 with engines made to his designs by Boulton and Watt and brought steam navigation for the first time to commercial success.

**7. Rise in Steam Pressure and Piston Speed.**—With improvements in the details of design and construction it gradually became practicable to use higher steam pressures and piston speeds and consequently to obtain not only greater efficiency but also a greater amount of power from engines of given bulk. The triple-expansion engine, introduced by A. C. Kirk in 1874, did not come into general use until after 1881. It became the normal type of marine engine, with pressures generally ranging from 150 to 200 psi, piston speeds generally of 500 or 600 ft. per minute (but sometimes as high as 900 or 1,000), and coal consumption of about $1\frac{1}{2}$ lb. per hour per indicated horsepower. The triple-expansion engine continues to be largely used in steamships that are not driven by turbines. In some instances quadruple expansion has been preferred, with somewhat higher pressures, but when the pressure is raised too greatly it has been the practice to abandon the piston engine in favour of the steam turbine. The gigantic concentration of steam power found in a great steamship or in a power station has been made practicable only by the introduction of the turbine. The introduction of turbines in 1907 as the motive engines of the "Lusitania" and "Mauretania" constituted a new departure in steam engineering. It was then a novelty to develop roughly 70,000 hp. in the engine room of a single ship.

**8. Introduction of the Steam Turbine.**—The invention of the steam turbine revolutionized marine engine practice with respect to the largest and fastest vessels. For the generation of electricity the turbine has a notable advantage in directly developing the high speed of rotation required by electric generators. In large sizes their efficiency is unrivaled by steam engines of any kind. To Sir Charles Parsons is owed not only the main idea of the modern steam turbine, but also the invention of many mechanical features and details essential to its practical success and general adaptation.

In the steam turbine, pressure, instead of being exerted on a piston, is employed to set the fluid itself in motion. There is a conversion of pressure energy into velocity energy as a preliminary step toward obtaining the effective work of the machine. If this were done in a single step it would involve immensely high velocities in the steam jet and in the vanes on which the jet acts. Attempts to design a steam turbine were made by numerous inventors, but they fell short of practical success mainly because of the difficulty of arranging for high enough velocity in the working parts to utilize a reasonably large fraction of the kinetic energy of the steam. There was a further difficulty in getting the energy of the stream into a suitable kinetic form, namely, to get the stream of issuing particles to take a single direction, without undue dispersion, when steam was allowed to expand through an orifice from a chamber at high pressure into a space where the pressure was much lower.

In 1889 Carl Gustaf de Laval introduced a form of steam turbine in which both of these difficulties were considerably overcome, partly by the special form of the nozzle used to produce the steam jet and partly by design features that allowed an exceptionally high speed to be reached in the wheel carrying the vanes against which the steam impinged.

Parsons attacked the problem at an earlier date and in a different way by his invention of the multistage turbine. He divided the whole expansion of the steam into a great number of successive and separate steps and thereby limited the velocity acquired at each step to such an extent as to make it comparatively easy to extract the greater part of the kinetic energy as work done upon the moving blades, without making the velocity of these blades inconveniently high. Moreover, in Parsons' compound turbine the range of pressure through which the steam expands in each step is too small to cause any difficulty in the formation of the jets. The guide blades, which form the jets, are distributed around the circumference of the revolving wheel, and all the revolving blades are consequently in action at once. The steam flows from end to end of the turbine through an annular space between a revolving drum and the casing that surrounds it. Parallel rings of fixed guide blades project inward from the casing at suitable distances, and between these are rings of moving blades that project outward from the drum and revolve with it. At each step in the expansion the steam passes through a ring of fixed guide blades, and the streams so formed impinge on the next ring of moving blades, and so on. The construction, which is of great simplicity, is described, along with others, in the article TURBINE. The turbine lends itself well to the generation of power on a large scale, especially where a fairly high speed of rotation is desired.

Parsons introduced his multistage steam turbine in 1884. For some years it was made in small sizes only, and the steam was discharged to the atmosphere without condensation. So long as this was done the steam turbine was sacrificing one of its most important advantages, namely, its exceptional capacity for utilizing the energy of low-pressure steam down to the lowest vacuum obtainable in a condenser. In 1891 it was first fitted with a condenser, and it then began to be used in electric generating stations. The first application to marine propulsion was in the "Turbinia" in 1897. The success of this little experimental vessel of 100 tons, which, with its horsepower of 2,100, made what was then a record in speed for any ship, was soon followed by the application of the turbine to warships and other steamers. In merchant vessels its use was at first limited to those of the highest speed, for the turbine shaft was directly coupled to the shaft of the screw propeller. But in 1910 Parsons introduced a mechanical reducing gear between the two that allowed the turbine shaft to run much faster than the propeller shaft, to the great advantage in efficiency of both turbine and propeller. Later he followed this up by a double-reduction gearing that allowed a still greater difference in speed of rotation between the propeller and the turbine. In most ships the single-reduction system is sufficient for the purpose, and its introduction greatly extended the range within which the turbine could be advantageously substituted for the three-cylinder or four-cylinder compound engine of the piston type in oceangoing steamships.

**9. Early Theory.**—In the early development of the steam engine inventors had little in the way of theory to guide them. Watt had the advantage of a knowledge of Joseph Black's doctrine of latent heat, but there was no philosophy of the relation of work to heat until long after the inventions of Watt were complete. The theory of the steam engine as a heat engine may be said to date from 1824, when N. L. Sadi Carnot published his *Réflexions sur la puissance motrice du feu et sur les machines propres à développer cette puissance,* a remarkable essay in which he showed that heat does work only in the process of descent from a higher to a lower temperature. But Carnot was not then aware that any of the heat disappears in the process, and it was not until the doctrine of the conservation of energy was established in 1843 by the experiments of James Prescott Joule that the theory of heat engines began a vigorous growth. From 1849 onward the science of thermodynamics was developed with extraordinary rapidity by Rudolf Clausius, W. J. Rankine, and William Thomson (Lord Kelvin) and was applied, especially by Rankine, to practical problems in the use of steam. Rankine's *Manual of the Steam Engine,* published in 1859, was the first attempt at a systematic treatment of steam-engine theory. It involved the assumption that the cylinder and piston might be treated as behaving to the steam like nonconducting bodies, in other words, that the transfer of heat between the steam and the metal might generally be disregarded. One effect of this was to treat the volume of steam consumed per stroke as corresponding to the volume of the cylinder up to the point of cutoff. When steam enters the engine cylinder, it finds the metal chilled by the previous exhaust, and a portion of it is at once condensed. This has the effect of increasing, often very largely, the volume of steam required per stroke. As expansion goes on, the water that was condensed during admission begins to be reevaporated, and this action is often prolonged into the exhaust. It is now recognized that exchanges of heat between the steam and its metal envelope cannot be ignored.

### B. ACTION OF RECIPROCATING ENGINES

Most reciprocating engines are double-acting; *i.e.,* steam from the boiler is alternately admitted to each side of the piston. In each double stroke, or revolution, there are four events for each end of the cylinder: (1) admission, which begins by opening a steam valve when the piston is at or very near the limit of its travel; (2) cutoff, at which the steam valve is closed and admission ceases. This may take place early in the stroke. The steam enclosed behind the piston then expands, with falling pressure, while the stroke continues, until (3) release occurs when an exhaust valve opens, allowing the steam to escape from the cylinder. Its discharge generally continues for a large part of the backstroke, until (4) the exhaust valve closes and compression begins. From there to the end of the backstroke, the steam remaining in the cylinder is compressed into the clearance space behind the piston. This compression of the residue of steam, called cushioning, assists smoothness of working as the piston passes what is called the dead point, at the limit of its stroke. The cushioning effect is often augmented by giving the steam valve lead; *i.e.,* causing it to open a little before the piston reaches the dead point.

**1. Distribution of Steam.**—Together, these various events of the stroke constitute what is termed the distribution of the steam. They are conveniently exhibited by drawing an indicator diagram of the action, such as that illustrated in fig. 5. There, on a base PQ, which represents the stroke, lines are drawn to show the continuous changes of pressure that go on within the cylinder during the whole action. Starting from the beginning of the stroke at a, for one side of the piston, steam is admitted up to the cutoff point b. At (or near) the end of the forward stroke c, the steam is allowed to escape. Compression, in the return stroke, begins at d. From b to c the steam confined in the cylinder is expanding, with falling pressure, doing work on the piston. The whole work done in the revolution, namely the average of the force acting on the piston and the distance through which it moves, is represented by the enclosed area of the indicator diagram, a-b-c-d.

The diagram is idealized in the sense that the events are shown as if they happened suddenly, giving sharply defined changes from admission to expansion and so on. In any real engine the events are necessarily gradual, for no valve—whatever its type—can close or open instantaneously.

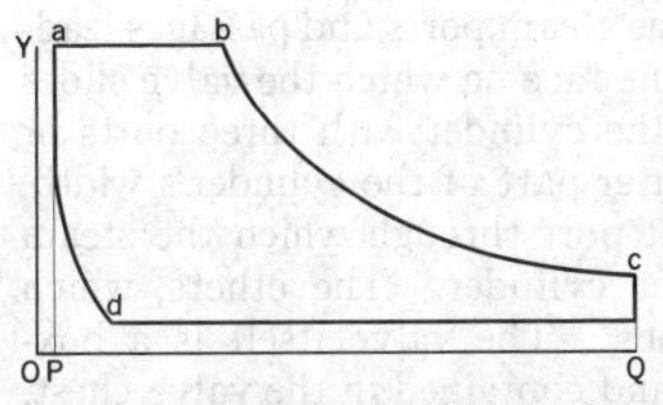

FIG. 5.—INDICATOR DIAGRAM SHOWING DISTRIBUTION OF STEAM (*see* TEXT FOR FURTHER INFORMATION)

A real indicator diagram accordingly has a smoother outline with rounded corners to mark the places of cutoff, release, compression, and admission. In practice, release always occurs before the piston has quite completed its stroke.

The distance PQ, which represents the stroke, may be interpreted as a volume, namely the volume swept through by the piston, and a point O behind P may be so taken that OP represents, on the same scale, the volume of the clearance. The distance measured horizontally from the line OY to any point of the curve represents the whole volume of steam behind the piston at that point, and the curve between admission and release exhibits the relation of the pressure to the total volume of the steam enclosed behind the piston throughout its process of expansion.

Actual indicator diagrams may be automatically drawn by attaching to the cylinder of the engine a device in which a pencil is made to rise or fall proportionally to the variations of steam pressure, while a paper, on which it inscribes a record, moves back and forth horizontally through distances proportional to the movement of the engine piston. Many forms of indicator have been designed to give a diagram in which the coordinates represent respectively the displacement of the piston and the pressure of the steam against it. From such diagrams it is easy to infer the mean effective pressure throughout the stroke and also to observe how the valves are working. By connecting the instrument successively to each of the two ends of the cylinder in a double-acting engine a complete record is obtained for the two strokes that make up a revolution. The indicated horsepower (ihp) is determined by the formula

$$\text{ihp} = \frac{nL(p_1A_1 + p_2A_2)}{33{,}000}$$

where $A_1$ and $A_2$ are the areas of the two sides of the piston, in square inches; $p_1$ and $p_2$ are the mean effective pressures on the two sides, in pounds per square inch, as determined from the diagrams; $n$ is the number of revolutions per minute, and $L$ is the stroke in feet. In steam engine trials such diagrams are taken during a considerable period. The amount and condition of the steam passing through the engine is observed by measuring either the quantity of water discharged from the condenser (if of the surface type) or the quantity of feed water required by the boiler to keep the water level constant. From these data it is possible to compare the power developed with the heat supplied. Measurements of the heat rejected may also be made by observing the quantity of condensing water used and its rise in temperature; together these figures give material for drawing up a balance sheet of the disposal of thermal energy.

**2. The Slide Valve.**—The admission and exhaust of steam, for each end of the cylinder, may be controlled by separate valves, but very commonly a single moving piece, called a slide valve, serves to control the events for both ends. A common form of the slide valve is illustrated in section in fig. 6, which also shows

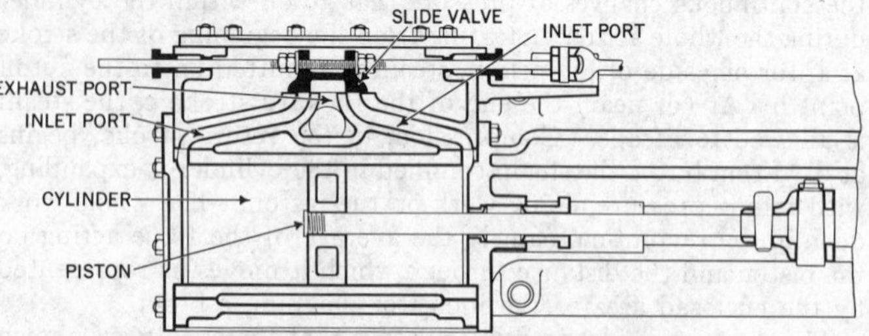


FIG. 6.—CROSS SECTION OF A SLIDE VALVE SHOWING THE EXHAUST AND INLET PORTS BELOW IT, AND CYLINDER AND PISTON

the cylinder, with the piston, and the steam ports and passages leading to each end of the cylinder. The face on which the valve slides is a plane surface on one side of the cylinder with three ports or openings extending across the greater part of the cylinder's width. The central opening is the exhaust port through which the steam escapes after doing its duty in the cylinder. The others, which are narrower, lead to the two ends. The valve itself is a box-shaped cover, sliding on the face, and contained in the valve chest, or chamber, to which steam is admitted from the boiler. When the valve moves a sufficient distance to either side of the middle position, steam is admitted to one end of the cylinder, past the outer edge. Similarly steam escapes from the other end of the cylinder, through the cavity of the valve, to the exhaust port. The valve takes its motion from an eccentric on the engine shaft, which is set more than 90° ahead of the crank, so that the valve has already begun to uncover the port on one side when the piston is at the corresponding dead point, with the result that steam passes from the steam chest above the valve into the space behind the piston. Fig. 7 shows a slide valve in its middle position and illustrates the internal lap i and the external lap e which the valve

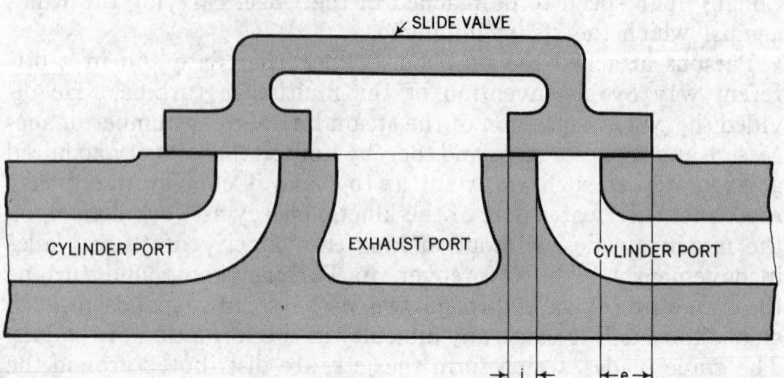


FIG. 7.—CROSS SECTION OF SLIDE VALVE IN MIDDLE POSITION: (i) INTERNAL LAP, (e) EXTERNAL LAP

must have to make expansive working possible. At the beginning of the stroke it has already passed its middle position by an amount at least equal to e, so that steam may enter. It continues to move farther, opening the port more widely, and then begins to return, while the piston is still advancing in the cylinder. At a particular point in its return the outer edge of the valve closes the port; this determines the instant of cutoff. The piston continues to advance, with expansion of the steam confined in the cylinder, while the valve continues to move back, until its inner edge begins to uncover the port, allowing steam from the cylinder to escape to the exhaust channel. This point, which depends on the internal lap i, determines the instant of release. The port then opens more widely to exhaust and remains open during most of the backstroke of the piston until the valve, again moving in the original direction, brings its inner edge again over the port, and compression begins. Similar events for the other end of the cylinder are determined by the other side of the valve. The positions of the piston when the several events occur depend on the amounts of the laps e and i and of the angular advance that exceeds 90° in the angle by which the eccentric stands ahead of the crank. If there were no laps and no angular advance, steam would be admitted during the whole forward stroke and exhausted during the whole backward stroke. By giving the valve laps and angular advance, expansive working becomes possible. The slide valve, however, is not too well adapted to effect a cutoff early in the stroke, and, when much expansion is desired, a separate expansion valve is added, or valves of a different type are used to control the distribution of the steam.

In many engines the events are controlled by using, at each end of the cylinder, separate valves for admission and exhaust (fig. 8). Sometimes these are double-beat drop valves in the sense that the valve, when it drops into its seat, simultaneously closes two passages. These are so arranged that the steam pressure tending to close or open the valve remains balanced, and no large force has to be exerted. Such

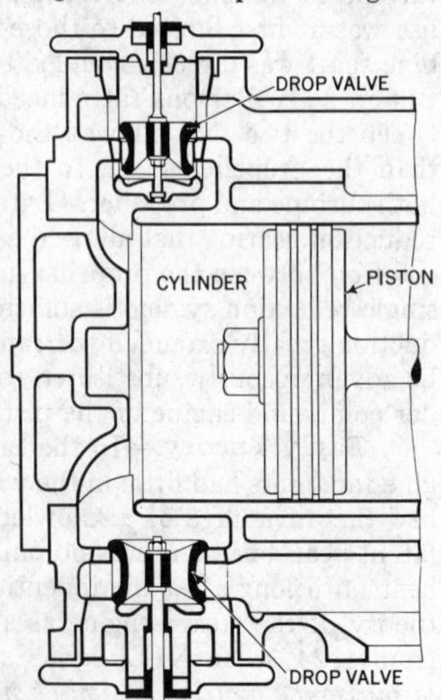


FIG. 8.—CROSS SECTION OF ONE END OF A CYLINDER SHOWING DROP VALVES

valves are often worked by cams and levers from a lay shaft alongside the cylinder and driven from the main shaft so as to turn in unison. Sometimes the admission valves are closed by a tripping device that is connected to the governor of the engine in such a manner that the cutoff comes earlier or later when the speed exceeds or falls short of the normal. Thus the engine automatically adjusts the amount of power it develops to suit changes in the demand made upon it by the mechanism which it drives.

Fig. 6 shows a slide valve form usual in locomotives and small engines, but in large sizes the unbalanced pressure of steam on the back of the valve would cause much friction and wear in the movement of the valve sliding over the working face. In large engines, such as those of steamships, it is usual to relieve the pressure of the valve on the working face by fitting the back of the valve with a relief frame, extending between the valve and the steam-chest cover, in order to prevent the steam of the steam chest from having access to the whole back surface of the valve.

Frequently used as a substitute for the flat form of slide valve is a piston form in which the effective sliding portions of the valve extend all around the surface of a cylinder and slide over cylindrical fixtures in the valve chest, around which the steam ports extend.

**3. Reversing Gears.**—The slide valve is a particularly convenient means of controlling the admission of steam when, as in locomotives or marine engines, etc., the engine's direction of motion must frequently be reversed. It is only necessary to provide means by which the valve may be actuated by either of two eccentrics, one set at the angle suitable for forward running and the other at the angle suitable for backward running.

In Stephenson's link motion, shown in fig. 9A, the engine shaft carries two eccentrics, one of which is set ahead of the crank at a suitable angle for one direction of running and the other at a suitable angle for the other direction. Their rods are connected to the ends of a link which gives its name to the contrivance. The link, a slotted bar curved to a circular arc, is capable of being moved up or down, being suspended from a rod that can be raised or lowered by means of the hand lever above. The valve rod ends in a block that slides within the link. This device allows either the forward eccentric or the backward eccentric to determine the motion of the valve and so allows the engine to be reversed. Moreover, if the link is set to an intermediate position, in which it takes its motion chiefly from one eccentric but partly from the other, the valve receives a motion virtually the same as that which it would get from a single eccentric of shorter travel and greater angular advance. The effect is to give a distribution of steam in which the cutoff is hastened and the expansion and compression are increased.

Thus besides allowing full forward and full backward gear the link may be notched up to give a much shorter admission of steam along with more compression, a matter of practical value in running a locomotive, where frequent large variations in the demand for driving effort have to be met.

Various other forms of link motion have been devised that share this advantage. It is also shared by a group of equivalent mechanical devices, called radial valve gears, in which only one eccentric is employed, but the valve can be moved and varied in the same way. Of these the most widely used is the Walschaerts gear, very common in locomotives, a diagram of which is shown in fig. 9B. There A is a projection moving with the engine piston. The valve V takes motion partly from it, through the rods AB and BV; but BV has a fulcrum at D, the position of which varies through the movement of the rod DG. That rod is supported by a suspension rod J, and its end at G can slide in a link HI rocking about a fixed fulcrum at O. There is one eccentric, CF, set at right angles to the crank CK, and giving motion to the rocking link HI by the rod FH. The block G can be shifted from near H to I by raising the suspension rod J. This reverses the motion and allows also for notching up to any intermediate position.

**4. Governors.**—To keep a steam engine running at a uniform speed, notwithstanding variations in the demand for power, an automatic regulator, or governor, is provided. Regulation may be effected in two ways: the steam may be throttled more or less on its way from the boiler to the engine, so that the pressure of admission is reduced when the speed tends to rise and increased when the speed tends to fall; or the point of cutoff may be varied, with the result of admitting a greater or smaller volume of steam in each stroke. In small engines the governor often acts on a throttle valve, but for high-efficiency engines it is preferable to govern by altering the cutoff. In such engines an early cutoff is employed to secure a proper amount of expansion, and a small change in the position of the cutoff largely affects the amount of steam admitted and consequently the amount of work done.

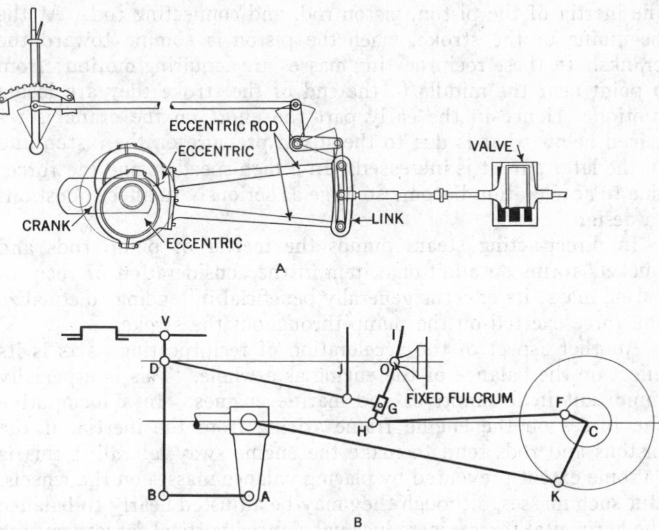


FIG. 9.—(A) STEPHENSON'S LINK MOTION; (B) WALSCHAERTS GEAR

Watt's original governor consisted of a pair of balls revolving about a vertical spindle as conical pendulums under the combined effect of their own weight and the centrifugal force due to their speed of revolution. Any increase of speed sufficient to overcome the slight friction of the attached gearing made them take up a higher position, and in so doing they partially closed a throttle valve. This went on until, at a slightly greater speed than before, equilibrium was established between the supply of steam and the demand for power. Here, as in all governors, the effect is not to maintain a strictly constant speed, but to prevent the variation, either way, from exceeding narrow limits.

In modern governors the centrifugal force of the balls generally acts not simply against their own weight, but against an extra load or against the force of a spring.

In many factory and other engines the governor determines the position of cutoff by means of a trigger action of the type already mentioned, in which the admission valve, which has been opened and held open by a cam turning with the engine shaft, is suddenly disconnected by the release of a trigger at a point depending on the exact height of the governor balls.

**5. The Flywheel.**—The function of the governor is, generally, to keep the engine running at a nearly uniform rate, measured in revolutions per minute; the function of the flywheel is to keep the rate nearly uniform within the limits of any one revolution. For this purpose it must act as a reservoir of energy, alternately storing and restoring the excess amounts that result from periodic variations of turning moment in the operation of the piston on the crank. At the dead points the piston's rate of doing work is zero, and it rises to a maximum at an intermediate point, the position of which may be much affected by an early cutoff. The flywheel is drawn upon for energy during those parts of the revolution in which the work done by the piston (or pistons) on the engine shaft is less than the work done by the shaft on the mechanism driven by the engine, and it takes up the surplus during the other parts of the revolution. To effect this alternate give and take of energy the flywheel must undergo small variations of speed, the magnitude of which may be kept down to any assigned amount by giving the rim a sufficient mass and speed.

**6. Inertia of Reciprocating Parts.**—The effective effort on the crank is greatly influenced, especially in high-speed engines, by the inertia of the piston, piston rod, and connecting rod. At the beginning of the stroke, when the piston is coming toward the crankshaft, these reciprocating masses are acquiring motion; from a point near the middle to the end of the stroke they are losing motion. Hence in the early part the effort on the crank is reduced below what is due to the steam pressure on the piston and in the later part it is increased. In a high-speed engine the forces due to acceleration become so large as seriously to affect questions of design.

In direct-acting steam pumps the inertia of pump rods and buckets forms an additional item in the consideration of reciprocating mass; its effect is generally beneficial in tending to equalize the force exerted on the pump throughout the stroke.

Another aspect of the acceleration of reciprocating parts is its effect on the balance of the engine as a whole. This is especially important in locomotives and marine engines. In a locomotive the forces on the engine frame arising from the inertia of the pistons and rods tend to make the engine sway laterally; this is to some extent prevented by placing balance masses on the wheels. But such masses, although they may be adjusted nearly to balance the horizontal forces, introduce unbalanced vertical forces, causing what is called hammerblow. In extreme cases these vertical forces might even lift the wheels from the rails. Short of that, however, they are objectionable in causing periodic variations in the pressure on the rails, which tend to set bridges into oscillation and may add substantially to the stresses for which the railway engineer must provide.

### C. Types of Reciprocating Engines

In classifying engines with regard to their general arrangement of parts and mode of working, account has to be taken of a considerable number of independent characteristics. There is first a general division into condensing and noncondensing engines, with a subdivision of condensing class into those acting by surface condensation and those using injection. Next there is the division into compound and noncompound, with a further classification of the former as double-, triple-, or quadruple-expansion engines. Again, engines may be classed as single- or double-acting, according to whether the steam acts on one or alternately on both sides of the piston. Also, a few engines—such as steam hammers and certain kinds of steam pumps—are nonrotative, *i.e.*, the reciprocating motion of the piston does work simply on a reciprocating piece, but generally an engine does work on a continuously revolving shaft. In most cases the crankpin of the revolving shaft is connected directly with the piston rod by a connecting rod, and the engine is then said to be direct-acting; in other cases, of which the beam engine is an historical example, a lever is interposed between the piston and the connecting rod. The same distinction applies to nonrotative pumping engines, in some of which the piston acts directly on the pump rod, while in others it acts through a beam. The position of the cylinder is another element of classification, giving horizontal-, vertical-, and inclined-cylinder engines. In most vertical engines the cylinder is above the connecting rod and crank. In oscillating-cylinder engines (a type still found in some riverboats) the connecting rod is dispensed with; the piston rod works on the crankpin, and the cylinder oscillates on trunnions to allow the piston rod to follow the crankpin around its circular path. In rotary engines there is no piston in the ordinary sense; the steam does work on a revolving piece, thus avoiding the need to later convert reciprocating into rotary motion.

**1. Beam Engines.**—In Newcomen's single-acting atmospheric engine the beam was a necessary feature; the use of water packing for the piston required that the piston should move down in the working stroke, and a beam was needed to let the counterpoise pull the piston up. Watt's improvements eliminated the need for the beam, and in one of the forms he designed it was discarded—namely, in the form of a pumping engine known as the Bull engine, in which a vertical inverted cylinder stands over and acts directly on the pump rod. However, the beam formed a convenient driver for pump rods and valve rods, and the parallel motion invented by Watt as a means of guiding the piston rod, which could easily be applied to a beam engine, was, in the early days of engine building, an easier thing to construct than the plane surfaces which are the natural guides of the piston rod in a direct-acting engine. In modern practice the direct-acting type has almost wholly displaced the beam engine.

**2. Direct-Acting Engines.**—Of direct-acting engines the horizontal arrangement has in general the advantage of greater accessibility, but the vertical arrangement saves floor space. In small forms the engine is generally self-contained, that is, a single frame or bedplate carries all the parts, including the main bearings in which the crankshaft with its flywheel turns. The frame often takes a girder shape, which brings a portion of it into a favourable position for taking the thrust between the cylinder and the crankshaft bearings and allows two surfaces to be formed on the frame to serve as guides for the crosshead. When a condenser is used with a horizontal engine it is often placed behind the cylinder, and the air pump, which may be within the condenser, has a horizontal plunger or piston on a tail rod or continuation of the main piston rod through the back cover of the cylinder. In large horizontal engines the condenser generally is in a well below, and its pump is driven by a mechanism linked with the crosshead.

**3. Coupled Engines.**—When uniformity of driving effort or the absence of dead points is important, two independent cylinders often work on the same shaft by cranks at right angles to each other. Such engines can start readily from any position. In some engines three cylinders, set to work on cranks 120° apart, cooperate in giving a still more uniform drive.

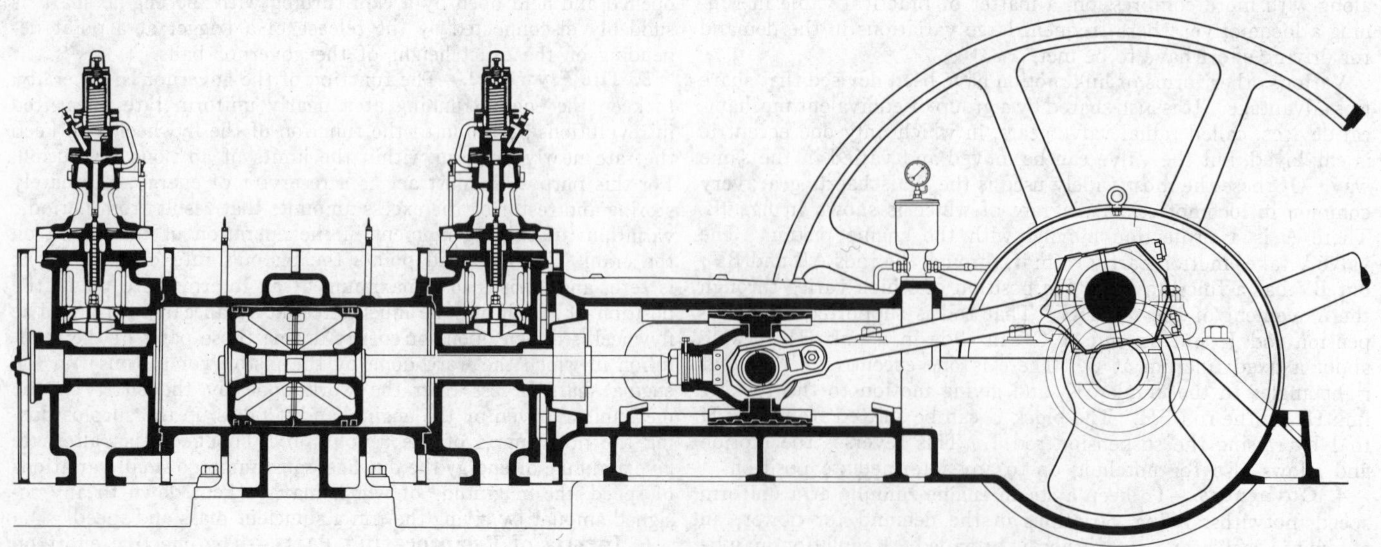

FIG. 10.—UNIFLOW ENGINE IN WHICH THE PISTON ACTS AS EXHAUST VALVE AND THE ADMISSION VALVES ARE IN THE CYLINDER ENDS

Winding engines for mines and collieries, in which ease of starting, stopping, and reversing is essential, are usually made by coupling a pair of cylinders on opposite sides of the winding drum.

**4. Compound Engines.**—Large direct-acting engines are usually compounded either by having a high- and a low-pressure cylinder side by side, with cranks at right angles, or by putting one cylinder behind the other with a common centre line. The latter is called a tandem arrangement. In a tandem engine, since the pistons agree in phase, the steam may expand directly from the small into the large cylinder. But the connecting pipe and steam chest form a receiver of considerable size, and it is preferable to cut off the supply of steam to the large cylinder at an earlier stage of the stroke. For mill engines the compound tandem and compound coupled types of engine are very usual. The high-pressure cylinder is often fitted with some form of trip gear.

The chief advantage of compounding is that it reduces the condensation that hot steam undergoes in the cylinder through contact with metal that has been chilled by the exhaust of the previous stroke. Compound working acts beneficially by narrowing the range through which the temperature periodically fluctuates in the metallic surfaces exposed to contact with the operative steam. The amount of steam that is at once condensed on admission depends on the extent to which the surface with which it comes in contact has been chilled during the previous exhaust. For this reason there is less loss through initial condensation in a compound engine giving the same total ratio of expansion.

**5. Uniflow Engine.**—The periodic give and take of heat between the steam and the metallic surfaces, which is a serious source of loss in any reciprocating engine, can be reduced by having separate valves for admission and exhaust, so that the same port surfaces and valve surfaces are not brought into contact with hot and comparatively cold steam. This idea is carried further in the uniflow engine (fig. 10) by an ingenious arrangement whereby the ends of the cylinder, where the steam is admitted, are always kept hot, the exhaust taking place at the middle of the cylinder through ports in the circumference which are uncovered by the motion of the piston.

The uniflow design is a conspicuously successful departure from earlier practice. It allows high-pressure steam to be expanded in a single cylinder without the drawbacks ordinarily entailed in noncompound operation. There is, however, still enough exchange of heat between the metal and the steam to make superheating highly advantageous.

**6. Condensation.**—In land engines a jet form of condenser is common, but surface condensation is resorted to when the available water supply is unsuited for boiler feed. When there is no large supply of condensing water a very fair vacuum can be obtained by using an evaporative condenser, consisting of a stack of pipes into which the exhaust steam is admitted and over which a small amount of cooling water is allowed to drip. This water is evaporated by the heat which the condensing steam gives up. Such a condenser is placed in the open, generally on a roof where the air has free access. The amount of water it uses need not exceed the amount of steam that is condensed, and it is a small fraction of the amount that would be required in a jet or surface condenser.

**7. High-Speed Direct-Acting Engines.**—Prior to the development of the steam turbine the demand for engines suitable for driving electric generators without the intervention of a belt led to the introduction of various forms of direct-acting engine adapted to run at a high speed. Some of these were single-acting, steam being admitted to one side of the piston only, generally the back, with the result that the rods could be kept in a state of thrust throughout the revolution and alternations of stress in the rods and at the joints thereby avoided, together with the knocking and wear of the bearing brasses. To assure, however, that the connecting rod should always push and never pull against the crankpin there had to be much cushioning during the outstroke because from about the middle of that stroke to the end the reciprocating mass was being retarded.

In engines of this class designed by P. W. Willans, which are now displaced by turbines, the cushioning was provided by means of a supplementary piston that compressed air during the outstroke. The energy spent by the reciprocating masses in losing their motion during the second half of the outstroke was stored in this air and was restored in the succeeding downstroke. The engine was entirely enclosed in a casing, the bottom of which formed an oil bath where the cranks splashed to ensure ample lubrication. This feature is retained in many modern high-speed engines.

**8. Pumping Engines.**—In engines for pumping or for blowing air it is not essential to drive a revolving shaft, and in many forms the reciprocating motion of the steam piston is applied directly to produce the reciprocating motion of the pump piston or plunger. Often an inverted vertical triple-expansion engine is used, resembling the usual marine form, with a pump plunger under each of the three cylinders. Most of the power is directly transmitted from the piston to the pump, but for each cylinder there is an auxiliary crank to drive a shaft with a flywheel to equalize the effort on the pump.

A familiar example of a direct-acting pump is the small donkey pump used for feeding boilers, in which the steam piston and pump plunger are on the same rod. In some of these pumps a rotative element is introduced, partly to secure steadiness of running and partly for convenience in working the valves. But many pumps of this class are entirely nonrotative, and in such cases the steam is generally admitted throughout the stroke without expansion. The valve may be actuated by tappets from the piston rod. In some cases a tappet worked by the piston as it reaches each end of its stroke throws open an auxiliary steam valve, which admits steam to one or the other side of an auxiliary piston carrying the main slide valve.

**9. Pulsometer.**—Hall's pulsometer, a peculiar pumping engine without cylinder or piston, may be regarded as the modern representative of the engine of Savery. The sectional view, fig. 11, shows its principal parts. There are two chambers, A and A′, narrowing toward the top, where the steam pipe B enters. A ball valve C allows steam to pass into one of the chambers and closes the other. Steam entering the right-hand chamber forces water out of it past the clack valve V into a delivery passage D, which is connected with an air vessel. When the water level in A sinks so far that steam begins to blow through the delivery passage, the water and steam are disturbed and so are brought into intimate contact; the steam in A condenses; and a partial vacuum is formed. This causes the ball valve C to rock over and close the top of A, while water rises from the suction pipe E to fill that chamber. At the same time steam begins to enter the other chamber A′, discharging water from it, and the same series of actions is repeated in each chamber alternately. While the water is being driven out there is comparatively little condensation of steam, partly because the shape of the vessel does not promote the formation of eddies and partly because there is a cushion of air between the steam and the water. Near the top of each chamber is a small air valve opening inward, which allows a little air to enter each time a vacuum is formed. When any steam is condensed, the air mixed with it remains on the cold surface and forms a nonconducting layer. The pulsometer is far from efficient as a thermodynamic engine, but its adaptability to situations where other steam pumps cannot easily be applied and the simplicity of its working parts sometimes make it useful.

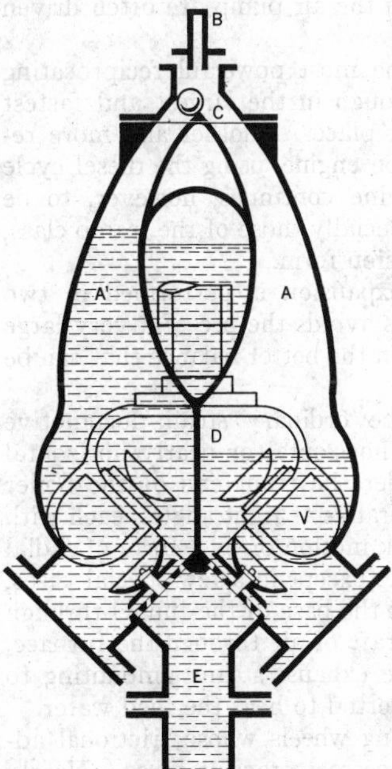

FIG. 11.—HALL'S PULSOMETER

**10. Marine Engines.**—The early steamers were fitted with paddle wheels, and the engines used to drive them were for the most part modified beam engines. Bell's "Comet" was driven by a species of inverted beam engine, and another form of inverted beam, known as the side-lever engine, was long a favourite with marine engineers. An old form of direct-acting paddle engine was the steeple engine, in which the cylinder was set vertically below the crank. Two piston rods projected through the top of the cylinder, one on each side of the shaft and of the crank. They were united by a crosshead sliding in vertical guides, and from this a return-connecting rod led to the crank. Most modern paddle-wheel engines are direct-acting engines of the ordinary connecting-rod type, with the cylinders fixed on an inclined bed and the guides sloping up toward the shaft.

When the screw propeller began to replace the paddle wheel in ocean steamers, the increased speed required was at first obtained by using spur-wheel gearing in conjunction with one of the forms of engines then usual in paddle steamers. Types of engines better suited to the screw were introduced later and were driven fast enough to be connected directly to the screw shaft. After passing through various forms, now obsolete, the marine engine settled into one that is now universal in all screw steamships that are not driven by steam turbine. This is the inverted vertical direct-acting engine, with two or more cylinders placed side by side directly over the shaft. It has the great advantage that the shaft can readily be put at the low level necessary for screw propulsion. Two, three, and four cranks are employed, the arrangement with four cranks being especially suitable when a balance of the engine at high speeds is needed. In vessels of high speed and power the engines are often arranged in twin sets, on two shafts with twin screw propellers.

The marine engine is always furnished with a surface condenser, consisting of a multitude of brass tubes about $\frac{3}{4}$ in. in diameter that are cooled by sea water circulated through the condenser by means of a pump. This pump and the air pump are often driven independently of the main engine.

It is in marine practice that the most powerful reciprocating engines are still to be found, although in the largest and fastest vessels the turbine has taken their place. Another and more recent rival is the internal-combustion engine, using the diesel cycle of action. The reciprocating engine continues, however, to be much used for seagoing vessels, especially those of the tramp class, most commonly in the triple-expansion form.

Often the third stage of the expansion is performed in two cylinders, making four in all. This avoids the use of a very large cylinder and secures an advantage in the better balance that can be obtained with four cranks.

**11. Locomotive Engines.**—The ordinary steam locomotive consists of a pair of direct-acting horizontal or nearly horizontal engines fixed in a rigid frame under the front end of the boiler and coupled to the same shaft by cranks at right angles, each with a single slide valve worked by a link motion or by a form of radial gear. The engine is noncondensing, except in a few special cases, and the exhaust steam, delivered at the base of the funnel through a blast pipe, serves to produce a draft of air through the furnace. In some instances a portion of the exhaust steam, amounting to about one-fifth of the whole, is diverted to heat the feed water.

On the shaft are a pair of driving wheels whose frictional adhesion to the rails furnishes the necessary tractive force. Nearly always a greater tractive force is secured by having two or more driving wheels on each side that are connected by a coupling rod between pins on the outside of the wheels.

Generally under the front of the engine there is a group of smaller wheels that do not form part of the driving system. These are carried in a bogie, that is, a small truck upon which the front end of the boiler rests by a swivel pin or plate. This allows the bogie to turn, so as to adapt itself to curves in the line, and thus obviate the grinding of tires and danger of derailment that would be caused by using a long rigid wheelbase.

In inside-cylinder engines the cylinders are placed side by side within the frame of the engine, and their connecting rods work on cranks in the driving shaft. In outside-cylinder engines the cylinders are spread apart far enough to lie outside the frame of the engine, and they work on crankpins on the outside of the driving wheels. Many modern locomotives combine the outside and inside arrangement in order to get greater power, placing one or in some cases two cylinders within the frame, as well as two outside. The principle of compounding has often been applied to locomotive engines, but without much advantage. *See* RAILWAY: *Locomotives.* (J. A. E.; RD. A. BR.)

### III. STEAM GENERATORS

With improvement of the steam engine there came a demand for higher pressure steam and for generators of increased capacity and efficiency. This stimulated the development of early versions of fire-tube and water-tube type boilers, forerunners of our present-day units.

**1. Fire-Tube Boiler.**—This type boiler is characterized by the use of tubes through which hot gases flow on their way to a stack or chimney. The tubes pass through a vessel, usually cylindrical in shape, and are surrounded by the water to be converted into steam. The most popular boiler of this type is the horizontal-return-tubular boiler. In early units the fuel, usually coal, was shoveled onto the grate by hand. Air for combustion was drawn in from underneath the grate by natural draft created by the stack. The hot products of combustion first passed underneath the horizontal boiler drum to the far end, where they entered the fire tubes for their return journey to the stack. The boiler drum was cylindrical in shape and arranged so that the steam generated could collect above the water level and be withdrawn through a dry pipe consisting of a tube with perforations near the top arranged so that leaving steam was forced to make a sharp turn in order to throw out entrained moisture. A safety valve, set to allow escape of steam at pressures somewhat above normal operating pressure, was also provided. This valve is an absolute necessity on all boilers since continued addition of heat to water in a closed vessel without means of escape will result in a rise in pressure and ultimate explosion of the boiler.

Fire-tube boilers of many varieties are still being built. However, because of limitations on the pressure which a drum of reasonable size can withstand and also because of the limited heating surface available, fire-tube boilers are employed only for pressures below about 250 lb. per square inch gauge (psig) and for steam capacities not exceeding about 25,000 lb. per hour. Modern installations are often of the package type, consisting of fully automatic shop-assembled units complete with boiler drum, furnace, forced-draft fan for supplying air for combustion, and all other necessary equipment for attendant-free operation. Designed to burn either oil or gas, they have the advantage of being easy to install and operate, less costly to manufacture, and more economical to operate. They are widely used for supplying steam to large apartment buildings, hotels, small factories, and other space-heating tasks.

**2. Water-Tube Boiler.**—The development of the steam turbogenerator early in the 20th century created a demand for large quantities of steam at pressures and temperatures far exceeding those possible with fire-tube boilers. This demand resulted in the evolution of modern water-tube boilers in which steam is generated inside water tubes from heat supplied on the outside by hot furnace gases. Boilers of this type are employed in a wide variety of sizes and designs and in capacities as high as 8,000,000 lb. of steam per hour and with pressures and temperatures as high as 5,000 psi and 1,200° F (648.8° C), respectively. The largest of these units are found in central-station power plants of public utilities. Other units of substantial size are employed in steel mills, paper mills, oil refineries, and large chemical and industrial manufacturing plants.

A typical central-station water-tube boiler employing pulverized coal fuel is illustrated in fig. 12. In this unit fuel stored in the bunker is fed into pulverizers, where it is reduced to dust size and blown into the burners with air supplied from a forced-draft fan located above the furnace. Additional preheated air is supplied around the burners. Combustion takes place in the huge rectangular furnace, which is completely surrounded by water tubes in which steam is generated. The hot gases pass up the

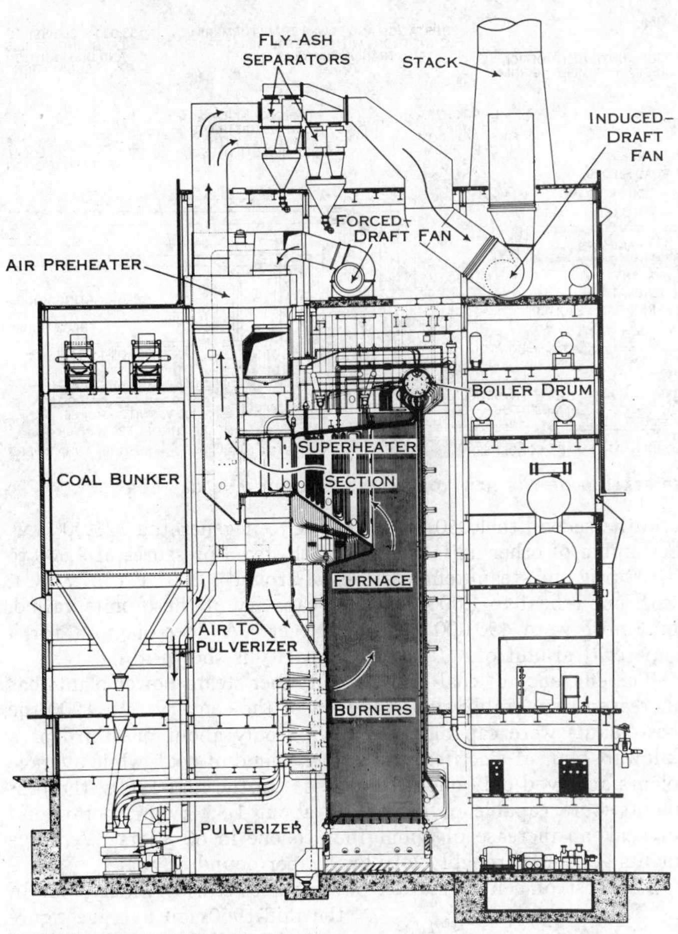


BY COURTESY OF THE BABCOCK AND WILCOX CO.

FIG. 12.—CROSS SECTION OF A TYPICAL CENTRAL-STATION BOILER

furnace and then over the superheater tubes. From this point they move up through the air preheater, in which a part of their heat is transferred to the air on its way to the burners. Leaving the air preheater the hot gases are drawn upward through fly-ash separators into the induced-draft fan and out the stack.

Circulation of water is natural. Water from the drum near the top of the unit is carried down to the lower level of the furnace in huge pipes called downcomers. Here the water is fed into the water-wall tubes surrounding the furnace cavity. Steam is generated in these tubes and is finally returned to the drum, where it is separated from the water by means of complex devices consisting of an array of steam separators, baffles, and scrubbers. The dry steam is then passed through superheater tubes before being piped to the turbogenerators for the production of electric power.

Beginning in the early 1950s pressures above the critical (see *Properties,* above) have been employed in some central-station power plants. In these installations natural circulation is no longer feasible, since at pressures above the critical, water does not boil. As a result there is insufficient difference in density between hot and cold water to effect natural circulation, and pumps must be used.

**3. Fuels.**—Principal fuels employed for the generation of steam are coal, oil, natural gas, coke oven gas, blast furnace gas, and wood. By far the major portion of coal used for this purpose is bituminous coal, although some lignite and anthracite also are burned where plentiful. Most central-station plants burn coal in pulverized form, but many smaller industrial and heating plants burn it in lump or crushed form on traveling grate, spreader, or other type stokers.

Oil and gas are burned in central-station power plants whenever or wherever they can be purchased more economically than coal. Many plants are equipped to burn pulverized coal in the winter and natural gas in the summer. Some are equipped with burners capable of operating with either oil, pulverized coal, or gas.

**4. Water Treatment.**—Water employed in modern steam generators must be completely free of all scale-forming or corrosive chemicals. It must also be free of dissolved oxygen and carbon dioxide. For this reason elaborate chemical treatment plants are necessary. In central-station power plants the water generated into steam is used over and over again so that only about 1 or 2% new treated water need be supplied to make up for losses resulting from leakage, contamination, blowdown, and other diversions.

The percentage of treated water added is called the makeup. In some industrial plants, such as oil refineries, nearly all steam generated is from makeup. This means that virtually 100% of the water going into the boiler must be treated.

**5. Efficiency.**—The generation of steam involves the transfer of heat from the fuel to the boiler fluid. In this process some of the heat released by the fuel is lost and is therefore not absorbed by the steam. The ratio of the heat actually absorbed by the steam to the heating value of the fuel employed is called the efficiency of the steam generator.

Because of high fuel costs, efforts to reduce heat losses to a minimum include the use of an economizer to preheat the feed water entering the boiler and an air preheater to preheat the air before being introduced into the furnace for combustion. Both of these items aid in cooling the hot flue gases to a lower temperature so that not so much heat is discharged from the stack. Other precautions involve the use of the exact amount of air for efficient combustion. This operation involves the supply of sufficient excess air to assure complete combustion of all carbon to carbon dioxide, yet not so much that excess heat is thrown away by heating unnecessary air. This air supply is governed by intricate controls that automatically maintain the correct air-to-fuel ratio for maximum overall steam-generator efficiency. In modern central-station plants, steam generators are capable of achieving efficiencies as high as 90% based on the higher heating value of the fuel, and average efficiencies of about 87% are common. For small steam generators not employing elaborate control apparatus, economizers, or air preheaters, efficiencies of the order of 70 to 80% are typical. *See* also BOILER.

## IV. STEAM POWER PLANTS

A steam power plant is a plant for the generation of electric power with steam. By far the major portion of electric power generated in the world comes from central-station power plants. In the United States in the mid-1960s total power generation amounted to slightly more than 1,000,000,000,000 kw-hr., of which about 91% was generated in electric utility plants. Of this total, 82% was generated in fuel-burning plants and 18% in hydroelectric plants. A breakdown of the types of fuel employed indicated that 66% of the power generated in fuel-burning plants was generated from coal, 27% from gas, and most of the remainder from oil and nuclear energy. Similar statistics, but on a smaller scale, would be true of other countries. All serve to emphasize the importance of steam power plants in our modern economy.

**1. Modern Power Plants.**—Fig. 13 illustrates a typical central-station power plant and the various items of equipment employed in the generation of electrical power from coal. Coal cars dump their contents into a hopper and then onto a coal conveyor. From there the coal is lifted onto a belt conveyor and deposited in huge coal bunkers from which it is automatically fed to the coal pulverizing mills as needed. From the pulverizing mills the coal is blown into the boiler furnace where it is burned with preheated air supplied by the forced-draft fan. The hot combustion gases formed pass over the various boiler heating surfaces, through the economizer, air preheater, precipitator, induced-draft fan, and finally to the stack.

In the particular plant shown the saturated liquid water from the condenser enters the condensate pumps and is pumped through the first heater into the deaerating heater, where any entrained air is expelled. From the deaerating heater it flows to the boiler feed pumps, which force it successively through three other feed-water heaters and then through the economizer into the boiler.

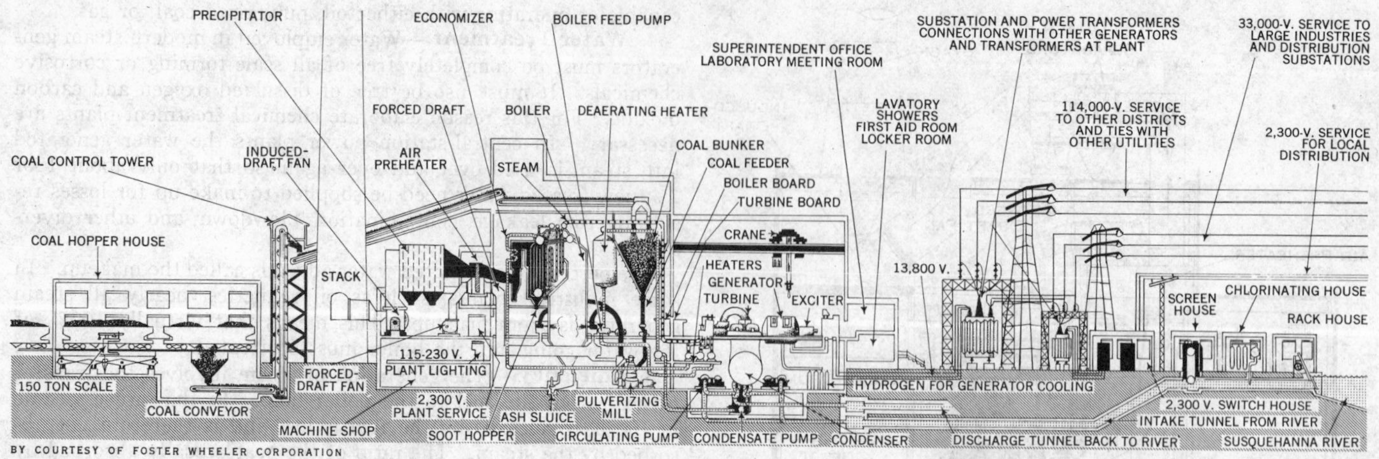


BY COURTESY OF FOSTER WHEELER CORPORATION

FIG. 13.—TYPICAL CENTRAL-STATION POWER PLANT, THE WESTOVER STATION OF THE NEW YORK STATE ELECTRIC AND GAS CORP.

Here it is generated into steam and after passing through the superheater flows into the turbine, where the power is generated. From the turbine the steam exhausts to the condenser, where it is divested of its latent heat by means of the circulating water pumped from a nearby river through the tubes of the condenser. The electric generator furnishes 60-cycle current at 13,000 v. In the substation, transformers are used to step the voltage up or down for transmission from the plant.

Modern steam power plants all employ regenerative cycles and many employ reheat. However, pressure and temperature conditions, number of heaters, and details of arrangement vary greatly. During the 1950s and 1960s the trend was toward higher pressures and temperatures, with a few supercritical units of huge capacity being built. One unit employed steam at 5,000 psig and 1,200° F (648.8° C), with two reheats, the first to 1,045° F (562.7° C) and the second to 1,050° F (565.6° C); it generated 325,000 kw. A number of other units operated with steam pressures of 3,500 to 4,500 psig and steam temperatures of around 1,000° F (537.8° C), with one reheat to 1,000° F. The capacity of these units varied, but most were 450,000 kw. and larger. A flow diagram for a supercritical unit of 450,000-kw. capacity is shown in fig. 14.

The efficiency of coal-burning and other steam power plants has increased remarkably since the turn of the century. In 1900 the best plants were capable of achieving only about one-third of a kilowatt hour of electrical energy per pound of coal, while average plants achieved only one-fifth or less. In the mid-1960s, the best plants were capable of generating about 1.33 kw-hr. per pound of coal, an increase of about four to one in 60 years. Average plants generated roughly 1.16 kw-hr. per pound of coal.

The cost of central-station power plants varies widely, but in the mid-1960s an average figure was about $150 per kilowatt of generating capacity. This means a typical modern central-station plant capable of generating 600,000 kw. would involve an investment of about $90,000,000 for the plant. To this must be added the cost of transmission, distribution, and miscellaneous capital equipment costs. From 1955 to 1965 the annual construction expenditures of U.S. electric power companies for plant, transmission, distribution, and miscellaneous equipment averaged about $3,500,000,000.

**2. Nuclear Power Plants.**—Following World War II the use of nuclear energy for the generation of power became feasible. A number of plants were built in the U.S., England, the U.S.S.R., and other countries. In these plants steam is still the motivating force and is generated with the aid of a reactor in which the controlled fission of uranium or plutonium furnishes the necessary heat for its vaporization. Thus the reactor takes the place of the steam generator of the conventional plant.

Problems associated with nuclear power generation are extremely complex and involve such considerations as shielding against radiation, disposal of fis-

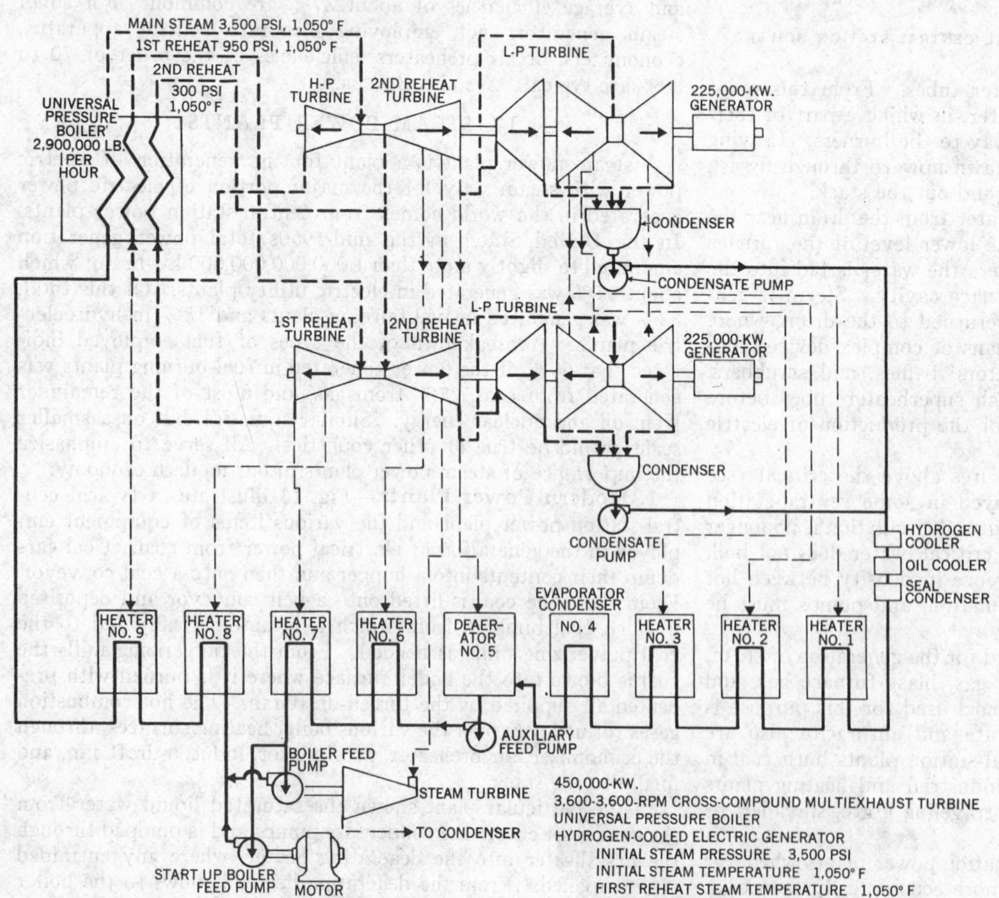


BY COURTESY OF MCGRAW-HILL PUBLISHING CO., INC.

FIG. 14.—FLOW DIAGRAM OF 450,000-KW. SUPERCRITICAL POWER PLANT sion products, hazard insurance, and high cost of construction. Because of these factors, early plants built in the U.S. were not economically competitive with coal-burning plants. However, with improved technology, plants of large size became competitive in certain locations in the U.S. in the mid-1960s. In 1964 about one-tenth of one per cent of the power generated in the U.S. was with nuclear fuel. As more experience is gained the use of nuclear fuel is expected to increase rapidly.

**3. Binary Cycle Plants.**—To achieve maximum efficiency, heat should be added to the cycle at the highest possible temperature. In conventional steam power plants a substantial portion of the heat is added at temperatures below the critical of 705.4° F (374.11° C). This is because the feed water supplied to the boiler must first be heated to the boiling point and then evaporated at the saturation temperature corresponding to the pressure. In the binary cycle plant this limitation is overcome by simultaneously employing two separate cycles, one a high-temperature Rankine cycle using mercury vapour, and the other a conventional steam cycle. The arrangement of the two cycles is such that most of the heat from the fuel is added at high temperatures to the mercury in a special boiler that need not withstand very high pressure. The mercury vapour is expanded through a mercury turbine and exhausted into a special condenser (called a condenser-boiler) that also serves as the boiler for the steam cycle. The condensing mercury thus supplies the latent heat of vaporization of the steam before it is pumped back into the mercury boiler. The steam generated is superheated in the furnace of the mercury boiler and then subjected to the conventional regenerative cycle, after which it is returned to the condenser-boiler for reuse. Although high efficiencies were obtained by this cycle, difficult design and heat-transfer problems limited its development. During the 1930s several large plants were constructed, but for economic reasons the binary cycle was abandoned in favour of high-pressure steam cycles employing multiple reheat.

**4. Combination Steam- and Gas-Turbine Cycles.**—Another means of increasing the efficiency and capacity of steam power plants is the use of a combination gas-turbine and steam-turbine cycle. There are a number of possible combinations but in general the objective is to direct the hot exhaust gases from a gas turbine, while they still contain approximately 15% oxygen, through the furnace of the steam generator, thus reducing the amount of preheated air required for combustion of the fuel. An increase of about 5% in thermal efficiency is realized by this means. By the early 1960s a number of units of this type had been built, but more were expected to be installed as improvements were made.

**5. Industrial Steam Power Plants.**—There are a wide variety of industrial plants that generate their own electrical energy. Usually such plants require a great deal of steam, and it is economical to generate this at higher pressure and temperature in order to permit passage through a noncondensing turbine before otherwise making use of it. In this manner by-product power may be obtained at low cost. Automatic extraction turbines are available for this purpose. With these, variable quantities of steam can be extracted at one or more desired fixed pressures, regardless of the electrical load carried. In industrial plants exhaust steam is also often used for space-heating purposes.

**6. Theory.**—As may be inferred from fig. 15, the generation of power from steam is accomplished by a cycle of events involving the addition of heat in a boiler and the rejection of heat in a condenser. For the sake of simplicity in developing the theory one may start with the simple Rankine cycle, named after the gifted Scottish engineer and scientist W. J. M. Rankine (*q.v.;* 1820–72) of Glasgow University. Fig. 15 illustrates the essential components of the Rankine cycle, together with an idealized diagram of the various processes involved as they would appear on a Mollier chart.

Starting at the outlet of the condenser the water enters the boiler feed pump in the saturated liquid state with enthalpy $h_{f2}$ and is pumped into the boiler at the enthalpy represented by $h_3$. In the boiler sufficient heat is added to vaporize the water into steam and superheat it to the enthalpy represented by $h_1$ on the chart. From here the steam flows into the turbine, through which

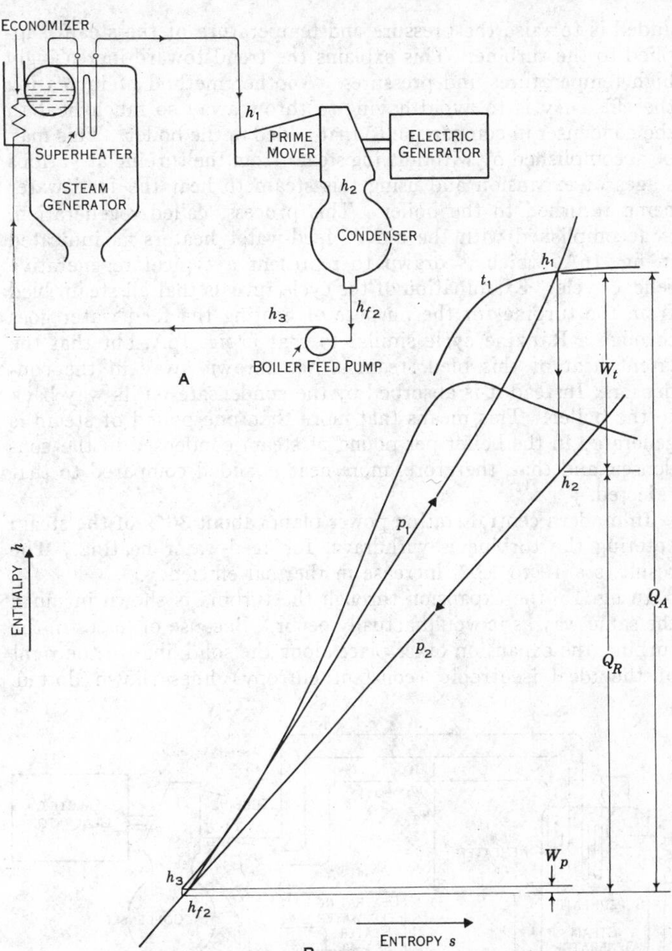


FIG. 15.—DIAGRAM AND MOLLIER CHART FOR AN IDEAL RANKINE CYCLE STEAM POWER PLANT

it expands to the enthalpy $h_2$ turning the rotor and electric generator. The steam then flows into the condenser, where it is converted into saturated liquid with an enthalpy $h_{f2}$. This is accomplished by transferring the latent heat of the steam to large quantities of circulating water flowing through the tubes of the condenser. From the condenser the water again enters the boiler feed pump to be returned to the boiler for generation into steam.

The thermal efficiency of any power plant cycle is equal to the net work performed divided by the thermal energy expended to perform that work. Since all energy must be accounted for, and also since energy is added only in the boiler,

$$\text{Thermal efficiency} = \eta_T = \frac{\text{net work performed}}{\text{heat added}} = \frac{\text{heat added} - \text{heat rejected}}{\text{heat added}} \quad (7)$$

Using the fact that heat added and heat rejected during steady-flow processes is equal to the change in enthalpy, one may write for the ideal Rankine cycle

$$\eta_{TR} = \frac{W_{\text{cycle}}}{Q_A} = \frac{W_t - W_p}{Q_A} = \frac{Q_A - Q_R}{Q_A} = \frac{(h_1 - h_2) - W_p}{(h_1 - h_{f2}) - W_p} \quad (8)$$

where for the cycle shown:

$\eta_{TR}$ = thermal efficiency of ideal Rankine cycle
$W_{\text{cycle}}$ = net work performed by the cycle, BTU per pound of steam
$W_t$ = work performed by the turbine, BTU per pound of steam
$W_p$ = work performed on the boiler feed water pump, BTU per pound of steam
$Q_A$ = heat added in the steam generator, BTU per pound of steam
$Q_R$ = heat rejected in the condenser, BTU per pound of steam
$h_n$ = enthalpy of the steam or water at the various sections indicated by subscripts, BTU per pound

Examination of equation (8) shows that the efficiency of the cycle can be increased by increasing the amount of heat added $Q_A$ relative to that rejected $Q_R$. One method of increasing the heat added is to raise the pressure and temperature of the steam supplied to the turbine. This explains the trend toward increasingly high temperatures and pressures. Another method of increasing the efficiency is to avoid having to throw away so much heat to the condenser in comparison to that added in the boiler. This may be accomplished by withdrawing steam from the turbine at various stages of expansion and using this steam to heat the feed water being returned to the boiler. This process, called regeneration, is accomplished with the aid of feed-water heaters as indicated in fig. 16A, which is drawn to represent a typical regenerative reheat cycle. Examination of the cycle reveals that all steam bled from the turbine for the purpose of heating the feed water goes through a Rankine cycle similar to that in fig. 16A, but that the latent heat of this bled steam is not thrown away in the condenser. Instead it is absorbed by the condensate on its way back to the boiler. This means that more than one pound of steam is generated in the boiler per pound of steam condensed in the condenser, and that, therefore, more heat is added compared to that rejected.

In modern central-station power plants about 30% of the steam entering the turbine is withdrawn for feed-water heating. The result is a 10 to 15% increase in thermal efficiency.

In fig. 16, the expansion through the turbine is shown in much the same way as it would actually occur. Because of losses in the turbine, the expansion takes place along the solid lines to the right of the ideal isentropic (constant entropy) lines shown dotted.

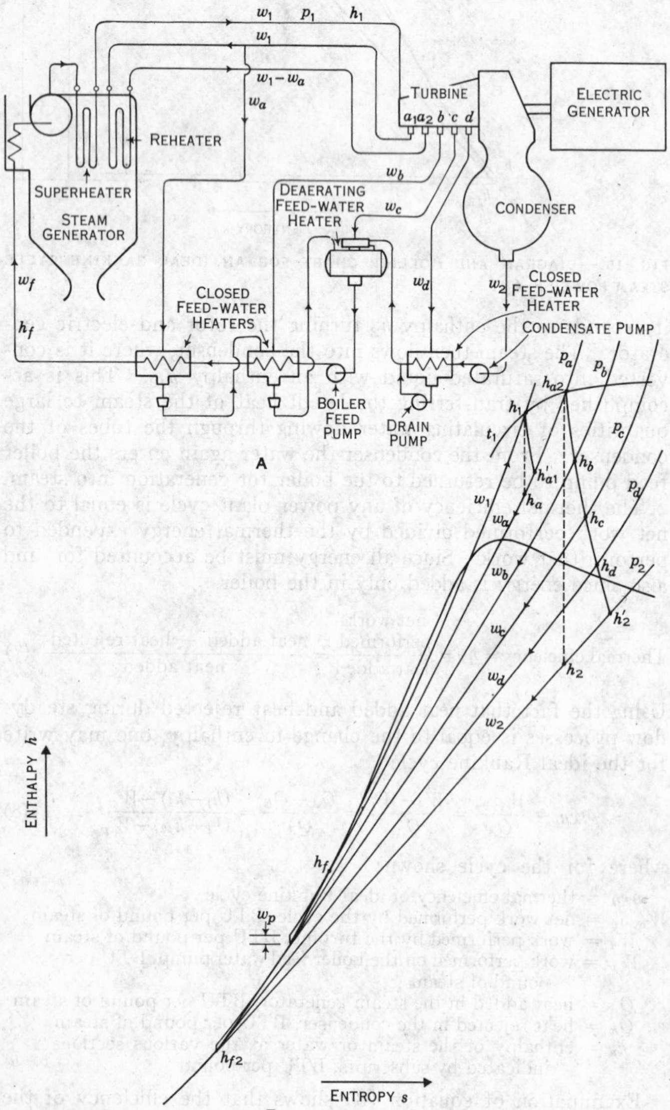

FIG. 16.—DIAGRAM AND MOLLIER CHART FOR A REHEAT-REGENERATIVE POWER PLANT CYCLE

Also one reheat is shown in which steam, after passing partway through the turbine, is returned to the boiler to be reheated before continuing its expansion through the remaining stages of the turbine.

From the diagram in fig. 16, and from the principle that work of expansion is equal to the weight of steam flowing times its change in enthalpy, the work performed by the steam in British thermal units per hour can be computed as follows:

$$W_{steam}=w_1(h_1-h'_{a1})+(w_1-w_a)(h_{a2}-h_b)+(w_1-w_a-w_b)(h_b-h_c)+(w_1-w_a-w_b-w_c)(h_c-h_d)+(w_1-w_a-w_b-w_c-w_d)(h_d-h'_2) \qquad (9)$$

where

$w_1$ = flow of steam to turbine, pounds per hour
$w_n$ = flow of steam from the various bleedpoints indicated by subscript $a$, $b$, $c$, and $d$, pounds per hour
$h_1$ = enthalpy of steam entering turbine, BTU per pound
$h'_{a1}$ = enthalpy of steam returned for reheat, BTU per pound
$h_{a2}$ = enthalpy of steam after reheat, BTU per pound
$h_n$ = enthalpy of steam flowing from the various bleedpoints indicated by subscript $a$, $b$, $c$, and $d$, BTU per pound
$h'_2$ = enthalpy of steam leaving turbine, BTU per pound

The net work of the power plant is obtained by subtracting the exhaust loss, mechanical loss, generator loss, and auxiliary power requirements of the plant, including pump work, from $W_{steam}$ (*see* TURBINE).

The heat added by the fuel is obtained by multiplying the steam flow through the boiler by its increase in enthalpy in the boiler, superheater, and reheater and dividing by the boiler efficiency. Thus,

$$Q=\frac{w_1(h_1-h_f)+(w_1-w_a)(h_{a2}-h'_{a1})}{\eta_{S+G}} \qquad (10)$$

where:

$h_f$ = enthalpy of boiler feed water entering the steam generator BTU per pound
$\eta_{S+G}$ = efficiency of steam generator, BTU per pound

The thermal efficiency of the regenerative-reheat power plant is therefore

$$\eta_{TP}=\frac{W_{plant}}{Q_A}=\frac{(W_{steam}-W_{ex}-W_M-W_G-W_{aux})\eta_{SG}}{w_1(h_1-h_f)+(w_1-w_a)(h_{a2}-h'_{a1})} \qquad (11)$$

where

$W_{ex}$ = exhaust loss, BTU per hour
$W_M$ = mechanical loss, BTU per hour
$W_G$ = generator loss, BTU per hour
$W_{aux}$ = auxiliary power including pump work, BTU per hour
$h_n$ = enthalpy at various points indicated by subscripts, BTU per pound
$\eta_{SG}$ = steam generator efficiency

Thermal efficiency of modern central-station power plants varies widely depending on steam conditions, number of feed-water heaters, and complexity. The range is from about 30% in the poorer stations to about 40% in the very best.

*See* also references under "Steam" in the Index.

BIBLIOGRAPHY.—H. L. Callendar, *Properties of Steam and Thermodynamic Theory of Turbines* (1920); J. H. Keenan and F. G. Keyes, *Thermodynamic Properties of Steam* (1936); G. S. Callendar and A. C. Egerton (eds.), *The 1939 Callendar Steam Tables*, 2nd ed. (1944); F. O. Ellenwood and C. O. Mackey, *Thermodynamic Charts*, 2nd ed. (1944); R. H. Thurston, *A History of the Growth of the Steam-Engine*, centennial ed. (1939); J. A. Ewing, *The Steam-Engine and Other Heat-Engines*, 4th ed. (1926); D. A. Wrangham, *Theory and Practice of Heat Engines*, 2nd ed. (1948); The Babcock and Wilcox Company, *Steam: Its Generation and Use* (1955); Combustion Engineering, Inc., *Combustion Engineering* (1951); O. Lyle, *Efficient Use of Steam* (1960); O. S. Lieberg, *High Temperature Water Systems*, 2nd ed. (1963); W. N. Barnard, F. O. Ellenwood, and C. F. Hirshfeld, *Heat Power Engineering*, vol. i, ii, and iii (1935); William H. Severns, H. E. Degler, and J. C. Miles, *Steam, Air, and Gas Power*, 5th ed. (1954); G. A. Gaffert, *Steam Power Stations*, 4th ed. (1952); J. K. Salisbury, *Steam Turbines and Their Cycles* (1950); F. T. Morse, *Power Plant Engineering and Design*, 2nd ed. (1942); P. J. Potter, *Power Plant Theory and Design* (1959); B. G. A. Skrotzki and W. A. Vopat, *Power Station Engineering and Economy* (1960); Alexander H. Zerban and E. P. Nye, *Power Plants*, 2nd ed. (1956).

(RD. A. BR.)

**STEAMSHIP:** *see* NAVAL ARCHITECTURE; SHIP.

**STEAMSHIP LINES:** *see* SHIPPING: *World Merchant Fleets.*

**STEARIC ACID** is one of the more important long-chain fatty acids (*see* CARBOXYLIC ACIDS) that occur in fats isolated from plants and animals. It is a predominant component of body fats; lard and tallow, for example, often contain up to 30% of stearic acid. Like other fatty acids, it does not occur in the free state but is normally found as an ester of glycerol (*i.e.*, as a glyceride) or as an ester of a long-chain alcohol. Tristearin is a typical example of a triglyceride; it is a triester of glycerol and stearic acid.

Stearic acid, $CH_3(CH_2)_{16}{\cdot}CO_2H$, is a colourless solid that exists in various crystalline forms of which that melting at 69.6° C is the most stable. It is a monocarboxylic acid and shows all the reactions typical of this class of organic compounds. Of chief importance are its metal salts and its esters.

Soaps are the sodium or potassium salts of long-chain carboxylic acids and are prepared by the alkaline hydrolysis of the glyceride components of natural fats. This process is often described as saponification. For the manufacture of soaps and edible fats, solid fats are preferable to liquids, and, since the compounds with lower melting points are unsaturated, hydrogenation of oils yields solid fats. This process is called hardening and is illustrated by the hydrogenation of the oil triolein (the triglyceride of oleic acid) to solid tristearin (melting point 71° C). *See* also OILS, FATS AND WAXES.

*See* K. S. Markley, *Fatty Acids: Their Chemistry, Properties, Production, and Uses,* 2nd ed., parts 1–3 (1960–64); A. E. Bailey, *Industrial Oil and Fat Products* (1945). (W. D. Os.)

**STEEL:** *see* ALLOYS; ARCHITECTURAL ENGINEERING; CONVERTER STEEL; HIGH-SPEED STEEL; IRON AND STEEL INDUSTRY; MANGANESE STEEL; MOLYBDENUM; NICKEL-CHROMIUM STEELS; NICKEL STEEL; NITRIDING; STAINLESS STEEL; STEELS, ALLOY; TOOL STEEL; WIRE; and other specific headings.

**STEEL CONSTRUCTION.** Steel fabrication of buildings and bridges has been a natural consequence of progress in the production of steel itself and of improved steel alloys. Even before the development of the Bessemer and open-hearth steelmaking processes in the latter half of the 19th century, which resulted in a rapidly expanding supply of cheap steel, cast and wrought iron had been used to a limited extent in bridge and building construction. As early as 1800 a technique had been developed for passing iron, heated to a plastic state, between rolls to form structural shapes. These shapes were small, however, and of a profile that limited their structural usefulness. It was not until the 1850s that rolled beams of wrought iron were used in floor construction, in the Cooper Union in New York City. Unlike the familiar I-beams of modern manufacture, these beams resembled in profile an inverted modern railroad rail. By the time structural steel became commercially available in the early 1880s, the basic structural shapes—I-beams, channels, and angles—had proved their adaptability to the builder's needs. When combined with plates of various widths and thicknesses, they could be fabricated into efficient members of any required size and strength, and these members could be joined together in the field, using hot-driven rivets.

**Steel-Framed Buildings.**—In 1889 the Eiffel Tower, designed as a latticed girder with a complete system of vertical diagonal bracing, was erected in Paris to a height of 984 ft. (1,056 ft. high from the base of the structure, including a 55-ft. television mast added later). Since it was an open steel-framework construction, the total wind pressure against it was much less than it would have been against the sides of an enclosed building of the same height. This tower was to remain the highest man-made structure for more than 40 years. During that time other systems of bracing for tall enclosed buildings were evolved, depending in part upon the use of diagonal bracing, which in effect formed upended cantilever trusses, and in part upon the bending stiffness of all the beams and columns, joined to one another by means of very rigid connections.

Use of the skeleton frame, with exterior curtain walls supported at each floor, released building construction from any height limitation due to the excessive thickness of masonry-bearing type walls. The most spectacular examples of this type of construction have been so-called skyscrapers, originally built to effectively utilize expensive urban real estate. (*See* ARCHITECTURE.) The Home Insurance Building, erected in Chicago in 1885 and torn down in 1931, has been generally acclaimed the forerunner of the modern skyscraper. It was the first multistoried building having masonry walls supported on a complete structural frame. The columns of the Home Insurance Building were cast iron. The first five floors were framed with wrought-iron beams, but the next five were framed in steel, which had only just become available and offered an attractive cost saving. In 1889 two more floors, framed in steel, were added. By mid-20th century hundreds of skeleton steel frame buildings higher than the Home Insurance Building had been erected in the United States.

The 102-story Empire State Building, which was completed in 1931 in New York City, exceeded the height of the Eiffel Tower by 266 ft. A 222-ft. television antenna mast, added in 1950, increased this height to 1,472 ft. This record height was exceeded in 1954, however, with the erection of a television antenna tower near Oklahoma City, Okla. Guyed with wire rope to provide lateral support, this structure rose 1,572 ft. above its ground-level foundations.

A number of interesting examples of steel dome construction can be cited. As early as 1894, for example, an exhibition building of spectacular clear span was constructed at Lyons, France. Its central portion consisted of a dome springing from a 361-ft.-diameter circle at ground level to an apex 180 ft. above ground. Encircling this large unobstructed area was a 131-ft. bay, having a roof that sloped down and away from the central dome. Another structure, the Dome of Discovery, constructed for the Festival of Britain in London (1951), utilized a steel tension ring 342 ft. in diameter, resting 48 ft. above the ground on steel supports battered outward slightly to form a 365-ft.-diameter circle at ground level. Both these structures were subsequently razed.

During the period from 1894 to 1951 the possibilities of steel dome construction, for enclosing large unencumbered areas suitable for assembly purposes, received scant attention. Since that time, however, a number of such structures have been erected. The record-breaking steel-framed roof enclosing the Harris County (Texas) Stadium, called the Astrodome (1965), provides a clear diameter of 642 ft. at its bottom tension ring. Covering over nine acres, it encloses a full-size playing field and seating area, with provision for air conditioning. The 400-ft. dome-shape roof over the Pittsburgh, Pa., Public Auditorium (1961) consists of six power-operated, retractable sections and two stationary sections, pie-shape in plan. The movable leaves are pivoted at the crown to an exterior supporting frame cantilevered out over the stationary portion of the roof. The bottom edge of these leaves is supported on wheels that travel on circumferential tracks. The sections are so constructed as to nest one inside of the next. The structural framework is covered by a stainless-steel sheath.

The aviation industry had been responsible for the construction of a number of very large buildings having wide areas free of supporting columns. Notable among these were the aircraft assembly building at Bristol, Eng., and the maintenance hangar at Kelly Air Force Base, San Antonio, Tex. The former, completed in 1948, provided three adjoining clear aisles 331 ft. wide and a clear height of 65 ft., serviced by overhead cranes of 12 tons' lifting capacity. Latticed box frames provided the necessary support for the roof and cranes. The maintenance hangar at Kelly Field covered a total area of approximately 23 ac., more than half of this in a single 300 × 2,000-ft. bay.

The Vehicle Assembly Building, erected for assembling space rockets at Cape Kennedy, Fla., is essentially a one-story structure 526 ft. high. Two 250-ton bridge cranes, spanning 150 ft. and located just under the roof, provide the means for lifting components from the ground floor and assembling them on a movable platform provided for transferring the completed rocket to its launching site.

**Steel Bridges.**—The first all-steel bridge, crossing the Missouri River at Glasgow, Mo., was erected in 1879, a century after the

Construction of the Vehicle Assembly Building on Merritt Island, near Cape Kennedy, Fla.: (left) 16-in.-diameter pilings being driven 150–170 ft. into bedrock; (above) the half-completed superstructure of steel girders; (below) aluminum and plastic panels being attached to the steel skeleton at its full height (526 ft.); (right) virtually completed building, the largest, by volume (129,000,000 cu.ft.), in the world

PHOTOS BY COURTESY OF UNITED STATES STEEL CORP.

first iron bridge had been constructed at Coalbrookdale, Eng. Since that time steel has been used in thousands of bridges, employing various structural systems (*e.g.*, suspension cables, cantilevers, and arches) to span great distances without intermediate support. The longest single span (4,260 ft.), that of the Verrazano-Narrows Bridge astride New York Harbor, which opened to traffic in 1964, exceeds by 60 ft. the main span of the Golden Gate Bridge (1937) in San Francisco, Calif. At least seven other suspension bridges have spans longer than any supported by other structural systems.

The two record-making 1,710-ft. spans of the Firth of Forth Bridge (Scot.), completed in 1890, each consist of a 350-ft.-long centre truss supported on 675-ft. cantilever arms. This cantilever-type construction was employed 28 years later to establish a new record with the 1,800-ft. main span of the Quebec Bridge in Canada. The earlier Firth of Forth Bridge was paralleled in 1964 by a suspension bridge having a 3,300-ft. centre span.

The Kill van Kull (Bayonne) Bridge in New York City, spanning 1,652 ft. between masonry piers, established a record as the longest single steel arch. Completed in 1931, it exceeded in length by only a few feet a similar structure spanning Sydney Harbour (Austr.), opened to traffic in 1932.

A bridge completed in Belgrade, Yugos., in 1957 contained the longest single-plate girder. Continuous for three spans, the load on its 856-ft. centre portion was largely counterbalanced by the weight of the 246-ft. end spans. This unusual span for a girder-type bridge was made possible by the use of a light deck construction consisting of stiffened steel plates covered by a relatively thin bituminous pavement, in lieu of a much heavier conventional structural concrete slab. This type of bridge deck, known as "orthotropic plate," was developed in Germany during the reconstruction period following World War II. Other outstanding examples of girder bridges include the Düsseldorf-Neuss continuous girder bridge with a 675-ft. centre span (1951), the Cologne-Mülheim suspension bridge with a 1,033-ft. centre span (1951), and the 1,200-ft. Port Mann arch bridge (1964) in Vancouver, B.C.

**Technological Advances.**—The use of welding made possible the introduction of lighter fabricated structural members. For example, open-web (latticed) steel joists were developed for use as floor beams and roof purlins in lieu of heavier rolled shapes. In Europe whole structures at mid-20th century utilized steel pipe and seamless tubing, welded together to form trusses, latticed columns and joists, and supplementary bracing. Welding was also used in the fabrication of heavier structural members and frames, frequently from flat plate. Neater connections being possible, exposed steelwork itself became a medium of architectural expression. High-strength bolts as a substitute for rivets in field connections meantime became popular in the United States.

With mass production techniques, steel floor and wall panels and roof decking came to play a major role in building construction. Cold-formed from light-gauge sheets, these products could span considerable distances with substantial saving in dead weight. Deeply corrugated for strength and stiffness, and backed up with a flat sheet, the cells of the panels thus formed were utilized as underfloor ducts for electrical wiring. Sandwichlike panels, consisting of one smooth and one ribbed or fluted sheet separated by a core of insulating material, were used extensively for the exterior walls of industrial buildings.

The facades of a number of modern office buildings consisted entirely of glass windows and stainless-steel panels bolted to the steel building frame. These panels, press-formed from light-gauge sheets to various designs and backed up with thermal insulation about four inches thick, were lighter, more durable, and less conductive of heat than older types of curtain wall construction. In one building alone the equivalent of 11 ac. of stainless-steel paneling was used in the exterior walls.

Approximately one-sixth of the world's steel production is used by the construction industry; only two-thirds of this amount, comprising those steel products required for structural purposes, comes within the category loosely referred to as steel construction. Of this amount, items fabricated from hot-rolled carbon steel structural shapes, bars, and plates (as for example, bridges, building frames, supports for industrial equipment, towers, and tanks) account for a larger tonnage of steel than all others combined.

Bibliography.—A. C. Bossom, *Building to the Skies: the Romance of the Skyscraper* (1934); J. F. Baker, *Steel Skeleton*, 2 vol. (1954–56); J. E. Lothers, *Design in Structural Steel*, 2nd ed. (1957); E. H. and C. N. Gaylord, *Design of Steel Structures* (1957); L. E. Grinter, *Design of Modern Steel Structures* (1941 and 1942); H. Sutherland and H. L. Bowman, *Structural Design* (1938); C. D. Williams and E. C. Harris, *Structural Design in Metals* (1949); L. Tall (ed.), *Structural Steel Design* (1964).

(T. R. H.)

**STEELE, SIR RICHARD** (1672–1729), Irish essayist, dramatist, and politician, who, with Joseph Addison (*q.v.*), wrote most of *The Tatler* and *The Spectator,* was born in Dublin, where he was baptized on March 12, 1672. His father died late in 1676, and his mother in the following year, but, under the guardianship of his uncle Henry Gascoigne, confidential secretary to the duke of Ormonde, he was sent to Charterhouse in 1684, and in 1689 to Christ Church, Oxford. At Charterhouse he met Addison, and this was the beginning of one of the most fruitful of all literary relationships, which lasted until political differences brought about an estrangement shortly before Addison's death in 1719. From Christ Church Steele went on to Merton in 1691 but left in 1692, without taking a degree, to join the army. He enlisted in the Life Guards, later transferring to the Coldstream Guards. He was commissioned in 1697 and promoted captain in 1699. In 1700 he was challenged to a duel by a fellow officer, Captain Kelly, and gravely wounded him; this incident inspired his hatred of dueling.

Steele's first major publication was a moralistic prose tract, *The Christian Hero* (1701), wherein he draws on his experiences of the "irregularity" of army life to advance the view that only the religious man is truly great. He was mocked for the contrast between his austere principles and his genially convivial practice, but he was unquestionably sincere, and this early work foreshadows much of his later writing. Aware of the jeers of his fellow officers, however, he wrote *The Funeral,* his first comedy, acted at Drury Lane in 1701 with "more than expected success." This was followed late in 1703 by *The Lying Lover,* one of the first sentimental comedies (*see* DRAMA: *Modern Drama: The Evolution of Middle-Class Drama*). With its sententious blank verse passages and priggish moralizing, it ran for only six nights, being, as Steele said, "damned for its piety"; but there is much of Steele in it: a protest against dueling, a regard for the qualities of "the fair sex," and a wry allusion to the gullible author's having been recently defrauded by an alchemist. Steele was, indeed, always ready to entertain moneymaking projects and later spent much time and energy on a scheme for transporting live fish in specially constructed boats.

Need for money dominated Steele's life: he found it easier to get than to keep, and actions for debt were always in the background, and often in the foreground, of his impulsively extravagant existence. His third play, *The Tender Husband* (1705), which Addison helped him to write, had some success, and in the next few years he secured various minor appointments, including that of a gentleman waiter to Prince George, and, more important, the office of gazetteer, editing a government-sponsored news-sheet at £300 a year. In 1705 he had married Margaret Stretch, a widow who owned land in Barbados; she died in 1706, leaving him what he estimated, overoptimistically, as an annual income of £850. In 1707 he married Mary Scurlock (d. 1718), the "Dear Prue" of his charming and lively correspondence. Of their four children only the eldest long survived her father.

The *Gazette* gave little opening for Steele's literary talents, and on April 12, 1709, he launched a thrice-weekly paper, *The Tatler.* This began a new chapter in the history of the periodical (*q.v.*). Steele wrote under the name "Isaac Bickerstaff," already made famous by Jonathan Swift (*q.v.*), and created the mixture of entertainment and instruction in manners and morals to be perfected in *The Spectator.* The essays were dated from different coffeehouses, so that Steele could effectively cover the interests of most of the fashionable and would-be fashionable world. Addison began to contribute with the 18th number and wrote about 46 papers in all, while some 36 were written by the two jointly; but the great bulk of the 271 issues were by Steele, and *The Tatler* enjoyed a prosperous run before it stopped, on Jan. 2, 1711. With the shift in power to the Tory Harley as chancellor of the exchequer, the Whig Steele had lost his gazetteership in October 1710 and came near to losing the post of commissioner of stamps, to which he had been appointed in the same year. During 1710 *The Tatler* had contained a good deal of political innuendo, some of it directed at Harley himself, and it may be that Harley brought pressure on Steele to discontinue the journal; certainly Addison seems not to have been consulted.

THE BETTMANN ARCHIVE

STEELE; PORTRAIT BY JONATHAN RICHARDSON, 1712

Whatever the cause of *The Tatler's* demise, its brilliant successor, appearing on March 1, 1711, was avowedly nonpolitical. *The Spectator* was a joint venture, and though Addison's contributions were perhaps more distinguished, Steele's was probably the more original and vivacious journalistic flair. He evolved many of the most successful ideas and characters, including Sir Roger de Coverley (*q.v.*), and his attractive, intimate style formed a perfect foil for Addison's more polished, erudite craftsmanship. Of the 555 daily numbers, up to Dec. 6, 1712, Steele wrote about 240.

He made many later ventures into periodical journalism, some purely political. The most notable were *The Guardian* (March 12–Oct. 1, 1713), with considerable assistance from Addison; *The Englishman* (Oct. 6, 1713–Feb. 11, 1714; July 11–Nov. 21, 1715); *The Lover* (Feb. 25–May 27, 1714), 40 of Steele's most attractive essays; and *The Reader, Town Talk,* and *The Plebeian,* all short lived but sometimes of considerable political importance. Steele became, indeed, the chief journalist of the Whigs in opposition, a writer of principle and integrity.

Many of his essays and pamphlets were collected in *Political Writings* (1715). These had stirred up enough storms to make his career far from smooth. He resigned as commissioner of stamps in 1713 and was elected member of Parliament for Stockbridge on Aug. 25; but after his pamphlets *The Importance of Dunkirk Consider'd* (1713)—following several *Guardian* papers calling on the Tories to honour the clause in the Treaty of Utrecht providing for demolition of Dunkirk—and *The Crisis,* defending the Hanoverian succession (1714), he was denounced in the Commons for seditious writings and expelled. Calmer weather followed with George I's accession, and Steele obtained various posts, most notable being that of a commissioner of Drury Lane Theatre (1714); shortly after this, he published his informative and dignified *Mr. Steele's Apology for Himself and His Writings.* In 1715 he was elected for Boroughbridge and knighted. In 1722 he changed constituencies and was elected for Wendover.

Steele's health was gradually undermined by his cheerful intemperance, and he was long plagued by gout. Nevertheless, he occupied himself conscientiously with politics and, more erratically, with the management of Drury Lane. One of his main contributions to its prosperity was his last and most successful comedy, *The Conscious Lovers* (1722); considered to be his best play, it is characteristic in its combination of vivacity and sentimentality, and its insistence on the value of the generous impulse.

In 1724 Steele retired to his wife's estate at Llangunnor in Wales and began to settle his debts. He suffered a paralytic stroke in 1726, and on Sept. 1, 1729, the genial and charming writer whose burly figure, brown face, and brilliant eyes had long been part of the London scene, died at Carmarthen.

BIBLIOGRAPHY.—*Editions: Dramatic Works* (1894), *The Tatler,* 4 vol. (1898–99), both ed. by G. A. Aitken; *The Spectator,* ed. by D. F. Bond (1962). A definitive edition of the complete works, by R. Blanchard, includes *The Christian Hero* (1932), *The Correspondence* (1941), *Tracts and Pamphlets* (1944), *Occasional Verse* (1952), *The Englishman* (1955), and *Periodical Journalism, 1714–16* (1959).

*Biography and Criticism: Lives* by G. A. Aitken (2 vol. 1889), and W. Connely (1934); G. S. Marr, *The Periodical Essayists of the 18th Century* (1923); E. Blunden, "Sir Richard Steele," *Times Literary Supplement* (Aug. 29, 1929); F. W. Bateson, *English Comic Drama, 1700–50* (1929); J. Loftis, *Steele at Drury Lane* (1952); A. R. Humphreys, *Steele, Addison and Their Periodical Essays* (1959); C. Winton, *Captain Steele: the Early Career of Richard Steele* (1964).

(R. P. C. M.)

**STEELS, ALLOY.** These steels generally cost more than the plain carbon types. Their importance stems from the fact that they have more to offer in terms of properties, chiefly higher hardness and strength within a part. This advantage helps to explain the growing popularity of these premium steels. Shipments by U.S. producers rose from 4,400,000 tons in 1960 to 7,000,000 tons by the end of the decade. Shipments of bars, by far the most popular alloy steel product, gained in excess of 33% during the same period. Technically, carbon content is the principal influence on hardness and strength in any steel, but alloying provides these properties to a desired depth within a part; and new properties, such as toughness and corrosion resistance, are available.

**Definition.**—Simply stated, alloy steels owe their enhanced properties to one or more special elements. In a more technical sense, the *Metals Handbook,* published by the American Society for Metals, defines an alloy steel as one "containing significant quantities of alloying elements (other than carbon and the commonly accepted amounts of manganese, silicon, sulfur and phosphorus) added to effect changes in the mechanical or physical properties." A more specific definition has been formulated by the American Iron and Steel Institute: "By common custom, steel is considered to be alloy steel when the maximum of the range given for the content of alloying elements exceeds one or more of the following limits: Manganese 1.65%; silicon 0.60%; copper 0.60%; or in which a definite range or a definite minimum quantity of any of the following elements is specified or required within the limits of the recognized field of constructional alloy steels: Aluminum, boron, chromium, up to 3.99%, cobalt, columbium, zirconium, or any other alloying element added to obtain a desired effect."

Steels that contain 4% or more of chromium are included in special types of alloys known as stainless and heat resistant steels, and they are discussed elsewhere (*see* STAINLESS STEEL). The other major groups of alloy steels to be covered here include: heat treatable constructional and automotive steels; high-strength low alloy steels; ultrahigh-strength steels, including maraging steels; alloy tool steels; and electrical (silicon) steels.

While it is difficult to draw a clear line of demarcation between alloy steels and other steels, formal definitions serve commercial interests for statistical and pricing purposes. The principal alloying elements are manganese, chromium, nickel, molybdenum, silicon, tungsten, and vanadium. Boron additions were being used increasingly in the late 1960s because in very small amounts (0.0005 to 0.005%) they enhance the ability to harden thick sections. Aluminum, columbium, copper, cobalt, titanium, and zirconium are also used in some alloy steels. The seven elements in the first group are by far the most important, and each element makes its own contribution to improving a specific property of steel. Fractional percentages of the alloying elements manganese and silicon also must be present in plain carbon steels.

**Production.**—Modern practices for producing alloy steels consist of far more than adding alloying metals to the liquid steel. The degree of refinement in production has been enhanced greatly with the adoption by steelmakers of vacuum melting, vacuum degassing, continuous casting, and carbon deoxidation in vacuum, which emphasize better control, greater uniformity, and result in steels virtually free from objectionable inclusions. Great strides are being made in nondestructive testing from the melt shop to the final inspection.

Before the steelmaker charges a single bucket of scrap or a ladle of hot metal into the alloy steel furnace, he generally has in mind "tailoring" the heat (batch) of steel by processing or composition to achieve a particular objective. More and more alloy steels are produced for special properties to enhance their behaviour in the later metalworking operations, including cold forming, welding, machining, and heat treatment. In fact, the steelmaker can provide most of the characteristics a fabricator could conceivably require. In other instances, aircraft landing gears for example, the emphasis may be on producing an alloy steel with the ultimate in cleanliness and impact strength.

**Historical Development.**—Michael Faraday, working with James Stodart, is credited with developing such commercial items as cutlery and razors from specifically prepared alloy steels, around 1820. He experimented with compositions containing nickel, chromium, and manganese, among others. Robert Mushet recognized tungsten as the essential element in air hardening tool steel (1871). Mushet's steel, containing about 7% tungsten, was rapidly adopted in machine shops. This was the precursor of modern, high-speed tool steels, which will be discussed in a subsequent section. Molybdenum, chemical cousin of tungsten, was unavailable until large U.S. deposits were developed in Colorado about 1918. In addition to being a substitute for tungsten, molybdenum is also an important element in fractional percentages in engineering alloy steels.

But the greatest advances were the discovery of manganese steel (1882) and silicon steel (1885) by Robert A. Hadfield. They ushered in the era of alloy steels. Manganese forms a very tough steel with the unusual property of increasing its hardness under repeated impact. Silicon steels assumed great importance in the electrical industry.

Chromium alloy steels were made commercially into hard grinding equipment and mining tools by Julius Baur, an American, in 1869, and they found their first structural use in arch members of the Eads Bridge (1874) across the Mississippi River at St. Louis, Mo. Chromium is now used in many steels for machine parts and high percentages (14 to 18%) impart corrosion and oxidation resistance (*see* STAINLESS STEEL).

Nickel, another common constituent of alloy steels, was first used by M. Marbeau in France in 1885; its properties were described in 1889 by James Riley. Nickel steel was adopted by the U.S. Navy for armour plate in 1891; it is said that in its first application in the mass-production industries armour plate was rolled into small bars for bicycle sprocket chains. This work with chromium and nickel in steels evolved into the realization that a combination of both elements in steel was superior to the use of only one. Nickel-chromium steels were made into projectiles that were effective in the Spanish-American War in 1898. Vanadium and chromium-vanadium steels were investigated in England by Arnold and J. Kent-Smith at the turn of the century; the latter, at Canton, O., in 1907 made the first alloy steel by the open-hearth process for the Ford Motor Company, which pioneered the use of alloy steels in mass production.

**Classification of Alloy Steels.**—The common alloying elements may be employed in various combinations and amounts to produce an infinite variety of alloy steels. Early in the 20th century a profusion of compositions appeared. Many were pioneered by the automobile makers. Commercial considerations of producers and consumers required a limitation of types. The Society of Automotive Engineers (SAE) led the way in 1911 by adopting chemical specifications for 7 carbon and 11 alloy steels. Since that time, the list of alloy steels has been extended greatly. In the late 1960s, 90 standard compositions were available. The American Iron and Steel Institute (AISI) also publishes a list of standard alloy steels that includes most of the SAE steels. The joint efforts of these groups in the standardization and simplification of thousands of compositions have been of great benefit to industry in the choice of alloy steels for various applications.

The classification of alloy steels by composition has been formalized by the AISI and SAE in a four-digit system of identification, with the exception of certain chromium containing steels for bearings that require five numbers. This numerical index partially describes the composition in percentage as shown below in the tabulation of the numerals for the various types of alloy steels.

| | |
|---|---|
| 13XX | manganese 1.75 |
| 40XX | molybdenum 0.20 or 0.25 |
| 41XX | chromium 0.50, 0.80, or 0.95; molybdenum 0.12, 0.20, or 0.30 |
| 43XX | nickel 1.83, chromium 0.50 or 0.80, molybdenum 0.25 |
| 44XX | molybdenum 0.53 |
| 46XX | nickel 0.85 or 1.83, molybdenum 0.20 or 0.25 |
| 47XX | nickel 1.05, chromium 0.45, molybdenum 0.20 or 0.35 |
| 48XX | nickel 3.50, molybdenum 0.25 |

| | |
|---|---|
| 50XX | chromium 0.40 |
| 51XX | chromium 0.80, 0.88, 0.93, 0.95, or 1 |
| 5XXXX | carbon 1.04, chromium 1.03 or 1.45 |
| 61XX | chromium 0.60 or 0.95, vanadium 0.13 or 0.15 minimum |
| 86XX | nickel 0.55, chromium 0.50, molybdenum 0.20 |
| 87XX | nickel 0.55, chromium 0.50, molybdenum 0.25 |
| 88XX | nickel 0.55, chromium 0.50, molybdenum 0.35 |
| 92XX | silicon 2 |
| 50BXX | chromium 0.28 or 0.50 |
| 51BXX | chromium 0.80 |
| 81BXX | nickel 0.30, chromium 0.45, molybdenum 0.12 |
| 94BXX | nickel 0.45, chromium 0.40, molybdenum 0.12 |

B denotes a steel containing boron.

The first digit indicates the type of steel. For example, a first digit of 5 is a chromium steel. For simple alloy steels, the second number usually indicates the percentage for the principal alloying element. The last two digits for a four-digit numeral and the last three digits for a five-digit numeral indicate the carbon content in "points" or hundredths of a percent. Thus, "5130" designates a chromium steel containing about 1% chromium (0.80 to 1.10%) and 0.30% carbon (0.28 to 0.33%).

A group of metallurgists working with Edgar C. Bain was influential in systematizing the information on alloy steels and in classifying the common alloying elements as to their basic functions in steel. These studies led to the practical conclusion that many of the alloy steels are interchangeable. It is now well established, however, that it is not realistic to attempt to correlate the mechanical properties of an alloy steel directly with the presence of alloying elements without considering the proportion of the element, the carbon content, and, above all, the heat treatment employed, as well as the final metallurgical structure that is achieved in the part made from the steel.

In essence, it would be misleading to say, without qualification, that any one element contributes such properties as hardness and toughness to steels without stating in what composition and after what heat treatment. An element does not simply by its presence contribute a property, as sugar imparts sweetness, without regard for the structure produced in the alloy under specific conditions of treatment.

**Hardenability of Alloy Steels.**—The highest mechanical properties of alloy steels are developed by heat treatment, that is, heating above the so-called critical point—a range of 725° to 825° C (1,335° to 1,515° F)—followed by quenching and tempering. Above the critical point, the crystal structure of iron (alpha ferrite) is transformed into a new one, gamma iron, which has far greater solubility for carbides. This high temperature solid solution of iron carbide (and alloy carbides) in gamma iron is called austenite. On slow cooling the reverse action takes place, and a fairly soft, ductile steel, called annealed, is reconstituted, except that the process may refine the grains that make up the metal structure. On very rapid cooling, as in quenching, austenite is trapped unchanged down to about 150° C (302° F), but then changes almost instantaneously to a hard needlelike structure called martensite, which appears to be alpha iron (ferrite) in which the iron carbide is dispersed in fine particles. This is the essence of the hardening action.

Plain carbon steels are said to have low hardenability. For example, if a two-inch diameter bar is quenched in cold water only the outer layers of steel are cooled fast enough to transform into martensite at low temperature. The inner core, cooling more slowly, is transformed at higher temperatures near the critical into a much softer structure, a mixture of laminated ferrite and carbide. The outer surface may be extremely hard, but the penetration of the hardness is low. To harden the bar more deeply, the cooling rate at the surface must be faster, so the interior of the bar will cool rapidly enough to avoid the high temperature transformation. Even the most drastic cooling, such as quenching in brines or vigorously agitated water, may be inadequate for through hardening.

All of the elements added to alloy steels (cobalt is an exception) both slow up the solution of carbides in the austenite on heating and also retard their precipitation on cooling. In practical terms, this means that alloy steels do not have to be cooled nearly so fast for the austenite to be trapped and transformed at about 150° C into hard martensite. Alloy steels thus have a higher hardenability. In the same quenching medium, an alloy steel bar will harden much more deeply than an equal-sized carbon steel bar of the same carbon content; or the alloy steel bar may be hardened in a milder (slower) quenching bath, such as oil, or even in air with less warpage and no danger of cracking. In the example of a steel containing 0.45% carbon, the addition of 1.25% nickel and 0.6% chromium doubles the hardenability.

Bain's classification of the relative effectiveness of alloys in respect to hardenability was: very strong, vanadium; strong, molybdenum and tungsten; moderate, chromium, manganese, and silicon; mild, copper, nickel, and phosphorus. Boron would now be placed at the top of the list. During World War II and the Korean War, boron was substituted for substantial quantities of nickel, chromium, and molybdenum in a group of alloy steels to conserve these elements, which are ordinarily used to increase hardenability. So-called boron-treated steels contain 0.0005 to 0.005% boron. This small amount is optimum for enhancing the hardenability of other alloying elements. Boron is most effective in low-carbon alloy steels; its action is greatly reduced as the carbon increases, and so it is not used in steels above 0.60% carbon.

When used in combinations, alloys may complement each other and produce greater benefits than they would if used singly in larger amounts. Thus, steels of the nickel, chromium, or molybdenum single alloy type are employed in smaller sections where through hardening and suitable mechanical properties can be realized. For parts with larger sections, the double and triple alloy types (nickel-chromium-molybdenum) are preferred because they harden deeper.

**Selection of Steels by Hardenability.**—Since there are many steels with standard and nonstandard analyses, the problems of selecting the right one for an application can be confusing if composition alone is the basis for comparison. The establishment of standard hardenability steels (H-steels) and hardenability bands by AISI and SAE committees offers a clear set of limits from which the user can calculate definite responses to heat treatment. The user is also assured that the steel he has selected will meet certain standard hardening and hardenability requirements.

The H-steel hardenability bands permit direct comparisons among various steels; and different steels can be grouped to meet hardenability requirements. This permits greater selectivity of steels to meet design and economic requirements, and also indicates to the engineer what steels are available in the higher or lower hardenability groupings if his part is under- or over-designed. Of all the factors affecting the selection of a steel for a part to be heat treated, hardenability is by far the single most important consideration. The depth to which a part is hardened not only affects the design and serviceability of the part but also influences the hardenability required and the cost of the part. As a general rule, hardening to 80% or more martensite at three-quarters the radius of the part is usually sufficient for automotive parts. This requirement applies to parts stressed in bending or torsion where the stress varies from a maximum at the surface to zero at the centre. For parts stressed uniformly in tension, such as fasteners, a general criterion is that parts quench out to a minimum hardness of Rockwell C 55 in the centre.

**Effects of Alloys in Tempering.**—The martensite structure that results from proper quenching is brittle; to achieve the engineering properties required for machine parts, it must be reheated or tempered. The purpose of tempering is to relieve the brittleness in the martensite structure and thus improve the degree of plasticity or toughness of the steel, which can be thought of as the ability to absorb rapid blows.

Improved toughness results from two effects of tempering. First, internal stresses set up during quenching are relieved; second, a structure of greater plasticity is developed in the steel due to crystallization or coalescence of iron and alloy carbides.

Alloying elements that increase hardenability assist in maintaining a lower level of internal stresses in quenched parts because they make it possible to achieve a martensitic structure with a less drastic cooling rate. Alloying elements, however, have a more significant influence on tempering, that of crystallization and coalescence of the carbides. The process is slowed up, which means that an alloy steel compared with a carbon steel may be reheated to a higher temperature or kept at temperature for a longer time and still retain its hardness. Evidently the sluggish diffusion of alloying elements trapped in solution in the freshly quenched martensite requires a higher temperature and a longer time before the complex carbides can reform, compared with the simple iron carbide that is present in plain carbon steels. Since the toughening from tempering is due largely to relieving the high internal stresses in freshly quenched steels, and since this stress relief is greater at higher temperatures or improves with length of time, it is evident that after proper heat treatment alloy steels are strong, hard, and unusually tough.

Toughness may be thought of as a desirable combination of hardness and ductility or plasticity. It is measured by a single-blow Charpy impact test. A 10-mm.-square bar, with a carefully machined V-notch on one side, is struck by a swinging hammer, and the energy for breaking the specimen is measured. Steels with various combinations of alloys respond differently to this test when they are quenched and tempered to the same hardness and strength level. For example, AISI type 5145 (0.45% C and 0.8% Cr) has 55 ft-lb. at 70° F (21° C) and 30 ft-lb. at −100° F (−73° C). AISI 4340 (0.4% C, 1.75% Ni, 0.8% Cr, and 0.25% Mo) has 70 ft-lb. at 70° F and 60 ft-lb. at −100° F. Both steels had equal hardness: 35 on the Rockwell C scale.

Such behaviour indicates why steels containing considerable alloys are preferred for applications at low temperatures and for shock-resisting parts such as aircraft landing gears and axle shafts for heavy automotive equipment. Generally speaking, the carbon steels have high transition temperatures, around 70° F (below which low impact strength is realized and brittle fracture may occur). Low alloy steels have a transition temperature of about −10° F. Higher alloy steels, such as AISI 4340, have a transition temperature of −100° to −200° F.

**Grain Refining.**—Certain elements added to steel have still another effect. They refine the grain structure by imparting a fine grain size and prevent grain coarsening at elevated temperatures used in heat treating. Steels containing vanadium show a fine structure, and the tendency for grains to grow in the heat treating range is minimized. Likewise, columbium (niobium), titanium, and zirconium are effective as grain-growth inhibitors.

Of all the alloying elements, aluminum is the most widely used for control of grain size. When added to a properly deoxidized steel, it apparently reacts with traces of oxygen and nitrogen and settles out as fine insoluble particles in the solidifying steel. These inclusions are effective obstructions to grain growth of the austenite in heat treatment. The advantage is that a fine-grained austenite, when quenched and tempered, has a desirable degree of toughness. Fine-grained steels are popular in the United States. They are especially useful for low-carbon alloy steels for carburizing. In the carburizing process, machined steel parts acquire a skin (called case) of high carbon content—for example, a case 0.05 in. deep is obtained in a five-hour exposure to a highly carbonaceous gas at 1,700° F (about 925° C). Even after such heating, the austenite remains so fine in grain size that the parts can be quenched directly from the carburizing heat to harden the high carbon case while the inner portion (core) remains fine grained and tough.

Aluminum is added to steels in amounts of about 1% to produce nitriding steels. A high surface hardness is obtained after treatment in an active nitrogen atmosphere at elevated temperature. The extremely high hardness of the nitrided case results from the formation of a hard aluminum nitride compound. The amount of aluminum in nitriding steels, however, is much higher than that used in alloy steels to maintain a fine austenitic grain size.

**Other Functions of Alloys.**—As has been noted, the principal function of alloying elements is to enhance the properties of steel through control of the structure, particularly in conjunction with heat treatments. Alloying elements increase the hardness of iron and thus are effective in increasing the strength of steel in the unhardened state, although the magnitude is small compared with that obtainable by changes in the dispersion of the carbide in the heat treating operation. This ferrite-strengthening effect of alloys is independent of their influence on microstructure and may be employed to increase the strength of steels that are not heat treated.

Each alloying element exerts its own effect in ferrite strengthening with phosphorus, silicon, manganese, and nickel being among the most effective, followed by molybdenum, vanadium, tungsten, and chromium in order of decreasing effectiveness. These strengthening elements are utilized to full advantage in the high-strength low alloy steels, discussed in a subsequent section, as is their ability to increase resistance to atmospheric corrosion, in which chromium, copper, and phosphorus are beneficial. Chromium in high percentages imparts extraordinary corrosion resistance to steels, and the stainless steels are based largely on this effect.

**Abrasion and Wear Resistance.**—Alloying elements employed in alloy tool steels form alloy carbides at heat treating temperatures that remain undissolved in the austenite. These hard carbides formed by tungsten, molybdenum, vanadium, titanium, and chromium thus increase the abrasion resistance of the steel. (See *Alloy Tool Steels,* below.)

Hadfield-cast manganese steel, discovered in 1882, is another class of abrasion resistant steels. The function of the alloying element, manganese, is to stabilize austenite to produce austenitic steels that harden on cold working. One characteristic of these commercial austenitic steels is that the austenite is not entirely stable. The small plastic movements in high manganese steel, associated with battering or attempted cutting, permit the martensitic reaction to occur in these restricted regions, causing intense hardness, which accounts for the wear resistance of these steels in rough service.

**Uses of Alloy Steels.**—Many factors must be considered in selecting or making a change in an alloy steel for a heat treated part whether it be for an automobile, truck, or aircraft. The effects of diverse factors must be balanced, including potential economies, the need for better properties, and possibilities of greater efficiency in production. As a consequence, long-term evaluation programs are needed to prove out a new material.

Even so, there was a general interest in the 1960s to reduce the alloy content or eliminate alloy steels in some applications, particularly in automotive parts, to reduce manufacturing costs. For example, medium carbon alloy steels were being replaced in some automotive applications by carbon-boron steels. Interest in the boron grades was sparked by hardenabilities comparable to those of alloy steels that cost much more. Each change must be carefully evaluated to ensure that product reliability is maintained. The usefulness of alloy steels is reflected by the facts that the tonnage produced increased steadily throughout the 1960s and their percentage of the total market also increased.

Because transmission gears need strength and fatigue resistance, auto and truckmakers usually employ forgings of alloy steels. In some instances, gears are machined from alloy steel bars or tubing. Most popular grades for transmission gears include SAE (or AISI) 5140, 5145, 8620, 5132, 4620, 1330, 4023, 4024, 4027, 8622, and 4820. Gears of medium carbon grades (0.30% C and over) have carbonitrided teeth; other gears are carburized. The machined gears are carburized by heating in contact with carbonaceous gases. One of the prime reasons for using alloy steels in gears is that the gear teeth are usually finish machined before heat treatment and the amount of distortion from heat treating must be held to a minimum. This means that the steel must have enough hardenability, achieved through alloying, to permit the slower cooling rates obtained from oil quenching. In carbonitriding a small amount of active nitrogen (as dissociated ammonia) is added to the carbonaceous atmosphere. Carbonitrided gears generally have a thinner case than carburized gears of lower carbon content.

The original conception of a gear tooth was that it should have a hard surface to resist wear and a tough centre or core to resist impact. After carburizing, steels low in carbon have an outer surface containing 0.9 to 1% carbon; and since surface hardness of the quenched gear depends on carbon, rather than on alloy content, gear teeth can be made file hard—that is, too hard to be nicked by a file whose hardness is Rockwell C 65. Experience has also shown that maximum resistance to abrasion is secured from such high-carbon cases on steel containing chromium or molybdenum carbides. In ring and pinion gears, the trend is to apply lower alloy steels.

Aircraft alloy steels are specially made to meet the exacting requirements specified by the industry for engine parts, airframes, and landing gears. In general, the nickel-chromium-molybdenum steels are the most widely used because their deep hardening characteristics assure satisfactory response to heat treatment and uniform properties in heavy sections. For airframes AISI series 4100 and 8600 are favoured because they are deep hardening with good welding characteristics. For landing gear forgings, steels of the AISI 4340 series with carbon in the 0.40% range have found wide application. AISI type 4340, also known as AMS (Aeronautical Material Specification) 6415, is used extensively. These steels can be heat treated to the ultrahigh-strength range (above 180,000 pounds per square inch [psi] yield strength) and are known as ultrahigh-strength steels.

**Ultrahigh-Strength Steels** are attractive because of their extremely high strength-to-density ratios, making it possible to save weight in components and structures of many types. Along with weight savings comes a variety of benefits including the opportunity to increase payloads, to reduce bulk, to decrease inertia in moving parts and structures, to reduce the cost of shipping components, and to decrease the cost of erecting large structures. In addition these steels are selected for numerous applications because of the great wear resistance they possess as a result of their high hardness and strength. Likewise, their extremely high compressive strength makes them outstandingly suited to a variety of tooling applications. In many instances, such as airframes, landing gears, and rocket motor cases, vitally important weight savings are brought about by specifying ultrahigh-strength steels. In other cases, these steels reduce the bulk of the component so that it will fit inside an envelope of fixed size. The reduced inertia that accompanies the decrease in weight is important in rotating or reciprocating mechanisms such as pumps, engines, actuators, and valves. In components of servomechanisms, their high hardness promotes resistance to wear.

Several types of high alloy steels were developed in the 1960s expressly for structural applications at ultrahigh-strength levels. One family comprises the high nickel maraging steels. Several 18% nickel variants within this family—which also contain substantial additions of cobalt, molybdenum, and titanium—are available in a wide variety of forms. These steels have a martensite structure as annealed, but because of their extra-low carbon and high nickel, the martensite is quite tough and ductile, and hence is amenable to forming, welding, and machining operations. A simple aging treatment at moderate temperatures on parts made of these steels brings about a tremendous increase in strength. Depending on composition, yield strengths between 180,000 and 350,000 psi can be attained on aging.

Another family of high alloy steels for ultrahigh-strength service is based on a 9% nickel, 4% cobalt composition. One grade with 0.25% carbon can be used at yield strengths up to 200,000 psi. With 0.45% carbon yield strength goes up to 250,000 psi. A steel containing 10% nickel with chromium, molybdenum, and cobalt has shown excellent toughness, weldability, and resistance to stress corrosion at yield strengths in the range of 180,000 to 200,000 psi.

Still another group of steels that has found application in the ultrahigh-strength structural field is the 5% chromium steels containing molybdenum and vanadium. These medium alloy steels, which can be heat treated by air cooling, are in essence aircraft quality versions of the 5% chromium steels used for hot work dies. Members of this group are for the most part proprietary and display considerable diversity of composition with reference to minor alloying elements.

**High-Strength Low Alloy Steels.**—The recognized yield strength (stress in pounds per square inch under which the metal extends with permanent set) of common structural carbon steels is 33,000 to 36,000 psi. The typical high-strength low alloy steels have yield strengths ranging from 45,000 to 65,000 psi, and common varieties of other types of high-strength steels go up to 100,000 psi. The latter, known in the trade as quenched and tempered constructional alloy steels, are represented by ten grades described in specifications developed by the American Society for Testing and Materials. Although not approaching the high-strength low alloy steels in tonnage production, these constructional alloy steels have provided the product designer with versatile materials for many applications. Special alloy steels containing 9% nickel have been developed for cryogenic service and are covered by specifications.

The method of specifying high-strength low alloy steels is in contrast to the usual method in which steels are classified on the basis of presence or absence of alloying elements, such as plain carbon or alloy and stainless. Because higher strength and other related characteristics can be realized by the addition of different combinations of alloying elements in relatively small quantities, high-strength low alloy steels may have different chemical compositions but each steel in the group must meet essentially the same minimum strength and other property requirements.

Since the introduction of Cor-Ten brand by United States Steel Corporation in 1933, the first of the present-day high-strength low alloy steels, many steel companies have developed their own grades, and many are on the market. Principal alloying elements in addition to carbon are manganese, phosphorus, silicon, copper, nickel, chromium, vanadium, columbium, molybdenum, and zirconium. The amount of each alloying element added is generally considerably less than 1%.

Copper in amounts up to about 0.35% is the most potent of the alloying elements in improving atmospheric corrosion resistance, another valuable property of many types of high-strength low alloy steels. This has led to the use of these steels in the bare condition for the exposed members of buildings and towers and in other exterior architectural applications to eliminate the cost of maintenance painting. Also, architects seem to like the rich, dark earthy colour that develops on the exposed steel. The protective film forms more rapidly in an industrial environment than it does in a rural area. Full weathering generally will require 18 months to 3 years. The improved corrosion resistance of high-strength low alloy steels and the adherent nature of the oxide film can reduce maintenance costs by making paint coatings more durable.

While there has been a growing use of high-strength low alloy steels in architectural applications, the original demand for them arose from the need for reducing the deadweight of transportation equipment, and this has been the largest field of application. Earliest uses were in construction of railroad freight and passenger cars, followed by applications in ore boats, tankers, earthmoving equipment, trucks, automobiles, and shipping containers. Bridge designers are giving more attention to reducing deadweight, particularly when spans are long. A reduction of weight in the centre through use of high-strength low alloy steels permits additional savings in the weight of supporting members.

**Electrical Steels.**—Around 1900 it was discovered that the addition of silicon substantially improved the magnetic (electrical) characteristics of steel. The property permitted the designer to improve the efficiency and reduce the size of electric motors and transformers. Steels used for transformer cores contain silicon up to 5% and have greatly increased electrical resistivity and, as annealed, high permeability. These properties result in greatly reduced core losses. Flat rolled electrical steel is produced in a wide variety of types and classes to meet the various combinations of magnetic and mechanical properties required for magnetic core materials needed in connection with the alternating current method of production, transmission, and use of electrical power.

Another example of alloy electrical steels is the magnet steel for permanent magnets. Here the outstanding property is the ability to retain magnetism. Cobalt, tungsten, and chromium are used to promote this characteristic.

**Alloy Tool Steels.**—The functions of the alloying elements in steels for cutting and forming tools are to increase hardenability; to form hard, wear-resistant alloy carbides; and to bear up under heat without softening as readily as plain carbon steel. As a class, tool steels are characterized by the fact that each grade has been designed for specific service conditions, although an AISI-SAE classification based on composition, heat treatment, mechanical properties, and specific applications has been developed. Excellent hardenability is desired for steels used for forging or hot-forming dies because they often must be hardened in large blocks. They must also be hard to resist wear and tough to withstand blows.

The tip of a lathe tool cutting at a high rate of speed is heated almost red hot by friction from the chip, yet it must retain useful hardness. It was pointed out earlier that Robert Mushet explored the properties of steels containing tungsten, but it remained for F. W. Taylor and M. White in America to discover (in about 1894) that if tungsten content is increased above the 7% of the old Mushet steel and if the quenching temperature is raised, a tool steel that remains hard even at dull red heat can be produced. This revolutionary product was called high-speed steel. Generally speaking, tungsten up to 18% and molybdenum, a useful substitute for tungsten at least in part (it can replace about twice its weight of tungsten), are ordinarily depended upon for retention of hardness when hot. Chromium and carbon assist in developing maximum hardness and wear resistance. Vanadium is the traditional element for refining the grain size, thus promoting shock resistance.

At the beginning of World War II the best-known and most universally used type was the so-called 18-4-1 (AISI-SAE T1 classification), which contained 18% tungsten, 4% chromium, 1.25% vanadium, and 0.70% carbon. The switch to molybdenum-bearing, high-speed steels was rapid during the early part of the war, and in recent years these steels have been further improved and refined. The advantages of both alloying elements are employed in a combination of 6.25% tungsten and 5% molybdenum, which imparts the same degree of red hardness as 18% tungsten. This is the popular 6-6-2 (AISI-SAE M2 classification), which, like the 18% tungsten grade, combines the most desirable red-hardness, hardenability, and wear resistance with suitable toughness for cutting tools.

*See* also references under "Steels, Alloy" in the Index.

BIBLIOGRAPHY.—Edgar C. Bain and Harold W. Paxton, *Alloying Elements in Steel* (1966); American Society for Metals, *Metals Handbook,* 8th ed., vol. 1 (1961), vol. 2 (1964), *Metal Progress Databook* (1968), *Metal Progress,* periodical (Aug. 1965, Oct. 1968, March 1969); Douglas Alan Fisher, *The Epic of Steel* (1963); American Iron and Steel Institute, *Steel Products Manual: Flat Rolled Electrical Steel* (1968); United States Steel Corp., *The Making, Shaping and Treating of Steel,* 8th ed. (1964); Robert F. Mehl, *A Brief History of the Science of Metals* (1948); Republic Steel Corp., *Republic Alloy Steels* (1961); G. A. Roberts, J. C. Hamaker, and A. R. Johnson, *Tool Steels* (1962). (AL. G. G.)

**STEEN, JAN HAVICKSZ** (1626–1679), after Rembrandt, the most varied and penetrating of the Dutch genre painters, was born at Leiden in 1626. His father was a brewer, and at various times Steen himself was a brewer and tavern keeper. He was a founder-member of the Leiden Guild of St. Luke in 1648. In 1649 he settled in The Hague and married Margareta van Goyen, daughter of the landscape painter. He moved to Delft in 1654 and to Haarlem in 1661. In 1670 he was back in Leiden; he married a second time in 1673. He was buried in Leiden, Feb. 3, 1679.

Steen's master was the Utrecht historical painter Nicolaus Knupfer, but there is little obvious influence of Knupfer even in his occasional history pieces, such as "Samson and Delilah" (Cologne) or the "Adoration of the Shepherds" (Rijksmuseum, Amsterdam). He is first and foremost a genre painter, heir to the "low life" tradition of Adriaen Brouwer and his school. In style and content he looks back on the one hand to the great early masters of genre, Hieronymus Bosch and Pieter Brueghel, and on the other adheres to the polished, colourful manner of his own generation, comparing favourably with Gerard Ter Borch and Gabriel Metsu in his delicacy of touch and his skill in rendering light and texture. However, his typical pictures are scenes of revelry, displaying a huge zest for living and a humour that ranges from subtlety to the crude or grotesque, or quieter scenes that yet pass a satirical comment on human character and behaviour, such as the numerous versions of "The Doctor's Visit." Often the coarse but engaging features of the painter himself grin familiarly at the spectator, inviting him to concur in this hilarious view of the world. The earthy jollity in Steen is balanced by an intellectual and literary element, with an extensive use of allegory, that is unique among the Dutch genre painters and gives a peculiar piquancy to his art.

*See* C. Hofstede de Groot, *Catalogue of Dutch Painters,* vol. i (1907); F. Schmidt-Degener and H. E. van Gelder, *Jan Steen,* Eng. trans. (1927); W. Martin, *Jan Steen* (1954). (R. E. W. J.)

**STEEPLECHASING:** *see* HORSE RACING AND BREEDING.

**STEEVENS, GEORGE** (1736–1800), English Shakespearean scholar, author of the first variorum edition, was born at Poplar on May 10, 1736, the son of a captain, later a director, of the East India company. He was educated at Eton and King's college, Cambridge, but left without taking a degree. He acquired a house on Hampstead Heath where he built up a great library, including over 30 early Shakespearean quartos and many Hogarth prints. Every morning he walked into London, visited his friend Isaac Reed, made a round of the booksellers and walked back to Hampstead. In 1766, when he was only 30, he published a reprint of 20 of the quarto editions of Shakespeare's plays, a notable achievement, especially at that time when the value of the quartos was not fully recognized. In 1773 he published a ten-volume edition of Johnson's *Shakespeare,* more fully annotated and including excerpts from other commentators. (Johnson's contributions to the edition were slight.) This therefore was an attempt at a variorum edition. In 1793, however, Steevens was persuaded by his jealousy of Edmund Malone to publish an edition of 15 volumes in which he used his wide knowledge of Elizabethan literature to offer many useful parallels from writers contemporary with Shakespeare. It is Isaac Reed's 1803 reissue of this edition, with additional notes left by Steevens, which is known as the first variorum edition.

Steevens was a learned man of an acrid and sometimes malignant humour. His practice of writing notes on obscene passages and expressions, which he signed with the names of clergymen he disliked, earned him the title of the Puck of commentators. He was one of the exposers of the Chatterton-Rowley and Ireland forgeries. He died at Hampstead on Jan. 22, 1800.

*See* D. Nichol Smith, *Shakespeare in the 18th Century* (1928).

**STEFAN, JOSEF** (1835–1893), Austrian physicist, who made original contributions to the kinetic theory of gases, hydrodynamics, and radiation, was born on March 24, 1835, at St. Peter near Klagenfurt and died on Jan. 7, 1893, in Vienna.

Stefan was educated in the University of Vienna, where he became doctor of philosophy in 1858, then *Privatdocent* in mathematical physics, in 1863 professor ordinarius of physics, and in 1866 director of the Physical Institute. He was a distinguished member of the Vienna Academy of Sciences, of which he was appointed secretary in 1875. Before Stefan's work, G. R. Kirchhoff had already described the perfect radiator as the "perfectly black body," namely, one that absorbed all the radiation that fell on it and reflected none, but emitted radiation of all wavelengths. Stefan showed empirically in 1879 that the radiation of such a body was proportional to the fourth power of its absolute temperature, a relationship since known as Stefan's Law or as the Stefan-Boltzmann Law after it had been deduced by L. Boltzmann in 1884 from thermodynamic considerations. Stefan's Law was one of the first important steps leading to the understanding of black-body radiation from which the quantum idea of radiation sprang (*see* further HEAT: *Radiation: Relation Between Radiation and Temperature*). (D. McK.)

**STEFANSSON, VILHJALMUR** (1879–1962), Arctic explorer, discovered large areas in the Canadian Arctic and became an authority on Eskimos. He was born on Nov. 3, 1879, at Arnes, Man., of Icelandic parents. He graduated from the University of Iowa and later studied theology and anthropology for three years at Harvard University. After two archaeological voyages to Iceland in 1904 and 1905, he turned to Arctic research, and in 1906–07 he visited the Canadian Arctic for the first time as ethnologist on an expedition to the Mackenzie River delta. The expedition ship, approaching from the west, was unable to penetrate the ice beyond Point Barrow, so Stefansson, who had traveled alone overland, never joined the expedition. Instead he spent a year living with the Eskimos, acquiring an intimate knowledge of their language and culture, and forming the belief, which he put into practice during his later travels, that Europeans could "live off the land" in the Arctic by following the pattern of Eskimo life. From 1908 to 1912 he and R. M. Anderson carried out ethnographical and zoological studies among the Mackenzie Eskimo and the Copper Eskimo of Coronation Gulf, including some groups hitherto unknown to Europeans.

He next led an expedition, sponsored by the Canadian government, spending five consecutive years (1913–18) north of the Arctic circle, exploring the western Canadian Arctic and discovering Borden, Brock, Meighen and Longheed islands. His knowledge of the Canadian Arctic gave rise to his profound belief in the potential economic importance of the area. In 1932 he became adviser on northern operations for Pan-American Airways. In World War II he served the United States government in an advisory capacity, surveyed defense conditions in Alaska, and prepared reports and manuals for the armed forces, becoming Arctic consultant to the Northern Studies program at Dartmouth College, Hanover, N.H., from 1947. He died in New Hampshire, Aug. 26, 1962. His principal publications are: *My Life with the Eskimo* (1913); *The Friendly Arctic* (1921); *The Northward Course of Empire* (1922); *The Adventure of Wrangel Island* (1925); *The Standardization of Error* (1928); *Unsolved Mysteries of the Arctic* (1939); *Greenland* (1942); *Arctic Manual* (1945); *Discovery* (1964). (L. M. Fs.)

**STEFFEN, ALBERT** (1884–1963), Swiss novelist and dramatist, was one of the leading writers of the anthroposophical movement founded by Rudolf Steiner (*q.v.*). Steffen was born at Murgenthal on Dec. 10, 1884. His early works were compassionate messages of alarm at the disastrous effects of modern technological civilization and secularized thought in human relations. Moved by these problems, he joined the anthroposophical movement in 1907, settling at its centre in Dornach, near Basel. (Steffen was later president of the Anthroposophical Society and was editor of its review, *Das Goetheanum.*) From that time his numerous writings became visions of a world permeated by metaphysical powers of good and evil, as revealed in old and esoteric European and Asiatic traditions. His novels include *Die Erneuerung des Bundes* (1913) and *Aus Georg Archibalds Lebenslauf* (1950); his plays, *Hieram und Salomo* (1927), *Das Todeserlebnis des Manes* (1934), and *Barrabas* (1949; Eng. trans., *Christ or Barrabas?,* 1950); and his essays, *Der Künstler zwischen Westen und Osten* (1925; Eng. trans., *The Artist Between West and East,* 1946). *Buch der Rückschau* (1939) is autobiographical. Steffen died at Dornach on July 13, 1963.

Bibliography.—A. von Sybel-Petersen, *A. Steffen* (1934); *Das A. Steffen-Buch,* ed. by P. Bühler (1944); F. Hiebel, *A. Steffen* (1960).
(A. Bx.)

**STEFFENS, HENRIK** (1773–1845), Danish philosopher and physicist, combined scientific ideas with German idealist metaphysics. He was born on May 2, 1773, at Stavanger, Nor., but spent his early years at Copenhagen, where he attended the university. He later studied at Kiel, Jena, and Berlin and by 1799 was an established figure in German literary and philosophical circles and on friendly terms with Schelling, Goethe, and Friedrich Schleiermacher. After publishing *Beiträge zur innern Naturgeschichte der Erde* (1801), he took up an academic career, beginning as a lecturer at Copenhagen in 1802 and becoming professor of mineralogy at Halle in 1804 and professor of physics at Breslau in 1811. Steffens spent almost all his adult life in Germany, which he regarded as his home, and was a fervent supporter of German nationalism. He fought with the Prussian Army against Napoleon in 1813 and 1814. Professor of physics at Berlin from 1832, he died there on Feb. 13, 1845.

Steffens did much sound scientific work as a physicist, but as a philosopher he was characterized by a fondness for using scientific fact as a basis for the construction of fanciful analogies and quite arbitrary metaphysical conclusions. His exposition of a philosophy of nature in *Grundzüge der philosophischen Naturwissenschaft* (1806) showed a typical combination of profound scientific knowledge and Schellingian speculation. He also wrote *Anthropologie,* 2 vol. (1824); an autobiography, *Was ich erlebte,* 10 vol. (1840–44); and some novels and poetry.

*See* I. Møller, *Henrik Steffens* (1948).

**STEFFENS, (JOSEPH) LINCOLN** (1866–1936), U.S. journalist, lecturer, and political philosopher, was a leading figure among the writers whom Theodore Roosevelt called muckrakers (*q.v.*), but his work was closer to documented sociological case study than mere sensational exposure. He was born in San Francisco, Calif., on April 6, 1866. After attending the University of California, he did graduate study with Wilhelm Wundt in Leipzig and with Jean Martin Charcot in Paris, which confirmed his basic positivist orientation. During nine years of New York newspaper work, Steffens discovered abundant evidence of corruption of politicians by businessmen seeking special privileges. In 1901 he became managing editor of *McClure's Magazine* and soon began to publish the influential articles later collected as *The Shame of the Cities* (1904). Many nationwide lecture tours won him recognition as an American Socrates. He raised rather than answered questions, jolting his audience by comic irony rather than moral indignation into awareness of the ethical paradox of private interest in public affairs. He revealed the shortcomings of the popular dogmas that connected economic success with moral worth and national progress with individual self-interest by showing that the Horatio Alger hero often won his position by corrupting the community—and himself.

Developments in Mexico and Russia turned Steffens' attention from reform to revolution. After a trip to Petrograd in 1917 he wrote a friend, "I have seen the future, and it works." His unorthodoxy lost him his American audience during the 1920s; he continued to study revolutionary politics in Europe and became something of a legendary character for the younger expatriates. After the great success of his *Autobiography* (1931), he supported many Communist activities but refused identification with any party or doctrine. He died on Aug. 9, 1936. His characteristic achievement, both as writer and as lecturer, was in persuading people to examine for themselves the character of contemporary civilization.

His *Letters* were edited by Ella Winter and G. Hicks, 2 vol. (1938). (R. D. H.)

**STEIERMARK** (Styria), a *Bundesland* (federal state) of Austria, borders on Yugoslavia, which lies to the south. Area 6,326 sq.mi. (16,384 sq.km.). Forming the southeastern part of Austria, the *Bundesland* shares in two of the country's main physical components, the Alps and the southeastern hill country. The principal regional division into Upper Steiermark and Lower Steiermark is based on this physical distinction. Upper Steiermark stretches in the north from the Limestone Alps to the eastern groups of the Central Alps and also embraces the valleys of the Salza, Upper Enns, Mur, and Mürz. Lower Steiermark is an upland and hill country consisting of: the middle Mur Valley with Graz "bay" in the centre; the Koralpe and Packalpe, which rise to just over 6,500 ft. (2,000 m.) in the west; and a hill country of uplifted Pliocene gravels, widely loam covered, with a number of volcanic necks in the east.

**History.**—The earliest traceable signs of man in the region belong to the Paleolithic Age (Dragon's Cave, near Mixnitz). In the Neolithic and Bronze ages human occupation spread over the lower part of the country, and some mining was done in the mountains. The country was eventually included in the Celtic kingdom of Noricum (*q.v.*), which was incorporated into the Roman Empire *c.* 15 B.C. After the collapse of Roman rule in the 5th century A.D., Germanic peoples overran the country, and in the 6th century it fell to the Avars (*q.v.*) and to their Slav subjects (Slovenes). After the breakup of the Avar dominion, the Slavs in the latter part of the 8th century were subjected by the Bavarians (*see* BAVARIA). With Bavaria, the country became part of the Frankish Empire. German colonization was intensified from 955 onward, and by *c.* 1300 Upper Steiermark was germanized. The southern countryside, however, remained predominantly Slav for several centuries.

The future Steiermark constituted the eastern part of the territory, which in 976 was detached from Bavaria to form the separate duchy of Carinthia (*q.v.*). Several of its northern countships, however, came in the 11th–12th centuries into the hands of the counts or margraves of the Traungau, whose main seat was at Styraburg, the modern Steyr (now in Oberösterreich); and in 1180 the whole area under this family was raised to the rank of a duchy (Steiermark or Styria) for Ottokar, the last member of the line. On his death the new duchy passed, in 1192, to the Babenberg duke of Austria, Leopold V (*see* BABENBERG). When the Babenberg family died out (1246), Steiermark was annexed by Bela IV of Hungary, but he had to cede the Traungau to Austria in 1254 and the rest of Steiermark to Otakar II of Bohemia in 1260. Otakar II in 1276 ceded his part of the country to the German King Rudolf I of the House of Habsburg (*q.v.*); and Rudolf in 1282 granted Austria (with the Traungau) and Steiermark jointly to his sons Albert I (the future German king) and Rudolf II. Thenceforward the history of Steiermark was merged with that of Austria (*see* AUSTRIA, EMPIRE OF), though from 1379 to 1439 and again from 1564 to 1619 it was not ruled directly by the senior branch of the House of Habsburg. The districts of Murau and Neumarkt (both west of Graz) and Cilli (Celje) were added to the duchy in the 15th century.

After World War I Austria in 1919 had to cede 2,329 sq.mi. (6,033 sq.km.) of southern Steiermark, including the towns of Marburg (Maribor), Cilli, and Pettau (Ptuj) to the new Kingdom of the Serbs, Croats, and Slovenes (later Yugoslavia). The rest of the country became a *Bundesland* of the Republic of Austria. On the *Anschluss,* or union of Austria and Germany (1938), Steiermark, apart from the Aussee district in the northwest but with the addition of the southern Burgenland, was constituted as a *Gau* (district) of the German *Reich;* and in 1941, during World War II, the territory lost in 1919 was restored to it. The boundaries of 1919 were reinstituted in 1945, when Steiermark again became a *Bundesland* of Austria.

**Population and Government.**—At the 1961 census the population was 1,137,865, with an overall density of just under 180 per sq.mi. (69 per sq.km.). Ethnically Steiermark is entirely German. The Slav heritage is represented only in place-names. About 90% of the inhabitants are Roman Catholic (included in the diocese of Seckau), and 6% are Protestant. The principal urban centres are: Graz (*q.v.*) (237,080), the capital and second town of Austria, Leoben (36,257), Kapfenberg (23,859), Bruck an der Mur (16,087), Knittelfeld (14,259), Eisenerz (12,435), Köflach (12,367), Mürzzuschlag (11,586), and Fohnsdorf (11,517). In the mountainous areas much ancient folklore, song, and dance are genuinely alive. The gray-green Steiermark suit is almost an Austrian national costume.

The *Bundesland* government consists of a governor and 8 members elected by, and responsible to, the provincial diet (*Landtag*), which has 56 members elected for five years by popular vote. The *Landtag* is a legislative body, but the acts it passes must be approved by the federal government. In the *Bundesrat* (federal upper house) Steiermark has seven votes. Administratively it is divided into 18 districts, including the city of Graz. Local government is in the hands of burgomasters and town and commune councils, which are elected for a five-year period.

**The Economy.**—Agriculture, which employs more than 40% of the working population, is important.

Steiermark's extractive industries are of prime importance. Most of Austria's iron ore is mined in the Erzberg. Brown coal is mined mainly at Fohnsdorf and Köflach, and magnesite in the Shale Alps. There is also a sizable production of graphite, talcum, gypsum, and common salt.

Heavy industry is concentrated in the Mur Valley below Fohnsdorf and in the Mürz Valley. Machine industries (including the production of motorcycles and railway rolling stock) and chemical, textile, leather, and food industries have been developed chiefly at Graz. Sawmills are numerous; the paper and cellulose industry is located largely in the Mur Valley between Leoben and Graz. Steiermark is self sufficient in electricity, which is generated in thermoelectric stations based on brown coal, as well as from waterpower derived from the Mur and other rivers.

*Communications.*—The most important routeway during the Middle Ages was the road from Italy via the Neumarkter Sattel (2,913 ft. [888 m.]), the westernmost crossing of the Central Alps below 3,281 ft. (1,000 m.), and then via the Semmering to Vienna. The main roads and railways followed the early routes. The Autobahn-Süd (projected) runs from Vienna through Steiermark to the Italian border via Graz and Klagenfurt. (K. A. S.)

**STEIN, SIR (MARK) AUREL** (1862–1943), Hungarian-British archaeologist, whose researches in central Asia revealed many aspects of that strategic region between eastern and western civilization, was born at Budapest, Hung., on Nov. 26, 1862, and became a British citizen in 1904. He was educated in Budapest and Dresden and at the universities of Vienna, Leipzig, and Tübingen; in Oxford and London (1884–87) Sir Henry Rawlinson influenced his studies in Oriental and classical archaeology and languages. In 1888 Stein went to India as principal of the Oriental College, Lahore, and registrar of the Punjab University. His friendship there with the Erasmian scholar P. S. Allen and Orientalist T. W. Arnold encouraged him in his geographical and archaeological research. In 1900 Stein published the *Chronicle of the Kings of Kashmir* and set out on the first of his central Asian expeditions, traveling to Khotan, north of the Kunlun Mountains. He went on four such expeditions between 1900 and 1930, tracing the caravan routes between China and the west and discovering the Cave of the Thousand Buddhas near Tun Huang.

As superintendent of the Indian Archaeological Survey (1910–29) Stein was interested especially in Greco-Buddhist remains and in tracing Alexander the Great's eastern campaigns; in 1926 he identified the site of Aornos at Pir-sar on the Indus River. He also investigated tells (ancient mounds) in Iran and Baluchistan to elucidate the relationships between the Mesopotamian and Indus civilizations. When political difficulties impeded work in Asia, Stein carried out two seasons of air photographic reconnaissance of the Roman frontier in Iraq (reported in the *Geographical Journal,* 1940). Stein had been created knight commander of the Indian Empire in 1912. He died at Kabul, Afg., on Oct. 26, 1943. His works include: *Ancient Khotan* (1907); *Serindia,* five volumes (1921); *Innermost Asia,* four volumes (1928); *On Alexander's Track to the Indus* (1929); *On Old Routes of Western Iran* (1940).

*See* C. M. Daugherty, *The Great Archaeologists* (1962). (J. M. WI.)

**STEIN, CHARLOTTE VON** (1742–1827), famous for her intimate friendship with Goethe (*q.v.*), was born at Weimar on Dec. 25, 1742, the eldest daughter of the *Hofmarschall* (master of ceremonies). When she was 15 she became lady-in-waiting to Duchess Anna Amalia, the mother of Karl August, the duke of Saxe-Weimar. In 1764 she married Freiherr Friedrich von Stein, master of the horse to the duke; they had seven children. Goethe, who moved to Weimar in 1775, was captivated by her and for more than ten years she was his constant companion and the inspiration of much of his poetry. On Goethe's return from Italy in 1788 this close relationship between them came to an end although their friendship was later renewed. Goethe's letters to Frau von Stein form one of the most interesting sections of his correspondence. She was also a friend of Schiller and his wife. Her husband died in 1793 and she continued to live at Weimar, where she died on Jan. 6, 1827.

BIBLIOGRAPHY.—Goethe's *Briefe an Frau von Stein aus den Jahren 1776–1820* was ed. by A. Schöll, 3 vol. (1848–51), 3rd ed. by J. Wahle (1899–1900); and also by J. Petersen (1923) and H. H. Borcherdt, 2nd ed. (1934). *See* also W. Bode, *Charlotte von Stein* (1910); L. Voss, *Goethes unsterbliche Freundin Charlotte von Stein* (1921); A. Nobel,

*Frau von Stein* (1939); M. Susman, *Deutung einer grossen Liebe, Goethe und Charlotte von Stein* (1951). (A. Gs.)

**STEIN, GERTRUDE** (1874–1946), expatriate U.S. author and one of the more colourful personalities of the post-World War I literary scene, was born in Allegheny, Pa., Feb. 3, 1874. She spent her infancy in Vienna and Paris and her girlhood in Oakland, Calif. At Radcliffe College, where she was a student from 1893 to 1897, she studied psychology under William James, and then attended Johns Hopkins Medical School from 1897 to 1902. Of independent means, she went abroad to live in 1903. For more than a generation her home in Paris at 27 rue de Fleurus was a centre for artists and writers. She was, in the words of one of her protégés, Bravig Ihms, a "vital, headstrong and cordial personality," with "an insatiable appetite for people." They came and went in an unending procession, year after year, some famous, some unknown, some to become famous later: Henri Matisse, Pablo Picasso, Juan Gris, Clive Bell, Wyndham Lewis, Carl Van Vechten, Sherwood Anderson, Ezra Pound, Ford Madox Ford, Ernest Hemingway, André Gide, John Reed, Elliot Paul, Jo Davidson, Paul Robeson, and scores of others.

CULVER PICTURES

GERTRUDE STEIN, PHOTOGRAPHED IN 1942

Despite her German-Jewish origin, Miss Stein continued living in Paris during World War II under Nazi occupation. She died in Paris July 27, 1946.

A literary "cubist," Gertrude Stein carried to extremes her weird, repetitious and seemingly nonsensical manipulation of words, one of her celebrated phrases being "Rose is a rose is a rose." "Widely ridiculed and seldom enjoyed," comments Edmund Wilson in a chapter about her in *Axel's Castle,* "she has yet played an important role in connection with other writers who have become popular." In *The Autobiography of Alice B. Toklas* (1933), Miss Stein, while ostensibly writing the life of her secretary and close companion since 1907, actually wrote her own. Alice Toklas, so the autobiography recounts, knew personally three geniuses in her lifetime: Picasso, Alfred North Whitehead, and Gertrude Stein.

Among Miss Stein's works are: *Three Lives* (1908); *Tender Buttons* (1915); *The Making of Americans* (1925); *Useful Knowledge* (1928); *Ten Portraits* (1930); *Lucy Church Amiably* (1930); *Before the Flowers of Friendship Faded Friendship Faded* (1931); *How to Write* (1931); *Operas and Plays* (1932); *Matisse, Picasso and Gertrude Stein* (1932); *Four Saints in Three Acts,* an opera libretto (1934); *Lectures in America* (1935); *Narration* (1936); *Picasso* (1938); *Ida* (1941); *Brewsie and Willie* (1946). Carl Van Vechten edited her *Last Operas and Plays* (1949).

BIBLIOGRAPHY.—D. Sutherland, *Gertrude Stein: a Biography of Her Work* (1951); H. R. Garvin, *Gertrude Stein: a Study of Her Theory and Practice* (1950); E. Sprigge, *Gertrude Stein: Her Life and Work* (1957).

**STEIN, KARL,** FREIHERR VOM UND ZUM (1757–1831), German statesman in the Prussian service, the sponsor of far-reaching reforms during the Napoleonic Wars, and a major benefactor of historical research. He was born at Nassau on Oct. 26, 1757, into a family of the knightly class, the son of a chamberlain in the service of the elector of Mainz. His ancestral tradition, as he himself declared, imbued him with "ideas of piety, patriotism, class and family honour, and the duty of devoting one's life to the community's needs and of acquiring the necessary proficiency for such purposes by diligence and effort." He grew up to feel a strong attachment to the old German *Reich* and to the imperial dynasty of the Habsburgs and a fervent German patriotism.

At the age of 16 Stein went to the school of law and political science at the University of Göttingen. From his reading there in early German history, in English literature and constitutional theory, and in the works of Montesquieu, he received impressions that were to be of significance for his later activity as a statesman. He then completed his training with experience in the institutional organs of the *Reich,* namely the Imperial Chamber at Wetzlar, the Imperial Court Council in Vienna, and the *Reichstag,* or Diet, of the empire at Regensburg. In 1780, however, he entered the Prussian government service.

**Service in Westphalia and the Ministry of 1804–07.**—Work in the direction of mining enterprises and in the provincial administration of Prussian Westphalia made Stein an expert in the practical detail of local government. In 1796 he was appointed head of all the Rhenish and Westphalian administrative districts; and in 1802–03 he was entrusted with the administrative execution of the merging of the secularized bishoprics of Münster and Paderborn into the Prussian state. On Oct. 27, 1804, he was summoned to Berlin to be minister for manufactures and excise; *i.e.,* for economic affairs. In this capacity he obtained an insight into the working of the central offices of the government, which moreover convinced him of the need for reform. Because of a momentary altercation with King Frederick William III (*q.v.*), who rejected his demands for a ministerial system free of interference from the king's personal cabinet, Stein was dismissed from office on Jan. 3, 1807, in the interval between the defeat of the Prussians by the French at Jena and Auerstädt (October 1806) and the Peace of Tilsit (July 1807; *see* NAPOLEONIC WARS).

**The Nassau Memorandum.**—Returning to his paternal house, Stein used his enforced leisure to compose, in April–June 1807, the so-called Nassau Memorandum (*Nassauer Denkschrift*). A comprehensive program for the reform of the Prussian state, this memorandum constitutes the best and most reliable account of Stein's ideas. His basic principle is that, for a healthy and efficient state, an organic relationship must be established between population and government and that citizens must be brought into responsible participation in the state's affairs. This view had long been developed, formulated, and modified in his mind through his preoccupation with the English system of self-government and through his objections to the theories of Montesquieu, of the Physiocratic School, and of the French Revolution; and experience had enriched and reinforced it. Seeking to give new life to the state from within, he hoped that the practice of self-government would generate "civic-mindedness" (*Bürgersinn*) and "community spirit" (*Gemeingeist*) in them, so that they would make its interests their own: a revived enthusiasm for "fatherland, independence, and national honour" should turn sources of energy, hitherto neglected or misapplied, into channels of positive activity.

**The Ministry of 1807–08.**—Under the Peace of Tilsit, which mutilated the Prussian state, Frederick William III had to dismiss his minister K. A. von Hardenberg (*q.v.*) at Napoleon's behest. He then invited Stein to be his chief minister, on Napoleon's recommendation. Stein arrived at Memel on Sept. 30, 1807, and after interviews with the king his new appointment was confirmed (Oct. 4). Confronted with the extraordinary situation of Prussia, the single-minded, uncompromising, and self-confident Stein saw the opportunity for fundamental reform. The old system of the state was quite obviously discredited; even the otherwise irresolute king could see that it was high time to put Prussia on a more up-to-date footing. Furthermore, Napoleon's demands on Prussia themselves necessitated incisive measures affecting the internal system. Last but not least, some of the liberally inclined members of the bureaucracy, inspired partly by Adam Smith, partly by Immanuel Kant, and partly by French Revolutionary ideas, were ready to collaborate with Stein.

Thus, from the earliest days of his tenure of office, Stein could launch his reform. On Oct. 9, 1807, a law was published "concerning the Emancipated Possession and the Free Use of Landed Property as well as the Personal Relationships of the Inhabitants," which freed the peasants from servitude. Though it did not furnish a satisfactory solution to a number of problems (foremost among them being that of the gradual transfer of economically exploited land to peasant ownership), this October Edict was a decisive step in the conversion of Prussia to civil liberty and to equality before the law. No less revolutionary were the economic implications: land, which nobles had been forbidden to sell to nonnobles, could henceforth be bought and sold freely, and men were free to follow the vocation of their own choosing.

Stein's Municipal Ordinance (*Städteordnung*) of Nov. 19, 1808, was of lasting importance. It introduced self-government for the urban communes, created the distinction between the salaried executive officials (mayor and magistrate) and the town councils, and so enabled the towns to deal with their local affairs largely through their own citizenry. Even so, the greater towns were put under the supervision of a police president directly responsible to the minister of the interior. Stein's ordinance pointed the way to the development of municipal life throughout Germany.

Stein effectively modernized the structure of the Prussian government as a whole. The irresponsible advisers of the absolute king, namely the so-called cabinet councilors, who had hitherto formed a sort of secret government behind the scenes, were discarded; and so also was the "General Directory," which had been set up as the central authority in Frederick William I's reign (1713–40). In its place Stein established departmental ministries (foreign affairs, internal affairs, finance, justice, and war) with unified competence for the whole Prussian territory. On the same principle he organized the activities of the intermediate administrations or *Regierungen* and created the post of *Oberpräsident,* or official head of a whole province, directly responsible for it to the central government.

Stein pursued his many-sided tasks with passionate determination, but much of his plan remained unexecuted. His schemes for agrarian and economic reform were taken up by Hardenberg from 1810 onward; but the latter applied them in a spirit more akin to that of the Enlightenment than to Stein's conservative sort of liberalism and without Stein's educative, ethicopolitical concern.

**Exile, and the War of Liberation.**—In August 1808 a letter in which Stein indiscreetly referred to the likelihood of war against France was intercepted by Napoleon's agents; and on Nov. 24, yielding to French pressure, Frederick William dismissed him from office. Next, when Napoleon had declared him a public enemy (Dec. 16), Stein had to take refuge on Austrian territory. In May 1812 he was summoned to the court of the Russian emperor Alexander I (*q.v.*), to be one of his political advisers. In the following winter, on the collapse of Napoleon's invasion (*see* again NAPOLEONIC WARS), he urged the pursuit of the retreating French Army beyond the Russian frontiers; and early in 1813 he not only helped to organize the raising of troops in East Prussia but also negotiated the Russo-Prussian Treaty of Kalisz, the formal signal for Prussia's rising against Napoleon. He used his moral authority, during the War of Liberation and the Congress of Vienna, to work for a political union of the German states.

**Monumenta Germaniae Historica.**—In 1816 Stein retired to his country property of Kappenberg in Westphalia. Even in his old age his energy did not desert him. German historical science, in fact, owes to Stein's efforts its most important enterprise of publishing. The Gesellschaft für ältere deutsche Geschichtskunde ("Society for Earlier German History") was founded on Jan. 20, 1819, at his house in Frankfurt am Main, with him as its head and its coordinating force. Thus the publication of the great documentary series *Monumenta Germaniae Historica,* which began in 1826, became the particular occupation of Stein's last years. As he himself said, he called the *Monumenta* into being "in order to give life to the savour of German history, to facilitate the study of its foundations, and thereby to contribute to the preservation of love of the common fatherland."

**Conclusion.**—Respected as marshal of the provincial Diet of the Westphalian Estates (from 1826), and honoured both as a landowner and as a family man, Stein died on June 29, 1831. He had been the greatest statesman concerned with Prussia's internal affairs since Frederick William I. His achievement consisted essentially in having so mitigated the authoritarian character of an absolute state as to introduce elements of liberalism and of constitutionalism. He had also been a political educator of the German people.

An edition of Stein's correspondence, memoranda, and notes, by E. Botzenhart, appeared in 1931–42, in eight volumes; a new edition of his letters and official writings, also by Botzenhart, began to appear in 1957. Other governmental and administrative documents of Stein's are edited by G. Winter, *Die Reorganisation des Preussischen Staates unter Stein und Hardenberg,* volume 1 (1931). There is an edition of Stein's autobiography by K. von Raumer (1955).

BIBLIOGRAPHY.—E. M. Arndt, *Meine Wanderungen und Wandelungen mit dem Reichsfreiherrn . . . vom Stein* (1858; new ed. by W. Steffens, 1957); M. Lehmann, *Freiherr vom Stein,* 3 vol. (1902–05); G. Ritter, *Stein, eine politische Biographie,* 2 vol. (1931; 3rd ed., 1 vol., 1958); F. Schnabel, *Freiherr vom Stein* (1931). Works in English are: Sir J. R. Seeley, *Life and Times of Stein* (1879); G. S. Ford, *Stein and the Era of Reform in Prussia, 1807–15* (1922); C. de Grunwald, *Baron Stein, Enemy of Napoleon* (1936). (E. W. Z.)

**STEINBECK, JOHN ERNST** (1902–1968), U.S. writer, who achieved fame in the 1930s for his powerful novels about agricultural workers in California and who received the Nobel Prize for Literature in 1962, was born in Salinas, Calif., on Feb. 27, 1902. He attended Stanford University intermittently between 1920 and 1926 but did not take a degree. His early novels, *Cup of Gold* (1929), *The Pastures of Heaven* (1932), and *To a God Unknown* (1933), were relatively unknown until *Tortilla Flat* (1935) brought him popularity. *In Dubious Battle* (1936) remains one of the best strike novels in the English language. *Of Mice and Men* (1937), a novelette about the strange, complex bond between two migrant labourers, was adapted for the stage and received the Drama Critics Circle award. His Pulitzer Prize winning novel, *The Grapes of Wrath* (1939), about the migration of a dispossessed family from the Oklahoma dust bowl to California and their consequent exploitation by a ruthless system of agricultural economics, remains his best-known work. The furor occasioned by this novel's realistic picture of migrant workers and what the public assumed to be its political and economic theories became a colourful national event.

ERICH HARTMANN—MAGNUM

JOHN STEINBECK, PHOTOGRAPHED IN 1962

During World War II Steinbeck wrote some effective pieces of propaganda, among them *The Moon Is Down* (1942) and *Bombs Away* (1942), and he also served as war correspondent for the *New York Herald Tribune.* His immediate postwar work—*Cannery Row* (1945), *The Pearl* (1945, 1947), *The Wayward Bus* (1947)—reflected a bitterness against the greedy, rapacious elements of society that had made the horrors of war possible. In *Burning Bright* (1950) and *East of Eden* (1952) Steinbeck turned away from the naturalistic preoccupations and techniques of the 1930s and asserted that all men are brothers, keepers of one another, and that each man has the power to choose between good and evil. His later books, including *Sweet Thursday* (1954), *The Short Reign of Pippin IV* (1957), *The Winter of Our Discontent* (1961), and *Travels With Charley* (1962), are comparatively slight works of entertainment and journalism, widely popular in their appeal. He died in New York City on Dec. 20, 1968.

Steinbeck's early reputation as a proletarian, naturalistic writer of sociological penetration, and his constant experimentation with materials and techniques, tended to obscure other facets of his writing, but under subsequent scrutiny much of his work has revealed itself rich in symbolic structures and mythopoeic qualities.

Bibliography.—E. W. Tedlock and C. V. Wicker (eds.), *Steinbeck and His Critics* (1957); Peter Lisca, *The Wide World of John Steinbeck* (1958); Warren French, *John Steinbeck* (1961); F. W. Watt, *Steinbeck* (1962); Joseph Fontenrose, *John Steinbeck* (1963). (Pe. L.)

**STEINER, JAKOB** (1796–1863), Swiss mathematician, one of the founders of modern synthetic geometry, was born at Utzenstorf, Bern, on March 18, 1796. He grew up without schooling; only at 14 did he learn to write. Against the wish of his parents, at 18 he went to the Pestalozzi school at Yverdon where his extraordinary geometric intuition was discovered. Later he went to Heidelberg and Berlin to study, supporting himself precariously as a tutor. The founding of August Crelle's *Journal* (1826) gave him an opportunity to publish his geometric discoveries. In 1832 he received an honorary doctorate from the University in Königsberg, and in 1834 was appointed extraordinary professor at the university in Berlin, a post he held until his death on April 1, 1863, in Bern (*see* Geometry: *Projective Geometry*).

Steiner was one of the great developers of projective geometry, and many of the basic concepts and results in this field are due to him. His writings were collected as *Gesammelte Werke,* 2 vol. (1881–82).

*See* J. H. Graf, *Der Mathematiker Jakob Steiner* (1897); L. Kollros, *Jakob Steiner* (1947). (O. Oe.)

**STEINER, RUDOLF** (1861–1925), Austrian philosopher, scientist, and artist, who formulated the philosophic theory known as anthroposophy, was born on Feb. 27, 1861, at Kraljevic, Aus., the son of a railway stationmaster. After an education, supplemented by much self-education, completed at the Technische Hochschule in Vienna, he edited an edition of Goethe's scientific writings, and from 1889 to 1896 worked on the standard edition of Goethe's works at Weimar. During this period he wrote *Truth and Science,* which secured his Ph.D., and his best-known philosophical work, *Die Philosophie der Freiheit* (1894). He then moved to Berlin where he was successively editor of the *Magazin für Literatur* and lecturer in a workingmen's college. Meanwhile he was developing a faculty for spiritual perception independent of the senses. The result of these researches, which he called anthroposophy and described as "knowledge produced by the higher self in man," brought him in 1902 into connection with the Theosophical Society (*see* Theosophy), but he found himself out of sympathy with its subsequent policy, and founded the independent Anthroposophical Society in 1912. Anthroposophy postulates the existence of a spiritual world comprehensible to pure thinking but fully accessible only to the higher faculties of knowledge latent in every man. Historically, Steiner regarded man as having originally participated in the spiritual processes of the world through a dreamlike consciousness out of which the more limited but awake consciousness of today has crystallized. He claimed that an enhanced consciousness can again achieve perception of spiritual worlds. In 1913 Steiner began to build the first *Goetheanum* at Dornach, near Basel, Switz., as a "school of spiritual science." This was burned in 1922, but Steiner immediately designed another, of molded concrete, which became the centre of the Anthroposophical Society. He died there on March 30, 1925.

Activities derived from Steiner's work include: the Waldorf School movement, by the late 1950s comprising some 60 schools and 25,000 children in Europe and America; homes and schools for defective and maladjusted children; a therapeutic movement with a central clinic at Arlesheim, Switz.; the biodynamic method of farming and gardening; centres for scientific and mathematical research; eurythmy, an art of movement to speech and music; and schools of drama, speech, painting, sculpture, and architecture. After World War I Steiner proposed a threefold organization of society as a solution of political, social, and economic questions.

Bibliography.—Of Steiner's numerous published works, which included lecture courses on man's relation to the earth and the universe, eurythmy, education, spiritual science, architecture, economics, and studies in the Gospels and Genesis, the following are the most important. Dates and titles are of the latest English edition; the original date of publication is given in brackets. *The Philosophy of Spiritual Activity* (1949 [1894]); *Goethe's Conception of the World* (1928 [1897]); *Theosophy* (1955 [1904]); *Occult Science: an Outline* (1950 [1913]); *Knowledge of the Higher Worlds and Its Attainment* (1932 [1909]); *The Threefold Commonwealth* (1920); *Story of My Life* (1924).

*See* also A. P. Shepherd, *A Scientist of the Invisible* (1954); E. Lehrs, *Man or Matter* (1951); C. Waterman, *The Three Spheres of Society* (1946); H. Poppelbaum, *Man and Animal* (1951); G. Wachsmuth, *Rudolf Steiners Erdenleben und Wirken* (1951), Eng. trans. (1955). (A. C. Hd.)

**STEINMETZ, CHARLES PROTEUS** (1865–1923), U.S. electrical engineer, one of the outstanding electrical geniuses of the United States, was born at Breslau, Ger., April 9, 1865. He was educated at Breslau, Zürich, and Berlin, specializing in mathematics, electrical engineering, and chemistry. His activities as a Socialist led him into difficulties with the authorities, and, after a short sojourn in other countries, he emigrated in 1889 to the United States and found work with the Osterheid and Eickemeyer factory at Yonkers, N.Y. In 1893 when that factory was absorbed by the General Electric Co., Schenectady, N.Y., he was given an appointment as consulting engineer. His knowledge won him speedy promotion. After 1902 he served also as professor of electrical engineering at Union College, Schenectady, N.Y. Steinmetz regarded his three greatest contributions to electrical science to be: (1) his investigations on magnetism, resulting in his discovery of the law of hysteresis, which enabled losses of electric power due to magnetism to be accurately forecast before starting the construction of motors, generators, transformers, and other electrical apparatus employing iron; (2) the development of his symbolic method of calculating alternating-current phenomena, which simplified an extremely complicated field, understood by few, so that the average engineer could work with alternating current, an accomplishment which was largely responsible for the rapid progress made in the commercial introduction of alternating-current apparatus; (3) his investigation of lightning phenomena, which resulted in his theory of traveling waves and opened the way for his development of lightning arresters to protect high-power transmission lines. Though primarily a mathematical genius and a student of theory, Steinmetz had about 200 patents to his credit, including improvements on generators, motors, transformers, in electrochemical operations, and the invention of the induction regulator, the method of phase transformation, and the metallic electrode arc lamp. He was the author of a number of standard textbooks, in addition to a large number of scientific papers.

THE GRANGER COLLECTION
STEINMETZ

Steinmetz died at Schenectady, N.Y., Oct. 26, 1923.

*See* J. W. Hammond, *Charles Proteus Steinmetz* (1924); J. N. Leonard, *Loki; the Life of Charles Proteus Steinmetz* (1929).

**STELLENBOSCH,** a town of Cape of Good Hope Province, Republic of South Africa, lies beside the Eerste River, 31 mi. (50 km.) E of Cape Town. Pop. (1960) 22,333, of whom 10,738 are white. Stellenbosch is attractively laid out: it has a number of stately houses dating from the 17th and 18th centuries, its streets are lined with oak trees, and there are numerous gardens and parks. It is generally regarded as one of the major centres of Afrikaans culture and learning, and among its educational institutions are the University of Stellenbosch, a training college, a theological seminary, research laboratories, and many schools. Stellenbosch is in the centre of a fertile farming area, and its chief industries are wine making, fruit production, and sawmilling. After Cape Town it is the oldest town in South Africa, founded in 1679 and named after the Dutch governor of the Cape, Simon van der Stel. (V. C. R. D.)

**STEM,** along with the root and leaf, is a characteristic vegetative organ of vascular plants (Tracheophyta; *q.v.*). Popularly, the stem is the stalk of a plant or the secondary limb of a tree;

botanically, it is the plant axis that bears the leaves. The stem conducts water, minerals, and food through vessels (xylem and phloem) and often serves as an organ of storage; green stems, like the green leaves they support, manufacture food for the plant (*see* PHOTOSYNTHESIS).

In most plants the stem is an obvious and dominant aerial shoot, but in some it may be considerably modified, resembling other plant parts. Plants with a distinct stem are caulescent; those with an inconspicuous or buried stem are acaulescent, as the primrose, cowslip, and dandelion.

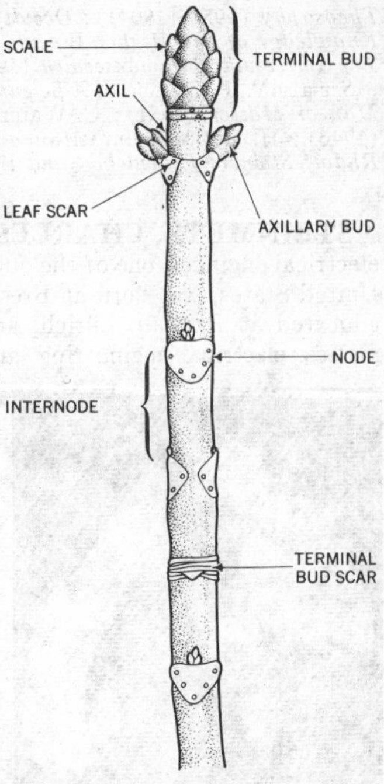

FROM H. L. STAHNKE, "BIOTIC PRINCIPLES"; CHARLES E. MERRILL BOOKS, INC.

**FIG. 1.—FEATURES OF A WOODY STEM**

**General Features.**—Many underground stems resemble roots, but they can always be distinguished by their terminal bud and evidences of leaf attachment (leaf scars) and by the absence of a protective cap for the growing tip (the rootcap of roots). Internally, the bundles or bands of vascular tissue are peripheral or scattered, never central or radial, as in the root. The relationship of the xylem and phloem is also diagnostic for stems (*see* PLANTS AND PLANT SCIENCE: *Vascular System*).

**Development.**—The first rudiment of the young shoot of the embryo appears from the seed after the radicle (young root) has protruded. It is termed the plumule and differs from the radicle in the absence of a rootcap and in its tendency to ascend (*see* SEED). The apical growing portion constitutes the terminal bud of the plant, and by continued development the stem increases in height; projections appear at intervals, which are the rudimentary leaves. Lateral buds are produced that develop into lateral shoots more or less resembling the parent stem, and by these the branching of the plant is determined. A bud may be found in the axil of a previously formed leaf or, in other words, in the angle formed between the stem and leaf. Such buds are called axillary and are produced like the leaves from the tissues of the stem. During their development vascular bundles are formed that are continuous with those of the stem. Ultimately branches are produced that in every respect resemble the axis from which the bud was differentiated. The place of origin of the leaf is called a node; the intervals between nodes are called internodes.

**Functions of the Stem.**—The primary functions of the stem are support of the leaves, conduction of water and nutrient substances to the leaves, and movement of elaborated foods from them. Other functions which may be performed by stems are storage of reserve food, photosynthesis, and vegetative reproduction. The regular arrangement of leaves on the stem distributes them in such a manner that they are equally exposed to the light, as is necessary for photosynthesis (*see* LEAF: *Arrangement or Phyllotaxy*). The stem also supports the flowers.

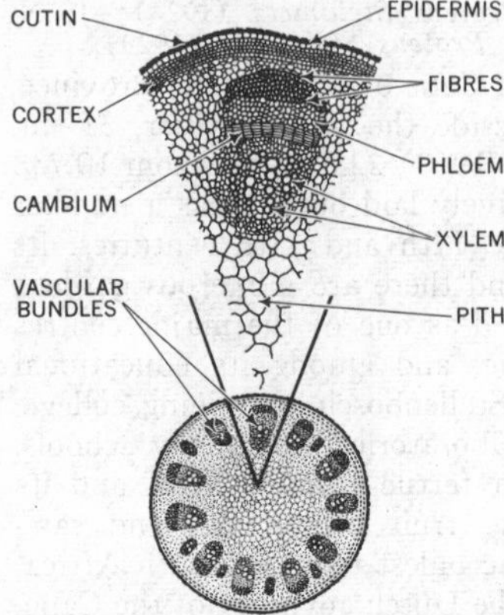


FROM "BIOLOGICAL SCIENCE: AN INQUIRY INTO LIFE"; BY PERMISSION OF THE BIOLOGICAL SCIENCES CURRICULUM STUDY

**FIG. 2.—MICROSCOPIC STRUCTURE OF A SUNFLOWER STEM**

Conduction of water and nutrient salts from regions of absorption in the roots to the leaves takes place through certain vascular elements of the xylem (vessels and tracheids), while the movement of synthesized foods from the leaves to other organs of the plant occurs chiefly through the phloem (*see* PLANTS AND PLANT SCIENCE: *Translocation of Water* and *Translocation of Solutes*). Radial movement of food within the stem may take place through ray and other parenchymatous cells. Storage of food and water frequently occurs in stems. Examples of food-storing stems are specialized forms, such as tubers, corms and rhizomes, and the woody stems of trees and shrubs. Water storage in stems is developed to a high degree in cacti.

All green stems carry on some of the photosynthetic work of the plant, but in most cacti this function is performed chiefly by the stem, the leaves being present often only for brief periods or as spines. Other plants in which food making is carried on in large measure by the stem are asparagus and various species of euphorbias. When the stem is specialized so that it is flattened and leaflike, it is termed a cladophyll, as in butcher's-broom or asparagus. Vegetative reproduction is accomplished by aerial stems like the stolons, or runners, of strawberries and by underground stems among the grasses and many members of the lily family.

**Growth and Bud Formation.**—Growth in length of the stem results from the activity of the apical meristem and elongation of the internodes. The zone of most rapid growth is at some distance below the apex; below this, the rate of growth gradually diminishes until the part is reached where growth in length no longer takes place. In some stems, as in those of grasses, growth in length persists for a longer time in a small region at the base of the internodes; this is known as intercalary growth. In shoots of limited growth, such as those of the larch, the internodes elongate only slightly and the leaves remain close together. Lateral buds give rise to branches, from which others, called branchlets or twigs, arise. The terminal bud sometimes dies at the end of one season, and the whole plant, as in annuals, perishes; or part of the axis is persistent and remains for two or more years, each of the leaves before its decay producing a bud in its axil, which continues the growth in the spring.

In ordinary trees, in which numerous lateral buds are formed, any injury done to a few branches is easily repaired; but in palms, which form mainly terminal buds and have no other provision for a lateral formation of them, destruction of the terminal bud results in no further growth of the tree. In the trees of temperate and cold climates the buds, which are developed during one season, lie dormant during the winter, ready to open in the spring. They are generally protected by specialized leaves in the form of scales, which frequently exhibit a firmer and coarser texture than the foliage leaves. They serve a temporary purpose and usually fall off sooner or later after the leaves are expanded. The bud is often protected by a coating of resinous matter, as in the horse chestnut and balsam poplar, or by a thick downy covering, as in the willow.

In plants of warm climates the buds are often devoid of any protecting appendages; such buds are called naked.

When the terminal bud is injured or arrested in its growth, the elongation of the main axis stops, and the lateral branches often acquire increased activity. By continually cutting off the terminal buds or branches, a woody plant is made to assume a bushy appearance, and thus pollard trees are produced. The peculiar bird's nest appearance often presented by the branches of the common birch depends on an arrestment in the terminal buds, a shortening of the internodes, and a consequent clustering of the twigs.

**Types of Stems.**—*Growth Habit.*—The character of the stem may be related to the longevity of the plant. Thus many herbaceous plants or herbs are annuals and complete their life cycle in one growing season, after which the entire plant dies. In biennial herbs the whole plant dies after two years; the lower part of the stem or crown persists after the first growing season and bears buds from which an erect stem arises the second season. In perennial herbs the short crown stem may produce new shoots for many years. Plants producing permanent woody stems are called trees and shrubs. The latter produce branches from or near the

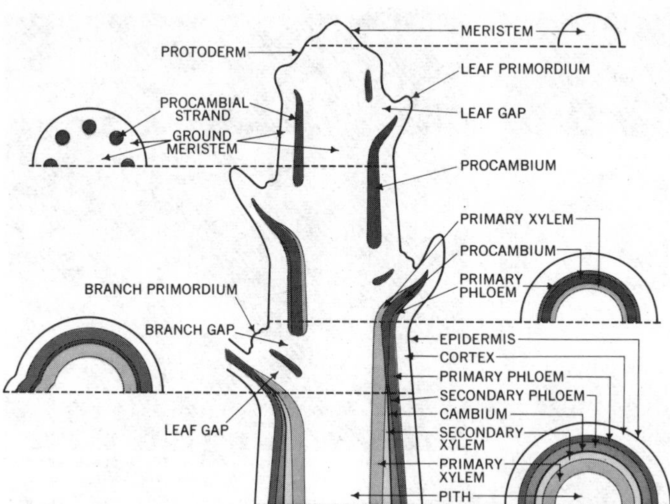


FROM H. J. FULLER AND O. TIPPO, "COLLEGE BOTANY"; HOLT, RINEHART AND WINSTON

FIG. 3.—DIAGRAMS OF LONGITUDINAL SECTION (CENTRE) OF A STEM TIP AND CROSS SECTIONS TAKEN AT DIFFERENT LEVELS AS INDICATED BY DOTTED LINES

ground, while the former have conspicuous trunks. Shrubby plants of small stature are called undershrubs or bushes. The limits between these different kinds of stems are not always well defined; and there are some plants occupying an intermediate position between shrubs and trees, sometimes called arborescent shrubs (*see* TREE). In general, the habit of the stem is erect or ascending, but it may lie prostrate on the ground, thus becoming procumbent, as in the sweet potato and strawberry. The scandent stem may climb on rocks or plants by means of rootlets, as in ivy; other vines have twining stems that twist around a supporting plant in a spiral manner, as in morning-glory, dodder, honeysuckle, and hop. In other cases, climbing plants are supported by tendrils, which may be specialized stems, as in the grape and passionflower. In warm climates twining plants often form thick woody stems and are called lianas, while in temperate regions they are generally herbaceous vines (*q.v.*).

In some plants the stem does not elongate during its early development but forms a short conical structure from which a crown of leaves arises. These may form a bulb (onion, lily), a head (cabbage, lettuce), or a rosette (dandelion, plantain). Later this type of stem may grow rapidly into an elongated axis. Subterranean stems include rhizomes, corms, and tubers.

*Rhizome.*—A rhizome or rootstock is a horizontal stem usually sending out numerous adventitious roots and leaf buds from its upper surface. It occurs in ferns, the iris, *Acorus* or sweet flag, ginger, the water lily, many species of *Carex,* rushes, grasses, anemone, etc. The leaves develop as scales. By the presence of leaf-scales and a bud at the apex, and by the absence of a root cap, a rhizome can be distinguished from a root.

A rhizome such as in Solomon's seal is not the product of a single bud but is composed of portions of successive axes, the aerial parts of which have died off, leaving scars. A rhizome sometimes assumes an erect form, as in *Scabiosa succisa,* in which the so-called praemorse root is in reality a rhizome, with the lower end decaying. The erect rhizome of water hemlock (*Cicuta virosa*) has hollow internodes, separated by partitions. In the coralroot orchid (*Corallorhiza*), which grows in soil rich in humus, no roots are developed, the corallike branching rhizome acting as the absorbing organ.

*Tuber.*—A tuber is a short thickened stem or branch in which there is little internodal elongation, as in the potato. The eyes of the potato are leaf buds. Tubers are sometimes aerial, occupying the place of branches. The ordinary herbaceous stem of the potato, when cut into slips and planted, sends off branches from its base, which assume the form of tubers.

Tubers frequently store up a quantity of starch, as in *Maranta arundinacea,* from which West Indian arrowroot is derived.

*Corm.*—Another form of thickened underground stem is the corm, as seen in the autumn crocus (*Colchicum*), gladiolus, etc. Structurally it is composed of a solid, more or less rounded axis covered by thin membranous scales.

A corm often persists for only one year, giving off buds annually in the form of young corms. In the axil of an upper leaf of one (or more) of the bud corms the flowering stem develops and bears the flowers. The flowering stem dies down and the bud corm, from which it arose, enlarges greatly at the expense of its parent corm, which thus becomes shriveled. In spring the corm that flowered the spring before sends out large leaves, which were mere rudiments the previous autumn. At the end of spring these leaves die down; only the bases of the lower ones remain as thin brown scales around the corm.

This corm, in its turn produces in the axils of its leaves new bud corms, which form rudimentary leaves in the autumn. The following spring one (or more) of these bud corms produces the flowering stem and, eventually, leaves and new bud corms; and thus the cycle goes on.

*Bulb.*—The bulb is a bud that is often subterranean. The axis in this case is much shortened, and the internodes are unelongated. The bases of the leaves rising from the stem are close together and become succulent and enclose the axis. In the lily the thick and narrow scales are arranged separately in rows, and the bulb is called scaly; while in the leek, onion, and tulip the scales are broad and enclose one another in a concentric manner, the outer ones being thin and membranous, forming a covering. In the axils of these fleshy scales new lateral shoots arise, forming new bulbs.

The lateral buds may remain attached to the axis and produce flowering stems, so that apparently the same bulb continues to flower for many years, as in the hyacinth and tulip; in other species the young bulbs form separate plants.

In the axil of the leaves of *Lilium bulbiferum, Dentaria bulbifera,* and some other plants, small conical or rounded bodies are produced, called bulbils or bulblets. They resemble bulbs and consist of a small number of thickened scales enclosing a growing point. These scales are frequently united closely together, so as to form a solid mass. The scales in bulbs vary in number. In *Gagea* there is only one scale; in the tulip and crown imperial they vary from two to five; while in lilies and hyacinths there are a great number of them.

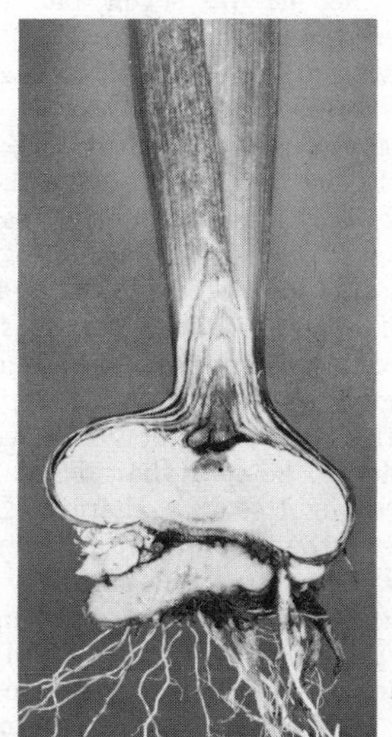

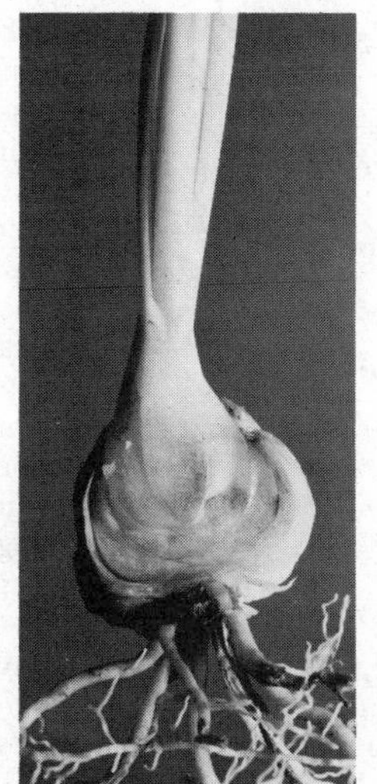

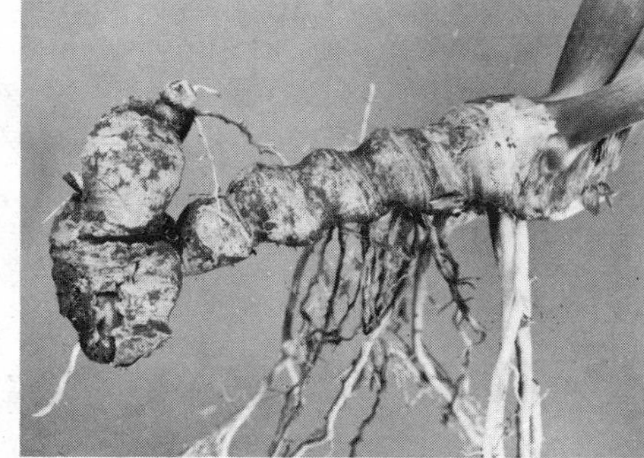

JOHN H. GERARD

(LEFT) CORM OF A GLADIOLUS; (CENTRE) BULB OF A MADONNA LILY; BOTH IN VERTICAL SECTION. (ABOVE) RHIZOME OF AN IRIS

*Other Modifications.*—Branches are sometimes long and slender and run along the ground, producing buds and adventitious roots at their extremity. This is seen in the runner of the strawberry. In the houseleek (*Sempervivum tectorum*) there is a similar prostrate branch of a shorter and thicker nature, known as an offset, producing a bud at its extremity capable of independent existence. In many instances the stem decays, and the young plant is separated from the parent plant.

(LEFT) ARTHUR W. AMBLER FROM NATIONAL AUDUBON SOCIETY, (RIGHT) MOLLY ADAMS FROM NATIONAL AUDUBON SOCIETY

TWO MODIFICATIONS OF AERIAL STEMS: (LEFT) THICK, WATER-STORING CACTUS, (RIGHT) PROPAGATIVE RUNNERS OF STRAWBERRIES

Gardeners propagate plants by the process of layering, which consists in bending a twig, fixing the central part of it into the ground and, after the production of roots, cutting off its connection with the parent. A stolon is a stem that curves toward the ground and, on reaching a moist spot, takes root and forms an upright stem and ultimately a separate plant. This is a sort of natural layering, and the plant producing such branches is called stoloniferous. In the rose and mint a subterranean branch arises from the stem, which runs horizontally to a certain extent and ultimately sends up an aerial stem, which may become an independent plant. Such branches are denominated rhizomes or suckers, and the gardener cuts the connection between the sucker and the parent stem to propagate these plants.

In asparagus and other plants that have a perennial stem below ground, subterranean buds are annually produced that appear above ground as shoots or branches covered with scales at first, and ultimately with cladophylls resembling true leaves. These branches are herbaceous and perish annually, while the main stem remains below ground to send up fresh shoots the following season.

In bananas the aerial stem is a shoot sent up by an underground stem and perishes after fruiting. Branches are sometimes arrested in their development and, in place of forming leaves, develop as spines or thorns, as in the hawthorn. Plants that have spines in a wild state, as the apple and pear, often are less spiny when cultivated; in some cases, as in the fire thorn (*Pyracantha coccinea*), a branch bears leaves at its lower portion and terminates in a spine.

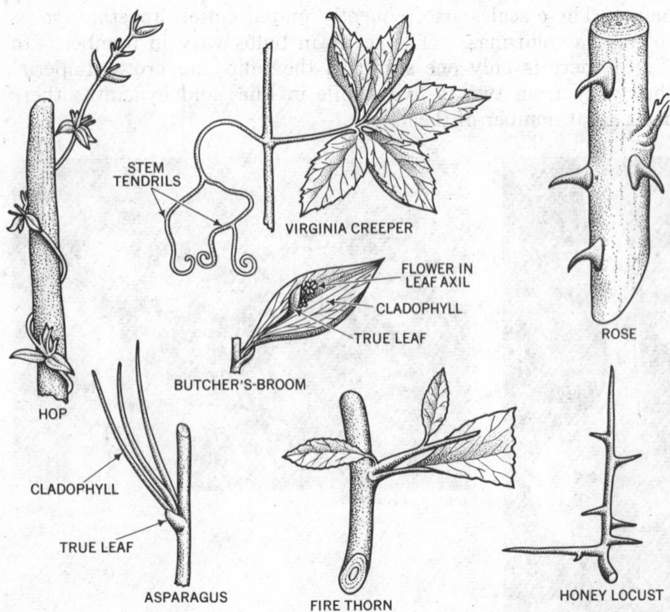


FROM W. W. ROBBINS AND T. E. WEIER, "BOTANY, AN INTRODUCTION TO PLANT SCIENCE"; JOHN WILEY & SONS, INC.

FIG. 4.—STEM MODIFICATIONS

*See* also references under "Stem" in the Index.

(H. E. HD.; K. E.; X.)

**STENDAL,** a town of East Germany in the *Bezirk* (district) of Magdeburg, German Democratic Republic, 70 mi. (113 km.) W of Berlin on the Uchte River. Pop. (1964) 35,931. It is a railway junction on the Hanover-Berlin line. There are many churches and gates in Gothic style, built in brick; the town hall is an imposing complex of buildings in Gothic and Renaissance styles. There are two parks, a zoological garden, and a museum. In front of the town hall is a 16th-century Roland's column, a symbol of municipal freedom. Stendal's industries include chemicals, metal goods, preserves, and sugar refining.

The town was once the capital of the Altmark. The first settlers were the Lower Saxons, the Wends, the Netherlanders, and the Rhinelanders. It was first mentioned in a charter of 1022 and was given municipal rights between 1150 and 1170 by Albert I, the Bear. As a member of the Hanseatic League, it rose to the height of its prosperity from the 13th to the 15th century by the weaving and trading of cloth. The archaeologist J. J. Winckelmann (1717–68) was born there. (A. Sz.)

**STENDHAL** (pseudonym of MARIE HENRI BEYLE) (1783–1842), one of the greatest French novelists, and the author of many original and entertaining works.

**Life.**—The elder child of a Chérubin Beyle and Henriette (*née* Gagnon), he was born on Jan. 23, 1783, at Grenoble, where he spent his first 16 years, of which he has left a vivid account in *La Vie de Henri Brulard*. He was devoted to his mother, who died when he was seven, but was always on bad terms with his father, whom he nicknamed "the bastard," and whom he suspected, unjustly, of deliberately keeping him short of money. His bitterness increased when he learned on his father's death in 1819 that, owing to business misfortunes, he would not inherit the fortune that he had confidently expected. Stendhal detested Grenoble—which he called "mudhole"—and its middle-class society with their monarchist sympathies. "My family," he wrote, "were the most aristocratic people in the town, which meant that I became a fanatical republican on the spot." He added that though he would do anything in his power "to ensure the happiness of the common people," he would prefer "to spend a fortnight of every month in prison rather than have to live with tradesmen." He claimed to be of Italian descent on his mother's side. This was long thought to be a characteristic piece of fantasy, but research suggests that there may be something in it. Stendhal used it as an explanation of his curiously contradictory nature. He was a mathematician and an adventurer, equally enthusiastic over the *logique* of the philosophers and what he called *espagnolisme* (the passionate ebullience typified for him by his maternal great-aunt).

At the École Centrale at Grenoble (1796–99), he was a brilliant pupil. He then went to Paris, ostensibly to study at the École Polytechnique, but in reality to escape from Grenoble. Although the heroes of two of his novels went to the Polytechnique, he himself found the entrance examination too much trouble and soon abandoned the idea. He fell ill and was befriended by his cousins, the Darus. Pierre Daru was a high official at the Ministère de la Guerre, where he obtained a clerkship for Stendhal. Later in 1799 Stendhal was posted to Milan during Napoleon's second Italian campaign. While he was there Daru secured him a commission in the 6th Dragoons. His enthusiasm for military life is famous, but in practice he found the army boring and disappointing. He soon became an expert in all the tricks of the "old sweat." His biographers have disproved the large claims made for him in army reports as a soldier, showing that he was never a combatant. He returned to France in 1802 and resigned his commission.

BY COURTESY OF THE MUSÉE STENDHAL, GRENOBLE; PHOTO, STUDIO PICCARDY

STENDHAL; PORTRAIT BY P. J. DEDREUX-DORCY

He had gone to Paris in the hope of achieving fame as a writer and happiness through love. Neither hope met with immediate success. Although he planned his conquests with the care of an 18th-century roué, he was a timid and bungling seducer who was rebuffed by most of his intended victims, including Mme Daru, his protector's wife. He announced, blithely and publicly, that he intended to become a "comic bard" and Molière's successor. He went assiduously to the theatre, attended a dramatic school, and hammered away intermittently for nearly 40 years at his plays. He complained of the difficulty of writing Alexandrines, but his genius was for prose fiction, not verse drama.

He became infatuated with an actress, Mélanie Guilbert, and in 1805 followed her to Marseilles, where for a few months he was a wholesale grocer. When the business failed, he returned to the Ministère as deputy to the *commissaire des guerres*. He spent two years (1806–08) with the army in Brunswick, applied unsuccessfully for a post in Spain, and took part, on the quartermaster's staff, in Napoleon's Russian campaign of 1812. He had a close view of the horrors of war in Russia and described them in some of his most brilliant letters. When the empire fell, he was angling for a prefecture. Seeing no prospect of employment under the new regime, he spent the years 1814–21 in Italy, six of them mostly at Milan, the home of Angela Pietragrua, who became his mistress in 1811, ten years after their first meeting, and provided him with material for several of his heroines.

In 1821 the Austrian police, who suspected him of espionage, asked him to leave Milan. This was a heavy blow. Italy was the land of his dreams; his love of it gives his novel *La Chartreuse de Parme* its youthfulness and spontaneity. He spent most of the next nine years in Paris, where he became a familiar figure in literary circles. He met Destutt de Tracy (*q.v.*), whose philosophy he greatly admired, and made friends with Prosper Mérimée. He also published his first two novels, *Armance* (1827) and *Le Rouge et le noir* (1830). In 1821 and 1826 he visited England and wrote engagingly of his visits in *Souvenirs d'égotisme* (1892).

Shortly after the July Revolution of 1830 he was appointed consul at Trieste, but Metternich refused him his exequatur, and he was sent instead to Civitavecchia in April 1831. It was not an exciting post but left him ample time for writing. While there, he wrote the romanticized autobiography *Henri Brulard* (1890), the novel *Lucien Leuwen* (1894), and part of the novel *Lamiel* (1889), all unfinished and posthumously published. In his later years, afflicted with boredom and poor health, he managed to wangle long leaves in Paris. During one of them, in the autumn of 1838, he wrote his masterpiece, *La Chartreuse de Parme* (1839), in only seven weeks.

He returned to France on sick leave in November 1841. On March 22, 1842, he attended a large official reception given by François Guizot at the Ministère des Affaires Etrangères in Paris. On his way home, he had an attack of apoplexy and died in the early hours of March 23. His death occurred at a moment when he seemed on the point of achieving fame: 18 months earlier Balzac had published his great panegyric of *La Chartreuse de Parme* in the *Revue de Paris;* and Stendhal had just negotiated an advantageous contract with the *Revue des deux mondes* for a series of short stories. Only three people, including Mérimée, followed the coffin to the cemetery of Montmartre.

**Works.**—According to the official bibliographies, Stendhal is the author of 33 works, of which 19 were published posthumously. They can be divided into four broad groups: criticism, travel, autobiography, and fiction. He began his career as a critic with a book on music, *Les Vies de Haydn, de Mozart et de Métastase* (published 1814). It set the pattern for much that followed. He plagiarized shamelessly and without acknowledgment, but the stolen material was enlivened by his own, very individual, comments and anecdotes. This work appeared under the pseudonym of L. A. C. Bombet. Stendhal's use of pseudonyms—scholars claim to have counted 171—is one of his more curious psychological quirks. It may be connected with his fondness for using a strange mixture of French and rudimentary English as a primitive form of code when making subversive comments on the regime in his autobiographies and diaries. The most famous of his pseudonyms, however, was borrowed from the small Prussian town of Stendal or Stendhal. It was the birthplace of J. J. Winckelmann, the famous German art critic and, since it was first used for *Rome, Naples et Florence,* was probably intended as a tribute to him. That this was Stendhal's first book to enjoy a modest success may explain his retention of this pseudonym. After his *Histoire de la peinture en Italie* (1817), he turned from painting to literature in *Racine et Shakespeare* (two pamphlets, published 1823 and 1825), in which he defends Shakespeare at the expense of the author whom he himself regarded as the archclassic. He went back to music with his *Vie de Rossini* (1823). His posthumous collections of criticism include *Molière, la comédie et le rire* (1930), *Écoles italiennes de peinture* (1932), *Mélanges de littérature* (1933), and a series of articles known as the *Courrier anglais* contributed to English magazines between 1822 and 1839.

Most of his criticism was frankly hackwork. This is also true of the travel books: *Rome, Naples et Florence* (1817; 3rd edition 1826), *Promenades dans Rome* (1829), *Mémoires d'un touriste* (1838), *Pages d'Italie* (1932), and *Voyage dans le Midi de la France* (1854). He made some pretense of providing serious information, extracted from other people's guidebooks, but his artistic judgments were erratic, and he was not above giving eyewitness accounts of events that he had not in fact witnessed. Nevertheless, what gives the best pages their sparkle is the author's personal touch: the shrewd, humorous observations on men and manners, and a sprinkling of amusing, though often scabrous, stories.

There is an autobiographical element in all Stendhal's works, which are, in differing degrees, assaults on the central mystery of the self. He was preoccupied from his early years with the problem of self-knowledge, and his method of tackling it was often remarkable. In pages that remind us of Proust on involuntary memory he tells us, in *Henri Brulard,* that many of the incidents described came back to him only in the act of writing, that in putting down his memories of childhood he was able to visualize, for example, the exact positions of members of the family group at his mother's funeral. *Henri Brulard,* the *Journal* (5 volumes, 1888, 1923–34), *Souvenirs d'égotisme,* and the splendid correspondence, particularly the touching letters to his sister Pauline, together cover almost his entire life. The result is paradoxical. Although he has written more about himself than almost any other Frenchman, he remains one of the most elusive of famous novelists, and this has proved both a gift and a temptation to psychological biographers.

There are two books that do not fit easily into any of the four groups: a biography of Napoleon and a treatise on love. Although he was a passionate admirer of Napoleon, his *Vie de Napoléon* (1929) is disappointing. The sources of *De l'amour* (1822) are partly literary, but the work is coloured by his own experiences, especially by the death of Mathilde Dembowska, the wife of a Polish general, whom he had loved in vain. It also contains the celebrated theory of "crystallization" (the growth of love compared to the dead branch of a tree that fell into a salt mine near Salzburg and became covered with sparkling crystals) that he was to use extensively in the novels.

Stendhal wrote five novels, two of them unfinished, and two volumes of *nouvelles: Chroniques italiennes* (1839) and *Romans et nouvelles* (1854). His novels can be fully appreciated only when regarded as parts of a single *oeuvre*. The central figure in all of them is the *étranger* (or "outsider"), the "singular" individual who is at odds with the society in which he is living and who ends by disrupting it. Stendhal uses the word *imprévu* to convey the disconcerting effect his heroes have on other people: the quality that "singles them out," making them both outcasts and superior beings, members of that small elite, "the happy few," for whom he claimed to write. All are passionate lovers, but the young men regard falling in love as a misfortune that can never overtake them, and love simply as a means of satisfying their ambitions. It is part of the fascination of the novels to watch the process of "crystallization" taking place in spite of themselves, and their horror when they discover what has happened. Stendhal put much of himself into his characters. Whatever their birth, their outlook is essentially aristocratic, and, though professing "progressive" views, they share their creator's contempt for their fellow progressives. They also reflect the contradiction at the heart of what is known as "Beylisme." For Stendhal projected into his principal characters his own "pursuit of happiness," a happiness which is of its nature inaccessible. It is because he was aware of this that in the last analysis Stendhal's view of life, for all its gaiety and wit, is a tragic one.

"Politics in a novel," Stendhal was fond of saying, "is like a pistol shot at a concert. It is something crude from which it is nevertheless impossible to withhold our attention." All his own novels are political novels in this sense. In them he examined the sociopolitical scene at different moments between 1814 and 1840: *La Chartreuse de Parme* is a remarkable study of a miniature police state that has survived into the Napoleonic era; *Armance* and *Le Rouge et le noir* are criticisms of the situation in 1827–30; and *Lucien Leuwen* is a devastating exposure of political corruption under Louis Philippe. He was not content with examining the scene at different moments; he also examined it from different angles by choosing his heroes from different social classes. Fabrice in *La Chartreuse de Parme* is an aristocrat; the heroes of *Armance* and *Lucien Leuwen* come from the upper-middle class; Julien Sorel in *Le Rouge et le noir* is born into the proletariat but succeeds in rising out of his class and laying the foundations of what might have been a brilliant career by way of the army and the church (the "scarlet" and "black" of the title). In his last novel, *Lamiel*, he varied the pattern and chose a woman "outsider" who was a gangster's "moll."

**Assessment.**—"I have bought a ticket in a lottery," Stendhal once said; "the prize may be described as this: to be read in 1935." He had it firmly in mind that he was writing not for his contemporaries but for posterity and thought that he might enjoy a little posthumous fame about 1880. He did not have to wait so long. Taine's essay (see *Bibliography*) brought fame in the middle of the century, and Paul Bourget records that by the '80s he had become a cult among the young. The cult has grown into an industry; patient scholars have deciphered and published everything down to his laundry bills. A similar revolution has taken place in critics' views of his style. Once regarded as a novelist who "wrote badly," he is now hailed as a "prince of language" whose prose style is a model of clarity and concision.

Praise of Stendhal's psychological insight has been a commonplace of criticism since Taine, but it does not convey the full measure of his originality. In the "outsider" he created a new psychological type that altered the perspective of European fiction. Because he appeals through his characters to the "outsider," and the spirit of rebellion latent in all of us, he is for his admirers not so much a novelist whom they read, as a writer who has become, mysteriously, a part of their being.

BIBLIOGRAPHY.—*Editions, etc.: Oeuvres complètes,* including 10 vol. of correspondence, ed. by H. Martineau, 79 vol. (1927–37); *To the Happy Few,* selected letters trans. by N. Cameron (1952); *The Private Diaries of Stendhal,* ed. and trans. by R. Sage (1955); H. Cordier, *Bibliographie stendhalienne* (1914); V. del Litto, *Bibliographie stendhalienne, 1938–60,* 5 vol. (1945–62). Most of Stendhal's works have been translated.

*Biography and Criticism:* P. Arbelet, *La Jeunesse de Stendhal* (1919); L. Blum, *Stendhal et le Beylisme,* 2nd ed. (1930); H. Martineau, *L'Oeuvre de Stendhal* (1945), *Le Calendrier de Stendhal* (1950), *Le Coeur de Stendhal* (1952–53); M. Bardèche, *Stendhal, romancier* (1947); M. Josephson, *Stendhal* (1946); J. Prévost, *La Création chez Stendhal,* 2nd ed. (1951); A. Caraccio, *Stendhal, l'homme et l'oeuvre* (1951; Eng. trans. 1965); F.-M. Albérès, *Le Naturel chez Stendhal* (1956); G. Blin, *Stendhal et les problèmes du roman* (1958), *Stendhal et les problèmes de la personnalité* (1958); R. M. Adams, *Stendhal: Notes on a Novelist* (1959); *Stendhal: a Collection of Critical Essays,* ed. by V. Brombert (1962); F. W. J. Hemmings, *Stendhal: a Study of his Novels* (1964). *See* also H. Taine, *Nouveaux essais de critique et d'histoire* (1865; 8th ed. 1905); M. Turnell, *The Novel in France* (1950), *The Art of French Fiction* (1959). (M. Tu.)

**STENO, NICOLAUS** (NIELS STEENSEN or STENSEN) (1638–1686), Danish naturalist, physician, and theologian, who made major early contributions to the science of crystallography and to the development of geologic theory, was born at Copenhagen on Jan. 10, 1638. He studied medicine at the University of Copenhagen, and in 1660 he went to Amsterdam and then to Leiden to continue his studies of anatomy. While at Amsterdam he discovered the parotid duct, also known as Stensen's duct. In 1664 he went to Paris, where he delivered a discourse on the anatomy of the brain that was printed in 1669. This paper was notable for its intelligibility and freedom from traditional interpretation. In 1665 he went to Florence, where he was appointed physician to the grand duke Ferdinand II.

Steno had time for travel and study in Italy and in 1669 published his geological observations in *De solido intra solidum naturaliter contento dissertationis prodromus* (translated into English with introduction by John G. Winter as *The Prodromus of Nicolas Steno's Dissertation Concerning a Solid Body Enclosed by Process of Nature Within a Solid* [1916]). In this short work he reported his discovery that quartz crystals that appear different from one another still have the same angles between corresponding faces (*see* CRYSTALLOGRAPHY: *Introduction*). He also was among the first to recognize fossils as remains of organisms and concluded that many rocks had formed in muddy marine or fresh waters. He rejected the idea that mountains grew, recognized the nature of volcanoes, and declared that some mountains had been shaped by running water. He attributed other mountains to "exhalations" and thought strata had been tilted and deformed as the roofs of great caverns collapsed. (*See* also GEOLOGY: *Development of the Science.*)

Steno became a Catholic in 1667 and soon abandoned science for religion. In 1676 he was made a bishop and was appointed apostolic vicar of northern Germany and Scandinavia. After a stormy career in Germany, he died at Schwerin in November 1686.

*See* R. Cioni, *Niels Stensen,* Eng. trans. by G. M. Camera (1962).
(M. A. F.; C. L. FE.)

**STENOTYPY,** a system of machine-recorded shorthand in which letters or groups of letters phonetically represent syllables, words, phrases, and punctuation marks. The stenotype machine, commonly used in business offices and in court reporting, is virtually noiseless and can be operated at speeds of more than 250 words per minute. It is composed of letter keys, a space key, a correction key (*), and a numeral bar that corresponds to the shift key on a typewriter. Four pairs of keys on the left side of the keyboard are initial consonants that print on the left side of a paper tape fed automatically through the back of the machine. Final consonants, five pairs of keys on the right, print on the right side of the tape. The four vowel keys centred below the consonants print in the centre of the tape.

The machine is operated with both hands, and several keys may be struck simultaneously to print a complete word with one stroke. The fingers of the left hand strike initial consonants, and the left thumb strikes two of the vowels. The right hand controls final consonants and the remaining two vowels.

Combinations of letters are substituted for letters or groups of letters; *e.g.,* TP on the left for an initial F sound, or, on the right, PL for a final M. Numerals are recorded by depressing the numeral bar and the key bearing the desired number.

In contrast with the variety of handwritten shorthand systems, stenotype recordings can be read by anyone familiar with the system, since it does not lend itself to individual modification.

*See* also SHORTHAND. (E. L. Y.)

**STEPHANITE,** which was an important ore of silver in the famous Comstock lode in Nevada, is a mineral consisting of silver, antimony, and sulfur, $Ag_5SbS_4$, containing 68.5% of silver. It occurs with other ores of silver in metalliferous veins. Under the name *Schwarzerz* (black ore) it was mentioned by G. Agricola in 1546. Stephanite has a hardness of 2.5 and is very brittle; the specific gravity is 6.3.

**STEPHEN, SAINT** (d. *c.* A.D. 36), the first Christian martyr, commemorated by the church on Dec. 26. He is the first named of the seven appointed for administrative duties when discord arose in the early Christian community about the neglect of Hellenistic widows (Acts 6–7). The choice of the men was determined by their endowment with the spirit and with wisdom, and their number corresponded with that of the seven elders chosen in Jewish synagogues. After their office had been suggested by the 12 apostles, who intended thus to be free to dedicate themselves to prayer and the ministry of the word, the seven were acclaimed by the whole community. Stephen, after performing "great wonders and signs," was accused by Hellenistic Jews before the Jewish high priest of blasphemy against the Temple and the Law. His speech of defense before the Sanhedrin served only to increase the fury of his accusers. Stressing the disobedience of the Jews, he traced God's guidance of them through their leaders Abraham, Isaac, Jacob, Joseph, Moses, and Joshua until they reached the Promised Land and Solomon built the Temple. He ended with a fierce denunciation of the Jews who had deviated from the way of God by resisting the Holy Spirit, persecuting the prophets, and murdering the Righteous One; *i.e.,* Jesus. He then received a vision of God's glory, which enraged his accusers still more; they threw him out of Jerusalem and stoned him to death as he prayed God to forgive them. Saul (later the apostle Paul) was present, consenting to the execution. After Stephen's death his fellow officers were compelled to flee, whereas the apostles remained in Jerusalem unscathed; this suggests that the seven were at that time the leaders of the Christian community.

The Hellenistic Jews of Jerusalem, among whom Stephen himself probably originated, did not hold liberal views, as is frequently assumed, but were a particularly active and zealous force for orthodoxy. They were drawn to Jerusalem by their attachment to the holy site, as well as by an intensive messianic eschatology. For them the two things went together: the appearance of the Messiah was to take place in the Temple. At both these points they came into conflict with Stephen. Stephen must have passed on and intensified the prophecy of Jesus regarding the approaching destruction of the Temple. Furthermore, he was the first to proclaim the Second Coming of Jesus (until then the early church had spoken only of his assumption), linking this thought so closely with eschatological expectation as to exclude an earthly, political Messiah. This is the background to the trial of Stephen.

Stephen's speech as reported in Acts, like other speeches in ancient historical works, is not to be taken as an exact summary of what he actually said. It is even possible that it originally had nothing to do with Stephen but was an account of the history of salvation that the author of Acts wished to insert at this point. Or it may be a modified version of Stephen's views compiled after his death by those who wished to show that the Jews were to blame for his execution. Most of its contents are unimpeachable from the Jewish point of view.

The account of Stephen's death contains elements that imply a mob execution. These can be explained best as evidence that pressure was put on the Sanhedrin to stone him to death as a blasphemer according to the Law, although by that time the right of capital punishment had passed from the Jewish authorities to the Roman procurator. For this reason it is likely that the execution took place after Pontius Pilate's recall (winter 36–37), during the vacancy in the procuratorship.

BIBLIOGRAPHY.—F. J. F. Jackson and K. Lake, *The Beginnings of Christianity,* 5 vol. (1920–33); W. Manson, *The Epistle to the Hebrews* (1951); A. von Schlatter, *The Church in the New Testament Period* (1955); M. Dibelius, *Studies in the Acts of the Apostles* (1956); Bo Reicke, *Glaube und Leben der Urgemeinde* (1957); M. Simon, *St. Stephen and the Hellenists in the Primitive Church* (1958); E. Haenchen, *Die Apostelgeschichte,* 2nd ed. (1959); P. Gaechter, *Petrus und seine Zeit* (1958); J. Bihler, *Die Stephanusgeschichte* (1963).

(E. BL.)

**STEPHEN,** the name of ten popes, sometimes numbered as nine, for reasons explained under *Stephen II.*

ST. STEPHEN I (d. 257), pope from 254 to 257, a Roman by birth, succeeded Lucius I. He is known principally from three controversies reported in the letters of St. Cyprian of Carthage. Stephen restored two Spanish bishops, accused of having "lapsed" under persecution (*libellatici*), and apparently he refused to depose Bishop Marcianus of Arles, accused of rigorism (Novatianism). Stephen also objected to the practice of rebaptizing heretics and threatened to excommunicate bishops in Africa (including Cyprian) and in Asia Minor unless they discontinued it. His death on Aug. 2, 257, almost coincided with a renewal of persecution under Valerian, but it is doubtful that he was martyred. His feast day is Aug. 2. (F. X. G.)

STEPHEN II (d. 752), a Roman, was elected March 24, 752, and died a few days later, before having been consecrated. He is listed neither in the *Liber pontificalis* nor in the catalogue of the popes. His successor, who also took the name Stephen, is called both Stephen II and Stephen III. Hence the succession of the popes with the name Stephen is somewhat irregular.

STEPHEN II (III) (d. 757), pope from 752 to 757, was a deacon when chosen in March 752 to succeed Zacharias in place of Stephen II. The central act of his pontificate was to free the papacy from Byzantium and to ally it with the Franks. Twice he appealed to the Frankish king Pepin III the Short for assistance against the Lombard king Aistulf, who was trying to conquer all Italy. In 754, before anointing Pepin at Saint-Denis, he obtained from him, at Quierzy, the donation whereby Pepin promised to "restore" to the church the lands taken by the Lombards. In 756 Pepin subdued the Lombards and conferred on Stephen territory in the exarchate of Ravenna, the duchy of Rome, and the districts of Venetia and Istria. Thus the papal states were founded, independent of any temporal power, and Stephen became their first temporal sovereign. He died in April 757.

STEPHEN III (IV) (d. 772), pope from 768 to 772, was a Sicilian and a Benedictine. He succeeded Paul I on Aug. 7, 768. His pontificate was mainly occupied with reaction to the antipapal policies of the Lombard king Desiderius, who attempted an alliance with the Franks against Stephen. He died in February 772.

STEPHEN IV (V) (d. 817), pope from 816 to 817, succeeded Leo III in June 816. Immediately after his consecration he ordered the Romans to swear fidelity to the emperor Louis the Pious, whom he personally visited in the following August. His crowning of Louis at Reims solidified the alliance between the papacy and the Franks. He died in January 817.

STEPHEN V (VI) (d. 891), pope from 885 to 891, succeeded Adrian III. In his dealings with both East (Photius and the Slavonic church) and West (Ravenna and Bordeaux) he acted with the utmost independence and authority.

STEPHEN VI (VII) (d. 897), pope from 896 to 897, succeeded Boniface VI. His conduct toward the remains of Pope Formosus, which he exhumed, placed on trial, degraded, and desecrated, ended in his own imprisonment and strangulation in August 897.

STEPHEN VII (VIII) (d. 931), pope from 929 to 931, was born of a Roman family and as cardinal priest of Saint Anastasia was active in the administration of the Roman Church before his election to the papacy. The history of his pontificate is practically unknown. He died in February 931.

STEPHEN VIII (IX) (d. 942), pope from 939 to 942, was a Roman elected on July 14, 939, to succeed Leo VII. His pontificate was dominated by the Roman prince Alberic, and Stephen had little opportunity for independent action. All his political efforts were directed toward the support of the last Carolingians. He died in October 942.

STEPHEN IX (X) (d. 1058), pope from 1057 to 1058, succeeded Victor II in August 1057, five days after the latter's death. His baptismal name was Frederick, and he was the brother of Godfrey, duke of Lorraine and marquis of Tuscany. Frederick, who had been raised to the cardinalate by Leo IX, acted for some time as papal legate at Constantinople and was with Leo in his unlucky expedition against the Normans. He showed great zeal in enforcing the law of clerical celibacy. During his pontificate the reform program became clearer, stronger, and more centralized. He died on March 29, 1058, at Florence.

*See* also PAPACY. (R. E. McN.)

**STEPHEN** (*c.* 1097–1154), king of England from 1135 to 1154, was the third son of Stephen, count of Blois and Chartres, and Adela, daughter of William I, the Conqueror. He was brought up in the household of his uncle Henry I of England, from whom he received knighthood, the county of Mortain in Normandy, and the honours of Eye and Lancaster in England. In 1118 he renounced his claims to Blois and Chartres in favour of his elder brother Theobald, and by marrying Matilda, heiress of Eustace III, count of Boulogne, he acquired (1125) not only the county but also the large estates in England which went with it. In 1127 and again in 1133 he was among the English magnates whom Henry I persuaded or forced to take an oath of fealty to his daughter the empress Matilda (*q.v.*) as heir to the throne and to recognize the hereditary right of her son Henry of Anjou, the future Henry II. A woman ruler married to Geoffrey, count of Anjou, was doubly repugnant to the Normans, and a queen regnant was unprecedented in England. Consequently, on Henry I's death (Dec. 1, 1135), despite their oaths of fealty, many of the bishops and great lords of England gave Stephen a friendly welcome when he speedily crossed the Channel, and with the help of the citizens of London, of his brother Henry of Blois, bishop of Winchester, and of the enormously influential Bishop Roger of Salisbury, he was crowned at Westminster by Archbishop William of Canterbury (*c.* Dec. 22, 1135). The succession was confirmed by the pope and at Easter 1136 a great council was attended by a widely representative body of prelates and feudatories. But in April Stephen was forced to issue a charter of liberties which made far-reaching concessions to both church and laity. Moreover, to meet the threat of Scottish invasion, he conceded to Henry, son of King David I, Carlisle and the honour of Huntingdon, and he allowed his strongest potential opponent, Robert of Gloucester, half brother of Matilda, substantial concessions in return for his homage. In 1137 Stephen missed an opportunity, which never recurred, of winning Normandy from Matilda and her husband, and in 1138 Robert of Gloucester took up arms in her support. The Angevin cause, however, made little headway. Thanks partly to speedy reinforcements from Stephen, David of Scotland, supporting Matilda, was badly defeated at the Battle of the Standard (1138). But in 1139, at the instigation of the powerful Beaumont family, the king arrested Roger of Salisbury and his nephews, the bishops of Lincoln and Ely, and deprived them of office. Insofar as there was a governmental machine at this time it was in the hands of Bishop Roger and his family. Their disgrace and ill-treatment not only drew the church, including Stephen's own brother Henry of Winchester, over to the Angevin side, it also deprived the king of an effective exchequer.

**Civil War.**—The crisis was Matilda's opportunity. She came to England in September 1139 with Robert of Gloucester, and they quickly made the West Country an Angevin stronghold. It was characteristic of the chivalrous Stephen that instead of arresting Matilda when she landed, he gave her an escort to take her to Bristol, which her half brother made into an Angevin capital to rival royalist London. It was also in character that the king besieged a string of castles in turn without having the singleness of purpose to capture any of them. Holding the triangle formed by Bristol, Gloucester, and Wallingford, the Angevins proved hard to dislodge and early in 1141, finding an ally in Ranulf, earl of Chester, they attacked and routed Stephen's forces at Lincoln. Stephen was made prisoner and Matilda's road to the throne lay open. But her arrogance offended Henry of Blois and also the citizens of London, from whom she had to flee. Stephen's mercenary captain William of Ypres returned to the fray and with Stephen's queen led a force which successfully routed the empress's supporters at Winchester (September 1141) and captured Earl Robert.

BY COURTESY OF KING'S COLLEGE, CAMBRIDGE, AND THE ROYAL ACADEMY OF ARTS

THE GREAT SEAL OF STEPHEN, SHOWING THE KING ON HORSEBACK AND FULLY ARMED

King and earl were soon exchanged (November) and gradually Stephen regained the upper hand. Oxford Castle fell to him in December 1142, Faringdon in 1145, and by 1147 when Earl Robert died Stephen seemed to be recognized as king over most of England from the Channel northward to the rivers Tyne and Ribble. North of that the king of Scots reigned supreme, despite his defeat in 1138.

**Weakness of Stephen's Rule.**—Nevertheless, Stephen failed utterly to keep the peace and dispense justice in those parts of England where he was recognized. He obtained the support of powerful lords only by lavish concessions, and he could not prevent the worst of them, such as Geoffrey de Mandeville, earl of Essex, from laying waste whole districts. It may be that life in many parts of England was not seriously disturbed during the "anarchy," but there is no doubt that scores of town and villages suffered dreadfully from the prevailing lawlessness. The monarchy itself suffered from Stephen's incompetence, losing ground both to the church and to the feudatories. Some great magnates made treaties of security with one another almost as though the king did not exist. Stephen was not always overruled. In 1140 he appointed his nephew William Fitz Herbert to the archbishopric of York and held his ground when the full weight of the reforming party in the church fiercely opposed the appointment. In spite of papal condemnation, Stephen's candidate ruled as archbishop for one year (1154). But the dispute finally ruptured any hope of reasonably good relations with the church, and Stephen failed to get his elder son Eustace crowned king in his own lifetime to ensure a peaceful succession.

**Last Years.**—In 1149 the 16-year-old Henry of Anjou made a serious but unsuccessful attempt to resume the Angevin military offensive. His next visit to England in 1153 was a much graver threat. Stephen was unable to prevent Henry, now duke of Normandy and Aquitaine, from traversing England from Bristol to the north Midlands and back to Wallingford, gaining en route numerous powerful adherents. A truce was arranged about the end of July, and Eustace's death in August made Stephen lose heart. A generous provision for the king's second son William made it possible for Stephen to reach firm agreement with Henry in November (Treaty of Winchester-Westminster, 1153) whereby Stephen would retain the throne till his death but Henry was recognized as his lawful heir. Stephen died at Dover on Oct. 25, 1154. Brave, generous, courteous, and not without energy, he had no political sense and lacked the ruthlessness essential for a strong king of 12th-century England. The *coup d'état* by which he won the throne is the most surprising episode in Stephen's career.

BIBLIOGRAPHY.—The chief authorities for the reign are the anonymous *Gesta Stephani, Regis Anglorum* and William of Malmesbury, *Historia Novella,* both trans. ed. by K. R. Potter (1955); John of Hexham's continuation of Simeon of Durham, *Historia Regum,* ed. by T. Arnold, 2 vol. (1882–85); the authors collected in *Chronicles of the Reigns of Stephen, Henry II and Richard I,* ed. by R. Howlett (1884–89); the Peterborough version of the *Anglo-Saxon Chronicle.* These and other sources may be found in translation in *English Historical Documents,* vol. ii, ed. by D. C. Douglas and G. W. Greenaway (1953–55). For Stephen's charters see *Regesta Regum Anglo-Normannorum,* vol. iii, ed. by H. A. Cronne and R. H. C. Davis (forthcoming). *See* also A. L. Poole, *From Domesday Book to Magna Carta 1087–1216,* 2nd ed. (1955). (G. W. S. B.)

**STEPHEN I** (SAINT STEPHEN; Hung. ISTVÁN) (977–1038), the first king of Hungary. A member of the Árpád dynasty, he was the son of the supreme chieftain Géza by his wife Sarolta. Brought up as a Christian, he had among his tutors the German priest Bruno, the Czech priest Radla, and an Italian knight, Theodatus of San Severino. In 996, he was married to Gisela, daughter of Duke Henry II of Bavaria. In 997 when his father died, the young Stephen was confronted by a formidable pagan insurrection in the country between the Drava River and Lake Balaton. Under the banner of St. Martin of Tours, whom he chose to be his patron saint, he routed the rebels at Veszprém (998). Immediately afterward he assumed the royal title. Doubt has been cast on the tradition (which seems to have started *c.* 1112 and was long developed) that in 1000 or 1001 he received a crown as a gift from Pope Silvester II with a letter addressing him as "Apostolic King" because of his missionary zeal. The struggle against the pagan nobles long continued to preoccupy him, so that he adopted a peaceful policy toward the Byzantine and the Holy Roman emperors alike. Even so, he defended his kingdom successfully when the emperor Conrad II attacked it in 1030.

In organizing his kingdom Stephen adopted German examples. He introduced the county system, founded bishoprics and abbeys, made the building of churches mandatory, and established tithing. He promoted agriculture, safeguarded private property with strict laws, and organized a standing army. A ruling class was brought into existence, consisting of the chieftains who acknowledged his royal authority, the sheriffs at the head of the counties, foreign knights, and liegemen. In addition, there were serfs: peasants and shepherds, the conquered Slavs, and people captured by the Magyars during military expeditions abroad. This organization of a feudal state was the greatest achievement of Stephen's reign; but he also brought the Magyars into the European cultural community, while saving them from German conquest.

Stephen died in 1038 and was canonized in 1083. Stronghanded and resolute, a careful and adroit diplomat, broad-minded, tolerant, and well aware of the contemporary European situation, this outstanding statesman had founded the Hungarian nation.

*See* Bálint Hóman, *King Stephen the Saint* (1938). (GE. GR.)

**STEPHEN** (ISTVÁN BÁTHORY) (1533–1586), king of Poland from 1575, after being prince of Transylvania from 1571. He was born at Szilágysomlyó (Şimleu Silvaniei) on Sept. 27, 1533, the son of István Báthory, governor of Transylvania (*q.v.*) for the Habsburg king of Hungary, the future Holy Roman emperor Ferdinand I. After studies in Italy (at the University of Padua), he went in 1552 to Ferdinand I's court; but when John Sigismund Zápolya became prince of independent Transylvania in 1556, Báthory entered his service. Eventually he became commander in chief of the Transylvanian Army. Sent by John Sigismund to Vienna in 1563 to negotiate a rectification of the frontier between Habsburg Hungary and Transylvania, he was arrested by the future emperor Maximilian II, who was then about to become king of Hungary; a year later Maximilian released him. On May 25, 1571, despite Maximilian's objections, the Hungarians elected Báthory prince of Transylvania in succession to John Sigismund.

In 1575, rejecting Maximilian's candidature, the Polish nobility elected Stephen Báthory king of Poland in succession to Henry of Valois (who had fled in 1574 to become king of France as Henry III). Having secured the election of his brother Christopher as prince of Transylvania instead of himself, Stephen hastened to Cracow, married the Jagiello princess Anna (sister of Henry's predecessor Sigismund II of Poland), and, on May 1, 1576, was crowned king. Only Gdansk, which supported Maximilian's cause, offered armed resistance; it was finally reduced by blockade to submission (Dec. 8, 1577). Meanwhile Stephen had concluded a truce with the Turks (Nov. 5, 1577). The Russian tsar Ivan IV, however, had tried to exploit the Polish interregnum in order to obtain access for Muscovy to the Baltic Sea through Polish Livonia. In 1579, therefore, with supplies voted by the *sejm* (Diet) of Warsaw, Stephen began war against Ivan. After three campaigns (during which he besieged Pskov in 1581), he forced Ivan to cede Polotsk and Livonia to Poland under the truce of Jam Zapolski (Jan. 15, 1582).

In internal affairs, Stephen sought to promote the Counter-Reformation and to strengthen the royal power. This policy brought him into conflict with his subjects. Even so, he cherished the ambition of uniting Poland, Muscovy, and Transylvania in one great state; and he was preparing a new war against Muscovy (intended also as the prelude to a crusade against the Turks) when he died near Grodno, on Dec. 12, 1586.

*See* Jan Dabrowski *et al., Étienne Báthory, roi de Pologne, prince de Transylvanie* (1935). (ST. HE.)

**STEPHEN** DUŠAN or DUSHAN (*c.* 1308–1355), king of the Serbs from 1331 and tsar, or emperor, from 1346, was the son of Stephen Uroš III (*see* SERBIA: *History*). He fought against Stephen Kotromanić of Bosnia in 1329 and took part in the victorious Battle of Velbuzhd (Kyustendil) against the Bulgars in 1330 before being put on the throne, in his father's place, in 1331.

In war against the Byzantine Empire, Stephen in 1334 conquered Strumica, Prilep, Ohrid, and Kostur (Kastoria) and had advanced to the gates of Salonika when peace was made. In 1342, during the civil war in the Byzantine Empire, he and John Cantacuzenus (*see* JOHN VI, emperor) started a joint offensive against Constantinople. This alliance did not last long, and Cantacuzenus then approached the Turks, who as his allies advanced to Serrai (Ser) in Macedonia. Stephen, who was in possession of all Albania in the summer of 1345, took Serrai in September. Soon afterward he proclaimed himself "emperor of the Serbs and Greeks." Having elevated the Serbian archbishopric to the rank of patriarchate, he had himself crowned emperor at Skoplje on Easter Day, 1346.

Epirus and Thessaly fell to Stephen in 1348, but he did not succeed in reconquering Hum (Hercegovina) from the Bosnians. Conscious of the menace of the Turks, he asked Pope Innocent VI to appoint him commander in chief of a crusade against them, but collaboration with the Holy See was interrupted by a Hungarian attack on Serbia in the summer of 1354.

Stephen's *Zakonik*, a code of law based on the Byzantine model (with some regulations taken over from earlier Serbian rulers) and valid for his whole empire, was promulgated at Skoplje in 1349; addenda were promulgated at Serrai in 1354.

Stephen died on Dec. 20, 1355. He had given Serbia the widest frontiers in all its history. (M. A. P.)

**STEPHEN** THE GREAT (d. 1504), prince or *voivode* of Moldavia from 1457, a figure of European importance because of his long resistance to the Ottoman Turks. The son of Prince Bogdan II (d. 1451), he succeeded his uncle, Prince Peter III, in 1457, four years after the fall of Constantinople to Sultan Mohammed II.

Mohammed launched an attack on Moldavia, but Stephen heavily defeated the invaders at Vaslui in 1475. For this success he received a letter of praise from Pope Sixtus IV and was hailed by the Polish chronicler Jan Dlugosz as "the first of the princes of the world to win so brilliant a victory over the Turks." There followed another victory at Valea Albă (1476) and, after some reverses in 1484–85, a further victory at Scheia (1486). The Turkish menace, and his concern for Moldavia's independence, motivated Stephen's negotiations with Matthias Corvinus, king of Hungary, and with Casimir IV, king of Poland. These culminated in alliances, which, however, brought no adequate help, material or military. Finally, in 1503, recognizing the economic and military superiority of Turkey, Stephen concluded a treaty with Sultan Bayazid II whereby Moldavia conserved its independence at the cost of paying an annual tribute to the Turks.

Stephen's internal policy was designed to establish a centralized state with the support of the freeholders, the townspeople, and the petty boyars. He promoted commercial and cultural development; his reign saw the building of the fortresses and market towns at Suceava, Baia, and Scheia, and also of many monasteries in the architectural style characteristic of Moldavia, as well as the writing of the Bistriţa and Putna chronicles.

**STEPHEN, SIR JAMES FITZJAMES** (1829–1894), English judge, law reformer and historian whose work in the codifying of criminal law was of wide and lasting influence, was born in London on March 3, 1829. He was the son of James Stephen, for many years undersecretary of state for the colonies, and an elder brother of Leslie Stephen, English philosopher and critic. Stephen was educated at Eton, London university and Trinity college, Cambridge. He was called to the bar in 1854, was made recorder of Newark in 1859, and became queen's counsel in 1868. In his early years at the bar, Stephen became one of the leading controversial publicists of his day. His miscellaneous writings, which encompass a wide range of topics, appeared frequently in such journals as the *Pall Mall Gazette* and the *Saturday Review*. Stephen's intellectual position may, in some respects, reflect the utilitarian tradition; but his thought was of a highly individual cast, and he was in no sense the disciple of any school. In 1863 he published his *General View of the Criminal Law of England,* a work of great importance, representing the first attempt since Blackstone to give systematic statement to the principles of English criminal jurisprudence. Ten years later, in reply to J. S. Mill's *On Liberty,* Stephen published *Liberty, Equality, Fraternity,* a work antidemocratic in tendency and displaying defects of expression and argument, which, nevertheless, remains one of the important statements of the conservative political philosophy.

In 1869 Stephen accepted the post of legal member of the viceroy's council in India and, like Macaulay and Sir Henry Maine before him, became engrossed in the reform and recodification of Indian law. He returned to England in 1872 and almost immediately became identified with the movement to codify the criminal law of England. His *Digest* of the criminal law (1877) was enthusiastically received. He was the principal draftsman of the Indictable Offences bill, which was, in effect, a criminal code. Because of powerful opposition, the bill was never introduced in parliament. Although failing of their immediate objectives, Stephen's efforts influenced the drafting of legislation in the nations of the British commonwealth, and, even today, are consulted in attempts to reformulate the criminal law of English-speaking countries. In 1883 Stephen published his great work, *History of the Criminal Law of England.* Although dogmatic in tone, often deficient in the critical handling of sources, and in many respects incomplete, the work represents a remarkable achievement which, on the whole, has never been surpassed.

In 1879 Stephen became a judge in the queen's bench division of the high court. He resigned in 1891, after a breakdown, and received a baronetcy in recognition of his services. He died in Ipswich on March 11, 1894. A selection of his letters, edited by his daughter, Caroline Emelia Stephen, was published in 1907.

BIBLIOGRAPHY.—Sir Leslie Stephen, *Life of Sir James Fitzjames Stephen* (1895) with bibliographical appendix, is one of the outstanding biographies in the English language; a shorter account by the same author will be found in the *Dictionary of National Biography. See* also Sir C. P. Ilbert, "Sir James Stephen as a Legislator," *Law Quart. Rev.,* x. 222; L. Radzinowicz, *Sir James Fitzjames Stephen,* Selden Society Lecture (1957). (F. A. A.)

**STEPHEN, SIR LESLIE** (1832–1904), English critic, man of letters and first editor of the *Dictionary of National Biography,* was born in London on Nov. 28, 1832, into a distinguished intellectual family. His grandfather was a member of the Clapham sect, his father a fine colonial servant, his brother a great criminal lawyer and Anglo-Indian administrator; the Venns and Diceys were his first cousins. He was educated at Eton, at King's college, London, and at Trinity hall, Cambridge, where he was elected to a fellowship in 1854 and became junior tutor in 1856. He won fame as a rowing coach and inaugurated the Oxford and Cambridge athletics contest; he also tried unsuccessfully to reform the outdated university curriculum. He had been ordained in 1855, but his philosophical studies, combined probably with the controversy that followed the publication of Charles Darwin's *Origin of Species* (1859), caused him to lose his faith; in 1862 he resigned his tutorship and two years later left Cambridge to live in London.

Through his brother, James Fitzjames, a contributor to the *Saturday Review,* Stephen gained an entry to the literary world, contributing to many periodicals. In politics he was a radical and supported the North during the American Civil War, and his articles in defense of agnosticism were republished in *Essays on Freethinking and Plainspeaking* (1873) and *An Agnostic's Apology* (1893). In 1871 George Smith offered him the editorship of the *Cornhill,* for which he wrote literary criticism later republished in the three series of *Hours in a Library* (1874–79). Stephen was the first serious critic of the novel and his work still deserves consideration by historians of literary criticism. Thomas Hardy, R. L. Stevenson, Edmund Gosse and Henry James were among those whom Stephen, as an editor, encouraged. After 11 years he resigned but continued to write for periodicals. *Studies of a Biographer* (4 vol., 1898–1902) and *Social Rights and Duties* (1896) contain the best of this work. He also wrote a short book on *Hobbes* (1904) and his Ford lectures, *English Literature and Society in the Eighteenth Century* (1904), were pioneer work in the sociological study of literature.

His greatest learned work was his excellently written *History of English Thought in the Eighteenth Century* (1876). *The English Utilitarians* (1900) was less compact and successful though it is still a useful source. His philosophical contribution to rationalist tradition, *Science of Ethics* (1882), attempted to wed evolutionary theory to ethics. His most enduring bequest to posterity is the *Dictionary of National Biography,* of which he edited the first 26 volumes and to which he contributed many biographies. In recognition of this service to letters he was created knight commander of the Bath in 1902 and received other honours.

Stephen was a leader among Victorian mountaineers and was president of the Alpine club (1865–68) and editor of the *Alpine Journal* (1868–71). Some of his more famous climbs are recorded in *The Playground of Europe* (1871). He was also the leader of "The Tramps," a club of intellectuals who enjoyed taking 30-mi. Sunday walks.

Stephen was highly respected in intellectual society and remembered for many acts of kindness to his friends. He was formidable in appearance, dispassionate in judgment and the enemy of whatever he considered to be cant or wilful obscurity which was designed to conceal the truth. He was shy and given to silence, the more so after the death in 1875 of his first wife Minny, the second daughter of Thackeray. In 1878 he married Julia Jackson, the widow of Herbert Duckworth, and among their four children were the painter Vanessa Bell and the novelist Virginia Woolf. He died in London on Feb. 22, 1904.

BIBLIOGRAPHY.—F. W. Maitland, *Life and Letters of Leslie Stephen* (1906); N. G. Annan, *Leslie Stephen: His Thought and Character in Relation to His Time* (1951); and—for a list of Stephen's writings—L. Stephen, *Men, Books and Mountains,* ed. by S. O. A. Ullmann (1956). (N. G. A.)

**STEPHENS, ALEXANDER HAMILTON** (1812–1883), vice-president of the Confederate States during the American Civil War, was born in Wilkes (now Taliaferro) County, Georgia, on Feb. 11, 1812. In 1828 Stephens was sent by the Georgia Educational Society to Franklin College (University of Georgia), where he graduated in 1832. After teaching in rural schools for approximately a year and a half he read law and was admitted to the bar in 1834.

BY COURTESY OF THE NATIONAL ARCHIVES
STEPHENS

In 1836 he was elected to the Georgia House of Representatives after a campaign in which he attacked the doctrine of nullification and opposed all extralegal steps against the abolitionists. He was annually reelected until 1841; in 1842 he was elected to the state Senate, and in the following year, on the Whig ticket, to the national House of Representatives. In this latter body he urged the annexation of Texas, chiefly as a means of achieving more power for the South in Congress. He vigorously supported the Compromise of 1850 and continued to act with the Whigs of the North until they, in 1852, nominated Gen. Winfield Scott for the presidency without Scott's endorsement of the compromise. In 1854 Stephens helped secure passage of the Kansas-Nebraska Bill.

He strongly opposed secession, but when Georgia seceded he followed his state and was elected vice-president of the Confederacy.

Throughout the war, Stephens was so concerned about states' rights and civil liberty that he opposed the exercise of extra-constitutional war powers by Pres. Jefferson Davis lest the freedom for which the South was fighting should be destroyed. His policy was to preserve constitutional government in the South and strengthen the antiwar party in the North by convincing it that the Lincoln administration had abandoned such government; to the same end he urged, in 1864, the unconditional discharge of Federal prisoners in the South. Stephens headed the Confederate commission to the peace conference at Hampton Roads, Va., in February 1865. In the following May, after the fall of the Confederacy, he was arrested at his home and taken to Fort Warren, in Boston Harbour, where he was confined until Oct. 12. In 1866 he was elected to the U.S. Senate but was not permitted to take his seat. He was a U.S. representative (1873–82) and governor of Georgia in 1882–83, dying in office, at Atlanta, on March 4, 1883.

From 1871 to 1873 Stephens edited the *Atlanta Southern Sun.* His published works include *A Constitutional View of the Late War Between the States* (1868–70), perhaps the best statement of the Southern position with reference to state sovereignty and secession; *The Reviewers Reviewed* (1872), a supplement to the preceding work; and *A Compendium of the History of the United States* (1875; new ed., 1883).

*See* Rudolph Von Abele, *Alexander H. Stephens* (1946).

**STEPHENS, JAMES** (1882–1950), Irish poet and storyteller whose pantheistic philosophy is revealed both in his fairy tales set in the Dublin slums and in his compassionate poems about animals, was born in Dublin on Feb. 2, 1882. He was a solicitor's clerk when *The Crock of Gold* (1912), with its fabulous Celtic theme, established his fame. But he also knew urban poverty (his theme in *The Charwoman's Daughter,* 1912), and his astringent irony suggests affinities with James Joyce. He wrote *The Demi-Gods* (1914) in a similar vein, and (having learned Gaelic) *Deirdre* (1923) in more formal, rhythmic prose. Short stories and lyric poems constitute the remainder of his work. Stephens was actively connected with the Irish nationalist movement. By 1940 he was living in London, and having discovered himself as a broadcaster of genius, was frequently on the air from 1939 until his death in London on Dec. 26, 1950. (P. At.)

**STEPHENSON,** the family name of three English engineers prominent in the development of railways.

George Stephenson (1781–1848), inventor and founder of railways, was born at Wylam, Northumberland, on June 9, 1781. His early life was spent in extreme poverty, but in 1804 he moved to Killingworth, Northumberland, supplementing his meagre income by repairing watches and clocks, and in 1812, after seriously considering emigrating, was appointed engine-wright of High Pit colliery at a salary of £100 per year. It was there that, in 1815, he designed and produced his version of the miners' safety lamp, while Sir Humphry Davy was still carrying out experiments. When Davy's lamp did appear there was violent controversy as to who should receive the credit for the invention.

About this time also Stephenson was given financial backing to produce for the colliery a "travelling engine" from pit-head to the port. It was a success and when, in 1822, the Stockton and Darlington railway was under construction, he persuaded the directors to use steam instead of animal traction. The railway opened on Sept. 27, 1825, and the first public passenger train in the world was drawn by Stephenson's "Active," later renamed "Locomotion." When the Liverpool and Manchester railway was nearing completion, Stephenson again persuaded the directors to try locomotives: a prize of £500 was offered for a suitable locomotive and was won by his "Rocket." Eight engines in all were employed when this line opened on Sept. 15, 1830, all having been built at Newcastle, in the works he founded with his cousin, Thomas Richardson, and a colleague, Edward Pease. Stephenson was engineer of many other railways in the midlands, but strongly disapproved of the "railway mania" which reached its climax in 1844. He was also consultant to many foreign companies, notably in Belgium and Spain. His last years were spent in retirement at Tapton house, Chesterfield, where he died on Aug. 12, 1848. (*See* also Railway: *Locomotives;* Steam.)

Robert Stephenson (1803–1859), who specialized in the construction of railway bridges, was born at Willington Quay, Northumberland, Oct. 16, 1803, the only son of George Stephenson. Educated at Bruce's academy, Newcastle upon Tyne, and Edinburgh university, in 1819 he was apprenticed to Nicholas Wood at Killingworth. In 1821 he assisted his father in a survey for the Stockton and Darlington and Liverpool and Manchester railways, but failing health in 1824 led to his accepting a mining appointment in South America. Recalled to England in 1827 to take up work on locomotives at Newcastle, he was able to overcome the problem of securing boiler tubes, a problem that had been giving much trouble to the designers, and he was responsible for most of the improvements to locomotives at this time. In 1833 he was appointed engineer of the London and Birmingham railway; while holding this appointment he carried out a number of engineering feats, such as the Blisworth cutting and the Kilsby tunnel. This railway proved to be a great success and was the first to run into London from the industrial north.

Robert Stephenson, however, was particularly concerned with the construction of tubular girder railway bridges and his work extended to Sweden, Denmark, Belgium, Switzerland and Egypt. The more notable examples were the Britannia tubular bridge over the Menai straits, the tubular bridge over the river Conway and the Victoria tubular bridge over the St. Lawrence river at Montreal. In 1847 he entered parliament as conservative member for Whitby, retaining the seat until his death in London on Oct. 12, 1859. (*See* also Railway.) (T. M. S.)

George Robert Stephenson (1819–1905), the nephew of George Stephenson (1781–1848), was born at Newcastle upon Tyne on Oct. 20, 1819. After working in colliery workshops near Manchester, he was sent to King William's school, Isle of Man. After his father's death in 1837 he worked for his uncle in the drawing office of the Manchester and Leeds railway. In 1860, when he was consulting engineer to the provincial government of Canterbury, New Zealand, the Lyttelton-Christchurch line was built under his direction. He returned to England and with Sir John Hawkshaw in 1864 built the East London railway. He was partly responsible for the construction of the Victoria tubular bridge across the St. Lawrence and designed many bridges in England and abroad. In 1859 he succeeded his cousin Robert Stephenson at the locomotive works at Newcastle upon Tyne, and at the Snibston and Tapton collieries. He died at Cheltenham on Oct. 26, 1905.

**STERCULIACEAE,** the cacao or chocolate family of plants, consisting of about 50 genera with 1,200 species of tropical or subtropical trees, shrubs and herbs. Five genera (*Ayenia, Fremontodendron, Hermannia, Melochia* and *Waltheria*) have representatives in southern United States. The leaves of Sterculiaceae are alternate and simple or palmately compound; flowers, often unisexual, are solitary or clustered and have three to five sepals and five or no petals. The usually numerous stamens are separate or joined into a column and the superior ovary has two to five cavities or separate parts. The fruit is fleshy, or dry and generally capsular. Important plants of the family include cacao (*Theobroma cacao*), source of cocoa (*q.v.*) and chocolate; cola (*see* Kola Nut) (*Cola nitida* and *C. acuminata*), which yields a stimulant used in cola drinks; and a few *Sterculia* species (especially, *Sterculia urens*), which yield karaya gum, an important substitute for tragacanth (*see* Gums, Plant). Species of a few genera are cultivated as ornamentals, notably bottle tree (*Brachychiton*), dombeya (*Dom-*

E. AUBERT DE LA RÜE

BOTTLE TREE (BRACHYCHITON RUPESTRIS), COMMON TO AUSTRALIA

*beya*), Chinese parasol tree (*Firmiana*), flannel bush (*Fremontodendron*) and sterculia (*Sterculia*).

In geologic times the family was distributed far beyond the limits of the present tropics and subtropics; *e.g.*, into Alaska.

(J. W. Tt.)

**STEREOCHEMISTRY.** Following are the main sections and divisions of this article:



## I. INTRODUCTION

The term stereochemistry (from Gr. "solid," + chemistry) is applied in a wide sense to all that part of physical science which deals with those properties of chemical compounds which are believed to be due to the relative positions of the different atoms within a single molecule, or to the relative positions of different molecules in a larger aggregate of material. In this article, however, the term is used in a narrower sense.

The following discussion is almost entirely limited to such aspects of the subject as are included in the field of stereoisomerism (*see* ISOMERISM), and it deals only with the stereochemical properties of individual molecules or ions. (For other aspects of the subject, which are largely ignored here, *see* CRYSTALLOGRAPHY: *Crystal-Structure Analysis;* ELECTRON DIFFRACTION; SPECTROSCOPY.)

One important goal of the structural theory of organic chemistry (knowledge of which is here assumed, *see* CHEMISTRY: *Organic Chemistry;* ISOMERISM) is to associate with the molecule (or with each of the ions, *see* MOLECULE) of each distinct compound a diagram, known as its structural formula or structure. The purpose of such a diagram is not to represent the true Euclidean geometry of the molecules of the substance; it is rather to specify the valences of the various atoms (*i.e.*, the numbers of lines which terminate at the corresponding atomic symbols) and the numbers of bonds between the various pairs of atoms (*i.e.*, the numbers of lines drawn between the corresponding pairs of atomic symbols).

About the middle of the 19th century, it was discovered that in certain instances the methods of structural chemistry led to the assignment of the same structural formula to more than one compound. It was, therefore, evident that the rules of structural chemistry were, in these instances, insufficient for the complete identification of the compounds in question. The theories of stereochemistry (in the narrower sense) were devised as the corrections necessary to remedy this defect. It proved possible to account for the number of distinct compounds to be associated with each structural diagram if two molecules of the same substance were assumed always to have not only the same structure, but also the same arrangement of their atoms in space. This geometrical interpretation has received independent support from the data derived from studies of X-ray and electron diffraction and of spectra. Consequently, although the possibility of an alternative, nongeometrical explanation of the observed numbers of isomers had not been seriously explored, the correctness of the geometrical interpretation was generally accepted without question in the 1960s. In the present article it is assumed explicitly.

For the sake of definiteness, but at the expense of anticipating and duplicating a small part of the discussion in subsequent sections, a specific example of the way in which stereoisomers are considered to differ geometrically may be given here. The two different 1,2-dichloroethylenes, which possess the same structure CHCl=CHCl, are thought to have the different geometrical forms represented by the following planar diagrams.

```
H     Cl          H     Cl
 \   /             \   /
   C                 C
   ‖                 ‖
   C                 C
 /   \             /   \
H     Cl          Cl    H
```

## II. EARLY HISTORY OF STEREOCHEMISTRY

**1. Optical Activity.**—The original approach to the subject of stereochemistry arose from a study of certain optical phenomena. In 1811 D. F. Arago discovered that crystals of quartz are optically active (*i.e.*, that they rotate the plane of polarization of plane polarized light). That this optical activity (or rotatory power) is not restricted to crystalline solids was demonstrated by J. B. Biot, who found in 1815, and later, that oil of turpentine and aqueous solutions of tartaric acid or of sugar are optically active, and in 1817 that even gaseous turpentine is also active.

**2. Specific Rotation.**—For the characterization of an optically active substance, the so-called specific rotation (introduced by Biot in 1836) has proved useful. This quantity is defined by the equation

$$[\alpha]_\lambda^t = \frac{\alpha}{ld}$$

where $[\alpha]_\lambda^t$ is the specific rotation for light of wavelength $\lambda$ at the temperature $t°$; and $\alpha$ is the rotation (in degrees) produced by passage of the light through a tube $l$ decimetres in length, which is filled with the optically active substance (either pure or in solution) at a concentration of $d$ grams per cubic centimetre. The rotation is taken with the positive sign if it is to the right (*i.e.*, in the sense which is clockwise when regarded in the direction contrary to that in which the light is traveling), and with the negative sign if it is to the left (*i.e.*, in the opposite, counterclockwise sense).

Ideally the specific rotation, as so defined, should be a characteristic property of the substance to which it applies, and its value should be independent of the experimental conditions. In practice, however, it varies somewhat in magnitude with the wavelength of the light, with the temperature, with the solvent (if any) and with the concentration. In a few instances, even the sign of rotation is found to change with conditions.

With colourless compounds, the variation in specific rotation with the wavelength of the light used is ordinarily small, but nevertheless great enough to make necessary the precise statement of the wavelength. The remaining variations are usually counteracted by standardization of the experimental procedure to as great an extent as possible. Thus, unless statements are made to the contrary, specific rotations are considered to apply to room temperature and to dilute solutions in specified solvents. Within these limitations, specific rotations may be employed for the characterization, identification and even quantitative analysis of optically active substances.

**3. The Work of Pasteur.**—After the discoveries of polarized light and of optical activity, the next important advance toward the modern stereochemical theories was made by Louis Pasteur in a series of investigations on tartaric and racemic acids, carried out chiefly during the years 1849–53. These two acids not only have identical chemical compositions but also possess the same structure $HO_2C$—CHOH—CHOH—$CO_2H$. Yet they show certain marked differences in properties. For example, racemic acid is much less soluble in water than tartaric acid and crystallizes with water of crystallization, whereas tartaric acid separates in anhydrous crystals; the most remarkable difference between the two substances, however, is in their effect on plane polarized light. Tartaric acid and its salts (the tartrates) are optically active; more specifically, they are dextrorotatory (*i.e.,* their aqueous solutions rotate the plane of polarization to the right). On the other hand, racemic acid and its salts (the racemates) are optically inactive.

Pasteur's discoveries arose out of a crystallographic investigation of tartaric acid. He observed that there was a certain lack of symmetry in the crystalline form of this substance of such a kind that the crystal was nonsuperposable on its mirror image.

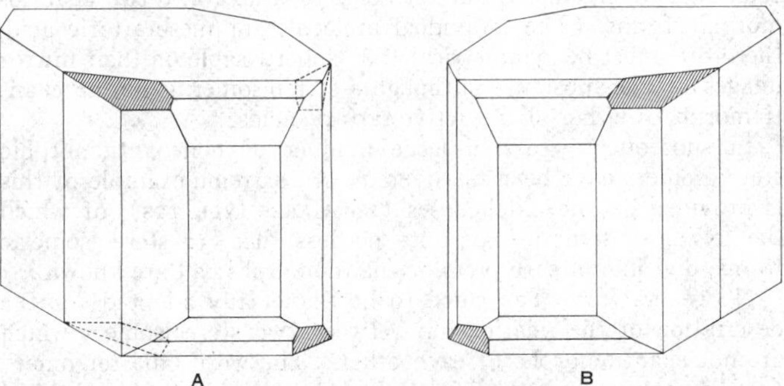


FROM STEWART, "STEREO-CHEMISTRY"; REPRODUCED BY PERMISSION FROM LONGMANS GREEN & CO.

FIG. 1.—(A AND B) ENANTIOMORPHOUS CRYSTALS OF SODIUM AMMONIUM TARTRATE

The crystal and its image thus differ in the same kind of way as the right and left hands. He prepared and examined 19 different salts of tartaric acid and found that each of these showed a similar lack of symmetry in its crystalline form. Thus fig. 1(A) represents the crystalline form of one of these salts, sodium ammonium tartrate. If the crystal possessed the full symmetry of the system to which it belongs, two faces, corresponding with the two shaded areas, should be found in the positions indicated by broken lines. These faces, instead of occurring eight times in the crystal, occur only four times (there are of course two corresponding faces on the back of the crystal not shown in the figure); such faces, occurring only half as frequently as the full symmetry of the crystal demands, are termed hemihedral faces. The sodium ammonium tartrate crystal, because of the presence of these hemihedral faces, is evidently nonsuperposable on its mirror image represented in fig. 1(B). In contrast to tartaric acid and the tartrates, racemic acid and such of its salts as Pasteur examined (with the exception of sodium ammonium racemate, *see* below) crystallize in symmetrical forms superposable on their mirror images. The optically active tartrates thus crystallize in dissymmetric forms, whereas the optically inactive racemates yield symmetrical crystals. (According to accepted terminology, an object is said to be dissymmetric if it is not superposable on its mirror image, and to be asymmetric if it possesses no element of symmetry whatever, *see* below. In discussions of stereochemistry, the word asymmetric is often used loosely in places where dissymmetric is intended; in the present article, however, the distinction is observed.)

Pasteur's chief discovery was made through investigating the exceptional racemate, sodium ammonium racemate, referred to above. Crystallized from water at a temperature below 28° C., this salt yields crystals which, unlike those of the other racemates, exhibit hemihedral faces; the crystals, however, are of two kinds. Some are identical in form with those of dextrorotatory sodium ammonium tartrate (fig. 1[A]) and are in fact crystals of that salt. The other crystals differ from these only in that their hemihedrism is in the opposite sense; they are thus the realization of the mirror image of sodium ammonium tartrate and have the form represented in fig. 1(B). When picked out from the mixture and dissolved in water, they give a levorotatory solution (*i.e.,* a solution which rotates the plane of polarization to the left). The acid obtained from these crystals has a crystalline form which is the mirror image of that of tartaric acid, and its solutions are levorotatory. It is to be regarded as a second variety of tartaric acid.

This new form of tartaric acid and the original one have exactly the same melting point and specific gravity; moreover, they exhibit exactly the same chemical reactivities toward all optically inactive reagents. Two substances related in this manner are said to be enantiomorphs of each other. (The further expressions antimers and optical antipodes are also frequently used.) A more detailed discussion of the ways in which such pairs of substances resemble each other, and of those in which they differ from each other, is given below (see *Enantiomorphs,* below).

On the basis of his discoveries, Pasteur postulated that, in consequence of the arrangement of their constituent atoms in space, the individual molecules of any optically active substance must be nonsuperposable on their own mirror images (*i.e.,* that they must be dissymmetric). Moreover, he postulated further that the molecules of any optically active substance must be superposable on the mirror images of the molecules of the enantiomorph of that substance. The situation visualized by Pasteur can be made more concrete with the aid of a rough analogy. The molecules of, say, dextrorotatory tartaric acid may be compared with right-hand gloves, whereas those of its levorotatory enantiomorph may be compared with left-hand gloves. No glove is identical with its own mirror image, but any right-hand glove is identical with the mirror image of any left-hand glove, and vice versa. If the analogy is carried a step further, a crystal of racemic acid can be compared with a large package of pairs of gloves; since each pair consists of one right-hand and one left-hand glove, the package as a whole may be considered superposable on its mirror image. These postulates of Pasteur form the basis of the following discussion; their justification lies in the fact that, as is shown below, they permit uniformly correct predictions to be made regarding the properties of, and relationships among, optically active substances.

## III. GENERAL DISCUSSION OF STEREOISOMERISM

**1. Symmetry Elements of Molecules.**—It is desirable at this point to examine the characteristics of a molecule which make it dissymmetric, or prevent its being so, as the case may be.

The symmetry of any rigid body can be described with the aid of its so-called symmetry elements. These elements are of several different kinds, of which only the following need be mentioned here. (1) An object is said to possess a plane of symmetry if a plane mirror can be imagined passing through it so that one half of the object coincides with the reflection in the mirror of the other half. The plane of the mirror is then the plane of symmetry. (2) An object is said to possess an $n$-fold axis (or an axis of order $n$) if it possesses an axis, about which rotation by $360°/n$ brings the object into a position indistinguishable from its original one. The order $n$ can take on any positive integral value, or it may be infinite if the object has, for example, the symmetry of a right circular cylinder. In general, $n$ rotations by $360°/n$ bring the object into a position identical with, and not merely indistinguishable from, the original one. Any straight line passing through any object is clearly a onefold axis; such onefold axes may usually be ignored, however, in discussions of symmetry since an infinite number of them are always present. (3) An object is said to possess a centre of inversion (or of symmetry, or of reflection) if it contains a point within it, such that any straight line through that point encounters exactly the same environment in each of its two directions. Further discussion, with examples, of each of these types of symmetry element is given in the article CRYSTALLOGRAPHY. A number of additional examples are also mentioned below.

The above-mentioned plane and centre of symmetry are examples of elements with what may be termed reflection symmetry. The most general type of element possessing this kind of symmetry is the so-called alternating (or mirror) axis, of which the plane and centre of symmetry are only special cases. Although no detailed description of alternating axes need be given here, mention should be made of the fact that an object may possess such an axis without having either plane or centre of symmetry. (*See* below.)

Mathematical analysis has shown that an object is superposable on its mirror image if, and only if, it possesses reflection symmetry of some sort. In stereochemistry, this rule finds its only important applications in those instances in which the molecules have either planes or centres of symmetry, or both. Not until 1955 was there reported (G. E. McCasland and S. Proskow) the preparation of an optically inactive substance with neither of these two symmetry elements, but with a fourfold alternating axis. Accordingly, the statement that a compound must be optically active unless it is a mixture of enantiomorphs (like racemic acid) or else its molecules possess either planes or centres of symmetry is adequate for most purposes. It is especially to be noted that the presence of simple (not alternating) axes of symmetry is not sufficient to ensure optical inactivity; or, in other words, that a molecule may possess an axis of symmetry and still be dissymmetric. (For an example of a dissymmetric molecule with both twofold and threefold simple axes, *see* the cobalt compound XXXII in the section below, *Elements of Co-ordination Number 6.*)

**2. Enantiomorphs.**—Since enantiomorphs have not only identical structures but also very similar configurations (*i.e.,* atomic arrangements in space), such pairs of substances should possess extremely similar properties. Indeed, in consequence of the mirror-image relationship assumed to exist between enantiomorphs, each property of either enantiomorph must be (in the sense discussed below) the mirror image of the corresponding property of the other enantiomorph; in other words, two enantiomorphs must be identical with respect to all those properties which are themselves (in this same sense) identical with their own mirror images, and can differ with respect to only those other properties which are different from their mirror images. For example, the melting point of any substance may be considered identical with that of its mirror image, since the temperature at which solid and liquid are in equilibrium must be the same whether the experiment is viewed directly or by reflection in a mirror. Consequently, two enantiomorphs must have identical melting points. In a similar way, it can be shown that two enantiomorphs must also have identical vapour tensions at any specified temperature, identical boiling points at any specified pressure, identical densities under the same conditions, identical solubilities in any specified optically inactive solvent, identical rates of reaction with any specified optically inactive reagent (or reagents), identical equilibriums in their reactions with any specified optically inactive reagent (or reagents), and so on. On the other hand, the mirror image of a rotation of the plane of polarization by a specified number of degrees to the right (or left) may be considered to be a rotation by exactly the same number of degrees to the left (or right), respectively. Consequently, two enantiomorphs, under identical conditions, must rotate the plane of polarization by equal amounts but in opposite directions. Similarly, the mirror image of right (or left) circularly polarized light is identical not with itself but instead with left (or right) circularly polarized light. Consequently, two enantiomorphs may be expected to possess different optical properties (*e.g.,* absorption spectra, indexes of refraction, etc.) when examined with circularly polarized light, but not when examined with ordinary light or even (except for the optical rotation) when examined with plane polarized light; conversely, the optical properties of a single optically active substance may be expected to be different with right and left circularly polarized light. The expected differences in spectrum have been observed experimentally (circular dichroism, Cotton effect); and the differences in index of refraction, although so small that their direct observation is difficult, are known always to exist since the observed angle of rotation by an optically active substance can be shown to be proportional to the difference in the indexes of refraction for right and left circularly polarized light. Also, measurable differences have been found in the rates and extents of adsorption (*q.v.*) of enantiomorphs upon optically active solid adsorbents, and in the rates and equilibriums of their reactions with optically active reagents (see *Asymmetric Syntheses and Decompositions,* below). Finally, the crystals of two enantiomorphs may be nonsuperposable mirror images of each other (*cf.* the enantiomorphic tartaric acids and tartrates, above); in many instances, however, the forms of the crystals of enantiomorphs are symmetrical and identical.

**3. Diastereomers.**—Examples of stereoisomers which are not enantiomorphs of each other are well known. In 1853 Pasteur discovered that the cinchonine (*see* CINCHONA BARK, ALKALOIDS OF) salt of either tartaric or racemic acid, when heated for several hours at 170° C., is transformed into the salt of still a different stereoisomeric acid. This acid, known as mesotartaric acid, resembles racemic acid in being optically inactive, but it differs from racemic acid in having a different melting point, different solubilities, etc., and also in not being separable into two enantiomorphic forms. The individual molecules of mesotartaric acid, therefore, must be symmetrical (*i.e.,* superposable on their mirror images). The substance, although a stereoisomer, is not an enantiomorph, of either of the active tartaric acids.

In subsequent years, a large number of nonenantiomorphic stereoisomers have been discovered. An extreme example of this is provided by the aldohexoses (*see* CARBOHYDRATES), of which the pyranose structure permits no less than 32 stereoisomeric forms, divisible into 16 pairs of enantiomorphs; all are known.

No general term has come to be universally adopted for the description of the relationship between two stereoisomers which are not enantiomorphs of each other. The word "diastereomer" (or diastereoisomer, or diamer) is often applied to certain, but usually not to all, such pairs of substances. For purposes of brevity and convenience throughout the remainder of this article, any nonenantiomorphic stereoisomer will be termed a diastereomer. It is to be noted, however, that, in this respect, the present article departs somewhat from the most customary terminology.

Unlike enantiomorphs, diastereomers (in the sense just defined) need not have closely similar physical and chemical properties. Indeed, they may differ as greatly as do structural isomers. For example, either of the optically active tartaric acids melts at 187° C., whereas mesotartaric acid melts at 143° C.

**4. Meso Forms.**—As with the tartaric acids, it frequently happens that a set of stereoisomers contains both optically active and optically inactive members. The inactive members of such sets are frequently distinguished from their active isomers by being called meso forms. (This is, of course, the significance of the name mesotartaric acid.)

**5. Racemic Modifications.**—A mixture of equal quantities of two enantiomorphs, which is optically inactive, is known as a racemic modification. The name is derived from racemic acid, the first example of such a mixture to be carefully studied. (This double use of the word racemic is found in practice to lead to little if any confusion.) Any process by which an optically active substance is transformed into the corresponding racemic modification is known as a racemization; conversely, any process by which a racemic modification is separated into the two enantiomorphs is known as a resolution. (See *Racemization* and *Resolution,* below.)

In the liquid and gaseous states, a racemic modification seems always to be merely a mechanical mixture of its two components. In the solid state, however, three different situations have been encountered. (1) Sometimes, as with sodium ammonium racemate crystallized from water at a temperature below 28° C. (*see* above), the solid is a conglomerate (or racemic mixture) consisting of separate crystals of the two enantiomorphic forms. (2) Sometimes, as with the dimethyl ester (*see* ESTERS) of racemic acid, the two enantiomorphs form a 1:1 compound (or racemate) with each other. Such compounds, however, decompose into their constituents at temperatures above their melting points. (3) Sometimes, as with camphor oxime (*see* OXIMES), the enantiomorphs form a solid solution (or pseudoracemic mixed crystal).

**6. A Word About Nomenclature.**—Dextrorotatory and levorotatory enantiomorphs were originally designated by the prefixes *d* and *l*, respectively, so that the dextrorotatory and levorotatory tartaric acids, for example, were called *d*-tartaric acid and *l*-tartaric acid, respectively. Somewhat later, however, these prefixes were made to refer also to the so-called optically active series to which the substances belonged, as well as to the directions of rotation. (For the significance of these series, see *Optically Active Series,* below.) As a result of this ambiguity in nomenclature, there were found to be many substances which had to be assigned the prefix *d* because they were dextrorotatory, and, at the same time, the prefix *l* because they belonged to the *l*-series (or the opposite). The confusion which was thus caused has been alleviated to some extent by the adoption of the convention that the prefixes D and L are used for the designation of the optically active series, and that the further prefixes (+) and (−) are employed to represent dextrorotation and levorotation, respectively.

Unfortunately, the convention just discussed is not always followed consistently by all chemists. If a substance does not belong to any of the accepted optically active series, the prefixes *d* and *l* are often used, as originally, to indicate the direction of rotation. Thus, the naturally occurring levorotatory quinine (*q.v.*) is often referred to as *l*-quinine rather than as (−)-quinine. No confusion can arise in such instances since no *d*- and *l*-series, or D- and L-series, have been defined for alkaloids like quinine. However, an expression like "*d*-lactic acid" may refer either to the dextrorotatory form, which belongs to the L-series (*see* above), or to its enantiomorph in the D-series. Consequently, such an expression is configurationally meaningless, unless accompanied by a statement as to which convention is being employed. In this article, the prefixes D and L are used to represent the optically active series, and the prefixes (+) and (−) are used to represent the direction of rotation (even for substances like quinine, for which no series have been defined).

Optically inactive meso forms are frequently designated by the prefix *i* (for inactive) or *m* (for meso). Thus mesotartaric acid may be called either *i*-tartaric acid or *m*-tartaric acid. Racemic modifications are similarly designated by the prefix *r* (for racemic) or (±) or DL (to indicate that the compound is a mixture of the two enantiomorphs). Thus, racemic acid may be called *r*- , (±)- , or DL-tartaric acid.

**7. Racemization.**—The ease with which an optically active substance can be transformed into the racemic modification varies within wide limits. On the one hand, the racemization of certain compounds (for example, an optically active paraffin hydrocarbon) is extremely difficult; on the other hand, the racemization of certain other compounds (for example, a tertiary amine, see *Stereochemistry of Nitrogen,* below) is so easily accomplished that the optically active forms cannot be obtained. With innumerable further compounds, however, the ease of racemization lies between these two extremes. Such compounds can be separated (see *Resolution,* below) into the active enantiomorphs, which can then be racemized more or less readily.

The experimental conditions under which the racemization of racemizable substances can be effected also vary widely. In all instances, however, the racemization is presumed to occur as a result of a reversible transformation into an unstable substance which is symmetric and so incapable of optical activity; the reverse transformation back from this hypothetical inactive intermediate then leads to the inactive (*i.e.,* racemic) modification of the original substance.

The transformations which thus lead to racemization are considered most commonly to involve chemical reactions of a familiar type, but occasionally to involve merely geometrical deformations.

**8. Resolution.**—Whenever a substance capable of optical activity is prepared under the usual experimental conditions from exclusively inactive reagents, the product obtained is always the inactive racemic modification. This is because, in view of the complete symmetry of the experimental situation, the probability that a molecule of the dextrorotatory enantiomorph will be formed is exactly the same as the probability that one of the levorotatory enantiomorph will be formed. Consequently, equal numbers of molecules of the enantiomorphs must be formed, so that the product must be racemic. If an optically active product is desired instead a resolution must therefore be performed.

The separation of a racemic modification into its two optically active components is made rather difficult by the close similarity of enantiomorphs in nearly all their properties. Two important methods of resolution were developed by Pasteur. The first of these, known as the method of spontaneous separation, has already been described in connection with Pasteur's work on sodium ammonium racemate. It can be employed if the solid racemic modification is a conglomerate composed of observably different crystals. Only a few instances in which this condition is satisfied have been reported in the organic chemical literature. Consequently, this method, although of great historical and theoretical interest, is seldom applicable.

Pasteur's second method of resolution is of much greater generality than his first, and it is the only one commonly used. It is based upon the transformation of the mixture of enantiomorphs into a mixture of diastereomers, which, since they differ in physical properties, can be separated relatively easily. This transformation requires the use of some previously obtained optically active substance. For example, Pasteur showed in 1853 that when racemic acid is treated with a naturally occurring optically active base, such as cinchonine, strychnine, brucine or quinine (*see* ALKALOIDS), the resulting salt is a mixture of diastereomers and no longer one of enantiomorphs. This is because (if, for definiteness, the base is assumed to be dextrorotatory) the salt formed from the (+)-acid and (+)-base is not the mirror image of the one formed from the (−)-acid and the same (+)-base. (The mirror image would instead be the salt formed from the (−)-acid and (−)-base.) The two salts present in the mixture may, therefore, be expected to have different solubilities and so to be separable by crystallization. After the separation has been carried out, the salt from the (+)-acid and (+)-base gives the pure (+)-acid when treated with a strong mineral acid, and the other salt gives the pure (−)-acid when treated similarly.

In the form just outlined, Pasteur's second method can be applied to the resolution of only racemic acids. Various modifications have been developed, however, and these permit it to be greatly extended. Thus, a racemic base can be resolved by means of salt formation with an optically active acid, a racemic aldehyde or ketone can be resolved by means of hydrazone formation with an optically active hydrazine, and so on. Moreover, a racemic alcohol can be resolved if it is first transformed into the acid ester of a dibasic acid (such as phthalic acid, *q.v.*), which is neutralized as before with an optically active base; the resulting ester salt can then be separated into the diastereomeric forms and finally hydrolyzed back to the alcohol.

Similar schemes of greater or less complexity can be devised for most remaining types of substance.

**9. Asymmetric Syntheses and Decompositions.**—If a compound capable of optical activity is prepared in a dissymmetric environment, the product obtained need not be completely racemic since factors are present which may favour the formation of one enantiomorph over that of the other. Such reactions are known as asymmetric syntheses (although dissymmetric syntheses might seem a more appropriate expression). For example, although the reduction of inactive phenylglyoxylic acid $C_6H_5$—CO—$CO_2H$ leads to completely racemic mandelic acid $C_6H_5$—CHOH—$CO_2H$, the reduction of the (−)-menthyl ester of the acid, followed by hydrolysis of the resulting menthyl mandelate gives a mandelic acid which is levorotatory although it contains a considerable amount of the (+)-enantiomorph. This slightly active acid can be separated by crystallization into the optically pure (−)-mandelic acid and *r*-mandelic acid. A different type of asymmetric synthesis is illustrated by the base-catalyzed reaction between benzaldehyde $C_6H_5$—CHO and hydrogen cyanide HCN to give mandelonitrile $C_6H_5$—CHOH—CN. Since the reagents are optically inactive, the product is necessarily racemic if the basic catalyst is also inactive; however, if an optically active catalyst, such as the alkaloid quinine, is used instead, the resulting mandelonitrile is somewhat optically active.

The asymmetric syntheses mentioned above are relative, since they require the previous existence of at least one optically active substance. A few absolute asymmetric syntheses, which are not subject to this requirement, have been reported. These syntheses are based upon photochemical reactions (*see* PHOTOCHEMISTRY) initiated by circularly polarized light; since circularly polarized light is not identical with its own mirror image (*see* above), it provides the necessary dissymmetric environment.

Asymmetric decompositions, either relative or absolute, can be performed under conditions analogous to those employed with the above asymmetric syntheses.

Asymmetric syntheses and decompositions are of especially great importance in biological reactions, since the reactions which occur in living systems are so frequently brought about by optically active reagents or are catalyzed by optically active catalysts (enzymes). For example, the fact that green plants are able to transform inactive water and carbon dioxide into active carbohydrates (*see* PHOTOSYNTHESIS) is due to the occurrence of asymmetric syntheses. Similarly, the fact that the natural D(+)-glucose is easily metabolized by animals and is fermented by yeast, whereas its enantiomorph undergoes neither reaction, must be attributed to the occurrence of asymmetric decompositions. An important application of such biological reactions was discovered by Pasteur, who found (1856–60) that the mold *Penicillium glaucum,* when allowed to grow in the presence of racemic (tartaric) acid, destroys the (+)-enantiomorph preferentially, so that the acid which remains becomes levorotatory. This method of obtaining optically active substances is of considerable generality since other microorganisms have been found to have similar effects, and since other racemic modifications have been made active in similar ways; it has, however, serious limitations since many substances are not attacked by any known organisms, and since often the organism destroys just the enantiomorph which is desired. It should be noted that the method cannot be called a resolution since one of the two enantiomorphs is always destroyed. (*See* also CARBOHYDRATES.)

**10. The Origin of Optically Active Substances in Nature.**—The frequent occurrence of optically active substances in animal and vegetable sources can be explained only as the result of asymmetric syntheses or decompositions. These reactions are made possible by the presence of pre-existing optically active substances, which must themselves have been made by asymmetric syntheses or decompositions; and so on. If life started on this earth many millions of years ago by the coming together of simple inorganic and optically inactive materials, there must have been a time at which the optical activity began. The question therefore arises how it came into being in the absence of any pre-existing optically active substance. (If life is assumed not to have started on this planet but to have come from some other body, the difficulty is merely pushed back in time and not avoided.) Naturally, the answer to this question is unknown, and possibly unknowable. Scientists have nevertheless speculated about it for many years.

Two types of theory have been advanced to explain the origin of optical activity. The first of these is based upon the fact of spontaneous separation. It is not inconceivable that an optically active substance produced in small amount in this way may have been involved somehow in the origin of life. An objection raised to this explanation is that it depends too much upon the operation of chance. The supposition that the universal and uniform occurrence of optical activity could have arisen in such a manner seems unlikely a priori.

The second kind of theory is based upon the existence of absolute asymmetric syntheses and decompositions. For example, since light can be circularly polarized by reflection, life may conceivably have started at such a time and place that the first organisms were more or less constantly subjected to the action of either right or left circularly polarized light. This theory avoids the difficulty of assigning too great a role to chance. It encounters a different one, however, in that the activities producible photochemically in the laboratory have always been extremely small, and also in that the natural circular polarization of light could at most be slight. A further theory, which assumes that the earth's magnetic field produced the necessary dissymmetric environment, enjoys a similar advantage, but it suffers from similar disadvantages.

## IV. THE STEREOCHEMISTRY OF CARBON

**1. The Tetrahedral Carbon Atom.**—The above extremely general considerations require no assumptions in regard to the actual geometrical forms of the molecules under discussion. Such assumptions become necessary, however, if the attempt is made to account for the numbers of stereoisomers corresponding to each structural formula. The first successful theory based upon explicit geometrical assumptions was brought forth simultaneously and independently in 1874 by J. H. van't Hoff and J. A. Le Bel. The ideas of van't Hoff were somewhat more definite than those of Le Bel, but they differed in no respect important to the present article. The following discussion makes no effort to follow either van't Hoff's or Le Bel's development very closely; it attempts instead to present the fundamental principles in logical rather than in historical order.

For the molecular formula $CH_4$, only the single structure I can be drawn (if, as usual, carbon and hydrogen are considered to be quadrivalent and univalent, respectively), and only the

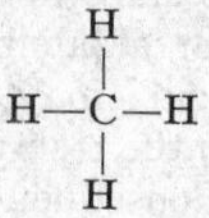

```
    H              H
    |              |
 H—C—H          H—C—H
    |              |
    H              Cl
    I              II
```

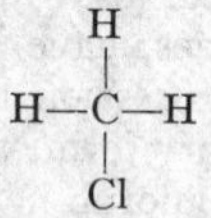

single substance, methane, is known. Similarly, for the formula $CH_3Cl$, only the single structure II can be drawn, and only the single substance, methyl chloride, is known. Now, if one hydrogen atom in methane were different from any one of the others in any respect, the substance produced by the replacement of the first hydrogen atom by a chlorine atom should be different from the one produced by the replacement of the second hydrogen atom. Consequently, at least two distinct substances, $CH_3Cl$, should exist. The fact that only one such substance is known strongly suggests, therefore, that all four hydrogen atoms of methane are completely equivalent to each other, not only structurally but also geometrically.

The requirement that all four hydrogen atoms of methane be geometrically equivalent restricts the atomic arrangements to the following: (1) The hydrogen atoms might lie at the corners of a rectangle, with the carbon atom at the centre, as in III. The dotted lines outlining the rectangle are given only for the sake of clarity; they do not represent valence bonds of any kind. This model is known as the planar model. (2) The hydrogen atoms might lie at the corners of the base of a square pyramid, with the carbon atom at the apex, as in IV. (It should be noted that,

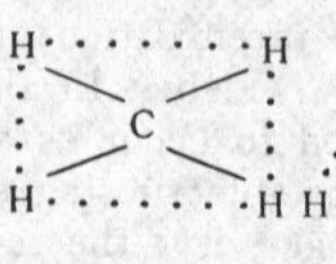

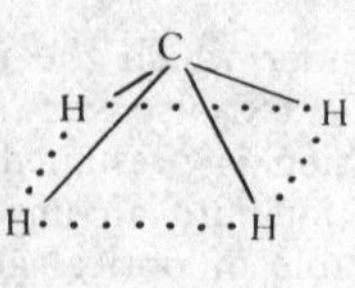

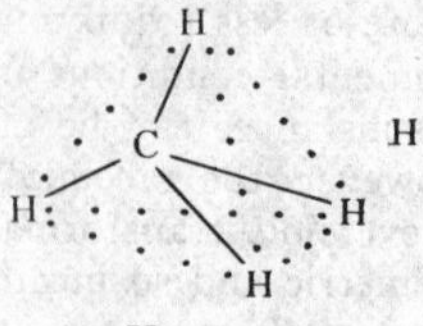

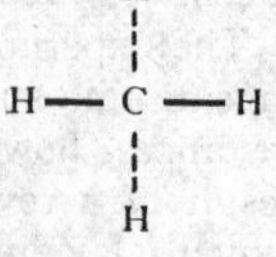

if the base of the pyramid were rectangular rather than square, two enantiomorphic forms of each monosubstituted derivative $CH_3R$ would be possible. Such a configuration can, therefore, be excluded.) The dotted lines are again given only for the sake of clarity. This model is known as the pyramidal model. (3) The hydrogen atoms might lie at the corners of a tetrahedron, with the carbon atom in the centre, as in V. The dotted lines which outline the imaginary tetrahedron are given, as before, only for the sake of clarity. A more convenient, but equivalent, representation of this so-called tetrahedral model, which is employed throughout the remainder of the article, is shown in the diagram VI. The two broken lines in this latter figure represent valence bonds to hydrogen atoms lying behind the plane of the paper; the two heavy lines represent bonds to hydrogen atoms lying in front of the plane of the paper.

The decision among the planar, pyramidal and tetrahedral models is made possible by a consideration of the numbers of isomeric substances $CH_2RS$, where R and S represent any two specified, but not necessarily different, atoms or groups. Only one known substance, methylene chloride, exists with the formula $CH_2Cl_2$; only one, chloroacetic acid, exists with the formula $CH_2Cl—CO_2H$, etc. For no formula of this type is more than a single substance known. Now, the planar model would lead to the three distinct spatial arrangements or configurations VII, VIII and IX, of which VII and VIII are identical if the rectangle

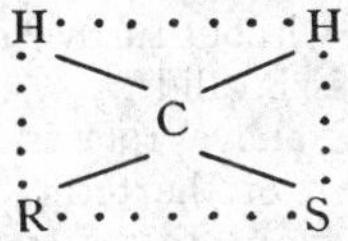

VII 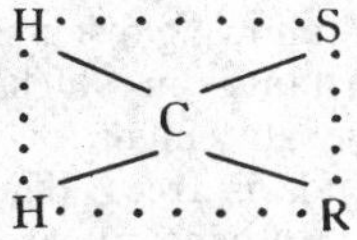 VIII 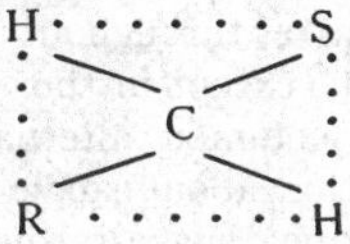 IX

is a square. Since IX cannot be identical with VII or VIII under any circumstances, however, this model requires the existence of at least two stereoisomeric forms and so can be excluded from further consideration.

The pyramidal model might be expected, like the square planar one, to permit two stereoisomeric substances. Thus, the two configurations X and XI are possible. If R and S are not identical, however, the configuration X is dissymmetric, and so its nonsuperposable mirror image (enantiomorph) XII represents still a third stereoisomer. Since stereoisomerism has never been observed with structures of the present type and, moreover, since optical activity has never been encountered, the pyramidal model must also be incorrect.

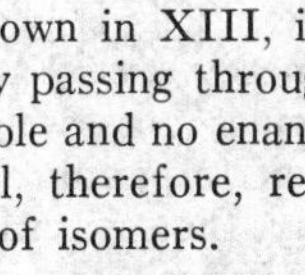

X 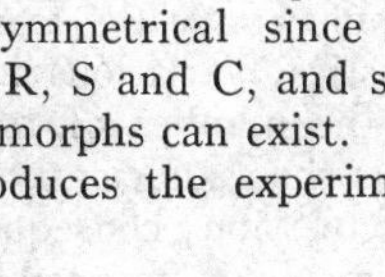 XI 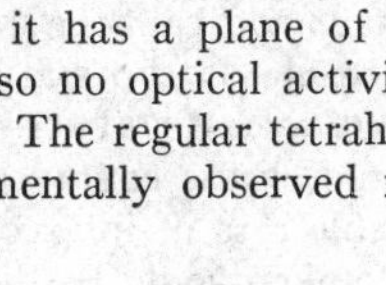 XII

Only the tetrahedral model remains. If the tetrahedron is regular, this model permits only a single substance $CH_2RS$, whether R and S are identical or different. In particular the configuration, as shown in XIII, is symmetrical since it has a plane of symmetry passing through R, S and C, and so no optical activity is possible and no enantiomorphs can exist. The regular tetrahedral model, therefore, reproduces the experimentally observed numbers of isomers.

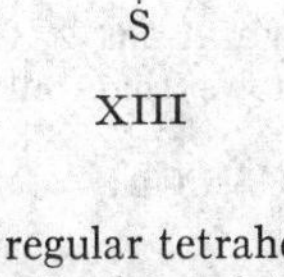

XIII 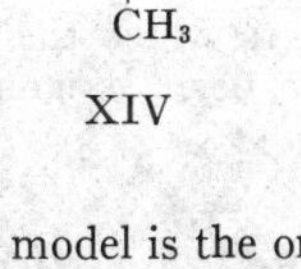 XIV 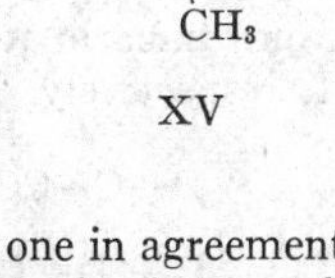 XV

The regular tetrahedral model is the only one in agreement with the observed numbers of isomers; consequently, it must be assumed correct. Confirmation of this model is provided by the fact that it correctly predicts the occurrence of optical activity, and hence also of enantiomorphs, with substances with the formula CPRST, where no two of the atoms or groups P, R, S and T are identical. Lactic acid, $CH_3—CHOH—CO_2H$, for example, occurs in enantiomorphic dextrorotatory and levorotatory forms. For the molecules of these substances, the nonsuperposable, mirror-image configurations XIV and XV are possible. One of these must therefore represent the molecule of the dextrorotatory lactic acid, and the other must represent that of the levorotatory form. Although it was long uncertain which of these two configurations belongs to each isomer, the problem was finally solved in 1951 by J. M. Bijvoet and his coworkers. By means of a complex and unusual modification of the methods of X-ray crystal-structure analysis, these authors showed that configurations XIV and XV describe, respectively, (−)- and (+)-lactic acid.

Physical evidence has confirmed the conclusions reached above. Studies of spectra and of X-ray and electron diffraction have shown that a saturated carbon atom is indeed tetrahedral, in the sense that the four single bonds which it forms are directed toward the corners of a tetrahedron, of which it occupies the centre. (The tetrahedron itself, of course, is only an intellectual construction without physical reality.) Moreover, the tetrahedron has been found to be regular, or very nearly regular, so that the angle between any two of the single bonds formed by the central carbon atom has the so-called tetrahedral value of 109° 28′, or very nearly that value. When the four atoms or groups joined to the carbon atom are of the same kind, as in methane $CH_4$ or carbon tetrachloride $CCl_4$, the tetrahedron seems always to be strictly regular, but, when the atoms or groups are not of the same kind, as in methylene chloride, $CH_2Cl_2$, some small distortions may occur.

**2. Asymmetric Carbon Atoms.**—A carbon atom is said to be asymmetric if it is joined by four different atoms or groups. Thus, of the three carbon atoms in lactic acid, the central one is seen to be asymmetric. (The terminology here is correct since an asymmetric carbon atom possesses no element of symmetry and so is actually asymmetric, and not merely dissymmetric.) The majority of all known optically active substances consist of molecules which contain one or more asymmetric carbon atoms. However, the presence of such atoms is neither necessary nor sufficient for optical activity. As will be discussed below, many substances containing no asymmetric atoms are active. Conversely, many containing asymmetric atoms are inactive. Optical activity arises from the dissymmetry of each individual molecule as a whole; the presence or absence of asymmetric atoms is important only insofar as it determines the symmetry or dissymmetry of the molecule.

**3. The Stereochemistry of Olefinic Compounds.**—Van't Hoff assumed that the carbon atoms in unsaturated compounds have the same tetrahedral form as those in the saturated substances. The configuration of ethylene, $H_2C{=}CH_2$, thus becomes XVI. If this configuration is correct, the six atoms in the molecule

XVI

lie in the same plane (the plane of the paper in XVI), the H—C—H bond angles have the tetrahedral value of 109° 28′, the C—C—H angles (or, more precisely, the angles between the carbon–hydrogen bonds and a straight line passing through the carbon atoms) are 125° 16′, and the carbon–carbon distance is 0.58 times that in ethane, $CH_3—CH_3$.

Although erroneous in some respects (*see* below), van't Hoff's configuration of ethylene appears to be correct in all essential stereochemical details. In particular, it leads to correct predictions of the numbers of stereoisomeric forms of suitably substituted ethylenes. Indeed, its significant features can be deduced directly, and without reference to the tetrahedral carbon atom, from considerations of isomer numbers. For example, with a molecule with the structure $HRC{=}CHR$, this planar model permits the two configurations XVII and XVIII. Now, XVII and XVIII must represent optically inactive diastereomers since, with each, the plane of the molecule is a plane of symmetry.

In the particular case in which R is the carboxyl group, $CO_2H$, two substances, fumaric and maleic acids (*q.v.*), are known; each of these acids is optically inactive, and the two differ markedly

```
H       H        H       R
 \     /          \     /
  C=C              C=C
 /     \          /     \
R       R        R       H
   XVII             XVIII
```

in nearly all their properties (*see* above). Consequently, they must be diastereomers and cannot be enantiomorphs. Since numerous further examples of similar type are known, and since optical activity has never been encountered in substances with the structure HRC═CHR (unless R represents a dissymmetric group), the necessary conclusion is that the planar model is correct, in agreement with van't Hoff. The configuration XVII is commonly said to be cis (Lat. *cis,* "on this side"), whereas XVIII is said to be trans (Lat. *trans,* "across").

From considerations of isomer number alone, no information can be obtained regarding the values of the bond angles or of the interatomic distances in ethylene and its derivatives; consequently, the angles and distances derived from van't Hoff's configuration, with the tetrahedral carbon atoms, cannot be verified by purely chemical procedures.

Physical investigations (*see* SPECTROSCOPY; ELECTRON DIFFRACTION) have shown, however, that it is precisely in such respects that van't Hoff's model is incorrect. Thus, in ethylene, the H—C—H and C—C—H angles are more nearly equal to 120° than to 109° 28′ and 125° 16′, respectively; and the carbon–carbon distance is more nearly 0.87 than 0.58 times that in ethane. Moreover, the modern quantum-mechanical picture of the double bond is rather different from that provided by the tetrahedral model XVI. Nevertheless, these defects in no way limit the usefulness of the simple model for the prediction and interpretation of the observed numbers of stereoisomers.

**4. The Stereochemistry of Acetylenic Compounds.**—Just as with ethylene, van't Hoff assumed that the carbon atoms in acetylene, H—C≡C—H, are tetrahedral. He accordingly wrote the configuration as XIX. This linear model is in agreement with

```
H — C ----- C — H
      XIX
```

the observed numbers of isomeric substitution products and also with recent physical evidence. Consequently, although van't Hoff's model of acetylene is inaccurate in several respects (analogous to those in which his model of ethylene is inaccurate, *see* above), it leads always to correct predictions of the numbers of isomers.

**5. Free Rotation.**—Certain limitations must be imposed upon the general statement that two molecules correspond to different substances unless they are exactly alike with respect to the relative positions in space of all their atoms. For the structure $H_3C—CH_3$, for example, an infinite number of geometrical arrangements (or conformations) are consistent with the assumption of tetrahedral carbon atoms; these include the two represented by XX and XXI, as well as all the further ones obtainable from

```
H            H        H            H
H --- C — C --- H     H --- C — C --- H
H            H        H            H
      XX                    XXI
```

either XX or XXI by rotation of one $CH_3$ group with respect to the other about the carbon–carbon bond. If each of these conformations represented a distinct substance, then an infinite number of stereoisomers with the structure in question should exist. Only a single substance, ethane, is known however. Similar considerations apply to nearly all further structures in which multivalent atoms are joined by single bonds. It is evident, therefore, that, if the geometrical interpretation of stereoisomerism is to be maintained, some further assumption, which restricts the predicted numbers of isomers, is required.

The assumption generally adopted for this purpose is contained in the rule that any two conformations (such as XX and XXI, or any other two of the infinite number of possible ones) are to be considered equivalent if they differ only by the rotation of one or more parts of the molecule about one or more single bonds. Thus, XX, XXI, etc. are equivalent; all these conformations correspond to the same substance, ethane, and all are said to represent the same configuration. Although this rule has a number of exceptions (see *Optically Active Biphenyls,* below), it is sufficiently general to find application throughout the entire field of stereochemistry. It has indeed already been assumed implicitly at several points of the preceding discussion, and it is assumed hereafter throughout the following discussion without further comment (except in those instances in which it is invalid).

A common alternative statement of the above rule is that rotation about single bonds is free. The use of the term "free rotation" suggests that, in ethane for example, no forces operate to make any one conformation more stable than any other, so that each molecule of the substance spends equal fractions of its time in each of its possible geometrical arrangements. This interpretation is obviously consistent with the fact that stereoisomeric forms of ethane, differing by rotation about the carbon–carbon bond, do not occur; nevertheless, it is probably incorrect. From a combination of spectroscopic and thermochemical data, the conclusion has been drawn that the "eclipsed" conformation XX is less stable (*i.e.,* has a higher energy) than the "staggered" one XXI by about 3,000 cal. per mole. If this conclusion is correct, most of the molecules at any one time must have arrangements rather close to the staggered one XXI. Stereoisomerism is still impossible, however, since each molecule must spend part of its time in each of the conformations, and since the transition from any one conformation to any other is rapid and easy.

In nearly all other substances for which data are available, the situation seems to be similar to that in ethane. Certain conformations always seem to be appreciably more stable than others differing from them by rotation about one or more single bonds, but stereoisomers are not encountered because the transition from one conformation to another is easy. In general, stereoisomers can be expected to occur only if there are two or more essentially different geometrical arrangements of the atoms, and if transitions between these arrangements are not easy. A transition may be considered easy at ordinary temperatures if it can be undergone by a molecule possessing an energy much less than about 20,000 cal. per mole above the average. This is because, as a result of the statistical variations in energy (*see* KINETIC THEORY OF MATTER), the number of molecules possessing the required excess energy is then sufficiently great to permit an appreciable rate of interconversion; consequently, the separation of the isomers would be difficult or impossible. Stereoisomerism is, therefore, impossible in ethane, since a molecule of this substance requires an excess energy of only approximately 3,000 cal. per mole for a complete rotation of 360° about the carbon–carbon bond. On the other hand, the existence of the stereoisomeric maleic and fumaric acids, to which the configurations XXII and XXIII, respectively, have been assigned, shows that only such

```
H—C—CO2H          H—C—CO2H
  ||                ||
H—C—CO2H        HO2C—C—H
   XXII              XXIII
```

molecules as possess at least 20,000 cal. per mole of excess energy can undergo the transition. Just as the nonexistence of stereoisomers in ethane (and the like) is attributed to the freedom of rotation about the carbon–carbon single bond, so also the existence of stereoisomerism between maleic and fumaric acids (and the like) is attributed to the lack of free rotation about the double bond.

It is interesting that van't Hoff's models of ethane and ethylene (XX and XVI, respectively) are consistent with the presence of free rotation about the single bond and the lack of it about the double bond. Since the two carbon atoms in ethane are joined by just one linkage, no forces exist in the model XX to favour any one conformation over any other. Consequently, rotation might be expected to be easy in the molecule also. On the other hand, since the two carbon atoms in ethylene are joined by two bonds, the model XVI is held rigidly in the planar form. Consequently, rotation might be expected to be impossible in the molecule. The modern quantum-mechanical pictures of the single and double bonds are rather different from those provided by the models of van't Hoff, but they are equally in agreement with the observed freedom and restriction, respectively, of rotation.

**6. Plane Projection Diagrams.**—The use of three-dimensional models of the sort employed by van't Hoff becomes extremely cumbersome if the molecule to be represented is even moderately complicated. Moreover, such models cannot be depicted very conveniently on a plane surface, such as a printed page; even the relatively simple diagrams XX and XXI, for example, are not too easily intelligible, and the situation rapidly becomes worse as the complexity of the molecule increases. Consequently, some simpler method of representation is highly desirable.

It has become conventional to represent the three-dimensional models by what are called plane projection diagrams or, more simply, plane configurations. Thus, by definition, the diagrams XXIV and XXV represent the dextrorotatory and levorotatory forms,

```
     CHO                 CHO
      |                   |
  H—C—OH             HO—C—H
      |                   |
     CH2OH               CH2OH
    XXIV                 XXV
```

respectively, of glyceraldehyde. It is to be noted that these diagrams do not in themselves specify the absolute configurations (*i.e.*, the true three-dimensional forms of the actual molecules). The diagram XXIV, for example could be considered the projection of either XXVI or XXVII; similarly, XXV can be considered the projection either of XXVIII (identical with XXVII) or of its enantiomorph XXIX (identical with XXVI). Nevertheless, the

```
    CHO          CHO           CHO          CHO
     |            :             |            :
 H···C···OH   H—C—OH      HO···C···H    HO—C—H
     |            :             |            :
    CH2OH        CH2OH         CH2OH        CH2OH
   XXVI         XXVII         XXVIII       XXIX
```

work of Bijvoet *et al.* (*see* above) has shown that the plane configurations XXIV and XXV actually correspond to the absolute configurations XXVII and XXIX, respectively.

The usefulness of plane configurations like XXIV and XXV lies in the fact that they make possible the unique representation of relative configurations. In other words, the plane projection diagrams define the configurations of the substances to which they refer by comparing them with those of the glyceraldehydes. Since the absolute configurations of the glyceraldehydes are now known, the relative configurations of other substances define the absolute ones.

Considerable care must be exercised in the use of the plane configurations, since errors and inconsistencies can easily be introduced. It might appear, for example, that the diagrams XXIV and XXV are identical since a rotation of 180° about a vertical axis lying in the plane of the paper would transform either into the other. Consequently, if XXIV and XXV are to represent enantiomorphs, a rotation which takes the figure out of the plane in which it is drawn must be considered to invert the configuration (*i.e.*, to change it into that of the enantiomorph). Although a rotation of 180° out of the plane of the paper inverts the configuration, as stated above, any rotation within the plane of the paper leaves the configuration unchanged. Thus, XXX, XXXI and XXXII are equivalent to XXIV and, like it, represent dextrorotatory glyceraldehyde.

```
          H               CH2OH          H       CHO
          |                 |             \     /
HOCH2—C—CHO          HO—C—H                C
          |                 |             /     \
          OH               CHO       HOCH2       OH
        XXX               XXXI           XXXII
```

It is to be noted that freedom of rotation does not in general exist about the single bonds in plane projection diagrams of the present type (see *Free Rotation*, above). This is because a rotation about any bond in such a diagram requires that that part of the diagram which is rotated leave the plane of the paper. If this part is dissymmetric, then, according to the convention adopted, it is inverted in the process, so that the resulting configuration is not equivalent to the original one. For example, a rotation by 180° of the lower part of XXIV about the upper carbon–carbon bond changes this configuration into the enantiomorphic one XXV. (The $CH_2OH$ group is not affected by the rotation since it is symmetric and so identical with its own mirror image.) These remarks do not imply any corresponding lack of freedom of rotation about the single bonds in the actual molecules or in the three-dimensional models; they have reference instead only to the conventions which must be adopted if the plane configurations are not to lead to self-contradictions.

If a molecule contains a ring of atoms, its configuration may be expressed on a plane surface in either of two ways. When one of these methods is used, the diagram is written as if no ring were present, and then the fact that a ring is present is indicated, more or less as an afterthought, by the drawing in of the necessary bonds as long, and frequently curved, lines. Thus, the configuration of α-D-glucose (*see* CARBOHYDRATES) is often written as XXXIII. When the second method of representation is employed, the ring is drawn as if it were a plane polygon approximately at right angles to the plane of the paper, and the substituents attached to the ring atoms are represented by the appropriate symbols above and below the plane of the ring. Thus, the configuration of α-D-glucose can be written as XXXIV; this diagram is to be considered equivalent to XXXIII. Plane projection dia-

```
      ┌──────┐
  H—C—OH     │                 CH2OH
      |      │                   |
  H—C—OH     │             H     C————O      H
      |      │             |   /  |     \    |
 HO—C—H      │             C      H       \  C
      |      │             |  \   OH    H  / |
  H—C—OH     │            HO   C—————C    OH
      |      │                 |     |
  H—C—O──────┘                 H     OH
      |
     CH2OH
    XXXIII                      XXXIV
```

grams like XXXIV do not imply knowledge of the corresponding absolute configurations. A molecule of glucose in which the upper horizontal line (of XXXIV) is in front of the paper, and the lower line is behind it, would be the enantiomorph of a molecule in which the upper line is behind the plane of the paper, and the lower line is in front of it. Nevertheless, since determination of the absolute configurations of the glyceraldehydes (*see* above) has shown that the hydrogen atoms and hydroxyl groups which are joined to the asymmetric carbon atoms lie in front of the plane of the paper in diagram XXXIII, consistency requires that the lower horizontal line of XXXIV be in front of, and that the upper horizontal line be behind, the paper. These diagrams do not imply that the rings are completely planar (see *Strain Theory,* below); they imply rather that the average positions of the atoms of the ring lie within a single plane.

The representation of an ethylenic compound is relatively easy since the two carbon atoms joined by the double bond, and the four other atoms joined by single bonds to these two, lie in the same plane. Consequently, diagrams like XXII and XXIII for maleic and fumaric acids, respectively, represent the absolute configurations. Such diagrams need no further discussion.

If a molecule contains several rings, several double bonds, or both rings and double bonds, the representation of its configuration may be rather difficult. In such instances, the conventional scheme just outlined often must be supplemented by the use of heavy and broken lines to represent bonds to atoms in front of and behind the paper, respectively, or by other devices analogous to those employed in preceding sections of this article. Examples of such molecules are given below.

**7. Use of Plane Projection Diagrams for the Prediction of the Number of Stereoisomers.**—The foregoing rather general considerations can be made more definite by a discussion of some specific examples of stereoisomerism. The dextrorotatory and levorotatory glyceraldehydes are represented by the diagrams XXIV and XXV, as has already been mentioned. That these two diagrams correspond to enantiomorphs is shown (according to the conventions adopted) by the fact that each can be considered identical with the reflection of the other in a mirror which is halfway between them and perpendicular to the plane of the paper. Since there is only one asymmetric atom in the molecule, and no further source of molecular dissymmetry, these two enantiomorphs are the only possible stereoisomeric forms.

A molecule of tartaric acid, $HO_2C—\overset{*}{C}HOH—\overset{*}{C}HOH—CO_2H$, has two asymmetric carbon atoms (the two designated by asterisks). Since there are two possible configurations about each such atom, one might anticipate altogether 2 × 2, or 4, distinct stereoisomers, which could be represented by the diagrams XXXV–XXXVIII. Of these, however, the first two are equivalent inasmuch as either is transformed into the other by a rotation

```
   CO2H          CO2H           CO2H          CO2H
    |             |              |             |
 H—C—OH       HO—C—H         H—C—OH       HO—C—H
    |             |              |             |
 H—C—OH       HO—C—H        HO—C—H         H—C—OH
    |             |              |             |
   CO2H          CO2H           CO2H          CO2H
  XXXV          XXXVI          XXXVII       XXXVIII
```

of 180° in the plane. Since these two equivalent diagrams are mirror images of each other, they must represent a substance which is identical with its own mirror image, and so optically inactive; they are, therefore, equivalent forms of the plane configuration of mesotartaric acid (*see* above). The optical inactivity of this substance follows also from the presence of a plane of symmetry in either of the two diagrams (*i.e.,* from the fact that the upper half of either diagram is identical with the reflection of the lower half in a mirror perpendicular to both the plane of the paper and the central carbon–carbon bond). On the other hand, the last two configurations, XXXVII and XXXVIII, are not equivalent since neither can be transformed into the other by any rotation in the plane. Since they are mirror images of each other, they must be enantiomorphs, and so one must represent the dextrorotatory, and one must represent the levorotatory, tartaric acid. In a way which cannot be described in this article, XXVII has been shown to belong to the dextrorotatory enantiomorph, and XXVIII has been shown to belong to the levorotatory one. Thus, the existence of the three known tartaric acids can be explained.

The trihydroxyglutaric acids, $HO_2C—\overset{*}{C}HOH—\overset{*}{C}HOH—\overset{*}{C}HOH—CO_2H$, have the three asymmetric carbon atoms marked by asterisks. (The central carbon atom may appear not to be asymmetric since two of the groups attached to it are structurally identical. It is customary, however, to regard such atoms as asymmetric since the attached groups may differ in configuration. Atoms of this type are sometimes said to be pseudoasymmetric.) One might expect $2^3$, or eight stereoisomeric forms, but, as with the tartaric acids, the number is reduced somewhat by the occurrence of meso forms. Only the four nonequivalent configurations XXXIX-XLII can be drawn, and, in agreement with prediction, only four stereoisomeric substances are known. It is easily seen that XXXIX and XL represent two different meso forms since each has a plane of symmetry (passing through the central CHOH group and perpendicular to the paper), and that XLI and XLII represent a pair of enantiomorphs.

```
   CO2H          CO2H           CO2H          CO2H
    |             |              |             |
 H—C—OH        H—C—OH         H—C—OH       HO—C—H
    |             |              |             |
 H—C—OH       HO—C—H          H—C—OH       HO—C—H
    |             |              |             |
 H—C—OH        H—C—OH        HO—C—H         H—C—OH
    |             |              |             |
   CO2H          CO2H           CO2H          CO2H
  XXXIX           XL             XLI          XLII
```

The aldohexoses (*see* CARBOHYDRATES) have five asymmetric atoms in the pyranose structure (*cf.* the configurations XXXIII and XXXIV of α-D-glucose). Since no meso forms are possible, $2^5$, or 32, different optically active stereoisomers should exist. As has already been mentioned, all these forms are known.

The cyclohexane-1,2-dicarboxylic acids, like the tartaric acids, contain two equivalent asymmetric carbon atoms; consequently, they also exist in two enantiomorphic forms, XLIII and XLIV, and one meso form XLV. It is readily verified that the configurations XLIII and XLIV are mirror images of each other, and that neither possesses a plane or centre of symmetry. On the other hand, XLV has a plane of symmetry perpendicular both to the ring and to the bond joining the two asymmetric atoms; it is, therefore, identical with its mirror image.

```
        CH2——CH2                          CH2——CH2
       /        \                        /        \
  H2C<   H    HO2C >CH2             H2C<  CO2H    H  >CH2
       \ |      | /                      \ |      | /
         C——————C                          C——————C
         |      |                          |      |
       HO2C     H                          H     CO2H
          XLIII                               XLIV

                      CH2——CH2
                     /        \
                H2C<   H     H  >CH2
                     \ |     | /
                       C—————C
                       |     |
                     HO2C   CO2H
                         XLV
```

The isomerism of the cyclohexane-1,2-dicarboxylic acids (as well as that of other analogous cyclic compounds) is frequently described by the statement that the optically active forms XLIII and XLIV are trans, whereas the meso form XLV is cis. This nomenclature is convenient since it expresses clearly and concisely the relative positions of the substituent groups with respect to the plane of the ring. However, it has given rise to much confusion since it suggests a false analogy with the cis-trans isomerism in ethylenic compounds like maleic and fumaric acids (*see* above).

In cyclohexane-1,4-dicarboxylic acid, cis and trans forms again exist. Here, however, both the cis form XLVI and the trans form XLVII have planes of symmetry and so are optically inactive. The isomerism of these two substances (like that of the 1,2-dicarboxylic acids) is not due to the rigidity of the ring; no conceivable rotation about any bond or bonds in the ring could

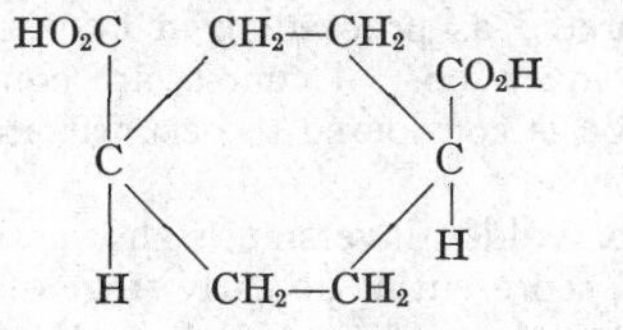

XLVI 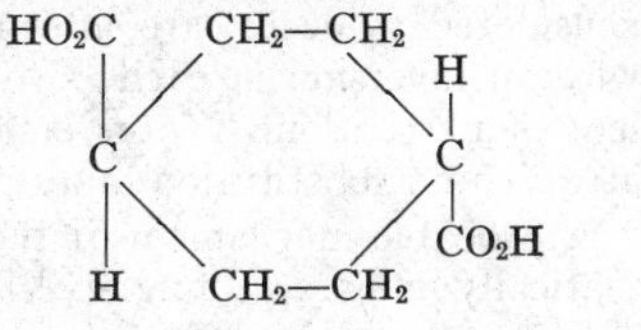 XLVII

transform either isomer into the other, even if the ring were perfectly flexible.

Alanine anhydride (dimethyldiketopiperazine), with a six-membered ring, exists in cis and trans forms. Here, the trans form XLVIII has a centre of symmetry (at the centre of the ring) and

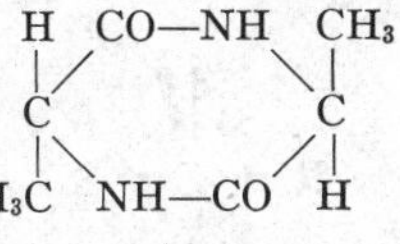

XLVIII

so it is optically inactive. (The presence of the centre of symmetry is apparent if the ring in XLVIII is visualized as lying in a plane perpendicular to that of the paper.) The cis form has neither plane nor centre of symmetry, and so it exists in the two enantiomorphic forms XLIX and L.

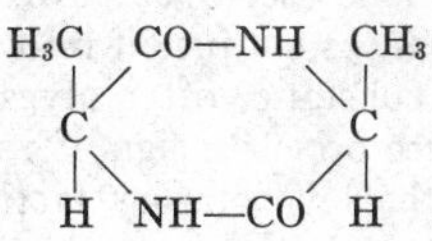

XLIX 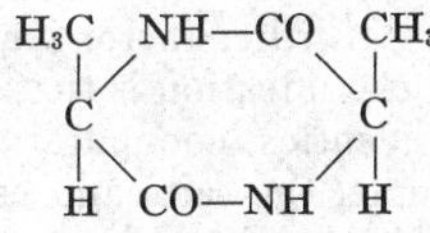 L

**8. Optically Active Allenes and Their Analogues.**—Van't Hoff pointed out that, if his tetrahedral model of the double bond (*see* above) is correct, the two $CH_2$ groups in allene, $H_2C{=}C{=}CH_2$, should lie in planes which are at right angles to each other; and that a substance with the structure RSC=C=CRS, where R and S are any two different atoms or groups, should exist in the enantiomorphic forms LI and LII. It was not until 1935, however,

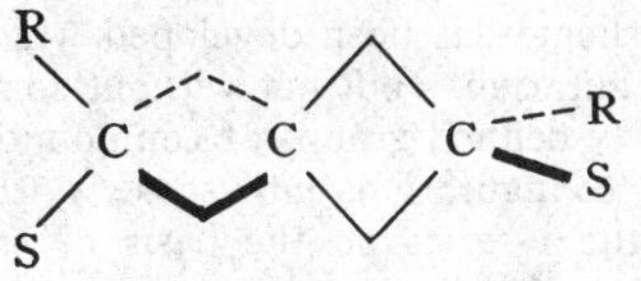

LI 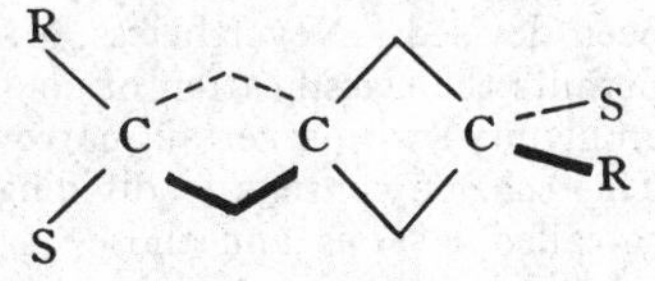 LII

that this prediction was verified by P. Maitland and W. H. Mills, who obtained the optically active diphenyldi-$\alpha$-naphthylallene LIII. In the same year, E. P. Kohler, J. T. Walker and M. Tishler reported the preparation of the similar optically active allene LIV.

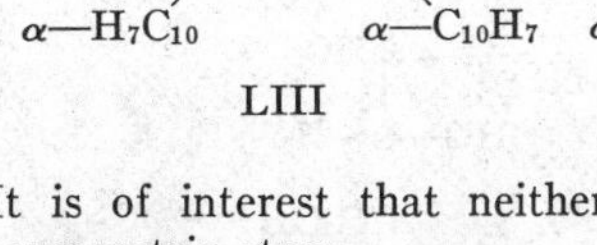

LIII 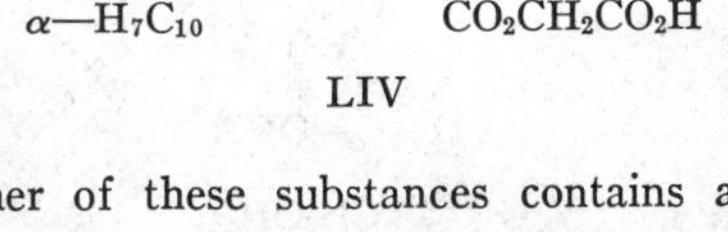 LIV

It is of interest that neither of these substances contains an asymmetric atom.

Although the existence of optically active allenes was not confirmed until comparatively recently, several analogous substances have been known for a longer time. These substances may be considered related to the allenes proper by the replacement of one or both of the two-membered rings (*i.e.*, double bonds) by larger rings. Two typical pairs of enantiomorphs are represented by the configurations LV and LVI, and LVII and LVIII. As with the allenes, none of these substances contains an asymmetric atom.

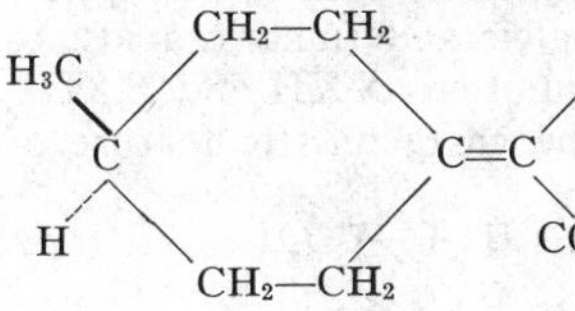

LV 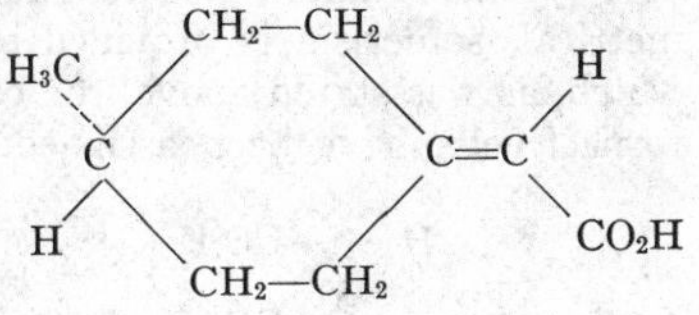 LVI

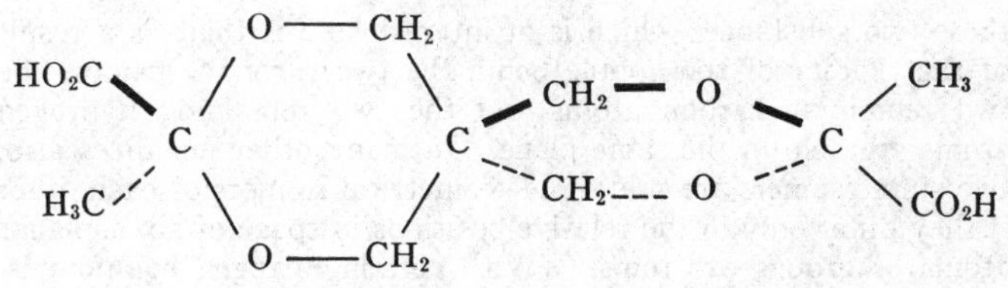

LVII

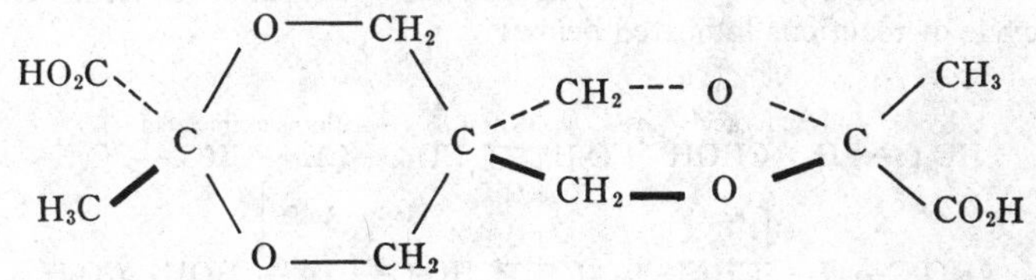

LVIII

**9. Optically Active Biphenyls.**—In 1922 G. H. Christie and J. Kenner found that the dinitrodiphenic acid LIX can be separated into a pair of enantiomorphs. The present interpretation of this fact is that the molecules of the two substances have the configurations LX and LXI. The two rings here are considered to lie in approximately perpendicular planes. Since a rotation of 180° about the central carbon–carbon bond would transform either enantiomorph into the other, such rotation must be assumed to be impossible. The factor responsible for this restriction of rotation is presumed to be the size of the four substituents attached to the rings. In order for a molecule to pass from one enantiomorphic form to the other, it must, at some time during

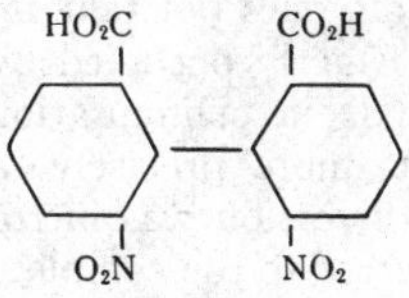

LIX 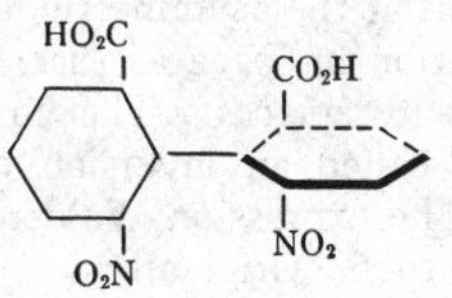 LX 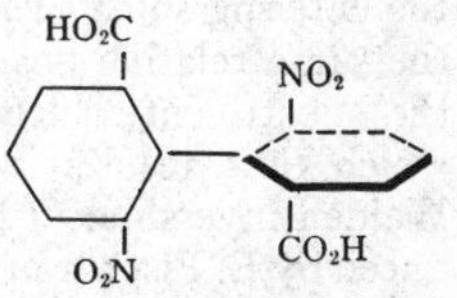 LXI

the process, assume a configuration in which the two rings are coplanar; if this should happen, however, the substituent groups mentioned would be forced to come so close together that they would get in one another's way. In other words, it is difficult, or impossible, for the large nitro and carboxyl groups to slip past each other.

As with the allenes and their analogues, neither this substance nor any of the numerous other ones similar to it possesses an asymmetric atom.

**10. Optical and Geometrical Isomerism.**—Stereoisomerism is often subdivided into optical and geometrical isomerism. The distinction between these two types of isomerism does not appear to be so significant as when it was first introduced; nevertheless, it has been retained by most chemists for historical reasons. A simple and precise definition of optical and geometrical isomerism appears to be impossible. On the one hand, many pairs of substances must be considered both optical and geometrical isomers of each other at the same time; and, on the other hand, there is no complete unanimity as to exactly where the dividing line between these two types of isomerism is to be drawn.

A typical example that is usually classified as illustrating geometrical isomerism is provided by maleic and fumaric acids, to which, as was stated above, the configurations XXII and XXIII, respectively, have been assigned. The characteristic feature of

```
H—C—CO2H        H—C—CO2H
  ‖               ‖
H—C—CO2H     HO2C—C—H
  XXII            XXIII
```

these two substances which is of interest here is that, as a result of the rigidity of the double bond, the two carboxyl groups, the two remaining carbon atoms and the two remaining hydrogen atoms are held in the same plane. In many other instances also, two stereoisomers are said to be geometrical isomers of each other if they differ only in the relative positions in space of six coplanar atoms or groups of atoms. (With certain nitrogen compounds, either one or two of these atoms or groups may be missing. See *Stereochemistry of Nitrogen,* below.)

**11. Walden Inversion.**—In 1893, P. Walden discovered the cycle of reactions indicated below:

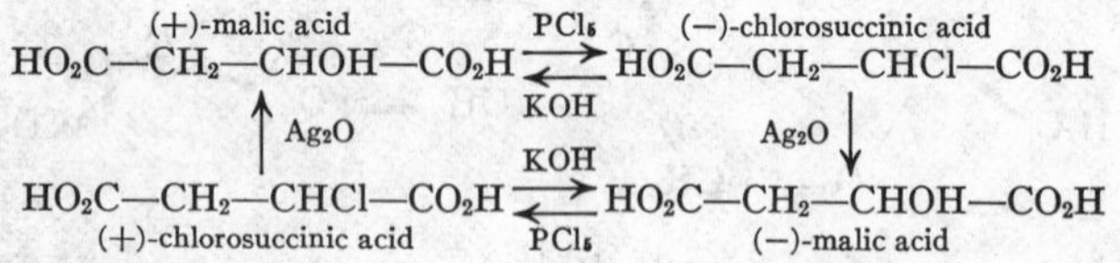

```
(+)-malic acid               PCl5        (−)-chlorosuccinic acid
HO2C—CH2—CHOH—CO2H  ⇄  HO2C—CH2—CHCl—CO2H
        ↑ Ag2O               KOH               Ag2O ↓
                             KOH
HO2C—CH2—CHCl—CO2H  ⇄  HO2C—CH2—CHOH—CO2H
(+)-chlorosuccinic acid      PCl5        (−)-malic acid
```

Thus, by treating either of the optically active malic acids first with phosphorus pentachloride (in chloroform solution) and then with silver oxide (in aqueous solution), he was able to transform it into its own enantiomorph; similarly, by treating either of the active chlorosuccinic acids first with silver oxide and then with phosphorus pentachloride, he was able to transform it also into its enantiomorph. (In each sequence of reactions, considerable racemization occurs, so that the activities of the final products are not great. In other similar sequences that have been discovered subsequently, however, relatively little racemization occurs.)

It is evident that, in one (and only one) reaction of the two in each of these sequences (*i.e.,* in either the reaction with silver oxide or the one with phosphorus pentachloride, but not in both), the entering substituent at the asymmetric atom does not take up the same relative position in space as that formerly occupied by the substituent which it replaces. The change in configuration which thus results is called an inversion or, more precisely, a Walden inversion. (The expression Walden inversion was introduced by E. Fischer in 1906. Originally it referred to the complete sequence of reactions by which the optically active substance is converted into its enantiomorph, and not to the single reaction in which the inversion of configuration occurs. Later, however, the expression seems more usually to refer to the single reaction; it is so used in this article.) The problem of identifying the particular reaction in which the inversion occurs is a difficult one. From evidence which cannot be described here, however, it has been shown that inversions occur in the reactions of the above scheme in which phosphorus pentachloride and potassium hydroxide participate, but that there is retention of configuration in the ones with silver oxide. It is to be especially noted that the fact that the sign of rotation changes in the first two types of reaction but not in the last is purely accidental; the sign of rotation often changes in reactions which are considered to proceed with retention of configuration, and, conversely, it often remains the same in reactions which are considered to proceed with inversion. No necessary general relation exists between the configurations and signs of rotation of nonenantiomorphic substances.

With relatively few exceptions every reaction in which one substituent atom or group is replaced by another is believed to be accompanied by an inversion of configuration about the atom at which the replacement occurs. Reactions, like that between chlorosuccinic acid and silver oxide, in which no net inversion is considered to occur, are interpreted as proceeding in two steps, with an inversion in each; two inversions, of course, are equivalent to a retention. No inversion is considered to occur at atoms at which no substitution takes place.

A probable mechanism of the Walden inversion is shown schematically in fig. 2. In fig. 2(A), representing an early stage of the reaction, the reagent R approaches the carbon atom from the side opposite the substituent S; in fig. 2(B), representing the midpoint of the reaction, the atoms or groups R and S are equidistant from the carbon atom, which is no longer tetrahedral; and in fig. 2(C), representing the conclusion of the reaction, the displaced substituent S is departing, and the entering one R has become attached to the carbon atom. In the process, the molecule has been "turned inside-out" like an umbrella in a high wind.

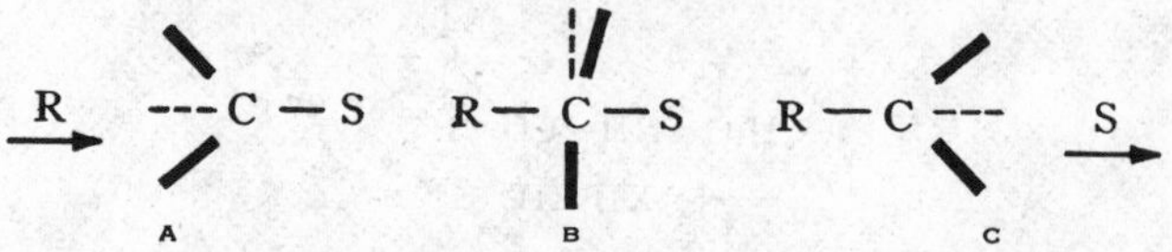

```
R →   ---C—S      R—C—S      R—C---    S →
        A            B           C
```

FIG. 2.—A PROPOSED MECHANISM OF THE WALDEN INVERSION
(A) An early stage; (B) mid-point; (C) conclusion

**12. Optically Active Series.**—The sign of the rotation produced by an optically active substance can occasionally be reversed by a change in the experimental conditions (see *Specific Rotation,* above). A further factor which introduces confusion into stereochemical classification is that a parent substance often gives derivatives of identical configuration but with opposite sign of rotation. For example, the salts and esters of the levorotatory lactic acid, $CH_3$—CHOH—$CO_2H$, are dextrorotatory; those of the dextrorotatory acid are levorotatory. For these reasons, it would seem desirable to include in the complete name of an optically active substance a symbol which refers directly to the configuration of the substance and is independent of the sign of rotation. This symbol would then remain unchanged when the substance, under different conditions, exhibits different signs of rotation, or when it forms derivatives of opposite rotation.

It may be doubted whether any completely general and completely unambiguous classification of configurations of the type desired is possible; certainly, no such classification has as yet been devised. Nevertheless, a scheme has been developed which permits the classification of configurations (but not without some ambiguity) within certain narrowly defined groups of compounds. This scheme consists in dividing configurations into those of the so-called D-series and those of the L-series on the basis of the genetic relationships among them. A substance is then said to belong to the D-series (or to the L-series) if it is a derivative of a substance belonging to the D-series (or L-series), respectively, and so on.

In order that an optically active series may be set up, some particular substance must be defined as belonging to the D- or L-series, so that the remaining substances may be related to it. Originally, Emil Fischer chose the naturally occurring sugars and their derivatives as the prototypes of the series. Later, the glyceraldehydes, XXIV and XXV, were chosen instead (M. A.

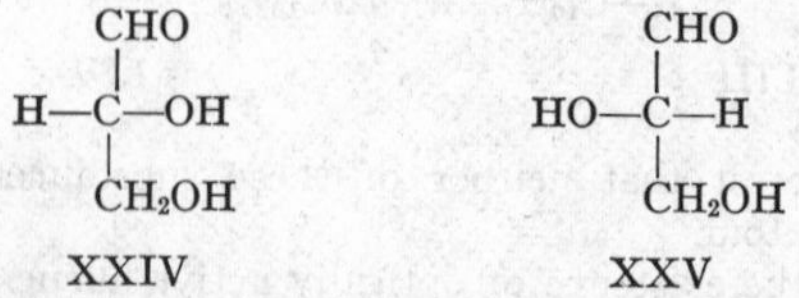

```
    CHO            CHO
     |              |
 H—C—OH        HO—C—H
     |              |
   CH2OH          CH2OH
   XXIV           XXV
```

Rosanoff, 1906); the two conventions lead to the same assignment of series, so that no ambiguity results.

The way in which the optically active series are built up can be illustrated by a few examples. As has been mentioned before,

(+)- and (−)-glyceraldehyde are by definition assigned the configurations XXIV and XXV, respectively. Also by definition, they are said to belong to the D- and L-series, so that their complete names are D(+)- and L(−)-glyceraldehyde, respectively. By well-known methods (*see* CARBOHYDRATES), the aldehyde group (CHO) of each of these substances can be changed into a CHOH—CHO group. Since this larger group contains an asymmetric carbon atom not present in the original, each of the glyceraldehydes can give rise to two products (which, not being enantiomorphs, need not be formed in equal amounts). Thus D(+)-glyceraldehyde gives rise to LXII and LXIII, which are, therefore, said to belong to the D-series. Similarly, L(−)-

```
   CHO            CHO             CHO             CHO
    |              |               |               |
H—C—OH        HO—C—H          H—C—OH         HO—C—H
    |              |               |               |
H—C—OH         H—C—OH         HO—C—H         HO—C—H
    |              |               |               |
   CH2OH          CH2OH           CH2OH           CH2OH
   LXII           LXIII           LXIV            LXV
```

glyceraldehyde gives rise to LXIV and LXV, which are said to belong to the L-series.

The procedure can be continued further. Each of the tetroses LXII-LXV can be transformed into two pentoses, each of which can in turn be transformed into two hexoses, and so on. In each reaction, the two products belong to the same optically active series as the substance from which they were made. In general, and without explicit reference to the sequence of reactions starting with the glyceraldehydes, the optically active series to which any monosaccharide belongs may be said to be determined by the configuration about the asymmetric carbon atom farthest removed from the carbonyl group (C=O); when the chain of carbon atoms is written vertically and with the carbonyl group at the top, the hydroxyl group upon the atom in question is to the right of the chain in the D-series, and to the left in the L-series.

If the glyceraldehydes are oxidized, they give the glyceric acids LXVI and LXVII. The first of these, even though it is levorota-

```
   CO2H            CO2H
    |               |
H—C—OH         HO—C—H
    |               |
   CH2OH           CH2OH
   LXVI            LXVII
```

tory, is said to belong to the D-series because of its genetic relationship to D-glyceraldehyde, it is accordingly called D(−)-glyceric acid. Similarly, the substance LXVII is called L(+)-glyceric acid.

With the $\alpha$-amino acids, and frequently also with the $\alpha$-hydroxy acids, the optically active series to which a given substance is assigned is determined by the configuration of the carbon atom adjacent to the carbonyl group, and not by that of the one farthest from this group. The two conventions are distinguished by the subscripts *s* and *g* which refer, respectively, to the simple amino acid serine, HO—$CH_2$—CN($N^+H_3$)—$CO_2^-$, and to the simple sugar, glyceraldehyde XXIV (or XXV). For example, the substance with configuration LXVIII may be described either as $D_s$- or as $L_g$-trihydroxybutyric acid.

```
   CO2H
    |
H—C—OH
    |
HO—C—H
    |
   CH2—OH
   LXVIII
```

**13. Strain Theory.**—In 1885 A. Baeyer called attention to the fact that nearly all the then known carbocyclic compounds (*i.e.*, cyclic compounds with only carbon atoms in the ring, or rings) contained either five- or six-membered rings. To explain this fact, he brought forth a group of ideas now called the strain theory. The angle between any two single bonds formed by a saturated carbon atom had been postulated by van't Hoff to have the tetrahedral value of 109° 28′ (*see* above). Consequently, Baeyer considered that an angle of this magnitude is most stable, so that, if one or more angles in a molecule were forced in some way to have a widely different value, the molecule would be "strained," and, therefore, unstable. Now, in cyclopropane LXIX, the C–C–C angles of the three-membered ring must be equal to 60°; since this value is much smaller than the preferred 109° 28′, the molecule is strained. Thus, Baeyer considered that the difficulty of preparing such a substance is accounted for. Similarly in cyclobutane LXX, the angles would have to be equal to 90° if the four-membered ring is planar; again considerable strain is present, and again the difficulty of preparing the substance appears to be explained. The minimum strain is reached with cyclopentane LXXI, in which the planar ring requires bond-angles of 108°, almost identical with the tetrahedral value. With still larger rings, the strain increases regularly with the size if, as before, the rings are considered to be planar. The six-membered ring of cyclohexane LXXII requires an angle of 120°, the seven-membered ring of cycloheptane requires one of 128° 34′, and so on. Thus,

```
                                                    CH2
                                                   /   \
                                   CH2          H2C     CH2
    CH2        H2C——CH2          /    \          |       |
   /   \        |     |       H2C      CH2      H2C     CH2
H2C————CH2     H2C——CH2        H2C————CH2          \   /
                                                    CH2
   LXIX          LXX             LXXI              LXXII
```

the least strain occurs in just those rings which are easiest to prepare and best known.

Baeyer's original ideas, although still considered essentially correct, have undergone extensive modification (H. Sachse, 1890). The strain postulated by Baeyer apparently exists only in the three- and four-membered rings, but no strain exists in the rings of six or more atoms. With the small rings, the least strain results if the rings are planar as assumed by Baeyer, but, with the larger rings, the strain can be relieved completely if the ring is permitted to be puckered. With cyclohexane, for example, two different strain-free configurations are possible; these are shown in LXXIII (the so-called boat-form or C-form) and LXXIV (the so-called chair form or Z-form). Transitions among the various

```
H2C ---CH2 --- CH2 --- CH2        H2C ---CH2 --- CH2 ---
   \                  /              \                 \
    CH2 ——— CH2                       CH2 ——— CH2 ——— CH2
        LXXIII                               LXXIV
```

forms of these puckered rings are so easy that isolation of stereoisomeric substances, differing only in the form of the ring, is impossible.

The assumption that the rings with six or more atoms are puckered and strain-free permits the conclusion that such large rings should be as stable as those with five atoms, and, in fact, as stable as the noncyclic chains. This conclusion is verified experimentally. There is no significant difference, referable to strain, between, say, cyclotriacontane, with 30 atoms in the ring, and cyclopentane, with only 5; nor is there any significant difference between either of these substances and any of the typical paraffin hydrocarbons (*see* PARAFFIN HYDROCARBONS). In particular, neither ring can be broken easily by ordinary chemical reagents, and the heats of combustion of the two cyclic substances (*see* THERMOCHEMISTRY), per $CH_2$ group, are practically identical. (In contrast, the three-membered ring in the strained cyclopropane LXIX is easily broken by reagents like bromine, hydrogen in the presence of a platinum catalyst, and hydrogen chloride, which have no similar effects upon cyclopentane, cyclotriacontane, or a paraffin hydrocarbon; and the heat of combustion of cyclopropane, per $CH_2$ group, is appreciably higher than that of either cyclopentane or cyclotriacontane.)

The reason that Baeyer was misled into believing the large rings to be strained was that, experimentally, such rings are difficult to prepare. More recently this fact has been interpreted differently. The difficulty of preparing cyclotriacontane, for example, is explained as the result, not of any assumed instability of the product, attributable to strain, but rather to the improbability that the two ends of a chain of 30 carbon atoms will happen to come close enough together to permit being joined to each other by a bond. The relative ease of forming the five-membered ring in cyclopentane, on the other hand, is attributed to the relatively great probability that the ends of a much shorter chain of only five carbon atoms will come close enough. In other words, the fact that the five- and six-membered rings are the most easily formed of all is explained as the result of two opposing effects: the strain, which operates against the formation of three- and (to a lesser extent) four-membered rings; and the probability factor, which causes the ease of formation to decrease more or less regularly as the size of the ring increases.

An important service performed by the strain theory consists in providing a reasonable explanation of the nonexistence of certain substances. For example, cyclopropyne LXXV is unknown although, as far as the ordinary rules of valence are concerned, it would appear to be a perfectly reasonable substance. However, if it existed, it would be extremely strained since the normal value of C—C≡C bond angles is 180°. Similarly, cyclohexene might be expected to be obtainable in cis and trans forms, analogous to maleic and fumaric acids, respectively. Only the cis form LXXVI is known; the trans form LXXVII would be too highly strained to be capable of existence. Moreover, camphor LXXVIII

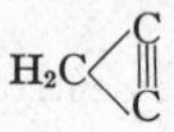

LXXV 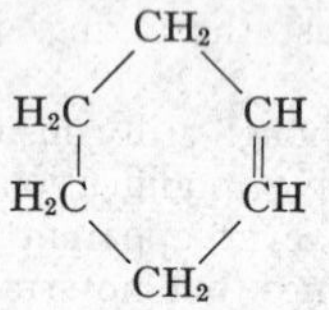 LXXVI 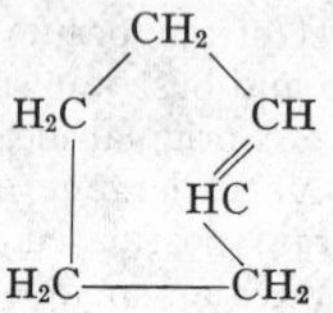 LXXVII

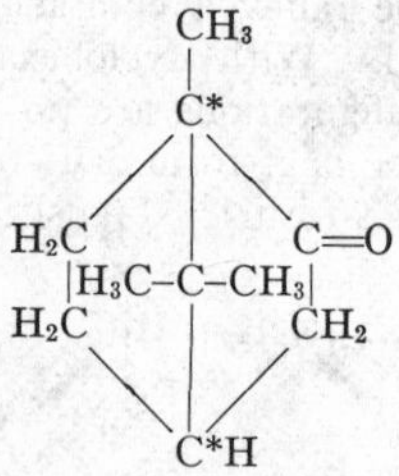

LXXVIII

(*see* CAMPHOR) has the two asymmetric carbon atoms marked with the asterisks. Since these atoms are nonequivalent, meso forms are impossible, and so two pairs of enantiomorphs might be expected. Only one such pair is known. This is the one in which the attachment of the —$C(CH_3)_2$— "bridge" to the outer six-membered ring is cis; the second pair of enantiomorphs, in which the attachment is trans, would be too strained to be capable of existence.

**14. Conformational Analysis.**—If the chair configuration LXXIV of cyclohexane is written more fully as LXXIX, the hydrogen atoms are seen to be of two geometrically different types. Six of these atoms are joined to the carbon atoms by bonds which are parallel to one another and perpendicular to the average plane of the ring; these atoms and bonds are commonly described as axial. On the other hand, the remaining six hydrogen atoms are joined to the carbon atoms by bonds which lie approximately in the average plane of the ring; these atoms and bonds are commonly described as equatorial.

If one of the hydrogen atoms of cyclohexane is replaced by a substituent, which may be explicitly a methyl group, a halogen atom, or the like, two conformations consistent with the Z-form

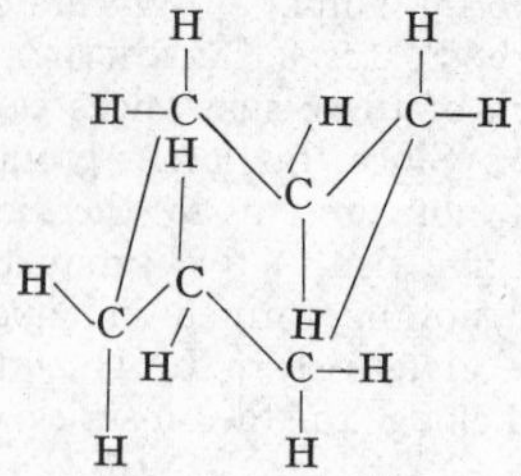

LXXIX

of the ring (*see* above) are possible inasmuch as this substituent may occupy either an axial or an equatorial position. Usually, however, the equatorial position is favoured because it permits the widest possible separation of the atoms that are not bonded to each other.

It will be possible here only to mention, without discussion, two of the many important applications of conformational analysis, which have been made since about 1950. (1) With a disubstituted cyclohexane, cis and trans isomers (*see* above) are possible. Of these, the trans form is usually the more stable when the substituents are either 1,2 or 1,4 with respect to each other, but the cis form is usually the more stable when the substituents are 1,3 to each other. The reason for these generalizations is that the favoured configurations are the ones permitting the maximum numbers of equatorial substituents. (2) When two or more saturated six-membered rings are fused together, as in decahydronaphthalene, the steroids and numerous other compounds, the molecules are often more or less rigid, so that substituents in given positions are required to be either axial or equatorial. The conformations of the substituents, determined in this way, have been related to the relative stabilities of stereoisomeric forms and to the observed differences in reactivity.

**15. Steric Hindrance.**—The rate of a chemical reaction is often decreased by the presence of nearby bulky substituents. For example, the esterification (*see* ESTERS) of benzoic acid (*q.v.*) becomes very slow if methyl groups, bromine atoms, or the like are introduced into the positions adjacent to the carboxyl group. This regularity is not limited to esterifications but is encountered throughout organic chemistry; an explanation for it was proposed by F. Kehrmann (1888) and by V. Meyer (1894). According to these authors, the substituents fill up the available space about the reactive centres and so make more difficult the approach of the reagent molecules.

This picture, although it clearly appears to contain important elements of validity, is far from complete, and undoubtedly represents a substantial oversimplification. Specific interactions of an electrostatic nature, effects attributable to resonance phenomena (*see* RESONANCE, THEORY OF), and so on, also would have to be taken into account in any complete treatment of the relation between structure and reactivity.

## V. THE STEREOCHEMISTRY OF NITROGEN

The general principles essential to the understanding of the stereochemistry of the elements other than carbon differ in no significant respect from those essential to the understanding of the stereochemistry of carbon itself. Since these principles are described in considerable detail in the preceding sections of this article, they need not be discussed further here. Moreover, since the factual material relating to the stereochemistry of the remaining elements is relatively restricted (although rather extensive in an absolute sense), a brief survey of the field is sufficient to bring out the important features.

In all optically active compounds known up to 1899, the molecular dissymmetry was dependent upon the spatial arrangement of the valencies of carbon. In that year, however, W. J. Pope and S. J. Peachey discovered that quaternary ammonium salts of the type $[NQRTZ]^+X^-$ (where Q, R, T and Z represent four dissimilar hydrocarbon radicals) could be resolved into enantiomorphs, and hence that the valency configurations of other elements besides carbon could have sufficient permanence to make their stereochemical investigation possible. (J. A. Le Bel had stated earlier that he had obtained an optically active substance of this type, but his work was shown to be incorrect.) Thus a wide field of research was opened. Further work on quaternary ammonium salts showed: (1) that, since molecular dissymmetry could no longer be demonstrated when two of the hydrocarbon radicals were identical, the ion $[NQRRT]^+$ probably has a plane of symmetry (no centre of symmetry is possible here, whatever the configuration about the nitrogen atom may be); and (2) that, since different methods of formation of a given salt, for instance $NQRT + ZX \rightarrow [NQRTZ]^+X^- \leftarrow NRTZ + QX$, never yielded isomeric modifications, the valencies linking the four hydrocarbon radicals to the nitrogen atom are most probably equivalent. Only two configurations of the ammonium ion satisfy these conditions, namely, the pyramidal configuration I and the tetrahedral configuration II; of these, the first has been definitely disproved by W. H. Mills and E. H. Warren (1925).

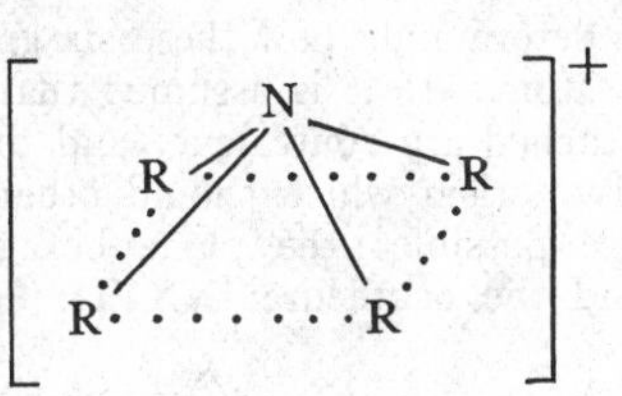

I 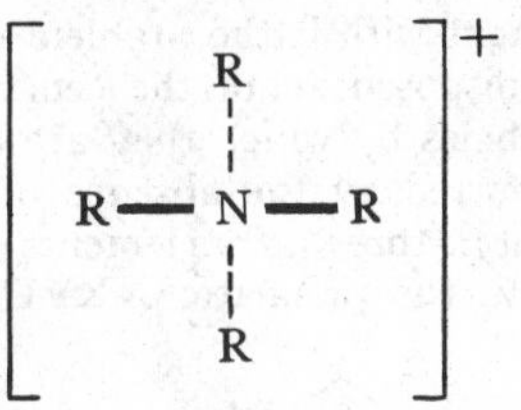 II

The amine oxides are another class of compound in which a nitrogen atom forms bonds to four distinct other atoms or groups. In these also, the radicals appear to be tetrahedrally disposed about the nitrogen atom, for amine oxides of the type III have been obtained in optically active forms by J. Meisenheimer (1908).

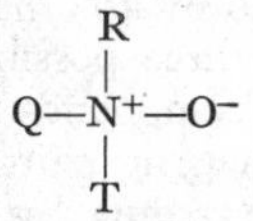

III

The configuration of the trivalent nitrogen atom is of special interest because of the number and importance of the compounds in which the element is present in this state. The numerous attempts made to obtain optically active compounds of the type NQRT have all given negative results, but it is not safe to conclude from this fact that these compounds have a planar configuration; it is possible that instead they have a dissymmetric pyramidal configuration but are racemized easily by passage through an intermediate planar configuration, thus

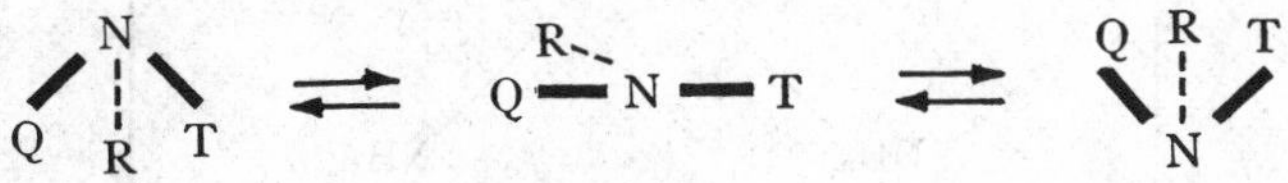

That this second explanation of the optical inactivity of amines of the form NQRT is the correct one has been shown by studies of spectra, of dipole moments, of crystal structure, and of electron diffraction.

In compounds of trivalent nitrogen of the type —X=N—Y, where the nitrogen atom is directly linked to only two other atoms, and, therefore, to one of them by a double bond, the stereochemistry of the nitrogen atom was established at an early date by the classical stereochemical methods (*i.e.*, by consideration of isomer numbers and not with the use of the physical methods employed with the amines). Thus, oximes can generally be prepared in two isomeric modifications if the two substituents attached to the carbon atom doubly bonded to the nitrogen are dissimilar. The two isomeric forms are represented by the configurations IV and V.

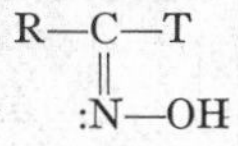

IV 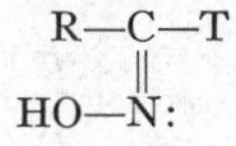 V

In these configurations the carbon, nitrogen and oxygen atoms, and the atoms of the groups R and T joined directly to the central carbon atom are considered to lie in the same plane. The situation is thus closely analogous to that in the ethylenic compounds considered previously, like maleic and fumaric acids; the only significant difference is that the nitrogen atom here forms three bonds whereas the corresponding carbon atom in the ethylenic compounds forms four. (Sometimes, the unshared pair of electrons on the nitrogen atom represented by the pair of dots, is said to act as a fourth valence bond.)

The above interpretation of the isomerism of the oximes, due to A. Hantzsch and A. Werner (1890), is confirmed by the optical activity of the cyclic oxime VI, demonstrated by W. H. Mills and A. M. Bain (1910).

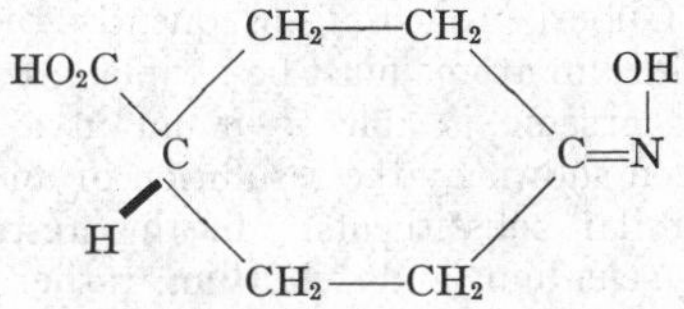

VI

Further examples of stereoisomeric nitrogen compounds, which owe their isomerism to restricted rotation about a double bond to the nitrogen atom, include the N-methyl oximes VII and VIII, the azo compounds IX and X and the azoxy compounds XI and XII. The so-called stable and labile diazohydrates (*see* DIAZO COMPOUNDS) were also considered by Hantzsch to be stereoisomers

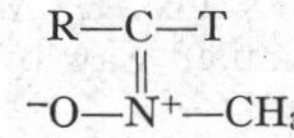

VII 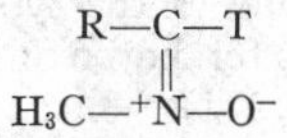 VIII 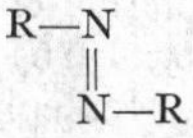 IX 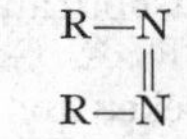 X

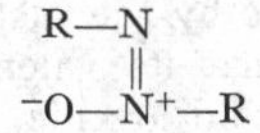

XI 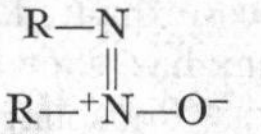 XII 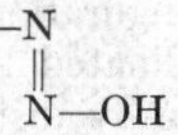 XIII 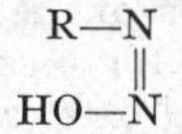 XIV

of each other with the configurations XIII and XIV, respectively; this view, although probably correct, has been contested by other authors.

## VI. THE STEREOCHEMISTRY OF THE REMAINING ELEMENTS

For reasons of convenience, the various remaining elements are classified below on the basis of their co-ordination numbers. In general, a given element in a given compound is said to have a co-ordination number N, or to be N-co-ordinated, if in the molecules of that compound each atom of the element in question is joined to N distinct other atoms by bonds that are not broken ionically in solution. For example, in sulfuric acid, $H_2SO_4$, the co-ordination number of sulfur is four, since each sulfur atom is joined to four oxygen atoms by bonds of the type stated; similarly, the co-ordination number of oxygen in the same substance is one, since the oxygen–hydrogen bonds are broken ionically in solution and so do not contribute to the co-ordination number. In those instances in which the nonionizable union between each atom and each of its neighbours consists of a covalent single bond, the co-ordination number of each atom is equal to its valence.

**1. Elements of Co-ordination Number 3.**—Sulfonium salts $[SQRT]^+X^-$, in which three dissimilar hydrocarbon radicals are linked to the sulfur atom, were shown to be dissymmetric by W. J. Pope and S. J. Peachey, and S. Smiles (1900); the sulfonium ion, therefore, has a nonplanar configuration as in XV. Other analogous compounds of sulfur are the sulfinic esters XVI, the sulfoxides

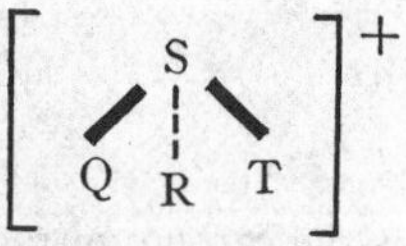

$$\left[ Q\diagup S(R)\diagdown T \right]^{+}$$

XV

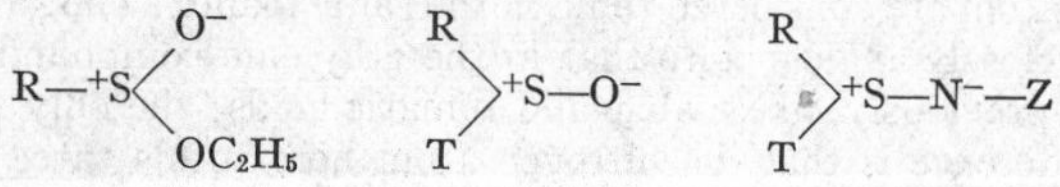

XVI  XVII  XVIII

XVII and the sulfilimines XVIII; each of these has been shown to have a similar nonplanar configuration, since optically active representatives of the three classes have been obtained, principally by H. Phillips and J. Kenyon (1925–27).

Optically active selenonium salts (analogous to the above sulfonium salts) were obtained by W. J. Pope and A. Neville (1902), and optically active telluronium salts were obtained by T. M. Lowry and F. L. Gilbert (1929). Consequently, the 3-co-ordinated selenium and tellurium atoms must be nonplanar.

That trivalent arsenic is able to maintain a pyramidal configuration has been shown by the resolution of an arsine, AsRQT, with three dissimilar substituents. In this respect, arsenic resembles sulfur, selenium and tellurium rather than nitrogen. Optically inactive stereoisomers of presumably the cis-trans type have been obtained when two trivalent arsenic atoms are present in a ring.

**2. Elements of Co-ordination Number 4.**—In the first short period (*see* Periodic Law), besides both carbon and nitrogen, the elements beryllium and boron can have co-ordination number four, and there is evidence that the atoms of each of these elements then have the four radicals tetrahedrally disposed about them. This was demonstrated for beryllium by the production of an optically active compound of the type XIX (W. H. Mills and R. A. Gotts, 1926), and for boron in a similar way by J. Böeseken and J. Meulenhoff (1924).

The molecular dissymmetry of silicon compounds of the type SiQRTZ has been established by F. S. Kipping, and the investigation of the configuration of 4-co-ordinated zinc by the method used for 4-co-ordinated beryllium has shown that its valencies are also tetrahedrally distributed. Phosphorus and arsenic, like nitrogen, have also been shown to have the tetrahedral configuration when 4-co-ordinated—phosphorus through the optical activity

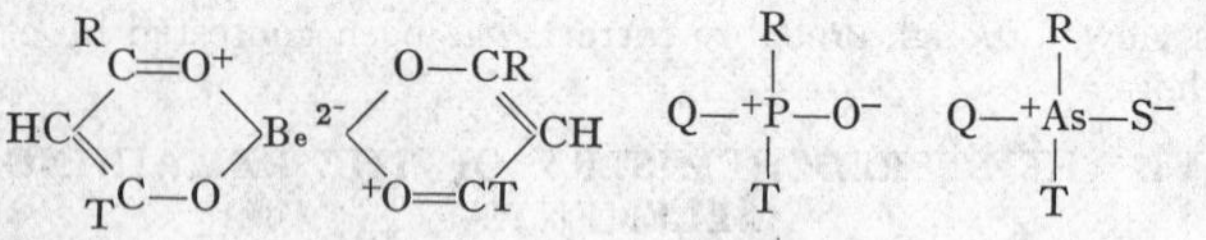

XIX  XX  XXI

of a phosphine oxide XX (J. Meisenheimer and L. Lichtenstadt, 1911), and arsenic through that of an arsine sulfide XXI. Optically active arsine oxides $RQTAs^{+}—O^{-}$ and arsonium salts $[RQTZAs]^{+}X^{-}$ are also known. The existence of diastereomers and of meso forms has been demonstrated with compounds containing two such asymmetric phosphorus or arsenic atoms.

It is not universally true, however, that when an atom is linked directly to four other atoms these must be arranged around it tetrahedrally. Thus, many compounds of 4-co-ordinated platinum containing a complex of the type $PtA_2B_2$ occur in two inactive, but evidently stereoisomeric, modifications; typical examples include the doubly charged cation $[Pt(NH_3)_2(C_5H_5N)_2]^{2+}$ and

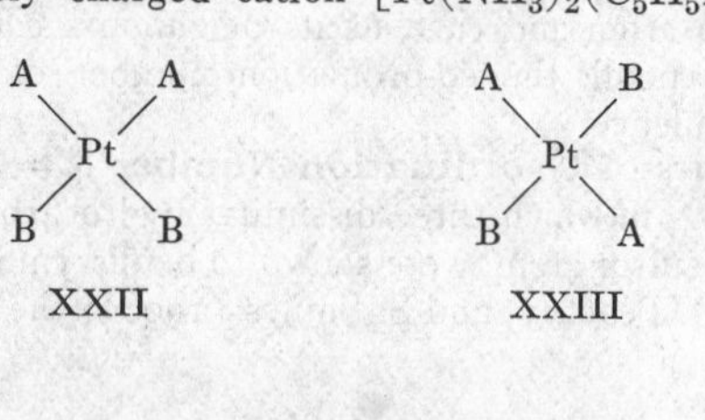

XXII  XXIII

the neutral molecule $Pt(NH_3)_2Cl_2$. This isomerism is clearly incompatible with a tetrahedral arrangement of the radicals about the platinum atom and is to be explained most simply by the supposition that 4-co-ordinated platinum has a plane configuration. The isomers are of the types XXII (cis) and XXIII (trans).

**3. Elements of Co-ordination Number 6.**—Werner's proof that substances like the compounds of metallic salts with ammonia (formerly regarded as "molecular compounds") are co-ordination compounds in which a certain number of atoms or groups, most frequently six, are directly attached to the metallic atom ($CoCl_3·6NH_3$, for example, having the structure XXIV)

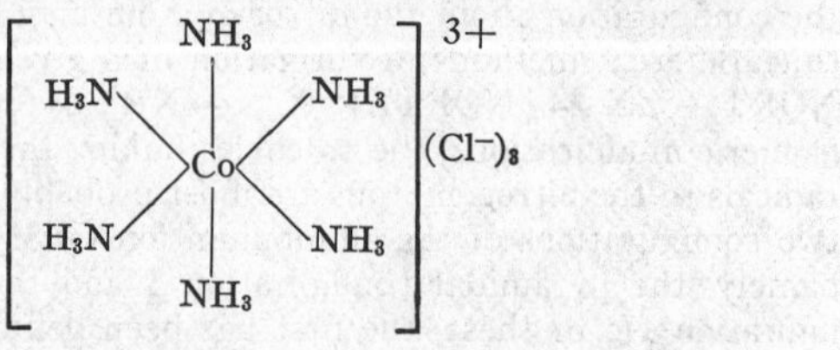

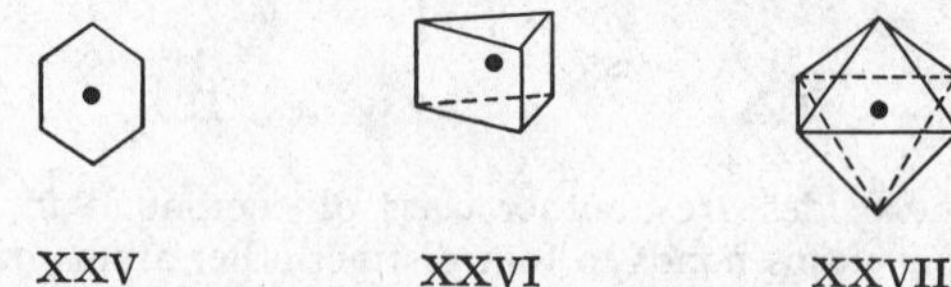

XXIV

brought with it the problem of determining how these six groups are disposed about the central atom. If it is assumed that the valencies by which they are attached are equivalent (and this is supported by the absence of isomerism which should otherwise occur), three arrangements are possible: the plane hexagonal XXV, the prismatic XXVI and the octahedral XXVII. (For

XXV  XXVI  XXVII

ease of visualization, the respective geometrical figures are outlined, the central atom is represented by a large dot and the valence bonds are not shown. A substituent is supposed to occupy each of the positions marked by a corner of the figure.)

A decision among these three possible configurations was obtained by investigating the compounds formed by linking the co-ordination positions together in pairs through four-membered chains, as can be done, for example, by the threefold replacement of two molecules of ammonia, $NH_3$, by one of ethylenediamine, $H_2N—CH_2—CH_2—NH_2$ (or of two nitrito groups, $NO_2^-$, by an oxalato group $—O_2C—CO_2^-$, or the like) so as to produce a complex in which the metallic atom forms a common member of three symmetrical five-membered rings, as in XXVIII. Since it seems

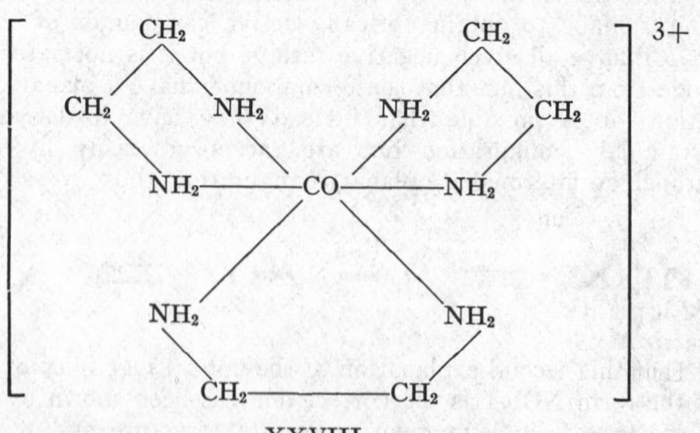

XXVIII

most probable that only adjacent co-ordination positions can be bridged in this way, the possible configurations for the tricyclic ion are those indicated by the dotted lines in the four different

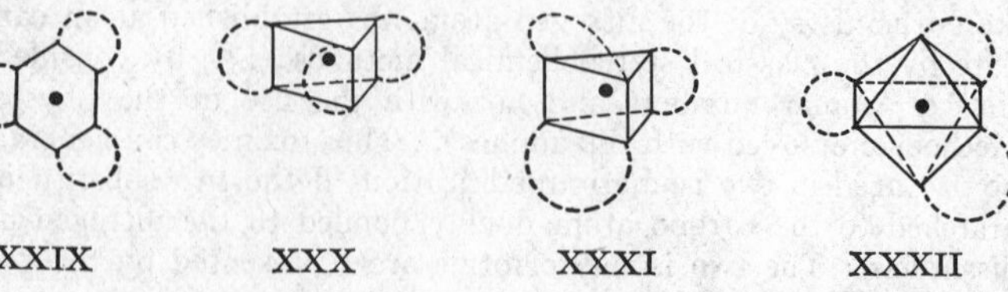

XXIX  XXX  XXXI  XXXII

diagrams XXIX–XXXII. Of these, the first three are evidently symmetrical, but the last is dissymmetrical, for it possesses only twofold and threefold axes of rotation. Experimental investigation of the salts of these tricyclic ions has shown that they can be produced in optically active forms. The ions are thus dissymmetric and must consequently have the last configuration XXXII. It is, therefore, to be concluded that in such compounds the six valencies of the central metallic atom are octahedrally disposed.

This conclusion is confirmed by the occurrence of a different type of stereoisomerism shown by complexes of the type $MA_2B_4$, such as are contained in the diacidotetrammine salts of cobalt and chromium. These compounds should exist in three isomeric forms if their configuration is hexagonal and in four if it is prismatic, but in only two if it is octahedral; the alternative arrangements are then those in which the two groups A lie at the ends

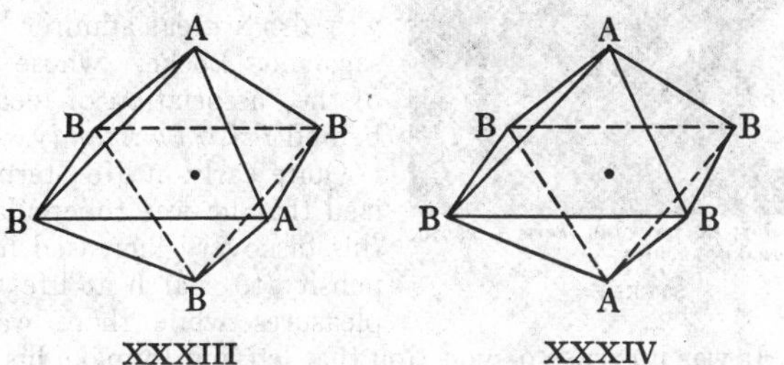

XXXIII XXXIV

(1) of an edge as in XXXIII (cis compound), and (2) of a diagonal as in XXXIV (trans compound) of the octahedron. The number of isomers actually found is two. Moreover, in dicyclic derivatives of this type like $[en_2CoCl_2]^+ Cl^-$, where *en* represents ethylenediamine, the isomer with the cis configuration can be obtained optically active, whereas the other, the trans isomer, cannot be resolved. These facts are in accordance with the con-

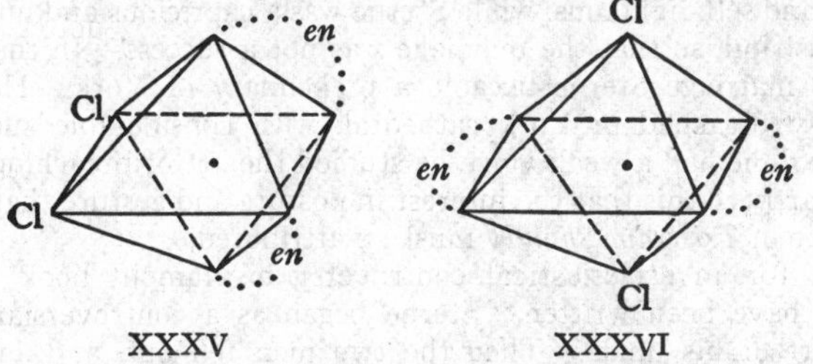

XXXV XXXVI

figuration XXXV for the cation of the cis isomer, and XXXVI for the cation of the trans isomer.

Bibliography.—J. H. van't Hoff, *La Chimie dans l'Espace* (1875), *Arrangement of Atoms in Space* (1877); A. Werner, *Lehrbuch der Stereochemie* (1904); F. M. Jaeger, *Lectures on the Principle of Symmetry* (1917); K. Freudenberg, *Stereochemie* (1933); R. L. Shriner, R. Adams and C. S. Marvel, "Stereoisomerism," ch. 4 of H. Gilman's *Organic Chemistry*, 2nd ed. (1943); G. W. Wheland, *Advanced Organic Chemistry*, 3rd ed. (1960); W. Klyne (ed.), *Progress in Stereochemistry* (1954); M. S. Newman (ed.), *Steric Effects in Organic Chemistry* (1956); J. Grundy, *Stereochemistry* (1964).

(G. W. Wd.; W. H. Mi.)

**STEREOTYPING,** in printing, is the process of making a duplicate metal or plastic printing plate cast from a mold or matrix of composed type. Invented in 1725 by William Ged (*q.v.*) of Edinburgh and almost forgotten, it was reintroduced in 1804 by Charles Stanhope, 3rd earl of Stanhope. Stereotyping was not markedly successful until after the introduction of the papier-mâché matrix by Claude Genoux, a French printer, in 1829. In the Genoux process, layers of wet blotting and tissue paper, called flong, were placed on the composed type and the wet paper was forced down around the type by beating with a broad, stiff brush. New and improved equipment was developed as a result of the adoption of the paper matrix. Paper molds of set type were prepared by revolving rollers or by direct-pressure machines. The curved casting box was developed in 1854 and, with the production of the curved plate, printing by rotary presses became practicable. For a description of the stereotype process used in letterpress printing, *see* Printing: *Letterpress Printing: Stereotypes*. *See* also Printing Press. (E. L. Y.; X.)

**STERILITY:** *see* Fertility and Fecundity; Reproduction; Reproductive System: *Diseases and Their Medical Treatment: Sterility; Spermatic Cord.*

**STERLING AREA,** a group of countries that keep most of their exchange reserves at the Bank of England and in return have access to the London capital and money market. Following the devaluation of sterling in September 1931, the United Kingdom and other countries that continued to maintain parity with sterling and to hold their reserves in London became known as the sterling bloc. When World War II brought exchange control and prospective exchange shortage, particularly of dollars, those countries with the closest ties to London adopted parallel policies of monetary collaboration. When sterling convertibility was gradually restored in the late 1950s, restrictions on long-term foreign investment were maintained, except for the overseas sterling area. Recurring financial crises in the 1960s caused these restrictions to be tightened. The overseas sterling area countries continued to receive preferential treatment.

There was never any formal constitution of the sterling area, which has no centralized administration or elaborate machinery. In the late 1960s, besides the United Kingdom and its few remaining dependencies and protectorates, the sterling area consisted mainly of countries then or formerly part of the Commonwealth. Canada was not a member; but Australia and New Zealand were, together with India, Pakistan, and Ceylon. Other Commonwealth members were Malaysia, Singapore, Hong Kong, Brunei, several former colonies in East, Central, and West Africa, the Bahamas, Bermuda, British Honduras and Guyana, Cyprus, and Malta. In addition, several Middle East former protectorates—Kuwait, Jordan, the Persian Gulf sheikhdoms, and Aden—as well as Libya, Ireland, Iceland, and Burma maintained their membership. South Africa, though no longer in the Commonwealth, sold most of its gold production to the Bank of England.

Former members of the sterling area included Egypt and Sudan, Palestine, Rhodesia, the Belgian Congo and Ruanda-Urundi, Syria and Lebanon, Iraq, and the Faeroe Islands.

The devaluation of sterling in November 1967 strained the area. Some members, notably Ireland and New Zealand, devalued their currencies. Others—notably Australia, Malaysia, Singapore, and Ghana—announced their intention not to devalue. The future of others remained doubtful.

The outlook for the sterling area was difficult even before the 1967 devaluation. The British balance of payments required curtailment of long-term investments in the area. These had been running high, and moreover could possibly serve as channels of capital flight to third countries. Many of the overseas sterling area countries that had been large contributors to the exchange reserves were building up their independent reserves of gold and dollars. The possibility that sterling balances belonging to the overseas members, especially the Arab oil-producing countries, might be withdrawn was an obstacle to acceptance of Britain's application to join the Common Market. It was probable that a realignment of currency relations was under way and that the devaluation of sterling would weaken, if not put an effective end to, the sterling area.

Periodic meetings of the finance ministers maintained liaison among the Commonwealth governments, and from 1947 the Sterling Area Statistical Committee facilitated the exchange of information, but administration was decentralized. Each government, even within the Commonwealth, retained control of its monetary policy. There was consultation among them; but London did not dominate. With the growing independence of the smaller countries, each tended to build up its own reserves and make its own contacts with the International Monetary Fund (*q.v.*). At the same time there was a growing body of opinion in the United Kingdom that the sterling area arrangements were ceasing to be an asset and becoming an encumbrance.

Bibliography.—Philip W. Bell, *The Sterling Area in the Postwar World* (1956); A. R. Conan, *The Sterling Area* (1952), *The Rationale of the Sterling Area* (1958), *Capital Imports into the Sterling Area* (1960); Susan Strange, *The Sterling Problem and the Six* (1967).

(J. B. Ce.)

**STERLITAMAK,** a town of the Bashkir Autonomous Soviet Socialist Republic in the Russian Soviet Federated Socialist Republic, U.S.S.R., stands on the left bank of the Belaya River, at its confluence with the Sterlya, about 75 mi. S of Ufa. Pop. (1959) 111,575. Founded in the 18th century, it only acquired importance with the industrialization of the Urals after the Revolution and especially with the development of the Second Baku oil field after World War II. It is a crossing point of railways southward from Ufa and westward from Magnitogorsk. Oil refining is important and other industries include machine building, production of synthetic rubber, soda (using local salt) and cement, flour milling, distilling, and leather working. (R. A. F.)

**STERN, OTTO** (1888–1969), German-U.S. theoretical physicist and Nobel Prize winner, was born in Sorau (now Zary, Pol.), on Feb. 17, 1888. He received the degree of doctor of philosophy in physical chemistry from the University of Breslau in 1912. He joined Albert Einstein at the University of Prague and followed him to the University of Zürich, where he received the *venia legendi* for physical chemistry. Early in 1914 Stern joined the faculty of the University of Frankfurt, where he remained until 1921 except for a period of military service during World War I.

After a short term as associate professor of theoretical physics at the University of Rostock, he was appointed to the chair of physical chemistry at the University of Hamburg in 1923. Resigning this position in 1933 he accepted shortly thereafter an invitation to join the Carnegie Institute of Technology in Pittsburgh, Pa., as research professor of physics. On retirement in 1945, he moved to Berkeley, Calif., where he died on Aug. 17, 1969.

Stern's earlier scientific contributions belong to the field of theoretical physics, the most important ones dealing with statistical thermodynamics. After 1919, however, his research was more experimental and was mostly devoted to the development and application of the molecular-beam method, a very powerful tool for the investigation of the properties of atoms, molecules, and atomic nuclei. A series of brilliant experiments designed to answer crucial questions of physical theory won him international recognition (*see* ATOMIC AND MOLECULAR BEAMS).

Stern was awarded the Nobel Prize for Physics in 1943 for the first measurement of the magnetic moment of the proton.

*See* T. N. Levitan, *Laureates: Jewish Winners of the Nobel Prize* (1960). (I. En.)

**STERNBERG, LEV YAKOVLEVICH** (1861–1927), Russian ethnographer, noted for his work on the Gilyak (Nivkh) people of Sakhalin Island and the neighbouring parts of the Siberian mainland. Born in Zhitomir in the Ukraine on May 3 (new style; April 21, old style), 1861, he studied at the University of St. Petersburg and later in the law faculty in Odessa. He was twice arrested for revolutionary activities and exiled to the island of Sakhalin. While in exile he began his studies of the Gilyak and Orok. After return from exile he remained under police surveillance in Zhitomir until in 1899 he was able to return to St. Petersburg to pursue his ethnographic studies (*see* GILYAK).

From 1902 through 1917 he continued his work, at the same time being active in Russian and Jewish social movements. He traveled to museums in Berlin, Leipzig and elsewhere, and he also studied the Ainu and the Tungus peoples. After the Revolution of 1917 he organized the teaching of ethnography at the University of Leningrad with V. G. Bogoraz. Sternberg died at Dudergof, near Leningrad, Aug. 14, 1927. (L. K.)

**STERNE, LAURENCE** (1713–1768), English novelist, the author of *Tristram Shandy,* was born at Clonmel, Tipperary, on Nov. 24, 1713. His father, Roger Sterne, was a poor and improvident soldier who belonged to a gifted and hardheaded family which had produced an archbishop of York, a great-grandfather of the novelist. Sterne disliked his mother, who was of partly French descent; but he idolized his father, and his early memories of him, and of the scenes of military life that he saw as he moved about with his mother after his father's regiment, were to serve him as inspiration later in life. In 1723 or 1724 he was sent to a school near Halifax, Yorkshire, and in 1733 he entered Jesus college, Cambridge, as a sizar. At Cambridge, where he is said to have "read a little, laugh'd a great deal" and amused himself by "puzzling his tutors," he became friendly with John Hall (later Hall-Stevenson), a wealthy young wit of dissipated habits whose home at Skelton castle (renamed "Crazy castle") he was often to visit. He delighted in exploring the extensive library there, which was rich in what booksellers term "curiosa." From an early age Sterne had been an inquisitive reader: from his own writings it is clear that he knew such writers as Rabelais, Cervantes, Burton, Montaigne, Erasmus, Horace and Swift. He was also a great admirer of "the sagacious Locke," whose theory of the "association of ideas" lies behind *Tristram Shandy*.

PORTRAIT BY AN UNKNOWN ARTIST; PHOTO, THE BETTMANN ARCHIVE

STERNE

Quite early in life Sterne realized that he was tubercular, and this discovery increased his propensity to snatch at life and its pleasures while there was still time. It was no sense of vocation that led him to make his career in the church, but rather the influence of his uncle Jacques, a pluralist who was both archdeacon of Cleveland and precentor of York.

Having taken his degree in 1737 Sterne entered the church the following year. Although his vicarage was at Sutton-on-the-Forest near York he preferred to live in York, then a centre of fashionable life and church politics. In 1741 he married a wealthy young woman, Elisabeth Lumley. She was a difficult woman, irritable and self-righteous, while Sterne was a capricious and unfaithful husband, so that the marriage was not a success. In the year of his marriage Sterne became a prebendary of York. He frequently preached in York cathedral, with considerable success: although he had a weak voice he studied the art of preaching, and it is partly to this that the interest in posture and gesture that is so evident in *Tristram Shandy* must be attributed.

But for an ecclesiastical controversy his famous book might never have been written. Sterne began as a controversialist in support of his uncle. Then the two men fell out, and Jacques Sterne managed to do his nephew permanent harm by spreading a story that the novelist's mother and sister were lodging in a debtor's prison because he was too mean to support them. For a while Sterne withdrew from ecclesiastical politics, but in 1758 he returned and wrote *A Political Romance,* published early in 1759 and later renamed *The History of a Good Warm Watch-Coat.* This satire on a Dr. Topham who had drawn into his own hands most of the legal offices connected with the diocese of York is a precursor of *Tristram Shandy,* and it must have been while he was writing it that he realized his genius for comedy and satire. At the beginning of 1759 he wrote the opening volumes of *Tristram Shandy,* which were published on Jan. 1, 1760.

Like *Hudibras* and *Don Juan* (two satires with which it has something in common), *Tristram Shandy* came out in parts (nine in all) and was never completed. The full title—*The Life and Opinions of Tristram Shandy, Gentleman*—gives one a hint of the nature of the book: this is not (like so many novels of the time) *The Life and Adventures* of somebody: it deals with opinions, not with things. The reason for this is given in the motto of the first two volumes: "It is not things, but opinions about things, that throw mankind into confusion." Talk rather than action constitutes the "plot" of the book. Thus *Tristram Shandy* could not possibly have been the first novel: it is (among other things) a sort of satire on its own precursors: it cocks a snook at the rigorous morality of Samuel Richardson, the careful plot-construction of Henry Fielding and the violent adventures of Tobias Smollett. Its own morality may best be described as "relaxed": it has (in the usual sense) no plot whatever: while its characters, so far from being involved in exciting adventures, seldom even venture out-of-doors. The book opens with an account of the begetting (not the birth) of its hero, so providing Sterne with a splendid occasion for a discussion of heredity, education and life in general. It takes the hero a long time to get born, but the time is most agreeably filled in by an account of the conversations of his father and Uncle Toby *de omnibus rebus et quibusdam aliis.* The most important structural device is that of the association of ideas: instead of limiting himself to one subject, as most writers do, Sterne allows his mind to wander freely from one topic to another, as happens in a state of reverie. The result is that his book, while it lacks all logic of the usual sort, has yet a subliminal logic of its own which gives it a remarkable hold on the minds of its readers.

On the publication of the first part of *Tristram Shandy* Sterne found himself famous, though many readers were shocked when they discovered that it was the work of a cleric. He moved to a new house near Stillington and went on with his book. He delighted in his celebrity, dining out constantly on his visits to London; but his health declined, and in 1762 he set out on an extended trip in France and Italy in search of the sun and a renewal of health. In France he found himself as famous as in his native country.

The main events during the remainder of his life were the publication of further installments of *Tristram Shandy* and his infatuation with Elizabeth Draper, possibly a deeper and more sentimental love affair than most in his life. *The Journal to Eliza,* which he wrote for her, reveals the complicated state of the emotions which inspired *A Sentimental Journey Through France and Italy* (1768), a travel book of a new kind in which Sterne concentrates on the effect of his travels on himself, dealing particularly with such "sentimental" experiences as the flirtations in which he became involved as he traveled about the continent. As a sort of riposte to Smollett's *Travels Through France and Italy,* Sterne concentrates on whatever had called forth his affections. The result is a work much slighter than *Tristram Shandy* which yet had a great influence on European literature and helped to give the word "sentimental" its international currency. He died in London on March 18, 1768.

Bibliography.—The first good edition of his *Works* (including his *Sermons* and *Letters*) appeared in 10 volumes in 1780. There is a 12-vol. edition by Wilbur L. Cross (1904). The only authentic text of *Tristram Shandy,* however, is that edited by J. A. Work (1940). The *Letters* were edited by L. P. Curtis (1934). *A Political Romance* is reprinted in I. Jack's edition of *Sterne's Sentimental Journey* and *The Journal to Eliza* (1968). J. Ferriar's *Illustrations of Sterne* (1798; rev. ed. 1812) is an interesting early study. The best biographical and critical studies are *The Life and Times of Laurence Sterne,* by W. L. Cross (1909; rev. ed., 1929) and *Laurence Sterne, de l'homme à l'oeuvre,* by H. Fluchère (1961). (I. J.)

**STEROIDS** in chemistry, biology, and medicine make up a large group of naturally occurring substances and their synthetic derivatives. All possess as a fundamental structure the four-membered hydrocarbon ring system known as cyclopentanoperhydrophenanthrene (I), for convenience represented by the diagram (II).

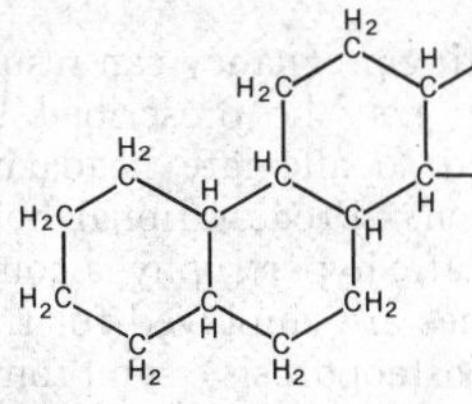

I

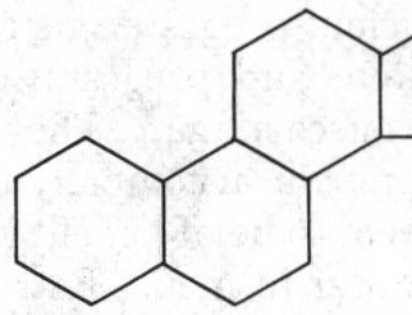

II

The steroids are colourless crystalline solids that differ among themselves in the nature of substituent groups attached to this basic nucleus. Steroid compounds are intimately concerned with a variety of life processes and may be divided into seven principal classes: sterols, bile acids, sex hormones, adrenal cortical hormones, insect hormones, cardiotonic agents, and sapogenins.

Because of the large variety of known steroid compounds, the problem of naming them is formidable. Two systems of steroid nomenclature are employed. So-called trivial nomenclature is based on the arbitrary names given to important natural steroids upon their discovery; compounds closely related in structure to these substances are named as derivatives thereof. Somewhat analogous to trivial names are the nonproprietary or generic names approved for new therapeutic steroid drugs by the United States Adopted Names (USAN) Council in cooperation with the World Health Organization. In systematic nomenclature compounds are designated as derivatives of certain reference hydrocarbons, and the systematic name denotes unambiguously the complete structure of the compound. Both types of names are employed in the following section; an explanation of steroid nomenclature is given in the section *Steroid Nomenclature* below.

## CLASSES OF STEROIDS

**Sterols.**—The sterols are constituents of the lipid material of the cells of practically all living organisms. In all these compounds the steroid nucleus is substituted with a β-hydroxyl group at position 3 and with a branched side chain containing eight, nine, or ten carbon atoms (see *Steroid Nomenclature*). The predominant sterol of the higher animals is cholesterol, whereas lower

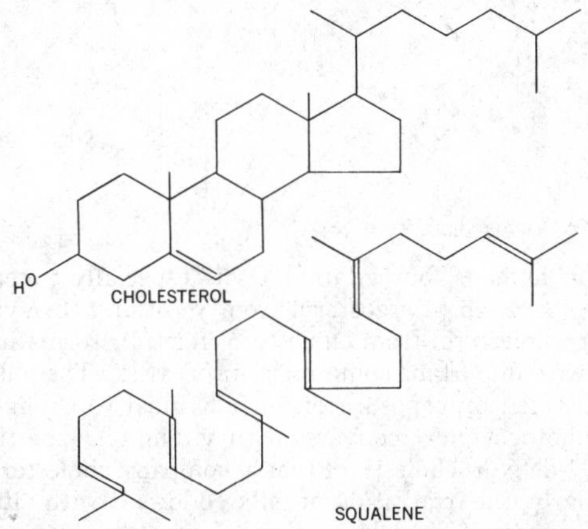

CHOLESTEROL

SQUALENE

animals and plants possess a variety of other sterols, most of them with the longer side chains. Some of the more than 30 different sterols that have been isolated from various species are listed as Table I.

Table I.—*Representative Sterols*

| Trivial name | Systematic name | Source |
|---|---|---|
| Cholesterol | cholest-5-en-3β-ol | animal cells |
| Cholestanol (dihydrocholesterol) | 5α-cholestan-3β-ol | animal cells |
| Coprostanol | 5β-cholestan-3β-ol | feces |
| Lathosterol | 5α-cholest-7-en-3β-ol | with cholesterol |
| 7-Dehydrocholesterol (provitamin $D_3$) | cholesta-5,7-dien-3β-ol | with cholesterol |
| Ergosterol (provitamin $D_2$) | ergosta-5,7,22-trien-3β-ol | yeast, ergot |
| Stigmasterol | stigmasta-5,22-dien-3β-ol | soybean |
| Lanosterol | 4,4,14-trimethyl-5α-cholesta-8,24-dien-3β-ol | wool fat, yeast, liver |
| Desmosterol (24-dehydrocholesterol) | cholesta-5,24-dien-3β-ol | chick embryo, rat skin, liver |

Cholesterol (*q.v.*) is particularly abundant in hair, neural tissue, adrenal glands, and egg yolk, occurring both in the free form and esterified with various fatty acids. Cholesterol is obtained commercially by extraction from the brains and spinal cords of cattle. In animals cholesterol is synthesized in the liver (and probably in other tissues as well) from acetic acid, which, by way of acetoacetic and mevalonic acids, is converted to five-carbon isoprenoid units. Six of these units combine to form the linear molecule squalene, which, by appropriate folding and ring closure, leads to lanosterol, desmosterol, and finally to cholesterol. Cholesterol is metabolized to cholestanol and coprostanol, which are excreted. One established biochemical function of cholesterol is to serve as a precursor for the biosynthesis of steroid hormones in the gonads and adrenal glands and of bile acids in the liver; other physiological functions of cholesterol remain obscure. In contrast to the cholesterol of most tissues, which is in continual metabolic turnover, the cholesterol of the brain and other neural tissue is metabolically inert.

In the pathological condition of atherosclerosis, the deposition of cholesterol occurs within the lining of the aorta and arteries, a situation that often leads to coronary thrombosis and death. The amount and nature of fat in the diet markedly influences this phenomenon, as do the steroid sex hormones, since this disease is much less common in premenopausal women than it is in men and in postmenopausal women (*see* ARTERIES, DISEASES OF).

Certain sterols that possess double bonds in both the 5 and 7 positions have an important relationship to vitamin D, a factor that is necessary for the proper deposition of calcium in the growing bone; absence of vitamin D leads to the pathological condition of rickets. On irradiation with ultraviolet light, ergosterol is converted to calciferol or vitamin $D_2$; 7-dehydrocholesterol similarly yields vitamin $D_3$, which differs from calciferol only in possessing the cholesterol ($C_8H_{17}$) rather than the ergosterol ($C_9H_{17}$) side chain. Both substances are of about equal anti-

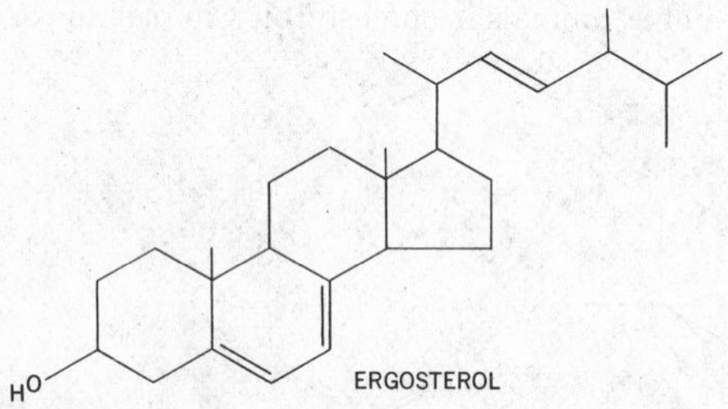

ERGOSTEROL

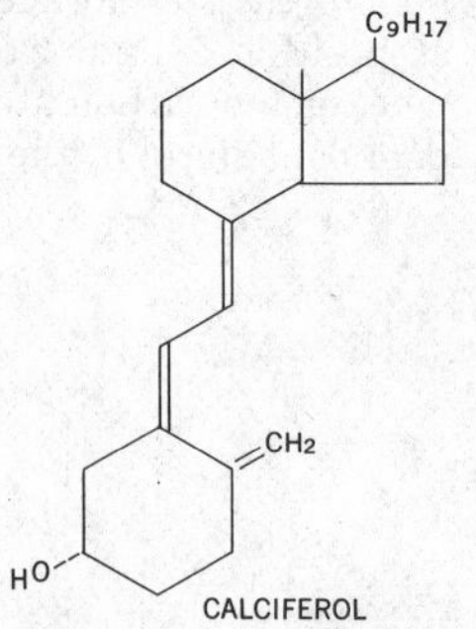

CALCIFEROL

rachitic potency in humans, but vitamin $D_3$ is especially potent in chicks. The preparation of ergosterol from yeast and the synthesis of 7-dehydrocholesterol from cholesterol for transformation to the D-vitamins are important commercial processes. The antirachitic effects obtained by exposure of an individual to sunlight result from the photochemical conversion to vitamin $D_3$ of the small amounts of 7-dehydrocholesterol that accompany cholesterol in the skin. Similarly, the irradiation of milk endows it with vitamin $D_3$ formed from the 7-dehydrocholesterol present.

**Bile Acids.**—The bile acids constitute a group of acidic steroids that are present in animal bile in the form of bile salts in which the bile acid is linked through a peptide bond to the amino acids glycine or taurine. The predominant bile acid in human or cattle

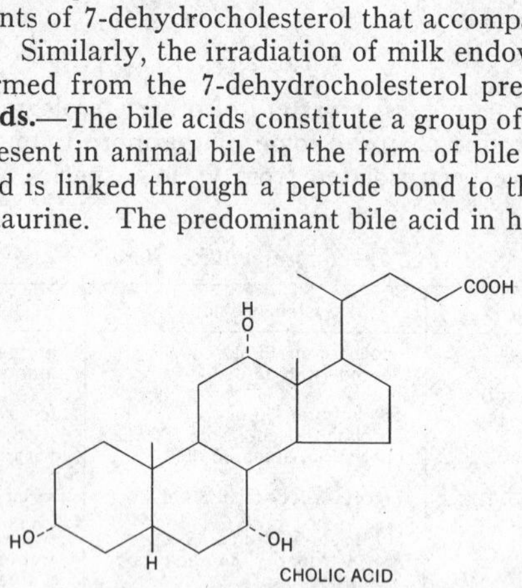

CHOLIC ACID

bile is cholic acid, which occurs chiefly as the glycocholate bile salt. The acids of human (and cattle) bile are listed as Table II; related bile acids have been isolated from other species.

TABLE II.—*Human Bile Acids*

| Trivial name | Systematic name |
|---|---|
| Cholic acid . . . . . | 3α,7α,12α-trihydroxy-5β-cholanic acid |
| Deoxycholic acid . . . . | 3α,12α-dihydroxy-5β-cholanic acid |
| Chenodeoxycholic acid . . . | 3α,7α-dihydroxy-5β-cholanic acid |
| Lithocholic acid . . . . | 3α-hydroxy-5β-cholanic acid |

The bile acids and salts are synthesized in the liver from cholesterol and are discharged with the bile into the duodenum. The bile salts are surface-active agents that promote the absorption of fats through the intestinal wall. In conditions such as obstructive jaundice when sufficient amounts of bile do not reach the intestine, absorption of lipids is impaired (*see* DIGESTION).

The bile acids are obtained commercially from cattle bile. Deoxycholic acid is an important raw material for one industrial process for the production of cortisol and other related anti-

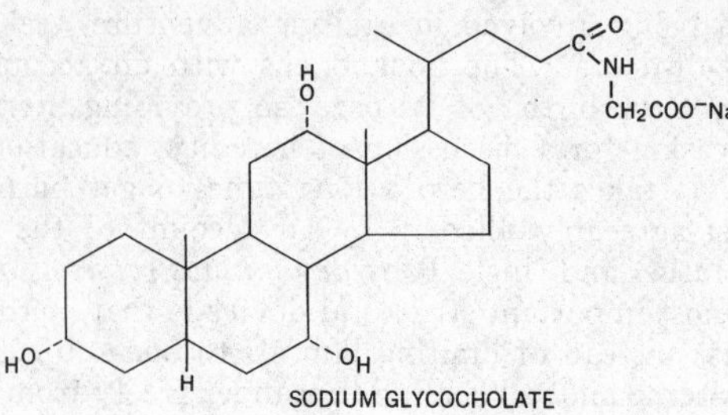

SODIUM GLYCOCHOLATE

inflammatory steroids. Cholic acid, the most abundant bile acid, can be transformed into deoxycholic acid by chemical removal of the 7α-hydroxyl group.

**Sex Hormones.**—The steroid sex hormones are produced primarily in the gonads (ovary in the female and testis in the male) under the stimulation of protein substances called gonadotrophins secreted by the pituitary. The sex hormones mediate the growth and development of the reproductive tract and accessory sex organs, and their maintenance and function.

Two types of hormones are produced at different stages of the ovarian cycle. The follicle containing the ripening ovum produces the estrogenic hormone estradiol (estra-1,3,5(10)-triene-3,17β-diol; British: oestradiol), which is primarily involved in the development of the female organs and the general feminine characteristics. After the mature ovum has been expelled into the fallopian tube, the wall of the ruptured ovarian follicle forms a yellowish body (corpus luteum) that secretes the progestational hormone progesterone (pregn-4-ene-3,20-dione). This substance exerts a marked stimulatory effect on the growth and secretion of the uterine lining. In combination with estrogen, it mediates the proper implantation of the fertilized ovum, the maintenance of pregnancy, and the preparation of the mammary gland for lactation. The high levels of estrogen and progesterone present during the latter stages of pregnancy are produced in the placenta.

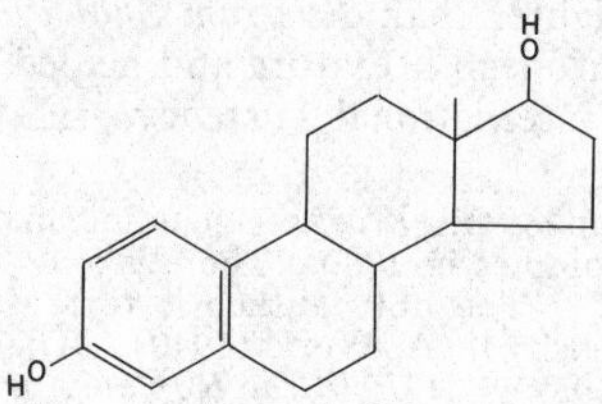

ESTRADIOL

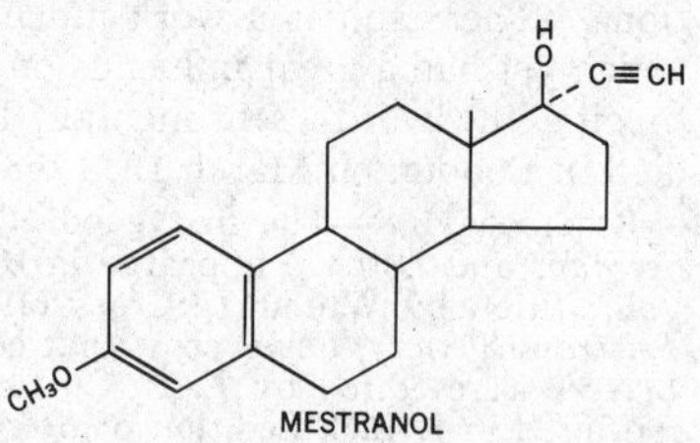

MESTRANOL

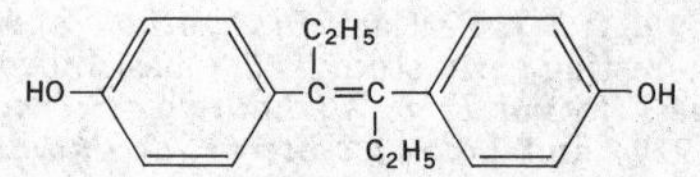

DIETHYLSTILBESTROL

The activity of an estrogenic hormone is evaluated by its effect in promoting growth of the uterus or in stimulating cellular changes in the vaginal epithelium of a castrated or immature rat or mouse. Progestational activity is determined by the extent of proliferation evoked in the uterine endometrium of a rabbit that has been previously stimulated with estrogen.

Insufficient progesterone production during pregnancy can result in abortion, and progestational hormones may be prescribed to prevent miscarriage. They are also used to alleviate headache and other pain accompanying menstruation. Progestational hormones seem to be of benefit in benign prostatic hypertrophy, a common disorder in men. Estrogenic hormones are employed for the relief of both psychic and physical (*e.g.*, osteoporosis) symptoms

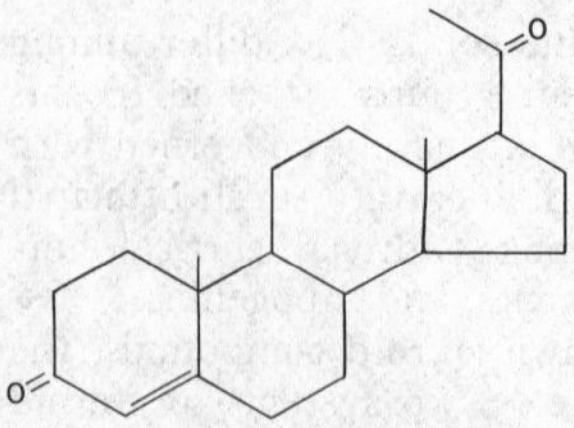

PROGESTERONE

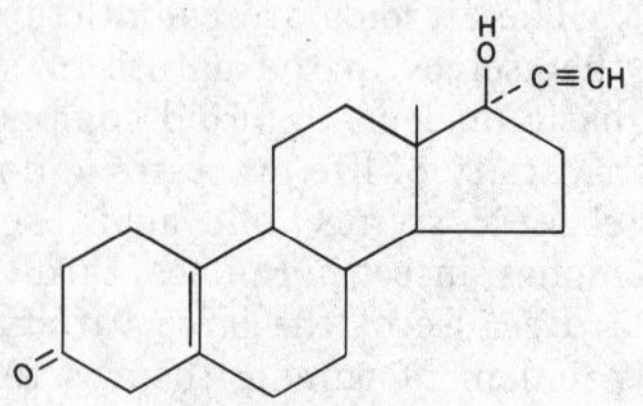

NORETHYNODREL

accompanying and following the menopause, for the suppression of lactation after pregnancy, and for the treatment of prostatic cancer and some types of breast cancer. Estrogenic hormones may help to prevent or ameliorate atherosclerosis. A combination of estrogenic and progestational hormones is used to treat ovarian hypofunction (amenorrhea), and to prevent ovulation by inhibiting the secretion of gonadotrophins by the pituitary.

Since neither estradiol nor progesterone is highly effective when given by mouth, synthetic derivatives are employed clinically for oral administration. The most widely used oral estrogens are 17α-ethynylestradiol, its 3-methyl ether known as mestranol, and a simple nonsteroid, diethylstilbestrol, which shows all the major physiological actions of estradiol. Widespread interest in orally active estrogen-progestin combinations as antifertility or birth-control pills prompted the development of a number of oral progestational agents: these are either chemically modified progesterones or 17-ethynyl derivatives of 19-norandrogens (*e.g.*, norethynodrel); that is, substances related to testosterone but lacking the angular methyl group at position 19. Typical oral progestins and progestin-estrogen combinations are listed in Table III.

TABLE III.—*Oral Progestational and Antifertility Agents*

| Nonproprietary name (Trade name) | Systematic name | Antiovulatory product (with estrogen E or M*) |
|---|---|---|
| 17-Hydroxyprogesterone caproate (Delalutin) | 17-hydroxypregn-4-ene-3, 20-dione, caproate | |
| Medroxyprogesterone acetate (Provera) | 17-hydroxy-6α-methylpregn-4-ene-3, 20-dione, acetate | Provest (E) |
| Megestrol acetate | 17-hydroxy-6-methylpregna-4, 6-diene-3, 20-dione, acetate | Volidan (E) |
| Chlormadinone acetate | 6-chloro-17-hydroxypregna-4, 6-diene-3, 20-dione, acetate | Lutoral (M), C-Quens |
| Ethisterone, 17-ethynyltestosterone | 17-hydroxy-17α-ethynyl-androst-4-en-3-one | |
| Norethindrone (Norlutin) | 17-hydroxy-17α-ethynylestr-4-en-3-one | Norinyl, Ortho-Novum (M) |
| Norethindrone acetate (Norlutate) | 17-hydroxy-17α-ethynylestr-4-en-3-one, acetate | Anovlar, Gestest, Norlestrin (E) |
| Norethynodrel | 17-hydroxy-17α-ethynylestr-5(10)-en-3-one | Enovid (M) |
| Ethynodiol diacetate | 17α-ethynylestr-4-ene-3β, 17-diol, diacetate | Ovulen (M) |
| Lynestrenol | 17α-ethynylestr-4-en-17-ol | Lyndiol (M) |
| Dimethisterone (Secrosterone) | 17-hydroxy-6α-methyl-17α-propynylestr-4-en-3-one | Ovin (E), Oracon |

*E=17-ethynylestradiol; M=mestranol.

The female sex hormones have certain important applications in livestock production. Estrogens are used to promote weight gain in sheep and cattle and to impart tenderness to the flesh of poultry. The compounds generally used are diethylstilbestrol and a closely related nonsteroidal estrogen, dienestrol diacetate, administered either as a feed additive or a subcutaneous implant. Progestins are finding increasing application for synchronization of estrus in sheep and cattle; by temporary retardation of ovarian function an entire herd can be brought into estrus when artificial insemination facilities are available.

The testis chiefly produces the androgenic hormone testosterone (17β-hydroxyandrost-4-en-3-one). Testosterone stimulates the development and function of the male sex organs, and such masculine characteristics as facial hair and deepening of the voice. In addition to promoting marked growth of specific sexual tissues, testosterone exhibits a general anabolic (tissue-building) effect. Androgenic activity is measured by the stimulation of growth either of the comb in chicks and capons or of the prostate gland and seminal vesicles of immature or castrated rats.

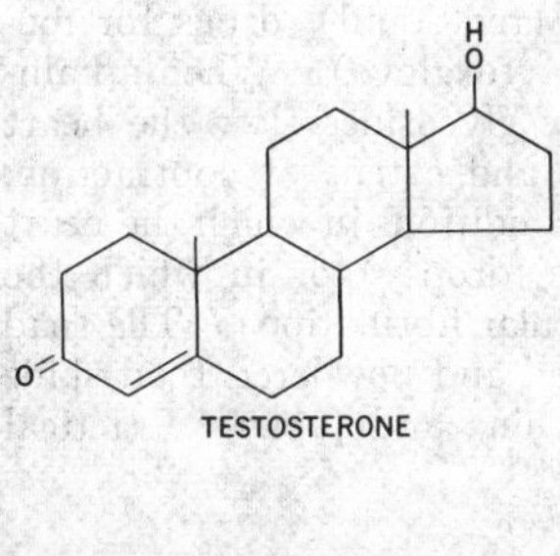

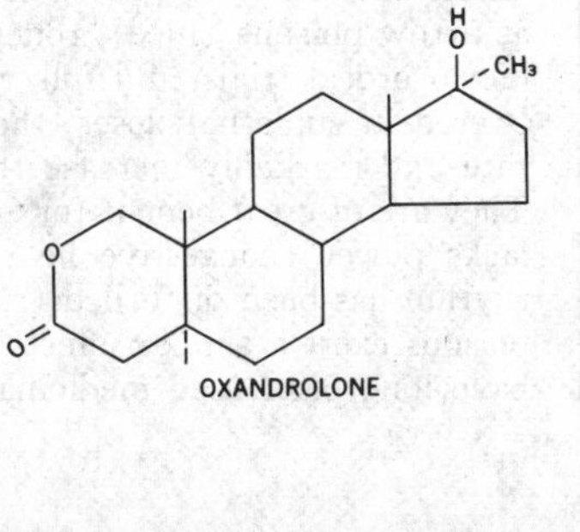

TESTOSTERONE

OXANDROLONE

Testosterone and similar androgenic hormones are used clinically for the treatment of testicular insufficiency (eunuchoidism), the suppression of lactation, the therapy of certain types of breast cancer, and the treatment of frigidity in women. Because of their general anabolic effect, androgenic hormones are employed to promote tissue building in debilitated conditions, or (in combination with growth hormone) for children whose growth is deficient. Testosterone is usually administered parenterally as an ester (*e.g.*, propionate); for oral administration a 17-methyl or ethyl derivative is employed (Table IV). Chemical modifications of the steroid structure have been effected (*e.g.*, oxandrolone) in an attempt to minimize masculinizing effects while retaining anabolic action.

TABLE IV.—*Androgenic and Anabolic Agents*

| Nonproprietary name (Trade name) | Systematic name |
|---|---|
| Testosterone propionate (Perandren, Neo-Hombreol) | 17β-hydroxyandrost-4-en-3-one, propionate |
| Testosterone enanthate (Delatestryl) | 17β-hydroxyandrost-4-en-3-one, heptanoate |
| Nandralone phenpropionate (Durabolin) | 17β-hydroxyestr-4-en-3-one, phenylpropionate |
| Methyltestosterone (Metandren, Oreton-M) | 17-hydroxy-17α-methylandrost-4-en-3-one |
| Methandrostenolone (Dianabol) | 17-hydroxy-17α-methylandrosta-1, 4-dien-3-one |
| Fluoxymesterone (Halotestin, Ultandren) | 9-fluoro-11β-17-dihydroxy-17α-methylandrost-4-en-3-one |
| Norethandrolone (Nilevar) | 17-hydroxy-17α-ethylestr-4-en-3-one |
| Oxymetholone (Adroyd, Anadrol) | 2-hydroxymethylene-17-hydroxy-17α-methyl-5α-androstan-3-one |
| Oxandrolone (Anavar) | 17-hydroxy-17α-methyl-2-oxa-5α-androstan-3-one |
| Stanozolol (Winstrol) | 17-hydroxy-17α-methyl-5α-androstano-[3, 2-c]-pyrazole |

The biochemical precursor of the natural sex hormones is cholesterol. Estradiol is converted metabolically to estrone (3-hydroxyestra-1,3,5(10)-trien-17-one), an active estrogen, estriol (estra-1,3,5(10)-triene-3,16α,17β-triol), and 16-epiestriol (estra-1,3,5(10)-triene-3,16β,17β-triol), all of which are excreted in the urine. During pregnancy, when large amounts of estrogens are being produced by the placenta, some of the estriol excreted may arise from a source other than estradiol. The high urinary level of estriol in the latter stages of pregnancy is an indication of placental function; a drop in the excretion of this steroid may be associated with death of the fetus unless prompt surgical delivery is effected. The principal urinary metabolite of progesterone is pregnanediol (5β-pregnane-3α,20α-diol), which furnishes a measure of progesterone production in an individual. During pregnancy, urinary pregnanediol levels usually are checked periodically to determine the need for additional progesterone to prevent abortion. Testosterone is converted metabolically to androsterone (3α-hydroxy-5α-androstan-17-one) and etiocholanolone (3α-hydroxy-5β-androstan-17-one), which are excreted in the urine; the latter substance is pyrogenic when administered to humans, and its production in abnormal amounts has been implicated in certain hitherto unexplained conditions of fever.

The steroid sex hormones are manufactured commercially from more abundant steroids, chiefly sapogenins; diethylstilbestrol is synthesized inexpensively from simple organic chemicals.

**Adrenal Cortical Hormones.**—When stimulated by a protein hormone from the pituitary called adrenocorticotropin (ACTH), the cortex or outer capsule of the adrenal gland converts cholesterol into a variety of steroid hormones. The major functions of these adrenal secretions are in regulating salt and water balance in the body by promoting the retention of sodium and excretion of potassium ions (mineralocorticoid activity) and in helping the individual cope with stress by promoting the rapid conversion of protein to carbohydrate (glucocorticoid activity). Unlike the sex hormones the adrenal secretions are necessary for life; no organism (including man) can survive adrenalectomy long unless adrenal hormones are administered.

The principal glucocorticoid secreted by the adrenal in the human, monkey, or dog is cortisol (hydrocortisone or compound F). In the rodent it is the corresponding 17-deoxy compound known as corticosterone or compound B. The principal mineralocorticoid is aldosterone. Other active steroids from adrenal tissue include

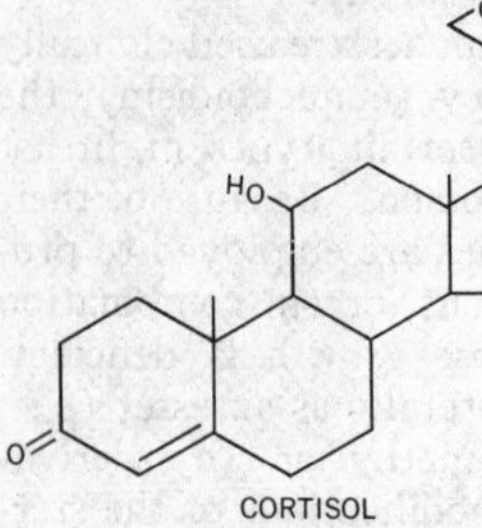

CORTISOL (HYDROCORTISONE)

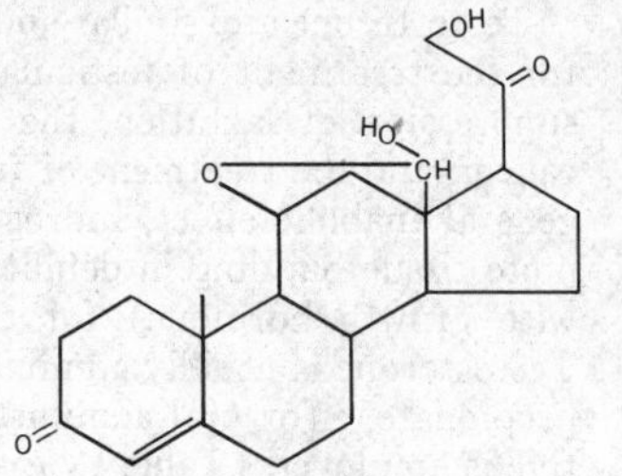

ALDOSTERONE

the 11-dehydro analogue of cortisol known as cortisone (compound E, 17,21-dihydroxypregn-4-ene-3,11,20-trione), which shows considerable glucocorticoid activity, and 11-deoxycorticosterone (DOC, 21-hydroxypregn-4-ene-3,20-dione, 21-hydroxyprogesterone), which exhibits a modest salt-retaining activity.

The glucocorticoid activity of an adrenal hormone is evaluated in the adrenalectomized rat by its action in accumulating glycogen in the liver, in involuting lymphatic tissue, in maintaining the ability of the leg muscle to do work, or helping the animal withstand cold. Mineralocorticoid activity is evaluated through its effect in keeping adrenalectomized animals alive or through sodium retention following salt administration.

The earliest clinical use of adrenal hormones was in Addison's disease, a typically fatal adrenal insufficiency. Crude extracts of beef adrenal glands were first used, since pure compounds were scarce. With the discovery (1949) that cortisone or cortisol could remarkably ameliorate rheumatoid arthritis and other inflammatory conditions, the resulting demand for adrenal steroids had profound effect on the pharmaceutical industry. An intensive effort toward large-scale synthesis of cortisone and cortisol involved the difficult task of introducing the 11-oxygenated substituent characteristic of the glucocorticoids. The original procedure starting with deoxycholic acid involves transfer of the hydroxyl group from $C_{12}$ to $C_{11}$ and is still utilized. Since the discovery that incubation with certain strains of mold or fungus can introduce a hydroxyl group directly into position 11, most processes for producing adrenal hormones involve fermentation of progesterone derivatives obtained from sapogenins or stigmasterol.

Since they inhibit immune response to foreign substances, glucocorticoids are used to treat allergies and (with radiation and other drugs) to combat rejection of transplanted organs such as kidneys. These steroids involute lymphatic tissue, offering temporary benefit in some forms of leukemia and other lymphomas.

Synthetic modifications of the cortisol structure have been found to yield markedly increased glucocorticoid and anti-inflammatory properties with reduced side effects. Such alterations include a

TABLE V.—*Corticoid Anti-inflammatory Agents*

| Nonproprietary name | Modification of cortisol structure | Trade name |
|---|---|---|
| Betamethasone | 1-dehydro-,9-fluoro-,16β-methyl- | Celestone |
| Dexamethasone | 1-dehydro-,9-fluoro-,16α-methyl- | Decadron, Deronil, Dexameth, Gammacorten, Hexadrol |
| Fluocinolone acetonide | 1-dehydro-,6α,9-difluoro-,16α-hydroxy-,16,17-acetonide | Synalar |
| Fludrocortisone acetate | 9-fluoro-,21-acetate | F-Cortef acetate, Alflorone acetate, Florinef acetate |
| Fluorometholone | 1-dehydro-,6α-methyl-,9-fluoro-,21-deoxy- | Oxylone |
| Fluprednisolone | 1-dehydro-,6α-fluoro- | Alphadrol |
| Flurandrenolone | 6α-fluoro-,16α-hydroxy-,16,17-acetonide | Cordran |
| Methylprednisolone | 1-dehydro-,6α-methyl- | Medrol, Wyacort |
| Paramethasone acetate | 1-dehydro-,6α-fluoro-,16α-methyl-,21-acetate | Haldrone |
| Prednisolone | 1-dehydro- | Delta-Cortef, Hydeltra, Meticortelone, Paracortol, Sterane |
| Prednisone | 1-dehydro-,11-dehydro- | Deltasone, Deltra, Meticorten, Paracort |
| Triamcinolone | 1-dehydro-,9-fluoro-,16α-hydroxy- | Aristocort, Kenacort |
| Triamcinolone acetonide | 1-dehydro-,9-fluoro-,16α-hydroxy-,16,17-acetonide | Aristocort acetonide, Aristoderm, Kenalog |

1,2 double bond, a 6α-methyl group, a 6α- or 9α-fluorine substituent, and a 16-hydroxy or 16-methyl group (*e.g.*, dexamethasone). Some of the clinically important corticoid drugs, which embody a combination of these molecular features, are listed as Table V. Some of these substances also are available as water-soluble 21-phosphate esters for intravenous injection.

Some chemically modified steroids inhibit the mineralocorticoid actions of aldosterone; thus spironolactone (trade name: Aldactone) is used to combat excessive salt and water retention in such disorders as congestive heart failure, nephrosis, cirrhosis, and some types of hypertension.

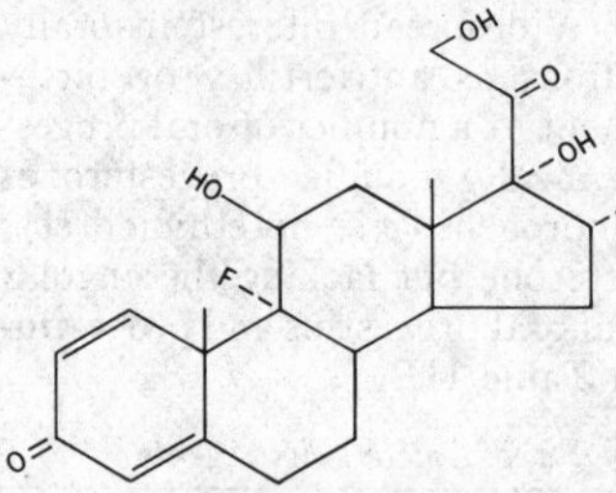

DEXAMETHASONE

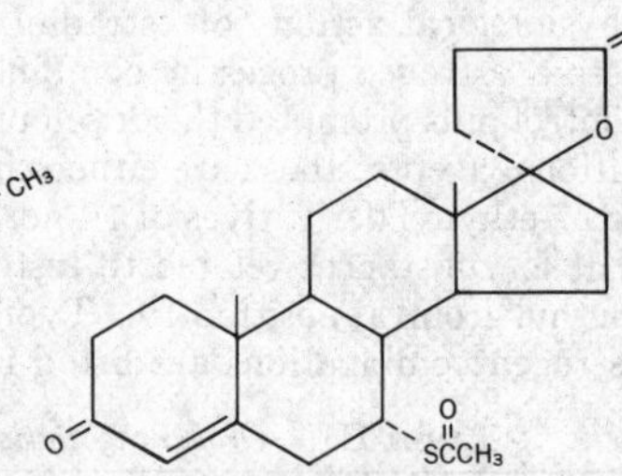

SPIRONOLACTONE

**Insect Hormones.**—In the 1960s it was found that ecdysone, the hormone that mediates insect metamorphosis of larva to pupa and pupa to moth, is a steroid. Isolated from the prothoracic glands of silkworm pupae, it is 2β,3β,14,22,25-pentahydroxy-5β-cholest-7-en-6-one. Probably other steroid hormones will be discovered to play a role in invertebrate organisms.

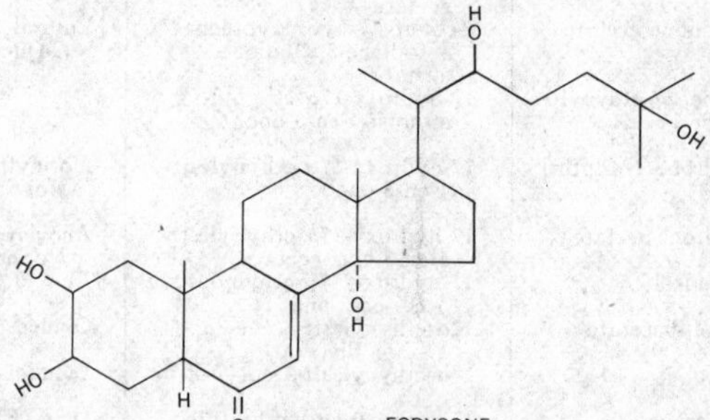

ECDYSONE

**Cardiotonic Agents.**—Two types of steroid found in nature exert a unique effect on the performance of the heart muscle in higher animals. These are the cardiac glycosides (illustrated by digitoxin) found in plants and consisting of a steroid genin or aglycone combined in glycosidic linkage through its 3-hydroxyl group with one or more molecules of a sugar; and the toad poisons (illustrated by bufotoxin) found in the skin and parotid gland secretions of toads and consisting of a steroid genin conjugated through its 14-hydroxyl group with suberylarginine, an amino acid derivative.

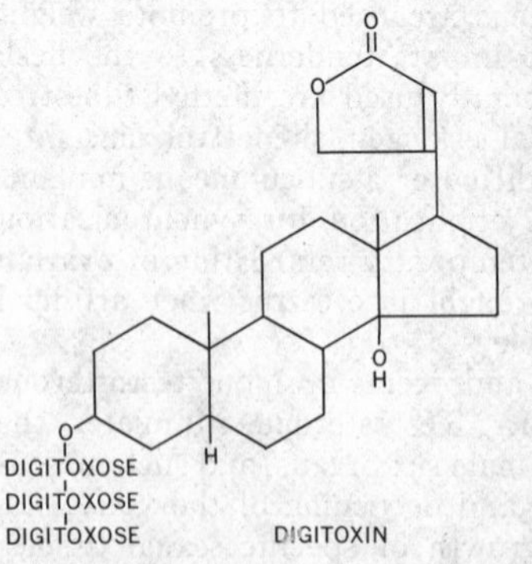

DIGITOXOSE–DIGITOXOSE–DIGITOXOSE

DIGITOXIN

The cardiac glycosides are found in the leaves, flowers, seeds, roots, and bark of a large variety of plants, including digitalis, *Strophanthus*, squill, oleander, and ouabaio. Extracts of such plants have long been recognized as toxic and have been employed as arrow poisons (inée), rodenticides (red squill), drugs for medieval ordeal trials, and folk remedies (foxglove). When administered in sublethal doses, the cardiac glycosides slow the heart rate and markedly increase the force and extent of contraction. They are of great benefit for treating conditions in which the heart lacks power (congestive heart failure, dropsy) or in which the rhythm has been disturbed (*e.g.*, auricular fibrillation). The toad poisons exert a similar effect, and dried and powdered toad skins have long been used medicinally in China and Japan. Practical

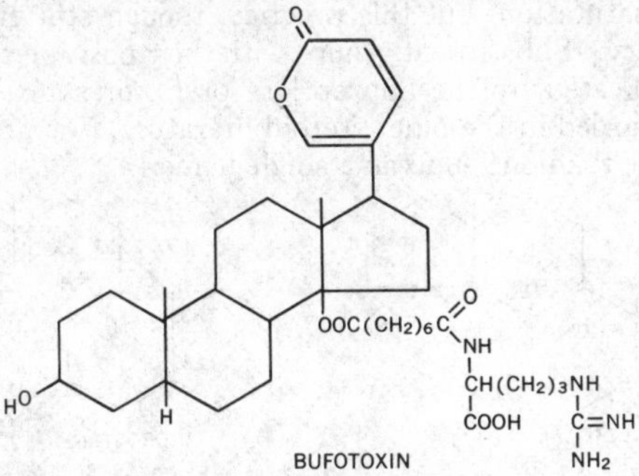


BUFOTOXIN

methods remain to be developed for the synthesis of cardiac aglycones and glycosides; material for clinical use is obtained by isolation from plant sources. Crystalline glycosides, as well as crude powders and extracts of digitalis leaves, find therapeutic use.

Hydrolysis of the cardiac glycosides by acid or by enzyme preparations removes the sugar groups and yields the steroid agly-

TABLE VI.—*Typical Cardiac Aglycones*

| Aglycone | Systematic name | From glycoside |
|---|---|---|
| Digitoxigenin . | 3β,14-dihydroxy-5β-card-20(22)enolide | digitoxin, digilanide-A |
| Periplogenin . | 3β,5,14-trihydroxy-5β-card-20(22)enolide | periplocin, periplocymarin |
| Sarmentogenin . | 3β,11α,14-trihydroxy-5β-card-20(22) enolide | sarmentocymarin |
| Digoxigenin . | 3β,12β,14-trihydroxy-5β-card-20(22) enolide | digoxin, digilanide-C |
| Gitoxigenin. . | 3β,14,16β-trihydroxy-5β-card-20(22) enolide | gitoxin, digilanide-B |
| Strophanthidin . | 3β,5,14-trihydroxy-19-oxo-5β-card-20(22)enolide | cymarin, k-strophanthoside |
| Ouabagenin . | 1β,3β,5,11α,14,19-hexahydroxy-5β-card-20(22)enolide | ouabain |
| Scillarenin . . | 3β,14-dihydroxybufa-4,20,22-trienolide | scillaren-A |
| Scilliglaucosidin. | 3β,14-dihydroxy-19-oxobufa-4,20,22-trienolide | scilliglaucoside |

cones. The simple aglycones are much less active physiologically than the complete glycosides. Some of the commonest aglycones are listed as Table VI. Characteristic features of this group of steroids are the unsaturated cyclic lactone side chain containing either four or five carbon atoms, 3β- and 14β-hydroxyl groups and the 14β ring junction that is unique among natural steroids.

**Sapogenins.**—The sapogenins are the steroid portions of glycosidic compounds (saponins) found in the leaves, seed, and roots of a number of plants (*Dioscorea,* yucca, agave, sarsaparilla, digitalis); they are called saponins because they form a soapy lather when mixed with water. Treatment of saponins with acid yields the sapogenins, characterized by a 3β-hydroxyl group and an eight-carbon side chain with two atoms of oxygen arranged in a bicyclic "spiroketal" structure (*e.g.,* diosgenin).

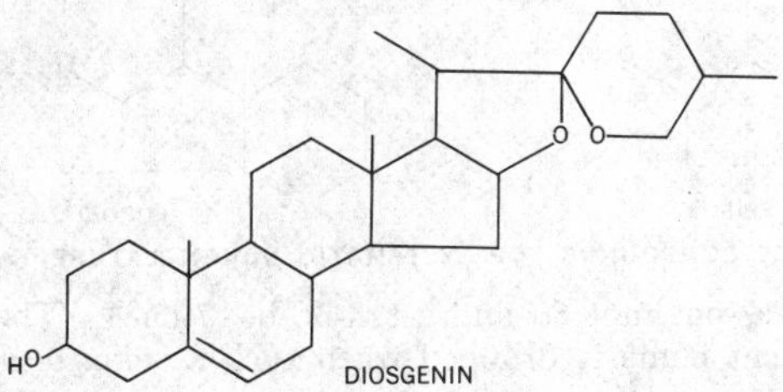


DIOSGENIN

On treatment with hot acetic anhydride, sapogenins are converted to the acetate esters of the so-called pseudo (ψ) sapogenins (*e.g.,* ψ-diosgenin), which can readily be cleaved at the 20,22 double bond to form 20-ketopregnane derivatives convertible to progesterone. Because of their abundance and ease of side-chain

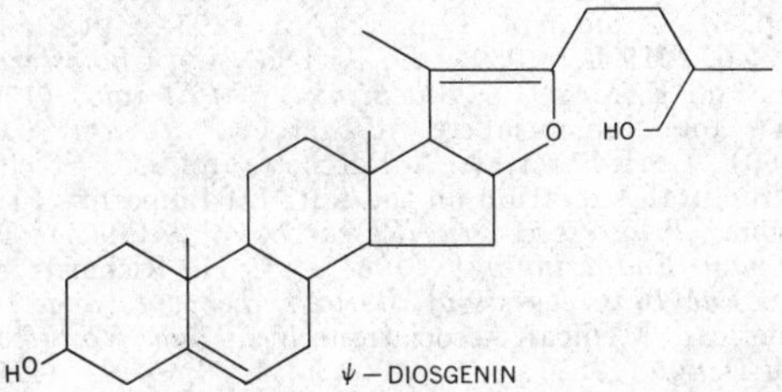


ψ – DIOSGENIN

TABLE VII.—*Typical Steroid Sapogenins*

| Trivial name | Systematic name |
|---|---|
| Diosgenin. . . . . . | 25α-spirost-5-en-3β-ol |
| Yamogenin . . . . . | 25β-spirost-5-en-3β-ol |
| Smilagenin . . . . . | 5β,25α-spirostan-3β-ol |
| Sarsasapogenin . . . . | 5β,25β-spirostan-3β-ol |
| Hecogenin . . . . . | 3β-hydroxy-5α,25α-spirostan-12-one |
| Botogenin . . . . . | 3β-hydroxy-25α-spirost-5-en-12-one |
| Gitogenin. . . . . . | 5α,25α-spirostane-2α,3β-diol |
| ψ-diosgenin . . . . . | furosta-5,20(22)-diene-3β,27-diol |
| ψ-sarsasapogenin . . . . | 5β-furost-20(22)ene-3β,27-diol |

degradation, the sapogenins are the chief raw materials for the manufacture of steroid hormones. Diosgenin, the most important substance in this regard, is obtained from the roots of a species of *Dioscorea* that abounds in southern Mexico. The structures of typical sapogenins are given as Table VII.

## STEROID NOMENCLATURE

**Numbering.**—The four rings of the steroid nucleus are desig-

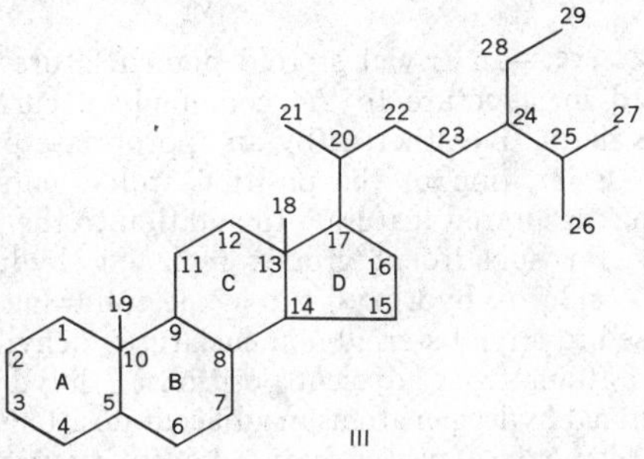

III

nated by letters and the individual carbon atoms by numbers (III). Naturally occurring steroids have an angular methyl group (18) attached at position 13, and most of them a similar methyl (19) at position 10; these are indicated in the formula by the short lines. Many steroids also have a side chain containing two, five, eight, nine, or ten carbon atoms attached to the nucleus at position 17 and numbered as shown.

*α* **and** *β* **Configuration.**—Since the four valence bonds of a carbon atom have a tetrahedral relationship, the single substituent (I) at each of the tertiary positions (ring junctions) of the steroid nucleus will project toward one side or the other of the approximate plane formed by the steroid ring system. At all other (secondary) positions, one of the two substituents will project toward one side of this plane and the other substituent toward the opposite side. When the steroid nucleus is represented in the conventional manner with the ring system lying in the plane of the paper, the configuration at $C_{13}$ in all the known natural steroids is such that the 18-methyl group projects upward. Substituents on the nucleus projecting in the same direction as the $C_{18}$ methyl group are said to have a β orientation and are denoted in the formula by attaching that group with a solid line (IV). Conversely, substituents projecting toward the opposite side of the molecule (downward) have an α orientation denoted by a broken or dotted line. Orientation at position 20 is defined according to the Fischer convention as β if the substituent projects toward the left, when the longest chain attached to this position is swung to the rear; and α if it projects toward the right. For the pregnanes, this is easily visualized in the usual representation (V) where a β-oriented substituent projects upward. For steroids with longer side chains, 20β configuration (Fischer convention) signifies that the $C_{21}$ methyl group projects toward the left when the $C_{22}$ chain projects toward the rear (VI); this means that the tertiary hydrogen atom at $C_{20}$ projects upward in the usual diagram (VII) as well as in the cyclic structures spirostan and furostan.

The Fischer convention is used in analogous fashion to denote configuration at other asymmetric positions in the side chain, such as $C_{24}$ in ergosterol and stigmasterol and $C_{25}$ in the sapogenins. There are two series of natural sapogenins differing in configuration at position 25; formerly these were called *a* or "iso" and *b* or "neo," but now that their stereochemistry has been established they can be designated as $\alpha$ (or $\alpha_f$ for Fischer) and $\beta$ (or $\beta_f$), respectively.

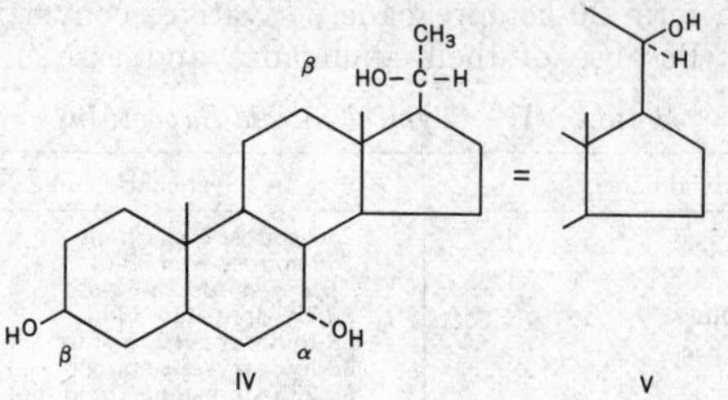

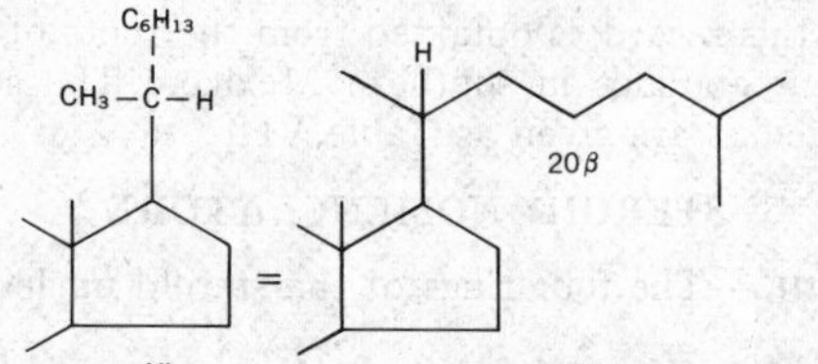

**Nomenclature.**—In trivial steroid nomenclature, compounds closely related in structure to the commonly occurring steroids are named as derivatives thereof by an appropriate prefix accompanied by a designation of the position and orientation of the added, missing, or altered feature. In addition to the usual chemical notations for substituent groups replacing hydrogen atoms (*e.g.*, methyl-, chloro-, hydroxy-, oxo-), the following prefixes are commonly used in trivial steroid nomenclature: dehydro- (lacking two hydrogen atoms from adjacent positions); dihydro- (possessing two additional hydrogen atoms in adjacent positions); anhydro- (lacking the elements of water from adjacent positions); deoxy- (hydroxyl group replaced by a hydrogen atom); epi- (differing in configuration at a secondary position); iso- (differing in configuration at a tertiary position); nor- (lacking one carbon atom); and homo- (possessing one additional carbon atom).

Systematic nomenclature, though often cumbersome, affords an unambiguous name for any steroid structure. Here compounds are designated as derivatives of reference hydrocarbons whose names imply the structure and stereochemistry of the complete carbon skeleton. Since certain classes of steroids possess characteristic oxygen-containing groupings in the side chain, it is convenient also to use certain reference structures that include such groups.

Except for cardanolide and bufanolide, which imply the 14$\beta$ configuration characteristic of the cardiotonic agents, these parent compounds have the "backbone" configuration common to most natural steroids: 8$\beta$, 9$\alpha$, 10$\beta$, 13$\beta$, and 14$\alpha$, as well as 17$\beta$ and 20$\beta$ in steroids with side chains. Thus configuration at any of these positions is not specified in the name or indicated in the formula unless it differs from that of the foregoing. Since compounds with both 5$\alpha$ or 5$\beta$ configurations are found in nature, the configuration at position 5 must be indicated, giving rise to two series of steroids for each parent hydrocarbon; 5$\alpha$-androstane, 5$\beta$-androstane, and so on. Until 1956 systematic nomenclature employed the names androstane and cholestane only for 5$\alpha$ compounds and used pregnane and cholane for 5$\beta$ compounds. 5$\beta$-Androstane was known as etiocholane or testane, 5$\beta$-cholestane as coprostane, 5$\alpha$-pregnane as allopregnane, and 5$\alpha$-cholane as allocholane. Names based on this former system are still encountered.

The presence of unsaturation is indicated by changing the syllable "ane" to "ene" for one double bond, "adiene" for two double bonds, and so on, and inserting before this syllable the number of the lowest numbered carbon atom attached to the double bond. If the other carbon atom is not the next higher numbered, its number is also given enclosed in parentheses. If there is no other numerical prefix to the parent name, it is common in the American but not the British literature to place the numbers locating the unsaturation before the name (*e.g.*, 4-androstene for androst-4-ene). Formerly, the symbol Δ was placed before the number to indicate unsaturation, but this practice, though still encountered, is unnecessary. Substituent groups with their position and orientation are indicated by the appropriate prefix or suffix. Although often disregarded in the older steroid literature, it is not proper to employ more than one suffix in a single name (*e.g.*, 3$\beta$-hydroxy-5$\alpha$-

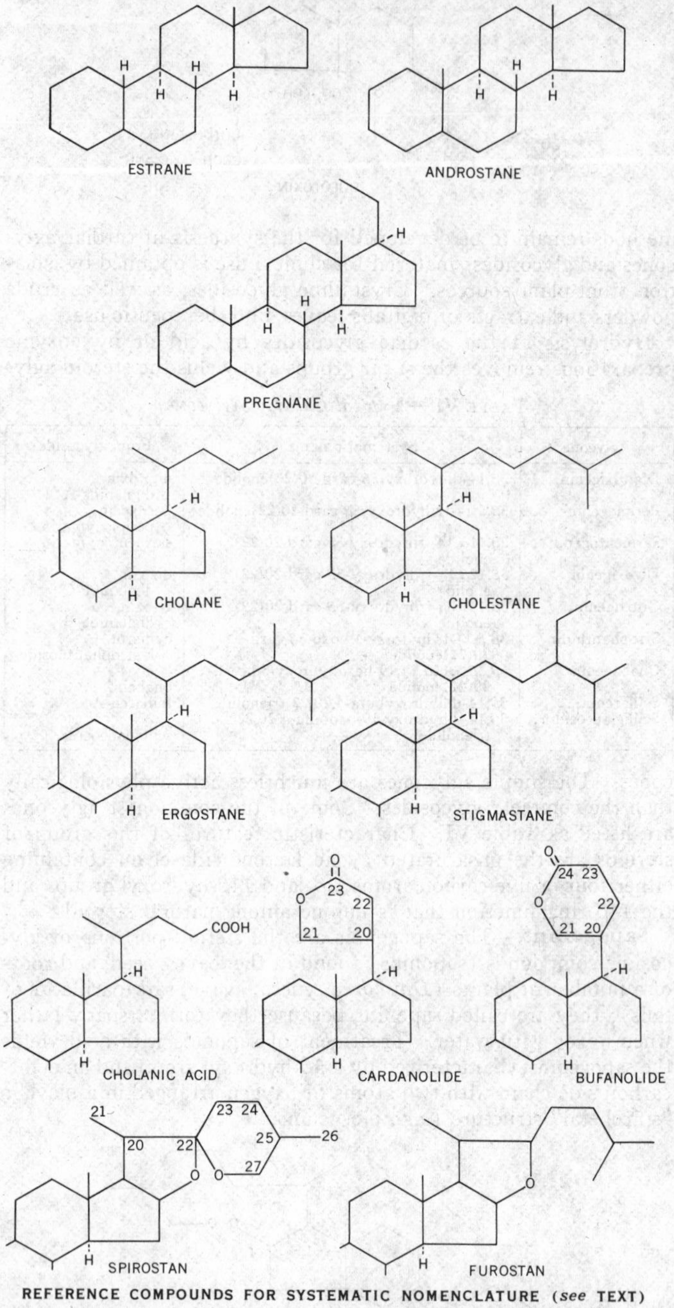

REFERENCE COMPOUNDS FOR SYSTEMATIC NOMENCLATURE (*see* TEXT)

androstan-17-one, not 5$\alpha$-androstan-3$\beta$-ol-17-one). The final "e" of the parent name is dropped when such a suffix begins with a vowel.

BIBLIOGRAPHY.—L. F. Fieser and M. Fieser, *Steroids* (1959); G. Pincus and K. V. Thimann (eds.), *The Hormones*, vol. i (1948), vol. ii (1950), vol. iii (1955); W. Klyne, *The Chemistry of the Steroids* (1957); C. W. Shoppee, *Chemistry of the Steroids*, 2nd ed. (1964); F. Radt (ed.), *Elsevier's Encyclopaedia of Organic Chemistry*, series 3, vol. 14, supp. 3, *Steroids*, pt. 1, p. 1347 ff. (1954), pt. 2, p. 1869 ff. (1956), pt. 3, p. 2215 ff. (1959); D. Kritchevsky, *Cholesterol* (1958); E. Heftmann and E. Mosettig, *Biochemistry of Steroids* (1960); "Definitive Rules for Nomenclature of Steroids," *J. Am. Chem. Soc.*, 82:5577 (1960); L. H. Sarett, A. A. Patchett, and S. L. Steelman, "The Effects of Structural Alteration on the Anti-Inflammatory Properties of Hydrocortisone," *Progress in Drug Research*, vol. 5 (1963); H. S. Kupperman, *Human Endocrinology* (1963); J. H. Richards and J. B. Hendrickson, *The Biosynthesis of Steroids, Terpenes and Acetogenins* (1964); American Medical Association, *New and Nonofficial Drugs* (1964), *New Drugs* (1965). (E. V. JE.)

**STESICHORUS** (*c.* 640–*c.* 555 B.C.), Greek lyric poet, born at Mataurus in southern Italy, but active mainly at Himera in Sicily. His works, which are said to have extended to 26 books (about 15,000 lines), were mainly narrative lyric poems dealing with stories from mythology. Plato records that his severe treatment of Helen of Troy's conduct in one of them led to an attack of blindness, which was cured only after he had composed his *Palinodia,* or recantation (*Phaedrus,* 243 a–b). Stesichorus is credited also with originating bucolic poetry (*Daphnis*), and other forerunners of the romantic poetry of Hellenistic times are ascribed to him (*Calyce, Rhadine*). He wrote in the Doric dialect, and his poems were serious enough for Horace (*Odes,* iv.9.8) to speak of his *graves Camenae,* and for Quintilian (x.1.62) to describe him as "upholding on his lyre the burdens of epic poetry"; but information about his work is mostly secondhand, for hardly 100 lines of his writings survive. It is not even certain if he used the triadic stanza (consisting of strophe, antistrophe, and epode) which some authorities credit him with inventing.

For fragments *see Poetae melici Graeci,* ed. by D. L. Page, pp. 93–141 (1962). *See* also C. M. Bowra, *Greek Lyric Poetry,* 2nd ed., ch. 3 (1961). (JN. A. D.)

**STETHOSCOPE,** a medical instrument used in listening to sounds produced within the body, chiefly in the heart or lungs (*see* DIAGNOSIS: *Auscultation*). It was invented in 1816 and described in 1819 by R. T. H. Laënnec (*q.v.*), who used a perforated wooden cylinder to transmit sounds from the patient's chest (Greek *stethos*) to the physician's ear. This monaural stethoscope was modified to more convenient forms but has been largely supplanted by the binaural type of two flexible rubber tubes attaching the chest-piece to spring-connected metal tubes with earpieces. In listening to heart sounds, in particular, it is necessary to use both a bell-shaped, open-ended chest-piece, which transmits low-pitched sounds well, and the flat chest-piece covered with a semirigid disk (diaphragm type), which detects sounds of higher frequency. Instruments having both types of chest-piece, arranged so that they can be rapidly interchanged by turning a valve, are widely used, especially in the United States. (H. B. SP.)

**STETTIN:** *see* SZCZECIN.

**STETTINIUS, EDWARD REILLY, JR.** (1900–1949), U.S. industrialist and statesman generally credited as one of the leading figures in the formation of the United Nations, was born on Oct. 22, 1900, at Chicago, Ill. Stettinius attended the University of Virginia, Charlottesville, but did not take a degree. In 1924 he was employed by a subsidiary of General Motors Corporation and by 1931 had risen to an executive position in the corporation. He joined the United States Steel Corporation and in 1938, at the age of 37, became chairman of the board of directors of that firm. He was named chairman of Pres. Franklin D. Roosevelt's War Resources Board (1939), Lend-Lease administrator (1941–43), and undersecretary of state (1943). Stettinius served as U.S. secretary of state in 1944 but he resigned the following year to become the first U.S. delegate to the General Assembly of the United Nations. Earlier, he had been one of President Roosevelt's chief advisers at the Yalta Conference, and he played a principal role in the Dumbarton Oaks meetings that laid the groundwork for the United Nations. He died at Greenwich, Conn., Oct. 31, 1949. (H. J. SG.)

**STEUBEN, FREDERICK WILLIAM AUGUSTUS,** BARON VON (1730–1794), German soldier who helped train American troops during the Revolution, was born at Magdeburg, Prussia, Sept. 17, 1730, the son of an officer in the Royal Prussian Engineers. From about the age of 16 Steuben led a soldier's life and during the Seven Years' War (1756–63) rose to the rank of captain in the Prussian Army and for a time was attached to the general staff. After the close of the war he was retired from the army and became court chamberlain for the prince of Hohenzollern-Hechingen, was made a knight of the Order of Fidelity in the neighbouring margravate of Baden-Durlach in 1769, and at some unknown date apparently was created a baron ("Freiherr"). In 1777 rumors were afloat that he had been obliged to leave Hohenzollern-Hechingen for extremely unsavoury conduct, which may account for the failure of his attempts to secure a post with the British East India Company, or in the service of France, Austria, or Baden. Finally, he obtained a letter from Benjamin Franklin and Silas Deane, agents of the United States in France, introducing him to Gen. George Washington as a "Lieut. Genl. in the King of Prussia's Service," fired with "Zeal for our Cause." Armed with this letter, he arrived in America in December 1777.

THE BETTMANN ARCHIVE

STEUBEN: PORTRAIT BY RALPH EARL

Impressed by his fictitiously high rank, his pleasing personality, and Washington's favourable comments, Congress, in May 1778, appointed Steuben inspector general of the army with the rank of major general. He trained the soldiers admirably, adapting Prussian military ideas to the needs of his pupils; but he made such a nuisance of himself by threatening to resign unless he was given command of a division of troops that by July 1778 Washington wished he had never appeared. When Washington called his bluff by refusing to yield, Steuben stayed on and continued to render valuable service throughout the war, including the drafting of *Regulations for the Order and Discipline of the Troops of the United States* (1779), which served as the official manual until 1812. In 1780 his wish for command was granted; he served as a division commander in Virginia and participated in the siege of Yorktown.

After the war Steuben lived for some years so extravagantly in and near New York City that, despite large grants of money from Congress and the grant of 16,000 ac. of land by the state of New York, he fell into debt. Finally, after ceaseless importunity and gross misstatements as to revenues in Germany lost to him in coming to America, Congress voted him in 1790 a life pension of $2,500 per year, which sufficed to maintain him on a farm he had cleared on his New York land grant, near present Remsen, N.Y. There, a bachelor to the end, he died Nov. 28, 1794.

*See* John McAuley Palmer, *General von Steuben* (1937), inadequate but valuable; Douglas S. Freeman, *George Washington,* vol. 5 (1952). (B. KN.)

**STEUBENVILLE,** a city of eastern Ohio, U.S., and the seat of Jefferson County, is on the Ohio River, 26 mi. N of Wheeling, W.Va. It is one of the state's oldest cities. The site was settled temporarily as early as 1765 by Jacob Walker and was occupied again with the building in 1786 of Ft. Steuben, named for Baron von Steuben, soldier and patriot of the American Revolution. The fort was abandoned with the outbreak of the Indian Wars in 1790. In 1797 a permanent settlement was laid out by two Pennsylvania land speculators, Bezaleel Wells and James Ross, who named it Steubenville. It was incorporated in 1805.

Adjacent to one of the nation's principal waterways in an area rich in coal and clay, the city early became an important manufacturing and commercial centre. The textile industry was its most important in the period after the War of 1812. Steubenville's economy centres upon the production of steel, chemicals, dinnerware, brick and tile, heaters, stoves, electrical equipment, paperboard, and ferroalloy metals. In the 1960 census Steubenville, with a population of 32,495, was named a central city of the Steubenville-Weirton standard metropolitan statistical area, comprising Jefferson County in Ohio and Brooke and Hancock counties in West Virginia, with a population of 167,756. For comparative population figures *see* table in OHIO: *Population.* *See* also WEIRTON. (P. R. S.)

**STEVENAGE,** a market town, urban district, and New Town of Hertfordshire, Eng., lies on the Great North Road 32 mi. (51 km.) N of Charing Cross, London, by road. Pop. (1961) 42,968.

The six hills along the Great North Road at the edge of the town are Romano-British burial mounds. The manor belonged to the abbot of Westminster at the time of the Domesday survey, and in 1281 the abbot obtained for the town a grant of a weekly market (now held twice weekly) and an annual fair, held in September. Stevenage was the first of the New Towns (*q.v.*) under the New Towns Act, 1946, and its population was scheduled at 80,000. In the New Town are an all-pedestrian-way shopping centre and interesting buildings such as St. George's Church, the girls' grammar school, and the County College. The old town contains St. Nicholas' parish church dating from the 12th century, old coaching inns, and a 16th-century grammar school. The predominant industry is electronics, but a variety of others includes engineering and a clearing bank.

*See* R. Trow-Smith, *The History of Stevenage* (1958).

**STEVENS,** the name of two U.S. inventors, father and son, who were prominent in developing marine and rail transportation in the 18th and 19th centuries.

JOHN STEVENS (1749–1838) was famous for his work in promoting the use of steam power in transportation. Born in New York City in 1749, he graduated from King's College (now Columbia University) in 1768, subsequently studied law, and was admitted to the New York bar in 1771. In 1776 he became a captain in the Revolutionary Army, and later colonel of his own regiment.

After the war, the problem of safe and speedy transportation across the Hudson River drew his interest to the possibilities of steam navigation. He developed designs for boilers and engines that were unique for the time, and in order to protect his inventions he petitioned Congress for a patent law, which he outlined and which was passed as the Patent Law of 1790, the foundation of the present U.S. patent system. In 1803 he received a patent for a multitubular boiler for use in his marine engines. He was the first to apply the principle of steam to screw propulsion for navigation, building in 1804 a steamboat with two underwater screw propellers that successfully crossed the Hudson. He then designed an engine for a paddle-wheeled, low-pressure steamboat, but before the project was completed, Robert Fulton in 1807 successfully launched his steamboat, the "Clermont." Though discouraged, Stevens launched the "Phoenix" several months later, and, since Fulton had received a monopoly grant of navigation rights on the Hudson, Stevens sent the "Phoenix" by sea to Philadelphia, Pa., the first voyage of a steamship on ocean waters. In 1811 he inaugurated the world's first steam-ferry service.

In an effort to apply the principle of steam engines to rail transportation and in order to enlist public support, Stevens published in 1812 an ingenious pamphlet entitled *Documents Tending to Prove the Superior Advantages of Rail-ways and Steam-carriages over Canal Navigation,* which outlined many phases of railway transportation, engineering features, and even construction costs. To prove the feasibility of the steam locomotive, at the age of 76 he designed and built the first American steam locomotive (1825), which ran on a circular track on his estate but was never used for actual service. In 1815 Stevens obtained from the New Jersey legislature the first charter for a railway ever granted in America, but it was not until 1830 that he formed the Camden and Amboy Railroad and Transportation Company, operated by his sons Edwin A. and Robert L. He died in Hoboken, N.J., March 6, 1838. (X.)

ROBERT LIVINGSTON STEVENS (1787–1856), noted as a mechanical engineer and ship designer, was born in Hoboken, N.J., on Oct. 18, 1787, the son of John. He designed the false bow for the "New Philadelphia," which so increased the speed of the steamboat that it was able to leave Albany, N.Y., in the morning and reach New York City before nightfall. In 1822 he built the ferryboat "Hoboken" on modern lines, and introduced the piled slip for ferry docks.

In 1830 Stevens designed the "T" railroad rail, now universally used. The famous "John Bull" locomotive, now in the Smithsonian Institution, was built to his specifications. He added the pilot and bogie trucks to locomotives and increased the number of driver wheels to eight in order to obtain better traction. He discovered that rails laid on log ties with crushed stone or gravel between them provided a more serviceable and comfortable roadbed than any previously used. He also invented the rail spike.

In 1844 Stevens, an ardent yachtsman, designed the "Maria," for 20 years the fastest yacht afloat. He died at Hoboken, N.J., April 20, 1856. (S. C. HR.)

**STEVENS, ALFRED GEORGE** (1817–1875), English designer, painter, and sculptor, notable for the Michelangelesque vigour of his work, was born on Dec. 30, 1817, at Blandford, Dorset. He traveled in Italy, 1833–42, spending a year under Bertel Thorvaldsen (*q.v.*) in Rome. In 1845–47 he taught at the new School of Design, Somerset House, London, and in 1850–52 designed cast-metal hearth furniture, stoves, etc., for Hoole and Company, Sheffield, some of which attracted attention at the 1851 Great Exhibition. In the 1857 competition for the Wellington monument in St. Paul's Cathedral, London, he was placed sixth, though his design was the only one adapted to the nave arch under which the monument was to stand.

In 1862, however, Stevens was given the commission and, despite vicissitudes, the complex marble structure with its allegories and bronze equestrian statue was nearly complete at his death (in Hampstead, London, May 1, 1875). For Dorchester House, London, Stevens carried out decorations in 1858–62 (caryatid mantelpiece and many drawings for Dorchester House and other projects now in the Tate Gallery, London), and these best display the freshness he brought to his forms. Stevens also painted portraits (*e.g.,* "Mrs. Leonard Collman," 1854, National Gallery, London), but is probably best remembered for his red chalk figure drawings.

BIBLIOGRAPHY.—Sir Walter Armstrong, *Alfred Stevens* (1881); H. Stannus, *Alfred Stevens* (1891); K. R. Towndrow, *Alfred Stevens, Architectural Sculptor, Painter and Designer* (1939) and (comp.) *The Works of Alfred Stevens at the Tate Gallery* (1952). (D. C. T. T.)

**STEVENS, THADDEUS** (1792–1868), U.S. political leader, was one of the most influential Radical Republicans after the Civil War. He was born in Danville, Vt., on April 4, 1792. After graduating from Dartmouth College in 1814, he moved to Pennsylvania, where he taught school and studied law until he was admitted to the bar (in Maryland). He practised as a lawyer in Gettysburg, Pa., from 1816 to 1842 and in Lancaster, Pa., from 1842 until his death. Meanwhile, he invested heavily in real estate and in the charcoal-iron business. An Anti-Masonic member of the Pennsylvania legislature between 1833 and 1842, he made himself conspicuous as a friend of banks, internal improvements, and public schools, and as a foe of Freemasons, Jacksonians, and slaveholders. A Whig congressman in the U.S. House of Representatives from 1849 to 1853, he advocated tariff increases and opposed the compromise measures of 1850, especially the fugitive-slave law. He joined the new Republican Party and from 1859 to 1868 again served in the House of Representatives, where he became, as James G. Blaine afterward said, "the natural leader, who assumed his place by common consent." He exerted this leadership by means of his sarcastic eloquence, his parliamentary skills, and his privileges as chairman of the Ways and Means Committee and later of the Appropriations Committee.

During the Civil War Stevens sponsored legislation for the issue of inconvertible paper money (greenbacks) and for other revenue measures. During the immediate postwar period he was one of the most extreme of the so-called Radical Republicans. He argued that the seceded states, having been defeated in war, were in the condition of "conquered provinces," to which the restraints of the constitution did not apply. When Congress met in December 1865 Stevens took the lead in excluding the senators and representatives from the South. As a member of the joint Committee on Reconstruction, he had an important part in the preparation of the 14th Amendment and the reconstruction acts of 1867. He introduced the resolution for the impeachment of Pres. Andrew Johnson and served as chairman of the committee appointed to draft impeachment articles. Throughout this period Stevens urged that southern plantations be taken from their owners and that part of the land be divided among the freedmen, the rest of it to be sold and the proceeds to be used toward paying off the national war debt; however, he failed to gain Congressional support for this

confiscation plan. He died at Washington, D.C., on Aug. 11, 1868, and was buried in a Lancaster cemetery amid the graves of Negroes. On his tombstone were carved the words he had composed, saying he had chosen this resting place so that he might "illustrate in death" the principle he had "advocated through a long life," namely, "Equality of man before his Creator."

*See* Richard N. Current, *Old Thad Stevens* (1942); Fawn M. Brodie, *Thaddeus Stevens* (1959). (R. N. Ct.)

**STEVENS, WALLACE** (1879–1955), U.S. poet whose work is characterized by subtle intellectuality and originality beneath a dandified and elegant manner, was born on Oct. 2, 1879, in Reading, Pa. He attended Harvard for three years, worked briefly for the *New York Herald Tribune,* then won a degree (1904) at the New York Law School. After practising law in New York City, he joined an insurance firm in Hartford, Conn., in 1916. In 1934 he became a vice-president.

In 1914 Harriet Monroe published several of his poems in *Poetry.* Thereafter he was a frequent contributor to the "little magazines." *Harmonium* (1923), his first book, sold poorly but received some favourable critical notices; it was reissued in 1931 and in 1947. Stevens thereafter published several volumes, including his *Collected Poems* (1954). A volume of critical essays, *The Necessary Angel* (1951), was devoted to the chief concern of his poetry—the relationship between "imagination" and "reality."

Late in life Stevens won major literary awards—the Bollingen Award (1949), the National Book Award (1950), and the Pulitzer Prize (1955).

Wallace Stevens died in Hartford, Conn., on Aug. 2, 1955. (W. V. O'C.)

**STEVENSON, ADLAI EWING** (1835–1914), vice-president of the United States (1893–97), was born in Christian County, Ky., on Oct. 23, 1835. At an early age he moved with his parents to Bloomington, Ill., where he attended Illinois Wesleyan University. He also studied at Centre College, Danville, Ky., where he met and married Letitia Green, daughter of the president of the college.

Stevenson prepared for the legal profession, was admitted to the bar, and began his practice in Metamora, Ill. His interest in politics was stimulated by the Lincoln-Douglas debates in 1858, and he soon became actively engaged in politics on both the local and national levels.

He was appointed to his first public office as a master in chancery in 1860, and in 1865 was elected state's attorney. He was a member of the 44th and 46th congresses; and in 1876–77 took a conspicuous part in the congressional debate protesting the manner of settlement of the contested Tilden-Hayes presidential electoral dispute. During Grover Cleveland's first administration (1885–89) he served as first assistant postmaster general.

CULVER PICTURES, INC

ADLAI E. STEVENSON

Stevenson was elected vice-president of the U.S. in 1892 on the Democratic ticket with Grover Cleveland. At the end of his term, in 1897, President McKinley appointed him chairman of a commission sent to Europe to work for international bimetallism. He was again nominated for vice-president on the ticket with William Jennings Bryan in 1900; and in 1908 he was unsuccessful as the Democratic candidate for governor of Illinois. He died in Chicago on June 14, 1914.

*See* his reminiscences, *Something of Men I Have Known* (1909). (A. E. St.)

**STEVENSON, ADLAI EWING** (1900–1965), U.S. lawyer, Democratic presidential candidate in 1952 and 1956, and U.S. representative at the United Nations (1961–65), was born in Los Angeles, Calif., on Feb. 5, 1900. He was the son of Lewis Green Stevenson, then an executive of Hearst newspapers in California, and the grandson of Adlai Ewing Stevenson (*q.v.*), vice-president of the U.S. during Grover Cleveland's second term (1893–97).

INGE MORATH—MAGNUM

ADLAI STEVENSON, PHOTOGRAPHED AT THE UNITED NATIONS IN 1962

After the family returned to its home in Bloomington, Ill., in 1906, Stevenson attended local public schools, and for college preparatory study was sent to the Choate School in Wallingford, Conn. During World War I he served for about a year as an apprentice seaman in the U.S. Naval Reserve. He then entered Princeton, where he graduated in 1922. After studying at Harvard Law School for the next two years, he returned to Illinois to become assistant managing editor of the *Bloomington Daily Pantagraph,* a newspaper that had been owned by his family for several generations. Meanwhile, he commuted to Chicago to continue his study of law at Northwestern University Law School, graduating in 1926.

In the same year Stevenson was admitted to the Illinois bar and began the practice of law in Chicago, but his legal work was frequently interrupted by periods of public service. During the years before World War II he served two terms as president of the Chicago Council on Foreign Relations, was chairman of the Civil Rights Committee of the Chicago Bar Association, and chairman of the Chicago chapter of the Committee to Defend America by Aiding the Allies. From July 1941 to April 1944 he was special assistant to the secretary of the navy and traveled extensively throughout the world on official business. Meanwhile, in 1943, Stevenson headed a Foreign Economic Administration mission to Italy to develop a U.S. program for relief and reconstruction after the invasion of Italy by the Allied armies. He became an assistant to the secretary of state in 1945 and was adviser to the U.S. delegation at the United Nations Conference on International Organization at San Francisco, Calif. He was named senior adviser to the U.S. delegation at the first meeting of the UN General Assembly in London in 1946, and was a U.S. delegate at the General Assembly meetings in New York, 1946–47.

In 1948 Stevenson was elected governor of Illinois by the largest majority any candidate had ever received in the state's history. His regime as governor was distinguished by far-reaching reforms, both legal and administrative; it included establishment of a merit system for state police, improved care and treatment of patients in state mental hospitals, greater state aid for public schools, and a revitalized civil service.

At the Democratic national convention held in Chicago in 1952, Stevenson, in spite of his refusal to seek the nomination, was chosen as the party's candidate for president. He waged a vigorous campaign and his speeches were widely applauded for their thoughtful eloquence and wit, but in the November election he was defeated by the Republican nominee, Dwight D. Eisenhower. In 1956 he was again his party's nominee for president and was again defeated in the election.

After this second defeat Stevenson returned to the practice of law and also traveled extensively throughout Africa and Europe, partly on business. In 1960, in company with William Benton with whom he was associated as a member of the Board of Directors of Encyclopædia Britannica, Inc., he traveled throughout Central and South America.

There was some support in the Democratic Party for nominating Stevenson for president in 1960 but the national convention held that year nominated Sen. John F. Kennedy of Massachusetts, and Stevenson supported him during the campaign. Shortly after his election, President-elect Kennedy announced that he would appoint Stevenson to be U.S. representative to the United Nations, with

cabinet rank and the title of ambassador. He served in that position until his sudden death in London on July 14, 1965.

Among Stevenson's published works were *Major Campaign Speeches of Adlai E. Stevenson, 1952* (1953), *Call to Greatness* (1954), *What I Think* (1956), *The New America* (1957), *Friends and Enemies* (1959), *Putting First Things First* (1960), and *Looking Outward: Years of Crisis at the United Nations* (1963).

ADLAI EWING STEVENSON III (1930– ), eldest of the three sons of Adlai Ewing II and Ellen Borden Stevenson, was born at Chicago, Ill., on Oct. 10, 1930. Like his father, he was active in politics, and in 1964 led the Democratic ticket for the Illinois legislature and in 1966 was elected state treasurer. In the 1970 election for the U.S. Senate, he won by a large majority.

(W. McC. B.; X.)

**STEVENSON, ROBERT LOUIS BALFOUR** (1850–1894), Scottish novelist, essayist and poet, was born at Edinburgh on Nov. 13, 1850, only son of Thomas Stevenson, prosperous civil engineer, and his wife Margaret Isabella Balfour. His poor health made regular schooling difficult, but he did attend Edinburgh academy and other schools before entering Edinburgh university at the age of 16. There he was expected to prepare himself for the family profession of lighthouse engineering. But Stevenson had no desire to be an engineer, and he eventually agreed with his father, as a compromise, to prepare instead for the Scottish bar.

He had early shown a desire to write, and once in his teens he set himself deliberately to learn the writer's craft by imitating a great variety of models in prose and verse. His youthful enthusiasm for the Covenanters led to his writing *The Pentland Rising,* his first printed work. During his years at the university he rebelled violently against his parents' religion and set himself up as a liberal Bohemian who abhorred the cruelties and hypocrisies of bourgeois respectability.

BROWN BROTHERS

ROBERT L. STEVENSON

In 1873, in the midst of painful differences with his father, he visited a married cousin at Cockfield, Suffolk, where he met Sidney Colvin, who became a lifelong friend, and Mrs. Fanny Sitwell (the future Lady Colvin). Mrs. Sitwell, an older woman of charm and talent, drew the young man out and won his confidence. Soon Stevenson was deeply in love, and on his return to Edinburgh wrote her a series of letters in which he played the part first of lover, then of worshiper, then of son. One of the several names by which Stevenson addressed her in these letters was "Claire," a fact which many years after his death was to give rise to the erroneous notion that Stevenson had had an affair with a humbly born Edinburgh girl of that name. The passion modulated eventually into a lasting friendship.

Later in 1873 Stevenson suffered severe respiratory illness and was sent to the French Riviera, where Colvin later joined him. He returned home the following spring. In July 1875 he was called to the Scottish bar, but he never practised. Stevenson was frequently abroad, most often in France. Two of these journeys produced *An Inland Voyage* (1878) and *Travels With a Donkey in the Cevennes* (1879). His career as a writer developed slowly. His essay "Roads" appeared in the *Portfolio* in 1873, and in 1874 "Ordered South" appeared in *Macmillan's*, a review of Lord Lytton's *Fables in Song* appeared in the *Fortnightly*, and his first contribution (on Victor Hugo) appeared in the *Cornhill,* then edited by Leslie Stephen. It was these early essays that first drew attention to Stevenson as a writer.

Stephen brought Stevenson into contact with Edmund Gosse, who became a good friend, and later, when in Edinburgh, Stephen introduced him to W. E. Henley. Henley and Stevenson became warm friends, and remained so until 1888, when a letter from Henley to Stevenson containing a deliberately implied accusation of dishonesty against the latter's wife precipitated a quarrel which Henley, jealous and embittered, perpetuated after his friend's death by a venomous review of Graham Balfour's biography.

While staying at Fontainebleau in 1876 Stevenson met Fanny Vandegrift Osbourne, an American lady separated from her husband, and the two fell in love. Stevenson's parents' horror at their son's involvement with a married woman subsided somewhat when Mrs. Osbourne returned to California in 1878, but it revived with greater force when Stevenson decided to join her in Aug. 1879. Stevenson arrived in California ill and penniless (the record of his arduous journey appeared later in *The Amateur Emigrant,* 1895, and *Across the Plains,* 1892). His adventures, which included coming very near death and eking out a precarious living in Monterey and San Francisco, culminated in marriage to Fanny Vandegrift (divorced from her first husband) early in 1880. About the same time a telegram from his relenting father offered much-needed financial support, and after a honeymoon by an abandoned silver mine (recorded in *The Silverado Squatters,* 1883) the couple sailed for Scotland to achieve reconciliation with the Thomas Stevensons.

Soon after his return Stevenson went, on medical advice (he had tuberculosis), to Davos in Switzerland, accompanied by his wife and his stepson, Lloyd Osbourne. They left there in April 1881 and spent the summer in Pitlochry and then in Braemar. There, in spite of bouts of illness, Stevenson embarked on *Treasure Island* (begun as a game with Lloyd), which started as a serial in *Young Folks*, under the title *The Sea-Cook,* in Oct. 1881. Stevenson finished the story in Davos, to which he returned in the autumn, and then started on *Prince Otto* (1885), a more complex but a less successful work. *Treasure Island* is an adventure presented with consummate skill, with atmosphere, character and action superbly geared to each other. The book is both a "rattling good yarn" for boys and a wry comment on the ambiguity of human motives.

In 1881 Stevenson published *Virginibus Puerisque,* his first collection of essays, most of which had appeared in the *Cornhill.* The winter of 1881 he spent at a chalet in Davos. In April 1882 he left Davos, but a stay in the Scottish Highlands, while it resulted in two of his finest short stories, "Thrawn Janet" and "The Merry Men," produced lung hemorrhages and in September he went to the south of France. There the Stevensons finally settled at a house in Hyères where, in spite of intermittent illness, Stevenson was happy and worked well. He revised *Prince Otto,* worked on *A Child's Garden of Verses* (first called *Penny Whistles*), and began *The Black Arrow,* a piece of "tushery" for *Young Folks.* In May 1885 he was again critically ill. On his recovery he went to England and eventually settled in Bournemouth. The Stevensons lived at Bournemouth from Jan. 1886 until July 1887, during which period his frequent bouts of dangerous illness proved conclusively that the British climate, even in the south of England, was not for him. The Bournemouth years were fruitful, however. There he got to know and love Henry James. There he revised *A Child's Garden* (first published in 1885) and wrote "Markheim," *Kidnapped* (1886) and *The Strange Case of Dr. Jekyll and Mr. Hyde* (1886). The poems in *A Child's Garden* represent with extraordinary fidelity an adult's recapturing of the emotions and sensations of childhood: there is nothing quite like them in English literature. In *Kidnapped,* the fruit of his researches into 18th-century Scottish history and of his feeling for Scottish landscape, history, character and local atmosphere mutually illuminate one another. But it was *Dr. Jekyll*—both moral allegory and thriller—that established his reputation with the ordinary reader.

In Aug. 1887 Stevenson set out for America with his wife, mother and stepson. In New York, he found himself famous, with editors and publishers offering lucrative contracts. He stayed for awhile in the Adirondacks, where he wrote essays for *Scribner's* and began *The Master of Ballantrae* (1889). This novel, another exploration of moral ambiguities, contains some of his most impressive writing, but it falls away in the contrived conclusion.

In June 1888 Stevenson, with his wife, his mother and his stepson, sailed from San Francisco in the schooner yacht "Casco," which he had chartered, on what was intended to be an excursion for health and pleasure; but in fact he was to spend the rest of his

life in the South Seas. They went first to the Marquesas, then to Fakarava atoll, then to Tahiti, then to Honolulu where they paid off the "Casco" and stayed nearly six months, leaving in June 1889 on the trading schooner "Equator" for the Gilberts and then to Samoa, where he spent six weeks.

During his months of wandering around the South Sea islands Stevenson made intensive efforts to understand the local scene and the inhabitants. As a result, his writings on the South Seas (*In the South Seas,* 1896; *A Footnote to History,* 1892) are admirably pungent and perceptive. He was writing first-rate journalism, deepened by the awareness of landscape and atmosphere such as that so notably rendered in his description of the first landfall at Nuku Hiva, in the Marquesas. Once, in his violent *Father Damien* (1890), passionately defending the memory of the priest who had given his life in the service of the lepers and as passionately attacking the Rev. Dr. Hyde, his detractor, Stevenson wrote in a wholly personal tone about South Seas affairs.

In Oct. 1890 he returned to Samoa from a voyage to Sydney, and established himself at Vailima, his house in Samoa, with patriarchal status, with his wife, mother, stepson and stepdaughter. The climate suited him; he led an industrious and active life; and when he died suddenly on Dec. 3, 1894, it was of a cerebral hemorrhage, not of the long-feared tuberculosis. His work during these years was moving toward a new maturity. While *Catriona* (U.S. title, *David Balfour;* 1893) marks no advance in technique or imaginative scope on *Kidnapped,* to which it is a sequel, *The Ebb-Tide* (1894), a grim and powerful tale written in a style of studied neutrality (it was a complete reworking of a first draft by Lloyd Osbourne) shows that Stevenson had reached an important transition in his literary career. The next phase was demonstrated triumphantly in *Weir of Hermiston* (1896), the unfinished masterpiece on which he was working on the day of his death. *The Beach of Falesa* (first published 1892; included in *Island Night's Entertainments,* 1893), a story with a finely wrought tragic texture, as well as the first part of *The Master of Ballantrae,* pointed in this direction, but neither approaches *Weir.* Drawing on the scenery of the Lowland hills and of Edinburgh for setting, using the character of Lord Braxfield as a central figure to set off the sensitive hero, his son; bringing in those plangent overtones of tragic destiny to be found in the Scottish border ballads—Stevenson achieved in this work a remarkable richness of tragic texture in a style stripped of all superfluous fat. The dialogue contains some of the best Scots prose in modern Scottish literature. Fragment though it is, *Weir of Hermiston* stands as a great work and Stevenson's masterpiece.

Stevenson was an indefatigable letter writer and his letters (edited by Sidney Colvin in 1899) provide a lively and enchanting picture of the man and his life. But Colvin omitted many of the most interesting letters, and compressed and dovetailed others, with the result that many important facts about Stevenson's emotional life remained unknown until the true text of all the letters was available. Colvin presented Stevenson's letters to Mrs. Sitwell to the Advocates' library (now the National Library of Scotland) with the proviso that they were not to be used until 1949; the revealing and often fascinating letters to Charles Baxter, given by Baxter to the Savile club, were much later acquired by Edwin Beinecke who deposited them (along with much other Stevenson material) in the Yale university library. Stevenson's biography suffered from his early canonizing; later writers built up a counter-picture, which eventually emerged as that of an immoral swaggerer restrained into reluctant respectability by a jealous wife. Access to the crucial letters yielded a picture of a Stevenson who is neither the "seraph in chocolate" against whom Henley protested, nor a low-living rake, nor an optimistic escapist, nor the happy invalid, but a sensitive and intelligent writer who had no illusions about life and wryly made the best of a world to which he did not profess to have the key.

His literary reputation has also fluctuated. The reaction against him set in soon after his death: he was considered a mannered and imitative essayist, or only a writer of children's books. But eventually the pendulum began to swing the other way, and by the 1950s his reputation was established among the more discerning as a writer of originality and power; whose essays at their best are cogent and perceptive renderings of aspects of the human situation; whose novels are either brilliant adventure stories with overtones of moral subtlety or original and impressive presentations of human action in terms of history and topography as well as psychology; whose short stories produce some new and effective permutations in the relation between romance and irony or manage to combine horror and suspense with moral diagnosis; whose poems, though not showing the highest poetic genius, are often skillful, occasionally (in his use of Scots, for example) interesting and original, sometimes (in *A Child's Garden*) valuable for their exhibition of a special kind of memory or sensibility.

Stevenson's other works include: *New Arabian Nights* (1882); *Familiar Studies of Men and Books* (1882); *Memories and Portraits* (1887); *Underwoods* (poems) (1887); *St. Ives,* completed by Sir A. Quiller Couch (1897). Stevenson's *Collected Poems* were edited by Janet Adam Smith (1950). The letters were edited by Sidney Colvin in 1899; *see* also *Vailima Letters,* to Sidney Colvin (1895) and, of great interest and importance, *R. L. S.: Stevenson's Letters to Charles Baxter,* ed. by De Lancy Fergusson and Marshall Waingrow (1956).

BIBLIOGRAPHY.—Bibliographies of the works of Stevenson were published by J. S. Slater (1894) and W. F. Prideaux (rev. by J. F. Livingston, 1917). *See* also *The Stevenson Collection of E. J. Beinecke, a Catalogue,* comp. by George L. Mackay (1950–52). Among the biographies and critical studies are Graham Balfour, *The Life of Robert Louis Stevenson* (1901); Rosaline Masson, *I Can Remember Robert Louis Stevenson* (1922); Lloyd Osbourne, *An Intimate Portrait of R. L. S.* (1924); G. S. Hellman, *The True Stevenson* (1925); G. K. Chesterton, *Robert Louis Stevenson* (1928); J. A. Smith, *R. L. Stevenson* (1927), *Henry James and Robert Louis Stevenson* (1948); A. B. Fisher, *No More a Stranger* (1946); David Daiches, *Robert Louis Stevenson* (1947); A. R. Issler, *Happier for His Presence* (1949); J. C. Furnas, *Voyage to Windward* (1951); Fanny Osbourne Stevenson, *Our Samoan Adventure,* with a diary by Mrs. Stevenson (1955).

(D. Ds.)

**STEVIN** (STEVINUS), **SIMON** (1548–1620), Dutch mathematician, who helped standardize the use of decimal fractions, was born in 1548 at Bruges and died in 1620, either at The Hague or in Leiden. He was director of the department for roads and waterways, and afterward quartermaster general. Stevin was known to his contemporaries by his military methods and inventions; he invented a defense by a system of sluices to release water through the dikes to flood land before the enemy which was of great importance to Holland. He also invented a carriage with sails which was used on the seashore and carried 26 passengers.

In his *Statics and Hydrostatics* (1586), he enunciated the important theorem of the triangle of forces. This gave a new impetus to the study of statics, which had previously been founded on the theory of the lever. He discovered the hydrostatic paradox that the downward pressure of a liquid is independent of the shape of the vessel, and depends only on its height and base.

In 1586 he published a pamphlet of a few pages, *Thiende,* in which he treated decimal fractions. Decimal fractions and fractions had been employed for the extraction of square roots five centuries before his time, but no one before Stevin had established their daily use. He declared that the universal introduction of decimal coinage, measures and weights would be only a question of time. His notation is rather unwieldy. He printed little circles round the exponents of the different powers of one-tenth. For instance, $237\frac{578}{1000}$ was printed 237 ⓪ 5 ① 7 ② 8 ③.

There are early editions of Stevin's works (1608, 1634); the first four volumes of a Dutch-English edition, with a biography, appeared in 1955–64. (O. OE.)

**STEWART** (STUART or STEUART), the surname of a Scottish family, the senior branch of which inherited the Scottish and ultimately the English crown. The first spelling of the name was undoubtedly Stewart, the old Scots version, but during the time of Mary, queen of Scots, when there was much intercourse with France, Stuart and Steuart were adopted owing to the absence of the letter *W* in the French alphabet.

The family can be traced back to 11th-century Brittany, where for at least four generations they were stewards to the counts of Dol. ALAN, the 4th steward of Dol, was a favourite of Henry I of England and is mentioned in English records as sheriff of

Shropshire from 1101. His younger sons WILLIAM (d. 1160) and WALTER FITZALAN (d. 1177) both held land in England; William, the second son, being lord of Oswestry and an ancestor of the earls of Arundel, his grandson JOHN FITZALAN (d. 1267) becoming "earl" of Arundel in 1243. Walter, the third son, in about 1136 entered the service of David I, king of Scots. He was given extensive estates in the west of Scotland, was appointed steward (or high steward) of Scotland to David, an office which was later confirmed to his family by Malcolm IV in 1157. His grandson WALTER (d. 1241), the 3rd steward, was appointed justiciar of Scotland in 1230 by Alexander II. Walter's eldest son ALEXANDER (1214–1283), the 4th steward, inherited by his marriage to Jean, daughter of James, lord of Bute, the islands of Bute and Arran and in 1263 led the Scots against King Haakon IV of Norway at Largs in Ayrshire.

Alexander had two sons, JAMES (*c.* 1243–1309), the 5th steward, and JOHN OF BONKYL. James was one of the six guardians appointed to rule Scotland on the death of Alexander III in 1286 in the name of Alexander's granddaughter, the infant Queen Margaret, the Maid of Norway. When Edward I of England established his suzerainty over Scotland in 1291, James became a leading opponent, fighting with William Wallace at the Battle of Stirling Bridge (1297) and supporting Robert I, the Bruce, who was crowned in 1306 as king of Scots. In 1314 James's second son WALTER (1292–1326), the 6th steward, at the age of 21 was placed with Sir James Douglas, "the Good," in command of one of the divisions of the Scottish Army at Bannockburn (1314), where he was knighted by King Robert on the field, and in 1315 he married the king's daughter Marjorie. Their only child ROBERT (1316–90), 7th steward, was declared heir presumptive to his grandfather in 1318, but shortly afterward the king had a son who succeeded in 1329 as David II. On David's death without issue in 1371 Robert, as Robert II, became the first Stewart king, his former title being thereafter held by the heir to the throne as prince and steward of Scotland.

The royal Stewarts had an unlucky history, for of the 14 crowned monarchs 4 were murdered or beheaded, 2 died in battle and 1 in exile, while 7 in succession came to the throne as minors. The direct male line of the family terminated with the death of JAMES V (1512–42). His daughter MARY (1542–87), queen of Scots, was succeeded in 1567 by her only son JAMES VI (1566–1625), who through his father HENRY STEWART, Lord Darnley (1545–1567), son of MATTHEW STEWART, 4th earl of Lennox, a descendant of John of Bonkyl, was also head of the second senior branch of the family. Meanwhile through the marriage of his great-grandparents JAMES IV (1473–1513) and Margaret Tudor, daughter of Henry VII of England, James VI became heir to the English throne, and on the death of Queen Elizabeth I in 1603 was proclaimed king of England as James I.

By the usurpation of Oliver Cromwell and the execution of James's son CHARLES I (1600–1649) the Stuarts were excluded from the throne until the restoration of his son CHARLES II (1630–1685) in May 1660. On the death of Charles II without legitimate issue, his brother JAMES (1633–1701) ascended the throne as James VII of Scotland and II of England, but he so alienated the sympathies of his subjects that after three years an invitation was sent to William, prince of Orange, to come "to the rescue of the laws and religion of England." MARY (1662–1694), James's elder daughter and next in line to her infant half brother JAMES (1688–1766), the Old Pretender, had married William, prince of Orange, son of Charles II's sister MARY (1631–1660), and they were proclaimed joint sovereigns as William III and Mary II of England on Feb. 13 and of Scotland on April 11, 1689. They left no issue and the Act of Settlement (1701), excluding Roman Catholics from the throne, secured the succession to ANNE (1665–1714), second daughter of James II, and, on her death without issue, to Sophia, electress of Hanover and her heirs, descended from Princess ELIZABETH (1596–1662), daughter of James VI and I, who married Frederick V, elector Palatine. James, the Old Pretender, had two sons, CHARLES EDWARD (1720–1788), the Young Pretender, known as Bonnie Prince Charlie, who died without legitimate issue, and HENRY (1725–1807), a cardinal and titular duke of York. With Henry, who on his death left his grandfather's coronation ring to George III, the legitimate male line of royal Stuarts came to an end. In the female line and senior to the House of Hanover was the royal House of Bavaria, descended from HENRIETTA ANNE (1644–1670), youngest daughter of Charles I, of whom the present head is Albrecht (1905– ), duke of Bavaria (*see* JACOBITES).

Apart from the royal Stewarts there were in Scotland many families of the name and there are few districts with which they have not been associated. The form of spelling of the name used by particular families is a matter of individual choice and does not necessarily indicate a special descent. As there is no legitimate heir male of the royal house, the families can be divided into two categories, the legitimate but preroyal, being those who came off the main stem before they became kings; and the royal but illegitimate descendants of the Stewart kings. From the first came, among others, the earls of Lennox, Galloway, Atholl, Traquair, the lords of Lorne, and Stewarts of Appin and Ardsheal, all descending from John Stewart of Bonkyl; the Stewarts of Ardvorlich and others who descend from ROBERT (*c.* 1340–1420), 1st duke of Albany and guardian of Scotland, brother to Robert III; and the Stewarts of Garth and others from the illegitimate issue of a third brother ALEXANDER (d. *c.* 1405), known as "the Wolf of Badenoch." From the second came, among others, the earls of Moray, and the marquesses of Bute. The Stewart descent is remembered in heraldry by variations either of the blue and silver fess chequey which was borne by the high stewards or of the rampant lion of the royal arms of Scotland.

*See* also references under "Stewart" in the Index.

BIBLIOGRAPHY.—D. Stewart, *A Short Historical and Genealogical Account of the Royal Family of Scotland . . . and of the Surname of Stewart* (1739); G. H. Johnston, *The Heraldry of the Stewarts* (1906); John Stewart of Ardvorlich, *The Stewarts* (1954); *The Stewarts, a Historical and General Magazine for the Stewart Society* (1902 to date). *See* also detailed bibliography in J. P. S. Ferguson, *Scottish Family Histories Held in Scottish Libraries* (1960). (J. M. MU.)

**STEWART, DUGALD** (1753–1828), Scottish philosopher, was one of the principal exponents of the philosophy of common sense (*see* further COMMON SENSE, PHILOSOPHY OF). He was born on Nov. 22, 1753, in Edinburgh, where his father, Matthew Stewart (1715–1785), was professor of mathematics. Dugald Stewart was educated at Edinburgh and Glasgow, began university teaching at the age of 19, and, from 1775, discharged all the duties of his father's professorship. In 1785 he succeeded Adam Ferguson in the chair of moral philosophy, which he held until 1820, although after 1809 ill health prevented him from performing his professorial duties. He died at Edinburgh on June 11, 1828.

Stewart's philosophy had little originality and was almost wholly a reproduction of the views of his master, Thomas Reid (*q.v.*). He was, however, a particularly brilliant exponent of the views of Reid and the common sense school and his classes at Edinburgh enjoyed great popularity. His principal work was *Elements of the Philosophy of the Human Mind* (3 vol., 1792, 1814, 1827); he also wrote *Outlines of Moral Philosophy* (1793); *Philosophical Essays* (1810); and *Philosophy of the Active and Moral Powers of Man* (1828). An edition of his complete works was prepared by Sir William Hamilton, 11 volumes (1854–58).

**STEYN, MARTHINUS THEUNIS** (1857–1916), president of the Orange Free State, South Africa, from 1896 to 1902, was born at Winburg, Orange Free State, on Oct. 2, 1857. Educated at the Grey College, Bloemfontein, and at Deventer in Holland (1877–79), he was called to the bar from the Inner Temple, London, in 1882. After practising as an advocate at Bloemfontein, he became state attorney and then a judge on the Free State bench in 1889.

Steyn defeated J. G. Fraser, chairman of the *Volksraad*, in the presidential election of February 1896. In the turbulent political atmosphere after the raid of L. S. Jameson (December 1895; *see* TRANSVAAL: *History*), he stood for closer ties with the Transvaal and as a defender of Dutch language rights against erosion by immigrant influences. In 1897 he concluded an alliance with the Transvaal. Ever watchful of Afrikaner solidarity, Steyn nevertheless strove for peace during the crisis of 1899 between Great Britain and the Transvaal, acting as host for the abortive Bloemfontein conference in June. He did not offer unequivocal support to the Transvaal until September, and did so then in the conviction that its cause was just. In the South African War (1899–1902) he fought to the bitter end and regretted the opening of peace negotiations in 1902.

The war ruined Steyn's health, and he never held political office again. After three years' medical care in Europe, however, he returned to the Orange River Colony in 1905 and became a power behind the scenes, opposing Louis Botha's conciliation policy in the Transvaal. He mellowed sufficiently to take part in the National Convention (1908–09), which led to the Union of South Africa (1910), but he lived to witness the Afrikaner rebellion of 1914, when his offer to mediate between the rebels and Botha proved unacceptable to the latter. He died at Bloemfontein on Nov. 28, 1916. *See* also ORANGE FREE STATE: *History*.

*See* N. J. van der Merwe, *Marthinus Theunis Steyn, 'n Lewensbeskrywing*, 2 vol. (1921). (T. R. H. D.)

**STEYR,** a town in the province of Upper Austria at the confluence of the Enns and Steyr rivers, 22 mi. (35 km.) SSE of Linz by road. Pop. (1961) 38,306. Steyr consists of an ancient centre and modern suburbs. In its old square, market place and narrow streets are many Gothic, Renaissance, and Baroque buildings, including the Bummerlhaus and St. Stephen's church (15th century), the museum (17th century), and the town hall (18th century). The castle was restored in the 17th and 18th centuries. In medieval times Steyr was the centre of Austria's iron industry. Present-day manufactures include trucks, automobiles, tractors, ball bearings, sporting guns, and iron goods. (W. H.)

**STIBNITE,** a mineral consisting of antimony sulfide, is an important ore of antimony. The powdered mineral was used by the ancients for darkening the eyebrows to increase the apparent size of the eyes. In addition to its use as an ore of antimony, it is employed in the manufacture of matches, fireworks and percussion caps. The formula of stibnite is $Sb_2S_3$. The crystals are prismatic in habit, longitudinally striated and usually terminated by acute pyramidal planes. There is a perfect cleavage parallel to the length of the crystals, and the basal plane is a plane of gliding; it is the latter property that facilitates the bending of the crystals, and stibnite crystals are often found in a deformed condition. The colour is lead gray and the lustre is metallic and brilliant; crystals become dull on prolonged exposure to light. The mineral is quite soft; hardness is 2 and specific gravity is 4.6. Thin flakes of the mineral transmit a small amount of red light, but are more transparent in the infrared. Stibnite is a photoconductive material which shows maximum sensitivity at 770 m$\mu$.

*See* also ANTIMONY. (A. J. F.)

**STICK INSECT** (WALKINGSTICK), an insect of the family Phasmatidae, so named because of its resemblance to twigs of trees and shrubs upon which most phasmids live and feed. The body and legs are long and slender, and the protective resemblance to twigs is enhanced by the usually brown, gray, or green coloration and the immobile attitudes assumed. Some species are further protected by an armature of sharp spines. Many are wingless; winged species have short, leathery wing covers (tegmina), but the hind wings are often large and beautifully coloured, though usually kept folded over the abdomen. As in the leaf insects (*q.v.*), to which phasmids are closely allied, the eggs closely resemble seeds. Stick insects attain their largest size and greatest profusion of species in the tropics: certain Asiatic *Palophus* and East Indian *Pharnacia* grow to be more than a foot long. A few smaller forms occur in southern Europe, and about 25 species are known from the United States, among them *Diapheromera femorata*, which, during heavy infestations, may defoliate oak forests. Phasmids freely regenerate amputated legs and antennae; under certain conditions the stump of an antenna will regenerate a leg.

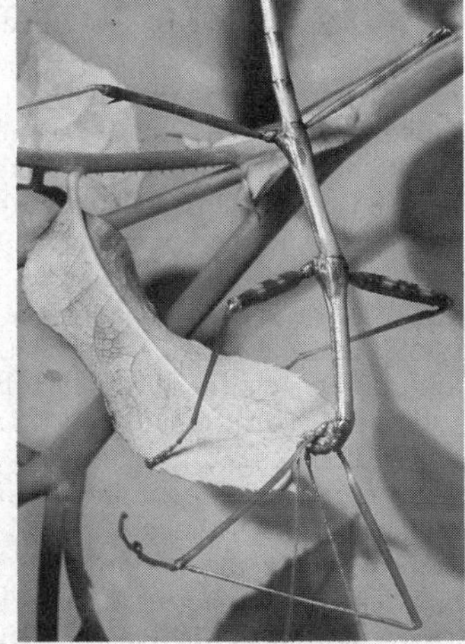

EDWIN WAY TEALE

AMERICAN STICK INSECT (DIAPHEROMERA FEMORATA), COMMONLY KNOWN AS WALKINGSTICK, FEEDING ON LEAF

*See* also ORTHOPTERA. (T. H. HL.)

**STICKLEBACK,** a small, aggressive bony fish with stout, pointed spines along the midline of the back, in front of the soft dorsal fin. Sticklebacks belong to the family Gasterosteidae. They occur in fresh and brackish waters as well as in coastal waters of the North Temperate Zone. The majority have a compressed, torpedo-shaped body, which in the marine species is longer. The mouth is moderately wide, oblique, and has small teeth. The head is protected by hard bone, the body by a series of bony plates along the sides. The spines are formed from the first dorsal fin; the ventral fins also include a stout erectile spine.

Sticklebacks are short-lived fishes, said to reach an age of three or four years. The widely distributed three-spined stickleback (*Gasterosteus aculeatus*) is a common and well-studied member of the family. It is green to brown above, blending to silvery on the belly, but in spring, at the start of the breeding season, the male displays a bright red belly and becomes active in the preliminaries to mating. He selects a territory and fashions a nest of stems of aquatic plants, which he binds together using a threadlike secretion from a part of his kidney. The male fiercely defends his territory against other males but actively invites females—often employing threats to drive them into his nest to lay eggs. He jealously guards the relatively large eggs, which begin to hatch after ten days, and cares for the hatchlings for a few days of their existence.

About 12 species of sticklebacks are known. The three-spined stickleback is found everywhere in the northern part of the Northern Hemisphere; in North America it occurs as far south as the Virginia coast. The nine-spined stickleback (*Pungitius pungitius* or *Pygosteus pungitius*) rarely exceeds two inches in length and may have 9 or 10 spines, rarely up to 13; its range nearly coincides with that of the preceding species but is more polar. The American, or four-spined, stickleback (*Apeltes quadracus*) is common along the North American east coast from Labrador to Virginia; it is commonly about one and one-half inches long. The sea, or fifteen-spined, stickleback (*Spinachia spinachia*), which attains a length of seven inches, is common along the British and European coasts.

**STIEGLITZ, ALFRED** (1864–1946), U.S. photographer, who devoted his life first to a fight for photography as an art, then to introducing modern painting to the United States, was born in Hoboken, N.J., on Jan. 1, 1864. Stieglitz was educated in New York and Germany, where he began photographing at the age of 19. His earlier work (*c.* 1883–1910), characterized by constant innovations believed impossible (*e.g.*, the first successful snow photographs), won over 150 important prizes. Having achieved public fame, his experimentation changed from preoccupation with techniques and wide subject matter to intense concentration on material closest to daily life. Two series, over 400 prints each (1917–37), are often considered his greatest photographs: the portrait of Georgia O'Keeffe (his wife) and the "Equivalents." His photographic prints were the first that U.S. museums acquired and housed with other graphic arts.

Stieglitz believed passionately that America could give rise to great works of art. His fostering of the work of others paralleled his own creative work, and is demonstrated through over 175 exhibitions in his three galleries (1905–46), many of which offered the public its first sight of modern art. Starting with Rodin and Matisse exhibitions in 1908 at his "291" gallery, Stieglitz followed with many other first U.S. exhibitions of equally important works (*e.g.*, African Negro sculpture as art, Cézanne, Picasso, Toulouse-Lautrec and others). When the public accepted modern European art, Stieglitz concentrated on U.S. artists, especially the five he showed most often in later years: Demuth, Dove, Hartley, Marin and O'Keeffe. *Camera Work* (1903–17), edited and published by Stieglitz, documents the history of these stormy years. He died on July 13, 1946, in New York city. (Ds. By.)

**STIEGLITZ, JULIUS** (1867–1937), U.S. chemist, was a pioneer in recognizing the value of the electron theories of valence to the interpretation of the behaviour and structure of organic compounds, and in applying to organic chemistry the methods and principles of physical chemistry. Born May 26, 1867, in Hoboken, N.J., he received his early schooling in New York, before attending the *Realgymnasium* in Karlsruhe, Ger., from 1881 to 1886. In 1889 he was awarded the Ph.D. in organic chemistry by the University of Berlin, where he had worked under Ferdinand Tiemann. Most of his professional career was spent at the University of Chicago, where he was chairman of the department of chemistry from 1915 to 1933. He was influential in the university as a whole as well as in the American Chemical Society, of which he was president in 1917. He died in Chicago, Jan. 10, 1937.

Stieglitz' research in organic chemistry dealt with four major topics: molecular rearrangements, for which he won the Gibbs medal in 1923; homogeneous catalysis; the theory of indicators; and the stereochemistry of organic nitrogen compounds. He was widely known as an inspiring teacher and, through his text on qualitative analysis (2 vol., 1911–12), the first to base that discipline on the theories of ionization and of chemical equilibrium. (H. I. Sr.)

**STIERNHIELM, GEORG** (1598–1672), Swedish poet and scholar, often called "the father of Swedish poetry," was born Aug. 7, 1598, at Vika, the son of a miner in Dalecarlia (Dalarna). After studying at Uppsala he spent several years at German universities (Greifswald, Wittenberg, Helmstedt). He returned to Sweden in 1626 and later obtained an official position in Dorpat. In 1631 he was raised to the nobility. From *c.* 1640 onward he was occasionally in Stockholm, as poet in attendance at the court of Queen Christina, although his home was in Estonia until 1656, when he fled before the Russian invaders. Thereafter he lived in Stockholm in straitened circumstances. In 1661 he was appointed councilor of war and in 1667 director of the college of antiquities. He died at Stockholm, April 22, 1672.

Stiernhielm's first poetic works in Swedish appeared during the 1640s. They included verses in celebration of the queen and three court masques adapted from the French, one of which, *Then Fångne Cupido* (1649), contains fine passages. His most important work is the allegorical, didactic epic, *Hercules* (written *c.* 1647; published 1658), a fine example of late Renaissance classicism, written in hexameters. Imbued with the spirit of humanism, it is a high-minded sermon on virtue and honour. The theme is developed with power and originality; the imagery is exuberant; the construction faultless. It had great influence on the development of Swedish poetry. Stiernhielm's poems were collected in *Musae Suethizantes* (1668).

Stiernhielm's scholarship was encyclopaedic, and in numerous writings, many unpublished, he dealt with philological, historical and philosophical problems. A great patriot, he claimed that Swedish was man's original language. In his fragmentary works of natural philosophy he expounded a cosmogony based on the platonic, mystical tradition of such thinkers as Paracelsus, Robert Fludd and Comenius.

Stiernhielm's *Samlade skrifter* were edited by J. Nordström, 12 volumes (1924 *et seq.*).

*See* also P. W. Wieselgren, *Georg Stiernhielm* (1948). (S. H. L.)

**STIFTER, ADALBERT** (1805–1868), Austrian narrative writer, one of the first of the middle-class realists. The quiet nobility of his work, with its exaltation of the humble virtues, and the classical purity of his style were only fully appreciated in the 20th century. Stifter was born in Oberplan in the Bohemian forest on Oct. 23, 1805, the son of a linen weaver and flax merchant. His background—the land, and the peasant craftsmen who were his ancestors—was lovingly transfigured in his work. He was educated at the Kremsmünster abbey school and Vienna University, where he matriculated as a law student but mainly attended scientific lectures and took no degree. For some years he made a precarious living as tutor, painter, and writer. From 1840 he began to publish stories in periodicals: *Der Condor* (1840), *Feldblumen* (1841), *Die Mappe meines Urgrossvaters* (1841–42), etc. The inner unity of landscape and people—a marked characteristic of Stifter's work—began to emerge in these stories, markedly in *Brigitta* (1844). *Studien* (1844–50), collections of his early stories in revised form, brought him fame. He followed it with *Bunte Steine* (1853), more stories (*Kalkstein* and *Bergkristall* probably the most compelling of them) with an important preface in which Stifter expounds his doctrine of the "law of gentleness" as the enduring principle.

In 1850 Stifter moved from Vienna, where he had been deeply stirred by political events, to Linz, becoming inspector of schools. In 1857 his great novel *Der Nachsommer* appeared. Like Goethe's *Wilhelm Meister,* of which it was a worthy successor, *Nachsommer* is a novel about the education and growth of a young man. The conquest of passion is here already a thing of the past and the work radiates a still and sun-soaked beauty, with flowing and unhurried pace, and restrained idealism set against the landscape Stifter loved. He then worked ten years on his epic *Witiko* (1865–67), a remarkable book in which medieval Bohemian history is the symbol of man's struggle for a just and peaceful order. Other stories followed (*Nachkommenschaft,* 1864; *Der Waldbrunnen,* 1866), but Stifter was too ill to complete his project of expanding *Die Mappe meines Urgrossvaters* into a novel; only the first volume was finished (1868). He died at Linz, on Jan. 28, 1868.

Bibliography.—*Werke und Briefe,* historical and critical edition by A. Sauer *et al.* (1901–60); *Gesammelte Werke,* ed. by M. Stefl, 6 vol. (1956–57); *Erzählungen in der Urfassung,* ed. by M. Stefl, 3 vol. (1950–52). *Biographies:* A. R. Hein, *Stifter,* 2nd ed. (1952); U. Roedl, *Stifter,* 2nd ed. (1958). Modern criticism includes J. Kühn, *Die Kunst A. Stifters,* 2nd ed. (1943); E. P. Lunding, *Stifter* (1946); H. Kunisch, *Stifter, Mensch und Wirklichkeit* (1950); E. A. Blackall, *Stifter* (1948); W. Rehm, *Nachsommer* (1951); F. Hüller, *Stifters Witiko,* 2nd ed. (1953); K. Steffen, *Stifter, Deutungen* (1955); J. Müller, *Stifter, Weltbild und Dichtung* (1956); K. G. Fischer, *A. Stifter, Pädagogik des Menschenmöglichen* (1962); U. Roedl, *A. Stifter* (1965). *See* also E. Eisenmeier, *A. Stifter Bibliographie* (1964). (Jm. M.)

**STIGAND** (d. 1072), archbishop of Canterbury, is probably Canute's priest of this name whom he placed over the minster of Ashingdon in Essex in 1020. He was consecrated bishop of Elmham in 1043, but was deposed later in the year when Queen Emma, mother of Edward the Confessor, fell into disgrace, because he was her adviser. He was reinstated in 1044. In 1047 he became bishop of Winchester, and Elmham was given to his brother Aethelmaer. Stigand mediated the peace between King Edward and Earl Godwin in 1052, and was made archbishop of Canterbury in place of the Norman, Robert of Jumièges, who had fled. He did not, however, relinquish Winchester. As he had been intruded into Canterbury while his predecessor was alive, his position was regarded as uncanonical; hence he did not receive the pallium until 1058, and then only from the antipope Benedict X, after whose deposition (1059) Stigand was excommunicated by Nicholas II. His continuance as archbishop was one of the reasons for the papal support given to William the Conqueror's invasion in 1066. Yet he was too powerful for William I to remove him at once, and he was not deposed until 1070. Domesday Book shows him to have had extensive lands and many men commended to him. He held some abbeys in plurality, as well as his two sees. He died on Feb. 22, 1072.

*See* Sir F. M. Stenton, *Anglo-Saxon England,* 2nd ed. (1947); F. E. Harmer (ed.), *Anglo-Saxon Writs* (1952). (D. Wk.)

**STIGMATIZATION,** in the religious sense, consists of the appearance, on the body of a living person, of wounds or scars (stigmata) corresponding to those of the crucified Christ—that is, on the hands, feet, and near the heart, and sometimes on the head (crown of thorns) or shoulders and back (carrying of the cross and scourging). Although cases of Protestants and unbelievers are known, the great majority of stigmatists are Roman Catholic mystics, and of these the majority are women. Some stigmatists are canonized saints, but the church, in canonizing a person, seeks proof of sanctity not in extraordinary phenomena such as ecstasies, visions, or stigmatization but in heroic virtue during his lifetime and in miracles after his death. Cardinal Prospero Lambertini (later Pope Benedict XIV) in his classical treatise on beatification and canonization declared that it is theoretically possible that God might accord stigmata to sinners and pagans, because stigmatization is a freely bestowed gift; hence, a person might have stigmata without being holy. Besides, the church in canonizing a stigmatist does not pass judgment on the question whether the stigmata are natural or supernatural. Among the more than 330 known stigmatized persons only some 60 are saints or beati.

Natural stigmata are commonly due to fraud or to auto- or heterosuggestion (*see* SUGGESTION). Medical and psychological evidence shows that stigmata may be the consequence of a strongly emotional state. Common experience indicates that emotions may be accompanied or followed by bodily changes and disturbances—increased rate of heartbeat, change of facial colour, trembling, sweating. Long-lasting or pathological emotional conditions may cause or aggravate organic disorders or lesions (*see* PSYCHIATRY: *History: Modern Schools: Psychosomatic Medicine*). Experiments made on hysterical women by the French psychiatrist Pierre Janet and the German physician Alfred Lechler have also shown that strong emotional states may result in such phenomena as bloody tears and stigmata. In these cases the psychophysiologic mechanism is set in motion by suggestion: an experienced psychiatrist or physician may work highly suggestible subjects to such an emotional pitch that the suggested idea of stigmata externalizes itself in their bodies. Since not only the psychophysiologic mechanism but also the initial cause is natural, stigmata so produced are called purely natural.

Roman Catholic authors admit also the possibility and actual existence of supernatural (divine) stigmata. These are stigmata whose initial cause is found in God, inasmuch as God may produce in certain persons an emotional condition that externalizes itself in the body. Stigmata that so result are natural insofar as they are the product of a natural state of emotion, but their initial cause is supernatural. This theory was advanced as early as the 17th century by St. Francis of Sales.

The criteria for deciding whether or not stigmata have divine origin are divinely inspired visions, spiritual fruits such as conversions of other persons, and miracles performed by the stigmatist.

*See* H. Thurston, S.J., *The Physical Phenomena of Mysticism,* posthumously ed. by J. H. Crehan, S.J. (1952); E. Amman, "Stigmatisation," in *Dictionnaire de théologie catholique,* vol. xiv, col. 2616–24 (1941). (J. H. V. D. V.)

**STILBITE,** a mineral of the zeolite group consisting of hydrated calcium aluminum silicate. The colour is usually white, sometimes red, and on the perfect cleavage (parallel to the plane of symmetry) the lustre is markedly pearly; hence the name stilbite (Gr. *stilbein,* "to shine") given by R. J. Haüy in 1796. After the separation of heulandite from this species in 1818, the name desmine (Gr. *desme,* "bundle") was proposed, and this name is employed in Germany. The composition is $CaAl_2Si_7O_{18}.7H_2O$. Usually a small proportion of the calcium is replaced by sodium. Crystals are monoclinic, and are invariably twinned, giving rise to complex groups and characteristic sheaflike aggregates. The hardness is 3.5 and the specific gravity 2.2. Stilbite occurs with other zeolites in the amygdaloidal cavities of basic volcanic rocks; it is sometimes found in granite and gneiss, and exceptionally in metalliferous veins. Beautiful, salmon-pink crystals occur with pale-green apophyllite in the Deccan traps near Bombay and Poona, India; white sheaflike groups encrust the calcite (Iceland spar) of Berufjördhur near Djúpivogur, Ice.; and crystals of a brick-red colour are found at Old Kilpatrick, Dumbartonshire, Scot. Good specimens of stilbite have been found in New Jersey and Nova Scotia. *See* also ZEOLITE.

**STILICHO, FLAVIUS** (*c.* A.D. 365–408), Roman general, the effective ruler of the Western Roman Empire from 395 until 408, was half-Roman and half-Vandal by birth. He made the army his career and in 383 served on an embassy to the Persian king Shapur III, afterward marrying Serena, the favourite niece of Theodosius I. He was appointed count of the domestics (commanding the emperor's household troops) *c.* 385, and then, in or before 393, master of both services (*i.e.,* commander in chief of the army), an office which he held until his death.

Little is known of Stilicho's military exploits during the lifetime of Theodosius. It is known that he became the enemy of Rufinus (*q.v.*) because of a difference of opinion about the treatment of some barbarian invaders in 389. Before his death Theodosius appointed Stilicho and Rufinus to be the guardians of his sons Honorius and Arcadius respectively. Stilicho had a great military advantage over his rival, for the army Theodosius had assembled to crush Eugenius (*see* THEODOSIUS) was still concentrated in the West under Stilicho's command when Theodosius died on Jan. 17, 395.

Before either Stilicho or Rufinus could attack the other, the Visigoths, who were living in Lower Moesia and who had suffered severe losses in the campaign against Eugenius, rebelled under the leadership of Alaric (*q.v.*) and began to devastate Thrace and Macedonia. Stilicho, who claimed the prefecture of Illyricum, disputed between the emperors, for the Western government, went with his army to Thessaly. But when he was about to engage Alaric there, he was ordered by Arcadius, acting on Rufinus' advice, to send a number of his troops to Constantinople. Stilicho obeyed and thus enabled Alaric to penetrate into Greece; but the troops who had been sent to Constantinople murdered Rufinus there on Nov. 27, 395. At this time the gifted poet Claudian began to publish his poems in praise of Stilicho, and his works are an important source of information about the politics of the time until 404, when the poet appears to have died (*see* CLAUDIANUS, CLAUDIUS).

In 397 Stilicho took another army to Greece but failed again to bring Alaric to battle and withdrew to Italy. In that same year Gildo, the count of Africa, rebelled against the Roman government and refused to allow the African grain ships to sail to Rome. Stilicho promptly imported grain from Gaul and Spain. In the following year he sent Mascezel, a brother of Gildo, to Africa with an army. Gildo was easily overthrown and put to death, but Mascezel died soon afterward and Stilicho was suspected of having had him murdered so that he might not become a rival to his own power. In 398 Stilicho's daughter Maria was married to the emperor Honorius, and Stilicho himself became consul in 400.

In 401 Alaric and the Visigoths invaded Italy and threatened Milan, where Honorius was then living. Stilicho summoned troops from the Rhine frontier and from Britain to strengthen his army, and in 402 he engaged the Goths at Pollentia (Pollenzo, near modern Bra). The battle was fought on Easter Sunday, April 6, and although Stilicho's victory was not complete he captured the Gothic camp. Alaric now marched toward Etruria but after negotiations agreed to withdraw from Italy. In 403, however, he entered Italy again and attacked Verona, where Stilicho once more engaged him successfully and pursued him northward toward the Brenner Pass. But again an understanding was reached, and Alaric, though his army was in bad condition, was allowed to escape.

Late in 405 Italy was menaced by new invaders, a vast host of Germans, mainly Ostrogoths, led by a pagan called Radagaisus. Terrified contemporaries believed that they numbered hundreds of thousands, though any such figure is impossible. They attacked Florence, but Stilicho compelled them to withdraw to Fiesole, where he cut off their supplies and massacred them. Radagaisus was executed on Aug. 23, 406, and in celebration of the victory a triumphal arch was erected at Rome, of which the inscription still exists.

Stilicho had never abandoned his aim of annexing the prefecture of Illyricum, and in 407 he was free to put his plans into operation. He closed the ports of Italy to all Eastern ships. He instructed Alaric to hold Epirus for Honorius, and he himself prepared to cross the Adriatic. But a false report reached him that Alaric was dead, and then he heard of the revolt of Constantine (*see* CONSTANTINE [d. A.D. 411]) in Britain. Once more his plans had to be abandoned. Alaric then marched to the province of Noricum and demanded compensation for the trouble he had been put to. His price was high—4,000 lb. of gold—but in spite of considerable opposition Stilicho persuaded the Senate at Rome to pay it.

By this time the empress Maria had died, but early in 408 Honorius married another daughter of Stilicho, Thermantia. But

Stilicho's influence had declined. It was rumored that he wished to have his son Eucherius elevated to the throne. Reports reached him, however, early in 408 that his army was disaffected. Then came the news of the death of the Eastern emperor, Arcadius, and Stilicho proposed to go to Constantinople. But a certain Olympius, a palace official, spread the rumour that Stilicho was preparing to put his own son on the Eastern throne, with the result that the troops in Ticinum (Pavia) killed nearly all the officials present there on Aug. 13. Stilicho went to Ravenna but was imprisoned on Honorius' orders. He was beheaded on Aug. 22, and Eucherius was put to death shortly after.

*See* J. B. Bury, *History of the Later Roman Empire,* vol. i, ch. 5 (1923); E. Stein, *Histoire du Bas-empire,* vol. i, ch. 6 (1959). (E. A. T.)

**STILL, ANDREW TAYLOR** (1828–1917), founder of osteopathy (*q.v.*), was born in Jonesville, Va., on Aug. 6, 1828. His family moved in 1837 to Macon County, Mo., and later to the Shawnee reservation near Kansas City, Kan. Still acquired some medical knowledge from his father and at a college in Kansas City; from 1849 onward he practised in various Kansas and Missouri communities. He took an active part in the antislavery cause in Kansas, and in 1857 was elected to the territorial legislature. After serving in the Civil War, and following the deaths of three of his children in an epidemic, Still began searching for means other than those of orthodox medicine to combat disease. After much experimentation he formulated his principles of osteopathy in 1874. He underwent a period of opposition, but finally, in 1892, founded the American School of Osteopathy at Kirksville, Mo., where he died on Dec. 12, 1917.

*See* E. R. Booth, *History of Osteopathy* (1924); M. A. Lane, *Dr. A. T. Still, Founder of Osteopathy* (1918). (F. L. A.; X.)

**STILL, WILLIAM GRANT** (1895– ), U.S. composer and conductor, the first notable American Negro composer, and the first Negro to conduct a professional symphony orchestra in the United States. Born at Woodville, Miss., on May 11, 1895, Still also had Spanish, Indian, Scottish, and Irish elements in his ancestry. Brought up by his mother and grandmother in Little Rock, Ark., he studied medicine at Wilberforce University, Wilberforce, O., before turning to music against his mother's wish. He first studied composition at Oberlin Conservatory of Music, Oberlin, O., then under the conservative George W. Chadwick at New England Conservatory, and later under Edgard Varèse during the latter's most radical avant-garde period. The diversity of Still's musical education was increased when, in the 1920s, he worked as an arranger for Paul Whiteman, W. C. Handy, and other prominent band leaders. In 1939 he married the white pianist and journalist, Verna Arvey, author of many of his librettos, and settled in Los Angeles.

Still's concern with the position of the Negro in U.S. society is reflected in many of his works, notably: the *Afro-American Symphony* (1931); the ballets *Sahdji* (1930), set in Africa and composed after extensive study of African music, and *Lenox Avenue* (1937); and in the opera *Troubled Island* (1938), libretto by the prominent Negro poet Langston Hughes.

Still's compositions from the mid-1930s show the jazz band as one of the greatest influences on his eclectic musical style. He makes considerable use of material in the Negro style—though rarely borrowing actual melodies—and prefers simple "commercial" harmonies and orchestration, the use of which is, however, characterized by the highest professionalism and seriousness of purpose.

Still is a prolific composer with a large number of operas, ballets, symphonies, and other works on large and small scale to his credit. The work that has probably met with widest acclaim is the *Afro-American Symphony,* which was hailed by some critics as "the most characteristically indigenous piece" to have come from the United States.

Bibliography.—V. Arvey, *William Grant Still* (1939); A. Locke, *The Negro and his Music* (1936); W. G. Still, "A Negro Composer's Point of View," in *American Composers of American Music,* ed. by H. Cowell (1933). (D. N. Fa.)

**STILLBIRTH:** *see* Abortion; Fetal Disorders.

**STILL-LIFE PAINTING** may be loosely defined as the depiction of inanimate objects for the sake of their qualities of form, colour, texture and composition. Still life has always existed in painting as a subsidiary element; it occurs in Roman wall decorations at Herculaneum in the 1st century A.D. and again in mosaics (Lateran museum, Rome) of the same date. Four centuries later it appeared as an independent decorative element in the ceiling mosaics at the church of Sta. Costanza, Rome. A significant change came in the 6th century when pure still life disappeared and was replaced by symbols with a specific religious connotation, as exemplified by the two fish on a plate in a mosaic of the Last Supper at S. Apollinare Nuovo, Ravenna. It was not until the rise of a wealthy merchant class, coupled with the prolonged effects of the Reformation, that a new demand grew for secular subjects in painting other than portraiture. Finally, the Renaissance artists' fresh interest in the material details of their environment led to a more naturalistic representation of these as well as of the human figure. Thus Raphael included an admirable still-life group of musical instruments in his "St. Cecilia" (Bologna) and Vittore Carpaccio devoted great care to the still life in his "St. Jerome in his Study" (S. Giorgio dei Schiavoni, Venice). Yet it was the northern artists who provided minutely detailed still life, and the exquisite draftsmanship of Jan van Eyck and of Albrecht Dürer was a part of the northern artistic tradition most suited to the development of still-life painting as a separate art.

However, the first signed and dated pure still life, of a dead partridge, gauntlets and arrow pinned against a wall (Munich), was painted in 1504 by an Italian, Jacopo de' Barbari, working in the north. Early still lifes were produced in Antwerp, where the Dutch painter Pieter Aertsen (1508?–75) spent a considerable part of his working life; a work by an unknown artist, produced in his environment (Boymans Museum, Rotterdam), has all the elements of the genre. On the table are an earthenware pot, a jug, a bowl, a sliced loaf, some pieces of cheese, and several fishes; all these are thrust forward in such a way that the spectator seems to be very close to the table and looking at them from only slightly above. The artist has concentrated on rendering the forms of the objects, which are accentuated by a strong light coming from a window on the left, but already the observation of tonal values of light and shade irrespective of local colour was becoming the chief preoccupation of the still-life painter. The austerity of this tightly composed painting may be contrasted with the work of Pieter Aertsen himself, who preferred the market stall and the kitchen larder, with their piles of vegetables and fruits, as his subjects. Figures are sometimes put into the background, as in "The Butcher's Shop" of 1551 (Uppsala), but interest is concentrated upon gory sides of beef, sausages, game and fish spread upon slabs or suspended from hooks. The composition is overcrowded; the picture literal to a point of nausea.

Giuseppe Arcimboldo (*c.* 1530–93) made a curious use of still life. Human heads and even whole figures are ingeniously fashioned out of various fruits, vegetables, fish and animals to symbolize the four elements or the four seasons. Examples of these fantasies are in the Vienna art gallery. One of the few great Italian masters to produce pure still life was Michelangelo da Caravaggio (1573–1610), and his still lifes in the Ambrosiana, Milan, and the Kress collection, Washington, D.C., show him to be a formidable rival of the Dutch and Flemish artists. Solidity of form and composition, brilliant colour and precise drawing are united with a superb feeling for light and atmosphere in his work, as in Francisco de Zurbaran's famous still life of 1633. Qualities such as these are the essence of still life; and during the 17th century many Netherlandish painters achieved a competence of this kind rarely surpassed. Mention need only be made of Willem Heda (1594–1680/82) and Willem Kalf (1622–93) who used goblets, nautilus shells, delicate porcelain and rich fabrics for much of their work. Kalf's technique, in particular, resembles Vermeer's; and, indeed, the interiors with figures painted by Vermeer partake strongly of the quality of still life. Kalf's pictures are usually simpler and less crowded than those of Abraham van Beyeren (1620–75), although each relied upon similar subjects, and the

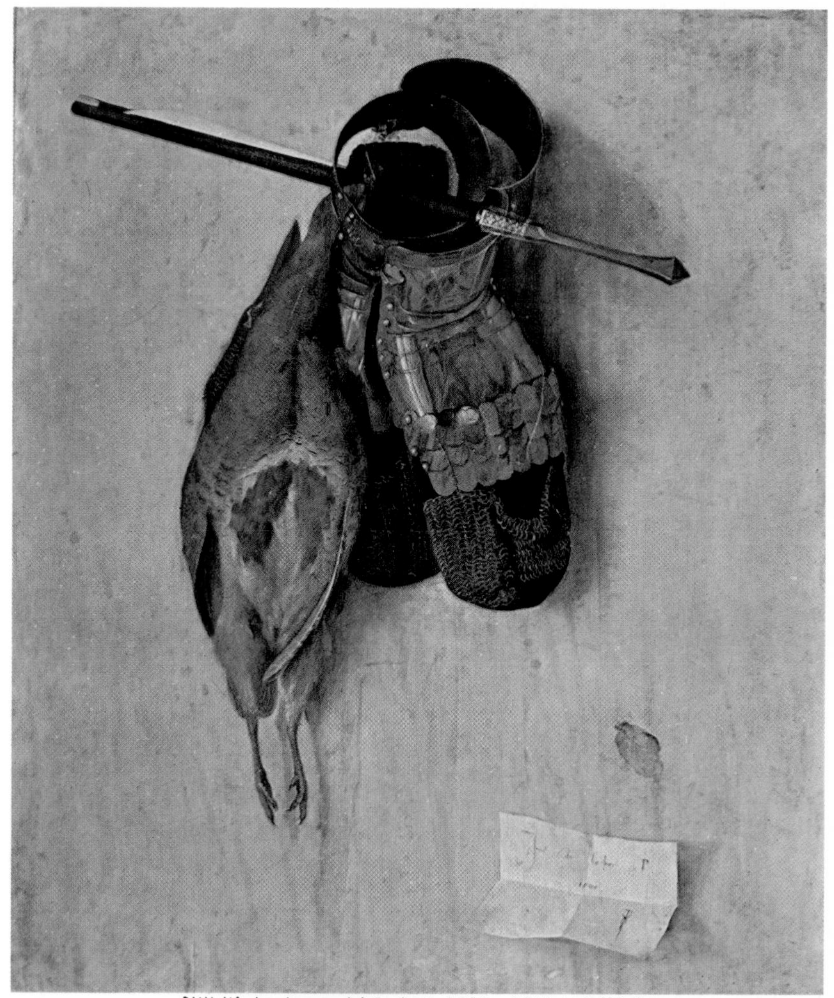
Still life by Jacopo de' Barbari, 1504. 19¼ × 16½ in.

"Shells, Lobster, Vase and Bird," Roman wall painting from Herculaneum, 1st century A.D.

### EARLY STILL LIFE

The challenge posed the artist by the form, colour and texture of inanimate objects has been a major inspirational force in Western art since the 1st-century Roman murals at Herculaneum (above), in which still life played an important but subsidiary role. Still life became an important independent art with the earliest known signed and dated work (left), painted in 1504 by Jacopo de' Barbari, an Italian who lived and worked in the north. The meticulous draftsmanship and fascination for detail that characterized 16th-century northern painting may be seen in the composition below, by an unknown Dutch artist

Still life by an unknown Antwerp master, about 1560–70. 13⅞ × 19⅛ in.

BY COURTESY OF (TOP LEFT) BAYERISCHE STAATSGEMÄLDESAMMLUNGEN, MUNICH, (TOP RIGHT) MUSEO NAZIONALE, NAPLES, (BOTTOM) MUSEUM BOYMANS-VAN BEUNINGEN, ROTTERDAM (ON LOAN FROM THE DIENST VOOR'S RIJKS VERSPREIDE KUNSTVOORWERPEN); PHOTOGRAPH, (TOP LEFT) JOACHIM BLAUEL

# STILL-LIFE PAINTING

"Basket of Fruit" by Michelangelo da Caravaggio (1573–1610). 18⅛ × 25⅜ in.

"Still Life" by Willem Kalf, (1622–93). 25⅜ × 21¼ in.

"Summer" by Giuseppe Arcimboldo, 1563. 29 × 19 in.

BY COURTESY OF (TOP) BIBLIOTECA AMBROSIANA, MILAN, (LEFT) NATIONAL GALLERY OF ART, WASHINGTON, D.C., GIFT OF CHESTER DALE, (RIGHT) KUNSTHISTORISCHES MUSEUM, VIENNA; PHOTOGRAPHS, (TOP) WALTER SCANSANI, (RIGHT) PHOTO MEYER

"The Butcher's Shop" by Pieter Aertsen, 1551. 48½ × 64½ in.

"Still Life with Lamb's Head" by Francisco Goya, about 1816–24. 18 × 24 in. In the Louvre, Paris

## 16TH- TO EARLY 19TH-CENTURY STILL LIFE

"Basket of Fruit" by Michelangelo da Caravaggio (Plate II, top) is an Italian painting which, in its precision, its solidity and its sense of light and atmosphere rivals the work of 17th-century northern masters like Willem Kalf (Plate II, bottom). The crowded butcher's shop scene by Pieter Aertsen (above) shows what was likely to occur when fascination with detail was allowed to overcome the northern artists' compositional sense. The 18th-century still life by Jean Baptiste Siméon Chardin (below) and the early 19th-century work by Francisco Goya (right) show a growing interest in the simplification and selection of important details. The fanciful caricature, which makes its own curious use of still-life elements, (Plate II, right) is the work of Giuseppe Arcimboldo, a 16th-century Italian Mannerist

"The Skate" by Jean Baptiste Siméon Chardin, 1728. 43¼ × 55 in. In the Louvre, Paris

# STILL-LIFE PAINTING

"The Stove" by Eugène Delacroix, *c.* 1830. 20 × 17 in. In the Louvre, Paris

"Vase of Flowers" by Claude Monet, about 1882. 39½ × 32 in.

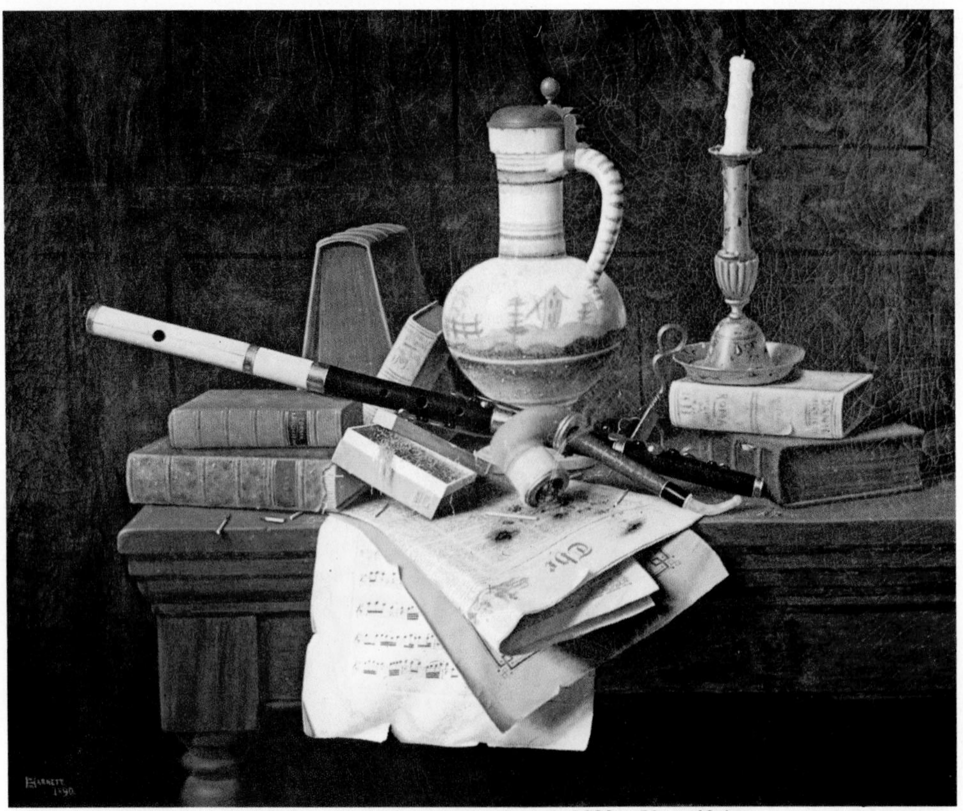

"Emblems of Peace" by William Harnett, 1890. 52 × 42 in.

### 19TH-CENTURY STILL LIFE

Still life was largely neglected during the neoclassical period. The bravura realism of Eugène Delacroix's painting "The Stove" (Plate IV, top left), painted in the 1830s, helped to reawaken interest among young artists like Gustave Courbet, one of whose finest still lifes appears at right. The "Vase of Flowers" by Claude Monet (Plate IV, top right) shows the Impressionists' interest in the effects of colour and light. Paul Cézanne (below) exploited spatial ambiguity in attempting to resolve one of the basic dilemmas of painting: how best to represent three-dimensional objects on a two-dimensional surface. The meticulously realistic grouping by W. Harnett (Plate IV, bottom) is an example of the Dutch-inspired, U.S. *trompe l'oeil* school

"Pomegranates" by Gustave Courbet, 1871. 10½ × 13¾ in.

"Still Life with Ginger Jar" by Paul Cézanne, *c.* 1888–90. 25½ × 32 in. In the Louvre, Paris

BY COURTESY OF (TOP) THE BURRELL COLLECTION, GLASGOW ART GALLERY AND MUSEUM; PHOTOGRAPH, (BOTTOM) CICCIONE—RAPHO

# STILL-LIFE PAINTING

"Chair and Pipe" by Vincent Van Gogh, 1888–89. 36 × 28 in.

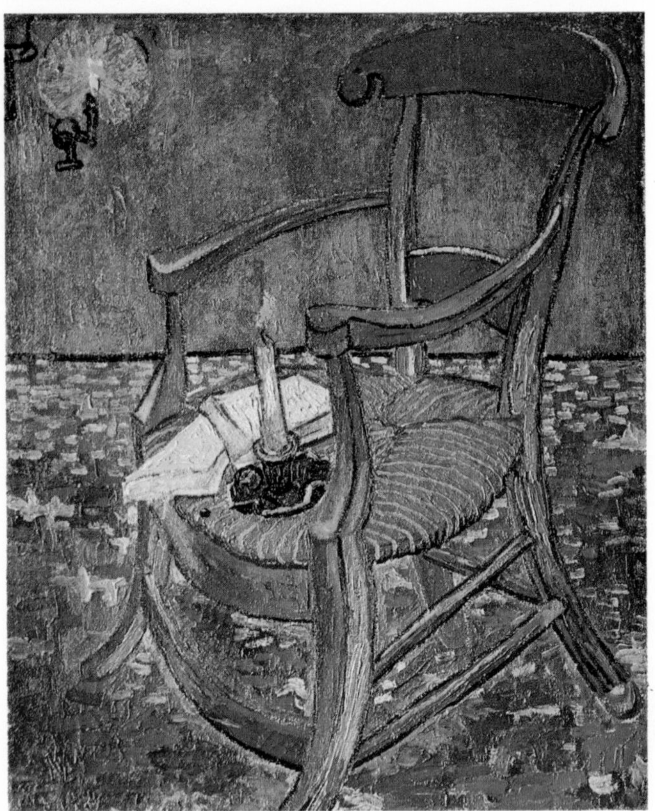

"Gauguin's Chair" by Van Gogh, 1888. 35¾ × 30¾ in.

"The Coffee" by Pierre Bonnard, about 1914. 28 × 41 in.

"Still Life: Death's Head, Leeks, and Pot" by Pablo Picasso, 1945. 15 × 20 in.

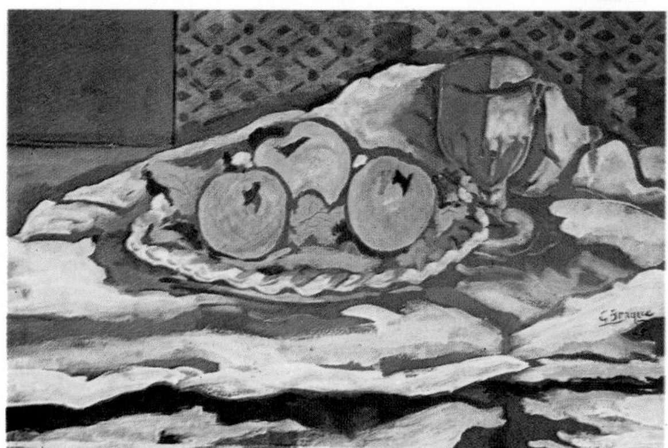


"Still Life" by Georges Braque, 1925. 15 × 23 in.

### LATE 19TH- AND EARLY 20TH-CENTURY STILL LIFE

The two paintings of chairs by Van Gogh (Plate VI, top left and right) show the range of emotion and invention that an inanimate object could produce in that impassioned painter. Both the *Nabis*, as Pierre Bonnard (Plate VI, bottom), and the *Fauves*, as Henri Matisse (right), employed unusual viewpoints and bright colours to produce brilliant two-dimensional patterns. Cubists Pablo Picasso (top) and Georges Braque (above) found in still life an ideal subject for their constructions, made up of complex fragmentations of form and multiple viewpoints

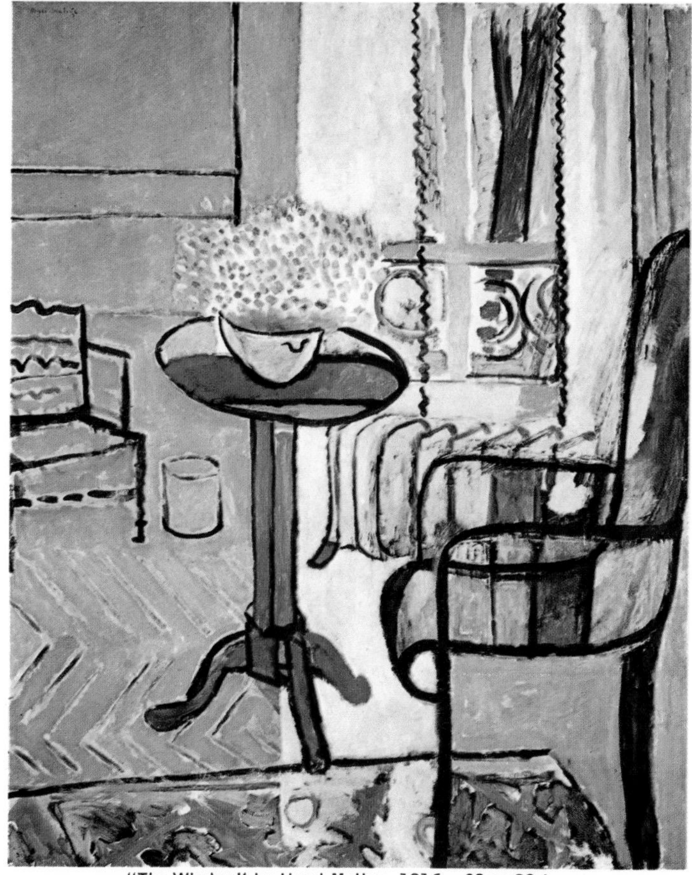

"The Window" by Henri Matisse, 1916. 30 × 20 in.

BY COURTESY OF IVAN LE LORRAINE ALBRIGHT

"Poor Room—There Is No Time, No End, No Today, No Yesterday, No Tomorrow, Only the Forever, and Forever, and Forever, Without End" by Ivan Le Lorraine Albright, 1959. Property of the artist

20TH-CENTURY STILL LIFE

inclusion of a partly peeled lemon was a favourite trick with many of these painters. Cornelis de Heem and Jan de Heem were the ablest of a large family of still-life painters, while Jan van Huysum (1682–1749) became pre-eminent as a flower painter, and often set his still life against a landscape background. Frans Snyders (1579–1657), along with Jan Fyt (1611?–61) and Jan Weenix (1640/44–1719) also did this, but chose to paint dead game, sometimes adding live birds and dogs for contrast. Melchior d'Hondecoeter (1636–95) also worked in this tradition.

Nothing of new artistic importance emerged from the Netherlands during the 18th century, for the country had become severely impoverished. Jean Baptiste Siméon Chardin (1699–1779) added peculiarly French qualities of lucidity and penetration to the enhancement of the art. He broke away from the outmoded conventions of A. F. Desportes (1661–1743) and J. B. Oudry (1686–1755), derived from the Netherlands; and the Louvre version of "The Skate" (1728) is notable for its broad treatment and thick, impasted highlights. There is an escape from the airlessness and overcrowding, the emphasis upon the inessential detail to the detriment of the whole, which often mars Dutch and Flemish painting. The figures and objects in a Chardin household seem timeless and inevitable; "La Fontaine" (National gallery, London) and "Le Bénédicité" (Louvre) are paintings that equal, if not surpass, the work of Gerard Terborch and Jan Vermeer. Something of Chardin's ease and simplicity appears in Francisco Goya's still-life paintings; for example, the "Still-Life With Lamb's Head" in the Louvre; and he, with Chardin, was to inspire 19th-century artists as diverse as I. H. Fantin-Latour and Edouard Manet.

After a momentary eclipse during the neoclassical period, interest in still life was reawakened by Eugène Delacroix's startlingly original "The Stove," painted in the 1830s. Casually composed, the painting shows a corner of the artist's studio with its stove and other bric-a-brac. There is a new quality of high-spirited realism, and even defiance, and it is significant that Paul Cézanne was to paint the same type of composition (Chester-Beatty collection, London) in the fierce, undisciplined style of his youth.

Fantin-Latour's early work is dry and sombre, with the accent upon one bright area, perhaps some roses in a glass, like the Tate gallery painting of 1861. He used a limited palette, and relied upon subtle gradations of tone to obtain plasticity. Influenced by the Impressionists, his colours became richer and his brushwork more lively and impasted, as in the 1881 "Bowl of Flowers" (Lady Lever gallery, Port Sunlight, Cheshire), but at no time did he approach the vigour and immediacy displayed in Gustave Courbet's "Fleurs dans un Panier," 1863 (Cargill collection, London), so reminiscent of Delacroix's painting of 1849, "The Over-turned Flower Basket in a Park" (Wildenstein gallery, New York city). Unhesitatingly, using broad, fluent strokes, Courbet captured the essential features of the objects before him, giving them tangible shape and glowing colour. "Pomegranates," 1871 (Burrell collection, Glasgow), and "The Trout," 1873 (Oeffentliche Kunstsammlung, Zürich), are two of Courbet's most powerful works. Even Manet's "Les Poissons" (Chester-Beatty collection, London), with its cool, brilliant colour, cannot quite rival it.

As might be expected, the still lifes by Claude Monet are flooded with a warm shimmering light. Form and space are revealed more by the acute perception and recording of hitherto unexplored colour harmonies, than by tonal variations and linear perspective.

Cézanne found landscape and still life particularly suited to his own artistic development. Still life acquired a new importance for him, allowing him to concentrate upon the fundamental, recurring problems of form, colour and space, undisturbed by irrelevant anecdotal or literary associations. By 1870, with "Still-Life With Black Marble Clock" (Wildenstein), he showed great originality of conception. Already he was fascinated by the abstract pattern formed by the folds in the tablecloth; the objects on the table, seen at a high eye level, seem to be in the same spatial plane as the clock on the mantelpiece. This spatial ambiguity is even more pronounced in the Louvre "Still-Life With Ginger Jar" (1888–90), where the jar and basket of fruit on the sharply tilted floor seem level with the objects on the table in the foreground. This deliberate use of different eye levels and viewpoints, combined with a slight "flattening" of elliptical shapes (*e.g.*, coffee pot, basket handle), was an attempt to limit the amount of recession into the picture, and to resolve the paradox of representing three-dimensional objects on a two-dimensional surface. Paul Gauguin also used those devices, but emphasized the decorative element, modeling his objects in broad planes of pure, bright colours; a development for which Van Gogh was also partly responsible.

Vincent Van Gogh's intensely personal vision, when applied to still-life painting, could bring a new emotional significance to such mundane objects as a row of peasants' boots, a Bible and a candle, or his "Bedroom Chair" (Tate gallery, London). Here, as in all his work, both the colours and the brush strokes used convey not only shape, but also much of this emotional fire. The contrast between the Tate "Chair" and "Gauguin's Chair" (V. W. Van Gogh collection, Amsterdam), with its fierce clashes of violet, green and red, surely illustrates Van Gogh's extremely wide evocative powers.

At the turn of the century, still-life painting was no longer the province of a few specialists. Between 1907 and 1909, the Cubists, led by Pablo Picasso and Georges Braque, carried Cézanne's ideas much further, and like him found still life to be the subject most suited to their experiments with perspective. Objects were reduced to their basic shapes, split open, flattened and reorganized into a complex, predominantly two-dimensional composition. The images made by the profile, top, bottom and oblique angles of one object might be superimposed upon each other in one painting. This is the so-called analytical Cubism. The colours were restricted to greens, grays and browns. Synthetic Cubism, or collage, came next, and pieces of material, newspapers, etc., were stuck to the board or canvas, and painted into the picture. These are gayer in colour, and often made rather witty visual paraphrases. Braque's "Still-Life" (Tate) of 1925, although still using Cubist formulas, is slightly more naturalistic. Although he worked in a more rigorous abstract style during the 1930s, unlike Picasso he did not use still life to convey violent changes of mood, such as found in the latter's somewhat disquieting "Death's-head with Leeks" (1945).

Contemporary with the Cubists were Henri Matisse, André Derain and Maurice de Vlaminck (*les Fauves*, "the Wild Beasts"), whose work is characterized by radiant colour, great decorative skill and *joie de vivre*. In still life, unusual viewpoints are sometimes chosen, partly for the variety of pattern they afford, and never for the purpose of deliberate distortion. Édouard Vuillard and Pierre Bonnard (*les Nabis*, "the Prophets"), less formalized in style than Matisse, were yet painters of extreme sensitivity and taste.

The Dadaists, and later the Surrealists, stimulated by modern psychoanalytical research, exploited still life in an unusual way. Attempting to explore and record something of the secret working of the subconscious, partially revealed in dreams, they juxtaposed in their paintings animate and inanimate objects which are quite unrelated to each other in normal circumstances. The disconcerting, haunting effect sometimes thus produced is intended as a pictorial approximation to this other (dream) reality. Salvador Dali's "Persistence of Memory," with its melting watches set on a rocky foreshore, is a typical example.

No British artist of note (excepting William Etty), had seriously attempted still life until W. R. Sickert, with the New English Art club, introduced a taste for the genre from France in the 1890s. Matthew Smith, Ben Nicholson, Edward Wadsworth and William Scott are representative modern English exponents.

Still-life painting in the United States stems primarily from the Dutch realist *trompe-l'oeil* tradition best exemplified by the work of the Peale family in the early 19th century and continued by William M. Harnett (1848–92). Harnett's reputation was established during the 1880s with works such as "Emblems of Peace" (1890, Springfield [Mass.] museum) in which he depicted commonplace objects with meticulous precision and deceptive realism. Of Harnett's several followers John F. Peto (1854–1907) was the most distinguished, his "Still Life With Lanterns" (Brooklyn [N.Y.] museum) might easily be confused in style with Harnett's "The Old Violin." For nearly 40 years Harnett's work lay forgotten until exhibited in 1939, when American Surrealists soon claimed him as a forerunner, reading into his sly whimsy a more profound psychopathic preoccupation than he could originally have intended. Surrealist overtones are more obvious in the work of Walter Tandy Murch (1907–67), who owes much to Harnett but paints more loosely and introduces a stronger feeling for atmosphere. Murch's "The Circle" (*c.* 1948, Brooklyn museum) represents an old gramophone seen cornerwise with a dead beetle pinned inconspicuously to an odd corallike object on the turntable. The paintings of Ivan Le Lorraine Albright (1897– ) are very different; he shows an almost overpowering, morbid interest in the minutiae of texture, and in "Self Portrait" (1935, Earle Ludgin collection, U.S.) the flesh seems about to dissolve. Bernard Perlin's "The Jacket" (1951, Whitney museum) represents yet another kind of careful, factual realism.

Bibliography.—H. Furst, *The Art of Still-Life Painting* (1927); M. J. Friedländer, *Landscape, Portrait, Still-Life* (1949); C. Sterling, *La Nature Morte de l'Antiquité à nos jours* (1955). (D. L. Fr.)

**STILLMAN, WILLIAM JAMES** (1828–1901), U.S. painter and journalist, was born at Schenectady, N.Y., June 1, 1828, and graduated from Union College, Schenectady, in 1848. He studied art under Frederick E. Church and early in 1850 went to England, where he fell under the influence of Rossetti and Millais. He studied art in Paris, returned to the United States and devoted himself to landscape painting on upper Saranac Lake in the Adirondacks and in New York City. There also he started the *Crayon;* when it failed for want of funds, Stillman moved to Cambridge, Mass. He returned to England, and afterward painted with Ruskin in Switzerland. He was in Normandy in 1861 when the American Civil War broke out and was appointed U.S. consul in Rome; he resigned in 1865, but immediately afterward was appointed to Crete. When in London he lived with D. G. Rossetti. When the insurrection of 1875 broke out in Hercegovina, he went there as a correspondent of the *Times* (London), and his letters from the Balkans aroused so much interest that the British government was induced to lend its countenance to Montenegrin aspirations. In 1877–83 he served as the correspondent of the *Times* at Athens; in 1886–98 at Rome. After his retirement he lived in Surrey, where he died on July 6, 1901. He wrote, among other books, *The Cretan Insurrection, 1866–1868* (1874), *On the Track of Ulysses* (1888), *Billy and Hans* (1897), and *Francesco Crispi* (1899). His *Autobiography of a Journalist* was published in 1901.

**STILLWATER,** a city of north central Oklahoma, U.S., 65 mi. N of Oklahoma City; the county seat of Payne County and the seat of Oklahoma State University. The first recorded mention of Stillwater was on Dec. 25, 1884, when an army officer reported that "about 200 men, armed with double-barreled shot guns and Winchesters," had located there on lands not officially opened to settlement. This was the last serious foray into the Indian territory of "boomers," persons from Kansas who had made raids into the territory in an effort to induce the federal government to open the lands. A permanent settlement was made in April 1889 in the first great Oklahoma land run. Stillwater was incorporated as a village in 1890 and as a town in 1891; the name is from Stillwater creek, known by that name before any settlement was made. The city secured the Oklahoma Agricultural and Mechanical College which opened in 1891. It was renamed Oklahoma State University in 1957. Industrial activity in the Stillwater region includes dairying, beef cattle, wheat, and oil.

For comparative population figures *see* table in Oklahoma: *Population.*

*See* B. B. Chapman, *The Founding of Stillwater* (1948). (B. B. C.)

**STILT,** a wading bird related to the avocet, with which it forms the family Recurvirostridae. Two species are generally recognized: the widely distributed common stilt (*Himantopus himantopus*), whose five or more geographic races are sometimes accorded specific rank; and the exclusively Australian banded stilt (*Cladorhynchus leucocephala*). Stilts are remarkable for the extreme length of their slender legs. The head is small, bill dark (and not upturned as in the avocet), neck long, and wings long and pointed. Their calls resemble the yelping of a pup. The black-necked stilt (*H. h. mexicanus*), breeding from the northwestern and southeastern U.S. to northern South America, winters from the southern U.S. to the southern limits of the breeding range. Its legs and the iris of the eye are reddish; wings and upper back, including the crown, are black; and underparts from throat to rump are white. This stilt builds a simple grassy nest on the edge of a pool or lake, where it can forage for its prey: crustaceans, insects, and other small animals. The clutch of three to five buffy and spotted eggs, laid in late spring, are incubated for almost a month by both parents; the young, brownish and downclad, leave the nest soon after hatching. The banded, or red-breasted, stilt, with chestnut chest band, yellow legs, and brown iris, nests along inland marshy ponds in the Australian interior.

ALLAN D. CRUICKSHANK FROM NATIONAL AUDUBON SOCIETY

AMERICAN BLACK-NECKED STILT AT NEST

**STIMSON, HENRY LEWIS** (1867–1950), U.S. lawyer and statesman who served as secretary of state in the early 1930s and as secretary of war throughout World War II. He was born in New York City on Sept. 21, 1867, the son of a successful and socially prominent banker and physician. He was educated at Phillips Academy (Andover, Mass.), Yale University (A.B., 1888), Harvard University (A.M., 1889), and Harvard Law School. Admitted to the New York bar in 1891, he joined the law firm of Elihu Root two years later.

From 1906 to 1909 he was U.S. attorney for the southern district of New York State; he distinguished himself especially for his devotion to the "trust-busting" policies of his friend and mentor, Pres. Theodore Roosevelt. At Roosevelt's request, he ran in 1910 as the Republican candidate for governor of New York, but was defeated. From 1911 to 1913 he was secretary of war in the cabinet of Pres. William Howard Taft. During World War I he served briefly as colonel of the 31st field artillery in France, and after the war he opposed Pres. Woodrow Wilson's plans for U.S. membership in the League of Nations. Stimson prospered as a lawyer during the 1920s, made some shrewd investments, and became, as he said, a "rich man." After 1927 his firm bore the name Winthrop, Stimson, Putnam & Roberts.

In 1927 he was recalled to public life by Pres. Calvin Coolidge, who sent him as a special commissioner to Nicaragua to mediate between Pres. Adolfo Díaz and the rebel leader José María Moncada. He arranged an armistice on the understanding that the United States should supervise the election of 1928. Appointed governor general of the Philippine Islands in December 1927, he opposed the Philippine independence movement and pursued a program of economic development of the islands with a view to converting them into "self-governing possessions or colonies whose citizens did not participate in our citizenship."

From 1929 to 1933 Stimson served as secretary of state in Pres. Herbert Hoover's cabinet. He led the U.S. delegation to the London Naval Conference in 1930. When, in 1931, the Japanese began military operations in Manchuria, he resisted efforts of the Chinese government and the League of Nations to obtain U.S. support against Japan. As the Japanese proceeded to overrun Manchuria, however, he took a stronger and stronger stand against Japanese aggression. He sent to Japan and China identical notes (Jan. 7, 1932) stating that the U.S. did not intend to recognize as legally valid any situation, treaty, or agreement impairing the treaty rights of the United States or brought about by means contrary to the Pact of Paris. This nonrecognition policy afterward became known as the Stimson doctrine. In January 1933 he took part in conferences on the international situation with President Hoover and President-Elect Roosevelt, and advocated close cooperation between the United States and the League in censuring and punishing Japan. Later, as an elder statesman, he urged cooperative international action against Italian and German as well as Japanese aggressions.

In 1940 Stimson, though a lifelong Republican, was appointed secretary of war by Pres. Franklin D. Roosevelt, who at the same time appointed another prominent Republican, Franklin Knox, as secretary of the navy. As secretary of war, Stimson guided the expansion and training of the U.S. Army throughout World War II. He also acted as President Roosevelt's and later as Pres. Harry S. Truman's chief adviser on atomic policy. To President Truman he recommended that atom bombs be dropped on Japanese cities that had military importance, and he afterward justified the bombing of Hiroshima and Nagasaki on humanitarian grounds. He wrote that use of the bomb accelerated the surrender of Japan and thus saved many more lives than it cost. He left office in September 1945 and died Oct. 20, 1950, in Huntington, N.Y.

In 1948 Stimson, aided by McGeorge Bundy, published an autobiographical work entitled *On Active Service in Peace and War*. Earlier books by Stimson appeared as follows: *American Policy in Nicaragua* (1927), *The United States and Other American Republics* (1931), *Pact of Paris* (1932), and *Far Eastern Crisis* (1936). (R. N. Ct.)

**STIPPLE AND CRAYON ENGRAVING:** *see* PRINTMAKING.

**STIRLING,** a midland county of Scotland, stretches from Loch Lomond in the west to the Firth of Forth in the east; the River Forth forms part of its northern border with the county of Perth, while the counties of Lanark and Dunbarton lie south and west. Area 451 sq.mi. (1,167 sq.km.).

**Physical Geography.**—The Highland boundary fault, running northeastward from near the southern end of Loch Lomond, limits the northwestern Highland prong of the county; there Dalradian schists form a bleak moorland ridge over 3,000 ft. (915 m.) high in parts (Ben Lomond 3,192 ft. [973 m.]), sloping to oak woods on the lake shores. Southeast of the fault, conglomerates of Lower Old Red Sandstone age, lapped unconformably by Upper Old Red Sandstones, form a depression which is a westerly continuation of Strathmore, Perth, interrupted by a low ridge which forms a Forth-Clyde watershed; Flanders Moss borders this zone along the Forth. Towering over this lowland, with abrupt drops of 1,000 ft. (305 m.) in places, are the intrusive volcanic porphyries of Carboniferous age comprising the Campsie Fells, the Fintry and Kilsyth hills, and filling the centre of the county; the successive lava flows are clearly seen. The Carron flowing to the Forth and the Endrick flowing to Loch Lomond subdivide the plateau with its rolling surfaces between 1,500 and 2,000 ft. (Earl's Seat 1,896 ft. [578 m.]), probably remnants of a once-continuous surface between the Highlands and Southern Uplands. Nardus moorland grazed by blackface sheep alternates with patches of peat bog. The county contains small portions of the Ochil Hills in the northeast and the Kilpatrick Hills in the southwest, both similar volcanic intrusions and separated from the Campsies by the Forth Valley and the Strathblane lowland respectively. These lowlands are linked by the narrow corridor which skirts the steep southern face of the central hills. This is Scotland's waist, used by all the major communication lines between the Forth and the Clyde. To the southeast lies part of the great syncline containing the coal measures of the Central Coalfield, rising to a bleak upland about 500 ft. (152 m.) round Slamannan. Ice moving south, then east, plastered the lowlands with boulder clay; at 50 and 100 ft., raised beaches flank the alluvial flats along the Forth.

The principal lochs include the greater part of the eastern waters of Loch Lomond, a small portion of the northern end of Loch Katrine, and Loch Arklet, in the northwestern area, which, with Loch Katrine, provides the water supply of Glasgow. The Carron Reservoir in the Denny Hills provides the water supply to the greater part of the county. The Forth and Clyde Canal (closed to traffic in the late 1960s) crosses the southeastern corner of the county from Grangemouth to Castlecary. Rainfall decreases from 100 in. (2,540 mm.) in the northwest highland to 30 in. (760 mm.) along the Forth; conditions are milder and wetter toward the west. (A. M. Le.)

**History.**—The Antonine Wall, built by Lollius Urbicus in A.D. 142 and connecting the Forth and Clyde, passes through the southeast of the county, in which it is locally known as Graham's Dyke. At Castlecary (where the Romans used coal in the fort) and Camelon many relics have been found. The Camelon Causeway ran northward to Stirling and the Forth, where there was a station near the present bridge of Drip. Then it crossed the river to Ardoch (Braco) in Perth. After the withdrawal of the Romans the native Picts gradually retired before the advance of the Saxons and Scots. By the time of Malcolm Canmore (d. 1093) the lowland area had become settled. Stirling, which received a royal charter from David I (*c.* 1130), became a trading centre. King James VI made Airth (1597) and Falkirk (1600) burghs of barony. The Stuart kings ruled from Stirling Castle until the union of the crowns. The county played a conspicuous part in the struggle for Scottish independence, being particularly associated with many of the exploits of Sir William Wallace and Robert I, the Bruce. The three great battles of the independence were fought in the county—Stirling Bridge (1297), Falkirk (1298), and Bannockburn (1314). James III was stabbed to death in a cottage in the village of Milton after the Battle of Sauchieburn (1488), but apart from the disastrous defeat of the Covenanters at Kilsyth (1645) and the transitory triumph which Prince Charles Edward won at Falkirk (1746), the history of the county practically centres in that of the county town. (*See* STIRLING [burgh].)

**Population and Administration.**—The population in 1966 of the administrative county was 200,180; 582 people spoke Gaelic as well as English. Falkirk (pop. 1966, 37,500) and Stirling (the county town and only royal burgh, 28,030) are large burghs, the small burghs being Grangemouth (21,380), Kilsyth (9,620), Denny and Dunipace (7,840), and Bridge of Allan (3,810).

The county, with the county of Clackmannan, sends three members to Parliament. It forms a sheriffdom with the counties of Dunbarton and Clackmannan; there are resident sheriff substitutes at Stirling and Falkirk.

**The Economy.**—Because of varying rainfall and different soils, Stirling has two types of agriculture. In the west, farms are largely used for dairying and feeding store cattle. In the east and northeast, and particularly on the (alluvial) Carse, a system of arable and stock feeding is practised. Wheat and beans grow well but the outstanding crop is timothy grass, which gives heavy yields as hay or produces seed of very good quality.

Hardy sheep are grazed on the hills. Stirling is the market centre for a wide area and has sales of lambs, sheep, and cattle.

Birches and conifers grow on the lower slopes of the mountains in Buchanan and Drymen, and oaks on the banks of Loch Lomond.

The coalfield of the southeast has been worked out and coal is chiefly produced in the central area at Fallin and Manor Powis. Firebricks are manufactured in large quantities at Bonnybridge and Whitecross, and there are ironworks at Carron, Falkirk (*q.v.*), Bonnybridge, Denny, and Larbert (*q.v.*).

Nails are made at Lennoxtown; carpets are manufactured at Bannockburn (*q.v.*); Grangemouth (*q.v.*) with a shipyard is the second port in Scotland and is one of the biggest centres for dyes and pharmaceuticals and has a modern oil refinery with an associated chemical industry producing plastics and synthetic rubber. Tanning, papermaking, brewing, and distilling are carried on at different places, and there is an aluminum mill in Falkirk. (J. D. K.)

*See* A. G. Ogilvie (ed.), *Central Scotland* in *Great Britain, Essays in Regional Geography* (1928); Land Utilization Survey of Britain, *Land of Britain*, pt. 21–23, *Lanarkshire, Dunbartonshire and Stirlingshire,* by L. D. Stamp (1946).

**STIRLING,** a royal, large, and parliamentary burgh, river port, and the county town of Stirling, Scot., on the right bank of the Forth, is 37 mi. (59.5 km.) NNW of Edinburgh and 27 mi. (43 km.) NNE of Glasgow by road. Pop. (1966) 28,030. The old town and castle occupy the slopes of a dolerite hill (420 ft. [128 m.] above the sea) terminating on the north and west in a precipice. The modern town was laid out on the level ground at the base, especially toward the south. Remains of a town wall exist at the southern end of the Back Walk. Formerly there were two main entrances—the South port and the "auld brig" over the Forth to the north, a high-pitched structure of four arches now used only by pedestrians. It dates from the end of the 14th century and was once literally "the key to the Highlands." Just below it is the bridge completed in 1831 from designs by Robert Stevenson, and below this again the railway viaduct. The castle crowning the hill is of unknown age, but from the time of Alexander I (d. 1124) until the union of the Scottish and English crowns in 1603, it was intimately associated with the fortunes of the Scottish monarchs. It is approached from the esplanade, on which stands a colossal statue of Robert Bruce. The main gateway, probably built by James III, gives access to the lower and then to the upper square, on the south side of which stands the palace, begun by James V (1540) and completed by his widow, Mary of Lorraine. The east side of the quadrangle is occupied by the Parliament House, a Gothic building of the time of James III, used as a barrack room and stores. On the north side of the square is the Chapel Royal, founded by Alexander I, rebuilt in the 15th century and again in 1594 by James VI (who was christened in it), and afterward converted into an armoury and finally a storeroom. The former banquet hall contains the regimental museum of the Argyll and Sutherland Highlanders. In the plain to the southwest were the King's gardens, now under grass, with an octagonal turf-covered mound called the King's Knott in the centre. Farther south lies the King's Park. On a hill of lower elevation than the castle and separated from the esplanade by a depression styled the Valley—the tilting ground of former times—a cemetery has been laid out where are the Virgin Martyrs' Memorial (in memory of Margaret Maclachlan and Agnes Wilson, who were drowned by the rising tide in Wigtown Bay for their fidelity to the Covenant [1685]), a large pyramid to the memory of the Covenanters, and the Ladies' rock, from which ladies viewed the jousts in the Valley.

Adjoining the cemetery on the south is the Church of the Holy Rude (Rood), portions of which may have formed part of the original church founded by David I. Following the Reformation it was partitioned into two churches, but was restored to its original condition in 1936–40. The choir (the old East Church) was added in 1494 by James IV, and the apse a few years later. At the west end is a battlemented square tower. The nave (the former West Church) is a transition between Romanesque and Gothic, with pointed windows. The main entrance to both churches was by the south transept, with its crow-stepped Gothic gable. The choir is in the Decorated and Perpendicular styles. Within its walls Mary Stuart, queen of Scots, was crowned in 1543, when nine months old; on July 29, 1567, James VI (then 12 months old) was crowned, John Knox preaching the sermon. James Guthrie (d. 1661), the martyr, and Ebenezer Erskine (1680–1754), founder of the Scottish Secession Church, were two of the most distinguished ministers. To the southwest of the church is Cowane's Hospital, founded in 1639 by John Cowane, dean of guild, and now used as a guildhall. Near the principal entrance to the esplanade stands Argyll's Lodging, the earlier part of which was erected about 1630 by William Alexander, 1st earl of Stirling, the founder of Nova Scotia. On his death in 1640 it passed to the 1st marquess of Argyll and later was made into a military hospital. It is a fine example of a baronial town house. Broad Street contains Mar's Work, the unfinished palace begun by John Erskine, 1st earl of Mar, about 1570, according to tradition, out of the stones of Cambuskenneth Abbey; the old town house, erected in 1701 to replace that in which John Hamilton, the last Roman Catholic archbishop of St. Andrews, was hanged in 1571 for alleged complicity in the murders of Lord Darnley and the regent Moray; the town cross, restored in 1891; and the house which was, as a mural tablet says, the "nursery of James VI and his son Prince Henry." The Smith Art Gallery and Museum in Dumbarton Road was founded in 1873 by Thomas Stewart Smith, an artist.

The Abbey Craig, across the Forth, an outlying spur of the Ochils, 1½ mi. NE of Stirling, is a thickly wooded hill on the top of which stands the National Wallace Monument (1869), a baronial tower, 220 ft. high, with a "Hall of Heroes" containing busts of eminent Scotsmen. Cambuskenneth Abbey, on the left bank of the Forth, about 1 mi. ENE of Stirling, was founded by David I in 1147 for Augustinian monks. Several Scots parliaments met within its walls. At the Reformation Mary Stuart bestowed it (1562) on the 1st earl of Mar, who is said to have used the stones for his palace in Stirling. All that remains of the abbey is the massive, four-storied tower, the west doorway and the foundations of some of the walls. The remains of James III and his queen, Margaret of Denmark, who were buried within the precincts, were discovered in 1864 and reinterred the next year under a tomb at the high altar at the expense of Queen Victoria.

Stirling was also known as Snowdoun, which became the official title of the Scots heralds. The Romans probably had a station there. The hill was in Pictish territory until their kingdom was merged with Dalriada after 843. Under Alexander I it became a royal burgh and later was one of the Court of Four Burghs (first mentioned in 1292 and lasting till the early 16th century). In 1174 it was promised to the English in security for the Treaty of Falaise, but was never exacted by Henry II. The earliest known charter existed *c.* 1130 and a later one was granted in 1226 by Alexander II who made the castle a royal residence. The fortress was repeatedly besieged during the wars of Scottish Independence and fell to the English in 1296. Recovered after the Battle of Stirling Bridge (September 1297), it fell again, with the town, to Edward I in 1304. The English held it for ten years, and it was in order to raise the Scottish siege in 1314 that Edward II risked the Battle at Bannockburn, 2½ mi. S. Edward Balliol surrendered it in 1334 in terms of his compact with Edward III, but the Scots regained it in 1339. From that time until the collapse of Queen Mary's fortunes after the Battle of Langside in 1568, Stirling almost shared with Edinburgh the rank and privileges of capital of the kingdom. It was the birthplace of James III. In 1571 an attempt was made to surprise the castle by Mary's adherents, the regent Lennox being slain in the fray, and seven years later it was captured by James Douglas, 4th earl of Morton. It was occupied in 1584 by the earls of Angus and Mar, the Protestant leaders, who, however, fled to England on the approach of the king. The next year they returned with a strong force and compelled James VI to open the gates, his personal safety having been guaranteed.

After the union of the crowns (1603) Stirling ceased to play a prominent part on the national stage. The Privy Council and Court of Session met in the town in 1637 because of the disturbed state of Edinburgh. In 1641 Charles I gave it its last governing charter, and four years later Parliament was held in Stirling because of the plague in the capital, but the outbreak of the pest in Stirling caused the legislators to move to Perth. During the Civil War the Covenanters held the town, to which the committees of church and state adjourned after Oliver Cromwell's victory at Dunbar (1650), but in August of the next year the castle was taken by General George Monck. In 1715 the 3rd duke of Argyll held it to prevent the passage of the Forth by the Jacobites, and in 1746 it was ineffectually besieged by Prince Charles Edward.

Stirling, with Falkirk and Grangemouth, returns one member to Parliament.

The most important industries are associated with agriculture: agricultural engineering; the production of farm and garden seeds and fertilizers; livestock marketing; sawmilling; bacon curing; and sausage making. Rubber, asbestos and fibre insulating materials are made; other industries include the manufacture of cigarettes, concrete, and carpets. Coal mining employs many of the inhabitants. There is some shipping from the small harbour which is accessible only at high water.

**STOA,** in Greek architecture, a long open building with the roof supported by one or more rows of columns parallel to the back wall. A row of rooms may open from the rear of the colonnade; a second story is often added. Stoae surrounded the market places and later the sanctuaries and served for nearly all public and private business, as well as for public promenade. Athens, Corinth, Delos, and the Asia Minor cities offer good examples, notably the reconstructed Stoa of Attalos at Athens. (L. T. Se.)

**STOAT,** a common name for the small northern weasel *Mustela erminea,* especially when it displays its summer pelage of brown upper parts and whitish under parts. These slender, agile, bloodthirsty mammals measure 7½ to 13½ in., approximately 40% of which is tail. In colder climates the winter coat is white, except for the black tail-tip; the animal in this colour phase is popularly called ermine, as are other winter-white weasels. In moderately cold climates the fur becomes only partially white. (The colour change is the result of molting and is an inherited hormonal response to the daily amount of light.)

Stoats occur from the Arctic southward in eastern America to Pennsylvania and in the west to northern New Mexico. They also extend from the British Isles to Japan and as far south as Algeria. They are versatile as to habitat but are most abundant in thickets and woodland, and in damp, grassy, semi-timbered areas. Females are smaller than males and northern races smaller than southern. Their diet consists of small mammals, birds, eggs, frogs, and occasional invertebrates. The prey is seized usually at the base of the skull, the sharp teeth penetrating the brain. Larger prey is seized by the throat and held with fierce tenacity. Stoats are preyed upon by larger carnivores and birds of prey. Mating takes place in late spring or early summer with gestation prolonged as much as 10 months because of delayed implantation of the egg. The 4 to 13 blind young are born in a burrow. They reach old age in 7 to 8 years.

JOHN MARKHAM

STOAT, OR ERMINE (MUSTELA ERMINEA), IN BROWN SUMMER COAT

The winter-taken pelts, prized for fineness and pure colour, are among the most valuable of commercial furs and are obtained mainly in northern Eurasia. (K. R. Kn.)

**STOCK,** a plant of the mustard family (Cruciferae), native to the Mediterranean area but widely grown in many horticultural varieties for its showy, fragrant flowers. It is *Matthiola incana,* a usually branched annual, biennial, or perennial that grows to three feet tall and has narrow, hairy leaves up to eight inches long. The flowers—white, blue, pink, purple, or yellowish—have four petals (more in double varieties). The fruit is a pod containing many flattened, winged seeds. Double stocks do not produce seeds. The night-scented stock, *Matthiola bicornis,* also native to the Mediterranean area, has purplish, night-blooming flowers and two-horned pods.

Stocks are easily raised from seeds and do well in ordinary soil. The two main groups are summer stocks (variety *annua*) and winter stocks. Summer stocks, or ten-weeks stocks, flower 7 to 14 weeks after sowing, which is usually done outdoors in April or under glass in March. Winter stocks, usually sown in June or July, bloom the following year, although some varieties will flower in autumn of the same year if sown early enough. (J. W. Tt.)

**STOCK** (Shares). The money invested by individuals in business corporations is divided into units called stock in the United States or shares in Great Britain. Such stock represents a permanent investment in the business. The investor receives a certificate as evidence of his ownership of a part of the corporation. The detailed contractual relationship between the corporation and its stockholders sets forth the division of the risk, income and control of the business. Stockholders have the right to share in the management of the corporation, to share proportionately in any dividends declared and in the assets of the business in case of liquidation, and to approve or disapprove proposed changes in the original contract. The stock certificate itself, which has been called both a negotiable and quasi-negotiable instrument, may be transferred from person to person. In Great Britain the discussion of the rights of shareholders is relatively simple because the Companies acts apply to the entire nation. In contrast, there are great diversities in the rights of stockholders in the United States because each state has its own corporation law.

By the middle of the 20th century virtually all large privately owned businesses and a large proportion of smaller businesses in the United States and Great Britain were organized as corporations and had issues of stock outstanding. The fact that the ownership of both large and small corporations is divided into shares makes any simple description of classes of stock and the rights of stockholders necessarily vague. Only by unreasonably stretching the legal fabric can the shares of the very large and very small businesses be included under the same cloak.

The Companies acts in Great Britain, the Securities act (1933) and Securities Exchange act (1934) of the United States, and the corporation laws of the individual states have tended to give more publicity to corporate affairs for the protection of the shareholders of public companies. The rights of minority interests are also protected by law. The rights of the shareholders of private or closely held corporations may be quite different from those of public companies. The right of the shareholder to transfer his shares is often restricted by agreement among the shareholders. Profits may be divided on the basis of private agreements. Shareholders' rights may become indistinguishable from those of partners. In the United States even one-man corporations are not uncommon. By the 1960s the laws governing the establishment of corporations in the United States and the rights of stockholders were beginning to recognize the differences between the problems of small businesses organized as corporations and large publicly owned businesses.

**Dividends.**—One of the basic rights of stockholders is to share in the profits of the corporation. These profits may be paid out to the investors in the form of cash dividends or retained in the business to help finance its growth. Stockholders have no right to receive dividends until they are declared by the board of directors. Dividends are usually declared as a certain amount per share by class of stockholder.

Cash dividends, with the exception of liquidating dividends, generally cannot be legally authorized if the effect of such a dividend payment would be to reduce the owners' equity in the business below their original contribution. However, such a limitation is of little importance to large corporations that have grown partly or wholly by "plowing profits back into the business." It is usually recognized that profits retained in the business in fact, if not legally, become a part of the permanent investment of the shareholders. Cash dividends generally cannot be paid if the corporation is insolvent or if the payment of the dividend would result in insolvency.

Dividends are sometimes paid in the form of additional common stock of the corporation rather than in cash. Such stock dividends, as they are called, give recognition to the fact that the profits retained in the business represent a permanent investment. Many rapidly growing, publicly held corporations have a policy of paying dividends partly in stock as well as in cash, thus conserving the firm's cash so that it may be used to help finance expansion. The stockholder may sell the stock received as dividends.

Small, closely held, rapidly expanding businesses usually pay little if any dividends until such time as they prepare for their first public issue of stock. At that time the retained earnings are transferred to the common stock account and the number of shares is increased or split so that the market price of the new shares will be in the popular trading range when they are sold. Stock splits of more than 1,000–1 are not uncommon in these circumstances. In one unusual case, the shares of Biophysical Electronics, Inc. were split 62,500–1 when the firm sold common stock to the public for the first time in 1959. The decision of a corporation to raise funds or finance by the use of equity shares rather than by borrowing is extremely complex. Some of the factors that influence the decision are: size and rate of growth of the business, distribution of shares of the business (whether closely held or publicly held), maintenance of voting control, stability of earnings, personal and corporate income tax rates, desire to avoid fixed contractual obligations for the payment of interest and principal on a debt, and availability and relative cost of debt and equity funds. *See* also Stock Exchange. (R. M. S.)

### UNITED STATES

As noted above, a share of stock is an ownership interest in a corporation. Each stockholder or shareholder has the fractional interest in the corporation that may be measured by comparing the number of shares he holds with the total number of the corporation's shares outstanding. This interest includes the right to share in the control of the organization's activities, to share in dividends as declared, to purchase additional shares when and if issued and to share in assets remaining after paying creditors upon termination of the corporation's existence. One or more of these rights, however, may be withheld or qualified by particular state laws or by the articles of incorporation.

As compared with partners in an unincorporated business, corporation stockholders have the advantage of limited liability but their freedom to withdraw assets from the firm is restricted. The restriction on owners' withdrawals creates the concept of "stated capital"—the portion of owners' interests which must not be withdrawn. The initial investments of stockholders usually exceed the amount designated in the articles of incorporation as stated capital. The legal term for this excess is "paid-in surplus" or "capital surplus." Profits accumulated as the corporation carries on its functions add to the owners' interests, while dividends paid by the corporation reduce the owners' interests in the corporate fund of assets as these assets are transferred to them. The excess of accumulated profits over dividends declared is called retained earnings or earned surplus. Thus, the owners' interests in corporate assets commonly arise from two sources—original investments and retained earnings—but the legal concept of stated capital requires a distinction between any part of the owners' original contributions that may be returned to them and the part that must be preserved.

Dividends and a rise in the price of the shares are the basic incentives for investing in an incorporated business by purchasing its stock. The payment of dividends entails the transfer of assets from the corporation to its stockholders, thus reducing both the total assets of the corporation and the owners' interests therein. The legal category of owners' interests that are reduced by dividends is partly regulated by law and partly at the discretion of the corporation's board of directors who have the responsibility for declaring dividends. Unless the corporation has covenanted with a specific group of creditors to restrict its dividends in some manner, the directors normally have the power to declare dividends which reduce retained earnings. Paid-in surplus is, in most states, available for reduction by dividends under certain circumstances. Stated capital, however, may not be reduced by dividends, although some states permit dividends not in excess of profits earned in the most recent fiscal period even if the stated capital of the corporation has been impaired by earlier losses. In such a case the earned surplus is negative and the total of the owners' interests is less than stated capital.

**Classes of Stock.**—Many corporations have only one class of stock, frequently referred to as capital stock or common stock in the United States or ordinary shares in Great Britain. Each share has full voting and dividend rights as well as the right to share in assets upon dissolution. The pre-emptive right to buy new issues of the corporation's stock is provided by law in some U.S. states or by articles of incorporation in others. The existence of two classes of stock means that one or more of these fundamental rights does not attach equally to the shares of all classes.

*Voting and Nonvoting Shares.*—Shares whose holders may not vote at all or may not vote on certain issues, such as the election of directors, may be referred to as nonvoting shares. The two classes are often officially designated as class A and class B shares.

*Preferred Stock.*—To appeal to investors who wish to be sure of receiving dividends regularly, many corporations issue a class of stock that gives its holders a preferential claim to dividends. The most common provision of this type is that no dividends may be declared on the common stock unless dividends of a stipulated amount per year have been declared on the preferred shares. Usually this preferred dividend is cumulative, meaning that any dividend omitted is added to future dividends payable on the preferred shares before the common shares may receive a dividend. Noncumulative preferred shares have a weak position legally because the board of directors is under no obligation to declare dividends on any class of stock even if earnings are ample.

Another type of preference that may be granted relates to the distribution of assets upon dissolution of the corporation. The articles of incorporation may provide that one class of stock shall rank before another class when assets are distributed at the end of the corporation's life. The amount of this preference must be specified; it may vary depending upon whether the liquidation is voluntary or involuntary.

*Convertible Preferred Stock.*—The major disadvantage of preferred stock is that the holder does not share in exceptionally good fortunes of the issuing corporation, because preferred shares rarely receive dividends in excess of the preferential rate. This shortcoming can be remedied by giving stockholders the right to exchange preferred shares for common shares in a stated ratio so that conversion may become attractive if the market price of the common stock increases by a modest percentage. For example, when the common shares are selling at $21, preferred shares convertible at the rate of four common for one preferred share may be issued at $100. If the company prospers and the price of the common shares rises to $30, the preferred stockholder may share in the prosperity by converting a share of preferred into four shares of common with an aggregate value of $120. Under such circumstances the market price of the preferred stock will also rise.

**Stock Values.**—Articles of incorporation must specify the maximum number of shares of stock to be issued by a corporation. The total stated capital to be attributed to this number of shares may also be set, in which case the total stated capital divided by the number of shares determines the par value of each share. Alternatively, the incorporators may exclude from the articles any reference to a maximum stated capital or par value per share, instead designating the shares as no-par shares. In such cases, either the stockholders as a group or the board of directors is charged with the responsibility for dividing proceeds from the issuance of shares between capital and paid-in surplus. No-par shares outstanding are said to have a stated value per share equal to the increase in stated capital recorded upon their issue divided by the number of such shares issued. The significance of the par or stated value of a share of stock is tied to the concept of stated capital and the dividend limitations connected therewith; par or stated value is unlikely to be related to the stock's market value.

The "book value" of a share of stock is the shareholder's equity in the corporation as indicated by the balance sheet. If only one class of stock is outstanding, the entire net worth—including stated capital, paid-in surplus and retained earnings—divided by the number of shares outstanding, is the book value per share. If both preferred and common shares are outstanding, the total liquidation preference of the preferred shares is subtracted from net worth before computing the book value of the common shares.

Shares of stock are assignable personal property and are frequently bought and sold in the stock market. The market value of a share subsequent to its issue date may be substantially different from its book value. The general reason for the purchase of stock is to obtain cash receipts in the future in excess of the purchase price. The anticipated receipts either take the form of dividends or occur upon resale to another party who purchases it to obtain dividends. The corporation's capacity to pay dividends over a long period is affected by factors other than the capital funds it employs; hence the market value of shares may be higher or lower than their book value.

**Changes in Capital Structure.**—Stock dividends can be declared by the board of directors if sufficient authorized but unissued shares are available. A 5% stock dividend involves the issuance for no consideration of one share for each 20 shares held. The net worth of the corporation is not changed by this step, which is sometimes characterized as dividing the pie into more pieces. Unlike a cash dividend, a stock dividend paid to a holder of common shares is not considered income to the shareholder. The stated capital of the corporation is increased by a transfer from retained earnings or paid-in surplus.

A stock split is similar to a stock dividend in that the net worth is unchanged but the number of shares is increased. However, stated capital is not increased by a stock split. An example is the splitting of 1,000,000 shares of $10 par value into 2,000,000 shares of $5 par value. Occasionally the number of shares is reduced and the stated capital relating to each increased by a reverse stock split.

When a corporation whose stockholders enjoy the pre-emptive right wishes to raise capital funds through the issue of additional stock it first offers the stock to its shareholders in proportion to their holdings. Thus, if the new shares will increase the number of shares outstanding by 20%, a stockholder who owns 100 shares is entitled to purchase 20 shares. In order to assure the success of the rights offering, the subscription price on the new shares is usually set below the current market price. Accordingly, the right to purchase the new shares is valuable in itself, and these rights are frequently bought and sold.

Treasury shares are shares acquired by their issuer and held pending reissue or retirement. The acquisition by a corporation of its own shares is strictly regulated by law in order to prevent the circumvention of the stated capital restriction by returning assets to owners through the purchase of their shares to the detriment of creditors. (G. J. St.)

### GREAT BRITAIN AND THE COMMONWEALTH

**Great Britain.**—In Great Britain the fundamental difference between stock and shares is a technical one only, though the two words have acquired overtones of meaning which tend to differentiate them in general usage. Since 1862, the term "stock" has signified a subscribed fund resolvable into parts as small as pounds, shillings and pence for use as corporate capital or a loan. Stock is therefore divisible and transferable in any amount desired not lower than a fraction specified by practical considerations. The term "share" on the other hand is used when the subdivision of the capital is of uniform amount. Thus a holding of stock is described as "£100 stock" or "£100 worth of stock," while a holding of shares is called "100 £1 shares." Furthermore, stock may be bought or transferred in odd amounts, *e.g.,* £10 8*s.* 5*d.* stock, whereas shares must always be subscribed or exchanged in multiples of the specified face value, be it £1, 10*s.*, 5*s.* or even 1*s.* Thus a sale of fractions of a share is not permitted.

Dividends payable on British shares are always expressed in one of two forms: "a dividend of 6*d.* (or so much) per share" or "a dividend of five (or so much) per cent," the latter meaning a dividend equivalent to the named percentage on the face value of each share. If the shares are £1 shares, 5% is equivalent to 1*s.* per share, but if they are 10*s.* shares, it is equivalent to 6*d.* per share. Dividends are normally paid annually or twice-yearly, those in the latter case being called interim and final payments.

The market price of stock or shares, which is related to the dividend payments, is normally expressed either in shillings and pence (*e.g.,* 11*s.* 6*d.* or 27*s.* 4½*d.*) or in pounds and fractions of pounds (*e.g.,* 13¼, meaning £13 5*s.* 0*d.*, or, in the case of stock, 87⅝, meaning £87 12*s.* 6*d.* per £100 stock).

In addition to the annual return the price of stock and shares depends on the degree of risk attached to the holding. Stock is a term normally applied in Great Britain to a loan or debenture repayable within or at a certain specified time and repaying a fixed rate of interest until that date. Shares, however, usually represent permanent capital as opposed to loans and debentures and fall into three main categories, each of which implies a different degree of risk to shareholders. These are preference, ordinary and deferred.

Preference shares, like loans and debentures, usually receive a fixed return only, although occasionally they participate with the ordinary shares in any further profits. They are then called participating preference shares. In all cases preference shares, as their name implies, have a prior claim to profits earned and rank ahead of ordinary and deferred shares, both as to the dividend and as to repayment of capital in the event of liquidation. Thus, if a company earns £100,000 and the preference dividend (say 5% on £2,000,000 of £1 preference shares) requires the full £100,000, then the holders of ordinary shares get nothing. If the preference shares are cumulative, any arrears of dividends on them are carried forward until a sufficient profit is earned to pay off the accumulated arrears; and this must be done before any payment is made on the ordinary shares. If preference shares are not cumulative, once a preference dividend is not paid in any one year, the shareholders have no claim in respect of that dividend on any future profits.

Ordinary shares rank after preference shares but, whereas the preference shareholder is entitled to a fixed rate of dividend only if profits are made and to the return of the nominal value of his shares only in the event of a liquidation, in both cases the ordinary shareholder receives what is left. If the company has also issued deferred shares, however, it is the ordinary shareholder who receives a fixed return only (sometimes with participating rights), while the deferred shareholder receives what is left. A company seldom issues all three classes of shares; normally two only will be issued and, if these should be the first and the third, they are frequently called preferred ordinary and deferred ordinary.

In no case are the directors of a company bound to pay a dividend, however, and in practice a company will normally pay only a portion of its earned profit in any one year, frequently putting the surplus into reserve funds or development expenditures. The profits made in any one financial year are often expressed as a percentage of the issued capital, this percentage being known as earnings.

A company increases its capital by issuing additional shares. These may be issued either free as a bonus to existing shareholders, often termed a scrip bonus issue (*e.g.,* two shares for every three held, frequently abbreviated to "two-for-three scrip"), or at a price below their current market price as a partial bonus to shareholders. In the latter case, for example, if the market price of £1 shares already in issue is 85*s.*, new shares may be offered at 45*s.*, a holder of two shares being entitled to buy one new one at the lower price, or to sell his right in the market to anyone who will buy it. This type of issue is known as a rights issue and the above example would be "a one-for-two rights."

Throughout the British Commonwealth the concept of stock and shares resembles closely that current in Great Britain both in terminology and practice. The one country providing a striking exception to this is Canada, which has in many respects followed the U.S. pattern.

**Canada.**—In Canada the term "stock" frequently takes the place of the English term "share." Thus, although preference shares form part of the capital structure of Canadian companies, the ordinary shares are known collectively as "stock" and investors in that company are "stockholders" and not "shareholders." Furthermore, the terms "ordinary" and "deferred" are not normally used, the equity being known as "common" stock. This common stock is frequently "bearer" stock, as opposed to the "registered" shares common in Great Britain; *i.e.,* ownership is vested simply in the bearer and no nominal registration of specific ownership is made in the company's books. Unlike British shares, Canadian stock does not always have a specific nominal or face value; it is frequently designated "of no par value" (commonly abbreviated to NPV). Common stock of Canadian companies may be divided into two sorts, class A and class B, the latter only carrying voting rights and the former carrying either a degree of preferential treatment with regard to dividends and liquidation, or participating rights, or sometimes both. Dividends are expressed in Canada as so many dollars (or cents) per share and not as a percentage, and are frequently issued together with trading information quarterly, not yearly or half yearly as in Great Britain. The most important Canadian stock exchanges are those of Toronto and Montreal.

**Australia and New Zealand.**—Australian and New Zealand shares bear a marked similarity to those in Great Britain, although the deferred share is not normally found. Australian companies, however, unlike their British counterparts, sometimes issue unsecured registered notes. These fulfill the same function as a debenture stock, representing a loan repayable at or within a specified period; they are, however, issued in units not of £100 but of small denominations. Unsecured notes normally pay a fixed rate of interest but sometimes carry participating rights also. Occasionally they are convertible into ordinary shares. The leading stock exchanges of Australia are those of Melbourne and Sydney, while the main centre of share dealing in New Zealand is at Wellington. Australian shares enjoy a sizable following in the stock exchanges at Singapore and Hong Kong. Both these markets follow closely the British pattern and the former is the home market for Malayan rubber shares in which active dealings take place in London.

### OTHER COUNTRIES

Stocks and shares have formed an integral part of the economic development of almost every country in the world, both in assisting their various governments to raise the finances necessary for their administrative program and in providing the capital required by private concerns in each country. Owing to the different rates of growth in economic and industrial development, however, the degree to which comprehensive trading of stocks and shares has been centralized and developed varies widely. In this respect the stock exchanges in London and New York had, by 1900, established a predominant position both in breadth and volume of trading and this position has since been consolidated, but the following cities also have stock exchanges which have gained international recognition: Tokyo, Cairo, Amsterdam, Paris, Brussels, Milan, Geneva, Frankfurt am Main, Düsseldorf, Munich, Lisbon, Stockholm, Oslo and Vienna.

On all these exchanges dealings take place in governmental and provincial securities and other private bonds and shares of a national character and the concept of a share in each case is fundamentally the same as that in Great Britain, although there are many minor technical and terminological differences in the case of European and Asian countries. The capital structure of many European companies, as well as that of Japan, shows a marked preponderance of ordinary shares over preference shares, the latter forming a much smaller proportion of the total share capital than is customary in Great Britain. As against this, however, it is not unusual to find among companies of other countries different denominations of both ordinary and preference shares, a feature not found in Great Britain and alien to the British definition of a share. For example, Philips' Incandescent Lamp works, the Netherlands company whose shares, together with those of Unilever and Royal Dutch, had by 1958 achieved perhaps the widest international circulation of any non-British or U.S. industrial share, has issued both preference and ordinary shares in denominations of 1,000*f*, 100*f* and 50*f*. In certain countries, notably Belgium, it is common to find shares with no par value, or nominal face value, as with Canada.

As in Great Britain, shares issued in other countries normally entitle their holders to vote in matters concerning the administration of the company, but in some European countries, particularly Switzerland and the Netherlands, comprehensive steps are frequently taken to ensure that voting control does not fall into the hands of non-nationals. This goal is achieved in spite of the fact that European companies tend to have a larger number of small shareholders than their counterparts in Great Britain and the United States.

In almost all European countries with the exception of Great Britain and Italy, shares are "bearer" shares and not "registered" shares. A "bearer" share certificate is, as its name suggests, a certificate vesting ownership simply in the bearer (as with an English pound note), whereas a registered certificate specifically designates the owner or subscriber by name and implies his specific registration by name in the books of the company. A bearer share certificate normally has dividend coupons attached to it; *i.e.*, perforated slips entitling the bearer to his dividend on presentation at a bank. Partly because of this and partly because of the smaller scope and less highly developed organization of many European and Asian stock exchanges, banks in Europe and Asia tend to take a bigger and closer part in investment and share dealing than they do in Great Britain or the United States.

South Africa is the home of many of the leading gold mining companies whose shares have an active following on the London stock exchange (where they are known as Kaffirs). The home market for these issues, together with many other shares of a national and local character, is Johannesburg, where the concept of stock and shares is very similar to that in London. Dividends, however, are always expressed in shillings and pence per share and not as a percentage. These are normally paid twice yearly, while gold mining companies also issue quarterly reports to shareholders.

*See* also references under "Stock" in the Index.

BIBLIOGRAPHY.—A. A. Berle and G. C. Means, *Modern Corporation and Private Property* (1948); J. B. Lindon *et al., Buckley on the Companies Acts,* 13th ed. (1957); H. G. Guthmann and H. E. Dougall, *Corporate Financial Policy,* 2nd ed. (1948); R. H. Code Holland, *Poley's Law and Practice of the Stock Exchange,* 5th ed. (1932).

(B. P. W.)

**STOCKBRIDGE,** a town of Berkshire county, Mass., U.S., on the Housatonic river, is located 116 mi. W. of Boston and 138 mi. N.E. of New York city. A summer and autumn resort and a region of historic interest, there are, within its area, the Stockbridge Bowl, a lake that provides opportunities for boating and fishing; Ice Glen (where caverns are lined with ice even in midsummer); Monument mountain (1,750 ft.); and most of Tanglewood, the home of the Boston Symphony orchestra's summer centre and the Berkshire Symphonic festival. Also located in the town is the Riggs Centre, a clinic for psychiatric research and treatment.

In 1734 a plantation 6 mi. square was laid out for the Mohican Indians who had come from the Hudson valley when white settlements encroached upon their territory, and among whom Rev. John Sergeant had established a mission in 1734. In 1739 this Indian town was incorporated as the town of Stockbridge; Jonathan Edwards was in charge of the Indian church and school from 1750 to 1758. By 1800 nearly all the Indians had moved west.

The resident population of Stockbridge is over 2,000.

(R. C. L. S.)

**STOCK EXCHANGE,** an auction market for the purchase and sale of securities such as shares, stocks and bonds. Stock exchanges, also known as bourses, play important roles in the economic life of all major industrial nations. Their primary function is to provide a convenient means for persons to invest money in business enterprises and to liquefy their investments at any time by selling their securities. (*See* also BROKER; CORPORATION; INVESTMENTS: INDIVIDUAL; STOCK.)

This article is organized according to the following outline:



### I. UNITED STATES

There are three national stock exchanges in the United States: the New York Stock exchange, the American Stock exchange (formerly the New York Curb exchange) and the National Stock exchange (opened in 1962), all located in the city of New York. These exchanges account for about 90% of the total trading on organized exchanges in the United States. In addition, there are regional exchanges located in many of the large cities. Securities are also bought and sold in the over-the-counter market, which consists of brokers and investment bankers in all parts of the country who arrange their transactions by telephone or telegraph. *See* further OVER-THE-COUNTER MARKET.

### A. HISTORICAL BACKGROUND

The first informal organization of the New York Stock exchange took place in May 1792, although there had been trading in government securities some time before. A group of 24 merchants and brokers decided to charge a commission for acting as agents for other persons and to give preference to each other in the purchase and sale of securities. They operated under a buttonwood tree on Wall street except during inclement weather, when they went into a coffee shop.

From 1792 to 1817, interest in stocks and bonds rose as a result of the increase in government obligations and the growth of banks and insurance companies. During this period there was no restriction as to the time of operation or the number of brokers who could transact business. When the number of brokers became large, a group of them decided to organize formally. They adopted a simple constitution comparable to that of a small-town social club and called themselves the New York Stock and Exchange board. They agreed to accept the regular brokers as members, but each new member had to be sponsored by one of the existing members and then approved by the entire membership.

The crowded conditions in the street influenced the members to take permanent quarters inside. They rented a room at 40 Wall street for $200 a year. New members were required to pay an initiation fee of not less than $25, the amount varying with the location of the seat in the room. Each member was assigned a seat and the chairman called roll each day. An absence without excuse resulted in a fine. Continued absence resulted in expulsion. If a member did not attend regularly, it became uneconomical for him to hold his seat. (The use of the phrase, "seat on the exchange," stems from this time, when members were assigned particular seats when admitted. There are no seats on the present exchange, yet the term continues to denote membership.) During the day the chairman would call the name of each stock once, and any bids or offers would be heard for that stock and transactions effected. If a member called for a stock that had already been called, he was fined. The procedure was orderly and unexciting.

The American Civil War created much interest in speculation and the number of brokers interested in gaining seats increased. Since the number of members was limited, an outside group of brokers organized a separate exchange called the Open Board of Brokers. This group operated in uptown New York.

Because of the increased activity, a need arose for more adequate quarters for the New York Stock and Exchange board. Through contributions from members, the first building was erected. The construction of the building raised the problem of the transferability of memberships. Before this time, memberships were not transferable. Seats of deceased members were sold at auction and the proceeds given to charity. But since members now had an equity in the building, seats were made transferable in 1868. The price of a seat at that time reflected the equity of a member in the real estate as well as the value of the trading privileges.

With the advent of transferable memberships it was necessary to limit the number to protect each member's equity. The maximum number of seats was set at 533. In the meantime, however, competition was being felt from the younger members of the Open Board of Brokers, who operated at night as well as during the day. The older group had previously decided to close at 3 o'clock each afternoon. In 1869, the two groups consolidated to form the present New York Stock exchange, with members of the Open Board of Brokers admitted without cost. This brought the total membership to 887.

At about the same time, 173 new memberships were sold for $1,000 each, bringing the total seats to 1,060. By 1879 the building had become inadequate and 40 new memberships were sold at current prices to pay for the enlargement of the building. This brought total membership to 1,100. Later admissions increased it to 1,375.

### B. ORGANIZATION OF THE NEW YORK STOCK EXCHANGE

The New York Stock exchange is organized as a nonprofit unincorporated association. The government of the exchange is vested in a board of governors consisting of members, the chairman, the president of the exchange, and representatives of the public. The principal powers of the board are to elect officers, establish rules governing trading, impose penalties for violations of rules, supervise member firms and consider applications for listing. The board has a chairman and vice-chairman, but the chief officer of the exchange is the president. He is a paid employee of the association and must not be a member of the exchange. Subject to the approval of the board of governors, he selects officers to whom he delegates authority vested in him by the board.

The organization of the exchange was completely revised in 1938 in substantial accordance with the recommendations of the Conway committee, which had been formed for that purpose in 1937. Previously, the administrative problems were handled by the members. Since 1938, in addition to the paid president, the exchange has had several paid vice-presidents and a total payroll of about 1,800. This staff, however, continued to be subject to the direction of the board of governors and its standing committees. They may not hold memberships on the exchange. There is a department headed by an officer of the exchange for each standing committee. These departments, at the direction of their committees, perform the functions necessary to the proper administration of the exchange. Final responsibility and authority for decisions, however, rest with the committees.

**1. Admission of New Members.**—The first requirement for acquiring membership on the New York Stock exchange is to be in a position to meet the existing offering price. This price varies from time to time, depending on the amount of trading activity. In 1929, for example, a seat was sold for $625,000; in 1942 a seat was sold for $17,000. Once a potential member agrees to meet the offering price he must appear before a subcommittee on admissions with two members who act as his sponsors. By the time he appears before the subcommittee the secretary's office has gathered as much information about him as possible. He must have a record of honesty in business affairs, a knowledge of the functions of the exchange, financial stability and a definite purpose for acquiring membership other than for speculation on his own account. The exchange guards carefully against speculation in the price of memberships. If the application is approved by the subcommittee it is posted on the bulletin board of the exchange. If within two weeks no member submits evidence to indicate that the applicant should not be admitted, the board of governors takes final action. If the applicant borrows funds to purchase the seat, the lender must agree to subordinate his claims against the membership or proceeds of its transfer to all claims of the New York Stock exchange or any of its members.

The exchange also provides for an unlimited number of allied members. They must pledge themselves to abide by the constitution and the rules and become general partners in member firms. An allied member may not go upon the floor of the exchange unless he has permission of the board to serve as an alternate for a partner who is a regular member.

**2. Board of Arbitration.**—To handle disputes that arise between members, between members and allied members, and between members and nonmembers, the board of governors appoints a board of arbitration. In disputes involving nonmembers, the board of arbitration may be composed of some members who do not own seats on the exchange. There is a panel of about 100 members and 100 nonmembers who may be drawn upon to serve as arbitrators in disputes. The secretary's office handles the technical aspects of the dispute. Certain procedures are followed in filing the complaint, selecting arbitrators, covering costs of arbitration, and selecting time and place for the hearing.

**3. Committees.**—The function of the Committee on Member Firms is to ensure that member firms observe the regulations of the exchange. Even though a firm finances the purchase of a seat for a partner, the membership represents a personal franchise of the partner. Should the member sell his seat either voluntarily or involuntarily while in debt to the exchange or one of its members, the proceeds of the sale will be used first to pay those debts. On the other hand, the partnership must sign an agreement to the effect that it will assume the risks of fluctuations in the value of the membership where the firm is financing, in part or in whole, its purchase. All members have a right to retain their memberships, subject to making agreed payments to their firms for their seats. These are but a few of the regulations governing member firms.

Trading on the floor of the exchange is governed by rules of the exchange and by rules of the Securities and Exchange commission (SEC). It is the duty of the committee on floor procedure to see that these rules are observed. For example, specialists (see *Classes of Members,* below) are required to file with the exchange a report of all their transactions. These reports are checked for infractions of trading rules.

As with many private corporations, the New York Stock exchange was late in recognizing the importance of its relations with the public. While the exchange has had a public relations department for some time, it originally was concerned only with internal information and relations. With a reorganization in 1938, the exchange showed concern about its relations with the public. It launched an advertising campaign to urge investors to be cautious. It told the public about the purpose of the exchange and how the public could invest in corporate enterprise through careful employment of savings.

The principal function of the Executive Committee is to coordinate the functions of all other committees. Its members participate in the policy decisions of the various departments.

**4. The Trading Floor.**—All trading takes place on the floor of the exchange where there are several large U-shaped posts. Each stock is traded at only one post. The selection of a post for a new issue is based on the relative activity around the several posts as well as the existing location of issues in the same industry as the new issue. In selecting this post, the exchange is interested primarily in preventing congestion on the floor. When, for example, a new aircraft issue is listed, a post is selected around which the activity is relatively light and where no other aircraft issue is traded.

Members who are interested in buying or selling a particular issue will congregate around the post where it is traded. These members constitute what is called a "crowd." The Chrysler crowd, for example, includes all members who are standing at the post where Chrysler stock is bought and sold, and who are participating in the auction process. Some will be bidding for Chrysler stock; others will be offering it for sale. When there is a meeting of minds, a transaction is effected.

Pages, the only other persons allowed on the floor, record transactions as they are effected in the crowd. If the members involved agree that the transaction as repeated by the page is correct, the page walks to the open end of the post and sends the report, via pneumatic tube, to another floor in the building where machines send the report to other cities. In this manner, reports of the latest transactions are flashed to brokerage houses throughout the country.

Along the sides of the floor are several hundred telephones over which clerks receive orders from member firms. Since the floor of the exchange is large, two huge boards on the walls provide a medium of communication between a clerk and his broker. Each member has a number assigned to him. When a clerk receives an order on the telephone he flashes the number of his broker on this board. His broker, observing the signal, goes to his booth, picks up the order, and takes it out into the appropriate crowd. Telephone clerks are not allowed on the floor.

### C. Classes of Members

**1. Commission Brokers.**—These members make up the largest group among the members of the New York Stock exchange. They are partners of member firms and own seats on the exchange in order to execute orders for their customers. They are their customers' agents; through them customers from all over the world can meet at one place and trade in securities. For their services they charge commissions which constitute the principal source of income for member firms.

**2. Specialists.**—Specialists are another group of members. For each stock listed there is a specialist. There may be more than one for one stock and several stocks may be handled by one specialist. For each stock the specialist has a book in which he enters all limited orders (see *Types of Orders,* below) given him by commission brokers as well as the time they were received. He stands at his post all day; therefore, if he specializes in more than one issue, they must all be located at his post. Whenever he executes an order for another broker, the specialist charges a commission, but a customer whose order is executed by a specialist does not pay this commission. Instead, the commission broker must pay it. Therefore, the latter will give orders to specialists only when he cannot himself gain an execution in a reasonable length of time. The origin of the function of the specialist dates back to the days when trading took place in the street. Some of the older brokers who could not stand the physical strain of hurrying from one place to another decided to stay in one place and specialize in the trading of one or more issues.

**3. Two-Dollar Brokers.**—A third group of brokers is the so-called two-dollar brokers. They are not associated with member firms; they make their livelihood by executing orders for commission brokers who may become too busy to handle all their orders quickly. Suppose a commission broker receives two orders at the same time, one to buy 500 shares of an automobile manufacturer and the other to buy 100 shares of an aircraft builder. Since the posts at which these two stocks are traded are some distance from one another, he elects to execute the larger order himself and gives the smaller order to a two-dollar broker to execute. The latter charges a commission for his services equal to those charged by the specialist. The two-dollar broker also executes orders for members while the latter take time out for lunch or while they are away from the floor for other reasons. Several members of the board of governors are two-dollar brokers.

**4. Odd-Lot Dealers.**—The fourth group includes odd-lot dealers and brokers. The dealers act as principals in making up so-called round lots—100 shares or multiples thereof—to trade in the auction market from the odd-lot orders—less than 100 shares—which are received by member firms. While they act as principals, their primary function is to service the odd-lot customer and their main source of income is the commissions they charge for this service.

**5. Traders.**—The traders represent the final group of members. They buy and sell stock for their own account with the hope of making speculative profits. They are small in number and account for only a small percentage of the total transactions.

### D. Types of Orders

The market for every security listed on an organized exchange is an auction market. At all times there is a quotation for these securities which consists of the best bid and the best offer. The best bid comes from that broker in the crowd who is willing to pay as much or more than any other person for that stock and the best offer comes from the broker who is willing to sell stock at a price below that of any other offer. These brokers are buying and selling stock for their customers, and the prices which they bid or ask are those specified by the customer. All stocks are quoted in terms of dollars per share. Except for very low-priced stocks and those traded on the National Stock exchange, the smallest change in price is one-eighth of a dollar. Thus, a stock could sell for 50, $50\frac{1}{8}$ or $50\frac{1}{4}$. All orders in the auction market are for 100 shares or multiples thereof, except for some inactive stocks traded at post 30 where the unit of trading is less than 100 shares. Every stock has a symbol which identifies it and which speeds the handling of orders and reports of transactions.

**1. The Quotation.**—Let us suppose that the last price for GM (symbol for General Motors) was 50 and that several brokers in the GM crowd want to buy it. The highest bid is made by one broker who is willing to pay $49\frac{3}{4}$. Since no other broker is willing to pay as much, this broker's bid constitutes part of the quotation, even though there may be others willing to pay $49\frac{5}{8}$ or below. There are other brokers in the crowd who want to sell GM. The one who is willing to sell at the lowest price constitutes the best offer. Suppose he offers GM at $50\frac{1}{4}$. Others may be offering to sell at $50\frac{3}{8}$ or above. The quotation for GM, however, is $49\frac{3}{4}$–$50\frac{1}{4}$, or the best bid and best offer received from brokers in the crowd. This quotation appears above the post where GM is traded and is kept up to date by the specialist or his clerk inside the post. If the spread between the bid and ask prices for GM is too great to constitute a good market for the stock, it is the duty of the specialist in GM to bid higher than the best bid or to offer to sell at a price below the best offer. It is possible that several brokers may be bidding for GM at $49\frac{3}{4}$. In this case, the broker whose bid came first is the one who will have the opportunity to purchase the stock if anyone offers to sell at that price.

A complete quotation includes the size or the amount of stock available at the best bid and at the best offer. If there were three brokers each offering to buy 100 shares of GM at $49\frac{3}{4}$ and two brokers willing to sell 100 shares at $50\frac{1}{4}$, then the complete quotation would be $49\frac{3}{4}$–$50\frac{1}{4}$, 300–200. The size of the orders does not appear on the post where the bid and offer are shown. A broker may wish to know the size, however, and he will ask the specialist for that information. The specialist will reply: "$49\frac{3}{4}$ for 300, 200 at $50\frac{1}{4}$." The size is often an important factor in measuring the strength or weakness of the market at any one time. If there are considerably more shares available at the best bid than at the best offer, the market is stronger than if the reverse were the case.

The quotation may change even before the next execution. One of the brokers in the crowd may better the best offer by asking $50\frac{1}{8}$. The quotation now becomes $49\frac{3}{4}$ for 100, 100 at $50\frac{1}{8}$, which narrows the spread between the bid and ask and brings an execution nearer to realization. The broker who offered to sell at $50\frac{1}{8}$ may now decide that he may be able to get a better price and cancels his offer. Since there is still one broker in the crowd who is willing to sell at $50\frac{1}{4}$, his offer now becomes the best offer and the quotation is changed to $49\frac{3}{4}$–$50\frac{1}{4}$. These are the two principal methods by which a quotation changes before an execution is realized—through a better bid or offer or through a cancellation. Most of these bids and offers are made by commission brokers on behalf of their customers. If a customer changes his mind and bids a higher price he tells his broker to change his bid and this order is sent to the floor of the exchange where the commission broker receives the instructions to change the bid.

Suppose a broker who is bidding for GM now decides to meet the best offer. If the quotation is $49\frac{3}{4}$–$50\frac{1}{4}$, the broker says: "$50\frac{1}{4}$ for 100," meaning he is willing to buy at that price. An execution is effected at $50\frac{1}{4}$, and the quotation now is changed to include the next best bid and offer. If another broker is willing to bid $49\frac{7}{8}$ while another offers at $50\frac{3}{8}$, and these constitute the best bid and offer, the quote is changed to $49\frac{7}{8}$–$50\frac{3}{8}$. It is possible, however, that an execution will leave the quotation unchanged, for there may be more bids and offers at the same price.

**2. Market Orders.**—The simplest type of order which a customer can enter is a market order. If a customer enters a market order to buy 100 shares of a certain stock the commission broker will take that order into the crowd and announce his willingness to buy at the best offer. If the quote is $49\frac{7}{8}$–$50\frac{3}{8}$, he will buy stock for his customer at $50\frac{3}{8}$, for he holds a market order and must meet the best offer. If a customer wishes to sell 100 shares at the market, the broker enters the crowd and sells 100 shares at $49\frac{7}{8}$, which is the best bid. This is the only course of action a broker may take when executing a market order. A customer who enters a market order receives the worst possible price, from his point of view, within the range of the quotation. The broker, on the other hand, dares not try to get a better price for his customer through the auction process without specific instructions to do so. If he decided not to execute the market order at $50\frac{3}{8}$, but instead bid something less, trying to get a better price for his customer, it is possible that no one would offer to sell at less than $50\frac{3}{8}$ and that, while he is holding the order, the broker who is offering to sell at that price cancels that offer and offers stock at $50\frac{1}{2}$ instead. If the offering price continues to advance without an execution, the customer's broker may be forced finally to meet an offering price higher than the one that existed when he entered the crowd. If this happened, the broker would be forced to account for the difference to his customer out of his own pocket. For example, if he is forced to buy at $50\frac{5}{8}$ because he withheld a market order which could have been executed at $50\frac{3}{8}$, he must make up $\frac{1}{4}$ of a dollar per share from his own funds. All orders are time-stamped when they reach the floor, and it is a simple procedure to check the quotation at the time the order was received. For this reason, a market order should be executed immediately. The customer who enters the market order should be aware, however, that he must meet the best offer, which is the highest price in the quotation range, if he wishes to buy stock and that he must meet the best bid, which is the lowest price in the quotation range, if he wishes to sell.

**3. Limited Orders.**—Any order other than a market order is called a limited order. Referring again to the hypothetical quotation of $49\frac{7}{8}$–$50\frac{3}{8}$, a customer may wish to buy 100 shares but does not want to pay $50\frac{3}{8}$, the price he would be forced to pay if he entered a market order. He is willing to pay no more than $49\frac{1}{2}$, so he enters a limited buy order at that price. When the telephone clerk receives this order on the floor, he may decide not to bother his broker, who may be executing market orders in other crowds, so he sends the order to the specialist via pneumatic tube. The specialist receives the order, time-stamps it, and enters it in his book. The order will not be executed until someone offers to sell at $49\frac{1}{2}$. This may take several hours or even days. The customer will be notified as soon as he gets an execution, but he cannot expect to get confirmation within a few minutes after he enters the order, as is the case for a market order. If he has decided that he is unwilling to pay more than $49\frac{1}{2}$ he must be willing to wait until someone offers stock at that price. It may be possible that he will get an execution below that price, for a limited order becomes a market order as soon as an execution of $49\frac{1}{2}$ is reached. It is a modified type of market order, however, for it cannot be executed above $49\frac{1}{2}$ but can be executed below that price. The procedure for executing a limited order to sell is exactly the same as that for limited buy orders. The former, of course, is entered above the market price, for the customer wants to receive more for his stock than the best bid. A customer who wants to buy stock but does not want to meet the best offer may nevertheless enter a limited order which betters the best bid, such as a limited buy order at 50. In this case, the quote would be changed to 50–$50\frac{3}{8}$, with the bid representing the customer's order. Under such circumstances, the broker might take the order into the crowd and bid 50, rather than give it to the specialist, in order to save the commission he would have to pay the specialist for executing it. Where a customer enters a limited order to buy at a price which is above the best offer, because he did not know the quotation at the time, the order will be executed as a market order.

**4. Stop-Loss Orders.**—Another type of limited order is called a stop-loss order. Suppose a customer buys 100 shares of a certain stock at 50 but is unwilling to take a loss of more than three dollars per share. He may protect himself by entering a stop-loss order at 47. This order is entered on the specialist's book. If the stock falls to 47 the specialist tries to sell it. This type of order, however, does not protect against a loss of more than three points, for it becomes a market order as soon as the stock drops to 47. If the stock continues to fall in price, it is likely that the best bid will be something less than 47 after an execution at that price. Since the stop-loss has become a market order, it will be executed at the best bid, which may be $46\frac{1}{2}$.

The stop-loss order is also used to protect profits. If stock bought at 48 goes to 53, the owner may wish to hold the stock and still protect part of his paper profit. In this case, he might enter a stop-loss order at 50. Should the stock fall back to 50, it will be sold at or near that price and the owner will realize some profit. If, on the other hand, the price of the stock continues to rise, the owner can enter stop-loss orders at progressively higher prices, thus protecting more of his profits while letting them increase.

It is also possible to enter a buy stop-loss order. This type is used to limit losses or protect gains when a customer has sold short. A customer sells short when he sells something he does not own. Of course, he must deliver stock when he sells it, and since he does not own it, he borrows some stock from someone who does and delivers this stock to the buyer. At some time in the future he will be forced to buy the same number of shares from someone else in order to repay the lender. An individual sells short when he believes a particular stock will fall in price. He sells short at a relatively high price and hopes to cover his short sale—buy the stock later to repay the lender—when the stock has fallen to a lower price.

Suppose an investor sells a certain stock short at 50. He decides to limit his losses to three dollars per share, so he enters a buy stop-loss order at 53. Should the stock rise to 53, his order will be executed. Should it drop to 45, however, he could enter a buy stop-loss order at 48, thus protecting two points' profit per share while letting his profits build up if the stock continues to fall.

**5. Stop Orders.**—Stop orders, of which stop-loss orders are a type, are often employed by chartists or persons who believe that a stock has resistance levels. An investor may feel that if a certain stock does not reach 50 it will probably go down to 40. He may also feel that if it does reach 50 or above it may go to 60. If the stock is selling at 48 the investor may enter a buy stop order at 51. This order is entered on the specialist's book. As soon as it reaches 51 the specialist will buy 100 shares. According to the analysis the stock will now probably go up to 60. If the stock does not reach 50, the specialist will not buy it and the stock, if it moves as anticipated, will go down to 40. The buy stop order differs from the limited buy order in that it is entered above the market while the latter is entered below the market. It differs from a buy stop-loss order only in its use. The former is used when one has no position in the stock. The latter is used when one is short in the stock. A sell stop order, on the other hand, is entered below the market and the procedure is reversed.

**6. Time Limits.**—A customer may wish to limit the length of time on a limited order. He may do so by telling his broker that the order is good for today only, good this week (G.T.W.), good this month (G.T.M.) or good until canceled (G.T.C.). If the order is not executed within the time limits, it will be canceled. A customer may cancel an order at any time, however, even though he did not so designate at the time it was entered. If orders do not carry a specific time limit, they are considered open orders. One danger of an open limited order is that the customer may forget about having entered it. It may be executed for him later, to his surprise. Most brokerage houses guard against this possibility by sending monthly notices to customers concerning open orders which they are holding for them.

The price of certain types of limited orders may be changed by the specialists when a stock sells "ex-dividend" (see *Glossary*, below.) If a stock is paying $1.25 every quarter, it will drop in price one and one-quarter points when it sells ex-dividend. This drop is exclusively due to the stock going ex-dividend, not to any fundamental or technical factors in the market. Therefore, on limited open buy orders and on limited open sell stop orders the specialist will reduce the price by one and one-quarter points. This accounts for the drop in the price of the stock due to its selling ex-dividend, and leaves the order, therefore, in exactly the same position as it was previously. Stop orders to buy or limited sell orders are not reduced. Where the dividend is in a fraction not divisible by the minimum trading range, the price is reduced to the nearest higher fraction.

*See* also LISTED SECURITIES; CURB MARKET. (F. GR.)

## II. GREAT BRITAIN

**1. Historical Background.**—London was once the greatest of the world's stock exchanges in the range and volume of its transactions; and even after New York's rise to rival importance in the 20th century the range of London's business covered every corner of the earth and every class and type of security. It was not until the latter part of the 18th century that the London stockbrokers definitely formed themselves into a stock exchange with premises of their own. They had been in the habit of meeting and doing business in the Royal exchange and neighbouring places, but in 1773 those who had hitherto met at Jonathan's (a coffeehouse in Change alley) moved to a room in Sweeting's alley to which the name of the stock exchange was formally given, the building becoming known as the Stock Exchange Coffeehouse or tavern. Business grew apace, and in 1801 a group of members raised £20,000 of capital in 400 shares of £50 each for the purpose of providing an adequate building and acquired a site in Capel court, Bartholomew lane.

The new building was opened in 1802. At that time the members of the stock exchange numbered about 500. Rules were drawn up for the conduct of business and for regulating membership of the house. It was provided that all future members should be admitted by ballot, and members were required to pay a subscription of ten guineas each for themselves and five guineas for their clerks. It was the general intention that the shares should be held by members, but there were always a large number of members who did not hold shares. The first extension was made in 1823 when the floor space was nearly doubled by the addition of a second room for dealings in foreign stock. In 1854 the two rooms with some small additions were rebuilt as one in the form of a dome with two transepts. Several subsequent extensions of this building were made, the principal one being in 1885 when another dome was added. In 1953 a public gallery was constructed. The stock exchange building occupies the greater portion of the triangular area formed by Throgmorton street, Bartholomew lane and Old Broad street.

**2. Organization.**—The control and administration of the assets and activities of the London Stock exchange have from June 1945 been in the hands of a body called the council of the stock exchange. After June 24, 1954, by which date the last ex officio members dating back to an earlier regime were compelled to retire, all members of the council (numbering from 30 to 36) were elected annually from and by the general membership. The introduction of the council to replace the earlier administrative bodies was accompanied by other revisions. Among these was the cessation of the earlier practice of distributing profits to the proprietors. In Dec. 1947, paid-up capital was reduced from £720,000 to £1,000 by writing down the paid-up capital value of each share from £36 to a nominal value of 1*s*. In compensation for the reduction of capital and surrender of rights to dividends on these 1*s*. shares, members received two £4 cumulative redeemable annuities for each share held. These annuities are redeemable by purchase at any time and any price, or by drawings after March 1, 1958, at £100 for each annuity; and they may be reissued any time. One important result of this change was that the purchase of a share qualification for membership was abolished. It was provided that each member should hold at least one share for voting purposes, to be obtained on application to the council.

The discipline of the stock exchange is very strict, and the council deals severely with members guilty of improper conduct. It has power to suspend or expel a member. The council also settles disputes between members and between members and their clients.

Securities cannot be quoted on the stock exchange except by permission of the council, and conditions have to be fulfilled before that permission is granted; this regulation marks a state of affairs sharply different from, and very much more satisfactory than, the ruling prior to World War I by which any security could be dealt in without permission and grave abuses occasionally arose.

**3. Membership.**—The annual income of the stock exchange is derived from the annual subscriptions of members and their clerks, entrance fees paid by new members and quotation fees. Since 1904, the only method by which a person may ordinarily become a member is to obtain a nomination (by purchase) from an existing member who must retire in his favour. Nominations may be obtained from a former member, or, if he has not disposed of his nomination, from the legal personal representative of a deceased member. Nominations, which are personal and nontransferable, are usually purchased, and the cost may range between £40 and £2,000. A candidate for membership must be recommended by three members, who become sureties for him during the first four years for £500 each, or £1,500 altogether. A certain number of clerks who have completed four years' service are admitted each year without nomination; for these, only two sureties of £300 each are needed, their liability extending for four years. Membership is for 12 months only, so that everyone who wishes to remain a member must apply to the committee for reelection. By the 1960s there were approximately 3,400 members of the stock exchange, employing more than 2,000 clerks (of whom about 1,200 had right of entry to the floor of the house).

**4. Business.**—By custom, each market has a special place allotted to it; for instance, the space immediately in front of the World War memorial is the market for British government securities and other gilt-edged stocks. Dealers or jobbers in these securities take up their posts in this space every day, and dealers in other classes of securities similarly occupy the floor space allotted to their particular markets. In this way the locality of a market can be readily and easily found by the brokers who go to the house to buy or sell securities for their clients. There is an important distinction between brokers and dealers. Brokers are not allowed to deal on their own account, nor can dealers act as brokers—this is the vital difference. The dealer or jobber occupies a position similar to that of the wholesale dealer in commodities. He deals in a particular group of securities, say oil shares, and his function is to buy oil shares when they are offered to him and to sell them if they are wanted. He quotes two prices for a share, his buying price, which is the lower, and his selling price, which is the higher, and the difference represents his profit. A broker acts for the public which desires to buy or sell securities. Ordinarily, both for buying and selling securities, though in certain circumstances only for buying, a commission is charged by the broker.

When a broker has bought or sold shares he usually enters on a printed slip the name of the shares and the price at which the business was done; he then signs the slip and drops it into one of the boxes provided for the purpose inside the house. These slips are all collected, and the prices are printed that evening in the official list. This is what is known as the marking of bargains.

Except in the gilt-edged market, every bargain that a broker executes for his client is "for the account," unless otherwise specified. This means that the bargain will be completed (*i.e.,* the stock handed over and paid for) on the next settling day. The usual period of the account is a fortnight, but there are four 21-day accounts in the course of a year. Settling days are usually fixed for a Tuesday; the passing of tickets—ticket day—takes place on a Wednesday; and making-up day is Tuesday, prices for the settlement of current securities being fixed in the morning. A broker on executing an order for a client sends him a contract note which sets forth the details of the transaction, the price obtained or to be paid, the amount of brokers' commission, stamp and transfer fee and the amount of the contract stamp. Later, as settlement day approaches, a further note is sent to a client who has bought stock, requesting him to forward the purchase money. The bargain may be "closed" in the same account, that is, stock purchased may be sold (and vice versa) before settlement is due; in this case the client is not required to pay the full consideration (or deliver the stock), but merely receives or pays the difference between the buying and the selling price.

This latter procedure is one of the commoner methods of speculation. Speculation differs from genuine investment in that the genuine investor normally buys for income purposes or steady capital appreciation, whereas the speculator operates in anticipation of a quick movement in the share price. He may buy in anticipation of a rise or sell in anticipation of a fall. He may do this in the hope of closing the bargain at a profit before he is called upon to pay for or to deliver the stock. Before 1930 facilities for buying and holding stock without paying for it (contango) and for lending shares to speculators who had sold them without possession (backwardation) were commonly employed. Since then, although these facilities are available, such transactions are less common. In 1958 reintroduction of options offered alternative facilities that largely replaced contango and backwardation.

(C. J. Mi.; E. Mt.; B. P. W.)

## III. OTHER EXCHANGES

There are three types of markets on the Paris bourse: the official market or *parquet;* the curb market or *marché des courtiers;* and the free market or *marché hors-cote.* The official stockbroker or *agent de change* on the *parquet* has a transferable monopoly (now subject to governmental sanction), must act only as an agent and must not recommend the purchase or sale of securities to his clients. He is a sworn government official, subject to close supervision. Business is divided into cash (*au comptant*) transactions and transactions for the term or for future delivery and settlement (*à terme*). Both investors and speculators use the more advantageous term market. At the end of each month, all open accounts are settled through the central liquidation service. On the curb market and the free market the *courtiers,* like the *agents de change,* have a transferable monopoly, which, however, covers securities not quoted on the official market. They are not government officials but only commission agents. The free market comprises all shares quoted neither on the *parquet* nor on the *marché des courtiers.* A new share is generally first quoted on the free market and then, as it steadies, rises to the *parquet.*

During their occupation of the Netherlands in World War II the Germans tried to disrupt business on the Amsterdam stock exchange as much as they could; not until 1953 were the old regulations re-established. The Stock Exchange union, though a private association, is subordinate to the minister of finance, who has the right to regulate the exchange's opening and closing and to approve the listing of new securities. The Amsterdam banks are members of the stock exchange, so that many transactions are effectuated not on the exchange itself but in the banks; such internal clearings, however, are based on the official quotations and governed by the regulations.

The most important Italian stock exchange is in Milan. The rules governing Italian stock exchanges are fixed by law; they are established and supervised by the government and the *agente di cambio* is a public official appointed by presidential decree, with a rate of commission fixed by the treasury. Direct negotiations by word of mouth can be conducted only by these *agenti* or their representatives. Methods of trading include: transactions *a contanti* (for cash), almost entirely confined to securities of fixed value; transactions *a termine* (for the term), concerned with shares, *i.e.,* the majority of business; and transactions *a premio,* of which option dealing alone is fairly widespread. Settlement takes place at the end of the month, through clearing houses.

## IV. GLOSSARY OF STOCK EXCHANGE TERMS

*Accounts.*—In British usage, accounts are the periods into which the stock exchange year is divided. Usually 24 in number, they are normally of 14 days' duration; sometimes they are of 21 days because of holidays.

*Arbitrage.*—The adjustment of anomalies in values between two different markets, *e.g.,* between London and Johannesburg. (*See* Arbitrage.)

*Bear.*—Originally a term limited in its application to a person who sold shares which he did not own, in the belief that he could buy them at a lower price when the time came for delivery. It has since been extended to cover any market operator who anticipates that prices will fall. Cf. *Bull.*

*Bearer Stock or Bond.*—Securities for which registration of ownership by the company concerned is unnecessary for a good title to pass from one person to another.

*Bid.*—Term indicating the price one is willing to pay for shares. Also the price which a buyer has declared that he will pay; commonly, therefore, the lower of the two prices quoted by a jobber or dealer.

*Blue Chip.*—An American expression also widely used in Britain to describe ordinary shares of the highest investment calibre.

*Bonus Issue.*—See *Capitalization Issue.*

*Bourse.*—A European term for a stock exchange, derived from French usage and first used for the Paris exchange.

*Bucket Shop.*—This term refers to a type of brokerage house that once flourished but is now illegal. It was not a brokerage firm in the true sense, for its operators merely accepted orders from customers without placing them on the market. The bucket shop operator gambled that customers were wrong in their judgment of the market, and that he would later be able to buy or sell the stock at more favourable prices.

*Bull.*—An investor who expects that prices will rise. The term was formerly used chiefly to describe speculators who bought shares which they hoped to sell at a profit before settlement day, when they would have to pay for them. A bull market is one in which prices are rising.

*Buying Limit.*—An order to buy shares at a price below the current market price. It is given to a broker to enable the would-be purchaser to take immediate advantage of a fall in price—which may be short-lived—without the necessity of the broker's referring to the client.

*Buy or Cancel.*—A customer may give his broker an order to buy today or cancel. If the order is not completed that day, the order is automatically canceled.

*Capital Gain.*—A profit from the sale of securities or other capital assets. *See* CAPITAL GAINS, TAXATION OF.

*Capitalization Issue.*—The official description in Great Britain of a scrip issue; also known as a bonus issue or, in the U.S., as a stock dividend. This expression means the issue by a company, to existing shareholders, of shares for which payment is not required. It represents the capitalization of reserves; to the extent that these have been accumulated from annual profits, it is a formal acknowledgment that the ploughing-back of profits in past years is the equivalent of the re-investment of those profits in the company.

*Chart Reader.*—Some investors and speculators employ charts which depict such data as the daily market averages, the market prices of individual stocks, or the volume of sales. They think they perceive patterns in formation, the completion of which can be anticipated profitably.

*Close to Close.*—A price made by British jobbers indicating that they are prepared to deal $\frac{1}{64}$ of a £ (*i.e.*, $3\frac{3}{4}d.$) either side of a specified price. For example, "seven-eighths close to close" = $17s.\ 2\frac{1}{4}d.$ to $17s.\ 9\frac{3}{4}d.$

*Closing.*—Buying or selling to close a bargain opened in the same account.

*Cum.*—Prefix meaning "with." "Cum all" means "with all advantages"; cum cap., "with capitalization rights"; cum div., "with dividend"; cum rights, "with rights."

*Customers' Man.*—The customers' man is the "contact man" for the brokerage firm by whom he is employed. He accepts and solicits orders from customers, advises them in their trading, and comments on the market outlook.

*Daylight Trading.*—Daylight trading refers to the practice of disposing of all stocks purchased during a single session.

*Dealing for New Time.*—A British term for the purchase or sale of securities during the two market days that precede the first day of an account. In "dealing for new time" the same stamp duty and commission concessionary rules apply as for "deals for the account." The jobber will, however, quote a higher price.

*Discretion.*—Concession of freedom by a client to a broker to act as he thinks fit, generally limited to a stated margin.

*Dollar Averaging.*—The investment of the same number of dollars in a given stock at regular intervals regardless of the price of the stock. Advocates of this procedure maintain that, over the long haul, it yields better results than the practice of waiting to buy until the stock seems to be low

*Dow-Jones Averages.*—In the United States, the average prices of three categories of stocks—industrials, railroads, and utilities. The industrial average is based on the selling prices of 30 well-known industrial stocks; the rail average is based on the prices of 20 representative railroad stocks; and the utility average on the prices of 15 utility stocks (gas and electric companies). There is also a comprehensive average of all the 65 stocks combined.

*Either Side.*—Term used to indicate that a quotation is $\frac{1}{32}$ (or $7\frac{1}{2}d.$) either side of a specified price. For example, "either side of the seven" means either side of $\frac{7}{16}$ and would indicate a range of from $\frac{13}{32}$ to $\frac{15}{32}$. If the "big figure" which (by implication) precedes it were 3, then the price quoted would be $68s.$ to $69s.\ 4\frac{1}{2}d.$

*Ex-dividend.*—When a company announces a dividend to stockholders of record as of a certain day, the books of the corporation are closed on that day for the payment of the dividend. Purchasers of the stock after the books are closed do not receive the dividend, and the stock is said to sell "ex-dividend."

*Flat.*—Bonds are usually quoted and sold "and interest." Bonds in default, however, are sold "flat," since no interest is being paid.

*Floating Supply.*—The floating supply is that portion of the outstanding stock which is usually held for speculative purposes, and which is available for trading purposes at or near the current market price.

*Gilt-edged.*—Originally, writing paper of the finest quality, and hence first-class bills of exchange. Now most commonly applied to British government securities, dominion and colonial government stocks, United Kingdom corporation issues, etc.

*Growth Stock.*—The stock of a company which gains in value over a period of time more than the general market. The company usually has sales and earnings growth prospects which are greater than those of the economy.

*G.T.C.*—This is an abbreviation for "good 'til canceled" and refers to a limited price offer which remains open until canceled.

*Kaffirs.*—Familiar name given to South African gold mining shares. The market in which they are dealt—the particular spot inside the stock exchange premises—is sometimes called the Kaffir circus.

*Loan Crowd.*—The loan crowd is composed of exchange members who are willing to borrow or lend stocks.

*Long.*—A buyer or holder of securities is said to be "long" of the market or "long" of stock if he has more of a particular security than he has contracts to deliver. The longs are usually those who have bought expecting a rise in prices.

*Margin.*—When a customer borrows money from his broker to buy stocks, he is said to have bought stock on margin. In the United States the federal reserve board sets limits as to how much a broker can lend on stock transactions. *See* MARGIN.

*Mixer.*—A security which, although too speculative to justify a large holding in relation to the size of the total portfolio, is recommended for "mixing purposes," *i.e.*, for raising the average yield.

*New Time.*—This British expression describes the account, also called "new account," following the one in which dealings are taking place. For the two days preceding the new account, brokers may deal for "new time" so that settlement does not take place until the settlement day of the following account.

*Not to Press (NTP).*—Short for "not to press for delivery"; expression used when a jobber sells shares which he has not got and which he believes may take him some time to acquire.

*Offer.*—A term indicating the price one is willing to sell his shares for. It is synonymous with "ask," and is distinguished from "bid," the price one is willing to pay for shares.

*Option.*—Literally, a right to choose. In stock exchange matters it refers usually to "single options" and "double options." Single option means the right (purchasable for a consideration) to choose whether or not at a given future date to buy ("call option") a given security for a given price; or, similarly, the right to choose whether or not to sell ("put option") a given security for a given price. In both cases the right must be exercised within a given period, normally three months. A double option, sometimes known as a straddle, gives the right to decide at the end of the period whether or not to buy or sell.

*Price-Earnings Ratio.*—The ratio between the selling price of a stock and the company's earnings per share. Many investors feel that a stock that sells for more than 20 times its earnings is overpriced.

*Rights Issue.*—An issue of shares to existing shareholders in a fixed proportion to those they already hold, to be purchased at a given price, which is generally below the market price of the existing shares.

*Selling Against the Box.*—When the holder of securities, possessing stocks which he is holding "long," sells an equal amount of stock "short," he is said to be "selling against the box."

*Short.*—A buyer or holder of securities is said to be "short" of the market or "short" of stock if he has contracted to deliver at some future date more of a particular stock than he holds. The shorts are principally those who have "sold short" in anticipation of a drop in prices, in which event they would buy at the lower price in time for delivery.

*Split.*—Frequently when the price of a stock rises to levels which discourage the average investor, the company may split its shares to reduce the price. For example, a stock selling at 200 may be split four shares for one and the price would drop to 50. The old stockholder now has four times as many shares but they are worth no more in total than before the stock split.

*Spread.*—The difference between the bid and asked prices.

*Stop-loss Order.*—The stop-loss order or stop order is an order to sell at the market if and when a transaction occurs at or below a stated price. By using "stops" holders of stocks limit their losses in a declining market.

*Ticker.*—A term used to describe the transmission of stock prices to brokerage offices all over the country. Appearing on the ticker tape are prices of securities which represent transactions completed only seconds before.

*Warrant.*—A certificate giving the holder the right to purchase a fixed number of shares of stock at some future time at a fixed price. It is properly known as a stock purchase warrant.

*Wash Sale.*—When two individuals agree to buy from or sell to each other securities to stimulate market activity, and where no intention to exchange goods or money is present, a wash sale is said to have been effected. This is an illegal transaction on the exchange floor and members are liable to expulsion when discovered engaging in it.

*Yield.*—Interest on bonds or dividends on stock expressed as a percentage of the amount invested on an annual basis.

*See* also references under "Stock Exchange" in the Index.

(B. P. W.; F. GR.)

*See* George L. Leffler and L. C. Farwell, *The Stock Market,* 3rd ed. (1963); C. A. Dice and W. J. Eiteman, *Leading World Stock Exchanges: Trading Practices and Organization* (1964).

**STOCKHAUSEN, KARLHEINZ** (1928– ), German composer and prominent theoretician of serial music. Born Aug. 22, 1928, at Mödrath, near Cologne, Stockhausen entered the Musikhochschule in Cologne in 1947 and, later, the university.

In 1950 he studied composition with Frank Martin, and in 1951 he met Herbert Eimert, who arranged performances of his works on the radio, and also at the summer course of contemporary music in Darmstadt. In 1951 he married a former fellow pupil, Doris Andreae, and they went to Paris. In Paris, Stockhausen studied with Olivier Messiaen, and also, for a time, with Darius Milhaud, and became interested in *musique concrète*. In 1953 he returned to Cologne, where, together with Eimert, he founded the celebrated electronic music studio, of which he became director in 1963. From 1954 to 1956, at the University of Bonn, he embarked on a study of phonetics, acoustics, and of information theory with H. Meyer-Eppler, and these ideas continued to influence his theories and practice. From 1957 he gave lectures at Darmstadt and, from 1958, gave concert and lecture tours in Europe and in North America. From 1955 he was coeditor of the theoretical journal for contemporary music, *Die Reihe* ("The Series").

His compositions include: *Kontrapunkte* (1952), for ten instruments; *Zeitmasse* (1955–56), for five woodwind instruments; *Refrain* (1959), for three players; *Zyklus* (1959), for one percussion player. His orchestral and choral works include: *Gruppen* (1957–59), for three orchestras; *Carré* (1959–60), for four orchestras and four choruses; *Momente* (1958), for soprano, four choruses, and 13 players. His electronic works include: *Elektronische Studien* I and II (1953); *Gesang der Jünglinge* ("Song of the Three Children"; 1956); text from the *Benedicite*, for five-track electronic tape, incorporating a prerecorded human voice; *Kontakte* (1960), *a*, for tape (four tracks), piano, and percussion, and, *b*, for electronic tape alone; and *Teletape* (1966), for electronic tape, incorporating prerecorded excerpts from Oriental, African, and Western music. He has also written a group of eleven piano pieces, *Klavierstücke I–XI*.

Stockhausen explored, in his theory and in his compositions, certain fundamental psychological and acoustical aspects of music, and has been relatively unconcerned with those aspects which stem from any particular historical tradition. "He who does not recreate traditions anew every day is three times dead," he has said. These preoccupations were intensified by the development of electronic music, and the vast extension of its musical possibilities rendered most traditional conventions obsolete; at the same time, as a counterbalance to the increasing mechanization of music, Stockhausen endeavoured to give performers an additional role in creating a composition afresh, even to the extent of determining the form of a piece.

In each work certain elements (or "parameters") are played off against one another, simultaneously and successively—as the titles of his compositions suggest: in *Kontrapunkte*, for instance, pairs of instruments and extremes of note values confront one another in a series of dramatic "cadenzas" and pedal points; in *Gruppen*, fanfares and passages of varying speed are flung from one orchestra to another, giving an extra dimension of an apparent movement in space; in *Zeitmasse* various rates of *accelerando* and decelerando oppose one another. In his electronic music these procedures are taken still further. In *Kontakte* there is "contact" between the instruments and the electronic sounds they respond to. In addition, there are points of contact between the different electronic sounds themselves: all of them are created in similar ways; one pitch (frequency) is set in motion and reiterated at a certain rate—if this reaches a certain frequency a new pitch is created. In this way every sound, and complex of sounds, or texture (*Momente*) can be heard in relation to the others.

In such works as *Klavierstücke XI*, the music consists of separate fragments, and the performer is given a certain freedom in regard to dynamics, attack, and even overall form; *i.e.*, the order or number of fragments played.

In *Plus-minus*, the number of players is free, and in *Mixture* there are "moments" for different groups—woodwind, brass, percussion, strings (*pizzicato*), and strings (bowed), and a selection may be made of these, in a variety of orders.

In these later works the influence of John Cage (*q.v.*) may be seen in the relaxation of Stockhausen's earlier preoccupation with rigid formal procedures.

*See* also MUSIC, 20TH-CENTURY.

BIBLIOGRAPHY.—K. Stockhausen, *Texte zur elektronischen und instrumentalen Musik*, 2 vol. (1963, 1964); Karl H. Wörner (ed.), "Karlheinz Stockhausen," no. 6 in the series *Kontrapunkte* (1963). *See* also prefaces by Stockhausen to scores of *Gruppen* and *Plus-minus*, and to phonograph records of *Zyklus* and *Kontakte*. (D. J. SI.)

**STOCKHOLM,** a *län* (county) of east central Sweden, surrounding the capital city, which is the seat of its *landshövding* (governor) but is administratively separate from it. Area 2,877 sq.mi. (7,452 sq.km.). Pop. (1965) 591,214. *See* STOCKHOLM (city).

**STOCKHOLM,** the capital city of Sweden, is in east central Sweden, at the junction of Mälaren (Lake Mälar) and Saltsjön (an arm of the Baltic). Pop. (1965) 787,183. Land area 72 sq.mi. (186 sq.km.). Greater Stockholm, which includes 18 surrounding communes, covers a land area of 522 sq.mi. (1,354 sq.km.). Pop. (1965) 1,190,685.

On a number of islands and peninsulas, the town is often called "the City on the Water" or "the Venice of the North." Its medieval heart, Gamla Staden (the Old Town) lies on Stadsholmen, a small island formed by two short streams through which the waters of Mälaren flow into the Baltic with its thousands of skerries (the Stockholm Archipelago). Stadsholmen and the adjacent Riddarholmen, Helgeandsholmen, and Strömsborg islet are known as the "town between the bridges." The Old Town still partly retains its medieval plan, with narrow streets and ancient buildings. There stand the Italianate Royal Palace (rebuilt, 1697–1754) of Nicodemus Tessin the Younger, Stockholm's cathedral, Storkyrkan, founded in the 13th century (but rebuilt later), Riddarhuset (the House of Nobility), from the mid-17th century, and the Stock Exchange—also the seat of the Swedish Academy—built in the 1770s. Along the eastern shore runs the old quay, Skeppsbron, with its trading houses mainly from the 17th and 18th centuries, where stands J. T. Sergel's statue of Gustavus III (1808). On Helgeandsholmen (the Island of the Holy Ghost) north of the palace are the late-19th-century Riksdagshuset (the House of Parliament) and Riksbanken (the National Bank). In the Old Town and on Riddarholmen to the west are most of the government departments, many being housed in 17th-century palaces. On the site of an old Franciscan monastery lies Riddarholmskyrkan, the royal memorial church since the time of Gustavus II Adolphus (d. 1632).

From the Royal Palace, the late-18th-century Norrbro (North Bridge) leads over to Norrmalm, the commercial centre of Stockholm with lively business streets, such as Drottninggatan, Regeringsgatan, Kungsgatan, Vasagatan, and Sveavägen. Opposite the palace, at the bridge abutment, is Gustav Adolfs Torg (square) with an equestrian statue of the king (1796), flanked by the Foreign Office (late 18th century) and the Royal Opera (opened 1898). East of the opera is Karl XII's Torg and Kungsträdgården (the King's Garden), a popular meeting place in the summer with concerts, variety performances, and exhibitions of modern handicraft. There are statues of Charles XII and Charles XIII, and the romantic Molin Fountain (1873). Alongside Kungsträdgården lie Jakobskyrkan (consecrated 1643), several large banks, and Stockholm's largest department store, Nordiska Kompaniet (NK).

BY COURTESY OF THE TRUSTEES OF THE BRITISH MUSEUM; PHOTO BY J. R. FREEMAN & CO.

THE ROYAL PALACE ON THE CITY ISLAND AS IT APPEARED IN THE EARLY 17TH CENTURY BEFORE IT WAS DESTROYED BY FIRE IN 1697; ENGRAVING FROM THE "INVENTARIUM SVECIAE" BY J. L. GOTTFRIED, 1632

(LEFT) GULLERS—RAPHO GUILLUMETTE; (RIGHT) LOUIS RENAULT—PHOTO RESEARCHERS, INC.

(LEFT) MODERN STOCKHOLM, SEEN FROM ROUGHLY THE SAME VANTAGE POINT AS IN THE 17TH-CENTURY ENGRAVING SHOWN ON PAGE 261; (RIGHT) NARROW STREET IN STADEN, THE OLDEST PART OF THE CITY

On the waterfront east of the opera are the Grand Hotel, with a magnificent view over central Stockholm, and the National Museum (1866), with large collections of Swedish and foreign art (chiefly 17th–19th centuries). A bridge leads to Skeppsholmen and Kastellholmen, formerly a naval base, where the Modern Museum of 20th-century art and the East Asia Museum are accommodated in old military buildings.

To the west of Lower Norrmalm, on the site of an old convent, the 16th-century (rebuilt) Klara Kyrka stands in a beautiful churchyard and contains the graves of several poets, including Carl Michael Bellman (*q.v.*). Farther west, in Vasagatan, is the Central Railway Station. During the late 1950s and early 1960s the central part of Norrmalm was entirely rebuilt as a modern shopping and business centre (Hötorgscity), featuring five 18-story office blocks and a pedestrian mall (Sergelgatan) with shops on two levels. In Hötorget (the Haymarket) stand the neoclassical Concert Hall (1926), with Carl Milles' famous Orpheus group in front, and the large department store PUB. Farther north are Handelshögskolan (the School of Economics) and the Town Library, both from the 1920s, and Stockholm University, accommodated in a number of buildings around the Old Observatory (*c.* 1750). At the northern end of Sveavägen is the Wenner-Gren Centre for international scientific research. West of Brunnsviken lie the Medical University (Karolinska Institutet) and Karolinska Sjukhuset (Caroline Hospital). Nearby is the large Haga Park with Gustavus III's pavilion, in late Gustavian style (1790). East of Brunnsviken are the Veterinary College, Forestry Research Institute, Royal Academy of Sciences, and the Natural History Museum.

On Kungsholmen, a large island to the west, separated from Norrmalm by a narrow channel, stands Ragnar Östberg's famous City Hall (1923). In the vicinity are the Seraphim Hospital (1752), the Royal Mint, and, farther away, Rådhuset (the Law Courts [1915]). There are also several large hospitals and schools. The main streets are Hantverkargatan, St. Eriksgatan, and Norr Mälarstrand, the last-named beautifully situated along Mälaren between the City Hall garden and the large modern Rålambshov Park with its playgrounds and open-air theatre.

On the Baltic side of Stockholm lies Östermalm, mainly a residential area from the latter part of the 19th century, intersected by boulevards and avenues, *e.g.*, Birger Jarlsgatan, Sturegatan, Karlavägen, Valhallavägen, Narvavägen, and Strandvägen. On the western side of Sturegatan is the town's largest inner park, Humlegården (the Hopgarden) in which is the Royal Library (1878). In Valhallavägen are the Technical University (1922), the Stadium (built for the 1912 Olympic Games), the Royal Central Gymnastics Institute (1945), the Royal Academy of Music's new school (1957), the School of Arts and Crafts (1959), and Swedish Radio's large establishment. Nearby, Gärdet, Stockholm's former drill ground, has been partly taken over for modern housing settlements. In Storgatan are the National Historical Museum and Royal Mint Collection (the latter containing many Anglo-Saxon coins), and in Riddargatan, housed in 18th-century military buildings, is the Army Museum. At Nybroplan, where Birger Jarlsgatan and Strandvägen meet, stands the white marble palace of the Royal Dramatic Theatre (1908), with the small Berzelii Park (commemorating the chemist J. J. Berzelius) on the Norrmalm side. Strandvägen, Östermalm's principal promenade, skirts Nybroviken and continues eastward past the Nobel Park along Djurgårdsbrunnsviken, a pleasant bay on which are situated the Ethnographical, Technical, and Naval History museums, and a number of embassies, including those of the United Kingdom and the United States. There also is the little English Church (1866), which until 1913 stood in Vallingatan.

South of this bay is Stockholm's largest park area, Southern Djurgården, which has oak trees 1,000 years old. In the immediate vicinity of Djurgårdsbron, which crosses the mouth of the bay from Strandvägen, is Nordiska Museet (the Nordic Museum [1907]) with the Royal Armoury, the former illustrating Swedish cultural history (folklore) and the latter recalling the history of Sweden and its kings from the 16th century. Connected with the Nordic Museum is Skansen, the world's first and largest open-air museum; both were founded by Artur Hazelius (1833–1901). There may be seen specimens of old buildings from different parts of Sweden; also there are a well-stocked zoo and several restaurants. Down by the shore of Saltsjön is the wharf accommodating the 17th-century warship "Vasa," which sank nearby on its maiden voyage in 1628 and was salvaged almost intact in 1961. Nearby is Grönalunds Tivoli, an amusement park. Farther out the shore is lined with villas. Waldemarsudde, the palace of the artist Prince Eugen (1865–1947), containing a collection of modern art, is open to the public, together with its extensive garden and park.

Södermalm is a large island rising boldly out of the Baltic. It is connected with the Old Town by the cloverleaf traffic junction at Slussen (the Sluice [1935]) and by the Söderström Bridge (1959). The main streets are Götgatan and Hornsgatan—the old southern exits from Stockholm—and Södergatan and Ringvägen. Along the Baltic lie the harbours of Stadsgården and Hammarby, and a number of industrial plants. The inner part of the island is mainly residential. Stockholm's City Museum is housed in the former city hall built by the Tessins in the 1680s. Above Årsta Bay, in the southwest, rises Södersjukhuset, a large modern hospital (built 1938–53). Three churches dominate Södermalm: the 16th-century Maria Magdalena (restored in 1825); Katarina, founded in 1656; and the modern twin-towered Högalidskyrka (1917–23).

The inner town is linked with the outer districts of Brännkyrka in the south and Bromma in the west by several modern, high bridges famous for their beauty. Early in the 20th century the town of Stockholm bought large properties there on which garden suburbs were erected between 1910 and 1930. Beyond these there were planned and erected during the 1940s and 1950s complete groups of suburbs with their own industrial areas, each individual suburb, with a population of from 10,000 to 15,000, being built around a local centre placed by an underground railway station. Within each suburban group (total population 50,000–100,000) one centre serves as main centre for the whole area. In the west, where this type of planning was first carried through, it is Vällingby (opened 1956). The main centres in the south are Farsta (1960) and Högdalen (1959). The construction of other centres continued during the 1960s. A feature of Farsta is that domestic heating is supplied by a nuclear power plant at Ågesta (½ mi. from Farsta), first used in 1964.

Immediately southwest of Bromma, on an island in Mälaren and outside Stockholm proper, lies the royal country palace of Drottningholm (17th–18th centuries). Noteworthy is the Court Theatre (1764–66), the auditorium, stage, and stage machinery of which are completely preserved; during the summer contemporary operas are performed there. In the park, laid out in French Baroque style, is the little rococo Kina Slott, a pavilion decorated and furnished in Chinese style.

In olden times, it was primarily the waterways that were used for communication between the various districts inside Stockholm, as well as with the rest of the country and the continent. In the late 1870s tramways were laid and subsequently extended to the garden suburbs mentioned above. The garden suburbs of Djursholm, Saltsjöbaden, and Lidingö, which came into being at the turn of the century, were immediately connected with Stockholm by rail. Because of the rapid growth in population and the increasing motor traffic, Stockholm has had to organize extensive traffic installations. Apart from the bridges mentioned above and Slussen, these include the elegant Västerbro (West Bridge [1935]) between Kungsholmen and the south, and the widening of streets in the inner town. During the early 1960s Klarabergsviadukten, a new link between Lower Norrmalm and Kungsholmen, and a new multilane motorway bridge to Lidingö were completed. The first section of Tunnelbanan, Stockholm's underground railway, was laid under Södermalm in the early 1930s. By the mid-1960s it linked the centre of the town with the new suburban districts to the south and west, and extension was continuing. Stockholm has, in addition, a growing number of bus lines which will probably eventually supersede the tramlines. The international airport is at Arlanda, 30 mi. (48 km.) to the north. Bromma Airport is used for internal services only. On the Baltic east of Gärdet are port installations, including the free port and oil harbour, the latter partly built from caissons used in the invasion of Normandy in 1944.

Stockholm city is an *överståthållarskap* (governorship) administratively separate from the surrounding *län* (county) of the same name. It is in the diocese of Uppsala but has a separate consistory presided over by the rector of Storkyrkan. Being the capital, it contains most of the government departments and also the large organizations within the labour market, commerce, and industry, such as the Confederation of Swedish Trade Unions (LO), the Swedish Employers' Confederation (SAF), and others. It is the seat of *högsta domstolen* (the Supreme Court of Justice) and of *Svea hovrätten* (the court of appeal for central Sweden and Gotland). Civil servants constitute an important element in the population, as do also the scientists and teachers attached to the large educational, cultural, social, and scientific institutions. Stockholm is the centre of the economic life of the country, particularly where wholesale trade is concerned. Building materials, fuel, and food are leading imports. In the Stockholm area are such internationally known industrial concerns as Telefon AB L. M. Ericsson, Atlas Copco, Elektrolux, Alfa-Laval, Gasaccumlator (AGA), and Gustavsberg's porcelain factory. The metal industry is the biggest employer of labour, followed by the printing industry.

According to tradition, Stockholm was founded by Birger Jarl about 1250. Its nucleus was a fortress built earlier in the century on Stadsholmen, at the site of the Royal Palace, and the city was surrounded by walls with fortified towers. The origin of the name "Stockholm" ("log island") is doubtful. Churches and monasteries were erected, and as early as 1288 the city was reported as being more populous than most other towns in the country. It had special importance during the Middle Ages for trade on the Baltic and was closely allied to the big Hansa towns. The country's most important articles of export in olden times, iron, copper, and Swedish tar, were shipped from Stockholm.

From the 15th century, Stockholm was the capital of the country. After conflicts lasting many years between the Danes and the Swedes, the town was liberated by Gustavus Vasa in 1523 and has never since been besieged or occupied. It experienced its biggest development about the middle of the 17th century. The central government departments were then placed there, and the population increased rapidly. The old city walls were torn down, and new districts grew up on the area between the old tollgates, north and south of the "town between the bridges." During the 18th century expansion slowed down, but Stockholm became the seat of culture, science, and letters. A new period of development began with industrialism in the mid-19th century, and the population again began to climb. In 1856 it exceeded 100,000, and in 1900, 300,000. During this time redevelopment took place in the area within the old tollgates, buildings were reconstructed, boulevards, avenues, and parks laid out, and many of the educational establishments, museums, libraries, hospitals, etc., were built.

The rapid increase in population continued during the 20th century, but the trend of planning and development during mid-century was to effect a transition from the old pattern of a dominating centre to a much larger urban district with several centres. Thus the population of the city began to decline after 1960, while that of Greater Stockholm continued to rise.

*See* further SWEDEN; *see* also references under "Stockholm" in the Index.

BIBLIOGRAPHY.—W. William-Olsson, *Stockholm: Structure and Development* (1960); S. Trenter and K. W. Gullers, *The Old Town of Stockholm* (1953); Burnett Anderson, *Stockholm, Capital and Crossroads* (1953). (B. NY.)

**STOCKMAR, CHRISTIAN FRIEDRICH,** BARON VON (1787–1863), Anglo-Belgian statesman, secretary to Prince Leopold of Saxe-Coburg (from 1831 King Leopold I of the Belgians) and unofficial adviser of Queen Victoria, was born at Coburg in Germany on August 22, 1787. He studied medicine and in 1816 became physician to Prince Leopold on his marriage with Princess Charlotte of England. After her death (November 1817) Stockmar became Leopold's secretary. He was active in the abortive negotiations (1829–30) to place Leopold on the throne of Greece and in promoting his successful candidature for the throne of Belgium (1830–31). Between 1831 and 1837 Stockmar acted mainly as Leopold's agent in England, where he helped to arrange the marriage (1836) between the widowed queen of Portugal and a Coburg prince.

With the accession of Queen Victoria to the throne of England in 1837, Stockmar's career entered a new phase. Leopold was Victoria's uncle, and planned a match between her and his nephew, Prince Albert of Saxe-Coburg-Gotha. Stockmar was employed to arrange the marriage (1840) and also to act as the queen's adviser. He now became attached rather to the English than to the Belgian court, and spent much of his time in England until 1857, when he retired finally to Germany. An ardent constitutionalist, his advice to the queen and prince, though somewhat theoretical at times, contributed greatly in the early years of the reign to their determination to act with strict constitutionality. He attended the German diets of Frankfurt (1848) and Erfurt (1850) and favoured the progress of Prussian influence. He died at Coburg on July 9, 1863.

See *Memoirs of Baron Stockmar by His Son, Baron E. von Stockmar*, 2 vol. (1872); F. Eyck, *The Prince Consort* (1959). (D. E. D. B.)

**STOCKPORT,** a municipal (1835), county (1888) and parliamentary borough, partly in Lancashire and partly in Cheshire, Eng., 7 mi. SE of Manchester and 38½ mi. NE of Chester by road. Pop. (1961) 142,543. Area 13.2 sq.mi. (34 sq.km.). The ancient town stood on the southern slope of a narrow gorge where the Tame and Goyt rivers meet to form the Mersey, but the modern town has spread over the more level ground above. The town hall (1908) and the war memorial building opposite, which is the art gallery, stand on high ground and are built of Portland stone. Close by is Stockport College (1887–89). The chief of the 48 parks and open spaces are Vernon and Woodbank Memorial parks, which lie along the banks of the Goyt.

It is recorded that in the rebellion of 1172 the castle of Stockport (later demolished) was held against Henry II by his son, Geoffrey. Sir Robert de Stokeport granted a charter to the town about 1220, making it a free borough. In 1260 an annual fair and weekly market was granted, to be held on the site of the present marketplace. Stockport's grammar school dates from the 15th century. The 14th-century Church of St. Mary, reconstructed in the 19th century, was built on an earlier foundation. During the rebellion of 1745 the defeated forces of Prince Charles Edward descended on the town whose bridge had been demolished. Stockport figures largely in the industrial disturbances of the early 19th century. Trade unionism increased as cotton spinning and weaving were transformed from cottage to factory industries. By 1800 local weavers were persistently pressing Parliament for the regulation of their wages, and in 1808 demanded a fixed minimum price for their goods. Distress was increased by the bankruptcy of the employers, and by 1812 serious disorders broke out. Later, during the Chartist demonstrations, a procession marched on Stockport workhouse and took forcible possession. By 1822 cotton spinning was already Stockport's staple industry. Its importance as a hat-making town dates at least from the 18th century. Today, engineering and the manufacture of chemicals have been added to these earlier industries.

**STOCKTON, ROBERT FIELD** (1795–1866), U.S. naval officer and public official who played an important role in events leading to the cession of California to the U.S. He was born in Princeton, N.J., Aug. 20, 1795, the grandson of Richard Stockton, signer of the Declaration of Independence. Robert Stockton attended Princeton College for a time but in 1811 joined the Navy as a midshipman. During the War of 1812 he served under Commodore John Rodgers, except for a brief period as aide to the secretary of the navy. After the war Stockton was transferred to the Mediterranean, where he participated (1815) in the war against the Barbary pirates. In 1821 he was dispatched by the American Colonization Society to Africa, where he was able to obtain for the society the land which later became Liberia.

From 1828 to 1838 he lived in Princeton, devoting his attention to founding the New Jersey Colonization Society, of which he was first president, and to the construction of the Delaware and Raritan Canal, which owed its existence to him. He was responsible for obtaining the charter for the canal, for financing it, and for directing it as president during the last years of his life.

In 1838 he went to sea again, as commander of the flagship of the Mediterranean fleet. Pres. John Tyler asked him to join his cabinet as secretary of the navy, but Stockton refused, preferring to remain on active duty. With John Ericsson, later designer of the "Monitor," he drew up plans for the "Princeton," the first warship to be driven with a screw propeller, designing himself one of its guns, the largest in the U.S. fleet. On one occasion in 1844, while many distinguished visitors were on board the ship, Stockton's gun was fired and exploded, killing the secretary of state and the secretary of the navy and wounding numerous other passengers. Stockton was later absolved of all blame for the tragedy.

In 1845 he was chosen by Tyler to sail in the "Princeton" to Texas to deliver to the state government the annexation resolution of the U.S. government, and later in the same year he commanded the "Congress" on its voyage from Norfolk to the Pacific, where he had been ordered to take command of the fleet. War with Mexico having broken out while he was en route, Stockton immediately took command of U.S. land and sea forces, capturing Los Angeles, the Mexican stronghold, on Aug. 13, 1846. Stockton set up a civil government, first naming himself as governor and later John C. Frémont (*q.v.*), who had been associated with him in the fighting. He subsequently fought and defeated the Mexicans at San Diego, San Gabriel, and La Mesa, after which Los Angeles, which the Mexicans had recaptured, again fell to the U.S. forces. The entire province of California was then ceded to the U.S.

Stockton returned east in 1847 and resigned from the Navy in 1850. He served in the United States Senate from 1851 to 1853 and after 1853 was president of the Delaware and Raritan Canal Company. He died in Princeton on Oct. 7, 1866.

**STOCKTON,** a city of California, U.S., the seat of San Joaquin County, is on the San Joaquin River, 78 mi. (125 km.) E of San Francisco, approximately in the centre of the great central valley of California. Although situated 88 nautical miles (163 km.) from the sea, Stockton is a deepwater port and has become a major shipping point for the produce of the rich interior valley. The city had a population of 86,321 in 1960, and is the centre of a standard metropolitan statistical area (San Joaquin County) with a population of 249,989 in 1960. (For comparative population figures *see* table in CALIFORNIA: *Population.*)

Stockton traces its origins to 1843 when Capt. Charles Weber, a German immigrant, endeavoured to develop a grant of 48,747 ac. of rich valley land which he and a Mexican partner had secured from the government of Mexico. The first settlement, named Tuleburg after the characteristic tules, or bulrushes, of the region, failed to attract settlers until the discovery of gold in the famous Mother Lode of the Sierra Nevada in 1848. As its position at the head of navigation on the San Joaquin River made it the most advantageous supply point for the mines, the community grew rapidly. By the summer of 1849 the one permanent building of 1848 was surrounded by a tent city of about 1,000 inhabitants, the great majority of whom catered to the needs of the miners. During the height of the gold rush the little port of Tuleburg was visited by ships from Europe, South America, and Asia, contemporary accounts telling of over 100 ships at anchor at one time.

In 1850 after fires virtually destroyed the original tent city and its ramshackle wooden successor, a planned community was begun by Captain Weber. Surveys were made, areas were set aside for schools, parks, and churches, and the name was changed from Tuleburg to Stockton in honour of Commodore Robert Stockton, whom Weber had met during the course of the war with Mexico. By 1853 the city had reached a population of 5,000.

With the coming of the Central Pacific Railroad in 1869 and the rapid settlement of the fertile interior valley, the economy of the area soon changed. Modern Stockton is a thriving trade centre but the wealth of the mines has long been superseded by the much greater wealth of the surrounding agricultural region.

As large steamships supplanted the small oceangoing craft of the mining days, the natural channel of the San Joaquin River soon proved inadequate and the growing commerce of the area was lost to San Francisco. As early as 1871 plans had been made for the construction of a deepwater channel to serve the city, but the financial burden prevented the undertaking until 1930 when federal assistance was secured. Since its completion in 1933 the Port of Stockton has been greatly enlarged and improved and is now one of the largest general cargo terminals on the Pacific coast. The 32-ft. (9.8-m.) channel and a 33-ac. (13-ha.) turning basin make it possible for any ship in the U.S. merchant marine to dock at Stockton. Among the facilities for handling the diversified cargoes are the 3,000,000-bu. capacity grain elevators and a fully automatic bulk ore terminal. The mid-20th century was a period of increasing industrialization of the Stockton area, particularly in those industries relating to agriculture and food processing. Several military establishments are located nearby, notably the Sharpe general depot with its atomic food processing plant, and a naval supply annex and west coast communications centre.

Stockton is the home of the University of the Pacific, founded by the Methodist Church in 1851 as California's first chartered institution of higher education. It is comprised of four liberal arts colleges, six professional schools (music, education, engineering, pharmacy in Stockton; dentistry in San Francisco; law in Sacramento) and a graduate school. The Stockton public-school system extends through junior college.

The city's program of cultural activities and recreational facilities includes the Haggin Art Gallery and Pioneer Historical Museum, a symphony orchestra, a successful civic theatre, and an extensive park system. Stockton established a council-manager form of government in 1923. (M. H. Mo.)

**STOCKTON-ON-TEES,** a former municipal borough incorporated in the county borough of Teesside (*q.v.*), Eng., since April 1, 1968, and a parliamentary constituency and port on the left bank of the River Tees, 11.5 mi. above its mouth and opposite Thornaby-on-Tees. Pop. (1961) 81,274. Area 8.5 sq.mi.

Stockton's first market charter was granted in 1310 and it is still a big market centre for cattle and agricultural produce. Because of the presence of iron ore in the Cleveland Hills to the south (which has long been mined) and the Durham coalfield to the north, it grew into a big industrial centre and the leading Tees port until superseded by Middlesbrough. The port has 980 ft. (300 m.) of quayage, a minimum depth of 12 ft. (3.6 m.) at low-water ordinary spring tide and 22½ ft. (6.9 m.) at high-water ordinary spring tide, and trades principally with Scandinavia and the Netherlands. The historic Stockton-Darlington Railway (opened 1825) was the first passenger-carrying railway. Stockton is interested in the development of diesel and electric locomotives. Many light industries are there and the Imperial Chemical Industries establishment at Billingham lies partly in Stockton.

Stockton grew up around the manor house and later castle of the bishops of Durham, to whom the town belonged. It is said that King John granted a charter in 1214, but no trace of this remains. The borough was first mentioned in 1283. Since 1867 Stockton has sent one member to Parliament.

**STOICHIOMETRY** (STOICHEIOMETRY), in chemistry, strictly denotes the determination of the proportions in which elements or compounds react with one another, and is occasionally extended to include the determination of atomic and molecular weights. The term, as used in analytical chemistry, refers to that branch of chemistry concerned with the weight relationships in gravimetric analysis, the volume relationships in volumetric analysis, and the calculations based on these relationships (*see* CHEMISTRY: *Analytical Chemistry*). The important stoichiometric relationships are expressed by the laws of constant composition, multiple proportions, and combining volumes. *See* also EQUIVALENT; REACTION KINETICS.

*See* E. T. Williams and R. C. Johnson, *Stoichiometry for Chemical Engineers* (1958); L. Mandelcorn (ed.), *Non-stoichiometric Compounds* (1963). (G. W. WD.)

**STOICS,** in Greco-Roman antiquity, were adherents of a particular philosophy, so named because their first master, Zeno, a citizen of Citium in Cyprus who arrived in Athens about 312 B.C., used to teach in the painted stoa, a colonnade on the north side of the marketplace there. Stoic philosophy may be divided into three periods: the Old Stoa, from 312 to 129 B.C.; the Middle Stoa, from 129 to 30 B.C.; and the New Stoa, from 30 B.C. to the end of the 2nd century A.D.

## THE OLD STOA (312–129 B.C.)

Zeno (*q.v.*) of Citium lived from *c.* 334 to 262/261 B.C. His pupils included Aristo of Chios; Persaeus of Citium, who lived till at least 243 B.C.; Sphaerus, who came from the north coast of the Black Sea and was at the court of Cleomenes III of Sparta between 235 and 222; and Cleanthes (*q.v.*) of Assus, who lived from *c.* 331/330 to 232/231. By far the most important philosopher of the Old Stoa was Chrysippus (*q.v.*), who came from Soli in Cilicia and died between 208 and 204 at the age of 73. Chrysippus modified and clarified Zeno's system. He was responsible to a large extent for the view that the *logos* (*see* below) was a power externally related to its environment and, since the intelligence of man was identified with the *logos,* for the concept of the free will and self-sufficiency of the Stoic wise man. To him also we probably owe the four Stoic categories (*see* below). The last important philosophers of the Old Stoa were Diogenes of Babylon, who was one of the three philosophers sent by Athens to Rome as ambassadors in 155; and Antipater of Tarsus, who must have been in Rome before 133 B.C., since he was a friend of Tiberius Gracchus.

Much has been made of the fact that Zeno was of Phoenician descent, and that the most prominent Stoics came from the East. The East, however, had been hellenized by the conquests of Alexander the Great, and Zeno himself was more decisively influenced by Athenian philosophy than by Eastern mysticism. Zeno studied under Crates the Cynic, under Stilpo the Megarian, and under Xenocrates and Polemon, both of the Academy, but may have been affected most strongly by the Peripatetic philosopher Theophrastus. No contact between Zeno and Epicurus can be discovered.

**The Stoic Categories.**—In their physical system the Stoics recognized four categories: substratum (*hypokeimenon*); qualified (*poios*); disposition (*pos echon*); and relative disposition (*pros ti pos echon*). The first category, substratum, was either primary or secondary. The primary substratum is substance without quality. Though it has no quality of its own, it always has some quality, just as wax is never without shape. It does not increase or decrease. The secondary substratum is the substance common to the genus or to the species.. For instance, two doves are one substance but two qualified entities. Similarly, according to Chrysippus, when our cosmos is destroyed by fire, Zeus, who alone of the gods is imperishable, will retire into foresight, and Zeus and foresight will continue to be in one substance, *aether;* so that Zeus, as a qualified entity, and foresight, a quality, have a common substance, *aether,* and this, in turn, is the secondary substratum. Stoic psychology may be explained in the same way: presentation, the act of assent, impulse, and reason are qualities of intelligence; intelligence, then, was a substance and a secondary substratum qualified by such things as impulse and reason. But since the intelligence was itself a quality, the analysis of Stoic physics is an analysis of qualities.

Each quality was a secondary substratum for another quality or differentiation. For example, Chrysippus in his book *On the Fact that the Virtues are Qualified* argued that the verbal adjectives "to be chosen," "to be done," and "to be confident" each indicated a different good. Moderation is virtue with the qualification "to be chosen," and courage is virtue with the qualification "to be confident." Virtue is "reason [*hegemonikon*] in a certain disposition," and soul (*psyche*) is "*pneuma* [breath, or spirit] in a certain disposition." Therefore the following secondary substrata are in ascending order: *pneuma,* soul, reason, virtue, and courage. All of these are qualities. There is some evidence that the differentiation, in turn, might be further qualified: sweet might be qualified by the sweet peculiar to a species (*e.g.,* the sweet of the apple as compared with that of honey), or by degrees of more or less.

The second category, qualified, included the particular qualified entity; *e.g.,* Socrates. Its secondary substratum was the species (*e.g.,* man) or the genus (*e.g.,* animal). It was the most important of the four Stoic categories for Chrysippus, since the quality (*poiotes*) was derived from the characteristics of the qualified object. For example, Chrysippus derived the quality manliness from manly and gentleness from gentle. He went so far as to recognize a whole flock of virtues corresponding to the age, sex, and circumstances of the person who had the characteristic.

The third category, disposition, had the meaning "in a certain disposition." It is always applied to the substratum: for example, soul is said to be *pneuma* in a certain disposition, and virtue is reason in a certain disposition. The substratum is also said to be in a certain disposition if it is qualified by powers such as sweet and bitter, or by differentiations which are not active, such as black and white. Whatever is indicated by the category "disposition" is always externally related to its environment. It is always of such a kind that it is not affected by a change in anything external to itself.

The fourth category, relative disposition, also had the meaning "in a certain disposition" and referred to the substratum, but it was limited to a few terms which were always internally related to, or affected by a change in something external to them. For example, part was internally related to whole, father to son, and right to left. The term "father" designated "man in a certain disposition and internally related to son."

Stoic physics thus rested primarily on substratum and qualification, since it was into these that all forms of reality could be analyzed. Since the two kinds of substratum denoted by the first two categories and the two types of disposition indicated by the last two were mutually exclusive, no quality or entity could be described by more than two categories.

**The Logos.**—At the heart of Stoic physics was the *logos.* It was the quality (*e.g.*, courage) and both the substratum and the differentiation of the substratum (*e.g.*, virtue and the differentiation "to be confident"); it was the particular qualified entity (*e.g.*, Socrates); and it was the differentiation or qualification (*e.g.*, hot). It makes each of these what it is. The *logos* is called hardness in iron, density in stone, and the white sheen in silver. It permeates both animate and inanimate matter. It is mind, soul, nature, and condition. As condition it is found in bones and sinews; as mind it is present in the intelligence and in the *aether*. Though each quality was a manifestation of the divine power which the Stoics termed *logos*, the *logos* was not limited to any one object, but was the totality of all qualities in the universe. Since, however, in its purest form it is found in rational intelligence, the Stoics argued that the virtue of God and of man was the same. As a seed the *logos* is present in primary matter and brings to birth the four elements, fire, air, earth, and water. After the destruction of our cosmos by fire, it will again produce a cosmos identical with our own. As a breath or *pneuma* the *logos* is said to be a "tensional motion." It is a stretching or tightness within the cosmos, as well as within each particular object, and is responsible for its cohesion. In the cosmos it binds together the four elements. In the human soul it is good or bad tension and is distinguished from the corresponding judgments. It is termed by Cleanthes force and strength and might perhaps be equated with character. The *pneuma* was also a tensional motion outward to the objects external to it (*see* below, *Psychology*).

Both Zeno and Chrysippus recognized the *logos* as corporeal and defined corporeal as that which can act or be acted upon. Since the qualities were the *logos*, the qualities also were corporeal. They were powers capable of producing an effect, or responsible for a predicate. The term "predicate" (*kategorema*) referred to an incorporeal action such as "living" or "being moderate." The predicates were classified as speech and were denoted by the articular infinitive (the infinitive preceded by a definite article) and by the finite verb. For example, Zeno named practical wisdom as the cause of being wise, soul as the cause of living, and moderation as the cause of being moderate; and Archedemus of Tarsus (2nd century B.C.) wrote that a cause was the cause of a predicate such as "is cut."

**Fate.**—The Stoics' concept of fate was based on their distinction between principal and initiating causes. The principal cause in Chrysippus' philosophy was the quality as a power externally related to its environment. On this the concepts of possibility and free will depended. A passage in Cicero's *De fato* is important in this connection: "You [Chrysippus]," Cicero wrote, "say that what is not going to happen can happen, so that this gem can be broken, even if it is never going to be, and that it would not have been necessary for Cypselus to reign at Corinth, though that had been prophesied by the oracle of Apollo a thousand years before." "This gem is broken" and "Cypselus will not reign at Corinth" were possible events. The predicates "is broken" and "will not reign" follow from the qualities "breakable" and "assent" since "breakable" is the cause of "is broken" and "assent" is the cause of "will not reign," in so far as Cypselus would be free to accept or to reject the occasion of reigning. Possibility is present in the principal cause (*e.g.*, breakable) as the cause of a predicate (*e.g.*, is broken or being broken) which may or may not be realized.

The principal cause, however, is not sufficient to bring about an actual event. Oedipus' decision (*i.e.*, the principal cause) to kill Laius was not the sole cause of the latter's death; a chain of circumstances, such as the fact that Oedipus had a weapon, that he met Laius on a narrow road, and that Laius refused to move aside, was also a cause. The actual event, therefore, requires two sorts of cause: (1) the principal cause, which is part of the nature of one of the factors of the event; (2) the antecedent or initiating cause or causes, which are external to that nature. Thus, if a man should push a cylinder or a cone, the push would be the initiating cause of its rolling movement; but the shape of the object would be the principal cause. Similarly, the presence of a visual object would be the initiating cause of sight, but the assent of the spectator to the visual impression would be the principal cause, and it is "in our power" to accord or to withhold such assent.

It is because of the initiating cause that every event is said to be according to fate. Cicero quotes Chrysippus again: "When we say that all things happen by fate according to antecedent causes, what we intend to be understood is this, namely that it is by accessory and proximate causes, not by complete and principal causes." Initiating causes of various types form a network external to the principal cause of any actual event; and this pattern of causes and effects—conditions in which the object is found and over which it has no control—is called fate.

The fulfillment of a true proposition in the future was not inevitable. This seems to be the basis of Chrysippus' treatment of oracles. The oracle was infallible, but it did not restrict the freedom of the individual. Though the oracle told Oedipus that he would murder his father, Oedipus was still free to murder Laius or to spare his life. The individual, by his free assent, made the decisions which fulfilled the oracles and was responsible for those decisions.

The Stoics saw the world as a total pattern in which the individual was only a small part. Chrysippus held that each particular and each event formed part of a plan which was good and which was not subject to any impediment. Each part fits into the whole. For instance, if a man is sick or maimed, his sickness is part of the common plan. Vice itself served some purpose in the whole. The good of the whole, moreover, might conflict with the good of the individual and even require the latter's destruction. The Stoic, then, may be portrayed as a man struggling against the fate which may destroy him but which is part of the total good. This is the meaning of Chrysippus' analogy that a man is like a dog tied behind a cart which he must follow willingly or reluctantly.

**Psychology.**—In Stoic philosophy the soul was regarded as corporeal, capable of acting and being acted upon. It permeated the whole body by mixture. The centre of perception and reason, which was called "the ruling part of the soul" (*hegemonikon*), was located in the heart and controlled the five senses, the generative parts of the body, and speech. The *hegemonikon* was the "*pneuma* in a certain disposition," and the movement of the *pneuma* between the sense organs and the *hegemonikon* was "tensional motion." The motion was both inward and outward: the movement toward the centre produced consciousness; the movement toward the periphery differentiated the sense perceptions. Knowledge was based on the sense perceptions. When these were tested by the reason and found to be trustworthy, they were termed "cataleptic" and received assent. Both assent and impulse were required for the initiation of an action. Zeno maintained that the four passions (*pathe;* sing. *pathos*), namely pleasure, pain, desire, and fear, were not the judgments themselves but the contractions and expansions of the soul which followed upon the judgments. Chrysippus, however, regarded the *pathos* as a change in the quality of the *hegemonikon* and identified this with judgment. Since perception and the passions were accompanied by judgment, all forms of evil could be reduced to incorrect judgments. In this way Chrysippus could assert the unity of man's soul.

**Ethics.**—Though only a few individuals, such as Socrates and Hercules, were recognized as wise men by the Stoics, the "wise man" was the ideal toward which every Stoic directed his efforts. The Stoics adopted the Socratic principle that injury is the doing rather than the receiving of injury and that, since the good man cannot be forced to act unjustly, the only person who can inflict injury on him is the good man himself. This is the basis of the Stoic concept of the self-sufficiency of the wise man. According to Zeno, the wise man would remain virtuous even if he lived under a tyrant; according to Persaeus, he would not be disturbed if he lost his property or family. In addition, the wise man was never tricked or deceived: because he did not give his assent to falsehood, his knowledge was infallible.

The Stoics did not recognize any distinction among the kinds of knowledge. Chrysippus argued that all knowledge was one and that it was not possible for a man to have practical knowledge and not to be experienced in human affairs, or to have an understanding of human activities and not to comprehend things pertaining to the gods. The Stoic possessed all knowledge, human and divine, but it was essentially practical and related to his duties as a member of society.

The concept of duty, which Zeno defined as "acts of which a reasonable account can be given," played a large part in Stoic philosophy. If a man were to serve in the army or to hold public office, such things as a good and a bad reputation, wealth and poverty, sickness and health were obviously of some concern; but so far as his virtue was concerned they were of no significance, and Zeno therefore termed them "indifferents" (*adiaphora*). He distinguished, however, between "things according to nature" and "things contrary to nature"—also called, respectively, "preferred" and "rejected." Chrysippus gave "things according to nature" an important place in his ethical system. "What shall I regard as the source of duty and the matter of virtue," Plutarch wrote in a passage probably based on Chrysippus, "if I pass over nature and things according to nature?" Chrysippus seems to have argued that a right choice among the "indifferents" would lead to a good habit-pattern and virtue, but that a bad choice would result in the loss of the virtue which the man already possessed. The "indifferents" possessed value, but it was of no significance compared with the value implicit in moral action itself.

Lack of emotion (*ataraxia*) and the capacity to bear whatever losses fortune might inflict was another characteristic of the Stoic wise man. If the Stoic experienced no emotion, did this mean that he felt no sympathy for those whom he was trying to assist? Was his duty merely a means of increasing his own virtue? Seneca, the philosopher of the New Stoa, suggested this when he wrote: "Why, then, do I make a man my friend? In order to have someone for whom I may die, whom I may follow into exile, against whose death I may stake my life and pay the pledge too." It seems clear, however, that the Stoics advocated the control of the emotions by reason rather than their eradication. The Stoic must always speak the truth, and his expression of sympathy must, therefore, be genuine.

All men were thought to have a natural disposition toward virtue. In their earliest years men strive for "the first things according to nature." The term denoted the instinctive capacity of man to find pleasure in those things which were advantageous to his own body and to reject those which were not. It was closely connected with *oikeiosis,* kinship or endearment. Chrysippus argued that what was most akin to every animal was its own constitution and its consciousness of this; and that, as soon as they were born, men were akin to themselves, to the parts of their own body, and to their offspring. The early Stoics made kinship the source of justice.

**Political Theory.**—The Stoics recognized a society of good men as well as a universal society of all men. In his *Republic,* Zeno described an ideal society so organized "that we may not live by cities or demes, severally divided according to our own ideas of what is just, but may consider all men our demesmen and fellow citizens, and that there may be one life and one world just as a herd feeding together nurtured by common law." Only the good, however, were citizens of Zeno's republic; they would not build temples, since the work of builders and craftsmen was neither of value nor sacred; and there would be no coinage or law courts. Zeno believed that elementary education was useless; he also advocated that all women should be held in common. Chrysippus put forward similar views in his own *Republic:* he maintained that bread and water should form the simple fare of the citizens; and he agreed with Zeno about women. Both works were strongly influenced by the Cynics, who argued that the individual could obtain freedom only if he reduced his physical needs to a minimum and ignored social convention.

Since Zeno, Cleanthes, and Chrysippus all maintained that the wise man should take part in public life, it is not surprising to find Stoic philosophers associated with rulers. Zeno was a friend of Antigonus Gonatas, king of Macedonia, who visited him in Athens and, after Zeno's death, promoted the request for his burial in the Ceramicus. Persaeus, Zeno's pupil and the author of a book on the constitution of Sparta, is said to have been powerful enough to dissuade Antigonus from restoring freedom to Eretria (*c.* 270 B.C.) and was Antigonus' general during the war between Macedonia and Aratus of Sicyon (after 250). Sphaerus, another of Zeno's pupils, was in charge of the gymnasia and of the syssitia, or communal messes, at Sparta under Cleomenes III; and the latter's reign (235–222 B.C.) was marked by a great redistribution of landholdings in pursuance of the drastic economic reform which had been initiated by his predecessor, Agis IV, and which was represented as a return to Lycurgus' system of rigorous discipline and simplicity (*see* SPARTA). Persaeus, Sphaerus, and Cleanthes all wrote books *On Kingship.*

The Stoics took a stand on social questions. Chrysippus attacked the concept of noble birth in his book *On Virtues* and argued that it made no difference whether a man was the son of a well-born father or not. In *On Concord* he defined the slave as a "hired man for life," a phrase which suggests that the slave was a man doing a piece of work but by nature not essentially different from his master. There is no evidence that the early Stoics ever actively supported the concept of the divinity of the monarch. Further, there is no indication that the Old Stoa regarded the mixed constitution as ideal (the passage in Cicero's *De republica* connecting the Stoics with this type of constitution seems to refer to the Middle Stoa).

**Religion.**—The most famous document in Stoic religion is Cleanthes' *Hymn to Zeus.* The opening lines, "Most glorious of the immortals, thou of many names, ever all-powerful, Zeus, ruler of nature, steering all things with law, hail," emphasize two important aspects of Stoic religion: the consciousness of a partnership between God and man, and an awareness of the moral and rational order of the universe. Zeus is omnipotent, as Cleanthes writes: "Nor is there any work upon the earth apart from thee, neither in the divine aetherial heavens nor in the sun except what evil men do in their own folly." Chrysippus carried this concept still farther and maintained that even the evil which men do served some purpose in the whole, and that the total pattern was good. Most of all, the *Hymn to Zeus* was a prayer for understanding: "Grant that we may find that judgment, in which thou trusting steerest all things with justice." For the Stoic, true religion was participation in the reason which guided the cosmos and which fulfilled his own nature.

Acceptance of the unity of the universe as a manifestation of the *logos* in its many forms, together with belief in a system of interlocking causes and effects, led the Stoics to accept oracles and divination of the future by natural signs (such as weather portents and the flight of birds). Chrysippus argued from belief in oracles to prove the existence of fate.

Though they believed that the rational part of the soul survived the body's death, the Stoics did not believe that it was immortal. Cleanthes argued that all souls endured till the destruction of the cosmos by fire, but Chrysippus held that only the souls of the wise could last that long.

**Dialectic (Logic).**—In dialectic, the Stoics developed a theory of signs in which they distinguished three factors: the sign, which is the sound of the word expressed; the significate, the meaning of the word; and that which exists, the externally existing object. The significate was classified under *lekton* (speech) and was regarded as incorporeal. From this the Stoics developed a logic of propositions, including an analysis of types of propositions and of the truth-conditions of propositions. They recognized five basic types of undemonstrated argument as valid inference-schemas. (*See* also LOGIC, HISTORY OF.)

**Rhetoric.**—The close connection between dialectic and rhetoric may be illustrated by Zeno's comparison of dialectic to a closed fist and of rhetoric to an open hand. Rhetoric was defined as the science of speaking correctly in question and answer. The thought or meaning expressed was the subject of both disciplines. According to the Stoics only the wise man was an orator, and the function of the orator was to teach; the best style, therefore, was that which agreed most closely with daily speech. Whereas P. Rutilius Rufus, a Roman of the Middle Stoa, described the style of Diogenes of Babylon as modest and sober, Cicero spoke derogatorily about Cleanthes' and Chrysippus' rhetoric books.

The Stoics recognized three kinds of speeches, namely deliberative, judicial, and eulogistic, and divided a formal speech into four parts, namely prooemium, narration, reply to opponents, and epilogue. They recognized four virtues of good style according to Cicero's testimony, namely hellenism (*i.e.,* purity), clarity, brevity, and propriety; five according to Diogenes Laërtius, who adds absence of vulgarity.

**Poetics.**—The Stoics analyzed a poem in terms of sound, style, and meaning. The sound-pattern in a good poem had a beneficial effect upon the hearer since it molded and formed the emotions by arousing pleasure and fear. The pleasure derived from poetry, however, was expected to be rational and controlled. The Stoics were interested in poetry from the ethical point of view.

Believing all names to be according to nature and so to imitate that to which they referred, the Stoics found a natural connection between words and their meanings. They introduced the trope (Gr. *tropos,* turn or manner), the use of a single word to express a concept which had no name of its own. Four of these tropes, namely onomatopoeia, metaphor, catachresis, and metalepsis, were much used in the Stoics' analysis of poetry. Catachresis was the application of the name of one thing to some nameless other thing; and metalepsis was the substitution of a partial synonym for the original word. Allegory, symbolism, and etymology were also used. By such devices as these, the Stoics were able to bring phrases and passages in Homer or in other poets into line with their own philosophy: Zeno tried to equate the names of the Titans with the elements of the universe, and Chrysippus used passages in Homer to prove that all things come about by fate. Recourse to the poets as teachers of virtue had been part of the educational tradition of the 5th century.

## THE MIDDLE STOA (129–30 B.C.)

**Panaetius.**—The year 129 B.C., when Panaetius (*q.v.*) of Rhodes succeeded Antipater of Tarsus as head of the Stoa at Athens, is conventionally taken as the point of division between the Old Stoa and the Middle because it is assumed that the attacks made by the Academic philosopher Carneades (*q.v.*), who incidentally died at about the same time, caused the Stoics to modify many of their doctrines. In many respects Panaetius' philosophy was a radical departure from the Old Stoa's. He deviated from the doctrine of the unity of the soul in reason and recognized a dualism of impulse and reason. He seems to have attached little importance to the concept of the wise man. Asked whether the wise man would fall in love, he is reported to have said: "So far as the wise man is concerned, we shall see; but as for you and me who are still a long way from being a wise man . . ." Virtue, he believed, was not sufficient for happiness. He rejected divination and expressed doubts about the destruction of the cosmos by fire.

Books I and II of Cicero's *De officiis* are based on Panaetius. Book II contains a discussion of *decorum,* a word which means "that which is fitting." *Decorum* is determined by the individual's nature, position, wealth, and age. The individual should give the impression of being severe and serious; speak on appropriate topics and in a good style; and live in a house which will be neither too much above nor too much below his income. Position, wealth, and age, which the Old Stoa regarded as indifferent, are used to determine the right kind of behaviour.

**Poseidonius.**—The other great philosopher of the Middle Stoa was Poseidonius (*q.v.; c.* 135–*c.* 50 B.C.). He denied the possibility of unqualified matter and argued that the elements always existed as the principles of the world. God did not have creative power but accommodated himself to what already existed. There was a threefold division of power: Zeus (reason) governs the universe; nature holds bodies together; and fate is the source of movement in matter. Soul gave plants, animals, human beings, and stars their unified structure. Poseidonius carried Stoic pantheism to an extreme by attributing desire and sensation to plants and arguing that the stars and the heavens were divine and alive. The universe itself was living and possessed soul and mind. Fate was the warm and light element which was the formative principle of matter.

Poseidonius based his ethical system on an understanding of the emotions, which were classified as follows: psychic (*e.g.,* desire, fear, and anger); bodily (*e.g.,* fever and coolness); concerning the soul but bodily (*e.g.,* lethargy and melancholy); concerning the body but psychic (*e.g.,* trembling and paleness). All were affected by changes in the body. From a correct understanding of the emotions there may be derived a discernment of things good and evil, of the virtues, and of the goal of life. Poseidonius considered health and wealth as good or bad in a positive sense, not as indifferent; and he recognized a rational and an irrational power in the soul—its good or bad demons. For him the goal of life was theoretical knowledge.

**The Middle Stoa and Rome.**—The philosophers of the Middle Stoa were associated with prominent Romans. Panaetius accompanied P. Cornelius Scipio Aemilianus (*see* SCIPIO) on his embassy to Alexandria in 140–139 B.C. and so may be supposed to have known the Scipios in Rome beforehand; and in book I of Cicero's *De republica,* where a group of friends is depicted at Scipio's home, Panaetius is mentioned several times in their discussion, though he is not cited as being present. Hecato of Rhodes, the pupil of Panaetius, was the friend of Quintus Aelius Tubero (*see* below). Blossius of Cumae, like Antipater of Tarsus, was connected with Tiberius Gracchus, but after the latter's death he joined the Attalid pretender Aristonicus in his revolt against the Romans in the province of Asia. Poseidonius visited Rome in 87 and in 51, and several anecdotes connect him with Pompey the Great.

A large number of Romans accepted Stoic philosophy. The known Stoics at Rome include Spurius Mummius (legate in 146 B.C.), Quintus Aelius Tubero (candidate for the praetorship in 129), Publius Mucius Scaevola (consul in 133), his son Quintus Mucius Scaevola (consul in 95), Gaius Fannius (consul in 122), Publius Rutilius Rufus (consul in 105), Sextus Pompeius (an uncle of Pompey the Great, not to be confused with the latter's son Sextus), the younger Marcus Porcius Cato (*q.v.;* Julius Caesar's adversary, who killed himself at Utica), and three eminent jurists, Servius Sulpicius Rufus, Aulus Ofilius, and Gaius Trebatius Testa.

Stoic philosophy moreover had a notable effect on Roman writers outside the ranks of professed Stoics throughout the lifetime of the Middle Stoa. Even earlier, it had had some influence on Terence (*q.v.*), whose *Adelphi* is thought to reflect the educational theories of the Scipionic circle. Its impact can be seen clearly in the works of Cicero (*q.v.*) and of some of the Augustan writers, who lived during the transition from the Middle Stoa to the New. Cicero's *De finibus, Tusculanae disputationes, De officiis, De natura deorum, De republica, De divinatione,* and *De fato* are the source of most of our information about the Middle Stoa and are also important philosophic works in their own right. Notwithstanding his eclecticism, Cicero very often takes Stoic doctrine as his starting point.

The emphasis which Livy (*q.v.*) puts on the acceptance of fate and on duty, responsibility, simplicity, and frugality is in accord with Stoic teachings.

Though there is much in the *Aeneid* which suggests Epicureanism, Virgil (*q.v.*) treated fate in the Stoic manner. Frequently in the *Aeneid* we find the expression "following fate," a phrase which denoted man's desire to bring his own actions into harmony with the total plan of the universe. Book ii shows Aeneas resisting fate (he joins battle after Hector's instructions to the contrary, is tempted to slay Helen, and is on the point of returning to the battle when his father Anchises refuses to accompany him); but as the epic progresses he becomes more submissive to fate till by book vi his actions are in accord with it. His early unwillingness may recall Chrysippus' comparison of a man to a dog behind a cart. Virgil is careful, however, to preserve the individual's free will: it is the decisions and actions of Aeneas which fulfill the plan of fate.

Horace (*q.v.*) pokes fun at the Stoic wise man in his *Epistles* (i, I, 106–108), but one of his odes (iii, 3), describing "the man just and tenacious of purpose," gives perhaps the most famous description of the Stoic wise man in all literature.

### THE NEW STOA (30 B.C.–A.D. 200)

The New Stoa is dated from Augustus' institution of the principate in Rome in the place of the old republic. As the new regime took root, Stoics became involved in palace intrigue, and many of them paid the price for their activities with their lives. Seneca, Barea Soranus, Rubellius Plautus, Thrasea Paetus, and Lucan died by their own hand during the emperor Nero's reign; Helvidius Priscus was put to death by the orders of Vespasian. Vespasian in A.D. 71 banished all philosophers from Rome, and Domitian between 89 and 95 banished them first from Rome and then from the whole of Italy. For the Stoics in this dangerous age life, death, and providence assumed a new meaning. The emphasis was on practical questions of ethics.

Lucius Annaeus Seneca (*q.v.;* 4 B.C.–A.D. 65) was born at Corduba (Córdoba) in Spain. He was banished from Rome by the emperor Claudius in 41, but was recalled in 49 to become Nero's tutor. When Nero became emperor in 54 Seneca enjoyed great influence, but gradually lost favour and in 65 received orders to end his life. Among his most important writings are *De ira, De clementia, De providentia,* and *Epistulae morales ad Lucilium.* His interest was almost entirely in ethics, and his discussion was concerned with standard topics; *e.g.,* the fear of death, the courage of the wise man, the kinship of all men, and fate or providence. He also wrote plays on subjects from Greek legend, illustrating the effect of the passions or interpreting questions of life and death, fate and free will.

Lucius Annaeus Cornutus (*q.v.*), who was banished from Rome toward the end of Nero's reign, has left a work on the interpretation of mythology according to the Stoic method and was the teacher of the poets Persius and Lucan (*qq.v.*). Lucan's *Pharsalia,* the most important work of imaginative literature produced under the influence of the New Stoa, contains many references to Stoic doctrine and constitutes a eulogy of Cato, the Stoic who by his suicide at Utica after Caesar's victory at Thapsus became the symbol of Roman republicanism.

Gaius Musonius Rufus was born in Volsinii in Etruria before A.D. 30. He was banished by Nero in 65 and later by Vespasian, but he was recalled by Titus and lived in Italy until his death *c.* 100. His interests were practical, as we can see from such discussions as "Should daughters receive the same education as sons?" and "That exile is not an evil."

Epictetus (*q.v.;* 1st–2nd century) was a Phrygian slave whose master allowed him to study with Musonius Rufus and eventually freed him. When the philosophers were banished by Domitian, he settled in southern Epirus. He addressed himself to the unhappy, since only those conscious of misery, he held, could profit by philosophy. He argued that wrongdoers were an object of pity rather than censure. He emphasized the self-sufficiency of the individual and maintained that death, pain, and illness were a matter of indifference. He advised the man who wanted to be free not to wish for anything or to avoid anything that was under the control of others, but to become adjusted to a simple life.

Marcus Aurelius Antoninus (*q.v.*) became Roman emperor in A.D. 161. The *Meditations* were his private notebooks written during military campaigns. He referred frequently to the universal city, of which all men are citizens, and to his constant effort to "live in accordance with nature." He regarded Rome's traditional gods as one god and conceived of the world as a unified organism. Preoccupied with death and with the uncertainty of fame, he wrote in a spirit of resignation, forbearance toward others, and longing to be rid of this life's troubles.

### THE LATER INFLUENCE OF STOICISM

Stoicism had a profound influence on Roman law: the concept of natural law (*q.v.; see* also JURISPRUDENCE) and the claims of equity versus the letter of the law are firmly based in Stoicism. Stoic influences can be seen moreover in Neoplatonism, in Neopythagoreanism, and in the patristic writings. Clement of Alexandria (born *c.* A.D. 150) adopted the teachings of Musonius Rufus in his *Paedagogus,* and Themistius in A.D. 364 referred to the *Meditations* of Marcus Aurelius. Of Cicero's writings, *De natura deorum* and *De republica* were well known to Lactantius (*c.* 240–*c.* 320) and to St. Augustine (354–430); *De officiis* was closely followed by St. Ambrose (337–397) in his *De officiis ministrorum;* and the "Dream of Scipio" from the *De republica* was preserved in a commentary by Macrobius.

In the middle of the 6th century St. Martin of Braga composed two ethical treatises, *De ira* and *Formula vitae honestae,* both adapted from the works of Seneca.

Cicero and Seneca were popular in the Renaissance, and through them Stoic teachings became familiar. In the Netherlands, Justus Lipsius published his *Manuductio ad Stoicam philosophiam* in 1604 and left also a *Physiologia Stoicorum,* which appeared in 1610. Lord Herbert of Cherbury's *De veritate* (1624) contained an account of Chrysippus' theory of sense perception. Traces of Stoic teachings can be found in Spinoza, in Descartes, and in Leibniz. Kant's concepts of duty and of imperturbability are drawn from Stoicism.

Concepts and ideas derived from Stoicism have become part of the Western heritage. The word Stoic has come to signify imperturbability and devotion to duty. The distrust of pleasure which is connected with the puritanical tradition may be traced back to the Stoics. The importance which is attached to the problems of fate and free will is, in part, Stoic. For the West, moreover, the whole concept of pantheism and that of the divinity of the common man have their origin in the teachings of Stoicism.

BIBLIOGRAPHY.—E. Zeller, *Die Philosophie der Griechen,* vol. iii, part 1, 5th ed. (1923); R. Hirzel, *Untersuchungen zu Ciceros philosophischen Schriften,* 3 vol. (1876–83); A. Bonhöffer, *Die Ethik des Stoikers Epiktet* (1894); E. V. Arnold, *Roman Stoicism* (1911); R. D. Hicks, *Stoic and Epicurean* (1910); J. von Arnim (ed.), *Stoicorum veterum fragmenta,* 3 vol. (1903–05); E. R. Bevan, *Stoics and Sceptics* (1913); K. Reinhardt, *Poseidonios* (1921), *Kosmos und Sympathie* (1926); E. Grumach, *Physis und Agathon in der alten Stoa* (1932); P. Barth, *Die Stoa,* 6th ed. (1946); J. Lukasiewicz, "Zur Geschichte des Aussagenskalküls," *Erkenntnis,* v (1935); M. Pohlenz, *Grundfragen der stoischen Philosophie* (1940), *Die Stoa,* 2 vol. (1948–49), *Stoa und Stoiker* (1950); M. van Straaten, *Panétius* (1946); A. Virieux-Reymond, *La Logique et l'épistémologie des Stoïciens* (1950); E. Bréhier, *Chrysippe et l'ancien Stoïcisme* (1951); B. Mates, *Stoic Logic* (1953); S. Sambursky, *Physics of the Stoics* (1959); L. Edelstein, *The Meaning of Stoicism* (1966). (M. E. R.)

**STOKE-ON-TRENT,** a city and a county and parliamentary borough of Staffordshire, Eng., 16 mi. (26 km.) NNW of Stafford and comprising the district known as the Potteries (*q.v.*). Pop. (1961) 265,306. Area 33.1 sq.mi. (86 sq.km.). The county borough was constituted in 1910 from a federation of the Potteries towns—Tunstall, Burslem, Hanley, Stoke-on-Trent, Fenton, and Longton. In 1922 it was considerably extended, in 1925 it became a city, in 1928 the chief magistrate became lord mayor, and in 1929 the boundaries were again extended. Of its six pre-federation town halls, that of Stoke-on-Trent is now the meeting place of the city council and the chief administrative centre.

The North Staffordshire Technical College contains the Solon Ceramic Library, and the British Ceramic Research Laboratories were opened in 1951. Stoke cooperated with the county council and Burton upon Trent to establish the University College of North Staffordshire, founded in 1949 at Keele, about 5 mi. W of Stoke. Next in importance to the potteries, which make almost every kind of ware, using local coarse clay for bricks, tiles, etc., and Cornish kaolin for finer work, come the coal mines. A statue of the great potter, Josiah Wedgwood (*q.v.;* 1730–95), faces the railway station. Other names made famous by local potteries are Spode, Minton, and Copeland. Arnold Bennett, who pictured the area in his novels of "the Five Towns" (there are in fact six), was born in Hanley. Stoke returns three members to Parliament.

**STOKE POGES,** parish and village in Buckinghamshire, Eng., about 2 mi. N of Slough. Pop. (1961) 3,886. It is a residential area. St. Giles's Church is of mixed architectural styles; Thomas Gray is buried in the churchyard, held to be the original of his *Elegy.* William Penn (*q.v.*) built the manor house, later a golf club.

**STOKES, SIR GEORGE GABRIEL,** 1ST BART. (1819–1903), British mathematician and physicist, who with James Clerk Maxwell and Lord Kelvin especially contributed to the fame of the Cambridge school of mathematical physics in the middle of the

19th century. Born on Aug. 13, 1819, at County Sligo, Ire., in 1837 he entered Pembroke college, Cambridge, where he became a fellow in 1841. He lost his fellowship when he married in 1857, but 12 years later, under new statutes, he was re-elected. In 1902 he was elected master. As Lucasian professor of mathematics (1849–1903), secretary (1854–85) and president (1885–90) of the Royal society, he held three offices which had only once before been held by one man, Sir Isaac Newton. He was a member of parliament for the university from 1887 to 1892 and was created baronet in 1889. He died on Feb. 1, 1903.

The greater part of Stokes's work was concerned with waves and the transformations imposed on them during their passage through various media. Stokes's first published papers, in 1842 and 1843, were on the steady motion of incompressible fluids and some cases of fluid motion; these were followed in 1845 by one on the friction of fluids in motion and the equilibrium and motion of elastic solids, and in 1850 by another on the effects of the internal friction of fluids on the motion of pendulums. To the theory of sound he made several contributions, including a discussion of the effect of wind on the intensity of sound and an explanation of how the intensity is influenced by the nature of the gas in which the sound is produced. These inquiries together put the science of hydrodynamics on a new footing and provided a key not only to the explanation of many common phenomena, such as the suspension of clouds in air and the subsidence of ripples and waves in water, but also to the solution of practical problems, such as the flow of water in rivers and channels and the skin resistance of ships. (*See* also CENTRIFUGE: *Effect on Liquids;* ELECTRON: *Oil Drop Measurement of* e.)

His best-known researches are perhaps those on the undulatory theory of light. His first papers on the aberration of light appeared in 1845 and 1846 and were followed in 1848 by one on the theory of certain bands seen in the spectrum. In 1849 his paper on the dynamic theory of diffraction showed that the plane of polarization must be perpendicular to the direction of vibration. Two years later he discussed the colours of thick plates; and in 1852 in his famous paper on the change of refrangibility of light, he described the phenomenon of fluorescence, as exhibited by fluorspar and uranium glass, materials which he viewed as having the power to convert invisible ultraviolet rays into rays of wavelengths which are visible (*see* LUMINESCENCE: *Early History: Fluorescence and Luminescence*). A mechanical model illustrating the dynamic principle of Stokes's explanation was shown in 1883, during a lecture at the Royal institution by Lord Kelvin, who said he had heard an account of it from Stokes many years before and had repeatedly but vainly begged him to publish it. In the same year, 1852, there appeared the paper on the composition and resolution of streams of polarized light from different sources, and in 1853 an investigation of the metallic reflection exhibited by certain nonmetallic substances. About 1860 he was engaged in an inquiry on the intensity of light reflected from, or transmitted through, a pile of plates; and in 1862 he prepared for the British association a valuable report on double refraction, which marks a period in the history of the subject in England. A paper on the long spectrum of the electric light bears the same date and was followed by an inquiry into the absorption spectrum of blood. (*See* also LIGHT: *Types of Polarized Light.*)

The discrimination of organic bodies by their optical properties was treated in 1864; and later, in conjunction with the Rev. W. Vernon Harcourt, he investigated the relation between the chemical constitution and the optical properties of various glasses, with reference to the conditions of transparency and the improvement of achromatic telescopes. A still later paper connected with the construction of optical instruments discussed the theoretical limits to the aperture of microscope objectives. In other departments of physics may be mentioned his paper on the conduction of heat in crystals (1851) and his inquiries in connection with the radiometer; his explanation of the light border frequently noticed in photographs just outside the outline of a dark body seen against the sky (1883); and still later his theory of Roentgen or X rays, which he suggested might be transverse waves traveling as innumerable solitary waves, not in regular trains. Two long papers published in 1849—one on attractions and Clairaut's theorem and the other on the variation of gravity at the surface of the earth—also demand notice, as do his mathematical memoirs on the critical values of the sums of periodic series (1847) and on the numerical calculation of a class of definite integrals and infinite series (1850) and his valuable discussion of a differential equation relating to the strains, stresses and other factors involved in the breaking of railway bridges (1849). (*See* also GEODESY: *Methods and Achievements of Physical Geodesy.*)

Many of his discoveries were only touched upon in lectures. An instance is his work in the theory of spectrum analysis. Some of Stokes's friends and pupils claimed that he had anticipated the work of G. R. Kirchhoff, but Stokes maintained that he had failed to see an essential step in the argument and disclaimed priority. As Lucasian professor, Stokes announced that he wished to help any member of the university in his mathematical studies, and pupils were glad to consult him, even after they had become colleagues. During the 30 years of his secretaryship to the Royal society he advanced the cause of mathematical and physical science not only by his own investigations but by suggesting problems for inquiry and encouraging men to attack them.

He received the Rumford medal in 1852 and the Copley medal in 1893. His numerous other honours included the Prussian order of merit.

Sir George Stokes's mathematical and physical papers were published in a collected form in five volumes; the first three (1880, 1883 and 1901) under his own editorship and the two last (1904 and 1905) under that of Sir Joseph Larmor, who also selected and arranged the *Memoir and Scientific Correspondence* of Stokes published at Cambridge in 1907. Stokes was the author of *Light* (1884–87) and *Natural Theology* (1891).

**STOLBERG, FRIEDRICH LEOPOLD,** GRAF ZU STOLBERG (1750–1819), German poet, known for his ballads, and of literary importance for his close association with the Göttingen *Hain* (*see* GERMAN LITERATURE: *The Age of Goethe*), was born at Bramstedt, Holstein, on Nov. 7, 1750. He studied law at Halle (1770) and Göttingen (1772). Enthusiasm for Klopstock, Greek literature, and nature led him to join the Göttingen *Hain;* his friendship with Goethe began when he and his brother, Christian (1748–1821), also a poet, arrived in Frankfurt in May 1775, dressed in "Werther costume" (blue coat, yellow waistcoat, and breeches), and invited Goethe to accompany them on a "sentimental" journey to Switzerland, of which there are accounts in Stolberg's *Tagebüchern* and Goethe's *Dichtung und Wahrheit.* During 1777–1800 he was mainly in the diplomatic service of the prince-bishop of Lübeck. In 1791 he traveled through Germany, Switzerland, and Italy before becoming president of the episcopal court at Eutin. In 1800 he retired to Münster, Westphalia; and in 1816 to his estate at Sondermühlen, near Osnabrück, where he died on Dec. 5, 1819.

Like other members of the Göttingen *Hain,* Stolberg wrote patriotic revolutionary odes extolling freedom and denouncing tyranny. His ballads form a link with the ballads of chivalry of the German Romantics, especially of the Swabian school. He also wrote satires and dramas, and excelled as a translator. His translations of Aeschylus (1782–83; published, after stylistic revision, in 1802), the Iliad (1778), and Plato (1796–97) helped to spread understanding of the Greek spirit in Germany. Schiller used the Aeschylus translations when working on the chorus in his *Die Braut von Messina.*

In 1800 Stolberg joined the Roman Catholic Church. This conversion, severely attacked by his former friend and benefactor J. H. Voss, led to his rejection of the spirit of the Enlightenment, of 18th-century Pietism, of the French Revolution, and, as he became more extreme, even of Schiller's attitude to the Greek gods. These cumulative rejections may be said to have initiated the trend toward Catholicism among the German Romantics.

BIBLIOGRAPHY.—*Editions and Correspondence: Der Brüder Chr. und F. L. Grafen zu Stolberg gesammelte Werke,* 20 vol. (1820–25; 2nd ed. 1827); selections in J. Kürschner's *Deutsche Nationalliteratur,* vol. 50 (1895); *Briefe an J. H. Voss,* ed. by O. Hellinghaus (1891); *Briefwechsel,* ed. by F. H. Jacobi (1825–27); *Briefe aus dem Stolbergschen Kreise,* ed. by H. Jansen (1932).

*Biography and Criticism:* T. Menge, *Der Graf F. L. Stolberg und seine Zeitgenossen,* 2 vol. (1862); J. H. Hennes, *Stolberg in den zwei letzten Jahrzehnten seines Lebens* (1875), and *Aus F. L. von Stolbergs Jugendjahren* (1876); J. Janssen, *F. L. Graf zu Stolberg,* 2 vol., 4th ed. rev. by L. V. Pastor (1910); W. Keiper, *F. L. Stolbergs Jugendpoesie* (1893); A. Beck, *Stolbergs Äschylos-Übersetzung* (1938). (W. I. L.)

**STOLBERG,** an industrial town of West Germany in the *Land* (state) of North Rhine-Westphalia, Federal Republic of Germany, lies 7 mi. (11 km.) E of Aachen. Pop. (1961) 37,462. The castle, founded in the 12th century, has been restored. The town is first mentioned in 1118 and was chartered in 1856. Its economic development began in the 17th century with the rise of the brass industry. Metal industries now include brass, copper, lead, zinc, tin, and iron. Glass, cables, rubber, textiles, lime, chemicals, soap, pharmaceutical goods, and furniture are produced, and there are spinning, brewing, and building construction enterprises.

**STOLE,** a liturgical vestment of the Roman Catholic Church, peculiar to the higher orders; *i.e.,* deacons, priests and bishops. Its equivalents in the Eastern Churches are the epitrachelion of priests and the orarion of deacons.

*See* Liturgy, Christian.

**STOLYPIN, PETR ARKADIEVICH** (1862–1911), Russian statesman, the sponsor of the last considerable reform envisaged before World War I and the Revolution. He was born at Dresden, in Saxony, on April 14, 1862, of an old noble family of Russian landowners, and was educated in St. Petersburg. Appointed governor of Grodno province in 1902, he was transferred to Saratov province in 1903. There in 1905 he attracted notice by his self-control and determination in quelling peasant disturbances. In May 1906 he was appointed minister of the interior, an office which he retained on becoming premier in July.

Stolypin set out to consolidate the new semiconstitutional regime by suppressing revolutionary violence and by improving the juridical and economic position of the peasants. His reform, inaugurated by a decree of Nov. 22 (new style; 9, old style), 1906, and given final legislative shape in 1910 and 1911, involved a radical transformation of Russia's agrarian structure. Peasants were encouraged to leave the commune and to secure their holdings as individual property; where possible, they were to consolidate their scattered strips of land into enclosed farms. This was designed to promote technical progress and to create a class of prosperous farmers who would constitute a bulwark of conservatism in the Russian countryside. The reform also comprised measures to expand credit facilities, to promote internal colonization (particularly in Siberia), to improve the machinery of local self-government, and to develop the educational system.

Stolypin sought the collaboration of the liberal opposition in realizing his program, but insisted on their accepting his terms. When the second Duma (*q.v.*) refused to endorse his policies it was dissolved in June 1907 and a new electoral law was promulgated without its consent, restricting the franchise. Stolypin was ready to disregard constitutional legality if he believed the government's vital interests to be at stake.

In the third Duma, Stolypin at first relied for support on the moderate (conservative) Octobrists, but a breach developed over his ruthless policy toward the Finns and other national minorities. He was a convinced Russian nationalist, and his zeal in this cause led in March 1911 to a constitutional crisis. He prevailed on the emperor Nicholas II to suspend both legislative chambers while he promulgated, as an emergency measure, a decree establishing *zemstva* (local assemblies) in the western provinces of the empire. This antagonized public opinion and also played into the hands of right-wing politicians who were intriguing against him with the emperor. Stolypin was now virtually isolated. On Sept. 14 (N.S.), 1911, at a Kiev theatre in the emperor's presence, he received bullet wounds from which he died four days later. His assassin was a former terrorist and police agent, Dmitri (Mordka) Bogrov. Mysterious features of the affair suggested that his death was not unwelcome to his highly placed enemies.

*See* Alexandra Stolypine, *L'Homme du dernier Tsar* (1931); V. Bogrov, *Dmitri Bogrov i ubiistvo Stolypina* (1931). (J. L. H. K.)

**STOMACH,** the baglike digestive organ which in man lies in the upper left part of the abdomen between the esophagus and the duodenum. For anatomical details *see* Gastrointestinal Tract. For the functions of the stomach *see* Digestion. For the diseases of the stomach in general *see* Gastrointestinal Tract, Diseases of; for particular ailments *see* Gastric and Duodenal Ulcer; Gastritis; Indigestion. *See* also references under "Stomach" in the Index.

**STOMACH, SURGERY OF.** The first successful major operations upon the stomach were performed by Theodor Billroth (1829–94) of Vienna. His procedures included two separate approaches for excisional therapy of cancer of the stomach: (1) partial removal of the stomach with reestablishment of direct continuity between the cut end of the stomach and the duodenum, and (2) partial removal of the stomach with construction of an indirect continuity between the stomach and the jejunum. Surgery of the stomach was not possible before Billroth chiefly because the required opening of the abdominal cavity (laparotomy; *q.v.*) was not feasible until general anesthesia and antisepsis were developed.

Stomach operations are performed mainly for (1) cancer of the stomach, (2) ulcer of the stomach or duodenum, and (3) hypertrophic pyloric stenosis.

**Cancer of the Stomach.**—Surgical treatment for this condition involves a subtotal or total removal of the stomach, reconstitution of the continuity of the intestinal tract so that food can again pass into the small intestine, and removal of the greater omentum, spleen, and surrounding lymph node areas. If there are obvious extensions into other organs that can be sacrificed (colon, left lobe of liver, pancreas, etc.) these are removed as well. When all the apparently cancerous tissue is removed, about one-third of the patients are still alive after five years. Surgery for cancer of the stomach has about a 10% mortality; without such treatment, fewer than 5% of the patients survive for three years.

**Ulcer of the Stomach or Duodenum.**—The aim of surgery for gastric or duodenal ulcers is different from that for cancer. The aim is not primarily to remove the ulcer but instead to reduce the secretion of acid by the parietal cells in the central portion (corpus) of the stomach so that the ulcer will heal. This may be accomplished by removing most of the corpus (*i.e.,* by subtotal gastric resection) or by cutting down on the strongest stimulators of acid secretion. These stimulators include nervous stimuli transmitted by the two abdominal branches of the vagus nerve, which may be cut bilaterally at the level of the diaphragm or selectively to the stomach only, and hormonal stimuli that arise from the lower portion (antrum) of the stomach; the hormonal stimuli may be eliminated by removing the antrum. Surgery for ulcer, therefore, usually involves one or more of the following procedures: cutting the vagal nerves, subtotal resection of the corpus, removal of the antrum, and often a sidetracking procedure to permit more easy exit of food from the stomach. Surgery for ulcer has about a 1–2% mortality and gives good results in 90% of cases.

While these principles apply to ulcers of both the stomach and duodenum, treatment of duodenal ulcer differs in that it is directed at the adjoining organ, the stomach, where the acid is secreted, rather than at the ulcerated duodenum itself. (*See* also Gastric and Duodenal Ulcer.)

**Hypertrophic Pyloric Stenosis.**—This condition represents a hypertrophy, or overgrowth, of the muscle that surrounds the pylorus (outlet) of the stomach. Its highest incidence is in first-born males, in whom it occurs at a rate of 1 in 300 at about the third week of life. If the condition is not treated surgically, the stomach contents cannot go through the narrowed ring and the mortality is 50–75%. The preferred method of surgery involves cutting the thickened muscular ring without cutting into the interior of the pyloric canal. This operation has about a 0.5% mortality and gives good results in 99% of cases.

*See* also Abdomen, Surgery of: *Gastrointestinal Surgery;* Gastrointestinal Tract, Diseases of: *Stomach.*

Bibliography.—L. R. Dragstedt, "Vagotomy for Gastroduodenal Ulcer," *Ann. Surg.,* 122:973–989 (Dec. 1945); Henry N. Harkins and Lloyd M. Nyhus (eds.), *Surgery of the Stomach and Duodenum*

(1962); N. C. Tanner, "The Indications for Surgery in Peptic Ulcer," *Edinburgh Medical Journal,* 58:261–278 (June 1951); O. H. Wangensteen, *Cancer of the Esophagus and the Stomach* (1951); R. Maingot, *Abdominal Operations,* 4th ed. (1961); R. W. Postlethwait *et al.* (eds.), *Results of Surgery for Peptic Ulcer* (1963). (H. N. Hs.)

**STONE, BARTON WARREN** (1772–1844), U.S. religious leader, one of the founders of the Disciples of Christ (*q.v.*), was born in Maryland on Dec. 24, 1772, and educated in academies of the Piedmont. Stone was ordained to the Presbyterian ministry in 1798, though he was more Arminian than Calvinist in his views and stressed primitive Christian thought and practice. He was preacher at Cane Ridge Church, near Paris, Ky., when it became the centre of the Great Revival (1801–03) and an immense camp meeting with many preachers participating (*see* REVIVALISM). In 1803 Stone and five colleagues left the Synod of Kentucky and formed the Springfield Presbytery. In 1804, after biblical study, they signed "The Last Will and Testament of the Springfield Presbytery," dissolving that body that it might "sink into union with the Body of Christ at large." This act on behalf of Christian unity furthered among churches of the Carolinas and Kentucky a movement toward congregational polity and the use of the name "Christian" only. Stone gradually became the leader of this movement west of the Allegheny Mountains, establishing the *Christian Messenger* (1826–37; 1839–45) to propagate his liberal views and to urge Christian unity. Stone's acquaintance with Alexander Campbell (*q.v.*) began in the 1820s, and in 1832 followers of the two men joined to form the Disciples of Christ or Christian Church. Stone's eagerness for the union is credited as the decisive factor in its achievement, but leadership fell upon the younger Campbell. Stone, always a frontier spirit, moved west, settling in Illinois. He died in Missouri on Nov. 9, 1844, and is buried at Cane Ridge, where his log church is enshrined.

BIBLIOGRAPHY.—W. G. West, *Barton Warren Stone* (1954); C. C. Ware, *Barton Warren Stone, Pathfinder of Christian Union* (1932); A. W. Fortune, *The Disciples in Kentucky* (1932); W. E. Garrison and A. T. DeGroot, *Disciples of Christ: a History* (1948). (W. B. BE.)

**STONE, EDWARD JAMES** (1831–1897), British astronomer, who improved the fundamental constants of astronomy, was born in London on Feb. 28, 1831. Educated at King's College, London, and Queen's College, Cambridge, in 1860 he became chief assistant to the astronomer royal at the Royal Observatory, Greenwich. Stone deduced the solar parallax, first from observations of Mars, obtaining 8.932″ and 8.945″, and then from the transit of Venus in 1869, which yielded 8.91″. He received the Gold Medal of the Royal Astronomical Society in 1869 and was appointed astronomer at the Cape Observatory, South Africa, in 1870. He was appointed Radcliffe observer at Oxford in 1878 and served as president of the Royal Astronomical Society from 1882 to 1884. Stone died at Oxford on May 9, 1897. (O. J. E.)

**STONE, HARLAN FISKE** (1872–1946), 12th chief justice of the United States, participated in making more of his dissenting positions become law than any other justice in history. He was born in Chesterfield, N.H., on Oct. 11, 1872, and died in Washington, D.C., on April 22, 1946. After graduating from Amherst College in 1894 and receiving his law degree from Columbia University Law School in 1898, he taught law there and practised in New York from 1899 until 1924. He was dean of Columbia Law School from 1910 until 1923. In 1924 Pres. Calvin Coolidge appointed him attorney general of the United States, and in 1925 associate justice of the U.S. Supreme Court. In 1941, Pres. Franklin D. Roosevelt appointed him chief justice.

BROWN BROTHERS

HARLAN FISKE STONE, PHOTOGRAPHED ABOUT 1938

His tenure on the Supreme Court was marked by three rather distinct areas of constitutional debate in addition to the perennial constitutional controversy concerning the authority of one state to regulate or tax persons or institutions connected with several states. During the first half of his tenure the great controversy involved the power of a state to make changes in its economic or legal order by regulations, prohibitions, or taxes. During most of this period he was associated with Justices Oliver Wendell Holmes and Louis Brandeis, and part of the time with Justice Benjamin Cardozo as one of three "great dissenters." A second period of his judicial career involved a controversy over the power of the national government to make changes in the economic or legal order of the nation. This was the period of the New Deal legislation. During his chief justiceship the great debate concerned the power of the popular majority to control matters touching affairs of conscience and expression.

In each of these areas, first as a dissenter and later writing for the majority, Stone made contributions to constitutional jurisprudence. The culmination of his views on the power of a state to regulate interstate commerce came in an opinion shortly before his death, *Southern Pacific Company* v. *Arizona,* 325 U.S. 761 (1945), in which he restated the historic position of the Supreme Court that the commerce clause of the Constitution gave the court power to invalidate local legislation affecting persons connected with several states. He rejected every mechanistic formula to determine how the court executed its power, such as the formula that if the burden of the regulation on interstate commerce was "direct," it was unconstitutional, but if "only indirect," the regulation was valid. The court, said Stone, must look to all facts and circumstances and determine for itself, without any help from Congress, whether state regulation imperiled the national interest in the free flow of commerce. This required the court openly to make a value judgment.

When the problem was the state's power under the due-process and equal-protection clause of the 14th Amendment to the Constitution to regulate economic enterprise, Stone adhered to the position developed earlier by Holmes and Brandeis that the court should abstain from invalidating the legislation, whatever the individual members thought about the policy of the legislation, as long as anyone could find a reasonable basis for supporting the statute. His unique contribution to the debate concerning the 14th Amendment came in a footnote to *United States* v. *Carolene Products Co.,* 304 U.S. 144 (1938), where he suggested that while the court should abstain from expressing judgment about economic regulation, it should, in matters concerning personal freedom and conscience and concerning the processes of democracy, such as voting, make a more searching inquiry into the reasonableness of the legislation. In application of this principle he was the lone dissenter in *Minersville District* v. *Gobitis,* 310 U.S. 586 (1940), wherein the majority held that the state could compel a member of Jehovah's Witnesses actively to participate in the flag salute ceremony. In 1943 the majority of the court switched to Stone's position and held, in *West Virginia Board of Education* v. *Barnette,* 319 U.S. 624, that such a compulsory flag salute was unconstitutional.

As chief justice during World War II, Stone presided over cases of martial law, military courts, and treason, many of which involved constitutional matters presented to the Supreme Court for the first time in U.S. history. The court was convened in special session that the German saboteurs might have their conviction reviewed without delay and in accordance with standards of due process. Later the court passed on the validity of the "war trial" of the Japanese General Tomoyuki Yamashita; the validity of the curfew for reasons of defense of the West Coast; and the question whether military tribunals could supersede civilian courts in Hawaii.

During his 22 years on the court, Stone wrote more than 600 opinions and dissents. While they cover the entire range of judicial business, the accidents of history projected him into the limelight for his work in the field of constitutional law.

In one of his more famous dissents, *U.S.* v. *Butler,* 297 U.S. 1 (1936), involving the constitutionality of the first Agricultural Adjustment Act of the New Deal, he expressed one of the great problems of judicial review of executive and legislative action when he said that "while unconstitutional exercise of power by the executive and legislative branches of the Government is subject to judicial restraint, the only check upon our own exercise of power is our own sense of restraint." Stone's conduct on the court indicated how thoroughly he subordinated self-interest and applied this principle. As Stone's biographers point out, some of Stone's passionate dissents, such as the one in the case cited above, found him upholding legislation which, if he had been a legislator, he would have passionately denounced.

Stone was stricken on the bench while reading a dissent in the case of *Girouard* v. *U.S.,* 328 U.S. 61 (1946), involving the question whether unwillingness to bear arms because of pacifistic religious belief was a bar to naturalization. In 1931, when this question had first come to the Supreme Court, Stone joined in a dissent declaring that the act of Congress should not be construed to bar naturalization. In 1946 the court changed its position to adopt Stone's original dissenting position, but he again dissented on the ground that subsequent consideration by Congress had confirmed the interpretation of the statute that he had earlier thought erroneous. Thus his last act on the Supreme Court was a dramatic illustration of his deference to the legislative will as he saw it.

*See* Alpheus Mason, *Harlan Fiske Stone: Pillar of the Law* (1956); Allison Dunham and Philip B. Kurland (eds.), *Mr. Justice* (1956). (A. DM.)

**STONE, LUCY** (1818–1893), U.S. women's rights leader, was born in West Brookfield, Mass., Aug. 13, 1818. Saddened by the inequalities then imposed upon women and determined to find out whether the scriptural texts regarding their subjection were correctly translated, she put herself through Oberlin, the only college then open to women, and graduated in 1847. The following year, already recognized as a gifted speaker, she was engaged as a lecturer by the Massachusetts Anti-Slavery Society, and soon obtained permission to speak part of each week for women's rights, on her own responsibility. She was instrumental in organizing women's rights conventions in the 1850s, including the first one of national character at Worcester, Mass., in 1850. In 1855 she married Henry B. Blackwell, an Ohio abolitionist. The couple issued at that time a public protest against the unequal laws applicable to married women, and agreed that she would retain her own name and be known as Mrs. Stone. Jointly working for suffrage as residents of New Jersey for over a decade, she and her husband were called to Boston in 1868 by the newly formed New England Woman Suffrage Association. In 1869 they helped establish the American Woman Suffrage Association, a nationwide organization that worked for woman suffrage by state legislation while the National Woman Suffrage Association urged a federal constitutional amendment. In 1870 Mrs. Stone and her husband helped found in Boston the *Woman's Journal,* a woman suffrage weekly, and assumed responsibility for editing it in 1872. Thereafter until 1917 this paper and *Woman Suffrage Leaflets,* both under Blackwell editorship, were major influences in extending the suffrage movement. Mrs. Stone also took a leading role in introducing suffrage articles into the metropolitan press of the country, while Mr. Blackwell initiated a movement to organize suffragists locally for political action. They thus paved the way for the educational, organizational, and political work of Carrie Chapman Catt (*q.v.*) after 1895. Mrs. Stone died Oct. 18, 1893.

BIBLIOGRAPHY.—Alice Stone Blackwell, *Lucy Stone* (1930); Elinor R. Hays, *Morning Star* (1961); Lois B. Merk, *Massachusetts and the Woman-Suffrage Movement* (microfilm, 1961, Library of Congress); *Woman's Journal* (1870–1917). (L. B. ME.)

**STONE, NICHOLAS** (1586?–1647), the most important English mason-sculptor of the early 17th century. A native of Woodbury, near Exeter, Devon, he was apprenticed in London to Isaac James, a Flemish refugee, and after 1606 spent seven years as a journeyman in Amsterdam with Hendrik de Keyser, the leading Dutch architect and sculptor, whose daughter he married. On his return he set up a workshop in London and quickly acquired a large practice as a tomb sculptor and mason. About 80 monuments are recorded in his notebook in the Soane museum, London. There is also an account book covering the years 1631–42, which throws interesting light on the organization of a big mason's yard.

Stone's earliest monuments—the Bodley monument at Merton college, Oxford (1615); Lady Carey (1617) at Church Stowe, Northamptonshire; or Sir Charles Morrison (1619) at Watford, Hertfordshire—show links with the style of the Low Countries and with late Elizabethan work. The architectural settings are florid, much use is often made of coloured alabasters and of brightly blazoned shields. The figure sculpture is, however, naturalistic and sensitively cut.

In the next decade Stone began to be aware of Italian art. From 1619 to 1622 he served as master mason under Inigo Jones at the Banqueting house at Whitehall and became master mason to the crown in 1632. He was concerned with the repairs of the antique sculpture bought by Charles I, and the knowledge he thus gained of classical art undoubtedly affected his style. Much of his later work, *e.g.,* the second Morrison tomb (1630) at Watford or the Lyttelton monument (1634) at Magdalen college, Oxford, is more classical both in the drapery treatment and in the architectural settings. Because of the extensive use of assistants, however, his later work is uneven in quality.

He also undertook a large number of masonry contracts for royal palaces. He could design as well as build—the gateway to the Botanic garden (1632), and probably the porch of St. Mary the Virgin, at Oxford are his, as were Goldsmiths' hall, London (now destroyed), and parts of Cornbury house, Oxfordshire. He built York Water gate, London, but whether he designed it is uncertain.

Nicholas Stone was an excellent craftsman and his best sculpture has some distinction, but he cannot be regarded as an artist of high rank. He died at his house in Long Acre, London, on Aug. 24, 1647.

*The Note-Book and Account Book of Nicholas Stone* was edited by W. L. Spiers (Walpole society, vii, 1918). (M. D. WY.)

**STONE,** as the word is most generally used, is a piece of rock (*see* PETROLOGY) or of the solid crust of the earth, and hence of natural origin and generally of inorganic composition.

By their resemblance to rock fragments, however, many objects that originate artificially are also called stone. Examples are commercial grindstones and whetstones (commonly made of crushed natural mineral substances cemented together artificially). A frequent but even more divergent use of the word is the medical one: gallstones and the like are physiologically secreted materials, also known as concretions (*see* URINARY SYSTEM; LIVER AND GALL-BLADDER, DISEASES OF). Because of their hardness, the seeds of some vegetables and fruits (*e.g.,* peaches) are called stones. Kinds of stones or rocks are distinguished by prefixes, *e.g.,* limestone, sandstone. To describe its use by man the word stone may have a prefix, *e.g.,* gemstone, millstone. The term is applied to markers used in surveying or building (*e.g.,* cornerstones).

Finally, stone is used somewhat archaically for units of weight, especially in Great Britain—the legal unit of measure, the stone (14 lb. avoirdupois), the stone of the wool weighers (formerly, and still in Scotland, 24; later usually 14 lb.), the Smithfield or butcher's stone (8 lb.; unofficial but still in use). The word has special meanings in certain trades, *e.g.,* a defect in glass, generally caused by foreign material, the glassmakers' stone, and a flat surface for assembling type known to printers as a stone for historical reasons.

### GENERAL USES OF STONE

When used for a fragment of rock, stone is widely applied to building material—for example, a house of stone, a stone wall. The stone may be crushed (crushed rock, crushed stone) or ground. Or the rock may be broken, quarried, cut or blasted, along natural lines of weakness. The resulting blocks, if large but irregular, are riprap; if more or less polygonal, thin slabs, they are flagging or flagstones. If sized to fairly definite dimensions, they are dimension stones, and if cut, cut stones. Boulders, pebbles or gravel are terms reserved, respectively, for the individual, generally large rounded pieces of stone, for such pieces when smaller and for masses of such boulders or pebbles, frequently embedded in sand or clay. Aggregate is used in the United States for pebbles, crushed stone or their natural or artificial substitutes which, when mixed with cement as binder, give concrete. Much stone is raw material for industrial processes. Important instances are in making glass and various refractories, in smelting several ores especially iron ore to make pig iron, in preparing cements notably portland cement, and in the chemical industries, where limestone is an inexpensive, widely available basic chemical material.

## BUILDING STONE

**Structural Features.**—Most stone will split along pre-existing or incipient planes of weakness. If originally laid down as a sediment, stone will part (after consolidation or cementation) parallel to bedding planes or stratification, though such planes may heal or be otherwise obliterated. The partings separating the beds may be closely or widely spaced, ranging from fractions of a millimetre to thicknesses of several feet. If the rock has been compressed in mountain building or folding, with or without heating, it may be dynamically metamorphosed and recrystallized (*see* METAMORPHISM). In such cases, cleavage planes are developed parallel to the most numerous and most flat surfaces of the constituent minerals. Examples are many schists and slates. Such parting planes, perhaps only millimetres apart, may transect the bedding at almost any angle. Slate also may have a much less well-defined tendency to fracture normal to the cleavage—the sculp or grain of quarrying. If once molten and later solidified in its present position—igneous rock, technically—stone may show some tendency to part along two ill-defined directions, rift and grain, normally about at right angles to each other and to the surface of the ground; further, it may have a tendency to part along nearly horizontal but gently curved planes (sheeting).

Almost all rocks have been slightly compressed or have been shrunken by drying or cooling and therefore show real or incipient parting, distinct from the planes already described. This may follow a regular pattern, giving jointing, which yields rectangular or rhombohedral blocks—forms obviously desirable for use in foundations, walls or pavements.

**Quarrying and Preparation.**—If the stone is to be used in bulk (as for ballast or chemical raw material), the quarry operation may be preceded by stripping useless material, followed by drilling holes into the rock and blasting it to size suitable for transport. Wherever possible, such operations are mechanized. They may be followed by crushing the rock in a gyrator, a heavy vertical spindle rotating within a hard metal collar, against which the rock is crushed. Or crushing may be by two metal jaws that close upon the rock as it is fed between them. Further stages of crushing or grinding, grading by screens or washing or a similar process may follow. If the stone must meet dimensions, the parting planes previously mentioned may be exploited in quarrying. Holes are drilled from the exposed surface to the level of an observed or inferred parting plane. Through these are introduced a gas or water under pressure, or explosives to make the rock break along the desired plane of weakness. Other surfaces are separated from the solid rock in like manner, until an approximately regular block of desired size is freed. Alternative methods of quarrying are by channeler, a chisellike blade rapidly forced against the rock, cutting a groove; by drilling a line of holes close together and broaching (breaking) the rock between; or by wire saw, a continuous wire which moves under tension dragging sand across the stone, thus sawing its way through. A block is next usually transported to a shed where it is sawed on a movable table or with a movable saw, toothed with hard alloys. Or the large block is cut, as in much marble production, with one or several parallel bands of hard steel swinging across one surface, sprayed with water and fed with abrasive sand. Such methods reduce the block to pieces approximating the desired thinness for possible use as facing (veneer). Blocks also may be trimmed to size and shape by hand or by smaller carborundum or other hard alloy saws, drilled if they are to be bolted in place, and polished. Polishing is on a sand bed, a rotating, horizontal disk, moving under the stone to be polished and carrying sand as abrasive. Another polishing device consists of one or several polishing heads that rotate while pressing against the slab from above and are operated manually or, more commonly, mechanically. Further processing depends upon special requirements—the more processing, the higher the unit value. (*See* also QUARRYING.)

**Natural Features Affecting Use.**—Factors affecting the use of stone for roadbeds, ballast, dam and embankment facing, construction of bridge piers, supporting walls, roofing or facing of buildings, surfacing of areas of much wear (like stairs) and of little wear (like shower stalls), decoration of tables and chairs, veneering of interiors of buildings and for statuary are as varied as the uses to which the stone is put. Special uses are mentioned below in discussing the appropriate stone.

Such properties as resistance to abrasion or sudden shock, and the tendency to fracture or spall when heated are normally considered in selecting the stone to be used for ballast or concrete aggregate. Various tests may be used to determine hardness, resistance to surface abrasion, or relative resistance to impact. Crushing strength tests are also used, especially with structural stone for foundations of dams, bridges and large buildings.

Porous rock may absorb water and, on the freezing of the water, will spall or chip with changes in temperature. Accelerated freezing tests, using some soluble compound that expands as it crystallizes and is introduced into the rock in solution, have proved useful in determining freezing resistance.

For decoration, critical properties are colour, texture and resistance to disfiguring developments (such as pitting, staining and spalling). Colour varies with the mineral constituents. Pink, red, brown and yellow are usually due to iron minerals, especially hematite and limonite. But granitelike stone is pinkish because of potassium feldspars. Grays may be due to carbon or dark minerals like amphiboles, pyroxenes and micas—silicates usually containing some iron. Green is usually from magnesium or iron silicates. Bluish gray and rare blue are commonly fundamentally black, but if iridescent, may indicate calcic or sodic feldspars, as in some of the iridescent peacock-coloured dark rocks from Scandinavia. White and light gray chiefly result from quartz, feldspars, calcite and clay minerals. Colours do not necessarily reflect major constituents; stones containing 99% white quartz may be rusty brown because of 1% iron oxide, a strong tinting agent.

Texture is important in many ways. Some rocks, such as certain lavas are extremely porous. Stone of mixed grain sizes does not polish as readily as one more uniform in grain. Marble too coarsely granular cannot be worked easily for statuary. Nevertheless, highly porous travertine with irregularly wavy pattern is at a premium as a decorative stone, and rocks with conspicuous veins, crystals, fossils or fragments (breccias) are valued for interior decoration. Similarly, sea-green and light-gray wavelike patterns in certain marbles are much in demand and so are matched panels, cut and set into patterned designs.

**Kinds and Sources of Stones.**—As suggested, building stones fall into three geologic classes: sedimentary, igneous and metamorphic. The first includes limestone (and its magnesium-bearing variety, dolomite), sandstone and the rarely used shale. Some marbles are properly limestones. Igneous building stones include granite and related light-coloured (acid) coarsely crystalline igneous rocks, basalt or trap and other dark-coloured (basic) igneous rocks, largely fine-grained but partly coarsely crystalline, like diorite and gabbro and fine-grained, light-coloured lavas and volcanic tuffs. Among the metamorphic rocks, marble, slate, gneiss, schist and serpentine are most used.

Of all types, limestone and dolomite, or magnesian limestone, find the largest and most versatile use. Being sedimentary rock, with the beds in many places essentially horizontal, these are commonly easily quarried. The uses of limestone and dolomite are highly varied—as a flux in metallurgy, particularly ironmaking, as a basic chemical raw material (if not too high in magnesium), as a source of coarse crushed stone, or road metal, and aggregate in concrete wherever available and as a satisfactory foundation, building and facing stone. Thus, limestone and dolomite yield more tons of stone in the United States than any other. Generally white to gray and fine textured, it may grade into the coarsely crystalline texture of marble. A major producing region is near Bedford, Ind. Characteristic of the Bedford limestones and those of southern England and northwestern France are the small pellets, or oölites, suggesting fish roe, composing them (*see* Oölite). Limestone is also available on tropical coasts in the form of coral-line lime if of corallike origin, and of coquina if composed of shell fragments.

Second in quantity used as building stone is sandstone. It ranges in colour from white through buff, red and dark brown. It consists of sand grains cemented with silica, calcium carbonate or clay. The porosity of certain sandstones makes them subject to water ingress and spalling. As coarseness increases sandstone grades into grit and finally conglomerate (cemented gravel). Sandstone is widely quarried for building, especially in western Europe and the United States (Ohio, New York, Wisconsin, Pennsylvania and New Jersey). Unlike limestone, it serves little use in industry except in glass and refractories.

Similar to sandstone in quantity used is granite (*q.v.*), a term loosely but inaccurately applied to most light-coloured, coarsely grained igneous stone. Granite is highly useful for crushed and building stone and for monuments and decoration. Its great variety of colours—from white through gray, pink, greenish and almost to black—and of coarseness of grain make it much in demand. Productive localities include especially the Scandinavian countries, Scotland, Canada and New England.

Many dark-coloured igneous rocks (gabbro, andesite, basalt, diabase) are collectively sold as trap and used chiefly in crushed stone for roads and aggregate. Typical localities of production are central France and western Scotland, and Washington, Oregon and New Jersey in the United States.

Marble is a recrystallized and commonly beautifully banded limestone. Its original layers may be greatly contorted, or shattered and recemented, resulting in strikingly contrasting colours and patterns. Its chief use is for decoration—mainly indoors—and for statuary. Famous sources are Italy, Greece, Egypt and Tennessee and Vermont.

Slate is a gray to red, green, mottled or black stone marked by closely spaced and splitting cleavage planes. It is used chiefly for roofing, blackboards, switchboards and partitions, but also as structural stone. Outstanding producing regions are Wales, France, Germany, Switzerland, Belgium, and the eastern United States (Pennsylvania, New York, Vermont and Maine). Similar foliated rocks with wavy cleavage, called schists, are locally used.

Serpentine and related types veined with white calcite (ophicalcite, verd antique) are massive and greenish, generally ranging from almost chartreuse to olive. They are used for counters and panels. Though widespread, large deposits are rare. Travertine, a hot-spring deposit, usually porous, and onyx, generally a precipitate from underground waters in caves, are other decorative stones.

*See* also separate articles on varieties of stone, as Granite; Limestone; Slate, etc.; and references under "Stone" in the Index.

Bibliography.—Oliver Bowles, *The Stone Industries* (1934), general, origin, technology, economics; American Institute of Mining, Metallurgical, and Petroleum Engineers, Committee on industrial minerals volume, *Industrial Minerals and Rocks,* 3rd ed. (1960), sections dealing with cement materials, crushed stone, dimension stone, granules, sand and gravel, slate; G. P. Merrill, *Stones for Building and Decoration* (1910), thorough but somewhat outmoded treatment; J. Hirschwald, *Handbuch der Bautechnischen Gesteinspruefung* (1921), numerous tables of extensive tests; U.S. Bureau of Mines, *Minerals Yearbook* (annual), production, trade, uses, and technology. (C. H. Be.)

**STONE AGE:** *see* Flint and Other Stone Tools; Archaeology: *Prehistory;* Paleolithic; Mesolithic; Neolithic.

**STONE CARVING:** *see* Sculpture; Sculpture Techniques.

**STONEHENGE,** a circular setting of large standing stones surrounded by an earthwork about 8 mi. (13 km.) N of Salisbury, Wiltshire, Eng., was built during Late Neolithic to Early Bronze Age (1800–1400 b.c.). Among the earliest references to it is that of Geoffrey of Monmouth, who related in *Historia regum Britanniae* (*c.* a.d. 1136) the legend that the stones were magically transported from Ireland by Merlin (*q.v.*). This legend perhaps enshrines a folk memory of the bringing from Pembrokeshire of the "bluestones" which form part of the monument. The supposed connection of Stonehenge with the Druids, which, though without foundation, has held the public imagination since the 17th century, originated with John Aubrey (1626–97), and was more particularly elaborated by William Stukeley in 1740 (*see* Druidism). The modern interpretation of the monument is based chiefly on excavations carried out by the Society of Antiquaries of London from 1919.

The monument consists of a number of structural elements, mostly circular in plan. On the outside is a circular ditch, broken by an entrance gap on the northeast, with a bank immediately within it.

Inside the bank is a ring of 56 pits, known after their discoverer as the Aubrey holes. Between these and the stones in the centre are two further rings of pits, now invisible on the surface, known as the Z and Y holes. The stone setting consisted of two circles (the outer of sarsen [Tertiary sandstone], the inner of bluestone) and two horseshoes of uprights (the outer of sarsen, the inner of bluestone), the outer circle and the outer horseshoe being capped by stone lintels. Additional stones include the Altar stone, lying on the axis southwest of the centre; the Slaughter stone inside the entrance of the earthwork; two Station stones just within the bank on the northwest and southeast; and the Heel ("Hele") stone, standing on the Avenue outside the entrance and surrounded by a narrow circular ditch.

Similar ditches enclose two flat areas on the inner edge of the bank, known as the North and South barrows, with empty stone-holes at their centres.

Excavations between 1950 and 1964 suggested three main periods of building (Stonehenge I, II, and III), the last of which can be divided into three phases (Stonehenge IIIa, IIIb, and IIIc).

Stonehenge I (built in the Late Neolithic about 1800 b.c.) comprised the circular ditch and bank, the Aubrey holes, and the Heel stone. There may have been some structure of stone or timber at the centre of the circle, but little or nothing of it is likely to have survived disturbance by treasure hunters. The bank, now reduced by weathering to a height nowhere more than 2 ft., has a mean diameter of 320 ft. (98 m.), and was broken by an entrance gap 35 ft. (10.7 m.) wide on the northeast side. It

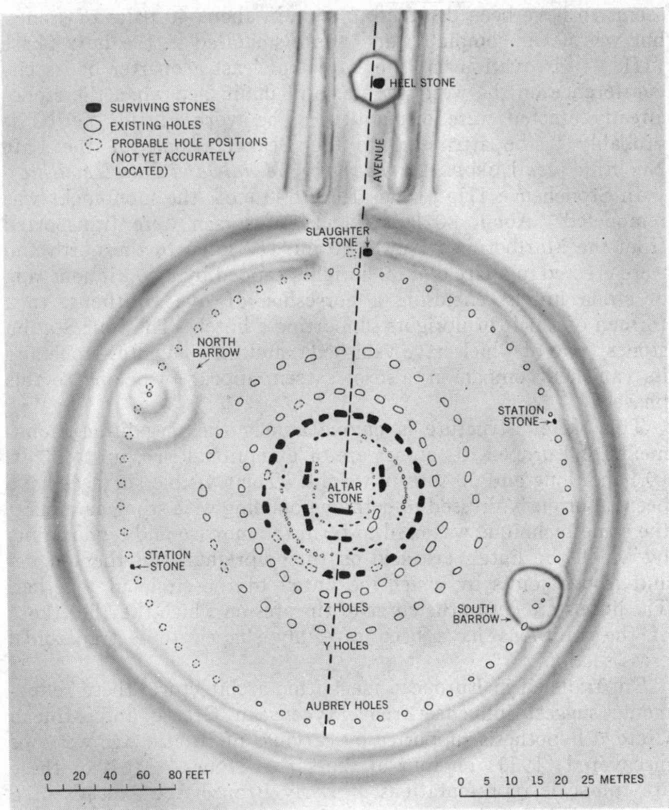


ADAPTED, BY PERMISSION, FROM MINISTRY OF PUBLIC BUILDING AND WORKS PLAN

STONEHENGE PLAN SHOWING STONES, EXCAVATED STRUCTURES, AND THE SOLSTITIAL ALIGNMENT OF THE AXIS OF SYMMETRY was built of chalk rubble quarried from the surrounding ditch. The latter is irregular in plan and depth, and consists of a series of interconnected pits up to 7 ft. (2.1 m.) deep, with steep sides and flat bottoms.

The Aubrey holes form a circle 288 ft. in diameter (87.8 m.). They are round pits up to 6 ft. (1.8 m.) in diameter and 4 ft. (1.2 m.) in depth, with steep sides and flat bottoms. They appear to have been deliberately filled soon after their excavation with the chalk rubble dug from them, some of which meanwhile had been burned. Many of them contain cremated human bones, in most cases inserted later as secondary deposits, though still within the first phase of the monument's history. Similar cremated remains form a cemetery of about 30 burials in the eastern half of the bank and the silting of the ditch.

The Heel stone, a 35-ton block of sarsen 16 ft. (4.9 m.) high, stands outside the entrance of the earthwork, but not on its axis of symmetry. West of it, astride this axis, four large postholes probably represent a former timber gateway. A pair of stones, later removed, appears to have stood centrally in the gap in the bank, northwest of the present position of the Slaughter stone.

In Stonehenge II (probably 17th century B.C.) the entrance of the earthwork was widened on the east side, and was joined to the River Avon (about 2 mi. [3.2 km.] to the east) by the Avenue, a processional way marked by parallel banks and ditches. This enclosed the Heel stone, which was now symbolically protected by the digging, and immediate refilling, of the ditch that surrounds it. At the same time a number of natural slabs and pillars of igneous rock (diabase, rhyolite, and volcanic ash) called bluestones were transported from the Prescelly Mountains in Pembrokeshire, southwest Wales, and erected in the centre of the site to form two concentric circles about 74 ft. and 86 ft. (22.6 m. and 26.2 m.) in diameter. Each radial pair of these stones stood at the ends of an elongated stone-hole straddling the line later followed by the bluestone circle (erected in period IIIc). The entrance of this earliest setting of bluestones was marked by additional inlying pillars, and was aligned approximately upon the sunrise at the summer solstice, the alignment being continued by the section of the Avenue nearest Stonehenge. The double circle seems to have been designed to contain about 40 pairs of stones, but was never completed and was dismantled in the next phase (IIIa). Excavation has shown that at least a quarter of its circumference on the west side was still unfinished when the stones already erected were dismantled. The work of this period is probably to be attributed to the Beaker people of the Late Neolithic (*see* EUROPE: *Archaeology: Middle and Late Neolithic*).

In Stonehenge IIIa (soon after 1600 B.C.) the monument was remodeled. About 80 large blocks of sarsen were transported from the Marlborough Downs 20 mi. (32 km.) to the north and were erected in a circle of 30 uprights capped by a continuous ring of stone lintels, enclosing a horseshoe of five trilithons, each formed of a pair of uprights supporting a lintel. The four Station stones (two of which have vanished), and the Slaughter stone and its vanished companion, also of sarsen, appear to belong to this phase.

This sarsen structure is unique among the megalithic monuments of Europe. Its stones are of exceptional size, up to 30 ft. (9.1 m.) long and 50 tons in weight. Their visible surfaces have been laboriously dressed smooth by pounding with stone hammers; the same technique was used to form the mortise-and-tenon joints by which the lintels are held on their uprights, and the tongue-and-groove joints by which the lintels of the circle fit together. The lintels are cut to the curve of the arcs on which they lie; those of the trilithons have been carefully shaped to a trapezoidal cross section.

Unparalleled in European megalithic architecture, these refinements suggest influence from Mycenaean Greece and Minoan Crete, a hypothesis supported by carvings of Bronze Age weapons discovered (1953) on four of the sarsen stones. Most of these are full-scale representations of Early Bronze Age axheads of a type current in Britain between 1600 and 1400 B.C.; but there is also a single carving of a hilted dagger that can best be matched with weapons from the shaft graves of Mycenae. This identification (though a matter of opinion) is supported by the presence of objects of Mediterranean origin in many of the rich barrow burials of the Early Bronze Age that cluster densely around Stonehenge. On this evidence the building of the sarsen structure may be assigned to the earlier half of the 16th century B.C., broadly confirmed by a radiocarbon estimate giving a probable range of 2000 to 1400 B.C. (*see* RADIOCARBON DATING).

In Stonehenge IIIb, which probably followed immediately, about 20 bluestones were selected from the dismantled components of Stonehenge II and dressed to shape with stone hammers. These were erected in an oval setting, largely coincident with the line of the present inner horseshoe of bluestones. This arrangement contained at least two bluestone trilithons with mortise-and-tenon

AEROFILMS LTD.

AERIAL VIEW OF STONEHENGE, SEEN FROM THE SOUTH; HEEL STONE AT RIGHT CORNER

joints, and a pair of contiguous pillars joined by a vertical tongue and groove. It seems to have been the intention to erect the remaining bluestones in the two circles of Y and Z holes, which are roughly concentric with the sarsen circle; but this plan clearly was never carried out. The holes on the southeast side were never completed; both circles were left open to silt up over the succeeding centuries.

The abandonment of this plan marks the end of phase IIIb and was probably followed at once by the final period of building (Stonehenge IIIc) likely to have been completed before the end of the Early Bronze Age about 1400 B.C. The phase IIIb oval structure of dressed and jointed bluestones in the centre was dismantled; and its bluestones, as well as those lying on or near the site since the dismantling of the phase II circles during phase IIIa, were rearranged into the bluestone circle and horseshoe whose remains can be seen today. Most of the components of the dismantled oval were reused as uprights in the final horseshoe, perhaps after some reshaping to give a sequence of straight-sided square pillars alternating with flatter, tapering obelisks. The Altar stone (of micaceous sandstone from the shores of Milford Haven in Pembrokeshire) apparently stood as a pillar at the focal point of the horseshoe, subsequently falling to cover its own stone-hole.

It is generally and probably rightly assumed that Stonehenge was constructed as a place of worship; but in the absence of contemporary documentary evidence the nature of the religion it served must remain conjectural. The solstitial alignment of the axis of symmetry of the sarsen structure (Stonehenge IIIa) has long been recognized, and is now known to have perpetuated a similar alignment in the earlier double circle of bluestones (Stonehenge II). In 1963 the existence of additional alignments on significant risings and settings of the sun and moon was suggested independently by C. A. Newham in England and by G. S. Hawkins in the U.S. These suggestions undoubtedly reinforce the popular belief that Stonehenge was a temple for sky worship, but should be considered with caution since most Christian churches are likewise astronomically orientated.

Hawkins also suggested that the circle of 56 Aubrey holes could have been used as a counting device for predicting significant risings of the moon, and eclipses of the moon and sun. The possibility cannot be denied, but its likelihood is open to question if only because the Aubrey holes (refilled very soon after they were opened) would have been ill-adapted as permanent markers over several centuries. They also belong to the first Stonehenge, representing a culture and technology markedly more primitive than that of the later stages of construction.

Between 1918 (when the monument was presented to the British nation) and 1964 more than half the surviving sarsen pillars were restored or straightened, and consolidated in concrete foundations, including stones that fell accidentally in 1797, 1900, and 1963. *See* also AMESBURY; WILTSHIRE.

BIBLIOGRAPHY.—R. J. C. Atkinson, *Stonehenge,* 2nd ed. (1960, with bibliography of principal publications to 1959); S. Piggott, article on radiocarbon dating in *The New Scientist* (July 30, 1959); C. A. Newham, article in *Yorkshire Post* (March 16, 1963), *The Enigma of Stonehenge* (1964); G. S. Hawkins, "Stonehenge Decoded," *Nature* (Oct. 26, 1963), "Stonehenge: a Neolithic Computer," *Nature* (June 27, 1964). (R. J. C. A.)

**STONY POINT,** a town of Rockland County, N.Y., U.S., lies in the scenic highlands along the west shore of the Hudson River and about 38 mi. (61 km.) from midtown New York City. Stony Point derives its name from the rocky promontory jutting into the Hudson. A part of Palisades Interstate Park lies within the town limits. At the town's northern point was anchored one end of the heavy chain stretched across the Hudson during the American Revolution to prevent the British fleet from ascending further, while at the southern limits stood the Treason (Joshua Hett Smith) house where Gen. Benedict Arnold and Maj. John André met on Sept. 21, 1780, to arrange for Arnold's betrayal of West Point to the British. At midnight on July 16, 1779, occurred the successful and daring storming of the strong British fortifications at Stony Point by Gen. Anthony Wayne and about 1,350 gallant, hand-picked American troops. Wayne's feat, with a loss of 15 killed and 83 wounded as against 63 British killed and 70 wounded, and the capture of 543 of the garrison, was a severe setback to the British. As the fort was undefendable against river bombardment, however, it was speedily dismantled and evacuated on July 18; the British thereupon reoccupied it a second time but abandoned it late in Oct. 1779, and the upper Hudson was thereafter safe for the Americans.

Major products include chemicals, traprock, and gypsum. Stony Point is governed by a town board consisting of a supervisor, two justices of the peace, and two councilmen.

For comparative population figures *see* table in NEW YORK: *Population.* (M. D. HH.)

**STOPES, MARIE CARMICHAEL** (1880–1958), British pioneer of the birth control movement, was born in Edinburgh, Scot., on Oct. 15, 1880. She graduated in botany and geology at University College, London, in 1903, obtained a doctorate in botany at the University of Munich in 1904, and became a lecturer at Manchester University. A specialist on fossil plants and problems of coal mining, she had established a considerable academic reputation when the failure of her first marriage, which was annulled in 1916, focused her thought on problems of marriage, and on birth control as an aid to marriage fulfillment and as a means to save women from the burdens of excessive childbearing. Humphrey Verdon Roe, the aircraft pioneer, whom she married in 1918, helped her in the crusade which she now began. Her *Married Love* and *Wise Parenthood,* both of which appeared in 1918, had many editions and translations. In 1921 Marie Stopes founded the United Kingdom's first birth control clinic. When her *Contraception: Its Theory, History and Practice* appeared in 1923 it was the most comprehensive work of its kind.

The fervour of Marie Stopes's writings and speeches evoked violent opposition, especially from Roman Catholics, which gave wide publicity to her movement and to herself. She did most to pave the way for the Church of England's change of stand on birth control, as reflected in the reports of successive Lambeth Conferences. After World War II she worked to promote birth control in Far Eastern countries, and continued her interest in coal research. She died at Norbury Park, near Dorking, Surrey, on Oct. 2, 1958. *See* also BIRTH CONTROL.

*See* K. Briant, *Passionate Paradox: the Life of Marie Stopes* (1962).

**STORACE, STEPHEN** (1762–1796), English composer who introduced the classical Italianate style of Vienna into English opera, was born in London on April 4, 1762. The son of an Italian double-bass player resident in Britain and of an English mother, he was trained at the S. Onofrio conservatory in Naples. From 1785 he periodically joined his sister, the singer Ann Selina (Nancy) Storace (1765–1817) in Vienna and took lessons there from Mozart. His first two operas, *Gli sposi malcontenti* (1785) and *Gli equivoci* (1786), were given in Vienna and later in Leipzig, Dresden, and other cities in Germany. The latter, the score of which survives, has an excellent libretto by Lorenzo da Ponte, based on Shakespeare's *The Comedy of Errors.*

In 1786 Nancy Storace created the part of Susanna in Mozart's *Nozze di Figaro,* and the family then returned to London, where Stephen spent the rest of his short life writing English operas for Drury Lane, in which his sister sang the lead. His masterpiece, *The Pirates* (1792), on a Neapolitan plot by James Cobb, is Mozartean in scale and sometimes in style. Of his other full-length operas the most successful was *The Haunted Tower* (1789), with a "Gothic" plot that anticipated the novels of Mrs. Radcliffe. *Dido, Queen of Carthage* (1792) was written in emulation of T. A. Arne's *Artaxerxes.* All Storace's other English operas have spoken dialogue. Of his afterpieces the most successful was *No Song, No Supper* (1790, reprinted, *Musica Britannica,* vol. xvi, 1959, edited by R. Fiske). Storace also published two early examples of the piano quintet, three Mozartean piano trios, and some songs. His anthology, *Storace's Collection of Original Harpsichord Music* (1787–89), includes many works he brought back from Vienna, and he was the first to publish Mozart's piano trio in G (K. 564). Storace's sound training and unrivaled knowledge of the continental repertory gave his music a style and professionalism lacking in that of his English contemporaries. He died in London on March 19, 1796.

*See* R. Fiske, "Stephen Storace," in *Proceedings of the Royal Musical Association,* 86th session (1959–60). (R. E. FI.)

**STORAGE BATTERY:** *see* BATTERY.

**STORK,** a large, long-legged, long-necked, large-billed bird related to the heron and ibis and placed with them in the order Ciconiiformes. The 17 species of true storks, which constitute the family Ciconiidae, include the white stork of popular fable, a bird that brings good luck and little babies.

In storks the voice box, or syrinx, is poorly developed, but many species are able to emit low grunts and hisses; they also clatter their bills. They fly with much soaring, the neck and legs being stretched to their limits. Storks feed during the day, mainly on small aquatic animals caught in marshes; some, like the marabou stork of Africa and the adjutant bird of India, feed primarily on carrion. Storks are found in flocks except during the breeding season when they pair off. The nest, a large twig platform built by both sexes, is constructed in trees, on rock ledges, or, in the white stork, on rooftops and chimneys, often in colonial groupings. Three to six chalky white eggs are incubated by both parents for a month or more; the down-clad young birds are cared for in the nest.

The white stork (*Ciconia ciconia*) breeds across Europe and Asia and winters south to the Cape of Good Hope. It is a stately bird, three to four feet long, with black flight feathers, a dark red bill, and reddish legs. To attract these harbingers of good fortune, the townspeople often put up ready-made platforms on their rooftops. The black stork (*C. nigra*), about the size of its congener and with red bill and legs, is black except for a white belly patch. It is more wary of man and nests in marshes and forest. Like the white stork, its population is decreasing, partly due to continuing destruction of its habitat by man.

The adjutant bird (*Leptoptilus dubius*) is distinguished by its dull plumage, black scabrous head, and enormous breast pouch; the last is of doubtful function, connected with the respiratory system. The bird is about 5 ft. tall. Related species are the lesser adjutant (*L. javanicus*), of southeast Asia, and the African adjutant, or marabou stork (*L. crumeniferus*). The original marabou feathers of commerce were the undertail coverts of the latter bird, but the name has come to be applied to large downy feathers of other birds as well.

The jabiru (*Jabiru mycteria*), an American stork found from

Mexico to the Argentine, stands between four and five feet high, with a massive black bill and white plumage. The head and neck are bare, and black and red in colour. "Jabiru" is often wrongly applied to the wood ibis, or wood stork (*Mycteria americana*), a smaller but somewhat similar bird ranging from Argentina to the coasts from Texas to Florida and North Carolina. These birds and the African wood ibis (*Ibis ibis*) belong to the subfamily Mycteriinae.

The shoebill, shoe-billed stork, or whale-headed stork (*Balaeniceps rex*), is a giant bird from the White Nile. Its affinities are doubtful and it is usually placed in its own family, Balaenicipitidae, either with the Ciconiiformes or the Pelecaniformes. In singularity of aspect few birds surpass the shoebill, with its gaunt gray figure, about five feet high, its large head surmounted by a little curled tuft, its scowling eyes, and its huge bill, in form not unlike a whale's head but tipped with a formidable hook. It forms large flocks and frequents dense swamps. The flight is heronlike, and the birds settle on trees. The food consists of any small animals or carrion. The nest is a hole in dry ground, roughly lined with herbage, and from 2 to 12 chalky white eggs are laid.

Another monospecific family in the Ciconiiformes is the Scopidae. It contains the African hammerkop, or hammer-headed stork (*Scopus umbretta*), a heavy-looking brownish bird about 20 in. long, with short black legs and long black bill, laterally compressed and slightly hooked. Most conspicuous is the long, backward-directed crest.

**STORM, (HANS) THEODOR WOLDSEN** (1817–1888), German writer, whose poems and *Novellen* are the outstanding expression of poetic realism in northern Germany. He was born on Sept. 14, 1817, at Husum, on the west coast of Schleswig, where he practised law until Schleswig's incorporation in Denmark made him move to Potsdam in 1853. In 1856 he was transferred to Heiligenstadt, Thuringia, as magistrate. When Denmark released Schleswig in 1864, Storm returned to Husum. In 1880 he retired to the village of Hademarschen, where he died on July 4, 1888.

Storm's lyrics (*Liederbuch dreier Freunde,* with T. and T. Mommsen, 1843; *Gedichte,* 1852) are songlike and direct in feeling, the work of a sensitive, fundamentally happy nature which inclined to melancholy resignation, however, in the face of reality. The main themes are love and friendship, a feeling for home, and an appreciation of nature. Only in his political poems, occasioned by the Danish occupation of Schleswig, is there any sense of antagonism. Although the mood of the early stories—notably *Immensee* (1852; first English translation, 1863), a moving story of the vanished happiness of childhood—is that of the lyrics, his *Novellen* soon surpassed his poetry in importance. In the 11 stories written at Heiligenstadt, of which *Im Schloss* (1861)—the portrayal of a decadent aristocracy—is the most notable, he achieved closer contact with life and a wider range of motifs. Then, after five barren years following his wife's death in 1865, he poured forth a succession of more mature *Novellen,* affirming life in both its lighter and its tragic aspects. They include *Viola tricolor* (1874; Eng. trans., 1956), *Pole Poppenspäler* (1875), *Aquis submersus* (1877; Eng. trans., 1910), and *Carsten Curator* (1878; Eng. trans., 1956). His last *Novelle, Der Schimmelreiter* (1888; Eng. trans., *The Rider on the White Horse,* 1917), with its objective approach, its terse style, and its forceful hero, is typical of Storm's later work and is probably his masterpiece.

BIBLIOGRAPHY.—*Editions, etc.: Sämtliche Schriften,* so-called Westermann ed., 19 vol. (1868–89), giving Storm's final arrangement of his writings; *Sämtliche Werke,* critical edition by A. Köster, 8 vol. (1919–20); *Ausgewählte Werke,* selections ed. by K. Hoppe, 4 vol. (1948–49); *Gesamt-Ausgabe,* ed. by H. Engelhard, 3 vol. (1958). Of the many editions of correspondence *see* G. Storm (ed.), *Briefe,* 4 vol. (1915–17); P. Goldammer (ed.), *Der Briefwechsel zwischen T. Storm und G. Keller* (1960).

*Biography and Crticism:* G. Storm, *T. Storm: ein Bild seines Lebens,* 2 vol. (1912–13); R. Pitrou, *La Vie et l'oeuvre de T. Storm* (1920); H. Heitmann, *T. Storm* (1940); E. O. Wooley, *Studies in T. Storm* (1943); F. Stuckert, *T. Storm: sein Leben und seine Welt* (1955); F. Böttger, *T. Storm in seiner Zeit* (1959). (K. HE.)

**STÖRMER, FREDRIK CARL MÜLERTZ** (1874–1957), Norwegian mathematician and geophysicist who developed a mathematical theory of auroral phenomena, was born at Skien, Sept. 3, 1874. Professor of mathematics at the University of Oslo, 1903–46, Störmer began his scientific work in pure mathematics, particularly number theory. In 1904 he became interested in experiments of the physicist Kristian Birkeland, in which aurora effects were obtained by electron bombardment of a terrella (a magnetized sphere to simulate the earth) in vacuum. Störmer calculated the trajectories of electrical particles in the field of a magnetic dipole and explained many of the peculiarities of the aurora borealis. The results are also applicable to cosmic rays (*see* AURORA POLARIS).

In 1910 he spent a winter at Bossekop, in the northernmost Norwegian county of Finnmark, observing auroras; later he organized a permanent network of stations in Norway to photograph and measure the heights of auroras and special types of clouds. Störmer was a member of numerous geophysical commissions and received a great number of scientific distinctions. He died at Oslo on Aug. 13, 1957.

*See* Carl Störmer, *The Polar Aurora* (1955); Royal Society of London, *Biographical Memoirs of Fellows of the Royal Society,* p. 257–279 (1958). (O. OE.)

**STORMONT,** the seat of the Northern Ireland government, is situated in a 300-ac. estate about 4 mi. E of the centre of Belfast. The parliament building (1928), built in the Greek classical tradition, has four main floors and accommodates the House of Commons and Senate chambers, together with offices for various administrative departments. The building is approached by a wide processional drive, about $\frac{3}{4}$ mi. in length, which is bordered by sweeping lawns and trees. The estate, most of which is open to the public, provides one of the most striking landscapes in Northern Ireland. It includes Stormont House, the official residence of the prime minister.

**STORNOWAY,** a small burgh on the island of Lewis-and-Harris (*q.v.*), Outer Hebrides, Scot., 53 mi. (85 km.) N of Portree, Isle of Skye, by steamer. Pop. (1961) 5,229. It is the biggest town in the county of Ross and Cromarty and is a natural harbour. There is about $\frac{3}{4}$ mi. of quayage and wharfage. The herring fishery, formerly much larger, declined when the shoals were depleted and the continental market collapsed. Stornoway's chief occupation is now the manufacture of Harris tweed, and the town is the service centre of the northern Hebrides. The parish of Stornoway was given to the people by the 1st Lord Leverhulme and is administered by the Stornoway Trust from offices in the burgh. The castle is a 19th-century building now used as a museum. There is daily steamship connection with Kyle of Lochalsh and Mallaig, air services with Glasgow and Inverness, and weekly cargo services to Aberdeen, Dundee, Leith, Glasgow, and Liverpool. (F. F. DG.)

**STORY, JOSEPH** (1779–1845), U.S. legal writer and educator, associate justice of the U.S. supreme court and a principal juristic supporter, with Chief Justice John Marshall (*q.v.*), of American nationalism, was born on Sept. 18, 1779, at Marblehead, Mass. One of the great figures in U.S. legal history, his influence on the development of U.S. law rivaled that of Marshall. After preparatory training at the Marblehead academy, he entered Harvard college in Jan. 1795, joining the class admitted the previous term and unsuccessfully contesting with William Ellery Channing (*q.v.*) for first rank in the class of 1798. Upon graduation, Story returned to Marblehead and began reading law with Samuel Sewall, who later became chief justice of the supreme judicial court of Massachusetts. In 1801, he moved to Salem and entered the office of Samuel Putnam, where he read law until July of that year when he was admitted to the bar.

From 1801 to 1811 Story practised law in Salem and occasionally argued cases in New Hampshire. In Massachusetts he became prominent in the Jeffersonian Republican (afterward called the Democratic) party and, in 1805, was elected to the state legislature. He also served part of one session (1808–09) in the U.S. congress. In 1810, he was counsel in the celebrated case of *Fletcher* v. *Peck,* in which the U.S. supreme court, for the first time, declared a state law invalid because it conflicted with the constitution. He was returned in 1810 to the Massachusetts legislature, becoming speaker of the state house of representatives in 1811.

**Supreme Court Appointment.**—Appointed an associate justice of the U.S. supreme court by Pres. James Madison in Nov. 1811 to fill the vacancy created by the death of William Cushing, Story was then 32 years old, the youngest justice ever to sit upon that court, and lacking in judicial experience. A leader in the Massachusetts Jeffersonian Republican party, he wrote shortly after receiving the life appointment, "I am no longer a political man." Although he was raised to the bench by Madison for the express purpose of contesting the nationalism of Chief Justice John Marshall, Story himself became a confirmed nationalist and a supporter of the Federalist views of the chief justice.

The supreme court was then composed of seven justices. One term of the court was held each year at Washington in a basement chamber of the old capitol building; in addition, each justice was assigned a "circuit" in which two terms of the court were held. Story's circuit consisted of Maine, Massachusetts, Rhode Island and New Hampshire. His circuit court decisions (reported by Gallison, Mason, Sumner and Story) in admiralty, prize, patent and copyright matters helped make United States law on these subjects.

**Notable Cases.**—The supreme court, which eight years previously had first declared a law of congress unconstitutional (*Marbury* v. *Madison*), was just entering upon its real importance when Story came to the bench, and many of the cases decided during his tenure established basic principles of U.S. public and constitutional law. Story's supreme court opinions, found in the reports of Cranch, Wheaton, Peters and Howard (1812–45), number more than 200.

In *Martin* v. *Hunter's Lessee* (1816), a decision that has been called "the keystone of the whole arch of Federal judicial power" (Charles Warren, *The Supreme Court in U.S. History,* p. 449, Little, Brown and Company, Boston, 1922), Story held that the supreme court's appellate civil jurisdiction embraces every case not otherwise to be decided initially and directly by way of its original jurisdiction; that there is no constitutional restraint upon the exercise of this appellate jurisdiction over state tribunals; and that sec. 25 of the Judiciary act of 1789, insofar as it granted such appellate jurisdiction, was constitutional. This decision established the supremacy of the supreme court over the highest court in any state in all civil cases where the federal constitution, laws and treaties were involved. (Five years later, Marshall's opinion in *Cohens* v. *Virginia* did likewise for state criminal cases.)

Although Marshall wrote the opinion of the court in *Dartmouth College* v. *Woodward* (1819), holding that charters of private corporations, as then issued, were contracts which could not constitutionally be impaired by the states granting them, Story concurred in a separate opinion—one of his most learned—which reviews English and U.S. authorities and reveals his devotion to higher-law principles. This decision gave stability to the rights of corporations and influenced subsequent economic developments in the United States.

In *Ogden* v. *Saunders* (1827), the first case in which Marshall was defeated on a constitutional issue, Story joined in a dissenting opinion written by the chief justice. They both took the position that the contract clause of art. i, sec. 10 of the constitution denounced state insolvency legislation concerning the prospective, as well as the retrospective, operation of contracts. This case marked the beginning of a trend away from the principles of economic conservatism which Marshall and Story had sought to entrench in U.S. law.

John Marshall died in July 1835. Story presided over the court while a successor was being chosen, but he was never chief justice. "I have never for a moment imagined that I should be thought of . . . ," he wrote on July 24, 1835. Roger Brooke Taney (*q.v.*) was commissioned chief justice in March 1836, and Story served under him until 1845.

Left over from the Marshall period were three cases, involving the constitutionality of state laws, that had been argued orally before the supreme court, but that had gone undecided: *City of New York* v. *Miln* (1837), *Briscoe* v. *Bank of Kentucky* (1837) and *Charles River Bridge* v. *Warren Bridge* (1837). In all of these cases, the Taney court upheld the state laws, and Story delivered dissenting opinions which lamented the death of Marshall and the passing of the "old order." He now referred to himself as the last of the "old race of judges," and he decided to resign. Friends, however, persuaded him to remain on the bench. Henceforth, on important constitutional issues, he was forced to dissent from the judgments of the Taney court, or to appear to agree in silence with doctrines which seemed to him at variance with his previous decisions.

Two cases decided during this final period, in which Story wrote the opinions of the court, were *Prigg* v. *the Commonwealth of Pennsylvania* (1842) and *Swift* v. *Tyson* (1842). In the Prigg opinion, Story held that since the constitution gave the federal government the power to deal with fugitive slaves, this power could not be exercised by the states, even if no conflict with federal laws was involved. Further, he expressed doubt that the federal government could compel state officers to enforce federal laws. In the Swift case, Story held that sec. 34 of the federal Judiciary act of 1789 did not require that local interpretations of general commercial law be followed in diversity cases in the federal courts. In 1938 the supreme court reversed this decision, holding that the law to be followed in such cases was the law of the state as interpreted by state courts.

**Story and Marshall Compared.**—Marshall, who was 24 years older than Story and versed mainly in constitutional law, disliked the labour of investigating legal authorities to support his judgments. Story, who was the master of several fields of law (including constitutional law), loved legal research, and his opinions drew heavily upon past authorities. If Marshall's opinions were businesslike, Story's were scholarlike; if the chief justice was concise and to the point in his judgments, his younger colleague was eager, luminous and had a tendency to be expansive. The difference between their judicial minds is seen in the Dartmouth college case, where opinions were written by both. Marshall served on the court just over 34 years; Story's tenure lacked only months of equaling that of the chief justice. In the field of constitutional law, they laboured together for nearly a quarter of a century in upholding the same legal doctrines.

**Harvard Professorship.**—In 1829 Nathan Dane founded a professorship of law at Harvard college, the duties of which were to prepare, deliver and revise for publication a course of lectures on the law of nature, the law of nations, commercial and maritime law, federal law and federal equity. By an express condition of the $10,000 endowment, Story became the first Dane professor of law at Harvard, which position he held, together with that of associate justice of the supreme court, until his death in 1845. Story's lectures on the designated subjects led to the publication of his nine great commentaries on the law, the first of which appeared in 1832. His first associate at the law school was John Hooker Ashmun, Royall professor of law, who died in 1833 and was replaced by Simon Greenleaf. The Story-Greenleaf period marked the beginning of the law school's growth to greatness. Story was exceptional as a teacher, and he devoted a great deal of time to the practical presentation of moot-court cases and arguments by his students. His annual salary at Harvard was $1,000.

In 1845 Story resolved to resign from the supreme court and devote his life to teaching and writing at Harvard. Early in September, however, before his letter of resignation was sent to Washington, he became ill, and on Sept. 10, 1845, he died at his home in Cambridge, Mass.

Story was married in 1804 to Mary Lynde Fitch Oliver, who died without issue; and in 1808 to Sarah Waldo Wetmore (1784–1855), the daughter of a Boston jurist, who bore him seven children, only two of whom survived childhood. A Calvinist, Story became a Unitarian and was several times president of the American Unitarian association.

**Writings.**—Story is best known as an author for a series of commentaries on *Bailments* (1832), *Constitution of the United States,* 3 vol. (1833), *Conflict of Laws* (1834), *Equity Jurisprudence,* 2 vol. (1836), *Equity Pleading* (1838), *Agency* (1839), *Partnership* (1841), *Bills of Exchange* (1843) and *Promissory*

*Notes* (1845). His works on equity were particularly important; with Chancellor James Kent (*q.v.*), he helped found equity jurisprudence in the United States. He also prepared *Commentaries on the Constitution,* one-vol. abridgment (1833), and *Constitutional Classbook* (1834). He wrote scholarly articles for *The American Jurist* and *The North American Review* and published biographical sketches of many prominent men. He drew up the bylaws of a bank, the *Report* of the Massachusetts Commission on Codification and the *Report on Salaries of the Judiciary* and prepared elaborate notes (for Wheaton's *Reports*) on prize, admiralty, etc. He drafted a bankruptcy law, a crimes act and a judiciary act. He published a volume of poems, constructed a portion of a legal digest and prepared an edition of the laws of the United States. He delivered many public addresses, some on literary, scientific and historical subjects, and participated in the convention called to revise the Massachusetts constitution.

Bibliography.—W. W. Story, *Life and Letters of Joseph Story,* 2 vol. (1851) and *Miscellaneous Writings of Joseph Story* (1835 and 1852); Roscoe Pound, "The Place of Judge Story in the Making of American Law," *American Law Review,* 48:676–697 (Sept.–Oct. 1914); W. Schofield, "Joseph Story, 1779–1845," *Great American Lawyers,* ed. by W. D. Lewis, 3:123–185 (1908); Mortimer D. Schwartz and John C. Hogan (eds.), *Joseph Story* (1959). Constitutional developments during the period are evaluated in: Carl B. Swisher, *American Constitutional Development* (1943); and W. W. Crosskey, *Politics and the Constitution in the History of the United States,* 2 vol. (1953). (Jn. C. H.)

**STORY, WILLIAM WETMORE** (1819–1895), U.S. sculptor and author, who is most famous for his statue "Cleopatra," was born in Salem, Mass., on Feb. 12, 1819. He graduated from Harvard College in 1838 and studied law under his father Justice Joseph Story. After his graduation from Harvard Law School in 1840 he decided while practising law in Boston to become a sculptor. In 1856 he settled in Rome and remained there for the rest of his life. He lived in the Palazzo Barberini, where he entertained famous literary, theatrical, and social figures of the day.

Story's "Cleopatra" was exhibited at the London Exposition in 1862 (a replica of it is in the Metropolitan Museum of Art, New York City). Nathaniel Hawthorne's description of this work in his novel *The Marble Faun* (1860) contributed greatly to its wide popularity in the United States and Great Britain.

In addition to his sculpture, Story wrote several volumes of poetry, essays, a biography of his father, and various legal works.

He died at Vallombrosa, Italy, on Oct. 7, 1895. Story's fame has been kept alive by the interest in Henry James's book about him titled *William Wetmore Story and His Friends* (1903; reprinted 1957).

*See* A. Gardner, *Yankee Stonecutters* (1945). (A. T. G.)

**STOSS, VEIT** (1438? or 1447?–1533), German sculptor whose style, developed from that of Nicholas Gerhaert, astonishes by its dramatic realism and emotional force no less than by the technical virtuosity of the carving. He was born in Swabia but reared in Nürnberg. From 1477 to 1496 he worked mainly in Poland, Bohemia, and Hungary. His principal works are the majestic high altar, carved in limewood and painted, of the church of St. Mary's in Cracow (1477–89) and the sculptured tombs of King Casimir IV and Archbishop Zbigniew Olesnicki in the cathedrals of Cracow and Gniezno. When he returned to Nürnberg, he was defrauded of his savings, attempted to regain them by forgery, was discovered and branded, and passed an embittered old age encumbered with civic disabilities. His work of this period includes important wood and stone sculpture in the churches of St. Sebaldus (1499, 1520) and St. Lorenz (1513, 1518) in Nürnberg, and a carved altar in Bamberg Cathedral (1523). He was active also as a painter and engraver. He died at Nürnberg in 1533.

*See* Eberhard Lutze, *Veit Stoss* (1938); Tadeusz Dobrowolski, *Wit Stwosz: Oltarz Krakowski* (1951). (D. Kg.)

**STOTHARD, THOMAS** (1755–1834), English subject painter, designer and book illustrator, was best known for his work in illustration. Born in London on Aug. 17, 1755, he was apprenticed in Spitalfields to a draftsman of patterns for silks and in 1777 became a student of the Royal Academy. He was elected associate in 1791 and full academician in 1794, being appointed librarian in 1812. He died in London on April 27, 1834.

In 1779 Stothard became a contributor to *Novelist's Magazine* and to Bell's *Poets.* Because he was so ill-paid he supplemented his income by designing plates for pocket books, tickets for concerts, illustrations for almanacs, portraits of popular actors—and into even the slightest sketches he infused grace and distinction. He is at his best in domestic or ideal subjects; the heroic and tragic were beyond his powers. He began to exhibit pictures in oil at the Royal Academy in 1778 and continued to do so until his death. His oils are usually small in size and free in handling, but their colouring is often rich and glowing. His best-known painting is "The Canterbury Pilgrims," the engraving from which attained immense popularity and heralds Pre-Raphaelite methods; the picture is connected, in an unfortunate way, with a painting on the same subject by William Blake (*q.v.*).

Stothard illustrated many books, including *The Adventures of Peregrine Pickle, Clarissa Harlowe, Tristram Shandy, Robinson Crusoe, The Pilgrim's Progress, The Vicar of Wakefield, The Rape of the Lock* and the works of Shakespeare, Byron, Milton and other poets. He also decorated the mansions of many of his wealthy patrons. (D. C. T. T.; X.)

**STOUR,** an ancient river name used for five English rivers in Suffolk, Kent, Hampshire, Worcestershire, and Warwickshire. The Suffolk Stour measures 47 mi. (76 km.) from its sources in the Chalk ridge of Cambridgeshire. It flows eastward along the county boundary between Suffolk and Essex through country made famous by the artist John Constable. At Manningtree it becomes a broad, shallow tidal estuary, and 10 mi. beyond enters the North Sea at Harwich. The Great, or Kentish, Stour is 40 mi. (64 km.) long. After uniting eastern and western headstreams in the Weald at Ashford, it breaks through the North Downs in a deep scenic valley to Canterbury. Downstream it traverses a series of lagoons caused by gravel working and colliery subsidence. From there the river is tidal. Its floodplain is a silted marine inlet, which as the former Wantsum Channel separated the Isle of Thanet from the mainland until the 14th century. The main discharge is south of Thanet to Pegwell Bay, while a small distributary, the Wantsum, debouches into the North Sea near Reculver. The final loop of the Stour is 7 mi. in length, but only 200 yd. (183 m.) across the neck, where an artificial cut assists flood control. The river is navigated to Sandwich by small timber vessels. The other three Stours are mere tributary streams. (A. M. Co.)

**STOURBRIDGE,** a municipal borough (1914) in the Dudley parliamentary division of Worcestershire, Eng., 12 mi. (19 km.) W of Birmingham by road. Pop. (1961) 42,631. Stourbridge glass, dating from 1556, is still made in the district, and the college of further education teaches glassmaking. At the Council House in Mary Stevens Park is a permanent glass exhibition. King Edward School (1430) was attended by Samuel Johnson; Oldswinford Hospital (bluecoat) School was founded in 1667. Manufactures include hollow ware, refractories, chains, tools, and leathers.

**STOUT, GEORGE FREDERICK** (1860–1944), British psychologist and philosopher, powerful critic of associationism and forerunner of Gestalt psychology, was by far the most influential British psychologist of the early 20th century. He was born Jan. 6, 1860, at South Shields, Eng., and educated at Cambridge. He was appointed reader in mental philosophy at Oxford in 1898 and professor of logic and metaphysics at St. Andrews in 1903. He spent the last eight years of his life in Australia, and died in Sydney, New South Wales, on Aug. 18, 1944.

Stout approached psychology primarily from a philosophical standpoint. His best-known works, *Analytic Psychology* (1896), *Manual of Psychology* (1898), and *Mind and Matter* (1931), provided a systematic theory designed to supplant the associationism of the 19th century (*see* Association, Mental). He firmly rejected the Cartesian dualistic conception of body and mind and reverted to a biological concept not unlike Aristotle's idea of the soul as the form of the body (*see* Body and Mind). Stout anticipated many of the principles later developed by the Gestalt School and by psychoanalytic writers such as Sigmund Freud. *See* also Consciousness: *As a Relation;* Gestalt Psychology: *Antecedents.*

*See* C. A. Mace, *George Frederick Stout* (1948). (Cy. B.; X.)

**STOUT:** *see* Beer; Brewing.

**STOW, JOHN** (1525–1605), the best known of the Elizabethan antiquaries, author of a famous *Survey of London* (1598; revised and enlarged, 1603), was born of a London family of tallow-chandlers in 1525. He became a tailor (freeman of the Merchant Taylors' Company, 1547), and practised his trade until *c.* 1565–70, after which he devoted his time and money to collecting rare books and manuscripts. He had already published an edition of Chaucer (1561) and a useful *Summary of English Chronicles . . .* (1565; many abridged versions). His first original work was *The Chronicles of England . . .* (1580), revised as *Annals of England . . .* (1592).

Self-educated, and with a passion for learning, he became the friend of famous antiquaries, and was employed by Archbishop Parker to edit medieval chronicles. Prosperous as a tailor, he became poor, traveling everywhere on foot in search of records. After 1579 he had a small yearly pension from the Merchant Taylors', and in 1603 received letters patent to collect alms. He died in London on April 6, 1605.

The *Survey,* cast in the form of a "perambulation" round the London wards, contains fascinating detail of the life, customs, buildings, monuments, government, and people of London at a time of transition from medieval to modern, with an account of the city's origins and growth. Stow sought out those who could describe past beauties and customs, and drew material from City and church records, from monastic cartularies, from early chroniclers, and from his own lifelong observation and retentive memory. Though his lack of linguistic learning sometimes resulted in faulty interpretation, his *Survey* is a pioneer work of scholarly devotion by a great Londoner to the city he loved.

Bibliography.—Some of Stow's manuscripts are at the British Museum, others at Lambeth Library. There were many 17th-, 18th-, and 19th-century "continuations" and editions of the *Survey;* the best modern edition is that from the 1603 text by C. L. Kingsford, 2 vol. (1908), *Additional Notes* (1927). There is a useful Everyman's Library edition (1965). *See* also the annual commemorative addresses given at St. Andrew's Undershaft, London, published in the *Transactions* of the London and Middlesex Archaeological Society. (Jl. H.)

**STOWE, HARRIET ELIZABETH BEECHER** (1811–1896), U.S. writer and philanthropist, is famous as the author of *Uncle Tom's Cabin.* She was born at Litchfield, Conn., on June 14, 1811, the daughter of the clergyman Lyman Beecher (*q.v.*). After her mother's death in 1815, she came most directly under the influence of her eldest sister Catharine, who a few years later set up a school in Hartford, where Harriet was first a pupil and afterward a teacher. In 1832 her father, who had for six years been the pastor of a church in Boston, accepted the presidency of the newly founded Lane Theological Seminary at Cincinnati, O. Catharine went with him and established a pioneer college for women, the Western Female Institute. Harriet was an assistant at the school, taking an active part in the literary and school life, contributing stories and sketches to local journals, and compiling a school geography, until the school closed in 1837. She was married Jan. 6, 1836, to one of the professors in the seminary, Calvin Ellis Stowe. In the midst of privation and anxiety, due largely to her husband's precarious health, she wrote continually, and in 1843 published *The Mayflower, or Sketches of Scenes and Characters among the Descendants of the Pilgrims.*

She lived 18 years in Cincinnati, separated only by the Ohio River from a slave-holding community, coming in contact with fugitive slaves and learning from friends and her own visits the life of the South. In 1850 her husband was elected to a professorship in Bowdoin College, Brunswick, Me., and moved his family there.

In Brunswick, Mrs. Stowe wrote, for serial publication in the *National Era,* an antislavery paper of Washington, D.C., the story of *Uncle Tom's Cabin; or, Life Among the Lowly.* The publication in book form (1852) was a factor which must be reckoned in summing up the causes of the Civil War. Her name was anathema in the South. The book sprang into unexampled popularity, and was translated into at least 23 languages; the dramatic adaptation was also immensely popular. Mrs. Stowe reinforced her story with *A Key to Uncle Tom's Cabin* (1853), in which she accumulated a large number of documents and testimonies against slavery and in defense of criticism of her accuracy. In 1853 when she made a journey to Europe she was lionized in England by people from all walks of life. (A magazine article published in 1869, "The True Story of Lady Byron's Life," detailing her charge that the poet had had an incestuous love for his sister, later turned British public opinion against her.) In 1856 she published *Dred: a Tale of the Dismal Swamp,* in which she threw the weight of her argument on the deterioration of a society resting on a slave basis. The establishment of the *Atlantic Monthly* in 1857 gave her a constant vehicle for her writings, as did the *Independent* of New York, and later the *Christian Union,* of which papers successively her brother, Henry Ward Beecher, was one of the editors.

THE BETTMANN ARCHIVE

HARRIET BEECHER STOWE

She thereafter led the life of a woman of letters, writing novels, of which *The Minister's Wooing* (1859) is best known, and many studies of social life in both fiction and essay. Her *Pearl of Orr's Island* (1862) was credited by the U.S. writer Sarah Orne Jewett with having revealed to her the literary value of the country folk. Mrs. Stowe published also a small volume of religious poems, and toward the end of her career gave some public readings from her writings. In 1852 Calvin Stowe accepted a professorship in the theological seminary at Andover, Mass., and the family made its home there till 1863, when he retired and moved to Hartford.

After the close of the Civil War, Mrs. Stowe bought an estate in Florida, and she spent many winters there. After the death of her husband in 1886, she lived in the seclusion of her Hartford home, where she died on July 1, 1896. She is buried by the side of her husband at Andover.

Bibliography.—The Riverside edition of Mrs. Stowe's works was published in 1899 and 1906 in 16 volumes (with an additional volume of biography). *See* also Annie Fields (ed.), *Life and Letters of Harriet Beecher Stowe* (1897); C. E. and L. B. Stowe, *Harriet Beecher Stowe: the Story of Her Life* (1911); F. Wilson, *Crusader in Crinoline* (1941); C. H. Foster, *Rungless Ladder: Harriet Beecher Stowe and New England Puritanism* (1954); and J. C. Furnas, *Goodbye to Uncle Tom* (1956). (H. E. S.; X.)

**STOWELL, WILLIAM SCOTT,** Baron (1745–1836), English admiralty judge, author of influential doctrines in international law, and brother of Lord Chancellor Eldon, was born on Oct. 17, 1745, near Newcastle upon Tyne. He was educated at the Newcastle grammar school and at Corpus Christi College, Oxford, from which he received his B.A. degree in 1764, his M.A. in 1767, his bachelor of civil law in 1772, and the doctor of civil law in 1779. He was an intimate friend of Samuel Johnson. He elected to practise in the admiralty and ecclesiastical courts and became advocate general for the office of lord high admiral in 1782 and in 1798 judge of the high court of admiralty. On the coronation of George IV in 1821, he was raised to the peerage as Baron Stowell. He died at Earley Court, Berkshire, on Jan. 28, 1836.

He stands in the front rank of English judges with Sir Matthew Hale and Lord Mansfield. His decisions in admiralty were the first of the English admiralty court to be published, and he was therefore free to be guided by writers on Roman, canon, and international law. His decisions were accepted by the United States courts through the work of Justice Joseph Story. The doctrines of international law with which the name of Lord Stowell are identified include: the perfect equality and entire independence of all states; the elementary rules of international law binding even semibarbarous states; the principles that a blockade, to be binding, must be effectual, and that a prize court is a court of the law of nations. (A. Dm.)

**STRABANE,** an urban district and market town of County Tyrone, Northern Ire., 14 mi. (23 km.) SSW of Londonderry by road. Pop. (1961) 7,783. Area 2.9 sq.mi. (7.5 sq.km.). The Rivers Mourne and Finn join there to form the Foyle. Shirt and collar making is the chief industry, with flax spinning at Sion Mills village.

**STRABO** of Amasya in Pontus, Greek geographer and historian whose *Geography* is the only general treatise on the subject surviving from antiquity, was born *c.* 63 B.C. Of distinguished family, especially on his mother's side, Strabo was sent abroad at an early age to study under well-known teachers at Nysa in Caria, Rome and perhaps elsewhere. Later he lived for long periods in Alexandria and in Rome. It is not known where he finally settled. He boasts of having traveled more widely than any of his predecessors, "east to west from Armenia to the Tuscan region facing Sardinia, and north to south from the Black sea to the borders of Ethiopia." With the one major exception of a journey up the Nile *c.* 25 B.C. in the retinue of the governor of Egypt, Aelius Gallus, there are practically no details of these journeys and there is no idea of their purpose. Strabo seems to have kept to a few main routes: he had seen little of Italy, and in Greece he had visited Corinth and probably Athens, but not Delphi or Mycenae.

Strabo was a Stoic, and he wrote (as he tells us) for the instruction of educated statesmen and other readers of high station. His belief in the importance of history and geography to such men derives from Polybius, who influenced him profoundly. His main work—a *History* in 47 books, lost except for a handful of small fragments—after four introductory books continued Polybius' *History* at least down to Caesar's death. The *Geography,* probably a long appendix to this work, survives almost in full. The first two books form a general introduction, the next eight deal with Europe, the following six with Asia, the last with Africa (its shape and size totally misconceived). Since little is said about events after 7 B.C., the work was probably completed about that date. A few notes were added about A.D. 18–19, and there is one reference (added by an editor?) to an event of *c.* A.D. 23. But the work was never systematically revised.

Although Strabo defends the orthodox picture of a spherical universe centred in a spherical earth, both divided into five zones, and although, in discussing his predecessors' theories, he has much philosophical argument, he defines the geographer's proper task as "to describe the known parts of the *oikoumene*" (inhabited portion of the earth). He stresses the geographer's need for mathematical and scientific knowledge and makes extensive use of Hipparchus; but his own inclination is clearly toward descriptive and historical geography. His knowledge is chiefly gathered from books: his reading was wide and critical. His work shows little sense of order, except that imposed by the subject, and is full of historical and mythological excursuses. His information is at best as good as that of his sources and can be far from recent: full of admiration for Homer, he bases his three books on Greece on Apollodorus' commentary on Homer's "Ships' catalogue."

The *Geography* had no influence on 1st-century writers. By the 6th century it was already a classic, and its reputation endured for centuries. To us its chief importance lies in the valuable source material (from Eratosthenes, Polybius, Poseidonius and others) that it transmits: without Strabo we could hardly begin to follow the development of ancient geography. The first good edition was by I. Casaubon (1587, revised 1620), by whose pages the text is normally cited. The Loeb edition (1917–32) by H. L. Jones with bibliography is very useful. The first volume (a general commentary) of a projected German edition by W. Aly, appeared in 1957. (E. BA.)

**STRACHAN, JOHN** (1778–1867), educator and first Anglican bishop of Toronto, whose principal achievement was to organize the church in Canada as a self-governing denomination within the Anglican communion, was born in Aberdeen, Scot., April 12, 1778. Educated at King's College, Aberdeen, he emigrated to Canada in 1799, was ordained (1803), and was appointed successively missionary at Cornwall, 1803; missionary at York (later Toronto), 1812; archdeacon of York, 1825; and bishop of Toronto, 1839. He fought a steady rear guard action to retain the privileged position of the church as a branch of the English establishment in the colony. As that position was gradually lost under colonial pressure, he created the first Anglican synod of clergy and laity in the British colonial empire (Toronto, 1851), raised endowment funds, subdivided his diocese, and presided over the first episcopal election by clergy and laity outside of the U.S. (1857). He was a controversial political figure, as member of the Executive Council of Upper Canada after 1815, and as the power behind the ruling Tory clique. His political power waned with the granting of responsible government to the colony.

In 1827 he secured a royal charter for the University of King's College, Toronto, and served as its first president. When the foundation was secularized as the University of Toronto, he founded the University of Trinity College in 1852 as a church institution. His published works, about 30 in number, are largely polemical. He died in Toronto on Nov. 1, 1867. (J. L. H. H.)

**STRACHEY, (GILES) LYTTON** (1880–1932), English biographer and critic, who revolutionized the writing of biography (*q.v.*), was born in London on March 1, 1880, the son of Sir Richard Strachey, the Indian administrator. He was at school in Derbyshire and at Leamington College, and studied history at Liverpool (1897–99) and at Trinity College, Cambridge (1899–1903). He then lived in London, writing for the *Spectator* and other reviews, and became a leading figure in the Bloomsbury group (*q.v.*).

In 1912 he published *Landmarks in French Literature,* and throughout his life he did much by his articles (collected in *Books and Characters,* 1922; and *Characters and Commentaries,* 1933) to make his countrymen appreciate the precision and delicacy of French poetry and prose. But his greatest achievement was in biography. He made his reputation with *Eminent Victorians* (1918) and *Queen Victoria* (1921) and added to it with *Elizabeth and Essex* (1928) and *Portraits in Miniature* (1931). Treating his subjects from a highly idiosyncratic point of view, he determined to create a work of art rather than a record of activities and events. He was fascinated by personality and motive and delighted in pricking the pretensions of the great and reducing them to somewhat less than life-size in a prose at once elegant, sinuous, and singularly ironical. His aim was to paint a portrait; and though this led to caricature and sometimes, through tendentious selection of material, to inaccuracy, he taught biographers a sense of form and of background, and he sharpened their critical acumen.

His many imitators lacked Strachey's detachment, taste, and Voltairean assurance. In his best work, *Queen Victoria,* he combined his gift for narrative with a power of analyzing characters with whom he had nothing in common. His defects as a biographer arose mainly from his limited vision of life. He did not love the past for its own sake; and he saw politics largely as intrigue, religion as a ludicrous anachronism, and personal relations as life's supremely important facet. Though bitterly attacked during his lifetime and after, Strachey remains a phenomenon in English letters and a preeminent humorist and wit. He died unmarried at Ham Spray House, near Hungerford, on Jan. 21, 1932.

BIBLIOGRAPHY.—Sir Max Beerbohm, *Lytton Strachey* (1943); R. A. Scott-James, *Lytton Strachey* (1955); Michael Holroyd, *Lytton Strachey: a Critical Biography,* 2 vol. (1967). (N. G. A.)

**STRADELLA, ALESSANDRO** (*c.* 1645–1682), Italian composer, singer, and violinist. The facts about his life are surrounded by mystery and much legend. He apparently lived for periods in Modena, Venice, Rome, and Florence in, as E. Allam says, "a kind of uncharted territory between the amateur and professional worlds." In Turin in 1677 an attempt was made to murder him, for reasons that are not definitely known, though it was believed to be at the instigation of a Venetian senator with whose fiancée Stradella had eloped. On Feb. 28, 1682, there was another, successful attempt on his life.

Stradella was one of the finest composers of chamber cantatas, of which he wrote more than 200; his fresh, mellifluous melodies are frequently supported by harmonies bolder than are usually found in music of this period. His instrumental music, both chamber and orchestral, is also worth reviving; particularly interesting is his novel application of *concerto grosso* texture to accompaniments of arias in some of his stage works and oratorios. But on the whole his dramatic works are not distinctive.

Stradella's legendary life, embroidered from suspicion and exiguous facts, was the subject of eight 19th-century operas and of at least one novel. (N. Fo.)

**STRADIVARI, ANTONIO** (?1644–1737), Italian violin maker, was associated throughout his life with the city of Cremona, where he brought the craft of violin-making to its highest pitch of perfection. He was still a pupil of Nicolo Amati in 1666, when he had begun to insert his own label on violins of his making. These at first followed the smaller Amati model, solidly constructed, with a thick yellow varnish. In 1684 he began to produce larger models, using a deeper-coloured varnish and improving the craftsmanship in many ways. His "long" models, dating from 1690, represent a complete innovation in the proportions of the instrument; while from 1700, after returning for a few years to an earlier style, he again broadened and otherwise improved his model. He also made some fine cellos and violas. The Stradivari

*Most Famous Instruments of Antonio Stradivari*

| Violins | | | | Violas | | Cellos | |
|---|---|---|---|---|---|---|---|
| Name | Date | Name | Date | Name | Date | Name | Date |
| Hellier | 1679 | Alard* | 1715 | Tuscan | 1690 | Archinto | 1689 |
| Sellière | before 1680 | Cessot | 1716 | † | | Tuscan | 1690 |
| | | Messiah | 1716 | Archinto | 1696 | Aylesford | 1696 |
| Tuscan | 1690 | Sasserno | 1717 | Macdonald | 1701 | Cristiani | 1700 |
| Betts | 1704 | Maurin | 1718 | Paganini | 1731 | Servais | 1701 |
| Ernst | 1709 | Lauterbach | 1719 | | | Gore-Booth | 1710 |
| La Pucelle | 1709 | Blunt | 1721 | | | Duport | 1711 |
| Viotti | 1709 | Rode | 1722 | | | Adam | 1713 |
| Vieuxtemps | 1710 | Sarasate | 1724 | | | Batta | 1714 |
| Parke | 1711 | Deurbroucq | 1727 | | | Piatti‡ | 1720 |
| Boissier | 1713 | Kiesewetter | 1731 | | | Baudiot | 1725 |
| Dolphin | 1714 | Habeneck | 1736 | | | Gallay | 1725 |
| Gillot | 1715 | Muntz | 1736 | | | | |

*The finest violin. †Two unnamed violas of 1696 formerly belonging to Philip IV of Spain. ‡The finest cello.

method of violin-making created a standard for subsequent times; but the secret of his varnish, soft in texture, and shading from orange to red, though much debated, has never been discovered. He died at Cremona on Dec. 18, 1737.

Stradivari's sons FRANCESCO (1671–1743) and OMOBONO (1679–1742) were also violin-makers. They are believed to have assisted their father, probably with Carlo Bergonzi, who appears to have succeeded to the possession of Antonio's stock-in-trade.

**STRAFFORD, THOMAS WENTWORTH,** EARL OF (1593–1641), English statesman, attempted to consolidate the sovereign power of Charles I by the so-called policy of "thorough," but was ultimately sacrificed by the king to appease Parliament. He was born in London on April 13, 1593, the eldest surviving son of Sir William Wentworth, a wealthy Yorkshire landowner. Educated at St. John's College, Cambridge, and at the Inner Temple, he was knighted by James I in 1611. His marriage to Lady Margaret Clifford, daughter of the impoverished earl of Cumberland, established a link with an ancient and noble family still influential in the north. Shortly after his marriage he completed his education by a leisurely journey through France, returning to England shortly before his father's death in 1614.

For the next years his conduct followed the familiar contemporary pattern for a young man of wealth and local influence seeking to make a career at the national level through court and Parliament. He represented Yorkshire in the Parliaments of 1614 and 1621, and Pontefract in 1624. In Yorkshire he was appointed *custos rotulorum* (keeper of the rolls) in 1615, an office which he refused to vacate two years later to make way for his powerful neighbour Sir John Savile, thus starting a personal feud which dominated Yorkshire politics for the next decade.

In the Parliament of 1621 his local influence secured the election as the other member for Yorkshire of the court candidate, the secretary of state Sir George Calvert, a service for which he received no special thanks from the court. In Charles I's first Parliament (1625) Wentworth, who was now resentful of the court and critical of the all-powerful favourite, George Villiers, first duke of Buckingham (*q.v.*), was again returned for Yorkshire. His election was challenged by Savile; Parliament decided in Wentworth's favour but not before he had been violently denounced in the House of Commons by Sir John Eliot for attempting to take his seat while his case was still under discussion.

BY COURTESY OF EARL FITZWILLIAM

"FIRST EARL OF STRAFFORD WITH A WOLFHOUND," PAINTED BY SIR ANTHONY VAN DYCK, 1636

Meanwhile, his first wife had died childless (1622) and he had married Arabella Holles, daughter of John, earl of Clare, a peer out of favour at court who brought Wentworth into touch with the critics of the king's and Buckingham's expensive and inefficient policy of war against Spain—and from 1627 against France. Along with other critics of the court he was prevented from sitting in the Parliament of 1626, having been appointed sheriff of Yorkshire in 1625; later in the year he refused to subscribe to the forced loan, imposed to pay for the war, and was for some time under arrest.

In the Parliament of 1628 he was one of the leading critics of crown policy in the Commons and advocated the measure in defense of the rights of the subject which was subsequently passed as the Petition of Right. But he did not join in the attack on Buckingham stimulated by Eliot in the last part of the session. During the recess he was approached by the court, now anxious to repair past neglect and to buy back his support, with the offer of a barony. Wentworth accepted. In December he was appointed lord president of the north, virtually governor of England north of the Humber. In the following year (1629) he was given a seat on the Privy Council.

Wentworth's return to the service of the court, coming so soon after his vehement opposition to it in Parliament, startled even some of his closest friends. His conduct was no doubt partly inspired by personal ambition, though he had logical reasons for his change of front since in the summer of 1628 the king gradually abandoned his war policy. The murder of Buckingham in August of that year made way for more sober policies in future. Though he certainly wanted power and the material fruits of office, Wentworth also had a vision of better government and there is no reason to doubt the sincerity of his claim, in his first speech as president of the north, that he came to serve his countrymen as "an instrument for good."

On the council Wentworth seems to have advocated the paternalist government which distinguished the early years of the king's personal rule: closer supervision of justices of the peace, more effective implementation of the poor law, of laws against enclosure, and of measures for dealing with famine, though he was not above privately making profit out of the corn shortage of 1631. As lord president of the north he quelled all defiance of his authority and made many enemies by his insistence on the honour due to him as the king's representative, but his administration was on the whole just and efficient; he supervised the local justices, curbed the often tyrannous excesses of local magnates, and, in the bad plague year of 1631, behaved conspicuously well at York. In the same year he was deeply distressed by the death of his much-loved wife, though he provoked scandalous rumours not long afterward by secretly marrying (October 1632) Elizabeth Rhodes, the young daughter of a neighbouring squire.

The king meanwhile had appointed him lord deputy of Ireland. Taking up his office in the summer of 1633, he immediately set himself to consolidate the royal authority, to break the power of the dominant clique of "new English" landowners, to extend English settlement, improve methods of agriculture, increase the productivity of the land, and stimulate industry and trade. His ultimate goal was to assimilate Irish law and customs to the English system and to make a prosperous Protestant Ireland into a source of revenue to the English crown. He made great use of the prerogative Court of Council Chamber to enforce his will and it may be that in this, as also in his masterful control of the Irish Parliament, he was consciously setting an example of the type of government that he hoped the king would achieve in England.

He was by this time on terms of close friendship with William Laud, archbishop of Canterbury, with whom he discussed his policy in a regular and very full correspondence. Between them they used the word "thorough" to describe the reformed efficient administration they wished to create.

Wentworth's policy in Ireland seemed at first successful. He cleared the sea of pirates, while the newly established conditions of peace with Spain were favourable to Irish trade. He took over personally the administration of the customs and greatly increased the revenue. He made some good appointments to the Irish bench. He established the king's right to settle the province of Connaught. He compelled the earl of Cork and other unscrupulous landowners to disgorge church property wrongfully appropriated. He created a small efficient army. He reformed Trinity College (to which he sent his son) and founded the first theatre in Dublin. But his methods were ruthless and at times unscrupulous. He alienated the Irish by extending English settlement, and the English by undermining their influence and interfering with their gains.

Although he greatly increased the revenues of the crown, he lost no opportunity of enriching himself, and his immense fortune laid him open to criticism. To get the administration of the customs into his own hands he eliminated the vice-treasurer, Lord Mountnorris, by trying him for treason before a court-martial, and he arrested the lord chancellor in full council. His conduct was criticized by his victims who had friends at court in England; the king did not always support him against them and even Archbishop Laud occasionally expressed doubts in his private letters.

In 1639, after the abortive attempt of King Charles to force episcopacy on Scotland and his defeat in the First Bishops' War, Wentworth was recalled to England for advice. He recognized that the Scottish revolt was a critical challenge to the king's authority and he advised the calling of Parliament which he believed by skilful management could be made to vote supplies for a war on Scotland. He guaranteed that the Irish Parliament would do so. Created earl of Strafford early in 1640, he returned to Dublin where he secured unqualified parliamentary support for the king. But on his return to London he found the English Parliament recalcitrant and had to vote with the rest of the Privy Council for its dissolution (May 1640). The disastrous Second Bishops' War followed. Though extremely ill, Strafford took command of the English army but failed to prevent the Scots from overrunning the northern counties. The king, unable to pay his own troops or to buy off the Scots, was compelled by joint English and Scottish action to call a new Parliament in November 1640.

Strafford was the chief target of attack from both nations. He was advised to leave the country, but the king relied on his help and assured him that he should not suffer in life or fortune. Detained by illness, he reached Westminster on Nov. 10 with the intention of impeaching the king's opponents in Parliament for treasonable correspondence with the Scots. The leader of the Commons, John Pym, acted first, by impeaching Strafford before he could take his seat in the House of Lords. His trial began in March 1641. The basic accusation was that of subverting the laws, supported by a charge that he had offered to bring over the Irish Army to subdue the king's opponents in England. More detailed charges rested on his administration in Ireland and the north. He conducted his defense with great skill and it looked at one time as though he might be acquitted. Pym therefore introduced a Bill of Attainder (*i.e.,* a summary condemnation to death by special Act of Parliament). The Commons passed it by a large majority, the Lords, intimidated by popular rioting, by a much smaller one. While an angry mob surged round Whitehall, Strafford wrote to the king releasing him from his promise of protection, and Charles, afraid for the safety of the queen, gave his consent to the bill. Strafford went to the scaffold on May 12, 1641, in the presence of an immense and jubilant crowd. In his last speech he once more professed his faith in "the joint and individual prosperity of the king and his people," for which, in his view, he had always worked.

He remains an enigmatic figure in English history, ambitious, greedy for power and wealth, ruthless, and sometimes dishonest, but with a vision of benevolent authoritarian government and efficient administration to which he often gave persuasive expression. He made innumerable enemies but his few close friends were deeply attached to him; he was a generous master to his servants, a good husband, and an indulgent father. In the last weeks of his life his dignity, eloquence, and loyalty to the king made a deep impression even on some of his enemies. Among Royalists he was subsequently elevated to the position of protomartyr for the royal cause.

BIBLIOGRAPHY.—*The Earl of Strafford's Letters and Despatches,* ed. by William Knowler, 2 vol. (1739–40); C. V. Wedgwood, *Thomas Wentworth, First Earl of Strafford: a Revaluation* (1961; replaces and entirely revises the same author's *Strafford,* 1935); William Laud, *Works,* vol. vii (1860); T. D. Whitaker, *Life and Original Correspondence of Sir George Redcliffe* (1810); J. P. Cooper, "The Fortune of Thomas Wentworth, Earl of Strafford," *Economic History Review,* 2nd series, vol. xi, no. 2 (1958); H. Kearney, *Strafford in Ireland, 1633–41* (1959); T. Ranger, "Strafford in Ireland: a Revaluation," *Past and Present,* no. 19 (1961); Aidan Clarke, *The Old English in Ireland, 1625–42* (1966); R. R. Reid, *The King's Council in the North* (1921).

(C. V. W.)

**STRAIN GAUGE.** The strain gauge has many scientific applications, particularly in engineering. In addition to the measurement of strain, the gauge has been applied as a transducer to determine magnitudes of forces, torques, pressures, accelerations and similar physical quantities. This wider application has resulted from the development of a gauge using electric phenomena, but mechanical and optical magnification are also employed to measure strain. If loads are applied to materials such as metals or glass, the deformations usually are not discernible to the eye. The function of a strain gauge is to magnify the small deformations on the surfaces of mechanical parts or structures to the point where they can be measured.

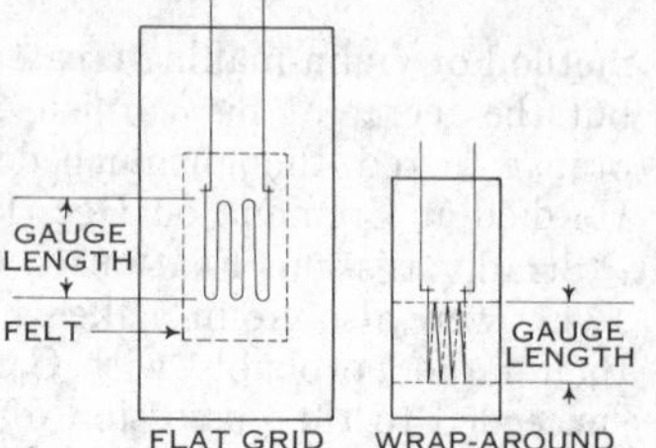

FIG. 1.—STRAIN GAUGES SHOWING CONSTRUCTION

In engineering, normal strain is defined as the deformation in a given direction divided by the gauge length in the same direction. If a 2 in. length, called the gauge length, is marked on a piece of rubber thread, it can be made to increase perceptibly when the thread is stretched. If the forces are such that the original length has increased to $2\frac{1}{4}$ in., the total deformation obviously is $\frac{1}{4}$ in., and the strain is $\frac{1}{8}$ in. per inch. The strain has the same value throughout the length of the rubber strip for a given force, regardless of the gauge length used, and increases as the force becomes greater.

If a block is shortened under a compressive load, compressive strains are developed. In parts of irregular shape which may be subjected to more complicated loading systems, the strain may vary from point to point, and a short gauge length therefore is required.

Engineers are interested in regions of high strain on parts or structures. If strains are known, properties of the material may be used to compute stresses, which are defined as forces per unit area. Conversely, if stresses are known, strains can be calculated. In design, mathematical equations are used to proportion the parts of a machine or structure so that the stresses caused by the applied loads are within the allowable limits of the materials specified. Strain gauges are applied to the actual structure or part to check these mathematical computations or to determine the strains at points when it is difficult or impossible to compute them.

One type of strain gauge widely used for this purpose is the bonded electric resistance strain gauge developed in 1938. This gauge consists of a length of fine wire, 0.001 in. in diameter, formed into a grid as shown in fig. 1 and cemented between two pieces of thin paper. Small and light, the gauge is made in many types, mostly in the size of a postage stamp. Gauge lengths as short as $\frac{1}{32}$ in. are available. The gauge is cemented to the part being tested. Many different cements have been used. As the part is loaded, the wire grid faithfully follows the deformations under it, either in tension or in compression, and the length and cross sectional area of the wire are changed. This causes the electrical resistance of the wire to change; even though this change is small—often a fraction of an ohm—electric circuits and instruments are available to detect the variation. A simple relation called the gauge factor exists between the unit change in resistance and the strain. This relation may be expressed mathematically by

$$\text{gauge factor} = \frac{\Delta R}{R} \Big/ \frac{\Delta L}{L} \qquad (1)$$

where $\Delta R$ is the change in resistance caused by strain, $R$ is the original resistance of the gauge, and $\Delta L/L$ is the strain under the grid.

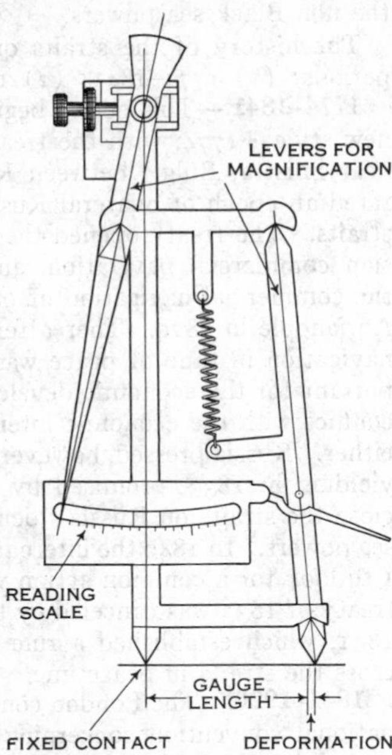


BY COURTESY OF A. U. HUGGENBERGER

FIG. 2.—A. HUGGENBERGER TENSOMETER LEVER SYSTEM (THE READING SCALE IS APPROXIMATELY 1 IN. LONG)

The manufacturer supplies the value of the gauge factor and the original resistance of each lot of gauges. If $\Delta R$ or a voltage change proportional to it is then measured, the strain can easily be calculated. The gauge is sensitive enough to detect strains as low as 0.000001 in. per inch and to measure strains as high as 0.03 in. per inch; special types can measure strains three times this value.

A gauge in which the grid is formed from metallic foil has been used to measure strains at temperatures as high as 1200° F.

Advantages are readily apparent. Many gauges have been bonded to structures and parts at strategic spots and their behaviour under load reported by wires leading to electronic instruments far removed from the test spots. Dynamic or rapidly changing strains occurring for example in freight car couplings or rocket firings have been recorded by oscilloscopes which handle strain variations as high as 50,000 cycles per second.

Strain gauges are used for measuring quantities other than strains. Load cells of various designs have been developed to measure force. Gauges have been bonded to short steel cylinders, the output of the gauges being calibrated in terms of the forces applied to them. Cells with capacities as high as 3,000,000 lb. have been built by the U.S. bureau of standards and calibrated in terms of force with an accuracy of 0.1%. Cantilever load beams have also been designed for force measurements. Gauges have been bonded to diaphragms, and the pressures on the diaphragms—static or variable—have been measured and recorded. Many other applications of the gauge have been made, especially to the measurement of accelerations. Other types of electric gauges—the unbonded resistance, electric inductance and electric capacitance gauges—have been utilized for the purposes described above.

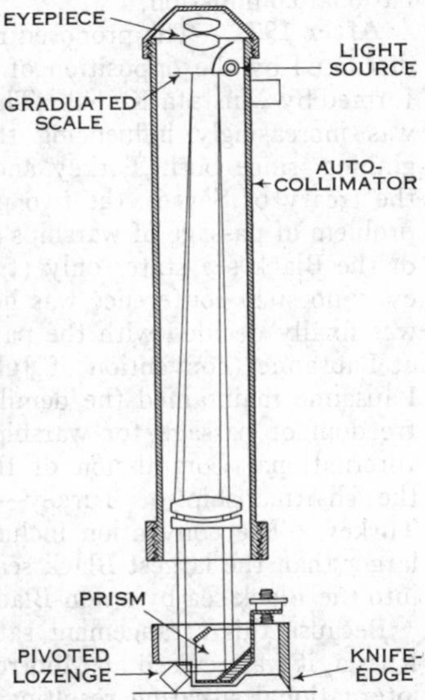

BY COURTESY OF AMERICAN INSTRUMENT CO. INC.

FIG. 3.—TUCKERMAN OPTICAL STRAIN GAUGE

Since 1870, many different types of instruments have been developed using a compound lever system for magnifying strains. The Huggenberger Tensometer shown in fig. 2 is of this type. The gauge length on most models is $\frac{1}{2}$ in. or 1 in., and magnifications of 1,200 to 1 are common. These instruments have been used to measure static strains with reliable accuracy. Their chief disadvantages are large size and inability to respond to dynamic strains. Other gauges employing levers, or levers and dial indicators, are the Whittemore, Berry and Porter-Lipp gauges.

The Tuckerman optical strain gauge was designed to use a beam of light as an optical lever for magnifying deformations. The gauge consists of an extensometer and an autocollimator as shown in fig. 3. The extensometer has a fixed knife-edge and a pivoted lozenge which are brought into contact with the part undergoing deformation. A one-inch gauge length is shown. One side of the Stellite lozenge is ground and lapped to an optically flat mirror surface. The autocollimator houses an optical system which can be adjusted above the gauge and is so designed that its distance above the extensometer is not critical. A beam of light from a lamp in the autocollimator is directed upon a prism in the extensometer, then reflected to the mirror surface of the lozenge and back to a graduated scale in the autocollimator. As the lozenge rotates, the reflected light beam from its mirror surface moves across the scale and may be viewed through an eyepiece in the autocollimator. The smallest deformation measurable is 0.00005 in. and for a gauge length of 1 in. this corresponds to a strain of 0.000002 in. per inch. The accuracy of the gauge is excellent, and it has therefore been regarded as a basic instrument for strain measurement.

Strain gauges of the types described above have been used in research laboratories and test stands of many companies, large and small, and in the control of manufacturing processes in refineries, steel mills and chemical industries.

*See* ELASTICITY.

BIBLIOGRAPHY.—M. Hetényi, *Handbook of Experimental Stress Analysis* (1950); C. C. Perry and H. R. Lissner, *The Strain Gage Primer*, 2nd ed. (1962); *Proceedings of the Society for Experimental Stress Analysis*, vol. i–xv, (1943). (E. O. ST.)

**STRAITS AND INTEROCEANIC CANALS.** In the geographic sense, a strait is a narrow stretch of the seas separating two land areas and linking two portions of the seas or a gulf with the high seas. In the legal sense, however, a strait is a point between two stretches of the high seas at which the territorial seas of two land areas meet and overlap. Since various states claim territorial seas ranging from three miles upward, it is impossible to fix a single generally accepted maximum breadth for a strait. A strait connecting the high seas with a gulf having one or more littoral states (such as the Straits of Tiran forming the entrance to the Gulf of Aqaba) is generally but not universally treated in the same way as a strait connecting two stretches of the high seas. Although interoceanic canals have occasionally been referred to as "artificial straits," they are not subject to the same legal regime as straits; their narrowness, length, and artificial character set them apart. Canals that connect two seas but are used for local traffic and are not traversed by large seagoing vessels (such as the Baltic-White Sea Canal in the U.S.S.R. or the Gota Canal, connecting the North Sea and the Baltic) are not of international significance.

**Straits.**—Approximately 30 straits are considered important routes for international traffic. Under customary international law, as enunciated by the International Court of Justice in the Corfu Channel case (1948), both merchant ships and warships have, unless otherwise prescribed by treaty, a right of free passage "through straits used for international navigation between two parts of the high seas without the previous authorization of a coastal state, provided that the passage is *innocent*." Save in this respect, the Geneva Convention of 1958 subjects the territorial sea in straits to the same regime as the territorial sea elsewhere. In time of war, a neutral littoral state may enforce reasonable measures to protect the neutrality of its territorial waters within a strait. Such measures may include the laying of mines and compulsory pilotage, but the strait must be kept open to free navigation. When a coastal state is at war, it may close the strait to enemy shipping and vessels carrying contraband to the enemy and may take all belligerent measures that it would be authorized to employ in its other territorial waters or on the high seas. Because of exceptional geographical and political circumstances, passage through certain straits is restricted by treaty. The most notable instance of such regulation is the Montreux Convention of 1936, which controls the passage of warships and merchant vessels through the Turkish straits and permits the closing of the straits when Turkey is at war. (*See* STRAITS QUESTION.)

**Interoceanic Canals.**—In the second half of the 20th century the three major interoceanic canals—Suez, Panama, and Kiel—were operated and maintained by the states with jurisdiction over the territory through which the canals passed. The three were opened to common usage by treaties that dedicated them to free navigation by the ships of all nations on a nondiscriminatory basis. Freedom of navigation through the Suez Canal was secured by the Convention of Constantinople of 1888 and was reaffirmed by the Egyptian government in its declaration of April 24, 1957; through the Panama Canal by the Hay-Pauncefote Treaty of 1901 between the United States and Great Britain, and the Hay-Bunau-Varilla Treaty of 1903 between the United States and Panama, giving the United States a permanent lease of the Canal Zone; and through the Kiel Canal by the Versailles Treaty of 1919. So long as the administering state is not at war, these canals must be left open to navigation by the warships and merchant ships of all nations. The passage of the shipping of belligerents is not, in the view of the Permanent Court of International Justice in the case of the SS "Wimbledon," inconsistent with the neutrality of the nation operating the canal. The treaties governing the Suez and Panama canals forbid belligerents using the waterways to take hostile measures in the canals or their approaches. The Panama Canal is the only one expressly "neutralized" by treaty, but all three have been fortified and defended by the powers in control of the adjacent territory when those nations have been at war. In case of a war to which the proprietor nation is a party, an interoceanic canal may be closed to enemy vessels and ships carrying contraband to the belligerents. The United Nations, however, condemned Egypt's closure of the Suez Canal to Israeli ships and cargoes on the ground that war could not lawfully exist between members of the United Nations. Passage through canals is at all times subject to the payment of tolls, but they must be equal for all states. They are fixed by the proprietor state, which assumes responsibility for the operation and maintenance of the waterway.

*See* Erik Brüel, *International Straits* (1947); R. R. Baxter, *The Law of International Waterways: With Particular Regard to Interoceanic Canals* (1964). (R. R. BR.)

**STRAITS QUESTION.** The straits question concerns the international status of the Black sea straits, *i.e.,* the Bosporus and the Dardanelles, which form the only existing passage from the Black sea into the Mediterranean and vice versa. In 1453 these straits became a part of Turkey and thus entered into the eastern question (*q.v.*) until the end of the Ottoman empire in 1920. It is not identical with the problem of Constantinople as the former capital of the Byzantine empire, although the two problems might have been connected in the past. Whatever the political aspirations of the antagonists of the Ottoman empire, including Peter the Great, there was no straits question before 1774, for until then the Black sea was an inland Turkish sea. From 1774 on, with Catherine the Great acquiring the northern shore of the Black sea, the straits question appeared, involving the interests of Russia, Turkey and the non-Black sea naval powers. These interests did not coincide: Russia's aim was to secure free passage for its warships through the straits but to close them to warships of non-Black sea powers; the latter, and especially Great Britain with its imperial lifeline, aimed at keeping the Russian navy from entering the Aegean sea, or at least at opening the straits to the warships of all nations. The Ottoman empire, resisting both pressures, saw in the control of the straits a guarantee of its independence and security, and this point of view remained that of the Turkish republic. From 1947 the control of the straits by Turkey was also considered as a major guarantee of their own security by the non-Black sea powers.

The history of the straits question can be divided into three periods: (1) 1774–1841; (2) 1841–1920; and (3) after 1921.

**1774–1841.**—This period begins on July 10 (old style; July 21, new style), 1774, with the treaty of Kuchuk Kainarji (a village near Silistra, Bulg.) between Russia and Turkey, which inaugurated an epoch of bilateral Russian-Turkish agreements as to the straits. The treaty opened the Black sea and the straits to Russian commercial navigation, and this privilege was extended to the commercial navigation of other states by the peace treaty of Adrianople in 1829. Thereafter the principle of free commercial navigation in time of peace was not challenged by Turkey. Important for the economic development of south Russia, it did not conflict with the economic interests of the non-Black sea powers either. Russia pressed, however, for naval privileges; and Turkey, yielding in 1833, promised by the treaty of Unkiar Skelessi to close the straits on Russia's demand to warships of all non-Black sea powers. In 1840 the international situation prompted Nicholas I to look for a common action with Great Britain in Turkey; the treaty of 1833 was canceled by the London convention of July 15, 1841, which established a rule that no non-Turkish navy might cross the straits in peacetime.

**1841–1920.**—The London convention was the first general international convention concerning the straits, and it inaugurated a period in which they became the common concern of all great powers. The regime of the straits agreed upon in the London convention remained without modification until World War I. The prohibition of passage for warships of all nations was confirmed in 1856 (treaty of Paris), in 1871 (treaty of London) and in 1878 (treaty of Berlin). During the Bosnian crisis of 1908–09 Russia attempted to get a straits' regime more favourable to the passage of its warships, but in spite of Russia's political alignment with France and England in European affairs at that time, the attempt ended in a failure. During World War I, Turkey having fought on the side of the Central Powers, the Allied Powers agreed to the inclusion of the straits, after the war, in the Russian empire (treaty of London, 1915). However, the leaders of the October revolution having canceled all the imperial secret treaties and renounced all annexations, the problem of the straits was solved after the war differently and without the participation of Russia. The peace treaty of Sèvres (1920), which never went into force, would have imposed on Turkey the disarmament of the straits and their opening to all foreign warships, while the zone of the straits would have passed under the administration of an international commission.

**After 1921.**—The proposed regime of the treaty of Sèvres was disrupted by the opposition of the national Turkish government formed by Mustafa Kemal. Thereafter, a forceful Turkish factor was increasingly influencing the straits question. In the beginning, since both Turkey and Soviet Russia were opposed to the treaty of Sèvres, the two powers agreed bilaterally that the problem of passage of warships should be decided by a conference of the Black sea states only (treaty of March 16, 1921). However, no such conference was held, and the regime of the straits was finally decided with the participation of the western powers at Lausanne (convention of July 24, 1923). The convention of Lausanne maintained the demilitarization of the straits and the freedom of passage for warships "under any banner"; also the International Commission of the Straits was maintained under the chairmanship of Turkey—a concession, among others, to Turkey. The convention included a clause that no naval force larger than the largest Black sea fleet might be sent in peacetime into the Black sea by a non-Black sea state.

Because this arrangement satisfied neither Turkey nor Soviet Russia, it was revised at Montreux on July 20, 1936, when a new international situation resulting from a more aggressive German and Italian policy made it appear dangerous also to Great Britain and France. The Montreux conference re-established the full right of Turkey to fortify the straits and disbanded the International commission. Reaffirming the already traditional freedom of navigation for commercial ships of all nations, the Montreux convention agreed to differentiate between the warships of Black sea states and those of non-Black sea states, giving to the former privileges the latter did not receive. With the exception of aircraft carriers and submarines, all warships of Black sea states were allowed to cross the straits unrestrictedly in peacetime; only light warships of non-Black sea states had this right under limitation of tonnage, number of units simultaneously present and duration of cruising time. In time of war the straits would be closed to all participants in the conflict if Turkey was neutral.

The Montreux convention (*q.v.*) was scheduled for revision in 1956 but the signatories were unable to agree on the premises of such a revision. In 1945 at Potsdam it was decided that each of the Big Three would communicate its views directly to Turkey concerning this revision. The U.S.S.R., although it had made demands on June 22, 1946, for joint control of the straits with Turkey, Great Britain and the U.S., backed Turkey in rejecting these demands as inconsistent with its independence and endangering its security. On May 30, 1953, the U.S.S.R. withdrew its demands of 1946.

*See* also TURKEY: *History: The Republic.*

BIBLIOGRAPHY.—A. Sorel, *La question d'Orient au XVIII^e^ siècle,* 2nd ed. (1889); P. P. Graves, *The Question of the Straits* (1930); L. Eisenmann, P. Renouvin (eds.), *Constantinople et les Détroits,* documents, 2 vol. (1930–32); B. H. Sumner, *Russia and the Balkans, 1870–1880* (1937); E. Brüel, *International Straits,* 2 vol. (1947); B. A. Dranov, *Chernomorskiya Prolivy* (1948); J. C. Hurewitz (ed.), *Diplomacy in the Near and Middle East,* 2 vol. (1956). (M. SL.)

**STRAITS SETTLEMENTS,** originally the collective name of four trading emporia, Penang, Singapore, Malacca, and Labuan, established or taken over by the English East India Company. Penang was founded by Francis Light in 1786, Singapore by Sir Thomas Stamford Raffles in 1819; Malacca, after temporary occupation by the British during the Napoleonic Wars, was finally transferred to the East India Company in 1824. These three territories were established as a crown colony in 1867. Labuan, which became part of Singapore Settlement in 1907, was constituted a fourth separate settlement in 1912.

The Straits colony ceased to exist in 1946. Labuan was incorporated in North Borneo (later Sabah), with which it became a part of Malaysia in 1963. Penang and Malacca were included in the Malayan Union (1946), the Federation of Malaya (1948), and Malaysia (1963). Singapore became a separate crown colony in 1946, attained full internal self-government in 1959, and became in 1963 a part of Malaysia, from which it was separated on mutually agreed terms in 1965 to become an independent republic.

*See* MALAYSIA; LABUAN; MALACCA; PENANG; SINGAPORE. (G. G. T.)

**STRALSUND,** a regional capital of East Germany in the *Bezirk* (district) of Rostock, German Democratic Republic. Pop. (1964) 67,888. The town, which is surrounded by water, is on the Strelasund, a strait between the mainland and Rügen Island. It is about 50 mi. (80 km.) NE of Rostock town by rail, and lines from Berlin and Rostock pass through it to the bathing and recreational centres on Rügen Island. The Rügen causeway connects Stralsund with the island. Fishing boats are built there; manufactures include fish-processing machinery, pipelines, furniture, sugar, and conserves; and there is fish smoking and brewing.

Stralsund received its municipal charter in 1234. The town was one of the leading members of the Hanseatic League. During the Thirty Years' War it was unsuccessfully besieged in 1628 by Wallenstein. After the Peace of Westphalia of 1648 it was transferred to Sweden; in 1815, after being occupied by France in 1807 and Denmark in 1814, it passed to Prussia. Although much damaged during World War II, it still retains its medieval centre, with Gothic buildings.

**STRANG, JAMES JESSE** (1813–1856), dissident Mormon leader, founder of the Strangite sect, a minute fragment of which still survives, was born at Scipio, N.Y., March 21, 1813. Admitted to the bar, he also taught school, edited a weekly paper, and was a country postmaster, before he followed his wife's family to Burlington, Wis., in 1843. Through his wife's brother-in-law, a Mormon, he visited Joseph Smith at Nauvoo, Ill., became a Mormon convert, and was ordained an elder by Smith in February 1844. After Smith's assassination, Strang exhibited a letter, purportedly written by Smith and naming Strang, a Mormon of less than five months' standing, as his successor. He also claimed to have had a vision appointing him "seer, revelator, and prophet" of the Mormon Church. He was out-generaled, however, by Brigham Young, and the Twelve Apostles denounced him as an impostor and forger and expelled him from the church. With a few of his 2,500 followers—one of whom was Joseph Smith's brother William—he moved to Voree (Vorhee, Vorree), Wis., where he caused himself to be crowned King James I after translating (with the aid of magic spectacles given him by an angel) *The Book of the Law of the Lord* from golden plates from the Ark of the Covenant. In 1849 the Strangites moved to Beaver Island, in Lake Michigan (40 mi. [64 km.] W of the Straits of Mackinac), and Strang received another revelation in the "plates of Laban." Under its rules polygamy was sanctioned, and he was married to four wives. The Strangites were the object of much persecution, but Strang was able to preserve the sect and to gain acquittal in the several lawsuits brought against him. He had more than 5,000 followers in Michigan and Wisconsin when he was shot on June 16, 1856, by two former Strangites. He was taken to Voree, where he died July 9, 1856. The Lake Michigan fishermen drove more than 2,000 of his believers from their homes and all but extinguished the Strangite branch of the Mormon Church.

**STRANRAER,** a royal and small burgh and seaport of Wigtown, Scotland. Pop. (1961) 9,250. It is situated at the head of Loch Ryan, an arm of the North Channel (Irish Sea), 52 mi. SSW of Ayr by road. It lies 39 mi. E by N of Larne in County Antrim, Northern Ireland, with which there is regular communication by mail steamer. Grain milling and nursery gardening are carried on, and there is a large trade in farm and dairy produce. Whitefish and herring are caught and there are oyster beds at Cairn Ryan on the east side of the loch. Stranraer, originally called St. John's Chapel, became a burgh of barony in 1596 and a royal burgh in 1617. In the centre of the town are the ruins of the castle of the 15th century, occupied for a time by John Graham of Claverhouse, Viscount Dundee, when he held the office of sheriff of Galloway (1682).

Three miles east of Stranraer is Lochinch, the residence of the earl of Stair, a modern structure (1870) in the Scots baronial style. The grounds include the White and Black lochs, and the ruins of Castle Kennedy on the isthmus between. This castle was erected in the reign of James VI for the earls of Cassillis, passed into the hands of the Stair family in the 17th century, and was burned down in 1716. The gardens, which contain the finest pinetum in Scotland, were restored in the middle of the 19th century.

**STRAPWORK,** in architecture and the decorative arts, a form of ornament developed in Germany, Flanders, and England during the latter half of the 16th and the 17th centuries and consisting of scrolls, straight lines, rectangles, and shield forms carved or modeled in flat relief, often with a raised fillet at the edge, and often pierced with circular or oval holes; the whole composition is usually formed of connected units, all upon the same plane, as though made by an elaborately cut out and pierced strap applied to a background. It is a development of certain Italian early Baroque motives, such as the multiple shield or cartouche frames, and certain approximations of it occurred in Italian metalwork as early as the silverwork of Benvenuto Cellini (1500–71); these forms are, themselves, Italian interpretations of the flat scrolls so common in Islamic metalwork. Strapwork was used extensively in the Renaissance woodwork of Germany and is occasionally found in stone, as in the Salzhaus at Frankfurt am Main (end of the 16th century). In Flanders and the Netherlands strapwork received an even more complete development, for although in Germany it was usually only a subsidiary motive, in the architectural woodwork and furniture of the Low Countries it often became the only type of ornament used. The form was introduced into England by the flood of Flemish and German woodworkers that came in in the latter part of the 16th and early 17th centuries. (T. F. H.)

**STRASBOURG,** a city of France and *préfecture* of the *département* of Bas-Rhin and of the region of Alsace (set up in 1964), lies 2 mi. (3 km.) W of the Rhine River, on the frontier between France and Germany. Pop. (1962) 225,964.

The city grew on an island between two branches of the Ill River. The Cathedral of Notre-Dame (11th–15th centuries) shows different styles, from Romanesque to late Gothic: the Romanesque crypt dates from 1015, the apse is Transitional, and the rest of the building Gothic. The cathedral is often considered to be typically German in style, but it was strongly influenced by French architecture, and the most strikingly German characteristic is probably its low proportions: for example the nave, completed in 1275, has a height of 107 ft. (32.6 m.) to a width of 53½ ft. (16.3 m.). The facade, with its rose window, was started about 1260 and not completed until much later. It is the work of several architects, but despite inconsistencies in its plan it has been much praised, notably by Goethe. It is asymmetrical, the north tower being completed by a remarkable 15th-century spire. At the entrance to the north transept is the Portal of St. Lawrence (1495–1505), designed by Jacob of Landshut. Many of the sculptures from the cathedral have been replaced by copies and some of the originals may be seen in the Maison de l'Oeuvre Notre-Dame. Near it is the Palais Rohan (1730), a former episcopal palace which houses three art museums. Also in the centre of the city are the Protestant Church of St. Thomas (13th–14th centuries), the Hôtel de Ville (1730–36), and the Chambre du Commerce (1582).

Strasbourg is a university city with an academy of music, and the headquarters of the Council of Europe. It is at the crossroads of routes from France to Central Europe and from the Netherlands to Italy, and it is linked by rail with Paris, Vienna, Berlin, Amsterdam, and Warsaw. There is an airport about 7 mi. (12 km.) from the city centre. The river port lies east of the city, on the Rhine, and by the mid-1960s dealt with well over 6,000,000 tons of traffic annually. From the port the Rhine is linked by canals with the Marne and the Rhône rivers. Many varieties of goods pass through the port including coal, food, wood, and metallurgical products. There are two modern petroleum refineries. Industries of Strasbourg include metallurgy, the manufacture of man-made textiles, tanning, brewing, food processing, and printing. Gutenberg made early experiments in printing there in 1436. The city's most celebrated product is *pâté de foie gras.*

Strasbourg has always been a place of great strategical importance. Originally a Celtic settlement, it was known to the Romans as Argentoratum. In the 4th century A.D. it was invaded by the Alamanni and in 357 it was the scene of a battle between the emperor Julian and the German tribes under Chnodomar. Julian's victory, due mainly to the superior discipline of the Roman infantry, resulted in the recovery of the Upper Rhine and the freeing of Gaul from barbarian invasions. Toward the end of the 5th century the town passed to the Franks, who gave it its present name. In 842 Charles the Bald and Louis the German took the Strasbourg Oath (*Serment de Strasbourg*), a text of which is the oldest written document in French. The town's connection with the German kingdom began in 923, through the homage paid by the Duke of Lorraine to the German king Henry I. The early history of Strasbourg consists mainly of struggles between the bishop and the citizens. This conflict was finally decided in favour of the citizens by the Battle of Oberhausbergen in 1262, and the position of a free imperial city which had been conferred upon Strasbourg by the German king, Philip of Swabia, was not again disputed. In 1332 there was an internal revolution, which resulted in admitting the guilds to a share in the government of the city.

In 1381 the city joined the *Städtebund,* or league of Swabian towns, and a century later it helped the Swiss confederates at Grandson and Nancy. The reformed doctrines were readily accepted in Strasbourg about 1523, and the city was skilfully piloted through the ensuing period of religious dissensions by Jacob Sturm von Sturmeck, who secured for it very favourable terms at the end of the War of the Schmalkaldic League. In the Thirty Years' War the town observed a prudent neutrality. In 1681, during a time of peace, it was suddenly seized by Louis XIV, and this unjustifiable action received formal recognition at the Peace of Rijswijk in 1697. At the French Revolution the city was deprived of its privileges as a free town. In the Franco-German War of 1870–71 Strasbourg, with its garrison of 17,000 men, surrendered to the Germans on Sept. 28, 1870. The city and the cathedral suffered considerably from the bombardment. Strasbourg remained German until 1918 when it once again became part of France. At the outbreak of World War II the city was evacuated and in 1944 it suffered heavily under Allied bombing. On Nov. 23, 1944, it was liberated by General Leclerc.

Strasbourg is the seat of a bishop. The bishopric originally embraced a large territory on both banks of the Rhine, but it was diminished by the creation of the bishoprics of Speyer (Spires) and Basel. The episcopal lands were annexed by France in 1789 and the subsequent Roman Catholic bishops of Strasbourg discharged spiritual duties only.

Rouget de Lisle composed "La Marseillaise" there in 1792.

*See* also references under "Strasbourg" in the Index.

**STRASBURGER, EDUARD** (1844–1912), German botanist, one of the first to realize the importance of the nucleus and chromosomes in heredity, was born in Warsaw, then in Russian Poland, on Feb. 1, 1844. He studied in Germany at Bonn and at Jena. He returned briefly to the university at Warsaw in 1868; he was professor of botany at Jena from 1869 to 1880 and thereafter at Bonn till his death.

Strasburger contributed to the advance of many branches of botany. His first work was concerned with the embryology of gymnosperms, then with the more minute details of the life history of angiosperms. Later he turned increasingly to the study of the cell, and made many contributions to the solution of problems of cell and nuclear division in plants. He also studied problems of water transport in plants, and in his last years the inheritance of sex differences in plants.

Strasburger was also the foremost botanical teacher of his day. He wrote a number of textbooks, among which the "Bonner Lehrbuch," *Lehrbuch der Botanik,* first published in 1894 in collaboration with others, established itself as the standard textbook for botanical students the world over and was widely translated. He died at Bonn on May 18, 1912. (G. H. Be.)

**STRATEGUS** (Greek Strategos), a word meaning strictly a general, but frequently in ancient Greece a state officer with much wider functions.

In Athens the board of ten strategi was originally a product of the reorganization of the tribal system under Cleisthenes (*q.v.*), each of the ten tribal units being represented in the army by a *taxis* (regiment) led by a strategus; but there is evidence (Aristotle, *Constitution of Athens,* xxii) against the view that Cleisthenes himself created the board. In any case, in 490 B.C., at Marathon, the head of the army was still the polemarch (*see* Archon), Herodotus' story of successive days of command being based on a misconception of the powers of strategi. After 487, however, when the archons came to be chosen by lot, command of the *taxeis* passed to taxiarchs subordinate to the strategi. In the 5th century, it was usual to appoint a number of strategi for a particular field of operations: while the chief command might be assigned to one of them, they often held coordinate powers (*e.g.,* in the Sicilian expedition) or exercised the chief command in turn (*e.g.,* at Arginusae). In crises, however, the whole board could be subordinated to one member (*e.g.,* Pericles at the outbreak of the Peloponnesian War, or Alcibiades in 407). At first each tribe elected a strategus from among its members; but in the second half of the 5th century there are examples of two strategi being elected from a single tribe (*e.g.,* Pericles and Glaucon in 433–432; Alcibiades and Adeimantus in 407–406); and in the later part of the 4th century the strategi were elected from the whole citizen body without regard to tribal divisions. The tribes, however, continued to elect the taxiarchs.

The political powers of the strategi were considerably increased in the 5th century, particularly in foreign affairs. Though apparently not members of the boule (council), they could attend its meetings, bring motions before it, and ask it for emergency meetings of the ecclesia (assembly), in which their business regularly took precedence of everything else. In concluding treaties, they acted on the voted resolutions of the ecclesia. The appointment of strategi for specified departments dates from the 4th century.

Two aspects of the office made it important: (1) it was elective, as opposed to the magistracies filled by lot; and (2) strategi were reeligible indefinitely. A man who commanded popular confidence (*e.g.,* Pericles) might thus not only obtain such commissions as could not be left to chance nominees but also be returned to power in subsequent years to profit from his experience. The board of strategi had no collective responsibility.

Military power prevailed over civil authority in the Greek world after Alexander the Great, and strategi became the supreme magistrates in most leagues and federations. Both in the Achaean and in the Aetolian League the strategus (helped by a commander of the cavalry or *hipparchus*) was the head of the state, being appointed for a year by the appropriate federal assembly: he was at once commander of the army, president of the federal assemblies, and foreign minister. The same man could not however be reelected in consecutive years; and in the Aetolian League the strategus was not allowed to make proposals about war or peace.

Alexander the Great appointed Antipater as strategus of Europe when he went to war against Persia. Polyperchon and Cassander filled the same position after Alexander's death; and Antigonus was sometime strategus of Asia. The governors appointed by the Macedonian kings over regions or cities of Greece were normally called strategi. In the Seleucid kingdom the provinces were governed at least in part by strategi, but details are controversial. There were provincial governors called strategi in other Hellenistic monarchies, and strategi appointed by the king are found in Pergamum. In Egypt the strategi became the civil governors of the nomes during the 3rd century B.C. (they almost completely lost their original military character); a special strategus governed the Thebaid; and there were strategi in the Ptolemaic territories outside Egypt. Under Roman rule strategi remained the heads of the Egyptian nomes until the 4th century A.D. There were officers with powers equivalent to those of strategi (and called strategi by Greek authors) in the Carthaginian state.

BIBLIOGRAPHY.—A. Hauvette-Besnault, *Les Stratèges athéniens* (1885); A. H. J. Greenidge, *Handbook of Greek Constitutional History,* pp. 180 ff. (1896); J. Sundwall, *Epigraphische Beiträge zur sozial-politischen Geschichte Athens,* pp. 19 ff. (1906); C. Hignett, *A History of the Athenian Constitution* (1952). For the Greek leagues, *see* G. Busolt, ed. by H. Swoboda, *Griechische Staatskunde,* part ii, esp. pp. 1527 ff., 1567 ff. (1926); A. Aymard, *Les Assemblées de la confédération achaïenne* (1938). For the Hellenistic monarchies, *see* H. Bengtson, *Die Strategie in der hellenistischen Zeit,* 3 vol. (1937–52).

(A. D. Mo.)

**STRATEGY,** narrowly defined, means "the art of the general" (from the Greek *strategus*). In a strictly military sense, the term first gained currency at the end of the 18th century, when warfare was still relatively simple and limited. In its military aspect, the term had to do with stratagems by which a general sought to deceive an enemy, with plans he made for a campaign, and with the way he moved and disposed his forces in war. Often defined as the art of projecting and directing campaigns, military strategy came to preempt almost the whole field of generalship, short of the battlefield itself. It also came to include the planning of naval warfare. To tactics (*q.v.*), military jargon reserved the art of executing plans and handling forces in battle.

The term strategy has expanded far beyond its original military meaning. As society and warfare have steadily grown more complex, particularly in Western civilization, military factors have become more and more inseparable from the nonmilitary in the conduct of war and in programs designed to secure peace. Nations have found it necessary to adjust and correlate political, economic, technological, and psychological factors, along with military elements, in the management of their national policy. The demarcation between strategy as a purely military phenomenon and national strategy of the broader variety became blurred in the 19th century, particularly in wartime. The distinction became even less clear in the 20th century when nations became more interdependent and the line between war and peace less clearly definable. As a result, the appearance of the term "grand strategy" (or "higher strategy"), meaning the art of employing all the resources of a nation or coalition of nations to achieve the objects of war (and peace), steadily became more popular in the literature of warfare and statecraft of the 20th century.

This broadened scope of strategy has tended to blur distinctions customarily drawn by earlier writers between strategy and statesmanship, and between garden varieties and higher or "grand" forms of strategy. Though there is still no agreed definition of the precise meaning of the term strategy, few students of the subject any longer accept the earlier narrow definition. Also, few contest that strategy, whether in its narrow or broad sense, will, by the very nature of its shifting bases, continue to be a changing art.

This article is divided into the following sections:



## I. FUNDAMENTALS OF STRATEGY

**1. The Search for Principles.**—The starting point of all strategic planning and action is national policy. Once the national aims are set forth by the leaders of the state, the commander sets about drawing up his plans. He must take many matters into account; for example, factors of space and time, the state of his own forces, the enemy's capabilities and intentions, and reactions at home and abroad to his projected moves. The strategist deals in many uncertainties and imponderables. Indeed, the art of the strategist is the art of the "calculated risk."

The growing complexity of modern warfare has led some students to take a fresh look at the principles that have traditionally guided military strategists in war. It has long been a favourite occupation of military theorists to seek to distill from the great mass of military experience simple but all-pervasive truths—lists of principles—to guide commanders. Usually they have derived such principles from a study of campaigns of the great captains of history; occasionally outstanding practitioners have set them down on the basis of personal experience. As far back as 500 B.C. Sun Tzu, a Chinese general, set forth 13 principles. The axioms range from Gen. N. B. Forrest's simple admonition about getting there first with the most men to Napoleon's 115 maxims. The stress varies from list to list. It ranges from the emphasis of the followers and interpreters of Karl von Clausewitz on the belief that the battle is all, and defeat of the enemy's armed forces the correct objective and path to victory, to that of exponents of "the strategy of indirect approach," of victory by indirect methods, such as B. H. Liddell Hart, eloquent advocate of the principle of "obliquity" in the 20th century.

Though there is no complete agreement on the number of principles, most lists include the following: the objective, the offensive, cooperation (unity of command), mass (concentration), economy of force, maneuver, surprise, security, and simplicity. The British have added one called "administration"; the Russians another, translated as "annihilation." Despite debate over their precise number and meaning, the principles of war are widely taught, and most military students accept them as basic concepts.

The individual authors of the lists have almost uniformly claimed the principles to be immutable. They have argued that success in military strategy in the past has been the result of adhering to them; that the advantages of the offensive, the concentration of force, the effort to achieve surprise, the proper movement of forces and their security from attack, sabotage, or subversion are in the province of modern as well as ancient warfare. Some authorities have even argued that since war is not the concern of soldiers only, the "principles" deserve a wider application throughout government—in grand as well as military strategy.

Other authorities have argued that the claim of immutability cannot be accepted literally; that there is little agreement as to what the principles are and mean; that they overlap; that they are fluid and require constant reexamination; that they are not comparable with scientific laws since no two military situations are ever completely alike; that the so-called principles are not really principles at all, but merely methods and common-sense procedures adopted by great commanders of the past; and that changes in the conditions of war alter their relative importance.

The debate over principles was renewed with the coming of the atomic era. Some theorists argued that the new weapons had destroyed whatever value the principles once had; others contended that the principles were as valid as ever, even more so. To some extent this was a debate over semantics. Defenders pointed out that each age must make its own applications of the "fundamental truths" of strategy. Opponents argued that there can be no set rules for the art; the so-called principles must by no means be interpreted as pat formulas for victory to be followed blindly and rigidly; the only sound guide in war and strategy is flexibility.

**2. Relation Between Strategy and Tactics.**—In the theory of warfare, strategy and tactics have generally been put into separate categories. The two fields have traditionally been defined in terms of different dimensions: strategy dealing with wide spaces, long periods of time, and large movements of forces; tactics with the opposite. Strategy is usually understood to be the prelude to the battlefield, and tactics the action on the battlefield itself. As a result, much of the literature and theory of strategy has in the past been preoccupied with the proper approach to the battlefield, the leading of troops up to the time of contact with the enemy. This situation explains the attention to strategic maneuver—aimed at putting one's army into the most favourable position to engage the enemy and compelling the enemy to engage at a disadvantage and depriving him of freedom of movement. Indeed, early writers on strategy dealt heavily in the so-called "geometrical strategy"—the angles formed by lines of movement and supply of opposing armies. Sir Edward Hamley in his *Operations of War* has well described all the various permutations and combinations of strategic maneuver.

Despite distinctions in theory, strategy and tactics cannot always be separated in practice. In fact, the language of strategic maneuver (for example, "envelopment," "penetration," "encirclement") is also largely the language of tactics (*see* TACTICS). Movement begets action, and action results in new movement. The one merges into the other. Strategy gives tactics its mission and wherewithal and seeks to reap the results. But tactics has also become an important conditioning factor of strategy, and as it changes, so does strategy. Battles and fronts are no longer necessarily restricted in space and time, and the distinction between battles and campaigns is no longer so clear-cut, as the experience of World Wars I and II with tridimensional warfare demonstrated. Indeed, in World War II, theatre commanders were as much concerned with the actual fighting of armed forces in battle as they were with larger strategic decisions—with relations to allies, economic problems and political questions on the ground. While in theory strategy continues to occupy a middle ground between national policy and tactics, in practice the line dividing it from the other two fields has become increasingly difficult to draw.

**3. Strategic Leadership and War Planning.**—Count von Schlieffen, the famous German military leader, once said, "A man is born, and not made, a strategist." But it is obvious that even a born strategist—if there be such a natural genius—has much to learn. In the old days strategic leadership was a relatively simple affair. J. F. C. Fuller, the British student of warfare, pointed out in *The Foundations of the Science of War* (1926), that until relatively recent times the death, capture or wounding of either of two opposing generals normally decided a conflict, "for the general *was* the plan." He could personally devise the plans and direct his troops. By mid-20th century this was rarely possible. As warfare has become complicated, strategic leadership has become more difficult. The art has taken on many more facets and systematic training is required to master them. The strategist has retired from the scene of battle, and large, specialized staffs have grown up to help him. While the responsibility for strategy remains the general's, many of his functions have been delegated to his planning staff. In modern states corporate leadership has become the rule in the management of military strategy, as in the direction of large business enterprises.

The example of an Alexander completing his advance planning and leaping into battle at the head of his troops, as at Arbela, would in modern warfare be considered most unusual. Napoleon was wont to make his plans and then retire with his retinue of trusted advisers to survey the battlefield on horseback from the top of a hill. Generals in World War I were often pictured in their offices in large headquarters—usually in a chateau behind the lines, studying a map on the desk and dispatching orders via the telephone and motorcar at hand. In World War II the headquarters staffs of commanders in the theatres of war grew even larger and more elaborate. Tridimensional warfare had enlarged the field of operations far beyond individual battlefields, and usually a high commander reached his decisions in a headquarters far removed from the field of battle and months before the battle itself took place. Far from striking the classic pose of the officer on a well-schooled charger, some of the greatest generals issued their orders from desks and fought their most important battles at conference tables. As strategic planning became a highly organized affair, planning committees and conferences in the capital cities of the warring powers made the blueprints for victory in the global, coalition struggle. In their capital command posts military leaders kept in touch with the manifold phases of the national government's war effort and dealt with the worldwide problems transcending those of the individual theatres of war. With the aid of new devices for rapid communication these leaders and their staffs sought to set the patterns of strategy and keep abreast of the movement of armies as the Caesars and Napoleons had done in earlier eras.

As war became more total, war planning became an increasingly significant peacetime function of governments. The manufacture of strategic plans has become a highly specialized industry in modern military establishments. At the same time, more and more governmental agencies have been drawn into the business of planning for national security. The plans they produce may vary from a simple design to shift a small task force to a danger spot to an elaborate plan for the conduct of war in its entirety. To be realistic, strategic plans and estimates must constantly be reexamined and brought into harmony.

Against this general background in the nature of the art, it is now possible to sketch the important contributions made in key periods to modern strategic theory and practice. It is important to remember that the art of strategy has changed from age to age, just as has war itself, and that each is the product of its own society and time.

## II. DEVELOPMENT OF STRATEGY

Though the serious and systematic study of modern strategy may be dated from the 18th century, various authorities have identified strategic precedents going back to earliest times. Students of warfare of primitive ages have associated with primitive tribes and clans a stratagem of surprise from darkness or by ambush, and they have identified a strategy of hunt and pounce, like that of a lion or tiger. The Bible points to the care with which Moses prepared his operations—an early form of advance planning. The ancient world developed a strategy of mass attack by phalanx, legion or cavalry. Alexander, Hannibal, and Caesar, who combined in their own persons political and military direction of the state, planned their famous campaigns far ahead. They have been singled out as forerunners of the modern art of grand strategy. Writers in modern times have used the campaigns of these great captains to illustrate practically every known "principle of war." But important as their attention to strategic considerations in war and especially to strategic approaches to the battlefield may have been, the foundations of the ancient art of warfare were tactics and battles. To a considerable extent battles—often short and furious—also held the centre of the military stage in the Middle Ages. Strategy was notably absent in the excursions of the Huns, the Muslims, and the crusaders. Far more important from a strategic viewpoint were the campaigns of Genghis Khan and his general, Sabutai, in the 13th century. Their advance planning and bold strategic maneuvers in broad sweeps from Mongolia across Asia and Europe showed an appreciation of strategic problems most unusual for their age.

In the transition to modern times two other figures who touched on the field of strategy are often mentioned—Niccolò Machiavelli in the realm of military thought and Gustavus II Adolphus in the field of generalship. Machiavelli's *Art of War* (1520) emphasized the larger aspects of war, particularly the close relationship between the civil and military spheres. A century later, Gustavus, ruler-general of Sweden, intervened in the Thirty Years' War, and, maneuvering skilfully, drove the imperial armies out of northern Germany.

**1. 18th-Century Warfare; Frederick the Great.**—After the death of Gustavus, warfare again settled down to a slower pace and a more stable mold. The 17th and 18th centuries saw the growth of professional armies loyal to the king. But the great cost of building and maintaining such armies led to a concern for their safety, a hesitation to risk them in bloody encounters and a preoccupation with defense and fortifications. Strategy was essentially of limited aim and was greatly concerned with the art of siegecraft, for which elaborate rules were prescribed. In Prussia of the mid-18th century, however, circumstances compelled Frederick the Great to try a new and aggressive approach and to break through the accepted military pattern of the day.

Confronted at the outset of the Seven Years' War (1756–1763) by a coalition of Austria, France, Russia, Sweden, and Saxony, Frederick found himself virtually surrounded. His task was to devise a strategy to defend his territory and not to dissipate his outnumbered troops. The strategy he evolved did not follow set rules or recipes. Indeed, never was the definition of strategy as a "system of makeshifts," offered in a later age by Count von Moltke, better demonstrated. In his planning Frederick capitalized on two valuable assets—his army, a superior and highly disciplined instrument of war, and a central position. He sought always to keep the initiative, to attack first one enemy and then another, to assemble at decisive points a force superior to that of his foe and to avoid long, drawn-out wars. Using his central position to concentrate against individual armies of the enemy before they could be reinforced by others, he developed the classical "strategy of interior lines." But even Frederick, the statesman-warrior, could not entirely escape the conditions imposed by the warfare of his times. Indeed, the statesman imposed caution on the warrior. He could not expose his costly armies to the risk of destruction and bloody decision by battle. His battles were not those of annihilation. In the end his wars were decided by reasons of state, and those wars left his nation exhausted.

The age that immediately followed Frederick chose to imitate his caution rather than his aim. Military theory was characterized by ideas of victory without battle, maneuvering for position, a system of lines and angles of operation. Geometric concepts and cunning tricks and artifices replaced the aim to destroy enemies. Great emphasis was put on terrain and the occupation of key geographic points. The 18th century, it must be remembered, was the era of enlightenment, and warfare conformed to the spirit of the age. Strategy, like all warfare, became "mathematical" and "scientific." Theorists optimistically maintained that a general who knew mathematics and topography could direct campaigns with geometrical precision and win wars without even fighting. But the new mode of warfare ushered in by the French Revolution and the Napoleonic era was soon to challenge these optimistic assumptions.

**2. Napoleonic Warfare; Clausewitz and Jomini.**—The French revolutionary and the Napoleonic periods witnessed great changes in the methods of war—the revolution in society accompanying and reinforcing the one in warfare. When Napoleon, the first great military strategist of the modern Western world, burst upon the European scene, the groundwork for a new age in warfare had already been laid. The French Revolution gave birth (1793) to the "nation in arms" and all Frenchmen became liable for military service. The patriotic citizen-soldier succeeded the mercenary professional. Skirmish tactics, or the loose formation, replaced the straight line; divisional organization came into use, along with lightweight artillery of great range and firing power. When Napoleon came to reap the benefits of these changes, he completely transformed strategy as well as tactics. He applied the same basic principle to the one as to the other—never to divide his forces, but to concentrate all his might against the enemy forces at the critical point. His emphasis was on careful preparation, on uniting his forces before the action, on overpowering weight of striking power, on shock attack, on great daring, and on bloody decision by battle. His methods were simple, direct, overpowering—even brutal; his aim was nothing short of the destruction of the enemy forces. Against such power, neat geometric calculations stood little chance and ordinary stratagems were helpless. Again and again he showed his military genius for bringing a mass to bear against the flanks of his enemy, for selection of battlegrounds advantageous to his forces, and for deploying his forces for battle. He gave supreme expression to the idea of victory by battle.

Though as a military leader, operational strategist and tactician of the battlefield he is regarded by many as unparalleled, in the larger field of national or grand strategy he showed shortcomings. Embodying in his own person the leadership of the state and its military affairs, he recognized the value of incorporating political and economic measures, along with military moves, to increase the chances of victory in war. But he could not successfully grasp and cope with the challenge finally put to him by Great Britain and its European allies. British strategy sought to meet the Napoleonic threat to Europe by using naval power to blockade the continent and by conducting a war of exhaustion on land through peripheral warfare, such as Wellington's famous campaign on the Iberian Peninsula. Napoleon's reply to the British naval blockade was the continental system prohibiting British goods from entering. But this helped bring his downfall, since he was needed everywhere—to hold the coast, fight in Spain, Holland, against Austria and Russia. His veteran French forces were dissipated and he had to rely on impressed nationalities of Europe. Eventually the coalition of his enemies was to use the methods and means of warfare that the French Revolution had introduced and Napoleon had perfected to reinvigorate their own forces and overwhelm him.

Despite his mistakes, Napoleon's preeminent place in the history of strategy is secure. His tactics and strategy influenced military leaders for a century. His maxims were widely studied and were said to have been carried in the saddlebag of the famous U.S. general, "Stonewall" Jackson. Students of strategy have long pointed to Napoleon's battles and campaigns for classical illustrations of "principles" of war—of surprise, mobility, concentration of force, and economy of force. Possibly more than that of any other general, his competent practice oriented modern military theory toward the search for underlying principles. Indeed, the art of strategy as evolved by theorists since 1800 may be traced largely to his operations.

For this development two great interpreters of Napoleonic strategy, Antoine Jomini and Clausewitz (*qq.v.*), were especially responsible. Clausewitz, a Prussian, the first great student of strategy and the father of modern strategical study, lived in the early 19th century. Trained in systematic study of philosophy in the school of Immanuel Kant, it was but natural for him to range widely over the whole field of military knowledge and to reduce Napoleonic warfare to a unified, philosophical conception. His famous work, *On War,* written as an outgrowth of his studies of Napoleon's campaigns, remains the best general study of the art of war. He died with his work unfinished, but his writings published after his death became the standard textbooks on war in Prussia and elsewhere. Their influence was felt profoundly in the Franco-Prussian War of 1870, and leading generals of World Wars I and II were brought up on them and on the works of his followers.

The contributions of Clausewitz to strategic thought are many and diverse. To some his work is the Bible of strategy, and, like that great book, susceptible to many conflicting interpretations. His work set forth fully and clearly for the first time the relationship between political and military leadership. He dwelt on decision by battle as the first rule of war; on seeking the destruction of the enemy's forces; and on achieving superiority at the decisive spot. Rejecting the optimism and rationalism of the 18th century, he held that war was not a scientific game but an act of violence. Mathematical and topographical factors, he held, were important in tactics, but less so in strategy. "We . . . do not hesitate," he asserted, "to regard as an established truth that in strategy more depends on the number and the magnitude of the victorious combats than on the form of the great lines by which they are connected" (*On War*, vol. 1, bk. 3, ch. xv, p. 223, Routledge & Kegan Paul, Ltd., London, 1940). The key to victory was battle, however bloody. Strategy he defined as the employment of battles to gain the end of war.

Clausewitz devoted much of his work to showing that war is both a social development and a political act. He went further and said that, "War is not merely a political act, but also a real political instrument, a continuation of policy carried out by other means" (Maj. Gen. Sir F. Maurice, *British Strategy*, p. 44, Constable & Co., Ltd., London, 1929). War was therefore not an independent phenomenon unto itself to be handed over to soldiers and sailors. Again and again he asserted that military and political strategy must go hand in hand. "War," he declared, "admittedly has its own grammar, but not its own logic" (*On War*).

Clausewitz' emphasis on the aim of strategy as the destruction of the enemy's forces on the battlefield has had a great influence on subsequent military thinking. His disciples, however, have generally overlooked the fact that he also recognized another strategical form—a strategy of limited aim for limited warfare, of wearing down an opponent. When Clausewitz wrote, warfare was conducted in two dimensions, and it was rarely possible for one nation to impose its will without first destroying the opposing army. But Clausewitz recognized clearly what many of his followers in subsequent generations forgot, that the destruction was only a means to enforce policy and not an end in itself.

In the history of military thought, the French general Jomini, one of Napoleon's staff officers and a contemporary of Clausewitz, presents a striking contrast to the Prussian philosopher of war. Lacking the philosophical bent of Clausewitz, Jomini concentrated his thinking on what he regarded as practical issues in war rather than on war as a whole. He became the chief expounder of Napoleonic methods, and out of his studies evolved a theory of strategy. Although he opposed "systems of war" purporting to provide for all contingencies, he nevertheless believed that in the field of strategy certain rules and general principles—eternally true—could and should be formulated "as a compass for the commander-in-chief of an army." To establish these principles, he believed, was the major problem of military science.

The heart of Jomini's theory lay in the theatre of war and the campaign. But he thought primarily of occupying all or part of the enemy's territory rather than of annihilating his army. This occupation was to be achieved by progressive domination of zones of territory. Jomini emphasized throughout his work the proper choice by the general of decisive maneuvering lines and their adaptation to geometrical configurations of zones of operation. Campaigns must be carefully planned in advance. The task of strategy is to make preliminary plans—to establish lines of operation and to bring military means into conformity with geographic realities of the chosen zone of operations. He laid down two basic principles: massing troops against fractions of the enemy by rapid movement, and striking in the most decisive direction.

Jomini's great contribution to military thought lay in his definition of the place of strategy in warfare. Probably more than any other work, his *Précis* fixed the major fields of modern military art. Subsequent wars were to cast doubt on much of his work, particularly on his conception of geographical campaigns and of the superiority of interior lines of operation. But, like Clausewitz in German strategic thinking, Jomini had an enduring influence on French military thought. His emphasis on planning for operations and on intelligence took root in military staffs and schools throughout Europe, and his work became the textbook for the conduct of the American Civil War. It has been said that the Civil War was fought with Jomini in the pockets of all the leading generals.

**3. American Civil War to World War I.**—Often called the first of the really modern wars, the American Civil War marked a transition to a new era in strategy. It gathered up new phenomena that had begun to influence warfare in the middle of the 19th century and whose fuller consequences were to be felt in the half century that followed. It was a period marked by refinement of the old in strategic theory and practice and by the addition of new strands—by such famous figures as Lee, Grant, and Sherman on the battlefield; Moltke, Schlieffen, Delbrück, and Mahan in the literature of strategy.

The Civil War is significant in the history of strategy in a number of ways. The basis of strategy—particularly factors of time and space—began to change. The use of steam power for land and water military transportation received its first major test. Railroads gave strategy a new speed of movement but tended to make strategy stick to straight lines and fixed routes. The Civil War also tested ironclad ships and heavy naval ordnance. The relation among the combat arms was completely upset by the introduction of the long-range infantry rifle. Artillery could no longer unlimber at case-shot ranges. The accuracy of long-range weapons in the hands of defending infantry shattered the effectiveness of the rapidly concentrated attack in which Napoleonic strategy had culminated. But, as so often has been noted in the history of warfare, armaments and weapons are more readily changed than ideas, and Napoleon's principles continued to be maintained, sometimes with disastrous consequences on the battlefield.

Aside from the effect of new inventions, the Civil War revealed the growing importance of the economy and manpower in war. Industry was called on more and more, and conscription was adopted to provide manpower. The war also revealed the impact of systematic West Point training received by the leading generals on both sides. In fact, it may be said that if the higher officers carried Jomini in their pockets, they carried in their minds the teachings of Dennis Hart Mahan, father of Alfred Thayer Mahan and one of the few outstanding U.S. students of strategy. Finally, the Civil War was long studied for classic examples of maneuver, and of offensive and defensive strategy, and for lessons in the relation among policy, strategy and means of war. Essentially the Civil War demonstrated local or theatre strategy and tactics. Though elements of grand strategy were at hand—political, economic, military and psychological—the art was still not well understood or consistently applied. Despite conscription and the partial mobilization of industry and the railroads, there was no well-worked-out grand design correlating the widely scattered forces and the war industries that supported them.

The strategies of the North and South were rooted in different political objectives. The objective of the North was to prevent the Confederate states from seceding from the Union; that of the South was to attain independence. Since the South was greatly inferior to the North in population and resources it could not hope to conquer the North. The dual purposes of its strategy were: (1) to convince the North that forcing the South to remain in the Union was not worth the cost; and (2) to bring about foreign intervention in favour of the South. Gen. Robert E. Lee, the great Southern leader, believed the best way to realize these objectives was to carry the war into the North and to defeat the Northern armies in their own territory. For a time, therefore, his strategy was essentially offensive. But after his defeat at Gettysburg he no longer had the wherewithal to continue the offensive, and at the same time it became obvious that foreign intervention would not be forthcoming. From that time to the end of the war his strategy was defensive, with the object of wearing down the patience, if not the power, of the North.

To achieve its political object, the North, on the other hand, developed another strategy. The Federal design had three main goals: (1) to isolate the Confederacy; (2) to cut it in two; and (3) to strike at Richmond, its capital. The blockade, though not completely effective, brought virtual commercial isolation to the South. Partition was gained by capturing Vicksburg, in July 1863, and by severing the east-west railroad connections. The capture of Vicksburg cut the South off from its sources of supplies beyond the Mississippi. Only gradually did the North change its design from that of attacking Richmond to that of striking at the main army of the Confederacy and the remaining sources of supply. Grant's elevation to the supreme command of the armies enabled him to put this concept into effect. The famous march of Gen. William T. Sherman through Georgia to the sea in 1864 was an outstanding example of strategic maneuver and surprise. Leaving his supply line, Sherman feinted against one city and attacked another, finally cutting off Lee's army in Virginia from its war resources in the South. The cooperation of the Federal eastern and western armies in a grand converging movement resulted in the evacuation of Richmond and, finally, in the surrender of Lee's army to Grant at Appomattox in April 1865.

The period from the close of the Civil War to the outbreak of World War I saw the further growth of trends already apparent. Space and time factors began to appear in a new light. A nation with a well-developed railway net gained significant advantages in war. The speed of mobilizing and concentrating armies became a basic element in strategic calculations and the timetable based on it the heart of staff plans drawn up in anticipation of war. Increased fire power in the machine gun, universal liability of able-bodied males for military service, rapid mobilization of reserve military units and increased potential of fortifications influenced military planning.

In strategic thinking the half century before World War I showed a remarkable diversity. To the Prussian-German school—Moltke and Schlieffen—the new trends in warfare seemed to reinforce Clausewitz' teachings about battles and the aim of defeating the enemy's armies. Battles, Moltke agreed, were the primary means of breaking the will of the enemy. But Moltke did not believe a strategist could follow a rigid set of rules. To him strategy was a system of "*ad hoc* expedients." It was "the art of action under the pressure of the most difficult conditions." No plan of operations, he believed, could look with any assurance beyond the first encounter with the main enemy forces. The offensive, according to Moltke, is "the straight way to the goal," whereas the defensive is "the long way around." He became famous for his skilful conduct of operations on the outer line leading to encirclement, and Königgrätz and Sedan (*see* SEDAN: *Battle of Sedan, 1870*) remain as supreme models of such strategy. In addition to exploiting the altered conditions of space and time created by the railroads and improved highways, he capitalized on the possibilities offered by the telegraph for handling armies of great size. Recognizing that the field of operations had become too vast to be surveyed by the eye of the commander, he introduced a new system of delegating power to subordinate commanders. Broad directives took the place of detailed orders. Moltke always fought with superior forces, and his wars, culminating in that against France in 1870–71, are regarded by some authorities as classical models of conception and execution in military strategy.

Field Marshal von Schlieffen, chief of the Prussian general staff before World War I and ablest of Moltke's successors, carried the strong line of strategic reasoning running from Napoleon through Clausewitz and Moltke to its logical conclusion in his conception of a "strategy of annihilation." Like Moltke, he stressed the military side of strategy, the concentration on decisive victory by battle. But, unlike Moltke, he could not count on superior forces and had to prepare for war on two fronts. The basis for German strategy before World War I as developed by him became that of the inner line—a conception that was embodied in the famous Schlieffen plan. The plan was extremely simple. The bulk of the German forces were to attack the nearest opponent, the one in the west, and to defeat him in a great battle; meanwhile, in the east the Germans would stand on the defensive. Schlieffen proposed to gain the decision in the great battle by means of an enveloping attack—if possible, by a double envelopment. Once the enemy in the west was defeated, the Germans would attack the foe in the east. This was the essence of the plan with which the Germans entered World War I.

Schlieffen's theories were to have wide influence, largely through his book, *Cannae.* Analyzing Hannibal's great victory over the Romans, he had developed his theory of the battle of annihilation by means of encirclement and double envelopment. The decisive German campaign at Tannenberg in Aug. 1914 was fought in this mold and Schlieffen's theories were studied exhaustively in the higher army schools of the United States and Europe after World War I. As Gen. Walter Bedell Smith, chief of staff to Gen. Dwight D. Eisenhower, supreme commander of the Allied Expeditionary Forces in World War II, pointed out, General Eisenhower and many of his staff officers, products of these schools, "were imbued with the idea of this type of wide, bold maneuver for decisive results."

Moltke and Schlieffen thought of war as military action—the speediest decisive defeat of the main opponent. But the closing years of the 19th and early years of the 20th centuries witnessed the emergence of new approaches and different emphases in strategy. Two thinkers looking to past history for light on the problems of their times made signal contributions to strategic theory—one, Alfred Thayer Mahan (*q.v.*), an American, in the field of naval strategy; the other, Hans Delbrück, a German, in the area of military strategy. Each recognized an intimate relationship between war and politics in every age; that political and military (or naval) strategy must be in harmony. Each showed an awareness of the growing importance of the economic bases of strategy, of state policy, geographic position, and available means as determinants of the mode of strategy; of accommodating strategic action to suit the particular times and needs.

Carrying forward a line of thinking already suggested by Clausewitz, Delbrück presented his theory of the "strategy of exhaustion"—of wearing down an opponent by a variety of means. Clausewitz had merely indicated the existence of two methods of conducting war—one aimed at annihilation of the enemy; the other, limited warfare. Delbrück expounded on the differences. The sole aim of the strategy of annihilation he identified as the decisive battle. The second type he called variously the "strategy of exhaustion" and "two-pole strategy." The commander could move between battle and maneuver; the political object of war could be obtained by other means than battle—by occupying territory, blockade, destroying crops or commerce. In Delbrück's view, Alexander, Caesar and Napoleon had been strategists of annihilation; Pericles, Gustavus Adolphus and Frederick the Great, equally great generals, exponents of the strategy of exhaustion. Holding that the strategy of exhaustion was just as valid as the strategy of annihilation—each depending on the political aims and means at hand—Delbrück's theories ran counter to the military thinking of his day and brought down a storm of criticism about his head. But he persisted in reminding his age, intent on victory by battle, of other important and forgotten aspects of Clausewitz' teachings.

While Delbrück was battling his military critics in Germany, a scholarly navy captain-teacher at the Naval War College in Newport, R.I., was quietly breaking ground in pursuing his brilliant researches in military and naval history and strategy. This pioneer was Alfred Thayer Mahan, indefatigable student of the strategy of Napoleon, Jomini and Nelson. His masterly works, *The Influence of Sea Power upon History, 1660–1783,* published in 1890, and *The Influence of Sea Power upon the French Revolution and Empire, 1793–1812,* published in 1892, marked a revolution in naval thought. While advances in technology were affecting naval architecture and weapons, and steam, armour plate, and rifled guns were coming into vogue, Mahan aimed to bring naval strategic thinking up-to-date. The books and articles that poured from his pen down to World War I about warfare of the second dimension—the sea—had a profound influence on the theory of warfare and on naval policy and strategy in the United States and abroad.

An advocate of a big navy, of overseas bases, of national greatness through sea power, he was the American apostle of "looking outward." Mahan emphasized the significance of commerce in war and of economic warfare through the application of sea power. His researches convinced him that the nation or group of nations that commanded the seas could best draw on the trade, wealth, and economic resources of the world and was the more likely to win wars. Strongly influenced by Jomini's teachings, he looked for fundamental truths and formulated "principles" of naval strategy. Naval strategy and sea power, he recognized, were conditioned by a nation's insular or continental situation. To Mahan a central position gave the same great advantages on the sea or on land—interior lines. Concentration of force he viewed as a fundamental principle of land and sea warfare. The backbone of fleet strength, in his opinion, was the battle- or capital-ship. Under Mahan's tutelage, command of the sea approaches took the place of the twin theories of coastal defense and commerce raiding that hitherto held sway in American naval strategy. His concepts of naval strategy and faith in preponderant naval power and the use of the navy as an instrument of national power were accepted by the U.S. Navy and Pres. Theodore Roosevelt. His doctrines stimulated the trend toward overseas expansion and growth of the navies of the world between 1898 and 1914. The resultant acquisition of an overseas empire almost overnight in 1898 greatly changed the strategic position and problems of the United States. Its emergence as a world power, beginning in these years, was to have important bearings on the strategic balance of power among the nations of the world, an equilibrium that World War I altered profoundly. (*See* further SEA POWER.)

**4. World War I.**—World War I, the first of the great coalition wars of the 20th century, was an important landmark in the story of the evolution of modern strategy. Never was the phenomenon of cultural lag as applied to warfare more clearly demonstrated. Beginning in the accepted mold of strategic planning popular since 1870, it soon ran head on into counter trends that were altering the very bases of strategic action and that strategic thinking in the intervening years had not yet fully grasped. Despite the experiences in the Boer and Russo-Japanese wars with the machine gun as a defensive weapon of tremendous fire power, French and German military leaders at the outbreak of the war continued to put their faith in the offensive. In fact, they were convinced that new weapons and methods of control, the radio and telephone, actually improved the offensive capabilities of their mass armies. The universal underestimation of the effect of modern firearms on the defense had important repercussions on strategy both during and after the war.

The first moves in the war began in 1914 as French and German strategists had planned—the Germans in accord with the Schlieffen plan, the French with their Plan XVII. In seven days the Germans concentrated over 3,000,000 men on the eastern and western fronts from mobilization points. In approximately the same time the French assembled 1,200,000 men on the western front. Both sides made heavy use of railroad lines to speed assembly of great masses of troops. Both sides were determined to attack. Out of the movements of mass armies came the first battles on the frontiers. As Schlieffen had planned, the Germans catapulted into Belgium, but the enveloping wing was not so strong as Schlieffen, who had died the previous year, had wished. It was compressed into a smaller corridor by the political decision not to violate Dutch neutrality. The anticipated six-week campaign of annihilation against France envisaged by Schlieffen could not be executed. The French attack also soon hit a snag. Though the French Army's right wing reached the Rhine, its centre was endangered by a German pincer movement. Only a hasty retreat and a counteroffensive at the Marne saved Paris. The so-called pinwheel strategy—each side attacking and driving the enemy back—had stalled badly. (*See* further WORLD WARS: *World War I: Eastern Front Strategy* and *Strategy of the Western Allies, 1914.*)

Meanwhile on the eastern front the German prewar strategy of holding until France had been quickly defeated was compromised by the desire of the Austrian ally to push against the Russians, partners of the French. The German victory at Tannenberg counterbalanced the Austrian defeat at Lemberg. The eastern front became stabilized.

By the close of 1914 the war had become a stalemate on both the eastern and western fronts. The conflict had resolved itself into trench warfare from Switzerland to the English Channel. Machine guns and artillery took over the battlefield. The conflict had settled down into a war of position, and strategic mobility was lost. World War I became a classic case of arrested strategy.

By the close of 1914 the first phase of the war was over. Prewar plans had failed; the war of movement, of mass offensives, had ceased. The big question thenceforth was how to dig the war out of the trenches. In answering that question important elements of grand strategy came into play. The heavy demands upon industry for munitions of war multiplied, and technology was called upon for new means—the tank and poison gas—of breaking the stalemate. Britain's naval blockade to starve Germany took on added significance. (*See* BLOCKADE.) The German countermeasures helped bring the United States into the war in 1917. But the United States, as usual in its military history, was not prepared for war. The buildup of its forces across the Atlantic was slow. The Germans, seeking in 1918 to forestall the full impact of U.S. might, put their resources into a great offensive which came close to succeeding. When the Americans, led by Gen. John J. Pershing, finally arrived in force, they played a valuable part in military strategy in reducing the salients within the Allied lines, such as that at St. Mihiel. Eventually the German allies defected, German armies reached a point of exhaustion and the homeland a stage of semistarvation. Germany asked for an armistice.

Though much has been written on World War I, the strategic lessons of that conflict for coalition warfare have not been fully comprehended. Never was the dependence of strategy on statecraft more clearly demonstrated. As political circumstances of the war changed, strategy changed. The Central Powers, led by Germany and Austria-Hungary, never had a common plan of campaign or effective unity of command. The Allied side achieved unity only under the pressure of necessity. Along with the military factors, economic and psychological considerations proved important in conducting the war and gaining the victory. Though the aim of annihilating the enemy was paramount with both sides—especially in the opening campaigns—the desire to exhaust him also influenced strategy, and fresh confirmation was given to Moltke's description of strategy as a "system of makeshifts."

Military leaders in World War I had to master three basic factors in strategic calculations: masses of men, technological advances, and wide areas. The movement of huge masses became an art in itself, for armies had taken on unprecedented dimensions. Millions of men were in action. Railroads and motor transport became important not only for concentration but also for establishing new strategic points on the fronts themselves. The arena of war embraced whole continents. Battles lasted for days and weeks, and the fighting continued even after the great battles were over.

New weapons came into play. Aerial reconnaissance enabled a commander to gain some insight into the enemy's intentions and movements. New means of communication—telephone, radio telegraphy, the automobile, and the airplane—promoted faster execution of orders and unified command over widely scattered forces. The overwhelming firepower of modern weapons checked the effectiveness of the attack, long considered the ideal path to victory. The tank, however, offered fresh possibilities in redressing the balance between the defensive and the offensive. Tactics became more than ever a prelude and conditioning factor of strategy, since without freedom of movement, strategy was only an academic exercise. Tactics came to mark the beginning rather than the conclusion of an operation.

But there were also larger strategic influences at work. If World War I was a war of masses, it was also a war of matériel. War was becoming increasingly total and cut deeper into the life of the nation. Some of the foremost leaders and students of World War I—notably Winston Churchill and Georges Clemenceau—recognized that military strategy had become but a part of a greater national strategy. Symptomatic of this thinking was Clemenceau's widely quoted statement that war was too important a business to be left to soldiers. More than ever strategy and politics would have to be correlated. The increasing totality of modern war would have to be matched by a broader national strategy. But the larger impact of the war in the international sphere—the effects of the defeat of Germany, the weakening of England and France, and the rise of the Soviet Union on the strategic balance of power in the world—could not yet be foreseen.

**5. Between World Wars I and II.**—The period between 1918 and 1939 saw strategy once more in process of flux. As an outgrowth of the experience of World War I, strategy came largely to mean defense. In France, particularly, a Maginot Line mentality began to take hold. The belief was strong that field fortifications aided by the machine gun would contain any attack. The huge losses of World War I would thereby be avoided.

But countertrends were soon to dispute this prevalent emphasis in strategic thinking. One strong challenge came from the new school of exponents of air power. In World War I the air arm had had its beginnings. The period between the end of World War I and the beginning of World War II saw it come into its own; air forces and air organization expanded greatly. Theorists began to develop the strategy of warfare of the third dimension. Foremost among these was the Italian Gen. Giulio Douhet. He first presented the doctrine that the air arm alone would decide wars of the future. In his view, land and sea forces would no longer be decisive. On the ground, armies could act henceforth only on the defensive, since attack, and with it the decision, could be gained only through the air. Air power could quickly conquer time and space. The air arm could circumvent every kind of ground resistance and nullify fortified positions and obstacles of terrain. It could strike at the enemy's sources of power before his armies could fire a shot. It could strike at his capital, industrial centres and communications. In short, it could so reduce his ability and willingness to resist that he would surrender. Douhet proposed to expand the air arm as much as possible, keep land and sea forces only as support for war in the air, and gain control of the air by defeating enemy air forces in battles or destroying them in their airfields. He made strategic bombing, and the industrial objective —strikes at the opponent's heart—the core of his doctrines.

Douhet's epoch-making ideas found many supporters in other countries, including the United States. This school of thought generally argued that huge armies would no longer be necessary. The opponent's will could be overcome even if his armed forces remained undefeated. Some of Douhet's adherents went further and demanded the abolition of land and sea forces altogether. In any event, the rise of air power accentuated the need of thinking of strategy as dealing with something more than the movements of armies on land, or of ships at sea. (*See* further AIR POWER.)

Meanwhile, army leaders began to advocate another solution to break the strategic stalemate of World War I. To overcome the superiority of the defensive, they put their faith in developing a modern cavalry of tanks and armoured, motor-driven vehicles. The best known among the great champions of mechanization and motorization that arose in Great Britain was Maj. Gen. J. F. C. Fuller (*q.v.*). These advocates saw in the armoured vehicle, combining firepower, extreme mobility and armoured protection, the best answer to overcoming defensive forces relying on machine guns. This system was particularly suited to needs of an insular country, protected by a strong air force and navy, and of a relatively small army intended primarily for expeditionary purposes in support of continental allies. But this solution on the ground found support in Germany, Russia, and the United States. In France, Charles de Gaulle bucked the strong tide of opinion and advocated tank warfare to restore a strategy of mobility and the offensive. (*See* also TANK.)

In the late 1930s the Germans combined air power and tanks into a new form of assault that also aimed to overthrow defensive superiority. Developing a highly mobile form of warfare for lightning strikes and mechanized attacks, they were to contribute the art of the blitzkrieg—the spearhead of a conquering, offensive strategy that Hitler unleashed in World War II.

In Germany, too, other influences supporting offensive strategy came to the fore. To overcome strategic stalemate of the World War I variety, Erich Ludendorff contributed his theory of total war. He envisaged total mobilization of a nation's manpower and resources for war. The nation at war would be led by a supreme military commander; strategy would dictate policy. The concept of total war moved geography and economics into prominent positions in Nazi thinking. Even before World War I the British geographer, Halford J. Mackinder, had posed the potential threat of a heartland power, in control of Eurasia, to sea power—a counter to Mahan's theory of control of the seas. Led by Karl Haushofer, the German geopoliticians after the war took over the "heartlands" concept. Through their teachings the concept of control of Eurasia became imbedded in Nazi statecraft. Their doctrines gave support to the main strands in Hitler's offensive strategy—continental expansion, autarky (national economic self-sufficiency), and *Lebensraum* ("living space").

Before war burst upon Europe in 1939, it was apparent that important changes were also brewing in naval strategy. All major sea powers were producing high-speed battleships and the aircraft carrier was becoming a significant and integral member of the fleet. In the crucible of World War II the emerging elements in ground, air, naval, and nonmilitary strategy were to take clearer shape.

**6. World War II.**—Strategy came into its own in World War II. Global and coalition warfare on an unprecedented scale required global and coalition strategy to match it. The new trends in military, air, and naval strategy were put to the test. At the same time the worldwide conflict lifted strategy out of the purely military sphere into the field of grand strategy and international relations. The war cut more deeply than ever into every phase of life. It touched all nations, directly or indirectly, all continents and oceans, the air, the land, and the sea. Political, economic, technological, and psychological factors were drawn into the web of the strategy of all-out effort. The strategy for war grown increasingly total was conditioned by massive armed forces, revolutionary scientific and technological advances, tridimensional warfare, and miracles of industrial production and logistics.

World War II began with independent offensive moves of the Axis nations, Germany, Italy and Japan. Though these nations formed a war coalition, they never formulated a common blueprint of strategy or achieved the degree of cooperation that the Allied coalition did. Nevertheless, the Axis war effort marked an epoch-making development in strategy. The Axis concept of total war, particularly as developed in Nazi philosophy, revealed more clearly than before that the traditional view of strategy—the art of employing military forces—was too narrow. Diplomacy, propaganda, "fifth columns" and espionage, geography, economics, technology, and morale all entered into the Nazi concept of strategy. In Nazi strategy, the line between war and peace could no longer be clearly defined. The course of Hitler's campaigns, before and after the outbreak of actual war in 1939, showed that military operations and battles were only the last resort against an enemy, to be applied after all other modes of conquest had failed. Hitler early recognized that armed forces are only one of many means available to grand strategy. Indeed, his greatest victories were the bloodless ones before Munich. After war was joined in Sept. 1939, following the invasion of Poland, military strategy perforce came into greater play. Like Caesar and Napoleon, Hilter combined in his own person the two functions of strategy and policy. But his reputation as a military strategist was not to compare with his early triumphs in political warfare.

Hitler gave the art of offensive strategy a new twist. Like Napoleon, he failed to master all the elements of grand strategy. But in developing and correlating an assortment of modern means of breaking an enemy's will, he showed himself to be far ahead of his opponents.

Despite great German blitzkrieg victories on the continent, successes in the Middle East, and strategic bombardment of England, the winter of 1941 found Germany still without the victory it sought. Though it had tried to avoid a two-front war, by June 1941 it had become embroiled with the U.S.S.R. In December the Japanese struck at Pearl Harbor and the United States came in to aid England and the U.S.S.R. against the Axis powers. The worldwide strategic contest was then joined in earnest. The Axis nations had the advantage of interior lines; the Allies, other than Russia, had to fight on exterior lines, and their lines of support had to fan out from the factories of Britain and the United States all over the world. Inevitably the Allies turned to the strategic weapon of blockade against the Axis powers, and Germany and Japan turned to submarine warfare to cripple the Allied lifelines.

The story of Allied strategy in World War II is the search for common denominators among three sovereign powers drawn together by a common bond of danger. That strategy was a product of many minds on both sides of the Atlantic, of diverse pressures and pulls, and of changing circumstances in the global war. It was the result of an evolutionary process and a series of compromises, and of a constant struggle to adjust ends and means. Above all, it was fashioned by powers with diverse national interests. If the national objectives sought by each of the participating powers were unchanging, the means and methods used by each to achieve them varied from time to time. In the process of planning and waging the war, moreover, the foundations of the alliance shifted and the relationships among the powers changed. These shifts are part and parcel of the strategy story.

That story falls into at least three phases. The first of these covers the period 1941–42. This phase saw the formation of the grand alliance and the emergence of divergent British and American concepts of strategic theory.

The grand alliance was a marriage of expediency, forged in war and cemented by the common bond of danger. But each member of the alliance expected different things from the partnership; each, because of its distinctive traditions, policies, interests, and position, looked at the war through different spectacles.

Great Britain, an island dependent upon sea lanes for its very existence and situated precariously on the edge of Hitler's European fortress, had for centuries put its faith in the balance of power. It was natural for it to seek to rally the smaller nations and oppose any strong power that threatened to upset the balance on the continent. It could be expected to intervene actively in the Mediterranean and the Middle East through which ran its lifeline to the empire in the East. But in any global war Great Britain's resources were bound to be stretched thin. Its economy, while highly industrialized, was small in comparison with that of the United States. Keenly conscious of its heavy losses in manpower during World War I, Britain would tend to avoid as long as possible large-scale ground battle on the continent. By necessity and choice, therefore, the leaders of Britain put their faith in the navy, the air force, and the mechanized and armoured forces. Experienced in war, diplomacy, and empire, Great Britain had a long history of alliances with European powers. Its admirals and generals were accustomed to working closely with the politicians and diplomats, and British strategy usually reflected political objectives.

Across the Atlantic lay the other major western power in the alliance, the United States—young, impatient, rich in resources, and highly industrialized. Traditionally opposed to becoming involved in European quarrels, it nevertheless had strong bonds with Europe, especially Britain. To most U.S. citizens war was an aberration; an unwelcome interruption to the normal course of events. Though its tradition in war had been first to declare, then to prepare, the country had between 1939 and 1941 gradually awakened to the dangers from without. It began to mobilize manpower and resources. Aid to Britain became official national policy in 1940, and lend-lease, a strategic weapon, was extended to Britain and other friendly powers in 1941. The strategic planners in Washington, laying aside their earlier academic exercises, began to think of global and coalition warfare. Without committing the administration, the military planners entered into staff conversations with their British opposites on possible ways of using U.S. forces in coalition strategy. For the first time in its history the United States entered a war well advanced in its military planning. The United States also had considerable interests in the Far East and a tradition of helping China. Throughout World War II the U.S. military staff and the president could not neglect the war in the East any more than the U.S. public could forget the attack on Pearl Harbor. One other factor that distinguished U.S. policy and strategy was the loose relationship between the president and the military. That relationship was in sharp contrast to the closely knit politico-military system of Great Britain.

The third major partner in the alliance against Germany was the Soviet Union, a land power with completely internal lines of communication. Though it possessed an enormous population and great resources, the Soviet Union's industrial facilities were still not fully developed. The U.S.S.R. represented an enigmatic force, devoted to a political and economic ideology different from that of the western partners. Born in revolution and come to power in a civil and foreign war, its policies seemed to combine Russian national socialism, Marxism, and tsarist imperialism. Dedicated to the proposition that war was inevitable in capitalistic society until the world revolution ushered in a new millennium, it had developed a strategy of revolution—based on the theories of Marx, Engels, and Lenin. In that theory, as in Nazi strategic theory, the line of demarcation between war and peace was not clearly drawn. Until attacked by Germany, Soviet policy was dominated by the twin notions of security and expansion. The Nazi invasion reinforced the Soviet desire to strengthen its position in eastern Europe—an objective whose roots lay deep in Russian history. But for almost two years after the German attack the Soviet Union was engaged in a desperate fight for existence. Lacking air and naval traditions, it relied on geography, the loyalty of its people, and the huge Red Army to see it through. Political and territorial ambitions were subordinated to military necessity. Still fearful of capitalist encirclement, suspicious of friend and foe, the Soviet Union held an uneasy position in what Gen. John R. Deane, head of the wartime military mission in Moscow, later so fittingly called "the strange alliance."

From the beginning, the inner web of the grand alliance was the close relationship between the United States and Great Britain. The Soviet Union's part in developing and directing the combined strategy of the war was to be relatively small. Compared with the worldwide demands facing the United States and Great Britain, its strategic problem was simple. Unlike the western partners, the U.S.S.R. would be at war on only one front at a time; it did not enter the conflict with Japan until the closing days of World War II. The Soviet relationship with its western partners consisted of demanding material aid and increased pressure against the common enemy. But collaboration was to prove difficult even in these areas. Actually the strategic decisions of the western powers were normally transmitted in general terms to the Soviet Union. The Russians took formal part in strategic decisions only at the international conferences at Moscow (Oct. 1943), Teheran (Nov. 1943), Yalta (Feb. 1945), and Potsdam (July 1945), and even these were called at the initiative of the western powers. Throughout World War II, the Russians remained outside the combined staff system, developed for the coordination of the western effort in the global war.

The basic procedures for formulating Allied strategy emerged in 1941 and 1942. Shortly before Christmas 1941, Prime Minister Winston Churchill and his principal military advisers arrived in Washington for the first of their great wartime conferences with Pres. Franklin D. Roosevelt and his staff. Out of this meeting —the Arcadia Conference—came the establishment in Washington, in Jan. 1942, of the Combined Chiefs of Staff (CCS), the agency for hammering out Allied strategy and for day-to-day conduct of the war. To supply U.S. opposites for the British in the combined organization, the United States Joint Chiefs of Staff (JCS) and joint staff planning system (army, air and navy) came into being. Since the three principal British military officers normally had to direct the operations of their services from London, they sent senior representatives to function for them in the Combined Chiefs of Staff. As finally constituted, the JCS was composed of the president's chief of staff and the senior officers of the Army, Navy and Army Air Forces.

The CCS was a unique organization in coalition machinery. Decisions were arrived at by common agreement; no votes were taken. The leaders concerted policies and plans, outlined strategies, discussed timing of operations, approved programs of allocations and measured requirements against resources. Their decisions were, of course, subject to the approval of the president and the prime minister.

The prime minister and the president, who were over and above the CCS system, were responsible for all decisions. Each wore two hats—one political, the other military. As political leaders they sometimes had more in common with each other than with their respective staffs. Advising Churchill at the summit of the

British system of intragovernmental planning was a war cabinet with which the chiefs of staff committee sat. While President Roosevelt could and did draw on the assistance of the war-born U.S. joint staff system, he never established anything remotely resembling the British war cabinet. The differences between the two politico-military systems—one loosely built, the other closely tied—were sometimes strikingly illustrated at the international war conferences.

The full-dress Anglo-American conferences usually came about when planning had reached a point where top-level decisions on important matters of Allied strategy and policy were necessary. The conferences and the CCS system provided the framework for the important decisions in European and Asiatic strategy. Decisions in the war in the Pacific against Japan were handled somewhat differently. The U.S. Joint Chiefs of Staff who were early given the responsibility for this war submitted their decisions on plans and operations against Japan to the conferences. There the combined chiefs usually gave their stamp of approval.

Beneath the top-level machinery, and funneling into it, was a whole network of specialized combined and joint planning agencies. At the bottom of the hierarchy lay the planning staffs of the individual services in the capitals. Unique among them on the American side was the War Department's Operations Division, which, under the army chief of staff, Gen. George C. Marshall, developed into the "Washington command post" to control the strategic deployment and activities of the army forces scattered all over the world. As the war progressed, the highly organized planning machinery in the capitals was supplemented by the big theatre headquarters staffs. Such theatre commanders as General Eisenhower in the European theatre and Gen. Douglas MacArthur in the Southwest Pacific began to play an increasingly important role in strategic decisions. The vast and speedy network of telecommunications circling the globe enabled strategic plans and decisions to be quickly made and executed. Never had the processes and machinery of strategic planning been so highly organized as in World War II.

Even though much of the Anglo-American discussions at the Arcadia Conference centred about the crisis in the Pacific, the western partners agreed that the first and major object of Anglo-American grand strategy must be the defeat of Germany. The principle of "Europe first" had actually been foreshadowed in staff conversations early in 1941. So had the corollary that, should Japan enter the war, military strategy in the East would be defensive. When war came to the United States in Dec. 1941, this strategy, despite the initial Japanese victories, was adopted.

Political expediency combined with geography and logistics in arriving at this decision—perhaps the single most important one made by the British and U.S. in World War II. British and Soviet power lay close to Germany. Great Britain offered a base for massing western air power; in the Mediterranean, operations against Germany could soon be undertaken. The Soviet Union and Great Britain could not wait for a decision in the war against Japan. Before the West could come to grips with Japan decisively, U.S. naval striking power would have to be restored, ships built, and advance bases and lines of communications extended across the far Pacific. It followed, therefore, that defeat of Germany should be the first major objective and that in the meantime the Japanese should be contained until the Allies could assemble enough strength to take the offensive in the Pacific.

The divergent approaches of the Allies were most clearly reflected initially in the conflict between U.S. and British strategy against Germany. The 1941–42 period saw the emergence of what may be called the peripheral theory, espoused by Churchill and the British staff, and the theory of mass and concentration, advocated by General Marshall and his staff. The British stood for hitting the German Army at the edges of the continent; the Americans, for concentration at the decisive point to defeat the main body of the enemy. In the peripheral concept, emphasis would be on swift campaigns of speed and maneuver, on probing soft spots, on a war of attrition. The cross-channel operation would follow as a last blow against a Germany already in process of collapse. The British concept was in accord with its small-scale economy and limited manpower, its experience in World War I, and the prime minister's predilections. The U.S. early thought of defeating the German Army decisively. This view reflected U.S. optimism, reliance on the industrial machine to produce the necessary wherewithal, and military faith in a large citizen army built and trained for offensive purposes. Both justified their theories and plans as ways of relieving the pressure upon the Russians. The divergent approaches lay behind the debate in 1942 over the notion of an early cross-channel attack versus the invasion of North Africa—Operation Torch. The British won out, the president overruling the U.S. staff, and October saw the start of Mediterranean operations.

The Torch decision, which so disappointed U.S. military expectations, also complicated relations with the Soviet Union. Stalin, locked in a death struggle on the eastern front, demanded a second front—and soon. Each Anglo-American postponement of this second front was to add fuel to the fire of his resentment.

The cross-channel versus Mediterranean debate of midwar was argued in and out of the big international conferences. North Africa led to Sicily (July 1943); Sicily, to the invasion and surrender of Italy (Sept. 1943). Always the prime minister urged operations in the Mediterranean that would bleed the foe and prepare the way for an eventual cross-channel operation. Always the U.S.—with Marshall as the foremost spokesman—urged the need for a definitely scheduled cross-channel operation in force and for tapering the Mediterranean effort. Both sides agreed on the need for strategic bombardment to pave the way. The series of Anglo-American decisions reached at the 1943 conferences—Casablanca in January, Trident (Washington) in May, Quebec in August, and Cairo-Teheran in November and December—reflected the compromises between opportunism and long-range commitments, between a war of attrition and a war of mass and concentration.

The meeting at Teheran in Nov. 1943, where, for the first time in the war, the president, the prime minister and their staffs met with Marshal Stalin and his staff, was the decisive conference for strategy. Churchill made eloquent appeals for operations in Italy, the Aegean, and the eastern Mediterranean, even at the expense of a delay in the cross-channel invasion—Operation Overlord. But Stalin, for reasons of his own, put Soviet weight squarely behind the U.S. concept of strategy. He asserted his full power as an equal member of the coalition and came out strongly in favour of Overlord. Further operations in the Mediterranean, he insisted, should be limited to the invasion of southern France in support of Overlord. In turn, he promised to launch an all-out offensive on the eastern front.

Stalin's stand put the capstone on Anglo-American European strategy and in a sense fixed western strategy. Germany was to be crushed by a great pincers—the Anglo-American drive on the west and a Soviet drive from the east. General Eisenhower was appointed commander for Overlord, and preparations for the cross-channel thrust began. The decision at Teheran marked a subtle but significant change in the relationship of the Allies. Britain was growing relatively weaker, the United States and the Soviet Union stronger. By way of the military doctrine of concentration the strategists of the Pentagon and of the Kremlin had found common ground.

The third phase of the strategy story—from the summer of 1944 to the surrenders of Germany and Japan—was the period of the payoff. In this period the problems of winning the war began to come up against winning the peace. The curtain began to lift on the divergent national objectives of the Allies—objectives hitherto obscured by the common military danger. The western drive unfolded according to plan. The thrust across France coincided with the invasion from the Mediterranean; the Rhine was crossed, the Ruhr encircled, and the drive across Germany met up with the Russian advance. But to Churchill, warily watching the swift Soviet advance into Poland and the Balkans, the war had become more than ever a contest for great political stakes. As the strategy unrolled in the field, the two approaches to the war boiled down to a question of military versus political maneuvers.

While the war in the West was drawing to a close, the strategy for defeating Japan had been taking gradual shape. As the war had advanced, Allied strategy in the Pacific shifted from the defensive to the offensive. Though firm, final plans had to await the defeat of Germany, the momentum of advances in the Pacific was so fast that it almost caught up with the European conflict. Island to island advance was gradually changed to island-hopping. The Battle of Midway in 1942 foreshadowed a new trend in naval strategy, in which opposing fleets did not get within gun range of each other, but dueled with their air power and submarines. Submarine warfare, amphibious assaults, task forces built around aircraft carriers, the strengthened American fleet—speeded the pace in midwar. A twofold approach—along the southwest and central Pacific axes—took the Allies to the threshold of Japan by the time the European war closed. Before final plans for invasion were put into effect, however, the Japanese surrendered. A multiplicity of factors led to this result—including the threat of invasion, the attrition of Japanese shipping, air bombardment, the entry of the Soviet Union into the war against Japan, and the dropping of two atomic bombs.

In retrospect, the strategy of World War II represented a curious mixture of old and new strands. Never had strategy had so vast a scope, for this was the first really global war. Never in history had two partners pooled their efforts and ideas so closely as had the Americans and British in the grand alliance. Once more the scales of war were tipped in favour of the offensive. To the age-old primary aim of seeking the defeat of the enemy's armed forces was added the objective of striking at his industrial heart. Both these aims, for example, were present in the directive given to General Eisenhower for the European campaign. In Pacific strategy, it long remained a question whether invasion and defeat of the enemy forces on their home grounds would even be necessary. Strategic bombardment and sea power gave support for a strategy of attrition and destruction of industrial capacity. But the thesis that the sole aim of strategy was to support air power in order to annihilate the enemy's industrial power was only partially tested. It had been impossible to put all production and manpower into the air strategy. Nor were ground and sea enthusiasts on the basis of World War II experiences disposed to yield the field of strategy completely to the new arm. Allied military strategy, despite attention to "principles," had been a hybrid product, largely hammered out on the anvil of necessity. Final answers in military strategy to the problems of proper aims and emphases, and of best combinations and permutations, were still not clear.

It was clear, however, that modern war had grown more total than ever, and that science, industry, diplomacy, and psychology all had to be harnessed to it. Campaign strategy could no longer be clearly differentiated from national strategy; military strategy —in the sense of disposing armed forces for battle—was overshadowed by grand strategy. Where all this would lead was still not clear at the end of World War II, for hanging over all society was the weapon that threatened to revolutionize all warfare, the atom bomb.

**7. Cold War in the Nuclear Age.**—A great debate over strategy arose in the postwar years. Underlying it were a number of crucial factors. World War II had further upset the balance of power in the world, earlier disturbed in World War I. Germany and Japan had been defeated, Britain and France further weakened, and the United States and the Soviet Union had emerged as the two strongest powers in the world. The growing rift between the East and West led some critics in the Western world to point to mistakes in Allied political and military strategy of World War II —especially to an overconcentration on military objectives at the expense of political aims, on gaining military victories rather than winning the peace. While part of this criticism seemed overly harsh and not always founded on well-established fact, it was clear from the growing flood of literature on World War II that political and military strategy in World War II had not been systematically meshed. At the same time the war had loosed a wave of nationalistic and revolutionary movements in the world with strategies of their own. The struggle by the committed powers to win the noncommitted was intense. Through coordinated political, economic, military, and psychological pressures, the Soviet Union sought to incline the new nationalistic and revolutionary movements toward its orbit. The growth of the cordon of Soviet satellite states in central and eastern Europe was one result of its postwar strategy; the Soviet link with Red China was another. Meanwhile the West, led by the United States, moved to shore up the weakened European powers. The Truman Doctrine, the Marshall Plan, and the emergence of the North Atlantic Treaty Organization (NATO) were diverse strategic weapons to counter the many-sided Soviet threat. The cold war moved strategy to all fronts—political, diplomatic, economic, propagandistic, as well as military—in both the East and West. New phrases entered the vocabulary of Western thought—"strategy of containment," "strategy of total war," "massive retaliation," "preventive war," "deterrence," "graduated deterrence," and "escalation" (increase in scope of a conflict).

Though the great concern in the cold war era was the possible outbreak of World War III, strategy also had to consider limited warfare. The Korean War (*q.v.*) brought the North Korean and Chinese Communist forces into conflict with the South Korean and United Nations forces. It demonstrated that warfare in the cold war could also be limited and "hot," and that strategy would have to be tailored to local as well as worldwide needs.

Meanwhile, on the military plane, the impact of science and technology on warfare was promising revolutionary changes in strategy. To the growing arsenal of powerful new weapons begun with the invention of the atom bomb was added the hydrogen bomb —a bomb that could wipe out a whole city. New developments such as atomic-powered air and naval craft, atomic artillery, guided missiles that could cross oceans and continents, chemical, biological and radiological weapons, supersonic speeds, and other revolutionary adaptations in communication and transportation pointed to many changes in the art of war and in strategy. A great debate was joined between those who placed primary reliance on the new methods and means of war, and those who championed more orthodox and conventional approaches supplemented by the new weapons. The debate was particularly sharp between the advocates of a national military strategy based upon air power alone and the defenders of traditional strategy. Some air enthusiasts felt that the defeat of an enemy's armed forces on the battlefield was no longer a primary aim of strategy; that a new atomic air strategy offered unparalleled opportunity to break an enemy's will to resist by paralyzing his industrial power. Some advocates believed that the new atomic air strategy could be superimposed on the old strategy based on land, sea, and air forces; others believed that a choice had to be made between the two. Inevitably, the new developments in warfare also led authorities to take a fresh look at the "principles of war." Some began to argue that dispersion rather than concentration had become a basic goal; others argued that concentration merely required new adaptation.

Still other theorists in the cold war period were pointing up other new trends in strategy. Some went so far as to assert that not only was conventional military strategy outmoded but, along with it, national strategy. This belief was based on the idea that the 20th century was the age of great coalitions. This condition had resulted from the shrinkage of the world, the growing interdependence of nations, and the nature of modern war.

Western theorists were groping to comprehend the implications of the new environment of strategy—the revolutions in technology, the rising expectations of the many new nations, exploding populations, the threat of national and international Communism, and the tensions among the Communist countries, especially China and the U.S.S.R., that became apparent in the 1960s. They were probing the options between coalition strategy and national policy, the impact of domestic budgets and politics in legislating strategic programs, the relations between the nuclear deterrent and civil defense, and the effect of the nuclear stalemate in encouraging limited or unconventional warfare. Beyond the growing complications of the earthbound world arena lay outer space, which man was beginning to explore, and theorists were beginning to reckon with the future possible military implications of space technology. The realization was growing that deterrence in the cold war must be as wide as the spectrum of conflict in all its possible forms and intensities. More and more attention was being given to "balanced," "integrated," and "flexible" strategy, and to a comprehensive system of deterrence—to tailor means to the particular threat and to give political leaders wider range of freedom of action. More attention was given to the theory and practice of so-called brush-fire wars, of wars of subversion, and of guerrilla and counterguerrilla warfare.

At the same time, strategy, it was felt, must be waged primarily with political, economic, and propagandistic means. Preparedness on all fronts—military and nonmilitary—became a significant factor in that strategy. The belief seemed to be growing that in the holocaust of all-out modern war all sides would lose. The ultimate aim of strategy in the cold war had become the achievement of national and international objectives without touching off World War III. Strategy had expanded into every phase of national endeavour, just as had war itself. The line of demarcation between war and peace had further broken down, and with it the broadest definitions of strategy yet offered were no longer adequate. From the stratagems of the commander in war, strategy had come to preempt more and more of the spheres of warfare and diplomacy. The line dividing it from policy had become indistinct, and its highest aim had become the defense and survival of civilization itself. *See* also LOGISTICS; compare, for further analysis of modern issues and dilemmas, INTERNATIONAL RELATIONS; also PEACE, INTERNATIONAL; WAR; and DISARMAMENT; and references under "Strategy" in the Index.

BIBLIOGRAPHY.—Hermann Foertsch, *The Art of Modern Warfare* (1940); Edward Mead Earle *et al.* (eds.), *Makers of Modern Strategy* (1943); Maurice Matloff and Edwin M. Snell, *Strategic Planning for Coalition Warfare, 1941–1942* (1953); B. H. Liddell Hart, *Strategy, the Indirect Approach* (1954); John C. Slessor, *Strategy for the West* (1954); John Ehrman, *Grand Strategy,* vol. v and vi (1956); Maurice Matloff, "The Soviet Union and the War in the West," *Proc. U.S. Nav. Inst.*, vol. 82, no. 3 (March 1956), and *Strategic Planning for Coalition Warfare, 1943–1944* (1959); Edgar J. Kingston-McCloughry, *Global Strategy* (1957), and *Defense: Policy and Strategy* (1960); Henry A. Kissinger, *Nuclear Weapons and Foreign Policy* (1957); Raymond L. Garthoff, *Soviet Strategy in the Nuclear Age* (1958); Bernard Brodie, *Strategy in the Missile Age* (1959); Raymond Aron, *On War* (1959); Samuel P. Huntington, *The Common Defense: Strategic Programs in National Politics* (1961); R. E. Osgood, *Limited War: the Challenge to American Strategy* (1957); Herman Kahn, *Thinking About the Unthinkable* (1962); W. W. Kaufmann, *McNamara Strategy* (1964); Michael Howard (ed.), *The Theory and Practice of War* (1965). (M. MF.)

**STRATFORD, JOHN** (d. 1348), archbishop of Canterbury (1333–48) and chancellor of England (November 1330–September 1334, June 1335–March 1337, April–June 1340), a leading counselor of the English king Edward III, was born at Stratford-upon-Avon, Warwickshire, and educated at Oxford University. By 1322 he was canon of York and of Salisbury, archdeacon of Lincoln, and in June 1323, while visiting Avignon, he was consecrated bishop of Winchester by Pope John XXII. Stratford, a doctor of civil law by 1312, gave legal advice to Edward II's council from 1317 and was a royal clerk by 1320. Stratford offered to mediate between Edward and Queen Isabella on her return from France in 1326, but he later drafted the so-called Articles of Deposition and helped to force Edward to renounce the throne. Although a councilor to the young Edward III, Stratford was opposed by Roger Mortimer and his ascendancy began only after Mortimer's fall (November 1330). Chancellor for about six of the following ten years and archbishop of Canterbury from 1333, Stratford accompanied Edward to France, Flanders, and Scotland. After the outbreak (1337) of the Hundred Years' War, Stratford had difficulty in providing the king with adequate financial supplies and in October 1339 and January 1340 failed to get a grant from Parliament. He was probably guilty of some mismanagement. Edward returned suddenly to England from Flanders in November 1340 and arrested many officials, John's brother Robert, who had succeeded him as chancellor, escaping only because he was a bishop. John retired to Canterbury, where he used his pulpit to rebut the charges made against him and at the Parliament of April–May 1341 he skilfully achieved a reconciliation with Edward. He did not regain his former influence, however. He died at Mayfield, Sussex, on Aug. 23, 1348, and was buried in Canterbury Cathedral.

*See* A. B. Emden, *A Biographical Register of the University of Oxford to A.D. 1500,* vol. iii (1959).

**STRATFORD DE REDCLIFFE, STRATFORD CANNING,** VISCOUNT (1786–1880), British diplomat notable for his influence in Turkish affairs, was born in London on Nov. 4, 1786, the fourth son of Stratford Canning, a merchant who had been disinherited following his marriage to Mehitabel Patrick. The elder Canning died in April 1787, endowing his family with little but the friendship of his nephew, George Canning (*q.v.*). The latter's influence enabled Stratford Canning to be educated at Eton and King's college, Cambridge. His studies there were interrupted when George Canning, then foreign minister, appointed him in 1807 as a précis writer at the foreign office and later to missions at Copenhagen and Constantinople. In 1810 he became chargé d'affaires at Constantinople and, without instructions from England, helped arrange the peace of Bucharest (1812) between Turkey and Russia, just as Napoleon was about to invade the latter. On returning home, poverty thwarted his ambition to enter political life, but Lord Castlereagh appointed him minister to Switzerland (1814–18) and used him at the Congress of Vienna as adviser on that country. He then went as minister to Washington (1819–23) and, although he sometimes clashed with John Quincy Adams, the U.S. secretary of state, on returning to London he negotiated a convention which was, however, refused ratification by the U.S. senate.

In 1824 George Canning appointed him ambassador at Constantinople, but sent him first to discuss North American frontier questions at St. Petersburg. He also raised, unofficially, the Greek issue. At Constantinople he joined the Russian and subsequently the French ambassadors, but the battle of Navarino (*q.v.*) on Oct. 20, 1827, forced all three to retire to Corfu. In 1828–29 Canning resumed negotiations concerning Greece at a conference at Poros and accepted an extension of its frontiers, which was however repudiated by the earl of Aberdeen, then foreign minister. Lord Palmerston sent him again to Constantinople in 1831, when he finally obtained these frontiers, chiefly because of the threat to the sultan from Mohammed Ali (*q.v.*), the pasha of Egypt. Palmerston, whom the cabinet prevented from accepting Canning's advice to protect the sultan, next appointed him ambassador to St. Petersburg. The tsar Nicholas I, for reasons still not completely explained, refused to receive him, so that henceforward there was a personal issue between the two.

During this controversy Stratford Canning was sent on a special mission to Spain (1832–33) which was not a great success, and then embarked on a political career. He had sat for the pocket borough of Old Sarum (1828) and Stockbridge (1831), both abolished by the Reform bill, and 1835–41 was member for King's Lynn, speaking in the house mainly on foreign affairs. He impressed little and although in 1851 Lord Stanley promised that he should be the next Tory foreign minister, Canning was never to hold office. Meanwhile he had accepted a fourth mission to Constantinople (1841–46), when he established a unique position of influence over the sultan and his ministers, and tried hard without much success to reform the Ottoman empire. Palmerston afterward dispatched him on missions to Switzerland and central Europe, and then began another period at Constantinople (1848–51), when he supported the sultan in retaining Polish and Hungarian refugees. Created viscount in 1852 he was reappointed (1853–58), and thus served throughout the Crimean War (*q.v.*). Contrary to the view often held by historians, research has shown that, though he saw the danger of the demands of Nicholas I, he worked for a peaceful solution but was thwarted by refusal of the sultan to accept his advice. During the war he strove to improve hospital and army administration. He was in continual controversy with the French, jealous of his influence which in fact declined over this period. Nevertheless he was given a magnificent farewell from Constantinople in 1858.

In 1816 Canning married Harriet Raikes (d. 1817) and in 1825, Eliza Alexander. From 1858 he lived quietly, occasionally speaking in the lords and publishing a few poems and books of devotion. He became a knight grand cross of the Bath in 1829, and received the Garter in 1869. He died on Aug. 14, 1880, in Frant, Sussex.

*See* also EASTERN QUESTION.

Bibliography.—S. Lane-Poole, *Life of Lord Stratford de Redcliffe* (1888); E. F. Malcolm-Smith, *The Life of Stratford Canning* (1933); H. W. V. Temperley, *England and the Near East: the Crimea* (1936).
(C. K. W.)

**STRATFORD-UPON-AVON,** a municipal borough in the Stratford parliamentary division of Warwickshire, Eng., 24 mi. S.S.E. of Birmingham and 91 mi. N.W. of London by road. Pop. (1969 est.) 19,110. Area 10.8 sq.mi. It stands mainly on the left bank of the river Avon at the point where it is crossed by a 14-arch stone bridge presented by Sir Hugh Clopton in the reign of Henry VII; there is also a 19th-century bridge. As *Æt-stretfordae* (signifying "the ford by which a Roman road crossed the river"), Stratford was mentioned as early as 691. The manor was granted by Offa to the bishopric of Worcester; and it was under the protection of the bishops of Worcester that the inhabitants of the town early assumed burghal rights. The Gild of the Holy Cross, founded in the 13th century for the support of poor priests and others, exercised authority over the town for many years. Its dissolution was the cause of the incorporation charter of Edward VI in 1553. Another charter, altering the constitution of the corporation, was granted in 1611. Other charters were granted in 1664 and 1674.

Stratford is a picturesque market town and road centre and has one or two industries, but its world fame arises from its connection with William Shakespeare, born there in 1564 and whose plays and sonnets contain many allusions to local scenes. Relatively little is known of Shakespeare's life, so that the few genuine local traditions have, as is understandable with so famous a man, become encrusted with picturesque legend. It was not until 1769, when David Garrick inaugurated the first of the annual birthday celebrations, that any attempt was made to preserve buildings and other memorials of Shakespeare's life in the town, but many valuable links had already vanished.

Shakespeare was born in a half-timbered house in Henley street, bought by public subscription in 1847 and later handed to the care of the Shakespeare Birthplace trust. Here are gathered a number of documents and relics and an early portrait of him. He attended the grammar school adjoining the chapel built in the 13th century by the Gild of the Holy Cross and rebuilt in the 15th century. The chapel has a well-restored medieval Doom painting and there is a reference to a schoolmaster there as early as 1295. The hall was used from time to time by traveling companies of actors and it may have been that in this room Shakespeare had his first introduction to the stage. In 1597 Shakespeare bought the house known as New Place, and there he died in 1616. The house was pulled down in 1759, and only the foundations remain. By it is Nash's house, a museum of both local and Shakespearean relics.

Shakespeare's grave is in Holy Trinity church, a fine cruciform building on the site of a monastery that existed before 691. The earliest parts of the church (transepts, tower and parts of the nave walls) date from 1189 to 1272; the aisles are Decorated, the chancel is Perpendicular. Here is the font in which it is said Shakespeare was baptized, and the chancel where he is buried, beside his wife and other relatives. On the adjoining wall is a monument with the well-known bust of Shakespeare by Gerard Johnson (Janssen).

The group of buildings by the river known as the Shakespeare Memorial comprise a library and art gallery (opened in 1881)—all that was left of the original memorial built in 1879—and a theatre (opened in 1932) designed by Elisabeth Scott to replace that destroyed by fire in 1926. The Memorial houses a valuable collection of Shakespeareana, including early folio editions of the plays and the famous "Droeshout print" of Shakespeare which was a frontispiece to the *Plays* of 1623. The library (10,000 vol.) is one of the most complete of its kind.

April 23—the date of Shakespeare's death and, approximately, also of his birth—is annually celebrated with a procession attended by distinguished representatives of many nations, and every year from March until October is the Shakespeare festival when his plays are acted at the Memorial theatre.

Hall's croft, a Tudor building with rare old furniture, was the home of John Hall, Shakespeare's son-in-law. The Quiney house was the home of Judith Shakespeare, the poet's youngest daughter. Harvard house (1596) was the girlhood home of the mother of John Harvard who endowed Harvard university in the United States. It is one of the few notable buildings (such as the 18th-century Town hall, Shrieve's house, rebuilt 1614, and Emm's court, dating from the 17th century) which are not connected with Shakespeare. Mason croft became in 1951 the Shakespeare institute of Birmingham university. At Shottery, 1 mi. W., is the thatched cottage which was the early home of Shakespeare's wife, Anne Hathaway. It was bought for the nation in 1892.

The poet's mother was Mary Arden, the name of an ancient county family that survives in the forest of Arden, which formerly covered a large area northwest of Stratford. Her birthplace, a Tudor farmhouse at Wilmcote (about 5 mi. N.W.), is preserved as a museum, and it has a collection of local farming implements.

**STRATHAVEN** (local pronunciation "Straven"), an upland manufacturing and market town in Avondale civil parish, Lanarkshire, Scot., on the Avon, 8 mi. S. of Hamilton by road. Pop. (1951) 4,288. It is the centre of a dairy-farming and pastoral country; industries include textiles (silk and hosiery), grain milling, agricultural engineering, printing and motor-coach building. The ruins of Avondale castle, which commanded the route into central Ayrshire, stand on a crag above Powmillion burn. At Drumclog, 6 mi. S.W., a school and a granite obelisk commemorate a victory of the Covenanters over Graham of Claverhouse on June 1, 1679. (G. P. I.)

**STRATHCLYDE,** the name given in the 9th and 10th centuries to the north British kingdom, which from the 6th century onward was probably confined to the basin of the Clyde, together with the adjacent coast districts, Ayrshire, etc., on the west of Scotland. Its capital was Dumbarton ("fortress of the Britons"), then known as Alclut. On the north the kingdom bordered on the Scots of Dalriada, and on the south on the Cymri (Lat. *Cumbri* or *Cumbrenses,* "Compatriots"), the name used by English writers since the 10th century to include Strathclyde, and surviving in the English Cumberland and in the Welsh name for themselves, *Cymry.* All were survivors of the British (Welsh) population, speaking one language (Welsh) and recognizing a common kinship, and the Cumbri extended southward into Lancashire and probably east of the Pennines. No vernacular written records survive from the Cymri, but much information about them is available from Scottish, Irish, and Saxon records, and from later Welsh literature derived from Cumbric oral tradition. Important for the early period are the *Historia Brittonum* of Nennius, the *Annales Cambriae,* the genealogies, and early Welsh poetry.

During the late Roman period the Cumbri emerge as a loose confederation of independent local princes, policing the northern frontiers of Roman Britain against Pictish aggression. Preeminent among them was the Strathclyde dynasty of Dumbarton which included Ceretic Guletic, generally identified with the Coroticus to whose soldiers St. Patrick's famous *Epistola* was addressed, and ancestor of Rhydderch, St. Columba's contemporary. Welsh tradition also records the arrival in the 5th century in North Wales from Lothian of a famous chief Cunedag (Cunedda) and his sons to dislodge Irish settlers. By the early 6th century Christianity was widely established in Cumbria. In the second half of the century the Cumbrian princes, including Rhydderch and a famous heroic chief Urien, probably from the Solway area, waged aggressive warfare against the Bernicians, while in 642 Owain, king of Strathclyde, defeated and killed the Scottish king of Dalriada, Domnall Brecc.

During the reign (641–670) of the Northumbrian king Oswiu the Anglian kingdoms established a supremacy over all Cumbria except Strathclyde, which maintained its independence till the year 756 when the kingdom suffered a crushing defeat from the Northumbrian king Eadberht and the Pictish king Angus mac Fergus. In 870 Vikings plundered and destroyed Dumbarton. Nevertheless, in 878 Eochaid of the Dumbarton dynasty seems to have gained a control over Dalriada lasting for 11 years; and some expansion of influence is traceable till 920 or 921 when the Anglo-Saxon king Edward the Elder, and in 927 his successor Aethelstan, received the submission of the Britons of Strathclyde, the Scots, the Bernicians, and the Danes of York. In 937 Strathclyde joined with the Scots and Norsemen in a combined attempt to overthrow the English supremacy, but were defeated at the Battle of Brunanburh.

During the first half of the 10th century kings were still reigning in Strathclyde; but in 945 the English king Edmund I harried the kingdom and leased it to Malcolm I, king of the Scots, who was thus the first Gaelic king to rule the Britons in southern Scotland. In 971, however, the Strathclyde Britons invaded Lothian, having evidently regained their independence, which they maintained under their own kings till the early 11th century. In *c.* 1016 (or 1018?) Owain of Strathclyde united his forces to those of Malcolm II, king of the Scots, in a triumphant campaign against the Anglian kingdom of Lothian, which ended in the overwhelming defeat of the English at the Battle of Carham. Owain died soon afterward, the last independent king of Strathclyde. Henceforth the ancient kingdom of Cumbria became a province of Scotland.

BIBLIOGRAPHY.—K. H. Jackson, "The Britons of Southern Scotland," *Antiquity*, vol. xxix (1955); H. M. Chadwick, *Early Scotland* (1949); W. F. Skene, *Celtic Scotland*, 2nd ed. (1886–90), (ed.) *Chronicles of the Picts and Scots* (1867). (N. K. C.)

**STRATHCONA AND MOUNT ROYAL, DONALD ALEXANDER SMITH,** BARON (1820–1914), Canadian fur trader, financier, railway promoter, and statesman. Born at Forres, Scot., Aug. 6, 1820, he was apprenticed to the Hudson's Bay Company in 1838 and, after serving at Lachine and Tadoussac for ten years, he was sent to Labrador, where he rose to the rank of chief factor. In 1870 he was appointed chief commissioner for the company in Canada, but relinquished this office in 1874 to head the land department. After becoming the principal shareholder, he was governor of the Hudson's Bay Company from 1889 until his death in London, Jan. 21, 1914.

In 1869 he represented the Canadian government in negotiations with the Red River insurgents for the peaceable transfer of the Hudson's Bay Company territory to Canada. A Conservative member of the new Manitoba legislature, 1870–74, he was elected to represent Selkirk in the Canadian House of Commons in 1871. By withdrawing his support of Sir John A. Macdonald during the Pacific Scandal, 1873, he contributed to the defeat of the Conservative ministry. With his cousin, George Stephen (later Baron Mount Stephen), and others, he successfully promoted the St. Paul, Minneapolis and Manitoba Railway, but because of Macdonald's antipathy he was not formally a member of the syndicate formed to build the Canadian Pacific Railway in 1880. Nevertheless his financial support was vital to the enterprise and he was accorded the honour of driving the last spike at Craigellachie, B.C., in 1885. He became president of the Bank of Montreal in 1887, and honorary president in 1905.

Defeated in Selkirk in 1880, he represented Montreal West in the House of Commons, 1887–96, but retired to become Canadian high commissioner in London, 1896–1914. Founder of Royal Victoria College for women at McGill University, he was elected chancellor of the University, 1889, and of Aberdeen University in 1903. He equipped and maintained Lord Strathcona's Horse in the South African War. Knighted in 1886, he was raised to the peerage in 1897.

*See* W. T. R. Preston, *The Life and Times of Lord Strathcona* (1914); Beckles Willson, *The Life of Lord Strathcona and Mount Royal* (1915). (A. R. TU.)

**STRATHNAIRN, HUGH HENRY ROSE,** 1ST BARON (1801–1885), British field marshal, the ablest of the galaxy of commanders who suppressed the Indian Mutiny (*q.v.*), was born on April 6, 1801, in Berlin. Commissioned in the 19th Foot (1820), he saw active service in Syria while on a mission to the Turkish Army, then opposing Mohammed Ali of Egypt. Under his regime as consul general in Syria (1841–48) order was restored, justice honestly administered, and tribal feuds repressed. In 1851 he became secretary to the embassy at Constantinople. Appointed British liaison officer at French headquarters he was present at all the battles of the Crimean War (1854–56). He was promoted major general in 1854.

At the beginning of the Indian Mutiny (1857) Rose was appointed to command the Central India force of two brigades and conducted the most difficult, vigorous, and successful operations of the war. After storming the fort of Rahatgarh (January 1858); he relieved Sagar (Feb. 3), captured the fort of Garhakota, forced the Malthon Pass, and seized Chanderi (March 7). These successes enabled him to lay siege to Jhansi, the principal hostile stronghold of the area, and despite the vigorous resistance of the garrison under the widowed rani of Jhansi, it was carried by assault (April 3–4) after a relieving army under Tantia Topi had been routed. Fierce heat rendered the operations toilsome and costly in losses from sunstroke and prostration; but they were pursued with vigour, and the enemy was driven from Kunch and from Kalpi. The campaign seemed over when Rose heard that the rani of Jhansi and Tantia Topi had seized Gwalior, the strongest fortress in central India, having won over the troops of its ruler, Sindhia. Rose at once moved against it and carried it by assault. He then took command of the Poona Division (June 1858) and later of the Bombay army (1860), with the delicate task of amalgamating the queen's and the East India Company's forces in that province. Returning to England in 1865, he was appointed commander in chief in Ireland (1865) and raised to the peerage (1866). He died, unmarried, in Paris on Oct. 16, 1885.

*See* O. T. Burne, *Clyde and Strathnairn* (1891). (E. W. SH.)

**STRATHSPEY,** a Scottish type of slow dance tune in common (4/4) time, characterized by frequent use of the "Scotch snap"; *i.e.*, a dotted quaver preceded by a semiquaver. Strathspeys appear to have originated *c.* 1700 in the valley (Scots: *strath*) of the River Spey. After *c.* 1745 strathspeys came into general use throughout Scotland as tunes for reels and country dances. *See* REEL. (T. M. FL.)

**STRATIFICATION,** as a term applied to rocks, refers to their layering. Strata or layers are distinctive features of most sedimentary rocks and are common also in those igneous rocks formed at the earth's surface—lava flows and volcanic fragmental deposits. No connotation of thickness is implied by the term and individual layers or strata may range from a fraction of an inch to many feet. Likewise the shapes of individual strata vary greatly according to the type of rock and the conditions of deposition. They range from thin sheets that cover many square miles to thick, lenslike bodies extending only a few feet laterally.

In sedimentary rocks the term stratum is not synonymous with the terms bed or lamination, although some geologists have used it in that sense. Both bed and lamina carry definite thickness connotations, beds referring to rock layers greater than one centimetre in thickness and laminations to layers that are one centimetre or less in thickness. Thus, both beds and laminations are varieties of strata; likewise bedding and lamination are terms restricted to stratification having definite thickness limitations.

Planes of parting or separation between individual rock layers commonly are referred to as stratification planes. They tend to be even and to be parallel to the strata that they bound, for they are essentially horizontal where sediments are deposited as flat-lying layers and they slope correspondingly where the deposits are laid down with an initial dip. Notable exceptions to the evenness of stratification planes develop where deposition takes place on irregular surfaces. In such situations the bottom surface of a stratum normally conforms roughly to the irregularities of the underlying surface, but the stratification plane above the stratum will tend to be nearly horizontal. In many places original, nearly horizontal surfaces of stratification planes have subsequently been destroyed by erosion during pauses or breaks in sedimentation.

Stratification in sedimentary rocks may result from changes in texture or in composition during deposition of the sediment; it also may result from pauses in deposition that allow the first deposits to undergo certain changes before additional sediments cover them. A sequence of strata, therefore, may appear as alterations of coarse and fine particles, as a series of colour changes resulting from differences in mineral composition or merely as layers of similar aspect, separated by distinct planes of parting. No direct relationship exists between the thickness and extent of strata and the rate of deposition or time represented; for example, a 1-in. stratum of limestone may take longer to form than a 10-ft. stratum of sandstone.

The most frequent cause of stratification is variation in velocity of the depositing agent. During transportation water and wind sort sediments according to size, weight and shape of particles and these sediments settle in layers of relative homogeneity. A second cause is differences in composition of sediments from different sources, illustrated by successive floods spreading over a flood-plain from several tributaries of a river. Still another cause is variation in sediment brought about by change in agents of deposition, as where muds of a delta plain are covered by wind-blown sands, or where limy ooze of the sea floor is buried beneath ash of a volcanic eruption. Thus, variations of any type that affect the uniformity of sediment being deposited result in stratification.

Stratification in sedimentary rocks varies greatly both in degree of prominence and in details of structure. In general, it is best developed in fine-grained sediments and is least apparent and least persistent in coarse-grained materials such as conglomerates. Two important and distinctive structural types are recognized as characteristic of particular environments. These types are: (1) current bedding or cross-stratification in which layers have been deposited at one or more angles to the original dip of the formation; and (2) graded bedding in which particles grade upward in a stratum from relatively coarse at the bottom to relatively fine at the top.

Cross-stratification is the product of deposition by wind or water currents as they lose velocity, whereas graded bedding results from simultaneous settling of coarse and fine sediments in waters of a comparatively quiet bottom.

Cross-stratification, which may consist of medium to thick layers (cross-bedding) or of very thin layers (cross-lamination), includes many variations, the most basic of which are the simple, planar and trough types. Simple cross-stratification involves sets of sloping layers formed by deposition only; planar cross-stratification results from alternating deposition and partial planation of the strata; trough cross-stratification, from deposition together with scouring or channeling. Cross-stratification is developed in a number of different depositional environments including the fronts of deltas, the lee sides of dunes, the channels of rivers and streams and various other places where initial dip is a characteristic feature. Commonly the nature of this environment can be recognized by analysis of the structures.

Graded bedding is typical especially of dark sandstones or graywackes and of conglomerates formed in areas of relatively rapid sedimentation under unstable crustal conditions that characterize the rapid sinking of a geosyncline or depositional trough. Under such conditions thick sequences of graded beds may accumulate. The mixing of coarse and fine particles has been attributed to submarine temblors (earthquakes), to movement by density currents down steep slopes and to other causes.

Seasonal deposits or varves of glacial lakes are another kind of graded bedding. In them light-coloured silt grades upward into dark-coloured mud forming a couplet a few millimetres thick. Each such couplet is the deposit of a single year and is separated from other, similar couplets by an abrupt change in colour.

Stratification in volcanic rocks differs in some respects from that in sedimentary rocks. Fragmental volcanic material, thrown into the air during violent eruptions, becomes stratified in flight under the influences of gravity and wind. Falling to the ground, it may form well-sorted layers. If it falls into lakes or the sea, it becomes layered like any other water-borne detrital matter; however, when a mixture of coarse, volcanic debris full of gas bubbles (pumice) and fine ash falls into quiet water, reverse graded bedding may result, with the finer but heavier grains at the bottom grading up into the coarser, lighter fragments. Stratification also may result from successive outflows of liquid lava or alternations between lava flows and ash falls. False stratification sometimes develops in flows due to contraction on cooling.

Not all sedimentary deposits are stratified. Those transported by ice, either pushed ahead of a glacier or carried by it, form unlayered deposits called till. They are piled up or dumped as the ice melts, forming moraines and other features lacking stratiform structure. Likewise materials accumulated through the force of gravity, such as talus deposits at the bases of cliffs and landslides, may exhibit no sorting and no stratification. Still other deposits are structureless because original stratification has been destroyed through the work of plant roots, or the borings of worms and various other animals, or by recrystallization. Residual soils and reefs built by organisms likewise have no stratification.

Stratification is one of the geologist's most useful tools. Its structure provides a clue to the environment in which the sediment or igneous material accumulated. Furthermore, where once-horizontal layers have been deformed, the record of past earth movements is preserved in the stratification. Folding, faulting and other forms of disturbance commonly are recorded by tilted or broken strata and these make possible the interpretation of geologic events. From this record such practical results as the location of mineral deposits, petroleum fields and ground water are obtained.

*See* also SEDIMENTARY ROCKS; GEOLOGY. (E. D. McK.)

**STRATIGRAPHY** is concerned with the sequence of strata formed in the earth by sedimentation (*e.g.*, from water, wind, ice, volcanoes, and human activity). Closely coordinated with petrology and paleontology (*qq.v.*), stratigraphy provides a basis for historical geology (the history of the earth's surface).

Leonardo da Vinci appreciated the concept of stratigraphy, but the scientific foundations were laid during the 19th century in England by Sir Roderick Impey Murchison, Adam Sedgwick, and William Smith (*qq.v.*); in Germany by A. G. Werner and F. A. Quenstedt; in Bohemia by J. Barrande; and in North America by Charles Schuchert. Since the upper of two layers usually has been deposited last (the so-called law of superposition) an age sequence can be established directly unless tectonic movements (*e.g.*, upheavals such as faulting, thrusting, and folding) have disturbed the sequence. In the analysis of such complicated cases the fossils contained in the strata are of paramount importance since different forms of life have been found to characterize specific periods of geologic time.

Thus investigations first delineated the stratigraphical sequence for the last 500,000,000 years, during which there was abundant life and many plants and animals were equipped with hard structures that are readily fossilized.

This sequence was divided into three major eras or groups: the Paleozoic, the Mesozoic, and the Cenozoic, each subdivided into periods or systems. The Paleozoic Era (divided into Cambrian, Ordovician, Silurian, Devonian, Carboniferous, and Permian periods) is known from the evidence of radioactivity to have lasted approximately from 500,000,000 to 200,000,000 years ago; the Upper Carboniferous was the time when coal was formed in swamp forests. The Mesozoic Era (divided into Triassic, Jurassic, and Cretaceous periods) lasted from about 200,000,000 to 70,000,000 years ago and was the time of dinosaurs and ammonites (*see* AMMONITE); in the Upper Cretaceous the chalk of Britain was laid down as a mud containing the skeletal remains of minute animals in the sea. The Cenozoic Era (divided into Tertiary and Quaternary or Pleistocene periods) covered the last 70,000,000 years (Pleistocene only 1,000,000); the Tertiary was the age of mammals; the Quaternary is the age of man.

These periods have been further subdivided into numerous epochs. Many were characterized by zone fossils that lived for only a brief time in many parts of the world; these made long-distance, even intercontinental, correlation possible.

Investigation of Precambrian times is aimed at establishing a sequence back to the origin of the earth's crust, roughly covering the last 3,500,000,000 to 500,000,000 years. Three eras are distinguished: the Proterozoic (Precambrian or Algonkian), the Archaean, and the Azoic. The Proterozoic has yielded fossils of organized forms of life; the Archaean indirect evidence of life; and the Azoic is the period before life appeared. The subdivisions of the Precambrian eras are based on breaks in the sequences produced by earth movements that served to identify specific periods in time.

The most recent application of stratigraphy has been to archaeology. The earlier part of prehistory, covering Paleolithic man living during the Pleistocene, is marked by fossil remains of man and his stone artifacts. When a site is excavated, details of stratification indicate climatic sequences into which the prehistoric industries can be fitted. Post-Pleistocene sites containing the products of early man are carefully excavated according to layers, starting from the top. The layers are studied to ascertain their petrological composition and the fossils they contain are identified and interpreted. The tells (occupation mounds) of Eastern countries (*e.g.*, ancient Jericho) have been investigated in this manner. These mounds consist of man-made deposits, later generations building their houses on the debris of earlier habitations (*see* ARCHAEOLOGY: *Mesopotamia: Stratigraphy and Relative Chronology*).

Archaeological stratigraphy has the advantage that tectonic disturbance is rare, but higher strata tend to cut into those below and the composition tends to be uniform throughout the sequence. Consequently, petrological methods are increasingly employed. *See* also GEOCHRONOLOGY; GEOLOGY; also references under "Stratigraphy" in the Index.

BIBLIOGRAPHY.—C. O. Dunbar, *Historical Geology,* 2nd ed. (1960); K. M. Kenyon, *Beginning in Archaeology,* rev. ed. (1953); J. F. Kirkaldy, *General Principles of Geology* (1954); P. Lake and R. H. Rastall, *Textbook of Geology,* 5th ed. (1941); R. E. M. Wheeler, *Archaeology from the Earth* (1954, 1962); F. E. Zeuner, *Dating the Past* (1958); M. Kay and E. H. Colbert, *Stratigraphy and Life History* (1965). (F. E. Z.; X.)

**STRATO** OF LAMPSACUS (d. *c.* 270 B.C.), Greek philosopher, became head of the Peripatetic school in succession to Theophrastus. As the main subject of his writings, apart from logic, was natural science, he was called Strato Physicus in antiquity.

Strato's theory was a combination of Aristotelian and atomistic elements. Thus he taught with Aristotle that there is only one world, instead of many; but he abandoned his master's teleological interpretation of nature and his hypothesis of a fifth element. The insistence on causality and the materialism that he shared with the atomists led him not only to remove every theological element but also to deny the immortality of the human soul.

Strato's writings as a whole are lost, but in antiquity he was highly esteemed and influential. His doctrine that all substances contain void and that differences in the weight of substances are caused by differences in the extension of void served as the theoretical base for the Hellenistic construction of air- and steam-engines as described in Hero of Alexandria's book.

*See* the fragments ed. by F. Wehrli, *Straton von Lampsakos* (1950), being part v of *Die Schule des Aristoteles: Texte und Kommentar;* G. Rodier, *La Physique de Straton* (1890). (F. WI.)

**STRATOSPHERE,** the second layer of the atmosphere, above the troposphere and below the mesosphere. Its lower boundary, the tropopause, is located where the tropospheric temperature decrease of about 6° C. per km. is replaced either by a much smaller decrease or, more often, by constant temperature or slight increase with elevation. Approximate heights and temperatures of the tropopause are shown in the table. These figures are averages along the meridian 80° W. but they are representative for other longitudes and for the southern hemisphere. The tropopause is lower at higher latitudes. It is not a continuous

*Heights and Temperatures of the Tropopause*

| Latitude | 90° N. | 60° N. | 30° N. | 0° |
|---|---|---|---|---|
| January | 8.5 km., −60° C. | 9 km., −55° C. | 12 km., −55° C.<br>17 km., −70° C. | 18 km., −80° C. |
| July | 9 km., −45° C. | 10 km., −50° C. | 16 km., −70° C. | 16 km., −73° C. |

surface between the poles and the equator. The polar tropopause extends to about 30° lat. in winter and 35° lat. in summer, while the tropical tropopause can be followed as far as 45° lat. There is thus a multiple tropopause at middle latitudes (indicated by the two values for 30° N. in the table). The polar tropopause is lowest in winter, the tropical tropopause in summer. The temperature in the stratosphere is generally highest in summer, except for one region at about 45° lat. between 14 and 18 km. where the temperature is about 2° C. higher in January than in July. The greatest seasonal warming in the stratosphere occurs at high latitudes because of the length of polar summer days.

The latitudinal temperature variation is smaller in the stratosphere than in the troposphere. At 20 km. elevation, for instance, the January temperature increases from about −70° C. at the equator to −55° C. or higher around 55° N. and then decreases to −75° C. at the north pole. In July, at the same height, the temperature rises continuously from −60° C. at the equator to −40° C. at the north pole. Above approximately 30 km. the temperature increases again because of the absorption of ultraviolet solar radiation by ozone and reaches a maximum of roughly 0° C. in the vicinity of 50 km. This is the level of the stratopause which separates the stratosphere from the next higher layer, the mesosphere, where the temperature decreases with elevation. Variations in space and time of the stratopause are not well known.

Outstanding features of the stratospheric winds in the northern hemisphere at 80° W. are: during January, a strong westerly jet with a maximum of 100 knots centred at the tropopause at 40° lat.; another strong west wind maximum, 80 knots, at 70° lat. and 25 km. altitude; and an easterly current with a maximum of 40 knots at 20° lat. and about 25 km. During the month of July the mid-latitude jet at the tropopause has a velocity maximum of only 50 knots, and the higher stratosphere has easterly currents at all latitudes.

The air density at 10 km. is about 30% of the sea level value, at 30 km. only slightly more than 1%. But the composition of the air, especially the relative proportion of the two main constituents, molecular oxygen and nitrogen, is the same as in the troposphere, indicating considerable vertical mixing. Ozone (*q.v.*) is more abundant than below. The water-vapour density is quite low because of the low temperature, and saturation seems to occur only rarely. Between 20 and 30 km. one occasionally observes clouds which are called mother-of-pearl or nacreous clouds because of their characteristic colouring.

The stratosphere is under more radiational control than the troposphere, where horizontal and vertical motions are of greater importance. The characteristic stratospheric temperature distribution is due mainly to the interaction of solar and terrestrial radiation. But strong atmospheric disturbances extend well up into the stratosphere and produce day-to-day changes there just as in the troposphere.

*See* also ATMOSPHERE; GEOCHEMISTRY: *Geochemistry of the Atmosphere,* and references under "Stratosphere" in the Index. (B. Hz.)

**STRAUBING,** a town of West Germany in the *Land* (state) of Bavaria, Federal Republic of Germany, lies on the Danube, 23 mi. (37 km.) SE of Regensburg on the rail route to Passau. Pop. (1961) 36,348. There were Neolithic settlements there, and the Celtic community on the site was taken over by the Romans and called Sorviodurum. In about 800 Straubing came into the possession of the cathedral chapter of Augsburg, which in 1180 built St. Peter's Church. The new town was founded west of the old in 1218; a tower (1316) marks its centre. Other churches include St. James's (15th century), and the Church of the Carmelites (1430). The main industries are brewing, electrical engineering, and the manufacture of tiles, and of clothing and hats. (I. Ro.)

**STRAUS,** a family of U.S. merchants, industrialists, and diplomats. LAZARUS STRAUS emigrated to the United States from Rhenish Bavaria in 1852. Two years later he was joined by his wife and four children. Lazarus and his son ISIDOR (1845–1912) formed the partnership of L. Straus and Son, which took over the pottery and glassware department of the R. H. Macy and Company department store in New York City. Two sons, NATHAN (1848–1931) and OSCAR SOLOMON (1850–1926), joined the firm in 1881. In 1888 Isidor and Nathan became partners in Macy's and in 1896 became its sole owners. Under their direction Macy's developed into one of the world's largest department stores. Isidor and Nathan also established a Brooklyn department store, Abraham and Straus. Isidor served a short term in the U.S. Congress as a result of a special election in 1893. Both Isidor and

Nathan had many philanthropic interests, Nathan being very active in public welfare work with a particular interest in child health. Isidor and his wife died in the sinking of the "Titanic" in 1912. Nathan's son NATHAN STRAUS (1889–1961) was active in public affairs and served as administrator of the U.S. Housing Authority (1937–42).

OSCAR SOLOMON STRAUS (1850–1926), although he spent some years in the family business, was primarily a lawyer, diplomat, and author. He graduated from Columbia Law School in 1873. From 1887 to 1889 and again from 1898 to 1900 he was U.S. minister to Turkey. He served as secretary of commerce and labour under Pres. Theodore Roosevelt. In 1909 he returned to Turkey as the first U.S. ambassador to the Ottoman Empire. He was appointed chairman of the New York Public Service Commission in 1915. He published several books on U.S. history and in 1922 published an autobiographical work, *Under Four Administrations: From Taft to Cleveland*.

JESSE ISIDOR STRAUS (1872–1936), son of Isidor, became an executive of Abraham and Straus, and from 1919 to 1933 served as president of Macy's. During the last few years of his life he was U.S. ambassador to France. PERCY SELDEN STRAUS (1876–1944), brother of Jesse Isidor, assumed the presidency of Macy's in 1933 and served in that capacity until 1940 when he became chairman of the board. In 1940 JACK ISIDOR STRAUS (1900– ), the grandson of one of the two Straus family members who were first partners in the Macy firm, and son of Jesse Isidor, became president, serving until 1956 when he became chairman of the board. Several other Straus family members served as vice-presidents of Macy's.

ROGER WILLIAMS STRAUS (1891–1957), son of Oscar Solomon, departed from the family business just as his father had before him. After graduating from Princeton in 1913 he joined the American Smelting and Refining Company. After holding various other positions with the company he became president in 1941 and chairman of the board in 1947. (H. J. SG.)

**STRAUSS,** Austrian family of musicians who achieved wide popularity throughout Europe in the 19th and 20th centuries as composers of waltzes, light music, and operettas in the Viennese style. Other 19th-century musicians bearing the name but having no direct connection with this family are Oscar Straus (1870–1954), composer of the operetta *Der tapfere Soldat*, based on G. B. Shaw's *Arms and the Man* (Vienna, 1908; given in New York as *The Chocolate Soldier*, 1909); Franz Strauss (1822–1905), horn player and composer of music for the horn; and the most prominent musician bearing this name, Franz's son Richard Strauss (*q.v.*).

JOHANN STRAUSS the Elder (1804–1849) was one of the principal composers of Viennese waltzes. Born in Vienna on March 14, 1804, he became a viola player in the dance orchestra of Michael Pamer, a composer of light music. Later he conducted the orchestra of Josef Lanner and in 1826 performed at the gardens of the "Zwei Tauben" the *Täuberlwalzer*, the first of many sets of Viennese waltzes named after the places where they were heard. In 1824 he married Anna Streim, the daughter of an innkeeper. He established his reputation as a composer of Viennese waltzes in 1830 by conducting at the "Sperl," a popular dance hall in the Leopoldstadt. There he was idolized to the extent of becoming known in the musical world as "the Austrian Napoleon." In 1834 he was appointed bandmaster to the 1st Vienna militia regiment and the following year was made director of the imperial court balls. He embarked in 1833 on the first of his many tours throughout Europe, visiting London in 1838. He died in Vienna on Sept. 25, 1849.

Strauss's complete works, including—besides waltzes—galops, polkas, quadrilles, and other dances, were published by his son Johann in 1889. Remarkable for their rhythmic verve and charm of melodic design, they represent the style of Viennese dance music at its best.

JOHANN STRAUSS the Younger (1825–1899), son of the above, developed the style of the Viennese waltz and became known for his operettas. Born in Vienna on Oct. 25, 1825, he started his career as a bank clerk, since his father wished him to follow a profession other than music. He studied the violin without his father's knowledge, however, and in 1844 conducted a dance band formed by himself at a Viennese restaurant. In 1849, when the elder Strauss died, Johann combined his orchestra with his father's and with it traveled all over Europe, including Russia (1865–66), and England (1869), winning great popularity. In 1872 he visited the United States and conducted concerts in New York and Boston. Earlier he had married Henrietta (Jetty) Treffz, a popular singer, and in the same year relinquished leadership of his orchestra to his brothers, Josef and Eduard, to spend his time writing music.

THE GRANGER COLLECTION
JOHANN STRAUSS THE YOUNGER, PHOTOGRAPHED ABOUT 1872

Strauss's most famous single composition is "An der schönen blauen Donau" ("The Blue Danube"; 1867), the main theme of which became one of the best-known tunes in 19th-century music. His many other melodious and successful waltzes include "Morgenblätter" (1864), "Künstlerleben" (1867), "Geschichten aus dem Wienerwald" (1868), "Wein, Weib und Gesang" (1869), "Wiener Blut" (1871), and "Kaiserwalzer" (1888). His waltzes number over 150, their popularity, which is still maintained, earning him the name "the Waltz King." Like his father he also wrote dances of several other kinds. Among his stage works, *Die Fledermaus* (1874) became the classical example of Viennese operetta. Other successful operettas were *Der Karneval in Rom* (1873), *Cagliostro in Wien* (1875), *Das Spitzentuch der Königin* (1880), *Der lustige Krieg* (1881), *Eine Nacht in Venedig* (1883), *Der Zigeunerbaron* (1885), and *Waldmeister* (1895). He died in Vienna, June 3, 1899. His second wife, Angelica, who long survived him, published his letters in 1926.

JOSEF STRAUSS (1827–1870), born in Vienna on Aug. 22, 1827, was the brother of Johann Strauss the younger. He was a composer and conductor of waltzes, among them *Dynamiden*, used by Richard Strauss for a theme in *Der Rosenkavalier*. He died in Vienna on July 21, 1870.

EDUARD STRAUSS (1835–1916), born in Vienna on March 15, 1835, was also a brother of Johann Strauss the younger. He deputized for his more famous brother during Johann's visit to Russia and succeeded him in 1870 as conductor of the imperial court balls. He died in Vienna on Dec. 28, 1916.

JOHANN STRAUSS (1866–1939), born in Vienna on Feb. 16, 1866, the son of Eduard Strauss, became known as a conductor of light music. He died in Berlin on Jan. 9, 1939.

BIBLIOGRAPHY.—A. Witeschnik, *Die Dynastie Strauss* (1939); J. Pastene, *Three-Quarter Time: the Life and Music of the Strauss Family* (1951); M. Corner, *The Waltz* (1948).

**STRAUSS, DAVID FRIEDRICH** (1808–1874), German theologian and biographer, author of one of the most sensational books on religion of the 19th century, the *Leben Jesu*, which first brought to wide public attention the new trends in biblical exegesis. He was born at Ludwigsburg, near Stuttgart, on Jan. 27, 1808, and studied at the University of Tübingen. After a short interval of teaching he went to Berlin (1831), where he was influenced by F. D. E. Schleiermacher and Hegel's followers. On his return to Tübingen he lectured for a time but soon found it necessary to give his whole energies to the preparation of the *Leben Jesu*. The work, published in 1835–36 (English translation, *Life of Jesus*, three volumes, 1846), produced an immense sensation since it applied the myth theory to the life of Jesus, denied the historicity of all supernatural elements in the Gospels, and interpreted the growth of primitive Christianity in Hegelian terms. In 1840–41 he published *Die christliche Glaubenslehre* (two volumes), the principle of which is that the history of Christian doctrines is their disintegration.

Strauss had been elected to a chair of theology in the University of Zürich, but so great was the hostility aroused by his *Leben Jesu* that the authorities pensioned him off before he was installed. With his *Glaubenslehre,* Strauss abandoned theology for 20 years, publishing during the period a series of biographical works that secured a permanent place for him in German literature. In 1864, however, he returned to theology with his *Leben Jesu für das deutsche Volk.* His *Der Christus des Glaubens und der Jesus der Geschichte* (1865) is a severe criticism of Schleiermacher's lectures on the life of Jesus. From 1865 to 1872 Strauss resided in Darmstadt, and in 1870 published his lectures on Voltaire. His last work, *Der alte und der neue Glaube* (1872; Eng. trans., *The Old Faith and the New,* 1873), caused some consternation among his friends; essentially it rejects Christianity in favour of scientific materialism, and like all his critical works it suffered from his lack of critical study of the texts. Strauss died on Feb. 8, 1874.

Strauss's works were published in a collected edition in 12 volumes by E. Zeller (1876–78) without his *Christliche Dogmatik.* His *Ausgewählte Briefe* appeared in 1895.

Bibliography.—E. Zeller, *David Friedrich Strauss in seinem Leben und seinen Schriften* (1874; Eng. trans., 1874); A. Hausrath, *D. F. Strauss und die Theologie seiner Zeit,* 2 vol. (1876–78); S. Eck, *D. F. Strauss* (1899); K. Harraeus, *D. F. Strauss, sein Leben und seine Schriften* (1901); T. Ziegler, *D. F. Strauss,* 2 vol. (1908–09); Albert Schweitzer, *The Quest of the Historical Jesus,* Eng. trans., pp. 68–120 (1910).

**STRAUSS, RICHARD GEORG** (1864–1949), German composer of orchestral works and operas illustrating the aesthetic of the Romantic movement at its final and farthest point of development, was born in Munich on June 11, 1864. His mother belonged to the Pschorr brewing family in Munich, and his father, Franz Joseph Strauss (1822–1905), was principal horn in the court orchestra there and the finest horn soloist in Germany. Strauss had his first piano lessons when he was four, and wrote his first composition, a Christmas carol, when he was six. He studied the violin from 1871 onward, and musical theory from 1875, but his formal education was a normal academic one, carried to university level with the study of philosophy, history, and aesthetics. He wrote music abundantly throughout his school years; the earliest of his works to be acknowledged was the orchestral *Festmarsch,* op. 1 (performed 1876). By 1880 his works were being performed in public, and before he graduated from Munich University a group of eight songs, op. 10, was published which include three—"Zueignung," "Die Nacht," "Allerseelen"—that were still favourites 80 years later.

After graduation Strauss spent some time in Berlin where he met Hans von Bülow. Having conducted Strauss's Wind Serenade, op. 7, Bülow asked him to compose a longer suite for the woodwind of the Meiningen Court Orchestra. This was included in the repertory of a tour by the orchestra, and Bülow invited Strauss to conduct the première of the work in Munich on Nov. 18, 1884. As a result of this debut, Bülow obtained for Strauss the post of assistant conductor at Meiningen. Here were laid the foundations of Strauss's secondary career, as an outstanding conductor, and at Meiningen, too, he was converted as a composer to the forward-looking ideals of Liszt and Wagner. When his stay at Meiningen ended in 1886 Strauss was appointed third conductor at the Munich Opera; his subordinate status irked him, but during this time he composed the symphonic poems *Aus Italien, Macbeth* (first version), and *Don Juan,* and began his first opera *Guntram.* He also met the singer Pauline de Ahna, whom he later married and with whom he often gave song recitals.

THE BETTMANN ARCHIVE

RICHARD STRAUSS, PHOTOGRAPHED IN 1949

From 1889 to 1894 he held the directorship of the Weimar Court Orchestra; the great success of *Don Juan* in 1889 was followed by *Tod und Verklärung* (1890), a revised *Macbeth* (1890), and, less successful, the Wagnerian *Guntram* (Weimar, 1894). Strauss then returned to a more senior post in Munich. The brilliant, uproarious *Till Eulenspiegel* (1895), *Also sprach Zarathustra* (1896), based on Nietzsche, and *Don Quixote* (1898), the finest and most elaborate of all these tone-poems, were all produced during this period. Strauss was now frustrated in Munich, and the fiasco of *Guntram* there turned him against his native city. As a result he wrote the satirical comic opera *Feuersnot* on a libretto by Ernst von Wolzogen, mocking small-town prudery and hypocrisy; its première (1901) was the first of many of his works introduced at Dresden. Fortunately Strauss, at the climax of his disenchantment with Munich, was appointed first conductor of the Prussian Royal Orchestra, and in 1898 moved to Berlin. There he spent fruitful years conducting concerts and opera, completing the autobiographical tone poems *Ein Heldenleben* (1899) and *Symphonia Domestica* (1904; a New York première during Strauss's tour of the U.S.), undertaking guest appearances in Germany and abroad, and establishing himself as Germany's foremost composer. The orchestral symphonic poems, completed with the *Alpine Symphony* (1915), proclaim an extraordinary mastery of the big post-Romantic symphony orchestra, an unrivaled descriptive power, and a remarkable ability to convey psychological detail in music. This last quality was particularly developed in his operas from *Salome* (Dresden, 1905; on the play by Oscar Wilde) onward.

**Collaboration with Hofmannsthal.**—*Elektra* (composed 1906–08) marked the beginning of a collaboration with Hugo von Hofmannsthal, which lasted until the poet's death in 1929, and produced many of Strauss's finest works. *Der Rosenkavalier* (Dresden, 1911), the second of their joint works, was the most successful of all Strauss's operas. *Ariadne auf Naxos,* at first designed to include a German adaptation of Molière's play *Le Bourgeois gentilhomme,* was produced in this form by Max Reinhardt (Stuttgart, 1912), and later revised as a self-sufficient opera with an explanatory prologue (Vienna, 1916). *Die Frau ohne Schatten* (Vienna, 1919), a symbolic fantasy on the relationship between the individual and society, is sometimes held to be their greatest joint work. *Die ägyptische Helena* (Dresden, 1928) is a fanciful drama on the subject of Menelaus and Helen on their return journey from Troy. Finally *Arabella* (Dresden, 1933), a Romantic comedy, was set in the Vienna of 1860. The libretto was completed shortly before Hofmannsthal's sudden death.

In 1908 Strauss settled at Garmisch-Partenkirchen in the Bavarian Alps, and was able to devote most of his time to composition. His other major works during the period of collaboration with Hofmannsthal are the ballet *Josephslegende* (scenario by Hofmannsthal and H. Kessler; Paris, 1914) for Diaghilev's Ballets Russes (Paris, 1914), the autobiographical comic opera *Intermezzo,* to his own libretto (Dresden, 1924), the entertaining ballet *Schlagobers* (Vienna, 1924), and a performing version of Mozart's *Idomeneo* (Vienna, 1930). In 1919 he accepted the post of musical director to the Vienna Opera, in collaboration with Franz Schalk, which he held until 1924, when difficulties caused by his frequent tours abroad forced his resignation. In recognition of his 60th birthday he was granted the freedom of the cities of Vienna and Munich, and given a villa in Vienna.

**Final Period.**—Hofmannsthal's death left Strauss in search of a librettist. Stefan Zweig provided him with an adaptation of Ben Jonson's *Epicoene,* produced at Dresden as *Die schweigsame Frau* (1935). But in Nazi Germany Zweig, a Jew, was unacceptable, and despite Strauss's protests of loyalty Zweig retired in favour of Joseph Gregor, who wrote (with much assistance from Zweig, and later from Clemens Krauss and others) the texts of three operas, *Friedenstag* (Munich, 1938), *Daphne* (Dresden, 1938), and *Die Liebe der Danae* (Salzburg, 1952). Strauss's position in Nazi Germany was ambivalent. He lacked political affiliations and interests to a point of naïveté. He disliked the philistine characteristics of Nazi officials, and made himself unpopular by his objections to government interference in artistic matters, especially when these concerned his own music.

Not wishing to leave home, he accepted Hitler's regime more or less passively. He served as president of the state music council (1933–35) and replaced Toscanini and Bruno Walter as conductor when they refused to work in Nazi Germany. After completing *Die Liebe der Danae* in 1940 he intended to retire from composition. But he wrote one more opera, *Capriccio* (Munich, 1942), based on an elegant Romantic discussion on the relationship between words and music in opera, the protagonists being Parisian characters of the period of Gluck. He himself wrote the libretto with Krauss and others. During his last years he found creative energy to return to orchestral music and to compose a series of cool, neoclassical works: a second horn concerto (1943), two works for wind band (1944, 1945), the sombre, meditative *Metamorphosen* for 23 solo strings (1946), the Oboe Concerto (1946), and Duet Concertino for clarinet and bassoon with strings (1948). His life's work was completed with the richly scored, poignantly retrospective *Vier letzte Lieder* ("Four Last Songs"; 1950) for soprano and orchestra.

During World War II Strauss had lived at home at Garmisch. After the war he lived in Switzerland. His health deteriorated but he was able to attend a Strauss festival in London in 1947. He returned to Germany for his 85th birthday celebrations, and in July 1949 he conducted an orchestra for the last time. After a heart attack, he died at Garmisch-Partenkirchen on Sept. 8, 1949.

Strauss was reared on the musical classics and on the early romantic composers up to the period of Schumann; so much may be gathered from his youthful works including the F minor symphony, op. 12, and the Violin Concerto, op. 8, the Horn Concerto no. 1, and the Violin Sonata, op. 18. He came under the influence of Berlioz, Liszt, and Wagner just when his technique and imagination were sharpened to make the most of their impact. From *Aus Italien* onward his style becomes recognizable as the big, bravura, flexible, post-Romantic panoply that dominated audiences and influenced composers as different as Bartók and Szymanowski. In *Elektra* Strauss occasionally broke the bounds of tonality, but this was to achieve special effects and not to establish a nontonal technique.

In *Der Rosenkavalier,* reflecting the outlook and the temper of 18th-century Vienna, Strauss regained his authentic manner. Thereafter he spent 38 years refining and polishing his style, writing often for small orchestras, partly out of practical considerations (to ensure, for instance, the audibility of sung words in the theatre), partly because large-scale Romantic textures were becoming less and less significant. In later years Strauss's style became more classical, in the Mozartian sense. In *Capriccio, Metamorphosen,* and the *Four Last Songs* he may be said to have achieved a perfect fusion of the Romantic German and the neoclassical manner. After *Elektra* his evolution as a composer was pursued in isolation and was hardly influenced by the course of music outside his own country.

BIBLIOGRAPHY.—Norman R. Del Mar, *Richard Strauss: a Critical Commentary on His Life and Works,* vol. i (1962); F. Trenner, *Richard Strauss Dokumente* (1954); Ernst Krause, *Richard Strauss: the Man and His Work,* Eng. trans. by John Coombs (1964); William Somervell Mann, *Richard Strauss: a Critical Study of the Operas* (1964).
(WI. S. M.)

**STRAVINSKY, IGOR FEDOROVICH** (1882– ), Russian-born composer, one of the most original, fertile, and influential figures in 20th-century music, was born at Oranienbaum, near St. Petersburg (now Leningrad), June 17 (N.S.; 5, O.S.), 1882. His father, Fedor (d. 1902), was a well-known operatic bass singer. Although Igor was not intended for a musical career, as a boy he was taught to play the piano and he frequented the opera and ballet performances at the Maryinsky Theatre. As a university student he read law but showed no special aptitude for his studies, having apparently made up his mind to devote himself to composition. When he was about 20 he consulted Rimski-Korsakov, who advised him not to enter an academy and agreed to give him private tuition himself.

For some years Stravinsky lived in St. Petersburg, where he married Catherine Nossenko in 1906; but the great success of *The Firebird,* his first commission for the Russian Ballet, led him to take his family to western Europe in 1910. The outbreak of World War I caught them in Switzerland; and the Russian Revolution of 1917 not only cut him off from his Russian property, but turned his temporary exile into a permanent one.

THE BETTMANN ARCHIVE

IGOR STRAVINSKY, INK DRAWING BY PICASSO, 1920

After the war he settled in France, becoming a French citizen in 1934. In 1939 his wife and mother died; and shortly after the outbreak of World War II he left France for the United States. In 1940 he married Vera de Bosset and settled in Hollywood; five years later he became a U.S. citizen. The disruptions of a long life, with two changes of nationality, are reflected in the quantity and varied style of his compositions.

Stravinsky's apprentice works, written under the supervision of Rimski-Korsakov, included a Symphony in E♭ (1905–07) and groups of songs. Shortly after Rimski-Korsakov's death in 1908, Stravinsky's *Scherzo Fantastique* and *Fireworks* were heard at an orchestral concert by Sergei Diaghilev, who was so favourably impressed that he asked him to write a ballet score for the 1910 season of the Russian Ballet. This was *The Firebird* (first performance, Paris, 1910), in which Stravinsky showed how fully he had assimilated the romantic idiom and orchestral palette of his master.

The success of *The Firebird* was so complete that he became known overnight as one of the most gifted of the younger composers, and Diaghilev was anxious to secure his continued cooperation. *Petrouchka* followed in 1911. The first performance of *The Rite of Spring* (Paris, May 29, 1913) caused a near-riot in the Théâtre des Champs-Elysées, but this, in the long run, did much to consolidate Stravinsky's growing reputation. The following year Diaghilev's company produced his first opera, *The Nightingale,* in Paris and London. The vocal score of *The Wedding,* a dance cantata based on Russian peasant wedding customs, was written during 1914–17, though it took another six years to discover the right instrumental formula.

World War I seriously disrupted the Russian Ballet's activities, and Stravinsky could no longer rely on it as a regular outlet for his new compositions. During these years of enforced exile he concentrated on chamber music of various kinds and produced two strikingly original stage works, *Reynard* (1915–16) and *The Soldier's Tale* (1918).

The compositions of his first maturity—from *The Rite of Spring* to the *Symphonies of Wind Instruments* (1920)—make use of a modal idiom based on Russian sources and are characterized by a highly sophisticated feeling for irregular metres and syncopation and by brilliant orchestral mastery. His postwar decision not to return to Russia led to a break in style. Diaghilev's request that he should adapt some music by Pergolesi for a *commedia dell'arte* ballet, *Pulcinella* (1919–20), helped him to review his attitude to the main European musical tradition, and the result was a series of works which seemed to be dominated by near-classical procedures. At the same time financial necessity forced him to develop a subsidiary career as pianist and conductor. The Concerto for piano and wind instruments (1923–24), *Capriccio* for solo piano and orchestra (1929), and the Concerto for two solo pianos (1934–35) were written to suit his ability as a solo pianist. The Violin Concerto (1931) was commissioned for Samuel Dushkin, the U.S. violinist, and Stravinsky conducted many performances of the work. Several ballet scores were written during this period: *Apollo Musagetes* (1928), the last ballet of his to be mounted by Diaghilev; *The Fairy's Kiss* (1928), after music by Tchaikovsky, and *Persephone* (1933–34), both commissioned by Ida Rubinstein for her ballet company; and *The Card Party* (1936), for the American Ballet. The two peaks of this early neoclassical period are the opera *Oedipus Rex* (1926–27), on a Latin libretto, and the *Symphony of Psalms* (1930) on extracts from the Vulgate.

The appearance of two important symphonies coincided with the beginning and end of World War II: the Symphony in C (1938–40) and the Symphony in Three Movements (1942–45). To the immediate postwar years belong the ballet *Orpheus* (1947), written for the Ballet Society of New York; the *Mass* (1944–48), and his only full-length opera, *The Rake's Progress* (1948–51), on a libretto by W. H. Auden.

Although the success of these works was not in dispute, Stravinsky seemed to feel that he had outgrown the particular neoclassical conventions in which he had been working for 30 years. He had recently met Robert Craft, a young conductor in New York; later he invited him to Hollywood, and in time Craft became invaluable to him as a musical assistant. Stravinsky welcomed the opportunity, afforded by Craft's interest in serial music, to familiarize himself with the compositions of Anton Webern and Arnold Schoenberg, and he became so interested in serialism that he gradually adopted it for his own purposes. (*See* DODECAPHONY.) His earliest serial essays, such as *In Memoriam Dylan Thomas* (1954), *Canticum Sacrum* (1955), and the ballet *Agon* (1953–57), all retained some kind of tonal framework: only with *Threni* (1957–58) and *Movements* (1958–59) did he become the complete serialist. The most ambitious work of this period is *The Flood* (1961–62); but this was written for television and makes a somewhat diffuse and patchy effect in the theatre or concert hall. More concentrated and more moving are the *Requiem Canticles* (1965–66), where each of the brief nine movements is carefully characterized and sharply differentiated.

Critics and the public have frequently been disconcerted by Stravinsky's various changes of style; but in the course of time, many idiosyncrasies that proved upsetting at a first hearing have fallen into proper perspective.

Stravinsky's literary works include an autobiography covering the first 52 years of his life, *Chronicle of My Life* (anon. Eng. trans., 1936); *Poetics of Music* (Eng. trans. by A. Knodel and I. Dahl, 1947); and five books in collaboration with Robert Craft: *Conversations* (1959), *Memories and Commentaries* (1960), *Expositions and Developments* (1962), *Dialogues and a Diary* (1963), and *Themes and Episodes* (1966).

*See* R. Vlad, *Stravinsky* (Eng. trans. by F. and A. Fuller 1960); Eric Walter White, *Stravinsky: the Composer and His Works* (1966). (E. W. WH.)

**STRAW,** the stalks of grasses, particularly of such cereal grasses as wheat, oats, rye, barley, and buckwheat. Used collectively, the term denotes such stalks in the aggregate after drying and threshing of the grain.

From ancient times man has used straw as litter and fodder for cattle, covering for floors, his own coarse bedding, and even clothing for his body. The thatched roof, still not without usefulness in some parts of the world, consists of straw laid down to a thickness of a foot or more and secured by strong cords, with the fibres running in the direction to be taken by rainwater.

Straw has its finer uses also, one of which is hat making. For this purpose cereals are specially grown and carefully selected for fine colour, lightness of weight, and toughness. Dunstable wheat straw provides an excellent plait that has long been important in English straw-hat manufacture. The middle part of the straw above the last joint is chosen and cut into ten-inch lengths that are split by machine into strips of required widths. One form of Dunstable plait is composed of 7 whole straws, while another consists of 14 split straws. Straw hats are also produced in the Orient. A justly famous hat-making plait is leghorn. A product of Tuscany in Italy, it is obtained from a special variety of wheat, *Triticum aestivum,* which is thickly sown and harvested before the grain is entirely ripe. The stalks are dried and sun bleached, and the upper part of the stalk down to the first joint is selected for making plaits. A finer, lighter, pearly-white straw is obtained from the lower part of the stalk from which the sheath is removed. Panama hats are not made from straw, but from the fibre of the *toquilla* leaf.

Straw, either in natural colouring or dyed in attractive hues, may be woven into matting for floor and furniture covering. Woven straw is also sometimes employed as a protective covering for fragile objects. One of the oldest and most attractive uses of straw is in basket making.

Chemically pulped straw is utilized in the manufacture of a coarse paper and a cardboard (strawboard) suited to the production of cheap paper boxes. Straw has also been used to fabricate adobe walls, where sun-baked brick made of clay is moistened and kneaded and combined with chopped straw. (E. L. Y.)

**STRAWBERRY,** well-known fruit plant with red fragrant, edible "fruit" (*see* below), of eight main species of the genus *Fragaria,* native to the temperate regions of the Northern Hemisphere and extending to Patagonia in the New World. In North America the meadow strawberry (*F. virginiana*) is native to the East and the beach strawberry (*F. chiloensis*) is found on the Pacific coast from Alaska down to the Andes of southern Chile. The woodland strawberry (*F. vesca*) is native to North and South America and Asia, where other species are found. In Europe the woodland strawberry is widely distributed, with the alpine strawberry (*F. vesca semperflorens*) being found at higher altitudes; there are two other less common species. All are very small fruited with fragrant but pippy berries.

JOHN MARKHAM

WOODLAND STRAWBERRY (FRAGARIA VESCA) IN FLOWER

**Plant Characteristics.**—The strawberry is a low-growing, herbaceous plant with a fibrous root system and a crown from which arise basal leaves. The leaves are compound, with three leaflets, sawtooth edged and hairy. The flowers, generally white, rarely reddish, are borne in small clusters on slender stalks that arise, like the surface-creeping stems (runners or stolons), from the axils of the leaves. As a plant ages, the root system becomes woody and the "mother" crown sends out runners that touch ground and root, thus enlarging the plant. Runner plants, removed and planted when their root system is sufficiently developed, are used to propagate named varieties.

**The Fruit and Its Composition.**—The strawberry fruit in the botanical sense is not a berry and is much more than a single fruit: it is the greatly enlarged stem end or receptacle, in which are partially embedded the many true fruits, or achenes (popularly called seeds). The achenes are dried ovaries containing the seeds.

Strawberries are 90% water by weight. One cupful of them yields 90 calories. They have more vitamin C than an equal quantity of lemons—a handful of fresh-picked strawberries supplies an adult man's entire day's need of vitamin C—and more vitamin A than the same weight of raisins.

**Cultivated Varieties.**—The cultivated, large-fruited strawberry originated in Europe in the 18th century. The woodland strawberry had long been cultivated in England, France, and Italy but no improvement in size and succulence occurred until species were introduced from the New World. Crosses of *F. chiloensis* and *F. virginiana* with *F. vesca* resulted in large-fruited types, an early one of which was the celebrated Ananassa strawberry raised in France probably from *F. virginiana* × *F. chiloensis.*

Most countries have their own varieties raised during the 19th century and often particularly suitable for the climate, day length, altitude, or type of production required. In Europe varieties are introduced from the horticultural institutes in England, Scotland, France, Germany, Holland, and elsewhere, and also by commercial firms. In the United States the Department of Agriculture frequently introduces new varieties, and in most states where the strawberry is an important crop some breeding work is undertaken. Field resistance to red core (red stele), a fungus disease, is an important advantage of some of the newer varieties, such as Stelemaster and Surecrop in the United States and Redgauntlet and Cambridge Vigour in Europe.

**Cultivation.**—The strawberry succeeds on a surprisingly wide range of soils and situations and, compared with other horticultural crops, has a low fertilizer requirement. Since it is susceptible to drought, it requires moisture-retaining soil or irrigation by furrow or sprinkler. Runner plants are planted in early autumn if a crop is required the next year. If planted in winter or spring, the plants are deblossomed to avoid a weakening crop the first year. Plants are usually retained for one to four years. Runners may be removed from the spaced plants, or a certain number may be allowed to form a matted row alongside the original parent plants. The spaced plants per acre varies from 7,000 to as many as 17,000.

J. HORACE MCFARLAND CO.

CULTIVATED VARIETY OF STRAWBERRY

In areas of north Europe and North America where severe winters are experienced, plants are put out in the spring and the established plantation protected during following winters by covering the rows with straw or mulches. Weeds, which have always been a problem in strawberry plantations, formerly required much hand labour. However, since World War II, herbicides (simazine, 2,4-D, chloroxuron) have been developed to control annual weeds. Chemicals can also be used for killing unwanted runner plants. The chief pathogens are root diseases, fruit rots, leaf blotches and mildews, virus diseases, and infestations from nematodes, leaf hoppers, and aphids.

The initiation of flowers and the production of runners is determined mainly by day length, probably through complex hormonal balance, but there are marked varietal differences. Most varieties produce flowers only in the spring and the fruit ripens about five weeks later. Some varieties produce further flowers and another crop later in the summer. True perpetual, everbearing, or remontant varieties produce flowers and fruit continuously from spring until frost, both on the parent plant and the runners of the same year. These varieties—including Progressive and Mastodon—are suitable for home cultivation.

Commercial production of strawberries is for immediate consumption, and for processing as frozen, canned, or preserved berries or as juice. In all countries, because of the perishable nature of the berries and the unlikelihood of mechanical picking, the strawberry is generally grown near centres of consumption or processing, and where sufficient labour is available. The berries are picked direct into small baskets, crated for market, or into trays for processing. Early crops can be produced under glass or plastic covering. Strawberries are very perishable and require cool (though not refrigerated), dry storage.

**Production.**—The United States produces over 250,000 metric tons annually, approximately equal to the entire production of western Europe. Winter and spring crops come from Florida and the Gulf and southeastern states. The main bulk of crops are grown in California with irrigation, but production is widespread near most consuming centres. Strawberries are grown in all European states, France, Italy, and the United Kingdom being the major producers. Production in Italy increased markedly after World War II mainly in the irrigated Po Valley. In England main production areas are in the southern and eastern counties, and in France in the Rhone Valley, in Brittany, and elsewhere. Bulgaria and Poland have increased production, mainly for export as processed pulp. There is a small production in southern and eastern Africa, where altitude provides sufficient winter chilling, in New Zealand, and in Victoria and New South Wales in Australia. Japan has increased production because of labour availability.

*See* Ministry of Agriculture [U.K.] *Bulletin 95, Strawberries* (1962); U.S. Department of Agriculture, *Farmers' Bulletins,* South Atlantic and Gulf Coast, *No. 1026* (1958), Eastern United States, *No. 1028* (1961). (H. M. H.)

**STREATHAM,** a residential and shopping district in Wandsworth, London, Eng. Streatham Common (67.75 ac.) rises to about 250 ft. (76 m.); there are several sports grounds in the area. Streatham Place, a house on the south side of Tooting Bec Common, pulled down in 1863, belonged to the brewer Henry Thrale (d. 1781). For many years Dr. Johnson (*see* JOHNSON, SAMUEL) spent long periods there; other notable visitors included Boswell, Fanny Burney, David Garrick, Sir Joshua Reynolds, and Edmund Burke.

**STREET, GEORGE EDMUND** (1824–1881), English architect noted for his many Gothic churches, was born at Woodford in Essex on June 20, 1824. He worked for five years with the architect Sir George Gilbert Scott in London and in 1849 began his own practice. In 1855 he published *The Brick and Marble Architecture of Northern Italy,* and in 1865 *The Gothic Architecture of Spain,* with beautiful drawings of his own.

Street's personal taste led him in most cases to select for his design the 13th-century Gothic of England or France. The majority of his buildings were for ecclesiastical uses, the chief being the convent of East Grinstead, the theological college at Cuddesden, and a large number of churches, such as St. Philip and St. James's at Oxford, St. John's at Torquay, All Saints' at Clifton, St. Saviour's at Eastbourne, St. Margaret's at Liverpool, and St. Mary Magdalene, Paddington. His largest works were the nave of Bristol Cathedral, the choir of the cathedral of Christ Church in Dublin, and the new courts of justice in London (not completed at the time of his death, on Dec. 18, 1881). Street was a friend of many of the pre-Raphaelite artists; he maintained an interest in various high church organizations within the Church of England, and was diocesan architect to Oxford, York, Winchester, and Ripon. He was professor of architecture at the Royal Academy, where he lectured on medieval architecture, and in 1881 he was elected president of the Royal Institute of British Architects. He was buried in the nave of Westminster Abbey.

**STREETCAR:** *see* ELECTRIC TRACTION.

**STREETER, BURNETT HILLMAN** (1874–1937), English theologian and biblical scholar, best remembered for his original contributions to knowledge of Gospel origins, was born Nov. 17, 1874, at Croydon. Most of his life was spent at Queen's College, Oxford, where he became chaplain in 1928 and provost in 1933. He was ordained in 1899, and for 15 years—from 1922 to 1937—was a member of the Archbishop's Commission on Doctrine in the Church of England. He wrote or contributed to a dozen volumes in the fields of philosophy of religion, comparative religion, and New Testament studies.

While Streeter regarded his work as primarily philosophical—the contemporary interpretation of religion—he is more widely known as a student of the New Testament. He contributed an important essay to the *Oxford Studies in the Synoptic Problem* (1911), but his most important work was *The Four Gospels: a Study of Origins* (1924). In this he originated a "four document hypothesis" (including a Proto-Luke) as a solution to the synoptic problem, and developed the theory of "local texts" in the manuscript transmission of the New Testament. (*See* GOSPELS: *The "Synoptic Problems."*) His section on the Caesarean text was very influential in subsequent studies in this field. This work was followed in 1929 by *The Primitive Church,* in which he argued that there were three (not one) systems of church government in the earliest Christian churches.

Streeter followed "the hue and cry after new discovery" into fields as diverse as *Foundations: a Statement of Christian Belief in Terms of Modern Thought, by Seven Oxford Men* (1912), *The Chained Library* (1931), *Reality: a New Correlation of Science and Religion* (1926), and *The Buddha and the Christ* (Bampton Lectures, 1932). He also was an enthusiastic follower of Frank Buchman and the Oxford Group. Streeter and his wife were killed in an airplane crash in Switzerland on Sept. 10, 1937.

(E. C. Co.)

**STRELTSY** (plural, from singular *strelets* "musketeer"), a Russian military corps that came into being in the middle of the 16th century and for about 100 years made up the bulk of the Russian Army. By the middle of the 17th century, the *streltsy* had developed into a hereditary military caste. In peacetime the Moscow *streltsy* provided the tsar's bodyguard and performed police and security duties. The municipal *streltsy* had a similar function in the border towns that they garrisoned. In the second half of the 17th century the government adopted a policy of substituting landholdings for the *streltsy's* payment in money and grain, and this was one of the causes of their discontent and consequent unreliability. The poorer *streltsy* more than once sided with the rioters or rebels whom they were supposed to quell. In spite of this, their number grew from about 40,000 in 1632 to 55,000 in 1681; 22,500 of them were stationed in Moscow. The *streltsy* lived in their own settlements (*slobody*) and were organized in regiments administered by the *streletski prikaz* ("office") in Moscow.

In 1682 the revolt of the *streltsy* against the family of Naryshkin (*q.v.*), which had been fomented by the rival family of Miloslavski, was skilfully exploited by the regent Sophia (*q.v.*) Alekseevna and by F. L. Shaklovity, whom Sophia had appointed chief of the *streletski prikaz* after the execution of the unreliable I. A. Khovanski. When in June 1698 the *streltsy* attempted to restore Sophia to power, they were defeated by Tsar Peter I's foreign mercenaries under Gen. Patrick Gordon (*q.v.*), while Peter himself was abroad (*see* PETER I the Great). Returning to Moscow early in September, Peter dealt ruthlessly with the *streltsy:* in the following six weeks 799 were either broken on the wheel or impaled, while 222 were deported. Though in 1702, in the first period of the Northern War, Peter saw fit to revive the *streltsy*, the Moscow *streltsy* were finally disbanded in 1713. (L. R. LR.)

**STREPSIPTERA,** an order of uncommon, usually minute insects, ordinarily referred to as stylops (after the name of a well-known genus), that are parasitic on other insects, especially wasps, ants, wild bees, and leafhoppers. The order contains six families and approximately 400 described species from various parts of the world. Some authorities regard these insects as constituting a peculiar and highly specialized family of beetles (*see* BEETLE: *Meloidea*).

They exhibit three principal sorts of parasitism. The basic type occurs in the genus *Mengenilla,* whose members, as larvae, attack young silverfish and later emerge from them as adults. The mature females are wingless, but the males have large, fanlike hindwings (folded at rest); short, clublike forewings; bulging eyes; and comblike antennae.

A more common and advanced type is exemplified by the genus *Stylops,* which parasitizes wild bees of the genus *Andrena.* Active young *Stylops,* bristly and long legged, are picked up from flowers by female *Andrena,* who transport them to their nests. Here, the *Stylops* penetrates the bee larva and becomes a sedentary saclike endoparasite. If the parasite is a female, it remains permanently in the host, but the head of the parasite protrudes from the bee's abdomen at maturity. The male comes out of the host as a winged adult and must locate and fertilize the female in situ through an opening behind her head. The *Stylops* young develop by the thousands inside the bee and emerge through the opening behind the mother's head. The cycle is completed when the larvae are carried to flowers by the bee. This mode of parasitism is so delicately adjusted that the host lives nearly a full life span; however, its reproductive organs do not develop.

A third type of parasitism is represented by the genus *Myrmecolax,* in which young destined to be males develop within ants, and those that will become females develop in katydids and related forms. In these cases, the females are permanently endoparasitic and may attain a length of nearly 1 in.; males of the same species are a conventional $\frac{3}{16}$ in. long.

*See* also INSECT: *Strepsiptera* (*Twisted-Wing Insects*). (R. M. Bo.)

**STRESA,** a town of Piedmont, Italy, in Novara Province, 673 ft. (205 m.) above sea level, lies on the west side of Lake Maggiore, 4½ mi. (7 km.) S of Verbania by water. Pop. (1961) 5,169. It is a health and tourist resort, and is frequently chosen as the site of congresses. A conference between Italy, Great Britain and France on European peace, called in an unsuccessful attempt to deal with Hitler's announcement that Germany would rearm despite the prohibitions contained in the Treaty of Versailles, was held there in 1935. Antonio Rosmini-Serbati, founder of the Institute of Charity, died in Stresa in 1855.

**STRESEMANN, GUSTAV** (1878–1929), German parliamentarian and statesman, chancellor of the *Reich* for a short time in 1923 and subsequently, as foreign minister from 1923 to 1929, the principal restorer of his country's international status after the Treaty of Versailles. He was born in Berlin on May 10, 1878, the son of an innkeeper with a small trade in bottled beer, and was the only one of the family to attend high school. Reading literature and history at Berlin University, he developed a strong interest in Goethe and in Napoleon; but his practical bent soon led him to study economics under Karl Bücher at Leipzig. He graduated as doctor of philosophy in 1902, with a dissertation on the development of the Berlin bottled-beer trade. A liberal Protestant of the Prussian sort, he grew up to believe in the military, political, spiritual, and moral superiority of Germany. His political idealism showed itself in a sentimental affection for the German Liberals of 1848 (*see* GERMANY: *History*) and in a romantically appealing turn of speech. An air of youthful carelessness distinguished his oratory even in later years.

RADIO TIMES HULTON PICTURE LIBRARY

STRESEMANN

**Political Beginnings.**—Unusually rapid success in commerce gave Stresemann a springboard for entry into politics. As assistant to the executive of the German Chocolatemakers' Union in Dresden (1901–04), he won a reputation as a brilliant organizer and as a clever businessman; and from 1902 to 1911 he was legal adviser to the Saxon Industrialists' Union, founded by himself. After an early inclination to the politico-social ideas of Friedrich Naumann (1860–1919) and collaboration with the latter's National Social Union (founded in 1896), he joined the National Liberal Party in 1903. His wife, whom he married in 1903, was a daughter of the Berlin industrialist Adolf Kreefeld. Of Jewish extraction, she was later to play a leading role in Berlin society under the Weimar Republic. She bore him two sons.

As editor of the Dresden paper *Sächsische Industrie* and as a Dresden city councilor (1906–12), Stresemann became thoroughly versed in commercial and municipal affairs. He was elected to the *Reichstag* as deputy for Annaberg from 1907 to 1912 and for Aurich from 1914 to 1918. His advocacy of the interests of middle-class tradespeople and his demand for further social legislation seemed too far-reaching to the powerful representatives of heavy industry on the right wing of his party. The consequent antagonism to him prevented his reelection to the presidium of the party in 1912; nor was he returned to the *Reichstag* by the elections of that year. Disappointed, he devoted his leisure to travel and study in the United States.

A member of the board of the Hansabund (from 1911), deputy chairman of his own Saxon Industrialists' Union (1911–18), executive member of the board of the German-American Commercial Union (1914–23), and chairman of the German Tea Industry's Union (1915–23), Stresemann ranked as one of the foremost figures in those great German business consortia which strove to influence politics. His financial independence, his acknowledged talent for organization, his skill at handling men, and his pronounced self-confidence paved the way for a brilliant political future. An active member of the Kolonialverein (under Pan-German inspiration) and a champion of Germany's naval program, he was an uncritical supporter of the *Weltpolitik* ("world policy") of William II's *Reich.*

**World War I.**—In World War I, Stresemann came forward as one of the most passionately vociferous exponents of Pan-Germanism and as a spokesman for extensive annexations of Polish, Russian, French, and Belgian territory. He made no secret of his hatred of the nations ranged against Germany. Over the National Liberals in the Reichstag he won ever-increasing influence as the closest collaborator of their leader, Ernst Bassermann (1854–1917). When Bassermann died, in July 1917, Stresemann succeeded to the leadership of the National Liberal group in the Reichstag, but leadership of the party as a whole passed to Robert Friedberg. In November, however, Friedberg was appointed vice-premier of Prussia, and Stresemann then succeeded to the party leadership also. Meanwhile, he had also been cooperating closely with the Supreme Command of the Army (Erich Ludendorff); and his ardent admiration for the navy had led him to call for unrestricted U-boat warfare. Likewise, as the parliamentary mouthpiece of the Supreme Command, Stresemann had struggled against the temperate policy of the chancellor, Theobald von Bethmann Hollweg (*q.v.*). The chancellor's downfall, in July 1917, was very largely brought about by Stresemann, in concert with Matthias Erzberger (*q.v.*); but Stresemann was unsuccessful in his plan to bring Bernhard von Bülow (*q.v.*) back to power. For a time Stresemann belonged to the Intergroup Committee (*Interfraktioneller Ausschuss*) in the Reichstag. This comprised prominent deputies of the Progressive, Centre, Social Democratic, and National Liberal parties who advocated a negotiated end to the war in accordance with the Peace Resolution voted by the majority of the Reichstag on July 19, 1917.

Notwithstanding the lack of unanimity among the National Liberals on the question of the Prussian *Dreiklassenwahlrecht* (whereby the voters in elections to the Prussian House of Deputies were divided into three classes according to the amounts paid in direct taxation) and the differences between the National Liberal group in the Reichstag and that in the Prussian *Landtag,* which stood farther to the right, Stresemann contrived to hold his party together. He declared himself in favour of abolishing the controversial *Dreiklassenwahlrecht,* hoping that the introduction of equal rights of voting would serve to strengthen the monarchy.

Up to the autumn of 1918, with most other German parliamentarians, Stresemann let himself be deceived about the seriousness of his country's military situation. While he had tacitly to renounce his former insistence on Germany's original war aims, he then brought his party to support the introduction of the parliamentary system with ministerial responsibility (*see* GERMANY: *History*). The "October Constitution" of 1918 corresponded to his ideas.

**The First Postwar Years.**—After the collapse of the imperial regime (November 1918), the versatile Stresemann accommodated himself soberly to the facts of a republican Germany. He remained active in politics. In December 1918, since the new German Democratic Party (led by Friedrich Naumann and Max Weber) did not want to receive into its ranks so well-known an annexationist and Pan-German as Stresemann, he took elements from the right wing of the National Liberals to form the German People's Party, a middle-class organization inclining still more to the right. In 1919 he was a member of the National Assembly, at Weimar, for the framing of a new constitution; and from 1920 onward he was a deputy in the new Reichstag. A convinced monarchist, hostile to the democracy of Weimar and to the Treaty of Versailles, Stresemann naturally disliked the republican constitution, to which he gave his assent only after an interval. The period from 1919 to 1923, which he spent mainly in opposition as a spokesman of nationalist opinion, was for him a time of preparation for greater tasks. During this period his German People's Party showed itself ready to enter into coalitions with the democratic parties; but at the time of Wolfgang Kapp's attempt to overthrow the regime (March 1920) Stresemann's attitude was highly ambiguous.

**Chancellorship.**—On Aug. 13, 1923, Stresemann became chancellor of the Reich at the head of a government of the "Great Coalition," comprising representatives of the Social Democrats, of the Centre, and of the German Democrats as well as of his People's Party. Whereas the crisis over the Ruhr (*q.v.*), with the "passive resistance" of the German population to the occupying forces of the Allies, had grown worse and worse under his predecessor Wilhelm Cuno and was precipitating the collapse of Germany's finances through inflation, Stresemann could read the situation correctly and brought the conflict to an end. For this decision he was vehemently attacked by the German National People's Party, which stood for the extremists of the right.

Communist attempts at insurrection in Saxony and in Thuringia were put down by Stresemann's dispatch of troops of the Reichswehr (national forces) into those states in October. In Bavaria, where the local commander of the Reichswehr, Gen. Otto von Lossow, aligned himself with the dissident government of the monarchist Gustav von Kahr, the authority of Stresemann's government was restored after the failure of Adolf Hitler's *Putsch* of Nov. 8–9. In the Rhineland and in the Palatinate, however, separatist movements received the backing of the French authorities and were more difficult for the government of the Reich to suppress. Meanwhile, with the Rentenmark, Stresemann's finance minister Hans Luther achieved a stabilization of the currency, an essential preliminary to the political rehabilitation of Germany.

When the Social Democrats, to the bitter distress of Pres. Friedrich Ebert, frivolously withdrew from the government, Stresemann on Nov. 23 was obliged to resign.

**Foreign Ministry.**—The next chancellor, Wilhelm Marx, a member of the Centre Party, took Stresemann as his foreign minister; and Stresemann remained in charge of foreign affairs under the successive chancellorships of Hans Luther, Wilhelm Marx again, and Hermann Müller, with their various coalition governments. Under his guidance Germany reached an understanding with the Western Powers by fulfilling to a considerable extent the obligations of the Versailles Treaty and by obtaining a reduction of its terms through negotiations. The beginning of reconciliation between Germany and France was especially notable, as Aristide Briand (*q.v.*) worked to the same purpose as Stresemann: the two statesmen shared the Nobel Peace Prize in 1926.

Stresemann was primarily concerned to solve the problem of reparations (*q.v.*) and to obtain security for Germany against any new application of sanctions like the French invasion of the Ruhr in January 1923. For him a general consolidation of the peace was a necessary preliminary to the restoration of Germany as a European Power. His immediate aim was to advance the eastern frontier at Poland's expense and to unite Germany and Austria; and his pursuit of this aim involved vigorous support of German minorities abroad. He saw clearly how Germany's central position in Europe furnished the possibility of alliance with the Western Powers or with the U.S.S.R.; and his realistic assessment of the international situation enabled him to exploit Anglo-French tensions in his diplomacy. He favoured the expansion of the Reichswehr beyond the numerical limits stipulated by the Versailles Treaty, as well as its clandestine rearmament and its development with Soviet help. In his efforts toward a rapprochement with the Western Powers he had the sympathetic collaboration of the British ambassador in Berlin, Lord D'Abernon.

Stresemann's success can be marked out in stages. In 1924 the Dawes Plan was signed, reorganizing the system of reparations on the basis of Germany's ability to pay. In 1925 the Pact of Locarno (*q.v.*) declared Germany's western frontier, as established in 1919, to be inviolable, under British and Italian as well as French and Belgian guarantee; provided for arbitration on matters in dispute; and gave assurances against further application of sanctions. The evacuation of the first zone of the Rhineland (*q.v.*) by the Allies ensued. In 1926 Germany was admitted to the League of Nations, and the Treaty of Berlin, between Germany and the U.S.S.R., strengthened the relationship which the Treaty of Rapallo had inaugurated. In 1927 the Inter-Allied Military Commission was recalled from Germany. In 1928 Germany subscribed to the Kellogg Pact (*q.v.*) renouncing war. Finally Stresemann procured a further revision of the system of reparations—which the Young Plan brought into effect, together with the evacuation of the Rhineland in advance of schedule, after his death.

Stresemann had to surmount formidable difficulties, including resistances in Germany itself. His last meeting with Briand, at Thoiry on Sept. 17, 1926, gave rise to exaggerated hopes, but thereafter Franco-German reconciliation came to a standstill. Neither Germany nor France was ready for a cleansing of their relationship. Even so, Stresemann was enthusiastic over Briand's plan of 1929 for a united Europe, supporting it with economic arguments.

Stresemann's prestige brought a certain stability to the internal politics of the Weimar Republic. He had to pay heavily for his success, however. In order to get the requisite parliamentary approval for his policy he had to make continual appearances in the *Reichstag,* apart from the burden of public speaking and writing articles for the press. While the parties of the "Weimar Coalition" (Social Democrats, German Democrats, and Centre) generally supported him, it was often very difficult for him to rally his own party's right wing, which was dominated by the leaders of heavy industry, to his cause. In 1924 disapproval of his policy prompted some deputies to secede from his parliamentary group and to form their own National Liberal Union. As a former Pan-German, Stresemann was constantly on the defensive against the extreme nationalists. To a large extent, moreover, opposition to him within his own party was an aspect of the struggle against the republic, of which he had paradoxically become the guardian and the symbol even though he was at heart a monarchist. He was more popular abroad than in his own country. He died suddenly in Berlin on Oct. 3, 1929.

Scarcely any other political figure typifies so aptly as Stresemann does the transition from monarchy to republicanism in Germany. Imbued with the traditions of the imperial regime and conditioned by National Liberalism, he had developed into a successful parliamentarian. Yet for all his efforts he failed in the task allotted to him in internal politics: that of converting the Liberals of the right—first and foremost the German People's Party—to the ideas of Weimar. Immediately after his death his party fell to pieces: its sponsors among the electorate turned to the German National Party and to the National Socialists. Stresemann's diplomatic talents and his success in foreign affairs are incontestable. As the exponent of "national realism" (*nationale Realpolitik*) against the "pacifist policy of renunciation," he worked consistently for the restoration of the *Reich* as a great power. His conception of the national state, one aspect of which (the incorporation of Austria) was unmistakably inspired by "Great German" ideology, reveals the limitations of his political thinking. It is quite unjustifiable to claim him as a precursor of any movement for European integration. He relied on further successes for the policy of peaceful revisionism which he had so promisingly inaugurated.

Stresemann is sometimes judged in a controversial way. After the enforced silence about him during the National Socialist period, a Stresemann revival set in from 1945, at first in propaganda, then in scholarly writing too, glorifying his foreign policy in terms of the later Pan-European idea. About 1950 with the opening-up of his voluminous papers, a one-sided portrait evolved of a nationalist politician cleverly pursuing his ambitious purposes under cover of slogans such as "League of Nations," "spirit of Locarno," "equality of rights." Later German research into his life and work show him as a master of politics who transcended his origins with extraordinary results. His published writings, catalogued by G. Zwoch, *Stresemann–Bibliographie* (1953), include *Macht und Freiheit* (1918), *Von der Revolution bis zum Frieden von Versailles* (1919), *Reden und Schriften,* 2 vol. (1926), and *Vermächtnis,* 3 vol. (1932–33).

Bibliography.—W. Görlitz, *Stresemann* (1948); H. Bretton, *Stresemann and the Revision of Versailles* (1953); H. W. Gatzke, *Stresemann and the Rearmament of Germany* (1954) and "Gustav Stresemann: a Bibliographical Article" in *The Journal of Modern History,* 36 (1964); F. Hirsch, *Gustav Stresemann* (1964); M. L. Edwards, *Stresemann and the Greater Germany 1914–1918* (1963); H. A. Turner, *Stresemann and the Politics of the Weimar Republic* (1963); L. Zimmermann, *Studien zur Geschichte der Weimarer Republik* (1956) and *Deutsche Aussenpolitik in der Ära der Weimarer Republik* (1958); M. Göhring, *Stresemann* (1956); A. Thimme, *Gustav Stresemann* (1957). (R. Mo.)

**STRETFORD,** a municipal (1933) and parliamentary borough of Lancashire, Eng., adjoining Salford and Manchester to the northeast. Pop. (1969 est.) 58,820. Area 5.5 sq.mi. (14.2 sq.km.). It contains a considerable part of the Trafford Park industrial estate, between the Bridgewater Canal and the Manchester Ship Canal (*see* Manchester). Old Trafford, the Lancashire County Cricket Club's ground, is in the town. Longford Hall houses the town's art collection and Longford Park is the biggest of Stretford's five parks. There is a civic theatre. The two manors of Stretford and Trafford have, since about 1260, descended in the family of de Trafford. The name of the town is a reference to the crossing of a ford by the Roman road (*strata*) from Chester to Manchester.

**STREUVELS, STIJN** (pseudonym of Frank Lateur) (1871–1969), whose novels and short stories are among the masterpieces of modern Flemish prose, was born at Heule, near Kortrijk, on Oct. 3, 1871. The nephew of the priest and poet Guido Gezelle (*q.v.*), he discovered his literary gifts while at school at Avelgem. He became a master baker there but found time to learn German, English, Danish, and some Russian and, after 1892, to write his first stories, stimulated by his reading of some French realistic stories and the revelation he found in Impressionist painting. He contributed to the periodical *Van Nu en Straks* (*see* Belgian Literature: *Flemish*) and, in 1899, achieved fame with his first collection of short stories, *Lenteleven* (*The Path of Life,* 1915). Deciding to devote himself to writing, in 1905 he settled in Ingooigem, a village near Kortrijk, where he spent the rest of his life. He died there on Aug. 15, 1969.

Streuvels finds his subjects in the village life of southwest Flanders between Scheldt and Lys—an isolated and agrarian Flanders that no longer exists—defining his chosen locality by precise reference to dialect and folklore. But he is no mere chronicler. His keen observation is enlarged and enriched by his imaginative power, his feeling for atmosphere, and his wealth of language. He creates a world of his own, at once elemental and true to life. In this world, nature is an ever-present force—a nature described with a visionary power resembling that of Van Gogh. Although his descriptions are often long, they are never irrelevant to his theme, for his characters are closely bound to the land (*e.g.,* in *Langs de Wegen,* 1902, Eng. trans. *Old Jan,* 1936; *Minnehandel,* 1903; *De Vlaschaard,* 1907). In his later works, where he deals with the conflict between nature and civilization, and with moral, religious, and social problems, he is less successful (*De teleurgang van den Waterhoek,* 1927; *Alma,* 1931; *Levensbloesem,* 1938). At his best he is a master of characterization, especially in his presentation of farmers and farm workers, who struggle against the land and against destiny (this is most clearly seen in *De Vlaschaard,* his masterpiece, and in *Het leven en de dood in den ast,* 1926), and of children, whose innocence introduces a note of tenderness into his cosmic and visionary view of life (*e.g.,* in "Lente," in *Lenteleven; Het Kerstekind,* 1911; and *Prutske,* 1922). His epic-lyrical prose style, perfectly suited to his subject, is among the best of its period.

Bibliography.—Streuvels' collected works appeared in 12 vol. (1957). For biography and criticism, *see* F. de Pillecijn, *S. Streuvels en zijn werk,* 2nd ed. (1943) and *S. Streuvels* (1958); E. Janssen, *S. Streuvels en zijn Vlaschaard* (1946); A. Demedts, *Streuvels* (1955); R. van de Linde, *Het oeuvre van Streuvels* (1958); G. Knuvelder, *S. Streuvels* (1964). (R. F. Ls.)

**STRICKLAND, WILLIAM** (1787–1854), U.S. architect and engineer, designed several public buildings and Washington's marble sarcophagus at Mount Vernon. Born in Philadelphia, Pa., in 1787, he first became known as an artist, although he studied architecture under Benjamin Latrobe. In 1810, however, he designed the Masonic Hall in Philadelphia and was thus well launched as an architect. Although the hall was Gothic in design, Strickland later turned to the neoclassical style, and his next important work, the United States Bank in Philadelphia, took the Parthenon for its inspiration. Strickland also designed the Merchants' Exchange building, the United States Naval Asylum, the United States Mint, and the United States Custom House, all in Philadelphia.

His engineering projects were nearly as well known as his architectural. In 1825 he was sent to Europe to study internal improvements and on his return did much to encourage the construction of the original line of the Pennsylvania Railroad Company, one of the first designed to carry passengers in the United States. He also constructed the Delaware Breakwater, a commission he received from the U.S. government. At the time of his death he was in Nashville, Tenn., superintending the construction of the state house, which he designed and which is regarded by many as his best work. He died in that city April 7, 1854, and by a special act of the state legislature was buried in the building.

He was the author of several technical publications relating to engineering and architectural projects which he headed.

**STRIGGIO, ALESSANDRO,** the Elder (*c.* 1535–1587), Italian composer and instrumentalist, one of the native masters who carried the Italian madrigal to its final perfection, was born in Mantua about 1535, of noble parentage. Apart from a stay in Florence (*c.* 1560–70) and a journey to England (1567), he spent his life in Mantua, where he died probably on Sept. 22, 1587. Striggio's fame lies in his seven collections of madrigals (1560–97) and his quasi-dramatic pieces, one of which depicts women chattering on washday. He was a brilliant violist, lutenist, and organist, and some of his *intermedi* and one of his few motets are early examples of Renaissance instrumentation.

*See* A. Einstein, *The Italian Madrigal* (1949). (B. L. Tr.)

**STRIJDOM** (Strydom), **JOHANNES GERHARDUS** (1893–1958), South African statesman and extreme advocate of the policy of apartheid (*q.v.*), was prime minister of the Union of South Africa from 1954 to 1958. Born at Willowmore, Cape Colony, on July 14, 1893, he was educated at Victoria College, Stellenbosch, and afterward joined his father, P. G. Strijdom, on his ostrich farm in the Willowmore district. He moved in 1914 to Pretoria, where he entered the public service and in 1917 qualified in law at Pretoria University. He set up as an attorney at Nylstroom, Transvaal, in 1918, and soon became active in the Nationalist Party. In 1929 he was elected member of parliament for Waterberg, Transvaal, a seat he held until his death.

Strijdom first became a national figure in 1934, when J. B. M. Hertzog, leader of the Nationalist Party, and J. C. Smuts, leader of the South African Party, joined forces to form the United Party, and Strijdom was the only Transvaal Nationalist member of Parliament to refuse to follow Hertzog. He afterward became the Transvaal leader of D. F. Malan's new Nationalist Party and was most energetic in building it up. When the Nationalists won the 1948 election, Strijdom became minister of lands and irrigation in Malan's Cabinet, where he devoted himself to maintaining white supremacy in South Africa. On the retirement of Malan in November 1954 he was elected leader by the parliamentary caucus of the Nationalist Party, in preference to Malan's candidate, N. C. Havenga, and became prime minister on Dec. 3, 1954. His succession marked the ascendancy of the extreme Transvaal wing of the party over the more moderate Cape wing.

Strijdom's government pushed vigorously ahead with apartheid, radically changed the composition of the Senate in 1955, and by thus gaining the necessary two-thirds majority in a joint sitting of both houses of Parliament, in 1956 placed the Cape Coloured voters on a separate electoral roll. Strijdom fell ill in December 1957 and died in Cape Town on Aug. 24, 1958. (L. M. T.)

**STRIKES AND LOCKOUTS.** Strikes (often called turnouts or sticks in the early 19th century) are concerted refusals by employees to work under the conditions required by employers. Lockouts, strictly speaking, are occasions on which employers close their establishments against their employees until they accept the terms offered them; but the word lockout is often used, especially by workers, to cover occasions on which the employer attempts to worsen the terms of employment and the workers abstain from work in protest. Lockouts in the strict sense became uncommon in the first half of the 20th century; in earlier years they occurred when an employer or group of employers was attempting to ban union membership and refused employment to workers who would not sign a pledge not to belong to a trade union. Later they arose most often when a body of employers retaliated against a strike at a particular works by closing all factories until the strikers returned to work. When the word lockout is used in its wider sense the distinction between it and a strike is often hard to draw, and workers will describe as a lockout what the employers call a strike. Statistically, no separation can be made, and strikes and lockouts are lumped together under the heading of work stoppages, or labour disputes.

Of the various types of strikes and lockouts, the simplest is the dispute about wages or conditions of employment, or about some special issue of discipline or labour union practice, when the strikers (or lockers-out) are the parties directly involved. Sympathetic strikes or lockouts are those in which persons or associations not directly involved in the original dispute go on strike or close their establishments in sympathy with one of the original parties. A jurisdictional strike is a dispute between two unions, both of which claim that certain work is within their exclusive jurisdiction. General strikes may be either very extensive sympathetic strikes or work stoppages over a wide range of industries for a common object. The political general strike belongs to the latter type: it can be either a mere protest strike, called for a single day or for a limited period, or a strike designed to last until it has achieved its purpose or failed, as in the German general strike against the Kapp *Putsch* of 1920. The British general strike of 1926 was simply an extended sympathetic strike in support of the Miners' federation, whereas the threatened strike of 1920 against British participation in the Soviet-Polish war belonged to the same class as the strike against the Kapp *Putsch*. A special variety of strike, which may belong to any of the foregoing categories, is the sit-down or stay-in strike (stay-down, in mining) in which the strikers occupy their places of employment and either do no work or attempt to carry on production on their own account (as in the Italian stay-in strikes after World War I). The stay-in strike was extensively used in France in the 1930s at the time of the popular front and is also a familiar technique among native workers in colonial areas. It was introduced into the United States in the 1930s.

The general strike as actually practised has to be distinguished from the general strike as aspiration—sometimes called the social general strike—which is a mass strike of workers designed to bring about a social revolution and the establishment of a workers' society. Its earliest advocates were the anarchist-communists (*see* A. Roller, *The Social General Strike,* 1905); and the idea was taken up by the French syndicalists. It was Georges Sorel, author of *Reflections on Violence* and other books of syndicalist theory, who introduced the idea of the general strike as a "social myth," inspiring working-class revolutionary feeling and giving a heightened meaning to ordinary strike action, even if in practice it never occurred. The French syndicalists also introduced the conception of *la grève perlée* (sometimes anglicized as "the strike with knobs on") by way of contrast with *la grève aux bras croisés* ("the strike with folded arms"), the former being accompanied by acts of sabotage or violence.

Strikes may be either spontaneous or organized. A great many strikes have begun as spontaneous reactions by a group of workers to a particular grievance, such as the dismissal of a fellow-worker whose "victimization" for union activity was suspected, or the employment of unskilled workers on jobs normally reserved for skilled workers, or the cutting of a piecework rate, or any of a hundred other things. Such sudden strikes may become organized subsequently, if a union takes them up, or sometimes if the strikers choose leaders of their own. Strikes may also be either official or unofficial: they are official when they are called or approved by a labour union, which takes control of the proceedings and of any negotiations designed to settle them; unofficial (wildcat) strikes are either strikes apart from unions, or strikes called by union branches or districts without the support of the union as a whole in accordance with its rules. Since, in many countries, organized national collective bargaining has been introduced into most industries and collective agreements have laid down procedures to be gone through before an official strike can be called, an increasing proportion of all strikes tends to be unofficial—for example, a group of workers, tired of waiting to have its grievance dealt with by dilatory negotiating procedures, strikes contrary to the provisions of a national or other collective agreement. The proportion of unofficial strikes is also increased when laws have been passed either forbidding strikes or imposing a compulsory period of delay for investigation before they can be lawfully called (the Lemieux system, used in Canada, and called after its proposer, Rodolphe Lemieux). Groups of workers will often dare to strike "against the law" when unions, fearful of having their funds attacked or their recognition by the state suspended or removed, hesitate to endorse a strike and so make it official. *See* further LABOUR LAW; GENERAL STRIKE. (G. D. H. C.)

**UNITED STATES STRIKES**

Even before the American Revolution a few strikes occurred in the American colonies. During the early years of the republic most labour disputes were on a small scale for higher wages or the ten-hour day. To maintain their standards of living during periods when the cost of living was on the increase, workers organized unions to gain financial and moral support in their struggles for higher wages. While prosperity continued, the workers' demands tended to be granted, but the financial panic of 1837, with its consequent unemployment, meant defeat for the trade unions on the economic front.

After the Civil War, unionism took on a national character. The first strike of nation-wide extent was on the Pennsylvania and the Baltimore and Ohio railroads in 1877, at the depth of a prolonged depression. The Pittsburgh freight yards of the Pennsylvania railroad were burned and looted. State troopers brought in from Philadelphia because of the inaction of local authorities and the unreliability of local state troopers were forced to surrender. The strike, which many feared might be the U.S. counterpart of the Paris Commune, was quelled by the dispatch of units of the U.S. army.

On May 1, 1886, approximately 340,000 workers went on strike in response to a call by the national trade union federation, which became the American Federation of Labor in 1886, to secure the eight-hour day. Explosion of a bomb in Haymarket square in Chicago, Ill., on May 4, 1886, supposedly by anarchists, and the consequent public clamour against radicalism and unionism was blamed by Samuel Gompers for seriously hurting the eight-hour-day movement. A revival of the demand for an eight-hour day occurred in 1890, when carpenters struck throughout the nation and were generally successful in achieving their objective.

Skilled organized workers at the Homestead, Pa., plant of the Carnegie Steel Co. in July 1892 refused to accept a wage reduction, and in the process gained the support of the unorganized workers. Thereupon Henry C. Frick, general manager of the company, shut down the entire plant and refused to negotiate any further with the Amalgamated Association of Iron, Steel and Tin Workers, until then the strongest union in the world. As the strike issue settled down to one of continued union recognition, Frick imported strikebreakers and armed guards. In the clash which ensued between the guards and strikers, several were killed on both sides. The strike ended in U.S. unionism's most decisive defeat. Organized labour's defeat in the American Railway union strike, or the so-called Pullman company boycott of 1894 was of another order. The union, young and weak, instituted a sympathetic strike to assist the Pullman local's resistance to a 25% wage cut. Violence and mass destruction of property occurred, centring in the Chicago yards. The railroad asked for federal intervention, and 2,000 federal troops were sent to Chicago. However, the strike was really broken by the issuance of injunctions in the federal courts secured at the insistence of the U.S. attorney general on the basis of the Sherman Anti-trust law as one of the grounds.

The successful strike of the bituminous coal miners in 1897 resulted in establishment of an agreement for the so-called central competitive field, with Illinois as the union's stronghold for decades thereafter. The collective agreement, after an apparently hopeless strike begun with an empty union treasury, founded an "industrial government" based on reciprocal rights and obligations of both parties and pointed the way in all of the coal industry and other industries as well. In 1902, 150,000 anthracite miners struck to achieve a reduction of hours, an increase in wages and recognition of their union. Violence occurred in areas where strikebreakers were hired to mine coal. To preserve order the national guard was sent to certain cities. As winter came, the situation grew worse, and Pres. Theodore Roosevelt intervened and arranged for arbitration. The miners won a 10% increase in wages and a shorter working day, but their union was not recognized. The outstanding figure of this struggle was the miners' leader, John Mitchell, who sustained the hope of his polyglot following and won public sympathy by his moderation.

The next big strike was that of the coat and suit makers (women's) in 1910. It produced a second major pattern of industrial government, added to that of the soft-coal miners. Following a two months' strike in New York, a "protocol of peace" established a tripartite board to settle differences between the manufacturers and the union under the agreement. Louis D. Brandeis, later on the United States supreme court, mediated in the strike and devised a compromise in the "preferential union shop" in lieu of the closed shop vainly demanded by the union. This proved a major invention. A four-months' strike against Hart, Schaffner and Marx in Chicago established a similar pattern in the men's division. In this strike, as in the working of the agreement, Sidney Hillman, later a major leader in U.S. unionism, made his debut.

Stable industrial government in the bituminous coal industry was constantly menaced by nonunion competition. Continuous efforts were made by the United Mine Workers to organize the West Virginia mines; but the operators, with state support, succeeded in repelling organization. Union members were evicted from company houses and forced to live in tent colonies, and in Feb. 1913, an armed railway train machine-gunned a miners' tent colony at night. A similar incident of industrial autocracy occurred in Colorado. In 1913–14 the national guard machine-gunned miners' tent colonies, and the miners retaliated by killing mine guards and destroying mine property. Federal troops were called to bring order in April 1914, but the strike was not called off until December.

An attempt made to organize the iron and steel industry during and immediately after World War I was a major effort to recoup labour's loss in the Homestead strike in 1892. About 350,000 responded to a strike started in Sept. 1919, but strike-smashing was employed extensively. The men held out for six weeks at the cost of 18 lives, and then mass surrenders began.

**The New Deal.**—With the New Deal, strikes began to evolve to a new pattern of diminishing violence because of a more considerate treatment of strikers by government and employers. Yet this may be said to date only from the "little steel" strike of 1937 and the La Follette committee investigation of denial of rights to wage earners.

A longshoreman's strike in San Francisco, Calif., in May 1934 developed into a general strike. Union recognition and control of the hiring halls, in essence the closed shop, and better wages and hours were the issues. Serious rioting began when the employers attempted to operate the docks by force. The California national guard was called out. Labour became steadily more embittered, and in July sympathetic strikes started, and the principal highways into the city were closed. The general strike called on July 16 lasted four days, but the strike committee permitted the entrance of food trucks. The longshoremen's leader in this strike was Harry Bridges, subsequently well known in Pacific coast and Hawaiian industrial relations.

To force "little steel" recognition of the Steel Workers' Organizing committee (C.I.O.), a strike was called in May 1937. The struggle was attended by considerable violence and, although "big steel's" recognition of the Steel Workers' Organizing committee had occurred early in 1937, "little steel" (the independent producers) continued to resist unionization for a few more years.

**World War II and After.**—Prior to the attack on Pearl Harbor two allegedly Communist-led strikes threatened to hold up the national defense program. In June 1941 leaders of the United Automobile Workers' local at the North American Aviation Co. in Inglewood, Calif., called a strike in violation of an interim agreement negotiated with the aid of the National Defense Mediation board. This unauthorized strike was broken through plant seizure by the government and a dispatch of troops. A strike at the Allis-Chalmers plant in Milwaukee, Wis. (1941), crippled vital defense production.

Production losses caused by wartime strikes were relatively small except for soft-coal mining. An outgrowth of two strikes during 1943 was the Smith-Connally or War Labor Disputes act.

With the termination of the no-strike pledge at the end of the war came renewed industrial warfare. The restriction of wage increases during the war, fear of unemployment and some reduction in income because of "cutbacks," and the conviction that organized labour was to be subjected to a concerted employer attack created a favourable climate for widespread strikes. It was expected that the events of World War I and its aftermath would be repeated. In that war the wartime truce had been followed by a triumphant employer counterattack which not only "contained" unionism but regained most of the ground lost by management. Just as 1919 had seen a new record in the number of strikers, it was expected that 1946 might approach that record and possibly bring about a comparable defeat for labour. What happened was something entirely different: prosperity held and the unions continued to gain in membership, notably in the newest of the New Deal-sponsored unions.

A number of the postwar strikes were industry-wide, and most of them were of considerable duration. During the 12-month period following V-J day, work stoppages resulted in almost 12,000,000 man-days of idleness. Strikes were called in the oil, lumber, auto, steel, electrical manufacturing, meat-packing, coal, railroad and maritime industries. A strike by the United Automobile Workers against General Motors began in Nov. 1945 and continued until March 1946. The leader of that strike, Walter Reuther, publicly championed the consumers' cause as well as that of the strikers. He said that he sought no wage increase that might result in a rise of the prices of cars—but he was certain that a wage increase could be met out of the corporation's accumulated profits. Debates between management and labour spokesmen about the ability of corporations to increase wages without at the same time increasing prices continued in following rounds of negotiation in the automobile and other basic industries, and the issue was still debated on the national level in the 1960s. The bituminous coal miners were on strike from April 1 to May 29, 1946, interrupted by a truce from May 13 to May 27. The railway trainmen and engineers struck on a nationwide scale for two days in May 1946 but were defeated by Pres. Harry S. Truman's radio appeal. Smaller but equally crucial strikes were those of the tugboat and building employees in New York and the public utility strike in Pittsburgh.

On the all-important wages question, the matter arranged itself in three "rounds" over 1946–48. Peculiar to this period was the importance of "pattern settlements." The first settlement reached in a mass-production industry tended to set a pattern which all other industries accepted. As the cost of living became stabilized, unions turned their attention to nonwage demands, such as employer-financed pension and social insurance programs. This demand was stimulated by the inability of unions to break the "little steel" wage formula during the war and gained added momentum from an agreement signed in 1946 between the United Mine Workers and the government in which a health and welfare fund was set up to be financed by a contribution of five cents on each ton of coal mined. From coal, "social security by contract" spread to the other basic industries.

The postwar years intensified the periods of industrial strife in the bituminous coal industry. Work stoppages were variously termed walkouts, memorial holidays, stabilization periods and just plain strikes. Since the industry was a "sick industry"—the coal demanded by the nation could be produced if the miners worked only three days a week—the union assumed responsibility for stabilizing production. Industrial government in the industry at times seemed to be dominated by a labour autocracy under John L. Lewis. But Lewis was careful to promote the welfare of his men. Action for contempt of court under the emergency provision of the Taft-Hartley act failed in the 1949–50 strike, as the union and its leaders gained immunity in complying outwardly with a court order to resume work, but without actually doing so.

The steel strike of 1949 typified the new day in industrial conflict. While the cost in dollars was great, the jails were empty. Not a cent was spent on strikebreakers, tear gas, riot guns or arms of any kind. There was no loss of human life. This absence of violence, formerly so prevalent in U.S. labour disputes, stemmed from the Wagner act, the rise of a new kind of employer and a well-disciplined union membership.

Following the outbreak of the Korean war, the number of work stoppages increased sharply. In 1950 there were 4,843 stoppages, as opposed to 1948 with 3,419 stoppages. There had been 4,985 in 1946, however. The demand for wage increases came to the forefront as unions proposed and obtained increases in anticipation of federal wage controls. Following the establishment of federal wage controls in 1951, the unions once again shifted their emphasis to demands for fringe adjustments (*e.g.,* vacation and holiday pay, shift differentials and overtime). This policy continued into 1952–53 as the cost of living became stabilized and started to decline. In the decade following World War II the peak in work stoppages occurred in 1953, with 5,091. The number dropped to 3,468 in 1954 and then rose to 4,320 in 1955.

Among the outstanding events of the period following the 1949 recession was the contract signed by United Automobile Workers, C.I.O., with the General Motors corporation. The five-year contract provided for cost-of-living adjustments in hourly wage rates, provided for a pension fund and established a union shop. These negotiations were harmoniously conducted and gave evidence of the effect that expanding business activity and sustained near capacity production levels had on labour-management relations. This settlement influenced the peaceful conclusion of wage agreements made by the Chrysler and Ford companies with the U.A.W. in 1950. Another important feature of labour-management relations after the outbreak of the Korean War was the active participation of the federal government in the settlement of labour disputes.

The Wage Stabilization board was authorized in April 1951 to investigate and recommend settlement in any dispute which was not resolved by collective bargaining or mediation, which threatened national defense, where the dispute was referred to the board by the parties involved or by the president of the United States. In 1951 the president referred five disputes to the board for settlement, in the copper refining and transport equipment industries. Also in 1951 the president referred the important steel dispute to the board. The steel union demanded an hourly wage increase and fringe benefits including shift premiums and holiday pay. The board recommended a wage increase and acceptance of some form of union shop. This recommendation was criticized by industry members because it threatened the anti-inflationary program of the federal government and it imposed a union shop on the industry. The union issued a strike notice in April 1952 when negotiations broke down. In an effort to avert the strike, the steel plants were seized by the federal government in April 1952. This seizure was declared unconstitutional by the U.S. supreme court in June 1952, and the president directed return of the mills to the owners. Immediately following the return of the mills the steel workers went out on strike.

This steel strike lasted 53 days and was responsible for one-half of the 55,000,000 man-days lost in 1952 through work stoppages. Steel production was not resumed until a new contract was signed granting an hourly wage increase and some of the fringe demands. Following the wage increase the acting defense mobilizer ordered the Office of Price Stabilization to authorize increases in the price of basic steel.

The government also participated directly in the settlement of two major railway disputes. Following an unsuccessful attempt to settle an 18-month dispute between the rail carriers and the major railway unions the government prevented a walkout by seizing the railways in Aug. 1950. The dispute centred about the unions' demands for a 40-hour week for yard workers and rules changes for road service employees. A settlement of the dispute between the railways and the switchmen was reached in Sept. 1950. The dispute with the trainmen ended in May 1951. However, an agreement between the railways and the other operating unions was not reached for another year. Consequently federal operation of the railroads ended in May 1952.

Strike activity in 1953 measured in total time lost by workers involved was relatively low but, when measured in the number of strikes, was high. Most of these strikes involved demands for wage increase. One notable exception was the strike of the United Hatters, Cap and Millinery Workers against the Hat Corporation of America to prevent the transfer of work from Norwalk, Conn., to another plant. It lasted more than a year, and a formula was finally found which guaranteed the right of the company to determine its production policy and gave the workers some protection against sudden shifts in operation.

The number of workers involved and the number of disputes rose markedly in 1955. Several disputes involved large numbers of workers and were bitterly contested. The strike against the Southern Bell Telegraph and Telephone company, which lasted 72 days, as well as the strike of nonoperating workers on the Louisville and Nashville railroad, which lasted 57 days, were attended by violence and bitter recriminations. The latter dispute hinged upon the refusal of the carrier to accept a health and welfare plan, and the former was over wages and arbitration of certain kinds of disputes. On the other hand, the strike of New England textile workers against a number of mills in that area which lasted 90 days at some mills was free from violence. One of the bitterest strikes in the 1945–55 period was that of 70,000 workers in the International Union of United Electric Workers against the Westinghouse Electric and Manufacturing Co. This strike lasted almost six months, and was bitterly fought on the picket line.

In 1959 the number of man-hours lost because of strikes rose to 69,000,000, the highest figure since 1946. The main reason for the high total that year was the prolonged steel strike that alone caused 42,000,000 man-days of idleness. In the 1960s Presidents Kennedy and Johnson both played prominent roles in preventing or terminating strikes. In 1962, for example, Kennedy invoked the emergency powers of the Taft-Hartley act to halt four strikes affecting major industries. President Johnson intervened to avert a strike over a long-standing dispute in the railroad industry and in 1965 did the same when a steel strike was threatened.

The impact of automation in the 1960s caused labour disputes in certain industries, particularly newspaper publishing where electronic computers for rapid automatic typesetting were introduced. In 1962–63 a strike stopped publication of the two leading newspapers in Cleveland, O., for 129 days. In New York city the leading papers were shut down by a strike that began on Dec. 8, 1962, and lasted 114 days. Another strike caused by the automation problem stopped publication of several New York papers in Sept.–Oct. 1965.

*See* also LABOUR LAW; HOURS OF LABOUR; LABOUR (TRADE) UNION; and references under "Strikes and Lockouts" in the Index.

BIBLIOGRAPHY.—Bureau of Labor Statistics, *Monthly Labor Review;* John R. Commons, *et al., History of Labour in the United States* (1921); Selig Perlman, *History of Trade Unionism in the United States* (1922); Selig Perlman and Philip Taft, *Labor Movements,* vol. iv in "History of Labor in the United States Series" (1935); Philip Taft, *Economics and Problems of Labor,* 2nd ed. (1948); A. M. Ross and P. Hartman, *Changing Patterns of Industrial Conflict* (1960); K. G. J. C. Knowles, *Strikes: a Study in Industrial Conflict; with Special Reference to British Experience Between 1911 and 1947* (1952); G. D. H. Cole, *Short History of the British Working-Class Movement, 1789–1947,* rev. ed., (1948). (P. TT.; X.)

**STRINDBERG, (JOHAN) AUGUST** (1849–1912), the greatest Swedish playwright, who exercised a profound influence on the drama, especially in Europe and the United States, novelist, short-story writer and poet, was born in Stockholm, Jan. 22, 1849. He was the son of a steamship agent and a former waitress, and had an unhappy childhood, marred by emotional insecurity, as he relates in his remarkable autobiography *Tjänstekvinnans son* (1886; Eng. trans., *The Son of a Servant,* 1913). He studied intermittently at Uppsala university, never taking a degree. He had to earn his living by working as a freelance journalist in Stockholm, among other occupations. Meanwhile he struggled to complete his first important work, the historical drama *Mäster Olof* (1872; Eng. trans., 1931), on the theme of the Swedish reformation, influenced by Shakespeare and by Ibsen's *Brand.* The Royal theatre's rejection of *Mäster Olof* deepened his pessimism and sharpened his contempt for official institutions and traditions. He continued to revise the play—later recognized as the first living piece of modern Swedish drama—for several years, and this delayed his development as a dramatist of contemporary problems.

BY COURTESY OF THE MUNCH-MUSEET, OSLO

STRINDBERG: LITHOGRAPH BY EDVARD MUNCH, 1896

In 1874 he became a librarian at the Royal library, and in 1875 met the Finno-Swedish Siri von Essen, then the wife of a guards officer; two years later they married. Their intense but ultimately disastrous relationship ended with divorce in 1891, when Strindberg, to his great grief, lost the custody of the children. At first, however, marriage stimulated his writing, and in 1879 he published his first novel *Röda rummet* (Eng. trans., *The Red Room,* 1913), a satirical account of abuses and frauds in Stockholm society: this was something new in Swedish fiction, and made its author famous.

He also wrote more plays, of which *Lycko-Pers resa* (1881; Eng. trans., *Lucky Peter's Travels,* 1931) contains the most biting social criticism. In 1883, after publishing *Det nya riket* ("The New Kingdom"), a withering satire on contemporary Sweden, Strindberg left Stockholm with his family and for six years moved restlessly about the continent. The first volume of his collection of stories *Giftas* (1884; Eng. trans., *Married,* 1913) led to a prosecution for blasphemy; he was acquitted, but the case affected his mind, and he imagined himself persecuted, even by Siri.

He returned to the drama with new intensity, and the conflict between the sexes inspired some of the outstanding works written at this period, such as *Fadren* (1887; Eng. trans., *The Father,* 1930), *Fröken Julie* (1888; Eng. trans., *Lady Julie,* 1930) and *Fordringsägare* (1888; Eng. trans., *The Creditor,* 1914). In these bold and concentrated works he combined the technique of dramatic naturalism with his own conception of psychology and thereby inaugurated a new movement in European drama. *Hemsöborna* (1887; Eng. trans., *The People of Hemsö,* 1959), a vigorous novel about the Stockholm skerries, always one of Strindberg's happiest sources of inspiration, was also produced during this intensively creative phase.

The years after his return to Sweden in 1889 were lonely and unhappy; in 1892 he went abroad again, to Berlin. His second marriage, to a young Austrian journalist, Frida Uhl, followed in 1893: they finally parted in Paris in 1895. A period of literary sterility, emotional and physical stress, and considerable mental instability, culminated in a kind of religious conversion, the crisis which he described in *Inferno* (1897; Eng. trans., 1912). Strindberg had earlier moved from Christianity to atheism by way of deism; scientific studies (1894–96) led to experiments with alchemy and to theosophy.

His new faith, coloured by Swedenborgian mysticism, recreated him as a writer. The immediate result was the drama in three parts, *Till Damaskus* (1898; Eng. trans., *The Road to Damascus,* 1939), in which he depicts himself as "the Stranger," a wanderer seeking and finally finding spiritual peace: another character, "the Lady" resembles both Frida Uhl and Siri von Essen.

By this time Strindberg had again returned to Sweden, settling first in Lund, then, in 1899, in Stockholm, where he lived (after 1908 in his apartment *Blå Tornet*—"the Blue Tower") until his death. The summers he often spent among his beloved skerries. His view that life is ruled by the "Powers," punitive but righteous, was reflected in a series of historical plays which he began in 1889. Of these *Gustav Vasa* (1899; Eng. trans., 1931) is the best, masterly in its firmness of construction and characterization and its vigorous dialogue. In 1901 he married the young Norwegian actress Harriet Bosse; in 1904 they parted, and again Strindberg lost the child, his fifth.

Yet out of this "spring in winter," as he called it, came *inter alia* the plays *Dödsdansen* (1901; Eng. trans., *The Dance of Death,* 1929), *Kronbruden* (1902; Eng. trans., *The Bridal Crown,* 1916) and *Drömspelet* (Eng. trans., *A Dream Play,* 1929), as well as the charming autobiography *Ensam* ("Alone," 1903) and some lyrical poems. Renewed bitterness after his parting from his wife provoked the grotesquely satirical novel *Svarta Fanor* ("Black Banners" pub. 1907), which attacked the vices and follies of Stockholm's literary coteries, as Strindberg saw them. *Kammarspel* ("Chamber Plays," 1907), written for the little Intima theatre, which Strindberg ran for a time with a young producer, August Falck, embody further developments of his dramatic technique: of these, *Spöksonaten* (Eng. trans., *The Ghost Sonata,* 1929) is the most fantastic, anticipating much in later European drama. His last play, *Stora Landsvägen* (Eng. trans., *The Great Highway,* 1954), a symbolic presentation of his own life, appeared in 1909.

Up to the last Strindberg debated current social and political ideas (returning to the radical views of his youth) in polemical press articles, while his philosophy was expounded in the aphoristic *Blå Böcker* (1907–12; Eng. trans., *Zones of the Spirit,* 1913). He died of cancer on May 14, 1912, in Stockholm, ignored in death, as in life, by the Swedish Academy, but mourned by his countrymen as their greatest writer. On Swedish life and letters he has exercised a lasting influence and is admired for his originality, his extraordinary vitality and his powerful imagination, which enabled him to transform autobiographic material into dramatic dialogue of characteristic brilliance.

The pregnant, colloquial style of Strindberg's early novels and, especially, of his short stories, brought about a long overdue regeneration of Swedish prose style, and *Tjänstekvinnans son* gave perhaps the strongest impulse since Rousseau's *Confessions* to the publication of discreditable self-revelations. His greatest influence however was exerted in the theatre, through his critical writings (such as the introduction to *Fröken Julie*), his plays and the devices of production which their staging enjoined. The continuous, brutal action and phonographic dialogue of *Fröken Julie* and other plays written between 1887 and 1893 reached the *ne plus ultra* of naturalistic drama, as presented simultaneously in André Antoine's Théâtre Libre in Paris. With the later phantasmagoric plays, such as *Till Damaskus, Drömspelet* and *Spöksonaten,* Strindberg then led that section of the revolt against stage realism issuing in the expressionist drama, which was developed mainly in Germany after 1912 by Fritz von Unruh, Franz Werfel, Ernst Toller and Georg Kaiser, but left notable traces elsewhere, as in the drama of Sean O'Casey, Elmer Rice, Eugene O'Neill, Luigi Pirandello and Pär Lagerkvist.

BIBLIOGRAPHY.—*Editions: Samlade skrifter,* ed. by J. Landquist, 55 vol. (1911–21); *Samlade otryckta skrifter,* ed. by G. Carheim-Gyllenskjöld, 2 vol. (1918–19).

*Letters: A. Strindbergs brev,* ed. by T. Eklund (1948 *et seq.*); *Från Fjärdingen till Blå Tornet,* ed. by T. Eklund, a selection (1946); *Strindbergs brev till H. Bosse* (1932).

*Bibliography:* R. Zetterlund, *Bibliografiska anteckningar om A. Strindberg* (1913); K. Lundmark and K. Kärnell—a bibliography in preparation.

*Criticism and biography:* E. Hedén, *Strindberg, en ledtråd vid studiet av hans verk* (1921); M. Lamm, *Strindbergs dramer,* 2 vol. (1924–26) and *Strindberg,* 2 vol. (1940–42); G. Ollén, *Strindbergs dramatik* (1948); G. Brandell, *Strindbergs Infernokris* (1950); see *Svensk Litteraturhistoria,* vol. iv, ed. by E. N. Tigerstedt (1956).

*Non-Swedish works:* K. Jaspers, *Strindberg und Van Gogh* (1922); M. Gravier, *Strindberg et le théâtre moderne* (1949); J. Bulman, *Strindberg and Shakespeare* (1933); E. Sprigge, *The Strange Life of August Strindberg* (1949); B. M. E. Mortensen and B. W. Downs, *Strindberg: an Introduction to His Life and Work* (1949).

(B. M. E. M.; B. W. D.)

**STRINGED INSTRUMENTS** owe their existence to the musical properties inherent in an elastic filament when it is made to vibrate regularly by being suitably energized while stretched between two fixed points. The tension, length, thickness and mass of the filament, or string, all affect the rate of vibration and consequently the note it will produce. The shorter or tenser the string, the higher the note; a heavy string produces a lower note than a lighter one of the same length and tension.

**Resonators.**—For musical purposes, the stretched string is not enough; it must, if the result is to be musically acceptable, be in contact with some sort of resonator that is capable of radiating vibrations. All stringed instruments therefore possess a resonant body, usually of wood, the essential feature of which is always the soundboard or belly, which lies directly under the strings and receives their vibrations through the bridge over which they are stretched. The form of the belly varies with the instrument, but it is in effect a thin diaphragm capable of responding to the vibrations transmitted by the bridge and of propagating them freely and instantaneously all over its area, which is made as large as practical considerations allow. Straight-grained pine is the favoured material for the bellies of the majority of European instruments on account of its excellent resonant properties and the rapid and even distribution of musical vibrations both along and across the grain. A stretched skin membrane has, however, been used, notably in the European banjo, the Indian *sarinda* and *sarangi* and the Arab *kamanga* and *rabab.* The wooden bellies of all developed instruments are reinforced in a variety of ways by crossbars glued to the underside; these bars serve as girder stiffeners and prevent the belly from sinking under pressure of the strings, while preserving its general flexibility and response. Such bars also assist in the propagation of transverse vibrations across the pine belly. The bowed stringed instruments, whose string tensions and bridge load are relatively high, employ a distinctive vertical strut, the soundpost, which not only gives greater support to the belly but also is a vital agent in the tonal adjustment of the instrument (*see* VIOLIN FAMILY).

With only a few primitive exceptions, the belly forms the "lid" of a box that is in fact the body of the instrument. If the air space thus enclosed is to resonate freely it must be in contact with the surrounding atmosphere, and it is usual to cut soundholes through the belly to ensure this. The form of the soundholes varies enormously, but to some extent their shape, position and area are functional, serving to regulate both the stresses to which the belly is subject and the effect of the resonant air space. In the violin family especially they have a marked influence on the over-all tone quality.

**String Supports.**—There must of course be two limiting supports between which a string is made to vibrate. The bridge has already been described. In practice the second "bridge," called the nut, is usually fixed rigidly to the fabric of the instrument beyond the area of the belly. Exceptions to this are the virginals and instruments of the dulcimer family, where both bridges stand on the belly and share the function of transmitting vibrations thereto. The upper extremity of the string is carried over and beyond the nut and there wound upon a peg for tuning. At the other end it is hitched to a string holder or a fixed pin attached to the instrument. Both these terminals are arranged below the level of the bridge and nut to secure a firm down-beating upon them when the string is tightened to its working tension. The bridge, and through it the belly, are then subject to a vertical pressure from the string that ensures sensitivity of response to its vibrations. This pressure bridge is the same type as used on the violin and other bowed instruments, on all keyboard instruments and certain plucked instruments (mandolin, banjo, cittern, etc.).

In keyboard instruments, with their many, carefully graded strings, the bridge is necessarily fixed to the belly, usually by glue. But bridges of the violin type are held in position only by the pull of the strings, thus allowing some latitude for adjusting their position to get the best result.

A contrast to the pressure bridge is the tension bridge. In this type the strings are attached direct to the bridge unit, which is glued to the belly. The pull of the strings is sustained by the bridge alone instead of by a separate anchorage beyond the bridge. Such bridges are found on instruments of the guitar and lute families, which are characterized by low-lying, rather slack strings and very thin, light bellies. In the harp the strings pull upward, away from the plane of the belly, the bridge being a central rail to which they are pinned.

**Production of Scales.**—The scale of notes that a stringed instrument will give is produced in one of two different ways: either by providing separate strings for every note or by "stopping" a given string somewhere along its working length, thus temporarily shortening the portion left free to vibrate and raising the pitch of the resultant note. Keyboard instruments, dulcimers and zithers belong to the first class, as also do harps, although for some centuries European harps have employed a limited form of stopping device for the chromatic alteration of some or all of the notes of the scale (*see* HARP).

In the majority of cases, stopping is accomplished by the player's fingers; he presses the string against a board (the fingerboard) that is either raised above the belly as in some forms of zither or, more characteristically, carried on a handle or neck extending beyond the belly to give the hand easier access to the strings. These necked instruments, which always carry the nut and tuning pegs in a head at the upper end of the fingerboard, exhibit a greater variety of form and size than any other type.

In many instances the fingerboard is fretted; that is, set with a number of raised markers, usually spaced at semitone intervals along the string so that each marker acts as an auxiliary nut when the string is pressed against it. Fretting is not, as is sometimes supposed, merely a guide to correct intonation in the early stages of learning to play the instrument; rather it is an integral part of the tone and technique of those instruments that use it. Among the common western instruments only the members of the violin family are not fretted; in that family the pressure of the fleshy part of the fingertip on a plain fingerboard seems to provide exactly the right kind of stop for a bowed string.

In instruments of the harp kind the many strings have to be graded in length and thickness from the lowest to the highest. None of the developed necked instruments derives the whole of its scale merely from stopping a single string all the way up. All employ several strings of the same length, laid close to each other on the fingerboard so that the same stopping technique may be used on all; but they are graded in thickness and tension in such a way that they may be tuned to widely spaced intervals. The number of strings and their tuning varies with particular instruments, but all have a common purpose: to produce the scale, or large parts of it, by a combination of finger-stopping and crossing from one string to the next above or below, the fingered notes bridging the gap or interval between a string and its neighbours. It is also possible, by stopping and sounding selected notes on different strings simultaneously, to produce chordal effects on such an instrument. Normally, the lowest-tuned string lies to the left of the neck, viewed from the front, and the highest to the right, those between being arranged in order of pitch. It is customary to refer to the highest-pitched string as no. 1 and to number the others in descending order.

**Methods of Inducing Vibrations.**—Musical strings may be set in vibration by applying energy in various ways, and it is of course the precise method employed, above all, that determines the character of the instrument and the kind of sound it produces. Energy may be applied either by plucking or by striking or by subjecting the string to continuous friction or wind pressure.

*Plucking.*—The first method of inducing vibrations is at once the most primitive and universal. If the string is pulled aside and suddenly released, it will continue vibrating until the initial energy stored by its elasticity is dissipated and it comes to rest. Such a note, consisting of a sharp *ictus* followed by a more or less rapid decay of loudness, does not really "sing," although the ear readily accepts the convention that it does, and both the performer's skill and the maker's craft are directed to sustain the illusion. Moreover, a wide variety of tone colour can be obtained even from a single string by altering the plucking point, or the nature of the material that does the plucking, or the string itself. The player's own fingertips pluck the strings directly in the lutes, guitars and harps and their derivatives, where the strings are mainly of highly elastic catgut and the playing of chords is an everyday occurrence, involving as it does the plucking of several strings at once with different fingers. For many wire-strung instruments, such as the mandolin, a plectrum is used. This is a small lozenge-shaped spatula of hard, flexible material, such as tortoise shell, held in the player's hand and struck across the strings. (For a description of the keyboard plucking mechanism of the harpsichord *see* the article HARPSICHORD.)

*Striking* with some form of hammer presupposes that the string shall offer rather more resistance to the blow than strings intended for plucking. Metal strings at comparatively high tension behave best under these conditions and afford the least latitude in the point of striking. What has been said above regarding the *ictus* and decay of the note applies equally here. This system of tone production is not adaptable to instruments with fingerboards, although for completeness it should be said that it has been so applied in one solitary instance, the short-lived English keyed guitar of Christian Clauss (1783). The basic type is rather the dulcimer, a struck version of the older plucked psaltery (*q.v.*). The dulcimer has separate strings (usually duplicated) for every note; the strings are stretched over a flat body or soundboard and are played with hand beaters. This ancient instrument survives in central and east Europe, the Hungarian *cimbalom* and Swiss *hackbrett* being best known. The classic example, however, is of course the pianoforte (*q.v.*) with its elaborate keyboard hammer mechanism.

*Friction or Wind.*—The application of continuous friction to the string in order to obtain sustained sound is the principle of the violin bow. The bow, which also is used with such other instruments as the oriental rebab and the European rebec, consists of a flat ribbon of resined horsehair that is kept under tension by a light, specially curved stick. The bow is drawn across the string at right angles to the string and rather near the bridge. The bow will naturally be designed to suit the weight and size of the instrument, and it is of course used in both directions of travel: downstroke when the hand is moving away from the strings and upstroke when moving towards them. Because of the nature of this technique the player has absolute control over the pressure of the bow on the string, its velocity in traveling across it, and of the exact point at which it is applied to the string. All of these factors are employed to vary not only the attack or articulation by which the note is started but also the volume and actual quality of the tone produced, and these varieties can, if necessary, be introduced within the duration of a single stroke. In its higher flights the bowed technique is probably capable of a wider range of musical effect than any other form of tone production.

A more mechanical application of the friction principle is that of the medieval *organistrum* or *symphony*, later to become known as the hurdy-gurdy (*q.v.*), in which a resined wheel turned by a handle passes over the strings. Nearly all such instruments, which have never died out at the folk level, have a system of touchpieces for stopping the strings, as opposed to the direct contact with the player's fingers, and are equipped with "drones" (one-note strings tuned to the prime tones of the piece being played) that form a simple and continuous accompaniment to the tune in bagpipe fashion. The hurdy-gurdy principle has been applied to keyboard instruments many times during the past four centuries but has met no general acceptance.

The final method of eliciting tone from strings is by wind pressure. This is the principle of the Aeolian harp (*q.v.*) and of one or two abortive keyboard instruments where a wind jet directed at the string sets it vibrating. Attractive though the resulting sound is, it is too uncontrollable in attack and duration to have any practical application.

*See* also SOUND: *Strings; the Helmholtz Resonator.* (E. HA.)

**STROBOSCOPE,** an instrument that provides a source of periodic, intermittent light. Such devices find common use in the observation of vibrating or rotating mechanical objects. The instrument is usually calibrated to indicate the frequency of vibration or rotation directly, when the rate of light interruption is so adjusted that the observed motion appears to stop. As an instrument for the measurement of speed of rotation, it can be considered a special type of tachometer. Originally a laboratory device, it is now widely used in industry, and in such fields as medicine and psychology.

A single flash of light, if short enough, will produce a motionless image of any moving object. With repetitive light flashes, if the number of flashes per minute is adjusted to correspond exactly to the number of revolutions per minute (rpm) in the motion, the object will be in the same phase of its rotation whenever it is illuminated and will appear to be stationary. Apparent ultraslow motion will result when the flashing rate and the rate of rotation are slightly different. The apparent motion will be forward if the light-flash rate is slightly less than the rotational rate of the object, backward if it is slightly greater.

Stroboscopic observation depends on persistence of vision on the part of the observer. Below about 50 cycles per second the observer is aware of the intermittent nature of the light, but, in spite of the flicker, he can still follow the action down to about 10 cycles per second. Below this he can see the object illuminated by each flash if the intensity of the flash is sufficient to outshine the continuous light of the surroundings (and if his eyes are focused on the desired spot when the flash occurs).

**History.**—The basic principle of the modern stroboscope is attributed to J. A. F. Plateau (1836). It had been used earlier in a less precise manner by Michael Faraday, and August Töpler (1866) was among the first to reduce the method to an exact science. In the early researches, particularly those concerned with observing acoustical vibrations, two types of procedure were employed. The first made use of intermittent vision; the second employed interrupted light. In both cases a spinning or vibrating disk equipped with a narrow slit allowed a view of the object at periodic intervals, or it permitted light to illuminate the body at successive instants. Thus, the object was exposed to view, or was illuminated, at precisely those times when it passed a given point in its motion. Such a disk device is called an episcotister.

Technical literature from the mid-19th century described many types of stroboscopic devices. Plateau's disk with radial slits was used to determine the rotational speed of wheels and shafts. The prongs of a stroboscopic tuning fork were equipped with slotted diaphragms to create periodic interruptions in a beam of light. Rotating and vibrating mirrors were used to produce periodic pulsing of light for stroboscopic observation.

Mechanical-shutter stroboscopes are particularly well adapted for outdoor use in sunlight and are still used. Most stroboscopes for indoor use now employ the method of successive light flashes from an electronic flash lamp, as explained below.

A direct outcome of the early stroboscopic experiments is the modern motion picture. The first motion pictures were a series of hand drawings viewed intermittently through slots that often were a part of the image-rotating system. Moving wagon wheels, when viewed on a motion-picture screen, provide a familiar example of stroboscopic effects. Here the camera shutter serves to produce intermittent vision. If the shutter frequency exceeds that of the successive passages of spokes, the viewer receives a visual impression that the wheels are turning slowly backward.

**Stroboscopic Effects.**—Disks bearing symmetrical patterns are often used to illustrate stroboscopic effects. Two such disks, which show interesting and useful illusions, are shown in fig. 1. Under stroboscopic light the top disk, for example, will show different rows of squares apparently moving in different directions at certain ratios of rotation speed and flashing frequency. Any one row will appear stationary when the following ratio holds: $F = kR/n$, where $R$ is the speed of rotation in rpm, $F$ is the frequency of the stroboscope in flashes per minute, $k$ is the number of repetitive patterns such as spokes of a wheel, and $n$ is any integer such as 1, 2, 3, 4, . . .

FIG. 1.—DISKS THAT SHOW STROBOSCOPIC EFFECTS WHEN ROTATED. (*see* TEXT)

A stroboscope can give several readings at which a rotating shaft appears to be stationary. For example, a shaft will seem stationary for one revolution per flash, for two revolutions per flash, and so on, and special methods are needed to identify the reading at which speed of rotation $R$ equals $F$.

One method is to increase the rate of flashing slowly, noting the frequencies that show a stationary fundamental pattern. The highest frequency found will correspond to the speed of rotation, since this is one flash per revolution. Any higher frequency will leave a multiple pattern on the shaft. For example, if $F = 2R$ there will be a double pattern on the shaft, since the stroboscope flashes twice per revolution.

Measurement of speeds above the highest frequency of the stroboscope can be calculated by using the multiple-image relationships mentioned above. Assume that the highest frequency of the stroboscope that gives a stationary single pattern is $F_1$ cycles per second. The next lowest stationary-pattern-producing frequency is $F_2$. Since these have a ratio of $F_1/F_2 = n/n-1$ where $F_1 = R/n$, the speed of rotation is $R = F_1F_2/F_1 - F_2$ rpm. This method permits the measurement of high-speed repetitive motion with a stroboscope of lower maximum flash speed.

**Stroboscope Circuits.**—The modern electronic stroboscope employs a capacitor to store energy and a gas-filled discharge tube as a lamp to produce very short, brilliant pulses of light. Typically, the tube comprises a cathode, anode, and trigger electrodes and is filled with xenon gas. The application of a low-energy high-voltage pulse to trigger electrodes ionizes the gas between the main anode and cathode initiating a high-energy discharge from the capacitor. In one commercial instrument, current in excess of 1,000 amperes and peak power of over 1,000,000 watts create intense flashes of white light of over 15,000,000 beam candles, lasting for about one microsecond.

The block diagram (fig. 2) shows the main elements of a stroboscope. The oscillator sets the flashing rate by controlling the generation of trigger-voltage pulses. The main high-voltage supply recharges the capacitor after each flash through the charging resistor, R.

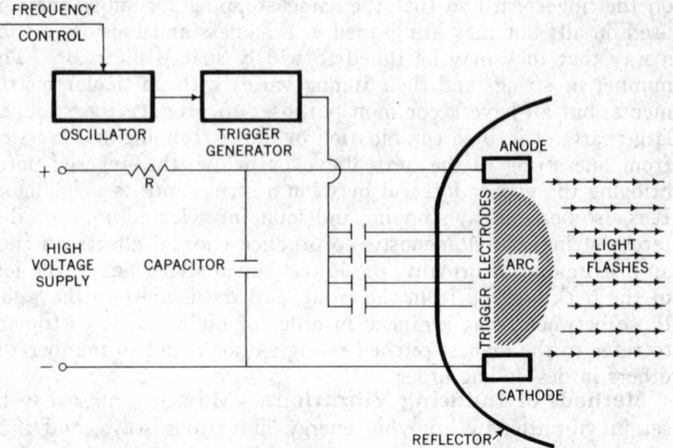


FIG. 2.—DIAGRAM OF A STROBOSCOPIC DEVICE

To observe modern textile twisting spindles and other high-speed mechanisms rotating up to 1,000,000 rpm, very high stroboscope flashing rates are desirable. Special techniques have been developed to ensure deionization of the flash lamp by means of a time delay and then to provide rapid recharge of the capacitor through an inductive charging circuit. By this means flashing rates of over 500,000 per minute have been obtained.

**Applications.**—The stroboscope has a great variety of applications for precise frequency determinations and for observations of moving parts. A familiar demonstration in the physics laboratory or in the study of musical instruments is the stroboscopic illusion of arresting the motion of a vibrating string to show the number and position of nodes and loops. Thousands of these instruments (fig. 3 shows one called a Strobotac) are in use in research laboratories and in industry. One typical model has a 1-microsecond flash duration and a speed range of 110,000–150,000 rpm.

*Slip-Speed Determinations.*—A common application of the stroboscope is the determination of the so-called slip speed in electrically driven induction motors (*see* MOTOR, ELECTRIC). The electrical currents in the stationary part of the induction motor produce magnetic fields that rotate in the air gap and link the windings in the rotating part. This magnetic field rotates at a speed of two poles per cycle of current. For example, a two-pole motor powered by a 60-cycle line will have a field that rotates 60 times per second (3,600 rpm). The speed of the two-pole induction-motor rotor, on the other hand, is less by an amount that depends upon the load. With no load, the rotor speed is very nearly the same as the speed at which the field rotates. As load on the motor is added, the speed decreases. The decrease is called the slip speed and can be measured directly with a stroboscope as follows.

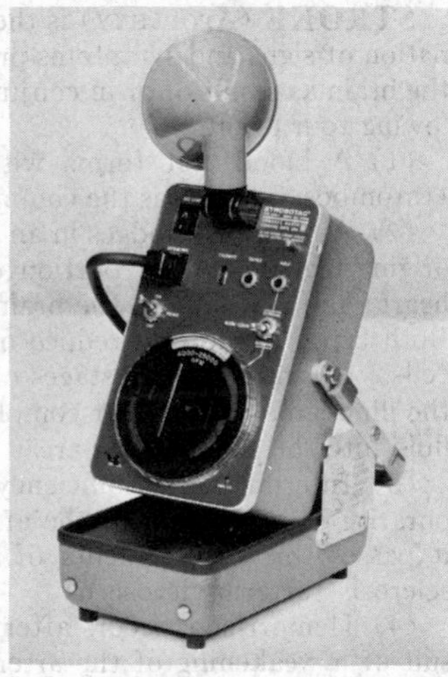

H. E. EDGERTON
FIG. 3.—COMMERCIAL STROBOSCOPE

A black circular cardboard disk with a single white spot near the edge is attached to the end of the induction-motor shaft for measuring slip. When the disk is illuminated by a pulsed source operated from the same 60-cycle line, with one flash per cycle, the disk appears to rotate slowly in a backward direction. If, for example, the observer sees one white spot for each pole pair, the spots will be equally spaced. Suppose the rotational frequency of the disk as determined by counting and by the use of a stopwatch is 36 rpm; then the shaft speed of the induction motor is 3,600 minus 36 or 3,564 rpm. The speed of the shaft for a particular motor load can thus be directly compared with the frequency of the alternating current supply, and the slip speed (in this case 36 rpm) is measured directly. The slip is given as a fraction of the slip speed to the synchronous speed; in this case, slip is .01.

*Synchronous-Motor Observations.*—The stroboscope also is most useful for the observation of the synchronous motor, since what is called the power angle can be seen and photographed both in the steady state and in transient conditions. The rotating part of a synchronous motor turns at the same speed (synchronously) as the rotating magnetic field set up by the currents from the line. There is a magnetic field that is stationary with respect to the rotating parts, produced either by a direct current in a winding, by magnetic induction (salient poles), or by permanent magnets. Without load these two fields, one arising from stator currents and the other from rotor currents, line up as a result of forces acting between them. A stroboscope that flashes in phase with the line voltage will show the rotor in a zero phase position in space in alignment with one of the fields. As load is applied, this phase angle (power angle) will increase until the so-called pullout torque is reached; *i.e.*, the motor speed will drop below synchronous speed, and the induction effects will supply the torque. A disk on the shaft marked in degrees permits the power angle to be read directly. Photographs taken with stroboscopic light on a moving film permit the plotting of data that vary so rapidly that they cannot be recorded by a human observer.

*Tachometer for Small Motors.*—The speeds of fractional-horsepower motors cannot be measured by ordinary means, because the load of a conventional tachometer would alter operating conditions. The stroboscopic tachometer, because it requires no mechanical or electrical connection to the motor, is ideal for this use. Speed can be measured under any driving or load conditions (*see* TACHOMETER).

*Miscellaneous Uses.*—The stroboscope has a wide range of additional applications. The following are typical examples.

1. Electric-motor operation can be studied, particularly as to brush action and vibration.

2. The stroboscope is used in the design of electric fans to discover sources of vibration. Chemical smokes introduced into the airstream permit study of air currents around blades.

3. Vibration patterns produced by a vacuum cleaner on a rug can be studied.

4. In industrial maintenance work, the operation of gears, cams, and other moving parts can be studied, and misadjustments, misalignment, wear, sources of noise, and so on, can be detected before damage occurs.

5. The reciprocating parts of internal-combustion engines can be studied when a stroboscope is flashed from a contactor on the crankshaft. To study the action of pistons and other enclosed parts a window in the side of an experimental engine is ordinarily used.

6. The stroboscope is used in the textile industry to adjust rotating and reciprocating machines for more efficient operation.

7. Vibration modes of loudspeakers, microphones, and ultrasonic transducers may be studied, as well as switch and relay bounce and closure time.

8. The effect of vibration on components intended for aircraft use can be observed under simulated service conditions.

9. In psychology and medicine, stroboscopic devices have been used in the diagnosis of epilepsy (since seizures may be induced by stimulating susceptible people with flickering light). Stroboscopes are also employed in measuring human critical flicker frequency (CFF, also called flicker-fusion frequency; *i.e.*, the stroboscopic frequency at which the flickering light appears continuous to the individual). CFF appears to be related to such factors as the individual's age, degree of introversion, level of fatigue (*q.v.*), brain-wave characteristics, and the degree of hardening of the arteries in his brain. It has also been reported that CFF gradually increased among U.S. Air Force personnel as they recovered from anxiety neuroses; when the level of anxiety was high, these men tended to perceive flicker only at low frequencies.

**Slow-Speed Stroboscopy.**—Very slow speeds such as those below 600 rpm are quite difficult to measure and observe, since people fail to retain the image during the interval between flashes.

For technical studies at slow speeds, which require a bright light, a more powerful electronic flash can be operated from the stroboscope. This device has been applied, for instance, in the observation of textile looms where the shuttle may make only one or two picks per second. An observer can see the shuttle with a single flash of light, but he must be in a dark environment and must have his eyes directed at the subject when the flash occurs.

**Photography with a Stroboscope.**—The brilliant, short-duration flash produced by the gas-discharge lamp developed for stroboscopic use is admirably suited for photographing rapidly moving objects. Single flashes with durations of one microsecond or less are used in scientific photography, while for ordinary photography flash durations of one millisecond are common. High-speed, single-flash photography is popularly called strobe photography, and the lamps are called strobe lights, although no stroboscopic effect is involved other than stopping motion with a single flash (*see* PHOTOGRAPHY: *Stroboscopic Photography*).

With the camera shutter open, a series of exposures resulting from successive flashes of a strobe light can be made. Thus a number of superimposed images on a single sheet of film show various stages of a continuous motion such as a golfer's swing.

*See* G. Kivenson, ***Industrial Stroboscopy*** (1965); General Radio Company, ***Handbook of Stroboscopy*** (1965). (H. E. ED.)

**STRODE, WILLIAM** (*c.* 1599–1645), English parliamentarian, one of the five members of the House of Commons whom Charles I tried to arrest in 1642, was the second son of Sir William Strode, of Newnham, Devon. Educated at the Inner Temple and at Exeter College, Oxford, he represented Bere Alston, in Devon, in every parliament from 1624 to his death. He consistently opposed Charles I and took a leading part in the proceedings in the House of Commons on March 2, 1629, when the speaker, Sir John Finch, was held down in his chair while three resolutions condemning the king's religious policy and the illegal levying of customs duties were carried. Prosecuted before the Star Chamber, Strode refused "to answer anything done in the House of Parliament but in that House." Sentenced to imprisonment during the king's pleasure, he was confined in various prisons for 11 years.

He was liberated in January 1640 at a time when Charles was trying to win support in England for a renewal of the war with the Scots. From this time Strode showed a deeply embittered spirit.

His long imprisonment gave him a reputation, which he might otherwise not have enjoyed, in the party opposed to Charles and his violent speeches and consistent hostility to the government established him among the opposition leaders. In the Long Parliament he proposed parliamentary control over ministerial appointments and the militia, and advocated annual parliaments. He supported the impeachment and trial of Thomas Wentworth, earl of Strafford, and the Grand Remonstrance of November 1641, and when Charles tried to arrest him for treason (January 1642) he was with difficulty persuaded to flee from the House of Commons. Opposing all suggestions of a compromise with the king, he urged on the preparations for war and was present at the Battle of Edgehill (Oct. 23). Bitterly opposed to Archbishop William Laud, on Nov. 28, 1644, he carried the Common's message to the Lords desiring that the ordinance for the archbishop's execution might be hastened.

Strode died at Tottenham, London, on Sept. 9, 1645, and by order of Parliament was buried in Westminster Abbey. His body was disinterred in 1661, following the restoration of Charles II. (S. R. Bt.)

**STROGANOV,** a wealthy Russian family of merchants, probably of Tatar origin, famous for their colonizing activities in the Urals and in Siberia (*q.v.*) in the 16th and 17th centuries. The earliest mention of the family occurs in 15th-century documents that refer to their trading in one of the provinces of Novgorod.

In 1515 Anika (Ioanniki) Stroganov started salt mining in Solvychegodsk; and in 1558 Tsar Ivan IV made a grant of lands along the Kama and Chusovaya rivers to Grigori Stroganov. The Stroganovs were allowed to attract inhabitants to those territories, to build towns, and to maintain their own armed forces for defense, and they were exempted from tax for 20 years. They engaged in salt and iron mining and in the timber and fur trades, and had extensive agricultural interests. They founded the town of Kankor in 1588 and that of Kergedan in 1564. In 1566 Yakov Stroganov petitioned Ivan IV to include the Stroganov estates in the *oprichnina; i.e.,* in the crown land administered under the personal control of the tsar. This request was granted in August 1566. A new grant of land in 1568 considerably increased their estates.

The Stroganovs traded with Siberia, but complications in their relations with the khan of Siberia, Kuchum, led to operations of a military nature. They also occasionally had to take arms against the indigenous inhabitants; *e.g.,* in 1572. In 1574 Ivan IV summoned the Stroganovs to discuss plans for the future of Siberia. Two months later they received a grant of land in Siberia along the Tura and Tobol rivers. In 1581 the Stroganovs equipped the expedition of Ermak Timofeevich (*q.v.*), which was to lay the foundation for Russia's annexation of Siberia.

During the Time of Troubles (*see* Russian History) the Stroganovs were of great assistance to the second levy raised by Prince D. M. Pozharski and Kuzma Minin, whose activities brought about the accession of Michael Romanov to the tsardom in 1613. The Stroganovs supported Michael's government, paying their taxes in advance and loaning large sums to the empty treasury. They were rewarded by a rise in rank and became answerable for their actions to the tsar alone.

In 1688 Grigori Dimitrievich Stroganov (1650–1715) became the sole owner of all the family's vast estates. He built and equipped two naval vessels for Peter the Great and aided him financially. He was made a baron. In 1798 the emperor Paul I raised Grigori Dimitrievich's heirs to the dignity of count. Throughout the 18th and 19th centuries the family produced statesmen and other men of eminence who continued the tradition of service.

The Stroganovs are also famous for their services to Russian art. Their patronage and commissions resulted in the building of many churches and in the creation of the so-called Stroganov school of icon painting in the 16th and 17th centuries. This school, to which such famous painters as Prokopii Chirin, Istoma Savin, and the latter's sons Nikofor and Nazari belonged, introduced the techniques of miniature painting as well as rich ornamentation and colouring and an extensive use of gold leaf. (N. An.)

**STROKE** (Apoplexy) is the term used to describe the combination of signs and symptoms produced by damage to a portion of the brain as result of or in conjunction with at least one of the following four events:

(1) A blood clot forms within a blood vessel of the brain (thrombosis). This is the commonest cause of strokes.

(2) A blood clot lodges in an artery supplying brain tissue after originating in another portion of the body (usually a damaged heart) and traveling to the brain. This is known as an embolism. Both types of clotting reduce or stop the flow of blood to brain cells. During the early stages of apoplexy from these two causes, the illness may be further complicated by the oozing of blood and fluid into the surrounding areas (edema).

(3) Intermittent insufficiency of specific arteries results temporarily due to spasm of the arteries or sludging of the blood as it passes through segments of the vessels narrowed by atherosclerosis (arteriosclerosis).

(4) Hemorrhage occurs after an artery ruptures, usually as result of a weakening of the arterial wall due to atherosclerosis or due to a thinning of the wall with bulging (an aneurysm), which may be congenital or develop later in life.

**Consequences.**—The initial onset may be massive in its effects, producing widespread paralysis, inability to speak, coma or death within a short time, usually within several hours or days. On the other hand the onset may be manifested by a series of transient "little strokes" during which the patient may experience weakness and numbness of an arm, leg or the side of his face. There may be temporary difficulty in speech, confusion of thought or visual disturbances. These may recur many times, but eventually they are usually followed by more widespread and permanent paralysis.

The groups of muscles involved are a direct reflection of the artery and brain tissues involved. Most commonly the left side of the brain (dominant side for most persons) is affected, producing paralysis of the right side of the body, because most of the nerves cross to the opposite side of the body from their origin in the brain. However, the combinations of signs and symptoms are innumerable.

Minute strokes may develop as result of closure of many tiny arterioles and produce gradual mental and physical deterioration.

Hemorrhagic strokes are commonly associated with high blood pressure. They frequently produce massive neurological signs, and death is commoner with them than with thrombo-embolic strokes. However, hemorrhagic strokes may be minute and recurrent, gradually producing widespread damage.

**Treatment.**—Precise history and physical examination, especially for neurological changes, are essential to differentiate apoplexy from tumours and brain injury from other causes. It is also important to determine whether the stroke is due to a thrombosis or embolism on the one hand, or hemorrhage on the other. Examination of the spinal fluid for evidence of blood is essential. X-ray studies following the injection of radiopaque substances may clarify the diagnosis. Establishing a differential diagnosis has become essential because anticoagulant drugs are now widely used in the treatment of strokes due to thromboses or emboli but are contraindicated when due to hemorrhage. A stroke may have both a clotting and a significant hemorrhagic factor present, and this presents difficulties.

Many strokes are due to closure of one of the two carotid arteries that supply the brain after passing up the sides of the neck from the aorta. If the closure involves only a small segment, surgery may be attempted to remove the obstruction or to place a graft or bypass using one of the synthetic materials such as Dacron.

Early and persistent efforts for rehabilitation are essential. These should begin within a day or two after the stroke so that muscle tendon contractures will not occur.

For most patients apoplexy or a stroke should not be considered as an isolated disease but as a chapter in the natural history of the over-all condition of atherosclerosis that tends to involve other organs. However, the outlook has been improved by modern treatment.

*See* Arteries, Diseases of; Brain: *Nutrition of the Brain;*

PARALYSIS: *Diseases That Produce Paralysis;* REHABILITATION, MEDICAL AND VOCATIONAL; THROMBOSIS AND EMBOLISM.

BIBLIOGRAPHY.—E. Hugh Luckey and Irving S. Wright, *Cerebral Vascular Diseases,* Transactions of First Conference (1956); Clark H. Millikan and Irving S. Wright, *Cerebral Vascular Diseases,* Transactions of Second Conference (1958); Clark H. Millikan, Robert G. Siekert and J. Whisnant, "Anticoagulant Drugs in Cerebral Vascular Disease: Current Status," *J.A.M.A.,* 166:587 (Feb. 8, 1958); Irving S. Wright, "The Pathogenesis, Diagnosis, and Treatment of Strokes: a Progress Report," *Ann. Intern. Med.,* 49:1004 (Nov. 1958). (I. S. W.)

**STROMNESS,** a small burgh and fishing port on the island of Mainland (Pomona), county of Orkney, Scot. Pop. (1961) 1,479. It is situated on the west side of a well-sheltered bay opening off Hoy Sound. Many of the houses are within tidal limits and are furnished with quays and jetties. The harbour admits vessels of all sizes. There is an egg-packing station, and eggs are exported to the Scottish mainland. The neighbourhood suffered much damage from the great storm of January 1953.

Stromness is a centre for visiting the magnificent scenery of the west coast of Mainland, including Black Craig (400 ft.) and the Hole of Row, a natural arch carved out by the ocean. At the southern edge of the bay of Skaill lies the prehistoric village of Skara Brae (*q.v.*).

**STRONTIANITE,** a mineral consisting of strontium carbonate and a principal source of strontium. It takes its name from Strontian in Argyll, Scot., where it appears to have been known as far back as 1764, but it was not recognized as a distinct mineral until later, when the examination of it led to the discovery of the element strontium (*q.v.*). The formula is $SrCO_3$. It crystallizes in the orthorhombic system and is isomorphous with aragonite ($CaCO_3$) and witherite ($BaCO_3$). Distinctly developed crystals are of rare occurrence; they are usually acicular with acute pyramid planes and are repeatedly twinned on the prism. Radiating, fibrous, or granular aggregates are more common. The colour is white, pale green, or yellowish brown. The hardness is 3.5 and the specific gravity 3.7. The mineral occurs in metalliferous veins in the lead mines of Strontian, abundantly in veins in calcareous marl near Münster and Hamm in Westphalia, in limestone near Barstow, San Bernardino County, California, and in geodes at Schoharie, N.Y. It is also found in Washington, Arizona, Texas, and other states.

It is used for producing red fire in highway and railway fusees, marine distress signals and pyrotechny, and for refining sugar. (CL. F.; X.)

**STRONTIUM,** a metallic element belonging to the alkaline earth family of elements in group two of the periodic table. Strontium (symbol Sr, atomic weight 87.62, atomic number 38) composes about .00019% of the igneous rocks and about .02% of the entire crust of the earth. It is distributed in small quantities in many different rocks and soils. Some is present in bones, in which it replaces small amounts of calcium. Its principal sources are strontianite $SrCO_3$ and celestite $SrSO_4$.

William Cruikshank in 1787 first detected the existence of the element in the strontianite found at Strontian in Argyll, Scot. The metal was isolated in 1808 by Sir Humphry Davy, who electrolyzed a mixture of the moist hydroxide or chloride with mercuric oxide, using a mercury cathode. It was obtained in a state of purity by heating the hydride in a vacuum to 1,000° C. It may be obtained in the form of sticks by the contact cathode method, in which a cooled iron rod, acting as a cathode, just touches the surface of a fused mixture of potassium and strontium chlorides and is raised as the strontium collects on it. Because calcium and barium, which it resembles closely, occur in much greater abundance, strontium is not produced in commercially important quantities.

There are four stable isotopes of the element; their mass numbers, in the order of abundance, are 88, 86, 87, and 84. Several radioactive isotopes are produced by nuclear reactions. Of these, the isotope having a mass number of 90 has received most attention because of its presence in the radioactive fallout from nuclear explosions (*see* further FALLOUT; RADIATION: BIOLOGICAL EFFECTS). The distribution of electrons in the levels and sublevels of the strontium atom is: $1s^2$, $2s^2$, $2p^6$, $3s^2$, $3p^6$, $3d^{10}$, $4s^2$, $4p^6$, $5s^2$.

**Properties.**—Strontium has a silvery white colour. It is malleable and ductile and acts as a good conductor of electricity. Other physical properties are listed below:

| | |
|---|---|
| Atomic radius | 2.13Å |
| Ionic radius | 1.13Å |
| Ionization potential (gaseous element) 1st electron | 5.69 v. |
| 2nd electron | 10.98 v. |
| Single electrode potential (between metal and molal solution of $Sr^{2+}$ ion) | 2.89 v. |
| Melting point | 757 ± 1° C |
| Boiling point | 1,366° C |
| Density | 2.60 g. per $cm^3$ |

The chemical properties of strontium are similar to those of calcium and barium, in keeping with its position in the periodic table, where it is above barium and below calcium. Generally speaking, its base-forming characteristics are somewhat less pronounced than those of barium but more pronounced than those of calcium. In its compounds, the element has a valence number of +2. As indicated by its atomic radius, ionization potential and single electrode potential, the atom of strontium easily loses the two electrons in the 5s level when it reacts with nonmetallic elements, thus forming the $Sr^{2+}$ ion. The element is an active reducing agent. It reacts readily with water to form hydrogen and the hydroxide $Sr(OH)_2$. It oxidizes rapidly when exposed to the air and burns brilliantly when heated in air, oxygen, chlorine, the vapour of bromine or the vapour of sulphur. With oxygen, the element forms the monoxide SrO and the peroxide $SrO_2$.

**Compounds.**—Compounds of strontium are not so extensively used as those of calcium or barium. The solubilities of the salts of the element, generally speaking, are intermediate with respect to the solubilities of the corresponding salts of calcium and barium.

The hydride $SrH_2$, obtained by A. Guntz on heating strontium amalgam in a current of hydrogen, is a white solid that readily decomposes cold water and behaves as a strong reducing agent. The monoxide or strontia SrO is formed by strongly heating the nitrate, or commercially from the hydroxide which is produced by heating the sulfide or carbonate in superheated steam (at about 500°–600° C). It is a white powder which resembles lime in its general character. By heating the powder in the electric furnace H. Moissan succeeded in obtaining crystals of the oxide. The compound readily slakes with water and the aqueous solution yields a crystalline hydrated hydroxide. It is used in the extraction of sugar from molasses, since it combines with the sugar to form a soluble saccharate, which is removed and then is decomposed by carbon dioxide. A hydrated peroxide, approximating in composition to $SrO_2 \cdot 8H_2O$, is formed as a crystalline precipitate when alkali is added to an aqueous solution of a strontium salt containing hydrogen peroxide. If all the solutions are above 50° C and concentrated, the anhydrous peroxide results.

Strontium fluoride $SrF_2$ is obtained by the action of hydrofluoric acid on the carbonate, or by the addition of potassium fluoride to strontium chloride solution. Strontium chloride $SrCl_2 \cdot 6H_2O$ is obtained by dissolving the carbonate in hydrochloric acid or, commercially, by fusing the carbonate with calcium chloride and extracting the melt with water. It crystallizes in small colourless needles and is easily soluble in water; the concentrated aqueous solution dissolves bromine and iodine readily. By concentrating the aqueous solution between 90° and 130° C or by passing hydrogen chloride into a saturated aqueous solution, a second hydrated form of composition, $SrCl_2 \cdot 2H_2O$, corresponding with dihydrated barium and radium chlorides, is obtained. The anhydrous chloride is formed by heating the hydrated chloride in a current of hydrogen chloride.

Strontium sulfide SrS is formed when the carbonate is heated to redness in a stream of hydrogen sulfide. It phosphoresces slightly when pure. Strontium sulfate $SrSO_4$, found as the mineral celestite, is formed when sulfuric acid or a soluble sulfate is added to a solution of a strontium salt. It is a colourless solid that is almost insoluble in water, its solubility diminishing with increasing temperature; it is appreciably soluble in concentrated sulfuric acid. When boiled with alkaline carbonates, it is converted into strontium carbonate.

Strontium nitride $Sr_3N_2$ is formed when strontium amalgam is heated to redness in a stream of nitrogen or by igniting the oxide with magnesium. It is readily decomposed by water, with liberation of ammonia. Strontium nitrate $Sr(NO_3)_2$ is obtained by dissolving the carbonate in dilute nitric acid. It crystallizes from water (in which it is soluble) in monoclinic prisms which approximate in composition to $Sr(NO_3)_2 \cdot 4H_2O$. It is used in fireworks (*q.v.*) to produce red colours.

Strontium carbide $SrC_2$ is obtained by heating strontium carbonate with carbon in the electric furnace. It resembles calcium carbide, decomposing rapidly with water, giving acetylene. Strontium carbonate $SrCO_3$, found as the mineral strontianite, is formed when a solution of a carbonate is added to one of a strontium salt. It loses carbon dioxide when heated above 1,250° C.

**Analysis.**—Strontium ion is colourless, almost tasteless, and feebly toxic. Volatile strontium salts impart a carmine colour to the flame. The spectrum of the element is characterized by the two prominent lines corresponding to wavelengths of 422 and 461 $\mu\mu$ ($10^{-6}$ mm.).

In the usual schemes of analysis, strontium is separated along with calcium, barium, magnesium, and the alkali metals; none of these ions is precipitated by sulfide ion in either an acidic or an alkaline solution.

After precipitation of all other positive ions by the sulfide ion, calcium, strontium, and barium are precipitated as carbonates in the presence of ammonium ion. The precipitate is then dissolved in acetic acid; and, in the usual procedure, barium is then separated by precipitation as the chromate, leaving strontium and calcium ions in solution. Strontium ion can then be separated from calcium by the addition of a dilute solution of sulfate ion which, because of the considerably greater solubility of calcium sulfate, precipitates strontium but not calcium. *See* also references under "Strontium" in the Index.

BIBLIOGRAPHY.—J. W. Mellor, *Comprehensive Treatise on Inorganic Chemistry,* 16 vol. (1922–37; Suppl., 1956– ); H. Rèmy, *Treatise on Inorganic Chemistry,* 2 vol. (1956). W. M. Latimer and J. H. Hildebrand, *Reference Book of Inorganic Chemistry,* 3rd ed. (1964); A. Engström *et al., Bone and Radiostrontium* (1958); F. C. Gran and R. Nicolaysen, *Radio Strontium Deposition in Humans* (1964).

(H. T. BE.)

**STROPHANTHUS,** a genus of poisonous plants of the dogbane family (Apocynaceae), comprises about 30 species of woody vines or small trees mainly of tropical Africa but extending into South Africa, with a few species in Asia, from eastern India to the Philippines and China. The name, from the Greek meaning "twisted tail," alludes to the long, twisted lobes of the petals, which in some species dangle a foot or more from the flower tube. Though a few species are grown for their showy blossoms, the genus is primarily of drug value. Among the few grown for flowers are *S. grandiflorus, S. courmontii,* and *S. speciosus.*

The seeds contain biologically active substances used as an arrow poison by some African tribes and as a cardiac stimulant when purified. The chief active principles are glycosides called strophanthins. Obtained from various species, they differ in chemical structure, and are named according to their source; thus K-strophanthin is from *S. kombe* and G-strophanthin is from *S. gratus.* G-strophanthin, also called ouabain, is an official drug in the British and U.S. pharmacopoeias, a pure, crystalline substance, whereas K-strophanthin is amorphous. The biological activity of both substances is similar, but in K-strophanthin the activity varies according to the composition.

The strophanthins have a digitalislike action on the heart, accounting for their value in the treatment of heart failure (*see* DIGITALIS). Toxic doses of the strophanthins cause nausea, vomiting, and gastrointestinal distress; headache and nervous irritability may precede the gastrointestinal effects. The heart becomes hyperirritable and ventricular fibrillation and death may result.

*Strophanthus sarmentosus* is a source of cortisone.

(K. P. DU.; X.)

**STRUCTURAL ENGINEERING:** *see* ARCHITECTURAL ENGINEERING.

**STRUENSEE, JOHANN FRIEDRICH,** COUNT VON (1737–1772), German doctor and reforming statesman, who by virtue of the control he exercised over King Christian VII was virtual dictator of Denmark from 1770 to 1772, was born at Halle in northern Germany, on Aug. 5, 1737. Educated at Halle University, in the 1760s he became town physician of Altona, then part of Denmark, and through his contacts with Danish courtiers was appointed traveling physician to the mentally unstable Christian VII during his European tour (1768–69). In 1769 Struensee was made court physician. By 1770 he was the lover of Christian's queen, Caroline Matilda, and rapidly gained authority in affairs of state. In December 1770 he abolished the council of state, dismissed the heads of the state departments, and abolished the office of *statholder,* or viceroy, of Norway. In June 1771 he induced the king to appoint him "privy cabinet minister" with supreme authority, and in July was made a count.

Influenced by the French philosophers, and a believer in enlightened despotism, Struensee began a radical reform of law and administration. Between March 1771 and January 1772 he issued more than 1,000 cabinet orders, or more than three a day. He introduced many useful and humane reforms, including the freedom of the press, a reduction in the labour services of serfs, the reform of the municipal government of Copenhagen and the abolition of the harsh penal laws against unmarried mothers. He also abolished the multiplicity of law courts in Denmark and replaced them by a single jurisdiction. However, many of his reforms were insufficiently prepared and were carried out too hurriedly. Opposition to him grew, aggravated by his disregard of national customs (all government decrees and regulations were issued in the German language), the dismissal without compensation of the staffs of public departments, and his affair with the queen. On Jan. 17, 1772, a conspiracy on behalf of the queen dowager, Juliana Maria, resulted in the arrest of Struensee and his supporters. A commission to interrogate him was set up on Jan. 20, 1772. He defended himself ably, but on Feb. 21 confessed that he was the queen's lover. On April 25 he was sentenced to lose his right hand, then to be beheaded, and his body to be quartered. The sentence was carried out at Copenhagen on April 28, 1772.

**STRUVE, FRIEDRICH GEORG WILHELM VON** (1793–1864), German astronomer, who made a systematic survey of the whole available sky for the discovery and measurement of visual double stars, was born at Altona on April 15, 1793. He attended the University of Dorpat, and was appointed to a professorship of astronomy and mathematics in 1813. He was summoned by Emperor Nicholas I of Russia in 1835 to superintend the building of the Pulkovo Observatory, near St. Petersburg, and became its director in 1839. He died on Nov. 23, 1864.

Struve was a highly skilful observer. The catalog in which his results were published, *Mensurae Micrometricae,* is one of the classics of double-star astronomy. (W. W. M.)

**STRUVE, OTTO** (1897–1963), Russian-born U.S. astronomer who made some of the major astronomical discoveries of the 20th century, was born at Kharkov, on Aug. 12, 1897. A fourth-generation member of a distinguished astronomical family (his great-grandfather was F. G. W. von Struve [*q.v.*]), he graduated from the University of Kharkov in 1919 and settled in the United States in 1921. He received the Ph.D. degree from The University of Chicago in 1923 and continued as a member of the staff of Yerkes Observatory, where he was director (1932–47). He became a U.S. citizen in 1927. He was director of the Leuschner Observatory of the University of California (1950–59), after which he became director of the National Radio Astronomy Observatory in Green Bank, W.Va. He died in Berkeley, Calif., on April 6, 1963.

Struve occupied a unique place in modern astronomy with respect both to his own discoveries and to the effect he had on other investigators. He was the first to demonstrate that a considerable percentage of stars of high temperature rotate rapidly on their axes. Struve showed that some blue stars have rotation periods as short as a day or less. Perhaps his greatest effect on astronomy was due to work on the nature and distribution of the gas located between the stars. Some of his earlier investigations showed that the interstellar calcium spectral lines strengthen in intensity with increasing distance. Later he discovered the large-scale distribution of hydrogen between the stars, a discovery basic to advances in radio astronomy and galactic structure. (W. W. M.)

**STRYCHNINE,** an alkaloid used as a rodent poison and (formerly) in medicine, was discovered in 1818 in Saint-Ignatius's-beans (*Strychnos ignatii*), a woody vine of the Philippines. It also occurs in other species of *Strychnos,* notably *S. nux-vomica,* a tree of India which is the chief commercial source. In its natural occurrence strychnine is generally accompanied by brucine (*q.v.;* dimethoxystrychnine). Strychnine crystallizes from alcohol in colourless prisms, which are practically insoluble in water and soluble with difficulty in the common organic solvents. It has an exceptionally bitter taste. Strychnine is a tertiary monoacid base giving an alkaline reaction.

Strychnine has been used in rodent poisons and in cathartic preparations, and these uses have led to considerable accidental poisoning in children. Suicidal use of the drug has been wide. As a drug, strychnine has no consistently beneficial effect on the cardiovascular system or on the gastrointestinal tract, although in small doses it increases the secretion of gastric juice, excites the motor areas of the spinal cord and increases their reflex irritability, and increases the sensibility of touch, sight, and hearing. Strychnine is partly detoxified in the liver and partly excreted unchanged by the kidneys.

**Strychnine Poisoning.**—Strychnine rapidly enters the blood, whether taken orally or by injection. It acts specifically on the central nervous system. Symptoms of poisoning usually appear within 20 minutes, starting with stiffness at the back of the neck, twitching of the muscles, and a feeling of impending suffocation. The patient is then seized with violent tetanic convulsions in which the body is arched and the head bent backward. After a minute the muscles relax, and the patient sinks back exhausted, heightened perceptiveness being preserved throughout due to sensory cortex stimulation. A touch, a noise, or some other stimulus causes the convulsions to recur; or they may recur spontaneously, often at intervals of a few minutes. Death from strychnine poisoning is ultimately the result of suffocation or exhaustion.

In treating strychnine poisoning, antidotes such as charcoal or egg white should be administered promptly. Emetics should be avoided as they tend to precipitate convulsions, as does morphine. The patient should be kept quiet and protected from external stimuli. The convulsions can be controlled best by intravenous barbiturates or general anesthesia. Artificial respiration may be necessary.

*See* also ALKALOIDS; POISON.

BIBLIOGRAPHY.—Frank E. Hamerslag, *The Technology and Chemistry of Alkaloids* (1950); Louis S. Goodman and Alfred Gilman, *The Pharmacological Basis of Therapeutics,* 3rd ed. (1965); Torald A. Sollmann, *A Manual of Pharmacology and Its Application to Therapeutics and Toxicology,* 8th ed. (1957); H. L. Holmes, "The Strychnos Alkaloids," in R. H. F. Manske and H. L. Holmes (eds.), *The Alkaloids* (1950). (W. J. V.; X.)

**STRYPE, JOHN** (1643–1737), English historian and biographer, whose works are a valuable source for Tudor church history, was born at Houndsditch, London, on Nov. 1, 1643. His uncle, Abraham van Strijp, from Brabant, was a founder of the Spitalfields silk trade, and his father, John van Strijp, was naturalized, and became a freeman of the City. Educated at St. Paul's School (1657–61), Strype entered Jesus College, Cambridge, in 1662, transferring to the more Protestant St. Catharine's Hall in 1663. In 1669, he became curate of Theydon Bois, Essex, but soon moved to Leyton. He was lecturer (*i.e.,* preacher appointed by the Puritans) at Hackney (1689–1724), and died there on Dec. 11, 1737.

A lifelong collector of documents, with a gift for acquiring manuscripts by various means (some not entirely scrupulous), he built up a valuable collection (many of which are in the British Museum). These formed the basis of works which, though often ill-arranged, lacking in literary style, and with innumerable appendices so crammed with documents that they earned him the nickname "Appendix Monger," are of great value to the historian. The most important are his lives of Archbishops Cranmer (2 vol. 1694; ed. by P. E. Barnes, 1853), Parker (3 vol. 1711), and Whitgift (1718); his little volumes on Sir Thomas Smith (1698) and Sir John Cheke (1705), still the best accounts of these paragons of the Indian summer of Edwardian humanism; his *Annals of the Reformation* . . . (4 vol. 1709–31; 3rd ed., with additions, 1735); and his *Ecclesiastical Memorials* . . . (3 vol. 1721, additional vol. 1733). The last two, as collections of primary sources, bridge the gap between those of John Foxe and Gilbert Burnet (*qq.v.*). Lack of critical sense prevents Strype from being classed as a true historian, but he belongs among the great chroniclers.

*See* his *Works,* 19 vol. (1812–24), index, 2 vol. (1828); also S. R. Maitland, *Notes on Strype* (1858). (E. G. RU.)

**STUART, ARABELLA** (ARBELLA STEWART) (1575–1615), first cousin of James VI of Scotland and next after him in the line of succession to Elizabeth I of England, was the daughter of Charles Stewart, earl of Lennox (a grandson of Margaret Tudor by her second marriage) and of Elizabeth Cavendish. To some Englishmen the fact that she was born and bred in England, while her cousin James was Scottish by birth and upbringing, gave her a greater claim to the English throne. She was, therefore, regarded with much suspicion, both by Elizabeth I and by the supporters of James, especially when her name was linked with plots in 1591 and 1597 to prevent his accession. However, when he became king of England as James I, in 1603, Arabella was invited to live at the royal court and was treated with outward respect.

The question of her marriage became a touchy issue. She had already received numerous marriage proposals, including one from Henry IV of France, but all of these had been vetoed by Elizabeth. The same policy was continued by James, who apparently thought her marriage to any foreign ruler or to any other claimant to the English throne would constitute a threat to himself. Hence, in December 1609, when she attempted to escape from the court to Scotland, probably with the intention of arranging a marriage with an obscure Balkan prince, she was arrested. Brought before the Privy Council (January 1610), she was released and apparently was given an assurance by James that he would not object to her marriage to one of his own subjects. She promptly fell in love with William Seymour (later duke of Somerset), a younger son of Edward, Lord Beauchamp, who also had a claim to the English throne.

When James heard of the romance, he forbade the lovers to marry. The command was disobeyed; on June 22, 1610, Arabella married Seymour at a private ceremony at Greenwich Palace. James's wrath was quickly felt. Seymour was imprisoned on July 8, in the Tower of London, while Arabella was committed to the custody of Sir Thomas Parry at his house at Lambeth. Later, when James learned that the couple were corresponding with one another, Arabella was ordered (March 1611) to be removed to Durham. On her way north she became ill and halted at Barnet, Hertfordshire. She returned to Highgate, near London, and while there made plans to flee to the continent with her husband. Seymour was to escape from the Tower, and they would meet on the coast where a French vessel would take them to Calais. The plan went awry. On June 4, Arabella reached the coast at Leigh in Essex, before Seymour, and at the urgings of her attendants, who feared pursuit, the ship sailed without him. Arriving at Leigh somewhat later, Seymour boarded another vessel which took him safely to Ostend. Arabella was not as fortunate. She was captured in the Straits of Dover, returned to London, and imprisoned in the Tower. Under the strain of imprisonment and separation from her husband, she lost her reason and finally died on Sept. 25 or 27, 1615. She was buried in Westminster Abbey.

*See* P. M. Handover, *Arbella Stuart* (1957). (R. C. JO.)

**STUART, GILBERT CHARLES** (1755–1828), U.S. painter, one of the great portraitists of his era and the creator of the most popular image of George Washington, was born on Dec. 3, 1755, in his father's snuff mill near Narragansett, R.I. He grew up in nearby Newport and there learned the rudiments of painting from Samuel King and Cosmo Alexander, a visiting Scotsman. He accompanied Alexander to Edinburgh about 1771, but returned home a year later. In 1775 he went to London and entered the studio of Benjamin West, with whom he worked for about six years. His mature style owed more, however, to Thomas Gainsborough and Sir Joshua Reynolds than to West. In 1782 he opened his own London studio and for five years enjoyed great success, but in 1787 he fled to Dublin to escape his creditors. After six years in Ireland he returned to the U.S. in 1793, worked for a year in New York, then settled in Philadelphia, then the political and cultural capital of the nation. He quickly established himself as the nation's leading portrait painter, a position he held until his death on July 9, 1828, in Boston, where he had settled in 1805.

Stuart's work was hailed by his contemporaries and subsequent critics have confirmed this judgment, especially praising its painterly brushwork, luminous colour, and psychological penetration. Of his nearly 1,000 portraits, undoubtedly the most famous is the unfinished head of George Washington (1796) at the Boston Athenaeum. (For a reproduction of this work *see* WASHINGTON, GEORGE.) Other fine portraits are those of Mrs. Richard Yates and "The Skater," both at the National Gallery, Washington; Mrs. Perez Morton, Worcester (Mass.) Art Museum; and John Adams, privately owned.

Although Stuart had no formal pupils, many young artists, including John Vanderlyn, Thomas Sully and John Neagle, availed themselves of the advice he freely gave. Less talented artists, including his own daughter Jane, simply reduced his style to a formula which gave a Stuartesque appearance to much U.S. portraiture of the succeeding generation.

BIBLIOGRAPHY.—Lawrence Park, *Gilbert Stuart: an Illustrated Descriptive List of His Works* (1926); William Sawitsky, "Some Unrecorded Portraits by Gilbert Stuart," *Art in America* (1932); James Thomas Flexner, *Gilbert Stuart* (1955); Charles M. Mount, *Gilbert Stuart* (1964). (D. H. W.)

**STUART, JAMES EWELL BROWN** ("JEB") (1833–1864), Confederate cavalry officer in the American Civil War, was born in Virginia on Feb. 6, 1833, and entered the U.S. Military Academy in 1850. When Virginia seceded from the Union, Stuart resigned his commission in the United States Army to share in the defense of his state. At the First Battle of Bull Run (1861) he distinguished himself by his personal bravery. Later in the year he was promoted brigadier general and placed in command of the cavalry brigade of the Army of Northern Virginia. Just before the Seven Days' Battle he was sent out by Lee to locate the right flank of McClellan's army; he not only successfully achieved his mission but rode completely around McClellan's army to deliver his report to Lee at Richmond. In the next campaign he had the good fortune, in his raid against General Pope's communications, not only to burn a great quantity of supplies but also to bring back a staff document from which Lee was able to discover the strength and position of the Union forces. Stuart, now a major general and commander of the cavalry corps, was present at the Second Battle of Bull Run (1862), and during the Maryland campaign he brilliantly defended one of the passes of South Mountain (Crampton's Gap), thus enabling Lee to concentrate his army in time to meet McClellan's attack. At Fredericksburg Stuart's horse artillery rendered valuable service in checking Franklin's attack on "Stonewall" Jackson's corps. At Chancellorsville Stuart was appointed by Lee to take command of the 2nd Army Corps after Jackson had been wounded. The next campaign, Gettysburg (1863), was preceded by the cavalry Battle of Brandy Station, in which for the first time the Federal cavalry showed themselves worthy opponents for Stuart and his men. The Confederates' march to the Potomac was screened by the cavalry corps, which held the various approaches on the right flank of the army, but at the crisis of the campaign Stuart was absent on a raid. He attempted to rejoin Lee during the battle, but was checked some miles from the field. Shortly after the opening of the campaign of 1864 Stuart's corps was drawn away from Lee's army by Sheridan; part of it was defeated at Yellow Tavern on May 11, and Stuart himself was wounded and died on May 12.

*See* J. W. Thomason, *Jeb Stuart* (1930).

**STUBBS, GEORGE** (1724–1806), outstanding English animal painter and anatomical draftsman, was born in Liverpool on Aug. 25, 1724, the son of a prosperous tanner. Apprenticed at the age of 15 to a local painter, Hamlet Winstanley, he remained only a few weeks with him and was thereafter virtually self-taught. At the age of eight Stubbs had already been making drawings from bones lent him by a local doctor, and an interest in anatomy proved one of the driving passions of his life. His earliest surviving works are 18 plates etched for Dr. John Burton's *An Essay Towards a Complete New System of Midwifery* (1751). After years of valuable experience in York he determined to make an exhaustive analysis of the anatomy of the horse. He rented a farmhouse in a remote Lincolnshire village where, over a period of 18 months, he undertook the painstaking dissection of innumerable specimens. From the many drawings executed at this time, after moving permanently to London in 1760, he etched the plates for his *Anatomy of the Horse* (1766), a major work of reference for natural scientists and artists alike. In the period immediately following its publication he established a reputation as the leading painter of portraits of the horse. His masterly depiction of hunters and racehorses brought him numerous commissions and his patrons included the duke of Richmond and the Lords Grosvenor, Torrington, and Rockingham. Perhaps more impressive than these single portraits are his informal groups of horses, such as "Mares and Foals in a Landscape" (Tate Gallery, London).

BY COURTESY OF THE TRUSTEES OF THE TATE GALLERY, LONDON

"MARES AND FOALS IN A LANDSCAPE" BY GEORGE STUBBS, *c.* 1760–70

Although Stubbs's fame was based on his paintings of horses, they were not his only animal subjects. He was familiar with many of the most eminent naturalists and natural scientists of the day, and in private menageries he could observe a wide variety of animals. Among his more striking subjects were the lion, tiger, giraffe, monkey, and rhinoceros.

Stubbs believed passionately in the importance of natural observation in art. According to the artist Ozias Humphrey he undertook a visit to Italy in 1754 only "to convince himself that nature was and is always superior to art." Skeptical of academic standards of excellence, he remained at the same time little affected by new tastes placing emphasis on the expressive and imaginative elements in painting, a circumstance which accounts for his lack of popularity in later life when Romantic precepts were becoming dominant. His treatment of the theme of the horse attacked by a lion, which occupied him in differing forms over a long period, is the nearest reflection in his work of this climate of ideas. Exploiting the emotive possibilities of the subject, the wild terror of the horse and predatory power of the lion, Stubbs's depictions of the encounter are nevertheless the product of a prolonged observation of both animals in captivity, studied as far as possible in similar attitudes.

For a brief period (about 1768) Stubbs attempted to participate in the creation of an English school of narrative painting. Dissatisfaction with his role as an animal painter led him to abandon his usual method of working from nature: his few history paintings are among his least successful works; much more convincing are his scenes of familiar country activities developed in an attractive series of paintings in the 1770s. At this time he was experimenting with the technique of enamel painting. Following the pattern of his anatomical studies, Stubbs's researches into the methods involved were painstakingly thorough and scientific.

In later life Stubbs encountered considerable hardship. A commission in 1790 for a series of portraits of famous racehorses, to be engraved for *The Turf Review,* petered out for lack of support in 1794. His last years were spent on a final work of anatomical analysis: *A Comparative Anatomical Exposition of the Structure of the Human Body, with that of a Tiger and Common Fowl.* Although never completed, Stubbs left over 100 drawings and 18 engravings for it which testify to his formidable vision and vitality in old age. He died in London on July 10, 1806.

Stubbs's reputation, already in decline at the end of the century, went into virtual eclipse after his death. The majority of his work was scattered in private hands, where much of it still remains, and it was not until the 1950s, with several important exhibitions, that he became widely known to the public. Now accepted as one of the outstanding British painters, Stubbs takes his place with William Blake and Turner as a dedicated and isolated master.

BIBLIOGRAPHY.—Ozias Humphrey, Manuscript Memoir, Picton Library, Liverpool; Sir Walter Gilbey, *Life of George Stubbs* (1898); E. R. Dibdin, "Liverpool Art and Artists in the Eighteenth Century," *Walpole Society,* VI (1917–18); W. S. Sparrow, *George Stubbs and Ben Marshall* (1929); Basil Taylor, *Animal Painting in England from Barlow to Landseer* (1955), *George Stubbs* (1969); R. B. F. Fountain, "George Stubbs (1724–1806) as an Anatomist," *Proc. R. Soc. of Med.,* lxi (July 1968). (S. E. B.)

**STUBBS, PHILIP** (*c.* 1555–*c.* 1610), English Puritan and pamphleteer. He seems to have spent some time at Cambridge but left without a degree. In 1586 he married Katherine Emmes, then aged 16, who about four years later died in childbed. To judge from his biographical account of her, *A Cristal Glasse for Christian Women* (1591) she was a more bigoted and narrow Puritan even than himself; on her deathbed she edified him by declaring her affection for a puppy to have been sinful vanity. However, Stubbs had probably recreated her in his own image. The chief works of this vigorous propagandist for a purer life and straiter devotion were *The Anatomie of Abuses* (1583), *A Rosarie of Christian Praiers and Meditations* (1583), *The Theatre of the Pope's Monarchie* (1584), *A Perfect Pathway to Felicitie* (1592), and *A Motive to Good Workes* (1593). The *Anatomie* proved the most popular of his books, probably because it consisted of a devastating attack on English habits in dress, food, drink, games, and especially sex. To do Stubbs justice, his outpourings on the subject of "whoredom" arose less from prurience than from genuine distress. At first inclined to condemn only excessive concentration on all these worldly pastimes, he eliminated such weakness from later editions and denounced all forms of them. As a writer he was third rate, his matter conventional, and his manner mainly pompous: it passes understanding how some scholars could ever have charged him with having had a part in the humour and satire of the Marprelate tracts. (G. R. E.)

**STUBBS, WILLIAM** (1825–1901), English historian, bishop of Oxford from 1888 to 1901, was founder of the systematic study of English medieval constitutional history, and his influence, even where unacknowledged or criticized, continues to pervade most works on this subject. Born at Knaresborough, Yorkshire, on June 21, 1825, the son of a solicitor, he went up to Christ Church, Oxford, graduating in 1848. Elected a fellow of Trinity College (1848), he was ordained priest (1850) and held the college living of Navestock, Essex, from 1850 to 1866. In 1862 he was appointed librarian at Lambeth Palace, and in 1866 regius professor of modern history at Oxford. Consecrated bishop of Chester (1884), he was translated to Oxford in 1888. He died at Cuddesdon, near Oxford, on April 22, 1901.

Stubbs's first publication was *Registrum sacrum anglicanum* (1858; rev. ed. 1897), tables of the successive holders of English bishoprics. His *Select Charters . . . From the Earliest Times to the Reign of Edward the First* (1866; 9th ed., rev. by H. W. C. Davis, 1913) was soon established as a textbook, and, revised, remains in use. Stubbs's contemporary fame, however, rested primarily on *The Constitutional History of England in its Origin and Development,* 3 vol. (1873–78; French trans., 1907), which reached a wide audience. This work, which traces the development of English institutions from the Teutonic invasions of Britain till 1485, is now much criticized, and Stubbs's best work is held to lie in the 19 volumes of editions of medieval English chronicles which, between 1864 and 1889, he contributed to the Rolls Series.

Stubbs's immense output caused many of the faults with which he has been charged. He consulted only printed sources, and sometimes, lacking sufficient evidence, reached erroneous conclusions. As an editor, he did not always adequately investigate the authority of his sources, and some critics accuse him of preconceived prejudice. Nevertheless, whether progress in English constitutional studies derives from following or from reacting against Stubbs's views, it is still impossible to neglect them.

BIBLIOGRAPHY.—*Letters of W. Stubbs, Bishop of Oxford,* ed. by W. H. Hutton (1904); J. G. Edwards, *William Stubbs* (1952); H. Cam, "Stubbs Seventy Years After," *Cambridge Historical Journal,* vol. ix, no. ii (1948); H. G. Richardson and G. O. Sayles, *The Governance of Mediaeval England* (1963).

**STUDEBAKER,** the family name of five brothers associated in the manufacture of wagons, carriages, and automobiles in the United States. CLEMENT STUDEBAKER (1831–1901) was born in Pinetown, Pa., March 12, 1831, and worked in his father's blacksmith shop in Ashland, O. In 1850 he moved to South Bend, Ind., to work as a schoolteacher, and there, two years later, with his older brother, HENRY STUDEBAKER (1826–95), he founded the firm of H. & C. Studebaker, blacksmiths and wagonmakers. In 1858 another brother, JOHN MOHLER STUDEBAKER (1833–1917), bought out Henry. The Civil War provided the firm with a large government contract, and in 1868 the company was incorporated as the Studebaker Brothers Manufacturing Co., at which time another brother, PETER EVERST STUDEBAKER (1836–97), joined the firm. A fifth brother, JACOB FRANKLIN STUDEBAKER (1844–87), joined the firm in 1870, the year in which the company opened its first branch office at St. Joseph, Mo., to outfit settlers moving West. At that time the firm was the largest manufacturer of horse-drawn vehicles in the world, and during its entire history it produced more than 750,000 wagons. With the advent of the automobile the firm began experiments in its manufacture in 1897. Soon after Clement's death, the firm started building electric (1902) and gasoline (1904) automobiles. Clement was succeeded as president by John. In 1911 the firm was absorbed by the Studebaker Corp., and in 1954 the Studebaker Corp. merged with the Packard Motor Car Co. Automobile production in South Bend ceased in 1963, though it continued on a reduced scale at the Studebaker plant in Hamilton, Ont.

*See* also SOUTH BEND; AUTOMOTIVE INDUSTRY. (W. H. D.)

**STUDENT AID** is an award, loan, or other form of assistance designed to help students obtain a higher education, usually at a college or university. In general, such awards are known as scholarships, fellowships, or loans; in European usage, a small scholarship is an exhibition, and a bursary is a sum granted to a needy student. Many awards are in the nature of long-term loans with low rates of interest. In a large number of countries student aid takes the form of government subsidies to reduce or eliminate tuition, room, board, and other fees and expenses. On most U.S. campuses, student employment services provide opportunities for students, especially men, to help pay their own way through part-time employment.

In Great Britain and on the continent, where colleges and universities are considerably older than those in the United States, marked differences appear in aims, traditions, and historical factors. In most countries student aids follow the pattern set in the United States or in Great Britain. The English educational system, with its medieval traditions, sought to provide grammar school facilities (secondary education) for only a small proportion of the population (*see* SECONDARY EDUCATION). University education was intended for a still smaller proportion, and until the 20th century relatively few students were selected by real or supposed merit. So the characteristic feature of the English system has been the scholarship, often quite generous in amount, but available only to the few after a fiercely competitive examination. (*See* EDUCATION, HISTORY OF; UNIVERSITY.) Despite vast increase in university and college provision in the United Kingdom, especially after World War II, the proportion of U.S. citizens taking full-time higher education was still much greater.

**Growing Needs.**—The growth of higher education throughout the world has constituted one of the major social revolutions of recent times. Nations with already well-developed systems of higher education have expanded them in response to growing student populations and demands to broaden higher educational opportunities. For example, the number of students enrolled in U.S. colleges and universities jumped from 2,250,000 in 1950 to approximately 4,500,000 by the 1960s; the number of university students in the Soviet Union more than doubled, rising from 1,250,000 to almost 3,000,000; French university enrollment increased from 150,000 to almost 250,000; and the number of Japanese students rose from approximately 400,000 to more than 700,000.

Developing nations, many newly independent, have also given high priority to the creation of college and university facilities. University enrollment in India, for example, soared from 425,000 in 1950 to almost 1,000,000 by the 1960s. Increases of even greater proportions have occurred in some newer countries where the student population, although still minuscule, has grown at an astronomical rate. Senegal, for example, which had only 250 university students in 1952, had ten times as many in the 1960s. In all, the world's university student population of about 14,000,000 more than doubled within the decade after 1950.

This striking growth in higher education has been in great part fostered by programs of scholarships, fellowships, loans, and other forms of financial assistance to students. These are provided by governments and academic institutions; business, industry, and labour organizations; foundations; religious, civic, and fraternal groups, and other private organizations; and by individuals. As a result of these financial aid programs, opportunities for higher education, once the prerogative of the economic and social elite in many lands, have become increasingly available to students who would otherwise be denied the opportunity. Indeed, although reliable statistics are not always available, it is clear that college and university students receiving some form of private or public support constitute in all countries an important, and in some countries an overwhelming, proportion of the university enrollment.

**Government Programs.**—In the great majority of countries, tuition at institutions of higher learning is either free or nominal. Generally, higher education is under the auspices of a government ministry, and although institutions jealously guard their academic autonomy, they are either directly or indirectly financed by government funds. Higher education is free in the Soviet Union and other Eastern European countries, the Scandinavian countries, the Republic of China (Formosa), and the People's Republic of China, to name only some. Tuition is either free or nominal throughout Latin America, and in most European, Asian, and Middle Eastern countries it is nominal. Even where tuition charges are appreciable, as in Great Britain, an extensive scholarship program supported by both government and the universities effectively underwrites this cost for most students. Students are also assisted to meet costs other than tuition, particularly living expenses, through stipends, loans, grants, and other financial aid.

In Austria and Japan about a quarter of the students receive government financial aid; in Denmark and Norway, more than half; and in the United Kingdom 90%. State aid for French students is very comprehensive. Indirect aid includes subsidies to students' quarters and student restaurants (half the cost of meals); contributions to students' social insurance; and the building of student hostels and restaurants. In the Federal Republic of Germany, about 30% of German university students receive aid from public funds. In Hungary, more than 60% of the students receive scholarships: government assistance includes provision of hostel accommodation (for about 50% of the total); and reduced-price meals (for 30%). Among the provisions for student aid in India is the Union Education Ministry's national loan scholarship scheme for future teachers. More than 18,000 of these loans are made annually to needy students following full-time courses of higher education or training. They vary in amount according to the course, a supplement being arranged for students following engineering and similar courses: repayment is called for at the rate of 10% a year.

Statistics on the number of U.S. students receiving government financial assistance are difficult to obtain, but it is estimated that on the graduate level alone, more than 70,000 fellowships and research assistantships are awarded annually.

Although the number of U.S. students receiving financial assistance from the government is proportionately less than in other countries, the scope of the U.S. government's support program nonetheless has become massive. Among the major scholarship programs financed by federal funds are those of the National Science Foundation, which annually disburses more than $30,000,000 to accelerate the training of promising students in science, mathematics, and engineering; the National Aeronautics and Space Administration, which disburses a somewhat smaller sum for fellowships in flight training, aeronautics, and special research; and the National Institutes of Health, whose grant program approaches $50,000,000 annually to support study in various fields of medicine and public health. More modest sums are provided by the Atomic Energy Commission and the Department of Health, Education, and Welfare to encourage competence in such fields as nuclear science and engineering mechanics, biology and medicine, vocational rehabilitation, and the teaching of the retarded. Less restricted as to field are the grants offered under the National Defense Education Act, which amount to more than $20,000,000 a year in scholarships and fellowships to increase the number of university teachers in all fields, but especially in modern languages, science, and international affairs. A student planning to teach may borrow up to $2,500 per year; and if he enters teaching after completing the program, up to 50% (10% per year up to five years) of the loan is forgiven. In all, the federal government appropriates more than $120,000,000 a year to support college and university study.

**College and University Aids.**—U.S. colleges and universities provide financial assistance in an amount at least equal to, if not greater than, that provided by the federal government. In some state and municipal institutions, tuition is free to students who are legal residents and some scholarships are provided by state governments. In the 1960s, U.S. academic institutions granted an estimated 320,000 scholarships and fellowships a year, more than twice as many as a decade earlier. The dollar value of these awards is estimated to be well in excess of $100,000,000. These grants, usually but not always provided to students of high ability without adequate financial resources, range from a mere reduction of tuition fees to grants covering all fees, tuition, and living expenses. Frequently, the recipient of a college or university grant is required to provide some service to the institution. An undergraduate may work as a clerk in a library or as a waiter in an eating hall, for example, and a graduate student may assist a professor in a laboratory. This arrangement is almost unique to the United States.

**Private Foundations and Corporations.**—Although corporations, foundations, religious, civic, and other groups provide funds for the support of students in many countries, and especially in Europe, nowhere does their involvement equal that in the United States. Led by the Ford, Rockefeller, Carnegie, Guggenheim, and Danforth foundations, U.S. philanthropic foundations contribute more than $50,000,000 annually to fellowships, scholarships, loans, and other programs of student aid. The Woodrow Wilson National Fellowship Foundation maintains the largest private program, offering 1,000 awards every year to future college teachers of the liberal arts. U.S. corporations, too, have taken an increasingly active interest in this form of philanthropy. Their contributions to student aid programs are estimated to be well over $30,000,000 a year.

The National Merit Scholarships Corporation (NMSC), a nonprofit organization, was established in the United States in 1955 through a $20,000,000 grant from the Ford Foundation and a $500,000 grant from the Carnegie Corporation of New York to operate a coordinated, nationwide scholarship program. Scholarships financed through the Ford Foundation grant are known as National Merit Scholarships; those provided by business corporations, foundations, unions, etc., usually bear the name of the sponsor—*e.g.,* Sears-Roebuck Foundation Merit Scholarships. More than 1,600 awards are granted each year on the basis of competitive examinations and school records; individual amounts depend on financial need.

Similar student aid programs are sponsored by other private organizations, including churches, foundations, unions, industries, trade and professional associations, fraternal groups, and clubs.

**International Exchange Scholarships.**—An especially significant development in the second half of the 20th century has been the growth of programs of international education, or the exchange of persons between nations for educational purposes. From the wandering scholar of classical times to the Fulbright fellow and the Rhodes scholar of the 20th century, men have ignored national boundaries in their search for knowledge. But it is only in recent years that educational exchange has enjoyed the interest and active support of governments, academic institutions, and other elements of society. As a result, educational exchange has added a new dimension to higher education, and to the conduct of foreign relations. This development has been in part a response to the need for education in emerging countries unable to provide training for their own people, and in part due to the hope, if not the conviction, that the exchange of students, scholars, artists, and others concerned with education in particular and culture in general contributes to international understanding and peace.

The dimensions of educational exchange may be suggested by the fact that by the 1960s there were approximately 250,000 students annually studying at institutions of higher learning in countries other than their own. To this number must be added thousands of scholars teaching and engaged in research at foreign institutions, as well as thousands of other individuals traveling abroad on short-term educational and cultural assignments. The United States, which has replaced Europe as the mecca of the exchange student, in the 1960s was host to more than 80,000 foreign students a year, about one out of every four exchange students, and twice as many as had been there a decade earlier.

Students participating in educational exchange are the beneficiaries of a wide and growing range of financial grants. Fully two-thirds of the foreign students in the United States receive support from one or more sources, including the United States or their own government, a college or university, or a foundation, corporation, or other private organization. Internationally, there are approximately 130,000 individual opportunities each year for subsidized international study and travel offered by more than 1,600 donor agencies in over 100 states and territories.

Because international education is considered an important factor in international relations, governments have played an especially important role in supporting it. Probably the best known government program is that of the United States, popularly known as the Fulbright program (after Sen. J. William Fulbright of Arkansas, who conceived it). The Fulbright Act of 1946 and subsequent legislation concerning educational exchange were consolidated and expanded in the Mutual Educational and Cultural Exchange Act of 1961, known as the Fulbright-Hays Act. The purpose of these programs is to increase mutual understanding between the people of the United States and the people of other countries by means of educational and cultural exchange. In less than 20 years, the Fulbright Program enabled more than 26,000 Americans to study abroad and brought almost twice that many foreign citizens to the United States at an expenditure of $330,000,000. The largest proportion of these 75,000 exchangees were students. But the Fulbright program also includes other categories: elementary and secondary school teachers; college and university professors and advanced researchers; and trainees and observers.

During one fiscal year, grants were issued to more than 5,000 citizens of 130 countries and territories allowing them to come to the United States for the following purposes: over 2,000 for university study, about 750 to lecture or conduct postdoctoral research at institutions of higher learning, 800 for observation and consultation, 850 to teach in elementary or secondary schools or for specialized training, 700 for special educational travel, and 650 for advanced training and practical experience in specialized and technical fields.

During the same period, 2,500 U.S. citizens were awarded grants to go abroad: 900 for graduate study, 700 to lecture or conduct postdoctoral research at institutions of higher learning, 600 to teach in elementary or secondary schools, or to attend foreign language summer seminars, and 300 for general lecturing or specialized consultation and advice.

All these categories of the exchange programs are administered by the Board of Foreign Scholarships, Bureau of Educational and Cultural Affairs, Department of State. A number of public and private agencies assist in administering the program. The Institute of International Education is responsible for the preliminary selection of U.S. student grantees and the placement and supervision of foreign student grantees. The elementary and secondary teacher program is under the supervision of the Teacher Exchange Section, Division of International Education, Office of Education. The Conference Board of Associated Research Councils is responsible for the program for university teachers and postdoctoral research candidates.

In more than 40 countries that have signed executive agreements with the United States on educational and cultural exchange, binational commissions or foundations have been established to assist in the administration of the program abroad. In other countries this activity is the responsibility of the United States Embassy.

Foreign student candidates for Fulbright grants, which are unrestricted as to field of study, must have a Bachelor of Arts degree or its equivalent and be under 35 years of age. There are two types of awards. A limited number provide round-trip transportation only. These must be supplemented by a scholarship or a fellowship from a college, private organization or other agency, or by the candidate's own funds.

As a rule, the U.S. candidate for a Fulbright grant must have a Bachelor of Arts degree or its equivalent, although if he is in the creative and performing arts, four years of professional study or experience will be accepted in lieu of a degree. Proficiency in the language of the country in which he plans to study, general maturity, scholastic competence, and the ability to promote the basic objectives of the Fulbright program are other qualifications. Preference is given to candidates between the ages of 20 and 35. The grants range from awards to cover round-trip transportation to awards covering all expenses, including transportation, tuition, books, maintenance, and insurance.

Among the private programs in international education are those sponsored by the Guggenheim Foundation, the Rotary International, the American Association of University Women, the International Association of Students in the Economic and Commercial Sciences, and, perhaps the most prestigious of all, the Rhodes Fellowship trusts.

Rhodes scholarships, established by Cecil John Rhodes (*q.v.*) in his will, have as their purpose the promotion of unity among the English-speaking peoples of the world. The scholarships are offered to male citizens of the British Commonwealth and colonies, the Republic of South Africa, and the United States, who are between the ages of 19 and 25, of high ability and character, and who are likely to use their talents in public service. (In the periods 1903–16 and 1930–39, the awards were also offered to citizens of Germany.) In the 1960s, 70 scholarships were awarded annually, 32 of them to United States citizens, by far the largest number assigned to any one country. The scholarships are tenable for two or three years at Oxford University and carry a stipend of £900. A Rhodes scholar may marry after his first year of residence at Oxford.

Other nations also support exchange programs for their own and foreign students. An estimated 10,000 students from developing countries and several thousand more from neighbouring Communist countries are studying under scholarships in the Soviet Union. A great majority of the more than 60,000 foreign students in Great Britain are indirectly subsidized by government funds, while all 30,000 foreign students in France receive free tuition, subsidized meals, social security services, and other benefits.

In Austria, the Minister for Education grants about 170 annual scholarships and about 50 summer scholarships for language courses, for which foreign students, including new graduates, are eligible, some of them under exchange schemes. Denmark offers eight-month exchange scholarships including contributions to travel expenses, to both graduate and undergraduate students of 13 Western European countries, including the United Kingdom, France, and the Federal Republic of Germany, and to nationals of the U.S.S.R., Czechoslovakia, Yugoslavia, Poland, Turkey, Japan, and the United States; scholarships for postgraduate study are offered to nationals of Belgium, Czechoslovakia, Italy, Poland, the U.S.S.R., and the United States; and about 235 unilateral scholarships of varying periods of tenure are offered to students from the developing countries.

The Federal Republic of Germany has many scholarships programs, both public and private, for foreign university students. The Deutsche Akademische Austauschdienst (German Centre for Academic Exchanges) awards more than 2,000 such scholarships and organizes exchanges of students in engineering, natural sciences, medicine, and occasionally in agriculture and political economy. The individual German *Länder* also offer scholarships; and a total of several hundred is awarded by Roman Catholic and Protestant institutions, by the Friedrich Ebert Foundation, and by the German associations of student unions. Exchange programs with foreign universities are founded partly on sponsorship and other links. Scholarships and exchange programs for foreign students are open to nationals of most countries of the world. In the 1960s about a quarter of the foreign scholarship holders came from Europe, and the remainder from the Far East, Latin America, Africa, the Near East, North America, and Australia. In Hungary, about 200 foreign students are granted scholarships each year by the government on the basis of cultural and other agreements with countries of Africa, Asia, and Latin America. The government of India awards each year nearly 500 scholarships and fellowships to students of certain Asian, African, European, and other countries. There are scholarship exchanges, under cultural exchange agreements, with a number of countries including Bulgaria, Greece, Poland, Rumania, Yugoslavia, the U.S.S.R., and the United Arab Republic. Other reciprocal scholarship schemes exist with other countries of Europe and South America. Under the Commonwealth Education Co-operation scheme, the government awards scholarships, fellowships, and bursaries to nationals of Commonwealth countries, some of them for postgraduate study, others for teacher training, for study or observation by senior educationists, and for the training of craft instructors. The awards vary in duration from three months to two years; those for craft instructors are open only to nationals of those Commonwealth countries not included in the educational exchange program conducted under the Colombo Plan.

**International Organization.**—International agencies, naturally, play a major role in supporting international studies. Such specialized agencies of the United Nations as the Food and Agriculture Organization, the World Health Organization, the United Nations Educational, Scientific, and Cultural Organization, and the International Atomic Energy Agency employ exchange programs to encourage proficiency in specialized fields and to assist the development of emerging countries. The fellowship awards are usually made to experienced individuals whose work in areas important to their home countries will be benefited by specialized training or study. The awards are granted for work in any country in which study or training may be effectively pursued. The grants usually include round-trip transportation, tuition, books, and a monthly maintenance allowance which varies according to the country to which the grantee is assigned.

Among the major agencies sponsoring such fellowships is the Food and Agriculture Organization, which provides grants to enable scientists and technicians from less developed countries to advance their training in various aspects of nutrition, agriculture, forestry, and other related fields. The World Health Organization maintains one of the largest fellowship programs, designed to improve standards of health and the level of teaching and training in countries throughout the world. It awards fellowships in public health, nursing, sanitation, child care, and related medical fields. The fellowship program of the International Atomic Energy Agency is one of the smallest but most highly specialized, concerned with such subjects as the development and use of nuclear energy for peaceful purposes and the theoretical and experimental aspects of the science and technology of nuclear energy.

Contrasted to the highly specialized program of the International Atomic Energy Agency is the United Nations Educational, Scientific, and Cultural Organization's program, which sponsors a broad fellowship program in the field of education, social science, cultural activities, mass communications, and the mutual appreciation of Western and non-Western cultural values. More than 2,000 persons a year are beneficiaries of UNESCO fellowships. In all, the various intergovernmental agencies of UNESCO provided more than 30,000 fellowships to nationals of developing countries by the 1960s.

Another major source of sponsorship of international educational programs is regional organizations, whose interest in underwriting such programs is, as in the case of UN agencies, to assist economic development and encourage international understanding. Since 1958 the Organization of American States has awarded up to 500 fellowships a year to candidates from member nations to allow study for between three months and two years in any other member country and in any field representing a basic need of their home country. These grants cover, at the maximum, tuition, maintenance, and transportation.

Similar in purpose to the OAS fellowship program, though far more modest in scope, are the programs sponsored by such regional organizations as the Southeast Asia Treaty Organization, the Organization for Economic Cooperation and Development, and the Colombo Plan. (G. K. H.)

Bibliography.—Institute of International Education, *Open Doors 1964: a Report on International Exchange, Handbook on International Study:* vol. i, *For Foreign Nationals;* vol. ii, *For U.S. Nationals* (1965); UNESCO, *Study Abroad* (biennial); S. N. Feingold, *Scholarships, Fellowships and Loans,* vol. i–iv (1949–62), with bibliography; university and college calendars, or catalogues, announcements, bulletins, etc., usually issued annually; publications of the U.S. Department of Health, Education, and Welfare, Office of Education; *Commonwealth Universities Yearbook* (annual); *Higher Education in the United Kingdom* (biennial). (W. J. Gr.; W. E. T.; G. K. H.)

**STUKELEY, WILLIAM** (1687–1765), English antiquary and physician, born at Holbeach, Lincolnshire, on Nov. 7, 1687, is remembered especially for his studies of such archaeological sites as the great stone circles of Avebury and Stonehenge (*qq.v.*). His surveys of these monuments in the 1720s are still of considerable interest, and he made extensive antiquarian travels recorded in his *Itinerarium curiosum* (1724). His accounts of Stonehenge and Avebury were published in 1740 and 1743 respectively, by which time Stukeley had developed extravagant theories relating the Druids to such stone circles. These views were widely and enthusiastically accepted in the late 18th century (*see* Druidism). He died in London on March 3, 1765.

*See* S. Piggott, *William Stukeley* (1950). (S. Pt.)

**STUMPF, CARL** (1848–1936), German philosopher and theoretical psychologist known principally for his work on the psychology of music, was born in Wiesentheid, Bavaria, April 21, 1848. A precocious child and a musical prodigy, he received his education at home, in the gymnasia of neighbouring towns, at Würzburg with Franz Brentano, and at Göttingen with Hermann Lotze, from whom he received his Ph.D. in 1868. After two years of further study with Brentano at Würzburg he habilitated as a dozent at Göttingen in 1870. In the spring of 1873 he published his first book, *Über den psychologischen Ursprung der Raumvorstellung* ("The Psychological Origin of Space Perception"), which won him the chair at Würzburg that autumn. During the next two decades, Stumpf changed his affiliation many times, moving to Prague (1879), Halle (1884), Munich (1889), and finally to Berlin (1894), where he held the chair in philosophy and the directorship of the laboratory until he retired in 1921. Stumpf was joint president of the International Congress of Psychology in Munich (1896); founded the *Beiträge zur Akustik und Musikwissenschaft* ("Contributions to Acoustics and Musicology," 1898); established the *Phonographische Archiv* of primitive music (1900); and served as rector of the university (1907–08). He died at Berlin on Dec. 25, 1936.

Stumpf's chief books are *Tonpsychologie*, 2 vol. (1883–90); *Über Leib und Seele* ("Body and Soul," 1897); *Philosophische Reden und Vorträge* ("Philosophic Speeches and Lectures," 1910); *Die Anfänge der Musik* ("The Origins of Music," 1911); and *Die Sprachlaute* ("The Sounds of Speech," 1926).

*See* H. S. Langfeld in the *Amer. J. Psychol.*, 49:316–320 (1937). (K. M. D.)

**STUMPF, JOHANNES** (1500–1578?), Swiss chronicler and theologian and one of the most important personalities of the Swiss Reformation. He was born in Bruchsal, Ger., on April 23, 1500, and in 1521 entered the order of the Knights of St. John in Freiburg im Breisgau, a year later being appointed prior at Bubikon, Zürich. He there declared himself for the Reformation and, as the friend of Zwingli, worked faithfully for the Reformers until his retirement in 1562. He died in Zürich between Martinmas (Nov. 11) 1577 and Martinmas 1578.

Stumpf's enduring fame rests upon his *Gemeiner loblicher Eydgnoschafft Stetten, Landen und Völkern chronikwirdiger Thaaten beschreybung* (1547–48), probably the most famous of Swiss chronicles. It remained a standard work until the 18th century. Like his many other books, it is marked by its combination of objectivity with intensity of participation.

*See* Stumpf's *Schweizer- und Reformationschronik*, ed. by E. Gagliardi, H. Müller, and F. Büsser, 2 vol. (1953–55) and his *Beschreibung des Abendmahlsstreites zwischen Zwingli und Luther*, ed. by F. Büsser (1959). (F. BÜ.)

**STUPA,** Buddhist religious building, also called a tope or dagoba, consisting of a solid mass of masonry, built above a receptacle containing a sacred relic. Although the origin of the stupa was probably the more primitive tumulus, or mound of earth over a grave, its development in historic times was toward greater and greater height and richness of treatment. Outside Tibet and China, a profile generally conical and of great height was developed, as in the famous gilded example in the centre of the Shwe Dagon, in Rangoon. The Tibetan form, developed to a great degree of beauty and richness in China, has a bulbous silhouette, wider near the top than at the bottom. The most famous of the Indian stupas is the largest of a group at Sanchi, which is generally attributed to the time of Asoka (3rd century B.C.). In it the stupa proper is surrounded by a circular walk, around which is a richly decorated stone fence, pierced by four richly sculptured gateways, the whole designed in forms manifestly reminiscent of wooden construction.

*See* also TEMPLE ARCHITECTURE; INDIAN ARCHITECTURE; and references under "Stupa" in the Index.

**STURDZA,** a great Rumanian boyar family that is recorded from the 15th century, when it owned land at Valea Berheciului in Moldavia. Several of its members were prominent at the court of the Moldavian princes in the 16th–17th centuries. In the 19th century it reached the zenith of its importance.

IOAN SANDU STURDZA was prince of Moldavia from 1822 to 1828, the first to hold that rank after the fall of the Phanariot regime. He supported the liberalism of the petty boyars, and his draft of a constitution was the first in Moldavian history, but in 1828 he was deposed by the Russians.

MIHAI, or MICHAEL, STURDZA (1795–1884) was prince of Moldavia from 1834 to 1849. He founded the high school at Iași known as the Academia Mihăileană, emancipated the gypsies from serfdom (1844), and forcefully suppressed the popular insurrection of 1848. His son GRIGORE (1821–1901) served with the Turkish Army in the Crimean War under the name and title of Muhlis Pasha and was a candidate for the princely throne of Moldavia in 1859.

ALEXANDRU STURDZA (1791–1854), a cousin of Prince Michael, was a diplomat in the Russian service. A champion of the Orthodox Eastern Church against Roman Catholicism, he wrote numerous philosophical works in Rumanian, many of which were translated into other languages. His sister ROXANDA (1786–1844), who as Countess Edling exercised some influence at the court of the Russian emperor Alexander I, wrote verse in French. Another writer was ALEXANDRU A. STURDZA (1867–1917), author of works in French on Rumanian historical subjects.

DIMITRIE ALEXANDRU STURDZA (1833–1914), statesman and four times prime minister of Rumania, was born at Miclăușeni, near Iași, on March 10, 1833. After studies in Germany, he became secretary to the Moldavian *divan ad hoc* of 1857 and then secretary to the commission of 1858 (*see* RUMANIA: *History*), which prepared the de facto unification of Moldavia and Walachia under Alexandru Ion Cuza (*q.v.*). He later opposed the agrarian reform sponsored by Cuza, whose abdication he helped to bring about. He then favoured the accession of Prince Charles of Hohenzollern-Sigmaringen to the Rumanian throne (*see* CAROL I). In the cabinets of Ion Ghica and Ion C. Brătianu, he was successively minister of public works, of finance, of education, and of foreign affairs. Chairman of the Liberal Party from 1892, he was prime minister in 1895–96, 1897–99, 1901–04, and 1907–09; he severely suppressed the peasant rising of 1907. He also published works on Rumanian foreign policy and on numismatics, and some major collections of historical documents; and from 1909 he was secretary-general of the Rumanian Academy. He died in Bucharest in October 1914.

**STURE,** the name of several Swedish noble families, only distantly related, to which belonged three regents of Sweden in the late Middle Ages, who to some extent epitomized national resistance to rule by Danish kings: the regents Sten Sture the Elder, Svante (Nilsson) Sture, and Sten Sture the Younger.

STEN STURE THE ELDER (*c.* 1440–1503) was appointed regent on the death (1470) of King Charles VIII and established himself in office by defeating the Danish king Christian I at Brunkeberg outside Stockholm (1471). Sten Sture gradually increased his power by ruthlessly playing off various factions in the *riksråd* (council) and nobility against each other. By the mid-1490s he had a firm grip on central and local administration, and had at his disposal the strongest castles in the country. He had deprived the *riksråd* of the possibility of independent intervention in governmental affairs. Then, because of the untenable external political situation—war on two fronts with Denmark and Russia—he was forced in 1497 to yield to the Danish king John (Hans). In 1501, through an uprising, he again became regent until his death in 1503. His administrative and military changes are regarded as the basis on which the Swedish monarchy achieved stability in the 16th century.

SVANTE (NILSSON) STURE (*c.* 1460–1512), succeeding as regent in 1503, tried to continue his predecessor's politics but lacked his fixity of purpose and energy. He mastered neither internal nor foreign affairs and was forced to make repeated concessions to the *riksråd*. The latter appeared to be gaining the upper hand when Svante Sture died suddenly in 1512.

STEN (SVANTESSON) STURE THE YOUNGER (*c.* 1492–1520) secured the regency for himself despite the opposition of the *riksråd*. He proved to be a master at neutralizing his political opponents by means of sudden coups, unscrupulous propaganda, and systematic persecution. He quickly restored the regency's former authority, then forced the *riksråd* into complete submission and subordinated the church to the state. Against Denmark he conducted a policy of procrastination which gave the country much-needed peace. When the war again broke out he warded off two Danish attacks, but in the third (1520) he himself was wounded and died. (G. T. WE.)

**STURGE, JOSEPH** (1793–1859), English philanthropist and political reformer, who was a leading member of the antislavery movement, was born at Elberton, Gloucester, on Aug. 2, 1793, the son of a farmer. After abandoning farming for corn dealing in 1814, he settled in Bewdley, Worcestershire. He came from a Quaker family and founded a branch of the Peace Society in Worcester in 1818 and organized the local antislavery movement. He moved to Birmingham in 1822 and became secretary of the Birmingham branch of the Anti-Slavery Society in 1826, but he soon went beyond Quaker politics and joined the Birmingham Political Union, founded by Thomas Attwood in 1829. His business interests prospered, but he retained his zeal for the antislavery movement even after the act of 1833 which abolished slavery in the British colonies. He toured the West Indies in 1836–37, collecting evidence of continued ill-treatment of Negroes, and in 1839 he was one of the founders of the new British and Foreign Anti-Slavery Society, designed to press for the abolition of slavery throughout the world.

From the antislavery movement he turned to the domestic battles for repeal of the corn laws and extension of the suffrage, and brought both causes together in the National Complete Suffrage Union, which he founded in 1842. He was unable, however, to unite repealers and Chartists in one common agitation, and the union failed in 1844 amid recriminations on both sides. Sturge failed to win a seat in Parliament but continued to support the causes in which he believed. He was an assiduous attender, for example, of world peace conferences, and in January 1854, on the eve of the Crimean War, he went as a Quaker emissary to Russia to plead with Nicholas I. In May 1858 he became president of the Peace Society. He died at Edgbaston, Birmingham, on May 14, 1859. (A. Bri.)

**STURGEON,** a sharklike bony fish of the family Acipenseridae, of ancient lineage. The more than 20 species are found only in the Northern Hemisphere. Several of them provide caviar (from eggs) and isinglass (from the swim bladders). Most sturgeons pass a great part of the year in the sea, but periodically ascend large rivers, some in spring to deposit their spawn, others later in the season; a few are confined to fresh water.

Sturgeons are identified by bony plates covering the head and by five rows of bony shields along the body, one along the back, one on each side above the pectoral fin, and one on each side near the belly. The tail fin is unequal, the upper lobe being longer than the lower. The toothless mouth, on the underside of the snout, is preceded by four fleshy feelers. The lips are protractile and have taste buds surrounding them. The form of the snout becomes more blunt and abbreviated with age.

Sturgeons are ground feeders that spend much time in foraging, dragging their tactile barbels over the bottom in search of food. They are found in the greatest abundance in the rivers of southern Russia during the two weeks of the upstream migration and in the freshwaters of North America. Early in summer the fish migrate into the rivers or toward the shores of freshwater lakes in large shoals for breeding purposes. The ova are small and numerous. The growth of the young is rapid. After the sturgeon attains maturity, growth continues for several years, but slowly. Some attain great age: observations made in Russia indicate that the hausen or beluga (*Huso huso*) may attain an age of between 200 and 300 years. Sturgeons ranging from 8 to 11 ft. (2 to 3 m.) in length are by no means scarce, and some species grow to a much larger size.

The common sturgeon (*Acipenser sturio*) occurs from Scandinavia to the Mediterranean. A very closely related form, considered by some authorities to be of the same species, occurs along the east coast of North America from the St. Lawrence River to the Gulf of Mexico. Females, which are larger than the males, reach a length of at least 12 ft. (4 m.); and specimens of 18 ft. (5.5 m.) have been reported. They feed on bottom-living invertebrates and fishes. They spawn in late spring and early summer.

*A. guldenstadtii* is one of the most valuable species of the rivers of the Soviet Union, extending from Russia eastward as far as Lake Baikal. It attains the same size as the common sturgeon and abounds particularly in the rivers of the Black and Caspian seas. A smaller species, the sterlet (*A. ruthenus*), inhabits the Black and Caspian seas.

*A. stellatus* occurs in abundance in the rivers of the Black Sea and of the Sea of Azov and the Caspian Sea. It has a long and pointed snout like the sterlet. Its flesh is highly esteemed and its caviar and isinglass bring the highest price.

The lake sturgeon of North America (*A. fulvescens*) occurs in the Mississippi Valley, the Great Lakes, and northward into Canada. A few thousand pounds a year are caught commercially. The white, Oregon or Sacramento, sturgeon (*A. transmontanus*) occurs on the Pacific coast of North America from Monterey to Alaska. It is identified by bony plates between the ventral fins and by small anal fins in two rows of 4 to 8. It is one of the three largest species, growing to nearly 2,000 lb., according to old accounts. Almost half a million pounds are caught annually.

The beluga is another of the large species, reaching a length of 24 ft. (more than 7 m.) and a weight of 3,000 lb. It inhabits the Caspian and Black seas, and the Sea of Azov. Its flesh, caviar, and air bladder are of less value than those of the smaller kinds.

The family Acipenseridae includes one other genus, *Scaphirhynchus,* the shovelhead or shovelnose sturgeon, distinguished by the long, broad, flat snout and the union of the longitudinal rows of scales posteriorly. All the species are confined to freshwater. One of them is common in the Mississippi and other rivers of North America; the other three occur in the larger rivers of eastern Asia.

The flesh of sturgeon is sold fresh, pickled, or smoked. Caviar consists of the eggs, which have been separated from the surrounding tissue of the roe, sometimes washed in white wine or vinegar, and pickled with salt. The largest production of sturgeon caviar is in the U.S.S.R. The inner membrane of the swim bladders, which is removed by a process of washing and air drying, is used in the preparation of isinglass, which is a very pure form of gelatin used for a variety of industrial purposes, *e.g.*, in clarification of wine and beer, for making jellies, and for special cements. (L. A. Wd.)

**STURGEON BAY,** the seat of Door County, in northeastern Wisconsin, U.S., 145 mi. (233 km.) N of Milwaukee, is a lake port. The city is on an inlet of the same name on the western or Green Bay side of the Door Peninsula in Lake Michigan. The federal government maintains a ship canal constructed across the peninsula in 1878. Activities of earlier days were sawmilling, which began in the 1850s, and the quarrying of limestone. The city derives income from the processing of red cherries, for which the surrounding region is famous; from manufacture of shoes and leatherwork; and from shipbuilding and the handling of water freight. The scenic beauty of the area makes the city the headquarters of an important tourist trade. It has one of the largest yacht storage facilities on the Great Lakes. For comparative population figures *see* table in Wisconsin: *Population.* (W. F. Ry.)

**STURGIS, RUSSELL** (1836–1909), U.S. architect and author of a number of books on art, was a perceptive critic of the architecture of his time, being, for example, one of the first writers on architecture to appreciate the work of Frank Lloyd Wright. Sturgis was born in Baltimore County, Md., on Oct. 16, 1836. He graduated from the Free Academy in New York (now the City College of New York) in 1856, studied architecture under Leopold Eidlitz and then for two years in Munich, returning to the United States in 1862. He designed the Yale University Chapel and the Farnham and Durfee dormitories at Yale, the Flower Hospital, New York, the Farmers' and Mechanics' Bank, Albany, N.Y., and many other buildings. He edited *A Dictionary of Architecture and Building,* 3 vol. (1901–02) and the English version of Wilhelm Lübke's *Outlines of the History of Art,* 2 vol. (1904), and wrote *European Architecture* (1896), *How to Judge Architecture* (1903), *The Appreciation of Sculpture* (1904), *The Appreciation of Pictures* (1905), *A Study of the Artist's Way of Working in the Various Handicrafts and Arts of Design,* 2 vol. (1905), and an unfinished *History of Architecture* (1906 *et seq.*). He died in New York City on Feb. 11, 1909.

**STURM, (JACQUES) CHARLES FRANÇOIS** (1803–1855), Swiss mathematician of Alsatian parentage, who was the originator of the Sturm theorem of equations, was born at Geneva on Sept. 29, 1803, and entered the university there in 1818. The death of his father meant that while there he had to support his family by private coaching. He visited Paris in 1823, as tutor to the de Broglie family, through whom he met many of the leading French men of science. He finally settled there in 1825. With Colladon, in 1826, he made the first accurate determination of the velocity of sound in water, and a year later wrote a prize essay on compressible fluids. The theorem which bears his name, regarding the number of real roots of a numerical equation included between given limits, was discovered in 1829 (*see* Equations, Theory of). His work on what is now called the Sturm-Liouville theory of differential equations of the second order was published in 1834 and won for him the Grand Prix des Sciences Mathématiques (*see* also Liouville, Joseph). He was elected to the

Académie des Sciences in 1836, and was appointed to the staff of the École Polytechnique in 1838. Finally he succeeded Siméon Denis Poisson in the chair of mechanics in the Faculté des Sciences in Paris in 1840. He died in Paris, on Dec. 18, 1855. His *Cours d'analyse de l'école polytechnique* (1857–63) and *Cours de mécanique de l'école polytechnique* (1861) were published posthumously. Although primarily an analyst, Sturm made significant contributions to projective geometry and to the differential geometry of curves and surfaces. (G. A. B.)

**ŠTURSA, JAN** (1880–1925), one of the leaders of the modern school of Czech sculpture, was born at Nové Město in Moravia on May 15, 1880. In 1899 he entered the Academy of Fine Arts at Prague as a pupil of the influential teacher J. V. Myslbek. His early works manifest the character of the symbolic literature of the period, and reflect also the plastic qualities of Rodin's sculpture. His individuality began to proclaim itself in such lyric works as "Puberty" (1905), "The Melancholy Girl" (1906), and "Primavera" (1907). A journey to Italy in 1907 was the opening of a new epoch in his development. "Eve" (1908, State gallery, Munich), "Hetaira" (1909), and the later "Gift of Heaven and Earth" demonstrate his sensitivity to feminine beauty as well as, stylistically, a tendency toward simplification of sculptural form and increasing expressive strength. Occasional excursions into extremes of sensuality, as in his monumental representation of the dancer "Sulamith Rahu" (1911, Venice), were not sustained. His decorative commissions, notably the groups for the pylons of the Hlavka bridge at Prague, are marked by intricate compositional massing restrained by strong, almost geometric, tensions. Štursa's war experiences gave to his mature style a tragic and more profound character, as in "Wounded Man" (1916), expressed in bold and vigorous sculptural terms. In 1916 he became professor in the Academy of Fine Arts at Prague, and in 1923–24 its director. He produced a number of portrait busts, the most noteworthy being "President Masaryk." Štursa died in Prague on May 2, 1925.

*See* A. Matějček and Z. Wirth, *Modern and Contemporary Czech Art* (1924). (N. L. R.)

**STURZO, LUIGI** (1871–1959), Italian priest and political organizer, promoter of the Christian Democratic movement in Italy, was born at Caltagirone, Sic., on Nov. 26, 1871. He studied at the Gregorian University, Rome, and became professor of philosophy and sociology in his native town. On the outbreak of World War I he went to Rome as secretary of Azione Cattolica (Catholic Action). In 1919 he founded the Partito Popolare and became its first political secretary. Sturzo and his party took their stand on papal encyclicals concerning the social order and advocated reforms of a radical nature, especially in agriculture.

At the elections of November 1919 the newly founded Partito Popolare secured 101 seats and became a dominant force in politics, if not with the Giolitti Cabinet certainly during the subsequent Bonomi Cabinet. After the Fascist "march on Rome" several Popolari entered the first Mussolini Cabinet, but soon the party joined the opposition. In 1923, however, the Vatican, subjected to pressure from Mussolini, withdrew its support from Sturzo in an attempt to reach some understanding with the Fascists. Sturzo's party had by now much shrunk as an outcome of Fascist electoral methods. He resigned the leadership in 1923 and left Italy in October 1924. Sturzo spent his 20 years of exile first in London and after the outbreak of World War II in the U.S. His party in Italy was driven underground, but after the overthrow of Fascism many of his ideas reemerged in the Christian Democratic Party, headed by Alcide de Gasperi and other followers of Sturzo, who revered him as the father of their ideas. He returned to Italy after the war and was made a senator for life in 1952. He died in Rome on Aug. 8, 1959. His books include *Italy and Fascism* (1927), *Church and State* (1939), *Italy and the Coming World* (1945), and other works not translated into English. (B. Wl.)

**STUTTERING:** *see* Speech Disorders.

**STUTTGART,** the capital of the *Land* (state) of Baden-Württemberg, Federal Republic of Germany, lies on both banks of the Neckar, a tributary of the Rhine, approximately 120 mi. (190 km.) N.W. of Munich and 70 mi. (110 km.) E.N.E. of Strasbourg in France. Stuttgart lies in the midst of woods, orchards and vineyards, but it is also an important industrial town and notable for its modern architecture. Some of the earliest work on the invention of the motorcar was done in Stuttgart and the oldest motorcar factory in the world is there. Pop. (1961) 637,539.

In the centre of the town is the Schillerplatz with a statue of Schiller by B. Thorwaldsen (1839), the old castle which dates from the 13th century (completed 1553–78) and now houses the state museum with its collection of prehistoric and historic objects, and the Stiftskirche (collegiate church), a 12th-century Romanesque basilica completed in the late Gothic style (1436–95). Immediately to the northeast is the Schlossplatz with its Jubilee column (1841–46), one of the most beautiful squares in Germany. In it is the new palace (1746–1807), built on a typical 18th-century plan; it was burned in 1944 and under reconstruction in the 1950s. Farther to the northeast are the Theater-Anlagen, with rose and other gardens, and the opera house of the Württemberg State opera along its eastern side. These gardens are continued northeast by the Schlossgarten Anlagen, with the main railway station on its west, to the Neckar, which there takes a right-angle turn to the northeast. On its left bank are the Wilhelma botanical and zoological gardens and the Rosenstein palace (1825–29), now the natural history museum. To the north and over the river is Bad-Cannstatt which, with Stuttgart-Berg on the other bank, has many mineral springs; the number of baths and swimming pools, mineral and otherwise, is a notable feature of the town. The city church in Bad-Cannstatt was built in 1471–1506. Along the east bank of the river lies the Cannstatter Wasen, a large sports ground with a sports stadium holding 100,000 spectators; every autumn the big Cannstatter folk festival is held there. The rococo Solitude palace (1763–67) stands in the wooded hills to the west of the town; Hohenheim palace (1768–85), housing the college of agriculture, is to the south. In the north of the city is the Höhenpark Killesberg, a large park with exhibition halls, an observation tower, chair lift and miniature railway, and adjoining it to the southeast is the Weissenhof estate, built in 1927 by 16 German and other architects. Other modern buildings include the town hall (1954–56) in the market place, south of the Schillerplatz; the television tower (1955), to the south, which is 633 ft. high with an observation platform and restaurant; the Stuttgarter Liederhalle (concert and congress hall) built in 1954–56. Not far from the market place is the late Gothic St. Leonard's church (1463–74), of special interest as being of the hall type with nave and aisles of the same height.

Stuttgart has a technical college and institutions for agriculture, music, art and architecture. The Staatsgalerie, in Neckarstrasse, has German paintings up to the 20th century and 15th- to 17th-century Dutch and Italian pictures. The Württemberg Land library in the Urbanstrasse contains the second largest collection of Bibles in the world. One of the most interesting of the museums is the Daimler-Benz automobile museum in Untertürkheim on the east bank of the Neckar. Gottlieb Daimler's tomb is in the Uff cemetery in Bad-Cannstatt and a memorial to him stands in the park there.

Stuttgart is an important transport junction at the centre of railway connections stretching all over Europe. It lies on two *Autobahnen* (Frankfurt-Munich-Salzburg and Stuttgart-Heilbronn) and has an airport 8 mi. from the city. The port, which is at the end of the Neckar, was opened in 1958 and will take shipping up to 1,200 tons. The city is the largest industrial centre in southwest Germany. Electrical engineering is of primary importance, followed by vehicle and machine construction. Textiles, clothing, precision tools, foodstuffs, luxury wooden and leather goods, shoes, musical instruments, chemicals and paper are manufactured. There are also large breweries. Stuttgart has a special reputation as a book centre, with numerous printing works and more than 200 publishing houses.

Settlements existed in the area of what is today Bad-Cannstatt in prehistoric times, and the Romans established a fort there. Stuttgart itself developed from a *Stuotgarten*, a *Gestüt* or stud farm, which was set up in about 950. It developed into a town about 1254 under Count Ulrich "the Founder." In 1495 it became the capital of the new dukedom of Württemberg, which in 1806 became a kingdom. With the industrial revolution, the court and administrative town quickly expanded, its population rising from 48,000 in 1850 to 177,000 in 1900 and 460,000 in 1939. (U. S.)

**STUYVESANT, PETER** (1610–1672), Dutch colonial governor who tried to resist the English seizure of New York, was born in Scherpenzeel, Friesland, son of a Calvinist minister. He began his career in the Dutch West India Company about 1632, and in 1643 became director in the company's colonies of Curacao, Aruba, and Bonaire. While he was unsuccessfully attacking the Portuguese island of Saint Martin, his right leg was severely injured and had to be amputated. Thereafter he wore a wooden leg. In 1645 he was selected by the company to supersede Willem Kieft as director general of all Dutch possessions in North America and the Caribbean. He arrived in New Amsterdam (later New York City) in 1647 and energetically set about renovating the government of the colony of New Netherland and the fortunes of the nearly bankrupt company.

Almost immediately began his lasting conflict with the burghers, who were alienated by his violent and despotic methods and his devotion to the interests of the company. In response to the demands for self-government he and the council in 1647 appointed an advisory board of nine, and in 1653 there was established the first municipal government for the city of New Amsterdam, modeled after that of the cities of Holland. These concessions, however, proved hollow, for Stuyvesant never ceased to dominate the government. He also aroused opposition because of his efforts to improve the system of defense and to prevent the sale of liquor and firearms to the Indians, and because of his persecutions of Lutherans and Quakers, to which the company finally put an end. In 1650 he sacrificed a large amount of territory in a settlement of the boundary between New Netherland and Connecticut. He succeeded, however, in dislodging the Swedes from their settlement in Dutch territory on the Delaware and in establishing peace with the Indians. In August 1664 the British, led by Col. Richard Nicolls with four ships and about 300 or 400 men, seized New Netherland, which Charles II of England had granted his brother, the duke of York. Stuyvesant was forced to surrender when the burghers refused to aid him. The West India Company made him the scapegoat for what actually were defects in company policies. He spent the remainder of his life on his New York farm, "the Bouwerie," from which New York City's "Bowery" takes its name. He died in February 1672 and was buried in a chapel on the site of which in 1799 was erected St. Mark's Church.

THE GRANGER COLLECTION

STUYVESANT, PORTRAIT PAINTED BY AN UNKNOWN ARTIST ABOUT 1660–70

*See* Henry H. Kessler and Eugene Rachlis, *Peter Stuyvesant and His New York* (1959). (E. S. By.)

**STYLE, LITERARY,** involves the selection and organization of the features of language for expressive effects, and includes all uses of sound patterns, words, figures of speech, images, and syntactic forms. In an absolute sense, the word "style" (Lat. *stilus,* "writing-rod") means a good or distinguished manner with language, as in: "Proust has style," or "Theodore Dreiser lacks style." Prose style only is treated here (*see* also POETRY; POETIC IMAGERY; PROSE; RHETORIC; ORATORY; FIGURES OF SPEECH; LANGUAGE: *The Structure of Language*).

**Views on Style.**—Aristotle, Cicero, and Quintilian treated style as the proper adornment of thought. In this view, which prevailed throughout the Renaissance period, devices of style can be catalogued. The essayist or orator is expected to frame his ideas with the help of model sentences and prescribed kinds of "figures" suitable to his mode of discourse.

Jonathan Swift's dictum on style, "Proper Words in Proper Places" (in *A Letter to a Young Gentleman, Lately Enter'd into Holy Orders,* 1721), stands midway between the idea of style as something properly added to thoughts, and the 20th-century ideas that derive from Charles Bally (1865–1947), the Swiss philologist. According to followers of Bally, style in language arises from the possibility of choice among alternative forms of expression, as for example, between "children," "kids," "youngsters," and "youths," each of which has a different evocative value. Any expression may give rise to a variety of effects, and the effect will be more forceful as the expression deviates from normal usage. Thus style depends on choice, evocation, polyvalency, and deviation in language. This theory emphasizes the relation between style and linguistics.

Style is also seen as a mark of character. Buffon's famous epigram, *"Le style est l'homme même"* ("Style is the man himself") in his *Discours sur le style* (1753), and Schopenhauer's definition of style as "the physiognomy of the mind" suggest that, no matter how calculatingly choices may be made, a writer's style will bear the mark of his personality. Style is "the mental picture of the man who writes," to quote Edmund Gosse's article "Style" for the 11th edition of *Encyclopædia Britannica* (1911). This view would account for the underlying consistency of individual styles. An experienced writer is able to rely on the power of his habitual choices of sounds, words, and syntactic patterns to convey his personality or fundamental outlook. Some effects of the possible choices are illustrated below.

**Syntax.**—Different expressive effects arise from every kind of phrase, clause, and sentence; from coordination and subordination, parallelism, word order, grammar, and other sentence features.

*Loose and Periodic Sentences.*—The distinction between the loose sentence (in which the main clause is completed early and other main clauses or subordinate ones follow) and the periodic (in which the main clause is not completed until the end) is central to style. Tacitus used the loose structure, with curt main clauses, for swift movement and smart concision: *"Quattuor principes ferro interempti: trina bella civilia, plura externa ac plerumque permixta: prosperae in Oriente, adversae in Occidente res: turbatum Illyricum, Galliae nutantes, perdomita Britannia et statim omissa"* ("Four emperors perished by the sword; there were three civil wars; there were more with foreign enemies; there were often wars that had both characters at once. There was success in the East, and disaster in the West. There were disturbances in Illyricum; Gaul wavered in its allegiance; Britain was thoroughly subdued and immediately abandoned"; *Historiae,* I, ii, *c.* A.D. 110). Sir Thomas Malory demonstrates the ease and flow of loose structure; Rabelais shows how flexible and informal it can be. Periodic structure is more apt to increase tension, heighten detail, and command attention, since the meaning is held in suspense. Cicero used a lengthy periodic structure to great emotional effect in the "grand style" (*genus grande*) of his oratory; Macaulay used a short variety, with dramatic twists in meaning, for surprise, as in "To this step, taken in the mere wantonness of tyranny, and in criminal ignorance or more criminal contempt of public feeling, our country owes her freedom" (*History of England,* 1848).

*Parallelism.*—Parallelism can be a means of ordering, emphasizing, or pointing out relations in the sentence; to some degree it is a feature of all good prose. In John Lyly's *Euphues* (1578) transverse alliteration is used to draw attention to parallel structure, as in "Ah my Philautus, if the *w*asting of our *m*oney might not *d*ehort us, yet the *w*ounding of our *m*inds should *d*eter us . . ." Such emphasis can cloy; but parallelism lends wit and authority to the antithetic aphorism, as in La Rochefoucauld's *"Nous aimons toujours ceux qui nous admirent, et nous n'aimons pas toujours ceux que nous admirons"* ("We always love those who admire us, but we do not always love those whom we admire"; *Maximes,* 1665). John Henry Newman, in his *Apologia pro vita sua* (1864), used chiasmic or inverted parallel structure for strong emphasis: "I have changed in many things: in this I have not."

*Word Order.*—Expressive effects of word order are most forceful when words are in prominent positions (*e.g.*, at the end of the sentence) or out of their usual order. In Thomas Love Peacock's sentence "King Gwythno had feasted joyously, and had sung his new ode to a chosen party of his admiring subjects, amidst their, of course, enthusiastic applause" (*The Misfortunes of Elphin,* 1829), humour results from the placing of the "of course" in a logical, rather than a conventional, position. Flaubert's word order can mirror psychological processes, as in *"Au milieu de cette ombre, par endroits, brillaient des blancheurs de baïonnettes"* (*L'Éducation sentimentale,* 1869). Here the order of the words follows the order of impressions as they occur to the onlooker: *"ombre"* (darkness), *"endroits"* (parts), *"brillaient"* (shone), *"blancheurs"* (whiteness), and *"baïonnettes"* (bayonets).

*Grammar.*—Different grammatical forms give rise to different expressive effects. In "Bill kissed Sally" and in "Sally was kissed by Bill" the same event is described; but the passive form focuses attention on Sally (and what happened to her) and the active on Bill (and what he did). In dialogue, and in psychological realism, grammatical conventions are sometimes violated for effect. For example, Dickens put into the mouth of his quick-witted scalawag, Mr. Alfred Jingle, such staccato asyntactical speeches as "Epic poem,—ten thousand lines—revolution of July—composed it on the spot—Mars by day, Apollo by night,—bang the field-piece, twang the lyre" (*The Pickwick Papers,* 1836–37). In such sentences as "Invent a story for some proverb which?" James Joyce depicted half-thoughts running through Mr. Bloom's mind in *Ulysses* (1922).

*Other Sentence Features.*—Complication in structure, sentence length, punctuation, and various typographical devices can all be expressive. Thomas Carlyle used heavy punctuation, italics, and many capitals in involuted sentences to underline his role as an original prophet, as in "All Anarchy, all Evil, Injustice, is, by the nature of it, *dragon's-teeth;* suicidal, and cannot endure" (*The French Revolution,* 1837).

**Words.**—*Word-forms.*—Although word-formation normally allows little scope for expressive choice, since most word-forms are fixed, some styles make effective use of it. Lewis Carroll's portmanteau word "chortle" ("chuckle" + "snort") is a device of comic wit; Gerard Manley Hopkins' "inscape" ("inside" + "landscape") expresses a new vision of reality. James Joyce, in *Ulysses,* freely compounded words (*e.g.*, "softcreakfooted," "husbandwords," and "swiftseen") for various rhythmic and emphatic effects. In *Finnegans Wake* (1939) he developed a system of "polyphonic" terms to delineate the subconscious mind, where meanings (often comically) merge and overlap: *e.g.*, "funnominal," "jinglish janglage," and "tellibly divilcult." Dickens, with such forms as "buzzums," "creetur," " 'umble," and "excuge," vigorously characterized the speakers in his novels; and misspellings, in fictional epistles and dialogue, for example, can be very expressive.

*Word-meanings.*—The widest scope for style is offered at the level of word-meanings. Phrases such as "the little house," "the diminutive house," and "the petite house" have overlapping or synonymous meanings, but "little" may suggest endearment as well as size; "diminutive," good construction; and "petite," prettiness. Synonymy enables the writer to choose the word that has the evocative value he wants. Samuel Johnson habitually used general, abstract, and nonemotive words: "This quality of looking forward into futurity seems the unavoidable condition of a being, whose motions are gradual, and whose life is progressive" (*The Rambler,* no. 2, 1750). Many English essayists have preferred particular, concrete, and emotive words; but great thoughts, Johnson claimed, "are always general." Evocative values are attached also to slang, technical, dialect, colloquial, formal literary, and standard contemporary words, as well as to archaisms and foreign expressions. George Meredith used the archaic "damsel" to suggest the immaturity of a heroine; Ronald Firbank, in "Mrs. Henedge lived in a small house with killing stairs just off Chesham Place" (*Vainglory,* 1915), characterized Mrs. Henedge with a colloquially used "killing," in stark and witty contrast to the standard words around it. Only a mention can be made here of imagery and ambiguity as rich sources of possibility in word style. In general, the gap between the image and the object is smaller in prose than in poetry; farfetched images are a mark of preciosity or inflated style (*see* also EUPHUISM).

**Sounds.**—*Rhythm.*—Aristotle maintained that while prose should not lack rhythm it should avoid metre; and metrical prose often has achieved only that "flatness" and "disenchantment" that R. L. Stevenson complained of. Lyly used the classical schemes of isocolon (like-length in phrases or clauses) and parison (like-length + like-form) to give close rhythmic order to prose, as in "I will to Athens there to toss my books, no more in Naples to live with fair looks" (*Euphues*), where rhyme is another device of order; and Dickens used isocolon for emphasis, as in "So I called myself Pip, and came to be called Pip" (*Great Expectations,* 1860).

Thomas Mann imitated the musical "leitmotiv" of Wagner by assigning special rhythms (and words) to recurrent characters and symbols, as in *"Die blonde Inge, Ingeborg Holm," "Inge Holm, die lustige Inge,"* and *"Ingeborg, die blonde Inge"* (*Tonio Kröger,* 1903). In general, except in prophetic writing (*e.g.*, Nietzsche, and parts of the Bible) and oratory (*e.g.*, Cicero, and Winston Churchill), good prose avoids insistent or obvious rhythms.

*Phonemic Pattern.*—The expressive effect of any phrase, clause, or sentence is partly determined by the pattern of its speech-sounds or phonemes. Alliteration lends dignity and force to the 14th-century devotional prose of Richard Rolle of Hampole, as in "It wanes in to wrechednes, þe welth of þis worlde." Later writers have also used alliteration to point out and underline relations in meaning, as in Jane Austen's simple "She watched him well" (*Emma,* 1815). Unobtrusive sound repetition is vital to euphony as well as to clarity. In Emily Brontë's sentence "She rang the bell till it broke with a twang; I entered leisurely" (*Wuthering Heights,* 1847), contrasting sounds fit contrasting actions, and euphony—in its fullest sense of "pleasing sound"—is perfectly achieved.

BIBLIOGRAPHY.—*General Works:* Walter Pater, "Style," in *Appreciations* (1889); C. Bally, *Traité de stylistique française,* 2 vol. (1909; 3rd ed., 1951); Otto Jespersen, *The Philosophy of Grammar* (1921); J. M. Murry, *The Problem of Style* (1922); Herbert Read, *English Prose Style* (1928; rev. ed., 1952); P. Beyer, "Stil" and "Stilistik," in Merker-Stammler, *Reallexikon der deutschen Literaturgeschichte,* vol. iii (1929); B. Dobrée, *Modern Prose Style* (1934; 2nd rev. ed., 1964); I. A. Richards, *The Philosophy of Rhetoric* (1936); R. A. Sayce, *Style in French Prose* (1953); F. L. Lucas, *Style* (1955; reissued, 1964); W. C. Booth, *The Rhetoric of Fiction* (1961); S. Ullmann, *Language and Style* (1964). For linguistic and grammatical details *see* also H. W. Fowler, *A Dictionary of Modern English Usage* (1926; revised by E. Gowers, 1965).

*Works with Essays on Particular Styles:* L. Spitzer, *Stilstudien,* 2 vol. (1928), *Linguistics and Literary History* (1948); E. Auerbach, *Mimesis* (1946; Eng. trans., 1953); S. Ullmann, *Style in the French Novel* (1957; 2nd ed., 1964); H. C. Martin (ed.), *Style in Prose Fiction* (1959); E. Staiger, *Stilwandel* (1963). (PK. H.)

**STYLITE,** Christian ascetic who lived standing on top of a column (Greek *stylos*). The first to do this was the 5th-century St. Simeon Stylites (*q.v.*) in Syria, and the best-known among his imitators are his Syrian disciple St. Daniel (409–493) in Constantinople, St. Simeon Stylites the Younger (517–592) on Mt. Admirable near Antioch, St. Alypius the Paphlagonian (7th century), St. Luke (879–979) at Chalcedon, and St. Lazarus (968–1054) on Mt. Galesion near Ephesus. Apart from these saints, of whom Greek lives exist, various other Stylites, named and unnamed, appear in ecclesiastical sources, living in Greece and the Middle East. John Moschus (d. 619) in his *Pratum spirituale* mentions several, including Monophysites, and references to women Stylites have been found. But the practice never spread to the West, where only an abortive attempt is recorded: St. Gregory of Tours in his *Historia Francorum* describes meeting St. Wulflaicus, then a deacon at Yvoi (near Carignan, Ardennes), who had tried living on a column but was soon forbidden by the bishops to pursue this extreme form of asceticism. The Stylite was permanently exposed to the elements, though he might have a little roof above his head, stood night and day in his restricted area, usually railed round, and was dependent for his scanty sustenance on what his disciples brought him by ladder. He spent most of his time in prayer but also did pastoral work among those who gathered around his column.

*See* H. Delehaye, *Les Saints stylites* (1923); Eng. trans. of life of St. Daniel in E. Dawes and N. H. Baynes, *Three Byzantine Saints* (1948).

**STYLOLITE.** A common feature in limestone, marbles, and similar rock is a series of relatively small, alternating, interlocked, toothlike columns of stone called stylolites. The term is taken from the Greek *stylos* meaning "pillar" or "column." The individual columns never appear singly but occur as a succession of interpenetrations which in cross section make a zigzag suture across the face of the stone. There has been much controversy over their origin since they were first described in 1751. However, geologists generally submit to the preponderance of field evidence supporting the theory of secondary origin resulting from differential chemical solution by ground waters circulating along some sort of a parting in hardened rock. (P. B. Se.)

**STYRENE** is a colourless, liquid, aromatic hydrocarbon, important chiefly for its marked tendency to undergo polymerization (*q.v.*). It was first produced commercially in 1935. Production thereafter increased steadily. Nearly all of it is used for synthetic rubber (*see* Rubber), molded plastic materials (*see* Plastics), or synthetic resins (*see* Resins). Styrene polymerizes slowly on standing, rapidly on heating, to form polystyrene, an inexpensive, clear, rigid plastic with excellent electrical and optical properties and with good strength and chemical resistance. Polystyrene is somewhat brittle; some of the copolymers of styrene are tougher.

Styrene was first found in storax balsam (Oriental sweet gum). It was isolated, analyzed, and named in 1839. It forms in the coking of coal and appears in small amounts in the crude xylene fraction. Styrene is produced by combining benzene (*q.v.*) from coal or petroleum with ethylene (*q.v.*) from the cracking of petroleum. The resulting ethylbenzene is then dehydrogenated to styrene. Styrene has the structure $C_6H_5—CH=CH_2$; a boiling point of 293° F (145° C), a freezing point of −23.1° F (−30.6° C), a specific gravity at 77° F (25° C) of 0.904, and a refractive index of 1.544. Styrene has a burning taste and a sweetish, penetrating, aromatic odour like manufactured (coke-oven) gas, in which it is present in very small amount. The reactive double bond in styrene participates readily in chemical reaction with halogens, halogen acids, oxygen, and other reagents. *See* Chemistry: *Organic Chemistry.*

Bibliography.—R. H. Boundy and R. F. Boyer, *Styrene: Its Polymers, Copolymers and Derivatives* (1952); W. C. Teach and G. C. Kiessling, *Polystyrene* (1960); P. Meares, *Polymers* (1965).
(Fk. R. M.)

**STYX,** in Greek mythology, one of the rivers of the underworld. The word *styx* literally means "hateful," and expresses loathing of death. In Homer the gods swear by the water of the Styx as their most binding oath, and this idea is elaborated in Hesiod's *Theogony:* Iris, the messenger of the gods, fetches water from the Styx which is poured out as a libation by the god concerned; if he perjures himself he is rendered insensible for a year and then banished from the divine society for nine years. Hesiod personifies Styx as the daughter of Ocean and the mother of Emulation, Victory, Power, and Might; she is described as an ally of Zeus in his struggle with Cronus.

In the classical period the Styx was identified with the stream now called Mavro Nero ("Black Water") near Nonacris in the Aroania Mountains (near modern Solos) in Arcadia, which plunges over a cliff into a deep gorge. Herodotus relates that Cleomenes I of Sparta attempted to found an Arcadian confederacy with oaths sworn by the water of Styx. According to popular superstition, the water of Styx was so poisonous that it would dissolve any vessel containing it except one made of a horse's hoof; there was a legend that Alexander the Great was poisoned by Styx water.

**SUAKIN** (Sawakin), once the major port of the Sudan, on the Red Sea coast in Kassala Province. It was abandoned in 1922, being replaced by Port Sudan, 36 mi. (58 km.) N. Pop. (1956) 4,228. Suakin was built on a coral island and connected by a causeway with El Geif, a suburb on the mainland. Because of the enlargement of the coral reef the harbour entrance is no longer safe for large vessels.

Suakin seems to have started about the 12th century as a rival port to 'Aydhab (Aidhab), still known as Old Suakin, farther north, since merchants from Yemen and India could trade there with the Beja tribesmen without paying the Egyptian dues levied at 'Aydhab. Toward the end of the 13th century Suakin came under Egyptian control for some time. It increased in importance after the destruction of 'Aydhab *c.* 1428. The pilgrim route to Mecca has crossed the Red Sea between Suakin and Jidda, on the Arabian coast, ever since. In the 16th century, Suakin was occupied by the Turks, and by the 18th century its prosperity had seriously declined, although pilgrims continued to pass through it from Sennar, and there was still an export of slaves, gold, and ivory. In 1821 Mohammed Ali, after conquering Sudan, leased Suakin from Turkey. This lease lapsed at his death (1849), but in 1865 Ismail Pasha reacquired the port for Egypt and it remained in Egyptian hands during the Mahdist theocracy (1881–98; *see* Mohammed Ahmed). Plans for its redevelopment as a major port were being considered in the 1960s. (A. J. Al.; I. C.)

**SUÁREZ, FRANCISCO** (1548–1617), Spanish theologian and philosopher, most important figure (*doctor eximius et pius*) of the second flowering of Scholasticism, and generally considered the greatest theologian of the Society of Jesus, was born in Granada on Jan. 5, 1548, to a family of jurists. He studied law in Salamanca and in 1564 joined the Jesuit order. After completion of his theological studies, he became (1571) instructor and professor of philosophy in Segovia, Valladolid and for a short time in Rome. From 1585 he taught theology in Alcalá and Salamanca. In 1597 he was appointed by Philip II *professor primarius* at Coimbra, where he died after a studious, yet humble and simple life, on Sept. 25, 1617.

Suárez' principal work in philosophy is the *Disputationes Metaphysicae,* in which he follows mostly Aristotle and Aquinas, yet taking in consideration the criticism of Duns Scotus and of late Scholasticism. He works out in some important points (*e.g.,* principle of individuation, potency and act) his own solution, and the points in which he departs from Thomism are considered by some scholars to be significant enough to warrant description as a separate system, called Suarezianism. The *Disputationes* was used for more than a century as the textbook in philosophy in most European universities, Catholic and Protestant alike, and Leibniz speaks of Suárez' philosophy as the *Philosophia recepta.* In theology Suárez intended to write a full commentary on the *Summa* of Thomas Aquinas in the form of treatises, but he did not succeed, since, upon the request of his general and of Pope Paul V, he had to write apologetic works on the religious state (*De Virtute et Statu Religionis,* 1608–09) and a *Defensio Fidei* (1613) against Anglican theologians, the oath of supremacy and the divine right theory of James I. In the grand dispute on the efficacy of divine grace, free will and predestination he took a stand, in the system called Congruism (*De vera intelligentia auxilii efficacis,* 1605, published 1655), more with Luis de Molina against Domingo Báñez.

Suárez' treatises *De Legibus* (1612), *De Bello et de Indis* and the "Defense of the Faith" contain his political theory and legal philosophy, in which he is both most original and personal. He refutes the divine right theory and explains that the people itself is the original holder of political authority: thus all constitutions can only be of positive law, neither of divine nor of natural law; the state must be thought to come into existence (ideally) by the consent (social compact) of those forming it. He argues strongly for the natural rights of the human person such as life, liberty and property, and repudiates the Aristotelian thesis of "natural slavery," affirming that all forms of servitude are only of human positive law. He criticizes most of the practices of Spanish colonization in the newly discovered Indies. These lands are for him sovereign states, members of the community of nations legally equal to Spain. Neither pope nor emperor as supposedly lord of the world (an absurd theory to him) nor Christian princes have the right to order an invasion or to conquer these states by reason of the idolatry or supposed backwardness of their citizens or for the propagation of Christianity. This would be against what Suárez calls for the first time the *jus inter gentes,* which, resting on natural law, contains customary and treaty law and, as the public law of the international community, is to be distinguished from the Roman *jus gentium,* which contained also private or civil law in addition to public law.

Suárez' collected works were published in 23 volumes at Venice (1740–51) and in 28 volumes at Paris (1856–78). Neither is complete; a complete and critical edition is in preparation.

BIBLIOGRAPHY.—R. de Scorraille, *François Suárez . . . d'après ses lettres, etc.,* 2 vol. (1912–13); J. H. Fichter, *Man of Spain* (1940); a full bibliography of and on Suárez is in *Atti del IV nascita di S.* (1949–50); Recasens Siches, *Legal Philosophy of Suárez,* in Spanish; H. Rommen, *Staatslehre des Suárez* (1927); J. Brown Scott, *Catholic Conception of International Law* (1934); G. Ambrosetti, *Philosophia delle Leggi di Suárez* (1950); Thomas U. Mullaney, *Suárez on Human Freedom* (1950). (H. A. Ro.)

**SUBDOMINANT,** in music, the 4th degree of the diatonic scale, as F in the scale of C. *See* SCALE.

**SUBIACO** (ancient SUBLAQUEUM), a town of Italy in Rome Province, Lazio region, on the Aniene River, 1,345 ft. (410 m.) above sea level and 45 mi. (73 km.) E of Rome. Pop. (1961) 8,595 (commune). Crowned by the Rocca Borgiana, originally built in the 11th century under Gregory VII, the town preserves its medieval form. Once a city of the Papal States, it has various buildings of Pius VI (who as cardinal was commendatory abbot), Gothic churches, medieval icons, and a 14th-century bridge. Its ancient name recalls its position below the three Neronian lakes (the Simbruina stagna of Tacitus). In the remains of Nero's lakeside villa was found the headless statue of a youth kneeling (an Ephebe?), now in the Museo Nazionale Romano (Museo delle Terme) at Rome. An inundation destroyed the lakes in 1305. St. Benedict (*q.v.*) retired (*c.* 494) as a hermit to a cave, Sacro Speco (Holy Grotto), above the lakes. The church dedicated to St. Scholastica, St. Benedict's sister, first built in 981, was destroyed by an earthquake (1228) and rebuilt in Gothic style. The present Neoclassical church, within the Gothic one, is by G. Quarenghi. The German monks Arnold Pannartz and Conrad Schweinheim set up in Sta. Scholastica the first Italian printing press in the 15th century.

The convent of St. Benedict on a mountain slope has 9th-century frescoes in the Grotta dei Pastori (Grotto of the Shepherds). St. Benedict's cave and the lower church contain 13th-century frescoes. In the upper church are scenes from the life of Christ by the Sienese School. In St. Gregory's chapel is the first portrait of St. Francis of Assisi, probably painted before 1224.

Agriculture is the principal industry. There are also a paper mill, an establishment for making spectacles, and a stone quarry. (GI. P.)

**SUBJECT,** in theory of knowledge and in psychology, means the knower or the perceiving mind or ego as opposed to the object of knowledge or sensation (*see* KNOWLEDGE, THEORY OF). In traditional logic (*see* LOGIC: *Traditional Logic*) the subject is that term (*q.v.*) of a categorical proposition that is distinguished from the predicate (*see* CATEGORY; PREDICABLES), as the "subject" of a sentence is in grammar.

**SUBJECTIVISM,** a philosophical term, applied in general to all theories that lay stress on the purely mental sides of experience, opposed to objectivism. In the narrowest sense, subjectivism goes to the logical extreme of denying that mind can know objects at all. Cf. SOLIPSISM; IDEALISM; SKEPTICISM. *See* also AESTHETICS, HISTORY OF: *The Subjective Approach;* ETHICS: *The Nature of Ethical Judgment;* ETHICS, HISTORY OF: *Ethical Relativity.*

**SUBMARINE,** a naval vessel capable of sustained operation underwater. Submarines first became a major factor in naval warfare during World War I (1914–18), when Germany employed them as commerce destroyers. They played a similar role on a larger scale in World War II (1939–45) in both the Atlantic and Pacific oceans. By the 1960s the nuclear-powered submarine capable of remaining underwater for months at a time and of firing medium-range nuclear missiles without surfacing had become a reality and was regarded by some naval strategists as the most potent of all naval weapons.

### HISTORICAL BACKGROUND

For centuries men attempted to find some way of descending beneath the surface of the sea for scientific observation, for salvage, or for attacking enemy ships in time of war. Herodotus, Aristotle, and Pliny the Elder all mentioned attempts to build diving bells or other such devices. The Greek mathematician and inventor Archimedes (*c.* 287–212 B.C.) laid the basis for a theoretical analysis of the matter by developing laws of floating bodies. A 13th-century French manuscript, "La Vrai Histoire d'Alexandre," describes an underwater venture by Alexander the Great (356–323 B.C.) in a glass barrel. Among the many inventions associated with the name of Leonardo da Vinci was a device for underwater exploration (*see* further DIVING, DEEP-SEA). But significant progress in this area had to await two inventions that were not made until the latter part of the 19th century: the internal combustion engine for surface propulsion and the electric motor (powered by storage batteries) for underwater propulsion.

Not until 1578 does any record appear of a craft designed to be navigated underwater. In that year William Bourne, a British mathematician and author of books on naval matters, published *Inventions and Devises,* in which the "18th Devise" was the design of a completely enclosed boat that could be submerged and rowed underwater. It consisted of a wooden frame covered with waterproof leather. It was to be submerged by reducing its volume by contracting the sides through the use of hand vises. Because Bourne did not actually build such a boat, it is to Cornelis Drebbel (or Cornelius van Drebel), a Dutch inventor, that credit is usually given for building the first submarine. Between 1620 and 1624 he successfully maneuvered his craft during repeated trials in the Thames at depths of from 12 to 15 ft. beneath the surface. On one occasion King James I is said to have gone aboard the vessel and taken a short ride. Drebbel's craft resembled that proposed by Bourne in that its outer hull consisted of greased leather over a wooden frame. Oars extending through the sides and sealed with tight-fitting leather flaps provided a means of propulsion either on the surface or underwater. Drebbel built his first boat in 1620 and followed it later with two larger ones built on the same principles.

Submarine boats seem to have been numerous in the early years of the 18th century. By 1727 no fewer than 14 types had been patented in England alone. An unidentified inventor, whose work was described in the *Gentleman's Magazine* of 1747, proposed an ingenious method of submerging and surfacing his submarine. His design called for attaching a number of goatskin bags to the hull with each skin connected to an aperture in the bottom. He planned to submerge the vessel by filling the skins with water and to bring it to the surface again by forcing the water out of the skins with a twisting rod. This was the forerunner of the modern ballast tank.

It was during the American Revolution that a submarine was first used as an offensive weapon in naval warfare. The "Turtle," a one-man submarine invented by David Bushnell, a student at Yale, was built of wood in the shape of a pear and was hand-operated by a screw propeller. In 1776 it attempted to sink a British man-of-war in New York Harbor. It was operated at the time by an army sergeant, Ezra Lee of Lyme, Conn., who had volunteered to make the attempt. The plan was to have the "Turtle" make its approach to the ship underwater, attach a charge of gunpowder to the ship's bottom with a screw, and quickly leave the scene before the charge was exploded by a time fuze. After repeated failures to force the screw through the copper sheathing on the hull of HMS "Eagle," the submarine gave up, released the charge, and withdrew. The powder exploded without result, except that the "Eagle" at once decided to shift to a berth farther out to sea.

Although his name is most often associated with the invention of the steamboat, Robert Fulton experimented with submarines several years before he sailed the "Clermont" up the Hudson. In 1800, while Fulton was in France, he built the "Nautilus" in hopes of helping France to destroy the British fleet. Made of wood covered with iron plates and in the shape of an elongated oval, the "Nautilus" was somewhat similar in structure to the modern submarine. A sail was provided for surface propulsion, and a hand-driven screw propeller drove the boat when submerged. A modified form of conning tower was equipped with a porthole for underwater observation, for the periscope had not yet been invented. Fulton tried to interest France, Britain, and the United States in his idea, but no nation ventured to sponsor the development of the craft, even though his model was superior to any submarine designed up to that time.

The first successful use of the submarine in war occurred in the American Civil War when the Confederacy developed a small type of semisubmersible vessel called "David." These were cigar-shaped craft, 50 ft. in length, steam-propelled, and carrying a crew of four. "Davids" were unable to attain complete submergence but cruised with the hatch and funnel exposed. Their armament consisted of a spar torpedo; *i.e.,* an explosive warhead attached to a long pole extending ahead of the vessel. On Oct. 5, 1863, a "David" successfully attacked the Union ironclad "New Ironsides" in the harbour at Charleston, S.C. The spar torpedo was too light to sink the ironclad, but it caused considerable damage.

Encouraged by the success of this attack, the Confederacy turned to the use of a true submersible, which had been designed and built at Mobile, Ala., and was named "H. L. Hunley" in honour of its chief financial backer, H. L. Hunley. Transported by railroad to Charleston, S.C., and subjected to several trial runs in the closing months of 1863, the "Hunley" on Feb. 17, 1864, operating on the surface at night, sank the Federal sloop "Housatonic" by means of a spar torpedo. The "Hunley" itself was lost.

Interest in improvement of the submarine continued after the American Civil War, but the lack of a suitable means of propulsion continued to limit progress. In 1880 an English clergyman, the Rev. George W. Garrett, successfully operated a submarine with steam from a coal-fired boiler that featured a retractable smokestack. The fire had to be extinguished before the vessel submerged, but enough steam remained in the boilers for traveling several miles.

During this same period, a Swedish gun designer, Thorsten Nordenfelt, also constructed a submarine that used steam and was driven by twin screws. His craft could submerge to a depth of 50 ft. and was fitted with one of the first practical torpedo tubes.

One of the pioneers in submarine development, Wilhelm Bauer, a noncommissioned officer in the Bavarian artillery, built two boats, "Le Plongeur-Marin" (1851) and "Le Diable-Marin" (1855). The former came to an untimely end, but the latter, built for the Russian government, achieved a measure of success, making 134 dives before she was lost at sea. Her most notable exploit occurred in September 1856 at Kronstadt when Bauer submerged his vessel with a small orchestra on board. The underwater rendition of the Russian national anthem was clearly heard by all ships in the harbour.

In an effort to overcome problems of propulsion, two Frenchmen, Capt. Siméon Bourgois and Charles Brun, built á 146-ft. submarine, "Le Plongeur" (1864). Powered by an 80-hp. compressed-air engine, the vessel quickly exhausted her air tanks whenever she tried to go anywhere. Considerably more successful was a small (30 tons displacement) experimental submarine, ordered by the French Navy and designed in part by the Frenchman Gustave Zédé, called "Gymnote" (1886, launched 1888). It was propelled by an electric motor and was extremely maneuverable but tended to go out of control when it dived. It was followed by the "Gustave Zédé," designed by Zédé and Romazzotti the next year. This 270-ton vessel, after initial difficulties were overcome, proved highly successful. In 1892 G. Pullino made successful dives in the "Delfino." The "Narval" (1899) designed for France by Maxime Laubeuf was a double-hulled vessel propelled by steam on the surface and by storage batteries when submerged.

Electric power was the only suitable answer to the problem posed by underwater operation, and with this in mind an all-electric submarine, the "Nautilus," invented in 1884 by two Englishmen, Andrew Campbell and James Ash, was built in 1886. It was propelled at a surface speed of six knots by two 50-hp. electric motors operated from a 100-cell storage battery. Because its battery had to be recharged and overhauled at short intervals its effective range never exceeded 80 mi.

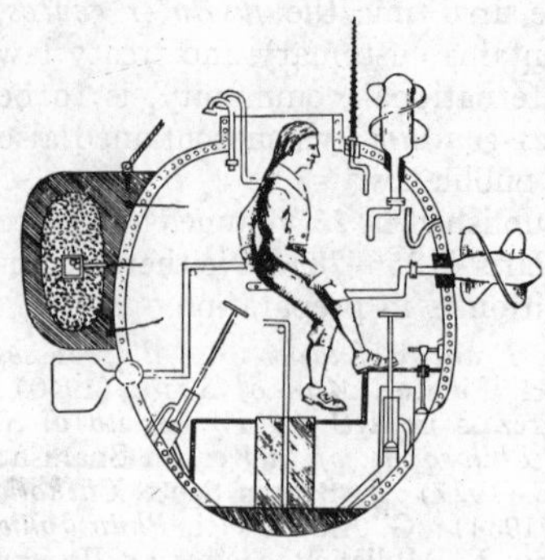

(Bottom left) Miniature from a 13th-century manuscript purporting to show Alexander the Great being lowered to the bottom of the sea in a glass barrel; (top left) 1885 drawing of David Bushnell's "Turtle," 1776, the first submarine used as an offensive weapon in naval warfare (the submarine had propellers different from those shown in the drawing); (above) John P. Holland, designer of the first operable U.S. Navy submarine, the "Holland," emerging from its conning tower

BY COURTESY OF (TOP LEFT) SUBMARINE LIBRARY, (ABOVE) GENERAL DYNAMICS; PHOTO, (BOTTOM LEFT) THE BETTMANN ARCHIVE

Antedating these efforts were the experiments of an American, John P. Holland of New Jersey, who launched his first boat in 1875. Although his early models embodied features that were discontinued as development progressed, many of his original ideas, perfected in practice, came into later use. Outstanding in importance was the principle of submergence by water ballast and the use of horizontal rudders to cause the boat to dive. Not until 1895, however, did Holland, in competition with Nordenfelt, finally receive an order for a submarine from the U.S. government. This vessel, named the "Plunger," was propelled by steam on the surface and by electricity when submerged. The original craft was redesigned frequently during construction and was finally abandoned altogether in favour of a newer model then being built at Elizabeth, N.J. This was Holland's ninth submersible and the first to be delivered to the U.S. government. It was accepted by the U.S. Navy in 1900, named "Holland," and served as the model for submarines to follow. It was 53 ft. long, 10 ft. in diameter, and displaced 74 tons. For underwater propulsion it used an electric motor, and for cruising on the surface it was equipped with a gasoline engine. The British Navy soon ordered several Holland vessels, and the submarine won a place for itself in naval warfare. As a result, Holland is now generally recognized as the "father of the modern submarine."

Another American, Simon Lake, who began building submarines in 1894, designed them primarily with peacetime uses in mind. He equipped his vessels with an air lock that permitted a passenger in a diving helmet to emerge from the hull to walk about in the water and explore. His first model, the "Argonaut, Jr.," was solely an experimental one. It was built of two layers of yellow pine with a sheet of canvas between them and was operated by hand.

It was followed in 1897 by the "Argonaut," a cigar-shaped hull 36 ft. long and powered by a 30-hp. gasoline engine. This craft could submerge to the bottom of a lake or river and roll along the bottom on three wheels. When not in use, the wheels could be raised and carried in pockets in the keel. In 1898 the "Argonaut" traveled under its own power through the heavy November storms from Norfolk to New York and was thus the first submarine to navigate extensively in the open sea. In 1906 Lake built the "Protector" and sold it to Russia. After it had successfully passed various severe tests there, Lake built a number of submersibles on contract for the Russian government. Thus the fundamental principles of construction and operation of submarine boats had been determined and demonstrated before the outbreak of World War I. By that time, too, internal-combustion engines, both gasoline and diesel, were available for use while the submarine was on the surface and could take in air freely. The invention of the periscope had materially increased the feasibility of underwater navigation (*see* PERISCOPE: *Submarine Periscopes*), and the primary weapon of the submarine, the torpedo, had been developed (*see* TORPEDO). Thus the preliminary development of the submarine was finished, and the vessel was ready to take its place as a major factor in naval warfare. *See* further *Submarine Warfare,* below.

### CONSTRUCTION FEATURES

While details of the construction of conventional submarines vary, the general principles of their design are similar. When a submarine rests on the surface, so little of it is seen above the water that it has the appearance of being longer and more slender than it really is. The typical U.S. submarine in World War II was 307 ft. long with a superstructure deck tapering almost to a point, both fore and aft, from its greatest width of approximately 16 ft. amidships. German and Italian submarines generally were smaller than those of the U.S. Navy while the Japanese were somewhat larger.

Beneath the superstructure deck is the all-welded hull, which actually consists of two hulls. Construction is on the basis of a cigar-shaped, watertight pressure hull subdivided into eight or more watertight compartments. Each compartment is a pressure vessel; that is, a watertight container or cylinder capable of withstanding great pressure. The pressure vessels, being subject to mechanical leverage, must be secured to one another by one common strength member (the keel) as well as by watertight connections (bulkheads).

In the double-hull type of submarine, the pressure hull is inside the outer hull; between the two hulls are the water and the fuel oil tanks. The pressure hull extends from the forward bulkhead of the forward trim tank to the after bulkhead of the after trim tank. Above the hull, and extending the length of the ship, is a nonwatertight superstructure that forms the main deck for use when surfaced. A watertight tower (the conning tower) extending up through the superstructure amidships is characteristic of conventional submarines but on nuclear boats has been replaced by the "sail," which floods on submergence. When surfaced the submarine is operated from a bridge atop the conning tower or sail. Submerged navigation is carried on in the conning tower or in a compartment known as the control room directly below it. In submerged operation a periscope extending from the conning tower may be used for making observations.

A submarine is built to withstand the pressure of a head of seawater, consistent with requirements as shown by battle experience and with naval specifications. The pressure is measured in actual submergence tests from the surface of the water to the axis of the vessel through its pressure hull. Watertight bulkheads are designed structurally and strengthened through reinforcements to withstand the pressure at test depths.

In addition to the mechanisms required to operate it on the surface, a modern submarine contains operating machinery and tanks that enable it to dive, surface, and proceed submerged. The pressure hull houses most of the ship's machinery and armament and provides living quarters for the crew. It is divided into watertight compartments that are connected by watertight, pressure-resisting doors.

The main deck is attached to the exterior hull by means of the framing and rounded sides. Holes in the sides allow seawater to enter all hollow spaces in the superstructure and the deck when diving and drain off when the submarine is surfacing. The midship section of the main deck is occupied by the conning tower, which is surmounted by the partially enclosed bridge "bubble," periscopes, and radar gear.

The bow is equipped with torpedo tube shutters and diving planes. The underside of the hull contains ballast tanks, flooding ports, and underwater soundheads for sonar and the fathometer. It may also contain a mushroom anchor recessed into a housing on the bottom.

The principal ballast in a submarine is water. The main ballast tanks make possible the controlled diving and surfacing of the vessel. When a submarine is on the surface the tanks are empty, and when it is submerged they are completely full. To flood the tanks rapidly there are large, power-operated vents at the tops of the tanks, and the tank bottoms are generally open to the sea, although some have large power-operated flood valves. The power for operating the vents (and flood valves, if installed) is usually hydraulic, although pneumatic equipment has been used.

To cause a submarine to dive, all vents (and flood valves, if fitted) are opened, allowing the trapped air to escape and seawater to enter the tanks. This has the effect of reducing the displacement of the submarine from that of the outer hull to that of the pressure hull. After leveling off at the desired depth, and ascertaining that the ballast tanks are completely flooded, the vent valves are usually closed. The submarine is then ready to be brought to the surface at any time by directing high-pressure air into the tanks and expelling the water.

To keep the submarine in a state of neutral buoyancy, trimming tanks are provided to compensate for changes in weights due to the consumption of food, ammunition, and fuel. One or more of these tanks are located approximately amidships and are used to control overall weight. The forward and after trimming tanks are used to correct any alteration in the longitudinal distribution of weight. These tanks are equipped with remote reading gauges, and the trimming system is designed to provide the greatest flexibility in shifting water ballast. There is also a negative buoyancy tank which, when flooded, permits the submarine to remain motionless on the sea bottom. It is also used in crash dives to enable the submarine to dive or gain depth quickly.

"Water around torpedo" tanks are fitted below the torpedo tubes and contain sufficient water to fill the spaces around the torpedoes when in the tubes. The torpedoes can thus be left dry in the tubes and can readily be withdrawn for examination. When it is desired to fire a torpedo, the tube is closed and the water from the "water around torpedo" tanks is blown into the tube; when the outer door of the tube is opened, no seawater enters because the tube is already full, and the weight of the submarine is unaltered.

The importance of air systems to a submarine cannot be overemphasized, for virtually every function in the diving and surfacing procedure is performed by air provided by one or more of the air systems. The main hydraulic system, for example, operates because of the air pressure maintained in the air-accumulator flask; torpedoes were formerly discharged by air pressure, and the diesel engines were started by air. Compressed air is necessary for the submarine to surface, submerge, attack, and cruise. Compressed air with oxygen added is used to revitalize the air in the ship after long periods of submergence. Compressed air is stored in tanks and is supplied by compressors located in the pump room, a cellarlike compartment located directly beneath the control room. Compressed air can be obtained also from a tender ship through outside connections.

A submarine is designed so that it can be kept under complete control while it dives or surfaces rapidly; it must be able to proceed on the surface or to submerge to specific depths at the desired rate of speed. To do so quickly and efficiently, it must maintain fore-and-aft balance by controlling the amount and distribution of water in the various tanks used for this purpose. Motor-driven pumps are provided for pumping out the submarine's tanks or bilges; they are capable of pumping against the water pressure at whatever depth the vessel is designed to reach and are also capable of pumping certain ballast tanks in case of compressed air failure.

The rudder of the submarine is similar to that of any surface vessel. Under normal operation the steering system has its own source of electrohydraulic power. The principal control units are assembled in the steering stand, located in the control room. To provide for every contingency, the steering system is planned so that three different methods of steering are available, based on three different sources of hydraulic power.

The hydroplanes, or bow and stern planes, which are actually horizontal rudders, are used for depth and angle control of the submarine when operating submerged. They are shaped like stubby aircraft wings and can be turned through 35° either up or down. The after pair, when in a neutral position, give the submarine a certain stability. The forward pair can be folded into the side of the superstructure; this decreases the water resistance, and the planes are not subject to additional strain when on the surface. The bow planes assist in submerging the vessel by overcoming the slight amount of buoyancy carried by the submarine when the negative buoyancy tank has not been flooded.

**Armament.**—Torpedoes were the main weapons of nonnuclear submarines. U.S. submarines had a maximum of ten 21-in. torpedo tubes and carried as many as 24 torpedoes. The tubes were arranged horizontally fore and aft and could be loaded from within the submarine. Each tube was fitted with doors at both ends so that the inner door could be opened when the outer door was closed, and vice versa. The tubes could be fired electrically or by hand when the submarine was on the surface or submerged. Submarine mines could also be laid through torpedo tubes.

Many advances in torpedoes after World War II greatly extended the capabilities of even the conventional submarine. In addition to magnetic and acoustic homing torpedoes, both widely used in World War II, experiments were made in combining rockets with torpedoes, so that a torpedo fired underwater would come to the surface, ignite its rocket engine, and fly some miles through the air before once again entering the water to seek out its target. (*See* further TORPEDO.)

**Periscopes.**—The periscope is the eye of the submarine. It was invented and developed to enable the submarine to view the surface without detection by surface craft. While it is basically simple in principle, it is a complicated piece of apparatus. The earliest submarines were built without provision for periscopes and when submerged were forced to grope their way blindly. In 1854 E. H. Marié-Davy, a Frenchman, designed a submarine sight tube containing two mirrors, one above the other, held at a 45° angle and facing in opposite directions. These mirrors provided some degree of sight to the submerged vessel but they were faulty at best, and in 1872 prisms were substituted for mirrors.

The essential function of a periscope is to give the person conning the submarine a view of the surface of the water while the vessel remains submerged. The instrument used on U.S. submarines is a 40-ft. tube about $7\frac{1}{2}$ in. in diameter, although the upper part tapers to a little more than one inch in diameter. It is equipped with a tilting head prism capable of elevating the line of sight 74.5° above the horizon and of correcting for the roll or pitch of the vessel. The most modern periscopes have an optical system that revolves independently of the casing, permitting the observer to remain in one position rather than moving around to scan the horizon. Periscopes may be fitted with camera attachments for photographic reconnaissance or with a periscope sextant for purposes of celestial navigation. *See* further PERISCOPE.

## PROPULSION SYSTEMS

**Diesel-Electric Propulsion Systems.**—The first U.S. submarines utilizing internal-combustion engines for propulsion were powered by 45-hp., two-cylinder, four-stroke-cycle gasoline engines produced by the Otto Company of Philadelphia, Pa. Early British submarines made use of 12- and 16-cylinder gasoline engines. The hazards accompanying the use of such a highly volatile fuel as gasoline were quickly realized. Stowage was a constant problem, and handling the fuel was extremely dangerous. Internal explosions were frequent; many of the engines gave off considerable carbon monoxide gas that was a menace to personnel. Because of the drawbacks associated with gasoline engines, the German firm Maschinenfabrik Augsburg-Nürnberg A.-G. (MAN) built and experimented with two-stroke-cycle diesel engines for submarine propulsion. However, insufficient progress had been made in metallurgy to provide metals capable of withstanding the greater heat and stress inherent in diesels. MAN then turned its efforts toward production of a four-stroke-cycle diesel engine capable of developing 1,000 hp. While fairly successful, these engines eventually developed structural weaknesses at the crankcase. Prior to 1930 the engines used in most submarines of all the larger naval powers with the exception of Great Britain were four-stroke-cycle diesels. The U.S. Navy, however, experimented with a two-stroke-cycle Busch-Sulzer engine and equipped a number of boats with this type. The U.S. Navy also turned to the use of solid-injection engines, with their advantage in weight reduction.

Along with the development of these engines there was experimentation in the method of transmitting the power of the engine to the propellers. Originally, engines were coupled to the propellers through friction clutches. With the advent of high-speed engines came reduction gears to keep propeller speed in an efficient range, and the mechanical clutch was replaced by electric drive. The power developed by the engine-driven generators was used in the two main motors for surface propulsion, or for charging batteries. The conventional submarine is usually driven by four main diesel engines, each capable of producing 1,600 hp. The four main generators each produce 1,100 kw. There are four slow-speed motors, driven by the generators or batteries, each producing about 1,375 hp. The auxiliary engine is rated at 450 hp. and drives a 300-kw. generator.

**Batteries.**—When submerged the diesels and generators cannot be used because they require a great deal of fresh air and a means of expelling exhaust fumes. Power for the motors is therefore supplied by storage batteries, which are recharged by the generators during surface operations.

Most older U.S. submarines have two main storage batteries of 126 cells each. Usually, the forward battery is installed belowdecks in the area of the wardroom while the after battery is located in the crew's space. Each cell weighs approximately 1,650 lb. Each battery is fitted with an exhaust ventilating system to remove battery gases and hydrogen that develop when the batteries are being recharged.

## ANCILLARY DEVELOPMENTS

**Escape Apparatus.**—For many years there were three vital pieces of gear used in escaping from a submerged submarine. The first of these, the marker buoy, was released by a disabled submarine to assist in guiding rescue parties to the area where the boat rested. If a properly equipped rescue party was able to locate the submarine, a second piece of gear, a rescue chamber, was lowered by cable over an escape hatch and the crew members of the submarine were removed in relays to the surface. However, if rescue parties were unable to locate the submarine, individual ascent was necessary. For many years this ascent was made with the assistance of an artificial lung of which the two main types were the Davis submerged escape apparatus, used by the British, and the Momsen lung, used by the United States. By the mid-1950s, however, the use of these lungs was abandoned by both British and American navies in favour of a buoyant ascent, in which the escapee is assisted only by a life jacket. As he begins his ascent, the escapee exhales all the air he can from his lungs and continues to exhale all the way to the surface. So long as he is exhaling, he is not subject to decompression "bends."

**Snorkel and Guppy.**—In the latter part of World War II the Germans adopted a radical change in submarine design known as the schnorkel—a Dutch invention. The spelling was reduced by the Americans to snorkel and further changed by the British to snort. The snorkel is a breathing tube that is raised while the submarine is at periscope depth; air for the diesels can thus be obtained from the surface. The snorkel enables the submarine to cruise on its diesel engines while almost totally submerged and to conserve its battery power for attack and evasive maneuvers.

At the end of World War II the United States Navy developed the guppy submarine, the name standing for "greater underwater propulsion power." It had the same type hull as the fleet-type submarine of World War II but the superstructure was radically

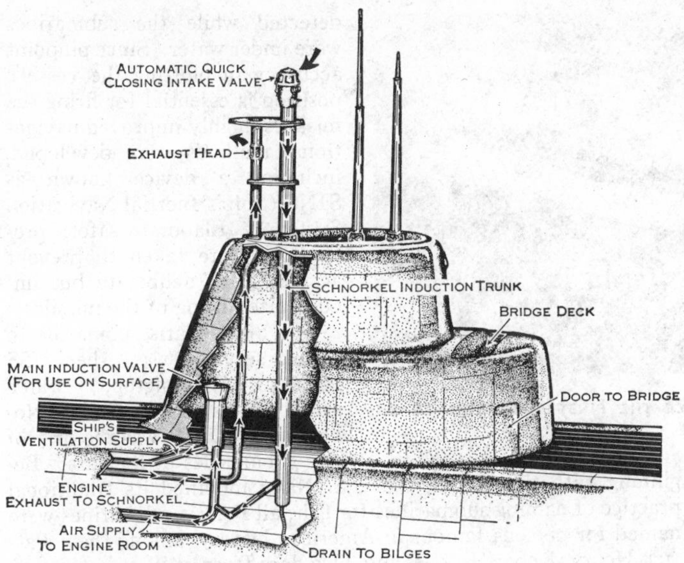


SCHEMATIC DRAWING OF THE SCHNORKEL WITH RETRACTABLE PERISCOPES AND MAST SHOWN HERE IN UP POSITION

modified by reducing the surface area and streamlining every protruding object. The lifelines and all guns were removed, the bitts were made retractable, and the periscope supports were enclosed in a streamlined metal fairing. The submerged speed of the new guppy was considerably greater than that of the fleet-type boat and nearly twice that of the old-style submarines.

**Developments After World War II.**—The lessons of World War II wrought great changes in submarine construction. Torpedoes came to be fired by hydraulic (water) pressure instead of compressed air as previously, eliminating any chance of telltale air bubbles escaping to the surface and betraying the submarine's location. Hulls were given greater strength for deeper diving. Hydraulic mechanisms (oil) were extensively employed throughout the ship for quieter and more efficient operation. Radar and sonar equipment increased in importance as it contributed to efficient operation. Torpedoes no longer had to be fired with sharpshooting accuracy; fire-control equipment and homing torpedoes (the torpedo that seeks its target) eliminated much of the guesswork and chance in firing torpedoes. Engines, electrical motors, and generators were made more compact.

During World War II, the Germans had conducted extensive experiments on the Type XXVI U-boat (the Walther boat), driven by a closed system of combustion that could be operated underwater by employing liquid hydrogen peroxide rather than air to supply the oxygen for fuel combustion. This system would permit greater submerged speed by allowing the use of the more powerful diesel engines while the submarine was completely submerged. Technical difficulties prevented this type of submarine from becoming operational during the war. After the war the German designs were revised and adapted by several navies, culminating in the development of the experimental British HMS "Explorer," accepted into service in 1956. In spite of the success of the "Explorer," the hydrogen-peroxide type was, generally speaking, obsolete by the time it was operational because of the development of the nuclear submarine.

Because World War II had shown that midget submarines had some value, several navies continued the development of this type. Probably the most extensive work was done by the British. Most midget submarines were about 50 ft. in length and carried a crew of five officers and men. Some carried as armament, in place of, or in addition to, torpedoes, limpet mines that were intended to be attached to the hulls of enemy vessels until detonated.

## NUCLEAR SUBMARINES

On Jan. 17, 1955, the USS "Nautilus" made history by getting underway on nuclear power. Here at last was the true submarine. The "Nautilus" could maintain submerged speeds in excess of 20 knots almost indefinitely, limited only by the endurance of her crew and her supply of provisions. The ship's air-conditioned interior was designed for the greatest possible comfort of the crew. Air was filtered and recirculated through carbon-dioxide scrubbers, and oxygen was added as required.

The power plant of a nuclear submarine consists of an atomic reactor that generates enormous heat. The reaction is controlled by inserting control rods into the core or removing them. When the rods are fully inserted the reaction stops, and when they are completely withdrawn the reaction is at its maximum. Surrounding the reactor core is a primary coolant, water pumped past the core by coolant pumps. The heated water of the coolant is forced into a boiler-heat exchanger. Since the coolant water is radioactive, it cannot be used directly in the propulsion system, so its heat is transferred to uncontaminated water on the secondary side of the boiler-heat exchanger. This uncontaminated water is thereby converted to steam, which passes through a control valve into the engine room where it is used to drive the ship's service turbogenerator (SSTG), the coolant turbogenerator (CTG), and the propulsion turbines. From there it passes through condensers into the feed water system. The water circulation on the reactor side (known as the primary system) is thus completely isolated from the propulsion side (the secondary system), so that no transfer of radioactivity takes place. On most nuclear submarines, reduction gears are used between the turbines and the shaft; others incorporate turbo-electric drive.

In the event of reactor failure, nuclear submarines are equipped with auxiliary electrical propulsion that can receive power from batteries, small diesel engines, or motor generators. Precautions against radioactive contamination of the vessel and exposure of the crew are so extensive that in a year's cruise crew members receive less than that set by the Bureau of Standards as the permissible radiation for a single week.

**Nuclear Submarine Developments.**—Experiments with the "Nautilus" and with the conventionally propelled experimental submarine USS "Albacore" led to great advances, both in power plant design and in hydrodynamics. The "Albacore," which was specially designed for hydrodynamic research, reached submerged speeds far in excess of any earlier submarine. Lessons learned from her design were adapted to the "Skipjack" class of attack

BY COURTESY OF U.S. NAVY

LOADING A TORPEDO ABOARD THE USS "NAUTILUS," THE FIRST NUCLEAR SUBMARINE

BY COURTESY OF U.S. NAVY

USS "TRITON," TWIN-REACTOR NUCLEAR SUBMARINE WHICH IN 1960 BECAME THE FIRST SUBMARINE TO ENCIRCLE THE GLOBE WITHOUT COMPLETELY SURFACING

nuclear submarines, and to some extent to all subsequent nuclear submarines. Other navies also worked to develop undersea nuclear craft. The Soviet Union built an undisclosed number of nuclear boats, and in 1963 Great Britain commissioned her first nuclear submarine, HMS "Dreadnought," perpetuating a distinguished name in the Royal Navy.

With nuclear propulsion, the development of atmosphere regeneration systems, and advances in the strength of pressure hulls, submarines increased their ranges of operation, design, and capabilities. During the period from Aug. 1–5, 1958, the "Nautilus," under the command of Comdr. William R. Anderson, made the first submerged polar transit from Point Barrow, Alaska, to the Greenland Sea, traveling 1,830 mi. under the polar ice cap. She crossed the geographic North Pole on Aug. 3. Several other submarines duplicated this feat, and some surfaced at the Pole. The USS "Triton," the world's largest submarine (at time of building) and the only one equipped with two reactors, on May 10, 1960, completed the first submerged circumnavigation of the world, following roughly the route taken by Magellan's fleet (1519–22). On this historic voyage she was commanded by Capt. Edward L. Beach.

The depth to which submarines can descend and their speed underwater are military secrets. Many U.S. submarines of the World War II variety could descend to 500 ft. and attain surface speeds greater than 20 knots. It was assumed that nuclear submarines in service in the 1960s could descend to greater depths and attain higher submerged speeds. When operating at such depths the submarine, of course, cannot use its periscope, radio, or radar, for they require operation at or near the surface.

Most nuclear submarines have been designated "attack submarines" and are designed to carry on the submarine's conventional role of destroying surface ships and other submarines. The USS "Tullibee" was especially designed as an antisubmarine submarine, and the USS "Halibut" was designed to fire the guided missile Regulus from the surface against either sea or land targets.

**Polaris Submarines.**—The most significant advance in the strategic employment of the submarine came about with the building of the Fleet Ballistic Missile (FBM) Polaris submarines in the 1960s. Each of these submarines could carry 16 Polaris solid-propellant, intermediate-range ballistic missiles, which could be fired when the submarine was completely submerged. The first successful firing of a Polaris missile from a submerged submarine, the USS "George Washington," occurred on July 20, 1960. Compressed air was used for the launching at that time, but later submarines employed steam-powered launchers. All of the 16 missiles could be fired in the short span of 15 minutes. The first Polaris missiles had a range of up to 1,200 mi., but this range was increased with the Polaris A-3 to more than 2,800 mi. Polaris submarines were kept almost continually at sea during the 1960s, two complete crews being designated for each one, so that at the end of a patrol of up to 60 days, the submarine could enter port, exchange crews, and depart again in a very short time. To insure communication with Polaris submarines at sea, powerful, ultra-low frequency radio transmitters were used so that the signals could be detected while the submarines were under water. Since pinpoint accuracy in plotting the vessel's position is essential for firing the missiles, highly improved navigational methods were developed, including a device known as SINS (Ship's Inertial Navigation System). Elaborate safety precautions were taken to prevent accidental or deliberate but unauthorized firing of the missiles.

The first Polaris submarine to enter service was the USS "George Washington," which sailed on its first patrol in November 1960. It was the first of five submarines of its class. Beginning with this vessel, the U.S. Navy modified its traditional practice of naming submarines for fish; all Polaris submarines were named for persons famous in American history, among them Patrick Henry, Robert E. Lee, and Theodore Roosevelt.

The "Ethan Allen," launched in November 1960, was the first of five additional Polaris submarines that were larger (6,900 tons standard displacement as compared with 5,600 tons for the "George Washington") and of a new hull design. The "Lafayette," first of its class of 31, was launched in May 1962. Submarines of this class were the largest of all U.S. submarines—7,250 tons standard displacement and 425 ft. in length.

The development of the Polaris submarine revolutionized the strategic role of the submarine. Its primary mission was no longer the destruction of enemy ships but the launching of nuclear missiles at land targets far inside the enemy's borders. Because the Polaris submarines could cruise for long periods underwater and launch missiles without surfacing, they constituted mobile missile launching platforms that were virtually undetectable. Nuclear submarines experienced a serious setback in April 1963 when the USS "Thresher" sank, with the loss of all on board, about 200 mi. off the New England coast while undergoing deep submergence tests. The cause of this disaster—the first for an atomic submarine and the worst in submarine history—was not determined.

By the 1960s the U.S.S.R. had apparently stabilized its submarine fleet at about 400 boats, retiring old vessels as new ones came into service. About 30 of these were believed to be nuclear powered. Those capable of launching medium-range missiles had to surface to do so. The U.S. had over 200 submarines, about two-fifths of them post-World War II, and half of those nuclear. Great Britain was the third largest submarine power with 65, including 20 built after World War II. France and Sweden, each with about 30, had significant submarine forces. (H. H. A.)

## SUBMARINE WARFARE

Submarine warfare is a relatively new form of naval warfare dating essentially from World War I (1914–18) and in this respect paralleling the history of air warfare and tank warfare. It was made possible by the technological development during the early years of the 20th century of the submarine itself and of the periscope, torpedo, and radio. The submarine gained greater stature as a strategic weapon in the 1950s and 1960s when nuclear power was successfully adapted for submarine propulsion and when means were devised for launching, from a submerged position, guided missiles capable of carrying nuclear warheads to targets 2,800 mi. away.

**World War I.**—Early in the 20th century France led in the development of submarines but it was Germany that first employed them in war as substitutes for surface commerce raiders. (For the legal aspects of this matter, *see* LAWS OF WAR: *Conduct of Hostilities.*)

At the outset of World War I, German U-boats, though numbering only 28, achieved notable successes against British warships; but because of the reactions of neutral powers (especially the United States) Germany hesitated before adopting unrestricted submarine warfare against merchant ships. The decision to do so in February 1917 was largely responsible for the entry of the United States into the war. The submarine campaign then became a race between German sinkings of merchant ships and the building of ships, mainly in the United States, to replace them. In April 1917, 430 Allied and neutral ships totaling 852,000 tons were sunk, and it seemed likely that the German gamble would succeed. However, the introduction of convoys, the arrival of numerous U.S. destroyers, and the vast output of American shipyards turned the tables. By the end of the war Germany had built 344 U-boats and had 226 under construction. The peak U-boat strength of 140 was reached in October 1917, but there were never more than about 60 at sea at one time. This comparatively small number of submarines accounted for nearly 90% of Allied shipping losses. The armistice terms required Germany and Austria to surrender all their U-boats, and the Treaty of Versailles forbade them to possess submarines in the future.

Because the German and Austrian surface warships were confined within the North Sea and the Adriatic Sea, respectively, and their merchant shipping was quickly swept off the seas, Allied submarines could never find plentiful targets. But British submarines penetrated into the Baltic in 1914–15, and into the Sea of Marmara during the Gallipoli campaign of 1915. In both cases a few submarines caused considerable disruption of supply traffic.

Submarines employed three types of weapons in World War I—the torpedo, the mine, and the gun. The torpedo was the submarine's natural weapon, for it could be launched while the submarine was fully submerged and was approaching its target unobserved; minefields could also be laid in the same stealthy manner. But to use its guns a submarine had to come to the surface where it was at a disadvantage against surface warships or armed merchantmen because it lacked protective armour and carried only a few small deck guns. At the very beginning of World War I submarines used gunfire against merchantmen but when the latter were armed the U-boats preferred not to face them, for the merchantmen usually mounted more powerful guns. (For antisubmarine operations *see* below.)

**World War II.**—At the end of World War I the lessons of the submarine campaign were well understood in the British and U.S. navies; but nonetheless they were gradually forgotten. Even after Germany had repudiated the Treaty of Versailles and had negotiated the right to build submarines up to the total British strength in 1935, it was believed that Germany would honour its signature of the London Protocol of 1936, whereby submarines were bound to conform to the established rules of international law. Thus Britain was ill prepared in 1939 for a resumption of unrestricted submarine warfare, and during the early months of World War II the U-boats, which at that time numbered only 57, again achieved great successes. The first phase, during which the U-boats generally operated singly, ended in March 1941, by which time many merchant ships were sailing in convoy, trained escort groups were becoming available, and aircraft were again proving their effectiveness as antisubmarine weapons. In the next phase the Germans, having acquired air and submarine bases in Norway and western France, were able to reach much farther out into the Atlantic, and their submarines began to operate in groups (called wolf packs by the British). One U-boat would shadow a convoy, summon others by radio, and then the group would attack, generally on the surface at night. These tactics succeeded until radar came to the aid of the escorts, and until convoys could be given continuous sea and air escort all the way across the Atlantic in both directions. In March 1943, as in April 1917, the Germans nearly succeeded in cutting Britain's Atlantic lifeline, but by May escort carriers and very-long-range reconnaissance bombers became available. After the U-boats lost 41 of their number during that month they withdrew temporarily from the Atlantic.

EUROPEAN

GERMAN U-BOATS USED IN THE EARLY PART OF WORLD WAR II

In the next phase U-boats were sent to remote waters where unescorted targets could still be found. Although at first they achieved considerable successes, especially in the Indian Ocean, the Allied strategy of striking at the U-boats' supply vessels and putting all possible shipping into convoy again proved successful. In the final phase the U-boats, then fitted with the schnorkel (snorkel or snort) breathing tube, which greatly reduced the effectiveness of radar, returned to the coastal waters around the British Isles; but they sank few ships and themselves suffered heavy losses.

Italian submarines, which numbered 115 in June 1940, had little influence on the Mediterranean campaigns. But when in 1941 the Germans sent U-boats into the Mediterranean, they sank a number of major British warships and offered a serious threat. Not until mid-1944 were U-boats mastered in the Mediterranean. British submarines, mostly based on Malta, did much to sever Axis sea communications with North Africa, but at a heavy price, 50 of them being lost.

In the Pacific the considerable Japanese submarine force (63 boats in December 1941) was deployed against major warships. Despite the dependence of the Allies on a long line of sea communications between the United States and the south Pacific the Japanese never organized a sustained attack on merchant shipping; nor did a brief cooperation with German U-boats in the Indian Ocean in 1942 yield significant results. The United States strategy was the precise opposite of the Japanese, and from the outset the U.S. Navy made Japanese seaborne traffic a major objective. Nor was this campaign inhibited by tender considerations regarding the legality of such attacks, for Germany and Italy, reluctantly followed by Britain, had already adopted what was in fact unrestricted submarine warfare. Moreover, by its vast industrial capacity the United States could easily outbuild Japan in submarines as in all other war supplies. Between 1942 and 1945 the U.S. Navy commissioned 205 new submarines, 170 being of the splendid "Fleet" type capable of prolonged patrols in distant waters. Furthermore the development of new weapons and equipment gave the U.S. submarines a decisive advantage, and Japanese failure to defend seaborne traffic by an organized convoy system contributed to the U.S. success. The U.S. Navy's submarines, which sank 1,153 Japanese merchant ships totaling 4,889,000 tons (57% of all Japanese losses), were the principal instrument of the blockade which, together with the defeat of Japan's main fleets in the series of major battles fought between April 1942 and October 1944, contributed greatly to bringing about the Japanese collapse and surrender.

In World War II Germany built 1,162 U-boats, of which 785 were destroyed and the remainder surrendered (or were scuttled to avoid surrender) at the capitulation. Of the 632 U-boats sunk at sea, Allied surface ships and shore-based aircraft accounted for the great majority (246 and 245 respectively). The submarine losses of the other belligerents were much smaller than those of Germany, totaling 74 British, 52 U.S., 84 Italian, and 127 Japanese. As in World War I, submarines inflicted by far the greatest proportion of all Allied shipping losses. Although U.S. warships and aircraft accounted for the great majority of Japanese submarines destroyed, it was Britain that bore the main burden of the second (as of the first) campaign against German U-boats. British naval and air forces sank 500 of the 632 U-boats sunk at sea, and more than three-quarters of the Allied merchant shipping destroyed came from the British merchant navy.

**Antisubmarine Operations.**—Many countermeasures were developed to defeat the submarine. Camouflage paint was used in World War I to render surface ships less visible or to distort their appearance and make it more difficult for the submarine to determine the target's course and speed, factors essential to successful torpedo fire. Steaming on a zigzag course also tended to confuse submarines. But camouflage and zigzagging were of limited value, for a ship might turn toward a submarine instead of away from it, and certain weather conditions might make camouflage paint stand out at great distances and actually attract submarines. Both camouflage and zigzagging were passive defense measures; more important were the active defense measures such as the use of depth charges, the practice of convoying ships, bombing submarine bases, and developing detection devices.

The primary antisubmarine weapon in both world wars was the depth charge (depth bomb in the U.S. Navy) which was operated hydrostatically and could be set to detonate at various depths down to 750 ft. Initially it could be dropped or fired only from surface ships, but in World War II it was adapted for use by aircraft. A ship attacking a submarine would endeavour to place a pattern of depth charges around it. But because a submarine could fairly easily evade an attack made by a single ship, in World War II it became normal for several ships to make coordinated attacks. The directing ship maintained asdic (sonar) contact continuously and signaled to the others when they reached the correct position to release their depth charges. This made it much more difficult for a submarine to avoid the pattern. Because aircraft could attack a submarine only on or near the surface they used a special shallow-firing depth charge. Antisubmarine contact bombs were developed by the British between the wars but proved ineffective. Other antisubmarine weapons are the torpedo (especially when fired from another submarine), the mine, and the guns of surface ships. Ramming was also used quite frequently against surfaced submarines in both world wars; but the toughness of a submarine's pressure hull was such that a lightly built antisubmarine vessel could incur severe damage from ramming, and the practice came to be discouraged. Mines proved an effective deterrent to submarine operations in waters shallow enough for minelaying, such as the Straits of Dover and the Malta Channel, and destroyed many submarines. Harbours and narrow channels were in some cases defended against passage by submarines by a detection device ("indicator loop") laid on the seabed. The loop indicated the passage over it of a steel vessel, enabling a controlled minefield to be fired from a shore station. Obstructions such as booms and nets were also placed across harbour entrances.

*Escort and Convoy.*—Strategically it was as commerce raiders that submarines exerted most influence in both world wars. However, they also achieved important successes against large warships, hence the mere threat of their presence compelled surface fleets to adopt constant antisubmarine escort. For this reason the torpedo-boat destroyer of World War I became, as the destroyer of World War II, primarily an antisubmarine vessel; other vessels such as frigates (destroyer escorts in the U.S. Navy), sloops, and corvettes were designed chiefly for the antisubmarine role. The world wars proved that a comparatively few submarines can force on the enemy a disproportionate effort in the provision of such vessels.

Much the most effective antisubmarine strategy was the adoption of escorted convoys (*see* CONVOY). A submarine must approach the convoy to attack it, and it thus affords the escorts an opportunity to strike back. Apart from the merchant ships they saved by this strategy, the convoy escorts were among the most effective submarine killers. In World War I the British opposed convoy, taking an exaggerated view of its difficulties. It was not adopted until losses of merchant ships became catastrophic in 1917; it then quickly proved effective. In World War II convoy was introduced without delay by both Britain and the United States, but Japan delayed the adoption of convoy until it was too late to prevent disastrous losses. Sea and air patrols and hunting groups, though frequently tried in both world wars, were much less effective than convoy escorts as submarine killers. In World War I the British deployed disguised merchantmen (Q-ships) on trade routes to lure U-boats within range of their concealed armament. They achieved a few successes, but the Germans soon became wary. The reintroduction of Q-ships by the British early in World War II was a total failure.

Both airships and airplanes were introduced for convoy escort toward the end of World War I. Though aircraft sank no U-boats in that war, their influence on the campaign was substantial. Aircraft could give early warning of a U-boat's presence and by forcing it to submerge they greatly reduced its effectiveness. In World War II air convoy escorts from aircraft carriers and from airfields made a decisive contribution. In the same conflict operational research was applied to antisubmarine warfare by Britain and the United States to furnish assessments of the optimum size of convoys, the speeds below which merchant ships should not be sailed independently, and the effectiveness of air escorts.

*Bombing Submarine Bases.*—In World War I, bomber aircraft were occasionally employed against U-boat bases, though without significant results. In World War II, a big effort was devoted by the RAF and USAAF to attacking U-boat bases, building yards, and associated factories. The Germans, however, mitigated the effects by dispersing production and by prefabricating U-boats, while in the operational bases they constructed enormously strong concrete pens to protect their U-boats. Strategic bombing undoubtedly delayed U-boat production, but not until the German air defenses finally collapsed were considerable numbers of completed U-boats thereby destroyed.

*Sonar and Radar.*—Detection has always been the cardinal problem in antisubmarine warfare, and evasion of detection the primary aim of the submarine. In World War I detection was possible only by visual sighting or by hydrophones; and the latter (capable of indicating approximate direction but not distance) were ineffective if other ships were nearby. But the development of the asdic (later sonar) ultrasonic detector in the 1920s greatly reduced the submarine's capacity for concealment. Unfortunately it also led in Britain to a belief that the submarine had been mastered. Moreover, between the wars naval establishments neglected to develop antisubmarine weapons with a performance to match the improved methods of detection. In World War II all submarines, as well as antisubmarine vessels, were fitted with sonar. But the most important antisubmarine development of the period was the shortwave (10 cm.) radar that enabled ships and aircraft to detect a surfaced submarine at a range of about 2,000 yd. Radar virtually eliminated the need to rely on sighting and deprived the submarine of its immunity from attack during darkness—the period when the submarine customarily moved on the surface and recharged its batteries.

*Controlling Antisubmarine Operations.*—In World War II the Royal Navy developed the control of antisubmarine operations to a fine art; the U.S. Navy adopted the same principles. The system was based on the centralized collection of intelligence, especially from the enemy's radio traffic. Widely separated direction-finding stations intercepted enemy signals, measured the bearing of the transmitting submarine, and signaled the bearings to the operational centre, where the resulting position was related to other intelligence. Orders to search were then sent to forces in the vicinity, and any convoys that appeared to be imperiled were diverted. Ship-mounted high-frequency direction-finding (H/F D/F) radio much improved the efficiency of the system, and a submarine's position could often be accurately plotted within seconds of its sending a message.

The potentialities of the submarine in an antisubmarine role were appreciated in World War I, but not until World War II were they fully exploited. Allied submarines then sank 21 U-boats, 18 Italian and 28 Japanese submarines.

*Ancillary Employment of Submarines.*—In both world wars submarines were frequently used in conjunction with the main fleets for reconnaissance and shadowing. Also they were used to supply beleaguered garrisons, notably by the British during the siege of Malta (1941–43) and by the Japanese during the Solomon Islands campaign (1942–43). But such employment is a diversion from the submarine's offensive role and was adopted only as an emergency measure. In World Wars I and II Germany used U-boats to pass strategic cargoes through the British blockade. Submarines were also used, especially by the British in World War II, as instruments of irregular warfare, such as landing agents or raiding parties.

*Minisubmarines.*—The use of small submersible craft for attacking ships in harbour was pioneered by the American David Bushnell in 1776 and continued by the Confederates in the American Civil War, but with little success in either case. Toward the end of World War I an Austrian battleship was sunk in Pola Harbour by an attack of this kind. In World War II, Britain, Germany, Italy, and Japan developed a variety of midget and pigmy submarines. Although they scored a few outstanding successes, such as the crippling by Italian frogmen of two British battleships in Alexandria harbour in December 1941 and the severe damage caused to the German battleship "Tirpitz" in a Norwegian fjord by British X-craft (4-man midget submarines) in September 1943, it is doubtful whether the results justified the considerable effort devoted to producing them.

**Developments After World War II.**—The profound influence of the submarine in World War II and the increased vulnerability of surface warships to air attack compelled maritime powers thereafter to foster developments in underwater warfare. Indeed, after 1945 the prevailing naval attitude toward the submarine, which only 25 years earlier had been deemed the weapon of the weaker power, changed fundamentally. Increase of diving depth and submerged speed, improved submarine weapons, and more efficient means of communication indicated that the influence of the submarine on naval warfare was still growing. The vulnerability of seaborne trade to submarine attack having been convincingly demonstrated in both world wars, it was natural that mercantile nations, including Britain, should pay close attention to antisubmarine defense. Sonar (the use of sound waves underwater on the radar principle) was greatly improved and made to record a submarine's depth as well as its range and bearing. (*See* SOUND: *Applications: Military: Underwater Detection.*) Automation was applied extensively to antisubmarine weapon control. Helicopters fitted with dunking (dipping) sonar and operated from surface ships greatly extended the range of detection; and antisubmarine guided homing torpedoes were developed to seek out their targets in the depths. Such developments undoubtedly reduced the lethality of the conventional submarine, despite its greatly improved performance. But the U.S. Navy's adoption of nuclear energy for propulsion in 1955 revolutionized all earlier submarine concepts, because the range and duration of operations were thereby rendered virtually unlimited; and the nuclear submarine at once became the most efficient and economical carrier for launching intercontinental missiles. Thus did the submarine become a major factor in deterrent strategy as well as conventional maritime strategy.

In the search for measures to restrict the dominance of submarines the U.S. and Britain both devoted considerable effort to developing hunter-killer nuclear submarines. These vessels, with improved means of detection and communication, and with new antisubmarine weapons such as rocket-propelled homing torpedoes, were expected to narrow the gap between defense and offense. Nevertheless, the submarine had firmly established itself as the capital ship of the nuclear era. Moreover, the scope for the employment of submarines on duties hitherto performed by surface ships or aircraft appeared to be limited only by the cost of submarine production. Indeed, the command of the surface sea, whereby a maritime power seeks to secure the uninterrupted passage of mercantile or military cargoes, seemed likely to depend increasingly on control of the waters beneath. (S. W. Ro.)

BIBLIOGRAPHY.—*History and Construction:* Robert H. Barnes, *United States Submarines,* 3rd ed. (1946); Wilbur Cross, *Challengers of the Deep* (1959); John Lewellen, *The Atomic Submarine* (1954); F. W. Lipscomb, *The British Submarine* (1954); E. B. Potter and Fleet Admiral Chester W. Nimitz (eds.), *Sea Power* (1960); Edward L. Beach, *Around the World Submerged: the Voyage of the Triton* (1962); David Thomas, *Submarine Victory* (1961); W. R. Anderson and Clay Blair, *Nautilus 90 North* (1959); Lydel Sims, "The Submarine That Wouldn't Come Up," *American Heritage* (April 1958); *Jane's Fighting Ships* (annual); Peter K. Kemp, *H. M. Submarines* (1952); Norman Polmar, *Atomic Submarines* (1963); William Jameson, *The Most Dangerous Thing* (1965). (H. H. A.)

*Submarine Warfare:* Sir Julian S. Corbett and H. Newbolt, *Naval Operations,* 5 vol. (1920–31); C. E. Fayle, *Seaborne Trade,* 3 vol. (1920–24); Lord Jellicoe, *The Crisis of the Naval War* (1920); R. H. Gibson and M. Prendergast, *The German Submarine War, 1914–1918* (1931); S. W. Roskill, *The War at Sea 1939–1945,* 4 vol. (1954–61); S. E. Morison, *The History of United States Naval Operations in World War II,* 15 vol. (1948–63); Karl Dönitz, *Memoirs: 10 Years and 20 Days* (1959); Friedrich Ruge, *Sea Warfare, 1939–45* (1957); C. W. Nimitz and E. B. Potter (eds.), *The Great Sea War* (1960); M. Hashimoto, *Sunk: the Story of the Japanese Submarine Fleet, 1941–1945* (1954); M. G. Saunders (ed.), *The Soviet Navy* (1958); A. Hezlet, *The Submarine and Sea Power* (1967). (S. W. Ro.)

**SUBMEDIANT:** *see* SCALE.

**SUBOTICA,** a town of Vojvodina Province, in the Socialist Republic of Serbia, Yugos., lies on the Belgrade–Budapest railway line about 100 mi. (160 km.) NNW of Belgrade. Pop. (1965) 78,000. It is the centre of the Bačka, a fertile agricultural district, and is also an important industrial town. Its chief manufactures are iron products, rolling stock, chemicals, and furniture. The Faculty of Economics of the University of Novi Sad is at Subotica.

The town was first mentioned in 1391. After the defeat of the Turks at the end of the 17th century, it was included in the Military Frontier. In later years many Serbs emigrated from Subotica to Russia, and large numbers of Hungarian settlers then moved in. Subotica joined Yugoslavia in 1918. During World War II it was occupied by Hungarian troops, and after 1945 it was restored to Yugoslavia. (V. DE.)

**SUBSIDY,** the promotion of private business enterprise by direct or indirect government action, frequently involving the granting of special privileges. Government subsidies to shipping, aviation, mining, agriculture, and other industries are granted in many countries throughout the world. *See* AGRICULTURAL ECONOMICS: *Agricultural Prices and Incomes;* AVIATION, CIVIL; SHIPPING: *International Problems.*

Though some subsidies may be criticized as obvious favours to special interest groups at the expense of the economy as a whole, others may serve to encourage activities that are generally regarded as socially desirable. Subsidies to aid the settlement of new lands, to support bona fide infant industries, to provide government statistical services, and to carry on basic scientific research (with results made available to all) are rarely questioned. On the other hand, paying above-market prices for certain metals, subsidizing irrigation when excess acreage already exists, making payments to a select group of growers of agricultural products, and giving favoured tax treatment to certain industries may be of dubious merit.

It is necessary to distinguish direct or visible subsidies, such as airmail subsidy grants, direct payments for ship construction, and payments to cover operating deficits, from indirect or concealed subsidies, which are more widespread but are often not recognized as subsidies. The latter include tariffs, quotas, and other trade restrictions that exclude foreign competitors; the provision of government services for which no charge is made; the sale of goods and services for which no, or an insufficient, charge is made; the purchase of goods and services for more than they are worth; government loans at lower than the market rate of interest; and the exemption of some enterprises from various forms of taxes that others in a similar position must pay.

It is obvious, of course, that the very existence of a government, which includes a legal system, a monetary system, and the establishment of standards and grades of quality, facilitates the conduct of business. A subsidy goes beyond such activities, however; its purpose usually is to maintain or improve the position of certain businesses or private interest groups, without commensurate public gains. In this sense, subsidies are an outgrowth of the protectionism of the mercantile system (*q.v.*), under which governments used special forms of regulation or restraint, particularly import duties, quotas, and fiscal expedients, in order to maintain, encourage, and promote "essential" industries that were endangered by foreign competition. Tariffs, import quotas, and other trade restrictions serve to exclude competitors from the home market or limit their access to it, thus enabling protected sellers to charge higher prices. The result is a transfer of income (or subsidy) from consumers of the protected goods to the favoured domestic producer.

In the case of industries that do not need protection to remain in business, tariffs and other restrictive devices merely enhance profits. Industry protection through trade restrictions causes a shift in the nation's resources from more productive to less productive uses. The objective underlying a policy of protection, aside from questions of national security and power, is to provide a balance of economic activities and power among various economic groups, both nationally and internationally. Use of such a doctrine to protect infant industries of a country until they expand sufficiently to attain an efficient level of operation often is extended to justify a variety of protectionist measures, without demonstrable public gains to either the domestic or international community. Once protectionist measures are justified on the ground that they benefit infant industries, they are often extended to cover lost markets (both real and imagined), as well as new markets. Thus, protectionist devices and subsidies are in reality practical expedients, not unlike other forms of controls designed to deal with specific problems or to accommodate special interest groups.

Nations have retreated in varying degrees from mercantilist protective measures toward freer trade, but other methods of protection, support, and promotion of private industry have become important in the functioning of economic systems of today. In the United States, where businessmen lay great stress on preserving the free-enterprise system, subsidy has become so pervasive as a means of effectuating public policy that it can properly be said the economy has entered an age of government by subsidy. In the 1960s, for example, up to $15,000,000,000 per year, or roughly 15% to 20% of the total U.S. budget, was allocated for benefits to interest groups, such as farmers, small and big businesses, veterans, and others, not including hidden subsidies covered under such items as interest, national security, federal highway program, and international affairs.

**Direct Subsidies.**—Railroads, transoceanic shipping companies, shipbuilders, and airlines have been given various forms of subsidy by almost all developed countries at one time or another. Direct gifts of land and construction funds were given to the railroads in connection with the settlement and development of the United States. In more recent years, railroad subsidies have consisted of authorization for railroads to amortize new investment more rapidly than usual, thus reducing their tax liability, and government guarantee of repayment of private loans to the railroads for the purchase of new equipment.

The most important subsidies in this field are for ship construction, payments for operation of transoceanic merchant vessels, establishment of cargo preferences for domestic lines, and exemption of profits from corporate income taxes under certain conditions. The U.S. government ship construction subsidy amounts to the differential between cost of construction in U.S. and in foreign shipyards, not to exceed one-half the cost (except where defense features are included). The liner "United States," for example, cost approximately $77,000,000, of which taxpayers provided $44,000,000. The subsidy to operators of transoceanic vessels, hidden for many years in excessive payments for carrying the U.S. mail, was brought out in the open during the 1930s as an "operating differential" between the cost assumed to be involved in operating under the U.S. flag rather than under a foreign flag.

Operating subsidies, or airmail subsidies, are fairly common as a means of promoting airlines. As early as 1924, for example, the British government provided a subsidy for Imperial Airways, Ltd., to develop air routes to the Commonwealth countries. During the 1950s the United States paid commercial airlines $500,000,000 in such subsidies.

Agriculture has received various direct subsidies, including gifts of land, export subsidies, and provision of a variety of services, such as market information, agricultural research and education, and protection from crop pests and animal diseases. Federal support for agricultural education and research alone have averaged several hundred million dollars per year in the United States.

**Indirect Subsidies.**—Indirect subsidies are the most widespread form of assistance to private enterprise, particularly in the United States. One type, the payment in excess of actual cost or market value, includes the purchase of silver for monetary purposes, the purchase of certain metals for stockpiling, and the purchase of agricultural commodities. Under domestic producer preference laws, government procurement officers must purchase goods made at home unless their price exceeds the price of goods made abroad by more than a specific percentage. The U.S. mining industry benefits from a federal law requiring the government to buy supplies at above market prices and in excess of its needs. For many years the entire domestic output of silver has been sold to the U.S. government at prices in excess of the international price; meanwhile the silver used by industry for commercial purposes was purchased from foreign sources at lower prices. Federal, state, and local governments all have provided subsidies to shipping by dredging rivers and building canals. Aviation has benefited from the construction of airports, provision of airways, traffic control equipment, weather-reporting facilities, radio beams, and instrument landing systems.

One of the most important subsidies in the United States is the price support program for 12 basic crops, with special emphasis on wheat, corn, and cotton. The subsidy operates through government "nonrecourse" loans: if market prices go above an arbitrary support level (minimum price), the farmer can pay off the loan and repossess his crop pledged as collateral. If prices fall below the support level, the farmer defaults on his loan, keeps the money loaned him, and the government takes the loss. These subsidies amounted to about $1,000,000,000 per year in the 1960s, with principal benefits accruing to the large, corporate-sized farms.

Indirect subsidies to farm operators also arise in connection with the building of farm-to-market roads, which in part are paid for with city gasoline tax revenues and federal support.

Other indirect subsidies consist of free or partially requited services, ostensibly available to all persons and businesses but actually of benefit to only a few enterprises. The trucking industry, for example, is subsidized indirectly to the extent that taxes imposed on trucks to cover the cost of highway construction and maintenance do not equal the benefits received. In addition, the tax burden falls heaviest on light, gasoline-powered vehicles (including passenger cars) as against heavy, diesel-powered vehicles.

Owners of irrigated farmlands are heavily subsidized; settlers are given long-term, low-interest loans that work out so that they pay only about one-half of the real cost to the government; in multipurpose water projects, the direct beneficiaries of federal irrigation pay only a minor part of their cost, the remainder being paid by taxpayers and other water users. Power companies receive subsidies in connection with the generation of electricity from atomic fuels; *i.e.*, in government-supported research, the price charged for the nuclear material, and the price paid by the government for nuclear wastes and residues.

Two other important types of indirect subsidies arise out of government guarantees and various kinds of special tax reduction to private industry. In the first, the government assumes a contingent liability on private investments, debts, and contracts, without requiring an equivalent public benefit, such as an equivalent reduction in price. Included here are guarantees on investments abroad, on loans to feeder or local-service airlines, on mortgage lenders' loans to home buyers, and on loans to small businesses, farmers, and railroads. Tax reduction as a subsidy includes the exemption of new businesses from local property taxes and of income from certain securities, accelerated amortization of plants (which as a minimum provides an interest-free loan), and the special "depletion" allowance for the mining industry. In the case of mining, not only are the costs of exploration and development deductible as current costs for tax purposes but mining companies also have the option of making an arbitrary deduction for the "depletion" of assets (in the United States at rates of from 5% of gross income for coal, sand, and gravel up to 27½% for oil and gas), instead of deducting the *actual* depletion through the estimated life of the assets. In the United States the depletion allowance is limited to a maximum of 50% of net income, but this can reduce corporate tax liability from 52% down to 26%.

Other indirect subsidies include the sale of war plants and merchant vessels to private industry at a fraction of their original costs and disposal of surplus commodities at less than buying prices plus storage and interest costs.

*See* also references under "Subsidy" in the Index.

BIBLIOGRAPHY.—Walter Adams and Horace M. Gray, *Monopoly in America: the Government as Promoter* (1955); James C. Nelson, *Railroad Transportation and Public Policy* (1959); Murray R. Benedict, *Can We Solve the Farm Problem?* (1955); J. C. Lessard, *Transportation in Canada* (1956); Otto Eckstein, *Water-Resource Development* (1958); Commission on the Organization of the Executive Branch of the Government, *Task Force Report on Lending Agencies,* (1949); Clair Wilcox, *Public Policies Toward Business* (1960); Howard S. Piquet, *Aid, Trade and the Tariff* (1953); Edmund Blair Bolles, *How to Get Rich in Washington* (1952); Eli Clemens, *Economics and Public Utilities* (1950). (R. F. LA.)

**SUBSTANCE.** In traditional philosophy a substance is a thing that exists independently and persists through change; but the notion has been developed in different ways by different philosophers, and it is impossible to judge of its value without a summary of its history.

**Origins of the Term.**—The Greek word sometimes translated as "substance" is *ousia.* Its earliest and most widespread use in Greek literature is for property or estate, but it is similar in origin to "being" and it was in fact used by Plato and Aristotle in a nontechnical way to signify being in the sense of "essence," being in the sense of "existence," and being as opposed to becoming. The beginning of the technical usage now rendered by "substance" is to be found in Aristotle's *Categories,* 5:

"Substance (*ousia*) in the . . . primary . . . sense of the word is that which is neither predicable of a subject nor present in a subject. . . . But in a secondary sense those things are called substances within which, as species, the primary substances are included. . . . Thus everything except primary substances is either predicated of primary substances or is present in them. . . . The fact that parts of substances appear to be present in the whole, as in a subject, should not make us apprehensive lest we have to admit that such parts are not substances: for in explaining the phrase 'present in a subject,' we stated that we meant 'otherwise than as parts in a whole.' . . . The most distinctive mark of substance appears to be that, while remaining numerically one and the same, it is capable of admitting contrary qualities. . . . The same individual . . . is at one time warm, at another cold. . . . This capacity is found nowhere else."

Use of "being" as a translation for *ousia* in this passage might perhaps give a clearer impression of Aristotle's intention. For he does not wish to fix the sense of a term that would otherwise be unintelligible. On the contrary, assuming that his reader knows the meaning of *ousia,* he asserts the existence of certain *protai ousiai* ("prime beings,"; *e.g.,* Socrates), presupposed by all talk of other things. Similarly, in his *Metaphysics* he announces that *ousia* is the principal subject of his study, as though everyone knew what he meant by that term, and then sets out to determine where it may be found. His conclusion in this work is similar to that in the *Categories,* but in his argument he attacks the doctrines of other philosophers (*e.g.,* Ionian theories about a primal stuff and Plato's assertion that "forms" exist independently), and he also makes a rather bewildering shift in his use of *ousia.* If we here translate the Greek by "substance," we must allow for a distinction between *a* substance (*i.e.,* an individual thing) and *the* substance of a thing (*i.e.,* what is fundamental in its being). According to *Metaphysics,* vii, the substance of a thing is what makes it what it is, and this is its form or essence (*i.e.,* the defining character of the species which in the *Categories* he described as a substance in a secondary sense). In addition to their form all ordinary substances have matter, and it is this which distinguishes them as individuals, though matter cannot exist without form. There are, however, some substances (God and the Intelligences in control of the planetary spheres) which have no matter; Aristotle does not explain how they are individuated.

The Latin word *substantia* appears first in the younger Seneca's *Epistulae,* 58, with the sense of "reality"; and slightly later occurrences show that at the end of the 1st century A.D. it had the whole range of uses of the Greek *ousia.* This exact correspondence is curious, since the etymology of *substantia* (literally "standing under" or "near") is different from that of *ousia,* but the circumstances in which *substantia* occurs suggest that it was not a deliberate neologism introduced for the purpose of translating the Greek. In later Latin *substantia* retains its wide range of usages: thus *consubstantialis* occurs in the Latin version of the Nicene Creed as a translation for the Greek *homoousios,* meaning "of the same essence." In English "substance" has acquired yet other meanings (*e.g.,* "kind of stuff"), but is now generally reserved by philosophers for Aristotle's "prime being," while other terms such as "essence" and "existence" are used for the other senses of *ousia.*

**Medieval and Modern Theories.**—Medieval Aristotelians, such as St. Albertus Magnus and St. Thomas Aquinas, retained the master's doctrine of substance for the most part unchanged; but they felt difficulties about individuation that had not distressed him. According to St. Thomas, angels are without matter (as Aristotle said of his Intelligences) and must therefore be distinguished one from another in respect of their forms; *i.e.,* must each be of a different species (*Summa theologica,* I, x, 6). The problem presented by human souls is even more serious. According to Aristotle's *De anima,* which St. Thomas followed, a soul is the form of the living body that it animates. This view may perhaps be reconciled with Christian doctrine, but what of the interval between death and the resurrection of the body? During that time, it seems, souls must continue to exist as separated forms, though this condition is unnatural for them (*Summa theologica,* I, lxxvi). These were among the difficulties that produced a reaction against Aristotelianism during the Renaissance; but to the founders of modern physics the most irritating feature of the system was that it deluded men into thinking that they had given an explanation of a fact when they had merely formulated it in a technical jargon. The statement that a substance originated through the reception of a form in matter might perhaps be defensible by an array of definitions, but it was useless for science.

This is not to say, however, that physicists of the 17th century had no use for the concept of a thing that existed independently of all else and persisted through change. On the contrary, many of them adopted the atomic theory suggested in antiquity by Democritus, and their reasons were a priori, like those of its ancient champions; for it was not until the time of John Dalton (1766–1844) that the atomic hypothesis was used in a scientific fashion to explain empirical generalizations. Since ordinary observable things come into being by the aggregation of parts and are destroyed by the separation of parts, it is plausible to suppose that there are very small things which never come into being or pass away but constitute all observable things by entering into close spatial relations with each other. This conclusion seems, indeed, to be required by the principle that nothing is made of nothing or resolved into nothing (Lucretius, *De rerum natura,* i, 147 ff.). Aristotle did not accept the atomic theory of his day and did not define substances as things that are everlasting; but there is a connection of thought between the atomist's belief in simple bodies and his doctrine of ultimate subjects. In a surviving fragment of his work *On Democritus,* he himself speaks of atoms as little substances, and it is not surprising that some philosophers of the 17th century came to think of atoms as the only genuine substances.

The new orthodoxy established at the end of the 17th century by Newton and Locke allowed for two kinds of basic things, atoms and souls; but there were some curious developments among philosophers who tried to take seriously the notion of a substance as something which requires nothing else for its own existence. Descartes (who gave this definition in his *Principia philosophiae,* i, 51) agreed with the demand for mechanical explanation of natural phenomena, but rejected atomism as self-contradictory (*ibid.*, ii, 20). According to his philosophy there is only one *res extensa,* though there are many *res cogitantes,* or minds. Spinoza went farther and argued that there could be only one substance, Nature or God, which comprised in its infinity the attributes both of extension and of thought. Whereas Descartes had allowed the title of substance by courtesy to things which were independent of all else except God, Spinoza denied the existence of created substances (*Ethica*). Frightened by this pantheism, Leibniz reverted to the view that there were many substances, but maintained that nothing extended could be a substance, since its existence presupposed the existence of its parts. According to his view, all substances must be conceived by analogy with minds, because these alone have the simplicity necessary for independence; and it must further be supposed that each has its experiences without being affected by any other, because causal interaction would be inconsistent with independence (*Discours de métaphysique; Monadologie*).

These surprising results were all derived from attempts to take the notion of independent existence in a much stricter way than Aristotle ever contemplated. So too the criticism which the doctrine of substance received a little later from Locke, Berkeley and Hume was based on a concept foreign to Aristotle. These philosophers all maintained that ideas must be derived from experience; but Locke held also that the ideas obtained in sense-perception were representative of the qualities of physical things and found himself driven to admit that he had no idea of a substance except that of a something-he-knew-not-what serving as support to qualities (*Essay Concerning Human Understanding,* I, iv, 18). It is not surprising that Berkeley declared talk of material substance to be meaningless, or that Hume went on to declare talk of a spiritual substance equally meaningless. Throughout the argument it was assumed that "substance" meant something standing under qualities. But Aristotle never taught that a substance was a featureless substratum of qualities; and apart from that, it is surely a mistake to speak of qualities as though they were drapings. (*See* QUALITIES.)

Hume, who held every impression or idea to be a distinct existence, says in one place that if anything may be called a substance which may exist by itself, then his perceptions are substances (*Treatise of Human Nature,* I, iv, 5). The remark is interesting because it had always been assumed without question that anything which satisfied Aristotle's first requirement must also persist through change. When he tried to rehabilitate the doctrine of substance after the attacks of the empiricists, Kant made this a matter of definition (*Critique of Pure Reason,* "First Analogy" of Experience). But it is difficult to be certain about the interpretation of Kant's doctrine; for he tried to justify it by saying that it was presupposed in our perception of change, suggesting also that it was the same as the principle of the conservation of matter. Clearly the continuants (to adopt a term from W. E. Johnson's *Logic*) which undergo perceived changes are themselves perceived, whereas the particles which scientists have supposed to be conserved through all change are not perceived.

In the 20th century Bertrand Russell ("The Philosophy of Logical Atomism," in *The Monist,* 1918–19) and A. N. Whitehead (*An Enquiry Concerning the Principles of Natural Knowledge,* 1919) made once more the distinction that Hume had indicated between Aristotle's two notions. According to their arguments, there must be simple and ultimate particulars which are the subjects of basic facts: Russell called them logical atoms. These satisfy Aristotle's first requirement for a substance, though it may be undesirable to call them by that name, since it suggests permanence, or at least persistence for a long time, whereas they are minimal events. To say that such events happen to a continuant can only mean that they form a temporal series in which each has a close resemblance to its neighbours and is causally connected with them.

**The Value of the Notion.**—There are undoubtedly substances such as Aristotle describes in his *Categories.* For according to his explanations a substance is just a thing, not in the sense in which things are contrasted with persons, but in the larger sense in which things are contrasted with attributes, such as manhood, with abstractions, such as grammar, and with the events that occur to them. It is not quite correct to say, as Aristotle does, that these things are the only subjects of change (for even Greek grammar has changed since his day); but they can undoubtedly change in respect of inessential characters. Are there also substances corresponding to the narrower definitions of later philosophers? In order to answer this question we must distinguish between the requirement of independence and that of permanence.

If we insist that nothing with parts shall be called a substance, we must agree with Leibniz that there can be no extended substances. This consideration is fatal to the a priori atomism of Democritus and also to that of Whitehead and of Russell. For in each case that which is offered as a substance is complex in the same way as entities disqualified for the title. There may, of course, be good scientific reasons for believing in physically indivisible particles or in events that are, so to say, natural units; but an a priori argument for atomism of either kind is fallacious in the same way as an argument from the principle of universal causation to the necessity of a first cause. It would be an equally serious mistake, however, to suppose that the extended world is composed of unextended substances. For although anything punctiform or instantaneous is not dependent for its existence on other things in the way in which a whole is dependent on its parts, it is dependent in another way, namely, in the way in which a boundary is dependent on that of which it is a boundary. There is, indeed, no absurdity in the suggestion that everything is dependent on something else in some way. Why should we suppose that some thing or things must be independent of everything in every way?

On the other hand, the search for something permanent through all change has been of the greatest importance in the development of science. For it has led not only to the primitive atomic theory of Democritus, but also to the principle of the conservation of energy (*q.v.*). Unlike the Democritean theory, the latter principle was formulated in connection with experimental inquiries, but it is a postulate that guides research rather than a generalization that might be refuted by a counterexample. Nature is intelligible only insofar as it is conservative, but it is not necessary for its intelligibility that what it conserves should be stuff.

*See* also ACCIDENT; CATEGORY; and references under "Substance" in the Index.

On Aristotle's doctrine *see* W. D. Ross, *Aristotle,* 5th ed. (1949). Some aspects of the later history are treated in E. Cassirer, *Substance and Function,* Eng. trans. (1923). (W. C. K.)

**SUBUKTIGIN** (*c.* 942–997), ruler of Ghazni (in modern Afghanistan) from 977 to 997 and father of the great conqueror Mahmud. Born in Barskhan, on the shores of the Issiq-Gol (Issyk-Kul'), of a Qarluq father, Subuktigin was captured by a neighbouring Turkish tribe and sold to a slave dealer who eventually took him to Bukhara. About 959 he was purchased by Alptigin, a Turkish military officer of the Samanid kingdom, and when in 962 Alptigin established himself as a semi-independent ruler at Ghazni he took Subuktigin with him. Marrying a local chief's daughter and becoming popular under Alptigin's successors at Ghazni, Subuktigin in 977 was accepted as ruler of Ghazni by the local Turkish soldiery. He did not, however, claim formal independence from the Samanids. His rule was notable for the extension of Ghazni's power in the direction of both Hindustan and Khurasan. His defeats of Raja Jaipal, of the Hindushanhiyya dynasty, in 986 and 987 led to the Hindushahiyyas' loss of control of the Kabul Valley.

In 994, as a reward for serving his Samanid overlord, Amir Nuh II, against rebels, Subuktigin acquired the governorship of Balkh. In 996 he so far forced his will upon Nuh as to conclude a peace for him with the Qara-khanid Turks of the steppe, a peace defining the mutual limits of their territories. At his death near Balkh in August 997, Subuktigin was in control of the Samanid provinces south of the Oxus (Amu-Darya), bequeathing a power that his son Mahmud (*q.v.*) of Ghazni was to make imperial. *See* also GHAZNI; SAMANIDS.

BIBLIOGRAPHY.—Muhammad Nazim, *Life and Times of Sultan Mahmud of Ghazna* (1931); V. V. Barthold, *Turkestan down to the Mon-*

*gol Invasion,* 2nd rev. ed. (1959); C. E. Bosworth, *The Ghaznavids: Their Empire in Afghanistan and Eastern Iran, 994–1040* (1963).
(P. H.)

**SUBWAY (UNDERGROUND RAILWAY),** an underground electric railway system used to transport large numbers of passengers within urban and suburban areas. Subways are usually built under city streets although they may cross under rivers and take shortcuts. Outlying sections usually emerge into the open, becoming elevated or conventional electric railways. Subway trains are usually made up of a number of cars operated on the multiple-unit system, as distinct from the single car or car and trailer of street railways (tramways).

**History.**—The world's first subway system was proposed for London by Charles Pearson, the city solicitor, as part of a city improvement plan shortly after the opening of the Thames Tunnel in 1843. After years of discussion, Parliament in 1853 and 1854 authorized the construction of 3.75-mi. (6.03-km.) underground railway between Farringdon Street and Bishop's Road, Paddington. Work on the Metropolitan District Railway began in 1860 by cut-and-cover methods, that is, by making great trenches along the streets, giving them brick sides, providing girders or a brick arch for the roof, and then restoring the roadway on top. This brick tunnel was 17 ft. (5.18 m.) high and, in order to take two tracks of the broad 7-ft. (2.13 m.) gauge, 28.5 ft. (8.68 m.) wide. The line was opened on Jan. 10, 1863, using steam locomotives that burned coke (later coal), and, in spite of the sulfurous fumes, the line was a success from the start, carrying 9,500,000 passengers in the first year of its existence.

In 1886 the City and Southwark Subway Co. (later the City and South London Railway) began work on their "tube" line, using a tunneling shield developed by J. H. Greathead (*q.v.*). This was an improvement over both the rectangular shield used by Sir Marc Isambard Brunel for the Thames Tunnel and the round shield of Greathead and Peter W. Barlow used on the Tower Subway of 1870. (This was a 7-ft.-diameter cross-river tube with a cable-hauled car, soon converted to a pedestrian subway.) The Greathead shield of 1886 used hydraulic jacks with a thrust of 200 tons to force its way through the ground by pushing against the cast-iron segments of the completed tunnel. It provided protection for the men excavating and lining the 10-ft. (3.05-m.) diameter single-track tunnels. Penetrating the London clay was fairly straightforward, but in wetter formations, such as gravels, compressed air was used. The tunnels were driven at such a depth as to avoid interference with building foundations or public utility works, and there was no disruption of street traffic. The original plan was for cable operation, but electric traction was substituted before the line was opened. Operation began on this first electric underground railway in 1890 with a uniform fare of twopence for any journey on the three-mile line. (*See* also TUNNEL.)

Charles Tyson Yerkes, a U.S. railway magnate, arrived in London in 1900 and was responsible for the construction of more tube railways and for the electrification of the cut-and-cover lines. Albert Stanley (later Baron Ashfield), at one time general manager of the Public Service Corporation of New Jersey, went to London to manage the Yerkes subways in 1907 and succeeded in establishing a single controlling authority when, in 1933, virtually all the London underground system was absorbed by the London Passenger Transport Board.

**The London Transport System.**—By the late 1960s London Transport trains were serving 277 stations spread over 254 route miles (409 km.), of which 98 mi. (158 km.) were underground (76 mi. [122 km.] in deep twin-tube tunnels and 22 mi. [35 km.] in cut-and-cover subsurface double-track tunnels). In 1969 the new Victoria Line, with 10.5 mi. of tube tunnels, was opened. Tube tunnels are generally about 12 ft. (3.66 m.) in diameter and lined with cast-iron segments except for sections of the Central and Victoria lines where reinforced concrete was used. The track gauge is the standard 4 ft. 8.5 in. (1.43 m.), although the original section of the Metropolitan Line retained its broad-gauge tunnel. Electric power at 630 v. DC for the multiple-unit trains comes mainly from London Transport's own generating stations. Automatic track-circuit signaling with coloured lights and train stops permits a theoretical maximum of 40 trains an hour each way, but with station stops the maximum peak-hour service is 32 to 35, carrying about 40,000 passengers per hour. The average speed, with stops, is 20 mph (32 kph), roughly double that of surface transport in peak hours. Speed-control signaling is employed on central area tracks with heavy traffic. The rolling stock is of two sizes: the tube cars have to fit the 12-ft. tunnels, but the subsurface cars are virtually of main-line cross section. Where tube and subsurface or main-line railways connect, safety devices guard against the larger cars' being driven toward a tube tunnel. Maximum length of trains is eight cars to carry 328 (tube) or up to 460 (subsurface) seated passengers plus up to about 1,000 standing. In the late 1960s the system carried each year about 671,000,000 passengers on an average journey of 4.6 mi. Because of the depth of the tubes, hydraulic and electric elevators (lifts) were provided at the stations, but since 1911 many of them have been replaced by escalators. In World Wars I and II tube stations performed an unintended function as air-raid shelters.

**Other British Systems.**—In 1886 the 4.75-mi. Mersey Railway was opened from an underground terminus under Liverpool Central Station through a double-track tunnel under the River Mersey to Birkenhead. In 1903 it became the first steam underground railway to be converted to electric traction. Since 1938 trains from the electrified Wirral suburban line have been projected over the Mersey Railway.

In 1886 2.75 mi. of a steam suburban line penetrated central Glasgow in a double-track tunnel. In 1891 work was begun on a 6.5-mi. subway loop, using both shield and cut-and-cover methods of construction. In 1894 there was a disastrous series of blowouts under the River Clyde, and work was temporarily abandoned, but the 410-ft. section under the river was later completed. The 4-ft. gauge trains were cable operated until 1935, when the line was electrified on a 570-v. DC third-rail system.

**Other European Systems.**—A 2.5-mi. electric subway in Budapest opened in 1896, using single cars with trolley poles; it was the first subway on the European continent. By using a flat roof with steel beams instead of a brick arch and, therefore, a shallower trench, considerable savings were achieved over earlier cut-and-cover methods.

The Paris system, called the Métro (*Chemin de Fer Métropolitain*), was started in 1898, and the first 6.25 mi. were opened in 1900. Rapid progress was attributed to the wide streets overhead and the modification of the cut-and-cover method devised by the engineer Fulgence Bienvenue. Vertical shafts were sunk at inter-

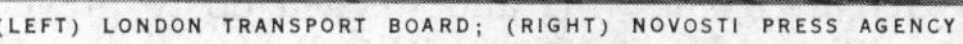

(LEFT) LONDON TRANSPORT BOARD; (RIGHT) NOVOSTI PRESS AGENCY

(LEFT) BAKER STREET STATION PLATFORM, LONDON, IN 1863; (RIGHT) MARBLE HALL AT KOMSOMOLSKAYA STATION, CIRCLE LINE, MOSCOW vals along the route, and from there side trenches were dug, with masonry foundations to support wooden shuttering immediately under the road surfaces. Construction of the roof arch then proceeded with little disturbance to street traffic. This method is still used in Paris but has not been copied to any great extent.

In the 1960s the Métro consisted of 14 lines with about 270 stations. In addition, the Sceaux Line had 28 stations, so that the system gave excellent coverage of Paris and its suburbs. With about 120 route miles, it was the third largest system in the world, and in number of passengers carried—more than 1,100,000,000 a year—it was second only to that of New York City.

A development on some lines in Paris has been the introduction of pneumatic-tired trains running on wood or concrete strips, with ordinary wheels and rails retained for emergencies and for running through switches. This system provides quieter running, faster acceleration, and improved speeds, while reduced vibration permits lighter construction.

Berlin's subway system, the U-bahn, opened in 1902, and by the 1960s there were in West and East Berlin 55.5 route miles, with 111 stations. The ten lines carried about 240,000,000 passengers each year. The Hamburg subway had 64 stations, 45.25 route miles, and 167,100,000 passengers a year.

Continental Europe's second largest system is the Moscow Metro, distinguished by its lavishly decorated and spacious stations. No two are alike, and they are finished in polished marble and granite, with decorations in mosaic and coloured glass and embellished with statuary. Work began in 1932, and the first line opened in 1935. Most lines are of tube construction, with twin tunnels 17 ft. in diameter and containing single 5-ft. gauge tracks. The Moscow subsoil proved far more difficult to penetrate than the London clay, but this did not prevent the extension of the system. By the 1960s there were 87 route miles with 82 stations carrying more than 1,000,000,000 passengers a year. Other European subways operate in Stockholm, Vienna, Madrid, Athens, Leningrad, Lisbon, Rome, Milan, Barcelona, Kiev, and Oslo. In the 1960s subway construction was proceeding in, among other places, Budapest and Rotterdam. Few of the European systems are entirely in tunnels; in some cases tracks run on the surface in outer districts, as in London, or there are urban elevated sections, as in Paris and Hamburg. Most of the lines have standard-gauge tracks, except those of the U.S.S.R. with a 5-ft. gauge and Spain with a 5-ft. 6-in. gauge. Nearly all have automatic signaling with coloured lights. In Stockholm all trains have cab-signaling indicating the correct speed for the section; if ignored, the brakes are applied automatically.

**North American and Other Systems.**—The first practical subway line in the United States was constructed on the cut-and-cover principle in Boston between 1895 and 1897. It was 1.5 mi. long and used trolley streetcars (tramcars). Later, Boston acquired conventional subway lines.

New York City tried to solve its transportation problem by constructing elevated railways, mainly because of the resistance of its subsoil to tunneling. However, in 1900 a subway program was started, and work progressed rapidly. The first experimental line, only 296 ft. (90.22 m.) in length, had been built in 1870 beneath Lower Broadway by Alfred E. Beach, editor of the *Scientific American.* Cars were propelled in a tube by compressed air, using the cars as a plunger and the tube as a cylinder. Financially the line was unsuccessful, and it closed after a few years. The first conventional line in New York City was built from City Hall to Dyckman Street for the Rapid Transit Commission, with William Barclay Parsons as chief engineer and John B. McDonald as contractor. The first section was opened on Oct. 27, 1904. Almost all subway construction in New York City was paid for by the city authorities and then turned over to two private companies, the Interborough Rapid Transit Company (IRT) and the Brooklyn-Manhattan Transit Corporation (BMT). However, in 1925 construction of a third subway was begun, the Independent city-owned subway (IND), to be operated by the city. The first IND line was opened in 1932–33 from Washington Heights, going south under Eighth Avenue. Unification of all lines under public auspices took place in 1940, and the system is now owned by the city and operated by the New York City Transit Authority, under the control of the state of New York. However, the Hudson Tubes, linking Manhattan and New Jersey, are run by the Port of New York Authority. New York City has the largest system in the world, consisting of 245.3 route miles with 495 stations carrying about 1,400,000,000 passengers a year.

WIDE WORLD
AIR-CONDITIONED TRAIN, PART OF THE LARGEST SUBWAY SYSTEM IN THE WORLD, STOPS AT THE 33RD STREET STATION IN NEW YORK CITY

Other subways in the United States are in Philadelphia, opened in 1907, and in Chicago, opened in 1943. Toronto, in Canada, opened a subway in 1954, and further construction was proceeding in the 1960s. For the second Canadian system, under construction in Montreal in the 1960s, Paris-type rubber-tired cars were to be used. In South America the Buenos Aires subway opened in 1913. Japan had lines in Tokyo (1927), Kyoto (1931), Osaka (1933), and Nagoya (1957).

**New Construction.**—The end of World War II heralded an impressive spate of construction, with new lines in Leningrad, Kiev, Milan, Lisbon, Toronto, Stockholm, Nagoya, Rome, Haifa, and Istanbul. Later construction was planned for Rotterdam, Warsaw, Oslo, Budapest, and Montreal. Existing systems, such as those in London, Moscow, and Berlin, built new extensions, while London, New York, and others modernized their lines and built new rolling stock. By the mid-1960s, 27 cities without subways were either considering them or had reached the stage of detailed planning. All this activity could be related to the increased needs of commuters, placing an increasing strain on surface transportation. Even in cases where subways might not be commercially successful in themselves, they could be justified by their contribution to the total economy.

**Construction Problems.**—The main problem of subway construction has always been the consideration of existing property. Utilities, including sewers, gas and water mains, telephone and power lines, steam mains, and mail tubes, must be avoided or else diverted. Apart from the early cut-and-cover lines in London, provision has usually been made for maintaining road traffic during construction. Interference with the foundations of buildings was a problem with the early subsurface and tube lines in London, but later lines were constructed sufficiently deep in the subsoil to avoid this problem. In Paris the wide boulevards helped the engineers avoid buildings. New York City has a high proportion of tall buildings, which, because of their weight, present special problems. Normal New York practice has been to retain the side walls of the trench with steel beams and horizontal wood lagging, with a temporary deck to carry traffic above it. However, some buildings that needed underpinning during subway construction led to development of the pretest pile by Lazarus White and Edmund A. Prentis. These piles are installed by jacking steel cylinders under a building to support it at a level below the subgrade of the subway. The piles are preloaded for the weight of the building and wedged up to prevent the elastic rebound of the earth. Many buildings that have been underpinned in this way now rest on the roof of the subway.

**Traffic Control.**—The signal system is a vital part of subway operation. Its purpose is twofold: to ensure safety with speed, especially by preventing conflicting movements, and to secure proper spacing of trains to maintain schedules and achieve maximum track usage. Train movements are controlled by coloured lights placed either at the side of the track or in the motorman's cab. The lights are operated automatically through track circuits, each circuit covering a short section of track and indicating its status to any approaching train. Interlocking devices at junctions prevent signalmen from setting up conflicting movements. Perhaps as a preliminary step to automatic trains, London Transport made considerable use of automatic traffic control. This was achieved by means of prepunched plastic "program rolls" carrying the day's train service, which passed through a machine operating signals and switches (points) by relays.

*See* also ELECTRIC TRACTION.

BIBLIOGRAPHY.—E. A. Course, *London Railways* (1962); T. C. Barker and M. Robbins, *A History of London Transport*, vol. i (1963); J. R. Day, *Railways Under the Ground* (1964); H. F. Howson, *World's Underground Railways* (1964). (E. A. Co.)

**SUCCINIC ACID** is an organic compound occurring in amber (3% to 8%), from which fossilized gum it is obtained by distillation. It is also found in other resins, in lignites, in fossilized woods and in many plants.

It is present at low concentration in a great variety of animal tissues, where it has an important function in intermediary metabolism (*see* KREBS CYCLE).

Chemically, succinic acid, or butanedioic acid, $CO_2HCH_2$-$CH_2CO_2H$, is a saturated dibasic acid which crystallizes in colourless prisms or plates melting at 186° C. and boils at 235° C. Its vapour readily loses water to form succinic anhydride (formula I), which crystallizes in plates melting at 120° C.

The acid itself is soluble in water, and its salts with the alkali and alkaline-earth metals are also soluble in water. Barium succinate is precipitated from aqueous solution by alcohol; ferric succinate is insoluble in water and is sometimes employed in the analytical separation of iron from other metals.

When heated with phosphorus trisulfide, sodium succinate yields thiophene.

Succinic acid is produced during the bacterial fermentation of ammonium tartrate or calcium malate. It may be prepared synthetically from ethylene, $C_2H_4$, through ethylene dichloride, $C_2H_4Cl_2$, ethylene dicyanide or succinonitrile, $C_2H_4(CN)_2$. The last compound yields the acid on hydrolysis.

Maleic acid, produced industrially by catalytic oxidation of benzene, yields succinic acid on reduction with sodium amalgam.

```
CH2CO            CH2COCl          CH2CO
|    \           |                |    \
|     O          |                |     NH
|    /           |                |    /
CH2CO            CH2COCl          CH2CO
  I                II               III
```

Succinyl chloride (formula II) is obtained by the interaction of phosphorus pentachloride and succinic acid. Succinic anhydride (formula I), also produced by heating the acid or its salts with acetic anhydride or by heating succinyl chloride with anhydrous oxalic acid, is employed as an intermediate in dye making. It is employed also in the manufacture of alkyd resins (*see* RESINS) and is an important reagent in organic chemical synthesis.

Succinimide (formula III), produced by heating succinic anhydride in ammonia, crystallizes in colourless octahedra melting at 125°–126° C. and readily soluble in water. This imide when distilled with zinc dust furnishes pyrrole (*q.v.*).

Succinonitrile, $CNCH_2CH_2CN$, obtained as above and also by electrolysis of potassium cyanoacetate, is a colourless solid melting at 54°–55° C. On reduction with sodium and alcohol it is converted into putrescine (tetramethylenediamine), $NH_2(CH_2)_4$-$NH_2$, and into pyrollidine (tetrahydropyrrole; *see* PYRROLE).

Methylsuccinic acid or pyrotartaric acid,

$$CO_2HCH_2CH(CH_3)CO_2H$$

formed during dry distillation of tartaric acid, by heating pyruvic acid with concentrated hydrochloric acid, or by the reduction with sodium amalgam of citraconic and mesaconic acids, is obtained in colourless prismatic crystals soluble in water and melting at 112° C. It forms an anhydride and its sodium salt heated with phosphorus trisulfide yields $\beta$-methylthiophene. Isosuccinic acid (methylmalonic acid), $CH_3CH(CO_2H)_2$, an isomeride of ordinary succinic acid, is obtained on hydrolyzing $\alpha$-cyanopropionic acid, $CH_3CH(CN)CO_2H$, or by the action of methyl iodide on ethyl sodiomalonate, $CHNa(CO_2C_2H_5)_2$. It crystallizes in prisms melting at 120° C. and is soluble in water. Unlike ordinary succinic acid, it does not yield an anhydride on heating, but loses carbon dioxide and passes into propionic acid.

*See* T. E. Thorpe, *Dictionary of Applied Chemistry*, vol. xi, 4th rev. ed. (1954); L. Weintraub *et al.*, "Novel Synthesis of Succinic Acid," *Chemistry and Industry*, p. 185 (Jan. 23, 1965). (G. T. M.; X.)

**SUCEAVA,** the capital of Suceava *regiune* (region) in the Socialist Republic of Rumania, lies on the Suceava River, 70 mi. (113 km.) NW of Iași (Jassy). Pop. (1963 est.) 24,856. The town was twice the capital of the historic province of Moldavia (1370–80 and 1564–68). Historical monuments include the ruined 14th-century Citadel and St. George's and St. Dumitru's churches (both in 16th-century Moldavian style). There is a museum, with important prehistoric and medieval collections, and a regional library. Chief industries are textile manufacture, timber working, and food processing.

SUCEAVA REGIUNE (area 5,309 sq.mi. [13,750 sq.km.]; pop. [1963 est.] 1,002,883) is about one-third mountainous (with hydropower potential) and more than one-third forested. To the east extends the Suceava Plateau and the northern part of the Jijia Depression, which is rich in chernozem. Extractive and mining industries are based on manganese, lignite, peat, and limestone. Arable land is devoted to maize (corn), wheat, sunflowers, potatoes, sugar beet, flax, and hemp. Chief towns, apart from Suceava, are Botoșani (*q.v.*), Cîmpulung Moldovenesc, Dorohoi, and Rădăuți.

**SÜCHOW** (HSÜ-CHOU, formerly T'UNG-SHAN), city in northwest Kiangsu province, China. Its site marks the approximate geographic border between the north China plain and the Yangtze delta plain, the meeting place of wheat and rice as staple crops, respectively. Twelve miles north is Wei-shan Hu, one of a series of long, narrow waterways into which the Grand Canal, 45 mi. E of Süchow, leads. Although walled, the city has had its historic struggles with Yellow River floods. Süchow is an important railway crossing where the north-south Tientsin–P'u-k'ou line meets the Lan-chou to Hai-chou (formerly the Lunghai) railway. This made it a strategic target during the Japanese attack on China, and at T'ai-erh-chuang, 30 mi. NE, the Chinese armies early in 1938 inflicted their first major defeat on the Japanese in a classic battle of manoeuvre that delayed the invaders' advance for two months and greatly raised the morale of the Chinese nation. A decisive battle in the Chinese civil war was also fought near Süchow from November 1948 to January 1949. Current industrial development is mainly in textiles and flour milling. Pop. (1958 est.) 710,000. (TE. H.)

**SUCKLING, SIR JOHN** (1609–1642), English poet, dramatist and courtier, best known for his lyrics, was born at Whitton, Middlesex, and baptized there on Feb. 10, 1609. He was the son of Sir John Suckling, secretary of state to James I. He was educated at Trinity college, Cambridge, to which he was admitted in 1623, and he inherited his father's considerable estates at the age of 18. He entered Gray's Inn in 1627 and left England to travel in France and Italy in 1628. Knighted on his return in the autumn of 1630, he joined the English volunteer force raised to serve under Gustavus Adolphus and appears to have been present at the battle of Breitenfeld in 1631. He returned to London in May 1632, and became a prominent figure at court with a reputation for being "the greatest gallant of his time, and the greatest gamester both for bowling and cards." He was a gentleman of the privy chamber to Charles I and the friend of the poets Thomas Carew, Richard Lovelace and William Davenant, as well as, rather surprisingly, the famous latitudinarian divine, John Hales. When the war with the Scots broke out in 1639, Suckling raised a troop of horse at his own expense and accompanied Charles I on his ill-fated expedition. The magnificent costumes of Suckling's gaudy warriors and their poor performance in the field were the subjects of much contemporary ridicule.

In May 1641 Suckling took an active part in the plot to rescue the earl of Strafford from the Tower. When the plot was discovered, Suckling fled to France and there is every reason to believe John Aubrey's statement that he committed suicide in Paris in 1642. According to Aubrey he invented the game of cribbage.

Suckling was the author of four plays, the most ambitious of which is the tragedy *Aglaura,* magnificently staged in 1637 and handsomely printed at the author's expense (1638), and the best, the lively comedy *The Goblins* (1638). They all contain echoes of Shakespeare and Beaumont and Fletcher. Richard Flecknoe's criticism of *Aglaura* that it seemed "full of flowers, but rather stuck in than growing there" applies to all Suckling's plays.

His reputation as a poet rests on his lyrics, the best of which justifies the description of him by Millamant in Congreve's *The Way of the World* as "natural, easy Suckling." He inherited from Donne the tradition of the "anti-platonic" deflation of high-flown love sentiment and uses it with a charming, gay insouciance in such poems as that which begins with the following lines:

Out upon it I have loved
 Three whole days together;
And am like to love three more,
 If it prove fair weather.

"A Session of the Poets" (1637; publ. 1646) is an amusing skit for which he probably took a hint from an Italian work by Traiano Boccalini; it is the prototype of a long line of similar works in the 17th and 18th centuries. He did his best work in the manner of popular poetry. His masterpiece is undoubtedly "A Ballad Upon a Wedding," in the style and metre of the contemporary street ballad. The description of the bride has an unsurpassed delicacy and grace:

Her feet beneath her petticoat,
Like little mice, stole in and out,
 As if they feared the light,
But O, she dances such a way
No sun upon an Easter-day,
 Is half so fine a sight.

Suckling's extant letters are in a lively, colloquial prose that anticipates that of the Restoration wits.

Bibliography.—The first published collection of Suckling's works was *Fragmenta Aurea* (1646; enlarged 1658). The so-called *Selections* published by Alfred Inigo Suckling in 1836 is in reality a complete edition of the works, of which W. C. Hazlitt's edition (1874, rev. ed. 1892) is little more than a reprint. A. I. Suckling's edition includes a valuable memoir and a portrait by Van Dyck. The best modern edition is *The Works of Sir John Suckling,* ed. by A. Hamilton Thompson (1910). For anecdotes of Suckling's life *see* Aubrey's *Brief Lives,* ed. by A. Clark, vol. ii, pp. 240–245 (1898) and for "A Session of the Poets" and its successors, *A Journal from Parnassus,* ed. by H. Macdonald (1937). There is important biographical information in "Sir John Suckling and the Cranfields" (*Times Literary Supplement,* Jan. 29, 1960) by Thomas Clayton. (V. de S. P.)

**SUCRE, ANTONIO JOSÉ DE** (1795–1830), was one of the most talented, successful and respected leaders of the Latin American war for independence from Spain. Born Feb. 3, 1795, at Cumaná, in eastern Venezuela, Sucre at the age of 15 was swept into the struggle against the Spaniards and loyalists and fought in many campaigns in Venezuela and Colombia. His skill and admirable character early attracted the attention of the revolutionary leader Simón Bolívar, and at the age of 26 with the rank of general, Sucre was assigned by Bolívar the mission of freeing southern Gran Colombia (Ecuador) from Spanish control. This he did by his victory at the battle of Pichincha, near Quito, in 1822.

Moving south to Peru, the central and southern portions of which formed the last stronghold of Spanish and loyalist forces in South America, Bolívar and Sucre organized an army which won the battles of Junín (Aug. 1824) and Ayacucho (Dec. 9, 1824). For his victory as field commander in the decisive engagement at Ayacucho, Sucre was given the rank of grand marshal of Ayacucho.

Early in 1825 Sucre was ordered by Bolívar to the region of Upper Peru (Bolivia) to occupy and organize the area. Bolívar joined him and the two leaders laboured to create a political structure, which took the form of a complicated constitution written by Bolívar. Under this constitution Sucre in 1826 was elected president of the new nation of Bolivia. Eager to retire from public responsibilities, he agreed to serve only two years of the lifetime tenure which he was offered. During this period Sucre attempted to provide Bolivia with institutions of government, including courts, a revenue system and schools. He sought to avoid excessive use of his great powers, but he became the target of mounting opposition born of political factionalism and ambition and complicated by Peruvian designs to absorb Bolivia. A mutiny at Chuquisaca in 1828, in which Sucre was wounded, and an invasion by Peruvian troops caused him to resign the presidency and retire to his chosen home in Ecuador. There he was called upon immediately to defend Gran Colombia against an invading force of Peruvians, whom he defeated in the battle of Portete de Tarqui early in 1829. The next year Bolívar again called Sucre from retirement, this time to preside over the "Admirable Congress" in Bogotá, a last effort to maintain the unity of Ecuador, Colombia and Venezuela within Bolívar's decade-old Gran Colombian federation. When this congress failed, Sucre started on the long ride home to Quito. At Berruecos, near Pasto in southern Colombia, he was assassinated in June 1830, probably by agents of José María Obando, an ambitious Colombian military chieftain who wished to be rid of the favourite lieutenant and possible successor of Bolívar.

Loyal, brave and modest, Sucre had been like a son or a younger brother to Bolívar, who was 12 years his senior. Among contemporaries Sucre gained the accolade, the "immaculate," for his high moral qualities. (T. F. McG.)

**SUCRE** is a northeastern coastal state of Venezuela, separated from Trinidad by the Gulf of Paria. Area 4,556 sq.mi. (11,800 sq.km.). Pop. (1961) 401,992. It is traversed by the northeastern highlands whose coastal range forms the two peninsulas of Paria and Araya on the east and west respectively. The eastern part of the state receives abundant rainfall while the western portion is relatively dry. Despite mountains and hills and excessive dryness in the western portion, Sucre is one of the more important states agriculturally. The rural population is very dense and the percentage of land under cultivation high; overcrowding and unemployment result in a high rate of out-migration from the rural areas to cities and to other states. Among the leading crops are bananas, cacao (half the national crop), coconuts (about 28%), coffee, corn, cotton, peanuts, sweet potatoes (almost half), sugarcane, tobacco, wheat, and cassava. Fishing is important in the adjacent waters of the Caribbean and an important seafood industry was developing in the 1960s—particularly in Cumaná, the state capital and an important commercial port. Cumaná, the oldest European settlement in South America, was in 1961 a town of about 70,000 people, and one of the largest cities of the northeast. With nine of the country's ten larger canneries, it ranks as the leading fish-canning centre of the nation. It also has textile mills, cigar factories, coconut-processing plants, garment and shoe factories. Mineral resources include asphalt from Lake Guanoco, salt from the Araya Peninsula, and gypsum from near Macuro. (L. We.)

**SUCRE,** legal capital of Bolivia, and seat of its supreme court. Pop. (1962 est.) 54,270. The city (elevation 8,530 ft. [2,600 m.]) is located in a fertile valley crossed by the Cachimayo River which flows into the wide Pilcomayo, and flanked by the majestic Churukella and Sicasica Hills. Its climate is mild with an average temperature of 16° C (61° F). A variety of fruits and vegetables are grown in the valley.

Known as the City of Four Names, the city at various times was called La Plata, Chuquisaca, Charcas and finally Sucre. It was founded by Pedro de Anzúrez in 1538 on the site of a Charcas Indian village. Numerous churches were built, including the magnificent 17th-century cathedral the Basilica Metropolitana. In 1561 it became the capital of the Charcas *audiencia* (Upper Peru) and in 1609 the seat of an archdiocese. Its University of St. Francis Xavier, one of the oldest in South America, was founded in 1624. Sucre was an early revolutionary centre; its citizens revolted against Spain on May 25, 1809. In 1839 it became the official capital of Bolivia and in 1840 was renamed Sucre in honour of Marshal Antonio José de Sucre, the first president of the Republic of Bolivia. In 1898 Sucre resisted efforts to move the capital permanently to La Paz and a civil war ensued. The outcome was a compromise; Sucre remained the capital in name and law but the executive and legislature moved to La Paz. (*See* BOLIVIA: *History*.)

A railroad to Potosí, a road to Cochabamba, a pipeline to the petroleum fields of Camiri, and secondary roads to nearby valleys made Sucre a commercial and agricultural centre of growing importance. Industrial establishments include an oil refinery and cement plant. (C. W. A.)

**SUDA LEXICON,** Greek lexicon of *c.* A.D. 1000. The title "Suda" is found in the manuscripts and in the earliest reference to it (in the commentary on Aristotle's *Rhetoric* by the 12th-century author Stephanus); the name "Suidas," by which the compiler is frequently known, is due to Eustathius (12th century), who arbitrarily hellenized the apparently barbarian title into a Greek (actually Thessalian) personal name.

The work is rather a combination of lexicon and encyclopaedia than a lexicon in the modern sense. It was compiled from a multitude of sources, lexicographical (principally the *Synagoge* also used by Photius, and the so-called *Lexicon Ambrosianum*), literary, biographical (principally an epitome of Hesychius of Miletus, *q.v.*) philosophical, historical, and religious. These sources were often inferior, and the compilation was prepared without adequate care or critical faculty; nevertheless, the lexicon is of immense value and is the most substantial of its kind extant. Especially important are the biographical entries on Greek classical and Byzantine writers, and the numerous quotations (over 5,000) from Aristophanes, for whose text the lexicon is an important authority.

*See* edition by A. Adler, 5 vol. (1928–38); Pauly-Wissowa, *Real-Encyclopädie der classischen Altertumswissenschaft,* 2nd series, vol. 4, col. 675–717 (1931). (D. M. J.)

**SUDAN** (BILAD AS SUDAN, "country of the Blacks"), as medieval Arab writers called the area south of the Sahara, stretches for more than 3,500 mi. (5,500 km.) across Africa from Cape Verde on the Atlantic to the highlands of Ethiopia and the Red Sea, between about latitude 8° and 16° N. It borders the Sahara on the north and extends southward to the forests of West Africa and the Congo Basin. Mean annual rainfall varies between 10 in. (250 mm.) in the north and 60 in. (1,500 mm.) in the south, with the hottest months usually from June to September and a pronounced, and often very prolonged, dry season. Temperatures are generally high throughout the year. Vegetation ranges from semidesert steppe and thorn-scrub near the Sahara through vast grass plains, loosely termed savannas, with numerous varieties of acacia and mimosa, to parkland country where low trees grow among tall grasses, and savanna forest that merges ultimately into equatorial rain forest.

During the dry season the trees shed their leaves, all but the largest rivers run dry, and bush fires which burn up the grass are common. Relative humidity may fall as low as 30%. The rainfall might be adequate for cultivation were it not for the very high rate of evaporation which makes irrigation essential in many areas.

Much of the Sudan is a plateau between 1,000 and 1,500 ft. (330–415 m.) above sea level, but there are many higher areas, sometimes exceeding 10,000 ft., as in northern Ethiopia and in the west of the Republic of the Sudan (Darfur). The principal rivers include the Senegal and Niger, draining to the Atlantic, and the Nile and its tributaries which derive much of their water from areas beyond the Sudan region. Lake Chad (*q.v.*) is a centre for interior drainage.

There has been considerable admixture with Hamitic peoples, the degree of Hamitic influence decreasing westward and southward toward the Gulf of Guinea. Many of the people are Muslims.

The density of population is generally low and many of the people are nomadic or seminomadic. Movement across the grasslands is generally uninterrupted, especially during the dry season and the continuity of a similar environment along the southern boundaries of the Sahara for vast distances has encouraged people to move from the north and east from early times. At first they traveled with the aid of horses and oxen but migration was greatly expanded and probably accelerated with the introduction of the camel in about A.D. 300, especially as camel caravans were able to cross the Sahara. Thus the Sudan was linked with the Mediterranean coastlands whose manufactured articles, together with Saharan salt, were exchanged for the gold, kola nuts, and slaves of Guinea.

From Arab historians something is known of some of the powerful states that were established by military rule, the largest and most enduring of which were associated in the western Sudan with the termini of the desert trade routes. Ancient Ghana was created by Jewish or Berber settlers about A.D. 300 in the area west of Tombouctou (Timbuktu), though its greatest years came when it was ruled by the Negro Sarakolé dynasty (*see* GHANA [ANCIENT]). Almoravid attacks in the 11th century reduced its power and led to its replacement by the Mali or Mandingo Empire, centred on the upper Niger. Mali in turn was overthrown during the latter part of the 15th century by the expansion of the Songhai or Gao Empire that developed from Berber settlements established on the lower Niger as early as the 7th century. In 1591 the Songhai towns of Gao, Tombouctou, and Jenné (Djenné) were occupied by Moroccan troops anxious to control both the lucrative caravan traffic and the long-established trade in gold. The empire was replaced by numerous Negro kingdoms, including the Mossi-Dagomba states, the Bambara kingdoms of Ségou and Kaarta, Bornu, and the small Hausa states that were later conquered by the Muslim Fulani early in the 19th century. European penetration was followed by the establishment of political control, principally that of the French and the British, which lasted until the emergence of independent states during the 1950s.

On the eastern side of the continent Egyptian links with the Sudan region were generally strong, notably with Nubia. After the Nubian Empire had been overrun by Muslims it was replaced by kingdoms such as those of Dongola, Darfur, and Sennar. Later there was invasion from Egypt and, in 1899, the establishment of the Anglo-Egyptian condominium. The independent Republic of the Sudan was created in 1956.

*See* CENTRAL AFRICAN REPUBLIC; CHAD, REPUBLIC OF; MAURITANIA, ISLAMIC REPUBLIC OF; NIGER, REPUBLIC OF THE; NIGERIA; MALI, REPUBLIC OF; SUDAN, REPUBLIC OF THE; UPPER VOLTA, REPUBLIC OF THE; NUBIA; *see* also references under "Sudan" in the Index. (R. W. SL.)

**SUDAN, REPUBLIC OF THE** (JUMHURIYAT AS SUDAN), an independent country of northeast Africa, bounded by Libya on the extreme northwest, by the United Arab Republic (Egypt) on the north, by the Red Sea and Ethiopia on the east, by Kenya, Uganda, and the Democratic Republic of the Congo (formerly Belgian Congo) on the south, and by the Central African Republic and the Republic of Chad on the west. Area 967,491 sq.mi. (2,505,805 sq.km.). Pop. (1955–56) 10,262,536; (1967 est.) 14,148,000. The Sudan was from 1899 under the joint sovereignty of Great Britain and Egypt and was known as the Anglo-Egyptian Sudan until its independence in 1956. The name Sudan is derived from the Arabic expression *Bilad as Sudan* ("country of the Blacks") which originally applied to a much wider area of Africa. The capital is Khartoum (*q.v.*).

This article contains the following sections and subsections:

## I. PHYSICAL GEOGRAPHY

**1. Relief, Drainage, and Geology.**—The Sudan is mainly made up of vast plains and plateaus drained by the Nile and its tributaries. The wide basin is bounded on the east by the Red Sea Hills (over 7,000 ft. [2,100 m.]), to the southeast by the Ethiopian Highlands and on the west by the Jabal Marrah group (highest peak 10,134 ft. [3,089 m.]), which rises over a lower rounded divide between the Nile and Chad basins, and, in the southwest, the Nile and Congo basins.

The Nile system is the dominant physical feature. The White Nile (Al Bahr al Abyad), entering the country as the Bahr el Jebel from the south through rapids at Nimule, has a very low gradient until it is joined by the Blue Nile (Al Bahr al Azraq) at Khartoum. The Blue Nile contributes most of the floodwater as much of the White Nile flow is lost in the sudd (swampy) region, and about half of its discharge to the north is from the Sobat, which, like the Blue Nile, rises in the Ethiopian Highlands. Throughout much of the country drainage does not reach the Niles; the rivers of the southwest infrequently reach the Bahr el Ghazal system, and to the north most hill groups initiate seasonal watercourses which are lost in the surrounding plains. An important inland delta is that of the Gash near Kassala. (*See* NILE.)

Igneous and metamorphic rocks of the Precambrian Basement Complex series underlie much of the Sudan and appear at the surface in the Red Sea Hills, the Nuba Mountains (Jibal an Nubah), the southern plateaus, and in scattered hills over the plains. Mesozoic Nubian sandstones unconformably overlie the older rocks over the northwestern Sudan and in the Gedaref area in the east. In Tertiary times volcanic outbursts gave rise to the Jabal Marrah group and to the many scattered volcanic hills of the northwest. Later events include the formation and alluvial infilling of the large depression (1,000 ft. [305 m.]) in the region of the White Nile (Umm Ruwabah series) and of a smaller depression (200 ft. [60 m.]) along the Blue Nile.

The northern region, between 16° N and the frontier (22° N), is a sand- or gravel-covered desert, diversified by the typical flat-topped *jabals* of Nubian sandstone and the islandlike steep-sided granite hills of the Basement Complex. To the south lie the great plains and plateaus of the Sudan. In the west these show evidence of former more arid climates in the relict, now stable, sand dunes and sheets of Kordofan. To the east the desert is replaced by clay plains at about the latitude of Khartoum extending southward to about 6° N and across the Nile into Bahr el Ghazal and Equatoria provinces. The soils on the clay plains are heavy and sticky during the rains but dry and cracked during the rest of the year. In the extreme south, tropical red earths and ironstone outcrops occur, particularly to the west of the Nile. Little percolation occurs in the clay plains and underground water is not easily obtained. The Nubian sandstone is the best aquifer where rainfall is sufficient or where water percolates from the Nile. Elsewhere local wells and bores are found near the foot of the scattered hill masses. Several streams in the Red Sea Hills have an appreciable flow, and Khor (Khawr) Arba'at supplies Port Sudan with surface and underground water.

**2. Climate.**—North of about latitude 19° N northerly winds prevail for most of the year and rainfall is rare; to the south of this the seasons are characterized by the oscillation, north and south, of the boundary between moist southerly air and dry northerly air. Abu Hamad is the normal northern limit of the rains; a short wet season at Khartoum provides an average rainfall of 7 in. (180 mm.); there is 15 in. (380 mm.) at Wad Madani (Wad Medani) and 44 in. (1,122 mm.) at Waw (a town in the southern Sudan on the Jur River). Most of the rainfall occurs in heavy thundery showers. Except for the Red Sea coast, where the most rain comes in autumn, 50–75% of the precipitation occurs in the three summer months, although at Juba in the far south there are only two really dry months.

Highest temperatures, which usually precede the rains, occur in July in the extreme north, in May–June in Khartoum, and in April, March, or February progressively farther south. A maximum of 52.2° C (126° F) has been recorded at Wadi Halfa and 47.7° (118°) at Khartoum, but in the south temperatures reach only 42–43° (108–109°). Haboobs (dust storms) occur in the northern and northeastern Sudan.

**3. Vegetation.**—Five major vegetation types can be distinguished: (1) the sparse desert vegetation of the north; (2) a zone of semiarid acacia scrub and short grassland farther south; (3) the woodland savanna of most of the southern half of the country; (4) the vegetation of the floodlands and swamps of the Nile; and (5) the flora of the mountain regions.

The desert, with less than 3 in. rainfall, supports permanent vegetation only near watercourses. Date palms are frequent along the Nile, and the doum palm, tamarisk, and coarse grasses are found where the banks are not cultivated. The semidesert (3–11 in. [76–280 mm.] rainfall) includes the Red Sea coastal plain and a zone running east-west across the country roughly between the latitudes of 'Atbarah (Atbara) and Wad Madani. Vegetation there is characteristically a mixture of grasses and herbs with scattered scrub and bare areas. *Acacia tortilis* is common, though not on clay soils, and *Blepharis* species with areas of grasses is the typical climax vegetation. On sands other acacias are more frequent. The woodland savanna—a mixture of grasses, bushes, and

THE REPUBLIC OF THE SUDAN SHOWING PROVINCES AND MAIN TOWNS

trees—has several distinct subdivisions. In the areas of the north where the rainfall is less than 30 in. (760 mm.) trees are thorny and acacias dominant. On the eastern clays *Acacia mellifera* is found merging into *A. seyal* in the south, while the Qoz (Qawz) sands support *A. senegal* (yielding gum arabic) and, in depressions between the dunes, baobab. With increasing rainfall *Combretum cordofanum* woodland develops with grasses, and in the wetter areas the natural vegetation would be the rain forest now found only in a few remnants. *Khaya,* or African mahogany, *Isoberlinia doka,* and *Anogeissus schimperi* are characteristic trees in the drier areas; *Terminalia glaucescens, Albizzia zygea, Vitex doniana* are among the larger trees found in wetter parts. Elephant grass is common. In the Nile Valley north of Juba and the widening swamps (sudd) to the north, papyrus is common along the waterways but grasses and the water plant *Pistia* are also important. The water hyacinth spread rapidly from 1957, infilling many of the side channels and lagoons. In each of the mountain groups, Jabal Marrah, Red Sea Hills, Imatong, Dongotona, and Didinga, distinctive assemblies and vegetation zones are found.

**4. Animal Life.**—The southern Sudan is one of the areas in Africa where the characteristic wildlife may be seen best. Most of the grassland animals (lion, leopard, cheetah, giraffe, zebra, antelope, etc.) are common; buffalo, hippopotamus, chimpanzee, and baboon are also abundant among a wide range of other species. Common birds include guinea fowl, bustards, geese, cranes, storks, pelicans, weaver birds, shrikes, and starlings. The rare shoebill is found in the Bahr el Ghazal region. Crocodiles are numerous on the Nile and many types of land lizard are found. Snakes are not abundant but many are poisonous. Mosquitoes are abundant on the rivers and blood-sucking horseflies are locally common. The tsetse fly occurs south of about 12° N.

*National Parks.*—There are 3 national parks, 14 game reserves, and 3 sanctuaries in the country. The Dinder (2,470 sq.mi. [6,397 sq.km.]) contains much game, while the Southern National Park (6,500 sq.mi. [16,835 sq.km.]) and the Nimule National Park provide sanctuary for elephant, white rhinoceros, buffalo, and the giant eland. (L. Be.)

## II. GEOGRAPHICAL REGIONS

Twelve regions may be distinguished:

1. The ironstone plateau of the south and southwest is largely forested. Along its northern margin, west of the Bahr el Jebel (Bahr el Jabal), Nilotic tribes, chiefly the Dinka, occupy their villages during the rainy season, when they graze their cattle and grow food crops. Farther south, and nearer to the international frontiers, agricultural tribes (or parts of tribes), practise shifting cultivation. Much of the centre and west is uninhabited.

2. The plateau of Darfur is remarkable for seasonal watercourses radiating from the Jabal Marrah. These have attracted almost all the permanent settlement in the province because of the proximity of cultivable land and the availability of water in wells after the rains. Between the main valleys the thin infertile soils of the plateau are lightly wooded and during the rainy season thickly carpeted by grass. Nomadic tribes graze their animals widely, but remain near the main watercourses during the dry season.

3. Jabal Marrah, and associated uplands, between 3,000 and nearly 10,000 ft. (900–3,000 m.) above sea level, are rugged and difficult of access. They are occupied by the Fur people who live in small villages and scattered farms. The Fur divert mountain streams into small gardens, make terraced fields and keep cattle, which they pen on their arable land after harvest.

4. The great clay plain is divisible into two parts. The southern and larger part is occupied by cattle-owning Nilotic tribes, who retreat to the margins or to small areas of relatively high land during the rainy season, when almost the entire surface is submerged. In the dry season they drive their herds to moist grazing close to the permanent rivers. The northern part receives less rain and therefore does not become a swamp in the rainy season, although at times movement is difficult. Bisected by the Blue Nile and bordered on the west by the White Nile, this part is sparsely inhabited in the south, but in the centre and along the two Niles a large population is supported both by cultivation depending on rain and by projects based on irrigation, growing cotton as the chief cash crop. The largest of these irrigation projects is the Gezira (*q.v.;* al Jazirah). More developed economically than other parts of the country since 1900, its population has increased rapidly and it has received many immigrants from the north and west. Also, it has a higher proportion of urban population. Farther north, where rainfall is still lower, agriculture gives way to nomadic grazing.

5. The eastern frontier, in principle, lies at the foot of the Ethiopian uplands; but locally, between the Atbara (ʻAtbarah) River and the Blue Nile near the Sobat River and in the far southeast, foothills or detached small uplands lie within the Sudan. All these areas are remote and have small populations.

6. The dunes (Arabic, *qoz,* or *qawz*) form a zone about 750 mi. (1,200 km.) long, from the White Nile to southern Darfur, and 125–250 mi. (200–400 km.) wide. Except along the northern fringe, it receives sufficient rainfall for agriculture; but tilled lands are discontinuous, because of lack of water supplies. Southwest Kordofan and much of eastern Darfur are used mainly by nomad cattle-owning pastoralists.

7. The Nuba Mountains, with the tableland from which they rise, are comparatively well populated. The Nuba peoples are expert at cutting rock cisterns in the veins of rotted granite, and sink wells at suitable places at the foot of the scarps. They have long been established in hill villages, surrounded by small terraced fields, and have been encouraged to settle in the piedmont areas and to cultivate more land, chiefly for cotton, in areas of silty soil.

8. The Red Sea Hills are near-desert except in the extreme south, and are occupied by the nomadic, camel-rearing Beja tribes.

9. The Red Sea coastal plain is also a near-desert and has practically no settlements except for Port Sudan (which depends for its water upon wells sunk in the bed of the Khor [Khawr] Arbaʻat, nearly 30 mi. [48 km.] N) and Tawkar (Tokar).

10. The semidesert zone is arid, but the slight rainfall sustains a sparse and discontinuous vegetation (chiefly in watercourses) which is grazed by camel-owning nomads.

11. The desert, in the northwest, is rainless, completely unproductive, and uninhabited.

12. The Nile Valley below Khartoum is a nearly continuous ribbon of land irrigated by the ancient shadoof (*shaduf*) and sakieh (*saqiya*) methods (*see* Egypt: *The Economy: Methods of Agriculture*) and the modern pump. It supports a peasant population, living in villages between the sown land and the desert behind, and several large towns, including Shandi, ʻAtbarah, Berber (Barbar), and Wadi Halfa. (J. H. G. L.)

## III. THE PEOPLE

The inhabitants of the Sudan are of widely varying ethnic origin. The republic is roughly divisible into the Muslim Arabic-speaking north and the pagan, partly Christianized, south, the boundary being the line of the Bahr al ʻArab (at about 10° N latitude). The amount of internal migration creates overlaps, but in the north only the pocket of Nuba, in the Nuba Mountains, is pagan. Physically the northerners are mostly of the stock generally called Semitic, although people of the types usually classified as Hamitic (the Beja tribes) are found in the east. Southerners are Nilotic (including Nuer, Dinka, Shilluk), Negroes (Azande, etc.), and Nilo-Hamites (Bari, etc.).

**1. Tribal Groups.**—Apart from the large agglomeration of the Three Towns (Khartoum, Khartoum North, and Omdurman) and of Port Sudan, the country is fairly described as rural and tribal although there are sizable market towns and administrative centres throughout.

The northern and central rural populations can be divided into nomadic camel owners, nomadic cattle owners, settled cultivators, riverain peoples, and participants in one or another of the rural development projects. The nomadic camel owners are mainly Kababish (*q.v.*), Kawahla, Hawawir, and Zaghawa (*q.v.*) of Kordofan and Darfur provinces and the Beja (*q.v.;* including the Hadendoa, or "Fuzzy Wuzzies") and the Shukria Arabs of

PHOTOS, CARL FRANK—PHOTO RESEARCHERS, INC.

(TOP LEFT) TATTOOED NILOTIC MAN OF THE SHILLUK TRIBE, SOUTHERN SUDAN; (TOP RIGHT) BEARDED SEMITIC MUSLIM, NORTHERN SUDAN; (BOTTOM) SHEPHERD AND FLOCK ON THE SHORE OF THE NILE

Kassala Province. The cattle-owning nomads are the Baggara (*q.v.*), or Baqqara, Arabs, comprising many different tribes who extend in a central belt westward from the White Nile through Darfur as far as Lake Chad but who share a similar way of life. The camel nomads and the Baggara each belong to tribes whose members regard themselves as being related to one another patrilineally. They move their herds each year over much the same ground, seeking the grass within their circumscribed tribal territories.

Between the camel and cattle owners there lies a belt of settled cultivators who depend on millet or the sale of gum arabic for their livelihood. The Nubians and Barabra (*q.v.*) of the Nile Valley grow and sell dates and export labour to the towns, largely in the form of domestic service, although many merchants in the towns and in tribal markets are Nubian in origin. They are forced out of their land by the continual fragmentation on inheritance of the small available riverain estates.

The development of the Gezira Plain, as well as the Baraka and the Gash projects and the new Khashm al Qirbah (el Girba) project on the Atbara River, afford poor rural populations some profit from cotton and other crops.

In the south the cattle folk (notably the Nuer and Dinka [*qq.v.*]) are the most numerous. Their climate is wetter and they move about less than the northern husbandmen. The difficulty in gaining access to the swamp land as well as the people's own resistance has delayed the development of this part of the country, although the Dinka are better educated and are more inclined to seek work in towns than are the Nuer. The Bari (*q.v.*), once primarily pastoral, were forced into a greater dependence upon agriculture by depredations in the 19th century.

**2. Languages.**—Arabic, the official language, was claimed at the 1956 census by more than half of the total population as their native tongue although it is spoken with considerable dialect variations. English is a common alternative. The Beja, Nuba, and some peoples of Darfur are large groups in the north with languages of their own, although many of them speak fluent Arabic as well (*see* NUBA; NUBIAN LANGUAGE AND WRITING). The south has a great language mixture, Dinka (over 1,000,000 speakers), Nuer (500,000), and Zande (250,000) being the languages most spoken. (*See* also SUDANIC LANGUAGES.)

**3. Religion.**—An estimated two-thirds of the population, mostly in the northern and central areas, profess Islam. There is a broad division on religious grounds between the followers of the Mahdi (*q.v.*) and his successors (largely accounted for by the western nomadic tribes) who follow an austere brand of Islam, and the rest. Leaders of the Mahdists, and the other important sect, the Khatmiya, became leaders of rival political parties that emerged before the Sudan's independence in 1956.

Pagan religions predominate in the south though there are considerable numbers of Christians (Catholic and Protestant), and since independence Islam has been making headway. Cattle play an important part in the religions of the Dinka and Nuer. The Azande (*q.v.*), who inhabit the Congo border, are known for their remarkable system of oracular divination, which regulates much of their daily lives. (*See* also *History*, below.)

**4. Population Distribution.**—The population of the Sudan, 10,262,536 at the first census in 1956, was estimated at 14,148,000 in 1967, an average annual increase of over 3% since 1956. The mean density is slightly more than 14 per sq.mi. (about 5 per sq.km.). Less than 10% of the population lives in urban centres, the largest of which are the Three Towns (Khartoum, Khartoum North, and Omdurman), Wad Madani, and al Ubayyid (El Obeid) in the central Sudan; Port Sudan on the Red Sea and 'Atbarah in the northern Sudan; Kassala in the northeast on the Eritrean border; al Fashir and Nyala in Darfur; and Malakal and Juba in the southern Sudan. Approximately a quarter of the country is completely uninhabited, including the desert in the north and northwest, a large area in the southeast divided between Upper Nile and eastern Equatoria provinces, and tracts in central and western Bahr el Ghazal. About a third is used only by migratory pastoralists. The areas containing a settled population account for less than a half of the total area and comprise, in order of importance: (1) the central rain lands, between about 10° and 15° N; (2) the southwestern margins of the southern clay plain and the adjoining fringe of the ironstone plateau; (3) the agricultural belt in the far south, close to the borders with the Republic of the Congo and Uganda; (4) the Nile Valley below Khartoum; (5) the areas containing patches of high land close to the Bahr el Jebel, the White Nile above Melut (Malut), and the Sobat, on which the eastern Dinka, Nuer, and Shilluk (*q.v.*) have their villages. In the mid-1960s, about 60,000 inhabitants from the Nile Valley villages (which were to be submerged by the lake forming behind the Aswan High Dam) were moved to the new irrigation area near Khashm al Qirbah in the Atbara Valley.

The extent of migratory modes of living is remarkable. About 14% of the population is wholly nomadic. These people live in the northern Sudan and include the Beja tribes of the Red Sea Hills, Arabs of northern Kordofan and Darfur, and the Baggara of south Kordofan and southern Darfur. The Nilotic tribes of the southern clay plain, although possessing permanent villages, normally migrate during the dry season for distances of from 5 to 50 mi. Some of the agricultural tribes living close to the southern and eastern frontiers practise shifting cultivation and abandon their old homesteads for new after a period varying between 5 and 15 years. Many cultivators in the central rain lands migrate during the dry season because local water supplies fail. Altogether, it can be estimated that nearly half of the population is migratory in varying degrees; and only slightly more than half is fully settled.

Tribal grouping is also very diverse. More than 570 tribes and many subtribes were registered at the 1956 census. Arab tribes accounted for about two-fifths of the population, but some other groups were also large. In northern and central Sudan the Arab tribes (Ga'alin, Guhayna, Baggara, and others) formed 39% of the population. Other major groupings were the Nuba (6%), the Beja (6%), and the tribes of western Darfur (9%). In the southern Sudan, the Dinka accounted for 8%, Azande for 2%, and Bari for 2%. An interesting indication of the sparse population was the presence of about 500,000 "westerners" from the countries that were formerly part of French Equatorial and West Africa who settled in Darfur, parts of Kordofan, and the Blue Nile Province. In the east, they were attracted by unused agricultural land and the demand for labour in agricultural projects. Some were Sudanese nationals, and altogether they comprised about 5% of the 1956 population. (J. H. G. L.)

## IV. ARCHAEOLOGY

With minor exceptions, it was only in the northern Sudan, where expeditions from many countries, all working under the auspices of UNESCO, were excavating sites doomed to be flooded by the Aswan High Dam reservoir, that there had been any scientific excavations by the mid-1960s (*see* NUBIA). Elsewhere in the Sudan archaeology remains in its infancy. No thorough archaeological surveys have been made, though from surface finds and from the observations of officials and others certain general lines are beginning to emerge. Roads by which foreigners obtained the products of the Sudan (particularly slaves, gold, and ivory) were always of paramount importance.

In the upper valley of the Atbara River in the eastern Sudan, fossils and Lower Paleolithic implements have been found, indicating one route by which the early Stone Age cultures of Egypt and east Africa were connected. In the desert in the northeastern Sudan gold was extensively mined from ancient Egyptian times down to the 11th century A.D. Stone-built huts, stone mortars, hammers, and circular grinding mills occur with pots at the ancient mines. The most important route in this area from the earliest historic period has been that which gave access from the Red Sea (south of Port Sudan) to the central Sudan by a route which passed north of the Ethiopian Massif to the Kassala area. The earliest pottery known in the Sudan, associated in the Khartoum area with barbed bone harpoons, has been found as far east as Kassala and as far west as Wanyanga (Ounianga) in Borku. From Qoz Regeb (Qawz Rajab) has come evidence of occupation from the protodynastic to the Christian period; and at Sarsareib and in the Kassala area are sites dating back to protodynastic and possibly earlier times. In the Red Sea Hills there are early occupation sites at Agordat in Eritrea (C Group and Pan-Grave) and at Erkowit. At 'Aqiq on the Red Sea coast are remains suggesting that this was the site of Ptolemais Therion, whence the Ptolemies obtained elephants for their army and which probably continued as a trade centre until the Aksumite period. In Roman times trade with India diverted attention from the African mainland; but Meroe and Aksum became affected by influences from India as a result of the development of that trade, and it was probably trade rivalry that led Aksum to destroy a degenerate Meroe *c.* A.D. 350. Early in the Muslim era Ptolemais was overshadowed by Badi on Airi Island (Jazirat ar Rih), where there is a ruined town with cisterns and where Muslim tombstones dating from the 10th and 11th centuries have been found. Similar tombstones dating from the 8th to the 10th centuries (the earliest is A.H. 153 = *c.* A.D. 790) have been found in Khawr Nubt, while early Muslim stone-built towerlike tombs occur at Ma'man east of Kassala and elsewhere. Circular stone graves with flat tops are probably those of the Muslim Beja.

In the Blue Nile Valley of the central Sudan fossils are found below the clay of the Gezira Plain, notably at Abu Hugar and Sinjah, where they include a proto-Bushman skull, contemporary with a crude Levalloisian culture. Ancient Egyptian expeditions must have penetrated far south of that part of the Nile Valley occupied by them during the New Kingdom. One such expedition to localities previously unidentified is recorded by Amenhotep II, one of whose scarabs was found 100 mi. E of Khartoum. The Blue Nile Valley from Khartoum to Al Roseires (Ar Rusayris; Er Roseires) was no doubt always the road to Beni Shangul (Ethiopia), whence came slaves and gold. Occupation sites occur all the way to Al Roseires, and no doubt the Napatan, Meroitic, Christian, and Fung (Funj) periods are represented. In the 6th century A.D. Aksum was trading with this area directly, bartering gold for iron at Fazughli. Finds of Napatan date were made at Sannar and Kusti, while at Moya (Jabal Mayyah) Sir Henry Wellcome excavated an occupation site and cemetery showing Negroes' trade connections with Napata. Finds of Meroitic date were made in and near Sannar. Rock pictures from this period occur at Geili (Jabal Jayli) east of Khartoum; and the artificial water reservoirs which are common as far south as the Jabal Mayyah area are probably the work of the kingdom of Meroe. A Meroitic ram, brought from Soba (Sawba) to Khartoum by Gen. C. G. Gordon, indicates that Soba was probably a Meroitic town before becoming the capital of the Christian kingdom of Aloa. Little now remains on the surface at Soba but red-brick fragments and the stone capitals of a Christian church; Old Nubian inscriptions have been found there in the past. Christian sites are reported from the Blue Nile between Khartoum and Sannar and from al Geteina (Qutaynah) on the White Nile. At Sannar the site of the Fung capital (A.D. 1500–1821) is being destroyed by the river. At Abu Jayli near Sannar, a site excavated for Wellcome in 1912, Fung pottery was recognized with considerable probability.

South of Kusti, occupation sites in the southern Sudan occur along the bank of the White Nile as far as Malakal. Shards of apparently early date have been found near Malakal, Doleib Hill, and Jabal Zaraf al Azraq, and a microlithic culture of Wilton type with pottery on Belli Island. Shards from a pre-Shilluk site near Kaka suggest a connection with Sannar and Meroe. Ancient occupation mounds have been reported from the Bahr el Ghazal in Aweil district, and polished celts of hematite near Yambio. This southern region must long have been the goal of traders seeking slaves and ivory, and copper mining probably began at Hofrat el Nahas (Hufrat an Nahas) at an early date. The Azande show evidence of cultural contact with ancient Egypt, and the Masai and the Kikuyu of East Africa seem to appear more than once, in scenes representing the arrival of the tribute of Cush, in the Tombs of the Nobles at Thebes.

In the western Sudan the most important road is that which runs west from the White Nile between the desert and the tropical forest through Darfur and past Lake Chad to West Africa. A few roads running north to south across the desert follow lines of water holes and link this great road with the North African coast. In early times the steppe country extended farther north, and finds of protodynastic date come from the southern Libyan desert. It may be that Tibesti is the source of the amazon stone common to the Neolithic cultures of the Fayyum and Shaheinab. From Wadi Howar come remains which suggest that the cattle-owning C Group people, first known to archaeologists in lower Nubia, once lived there. The 6th-dynasty inscriptions on Harkuf's tomb at Aswan suggest that the ancient Egyptians used donkey caravans on the Darb al Arba'in. The earliest traditional rulers of Darfur were the Dagu (otherwise Daju, Tajo, Tago), and some of the brands used till recently by the Dagu sultans of Dar Sila may have a hieroglyphic origin. The extent to which the ancient Egyptians and, later, the kingdoms of Napata and Meroe controlled the great east-west road is unknown.

Meroitic "archer's looses" were found in Darfur and at Jabal Harazah. That, after the fall of Meroe itself, the Meroitic royal family may have carried on in the west is suggested by an Old Nubian graffito at Audun, a tumulus near Kaboija in Jabal Maydub (said to be the grave of a queen who brought the Meidob-Kagiddi people from the Nile) and also by the survival of Kash (Cush), the old name of the kingdoms of Napata and Meroe, in the modern tribal names Kagiddi, Kaja, and Kajar (Birgid).

There are many stone-built ruins in the hills of Darfur. A few are attributed to the Dagu. The red-brick ruins at 'Ein Fara ('Ayn Fa'rah) in northern Darfur were proved to have been a monastery and two small churches (one, domed), indicating that between the 9th and 13th centuries, if not earlier, Darfur was within the sphere of influence of the Christian kingdom of Mukurra (from which the tribal name Tungur is derived). That sphere probably once extended as far as Lake Chad. The fine date palms and hill-terracing near 'Ein Fara suggest that the Tungur originated the excellent terracing and good agriculture of the Darfur Hills. They still maintain their connections with the Bideyat (Bedyat) of the Ennedi Plateau (who were once Christian). The walled stone town containing two royal residences at Jabal Orrei (Uri) probably dates from the same period. Rock pictures of horsemen in the Tungur Hills (Jabal Tungwa) and at Jabal al 'Afarit in Kordofan are probably crude copies of Christian saints on horseback as represented in the church of Abd al Qadir at Wadi Halfa. The red-brick ruins at Abu Sufyan and Jabal Zankor in northern Kordofan no doubt date from this period, and there are rectangular stone Christian graves in the Wadi Muqaddam. The influence of Christian Nubia in Darfur must have been destroyed by the advancing power of the Muslim kingdom of Kanem, which by A.D. 1240 controlled the trade route between Kanem and Nubia. From that date to the 16th century, the influence of the medieval kingdom of Bornu was predominant in Darfur and Kordofan and is responsible for the many stone compounds between Kordofan and Dongola, and no doubt for some stone buildings in the Darfur Hills. The most recent stone forts in Turrah at the northern end of the Marrah Massif are traditionally associated with the early Fur sultans. *See* also EGYPT: *Archaeology*. (A. J. AL.)

## V. HISTORY

**1. Early History.**—The name Sudan, short for *Bilad as-Sudan*, "The Land of the Blacks," was not commonly used before the 19th century by Europeans who usually called the region Ethiopia or Nubia. Though vaguely known to geographers since ancient Egyptian times, largely through their interest in the sources of the Nile, the southern Sudan was virtually unknown until the coming of European and American explorers in the 19th century.

The northern, and to a lesser extent the central, Sudan has a long recorded history though much of it is still controversial. Archaeological evidence suggests that the introduction of Egyptian culture into the northern Sudan began as early as *c.* 3000 B.C. Between *c.* 2150 B.C. and *c.* 1580 B.C. the pharaohs planted fortified settlements up to the 4th cataract to protect Upper Egypt from raids, expand trade, and exploit the gold deposits. From 725 B.C. to A.D. 350 an independent, highly egyptianized power of unascertained origin ruled in the north with its capital first at Napata at the 4th cataract and, from *c.* 590 B.C., at Meroe, between the 5th and 6th cataracts. Its kings (including Taharqa, the Tirhakah of the Bible) conquered and held Egypt itself, *c.* 730 B.C.–*c.* 660 B.C. Meroitic civilization became progressively negroid in character and suffered a long period of decline and finally disaster when Meroe was destroyed in A.D. 350 by King Aeizanes of Aksum. Out of the ensuing chaos three kingdoms eventually emerged: a northern state, Nobatia, whose capital was Faras, now submerged under Lake Nasir; Mukurra (Muqarra), with its capital at Old Dongola (Dunqula), which shortly afterward united with Nobatia; and a southern state, less advanced culturally but larger and wealthier than its northern neighbours, Alodia (Arabic, 'Alwa), centred on Soba (Sawba) near the confluence of the Blue and White Niles. Contemporary writers described the people of all three kingdoms as Nubians.

Christianity, both Orthodox and Monophysite, came to Nubia *c.* 543 when the efforts of Monophysite missionaries prevailed. The new church owed spiritual allegiance to the Coptic patriarch of Alexandria. Mural paintings in the cathedral at Faras, recently excavated, reveal a fusion of Byzantine and Coptic art forms of a high order. Ruins of churches occur widely in the Sudan.

The conquest of Byzantine Egypt by the Arabs in 640–642 brought triumphant Islam to the northern border of the Sudan and isolated the people from Christendom. In 651–652 a treaty was made between the Arab governor of Upper Egypt and the Christian ruler of Nubia, possibly in continuation of a previous treaty with Byzantine Egypt, which was observed fitfully for several centuries. The gradual withering away of Christian civilization in Nubia and the extinction of the state *c.* 1300 have been ascribed to the lack of religious vitality outside the court, to internal political disunity, and, more immediately, to intermarriage with wandering Arab tribes edged out of Egypt by unsympathetic Muslim but foreign rulers. A contributory factor lay in foreign relations. So long as the Arabs were masters of Egypt relations with Nubia were not unfriendly, but after the Arab governors were succeeded by non-Arab mercenaries relations with Egypt worsened.

The southern kingdom of 'Alwa, which survived until *c.* 1500, endured the same long process of erosion at the hands of marauding Arab nomads and was finally overpowered in circumstances which remain obscure, leaving in the central, as in the northern, Sudan a mixed Arab and native stock having a culture distinctly Arab and Islamic. One tribe, the 'Abdallab, early evolved a sedentary political community and later became associated with an immigrant group, the Fung (Funj) (*q.v.*), whose origin is disputed by historians who variously place their homeland in Ethiopia, the Shilluk country of the White Nile, and the region of Lake Chad. The Fung themselves claimed descent from the Arab tribe to which the Omayyad caliphs of Damascus belonged. They established their capital at Sennar (Sinnar) on the Blue Nile. They ruled directly only the peninsula between the two Niles (*Al Jazirat Sinnar*) and left the district immediately to the north to 'Abdallab viceroys, who had their seat at Qarri at the 6th cataract. The sultanate was a loose confederation divided into tribal units each represented by a *makk,* the more important of whom enjoyed considerable autonomy and received the title of *manjil.* The latter were invested with the ceremonial stool and horned cap, symbols of the sultan's warrant.

Though they encouraged trade, the Fung sultans struck no coins. The spread and consolidation of Islam followed in the wake of settled rule. The sultans welcomed immigrant Muslim scholars and missionaries of the Sufi orders by generous patronage. Militarily the sultanate was unaggressive. The Ottoman Turks under Selim I, who conquered Egypt in 1517, soon pushed south into the Sudan and established a garrison at Say, defeating a Fung army at Hannik (Hannek). Under Selim's successor, Suleiman I, Özdemir Pasha, beylerbey of Yemen, occupied the ports of Suakin (Sawakin) and Massawa (Mitssawa), which became part of the Ottoman coastal province of Habash. The sultanate was affected by a series of internal crises leading in 1788–89 to the usurpation of the government by chiefs of the Hameg (Hamaj) tribe (*q.v.*), a people of indeterminate origin whose regents ruled behind a facade of puppet sultans. The state lapsed into political fragmentation. In 1812 Dongola, which had long thrown off Fung hegemony, was seized by Mameluke fugitives from the *vali* Mohammed Ali's massacres in Egypt who set up a precarious bandit state.

**2. Egyptian Occupation, 1820–81.**—Mohammed Ali decided to drive out the Mamelukes from Dongola and, as part of a larger operation, to occupy Sennar and Kordofan (Kurdufan). Sennar was in a state of anarchy; Kordofan was ruled by a regent of the sultan of Darfur. The pasha never disclosed the reasons for his invasion and appears to have kept the Sublime Porte ignorant of his intentions. Europeans presumed that his objectives were the gold and slaves of the Sudan. Mohammed Ali set in motion two columns. The first, commanded by his son Ismail, defeated the Shayqiya and in 1821 occupied Sennar. The second, under Mohammed Bey Khosrau, called the *daftardar,* his son-in-law, crossed the Bayuda steppe (Sahra Bayyudah) and defeated and killed Musellim, the Fur regent, at Barah, and entered Al Ubayyid (El Obeid), in the same year. Ismail's murder by an aggrieved Sudanese chief at Shandi in 1822 was the signal for a widespread Sudanese revolt which the *daftardar* cruelly suppressed. After five years of military misrule Ali Khurshid Pasha was sent from Egypt to the Sudan as its first governor-general with full civil and military powers. He converted Khartoum from a military base to an administrative capital and, despite several short periods of decentralization, it remained the administrative centre. He created the framework of provincial government, placed slave raiding on a systematic basis as a source of recruits for the army, and conscientiously tried to implement Mohammed Ali's plans for economic development.

The Sudan was then ruled by an Ottoman type of government which was the first sustained Ottoman experiment in colonial administration. The political structure partly embodied Egyptian models and was partly the result of improvisation, for the indiscriminate application of Ottoman institutions to the Sudan was impracticable. A governor-general and central services were located at the capital. Each principal territorial subdivision was ruled by a governor. The governorates were divided into districts each under a district officer. As under the Fung, each tribe was represented by a sheikh; a paramount sheikh was given the title of *shaykh al-mashayikh*, literally "sheikh of sheikhs." During the reign of Khedive Ismail technical departments responsible for steamers and posts and telegraphs were added to the central services. The Egyptian authority in the Sudan early conciliated the important official representatives of Islam, the *'ulama'*, and the leading tribal chiefs of the Nile Valley. Its greatest failure was in its relations with the nomads; these remained actively or passively hostile until the end.

The forces which took part in the original invasion were composed of Turkish-speaking troops of many races in the Ottoman dominions, and Arab irregulars. Climate and economy dictated the conscription of Negroes who were captured in the annual slave raids conducted by the government and the Arab tribal chiefs or accepted from the Arabs as taxes in kind. For, with the exception of the Shayqiya volunteers in the irregular cavalry, the Arabs had the greatest aversion to regular military service. By 1843 the Sudan garrisons were composed almost wholly of ex-slave regular infantry, irregular Shayqiya and Turkish cavalry, and Turkish artillery. Infantry officers were at first Turks with two or three French instructors. After 1835 selected Sudanese youths were given commissions until in 1872 Adam Pasha at-Taqalawi rose to be acting governor-general. Under Khedive Ismail the army was modernized and equipped with Remington rifles and Krupp artillery. In 1863–66 a Sudanese infantry contingent campaigned with Marshal Achille François Bazaine's army in Mexico. Its battle-scarred officers were afterward to receive high commands under Gen. Charles George Gordon (*q.v.*).

The area of Egyptian rule was extended by successive stages. In 1840 the Egyptians defeated the Hadendowa tribesmen of Taka and established the province since known as Kassala. The ports of Suakin and Massawa (the latter now in Ethiopia) were leased to Egypt in 1846 and ceded in 1865. In 1869, in the name of the Egyptian government, Sir Samuel White Baker annexed to Egypt the region between Gondokoro and the Great Lakes. Baker's mission was an expensive failure, and Gordon, his successor in the Equatorial Province, withdrew the Egyptian garrisons from most of the area. The Egyptians extended their authority down the Red Sea and Somali Coast and would probably have annexed Kismayu (Somalia) if Britain had not intervened. The final stage of Egyptian expansion was completed in 1874 with the conquest of Darfur by a private army led by az-Zubayr Pasha Rahma Mansur al-'Abbasi. Ismail's efforts to gain territory from Ethiopia failed when two Egyptian invading armies were defeated in 1875 and 1876.

Egyptian rule brought many changes to the Sudan. For the first time in its history a single government was imposed over the whole country. Practices foreign to Sudanese religious traditions were introduced. The Sudanese Muslims followed the Maliki discipline, whereas the Egyptian judges administered the Hanafi discipline which was official throughout the Ottoman Empire. At first the judges and the higher *'ulama'* were Egyptian, but later the Sudanese took an increasing part in judicial work. The cultural influence of Egypt was nevertheless confined to the small assimilated class in the larger towns where in the time of Khedive Ismail primary schools on the Egyptian pattern were established. There was no large-scale immigration of Egyptian settlers, though there was much intermarriage with Sudanese in the garrison towns. The way of life of the mass of the Sudanese people was unaffected by the Egyptian presence.

**3. Mahdist Theocracy, 1881–98.**—On June 29, 1881, at Aba on the White Nile, Mohammed Ahmad ibn as-Sayyid 'Abdullah proclaimed himself as the expected Mahdi who had been divinely appointed to restore Islam. His revolt was partly a protest against an alien rule, for the senior posts in the Egyptian administration, though Ottoman in character, were staffed by members of the europeanized, Turkish-speaking Egyptian ruling class whose way of life scandalized the religious-minded, austere-living Sudanese. A more immediate cause for discontent was the rough-handed attempt to suppress the slave trade. Islam tolerated slavery, but whereas in Egypt slavery had become an anachronism, the Sudanese economy was still based on it. When Ismail recruited European officers to carry out his policy more effectively, the Sudanese concluded that he had sold himself to the European unbelievers and was undermining Islam. Another cause lay in the nature of Sudanese Islam itself, which found corporate expression in the Sufi religious orders. The Mahdist movement was not, as Egyptian and European writers of the time termed it, a revolt of dervishes against orthodox Sunnite Islam. The Mahdi was no dervish and expressly forbade the use of the term by any of his followers. The movement was intended rather to restore primitive Islam and to cleanse it from innovation and superstition. The Mahdi's immediate enemy was the Egyptian government which in his view had lapsed into unbelief.

The governor-general at the time, Mohammed Ra'uf Pasha, underestimated the strength of the movement. After massacring a small government force sent to arrest him, the Mahdi and his followers retired to the Nubah Mountains where in December 1881 and May 1882 they annihilated two columns sent against them. In 1882–83 they won a series of spectacular victories over the Egyptian garrisons, and the expeditions sent for their relief.

During 1884 the Mahdist horde closed in on Khartoum. On Jan. 26, 1885, the capital fell and its redoubtable commander, Gordon, was killed. Four days later the Mahdi solemnly led the Friday prayers in the city mosque. Within the next few months the surviving Egyptian garrisons in the Sudan were evacuated or forced to surrender. The Anglo-Egyptian power, which had vainly attempted the relief of Khartoum in the winter of 1884–85, retired from Dongola. Only Wadi Halfa, Suakin, and part of the Equatorial Province remained in Egyptian hands. The Mahdi died at Omdurman (Umm Durman), which he had made his capital, on June 22, 1885, and the control of the Mahdist state fell to the Khalifa 'Abdullahi (*see* KHALIFA, THE).

**4. Anglo-Egyptian Condominium, 1899–1955.**—The Mahdist power was broken by an Anglo-Egyptian army commanded by Sir Herbert (afterward Lord) Kitchener. The occupation of the Nile Valley up to Khartoum was completed by the Battle of Omdurman on Sept. 2, 1898, but an extensive area of the country remained either unoccupied or in disputed ownership. However,

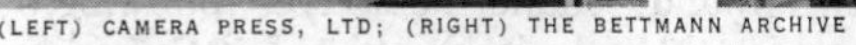

(LEFT) CAMERA PRESS, LTD; (RIGHT) THE BETTMANN ARCHIVE

(LEFT) TOMB OF THE MAHDI AT OMDURMAN; (RIGHT) GEN. CHARLES GEORGE GORDON DIRECTING FIRE AGAINST THE MAHDI'S FORCES NEAR KHARTOUM, 1885 (19TH-CENTURY ENGLISH NEWSPAPER ENGRAVING)

disagreements with the French which had led to the Fashoda incident (*see* Egypt: *History*) were settled by an Anglo-French declaration of March 21, 1899, whereby the French recognized the Nile-Congo watershed as the eastern limit of French interest, while the Belgians, who had occupied the country between the Nile-Congo watershed and Lado on the upper White Nile, agreed in 1906 that the Lado Enclave (*q.v.*) should revert to the Sudan after the death of King Leopold II (1909). By the Anglo-Egyptian Condominium agreements of January 19 and July 10, 1899, the northern border of the Sudan was fixed at latitude 22 N with enclaves to include some villages north of Wadi Halfa and some Beja grazing grounds. The Italians who had wrested Kassala from the Mahdists in 1894 handed it back to the Egyptian Army in 1897. On Nov. 24, 1899, Sir Francis Reginald Wingate's column defeated and killed the Khalifa 'Abdullahi at Umm Diwaikarat, and in December another Egyptian column reoccupied Al Ubayyid. In 1898 a scion of the former royal house of Darfur, 'Ali Dinar, hastened to Al Fashir and seized the throne. In 1901 the Khartoum government accorded him recognition as a tributary sultan.

The condominium devised by Lord Cromer established the future form of government. The British and Egyptian flags were to fly side by side. Supreme civil and military powers were to be vested in a governor-general appointed by the khedive on the recommendation of the British government. The Sudan was to be excluded from the capitular regime and consular jurisdiction then in force in Egypt. Structurally the condominium was built on Egyptian foundations. The governor-general's office was left unchanged. Most of the provincial capitals and boundaries were retained as was the nomenclature of administration. The Islamic law, confined as in Egypt to the realm of personal status, was administered by a grand *qadi* (judge of the Islamic law) and a system of central and provincial courts. In one respect there was a legal revolution: for the first time secular law became the law of the land when criminal and civil codes, based on Indian practice, were introduced in 1899–1900. The first governors and inspectors were British officers of the Egyptian Army, but, as these were always likely to be recalled, a few graduates of British universities were appointed to form the nucleus of a civil (later renamed political) service. The Sudan Medical Service grew out of the Army Medical Corps; the Veterinary Service had a similar military beginning. Education under Mahdist rule had been confined to the teaching of Arabic and religion in Koranic schools. In 1898 Kitchener opened an appeal for funds to build Gordon Memorial College, Khartoum, which was opened as a primary school in 1902. By 1907 there were 6 primary and 20 elementary schools functioning, and in 1906 at Rufa'ah a Sudanese sheikh, Babikr Badri, opened the Sudan's first girls' school. By 1913 Gordon College was providing a secondary education with special courses for future judges of the Islamic law, engineers, and teachers. Sudanese communications expanded steadily. The Egyptian telegraph network, destroyed during the Mahdist rule, had to be entirely reconstructed. The core of the railway system was the 3-ft. 6-in.-gauge military line built from Wadi Halfa to Khartoum North in 1897–99. The Red Sea railway linking Atbara ('Atbarah) with Suakin in 1904–05, and completed to Port Sudan shortly after, gave a deep-sea outlet to the Nile Valley. Port Sudan was built on a deep harbour 30 mi. N of Suakin during 1906–08. A railway extension southward from Khartoum reached Al Ubayyid in 1911.

Kitchener was succeeded in December 1899 by Wingate, who as governor-general until 1916 saw the government through its pioneering years. Poverty dogged the annual budgets. In 1898 the total revenue amounted to £35,000 against expenditure of £235,000. The Egyptian Treasury met the annual deficit, and the Sudan was not solvent until 1913.

During World War I the Sudan enjoyed internal tranquility and economic prosperity. Though Turkey was at war with Britain the sultan's claim to the caliphate of Islam was not recognized in the Sudan. The Arab revolt in the Hejaz (Saudi Arabia) found much sympathy in the Sudan, which formed a supply base for the Arab insurgents in the first phase of hostilities. In 1916 Sultan 'Ali Dinar of Darfur, who was already troubled by French encroachments on the buffer states on his western border, revoked his nominal allegiance to the Sudan government. A force commanded by Lieut. Col. (afterward Brig. Gen.) P. J. V. Kelly routed the Fur Army near Al Fashir on May 22. 'Ali Dinar fled to Jabal Marrah, where he was killed on Nov. 6. Darfur was incorporated in the Sudanese administrative system, but the western frontier with the French was not demarcated until 1924.

Experiments at a small plantation at Az Zaydab and in the Blue Nile Valley proved that Egyptian long-staple cotton (which originated in the Sudan) could be profitably grown in the Gezira (Al Jazirah) and at other sites in the Nile Valley. A dam across the Blue Nile at Sennar was brought into use in 1926 for the purpose of irrigating a vast cotton plantation in the eastern Gezira which, with the considerable westward extension at Al Manaqil, the first phase of which opened in 1958, provided the Sudan with its principal cash crop and with a great addition to its grain acreage. The cotton plantation at Tawkar (Tokar) near the Red Sea coast was reconditioned in 1922, and a new plantation was established in the Qash (Gash) Delta near Kassala, a project made possible by the building of a railway from Hayya to Kassala in 1924. This line was extended to Sennar in 1929. An international commission was set up in 1925 to report on irrigation works in the Sudan which could be undertaken without detriment to Egypt's rights. Its findings were incorporated in the Anglo-Egyptian Nile Waters Agreement of May 7, 1929.

*The Growth of Sudanese Nationalism.*—The first sign of a nationalist movement in the modern sense appeared in May 1922 with the publication of a manifesto entitled *The Claims of the Sudanese Nation,* by 'Ali 'Abd al-Latif, a junior officer of a Sudanese battalion of the Egyptian Army who in 1924 founded the White Flag League. After his arrest and imprisonment in June 1924, cadets of the military school paraded the streets of Khartoum, and at Atbara the Egyptian Railway battalion mutinied. On Nov. 19 Sir Lee Stack, governor-general of the Sudan and sirdar of the Egyptian Army, was assassinated in Cairo. The resulting British ultimatum to Egypt included a demand for the immediate withdrawal from the Sudan of all Egyptian officers and purely Egyptian units of the Egyptian Army. After disorders in Khartoum where Sudanese mutineers killed British, Egyptian, and Syrian patients in a hospital, the Egyptian withdrawal was carried out. The Sudanese units of the Egyptian Army were then embodied in a Sudan Defense Force with British and Sudanese officers under a commandant responsible to the governor-general.

The negotiations which led to the Anglo-Egyptian Treaty of 1936 were closely followed by the educated minority in the Sudan, and the next stage of nationalist development was reached in 1938 with the formation of a Graduates' General Congress. Ismail al-Azhari became secretary to the Congress in 1939 and its president in 1940. Meanwhile the Sudan was heavily involved in World War II. In 1940 the Sudan Defense Force took the strain of the Italian pressure on the frontier and in 1941 assisted in the rout of the Italian forces in Eritrea and Ethiopia. Sudanese troops also took part in the North African campaigns.

The war years saw a further growth of national awareness. War brought a shortage of imported goods and so promoted a drive for economic self-sufficiency and the training of men in new industrial skills. On the political plane an Advisory Council, created in 1944, presaged further constitutional change. Municipal development was slow, and it was not until 1942 that the first town council with full control over its budget was installed, but the number of municipal authorities increased in later years. An ordinance of 1951 increased the representative element in local government. The development of education was a powerful contributing factor toward awakening a sense of nationhood. Gordon College, Khartoum, became a University College in special relationship with the University of London in 1945 and an independent university in 1956. Newspapers and broadcasting popularized the conception of the Sudan as a nation. Even the religious orders found themselves following political paths. The Khatmiya, under the leadership of al-Sayyid Sir 'Ali el-Mirghani, whose family was traditionally loyal to Egypt, adopted a position friendly to Egypt's claims in the Sudan, while the Ansar, the Mahdist confraternity, under al-Sayyid Sir 'Abd ar-Rahman, posthumous son of the Mahdi, championed the cause of absolute Sudanese independence. After 1946 two main political parties reflecting these two divergent points of view emerged. In 1947 Anglo-Egyptian negotiations broke down on the issue of the Sudan, and in July Egypt referred the dispute to the UN Security Council but got no satisfaction. In the absence of a settlement the governor-general announced a program of constitutional advance including the creation of an Executive Council and a Legislative Assembly which met in December 1948. The preceding elections had returned the Umma Party, the political expression of neo-Mahdism, to power with 'Abdullah Khalil, a retired brigadier, as leader of the Assembly. On Oct. 8, 1951, Egypt unilaterally abrogated the treaty of 1936 and proclaimed King Faruk as king of Egypt and the Sudan, a pronouncement which made no impression upon Sudanese opinion.

The Egyptian *coup d'état* of July 1952 radically altered Sudanese-Egyptian relations. On Nov. 2 Gen. Mohammed Naguib, himself half Sudanese, publicly recognized the Sudan's right to self-determination. On Feb. 12, 1953, Britain and Egypt signed an agreement by which the Sudan would attain self-government within three years. In the elections held later in the year the National Unionist Party won a victory, and Ismail al-Azhari was elected prime minister. Though he came to office on a political program favourable to Egypt, relations with Cairo worsened during 1955. The final steps toward independence were then taken. By the end of 1954 almost all the British officials had handed over their duties to their Sudanese colleagues when a tragedy in the south Sudan occurred. A mutiny in the Equatorial battalion of the army broke out in August 1955, accompanied by serious disturbances and loss of civilian lives. A Commission of Inquiry which issued its reports on Oct. 19 advanced seven causes for the outbreak, among them fear in the non-Muslim south of the political domination of the Muslim north, the circulation of false rumours, and official maladroitness.

**5. Republic of the Sudan.**—British and Egyptian troops handed over defense to the Sudanese armed forces and left the country by Jan. 1, 1956, when the Sudan proclaimed its independence. The new ruling institution, however, lacked stability. Azhari's broadly based government was wrecked in July by defecting ministers with the result that 'Abdullah Khalil (Umma Party) became prime minister of a coalition government. An Egyptian-Sudanese incident arose from the disputed ownership of two frontier enclaves. The dispute was settled by direct agreement of the two states. Khalil's term of office was compromised by an economic crisis and Cabinet dissensions.

In the troubled atmosphere a military *coup d'état* was carried out bloodlessly on Nov. 17, 1958, when a body of officers headed by Gen. Ibrahim 'Abboud took over power from the civilians and suspended the constitutional life of the country. Disharmony within the military junta led to three attempts within the following 12 months to overthrow the regime. In spite of the apparent stability which it imposed on the country and its international reputation for sound financial policy, the military government encountered increasing unpopularity culminating in October 1964 with a fracas between police and students which was followed by the fall of the Supreme Council for the Armed Forces and the formation of a provisional government with Sirr al-Khatim al-Khalifa, a civil servant, as prime minister. On Feb. 23, 1965, Khalifa, who had resigned office, was recalled by the revived Council of Sovereignty (see *Administration and Social Conditions,* below) to head a coalition ministry. General elections were held in April–May resulting in a return of the Umma Party in force followed by the National Unionists. The two parties formed a coalition with Mohammed Ahmad Mahgoub (Umma) as prime minister and Ismail al-Azhari (National Unionist) as president of the Council of Sovereignty. In July 1966 the Mahgoub coalition fell, and a new government, led by as-Sadiq (Sadik) al-Mahdi and formed from the same parties as the outgoing ministry, remained in power until May 1967 when Mahgoub returned to office. Two measures passed by Parliament reflected the influence of the Mahdists and the Muslim Brothers: a measure to make the Sudan a democratic socialist republic guided by Islamic principles, passed in April 1967, and the continuance of the ban on the Communist Party imposed in December 1965.

In spite of the reunion of the two factions of the Umma Party, led respectively by the Imam al-Hadi al-Mahdi, head of the Mahdist community, and his nephew, as-Sadiq al-Mahdi, political life by the opening of 1969 had degenerated into altercations between Communists and Muslim Brothers. There grew a feeling among civil servants, the professions, and the university that the conventional politicians had diverted the revolution of 1964, which had promised so much, into triviality and party bickering while they were ruining the economy by their technological ineptitude.

A group of officers of the middle and junior ranks, led by Col. (afterward Maj. Gen.) Gaafar Muhammad al-Nimeiry, seized power on the night of May 24–25, 1969. The officers suspended the provisional constitution, the Supreme Council, and the Constituent Assembly, abolished political parties, and detained government leaders. A Council of the Revolution was appointed with General al-Nimeiry as chairman. Abubakr Awadallah, a former chief justice, was made prime minister. The new Cabinet was drawn mostly from young civilians including two southern Sudanese and three Communists. When differences on policy became a major problem in the Cabinet, General al-Nimeiry himself took over as prime minister.

The government announced itself as the inheritor and guardian of the revolution of 1964. It was essentially a government of intellectuals. Its program followed a leftward direction: in foreign policy, alignment with the Arab states. Thus East Germany was given diplomatic recognition while relations with the U.S. and West Germany, both previously broken off on account of the Arab-Israeli dispute, were not resumed. In domestic policy the government adopted a program of state socialism akin to that of the United Arab Republic (U.A.R.), and reconciliation with the southern Sudanese. In March 1970 the Imam al-Hadi Ahmed al-Mahdi, who had been attempting to overthrow the new regime, tried unsuccessfully to assassinate al-Nimeiry. The Imam was slain during a fight that ensued when he and his followers attempted to escape into Ethiopia.

*The Southern Provinces.*—Successive governments failed to conciliate the south. In 1959 Christian mission schools were nationalized, and during 1962–64 foreign missionaries were expelled from the southern provinces. An outbreak of armed revolt was met by bloody reprisals by the northern forces. The dissidents were themselves divided in their political aspirations between independence and some form of federation with the north. An initiative by the government to hold a conference with southern representatives in March 1965 failed. However, elections were held in March 1967 in areas under effective government control, and agreement over procedure was reached between the northern parties and those southern parties willing to cooperate. In 1969 the government took active steps toward a permanent settlement of southern claims.

*Economics and Finance.*—A Sudanese-Egyptian agreement signed in Cairo in 1959 superseded the Nile Waters Agreement of 1929 between Britain and Egypt. The Sudan consented to the building of the High Dam near Aswan (*q.v.*) by Egypt while the latter compensated the Sudan for the loss of towns and land flooded by the new reservoir commanded by the Aswan High Dam. Dams for irrigation and hydroelectric power were built at Khashm al Qirbah on the 'Atbarah and at Ar Rusayris on the Blue Nile. Both irrigation schemes were completed in 1966 while a vast westward extension to the central cotton plantation at al Jazirah watered by the Sennar Dam was already in operation. Communications developed rapidly after 1945 with railway extensions to Ar Rusayris in 1958, to Nyala in Darfur in 1959, and to Waw on the Bahr el Ghazal in 1962.

A new state-owned Merchant Navy commissioned its first two seagoing ships in 1962. Nevertheless the financial strain of the rapid pace of economic expansion became apparent in 1967. This, combined with a decline in foreign currency reserves and the trading dislocation consequent upon the closure of the Suez Canal in June 1967 by the Arab-Israeli war, bore heavily upon the national economy. (R. L. Hl.)

## VI. ADMINISTRATION AND SOCIAL CONDITIONS

**1. Government.**—The Anglo-Egyptian Condominium began in 1899 and ended on Dec. 31, 1955. It was terminated after a transitional period under the terms of the Anglo-Egyptian agreement of February 1953. For nearly three years the new republic was governed by a council of ministers based upon a majority in the House of Representatives; there was also a senate and a five-man commission which functioned as chief of state.

From November 1958 to 1964 the commander of the Sudan Army, Gen. Ibrahim 'Abboud, was head of state and head of the government; but after unrest and disturbances in the autumn of 1964, a civilian government was formed and the central and provincial councils created by the military government were abolished. In December, in accordance with the provisional constitution of 1956, the Five-Man Commission (Council of Sovereignty) was revived to perform the function of the head of state, and in April 1965 a general election was held in the north. The Umma Party won 75 seats, the National Unionist 54, the Beja Tribal Association 10, the Islamic Front 5, the People's Democratic 3, and the Communists 11. Independents won 15 seats. In December 1965 a law was passed to prevent communists from sitting in the House. A cabinet of nine ministers (three representing the south) was formed in June 1965 but much of Equatoria and Bahr el Ghazal had been in a state of insurrection since 1963 and was no longer effectively administered (see *History,* above).

**2. Administration.**—The Sudan is divided into nine provinces. The provinces were formerly divided into districts, at first administered directly by district commissioners; but devolution to local authorities began in 1918 and passed through further stages in 1937 and 1954. Provinces and districts have some powers of taxation, and responsibilities in the spheres of health, education, and veterinary services. Governors of provinces are responsible to the Ministry of Local Government.

Khartoum is the capital of the republic and in 1956 had a population of 93,103; (1967 est.) 188,000. The total population (1967 est.) was over 14,000,000, with an increase mainly in the north. In the south there was widespread depopulation as the result of civil war and the emigration of tribes to Uganda, the Congo, and the Central African Republic.

*Provinces of the Republic of the Sudan*

| Province | Capital | Area (sq.mi.*) | Population (1965 est.) |
|---|---|---|---|
| Bahr el Ghazal | Waw | 82,529 | 1,274,000 |
| Blue Nile | Wad Madani | 54,879 | 2,801,000 |
| Darfur | Al Fashir | 191,648 | 1,509,000 |
| Equatoria | Juba | 76,495 | 1,161,000 |
| Kassala | Kassala | 131,527 | 1,452,000 |
| Khartoum | Khartoum | 8,097 | 771,000 |
| Kordofan | Al Ubayyid | 146,929 | 2,079,000 |
| Northern | Ad Damir | 184,198 | 1,009,000 |
| Upper Nile | Malakal | 91,189 | 1,142,000 |

*1 sq.mi.=2.59 sq.km.

**3. Living Conditions.**—According to the 1956 census the labour force comprised about 3,800,000 (37% of the population), the majority of whom were engaged in farming, and animal husbandry. In industry, commerce, and public administration there is legislation to cover employment exchanges, conditions of employment in factories and in domestic service, and workmen's compensation. Trade unions have been recognized since 1948, and negotiate with employers (including the government) on wages and working conditions. Under an amending ordinance of 1960, provision is made for closer control by the labour commissioner. Another ordinance of 1960 prescribed that disputes should be compulsorily arbitrated when negotiation and conciliation fail. Under legislation applying to cooperative societies, many such bodies have been registered, of which about 150 are agricultural and more than 100 are for marketing and credit.

Towns are planned so that there are separate first-, second-, and third-class residential areas, as well as commercial and industrial zones. Buildings must be erected in conformity with regulations governing materials to be used, number of stories, etc. Outside the limits of towns are *deims* (*dayms*) where unregulated houses, *i.e.,* shacks and native huts, may be erected. In rural areas generally, where the population is sedentary, housing conforms to tribal custom and usually comprises square flat-roofed, mud-brick dwellings (in the north) or circular grass huts with conical thatched roofs. The nomads live in tents.

**4. Public Health.**—Early in the 20th century the Sudan was reputed to be very unhealthy, and epidemics of sleeping sickness, cerebrospinal meningitis, and yellow fever were frequent. The progress of medical and sanitary services under the Sudan Medical Service (later the Ministry of Health), supplemented in many places by missionary institutions, has reduced mortality. By 1965 there were about 70 government hospitals of different grades, located in all important centres. Rural areas were served by more than 1,000 dispensaries and dressing stations under medical assistants. There are doctors in private practice in larger towns and a rural midwife service.

**5. Justice.**—Civil justice is administered through the High Court of Justice in Khartoum, province courts, and lower courts. There is a body of civil law; but where there is no special enactment, cases are decided according to "justice, equity, and good conscience." The criminal code is based upon the Indian Penal Code and is dispensed in major, minor, and magistrate's courts. There are also local courts, constituted under the Native Courts Ordinance (1932) and the Chiefs' Courts Ordinance (1931), which try a substantial proportion of civil and criminal cases. Muslims in the north are subject to the Shari'a, or religious law of Islam, in questions of inheritance, marriage, divorce, family relationship, and charitable trusts.

**6. Education.**—In the Muslim areas of the north, boys have long been instructed in religious subjects according to traditional methods. During the Condominium, and as the outcome of an appeal by Kitchener in 1898, modern primary education was begun in the northern Sudan, and secondary education commenced in 1913 (see *History,* above). Post-secondary schools in arts and science, agriculture, veterinary science, engineering, and law were established between 1938 and 1941. In 1947 these schools were brought together within Gordon Memorial College, which was linked in special relationship with the University of London until 1959. Education in medicine began in 1923, at the foundation of the Kitchener School of Medicine which in 1951 was united with Gordon Memorial College in the University College of Khartoum (which in 1956 became the University of Khartoum).

In the south, missionaries were responsible for education, with the consent and support of the government, until 1957, when the government assumed direct control, as a result of which Arabic was given greater prominence in the curriculum. But education was later to suffer severely from the civil war.

The census of 1955–56 disclosed that over 85% of the total population aged five years and above had never attended any school. In the mid-1960s there were about 3,100 government schools with 520,000 pupils, and more than 170 nongovernment schools, of all grades, with about 46,500 pupils. There were also 37 intermediate and secondary religious (Muslim) schools, attended by over 6,300 pupils. The *Maahad Ilmi* in the mosque at Omdurman, attended by pupils from Muslim areas, provides theological education and trains the religious leaders (*ulema*) and lawyers (*qadis*). The principal centre for the training of intermediate school teachers is the Institute of Education at Bakht ar Ruda, near Ad Duwaym, for men, and at Omdurman for women. Secondary school teachers are trained at a Higher Teachers College at Omdurman.

The University of Khartoum has faculties of agriculture, arts, science, economics, engineering, law, medicine, and veterinary science. English is the medium of instruction in the university and the secondary schools, but it is being replaced by Arabic in the secondary schools. A branch of Cairo University in Khartoum provides facilities for evening classes in arts, law, and commerce. The classes are conducted in Arabic. The Khartoum Technical Institute was founded in 1950.

**7. Defense.**—The Sudan Army had its origin in the Sudan Defense Force, founded in 1925. The total rifle strength in 1955, when the British officers left, was between 4,000 and 5,000, and it remained at about 5,000. There are also technical corps based on

Omdurman and Khartoum, and artillery is based on ʻAtbarah. Some light aircraft have been acquired, and there is a small naval force on the Red Sea composed mainly of patrol boats.

## VII. THE ECONOMY

The Sudan's economy depends almost wholly upon agricultural and pastoral products. Minerals and sources of power are lacking, and industrial development was in its infancy in the mid-1960s. Commercial development has been mainly in the north and east. The closure of the Suez Canal from June 1967 caused some economic hardship and compelled the diversion of most Sudanese imports and exports, other than oil, to other routes.

**1. Agricultural and Pastoral Production.**—In the west and south both crops and livestock are produced mainly for subsistence, and little is sold. In the north and east surpluses are available and are moved to towns or exported. The only capitalized agricultural production, applying modern technical knowledge, is from the irrigated areas close to the Nile in the northeast and some areas under rain cultivation near al Qadarif.

The chief food crops are the common millet (durra) and bulrush millet (*dukhn*). The latter flourishes on the sands of the dunes. Millet cultivation extends across the country in an east-west zone —the central rain lands—between latitudes $10\frac{1}{2}°$ N and 14° N, but is also grown by Nilotic peoples near their permanent villages. In the far south, finger millet (eleusine) and corn (maize) are preferred. The area under durra and *dukhn* has increased in the northeastern Sudan concomitantly with the population in the 20th century; this has been true especially in the clay plain (since World War II) as a result of the provision of new roads and perennial water supplies from *hawafir* or excavated reservoirs. Near al Qadarif, the introduction of mechanized production has proved profitable. Durra also enters into the rotation of crops in irrigated areas. Yields of millets fluctuate mainly according to rainfall, and in years of poor harvests the supplies to towns and deficiency regions cause the government anxiety; but the cultivator makes use of underground storage in pits and in lean years draws upon his reserves. In good years some grain is exported. Wheat is grown as a winter crop along the Nile in Northern Province.

Sesame and peanuts are also important; both are normally exported. A bean known as *lubia affin* (*Dolichos lablab*), a clover (*berseem higazi*), and alfalfa are grown for fodder on irrigated land. Tobacco is widely grown in Darfur and is the only crop which can justify the cost of transport from that remote part of the country. Medium- and low-quality dates are a traditional product of the Nile Valley north of Shandi and find a market throughout the northern Sudan. Citrus fruits, especially limes and grapefruit, are produced at Kassala, in irrigated gardens along the Nile and near some towns in both north and south. Market gardening is also established in some areas but does not produce an adequate supply of fresh vegetables. In the southern Sudan tobacco, coffee, sugar, rice, and the oil palm have all been cultivated experimentally, but commercial output has been negligible.

Cotton is the major cash crop and, after the completion of the Sennar Dam in 1925, became the mainstay of the Sudan's economy. Until about 1960 the long-staple Sakellarides varieties were dominant because they commanded higher prices in the world market. But lessened demand for these types of cotton has prompted increase in production of medium- and short-staple varieties and the diversification of cash crops generally. New pump projects and the al Manaqil extension to the Gezira (al Jazirah) project have greatly increased the area under cotton. In 1965 this exceeded 1,000,000 feddans (1 feddan = 1.038 ac.), of which about 300,000 were unirrigated, mainly in Kordofan and Kassala provinces. The production of long-staple seed cotton, almost wholly from irrigated land, amounted to about 386,000 metric tons and of short-staple (rain grown) seed cotton to about 43,000 metric tons. The Sudan Gezira Board (established 1950) controls most of the cotton production. Since the completion in 1966 of the first stage of the Al Roseires (Ar Rusayris) Dam on the Blue Nile, an extension to irrigated farming (the Kinanah Scheme) has been undertaken.

*Livestock.*—Pastoral activities extend throughout the country, except on the ironstone plateau of the southwest, which is infested by the tsetse fly, and on the desert of the north and northwest. In 1967 there were about 4,000,000 camels, owned by Beja, Arab, and nomadic tribes of the north and west, which graze over the desert margin scrub. About 12,000,000 cattle were bred mainly in the central rain lands, especially by the Baggara tribes of southwest Kordofan and southern Darfur. Cattle also form the chief wealth of the Nilotic tribes. There were an estimated 1,100,000 sheep and 8,000,000 goats, associated with both camel and cattle rearing in the north. Goats are also numerous in the towns as milk suppliers. Camels and small numbers of cattle are exported to Egypt, and sheep to Saudi Arabia; there is also sale for slaughter to towns. A corned-beef factory established at Kusti in 1950 was forced to close for lack of regular and adequate supply of animals despite the improvement of drove roads from the west and the possibility of transporting animals by air. Since 1945 the preparation and export of hides has been encouraged, with some success.

The growth of population and the settlement in new areas during the Condominium, together with control of animal diseases by veterinary services, have greatly increased the use of cultivable land and natural grazing. In some areas land is losing its fertility,

(LEFT) BEN KENTRY—BLACK STAR; (TOP) GEORGE RODGER—MAGNUM; (BOTTOM) CAMERA PRESS—PIX FROM PUBLIX

(LEFT) SORTING COTTON IN A SUDANESE COTTON GIN; (BELOW) GIRL CLEANING GUM ARABIC; (ABOVE) SCHOOLBOYS HURRYING TOWARD A VILLAGE SCHOOLHOUSE IN SOUTHERN SUDAN

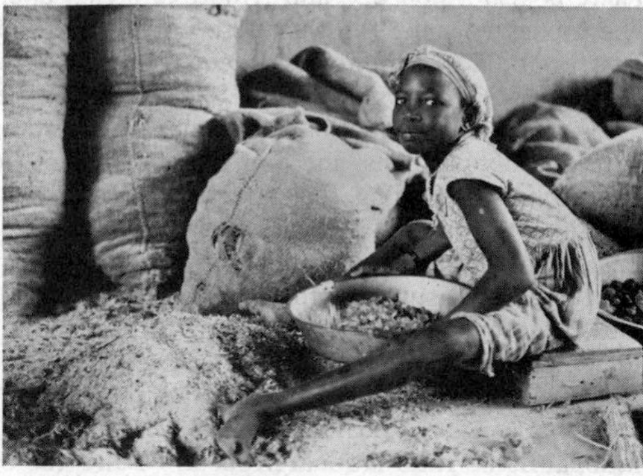

and the best fodder plants are disappearing. The provision of new water supplies (wells and *hawafir*) has been the chief conservation measure, rendering new areas of pasture and cultivable land available for use. Further methods of control are desirable, and are under study by the Rural Water Corporation.

*Fisheries.*—The Nile system, and especially the White Nile above Kusti and the Bahr el Jebel, is an important source of fish, particularly Nile perch, for riverine peoples. Small quantities are sold in the towns, and a little is dried and salted.

**2. Forestry.**—The Sudan is one of the world's chief suppliers of gum arabic, chiefly *hashab* gum, which is collected from *Acacia senegal* in the central rain land zone from Darfur to Kassala; it is bought by exporting companies at government auctions. Timber is produced mainly in the south, apart from the dense hardwood known as *sunt* (*Acacia nilotica*), exploited in the Blue Nile and Dindar (Dinder) valleys. There are sawmills near Waw, Loka, and Katire, producing mahogany and other hard and soft timbers. The forests are the local sources of firewood and charcoal, and cutting is supervised; but severe inroads have been made into the more meagre woodlands of northern Sudan. The growing use of oil fuels is proving to be an ameliorative.

**3. Minerals.**—No large mineral deposits have been discovered, but gold, iron ore, manganese, limestone, mica, and chromite are exploited on a small scale. Salterns at Port Sudan supply unrefined salt for the country's needs and for export.

**4. Industry and Power.**—Oil milling and soap making are established in some northern towns; Khartoum and Port Sudan have factories of moderate size. There is a cement works at 'Atbarah. Steel and aluminum are fabricated into utensils in Khartoum and Wad Madani. A modern brewery operates in Khartoum North, and there are two distilleries in the Three Towns. Factories for shoes, paints, glass, knitwear, sweets, and cigarettes also operate in Khartoum. Khartoum North and Omdurman each have a cotton-spinning and weaving mill. There are motor-maintenance workshops and tire-retreading works in Khartoum and elsewhere. The railway workshops at 'Atbarah are the largest industrial unit in the country. River steamers and barges are repaired in the dockyards at Khartoum North and Kusti. Local craftsmen make leather goods, clothes, pottery, furniture, household utensils, jewelry, and implements in the bazaars of northern towns.

A Sudanese-Egyptian Agreement signed in 1959 superseded the Nile Waters Agreement of 1929 between Great Britain and Egypt. Under the new agreement dams for irrigation and hydroelectric power were built at Khashm al Qirbah on the Atbara ('Atbarah) and near Ar Rusayris (Roseires) on the Blue Nile. The first phase of both schemes was completed in 1966. A power station on the Sennar Dam supplies the Gezira and Khartoum with electricity.

**5. Trade and Finance.**—The principal exports of the Sudan are cotton and cottonseed, peanuts, gum arabic, and sesame. The principal imports are textiles, petroleum products, machinery, refined sugar, base metals and manufactures, and vehicles. In 1965 the chief receiving countries were Germany, Italy, and the U.K. Chief sources of supply were the U.K., Japan, and India.

Indirect sources of revenue include import duties, royalties on exported products, and the profits of trading concerns such as the cotton projects and the sugar monopoly. Direct taxes include those on date-palms, animals, land, crops, houses, and income. There is also a poll tax, and tribute is levied upon certain tribes. The monetary unit, the Sudanese pound (£S), divided into 100 piastres and 1,000 milliemes, is equal to £.837 sterling.

In 1966–67 the revenue was £S79,000,000 and expenditure was £S83,000,000. From 1945 additional development budgets financed five-year plans, and annual development budgets provided for projects, including the dam at Al Roseires, the Khashm al Qirbah ('Atbarah or Atbara River) scheme, the al Manaqil extension to the Gezira scheme, the Sennar hydroelectric scheme, and the Junayd sugar factory. A ten-year development plan for 1961–71 provided £S287,300,000 to be used for social and economic development.

The external public debt stood at about £S44,000,000 at the beginning of 1965. Loans or credits were obtained from the International Bank, International Monetary Fund, the United Kingdom, the Federal Republic of Germany, Yugoslavia, and Kuwait (for railway development). A credit under the American aid agreement (1952–59) was principally for establishing a textile industry in the northern Sudan and for railway extension and improvements. Under an agreement with the U.S.S.R. (1961) financial and technical aid was provided for the construction of food-processing factories.

*Banking.*—Until 1960 banking was provided by foreign concerns, led by Barclays Bank D.C.O. (Dominion, Colonial, and Overseas) and the National Bank of Egypt. The latter was acquired by the state, renamed the Bank of Sudan, and reorganized as the central bank for the country. The state-owned Agricultural Bank of Sudan provides agricultural credit. The Industrial Bank of Sudan was officially inaugurated in 1962. In May 1970 the government announced the nationalization of all banks operating in the Sudan, including foreign banks.

**6. Transport and Communications.**—Communications in the north are provided by the Sudan railways. The line from Wadi Halfa to Khartoum was built in 1897–99; the 'Atbarah-Port Sudan branch was opened in 1904–06; and the main line from Khartoum (via Sennar and Kusti) to al Ubayyid was extended in 1906–11. Except for the Kassala-Hayya loop, completed in 1929, railway building ceased until 1950. A branch from Sennar to Al Roseires was completed in 1956, and a westward extension from Ar Rahad via Abu Zabad and Ad Du'ayn to Nyala in 1959. A branch line from Babanusah (on the latter extension) southwestward across the Bahr al 'Arab to Waw was completed in 1962. This railway system facilitates the economic advance of the north by providing the means for bulk movement of cotton, oilseeds, hides, and gum arabic, as well as the distribution of imported goods.

In the south the White Nile and the Bahr el Jebel, between Kusti and Juba, and the Bahr el Ghazal as far as Mashra' ar Raqq are navigable throughout the year and have regular passenger and freight services. The Jur River is navigable from its confluence with the Bahr el Ghazal to Waw from July to October, and the Sobat from May till December. From ports on these rivers an all-weather road system serves the provinces of Bahr el Ghazal and Equatoria (on the ironstone plateau); but Upper Nile, on the clay plain, possesses only dry-weather tracks, and porterage is still necessary away from the rivers except between December and May.

There are no improved roads in the northern Sudan; but motorable tracks (with locally improved stretches to ensure continuity over soft, rocky, or marshy ground) are used by trucks and estate and heavier cars, except after heavy rainfall between July and September. The soft sand of the dunes impedes motor transport in central and southwestern Kordofan and eastern Darfur.

Khartoum is a stopping place on the main air route from Cairo, to East Africa, with feeder services to the east (Ethiopia and Aden) and to the west. The government-owned Sudan Airways operates internal air services between the Three Towns and most provincial capitals and external services to Egypt, Aden, Jidda, Jordan, Eritrea, Nairobi, Lebanon, Athens, Frankfurt, Rome, and London.

*Telecommunications.*—The telegraph system serves most settled parts of the country. A telephone service exists in the north and east. In the south, and in Darfur, radio transmission is employed instead of land lines. Communications abroad are by means of cable, land line, and radio (telegraphy and telephony). The government-controlled Sudan Broadcasting Service at Omdurman broadcasts in Arabic and English. *See* also references under "Sudan, Republic of the" in the Index. (J. H. G. L.)

BIBLIOGRAPHY.—R. L. Hill, *Bibliography of the Anglo-Egyptian Sudan* (1939); A. R. el Nasri, *A Bibliography of the Sudan, 1938–1958* (1962). *Geography and Botany:* K. M. Barbour, *The Republic of the Sudan* (1961); A. F. Broun and R. E. Massey, *Flora of the Sudan* (1929); F. W. Andrews, *Flowering Plants of the Anglo-Egyptian Sudan*, 3 vol. (1950–56); J. H. G. Lebon, *Land Use in Sudan* (1965). *The People:* H. A. MacMichael, *History of the Arabs in the Sudan,* 2 vol. (1922); S. F. Nadel, *The Nuba* (1947); J. S. Trimingham, *Islam in the Sudan* (1949); D. Forde (ed.), *Ethnographic Survey of Africa, East Central Africa* (1960): Part IV, *Nilotes;* Part VI, *Northern Nilo-Hamites;* Part VII, *Central Nilo-Hamites;* Part IX, *Azande;* this series contains full annotated bibliographies; *Sudan Notes and Records* (1918– ).

*Archaeology:* A. J. Arkell *et al., The Pleistocene Fauna of Two Blue*

*Nile Sites* (1951); C. R. Lepsius, *Denkmäler aus Aegypten and Aethiopien,* Ab. vi. (1849); F. Cailliaud, *Voyage à Méroé, au Fleuve Blanc,* etc. (1823–27); E. A. Wallis Budge, *The Egyptian Sudan,* 2 vol. (1907); *The Wellcome Excavations in the Sudan,* vol. i and ii, *Jebel Moya,* by F. Addison (1949), vol. iii, *Abu Geili and Saqadi and Dar el Mek,* by O. G. S. Crawford and F. Addison (1951); O. G. S. Crawford, *The Fung Kingdom of Sennar* (1951); *Kush, Journal of the Sudan Antiquities Service* (1953– ); *The Journal of Egyptian Archaeology* (1914– ). *See* also works cited under NUBIA.

*History:* R. L. Hill, *Egypt in the Sudan, 1820–1881* (1959), *Sudan Transport: a History of Railway, Marine and River Services in the Republic of the Sudan* (1965); P. L. Shinnie, *Meroe* (1967); A. J. Arkell, *A History of the Sudan: From the Earliest Times to 1821* (1955); Y. F. Hasan, *The Arabs and the Sudan* (1967); M. F. Shukry, *The Khedive Ismail and Slavery in the Sudan, 1863–1879* (1937); M. Sabry, *Le Soudan égyptien, 1821–98* (1947); B. M. Allen, *Gordon and the Sudan* (1931); M. E. T. Shibeika, *The Independent Sudan* (1959), *British Policy in the Sudan, 1882–1902* (1952); P. M. Holt, *The Mahdist State in the Sudan, 1881–1898* (1958), *A Modern History of the Sudan* (1961); R. A. Gray, *A History of the Southern Sudan, 1839–1889* (1961); R. O. Collins, *The Southern Sudan, 1883–1898* (1962); M. Abbas, *The Sudan Question: the Dispute over the Anglo-Egyptian Condominium, 1884–1951* (1952); K. D. D. Henderson (ed.), *The Making of the Modern Sudan: the Life and Letters of Sir Douglas Newbold* (1953), *Sudan Republic* (1965); A. B. Theobald, *'Ali Dinar, Last Sultan of Darfur* (1965); M. A. Rahim, *Imperialism and Nationalism in the Sudan* (1969).

*Administration and Economy: Annual Reports on the Administration, Finances and Condition of the Sudan* (1899–1956); V. L. Griffiths, *An Experiment in Education* (1953); M. O. Beshir, *Educational Development in the Sudan, 1898–1956* (1969); F. Saad al-Din Fawzi, *The Labour Movement in the Sudan, 1946–1955* (1957); H. C. Squires, *The Sudan Medical Service* (1958); J. D. Tothill (ed.), *Agriculture in the Sudan* (1948); A. Gaitskell, *Gezira: a Story of Development in the Sudan* (1959); Central Office of Information, The Republic of Sudan, *Sudan Almanac* (annually); *Annual Reports of Survey, Forests and Land Use Departments.*

**SUDANIC LANGUAGES.** The term Sudanic has been used to designate many African languages spoken from Ethiopia in the east to Nigeria in the west. Totally unrelated languages have been included in the various groupings listed as Sudanic, either on geographic or other nonlinguistic grounds. A more satisfactory classification is that of Joseph H. Greenberg, which is based upon strictly linguistic relationships.

Chari-Nile (or Macro-Sudanic) includes Central Sudanic, Eastern Sudanic, Berta, and Kunama. Even this broad grouping is tentative. Central Sudanic includes the Moru-Madi group (in the Sudan, northeast Democratic Republic of the Congo, and northwest Uganda) and the Bongo-Baka-Bagirmi group (largely in Cameroon, Chad, and the Central African Republic but extending east into the Sudan). Eastern Sudanic (on the upper Nile, largely in the Sudan, Uganda, and Kenya but extending into Tanganyika) has seven branches: Nubian, Beir-Didinga, Barea, Tabi, Merarit, Dagu, and Southern.

Old Nubian is known from medieval records ranging from the 8th to the 11th centuries. The Southern branch includes (1) Nilotic proper or West Nilotic, including Shilluk, Nuer, Dinka, Lango, and Acholi; (2) East Nilotic, including Bari, Masai, Turkana, and Lotuko; and (3) South Nilotic (Nandi-Suk).

*See* also AFRICAN LANGUAGES.

BIBLIOGRAPHY.—A. N. Tucker, *The Eastern Sudanic Languages* (1940); Joseph H. Greenberg, *Studies in African Linguistic Classification* (1955). For the older type of classification *see* A. Meillet and M. Cohen, *Les Langues du Monde,* rev. ed. (1952). (C. T. HE.)

**SUDBURY, SIMON OF** (d. 1381), archbishop of Canterbury (1375–81), the most distinguished victim of the peasants' revolt, was the son of Nigel Thebaud (Theobald or Tybald) of Sudbury, Suffolk. His appointment to the See of London by Pope Innocent VI in 1361 was a reward for service at the papal curia; he was an auditor of the Rota for 12 years and in 1359 the pope sent him to England in an attempt to persuade Edward III to open peace negotiations with France. Capable and efficient, he was a conscientious and popular bishop. Translated to Canterbury in May 1375, he crowned Richard II on July 16, 1377; as primate, he avoided conflict with the state but showed firmness in his dealings with his suffragans. John Wycliffe appeared before him in February 1378 to answer charges of heresy. He became chancellor in January 1380. In 1381 the Kentish rebels held Sudbury and the lord treasurer, Sir Robert Hales, responsible for the hated poll tax. When the Tower of London was surrendered to Wat Tyler's insurgents on Friday, June 14, Sudbury, Hales, and two other men were beheaded on Tower Hill. The archbishop's head was displayed on London Bridge for several days and is now preserved in St. Gregory's, at his birthplace, Sudbury.

BIBLIOGRAPHY.—*Registrum Simonis de Sudbiria, 1362–75,* ed. by R. C. Fowler (1927–38); W. L. Warren, "A Reappraisal of Simon Sudbury," *The Journal of Ecclesiastical History,* vol. x, no. 2 (1959). (T. B. P.)

**SUDBURY,** a city in southeastern Ontario, Can., 264 mi. (425 km.) NW of Toronto and the seat of Sudbury District. Pop. (1966) 84,888. The chief retail and wholesale centre for the area known as Northern Ontario, Sudbury began with the arbitrary location of a station on the new Canadian Pacific Railway. Copper-bearing ores containing large quantities of nickel were unearthed in 1883 during construction of the railway, but it was not until the metallurgy of copper-nickel separation was solved that development started and the major growth of the city began.

By the end of 1945 over $1,000,000,000 worth of nickel and $500,000,000 worth of copper had been produced. In the 1960s Sudbury still produced about 50% of the world's nickel and almost all of Ontario's copper. The huge concentrator and smelter of the International Nickel Company is at Copper Cliff, 4 mi. W of Sudbury. Falconbridge Nickel Mines Ltd. operates a nickel-copper mine, concentrator, and smelter at Falconbridge, about 12 mi. NE of Sudbury. More than three-quarters of those gainfully employed work in mining and metallurgy, earning a higher average wage than the workers of any other Canadian city.

Sudbury was incorporated as a town in 1893 and as a city in 1930. Modern Sudbury is a well-built city with more than 20 mi. of paved streets. It has an extensive business section with many stores, hotels, and large office buildings, as well as many fine churches and schools.

The Laurentian University of Sudbury, a bilingual nondenominational university, was established in 1960. (F. A. CK.)

**SUDBURY,** a municipal borough of West Suffolk, Eng., lies on the River Stour 22 mi. (35 km.) W of Ipswich by road. Pop. (1969 est.) 8,000. One of the medieval wool towns, it has many beautiful half-timbered buildings and three Perpendicular churches: All Saints, with a fine oaken pulpit dating from 1490; St. Peter's, with a carved nave roof; and St. Gregory's, once collegiate, which contains a rich, spire-shaped font cover of wood, gilded and painted. The grammar school was founded by William Wood in 1491 (rebuilt 1857). The artist Thomas Gainsborough (1727–88) was born there in a house that is now an art centre. An earlier native was Simon of Sudbury, or Simon Tybald, archbishop of Canterbury, who was murdered in Wat Tyler's rebellion and whose head is preserved in St. Gregory's. Before the Conquest the borough was owned by the mother of Morcar, earl of Northumbria, from whom it was taken by William I. It probably then passed to Robert, earl of Gloucester, and in the 1270s Gilbert de Clare, earl of Gloucester, gave the burgesses their first charter confirming their ancient liberties. Sudbury was incorporated in 1554.

**SUDERMANN, HERMANN** (1857–1928), one of the leading writers of the German Naturalist movement, was born at Matziken, East Prussia, on Sept. 30, 1857, of a Mennonite family. Though first apprenticed to a chemist, he was eventually able to attend Königsberg University. After a short period as tutor in Berlin he worked as a journalist, then turned to novel writing. *Frau Sorge* (1887; English translation, *Dame Care,* 1891), a keenly observed description of the growing up of a sensitive youth, and *Der Katzensteg* (1880; Eng. trans., *Regine,* 1894) are the best known of his early novels. He won fame, however, with his plays. *Ehre* (1890; Eng. trans., *What Money Cannot Buy,* 1906), first performed in Berlin on Nov. 27, 1889, only a month after Gerhart Hauptmann's *Vor Sonnenaufgang,* was, like Hauptmann's play, a milestone in the Naturalist movement (*see* HAUPTMANN, GERHART), although to later criticism it seems a rather trite and slick treatment of class conflicts in Berlin. *Heimat* (1893; Eng. trans., *Magda,* 1896) carried his fame throughout the world and provided the favourite role for many prominent actresses. Influenced by Ibsen, Sudermann sought to champion the equality of women, but the play is marred by a sickly sentimentality. His plays, notably *Das Glück im Winkel* (1896; Eng. trans., *The Vale of Content,* 1915), *Morituri* (1896; Eng. trans., 1897), *Es lebe das Leben!* (1902; Eng. trans., *The Joy of Living,* 1902), *Der gute Ruf* (1913; Eng. trans., *A Good Reputation,* 1915), were almost all successful on the stage of his time, for Sudermann's dramatic construction is skilful, his dialogue convincing, and his language simple; but when he seeks to depict passion, he often becomes sentimental, and his criticism of contemporary society—a recurrent motif—is superficial. Consequently, his plays are seldom staged today. Among his later prose writings, *Litauische Geschichten* (1917), a collection of stories, is powerful because he knows how to build up tension and describe the life of simple people convincingly. *Das Bilderbuch meiner Jugend* (1922; Eng. trans., *Book of My Youth,* 1923) is a vivid account of his early years in East Prussia. He died at Berlin-Grunewald on Nov. 21, 1928.

Bibliography.—*Dramatische Werke,* 6 vol. (1923); *Romane und Novellen,* 6 vol. (1919). *See* also H. Schoen, *H. Sudermann, Poète dramatique et romancier* (1904); I. Leux, *H. Sudermann* (1931); T. Duglor, *H. Sudermann, ein Dichter an der Grenzscheide zweier Welten* (1958). (H. S. R.)

**SUE, EUGÈNE** (Marie-Joseph Sue) (1804–1857), French novelist and a leading exponent of the *roman-feuilleton* ("newspaper serial"), was born in Paris on Jan. 26, 1804. His early experiences as a naval surgeon prompted several highly coloured sea stories (*e.g., Plik et Plok,* 1831). He also wrote a number of historical novels.

Having inherited a fortune from his father, Sue became a well-known dandy. His carriage and horses, pack of beagles (a present from his friend Count d'Orsay), and displays of luxury made him the talk of Paris. He was one of the first members of the French Jockey Club (1834). He depicted contemporary "high life" in *Arthur* (1838) and *Mathilde* (1841). The latter showed Socialist tendencies, and Sue turned in this direction in *Les Mystères de Paris* (1842–43), which influenced Hugo's *Les Misérables,* and *Le Juif errant* (1844–45). Published in installments, these long but exciting novels vastly increased the circulation of the newspapers in which they appeared. His later works were less successful.

After participating in the 1848 Revolution, Sue was elected Socialist deputy for the Seine in 1850. He opposed Louis Napoleon's *coup d'état* in 1851, went into voluntary exile at Annecy, and remained there until his death on Aug. 3, 1857.

Bibliography.—N. Atkinson, *E. Sue et le roman-feuilleton* (1929); J. Boulenger, *Sous Louis-Philippe: les Dandys,* new ed. (1932); J.-L. Bory, *E. Sue. Le roi du roman populaire* (1962). (S. C. Gd.)

**SUEBI** (Lat. Suebi, Suevi; Span. Suevos; Eng. Sueves), a group of Germanic peoples (*q.v.*), including the Marcomanni and Quadi, Hermunduri, Semnones, and Langobardi (Lombards). In the late 1st century A.D. most of these tribes lived around the Elbe River, but some of them had already migrated from this area. Several Suebic tribes have their own separate history (*see* Marcomanni; Lombards). Some Suebi were among the Alamanni (*q.v.*) and some gave their name to Swabia (*q.v.*). This article deals with the Suebic kingdom in Spain.

Dislodged by the Huns, some Suebi, together with two hordes of Vandals and the Alani, reached Mainz in 406, crossed the Rhine, and in 409 entered Spain. The Suebi settled mainly in the northwest (Galicia), their capital being Bracara Augusta (Braga, Port.). Their expansion was hindered by the campaigns of the Visigothic king Wallia in Spain (416–418) and the defeat of a Suebic army by the Vandals near Augusta Emerita (Mérida) in 429; but by 447, under their king Rechila, the Suebi had spread over Lusitania and Baetica. The Suebi entered Spain as pagans, and as late as the 6th century they retained several pagan superstitions. Rechila's son Rechiarius (445–456) was, however, converted to Catholicism. He attacked the Romans in Tarraconensis but was defeated by the Visigoths under Theodoric II in 456.

This was described by the contemporary Hydatius, bishop of Aquae Flaviae (Chaves), in his *Chronicon,* as the end of the Suebic kingdom, but remnants of the Suebi survived under Maldras (456–460) and rival kings. Remismund, who became sole king of the Suebi in 464, converted his people to Arianism during a temporary *rapprochement* with the Visigothic king. For the 90 years following 468 (when Hydatius' *Chronicon* ends) this history of the Suebi is obscure. King Theodomir (558–570) was converted to Catholicism by St. Martin, bishop of Braga. The reigns of Theodomir's two successors were disturbed, and *c.* 585 the kingdom was annexed to the Visigothic state.

*See* L. Schmidt, *Geschichte der deutschen Stämme: die Westgermanen,* 2nd ed. (1938–40); R. Menéndez Pidal (ed.), *Historia de España,* vol. iii, esp. part 1, ch. 2–3 (1940).

**SUESS, EDUARD** (1831–1914), Austrian geologist who, among his contributions to the theory of continental origins, postulated the existence of Gondwanaland (*q.v.*), was born at London on Aug. 20, 1831. He was educated at the universities of Prague and Vienna, specializing in invertebrate paleontology. In 1852 he became assistant in the Hofmuseum, Vienna, and in 1857 extraordinary professor of geology at the University of Vienna, becoming ordinary (or full) professor in 1867, a position he held until 1901.

While connected with the Hofmuseum, Suess published papers on the anatomy and classification of brachiopods, established the classification of ammonites, and described fossils belonging to several other groups.

After 1857 he turned to geology proper. In 1875 he published a small book on the origin of the Alps, in which he denied vertical uplift of mountains and continents, limited the rǫle of vulcanism in mountain building, and declared that the Alps and related mountains had been formed by thrusting movements that crumpled and broke outer portions of the earth's crust. He also emphasized the existence of unyielding continental areas composed of very old mountain masses, now generally called shields.

His major work, *Das Antlitz der Erde,* published between 1885 and 1907, achieved great influence and was translated into Italian and French, and into English as *The Face of the Earth.* In it he expounded his interpretation of the earth's surface in terms of ancient changes in continents and seas. He also dealt with fluctuations of ancient seas, the rise of magmas, and other subjects related to his main thesis.

Suess became a member of the *Landtag* of Lower Austria in 1869, and in 1873 entered the lower house of the *Reichsrath,* where for more than 30 years he was Liberal deputy from Vienna. He died at Vienna on April 26, 1914. (M. A. F.; C. L. Fe.)

**SUETONIUS TRANQUILLUS, GAIUS** (b. *c.* A.D. 70, d. after A.D. 122), Roman biographer and antiquarian, is best known for his *De vita Caesarum* (*Lives of the Caesars*). Probably born in Rome, he was of equestrian family, a friend and protégé of the younger Pliny. He seems to have toyed with the law as a career but abandoned it; and having secured through his friend a military tribunate, he relinquished that also. It is possible, though not certain, that he accompanied Pliny on his mission to Bithynia (*c.* 110–113). After Pliny's death Suetonius found another patron, Septicius Clarus (to whom Pliny had dedicated his letters, and to whom Suetonius himself was later to dedicate the *De vita Caesarum*); upon the accession of Hadrian, Septicius became praetorian prefect, and, either then or a little before, Suetonius entered the imperial service. He held, probably simultaneously, the posts *a studiis* and *a bibliothecis,* controlling the Roman libraries, keeping archives and advising the emperor on cultural matters. In 121 Hadrian began his first grand tour of the empire, and probably at this time Suetonius was promoted to be *ab epistulis,* secretary of the imperial correspondence, in which capacity he traveled (along with his patron) in the emperor's suite. Both men were dismissed for neglect of court formality; the incident is recorded in the context of Hadrian's visit to Britain in 122, but may have taken place somewhat later. Presumably Suetonius devoted himself thenceforward to literary pursuits. The date of his death is unknown.

**Works.**—A list of writings of Suetonius is given in the Suda Lexicon (*q.v.*). Most of them were antiquarian; their titles indicate that they dealt with Greek pastimes, the history of Roman spectacles and shows, the Roman year, critical signs in books, the terminology of clothing, oaths and imprecations and their origin, Roman customs and a defense of Cicero's *De republica* (probably of its style, not its politics). Other sources refer to similar works on famous courtesans, physical defects, the growth of the civil service, and on kings. An encyclopaedia like Pliny's *Natural History,* called *Prata* ("Meadows"), was attributed to him and often quoted in late antiquity; some of the works mentioned above may have been subsections of this.

However, Suetonius' main works were biographical: the *De vita Caesarum* and the *De viris illustribus*. The latter was a collection of short biographies of celebrated literary figures of Rome, divided into books on poets, orators, historians, teachers (*grammatici* and *rhetores*) and perhaps philosophers. There survive the whole of the *De grammaticis* and the preface and first five lives of the *De rhetoribus;* in addition, the lives attached to manuscripts of several famous poets derive from Suetonius' book, especially those of Horace and Lucan. The life of Terence that begins Aelius Donatus' commentary on Terence comes from the same source, and so do the facts (but not the padding) in Donatus' life of Virgil. Since, in addition, the notices about writers inserted by St. Jerome in his Latin version of Eusebius' chronicle come from Suetonius, it is fair to say that almost all of what little is known about the lives of Rome's eminent authors is owed to him.

*Lives of the Caesars.*—Nevertheless, it is for the *Lives of the Caesars,* from Julius Caesar to Domitian, that Suetonius is famous. Upon them (along with the works of Tacitus) is largely based that vivid picture of Roman society and its leaders, morally and politically decadent, which dominated historical thought until modern times when the discovery of nonliterary sources of evidence did something to modify it. Moreover, under the influence of the *Lives,* much of later Roman historical writing was directed, to its detriment, into the biographical channel. They are organized not chronologically but by topics (the family background of the emperor, his career before accession, his public actions, his private life, appearance and personality and his death), a procedure more antiquarian than historical; they are full of scandalous gossip; and on the empire in general—its growth, administration and defense—they are largely silent. However, Suetonius exhibits compensating merits, quite apart from the fact that he was not aiming to write history and that the gossip and the lampoons are, in their way, valuable historical evidence. He is free from the bias of the senatorial class which distorts much Roman historical writing, and he is commendably willing to quote documents verbatim.

The earlier *Lives* down to Nero (especially the first two) are much the fullest; for that period a mass of sources was available, already collected and published, whereas for the Flavian period original research had to be done. It is surprising that Suetonius, who, in his position *a studiis,* was ideally placed for the necessary research, should have failed just in this (he quotes no original sources in his account of the Flavians); and the opinion is held by some that he made no attempt to investigate any sources himself but took everything from existing collections. However, it may be that as an antiquarian he was drawn to the documentary byways of the earlier age and had less interest in the Flavian emperors, and it seems likely that posterity owes to his brief tenure of the post *a studiis* such immensely valuable pieces of historical material as imperial wills and private letters.

Suetonius was not incapable of critical analysis of his sources, but he exercised it only on minutiae. He was trying to evaluate the personalities of individuals in terms of the standards and traditional interests of Roman public life and society; and he was ready, like Plutarch, to press into service the "characteristic anecdote," without exhaustive inquiry into its authenticity. His pen pictures of the habits and appearance of the emperors are invaluable; but the "rubric" method of composition made it impossible for him to analyze the development of their different characters.

The *Lives* are exciting to read. Suetonius avoids the excesses of archaism and preciosity to which many authors of his day were prone. He writes with firmness and brevity; he loves the *mot juste,* the Greek word for a Greek thing, the correct technicality (this was the direction in which his interests lay, as can be seen from the titles of his lost works); and his use of this precise vocabulary enhances his pictorial vividness. Above all, he is unrhetorical and unpretentious, not shrinking from bald lists of facts where they are appropriate, but capable of molding complex events into lucid, well-designed periodic sentences.

Bibliography.—*Editions:* For the whole extant works, *see* K. L. Roth (ed.), in the "Teubner Series" (1858); for the *Lives of the Caesars,* see M. Ihm (ed.), in the "Teubner Series" (1907; minor ed., 1923); J. C. Rolfe (ed.), in the "Loeb Series," with Eng. trans., 2 vol. (1914); H. Ailloud (ed.), in the "Budé Series," with French trans. (1931–32). All the minor works were edited by A. Reifferscheid (1860); the *De grammaticis* and *De rhetoribus* by R. P. Robinson (1922); the *De poetis* by A. Rostagni (1956); *Index verborum* by A. A. Howard and C. N. Jackson (1922).

*English Translations:* The *Lives of the Caesars* were translated by Philemon Holland (1606; often reprinted) and R. Graves (1957).

*General:* On Suetonius' life, works and place in the history of ancient biography *see* A. Macé, *Essai sur Suétone* (1900); G. Funaioli in Pauly-Wissowa, *Real-Encyclopädie der classischen Altertumswissenschaft,* vol. iv, 2nd series (1931); W. Steidle, "Sueton und die antike Biographie," in *Zetemata,* vol. i (1951); R. Syme, *Tacitus,* pp. 501–502, 778–782 (1958). (J. A. Cr.)

**SUEZ** (as Suways), the name of a town and governorate in Egypt, and of a gulf of the Red Sea at the head of which they are situated. With Bur Tawfiq (Port Tewfik, included in the governorate) they lie at the southern terminus of the Suez Canal (*q.v.*), where it joins the Gulf of Suez.

**Governorate and Town of Suez.**—The area of the governorate is 119 sq.mi. (307 sq.km.), and the population (1960 census) was 203,610. The governorate is surrounded by desert and for its water supply relies upon the Sweet Water Canal (opened 1863), which leaves the Nile at Cairo as the Ismailia Canal (Tur'at al Isma'iliyah). Bur Tawfiq, connected with Suez by an embankment, is a creation of the former Suez Canal Company. The harbour is built on land reclaimed from the sea and includes a dry dock 410 ft. (125 m.) long, 100 ft. (30 m.) wide, and 36 ft. (11 m.) deep. There are large quays and separate basins for warships and merchant ships, and the roadstead at the mouth of the canal provides ample room for the assembly of convoys for transshipment.

The site of Suez as a terminus to the old route between Cairo and the Red Sea has long been settled. The Greek settlement of Clysma became in the 7th century the Muslim Kolzum, standing at the southern end of the canal then joining the Red Sea and the Nile. After the Ottoman conquest of Egypt in the 16th century, Suez became a naval as well as a trading station, where fleets were equipped that rivaled the Portuguese for mastery of the Indian Ocean.

An overland mail route from Egypt to India (organized by Thomas Waghorn), including the desert section from Cairo to Suez, was opened in 1837, and in 1857 a direct railway over this route was completed. A further rail link with Cairo via Ismailia was constructed in 1868; this, with the opening of the Suez Canal in 1869, gave new life to the declining settlement. A road now parallels the direct railway. Two pipelines convey refined products and crude oil to Cairo from the refineries and bunkers at Suez. The expansion of the workshops of the Suez Canal Company and the establishment of two oil refineries and an artificial fertilizer factory have brought some diversification to the economy. Most of the 150,000,000 tons of shipping handled annually by Bur Tawfiq is in transit through the canal.

Suez is the port of departure for the pilgrims' sea voyage to Jidda (the port for Mecca, on the Arabian coast), and Ash Shatt, opposite Bur Tawfiq, is a quarantine station for pilgrims returning from Mecca.

**Gulf of Suez.**—This northwesterly arm of the Red Sea separates Africa proper from the Sinai Peninsula and is linked to the Mediterranean by the Suez Canal. Its length, from its mouth at the Strait of Jubal to its head at the town of Suez, is 195 mi. (314 km.). The width of the Strait of Jubal, between Cape Muhammad, the most southerly point of the Sinai Peninsula, and Shadwan Island, is 20 mi. (32 km.; from mainland to mainland, 42 mi. [68 km.]). The gulf is shallow, its maximum depth being about 120 ft. (37 m.). It narrows in four places, being at its narrowest 12 mi. wide.

The Gulf of Suez dates initially from the Oligocene Period,

when sporadic elevations of the land accompanied by great fracturing began the formation of the Red Sea Basin. The great structural depression of the Red Sea-Gulf of Aqaba-Gulf of Suez, between the two ancient Archean blocks of Arabia and North Africa, was formed in the subsequent Miocene and Pliocene periods of the Tertiary Age. The Gulf of Suez, a submerged rift valley, is a continuation of the main Red Sea rift, which is part of the rift system extending from Syria south to Malawi (*see* GREAT RIFT VALLEY). Igneous and metamorphic rocks of the Archean basement flank the southern half of the gulf, although for the most part they are masked by younger limestones and sandstones. Step faulting is severe on the Sinai side, while the strata of the African mainland sag rather than fracture. The shallow Gulf of Suez slopes down regularly to the Red Sea, where, at the Strait of Jubal, there is a sudden drop to a depth of over 3,000 ft. Coral reefs have been built up in the shallow coastal waters, and barrier reefs fringe the island groups at the entrance.

The shores of the gulf are steep only where the older rocks outcrop, as along the central Sinai coast; for the most part the bordering high land is fringed by a waterless coastal plain up to 15 mi. wide dissected by the wadis of occasional or relict streams. There are few harbours, but some capes afford shelter. Settlements are confined to a few fishing and mining villages, notably, on the African mainland coast, Al Ghurdaqah (Hurghada; pop. 4,300) and Ras Gharib (3,800) serving the nearby oil fields. On the Sinai coast the harbour of Abu Zanimah, considered the best on either side of the gulf, serves (by wire ropeway) the neighbouring Umm Bogma (Bujmah) manganese mines. (A. B. M.)

**SUEZ CANAL,** a sea-level waterway, cut through the Isthmus of Suez in the United Arab Republic and connecting Suez on the Red Sea with Port Said on the Mediterranean. It is the shortest maritime route between Europe and the lands lying round the Indian and western Pacific oceans and is normally one of the world's most heavily used shipping lanes.

In ancient Egyptian times, possibly in the reign of the pharaoh Sesostris I (early 20th century B.C.), a freshwater canal was dug from the Nile Delta to a point on the Red Sea near the present port of Suez. Its restoration was begun by the pharaoh Necho II about 600 B.C. and completed about 500 B.C. by the Persian conqueror Darius I. During the succeeding Ptolemaic and Roman occupations this canal was several times restored and abandoned. In the 7th century A.D. the Arab commander of Lower Egypt, Amr ibn al-As, reopened this ancient waterway to facilitate the transport of grain from the Nile Valley for shipment to Mecca. In the 8th century the caliph al-Mansur had part of it blocked for military reasons, and the whole canal thereafter fell into final disuse.

**Maritime Canal Projects.**—Among the Venetians in the 15th century and the French in the 17th and 18th centuries were writers who speculated upon the possibility of making a canal through the isthmus. A canal there would make it possible for ships of their nations to sail directly from the Mediterranean to the Indian Ocean and so dispute the monopoly of the East Indian trade that had been won first by the Portuguese, then by the Dutch, and finally by the English, all of whom used the route around the Cape of Good Hope. These schemes came to nothing.

It was not until the French occupation of Egypt (1798–1801) that the first survey was made across the isthmus. Bonaparte, commander of the French expedition, and a group of French officers and scientists spent several days there. J. M. Le Père, Bonaparte's chief lines-of-communication engineer, made a superficial survey of the country between Suez and the site of the ancient city of Pelusium, 20 mi. (32 km.) SE of the present Port Said. He erroneously calculated that the level of the Red Sea was 32 ft. 6 in. (10 m.) higher at high tide than the Mediterranean at low tide. Considering the adverse conditions under which the French surveyors worked, and the prevailing belief in the disparity of levels of the two seas, the error was excusable. Le Père's assumption that there was a considerable difference in the levels of the two seas, and that the construction of a lockless canal was therefore impossible, was uncritically accepted by a succession of subsequent authors of canal projects.

The advent of the steamship and the increasing tonnage and speed of steam vessels drew attention to the advantages of a Suez canal. Technical opinion was long divided between the merits of a saltwater canal through the narrowest part of the isthmus and a freshwater canal, supplied from the Nile, between Alexandria and Suez. A third proposed means of communication between the two seas was by a composite river and road route. The opening of the Mahmudiya Canal in 1820 placed Alexandria in direct river

THE SUEZ CANAL

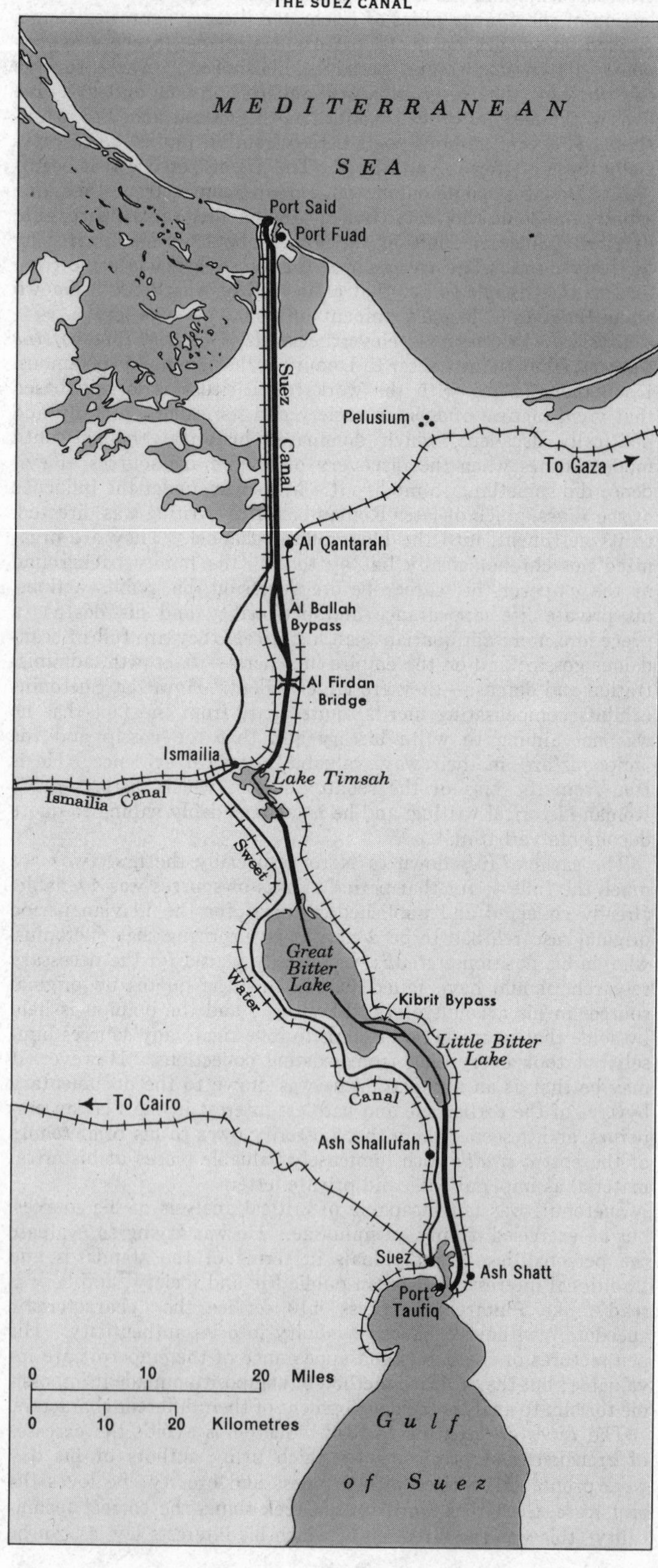

communication with Cairo and made this overland route, pioneered in 1829 by Lieut. T. Waghorn, a serious, if temporary, competitor to the canal project. In 1830, however, the British government sent Capt. (afterward Gen.) F. R. Chesney to survey the terrain and report on the feasibility of a ship canal. Chesney found only a slight difference in levels between the Red Sea and the Mediterranean, proving that a lockless canal was an engineering possibility. But his report, laid before a select committee of the British Parliament, was for the time forgotten.

A group of engineers, followers of the sociological principles of Claude Henri de Rouvroy Saint-Simon (*q.v.*), with Barthélemy Prosper Enfantin (*q.v.*) at their head, went to Egypt in 1833 and placed before the viceroy a proposal for a Suez canal which the viceroy rejected. In 1841 Arthur Anderson, managing director of the Peninsular and Oriental Steam Navigation Company, with L. M. A. Linant de Bellefonds (Linant Bey), the future Egyptian minister of public works, and two merchants in Egypt, the brothers J. and G. Gliddon, formed a company to make a technical study for the construction of a sea-level canal between Suez and a site on the Mediterranean near Pelusium. The company based its proposals on the detailed surveys of Linant, who confirmed the accuracy of Chesney's conclusions. Anderson's pamphlet *Observations on the Practicability and Utility of Opening a Communication Between the Red Sea and the Mediterranean by a Ship-Canal* (1843) impressed world shipping opinion.

A public company of international composition, the Société d'Études pour le Canal de Suez, was formed on Enfantin's initiative in 1846 with an initial capital of Fr. 150,000. Among its 12 directors was Robert Stephenson, a British engineer; Alois von Negrelli, a distinguished Austrian railway engineer of Italian descent; and Linant. The company divided itself into national groups, the British with Stephenson as their engineer, the Austro-German with Negrelli, and the French with Paulin Talabot supported by the chambers of commerce of Lyons and Marseilles. The British group failed to send a surveyor to the site, but Stephenson sent plans. With his subsequent appointment as engineer in chief of the Alexandria-Cairo Railway construction he ceased his somewhat passive connection with the canal project. Talabot projected a freshwater canal between Alexandria and Suez via the Nile barrage slightly downstream of Cairo. Two other Frenchmen, the brothers A. and E. Barrault, preferred a trace which would describe a great arc from Alexandria eastward through the Nile Delta inland then southward, following the route of the present canal, from Al Qantarah to Suez. Of all the alternative routes suggested to the company, that of Negrelli came nearest to the plan finally adopted.

**The Suez Canal Company Formed.**—At this point Ferdinand Marie, vicomte de Lesseps (*q.v.*), enters the story of the canal. He had served in Egypt as a junior member of the French diplomatic service during 1833–37 and had befriended Mohammed Said Pasha, the future viceroy of Egypt. He had met Waghorn and had been inspired by the imaginative engineering genius of Enfantin. Further, he had studied the surveys of Linant and Negrelli. His opportunity came in 1854 when Said succeeded to the viceroyalty of Egypt. Lesseps, who had retired from the French diplomatic service, hurried to Egypt to congratulate the new viceroy and gain his support for a Suez canal. On Nov. 15, 1854, he unfolded his plan to Said, who at once accepted it. On November 30 a preliminary draft of a concession was signed, subject to ratification by the Ottoman government. The original Turkish text of this agreement accorded less sweeping powers than did the French version. Lesseps' plan closely followed that of Negrelli for the Société d'Études of 1846. The concession provided for the creation of an international enterprise, a Compagnie Universelle du Canal Maritime de Suez, with a chairman appointed by the Egyptian government and a board of directors to be drawn from the chief subscribing nationalities. The French emperor Napoleon III offered Lesseps encouragement and, if necessary, support.

Lesseps well understood the importance of public sympathy, and his pamphlet *The Isthmus of Suez Question,* published in French and English in 1855, was well received. In 1856 the Suez Canal Company, as it came to be known in the English-speaking world, issued its own journal, *L'Isthme de Suez,* which changed its title in 1869 to *Le Canal de Suez.* With skilful diplomacy the company wooed shipping interests and chambers of commerce and in 1855 invited an international commission of eminent engineers and naval officers to pronounce upon the practicability of the project. The commission met in October of that year and sent a subcommittee to Egypt to make studies on the site.

The plans drawn up by Linant and E. Mougel the year previously were for a canal 91 mi. (146 km.) long, from Suez through the Bitter Lakes to Pelusium, with a lock at each end, which would give a minimum draft of 26 ft. (7.9 m.). The acceptance of their plan would have rendered subsequent widening difficult, and severely limited the size of ships using the canal. In January 1856 the commission presented Said Pasha with a report, published in 1857, in which they recommended a sea-level lockless canal between Suez and the Gulf of Pelusium at an estimated cost of not more than Fr. 200,000,000. Their report removed any lingering doubts as to the technical practicability of the project.

The original act of concession of 1854 was replaced by a more precise and detailed document dated Jan. 5, 1856, to which the statutes of the Suez Canal Company were annexed. By the new act the canal, subject to the approval of the viceroy's sovereign, the Ottoman sultan, was to be open at all times to all merchant ships without distinction or discrimination. The company was empowered to fix and levy transit dues at defined maximum rates. The concession was to run for 99 years from the date on which the canal was opened for navigation, at the end of which period, in the absence of other subsequent arrangements, the canal was to pass to the ownership of the Egyptian government. In addition to the excavation of the maritime canal, the company undertook to excavate a freshwater canal from the Nile to the canal zone. The company's central offices were to be located at Alexandria with administrative headquarters in Paris. The capital of the company was fixed at Fr. 200,000,000 divided into shares of Fr. 500 each. The Egyptian government was to receive 15% of the net profits as a first charge on the company's revenues. The stock issue was only partly successful. France provided half the capital; neither Britain nor the United States subscribed at all, and Said came to the rescue by subscribing Fr. 60,000,000. The response was sufficient to provide the company with its minimum capital requirements, and the directors decided not to wait for the sultan's approval. On April 25, 1859, Lesseps turned the first spadeful of sand at the site of the future Port Said.

**Construction of the Canal.**—The British government, anxious for the security of its communications with India and suspicious of French intentions, opposed the construction of the canal by every means within its power, despite the generally favourable attitude to the canal adopted by British shipping and engineering interests.

The Sweet Water Canal, to supply the installations and towns under construction in the canal zone, was dug during 1858–63 from the Nile at Bulaq, a part of Cairo, to Ismailia, whence a branch was extended southward to Suez. This canal not only provided a channel for the navigation of small ships but also made possible the irrigation of much fertile land along its course.

Preliminary work occupied the first two years, 1859–61, except at Port Said, where land reclamation and harbour work were begun in 1859 by the engineer F. A. T. Laroche. The site chosen for the Mediterranean entrance to the canal, though not the nearest point to Suez, possessed a deeper sea approach than any other site along the neighbouring coast. The quay walls were faced by stone quarried near Alexandria and brought expensively by sea. Concrete blocks for the breakwaters were made at Port Said by Dussaud Frères of Marseilles. By 1868 two breakwaters had been built, on the western mole of which was later placed a colossal statue of Lesseps by E. Fremiet; it was unveiled in 1899 and demolished by the Egyptians in 1956. Water for the workers at Port Said was first produced by condensers, but during 1864–66 two ten-inch (254-mm.) pipes were laid along the artificial causeway from pumps on the Sweet Water Canal at Ismailia. In 1885 these were replaced by an extension of the Sweet Water Canal (named the Abbasiyah Canal) from Ismailia to Port Said.

Said's death in 1863 removed a staunch, if not altogether uncritical, ally from Lesseps' side. Though enthusiastic for the canal project and personally friendly to Lesseps, Said's successor, Ismail, sought to secure from the Suez Canal Company better conditions for Egypt and himself than were obtained under Said's concession. The company resisted Ismail's demand for the cancellation of Said's undertaking to provide free labour by relays of conscripted Egyptian peasants. With the agreement of the Ottoman government the two parties submitted the dispute to the arbitration of Napoleon III. Under the terms of the arbitration award of July 1864, confirmed by an agreement of Feb. 22, 1866, between Ismail and the company, the latter abandoned its title to 148,000 ac. (approximately 60,000 ha.) of irrigable land and subsidiary freshwater canals and its claim to free labour against a total compensation of Fr. 84,000,000 repayable over a period of 15 years. Though the award was criticized at the time and later as unduly favourable to the company, the finances of which were thereby stabilized, Egypt gained by the company's surrender of property in the canal zone which might well have proved a considerable political embarrassment to both parties. After long delay the sultan ratified the award on March 19, 1866. The company's position was then finally legalized, and the British government, the last powerful opponent of the project, conceded defeat and made active preparations for the opening of the canal by strengthening the dockyard and defenses of Malta.

The organization of work was modified as the construction proceeded. The company retained control of administration and technical management, planning, and the provision of major equipment, while excavation and masonry were entrusted to contractors. At first the company intended to hand over the entire construction to A. Hardon as contractor in chief, but this proved unsatisfactory. The Hardon contract was canceled in 1863, and Hardon was indemnified. From 1862 the technical direction was under F. P. Voisin Bey as chief administrator. After a brief period during which the company undertook direct work, the construction was shared among four contracting firms, each of which undertook to excavate a section of the canal. The first, Dussaud Frères, undertook the harbour works at Port Said; the second, W. Aiton, a Clydeside contractor, was entrusted with the excavation of the 37 mi. (60 km.) of canal south from Port Said; the third contract, 8 mi. (13 km.) of difficult, rocky terrain, was given to A. Couvreux; and the fourth, the largest contract, the excavation of the section between Lake Timsah and Suez, was given to the firm of P. Borel and A. Lavalley, which later took over Aiton's contract as well.

Before the arbitration award of 1866 was promulgated, a maximum labour force of 25,000 Egyptian workmen was employed. After the award, mechanical dredgers of a total of 10,000 h.p. and capable of moving 2,615,900 cu.yd. (2,000,000 cu.m.) of earth a month drastically reduced the number of labourers needed. From then on, an average force of 10,000 labourers and 8,000 European artisans was maintained. The partial substitution of voluntary labour and machines for low-grade forced labour and manual work made it possible to employ more efficient methods. As dredging was found to be cheaper than dry excavation, Borel and Lavalley first flooded sections with water and then dredged. At one time this firm was operating 60 dredgers. Special machinery, such as long-arm dredgers and machines for cutting rock under water, was devised. A particularly difficult section, the rock shelf at Ash Shallufah at the south end of the canal, was removed by 1,300 Sardinian quarrymen. The construction of the canal attracted skilled and unskilled labour from all parts of the Mediterranean and the Middle East.

In February 1862 the Sweet Water Canal reached Lake Timsah and made possible the establishment of a large construction camp at Ismailia. A small pilot saltwater canal from Port Said reached the lake in the following November, by which time excavation was in full swing along the entire construction. On March 19, 1869, the waters of the Mediterranean were admitted to the Bitter Lakes, which within a few weeks became filled and thereby converted into a navigable channel between the two excavated extremities of the canal. By the early autumn, construction was virtually completed from Port Said to Suez. A total of 97,000,000 cu.yd. (74,162,000 cu.m.) of earth had been excavated. The estimated cost of construction had been not more than Fr. 200,000,000; the actual cost to the end of 1869 was almost Fr. 433,000,000. The work had taken ten years, against an estimate of six.

On Nov. 17, 1869, the canal was officially opened in the presence of foreign sovereigns and princes, statesmen, and notables. A procession of ships headed by the French imperial yacht "l'Aigle," with the empress Eugénie on board, passed through the canal. Several thousand guests representing a cross section of European and Middle Eastern society were invited to the celebrations by the khedive Ismail. Among them were the Algerian patriot and exile 'Abd-el-Kader, the playwright Henrik Ibsen, the novelist Théophile Gautier, and the painter Eugène Fromentin, with a crowd of journalists, military and naval officers, and a representative of the Jockey Club de Paris. Besides a series of lavish celebrations in the canal zone and tours in the Nile Valley, an operatic season was arranged in Cairo, and Verdi's opera *Aida* was commissioned for the occasion, though it was not produced until 1871.

The opening of the Suez Canal deprived the Cairo-Suez Railway of most of its economic justification. It was abandoned in 1868 in favour of a new line, longer but serving fertile country, from Cairo to Suez by way of Ismailia, which was opened in the same year. The subsequent growth of the trade of Suez, however, caused the abandoned direct line to be restored in 1930.

After a short period of uncertainty the tonnage of general shipping using the canal steadily increased. In 1892 a new class of traffic appeared when a tanker passed through the canal with a cargo of oil from the Caucasus to the Far East. In 1900 the annual tanker transits had risen to 88.

**International Status.**—The international status of the Suez Canal was long undefined. In 1875 the British government, on the initiative of the prime minister, Lord Beaconsfield, acquired 176,602 Suez Canal shares held by the khedive Ismail for £4,080,000, thus making Britain the largest single shareholder in the company. During the Egyptian nationalist revolt led by Arabi Pasha in 1882, British forces landed at several points on the canal, which for three days was denied to the passage of merchant ships. Although the British action was legalized by a decree of the khedive of Egypt authorizing the British to occupy all the points necessary for the reestablishment of order in the country, Lesseps instructed the canal employees to abandon their work and protested against the British action.

The operation of the canal was complicated by problems arising from the increase of traffic passing through and by disputes between shippers and the company regarding dues. A petition representing over half of the tonnage of shipping using the canal was presented to the British government in 1883 with a request for the construction of a second canal to accommodate the increasing traffic. The government decided in favour of widening and deepening the existing channel, a solution which the company adopted. This, however, still left the international status of the canal unsettled. In 1883 the British government proposed that the canal should remain unfortified, free for the passage of all ships in peace and in war, but that during hostilities there should be a limitation of the period during which a belligerent warship could remain in the canal. A conference of international experts met in 1885 to settle the canal's international status but failed to reach agreement. After lengthy negotiations a convention was signed at Constantinople in 1888 by which the canal was made a corridor for all ships of all nations in peace and in war; acts of hostility in its waters were forbidden.

Britain was not at first a party to the whole 1888 convention, and it was not until the signature of the Anglo-French Agreement of 1904 that it declared its complete adhesion. Spanish warships had been denied transit through the canal during the Spanish-American War of 1898, and a testing time for the agreement came in 1905 during the Russo-Japanese War when a squadron of the Russian Navy passed through the canal without incident, an operation repeated by Italian vessels during the Italo-Turkish War of 1911–12.

The canal was in theory open to all belligerents during World

Wars I and II. In fact, however, the naval and military superiority of the Allied forces in Egypt and the canal zone, and the Allies' decision that there should be no right of asylum within its waters, denied the effective use of the canal to enemy shipping. In the face of much difficulty the Suez Canal Company endeavoured to maintain neutrality during both wars. During World War I, in February 1915, there was heavy ground fighting on the east bank between Ismailia and Suez when a Turkish expedition endeavoured to penetrate the canal defenses. In the course of World War II the canal was repeatedly attacked from the air, with surprisingly little delay to traffic or damage to ships. After the armistice between Israel and its Arab opponents in 1949, Egypt denied Israeli ships access to the canal and detained ships suspected of carrying cargoes to and from Israeli ports. Though at the end of both wars the canal defenses were removed and the canal zone was unfortified, British troops were maintained in the zone in varying strengths until 1956.

**Relations with Egypt.**—Relations between the Suez Canal Company and the Egyptian government were from time to time complicated by the presence on Egyptian soil of an international undertaking not fully accountable to Egypt. In 1909 the company applied for an extension of the canal concession for a further period of 40 years from 1968, but the Egyptian government rejected the application. Although the Egyptian representation on the board of the company had progressively increased, there were in 1955 only 5 Egyptian directors as compared with 16 French, 9 British, one Dutch, and one U.S. director.

It was not until July 26, 1956, that a major crisis arose between the parties. On that date, without prior warning, the Egyptian government, under the leadership of Pres. Gamal Abd-al-Nasser (*q.v.*), announced the nationalization of the assets in Egypt of the Suez Canal Company, a unilateral act of seizure embodied in Egyptian Law No. 285 of that year. The management of the undertaking was vested in a state organ created for the purpose, the Suez Canal Authority, which absorbed all the functions of the former company in Egypt. As a result of the long experience of Egyptian technical administrators, technicians and artisans, floating and shore staff, in maintaining public works in the Nile Valley and harbour installations at the Egyptian ports, the transfer of control was effected with ease.

Twice within 11 years, in 1956 and 1967, the canal was closed to the world's shipping by the effects of war. The story of these events is told in full in EGYPT: *History* and ISRAEL: *History*.

The physical result on the canal of the 1956 closure was that for several months it was blocked by sunken ships. After the UN expeditionary force had arrived in the canal zone in November 1956 the Egyptian government appealed to the UN for help in clearing the canal. The task was carried out with the utmost expedition under the direction of Lieut. Gen. R. A. Wheeler, formerly of the U.S. Army Corps of Engineers. By April 1957 all obstacles had been removed and the canal was open to traffic.

In July 1958 the former Compagnie Universelle du Canal Maritime de Suez (Suez Canal Company), renamed Compagnie Financière de Suez (Suez Finance Company), registered in Paris, concluded an agreement with the Egyptian government on compensation. The company was awarded slightly over £E.28,000,000 for the loss of the canal. On Jan. 1, 1963, the United Arab Republic paid the company the final installment of £E.4,000,000.

The outbreak of war between Israel and the U.A.R. in June 1967 had an immediate and disastrous effect upon the operation of the canal. On June 6, the day following the outbreak of hostilities, the U.A.R. government closed the canal, which was again blocked by the sinking of ships, trapping a number of neutral vessels which were in transit at the time.

**Facts About the Suez Canal.**—The Suez Canal is 101 mi. (162.5 km.) long. The length of the excavated section is 92 mi. (148 km.). The distance of 9 mi. (14 km.) through the artificially raised water level in the Bitter Lakes required little or no dredging. When first opened, the minimum depth along $2\frac{1}{2}$ mi. of the canal was less than 23 ft. (7 m.) at low tide, and the minimum width was 72 ft. (22 m.). After successive widenings and deepenings, the width in 1963 was nowhere less than 179 ft. (55 m.) at a depth of 33 ft. (10 m.) at the banks, and the minimum depth in the channel at low tide was 40 ft. (12 m.). Except in the Bitter Lakes the canal is lined by revetments to protect the banks from ships' wash. The channel allows the passage of vessels having drafts up to 37 ft. (11 m.), and dredging has been undertaken to increase the maximum draft to 40 ft. The maximum permissible speed for laden tankers is 8 mi. (13 km.) an hour and for vessels in cargo or ballast 8.6 mi. (14 km.) an hour. The average transit time has been reduced over the years from 48 to about 15 hours. Bypasses for ships are at Port Said, Al Ballah, and Kibrit. The development plans disrupted by the Israeli-Arab War of 1967 envisaged a waterway capacity for fully laden oil tankers of about 110,000 tons with provision for tankers of up to about 200,000 tons to transit the canal in ballast.

For years after the opening of the canal Port Said was without railway communication with the rest of Egypt. In consequence the channel between Port Said and Ismailia was impeded by numerous small pilotage and passenger craft which became a danger to ships using the canal. In 1891 the Egyptian government authorized the Suez Canal Company to lay a private narrow-gauge railway between Port Said and Ismailia, the nearest station on the state railway, for carriage of passengers, mail, and company's supplies. The light railway was opened for traffic in December 1893. In 1902 the government replaced it by extending the main line northward from Ismailia. The railway track from Cairo was doubled to Ismailia by 1916 and to Al Firdan by 1917. The railway to As Salihiyah was extended to Al Qantarah in 1916 but was dismantled in 1918.

A swing bridge over the canal carrying a railway toward Palestine was erected in 1916 and removed at the request of the Suez Canal Company after the armistice in 1918. The bridge was reerected during World War II and, after the war, once again removed; railway vehicles thereafter were ferried across the canal. A road and rail swing bridge at Al Firdan, at kilometre 68, carrying the railway to Gaza, was opened in 1954. As the distance between the two piers of the bridge gave an opening of only 197 ft. (approximately 60 m.) for the passage of ships, the bridge formed a bottleneck in the canal and stultified the widening of the channel. It was therefore replaced by a second road and rail bridge, opened in 1964, with approaches sufficiently wide to allow a navigable channel of approximately 485 ft. (148 m.) width.

Ismailia (*q.v.*), laid out in 1863, is the headquarters of the Suez Canal Authority and the location of various installations, including a pilotage tower and a research centre.

The table shows the number and tonnage of ships and the weight of goods that passed through the canal in selected years:

*Shipping Through the Suez Canal*

| Ships and Cargoes | 1913 | 1938 | 1955 | 1965 | 1966 |
|---|---|---|---|---|---|
| Ships in transit | | | | | |
| Number of transits | 5,085 | 6,171 | 14,666 | 20,289 | 21,250* |
| Net tonnage (in 000s) | 20,000 | 34,418 | 115,756 | 246,817 | 279,331 |
| Goods in transit (in 000 metric tons) | | | | | |
| Southward | 11,320 | 7,768 | 20,082 | 42,001 | 47,700 |
| Northward | 14,455 | 21,011 | 87,426 | 183,441 | 194,200 |
| Total | 25,775 | 28,779 | 107,508 | 225,442 | 241,900† |

*Compared with 12,013 transits through the Panama Canal.
†Compared with 81,713,000 long tons through the Panama Canal (1 metric ton=2,204 lb.; 1 long ton=2,240 lb.).

A marked feature of canal traffic since 1914 has been the increasing number and size of big ships and the increasing percentage of oil carried. In 1966 no fewer than 907 vessels exceeding 40,000 tons passed through the canal while 166,718,000 tons of petroleum products passed through northward and 8,953,000 tons passed southward. Receipts from canal dues and services in 1966 reached the figure of £E.95,167,000 (£76,137,000).

*See* also references under "Suez Canal" in the Index.

BIBLIOGRAPHY.—J. M. Le Père, "Mémoire sur la communication de la mer des Indes à la Méditerranée par la mer Rouge et l'isthme de Soueys," *Description de l'Égypte: État moderne,* tom i (1809); F. M. de Lesseps, *Percement de l'isthme de Suez, exposé et documents officiels,* 6 vol. (1855–69); J. Charles-Roux, *L'Isthme et le canal de Suez,* 2 vol. (1901); F. P. Voisin, *Le Canal de Suez,* 6 vol. (1902–06); A. T. Wilson, *The Suez Canal: Its Past, Present and Future,* 2nd ed. (1939); B.

Avram, *The Evolution of the Suez Canal Status from 1869 up to 1956: a Historico-Juridical Study* (1958); J. A. Obieta, *The International Status of the Suez Canal* (1960); B. B. Broms, *The Legal Status of the Suez Canal* (1961); E. Lauterpacht (ed.), *The Suez Canal Settlement: a Selection of Documents Relating to the Settlement of the Suez Canal Dispute . . . 1956– . . . 1959* (1960); J. Marlowe, *World Ditch: the Making of the Suez Canal* (1964); periodical reports of the Compagnie Universelle du Canal Maritime de Suez (1859–1956) and of the Suez Canal Authority (1957– ). (R. L. Hl.)

**SUFFOLK, EARLS AND DUKES OF.** The 1st earl of Suffolk, ROBERT DE UFFORD (1298–1369), was one of six new earls created by Edward III in 1337. After taking part in the arrest of Roger Mortimer, earl of March, at Nottingham Castle in October 1330, he became one of the king's most trusted commanders, diplomats, and councilors. The Uffords were a Suffolk landowning family recently risen to prominence; the 1st earl's father, Robert (1279–1316), who was summoned to Parliament as a baron in 1309, was the son of Robert de Ufford (d. 1298), twice justiciar of Ireland in Edward I's reign. Earl Robert fought at Crécy (1346) and Poitiers (1356) and served in almost every campaign between 1340 and 1360. His heir, WILLIAM (1339–82), 2nd earl, narrowly escaped capture by the East Anglian rebels in the Peasants' Revolt of 1381 and later took the lead in suppressing the insurrection in Suffolk. All Earl William's five children predeceased him; on his death the earldom became extinct, and the bulk of the de Ufford estates escheated to the crown.

The extinction of the de Ufford earls made possible the rapid rise of the de la Poles to magnate status; in August 1385, Richard II created MICHAEL DE LA POLE (*c.* 1330–1389) earl of Suffolk. Pole was the trusted adviser of Richard II, but was dismissed from his office of chancellor, impeached and sentenced to death. He escaped to France, however, where he died. In 1399 the earldom of Suffolk was restored to his son MICHAEL (*c.* 1361–1415), the third earl, who was killed at the battle of Agincourt. The earldom passed to his brother William. WILLIAM (1396–1450), 4th earl, was made a marquess in 1444 and duke of Suffolk in 1448 (*see* POLE; SUFFOLK, WILLIAM DE LA POLE, Duke of). JOHN DE LA POLE (1442–91/92), 2nd duke of Suffolk, was the son of the 1st duke by his wife, Alice Chaucer, granddaughter of the poet; he married Elizabeth (d. *c.* 1503), sister of the future Edward IV and Richard III, and survived the Wars of the Roses, having supported in turn Edward IV, Richard III, and Henry VII. His second but first surviving son, EDMUND (1471/72–1513), surrendered the dukedom in 1493 and became earl of Suffolk; he was attainted in 1504 (*see* POLE, RICHARD DE LA). The male line ended when William, the last survivor of Duke John's seven sons, died in the Tower of London in 1539.

The title of duke of Suffolk, revived by Henry VIII in 1514 for his favourite, CHARLES BRANDON (*c.* 1484–1545; *see* SUFFOLK, CHARLES BRANDON, 1st Duke of), became extinct on the death from the sweating sickness of Brandon's sons (by his fourth wife, Katherine Willoughby), Henry and Charles, on July 14, 1551. Frances, Brandon's elder daughter by his third wife, the king's younger sister Mary Tudor (d. 1533), had married HENRY GREY (1517–54), 3rd marquess of Dorset, a great-grandson of Edward IV's queen, Elizabeth Woodville. Well-educated and a strong Protestant, Dorset was a weak and ambitious man; he belonged to the party of John Dudley, duke of Northumberland, and was created duke of Suffolk on Oct. 11, 1551. He supported Northumberland's attempt to make his daughter Lady Jane Grey (1537–54) queen in July 1553, but he was quick to abandon her cause when the plot failed and was pardoned by Queen Mary. His opposition to the queen's plans for her Spanish marriage involved him in Sir Thomas Wyat's Rebellion in 1554; the dukedom again became extinct after his execution for treason on Feb. 23, 1554.

In 1603 THOMAS HOWARD (1561–1626), Lord Howard de Walden, second son of Thomas Howard (1538–72), 4th duke of Norfolk, was created earl of Suffolk by James I (*see* SUFFOLK, THOMAS HOWARD, 1st Earl of), and that branch of the Howard family has held the title ever since.

BIBLIOGRAPHY.—R. E. Chester Waters, *Genealogical Memoirs of the Extinct Family of Chester of Chicheley* (1878); G. H. Orpen, *Ireland Under the Normans,* vol. iii–iv (1911); J. G. Nichols (ed.), *The Chronicle of Queen Jane and of Two Years of Queen Mary* (1850).
(T. B. P.)

**SUFFOLK, CHARLES BRANDON,** 1ST DUKE OF (*c.* 1484–1545), English courtier, a personal friend of King Henry VIII, was the husband of Henry's sister Mary and grandfather of Lady Jane Grey. He was the younger son of William Brandon, Henry VII's standard-bearer, killed at the Battle of Bosworth (Aug. 22, 1485), allegedly by Richard III in person. A large, athletic man, young Brandon proved to be about the only member of Henry VIII's entourage capable of standing up to the king in the tourney, a fact which cemented their youthful friendship. On May 15, 1513, Brandon was created Viscount Lisle because (after the death in 1511 of his second wife, Anne Brown) he had contracted to marry Elizabeth Grey, viscountess Lisle in her own right. However, when she came of age she married Henry Courtenay, earl of Devon, to whom the viscountcy was transferred, and Henry instead made Brandon duke of Suffolk on Feb. 1, 1514.

The duke's matrimonial situation remained complicated. In October 1514, Henry VIII's sister Mary married the elderly Louis XII of France, who died within a few months. The English government then hoped to marry her to the new French king, Francis I, and early in 1515 sent Suffolk to promote the match. The choice was unfortunate, for Mary and Suffolk had long been in love, and Mary believed herself to have received a promise from Henry that after her first political marriage she should have a free choice. The pair married (1515) in Paris secretly, thereby incurring the dangers of the English treason law. Henry's wrath was apparently assuaged by Thomas Cardinal Wolsey (or so Wolsey later claimed), and Suffolk soon returned to favour. He had, however, to resolve the difficulty caused by his marriage to his first wife, Margaret Mortimer, who was still alive. Although this first marriage was declared null (*c.* 1507) by the London Archdeanery Court on the grounds of an alleged consanguinity, it was not until 1528 that a papal bull resolved the complications and secured the legitimacy of his marriage to Mary.

Suffolk's interests were those of a knightly courtier with military ambitions; all the evidence suggests that he was a handsome giant of solid stupidity. He proved his personal courage in the 1513 campaign against France; but given military command in 1523 and 1542–44 he displayed only incompetence. He played little part in politics or government, though he assisted in the move to overthrow Wolsey in 1529 and for a few years thereafter appeared to be among the leaders of the king's council. Henry made Suffolk responsible for controlling the shire from which he took his title and used him to balance the powerful interest of the Howard family in East Anglia. The dissolution of the monasteries (1536–40) enabled him to build up a sizable territorial estate in Suffolk, but by 1551 his three sons, one by Mary (d. 1533), and two by his fourth wife, Katherine Willoughby, were all dead, and the Brandon interest passed to the descendants of his paternal aunts. Frances, his eldest daughter by Mary, married Henry Grey, 3rd marquess of Dorset, and was the mother of Lady Jane Grey, *de facto* queen of England on Edward VI's death. Suffolk became lord president of the council in 1529 and great master of the household in 1540. He died at the palace in Guildford, Surrey, on Aug. 24, 1545. (G. R. E.)

**SUFFOLK, THOMAS HOWARD,** 1ST EARL OF (1561–1626), second son of Thomas Howard, 4th duke of Norfolk, was born on Aug. 24, 1561. He behaved very gallantly during the attack on the Spanish Armada. He commanded the expedition on which Sir Richard Grenville and the "Revenge" were lost (1591) and held commands in the Cadiz and Islands voyages (1596–97). Created Baron Howard de Walden in 1597 and earl of Suffolk in July 1603, he was lord chamberlain of the royal household from 1603 to 1614 and lord high treasurer from 1614 to 1618, when he was deprived of his office on a charge of misappropriating money. He was tried in the Star Chamber and was heavily fined.

Suffolk's second wife was Catherine (d. 1633), widow of Richard Rich, a woman whose avarice was partly responsible for her husband's downfall. She shared his trial and was certainly guilty of taking bribes from Spain. One of his three daughters was the notorious Frances Howard, who instigated the poisoning of Sir Thomas Overbury (*q.v.*). The earl died on May 28, 1626, in London. (R. B. Wm.)

**SUFFOLK, WILLIAM DE LA POLE,** DUKE OF (1396–1450), second son of Michael de la Pole, 2nd earl of Suffolk, served the early part of his career in the wars against France and the later years of his life in seeking peace with that country. He was born on Oct. 16, 1396, at Cotton, Suffolk. Suffolk served in all the later French campaigns of the reign of Henry V, and in spite of his youth held high command on the marches of Normandy in 1421–22. In 1423 he joined the earl of Salisbury in Champagne and shared his victory at Crevant. He fought under John, duke of Bedford, at Verneuil on Aug. 17, 1424, and throughout the next four years was Salisbury's principal lieutenant in the direction of the war. When Salisbury was killed before Orléans on Nov. 3, 1428, Suffolk succeeded to the command. After the siege was raised, Suffolk was defeated and taken prisoner by Jeanne d'Arc at Jargeau on June 12, 1429. He was soon ransomed, and during the next two years was again in command on the Norman frontier. He returned to England in Nov. 1431, after more than 14 years' continuous service in the field.

In the next decade, as a royal household official and a supporter of the predominant faction of Cardinal Beaufort, Suffolk acquired a considerable influence in the government, which he used mainly to further his own interests. Greedy and unscrupulous, he showed himself unusually grasping even in that mercenary age. He acquired a large number of wardships and offices of profit in the king's gift, and his agents made the heavy hand of his lordship felt throughout East Anglia, where his principal estates lay. It was not until 1443 that the retirement of Cardinal Beaufort brought Suffolk reluctantly to the forefront of politics. Like Beaufort, Suffolk had a genuine desire to achieve a peaceful settlement with France, but he had no clear and practical plan for obtaining peace without disgrace, and he shirked necessary but unpopular decisions. His first success (for which he was made a marquess) was the securing in 1444 of a two years' truce and the hand of Margaret of Anjou for Henry VI. Yet soon afterward the English government was forced to surrender Anjou and Maine in return for a further extension of the truce, a concession which increased Suffolk's growing unpopularity at home. Rumour, though without sufficient reason, made Suffolk responsible for the death of his rival, Humphrey, duke of Gloucester, in Feb. 1447. Another critic of the government, Richard, duke of York, was replaced in his French command by the incompetent Edmund Beaufort, duke of Somerset. Suffolk's promotion to a dukedom in 1448 marked the height of his power.

The difficulties of his position may have led him to give some countenance to a treacherous attack on Fougères during the time of truce (March 1449). The renewal of the war and the loss of all Normandy were its direct consequences. When parliament met in Nov. 1449, the whole Suffolk administration came under attack. The treasurer, Adam Moleyns, bishop of Chichester, was forced to resign, and on Feb. 7, 1450, the commons presented articles of accusation against Suffolk himself, dealing chiefly with alleged maladministration and the ill success of the French policy; there was a charge of aiming at the throne by the betrothal of his son to the little Margaret Beaufort. Suffolk denied the accusations. Ultimately the king sentenced him to banishment for five years. Suffolk left England on May 1. He was intercepted in the channel by the ship "Nicholas of the Tower," and next morning was beheaded in a little boat alongside.

Popular opinion at the time, followed by Yorkist chroniclers and Tudor historians, judged him a traitor, and later legend made him a paramour of Margaret of Anjou. These charges are not supported by any reliable evidence, and probably Suffolk was unfortunate in being made a scapegoat for an unpopular and corrupt administration and policies for which others were as much responsible as he.

Suffolk's wife, Alice, was widow of Thomas, earl of Salisbury, and granddaughter of Geoffrey Chaucer. By her he had an only son John, 2nd duke of Suffolk.

BIBLIOGRAPHY.—Suffolk's character and policy have been the subject of much discussion: *see* W. Stubbs, *Constitutional History of England* (1880); C. Oman, *The Political History of England,* vol. vi (1906); C. L. Kingsford, *Prejudice and Promise in Fifteenth Century England* (1925); K. B. McFarlane in *Cambridge Medieval History,* vol. vii (1936). Besides the authorities for his career listed in the *Dictionary of National Biography,* reference should be made to the series of *Calendars* of Patent and Close Rolls. (C. D. R.)

**SUFFOLK,** an eastern county of England, is bounded north by Norfolk, south by Essex, west by Cambridgeshire and the Isle of Ely, and east by the North Sea. Its area is 1,481.7 sq.mi. including Ipswich, the county town.

**Physical Geography.**—The general contour of the county is that of a low-lying plateau, but near Denston, in the southwest, the ground rises to over 400 ft. (122 m.). The scenery is varied. In the northwest is the Breckland where the Upper Chalk escarpment of the Chilterns, which continues through Suffolk and on to the Lincolnshire Wolds, is covered by light sands which would be blown away but for their covering of heath. Many plants and insects native to this area are found nowhere else, and the abundance of flints made Brandon for centuries the centre of a flint-knapping industry, now obsolete. The heath is in part giving place to the coniferous plantations of the Forestry Commission.

To the east the chalk is overlaid by the London clay and the crag deposits of the Pliocene, the rich and specialized fauna of which attracts paleontologists throughout the world. These formations are themselves overlaid first by a broad belt of glacial boulder clay running from the northeast to the southwest of the county, and second, near the coast, by sands and gravels. The boulder clay region, known in part as "High Suffolk," was once blanketed by forest but is now fertile farmland. It is intersected by many shallow river valleys and is notable for its fine villages and small towns such as Chelsworth, Kersey, and Lavenham in the Stour (*q.v.*) Valley, made famous by the paintings of John Constable; Beccles (*q.v.*) and Bungay in the Waveney Valley; Framlingham (*q.v.*), and Peasenhall. The coastal region, known as the sandlings, like the Breckland, is marked by great stretches of heath and conifers. It is divided up by broad tidal estuaries bordered by alluvial deposits, such as the Stour, Orwell, and Deben, formed by the subsidence, begun in Neolithic times and possibly still continuing, which extended the tidal range of the sea far inland. Over a thousand acres have been protected as nature reserves; areas of special scientific or historic interest, such as Minsmere, Staverton Thicks, a remnant of the primeval forest, and Havergate Island, the only British home of the avocets, are also protected. (In 1963 the National Trust owned 2,000 ac. and protected 267 ac.) The coastline is very sensitive to tidal action, particularly erosion, which has since the 14th century led to the virtual extinction of the once flourishing port of Dunwich (*q.v.*). The last millennium has seen the formation of the ten-mile-long spit of shingle extending from the mouth of the Alde to Weir Point.

**History.**—Excavations at Hoxne provide definite evidence that Paleolithic man occupied the region as early as the Great Interglacial Period (*c.* 250,000 B.C.). The culture was Acheulean. Upper Paleolithic, Mesolithic, and Neolithic are found at various sites. At Creeting St. Mary, Neolithic Rinyo-Clactonian ware was associated with cremations. The Beaker folk are found both near Ipswich and in the Breckland. The Bronze Age saw a penetration from the west along the Icknield Way; barrows of the Middle Bronze Age have been excavated at Brightwell, and Later Bronze Age urnfields demonstrate a spread from the east by way of the valleys. Iron Age "A" settlements are found principally on the light lands, and Iron Age "B" is represented by a chariot burial near Mildenhall (*q.v.*). Notable Belgic finds come from a cemetery at Boxford and a settlement at Burgh, near Woodbridge.

Along with Norfolk, Suffolk formed part of the kingdom of the Iceni. A bronze head of the emperor Claudius I, dredged from the River Alde at Rendham, may represent jettisoned spoil from the sack of Colchester during the rebellion of Boadicea (Boudicca) in A.D. 60. Excavations near Baylham have revealed a Claudian settlement beneath the Roman road from Colchester to Venta Icenorum; air photography disclosed a camp, possibly of this period, near Ixworth, in an area containing several villa sites. A statuette of Nero from Baylham and a plaque of Mithras from Whitton (Ipswich) have a religious connotation. The notable Mildenhall treasure (in the British Museum, London) was buried at the time of the Saxon raids. Burgh castle still stands, a fort of the Saxon shore, and a print of the 18th century shows such a fort at Walton (Felixstowe).

The earliest evidence of Saxon settlement comes from the pagan burial grounds at Ipswich and Lackford. The remarkable ship burial at Sutton Hoo (*see* SUTTON HOO SHIP BURIAL), near Rendlesham, seat of the East Anglian monarchs, throws new light on the aesthetic standards of the time and, along with the pottery evidence, stresses the importance of the continental contacts of the 7th century. The effects of the Danish invasions of the late 9th century, and of the Viking invasions of the late 10th, though locally severe, seem to have stimulated rather than retarded the development of Suffolk, and by the Norman Conquest Suffolk and Norfolk together formed the most populous and prosperous region of England. During this period the famous abbey of Bury St. Edmunds (*q.v.*), the ruins of which are still extant, was founded as a resting place for the bones of King Edmund, martyred by the Danes in 869. The jurisdiction of the abbey extended over eight and a half hundreds, now forming the basis of the administrative county of West Suffolk. At about the same time a "liberty" consisting of five and a half hundreds in East Suffolk was granted to the prior and convent of Ely which passed to the dean and chapter of Ely Cathedral in 1541. The remaining hundreds, called the "Geldable," were under the jurisdiction of the sheriff who was appointed jointly for Norfolk and Suffolk until 1575. (*See* also EAST ANGLIA.)

The centuries immediately following the Norman Conquest saw the construction of a number of castles, two of which, Eye and Clare, became the centres of great honours. The most important remains are to be found at Framlingham and Orford (both in the custody of the Ministry of Works), Wingfield, and Mettingham. A number of small religious houses were also founded, including Clare Priory, which was dissolved in the 16th century and reoccupied in 1953, after a lapse of 400 years, by the Order of St. Augustine. Little Wenham Hall is a notable example of a 13th-century fortified dwelling house.

Cloth weaving, based on a supply of local wool, flourished from the 14th to the 16th century, and Lindsey and Kersey woolens were famous throughout Europe. The prosperity engendered by this industry is apparent in the churches, the majority of which are of the Decorated and Perpendicular periods, with open roofs, good woodwork, and fine fonts. Long Melford, with its remarkable Lady Chapel, Lavenham, Blythburgh, and Southwold are magnificent examples. In the main the churches of all periods are constructed of flint, and no less than 41 have early round flint towers, the most notable at Little Saxham and Wortham.

There were serious uprisings in West Suffolk against Bury Abbey in the 14th century, but the county was relatively unaffected by the Wars of the Roses in the 15th century, in spite of the strong Yorkist flavour imparted by the presence of one of the chief seats of the dukes of Norfolk at Framlingham.

Though strong Protestant influences penetrated the county through Ipswich in the early 16th century, Mary Tudor derived much of the support for her claim to the throne from Suffolk. However, Puritanism did establish itself as a dominant force in the later 16th century and many families emigrated to the New England colonies of America for religious as well as economic reasons. During the Civil War the county was strongly parliamentarian and the local gentry actively supported the Association of the Eastern Counties. Hengrave and Helmingham halls, both of the early 16th century, are fine examples of the domestic architecture of the period.

The 17th and 18th centuries saw the rapid decline of cloth weaving, but the prosperity of agriculture led to the building of such fine houses as Heveningham, designed by James Wyatt, with its superb interior decorations, and Ickworth (since 1956 owned by the National Trust), built about 1794–1830 by the 4th earl of Bristol, bishop of Derry, with its rotunda and great curving wings.

As a coastal county, the history of Suffolk has been much influenced by the sea. Fishing fleets left the ports for cod and ling from Iceland, and herring and mackerel from the North Sea. A big fish trade was carried on with Flanders. It was from Orwell Haven that Edward III sailed in 1340 to win the Battle of Sluys against the French; Thomas Cavendish of Trimley St. Martin was the third man to circumnavigate the world; and in the 17th century Suffolk was the base for sea operations against the Dutch. The threat of invasion during the Napoleonic period led to the erection of the many surviving Martello towers, for example, at Aldeburgh and Felixstowe (*qq.v.*).

**Population and Administration.**—Suffolk is divided into three major administrative units: East Suffolk covering 855.3 sq.mi. with a population (1961) of 225,661; West Suffolk covering 610.8 sq.mi. with a population (1961) of 128,918; and Ipswich covering 15.6 sq.mi. with a population (1961) of 117,395.

East Suffolk has five municipal boroughs, seven urban and seven rural districts; West Suffolk has two municipal boroughs, three urban and six rural districts. Ipswich, in East Suffolk, is a county borough and the county town.

Prior to the Reform Act of 1832 the county returned 2 members to Parliament and 14 members from its seven boroughs. By this act the boroughs of Orford, Aldeburgh, and Dunwich were disfranchised. From 1948 the county constituted five divisions, each returning one member. Until 1872 the county had a single commission of the peace and quarter sessions were held in four divisions, one each for the liberties of Bury St. Edmunds and St. Etheldreda, and one each for the two parts of the "Geldable" based on Beccles and Ipswich, respectively. After 1872 the numbers were reduced to two, namely East and West Suffolk. Since 1951 separate commissions of the peace have been in force for East and West Suffolk. There are separate commissions for Ipswich and Bury St. Edmunds. Since 1888 East and West Suffolk have been governed by their own county councils.

In 1837 the archdeaconry of Sudbury (*q.v.*), roughly covering the area now known as West Suffolk, was transferred to the Ely diocese. In 1914 the present diocese of St. Edmundsbury and Ipswich was founded and comprises the whole of Suffolk less the deaneries of Lothingland and Flegg.

**The Economy.**—Agriculture was, and still is, the greatest employer of labour in Suffolk. After the breakup of much of the pasture during the Napoleonic Wars, it became one of the principal grain-growing counties. More than half the land is arable, and the numbers of cows, sheep, and pigs fluctuate considerably. The main crops, in order of importance, are barley, wheat, oats, sugar beet, clover and grass (for hay), mangels (with turnips and swedes), peas, and beans. Horse breeding is declining—including the famous Suffolk Punch—but Newmarket (*q.v.*) retains its preeminence as the centre of the bloodstock and racehorse industry.

The cloth industry was replaced during the 18th and 19th centuries by textiles such as sailcloth, coconut fibres, horsehair, and clothing. Besides textiles the most important manufactures relate to agriculture. Agricultural machinery is especially important at Ipswich, Bury St. Edmunds, and Stowmarket. Grain milling and malting are extensive and fertilizers are made at Ipswich. There are sugar-beet factories at Sproughton and Bury St. Edmunds, and quick frozen foods are processed at Lowestoft (*q.v.*). Heavy engineering is also found at Ipswich, and shipbuilding at Lowestoft. Ipswich, Beccles, and Bungay are important for printing. Paint is manufactured at Stowmarket, and at Brantham a large plastic works has been established. Fishing is mainly concentrated at Lowestoft. In 1962 the building of a nuclear power station for the Central Electricity Generating Board was begun at Sizewell on the coast, 2 mi. E of Leiston. The port of Ipswich takes vessels of up to 25 ft. draught, and with Lowestoft Harbour and the reopened Felixstowe dock, handles a considerable import trade. British Railways (Eastern region) serves the county with a main line from London (Liverpool Street) to Ipswich, and branch lines to other parts. There are civil aerodromes at Ipswich and Newmarket Heath (a private landing ground).

BIBLIOGRAPHY.—A. Suckling, *The History and Antiquities . . . of Suffolk,* 2 vol. (1846–48), and Index (1952); W. White, *History, Gazetteer, and Directory of Suffolk, . . . ,* 3rd ed. (1874); J. Kirby, *The Suffolk Traveller . . .* (1735); A. Page, *A Supplement to the Suffolk Traveller,* 5 vol. (1844); *Victoria County History of Suffolk,* 2 vol. (1907–11); L. J. Redstone, *Suffolk* (1930); Ipswich and East Suffolk Record Office, *East Suffolk County Plan 1951: the Report of the Survey, West Suffolk County Plan 1951: the Analysis of the Sur-*

*vey;* J. G. Hurst and S. G. West, "Saxo-Norman Pottery in East Anglia," *Proceedings of the Cambridge Antiquarian Society,* vol. 2 (1957). (D. Cn.)

**SUFFREN, PIERRE ANDRÉ DE** (1729–1788), French admiral noted for his contribution to the advancement of French naval strategy and tactics. Born at Saint-Cannat, near Aix-en-Provence, on July 13, 1729, into the noble family of Suffren de Saint-Tropez, he was very early admitted into the Order of the Hospital of Saint John of Jerusalem (Knights of Malta), in which he eventually rose to the rank of bailli. Entering the French corps of *Gardes de la Marine* (naval guards) as a cadet in 1743, during the War of the Austrian Succession, he was soon sent to sea. In 1747 he was impressed by Adm. Edward Hawke's concentration of fire on the French rearguard in the Battle of Cape Finistère, in which Suffren was among the prisoners taken. Released on the peace of 1748, he went to serve with the Maltese galleys. In the French service again at the start of the Seven Years' War (1756), he saw, in action off Minorca, how opportunities were missed by rigid adherence to "line ahead" formation.

In April 1778, as captain of a ship in the squadron under Adm. C. H. d'Estaing (*q.v.*), Suffren sailed from Toulon for North America to help the insurgent colonists against the British. In his private letters he sharply criticized his admiral's conduct.

Suffren's own ideas, inspired by the example of the 17th-century Dutch admiral De Ruyter, were clear enough: sea warfare can play a decisive part in strategy; and in naval engagements the essential factors are retention of the initiative, speed, and watchfulness for the means and opportunity of concentrating a maximum of strength against a fraction of the enemy's line. He reacted, just as Hawke and Samuel Hood on the British side did, against the sterile caution of engagements in line and against the failure to appreciate the strategic role of a fleet. A man of violent temper and of prodigious energy, explosively choleric, and vulgar in his manner, Suffren nevertheless had a quick and subtle mind and a kind heart. His boundless ambition was directed only toward the glory of achievement.

A mission to the Indian coast gave him a chance of proving his ability, with means so limited that he had often to resort to improvisation. On his way out (April 1781), he attacked a British fleet anchored at La Praya (Praia), in the Cape Verde Islands: his motive—surprising to contemporary strategists—was to promote the success of a land enterprise, the French occupation of the Cape of Good Hope, which the British fleet was going to contest. In Indian waters he fought engagements off Sadras (near Tirukkalikkunram; in February 1782), off Provédien (in April), off Negapatam (Nagapattinam; in July), off Trincomalee (in September), and off Cuddalore (in June 1783). In this remarkable series of engagements he tried to teach his captains how to isolate groups of enemy vessels and thus destroy a squadron piecemeal. His efforts were not invariably successful, and their originality was scarcely understood by his superiors: but public opinion in France was enthusiastic for him. On his return after the peace of 1783 he was made a vice-admiral.

Suffren died in Paris on Dec. 8, 1788, in circumstances still debated by historians (whether from apoplexy or from a duel).

*See* R. Boutet de Monvel, *La Vie martiale du Bailli de Suffren* (1929); E. Davin, *Suffren* (1947). (L. Ni.)

**SUFISM** (Tasawwuf), the name by which Islamic mysticism came to be known in the 8th or 9th century A.D., is formed from the Arabic word *sufi,* meaning "wearer of wool," woolen dress having been strongly associated with spirituality even in pre-Islamic times. The Sufis are also generally known as "the poor [in spirit]," *fuqara,* plural of *faqir,* in Persian *darwish,* whence the English words "fakir" and "dervish."

**Sufi Doctrine and Practice.**—All Muslims must believe that there is no absolute reality but God (*see* Islam: *Muslim Theology*) but only the Sufi carries this doctrine to its ultimate conclusion. For him, reality (*al-Haqq*) is that which is as opposed to that which is not. Therefore God alone is, whence the term "oneness of being." The doctrine of the oneness of being, which Western scholars term monism, is expressed by several verses of the Koran, such as "Wheresoe'er ye turn, there is the face of God" (2:115) and the all-inclusive definition of God: "He is the first and the last and the outwardly manifest and the inwardly hidden" (57:3). This last verse cannot, however, be taken pantheistically, nor does any Sufi imagine God to be the sum of all existing things, for it is an essential aspect of God's oneness that he has no parts. The doctrine of oneness of being means that each apparently separate thing is an illusory veil over the one indivisible plenitude of the absolute, infinite, and eternal truth. A 13th-century Sufi, 'Abd Allah al-Balyani, said, "When the secret of an atom of the atoms is clear, the secret of all created things both external and internal is clear, and thou dost not see in this world or the next aught beside God."

The veil of illusion cannot be pierced by any human faculty, but vision of the truth is nonetheless possible because, owing to the extreme nearness of God, expressed in the koranic verse "We [God] are nearer to him [man] than his jugular vein" (50:16), human sight is liable to be overwhelmed by the divine sight. "The sight o'ertaketh him not, but he o'ertaketh the sight" (6:103); "God cometh in between a man and his own heart" (8:24). The key to inward vision lies in the verse "All things in creation suffer extinction and there remaineth the face of thy Lord in its majesty and bounty" (55:26–27). It is on this verse, continually quoted by the mystics of Islam, that the Sufi doctrine of extinction (*fana'*) is based.

The path of Islamic mysticism may be said to consist in anticipating the inevitable ultimate extinction of all things other than God. The prostration in the ritual prayer, which for the average Muslim symbolizes an undefined humility before God, is for the Sufi no less than the absolute humility of extinction of the ego so that only God, the true self, will remain. Similarly, when he performs the ritual ablution the Sufi aspires to absolute purification through the washing away of everything except God. In reciting the Koran he aspires to be as it were drowned in the koranic ocean of uncreatedness, one of the basic tenets of Islam being that the Koran is the uncreated Word of God. These examples show that in practice as well as in doctrine the difference between the Sufi and the average Muslim is not one of form but of the understanding and aspiration that lie behind the form.

The whole of Sufism as regards both doctrine and practice is summed up in the saying of the Prophet (called a "holy tradition," or *hadith qudusi,* because in it God speaks in the first person) quoted by the great traditionist al-Bukhari:

> Nothing is more pleasing to me as a means for my slave to draw near to me, than the worship that I have made binding upon him. And my slave ceaseth not to draw near to me with added devotions of his free will until I love him. And when I love him I am the hearing wherewith he heareth and the sight wherewith he seeth and the hand wherewith he smiteth and the foot whereon he walketh.

As this tradition implies, the practices of the Sufis are of two kinds: the obligatory forms of worship that are binding on all Muslims, namely the five daily ritual prayers, paying the legal alms, fasting in the month of Ramadan, and making the pilgrimage to Mecca if possible; and voluntary worship, such as reciting the Koran and litanies, fasting apart from Ramadan, keeping vigils, making spiritual retreats, and above all invoking the name "Allah" and other divine names. All these practices, the voluntary as well as the obligatory, were undoubtedly the practices of the Prophet and his chief companions.

**Historical Development.**—It is only in secondary respects that there can be said to have been any development in Sufism, or for that matter in Islam as a whole, since the time of the Prophet. The first Islamic community, not unlike the first Christian community, was a fairly homogeneous whole with a strong mystical bias. But, as the historian Ibn Khaldun points out, in and after the second generation the spread of worldliness caused a general falling away, which left the mystics a much more distinct class than they had been before; hence the need of a special name to denote them. Different groups were soon formed in Sufism, which led finally to the formation of orders or brotherhoods (sing. *tariqa;* pl. *turuq*), which became more and more fully organized as time went on.

As regards certain details of Sufi observance, Mohammed had

recommended the recitation of several litanies a specified number of times. From the need to keep count, the Sufis quickly took to using knotted cords and then beads. The repetition of formulas not only leads to the use of rosaries but is also conducive to rhythmic movements of the body. Some of the collective dances practised in many of the Sufi orders are so simple that they could have easily crystallized in one generation from the spontaneous isolated movements of single individuals; and once such practices had been established, it was natural that here and there more complex dance movements should be developed. The Mawlawi order of Sufis, founded by Jalal-ud-din Rumi (*q.v.*), is better known to the West as the "whirling" or "dancing dervishes" because of the dance their founder prescribed for them. Such practices, however, have never been considered as more than aids to concentration.

It was not long before the Sufis began to write treatises. In one of these al-Kalabadhi (d. A.D. 995) says: "Then [after the second generation] spiritual desire diminished and purpose flagged: and with this came the spate of questions and answers, books and treatises." What Western scholars tend to take as a mark of progress was clearly not considered so by the Sufis themselves. "Take knowledge from the breasts of men, not from words" and "Whoso knoweth God, his tongue flaggeth" are among the most often repeated Sufi maxims.

But words are sometimes necessary. Conscious that the rest of the community had ebbed away from them, and themselves struggling against the current of this ebb, the Sufis of the 9th and 10th centuries felt driven to go to lengths previously unknown in Islam, not only as regards asceticism but also as regards doctrinal formulation. Abu Yazid al-Bistami in the 9th century went so far as to say "Glory be to Me! How great is My majesty!" Such utterances were liable to bring the Sufis into conflict with the more exoteric authorities, and in A.D. 922 al-Hallaj (*q.v.*) was put to death for saying "I am the Truth."

On the other hand, the inevitable chasm that exists between mysticism and the more external aspects of religion has been bridged in every Muslim generation by men who were at the same time members of Sufi orders and eminent authorities in one or more of the outer domains of Islam. The most famous of these "bridges" is probably al-Ghazzali (*q.v.*), the great canonist and theologian, who devoted his latter years to the mystic path and wrote among other things a treatise in praise of Sufism as the highest kind of life and as the only sure antidote to skepticism. His much younger contemporary, 'Abd al-Qadir al-Jilani (d. A.D. 1166), "the sultan of the saints," founded the Qadiri order, which within one generation after his death had spread to most parts of the Islamic world. Today the largest Sufi brotherhoods are the Qadiri and the Shadhili, the latter founded by Abu'l-Hasan al-Shadhili (d. A.D. 1258).

Even the most summary account of Sufism would not be complete without a mention also of the Spanish-born mystic Ibn Arabi (*q.v.*), known as "the greatest sheikh," who in a sense belongs to all the orders in virtue of his writings, a vast and much drawn on treasury of mystical prose and poetry. Perhaps the two greatest poets of Sufism, however, are his two contemporaries, the Arabian Ibn al-Farid (*q.v.*), known as "the sultan of the lovers," whose famous wine song begins with the words "We have drunk to the memory of the beloved a wine wherewith we were made drunk before the vine was created"; and the founder of the "whirling dervishes," Jalal-ud-Din Rumi (*q.v.*), whose *Mathnawi* is considered to be one of the finest works in Persian poetry. One of the works most consulted by Sufis themselves is 'Abd al-Karim al-Jili's early-15th-century treatise *al-Insan al-kamil* ("Universal Man"), which presents all that is essential to Sufi doctrine in a remarkably clear and accessible form. To al-Jili is owed the illuminating symbolism of water and ice as representing, respectively, God and creation in their apparent difference and secret identity.

**Sufism Today.**—Such deviations as drug taking, sorcery, jugglery, snake charming, and fire eating, the features most associated with Sufism by many Westerners, have affected only a small fraction of the whole. The orders still comprise thousands of deeply serious and devout men and women in nearly every Islamic country, and of all Muslims these are probably the most aloof and inaccessible to Europeans. Only in Turkey and in Saudi Arabia are the orders officially forbidden, for almost opposite reasons. Mustafa Kemal Atatürk banned them (1925) as the most conservative element in Islam, knowing that they would be a great impediment to his secularization of Turkey. On the other hand, the puritanical Wahhabi sect that rules Saudi Arabia is hostile to the orders because their conservatism is not narrow enough and because, in particular, they encourage people to visit the tombs of the saints.

Of the approximately 70 Sufi orders in existence today, the following are among the most important:

'Alawi, branch of the Darqawi-Shadhili, in Algeria, Morocco, Syria, Jordan, Israel, Aden, and Ethiopia
Bektashi, originally in Turkey, now chiefly in the Balkans
Burhani, in Egypt
Darqawi (Derqawa), a branch of the Shadhili, in Morocco, Algeria, Egypt, Lebanon, Ceylon
'Isawi, a branch of the Shadhili, in Morocco, Algeria, and Tunisia
Khalwati, a branch of the Suhrawardi, originally in Khurasan, with branches in various parts of the Islamic world
Madari, in India-Pakistan
Mawlawi (Mevlevi in Turkish), originally in Turkey, spread to other parts of the former Ottoman Empire
Naqshabandi, originally in Turkistan, with branches in all Islamic countries of the Near East and in central Asia, China, India-Pakistan, and Indonesia
Ni'matallahi, in Iran, a descendant of the Qadiri
Qadiri, originally in Baghdad, with branches all over the Islamic world
Rahmani, a branch of the Khalwati in Algeria
Rifa'i, originally in southern Iraq, with branches in Syria and Egypt
Sanusi (*see* SENUSSI)
Shadhili (Shazili), with branches all over the Islamic world
Shattari, in India-Pakistan, Malaya, and Indonesia
Suhrawardi, founded in Baghdad, now in Afghanistan and India-Pakistan, with many branches elsewhere
Tijani, in North and West Africa and Sudan

**Influences Received and Exerted.**—The influences on Sufism from outside have been enormously exaggerated. Probably the chief influence was Neoplatonism, but even this was confined mostly to terminology and to methods of doctrinal exposition.

As regards the influence exerted by Sufism on non-Islamic communities, it has made many converts to Islam. The Tijani order, for example, may be said to have taken parts of West Africa by storm, and some Muslim communities there are Sufi almost to a man. It was also through Sufism, as representing the most intellectual aspect of the religion, that many Hindus were converted to Islam. Dara Shikuh, the Sufi brother of the 17th-century Mughal emperor Aurangzeb, remarked that the only difference between the Hindu doctrine of *advaita* (nonduality) and the basic doctrine of Sufism is one of terminology.

Today, with the vast increase in Western knowledge of Islamic mysticism, more than one attempt has been made to start non-Islamic Sufi movements in the West, but the real Sufis would not recognize in this anything but dilettantism.

Apart from conversions, the influence of Sufism on other mysticisms is impossible to assess. All mysticism is fundamentally the same, and two forms may correspond closely even in details without being in any way mutually indebted. (*See* MYSTICISM.) There was no doubt a certain interchange of ideas between Sufism and Christianity. The Knights Templar, for example, almost certainly made intellectual contacts with the Sufis; so did St. Francis, it is said; and al-Ghazzali was well known to Western Europe in the Middle Ages, and some of his works were widely read in Latin translations.

BIBLIOGRAPHY.—F. Schuon, *Understanding Islam* (1963); T. Burckhardt, *An Introduction to Sufi Doctrine* (1959); M. Lings, *A Moslem Saint of the Twentieth Century* (1961); A. J. Arberry, *Sufism* (1950); S. H. Nasr, *Three Muslim Sages* (1964); L. Massignon, *Essai sur les origines du lexique technique de la mystique musulmane*, new ed. (1954), *La Passion d'al-Hallaj* (1922); A. Siraj ul-Din, *The Book of Certainty* (1952), "The Origins of Sufism," *Islamic Quarterly*, 3:53–63 (1956); M. Smith, *Rabi'a the Mystic* (1928), *An Early Mystic of Baghdad* (1935).

(M. LI.)

**SUGAR.** The familiar white crystalline substance known as sugar is the organic chemical compound sucrose having the formula $C_{12}H_{22}O_{11}$. Chemists designate a large group of related compounds as sugars but these are usually referred to by specific names: corn sugar (glucose, dextrose), fruit sugar (fructose, levulose), milk sugar (lactose), etc. All sugars are members of the larger group known as carbohydrates (*q.v.*). Of the more than 70,000,000 short tons of sugar (sucrose) produced annually in the world, about 60% comes from sugarcane and 40% from sugar beets. Minor sources of sucrose are the maple tree *Acer saccharinum,* sorghum cane (known by many different names), and certain classes of palms, primarily the wild date palm *Phoenix sylvestris;* all are produced on a small-farm basis largely for local consumption, although the total output may reach fairly large proportions (*see* MAPLE SYRUP; SORGHUM; DATE PALM; PALM).

Sugar in the mature cane or beet has the same chemical composition as the product that reaches the consumer; that is, the basic character of the sucrose remains unchanged from field to final product. Sugar is formed in the stalk of the cane and the root of the beet by the process of photosynthesis by which the action of sunlight on the chlorophyll of the leaves combines carbon dioxide from the air and water from the soil, giving off oxygen in the process.

## SUGARCANE

**History.**—Although the beet as a source of sugar is a development of the past 150 years, utilization of sugarcane dates from antiquity. Authorities now generally agree that sugarcane originated in New Guinea and was transported to southern Asia in prehistoric times. The first references in the literature relate to the growth of sugarcane in northern India in the 4th century B.C. The word "sugar" is derived from the Sanskrit *śarkarā,* which may be traced to practically all modern languages. The Sanskrit for solidified sugar is *khanda,* from which comes the word "candy." The first positive evidence of sugar in solid form dates from Persia, about A.D. 500.

The Arabs spread the culture of sugarcane through northern Africa and southern Europe at the same time that the Chinese, who introduced methods of extracting sugar from the cane, carried it to Java and the Philippines. Commercial manufacture developed in Egypt during the 9th and 10th centuries, but not until the "Age of Discovery" made sugar from the Americas available in large supply did it cease to be a scarce luxury dispensed by apothecaries. Practically every newly discovered area was promptly supplied with cane for planting. Columbus carried sugarcane to Santo Domingo on his second voyage in 1493 and the culture spread to Cuba and other islands of the Caribbean. Cortés, Pizarro, and other explorers took cane to the mainland of Central and South America, with the result that by the year 1600 raw sugar production in tropical America was the largest industry in the world of that day. The close relationship between cane culture and Negro slavery has been traced by many historians. Cane growing in Louisiana was not successful until 1795, and Australia in 1817 became the last of the large sugar-producing areas to establish the culture.

**Description.**—Sugarcane is a giant perennial grass of the genus *Saccharum,* cultivated in tropical and subtropical regions throughout the world. The plant consists of clumps of solid stalks with regularly spaced joints or nodes, at each of which occurs a single bud or eye. The graceful sword-shaped leaves are similar to those of corn, and the leaf sheath folds around the stem, protecting the bud. Mature canes reach a height of 10 to 20 ft. (3 to 6 m.) and are generally 1½ to 2 in. (3½ to 5 cm.) in diameter, the dimensions varying with local conditions, length of growing period, and the variety of cane. The colour of the cane ranges from almost white, through yellow to deep green, purple, red, or violet. Some varieties have striped or ribbon canes of variegated colours. Until the widespread introduction of seedling canes about 1920, most authorities ascribed all cultivated canes to one species, *Saccharum officinarum,* the so-called native canes or noble canes that had been propagated in their particular areas for many generations. Four other species of "wild" canes are now recognized, which have been crossbred with the native canes to give seedling variety canes now in wide cultivation.

**Seedling Canes.**—Sugarcane comes into flower under the influence of shortening days—in the Northern Hemisphere from September to December, in the Southern Hemisphere from March to June—when the mature plant under favourable climatic conditions produces a "tassel," or "arrow," a handsome plumelike panicle that bears many hundreds of small spikelets with inconspicuous flowerets (*see* GRASSES: *Andropogoneae*). It was long known that the "arrows" contained minute seeds (so small that nearly 100 would be required to equal the weight of a single grain of wheat), but these were believed to be sterile until about 1888 when J. B. Harrison and J. R. Rovell in Barbados and F. Soltwedel in Java, working independently, announced the growth of cane from seed. This started an intensive search in various parts of the world for new varieties, which has resulted in an immense number of seedlings. The occurrence of disease epidemics among the existing varieties in Java prompted that country to become the first of the cane-growing areas to substitute seedling varieties for the older "noble" strains. New, experimentally bred varieties were developed that far surpassed the old varieties in vigour, disease resistance, and yield of sucrose, and practically all cane-producing countries began to plant the new strains soon after World War I, with the result that many have entirely eliminated the native canes. The Australian cane breeders estimate that 10,000 to 20,000 seedlings and about 10 years' time are required to produce one or two varieties that are successful in commercial culture.

**Diseases and Pests.**—The cultivated sugarcane plant is attacked by numerous diseases and pests that have been transported from one country to another with seed canes. In Java, Argentina, Puerto Rico, Louisiana, and many other cane areas the highly destructive mosaic disease threatened to destroy the industry entirely, necessitating the prompt introduction of new canes resistant to mosaic. Gumming disease (*Bacterium vasculorum*) has assumed great importance in such widely separated areas as Brazil, Australia, and Mauritius. Other parasitic diseases are leaf scald (*Xanthomonas albilineans*) and Fiji disease (a virus), both preva-

(RIGHT) BY COURTESY OF THE CATERPILLAR TRACTOR CO.; PHOTO, (LEFT) MAX HUNN

FIG. 1.—(LEFT) FLOWERS OF THE CANE, CALLED TASSELS OR "ARROWS," CONTAIN MINUTE SEEDS; (RIGHT) HARVESTING CANE BY HAND lent in the Pacific area. Of the insect pests, various moth borers have been especially destructive in the Western Hemisphere, and to some extent in India, Java, and the Philippines. The white grubs of several species of beetles have caused severe damage in Australia and in other regions of the Pacific but are controlled by chemical insecticides. The woolly aphid, froghoppers, and sap-sucking leafhoppers are among other insect pests. Rigid quarantine controls regulating the importation of cane cuttings and other plant carriers into various countries have been effective in preventing the spread of cane diseases and pests.

**Cultivation and Growth.**—Commercial sugarcane is grown from cuttings, never from seed. Pieces of stalks about a foot long, each including several joints or nodes, are planted in a shallow furrow and lightly covered with soil, either by hand or by a mechanical planter. Each bud or "eye" located at the nodes produces a plant consisting of several shoots that grow into a clump or stool of six or eight stalks. Cultivation carried out in the early growth stage is principally for the control of weeds. Chemical fertilizers in relatively large amounts are necessary to maintain yields at economic levels. Loam, clay loam, or muck soils are preferred, sandy loams requiring more moisture and fertilizer. After the cane is cut to the ground at harvest time, new plants, termed ratoons, spring up from the stubble to form a second crop, and in virgin soil this may be repeated for many years without replanting, although one or two years of ratoons are frequently the limit. Louisiana plants every second or third year, while Florida plants every fourth year only. Sugarcane grows best in moist hot climates where a period of heavy rainfall is followed by a dry season. These conditions are met in a belt extending from somewhat north of the Tropic of Cancer to slightly south of the Tropic of Capricorn. Where sufficient rainfall is not available, irrigation is resorted to as in Hawaii, Peru, and some parts of Australia. Transpiration is enormous, and irrigation records show crops requiring more than 100 in. (3 m.) per ac. annually for maximum growth. The length of the growing period varies greatly in different countries, Louisiana and other subtropical areas being limited to 7 or 8 months. Cuba and Puerto Rico average 12 months; Hawaiian crops grow for 18, 20, or even 24 months. The plant matures and sucrose increases with the approach of cool or dry weather. The leading producing countries are Cuba, Brazil, India, the United States (Hawaii, Louisiana, and Florida), Australia, the Philippines, and Puerto Rico, but sugarcane is also an important crop in Mexico and throughout Latin America (the Caribbean area and northern South America), Africa (led by South Africa, Mauritius, and Egypt), and Asia (including mainland China, Formosa [Taiwan], Indonesia, Thailand, and Pakistan, in addition to India and the Philippines).

**Harvesting and Transport.**—The greater portion of the world's cane supply is harvested by hand, heavy knives of the machete type being commonly used. The stalk is cut close to the ground, topped just above the uppermost coloured joint, and the remaining leaves stripped off. In some areas the three top joints are reserved for planting. Where labour is scarce, as in Hawaii, the cane while still standing is burned to remove the leaves, and the practice has spread elsewhere because of high costs. Burning does not injure the cane, but deterioration is accelerated and burned cane must be harvested and ground promptly to avoid heavy loss of sucrose. Mechanical harvesting has become more prevalent with increased labour costs, entirely replacing hand-cutting in Hawaii, Louisiana, and in many parts of Australia. Mechanical harvesting, however, results in much trash and dirt in the harvested cane, which have an adverse effect on mill performance.

The methods of transport from field to factory vary greatly with local conditions. In many regions, bullock carts collect the cut cane. In the Pacific areas, portable railway tracks are laid in the fields, and many countries where rain is prevalent use motor-trucks with large pneumatic tires. Fluming in mountain streams is practised in some regions, and where waterways are available barges or punts are used for transport. Factory-owned narrow-gauge railways still carry the greater proportion of cane but motor transport has become increasingly important.

The manufacturing season necessarily corresponds to the harvesting period, since cane cannot be stored in hot climates for more than a few days without serious loss of sugar. In the irrigation areas grinding may continue for the greater part of the year. The Louisiana season is limited by frosts to the late fall months, and in the West Indies the period is from January to June. The factories of Indonesia grind from May to November, which corresponds to the season in most areas in the Southern Hemisphere.

## THE SUGAR BEET

The second major source of the world's sugar supply, the sugar beet (*Beta vulgaris*), presents several contrasts to the sugarcane. The beet is grown in temperate or cold climates, in populated and well-developed areas where much of the product is consumed, as compared with the remote tropical regions of cane culture; the sugar is stored in the root instead of in the stalk; seeds are planted annually; and beet culture is a development of comparatively recent time. (For botany, culture, and production, *see* BEET.)

**History.**—The sugar beet was grown as a garden vegetable and for fodder long before it was valued for its sugar content. Sugar was produced experimentally from beets in Germany in 1747, but the first beet sugar factory was built in Silesia in 1803. Napoleon became interested in 1811 because the English blockade had cut off the raw sugar supply from the West Indies, and under his influence and encouragement 40 factories were established in France. The industry collapsed after his defeat at Waterloo (1815) and did not prosper again until slavery was abolished in the West Indies in 1843. After that, beet sugar production increased so rapidly throughout Europe that by 1880 the tonnage had surpassed that of cane sugar, and from then until World War I the world production of cane and beet was approximately equal.

Beets are grown on nearly all types of soil, with a fairly deep loam, moist but well drained, preferred. They have a wide range in the temperate mid-latitudes, but sugar content develops best in areas with moderate summer temperatures averaging 63°–73° F (about 17°–23° C) for the three summer months and with well-distributed rainfall during the growing season, unless irrigation is practised. Large quantities are grown in the U.S.S.R. and throughout Europe, especially in France, West Germany, Italy, the U.K., and Poland. Many other countries have increased sugar-beet production in the second half of the 20th century, including Chile, Uruguay, Iran, Turkey, mainland China, and Japan. In the United States the sugar-beet industry as a successful commercial enterprise began about 1890 with the establishment of factories in California and the Rocky Mountain states, although sporadic attempts had been made in many other states for half a century before that. Beet production in Great Britain is a development of the years following World War I.

**Beet Cultivation and Harvesting.**—Beet seeds are generally planted in the spring, the time depending on the weather and the proposed harvest date. Spacing of rows is from 20 to 28 in. (50 to 70 cm.). After the seedlings attain a height of 4 in., they are thinned and blocked out to allow a space of 8 to 10 in. between plants, which results in about 30,000 plants to the acre. Weed control is by hand hoeing, machine cultivation, and chemical weed killers. Fertilizers are added either to the seedbed or with the seed at the time of planting, or by side-dressing the rows of plants. Irrigation is practised in the far western United States, but in most of Europe and in the Great Lakes area of the U.S. and Canada natural rainfall supplies the needed water. At the end of the growing season, usually with the approach of cold weather, the crop is harvested by machine or by hand by lifting the beets and cutting off the leaves and part of the crowns. The tops are used for cattle feed. The topped beets are collected and carried to the factory, where they are processed or stored in large piles. The operations from planting to harvesting and handling the beets, both in transit and in storage, are becoming increasingly mechanized.

**Beet Seed Production.**—The breeding and selection of sugar beets for seed has resulted in the steady improvement of the quality of beets as to both tonnage and sucrose content and is one of the great scientific agricultural achievements. The amount of sugar produced per acre has more than tripled since the early days of the industry in Europe. Until World War I practically all beet seeds were produced in Europe, but the United States is now producing seed especially suitable for the areas in which it is to be grown. Until 1942 whole beet seeds were planted, but since then the outer corky layers have been removed and the seeds screened to reduce the number of seed germs per seedball; this process has developed so that single, or "segmented," seeds can be produced, greatly reducing the costs of thinning.

**Pests and Diseases.**—Insect damage and disease have been almost as destructive as with sugarcane. Beet armyworms, wireworms, cutworms, nematodes, and the larvae of certain beetles occur in the fields at the time of planting. Migrating pests that feed chiefly above ground include the beet leafhopper, adult beetles, grasshoppers, thrips, and webworms. Soil fumigation, crop rotation, weed control, counterattack by parasitic insects, and development of resistant strains, together with spraying and dusting with DDT and other chemical insecticides, are the usual control measures. Fungus diseases of seedlings have caused serious damage but treated seeds and soil treatment with fungicides are effective means of control. Curly top, a virus disease carried by one of the leafhoppers, is controlled by the use of resistant varieties and by control of the leafhopper that carries it. Sugar-beet mosaic is widespread but is not so serious as its counterpart in sugarcane. Various forms of rootrot may cause heavy damage in susceptible areas.

## MANUFACTURE

**History.**—The production of raw cane sugar in the tropics by open-kettle boiling methods changed little through the centuries until the introduction of modern machinery. Sugar refining began as a small-unit operation, depending upon several boilings for purification by recrystallization. In the 17th and 18th centuries literally hundreds of refineries dotted the larger ports of Europe and Great Britain, where the final product was molded into conical shape and hardened by baking.

The invention of the vacuum pan, by E. C. Howard of England about 1813, was an enormous step forward in processing a heat-sensitive material, such as sugar, and vacuum boiling spread fairly rapidly from English refineries to other branches of the industry. All modern sugar boiling, both beet and cane, takes place in vessels similar to the type that Howard introduced. The use of granular bone char (bone black) for the decolorization of refinery "liquors" was another innovation of that period. As an outgrowth of Howard's patent, Norbert Rillieux, a "free man of colour" of Louisiana, built the first multiple-effect evaporator for concentrating cane juice near New Orleans about 1845, resulting in savings in fuel, labour, and sugar that revolutionized the raw-sugar process. The plate-and-frame filter press and the suspended centrifugal were other developments of this general period. All these scientific and technical advances in which the sugar industry pioneered were later adopted or modified for other unrelated industries. The centralization of factories and refineries, so evident in modern practice, began about 1900. In Louisiana in 1880, more than 1,000 small plantation sugar factories produced 135,000 tons of sugar; within 25 years, 200 factories produced more than 400,000 tons. The concentration of the raw-sugar industry in Cuba and Puerto Rico was even more marked during these years.

The delivery of sugarcane and sugar beets to the factory scale for weighing marks the beginning of present-day manufacturing processes. Many steps in the elaboration of cane and beet sugar are similar, but marked differences also exist, especially where beet sugar production is a one-stage process, as in the United States and in many parts of Europe. Raw cane sugar is necessarily manufactured in the cane-producing areas, but refining generally takes place in the great population centres.

### Cane Sugar Manufacture

**Juice Extraction.**—The milling of cane by crushing and grinding is a highly developed process, the purpose being to rupture the plant cells by pressure to release the sugar-bearing juice. With few exceptions, the cane is weighed for economic and control purposes, generally in the railway cars, motortrucks, or carts in which it is transported to the mill. In the well-equipped modern factory the cane is unloaded and handled mechanically, traveling on endless conveyors to the crushing equipment.

The high capacities of the mill trains and the tough nature of the material to be ground require machinery of massive construction. Multiple mills arranged in triangular form are universal. Rapidly revolving cane knives, first used in Hawaii, cut the cane into chips to level and compact the bed of cane on the carrier but do not extract any juice. The carrier delivers the cane to a two-roller crusher that separates out about 50% of the juice by breaking and crushing the stalks or chips. Shredders of the hammer mill type shred the cane but extract no juice. In addition to crushers or shredders or both, a modern mill train or "tandem" may consist of from four to seven sets of three-roller combinations, with a capacity of 5,000 tons or more in 24 hours. The individual rolls are peripherally grooved, about 3 ft. in diameter and 5–7 ft. long, and are driven by meshing pinions at the end of the mill shafts. Larger gears connect these pinions with the motive power, which may be steam engines, turbines, or electric motors. Pressures up to 500 tons are applied to the top rollers by hydraulic rams. Two-tandem factories are fairly common, though the largest sugar factories have three tandems. To increase extraction, water or thin juice is sprayed on the blanket of crushed cane between one set of mills and the next. The terms "maceration," "imbibition," or "saturation" are applied interchangeably to this leaching process. Compound maceration, the most efficient system, is illustrated in fig. 2 (fourth mill juice behind second mill, third mill juice behind first mill, water following third mill). The combined juice from the crusher and first mill goes to process for clarification (purification).

Continuous diffusers, similar to those used in beet manufacture, but modified to handle shredded cane, came into commercial service in Hawaii in 1965. In comparison with mills the diffusion process gives higher sucrose extraction, uses less power, and has a lower initial cost.

The "raw juice" going to process contains from 93 to 97% of the sugar originally in the cane, depending on the quality of the cane, the degree of milling, and other related factors. The juice is turbid and dirty, greenish in colour, and acidic. The sucrose content ranges from 10 to 16%, with a purity (percent sucrose in dissolved solids) varying from 80 to 90, mature tropical canes generally yielding richer juice than those in subtropical regions. The nonsucrose solids in the juice consist of reducing sugars (levulose, dextrose); mineral matter, of which potash is the largest constituent; and organic nonsugars, such as nitrogenous bodies, fats, waxes, and pectins or gums. The percentage of these nonsucrose impurities varies with the variety of cane, the growth period, soil conditions, climate, and intensity of milling.

**Bagasse.**—The residue from the milling process, amounting to about 25% of the cane ground, is called bagasse in most cane-grinding countries, but megass in Australia and other British Commonwealth areas. It consists of woody fibre, some unextracted juice, and 40–50% of water. In most factories the bagasse is conveyed directly to the boilers, a ton of wet bagasse having the fuel value of about one barrel of fuel oil or $\frac{1}{4}$ ton of coal. In 1920 in Louisiana the manufacture of wallboard and insulating board from bagasse was begun, a practice since extended to Australia and Hawaii. Factories in Louisiana also pioneered in the manufacture of plastics and tile from bagasse and in the use of the dried and screened fibres for chicken litter, cattle bedding, and plant mulch. Bagasse fibre had long been recognized as a possible base for paper manufacture, but commercial success was not achieved until 1953. Factories producing bagasse paper now operate in Louisiana, Peru, Brazil, Hawaii, Spain, and the Philippines. Furfural from bagasse, formerly produced in the Dominican Republic, is now made in Florida. Potential uses include the production of lignin and alpha-cellulose.

**Clarification.**—Purification of the juice, termed clarification or defecation, is primarily designed to remove the maximum quantity of impurities that will result in a clear juice of proper

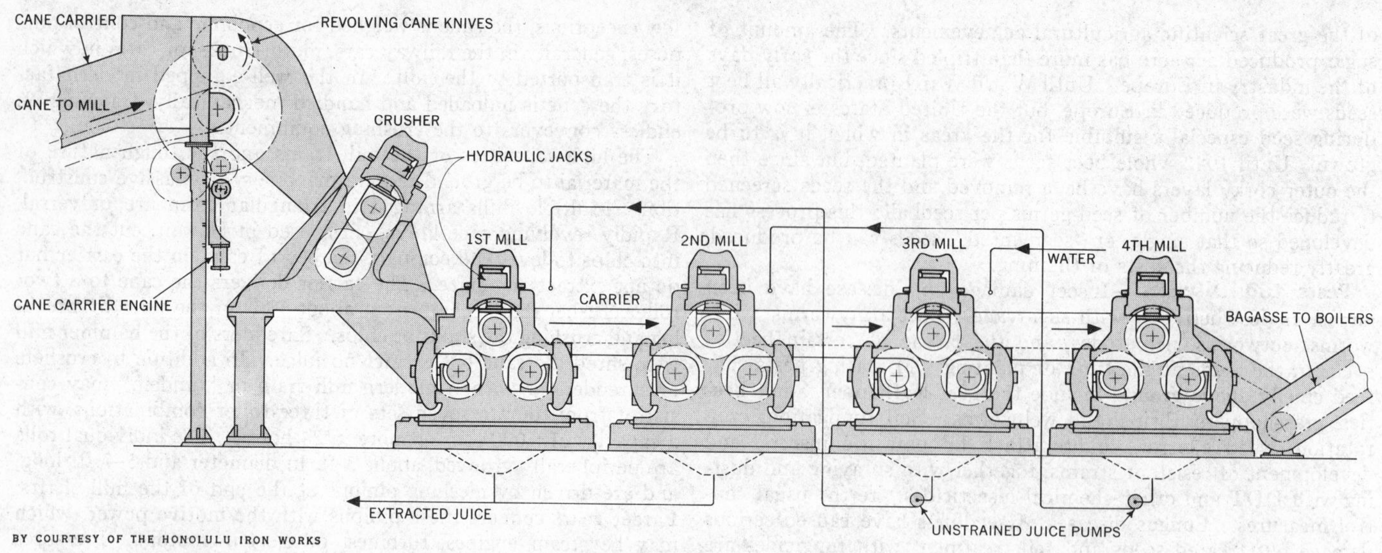


BY COURTESY OF THE HONOLULU IRON WORKS

FIG. 2.—CANE MILLING PLANT

reaction (about neutral, pH 7). Lime and heat have served as clarifying agents for several centuries, and this "simple defecation" is still accepted procedure throughout the world. The addition of lime (about $1\frac{1}{2}$ lb. per ton of cane) neutralizes the organic acids naturally present, after which the juice is heated to the boiling point or higher. The lime salts, mostly calcium phosphate, together with coagulated albumin and some fats, waxes, and gums, form a feathery precipitate that entraps finely suspended matter and part of the colloids. By settling, this defecated juice separates into scums, muds, and clear juice. The hot limed juice is allowed to separate in various forms of subsiders and is then decanted, leaving the scums and muds to be filtered.

The heat-and-lime treatment has been modified in numerous ways but without altering the basic process. The earliest system of removing impurities was by skimming the limed juice during boiling in open kettles, but intermittent batch settling replaced this boil-and-skim method many years ago. Since 1920 various types of continuous clarifiers have come into use, the usual form consisting of an enclosed series of shallow trays on which the precipitated materials in the stream of hot juice settle. Revolving arms sweep the muds to a central or peripheral draw-off well (fig. 3). Automatic addition of lime and control of the hydrogen-ion concentration (pH) are customary with continuous clarification systems. A well-clarified juice is a clear dark brown and has the same general composition as the raw juice. Muds and scums are treated by dilution with water, reliming and reheating, followed by filtration through plate-and-frame filter presses, or more generally on rotary-drum vacuum filters. The press juice goes to process, but the press cake is discarded (fig. 4).

**Direct Consumption Sugars.**—The production of white or off-white sugars direct from cane syrup requires more elaborate clarification. Impregnating the juice with sulfur dioxide before liming, formerly a process quite general in Louisiana, U.A.R., and South Africa, is on the decline. Carbonatation (carbonation), which involves excess liming and precipitation with carbon dioxide gas as described below for purification of beet juices, is extensively employed in Indonesia (Java). In Formosa and other Far Eastern countries the production of white sugar from cane syrup by carbonatation has greatly increased since 1950.

**Evaporation.**—The clarified juice, with a water content between 80 and 90%, goes to the evaporators without further treatment. Multiple-effect vacuum evaporators, in which the latent heat of the vapours is made to do duty several times, consist of a number of cells or bodies arranged in series so that each succeeding body has a higher vacuum, and therefore a lower boiling temperature, than the one preceding it (fig. 5). The heating unit in each body is a "calandria," or bank of tubes, generally vertical, into the first of which low-pressure steam is admitted. The vapour from the boiling juice passes over to the calandria of the second body, where, because of the higher vacuum, the juice boils at a lower temperature, releasing vapour for boiling the material in the third body and so on, the vapour from the final body going to the condenser. Each pound of steam admitted to the first body evaporates almost a pound of water for each multiple-effect body; *i.e.*, in a quadruple-effect evaporator the steam does nearly four times the work that it would do in direct boiling. The juice moving continuously from one body to the next becomes successively denser, until in the final body about 75% of the original water has been removed, leaving a syrup containing 60% or more solids of much the same composition as the clarified juice.

**Crystallization.**—Further evaporation of the syrup in single-effect vacuum pans results in the formation of sugar crystals. Vacuum pans having a capacity of 1,000 cu.ft. or more, essentially like a single body of a multiple-effect evaporator, work in batch operations at high vacuum (26 in., 130° F [about 54° C] boiling point). Pan boiling is a highly skilled industrial art that has only recently been simplified in modern installations by the application of control instruments. The pan boiler controls the amount and size of grain by regulating the vacuum, temperature,

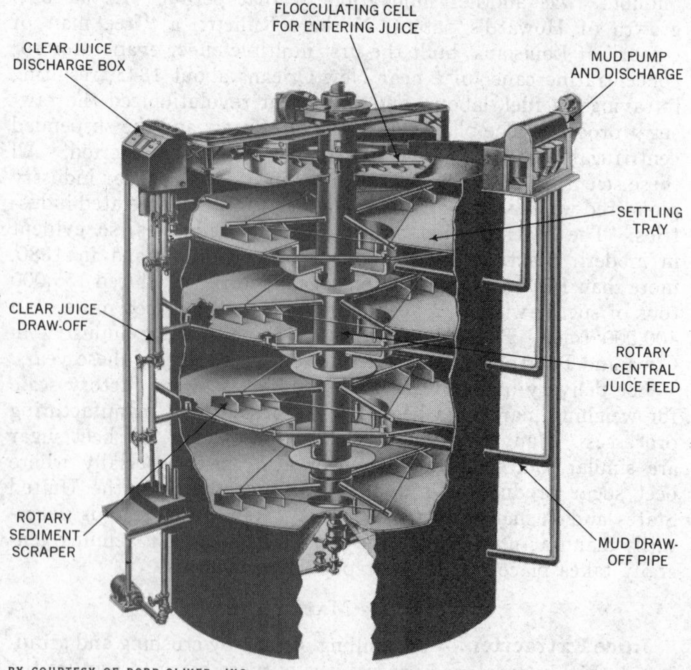


BY COURTESY OF DORR-OLIVER, INC.

FIG. 3.—CANE JUICE CLARIFIER

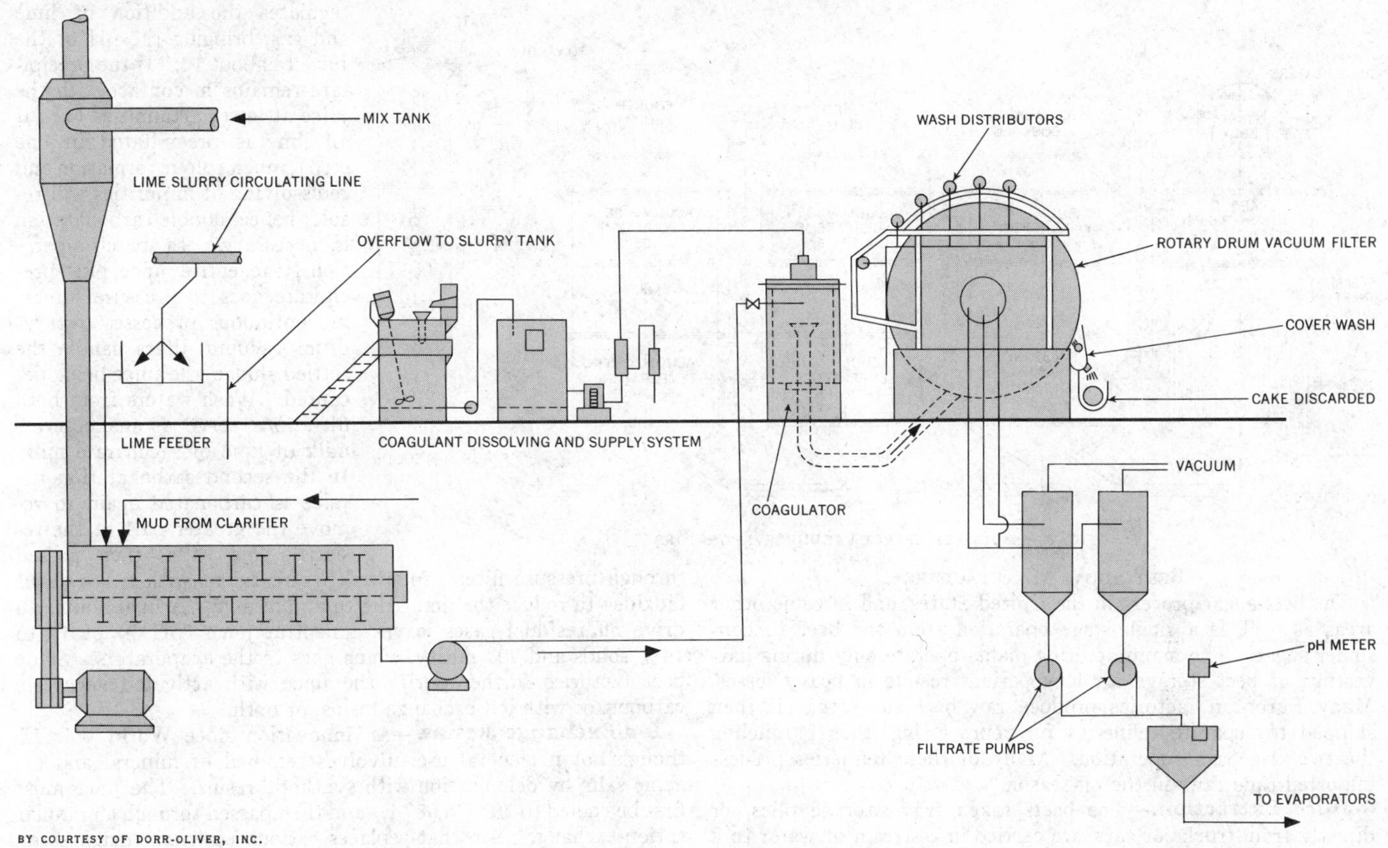


BY COURTESY OF DORR-OLIVER, INC.

FIG. 4.—FILTRATION PROCESS FOR CANE MUDS

speed of evaporation, and amount of syrup drawn into the pan. Older style "coil pans" have banks of serpentine copper coils heated by high-pressure steam (50–90 lb. per sq.in.[psi]), but calandria pans using exhaust steam now predominate (fig. 6). The first charge of syrup, about one-third of a panful, is boiled rapidly until supersaturation is reached. At the proper moment, determined either by instruments or from samples drawn by an instrument known as a proof stick, "grain" is made to form either by lowering the temperature or more generally by adding seed crystals of fine sugar. The boiling progresses with further additions of syrup until the finished "strike" or panful is completed. The operator then discharges the massecuite, a dense mixture of crystals and molasses, to the mixer or crystallizer.

**Centrifuging.**—The method of separating the crystals and surrounding mother syrup in all sugar processes is by "purging" in centrifugal machines. The suspended type of machine has a revolving cylindrical "basket," hung by a vertical shaft, or "spindle," and driven by belt or direct-connected motor. The basket has perforated metal sides lined with wirecloth and an inner perforated sheet (fig. 6). As the basket spins at high velocity, the crystals are retained by the lining, while the molasses passes through to the "curb," or container. After the purging is complete, the sugar may be sprayed with water before discharge to conveyors. The older centrifugals, which were 40 in. in diameter and revolved at 1,000 rpm, required manual filling and discharging. Newer high-speed machines are 48 in. in diameter and run at 1,400 to 2,000 rpm, usually with complete automatic control, timing, and operation. Continuous centrifugals came into general use in the 1960s. The newer types require less power and fewer automatic controls. Less floor space and headroom are necessary than with the more expensive automatic batch machines.

**Reboiling Molasses.**—The purged molasses from syrup strikes must be reboiled to reclaim further sugar. Modern cane factories produce only one grade of raw sugar, and, to accomplish this, complex boiling systems have been developed. One system commonly used incorporates the washed grain from the lowest grade, or "C" boiling, into a magma with cane syrup, which is used as a "footing" of seed crystals for the first, or "A" boiling, composed entirely of syrup. The "A" molasses is boiled on a similar footing of "C" sugar to form "B" massecuite, and the mixed "A" and "B" sugars constitute the commercial output of raw sugar. The "C" massecuite is grained on syrup to ensure a clean nucleus for the seed crystals and is completed with "B" molasses. This "C" massecuite goes to a crystallizer, generally a horizontal closed vessel with slowly revolving arms, to agitate the mixture of crystals and molasses during a cooling period of several days. As the massecuite cools, the crystals "grow," reducing the crystallizable sugar in the molassses to a minimum. Modern crystallizers include coils in which water circulates for rapid cooling (fig. 6). Sugar purged from the "C" massecuite serves as seed for high-grade strikes as described, and the "C" molasses is called "blackstrap," the final end product or by-product of the process.

The commercial raw sugar, the raw material for the refining process, is either packed in jute bags or shipped in loose bulk. Practically the entire output of Hawaii, Puerto Rico, Australia, and Louisiana is handled in bulk, and other areas are adopting the practice. The raw sugar contains from 96 to 98% sucrose, 1% or less of reducing sugars, 0.5% ash, less than 1% moisture, and the remainder organic nonsugars.

**By-Products.**—The heavy viscous final molasses, blackstrap, varies in composition with country of origin, maturity of cane, extent of milling, and methods of manufacture. Tropical molasses averages about 35% sucrose, 20% reducing sugar (levulose and dextrose), 10% ash, 15% organic nonsugars, and 20% water. The world output (50 gal. for each ton of raw sugar) is used commercially for cattle feed, for fermentation into alcohol, and, to a lesser degree, for the production of yeast and organic chemicals.

Another by-product of cane milling is cane wax, extracted by organic solvents from the clarification muds. Sugarcane wax has been refined commercially in Louisiana since 1948. Aconitic acid has been commercially extracted from cane molasses in Louisiana. The uses of bagasse, the by-product of milling, were described above. The bagasse from the diffusion process has the same composition as that produced by milling.

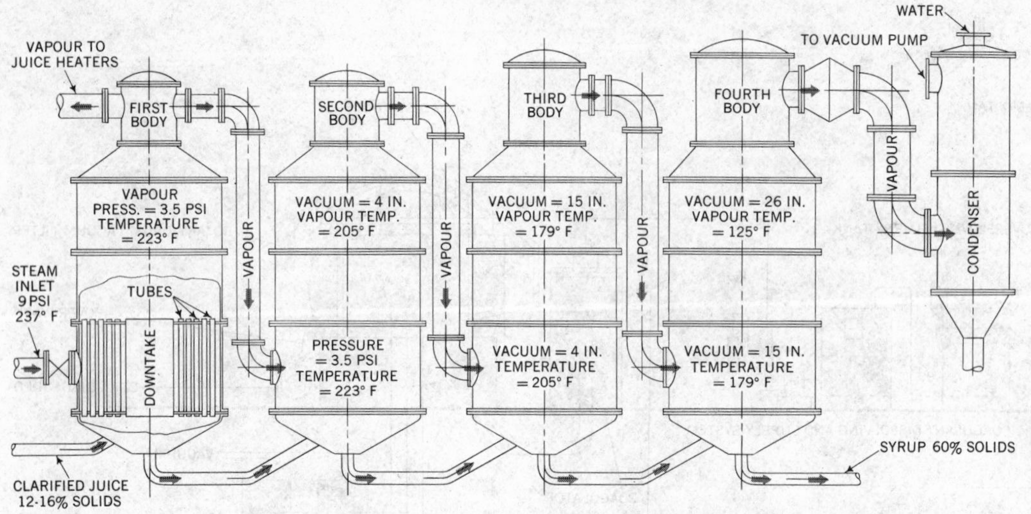


FIG. 5.—MULTIPLE-EFFECT VACUUM EVAPORATORS

### Beet-Sugar Manufacture

The beet-sugar process in the United States, and in some other areas as well, is a single-stage operation from the beet to consumer sugar. The manufacturing plants operate only during harvesting, as beet storage for long periods results in heavy losses. Many European factories produce raw beet sugar that is then shipped to separate refineries for reprocessing, thus paralleling the two-stage cane operation. Many of these refineries process imported cane raws in the off-season.

**Juice Extraction.**—The beets taken from storage piles, or directly from trucks or cars, are carried in a stream of water to a washer to remove dirt, after which they are weighed. Sugar is extracted by membrane diffusion, a process in sharp contrast to the crushing and grinding of cane, where the object is to rupture the cells. The beets are sliced into thin V-shaped chips or long narrow strips called cossettes by a series of knives on the inner periphery of a revolving drum that acts somewhat like a kitchen vegetable slicer. Batch diffusion, rare except in older factories, consists of a battery of 12 or 14 vertical cylindrical tanks or cells connected in series where the sugar is extracted countercurrently with water. Fresh water is added to that cell in which the cossettes are almost exhausted of sugar, and a fresh batch of cossettes is treated in the last cell with the most concentrated sugar juice. The extracted juice becomes successively stronger as it progresses through the battery, and the sliced beets that have been exhausted of sugar are discharged as pulp when the process is completed. This pulp is then dried and sold as cattle feed. Temperatures are maintained at about 85° C (185° F) by heating the juice as it passes from one cell to the next. After World War II continuous diffusors of various types were widely introduced. In general, they are either of horizontal rotary-drum design or of a chain-drag type that carries the cossettes on wide perforated trays, the travel of juice and cossettes in the two types being mainly countercurrent, though not entirely so.

The diffusion juice that goes to process is very dark in colour, contains from 10 to 15% sucrose and only traces of reducing sugars (levulose and dextrose), and is higher in mineral matter and nitrogenous bodies than cane juice. The purity (percent of sucrose in dissolved solids) is about 88, and the quantity of juice varies from 100 to 150% of the weight of sliced beets.

**Juice Purification.**—Carbonatation (carbonation) is universal in the beet industry. The active clarifying agents are an excess of $Ca(OH)_2$ (lime) and $CO_2$ (carbon dioxide gas), which form a precipitate of $CaCO_3$ (calcium carbonate) that is readily filtered. The beet process uses much more lime than the cane sugar processes. The high alkalinity (pH 10) has no adverse effect, since beet juices contain practically no reducing sugars.

Carbonatation invariably takes place in two stages. First the heavily limed juice is "gassed" with carbon dioxide. Temperatures of 70° C (158° F) are maintained, and accurate pH control regulates the addition of lime and gas, bringing the pH of the juice to about 10. If the precipitate remains in contact with the juice at lower alkalinities (*i.e.*, if all lime is precipitated in one step), much colour formation and redissolving of impurities will result; hence, double carbonatation is necessary. In batch operations, the entire juice plus precipitate goes to pressure filters; in continuous processes, rotary-drum vacuum filters handle the settled sludge, the juice being decanted. Wash waters from both filtrations serve as makeup for milk of lime or saccharate milk. In the second carbonatation the juice is carbonated again to remove the greater part of the residual lime salts, then passed through pressure filters, followed by treatment with $SO_2$ (sulfur dioxide) to reduce the lime salts to a minimum. A final boiling to drive off residual gases leaves a neutral juice (pH 7) of 13 to 14% solids and 90° purity, which goes to the evaporators. Some beet factories further purify the juice with activated vegetable carbons, or with ion-exchange resins, or both.

**Ion-Exchange Resins.**—An innovation since World War II, though not in general use, involves removal of mineral and organic salts by deionization with synthetic resins. The juice must first be cooled to 20° C (68° F) and then passed through a granular cation-exchange resin that replaces cations (calcium, magnesium, sodium, etc.) with hydrogen ions. To prevent inversion of sucrose, the free acid thus formed must be removed promptly by anion-exchange resins that leave the juice almost ash free. Organic nonsugars are also removed so that the purity of the juice improves 6 or 8%. The main disadvantages of this process are heavy capital outlay, the high cost of regenerating the resins, high fuel and water consumption, and appreciable bacterial and inversion losses. Some cane sugar refineries also employ ion-exchange resins to remove mineral salts from liquid sugars, but in general the exchange resins have not attained the promising results predicted for the sugar industry.

**Evaporation, Crystallization, and Finishing.**—The beet process in its final stages closely parallels the steps used in cane sugar manufacture and refining. The clarified thin juice goes to multiple-effect, frequently quintuple-effect, evaporators. Single-effect vacuum pans crystallize the sugar, and separation of crystals and molasses takes place in centrifugal machines. Boiling systems are complex, involving many features common to cane processes. Drying, screening, and packaging are accomplished by standard methods. Beet sugar is generally marketed in the form of table-granulated sugar, but production of specialty sugars is increasing. Because of the short manufacturing season, storage in huge silos and packaging throughout the year to meet market requirements are common.

Desugarization of molasses, which is peculiar to the beet industry, is made possible because of the absence of reducing sugars in the juices. The Steffen process involves the addition of finely powdered lime to cold diluted molasses of about 50 purity and 12° Brix (by weight, the percentage of sucrose in a pure sugar solution), with vigorous stirring. The lime combines with the sugar (sucrose) to form insoluble calcium saccharate, which is reclaimed on rotary vacuum filters. On heating the filtrate another insoluble saccharate appears. The combined cold and hot saccharates in the Steffen process that are slurried in sweet waters make up the "saccharate milk" used as the liming agent for carbonatation, the sucrose being released to the juice as the lime is precipitated by carbon dioxide.

**By-Products.**—Beet pulp has always been used as livestock food. Because wet pulp that has been stored in silos or pits develops offensive odour and hence heavy losses, United States practice is to dewater by mechanical pressing, then dry in direct-fired rotary drums. This produces a highly concentrated cattle feed that is frequently mixed with molasses either before or after evaporation. Concentrated Steffen wastes are a source of monosodium glutamate, used as a condiment, and to a lesser extent as a source of betaine and other amino acids. Potash has been recovered from these wastes in war periods. Beet molasses serves as stock feed (normally mixed with beet pulp) and as a base for alcoholic beverages and for yeast manufacture.

## SUGAR REFINING

Sugar refining generally takes place in large plants that have easy access to great market areas. All refined cane sugar in the United States comes from about 20 refineries situated in or near large seaports. British refineries are located in London, Liverpool, and Greenock, Scot. Modern refineries can refine beet or cane raws simultaneously, but in the United States refining as a separate operation is limited to cane sugar. Handling of raw sugar is largely mechanical; bags of sugar are emptied onto conveyor belts soon after delivery from ships, and bulk sugar travels by the same conveyors to storage bins or to process.

**Affination.**—Raw sugar, mixed with heavy syrup in a mixer-type scroll conveyor termed a "mingler," forms a magma that loosens the adhering film of molasses on the raw crystal. The magma (usually warmed) is purged of syrup in conventional centrifugal machines, and the sugar is washed with a spray of warm water before leaving the machine. This yields about 90 lb. of 99-purity sugar per 100 lb. raw melted, and an affination syrup of about 80 purity and 75° Brix. The washed sugar is dissolved in about one-half its weight of hot water, or high-test sweet waters from process, and pumped to the clarification station. Part of the affination syrup goes back to the mingler for mixing with incoming raws, the excess being pumped to process, either for boiling to "remelt sugar" or for clarification and char filtration. Modern affination stations are completely automatic.

**Clarification.**—The clarification (defecation) process prepares the solution of washed sugar, or washed sugar liquor, for char filtration or other decolorization. Three different refinery clarification systems are in use. (1) *Pressure filtration* adds sufficient lime to neutralize acidity (pH 7.4), then heats to 85° C (185° F), adds diatomaceous earth (kieselguhr) as a filter aid (three to six pounds per ton of melt), then passes the treated liquor through leaf-type filters to remove insolubles, some of the colloids and gums, but little or no colour. (2) *The Williamson System,* invented by George B. Williamson in 1918, consists essentially of defecation with phosphoric acid and lime and air-flotation of the precipitated calcium phosphate by impregnation with air bubbles and heating to 95° C (203° F) in troughlike continuous clarifiers. The air bubbles expand, floating the precipitate to the surface to form a blanket of mud. The clear liquor is drawn off without filtration, and the mud blanket removed, all continuously. The phosphate treatment removes 30% of the colour, largely colloidal. All vegetable-carbon plants and most bone char refineries employ phosphate-lime defecation with some modified form of the clarifier. (3) *Carbonatation,* which is universal in beet sugar work, involves precipitation of an excess of lime with carbon dioxide gas. All cane refineries in Great Britain, Australia, and Canada, and at least one large refinery in the United States, employ carbonatation. The calcium carbonate ($CaCO_3$) formed is easily filtered and washed free of sugar. About 70% of all colour is removed, as well as other impurities, so that a much smaller decolorizing station is required than with other systems.

**Mud Treatment.**—The muds from the pressure filters and from the Williamson System are diluted and filtered to recover the retained sugar, the high-test sweet waters serving to melt the washed raw sugar. The Williamson filter cake is always discarded, but several large United States refineries regenerate the kieselguhr cake in special furnaces for continued reuse.

**Decolorization.**—The clear yellow to golden brown clarified washed sugar liquor contains about 65% solids (Brix) of 99° purity. Most of the world's large refineries decolorize with bone char; *i.e.,* with granular bone particles carbonized in the absence of air at about 700° C (1,292° F). The liquors percolate through the char in cisterns of 25 tons capacity, 20 ft. deep. The char removes practically all the colouring matter, as well as the ash and organic nonsugars in the liquor, by the physicochemical action known as adsorption. The filter cycle (100 hours or more) consists of: (1) filling the filter with revivified char and liquor; (2) filtration proper, first with washed sugar liquor, then with successively lower grades; (3) "sweetening off" with hot water for several hours to obtain "char sweet water"; (4) washing the char to remove the last traces of sugar and soluble matter; (5) draining and discharging the wet char to the dryers and kilns; (6) revivification in retort kilns or special furnaces at 600° C (1,112° F) with air excluded; and (7) return to the filters for reuse. A patented process called "Continuous Adsorption Process" (CAP) used with either bone char or granular carbon was developed about 1960. The continuous operation is countercurrent. Automatic control replaces the manual regulation of the conventional char system. Liquors flowing from the filter outlets are distributed to proper channels at the "liquor gallery," some for refiltration, others to the vacuum pans for crystallization.

**Activated Carbons.**—The commercial development of decolorization by activated vegetable carbons made from various fibrous wastes (rice hulls, seaweed, peat moss, bagasse, etc.) dates from World War I. About 0.5% of carbon on solids serves to decolorize phosphate-lime defecated washed sugar liquor, generally in a two-stage process in which the carbon is discarded rather than revivified. Leaf-type pressure filters remove the carbon, resulting in a much simpler process requiring less equipment, less water, and a smaller capital outlay than required with bone char. Granular carbon, having properties similar to bone char, has been

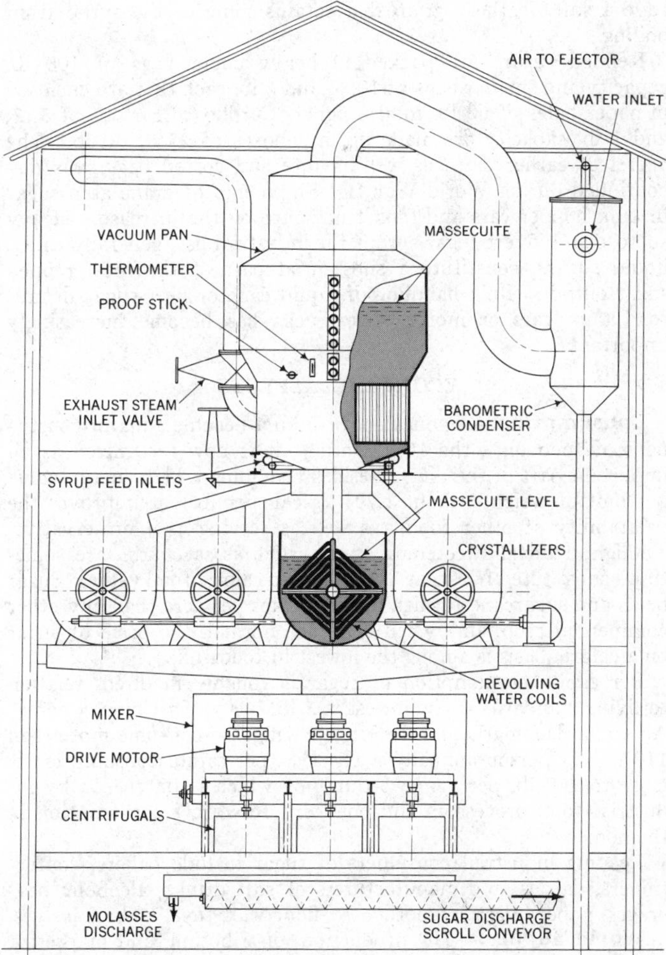

BY COURTESY OF THE HONOLULU IRON WORKS

FIG. 6.—CROSS SECTION THROUGH RAW SUGAR BOILING HOUSE

substituted for the powdered form, but bone char continues to be preferred by refiners because of lower cost, ash removal, and durability.

**Crystallization and Finishing.**—The char-filtered or carbon-treated liquors, water-white or nearly so, are crystallized in vacuum pans similar to those used in raw-sugar factories. Vacuum pans in modern refineries are generally of large capacity and operate with instrument control. Centrifugal machines, generally automatic, separate crystals and syrups. A spray of hot water in the centrifugal removes the syrup film from the white sugar crystals, and the washed moist crystals are air dried in large horizontal atmospheric dryers called granulators. Mechanical screening removes lumps and fines, leaving the dry screened product ready for packaging. Syrups from the centrifugals are boiled several times, the darker granulated syrups being returned for refiltration through bone char. Affination syrups are boiled to remelt sugar that goes through the process again with the washed raw sugar. Refinery final molasses, end-product of this complex boiling system, is sold for fermentation and cattle feed, as is cane blackstrap, which it resembles.

**Packaging.**—Since the output of a large refinery includes numerous grades of sugar, packaging depends to a large extent on the type of sugar, and its use for industry or domestic consumption. Commercial grades of sugar range from the large "coffee crystals" popular in England, through several coarse grades used by confectioners and other manufacturers, to the familiar "table granulated" sugar that makes up the greatest portion of the product. Very fine crystals are termed Fruit Sugar, Dessert Sugar, or Superfine. Confectioners' and powdered (icing) sugars are pulverized in hammer mills with 3% cornstarch to prevent caking. Tablet and cube sugars are made from mixtures of crystals and sugar syrups molded into the desired form, then dried or baked. Brown and yellow sugars, styled "soft sugars" by the refiner, have a soft, feathery grain that retains some of the syrup from boiling.

Refined sugars are packed in heavy paper bags of 100 lb. capacity and smaller bags of 10, 5, and 2 lb. each that are enclosed in paper bales of 60 lb. total weight. Cardboard cartons of 5, 2, and 1 lb. capacity are made up into boxes of 25 or 50 lb. The barrel of earlier days, as well as jute and cotton bags, was discontinued during World War II. Shipments of granulated sugar in bulk hopper cars and tank trucks are on the increase. Heavy sucrose and invert sugar syrups for industrial use, generally called liquid sugars, constitute a substantial part of the total refined sugar output. Bulk handling of liquid cane or beet sugar in railroad tank cars or motor tank trucks has become increasingly important.

## ECONOMIC ASPECTS

**Consumption.**—Though sugar did not become a major constituent of food until the 19th century, it is now recognized as an important part of the diet. Besides providing a high energy value per unit of weight (about 1,794 kg-cal. per lb.), it improves the palatability of other foods, as well as serving as a preservative. Though artificial sweetening agents, such as saccharin, are sometimes substituted for sugar, they have no caloric food value. Sugar beets and sugarcane furnish more calories per acre than any other commercial crop, and, when costs are normal, the price of sugar on a caloric basis is among the lowest in foodstuffs.

Per capita consumption of sugar is roughly in direct relation to living standards. The lowest is 3 lb. per yr. in China, whereas Australia, Denmark, and the United Kingdom consume more than 110 lb. per person annually. The U.S. per capita consumption is close to 100 lb. per yr., two-thirds of which is purchased by industrial food processors and one-third for direct consumption in the home.

Leading industrial consumers of sugar include bakers, confectioners, dairies, and manufacturers of soft drinks, alcoholic beverages, paper, plastics, toothpaste, floor wax, toys, and explosives.

**World Supply.**—The production, distribution, and marketing of the world's sugar supply depend on many factors not directly related to supply and demand. Political considerations, such as tariff restrictions, preferential markets, rationing, and government-established quotas, bounties, and taxes, as well as voluntary international agreements to regulate prices, all play a large part. Wars and their aftermaths have affected the industry enormously. The Japanese occupation of the Philippines and Java (Indonesia) during World War II practically destroyed cane production in these two important areas, although both revived rapidly. The beet fields of Europe were the battlegrounds of both World Wars, causing destruction of crops and disruption of production for several years after.

On the other hand, Cuba, and to a lesser extent other war-free areas, stepped up production during the war years and the subsequent years of shortage. As an example of these fluctuations, Cuba produced only 2,700,000 short tons in 1940–41, but approached 8,000,000 short tons during the Korean War. The revolution led by Fidel Castro (1959) and his subsequent Communist government, which expropriated and nationalized all sugar plantations and mills (1960), and the flight of much skilled labour from the country, disrupted the industry. In addition, there was extensive hurricane damage, with the result that Cuba's sugar production was reduced to about 4,000,000 short tons in the early 1960s. Cuban production later increased to about 6,000,000 short tons annually, and the nation remained the world's leading exporter.

About 85% of the world's beet sugar, which in the mid-1960s exceeded 30,000,000 short tons, is produced in the countries extending across Europe and Asia from Ireland and Great Britain to the U.S.S.R., including Siberia. In the mid-1960s the U.S.S.R. ranked first with about 10,000,000 short tons, followed by France, West Germany, Italy, and the United Kingdom. Practically all the beet sugar not produced in Europe and northern Asia comes from the United States (Michigan to California) and Canada. Most European countries produce their own sugar supply, except Great Britain, which imports large quantities of cane sugar, mostly from the Commonwealth nations.

In contrast to the somewhat limited area of beet culture, sugarcane grows around the world, generally between latitudes 30° N and 30° S. At least two-thirds of the total cane production (more than 40,000,000 short tons in the mid-1960s) comes from Cuba, India, Brazil, Australia, the Philippines, Taiwan (Formosa), Indonesia, Hawaii, Puerto Rico, and the British West Indies. Also of importance as cane producers are Argentina, South Africa, the Dominican Republic, Peru, Egypt, and Mauritius. Cane culture in the continental United States is, for the most part, limited to Louisiana and Florida, but the combined output of beet and cane, including Hawaii and Puerto Rico, exceeded 6,500,000 short tons in the mid-1960s. The United States also imported another 4,500,000 short tons, making it the world's largest sugar consumer.

Possibly 10% of the world's sugar is consumed locally and does not enter into general market channels. India has sometimes produced more cane than Cuba, but the output is largely a low-test sugar that may total several million tons. Latin-American countries and the Philippines also produce these low-grade sugars.

World markets are largely controlled by the International Sugar Agreement, which has been periodically ratified since 1932 by more than 40 nations. Quotas are assigned and adjusted from time to time, depending on the price of sugar. Similar measures have been adopted by the Commonwealth Sugar Agreement. The United States substantially controls its domestic prices through the quota system established by the Sugar Act of 1934, under the direction of the Department of Agriculture.

*See* also entries under "Sugar" in the Index.

Bibliography.—Noël Deerr, *The History of Sugar,* 2 vol. (1949 and 1950); B. C. Swerling and V. P. Timoshenko, *World's Sugar: Progress and Policy* (1957); W. R. Aykroyd, *The Story of Sugar* (1967); J. Henry (ed.), *Technological Value of the Sugar Beet* (1962); Pieter Honig, *Principles of Sugar Technology,* 3 vol. (1953–1963); A. C. Barnes, *The Sugar Cane* (1964); C. G. Hughes *et al., Sugar Cane Diseases of the World,* vol. 2 (1964); G. C. Stevenson, *Genetics and Breeding of Sugar Cane* (1965); G. P. Meade, *Cane Sugar Handbook,* 9th ed. (1963); R. A. McGinnis (ed.), *Beet Sugar Technology* (1951); G. H. Jenkins, *Introduction to Cane Sugar Technology* (1966). *See* also International Sugar Council, *Sugar Yearbook* (annual). (G. P. Me.)

**SUGER** (*c.* 1081–1151), abbot of Saint-Denis and famous counselor of the French kings Louis VI and Louis VII, epitomizes the type of humbly born administrator increasingly employed by French and English kings from the 12th century onward. Born probably at Saint-Denis or at Argenteuil, Suger was vowed to the Abbey of Saint-Denis in 1091, and from 1094 to 1104 was a fellow pupil at the Prieuré de l'Estrée with the future King Louis VI. While continuing his studies, probably at Marmoutiers, Suger was already gaining the reputation of a skilful advocate and at La Charité-sur-Loire in 1107 ably and successfully defended his abbey's privileges against the claims of the bishop of Paris. He was made provost of Berneval in Normandy (1107) and moved to Toury in Beauce (1109). Soon afterward Louis, who had become king in 1108, began to employ Suger on special missions; he was sent to the Lateran Council of 1123 and went on an embassy to Pope Calixtus II in 1122.

ARCHIVES PHOTOGRAPHIQUES

PORTRAIT OF ABBOT SUGER IN STAINED GLASS FROM THE 12TH-CENTURY "LIFE OF THE VIRGIN" WINDOW IN THE ABBEY CHURCH OF SAINT-DENIS

While returning from Italy, Suger heard that in his absence he had been elected (1122) abbot of Saint-Denis in succession to Abbot Adam. Some years later, influenced by St. Bernard of Clairvaux, he reformed the abbey, expelling seculars from its precincts and restoring the observance of the strict Benedictine rule (1127). At this period Suger was less at court, attending only on occasions particularly important to the royal family. In 1137 he accompanied the future Louis VII to Aquitaine for the prince's marriage with the heiress Eleanor. A year later Suger was with Louis VII on an expedition to Poitou, but at this period his influence was opposed by the seneschal Ralph of Vermandois and by the queen mother Adelaide. However, with St. Bernard, he worked for peace within France, reconciling the king with his chancellor Algrin (1140) and with Count Thibaut of Blois and Champagne (1144). When Louis set out on the Second Crusade (1147), Suger was appointed regent of France. Ralph of Vermandois and the archbishop of Reims were associated with him, but the main responsibility fell on Suger, whose tenure of office was particularly notable for his brilliant administration of the finances and of the royal demesne. As a result of his excellent management, the increasing wealth and good order of the king's territories made Louis VII, in fact as well as in name, the most powerful prince in France.

Suger's most famous work is his *Vita Ludovici regis* ("The Life of Louis VI"), which is, however, of literary rather than historical interest. He also wrote the first pages of a life of Louis VII. His rebuilding of the abbey church of Saint-Denis was completed in 1145. Reputedly small and with the appearance of a weakling, Suger yet reached his 70th year, dying at Saint-Denis on Jan. 31, 1151.

BIBLIOGRAPHY.—Suger, *Vie de Louis VI le gros,* ed. by H. Waquet (1929); M. Aubert, *Suger* (1950); M. Pacaut, *Louis VII et son royaume* (1964). (M. PAC.)

**SUGGESTION,** in psychology, is a process of human communication that leads the subject to respond uncritically; *e.g.,* in belief or in action. The mode of suggestion, while usually verbal, may be visual or may involve any other sense. The suggestion may be symbolic: a person who is allergic to roses may develop an attack of asthma from looking through a seed catalogue. The tendency to respond to suggestion is not always generalized: a man may be very critical in his business judgments, very suggestible as regards his health.

Most advertisements involve direct suggestion. Subliminal stimulation, the presentation of stimuli too faint or too brief to be perceived, has been offered as an example of indirect suggestion; for example, although the claim has been disputed, popcorn sales were reported to increase by subliminal suggestion via the motion-picture screen.

In prestige suggestion effectiveness depends largely on the credibility of the source. It is often assumed that an authority in nuclear physics, for example, is equally competent in politics or town planning; his prestige in one field may give unwarranted importance to his opinions in an unrelated field (*see* also PSYCHOLOGY, SOCIAL: *Simple Group Effects*).

Suggestion can stimulate both positive and negative reactions. An invitation for a drink extended to a teetotaler will evoke a negative response. Similarly, statements on racial issues will touch off positive or negative reactions according to the background of the person receiving them (*see* ATTITUDE).

If the surrounding environment provides the stimulus, the process is called heterosuggestion. In autosuggestion the person himself is the source. Such physiological factors as fatigue, malnutrition, and drugs may increase suggestibility but are of relative unimportance in daily life. Brainwashing (*q.v.*) techniques are examples of the part unusual physiological conditions may play in suggestibility. Such drugs as thiopental sodium and scopolamine increase suggestibility and have been used as aids in inducing hypnotic states (*see* HYPNOSIS).

BIBLIOGRAPHY.—H. Bernheim, *Hypnosis and Suggestion in Psychotherapy,* 2nd rev. ed., trans. by C. A. Herter (1964); J. V. McConnell, R. L. Cutler, and E. B. McNeil, "Subliminal Stimulation," *Am. Psychol.,* vol. 13 (1958); K. G. Stukát, *Suggestibility* (1958); P. Chauchard, *Hypnosis and Suggestion* (1964); M. Teitelbaum, *Hypnosis Induction Technics* (1965). (G. H. E.; X.)

**SUHL,** a town of East Germany and capital of Suhl *Bezirk* (district), German Democratic Republic. The town (pop. [1964] 28,177) is a railway junction 25 mi. (40 km.) S of Gotha. It produces vehicles, machinery, sporting guns, precision measuring instruments, electrical appliances, metalwork, tools, and toys. First mentioned in 1239, it was noted from the 16th century for making firearms.

SUHL *Bezirk* (pop. [1964] 548,949; area 1,489 sq.mi. [3,856 sq.km.]) extends along much of the Thuringian Forest (Thüringer Wald) and the upper Werra Valley. The development of engineering, vehicle-building, and small iron industries was favoured by local potash deposits and iron ore mines. Electrotechnical, glass, wood, textile, and toy-making enterprises are found in the forest valleys.

**SUI,** a village in the foothills of the Sibi District of West Pakistan, about 60 mi. (97 km.) NE of Jacobabad, which suddenly became of great importance in 1950–51 through the discovery by drilling of immensely rich deposits of natural gas. As Pakistan has only a few oil fields and some poor coal deposits, this discovery changed the whole economic position of the country, providing a cheap source of fuel and power. A pipeline to Karachi was laid down in 1955, a length of 347 mi. (558 km.) being completed in 165 days. Another pipeline reached Multan in 1958 and was subsequently extended to Lahore. The first six wells drilled yielded 70,000,000 cu.ft. (2,000,000 cu.m.) of gas a day. Reserves were estimated to be at least 4,000,000,000,000 cu.ft. (113,000,000,000 cu.m.). The gas is likely to be of particular benefit to the country in the manufacture of chemical fertilizers. (L. D. S.)

**SUICIDE** is the act of voluntary and intentional self-destruction. This definition, however, has at various times and in different places been subject to legal qualification. Thus, in England the term once covered an act of self-destruction committed only while the deceased was of unsound mind; if committed with sound mind, the act was termed *felo-de-se,* a crime which before 1870 could entail forfeiture of the deceased's estate to the crown, and until 1961 any survivor of an attempt was subject to criminal penalty (*see* FELO-DE-SE). In the United States only a few states regard suicide as a criminal act, although it may be criminal to influence or assist in a suicide.

**Religious and Cultural Valuations.**—Suicide has been both condemned and honoured. The Koran severely censures suicide as a graver crime than homicide. The Talmud emphasizes the sacredness of life and condemns suicide as sinful. From the time of the early church, Christianity has opposed self-destruction, though for a time it was debatable whether or not a Christian woman might commit suicide to avoid rape; St. Augustine, however, condemned even this act, and he has been supported by many other Christian writers since. In the Middle Ages, some countries prescribed mutilation of the body and confiscation of the property of a suicide.

The Brahmans of India, however, honoured the person who voluntarily freed himself from his body; hence, the Hindu widow who perished on the funeral pyre of her husband was greatly praised (*see* SUTTEE). The Greeks permitted some convicted criminals to take their own lives, a notable example being Socrates' drinking the hemlock. In Japan, *seppuku* (*hara-kiri; q.v.*), or self-disembowelment, was practised as a ceremonial rite: noblemen were granted the privilege of punishing themselves in this way for wrongdoing; and it was also used to escape the humiliation of failure, to shame one's enemies, to demonstrate loyalty to a recently dead master or emperor, and for other reasons. In World War II, the indoctrination of Japanese soldiers included banzai (suicide charges) and the indoctrination of pilots kamikaze (suicide dive bombing). Spies, and sometimes others in possession of secret information, may be expected to commit suicide if necessary to prevent capture. In Southeast Asia, Buddhist monks and nuns have committed sacrificial suicide by burning themselves alive as a form of social protest, as, for example, in Vietnam.

Few systematic studies have been made of suicide in primitive societies. Anthropologists have claimed that to some peoples, the Zuñi of New Mexico and the Andaman Islanders, for example, the idea of suicide is incomprehensible, and some writers have concluded that suicide rates are very low in primitive societies; other writers have held that rates are much higher in some groups, among the Navaho of North America and the Fiji Islanders, for example, than in most modern societies. Variation in rates of suicide among primitive peoples is probably at least as great as it is among more complex societies. (*See* also MORALITY, PRIMITIVE.)

**Statistics.**—The information available on the numbers and categories of people who commit suicide is not uniformly accurate. Suicide statistics are subject to problems of faulty and incomplete record keeping, attempts at concealment, and differences in definition. Statistics are completely unavailable for many peoples, and only spotty at best for most. One authority estimated that even the best figures available exclude as much as two-thirds of the suicides committed. On the other hand, most authorities argue that the data available, even though they may be incomplete, are approximate representations of trends. Since the early days of the 19th century, it has been recognized that differences in rates between countries are too great to be explained away in terms of differential accuracy of registration. The suicide rates of some countries in Europe, for example, are more than five times as high as those of others. Ireland has consistently shown one of the lowest rates in Europe, and in the world (less than 3 per 100,000 population). The rates of Denmark, Austria, and Hungary have been among the highest (over 20). The rates of France, West Germany, and Sweden are between 15 and 20; those of the United States and England and Wales between 10 and 12; and of Spain, Italy, and Norway between 5 and 10. Chile ranks with Ireland (less than 3); Uruguay's rate is over 10. Japan was for a long time the only country outside Europe to rank consistently among the nations with the highest suicide rates, but in the 1960s the Japanese rate declined to 15 per 100,000. (*See* also VITAL STATISTICS.)

**Who Commits Suicide?**—*Age.*—Studies made in Europe and in the United States at widely different periods of time all show that virtually no children below the age of 15 commit suicide, and that the rate for the later teens is low. The rate tends to increase steadily into old age, especially among males. The rate in old age (over 25 per 100,000 population after age 65) is approximately four times the rate in young adulthood.

*Sex and Marital Status.*—The rates for males are consistently higher than those for females, in different countries, at widely different periods of time, and at all ages. The male rate is about three to five times the female rate. Women, however, make more unsuccessful attempts at suicide than do men. Data from Europe and the U.S. have repeatedly demonstrated that divorced persons and the widowed have much higher suicide rates than married people and those who never married. Having children also appears to be a deterrent to suicide, especially among women.

*Religion and Nationality.*—Roman Catholics characteristically have lower suicide rates than Protestants. Jews tend to have rates as low as or lower than the Catholic rate, but statistics here are less consistent; for example, between 1849 and 1907, the suicide rate among German Jews rose from the lowest to the highest among the three major religious categories in Germany. In general, the predominantly Catholic countries have low suicide rates. The low rates for Catholic Chile, Ireland, Spain, and Italy have been cited under *Statistics,* above; but France has a relatively high rate, while Protestant Norway has a low rate. Most immigrant groups to the U.S. show higher rates than native-born Americans.

*Race and Occupation.*—Negro Americans have consistently produced suicide rates only about one-third as high as the white Americans' rates; the differences between the males of the two races are usually greater than the differences between the females. Data from England and Wales, where the former occupations of suicides are recorded, indicate that persons in the higher status occupations —professionals, managers, and the like—are more prone to suicide than those of lower status; on the other hand, the lowest status, unskilled workers, shows somewhat higher rates than middle-status categories. Data from the records of U.S. insurance companies reveal the same relationship of occupational status to suicide rates.

**Means of Suicide.**—Means of suicide vary according to such factors as the availability of fatal compounds and weapons, the social customs and fads, and the characteristics of the victim. Various typical and fairly stable differences are found between different societies. In England and Wales, for example, gas (most commonly carbon monoxide) poisoning, other forms of poisoning (mostly by narcotics or "sleeping pills"), hanging, and drowning lead the list. In the United States, on the other hand, shooting is the most common method. A major reason for this appears to be that firearms are much more readily accessible in the United States than in England. It is evident, however, that other factors also influence the means used: it is generally found, for example, that violent methods of self-destruction are more commonly used by men than by women.

**Conditions Surrounding Suicide.**—*Urban-Rural Residence.* —Almost invariably urban suicide rates have proved higher than rural rates. The notable exceptions have been the rates in the Netherlands, where the high rate among the rural aged causes the rural rates to supersede the urban rates. Within large urban centres suicide rates are highest in the central residential areas bordering on and interspersed among commercial and industrial districts, and decrease out to the periphery. Exceptions to this general trend in the United States are the low rates of those districts that are inhabited predominantly by Negroes, although increasing urbanization of Negroes is raising even the generally low Negro suicide rate.

*Business Conditions.*—Suicide rates tend to rise during times of business depression; the greater portion of the increase is among men in higher status occupations. The peaks of suicide rates have been noticed to occur during the deepest points of economic downturns; the rates begin to drop to their lowest level just prior to the highest points of prosperity.

*War.*—Trend data associated with several wars indicate that wars tend to depress suicide rates even though men in the military services ordinarily have higher suicide rates than civilians, and, of course, more men are in the service during wartime; it seems that, in wartime, suicide rates drop among career military men as well.

*Seasons.*—Data compiled over long periods of time show that suicide rates increase in the late spring and the early summer, although there are great variations in this trend from year to year. That this trend cannot be accounted for by weather conditions has been demonstrated in several ways: geographic areas that characteristically enjoy mild weather do not necessarily have higher rates; nor do changes in temperature or humidity themselves correspond regularly with changes in the suicide rate. (M. Gd.)

**Attempted Suicide.**—Statistics on attempted suicide are far more unreliable than those on actual suicide, but rates are undoubtedly many times higher than rates of completed suicide. The distribution of attempted suicide differs in several ways from that of actual suicide. The relative frequency of methods used is different: narcotic poisoning (barbiturates, "sleeping pills") heads the list for attempted suicide in Western European countries. The age and sex ratios are also different. While suicide is nearly everywhere more common among men than women, the reverse is true of attempted suicide. For both sexes, rates of attempted suicide reach a peak between about 25 and 40 years of age, while the peak for suicide is over 50. Thus, most attempted suicides do not seem to represent simply suicides that "accidentally" fail; many appear to represent a "cry for help." Some communities, among them, in the United States, Los Angeles, Boston, Chicago, New York, and Miami, have established suicide prevention centres. These are staffed around the clock by psychiatrists, psychologists, psychiatric social workers, and trained laymen whom the person contemplating suicide can call for help to prevent him from committing the act.

**Causes of Suicide.**—The association of such factors as old age, urban residence, and Protestantism with suicide rates does not necessarily indicate that each is a separate cause of suicide. Theorists have proposed that these associations are evidence for certain underlying causes of suicide, but there is still disagreement about what these underlying causes are.

Sociologist Émile Durkheim, in a major work on suicide (1897), identified two major types of suicide, egoistic and anomic, as characteristic of modern societies, and one type, altruistic, as characteristic of traditional and primitive societies. Egoistic suicide results from lack of integration of the individual into society; a person without close family ties or similar interpersonal connections is not so much deterred from suicide. Thus, according to Durkheim, the suicide rate is lowest among Catholics who are part of a collective religious institution and highest among Protestants, among whom there is greater emphasis on individualism. Anomic suicide results from the failure of normative social standards to regulate individual behaviour; an individual may take his life when his habitual norms are no longer appropriate to his situation. This type of suicide is most common in periods of economic depression, not because of the sheer poverty involved but because of the resulting state of *anomie*, or normlessness.

English sociologist Peter Sainsbury, emphasizing Durkheim's anomic type of suicide, held that individuals are more prone to suicide when they live in, but apart from, a social group that neither acknowledges nor provides means for satisfying their needs. Where mobility and social isolation are pronounced, community life will be unstable, without order or purpose, and this will be reflected in the suicide rates.

Altruistic suicide results from too much integration of the individual into society so that the individual takes his own life in obedience to the customs of his society, in which suicide in certain situations is regarded either as obligatory or as an honourable act. Durkheim believed this type of suicide to be most common in primitive and traditional societies.

In psychological theory, suicide has commonly been related directly to mental disorder, which has often been held to be "the cause" of suicide. However, nothing like a complete correspondence between suicide and accepted forms of mental disorder has ever been demonstrated. The most profitable approach would seem to be to recognize that the cause of suicide and the causes of mental disorder partly overlap, so that a theory of suicide must link up closely with what is known about relevant types of mental disorder. Thus, virtually the only important theoretical approach to suicide in psychology, based on ideas suggested by Freud, links the causes of suicide closely with the causes of depression. According to this theory, depression and suicide can be understood in terms of hostile impulses that, although first directed against others, become turned back against the self. The depressive individual is held to be characterized by an excessively strong and repressive conscience (superego), which does not allow him to express his aggressive feelings externally, but which redirects them against the ego. Suicide is seen as an extreme upon a continuum of self-aggression ranging from verbal self-derogation to attempts at self-destruction.

Since the conscience is supposed to be the outer-voice-become-inner of some important figure in the person's life, usually a parent, suicide in this theory takes on the meaning not only of self-destruction but also of murdering an accuser; thus, Karl A. Menninger suggested that every suicide has three elements: (1) the wish to kill, (2) the wish to be killed, and (3) the wish to die. Similarly, Louis I. Dublin proposed that suicide is caused by feelings of fear, inferiority, and death wishes against another with whom the individual identified; guilt is almost invariably present.

Andrew F. Henry and James F. Short are among those theorists who have held that the act of suicide is a manifestation of the general principle that the frustration of any desire is likely to cause aggression. The suicide, according to Henry and Short, turns his aggression inward against himself rather than outward against others (homicide) for reasons associated with his social position and the manner in which he was raised in childhood.

It is clear that no one theory has adequately and completely explained suicide. Hope for a general theory of suicide probably lies in a continuation and development of ideas suggested in the sociological and psychological approaches to the explanation of suicide and embracing a range of factors including individual wishes and attitudes, personal life crises, societal beliefs and practices, and social and economic conditions. In spite of well over a hundred years of research in the field, knowledge of the etiology of suicide is still on a rudimentary level. One reason for this is the obvious difficulty of obtaining adequate and controlled data through which theoretical ideas can be tested.

Bibliography.—É. Durkheim, *Suicide* (Eng. trans. by G. Simpson and J. A. Spaulding, 1951); L. I. Dublin and B. Bunzel, *To Be or Not To Be* (1933); S. Freud, "Mourning and Melancholia" (1917), *Collected Papers,* vol. iv (1924); M. Halbwachs, *Les Causes du suicide* (1930); R. S. Cavan, *Suicide* (1928); K. A. Menninger, *Man Against Himself* (1938); P. Sainsbury, *Suicide in London* (1955); A. F. Henry and J. F. Short, Jr., *Suicide and Homicide* (1954); E. Stengel and N. G. Cook, *Attempted Suicide* (1958); P. Bohannan (ed.), *African Homicide and Suicide* (1960); E. S. Shneidman and N. L. Farberow (eds.), *Clues to Suicide* (1957), *The Cry for Help* (1961); L. I. Dublin, *Suicide* (1963); E. Stengel, *Suicide and Attempted Suicide* (1965).
(M. Gd.; Ay. G.)

**SUIR,** a river in the Republic of Ireland that has considerable variety in its 114-mi. (183 km.) course. It rises in the Devil's Bit Mountains and flows south across the lowland of County Tipperary through the town of Thurles and past the ruins of the 12th-century Cistercian abbey of Holycross to the foot of the Knockmealdown Mountains. There, in a wide fertile lowland, it receives an east-flowing tributary, the Tar, bends through an elbow-shaped loop, and flows north around the western edge of the Comeragh Mountains, forming part of the Tipperary–Waterford county boundary. Having now passed through more than half its course, the river enters a long west-east valley guarded on the south by the Comeraghs and consisting of limestone lowlands on the north, except for Slievenamon, another line of hills. The contrast between north and south is well seen at Clonmel (*q.v.*), which has a promenade on the north side of the river giving fine views of the Comeraghs.

In the 1760s the river was made navigable to Clonmel, but the tidal limit is at Carrick-on-Suir (*q.v.*), 15 mi. downstream. There is no water traffic now. Finally the river broadens into an estuary and passes through Waterford (*q.v.;* from Norse times a port and still a major town); a little farther east it is joined by the Barrow and the Nore, all three rivers discharging into the wide estuarine bay called Waterford Harbour. (T. W. Fr.)

**SUITE,** in music, from the French *suite de pièces,* a group of self-contained instrumental movements of varying character, usually in the same key. During the 17th and early 18th centuries, the period of its greatest importance, the suite was comprised principally of dance movements. In the 19th and 20th centuries, however, the term was used in a more general sense to cover almost all sets of instrumental pieces, mainly in forms smaller than those of the sonata, including selections for concert performance of music from ballets or from incidental music to plays.

The principle of related dance movements may be said to have its origins in the paired dances of the 14th century; *e.g.*, the saltarello and rotta. The practice of grouping dances of related key but contrasting tempo and metre continued, but by the 16th century the order of the dances had begun to be dictated more by considerations of music than of dance. By the middle of the 17th century French composers had established the principal features of the suite. This essentially French form of the genre was to remain the model for composers of all countries for 100 years.

The classical suite of the time of Bach and Handel consists essentially of four principal dance movements, with one to three lighter movements inserted before the final principal one:

1. The Allemande. The first movement of the classical suite, it is a staid dance in $\frac{4}{4}$ time with a characteristically rich, flowing rhythm; it frequently begins with either one or three short notes before the first full bar.

2. The Courante. The second movement is of two kinds, the French and the Italian. The French courante begins with either one or three short notes before the first full bar. It is a dignified dance in an ambiguous rhythm that alternates between $\frac{3}{2}$ and $\frac{6}{4}$.

3. The Saraband. The slow third movement is in triple time, traditionally beginning on the full bar. The Italian type (the corrente) is a brilliant, continuously running piece in a quick $\frac{3}{4}$ or $\frac{3}{8}$.

4. The Gigue. The concluding movement is an animated dance in a triplet rhythm ($\frac{12}{8}$, $\frac{6}{8}$, or $\frac{3}{8}$), lightly fugal in style.

Bach's French suites may be said to mark the end of the classical suite in the French style. His English suites and *partitas* (German suites) are on a larger scale and show a tendency toward a symphonic conception. This is apparent in the scope of the long and characteristic first movement, the prelude. Some of Bach's large-scale suites end with a finale after the gigue.

**SUKARNO** (SOEKARNO) (1901–1970), first president of Indonesia, was born June 6, 1901, at Surabaja, Java, and graduated in engineering from the Bandung Technical Institute in 1925. By 1928 he had become Indonesia's foremost nationalist leader, advocating noncooperation with the colonial government and independence for an Indonesia whose economy was to be organized along socialist lines. He was arrested by Dutch authorities in December 1929 and jailed for two years. His further arrest in July 1933 was followed by a nine-year exile in Flores Island and at Bengkulu in Sumatra. In 1942 he was released by the Japanese, with whom he cooperated in return for concessions providing greater scope in organizing the nationalist movement. Sukarno proclaimed Indonesia's independence on Aug. 17, 1945, becoming its president and a foremost leader in the ensuing struggle for independence.

His synthesis of Marxism, nationalism, and traditional Javanese concepts provided the basis for a national Indonesian ideology—*Marhaenism*. His magnetic personality, which he injected into mass-attended speeches, did much to spread this ideology and his political formulations throughout Indonesia. While sympathetic to much in the program of Indonesian Communists and to the accomplishments of the Chinese Communists, Sukarno opposed proletarian dictatorship and Marxist class analysis. He was a political eclectic insisting upon an ideological synthesis of his own, attuned to the particular conditions existing in Indonesia.

The ineffectiveness of party government during 1950–56 increased Sukarno's long-held reservations concerning the appropriateness of parliamentary democracy for Indonesia. To replace it he advocated a "truly Indonesian" system—"Guided Democracy." This called for temporary representation in government of all major political parties and social groups, to be followed by the dissolution of political parties into a monolithic national front, controlled by him and dedicated to greater national unity and economic progress. Though the National Front never assumed real importance, and it proved impossible for Sukarno to develop Guided Democracy in accordance with his original con-

FRED MAYER FROM MAGNUM

SUKARNO

cept, he did assume, beginning in 1957, an increasingly active role in government. His growing ascendancy was challenged in 1958 by military commanders in Sumatra and Celebes and some influential Islamic political leaders, but following their defeat his position became stronger. In 1960 he dissolved the elected Parliament and replaced it with one appointed by him. He was still obliged to share power with the armed forces, but by 1962 he was clearly the dominant partner. To help ensure his ascendancy he gave the Communist Party (which he regarded as subservient to neither Peking nor Moscow) enough scope for growth to ensure that it would remain a counterweight to the army. Increasingly, significant aspects of his policies paralleled those advocated by the Indonesian Communists; while insisting that they be represented in government, however, he refused them key positions.

Sukarno's attitude toward the U.S. and Great Britain was much affected by foreign policy issues, but the most important factor in determining his hostile attitude toward the U.S. was the covert American support given to the anti-Sukarno rebels in 1958. In the 1960s he showed increasing interest in assuming a role as the principal world leader in a struggle against old and "neo" colonial forces. In 1965 he took Indonesia out of the United Nations and, with the support of Peking, laid plans for establishment of a rival world organization to be known as CONEFO (Conference of New Emerging Forces). On Oct. 1, 1965, an attempted coup by army elements, largely drawn from central Java and supported by part of the air force and some armed members of the Communist Youth, resulted in the killing of six top generals. As a consequence, the Communist Party was outlawed and several hundred thousand adherents massacred. With the elimination of the Communist Party the balance of power was drastically altered in favour of the army, and Sukarno's position was further weakened because it was alleged that he, as well as Communist leaders, was involved in planning the coup. On March 11, 1966, Sukarno was obliged to delegate wide powers to the army commander, General Suharto. There followed a rapid reversal of many of Sukarno's domestic and foreign policies (with Indonesia reentering the United Nations) and an attempt to win Western support for a program of economic recovery. On March 12, 1967, the Provisional People's Consultative Congress transferred Sukarno's remaining powers to Suharto, who became acting president and prime minister. Because of fear of civil war, Sukarno was not brought to trial but was kept under house arrest and banned from political activity. While still under house arrest he died on June 21, 1970.

*See* also INDONESIA, REPUBLIC OF.

BIBLIOGRAPHY.—Herbert Feith, *The Decline of Constitutional Democracy in Indonesia* (1962); Louis Fischer, *The Story of Indonesia* (1959); Bruce Grant, *Indonesia* (1964); Donald Hindley, *The Communist Party of Indonesia, 1951–1963* (1964); George McT. Kahin, *Nationalism and Revolution in Indonesia* (1952); *Sukarno: an Autobiography, as Told to Cindy Adams* (1965). (G. McT. K.)

**SUKENIK, ELEAZAR LIPA** (1889–1953), Israeli archaeologist who identified the antiquity of the Dead Sea Scrolls (*q.v.*) and secured the first lot for the Hebrew University of Jerusalem. Born on Aug. 12, 1889, in Russia at Bialystok (now in northeastern Poland), he attended the Hebrew Teachers Seminary and the École Biblique et Archéologique Française at Jerusalem, Berlin University, and Dropsie College, Philadelphia, Pa. He returned to the Hebrew University as field archaeologist (1926), subsequently becoming (1935) lecturer in and then (1938) professor of the archaeology of Palestine. He was also director of the Museum of Jewish Antiquities. His numerous excavations and investigations led to remarkable discoveries. At Tell Jerishe he found remnants of an important Hyksos fortification. Together with L. A. Mayer he published *The Third Wall of Jerusalem* (1930), based on their excavations, which solved a vexed problem of topography. His Schweich Lectures of 1930 were published as *Ancient Synagogues in Palestine and Greece* (1934). His publication *The Ancient Synagogue of Beth Alpha* (1932) made famous the mosaic pavement he had unearthed and opened a new page in the history of Jewish art. Keen interest in numismatics led to his discovery of the formerly misinterpreted oldest Jewish coins of the Persian period. Sukenik's familiarity with the script of the epitaphs of the Jewish necropolis in Jerusalem, dating from the last century (*c.* 30 B.C.–A.D. 70) of the Second Temple, enabled him to recognize that the scrolls found in the first Qumran cave in 1947 dated from the same period. His book *The Dead Sea Scrolls of the Hebrew University* (1955) appeared after his death at Jerusalem on Feb. 28, 1953. (N. Av.)

**SUKHOTHAI,** the first independent Thai kingdom. The Thais originally peopled the Yangtze valley, where they founded the empire of Nanchao. Long before the fall of Nanchao, they began to drift southward along the rivers of the Indochinese peninsula, forming small principalities that came under the suzerainty of the Khmers from Cambodia. In 1238 two Thai chieftains from Chiangrai and Chiangmai waged a successful war of independence against the Khmers. One of them assumed the Khmer title of Sri Indraditya and proclaimed himself king. He established at Sukhothai the capital city of what was to become a mighty and vigorous, though short-lived, Thai state.

Indraditya's third son, Ramkhaeng or Rama the Great (1275–*c.* 1317), gave Sukhothai its period of greatest glory. He extended his dominion to the Bay of Bengal, Luang Prabang, and down the Malay peninsula as far as Ligor. He maintained relations with the Mongol court in China, receiving emissaries from Kublai Khan and sending numerous tributary missions to Peking. Political disintegration of Sukhothai followed the death of Ramkhaeng, or Phra Ruang, as he is popularly known, and the centre of power shifted southward to the succeeding Thai kingdom of Ayutthaya.

From many peoples and civilizations, the Sukhothai kings drew the elements that went into the making of their own society. Religious missions, objects of Buddhist art, and the basic religious beliefs of Theravada Buddhism came from Ceylon. The pattern of political organization, the Brahmanistic ceremonials associated with kingship, and the alphabet first used to write the Thai language were adopted from Cambodia. Art, sculpture and literature were introduced from India and highly skilled artisans in ceramics were imported from China. The Sukhothai period is known as the golden age in the development of Thai culture.

*See* also THAILAND: *History*. (C. A. B.)

**SUKHUMI,** seaport and capital of the Abkhaz Autonomous Soviet Socialist Republic in the Georgian S.S.R., U.S.S.R., on the coastal railway about 100 mi. (160 km.) NNW of Batumi. Pop. (1959) 64,730. Its Black Sea location, on the north of a broad, shallow bay with sandy beaches, and subtropical climate have made it one of the most popular of Soviet resorts. There are many sanatoria and holiday camps. Shipping services run to other Black Sea ports. Industries are based on local agricultural products and include fruit canning and wine making, and the production of tobacco, leather goods, and footwear. The town has a botanical garden, a pedagogic institute, and the Institute of Abkhaz Language, Literature, and History. (R. A. F.)

**SUKKOTH:** *see* JEWISH HOLIDAYS.

**SUKKUR,** a town in the Khairpur division of West Pakistan, and the headquarters of the district of the same name, is situated on the right bank of the Indus River, about 225 mi. (362 km.) NNE of Karachi. Pop. (1961) 103,216. A cantilever bridge connects Sukkur with Rohri on the other bank. Midstream between the two towns lies the island fortress of Bukkur. The newer part of Sukkur is partly built on a rocky site connected with a low limestone hill. In the old town there are ruins of many tombs and mosques. On the western side, overlooking the river, is the lofty minaret of Mir Masum Shah, erected about 1607. Other antiquities include the white tomb of Adam Shah, the first of the Kalhoras, and the blue tomb of Shah Khairuddin, the founder of a spiritual order. Sukkur also possesses a degree college. The town is an important trade and industrial centre, with cotton and silk textile and hosiery mills, and biscuit, oil, flour, and other factories. It is also noted for cotton handloom weaving. The Sukkur industrial trading estate was developed in the 1950s to provide facilities for factories using local materials, such as wool, oilseeds, and hides and skins.

SUKKUR DISTRICT has an area of 5,531 sq.mi. (14,325 sq.km.). Pop. (1961) 836,867. It consists of an alluvial plain broken only at Sukkur and Rohri by limestone hills that provide firm banks for the Indus. The eastern section of the district, known as Registan, forms a part of the Thal Desert and is covered with sand dunes. The principal crops are rice, wheat, gram, and millets. Earthen-, leather-, and metalware, cotton cloth, and tussah silk are manufactured, also pipe bowls, snuffboxes, and scissors. Sukkur is the site of the Lloyd Barrage, completed in 1932. The barrage, about one mile long, crosses the Indus and feeds four main canals on the left bank and three on the right. The canals cover a cultivable area of 5,400,000 ac. (2,185,000 ha.) and a gross area of 8,300,000 ac. (3,359,000 ha.). Numerous ferries cross the Indus at different places, the exact positions of the crossings varying with the changes in the course of the river. Rohri and Shikarpur are the only other important towns. At Shikarpur (pop. [1961] 53,910) brassware and locks are manufactured. The town also has a degree college affiliated with Sind University. Rohri (pop. [1961] 19,072) is an important railway junction and has a cement factory. (K. S. AD.)

**SUKUMA** (BASUKUMA, WASUKUMA), a Bantu people who inhabit the area southwest of Lake Victoria between Smith Sound and the Serengeti Plain in Tanganyika, Tanzania. Numbering about 1,000,000 in the 1960s, and traditionally divided into many small chiefdoms, they combined as a political federation that operated from 1964 as a unit under the government of Tanzania. Linguistically they are closest to their southern neighbours the Nyamwezi (*q.v.*), but some Sukuma chiefs claim descent from the Hima people to the northwest (*see* NKOLE). Traditional Sukuma economy is based on cattle, millet, and sorghum; cotton was added as a cash crop in recent times.

Historically the Sukuma chief (*Ntemi*) was advised by a group of hereditary councilors and ruled through hereditary village headmen. Adult males were divided into two clubs or lodges: one specialized in divination (*q.v.*) and advised the headmen; the other was in charge of land administration and communal labour. Numerous other societies were devoted to mutual aid in cultivation. Inheritance of property and succession to office are usually patrilineal; however, the office of chief passes to one of his sisters' sons, while the children of a woman married without bridewealth (*q.v.*) inherit from her family instead of from their father's. Traditional religion mainly involved communicating with and propitiating ancestral spirits.

*See* also BANTU (INTERLACUSTRINE). (L. A. Fs.)

**SULAIMAN RANGE,** a range of mountains in West Pakistan, stretching for about 250 mi. (400 km.) from the Gumal Pass (which gives access from northern Baluchistan to Dera Ismail Khan and the upper Indus) to the Marri and Bugti tribal country north of Jacobabad and the lower Indus. The height of the range gradually decreases toward the south. In the northern part, pale, marine coral limestone rests on Cretaceous Sandstone, while, in the south, sandstone, clays, and marble predominate. Edible pines abound in the higher northern part and olives in the centre, but vegetation is scarce in the south. The northern part is transversely cut by very narrow gorges that provide means of communication across the range, the principal routes being through the Ghat, Zao, Chuharkhel Dhana, and Sakhi Sarwar passes. In the southern part, about 60 mi. (97 km.) from Dera Ghazi Khan lies the hill station of Fort Munro (6,303 ft. [1,921 m.]). The highest point of the range is the twin peak known as Takht-i-Sulaiman, or Solomon's Throne (the higher one being 11,290 ft. [3,441 m.]), at the northern end, which legend connects with Solomon's visit to Hindustan. It has a *ziarat*, or shrine, which, though difficult of approach, is visited annually by many pilgrims. On both sides of the Takht-i-Sulaiman dwell the Shirani Pathans, those on the eastern slope being known as the Largha and those on the western as the Bargha. (C. C. D.; K. S. AD.)

**SULA ISLANDS,** a chain of islands east of Celebes (Sulawesi), Indonesia, physically an extension of the eastern peninsula of that island, and administratively forming part of the Maluku Utara (North Moluccas) *kabupaten* (regency). The population (1957 est.) was 30,779. There are three large islands, Taliabu, Mangole, and Sanana (also known as Sula Besi), and several smaller ones. Taliabu and Mangole, separated by the narrow Tjapalulu Strait, extend (with Lifamatola) about 135 mi. (217 km.) east and west. Both are narrow, mountainous, thickly forested, and thinly populated. Taliabu, the largest in area and little known, is said to contain hot springs and mountains 3,000–4,000 ft. (900–1,200 m.) high. Mangole, much narrower than Taliabu, has Mt. Buja in the west. Sanana, the smallest of the three, is well populated and cultivated.

The naturalist A. R. Wallace considered that the approximation between the birds of the Sula Islands and those of Buru Island, in the Moluccas, indicated that there had once been a land bridge between them. The babirusa and crested baboon of Buru are also found in the Sulas. The islands produce timber for shipbuilding, and the inhabitants are good navigators. Damar is collected in the forests; rice, maize, tobacco, and sugarcane are grown on Sanana, where cultivation is far superior to that of the other islands. The sago palm is common, forming the staple food on Taliabu and Mangole. Coal of inferior quality is found on Sanana, and the people weave sarongs and plait mats.

The people of the Sulas resemble the inhabitants of Buru and Ceram (*q.v.*) and may be of Malayo-Polynesian stock from eastern Celebes. Most of them are pagan, but Muslim elements are increasing. The town of Sanana on the northeastern coast of Sanana Island is the chief town and the residence of the local administrator of the islands. The town, formerly the haunt of pirates, has a good roadstead and is a port of call for vessels.

The Banggai or Peleng islands, off the western end of Taliabu, are little known; Peleng itself is mountainous and well forested, with bays affording anchorage but also with reefs. They supply trepang and turtle. The people, who are also either pagan or Muslim, live along the coast.

The Sula and Banggai isles once formed part of the territory of the sultan of Ternate and came under Dutch influence when the Dutch took over the sultan's possessions in 1683. The Sula Islands were occupied by Japan in World War II.

(E. E. L.; J. O. M. B.)

**SULAYMANIYAH,** a town and administrative centre of Sulaymaniyah *liwa'*, Iraq, lies about 30 mi. (48 km.) W of the Iraqi-Iranian frontier in a fertile basin situated between two mountain ranges, the Baranand Dagh and Azmar Dagh, and drained by the Av-i Tanjero, one of the main headstreams forming the Diyala River. Sulaymaniyah itself lies mostly on the lower slopes of the Azmar Dagh and is surrounded on all sides except the southeastern by bare and wild hill country that culminates in the Pir-i Makurun (8,600 ft. [2,621 m.]), 20 mi. NE. Climatic conditions are relatively severe, with cold winters (snow on 50–60 days) and hot but variable summers. Pop. (1961 est.) 42,000.

Sulaymaniyah is somewhat unusual in Iraq, having an extensive open square, and many houses, generally flat roofed, standing in walled compounds or gardens. It is a market centre for cereals (wheat, barley, and some rice) grown in the Tanjero valley and for the gum and pastoral products (wool, skins, and dairy produce) of the mountain zone. Lying on the trade route from Baghdad to Tabriz, it has an important merchant community. The inhabitants are mainly Kurds (*q.v.*), and the town is a centre of Kurdish nationalism.

The whole region was for long in dispute between Ottoman Turkey and Persia; the present town was established by a local ruler in 1781 and named after the contemporary Ottoman pasha of Baghdad.

SULAYMANIYAH LIWA' comprises not only the headstream zone of the Diyala River but part of another basin, that of the Lesser Zab. Area 4,630 sq.mi. (11,992 sq.km.). Pop. (1965) 408,220.

(W. B. FR.)

**SULEIMAN I,** known to the Turks as KANUNI, "the Lawgiver," and to the Christian world as THE MAGNIFICENT (1494/1495–1566), sultan of the Ottoman Empire from 1520 to 1566, whose reign witnessed the unfolding of all that was most characteristic and brilliant in Ottoman civilization, was the only son of Sultan Selim I. He became Sanjak Beg of Kaffa in the Crimea during the reign of his grandfather Bayazid II and Sanjak Beg at Manisa in western Asia Minor in the reign of Selim I.

BY COURTESY OF THE ALBERTINA, VIENNA

SULEIMAN I

Engraved portrait from life by a Danish artist, Melchior Lorichs, who visited Constantinople in 1559

Suleiman succeeded his father as sultan in September 1520. Belgrade fell to him in 1521 and Rhodes, long under the rule of the Knights of St. John, in 1522. At Mohács, in August 1526, Suleiman broke the military strength of Hungary, the Hungarian king, Louis II, losing his life in the battle. The vacant throne of Hungary was now claimed by Ferdinand, the Habsburg archduke of Austria, and by John Zápolya, who was voivode of Transylvania and the candidate of the "native" party opposed to the prospect of Habsburg rule. Suleiman agreed to recognize Zápolya as a vassal king of Hungary, and in 1529, hoping to remove at one blow all further intervention by Austria, he laid siege to Vienna. Difficulties of time and distance, of bad weather and lack of supplies, no less than the resistance of the Christians, forced the sultan to raise the siege. The campaign was successful, however, in a more immediate sense, for Zápolya was to rule thereafter over most of Hungary until his death in 1540. A second great campaign in 1532, notable for the brilliant Christian defense of Güns, ended as a mere foray into Austrian border territories. The sultan, preoccupied with affairs in the East and convinced that Austria was not to be overcome at one stroke, granted a truce to the archduke Ferdinand in 1533.

The death of Zápolya in 1540 and the prompt advance of Austrian forces once more into central Hungary drove Suleiman to modify profoundly the solution that he had imposed in the time of Zápolya. The great Ottoman campaigns of 1541 and 1543 led to the emergence of three distinct Hungaries—Habsburg Hungary in the extreme north and west; Ottoman Hungary along the middle Danube, a region under direct and permanent military occupation by the Ottomans and with its main centre at Buda; and Transylvania, a vassal state dependent on the Porte and in the hands of John Sigismund, the son of Zápolya. Between 1543 and 1562 the war in Hungary continued, broken by truces and with few notable changes on either side; the most important was the Ottoman capture of Temesvár (Timişoara) in 1552. After long negotiations a peace recognizing the *status quo* in Hungary was signed in 1562.

Suleiman waged three major campaigns against Persia. The first (1534–35) gave the Ottomans control over the region of Erzurum in eastern Asia Minor and also witnessed the Ottoman conquest of Iraq, a success that rounded off the achievements of Selim I. The second campaign in 1548–49 brought much of the area around Lake Van under Ottoman rule, but the third (1554–55) served rather as a warning to the Ottomans of the difficulty of subduing the Safavid state in Persia. The first formal peace between the Ottomans and the Safavids was signed in 1555, but it offered no clear solution to the problems confronting the Ottoman sultan on his eastern frontier.

The naval strength of the Ottomans became formidable in the reign of Sultan Suleiman. Khair ed-Din, known in the West as Barbarossa (*q.v.*), became *kapudan* (high admiral) of the Ottoman fleet and won off Preveza a sea fight (1538) against the combined fleets of Venice and Spain, which gave to the Ottomans the naval initiative in the Mediterranean until the Battle of Lepanto in 1571. Tripoli in North Africa fell to the Ottomans in 1551. A strong Spanish expedition against Tripoli was crushed at Djerba in 1560, but the Ottomans failed to capture Malta from the Knights of

St. John in 1565. Ottoman naval power was felt at this time even as far afield as India, where a fleet sent out from Egypt made an unsuccessful attempt in 1538 to take Diu from the Portuguese.

The later years of Suleiman were troubled by conflict between his sons. Mustafa had become by 1553 a focus of disaffection in Asia Minor and was executed in that year on the order of the sultan. There followed during 1559–61 a conflict between the princes Selim and Bayazid over the succession to the throne, which ended with the defeat and execution of Bayazid. Suleiman himself died during the night of Sept. 5/6, 1566, while he was besieging the fortress of Szigetvár in Hungary.

The great figures who surrounded the sultan contributed much, no doubt, to the splendour of the reign: men like Ibrahim Pasha, Rustem Pasha, and Mehmed Sokollu Pasha in the field of statecraft; like Baki, the prince of Ottoman poets, and Mimar Sinan, the most renowned of Ottoman architects; or like Abu Su'ud in the field of law. Suleiman himself was, to his subjects, the "Lawgiver," due to the fact that his long reign saw a sustained effort to adjust the complex structure of the Ottoman state to the circumstances of a new age. To his contemporaries in Europe Suleiman was "il magnifico," "the magnificent sultan." It was the Venetian Andre Navagero who paid him the rarest of compliments when he wrote that Suleiman, provided he were well informed, did injustice to no one. *See* also TURKEY: *History;* and references under "Suleiman I" in the Index.

*See* R. B. Merriman, *Suleiman the Magnificent* (1944); *The New Cambridge Modern History,* ch. xvii (1958). (V. J. P.)

**SULEIMAN II** (1642–1691), a sultan of the Ottoman Empire, was born in Istanbul on April 15, 1642, and succeeded his brother Mohammed IV in 1687. An enforced retirement of 46 years qualified him for the cloister rather than for the throne, and his first feeling when notified of his accession was one of terror of his brother's vengeance. Nor were the circumstances of a nature to reassure him. Immediately following his elevation to the throne occurred one of the most violent revolts of the janizaries, which ended in the murder of the grand vizier and the brutal mutilation of his family, with massacre and pillage throughout Istanbul. Yet Suleiman, in spite of his poor physique and unsuitable upbringing, possessed a martial spirit, and he twice took the field with his troops. The war with Austria (begun before Suleiman's accession) was for Turkey a succession of disasters, but, fortunately for the Ottoman Empire, a third great Koprulu (Mustafa) arose at this time and reestablished order in the sorely tried state. (*See* KOPRULU.) In the reforms that followed, which greatly improved the situation of the Christian subjects of the Porte, Suleiman is at least to be given the credit of having allowed Mustafa Koprulu a free hand. With an improved administration, Turkey's fortunes in the Austrian war began to revive, and the reconquest of Belgrade late in 1690 was the last important event before Suleiman's death at Edirne on June 23, 1691. *See* also TURKEY: *History.*

(G. L. L.; X.)

**SULEYMAN CHELEBI** (d. 1422), Turkish poet, was the author of one work only, the great religious poem *Mevlid.* The son of a vizier, he was born in Bursa and became imam of the great mosque there. The *Mevlid* tells the story of the Prophet's life and death, his miracles, and his heavenly journey. Though written in simple language it is inspired with religious fervour and is often recited at religious ceremonies, particularly funerals. Suleyman Chelebi seems to have made use of the legends on Mohammed which spread through Islamic literature. Further, a few verses of Ashik Pasha's *Garibname* (1329) are reproduced in the *Mevlid,* and the passage on the birth of the Prophet is closely inspired by a corresponding passage in Mustafa Darir's verse and prose translation of Ibn Ishaq's biography.

*See* F. Lyman MacCallum, *The Mevlidi Sherif,* with Eng. trans. (1943) and edition by Ahmed Atesh (1954). (F. I.)

**SULFA DRUGS:** *see* SULFONAMIDES.

**SULFONAMIDES,** a group of chemicals used chiefly in combating infectious disease. Initially, the "sulfa" drugs were produced for treating bacterial infections, but they have come to be used also in treating histoplasmosis and South American blastomycosis (fungus-caused diseases) and diabetes mellitus (a metabolic disorder), and as antihypertensive and diuretic agents.

The sulfonamides have as their basic structure *p*-aminobenzenesulfonamide. From the parent substance, designated sulfanilamide, various related compounds are made, usually by substituting or adding various groups to the sulfone radical (*see* below).

**History.**—In 1932 Gerhard Domagk (*q.v.*) reported to the chemists Fritz Mietzsch and Joseph Klarer that the compound Prontosil, which they had prepared for study, had a curative action in many experimental streptococcal infections. Several years later, Domagk described experiments which demonstrated that Prontosil was a dye of low toxicity, and that when it was administered to mice infected with streptococci, it prevented death. This dye was also effective in controlling staphylococcic infections in rabbits, but it was ineffective in pneumococcic and other experimental infections. These studies by Domagk excited interest in chemotherapy in France, England, and the United States. Within a relatively short period of time it was demonstrated that Prontosil was not only effective in experimental infections in animals but that it also had a powerful effect upon the course of streptococcic diseases in man, including meningitis and puerperal sepsis. It remained for French investigators to point out that the azo dye Prontosil opened up in the tissues, and that it was broken at the azo linkage to *p*-aminobenzenesulfonamide. Moreover, they suggested and later proved that the active principle in Prontosil was sulfanilamide.

In the United States the first important observations were made by P. H. Long and E. A. Bliss in Baltimore; they were soon followed by those of others. Experimental and clinical observations on patients were placed on a sound basis by E. K. Marshall and his associates through the development of chemical methods for determining the amount and distribution of these drugs in the body after they are given by mouth or injected into the bloodstream. To Marshall and his colleagues belongs the credit for placing bacterial chemotherapy on a sound and rational basis, since clinicians, by using their methods of chemical analysis and knowing the pharmacology of these substances, could use objective methods in following patients undergoing such treatment.

As new sulfonamides have been synthesized and applied in the study of infections and other diseases in man and animals, more effective and less toxic agents have been discovered. Also, some compounds have been developed that exert their main effect locally in the gastrointestinal tract and are not absorbed. Others are absorbed slowly or excreted slowly, so that they are longer acting.

The sulfonamides have come to be used most widely in the treatment of urinary tract infections, for the treatment and prevention of meningococcic meningitis, for bacillary dysentery, for pneumococcic pneumonia, and for prophylaxis of streptococcic infections. They are combined with antibiotics to broaden the spectrum of activity and to delay the emergence of resistant bacteria, especially in *Hemophilus influenzae* and *Pseudomonas aeruginosa* infections of the meninges.

Scarcely a year goes by that new sulfonamides are not synthesized and tested. A large number of drugs have been tested and found to be effective, among them sulfapyridine, sulfathiazol, sulfadiazine, sulfapyrazine, sulfamerazine, sulfaguanidine, sulfasuxadine, sulfisoxazole, sulfamethoxypyridazine, sulfachloropyridazine, and sulfisomidine. The most widely used of all these sulfonamides are sulfadiazine, sulfisoxazole, and sulfasuxadine. (C. S. KR.)

**Mode of Action.**—The sulfonamides inhibit the growth of susceptible microorganisms by preventing the formation of folic acid, a member of the B-group of vitamins present in all living cells and functioning as a coenzyme in the synthesis of many important constituents of protoplasm. Most bacteria make their own folic acid from simpler starting materials, while man and other higher animals must have folic acid supplied in the diet. Thus, the sulfonamides can inhibit the growth of invading microorganisms without harming the host, since the enzymatic reaction these drugs inhibit does not take place in the host.

T. C. Stamp provided the first clue to the mode of action of the sulfonamides by discovering in 1939 an unknown substance in yeast that antagonized the antibacterial effect of sulfanilamide.

A year later, D. D. Woods identified this substance as *p*-amino-

$$\underset{\text{(A)}}{p\text{-}NH_2C_6H_4COOH} \qquad \underset{\text{(B)}}{p\text{-}NH_2C_6H_4SO_2NH_2}$$

benzoic acid (*see* formula A), which closely resembles sulfanilamide (*see* formula B) in structure. Woods's explanation of how *p*-aminobenzoic acid reverses the inhibitory effect of sulfonamides had far-reaching effects in chemotherapy, nutrition, and enzymology. Although *p*-aminobenzoic acid had never before been found in living cells, Woods postulated that it was essential for the multiplication of the bacterial cell and that the sulfonamides inhibited enzymes involved in its utilization by virtue of their close structural resemblance to *p*-aminobenzoic acid.

His prediction was soon verified by the discovery of *p*-aminobenzoic acid as a growth factor for several microorganisms and as a portion of the folic acid molecule. Thus, it is apparent that the sulfonamides act by being absorbed to folic acid-synthesizing enzymes in place of *p*-aminobenzoic acid and thus preventing folic acid formation. (J. W. Mr.)

**Sulfonamide Resistance.**—Bacteria become increasingly resistant to the sulfonamides after exposure to them. These agents are principally bacteriostatic, *i.e.*, they inhibit the growth and multiplication of bacteria; and with the body's defense mechanism they act to control infection. When the action of the sulfonamides is interfered with by pus or chemicals such as procaine or para-aminobenzoic, then strains of bacteria that are resistant to their action emerge and survive. Also, the bacteriostatic action of sulfonamides is diminished by acetylation, a process in which an acetyl group is substituted for one of the hydrogens of the para-amino group of the sulfonamide molecule.

The problem of sulfonamide resistance is of importance in the management of infections. When sulfadiazine was used in mass prophylaxis during World War II in an attempt to control the spread of hemolytic streptococcic infections and thus prevent tonsillitis, scarlet fever, and their consequences (rheumatic fever and acute nephritis), it was found that resistant strains soon appeared in the population being treated. From patients harbouring sulfonamide-resistant strains the organisms spread to others in the community; thus new outbreaks of sulfonamide-resistant streptococcic disease were observed.

**Triple Sulfonamides.**—In an attempt to increase the solubility of sulfonamides and decrease their toxicity and their capacity to produce hypersensitivity, sulfonamide mixtures have been advocated and widely used. O. Lehr pointed out that several sulfonamides can be dissolved simultaneously in the same medium almost to the full extent of their saturation level without the occurrence of precipitation. Moreover, he showed that mixtures of partial dosages of several sulfonamides showed substantially less tendency toward the development of renal obstruction by intratubular deposition of crystals than do any of the single components of the mixture in equal total dosage.

Highly soluble sulfonamides, or sulfonamide mixtures that are more soluble than individual members of the mixture, have been found to be effective in the prevention and treatment of renal complications.

**Toxic Effects.**—All the sulfonamides are capable of causing drug intoxication, and some patients are hypersensitive to them. It is advisable that these drugs be taken only under the direction of a physician and for no longer a period than necessary. The commonest side effects are nausea, vomiting, and mental confusion. The signs of hypersensitivity are fever and skin eruptions. Other signs of intoxication are anemia resulting from destruction of red blood cells and leukopenia from destruction of white blood corpuscles. Irritation of the kidneys and obstruction of the free flow of urine are undesirable reactions that can be avoided by using the triple sulfonamides and keeping the reaction of the urine alkaline or by using the highly soluble bacterocyclic derivatives of sulfanilamide and maintaining urinary output at a quart to a quart and a half a day.

All the signs of drug intoxication should be watched for in patients receiving sulfonamide drugs, and if any signs occur the drug should be discontinued at once.

*See* Chemotherapy. *See* also references under "Sulfonamides" in the Index.

Bibliography.—"Toxic and Other Special Features of Sulfonamide Therapy" in Harry Beckman, *Treatment in General Practice,* 6th ed. (1948); F. Hawking and J. S. Lawrence, *The Sulphonamides* (1950); P. H. Long and E. A. Bliss, *The Clinical and Experimental Use of Sulfanilamide, Sulfapyridine and Allied Compounds* (1939); T. S. Work and F. Work, *The Basis of Chemotherapy* (1948); "Sulfonamide Therapy," *Merck Manual,* 10th ed. (1961); A. Smith and P. L. Wermer, *Modern Treatment* (1953); D. W. Woolley, *A Study of Antimetabolites* (1952). (C. S. Kr.)

**SULFONIC ACIDS,** organic acids containing sulfur and having the general formula $RSO_3H$, where R is either an alkyl (*e.g.,* methyl) or an aryl (*e.g.,* phenyl) radical.

**Aromatic Sulfonic Acids.**—The acids of this more important group are obtained generally by treating aromatic compounds with concentrated sulfuric acid, the process being called sulfonation. Such operations are frequently conducted on a manufacturing scale as in the preparation of the sulfonic acids of benzene (*q.v.*), naphthalene (*q.v.*), and anthraquinone (*q.v.*). The sodium salt of benzenesulfonic acid is of importance since on fusion with sodium hydroxide it yields sodium phenoxide, from which phenol is liberated by a strong acid. During World War I large quantities of synthetic phenol were made by this process in order to eke out the supply of coal-tar phenol, which was then insufficient for the wholesale production of the explosive, picric acid (*q.v.*). From then, the process retained its importance in consequence of the large demand for phenol in the manufacture of synthetic resins and plastics (*q.v.*). Benzenedisulfonic acid, made from oleum (fuming sulfuric acid) and benzene, yields by alkali fusion the important dye intermediate, resorcinol.

The sulfonic acids of naphthalene are manufactured on an extensive scale. Anthraquinone, the oxidation product of anthracene (*q.v.*), when sulfonated with oleum at high temperatures yields anthraquinone-$\beta$-sulfonic acid, the sodium salt of which ("silver salt") is an important intermediate used in the manufacture of alizarin (*q.v.*) and the indanthrene vat dyes. Sulfonation of anthraquinone is facilitated by a mercuric sulfate catalyst. Sulfonation may be effected also by chlorosulfonic acid whereby sulfonyl chlorides are formed. (*See* Saccharin.)

Sulfonic acids of aromatic hydrocarbons are very soluble in water, and in the crystalline form are extremely hygroscopic. With phosphorus pentachloride they yield sulfonyl chlorides, which are reducible to thiophenols.

Sulfanilic acid, a sulfonic acid of aniline, is sparingly soluble in cold water and is to be regarded as an internal salt

$$\overset{+}{N}H_3C_6H_4\overset{-}{S}O_3$$

Its amide is important as the simplest member of the medically important sulfonamides (*q.v.*). Sulfanilic acid and the similar naphthylamine sulfonic acids are important dye intermediates.

**Aliphatic Sulfonic Acids.**—These are less important than those of the aromatic series. They are obtained generally (1) by oxidation of mercaptans, alkyl disulfides, alkyl thiocyanates or alkyl sulfinic acids; (2) by the interaction of alkyl iodides and metallic sulfites; (3) by the action of sulfuryl chloride $SO_2Cl_2$ upon a saturated hydrocarbon in the presence of light and of a catalyst such as pyridine; (4) by the action of sodium bisulfite upon an olefin in the presence of oxygen or other oxidizing agent. They are either viscous liquids or crystalline solids, converted into sulfonyl chlorides by phosphorus pentachloride.

**Hydroaromatic Sulfonic Acids.**—Camphor yields a characteristic sulfonic acid on sulfonation with sulfuric acid in acetic anhydride. The optically active camphor sulfonic acids from dextro- and levo-modifications of camphor have been very useful in the resolution of racemoid bases. *See* Stereochemistry.

(G. T. M.; X.)

**SULFONMETHANE GROUP,** a group of hypnotic drugs, formerly popular but now seldom used. These disulfone compounds were introduced into therapeutics between 1884 and 1888 by Eugen Baumann and Alfred Kast. Sulfonmethane (Sulfonal) is slowly absorbed from the intestinal tract. Depression after awakening is common and may be severe. Because the drug is slowly excreted, cumulation may occur during continuous administration, producing toxic effects. Death from overdosage is a result of failure of respiration and circulation. Chronic poisoning causes mental and gastrointestinal symptoms and urinary changes. Other toxic manifestations may appear in the skin, liver, and kidneys.

Sulfonethylmethane (Trional) and sulfondiethylmethane (Tetronal) are other members of the group. Trional is absorbed more rapidly than Sulfonal, Tetronal more slowly. (A. E. SH.; X.)

**SULFUR,** a nonmetallic chemical element, is used in making sulfuric acid, carbon disulfide, sulfur monochloride, and many other sulfur compounds important to an industrialized society. It is readily recognized in its native or free state and is widely disseminated in many forms in the lands bordering the Mediterranean Sea, the area in which civilization began; it evidently has been known to man for a very long time. Prehistoric man must have noted sulfur burning in the vicinity of volcanoes or hot sulfur springs, and it may be assumed that man came to know and utilize sulfur at that stage of his civilization when he learned the use and control of fire.

In ancient times sulfur was employed in religious ceremonies, in witchcraft, and in sorcery. The Egyptians used it as early as 2000 B.C. as a medicine, in bleaching cloth and straw, in the preparation of pigments and cosmetics, and in decorating weapons with niello. The Bible refers to the destruction of Sodom and Gomorrah by a rain of sulfur. Relics found in caves in southern Scandinavia indicate that the people in Paleolithic times made fire by striking iron disulfide (pyrite) with flint.

In the Middle Ages incendiary materials (Greek fire) were prepared with sulfur. The Chinese in 1232 mixed sulfur and saltpetre in the preparation of bombs and rockets. Sulfuric acid, often called the workhorse of the chemical industry, probably was made as early as 700 B.C., but it was not until 1745, when the lead-chamber process of making sulfuric acid was developed, that this acid and sulfur assumed their prominent roles in the development of the Industrial Revolution and the initiation of the chemical industry. During the Middle Ages, also, the alchemists regarded sulfur as the principle of combustibility (phlogiston). Antoine Lavoisier classified it as an element in 1777, but many of his contemporaries considered it a compound of hydrogen and oxygen. Joseph Gay-Lussac and Louis Thénard finally proved it to be an element.

### OCCURRENCE

Some have estimated that sulfur is the ninth most abundant element in the universe—one atom out of 20,000 to 30,000 being sulfur. It has been detected in certain stars, novae, cosmic clouds, and the sun. It is present in the meteorites that come to earth from cosmic space and is found in the oceans, the atmosphere, in fossil fuels—coal, petroleum, and natural gas—and in practically all plant and animal life.

Sulfur is present in the earth's crust, which, according to the classic studies of geochemist F. W. Clarke, contains 0.06% sulfur as sulfides, sulfates, and elemental sulfur. But most of it lies deep in the earth associated with silicates and metals. There is a continuous stream of sulfur rising from the interior of the earth. Some of this is the result of fluxing processes; some is hydrogen sulfide vented by volcanoes.

Elemental or native sulfur occurs chiefly in sedimentary and volcanic deposits. Most of the world's production of sulfur comes from sedimentary deposits and the majority of that from the calcareous horizons of the cap rock of shallow salt domes in the U.S. coastal region of Texas and Louisiana, and the Isthmus of Tehuantepec, Mexico. Other sedimentary deposits of commercial interest are located in western Texas; Italy (chiefly Sicily); Iraq; in the Miocene sediments under the glacial outwash and alluvium of the Vistula River in Poland; and in the U.S.S.R. in the Rozdol mine of the Ukraine, in the Gaurdak mine of Turkmenistan, and the Shorsu mine of Tadzhikistan. Discoveries in the late 1960s in the Sverdrup Basin in Canada's far northern Arctic archipelago revealed large deposits of elemental sulfur.

Volcanic sulfur, widely distributed throughout the world, occurs as a sublimate on the walls of vents or penetrating porous lava and ash beds. Chief occurrences are in Japan, the Andes Mountains (especially in Chile), and Indonesia. Smaller deposits, formed at or near the surface by atmospheric oxidation, are also widely distributed throughout the world, in almost any type of rock, but they are of minor commercial importance.

After oxygen and silicon, sulfur is one of the most abundant elements in minerals. In combination, it occurs chiefly as sulfides and sulfates. The former are important as a source of sulfur; *e.g.*, pyrite, or iron pyrites, marcasite, pyrrhotite, chalcopyrite, galena, and sphalerite. The chief sulfates are anhydrite, gypsum, and barite, also known as barytes or heavy spar.

### PRODUCTION

Ancient producers described their method of obtaining sulfur from ores as purification by fire. Similar methods are still used in Sicily, where native sulfur ore, mined by conventional methods, is piled in open cylindrical kilns (*calcaroni*), covered with spent ore, and ignited. Heat from burning about one-third of the sulfur melts the remainder, which drains from the kilns and is cast into blocks. Somewhat better sulfur recovery is obtained in other kilns (Gill furnaces), constructed so that combustion gases from one kiln can be used to preheat the ore in another. In Japan, sulfur is usually distilled from the ore in retorts. Sulfur ore also may be heated with steam or superheated water in autoclaves. The sulfur melts, drains from the gangue (worthless rock), and is recovered in the liquid state. Flotation processes usually yield a product containing excessive quantities of ash.

Before the start of the 20th century, Sicily monopolized the sulfur trade. By 1886 iron pyrites had largely replaced sulfur as a source because of increases in the price of Sicilian sulfur. It remained for Herman Frasch to expand the role of sulfur in industry with his process. After several failures in conventional mining, Frasch successfully mined sulfur at Sulphur Mine, La., in 1894 by a novel hot-water melting process. In 1895 the Union Sulphur Company, organized with his help, was the first to produce what is known as Frasch process sulfur. Other companies followed suit and began its production from deposits located near the Gulf of Mexico in Texas and Louisiana.

**Frasch Process.**—With the exceptions of the Frasch process deposits in western Texas and Poland, all of the sulfur deposits mined by this process occur at depths of from 100 to 3,000 ft. in the cap rock of salt domes. In horizontal section the domes are circular to elliptical in shape. Surrounding and overlying the domes are clay, sand, and gumbo. The upper portion of the dome consists of a porous cap rock which is largely anhydrite, limestone, and gypsum, with an occasional trace of sand, shale, and iron pyrites. The sulfur occurs in the porous limestone in the form of rhombic crystals. Below the limestone is a stratum of massive anhydrite that overlies the rock-salt core of the dome.

Natural sulfur melts at about 116° C (about 240° F). The Frasch process takes advantage of this fact and melts the sulfur underground by pumping water heated above this temperature into the deposit. The liquid sulfur, which is almost chemically pure, collects in a pool from which it is pumped to the surface.

In mining, wells are drilled into the sulfur formation with rotary rigs such as those employed in the petroleum industry. Typically, the wells (*see* illustration) consist of concentrically placed pipes that reach from the surface of the ground into the sulfur deposit. A 6-in. pipe extends through the sulfur-bearing stratum and rests in the upper portion of the underlying calcium sulfate, or gypsum. A 3-in. pipe is placed inside the 6-in. pipe, reaching nearly to the bottom of the sulfur-bearing rock but resting on a collar set within the 6-in. pipe, sealing the annular space between the two. Finally, a 1-in. air pipe, inside the 3-in. pipe, extends to a depth slightly above the collar. The 6-in. pipe is perforated at two levels, separated by the collar, the upper set of holes permitting the escape of the hot water and the lower set permitting

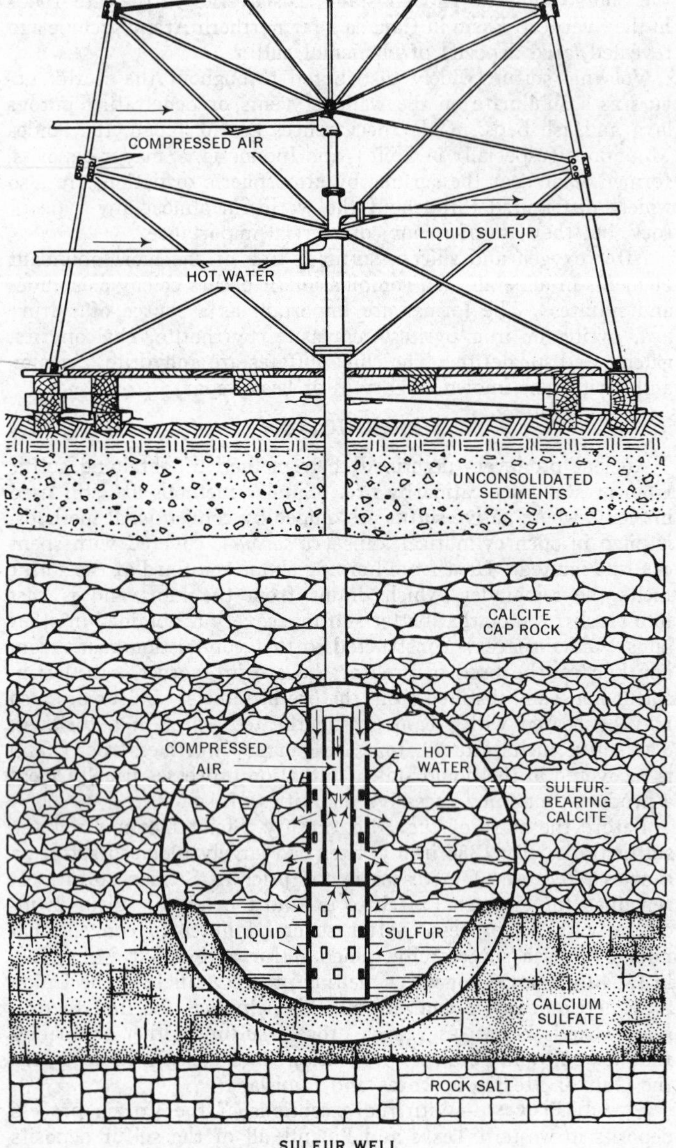


SULFUR WELL

the entrance of liquid sulfur. Hot water is pumped down the annular space between the 6-in. and 3-in. pipes and is discharged into the porous formation through the perforations. The entire region through which the water circulates is raised to a temperature above the melting point of sulfur. The melted sulfur, being heavier than water, settles and forms a pool around the foot of the well and, entering the lower set of perforations, rises in the 3-in. pipe. Compressed air, released at the bottom of the central 1-in. pipe, then raises the liquid sulfur to the surface, where it is collected in heated storage tanks for shipment in insulated tank cars, tank trucks, barges, and oceangoing tankers to the world's markets.

**Recovered and By-Product Sulfur.**—The sulfur production previously described is that obtained in elemental form from natural deposits. In addition, increasing quantities of elemental sulfur are recovered from pyrites and from industrial gases such as coke-oven gas, "sour" natural gas, petroleum refinery gases, and from smelter gases from the processing of zinc- and copper-sulfide ores.

Hydrogen sulfide is naturally present in "sour" natural gas and is a contaminant of gases produced in refining petroleum and in making coke-oven gas. The hydrogen sulfide in such gas is removed by absorption in a solvent, and concentrated by vaporizing it from the solution. The recovered hydrogen sulfide is then converted to elemental sulfur.

In smelter gases, sulfur is present as sulfur dioxide. Only in a few instances has by-product elemental sulfur been recovered economically from smelter gases by the use of reducing agents. Many investigators have searched for economic ways of using coal, coke, natural gas, hydrogen, and liquid hydrocarbons to convert the sulfur dioxide in smelter gases to elemental sulfur, but with very limited success. By-product sulfur has also been produced directly from sulfide ores by reductive smelting.

With increased attention being given to the control of atmospheric pollution, research efforts have been directed to desulfurization of fuels (coal and petroleum) and to the removal of sulfur dioxide from stack gases. Efforts to reduce the sulfur content of coal have been economically discouraging, but similar work with crude petroleum has been successful. It has been proven technically feasible to remove and/or recover sulfur dioxide from flue gases. Eventually, air pollution control may yield substantially more by-product sulfur for industrial use.

**Commercial Forms of Sulfur.**—Elemental sulfur is sold on the basis of the long ton (2,240 lb.). A number of grades or terms used to describe the commercial products are set forth in the list below.

*Native sulfur* is sulfur found in elemental form in nature. When mined by the Frasch hot-water process, it is termed Frasch sulfur.

*Recovered sulfur* is elemental sulfur produced from hydrogen sulfide obtained from "sour" natural gas, petroleum refinery gas, and other fuel gases.

*Crude domestic bright sulfur* (bright yellow in colour) on the U.S. market is 99.5–99.9% pure and commercially free from arsenic, selenium, and tellurium.

*Crude domestic dark sulfur* on the U.S. market analyzes more than 99% sulfur. It contains small quantities of hydrocarbon derivatives of petroleum which impart a dark brownish colour.

*Virgin block sulfur,* or broken-rock brimstone, is sublimed or refined sulfur broken and sold as a mixture of fines and lumps.

*Roll sulfur,* also known as stick or cannon sulfur, is refined sulfur cast into convenient shapes and sizes.

*Flowers of sulfur* is crude sulfur refined by sublimation.

*Amorphous sulfur,* used in the vulcanization of rubber, is the insoluble residue produced by extracting flowers of sulfur with carbon disulfide.

*Commercial flour sulfur* is produced by grinding crude sulfur.

*Colloidal sulfur* is a suspension of fine sulfur particles in water.

*Wettable sulfur* is sulfur treated so that it readily disperses in water.

*Precipitated sulfur* is sulfur precipitated from calcium polysulfide solutions by hydrochloric acid and washed to remove all calcium chloride.

Crude sulfur shipped in solid form contains about 50% fines with lumps up to eight inches in size. Liquid shipments of crude sulfur began domestically about 1945 and in the early 1970s constitute about 90% of the sulfur transported in the United States.

**World Production.**—During the 1960s world production of elemental sulfur grew at an average annual increase of 7.4%. The United States, which in 1913 took world leadership in sulfur production, in the late 1960s supplied 62% of the world's production of native sulfur, about 21% of recovered elemental sulfur, and 3.5% of iron pyrites, producing annually 7,458,000 long tons of Frasch process sulfur and 1,354,000 long tons of recovered sulfur.

Mexico, with an annual production of 1,582,000 long tons of Frasch process sulfur in the late 1960s, was the world's second largest producer, and Poland, with an estimated 788,000 long tons per year in the same period, was the world's third largest Frasch producer. Canada led the world in production of recovered sulfur, producing annually an estimated 3,108,000 long tons, and France held second place with an estimated 1,589,000 long tons.

## USES AND CONSUMPTION

**Uses.**—Uses of sulfur are so widespread that its consumption has been taken by some as a reliable indicator of industrial activity. Most of the sulfur used seldom appears in the final product.

The largest single use of sulfur is in the manufacture of fertilizers—phosphates and ammonium sulfate. Other important uses include inorganic pigments, cellulosic fibres, nonferrous metallurgy, pulp and paper, and petroleum refining. An enormous variety of other products, such as cements, dyes, food preservatives, photographic materials, sugar, and textiles, depend on its use in their manufacture.

Sulfur also is indispensable in plant and animal nutrition. In the form of organic matter and sulfates it improves soil structure, increases water-holding capacity, modifies soil reaction, makes other basic elements available to plants through ion exchange, and stimulates growth of soil microorganisms. Plants assimilate the sulfate ion and convert it into complex organic sulfur-containing compounds such as amino acids (methionine), sulfur-containing proteins, and sulfur-containing substances from which vitamins are formed.

Humans and animals derive all of their sulfur supplies from plants. Protein, as far as human nutrition is concerned, is synthesized from ten basic amino acids, one of which is methionine. This acid cannot be synthesized by the human body, and, if withdrawn from the diet, growth ceases or is retarded. Another sulfur-containing amino acid is cystine, which constitutes a large part of the skin, hair, and nails. Sulfur-containing protein material or certain amino-acid derivatives are also essential parts of many of the enzymes and hormones that regulate complex biological reactions. Thiamin (vitamin $B_1$), an important sulfur complex, is essential for the well-being of every living cell and for the normal growth of all species of animals, yeasts, molds, and higher plants.

**Consumption.**—The United States consumes more sulfur (in all forms) than any other nation: the estimated per capita consumption was 33.8 lb. in 1920, as compared to 106.3 lb. in 1967. About 87% was consumed as sulfuric acid, 11% as elemental, and 2% as hydrogen sulfide and sulfur dioxide in the late 1960s. In 1969, for the first time since 1962, world consumption was less than production.

## PHYSICAL PROPERTIES

The element sulfur, chemical symbol S, exhibits nonmetallic properties. It occupies the position immediately below oxygen in Group VI of the periodic table. Four stable isotopes are known, each with a nucleus containing 16 protons, but differing by having 16, 17, 18, and 20 neutrons respectively. The respective mass numbers are 32, 33, 34, and 36, and the normal composition of sulfur is given as $S^{32}$ (95%), $S^{33}$ (0.75%), $S^{34}$ (4.2%), $S^{36}$ (0.017%). Four radioactive isotopes, $S^{31}$ (half-life 2.4 sec.), $S^{35}$ (half-life 87 days), $S^{37}$ (half-life 5 min.), and $S^{38}$ (half-life 172 min.), have been prepared.

Pure sulfur has a pale yellow colour but its naturally occurring forms may be bright greenish-yellow, straw or honey yellow, yellowish brown, greenish or reddish to yellowish gray. Just above the melting point sulfur is a transparent yellow liquid which, with increasing temperature, turns dark red and becames black at about 250° C. At the boiling point 444.6° C, vapours are generated which turn deep red at 500° C and a straw yellow at 850° C.

Sulfur is tasteless and odourless. It has no action on the skin. It is insoluble in water, highly soluble in carbon disulfide, moderately so in aromatic solvents, and indifferently so in aliphatics. The liquid density varies from 1.808 g. per millilitre (ml.) at 115° C to 1.599–1.614 g. per ml. at the boiling point.

At the normal boiling point the vapour density corresponds closely to $S_8$ molecules, at about 900° C to $S_2$, and above 1,800° C to monatomic sulfur. Reducing the pressure lowers the temperature at which sulfur vapour dissociates from the octatomic form to the molecules with fewer atoms.

Sulfur is a poor conductor of both heat and electricity and becomes charged negatively if rubbed with glass, fur, silk, wool, or hard rubber. On Mohs' scale, its hardness varies from 1.5 to 2.5. The vapour pressure varies from 0.00005 mm. of mercury at 50° C to 2,896 mm. at 550° C. The coefficient of thermal expansion continuously increases with temperature for the solid, while that for the liquid passes through a minimum value. The bond angle, the interatomic distance, and the atomic radius for crystalline $S_8$ are 105°, 2.12 Å (Å, the angstrom unit = $10^{-8}$ cm.), and 1.04 Å, respectively. For the $S_8$ gas the bond angle is 100° but the interatomic distance and the atomic radius are the same as for the solid. The ignition temperature for sulfur in air is 261° C.

A number of crystalline forms of sulfur have been identified by their external appearance and optical properties. These forms differ in external appearance, crystal structure, and physical properties; *e.g.,* density, solubility, and melting point. Of the allotropic forms, the two most important are rhombic and monoclinic. Thermodynamically, rhombic sulfur is stable at room temperature and is readily obtained by crystallization from solution in carbon disulfide. It is a yellow solid with a density of 2.07 g. per ml. and melting point of 112.8° C (if heated rapidly). Above 95.5° C, the transition temperature, the crystals become opaque and consist of aggregates of the monoclinic form. An X-ray investigation of rhombic crystals has shown that the unit cell is composed of 16 puckered rings of $S_8$ molecules arranged approximately in layers perpendicular to the C-axis.

Monoclinic sulfur is obtained when liquid sulfur is cooled slowly. On breaking the surface crust and pouring off the still liquid sulfur, the interior of the cooled mass will be found to be filled with needlelike, monoclinic crystals. The density of the monoclinic sulfur is 1.96 g. per ml. Pure crystals melt at 118.9° C. The two forms can coexist only at a definite temperature for any particular pressure (*i.e.,* the transition point), and if the pressure is raised while temperature is kept constant, the rhombic form is produced since it is the more dense. The balanced state continues to 151° C and 1,288 atm.; above this temperature and pressure the monoclinic form cannot exist. The heat of transition is 2.992 cal. per g.

On standing at room temperature, monoclinic sulfur slowly changes into rhombic sulfur but the outward monoclinic crystalline form is preserved, each monoclinic crystal consisting of an aggregate of very small crystals of rhombic sulfur. Commercial varieties of sulfur such as ordinary brimstone, roll sulfur, and flowers of sulfur consist mainly of the rhombic form and a small amount of insoluble or amorphous sulfur.

Carbon disulfide dissolves both rhombic and monoclinic sulfur. The molecular weight of both forms in this solvent corresponds to $S_8$. Another good solvent for rhombic or monoclinic sulfur is sulfur monochloride, $S_2Cl_2$.

Rhombic sulfur melts at 112.8° C, monoclinic sulfur melts at 118.9° C to lambda liquid, but the natural melting point of commercial sulfur is a few degrees lower. This is because liquid sulfur consists of a mixture of two or three molecular species and time is required before equilibrium is established between them. At 120° C liquid sulfur has a viscosity of approximately 10 centipoises; further heating causes the viscosity to drop to a minimum at about 157° C. At 159° to 160° C the viscosity increases rapidly to a maximum of 932 poises at 186° to 188° C, after which it again decreases.

Various explanations have been given for the peculiar viscosity of liquid sulfur. At lower temperatures near the melting point, it is supposed that the $S_8$ molecule predominates. As the temperature increases to 160° C, the eight-membered ring molecules rupture, giving an equilibrium mixture of rings and eight-membered chains. The increasing concentration of these eight-membered chains causes polymerization to long unbranched chains. In addition to the long straight chains, it is possible that side chains of varying lengths exist. A maximum chain length of 12,000 to 27,000 atoms is attained at approximately 187° C, above which the polysulfur chains break into shorter chains.

If hot molten sulfur is poured into water it forms a soft, sticky, elastic mass known as plastic sulfur. X-ray analyses show a fibre diagram, and it is believed that long chains of sulfur atoms are arranged parallel to the direction of stretching. The stress/strain curves for these elastic chains appear very similar to those given by raw rubber. Plastic sulfur becomes opaque and brittle after a few days because of the conversion of most of the $S_8$ and some of the polymer into crystalline rhombic sulfur. When treated with carbon disulfide, only part of this hardened sulfur will dissolve, leaving amorphous or insoluble sulfur.

### CHEMICAL PROPERTIES

All the metals except gold and platinum combine with sulfur to form sulfides and, in most cases, heat is given off during the union. Moist sulfur is slowly oxidized at ordinary temperatures to sulfurous and sulfuric acids. Sulfur is an oxidizing agent as well as a reducing agent.

Hydrogen sulfide ($H_2S$) is formed by the reaction of hydrogen with liquid sulfur at 200° to 400° C and with sulfur vapour at temperatures up to 800° C. It is also formed by the action of acids on metallic sulfides such as ferrous sulfide; by putrefaction of organic substances containing sulfur; by bacterial action on sulfates; by the destructive distillation of coal; and by heating sulfur with hydrocarbons such as paraffin, petroleum oil, and methane.

Hydrogen sulfide, a colourless gas having the odour of rotten eggs, is fairly soluble in water, giving a feebly acid solution which slowly deposits sulfur when exposed to air. This gas, poisonous when inhaled, burns in air with a pale-blue flame to give sulfur dioxide and water. It can be liquefied at 18° C by a pressure of 17 atm., the liquid boiling at −60.1° C under atmospheric pressure and solidifying at −82.9° C. Hydrogen sulfide, often used as a reducing agent, is oxidized by chlorine, bromine, and iodine to sulfur, excess halogen oxidizing the sulfur to sulfuric acid; by hydrogen peroxide slowly to thiosulfate and finally, to sulfate; and by concentrated sulfuric acid to sulfur and sulfur dioxide. Hydrogen sulfide is thermodynamically stable with respect to hydrogen and all forms of sulfur, up to 1,550° C. It can, however, be converted to elemental sulfur in good yield by the Claus process, the overall reaction of which is $2H_2S + O_2 \rightarrow 2S + 2H_2O$. This process is increasingly used to produce sulfur from "sour" gas and oil.

Hydrogen polysulfides, also called hydrogen persulfides or sulfanes, have been synthesized by different methods such as the reaction of hydrogen sulfide gas with liquid sulfur, the reaction of liquid hydrogen sulfide with bromine, sulfur dichloride, and sulfur monochloride, and by acidification of aqueous solutions of sodium polysulfides.

The hydrogen atoms in hydrogen sulfide can be replaced by metals to form the normal sulfide, $M_2S$, or the acid sulfide, MHS. Sulfides of the alkali metals dissolve readily in alcohol and in water and are used in the paper and leather industries. Many sulfides, those with high heats of formation, can be made by grinding the metal and sulfur. Others require heating; in some instances a high temperature is necessary to start the reaction. Sulfates, especially those of alkali and alkaline earth metals, can be reduced to the sulfides by heating with carbon. Heavy-metal sulfides, which are all highly insoluble in water (being among the most insoluble of all substances), also can be made by passing hydrogen sulfide through solutions of metal salts. This precipitation with hydrogen sulfide is used in qualitative analysis.

The sulfides of the heavy metals have a characteristic appearance and colour. Some are volatile at moderate temperatures, mercuric sulfide subliming at 446° C. They can be oxidized in air. Some metallic sulfides containing small amounts of heavy metal salts are phosphorescent. Zinc sulfide is used in luminous paints and, combined with traces of a radium salt, it is used for painting hands and figures on luminous watch dials.

Metallic sulfides react with sulfides of the more negative elements ($3Na_2S + P_2S_5 \rightarrow 2\ Na_3PS_4$) to give thio salts or sulfosalts. This reaction is used analytically to separate As, Sb, and Sn from Cu, Pb, Bi, Cd, and Hg.

Sulfur combines with simple sulfides like $Na_2S$ or NaSH to form polysulfides having the general formula $Na_2S_x$ in which x varies from 2 to 5. (Some $Na_2S_6$ is formed in liquid ammonia solution.) The polysulfides, well-crystallized hygroscopic solids which are oxidized by air to form thiosulfates, are used by the tanning industry. Lime-sulfur solution, consisting of calcium sulfide and polysulfides, is made by boiling sulfur with a suspension of lime and is used both as an insecticide and as a fungicide.

The sulfides of carbon, silicon, and boron are obtained by direct union of sulfur with these elements at high temperatures. Carbon disulfide is unimolecular. It boils at 46.25° C, while $SiS_2$ and $B_2S_3$ are solid compounds which are difficult to volatilize. Both of the latter, in contrast to carbon disulfide, burn in oxygen with difficulty. $SiS_2$ and $B_2S_3$ are hydrolyzed by water. Carbon disulfide is important commercially, being used in the preparation of viscose rayon and carbon tetrachloride and as a solvent. Other sulfides such as CS, $C_3S_2$, and SiS are also known. The first, a solid, is prepared by the action of a silent electric discharge on the vapour of $CS_2$. Carbon and silicon also form sulfides which contain oxygen or a halogen. Carbon oxysulfide, COS, may be formed when carbon, oxygen, and sulfur are brought together at high temperatures. In its physical properties, carbon oxysulfide is intermediate between $CO_2$ and $CS_2$. It is a colourless, odourless gas which condenses to a liquid at −47.5° C.

Another series of compounds is the sulfides of nitrogen. Nitrogen sulfide, $NS_2$, is a red liquid. The tetrasulfide, $N_4S_4$, a yellow or orange-yellow solid, melting point 179° C, is prepared by passing ammonia through $SCl_2$ dissolved in benzene, or by dissolving sulfur in liquid ammonia at −15.5° C. The material explodes when struck. The pentasulfide, $N_2S_5$, a red liquid with a melting point of 10° C, is obtained when the tetrasulfide is boiled with $CS_2$. Nitrogen tetrasulfide has been suggested for use as an ignition promoter in diesel fuels, and as an insecticide and fungicide.

Sulfur burns readily in air to form $SO_2$ and traces of $SO_3$. Sulfur dioxide may also be easily prepared by treating sulfites, thiosulfates, or bisulfites with a strong acid. It is available in the liquid form, boiling point −8° C, at low cost in steel cylinders. It has many important commercial uses, being used as a bleaching or reducing agent, a refrigerant, and a solvent.

Sulfur trioxide, $SO_3$, is formed by heating $SO_2$ and oxygen in the presence of a catalyst such as finely divided platinum, nickel or cobalt sulfates, or oxides of vanadium, tungsten, molybdenum, chromium, or iron. The conversion is favoured by low temperatures. This reaction is the basis of the contact process for the manufacture of sulfuric acid. Sulfur trioxide may also be prepared by heating anhydrous ferric sulfate, $Fe_2(SO_4)_3$, to 600° or 700° C or by allowing $SO_2$ and ozone, $O_3$, to come together at room temperature. Two other oxides of sulfur, $S_2O_3$ and $SO_4$, are known, and $S_2O_7$ has been described. The sesquioxide, $S_2O_3$, is formed on adding powdered sulfur to liquid sulfur trioxide at 15° C. It is a blue-green solid which decomposes slowly into $SO_3$, $SO_2$, and S. Sulfur tetroxide, $SO_4$, a white solid, is prepared by subjecting a mixture of $SO_2$ and $O_2$ to a silent electric discharge. In the gas phase, $SO_3$ consists of monomeric molecules, but in the liquid state, boiling point 46° C, it consists of a mixture of $SO_3$ and $S_3O_9$ molecules and perhaps others. It also exists in several low-melting asbestoslike modifications and the gamma or high-melting asbestoslike form. Sulfur trioxide reacts energetically with organic matter to form sulfonic acid derivatives of carbon and $SO_2$, and with basic oxides to form sulfates. In liquid form it combines with $NO_2$ to form oxynitroso sulfuric anhydride, $(NO_2SO_3)_2$, and with water to form a series of hydrates of sulfuric acid.

The oxides of sulfur dissolve in water to form acids—$H_2SO_2$ sulfoxylic, $H_2S_2O_4$ hyposulfurous, $H_2SO_3$ sulfurous, $H_2S_2O_5$ pyrosulfurous, $H_2S_2O_6$ dithionic, $H_2SO_4$ sulfuric, $H_2S_2O_7$ pyrosulfuric, $H_2S_2O_3$ thiosulfuric, $H_2SO_5$ peroxymonosulfuric, $H_2S_2O_8$ peroxydisulfuric, $H_2S_nO_6$ polythionic where n = 3, 4, 5, 6 in Wackenroder's solution.

The sodium salt of hyposulfurous acid, sodium hyposulfite, is an article of commerce and is used as a reducing agent in the dye industry. Sulfurous acid and its salts are excellent and cheap reducing agents and are also used as disinfectants and food preservatives. Calcium bisulfite and magnesium bisulfite are used to extract lignin from wood in the preparation of wood pulp. Thiosulfates are used extensively in photography.

The halides and oxyhalides of sulfur possess certain properties in common. They are all readily prepared, usually by several methods. All are either gases or volatile liquids. Except for the fluorides, which exhibit great stability, all hydrolyze readily to give acid products which are irritating to mucous membranes.

Again, except the colourless, tasteless fluorides, these compounds possess a pungent odour. As one might expect, the physical properties, reactivity, and stability of these materials vary regularly with the position of the halide in the periodic table. Sulfur monochloride and sulfur dichloride are used to vulcanize rubber. The oxychlorides are useful reagents for the introduction of sulfoxides, sulfone, or chlorine groups into organic molecules. Chlorosulfonic acid, $HSO_3Cl$, prepared by reacting HCl directly with sulfur trioxide, reacts readily with water to form sulfuric and hydrochloric acids. It fumes in air and has found application as a smoke producer in military operations. Its most useful application is in organic chemistry where it serves as a sulfonating agent.

The organic chemistry of sulfur may be divided into reactions which occur under reducing conditions and reactions which occur under oxidizing conditions. The first type is encountered when elemental sulfur is heated with petroleum hydrocarbons, rubber, or other organic substances. The organic material is sulfurized and hydrogen sulfide is formed as a consequence of sulfur's action as a dehydrogenating agent. The hydrogen sulfide, being a reducing agent, may induce further reactions, particularly with unsaturated compounds, to yield mercaptans and thiophenols which, in turn, may be alkylated to sulfides; *e.g.*, mustard gas. All such sulfur compounds are analogous to similar compounds of oxygen, but differ from them because of dissimilarities in the respective molecular weights and electronic structures. The additional shell of electrons possessed by sulfur may lead to the formation of polysulfides such as the thiokol-type synthetic resins. The resistance of these resins to attack by gasoline has led to their use as linings for aircraft fuel tanks. The aromatic sulfur compounds, usually nitrogen derivatives, find extensive use as accelerators in the vulcanization of rubber. The second type of reaction, oxidation of organic sulfur compounds, yields materials which, with the exception of the disulfides and the peroxides, are not analogous to oxygen compounds with respect to structure. The most important of these compounds are the sulfuric acids, alkyl sulfates, and their derivatives which are used extensively as medicinals (sulfa drugs), detergents, lubricants, and dyestuff intermediates.

### ANALYTICAL METHODS

Moisture in commercial sulfur is determined by drying a 50 g. sample at 80° C for 16 to 24 hours in a widemouthed weighing bottle or for four hours at 105° C.

Ash in commercial sulfur is determined by burning 10 to 50 g. of the sample in a porcelain crucible, using sufficient auxiliary heat to keep the sulfur burning and finally igniting the crucible to destroy all organic matter.

Arsenic, selenium, and tellurium in sulfur are determined by first oxidizing the sulfur to sulfuric acid through use of bromine and nitric acid. Arsenic is then determined by the Gutzeit method, selenium by reduction with hydrazine sulfate, and tellurium by reduction with stannous chloride solution.

Acid and chlorides in sulfur are determined by shaking 100 g. of ground sulfur with 100 ml. $CO_2$-free distilled water, titrating an aliquot portion of the filtered solution to neutrality with alkali, and titrating with standard silver nitrate solution using potassium dichromate as the indicator. Isopropyl alcohol may be added to the water if the sulfur is difficult to wet.

Organic carbon in sulfur is determined by burning the sulfur and absorbing and weighing the carbon dioxide which is formed, or by boiling the sulfur to convert the organic carbon to a carbon-sulfur complex.

BIBLIOGRAPHY.—F. W. Clarke, *The Data of Geochemistry,* 5th ed., U.S. Geological Survey Bulletin 770, (1924); D. M. Yost and H. Russell, *Systematic Inorganic Chemistry of the Fifth-and-Sixth-Group Nonmetallic Elements* (1944); Fritz Ephraim, *Inorganic Chemistry,* 6th ed., rev. and enlarged by P. C. L. Thorne and E. R. Roberts (1954); W. N. Tuller, ed., *The Sulphur Data Book* (1954); E. E. Reid, *Organic Chemistry of Bivalent Sulfur,* 6 vol. (1958–65); L. Young and G. A. Maw, *Metabolism of Sulphur Compounds* (1958); F. Challenger, *Aspects of the Organic Chemistry of Sulphur* (1959); Williams Haynes, *Brimstone: the Stone That Burns* (1959); M. C. Sneed *et al.*, *Comprehensive Inorganic Chemistry,* vol. 8, R. C. Brasted, ed., *Sulphur, Selenium, Tellurium, Polonium and Oxygen* (1961); W. A. Pryor, *Mechanisms of Sulfur Reactions* (1962); C. C. Price and S. Oae, *Sulfur Bonding* (1962); Beat Meyer, ed., *Elemental Sulfur: Chemistry and Physics* (1965); G. Nickless, ed., *Inorganic Sulphur Chemistry* (1968); A. V. Tobolsky and W. J. MacKnight, *Polymeric Sulfur and Related Polymers* (1966); A. V. Tobolsky, ed., *The Chemistry of Sulfides* (1968); L. C. Schroeter, *Sulfur Dioxide: Applications in Foods, Beverages, and Pharmaceuticals* (1966); F. Tuinstra, *Structural Aspects of the Allotrophy of Sulfur and Other Divalent Elements* (1967).

(W. W. D.; J. R. WT.)

**SULFURIC ACID,** $H_2SO_4$, is one of the most widely used of all commercial chemical substances. It is made from sulfur (or compounds of sulfur), water, and oxygen from the air. Although rarely used or even seen by the layman, sulfuric acid is employed in some stage of the manufacture of practically all industrial products. Annual production in the late 1960s was approximately 28,000,000 tons in the U.S. and 4,000,000 tons in the U.K., all short tons, 100% $H_2SO_4$ equivalent.

Sulfuric acid occupies its unique position of usefulness because it can be employed for an unusually wide range of purposes and because it is one of the cheapest of the industrial chemicals to produce. Its great affinity for water makes it a powerful dehydrating agent. It is a valuable electrolyte, a strong oxidizing agent, and a solvent in which many important reactions can be brought about. It is also an effective catalyst for various chemical reactions. It is used in varying concentrations from extremely dilute solutions for control of acidity or alkalinity to highly concentrated fuming acids prepared for the manufacture of drugs, dyes, and explosives. It is made in various grades from those of high purity for the rayon and pharmaceutical industries to those of relatively low grade for the manufacture of normal superphosphate and ammonium sulfate for the fertilizer industries. The same batch of acid is often used for several purposes in succession. After an initial use in the petroleum, explosives, drug, or dye industries, for instance, it is frequently recovered in a solution too dilute or impure for further use in the same process but still usable for the pickling of steel or manufacture of fertilizer. Sulfuric acid is made by two very different processes: the contact process and the lead-chamber process. (See *Manufacture,* below.) For use in either process a large variety of sulfur-containing raw materials is available.

**Properties.**—Pure (100%) sulfuric acid is a colourless liquid that is sometimes called monohydrate of sulfur trioxide because its anhydride, sulfur trioxide ($SO_3$), and water are combined in equimolal quantities ($SO_3 + H_2O \rightarrow H_2SO_4$). Its specific gravity is 1.830 at 25° C (77° F), freezing point 10.37° C (50.7° F) and at one atmosphere it boils at about 340° C (644° F) but undergoes decomposition into sulfur trioxide and water. The former escapes as a vapour until the concentration has fallen to 98.54%, which is the composition of the constant-boiling mixture of sulfuric acid and water at atmospheric pressure. The solution then distills at 317° C (603° F), the boiling point of the mixture. The freezing point of the acid is lowered markedly by the addition of either sulfur trioxide or water.

The existence of the following crystalline phases has been established by the study of freezing temperatures and other properties: $SO_3$, $(SO_3)_2 \cdot H_2O$; *i.e.*, $H_2S_2O_7$, $H_2SO_4$, $H_2SO_4 \cdot H_2O$, $H_2SO_4 \cdot 2H_2O$, $H_2SO_4 \cdot 4H_2O$, $H_2SO_4 \cdot 6.5H_2O$, and $H_2SO_4 \cdot 8H_2O$. The hydrate containing 6.5 molecules of water per molecule of anhydrous acid (13 molecules of water for 2 molecules of acid) was believed, prior to publication of careful measurements by J. E. Kunzler and W. F. Giauque, to be a hexahydrate. It is possible (though not likely) that the octahydrate may not have exactly the composition ascribed to it. It is known, however, that the ratio of $H_2O$ molecules to $H_2SO_4$ molecules is less than nine.

Sulfuric acid is dibasic; that is, its molecules each contain two hydrogen atoms and ionize in two steps: $H_2SO_4 = H^+ + HSO_4^-$ and $HSO_4^- = H^+ + SO_4^{2-}$. The second stage of the dissociation is moderately weak, the constant being 0.010 at 25° C. Solutions of various concentrations of the acid therefore may contain in addition to hydrogen ions ($H^+$ or $H_3O^+$), molecules of the acid ($H_2SO_4$), bisulfate ions ($HSO_4^-$), and sulfate ions ($SO_4^{2-}$) in proportions which vary with the dilution. In very dilute solutions the concentration of the $SO_4^{2-}$ ion is equal to the stoichiometric concentration; that is, there is an $SO_4^{2-}$ ion for practically every molecule of $H_2SO_4$ which was originally added to the water. As the concentration of the solution is increased, the concentration of the $HSO_4^-$ rises rapidly; that of the $SO_4^{2-}$ increases more slowly and reaches a maximum value of two molar at a stoichiometric concentration of about seven molar. It then decreases to a very small value, virtually zero, in a solution of high concentration (14 molar). At this same high concentration (14 molar) the $HSO_4^-$ is at a maximum value of 14 molar, that is, practically all of the acid has undergone primary ionization but no secondary ionization. At still higher molarities the $HSO_4^-$ ion concentration diminishes as the $H_2SO_4$ increases.

As a result of these variations in the concentrations of the various molecular species, the properties of aqueous sulfuric acid solutions undergo interesting changes; *i.e.*, the specific conductance reaches a maximum in the 4-molar acid, the specific conductance-viscosity product attains a maximum in the 9-molar solution, and the surface tension reaches a maximum when the stoichiometric concentration is about 6.5 molar. At low temperatures (0° C) there is a minimum in the surface tension-concentration curve at about one molar concentration. Other properties such as density, heat of dilution, and heat capacity are also affected by the changes in the concentration of the various components that result from the dissociation of the $H_2SO_4$ molecules.

Dilute sulfuric acid reacts with the more electropositive metals such as zinc, magnesium, and iron with the evolution of hydrogen. It also reacts with metal oxides and hydroxides forming sulfates. Because of its high boiling point the concentrated acid is used to manufacture volatile acids (some of them stronger than sulfuric acid) from their salts. It liberates hydrogen chloride gas (hydrochloric acid in water solution) from sodium chloride, nitric acid from nitrates, and hydrofluoric acid from calcium fluoride. It is also used to convert calcium phosphate to a more soluble acid phosphate for fertilizer and in solution displaces numerous weak acids; *e.g.*, acetic and boric acids from their respective salts. Since bromide ion and iodide ion are oxidized by the concentrated acid, it cannot be used for the manufacture of hydrobromic and hydriodic acids.

In sulfuric acid the sulfur is at its maximum oxidation state of +6; it may therefore function as an oxidizing agent and be reduced to the $+4(SO_2)$, zero (S), or $-2(S^{2-})$ state. The dilute acid is not an effective oxidizer but the hot concentrated acid oxidizes less active metals (*e.g.*, copper and silver) as well as the nonmetals carbon and sulfur, and is itself reduced to sulfur dioxide. With stronger reducing agents as zinc or iodide it is reduced to hydrogen sulfide, which under favourable conditions may escape before being oxidized by more of the sulfuric acid. It removes by oxidation the tars and organic sulfides present in petroleum and serves as a catalyst in the sulfuric acid alkylation processes involved in the manufacture of high-octane aviation gasoline.

The concentrated acid has great affinity for water and serves as an excellent drying agent and as a dehydrating agent, not only removing moisture from gases and liquids that do not react with the acid but extracting water from compounds. Thus it chars many organic compounds such as wood, paper, cloth, starch, and sugars. For the same reason, the acid becomes brown in colour if it comes in contact with traces of oil, grease, or atmospheric dust. It is essential in the manufacture of explosives, celluloid, lacquers, etc., for the nitration operations involved in these processes liberate water which is removed by the sulfuric acid, thereby permitting the reactions to go to completion. Its value to organic chemistry is due also to its reaction with many aromatic compounds to form sulfonic acids. (*See* DYES AND DYEING; NAPHTHALENE; PHENOLS; SULFONIC ACIDS.)

**Sulfates.**—Since sulfuric acid is dibasic, it forms both normal or neutral salts ($Na_2SO_4$) and acid salts ($NaHSO_4$). The latter show acid properties in solution because of the ionization of the $HSO_4^-$ ion and are sometimes employed for purposes requiring moderate acidity. The common sulfates are soluble in water with the exception of those of lead, strontium, barium, and calcium. Many of the sulfates have important industrial uses: barium and lead sulfates in the manufacture of paints; sodium sulfate in the manufacture of paper, and its hydrate, $Na_2SO_4 \cdot 10H_2O$ (Glauber's salt), in medicine; copper sulfate, $CuSO_4 \cdot 5H_2O$, in insecticides and its solution as an electrolyte in the electrolytic refining of copper; gypsum, $CaSO_4 \cdot 2H_2O$, and plaster of paris, $(CaSO_4)_2 \cdot H_2O$, in the building industries. The sulfates of potassium and aluminum crystallize from solution as a double salt, $K_2SO_4 \cdot Al_2(SO_4)_3 \cdot 24H_2O$, which is called alum (*q.v.*). The term is also applicable to other double sulfates of similar crystalline form in which the potassium ions are replaced by other univalent ions (*e.g.*, those of sodium or ammonium) and the aluminum ions by other trivalent ions (*e.g.*, those of chromium or iron).

**Grades and Terminology.**—Since there is a linear relationship between the concentration and density of sulfuric acid in the range from 0% to 93.19%, the concentration within this range may be determined fairly accurately with the aid of a hydrometer. The Baumé (Bé.) hydrometer, American modulus, is used by the industry in the U.S., while in continental Europe it is employed with a different modulus. The Twaddell hydrometer is used in the United Kingdom although there is an increasing tendency to express the concentration directly in percentage of $H_2SO_4$ or of $SO_3$ rather than in the degrees of the hydrometer scale. Temperature corrections must be made for all hydrometer readings (*see* HYDROMETER).

Except in warm climates 100% $H_2SO_4$ is rarely shipped because of its high freezing point (*see* above); the 98–99% acid which is produced in the contact process is frequently used and because of its somewhat lower freezing point may be shipped if care is exercised in winter.

The 93.19% acid is a sirupy, oily liquid whose freezing point is −34° C (−29° F) and boiling point 281° C (538° F); at 15.6° C (60° F) its specific gravity is 1.835 and its viscosity 24 times that of water at the same temperature. It is one of the most popular shipping concentrations because of its low freezing point and the fact that it does not substantially react on and corrode economical steel containers at atmospheric temperatures. The name oil of vitriol (o.v.) is often used in the U.S. to designate this concentration of the acid because of its appearance and oily, corrosive characteristics. In the United Kingdom and Europe, however, the term is used generally to mean simply sulfuric acid. Thus, in the British Isles the following designations are used: brown oil of vitriol (b.o.v.), ordinary commercial 77–80% acid; best brown oil of vitriol (b.b.o.v.), the commercial 77–80% acid relatively free from arsenic and other impurities; concentrated or rectified oil of vitriol (c.o.v. or r.o.v.), 93–96% acid now usually made by the contact process rather than by concentration or rectification of the more dilute chamber acid. The term chamber acid may refer either to any acid produced by the lead-chamber process or to the acid of the particular concentration 62–78% otherwise produced. Dilute acid if much below 78% reacts with steel containers and is therefore rarely shipped in quantity. The term 50° Bé. acid (62.18%) is sometimes used for statistical purposes in the U.S. Acids of still lower concentrations are sometimes prepared by dilution but must be shipped in expensive glass carboys or bottles or in alloy, lead, or rubber-lined containers.

Another popular shipping strength is the approximately 78% acid because it is the maximum strength made by the chamber process and because its freezing point, −10.8° C (12.6° F), is low. In cold climates the shipping concentration is often changed to 76%, which acid has a still lower freezing point. The 76–78% acid is not seriously corrosive to steel tank cars or tank trucks. The fertilizer industry, one of the largest consumers of sulfuric acid, requires acid of only 78% concentration for the manufacture of normal superphosphate.

Oleum or fuming sulfuric acid (also known in some countries as Nordhausen acid) is a solution of sulfur trioxide, $SO_3$, in 100% sulfuric acid. Its concentration is usually expressed as "percent oleum," *i.e.*, the percentage of free $SO_3$ dissolved in the acid, but occasionally as the percentage of "equivalent $H_2SO_4$," which includes both the free oxide and that combined with water in the $H_2SO_4$. Thus 100 lb. of 40% oleum contains 40 lb. of $SO_3$ and 60 lb. of 100% $H_2SO_4$, or a total of 89 lb. (89%) of $SO_3$ free and combined. Addition of 9 lb. of water to the 100 lb. of 40% oleum yields 109 lb. of 100% $H_2SO_4$. For this reason oleum has an equivalent acid concentration greater than 100% $H_2SO_4$, that of the 40% oleum being equivalent to 109% $H_2SO_4$. As sulfur trioxide dissolves in sulfuric acid in all proportions, the resulting oleums may have a wide range of concentrations. When the two combine in equimolal proportions, pyrosulfuric acid, $H_2S_2O_7$, is formed. This acid has the maximum melting point, 36° C (96.8° F), of all the compounds of the $H_2O–SO_3$ system.

Sulfuric acid may also be designated by terms which refer to its purity, origin, or use rather than to its concentration. Thus battery acid and electrolyte refer to acid of a quality suitable for accumulators or storage batteries; in the U.S. the concentrations sold are either 50% $H_2SO_4$ (specific gravity 1.40) or 93.19% (specific gravity 1.835). Brimstone (or sulfur) acid refers usually to acid produced from sulfur rather than from less pure raw materials such as pyrites, spent oxide, etc.

Mixed acid consists of nitric acid and concentrated sulfuric acid. Spent acid is that which has been used once and is usually dilute and impure. Sludge acid is the residue of the acid used in the refining of petroleum. It is contaminated with organic impurities and is frequently made usable by further dilution, to separate as many of the impurities as possible, followed by concentration; or it may be decomposed by heat, the organic material oxidized, and the sulfur dioxide recovered for use in the manufacture of more acid. Spent alkylation acid is a by-product of sulfuric acid alkylation processes for the manufacture of high-octane aviation gasoline. It is of a higher purity than sludge acid, usually containing 85–90% $H_2SO_4$, and is frequently reused in the petroleum refinery or elsewhere.

Like other chemicals, sulfuric acid is graded by standards stipulated by the appropriate scientific societies or industries. The technical grade is usually intended for large-scale industrial use and need not be of high purity. The U.S.P. label designates acid that meets the specifications of the *United States Pharmacopeia*, while C.P., chemically pure, refers to acid of a higher grade usually prepared by distillation of a commercial grade acid. The purest grades, suitable for analytical and research purposes, are designated as reagent, analyzed, and so on.

**Materials of Construction of Containers.**—Of the common metals, only lead is satisfactorily resistant to cold sulfuric acid of nearly all concentrations up to 100% and to hot acid of concentrations up to about 70%. Generally the metals are less resistant to the hot and the more concentrated acids, but steel and cast iron are exceptional in that they are resistant to cold acid of concentrations higher than about 78% because of the formation of a protective scale and are attacked with increasing effect as the concentration decreases. Cast iron is more resistant than mild steel to acid of most concentrations and has a satisfactory life even with very hot acid, provided its concentration exceeds 90%. However, cast iron should never be used as a container for oleum or for sulfur trioxide gases, since it may crack with explosive violence when in contact with sulfur trioxide. Mild steel should not be used at temperatures in excess of approximately 49° C (120° F) regardless of the concentration of the acid but it has a satisfactory life for acid of concentrations exceeding 20% oleum even though hot. Cast steel, malleable iron, and many resistant alloys are available for specific concentrations, temperatures, and applications; in some instances acid-resistant brick linings are used.

The U.S. Department of Transportation specifies the type and materials of construction allowable for all containers to be used for shipment of sulfuric acid of various concentrations.

Moisture should be carefully excluded from iron or steel containers, since dilution of the acid at any point prompts rapid corrosion. Sparks or open flames must be kept away from any closed vessel, which should not be opened unless it is previously washed and the residual acid neutralized. The vapour space over the acid may contain explosive hydrogen and poisonous arsenic, nitrogen, or sulfur compounds.

**Manufacture.**—The date of the discovery of sulfuric acid is lost in antiquity; it was probably first prepared by Arabian chemists (8th century A.D.) and was apparently well known to the alchemists. Near the end of the 15th century Basil Valentine described a method of preparation in which the acid was distilled from a mixture of green vitriol ($FeSO_4 \cdot 7H_2O$) and silica and another method whereby the acid was obtained by burning sulfur with saltpetre ($NaNO_3$). The older of the two commercial methods, the lead-chamber process, was introduced in England in 1746 although the principles of the process had been used much earlier. It was first manufactured on a commercial scale from weathered pyritic shales in Bohemia and at Nordhausen in Germany.

The first step in the manufacture of sulfuric acid is to prepare sulfur dioxide ($SO_2$) gas by burning elemental sulfur, or from various other sulfur-bearing materials. In the late 1960s approximately 75% of the sulfuric acid production in the U.S. was derived from elemental sulfur and the rest from smelter gases, hydrogen sulfide ($H_2S$), pyrites, thermal decomposition of acid sludge, and regeneration of spent acid. In the U.K. approximately 58% of the production was from elemental sulfur, 21% from anhydrite ($CaSO_4$), 9% from pyrites, 7% from zinc smelter gases, and 5% from miscellaneous sulfur-bearing materials, mainly spent oxide.

The raw material used in a given plant is determined by a number of complex considerations that may include plant location, type of process employed, grade and concentration of acid to be produced, and cost.

The next step in the production of the acid is to oxidize the $SO_2$ to $SO_3$. This is done by two different processes, both employing catalysts. The lead-chamber process yields acid of a concentration of not more than 78%, and unless a pure raw material (*e.g.*, sulfur) is used, the product is impure. The newer contact process was developed on a commercial scale in the 1890s and is used to produce acid of any desired concentration and of high purity regardless of the quality of raw materials.

Because of the increasing demand for acid of high concentration and purity, the latter process has steadily gained and by the early 1970s over 97% of the acid produced in the U.S. and much more than one-half of that produced in the U.K. was manufactured by the contact process.

*Contact Process.*—Contact plants are of two main types. The much simpler type, often known as a sulfur or hot-gas purification unit, was developed for use with vanadium pentoxide ($V_2O_5$) catalysts, which are relatively immune to impurities in the gas stream, and with sulfur as the raw material. The second type, known as a cold-gas purification unit, is used when the $SO_2$ gas contains various solid, liquid, and gaseous impurities from the sulfur-bearing ores or other raw materials.

*Sulfur-Burning Contact Plants.*—In these plants the sulfur is melted to remove moisture and to permit the major portion of the dust or ash which may be present to settle. The molten sulfur with or without subsequent filtration is pumped to the burner. Combustion air, which has been dried by concentrated sulfuric acid, is supplied to the burner by a blower at a pressure up to 7 lb. per square inch greater than that of the atmosphere. The entire plant is thus maintained under a slight pressure and no moist air from the atmosphere can infiltrate into it. The $SO_2$-air mixture containing 8 to 11% of $SO_2$ leaves the sulfur burner at temperatures that range from 760° to 1,200° C (1,400° to 2,200° F), the temperature being proportional to the percentage of $SO_2$ in the gases and to the level of heat energy in the molten sulfur and in the combustion air. Except in very small plants the gas is cooled by a waste-heat boiler, usually to approximately 400° C (750° F), and in some cases is passed through a hot-gas filter to remove remaining dust or ash before it comes into contact with the catalyst. The catalyst is usually in the form of pellets of a porous siliceous material impregnated with $V_2O_5$ and a potassium compound.

The catalyst is usually placed in layers on horizontal temperature-resistant cast iron or alloy gratings in an insulated vessel called a converter. The reaction, $2SO_2 + O_2 \rightleftarrows 2SO_3 + 45$ kilocalories, takes place at an almost imperceptible rate without a catalyst. However, the rate is enormously increased by surface catalysts such as $V_2O_5$ or platinum, the forward acceleration being proportional to the temperature in the approximate range of 400° to 600° C (750° to 1,100° F). Above 600° C the reaction begins to go in the reverse direction. After 1925 $V_2O_5$ gradually replaced platinum in substantially all plants. To avoid excessively high temperatures from the exothermic reaction, which would reduce the yield of $SO_3$ and damage catalyst and equipment, the conversion is carried out in stages with removal of part of the heat of reaction by waste-heat boilers or other cooling means between the stages. The gas leaves the final layer or stage of catalyst at temperatures between 438° C (820° F) and 450° C (842° F). By the early 1970s, in newer plants extremely high efficiencies had been achieved whereby 98 to 99.5% of the $SO_2$ was converted to $SO_3$.

Sulfur-burning contact plants with capacities in a single train of equipment up to 2,600 tons per 24 hours and sometimes requiring only one operator have been built. Considerably more than a ton of high-pressure, saturated, or superheated steam may be generated for every ton of 100% acid produced. The required electric power is usually less than 35 kw-hr. per ton of 100% acid and the cooling water about 4,000–5,000 U.S. gal. per ton of acid. Except in very cold climates, no buildings are essential for housing of equipment.

*Cold-Gas Purification Types of Contact Plants.*—For production of $SO_2$ from low-grade sulfur-bearing materials, a large variety of furnaces or roasters is available. It is desirable to select a roaster that will remove the maximum quantity of sulfur from the raw materials with a minimum carry-over of dust or other impurities into the effluent gas and that will produce gas with a maximum $SO_2$ concentration at minimum operating and repair costs. It is also desirable to avoid oxidation of $SO_2$ to $SO_3$ in the roaster and the consequent formation of acid mist. The concentration and purity of the $SO_2$ gas from the roaster determines the size, quantity, and cost of subsequent gas-purification equipment.

The gas usually leaves the roaster at temperatures between 650° and 1,100° C (about 1,200° to 2,000° F) and may be cooled by waste-heat boilers or other means. It is important to remove the dust at this stage to prevent its deposit in subsequent equipment. This is done by various methods: about 80–90% may be removed in cyclone centrifugal collectors and 90–99% of the remaining dust in electrical precipitators that operate at 50,000 to 70,000 v. and at 150°–430° C (about 300°–800° F). Precipitators have the advantage of low pressure drop, low power consumption, and of recovery of dust in dry form but at the disadvantage of relatively high cost. This equipment may be built of steel or of steel lined with firebrick, as the gas is normally so hot that no corrosive acid can condense. Some plants have replaced precipitators with proprietary gas washers that have as high or higher efficiencies in removal of dust and have the additional advantages of removing a large portion of other impurities such as metallic fume, arsenic, and acid mist while simultaneously cooling the gas. They have the disadvantage of relatively high pressure drop, as do cyclone dust collectors. They necessitate recovery of dust in the wet condition but in many cases this is considered an advantage.

After removal of the dust the gas must be cooled to permit removal of other impurities such as metallic fume, acid mist, and fluorine, chlorine, or arsenic compounds. They must be removed to the point where they do not clog or damage subsequent equipment and do not adversely affect the quality of the product acid for the purpose for which it is to be used. Cooling of the gas is necessary not only to remove impurities but also to condense and thus remove part of the water vapour in the gases. If all of the water vapour were allowed to remain in the gas, it would make the product acid in many cases more dilute than desired.

After cooling and removal of impurities, the $SO_2$ gas is dried with concentrated sulfuric acid. Equipment after the drying tower is much the same as in sulfur-burning plants with the single exception that waste-heat boilers cannot be employed to recover the heat evolved in the converter. As a result of its purification, the gas in this process is cold, instead of hot as in sulfur-burning plants, and must be heated to the temperature at which the catalyst begins to function. The energy evolved in the converter is utilized for this heating by passing the hot $SO_3$ gas and the cold $SO_2$ gas through a series of insulated tubular heat exchangers built of steel. The $SO_2$ gas is thus heated and the $SO_3$ gas cooled.

Contact plants of this type have been built with a single purification line that can produce 1,400 tons of 100% acid per 24 hours. The labour, cooling water, power, and maintenance requirements are much higher than in sulfur-burning plants because of the additional roasting and purification equipment. However, in many cases the $SO_2$ gas is obtained at little or no cost from copper and zinc smelters or from other low-cost raw materials and the cost of the product acid may be substantially less than that from sulfur-burning plants.

*The Lead-Chamber Process.*—This process derives its name from the use of large chambers of sheet lead and differs radically from the contact process, particularly in its use of gaseous oxides of nitrogen whose function may be considered to be catalytic. The chemical reactions which occur in the lead-chamber process are more complex than those in the contact process, and there is not unanimity of opinion as to their mechanisms. It is thought that the catalyst reacts with $SO_2$ gas, oxygen, and water vapour to form the intermediate compound, nitrososulfuric acid ($ONHSO_4$), which in turn reacts with water to form sulfuric acid and the oxides of nitrogen (NO and $NO_2$). Thus the catalyst goes through repeated cycles, combining with the $SO_2$, $O_2$ and $H_2O$ to form the intermediate compound and being set free again with the simultaneous formation of $H_2SO_4$.

The $SO_2$ gas is generally produced in the same manner as in the contact process. However, if it is impure, *i.e.*, obtained by the roasting of ores or by the burning of spent oxide, the purification is carried out only to the extent that the dust and other impurities are not present in quantities sufficient to clog the equipment. This less efficient purification obviates the necessity of cooling the gas which is needed in the next stage of the process at a high temperature, preferably in excess of approximately 600° C (1,100° F), and is necessarily at the expense of the quality of the product acid.

After the hot sulfur dioxide-air mixture has undergone the necessary purification, it is passed in succession upward through the Glover tower, through the lead chambers, and upward through the Gay-Lussac towers, nearly all of the $SO_2$ being removed in the first two steps. The Glover tower is a large masonry structure in some instances sheathed outside with lead. It is packed with lumps of loose quartz, acid-resisting brick, or ceramic shapes so that the hot gases are brought into intimate contact with acid that trickles downward through the packing.

The Glover tower has two main functions: (1) to concentrate the approximately 65% acid made in the chambers to 78% acid, the water vapour thus released entering the chambers with the gas stream; (2) to remove the nitrogen oxides from the 78% acid (nitrous vitriol) that has been used in the Gay-Lussac tower to absorb these oxides released at the end of the process and to return them to the cycle. The denitrification is accomplished by dilution of the 78% nitrous vitriol with the less concentrated chamber acid and by the elevation of the temperature of the mixture by the entering hot gases. The gases also begin to react and a substantial amount of sulfuric acid is formed in the Glover tower. The 78% acid drawn off at this point is hot and contains only traces of the oxides of nitrogen. After cooling, part is transferred to the Gay-Lussac towers where it is used to absorb the oxides of nitrogen released from the chambers. The balance represents the plant production and is delivered to steel storage tanks.

The cooled gases leaving the Glover tower proceed to the box-like lead chambers which may vary in size from 5,000 to 500,000 cu.ft. and in number from 1 to 20. The large chambers afford sufficient space and time for the gases, which do not mix rapidly, to react completely. The additional water necessary for the reactions is supplied through atomizing nozzles in the tops of the chambers. The sulfuric acid forms as a rain, drops to the bottom of the chambers, and is pumped to the Glover tower. A large amount of energy is evolved by the reactions and cooling is by the natural circulation of air around the chambers, which are set well above the ground. The chambers are usually housed in a building to lessen the effect of varying atmospheric conditions on the operation. As the gases pass through the Glover tower and the chambers, their $SO_2$ content gradually decreases to 0.1% or less, this amount being desirable for the optimum recovery of the nitrogen oxides in the Gay-Lussac towers.

The Gay-Lussac towers, usually two arranged in series, are similar in construction to the Glover tower but are taller and of smaller diameter. They have thinner walls and linings because they receive relatively cool gases. Their only function is to recover the nitrogen oxides in the spent gases and for this purpose cool 78% acid is used. The recovery is incomplete, and usually 10–15% of the oxides are lost, constituting an appreciable item of expense. Hence, fresh oxides of nitrogen must be constantly supplied to the process. In some plants the fresh nitrogen oxides are made from sodium nitrate and 78% sulfuric acid that is heated in an iron pot either by the hot $SO_2$ burner gases or by fuel. This method is obsolete at most plants and "nitre pots" have been superseded by ammonia oxidation units. Such units produce oxides of nitrogen by catalytic action of an incandescent platinum alloy gauze on a mixture of air and ammonia (about 9%). The oxides of nitrogen are then introduced into the process usually at the Glover tower inlet or outlet. The gases may be propelled through the chamber plant by the natural draft created by the final Gay-Lussac tower and its exit stack but usually one or more lead or alloy fans are employed. Such a fan may be located between the Glover tower and the first chamber, after the last chamber, or at both points.

Because of the considerable lead and space requirements of the chambers, the lack of efficient cooling, and the necessity for a large building, many variations of the process are in existence in which the boxlike chambers have been superseded by towers or by chambers of other shapes designed to promote more intensive gas mixing. Some are water cooled externally while some depend on cooling by the internal circulation of large quantities of acid. The principal successor in the U.S. is the Mills-Packard water-cooled chamber constructed in the shape of the frustum of a cone and first developed in England in 1914. By this means the chamber space required was reduced from 6 to 9 cu.ft. (.2 to .3 cu.m.) per pound of sulfur burned, in the case of air-cooled box chambers, to 2.0–3.5 cu.ft. (.05 to .10 cu.m.). No building is required for the Mills-Packard chambers. In the U.K. the Gaillard-Parrish chamber replaced the box chamber in some instances. It is relatively tall but cylindrical in shape and is cooled by a spray of 65% acid from a horizontal rotating disk (disperser) through the closed top. The Gaillard disperser has also been used in the tops of box chambers to increase their acid-making capacity. Various processes have also been evolved in which a series of packed towers take the place of the box chambers and in which the oxidation of $SO_2$ takes place largely in the liquid phase. Among these may be mentioned the Opl, Kachkaroff-Guareschi and Petersen processes, much used in Europe but not in America.

**Concentration.**—Concentration of sulfuric acid by evaporation of the water is gradually decreasing, except in time of war, and is practised in the U.S. in only a few industries. A variety of types of equipment may be used; in the U.S. the main types are the Simonson-Mantius vacuum and the Chemico drum concentrators. In the Simonson-Mantius type the acid is heated indirectly by steam in a closed vessel under vacuum so that any possibility of atmospheric pollution is essentially nonexistent. In the Chemico drum type the acid is brought into direct contact with hot gases from combustion of a fuel. The exit gases contain substantial quantities of acid mist which must be recovered, usually in electrical precipitators or scrubbers.

In countries other than the U.S., concentration is practised to a somewhat greater extent but smaller tonnages are involved. In addition to the vacuum and drum types, direct-fired pot concentrators with reflux condensers are frequently used.

**First Aid.**—The best first-aid measure for a sulfuric acid burn is "a lot of water quickly." Speed in removing the acid is of utmost importance, but small amounts of water must not be used because much heat is generated by dilution of the acid and the burn is thus made more severe. Neutralizing agents and ointments are dangerous and should never be used until the burned area has been washed completely free of acid with water. After this has been done the burn may be treated in the same manner as a heat burn.

**Environmental Pollution.**—In the past, many sulfuric acid plants emitted objectionable amounts of $SO_2$ and acid mist. However, by the early 1970s most plants normally converted 98 to 99% of the sulfur entering the process to usable sulfuric acid. In the late 1960s in the U.K. the total permissible amount of sulfur compounds, expressed as sulfur, in the effluent gases of a sulfuric acid plant was 2% of the sulfur burned in sulfur-burning plants, but 4% in plants using pyrites or spent oxide. In the case of pyrites, however, spent oxide, or any other raw material, except sulfur, there is an overriding maximum for sulfur compounds in the undiluted effluent gases of four grains, expressed as $SO_3$ per cu.ft. measured at standard conditions of 60° F and 30 in. mercury barometer. In the U.S. regulation was under control of the individual states. In California in the late 1960s the maximum allowable discharge in stack gases of all sulfur compounds, expressed as $SO_2$, was 0.2% $SO_2$ by volume. Two other states permitted a maximum of only 0.05% $SO_2$.

A conversion efficiency of 98% is usually adequate to achieve 0.2% $SO_2$ or slightly less; but to achieve 0.05% a minimum of 99% conversion is needed. To meet the 0.05% maximum either a stack gas scrubbing system or a recent development known as "inter-pass absorption" must be employed. Inter-pass absorption involves absorption of $SO_3$ between the converter stages, thus shifting the equilibrium of the reaction in the final catalyst pass in favour of more $SO_3$ formation. While doubtless desirable, these ever more stringent restrictions against escape of sulfur compounds into the atmosphere do greatly increase the cost of sulfuric acid.

Water pollution from sulfuric acid plants is almost never encountered. *See* also references under "Sulfuric Acid" in the Index.

BIBLIOGRAPHY.—Don M. Yost and Horace Russell, Jr., *Systematic Inorganic Chemistry of the Fifth-and-Sixth-Group Nonmetallic Elements* (1944); H. S. Harned and B. B. Owen, *The Physical Chemistry of Electrolytic Solutions,* 2nd ed. (1950); R. A. Robinson and R. H. Stokes, *Electrolyte Solutions* (1955); American Institute of Physics, *Handbook* (1957); W. W. Duecker and J. R. West, *The Manufacture of Sulfuric Acid* (1959); M. W. Kellogg, "Cascade Sulfuric Acid Process," *Oil and Gas Journal,* vol. 63 (1965); Manufacturing Chemists' Association and U.S. Public Health Service, *Atmospheric Emissions from Sulfuric Acid Manufacturing Processes* (1965); Stanford Research Institute, *Chemical Economics Handbook* (1967).

(T. F. Y.; C. M. D.)

**SULLA, LUCIUS CORNELIUS** (138–78 B.C.), Roman general and dictator, wrought great constitutional reforms. As quaestor, in 107 he joined the staff of Gaius Marius in Africa and in 105, by a piece of trickery, contrived the capture of the Numidian king Jugurtha. Though by this he attracted attention to himself and earned Marius' jealousy, he continued to serve on Marius' staff in the war against the Cimbri and Teutones in Gaul. After his praetorship in 93 he governed Cilicia in 92 and secured from Mithradates VI Eupator, king of Pontus, the restoration to Cappadocia of King Ariobarzanes, whom Mithradates had expelled. Sulla returned to Italy to fight in the Social War against the Italian *socii,* or allies, and was elected consul for 88, in which year he contracted important alliances by marrying, as his fourth wife, Caecilia Metella, widow of M. Aemilius Scaurus. As consul he received command of the war against Mithradates (*q.v.*).

The tribune P. Sulpicius Rufus, however, in the interest of the party of the Populares, carried a bill at Rome transferring the command in this war from Sulla to Marius. Sulla went at once to his legions in Campania and marched on Rome. Sulpicius was killed, Marius escaped, and measures were hurriedly improvised to prevent a recurrence of this type of tribunician interference. Sulla then set out for the east. Athens, which had joined Mithradates, was captured after a long siege in 86, and Mithradates' general Archelaus was defeated at Chaeronea and Orchomenos. Negotiations followed; and in August 85, Sulla offered Mithradates terms, which he accepted. He had to abandon all captured territory, to surrender his fleet, and to pay an indemnity. After imposing a heavy fine of 20,000 talents on the province of Asia and introducing emergency measures for the reinstitution of Roman taxation in the province, Sulla in the summer of 83 returned to Italy with 40,000 men and with plunder that included, from Athens, the works of Aristotle, most at that date unpublished.

During his absence the Popular Party had had its own way under L. Cornelius Cinna, Marius having died in 86. Sulla's political measures of 88 had been rescinded; Sulla had been declared a public enemy (86), and the former consul L. Valerius Flaccus had been sent to replace him. Flaccus, however, was murdered. On his return to Italy Sulla was joined by opponents of the Popular regime who had saved their lives by going underground during his absence, notably by Gnaeus Pompeius whom three years later he was to salute as "Magnus"—Pompey the Great. Cinna having been murdered in 84, Sulla's opponents were Gnaeus Papirius Carbo and the younger Marius, consuls for 82. There followed the first full-scale civil war in Roman history, ended in 82 by Sulla's victory in the Battle of the Colline Gate (in the northern suburbs of Rome) and by the siege and capture of Praeneste (Palestrina), held by the young Marius, who committed suicide after the surrender. The infamous proscriptions followed.

The *Lex Valeria* of 82, whereby Sulla was appointed dictator, was contrary to precedent in that it set no limit of time on his tenure of the office. He celebrated a spectacular triumph for his successes in the east; and as dictator in 81 and as both dictator and consul in 80, he carried through a vast program of constitutional reform, a series of *Leges Corneliae,* mainly designed to reestablish the supremacy of the Senate in the Roman constitution. Much of this reform was statesmanlike and survived to the end of the republic: in particular, a new treason law, the *Lex Cornelia maiestatis,* designed to check insubordination on the part of provincial governors and army commanders; an increase in the number of standing courts for criminal trials, the *quaestiones perpetuae;* and an arrangement by which the 20 quaestors elected each year should pass automatically into the Senate. Worst of all was the ruthless manner in which Sulla's discharged troops and supporters were settled in the Italian countryside, whether in colonies (for instance, Pompeii) or in districts from which the existing inhabitants were evicted. These settlers were the much hated "Sullani."

In 79 Sulla startled Rome by resigning the dictatorship and retiring into private life. He lived for a year longer, in Campania, writing the memoirs of which Plutarch was to make such extensive use. This resignation constitutes a puzzle that has never been solved. The evidence does not fully support J. Carcopino's hypothesis that Sulla had all the time been aiming not at the restoration of republican government but at establishing something like the principate that Augustus was to establish later; and that, his scheme detected, his most powerful backers, led by the Caecilii Metelli, turned on him and forced him to resign, using as instruments Pompey, who was certainly on bad terms with Sulla at the end, and Cicero, whose first important speech, *Pro Roscio Amerino,* in 80 or 79 was a bold attack on the Sullan regime.

Sulla was most superstitious, believing himself to be the object of divine favour. He expressed his belief in his own luck by assuming, late in 82, the name Felix (in Greek, Epaphroditus).

For portrait *see* article ROMAN HISTORY. *See* also references under "Sulla, Lucius Cornelius" in the Index.

BIBLIOGRAPHY.—*Ancient Sources:* Appian, *Bellum Civile,* i; Plutarch, *Marius* and *Sulla;* Sallust, *Bellum Iugurthinum;* Cicero, *Pro Roscio Amerino. Modern Works: Cambridge Ancient History,* vol. ix, ch. 4–6 (by Hugh Last, R. Gardner, and M. Rostovtzeff), with extensive bibliography (1932); J. Carcopino, *Sylla ou la monarchie manquée* (1931); F. Fröhlich in Pauly-Wissowa, *Real-Encyclopädie der classischen Altertumswissenschaft,* iv, 1522–66 (1900); Carolina Lanzani, *Lucio Cornelio Silla dittatore* (1936). On Sulla's memoirs *see* H. Peter, *Historicorum Romanorum reliquiae,* i, 2nd ed., cclxx–cclxxx, 195–204 (1914). On his religious views and his title "Felix" *see* J. P. V. D. Balsdon, "Sulla Felix," *Journal of Roman Studies,* 41:1–10 (1951); and H. Erkell, *Augustus, Felicitas, Fortuna* (1952). (J. P. V. D. B.)

**SULLIVAN, SIR ARTHUR SEYMOUR** (1842–1900), English composer who, with W. S. Gilbert, established the distinctive national form of the operetta. Born in London on May 13, 1842, he was the son of an Irish musician who became bandmaster at the Royal Military College; his mother was of Italian descent. He joined the choir of the Chapel Royal and later held the Mendelssohn Scholarship at the Royal Academy of Music, London, where he studied under Sir W. Sterndale Bennett and Sir John Goss. His studies were continued at the Leipzig Conservatory. In 1862 his music to *The Tempest* achieved great success at the Crystal Palace. Then followed his *Kenilworth* cantata (1864), a ballet, *L'Île Enchantée,* produced at Covent Garden, a symphony, and a cello concerto, the *In Memoriam* and the *Di Ballo* overtures, and numerous songs, including "Orpheus with His Lute."

THE BETTMANN ARCHIVE
SIR ARTHUR SULLIVAN

Sullivan's first comic opera was his setting of F. C. Burnand's *Cox and Box* (1867). An operetta, *The Contrabandista,* also on a libretto by Burnand, was produced in the same year. *Thespis* (1871), the first work in which Sullivan collaborated with W. S. Gilbert, met with little success when produced at the Gaiety Theatre. It was Richard D'Oyly Carte (*q.v.*), then manager of the Royalty Theatre, who brought the two men together again in 1875; the result was *Trial by Jury,* which, originally put on as an afterpiece to an Offenbach operetta, won instant popularity and ran for more than a year. Carte thereupon formed the Comedy Opera Company with a view to presenting full-length operettas by Gilbert and Sullivan. The first of these, *The Sorcerer* (1877), was succeeded by *H.M.S. Pinafore* (1878), whose eventual success was phenomenal. It was pirated in the United States, where Carte, together with the author and composer, produced an "official" version in 1879. The U.S. rights for their next operetta, *The Pirates of Penzance,* were secured by a production of this work in New York City, shortly before the London production in 1880. During the run of *Patience* (1881), Carte transferred the production to his newly built Savoy Theatre, where the later operettas were presented. These were *Iolanthe* (1882), *Princess Ida* (1884), *The Mikado* (1885), *Ruddigore* (1887), *The Yeomen of the Guard* (1888), and *The Gondoliers* (1889). In all these Gilbert's satire and verbal ingenuity were matched by Sullivan's unfailing melodiousness, resourceful musicianship, and sense of parody.

From time to time, however, Sullivan protested against the artificial nature of Gilbert's plots; this led to a disagreement between them that came to a head when Sullivan supported Carte in a minor business dispute. Sullivan's next opera, *Haddon Hall* (1892), had a libretto by Sydney Grundy, and subsequent collaboration with Gilbert, in *Utopia Limited* (1893) and *The Grand Duke* (1896), did not reach their former standard. Three other operettas were completed by Sullivan: *The Chieftain* (1894), largely an adaptation of *The Contrabandista;* the *Beauty Stone* (1898), with a libretto by A. W. Pinero and J. Comyns Carr; and *The Rose of Persia* (1899), with Basil Hood, who also wrote the libretto for *The Emerald Isle,* left unfinished by Sullivan and completed by Edward German.

Sullivan's more serious and ambitious compositions, such as *The Prodigal Son* (1869), *The Light of the World* (1873), *The Martyr of Antioch* (1880), *The Golden Legend* (1886), and the "romantic opera" *Ivanhoe,* written for the opening of the Royal English Opera House (now the Palace Theatre), built by Carte in 1891, were not maintained in the repertory, though they were acclaimed in their day. He also wrote many hymn tunes, including a famous one for "Onward, Christian Soldiers"; and his song "The Lost Chord" attained great popularity. In 1876 he accepted the principalship of the National Training School for Music (later the Royal College of Music), which he held for five years; he was active as a conductor, particularly at the Leeds festivals (1880–98). Knighted in 1883, he died in London on Nov. 22, 1900.

*See* also GILBERT, SIR WILLIAM SCHWENCK.

BIBLIOGRAPHY.—H. Sullivan and W. N. Flower, *Sir Arthur Sullivan,*

*His Life, Letters and Diaries* (1927); T. F. Dunhill, *Sullivan's Comic Operas* (1928); L. Baily, *The Gilbert and Sullivan Book* (1952); G. Hughes, *The Music of Arthur Sullivan* (1960). (H. Ru.)

**SULLIVAN, HARRY STACK** (1892–1949), U.S. psychiatrist who contributed an influential conception of psychiatry as the study of interpersonal relations, was born at Norwich, N.Y., on Feb. 21, 1892. His views quickly became controversial, stimulating much study of the relation between social processes and psychiatric disorder.

Sullivan received his medical degree in 1917 and began his psychiatric work under William A. White at St. Elizabeth's Hospital, Washington, D.C., in 1919; he turned to clinical research at Sheppard and Enoch Pratt Hospital, Towson, Md., from 1923 to 1930. There he developed his formulation of psychiatry and applied it by organizing what became a celebrated special ward for the group treatment of schizophrenic patients. After 1930 he devoted himself to elaborating his theoretical analysis, teaching, helping establish the Washington School of Psychiatry (1936), and writing. Conceiving of anxiety as arising in the infant as a disturbance in relations with the mothering one, he taught that the child develops a self-dynamism that functions to guide behaviour in diminishing anxiety; and that anxiety acts in opposition to tendencies to integrate activities with others. Personality characteristics and the "dynamisms of difficulty"—psychiatric disorders—were seen as interpersonal phenomena. Sullivan explicitly asserted the unique individual personality to be a myth.

Following World War II, Sullivan made energetic efforts to apply psychiatric concepts to international tensions. He died suddenly in Paris, Jan. 14, 1949, of apoplexy. His major works include *The Interpersonal Theory of Psychiatry* (1953), *The Psychiatric Interview* (1954), *Clinical Studies in Psychiatry* (1956), and *The Fusion of Psychiatry and Social Science* (1964).

*See* Patrick Mullahy (ed.), *Contributions of Harry Stack Sullivan: a Symposium of Interpersonal Theory in Psychiatry and Social Science* (1952); Edith Jacobson, "Sullivan's Interpersonal Theory of Psychiatry," *J. Am. Psychoanal. Ass.,* 3:149–156 (1955), a critical review. (A. H. Sn.; X.)

**SULLIVAN, JOHN** (1740–1795), American soldier and political leader who played an important part in the Revolutionary War, was born in Somersworth, N.H., on Feb. 17, 1740. He practised law at Berwick, Mass. (now Maine), and at Durham, N.H., was a member of the New Hampshire Provincial Congress (1774), and also served in the First Continental Congress. In June 1775 he was appointed brigadier general in the Continental Army and aided in the siege of Boston. In April 1776 he was ordered to Canada and, on the death of Maj. Gen. John Thomas, commanded the American troops on their retreat to New York. Superseded in command by Gen. Horatio Gates, Sullivan rejoined Washington's army. He was promoted to major general in August 1776 and took part in the Battle of Long Island, where he was taken prisoner. Exchanged in December, he led the right column of Washington's successful attack at Trenton, and in August 1777 led an unsuccessful night attack against the British and Loyalists on Staten Island. He commanded the American right flank in the Battle of Brandywine and took part in the Battle of Germantown. In 1778 he commanded the troops who were to join with the French fleet under Count d'Estaing in an attack on Newport, but the project failed when d'Estaing withdrew to Boston. Indian raids against colonists in western New York resulted in a retaliatory expedition against them led by Sullivan in 1779; with about 4,000 men, he defeated the Iroquois and their Loyalist allies near present-day Elmira, N.Y., burned their villages, and destroyed their orchards and crops. Thanked by Congress in October 1779 for his conduct in this expedition, he resigned from military service soon afterward because of ill health.

Sullivan was again a delegate to the Continental Congress in 1780–81, and from 1782 to 1786 was attorney general of New Hampshire. He was president of the state in 1786–87 and again in 1789, and in 1786 suppressed an insurrection at Exeter immediately preceding Shays's Rebellion in Massachusetts. He presided over the New Hampshire convention that ratified the federal Constitution in June 1788.

From 1789 until his death at Durham on Jan. 23, 1795, he was United States district judge in New Hampshire.

*See* Charles P. Whittemore, *A General of the Revolution, John Sullivan* (1961). (B. Kn.)

**SULLIVAN, JOHN L.** (Lawrence) (1858–1918), U.S. professional boxer, known as the "Great John L." and the "Boston Strong Boy." Born on Oct. 15, 1858, at Boston, Mass., Sullivan attended school there and for a time studied at Boston College. At the age of 19 he launched his professional boxing career. Sullivan was supreme at the rough-and-ready style and in 1882 knocked out Paddy Ryan in nine rounds to win the world heavyweight championship. He held the title until Sept. 7, 1892, when James J. Corbett knocked him out in 21 rounds at New Orleans, La. In the last bare-knuckle fight of professional boxing, Sullivan knocked out Jake Kilrain in 1889 in a 75-round battle that lasted 2 hr. 15 min. 25 sec. Sullivan, who had earned more than $1,000,000 as champion but dissipated it all, later became an advocate of prohibition and gave many lectures on the subject before his death in modest circumstances on Feb. 2, 1918. (J. P. D.; X.)

**SULLIVAN, LOUIS HENRY** (1856–1924), was one of the pioneers of the modern movement in architecture. Born in Boston, Mass., on Sept. 3, 1856, he studied at the Massachusetts Institute of Technology, Cambridge, and at the École des Beaux-Arts in Paris. He worked as a draftsman in various offices, including those of Frank Furness in Philadelphia, Pa., and William Le Baron Jenney in Chicago, Ill., in 1873–74. A decade later Jenney, an engineering genius, invented the principle of skyscraper construction. (*See* Architectural Engineering.) Sullivan was much interested in the many structural innovations made in Chicago during the generation after the fire of 1871. Dissatisfied with the widespread imitation of past styles that had prevailed during the preceding century, he sought to create a new architectural style, expressive of the functional problems and engineering advances of his day.

Sullivan's greatest work was done during his partnership with Dankmar Adler (1881–95). During those years the firm designed more than 100 structures. Outstanding were the Auditorium Building (acquired by Roosevelt University), Chicago; the Transportation Building at the Chicago Columbian Exposition of 1893; the Gage Building, Chicago; and two great skyscrapers, the Wainwright Building in St. Louis, Mo., and the Prudential Building in Buffalo, N.Y. In his steel-frame office buildings and skyscrapers Sullivan created designs harmonious with the purpose of the structure and appropriate to the new materials being used. During the years 1887–93 Sullivan was assisted by Frank Lloyd Wright (*q.v.*), who entered the office at 18 and became an ardent disciple of the older man, to whom he always referred as "the Master."

After the dissolution of the partnership with Adler, Sullivan's practice fell off drastically, but the score or more buildings he produced before his death included his masterpiece, the Carson Pirie Scott department store building in Chicago (1899–1904), and a number of fine banks in small midwestern towns, notably National Farmers' Bank (later the Security Bank and Trust Company of Owatonna), Owatonna, Minn.

BROWN BROTHERS

LOUIS H. SULLIVAN

More influential than his buildings was his philosophy of architectural design, which he set forth in books, magazine articles, and lectures. In these he bitterly attacked the imitation of historic styles—the architectural eclecticism of the 19th and 20th centuries—and called for a modern style expressive of the facts and spirit of the 20th century. Sullivan's theory of "functionalism" is but baldly stated in his slogan "form follows function." He believed that the architectural style of a building should be derived from and expressive of its function and structure. He believed that "each problem contains and suggests its own solution," that each building should have its own identity of beauty and that this must necessarily reflect its origin in present-day conditions, social, technical and spiritual. Another mainspring of Sullivan's thinking was an ardent belief in United States democracy, eloquently expressed in his Whitmanesque prose poetry and basic to his conviction that architecture is a democratic social art. Sullivan's most important published books were *Kindergarten Chats* (1901–02) and *The Autobiography of an Idea* (1924).

Sullivan died in almost complete poverty on April 14, 1924, in Chicago. After his death he came to be recognized, in both the United States and Europe, as one of the great pioneers of modern architecture. In 1943 he was posthumously awarded the gold medal of the American Institute of Architects. In 1956 the centennial of his birth was widely celebrated and an exhibition of his work was prepared at the Art Institute of Chicago for national and international showings. *See* also MODERN ARCHITECTURE.

*See* H. Morrison, *Louis Sullivan, Prophet of Modern Architecture* (1935); J. Szarkowski, *The Idea of Louis Sullivan* (1956); W. Connely, *Louis Sullivan as He Lived* (1960); S. Paul, *Louis Sullivan: an Architect in American Thought* (1962). (HH. M.)

**SULLY, MAXIMILIEN DE BÉTHUNE,** DUC DE (1559–1641), French statesman who, as the trusted minister of Henry IV, substantially contributed to the rehabilitation of the state after the Wars of Religion. He was born in the château of Rosny, near Mantes, on Dec. 13, 1559, the son of François de Béthune, baron de Rosny (1532–75). Brought up as a Huguenot, he was early sent to the court of Henry of Navarre (the future Henry IV of France), who took him to Paris in 1572. A student at the Collège de Bourgogne there, he escaped death in the Massacre of St. Bartholomew's Day by carrying a Catholic Book of Hours under his arm. In the civil war of 1575–76, Rosny, as he was called, served in Henry's forces; but in 1580 he went to the Netherlands, in the hope of recovering ancestral lands there. Disappointed, he went back to Henry of Navarre in Guienne. In 1583 he was Henry's special agent in Paris. In 1584 he married a rich heiress, Anne de Courtenvaux (d. 1589). On the renewal of civil war (1585) he rejoined Henry of Navarre. In the Battle of Ivry (1590), during Henry's struggle for the French crown, Rosny was wounded. He was in favour of Henry's conversion to Roman Catholicism but refused to change his own religion. He helped arrange Henry's marriage to Marie de Médicis (1600) and to negotiate peace with Savoy (1601); in 1603 he was ambassador extraordinary to James I of England.

PHOTO BULLOZ

SULLY, PORTRAIT BY FRANÇOIS QUESNEL IN THE MUSÉE CONDÉ, CHANTILLY

Rosny, who became a member of the king's Council of Finance in 1596, seems to have been sole superintendent of finances by 1598. In this capacity, though he was not strictly an economist, he had the practical sense and the resolution to discern and to impose the most efficacious measures. He authorized the free export of grain and wine; reduced the legal rate of interest on loans from $8\frac{1}{3}$ to $6\frac{1}{4}\%$; set up a special court to try cases of peculation; stopped various abuses of tax collecting, including the raising of money by provincial governors on their own authority; and abolished some superfluous public offices. It was he, moreover, who in 1604 sponsored the adoption of the system of the "annual right" or *droit annuel,* which assured the state of a predictable revenue, at the cost of making offices in fact hereditary: under this system, officeholders by paying annually one-sixtieth of the sum that they had originally paid for their office could secure the right to transfer it as they might see fit, whereas previously any transfer that they might have made, by sale or by bequest, could be annulled if they died within 40 days of making it. Altogether, through honest and rigorous conduct of the finances, an average of 1,000,000 livres a year was saved between 1600 and 1610.

The chancellor Pomponne de Bellièvre, who stood for the old tradition of the French monarchy (with the various councils and the *parlements* playing a considerable role in public affairs), was eventually eclipsed by Rosny, who was indeed "the king's man" and who subordinated private and particular interests to the authority of the state. Rosny's loyalty was copiously rewarded. He was appointed grand commissioner for highways and public works in 1597; superintendent of fortifications and grand master of the artillery in 1599; governor of Mantes and of Jargeau, captain general of the queen's *gens d'armes,* and governor of the Bastille in 1602; and governor of Poitou in 1603. Finally, in 1606, he was created duc de Sully and a peer of France.

For the internal economy, Sully encouraged agriculture and stock raising, urged the free circulation of produce, checked the destruction of the forests, promoted road building and the draining of marshland, and planned a great canal system (the Briare Canal was actually started). He did little for industry, except to establish some silk factories, on which the king himself insisted; and he was unsympathetic to the king's colonial policy. He strengthened the military establishment and directed the construction of frontier defense works.

Sully's political role came practically to an end with the assassination of Henry IV on May 14, 1610. Though Marie de Médicis, as regent for Louis XIII, at first retained him in her council, his colleagues were impatient of his domineering leadership, and on Jan. 26, 1611, the queen accepted his resignation. He then retired into private life. In 1634 he was created a marshal of France. He died at Villebon on Dec. 22, 1641.

Sully's curious and lengthy *Mémoires,* otherwise known as the *Économies royales* (1638; numerous editions down to 1837; modern ed. by L. R. Lefèvre, 1942), are remarkable for their often reprinted account of the "Great Design," which he attributes to Henry IV—a European confederation or "Christian Republic" to be established after the defeat of Austria and Spain.

BIBLIOGRAPHY.—Apart from H. Carré, *Sully* (1932), and H. Pourrat, *Sully et sa grande passion* (1942), the best works are those listed under HENRY IV; *see* especially R. Mousnier, *La Vénalité des offices . . .* (1946) for the new light that it casts. For the "Great Design," *see* C. Pfister, article in the *Revue historique,* vol. 54 and 56 (1894); and A. Puharré, *Les Projets d'organisation européene d'après le Grand Dessein* (1954). (V. L. T.)

**SULLY, THOMAS** (1783–1872), U.S. painter, one of the best early American portrait painters, was born at Horncastle, Eng., on June 8 (or 19), 1783, of actor parents. They moved to the United States when Sully was nine years old, settling at Charleston, S.C. He was a pupil of Gilbert Stuart in Boston, and in 1809 he entered the studio of Benjamin West in London. After 1810 he made Philadelphia his home, but in 1837 again visited London, where he painted a full-length portrait of Queen Victoria for the St. George's Society of Philadelphia. He died in Philadelphia on Nov. 5, 1872. Though Sully left about 500 subject pictures, he is best known for portraits. Among his 2,000 portraits are those of Stephen Decatur, the actor George Frederick Cooke as Richard III and Lafayette, and Thomas Jefferson. Many others are in galleries throughout the U.S.

**SULLY PRUDHOMME** (real name RENÉ FRANÇOIS ARMAND PRUDHOMME) (1839–1907), French poet connected with the Parnassian school, winner of the Nobel Prize for Literature in 1901, was born in Paris, March 16, 1839. Throughout his life he suffered from a feeling of loneliness. Ophthalmia prevented him from taking up scientific studies, and he worked as a clerk in Paris (1860). His first published poem, "L'Art," appeared in *La Revue nationale et étrangère* (1863). In 1864 he met Leconte de Lisle and contributed to *Le Parnasse contemporain* (1866, 1871, and 1876). Like the Parnassians, he concentrated on technique but differed in expressing personal feelings—fleeting joys and sorrows in *Stances et poèmes* (1865) and *Les Épreuves* (1866), craving for affection in *Les Solitudes* (1869) and *Les Vaines tendresses* (1875). This sentimental verse, of which "Le Vase brisé" is typical, was widely acclaimed, whereas little interest was aroused by his attempts to create a new type of philosophic and scientific poetry—

*Les Destins* (1872), *Le Zénith* (1876), *La Justice* (1878), and *Le Bonheur* (1888). His last works were in prose—*Testament poétique* (1901) and *La Vraie Religion selon Pascal* (1905). In 1882 he was elected to the Académie Française. He died at Châtenay, near Paris, Sept. 7, 1907.

BIBLIOGRAPHY.—C. Hémon, *La Philosophie de M. Sully-Prudhomme* (1907); E. Estève, *Sully-Prudhomme* (1925); P. Flottes, *Sully-Prudhomme et sa pensée* (1930). (E. M. So.)

**SULMAN, HENRY LIVINGSTONE** (1861–1940), English metallurgist, one of the originators of the froth flotation process for concentrating ores preliminary to the extraction of metal from them, was born in London on Jan. 15, 1861. From 1878 to 1881 he studied chemistry at University College, London, gaining a number of medals and other awards. After graduation he served as chemist or manager of various chemical plants in Bristol and London and subsequently engaged in consulting work. In 1898 he entered into partnership with H. F. K. Picard as metallurgical consultants in the City of London, work that involved travel to South Africa, Australia, Malaya, Japan, and Canada. He was the inventor, or co-inventor, of several processes for the extraction of gold, including treatment with bromocyanide. Later, and in conjunction with his partner Picard, he introduced the froth flotation process. The Institution of Mining and Metallurgy, of which he was president 1911–12, awarded him its Gold Medal in 1919. He also received the Gold Medal and premium of the Consolidated Gold Fields of South Africa in 1920. He died at Croydon, Surrey, on Jan. 31, 1940. *See* also METALLURGY: *Ores and Ore Treatment*. (C. W. D.)

**SULMONA,** a town in L'Aquila Province, Abruzzi, Italy, 30 mi. (48 km.) SW of Pescara and a railway junction on the Rome–Pescara line. Pop. (1969 est.) 21,439. Remains include an aqueduct (1250) that supplied water to a 15th-century fountain. The Palazzo dell'Annunziata, founded in 1320, has a facade in both Gothic and Baroque styles. The 13th-century Church of S. Francesco della Scarpa was damaged by earthquakes but retains an imposing Romanesque portal; Sta. Maria della Tomba (15th century) has a Romanesque-Abruzzese front and a rose window; the Palazzo Tabassi has a fine 15th-century Gothic double window. There are collections of ancient marble and medieval Baroque jewelry in the museum.

The poet Ovid was born in Sulmona in 43 B.C.; part of his villa still remains. Pope Innocent VII was also a native of the town. Manufactures include confectionery (sugared almonds) and copper and wrought-iron work; trade in agricultural products is important. (M. T. A. N.)

**SULPHUR.** For a description of this element and its commercially important acid, *see* SULFUR; SULFURIC ACID.

**SULPICIUS RUFUS, PUBLIUS** (*c.* 124–88 B.C.), outstanding Roman orator and politician who supported the reforms of his friend the younger M. Livius Drusus (91 B.C.) and inherited his policy of generous concessions to the Italian allies. Though he renounced his patrician status to become a tribune of the plebs, he had shown, by prosecuting the tribune Gaius Norbanus for treason *c.* 94, that his political attitude was moderate, and he had a subordinate command for at least one year (89) in the Social War against the allies (*socii*). As tribune in 88 he introduced several laws: (1) to unseat all senators who were more than 2,000 denarii in debt; (2) to recall all men exiled under the *Lex Varia* of 90 B.C. (a measure that he himself had opposed earlier); (3) to transfer the command in the war against Mithradates from Sulla, the Senate's nominee, to Marius; and (4) to distribute freedmen and the newly enfranchised Italians among the 35 tribes (so as to make their voting power effective). Sulpicius' chief aim was probably championship of the new Italian citizens, but to implement this he needed wide support: hence his other measures, which would secure for him the backing of the people, of Marius, and of the equites. This bold challenge to the Senate led to violence, and Sulpicius is said to have organized a group of 600 young equites and a larger bodyguard of 3,000 armed men. The consuls, Sulla and Q. Pompeius Rufus, declared some form of cessation of public business (perhaps a *justitium*), which Sulpicius denounced as illegal. Disturbances followed in the Forum, and Sulla was forced to call off the *justitium*; he then joined his army in Campania. At Rome Sulpicius' measures were carried. Sulla then marched on Rome and won the city. Marius and Sulpicius fled and were declared outlaws, and Sulpicius was caught and killed at Lavinium. His laws were declared invalid, as passed "by force."

Sulpicius' policy is obscure, but he may well have been a liberal optimate, whose championship of the Italians led his enemies to depict him as a revolutionary demagogue rather than as a moderate reformer forced by circumstances to go to greater lengths than he probably wished. He was an outstanding orator, though his speeches are lost, and was much admired by Cicero, who made him a speaker in his *De oratore*. (H. H. SD.)

**SULPICIUS RUFUS, SERVIUS** (*c.* 106–43 B.C.), Roman jurist, who left nearly 180 treatises on law and is often quoted in the *Digest* of Justinian, although direct extracts from his works are not found. He studied rhetoric with Cicero and went with him to study in Rhodes in 78 B.C. Deciding that he would never be a first-class orator, he gave up rhetoric for law. In 63 he was a candidate for the consulship of 62 but was defeated by L. Licinius Murena, whom he subsequently accused of bribery; Cicero successfully defended Murena. In 51 Sulpicius became consul. In the civil war, after considerable hesitation, he threw in his lot with Julius Caesar, who made him proconsul of Achaea in 46. He died in 43 while on a mission from the Senate to Mark Antony at Mutina. He was accorded a public funeral, and a statue was erected to his memory in front of the Rostra.

Two letters from Sulpicius to Cicero are preserved (Cicero, *Ad familiares*, iv, 5 and 12); the first is his famous letter of consolation on the death of Cicero's daughter Tullia. Quintilian mentions three orations by Sulpicius (now lost); one of these was the speech against Murena, another *Pro* (or *Contra*) *Aufidia*, of whom nothing is known. He is also said to have been a writer of erotic poems, though this may refer to his son. The poetess Sulpicia was probably Sulpicius' granddaughter.

**SULPICIUS SEVERUS** (fl. *c.* A.D. 400), a Christian ascetic, one of the chief authorities for Gallo-Roman history of his own times and the most graceful writer of the age, was born in Aquitaine (southwestern France) of good family not earlier than 353. Trained for the bar in the best period of Gaulish rhetoric, he devoted himself after the early death of his wife to local church building and to the life of a literary recluse in Aquitaine, forwarding the interests of the church in the West, and especially the ascetic monasticism recently introduced into Gaul. To the friendship and generosity of his mother-in-law, Bassula, in Trier he owed his pecuniary independence and doubtless much of his knowledge of current affairs. The biographer Gennadius (*c.* 500) refers to him as a priest whose orthodoxy was suspect, and he was not in good relations with the Gaulish bishops; but the references to him by St. Augustine and St. Jerome are friendly, and 13 extant letters are addressed to him by his friend St. Paulinus of Nola, one of the choicest Christian spirits of the age. Severus died probably in the first quarter of the 5th century.

Severus' most famous work, the *Vita S. Martini*, was in first draft before the death of St. Martin in 397; but supplementary matter relating to Martin is added in all his subsequent writings, including three authentic surviving letters. In 400 he wrote and *c.* 402–404 published his *Chronica* ("Sacred Histories") in two books, from the creation to his own time, but omitting the Gospels. It is unusually readable, and the latter portion is a valuable contemporary document, especially for the tragic history of the Priscillianists (*see* PRISCILLIAN). The *Dialogi*, which appeared in 404, are a literary masterpiece in which the relative merits of Martin's monastery are debated by one of its inmates with a traveler newly returned to Aquitaine from the ascetics of the North African desert, while Severus presides and prompts the speakers.

BIBLIOGRAPHY.—Works ed. by C. Halm, *Corpus scriptorum ecclesiasticorum Latinorum*, vol. i (1866). Complete Eng. trans. by A. Roberts in *Nicene and Post-Nicene Fathers*, 2nd series, vol. xi (1894); select Eng. trans. by B. Peebles in *The Fathers of the Church* (1949); Eng. trans. of *Dialogi* and three letters in *The Western Fathers*, ed. by C. Dawson (1954). *See* also Pauly-Wissowa, *Real-Encyclopädie der classischen Altertumswissenschaft*, 2nd series, vol. iv, col. 863–871 (1931). (N. K. C.)

**SULTANPUR** (formerly KUSAPURA or KUSHBHAWANPUR), a town of Uttar Pradesh, India, and the headquarters of the district of the same name, is on the Gumti River, 83 mi. (134 km.) SE of Lucknow. Pop. (1961) 26,081. Sultanpur is an ancient town, although little is known about its origins. Destroyed and rebuilt several times, it passed into the hands of the sultans, possibly in the 12th century. The Muslim town was finally razed to the ground in 1857. The present town grew as a military settlement during the early British occupation.

SULTANPUR DISTRICT (area 1,713 sq.mi. [4,437 sq.km.]; pop. [1961] 1,412,984) forms a part of the Ganges-Ghaghra Doab west, traversed by the Gumti and its tributary, the Sai. The surface in general is level, except for some patches of ravines and *usar* lands. The chief crops are rice, wheat, barley, and millets. There is a degree college at Amethi affiliated to Agra University.

(R. L. SI.)

**SULU,** a province and archipelago in the Philippines extending about 170 mi. (274 km.) SW from the southwestern tip of Mindanao. Its area of 1,037 sq.mi. (2,686 sq.km.) is divided into hundreds of islands, some volcanic and some coral, of which the most important are Jolo, Tawi Tawi, Sanga Sanga, Sibutu, Siasi, and Cagayan Sulu. The 1960 provincial population of 326,898 was about 95% Muslim. These Muslim tribes, known as Moros, historically were fiercely independent (*see* MORO). During the Spanish occupation of the Philippines a troop garrison was stationed at the town of Jolo but Spanish rule never extended far beyond the fort. During the early period of U.S. rule, which began in 1899, several battles were fought against the Moros. The archipelago became part of Moro Province (1903) and civil government was established in 1914. On March 11, 1915, the reigning sultan of Sulu agreed to abdicate his rights of sovereignty and to retain only his right to be head of the Islamic sect. Following this agreement sporadic fighting continued between government forces and outlaw bands. A treaty signed April 1940 abolished the sultanate, and Sulu became part of the Commonwealth, later the Republic, of the Philippines.

Cassava, coconuts, and rice are the main agricultural products, but rice is not produced in sufficient quantity and some must be imported. Fishing and gathering seashells (for the manufacture of buttons) are important activities. The Turtle Islands are famous as a source of turtle shells and eggs. Considerable illegal trade is carried on between Sulu and Borneo. The capital and chief port and trading centre is the town of Jolo on Jolo Island.

(R. E. HE.)

**SULU SEA,** a large, very deep interisland sea, located between the southwestern Philippine Islands and northeastern Borneo. About 350 mi. (563 km.) from north to south, 425 mi. (684 km.) in east to west dimension, and 135,000 sq.mi. (349,650 sq.km.) in area, the Sulu Sea is enclosed by various islands of the Philippines: Palawan on the west and northwest, Dalanganem and Cuyo Islands on the north, Panay and Negros on the east, Mindanao and the Sulu archipelago on the southeast, and Sabah on the southwest. The sea occupies a downfaulted block, in some places almost 3,000 fathoms (18,000 ft. [5,486 m.]) deep. The edges of this enclosed basin are seen in the bordering islands, particularly in the northeast-southwest orientation of Palawan and the Sulu archipelago. The sea is bisected by another northeast-southwest fracture line which is evidenced by the coral atolls of the Cagayan Islands, the Tubbataha reefs, and the volcanic cones of the Cagayan Sulu group. The sheltered sea is extensively used for interisland trade. Fishing is an important occupation and marine products include pearls, pearl shells, *bêche-de-mer,* shark fins, and turtle eggs. Copra, timber, and forest products of the surrounding islands provide the other commercial activities of the area.

The Sulu Sea was long the stronghold of the fierce Moro pirates of the Sulu archipelago, who raided shipping as far away as Malaya. Punitive campaigns, started by the Spanish in the mid-19th century and terminated by U.S. troops in 1906, broke the power of the Muslim Moros and brought peace to the area. (L. A. P. G.)

**SUMAC,** the popular name for shrubs and small trees of the genus *Rhus* (family Anacardiaceae) with perhaps 50 species in southern Europe, Asia, and eastern North America. They have a resinous, milky sap that hardens in the air; a few staghorn branches; alternate, pinnate leaves; terminal clusters of small flowers with parts in fives; and small, one-seeded, hairy, red fruits. Closely related to and often included in *Rhus* is the genus *Schmaltzia* with about 30 species of many-branched shrubs with spikelike clusters of flowers and fruit and variously compound or simple, deciduous, or evergreen leaves. The distribution of *Schmaltzia* centres in Mexico.

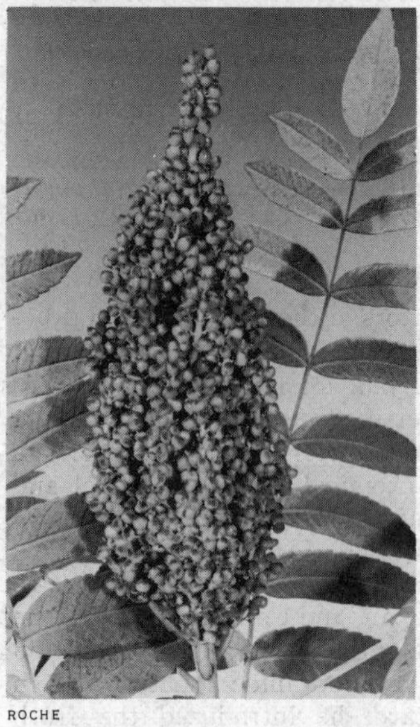
ROCHE
SMOOTH SUMAC (RHUS GLABRA)

The name sumac is given also to the commercial preparation of the dried and ground leaves of the Sicilian or tanners' sumac (*R. coriaria*) of southern Europe, long used in tanning leather. Several of the eastern North American species also were used in tanning. Among the most attractive North American shrubs are the staghorn sumac (*R. typhina*), sometimes a tree 30 ft. (9 m.) high, and the smooth sumac (*R. glabra*), sometimes 20 ft. high, both of which in autumn display highly coloured fruit and foliage. The dwarf or shining sumac (*R. copallina*) is a small shrub in the north and a tree 30 ft. (9 m.) high in the south. Best known in *Schmaltzia* is the aromatic sumac (*S. crenata*), 3 to 8 ft. (0.9 to 2.4 m.) high, with pleasant-scented foliage, which occurs in the eastern U.S., and its western counterpart, the skunkbush or squawbush (*S. trilobata,* perhaps better treated as a subspecies of *S. crenata*), with ill-scented foliage, found from Illinois to Oregon and southward. The mahogany sumac, or sourberry (*S. integrifolia*), and the sugarbush (*S. ovata*) are elegant shrubs of southern California.

The laurel sumac of the same area is sometimes placed in another segregate genus, *Malosma* (*M. laurina*).

The swamp-dwelling poison sumac (*Toxicodendron vernix*) is closely related to poison ivy (*q.v.*) and poison oak. Poison sumac can be distinguished from other sumacs by its persistent white or grayish fruits.

In addition to their value in tanning, sumacs were used by the American Indians as sources of orange dyes, medicines, fuel, twigs for basket-weaving (*S. trilobata*), and fruit for cool drinks in summer and hot drinks, with maple sugar, in winter. *R. chinensis* of eastern Asia and *R. typhina* and *R. glabra,* especially the narrow-leaved varieties, are planted for their ornamental foliage. Sumacs are valuable as sand binders, game cover, and pioneers in the revegetation of denuded areas. (R. F. TH.)

**SUMATRA** (SUMATERA), an island in the Republic of Indonesia lying between 5°39′ N and 5°57′ S, so that the Equator divides it into two nearly equal parts. Sumatra is the westernmost and, after Borneo, the second largest of the Greater Sunda Islands of the Malay Archipelago. It is separated in the northeast from the Malay Peninsula by the Strait of Malacca and in the south from Java by the Sunda Strait. It is 1,069 mi. (1,722 km.) long, and its greatest width is 324 mi. (521 km.). With its adjacent islands, Sumatra has an area of 182,859 sq.mi. (473,606 sq.km.). In 1961 the population was 15,739,363 (about one-sixth of the Indonesian total of 97,018,829).

## PHYSICAL GEOGRAPHY

**Relief and Drainage.**—Sumatra consists of a high mountain chain which runs along the western coast, descending eastward to a huge tract of flat, alluvial land, drained by many large rivers and their scores of tributaries. Its mountain chain is part of the great mountain system which occurs in Lower Burma and continues via Preparis, the Great Coco Islands, the Andaman Islands, and the Nicobar Islands to Sumatra and then swings east through Java and the Lesser Sunda Islands to the Moluccas. The Sumatran chain, running northwest-southeast through the island, extends for a distance of more than 1,000 mi. (1,609 km.) and contains numerous volcanic peaks up to more than 12,000 ft. (3,658 m.). The whole system, known as the Pegunungan Barisan ("Parade of Mountains"), consists in general of two or more folded chains running parallel to each other, with a valley between, which is broken up into separate sections by the intrusion of volcanic massifs. Along this valley lies a string of mountain lakes, from south to north—Ranau, Kerintji, Singkarak, Manindjau, and Toba. By far the largest of these is Lake Toba, which is 56 mi. (90 km.) long and 19 mi. (30 km.) wide, of great depth, and has a large island, Samosir.

The line of volcanic peaks stretches through Sumatra from Abongabong (9,892 ft. [3,015 m.]) and the mountains of Atjeh to the islet of Krakatau (*q.v.*) at the southern end of the island. It includes Leuser (Loser; 11,548 ft. [3,520 m.]), Talakmau (Mt. Ophir; 9,554 ft. [2,912 m.]), Kerintji (Indrapura, 12,483 ft. [3,805 m.], the highest point in Sumatra), and Dempo (10,364 ft. [3,159 m.]). In all, 90 volcanoes have been counted, 12 active.

Sumatra, like Java and Borneo, is formed largely of strata of the Tertiary Period, although it contains also two schistose formations, one of which is pre-Carboniferous. The Tertiary series are more complete than in Java; the volcanoes, so characteristic of the whole archipelago, were formed during the Quaternary Period. The western mountain system is composed largely of Archean rocks, with occasional longitudinal bands of Jurassic and Cretaceous rocks. The whole ridge is metalliferous, and erosion of the ranges exposes their mineral contents. The crystalline rocks (including granites and basalts) are of various geological ages; they are exposed by denudation, or pushed through by intrusion. Extensive petroleum deposits occur in the Tertiary rocks underlying the eastern lowland.

The river system of Sumatra is extensive and of great value to the country. On the west coast, where the mountains approach the sea, the rivers run in valleys with a steep slope, have a very short lower course, and are unnavigable, except near the mouth in the case of a few. The eastern rivers (often impeded by silt) run through alluvial plains, have extensive drainage areas, and form the principal and often the only means of communication. The important rivers lie south of 3° N: the Asahan, which drains Lake Toba, navigable by steamers for a portion of its length; the Panai (Bila and Barumun), with a very wide mouth; the Rokan, about 140 mi. (225 km.) long and flowing into the Strait of Malacca through a wide, muddy estuary, navigable for 70 mi. (113 km.) inland; the Siak, with the port of Pakanbaru 90 mi. (145 km.) upstream; the Kampar and the Inderagiri, both partly navigable for ocean steamers; the Hari, the longest river of Sumatra, having a maximum navigability of 300 mi. (483 km.); and the Musi (*q.v.*), on which oceangoing vessels can reach Palembang, 56 mi. (90 km.) upstream, while steam launches and motorboats are able to go farther inland.

JULES BUCHER—PHOTO RESEARCHERS, INC.

LAKE TOBA, THE LARGEST OF A STRING OF MOUNTAIN LAKES IN NORTH SUMATRA

On the west coast there are small semicircular bays but few large indentations, immunity from the southwest monsoon being provided for harbours only between Tapanuli Bay and Indrapura. The north coast has precipitous cliffs crowned with dense vegetation in some parts; in other sections there are sandy beaches and well-cultivated plains, while the Bay of Uleelheue gives shelter for shipping. The south coast consists, mainly, of two large indentations, Lampung Bay and Semangka Bay. The eastern shore of Lampung Bay is mountainous and little indented, the western much cut up; the centre of the bay has a good harbour (Telukbetung). Semangka Bay has a mountainous coastline, with little indentation.

The whole of the east coast is formed of morasses and sandbanks, which break up into innumerable islands, large and small, particularly about the central portion; and the coastline is deeply indented in many places and very irregular. The indentations are not permanent, the coast is constantly advancing, and it is difficult to establish practicable ports or landing places.

Sumatra has a chain of islands off the west coast which arise from the edge of the submarine platform and serve as a kind of outer barrier. They have an aggregate area of 5,769 sq.mi. (14,941 sq.km.). Several are densely populated, and some are of considerable size; most have rocky, reef-bound coasts, dangerous of approach. Between south Sumatra and Malaya, athwart the entrance to the Strait of Malacca, lie the innumerable islands of the Riouw Archipelago (*q.v.*).

**Climate.**—The climate of Sumatra resembles that of Java and is hot and extremely moist, but in most eastern coastal districts and often for many miles inland the heat is tempered by cooling land and sea breezes, the wind generally being northeast by day and southwest by night throughout the year. The wind system of northern Sumatra differs from that of the greater part of Indonesia, the northeast monsoon blowing from December to March, and the southwest monsoon from May to October. During the southwest monsoon strong squalls from the northwest, known as Sumatras, which are accompanied by thunder, lightning, and rain, blow in the Strait of Malacca; they have been known also to occur during the northeast monsoon. On the west coast the influence of the northeast and southwest monsoons is felt as far south as 4° N. Between 4° N and 2° N there is a region of calms and light variable winds, which have a westerly tendency from March to November, when the northwest monsoon is blowing along the remainder of the west coast (*i.e.*, from 2° N to 5°57′ S), and an easterly tendency from May to September, the period of the southeast monsoon on the west coast. Southern Sumatra has the highest temperatures, and the mean annual temperature for the lowlands is about 26.6° C (80° F). At Toba, in the Batak country (3,772 ft. [1,150 m.]), this is 21° C (69.6° F), and higher altitudes show a corresponding reduction. On the whole, temperature in Sumatra is slightly higher than in Java. March, April, and May are the hottest months; January and February the coolest, but the difference does not exceed 2° F. The different wind distribution causes a variation of the seasons. Thus in northern Sumatra October is the wettest month and February and March are the driest, while elsewhere the wettest months are December, January, and February, and from July to September is the dry period. Accordingly, the rainfall varies considerably. The annual average rainfall for northern Sumatra is 95 in. (2,413 mm.), for eastern Sumatra 106 in. (2,692 mm.), and for western Sumatra 122 in. (3,099 mm.). The west monsoon gives the heavier rainfall, and the fall is accentuated in western Sumatra by the high mountains.

**Vegetation.**—The vegetation of Sumatra bears a strong resemblance to that of India and of the Malay Peninsula in the northern part of the island and to that of Java in the southern, but it has also many varieties distinct from either, and not only different varieties but different genera from those of Java. The pine, *Pinus merkusii,* in the mountains of the north is not found elsewhere in the Malay Archipelago but occurs as far south as the Equator. One of the most striking flowers is the huge parasitic monster flower, *Rafflesia,* with blossoms up to three feet across, growing on big lianas on the ground in the forests. There are immense areas of savanna country, covered with coarse grasses which stifle other forms of vegetation and give shelter to hordes of wild animals. These tracts occur as low as within 700 ft. (200 m.) of sea level. Myrtles, bamboo, rhododendrons, moss-loving orchids, and palms are common. There are zones of vegetation differing with altitude, but the general tendency is for all forms to grow at a lower level than is the case in Java. The Sumatran forest begins at a height of from 300 to 400 ft. (90–120 m.) and extends to all but the highest mountain peaks, giving a wealth of vegetation that produces very beautiful mountain scenery. The forests contain the finest timber-producing woods in the archipelago; there is not only a great variety of trees, but they possess both stature and beauty. Deciduous trees such as the oak, chestnut, etc., grow on lower slopes than in Java; and apart from ebony, ironwood, camphorwood, and sandalwood there are also many species of resin and wild rubber-producing trees.

**Animal Life.**—Notwithstanding the proximity of the island to Java the fauna of Sumatra shows a greater resemblance to that of Borneo than to that of Java, this being particularly noticeable as regards the fauna of the east coast of Sumatra (that of the west coast and of the islands adjacent is more allied to the Javanese fauna). This striking difference in species between the fauna of Sumatra and Java led A. R. Wallace to assert that the first severance of Sumatra from Java is very ancient; that since the epoch of the first (volcanic) disturbance several distinct elevations and depressions may have taken place, the islands having perhaps been more than once joined with each other or with the mainland (of Asia) and again separated; and that successive waves of immigration may thus have modified the fauna and led to those anomalies in distribution which are so difficult to account for by any single operation of elevation or submergence.

The orangutan, common to Sumatra (in the northeast) and Borneo, is unknown in Java; the siamang is found in Sumatra and in the Malay Peninsula but not in Borneo or Java; there are ape species common to Borneo and Sumatra, also the elephant (introduced into Borneo), tapir (indigenous also in the Malay Peninsula), and Malayan bear, all of which are unknown in Java, though, on the other hand, Sumatra shares the tiger with Java, while it is unknown in Borneo. The one-horned rhinoceros of Java is known also in Sumatra, which shares a two-horned variety with Borneo, but the rhinoceros is now dying out. The Sumatran fauna also includes among primates the gibbon, the banded leaf monkey and the pig-tailed macaque, both common to Borneo also; the silvered leaf monkey and crab-eating macaque, common to Borneo and Java; the slow loris; tree shrews; and the flying lemur, bats, flying squirrels, rats, and mice; the sambar and the serow; wild dog; wild boar; and civet cat.

There is no genus of birds peculiar to Sumatra, but there are a few species and many subspecies. The birdlife is very similar to that of the Malay Peninsula; in the extreme south a few Javanese forms are found. Among birds found in Sumatra but not in Java are the great Argus pheasant, the fireback and other pheasants, and various partridges, the little Malay parrot, the helmeted hornbill, and the red-breasted bee-eater. Other Sumatran birds include woodpeckers, pigeons, and trogons. Insects, which also show a marked difference from those of Java, comprise many beautiful butterflies; the *Kallima* butterfly imitates the leaf of a certain plant so closely as to secure itself from the attacks of enemies. Lizards, large and small, frogs, tortoises, and turtles abound; crocodiles frequent the mouths of rivers and are also found upstream; there are many varieties of poisonous snakes; the rocks around the coast yield many kinds of shellfish; and the sea, ponds, and rivers, numerous sorts of edible fishes.

(E. E. L.; J. O. M. B.)

### THE PEOPLE

The inhabitants of Sumatra belong to the Oceanic or southern branch of the Mongoloid race, and to the Malayo-Polynesian linguistic family. They form several groups, each with its own language and distinctive cultural traits. In the lowlands of northwest Sumatra live the Achinese (*q.v.*), who are intensely devoted to Islam. Marriage is matrilocal and the position of the woman is high. The Gajo (*q.v.*) and Alas peoples live in the mountainous north-central portion between the Achinese and Bataks. They are Muslim, with a substratum of animism, and dwell in well-built stilt houses of wood, in small scattered villages. Their chief crop is rice; they rear cattle and horses and collect forest products. The Batak (*q.v.*) inhabit the mountainous region around and south of Lake Toba. Nearly one-third are Muslim, well over one-third Christian, and the rest animist. The Batak possess a written language of their own; they build large houses on piles, with horned roofs, each house occupied by many families, and have rice barns and a communal hall.

The houses are beautifully decorated, the Batak being clever craftsmen in wood, ivory, and copper. They are also good agriculturists (rice cultivation, wet and dry, being their chief occupation), and they raise horses, cattle, buffalo, and pigs. They have keen minds and great energy; most of them are literate and many have become traders and shopkeepers, teachers, and even doctors.

South of the Batak, in the Padang Highlands and vicinity, are the Menangkabau (*q.v.*), the largest ethnic group in Sumatra. Although converted to Islam, the Menangkabau have retained their ancient custom of the matrilineate (*i.e.,* descent and inheritance through the female line). A wife remains with her maternal relatives after marriage, and the husband, having no home of his own, only visits his wife and resides in his mother's house; names, privileges, and property derive from the mother's side; the eldest man of the elder female line is termed *mamak* and is the keeper of all the family possessions.

Houses, raised high above the ground, are very ornate, with horned ridge poles and finely carved wooden fronts, sometimes painted. Several families bearing the same patronymic live in the same house; and several houses, their rice barns, a communal house, a mosque, a school, an inn, and a market form a village. The Menangkabau are skilful farmers (as evidenced by their terraced mountain slopes), excellent woodcarvers, metalworkers, and weavers. Whether it was to escape the limitations of highland agriculture, or those of matriarchy, many men of the Menangkabau have settled in other areas and achieved much, helped by Western education which the Menangkabau accepted several generations ago.

The Lampong (*q.v.*) languages are spoken south of the Menangkabau, along the west side of Sumatra to its southern tip. The people of this linguistic group, such as the Redjang and Lebong in the mountains and the Lampong proper in the southern lowland, have all undergone Hindu influence. In addition to rice for food, pepper and coffee are grown for export. Since the 1930s there has been considerable resettlement of Javanese in the southern lowland (see *Population,* below).

On the east coast of Sumatra live the Malays (Melayu), essentially a coastal and riverine people (*see* also MALAY). In the north, next to the Achinese, they occupy a narrow strip in front of the upland Batak, and in the wide southern plains they inhabit a broad territory. Their seafaring has carried them to many islands, and they have settled not only the adjacent islands but also the coastal regions of west Malaya and of Kalimantan (Indonesian Borneo).

Their speech became the lingua franca of the archipelago and now forms the basis for the Indonesian national language. Generally speaking, they are indifferent farmers but good fishermen. Their houses, simple in style, are rectangular and built on piles, for single families. All are Muslims. Among them, deep in the forests, live small bands of the shy nomadic Kubu, their frizzled hair and dark skin denoting Negroid affinities. They live by gathering, hunting, and fishing. For the western islands *see* NIAS; MENTAWAI.

(J. O. M. B.)

## PREHISTORY

There has been little archaeological research on the prehistory of Sumatra but stray finds and the little systematic research done present some idea of it. There is no reliable dating.

Monofacial pebble tools found in Sumatra indicate relationship with Northern Malaya and the rest of mainland Southeast Asia (probably Middle Paleolithic and later). Following in this tradition, the Sumatraliths and associated stone tools found in extensive middens and surface stations in Northern Sumatra show close similarities to the Hoabinhian-type tools found in Northern Malaya and Thailand, and many other locations on the mainland. Probably overlapping in time with the people making the Sumatraliths were people making flake tools of obsidian. These remains have been found in Central and Southern Sumatra, with similar industries known to the east in other Indonesian islands.

The use of domesticated plants and animals probably entered Sumatra from Northern Malaya several thousand years before the Christian era but the only evidence of this is numerous finds of polished stone tools similar to Neolithic stone tools found in Malaya and Thailand (adzes: cross section rectangular, oval to lenticular; and triangular pick adzes). Later, the practice of using large stone monuments came in. These included large zoomorphic and anthropomorphic images, dolmens, and stone troughs (perhaps sarcophagi) with geometric-natural painted designs.

(W. G. So.)

## HISTORY

**Indian Influence.**—Trade between India and China, through the Strait of Malacca, developed about 2,000 years ago, and thus Sumatra became known to the outer world. Thereafter its relations with India were close, and expressed themselves in the deep impact of Indian culture; those with China, although economically and politically significant, had little if any direct cultural effect. Knowledge of Sumatra's early history is very fragmentary, since it rests on a few Chinese reports and some local inscriptions. Moreover, there is uncertainty whether the foreign sources using "Yawa" or some such name refer to Java or Sumatra.

Chinese reports of the early 5th century leave no doubt about the existence of a hinduized aristocracy. Sanskrit and the Pallava script of south India were used, and Buddhism was at that time gaining ascendancy over the Shivaistic rites of Brahmanism. In the 7th century there were at least two hinduized kingdoms in Sumatra. The northern one, Malayu, had its capital on the Hari River at the site of modern Jambi (Djambi). It was overshadowed, and before long conquered, by Sri Vijaya, with its capital on the Musi River at Palembang. Palembang was a centre of Buddhist scholarship, and a meeting place for Chinese pilgrims (among them I-tsing, *c.* A.D. 680) going to or coming from India. In the 8th century Sri Vijaya came under a branch of the Shailendra (Cailendra) dynasty, well known in the history of Java (*q.v.*), but the Sumatran rulers appear soon to have become independent of Java. At first, relations between the two houses were good, but as Sri Vijaya rose to be a mighty empire friction developed. The Sumatran kingdom came to dominate not only most of Sumatra but also Malaya, including the Isthmus of Kra, thus controlling the sea trade through the straits as well as the land passage across the neck of the peninsula. Its influence reached to southern Indochina as well as to Ceylon. It reached the zenith of its power toward the end of the 10th century. The Sumatrans not only beat off an attack from the East Javanese kingdom of Mataram but counterattacked, killing the king of Mataram and destroying its capital (1006).

In the early 11th century there were several wars for naval hegemony between Sri Vijaya and the Chola king, Rajendracola Deva I, whose kingdom was on the Coromandel coast of India. He conquered the key cities of the Sumatran empire on one of his expeditions; Sri Vijaya survived the attacks, but its power diminished gradually after this period. It was at this time still a prominent centre of learning; the reformer of Tibetan Buddhism, Atisha, studied in Sumatra *c.* A.D. 1020 under the priest Dharmakirti, who was considered the greatest scholar of his time. The name of the Shailendra dynasty, which had ruled Sri Vijaya since the 8th century, disappeared in the early 12th century. Resistance in Ceylon and the expansion of the Siamese toward the Isthmus of Kra put severe pressures on Sri Vijaya's resources. Malayu (Djambi), independent from about 1150, was conquered in 1275 by the Javanese king Kritanagara and made into a vassal state under a Javanese-educated Sumatran prince, thus placing the Palembang kingdom under close threat.

Soon after this date, Sri Vijaya became a vassal state and then, in 1377, a province of Java's Hindu Majapahit Empire, and was directly ruled by a Javanese governor. The ruling prince of Majapahit's vassal state Malayu, Adityavarman, on the other hand, gained greater autonomy by moving his residence to the highlands (*c.* 1350), among the Menangkabau. Hindu influence in the Padang Highlands dates back to the 8th century, but the rise of a strong Menangkabau kingdom seems related to the penetration of Hindu-Javanese influence in the 14th century. For a while Malayu had considerable power in Sumatra, but it did not challenge Java's hegemony.

**The Advent of Islam.**—In 1292 Marco Polo visited Sumatra. He mentioned Malayu, but not Sri Vijaya, among the kingdoms on this island. More important, he noted that the port town of Perlak (Keudepeureulak), in North Sumatra, was Islamic in religion. A few years later there was a Muslim state at the north tip called Samudra, which probably gave rise to the modern name of the island. The first great Muslim power was the city-state of Malacca across the straits. It had its beginnings as a Javanese-Sumatran trade centre in the twilight zone between the dominions of Majapahit and Siam, and sought protection from China when Siamese pressure became dangerous. In 1414 it had its first Muslim sultan, and from then on the attraction of Malacca's trade relations with the Middle East, India, and China drew ever more merchants in Sumatra and Java into the Muslim faith.

In the 16th century Atjeh arose as the main power in Sumatra. From the core area in the north tip, its sultans subdued in a series of holy wars the adjacent eastern and western coasts and even the Menangkabau, converting them to Islam. In the process Atjeh gained control over the pepper-growing districts of northern Sumatra. After the Portuguese had conquered Malacca (1511) the Achinese (Atjehnese) tried repeatedly to dislodge them, but without success. Atjeh, however, extended its influence over some other parts of the peninsula, especially Kedah and Perak which had valuable tin mines. From the tin and the pepper monopoly Atjeh grew rich. Under Iskandar Muda (1607–36) Atjeh might have become the great new sea power of the straits, had its fleet not been defeated (1629) by the allied naval forces of Portugal, Malacca, Johore, and Pattani.

**The Dutch Period.**—The first Dutch ships to visit Sumatra arrived in 1599 on the roadstead of Atjeh, where they were attacked. Their leader, Cornelis de Houtman, was killed, and his brother taken prisoner. Later, however, the Dutch East India Company (formed in 1602) was permitted to establish a factory there (1616) and the Achinese helped the Dutch in ousting the Portuguese from Malacca (1641). Then the Dutch turned on Atjeh, blockading its coasts and fomenting revolts among the peoples which Atjeh had subjected to its rule. By the Treaty of Painan (1662) the west coast principalities of Indrapura, Tiku, and Padang placed themselves under the protection of the company, which guaranteed their independence from Atjeh in exchange for the trade monopoly in these principalities, with pepper as a particularly rich prize. On the east coast the Dutch had a monopoly of the pepper trade by responding to requests from the sultans of Djambi (1615) and Palembang (1616) for military protection against threats from Atjeh and from Bantam of West Java respectively. The chieftains of Bangka and Billiton (Belitung) also sought the protection of the company, but the Dutch showed little interest until tin was discovered there in the 18th century. Bengkulu, founded in 1685, remained British until 1824.

Increasing British interest in East Asia, and thus in the Strait of Malacca, had been evident since the latter part of the 18th century. After the Napoleonic Wars England returned the East Indies to the Netherlands, but Sir Thomas Stamford Raffles, on his own initiative, purchased the island of Singapore (1819) from the sultan of Johore, although the latter had recognized the overlordship of Batavia over all islands of the Riouw Archipelago. This and other acts led to disputes with the Netherlands, which were settled in 1824 by the Treaty of London The British gave up Bengkulu and their claims on Billiton, in return for Malacca and Dutch recognition of Singapore as a British possession. Furthermore, to remove the danger of the Dutch controlling the straits, the British obtained a promise from the Netherlands that it would respect the independence of Atjeh.

Until the latter half of the 19th century, the Netherlands colonial government exercised effective authority only in a few areas of Sumatra, and economic development was slow. In 1863, however, tobacco planting was started by private enterprise in Deli on the northeastern coast. This was the beginning of a remarkable transformation of this area from almost empty forest land to one of the most important estate areas in the Indies. The Padang Highlands were in tumult for decades because of a religious conflict (the Padri War), which ended only in 1845. Here exploitation of coal in the interior, and the building of railroads and of harbour works at Padang, stimulated economic progress in the last quarter of the 19th century. At the same time the Batak Highlands were opened up, and missions were established there. The only area that resisted Dutch control until the early 20th century was Atjeh.

In World War II Japanese troops seized Sumatra during February–March 1942. After the capitulation of Japan in 1945 the Dutch tried to reestablish their authority. A period of confusion followed. National independence movements blended in some regions with local revolutions, in which new leading groups eliminated the ruling aristocracies. Finally in 1949 the Netherlands transferred full sovereignty to the United States of Indonesia into which Sumatra was merged. In 1950 this federation was abolished and Sumatra became part of the Republik Indonesia, a centralized state with capital at Jakarta. Dissatisfaction with the policies of the central government in Jakarta, however, led in later years to several regional movements and insurrections in Sumatra. (See *Administration and Regionalist Movements,* below.) During 1964–65, in Indonesia's war of "confrontation" against Malaysia (*q.v.*), islands off Sumatra's east coast were used as bases for attempts to infiltrate saboteurs and guerrillas into the Malayan mainland. *See* also MALAYSIA: *History;* JAVA: *History;* INDONESIA, REPUBLIC OF: *History;* MALAY ARCHIPELAGO. (J. O. M. B.)

THOMAS HÖPKER, "STERN"—BLACK STAR

RICE FIELDS IN NORTH SUMATRA

## POPULATION

The population of Sumatra in 1961 was 15,739,363. The last detailed census was taken in 1930, establishing a population of 8,254,500, of whom 7,745,000 were Indonesians, 28,500 Europeans (mostly Dutch), 448,000 Chinese, and 33,000 other Asians. All Dutch citizens left the island in 1957, but there are groups of American and British people in estate and petroleum enterprises along the east coast. The Chinese are concentrated on the east coast and in the tin-producing islands of Bangka and Billiton. The highest density of population, about 400 per sq.mi. (155 per sq.km.), is in the estate district around Medan in North Sumatra. Densities between 200 and 400 per sq.mi. are characteristic of the Padang Highlands, the north coast of Atjeh, and the upland zone between Medan and Lake Toba, all being well-developed agricultural areas. At the other extreme are the malaria-ridden equatorial forests of Sumatra's broad eastern coastal plain (Jambi, Riouw, Siak), where the population averages less than 15 per sq.mi. (6 per sq.km.). The largest ethnic group is that of the Menangkabau, estimated (1961) at 3,500,000. The Batak number about 2,000,000, the Achinese 2,000,000; the remaining half of the population are Malays, Palembangs, Lampongs, and other related groups. Nine-tenths of the total population live in rural villages or small towns. The main cities are Palembang (1961 pop. 474,971), Medan (479,098), and Padang (143,699).

The relatively sparse population, compared to that of Java, is related to infertile old acidic soils covering much of the higher plain, and to the extensive marshes along the coast. More intensive use of land is possible, however, as shown by the Javanese colonization in south Sumatra. Dutch attempts to alleviate overpopulation in Java by resettling the Javanese in Sumatra date from 1905, but it was not until the 1930s that the movement gathered momentum. The main area of colonization was that of the Lampong. In the southern lowlands of the Lampong district the soil had been enriched by the volcanic ash cover from Krakatau. Farther northward the acidic soils of the upper plain proved good if irrigated with water transporting silt from the andesite highlands, such as the lands along the middle Sekampung River, north of Telukbetung. In 1940 there were 160,000 Javanese in this area and several thousands near Palembang and Bengkulu. After independence resettlement was resumed, providing homes for an estimated additional 300,000 Javanese in south Sumatra.

## ADMINISTRATION AND REGIONALIST MOVEMENTS

Under the Dutch regime Sumatra, with adjacent islands, was divided into ten residencies. After independence, the residencies were eliminated and replaced by three provinces of North, Central, and South Sumatra. Later six provinces were created, each with a presidentially appointed governor and an appointed regional legislative council of representatives. The provinces with their capitals are: Atjeh (Kutaradja); Sumatera Utara or North Sumatra (Medan); Djambi (Jambi); Riouw (Pakanbaru); Sumatera Barat or West Sumatra (Bukittinggi); and Sumatera Selatan or South Sumatra (Palembang).

The increase in the number of provinces was brought about by the realization that the old units were too large to accommodate the regional diversity. Atjeh (*q.v.*) in North Sumatra was in armed revolt from 1953 to 1957; at least one of the aims of its leaders was autonomy, which was granted in 1956. Regional movements and open insurrections also occurred in other parts of Sumatra. Their purpose, as announced, was not secession from the Republic of Indonesia, but concern for local welfare which, according to the regional leaders, had been neglected by the central government in Jakarta. Among the orthodox Muslims of Sumatra there also was suspicion of leftist leanings in the central government. In December 1956 the regional military commanders, taking over the civil administration, set up revolutionary committees (Banteng ["wild buffalo"] councils) in Medan and Padang, and proceeded to obtain funds by diverting trade revenues from Jakarta to local treasuries. The Banteng Council of Central Sumatra in early 1957 acceded on its own initiative to the claims of Jambi and Riouw for separate status (this was later legalized by the central government). In February 1958 the regionalists formed a Revolutionary Government of the Republic of Indonesia, which included several former cabinet ministers and prominent military leaders. In March–May 1958 the rebels were attacked and defeated by the Indonesian armed forces. The roots of dissatisfaction, however, persist. Sumatra, earning most of the foreign exchange of Indonesia, desires a greater return in the form of schools, roads, and other public works. Within the island the diverse social groups demand reorganization. (*See* also INDONESIA, REPUBLIC OF: *Administration and Social Conditions*.)

## THE ECONOMY

Sumatra, not having the excessive population of Java, and possessing rich natural resources, contributes well over half of the exports of raw materials from Indonesia.

**Agriculture.**—The soils derived from young basic and neutral volcanic ejecta are very fertile. They occur in the Batak Highlands and coastal areas of north Atjeh and the adjacent zone around Medan, along the central west coast and in the Padang Highlands, and farther south in the Palembang Highlands and the Lampong district. In these areas cultivation gives good yields. In other areas the soils are derived from deeply leached parent materials or, if volcanic in origin, from acidic ejecta, which are, on the whole, of low fertility. For these reasons much of the broad east coast plain is of limited value for most crops. Agriculture in Sumatra is of two types: indigenous as practised by smallholders, and European on large estates.

*Smallholder Agriculture.*—The smallholder (small owner) is first and foremost a producer of foodstuffs for domestic consumption, and only secondarily of export commodities. Rice is the predominant crop, raised on permanent fields by flooding or irrigation (*sawah*) or on temporary clearings in the forest (*ladang*). Large quantities of rice have to be imported to feed the labour force on the estates and the urban population. In the hope of increasing rice yields the Indonesian government established pools of equipment from which smallholders could borrow tractors and other kinds of machinery. Other crops exclusively grown for home consumption are maize (corn), root crops, and vegetables. The surplus farm commodities, such as coffee, copra, tobacco, betel nuts, kapok, and peanuts, are exported. The government encourages the production of ramie fibre, which has to some extent superseded that of sisal. Two important export crops are pepper and rubber, the former a traditional cash crop, now overshadowed by rubber, which was quickly adopted by the Indonesians after introduction on estates in the early 20th century. The hevea tree, not needing rich soil, has proved a special boon to the people of the eastern plain, though rubber is grown in all lowland areas and Sumatra produces about two-thirds of Indonesia's smallholder rubber. But in the mid-1960s yields were decreasing because most hevea trees were old and little replanting had been done since 1940. The farmers in Sumatra are better off than their counterparts in Java; their holdings are larger, affording the space for cash crops, which the Javanese often lack. In Sumatra the Chinese middleman has a minor role, thus leaving much of the local trade in Indonesian hands. Income per capita in Sumatra is probably more than double that of Java.

*Estates.*—European estates, or plantations, were established on Sumatra in the latter part of the 19th century. As labour was scarce, estates either specialized on a commodity that required relatively little care, such as rubber, or they imported labour, first from China, later from Java, for the intensive cultivation of tobacco and tea. Estates are found in almost all parts of the island, but the great concentration is in the so-called east coast, actually a zone centring on Medan, from about Aru Bay in the northwest to the Barumun River in the southeast, composing the former principalities of Langkat, Deli, and Asahan in the plain and Simelungun and Karo lands in the hills north of Lake Toba. Cultivation of high-grade wrapper tobacco started in the 1860s. Thirty years later, coffee estates were added. Then, in the early 20th century hevea rubber was introduced, and in the next decade this became the main commodity. Later estates for tea, palm oil, and sisal were established.

MIRIAM BUCHER—PHOTO RESEARCHERS, INC.

PREPARATIONS FOR DRILLING AT AN OIL FIELD IN CENTRAL SUMATRA

The number of estates greatly declined during and after World War II. Under the Japanese occupation large areas of estate lands were turned over to the idle workers for food production. Deterrents to production in postwar rehabilitation were the disturbed political conditions, changed labour relations, and stringent foreign exchange controls. Most estates were Dutch-owned and in late 1957 these were seized by the Indonesian government, in retaliation for Dutch unwillingness to hand over West New Guinea (Irian Barat), and placed under Army control. The Basic Agrarian Act of 1960 placed restrictions on all remaining foreign estates.

**Forest Products.**—Over 60% of Sumatra is forest-covered. The local population obtains construction materials, firewood, and charcoal from them. There is good hardwood timber, such as various species of dipterocarps, but exploitation is hampered because the forests are mixed. Commercial production on a small scale is mainly in accessible areas along the rivers in the eastern lowland. Somewhat larger enterprises, including sawmills, are along the coast and in the Riouw Islands, where the Chinese have concessions. From there logs, firewood, and charcoal are normally exported to Singapore. The timber cut in Sumatra is about 1,000,000 cu.m. (rough timber equivalent), one-third of Indonesia's total output. The forests also yield gums and resins, such as jelutong (used in chewing gum), gutta-percha, damar, benzoin, camphor, and copal.

**Fisheries.**—As fish is the common animal protein accompanying the rice diet, fishing is widespread in the rivers and coastal waters. Intensive fish-raising in ponds, as on Java, is rare. The largest catch comes from the Strait of Malacca and the waters surrounding the Riouw Archipelago. The great fishing port of Sumatra is Bagan-Siapiapi, at the mouth of the Rokan, which handles an annual catch of about 80,000 metric tons, almost two-thirds of the sea fisheries' yield of Sumatra. There a large part of the catch is cured, smoked, or dried, and forwarded to Java. Besides fish, trepang (sea slugs), prawns (from which the delicacy *krupuk* is made), and other shellfish are caught. Other fishing centres are near Telukbetung, at Bengkulu, and on Bangka Island.

**Minerals.**—Sumatra with its adjacent islands is rich in minerals, among which petroleum, tin, bauxite, and coal are foremost, and gold, silver, tungsten, iron, clay, and limestone are of minor importance.

Petroleum is recovered from long, narrow anticlines in the Late Tertiary sediments east of the mountains, from Palembang to Atjeh. Sumatra is the richest producer of crude oil in Indonesia, with about 70% of the total production (over 160,000,000 bbl. in the early 1960s). Palembang, in South Sumatra, is the main refining centre; there are refineries in Sungaigerong and in Pladju, both connected by pipelines to the oilfields west and southwest of the city. A field in the Lirik region, central Sumatra, is also exploited. There are wells north and northwest of Pakanbaru between the Siak and Rokan rivers. Until 1959 all crude oil was piped to the Siak River and then into river tankers which carried it 93 mi. (150 km.) to the terminal at the seaport of Pakning. Since then 30-inch pipelines connect the fields (Minas, Pungut, and

Duri) with a new ocean harbour at Dumai on Rupat Strait, equipped to receive oil tankers up to 84,000 tons capacity, as well as oceangoing cargo ships.

Tin occurs in the Riouw Archipelago and on the islands of Bangka and Billiton, but only the latter two and Singkep in the Riouw group are significant producers. Ore lodes occur, but most of the tin is extracted from the alluvium in the valleys and their continuation in the drowned continental shelf. Tin mining started in Bangka in the 18th century and in Billiton in 1852. The mines are operated by the government. The rich deposits of tin in these islands have made Indonesia the second largest tin-producing country. As the smelters existing before the war have not been rehabilitated, the concentrates are shipped abroad.

Bauxite was discovered shortly before World War II in the Riouw Archipelago, where it covers large areas to a shallow depth and in varying concentration. The ore, a weathering product of granite and diorite, is dug in open-pit mines on Bintan and the adjoining small islands. Bauxite is shipped abroad for processing, mainly to Japan.

The coal deposits on Sumatra are of Tertiary age. The Umbilin field in central Sumatra near Sawahlunto (in the Padang Highlands) is of Eocene age and covers about 40 sq.mi. (104 sq.km.). In south Sumatra some Miocene lignite beds have been transformed into excellent coal by intruding andesite plugs. Here lies the Bukit Asem mine, south of the Muaraenim. Both are government owned and operated and produce more than three-quarters of the total output of coal in Indonesia. Production is far less than in prewar years, causing a shortage for the railroads, which are the main consumers. The coal is not suitable for coking. Gold and silver occur in the Redjang-Lebong highlands and in some other sections of the island, but production is negligible.

**Transport and Communications.**—The estate area on the east coast, the Padang Highlands, and south Sumatra have fairly good land transportation networks but the remainder of the island depends on mountain trails and rivers. The main road from Medan to the west coast runs past Pematangsiantar to the resort town of Prapat on Lake Toba and descends to the small port of Sibolga on the west coast; from there it runs through mountain valleys and connecting pass routes to Bukittinggi (formerly Fort de Kock) and Padang (*qq.v.*). The plain of central Sumatra has few roads apart from those built by the petroleum companies. In the south most of the large towns are linked by main roads.

The railways are divided into three sections. In north Sumatra a narrow-gauge line runs northwest from Medan to Kutaradja, the capital of Atjeh, and to its port Uleelheue, serving rubber plantations and pepper gardens. Southward from Medan the line runs through the tobacco, rubber, and oil palm estates, to Rantauparapat, with a branch line from Tebingtinggi to Pematangsiantar, through tea plantations in the foothills north of Lake Toba. Belawan, connected by a 12-mi. (19 km.) railway to Medan, is the chief ocean port of the estate district; Tandjungbalai, on the Asahan River, also serves as a shipping point. In central Sumatra steep-gradient railways with many tunnels connect the port of Padang on the west coast with the Umbilin mine in the highlands to the east and with Bukittinggi and Pajakumbuh toward the north, where coffee is grown.

In south Sumatra Pandjang on Lampung Bay (export of rubber and pepper) and the commercial centre of Telukbetung are connected by rail with Palembang on the Musi River, the shipping point for petroleum products, rubber, coffee, and forest products. Palembang is also connected with the hinterland by a branch line from Perabumulih, which runs southwestward past Muaraenim (with a spur to the Bukit Asem coal mines) and Tebittinggi, to Lubuklinggau. Each river has its port, several of them well inland. The tin islands have several ports: Pangkalbalam, Belinju, and Muntok on Bangka, which ship pepper in addition to tin; and Tandjungpandan on Billiton. The main trade centre on Bintan is Tandjungpinang. The larger cities of Sumatra are served by the Garuda Indonesian Airways.

*See* also references to "Sumatra" in the Index. (J. O. M. B.)

BIBLIOGRAPHY.—A. N. J. T. à T. van der Hoop, *Megalithic Remains in South Sumatra,* Eng. trans. by W. Shirlaw (1934); H. R. van Heekeren, *The Stone Age of Indonesia,* and *The Bronze-Iron Age of Indonesia,* "Verhandelingen van het Koninklijk Instituut voor Taal-, Land- en Volkenkunde Series," vol. 21 and 22 (1957 and 1958); W. Marsden, *The History of Sumatra,* 3rd ed. (1811; reprinted, with introduction by J. Bastin, 1966); O. J. A. Collet, *Terres et peuples de Sumatra* (1925); E. M. Loeb, *Sumatra: Its History and Peoples* (1935); J. Mossman, *Rebels in Paradise: Indonesia's Civil War* (1961).

For general information on the geography, history, and economy of Sumatra, consult the books cited in the bibliographies to the articles MALAY ARCHIPELAGO; INDONESIA, REPUBLIC OF.

(M. W. F. T.; J. O. M. B.)

**SUMBA** (also known as SANDALWOOD), one of the Lesser Sunda Islands in East Nusa Tenggara Province, Indonesia, lies west of Timor and south of Flores, from which it is separated by the Sumba Strait. Area 4,306 sq.mi. (11,153 sq.km.). It is dominated by heights of 2,200–4,000 ft. (670–1,220 m.); unlike the islands to the north, Sumba has no volcanoes. Several bays on the north coast give good anchorage, the best being that of Waingapu, the chief town (pop. [1960 est.] 5,000). The rivers, most of which are unnavigable, are important for agriculture. The average annual rainfall is 63.7 in. (1,618 mm.), resulting in only light forest and much grassland. Most of the sandalwood is gone. On the island's grazing grounds are bred some of the finest horses in the country—the Sandalwood breed—and fine cattle (Ongole), both of which formerly figured largely as exports. Maize is the main crop; in addition, rice, coffee, tobacco, coconuts, vegetables, and fruit are grown in a primitive manner, copra being exported. The woven cloth of Sumba, adorned with animal patterns, is famous for its artistic quality.

The population (1961) was 251,126, consisting, apart from the indigenous Sumbanese, of people from Flores, Sawu, and Roti islands; they are mostly animist, though some are Muslim. Traditional customs include marriage by dowry, and polygamy is fairly common among the upper classes. There is no written form of the Sumbanese language, which is allied to that of Sawu. Sumba has numerous megalithic monuments.

The sandalwood of Sumba attracted attention to the island in the 17th century, when Sumba appears to have been a tributary of the state of Bima, in Sumbawa. Later Sumba became independent of Sumbawa, and treaties were concluded in 1756 with the Dutch. Between 1856 and 1874 new treaties were made, but there were frequent difficulties with the inhabitants because of piracy and slave raids. In 1901 and 1914 the Dutch landed troops on the island. (E. E. L.; J. O. M. B.)

**SUMBAWA,** one of the Lesser Sunda Islands in East Nusa Tenggara Province, Indonesia, lies between Lombok and Flores islands, separated from the former by Alas Strait and from the latter by Sape Strait and Komodo Island. Pop. (1961) 407,596. Sumbawa is 175 mi. (282 km.) long by 55 mi. (89 km.) at its widest, but deep coastal indentations divide the island into several peninsulas. The largest bay is that of Saleh on the central north coast with Mojo Island at its mouth. More to the east is the narrow and deep Bima Bay, an excellent natural harbour.

The island is very mountainous, with rocky coasts and only a few small plains. Some of the mountains are volcanic, the highest being Mt. Tambora (9,350 ft. [2,850 m.]), whose tremendous eruption in 1815 caused the death of about 50,000 inhabitants and the emigration of about 35,000 to other islands. The average annual rainfall is 90 in. (2,286 mm.) in the central mountains and 50 in. (1,270 mm.) along the north coast; little rain falls in the east monsoon, from June to September. Dense forest occurs only on the mountains of the central watershed. The sappan (red dye) wood, formerly exported to China, has largely been depleted. Because of shifting cultivation, followed by grazing, large areas are now covered by thorn brush.

The people of the western part of the island are of Malay stock, but in the eastern interior Papuan (Oceanic Negroid) traits are quite strong. Islam is the prevailing religion.

Agriculture consists of wet rice cultivation on a small scale on permanent fields along the north coast, but most crops (maize, beans, tubers) are raised on temporary fields. Some coffee is grown in the highlands; coconut palms in the coastal zone yield copra for export. Raising of cattle, goats, and horses is an important feature of the economy, partly for export. A fair-weather motor road traverses the northern part of the island, from Sumbawa-Besar (with an airfield) to Bima. These two towns and Taliwang (on the west coast) are ports of call for ships of the interisland service.

Sumbawa was once a part of the Javanese Majapahit kingdom (*see* JAVA: *History*). Later it came under the suzerainty of the sultanates of South Celebes. The defeat of the sultan of Gowa (1668) brought Sumbawa under Dutch authority. From 1701 onward a Dutch representative resided at Bima, but the island was not brought under effective control until 1905. Sumbawa was occupied by Japanese troops during World War II and became part of the Republic of Indonesia in 1949. (J. O. M. B.)

**SUMERIAN LANGUAGE.** Sumerian is the oldest written language in existence. First attested about 3100 B.C. in southern Mesopotamia, it flourished during the 3rd millennium B.C. It was replaced about 2000 B.C. as a spoken language by the Semitic Akkadian (Assyro-Babylonian), but it continued in written usage almost to the end of the life of the Akkadian language (*q.v.*), around the beginning of the Christian era. Sumerian never extended much beyond its original boundaries in southern Mesopotamia; the small number of its native speakers was entirely out of proportion to the tremendous importance and influence Sumerian exercised on the development of the Mesopotamian and other ancient civilizations in all their stages.

**History.**—Four periods of Sumerian can be distinguished. Archaic Sumerian, Old or Classical Sumerian, New Sumerian, and Post-Sumerian.

Archaic Sumerian embraced a period from about 3100 B.C., when the first Sumerian records make their appearance, down to about 2500 B.C. The earliest Sumerian writing is almost exclusively represented by texts of business and administrative character. There are also school texts in the form of simple exercises in writing signs and words. The Archaic Sumerian language is still very poorly understood, partly because of the difficulties surrounding the reading and interpretation of early Sumerian writing and partly because of the meagreness of sources.

The Old or Classical period of Sumerian lasted from about 2500 to 2300 B.C. This period is represented mainly by records of the early rulers of Lagash. The use of the Sumerian language is attested not only in business, legal, and administrative texts but also in royal and private inscriptions, mostly of votive character, letters, both private and official, and incantations. These sources are much more numerous than those of the preceding period, and the writing is explicit enough to make possible an adequate reconstruction of Sumerian grammar and lexicon.

During the period of the Sargonic dynasty, the Semitic Akkadians took over the political hegemony of Babylonia, marking a definite setback in the progress of the Sumerian language. During this period, the Akkadian language was used extensively throughout the whole area of the Old Akkadian empire, while the use of Sumerian was gradually limited to a small area in Sumer proper. Toward the end of the dynasty the Sumerian elements came again to the fore, marking in turn a setback to the progress of Akkadian. The New Sumerian period came to an end about 2000 B.C., when new inroads of the Semitic peoples from the desert succeeded in destroying the supremacy of the 3rd dynasty of Ur and in establishing the Semitic dynasties of Isin, Larsa, and Babylon. The New Sumerian period is characterized by an extraordinary number of administrative texts.

The period of the dynasties of Isin, Larsa, and Babylon is called the Old Babylonian period, after Babylon, which became the capital and the most important city in the country. During this period the Sumerians lost their political identity, and the Sumerian language gradually disappeared from spoken use. However, it continued in written usage to the very end of the use of cuneiform writing. This is the last stage of the Sumerian language, called "Post-Sumerian."

In the early stages of the post-Sumerian period the use of written Sumerian is extensively attested in legal and administrative texts, as well as in the royal inscriptions. The latter are often bilingual, that is, in Sumerian and Babylonian. Many Sumerian literary compositions, which came down from the older Sumerian periods by way of oral tradition, were put down in writing for the first time in the Old Babylonian period. Many more were copied by industrious scribes from originals now lost. The rich Sumerian literature is represented by texts of varied nature, such as myths and epics, hymns and lamentations, rituals and incantations, and proverbs and the so-called "wisdom" compositions. For many centuries after the Old Babylonian period, the study of Sumerian continued in the Babylonian schools. As late as the 7th century B.C., Ashurbanipal, one of the last rulers of Assyria, boasted of being able to read the difficult Sumerian language, and from an even later period, in Hellenistic times, there are some cuneiform tablets which show Sumerian words transcribed with the letters of Greek writing.

ARCHIVES PHOTOGRAPHIQUES

SUMERIAN INSCRIPTION, DETAIL OF A DIORITE STATUE OF GUDEA OF LAGASH, 22ND CENTURY B.C. IN THE LOUVRE, PARIS

**Rediscovery.**—At the time of Christ, all knowledge of Sumerian disappeared along with cuneiform writing, and in the succeeding centuries even the name Sumer vanished from memory.

Unlike Assyria, Babylonia, and Egypt, whose histories and traditions are amply documented in biblical and classical sources, there was nothing to be found in non-Mesopotamian sources anywhere to make one even suspect the existence of the Sumerians in antiquity, let alone to appreciate fully their important role in the history of early civilizations.

When the decipherment of cuneiform writing was achieved in the early decades of the 19th century, three languages written in cuneiform were discovered: Semitic Babylonian, Indo-European Persian, and Elamite, of unknown linguistic affiliation. Only after the texts written in Babylonian had become better understood did scholars become aware of the existence of texts written in a language different from Babylonian. When the new language was discovered it was variously designated as Scythian or even Akkadian, that is, by the very name now given to the Semitic language spoken in Babylonia and Assyria. As knowledge of the new language grew, it was given the correct name of Sumerian.

**Characteristics.**—The linguistic affinity of Sumerian has not yet been successfully established. Ural-Altaic (which includes Turkish), Dravidian, Brahui, Bantu, and many other families of languages have been compared with Sumerian, but no theory has gained common acceptance. Sumerian is clearly an agglutinative language in that it preserves the root intact while expressing the various morphemic changes, through the concatenation principle, by means of prefixed, infixed, and suffixed elements. The difference between nouns and verbs, as it exists, *e.g.*, in the Indo-European or Semitic languages, is unknown to Sumerian. The word *dug* alone means both "speech" and "to speak" in Sumerian, the difference between the noun and the verb being indicated by syntax and different affixes.

The phonemic system of Sumerian consisted of four vowels *a, i, e, u,* and fifteen consonants, *b, d, g, h, k, l, m, n, p, r, s, ś, š, t, z.* In the noun gender was not expressed. Plural number was indicated either by the suffixes *-me* (or *-me* + *esh*), *-hia,* and *-ene* or by reduplication, as in *kur* + *kur,* "mountains." The relational morphemes of the noun, corresponding approximately to the cases of the Latin declension, are: *-e* for the subject (nominative), *-a(k)* "of" (genitive), *-ra* "to," "for" (dative), *-a* "in," *-ta* "from" (ablative), *-da* "with" (commitative), and *-sh(e)* "for (a period of time)," "for (the purpose of)," etc.

The Sumerian verb, with its concatenation of various prefixes, infixes, and suffixes, presents a very complicated picture. The elements connected with the verb follow a rigid order: modal elements, tempo elements, relational elements, causative elements, object elements, verbal root, subject elements, and intransitive present-future elements. In the preterit transitive active the order of object and subject elements is reversed. The verb can distinguish, in addition to person and number, transitive and intransitive, active and passive, and two tenses, present-future and preterit.

Several Sumerian dialects are known. Of these the most important are *eme-KU,* the official dialect of Sumerian, and *eme-SAL,* the dialect used often in the composition of hymns and incantations.

*See* also CUNEIFORM; WRITING: *Phonography;* BABYLONIA AND ASSYRIA: *Language and Literature.* (I. J. G.)

BIBLIOGRAPHY.—Cyril J. Gadd, *Sumerian Reading-Book* (1924); Arno Poebel, *Grundzüge der sumerischen Grammatik* (1923); Anton Deimel, *Sumerische Grammatik,* 2nd ed. (1939); Adam Falkenstein, *Grammatik der Sprache Gudeas von Lagaš* (1949); Edward Chiera, *Sumerian Lexical Texts from the Temple School of Nippur* (1929), *Sumerian Texts of Varied Contents* (1934); Samuel N. Kramer, *The Sumerians* (1963).

**SUMMARY JURISDICTION,** in Anglo-American law, ordinarily designates the jurisdiction of a magistrate or judge to conduct proceedings resulting in a conviction or order without trial by jury. Since in the later common law the only recognized mode of trial, except in cases of contempt, was jury trial, summary jurisdiction is almost entirely a creature of statute. In the United States, despite federal and state constitutional provisions guaranteeing trial by jury, it is generally held that certain petty offenses may be tried summarily. The trial of such cases is usually more informal and expeditious than those for more serious offenses. Civil suits in which the amounts involved are small may also be tried without right of jury trial. In England crimes are classified as either summary offenses, which are tried by magistrates' courts, or indictable offenses, to which the right of jury trial attaches. There is also a class of offenses that are both summary and indictable. Under the terms of the Magistrates' Courts Act, 1952, most petty offenses punishable by imprisonment for more than three months may, however, be tried on indictment. Provision is also made for the summary trial of some common indictable offenses when certain conditions are satisfied. The English law includes some civil proceedings within the summary jurisdiction of the magistrates. *See* also COURT. (F. A. A.)

**SUMMIT,** a city and suburban residential community of New Jersey, U.S., in Union County, on an escarpment of Watchung Mountain adjacent to Springfield, Millburn, and Chatham, is 10 mi. (16 km.) SW of Newark and 19 mi. (31 km.) W of New York City. Founded as Turkey Hill in 1710, it was renamed Summit in 1837 and incorporated as a city in 1899. The site of a lookout post and signal tower for General Washington's troops alerting them to any movement of the British in the Revolutionary War is commemorated by a marker showing the location of the alarm gun "Old Sow." Summit's chief industries are chemicals, pharmaceuticals, textiles, and floristry.

For comparative population figures *see* table in NEW JERSEY: *Population.* (D. N. A.; M. P. M.)

**SUMNER, CHARLES** (1811–1874), U.S. statesman, a leader of the antislavery forces before and during the Civil War, was born in Boston, Mass., on Jan. 6, 1811. He graduated in 1830 from Harvard College and in 1834 from Harvard Law School. He interrupted his law practice when he was 26 for a three-year sojourn in Europe (1837–40), which resulted in friendships with many influential Europeans. Upon his return he devoted much time to lecturing at Harvard and to editing legal works. He crusaded for many reforms, including prison reform, world peace, and Horace Mann's plans for educational improvement. His especial dedication to "absolute human equality, secured, assured, and invulnerable," made him an effective champion of the abolition of slavery.

THE GRANGER COLLECTION

CHARLES SUMNER, PHOTOGRAPHED BY MATHEW BRADY

In 1851 Massachusetts Free Soilers and Democrats nominated Sumner for the U.S. Senate, and after a heated contest in the legislature he was elected. As a U.S. senator he was in an arena well suited to his talents and soon became famous. On Aug. 26, 1852, he delivered the first of many philippics: "Freedom national; Slavery sectional." In this slashing tirade he flayed the Compromise of 1850 and those who supported it, gave hope to abolitionists, and alarmed all compromisers. On May 19–20, 1856, he denounced the "Crime against Kansas" (the Kansas-Nebraska Act) as "in every respect a swindle" and characterized its authors, Senators Andrew P. Butler and Stephen A. Douglas, as myrmidons of slavery. Two days later Congressman Preston S. Brooks of South Carolina invaded the Senate, labeled the speech a libel on his state and on his uncle, Senator Butler, and then severely beat Sumner with a cane. It took three years for him to recover from the beating. He was meanwhile reelected to the Senate where his empty seat was regarded as an effective symbol of freedom of speech and the abolition movement.

His prominent role in organizing the Republican Party and his Senate seniority earned for Sumner the chairmanship of the Senate Foreign Relations Committee on March 8, 1861. Close acquaintance with Cobden, Bright, Gladstone, and the duke and duchess of Argyll, and with many other influential Europeans, gave weight to his views abroad. Sumner used his knowledge of European views to persuade President Lincoln to give up Confederate commissioners James M. Mason and John Slidell after their capture aboard the "Trent" in November 1861. This mediation helped to preserve peace between Britain and the United States.

Following the Civil War, Sumner became an implacable foe of Pres. Andrew Johnson and Johnson's plan for reconstruction of the South. As a prerequisite for readmission to the Union, he believed that the Confederate states should provide constitutional guarantees of equal voting rights to Negroes, and he secured congressional approval of this scheme.

In 1870 Sumner led the opposition that defeated Pres. Ulysses S. Grant's plan to annex Santo Domingo. As a result, Grant apparently brought about Sumner's removal (March 10, 1871) from the chairmanship of the Foreign Relations Committee. The blow almost broke Sumner, but he nevertheless used his influence to win approval by the Senate in 1871 of the Treaty of Washington, which helped improve and stabilize relations between the U.S. and Great Britain.

Sumner's last years were saddened by varying misfortunes. His marriage in October 1866 ended in divorce within a year. His greatest act of magnanimity in the Senate was doomed to misunderstanding. In 1872 he introduced a resolution providing that the names of battles with fellow citizens should not be placed on the regimental colours of the U.S. Army. The Massachusetts legislature censured this resolution as "an insult to the loyal soldiery of the nation" and asserted it met "the unqualified condemnation of the people of the Commonwealth." But early in 1874 the legislature rescinded its action. On March 10, 1874, acting against his doctor's orders, Sumner went to the Senate to hear his colleague report that the censure had been rescinded and that he had been absolved. Stricken that night with an attack of angina pectoris, Sumner died the next day.

Wrong in some things, careless with personal invective, stubborn and uncompromising, Sumner nonetheless ranked as one of America's best crisis leaders. He stood always for principle and honesty, and perhaps that explains his estrangement from the postwar age.

BIBLIOGRAPHY.—*Complete Works,* with an introduction by G. F. Hoar (1900); G. H. Haynes, *Charles Sumner* (1909); W. A. Dunning, *Reconstruction, Political and Economic* (1907); H. K. Beale, *The Critical Year* (1930); David Donald, *Charles Sumner and the Coming of the Civil War* (1960). (F. E. V.)

**SUMNER, JAMES BATCHELLER** (1887–1955), U.S. biochemist who discovered that enzymes can be crystallized, was awarded the 1946 Nobel prize in chemistry with W. M. Stanley and J. H. Northrop. Born Nov. 19, 1887, in Canton, Mass., Sumner received his bachelor's degree in 1910 and his doctor's degree in 1914 from Harvard university. He taught at Mt. Allison college, Sackville, N.B., and at Worcester Polytechnic institute. In 1914 he became assistant professor and in 1929 professor of chemistry at the medical college of Cornell university, Ithaca, N.Y., where he remained until his retirement in July 1955. He had studied in Brussels, Stockholm and Uppsala. He was a member of the commission for relief in the Belgian Educational foundation 1921–22. He was awarded the Scheele medal at Stockholm in 1937. In 1947 he became the director of the Cornell laboratory of enzyme chemistry, established by the trustees of the university in recognition of his investigations.

Sumner's early work included the study of urea formation and the estimation of sugar in urine. In 1926, after chemists had hoped to isolate an enzyme, Sumner observed urease, an enzyme essential to the nitrogen cycle. The first enzyme to be prepared in a laboratory, it was a remarkable contribution. In 1937 Sumner crystallized the important enzyme catalase, which influences reactions involving hydrogen peroxide and protects the living cells from this compound, which they produce during their respiratory process. Sumner contributed to the purification of coenzyme I, lipoxidase and saccharase. He published *Biological Chemistry* in 1927. With G. F. Somers he wrote three editions of the two books *Chemistry and Methods of Enzymes* and *Laboratory Experiments in Biological Chemistry,* and with Karl Myrbäck compiled four books on *The Enzymes: Chemistry and Mechanism of Action* (1950–52). He died Aug. 12, 1955.

*See* E. Farber, *Nobel Prize Winners in Chemistry, 1901–1961* (1963). (V. Bw.)

**SUMNER, WILLIAM GRAHAM** (1840–1910), U.S. social scientist, an influential teacher and prolific publicist, was born in Paterson, N.J., on Oct. 30, 1840. He studied at Yale (A.B., 1863); and at Geneva, Göttingen and Oxford (1863–66); tutored at Yale (1866–69); served as a priest in the Episcopal Church (1869–72); and was professor of political and social science at Yale (1872–1909). He was president of the American Sociological society in 1909. He died in Englewood, N.J., April 12, 1910.

Like Herbert Spencer, Sumner expounded in many essays on current issues his firm belief in *laissez faire,* individual liberty and the innate inequalities among men. As a social Darwinist he viewed competition for property and social status as resulting in a beneficent elimination of the ill-adapted and the preservation of racial soundness and cultural vigour. For him the middle class Protestant ethic of hard work, thrift and sobriety exemplified those virtues conducive to wholesome family life and sound public morality. Foreseeing the drift toward the welfare state, but viewing poverty as the natural result of inherent inferiorities, he opposed all proposals that smacked of paternalism because they impose unequal burdens on that class, his "forgotten men."

In his famous *Folkways* (1906), he found the origin of customs and morals in instinctive responses to the stimuli of hunger, sex, vanity and fear, selectively guided by pain and pleasure. He emphasized their inherent irrationality and resistance to reform. His notes became the basis of *The Science of Society,* 4 vol. (1927–28), edited by A. G. Keller.

*See* ETHICS, HISTORY OF: *Ethical Relativity.* (F. H. Hs.)

**SUMPTUARY LAWS,** a term originally used to denote regulations designed to restrict extravagance in food, drink, dress, household equipment and the like, usually on religious or moral grounds. More recently, the term has been applied to laws which either directly prohibit the manufacture or consumption of certain commodities or which influence their consumption indirectly through excise taxes. In the case of this more recent usage, the regulations are ordinarily defended on religious or moral grounds or on the grounds of public welfare.

Sumptuary laws have an ancient origin; numerous instances are to be found in ancient Greece. All the inhabitants of Laconia, for example, were forbidden to attend drinking entertainments and the Lacedaemonians were forbidden to possess a house or furniture that was the work of more elaborate implements than the axe and saw. The possession of gold or silver was forbidden to the citizens of Sparta and the use of iron money alone was permitted by the Lycurgean legislation. A system of sumptuary edicts and enactments was extensively developed in ancient Rome. The code of the Twelve Tables included provisions limiting expenditures on funerals. A series of laws beginning in 215 B.C. governed the materials of which garments could be made, the number of guests at entertainments and the sums to be expended on entertainments, and forbade the consumption of certain foods.

In later times, sumptuary laws were enacted in many countries of Europe. For example, in France, Philip IV issued regulations governing the dress and the table expenditures of the several orders of men in his kingdom and Charles V forbade the use of long-pointed shoes. Under later French kings the use of gold and silver embroidery, silk stuffs and fine linen was restricted. In England during the reign of Edward II a proclamation was issued against the "outrageous and excessive multitude of meats and dishes which the great men of the Kingdom had used, and still used, in their castles." Edward III in 1336 attempted to legislate against luxurious living and at the same time when costumes were regulated it was held that servants of gentlemen, merchants and artificers should have only one meal of flesh or fish per day. Another illustration may be found in 1433 in an act of parliament meeting at Perth which prescribed the manner of living of all orders in Scotland, even going so far as to limit the use of pies and baked meats to those who held the rank of baron or higher. Such legislation was brought to some of the American colonies in the 17th century. It appears, however, that most such legislation was not strictly enforced in the colonies.

In Japan sumptuary laws were passed with a frequency and minuteness of scope that had no parallel in the history of the western world. At the beginning of the 11th century an imperial edict regulated the size of houses and imposed restrictions as to materials that could be used in their construction. During the Tokugawa period sumptuary laws were passed in bewildering profusion regulating the most minute details of personal life.

In more modern times sumptuary laws have generally not gone as far as did the ancient enactments. An exception is to be found in the 18th amendment to the U.S. constitution (in effect 1919–33) that prohibited the manufacture, transport and sale of alcoholic beverages. Many additional illustrations are to be found of laws having the effect of sumptuary laws indirectly although enacted primarily for raising revenue. Excise taxes on tobacco, alcoholic beverages, jewelry, watches and other articles that are viewed as luxuries are levied in many parts of the world and are frequently defended, in part, on the ground of their beneficial moral effect.

*See* F. Baldwin, *Sumptuary Legislation and Personal Regulation in England* (1926). (FK. L. K.)

**SUMTER,** a city of South Carolina, U.S., seat of Sumter County, is 40 mi. (64 km.) E of Columbia. Founded as Sumterville in 1799, and named after the Revolutionary general Thomas Sumter, it was long a typical cotton plantation village in the heart of the low-country sand hills. Furniture, lumbering, and textile industries came slowly, and the village was chartered as Sumter in 1887. It claims to be the first city to have successfully adopted, in 1912, the council-manager form of government.

Essentially a town of the new South rather than the old, it

maintains a leisurely Southern atmosphere. Wide streets are lined with oak trees covered with Spanish moss. The iris gardens in the city are known for the old cypress trees, azaleas, and camellias, as well as iris.

For comparative population figures *see* table in SOUTH CAROLINA: *Population.* (G. H. CT.)

**SUMY,** a town and *oblast* of the Ukrainian Soviet Socialist Republic, U.S.S.R., in the northeast of the Ukraine. The *oblast* lies along the southwestern edge of the Central Russian upland from which the land slopes gently toward the Dnieper River. Area 9,382 sq.mi.; pop. (1959) 1,513,718.

Drainage of the *oblast* is by tributaries of the Dnieper, notably the Seim, Sula, and Psel rivers. In the north part its boundary lies along the Desna River, the basin of which is in the mixed forest zone, with extensive areas of marsh. South of the Seim the *oblast* is in the forest-steppe zone, but most of the former areas of oak forest have been cleared for cultivation and occupy not more than 5% of the surface. In the Desna basin soils are sod-podzols and elsewhere chernozems of high fertility. Two-thirds of the population are rural dwellers and agriculture dominates the economy.

The main crops are grains, sugar beet, tobacco, hemp, and potatoes. Sugar refining is a major industry and the beet waste helps to maintain the large number of cattle.

There are 12 towns and 20 urban districts in the *oblast*. All the towns are small, the main industry being food production. Romny, in the southwest, dates from the early 10th century. Konotop and Shostka are minor industrial centres. During World War II the area was occupied (1941–43) by German troops.

The town of Sumy, the administrative centre of the *oblast*, is on the upper Psel River, about 68 mi. SW of Kursk. Pop. (1959) 98,015. Industries include manufacture of machinery for the chemical, coal-mining and metallurgical industries, sugar refining, shoemaking, and the production of superphosphates. There is a teacher training college. Railways connect Sumy with Kharkov and the main Kiev-Kursk line. The town was founded as a Russian settlement in 1652 but there had been an earlier Slav settlement there in the 8th–9th centuries. (R. A. F.)

**SUN.** The sun is apparently the largest and brightest of the stars visible to the naked eye, but it is actually among the smallest and faintest. The illusion arises from its comparative nearness—the next nearest star is, in fact, nearly 300,000 times as far away.

## TELESCOPIC INVESTIGATION

**General Characteristics.**—The sun presents to the telescopic view a dazzling white, circular disk with a sharp edge, whose diameter is an angular distance in the sky of about ½°. Slight systematic variations of the angular diameter reveal that the distance from earth to sun is not constant, and that the earth's orbit is an ellipse with the sun at one of the focuses. Several methods have been employed to measure the distance of the earth from the sun in miles or other terrestrial units. The mean value throughout the year (from which the actual distance departs by less than 2%) is found to be about 93,000,000 mi. (149,664,900 km.). This is expressed astronomically by saying that the solar parallax is 8.79 (*i.e.*, 8.79 sec. of arc), the solar parallax being the difference in direction of two ends of the earth's equatorial radius as viewed from the sun.

The sun's linear diameter, in miles, follows at once from its distance and the observed angular diameter. It is approximately 865,000 mi.—about 109 times the diameter of the earth, but much smaller than many stars, some having diameters 800 times that of the sun.

Its mass is calculated from the force of mutual attraction of the earth and sun, the mass of the earth having been independently determined (*see* EARTH). The result ($2 \times 10^{33}$ g. or $2 \times 10^{27}$ tons) is 333,000 times the mass of the earth and about at the middle of the range of stellar masses. Mass and diameter are sufficient data for the estimation of the mean density of the sun, viz., 1.41 times that of water. The density of the sun actually varies from a value in its outer layers much less than that of air to about 60 times the density of ordinary rocks at its centre.

Comparison of measurements of the positions of the stars made over long periods shows that in the direction of the constellation Hercules the stars appear on the whole to be getting farther apart; in the opposite direction (the constellation Columba), they appear to be drawing together. This indicates that the sun and the members of the solar system are moving as a group with respect to the stars.

*Surface Features.*—The mensurational characteristics are supplemented by a voluminous body of physical data. When the surface of the sun is carefully observed through a telescope it is found to present a mottled or grainy structure. The brightness of the disk is not uniform; the region near the circumference, or limb, is appreciably less bright than the centre of the disk—a fact which appears most obvious in photographs. Sunspots, which are frequently visible to the eye when viewed through a densely smoked glass, are the most easily observed markings on the sun.

A sunspot consists of a central, apparently black, umbra, surrounded by a less dark penumbra. Each of these regions is in fact

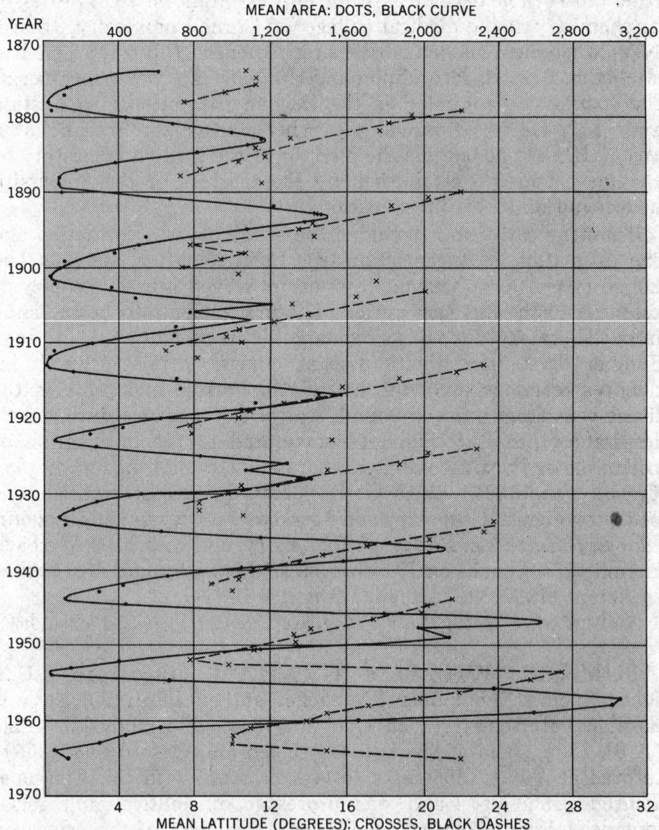


**MEAN AREAS AND HELIOGRAPHIC LATITUDES OF SUNSPOTS FOR EACH YEAR, 1874–1965**

**Areas in millionths of the visible hemisphere, heliographic latitudes in degrees**

exceedingly bright, and appears dark only by contrast with the still brighter solar disk. Spots often are clustered together in groups, often in pairs or pairs of groups, and only rarely appear outside two zones on either side of the solar equator, extending about halfway toward the sun's north and south poles of rotation. The spots move steadily across the face of the sun so as to leave no doubt that the motion is caused by rotation of the sun about an axis. The sun, since it always appears circular in the sky, must be spherical, and its bright visible surface is called the photosphere. A remarkable feature of the sun's rotation is its variation with latitude; *i.e.*, the sun does not rotate as a rigid body: the nearer to its equator, the faster the rotation. Near the equator, the mean rotation period is 24.65 days; at solar latitude 20°, it is 25.19 days; at 35°, 26.63 days; and at 60°, 30.93 days.

Individual sunspots appear spasmodically, remain visible for periods varying from a few hours to several months and then disappear. This apparently capricious behaviour becomes a striking regularity when large numbers of spots and great lengths of time are considered. If the number of spots appearing per year (or the total area covered by them) is plotted against time, as in the diagram, a nearly periodic relation is shown, the annual number reaching a maximum approximately every 11th year. A similar regularity characterizes the location of the spots. At a time of minimum those of a new cycle begin to appear in the higher latitudes, both north and south, of their appointed belts, and as the cycle progresses the place of outbreak gradually moves toward the equator. The thin lines in the graph illustrate this.

Sunspots are always accompanied by exceptionally bright areas on the photosphere, known as faculae. They are most easily seen near the limb, where the brightness of the photospheric background is diminished. Although they are less conspicuous than the spots, their study is equally important for an understanding of the sun.

On the comparatively rare occasions on which the sun is observed in total eclipse, small red clouds are seen apparently floating above various points on the circumference of the dark moon. They belong in reality to the sun, and are known as prominences. Prominences are not seen through an ordinary telescope in full daylight because the intense photospheric light, diffused by the earth's atmosphere and the optical parts of the telescope as by a ground glass, acts as a veil through which prominences and faint stars alike are invisible as individual objects. Prominences assume various shapes and sizes, sometimes reaching heights of hundreds of thousands of miles above the photosphere. The larger prominences can easily be seen during eclipses.

Prominences seem to be extensions of an outer solar atmosphere that is directly revealed at the beginning and ending of each total eclipse. When the moon is just covering the last remnant of the photosphere, a crescent of atmosphere remains exposed for a few seconds. It is easily seen in a small telescope as a brilliant red layer, and has been named the chromosphere.

The most striking solar eclipse phenomenon is the corona, a pearly white halo enveloping the sun and extending in more or less definite rays or streamers to distances of many solar radii. The brilliance of the corona diminishes very rapidly with distance from the sun's limb, and although its total brightness is about one-half that of the full moon, it is much fainter, area for area, than the solar prominences. No two aspects of the corona seen at different eclipses are identical; however, there is a relation between the shape of the corona and the sunspot period. At sunspot maximum the corona appears to extend equally in all directions from the sun's limb and appears round. At sunspot minimum, the poles of the sun are marked by comparatively small tufts of light, while from the equatorial regions long streamers extend to enormous distances.

A special type of telescope, called a coronagraph, can be constructed so that it diffuses almost no light and intercepts the image of the photosphere with a metal disk. On high mountain tops, where diffusion by the earth's atmosphere is negligible on days of exceptional clarity, the innermost, brightest portions of the corona can be observed directly with this instrument.

## SPECTROSCOPIC INVESTIGATION

**General Considerations.**—The spectroscope is the most important of the auxiliary instruments used with the telescope for the investigation of the sun because it can select minute portions of the flood of solar radiation for intensive study. (*See* SPECTROSCOPY; SPECTROSCOPY, ASTRONOMICAL.)

Nearly all solar research depends at some point on a device for sorting radiation by its wavelength. This results in the familiar sequence of colours seen in the rainbow. The word spectroscope in its most general meaning is used to indicate such a device. The human eye is sensitive to only a small band out of the vast range of wavelengths represented in the total radiation of the sun, but over this restricted range, the word "wavelength" is analogous to a precise specification of colour. The spectrum, or ordered arrangement of radiation obtained from a spectroscope, of the sun's radiation consists mainly of a continuous bright background on which dark lines appear. This is called an absorption spectrum, and it confirms the direct eclipse observation that the photosphere is covered by a layer of glowing gases. The dark lines are evidence that the glowing gases are relatively cool. A qualitative spectroscopic chemical analysis of the sun's outer envelopes may be made by comparing the positions, or wavelengths, of the absorption lines with those of emission lines produced by known substances in the laboratory. In this manner the presence on the sun of 67 elements known on earth, and 18 chemical compounds, has been established. The spectroscopic chemical analysis of the sun can also be made quantitative by directing attention to the total amount of radiation extracted from the continuous background by the dark lines. The darkness of a line is related in a complicated way to the amount of material that produces it, but with the aid of laboratory calibrations of line strengths, the relative abundance of the chemical elements has been determined for the sun. The chemical constitution of the sun resembles that of the earth, with the exception that the lighter elements, especially hydrogen and helium, account for almost all its mass.

The spectrum of individual features of the sun may be studied, as well as the light of the entire solar disk. Just at the start of, or just before the end of, the total phase of a solar eclipse, when the chromosphere still remains exposed for a few seconds, the spectrum of its light shows bright rather than dark lines, since this layer of the sun is semitransparent and there is no bright photospheric background to provide a source of radiation to be absorbed. Because of its evanescence, this spectrum is known as the flash spectrum, and it is essentially identical with the absorption spectrum in the position of its lines. The heights reached by the various substances have been determined from special observations at such times. The majority are confined to the lowest atmospheric layers, not more than 500 mi. high, near the top of the photosphere or the bottom of the chromosphere. Hydrogen, helium, and ionized calcium can be traced to great heights, extending up to 8,000 or 9,000 mi. The radiation of hydrogen is the source of the intense red colour of this part of the sun's atmosphere—the chromosphere.

The chromosphere is so bright when viewed during a solar eclipse that it seems reasonable to expect success in the observation of its bright-line spectrum in full daylight. The observation is difficult because the photospheric light diffused by ordinary telescopes and the earth's atmosphere spreads over and drowns the chromospheric radiations. Nevertheless, the hydrogen and helium emission lines are easily observable with very modest telescopic and spectroscopic equipment, but the fainter lines can be seen only with very powerful instruments fed by clean (nondiffusing) telescopes, such as the coronagraph, and located where the scattering of light by the earth's atmosphere is as small as possible.

When the spectroscope is directed toward the corona, at eclipse time or with the aid of a coronagraph, it is found that a great deal of the coronal radiation yields the ordinary solar spectrum and seems to be only reflected sunlight. Actually, radiation from the corona contains four main components: a continuous spectrum which is sunlight scattered by electrons; an absorption spectrum, which is sunlight diffracted by interplanetary dust particles; a series of bright emission lines which have not yet been produced in terrestrial laboratories; and radiation that can be detected using radio methods. The bright emission lines of the corona can be identified with radiations emitted by isolated and very highly ionized atoms of iron, nickel, and calcium (*see* CORONA).

**Spectra and Physical Conditions.**—The spectrum of the solar corona is one of the best examples of the results of physical conditions in modifying the radiation emitted from various regions of the sun. After the effects on line spectra of temperatures, pressures, magnetic and electric fields, and motions of the sources of light had been established through terrestrial spectroscopic studies, these and other physical parameters could be investigated on the sun by means of detailed investigation of the solar spectrum lines. Three of the more important applications to the sun have produced knowledge of temperatures, magnetic fields, and motions.

An early spectroscopic laboratory result classified spectrum lines into high-temperature and low-temperature lines. This classification had an important application when spectra of the photosphere and of a sunspot were compared. The spectrum of a spot contains evidence of compounds, of which only the separated elements contribute to the photospheric spectrum, and the spot spectrum shows a strengthening of low-temperature and a weakening of high-temperature lines when compared with the spectrum of the photosphere. The conclusion is that the sunspot region has a temperature 2,000° C lower than the rest of the solar atmosphere.

A source of light placed in a magnetic field (*i.e.*, a region such as the neighbourhood of the poles of a magnet) has many of its spectrum lines split into a number of component lines, lying closely side by side. Unless the field is very strong, the components are too close together to be seen as distinct individual lines, but the original line may appear to be broadened. By means of special appliances very slight broadenings produced by weak magnetic fields can be detected. The lines in the spectrum of a sunspot show just the composite character that would result from the existence of a magnetic field in the spot in a direction perpendicular to the sun's surface.

Many years of observation show that all sunspots are magnets, some presenting a north, others a south pole to the surrounding space. In each pair of spots, or spot groups, the leaders and followers in the journey around the sun's axis have opposite polarities. Many apparently single spots have invisible companions which can be found by the magnetic splitting of the spectrum lines.

There is a reversal of polarity in the southern solar hemisphere with respect to the northern; thus, if the leader of a pair were a north pole in the northern hemisphere, it would be a south pole in the southern hemisphere, and vice versa; and, with few exceptions, this order would characterize all spots from one minimum to the next of a sunspot cycle. During the next cycle this order would be reversed, so that the approximate period from north pole preceding in the northern hemisphere to north pole preceding in the northern hemisphere is 22 years, just twice the interval between sunspot maxima.

More refined investigations have shown that weak magnetic fields are widespread over the solar surface. At times, these fields, which are much weaker than those of the spots, and generally only a few thousandths of the field in extremely large spots, give the impression that the sun as a whole is a magnet like the earth. (*See* GEOMAGNETISM.) Continued observation of the sun's weak fields has shown that they vary in a complicated, quite disorganized fashion and produce no resultant general magnetic field for the sun. Among the weak fields, the stronger show a gross structure closely related to the forms of the facular regions, but there is no obvious connection between brightness variations, motions, and the general background of weak fields in the photosphere.

Relatively rare measurements of magnetic fields in the chromosphere indicate a weak correlation between magnetic fields and motions in this layer of the solar atmosphere. A fairly close relationship between brightness, motions, and magnetic fields may exist in the corona, but the technical difficulties of achieving direct, simultaneous observation of these quantities are enormous.

The effect on a spectrum line of relative motion of the source and observer along the line of sight (*see* DOPPLER, CHRISTIAN JOHANN; SPECTROSCOPY, ASTRONOMICAL) has had many and varied applications. The amount and direction of displacements of the spectrum lines relative to their normal positions indicate velocities of approach or recession.

Spectroscopic measurement of line shifts in stellar spectra has been used to find the speed of the sun's motion among the stars. Analysis of the line displacements shows that the solar system is moving at a speed of 12 mi. per second with respect to the local stellar system.

Another application to the sun consists in the observation of line shifts in spectra of the east and west limbs of the sun. These show that the east limb is approaching the earth and the west limb receding. The deduced values of the speed of rotation agree very well with those indicated by the spots, and the spectroscopic observations can be extended beyond the narrow belts to which the spots are confined. Similar spectra can be used for determining what lines in the solar spectrum properly belong to the sun, and which are produced by absorption in the earth's atmosphere. The atmosphere of the earth contains much water vapour and other constituents that produce many absorption lines. These are not only intermingled with the solar lines, but are crowded so closely together in long ranges of the spectrum that no sunlight at all reaches the earth in these wavelengths. Such lines, however, occupy identical positions in the spectra of the two solar limbs and are therefore readily distinguished from the displaced lines of the sun.

One of the most difficult and important applications of the shifts arising from motions along the line of sight seeks to detect atmospheric currents in the sun. Solar storms sometimes occur, of incomparably greater fury than the hurricanes and tornadoes of the earth, but quite inconsequential as far as the sun is concerned, and the stormy motions of the solar atmosphere are revealed by distortions and displacements of the spectrum lines. Prominences are sometimes ejected from the sun as a result of such activity, and bits of the solar atmosphere can be projected from sun to earth, where they may produce auroras and magnetic storms. However, there are systematic movements which have been observed, and of these perhaps the most interesting are those occurring near sunspots. At the lower atmospheric levels gases move upward and outward from a spot, while in the higher levels the movements are inward and downward, as if a spot were a sort of whirlpool into which the high-level gases are drawn. Indeed there is definite evidence of high-level circulatory movements around the axes of spots, which points strongly to the same conclusion.

Away from the spots, the solar atmosphere is in a constant, random, bubbling motion in rather strong contrast to the organized movement enforced by a sunspot region. Close to sunspots and their surrounding faculae, the bubbling, or twinkling, motions of small regions in the solar surface are strongly suppressed, possibly because of the action of magnetic fields.

## SPECTROHELIOGRAPHIC INVESTIGATION

The spectroheliograph is an instrument that uses a spectroscope as a light filter to reject all radiation but that in the centre of a dark absorption line or other small regions of the spectrum. The radiation transmitted by a spectroheliograph is used to form a monochromatic picture of the sun. (For construction and method of operation of this instrument, *see* SPECTROHELIOGRAPH.) A variant of the spectroheliograph, the spectrohelioscope, can be employed for direct visual examination of the sun using light from any selected wavelength in the visual part of the spectrum.

Somewhat similar photographs and views of the sun can be obtained through polarizing monochromatic filters, or multilayer interference filters. These devices are used to select small regions of the spectrum, and may be properly regarded as forms of the spectroscope in the general sense. The filters transmit a complete picture rather than dissecting it into lines and then reassembling it as is the case in the spectroheliograph, and they have found wide application in the production of monochromatic solar pictures.

The observation of the solar atmosphere with the instruments mentioned points the way to a fairly complete knowledge of the appearance of the sun in the radiation of various spectral lines and regions of the continuous spectrum. The observations verify and extend the evidence of the complicated structure of the sun which the ordinary telescope provides. The upper part of the sun's atmosphere is composed of minute prominences that form, disappear, and re-form repeatedly, so that on the average the monochromatic view of the sun shows a rather permanent mottling. In the region of spot groups, bright plage regions, the monochromatic aspects of the faculae, are revealed, and the spectroheliographic studies have shown that sunspots always appear only in the plages. The plages form before the sunspots and persist long after the spots have vanished.

Solar flares, the sudden, short-lived brightenings of small parts of the solar surface, also appear only in plages. The word "sudden" must be emphasized in the definition of a flare since the larger plage regions often change brightness at a slow rate. Among the markings on the sun's surface, revealed by monochromatic observation, flares are the most significant from the standpoint of

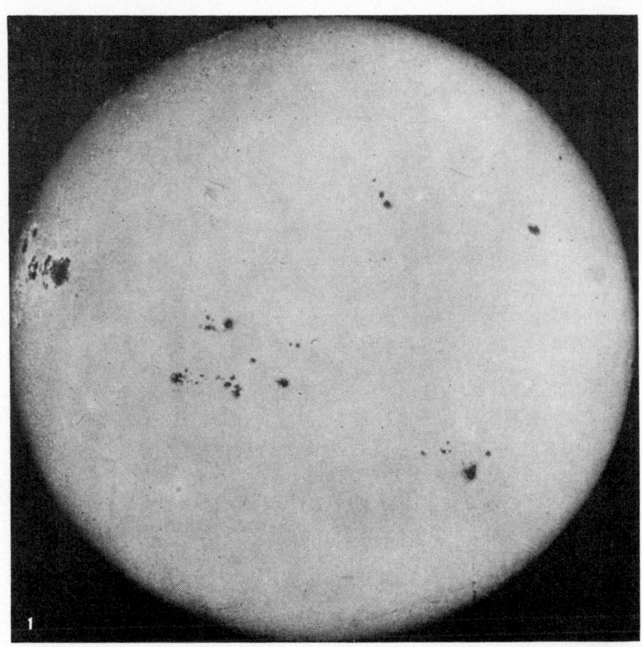

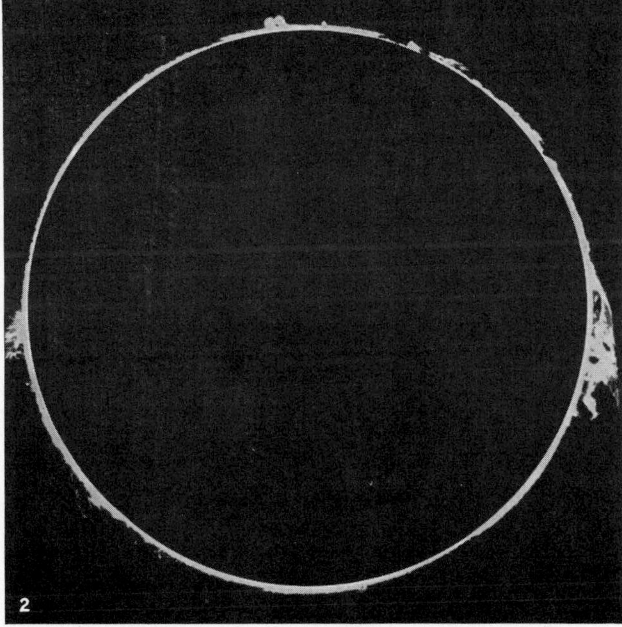

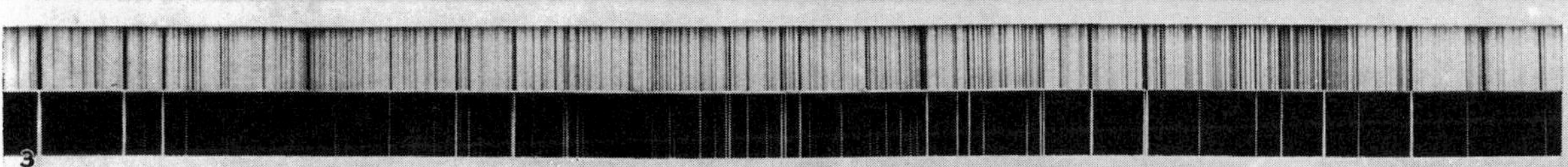


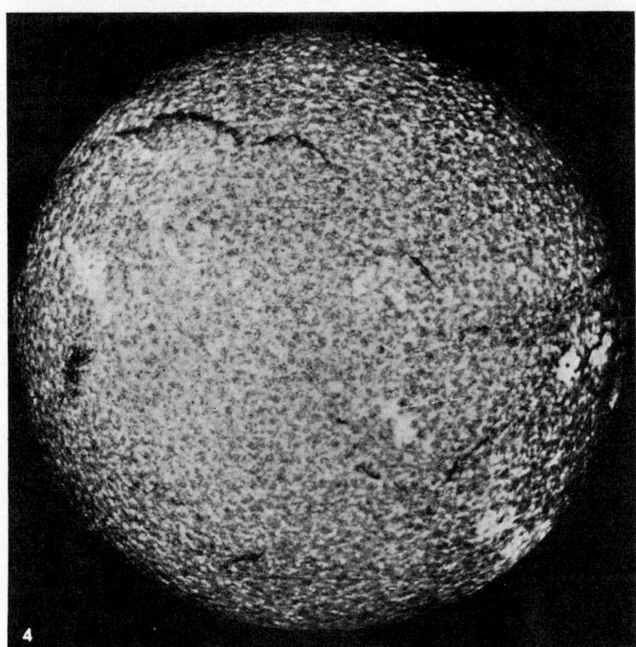

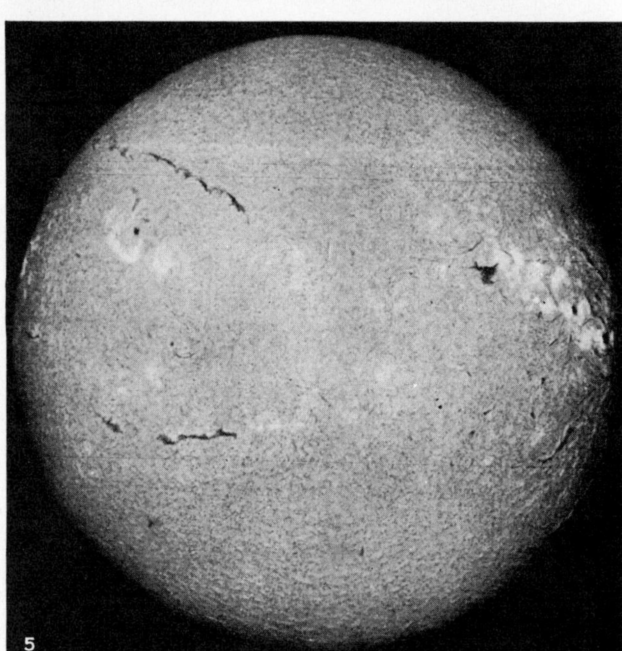

**PHOTOGRAPHIC STUDIES OF THE SUN**

1. The photosphere of the sun, showing an unusually large number of spots, faculae, and darkening at the limb (Rutherfurd)
2. Photograph taken in calcium light, the image of the photosphere having been artificially covered. Shows Chromosphere and Prominences (Evershed)
3. Comparison of solar spectrum with laboratory spectrum of iron (violet region). Presence of iron in the atmosphere of the sun is indicated by coincidence in positions of lines (Imperial College)
4. Spectroheliogram (photograph of sun made by monochromatic light) showing distribution of high-level calcium in the solar atmosphere (Deslandres)
5. Spectroheliogram showing distribution of hydrogen in the solar atmosphere (Deslandres)

# SUN

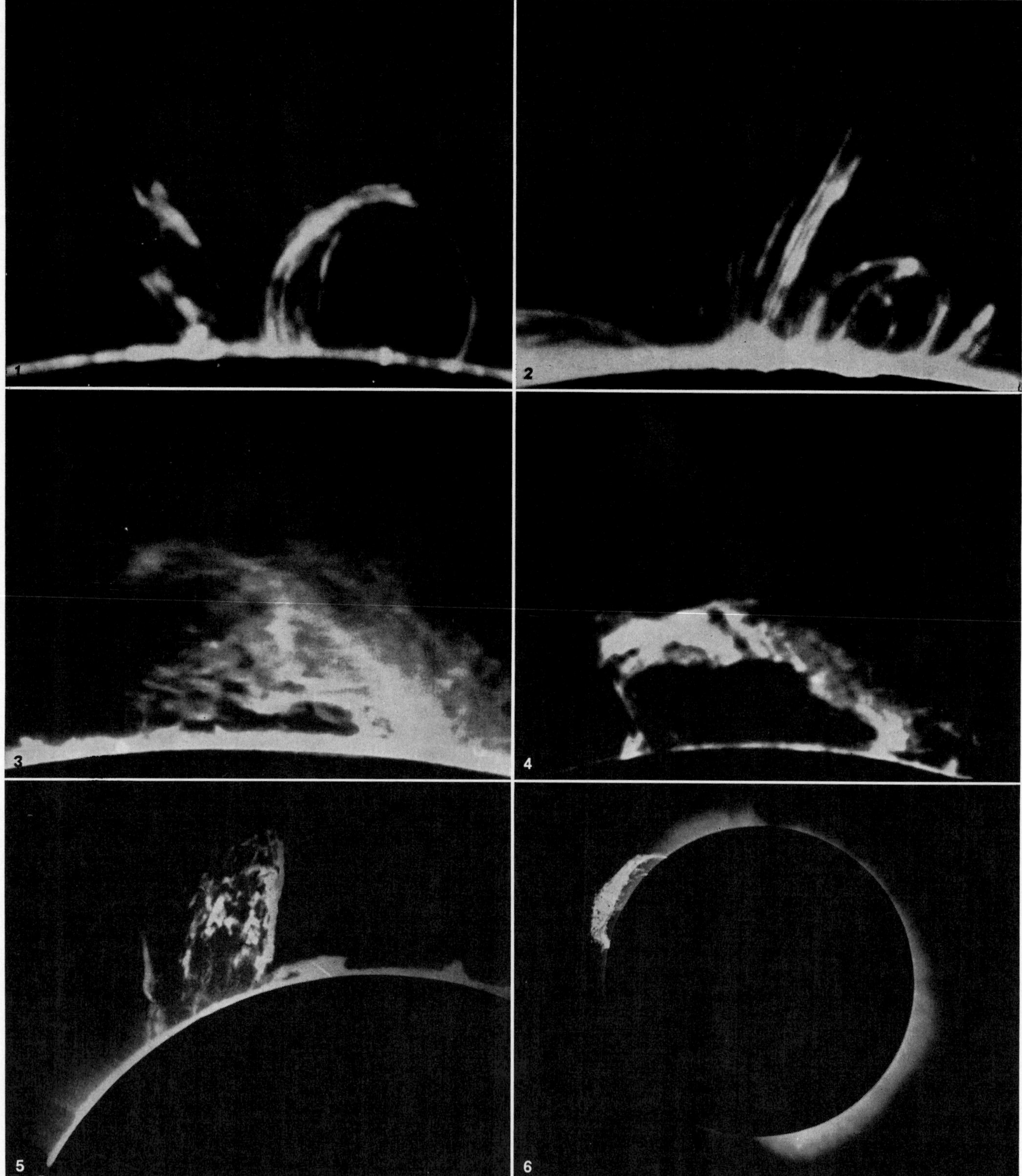


BY COURTESY OF (1-4) THE MC MATH-HULBERT OBSERVATORY OF THE UNIVERSITY OF MICHIGAN, (5) J. EVERSHED, (6) THE ASTRONOMER ROYAL

## STUDIES OF SOLAR PROMINENCES

1. Prominence of Sept. 21, 1939, an example of the sunspot-type classification. All detectable motions were downward (*i.e.*, toward the surface of the sun). The photograph shows a loop formation that measured approximately 90,000 mi. in height and 105,000 mi. in width at the start of the record. The overall dimensions increased about 25% during the period of observation
2. Sunspot-type prominence of Sept. 7, 1939, recorded in a remarkable motion-picture scene of continuous and varied activity. As the scene progressed, the general pattern became intricate, developing a background of faint gigantic loops and many small condensations moving at high velocities toward the chromosphere. The longest streamer extended more than 150,000 mi. above the edge of the sun
3. Quasi-eruptive prominence of Aug. 24, 1939, photographed in the light of ionized calcium. The prominence was about 105,000 mi. high and extended about 155,000 mi. along the edge of the sun
4. The same prominence as in (3), photographed the next day
5. Prominences of the sun observed May 26, 1916, at Srinagar, Kashmir, India
6. Inner corona and prominence photographed during a total solar eclipse, May 29, 1919, observed at Sobral, Brazil. The red flame rose from a height of 130,000 mi. to more than 500,000 mi. above the surface of the sun in less than seven hours

BY COURTESY OF (1) MRS. E. W. MAUNDER, (2) THE ASTRONOMER ROYAL, ROYAL ASTRONOMICAL SOCIETY, LONDON, (3) J. E. WILLIS, U.S. NAVAL OBSERVATORY, NATIONAL GEOGRAPHIC SOCIETY, (4) THE LICK OBSERVATORY

## CORONAE AT VARIOUS STAGES OF SUNSPOT ACTIVITY

1. Corona, May 18, 1901, near time of minimum sunspot activity. Characteristic sunspot minimum with short polar brushes and long equatorial streamers
2. Corona, Aug. 30, 1905, near time of maximum sunspot activity. The circular corona characteristic of a sunspot-maximum period and the long equatorial streamers which give it its typical form are here visible
3. Corona during total eclipse of June 8, 1937, characteristic of maximum sunspot activity. Photograph taken at Canton Island
4. Solar corona, Alhambra, Sp., Aug. 30, 1905. Photograph taken with 40-ft. telescope; exposure time 25 seconds

NOTE: THE RANGE OF BRIGHTNESS IN THE CORONA IS SO GREAT THAT ANY ONE PHOTOGRAPH CAN SHOW DETAIL EITHER OF THE INNER OR OUTER CORONA ONLY. FIGS. 1 AND 2 ARE FROM COMPOSITE DRAWINGS MADE FROM ORIGINAL NEGATIVES, WITH CONTRAST REDUCED

# SUN

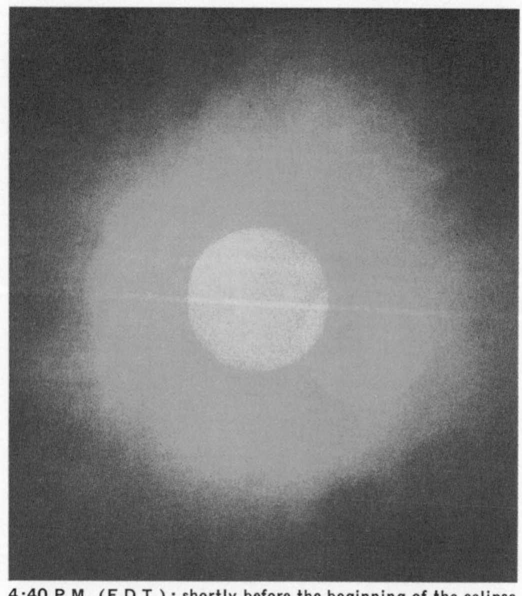

4:40 P.M. (E.D.T.) ; shortly before the beginning of the eclipse

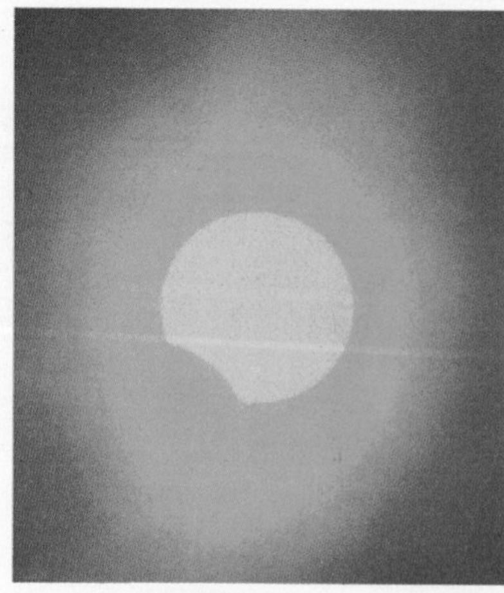

5:15 P.M.; onset of the eclipse

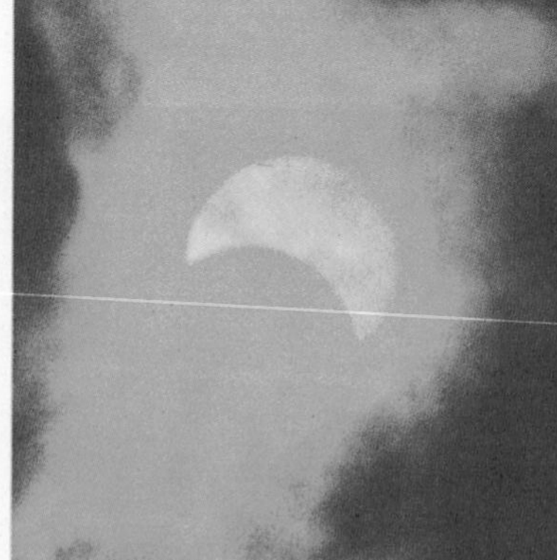

5:35 P.M.

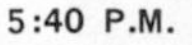

5:40 P.M.

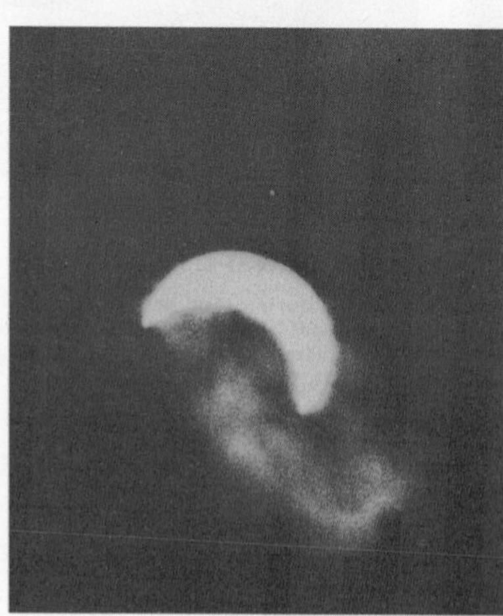

5:45 P.M.

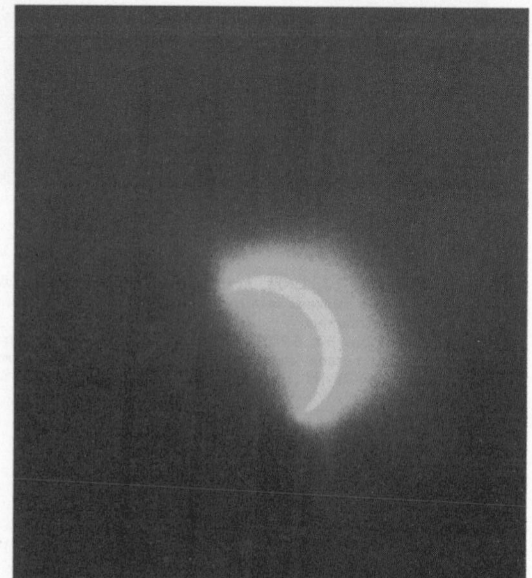

6:00 P.M.

ECLIPSE OF THE SUN, JULY 20, 1963, AS PHOTOGRAPHED FROM NEW YORK CITY

PHOTOGRAPHS, (ALL) PAUL GREENWALD FROM SHOSTAL

the direct effects of the sun on earth. The outbreak of a flare, visible in hydrogen light and accompanied exactly at the start of the visible disturbance by a sudden large increase in the solar radiation in the radio region of the spectrum, often is followed by a magnetic storm on earth after a delay of one to three days. Magnetic storms are accompanied by auroral displays, and it is assumed that the flares in some way eject nuclei of hydrogen atoms (or protons) and electrons and these, traveling at rather modest speeds of 400 to 600 mi. per second, impinge upon the earth's atmosphere about 50 hours after the flare outbreak to produce the observed terrestrial disturbances. The connection between solar flares and the electrical equilibrium of the earth's ionosphere has been established so firmly that observations of the flares are important elements in the prediction of favourable or unfavourable conditions for the sending of long-distance radio messages. *See* also INTERNATIONAL GEOPHYSICAL YEAR.

## INVESTIGATION OF THE SUN'S RADIATION

**The Sun's Total Radiation.**—Of the $3.8 \times 10^{33}$ ergs emitted by the sun every second in the form of electromagnetic radiation, its attendant planets and their satellites receive about 1 part in 120,000,000, so that the significance of the process is primarily cosmic, even though of dominant importance for the thermal environment of the earth. The first step in seeking further knowledge of this fundamental process is the measurement of the rate of radiation with as great precision as possible. Various instruments must be used in this endeavour, since one must measure X-rays, ultraviolet radiation, light, infrared radiation, and radio emissions.

Only the radiation received by a small area near the earth can be measured, but, knowing the dimensions of the solar system, the total amount can be deduced. A general method is to convert the sun's radiation into heat, which can be accurately measured. The result is called the solar constant: the amount of energy which would fall perpendicularly per square centimetre per minute on a surface placed outside the earth's atmosphere at the earth's mean distance from the sun. The value of this constant is about 2.0 cal.

The results of measurement of the solar constant can be combined with similar laboratory measurements for obtaining an estimate of the sun's temperature. Extrapolations from experiment have shown that an ideal emitter of electromagnetic radiation—a black body—would radiate energy at a rate strictly proportional to the fourth power of its temperature. The assumption that the sun radiates like a black body is an oversimplification, yet it makes possible a temperature estimate which is an important clue to solar radiative processes. Since the sun is visible, energy is flowing out of it from hotter to cooler regions, and it cannot be uniform in temperature. It is necessary to consider what region of the sun has the temperature that is determined by the black-body assumption. Because the greatest part of the radiation is in the form of light, this region must be the photosphere: the relatively thin visible surface of the sun, and the temperature estimated from the total radiation is that of this layer. The temperature is called the effective temperature, and has a value of 5,800° K (absolute centigrade degrees).

**The Sun's Analyzed Radiation.**—The same instruments that are used in the measurement of the sun's total radiation can be employed in other ways to provide data for a slightly different method of estimating a temperature of the sun. The radiation from a black body is distributed among the various wavelengths in its continuous spectrum in a manner definitely related to the temperature. Therefore, if a photoelectric cell be passed along the solar spectrum, and the amount of energy at each point in the continuous background be measured, the distribution of energy throughout the spectrum is obtained and the absolute temperature follows. There are several methods of analyzing such observations to derive a temperature, and values are obtained in the range 4,500° to 6,300° K (absolute). If the sun radiated exactly like a black body, the several temperatures would agree with one another and with the result obtained from the solar constant. The slight departures from agreement indicate that the sun is not quite in the ideal equilibrium demanded for a black body, but is sufficiently close to ensure that the physical phenomena near its surface are similar to those expected in an enclosure at a temperature of 5,000° to 6,000° K.

Although the assumption of black-body conditions provides a close representation of measurements of radiation made with ordinary and infrared light, there are two regions of the spectrum which are extraordinary in appearance and show large differences from expectations based on a solar model radiating perfectly at a temperature of 5,000° K. The two regions are: in the extreme ultraviolet, where observations must be made from rockets, or other space vehicles, far above the earth's atmosphere; and in the radio region, where special types of antennae and receivers make investigation possible from the earth's surface.

*The Sun's Radiation in the Extreme Ultraviolet.*—In the extreme ultraviolet (wavelength less than 0.00015 mm.), the continuous background of the sun's spectrum is undetectable and only bright lines appear. The principal line is the fundamental line of hydrogen. The character of this line indicates that it is formed in a region of the chromosphere where the temperature is increasing rapidly with height above the photosphere. Other bright, high-temperature lines are present to support this deduction. Thus the chromosphere, which is the source of the bright lines in the extreme ultraviolet part of the solar spectrum, is a most unusual region, in which the temperature increases with distance away from the sun, and atoms are observed in motion at unexpectedly high speeds.

*The Sun's Radiation in the Radio Region.*—The result derived from the observations in the extreme ultraviolet is confirmed by measurements of the sun's radio radiation. In the ultraviolet part of the solar spectrum the wavelengths of solar radiation are less than 0.00015 mm.; in the radio region the wavelengths are in the range 5 mm. to 10,000 mm. The shortest wavelengths originate near the base of the chromosphere, but the longest can only come from far out in the corona. Energy observed at the various wavelengths can be equated to the energy radiated from a black body of the same size as the sun's visible disk in order to derive an apparent temperature. Apparent temperatures, based on measurements of the radio energy received from the sun, range from about 6,400° K for the shortest waves originating in the chromosphere near the sun's visible surface to 1,200,000° K for wavelengths of tens of metres originating entirely in the solar corona, more than 1,000,000 mi. above the visible surface.

On earth lightning flashes are the only natural sources of radio waves, but there are at least five different kinds of radio energy generated on the sun: (1) The continuous, nearly invariable component from which the apparent temperatures are computed; (2) The continuous and steady contribution that is associated with the presence of plages on the sun's visible surface; (3) Erratic increases in energy of very short duration, but following closely upon one another, often so closely that they overlap; these may be accompanied by an increase in the steady component; (4) Sudden, very great, nonrecurrent increases beginning at the start of solar flares and associated with them; (5) Occasional isolated increases of very short duration. Sometimes the variable portion of the sun's radio energy quite overwhelms the continuous background. This is completely different from the situation in the visible spectrum, where the variable features are difficult to detect. *See* also TELESCOPE, RADIO.

## THEORIES OF SOLAR STRUCTURE AND EVOLUTION

**Structure of the Sun.**—A mathematical model of the structure of the sun can be based on data from observations similar to those described above, and data from terrestrial physics laboratories dealing with the behaviour of matter at temperatures, pressures, and densities that range from the extremely high to the almost vanishingly small. According to these models, the temperature at the centre of the sun is about 20,000,000° K. Going out from the centre of the sun toward the surface about 4,200° K is reached at the very top of the photosphere. In the chromosphere the temperature starts to rise, at first very slowly and then more rapidly, until at the beginning of the corona, about 9,000 mi. above the photosphere, the temperature is 500,000° K. In the outer parts of the corona, 1,500,000 mi. from the centre of the sun, the radio observations are best fitted by a temperature of 1,500,000° K. Pressures start at 6,000,000,000,000 lb. per sq.in. at the centre, decrease to about atmospheric near the visible surface, and become inappreciable in the upper chromosphere and corona. The mathematical model indicates that 99% of the mass of the sun is concentrated within 0.6% of its radius; thus, the density of the sun decreases rapidly away from the centre.

Only the most elemental forms of matter can exist at the temperatures encountered near the centre of the sun. Atomic nuclei must be stripped almost bare of their satellite electrons and the rates of motion of the elementary particles must be in the range 100 to 1,000 mi. per second. All of the bits of matter—electrons, neutrons, and protons—that exist at the sun's centre participate in a process of continual interchange of energy between radiation and motion of particles. But there is an important difference in the behaviour of the atoms and electrons on one hand and the radiation on the other. The motions of the particles are kept within a limited range by the gravitational equilibrium of the whole sun, while electrostatic forces preserve a constant proportion between the number of nuclei and the number of electrons in each region. Radiation, however, is not so controlled. It works its way from the centre, where it is most intense, out to the surface and thence to space at the observed rate of $3.8 \times 10^{33}$ ergs per second. The sun loses radiation at this prodigious rate, and has been doing so for many millions of years, while the electrons and atomic nuclei remain chained within its boundaries.

**Source of the Sun's Radiation.**—It has been realized for many years that the observed rate of energy loss by leaking of radiation from the solar surface must be balanced rather exactly by the rate of energy generation in the interior, since there is little evidence that the sun is heating or cooling rapidly. Because other sources of energy are insufficient, astronomers have sought a series of nuclear transformations which would liberate radiation at the required rate. The transformation of 1% of the sun's mass from hydrogen to helium supplies enough energy to keep it shining for fully 1,000,000,000 years. There are other conditions that must be satisfied in the selection of possible energy sources. The sun must not only be in balance as regards the flow of radiation; it must simultaneously be in mechanical equilibrium. The pressure, which is primarily determined by the temperature, must exactly balance the weight of the overlying layers at every point throughout the sun. Restrictions such as these on the possible choices have directly led to the conclusion: fusion between hydrogen nuclei, or protons, to produce helium is the source of the sun's energy. The discovery of a satisfactory means of generating the required enormous energies and advances in knowledge of nuclear reactions have made possible the computation of a probable course of evolution for the sun.

**Mathematical Models of Detailed Features of the Sun.**—The general concepts involved in the computation of plausible models for the interior of the sun and the choice of a method of energy generation, if complete, would imply the existence of sunspots, the chromosphere and the prominences, the plages and the flares, the corona, the weird law of solar rotation, the magnetic fields—in short, all of the detailed and transient features that still require continuous observation. Considerable progress has been made in the study of solar details, but mutually consistent theories for the different structures do not exist. Perhaps a reason can be found in the realization that the observed deviations from equilibrium represent trifling phenomena on a solar scale, despite their remarkable effects on earth, and the idea of the sun as the perfectly calm, unchanging star of the mathematician and poet is an amazingly good approximation to the truth. *See* also STAR; and references to "Sun" in the Index.

BIBLIOGRAPHY.—General accounts of the sun are contained in Giorgio Abetti, *Solar Research* (1963); W. M. Baxter, *The Sun and the Amateur Astronomer* (1963); A. Dauvillier, *Physique Solaire et Géophysique* (1962); G. Gamow, *A Star Called the Sun* (1964); D. H. Menzel, *Our Sun*, rev. ed. (1959); H. W. Newton, *The Face of the Sun* (1958); for more technical treatment *see* R. J. Bray and R. N. Loughhead, *Sunspots* (1964); J. W. Evans (ed.), *The Solar Corona* (1963); G. P. Kuiper (ed.), *The Sun* (1953); M. R. Kundu, *Solar Radio Astronomy* (1965); H. J. and E. v. P. Smith, *Solar Flares* (1963); R. N. Thomas, *Physics of the Solar Chromosphere* (1961); A. Unsöld, *Physik der Sternatmosphären* (1955). (H. D.; O. C. M.)

**SUNBIRD,** a group of small perching birds of more than 100 species forming the family Nectariniidae. They are the Old World counterparts of the hummingbirds. Africa is richest in species, then southern Asia, nearby islands, and Australia. They are forest-, brush-, and garden-dwelling birds. The males of many species have brilliant colours; iridescent blues, purples, and greens with patches of yellow, red, and black are common. However, some species are dull coloured, as the females usually are.

Sunbirds are characteristically flower birds, flitting about and perching among blossoms, probing into the flowers for small insects and nectar. For this they have long, slender, curved bills and extensible, more or less tubular tongues. The usual type of nest is an oval, hanging structure attached to a twig. The entrance is at the side near the top, over which a roof projects. The eggs are usually spotted and two in number. (A. L. RD.)

**SUN BITTERN,** a bird, *Eurypyga helias,* of Central and South America, placed in a family by itself, the Eurypygidae. It is distantly related to such birds as the kagu of New Caledonia and the rails and cranes and is grouped with them in the order Gruiformes. The sun bittern is a slender bird about 17 in. long, somewhat raillike but with full wings; a long, ample tail; and plumage variegated with browns, yellows, black, and white. In courtship, its beautifully marked golden wings and tail are fully spread. It lives on the ground in wet forests and feeds on insects. The flight is buoyant. It builds a bulky nest in trees and lays two or three rust to brownish eggs, with darker blotches. (DN. A.)

**SUNBURY,** the seat of Northumberland County, Pa., U.S., is an industrial and agricultural centre on the Susquehanna River, 40 mi. (64 km.) N of Harrisburg, on the site of an old Indian village. Sunbury was surveyed in 1772, incorporated as a borough in 1797, and became a city in 1922. Ft. Augusta, erected 1756, where the French were defeated during the French and Indian War, and the nearby home of Joseph Priestley, the discoverer of oxygen, are tourist attractions. In July 1883 Thomas Edison began operating in Sunbury the world's first three-wire central electric-lighting station. For comparative population figures *see* table in PENNSYLVANIA: *Population.* (A. J. FO.)

**SUNBURY-ON-THAMES,** an urban district in northwest Surrey, Eng.; until 1965 it was in the former Middlesex County. It comprises Sunbury, Sunbury Common, Ashford Common, Charlton, Littleton, Shepperton, Shepperton Green, and Upper and Lower Halliford. Pop. (1961) 33,437. The district has a frontage to the River Thames of about eight miles. A vast reservoir of the Metropolitan Water Board is at Littleton, and other properties of the board and of the Thames Conservancy are elsewhere in the locality. Sand and gravel are excavated on a considerable scale. There is an extensive petroleum research centre in the district. Large film studios are at Shepperton, and race meetings are held at Kempton Park. Some market gardening is carried on.

Thomas Love Peacock, the poet and novelist, who lived in Lower Halliford for many years, is buried in Shepperton Cemetery.

**SUNDA ISLANDS AND STRAIT.** The Sunda, or Soenda, Islands extend from the Malay Peninsula to the Moluccas and include the Greater Sunda Islands (Sumatra, Java, Borneo, Celebes, and adjacent smaller islands) and the Lesser Sunda Islands (Bali, Lombok, Sumbawa, Sumba, Flores, Timor, Alor, Wetar, etc.). With the exception of Borneo, eastern Sumatra, and nearby areas, they belong to the geologically unstable zone of island arcs, undersea ridges and active volcanism lying between Asia and Australia. The Sunda Islands include most of the land area of Indonesia. Only northern and northwestern Borneo and eastern Timor are not under Indonesian political control. Malaysian cultures and languages predominate in the area.

Sunda Strait separates Java and Sumatra. At its narrowest the island of Sangiang divides it into two channels, each about four miles wide. Although overshadowed in commercial and strategic significance by Malacca Strait, it remains an important passage uniting the Indian Ocean and eastern Asia. The spectacular eruption of Krakatau (*q.v.*) took place in Sunda Strait in 1883.

*See* also INDONESIA, REPUBLIC OF and articles on the individual islands. (J. M. BT.)

**SUN DANCE,** the most spectacular and important religious ceremony of the Plains Indians (*q.v.*) of the 19th century. Ordinarily held by each tribe once a year in early summer, it was an occasion when all could gather with guests from other tribes and reaffirm their basic beliefs about the universe and the supernatural through words, ceremonies, and symbolic objects.

The ceremony was most highly developed among the Arapaho, Cheyenne (*qq.v.*), and Oglala Sioux (and may have originated with these tribes). By the end of the 19th century, it had spread with local variations to include most (26) of the tribes from the Plains Ojibwa in Saskatchewan south to the Kiowa (*q.v.*) in Texas. The sun dance is a good example of the many individual quests for power or aid from the supernatural that became elaborated as tribal ceremonies. In many instances it was a private experience involving just one votary, or a small group of them. The development of total tribal participation, widespread cooperative effort, direction by such officials as tribal leaders and shamans, and elaboration beyond the immediate sun dance indicate the meaning of this ceremony in terms of tribal aspirations (secular and religious) and in the reinforcement of social control.

In the most elaborate versions a great camp circle was formed, preliminary instruction was given to the pledger and his associates, necessary supplies were gathered, and a dance structure was erected with a central pole to symbolize a source of supernatural power (*e.g.,* the sun). Preliminary dances by others and the erection of an altar were followed by the sun dance itself. This continued intermittently for several days and nights; during this time those dancers who were fulfilling a vow or seeking power neither ate nor drank, their sacrifice ending in frenzy and exhaustion (among some tribes in self-torture and mutilation). In one version skewers tethered to the central pole were thrust through the flesh of the dancer's breast or back and torn away to end the rite, the camp site then being immediately abandoned.

In an effort to curb such practices the U.S. government outlawed the sun dance (1904). Among some tribes benign forms of the ceremony continued, usually as part of Fourth of July celebrations. A few tribes, however, have attempted to revive the sun dance in its original form and meaning.

BIBLIOGRAPHY.—L. Spier, "The Sun Dance of the Plains Indians," *American Museum of Natural History Anthropological Papers,* vol. 16 (1921); J. W. Bennett, "Development of Ethnological Theory as Illustrated by Studies of the Plains Sun Dance," *Am. Anthrop.,* vol. 46 (1944); F. W. Voget, "A Shoshone Innovator," *Am. Anthrop.,* vol. 52 (1950); D. B. Shimkin, "The Wind River Shoshone Sun Dance," *Bureau of American Ethnology Bulletin 151* (1953); J. A. Jones, "The Sun Dance of the Northern Ute," *Bureau of American Ethnology Bulletin 157* (1955). (W. H. KE.)

**SUNDANESE,** a highland people of West Java (Republic of Indonesia), numbering about 12,000,000. Historically they were first recorded under the Indo-Javanese Brahmanical states (8th century A.D.) and subsequently accepted the Mahayana (*q.v.*) Buddhism adopted by the Shailendra kings (*see* JAVA: *History*). Muslim trade influenced them to accept Islam in the 16th century, the people of Bantam (*q.v.*) being especially fervent; however, animistic and Hindu influences survive.

The Sundanese village is ruled by a headman and a council of elders. Single-family houses of wood or bamboo are raised on piles. Close to the settlement are individually owned lands largely devoted to terraced rice fields. Rice culture and ironworking, as well as marriage, birth, and death ceremonies, conform closely to the Indonesian pattern, although often mixed with elements of more elaborate Indian ceremonies.

The opening of roads into the highlands, development of government- and foreign-owned plantations, and the establishment of village schools tended to erase differences between other Javans and the Sundanese. They have spread into neighbouring districts of Java and into the Lampong area of southern Sumatra.

(F. C. CE.; P. E. DE J. DE J.)

Except for Javanese, the most widely spoken Malayo-Polynesian language is Sundanese (with a number of dialects; that spoken in Priangan Province has the highest prestige). Like Javanese, Sundanese has status styles: *kasar* (informal), *lemes* (deferential), and *panengah* (a middle style). The Javanese alphabet (the earliest used to write Sundanese) and one adapted from Latin are most commonly employed. A modified Arabic system is usual in religious writings. Publication in Sundanese has been meagre, the major city of Bandung (*q.v.*), for example, having only one newspaper. The limited Sundanese literature is strongly affected by that in Javanese. *See* also JAVA: *Population.* (I. DN.)

BIBLIOGRAPHY.—Hasan Mustafa (Haji), *Over de gewoonten en gebruiken der Soendaneezen* (1946); A. E. Kramer, *West Indonesien* (1927); P. J. Veth, *Java,* 4 vol. (1896–1907); H. G. Q. Wales, *The Making of Greater India* (1951); E. M. Uhlenbeck, *A Critical Survey of Studies on the Languages of Java and Madura* (1964).

**SUNDARBANS** (formerly SUNDERBUNDS), a tract of country in the India-Pakistan subcontinent, forming the seaward fringe of the Gangetic Delta. It extends for about 170 mi. (274 km.) along the coast of the Bay of Bengal, from the estuary of the Hooghly River (India) on the west to that of the Meghna (East Pakistan) on the east. It is intersected from north to south by large tidal rivers or estuaries, which are connected by numerous interlacing channels. The whole tract is a network of estuaries, rivers, and creeks, which enclose a large number of flat, marshy islands. Most of these are covered with forest standing in soft mud, usually under water at high tide. Formerly the Sundarbans ran inland from 60 to 80 mi. (97 to 129 km.). The characteristic tree is a large mangrove, the sundari (*Heritiera littoralis*), from which the name of the tract probably derives. Along the coast the forest passes into a mangrove swamp of other, smaller species, which in some places is separated from the sea by a line of sand dunes. South of the northern area of cultivation the Sundarbans are almost uninhabited, but wild animals are numerous, and crocodiles infest the estuaries. (L. D. S.)

**SUNDARGARH,** a town of Orissa state, India, and the headquarters of the district of the same name, is 45 mi. (72 km.) N of Sambalpur and 120 mi. (193 km.) SW of Ranchi. Pop. (1961) 11,329. The town has a science college affiliated to Utkal University in Cuttack.

SUNDARGARH DISTRICT (area 3,571 sq.mi. [9,715 sq.km.]; pop. [1961] 758,617), created in 1949 by the merger of the former princely states of Gangpur and Bonai, occupies the northwestern part of Orissa and is bounded west by Madhya Pradesh and north and east by Bihar. Gangpur is a plateau 700 ft. (213 m.) above sea level with a belt of forest in the north. Bonai is a thickly wooded region surrounded by low hills. The chief rivers are the Ib, the Samkha, and the Koel. The majority of the population is engaged in agriculture, and the main crops are rice, pulses, mustard, gram, sugarcane, potatoes, and jute. The district has valuable deposits of coal, iron ore, limestone, manganese, and dolomite, however, and is rapidly being industrialized. The main industrial centre is the town of Rourkela (pop. [1961] 90,287), the site of the Hindustan steel plant. Built with aid from West Germany, the plant has an annual output of more than 1,000,000 tons of steel. (MA. M.; N. K. S.)

**SUNDAY, BILLY** (WILLIAM ASHLEY SUNDAY) (1862–1935), U.S. evangelist, whose sermons gave vivid expression to the emotional upheaval caused by the transition from a rural to an industrial society in the United States, was born at Ames, Ia., on Nov. 19, 1862. The son of a brickmason who died a private in the Union Army (1862), Sunday spent four years in an orphans' home, grew up on a farm, completed high school, and worked as an undertaker's assistant before entering professional baseball in 1883. He gave up baseball in 1891 to become a YMCA worker. From 1896 until his death he conducted religious revivals in major cities throughout the United States. He was ordained in the Presbyterian Church in 1903. His theology was Fundamentalist.

Following in the footsteps of Dwight L. Moody (*q.v.*), and with the aid of a choir leader, Homer A. Rodeheaver, and a score of revival "specialists," Sunday conducted more than 300 revivals with an estimated total attendance of 100,000,000. Sunday claimed that 1,000,000 "hit the sawdust trail" to profess their conversion; he received more than $1,000,000 in "free-will offerings." Despite his sensationalism, Sunday was enthusiastically supported by the evangelical churches and by influential laymen. He played a prominent part in the prohibition movement and reached the peak of his fame in 1917 in his New York City revival. He died at Chicago, Ill., on Nov. 6, 1935. *See* REVIVALISM.

BIBLIOGRAPHY.—Elijah P. Brown, *The Real Billy Sunday* (1914); William T. Ellis, *Billy Sunday: the Man and His Message* (1936), which contains Sunday's brief autobiography; Homer A. Rodeheaver, *Twenty Years with Billy Sunday* (1936). The only analytical study of Sunday's career is that of William G. McLoughlin, Jr., *Billy Sunday Was His Real Name* (1955). (W. G. McL.)

**SUNDAY,** the first day of the week, called in Christian terminology the Lord's day (*kyriake* in Greek and *dies dominica* in Latin; hence *domenica* in Italian, *domingo* in Spanish, *dimanche* in French). But it is not the Lord's day in the same sense as the Jewish sabbath (*q.v.*), on which the sovereign lordship of God is acknowledged by abstention from work. Sunday is the day not of Yahweh but of Christ, the Lord in virtue of his resurrection from the dead (hence the Russian word for Sunday, *Voskresenye,* derived from the word for "resurrection"). Sunday is the weekly memorial of the Easter mystery and of the rebirth of Christians, the day both of Christ the Lord and of the people whom he bought with his blood. The essence of its celebration is the gathering of the baptized around the Lord's table (*see* EUCHARIST; LITURGY, CHRISTIAN). Thus the Constitution on the Sacred Liturgy (1963) of the second Vatican Council says: "The Lord's day is the original feast day," which should be observed "as a day of joy and of freedom from work."

**The Weekly Easter.**—The keeping of Sunday is based on the Gospel accounts of the resurrection of Christ and his first appearance to his disciples thereafter. It was on "the first day of the week" that the Lord rose again (Matt. 28:1; Mark 16:9; Luke 24:1; John 20:1) and showed himself to his friends; that he was recognized by the disciples at Emmaus "in the breaking of the bread" (Luke 24:35); and that he appeared among the assembled apostles, ate with them (Luke 24:41–43), and said to them "As the Father has sent me, even so I send you" (John 20: 21–23). The first commemoration of the resurrection took place eight days later (by biblical methods of counting), on the following Sunday, when the disciples were met together and Jesus showed himself again, stood among them, and invited Thomas to place his hand in his wounded side (John 20:26–27).

The apostolic generation at once grasped the importance of the first day, linked to the remembrance and the presence of the risen Lord. St. Paul, writing at Easter in about the year 57, connects the collection for the brethren in Jerusalem with the weekly meeting (I Cor. 16:2), and in Acts there is a description of the group with Paul at Troas on "the first day of the week, when we were gathered together to break bread" (Acts 20:7). Before the end of the 1st century A.D., the author of Revelation gave the first day its name of the "Lord's day": "I was in the Spirit on the Lord's day" (Rev. 1:10).

But Easter for Christians is a day not merely of remembrance but also of hope. For this reason the Lord's day has always been kept as an anticipation of the return of Christ in glory; the Lord's Eucharist brings together the royal and priestly people until he comes (I Cor. 11:26). The church fathers therefore called Sunday the eighth day. In the words of St. Augustine, "The day which was first shall be the eighth, so that the first life will not be taken away but made eternal." After the present age, with its rhythm of seven days in the week, comes the eternal day, the day beyond weeks, the day of the consummation of Easter.

**The Day of the Church.**—Sunday is the church's day, because on it the people of God meet together. The text from Acts quoted above shows the local community thus assembled. A little later (perhaps late 1st century A.D.) the author of the *Didache* said, "Having met together on the Lord's day, break bread and give thanks." Justin (mid-2nd century) gave the first description of this liturgical assembly: "On the day called the day of the sun all our people living in town or country meet together in one place. The memoirs of the apostles are read, or the writings of the prophets." After the reading of the Word of God came the homily of the presiding minister, common prayer, and the celebration of the Eucharist.

As the day of the church, Sunday is also the day of baptism (as can be seen from the *Apostolic Tradition* of Hippolytus, written at the beginning of the 3rd century), of ordinations, and of church dedications. Baptism marks the entry of newcomers into the people of God, represents the death and resurrection of Jesus Christ (Rom. 6:3–5), and is the first moment of Christian initiation, which is achieved in communion at the Saviour's meal celebrated in the Lord's assembly.

**A Day of Joy.**—As the weekly Easter, and the day of the Saviour and of his church, each Sunday ought to be full of joy and charity; hence the early custom of standing to pray (no longer entirely observed in the West) and of not fasting on Sunday. "On Sunday be always joyful, for he who is afflicted on Sunday commits a sin," says the 3rd-century *Didascalia apostolorum.* This command is echoed by the whole church tradition. (PI. J.)

**Sunday Observance.**—In the early church, which had no legal standing in the Roman Empire, Sunday was a day not only of joyful worship but also of ordinary work. Constantine I introduced the first civil legislation (321) making Sunday a day of rest when he decreed the cessation of work on Sunday for the legal profession and for townsfolk, though farmers were not compelled to remain inactive because of the dependence of agriculture on the weather. This law, aimed at providing time for worship, was followed later in the same century and in subsequent centuries by further restrictions on Sunday activities.

At first no connection was made between the Jewish regulations governing the sabbath and the Christian laws of Sunday abstention from work, but parallels between them began to be drawn in the 6th century and by the 9th century the commandment in the Decalogue which forbids work on the sabbath was explicitly cited in a Roman synod as a justification for undertaking no servile labour (*i.e.,* such as a slave would do) on Sunday. There was no identification of the sabbath with Sunday in the medieval West, however, and the parallel was not pushed to its logical conclusion until after the Reformation in some Protestant countries. Hence Sunday in Roman Catholic countries tends to be a day of both worship and enjoyable recreation.

The great Reformers themselves, including Luther and Calvin, held that Sunday did not replace the Jewish sabbath. But the Puritans, with their desire to regulate life by the Bible, and in the absence of any clear commands in the New Testament about Sunday observance by Christians, applied the Old Testament sabbath regulations to Sunday. A book by the English rector Nicholas Bownde (Bound), *The Doctrine of the Sabbath* (1595), which identified Sunday with the sabbath, was of great influence in this connection. In 17th-century England and Scotland, and hence also in parts of colonial North America, laws were passed forbidding public entertainments, sports, buying and selling, and traveling on Sunday, in addition to the time-honoured prohibition on unnecessary work. Together with this went the strict practice in private life of confining the day to godly pursuits alone, alongside church worship. Restriction of public activities continued to be the subject of legislation, to facilitate opportunities for worship and keep the day holy. (*See* SABBATARIANISM.)

In the changed conditions of the 20th century, however, Sunday legislation has often been relaxed. Yet Sunday generally remains a day of legal cessation of many forms of labour, and for Christians a day primarily of worship.

BIBLIOGRAPHY.—J. A. Hessey, *Sunday,* 5th ed. (1889); H. Dumaine in F. Cabrol (ed.), *Dictionnaire d'archéologie chrétienne et de liturgie,* vol. 4, col. 858–994 (1920); P. Jounel in A. G. Martimort (ed.), *L'Église en prière,* pp. 673–686 (1961); H. B. Porter, *The Day of Light* (1960); H. H. Ward, *Space-Age Sunday* (1960); W. A. Rordorf, *Der Sonntag . . . im ältesten Christentum* (1962).

**SUNDBYBERG,** a town of Sweden in Stockholm *län* (county), on the northwestern outskirts of Stockholm. Pop. (1965) 28,190. Founded in 1877 as one of Stockholm's first residential suburbs, it received its charter in 1927 and has become an important industrial centre. The church (1909–11), beautifully situated in a park, has some notable stained glass. Among other imposing buildings are those of the large Marabou chocolate factory, while around Storskogen Park is a district of modern multistory apartment blocks. Electrical and chemical equipment, building materials, outboard motors, and other products are manufactured. Immediately to the southwest is Bromma Airport for internal services.

**SUNDERLAND, CHARLES SPENCER,** 3RD EARL OF (*c.* 1674–1722), English statesman, first lord of the treasury from 1718 to 1721, originated the financial schemes that resulted in the South Sea Bubble (*q.v.*). The second son of Robert, 2nd earl of Sunderland (*q.v.*), he succeeded to the earldom in 1702. When Spencer's first wife, Arabella, died in 1698, Sidney Godolphin (*see* GODOLPHIN, SIDNEY GODOLPHIN, Earl of), the reigning exponent of court politics, arranged a match for him with Lady Anne Churchill, second daughter of Godolphin's ally the earl (later duke) of Marlborough. The marriage was celebrated in 1700. Sunderland, however, devoted his skill in intrigue to the Whig Junto, and his marriage in the long run drew Marlborough and Godolphin toward the Whigs. In 1706 the Junto, as the price of their support, forced Sunderland upon Godolphin's ministry as secretary of state for the southern department. Sunderland's ungovernable extremism, and his violent support of the impeachment of Henry Sacheverell in 1710, were met by the rooted antipathy of Queen Anne, and his dismissal in June 1710 heralded the overthrow of the Whig government.

Sunderland conducted factious negotiations with the Hanoverian court, but on the accession of George I in 1714 he was bitterly disappointed by his relegation as lord lieutenant of Ireland. Currying favour with the king's mistress the baroness von Schulenburg (later duchess of Kendal) and with his German ministers, he became lord privy seal in 1715 and in 1716 went to the king in Hanover to foment the misunderstandings between the king and some London ministers over the delay in the conclusion of the Triple Alliance between Great Britain, France, and Holland. Sunderland succeeded in ousting Robert Walpole and Charles Townshend from office and established a new ministry in which as northern secretary (1717), lord president of the council (1718), and first lord of the treasury (1718) he shared chief influence with James Stanhope (created Earl Stanhope in 1718). Sunderland's plan to maintain a permanent majority in the Lords by his Peerage Bill (1719) and his South Sea scheme (1720) both failed disastrously (*see* ENGLISH HISTORY). Stanhope died in February 1721, and in April Sunderland had to yield office to Walpole and accept his protection from political attack. Sunderland died unexpectedly in London on April 19, 1722. (W. R. WD.)

**SUNDERLAND, ROBERT SPENCER,** 2ND EARL OF (1641–1702), English statesman who held high office under Charles II and James II and who was one of William III's closest advisers, was the son of Henry, 3rd Lord Spencer (afterward earl of Sunderland), and Dorothy Sidney, daughter of Robert, 2nd earl of Leicester. He was born in Paris on Sept. 5, 1641, and succeeded to his father's titles on the latter's death at the Battle of Newbury in September 1643. He was ambassador to Madrid (1671–72) and to Paris (1672–73). He was sent to Paris again, as an envoy extraordinary, in July 1678, but he returned to London in October at the beginning of the crisis caused by the move to exclude James, duke of York (later James II), from succeeding Charles II. Sunderland was appointed secretary of state in February 1679.

His policies were not at first incompatible with his loyalty to his old patron the duke of York. With his uncle Henry Sidney (later earl of Romney) and his friends Sir William Temple and Arthur Capel, earl of Essex, he was soon identified with the group that supported Princess Mary (later Mary II) and her husband William of Orange (later William III) and rejected the claims of James, duke of Monmouth, to the succession. By 1680 he had emerged as one of the chief ministers of Charles. On the assembly (October 1680) of the Parliament that brought in the second exclusion bill, he decided that the duke of York must be sacrificed to prevent the complete triumph of Monmouth and the Whig opposition, and, although he could not convert the king to his views, he voted for the exclusion bill (November 1680). For this he was dismissed from his offices in disgrace in January 1681, but his abilities as an administrator and his knowledge of foreign affairs were such that he could not be permanently discarded, and the following year, aided by the influence of the king's mistress, Louise de Kérouaille, duchess of Portsmouth, he was reconciled with the king and the duke of York and returned to court in July 1682. He was reappointed secretary of state in January 1683.

From 1683 until the Revolution in 1688 Sunderland was associated with the authoritarian, pro-French, pro-Catholic policy that was a feature of this period. In December 1685, soon after James II's accession, he was appointed lord president of the council, and the dismissal of his chief rival and political opponent, Lawrence Hyde, earl of Rochester, in January 1687, left him as the chief minister. There is some evidence to show that he tried to moderate James's more extreme policies, but his own position at court was never strong enough for him to make a stand, even if his rather attenuated moral principles had dictated it. In June 1688 he felt obliged to turn Roman Catholic. On the other hand, there is no evidence to support the legend that he betrayed James by offering his support to William of Orange, and the probabilities are against it; though William always retained a high regard for him, which was manifested after the Revolution.

Dismissed in October 1688, Sunderland fled to Holland in December and was exempted from both James II's and William III's proclamations of pardon. He returned to England in May 1690, having abandoned the Roman faith, and in two years established himself as one of William's most valued political advisers and the principal intermediary between him and the parliamentary leaders. It was mainly his pressure that obliged William to form a new war ministry round the Junto Whigs in 1693. But the loathing with which the public, and many practising politicians, regarded him reached its peak in April 1697, when he made the mistake of accepting William's pressing offer of the lord chamberlainship. The hostile reaction of the House of Commons drove him to resign in December, and the king did not easily forgive his "desertion"; however, William was happy to consult him on the formation of a new ministry in 1700 and again in 1701. Sunderland did not long survive the king, dying at Althorp, Northamptonshire, on Sept. 28, 1702.

He married Anne Digby, daughter of George, 2nd earl of Bristol, in 1665. Their only surviving son, Charles, 3rd earl, married Anne Churchill, second daughter of the great duke of Marlborough, and their grandson Charles, 5th earl of Sunderland, succeeded as the 3rd duke of Marlborough in 1733. From him is descended the Spencer Churchill family.

*See* J. P. Kenyon, *Robert Spencer, Earl of Sunderland 1641–1702* (1958). (J. P. K.)

**SUNDERLAND,** a seaport, municipal, county and parliamentary borough situated at the mouth of the Wear river in County Durham, Eng., 13 mi. (21 km.) NE of Durham by road. Pop. (1961) 189,686. Area 13.4 sq.mi. (34.7 sq.km.). It is a great shipbuilding centre (shipbuilding was recorded as early as 1346) and has also big ship-repairing and marine-engineering works. Coal was first shipped from the port in 1396 and the tonnage exported per year from Wearmouth and other collieries had reached 5,000,000 before World War II. There are several foundries and the largest ships' anchors are made there. Other manufactures include telecommunication equipment, ropes, aircraft engineering, furniture, clothing, confectionery, pottery (the Sunderland lustreware was an early product), glass, beer and many more.

The Wear river commissioners administer the port of Sunderland which has a well-equipped deep-water quay and several wet and dry docks. The two curved piers at the entrance, on one of which stands a lighthouse, enclose about 130 ac. In addition to coal and coke Sunderland exports iron and steel, machinery, paper, coal tar, pitch, glassware, etc. The main imports are timber, grain, sisal and hemp, esparto, iron ore, wood pulp, fuel oil and petroleum. Within the borough are the seaside resorts of Roker and Seaburn, with fine sands.

In Sunderland there are a technical college, affiliated to Durham university and specializing in electrical engineering and other subjects, a teachers' residential training college and a college of art. There is a museum and art gallery.

**History.**—In 674 a monastery was established on the north side of the river by St. Benedict Biscop and a church built, dedicated to St. Peter. The church is still in use and retains parts of the original building. The Venerable Bede was born at Wearmouth about 673 and studied at the monastery. Biscop brought over skilled Frankish workmen who made glass for the windows of the church—the first recorded instance of glassmaking in England.

The area in which the monastery was located became known as Monkwearmouth. Sunderland was the part "sundered" from the monastery by the river. Bishopwearmouth, immediately west of Sunderland, had been granted in 930 to the bishops of Durham, by Aethelstan. In 1382 there was probably a dock there and from the 16th century Bishopwearmouth seems to have been completely identified with Sunderland. In 1567 Wearmouth was one of the three ports in Durham where precautions were to be taken against pirates, while no mention is made of Sunderland. Monkwearmouth remained purely agricultural until 1775, when a shipbuilding yard was established and prospered to such an extent that by 1795 five similar yards were at work. Prosperity continued until the depression of the 1930s caused severe unemployment—41% of the insured population in 1934.

From the 9th to the 11th century the district suffered from successive raids from the Danes and the Scots. Hugh Pudsey, bishop of Durham, granted a charter toward the end of the 12th century, elevating Sunderland to borough status. In 1634 Bishop Thomas Morton granted a further charter. During the Great Rebellion Sunderland supported the parliamentary cause. Newcastle took the royalist side and an embargo on ships leaving the Tyne resulted in increased shipments from the Wear. In 1717 a board of harbour commissioners was appointed to develop the port.

In 1796 the river was spanned by what was then the longest single-span cast-iron bridge in the world (an aluminum alloy bridge opened in 1948 also created a record). Sunderland was incorporated in 1634 and became a parliamentary borough in 1832. It returns two members to parliament.

**SUNDEW,** an insectivorous plant of the genus *Drosera,* of which there are more than 90 species with worldwide distribution. There are four species in North America and three in Europe. The most extraordinary development of this genus is attained in Australia and south Africa, where, in addition to the low, soft, herbaceous plants found elsewhere, occur tall plants attaining a height of three feet, with wiry stems that climb by the aid of adhesive leaf blades.

All species are carnivorous. They catch their prey by means of tentacles that spring in a regular pattern from the upper surface of the leaf blade. As many as 400 tentacles have been counted on a leaf of *D. rotundifolia* 0.9 cm. in diameter. The tentacles vary in size, shorter in the middle of the blade and much longer (0.6 cm.) along and near the margins. In some species with linear leaves there is little or no difference in size. Each tentacle consists of a stalk, broader at the base and tapering to the top, which supports an oval or rounded gland of rather complex structure. The middle of this gland is occupied by a cylindrical mass of water vessels enclosed within a bell-shaped layer of flat cells. The cells that form the edge of the bell extend to the outer surface of the gland. Covering this bell are two courses of cells normally filled with red or purplish sap. Each gland secretes and supports a droplet of mucilage, which accounts for the dewy appearance of the leaf. The red point of colour shining through the clear mucilage presents an appearance of rare beauty, which appears to attract insects. Connecting the gland with the vascular tissues of the leaf is a strand of vascular tissue extending through the stalk and base to the veins of the blade.

The tentacles are capable of motion. Darwin was the first to make extensive experimental studies on the matter. When a small insect alights on the leaf, its escape is prevented by the mucilage, which smears and smothers it during its struggles to escape. The presence of an insect provides a stimulus to neighbouring tentacles, which bend toward the prey and attach themselves to it by their mucilage, bringing a large contact surface to bear. A digestive ferment is secreted that attacks the nitrogenous content of the prey. The products of this digestion are then absorbed by the same glands. The movements of the tentacles are complex, but the net result is to bring the body of the prey toward the middle zone of the leaf blade, which itself can bend to surround the prey. There are also many minute sessile glands, scattered over both leaf surfaces, whose function is problematical. The leaf blade may be nearly orbicular, or linear and rushlike (it is then nonmotile), with various intermediate forms. Some are peltate (*i.e.,* having the stalk attached to the underside rather than to the base of the leaf) and circular, bowl shaped, or lunate, others variously ovate to large strap shaped.

Reproduction takes place not only by seeds but also by leaf buds, which spring normally from the bases of the tentacles, more abundantly on leaves that have been detached. In one or two species buds, in the form of gemmae, spring from the apex of the stem after the foliage leaves have been produced. Some species produce "droppers," special branches with negative geotropism, which penetrate the substrate. Their ends then enlarge into tubers. Closely related to *Drosera* are the genera *Drosophyllum* and *Byblis,* both carnivorous, and *Roridula,* which traps insects but does not utilize them as food.

*See* also CARNIVOROUS PLANTS.

*See* C. Darwin, *Insectivorous Plants* (1875; reprinted); F. E. Lloyd, *The Carnivorous Plants* (1942). (F. E. L.)

**SUNDIAL,** a device which indicates divisions of the day by the motion of the shadow of some object on which the sun's rays fall. It is one of the earliest examples of the application of man's knowledge of the apparent motion of the sun across the sky, and is constructed in various ways.

**History.**—The first device used was probably the gnomon. This consisted of a vertical stick or pillar, and the length of the shadow which it cast gave an indication of the time of day. By the 8th century B.C. it is clear that more precise devices were in use, and the earliest known sundial still preserved is an Egyptian shadow clock of green schist dating at least from this period. This clock consists of a straight base and a crosspiece set at 90° to it. The base was placed in an east–west direction and the shadow of the crosspiece fell across the base, upon which was inscribed a scale of six time divisions. Clocks of this kind are still in use in primitive parts of Egypt; they are positioned so that the crosspiece lies to the east before noon and to the west after noon.

Another early device was the hemispherical sundial or hemicycle. It is attributed to the Babylonian astronomer Berossus (Berosus, fl. *c.* 300 B.C.). Made of stone or wood, the instrument consisted of a cubical block into which was cut a hemispherical opening; to this was fixed a pointer or style, the end of the style lying at the centre of the hemispherical space. The path traced by the shadow of the style was, approximately, a circular arc. The length and position of the arc varied according to the seasons, so an appropriate number of arcs was inscribed on the internal surface of the hemisphere.

Each arc was divided into 12 equal divisions and each day, reckoned from sunrise to sunset, had therefore 12 equal intervals or hours. Because the length of the day varied according to the season, these hours likewise varied in length from season to season and even from day to day, and were consequently known as temporary hours. The dial of Berosus was widely used for many centuries, and, according to the Arab astronomer al-Battani (Albategnius, *c.* A.D. 858–929), was still in use in Muslim countries during the 10th century.

The Greeks, with their geometrical prowess, developed and constructed sundials of considerable complexity. Apollonius of Perga (*c.* 250 B.C.) developed the hemicyclium by using a surface of conic section upon which the hour lines were inscribed; this arrangement gave greater accuracy. Ptolemy used the analemma, a device which enabled shadows to be projected geometrically on to flat surfaces inclined at various angles to the horizontal. In general it appears that the Greeks constructed instruments with either vertical, horizontal or inclined dials, indicating time in temporary hours. The Tower of the Winds in Athens, which was octagonal in shape and dates from about 100 B.C., contains eight sundials. It is therefore clear that dials facing various cardinal points were in use for a long time.

The Romans also used sundials with temporary hours. The first dial set up in Rome in 290 B.C. had been captured from the Samnites, but it was not until almost 164 B.C. that a sundial was actually constructed for the city. In his great work *De Architectura,* M. Vitruvius (1st century B.C.) mentions many types of sundials, including portable ones.

The Arabs attached much importance to the study of sundials, the principle and design of which they derived from the Greeks. They increased the variety of designs available and, at the same time, simplified the processes of design and construction by using the principles of trigonometry. Abu'l Hasan, at the beginning of the 13th century A.D., wrote on the construction of hour lines on cylindrical, conical and other surfaces and is credited also with introducing equal hours, at least for astronomical purposes. With the advent of mechanical clocks in the early 14th century sundials with equal hours gradually came into general use.

During the Renaissance the construction of sundials flourished; there was a great diversity of forms, and some dials of considerable artistic merit were produced. The making of sundials was a profitable business and required not only considerable manual skill but also some understanding of the theoretical principles of the apparent motion of the sun; in consequence, the methods of sundial design and construction were jealously guarded trade secrets. From the 16th century onward, however, the growing spirit of inquiry into natural phenomena caused this secrecy to give way to open discussion, and in Basel in 1531 the German cosmographer Sebastian Münster (1489–1552) published his *Compositio Horologiorum,* which contained details of sundials and also of a moondial.

By the 17th century the study of dialing, as it was then called, formed a branch of education. The German Jesuit astronomer Christopher Clavius (1537–1612) published in 1581 the *Gnomonices,* in which he virtually summed up all knowledge on dialing at that time. Universal sundials, adjustable for use in any latitude, were a feature of the 18th century, although such instruments had been constructed earlier.

The increasing accuracy of clocks and watches eventually made the sundial obsolete. By the 19th century sundials were, in general, used only as ornaments in gardens, although it is to be noted that certain instruments of a very precise kind, such as the heliochronometer, were designed and used for scientific purposes.

CROWN COPYRIGHT, SCIENCE MUSEUM, LONDON

FLORENTINE CUBICAL SUNDIAL SHOWING ITALIAN HOURS, *c.* 1560

**General Principles.**—Timekeeping by sundial depends on the changing position of the sun in the sky. As is well known, this apparent motion is caused by the diurnal rotation of the earth and by the motion of the earth in an elliptical orbit about the sun. The diurnal motion causes the sun to appear to rise in the east and to set in the west. The orbital motion gives rise to three other factors which the designer of a sundial has to take into account if correct time indications are to be obtained. The first of these is due to the earth's motion about the sun as a focus; because of this the apparent motion of the sun is retarded, so that it takes four minutes longer to move across the sky than do the stars.

The second factor is due to the elliptical nature of the earth's orbit. This causes the earth to move more slowly when far from the sun than when near to it, so the velocity of the sun's apparent motion varies according to the time of year. Third, the inclination of the axis of diurnal rotation is inclined by 23° to the plane of the earth's orbit; therefore in summer the apparent path of the sun (the ecliptic) is higher in the sky than in winter and the duration of sunlight is longer. There is also the latitude of the observer to be considered; this affects the maximum height which the sun reaches above the horizon, and thus the inclination of the style or the position of the hour lines on a sundial.

Although it was not until the 17th century that the earth's orbit was correctly understood, sundials of considerable accuracy could nevertheless be constructed because dialing is concerned with the apparent motion of the sun. Temporary hours were sufficient until the advent of mechanical clocks, when reckoning of time in equal hours became necessary. Such equal hours give a mean solar time compared with the apparent solar time of temporary hours.

Mean solar time is based upon the behaviour of a fictitious body called the mean sun, which is assumed to travel along the celestial equator at a uniform speed. The mean sun coincides with the true sun at the equinoxes and solstices. The time difference between the two is known as the equation of time and is defined as mean solar time minus true solar time. The greatest numerical value of the equation of time, of the order of 16 minutes, occurs at a point between each equinox and solstice.

CROWN COPYRIGHT, SCIENCE MUSEUM, LONDON

IVORY TABLET SUNDIAL BY HANS DUCHER, 1574

For indicating true solar time a sundial is oriented so that the style lies in the meridian and, in the cases of vertical, horizontal and inclined dials, with the style parallel to the earth's polar axis, *i.e.,* inclined to the horizontal by an angle equal to the latitude of the place at which the dial is to be used. At local noon as indicated by the true sun, the shadow cast by the style should fall on the noon mark engraved on the appropriate hour line. A sundial may be oriented by means of a compass or, if a compass is not available, by a plumb line fixed to the end of the style. The shadows cast by the style and the plumb line should coincide over the noon mark at local noon. Local noon as indicated by the true sun may be obtained by taking the zone time and making due allowance for the equation of time and for the longitude of the place at which the sundial is being set up.

Sundials for use in the southern hemisphere are like those for use in the northern, except that the hour lines are inscribed in the opposite direction. The noon mark and orientation are obtained in a similar manner.

**Types of Sundial.**—*T-Shaped Dials.*—These dials were used in Egypt in very ancient times. They usually consisted of either a simple inscribed bar with a perpendicular endpiece or a central block with two sloping sides cut in steps and with a perpendicular rectangular block at each end. In the latter form the steps did duty for hour lines and the instrument was not, of course, reversed at midday.

*Hemispherical Dials.*—In the original form of these dials the hemispherical depression was cut in a block of stone, but later only part of the hemisphere was cut and the depression was situated at one end of the block to allow for easier fabrication. As noted, Apollonius of Perga used a conically shaped depression which gave greater accuracy. This type of sundial was revived in the late 16th century in Italy and Germany and took the shape of a cup or goblet. There the style was vertical and the hour lines were inscribed on the interior.

*Sunken Dials.*—In fashion during the Renaissance, sundials of this kind were usually made of stone. They were in essence a variation of the hemispherical dial, but the sunken depression took a great variety of forms. On one and the same dial cylindrical, triangular and heart-shaped depressions were sometimes cut, and it became popular to cut depressions of this kind into the buttresses of churches and into tombstones and other monumental stonework.

*Cubical Dials.*—Generally of painted wood and fixed to a stand, these sundials had a style set perpendicularly to the various faces. Different time scales were indicated on these faces; for example, a well-preserved cubical dial made in Florence about 1560 indicates "old Italian hours" (24 equal hours between sunset and sunset) on its north and south faces, "Babylonian" hours (24 hours between sunrise and sunrise) on its top face and the old Jewish system (12 hours between sunrise and sunset and 12 hours of different duration between sunset and sunrise) on the east and west faces.

*Column Dials.*—Sundials of this type had a cylindrical column on the top of which was a horizontal style fixed to a cap which could be rotated to allow for the sun's position at different seasons. The instrument was oriented so that the shadow of the style fell vertically, and time was indicated by the shadow of the tip of the style on hour lines inscribed on the cylinder. In order to set up the sundial it was necessary to know whether the sun was east or west of the meridian and, in consequence, a compass was often fitted to the base of the mounting. Column dials date at least from the 16th century, and some 17th-century portable dials are known. In Tibet varieties called "time sticks" have been discovered. In these, the gnomon is placed in a hole for the appropriate month. An example of a similar type, dating from the 10th century, was discovered during excavations in the cloister yard of Canterbury cathedral in 1939. This was of gold and silver and had a chain by which it could be suspended vertically. It is known as St. Dunstan's dial and may have been made by him. In both this and the Tibetan type of dial the shadow had to be vertical for a correct reading to be obtained.

*Ring Dials.*—The basis of such a sundial was a metal ring, usually of about 3-in. diameter and 1-in. width. Sunlight passed through a pin hole in the rim on to the inside surface of the ring, on which were inscribed a series of vertical circles corresponding to the various seasons, time being indicated on inclined hour lines. Such dials were suspended from a shackle on the rim. Ring dials appear to have been constructed first in the late 17th century, and some were elaborately designed with various refinements permitting adjustment for any latitude.

*Tablet Dials.*—These were made from two rectangular pieces or tablets of ivory, metal or wood, hinged together at one end. The gnomon was usually a string which, when the two tablets were opened out at about 90°, became taut. In orienting this kind of sundial, it was necessary to ensure that the shadow of the string fell at similar hour markings on both of the tablets. A compass was often included. Such dials were widely used in the 16th century.

*Flat Dials.*—Perhaps the best-known modern form of this type of sundial is that in which the dial is horizontal and the style is inclined from it by an angle equal to the latitude of the place where the dial is set up. Of such a kind is the garden sundial. Flat dials may, however, be so constructed that the dial is vertical or inclined by any amount to the horizontal. For any inclination the hour lines must be separately constructed.

GARDEN SUNDIAL, 1718

*Scratch Dials.*—These, to be found on many early English church walls, consisted of a horizontal gnomon with hour lines scratched into the surrounding stonework. In the simplest type the day is divided into four "tides" of three hours each. A good example may be seen at Daglingworth. In the 7th-century dial on Bewcastle cross, hour lines have been intercalated between the early tide lines, which are marked with crosses.

*Portable Sundials.*—Many sundials of this kind have been made at different times. The requirements for such a dial are that it should not be too large, that it should be capable of adjustment in azimuth and also of adjustment for latitude if it is to be portable over considerable distances. Such was the "ham" dial (1st century A.D.), which consisted of a piece of metal shaped like a ham; the gnomon or style was a vertical arm, and the hour lines were engraved on the metal body. In use it was suspended vertically from a chain. Other examples are column, ring and tablet sundials.

PORTABLE UNIVERSAL RING DIAL, *c.* 1800

*Scientific Sundials.* — During the 19th and early 20th centuries various sundials were developed to give results of an accuracy sufficient for scientific purposes. Of these perhaps the most notable were the solar chronometer made by the Scottish astronomer James Ferguson (1710–1776) and a universal heliochronometer of the early 20th century. The former consisted of two pointed rods parallel to the polar axis and close to each other, the shadow of these rods falling on a card mounted in a frame forming part of a cylinder of which the rods themselves were the axis. The hour lines on the card were so curved that an allowance was automatically made for the equation of time. Latitude and longitude corrections could also be made. The heliochronometer consisted of a disk set, by means of a quadrant, parallel to the celestial equator and mounted about a polar axis. Sunlight passed through a hole in one plate or on to a line on another plate, the time being indicated on the equatorial disk. The equation of time was allowed for by a cam which offset the first plate with respect to the second.

BIBLIOGRAPHY.—Ptolemy, *Almagest* bk. ii; *The Analemma;* M. Vitruvius, *De Architectura;* Johann Müller (Regiomontanus), *Kalendarium* (1489); A. Schöner, *Gnomonice . . . De descriptionibus horologiorum . . . omnis generis* (1562); S. Münster, *Compositio horologiorum* (1531); J. Delambre, *Astronomie ancienne* (1817); A. Gatty, *The Book of Sundials,* rev. ed. by H. K. F. Eden and E. Lloyd (1900); R. N. and M. L. Mayall, *Sundials,* 2nd ed. (1958); F. A. B. Ward, *Time Measurement,* pt. i, 2nd ed. (1958), pt. ii (1955); R. K. Marshall, *Sundials* (1963). (CN. A. R.)

**SUNDSVALL,** a seaport of Sweden in the *län* (county) of Västernorrland, lies at the mouth of Selångerån on the Gulf of Bothnia, 257 mi. (414 km.) N of Stockholm by rail. Pop. (1960) 29,355. It is the centre of one of the world's most important cellulose-producing regions and has aluminum and engineering plants. Chartered in 1621, it was burned by the Russians in 1721 and suffered further disastrous fires in 1803 and 1888. The town centre dates largely from the 1890s, when it was entirely rebuilt in brick and stone. Sundsvall is the seat of the Court of Appeal for Lower Norrland. (HE. WE.; X.)

**SUNFISH,** a name applied to several genera of North American perchlike freshwater fishes of the family Centrarchidae and also applied to an unrelated group of marine species of the family Molidae, the ocean fishes often seen sunning or resting in the surface waters of temperate and tropical seas.

**Freshwater Sunfishes.**—Among the many kinds of freshwater sunfishes, the bluegill (*L. macrochirus*) and the pumpkinseed (*L. gibbosus*) are the well-known plucky fighters prized by many fishermen. In general, the body, deep and rather compressed laterally, varies from a brilliant green to olive and, except in the bluegill, usually has orange or reddish spots on the sides; most species have a conspicuous dark membranous flap at the upper corner of the gill cover.

Sunfish inhabit ponds, lakes, and quiet streams. They mature in spring and early summer, at which time the female excavates, using her body and tail, a shallow nest about two feet across. After the eggs are deposited and fertilized, the male drives the female away and guards the nest till the eggs hatch and the young are able to shift for themselves. The bluegill sunfish, which may grow to be 12 to 14 in. and about 1½ lb., averages about 7–8 in. and less than ½ lb. It becomes quite stunted, however, when the food supply—crustaceans, snails, insects, and larvae—is limited, as in an overpopulated body of water. The bluegill sunfish has been widely introduced where ecological conditions are favourable, often in farm ponds in combination with black bass.

**Marine Sunfishes.**—The Molidae are curious oval-shaped fishes that appear tailless, the body ending abruptly behind the high, single dorsal and anal fins. They have a cosmopolitan distribution in the warm seas. The common ocean sunfish (*Mola mola*) and the sharp-tailed sunfish (*Masturus lanceolatus*) are large, stout, deep-bodied fishes. They reach a length of nearly 11 ft. and a weight of perhaps two tons. They feed on a variety of pelagic and bottom-living invertebrates and on small fishes. The oblong sunfish (*Ranzania truncata*) is longer in proportion to its depth and more compressed. It grows to be about 2 ft. long.

(L. A. Wd.)

**SUNFLOWER,** a coarse plant with sunburst flowers, belonging to the genus *Helianthus,* especially the common sunflower (*Helianthus annuus*). Sunflowers, of the family Compositae (*q.v.*), are native to North America, primarily the Great Plains region of the U.S. The common sunflower is an annual herb with a rough hairy stem 3 to 15 ft. high, broad, coarsely toothed, rough leaves 3 to 12 in. long, and heads of flowers 3 to 6 in. wide in wild specimens and often 1 ft. or more in cultivated types. The plant is valuable from an economic as well as from an ornamental point of view. The leaves are used as fodder, the flowers yield a yellow dye, and the seeds contain oil and are used for food. It is cultivated in the U.S.S.R., England, and other parts of Europe, in Egypt, and on the subcontinent of India for the seeds, the yellow sweet oil obtained by compression being considered about equal to olive or almond oil for table use. Sunflower oilcake is used for stock and poultry feeding and is ordinarily exported from the U.S.S.R. to Denmark, Sweden, and elsewhere.

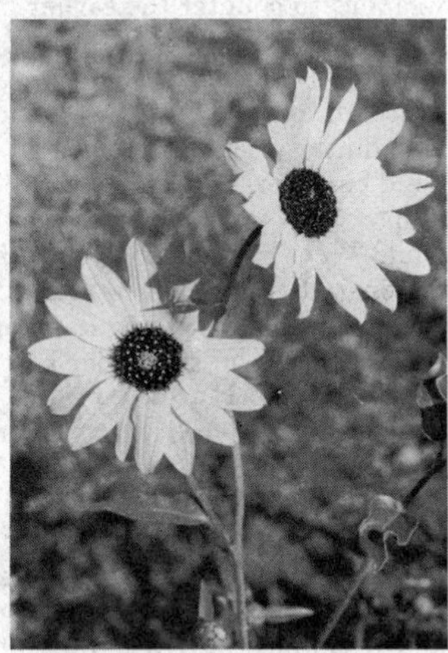

JOHN H. GERARD

PRAIRIE SUNFLOWERS (HELIANTHUS PETIOLARIS)

Of the approximately 60 species of *Helianthus* only a few are cultivated, some for their spectacular size. They are tall, hardy annual or perennial herbs, several of which are grown in gardens with moderately good soil. *H. decapetalus* is a perennial about 5 ft. high with solitary heads about two inches across in slender twiggy branchlets; *multiflorus* is a beautiful species with several handsome double varieties; *H. orygalis* is a graceful perennial 6 to 10 ft. high, with drooping willowlike leaves and numerous comparatively small yellow flower heads. *H. atrorubens* is a smaller plant, 2 to 5 ft. high, the flower heads of which have a dark red or purple disk and yellow rays. There are many fine forms of this, some of which grow 6 to 9 ft. high and have much larger and finer flowers than the parent species. Other fine species are *H. giganteus,* 10 to 12 ft. (3 to 4 m.), and *H. mollis,* 3 to 5 ft. (0.9 to 1.5 m.). *H. tuberosus* is the Jerusalem artichoke.

**SUNG,** a great Chinese dynasty and cultural period (960–1279) that marked one of China's most brilliant ages. The founder of the dynasty, Chao K'uang-yin (*q.v.*), named it for the ancient feudal state of Sung. It is sometimes called the Chao Sung to distinguish it from the Sung dynasty of the Liu house which ruled briefly in southern China (420–479). The era before 1127, when the capital was at K'ai-feng near the junction of the Grand canal and the Yellow river, is often called the Northern Sung, while the following period, when the Yellow river valley was lost to the Jurchen empire and the capital was normally at Hangchow in Chekiang, is called the Southern Sung. The founder and his successors, scholarly in tastes and educated under strong Confucian influence, proved unusually conscientious in promoting the stability, prosperity and intellectual life of their empire. The Sung brought to full flower trends of development begun in the T'ang (618–906). Its life, interests and accomplishments in many ways resembled those of Europe in the Renaissance.

**Sung Civilization.**—A characteristic of the age was the rise of commercial cities clustered along the principal canals and rivers and the southeast coast. Some were uniquely great for their times: Hangchow attained a population of 1,000,000 or more. These cities were walled and often symmetrically planned, with canals, broad avenues, market places, private gardens and public parks. Marco Polo described them soon after the dynasty's fall, when many of their features and customs were still preserved. Around the palaces and public buildings were the establishments of merchants, craftsmen, money-changers, dealers in intercity credit certificates, pawnshops, teahouses and wineshops. Citizens enjoyed the protection of state police and fire-fighting services, public baths, state relief, hospitals, orphanages and homes for the aged and destitute.

The canal system was extended to supplement the roads in linking the cities and to irrigate new farmland. Sea navigation served both internal and foreign trade—the size of the junks impressed even the Venetian Marco Polo. Long-distance exchange of common commodities made possible regionally specialized industries and agriculture. Improved strains of rice were introduced from Indochina and industrial entrepreneurs organized shops employing hundreds of workers. Iron, apparently smelted with the aid of coal, was cast in the form of pagodas and other objects of similar scale. Commerce was facilitated by a volume of copper coinage unparalleled in China before the 19th century and by the printing of paper money, whose circulation was successfully controlled until late in the 11th century.

With economic growth came social change. Merchants suffered less social stigma than before, and their progeny entered the bureaucracy more freely. Widespread printing of the classics and other writings from the 10th century, facilitated by the use of movable type in the 11th, opened the door to education for greater numbers. The private academies that flourished in more populous regions and state schools in several hundred prefectures and subprefectures prepared students for the national university at the capital. By increasing the numbers trained for governmental service, these developments broadened the distribution of influential offices, which during the earlier T'ang period had been largely monopolized by a few eminent families of north China.

The growing competition for bureaucratic positions encouraged a wider use of civil service examinations. Candidates were subjected to successive elimination through written tests on three levels, more than a hundred beginning the ordeal for each one who emerged successful; yet the numbers thus recruited rose from a yearly average of under 20 to over 200. The effort to devise objective and meaningful tests for practical qualities led to long contentions over subject matter and testing methods. To preserve the anonymity of the candidate and ensure fairness in grading, examination papers were copied by clerks, examinees were identified by number only and three examiners read each paper. Higher officials were privileged to nominate junior relatives for admission to the bureaucracy, but the great stress on examination grades in promotion and the practice of recruiting many lower officials from the ranks of the clerical service ensured a considerable freedom of opportunity. Promotion of the more able and reliable was sought through legally guaranteed recommendation by higher officials and by annual merit ratings.

The bureaucracy was successful in drawing into its ranks nearly all of the ablest educated men. As a result, the outstanding achievements in fields of the greatest diversity were by men active in government and politics. The "universal man" was the typical figure of the time. A leading official might be creatively concerned with philosophy, history writing, poetry, science or painting, and most often with several of these: Ou-yang Hsiu, Fan Chung-yen, Ssu-ma Kuang, Wang An-shih, Shen Kua, Su Tung-p'o, Chu Hsi, Lu Hsiang-shan and Wen T'ien-hsiang were but a few of the most famous. Women were represented by such examples as the poet-archaeologist Li Ch'ing-chao. The emperor Hui Tsung —painter of the first rank, calligrapher, patron of art and archaeology—was the best-known instance of such versatility among the Sung emperors, but not the only one.

**Political History of the Dynasty.**—The character of officialdom and the tradition of the ruling house created an atmosphere favourable to spirited political debate. After the vigorous rule of Chao K'uang-yin (960–976), who took the reign title of T'ai Tsu, and his brother T'ai Tsung (976–997), both circumstances and the rulers' personalities tended to confine their role to that of selecting the chief officials and resolving divergences over policy. The emperor Chen Tsung (997–1022) was unsettled in mind during his later years; on the accession of the 11-year-old Jen Tsung (1022–63) the empress dowager ruled as regent; his successor, Ying Tsung (1063–67), was an invalid during his short reign. The authority deputed to the councilors of state was tempered by the influences of the censorate, the bureau of policy criticism and the bureau of academicians, and discussions at court on questions of policy often ranged officials of these and other bureaus in opposing groups. While more ardent followers of Confucius were never satisfied that his precepts of government through moral principle, character and reason were fully applied, the early Sung perhaps came closer than any other period to realizing the Confucian political ideal in practice.

But factional divisions grew acrid as economic and military problems became pressing. Rising farm population and equal land inheritance aggravated the burden of heavy taxes for the small farmer, who often lost his lands to larger landholders who could keep their lands in better condition and farm them more effectively. While the government depended increasingly on state monopolies or excises—salt, metals, wine, alum, aromatics and foreign imports —the total state income had begun to decline. Fan Chung-yen and others had proposed and sometimes implemented schemes to deal with some of these problems, but the difficulties increased. Wang An-shih (*q.v.*) offered a more radical and comprehensive program to deal with the mounting difficulties. He advocated increased economic planning by the government and urged that the training of government officials be made more practical and technical. Firm support by the emperor Shen Tsung (1067–85) enabled Wang to carry out his program despite the antagonism of his leading contemporaries, which he invited by impatiently ousting from office all who questioned the prudence of any new measure. The magnitude of the problem and the bureaucrats' ineptness in applying the new laws limited their success. They were repealed under the regency of the empress dowager Hsuan-ho early in the reign of Che Tsung (1085–1100) and restored when the emperor assumed personal power. Despite the moderating efforts of the following ruler, Hui Tsung (*q.v.;* 1100–25), the struggle of the pro-Wang and anti-Wang factions continued for several generations, during which one or the other party was sometimes declared anathema and barred from all official rank or function.

In the meanwhile the military situation had further deteriorated. After the initial achievement of recovering from the Khitan (Liao) empire all that it had seized of north China excepting a small strip within the Great Wall, and the subjection of the independent principalities in south China, the rulers curtailed the powers of their commanders to forestall a recurrence of the war lordism that had destroyed the T'ang. The peace of the 11th century was unbroken until midway in Jen Tsung's reign when the new Tangut (Hsi-hsia) empire invaded the northwest frontier, and the Khitans in the north were kept neutral only through appeasement payments. The regular troops were softened by ease, and the enemy was repelled only by the raising of militia corps. Wang An-shih included in his program a provision for regular militia reserves and for army horses to be kept by farmers. The inadequacy of this was shown when the Jurchen (Chin) empire, after overthrowing the Khitan in alliance with the Sung, invaded China and attacked K'ai-feng. After a humiliating peace and the abdication of Hui Tsung to his son Ch'in Tsung (1125–27), the Jurchen renewed the fight, took both emperors captive and invaded the Yangtze valley. Under Kao Tsung (1127–62), who established the capital of the Sung at Hangchow, the Chinese responded to the emergency. Led by Yueh Fei and other generals they threw the invaders back. Perhaps for economic reasons, the councilor Ch'in Kuei nevertheless determinedly renounced the reconquest of the north, made peace with the Jurchen in 1141 and executed the recalcitrant Yueh Fei who was revered thereafter as China's national hero. Despite the fervid national spirit that could be aroused in times of crisis, the Chinese of the Sung had grown less martial and depended increasingly for military success on the technical development of weapons. Incendiary projectiles had long been used; explosive grenades appeared by the 13th century and by the end of the dynasty it appears that cannons were also employed. Such weapons also armed the large navy that was built up in the Southern Sung.

With such help the Sung Chinese enjoyed another century of relative prosperity and intellectual flowering, despite accumulating difficulties with monetary inflation and an unsolved farm problem, under the reigns of Hsiao Tsung (1162–89), Kuang Tsung (1189–94) and Ning Tsung (1194–1224). But China's security was precarious. The Jurchen, and then the Mongols who conquered them, in time discovered the secrets of China's new weapons, and technicians from occupied north China could copy them. Chinese technical skill was forced to surpass itself in creating still newer weapons to counter the earlier ones. Beginning in the second decade of the reign of Li Tsung (1224–65) and continuing through that of Tu Tsung (1265–74), the key fortresses guarding the northern approach by the Han river fell after a prolonged siege, and during the brief reigns of Kung Tsung (1274–76) and the child emperors Tuan Tsung (1276–78) and Ti-ping (1278–79) the Sung court sought successive refuges near the Canton estuary while Wen T'ien-hsiang and other loyal leaders fought defensive actions; it was believed that after a last unsuccessful naval engagement the Sung admiral perished in the sea with the infant ruler rather than surrender him to the Mongols.

**Intellectual and Artistic Achievements.**—In its cultural life the Sung dynasty was a time of beginning in some respects and of culmination in others. The rise of cities, new wealth and wider availability of education called into being new forms of entertainment to please simpler tastes and led a larger number to pursue more sophisticated forms of intellectual satisfaction. To the amusements of acrobatic troupes and displays of fireworks were added simple theatrical presentations that were to develop into the drama of later dynasties and itinerant storytellers whose prompting books held the plots of later historical and picaresque novels. The forms of verse developed by the great T'ang poets were employed subtly and elegantly as the habitual expression of educated men, reaching greatness at the hand of Su Tung-p'o, and a new form of poetry was brought to perfection—the writing of lyrics to well-known melodies. Great skill was devoted to artistic craftsmanship, and the manufacture of porcelain, while it did not reach the technical dexterity of the Ming and Manchu periods, attained perhaps its highest aesthetic perfection. Buddhist sculpture found its fullest grace; landscape painting, at the brushes of masters like Kuo Hsi, Hsia Kuei and Liang K'ai, attained successive heights of expressiveness, subtle mood and mysticism that were scarcely to be touched again.

While Buddhism had passed its intellectual prime in China, its past attainments challenged reviving Confucianism to create a metaphysical system that could answer the problems the Buddhists had raised. Freedom of speculation prevailed, and private academies taught a diversity of interpretations; the two most influential formulations were those reached in the 12th century by Chu Hsi (*q.v.*), whose discipline stressed the extension of knowledge, and the more mystical Lu Hsiang-shan. While the system of Chu would become orthodox in later times, that of Lu was the forerunner of Wang Yang-ming's heterodoxy. The explanation of nature concerned systematic thinkers like Chu Hsi, and men like Shen Kua combined active interests in mathematics, theoretical speculation and the many advances that Chinese were making in practical technology, ranging from new medical practices to the development of the mariner's compass.

Ssu-ma Kuang and Li Tao typify the many historians who applied more critical methods, created new forms of historiography to present the causation and relationship of events and treated recent history in works impressive for size and detail. The thought of the time is expressed also in the popularity of the essay; and the individual personalities of the period are well preserved in the many collections of letters and other smaller pieces that were first published in large numbers.

*See* also China: *History;* and references under "Sung" in the Index.

Bibliography.—A. C. Moule, *Quinsai: With Other Notes on Marco Polo* (1957); J. P. Lo, "The Emergence of China as a Sea Power," *Far Eastern Quarterly*, xiv, 489–503 (1955); E. A. Kracke, Jr., *Civil Service in Early Sung China, 960–1067* (1953); J. T. C. Liu, *Reform in Sung China* (1959); Clara Candlin, *The Herald Wind, Translations of Sung Dynasty Poems, Lyrics, and Songs* (1955); Laurence Sickman and Alexander Soper, *The Art and Architecture of China*, pp. 94–145, 255–268 (1956). (E. A. Ke.)

**SUNN** (Sann, Sunn hemp) is *Crotalaria juncea* of the pea family (Leguminosae), a well-known source of a stem fibre. *Crotalaria*, a large genus of tropical herbs and shrubs, mostly serves as forage plants. Sunn is probably native to India (although no longer found wild there); most species of *Crotalaria* are African, a few of them in addition to sunn being used locally for fibre. In India sunn is second only to jute as a source of bast fibre (stem fibres derived from the inner bark like hemp, rather than from leaf strands like sisal, or from seed hairs like cotton). Sunn fibre is used mainly for cordage. It is resistant to deterioration in water and so is well-suited for making fishing nets. Sacking, rope shoe soles, and stuffing are other local uses, and small amounts are imported into Great Britain for making paper, and into the United States for making cigarette paper. Sunn fibre is stronger than jute, but not quite so strong as hemp for which it sometimes substitutes. Production is almost entirely from India, and amounts to about 100,000 tons annually.

Sunn is unusual among legumes in having a simple leaf; most members of the family, such as clover, beans, locusts, and the vetches, have several leaflets. It is a shrubby annual from three to ten feet tall, with a deep taproot and showy, yellowish flowers. The swollen pods, about one inch long, contain several kidney-shaped blackish seeds, which are used to propagate the crop. At maturity the seeds rattle, giving rise to the name *Crotalaria*, from the Greek word meaning "rattle." The fibres are freed from the softer surrounding bark tissues by retting, as with jute. Retting involves decomposition or "rotting" of the thin-walled surrounding cells under moist conditions. The resistant fibre bundles can be sloughed free of decomposing bark and woody core. The strands are dried and marketed as yellowish hanks about four feet long. Sunn fibres are essentially pure cellulose, and so contribute no "off flavours" upon burning, making them suitable for cigarette paper. (R. W. Sy.)

**SUNNISM:** *see* Islam.

**SUNNYVALE,** a city of Santa Clara County in northern California, U.S., 39 mi. S of San Francisco, is noted primarily for its two major industries, electronics and guided missiles. Incorporated in 1912, the city adopted the council-manager form of government in 1949. Originally a part of the Mariano Castro land grant, it was known as Murphy's Station from 1850 to the turn of the century and then briefly as Encinal; the name Sunnyvale was officially adopted in 1912. Between World Wars I and II it was chiefly a cannery centre processing the fruit of the extensive orchards nearby. Industry came to the area during World War II and the Korean War; its population rose from 4,373 in 1940 to 52,898 in 1960. For comparative population figures *see* table in California: *Population.* (J. J. Ha.)

**SUNSHINE,** the sun's light; the direct rays neither scattered nor reflected; hence the warmth and light given by the sun's rays. Sunshine includes not only the visible portion of radiation from the sun, but also invisible ultraviolet and infrared rays (*see* also Sun). Radiation from the sun is the ultimate source of nearly all energy that is essential for the maintenance of plant and animal life on the earth and the operation of most natural phenomena on the surface of the earth. In particular, the amount and distribution in time and space of the solar radiation which is intercepted by the earth are the prime cause of weather and climate. (For man's attempts to harness the energy of the sun, *see* Solar Energy, Utilization of.)

The energy output of the sun has its peak at 0.47$\mu$ (0.00047 mm.) and radiates 8 kw. per square centimetre into space. At the earth's surface the amount received is on an average 1 kw. per square metre. The energy measured at the outer boundary of the atmosphere, the so-called solar constant, is 2 cal. per square centimetre per minute on a surface normal to the rays at the mean distance between sun and earth. The amount of possible sunshine for each point on the earth's surface is determined by latitude and season, as shown in Table I.

Table I.—*Possible Duration of Sunshine in Various Northern Latitudes (Hours:Minutes)*

| Date | 10° | 30° | 50° | 70° | 90° |
|---|---|---|---|---|---|
| Feb. 15 | 11:49 | 11:10 | 10:07 | 7:20 | 0:00 |
| April 15 | 12:21 | 12:53 | 13:44 | 16:06 | 24:00 |
| June 15 | 12:42 | 14:04 | 16:21 | 24:00 | 24:00 |
| Aug. 15 | 12:28 | 13:16 | 14:33 | 18:26 | 24:00 |
| Oct. 15 | 11:55 | 11:28 | 10:47 | 9:03 | 0:00 |
| Dec. 15 | 11:32 | 10:14 | 8:05 | 0:00 | 0:00 |
| Longest day | 12:35 | 13:56 | 16:09 | 24:00 | 24:00 |
| Shortest day | 11:25 | 10:04 | 7:51 | 0:00 | 0:00 |

**Duration.**—At the surface of the earth cloudiness is the primary factor governing the amount of sunshine actually received, but even through dense clouds or fog some diffuse radiation still penetrates. The insolation received through various cloud types (in percent of clear sky radiation) is: cirrus 83%, cirrostratus 78%, altocumulus 49%, altostratus 41%, stratocumulus 32%, stratus 25%, nimbostratus 20%, fog 18%.

The distribution of sunshine over the earth varies from over 4,000 hours per year; *i.e.*, more than 90% of the possible, to less than 2,000 hours in the storm belts. The Sahara Desert gets the largest amount, areas around Iceland and Scotland are among those getting least.

In the conterminous United States, Arizona shows the greatest amounts of sunshine, the Pacific northwest coast receives least. The variation throughout the year in terms of the possible duration in various parts of the world is given for a selection of representative stations in Table II.

The sunshine shows in most places a rather regular variation throughout the day. A common situation, representative of many parts of the U.S. and other moderate latitudes, is cloudiness in early morning, fewer clouds in late morning and early afternoon, and an increase in cloudiness again in late afternoon.

**Quality.**—The major portion of sunshine which penetrates through the atmosphere ranges in wave length from 0.29$\mu$ to 2.5$\mu$. Ordinarily, sunshine is broken down into three major components: (1) the visible, or that part between 0.4$\mu$ and 0.8$\mu$ (one octave of wavelength); (2) the ultraviolet, or that portion with wavelengths shorter than 0.4$\mu$; and (3) the infrared with wavelengths longer than 0.8$\mu$.

Because of a continual shift in the position of the maximum of the solar energy curve, no one factor can be used accurately to convert values in gram calories to values in footcandles. However, the value of 6,500 footcandles per gram calorie suffices for most practical purposes.

*Visible Radiation.*—Visible radiation is commonly termed light; however, the word light now has a broader meaning and includes the ultraviolet, or that invisible portion immediately adjoining the shortest wavelength of visible radiation. The visible portion comprises nearly one-half of the total radiation received at the surface of the earth.

TABLE II.—*Monthly and Annual Sunshine* in Various Parts of the World*

| Area | Station | Jan. | Feb. | March | April | May | June | July | Aug. | Sept. | Oct. | Nov. | Dec. | Annual |
|---|---|---|---|---|---|---|---|---|---|---|---|---|---|---|
| U.S. Atlantic | Boston, Mass. | 47 | 56 | 57 | 56 | 58 | 63 | 64 | 63 | 61 | 58 | 49 | 49 | 57 |
| | New York, N.Y. | 51 | 58 | 59 | 60 | 60 | 64 | 65 | 63 | 64 | 63 | 56 | 53 | 60 |
| | Washington, D.C. | 46 | 54 | 56 | 57 | 61 | 63 | 64 | 62 | 62 | 61 | 53 | 46 | 58 |
| | Miami, Fla. | 65 | 72 | 73 | 72 | 68 | 61 | 65 | 67 | 62 | 61 | 64 | 65 | 66 |
| U.S. Central | Chicago, Ill. | 44 | 59 | 53 | 56 | 63 | 69 | 73 | 70 | 65 | 61 | 47 | 41 | 59 |
| | St. Louis, Mo. | 48 | 49 | 56 | 59 | 64 | 68 | 72 | 68 | 67 | 65 | 54 | 44 | 61 |
| | Little Rock, Ark. | 45 | 53 | 57 | 62 | 67 | 72 | 74 | 74 | 68 | 66 | 58 | 46 | 63 |
| | New Orleans, La. | 49 | 50 | 57 | 63 | 68 | 65 | 58 | 59 | 64 | 69 | 60 | 46 | 59 |
| U.S. Mountains | Rapid City, S.D. | 58 | 63 | 63 | 62 | 61 | 66 | 74 | 74 | 69 | 66 | 58 | 54 | 64 |
| | Denver, Colo. | 67 | 67 | 65 | 63 | 61 | 69 | 68 | 68 | 71 | 71 | 65 | 65 | 67 |
| | Albuquerque, N.M. | 71 | 72 | 73 | 76 | 79 | 84 | 77 | 76 | 80 | 81 | 80 | 71 | 77 |
| | Phoenix, Ariz. | 76 | 78 | 82 | 87 | 93 | 94 | 83 | 84 | 89 | 88 | 84 | 76 | 85 |
| U.S. Pacific | Anchorage, Alaska | 41 | 47 | 55 | 58 | 50 | 50 | 45 | 39 | 32 | 28 | 35 | 28 | 44 |
| | Seattle, Wash. | 25 | 35 | 43 | 50 | 53 | 53 | 64 | 58 | 51 | 35 | 23 | 22 | 46 |
| | San Francisco, Calif. | 53 | 57 | 63 | 69 | 70 | 75 | 68 | 63 | 70 | 70 | 62 | 54 | 66 |
| | Los Angeles, Calif. | 70 | 69 | 69 | 67 | 65 | 69 | 78 | 80 | 78 | 76 | 79 | 73 | 72 |
| | Honolulu, Hawaii | 62 | 64 | 60 | 62 | 64 | 66 | 67 | 70 | 70 | 68 | 63 | 60 | 65 |
| Canada | Quebec, Que. | 30 | 47 | 40 | 41 | 41 | 44 | 48 | 48 | 42 | 36 | 25 | 26 | 39 |
| | Montreal, Que. | 30 | 37 | 43 | 47 | 48 | 52 | 57 | 55 | 50 | 40 | 27 | 23 | 42 |
| | Toronto, Ont. | 37 | 37 | 41 | 47 | 50 | 57 | 61 | 59 | 55 | 45 | 29 | 24 | 45 |
| | Vancouver, B.C. | 18 | 28 | 37 | 43 | 49 | 46 | 60 | 59 | 47 | 33 | 20 | 15 | 38 |
| Europe | Edinburgh, U.K. | 21 | 29 | 31 | 33 | 35 | 35 | 32 | 32 | 31 | 31 | 25 | 20 | 31 |
| | London-Kew., U.K. | 17 | 22 | 29 | 38 | 42 | 40 | 40 | 41 | 38 | 28 | 20 | 17 | 33 |
| | Paris, France | 21 | 31 | 36 | 39 | 49 | 47 | 50 | 50 | 42 | 33 | 23 | 20 | 37 |
| | Vienna, Aus. | 23 | 25 | 34 | 42 | 47 | 50 | 55 | 55 | 41 | 36 | 24 | 17 | 40 |
| | Rome, Italy | 38 | 45 | 42 | 44 | 50 | 62 | 76 | 73 | 59 | 47 | 44 | 37 | 53 |
| Near East | Cairo, Egy. | 61 | 62 | 62 | 67 | 76 | 85 | 85 | 86 | 77 | 71 | 70 | 62 | 73 |
| East Asia | Tokyo, Jap. | 61 | 55 | 50 | 48 | 46 | 35 | 44 | 50 | 38 | 40 | 55 | 61 | 49 |
| Caribbean | San Juan, P.R. | 64 | 68 | 70 | 65 | 59 | 61 | 64 | 66 | 60 | 63 | 62 | 64 | 64 |

*In percent of possible.

*Ultraviolet Radiation.*—While ultraviolet light comprises only a very small proportion of the total radiation, this component is extremely important. It produces vitamin D through the activation of ergosterol. It also is an important germicidal agent. Unfortunately, the contaminated atmosphere over large cities robs radiation of practically all the shorter wavelengths.

Ultraviolet and the near ultraviolet rays comprise the so-called actinic rays which are very potent in effecting chemical changes on photographic films.

*Infrared Radiation* has its chief merit in its heat-producing quality. Close to one-half of total solar radiation received at the surface of the earth is infrared. The spectrobolometer is the most important instrument for measuring small components of sunlight. Solar rays of different wavelengths are refracted on entering and emerging from a prism, the shorter wavelengths being refracted more than the infrared rays. It was through the use of the spectroscope and matched absorption bands that knowledge of the composition of the sun was determined.

The sunshine reaching the outer edge of the earth's atmosphere is closely equivalent to the radiation of a black body at a temperature of 5,800° to 6,000° C. On its path through the atmosphere this radiation is absorbed and weakened by various constituents of the atmosphere. It is also scattered by air molecules. This scattering, which occurs in the shorter wavelengths, causes the light-blue colour of the sky at the earth's surface. In the stratosphere, with fewer air molecules above the observer, the sky appears dark.

An effective absorber of solar radiation is ozone, which forms by a photochemical process at heights of 20 mi. and filters out most of the radiation below $0.3\mu$. Equally important as an absorber in the longer wavelengths is water vapour. A secondary absorber in the infrared range is carbon dioxide. These two filter out much of the solar energy longer than $1\mu$.

In the low layers of the atmosphere, dust scatters and absorbs effectively. At sunrise and sunset sunlight has a long path through the turbid air. The light is much attenuated and the short wavelengths are scattered. This causes the red colour of the sun at those times and permits one to look directly into the sun.

**Measurement of Sunshine.**—Several devices are used to record sunshine.

*The Campbell-Stokes Sunshine Recorder.*—This instrument consists essentially of a segment of a spherical metal bowl, having a glass sphere placed concentrically within it and centred so that the sun's rays are focused on a card lining the bowl. Direct sunshine burns a spot or a line on the card. Differentiation between a record of a few seconds and a minute of intense sunlight is difficult because the two traces are similar. Also, when the sun is barely visible through smoke or thin clouds, its rays are too weak to make a record.

Modified forms of sunshine recorders use blueprint paper mounted on a cylinder. The Jordan type contains two semicylinders with narrow slits in their narrow sides and, like the Campbell-Stokes recorder, maintains its own time record.

*The Marvin Sunshine Recorder.*—This is an air thermometer in which an electrical circuit is closed through the expansion of mercury by thermal action of the sun.

The instruments so far mentioned merely indicate when the sun shines.

*The Eppley Pyrheliometer.*—This unit accurately responds to nearly all the radiation which reaches the surface of the earth on a horizontal surface and gives quantitative results. The instrument consists of two concentric rings of equal area, one blackened and the other white coated. The hot junctions of a multiple thermopile of gold-palladium and platinum-rhodium alloys are attached to the lower side of the black ring, and the cold junctions are fastened to the lower side of the white ring. The differential in temperature between the two rings when radiation falls upon them creates an electromotive force that is nearly proportional to the amount of radiation received. The rings are mounted horizontally in the centre of a thin spherical glass bulb which is sealed to prevent deterioration of the receiving surfaces and also to prevent moisture from condensing within. The electromotive force generated by the receiver is recorded on a potentiometer and reduced to values in gram calories per minute per square centimetre.

For information regarding the biological effects of the sun's radiation, *see* RADIATION: BIOLOGICAL EFFECTS: *Radiation and Human Health: Effects of Hertzian Waves and Infrared Rays* and *Effects of Visible and Ultraviolet Light.*

*See* also METEOROLOGY: *Solar and Terrestrial Radiation;* and references under "Sunshine" in the Index.

(I. F. H.; H. E. LG.)

**SUNSTONE,** a variety of the mineral feldspar (*q.v.*) exhibiting a brilliant spangled appearance in certain directions, caused by minute scales of iron oxide arranged parallel to a cleavage. It is somewhat similar to aventurine. The best-known locality is in Tvedestrand, Nor. It is also found near Lake Baikal, Sib., and at several localities in the U.S., especially at Middletown, Pa., and Statesville, N.C.

*See* also AVENTURINE.

**SUNSTROKE:** *see* HEATSTROKE.

**SUN TZU,** reputed author of the first Chinese treatise on the art of war, probably lived in the early part of the 4th century B.C. His classic *Ping Fa* (*The Art of War*) is thus one of the earliest known compilations on the subject of war and strategy.

For centuries, the Chinese have accorded to the Sun Tzu *Ping Fa* preeminent position in their martial canon, and, throughout China's long recorded history, its military leaders have without exception been assiduous students of these succinct and perceptive essays.

The Chinese historian Ssu-ma Ch'ien, whose monumental *Shih Chi* (*Historical Records*) was completed shortly after 100 B.C., believed that Sun Tzu lived in the 6th century B.C., and that he served Ho Lü, king of the semi-barbarous state of Wu, as a strategist and general. This supposition, based entirely on folklore and legend, cannot be substantiated. Textual analysis indicates reasonably clearly that *The Art of War* was, in fact, completed several hundred years after the "Great Historian" believed it was. This opinion is shared by most Chinese scholars and literary critics, including several who are today prominent in the intellectual hierarchy of the Chinese People's Republic.

Sun Tzu lived during one of the most dynamic periods in Chinese history, a period in which five or six major states contested savagely for empire. War was not sporadic; it was endemic. It consumed the energies and resources of the states implacably, as their rulers attempted in turn to establish hegemony—to "roll up All-Under-Heaven like a mat and put the four seas in a bag."

These aspirations were encouraged by itinerant strategists, who wandered from one court to the next, propounding all sorts of novel schemes to rulers absorbed by ambition to create a universal state. Sun Tzu was no doubt one of these traveling "experts" or "consultants."

Of *The Art of War,* Capt. Sir Basil Liddell Hart, the strategist and historian, has written that Sun Tzu's essays on war "have never been surpassed in comprehensiveness and depth of understanding. They might well be termed the concentrated essence of wisdom on the conduct of war."

*See* Sun Tzu, *The Art of War,* trans. by Samuel B. Griffith II (1963). (S. B. G.)

**SUN WORSHIP.** The sun, as the most prominent representative of the heavens, plays a central role in primitive man's life. It regulates the change between day and night and is the benevolent giver of warmth as well as the terrible sender of unsupportable heat. In the ancient high cultures, as well as among preliterate peoples, the sun was an object of worship.

**Ancient Egyptian Religion.**—In Egypt the sun-god Re (*q.v.*) was the dominating figure among the high gods and kept this position from the most remote times. However, the sun was worshiped also by other names—as Kheper in the symbol of the scarab and as Horakhte, "the Horus of the Horizon." In the myth relating the voyage of the sun-god over the heavenly ocean, the sun sets out as the young god, Kheper; appears at noon in the zenith as the full-grown sun, Re; and arrives in the evening at the western region in the shape of the old sun-god, Atum. The right eye of the god, the Horus eye, as the "Sun-Eye," was the central figure of mythical speculation (*see* HORUS). When Ikhnaton (*q.v.*) reformed Egyptian religion, he took up the cult of the ancient deity Re-Horakhte under the name of Aton, an older designation of the sun's disk. The hymns of this age, the Amarna period, give insight into the deeper aspects of solar religion. Above all, the sun's qualities as creator and nourisher of the earth and its inhabitants are glorified. The great importance of the so-called Aton hymns is shown by their influence on Hebrew cult lyrics, as, for example, Psalm 104. (*See* further EGYPT: *History: Ancient Religion.*)

**Sumerian and Semitic Religion.**—The sun-god occupied a central position in both Sumerian and Akkadian religion, but neither the Sumerian Utu nor the Semitic Shamash (*q.v.*) was included among the three highest gods of the pantheon. In religious literature Shamash is above all a guardian of justice and punisher of evil. In the Epic of Gilgamesh he is the constant supporter of the hero. He sees everything and foretells the future, and for this reason the seers are attached to him. (*See* further BABYLONIA AND ASSYRIA: *Religion.*)

Shamash belongs to the oldest Semitic pantheon. As Shemesh he was worshiped among the western Semites, as is shown by many Palestinian place-names; and as the goddess Shapash, the same deity plays a certain role in the mythical epics found in the excavation of Ras Shamra (ancient Ugarit). The female character of the sun deity recurs also in Arabia, where Shams enjoyed a widespread worship. Traces of the male deity are found also in the Old Testament (Ps. 19:4–6).

**Indo-European Religion.**—The sun was one of the most popular deities of the Indo-European peoples and a symbol of divine power. Sūrya is glorified in the Vedic hymns of ancient India as the all-seeing god who observes both good and evil actions. He expels not only darkness but also evil dreams and diseases. His existence is attested as early as the Kassites of Mesopotamia, among whom Suriyash is found, as well as in the Mitanni kingdom of northern Mesopotamia, where the proper name Shuwardata, "Given by the Sun," occurs. The Indian Sūrya has a female consort, Sūryā, who is thought of sometimes as the daughter of Sūrya, and sometimes as the daughter of Savitar, apparently only an aspect of Sūrya. Sun heroes and sun kings also occupy a central position in Indian mythology, where Vivasvant, the father of Yama, corresponds to the Iranian Vivahvant, the father of Yima. There is a dynasty of sun kings, characterized by peaceful character, quite distinct from the warlike moon kings. This contrast returns in ancient Iran, where Yima is the peaceful sun king. The symbolic animal of the sun in Indo-Iranian culture is above all the horse. After an interregnum, when a new king had to be appointed, he was chosen at sunrise by the neighing of a horse. The sun horse obviously played a great role all over the Indo-European culture area and is attested also in Baltic folk songs.

Many of the gods in Indo-European religion show traces of solar qualities—among them, Mitra-Mithra (*see* MITHRAISM) in India and Iran, and Apollo (*q.v.*) in Greece—but the worship of the visible sun itself seems early to have faded from official religion. The deities possessing names derived from *svar-*, the root of Sūrya, such as *hvar* in Iran, Helios (*q.v.*) in Greece, Sol (*q.v.*) in Rome, and the visible sun in Germanic religion, are not included among the highest gods. Nevertheless their worship must once have been more important. A special Zoroastrian hymn is devoted to praise of the sun. Helios and Sol play considerable roles. Caesar (1st century B.C.) says that the Teutons worshiped the sun as a deity (*De bello Gallico,* 6, 21), and they celebrated sun festivals at those times of the year when the sun's appearance is of special purport.

In medieval Iran, sun festivals were celebrated as a heritage from pre-Islamic times. Such feasts are known also from India and Europe, where survivals are still found in popular customs. The centre of such festivals is occupied by fire rites and certain phallic ceremonies. The Indo-European character of sun worship is also seen in the conception of the solar deity, drawn in his carriage, generally by four white horses, common to many Indo-European peoples, and recurring in Indo-Iranian, Greco-Roman, and Scandinavian mythology.

During the later periods of Roman history sun worship gained in importance and ultimately led to what has been called a "solar monotheism." Influence from Oriental sun cults contributed to an already existing tendency. Nearly all the gods of the period were possessed of solar qualities, and both Christ and Mithra acquired the traits of solar deities. The feast of *Sol Invictus* (unconquered sun) on Dec. 25 was celebrated with great joy, and eventually this date was taken over by the Christians as Christmas, the birthday of Christ.

**Other.**—The most famous type of solar cult is the sun dance (*q.v.*) of the Plains Indians of North America, a complex conglomeration of rites, very important for the understanding of the position occupied by the sun in the religion of North America. In the pre-Columbian civilizations of Mexico and Peru, sun worship was a prominent feature. In Aztec religion extensive human sacrifice was demanded by the sun gods Huitzilopochtli (*q.v.*) and Tezcatlipoca (*see* also AZTEC; ANDEAN CIVILIZATION: *Inca Culture*). The ball games found both in pre-Columbian civilization and among the Indians of modern times symbolize the movements of the sun and possessed ritual significance. In both Mexican and Peruvian ancient religion the sun occupied an important place in myth and ritual. The ruler in Peru was an incarnation of the sun god, Inti, the divine ancestor of the deity. In Japan the sun goddess, Amaterasu, who played an important role in ancient mythology and was considered to be the supreme ruler of the world, was the tutelary deity of the imperial clan, and to this day the sun symbols represent the Japanese state (*see* JAPANESE MYTHOLOGY).

BIBLIOGRAPHY.—G. A. Dorsey, *The Arapaho Sun Dance* (1903), *The Cheyenne,* part 2, "The Sun Dance" (1905); F. Cumont, "La Théologie solaire du paganisme romain," *Mémoires présentés à l'Académie des Inscriptions,* vol. 12 (1909); F. Cumont, *Astrology and Religion Among the Greeks and Romans* (1912); W. Krickeberg *et al., Die Religionen des alten Amerika* (1961). (G. Wi.)

**SUN YAT-SEN** (1866–1925), the leading figure in the Chinese revolution of 1911 and a national hero for all factions in modern China, was born in a farming village in Kwangtung province, near Canton. When he was 13 years old an elder brother who had emigrated to Hawaii sent for him; there he was educated and converted to Christianity in an Anglican school. After a brief return to his village, where he showed himself impatient with traditional practices and beliefs, Sun left for Hong Kong in 1883. He completed training in medicine there in 1892, and practised briefly in Macao, but his real interests lay in politics, not in medicine. His experience in Hawaii and Hong Kong, his belief in Christianity, and his western education combined to make him eager for change in China. Because Sun Yat-sen was poorly grounded in the classical tradition of Chinese culture he drew his support from Chinese who were western-oriented as he was. He traveled constantly to recruit followers and solicit funds from Chinese living in southeast Asia, Japan and the western world. He also had many close friends in England and the United States. For a decade, during much of which he used the name Nakayama, Japan provided help for some of his many abortive revolts, and at the end of his life he looked to the Soviet Union for aid.

BROWN BROTHERS

SUN YAT-SEN

**Revolutionary Activities.**—In 1894 Sun Yat-sen made an unsuccessful attempt to present a memorial to the Viceroy Li Hung-chang urging reforms. The following year came the Japanese victory over China, and in its wake came Sun's first effort at rebellion in Canton. From then until the collapse of the Manchu (Ch'ing) dynasty he tried time after time to bring about a revolution. His tactics formed a link between the conspiratorial techniques of the old secret societies, which had always been strong in south China, and the more broadly based nationalist movements of modern times. Until 1911 Sun's program was dominated by a determination to rid China of the Manchus. To this end he allied himself with many other discontented groups. Japan, where thousands of Chinese students were to be found, was the scene of the organization of the T'ung-meng-hui (Combined League Society) in 1905. Although a broad program was set forth for the organization, its members were most firmly united on the nationalist, anti-Manchu goal.

**Early Years of the Republic.**—Sun Yat-sen was abroad when the Manchu dynasty fell, late in 1911; he returned to China a national hero. After a brief period as president of the Chinese republic, he resigned in favour of Yüan Shih-k'ai (*q.v.*), whose military strength forced the revolutionaries to compromise with him. It then became clear that Sun's republican associates could not agree on a political program. Sun trusted in the new constitutional machinery to control Yüan, but the latter, who enjoyed the financial support of international loan consortiums, was able to flout the will of the revolutionaries. In 1913 Sun staged an unsuccessful revolt against Yüan. Thereafter, once again a fugitive and conspirator, Sun entered upon a discouraging period during which he bargained desperately for foreign support. Henceforth he was less confident and trusting, and more concerned with practical politics and the strategy of power.

After Yüan Shih-k'ai's death in 1916 China entered the chaotic period of war-lord rule. By dealing with war lords in the Canton area Sun was able to set up a government there. But his real strength lay not with the war lords but with the students, merchants and workers of the modern cities, for whom he was becoming the best-known and most articulate representative of the new spirit of nationalism. When the Soviet Union turned its attention to China, Sun's movement seemed to offer the best prospects for a "united-front" drive against imperialism. By agreement with a communist agent in 1923 Sun received Soviet support for the reorganization of the Kuomintang (*q.v.*). The party was recast on communist lines, with leadership securely in the hands of the central executive committee. Soviet military advisers trained and equipped the new army headed by Chiang Kai-shek, and Chinese communists, who joined the Kuomintang as individuals, contributed their organizational skills and propaganda to undermine the war lords in preparation for the northern expedition that was to bring national unification.

Sun did not live to carry out this program. Shortly before the northern expedition was to begin he made one last attempt to negotiate with the war lords. After his death in Peking on March 12, 1925, his last testament, a moving document that instructed his followers to carry on his work, became his legacy to modern China. Acclaimed as the leader of the Kuomintang and father of his country, he was for a time the centre of a state cult. In character and personality he was ideally suited for such a role, for his integrity, idealism, courage and sincerity had played a large part in bringing about the final victory. But the choice of Sun's writings as the centre of a new ideology was less fortunate.

**Writings.**—Sun had read widely and had drawn his ideas from many sources, but he was primarily an activist, intent upon the selection of materials suitable for the needs of the moment. His revolutionary program had begun to form in 1905 when he first enunciated the Three Principles of the People (*San Min Chu I*). "People's Rule" (nationalism), "People's Authority" (democracy) and "People's Livelihood" (sometimes given as socialism) became the slogans of the revolutionary movement. These principles received their fullest treatment in lectures Sun delivered at Canton shortly before his death. Under nationalism he denounced foreign controls on China and called for a rise in national spirit. His approach to livelihood owed much to the single-tax doctrines of Henry George (*q.v.*). Most significant was his treatment of democracy. He saw his party, the Kuomintang, acting as an elite, preparing the Chinese people for democracy against the day when they would be able to take over the task of governing themselves. There again Sun's ideas were garnered from many sources. He distinguished between the four powers of the people (election, recall, initiative and referendum) and the five powers of the government (legislative, executive, judicial, civil service examinations and censorate). The skilled elite would run this elaborate machinery just as an engineer would run a railroad train. Clearly this acceptance of the necessity of a period of one-party rule would defer indefinitely the establishment of democracy in China.

Perhaps because of the lack of a systematic treatment of these topics, Sun Yat-sen's writings were later made to serve many purposes. His mantle was claimed by Wang Ching-wei, who headed the puppet government at Nanking during the Japanese occupation, and also by Chiang Kai-shek, who carried the northern expedition to completion and headed the new Nationalist regime. Sun Yat-sen's widow, who was the sister of Mme Chiang Kai-shek, professed to find the program of the Communist government, which she served in high posts, in harmony with her husband's views. But it was above all the Nationalist government of Chiang Kai-shek that laid claim to Sun's memory. Sun Yat-sen's son by his first marriage, Sun Fo, held many important positions in the Nationalist administration. A magnificent mausoleum for Sun Yat-sen was erected on Purple mountain outside Nanking, and Sun's title as Kuomintang Leader, *Tsung-li*, remains his in perpetuity. *See* CHINA: *History; see* also references under "Sun Yat-sen" in the Index.

BIBLIOGRAPHY.—Sun Yat-sen, *Kidnapped in London* (1897), *The International Development of China*, 2nd ed. (1929), *Memoirs of a Chinese Revolutionary* (1927), *The Three Principles of the People* (1927); P. M. W. Linebarger, *Sun Yat Sen and the Chinese Republic* (1925); Lyon Sharman, *Sun Yat-sen: His Life and Its Meaning* (1934; repub. 1965); Marius B. Jansen, *The Japanese and Sun Yat-sen* (1954); T. C. Woo, *The Kuomintang and the Future of the Chinese Revolution* (1928), *Tsung-li ch'üan-chi* ("Complete Collected Works of the Leader") ed. by Hu Hanmin (1930). (M. B. J.)

**SUPERCONDUCTIVITY:** *see* LOW-TEMPERATURE PHYSICS: *The Phenomenon of Superconductivity.*

**SUPERFLUIDITY:** *see* LOW-TEMPERATURE PHYSICS: *Areas of Low-Temperature Research: The Behaviour of Liquid Helium.*

**SUPERIOR,** the most northwesterly city of Wisconsin, is situated between the bays of St. Louis and Allouez on Lake Superior; it is the seat of Douglas County. With its twin port, Duluth (*q.v.*), it forms the western terminus of the St. Lawrence Seaway; through the natural harbour shared with Duluth are shipped iron ore, coal, grain, and crude oil. The Superior harbor shipping facilities include four ore docks, averaging 2,250 ft. (686 m.) in length and 80.5 ft. (24.5 m.) in height, with a total capacity of 500,000 gross tons; eight grain elevators with a 30,500,000-ton capacity; and ten coal docks with a capacity of more than 3,500,000 tons. Crude oil arrives at Superior from Canada through a 1,127-mi. (1,814 km.) pipeline to be refined. Other industries include shipbuilding and the manufacture of coal briquettes, flour, beer, and dairy and wood products.

Pop. (1960) city 33,563; Duluth-Superior standard metropolitan statistical area (St. Louis County, Minn., and Douglas County, Wis.) 276,596. For comparative population figures, *see* table in WISCONSIN: *Population.*)

The Superior area was occupied originally by the Sioux (Dakota) and Chippewa Indians. In 1655 the Jesuit Father Claude Allouez built a mission near the bay that bears his name. Pierre Esprit Radisson and Médard Chouart des Groseilliers arrived in 1661. Trading posts were established about 1678 by Daniel Greysolon, Sieur Dulhut (or Duluth) and about 1820 by the Hudson's Bay Company. Permanent settlement did not take place until 1853, one year after the government survey made by George R. Stuntz. Lands were purchased, and settlement was made at the eastern end of present Superior, the Allouez Bay area, where names of avenues recall early speculators, such as William Wilson Corcoran, former Sen. Robert J. Walker, and Congressman John C. Breckinridge. A second settlement was made in 1882 by Gen. John H. Hammond; he organized the Land and River Improvement Company, which platted the townsite of West Superior on St. Louis Bay. The third townsite was South Superior. Both West and South Superior were joined with the original East End settlement, and the united municipality was incorporated as the City of Superior in April 1889. Between 1941 and 1959 the city was administered by a city manager and seven councilmen; then the mayor-council form of government was adopted.

Superior is the site of a Wisconsin State University, opened in 1896. The city has public and parochial high schools, a Carnegie Library with several branches, and the Douglas County Historical Museum.

Proximity to Lake Superior, numerous small lakes, and Brule River, famous for trout fishing and canoeing, make the area a tourist haven. Along the St. Louis River is Billings Park. Manitou Falls, the largest in Wisconsin, is 14 mi. S of Superior.

(E. F. GR.)

**SUPERIOR, LAKE,** named from the French *Lac Supérieur,* meaning "Upper Lake," and the most northwesterly of the five Great Lakes of North America, is the largest body of fresh water in the world. It is bounded on the east and north by the province of Ontario, on the west by the state of Minnesota and on the south by Wisconsin and Michigan. The general form of Lake Superior is that of a wide crescent convex toward the north. It is 383 mi. (616 km.) long (on a straight line) in an east-west direction and its greatest width is 160 mi. (257 km.). The surface area of the lake is 31,800 sq.mi. (82,362 sq.km.) and the area of its drainage basin, exclusive of lake area, is 48,200 sq.mi. (124,838 sq.km.). The mean height of the lake above sea level is 600 ft. (183 m.), 22 ft. (6.7 m.) above that of Lake Huron, to which it is joined at its eastern extremity by the St. Marys river. Its maximum recorded depth is 1,333 ft. (406 m.), 733 ft. (223 m.) below sea level. (For comparison with the other Great Lakes, a discussion of their origins, connections, utilization, etc., *see* GREAT LAKES, THE.)

**History.**—Pierre Radisson and Médard des Groseilliers traveled extensively on Lake Superior in 1659–60 and returned to the east with a valuable cargo of furs. Father Claude Jean Allouez circumnavigated the lake by canoe in 1667 and prepared a map of the lake which was the most accurate drawn until recent times.

Daniel Greysolon, Sieur Dulhut, known as Duluth, opened Lake Superior to active trading in 1679. Fur trading by the French then flourished at intervals, but in 1763 the entire region was ceded to Great Britain. Lake Superior was under formal British control until the close of the American Revolution in 1783; after that, trade continued in the hands of the British until 1817 when John Jacob Astor's American Fur Company took control of trade south of the international boundary line.

**Physiography.**—The lake receives the drainage of approximately 200 rivers. The largest tributary is the Nipigon river, entering from the north and draining Lake Nipigon, and the second largest is the St. Louis river, entering from the west at Duluth. Other principal rivers of the north shore are the Pigeon, which forms the international boundary northwestward from the lake, the Kaministikwia, which enters Thunder bay at Fort William, the Pic, the White and the Michipicoten. No large rivers empty into the lake from the south. The outlet, the St. Marys river, carries a mean annual discharge of 73,100 cu.ft. per second.

Going outward from the lake in any direction except the southeast, one soon comes to an escarpment above which is a distinct upland overlooking the lake basin. At many places the escarpment, 400 to 800 ft. (122 to 244 m.) high, descends into water 500 to 800 ft. (152 to 244 m.) deep. The coast line is picturesque, the north shore particularly being indented by deep bays surrounded by high cliffs. The principal islands in the lake are Isle Royale, 44 mi. (71 km.) long, near the northwestern shore, which is a U.S. national park; Michipicoten, 17 mi. (27 km.) long, in the eastern part; and the Apostle Islands, a group off the Wisconsin shore in the southwest. Abandoned shore lines indicate that the lake once stood about 200 ft. (61 m.) higher and drained southwestward to the Mississippi river while glacial ice occupied the eastern part of the basin, and that later the lake discharged into Green Bay of Lake Michigan before its present outlet was uncovered by melting of the ice sheet.

The ancient (Precambrian) rocks which nearly surround Lake Superior contain valuable mineral deposits. For many years the Lake Superior district was the largest producer of copper in the United States. Iron ore was mined and smelted locally in the Negaunee and Marquette areas during 1848–54. The opening in 1855 of the ship canal along St. Marys river (*see* SAULT SAINTE MARIE) was followed by regular shipment of iron ore from the Marquette district to the lower lakes. Subsequently iron was produced from many parts of the Lake Superior district, including the Mesabi range in Minnesota (*see* IRON AND STEEL INDUSTRY). By the second half of the 20th century high-grade iron ores were becoming scarce but improved technology permitted the use of abundant taconite and other low-grade ores.

**Harbours and Commerce.**—Lake Superior is fairly well provided with natural harbours, and works of improvements have created additional harbours at various points. Fort William at the mouth of the Kaministikwia river and Port Arthur, 4 mi. (6.4 km.) distant, with an artificial harbour, are the lake terminals of two Canadian transcontinental railway systems and they ship grain from the western prairies. Taconite Harbor, Minn., formed by joining two islands to the shore with breakwaters, and Two Harbors, Minn., on a natural bay improved with breakwaters, are important shipping points for iron ore. Duluth, Minn., and Superior, Wis., are located at the western end of the lake on a large natural harbour, formed by a sand bar across the mouth of the St. Louis river, with two entrances maintained by piers. This port ships a large tonnage of iron ore, grain and flour. The principal ports along the south shore of the lake are Ashland, Wis., with a harbour formed by a breakwater; Houghton and Hancock, Mich., located on a 25-mi. (40 km.)-long canal across the Keweenaw peninsula; and Marquette, Mich., with an artificial harbour. These ports ship large tonnages of ore. The traffic to and from Lake Superior via the United States and Canadian locks at Sault Ste. Marie amounts to approximately 100,000,000 tons annually.

A large part of the land surrounding Lake Superior is very sparsely settled and much of it is a wilderness. Extensive forests are held in federal, state, provincial and private timber lands.

Hunting and sport fishing in season and tourism in the summer months form the basis for an increasingly important recreation industry in the region.

Bibliography.—Canadian Hydrographic Service, *Great Lakes Pilot,* vol. iii and charts (annually); U.S. Army Corps of Engineers, U.S. Lake Survey, *Great Lakes Pilot* and charts (annually); G. L. Nute, *Lake Superior* (1944). (J. L. Hh.)

**SUPERNATURALISM,** a belief in an otherworldly reality that, in one way or another, is found in all forms of religion.

The idea of nature is unknown to primitive man, who inhabits a wonder world charged with the sacred power of *mana* (*q.v.*) and spirits. Primitive man associates the uncanny, the unusual or the powerful of any kind (including so-called natural phenomena such as the rising of the sun and the prowess of a warrior) with the presence of a sacred power.

In the higher religions, a gulf usually is created between the supernatural and natural realms. Thus, for example, Christianity distinguishes between this world and the Kingdom of God, or nature and grace, or earth and heaven. Hinduism in its various forms draws a polar distinction either between nature and spirit or between *samsara* (the world) and Brahman-Atman (the deity); and in the Vedanta school of Hinduism the world becomes *maya* (illusion).

Early Buddhism drew a radical distinction between the world as pain and suffering (*samsara*) and the redemptive goal of the disciple (*nirvana*), while refusing to look upon *nirvana* as a supernatural realm of existence. Certain later schools of Mahayana Buddhism postulated a mystical and paradoxical identification of *nirvana* and *samsara.* This identification of the world and the Beyond, the profane and the sacred, is virtually unique in the history of religions, although it has a parallel in the Hasidic school of Jewish mysticism.

Far eastern religions have never abandoned their primitive roots; and in Confucianism, Taoism and various sects of Chinese and Japanese Buddhism no genuine distinction is made between the natural and the supernatural.

The secularization of modern western civilization has created a gulf between the natural and the supernatural resting upon the idea of an autonomous nature existing apart from the influence or control of God. Here, the world becomes a profane reality wholly isolated from the sacred. This situation led to Nietzsche's proclamation of the "death" of God and his condemnation of Christianity as a flight from reality and an escape to an otherworldly nothingness.

So pervasive is the modern experience of the unreality of the supernatural realm that certain schools of Protestant theology have collapsed the distinction between the natural and the supernatural. This is fully apparent in process theology, as exemplified by H. N. Wieman, and partially so in the existentialist school of dialectical theology led by Paul Tillich and Rudolf Bultmann (*see* Neo-orthodoxy). In the one case is found an affirmation of a rational and scientific universe that will admit the existence neither of a supernatural realm nor of a God who exists wholly apart from the world; in the other, a dialectical conception of faith that conceives it as leading the believer in some sense beyond the world while at the same time insisting that true faith leads the Christian into the depths of his present existence in such a way as to exclude the possibility of a belief in an actual supernatural realm.

Bibliography.—R. R. Marett, *The Threshold of Religion* (1914); Rudolf Otto, *The Idea of the Holy* (1923); Mircea Eliade, *Patterns in Comparative Religion* (1958); H. N. Wieman, *The Source of Human Good* (1946); Paul Tillich, *The Protestant Era* (1948). (T. J. J. A.)

**SUPERNOVA:** *see* Nova and Supernova.

**SUPERSTITION,** an irrational belief, half belief, or practice. Those who use the term imply that they have certain knowledge or superior evidence for their own scientific, philosophical, or religious convictions (*see* Knowledge, Theory of). But the word is ambiguous, and it seems likely that it cannot be used except subjectively. With this qualification in mind, superstitions may be classified roughly as religious, cultural, and personal.

Every religious system tends to accumulate superstitions as peripheral beliefs—a Christian, for example, may believe that in time of trouble he will be guided by the Bible if he opens it at random and reads the text that first strikes his eye. Over and beyond these, however, one man's religion is another man's superstition: Tacitus called Christianity a pernicious superstition; Constantine called paganism superstition; Catholic veneration of relics, images, and the saints appears superstitious to many Protestants; Christians regard many Hindu practices as superstitious; adherents of all "higher" religions may consider the Australian aborigine's relation to his totem superstitious; and all religious beliefs and practices may seem superstitious to the person without religion.

Superstitions that belong to the cultural tradition (in some cases inseparable from religious superstition) are enormous in their variety. Nearly all men, in nearly all times, have held, seriously or half seriously, "irrational beliefs" concerning methods of warding off ill or bringing good, foretelling the future, and healing or preventing sickness or accident. A few specific beliefs, such as that in the evil eye or in the efficacy of amulets, have been found in most periods of history and in most parts of the world. Others may be limited to one country, or one region, or one village, to one family or one social or vocational group. Some of them stem from a body of outmoded learning (such as astrology), from a superseded religion (as, according to Margaret Murray, the medieval witch cult in Europe, traces of which probably can still be seen, represents the remains of pre-Christian pagan religion), from magical practices whose original significance has been long forgotten (as touching wood when mentioning a run of good fortune), or merely from a conservatism that continues to accept without question explanations or ideas once they have become current.

And, finally, people develop personal superstitions: a schoolboy writes a good examination paper with a certain pen, and from then on that pen is "lucky"; a horseplayer may be convinced that gray horses run well for him.

Superstition, defined as above, has been deeply influential in world history. It would be impossible to estimate how many people have been hanged or burned as adults or drowned in infancy, how many battles have been fought, drawn, or evaded, how many journeys undertaken or withdrawn from because of superstition. Being irrational, superstition, one would say, must recede before education and, especially, science. Once an astronomer has been able to provide a natural explanation for solar eclipses and predict to the day and minute the occurrence of the next one, those who are within reach of his voice or his writings are much less likely to believe that an eclipse is a sign of the gods' disapproval of some act of man. Many superstitious observances are little more than automatic habitual reactions: a physicist may comment on a black cat's crossing his path; a cultured Chinese may consult his astrologer, or an educated American may glance at the horoscope in his newspaper every day. Others may represent nothing more than an unvoiced notion that one might as well not invite trouble—it is just as easy to walk around a ladder as under it. If the question is put to him seriously, the boy will acknowledge that the pen is no more lucky than any other, and the horseplayer will admit that gray horses have failed him. But even in a day when objective evidence is valued very highly, there are few people who, if pressed, would not admit to cherishing secretly one or two irrational beliefs, or superstitions.

*See* also Amulet; Divination; Evil Eye; Magic; Magic, Primitive; Witchcraft; and references to "Superstition" in the Index. (K. S. Ra.)

**SUPERTONIC,** in music, the second degree of the diatonic tonal scale, as D in the scale of C, that is, the note next above the tonic, whence its name. *See* Scale.

**SUPILO, FRANO** (1870–1917), Croatian patriot who played a significant role in the conflicts preceding the birth of an independent South Slav state. He was born into a peasant family on Nov. 30, 1870, at Cavtat in Dalmatia. From 1900 he edited *Novi List,* a Croatian newspaper at Rijeka, which strongly opposed Austrian and Hungarian encroachment on Croatian interests. In 1905, together with Pero Čingrija and Josip Smodlaka, he drew up the Rijeka Resolution, which led to the formation of a new political group, the Croato-Serb coalition. Supilo became the first president of this group and the instigator of anti-Austro-Hungarian activities in Croatia. In order to discredit him the Austrian Foreign Office supplied documents, allegedly proving his collusion with Serbia, to the publicist Heinrich Friedjung (*q.v.*); but Supilo and other coalition leaders then sued Friedjung for defaming them, and they were vindicated at a sensational trial in Vienna (December 1909), when the documents were shown to be forgeries. Even so, Supilo gave up his presidency, and the coalition adopted an opportunist attitude toward Budapest.

During World War I, Supilo went over to the Allied side and, together with Ante Trumbić and Ivan Meštrović, started the movement for the liberation of the South Slavs. From a talk with S. D. Sazonov, the Russian foreign minister, he learned of the negotiations between the Allies and Italy. The Allies were promising that extensive territories along the eastern Adriatic coast, to be taken from Austria-Hungary, should go to Italy. Supilo and his friends, who had formed the Yugoslav Committee, warned the Allied leaders against this and propagated the idea of establishing a South Slav state. Favouring a federalist constitution for this union as a security valve against Serb predominance, he came into conflict with Nikola Pašić (*q.v.*). Supilo proposed that agreement with Serbia on the constitution of the future Yugoslavia should precede all efforts for unification. Outvoted on this point, he resigned from the Yugoslav Committee; but shortly before his death, which took place in London on Sept. 23, 1917, he endorsed the Declaration of Corfu of July 20, which Trumbić and the committee had negotiated with Pašić.

*See* Josip Horvat, *Frano Supilo* (1938). (A. S. PA.)

**SUPPÉ, FRANZ VON** (real name FRANCESCO EZECHIELE ERMENEGILDO SUPPÉ DEMELLI) (1819–1895), Austrian composer of light operas written in the style of Offenbach, who greatly influenced the development of Austrian and German light music up to the middle of the 20th century. Born at Spalato (Split) on April 18, 1819, he came from a family of Belgian origin that had lived in Italy for two generations. In his youth he went to Vienna, where he studied composition with S. Sechter and I. X. Seyfried and took advice from Donizetti. Later he conducted at the Theater an der Wien, the Josephstadt, and other theatres in Vienna. In 1841 he wrote the incidental music for a play at the Josephstadt Theatre and thereafter wrote numerous comic operas and operettas, as well as incidental music, including the overture for the play *Dichter und Bauer* ("Poet and Peasant," Vienna, 1846). His most successful comic operas were produced in Vienna and include *Leichte Kavallerie* (1866), *Fatinitza* (1876), and *Boccaccio* (1879). He also wrote choral works, a symphony, and string quartets. He died in Vienna on May 21, 1895.

*See* O. Keller, *Franz von Suppé der Schöpfer der deutschen Operette* (1905); E. Rieger, *Offenbach und seine Wiener Schule* (1920).

**SUPPLY AND DEMAND.** The celebrated "law of supply and demand" in economics can be formulated simply by saying that for each commodity some price must exist that will cause the supply and the demand for any commodity or source to be just equal. Such a price will "clear the market." This principle of supply and demand was called the "first, greatest, and most universal principle" of political economy by one of the early giants among economists, Thomas R. Malthus. His enthusiasm may have carried him a little too far, but probably not by very much.

Supply and demand can be spoken of in two possible contexts, one that concerns individual commodities, and another that considers the aggregate of all commodities taken together. In discussing individual commodities the first point to be made clear is that supply, or demand, should be thought of not in terms of what is actually supplied, or demanded, in any given instance but rather in terms of schedules of potential supplies, at various possible prices, and of potential demands. One would indicate the willingness of suppliers to sell at various prices, the other the willingness of potential customers to buy. At any one price the two may or may not match. It is the function of markets to make them match.

**Characteristics of Demand.**—A curve relating willingness to buy to various prices is usually drawn with a "negative" slope, indicating that this willingness declines as prices rise. The justification for this practice can be seen if the two major types of markets are considered separately, first the market for consumer goods and services, then the market for services of the factors of production, land, labour, and capital. In the first it is discovered that as the price of a certain commodity rises, more of any consumer's income will be lost on it should the consumer maintain the volume of his purchases. Less would be left over for other commodities, whose purchases must therefore decline.

But as purchases of some alternative commodity decline, the alternative commodity becomes scarcer—and hence more valuable —in the eyes of the consumer. It is likely, therefore, that the consumer will become increasingly reluctant to sacrifice more of it, and prefer to reduce instead his purchases of the commodity whose price has risen. This causes the "demand curve" to have a negative slope in the market for each individual consumer good.

What causes the demand curve in the market for productive factors to have a similar slope? Naturally an enterprise would not hire any such factor unless its contribution to the revenues of the firm were sufficient at a minimum to cover the cost of that factor. For example, in the case of labour, an employer seeking to maximize profits for his firm would have to continue to hire labourers as long as—for each additional workman—the product exceeded the wage. Suppose, however, that each additional worker's contribution to the product tended to decline, due to the operation of the law of diminishing returns. Then the demand for labour, and employment, could continuously increase only if the wage continuously fell. That fact accounts for the negative slope of the demand.

The steepness of such curves reflects what has come to be known as the "elasticity" of the curve, or better, the "responsiveness" of demand to changes in price. If, for example, a 1% decline in price causes demand to increase by 2%, the elasticity of demand is said to be equal to two—that is, equal to the ratio of the percent change in demand to the percent change in price. This elasticity depends in the first instance on the availability of substitutes.

**Characteristics of Supply.**—Curves relating willingness to sell individual commodities to some range of possible prices are customarily drawn with a "positive" slope, indicating that this willingness increases as prices increase. In the commodity market, one justification for this practice runs as follows. Productive resources are deployed in such a way that producers make the highest possible profit. Should prices rise in a certain line, say ladies' hats, profits there would rise and attract resources away from competing uses. In these competing lines, supplies would therefore fall, driving up prices there. Should competing prices rise very quickly, the redeployment of resources to the production of hats would not go very far, unless the price of hats was increased still further. There is, therefore, a positive correlation between the supply and the price of hats.

In the factor markets supply curves are drawn similarly, and for similar reasons. If a certain factor has been earning a given return in a particular employment, it can be attracted to any other —"new"—line only by the offer of a higher return. As the transfer proceeds, the supply of factors in old employments falls, the marginal products there rise, and the returns foregone by shifting into the "new" line increase progressively. To keep attracting more and more factors, "new" lines will have to keep offering progressively higher returns. The supply, again, is positively correlated with the return; *i.e.*, with the price offered.

**Equilibrium.**—Schedules of willingness to buy and sell generally reveal some price at which the two come out to be equal. This is the "equilibrium" price; at this price all sellers can find buyers and all buyers sellers. Suppose a price obtains such that some sellers cannot find buyers. Disappointed sellers will then cut prices in order to lure buyers away from their competitors. Suppose, on the other hand, a price obtains at which some would-be buyers cannot find sellers. They will then offer to pay higher prices to divert supplies away from their rivals. Any departure from an equilibrium price seems, therefore, automatically to be corrected by market forces pushing the price toward equilibrium.

This happy result is sometimes destroyed by speculation. Suppose that demand rose above supply; the price would then show a tendency to rise. If all went properly, any rise in price should lower demand and raise supplies. If, however, an initial increase in price leads speculators to believe that prices will continue to rise, then they may withdraw more supplies from the market rather than add to them, hoping to do better by themselves later, when prices are yet higher. It is easy to see that this sort of thing may lead to a greater disequilibrium rather than to a restored balance between supply and demand. Where there is the possibility of such speculation, any equilibrium is spoken of as being "unstable."

**Aggregates.**—The problem of the supply and demand for all commodities taken together is very complex, and, therefore, a few points only are discussed here.

Aggregate supplies depend on the inducements offered to productive factors to produce. In the case of labour, it could be argued that increases in total labour hours worked involve reductions in the leisure enjoyed by the working population. The less leisure left to them, the higher the compensation for additional reduction would have to be. Once every man is employed this probably holds true. With unemployment, however, changes in labour hours supplied involve changes in the number of men working rather than in the division of time between work and leisure for each man. In that case, more men could probably be hired at the going wage, and the supply curve of labour would have to be drawn as a horizontal line up to the point of full employment.

The same would hold for other factors of production, such as land and capital. The overall supply of land would stay more or less fixed. Its supply curve past full employment would therefore be vertical. The supply of capital could grow as long as people were willing to produce capital rather than consumer goods. The rate of growth of capital probably depends, in part at least, on the inducement offered to potential investors to reduce consumption. The lower their consumption levels are pushed, the higher would have to be the compensation offered for further reductions.

In considering aggregate demand and what determines the total of expenditures on goods and services it is clear that since the total of expenditures determines the total of incomes, demand curves can no longer be drawn in relation to "price" with incomes constant, as was done with individual commodities. Instead, economists have examined the determinants of three broad classes of expenditures, those of consumers, those of investors in capital goods, and those of the government. The first seems on the whole to be related to the (changing) level of income, the second to expectations of future markets, and the last to political considerations. Once these demands, added up, are brought to bear on available supplies, supply and demand again determine a price—this time the price level. It is debatable, however, whether this is an equilibrium price in quite the same sense as before.

*See* also references under "Supply and Demand" in the Index.

(H. O. S.)

**SUPREME COURT OF JUDICATURE,** in England, a court established by the Judicature Act, 1873, consisting of the Court of Appeal and the High Court of Justice (*q.v.*). *See* also COURT: *England: Civil Courts: The Supreme Court.*

**SUPREME COURT OF THE UNITED STATES, THE,** stands at the apex of a dual system of courts: state and federal. This position accounts for the distinctive and even paradoxical character of the court's function: it is a conventional tribunal whose authority can be exercised only in the decision of ordinary lawsuits, and at the same time, as the final expositor of the United States constitution, it is the voice and symbol of the aspirations of the nation. Within the framework of litigation, the supreme court marks the boundaries of authority between state and nation, state and state and government and citizen.

## ORGANIZATION AND POWERS

**Establishment and Membership.**—The articles of confederation, which held together the American states from 1781 until adoption of the constitution, did not provide for a supreme court. But the articles did authorize congress to appoint courts of appeal in cases of naval captures, and such a court functioned until 1787, deciding more than 100 appeals from state courts. In a limited sense this tribunal was a precursor of the present supreme court. The framers of the constitution in 1787 concluded that a supreme judicial tribunal was required in a political system that gave limited powers to the centre and that, even before the adoption of the Bill of Rights through amendments, imposed specific prohibitions on the state and national governments. Article iii, section I, of the constitution provides:

> The judicial Power of the United States shall be vested in one supreme Court, and in such inferior Courts as the Congress may from time to time ordain and establish. The Judges, both of the supreme and inferior Courts, shall hold their Offices during good Behavior, and shall, at stated Times, receive for their Services, a Compensation, which shall not be diminished during their Continuance in Office.

The jurisdiction of the federal courts is defined in succeeding provisions of article iii. The major heads of jurisdiction reflect the special mission of these courts conceived as tribunals relatively detached from local pressures and biases. The authority of the federal courts extends to cases arising under the constitution, laws or treaties of the United States, controversies to which the United States is a party, controversies between states or between citizens of different states, cases of admiralty and maritime jurisdiction and cases affecting ambassadors, other public ministers and consuls. Of these courts, only the supreme court is given by article iii a status independent of the will of congress. Since the constitution is silent on such matters as the size of the court and the scope of its appellate jurisdiction in the judicial hierarchy, however, the supreme court itself is subject in important respects to congressional action.

The first Judiciary act, passed on Sept. 24, 1789, provided for a chief justice and five associate justices. In 1807 the membership was increased by law to seven, in 1837 to nine and in 1863 to ten. In 1866, as part of the effort by congress to curb the appointing power of Pres. Andrew Johnson, a statute reduced the membership to seven as vacancies should occur, and actually the court declined to eight members. But in 1869 an increase to nine was provided, at which the size of the court has remained. Tenure is during good behaviour, subject to expulsion by conviction on impeachment as provided in article ii, section 4, of the constitution. One justice of the court has been impeached—Samuel Chase, who was acquitted in 1805. By an act of 1937, a member of the court who has served for ten years or more may retire with full compensation upon reaching the age of 70.

Appointments to the supreme court, as to the lower federal courts, are made by the president with the advice and consent of the senate. Eleven nominations have been rejected by the senate, the latest being in 1969 and 1970. All appointees have been lawyers, but there has been no other pattern of selection. It can be said that geographic distribution has been a factor as well as the political outlook of the nominees: not so much their partisan affiliation as an outlook on problems of statecraft congenial to the chief executive and the senate. A number of justices, enjoying the emancipation of the robe, have surprised and disappointed those responsible for their appointment, as in the case of Abe Fortas, appointed to the court in 1965 by Pres. Lyndon Johnson. After publicity about outside financial activities on his part, Fortas resigned in 1969 under pressure, becoming the first justice in the history of the court to do so.

Chief justices, with terms of service, are as follows:

John Jay (1789–95)
John Rutledge (1795)
Oliver Ellsworth (1796–1800)
John Marshall (1801–35)
Roger B. Taney (1836–64)
Salmon P. Chase (1864–73)
Morrison R. Waite (1874–88)
Melville W. Fuller (1888–1910)
Edward D. White (1910–21)
William H. Taft (1921–30)
Charles E. Hughes (1930–41)
Harlan F. Stone (1941–46)
Fred M. Vinson (1946–53)
Earl Warren (1953–69)
Warren E. Burger (1969– )

Associate justices, with terms of service, are as follows:

John Rutledge (1789–91)
William Cushing (1789–1810)
James Wilson (1789–98)
John Blair (1789–96)
James Iredell (1790–99)
Thomas Johnson (1792–93)
William Paterson (1793–1806)
Samuel Chase (1796–1811)
Bushrod Washington (1798–1829)
Alfred Moore (1800–1804)
William Johnson (1804–34)
Brockholst Livingston (1806–23)
Thomas Todd (1807–26)
Joseph Story (1811–45)
Gabriel Duval (1812–35)
Smith Thompson (1823–43)

Robert Trimble (1826–28)
John McLean (1829–61)
Henry Baldwin (1830–44)
James M. Wayne (1835–67)
Philip P. Barbour (1836–41)
John Catron (1837–65)
John McKinley (1837–52)
Peter V. Daniel (1841–60)
Samuel Nelson (1845–72)
Levi Woodbury (1845–51)
Robert C. Grier (1846–70)
Benjamin R. Curtis (1851–57)
John A. Campbell (1853–61)
Nathan Clifford (1858–81)
Noah H. Swayne (1862–81)
Samuel F. Miller (1862–90)
David Davis (1862–77)
Stephen J. Field (1863–97)
William Strong (1870–80)
Joseph P. Bradley (1870–92)
Ward Hunt (1873–82)
John M. Harlan (1877–1911)
William B. Woods (1880–87)
Stanley Matthews (1881–89)
Horace Gray (1881–1902)
Samuel Blatchford (1882–93)
Lucius Q. C. Lamar (1888–93)
David J. Brewer (1889–1910)
Henry B. Brown (1890–1906)
George Shiras, Jr. (1892–1903)
Howell E. Jackson (1893–95)
Edward D. White (1894–1910)
Rufus W. Peckham (1896–1909)
Joseph McKenna (1898–1925)
Oliver W. Holmes (1902–32)
William R. Day (1903–22)
William H. Moody (1906–10)
Horace H. Lurton (1909–14)
Charles E. Hughes (1910–16)
Willis Van Devanter (1910–37)
Joseph R. Lamar (1911–16)
Mahlon Pitney (1912–22)
James C. McReynolds (1914–41)
Louis D. Brandeis (1916–39)
John H. Clarke (1916–22)
George Sutherland (1922–38)
Pierce Butler (1922–39)
Edward T. Sanford (1923–30)
Harlan F. Stone (1925–41)
Owen J. Roberts (1930–45)
Benjamin N. Cardozo (1932–38)
Hugo L. Black (1937– )
Stanley F. Reed (1938–57)
Felix Frankfurter (1939–62)
William O. Douglas (1939– )
Frank Murphy (1940–49)
James F. Byrnes (1941–42)
Robert H. Jackson (1941–54)
Wiley B. Rutledge (1943–49)
Harold H. Burton (1945–58)
Tom C. Clark (1949–67)
Sherman Minton (1949–56)
John M. Harlan (1955– )
William J. Brennan (1956– )
Charles E. Whittaker (1957–62)
Potter Stewart (1958– )
Byron R. White (1962– )
Arthur J. Goldberg (1962–65)
Abe Fortas (1965–69)
Thurgood Marshall (1967– )
Harry A. Blackmun (1970– )

Two chief justices, Edward D. White and Harlan F. Stone, were advanced to that office while serving as associate justices. Charles Evans Hughes (chief justice 1930–41) served as associate justice before resigning in 1916 to run for president. John Rutledge was an associate justice (1789–91) but resigned to become chief justice of the supreme court of South Carolina; he received a recess appointment as chief justice of the U.S. supreme court in 1795, but his nomination for an unlimited term was rejected by the senate. The longest tenure, 34 years and 8 months, was that of Stephen J. Field.

**Basic Functions.**—In maintaining the constitutional order, the supreme court from an early date has exercised the power of declaring acts of congress or of the state legislatures to be unconstitutional. Neither branch of this power of judicial review is expressly conferred by the constitution, and neither was established without intense partisan and sectional resentment.

Judicial review of acts of congress, assumed to be proper in a case in 1796, was established as a function of the court in 1803 in the celebrated case of *Marbury* v. *Madison.* The opinion of Chief Justice Marshall, adopting in substance the argument of Alexander Hamilton in no. 78 of the *Federalist,* deduced the power as a logically inevitable element of the judicial process: if in the decision of a case it appears that a statute and the constitution are in conflict, the court, which is bound to decide according to law, must prefer the higher to the inferior law. This analysis, assuming as it does that the court rather than congress or the electorate has the controlling judgment on such issues of conflict, is not free of the question-begging fallacy, as is suggested by the practice in the Swiss federation, where the constitutional validity of acts of the federal legislature is not examinable by the supreme court. But this is by no means to countenance the charge of usurpation that has sometimes been leveled at Marshall. There were precedents for judicial review of legislation in the practice of the privy council in relation to the colonies and of U.S. state courts after the Revolution. Moreover, there were references in the Constitutional Convention, though oblique, to the function of judicial review in litigation as a preferable alternative to a council of revision exercising a kind of veto power over legislation deemed invalid.

The doctrine of judicial review was made more palatable to the anti-Federalist critics of Marshall by the actual consequence of the doctrine in the Marbury case itself: an act of congress which the supreme court read as conferring original jurisdiction on the court beyond the warrant of article iii was declared invalid, the case was therefore dismissed for lack of jurisdiction, and a direct clash with the defendant, Pres. Thomas Jefferson's secretary of state, was averted. The irony of this act of abstention tended to blunt in popular consciousness the immediate effect of the court's assertion of power.

Judicial review of legislation of the states brought more severe immediate repercussions. Indeed the very power of the court to review decisions of state courts was vigorously challenged when it was laid down in an opinion of Justice Joseph Story in 1816, in the case of *Martin* v. *Hunter's Lessee.* For a number of years thereafter efforts were made in congress to repeal the section of the Judiciary act that conferred on the supreme court this appellate jurisdiction over state tribunals in cases turning on constitutional issues. No state or section had a monopoly on this spirit of resistance. Originally centred in the southern states, it was echoed on occasion in the North, as when in the period before the Civil War the state courts were held to the enforcement of the federal Fugitive-Slave law. A further ironic turn, in a subject studded with ironies, is that after the Civil War the power of judicial review served as an instrument of reconciliation, for the court declared unconstitutional, as bills of attainder, federal and state laws imposing test oaths intended to disqualify Confederate sympathizers from holding office or practising the professions.

Judicial review of legislation is not the only method whereby the court serves to maintain the constitutional order. Executive, administrative and judicial action also are subject to review in the supreme court. Moreover, some of the frictions and confusions of authority incident to a federal system are resolved in the court through the adjudication of controversies between states themselves, as for example those over boundaries or the allocation of water rights in interstate rivers. In this arbitral capacity the court serves as a substitute for diplomacy or war. Still another unifying function of the court is the interpretation of federal statutes, which would otherwise be subject to divergent applications in the lower courts.

For a time the supreme court attempted a further unifying role, that of developing a body of federal common (nonstatutory) law in cases arising in the diversity-of-citizenship jurisdiction of the federal district courts, but this enterprise introduced some anomalies of its own and it came to an end in 1938 with a decision holding that in such cases the common law to be applied is that of the state in which the federal district court is situated.

**Jurisdiction and Procedure.**—Since the functions of the court are performed within the framework of ordinary litigation, it is necessary to outline the procedures by which cases reach the court and are there decided. Relatively few cases are brought in the original jurisdiction of the court. These are controversies between states, between a state and the United States or between a state and citizens of another state, and cases affecting ambassadors, other public ministers and consuls. The great bulk of the court's business comes to it in its appellate jurisdiction. Depending on the nature of the decision in the state or lower federal court, the route to the supreme court is by appeal or certiorari. The difference between the two is that an appeal invokes the obligatory jurisdiction of the supreme court, certiorari its discretionary jurisdiction.

The development of this bifurcated jurisdiction reflects a response by congress to a long struggle by the court to cope with the volume of cases annually docketed. In 1891 a measure of relief was afforded by the Circuit Court of Appeals act, setting up intermediate courts (of which there are 11, in ten circuits and the District of Columbia) having final authority over appeals from federal district courts save in cases of exceptional public importance. The same act put a belated end to the circuit-riding duties of supreme court justices. The Judiciary act of 1925 carried the reforms further. Sponsored by the court itself, under the aegis of Chief Justice Taft, the act greatly limited the obligatory jurisdiction and gave the court a large measure of control of its business by subsuming most classes of cases under the head of review by certiorari; these can be disposed of on the moving papers, without full briefs or oral argument, where they do not qualify by their importance for an exercise of the court's discretionary power of review. Each member of the court votes on each petition for certiorari, as in other actions of the court. The affirmative vote of four justices suffices for the granting of certiorari, since at that stage the question is simply the appropriateness of the case for review. The number of cases that are filed annually in the court exceeds 3,000. Of this total, about five-sixths are disposed of summarily, mainly by the denial of petitions for certiorari.

The cases not thus disposed of are set down for oral argument after the filing of briefs. The time allowed for oral argument is limited, ordinarily to one hour for each side. At a conference of the justices following a week of oral arguments the cases heard during that week are decided, and the responsibility of writing the opinion of the court in each is assigned among the justices by the chief justice (or by the senior associate justice if the chief justice is in the minority in a case). The practice of writing dissenting opinions has been followed since the time of the Marshall court; the first resolute dissenter was Marshall's colleague William Johnson. In this tradition the supreme court stands midway between the British house of lords sitting as a court, where each participating member delivers an opinion, and the judicial committee of the privy council, where customarily only a single opinion has been given.

## ROLE IN AMERICAN LIFE

**Changing Contributions and Conflicts.**—Any assessment of the unifying forces in United States society must ascribe an important role to the supreme court. Judicial review of state legislation takes its place in this regard with such physical factors as transportation and communication, and such political factors as national parties and presidential leadership. The chief technical instrument employed by the court in this aspect of its work has been the commerce clause, which conferred power on congress to regulate commerce among the states. This clause has been applied from the time of Marshall to nullify state laws of taxation or regulation that discriminate against or unduly burden interstate commerce. The common national market has thereby been maintained against the grosser demands of local commercial protectionism. The process has been one of accommodation, requiring in each case an appraisal of the state law in the light of local need compared with the inroad on the common market. Marshall's court tended to stress the national imperative, Taney's the concerns of local welfare. At no time in its history, however, has it been possible for the court to avoid making close judgments on a pragmatic basis.

The assertion of national interest that spelled the doom of many state laws has served ultimately to vindicate national power when congress has legislated. Beginning with the Interstate Commerce act of 1887 and the Sherman Anti-Trust act of 1890, congress increasingly took over the regulation of sectors of the economy that previously were regulated ineffectively or not at all because of judicial restraints and practical inhibitions on the states.

A series of decisions, of which the child labour case in 1918 was the most conspicuous, threatened for a time to create a no man's land in which neither the federal nor state governments would have constitutional power to legislate effectively—the federal government denied power because the objective of the law was employment practices, the state governments denied power because the interstate importation of articles of commerce is immune from state prohibition. Not until the overruling of the child labour case in 1941 was the federal power over commerce placed on a firm basis. Subsequently the court sustained far-reaching applications of the commerce power by congress, of which perhaps the most striking was the setting of maximum acreage quotas for the production of wheat, including wheat that is consumed on the farm.

As the commerce clause has been the chief doctrinal source of national power over the economy, the due-process and equal-protection clauses have been the principal sources of protection of persons and corporations against arbitrary or repressive acts of government. The guarantee of life, liberty and property against deprivation without due process of law, enforceable against the states by virtue of the post-Civil War 14th amendment, has been interpreted by the court to protect against the substance of legislation as well as against arbitrary procedures. Accordingly, during the first third of the 20th century the court invalidated important social and economic measures, including laws of the states setting minimum wages and maximum prices. Liberty of contract was construed in light of a laissez-faire philosophy shared by a dominant majority within the court. Against this paralyzing judicial treatment of experimental legislation Justices Oliver Wendell Holmes and Louis D. Brandeis voiced a current of powerful dissents. Beginning about 1940 the doctrine embodied in these dissents became the law of the land, and thereafter no significant economic legislation was found repugnant to the constitutional guarantees.

The field of civil liberties has had a markedly different history. Not until the 1920s was it established that the rights safeguarded against federal incursion by the first amendment—the rights of freedom of speech, press, assembly and religious exercise—are safeguarded also against action by the states, as part of the liberty guaranteed by the 14th amendment. As the court has become more tolerant of economic controls, it has taken a more stringent view of laws that curtail the first-amendment liberties and the procedural guarantees of the Bill of Rights. Insofar as these changing standards of judicial review have been rationalized, the warrant is that the special concern of the court is with process and structure; that political liberties are at the base of representative self-government; and that if normally the people must look to political processes for the correction of harsh or unwise legislation, the court for that very reason must remain vigilant to strike down those measures that repress the political process itself.

The guarantee of equal protection of the laws in the 14th amendment has had a development similar to the evolution of due process of law. Originally designed for the benefit of the emancipated Negroes, soon utilized as a shield against social legislation, it came at mid-20th century to serve its historic purpose as a barrier to racially discriminatory laws.

In a steady series of cases the court invalidated a variety of restrictions directed at Negroes: exclusion from voting in party primary elections, racial zoning, enforcement of restrictive covenants in real-estate deeds, exclusion from state-maintained universities, and enforced segregation in public schools and on public conveyances.

It is hardly surprising that a tribunal exercising authority of such gravity, delicacy and finality has frequently found itself the object of popular or partisan attack. Given the generality of the great constitutional provisions and the task of applying that document to an evolving social, economic and political order, the court cannot escape the responsibility of rendering judgments that provoke dissatisfaction in some quarters and for some time. Whether a judgment is viable will depend on whether it is the court or its critics who have more truly sensed the climate of the age rather than the weather of the day.

A number of the strongest presidents have been pitted at one time or another against the court. Thomas Jefferson and Andrew Jackson found certain of Marshall's opinions decidedly distasteful. Abraham Lincoln, faced with the Dred Scott decision, called for its re-examination, though he was careful to counsel against resistance to the decree itself. Theodore Roosevelt, irked by judicial invalidation of social legislation, urged in 1912 popular recall of judges and popular referenda on judicial decisions. Franklin D. Roosevelt, confronted with a supreme court that had upset a large part of his recovery program, generally by divided decisions, proposed a reorganization of the federal courts. His plan, presented to congress in 1937, provided for the appointment of an additional judge for each judge who remained on the bench after having served ten years and reached the age of 70; the maximum size of the supreme court was to be fixed at 15. The plan was defeated in congress. Meanwhile, however, the supreme court had given clear signs in its intervening decisions that it would take a more hospitable view of the scope of governmental power under the constitution.

**Self-Limitation.**—Cognizant of the risks of ill-advised decisions, the court has developed canons of self-limitation. It will not render advisory opinions, or decide a constitutional question when the case can be disposed of on another ground, or render a constitutional decision broader than required by the facts of the case before it or at the instance of a litigant whose interests are not actually in jeopardy.

A category of "political" questions has been evolved, moreover, which will be left for resolution by other departments of government without judicial review. Some of the most unfortunate decisions of the court have been marked by a disregard of the court's own canons.

Writing in 1928, Charles Evans Hughes characterized three ill-starred decisions as self-inflicted wounds: the Dred Scott case, the first legal tender cases and the income-tax cases. (*See* Hughes, *The Supreme Court of the United States,* p. 50, 1928.) Each of these was in time uprooted: the first by the Civil War, the second by an overruling decision, the third by the 16th amendment to the constitution. Each was a needlessly precipitate decision: the first because it could have been resolved on a nonconstitutional ground of state law; the second because one member of the court, holding a decisive vote, was on the verge of retirement for disability; the third because the interests of the complainants, corporate stockholders, did not require the relief that the court granted. It is noteworthy that judges who have been deeply sensitive to the demands on constitutional law made by a changing social order—Justice Brandeis most conspicuously—have also been most insistent on the court's observance of its professed canons of self-limitation.

**Important Decisions.**—The Marshall court laid the basis for a federal union capable of effective government. In *McCulloch* v. *Maryland* (1819), upholding the second Bank of the United States, the court gave a liberal interpretation to the necessary and proper clause of the constitution and thus equipped congress with ancillary powers of great potentiality. A counterpart was the decision in *Gibbons* v. *Ogden* (1824), holding that a state could not confer a monopoly of interstate steamboat traffic, thus establishing the court as a guardian of the free national market against local commercial self-interest.

The Taney court, although on the whole more sympathetic to the concerns of the states, by no means reversed the current. *Bank of Augusta* v. *Earle* (1839) established the capacity of a corporation chartered in one state to do business in another; and the *Charles River Bridge Co.* v. *Warren Bridge Co.* case (1837), while sustaining the power of a state to charter a company in competition with one operating under a prior grant from the state, served to stimulate the development of new forms of interstate transportation. The *Genesee Chief* (1851) extended federal admiralty jurisdiction to inland navigable lakes and rivers, rejecting the English rule that such jurisdiction was confined to tidewaters. Pointing out the divergence between the English and American topography, Taney's opinion is at once a declaration of independence and an avowal that constitutional interpretation should conform to the facts of life.

Unhappily, Taney's reputation was derived too largely from the *Scott* v. *Sanford* (Dred Scott) case (1857), whose holding that congress lacked power to prohibit slavery in the territories foreclosed one avenue of compromise and helped to precipitate the Civil War. The war itself produced the *Ex parte Milligan* case (1866), a notable landmark in the field of civil liberties, holding that trial of civilians by military commission is unlawful outside the theatre of military operations while the civil courts are capable of functioning.

The post-Civil War amendments to the constitution were construed in the *Slaughterhouse* cases (1873) and the *Civil Rights* cases (1883) not to have worked a radical transformation in the basic structure of U.S. federalism. The first of these decisions ruled that the privileges and immunities of citizens of the United States, safeguarded by the 14th amendment, must be narrowly interpreted to include only those privileges peculiar to national citizenship and not such asserted rights as the opportunity to engage in common callings. The second decision established the position that the amendments provide a federal guarantee against racial discrimination by state and not private action.

The due-process clause of the 14th amendment was used in the late 19th and early 20th centuries to strike down economic legislation which did not commend itself to the social philosophy of a majority of the justices. Perhaps the high-water mark was reached in *Lochner* v. *New York* (1905), invalidating a law which limited the workday of bakers to ten hours: in time the case became less notable for the decision than for the stinging dissent of Justice Holmes. The dissenting position was definitely established as the law of the land in *Nebbia* v. *New York* (1934), a decision that gave broad scope to economic legislation affecting prices, wages and the hours of labour by renouncing the view that there is a closed category of businesses so affected with a public interest that for them alone is such regulation constitutionally permissible.

The New Deal program of Pres. Franklin D. Roosevelt at first foundered on restrictive constitutional decisions of the court. But the tide turned with the *National Labor Relations Board* v. *Jones and Laughlin Steel Corp.* case (1937), upholding federal authority over collective bargaining in industries in which work stoppages would affect interstate commerce. The opinion of Chief Justice Hughes was able to draw support from an earlier opinion of his in the Shreveport case (1914), where federal authority over intrastate railroad rates was sustained on a showing of their effect upon competitive interstate traffic. Congressional power over industry and agriculture has been validated to an extent ample for legislative purposes. Restraints in the interest of the states have become a matter of congressional discretion rather than constitutional compulsion.

The decision in *Brown* v. *Board of Education* (1954), holding that separate but equal facilities for Negroes in public schools do not meet the constitutional standard of equal protection of the laws, created the greatest problem of compliance faced by the court since the Marshall period. But the court as an arbitral institution meanwhile won firm acceptance if not always equal understanding.

In *Baker* v. *Carr* (1962) and succeeding cases the court invalidated, under the equal-protection clause, grossly disproportionate state legislative districts, over the dissent of Justice Frankfurter, who warned that the court was entering a "political thicket." The political process was safeguarded in a different way when the court held in *N.Y. Times Co.* v. *Sullivan* (1964) that the guarantee of freedom of the press protected a newspaper from liability for defamation of a public official provided the falsehood was not published knowingly or recklessly. In another series of cases the court applied various provisions of the federal Bill of Rights to state criminal trials, under the due-process guarantee of the 14th amendment. *Mapp* v. *Ohio* (1961) required the exclusion of evidence obtained through an unconstitutional search and seizure; *Miranda* v. *Arizona* (1966) required the exclusion of confessions secured from a person under arrest without giving him an opportunity to consult counsel or offering to provide counsel if he is indigent. These lines of cases indicate how the court exercises the power of judicial review with increasing intensity to assure more responsive and responsible government.

**Symbolic and Pragmatic Role.**—It has been argued with some force that the functions vested in the supreme court are tolerable only in a country that is agreed on its fundamental premises; that judicial review on the United States model would be impossible where there are deep philosophic cleavages; and that the U.S. practice is a corollary of the pragmatic American spirit. It can be said, however, that the relation is one of interaction. The practice of judicial review, by a reflexive effect, serves to soften the edges of ideological weapons and to promote accommodations on a working basis. The court operates in the context of specific facts; it does not so much choose between absolutes as endeavour to reach a mediating solution; and it holds itself open for reconsideration of doctrine in the light of changed circumstances and fuller experience.

By virtue of the reasoned elaboration of its opinions and the tradition of dissent it serves continually to clarify, refine and test the large philosophic ideals that are written into the constitution, and so to translate them into working principles for a federal union under a rule of law. Beyond its specific contributions, this symbolic and pragmatic function may be regarded as the most significant role of the supreme court in the life of the nation.

For the role of the United States supreme court in the development of the U.S. federal system and the history of judicial constitutional construction, *see* AMERICAN LAW and CONSTITUTION AND CONSTITUTIONAL LAW. *See* also UNITED STATES (OF AMERICA): *History;* COURT; and APPEAL.

Important decisions of the court are covered in detail in separate articles on various legal subjects of special interest, for example CIVIL RIGHTS AND LIBERTIES; CENSORSHIP; INTERSTATE COMMERCE; LABOUR LAW; and PUBLIC UTILITIES: *Regulation in the United States.*

*See* articles on famous justices, such as BRANDEIS, LOUIS DEMBITZ; CARDOZO, BENJAMIN NATHAN; HOLMES, OLIVER WENDELL; JAY, JOHN; MARSHALL, JOHN; STONE, HARLAN FISKE; and STORY, JOSEPH.

*See* also references under "Supreme Court of the United States, The" in the Index.

BIBLIOGRAPHY.—Charles Warren, *The Supreme Court in United States History,* 2 vol., rev. ed. (1935); Carl B. Swisher, *American Constitutional Development* (1943); Paul A. Freund, *The Supreme Court of the United States* (1961); Robert H. Jackson, *The Struggle for Judicial Supremacy* (1941) and *Supreme Court in the American System of Government* (1955); Felix Frankfurter, *Of Law and Men* (1956); William O. Douglas, *We the Judges* (1956); Alan F. Westin (ed.), *The Supreme Court: Views from Inside* (1961); Robert L. Stern and Eugene Gressman, *Supreme Court Practice,* 3rd ed. (1962).

(P. A. F.)

**SURABAJA,** capital of East Java Province and the second port (after Jakarta) of Java, Indon., lies at the mouth of the Kali Mas, a branch of the Brantas River, on the Surabaja Strait (which separates Java from Madura Island), 420 mi. (675 km.) ESE of Jakarta. Pop. (1961) 1,007,945. Surabaja has modern houses and offices, hotels, motion-picture theatres, and shops. In contrast to these are the street markets and the crowded downtown districts. The Kali Mas River is canalized, and the canal flows through the centre of the city. From a lookout station at the mouth of the river the railway and road run southward inland, past the old fort (formerly called Fort Prins Hendrik) to the old town, then to the upper town, and beyond that to the suburbs of Gubeng and Wonokromo, where a new residential sector of the city was developed. The naval station is on the south side of the canal, and opposite are the commercial docks; these, destroyed by the Dutch during the Japanese invasion in 1942, have been rebuilt. Notable buildings include a large mosque (1868); the Airlangga University (1954), with faculties of law, medicine, and dental surgery in the city; the Institute of Technology, with university status; and a naval college.

The area around the city is flat and, protected from extremes of climate by Madura Island, is a rich agricultural region. Sugarcane is chiefly grown, other crops including tobacco, maize, and rice. Tapioca, coffee, and cocoa are also produced locally. Cattle are bred, and there is a large fishing fleet.

Surabaja is the largest naval base of Indonesia, as well as a major commercial port and an important industrial centre, with several heavy industries. There are railway locomotive workshops, shipbuilding and ship-repair yards, textile mills, and glass, cigarette, and shoe factories. There is an oil refinery in Wonokromo. The bulk of Java's chief product, sugar, is shipped from Surabaja. Other goods exported include coffee, tobacco, rubber, spices, and petroleum products.

Surabaja is linked with the railway system that connects the eastern and western coasts of Java and is thus in communication with Jakarta, Semarang, Jogjakarta, and the other chief towns of the island. There is shipping communication with the chief ports of the world; Surabaja also lies on the main sea route from Singapore and Jakarta to Australia. From the airport at Tandjungperak, 5 mi. (8 km.) from the city, there are flights to various airports in the island, including Jakarta, and thence to the principal cities in Asia and Europe.

Surabaja was one of the chief centres of resistance to Dutch and British forces during the Indonesian war of independence (1945–49).

**SURAKARTA** (also known as SOLO), a town of Central Java Province, Indon., lies on the Solo River about 260 mi. (420 km.) ESE of Jakarta. Pop. (1961) 367,626. It was the capital of the protected principality of Surakarta, which constituted a government (status given to major units of administration) of the former Netherlands Indies. The principality, occupied by the Japanese during World War II, was eliminated after independence and incorporated in the Republic of Indonesia. (*See* JAVA: *History.*)

The town has broad, tree-lined streets with many modern buildings in addition to the old quarter and busy markets. Traffic is dominated by the *betjak* (tricycle taxi). Notable buildings include the palace of the Susuhunan (1745); the court of Prince Mangku Negoro (1788); the mayor's residence, known as Lodji Gandrung, which accommodates distinguished guests; and the old Dutch fort of Vastenburcht (1779), now a garrison headquarters. More modern are the town hall, the telephone exchange, the post office, a rehabilitation centre with its workshop, and an institute for crippled children. Public parks include Sriwedari Park, in the middle of the town, with its zoo, *wajang orang* (drama) performances, motion-picture theatre, and stadium. Long famous as a cultural and educational centre, Surakarta has several private universities, including the Islamic University of Indonesia and faculties of the 17th August 1945 University, including law, agriculture, social sciences, economics, teachers' training, and religion, and there is an academy of art. The Radyapustaka houses the museum and a library.

The town is a market for the surrounding agricultural area, which produces tobacco, sugar, rice, cassava, coconuts, and fruits and vegetables. The making of batik cloth is the main industry, followed by the manufacture of cigarettes, furniture, and textiles; and there is a metal foundry. Local handicrafts include pottery, wood and bone carving, and the making of musical instruments. Surakarta is linked by rail and road with Jakarta, Surabaja, Semarang, and Jogjakarta. (MA. J.)

**SURAT,** a city of Gujarat state, India, and the headquarters of the district of the same name, lies near the mouth of the Tapti River, about 160 mi. (260 km.) N of Bombay. Pop. (1961) 288,026. Surat is a city with narrow, winding lanes and densely packed houses. Buildings of historical interest include the Nav-Saiyed Saheb's mosque on the Gopi Tank (now dry) and the nine tombs beside it; the mosque built by Khudawand Khan (1540) and his tomb; the castle (1546); Idrus' Mosque (1639); and Gosavi's Temple (1695), destroyed by fire and restored. The city has eight colleges affiliated to Gujarat University. Fine cotton and silk goods are woven in Surat, and its brocades and gold- and silverware are famous. The ancient art of manufacturing superfine muslins, which had died out in the 19th century, was revived in the mid-1950s.

The origin of the town is not clear. It is believed that a Brahmin named Gopi built the Gopi Tank in 1516 and named the area Surajpur or Suryapur, the name being changed to Surat in 1520. Records show, however, that a town existed much earlier. In 1194 Qutb ud-Din Aibak, general of Mohammed of Ghor and one of the founders of Muslim rule in India, invaded the Surat region, and in 1347 Mohammed Tughlak, sultan of Delhi, plundered the town. His successor, Firuz Shah Tughlak, built the fort in 1373. In 1514 the Portuguese traveler Duarte Barbosa described Surat as a leading port. The Portuguese burned the town in 1512 and in 1530. The fort was rebuilt by the sultan of Gujarat in 1546.

In 1573 the Mughal emperor Akbar conquered Surat, and for nearly 100 years it enjoyed peace. It became the emporium of India, with a considerable trade in silks, muslins, brocades, and gold with Mocha in Yemen, Basra (Iraq), and Achin (Atjeh) in Sumatra. Its major industries were textile manufacture and shipbuilding. In 1608 the British established their first factory in

India at Surat. Surat's gradual decline was due to a number of causes—the raids of the Marathas (1664–84), the rise of Bombay and the ascendancy of the British, the decline of the Mughals after 1707, the loss of the Basra trade in 1776, and internal strife. The British and the Dutch played one party against another, and in 1800 the administration passed to the British. By the mid-19th century Surat was a decayed town of 80,000 inhabitants. Its revival came with the opening of the railways.

SURAT DISTRICT has an area of 2,849 sq.mi. (7,379 sq.km.) and a population (1961) of 1,313,823. In 1948 the former states of Dharampur, Sachin, and Bansda and the Navsari district of the former Baroda state (with the town of the same name, an old Parsee settlement) were absorbed into the district. Except for a barren coastal stretch of 80 mi. (135 km.), the district is highly cultivated. The chief crops are cotton, millet, pulses, and rice. (V. A. M. J.)

**SURENDRANAGAR,** a town and district of Gujarat state, India. The town, headquarters of the district, lies 60 mi. NE of Rajkot. Pop. (1961) 48,602. It is a trade centre for grain and cotton.

SURENDRANAGAR DISTRICT, formerly Zalawad, is one of the six districts that make up most of the Kathiawar (*q.v.*) Peninsula. Area 4,006 sq.mi. (10,376 sq.km.). Pop. (1961) 663,206. It is composed of 21 former princely states, the chief being Limbdi, Lakhtar, Wadhwan, Chotila, and Dhrangadhra. The land is uneven but partly flat. The majority of the population are farmers, the principal crops being cotton and cereals. Industries include manufacture of salt, soap, copper- and brassware, pottery, and textiles. The district is crossed by a network of railways, linking it with Rajkot, Junagadh, and other towns on the peninsula and with the main Western Railway line via Ahmedabad. Main towns besides Surendranagar are Dhrangadhra (pop. [1961] 32,477), Wadhwan (27,104), and Limbdi (21,801). (M. R. P.)

**SURFACE CHEMISTRY** is concerned with chemical events at the area of contact, called the interface, between immiscible materials of different or like phase; *e.g.*, a liquid with a gas, or a solid with another solid. *See* ADSORPTION; SURFACE TENSION. *See* also PHASE EQUILIBRIA.

**SURFACE HARDENING,** a heat treatment of steel in which only the surface is hardened. Other surface-hardening treatments include facing, by fusing a hard metal onto a soft one, and shot peening (*see* BLAST CLEANING AND SHOT PEENING). The conventional quenching of hot steel in water or oil is literally surface hardening; however, it usually hardens not only the surface but some or all of the interior, too, depending on the size of the piece. The phrase "surface hardening" usually implies processes other than merely quenching, such as carburizing, nitriding and induction hardening. The combination of a hard surface and soft interior is of inestimable value in modern engineering practices. Great strength and toughness in the core and extreme surface hardness result in a composite structure capable of withstanding certain kinds of stress to a high degree such as in gears or antifriction bearings. For less exacting requirements, low or moderate core properties and a high surface hardness can be obtained with cheaply fabricated, low-priced steels.

**Carburizing.**—One of the most important surface-hardening processes is carburizing in which steel is held at a high temperature (1,600° F. is common) for a long time (six hours, for instance) in a carbonaceous environment, usually a gas mixture of carbon monoxide and carbon dioxide, with or without hydrocarbons such as methane. This treatment causes carbon to diffuse into the steel to a depth of several thousandths or hundredths of an inch and leaves the carbon content of the surface much higher than that of the core; *e.g.*, 1.5% carbon compared with about .25%. When the carburized steel is quenched it becomes harder and more wear-resistant than similar steel of lower surface carbon content similarly quenched.

**Carbonitriding and Cyaniding.**—Carbonitriding, a variant of carburizing, is the same except that nitrogen as well as carbon diffuses into the steel. The nitrogen comes from ammonia introduced into the furnace atmosphere along with the carbonaceous gas. The cyaniding process gives a similar result; both carbon and nitrogen are supplied to the steel by diffusion from a liquid cyanide salt (usually potassium cyanide, KCN) in which the steel is immersed at about 1,600° F. Cyanides are violent poisons requiring rigid safety precautions when using the cyanide process of surface hardening.

**Nitriding.**—Another diffusion process producing hard surfaces is nitriding (*q.v.*) in which, by using ammonia without a carbonaceous gas, nitrogen goes into the steel and combines with other elements, principally chromium, already contained in the steel to form nitrides that are extremely hard and wear-resistant without the necessity for quenching the steel. Elimination of the quenching process is an advantage because dimensional changes that occur during quenching are avoided.

**Induction Hardening.**—From about 1935, another process of surface hardening became important—induction hardening. In this process, steel is briefly heated by electrical induction so that only the surface portion has time to get hot. It is immediately cooled or quenched and the portion that was heated above the critical temperature (about 1,500° F.) becomes hard while the rest of the steel which was not heated by the brief flow of induced current remains unaffected. Induction hardening has become common in mass-production industries since World War II because it is a rapid process—heating time per piece may be five seconds or less—and because it often permits the use of a less costly steel than other hardening processes.

**Flame Hardening.**—Flame hardening, like induction hardening, involves no change in the chemical composition of the steel surface. In flame hardening, a high-temperature flame impinges directly on the work for a short time, heating the surface but not the interior of the piece. The depth of hardening is usually $\frac{1}{32}$ in. or greater. Bulky pieces are often hardened by this method.

**Choice of Methods.**—The choice of a surface-hardening method depends on the design of the part, composition of the steel, type and depth of case needed, permissible distortion, production volume, initial investment and operating cost. Usually a given steel and treatment are compared with another steel-treatment combination. The selection of case depth is also important because a deeper case usually costs appreciably more and may even be undesirable, especially on thin pieces, which become more brittle as the case depth is increased. (T. LY.)

**SURFACES.** Intuitively, a surface in three-dimensional space (three space) is a two-dimensional set of points selected in a smooth fashion. The simplest examples are planes and spheres. In terms of a Cartesian coordinate system in three space, a plane is the set of points whose coordinates satisfy the equation $a(x - x_0) + b(y - y_0) + c(z - z_0) = 0$, the numbers $a,b,c$ not all zero. The plane passes through the point $(x_0, y_0, z_0)$ and is perpendicular to the vector $(a,b,c)$. A sphere is the set of points whose coordinates satisfy the equation $(x - x_0)^2 + (y - y_0)^2 + (z - z_0)^2 - r^2 = 0$; *i.e.*, the locus of a point whose distance from the fixed point $(x_0,y_0,z_0)$ is $r$, a fixed positive number. More generally, if $f(x,y,z)$ is a smooth function in three space not all whose partial derivatives vanish at any point, the set of points where $f(x,y,z)$ is zero, *i.e.*, satisfying the equation $f(x,y,z) = 0$, constitutes a surface. To see that this point set is two-dimensional, observe that if $\frac{\partial f}{\partial z}$ does not equal 0 at some point $(x_0,y_0,z_0)$, the equation $f(x,y,z) = 0$ can be solved for $z$ as a function $g$ of $x$ and $y$. Thus the surface in the vicinity of $(x_0,y_0,z_0)$ can be represented by the equation $z = g(x,y)$ and consists of the points with coordinates $(x,y,g(x,y))$.

This way of representing a surface in the vicinity of a point is quite general. If $Q$ is a fixed point on the surface and if $R$ and $S$ are arbitrary points on the surface, the smoothness assumption guarantees that the plane through $Q$, $R$, and $S$ approaches a limiting plane through $Q$ as $R$ and $S$ are taken closer and closer to $Q$. The limiting plane is called the tangent plane at $Q$, and the perpendicular line is called the normal at $Q$. If the coordinate system in three space is chosen so that the tangent plane is the $xy$ plane and the normal line is the $z$ axis, then distinct points on the surface near $Q$ project along the $z$ axis onto distinct points of the tangent plane. If $g(x,y)$ is the signed distance of a point on the surface to its projection with coordinates $x,y$, then the surface in the vicinity of $Q$ can be represented by the equation $z = g(x,y)$. The $x$ and $y$ coordinates of the projection of a point are smooth functions in the vicinity of $Q$ and serve as a system of coordinates near $Q$. The coordinate curves are those on which either $x$ or $y$ is constant.

The notion of surface can be freed from its embedding or position in three space. An abstract surface (two-dimensional manifold) is a collection of points together with a family of pairs of functions (*see* MANIFOLDS). Every point $Q$ of the manifold has defined in its vicinity a pair of functions that play the role of coordinate functions in this neighbourhood of $Q$. The smoothness condition requires that in overlapping neighbourhoods each pair of coordinate functions be expressible as smooth functions of any other pair. The set $\mathfrak{P}$ of all planes passing through the origin in three space is an example of such an abstract surface. Any such plane $P$ in $\mathfrak{P}$ can be represented by the equation $ax + by + cz = 0$, so that the three numbers $(a,b,c)$ not all zero and depending on $P$ characterize this plane up to a nonzero scale factor. If, say, $a \neq 0$ for a fixed plane $P$, nearby planes will also have $a \neq 0$. The functions $b/a, c/a$ are coordinate functions in the vicinity of $P$ but are not well defined for all of $\mathfrak{P}$ since $a = 0$ for the plane $z = 0$. Nevertheless one of the pair $b/a, c/a$ or $c/b, a/b$ or $a/c, b/c$ will serve as coordinate functions near any element of $\mathfrak{P}$. This particular surface is called projective space and is not realizable as a surface in three space.

Surfaces can be considered from several points of view. Depending on how much additional structure is put on the surface, one studies their topological, metric, conformal, or algebraic properties. Two abstract surfaces are topologically equivalent if a one-to-one correspondence can be found between the points of each surface in such a way that a sequence of points $Q_n$ gets closer and closer to a point $Q$ of the first surface if and only if the corresponding points $Q'_n$ get closer to $Q'$ in the second surface. Intuitively such a correspondence between surfaces need not preserve any distances imposed on the surfaces. It allows stretching but no tearing. As a result, this aspect of surface theory is called rubber-sheet geometry (*see* fig. 1). Compact, orientable surfaces

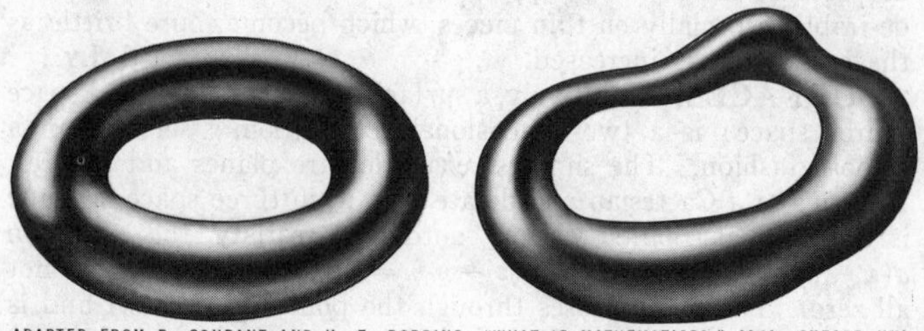

ADAPTED FROM R. COURANT AND H. E. ROBBINS, "WHAT IS MATHEMATICS?," 1941, OXFORD UNIVERSITY PRESS

**FIG. 1.—EACH TORUS IS TOPOLOGICALLY EQUIVALENT TO THE OTHER**

are easily classified. A surface is compact if every infinite sequence of points of the surface has a subsequence that comes closer and closer (converges) to a point of the surface. A surface is orientable if the family of coordinate functions can be so chosen that on overlapping neighbourhoods the Jacobian (determinant) expressing one pair as a function of the other is positive. A long strip of paper with the ends joined after a half twist is a simple example of a surface that is not orientable; the projective space described previously is another. Besides the sphere, the simplest example of a compact surface is a torus; *e.g.*, a rubber tire. It can be realized in three space by revolving the circle $x^2 + y^2 = 1$ in the $xy$ plane about the line $x = 2$. It is topologically equivalent to putting a handle on a sphere; *e.g.*, cutting two circular holes in a spherical ball and connecting them by a tube. The most general compact, orientable surface is topologically equivalent to a sphere with $n$ handles (fig. 2). Noncompact surfaces are harder to classify; however, those for which loops can be continuously deformed to a point are topologically equivalent to a plane (*see* TOPOLOGY, ALGEBRAIC; TOPOLOGY, GENERAL).

The metric or Riemannian structure imposed on a surface involves the notion of the distance between two points of a surface. For a surface in three space, the distance between two points $Q$

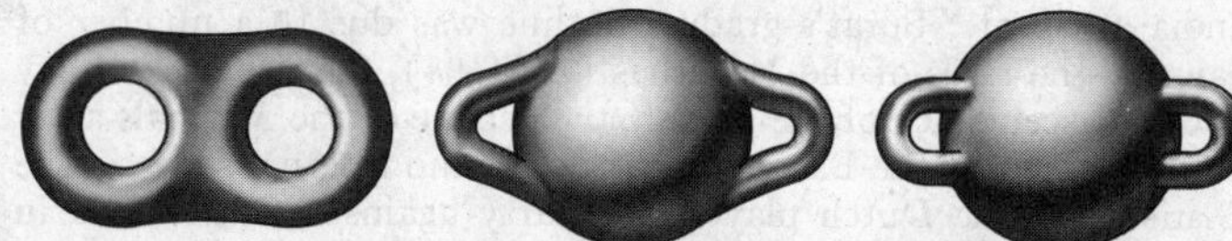

ADAPTED FROM R. COURANT AND H. E. ROBBINS, "WHAT IS MATHEMATICS?," 1941, OXFORD UNIVERSITY PRESS

**FIG. 2.—TOPOLOGICALLY EQUIVALENT FORMS OF A SPHERE WITH TWO HANDLES**

and $R$ is the greatest lower bound of the arc lengths of all curves on the surface beginning at $Q$ and ending at $R$. Since the arc length of a curve with given parameters is the integral of the lengths of its tangent vectors, the lengths of vectors tangent to the surface determine the distance between points. The function that assigns to each tangent vector the square of its length is called the first fundamental form or Riemannian metric of the surface (*see* RIEMANNIAN GEOMETRY). The Riemannian metric not only determines distance, length of tangent vectors, and the angle between vectors but gives other geometric invariants of the surface. The notion of parallel transport of a vector along a curve can be defined geometrically as a field of vectors tangent to the surface at each point of a curve with derivatives in three space that are always normal to the surface. Geodesics are curves on the surface with tangent vectors that are parallel transports of themselves. They are also curves whose small arcs are curves of shortest length between their extremities. The Gaussian curvature at a point of the surface is the limit of the amount of turning a vector undergoes when it is transported around smaller and smaller rectangles. The geometric entities definable in terms of the first fundamental form are called intrinsic invariants of the surface.

Each point of an abstract surface also has a tangent space: the space of directional derivatives of the family of functions on the surface smooth near the point. If lengths and angles between vectors are imposed on each such tangent space, the abstract surface gains a Riemannian metric, and the geometric notions of the previous paragraph are valid. Two surfaces with Riemannian structures are isometric if there is a smooth one-to-one correspondence of their points preserving their Riemannian metric. An abstract Riemannian structure is more general than one in three space. For example, a torus can be endowed with a metric that has zero Gaussian curvature at every point, while a torus in three space has a first fundamental form giving a Gaussian curvature not identically zero. However, every surface with Riemannian metric is embeddable in a Euclidean space of sufficiently high dimension in such a way that its metric is the one it inherits from the embedding.

Aside from the intrinsic invariants, an additional measurement is needed to describe how a surface lies in three space. For example, a twisted sheet of paper can be straightened into a flat sheet without changing distances; thus the twisted form is metrically equivalent to a portion of a plane. Yet the position of the twisted sheet in three space is entirely different from that of a plane. This difference is completely described by the second fundamental form. Two isometric surfaces with the same second fundamental form at corresponding points differ only by a motion of three space, that is a translation followed by a rotation. The second fundamental form measures the rate at which the normal directions change at a point moving about the surface. It is the function on the tangent space whose value on a vector $v$ is the scalar product of $v$ with $N_v$ (the rate of change in the direction of $v$ of the unit normal). $N_v$ lies in the tangent space and the transformation $S$ sending $v$ into $N_v$ is a symmetric transformation that becomes a $2 \times 2$ symmetric matrix (*q.v.*) in the presence of a coordinate system. The determinant of $S$ turns out to be the Gaussian curvature so that the second fundamental form gives a nonintrinsic characterization of this curvature. If the surface is of the form $z = g(x,y)$ in the vicinity of the origin with the $xy$ plane as tangent plane as previously described, then the matrix of $S$ is

$$\begin{pmatrix} \frac{\partial^2 g}{\partial x^2} & \frac{\partial^2 g}{\partial x \partial y} \\ \frac{\partial^2 g}{\partial y \partial x} & \frac{\partial^2 g}{\partial y^2} \end{pmatrix}$$

As a result, if the Gaussian curvature is positive, the surface lies on one side of the tangent plane; at such a point the surface is elliptic. If the Gaussian curvature is negative, part of the surface is on one side, part on the other side of the tangent plane, and the surface has a saddle in the vicinity of the origin; such a point is called hyperbolic (fig. 3). At a parabolic point the Gaussian curvature is zero. One half the trace of $S$ is called the mean curvature of the surface at the point; the eigenvalues of $S$ are called the principal curvatures; and the eigenvectors of $S$ are called the directions of principal curvature (*see* DIFFERENTIAL EQUATIONS, PARTIAL; OPERATORS, THEORY OF). A line of curvature is a curve on the surface with tangent vectors that lie in a direction of principal curvature. If the eigenvalues of $S$ are distinct at a point, the lines of curvature form a two-parameter orthogonal family of curves in the vicinity of this point. An umbilical point is one where the two eigenvalues of $S$ coincide.

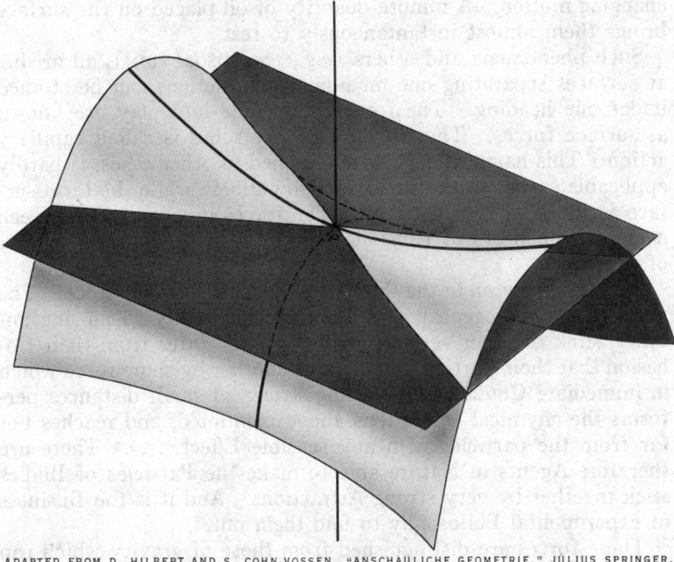



ADAPTED FROM D. HILBERT AND S. COHN-VOSSEN, "ANSCHAULICHE GEOMETRIE," JULIUS SPRINGER, BERLIN, 1932; COPYRIGHT INTERESTS HAVE BEEN VESTED IN THE ATTORNEY GENERAL OF THE U.S. PURSUANT TO LAW AND ARE PUBLISHED BY PERMISSION

FIG. 3.—SADDLEPOINT (AT $P$)

The second fundamental form also measures the amount of turning a curve on the surface does in the normal direction. The curvature vector at a point of a curve in three space is the derivative of its tangent vectors. If the curve lies on a surface, its curvature vector is the sum of a tangent vector (the geodesic curvature vector) and a normal vector (the normal curvature vector). Two curves on the surface with the same tangent vector $v$ have the same normal curvature vector. The length of the normal curvature vector is the ratio of the second fundamental form over the first fundamental form evaluated at $v$ and is called the normal curvature. The extreme values of the normal curvatures at a point occur at the principal curvature directions.

Of special interest are surfaces in three space with constant Gaussian curvature. If the curvature is zero, the surface is called developable, for any small portion of such a surface is isometric (can be developed onto) to a portion of a plane. Locally a developable surface consists of a one-parameter family of straight lines with the property that the tangent planes along one line coincide, so that the collection of tangent planes forms only a one-parameter family. An example of a developable surface is the tangent developable consisting of the family of tangent lines to a smooth curve (*see* CURVES). Developable surfaces are special cases of ruled surfaces; *i.e.,* those made up of straight lines (*see* MATHEMATICAL MODELS). If the curvature is a constant positive number $a^2$, small regions of the surface are isometric to a region on a sphere in three space of radius $\frac{1}{a}$. Nevertheless, such a surface in three space need not be on a sphere. If, however, the surface is compact, then it is in fact a sphere of radius $\frac{1}{a}$. It is said that the sphere is rigid; *i.e.,* its shape in three space cannot be distorted without changing its curvature. Any compact surface with positive but not necessarily constant curvature is also rigid.

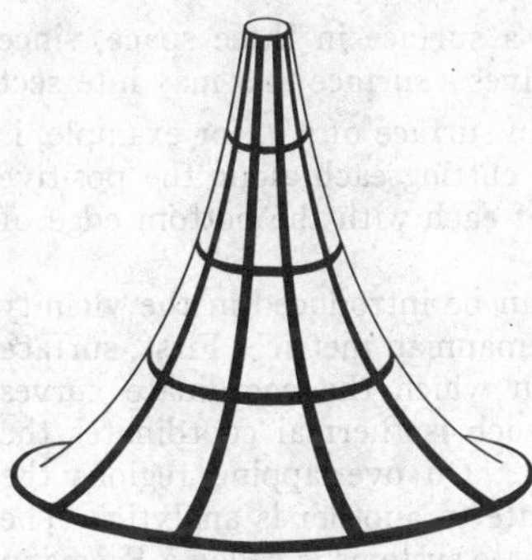

ADAPTED FROM D. HILBERT AND S. COHN-VOSSEN, "ANSCHAULICHE GEOMETRIE," JULIUS SPRINGER, BERLIN, 1932; COPYRIGHT INTERESTS HAVE BEEN VESTED IN THE ATTORNEY GENERAL OF THE U.S. PURSUANT TO LAW AND ARE PUBLISHED BY PERMISSION

FIG. 4.—PSEUDOSPHERE

Surfaces with constant negative curvature are harder to visualize. The simplest example with curvature $-a^2$ is the pseudosphere obtained by rotating the curve $y = f(x)$ in the $xy$ plane around the $y$ axis where $f'(x) = (a^2/x^2 - 1)^{1/2}$, $x$ strictly between 0 and $a$ (fig. 4). A small region of any surface with constant negative curvature $-a^2$ is isometric to a region on the pseudosphere. Geodesics on surfaces in three space with curvature $-a^2$ are not all infinitely extendable. Some must approach a boundary or singularity of the surface. On the pseudosphere this happens as $x$ approaches $a$.

The surfaces of constant curvature form models of non-Euclidean geometries, geometries in which Euclid's fifth or parallel postulate does not hold (*see* GEOMETRY: *Non-Euclidean Geometry*). On a surface, interpret straight line to mean geodesic, angle between intersecting lines as the angle between tangent vectors of intersecting geodesics, and parallel lines as geodesics that do not meet. Then a sphere with opposite points identified is an example of an elliptic non-Euclidean geometry in which every pair of lines meet; *i.e.,* every pair of geodesics (great circles) meet. A hyperbolic geometry is one in which there are many lines through a given point parallel to a given line. Examples of such a geometry stem from surfaces of constant negative curvature. A simple model is the interior of the circle in the plane of radius one. A metric structure can be placed on this set in such a way that the curvature is constantly $-1$ and geodesics are arcs of circles perpendicular to the given circle. Since there are many such arcs through a given point that do not meet a given arc, this space gives a hyperbolic geometry (fig. 5).

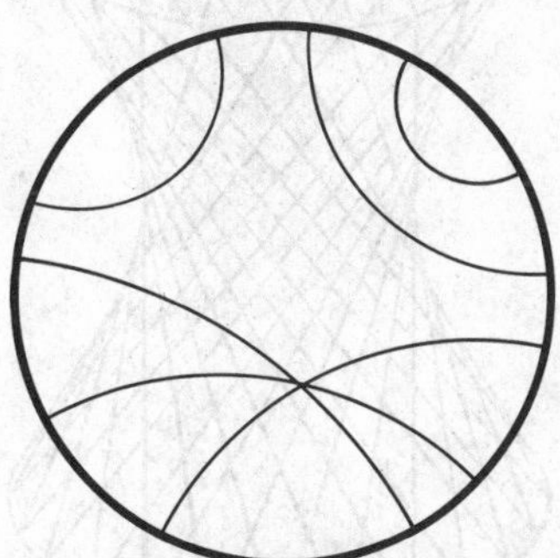

ADAPTED FROM R. COURANT AND H. E. ROBBINS, "WHAT IS MATHEMATICS?," 1941, OXFORD UNIVERSITY PRESS

FIG. 5.—POINCARÉ MODEL OF HYPERBOLIC GEOMETRY

The conformal structure of a surface is described in terms of the angle between vectors, ignoring vector lengths. Consideration of a conformal structure on a surface originated in the theory of analytic functions of a complex variable (*see* ANALYSIS, COMPLEX). If $f(z)$ is an analytic function in the complex plane, its differential sends tangent vectors at $z$ into tangent vectors at $f(z)$ so that the angle between corresponding pairs of vectors is the same; lengths of corresponding vectors need not be the same.

Suppose $f(z)$ is a multiple-valued function analytic on a portion of the complex plane; $\sqrt{z}$, for example. To find the largest domain in which it is analytic, in fact, to construct a set on which it is single valued, start with a single-valued branch of the function in a region of the plane and analytically extend or continue the function along curves as far as possible. When a region is reached in which the function has already been defined, this region is not identified with the original one unless the new function obtained agrees with the old function. In this way a surface (the Riemann surface) is constructed of the function $f(z)$ on which an extension of $f(z)$ is single valued. Since every sufficiently small portion of this surface is the same as a region in the plane, the complex coordinate $z$ is well defined on this portion. A function on this Riemann surface is analytic if it is an analytic function in every small region of the complex coordinate $z$. The Riemann surface of $f(z)$ is hard to visualize in three space and in general is not a surface in three space, since the analytic continuation process gives a surface that may intersect itself in three space. The Riemann surface of $\sqrt{z}$, for example, is constructed by taking two planes, cutting each along the positive axis, and pasting the upper edge of each with the bottom edge of the other.

A complex coordinate system can be introduced in the vicinity of any point of a surface with Riemannian metric. First, surface coordinate functions are found in which the coordinate curves are orthogonal. If $u$ and $v$ are such isothermal coordinates the complex coordinate is $z = u + iv$. On overlapping regions the change from one complex coordinate to another is analytic. The surface with these complex coordinate systems is called a Riemann surface or complex manifold. Two metrics on a surface give the same Riemann surface if their first fundamental forms differ only by a scale factor possibly varying from point to point. Two Riemann surfaces are conformal or analytically equivalent if there is a one-to-one correspondence between them that preserves angles. For example, the sphere with the north pole deleted is conformal with the plane. A particular conformal correspondence of the sphere with the plane useful in making flat maps of the earth is the Mercator projection (*see* MAP).

An algebraic surface in three space is one whose equation is $f(x,y,z) = 0$, with $f(x,y,z)$ a polynomial (*q.v.*) in $x,y,z$. The order of the surface is the degree of the polynomial equation. If the surface is of the first order, it is a plane. If the surface is of order two, it is called a quadric surface. By rotating the surface, its equation can be put in the form

$$Ax^2 + By^2 + Cz^2 + Dx + Ey + Fz = G$$

If $A,B,C$ are all not zero, the equation can generally be simplified to the form $ax^2 + by^2 + cz^2 = 1$. This surface is called an ellipsoid (*q.v.*) if $a$, $b$, and $c$ are positive. Its Gaussian curvature is positive at every point. If one of the coefficients is negative, the surface is a hyperboloid (*q.v.*) of one sheet (fig. 6); if two of the coefficients are negative, the surface is a hyperboloid of two sheets. A hyperboloid of one sheet can be visualized by rotating the hyperbola $x^2 - y^2 = 1$ about the $y$ axis. The surface has a saddle point at $x = 1$, $y = z = 0$. If the hyperbola is rotated about the $x$-axis, it generates a hyperboloid of two sheets. If $A,B,C$ are possibly zero, cylinders, cones, interesting planes, and elliptic or hyperbolic paraboloids may be produced (*see* PARABOLOID). Examples of the latter are $z = x^2 + y^2$ and $z = x^2 - y^2$, respectively. Through every point of a quadric pass two straight lines (possibly imaginary) lying on the surface. A cubic surface is one of order three. Its most remarkable property is that 27 lines lie on it, each one meeting 10 others. In general, a surface of order four or more contains no straight lines.

ADAPTED FROM R. COURANT AND H. E. ROBBINS, "WHAT IS MATHEMATICS?," 1941, OXFORD UNIVERSITY PRESS

FIG. 6.—HYPERBOLOID OF ONE SHEET

*See* also SOLIDS, GEOMETRIC.

BIBLIOGRAPHY.—L. Bianchi, *Lezioni di geometria differenziale* (1894); W. Blaschke, *Einführung in die Differentialgeometrie I* (1930); J. G. Darboux, *Leçons sur la théorie générale des surfaces* (1887); D. Hilbert and S. Cohn-Vossen, *Anschauliche Geometrie* (1932); D. J. Struik, *Differential Geometry*, 2nd ed. (1961); I. I. Trokhimchuk, *Continuous Mappings and Conditions of Monogeneity* (1965). (I. M. S.)

**SURFACE TENSION,** a force that gives liquid surfaces filmlike characteristics. Thus a thin razor blade or a water beetle can ride the surface of water without breaking through. The tension is explained as resulting from an attraction between molecules of the liquid. The following examples of other surface phenomena are explained in a similar way.

The surface of water (or other liquid) in a tank is not perfectly level but becomes curved where the liquid comes in contact with the wall of the tank.

If a tube with a very narrow bore (*see* CAPILLARY TUBE) is placed with one end in the water, the liquid rises above the level of the outer surface. The rise is greater the smaller the diameter of the bore. The rise of oil through a wick is a phenomenon of the same kind.

If a small quantity of mercury is poured on a horizontal plate, it forms a drop. Very small drops are nearly spherical; larger ones tend to have flat tops and rounded edges.

A drop of oil placed on a clean water surface spreads rapidly to form a very thin film. The thinness of the film can be judged from the size of the area covered by even a small drop. Soap bubbles and froth are other familiar examples of thin films.

Camphor fragments on a clean surface of water show rapidly changing motion. A minute quantity of oil placed on the surface brings them almost instantaneously to rest.

Such phenomena and others (*e.g., see* ADSORPTION), all arising at surfaces separating one medium from another, can be studied under one heading. The forces that come into play are known as surface forces. The rise in capillary tubes is called capillary action. This name, though often applied in other cases, is hardly applicable except to the case of narrow tubes; while the term surface action is applicable in all. The forces involved act between neighbouring parts of substances; they also produce the effects of cohesion.

Sir Isaac Newton in the third edition of his *Opticks* wrote: "The parts of all homogeneal hard Bodies, which fully touch one another, stick together very strongly . . . I . . . infer from their Cohesion that their Particles attract one another by some force which in immediate Contact is exceeding strong, at small distances performs the chymical Operations above mention'd, and reaches not far from the particles with any sensible Effect. . . . There are therefore Agents in Nature able to make the Particles of Bodies stick together by very strong Attractions. And it is the Business of experimental Philosophy to find them out."

These forces are distinguished from those of gravity which can act over very great distances (*see* FORCE). Cohesion acts to any measurable extent only over minute distances. If a stick of chalk is broken, the two parts no longer stick together; the neighbouring particles are still so far apart as to exert no sensible attraction. High pressure is needed to bring them close enough for this.

In some applications it is desirable to reduce the forces of cohesion; for example, great sums of money and considerable effort are devoted to the preparation of materials that act to reduce the surface tension of water. Such additives substantially increase the effectiveness of laundering, facilitate chemical reactions in manufacturing, and allow efficient recovery of petroleum from shale deposits (*see* DETERGENTS AND WETTING AGENTS).

**History.**—(The following historical summary is taken from James Clerk Maxwell's classical article in the 9th ed. of *Encyclopædia Britannica*, as modified by the 3rd Lord Rayleigh in the 10th ed.) According to J. C. Poggendorff (*Pogg. Ann.* ci. p. 551), Leonardo da Vinci must be considered as the discoverer of capillary phenomena, but the first accurate observations of the capillary action of tubes and glass plates were made by Francis Hauksbee (*Physico-Mechanical Experiments*, London, 1709, pp. 139–169; and *Phil. Trans.* 1711 and 1712), who ascribed the action to an attraction between the glass and the liquid. He observed that the effect was the same in thick tubes as in thin, and concluded that only those particles of the glass which are very near the surface have any influence on the phenomenon. Dr. James Jurin (*Phil. Trans.*, 1718, p. 739, and 1719, p. 1083) showed that the height at which the liquid is suspended depends on the section of the tube at the position of the meniscus, and is independent of the form of the lower part. Sir Isaac Newton devoted the 31st query in the last edition of his *Opticks* to molecular forces, and instanced several examples of the cohesion of liquids, such as the suspension of mercury in a barometer tube at more than double the height at which it usually stands. This arises from its adhesion to the tube, and the upper part of the mercury sustains a considerable tension, or negative pressure, without the separation of its parts. He considered the capillary phenomena to be of the same kind, but his explanation is not sufficiently explicit with respect to the nature and the limits of the action of the attractive force.

It is to be observed that, while these early speculators ascribe the phenomena to attraction, they do not distinctly assert that this attraction is sensible only at insensible distances, and that for all distances which we can directly measure the force is altogether insensible. The idea of such forces, however, had been distinctly formed by Newton, who gave the first example of the calculation of their effect in his theorem on the alteration of the path of a light-corpuscle when it enters or leaves a dense body.

Alexis Claude Clairaut (*Théorie de la figure de la terre,* Paris, 1808, pp. 105, 128) appears to have been the first to show the necessity of taking account of the attraction between the parts of the fluid itself in order to explain the phenomena. He did not, however, recognize the fact that the distance at which the attraction is sensible is not only small but altogether insensible. J. A. von Segner (*Comment. Soc. Reg. Götting.* i. p. 301) introduced the very important idea of the surface tension of liquids, which he ascribed to attractive forces, the sphere of whose action is so small that it cannot be perceived ("ut nullo adhuc sensu percipi potuerit").

In 1756 J. G. Leidenfrost (*De aquae communis nonnullis qualitatibus tractatus,* Duisburg) showed that a soap bubble tends to contract, so that if the tube with which it was blown is left open the bubble will diminish in size and will expel through the tube the air which it contains.

In 1787 Gaspard Monge (*Mémoires de l'Acad. des Sciences,* 1787, p. 506) asserted that "by supposing the adherence of the particles of a fluid to have a sensible effect only at the surface itself and in the direction of the surface it would be easy to determine the curvature of the surfaces of fluids in the neighbourhood of the solid boundaries which contain them; that these surfaces would be *linteariae* of which the tension, constant in all directions, would be everywhere equal to the adherence of two particles, and the phenomena of capillary tubes would then present nothing which could not be determined by analysis." He applied this principle of surface tension to the explanation of the apparent attractions and repulsions between bodies floating on a liquid.

In 1802 John Leslie (*Phil. Mag.,* 1802, vol. xiv, p. 193) gave the first modern explanation of the rise of a liquid in a tube by considering the effect of the attraction of the solid on the very thin stratum of the liquid in contact with it. He did not, like the earlier speculators, suppose this attraction to act in an upward direction so as to support the fluid directly. He showed that the attraction is everywhere normal to the surface of the solid. The direct effect of the attraction is to increase the pressure of the stratum of the fluid in contact with the solid, so as to make it greater than the pressure within the fluid.

In 1804 Thomas Young (essay on the "Cohesion of Fluids," *Phil. Trans.,* 1805, p. 65) founded the theory of capillary phenomena on the principle of surface tension. He also observed the constancy of the angle of contact of a liquid surface with a solid, and showed how from these two principles to deduce the phenomena of capillary action. His essay contains the solution of a great number of cases, including most of those afterwards solved by Laplace, but his methods of demonstration, though always precise, and often extremely elegant, are sometimes rendered obscure by his scrupulous avoidance of mathematical symbols. Having applied the secondary principle of surface tension to the various particular cases of capillary action, Young proceeded to deduce surface tension from underlying principles. He supposed the particles to act on one another with two different kinds of force, one of which, the attractive forces of cohesion, extends to particles at a greater distance than those to which the repulsive force is confined. He further supposed that the attractive force is constant throughout the minute distance to which it extends, but that the repulsive force increases rapidly as the distance diminishes. He thus showed that, at a curved part of the surface, a superficial particle would be urged towards the centre of curvature of the surface, and he gave reasons for concluding that this force is proportional to the sum of the curvatures of the surface in two normal planes at right angles to each other.

The subject was next taken up by Pierre Simon Laplace (*Mécanique céleste,* supplement to the tenth book, pub. in 1806). His results are in many respects identical with those of Young, but his methods of arriving at them are very different, being conducted entirely by mathematical calculations. For those who wish to study the molecular constitution of bodies it is necessary to study the effect of forces which are sensible only at insensible distances; and Laplace has furnished us with an example of the method of this study which has never been surpassed. He found for the pressure $p$ at a point in the interior of the fluid an expression of the form

$$p = \mathrm{K} + \tfrac{1}{2}\mathrm{H}(1/R + 1/R')$$

where K is a constant pressure, probably very large, which, however, does not influence capillary phenomena, and therefore cannot be determined from observation of such phenomena; H is another constant on which all capillary phenomena depend; and $R$ and $R'$ are the radii of curvature of any two normal sections of the surface at right angles to each other.

The next great step in the treatment of the subject was made by J. C. F. Gauss (*Principia generalia Theoriae Figurae Fluidorum in statu Aequilibrii,* Göttingen, 1830, or *Werke,* v. 29, Göttingen, 1867). The principle which he adopted is that of virtual velocities, a principle which under his hands was gradually transforming itself into what is now known as the principle of the conservation of energy. Instead of calculating the direction and magnitude of the resultant force on each particle arising from the action of neighbouring particles, he formed a single expression which is the aggregate of all the potentials arising from the mutual action between pairs of particles. This expression has been called the force function. With its sign reversed it is now called the potential energy of the system. It consists of three parts, the first depending on the action of gravity, the second on the mutual action between the particles of the fluid, and the third on the interaction of the particles of the fluid and the particles of a solid or fluid in contact with it.

The condition of equilibrium is that this expression (which we may for the sake of distinctness call the potential energy) shall be a minimum. This condition when worked out gives not only the equation of the free surface in the form already established by Laplace, but the conditions of the angle of contact of this surface with the surface of a solid.

In 1831 Siméon Denis Poisson published his *Nouvelle Théorie de l'action capillaire.* He maintained that there is a rapid variation of density near the surface of a liquid, and he gave very strong reasons, which have been only strengthened by subsequent discoveries, for believing that this is the case.

The result, however, of Poisson's investigation is practically equivalent to that already obtained by Laplace. In both theories the equation of the liquid surface is the same, involving a constant H which can be determined only by experiment. The only difference is in the manner in which this quantity H depends on the law of the molecular forces and the law of density near the surface of the fluid, and as these laws are unknown to us we cannot obtain any test to discriminate between the two theories.

We have now described the principal forms of the theory of capillary action during its earlier development. In more recent times the method of Gauss has been modified so as to take account of the variation of density near the surface, and its language has been translated in terms of the modern doctrine of the conservation of energy. *See* Enrico Betti, *Teoria della Capillarità: Nuovo Cimento* (1867); a memoir by M. Stahl, "Ueber einige Punckte in der Theorie der Capillarerscheinungen," *Pogg. Ann.* cxxxix. p. 239 (1870); and J. D. Van der Waals' *Over de Continuiteit van den Gas- en Vloeistoftoestand.* A good account of the subject from a mathematical point of view will be found in James Challis's "Report on the Theory of Capillary Attraction," *Brit. Assn. Report,* iv. p. 235 (1834).

J. A. F. Plateau (*Statique expérimentale et théorique des liquides,* 1873), who made elaborate study of the phenomena of surface tension, adopted the following method of getting rid of the effects of gravity. He formed a mixture of alcohol and water of the same density as olive oil, and then introduced a quantity of oil into the mixture. It assumes the form of a sphere under the action of surface tension alone. He then, by means of rings of iron wire, discs, and other contrivances, altered the form of certain parts of the surface of the oil. The free portions of the surface then assume new forms depending on the equilibrium of surface tension. In this way he produced a great many of the forms of equilibrium of a liquid under the action of surface tension alone, and compared them with the results of mathematical investigation. The debt science owes to Plateau is not diminished by the fact that, while investigating these beautiful phenomena, he never saw them, having lost his sight about 1840.

G. L. van der Mensbrugghe (*Mém. de l'Acad. Roy. de Belgique*, xxxvii., 1873) devised a great number of beautiful illustrations of the phenomena of surface tension, and showed their connection with the experiments of Charles Tomlinson on the figures formed by oils dropped on the clean surface of water.

Athanase Dupré in his 5th, 6th, and 7th memoirs on the mechanical theory of heat (*Ann. de Chimie et de Physique*, 1866–68) applied the principles of thermodynamics to capillary phenomena, and the experiments of his son Paul were exceedingly ingenious and well devised, tracing the influence of surface tension in a great number of very different circumstances, and deducing from independent methods the numerical value of the surface tension. The experimental evidence which Dupré obtained bearing on the molecular structure of liquids must be very valuable, even if our present opinions on this subject should turn out to require modification.

## GENERAL THEORY OF CAPILLARY ACTION

It is found by experiment that the forces between molecules to which cohesion is due only act perceptibly across very short distances. If we regard the forces between two particles as acting according to a law depending only upon their positions it must vary inversely as the distance according to a higher power than that of the inverse square which is obeyed by gravitation. The experiments of G. H. Quincke and others show that the extreme range through which sensible effect is produced by them is certainly much less than a thousandth of a centimetre and it is probably less than one millionth.

In order to illustrate the important bearing of this limitation in range, consider a molecule $A$ well within a substance (fig. 1).

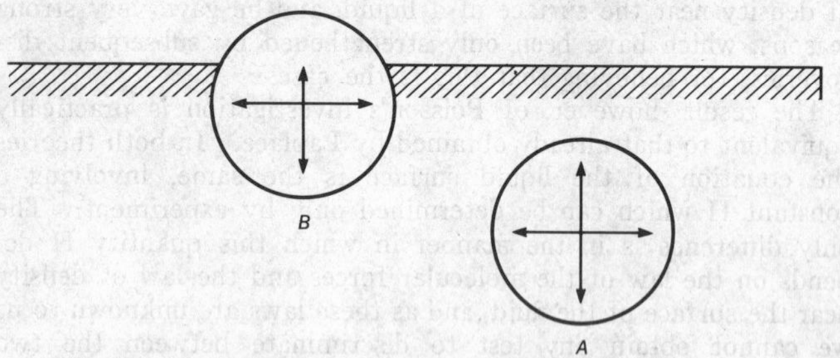


FIG. 1

A sphere of a thousandth of a centimetre radius may be drawn round it and the molecules outside this sphere will have no sensible influence on $A$. Those within the sphere attract $A$ but in the case of a homogeneous isotropic body their pulls will be uniformly distributed and the resultant force on $A$ will be zero. There will, however, be a pressure throughout the sphere due to the attraction; each spherical layer, being attracted, will compress the particles lying inside it. But if we consider a particle $B$ very near the surface—nearer in fact than the range of action—the state of things will be found to be different. There will be more particles pulling $B$ downwards than upwards so that all such particles as $B$ will undergo a resultant force downwards. There will also be a pressure at $B$ but its value is less the nearer $B$ is to the surface. There is, therefore, a thin, indefinitely bounded layer near the surface which is in a different condition from the main body of the substance. Many of the properties will be different in this surface layer from elsewhere. For example, corresponding to the different pressure, the density will be different. Since work is done in producing compression the potential energy will differ in the two regions. In the main body it can be written

$$\int \chi_0\rho_0 dV = \chi_0\rho_0 V_0$$

where $V$ = volume, $\rho$ density, and $\chi$ the potential energy per unit mass; in the film, owing to its minute thickness $e$ (which we divide up into still thinner layers $de$), and surface (area) $S$ we write total mass $M$ as

$$M = V\rho_0 - S\int_0^e (\rho_0 - \rho)\, de$$

while the total potential energy $E$ (in terms of $\chi$ its value per unit mass) is written

$$E = \int \chi\rho dV$$

or

$$E = V\chi_0\rho_0 - S\int_0^e (\chi_0\rho_0 - \chi\rho) de$$

Multiplying the total mass $M$ by $\chi_0$ and subtracting from the last expression

$$E - M\chi_0 = S\int_0^e (\chi - \chi_0)\rho de$$

The right-hand side is therefore an expression for that part of the energy which depends upon the existence of a surface $S$. The integral which multiplies it is the constant (or rather, factor) known as the surface tension. This integral is a measure of the work done in increasing the area of the surface. It must be carefully distinguished from the corresponding increase in the total energy because heat energy is drawn in simultaneously if the change takes place at constant temperature.

By the principles of energy the potential energy (at constant temperature) tends to a minimum; in other words, any change that takes place spontaneously involves a diminution of this energy. Hence whenever the surface tension is positive there will be a tendency for the surface to decrease, and the diminution will in fact take place unless it is resisted by other forces. This diminution takes place not by a contraction of the liquid but by a passage of the surface molecules into the body of the liquid. The properties of the body are not changed thereby. In this respect the phenomenon is quite different from the case of a stretched india-rubber film. For the liquid the surface tension remains constant during the contraction of the surface area; in the case of the stretched india-rubber it diminishes with the contraction.

We may express it otherwise by saying that if an imaginary straight line be drawn anywhere in the surface, when equilibrium exists there must be a force acting across the line in such a direction as to prevent further contraction of area. It may be shown that this force per unit length of line is numerically the same as the surface tension as defined above.

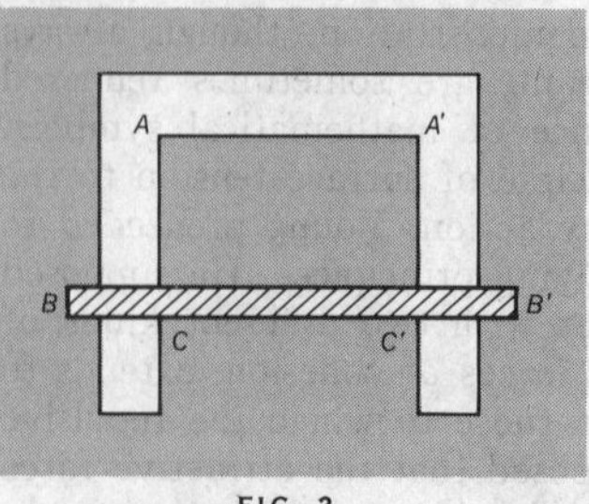


FIG. 2

The surface tension of a liquid film may be illustrated with a piece of sheet metal cut in the form $AA'$ (fig. 2). A very fine slip of metal is laid on it in the position $BB'$ and the whole is dipped into a solution of soap. When it is taken out the rectangle $AA'CC'$ is filled by a liquid film. This film tends to contract on itself and the loose strip of metal will, if let go, be drawn toward $AA'$. If $S$ is the area of one face of the film the potential energy is $\sigma S$. If $AA' = b$ and $AC = a$ it is equal to $\sigma ab$. Hence if $F$ is the force by which the slip is pulled toward $AA'$, $F = \frac{d}{db}(\sigma ab) = \sigma a$;

so that the force per unit length for one face is $\sigma$. Hence $\sigma$ is either the force per unit length or the potential energy per unit area.

It must be added that we have only considered one of the two faces and the force due to it. There is an equal force on the strip due to the second surface so that the total force is twice as great as the value taken. But the total area is twice as great also so that the conclusion remains unchanged.

There are other ways of illustrating the existence of the tension. Form a film as before but in a fixed frame. Tie a short length of fine unspun silk to form a flexible ring. If it is placed carefully on the film it usually takes an irregular shape. If the film inside the ring is destroyed by piercing it with a hot wire the silk opens into a circular form, this being the form that minimizes the surrounding surface for a given length of thread. Again, a small drop of mercury or a falling raindrop is practically spherical—the sphere being the form with the smallest area for a given volume. A large drop fails to be spherical because gravitational forces are then strong enough to compete successfully with surface forces. Sometimes a difficulty is felt in connection with the assertion that the surface tension is constant. Take a film such as we considered and place it vertically. The upward force on $AA' = 2\sigma a$ for the two faces, the downward force at the level $CC'$ is also $2\sigma a$. The remaining force on the portion of the film between these lines is its weight. Hence the resultant force on the mass of the film is its weight and its acceleration should therefore be that of a freely falling body. Yet whatever may be found for a pure substance, it does not hold in general that the tension is the same at all parts of a large area. In the case of a soap film some adjustment automatically occurs (either by alteration of concentration or otherwise) which makes the upper tension a little greater than the lower. This produces a durable film that otherwise would fall to pieces.

**Theory of Cohesion.**—Cohesion was once explained by assuming forces between elements (*i.e.*, infinitesimal volumes) of matter; it was supposed that the substance of a body is distributed continuously instead of being partitioned into molecules. Such was the mode in which Laplace regarded it. The reasoning ran as follows:

Let the force between two elementary volumes be supposed proportional to the product of the volumes and inversely as the $n$th power of their distances apart. The force required is that across unit area drawn anywhere well inside the body arising from the volumes on each side of it.

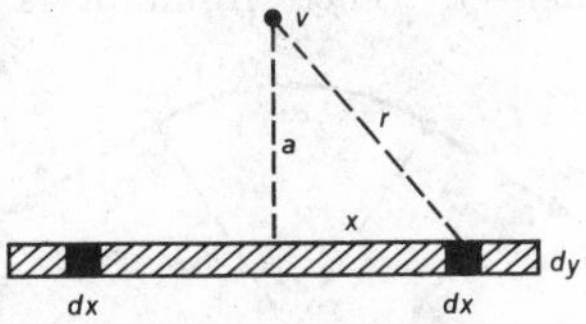

FIG. 3

Take a lamina of thickness $dy$ (fig. 3). The force on an elementary volume $v$ due to a zone of radius $x$ and width $dx$ is $v \cdot \frac{2\pi x dx}{r^n} \cdot \frac{a}{r}\, dy$ since the tangential components will cancel each other. Hence the whole lamina attracts the element with a force

$$2\pi va \int_a^\infty \frac{x dx}{r^{n+1}}\, dy = 2\pi va \int_a^\infty \frac{dr}{r^n}\, dy$$

This becomes $\frac{2\pi va}{(n-1)a^{n-1}} dy$ or $\frac{2\pi v}{(n-1)a^{n-2}} dy$ since we assume the forces to vanish at infinity.

Let $v$ be an element in a parallel lamina of thickness $da$. Then the total force per unit area on such a lamina is obtained by putting $v = da$. Hence we find the force on a semi-infinite solid above lamina II due to lamina I shown in fig. 3 by integrating from 0 to $\infty$; that is

$$\text{Force on semisolid (per unit area)} = \frac{2\pi dy}{n-1} \int_0^\infty \frac{da}{a^{n-2}}$$

$$= \frac{2\pi}{(n-1)(n-3)} \left| \frac{1}{a^{n-3}} \right|_0^\infty$$

The force (per unit area) on such a semi-infinite body due to a semi-infinite body in contact with it is obtained by integrating with respect to $y$ from $y = 0$ to $y = \infty$. This force is the cohesion per unit area and is given by

$$K_0 = \frac{2\pi}{(n-1)(n-3)(n-4)} \left| \frac{1}{a^{n-4}} \right|_0^\infty$$

The unit of force used is that between two unit volumes separated by unit distance.

Lord Rayleigh noted: "The pressure will therefore be infinite whatever $n$ may be. If $n-4$ be negative the attraction of infinitely distant parts contributes to the result; while if $n-4$ be positive the parts in immediate contiguity act with infinite power. For the transition case, discussed by W. Sutherland (*Phil. Mag.* xxiv. p. 113, 1887) of $n = 4$, $K$ is also infinite. . . . It seems therefore that nothing satisfactory can be arrived at under this head."

It was later realized that to treat the body as a continuum is bound to give erroneous results; and modern explanations are based on the notion of discrete units (molecules). If we assume the existence of attractions depending on the distance between the centres of the molecules it is at the same time necessary to recognize that the two halves of the body can never approach to absolute contact. The lower limit in the last integration should be the least distance of separation between the lines of centres of contiguous layers. This will be a magnitude comparable with the molecular diameter $s$. The value we seek then becomes

$$K_0 = \frac{2\pi}{(n-1)(n-3)(n-4)} \cdot \frac{1}{s^{n-4}}$$

There is now no objection on the above grounds to the power law provided that $n > 4$.

There can be no doubt that if the amount of matter compressed into unit volume (*i.e.*, the density $\rho$) be increased the value of the intrinsic pressure would be increased. Moreover, a factor $\Gamma$ (akin to the gravitation constant) is also needed if $K$ is to be expressed in ordinary dynamic units. Hence finally

$$K = \Gamma \cdot \frac{2\pi\rho^2}{(n-1)(n-3)(n-4)} \cdot \frac{1}{s^{n-4}}$$

The quantity $K$ is called the Laplace pressure or intrinsic pressure. More generally we could assume that the force between elementary volumes is $f(r)$. The successive integrals then become

$$2\pi a \int_a^\infty f(r) dr dy = 2\pi a\phi(a)\, dy$$

$$2\pi dy \int_y^\infty a\phi(a)\, da = 2\pi dy\, \psi(y)$$

$$K_0 = 2\pi \int_s^\infty \psi(y)\, dy$$

where $\phi a$, $\psi y$ are written as the values of successive integrals. Finally $K$ is obtained in ordinary units by multiplying by $\Gamma\rho^2$. For example if $f(r) = e^{-kr}$ where $k$ is a constant we have

$$\psi(s) = \frac{ks+1}{k^3} e^{-ks}$$

The difficulty in testing these equations arises from the occurrence of three variables ($k$, $s$, $\Gamma$). The only one whose value is known independently is $s$ which for liquids must be of the same order as the molecular diameter. Caution is necessary in considering forces that vary as greatly with distance as cohesive forces undoubtedly do. A small error in the assumed value for $s$ would lead to very considerable error in $k$ and $\Gamma$. The intrinsic pressure at the breaking point of a solid in tension should be the breaking stress itself. The latter as actually measured is, however, only a lower limit of $K$ since flaws in the material and irregularities in the application of the tension will lead to fracture occurring at a value lower than the ideal stress (*see* SOLID STATE PHYSICS). The effect of cohesion on the characteristic equation of a gas was allowed for by van der Waals who, following Laplace, took the intrinsic pressure as varying with the density square alone. The equation becomes

$$(p + ap^2)(v - b) = RT$$

where at the same time $b$ is introduced to represent the fact that the volume of the gas cannot be reduced to zero. Here $K = a\rho^2$ which for water at ordinary densities is between 10–20 atmospheres. The fact that the equation turns out to be approximate only makes caution necessary. Moreover $a$ is found to vary nearly inversely as the absolute temperature. We are obliged to assume, therefore, either that $\Gamma$ is a function of the temperature or, what is more likely, that $s$ is such a function. The latter assumption is indeed a very plausible one, for the least average distance of approach of the molecules must be affected by the motion of agitation amongst them and this increases as the square root of the absolute temperature.

Besides these considerations it must be pointed out that this modification only partly allows for the effects arising from the molecular character of matter. If the forces between two molecules at a given distance apart are known, the actual value of the intrinsic pressure could only be correctly obtained by summing up the components (normal to the interface at which the pressure is being calculated) of all the forces between every pair of molecules, each being calculated for the actual instantaneous positions of the molecules. With forces that vary so fast with distance the important molecules are those that are fairly near any given point; the contributions of the remainder may be estimated by an approximate method such as that followed by Laplace. If it is assumed (as experiment suggests) that the force may vary up to the inverse seventh power of distance, the force between molecules that are neighbours and those that are next door to neighbours will be as $2^7$ to 1 (*i.e.*, in the ratio 128 to 1) or that between any layer and the next and next but one contiguous layer as $2^6$ to 1 (*i.e.*, in the ratio of 64 to 1). Hence all but a small percentage of the intrinsic pressure is due to the molecules in a small volume surrounding the point. This conclusion signifies that in any material (gas, liquid, solid) the intrinsic pressure will be uniform at all points except for a thin layer of usually negligible volume near its boundary.

**Theory of Surface Forces.**—This surface layer has theoretically no inner boundary but it may be taken, for most purposes, as being only a few molecules thick (molecular diameter is of the order of $10^{-8}$ cm.). The most prominent peculiarity is that it possesses more potential energy than the rest of the body per unit volume.

Now increase of so-called free (Gibbs) energy (*see* THERMODYNAMICS) at constant temperature is equal to the external work done on a system. If we write $dW = \sigma dA$, $\sigma$ is called the surface tension. To determine its value theoretically we estimate $dW$ for the formation of a surface of unit area. Now if a body is split by a plane section and the two halves separated, a fresh surface is formed. The attraction per unit area between the halves at any distance $x$ may be given as

$$2\pi \int_x^\infty \psi(y)dy = K(x)$$

The total work of separation is $\int_s^\infty K(x)\,dx$ and in the process a fresh area of 2 units is formed. Hence expressing the work done in ordinary units

$$2\sigma = 2\pi\Gamma\rho^2 \int_s^\infty K(x)dx$$

If a power law is taken as the law of force between molecules it follows that

$$\sigma = \frac{\pi\rho^2\Gamma}{(n-1)(n-3)(n-4)(n-5)s^{n-5}}$$

This law may be combined with that for $K$ with the result that

$$\frac{K}{\sigma} = \frac{2(n-5)}{s}$$

For water at ordinary temperature (approximately)

$K = 10{,}000$ atm. $= 10^{10}$ dynes/cm.$^2$

$\sigma = 75$ dynes/cm.

$s = 4 \times 10^{-8}$ cm.

Whence, $n - 5 = \dfrac{10^{10} \times 4 \times 10^{-8}}{2 \times 75} = \dfrac{8}{3}$

and $n = 7.67$

It must not be forgotten, however, that $K$ and $s$ are obtained by very approximate methods only.

**Interfacial Tensions.**—When liquids 1 and 2 (composed of different species of molecule) are in contact, there is in general a surface tension at the interface which is called interfacial tension. Denoting this as $\sigma_{12}$, the tensions of the liquids as $\sigma_1$ and $\sigma_2$ respectively, and carrying out a separation of the two liquids, the value of $\sigma_{12}$ can be determined. In the above process the interface between 1 and 2 disappears and two fresh surfaces appear at which the tensions are $\sigma_1$ and $\sigma_2$. Hence

$$\sigma_2 + \sigma_1 - \sigma_{12} = 2\pi\rho_1\rho_2 \int_{\frac{s_1+s_2}{2}}^\infty K(x)dx$$

where the lower limit is the sum of the radii of the two kinds of molecule. Hence

$$\sigma_{12} = \pi\rho_2^2F(s_2) + \pi\rho_1^2F(s_1) - 2\pi\rho_1\rho_2F\left(\frac{s_1+s_2}{2}\right)$$

If the power law is valid and is the same law for different substances the equations given here lead to

$$\sigma_{12} = \left(\frac{\rho_2^2}{\sigma_2^{n-5}} + \frac{\rho_1^2}{\sigma_1^{n-5}} - \frac{2\rho_1\rho_2}{\left(\frac{s_1+s_2}{2}\right)^{n-5}}\right)\frac{\pi}{(n-1)(n-3)(n-4)(n-5)}$$

All surface tensions with which we have to deal are interfacial tensions since a liquid is always in contact with its own vapour or the gas in which it is immersed. The effect due to the gas is known, however, to be very small.

The normal pressure to be expected from the existence of a superficial tension may be given in the example of a cylinder. Consider an element of surface $ds$; the tensions acting at its extreme edges are inclined to one another and have a resultant inwards (fig. 4). Their resultant is a normal force $2\sigma\sin\frac{d\theta}{2}$ or in the limit $\sigma d\theta$. But $\frac{ds}{d\theta} = R$ (the radius of curvature); hence the normal force is $\sigma\frac{ds}{R}$. Since this acts over an area equal to $ds$, the normal pressure is $\sigma/R$.

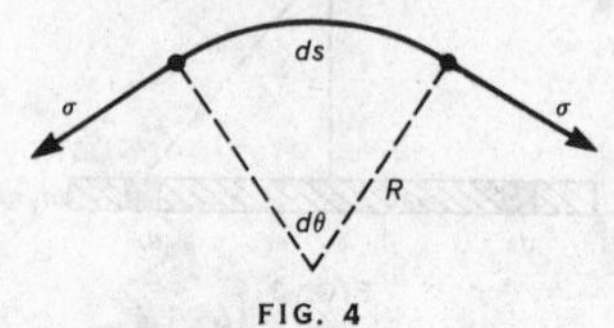

FIG. 4

If we take a body of any shape and select a square-bounded element of the surface, the tensions in the plane of the diagram are equivalent to a normal force $\sigma ds_1 \times \frac{ds_2}{R_1}$ and those acting on the other two edges to $\sigma ds_2 \times \frac{ds_1}{R_2}$. Hence per unit area

$$p = \sigma\left(\frac{1}{R_1} + \frac{1}{R_2}\right)$$

Here $R_1$ and $R_2$ are the radii of curvature in two planes at right angles. Owing to Gauss's theorem of integral curvature the sum of two such curvatures at a point is a constant. The above theorem therefore holds whether the two rectangular planes considered are principal planes or otherwise. In the case of a sphere

$$p = \frac{2\sigma}{R}$$

**Effect of Temperature.**—The variation of surface tension with temperature was not taken into account in Laplace's theory. The forces between molecules were taken, like gravitational forces, to be independent of temperature. The rise in a capillary tube was supposed to vary merely because the density varied. Experiment has shown, however, that the tension itself in all cases diminishes with rise in temperature. That it will tend to diminish to zero can be inferred from the notion that at the critical state a liquid and its vapour will become identical; the tension at the interface must then be zero. R. Eotvös introduced the conception of molecular surface tension. By somewhat doubtful reasoning he concluded that $\sigma(Mv)^{\frac{2}{3}}$ (where $Mv$ is the molecular volume) plotted against temperature should give the same kind of curve for different substances, and he found that it was representable by $K(T_c - T)$ where $T_c$ is the critical temperature and $K$ a constant. Empirically, however, $K$ varies between 1.5 and 2.6 and it is necessary also to change $T_c - T$ to $T_c - T - \delta$ where $\delta$ is a small constant, so that the law is only a rough one. According to this equation the curve would be a straight line cutting the temperature axis a few degrees below the critical point.

In connection with this, remember that $\sigma$ is only the so-called free energy per unit area and not the total energy per unit area $(u)$. Lord Kelvin was the first to show that, in the variation of $\sigma$ with temperature, $u$ must be greater than $\sigma$; in other words, when an expansion of the surface takes place heat energy must be added to keep the temperature constant. The connection between these quantities he showed thermodynamically to be $u = \sigma - T\frac{d\sigma}{dT}$. Now, at the critical point, $u$ (which is only the extra energy due to the existence of unit surface and not the total energy of the whole body) must also vanish. But if both $u$ and $\sigma$ are then zero so also must $T\frac{d\sigma}{dT}$ be zero.

Hence, if our conceptions of the critical state are correct the curve of $\sigma$ plotted against $T$ instead of being a straight line must become horizontal at the critical point. In 1894 van der Waals showed that a formula of the type $\sigma = A(T_c - T)^n$ was to be expected and gave the average value of $n = 1.27$ as deducible from the experimental values. In 1916 A. Ferguson (*Phil. Mag.*, Jan. 1916), examining the data for 14 different organic substances, showed that the best values of $n$ ranged from 1.187 to 1.248. The advantageous character of this power equation is that it makes $\sigma$, $u$, and $\frac{d\sigma}{dT}$ all equal to zero at the critical point and it thus satisfies all that is required of it theoretically.

Liquids, however, do not follow the above simple law. The surface energy $u$ also falls to zero at the critical point, but according to a different law. For taking the equation $u = \sigma - T\frac{d\sigma}{dT}$ it follows that $u = A(T_c - T)^{n-1}(T_c + [n-1]T)$. Curve B for $\sigma$ and curve A for $u$ are shown in fig. 5 for the case of benzene. The figure shows how nearly a straight-line law satisfies the values of $\sigma$ until the critical point is closely approached. An interesting relation was given by E. T. Whittaker between $u$ and the latent heat (internal) of evaporation. The internal latent heat $(L_i)$ is obtained by subtracting the external work done from the ordinary latent heat. The relation in question is that $\frac{T_c}{T} \cdot \frac{u}{L_i}$ is nearly a constant, and that (in cgs units) this constant is about unity for ethyl oxide, methyl formate, benzene, and chlorobenzene, and about 2 for carbon tetrachloride. The degree of constancy is indicated in the following table for benzene (critical temperature about 561.5° K).

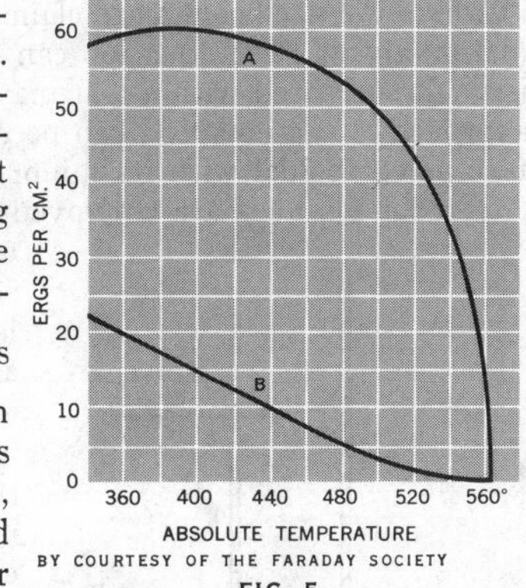

BY COURTESY OF THE FARADAY SOCIETY

FIG. 5

| $T°K$ | $\frac{T_c u}{T L_i}$ | $T°K$ | $\frac{T_c u}{T L_i}$ |
|---|---|---|---|
| 353 | 1.106 | 493 | 1.089 |
| 403 | 1.100 | 503 | 1.106 |
| 453 | 1.067 | 513 | 1.129 |

The relation indicates a close connection between the surface energy and the volume energy of the substances.

**General Properties of Surface Tension.**—The tension of a liquid across any straight line drawn on the surface is normal to that line and is the same for all directions of the line. It is measured by the force across an element of the line divided by the length of that element.

For any given homogeneous liquid surface, as the surface that separates water from air or oil from water, the tension is the same at every point of the surface and in every direction. In the case of mixtures, however, when circumstances demand it (*e.g.*, when the surface is inclined and the effects of a gravitation field require consideration) the concentration at the surface may adjust from point to point to produce a corresponding variation in surface tension to produce equilibrium. This effect is very minute and in most problems may be ignored.

When the surface is curved the effect of the surface tension is to make the pressure on the concave side greater than that on the convex side by $\sigma(C_1 + C_2)$ where $C_1$ and $C_2$ are the curvatures in mutually perpendicular normal planes.

The tension of the surface separating two liquids cannot be deduced by any reliable method from the tensions of the liquids when separately in contact with air.

The experiments of C. G. M. Marangoni, van der Mensbrugghe, and Quincke show that the common surface between two liquids has a tension always less than the difference of the tensions of the separate liquids. This is usually referred to as Marangoni's rule.

If three liquids meet along a line the interfaces at the common edge must be parallel to the sides of a triangle proportional to the three tensions $\sigma_{12}$, $\sigma_{23}$, $\sigma_{31}$; otherwise equilibrium cannot obtain (Neumann's rule). This triangle cannot exist unless two of the interfacial tensions are greater than the third. Marangoni's experimental rule shows that the triangle is always imaginary. Hence three pure fluids (of which one may be a gas) accordingly cannot remain in contact. If a drop of oil stands in a lenticular form upon a surface of water, it indicates that the water surface is already contaminated with a greasy film.

When a solid body is in contact with two fluids (fig. 6) the surface of the solid cannot alter its form but the angle at which the surface of contact of the two fluids meets the surface of the solid will depend on the values of the three surface tensions. For equilibrium

$$\sigma_{31} - \sigma_{32} = \sigma_{21} \cos \alpha$$

The angle $\alpha$ is known as the angle of contact. For pure substances the angle of contact varies from 0° (or very nearly so) for liquids that "wet" the solid to 130° or 140° for mercury in contact with glass.

3 1 α 2

FIG. 6

In regard to the experimental behaviour of water on mercury the wealth of papers is equalled by the remarkable lack of uniformity in the results obtained even when elaborate precautions are taken. A drop of water that fails to spread when placed on a mercury surface often will spread when the mercury is poured out of the dish—thus involving the production of a new surface.

**Form of a Capillary Surface.**—The form of the surface of a liquid acted on by gravity may be determined if it is assumed that near the liquid-solid interface it is straight and horizontal. This will be the case, for example, near a flat plate dipped into the liquid.

Let $A_2P_2$ in fig. 7 be the vertical plate supposed to be so wide that the edge effects do not count. Consider the forces per unit depth (perpendicular to the paper) and consider $A_1A_2$ as the standard level of the liquid far from the plate. The curvature of the surface at the point $x, y$ $(P_1)$ is

$$\frac{d\theta}{ds} = \sin\theta\frac{d\theta}{dy} = -\frac{d(\cos\theta)}{dy}$$

and consequently the pressure in the liquid at that point is less than the pressure outside it by $-\sigma\dfrac{d(\cos\theta)}{dy}$. But the pressure is less than that at a distant point where the surface is flat by $g\rho y$ or $g(\rho-\rho_0)y$ if allowance is made for the surrounding gas. Hence the differential equation for the surface is

$$-\frac{d(\cos\theta)}{dy}=\frac{g(\rho-\rho_0)}{\sigma}y$$

the integral of which is $1-\cos\theta=2\sin^2\dfrac{\theta}{2}=\dfrac{g(\rho-\rho_0)}{\sigma}\cdot\dfrac{y^2}{2}$. The shape of the surface is therefore the elastica; *i.e.*, the form taken by a uniform spring when equal and opposite forces are applied at its ends. The equation might have been found by considering the elementary volume $dx$ of a strip of liquid sustained above the normal level of the liquid by the surface forces at its outer and inner edges. The difference of the vertical component of these is $\sigma d(\sin\theta)$ and the weight of the strip is $g\rho y dx$ but since $\dfrac{d(\sin\theta)}{dx}=\dfrac{d(\cos\theta)}{dy}$ the same result is obtained.

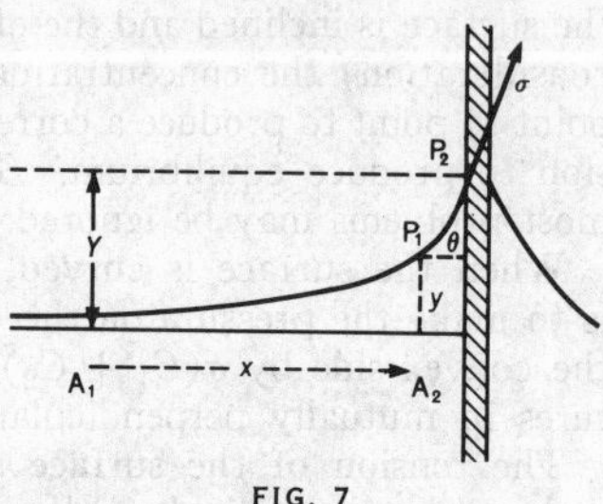

FIG. 7

If the angle of contact is $\alpha$ the value of $\theta$ at the plate is $\dfrac{\pi}{2}-\alpha$; hence

$$1-\sin\alpha=\frac{g(\rho-\rho_0)}{\sigma}\cdot\frac{Y^2}{2}$$

which gives the greatest height through which the liquid is raised. A thin sheet of glass suspended from the arm of a balance and just dipping into a liquid provides a simple way of determining the surface tension.

The increase in the apparent weight of the sheet when the liquid has been raised by capillarity is $\sigma$ multiplied by twice the horizontal length of the sheet. An unusually sensitive form of this apparatus is known as Worthington's multiplier, a special piece of equipment in which the strip is rolled into a vertical cylindrical spiral.

**Ascent up a Capillary Tube.**—A capillary tube dipped in a liquid provides a simple method of determining surface tension. To connect the surface tension with the rise (or descent) of the liquid in the tube measured from the level part of the outside surface, equate the effective weight of the liquid raised to the total force due to the tension. The effective weight (with the symbols shown in fig. 8) is

$$g(\rho-\rho_0)\int_0^x 2\pi x(h+y)dx$$

for an inner cylinder of radius $x$ where $\rho$ is the density of the liquid and $\rho_0$ that of the surrounding gas or vapour. The vertical component of the surface force acting all around the edge of the liquid surface of this cylinder is $2\pi x\sigma\sin\theta$ or $2\pi x\sigma\cos\alpha$ where $\theta$ is the angle between the surface and the horizontal and $\alpha$ is the contact angle which is measured with respect to the solid surface (in this case the vertical). These two expressions are to be equated to one another.

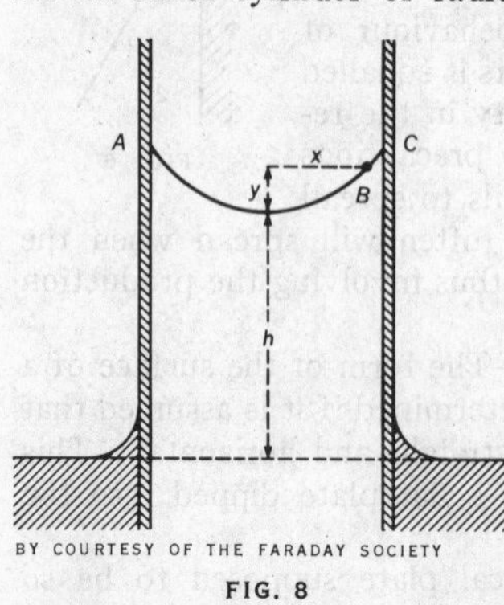

BY COURTESY OF THE FARADAY SOCIETY

FIG. 8

Neglecting $y$ altogether compared with $h$ and integrating between the limits 0 and $r$ gives $2\pi r\sigma\sin\theta=g(\rho-\rho_0)\pi r^2h$ whence $\sigma\sin\theta=\frac{1}{2}g(\rho-\rho_0)rh$. For a better approximation first differentiate the two sides of the equation; whence

$$\frac{d(x\sin\theta)}{dx}=\frac{g(\rho-\rho_0)}{\sigma}x(h+y)=\frac{x(h+y)}{\beta^2}$$

This may be considered as the standard exact equation. The left side is $\dfrac{x d\sin\theta}{dx}+\sin\theta$ or $x\left(\dfrac{\cos\theta d\theta}{dx}+\dfrac{\sin\theta}{x}\right)$

But $\cos\theta\dfrac{d\theta}{dx}=\dfrac{d\theta}{ds}$ (where $ds$ is an element of the curve $AC$) and is therefore the curvature in the plane of the diagram at $B$; and $\dfrac{\sin\theta}{x}$ is the curvature of the surface at $B$ in a plane at right angles to the diagram. Hence, calling these curvatures $\dfrac{1}{R_1}$ and $\dfrac{1}{R_2}$,

$$\sigma\left(\frac{1}{R_1}+\frac{1}{R_2}\right)=g(\rho-\rho_0)(h+y)$$

Both of the terms here are expressions for the difference of pressure between the two sides of the surface at the point $B$.

**Narrow Tubes.**—The equation shows that the sum of these curvatures increases with the height; but when $h$ is large and $y$ small, as it is for a very narrow tube, the sum is nearly constant. Going back to the differential form of the equation and taking the case where the liquid wets the tube, the curve may be considered as practically circular, of radius $r$; the corresponding value of $y=r-\sqrt{r^2-x^2}$ and

$$\frac{d(x\sin\theta)}{dx}=\frac{1}{\beta^2}(h+y)x=\frac{x}{\beta^2}(h+r-\sqrt{r^2-x^2})\text{ nearly whence,}$$

by integration

$$x\sin\theta=\frac{1}{\beta^2}\left[\frac{hx^2}{2}+\frac{rx^2}{2}+\tfrac{1}{3}\{(r^2-x^2)^{\frac{3}{2}}-r^3\}\right]$$

or since $\sin\theta=1$ when $x=r$

$$1=\frac{r}{2\beta^2}\left(h+\frac{r}{3}\right)$$

By putting the radius of the circle as $R=\dfrac{r}{\cos\alpha}$ when the angle of contact is $\alpha$ instead of zero this becomes

$$\cos\alpha=\frac{r}{2\beta^2}\left[h+\frac{r}{3\cos^3\alpha}\{1-3\sin^2\alpha-2\sin^3\alpha\}\right]$$

By calculating $\tan\theta$ from $\sin\theta$ and noting that

$$\tan\theta=dy/dx,$$

we can by subsequent integration obtain a closer value of $y$ in terms of $x$ which can, in turn, be introduced into the differential equation, and so on. By such successive approximations Lord Rayleigh obtained the equation for the case $\alpha=0$ in the form

$$\sigma=\tfrac{1}{2}g(\rho-\rho_0)hr\left[1+\frac{1}{3}\frac{r}{h}-0.1288\frac{r^2}{h^2}+0.1312\frac{r^3}{h^3}\right]$$

in which the coefficients are claimed to be correct to the approximation given. The equation can only be used in the case when $r$ is small compared with $h$. It may be mentioned that a very near approach to the equation can be obtained by considering the surface as ellipsoidal with its minor axis vertical.

Various methods are employed for determining surface tension experimentally:

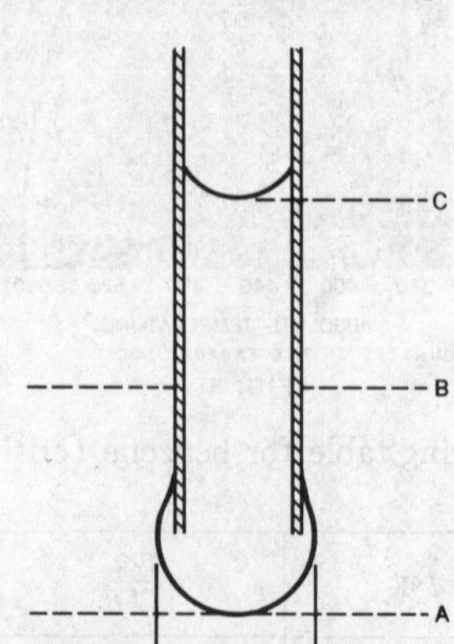

BY COURTESY OF THE FARADAY SOCIETY

FIG. 9

(*a*) From the rise in a capillary tube making use of the above equation.

(*b*) *Sentis' Method.*—A capillary tube is partly immersed in the liquid. It is then withdrawn vertically and a drop remains clinging to the lower end; the position A of the vertex of the drop is noticed (fig. 9). The liquid in the vessel is then raised until it touches the vertex (when the column falls) and then raised further till the upper surface is at the same level C as at first. The liquid in the vessel is then at the level B. The vertical distance AB corresponds to $h$ in the ordinary method but in the correcting terms $h$ must be put negative. The width of the drop is in this case to be small compared with $h$.

(*c*) *Jaeger's Method.*—In this method an orifice (a "tip") is placed just under the surface of the liquid and the pressure of gas is increased until bubbles form. The maximum pressure of the gas (which is fairly sharply marked) is observed. The deduction of the applicable equation is a somewhat delicate matter because the problem is really kinetic, not static. The formula employed is

$$\sigma = \frac{p_{\max} r}{2}\left[1 - \frac{2}{3}\frac{r}{h}\right]$$

where $p_{\max}$ is the maximum difference of pressure between the level of the end of tube inside and outside, and $r$ is the internal radius of the tube. The bubble is assumed to form within the internal circumference. In practice, however, it sometimes forms on the outside circumference. To obviate the uncertainty it is recommended to make the two circumferences as nearly equal as possible, but this is an experimental matter of great difficulty. The final accuracy depends chiefly on the measurement of the radius $r$.

(*d*) *Drop-Weight Method.*—This method is connected with the preceding one because the drops considered are those issuing from a narrow tube. Other things being the same, the weight of a drop of liquid is proportional to the diameter of the tube in which it is formed. Quincke gave the value $2\pi r\sigma$ as the weight of the suspended drop just before falling provided that the inflow of liquid is sufficiently slow. A portion of the drop is always left behind when the main part falls; but he considered that it might be neglected in the case of very small drops.

Lord Rayleigh discussed the question from the dimensional point of view (*see* DIMENSIONAL ANALYSIS). Assume that the mass $M$ of the drop depends only upon the surface tension $\sigma$, the value of acceleration due to gravity $g$, the density of the liquid $\rho$, and the inside radius $a$ of the tube. Rayleigh showed that $\sigma a/g$ has the same dimensions as a mass and that $\sigma/g\rho a^2$ is a dimensionless number. Since quantities that can be equated must be of the same kind, it follows that $M \propto (\sigma a/g)F(\sigma/g\rho a^2)$ where there is no restriction, imposed by this method of inquiry, on the function $F$. Rayleigh found by experiment that $gm/\sigma a$ is fairly constant for wide ranges in the diameter of the tube. For thin-walled tubes in the case of water the following values were obtained:

| $\frac{\sigma}{g\rho a^2}$ | $\frac{gM}{\sigma a}$ | $\frac{\sigma}{g\rho a^2}$ | $\frac{gM}{\sigma a}$ |
|---|---|---|---|
| 2.58 | 4.13 | .277 | 3.78 |
| 1.16 | 3.97 | .220 | 3.90 |
| .708 | 3.80 | .169 | 4.06 |
| .441 | 3.73 | | |

The mean value of the constant is thus about 3.8 instead of $2\pi$ as estimated by Quincke. Further experiments by others showed that the constant approaches Quincke's value as the diameter becomes very small.

As a means for measuring surface tension this method is obviously not satisfactory; but for rough comparative values for liquids of like kind it is very quick and easy. When $a$ is not small the approximations made for narrow tubes are not suitable.

**Bubbles and Drops.**—These can be dealt with by similar methods. Minute air bubbles in a liquid are nearly spherical; they tend to become flat with increasing size (fig. 10). The excess pressure $p - p_0$, which can be found by experiment, determines the total curvature at the lowest point $N$; the curvature is equal to $2/R$. If $y$ is reckoned upward as before, then

$$\frac{d\,(x \sin\theta)}{dx} = \left(\frac{2}{R} + \frac{y}{\beta^2}\right)x$$

thus $2/R$ replaces $h/\beta^2$ in the previous problems. For very large bubbles, as for wide tubes, a good approximation can be obtained by neglecting the second curvature and also $2/R$, so that

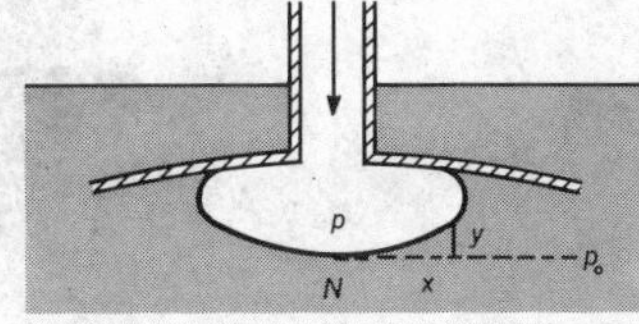

BY COURTESY OF THE FARADAY SOCIETY

FIG. 10

$$(1 - \cos\theta) = \frac{y^2}{2\beta^2} = 2\sin^2\frac{\theta}{2}$$

If $H$ is the value of $y$ for which the tangent to the curve becomes vertical, then $H = \sqrt{2}\beta$. This method was used by Quincke and others but not always with bubbles large enough to justify the approximation. The bubble is conveniently formed under a slightly concave surface to prevent it from escaping. Drops of mercury are easily formed above a concave surface. If $y$ is measured downward from the summit the same equations hold as for bubbles.

These methods have been used in determining surface tension. Through infinite series calculated for each of the variables each term in the differential equation can be calculated to very high accuracy, and tables are drawn up from which the form can be determined for given weights of material and given surface tensions.

**Thin Films.**—One group of thin films consists of those in which the substance forms a thin sheet with gas on both sides, as for example, a soap bubble. In this case there are always two surfaces to consider. When the thickness is considerably greater than the value of the range $e$ of molecular forces, the two surfaces are independent of one another; the surface tension must then have the usual value for each. For very thin films this will not hold. If the thickness is less than the range $e$, the tension for each surface will be less than the normal value. When the variation of density at different levels in the film is taken into account, reduction in surface tension will begin when the thickness is twice $e$.

A soap film is a small quantity of soap solution spread out to present a large surface to the air. The addition of glycerol and resin permits more permanent films to be prepared. Bubbles may easily be blown 20 in. in diameter in the open air using a clay pipe or a small glass funnel. Sir James Dewar obtained bubbles that lasted almost indefinitely, preventing evaporation by blowing them in a confined space saturated with water vapour.

The pressure inside a bubble is greater than that outside by $2\sigma\left(\frac{1}{R} + \frac{1}{R}\right)$; *i.e.*, by $4\sigma/R$ where $R$ is the radius of curvature. The factor 2 arises because both surfaces give rise to normal components of forces. This result is obtained by considering the equilibrium of each half of the bubble. The force at the cut edge is $2\sigma \cdot 2\pi R$, and this is balanced by the excess pressure acting over the plane area $\pi R^2$. Hence the excess pressure is

$$\frac{2\sigma \cdot 2\pi R}{\pi R^2} = \frac{4\sigma}{R}$$

If the end of the pipe or funnel is opened, the bubble will contract because of the escape of high pressure air from inside. As it contracts, the pressure paradoxically increases. It may be added that (neglecting gravity) the bubble is spherical, since this shape minimizes the surface area (and therefore the potential energy) for a given volume.

If bubbles are blown on the expanded ends of two funnels (the stems being stopped by the fingers), they can be made to coalesce by carefully bringing them into contact. (A slightly electrified rod brought not too near will assist the coalescence.) On drawing the funnels slowly apart a cylindrical bubble is obtained. The excess pressure is now $2\sigma/R$ where $R$ is the radius of the opening of the funnel. On further separation the cylinder will contract in the middle; one of the two curvatures is now negative, giving what is called an anticlastic surface. With further extension of length the surface becomes unstable and the film collapses. It has been shown by Maxwell that a cylindrical film becomes unstable when its length is greater than its circumference.

**Films on Liquids.**—In another group of thin films a liquid or solid is on one side and a gas on the other. To this group belong all cases of the spreading of oil or other substance on water or other liquid or solid. This old familiar subject has great importance in its bearing on molecular structures. The first

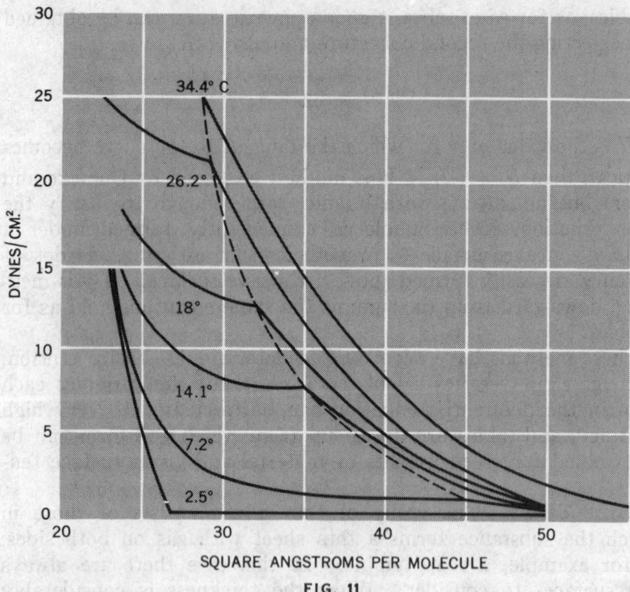

FIG. 11

to experiment in detail on such films was F. H. R. Lüdtge, who showed how a film of high surface tension is replaced by one of lower surface tension. Akin to these are experiments made on the erratic movements observed when fragments of camphor are sprinkled on a clean water surface. A trace of grease as communicated to the surface by dipping a finger in the water can practically stop this motion. The thickness of oil that is required has been called the camphor point. Lord Rayleigh showed that the thickness of a film of olive oil that corresponds to the camphor point is about $2 \times 10^{-6}$ mm.; *i.e.*, it is only a moderate multiple of the diameter of a gaseous molecule and scarcely exceeds the diameter of a molecule of oil.

By means of a movable slider on water (the surface tension being measured by means of the attraction on a small disc) the contaminating material on the surface can be squeezed. Such experiments indicate that the water surface can exist in two sharply contrasted conditions: the normal condition, in which the displacement of the partition makes no impression on the tension; and the anomalous condition, in which every increase or decrease (of the surface) alters the tension. Lord Rayleigh used a similar apparatus to conclude that the first drop in tension corresponds to a complete layer one molecule thick and that the diameter of a molecule of oil is about $1.0 \times 10^{-6}$ mm.

By measuring the surface area that can be completely covered by a weighed quantity of material, I. Langmuir determined both the cross-sectional area and the length of a molecule and showed that the length for organic molecules like those of palmitic, stearic, and cerotic acids is nearly five times the breadth, while in cetyl palmitate it is nearly ten times. He and N. K. Adam measured the amount of "oil" and measured directly the force required to compress the oily surface to any given area with a floating barrier. It was found that when the molecules in the film are widely separated from one another the force due to the film is an expansive one.

This cannot be explained through Laplace's theory; it is necessary to allow for the effects of thermal motion; the film in such a case is analogous to a two-dimensional gas. If the barrier is moved gradually to compress the film, successive changes take place. Fig. 11 shows these for a film of myristic acid on weak HCl (N/100). The unit of area is a square angstrom (*i.e.*, $10^{-100}$ sq.m.), and the area specified is that occupied by one molecule of the acid. The ordinates of the curves are the difference of the tensions on the two sides of the barrier. The curves are isothermals extending from 2.5° to 34.4° C. They exhibit some of the characteristics of the $p,v$ curves for a condensible substance. At high temperatures the curves appear to be approximately rectangular hyperbolas. For small values of the area they approach the form for liquids. At intermediate stages, however, there is no constant pressure isothermal as in the analogous case of the vapour pressure of a liquid below the critical point. The form is more nearly that for the vapour pressure of a mixture of two liquids (*see* SOLUTIONS). This suggests that the underlying water takes a part in the changes.

It is not to be expected that there should be complete correspondence between the two classes of phenomena. However, the effects of thermal motions in the films cannot be neglected. The analogy with liquids and gases can be further illustrated by plotting $AF$ against $F$, where $F$ is the force applied per unit length. It is clear from fig. 11 that a film of myristic acid can be squeezed up until a molecule occupies less than 24 square angstroms. At the opposite end where the behaviour approaches that of a gas it is to be expected that the equation will take the form $AF = RT$ where the value of $R$ (allowing for only two degrees of freedom) should be 1.372 per molecule; at room temperature, therefore, $AF$ should be about 400. This has been experimentally verified as a limiting value for very low surface pressures. With the long-chain fatty acids, esters, and nitriles it is approached within 25%, the pressure being below 0.1 dyne per square centimetre. With the dibasic ester $C_2H_5OOC(CH_2)_{11}COOC_2H_5$ it has been verified within 10%.

A simple gas analogy should not be pressed too far, however. A thin film on a body of different material cannot be treated as being in a similar state to the molecules in the body of a gas. Forces between the film and the liquid beneath must also be considered. These may account for the fact that some films do not spread indefinitely as a gas expands into a vacuum. Further, the most compressed state can only give an upper limit to the least cross-sectional area of the molecule. The molecules are resting on the rapidly moving molecules beneath them and share in their agitation. Still, these investigations throw light on the nature of films and on the dimensions of molecules. Where corroboration is possible, measurements made by X-rays are in good accord with those obtained by this method.

*See* MOLECULE.

BIBLIOGRAPHY.—C. V. Boys, *Soap Bubbles and the Forces Which Mould Them* (1959); American Chemical Society, *Contact Angle, Wettability, and Adhesion* (1964); H. Lange, "Dynamic Surface Tension of Detergent Solutions at Constant and Variable Surface Area," *J. Colloid Sci.*, vol. 20 (1965). (A. W. Po.; X.)

**SURF RIDING,** a sport originating in Hawaii, is now enjoyed on the open ocean coastlines throughout the world. Best conditions occur where large, smooth ocean swells in deep water peak up into steep-sided sets of waves or breakers as they encounter a shelflike reef or sandbar 100 to 1,000 yd. out while approaching the shore. The lee side of a point of land or a jetty often has the proper bottom contour for good surfing waves. Under ideal conditions, as at Makaha, Hawaii, with 14-ft. waves, rides of over half a mile are obtained.

Where surf is light, flat boards 4 to 6 ft. (122 to 183 cm.) long by a foot wide are used. For waves up to 20 ft. (610 cm.) in height, a tapered hollow surfboard 10 to 12 ft. (305 to 366 cm.) long and

BRUCE DAVIDSON—MAGNUM
SURF RIDING IN CALIFORNIA

2 ft. (60 cm.) wide, with a stabilizing fin, or skeg, near the back, is used. The rider first swims out to the point where the larger rollers peak up, but before the crest breaks. As the wave approaches him, he paddles his board toward shore to attain sufficient speed to start to coast down the face of the wave. Once he has caught the wave, he may rise to a standing position and ride it until it dies out near the beach. To increase speed and distance experts ride diagonally toward shore.

National and international competitions have been held on both coasts of North America, Peru, Hawaii, and eastern Australia. Groups of 5 to 12 competing surfers with numbered shirts perform in the same area. They are judged on a point system for takeoff, turns, length of ride, and difficulty of wave selected.

The wakes of heavier outboard and inboard motorboats driven at speeds of 9 to 13 mph provide waves of sufficient strength for less difficult "surfing" on inland lakes and rivers. This inland surfing, in which a whole family can participate, plus the development of plastic foam, fiberglass coated boards at popular prices accounted for rapid growth in popularity of the sport. For wake riding, boards about 8 ft. long are used. The rider starts with a towline from the boat and lets it go when he feels the wake pushing him. (J. An.)

**SURGE,** in general terms, is a sudden increase to an excessive or abnormal value and a subsequent fall from such a value. In meteorology, "surge" is the name applied to those long-period progressive changes of barometric pressure that occur simultaneously at many locations over a wide region and that are superimposed on short-period pressure fluctuations of a diurnal nature or variations caused by traveling atmospheric disturbances of a local character. A pressure rise or fall of two millibars in 24 hours that occurs simultaneously within an area of 3,000,000 sq.mi. (7,750,000 sq.km.) corresponds to the order of magnitude of the phenomenon. Such pressure surges are commonly noted in regions close to the large semipermanent pressure centres of the earth, such as the high-pressure area of the southern North Atlantic Ocean. "Surge" is also a meteorological term often applied to a sudden increase in velocity of the large atmospheric wind streams, especially in the tropics. Such a wind surge occurs simultaneously over a large area and frequently spreads from place to place so that its progress can be followed on weather maps. In the trade-wind belts, meteorologists frequently refer to this event as the "surge of the trades" and, in the regions of the monsoon currents, as the "burst" or "surge of the monsoon." At a given location, an increase of wind speed from about 10 to 35 mph (16 to 56 km.ph) or more at all levels from the ground up to approximately 15,000 ft. (4,600 m.) can be expected in connection with a well-marked surge of the trades. (D. C. McD.)

**SURGERY (ARTICLES ON):** *see* Medicine and Surgery (Articles on).

**SURGUJA,** a district in the northeastern part of Madhya Pradesh, India. Area 8,626 sq.mi. (22,341 sq.km.). Pop. (1961) 1,036,738. In the central part there is fairly well-cultivated country, surrounded on the north, east, and south by massive hill barriers and tablelands. A long, winding ridge, the Jamirapat, forms part of the eastern boundary and separates the district from the Chota Nagpur Plateau. The southern barrier of Surguja is the Mainpat tableland, which rises to a height of 3,700 ft. The majority of the population is made up of a great variety of aboriginal tribes. The chief town is Ambikapur (pop. [1961] 15,240). Crops include rice and oilseeds, mainly in the valleys of the southwest. There are considerable coal deposits, and iron ore, limestone, and bauxite are also found. The Ramgarh Hill, a rectangular mass of sandstone rising abruptly from the central plain, contains a remarkable natural tunnel, many rock caves, and remains of temples made of enormous blocks of stone. Most important among its antiquities are the Sitabenga and Jogimara caves, which contain inscriptions in the Brahmi script dating from the early 1st century B.C. and wall paintings of similar age. These paintings are thought to be among the oldest surviving in India. Other ruins in the jungles indicate a high state of civilization in later centuries, but these have never been described adequately. Surguja, formerly one of the Chhattisgarh states, ruled over by a Rajput family, was merged with Madhya Pradesh in 1948. The state had been ceded to the British in 1818. (F. R. A.)

**SURINAM** (Suriname in Dutch), Dutch Guiana, or Netherlands Guiana, a fully autonomous part of the Netherlands Realm, lies between Guyana and French Guiana. Its area is 63,251 sq.mi. (163,820 sq.km.), and its Atlantic coastline is about 196 mi. (315 km.) long.

**Physical Geography.**—The geology, topography, and drainage of Surinam are similar to those described for Guyana (*q.v.*), but the area of elevated sandstone within Surinam is limited to the Tumuc-Humac Mountains (Serra de Tumucumaque) on the extreme southern frontier and its northward projection, the Eilerts de Haan Mountains, at about 2,500 ft. (760 m.). Except for the coastal area, the territory therefore consists of an ancient crystalline plateau, rarely over 500 ft. (150 m.) above sea level, intensely folded, sloping gently seaward. It is crossed by large parallel rivers, notably the Courantyne (Corantijn), Saramacca, Suriname, and Tapanahoni, which are interrupted by rapids formed by igneous intrusions into the crystalline complex. The plateau is almost wholly covered with dense forest.

The coastal deposits are of marine origin, distributed by currents from the direction of the Amazon. The lower courses of the main rivers have a northwesterly alignment in consequence. The coastal zone is varied by sand dunes and shelly and peaty deposits and is swampy except where it has been drained and made cultivable near the sea and the lower rivers. This limited area remains the chief source of agricultural wealth, though much of it needs rehabilitation of its drainage works.

The climate is tropical, similar to that of Guyana though the coast is slightly wetter. The vegetation and animal life are also similar. For a full discussion, *see* Guyana, Republic of: *Physical Geography*.

**History.**—(For history before 1815, *see* Guyana, Republic of: *History*.) Political affairs before 1900 were uneventful. From 1828 to 1848 Surinam and the Dutch West Indian Islands were under a single governor at Paramaribo. About 300,000 West Africans were brought into Surinam between 1650 and 1820.

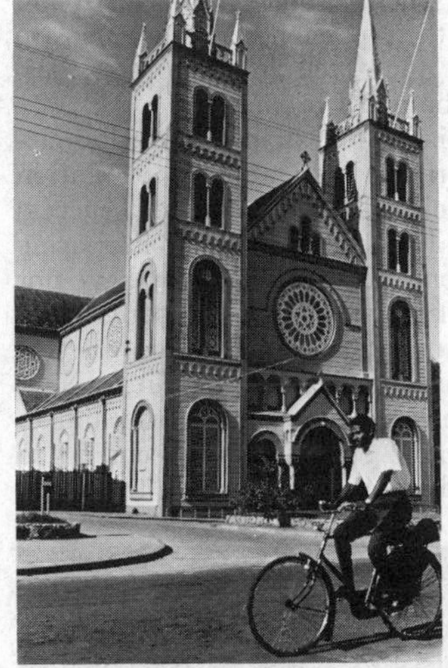

CARL FRANK FROM PHOTO RESEARCHERS

CHURCH IN PARAMARIBO, SIMILAR TO THOSE IN THE NETHERLANDS

In the early 19th century Moravian and Roman Catholic missions were active in Surinam, and when slavery was abolished in 1863, almost all the slaves were nominally Christian. For the ten years after emancipation the rights of the freed slaves were severely limited. Thereafter, they could own land, and former plantations were parceled out. Lack of central control, however, led to a breakdown of irrigation and drainage, and this helped drive large numbers of the former slaves into town life, the mining of bauxite, and emigration. An arrangement with the British for the control of immigrants from India was drawn up in 1870, and the first indentured labourers arrived in 1873. Between then and 1917, when the treaty was abrogated, 34,304 persons arrived, about one-third of whom later returned to India. After 1895 the Surinam government made land ownership possible for these immigrants, and this proved an effective method of keeping them in the country, especially after the introduction of rice growing in 1913. Javanese immigration began in 1890, giving the country a useful body of small farmers. From 1930 to 1939 there was an influx of nonindentured Javanese.

During the 19th century the colony suffered from the concentration of Dutch energies on the East Indies, and there was little real development before 1900. At that date, 90% of all agricultural products were grown on plantations and 10% on small farms; but these figures were completely reversed in the subsequent half-century, and the plantation crops of cocoa, coffee, sugar, and cotton were replaced by rice and fruit.

The amount of reclaimed land diminished as plantation agriculture declined, but there was considerable development in other directions, stimulated by the influx of financial and technical resources diverted from the East Indies after 1945. In 1954 Surinam became a self governing part of the kingdom of the Netherlands. It also joined the European Economic Community as an Associated Overseas Territory. A ten-year plan, inaugurated in 1955, stressed the economic and social development of the country, and it was in general very effective.

**Population and Peoples.**—The population at the 1950 census was 183,681, and in addition there were about 26,000 Amerindians and Bush Negroes. The provisional total for the census of March 1964 was 324,211, with about 38,000 Amerindians and Bush Negroes. At least seven-eighths of the people lived on the coast and no less than 34% in Paramaribo (pop. 1964, 110,867). The next town in size was Nieuw Nickerie (pop. 1964, 7,396).

The increase in population has been striking; in 1900 the total was less than 70,000. Bush Negroes (Djukas), the descendants of escaped slaves, have been increasing for many years. The Amerindians numbered about 5,000 in the mid-1960s as against about 2,000 in 1942. As in Guyana, Asian Indians were the most rapidly increasing group; they formed about 30% of the total in 1964. The approximate proportions of other racial groups were: Creoles (former African slaves) 41%; Indonesians 13%; Bush Negroes 9%; Amerindians, Chinese, and Europeans about 1.5% each; others 2.5%.

The three main ethnic groups maintain marked differences in social and cultural life. Creole culture, especially in its loose family structure and its matrilocal emphasis, is essentially derived from slave conditions. The Creoles have generally been less successful in smallholding and commerce than the Indians but have made good labourers and artisans. Their readiness to move around the country and to emigrate and their passion for education are important assets, and they have done well in the professions. Creoles preponderate in Paramaribo and Coronie.

The Asian Indians are mostly Hindus but include a Muslim element. In their early years in Surinam they were, as plantation labourers, separated from the Creoles. Their subsequent success as merchants and smallholders, and the threat of their increasing numbers, have kept them apart from the Creoles. They have not assimilated European culture as the Creoles have, and remain a frugal farming and trading community, speaking their own languages and living in strongly organized patriarchal families. Nevertheless, there have been big changes even among the Indian community since 1945, and economic opportunity is tending to make them more assimilated. Indians preponderate in the country areas of Nickerie, Saramacca, and Suriname, and their farms are mostly of 12 to 124 ac. (5–50 ha.).

CARL FRANK FROM BLACK STAR

BUSH NEGROES IN A DUGOUT CANOE ON THE MARONI RIVER

The Javanese cultivate smallholdings mainly of less than 10 ac. (4 ha.), most of which are in Commewijne and Suriname. They are the least affected by Western culture of the three main racial groups. They are rice growers and have generally shown little ambition to do anything else. Their religion is nominally Muslim but is intensely ritualistic and has strong pagan overtones. They are generally ignorant of languages other than their own.

**Government and Administration.**—Surinam became part of the Netherlands in 1948. The present constitution was defined by the Realm Statute, effective from Dec. 29, 1954, which confirmed and amplified an interim order of Jan. 20, 1950. Surinam was given self-government except in foreign affairs and defense, but has certain rights of choice in international commitments.

The governor, representing the sovereign, is head of the government. He appoints an advisory council of five for life, and a council of nine ministers from the Legislative Assembly (*Staten van Suriname*), which has 36 members elected for four years by adult suffrage. The country is divided into eight districts, of which Paramaribo (*q.v.*), the capital and chief port, is one.

**Social Conditions.**—Of a total labour force of about 100,000, more than half were engaged in agriculture in the mid-1960s, but as smallholdings and family working predominated, figures were very unreliable. Of more than 16,000 holdings, no fewer than 12,000 were less than 10 ac. (4 ha.). Asian Indians farmed 45% of the holdings, Indonesians 14%, and Creoles the rest.

Surinam has a relatively high literacy rate, there having been compulsory education for children 7–12 years of age since 1876. The government provides some schools and aids others. More than half the primary and secondary schools are denominational. There are also a medical school, a law school, technical schools, teacher-training colleges, agricultural courses, domestic science schools, and special schools. Provision is made for children in remote areas, and the needs of children whose mother tongue is not European get special attention.

The health of Surinamers is good by the standards of tropical countries. The crude death rate in the 1960s was about 8.5 per 1,000 of the population.

**Economy.**—About 89,000 ac. (36,000 ha.) of land are under cultivation, of which 49,000 ac. (20,000 ha.) are irrigated. About 15,500 ac. (6,300 ha.) are used as pasture. Perhaps another 155,000 ac. (63,000 ha.) are suitable for crops but are unused. There has been no development of the far interior savanna comparable to that in Guyana.

Of the cultivated area, 75% is devoted to growing rice, which is not only a staple of local diet but forms more than half of the agricultural exports. The main crop is sown from late March to May and is harvested about 140 days later. A second crop is planted on about one-fifth of farms in October or November. Nickerie is the centre of the main rice-growing area.

Citrus fruits (mainly oranges and grapefruit), coffee, cocoa, sugar, and bananas are the other main crops. Only two plantations grow sugarcane, but both are large and well-equipped. Surinam does not possess the labour or skill to compete successfully in world markets for fruit. A great variety of crops is grown for domestic consumption, including coconuts, corn (maize), peanuts, and soybeans, and domestic trade is mainly in foodstuffs. Even so, there is not enough food grown for the town populations, and Surinam must import vegetables and peanuts.

Bauxite is mined in opencast workings at three main sites at Paranam, Onverdacht, and Moengo. The first two are worked by Suralco, a subsidiary company of Alcoa (The Aluminum Company of America), and the third by the Billiton Company, which originally mined tin in the East Indies. The bauxite is mainly exported to the U.S. It is loaded directly to ocean-going vessels at Paranam and Smalkalden, about 20 mi. (32 km.) above Paramaribo; and at Moengo, which is 17 mi. (27 km.) up the Commewijne River and another 69 mi. (111 km.) up the Cottica, involving the navigation of awkward bends. The government and Suralco undertook construction of an aluminum smelter at Brokopondo, using hydroelectricity from the Afobaka dam. Bauxite is

CARL FRANK FROM PHOTO RESEARCHERS

PLANTING RICE, THE LEADING AGRICULTURAL PRODUCT OF SURINAM

the only mineral of economic consequence. It forms 80% by value of Surinam's exports, and the territory is among the world's chief sources of the mineral.

The other principal exports are plywood and rice. Imports, chiefly machinery, fuel oil, construction materials, and foodstuffs, are mainly from the U.S. and the Netherlands. Local industries are numerous but small. They include logging, rice mills, and a modern clothing industry.

A ten-year plan, launched in 1955, envisaged the expenditure of 117 million Surinam guilders (later raised to 207 million Surinam guilders) on agriculture, industry, communications, education, and social services. The plan accomplished much in its efforts to make Surinam more independent economically. Schemes successfully completed included the Afobaka-Brokopondo project already mentioned; the reconstruction of irrigation works; the reclamation of new land; housing; a complete geological survey; and a number of new roads.

The currency unit is the Surinam guilder (gulden or florin; 1.89 Surinam guilders = U.S. $1). The Centrale Bank van Suriname, established in 1956, is government sponsored and acts as a clearing house, supervising the monetary system. In addition there are several commercial banks and a number of investment and mortgage banks.

In spite of modern improvements the road system remained inadequate. There were in the mid-1960s about 975 mi. (1,569 km.) of "all-weather" roads, of which about 290 mi. (466 km.) were asphalted and the rest topped with shell and bauxite. The main east–west road, 220 mi. (354 km.) from Albina on the Maroni (Marowijne) to Nieuw Nickerie on the Courantyne (Corantijn), was completed in 1965. The main north–south road in the mid-1960s was asphalted for 18 mi. (29 km.) from Paramaribo to Paranam, and continued an additional 45 mi. (72 km.) with a bauxite surface to Afobaka.

The other main road extended 28 mi. (45 km.) from the capital to Zanderij airport. The airport, one of the best in the Caribbean area, maintained international and domestic services. There was one single-track railway, from Paramaribo to Republiek, Zanderij, and Kabelstation (83 mi., 133 km.).

Internal transport depended heavily on waterways. A singularly complete system on the coastal plain required only the single artificial link of the Saramacca Canal to provide a through waterway from the east to the west border of the country. Paramaribo, which has more than 2,000 ft. (609 m.) of wharf, has regular sailings to Caribbean, U.S., and European ports.

BIBLIOGRAPHY.—J. Warren Nystrom, *Surinam* (1942); P. H. Hiss, *Netherlands America* (1943); G. J. Kruyer, *Suriname en zijn buurlanden* (1960); International Bank for Reconstruction and Development, *Surinam: Recommendations for a Ten-Year Development Program* (1952); Organization for European Economic Development, *Economic Development of (Associated) Overseas Countries* (annually); Government Information Service, Paramaribo, *Facts and Figures about Surinam* (1960). (G. LN.)

**SURINAM TOAD,** a tongueless, tailless amphibian unusual in several respects. It is *Pipa pipa* (or *P. americana*), one of several species of the family Pipidae. It inhabits South America east of the Andes and north of the Amazon and is strictly aquatic, feeding largely on fish in quiet pools. It has a flat body and an extremely flattened head. The snout and the angles of the jaws bear several loose skin flaps, the fingers of the forelimbs terminate in small star-shaped appendages, and the eyes are minute and without lids. The hind limbs end in large fully webbed feet.

These toads exhibit a remarkable method of mating and parental care. Pairing takes place in the water, the male clasping the female round the waist. During oviposition the female extends from the cloaca a long bladderlike pouch, which the male carries forward between his breast and the gelatinous-covered back of the female. As each egg is released, it is fertilized and attached by a natural adhesive to the female's back. The skin thickens and grows round the eggs until each is enclosed in a dermal cell, which is finally covered by a horny lid. The eggs may number about 100 and measure 5–7 mm. in diameter. They develop for about 80 days entirely within these pouches, and the young hop out as miniatures of the adult.

**SURKHAN-DAR'YA,** an *oblast* of the Uzbek Soviet Socialist Republic, U.S.S.R., is bordered south by the Amu-Darya (Oxus River), which forms the frontier with Afghanistan. Area, 8,031 sq.mi. (20,800 sq.km.). Pop. (1967 est.) 581,000, of which more than 15% is urban. In the centre and south is an upland plain bordered east, north, and west by mountains rising to 17,000 ft. (5,180 m.). The climate is continental with very hot summers (July average 21.9° C [71.6° F]). There are two towns, Termez (*q.v.*), the capital, and Denau. The economy is mainly agricultural, based on cotton in the irrigated valleys of the Surkhandar'ya and Shirabad, wheat on the hillsides, and the raising of karakul sheep and goats in the plains. (G. E. WR.)

**SURMA** (BARAK), a river of Assam, India, and East Pakistan. It rises in the Barail Range in the union territory of Manipur, in northeast India, its source being among the southern spurs of Mt. Japvo. Thence its course is south, with a slight westerly bearing, through the Manipur Hills. The name "Barak" is given to the upper part of the river, in Manipur and the Cachar district of Assam. A short distance below Badarpur in Cachar it divides into two branches, which then flow into East Pakistan. The northern, which passes Sylhet, is called the Surma. The southern, called the Kusiyara, subdivides into two branches, one called the Bibiyana or Kalni, and the other the Barak, both of which rejoin the Surma. At Bhairab Bazar, in the Mymensingh district of Dacca, the Surma unites with an old channel of the Brahmaputra and becomes known as the Meghna until it joins the Ganges between Narayanganj and Chandpur. The river is navigable by steamers as far as Silchar in the rainy season. The total length is about 560 mi. (900 km.). (L. D. S.)

**SURPLICE,** a liturgical vestment of the Christian Church. It is a loose tunic of white linen or cotton material, with wide sleeves, worn as a choir vestment in the Roman Catholic Church (in which it is proper to all clerics) and as a eucharistic vestment in the Anglican Church and in some Lutheran and Free churches. The surplice appeared first in the Middle Ages, and it has no counterpart in the Eastern Churches. *See* LITURGY, CHRISTIAN.

**SURREALISM,** a widespread revolutionary movement in the arts, promoted by the poet André Breton. The word itself was coined by the poet Guillaume Apollinaire, and the movement had its heyday, primarily in Paris, from 1918 to 1939, attacking tradition in all forms. It was an assertion of the belief that the world of the unconscious mind—as expressed by fantasies and dreams—has a reality superior to that of the phenomenal world. Surrealist expression aimed at a creative integration of both realities into a "super-reality." The theory owed much to the research of Sigmund Freud, whose technique of probing the unconscious mind for the ultimate truth of human behaviour compares with the surrealist method of penetrating the depths of human personality to tap the inexhaustible sources of the imagination. In *Manifeste du surréalisme,* published in 1924 in Paris, Breton's own definition of surrealism was: "Pure psychic automatism, by which it is intended to express whether verbally or in writing, or in any other way, the real process of thought. It is the dictation of thought, free from any control by the reason and of any aesthetic or moral preoccupation."

Submission to mental promptings, appropriate as means of spontaneous writing, could apply only to the initial, conceptual phase of a painting. Since the movement was largely a literary expression, surrealist painting was, therefore, an illustrative art based on literary themes, using realistic and recognizable means and expressions. In abandoning rational, moral, and aesthetic considerations, it echoed Dadaism (*q.v.*); but it was dissimilar in having a positive intention, namely to create a new, authentic vision of life by releasing dormant sensibilities. The release found infinitely varied expression in a fantastic art which, unprecedented as a movement, had affinities with the weird images of individual painters like Hieronymus Bosch (*q.v.*) or Giuseppe Arcimboldo. The emergence of surrealism in art was assisted directly by such notable pioneers as Kurt Schwitters, whose collages established strange relationships between disparate objects in juxtaposition; Marcel Duchamp (*q.v.*), whose "ready-mades" revealed the extraordinary significance of objects in abnormal contexts; and indirectly by Giorgio de Chirico, Paul Klee, and Pablo Picasso (*qq.v.*). Exponents of surrealist art were Hans Arp, Salvador Dali (*q.v.*), Paul Delvaux, Jean Dubuffet, Matta Echaurren, Max Ernst, Morris Graves, René Magritte, André Masson, Joan Miró (*q.v.*), Francis Picabia (*q.v.*), and Yves Tanguy.

Surrealist expression also found outlet in literature (Jean Cocteau, Paul Éluard, Guillaume Apollinaire [*qq.v.*], and Louis Aragon), in sculpture (Alberto Giacometti), and in photography (Man Ray). The spirit of surrealism is also to be seen in advertising techniques where objects apparently unrelated are juxtapositioned.

BIBLIOGRAPHY.—A. Breton, *Manifeste du Surréalisme* (1924), *Poisson soluble* (1924) and *Le Surréalisme et la peinture* (1928); Alfred H. Barr, ed., *Fantastic Art, Dada, Surrealism* (1936); Alfred Schmeller, *Surrealism* (1956); M. Nadeau, *Histoire du Surréalisme* (1945); Y. Duplessis, *Le Surréalisme* (1950); D. Gascoyne, *A Short Survey of Surrealism* (1935).

(F. W. W.-S.)

**SURREY, EARLS AND DUKE OF.** The English title of earl of Surrey was created in the 11th century and since 1483 has been held by the Howards, earls and dukes of Norfolk. WILLIAM DE WARENNE (d. 1088), a Norman baron who fought with William the Conqueror at Hastings in 1066, was created earl of Surrey by William II in 1088. His immediate successors were generally known as earls de Warenne (for the earls of the Warenne family *see* WARENNE). On the death without issue of JOHN DE WARENNE (1286–1347), 8th earl, the title passed to his nephew RICHARD FITZALAN (*c.* 1313–76), 3rd earl of Arundel, the son of Edmund Fitzalan and Alice, sister of the 8th earl. Richard styled himself earl of Surrey in 1361 on the death of his aunt, the dowager Countess Joan. The title was forfeited when Richard's son RICHARD (1346–97), 10th earl of Surrey and 4th earl of Arundel, was beheaded for conspiring against Richard II (*see* ARUNDEL, EARLS OF).

THOMAS DE HOLAND (*c.* 1371–1400), earl of Kent, was created duke of Surrey in 1397 for supporting Richard II against the lords appellant (*see* ENGLISH HISTORY). He was degraded from the dukedom and forfeited the title in November 1399 and was beheaded in January 1400 for conspiring against Henry IV. The earldoms of Surrey and Arundel were restored in October 1400 to THOMAS FITZALAN (1381–1415), son of the 10th earl, but on his death without issue the Surrey earldom reverted to the crown. JOHN MOWBRAY (1444–76), son of John (1415–61), 3rd duke of Norfolk of his line, was created earl of Surrey in 1451, but the title again became extinct on his death. It was revived in 1483 for THOMAS HOWARD (1443–1524), son of John (*c.* 1430–85), 1st duke of Norfolk of his line. The title has since been held by the Howard family (*see* NORFOLK, EARLS AND DUKES OF). The present holder of the title is BERNARD MARMADUKE FITZALAN-HOWARD (1908– ), 16th duke of Norfolk.

**SURREY, HENRY HOWARD,** EARL OF (1517–1547), English poet who, with Sir Thomas Wyat (*q.v.*), introduced to England the styles and metres of the Italian Humanist poets and so laid the foundation of a great age of English poetry. He was born early in 1517, perhaps at Hunsdon, Hertfordshire, the grandson of Thomas Howard, earl of Surrey and duke of Norfolk, who defeated the Scots at Flodden in 1513; and the eldest son of Lord Thomas Howard. In 1524, when his father succeeded as 3rd duke of Norfolk, he took the courtesy title of earl of Surrey.

IN WINDSOR CASTLE; BY THE GRACIOUS PERMISSION OF HER MAJESTY, QUEEN ELIZABETH II

HENRY HOWARD, EARL OF SURREY: PORTRAIT BY HANS HOLBEIN THE YOUNGER, DRAWN AFTER 1532

In his early years Surrey was influenced by the Humanist John Clerk and learned Italian as well as Latin. From 1530 until 1532 he lived at Windsor with his father's ward, the bastard son of Henry VIII, who had been created duke of Richmond in 1525. After talk of a marriage with the princess Mary, in April 1532 he married Lady Frances de Vere, the 14-year-old daughter of the earl of Oxford; they did not live together until 1535. [In October 1532 he went with Richmond to the Field of Cloth of Gold and then to the French court, where his behaviour seems to have been free from the rashness and occasional boasting that marked it later.] Despite his marriage an alliance between him and the princess Mary was still discussed. It was Surrey's fate, because of his birth and connections, to be constantly, though usually peripherally, involved in the jockeying for place that accompanied Henry VIII's policies. In 1533 Richmond married Surrey's sister Mary, but the two did not live together, and Richmond's death in 1536 postponed the trouble that was to come of this connection.

In 1537, however, Surrey was confined at Windsor after being charged by the Seymours (high in favour since the king's marriage to Jane Seymour in 1536) with having secretly favoured the Catholics in the rebellion of 1536 known as the Pilgrimage of Grace. He had in fact joined his father against the insurgents (*see* NORFOLK, THOMAS HOWARD, 3rd duke of), and in anger he struck his accuser. His punishment for breaking the peace ended in 1539. In May 1540 he was a champion in court jousts, and in August his prospects were further improved by the marriage of his cousin Catherine Howard to the king. Though he was imprisoned in 1542 for quarreling, and for breaking Londoners' windows with Thomas Wyat the younger in 1543, these confinements were short, and he was free to serve in the campaign in Scotland in 1542 and in France and Flanders from 1543 to 1546. He showed something of his grandfather's military abilities, acted as field marshal in 1544, and won royal approval.

This was the end of his period of favour. Returning to England in March 1546, he found the king dying and his old enemies the Seymours further incensed against him by his interference in the projected alliance between his sister the duchess of Richmond and Sir Thomas Seymour; he made matters worse by his assertion that the Howards were the obvious regents for Prince Edward. The Seymours, alarmed, accused Surrey, with his father, of treason and called the duchess of Richmond to witness against him; Surrey was said to have quartered the arms of Edward the Confessor with his own. He defended himself unavailingly and was executed on Tower Hill on Jan. 19, 1547. His father was saved only because the king died before he could be executed.

No historical credence can be given to the account in Thomas Nashe's *The Unfortunate Traveller* (1594) and Michael Drayton's *Englands Heroicall Epistles* (1598) of Surrey's love for Lady Elizabeth Fitzgerald. She was the "Fair Geraldine" of his love poetry, but she was a child when he wrote about her, and the lady Geraldine is clearly a fanciful creation on the ground of an interest in her charm.

Most of Surrey's poetry was probably written during his confinement at Windsor; it was nearly all first published in 1557. He acknowledged Wyat (on whom he wrote an epitaph) as a master, and certainly followed him in adapting Italian forms to English verse. He translated from Petrarch a number of sonnets already translated by Wyat, and a comparison of their translations shows that Surrey achieved a greater smoothness and firmness, qualities that were to be important in the evolution of the English sonnet (*q.v.*). Surrey was the first to develop the form used by Shakespeare. His smoothness often degenerates into monotony, but at least one sonnet, "The soote season," is memorable for its sweet fresh grace.

His other short poems have less intensity and metrical subtlety than most of Wyat's but are remarkable in ranging over a wider field of emotional experience than most poetry of the time. He writes not only on the usual early Tudor themes of love and death but also a satire on London, and of friendship, and musing memories of happy youth. Emotion is freshly conveyed when "Prisoned in Windsor, he recounteth his pleasures there passed":

So cruel prison how could betide, alas,
As proud Windsor? where I in lust and joy,
With a king's son, my childish years did pass,
In greater feast than Priam's sons of Troy.

The love poems have little force except when, in two "Complaint(s) of the absence of her lover being upon the sea," he writes, unusually for his period, from the woman's point of view:

When other lovers in arms across,
Rejoice their chief delight,
Drowned in tears to mourn my loss
I stand the bitter night
In my window where I may see
Before the winds how the clouds flee.
Lo, what a mariner love hath made me!

The short poems were printed by Richard Tottel in his *Songes and Sonettes written by the ryght honorable Lorde Henry Haward, late Earle of Surrey and other* (1557; usually known as *Tottel's Miscellany*). "Other" included Wyat, and critics from George Puttenham (*q.v.*) onward have coupled their names.

In the same year *Certain Bokes of Virgiles Aenaeis* was published, and this translation of Books II and IV of the *Aeneid* marks the first use of blank verse (*q.v.*) in English. Surrey adopted the metre from Giangiorgio Trissino and others, but the importance of its introduction into English cannot be overestimated. The actual writing is often stiff in phrasing and syntax, but it established what was to become the staple metre for long poems in English, developed with infinite richness and variety by the greatest poets.

BIBLIOGRAPHY.—*Editions:* Surrey's *Works,* ed. with those of Wyat, by G. Sewell (1717), and by G. F. Nott, 2 vol. (1815–16); with those of Sackville and others by R. Bell (1854); and by F. M. Padelford (1920; rev. ed. 1928), and E. Jones (1964). Shorter poems in G. Bullett (ed.), *Silver Poets of the XVIth Century* (1947). *Aeneid IV,* ed. by H. Hartmann (1933); *The Aeneid of Henry Howard Earl of Surrey,* ed. by F. H. Ridley (1963).

*Biography and Criticism:* E. Bapst, *Deux Gentilshommes—Poètes de la Cour de Henry VIII* (1891); O. F. Emerson, on Surrey's use of blank verse, in *Modern Language Notes,* IV (1889); O. Fest, "Über Surreys Virgilübersetzung," in *Palästra,* xxxiv (1903); F. M. Padelford, *The Manuscript Poems of Henry Howard, Earl of Surrey* (1906); G. D. Willcock, on the Aeneid version, in the *Modern Language Review,* xiv, xv, xvii (1919–22); E. Casady, *Henry Howard, Earl of Surrey* (1938); Hester W. Chapman, *Two Tudor Portraits* (1960). (C. M. I.)

**SURREY,** a southeastern county of England, is bounded on the northeast by Greater London, east by Kent, south by Sussex, west by Hampshire, and northwest by Berkshire and Buckinghamshire. The area of the administrative county is 649.8 sq.mi. (1,683 sq.km.) and comprises 4 boroughs, 14 urban districts, and 5 rural districts.

The north of the county adjoining the Thames is low lying, and the soil consists largely of brick earth overlying London Clay. To the west, on the edge of the Thames Basin, Bagshot Sands outcrop at Chobham Common, and Bagshot Heath and Chobham Ridges (400 ft. [122 m.]) are capped by plateau gravels. Across the middle of the county, from east to west, run the chalk North Downs. In the east they form a wide band, rising to a height of 852 ft. [260 m.], but westward they narrow into the Hog's Back. The line of the Downs is broken by the River Mole between Dorking and Leatherhead, and by the Wey at Guildford. These are the county's two chief rivers, and they join the Thames at Molesey and Weybridge, respectively. To the south of the chalk Downs is a wide band of Lower Greensand, which narrows eastward. On this greensand is found the highest land in the county, Leith Hill (965 ft. [294 m.]) near the centre, and Hindhead (895 ft. [273 m.]) in the west. The rest of the county, except for a small triangle of Hastings Beds in the extreme southeast, is composed of Weald Clay. The National Trust owned 11,798 ac. (4,774 ha.) in Surrey and protected 586 ac. (237 ha.) in 1964. In 1958 about 160 sq.mi. (414 sq.km.) in the Surrey Hills was established as "an area of outstanding natural beauty" under the National Parks and Access to the Countryside Act, 1949. At Wisley are the gardens of the Royal Horticultural Society.

**History.**—This discussion embraces certain places once in Surrey but now in Greater London (for boundary changes *see* below).

Paleolithic implements were found in the gravel beds of the Wey, the Mole, the Wandle, and the Thames (for example, near Farnham, Guildford, Godalming, Mortlake, and Wandsworth), and at older gravel plateaus, such as Warlingham and Wimbledon Common. At Blackheath near Albury there is evidence of Neolithic man. Hoards of bronze implements have been found at a number of places. Iron Age earthworks cover a wide area and include mounds at Weybridge, Farnham, Holmbury, and one, the largest of all, near Lingfield.

It was an area of forest, swamp, heath, and open downland through which the Romans passed at the time of the invasion of Julius Caesar (55 B.C.), using perhaps the ancient track along the Downs, later known as the Pilgrims' Way. Romanization, however, did not come until the time of the emperor Claudius I (A.D. 43). For the next four centuries Surrey was ruled by the Romans, and though Roman remains are relatively few, the largest settlements appear to have been at Southwark, Kingston upon Thames, Farley Heath near Albury, and Woodcote near Croydon. Remains of about two dozen villas lie, for the most part, along the northern and southern edges of the Downs and include that of Ashtead to the north and Titsey to the south. The Thames was bridged at Southwark as part of Watling Street, leading from Dover and Canterbury. Stane Street, from Chichester to London, was probably not constructed till the 3rd century; it ran via Ockley, Dorking, and Merton. No Roman town survived the Saxon settlement of Surrey, and there are few place-names of Roman origin. Surrey was never an independent Saxon kingdom. The name itself means southern district. Nearly all place-names are of Saxon origin, a large proportion pagan, such as Friday Street (commemorating the goddess Frigg [Frea]). The scantiness of the population is indicated by the small number of hundreds (14) compared with neighbouring counties. The tithings into which they were divided generally became parishes after the establishment of Christianity. Coronations of West Saxon kings at Kingston during the 10th century are referred to by chroniclers. A coronation stone is preserved there.

During the reign of Edward the Confessor, Godwin, earl of Wessex, and members of his family, including Harold, held many manors in Surrey. After the Battle of Hastings (1066) William I took these for himself or for his Norman followers. Held back in Southwark from entering London, he turned southward to the Pilgrims' Way. Domesday Book shows the extent of the ravaging of the Normans through Limpsfield, Godstone, and Gatton, and then westward through Albury, Shalford, and Farnham along the road to Winchester. The bishop of Winchester retained Farnham.

Chertsey Abbey, according to the 13th-century cartulary, was founded in 666 by St. Erkenwald, who became its first abbot. It was burned during the Danish wars (*c.* 871). Refounded for Benedictines in the 10th century, it maintained a prominent position and held many manors, including Chertsey, Egham, Thorpe, Chobham, Cobham, Epsom, Sutton, and Coulsdon, until it was dissolved in 1537. Later foundations include the Cluniac priory of Bermondsey (1082), the Cistercian abbey of Waverley (1128), the Augustine priories of Merton (1117), Newark (*c.* 1190), Tandridge (*c.* 1200), and Reigate (1220).

Even in the 13th and 14th centuries there probably was a strong contrast between the outlying forests and the suburban parts of Surrey, Southwark, Lambeth, and Bermondsey, with their great suburban houses of ecclesiastical dignitaries, sharing in the life of London. Kingston, with its bridge over the Thames, was a market town, as was Guildford with its manufacture of cloth. As elsewhere the ravages of the Black Death intensified commercial depression and religious agitation, which led to the Peasants' Revolt of 1381.

Sheen already had royal importance when Richard II pulled down the palace after the death of his first queen. Henry V rebuilt it, founding at the same time a Carthusian house. Following the insurrections of the 15th century, Surrey under the Tudors became a county of royal residences. Henry VII rebuilt the palace of Sheen, renaming it Richmond. Henry VIII and Elizabeth I resided there, and Henry VIII received Hampton Court, just across the Thames, from Cardinal Wolsey. This brought court officials to the villages on the Surrey side. After the dissolution of the monasteries (1536–39), Henry built a flamboyant hunting lodge in Surrey, Nonsuch (near Ewell). This was built partly of materials from the dissolved priory of Merton and on the site of the village of Cuddington, which he destroyed. Stones from Waverley Abbey were used in building Loseley House, and Oatlands Palace (Weybridge), now in ruins, had stones from Chertsey Abbey. The manors of the religious houses fell into the king's hands or were sold by him or his successors. Reigate Priory was granted to William Howard (later Lord Howard of Effingham; *see* HOWARD); and his son, who was commander in chief against the Spanish Armada (1588), is buried in Reigate Church. No reference to the Tudors could ignore the theatres of Southwark, more especially Shakespeare's Globe.

In the Middle Ages sheep were important in rural Surrey, and by the 16th century a cloth trade was growing, for example, at Guildford, Godalming, and Farnham. Fuller's Earth was already known at Nutfield and until the 19th century was used mainly in the woolen industry. In the 16th century iron smelting with charcoal in the Weald areas was further developed because of the demand for cannons. Charcoal was also needed to make gunpowder. Powder mills were established before 1570 at Rotherhithe, Wotton, Albury, and Chilworth (the latter closed only during World War I), and at Godstone in 1589. Glassmaking at Chiddingfold flourished until the beginning of the 20th century; it may have begun during the Roman occupation.

Surrey, like London, was overwhelmingly parliamentarian during the Civil War. It was not a major battleground, though there was fighting in the county, for example during the Royalist reversals leading to the stand at Kingston Common (July 7, 1648).

By 1653 the canalization of the Wey from Guildford to the Thames, planned by Sir Richard Weston of Sutton Place, was completed. This facilitated the transport to London of timber, grain, iron, gunpowder, and the produce of market gardens. Daniel Defoe in the early 18th century described Farnham as the greatest corn market in England, London excepted, grain being brought along the Wey to be ground and sent onward to London by water.

Surrey quarter sessions records that survive from 1659–60 contain numerous references to Quaker meetings and religious dissent generally. At the July sessions, 1665, during the plague, it was ordered that the wells at Epsom be locked for the summer to discourage visitors from London and thereby prevent the spread of disease. Samuel Pepys and John Evelyn, both Surrey men, have many references to the county in their *Diaries,* including Epsom at its height as a spa. It was then that horse racing on the Downs became fashionable. It was already possible to go from London for the day. John Evelyn was also a great gardener, expert on trees, and pioneer planter of conifers.

In Surrey much land was enclosed before the 18th century. Market gardens were a feature in the west and along the Thames, as at Mortlake, at Mitcham, with its lavender and physic gardens, in Bermondsey, and Camberwell. These gave place to housing developments. Godalming and Guildford declined as industries moved to the Midlands or to Yorkshire. Maps of the 18th and 19th centuries show copper, iron, oil, grain, paper, snuff, and calico printing mills, mainly along the Wandle. Elsewhere were chalk, gravel, and stone quarries, brickworks, and lime kilns.

The middle decades of the 18th century saw the beginning of improved roads in Surrey, under turnpike trusts. Navigations included the improved canalization of the Wey as far as Godalming (1762); the Basingstoke Canal (1796), originally constructed to link the industrial town of Basingstoke with the port of London; and the Wey and Arun Canal (1816). The development of railways brought to an end the turnpike road system and canal building. The Surrey Iron Railway, from Wandsworth to Croydon and then to Merstham, worked by horses and intended to convey materials such as chalk and stone to the Thames, was the first public railway sanctioned by Parliament (1801). Freight was carried on payment of a toll. The first railway for steam trains to pass through Surrey was the London and Southampton, opened as far as Woking in 1838. This was followed by the London and Brighton in 1841. The railways brought the county, particularly north of the Downs, continually nearer to London and resulted in intense house building, as at Wimbledon, or at Caterham after the building of the Caterham Valley Railway, sanctioned in 1854.

William Cobbett (born at Farnham, 1763) in his *Rural Rides* observed political and social conditions in the 1820s. These must be viewed against the background of the wars with France and shortage of wheat. A wet summer and poor harvest helped intensify the crisis of the autumn of 1830. In 1848 the Chartist Rising ended at Kennington Common.

Until the 19th century the county lay in the diocese of Winchester, apart from those parishes belonging to Canterbury. In 1905 the diocese of Southwark was created. Parishes that had previously been transferred to the see of London and those that in 1877 had been transferred to Rochester were transferred to Southwark. In 1927 the west of the county passed to the new diocese of Guildford. Its cathedral, begun in 1936 and consecrated in 1961, stands on Stag Hill. It was designed by Sir Edward Maufe and contains sculpture by Eric Gill (d. 1940). Croydon remains in the diocese of Canterbury.

There are racecourses in the county at Epsom Downs, where "the Derby" is run, Sandown Park (Esher), Kempton Park, and Lingfield Park; the All England Lawn Tennis Club has its headquarters at Wimbledon; Bisley is a centre for rifle shooting; the headquarters of the Surrey County Cricket Club is the Oval in Kennington, Lambeth, but some matches are played at Guildford.

The development of the county has been greatly influenced by its proximity to London; its good transport facilities have made it attractive both as a residential and recreational area.

*Boundary Changes.*—The Reform Act of 1832 disfranchised three boroughs and divided the county into two divisions, each returning two members. Lambeth became a borough and was extended. Rotherhithe and Bermondsey were included in the borough of Southwark. Further changes were made by the Reform acts of 1867 and 1885. By the second act the boroughs of the northeast, including Southwark, Lambeth, and Croydon, were divided into 17 single-member districts. Apart from Croydon (which remained a county borough until 1965) these boroughs became in 1889 part of the new county of London and a new phase in the history of Surrey County, with its administrative headquarters at Kingston, began.

Until 1889, when the administrative counties (including London) created under the Local Government Act 1888 came into being, Surrey stretched along the south bank of the Thames as far east as Rotherhithe and embraced ancient parishes, including Wandsworth, Lambeth, Camberwell, and Southwark, which were in the hundred of Brixton, and under the act became a part of the administrative county of London.

Under the terms of the London Government Act 1963, the administrative county of London and most of Middlesex, with the addition of certain areas from adjoining counties, including Surrey, became Greater London on April 1, 1965. The county of Surrey was altered by the addition of the urban districts of Staines and Sunbury-on-Thames (from Middlesex) and the loss to Greater London of the boroughs of Barnes, Beddington and Wallington, Kingston upon Thames, Malden and Coombe,

Mitcham, Richmond, Surbiton, Sutton and Cheam, Wimbledon, and the urban districts of Carshalton, Coulsdon and Purley, and Merton and Morden. Croydon, the only county borough in Surrey, also became part of Greater London. The county's total area was reduced from 702 sq.mi. (1,818 sq.km.) (1961) to 649.8 sq.mi. (1,683 sq.km.). (*See* LONDON; CROYDON; MERTON; SUTTON; KINGSTON UPON THAMES; RICHMOND UPON THAMES.)

**Population and Administration.**—The population of the present administrative county (based on the 1961 census) was 902,691. The population of the 4 boroughs was: Epsom and Ewell 71,159; Godalming 15,780; Guildford 53,976; Reigate 53,751; of the 14 urban districts 2 had a population exceeding 50,000: Esher 60,610; and Woking 67,519. The 5 rural districts, one of which had a population exceeding 50,000, contained 69 civil parishes.

The headquarters of the Surrey County Council are at County Hall, Kingston upon Thames in Greater London. Assizes and quarter sessions are both held at County Hall. Guildford has separate sessions. There are magistrates courts for nine petty sessional divisions and also for the boroughs of Guildford and Reigate.

The northern part of the county (as far south as Epsom) is in the Metropolitan Police Area. The Surrey Constabulary, covering the rest of the county, is divided into eight divisions. The parliamentary constituencies in the administrative county under the Representation of the People Act 1948 (as amended) consist of nine county constituencies and parts of two others.

**Industries and Communications.**—The total acreage under crops and grass in the early 1960s exceeded 180,000 ac. (72,840 ha.), of which more than 110,000 were arable land. This represented about 25% of the total area (excluding water) of the county, compared with about 9% in 1939. Wheat and oats are the chief grain crops. The cattle are mainly of the dairy type. There are extensive market and nursery gardens in the fertile brick-earth plain beside the Thames and in the Bracklesham Beds at Chobham and Bagshot.

The level land adjoining the main roads and railways attracted groups of miscellaneous industries along the Kingston Bypass near Raynes Park and Tolworth, and also at Addlestone and Salfords. More recently there has been industrial development at Camberley. Kingston upon Thames and Weybridge are important centres of general engineering and aircraft industry, while miscellaneous industries in the Wandle Valley at Mitcham, Merton, and Hackbridge are the modern development of the old watermill industries for which the Wandle was once well known.

The main roads from London to Penzance, Portsmouth, Brighton, and the south coast pass through Surrey, which is served also by the Southern Region main and suburban lines of British Rail. The London Underground extends to Morden, Wimbledon, and Richmond. Bus and coach services cross the county. The civil airport at Gatwick was opened in 1958.

BIBLIOGRAPHY.—J. Aubrey, *Natural History and Antiquities of the County of Surrey*, 5 vol. (1719); D. Lysons, *The Environs of London*, vol. i (1792–96); O. Manning and W. Bray, *The History and Antiquities of the County of Surrey*, 3 vol. (1804–14); also, in the British Museum, London, a 30 vol. edition, expanded by more than 6,000 illustrations, maps, etc., entitled *The History and Topography of the County of Surrey* (1847); Surrey Archaeological Society, *Surrey Archaeological Collections* (1858 *et seq.*); *The Domesday Book for the County of Surrey* (1876); E. W. Brayley, *A Topographical History of Surrey*, 4 vol., ed. and rev. by E. Walford (1878–81); *Victoria County History of Surrey*, 4 vol. (1902–14); J. E. B. Gover *et al.*, *The Place-names of Surrey* (1934); F. J. C. Hearnshaw, *The Place of Surrey in the History of England* (1936); Land Utilisation Survey of Britain, *The Land of Britain*, ed. by L. D. Stamp, pt. 81 (1941); *Publications* of the Surrey Record Society (1913 *et seq.*); *The Diary of John Evelyn*, ed. by E. S. de Beer (1955); W. Cobbett, *Rural Rides in the Counties of Surrey . . .*, ed. by E. W. Martin (1958); Surrey County Council, *Surrey Development Plan* (1958) and *Review of Development Plan* (1965); *Census 1961 England and Wales: County Report, Surrey;* Surrey County Council, *Antiquities of Surrey*, 5th ed. (1965), Surrey County Council, *General Reference Book*, 6th ed. (1965).

(W. W. R.; M. Gz.)

**SURTEES, ROBERT SMITH** (1805–1864), English novelist of the chase and the creator of "Mr. Jorrocks," the fox-hunting London grocer, was born at The Ridings, Northumberland, on May 17, 1805, of an ancient Durham family. He was educated at Durham grammar school, articled to solicitors in Newcastle and London, and admitted in 1828 but never practised law. From the days when he followed his father's hounds, hunting was his passion, but he had a taste for scribbling and took his writing seriously. A contributor to the *Sporting Magazine*, he broke away and, with Rudolph Ackermann as publisher, launched the *New Sporting Magazine* (N.S.M.) in 1831, editing it till 1836. He stood for Parliament unsuccessfully as a Conservative in 1837, took over the family seat, Hamsterley Hall, on his father's death in 1838, and was appointed a magistrate, deputy lieutenant for the county of Durham (1842), and high sheriff (1856).

Surtees' novels appeared as serials in the *N.S.M.* or elsewhere, or in monthly parts before final publication in book form, and these first and last dates are given after their titles. *Jorrocks' Jaunts and Jollities* (1831, 1838), a collection of tales; *Handley Cross* (1843 in 3 vol., expanded 1854), Surtees' own favourite; and *Hillingdon Hall* (1843, 1845) all immortalize Mr. Jorrocks, one of the great comic characters of English literature, as blunt as John Bull and entirely given over to hunting. There followed *Hawbuck Grange* (1846, 1847), *Mr Sponge's Sporting Tour* (1849, 1853), *Ask Mamma* (1857, 1858), *Plain or Ringlets?* (1858, 1860), and *Mr Romford's Hounds* (posthumous, 1865). Connoisseurs generally put first the chronicles of Soapey Sponge and Facey Romford, two cool horsemen and near-blackguards, whose chief business it is to pass off dangerous horses as tractable animals. In nearly all these books Surtees was fortunate to have two such illustrators as John Leech and Hablot K. Browne ("Phiz").

Surtees' style is plain, even slapdash, and his books have their *longueurs*—reiterated lectures on hunting and land management; imagination burns low, but the ear for dialogue is acute and the observation telling. In fact, Surtees is a surprisingly mordant satirist, and the snobbery, envy, malice, greed, avarice, and ignorance that consume so many of his characters are set down with no particular geniality; the picture he paints, mainly of provincial England just leaving the coaching for the railway era, is an unamiable one of boredom, ill manners, discomfort, and horribly coarse food, and its very matter-of-factness, with detail as clear as that of a sporting print, makes admirable social history. Yet the descriptions of fast runs with hounds over open country—perhaps the next best thing to a day in the open air—leave the most lasting impression.

The novelist Thackeray, Surtees, and John Leech, three close friends, died within ten months of each other, Surtees at Brighton on March 16, 1864.

BIBLIOGRAPHY.—E. D. Cuming, *R. S. Surtees* (1924); Frederick Watson, *R. S. Surtees* (1933); Leonard Cooper, *R. S. Surtees* (1952).

(Ro. M. G.)

**SURVEYING** is the science that deals with relatively large-scale, accurate, geometrical measurement. It includes the determination of the measurement data, the reduction and interpretation of the data to usable form, and, conversely, the establishment of relative position and size according to given measurement requirements. Thus surveying has two similar but opposite functions: (1) the determination of relative horizontal and vertical position, such as that used for the process of mapping; and (2) the establishment of marks to control construction or to indicate land boundaries.

When highly accurate surveying is used in connection with the construction of large products or the jigs and fixtures used to make them, it is called optical tooling or optical metrology.

Surveying has been an essential element in the development of man's environment for so many centuries that its importance is often forgotten. It is an imperative requirement in the planning and execution of nearly every form of construction. Surveying was essential in the great waterworks created at the dawn of history, and some of the most significant scientific discoveries could never have been implemented were it not for its far-reaching achievements. Its greatest fields are transportation, building, apportionment of land, and communications.

**History.**—It is very probable that surveying had its origin in ancient Egypt. In the tomb of one Menna at Thebes there is a representation on the walls of two chainmen surveying a field of corn, and in Ptolemaic and Roman papyruses in the same country, measurements of plots of land are described. That the early Egyptians could carry out measurements with a considerable degree of accuracy is certain from a study of the dimensions of the Great Pyramid.

In Roman times the groma, which consisted of two pairs of plumb lines suspended from the ends of two horizontal rods placed at right angles to each other, was used to lay out lines at right angles. An early groma of the same type, but rougher construction, has been found in Egypt. The Romans certainly made use of an instrument not unlike the plane table for determining the alignment of their roads. The Greeks used a form of log line for recording the distances run from point to point along the coast while making their slow voyage from the Indus to the Persian Gulf about 325 B.C. Still earlier (as early as 1600 B.C.) it is said that the Chinese knew the value of the lodestone and possessed some form of magnetic compass. The earliest maps were based on inaccurate astronomical determination, but not until medieval times, when the Arabs made use of the astrolabe, could nautical surveying really be said to begin. In 1450 the Arabs were aided by the compass in charting the coastlines of those countries that they visited. Plane tables were in use in Europe in the 16th century, and the principle of graphic triangulation and intersection was practised by surveyors in England and elsewhere. In 1615 Willebrord Snell, the Dutch mathematician, measured an arc of meridian by instrumental triangulation.

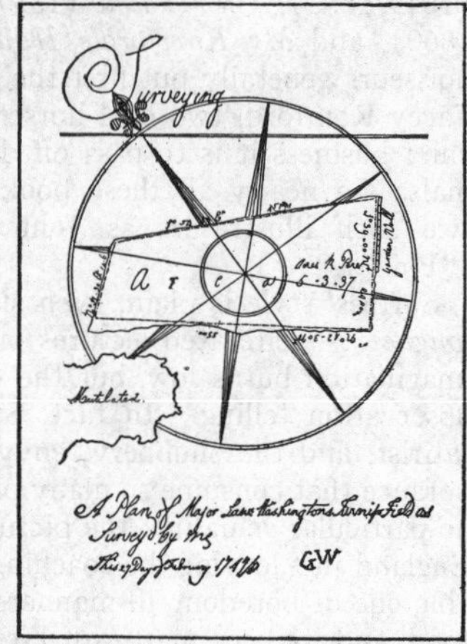


BY COURTESY OF THE U.S. BUREAU OF RECLAMATION

FIG. 1.—A PLAN MADE BY GEORGE WASHINGTON IN 1746, INSCRIBED IN HIS OWN HANDWRITING

Modern developments in electronics, optics, photography, reproduction, and aviation greatly influenced modern surveying. During World War II, the U.S. Army Map Service and its affiliated organizations prepared more than 30,000 different maps and reproduced more than 500,000,000 individual map sheets.

**Fundamentals.**—In contrast to other types of metrology (*q.v.*), nearly all surveying measurements are made either perpendicular to the direction of gravity (designated as horizontal) or in the direction of gravity (designated as vertical). When not so made, the quantities are immediately reduced mathematically to their horizontal or vertical equivalents. Thus the direction of gravity must be determined whenever a surveying measurement is made. It follows that only four types of measurements are determined: (1) horizontal lengths or distances; (2) vertical lengths or differences in height or elevation; (3) horizontal angles measured in planes horizontal at the vertex; and (4) vertical angles measured in vertical planes.

Horizontal lengths, with few exceptions, are measured in short, straight sections, which together are practically equivalent to an arc everywhere perpendicular to gravity.

Vertical measurements use as a reference a level surface, which, in considering the earth, is a curved surface everywhere perpendicular to gravity, such as the surface of still water. The surveyor's level, when properly operated, is an instrument that establishes a line of sight that is very nearly perpendicular to gravity at the instrument and maintains this angle without change in whatever direction it is pointed. At equal distances from the instrument the line of sight marks the position of a certain level surface. Thus the difference in height between two points is the vertical distance between the level surfaces that pass through them (see *Orthometric Corrections,* below). To determine the difference in height, the level is placed equidistant between the two points, and the graduations are read on a rod held vertically on each in turn. For less accurate results, the equality of horizontal distances need not be very accurately maintained. Variations in atmospheric refraction restrict the distances from the instrument to the points observed so that the difference in height between widely separated points is determined by a series of measurements over temporary points. This operation is called leveling, or running a line of levels.

Within any strip on the earth's surface about 12 mi. (20 km.) wide, and without large differences in altitude, the differences are negligible between the horizontal or vertical measurements made as described above and the same measurements reproduced on, or from, a plane surface where the directions of gravity would be parallel. Thus the results of such surveys are computed by plane trigonometry, and the whole process is called plane surveying.

For surveys outside these limits, geodetic computation must be used if geometric inconsistencies are to be avoided; this process is called geodetic surveying. Since geodetic surveys must be very accurate, the instruments used must be unusually precise, and they are often called geodetic instruments, even though they may be used for other types of accurate surveys.

**Units of Measure Used in Surveying.**—The metre is the fundamental unit of length used throughout the world. In 1889 the length of the metre was defined in terms of the International Prototype Metre, a platinum-iridium bar kept at the International Bureau of Weights and Measures at Sèvres, France. In October 1960, the length of the metre was redefined as equal to 1,650,763.73 times the wavelength of krypton-86 under specified conditions. This stabilized but did not effectively change the length of the metre.

From 1893 until 1959, the foot used in the United States equalled $\frac{1{,}200}{3{,}937}$ m., or 0.30480061 m. It was not quite the same length as the foot used in other English-speaking nations, as these were based on the imperial yard, whose relationship with the metre apparently varied slightly from time to time.

In 1959 it was agreed by representatives of the English-speaking nations to base the foot on the metre according to the exact ratio: 1 ft. = 0.3048 m. This shortened the foot used in the United States by about 2 parts in 1,000,000 and lengthened the contemporary British foot by about $\frac{1}{3}$ part in 1,000,000.

The U.S. Coast and Geodetic Survey, which maintains the fundamental survey control systems in the United States, measures in metres. Since 1893, this survey has converted to values in feet by the ratio $\frac{1{,}200}{3{,}937}$ in all publications in which the foot appears. It was necessary, in order to avoid confusion, to retain this value of the foot until such time as all vertical and horizontal control systems should be readjusted. Accordingly, this foot was named the U.S. Survey Foot.

Today, except in rare instances, the only unit of length used in surveying, in addition to metric units, is the foot (*e.g.,* 1 station = 100 ft., and decimals of tenths, hundredths, and thousandths of a foot are used instead of inches and fractions). In optical tooling, the inch and decimals of an inch are used exclusively (*e.g.,* 20 ft. would be termed 240 in.).

Two types of angular measure are used throughout the world as follows:

| *Sexagesimal System* | *Centesimal System* |
|---|---|
| 1 circle = 360 degrees (°) | 1 circle = 400 grads ($^g$) |
| 1 degree = 60 min. (′) | 1 grad = 100 min. (`) |
| 1 min. = 60 sec. (″) | 1 min. = 100 sec. (``) |

Directions are given in azimuths or bearings. Azimuths are clockwise angles from the north, or occasionally from the south. Equivalent values are the following:

| | | | | |
|---|---|---|---|---|
| Azimuth from North | 50° | 120° | 200° | 310° |
| Azimuth from South | 230° | 300° | 20° | 130° |
| Bearing | N 50°E | S 60°E | S 20°W | N 50°W |

**Surveying Instruments.**—There are four fundamental surveying instruments: the steel tape, the theodolite (or transit), the compass, and the level. Each requires supplementary equipment, and each has a number of forms for special purposes.

*The Steel Tape,* which consists of a graduated steel ribbon, or a flat wire, with handles at each end, is the basic means of measuring distance. Its length is taken as the straight-line distance between the two end marks at 68° F (20° C). Thus its length is different with different types of support and under different tensions. When compared to a standard to determine its length, tensions and types of support are used which are likely to be used in the field. In the field, if accuracy is desired, the type of support, the tension, the temperature, and the difference in height of the two end marks must be recorded and the measured length corrected accordingly.

In most routine surveys, the tape is held by hand at the ends, kept high enough to clear ground objects, made horizontal by estimation, and placed in the direction of measurement by eye or with an instrument. The desired tension is estimated, and the positions of the graduations are brought to the ground marks by plumb bobs. Sometimes the air temperatures are recorded. For higher accuracy, tripods or other more definite types of support are employed, or the tape is fully supported on smooth surfaces. The slopes of the tape are measured directly or determined by leveling, and tape temperatures are ascertained by thermometers with their bulbs in contact with the tape. The tension is regulated with a spring balance, and the tape is in actual contact with the surfaces where the marks are placed.

Accurate electronic distance-measuring devices are often used to measure long traverse courses, long triangulation base lines, and for trilateration, which is the measurement of the sides of a system of triangles. When supported in an airplane, these electronic devices are used to measure distances over water where the earth's curvature prevents triangulation.

*The Theodolite* (*Transit*) is used to measure horizontal and vertical angles. It often has a compass for determining magnetic bearings and a spirit level containing a bubble in a liquid attached to the telescope for establishing a horizontal plane and for running levels. The telescope objective lens forms an image on the plane of the reticle, where a pattern, etched on glass, or cross hairs mark a point. An eye-piece (ocular) magnifies both the image and the cross hairs so that the observer sees the cross hairs on the object sighted, at the point of aim (on the line of sight), while the view is magnified about 20 to 30 diameters.

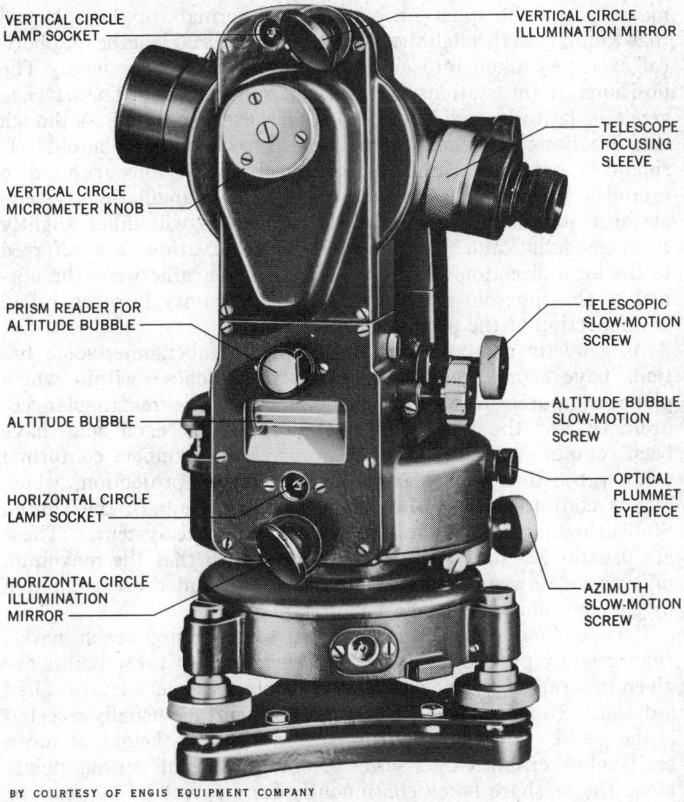

BY COURTESY OF ENGIS EQUIPMENT COMPANY

FIG. 2.—THEODOLITE

The telescope turns vertically through 360° on a horizontal (elevation) axis established by bearings in two uprights (standards). A graduated vertical circle turns with the telescope past an index on a standard and thus measures vertical angles.

The standards are mounted on a horizontal plate which carries one spirit level, or two at right angles, and usually two indices 180° apart for reading a horizontal graduated circle. The average of the two readings is free from the effects of eccentricity in the circle graduations. The plate is mounted on a vertical spindle that allows it to turn in a horizontal plane about a vertical axis (azimuth axis), and the horizontal axis is adjusted so that it is perpendicular to the vertical axis. The parts so far described are called collectively the alidade.

In nearly all European instruments and in special U.S. instruments the spindle turns in a bearing in the base, or leveling head, and the graduated horizontal circle for measuring horizontal angles turns in a separate bearing also in the leveling head. The rotation of the alidade with respect to the leveling head is controlled by a clamp and a tangent screw that permits slow motion. The circle is held in directional position by friction, but it can be turned by hand to approximate settings so that various parts of the circle can be used to measure an angle; thus the effects of circle-graduation inaccuracies can be reduced by averaging. This instrument is called a directional theodolite, or merely a theodolite.

The American instrument has a unique feature known as the double centre, on which the circle is mounted. It can be visualized as a thick, vertical, conical tube. The inner surface provides the bearing for the alidade spindle, and the outer surface turns in a bearing in the leveling head. An upper clamp and tangent screw (the "upper motion") control the rotation between the alidade and the circle, while a similar "lower motion" controls the rotation between the circle and the leveling head. With this arrangement, the alidade index can be set at zero on the circle by operating the upper motion. By using the lower motion, the line of sight can then be turned to the target that marks the first side of the angle without disturbing the zero setting. When the telescope is turned to the second side of the angle, by means of the upper motion, the alidade index will read the value of the angle. Furthermore, by returning the aim to the first target with the lower motion and repeating the process, a second value of the angle is added, and this can be continued indefinitely. When the final angle reading is divided by the number of times the angle is turned off, a very accurate value of the angle is obtained. This instrument is known as a repeating transit, or merely a transit.

The base of the leveling head of a theodolite or a transit is screwed on a tripod or some other support. The bearings for the alidade can be tilted slightly by either three or four leveling screws, thus placing the vertical axis in the direction of gravity according to the spirit level or levels on the plate.

Three-screw leveling heads are much easier and faster to use, but they sometimes allow the circle to rotate a little. Four-screw types, though safer, are more difficult to use, and they tend to deform the vertical bearing slightly.

A plumb bob or a vertical sighting device is used to place the instrument centre over the point of observation. The instrument can be shifted laterally for final positioning.

Originally all horizontal-angle measuring instruments were called theodolites. The poorer optics of earlier times required a very long telescope. To eliminate the effect of residual errors in the adjustment of the horizontal axis, or to prolong a line, the telescope had to be reversed in direction by lifting it out of its bearings and turning it around. With improvement in optics, the telescope was made short enough to be reversed by turning it in its bearings vertically through the zenith, that is, causing it to transit (hence the name "transit theodolites"). Today the name "transit" is usually reserved for repeating instruments.

Directional instruments (theodolites) can give results very rapidly in triangulation. For this purpose highly precise circle-reading devices are required. Modern instruments contain glass circles and micrometers with glass scales, both of which are illuminated from below.

Repeating instruments (transits) are equipped with vernier indices (scales). Single angles can be measured to the same accuracy and in about the same time as with theodolites. However, they are somewhat difficult to read. On the other hand, transits are much better than theodolites for staking purposes.

In an effort to compete with the American transit, European theodolite manufacturers have introduced a snap clamp that locks the circle to the alidade. This makes it possible to start at zero when measuring an angle and to repeat angles. Unfortunately, operating the clamp changes the setting slightly, and, since both the circle bearing and the alidade bearing are used simultaneously, the eccentricity between them introduces small errors that do not occur in transit operation.

*Compasses* of two needle-types are used: box compasses and circular compasses. Box compasses must be used with angle-measuring instruments, as they operate only when the line of sight points toward magnetic north. The bearing desired must then be measured from this direction.

Circular compasses can be mounted on theodolites and are often permanently mounted on transits. When provided with open sights, they can be used alone either mounted on light tripods or held in the hand.

*Surveying Levels* are of three types: (1) the wye or the dumpy level; (2) the tilting level; and (3) the self-leveling level. The first type consists of a telescopic sight, like that of a transit but usually of slightly higher magnification, to which a long spirit level is attached and adjusted so that the bubble centres when the line of sight is horizontal. The whole is mounted on a spindle in a leveling head so that it can be turned in direction. The telescope of the wye level can be rotated and changed end for end in the wyes for adjustment.

The tilting level is similar but the telescope can be tilted with respect to the spindle by means of a micrometer screw. The spindle is set nearly vertical with a circular spirit level, and the main bubble is centred with the micrometer screw.

The self-leveling level is similar to the tilting level, except that it has no micrometer screw. Instead, it contains an optical part that is operated by a pendulum in such a way that the line of sight is made horizontal automatically. Some types are extremely accurate, and all eliminate the time-consuming operation of centring the main bubble.

For very accurate work, tilting levels are equipped with coincidence-reading bubbles. By an optical device the bubble is split in half longitudinally, and the ends are shown with their centre-lines adjacent. When the two ends are made to coincide, the bubble is precisely centred. Often tilting and self-leveling levels have three horizontal cross hairs so that three readings of the staff (rod) can be taken and averaged. Also used are optical micrometers, which consist of thick glass disks with parallel optically flat surfaces usually mounted in front of the telescope. When these micrometers are rotated on a horizontal axis, they move the line of sight up or down and parallel to itself. A graduated drum indicates the distance moved from their normal position so that when the line of sight is placed exactly on a rod graduation, they read the very small additional quantity to be applied.

**Survey Control.**—The accuracy of survey measurements can be increased almost indefinitely, but only at increased cost. Accordingly, control surveys are used; these consist of a comparatively few, accurate measurements that cover the area of the project and from which short, less accurate measurements are made to the objects to be located. The simplest form of horizontal control is the traverse, which consists of a series of marked stations connected by measured courses and the measured angles between them. When such a series of distances and angles returns to its point of beginning, or begins and ends at stations of superior (more accurate) control, it can be checked and the small errors of measurement adjusted for mathematical consistency. By assuming or measuring a direction of one of the courses and rectangular coordinates of one of the stations, the rectangular coordinates of all the stations can be computed.

*Superior Horizontal Control* usually consists of a system of triangles. All of the angles and at least one side, called the base, are measured. Though several arrangements of triangles are used, one of the best is the quadrangle, or a chain of quadrangles. In each quadrangle, the four sides and the two diagonals are used so that eight angles are measured. To be geometrically consistent, the angles must satisfy three so-called angle equations and one side equation. The slight departures from these requirements are adjusted, usually by the theory of least squares, so that the results are very close to the true values. Rectangular coordinates are usually established as for traverses.

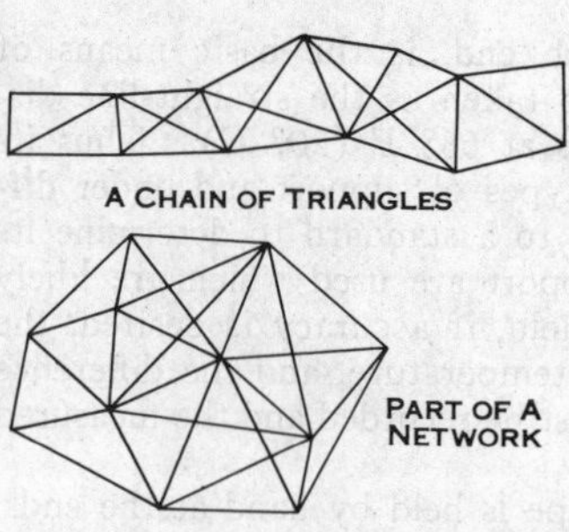


FIG. 3.—SYSTEMS OF TRIANGULATION

Since a number of sight lines extend from each triangulation station, it is difficult to find positions where triangulation stations can be located without the use of special towers. However, traverse stations can usually be successfully placed at ground level. This consideration often dictates which type of control is selected.

When the survey is so large that geodetic computation is necessary, a mathematical figure of the earth must be chosen as a reference surface. A level surface at mean sea level is considered to represent the earth's size and shape, and this is called the geoid (*see* also GEODESY). Due to gravity anomalies, the geoid is irregular; however, it is very nearly the surface generated by an ellipse rotating on its minor axis, *i.e.*, an oblate ellipsoid of revolution. The exact size and shape of such a figure are completely defined by the lengths of its two axes. An ellipsoid that nearly represents the geoid can be deduced from the results of triangulation systems which extend a considerable distance north and south and from astronomical observations connected with them. Such a figure is called a spheroid. Several have been computed by various authorities, but that usually used as a reference surface by English-speaking nations is known as Clarke's spheroid of 1866.

All length measurements are reduced to their sea-level equivalents, *i.e.*, to the geoid. These are assumed to be the distances, measured on the spheroid, between the normals to the spheroid that would pass through the ends of the measured lengths. Spherical excess is taken into account in angular computations. The positions of the stations are given in spherical coordinates (*i.e.*, geodetic latitude and longitude) which are computed as though the directions and distances were measured on the spheroid. It should be noted that, while astronomical observations are used to establish the position and orientation of a triangulation system, at most stations astronomical determinations will differ slightly from geodetic values, as astronomical observations are referred to the local direction of gravity. The difference between the normal to the spheroid and the direction of gravity is often called the deflection of the plumb bob.

As geodetic computation is somewhat cumbersome, some nations have established a series of strips (zones) within which plane computations can be made. The plane rectangular coordinates for the triangulation stations within each zone have been computed, usually on some form of the Lambert conformal conic projection or the transverse Mercator projection, which also is conformal (*see* MAP: *Map Projections*). In the United States these are called the state plane coordinate systems. These are usually 125 mi. wide and are arranged so that the maximum differences between lengths on the spheroid and those computed by the coordinates are 1 part in 10,000.

*Vertical Control* consists of marked points, called bench marks, connected by precise leveling. The elevations of these points are given in terms of their heights above a selected level surface called a datum. In large level surveys the level surface usually selected is the geoid. The elevation taken as zero is the height of mean sea level determined by a series of observations at various points along the seashore taken continuously for a period of 19 years or more.

*Orthometric Corrections* must be applied to long lines of levels at high altitudes that have a north-south trend. Since the level surfaces, determined by leveling, converge slightly toward the earth's poles due to the reduction in centrifugal force and the increase in the force of gravity at higher latitudes, the distances between the surfaces and the geoid do not exactly represent their height above the geoid.

Trigonometric leveling is often used where accurate elevations are not available or when the elevations of inaccessible points must be determined. From two points of known position and elevation, the horizontal position of the unknown point is found by triangulation, and the vertical angles from the known points are measured. The differences in elevation from each of the known points to the unknown point can then be computed trigonometrically.

When large areas must be mapped where accurate control is lacking, positions are determined astronomically, and elevations are measured by barometric pressure, usually determined by sensitive aneroid barometers (altimeters) or by hypsometers, which determine the temperatures of boiling water. Readings must be compared to those of a base instrument at a known elevation and corrected for air density estimated from the barometric pressure and the values of temperature and humidity. When two or more bases are used at well-separated elevations, proportional interpolation of results automatically eliminates the need for air-density corrections.

Finally, elevations are measured from aircraft by determining the height above the ground with electronic devices and the elevation of the aircraft by altimeter or trigonometric leveling.

**Maps and Charts.**—A complete map or chart shows the horizontal size, position, and elevation of natural and man-made topographic features according to a scale or, if the earth's curvature is considered, according to a mathematical projection. The shape of the ground in elevation is shown by contour lines that connect points of equal elevation; water depths are shown by spot depths and sometimes by lines of equal depth. Small-scale maps and charts show lines of latitude and longitude; large-scale maps show an indication of geodetic, astronomic, or magnetic north and often the lines of a rectangular coordinate system. Maps or charts made for special purposes omit many of these features.

A profile is a line which shows to scale, by its height, the elevation of the ground or other features along a selected route. Frequently the profiles of several features are shown on the same drawing.

Due to the immense importance of maps and charts, large areas of the earth have been surveyed, mapped, and charted, with the results published by government agencies. Government triangulation systems cover most of the world and are connected over oceans by wireless time, observations of moon occultations, ordinary astronomical observations, and satellite triangulation. Smaller bodies of water, where the earth's curvature prevents ground triangulation, are crossed by trilateration measured with electronic devices or triangulation by simultaneous observations to flares dropped from an airplane. Level nets (interconnecting networks of level circuits) based on mean sea level give elevation control. Secondary triangulation and levels are established where the mapping will be carried out. Photogrammetry (*q.v.*) is used almost exclusively for supplying detail. The photographs are usually connected to the control by transit-stadia and plane-table measurements to ground objects shown on the photographs.

Stadia is a method of measuring distance, direction, and difference in height by observing a graduated rod with a transit telescope or the telescope of a plane-table alidade. The telescope has two supplementary horizontal cross hairs in the reticle, equally spaced above and below the central horizontal cross hair. They are spaced so that they intercept on the rod, usually $\frac{1}{100}$ of the distance from a point at the instrument to the rod. This intercept, the direction, and the vertical angle are read and then reduced to the desired values by slide rule or tables.

The plane table consists essentially of a drawing board mounted on a tripod. The alidade is a telescope with a vertical-angle circle that is mounted on standards attached to a straightedge. Once aimed, the stadia intercept and the vertical angle are read, and the direction is recorded by drawing a line along the straightedge. Thus points are located and a map can be drawn as the work progresses.

Surveys for smaller maps are usually based on traverse and sometimes triangulation with a rudimentary level net to control elevations. Detail is filled in by transit-stadia on the plane table. Where elevations are important, the area is laid out in squares and the elevations of the intersections are determined with a level.

**Route Surveys.**—Route surveys are required for all forms of transportation, but those for canals, railways, and highways require the greatest accuracy. A strip map is made of the most probable route, which is controlled by a traverse and a single line of levels, and photogrammetry is usually used for details. For small surveys, profiles are measured at right angles to the traverse, and contour lines are drawn connecting them. Other details are located by right-angle distances (offsets) from the traverse and the distance along the traverse to the foot of the perpendicular.

The centreline of construction, composed of straight lines (tangents) and circular curves, is laid out on the map and then marked on the ground where the required limits of rate-of-grade and curvature can be met with the greatest economy. Changes in rate-of-grade are connected by vertical curves, which are parabolas with vertical axes. Occasionally, in the final layout, spirals are used to connect curves with tangents or other curves.

Detailed construction is usually laid out by measurements from the centreline and the original line of levels. Often the centreline is represented by a base line parallel to it.

The computation of earthwork volumes and the complicated computations required for highway interchanges are nearly always handled by electronic computers.

**Nautical Charts.**—Horizontal control for a chart usually consists of triangulation established on land and on stationary positions in the water, such as lighthouses. Traverse is frequently used on land, and usually special land targets are built to mark ranges from which the positions of soundings can be determined. These targets, the shore line, and other objects used for navigation or construction are located from the control.

Water depths, which are recorded in feet or fathoms (units of six feet), are measured by soundings with poles, weighted lines, or Fathometers, which time the interval between the emission of a sound near the water surface and the return of the echo from the bottom. Isolated rocks, wrecks, or other obstructions are found by a wire drag, which is held level by buoys at the desired depth and towed over the area.

In tidal waters, one or more automatic tide gauges are established to make a continuous record of the height of the water against time. The time of each sounding is recorded so that the depths measured can be reduced to a selected datum, usually mean low water or lower low water. The datum is established by a comparison of the tide gauge records and those of the nearest permanent tidal station.

The horizontal positions of soundings are determined by triangulation from shore, timing on ranges, stadia, wire-line measurements, timing sound impulses through the water, electronic measuring devices, and by the simultaneous measurement from the sounding craft of the two angles between three targets on shore. A sextant (*q.v.*) held on its side is used to measure these angles.

**Property Boundary Surveys.**—These surveys constitute a large, highly specialized branch of surveying known as land surveying. Not only must a land surveyor be thoroughly versed in surveying techniques, but he must thoroughly understand real property law, be very familiar with property lines within the area of his work, and be able to make decisions that he can justify in court when appearing as an expert witness.

In general, property boundary lines must be shown by marks on the ground (landmarks), often called monuments. These usually consist of ridges, streams, blazed lines, ditches, walls, fences, trees, field stones, stakes, iron pipes or rods, or prepared square concrete or stone posts sunk vertically into the ground.

Land surveying as we know it was first used to determine acreage. The directions of the boundary lines were determined by compass, and their lengths were determined usually by an actual chain made of wire links. These lengths and bearings were used to compute the acreage and were included in land descriptions to aid in identifying monuments. The chain used in most English-speaking nations is Gunter's chain, 66 ft. long and made of 100 links. Ten square chains equal one acre. Other units associated with the chain are the rod, pole, or perch, each 25 links long, and a square chain contains 4 roods. One rood equals 40 perches or square rods. The United States and Canadian public land systems are based on the chain, and many land descriptions there and elsewhere contain this unit.

FIG. 4.—BENCH MARK TABLET USED IN THE UNITED STATES

With the introduction of the transit and tape, it became possible to locate land boundaries accurately by measurement from any monumented line so that the recorded measurements gained in importance and fewer monuments were used.

Since the cost of a survey increases with its accuracy, surveys of low-priced land are seldom very accurate. When placed together, they overlap or gap, often containing errors or omissions, and frequently the same line in abutting parcels is recorded with different directions and lengths in the two descriptions. Moreover, monuments disappear and natural monuments, such as trees or field stones, are often destroyed or cannot be identified. In localities where land is increasing in value, an almost universal condition, these inconsistencies must be eliminated. While the power of decision rests with the court, the land surveyor must reach a solution based on his experience, his estimate of the accuracy of the work of the previous surveyors, his familiarity with the property lines in the vicinity, and his knowledge of the law.

*See* also CHART; LAND DESCRIPTION; MAP; METROLOGY; PHOTOGRAMMETRY; RANGE FINDERS; TACHEOMETRY; and references under "Surveying" in the Index.

BIBLIOGRAPHY.—H. C. Mitchell, "Definitions of Terms Used in Geodetic and Other Surveys," U. S. Coast and Geodetic Survey, *Special Publication 242* (1948); J. C. Tracy, *Surveying: Theory and Practice* (1947); Philip Kissam, *Surveying: Instruments and Methods,* 2nd ed. (1956), *Surveying for Civil Engineers* (1956), *Optical Tooling* (1962); H. C. Ives and P. Kissam, *Highway Curves,* 4th ed. (1952); C. B. Breed, G. L. Hosmer, and A. J. Bone, *Principles and Practice of Surveying,* vol. i (Elementary), 9th ed. (1958), and vol ii (Higher), 8th ed. (1962); F. R. Gosset, "Manual of Geodetic Triangulation," U. S. Coast and Geodetic Survey, *Special Publication 247,* (1950); "Formulas and Tables for the Computation of Geodetic Positions," U. S. Coast and Geodetic Survey, *Special Publication 8,* 7th ed. (1933); H. S. Rappleye, "Manual of Geodetic Leveling," U. S. Coast and Geodetic Survey, *Special Publication 239,* (1948), Manual of Leveling Computation and Adjustment, *Special Publication 240,* (1948); K. T. Adams, "Hydrographic Manual," U. S. Coast and Geodetic Survey, *Special Publication 143* (1942); R. H. Skelton, *Legal Elements of Boundaries and Adjacent Properties* (1930); W. C. Wattles, *Land Survey Descriptions* (1956); C. M. Brown and W. H. Eldridge, *Evidence and Procedures for Boundary Location* (1962). (P. K.)

**SURVILLE, CLOTILDE DE,** supposedly a 15th-century French poet and author of the so-called *Poésies de Clotilde.* Legend has it that the poet's full name was Marguerite Éléonore Clotilde de Vallon-Chalis, born in 1405 in the chateau of Vallon and married in 1421 to Bérenger de Surville, who was killed at the siege of Orléans in 1428. Her poems are said to have been inspired by her husband's absence and death in the war. Research has shown, however, that Bérenger married a widow, Marguerite Chalis from Privas, on Jan. 4, 1428, and that he was still alive in 1448.

The *Poésies de Clotilde,* about 50 poems treating of love and war, were first published partly by Charles Vanderbourg (1803) and partly by De Roujoux and Charles Nodier (1827) from alleged copies of manuscripts made by a descendant of Clotilde, the marquis Joseph-Étienne de Surville (1755–98). They were quickly recognized as spurious; both in form and allusion (*e.g.,* to Copernicus) they are out of keeping with their supposed period. They were almost certainly written by the marquis himself, a man with literary ambitions, who published similar poems of his own.

*See* A. Mazon, *Marguerite Chalis et la légende de Clotilde de Surville* (1873); W. Koenig, *Étude sur l'authenticité des poésies de Clotilde de Surville, poète français du XVe siècle* (1875). (F. J. WE.)

**SUSA** (SHUSHAN, SHUSH), capital of Susiana (Elam, *q.v.*) and chief residence of Darius I and his successors from 521 B.C. It lay at the foot of the Zagros Mountains at about latitude 32° N, near the bank of the Karkheh (Choaspes) River, and close to the Karun River in what is now Iran (*see* IRAN: *Archaeology*).

The site, identified (1850) by W. K. Loftus, has on it four mounds. One, rising about 38 m., holds the citadel. A second to the east represents the palace of Darius I and was excavated by M. Dieulafoy. The enameled bricks taken from its walls are in the Louvre, Paris. A third mound to the south contains the royal Elamite city, while the fourth mound consists of the poorer houses. Excavation of the citadel was begun by J. de Morgan in 1897. It yielded the obelisk of Manistusu, the stele of King Naramsin, and the code of Hammurabi (the latter in the winter of 1901–02).

The finest pottery came in the lowest strata, 25 m. below the surface and belongs to two different civilizations, both Neolithic. The earlier is characterized by vases of fine red clay, wheel made, in a few well-defined shapes, and all with thin, polished sides. The decorations applied in black paint or red-brown ferruginous (iron-bearing) earth consist of bold geometrical patterns, often combined with spirited studies from nature. The pottery of the second period shows a retrogression, being coarser and porous.

Above the early strata come remains of Elamite and early Babylonian civilizations, inscribed objects from the latter bearing pictorial characters from which the cuneiform (*q.v.*) was evolved. The upper portions of the mounds disclosed inscribed Achaemenian monuments, Greek pottery and inscriptions of the 4th century B.C., coins of the kings of Elam, and Parthian and Sasanian relics. Muslim tradition says that the tomb of the prophet Daniel lay in the bed of the Karkheh River, and a mosque was built on the bank opposite the supposed spot. Until after the 14th century the city was a flourishing centre of a district famous for silk, sugarcane, and oranges.

*See* also PERSIAN HISTORY and references under "Susa" in the Index.

BIBLIOGRAPHY.—W. K. Loftus, *Travels and Researches in Chaldaea and Susiana* (1857); M. Dieulafoy, *L'Art antique de la Perse* (1884–85), *L'Acropole de Suse* (1890); A. Billerbeck, *Susa* (1893); J. de Morgan, *Mémoires de la délégation en Perse,* vol. i–xxxii (1899); H. Frankfort, *Studies in Early Pottery of the Near East* (1924); E. E. Herzfeld, *Archaeological History of Iran* (1935), *Iran in the Ancient East* (1941); G. G. Cameron, *History of Early Iran* (1936); A. E. Christensen, *L'Iran sous les Sassanides* (1936); A. T. Olmstead, *History of the Persian Empire (Achaemenid Period)* (1948; 1949); R. Ghirshman, *Iran: Parthians and Sassanians* (1962), *Persia: From the Origins to Alexander the Great* (1964). (R. LEV.; T. C. Y.)

**SUSAH** (French SOUSSE), a town and port of eastern Tunisia and seat of a governorate, is the centre of the Sahel (As Sahil) region. Pop. (1963 est.) 52,000. The old town (*medina*), enclosed in ramparts that date from the Byzantine period and from the Aghlabid dynasty (9th century), and dominated by a kasbah, is on the side of a hill that leads down to the port. It encloses the Great Mosque and the Ribat (religious house), which date from the 9th century, the *suqs* (market places), and some Muslim quarters. Newer quarters have advanced for a long way to the north (on either side of the railway station), to the northwest, and to the south (the industrial quarter). The west is occupied by the army camp. The town is linked by rail and road to Tunis, Sfax (Safaqis), Gabès (Qabis), and Gafsa (Gafsah), and by roads to the hinterland.

Two-fifths of the inhabitants of Susah are engaged in industry, which includes flour mills, olive oil and residuum plants, food preservation factories, mechanical workshops, a motor vehicle assembly plant, and cotton spinneries. Plastics are also manufactured. But its trade is limited by the competition from Mahdia (Al Mahdiyah), in the south of the Sahel, and by the growing attraction of Tunis and Sfax. Exports from the port of Susah are chiefly oils, followed by esparto grass, salt, and preserved fish. Imports, in unequal competition with goods arriving from Tunis by road and railway, are restricted to cotton thread and cloths, machinery, grain and sugar, some petroleum products, and building materials. The port also has a small fishing fleet.

Susah is the successor of the Phoenician (or Carthaginian) Hadrumetum (*q.v.*). It declined under the Arab conquest but was revived by the Aghlabid rulers of Kairouan (Al Qayrawan), whose port it became and remained until the invasions of the Bedouin Arabs in the 11th century (*see* TUNISIA: *History*). These incursions ruined Kairouan and Tunisia and greatly restricted the activity of Susah. Its revival, after two centuries of decline, was thereafter associated with that of the Sahel. Susah is actually the centre for a region of over 600,000 inhabitants, which, with its lightly undulating landscape and nucleated villages, has an old tradition of olive cultivation. It was gradually reestablished from the 13th century and developed greatly under the French protectorate (1881–1955); it had 50 villages and 9,000,000 olive trees. Its surplus population, however, has been emigrating to Tunis.

*See* J. Despois, *La Tunisie orientale: Sahel et Basse Steppe*, 2nd ed. (1955). (J.-J. Ds.)

**SUSANNA** (SUSANNAH), an Old Testament writing not included in the Hebrew Bible, hence counted apocryphal by Protestantism. The story comprises ch. 13 of the Book of Daniel in the Vulgate (Latin) Bible and in English Bibles descended from it. *See* APOCRYPHA, OLD TESTAMENT (for status of the Standard Apocrypha); DANIEL, BOOK OF.

**SU SHIH:** *see* SU TUNG-P'O.

**SUSO** (SEUSE), **HEINRICH** (*c.* 1296–1366), Swabian mystic, the most renowned pupil of Meister Eckhart (*q.v.*) and read and admired by Thomas à Kempis, was born at Überlingen, on the German shore of Lake Constance, or possibly at Constance itself. At the age of 14 he joined the Dominican Order in Constance, where, five years later, he underwent a religious experience that gave a lasting and distinctive character to his spiritual life, all of which is marked by his self-dedication, made at that time, to the Eternal Wisdom. (Testimony of the so-called *Life of the Servant* concerning the early decades of his religious life is open to serious reserves.) Sometime before 1327 he went to Cologne for further theological studies and, together with Johann Tauler, was a pupil of Meister Eckhart. His first work, the *Little Book of Truth* (*c.* 1329), was occasioned by the controversies stirred up by the trial of his teacher. About ten years later he composed in Latin the *Horologe of Wisdom*, the most durably popular and influential of his writings. The *Little Book of Eternal Wisdom* (of which, at one time, the *Horologe* was thought to be a free translation) seems to come from the period of his maturity, about 1348. The most attractive of the Rhineland mystics and the easiest to comprehend, Suso presents a doctrine, Neoplatonic and Thomist, which in orientation is Eckhartian but in content quite his own.

He died at Ulm on Jan. 25, 1366. He was beatified in 1831, and his feast is celebrated on March 2.

The most reliable text of the German writings is that established by K. Bihlmeyer, *Heinrich Seuse: Deutsche Schriften* (1907); of the *Horologe* it is *Colloquia Dominicana . . . a Beato Henrico Susone dictata* (1923). The best English translations are those of J. M. Clark: *The Life of the Servant* (1952) and *Little Book of Eternal Wisdom* and *Little Book of Truth* (1953).

*See* C. Gröber, *Der Mystiker Heinrich Seuse* (1941); J. A. Bizet, *Henri Suso et le déclin de la scholastique* (1946); J. M. Clark, *The Great German Mystics*, pp. 54–74, with bibliography, pp. 114–117 (1949). (E. O'B.)

**SUSQUEHANNA,** the longest river in the eastern United States, rises in Otsego Lake, central New York, and flows southwestward into Chenango County, N.Y., where it heads southward into Susquehanna County of northeastern Pennsylvania. The river then changes its direction northwestward and enters south-central New York for a short distance before again turning southward into Bradford County, Pa. After flowing southeastward through the Allegheny Plateau it enters the Ridge and Valley Province north of Wilkes-Barre and changes its course southwestward, following one of the major longitudinal valleys. At Sunbury this part of the river, called the North Fork, is joined by the West Branch. The stream then turns southeastward, crossing five ridges and forming water gaps, after which it traverses the Piedmont plateau and empties into Chesapeake Bay at Havre de Grace, Md.

Prior to the Pleistocene ice age the Susquehanna drained most of central New York state, but due to morainal deposits across the state the northern tributaries were blocked. At the mouth of the Susquehanna a submarine channel extending eastward across the Continental Shelf indicates the presence of the former valley of the river.

The West Branch of the Susquehanna, 160 mi. in length, rises in the Allegheny Plateau of Indiana County, west-central Pennsylvania. The river flows northeastward to Williamsport and then turns southward to Sunbury. The North Fork falls 1,923 ft. and the West Branch falls 688 ft. The major tributaries are the Chemung and Juniata rivers.

Important cities on the Susquehanna river are Binghamton, N.Y., and Wilkes-Barre, Berwick, Sunbury, and Harrisburg, Pa. Williamsport is the major city of the West Branch. Due to rock obstructions and rapids the Susquehanna is not navigable; an abandoned canal at its mouth once made the river navigable for a short distance. The Susquehanna presents the greatest water-power potential of rivers in the eastern United States. There are hydroelectric power plants at Holtwood and Safe Harbor, Pa., and Conowingo, Md. (E. W. MI.)

**SUSSEX, EARLS AND DUKE OF.** The English title of earl of Sussex has been held by several families since its creation in the 12th century. The dukedom was created in 1801. The early history of the earldom is involved in some obscurity, for in the 12th and 13th centuries the same person is sometimes described as earl of Sussex, sometimes as earl of Chichester (the chief town of the county), and sometimes as earl of Arundel (the principal seat). Roger de Montgomery (d. 1094), who was created an earl in 1067 and received a large part of Sussex from William the Conqueror, was the first to be known as earl of Sussex, but the title of earl of Sussex was formally created by King Stephen in 1141 for WILLIAM D'AUBIGNY (d. 1176). He was the husband of Adelaide, widow of Henry I, who had received the Sussex estates after 1102 when Montgomery's son Robert, 3rd earl of Arundel, was attainted and the estates were forfeited to the crown. William and his descendants were usually styled earls of Arundel (*see* ARUNDEL, EARLS OF). William's grandson WILLIAM (d. 1221), 3rd earl, was a favourite of King John and was one of his sureties for the observance of Magna Carta. On the death without issue of his second son, HUGH (d. 1243), 5th earl, the earldom reverted to the crown. John de Warenne (1231–1304), 7th earl of Surrey, the brother of Hugh's wife Maud, and John's grandson John (1286–1347), 8th earl of Surrey, were sometimes styled earls of Sussex, but neither possessed the earldom. (*See* WARENNE.)

**Radclyffe Earls.**—There was no earl of Sussex from 1243 until 1529 when the title was conferred on ROBERT RADCLYFFE (Ratcliffe; *c.* 1483–1542). Created Viscount Fitzwalter in 1525, he became great chamberlain of England in 1540. His grandson THOMAS (*c.* 1525–83), 3rd earl of his line, was lord lieutenant of Ireland (*see* SUSSEX, THOMAS RADCLIFFE, 3RD EARL OF). Thomas' brother HENRY (*c.* 1532–93), 4th earl, served in Ireland from 1556 until about 1565. ROBERT (1573–1629), 5th earl, Henry's only son, died without legitimate living issue, and on the death of EDWARD (1559–1643), 6th earl, the son of Humphrey, third son of the 1st earl, the title became extinct.

**Savile, Lennard, and Yelverton Earls.**—THOMAS SAVILE (1590–*c.* 1659), son of John (1566–1630), 1st Baron Savile of Pontefract, was created earl of Sussex in 1644. His fluctuating allegiance in the English Civil War led to his imprisonment for a short time by both Charles I and by Parliament. The title became extinct on the death of his son JAMES (1647–71), 2nd earl of his line. It was revived in 1674 for THOMAS LENNARD (1654–1715), 15th Baron Dacre, soon after his marriage to Anne, the daughter of the duchess of Cleveland probably by Charles II. The title became extinct on the death of Thomas and was conferred in

1717 on TALBOT YELVERTON (1690–1731), 2nd viscount de Longueville, from whom it descended to his sons GEORGE (1727–58), 2nd earl of his line, and HENRY (1728–99), 3rd earl, on whose death it became extinct.

**Dukedom and Royal Earls.**—AUGUSTUS FREDERICK (1773–1843), the sixth son of George III, was created earl of Inverness and duke of Sussex in 1801. A supporter of the Liberals, he gave active help to the movements for the abolition of the slave trade, Catholic emancipation, and parliamentary reform. He was president (1816–43) of the (Royal) Society of Arts and (1830–39) of the Royal Society. The dukedom became extinct on his death in 1843.

The earldom was revived in 1874 for ARTHUR WILLIAM PATRICK ALBERT (1850–1942), third son of Queen Victoria, who at the same time was created duke of Connaught and Strathearn (*see* CONNAUGHT, ARTHUR WILLIAM PATRICK ALBERT, DUKE OF). He was succeeded by his grandson ALASTAIR ARTHUR (1914–43), who died unmarried, when the titles became extinct.

**SUSSEX, THOMAS RADCLIFFE** or RATCLYFFE, 3RD EARL OF (*c.* 1525–1583), was lord lieutenant of Ireland and lord lieutenant of the north under Queen Elizabeth I. The eldest son of Henry, 2nd earl of Sussex, he was born about 1525, and after his father's succession to the earldom in 1542 was styled Viscount Fitzwalter. After serving in the army abroad, he was employed in 1551 in negotiating a marriage between Edward VI and a daughter of Henry II, king of France. His prominence in the kingdom was shown by his inclusion among the signatories to the letters patent of June 16, 1553, settling the crown on Lady Jane Grey; but he nevertheless won favour with Queen Mary, who employed him in arranging her marriage with Philip of Spain, and who raised him to the peerage as Baron Fitzwalter in Aug. 1553.

BY COURTESY OF BARON FITZWALTER

THOMAS RADCLIFFE, 3RD EARL OF SUSSEX, ABOUT 1565 BY AN UNKNOWN ARTIST

In April 1556, Fitzwalter was appointed lord deputy of Ireland. The measures enjoined upon Fitzwalter by the government in London comprised the reversal of the partial attempts that had been made during the short reign of Edward VI to promote Protestantism in Ireland, and the "plantation" by English settlers of that part of the country then known as Offaly and Leix. But Fitzwalter first of all found it necessary to make an expedition into Ulster. Having defeated Shane O'Neill and his allies the MacDonnells, the lord deputy, who by the death of his father in Feb. 1557 became earl of Sussex, returned to Dublin, where he summoned a parliament in June of that year. Sussex then took the field against Donough O'Conor, whom he failed to capture, and afterward against O'Neill, whose lands in Tyrone he ravaged, restoring to their nominal rights the earl of Tyrone and his reputed son Matthew O'Neill, baron of Dungannon. (*See* O'NEILL.) In June of the following year Sussex turned his attention to the west, where the head of the O'Briens had ousted his nephew Conor O'Brien, earl of Thomond, from his possessions, and refused to pay allegiance to the crown; he forced Limerick to open its gates to him, restored Thomond, and proclaimed Donnell O'Brien a traitor. He took part in the ceremonial of Queen Elizabeth I's coronation in Jan. 1559; and in the following July he returned to Ireland with a fresh commission, now as lord lieutenant, from the new queen, whose policy required him to come to terms if possible with the troublesome leaders of the O'Neills and the MacDonnells. Sussex was recalled, at his own request, in Oct. 1565. His government of Ireland had not, however, been without fruit. Sussex was the first representative of the English crown who enforced authority to any considerable extent beyond the limits of the Pale.

On his return to England, Sussex immediately threw himself into opposition to the earl of Leicester. In 1566 and the following year Elizabeth employed him in negotiations for a marriage with the archduke Charles. When this project failed Sussex returned from Vienna in March 1568. In July he was appointed lord president of the council of the north and in 1569 lord lieutenant of the north in which office he had to deal with the rebellion of the earls of Northumberland and Westmorland. In 1570 he laid waste the border, invaded Scotland, and raided the country round Dumfries, reducing the rebel leaders to complete submission. In December he became a privy councillor and in July 1572 lord chamberlain. He was henceforth in frequent attendance on Queen Elizabeth, both in her progresses through the country and at court. He favoured her proposed marriage to Francis, duke of Anjou, and was an advocate of a conciliatory policy toward Spain. He died in London on June 9, 1583.

The earl of Sussex was a patron of literature and of the drama. He was twice married: first to Elizabeth, daughter of Thomas Wriothesley, earl of Southampton; and secondly to Frances, daughter of Sir William Sidney. His second wife was the foundress of Sidney Sussex college at Cambridge, which she endowed by her will. The earl left no children, and at his death his titles passed to his brother Henry. (R. B. WM.)

**SUSSEX,** a county of southern England bounded on the south by the English Channel, on the west by Hampshire, and on the north by Surrey and in part by Kent, which bounds it on the east. The geographical area is 1,457 sq.mi. (3,774 sq.km.).

**Physical Geography.**—From the chalk hills of the western border, the South Downs (average height 500 ft. [150 m.]; Ditchling Beacon, 813 ft. [248 m.]) lead east-southeast to meet the sea between Brighton and Eastbourne as bold cliffs, notably Beachy Head. Farther east, between the rich alluvial pastures of Pevensey Levels and Walland Marsh (part of Romney Marsh), the Hastings Sands reach the sea, stretching back in a broken range northwest to the Forest Ridge of Ashdown Forest (837 ft. [255 m.] at Crowborough) and St. Leonard's Forest. The South Downs slope gently to the south, with zones of greensand and gault leading to a belt of fertile brick-earth loam extending from near Shoreham-by-Sea to Hampshire and broadening out south of Chichester into the flat headland of Selsey Bill. The northern slopes of the Downs are abrupt, and there the greensand and gault belts lead to the heavy clay of the Weald (*q.v.*). The coastline has changed within historic times, the land being constantly eroded by the sea, particularly around Selsey, where the site of the Saxon cathedral is now probably a mile out to sea. The lagoon of Pagham Harbour was partly reclaimed at an early date but was inundated by the sea about 1300, recovered in 1876, and again lost to the sea in 1911. The drift of shingle tends to force eastward the mouths of the rivers that rise in the Forest Ridge and flow south through gaps in the Downs, but new outlets have in some instances been made by storms, as at Newhaven in *c.* 1590, or by dredging, as at Shoreham-by-Sea in 1815. Wide deposits of shingle now separate the sea from the medieval ports of Winchelsea and Pevensey. (L. F. S.)

**Archaeology.**—The influence of geology on the distribution of human activities at different stages of culture is striking, and Sussex has an important record of prehistoric sites and discoveries. The Paleolithic period is poorly represented, especially since the Piltdown discoveries, world famous for 40 years, were proved fraudulent in 1953. A few implements have been found in the raised beaches, especially at Slindon, and in the river gravels near Pulborough. The Mesolithic food-gatherers left a scatter of remains along the sand ridges of the Weald and on Tertiary deposits near Peacehaven. Primitive agricultural communities from the Neolithic to the Roman period preferred the chalk, though they hunted in the Weald. Four of the rare Neolithic "causewayed camps" lie on the Downs, the two larger ones being at Whitehawk (Brighton racecourse) and the Trundle (inner ring) at Goodwood. There is also a group of flint-mining sites near Worthing, including the well-known Cissbury and Harrow Hill flint mines. The Early and Middle Bronze Ages are poorly represented but include bell barrows on Bow Hill and on Monkton Down, Treyford, as well as the vanished Hove Barrow, which yielded a magnificent amber cup and other objects. Remains of the Late Bronze Age are abundant, including several examples of the earliest identifiable farm sites with their field systems, notably at Plumpton Plain near Brighton, New Barn Down near Worthing, and Itford Hill near Lewes. Many bronze implements have been found, singly and in hoards, as well as gold ornaments, including the lost Mountfield treasure near Battle. The Iron Age is notable for the hill forts on the Downs, especially the Trundle (outer ring) at Goodwood, Cissbury near Worthing, and the Caburn near Lewes. The first two were constructed perhaps in the 3rd century B.C. and abandoned before the Roman occupation; the Caburn was rather later and appears to have been captured by the Romans soon after A.D. 43. Farm sites of the Iron Age have been found on Park Brow near Cissbury and elsewhere, and many gold coins of the Belgic kings of the Commius dynasty have been found at Selsey.

(Et. C. C.)

**History.**—About the beginning of the Christian era a dynasty of British chieftains was established in the peninsula of Selsey. When the Romans invaded Britain in A.D. 43, the last of these chiefs, Cogidumnus, proved so useful an ally that he was made *legatus,* or official administrator, and given an extended kingdom (*regnum*). His centre, Noviomagus (Chichester), was developed as a tribal capital by the Romans, who made a great road (Stane Street) to London and others to Calleva (Silchester) and Venta Belgarum (Winchester), and minor roads connecting the downland corn districts and the Wealden iron mines with London. The fertile coast and downland area west of the Pevensey lagoons was developed with many villas or large farms. During the 3rd and 4th centuries fortresses were built for defense against pirates, one being at Anderida (Pevensey, where half the 20-ft. [6 m.] high walls still stand). After the Roman troops left Britain, about 410, civilization decayed, and in 477 a band of Saxons under Aella (Ella) and his three sons landed near Selsey and occupied the country, slowly fighting their way eastward until in 491 they stormed the last stronghold of Andredesceaster—usually assumed to be Pevensey—and massacred its defenders. The South Saxon conquest seems to have been ruthless and complete: no Celtic place-names survived, except those of three rivers—Tarrant (later Arun), Lavant, and Limene (later Rother). Aella's son Cissa probably occupied the walled Roman city called Chichester after him; but Sussex, the land of the South Saxons, soon fell under the control of Wessex, except for a (probably later) settlement in the east near Hastings, which seems to have retained some independence until 1011, when the Danes are said to have overrun it and the rest of Sussex.

In 681 Aethelwalh, one of the semi-independent kings, received the exiled Bishop Wilfrid, gave him large estates, and encouraged or ordered his subjects to accept Christianity. Wilfrid established a monastic bishopric at Selsey, and during the next two centuries churches were built and endowed throughout the county. Estates on the coast of Sussex were granted to Norman monasteries, notably to the abbey of Fécamp. In 1066, when Harold II was elected king, William I landed at Pevensey and marched to Hastings, near which town the decisive Battle of Hastings was fought on Oct. 14. On the site William built his votive Battle Abbey. Probably in order to secure his communications between Normandy and London, William divided Sussex into five blocks, each running from the coast, with a port, to the northern bounds of the county. Each of these districts, known as rapes, *i.e.,* districts that were "roped off," was in the hands of a trusted Norman lord, whose castles were built at Hastings, Pevensey, Lewes, Bramber, and Arundel. Later, about 1250, a sixth rape, Chichester, was separated for administrative purposes from Arundel. In the Domesday Book of 1086 the liberty of the abbot of Battle is also called a rape, but in all other records it is called the lowy. The boundaries of the rapes ran roughly parallel from north to south, and each rape contained a river, a castle, and a forest. From Domesday it is clear that the northern boundary of Sussex was still uncertain and that scarcely any villages existed in the wooded districts of the Weald, though many areas there were attached to manors in the settled south, serving at first as pastures for swine but being gradually cleared and settled. In 1086 the chief towns were Chichester, to which city the cathedral see had been moved from Selsey in 1075, and Lewes, which as early as 930 had been one of the few boroughs in England to be allowed two mints. Of Hastings, then an important harbour and one of the Cinque Ports (*q.v.*), no details are given. The Norman Conquest brought much building of churches and the foundation of the great Cluniac priory of Lewes and of "alien priories" (cells of Norman abbeys) at Boxgrove, Sele, and Wilmington.

During the reign of Henry III the see of Chichester was occupied by Bishop Richard de Wyche, whose saintly character led to his canonization in 1262, the shrine of St. Richard in the cathedral becoming a centre of pilgrimage. Although the castles of Sussex were held by supporters of King Henry III, it was on the Downs above Lewes that the royal forces were decisively defeated by Simon de Montfort in 1264; but Pevensey Castle held out until the king was restored to power. About this time a series of storms damaged the Cinque Port of Hastings and threatened to destroy the "ancient town" of Winchelsea. Accordingly, Edward I removed the inhabitants of Winchelsea to a safer site, where he laid out a town on a plan of rectangular blocks. The coast, however, soon suffered other assaults, the Hundred Years' War bringing constant raids by the French, who burned Hastings, Rye, and Winchelsea. The plague known as the Black Death hit the county heavily in 1349, killing about a third of the population, and there were further outbreaks in 1361 and 1366. Distress and misgovernment led the men of Sussex to support the Peasants' Revolt in 1381 and to take a prominent part in Jack Cade's Rebellion in 1450.

The Tudor period brought increased prosperity, but its importance in Sussex lies mainly in the realm of religion. On the whole, Sussex accepted the Protestant reform, so much so that during the short reign of Mary I, 30 men and women were burned, at Lewes and elsewhere, as heretics. The memory of these martyrs gave a strongly antipapal, and later puritan, tinge to popular feeling, though there were pockets of Roman Catholicism in the county. The county was therefore predominantly on the side of the Parliament during the Civil War, though Arundel Castle and the city of Chichester were for a time held for the king, and it was from Brighton that Charles II escaped to France after his defeat at Worcester. Puritan tendencies in the diocese are shown by the resignation or expulsion of more than 60 incumbents under the Act of Uniformity in 1662 and by the growth of the Quakers in spite of persecution.

During the last quarter of the 18th century, troubles with France led to the formation of local volunteers, and the movement was speeded up by the French Revolution, many of whose victims sought shelter in the Sussex coastal towns. A great camp was established in 1793 on the Downs near Brighton, and others near Eastbourne and Bexhill; when Napoleon I threatened invasion the coast was fortified by a chain of Martello towers, of which the westernmost was at Seaford. Brighton had since 1750 been developing into a fashionable watering place, especially from the first visit (1783) of the Prince Regent (afterward George IV) and the building of the Royal Pavilion. With the cult of sea bathing other towns developed at Bognor (*see* Bognor Regis), Hastings (*q.v.*), and St. Leonards, Eastbourne (*q.v.*), and Worthing (*q.v.*).

The growth of coastal resorts, the urbanization of almost the whole coast, and the conversion of much of it into "dormitory towns" for London were the main features of the history of Sussex after the beginning of the 19th century.

**Architecture.**—Of monastic remains the chief are those of Battle Abbey, with its splendid gatehouse, Bayham Abbey, and Lewes Priory. Extensive remains of Robertsbridge Abbey and of the Augustinian priories of Michelham and Shulbrede and the alien priory of Wilmington are incorporated in modern houses. The friary chapels of Chichester, Winchelsea, and Rye are important, as is the medieval hospital of St. Mary at Chichester. Sussex is rich in churches built before or shortly after the Norman Conquest, such as Bosham, Sompting, and Worth. There are many mural paintings; an early group arose under the influence of Lewes Priory.

Pevensey Castle, built within the impressive walls of a Roman fortress, has an early Norman keep but was mostly built about 1250. At Lewes the early keep and later barbican are noteworthy; at Arundel only the keep is ancient, and Hastings and Bramber are mere fragments. Amberley Castle dates from 1377 and the lovely moated castle of Bodiam from 1386. Herstmonceux Castle (now occupied by the Royal Observatory), a brick building completed *c.* 1444, was rather a defensible great house than a true castle, in this resembling the ruined early Tudor house of Cowdray. Of later great houses, Parham, Petworth, and Up Park (the last two belonging to the National Trust) are outstanding. But it is in its wealth of minor houses that Sussex is particularly strong. The medieval examples are mostly timber framed; later building is mainly in brick, *e.g.*, at Chichester and Lewes; and the good tradition, come down through the charming Regency buildings of Brighton, was revived in the planning of many council estates. (*See* also BATTLE; BEXHILL; BRIGHTON; CHICHESTER; HASTINGS; HERSTMONCEUX; LEWES; PETWORTH; PEVENSEY; RYE; SEAFORD; SHOREHAM-BY-SEA; WINCHELSEA.)

**Population and Administration.**—At the first census in 1801 the population was, in round figures, 159,500; in 1851, 337,000; in 1901, 605,000; in 1951, 937,339; and in 1961, 1,077,517 (East Sussex 665,904, West Sussex 411,613). The respective figures for Brighton were: 7,300; 65,500; 102,300; 156,486; 163,159; and for Hove: 100; 4,100; 29,700; 69,535; and 72,973, showing the progressive urbanization of the county. In East Sussex are three county boroughs: Brighton, Eastbourne (1961, 60,918), Hastings (66,478); four municipal boroughs: Bexhill (28,941), Hove, Lewes (13,645), Rye (4,438); and six urban and five rural districts. West Sussex has three municipal boroughs: Arundel (2,617), Chichester (20,124), Worthing (80,329), and five urban and six rural districts. Crawley New Town, designated in 1946, had a population of 54,047 in 1961.

The formation of the two administrative counties of East and West Sussex in 1889 regularized a division that is traceable in Saxon times, corresponding to the two archdeaconries of Lewes and Chichester. The creation of five rapes, each originally with its own sheriff in addition to the king's sheriff of the whole county, obscured this division, but a long struggle over whether the County Court should be held at Chichester or Lewes was compromised in 1504 by an order for alternate sessions. From the reign of Elizabeth I, Quarter Sessions records were kept separately for East and West Sussex, with one joint session yearly. After the grant of the honour of Pevensey to John of Gaunt in 1372, this district became part of the duchy of Lancaster; the privileges of the manor of Bosham and of the Cinque Ports, the ecclesiastical lowy of Battle Abbey, and the peculiars of the archbishop of Canterbury complicated the medieval jurisdiction of the county.

From 1295, members of Parliament were returned more or less regularly by the city of Chichester and the boroughs of Arundel, Bramber, East Grinstead, Horsham, Lewes, Midhurst, Shoreham-by-Sea, and Steyning, and the Cinque Ports of Hastings, Rye, Seaford, and Winchelsea. Many of these constituencies were small and very corrupt, and under the Reform Act of 1832 five lost both members and four lost one, but Brighton was assigned two members. There are four county and four borough constituencies in East Sussex. West Sussex returns four members to Parliament. Brighton returns two members, Eastbourne one, and Hastings one. The University of Sussex was founded at Brighton in 1961, with its headquarters in the 18th-century Stanmer House.

**The Economy.**—Sussex is still heavily wooded; in early times the Weald was tree covered, the clay producing oaks and the lighter soils favouring beech. The small fields there became good corn-growing areas, after improved drainage was provided. Most arable land, however, has always lain on chalk and greensand and along the coastal plain. This last, especially near Worthing, became a centre of market gardening. Hops are grown in the east, though less widely than formerly. Under John Ellman of Glynde between 1780 and 1830 the breed of Southdown sheep became famous, but since 1870 sheep have almost vanished from the Downs. Cattle have increased, particularly for dairy herds, and the rearing and fattening of poultry is also an active industry. Nor is the harvest of the sea negligible, though less important than in medieval times, when Winchelsea was famous for plaice, Arundel for mullet, and Selsey for cockles, and the Cinque Ports were as much concerned with herring as with naval transport and piracy.

The sea was once the source of the salt industry; a quarter of all salt pans recorded in Domesday Book were in Sussex. Salt boiling depended on fuel, and the Sussex woods supplied fuel also for glassworks round Kirdford and Wisborough Green from the 13th to the 17th century, as well as for pottery, tile, and, later, brick kilns. Sussex oak was in demand for naval and other shipbuilding. The plentiful supply of fuel and iron ore made the county a centre of the iron industry from Roman times until the end of the 18th century. From Tudor times Sussex cast-iron ordnance, as well as domestic objects, were in demand; but when it became possible to use pit coal for smelting, the industry moved north to the coalfields.

Although the Weald was not impenetrable, Sussex roads were notoriously bad, and in winter often impassable, until the coming of turnpike roads toward the end of the 18th century. A railway from London to Brighton was opened in 1841, and the county is now served by the Southern Region of British Railways. A regular cross-channel service to Dieppe is maintained from Newhaven.

Kingley Vale and Lullington Heath are nature reserves; 10,618 ac. (4,297 ha.) of Sussex were owned by the National Trust in 1963 and 1,414 ac. (572 ha.) protected; 15 areas belonged to the Forestry Commission.

BIBLIOGRAPHY.—J. Dallaway and E. Cartwright, *A History of the Western Division of Sussex* (1815–32); T. W. Horsfield, *The History, Antiquities, and Topography . . . of Sussex*, 2 vol. (1835); Sussex Archaeological Society, *Sussex Archaeological Collections* (1846 *et seq.*); M. A. Lower, *The Worthies of Sussex . . .* (1865); W. D. Parish, *A Dictionary of the Sussex Dialect . . .* (rev. 1958); Sussex Record Society Publications (1901 *et seq.*); *Victoria County History of Sussex*, 6 vol. (1905 *et seq.*); A. Mawer, F. M. Stenton, and J. E. B. Gover, *Place-names of Sussex*, 2 vol. (1930); E. Straker, *Wealden Iron . . .* (1931); H. C. K. Henderson and W. H. Briault, *Sussex*, "Land of Britain Series," no. 83 and 84 (1942); I. D. Margary, *Roman Ways in the Weald* (1948); E. C. Curwen, *Archaeology of Sussex*, 2nd ed. rev. (1954). (L. F. S.)

**SUSSEX, KINGDOM OF** (*Suð Seaxe, i.e.*, the South Saxons), one of the kingdoms of Anglo-Saxon Britain, the boundaries of which coincided by the end of the period with those of the modern county, though as late as 1011 a distinction can be drawn between Sussex and Hastings; *i.e.*, an area of East Sussex whose name survives as that of a town. According to the tradition given in the *Anglo-Saxon Chronicle*, a certain Aelli and his three sons landed in 477 at Cymenesora, a place now covered by the sea, south of Selsey Bill, and defeated the Britons. He fought again in 485 near a stream called Mearcredesburne and in 491, with his son Cissa, captured Anderida (Pevensey) and killed all the inhabitants. Bede names Aelli as the first king of the English to hold a supremacy over all the peoples south of the Humber. No later king of Sussex held this eminence.

The history of Sussex is then blank for about two centuries, except for a war with Ceolwulf of Wessex in 607. In 681 Bishop Wilfrid, expelled from Northumbria, went to Sussex. He found the people heathen, though their king, Aethelwalh, had been baptized in Mercia and had been given by his sponsor, King Wulfhere, the Isle of Wight and the district about the River Meon in Hampshire. Wilfrid stayed five years converting the South Saxons. He received a grant of 87 hides at Selsey for a monastery, and this became the episcopal see for the South Saxons, probably about 709. The see was moved to Chichester after the Norman Conquest.

At the end of 684, the South Saxons sent an army to help a Kentish aetheling, Eadric, to drive out his uncle King Hlothere. Soon after, a West Saxon exiled prince, Ceadwalla, ravaged Sussex and killed King Aethelwalh, and, though he was then driven out, he subjugated Sussex after he became king of Wessex in 685. Sussex was later divided among several kings. One called Nothhelm, or Nunna for short, made in 692 a grant to his sister Nothgith that was witnessed by a King Watt; a later charter of Nunna is witnessed by King Aethelstan and Queen Aethelthryth, and another by King Aethelberht. Nunna is described as a kinsman of Ine of Wessex, when in 710 he helped him fight Geraint, king of the West

Welsh; but Ine fought against the South Saxons, who were harbouring a West Saxon aetheling, Ealdberht, in 722 and again in 725, when he killed Ealdberht. There were still kings in Sussex early in the reign (757–796) of Offa of Mercia; he confirmed between 757 and 770 grants by kings called Aldwulf and Osmund; Aldwulf's charter is witnessed by a King Aelhwald and, probably, a King Oslac, though the name is bungled. Later, however, Aldwulf, Osmund, and Oslac attest as *duces* (ealdormen), and no further mention is made of kings. Offa captured the area of Hastings in 771. In 825 the South Saxons submitted to Egbert of Wessex, and henceforth were ruled by West Saxon kings. Sussex sometimes had an ealdorman of its own. It was divided into rapes, which, although they are not mentioned in pre-Conquest sources, are held to be very ancient administrative divisions.

BIBLIOGRAPHY.—*Anglo-Saxon Chronicle;* Bede, *Historia Ecclesiastica,* bk. ii. ch. 5, bk. iv. ch. 13; *The Life of Bishop Wilfrid by Eddius Stephanus,* ed. by B. Colgrave (1927); W. de G. Birch, *Cartularium Saxonicum,* 3 vol., no. 78, 132, 145, 197, 198, 206, 208, 212, 1334 (1885–93); F. M. Stenton, *Anglo-Saxon England,* 2nd ed. (1947).

(D. WK.)

**SUSU,** a Negro people of West Africa living in the coastal regions of southern Republic of Guinea (250,000) and the northwestern parts of Sierra Leone (50,000 in the 1960s). Their language is classed with the Mande-fu group (*see* MANDINGO), but ethnically there appear to be three stocks: Dialonke, deriving from the indigenous peoples expelled from Fouta Djallon by the Fulani (*q.v.*); a very old semi-Bantu stock linked with Baga, Landuman (*qq.v.*), Nalu, and Mandenyi; and a Mandingo stock probably of more recent origin.

From what is known of these tall, slender people authority would seem to be vested in a family head (*kabilé koundji*), rather than in a village chief. In Sierra Leone villages are grouped under a paramount chief into small chiefdoms (of about 3,000–6,000 people each) represented on district councils. Every Susu belongs to one of the patrilineal clans identified by name and totem animal. Marriage between cross-cousins is favoured, and polygynous unions are common. Shoemakers, jewelers, musicians, smiths, and carpenters used to constitute separate castes and were said to be descended from slaves. There were no marriages between them and members of free lineages, but such restrictions are of little importance now. Traditionally the Susu were animists but are now largely Muslim.

BIBLIOGRAPHY.—M. Houis, "Que sont les soso?," *Études Guinéenes,* vol. 6 (1950); M. McCulloch, *Peoples of the Sierra Leone Protectorate* (1950); H. Frechou, "Le régime foncier chez les Soussous du Moyen-Konkouré," *Cahiers Inst. Sci. écon. appliquée,* Supp. 129 (Sept. 1962), summarized in *African Abstracts,* vol. 15, abstract no. 37 (Jan. 1964).

(M. P. BN.)

**SUTHERLAND, EARLS AND DUKES OF.** From the time of its creation in the 13th century, the Scottish title of earl and later of duke of Sutherland has been held in the same family, although twice descending through the female line. The first earl is generally held to have been WILLIAM (d. *c.* 1248), whose father, Hugh Freskin (d. *c.* 1214/22), had large possessions in Sutherland before 1211. William was probably created earl in 1235. His great grandson WILLIAM (d. *c.* 1370), 5th earl, married Margaret, daughter of Robert I, the Bruce, and sister of David II. He fought against the English at the Battle of Neville's Cross (1346) and in 1357 was a hostage for the payment of the ransom for David, who had been captured at the battle. William's descendant JOHN (d. 1514), 9th earl, died unmarried and was succeeded by his sister and heir ELIZABETH (d. 1535), countess of Sutherland, wife of ADAM GORDON (d. 1538), the second son of George Gordon, 2nd earl of Huntly. Adam was styled earl of Sutherland from 1515 by right of his wife. He was succeeded by his grandson JOHN (1525–67), 11th earl, known as "the Good Earl John," who was poisoned by Isabel Sinclair, widow of his uncle Gilbert Gordon of Garty, in an attempt to secure the earldom for her son. She failed, however, to poison John's son ALEXANDER (1552–94), who succeeded as 12th earl.

Alexander's grandson JOHN (1609–79), 14th earl, was a leader of the Covenanters and fought against the marquess of Montrose at the Battle of Auldearn in 1645. He was keeper of the privy seal in Scotland (1649–51). His grandson JOHN (1661–1733), 16th earl, supported the Revolution in 1688 and was a commissioner in 1706 for the union of England and Scotland. In 1715 he became lord lieutenant of the six northern counties of Scotland and was active in putting down the Jacobite Rebellion in that year. About 1690 he took the surname of Sutherland instead of Gordon. He was succeeded by his grandson WILLIAM (1708–50), 17th earl, who helped suppress the Jacobite Rebellion of 1745.

His son WILLIAM (1735–66), 18th earl, died without male issue, and in 1771 the House of Lords confirmed the claim of this William's second daughter, ELIZABETH (1765–1839). She married in 1785 GEORGE GRANVILLE LEVESON-GOWER (1758–1833), who succeeded his father as 2nd marquess of Stafford in 1803. In addition to the estates of this title, he also inherited the Bridgwater Canal and estates from his maternal uncle Francis Egerton, 3rd duke of Bridgwater, and these properties, together with his wife's estates, made him a "leviathan of wealth" (Charles Greville, *Memoirs,* 1st series, [1874], vol. iii, p. 19). An "improving" landowner, he constructed roads and bridges in Sutherland and was also responsible for the Sutherland clearances, establishing extensive sheep runs by removing large numbers of his tenants from the interior to new coastal fishing villages. This aroused much bitterness and criticism. He was created duke of Sutherland in 1833. His son GEORGE (1786–1861), 2nd duke, assumed the additional surname of Sutherland in 1841. On the death without issue of the 2nd duke's great-grandson, GEORGE (1888–1963), 5th duke, the dukedom passed to his kinsman, JOHN SUTHERLAND EGERTON (1915– ), 5th earl of Ellesmere, who was descended from the brother of the 1st duke; the earldom of Sutherland passed to the 5th duke's niece, ELIZABETH MILLICENT (1921– ).

*See* Sir Robert Gordon, *A Genealogical History of the Earldom of Sutherland . . . to the Year 1651* (1813).

**SUTHERLAND, GEORGE** (1862–1942), U.S. Supreme Court justice from 1922 to 1938, was often spokesman for the court when it nullified social legislation. Brought to Utah soon after he was born in Buckinghamshire, Eng., on March 25, 1862, Sutherland attended Brigham Young University and the University of Michigan Law School. He was admitted to the bar in 1883. Subsequently he settled in Salt Lake City and became active as a Republican in Utah politics, becoming in 1896 a member of the state senate. He was widely supported by members of the Church of Jesus Christ of the Latter-day Saints although he himself was not a member.

From 1901 to 1903 Sutherland was a member of the U.S. House of Representatives, and from 1905 to 1917 he served in the U.S. Senate, his principal legislative accomplishment being the impetus he gave to the 19th (woman suffrage) Amendment to the U.S. Constitution. He was an ardent exponent of workmen's compensation and legislation for the benefit of seamen. In the 1920 presidential campaign and thereafter until his appointment to the court in 1922, he was an intimate adviser of Pres. Warren G. Harding. On the court, Sutherland quickly became identified with the conservative majority, writing the opinion outlawing the minimum wage (*Adkins* v. *Children's Hospital,* 261 U.S. 525 [1923]). Paradoxically, despite his hostility to governmental action, his most enduring contribution is probably his conception of the foreign relations power; it was, he successfully argued, not subject to the usual constitutional limitations (*U.S.* v. *Curtiss-Wright Export Corp.,* 299 U.S. 304 [1936]). He retired from the Supreme Court on Jan. 5, 1938, and died on July 18, 1942, in Stockbridge, Mass.

*See* J. F. Paschal, *Mr. Justice Sutherland* (1951). (J. F. PL.)

**SUTHERLAND, GRAHAM VIVIAN** (1903– ), English painter, whose imaginative landscapes and other works can be seen in galleries throughout the world, was born in London on Aug. 24, 1903. His early work as an etcher and engraver owes much to the romatic painter Samuel Palmer, but he was influenced at different times by the work of William Blake, Paul Nash, Henry Moore, and Picasso. It was not until 1935, after a visit to Wales, that he decided to become a painter. Although primarily interested in landscape, Sutherland's best-known works are remarkably diverse. His paintings as an official war artist (1941–44) provide a record of desolation both factual and evocative. His "Crucifixion" of 1946 in St. Matthew's Church, Northampton, uses the thorn motif, which recurs frequently in later work, for its expressionistic power, while the hard spiky shapes of fossils provided the theme of his large "Origins of the Land," painted for the 1951 Festival of Britain. His portrait of Somerset Maugham (Tate Gallery, London, 1949) was the first of a short but impressive series of portraits. In 1954–57 he designed the enormous tapestry for the new Coventry Cathedral. Important retrospective exhibitions were held at Venice (1952), London (1953), and Turin (1965). In 1960 he was elected to the Order of Merit.

BIBLIOGRAPHY.—E. Sackville-West, *Graham Sutherland*, 2nd ed. (1955); Robert Melville, *Graham Sutherland* (1950); D. Cooper, *The Work of Graham Sutherland* (1961). (D. L. FR.)

**SUTHERLAND,** a county of Scotland, forms an irregular pentagon with its apex pointing into the Atlantic at the Cape Wrath cliffs, the northwesterly point of the Scottish mainland. From Cape Wrath the rugged north coast runs east to the eastern boundary with Caithness and the somewhat similar but island-girt west coast runs southwest to the southern boundary with Ross and Cromarty. The fifth, southeastern, side is the North Sea shore running northeast-southwest, gentler and indented only in Dornoch Firth at the southern boundary and in the partially reclaimed Loch Fleet. The land area is 2,028 sq.mi. (5,253 sq.km.).

**Physical Characteristics.**—Mean annual rainfall in the east is about 25–30 in. (640–760 mm.), with dry springs; it rises gradually to 80–90 in. in the western Highlands, declining to 40 in. on the littoral. Associated contrasts in landscape from east to west include: (1) a narrow coastal belt of arable stock farms and estate woodlands mainly on postglacial raised beaches, etc., and on the downfaulted Jurassic marls, limestones, and coal around Brora; (2) hills of granite (Ben na Meilich, 1,940 ft. [590 m.]) or Old Red Sandstone conglomerate (Beinn Dhorain, 2,060 ft.) clad in heather—*nardus* moor; (3) a belt 30–40 mi. (48–64 km.) wide of bleak moors at 500–1,000 ft. planed across metamorphic Moine (Gaelic "moorland") schists, the root of Caledonian folding—this surface cut by glens, molded by ice, some a ribbon lake (Loch Shin), some with glacial and fluvio-glacial deposits carved by modern streams (*e.g.*, near Inchnadamph); above the main moorland surface stand isolated hills in schists (Ben Hope, 3,040 ft.) or granite (Ben Loyal, 2,504 ft.); (4) a series of narrow north-south belts in the west: the Moine thrust plane from Loch Eriboll to Loch Ailsh in Glen Oykell, bounding the schists to the east and, to the west, the white Cambrian quartzites and scarped, sweet-grassed Durness limestone, the massive red-brown Torridonian sandstone, and the ice-scoured hummocks and lochans (small lochs) of the Archean Lewisian Gneiss. This complex zone includes the Ben More Assynt massif (3,273 ft.; 998 m.) of Lewisian Gneiss capped by gleaming Cambrian quartzite, and was a major centre of dispersal of Quaternary glaciers; lower slopes carry extensive acid sheep pastures (fescue-purple moorgrass). Fauna includes red deer, pine marten, wild cat, and ptarmigan, with salmon in the prized and high-rented streams; (5) a coast with spectacular cliffs (Cape Wrath), sea-lochs, and sandy bays.

**History.**—There are a number of prehistoric remains, comprising chambered cairns, standing stones and stone rows, hill forts, settlements, and brochs (round towers). The majority are in the southeast, in particular near the Dornoch Firth but also northward as far as Helmsdale. Other groups are on the north coast, near Bettyhill, Tongue, and Portskerra; and in the west, near Inchnadamph, Lochinver, and Scourie. Near Inchnadamph, on the northern side of Loch Assynt, is the ruined Ardvreck Castle, in which James Graham, marquess of Montrose (*q.v.*), was held for a few days in 1650 by Neil Macleod of Assynt.

In the first half of the 11th century, Sutherland and Caithness were held by Thorfinn (d. *c.* 1065), the Norse jarl of Orkney, whose mother was a daughter of the Scottish king Malcolm II. It was the Norse who named the area (in relation to their settlements in Orkney and Shetland) *Sudrland* (southern land). After conquering the district, King William the Lion (reigned 1165–1214) seems to have granted land in Sutherland to a Hugh Freskin, whose son William was probably created earl in 1235. *See* also SUTHERLAND, EARLS AND DUKES OF.

George Granville Leveson-Gower (1758–1833), who had married (1785) Elizabeth (countess of Sutherland in her own right), succeeded his father as marquess of Stafford (1803), and was created duke of Sutherland (1833), was responsible for the notorious Sutherland Clearances (*c.* 1810–20), though also for road building. Advised that the interior of Sutherland was best suited for sheepraising and little fit for human habitation, he evicted thousands of families, burning their cottages and establishing large sheep farms. The evicted tenants were resettled in small coastal crofts, where their livelihood was to depend upon fishing and kelp-burning (until the latter was brought to an end by the development of the alkali industry). From the time of the potato famine of 1846, emigration has been continuous, despite various measures designed to help the crofters. Karl Marx in *Das Kapital* gave a striking, though polemical, description of these events.

**The Economy.**—Only about $1\frac{1}{2}\%$ of the total area is arable, the lowest proportion in Scotland. The best land adjoins Dornoch Firth, where farming is advanced and on fertile valley flats. Crofters still predominate, and the average holding of crops and grass (*i.e.*, rough grazings excluded) is 14 ac. (5.7 ha.), the smallest in Scotland excepting the Shetland Islands. Oats, turnips, swedes (rutabagas), and potatoes are grown. The raising of sheep, mostly Cheviot, is the county's staple business, and cattle are also kept. Next to agriculture, the sea fisheries and the salmon fisheries in the estuaries are the most important industries. A new growth industry is forestry, and large areas have been planted by both the Forestry Commission and private owners. An increasing activity, centred on Dornoch, is the collection, slaughter, and packaging of beef and mutton for sale in Scottish and English markets. Kinlochbervie and Lochinver are west-coast fishing ports, landing high quality whitefish, prawns, and lobsters. Brora makes whisky, woolens, and bricks, and some coal is mined. The extensive deer forests and grouse moors and lochs and rivers attract many sportsmen; Dornoch (*q.v.*), Lochinver, Golspie (*q.v.*), and Brora are holiday resorts. The railway enters the county from Ross and Cromarty at Invershin and leaves it for Caithness beyond Forsinard.

**Population and Administration.**—The population in 1921 was 17,802; in 1961 it was 13,507, of whom 2,349 spoke Gaelic and English and 5 Gaelic only. In 1966 it was 13,650. The population density is the lowest in the U.K. Dornoch (pop., 1966, 970) is the county town and the only burgh; the county offices are at Golspie. There are six county districts. The shire (with Caithness) returns one member to Parliament and forms a joint sheriffdom with Ross and Cromarty, with a sheriff-substitute resident in Ross-shire.

BIBLIOGRAPHY.—F. T. Smith, *Sutherland*, "Land of Britain Series" no. 3 (1939); D. Beaton (ed.), *History of the Province of Cat . . . to the Year 1615* (1914); J. Mackay and A. Gunn, *Sutherland and the Reay Country* (1897); Society for the Benefit of the Sons and Daughters of the Clergy, *The New Statistical Account of Scotland*, vol. xv (1845); R. W. Feachem, *Guide to Prehistoric Scotland* (1963); H. Fairhurst, "Scottish Clachans," *Scot. Geog. Mag.*, vol. 76, pp. 67–76 (1960). (A. T. A. L.; X.)

**SUTLEJ** (ancient Greek ZARADROS, Vedic SUTUDRI or SATADRU), one of the "five rivers" of the Punjab, rises in southwestern Tibet in Rakas Tal Lake (which receives water from Manasarowar Lake lying just to the east), at an elevation of more than 15,000 ft. (4,600 m.). It threads its way in a northwesterly direction through the Himalayan gorges, with heights of 20,000 ft. (6,000 m.) on either side, crosses the Indian union territory of Himachal Pradesh, and enters the Hoshiarpur district of Punjab. Thence it flows through the plains of the Punjab, receiving the Beas on its north bank in the southwest of Kapurthala district and forming for 65 mi. (105 km.) the Indo-Pakistan frontier before entering West Pakistan. It joins the Chenab (*q.v.*) 40 mi. (64 km.) W of Bahawalpur after a course of 850 mi. (1,368 km.). The two rivers there form the Panjnad ("five streams"), the link between the five rivers and the Indus.

As the river flows through an area of precarious rainfall, dams have been built all along it. Works include the Bhakra-Nangal multipurpose project; the Sirhind Canal; and, below Ferozepur, on both banks in India and Pakistan, the Sutlej Valley Project. Of the five rivers it has the largest catchment area (18,500 sq.mi.

[47,900 sq.km.]), but in relation to its size the poorest discharge. From 1947 until the agreement between India and Pakistan in 1960 the use of the Sutlej waters was a source of serious friction.

*See* also PUNJAB; PÚNJAB (India); PAKISTÁN: *History*.

(L. D. S.)

**SUTO** (BASUTO), the occupants of Lesotho (formerly Basutoland) and neighbouring areas in South Africa. They are not all of one ethnic stock but consist of those who accept the authority of the paramount chief or king of Lesotho. The Basuto nation was created by the chief Moshoeshoe (known to Europeans as Moshesh) in the 19th century (*see* LESOTHO: *History*). The majority are of southern Sotho linguistic stock, with a small minority from the Nguni-speaking tribes (about 15%). By the early 1960s they numbered about 500,000, though about 45% of the adult males were absent from the country as labour migrants.

The people live in small hamlets, which are grouped into parishes under hereditary headmen possessing administrative and judicial powers. Parishes are grouped into chiefdoms with hereditary chiefs, and these form provinces under chiefs, most of whom are close kin of the paramount. Authority at all levels is held by the genealogically senior man of the patrilineal line of descent that is regarded as the founding line of the settlement or chiefdom, the members of which regard their chief as a senior kinsman rather than as a mere administrative official.

The paramount is the senior patrilineal descendant from Mamohate, the senior wife of Moshoeshoe. He is advised both by a council of his close kin and by the national assembly, the *pitso*. He acts as head of the nation in all affairs, as final court of appeal and as ritual guardian of the country.

Corn (maize) is the staple food of the people; sorghum in the lowlands and wheat in the mountain areas are also important crops.

Initiation and formal instruction at puberty are practised, but the Basuto have no age-set system. Marriage is by transfer of bridewealth and cross-cousin marriage is preferred, although marriage with a parallel cousin is also permitted.

Most Basuto have become Christian. The central feature of the traditional religion is a cult of ancestors worshiped by their descendants. Modern cultists believe in a supreme being, but this is probably taken from Christian missionaries. *See* also AFRICA: *Ethnography (Anthropology): Southern Africa;* LESOTHO: *The People*.

BIBLIOGRAPHY.—V. G. J. Sheddick, *The Southern Sotho* (1953); E. H. Ashton, *The Basuto* (1952); I. Schapera, *Government and Politics in Tribal Societies* (1956); P. Duncan, *Sotho Laws and Customs* (1960); G. M. Theal, *Basutoland Records . . .*, 2nd ed. (1964).

(J. F. M. M.)

**SUTTEE** (SATI), the former Indian custom of immolating a widow along with her dead husband (*saha-marana*) or soon after his death (*anu-marana*); sometimes the wife was immolated before the husband's expected death in battle (*jauhar*). The Indian term *sati* means "chaste wife" and does not refer to the act of immolation. The custom probably originated in the belief that the great ones needed their companions in the afterlife as well as in this world. It was thus originally confined to royalty and nobility, and it never became a common practice. The first reference to it in a Sanskrit text is in the Mahabharata (*c.* A.D. 400), where some queens undergo *sati;* but it is mentioned by the 1st-century B.C. Greek author Diodorus Siculus in his account of the Punjab in the 4th century B.C. That it was practised among royalty and the fighting classes from *c.* A.D. 500 is confirmed by extant *sati* stones, memorials to widows who died in this way.

In the Muslim Period the Rajputs practised *jauhar* to save the women from dishonour by foes (*see* CHITTORGARH). The larger incidence of *sati* among the Brahmans of Bengal, particularly during 1680–1830, was due indirectly to the *Dayabhaga* system of law (*c.* 1100 A.D.), which prevailed in Bengal and which gave inheritance to widows. At its best *sati* was committed voluntarily on the widow's part, but cases of compulsion, escape, and rescue are known. Steps to prohibit it were taken by the Mogul rulers Humayun and his son Akbar, and it was abolished in British India by Lord William Bentinck in 1829. Instances of it continued to occur in Indian states for more than 30 years.

*See* Edward Thompson, *Suttee* (1928). (VE. R.)

**SUTTER, JOHN AUGUSTUS** (1803–1880), pioneer settler in California on whose land gold was discovered in 1848. He was born Feb. 15, 1803, in Kandern, in the Grand Duchy of Baden, of Swiss parentage. He went to America in 1834, fleeing from bankruptcy and abandoning his wife and children. After traveling widely and experiencing further financial failures he reached California in 1839. By sheer charm and vivacity, supplemented by a claim to military rank that never existed, he persuaded the Mexican governor to grant him lands on the Sacramento River, where he was to establish a fortified settlement. There, at its junction with the American River, he established New Helvetia, later to become the city of Sacramento. He built "Sutter's Fort," set up frontier industries, cultivated the land, and increased his herds. His debts were enormous and his tenure precarious, but when trappers and immigrants came to his fort they were received with lavish hospitality.

At the outbreak of the war with Mexico (1846) the fort was taken over by U.S. forces commanded by John C. Frémont, who was unappreciative of Sutter's former kindness to American settlers. Sutter, nevertheless, gave invaluable aid to the conquerors and became an American citizen. Then, just as his fortunes seemed restored, the discovery of gold on his land ironically brought colossal disaster. On Jan. 24, 1848, James W. Marshall, who was building a sawmill for Sutter at Coloma, 50 mi. up the American River, arrived at Sutter's Fort and with great secrecy showed Sutter flakes of gold. The two men tried to keep the discovery secret but the news leaked out, and shortly there was wholesale desertion from New Helvetia, followed by swarms of gold seekers from San Francisco. Sutter saw his lands overrun, his herds slaughtered, and his property stolen. His downfall was completed when the courts denied title to his Mexican land grant. By 1852 he was bankrupt. There followed brief periods of hopefulness and illusory grandeur, but the rest of his life was one of continued disappointment and frustration. The family he had abandoned in Switzerland joined him after 16 years, only to share in his misfortunes.

Sutter died in Washington, D.C., on June 18, 1880, heartbroken at the failure of Congress to act for his relief. Sutter Street, in San Francisco, and Sutter County commemorate his name; in Sacramento there is a restoration of his fort.

BIBLIOGRAPHY.—J. A. Sutter, *New Helvetia Diary* (1939); Erwin G. Gudde, *Sutter's Own Story* (1936); J. P. Zollinger, *Sutter: the Man and His Empire* (1939). (F. P. F.)

**SUTTNER, BERTHA FÉLICIE SOPHIE,** BARONESS VON (1843–1914), Austrian novelist, notable female pacifist, and winner of the Nobel Prize for Peace in 1905, was born at Prague on June 9, 1843, the daughter of Count Franz von Kinsky, Austrian field marshal. In 1876 she was hired as a secretary-housekeeper by Alfred Nobel, the munitions maker, but soon married Baron Arthur Gundaccar von Suttner, whose family disapproved of the match because she was seven years his senior and of a poor family. The couple lived at Tiflis in the Caucasus until 1885, when the Von Suttner family was reconciled to the marriage. Though she saw Nobel only twice more, she corresponded with him and is credited with influencing him in the establishment of the Nobel Prize for Peace.

Of her novels, *Die Waffen nieder!* (1889; best Eng. trans. by T. Holmes, *Lay Down Your Arms!*, 1892) was second in popularity in the 19th century only to Harriet Beecher Stowe's *Uncle Tom's Cabin*. *Das Maschinenzeitalter* (1899) reflects the scientific and free-thinking basis of her pacifism as derived from H. T. Buckle, Spencer, and Darwin. She founded the Austrian Society of Peace-Lovers in 1891 and edited the international pacifist journal *Die Waffen nieder!* from 1892 to 1899. She died in Vienna on June 21, 1914.

*See* Ellen Key, *Florence Nightingale und Baroness von Suttner* (1919); H. Schück *et al.* (ed.), *Nobel, the Man and His Prizes* (1962).

**SUTTON,** one of the 32 boroughs constituting Greater London, forms part of its southern perimeter. Area 16.7 sq.mi. (43.3 sq.km.); pop. (1961) 166,790. It is mainly residential but has some industries, including the manufacture of plastics, chemicals, radio components, and paper goods.

Historic buildings include All Saints Church at Carshalton, dating from the 12th century (restored 1893); the Lumley Chapel of the old St. Dunstan's Church at Cheam; Beddington Church (14th century); and the Great Hall of Beddington Place with a fine Tudor hammerbeam roof. In Cheam are a number of old timber-framed houses, including Whitehall (early Tudor).

The River Wandle rises in the borough and flows north to the Thames. Landscaped parks include Cheam Park (adjoining Nonsuch Park), and the Oaks, the estate once leased to the 12th earl of Derby which gave its name (1779) to the Oaks horse race. This, with the Derby (1780), is run annually on nearby Epsom racecourse. Within the borough is most of the former Croydon Airport, unused from 1959; the site is being developed as a residential neighbourhood. Sutton Station is an important suburban railway junction, and there are twelve other stations in the borough that provide rail links to Central London and the south coast. The southern terminus of the London Underground's Northern Line is at Morden, near the borough's northern boundary, which is approximately 12 mi. S of Charing Cross.

The London Borough of Sutton was created by Royal Charter in 1964 under the London Government Act 1963 (*see* LONDON) through the amalgamation of the former boroughs of Sutton and Cheam and Beddington and Wallington, and the urban district of Carshalton. These localities have long histories, and all appear in the Domesday Book. Medieval holders of manors were the Carew family (Beddington); the Dymoke family (Wallington); Christchurch Priory (West Cheam); the archbishop of Canterbury (East Cheam); and Chertsey Abbey (Sutton).

Distinguished residents were John Radcliffe (1650–1714), the well-known physician and benefactor to the University of Oxford; Philip Yorke, 1st earl of Hardwicke (1690–1764), the celebrated lord chancellor; and Gen. John Burgoyne (1722–1792).

(T. M. H. S.)

**SUTTON COLDFIELD,** a municipal borough (1886) in the Sutton Coldfield Parliamentary Division of Warwickshire, Eng., 7 mi. NNE of Birmingham. Pop. (1961) 72,165. Area 21.8 sq.mi. It is a residential district with a few light industries, and the British Broadcasting Corporation's television transmitter mast (750 ft.) is a landmark. It was at Sutton Coldfield that John Wyatt, a native, invented a mechanical device in 1733 for spinning cotton. The parish church of Holy Trinity was built in the 14th century and contains the tomb of Bishop Vesey (d. 1555), a great benefactor of the town. The Vesey Memorial Gardens were laid out in 1938; his birthplace, Moor Hall, is a private house. Other old houses are New Hall at Walmley, the Moat House (Queen Anne) and the grove at Wishaw (14th century). Bishop Vesey's grammar school was founded in 1541 and the Roman Catholic seminary of Oscott College in 1785. Its first charter of incorporation (1528) gave the town the right to be described forever as the Royal Town of Sutton Coldfield and also gave 2,400 ac. (including 75 ac. of water) of Sutton Forest, now Sutton Park, to the town.

**SUTTON HOO SHIP BURIAL,** an early Anglo-Saxon king's grave containing a ship fully equipped for the afterlife (but no body), which came to light in 1939 with excavations at Sutton Hoo, an estate near Woodbridge, Suffolk, Eng. Richest Germanic burial found in Europe since the 17th century, it throws important light on the wealth and contacts of early Anglo-Saxon kings and is particularly valuable because burial of the dead in a ship is rare in England, although described in *Beowulf* (*q.v.*).

The ship's timbers had rotted away, but their impression in the sand and the rivets that remained showed it to be a mastless clinker-built rowboat more than 80 ft. long. The grave goods, laid out amidships, included a sword with a gold and garnet pommel, a gold-mounted shield, a visored helmet enriched with silver inlay, a mail coat, an iron-handled ax, three angons (throwing javelins), four spears, and a knife. Ceremonial objects, showing that the deceased was a king, were a wrought iron stand surmounted with a stag, which is explained as a unique Anglo-Saxon standard, and a great whetstone, 2 ft. long, carved with bearded faces.

The wealth of the obscure kingdom of East Anglia (*q.v.*) is shown by 41 items of solid gold, the fittings for a baldric, and ceremonial regalia. These include a magnificent purse lid decorated with seven ornamental plaques, and a pair of curved and hinged epaulettes whose ornamentation of interlaced beasts and checker patterns is reminiscent of Hiberno-Saxon manuscript art. Small buckles and strap mounts, buttons, and pyramid studs for the sword knot are all lavishly decorated with garnets, and there is an impressive gold buckle weighing more than 14 oz.

Besides the gold cloisonné jewelry, probably made in a single English workshop, there was a quantity of imported silverware. One great silver dish bears the control stamp of the emperor Anastasius I (491–518) and is the only demonstrably Byzantine object so far found in England. In addition, there are a fluted bowl, a set of nine shallow bowls, a plain silver bowl, a ladle cup, and two spoons, probably christening presents, inscribed in Greek with the names Paul and Saul. A bronze bowl of Near Eastern manufacture and six small vessels made from gourds show wide East Anglian trading connections. The skill of the Celtic west is represented by three hanging bowls ornamented with enameled escutcheons, and inside one of these was found the remains of a small rectangular harp, the earliest postclassical instrument known. Domestic objects included bronze cauldrons, ironbound buckets, drinking horns, a pottery bottle, and textiles.

There was no body or cremated remains in the grave, and it is not certain whose cenotaph this was; its richness indicates a king, and Merovingian coins found in the grave date the deposit 650–670. In that period three kings of East Anglia died: Anna (d. *c.* 653), Aethelhere (d. 654), and Aethelwald (d. 662–663). A pagan burial, albeit with such Christian elements as the spoons, is, however, surprising for any of the kings, especially the latest. Anna was a notable Christian; his body was buried at Blythburgh, Suffolk, but the memorial could have been put up to placate some of his heathen followers. Aethelhere, however, seems the most likely candidate; he died fighting at the River Winwaed for Penda, the pagan king of Mercia, and his body was probably not recovered from the battle where Bede says many perished by drowning.

The rite of ship burial and certain items in the grave are most closely paralleled in Sweden and postulate a hitherto unsuspected Swedish origin for the East Anglian royal dynasty.

The grave goods are now in the British Museum.

BIBLIOGRAPHY.—R. L. S. Bruce-Mitford, *The Sutton Hoo Ship-Burial* (1947), "The Sutton Hoo Ship-Burial," *Proceedings of the Suffolk Institute of Archaeology,* vol. xxv, part 1 (1950), and "The Sutton Hoo Ship-Burial," in R. H. Hodgkin, *A History of the Anglo-Saxons,* 3rd ed., vol. ii (1952); C. W. Phillips, "The Excavation of the Sutton Hoo Ship-Burial," *The Antiquaries Journal,* vol. xx (1940); Francis P. Magoun, Jr., "The Sutton Hoo Ship-Burial: a Chronological Bibliography," *Speculum,* vol. xxix (1954); Jess B. Bessinger, Jr., "The Sutton Hoo Ship-Burial: a Chronological Bibliography, Part 2," *Speculum,* vol. xxxiii (1958). (R. J. CR.)

**SUTTON-IN-ASHFIELD,** a market town and urban district in the Arkfield parliamentary division of Nottinghamshire, Eng., 12 mi. N.N.W. of Nottingham by road. Pop. (1961) 40,441. Area 16.4 sq.mi. The neighbourhood contains remains of Sherwood forest. Formerly the town relied solely on textiles but after the discovery of coal in the vicinity a variety of manufactures was introduced although its chief trade is still hosiery.

**SU TUNG-P'O** (regular name SU SHIH) (1036–1101) was one of China's greatest poets, painters and prose masters. He pioneered in the Sung school of Chinese painting. He excelled in dignified historical essays as well as in light, whimsical pieces. He was an authority in medicine who picked his own herbs, a great winebibber and maker of wines, a judge who sympathized with his prisoners, an inventor of such famous dishes as "Tung-p'o pork," an inkmaker, a renowned calligraphist whose every scribbled note was carefully preserved and whose family letters were inscribed in stone in his own lifetime. Wherever he was stationed as a magistrate, he dredged lakes, built canals, fought floods and constructed dams. He instituted hospitals and dispensaries, and was the first man to start the system of prison physicians because he could not stand the condition of the prisons. Alone, he fought the drowning of girl babies. He worked for famine relief and wrote successive letters to the empress dowager begging for forgiveness of tax to the poor. He forgave his friend who sent him to exile in Hainan Island, then almost outside the pale of civilization. All these actions made him indubitably the most loved and admired scholar of his and later days.

Of the eight prose masters of the T'ang and Sung dynasties, the Su family accounted for three, Tung-p'o himself, his brother Su Tse-yu and his father, Su Hsün (1009–66). When he went to the capital to take his examinations, Ou-yang Hsiu, the acknowledged leader of the scholars, said when he read his writings, "I must give place to this young man." His reputation was established. Later the court attendants reported that whenever they saw the emperor's chopsticks stop moving in the midst of eating, they knew it was a memorandum by Su Tung-p'o he was reading. It was his misfortune that the emperor listened to Wang An-shih (*q.v.*), the social reformer, who banished all opposition to exile. Su Tung-p'o was first banished to Huangchow for four years (1080–84). With the emperor's death, during the regency of the empress dowager (1085–93), he was successively secretary to the emperor, governor of Chekiang, minister of civil service, of war, of education, and governor of Hopei. On the death of the empress dowager, he was banished to Huichow, in Kwangtung, and again to Hainan, whence he returned to China in 1101, one month before his death.

Tung-p'o's position and popularity came from a combination of literary brilliance and political integrity and his fearless championing of the people. His honesty with himself was the "bone" of his stature, while the charm of his personality, his wit, his gaiety and his literary accomplishments were the "skin and flesh" which gave to him the great charm which has endeared him to admirers throughout the generations.

*See* Lin Yutang, *The Gay Genius* (1947); *Selections from the Works of Su Tung-p'o,* trans. by C. D. LeGros Clark (1931); Burton Watson (trans.), *Su Tung-p'o: Selections from a Sung Dynasty Poet* (1965). (L. Y.)

**SUVA,** the capital, chief port and commercial centre, and largest town of the British colony of Fiji (*q.v.*), near the mouth of the Rewa River on the southeast coast of Viti Levu, or "great Fiji," the principal island. First occupied by European settlers in 1870, it was selected for the new capital in 1877 although the actual move from Levuka on the island of Ovalau was delayed until 1882. From the original site on the western side of the Suva Peninsula the town has spread to the north, west, and south, while reclamation has provided space for the expansion of warehouses, factories, wharves, and slipways. The rapidly increasing population reached 37,371 in 1956 and included 19,321 Indians, 9,758 Fijians, 3,394 Europeans, 2,094 part-Europeans and 1,647 Chinese.

Administration is by an elected municipal council. Secondary schools and a teachers' training college serve all ethnic groups. The central medical school provides medical and dental courses for native students from Pacific islands as far distant as New Guinea. Besides a general hospital there are hospitals for mental and tuberculosis cases. Newspapers and periodicals are published in English, Hindustani, and Fijian. Industry includes cigarette and soap manufacture, copra-crushing, baking, and brewing. Electric power is generated locally. Slipway facilities are used by vessels from surrounding islands. (R. M. Fr.)

**SUVOROV, ALEKSANDR VASILIEVICH,** Count (1730–1800), Russian military commander whose genius created a lasting tradition, was born in Moscow on Nov. 24 (new style; 13, old style), 1730, of a noble family, Swedish in origin. His father, V. I. Suvorov, had served under Peter the Great, reaching the rank of general. At the age of 12 Suvorov was enlisted in the Semenovski Life Guards Regiment, but until the age of 17 he remained at home, studying military subjects under his father's tutelage. He began serving in 1748 and spent about seven years as a guardsman before receiving his commission. He first saw action during the Seven Years' War (1756–63) and, having won rapid promotion to lieutenant colonel, took part in the Battle of Kunersdorf (1759) and in the advance on Berlin in the following year.

A dedicated soldier, Suvorov worked out new tactics and strategy, which proved effective against the Confederation of Bar and in the Russo-Turkish War of 1768–74, when he served under the outstanding Russian commander Count P. A. Rumyantsev and won promotion to general. In August 1774 the empress Catherine II, who was his friend, sent him to command a small detachment of troops to support Count P. I. Panin in suppressing the peasant revolt led by Emelyan Pugachev (*q.v.*). Defeated before Suvorov could set out for Tsaritsyn, Pugachev was betrayed into Suvorov's hands in September 1774 and brought by him to Moscow.

During the Russo-Turkish War of 1787–91, Suvorov proved himself a brilliant commander. He successfully defended the shores of the Black Sea from Kherson to the Crimean Peninsula; and when on Oct. 12, 1787, the Turks tried to occupy Kinburn, in the Dnieper estuary, Suvorov, although twice wounded and far outnumbered, expelled them. His most resounding victories in this war, however, were in Moldavia: operating with an Austrian corps under Prince Josias of Saxe-Coburg, Suvorov used surprise tactics to defeat a greatly superior Turkish Army and took Focşani (Aug. 1, 1789); then, advancing with only 8,000 men to relieve an Austrian Army of 25,000, threatened by the Turkish Army, 115,000 strong, on the Rîmnic River, he attacked and inflicted a major defeat (Sept. 22, 1789). He was created Count Rymnikski by Catherine II and a count of the *Reich* by her ally the Holy Roman emperor Joseph II in recognition of this heroic exploit. The capture of Izmail, in Bessarabia, on Dec. 22, 1790, crowned Suvorov's victories in this war, although, as with so many of his successes, it was marked by heavy losses of life, about 8,000 Russian and 10,000 Turkish troops perishing in the storming.

In August 1794 Suvorov commanded the army sent into Poland to suppress the insurrection led by Tadeusz Kosciuszko. The Poles had concentrated most of their forces at Praga, the eastern suburb of Warsaw, but Suvorov took it by storm on Nov. 4, giving it over to a massacre in which about 23,000 men and women perished. While Suvorov was a soldier of genius, he could also be, as one contemporary wrote, "a most barbarous warrior." Catherine II rewarded him with the baton of a field marshal.

Suvorov was next appointed in command of the armies in the south, where troops were assembling to march against the French Republic. At his headquarters at Tul'chin in the Ukraine (1796–97), he wrote his treatise *Nauka pobezhdat* ("The Science of Conquering"), setting out clearly and forcefully his principles of warfare and his views on the training of troops. This treatise became the manual of all Russian army commanders and has exercised a strong influence on Russian military thought.

On the death of Catherine II (November 1796) and the accession of Paul I, Suvorov fell from favour and went into exile on his estate in the Novgorod Province. When Russia joined the coalition against France (1798), he was recalled to command the army destined to operate against the French in Italy. In a series of rapid victories (April–August 1799), he expelled the French from Italy, except for a small force under Jean Moreau, gathered near Genoa. Suvorov was rewarded with the title of Prince Italiiski in recognition of these victories; and in October 1799 he was appointed generalissimo of the Russian forces. (*See* French Revolutionary Wars.)

At this juncture the allied command ordered Suvorov to march his army into Switzerland. He objected that conditions in the late autumn in the Alpine passes made such an operation excessively difficult. Both the Russian and the Austrian governments, however, overruled his objections. Suvorov hurriedly trained his troops in mountain warfare and made extensive plans to ensure his supplies, but difficulties mounted against him. His chief lieutenant, Gen. A. M. Rimski-Korsakov, was defeated by the French at Zürich. Then the French army, 80,000 strong, seized all mountain passes, thus surrounding Suvorov and his small army of about 22,000 men, but the wily old field marshal managed to extricate himself and to save his army. This Swiss expedition of 1799, in which Suvorov marched over the Alps, was his last and most brilliant exploit.

Suvorov, ill and exhausted, returned to Russia to find himself again in disgrace. The emperor Paul canceled the ceremonial welcome prepared some months earlier, and Suvorov was brought by night into St. Petersburg, the capital, to the house of a relative, where a fortnight later, on May 18 (N.S.; 6, O.S.), 1800, he died. There was a spontaneous demonstration of respect by the guards and people at his funeral, and within a year the emperor Alexander I erected a statue to his memory.

A small wiry man, Suvorov was incredibly brave, ruthless, and eccentric almost to the point of madness, but a military commander of genius. He was austere in habit, modest, but dry and sarcastic in speech, except to his troops who were as his children. He welded his regiments into indivisible units that he as their commander understood intimately, and he almost invariably led them into the attack himself. Swift in decision, Suvorov had an intuitive appreciation of the military factors before him.

BIBLIOGRAPHY.—G. P. Meshcheryakov (ed.), *A. V. Suvorov: Dokumenty,* 4 vol. (1949–53); P. Longworth, *The Art of Victory; The Life and Achievements of Generalissimo Suvorov* (1965). (I. GY.)

**SUWANNEE RIVER,** the river of Stephen Foster's song "Old Folks at Home," rises in the Okefenokee Swamp in southeast Georgia. As the river moves southward through Florida it is augmented by the discharge of many springs, and also receives the Withlacoochee, Alapaha, and Santa Fe rivers. The channel is dredged 135 mi. (217 km.) inland from the Gulf to junction with the Withlacoochee; 250 mi. (402 km.) from its headwaters the Suwannee empties into the Gulf of Mexico, 22 mi. (35 km.) S of Cross City, Fla. All but 35 mi. (56 km.) of the river's course is in Florida. In north Florida the Suwannee flows over shoals and boulders between high limestone banks lined with second-growth cedar. In its middle course it moves quietly through wild hammock and forested areas; in dry weather it forms only a narrow channel in a river bed of limestone strata which have been eroded into numerous curious forms. The banks of the river are heavily wooded with cypress and live oaks. Exotic flowers including gardenia, orchids, and ixia are abundant. Bass, perch, catfish, bream, and small game are plentiful.

In the 1780s the secluded bays and inlets of Suwannee Sound were rendezvous points for pirates. Tales of buried treasure still persist. The Suwannee was the boundary between the Timucua and Apalachee Indian tribes when northern Florida was explored. They called it the Guasaca Esqui, meaning "River of Reeds." The present name is thought to be a Negro corruption of San Juanee, meaning "little St. John." (M. C. P.)

**SUWAYDA', AS** (ES SUWEIDA; SOUEIDA; SWEIDA), a town and governorate of the Jebel Druze in the southern part of Syria. The town, which is the administrative centre of the governorate, is 55 mi. (89 km.) SSE of Damascus by road. Area (governorate) 2,143 sq.mi. (5,550 sq.km.); pop. (governorate, 1960) 99,519, (town, 1960) 18,154. The ancient name for the Jebel Druze was the Hauran. This area originally marked the boundary between Palestine and Syria. The northern part is known as El Lejja ("the refuge"), as robbers and rebels from the surrounding countries made it their hiding place. The volcanic soil is extremely fertile, and wheat, barley, vetches, and lentils are grown.

The town, whose ancient name was Soada or Dionysias, is said to have been founded by the Nabataeans but may date from an earlier period. The Nabataeans built a temple there to their god Dusares (later probably erroneously identified with Dionysus). The town came under Roman rule in the 1st century B.C., and Augustus handed it over to Herod the Great, whose family held it till A.D. 100. About 15 mi. (24 km.) SSW of As Suwayda' is the ancient site of Bozrah (*q.v.*). (M. V. S.-W.)

**SUYUTI, AL-** (ABU AL-FADL ABD AL-RAHMAN IBN ABI BAKR JALAL AL-DIN AL-SUYUTI) (1445–1505), Arabic encyclopaedic author, whose works deal with almost every subject, the Islamic religious sciences predominating. He was the son of a judge of Asyut in Egypt. Tutored by a Sufi friend of his father's, he was already a teacher in 1462. In 1486 he was appointed to a chair in the mosque of Baybars in Cairo. From 1501 onward he worked in seclusion on the island of Rauda on the Nile in Cairo.

His works number several hundred—many of them short booklets, others large-scale works. He was co-author of *Tafsir al-Jalalain,* a word-by-word commentary on the *Koran,* the first part of which was written by Jalal al-Din al-Mahalli (1389–1459). His *Itqan fi 'Ulum al-Koran* is a well-known work of koranic exegesis. Among his historical works is a history of the caliphs. His *Bughyat al-Wu'ah* is a biographical dictionary of grammarians and lexicographers, abridging and completing similar previous compilations.

Al-Suyuti was a compiler of genius: it is precisely his ability to select and abridge which makes his books so useful. This faculty, together with his keen, analytical mind, characterizes his best work, *al-Muzhir fi 'Ulum al-Lugha,* a guide to the Arabic science of lexicography or philology, in which the subject is treated in 50 aspects or categories. The work has been much used by European Arabists, especially by E. W. Lane (*q.v.*) in the introduction to his lexicon.

*See* C. Brockelmann, *Geschichte der arabischen Litteratur,* vol. ii, 2nd ed., pp. 180–204 (1949), and supplement ii, pp. 178–198 (1938). (J. A. HD.)

**SUZDAL, PRINCES OF.** In Russian history the area between the Oka River and the Upper Volga was called the Suzdal land or *zemlya Suzdalskaya.* In the 10th and 11th centuries A.D. it was a remote corner of the Russian world, but during the 12th and 13th centuries it grew rapidly in political and economic importance, becoming a cradle of the Great Russian nationality. There the immigrants from the Russian south, which was devastated by nomadic invasions, found a quieter life and gradually merged with the scattered and peaceful indigenous Finnish tribes to form the bulk of the Russian peasantry.

The first important prince of the region was Andrew (*q.v.;* Russ. Andrei Yurievich) Bogolyubski, who ruled from 1157 to 1174. He moved his capital to Vladimir on the Klyazma River and successfully colonized and organized the area, becoming the most powerful among the contemporary Russian princes. His brother Vsevolod III (1176–1212) successfully continued Andrew's policies. Vsevolod's power and influence were felt by other Russian princes, as well as by the city-state of Novgorod the Great, which depended on Suzdalia for grain supply. But the political structure erected by Andrew and Vsevolod did not endure. The Suzdal princes regarded their territories as their private property and, accordingly, divided them by testaments among their sons. During the 13th and 14th centuries Suzdalia thus disintegrated gradually into several lesser principalities, which recognized the seniority of the grand prince of Vladimir only nominally. The Tatar conquest (in 1237–40) made the grand prince of Vladimir, as all other Russian princes, an obedient vassal of the Tatar khan.

Prince Konstantin Vasilievich (1332–55) succeeded in building the grand principality of Suzdal and Nizhni Novgorod, with the capital in Nizhni Novgorod (now Gorki) from 1350; and his son Dimitri even became grand prince of Vladimir in 1359–62. Soon, however, the throne of Vladimir returned to the grand prince of Moscow (*q.v.*); and in 1392 Prince Vasili I Dimitrievich of Moscow, empowered by the khan Tokhtamysh, seized the region of Nizhni Novgorod and annexed it. (S. G. PU.)

**SUZUKI, DAISETZ TEITARŌ** (1870–1966), renowned Buddhologist, the chief interpreter of Zen Buddhism to the West. Born in Kanazawa, Japan, on Oct. 18, 1870, he studied English literature during his college days in Tokyo and was greatly influenced by Ralph Waldo Emerson. He was also interested in Japanese literature and was a close friend of the writer Natsume Sōseki (*q.v.*). His philosophical interests covered classical Chinese philosophy, Buddhist philosophy (especially in the tradition of the Kegon school), and Western philosophy. His friendship with the foremost modern Japanese philosopher, Nishida Kitarō (*q.v.*), lasted until Nishida's death. Suzuki was also an admirer of Emanuel Swedenborg (*q.v.*), whom he introduced into Japan by publishing his biography and translating four of his major works. Also, while Suzuki was a convinced follower of Zen Buddhism and trained under two great Zen masters, Imakita Kōsen and Shaku Sōyen, he had a profound appreciation of Shin Buddhism (*see* BUDDHISM: *Regional Variations in Buddhism: Japan*).

In 1893 Suzuki's Zen master, Shaku Sōyen, abbot of the Engaku-ji (temple) at Kamakura, represented Mahayana Buddhism at the World Parliament of Religions, held in Chicago. There he met Paul Carus (1852–1919), a philosopher and editor of the *Monist* and the *Open Court.* Carus was then interested in Chinese and Buddhist philosophies, and through Shaku Sōyen he secured Suzuki as his assistant. Suzuki thus went to LaSalle, Ill., where Carus lived, and there he remained until 1908, translating Aśvaghosha's *Discourse on the Awakening of Faith in the Mahayana* (1900),

*T'ai-Shang Kan-ying P'ien: Treatise of the Exalted One on Response and Retribution* (1906), and *Sermons of a Buddhist Abbot* (1906) and completing *Outlines of Mahayana Buddhism* (1907).

Upon his return to Japan in 1909, he taught English at the Peers' School and at Tokyo Imperial University. In 1911 he married Beatrice Lane (d. 1939), author of many works on Buddhism and Japanese art. In 1921 he accepted the chair of religious studies at Ōtani University (emeritus 1960), Kyoto, a Shin sectarian institution, where he also served for 20 years as editor of an English-language journal, *The Eastern Buddhist.* In 1934 he traveled through Korea, Manchuria, and China, and in 1936–37 the Japanese government sent him to lecture on Zen and Japanese culture in Europe and America. Some of his most famous works in English were written during his days in Kyoto—*e.g., Essays in Zen Buddhism,* 3 vol. (1927–34), *Studies in the Lankavatara Sutra* (1930), *An Index to the Lankavatara Sutra* (1933), *The Training of the Zen Buddhist Monk* (1934), *An Introduction to Zen Buddhism* (1934), the critical edition of *The Gandvyuha Sutra* (with H. Idzumi, 1934–36), *Manual of Zen Buddhism* (1936), *Buddhist Philosophy and Its Effects on the Life and Thought of the Japanese People* (1936), *Japanese Buddhism* (1938), and *Zen Buddhism and Its Influence on Japanese Culture* (1938).

In 1946 Suzuki established the Matsu-ga-oka ("Pine Hill") Library at Kamakura, and with a collaborator began publication of an English-language journal, *Cultural East.* He was made a member of the Japan Academy and was decorated by the Japanese government in 1949. In 1950, at the age of 80, Suzuki accepted the invitation of the Rockefeller Foundation to deliver lectures at several universities in North America. Except for intermittent visits to Europe and Japan, he was in the United States until 1958, mostly at Columbia University. The writings of his later years are interpretive rather than original: *e.g., The Zen Doctrine of No-Mind* (1949), *A Miscellany on the Shin Teaching of Buddhism* (1949), *Living by Zen* (1949), *Studies in Zen* (1955), *Mysticism: Christian and Buddhist* (1957), *Zen and Japanese Buddhism* (1958), *Zen and Japanese Culture* (1959), and (with Erich Fromm and Richard De Martino) *Zen Buddhism and Psychoanalysis* (1960).

After a tour of India in 1960, made at the invitation of the Indian government, he remained in Japan until his death on July 12, 1966. (S. Fu.; J. M. Ka.)

**SVALBARD** is part of the kingdom of Norway and comprises all islands in the Arctic Ocean between longitude 10° and 35° E and latitude 74° and 81° N. The main group of islands, known as Spitsbergen, consists of Vestspitsbergen, Nordaustlandet (North East Land), Edgeøya (Edge Island), Barentsøya (Barents Island), Prins Karls Forland (Prince Charles Foreland), and numerous smaller islands. Fringing the Spitsbergen group from north to south on the east are Kvitøya (White Island, or Gilles Land), Kong Karls Land (King Charles Land, or Wiche Islands), and Hopen (Hope Island). Further to the south is Bjørnøya (Bear Island). The total area of Svalbard is 23,958 sq.mi. (62,050 sq.-km.); that of the Spitsbergen group is 23,641 sq.mi. (61,229 sq.km.), with Vestspitsbergen 15,075 sq.mi. (39,044 sq.km.). Other areas are: Nordaustlandet 5,610 sq.mi. (14,530 sq.km.); Edgeøya 1,942 sq.mi. (5,030 sq.km.); Barentsøya 514 sq.mi. (1,330 sq.km.); Prins Karls Forland 247 sq.mi. (640 sq.km.); Kong Karls Land 128 sq.mi. (331 sq.km.); Kvitøya 102 sq.mi. (265 sq.km.); Bjørnøya 69 sq.mi. (178 sq.km.); and Hopen 18 sq.mi. (47 sq.km.). There are no indigenous inhabitants. The population, consisting of miners and administrative staff living at the Norwegian and Soviet mining towns (*see* below), and some trappers and radio operators, changes seasonally; in the winter of 1965 it was about 1,000 Norwegians and 1,600 Russians and others. The administrative centre is Longyearbyen in Vestspitsbergen.

**Physical Features.**—Nearly 60% of Svalbard is covered by ice. The mountains along the west coast of Vestspitsbergen are rather wild with sharp ridges and peaks formed by folded and metamorphic pre-Devonian sediments. The eastern part of the island and Edgeøya and Barentsøya have plateau-formed mountains built up of nearly horizontal, younger sediments. In the northern part of Vestspitsbergen and Nordaustlandet there are more rounded mountains built up partly of granites and gneisses. The highest peaks are in Ny Friesland, where Newtontoppen reaches 5,633 ft. (1,717 m.). In the southern part of Vestspitsbergen, Hornsundtind (4,695 ft. [1,431 m.]) is the highest mountain. Many large fjords penetrate the west and north coasts of Vestspitsbergen. The most important are Hornsund, Bellsund with Van Mijenfjorden and Van Keulenfjorden, Isfjorden with several branches, Kongsfjorden, and Krossfjorden on the west coast, and Woodfjorden and Wijdefjorden on the north coast. The west and north coasts of Nordaustlandet are also indented by fjords, but the east coast of this island is formed by the front of the inland ice. Many of the glaciers reach the sea, but in Vestspitsbergen there are also large ice-free valleys, such as Sassendalen, Adventdalen, Colesdalen, and Reindalen. In many parts of the coast there are extensive coastal plains, formed by the sea when its level was higher. Bjørnøya consists of an ice-free plain with many lakes, rising to Miseryfjellet (1,759 ft. [536 m.]) in the southeast.

*Structure and Geology.*—The principal features of the geology are known. Most formations from early Paleozoic, and perhaps Archean, to Recent, occur. The oldest rocks appear chiefly on the west and north, including Prins Karls Forland and Nordaustlandet. They are the Heclahuken (Hecla Hoek) series of Pre-cambrian, Cambrian, and Ordovician dolomites, limestones, shales, and quartzites which form the Caledonian folds and overthrusts of the west. The folds can be traced as far east as the west of Nordaustlandet. Granite and gneiss were probably involved in the Caledonian foldings. The metamorphosed Hecla Hoek series and eruptives are in the northwest unconformably overlain by Devonian sandstones and shales. These are uncomformably followed by Lower Carboniferous sandstones and shales with some coal, Middle Carboniferous or Upper Carboniferous limestones, Permocarboniferous cherts, and Permian sandstones and shales. Next come Triassic, Jurassic, and Cretaceous sandstones, and shales with some small coal seams. Unconformably, Teritary sandstones and shales with several coal seams follow. Tertiary folding is obvious in the west against the Hecla Hoek beds. In the central part of southern Vestspitsbergen the Tertiary beds form a large syncline. Heavy faulting also occurred in Tertiary times. Intrusions of dolerites and basalt were probably of Cretaceous (Neocomian) date. An extinct volcano and several hot springs (28° C [82° F]) in Bock Bay are Quaternary. The *strandflat* is well developed up to 180 ft. (55 m.), and postglacial raised beaches are marked. Glacial and postglacial debris on low ground generally mask the solid rock, and loose screes form fans on the lower slopes. Many Devonian and later deposits in Svalbard are extremely rich in fossils.

*Climate and Ice Conditions.*—The sea around Spitsbergen is shallow, and the ice readily accumulates round the shores. Pack ice prevents access to most shores except for a few months in the year. However, the warm North Atlantic drift sends a branch to the western shores of Spitsbergen, moderating its climate and leaving an open passage that permits vessels to approach the western coast during most months of the year. The fjords are frozen from October or November to May or June.

February and March temperature means are about −15° C (5° F) and July means are about 6° C (43° F). Extreme temperatures may rise to more than 21° C (70° F) in summer and fall below −40° C (−40° F) in winter. Records, though incomplete, indicate a marked rise in mean temperatures, especially for the winter months, during the first half of the 20th century. In September, autumn sets in. The Arctic night begins in October and lasts until the end of February. The annual precipitation at Grønfjorden (Green Harbour) is 11.6 in. (295 mm.); precipitation is often less in the interior. Winds are generally light except on the west coast. There is mist in the west.

*Vegetation.*—The only trees are the polar willow, which does not exceed two inches in height, and the rare dwarf birch (*Betula nana*). The vegetation consists mostly of lichens and mosses, variegated with the golden-yellow flowers of the ranunculus, the large-leaved scurvy grass, the cuckoo flower, many saxifrages, foxtail grass, etc.; while on the driest spots yellow poppies, whitlow grasses, and mountain avens are found—poppies sometimes even on the higher slopes, 2,500 ft. (760 m.) or more above the sea. In all, about 130 species of flowering plants have been collected. The distribution is suggestive: most species are found in Europe and 117 are circumpolar. In the ice-free valleys of Vestspitsbergen there is a comparatively rich vegetation of *Salix polaris,* grasses, moors with cotton grass, and Arctic flowers.

*Animal Life.*—According to the English explorer William Scoresby, no fewer than 57,590 whales were killed between 1669 and 1775. Reckless extermination of seals also took place. Walruses are now rarely seen in the waters west of Spitsbergen. There is a rich bird life. The fulmars, the glaucous gull or burgomaster, little auks, black guillemots, ivory gulls, and kittiwake gulls breed on the cliffs, while Arctic (Brünnich's) guillemots, puffins, pink-footed brant and barnacle geese, purple sandpipers, red-necked phalarope and other waders, and Arctic terns frequent the tundra and its pools. The commonest passerine bird is the snow bunting. The eider duck breeds on the islands, but its numbers have become noticeably reduced. These birds, however, are only summer visitors, the ptarmigan being the only species which stays permanently. In all, about 70 species have been recorded in Svalbard, of which about 30 breed there. Red char are the only fish found in the rivers and lakes. Land mammals are the polar bear, reindeer, and Arctic fox (both blue and white). There was heavy slaughter of reindeer before they became protected in 1925. The musk-ox, introduced from Greenland in 1929, is also protected, and has thrived, unlike the Arctic hare, another import from Greenland.

**History.**—*Exploration.*—It is probable that the Svalbard ("cold coast") discovered in 1194, according to Icelandic annals, and mentioned in the *Landnámabók* (*see* ICELANDIC LITERATURE) was Spitsbergen; modern knowledge of Svalbard, however, dates from its discovery by Willem Barents and Jacob van Heemskerck in June 1596. They first discovered Bjørnøya and later saw the northwest coast of Vestspitsbergen. After visits by Stephen Bennett in 1603, Henry Hudson in 1607, and Thomas Marmaduke in 1609, the Muscovy company sent an expedition in 1610, which resulted in the setting-up of the whaling industry in 1611, in which English and Dutch whalers took part. Later, French, Hanseatic, Danish, and Norwegian whalers also participated, and the king of Norway-Denmark laid claim to "this part of Greenland," as it was then considered. Quarrels among the whalers resulted in the division of the coast. The English had whaling rights south of latitude 79° N, whereas the Dutch erected their cookeries at Smeerenburg on Amsterdamøya, where more than 1,000 persons might be assembled in summer. The French were driven away from the coast in 1632 and had to boil their blubber on board their ships. After about 1640 the whales began to withdraw from the fjords and had to be caught off the coast. English whaling at Spitsbergen ceased in 1660, and Dutch whaling in about 1800, by which time the Greenland whale had been exterminated. English whalers were the first to winter in Spitsbergen, in 1630–31. Probably it was not until about 1715 that the Russians first visited Spitsbergen, wintering there to hunt walrus, seal, bear, fox, and reindeer. Many of them were sent out by the Solovetskiy monastery. Russian activity ceased in about 1850, but already at the end of the 18th century Norwegian sealers from Tromsø, Hammerfest, and other towns had been hunting in the Spitsbergen waters, and from 1822 they also wintered there to trap fur-bearing animals. This wintering was, however, not regular until the last years of the 19th century.

Many expeditions have made Spitsbergen their base for polar exploration, as C. J. Phipps in 1773, D. Buchan and John Franklin (*q.v.*) in 1818, D. C. Clavering and Edward Sabine (*q.v.*) in 1823, and William Edward Parry (*q.v.*), who in 1827 reached 82°45′ N. In the same year the Norwegian geologist B. M. Keilhau visited the islands, and in 1837 Swedish exploration began with Sven Lovén's expedition. This was followed by many Swedish expeditions, including those of Otto Torell in 1858, Adolf Erik Nordenskiöld (*q.v.*) in 1864, 1868, and 1872–73, A. G. Nathorst, Gerard De Geer, and others, which were the foundation for later exploration. Other 19th-century exploration included the German expedition under K. Koldewey to the eastern part in 1868, that of Sir Martin Conway (*see* CONWAY OF ALLINGTON, [WILLIAM] MARTIN CONWAY), who crossed Vestspitsbergen in 1896–97, and the Swedish-Russian expeditions of 1898–1902. In 1896 the Norwegians built a hotel on Hotellneset at Adventfjorden and started weekly trips by tourist steamers. In the first half of the 20th century Spitsbergen was visited by numerous scientific and exploring expeditions. In 1906 and 1907 the prince of Monaco sent a party, led by W. S. Bruce, who worked on Prins Karls Forland, and another party, led by Gunnar Isachsen, began mapping the northwestern part of Vestspitsbergen. This led to Isachsen's expeditions of 1909–10, and later to Norwegian expeditions under the leadership of Adolf Hoel, A. Staxrud, and others. After 1948 this work was continued by the Norsk Polarinstitutt, Oslo. From the early 1920s many British expeditions, associated particularly with the Oxford University Exploration Club, visited Spitsbergen, and some wintered there.

Spitsbergen has also been used as a base for polar flight. The first (fatal) attempt was in 1897, when the Swedish scientist S. A. Andrée and two companions set off by balloon from Danskøya; their remains were found on Kvitøya 33 years later. Roald Amundsen (*q.v.*) started from Ny-Ålesund on his unsuccessful flight to the pole in 1925 and on his flight with Lincoln Ellsworth and Umberto Nobile (*qq.v.*) in the dirigible "Norge" across the pole in 1926. Richard E. Byrd (*q.v.*) also started from Ny-Ålesund on his transpolar flight in 1926. Sir George Hubert Wilkins (*q.v.*) landed at the entrance of Isfjorden in April 1928 after his flight from Alaska, and, in May, Nobile started there in the dirigible "Italia," which met disaster north of Nordaustlandet.

*Political History.*—Despite diverse interests in, and claims to, the islands by British, Dutch, Norwegians, Swedes, Danes, Russians, and Americans, the question of sovereignty was long unsolved, and Spitsbergen was a *terra nullius.* Norway initiated a conference on the matter in Christiania (Oslo) in 1910, which was followed by others in 1912 and 1914, all without result. In 1919 F. H. H. Wedel Jarlsberg persuaded the Allied Supreme Council to grant Norway sovereignty over Spitsbergen, Bear Island, and all the lands lying between 74° and 81° N and between 10° and 35° E. This was put into effect by a treaty of Feb. 9, 1920, signed by Great Britain and the British dominions, the United States, France, Italy, Japan, the Netherlands, Denmark, Norway, and Sweden; the U.S.S.R. adhered later. Norway took formal possession on Aug. 14, 1925, and declared the region a part of the kingdom of Norway, under the old name of Svalbard.

The 1920 treaty forbade the erection of any naval base or fortress within Svalbard. Nevertheless, during World War II Spitsbergen was the scene of serious operations. In August–September 1941 an Allied force destroyed the radio stations, power stations, stocks of coal and oil, etc., and evacuated all Russians to the U.S.S.R., and Norwegians to Scotland. In the autumn the Germans erected a meteorological station in Longyearbyen. In May 1942 two vessels, "Isbjørn" and "Selis," were sent from England to prevent the mines from falling into German hands, but on reaching Grønfjorden they were destroyed by German aircraft. A small Norwegian force from England landed in July 1942 and occupied Barentsburg, Longyearbyen, and Sveagruva. After a German meteorological station had been destroyed in Krossfjorden in 1943, a large German force consisting of the "Tirpitz," the "Scharnhorst," and about ten destroyers entered Isfjorden on Sept. 8, 1943, and totally demolished the mining towns of Barentsburg, Grumantbyen, and Longyearbyen. In 1944 a German submarine set fire to Sveagruva. The Norwegian garrison was, however, maintained throughout the war. After the war all towns were rebuilt.

**Administration.**—Svalbard is administered by a governor (*sysselmann*), who is also district judge, chief of police, notary public, and revenue officer, and has his residence in Longyearbyen. An inspector of mines (*bergmester*) supervises mining activities. A 4% income tax is payable by Russians as well as by Norwegians. There are primary schools for children.

**The Economy.**—*Mining.*—Except for coal deposits, ore and mineral deposits are rather poor and scanty. Deposits of anhydrite with gypsum, marble, iron ore, asbestos, galena, zinc blende, and pyrites have been found, but they have seemed too small or too poor to render mining profitable. Coal has been known since 1610, but it was not until the beginning of the 20th century that the deposits were thoroughly surveyed. From 1898 to 1920 many areas, most of them containing coal seams, were claimed by companies and persons from various countries. When Norway took over the sovereignty, a Danish commissioner was nominated to decide upon the ownership of these claims. He recognized a total area of 1,631 sq.mi. (4,223 sq.km.) as private property, of which by the early 1960s 6% belonged to the U.S.S.R. and the remainder to Norway. All other land is the property of the Norwegian government and may not be transferred into private possession, but the subjects of all signatory powers to the treaty of 1920 have equal rights to exploit mineral deposits. Coal mining on a commercial scale was started by John M. Longyear's Arctic Coal Company (Boston, Mass.) in Longyeardalen south of Adventfjorden in 1906 and by an English company on the north side of this fjord. The U.S. company exported 147,000 tons of coal between 1907 and 1915. In 1916 the property was sold to a Norwegian group that established Store Norske Spitsbergen Kulkompani A/S. A Swedish mine that was worked during 1917–25 at Sveagruva on the north side of Braganzavågen was sold to Store Norske in 1933. A Dutch company worked the mines at Barentsburg on the east side of Grønfjorden till 1926, but sold the property to the Soviet company Arktikugol in 1932. This company also took over the properties at Grumantbyen and Pyramiden. The only mines worked in the mid-1960s were Store Norske's in Adventdalen and Arktikugol's at Barentsburg and Pyramiden.

During the early 1960s coal exports from Norwegian mines exceeded 400,000 tons a year, from Soviet mines 200,000 tons. Shipment takes place mainly between the middle of May and the end of October.

Apart from mining, the only economic activity is trapping and hunting fox, polar bear, and seal, but since 1960 there has been increasing activity by U.S., Soviet, and Norwegian oil prospectors.

*Communications.*—Besides the coal steamers, a mail and passenger steamer makes eight trips during the summer from Tromsø to the Vestspitsbergen harbours. In summer Svalbard is also visited by large tourist steamers and many sealers. There are navigation lights and radio beacons in Bellsund-Van Mijenfjorden, Isfjorden, and Kongsfjorden, and Isfjord Radio at Kapp Linné provides a radar service. Svalbard Radio, situated in Longyearbyen, is linked with Norway; the other mining towns have local stations. *See* also ARCTIC. THE. (A. K. O.)

**SVEDBERG, THEODOR** (called "THE") (1884– ), Swedish chemist and Nobel Prize winner in 1926, developed physicochemical methods of studying colloids and macromolecules, particularly that of ultracentrifugation. He was born at Fleräng, near Valbo, Swed., on Aug. 30, 1884. From 1904 he studied chemistry at Uppsala University, where he became professor of physical chemistry (1912–49), professor emeritus (1949), director of the Institute of Physical Chemistry (1931–49) and director of the Gustaf-Werner Institute of Nuclear Chemistry (1949).

The development of the ultracentrifuge made a profound and timely contribution to the study of large molecules. In this instrument the migration of large molecules in solution under the influence of a strong centrifugal force (up to 100,000 times gravity) can be observed and related to the molecular size and shape. By this means Svedberg demonstrated that the molecules of certain pure proteins are all of one size. Thus, the ultracentrifuge can sometimes, in the characterization of a new protein, show the presence of contaminating substances. In the field of high polymers the behaviour of long chain molecules, particularly cellulose, in the ultracentrifuge has contributed to the elucidation of their properties. For his studies in colloidal systems Svedberg was awarded the Nobel Prize. *See* also CENTRIFUGE. (K. A. SY.)

**SVERDLOV, YAKOV MIKHAILOVICH** (1885–1919), Russian Communist leader and a key figure in the formative period of the Bolshevik Party's organization, was born in Nizhni-Novgorod (now Gorki) on June 3 (new style; May 22, old style), 1885, the son of an artisan. He joined the All-Russian Social-Democratic Labour Party in 1901 and was a "professional revolutionary" from 1902, always strictly following Lenin's policy. He took part in conducting Bolshevik activities in the Urals in the Revolution of 1905–07 and was later active in various parts of central Russia, being several times arrested and banished to Siberia. When in exile he was co-opted in January 1912 into the Central Committee of the party. From December 1912 to February 1913, having fled from Siberia, he directed the Bolshevik group in the Fourth Duma. Arrested again and deported to the Turukhan province in the polar circle, he remained there until the outbreak of the March Revolution in 1917. Returning to Petrograd he was sent to Yekaterinburg (now Sverdlovsk), becoming the principal Bolshevik leader in the Urals. He returned to Petrograd as a delegate to the April conference of the party, was reelected to its Central Committee and appointed its secretary, becoming the party's chief organizer. In November 1917 he was elected chairman of the All-Russian Central Executive Committee, thus becoming titular head of state. He took an active part in the preparation of the first Soviet constitution, supported Lenin against Trotski in the great debate over the peace treaty of Brest-Litovsk and, at the beginning of March 1919, was among the principal delegates to the first conference of the Communist (or Third) International. He died in Moscow on March 16, 1919. (L. B. SC.)

**SVERDLOVSK,** an *oblast* of the Russian Soviet Federated Socialist Republic, U.S.S.R., was formed in 1934. Pop. (1959), 4,044,416. Area 75,174 sq.mi. (194,700 sq.km.). The *oblast* is triangular, with its western side lying along the crest line of the Urals, which within the *oblast* reach a maximum height of 5,148 ft. (1,569 m.) in Gora Konzhakovski Kamen. The *oblast* includes the eastern slope of the Urals and stretches out to the West Siberian plain (Zapadno-Sibirskaya Nizmennost). Its southwestern corner extends to the western flank of the Urals in the upper Ufa basin. The main rivers draining eastward are the Tavda, with its headstreams Lozva and Sosva, and the Tura, with its tributaries Nitsa and Pyshma. The climate is sharply continental, January temperatures ranging from −16° C (3° F) in the southwest to −20° C (−4° F) in the north, and July averages about 16°–17° C (61°–63° F). Rainfall is about 16 in. (41 cm.) a year on the lowland; 24 in. (61 cm.) on the Urals. Almost the entire *oblast* is covered in taiga forest of pine, stone pine, birch and larch; spruce, fir and oak appear in the southwest. Only the highest summits of the Urals are bare; in the extreme south the *oblast* enters the forest-steppe zone, with alternating birch groves and grass steppe.

Of the 1959 population, more than three-quarters were urban dwellers, a reflection of the *oblast's* role as part of the Urals industrial region. The largest of the 39 towns and 88 urban districts are the administrative centre Sverdlovsk (778,602), Nizhni Tagil (338,501), Kamensk-Uralski (141,019), Serov (97,882), Pervouralsk (90,424), Krasnoturinsk (61,990), Asbest (60,053), and Revda (54,870).

Like all the Urals region, the *oblast* is exceptionally rich in the range and quantities of minerals. Iron ore is mined in the Serov-Ivdel area, at Nizhni Tagil and at Kushva. Manganese occurs at Ivdel; chromium at Kluchevsk; cobalt, nickel, tungsten and vanadium near Sverdlovsk; beryllium near Asbest. Copper is mined at several places including Alapayevsk, Degtyarsk, Krasnouralsk and Kirovgrad. Asbest has the largest deposits of asbestos in the U.S.S.R. Bauxite is found at Kamensk-Uralski and Serov, and Polevskoi is a major producer of artificial cryolite. Platinum and gold are widespread, and zinc and sulfur deposits are worked. Coal and lignite are of inferior quality. Based on these minerals a large metallurgical industry developed in the 1930s and received further impetus during World War II. Nizhni Tagil has one of the largest iron and steel plants of the Soviet Union and smaller works are located at Serov, Kushva, Pervouralsk, Revda and Severski. Sverdlovsk and Nizhni Tagil are centres of large-scale heavy engineering. Nonferrous metals are processed in Krasnoturinsk, Krasnouralsk, Kirovgrad, Kamensk-Uralski and Revda (copper). There is a thriving chemical industry producing industrial chemicals, plastics, fertilizers and medical preparations. Timber working is widespread and well developed. The chief lack of the *oblast* is fuel. Coking coal is brought from Karaganda (Kazakh S.S.R.) and the Kuzbass (Kuznetsk basin) and natural gas is piped from Berezovo in the northern Urals. Agriculture is relatively unimportant and largely confined to the southeast (around Irbit), where grains and potatoes are grown. Market gardening is important around the towns.

All the main centres are connected by a rail network which is linked to the Trans-Siberian railroad. (R. A. F.)

**SVERDLOVSK** (formerly YEKATERINBURG), a town and administrative centre of the *oblast* of the same name in the Russian Soviet Federated Socialist Republic, U.S.S.R., lies on the eastern slope of the Ural Mountains on both banks of the Iset River, a tributary of the Tobol, 850 mi. (1,368 km.) E of Moscow. Pop. (1969 est.) 1,001,000. The town has two 18th-century cathedrals and is the leading cultural and educational centre of the Urals region. It has a musical *conservatoire* and opera and dramatic theatres; a polytechnic; and institutes of mining, forestry, agriculture, medicine, law, and teaching. It is also the seat of the Urals A. M. Gorki State University (founded 1920) and of the Urals branch of the U.S.S.R. Academy of Sciences.

Sverdlovsk is an important railway junction. Seven lines radiate from it to all parts of the Urals and the rest of the Soviet Union, including Moscow, Leningrad, and Omsk. Its chief importance lies in heavy engineering, for which it is one of the largest centres of the U.S.S.R. Among its wide range of products are machines for the metallurgical and chemical industries; mining and oil drilling equipment; turbines, diesels, ball bearings, electrical equipment, cables, precision instruments, refrigerators, and bicycles. The chemical and rubber industries (plastics, tires) are well developed. Steel manufacture, utilizing pig iron from other centres and scrap, is still maintained but is less important than in other Ural centres. Light industrial products include footwear and other leather goods, clothing, tobacco, and foodstuffs. A traditional craft is the cutting of gems.

Sverdlovsk has its origin in the establishment there in 1721 of the Verkhne-Isetski (Upper Iset) ironworks and fortress by V. N. Tatischev, historian, traveler, and government functionary; and the settlement became the administrative centre for all the ironworks of the Urals. It was named Yekaterinburg in 1723 for Catherine I, wife of Peter I the Great. Other ironworks developed in the vicinity, and its industrial and administrative importance was increased from 1783 when the Great Siberian Highway was built through it. The first railway arrived from Perm in 1878 and several other lines were laid from it during the next fifty years. After the Revolution Yekaterinburg was the last place of imprisonment of the tsar Nicholas II and his family, who were shot there on July 16–17 (N.S.), 1918. Yekaterinburg then fell to the White troops but was recaptured by the Red Army in July 1919. It was renamed Sverdlovsk for the Bolshevist Yakov Sverdlov in 1924. Evacuation of industry to the Urals during World War II gave further impetus to expansion. (R. A. F.)

**SVERDRUP, JOHAN** (1816–1892), Norwegian statesman, first leader of the Venstre (the Left) Party, and prime minister from 1884 to 1889, was born at Jarlsberg on July 30, 1816. Educated as a lawyer, Sverdrup entered the *storting* (legislative assembly) in 1851 and became leader of the opposition group of city liberals. He was president of the *odelsting* (the lower division of the legislative assembly) from 1862 to 1869 and president of the *storting* from 1871 to 1884. Allied with Søren Jaabaek, leader of the Peasant Party, Sverdrup created (1869) a unified liberal and national opposition, the Left. He was its undoubted leader during the long fight (1872–84) against the government over the admission of ministers to the *storting* (*see* NORWAY: *History*).

The victory of the *storting* in 1884 brought Sverdrup the office of prime minister in Norway's first Left ministry. Many reforms for which he had worked since 1851 were now authorized, notably an extension of the franchise (1884) and the introduction of trial by jury and of universal conscription (1887). Soon, however, Sverdrup found himself at issue with the radical majority of his party on questions of religious toleration and church reform and on the handling of the problems of the Swedish-Norwegian union. A controversial church reform bill, introduced by Sverdrup's nephew Jakob Sverdrup, minister of ecclesiastical affairs, was defeated in 1887. In the elections of 1888 Sverdrup lost his absolute majority, and when a motion of no confidence in his government was proposed in the *storting* in June 1889, he resigned. He died at Christiania (now Oslo) on Feb. 17, 1892. (D. MA.)

**SVERRE** (d. 1202), king of Norway from 1177 to 1202, was one of the most remarkable kings and controversial figures of medieval Norway. He was born in the Faeroe Islands, supposedly in 1149, and was ordained as a priest at an unusually early age by Hrói, bishop of the Faeroes. His mother was a Norwegian, Gunnhild, married to a Faeroe man, Unas the Combmaker. But, according to Sverre's own story, his mother had confessed to him that she had begotten him, not with Unas, but with Sigurd II Munnr (d. 1155), a former king of Norway. There are good reasons to doubt the truth of this story, but if Sverre was, in fact, the illegitimate son of Sigurd, he had a valid claim to the throne.

In 1174 Sverre left the Faeroes for Norway. At this time Norway was ruled by Erling the Crooked and his son Magnus IV, whose claims to the throne were somewhat doubtful. Their rivals, called the Birchlegs, were now in severe straits, and their pretender, Eystein, was killed after a crushing defeat in January 1177.

The remnants of the Birchlegs gathered round Sverre, imploring him to lead them. Within a few months, Sverre had seized Trondheim, where he was proclaimed king. During the next years his fortunes varied, but he showed military skill, as well as the power of leadership, and in 1179 he won a great victory in which Erling was killed and his son Magnus put to flight. In 1184 Sverre met Magnus at Fimreite, in the Sognefjord, and Magnus fell in the ensuing battle, leaving Sverre virtual ruler.

Sverre's relations with the church are particularly interesting, and it is plain that he represented the national, as opposed to the universal, church movement. In 1180 Eystein Erlendsson, archbishop of Trondheim, who had consistently sided with King Magnus, fled to England, where he remained three years. He then returned to Norway, where he died in 1188. Eystein was succeeded as archbishop by Erik Ivarsson, with whom Sverre's differences were graver, culminating in the archbishop's refusal to crown Sverre and his flight to Denmark in 1190. In 1194 Sverre was crowned by bishops who had remained in Norway, but later Pope Innocent III intervened on the side of the exiled archbishop. He solemnly excommunicated the bishops who had assisted at Sverre's coronation and in a series of bulls anathematized Sverre as an apostate, excommunicate enemy of God and the saints and condemned all who associated with him. Norway was, in fact, under interdict.

In his latter years, Sverre contended successfully against new claimants to the throne. He died in his bed, as few kings of Norway had done, at Bergen, on March 9, 1202.

The life of Sverre (*Sverris Saga*) was written in part by the Icelandic abbot Karl Jónsson, under the direction of the king himself. It was later completed by other Icelandic scholars. Sverre is depicted as a consummate orator, and as something of a mystic, with an implicit faith in his own destiny and especially in dream symbolism.

*See* G. M. Gathorne-Hardy, *A Royal Impostor* (1956); F. Paasche, *Kong Sverre* (1920). (G. T.-P.)

**SVEVO, ITALO** (ETTORE SCHMITZ) (1861–1928), Italian novelist, was a pioneer of psychological fiction. He was born in Trieste on Dec. 19, 1861—his real name was Ettore Schmitz, the pseudonym meaning "Italus the Swabian"—the son of a Triestine Jewish glassware-merchant of German ancestry and an Italian mother. He was sent to boarding school in Bavaria, and then became a student at the Istituto Superiore Commerciale Revoltella in Trieste, at which period he was already dabbling in playwriting. In 1880, however, as a result of his father's financial difficulties, he had to abandon his studies and take a job as a clerk in the Unionbank. In his spare time he did editorial work and wrote reviews for *L'Independente,* the local organ of the pro-Italian irredentist movement (Trieste then being part of the Austro-Hungarian empire). In 1892 he published a novel, *Una vita* (trans. *A Life,* 1963). This was a powerful but rambling Zolaesque study (much influenced also by Schopenhauer) of a country boy employed in a city bank who becomes involved with his director's daughter and, having ruined this and all his other chances through indecision, finally shoots himself. The novel fell almost completely flat, as did its successor, *Senilità* (1898; trans. *As a Man Grown Older,* 1932), a masterly ironic study of another ineffectual hero. The latter, an undistinguished employee in an insurance office, living with his sister, embarks on a love affair with a working-class girl and becomes so absorbed in his own frenzied, and largely farcical, drama that he fails to notice the grim tragedy overtaking his sister.

In 1896 Svevo married a young cousin, Livia Veneziani, whose father was a prosperous manufacturer of marine paint. A daughter, Letizia, was born in 1897. He joined his father-in-law's firm shortly afterward and thereupon formally renounced literature, a vow which he kept for some 20 years, though continuing to write little fables and an occasional play and story for his own amusement. His new post entailed frequent visits to England, where a branch factory had been set up at Charlton, London (to supply the Royal Navy), and in 1907 he engaged the services of an English teacher. The teacher was the writer James Joyce, then living in Trieste, and the two became warm friends, Joyce being the first person to express strong admiration for his novels.

His enforced idleness during World War I, the experience of reading Freud, and excitement at the Italian annexation of Trieste in 1918 led Svevo to return to writing, and in 1923 he published his most famous novel, *La coscienza di Zeno* (trans. *The Confessions of Zeno,* 1930), a comic fantasia on the theme of psychoanalysis—a work of great ironic complexity and originality of form, exploring the paradoxes of unconscious motivation with profound insight mixed with extravagant farce.

The novel fell as flat as its predecessors, but a year or two later, at the instigation of Joyce, Svevo was finally discovered and acclaimed by French critics. He now made various visits to Paris, enjoying his long-delayed celebrity, and a number of the periodical *Le Navire d'Argent* was devoted to him. His fame spread more slowly in his own country, where critics were alienated by his prose style—a graceless "business" Italian, frequently falling into Germanic turns of phrase. However, he became increasingly regarded as the founder of the "modern" novel in Italian.

He died at Motta di Livenza near Treviso on Sept. 13, 1928, as the result of a car accident, while engaged on a successor to *Zeno.* Fragments of this, short stories, and essays were published after his death. His novels have been translated into many languages.

BIBLIOGRAPHY.—*Works: Opere,* ed. B. Maier (1954); *Corto viaggio sentimentale e altri racconti inediti,* ed. U. Apollonio (1949); *Saggi e pagine sparse,* ed. U. Apollonio (1954); *Commedie,* ed. U. Apollonio (1960); *Epistolario,* ed. B. Maier (1966). *Translations:* Uniform edition, 1962– : *The Confessions of Zeno,* trans. B. de Zoete (1962); *As a Man Grows Older,* trans. B. de Zoete (1962); *A Life,* trans. A. Colquhoun (1963); *Short Sentimental Journey and Other Stories,* trans. by various hands (1967). *Criticism and biography:* Livia Veneziani Svevo, *Vita di mio marito* (1950; 2nd ed. with important additions by Anita Pittoni, 1958); P. N. Furbank, *Italo Svevo: the Man and the Writer* (1966). References to important critical articles will be found in the bibliographies to both these, as well as in that to Maier's edition of the *Opere.* (P. N. F.)

**SVINHUFVUD, PEHR EVIND** (1861–1944), Finnish statesman, first head of state of independent Finland in 1918 and president of the republic in 1931–37, was born at Sääksmäki on Dec. 15, 1861, a member of a noble family. Having completed his studies in law (1886), he entered the Finnish Diet in 1894 as representative of his family in the House of Knights and soon became known as a steadfast Constitutionalist (*see* FINLAND: *History*). During the great strike (1905) he coordinated the activities of the Constitutionalists and the Social Democrats. After the reform of the Diet he was its speaker from 1907 until the end of 1912. He was exiled to Siberia in 1914, returning after the Russian Revolution of March 1917. Uncompromisingly anti-Russian, he was elected prime minister by the votes of the bourgeois parties of Finland on Nov. 27. When the Red Guard forces seized power in southern Finland, he managed to escape to Ostrobothnia, whence he conducted the government during the war of independence. Elected regent of Finland on May 18, 1918, he was in favour of having a German prince as king; and his policy led to his resignation, on Dec. 12, after Germany's collapse at the end of World War I. When the parties were regrouped, Svinhufvud joined the national coalition.

Prime minister from July 5, 1930, to Feb. 16, 1931, and president from March 2, 1931, to Feb. 28, 1937, Svinhufvud saw to it that the demand of the right-wing Lapua movement for the banning of the Communist Party was carried through but used his presidential authority to prevent the movement from overthrowing democratic institutions. He died at Luumäki, on Feb. 29, 1944.

*See* E. Räikkönen, *Svinhufvud: the Builder of Finland* (1938); E. W. Juva, *P. E. Svinhufvud,* 2 vol. (1957–61). (E. K. I. J.)

**SVYATOSLAV I** (SVYATOSLAV IGOREVICH, d. 972), grand prince of Kiev from 945 and a hero of early Russian history, was the son of Igor and Olga (*qq.v.*). After coming of age, he dedicated all his efforts to bold military expeditions, leaving his mother, Olga, in Kiev to take care of the internal affairs of the state until her death in 969. The Russian chronicle describes the last heathen Russian prince, who "stepping light as a leopard . . . carried with him neither wagons nor kettles . . . nor did he have a tent. . . . He sent messengers to the other lands announcing his intention to attack them." Between 963 and 965 he defeated the Khazars on the lower Don and the Ossetians and Circassians in the northern Caucasus and stormed the capital of the Volga Bulgars. When the Byzantine government, engaged in a war against the Balkan Bulgars, asked Svyatoslav for help, he invaded Danubian Bulgaria in 967 and defeated the Bulgars. He then refused to cede his conquests to the Byzantines, declaring his intention of establishing his capital in Pereyaslavets (Pereyaslav-Khmelnitski) on the Danube and founding a Russo-Bulgarian empire. The Byzantine emperor John I Tzimisces, having gathered overwhelming forces, defeated Svyatoslav's relatively small army and forced him to abandon any claims to Balkan territory (971). In the spring of 972, while Svyatoslav was returning to Russia with a small retinue, he was ambushed by the Pechenegs near the cataracts of the Dnieper and killed.

See *The Russian Primary Chronicle,* Eng. trans. (1953); G. V. Vernadsky, *Kievan Russia* (1948). (S. G. PU.)

**SWABIA** (German SCHWABEN), the historical name for the southwesternmost part of the old German kingdom or *Reich,* comprising, in 20th-century terms, not only the southern part of the German Federal Republic's *Land* Baden-Württemberg, together with the southwestern part of the *Land* Bavaria, but also eastern Switzerland and Alsace (*qq.v.*). The present article covers (1) the Duchy of Swabia; (2) the Swabian leagues of the 14th–16th centuries; and (3) the Swabian Circle of the *Reich.*

**The Alamanni and the Duchy.**—The name Swabia is derived from that of the Suebi (*q.v.*), a Germanic people. With the Alamanni (*q.v.*), some Suebi in the 3rd century A.D. moved into the Roman territory between the upper Rhine and the upper Danube and along the Neckar River. Further expansion, westward over the Rhine, southward beyond Lake Constance, and eastward to the Lech River, led to the consolidation of a territory known at first as Alamannia. From the 11th century this name was superseded by Swabia.

The Alamanni were subdued by the Frankish king Clovis between 496 and 506, and Frankish supremacy over their dukes was reinforced by Charles Martel in 730. The people lived under the *Lex Alamannorum,* a code of law dating from the 6th–8th centuries (edited in the *Monumenta Germaniae Historica,* 1888). Promulgated by their Frankish overlords, this law nevertheless shows deep respect for the traditions of the Alamanni—whereas the later *Schwabenspiegel* (drafted in Augsburg in 1274–75; edited by H. Planitz and A. Benna, 1956) has no specifically Swabian characteristics in its approach to legal matters. The Alamanni long remained pagan, but in the 7th century the process of converting them to Christianity started; it was achieved mainly by Irish missionaries. The bishoprics of Basel, of Constance, and of Augsburg and the abbeys of St. Gall and of Reichenau began to play an important role.

Swabia emerged, together with Saxony, Franconia, Bavaria, and Lotharingia (Lorraine), as one of the five great duchies of the East Frankish or German Kingdom (*see* GERMANY: *History*). At the turn of the 9th–10th century the counts of Raetia temporarily obtained the Swabian dukedom, but there followed a rapid succession of dukes belonging to other families. Rudolf of Rheinfelden, duke of Swabia from 1057, was set up as German king in opposition to King Henry IV in 1077 (*see* RUDOLF), but in 1079 Henry enfiefed his own son-in-law, Frederick of Hohenstaufen, as duke of Swabia. The latter's grandson became German king, as Frederick I, in 1152, and the duchy of Swabia remained in the hands of members of the Hohenstaufen dynasty till the extinction of its legitimate male line in 1268. Thereafter local nobles, in particular the counts of Württemberg (*q.v.*), encroached on the royal and ducal lands. The German king Rudolf I, of the Habsburg dynasty, was able to consolidate what was left of Swabia as a duchy for his son Rudolf II of Austria; but the latter died in 1290, and his posthumous son, John, was only nominally duke of Swabia. With his death (1313) the title fell out of use.

**The Swabian Leagues.**—From the emperor's court of justice at Rottweil attempts were made to assert the authority of the *Reich* over the numerous lordships of the Swabian nobility. In 1331 a league was formed by 22 Swabian free towns or Imperial cities (*q.v.*), including Ulm, Augsburg, Reutlingen, and Heilbronn, to support the emperor Louis IV in return for his undertaking not to mortgage any of them to a vassal. Count Ulrich III of Württemberg (d. 1344) was induced to join this league in 1340; but during the emperor Charles IV's reign the Swabian knights in 1366 formed a league of their own, the Schleglerbund (so named from the hammer or mallet, Ger. *Schlegel,* in its insignia), in opposition to the towns and to the greater territorial princes alike. Civil war ensued; Charles tried to set up a league under his own control for the maintenance of the public peace; and finally Ulrich's son and successor, Eberhard II of Württemberg (d. 1392), with the help of the Schleglerbund, defeated the towns' league in 1372.

A new Swabian towns' league, led by Ulm and comprising 14 Imperial cities, was formed on July 4, 1376. Its aim was to protect its members' status against any threat of mortgaging, to safeguard their commercial interests, to resist excessive taxation, and to preserve the public peace. After its victory over Count Eberhard's son Ulrich at Reutlingen on May 14, 1377, it spread its influence into Bavaria, Franconia, and the middle Rhineland, as well as the outlying Swiss and Alsatian areas of the old Swabia; after its declaration of war against the dukes of Bavaria, however, the new league was also defeated by Eberhard II of Württemberg at Döffingen (August 1388).

The Schleglerbund was overthrown when Eberhard III of Württemberg captured its stronghold of Heimsheim on Sept. 24, 1395.

The Swabian League that was founded at Esslingen on Feb. 14, 1488, was a more comprehensive organization than the 14th-century leagues. Promoted by the emperor Frederick III, it comprised not only 22 Imperial cities but also the Swabian knights' League of St. George's Shield and the local prelates. Sigismund of Tirol and Eberhard V of Württemberg were promptly brought into it; the Palatinate, Mainz, Trier, and Baden soon acceded; and Hesse and Bavaria, as well as Ansbach and Bayreuth in Franconia, eventually became members.

A federal council, with princes, towns, and knights represented in three "colleges," was constituted for the league; and provision was made for an army of 13,000 men to maintain order, under an appointed captain. The league helped rescue Frederick's son, the future emperor Maximilian I, from captivity in the Netherlands in 1488, forced Duke Albert of Bavaria to renounce Regensburg in 1492, and was the mainstay of Habsburg authority in southwestern Germany throughout Maximilian's reign. When Duke Ulrich I of Württemberg seized Reutlingen (1519), the Swabian League expelled him from his duchy, which it then sold to the emperor Charles V (1520). It cooperated in the overthrow of Franz von Sickingen (*q.v.*) in 1523 and in the suppression of the peasants' rebellion of 1524–25. The Reformation, however, led to the expiry of the Swabian League (which had been several times formally renewed) in February 1534. Attempts to revive it, by the Bavarian chancellor Johann Eck in 1535 and by Charles V in 1547, came to nothing.

**The Swabian Circle.**—The name of Swabia was perpetuated in that of the Swabian Circle of the Empire (*Schwäbischer Reichskreis*), one of the zones into which Germany was divided, from the 16th century onward, for purposes of Imperial administration. First organized in 1500, this circle was finally established in 1555 and lasted till the dissolution of the Holy Roman Empire in 1806. It was bounded west by the Upper Rhenish Circle, north by the Electoral Rhenish and by the Franconian, east by the Bavarian, and southeast by the Austrian, which had numerous exclaves within it. There was also a Swabian Towns' Bench (*Schwäbische Städtebank*) in the old *Reichstag* or Diet of the Empire.

BIBLIOGRAPHY.—P. F. Stälin, *Geschichte Württembergs,* vol. 1 (1882–87); K. Weller, *Besiedlungsgeschichte Württembergs . . .* (1938), *Geschichte des schwäbischen Stammes . . .* (1944); H. Tüchle, *Kirchengeschichte Schwabens,* 2 vol. (1950–54). For the leagues *see* H. Blezinger, *Der Schwäbische Stadtebund* (1954); E. Bock, *Der Schwäbische Bund und seine Verfassungen* (1927); K. S. Bader, *Der deutsche Südwesten in seiner territorialstaatlichen Entwicklung* (1950).

(K. RE.)

**SWAHILI LANGUAGE.** Swahili (Kiswahili) is a Bantu language spoken primarily on the east coast and islands of Africa between Lamu Island, Kenya, in the north and the mouth of the Ruvuma River (southern border of Tanzania) in the south. It is spoken sporadically as far north as Mogadishu, Somali Democratic Republic, and there appear to be Swahili-speaking enclaves in the French Territory of Afars and Issas (the former French Somaliland); it has also been heard as far south as Mozambique. A form of Swahili is also spoken on the west coast of Madagascar (Malagasy Republic).

People who speak Swahili as their sole mother tongue are usually referred to as Waswahili, but this name refers to their language only and does not denote any one tribal unit. At the coast there is considerable Arab influence, both racial and cultural, and Islam is the dominant religion. There are about 15 main Swahili dialects, as well as several pidgin forms in use.

Swahili as a lingua franca is current in: (1) Tanzania, *i.e.,* Tanganyika and Zanzibar, where it is the language of administration and primary education; (2) Kenya, where it is, after English, the main language for these purposes, though alternative languages have been recognized in certain parts of the country; (3) Uganda, where it is in competition with local languages—the main language being again English; (4) the Democratic Republic of the (former Belgian) Congo, where a form of Swahili (sometimes called Kingwana) is one of the four languages of administration—the main language for both administration and education being French. There are a few communities in the Eastern Congo where Swahili appears to be the mother tongue. Swahili is regarded, with Nyika (including Giryama), as a language group closely related to the Taita language group. Although modern Swahili contains an enormous vocabulary of Arabic borrowings (as well as borrowings from Persian, Hindi, Portuguese and English), in its grammatical behaviour it is characteristically Bantu; *i.e.,* (1) it has a large vocabulary of word roots traceable to a common Bantu stock; (2) its nouns are divided into classes, distinguished by typical prefixes, for the most part groupable in pairs denoting singular and plural; *e.g., m-tu,* pl. *wa-tu* ("person"), *ki-tu,* pl. *vi-tu* ("thing"), etc.; (3) verbs, adjectives, demonstrative and possessive forms are brought into agreement with nouns by means of prefixes; *e.g., wa-tu w-etu wa-le wa-kubwa wa-mekuja* ("those big people of ours have come"); (4) verb stems may be extended by means of varying suffixes, each one with its particular nuance of meaning; *e.g., funga* ("shut"), *fungwa* ("be shut"), *fungika* ("become shut"), *fungia* ("shut for"), *fungisha* ("cause to shut"), *fungua* ("open"), etc.

**Origin and History.**—The name Swahili is derived from the Arabic *sawāhilī* ("coastal"). Contact between Arabia and the east coast of Africa was made as early as the 1st century A.D. when, according to the *Periplus of the Erythraean Sea,* the people of Muza (in southern Arabia) "sent thither many large ships, using Arab captains and agents, who are familiar with the natives and intermarry with them." But the earliest known settlement at Pate is said to have been founded in A.D. 689. During the next 600 years other cities such as Lamu, Malindi, Mombasa and Kilwa were founded and reached a high level of civilization, until eclipsed by the Portuguese conquests in the early 16th century. After the

Arabs had returned and ousted the Portuguese in the early 18th century and transferred their court from Oman to Zanzibar in 1832, Swahili came into its own, enhanced by the intermarriage of the Arab overlords with the coastal people.

During the early 19th century the spread of Swahili inland received a great impetus through its being the language of the Arab ivory and slave caravans, which penetrated as far north as Uganda and as far west as the upper reaches of the Congo (Lualaba) river. It was later adopted by Europeans, especially the Germans, who used it extensively as the language of administration in Tanganyika, thus laying the foundations for its ultimate adoption as national language of Tanzania after independence. In Kenya and especially Uganda other local languages were also officially encouraged during the colonial period, but the tendency now in these territories is to put a greater emphasis on Swahili.

**Literature.**—The oldest preserved Swahili literature, written in the Arabic script, dates from the early 18th century. This form of literature still exists and is expanding in certain areas, though only a fraction of it has been printed. In the latter half of the 19th century, the roman alphabet was successfully applied to Swahili by missionaries and the first complete Bible was produced by 1891 in the Mvita (Mombasa) dialect. There was strong rivalry between this dialect and that of Zanzibar (Unguja), until the latter obtained official recognition as "standard" in the 1920s. Afterward the written language progressed apace, under the encouragement of the Interterritorial Language (Swahili) committee—later the East African Swahili committee. Besides further Bible translations (including the "Union Version" of 1950) and a spate of government-inspired textbooks for schools and adult literacy campaigns, there are about 60 Swahili newspapers and broadsheets in East Africa and a dozen in the Congo area. Indigenous authors have gradually come to the fore, among whom the late Shaaban Robert and Amri Abedi are outstanding.

*See* also BANTU LANGUAGES.

BIBLIOGRAPHY.—J. L. Krapf, *Dictionary of the Suahili Language* (1882); W. E. Taylor, *African Aphorisms* (1891); C. Sacleux, *Grammaire des dialectes swahilis* (1909) and *Dictionnaire swahili-français et français-swahili,* 3 vol. (1939–41); A. E. Burt, *Swahili grammar and vocabulary* (1910) (Mvita dialect); C. Velten, *Suaheli Wörterbuch,* 2 vol. (1910–33); E. Steere, *A Handbook of the Swahili Language,* rev. by A. B. Hellier (1943); G. W. Broomfield, *Sarufi ya Ki-Swahili* (1931); F. Johnson, *Kamusi ya Kiswahili* (1935) and *Standard Swahili-English Dictionary, Standard English-Swahili Dictionary,* 2 vol. based on the dictionaries of A. C. Madan (1939); A. Seidel, *Suaheli Konversations-Grammatik* (1941); A. N. Tucker and E. O. Ashton, *Swahili Phonetics* (1942); E. O. Ashton, *Swahili Grammar (with Intonation)* (1944); F. van den Eynde, *Swahili Spraakkunst* (1949); D. V. Perrott, *Teach yourself Swahili* (1951) and *The E.U.P. Concise Swahili and English Dictionary* (1965); R. A. Snoxall, *A Concise English-Swahili Dictionary* (1958); D. A. Olderogge, *Kamusi ya Kiswahili-Kirusi, Suakhili-Russkij Slovar* (1961); E. W. Stevick, J. G. Mlela and F. N. Njenga, *Swahili Basic Course* (1963) (accompanied by tape recordings); A. Loogman, *Swahili Grammar and Syntax* (1965); E. G. C. Polomé, *Swahili Language Handbook* (1967). J. and L. F. Whitehead, *Manuel de Kingwana* (1928); J. Wegsteen, *Ki-Swahili* (1953), and A. Verbeken, *Petit cours de Kiswahili (Kingwana) pratique* (8th ed., 1958), deal with Congo Swahili. (A. N. T.)

**SWALLOW,** among the best-known of birds, an accomplished flier that captures its insect food on the wing, with much graceful twisting and turning. About 74 species of small to medium-sized songbirds constitute the almost cosmopolitan family Hirundinidae, but three species are particularly well known: *Hirundo rustica,* the common, or barn, swallow; *Riparia riparia,* the bank swallow; and *Petrochelidon pyrrhonota,* the cliff swallow. Swallows have long been celebrated in both literature and song as the epitome of diligence and hopefulness; in Christian symbolism they represent suppliant prayers, perhaps because swallows always seem to be hungry.

Contrary to popular legend, the cliff swallows that have built their mud nests in the ruins of the Mission San Juan Capistrano in California since Spanish colonial times do not leave on the same day each autumn (Oct. 23, St. John's Day) nor do they return on the same day each spring (March 19, St. Joseph's Day); food supply and weather greatly influence their migrations.

Swallows share superficial features with the unrelated swifts; these adaptations to a predominantly aerial life include long, pointed wings, small feet suited more for perching than for walking, short broad bill, and wide gape. Most swallows have notched tails, but the barn swallow's is deeply forked and the cliff swallow's is squared. Their colours are not gaudy, but many species have rufous or glistening white and iridescent deep-blue or green in the plumage. The species breeding far north and south are strongly migratory, and some make long journeys across the Equator to reach their winter quarters.

Swallows like company. They gather to feed in favourite spots; great numbers may assemble in the late afternoon to roost together during the night, and many species nest in colonies. Certain species come commonly about human habitations and nest on buildings or in nest boxes prepared for them. Though hardly songsters, their twitterings and chirping notes are pleasant, and this, plus their familiar habits and their returning to temperate climates with the spring, has given them a friendly place in people's minds and in literature. Their nesting is various: in a hole in a tree or bank, in a burrow dug by themselves in an earthen bank, a saucer-shaped structure on a ledge of rock or a building, or a retort-shaped structure of mud pellets stuck to the side of a cliff, cave, or building. There may be up to six eggs, pure white or spotted. (A. L. RD.; X.)

**SWAMMERDAM, JAN** (1637–1680), Dutch naturalist and biologist, first described the red blood corpuscles and made one of the finest collections of microscopic observations ever published. He was born on Feb. 12, 1637, at Amsterdam. His father was an apothecary and naturalist who had a museum of curiosities, and Swammerdam started his career by helping with the museum. He went to Leiden University in 1661, graduating in medicine in 1667. Neglecting his practice, he became a pioneer of microscopy. He made a comparative study of insect life histories, which he classified according to the type of metamorphosis. He went into minute details of the internal anatomy of the mayfly and the bee; observed the cleavage of the frog's egg and studied the anatomy of tadpole and adult; described the ovarian follicles of mammals in the same year as Regnier de Graaf (*q.v.;* 1672); and evolved improved techniques of injection, which aided his study of human anatomy. Swammerdam discovered the valves of the lymphatic vessels. His description of the red blood cells was made in 1658. By a well-devised experiment he showed that the muscles alter in shape but not in size during contraction; this contradicted the current theory that a material fluid passed down the nerves to cause movement. He was the first to draw the sporangia of a fern. Deeply religious and somewhat unstable, he became for a time, after a quarrel with his father, a disciple of Antoinette Bourignon (*q.v.*).

Swammerdam died in Amsterdam on Feb. 15, 1680, after a period of deep spiritual and bodily misery. (A. C. CE.; X.)

**SWAMP:** *see* MARSHES AND SWAMPS.

**SWAN, SIR JOSEPH WILSON** (1828–1914), English physicist and chemist who invented the dry photographic plate and a prototype of the electric light, was born at Sunderland, in County Durham, on Oct. 31, 1828. After serving his apprenticeship with a druggist in his native town, he became first assistant and later partner in a firm of manufacturing chemists in Newcastle.

Among its operations was the manufacture of photographic plates, and thus Swan was led to begin the production of dry plates, the outcome of an original observation made by him on the effect of heat in increasing the sensitiveness of a gelatine bromide of silver emulsion. In 1864 he patented the first commercially practicable process for carbon printing in photography (*see* PHOTOGRAPHY). In 1879 he patented bromide paper.

In 1860 he produced an electric lamp with a carbon filament which was formed by packing pieces of paper or card with charcoal powder in a crucible and subjecting the whole to a high temperature. The carbonized paper thus obtained he mounted in the form of a fine strip in an evacuated glass vessel and connected it with a battery to Grove's cells, which, though not strong enough to raise it to complete incandescence, were sufficient to make it red-hot. This was substantially the method adopted by Thomas A. Edison nearly 20 years later (*see* LIGHTING).

Subsequently Swan devised a cotton thread parchmentized

by the action of sulfuric acid, and on Oct. 20, 1880, he gave at Newcastle the first public exhibition on a large scale of electric lighting by means of glow lamps. In another method devised by him, first exhibited in 1897, collodion was squirted into a coagulating solution and the tough threads thus obtained carbonized by heat (*see* FIBRE: *Man-made Fibres*). He also devoted attention to apparatus for measuring electric currents, to the improvement of storage batteries, and to the conditions governing the electrodisposition of metals.

Swan was knighted in 1904. He died at Warlingham, Surrey, on May 27, 1914.

*See* K. R. Swan, *Sir Joseph Swan* (1947); C. Singer *et al.* (eds.), *A History of Technology,* vol. v (1958).

**SWAN,** a well-known relative of geese and ducks and one of the largest of waterfowl. As symbols of beauty, dignity, and immortality, swans figure widely in song, story, and mythology. Especially prominent are the stories of the swan maidens—half mortal, half supernatural—whose alliances with mortal men are romantic but invariably poignant and troubled. The last achievement of an artist is called a "swan song" in allusion to the plaintive song a swan, mute in its lifetime, is fabled to sing when dying.

Swans constitute the subfamily Cygninae in the family Anatidae. Although gooselike in appearance, they are much larger (up to six feet long in the trumpeter swan) and have longer necks. They are most at home on water, where they feed on aquatic plants, but they also venture awkwardly onto land in search of grass and grain. The sexes have similar plumage. A cob (male) and pen probably mate for life. The nest, a bulky mound of vegetation on the ground, contains several pale-coloured eggs, which, after about 35 days of incubation by both parents, hatch into brownish-white down-clad cygnets. Swans, like other anatids, are gregarious and form flocks except when breeding; they often fly in V-formation, especially when migrating.

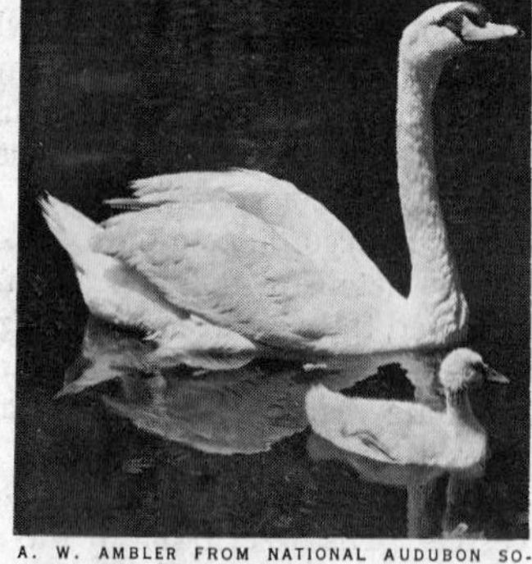

A. W. AMBLER FROM NATIONAL AUDUBON SOCIETY

MUTE SWAN (CYGNUS OLOR) AND CYGNET

Five white species live in the Northern Hemisphere; a black-necked swan, *Cygnus melancoriphus,* lives in southern South America; and a black one, *Chenopis atrata,* lives in Australia and New Zealand, having been introduced into the latter country.

The common swan of ornamental ponds everywhere is the mute swan (*Cygnus olor*), up to five feet long, native to northern Europe and Asia and easily recognized by the knob on its forehead. It became a wild bird in Long Island, N.Y., after it escaped from estate ponds. Because of its pugnacious disposition and voraciousness, it poses a threat to other waterfowl.

American species are the Arctic-nesting whistling swan (*Olor columbianus*), a race of the Bewick's swan (*Cygnus bewickii*) of Eurasia, and the rare trumpeter swan (*O. buccinator*) of Montana, Wyoming, and western Canada. The latter was threatened with extinction but has increased and extended its range into southern Alaska. The whistling swan winters in large numbers in the Currituck Sound area of North Carolina and Virginia. On northward migration, flocks occasionally alight in the Niagara River and, unable to take flight as they are swept through the rapids, pass over the falls to their destruction. (DN. A.; X.)

**SWANAGE,** a seaside holiday town and urban district in the South Dorset parliamentary division of Dorset, Eng., 27 mi. (43 km.) ESE of Dorchester by road. Pop. (1961) 8,120. Area 4.3 sq.mi. It lies in a sandy bay backed by precipitous chalk cliffs with numerous caves. Swanage Bay was the scene of Alfred the Great's naval victory over the Danes in 877. Purbeck marble is still extracted from quarries first mentioned in 1250.

**SWANSEA** (ABERTAWE), a municipal, county, and parliamentary borough and seaport of Glamorgan, Wales, lies at the mouth of the river Tawe on the north side of Swansea Bay. Pop. (1961) 167,322.

The Via Julia from Nidum (Neath) to Loughor probably passed through the north of the borough, where Roman coins were found in 1835. The name Swansea stands for Sweyn's "ey" or inlet, and may have been derived from Sweyn I (Forkbeard), king of Denmark, who certainly visited the Bristol Channel. The earliest known form of the name is Sweynesse, which occurs in a charter granted by William, earl of Warwick, some time previous to 1184; in King John's charter (1215) it appears as Sweyneshe, and in the town seal, of medieval origin, it is given as "Sweyse." The Welsh name, Abertawe, first appears in Welsh poems of the beginning of the 13th century. The town grew up around the castle that Henry de Newburgh (or Beaumont) built in the early 12th century on the west bank of the Tawe. (*See* GOWER.) In the Civil War the town was Royalist until the autumn of 1645 when Colonel Philip Jones became its governor. The older part of the town (the whole of the municipal borough previous to 1836) occupies the west bank of the Tawe near its mouth and is now wholly given up to business. Stretching inland to the north along the river for about 6 mi. through Landore to Morriston, and also eastward along the sea margin toward Neath, is the industrial quarter, while the residential part occupies the sea front and the slopes of the Town Hill (573 ft. [175 m.] high) to the west, stretching out to Sketty. The attractive seaside resort of the Mumbles or Oystermouth and a large part of the Swansea rural district were included in the borough in 1918. The east side of the river is known as St. Thomas and Port Tennant.

The 12th-century castle has entirely disappeared, but portions of the new castle, which was probably intended only as a fortified house, are incorporated in certain town buildings. The remains include a tower, a so-called keep with the curtain wall connecting them, and a fine embattled parapet with an arcade of pointed arches in a style similar to that of the episcopal palaces of St. David's and Lamphey built by Henry de Gower (d. 1347), bishop of St. David's, to whom the building of the new "castle" is also ascribed. Traces of St. David's Hospital, built by the same prelate in 1331, are still to be seen at Cross Keys Inn. The parish church of St. Mary was entirely rebuilt in 1896–98, only to be destroyed in 1941 by an air raid. It has since been restored and was reopened in May 1959. Within the parish of St. Mary was St. John's, a church once owned by the Knights Hospitallers. This church, which was entirely rebuilt in 1820, was renamed St. Matthew in 1880, when a new St. John's was erected within its own parish. The Royal Institution of South Wales, founded in 1835, possesses a museum in which the geology, mineralogy, botany, prehistoric, and later antiquities of the district are well represented. Its library is rich in historical and scientific works relating to Wales and Welsh industries. The free library and Glynn Vivian Art Gallery (opened 1911) contain exhibits of local and general Welsh interest. Near the shore at the west end of the town is the new guildhall, opened in 1934. It is notable as containing Sir Frank Brangwyn's 16 panels depicting the peoples, flowers, fruits, and animals of the British Empire, originally painted for the royal gallery of the House of Lords as part of a peers' war memorial. The grammar school, founded in 1682 by Hugh Gore (1613–91), bishop of Waterford, was destroyed during an air raid (1941); a new Bishop Gore School was opened in 1952. The University College of Swansea was founded in 1920. Beau Nash, the dandy, was born in Upper Goat Street in 1674. The town has about 3,000 ac. (1,214 ha.) of open spaces.

**Industrial Development and Port Facilities.**—William de Braose's charter of 1306 gave the burgesses the right to take from the lord's woods sufficient timber to make four great ships at a time and as many small vessels as they wished. Cromwell in his charter of 1655 recognized Swansea as "convenient for shipping and resisting foreign invasions."

From about 1768 to 1850 Swansea had a famous pottery. Beginning with earthenware which twenty years later was improved into "opaque china," it produced from 1814 to 1823 superior, beautifully decorated porcelain.

During the 18th century coal (which had been worked in the district as early as the 14th century) began to be mined at Llansamlet, and copper smelting (begun at Swansea in 1717, though at Neath it dated from 1584) assumed large proportions. The coal was conveyed on the backs of mules and later by means of a private canal. Under an act of 1791 harbour trustees cleared the river bed and built a long pier on either side of it. A canal connecting the tidal part of the River Neath with the mouth of the Tawe was made in 1789, and also a small dock, Port Tennant or Salthouse Dock, near the east pier, which continued to be used till 1875. By 1798 the entire coal-producing Swansea Valley had been connected with the port by a canal 16½ mi. (27 km.) long (acquired by the Great Western Railway in 1872). In 1845 the river was diverted eastward into a new channel (called the New Cut), and its old channel was locked and floated in 1852, thereby forming the North dock. (Area 11½ ac., and a half tide basin 2½ ac. [1 ha.]. Length of quays 5,500 ft. [1,676 m.].) The South Dock, begun in 1852 and opened in 1859, is mainly used for shipping coal and general cargo and for discharging timber and fish. It has an area of 18½ ac. (7.5 ha.); length of quays 6,550 ft. (1,996 m.); depth of water in lock 34 ft. (10 m.).

The next development was in the east side of the river where the shore of Fabian's Bay, inside the harbour mouth, was extended for the construction of the Prince of Wales Dock (authorized 1874, opened October 1881, and subsequently extended), area 28 ac. (11 ha.); length of quay 6,872 ft. (2,095 m.). The very rapid increase in the demand for anthracite coal (for the shipment of which Swansea has practically a monopoly) soon necessitated still further accommodation, and in July 1904 was begun the King's Dock, which lies farther east and has an entrance direct from the bay. By means of the embankment made in connection with it, 400 ac. (162 ha.) were reclaimed from the sea. King's Dock and basin is 221 ac. (89 ha.); depth of water 40 ft. (12 m.) (high tide); length of quays 14,050 ft. (4,282 m.). The Queen's Dock, exclusively an oil dock, occupies 150 ac. (61 ha.). There are three dry docks, and the entire harbour has approximately 270 ac. (109 ha.) of deep water, more than 6 mi. of quays, and 130 mi. (209 km.) of railway sidings. Imports include crude oil, copper, nickel, iron, timber, grain, and rubber. Exports include coal, patent fuel, refined oil, coke, tin plate, and large quantities of manufactured goods.

Formerly acknowledged as "the metallurgical capital of Wales," Swansea is still an important seat of the copper, tin plate, and spelter or zinc industries. Three-fourths of the tin plate manufactured in Great Britain and a very high proportion of the spelter are made in the district. There are also important steel works, and light industries have been developed, notably on the Fforestfach industrial estate. In 1918 Swansea became an important centre for the distribution of oil, extensive storage and refining facilities (since enormously extended) being opened at Llandarcy.

**Administration.**—The town claims to be a borough by prescription because (although its charter of creation cannot be found or established) its status may be inferred from King John's charter of 1215 in which the inhabitants are addressed as "our burgesses of Sweyneshe." Its first grant of municipal privileges may have been in the charter of William, 3rd earl of Warwick, granted some time before 1184. In 1208 King John granted Gower by charter to William de Braose, whose descendant gave Swansea and Gower various liberties by a charter of 1306 (*see* above). These were confirmed by the earl of Worcester's charter in 1532. Cromwell's charter of 1655 changed the title of portreeve into mayor, but this lasted only until 1659 when the title of portreeve was resumed.

From 1535 to 1832 (with the exception of 1658–59) Swansea was one of several contributory boroughs sending only one member to parliament. In 1832 Swansea, with four other contributory boroughs known together as Swansea District, was again represented by one member. In 1885 the district was split into two divisions, Swansea Town and Swansea District, each returning one member. In 1919 a different division was made which still remains: Swansea West and Swansea East.

The assizes and quarter sessions for the administrative county of Glamorgan are held at Swansea and Cardiff alternately, but the borough has its own separate commission of the peace and quarter sessions. It became a county borough in 1888, and in 1923 the Church in Wales created a bishopric of Swansea and Brecon. In February 1941 the whole business centre of the town (about 25 ac. [10 ha.]) was destroyed by air raids. It has now been rebuilt on modern lines. The main thoroughfares are the Kingsway, running east to west, and Princess Way, north to south. Shops and stores have been erected on these highways and have made Swansea the principal shopping centre for an area populated by 500,000 people.

The corporation has acquired and is operating an airport at Fairwood Common. This has been equipped with up-to-date appliances and is capable of dealing with all types of air traffic.

(I. J. W.)

**SWANTON, JOHN REED** (1873–1958), U.S. anthropologist, a foremost student of American Indian ethnology, was born on Feb. 19, 1873, in Gardiner, Me. He was educated at Harvard University (A.B. in 1896 and Ph.D. in 1900). Associated during the following 44 years with the Bureau of American Ethnology, Smithsonian Institution, Swanton's first important field work was among the Haida and Tlingit Indians in 1901 and 1904 (Jesup expedition). He became the leading authority on tribes of the southeastern U.S., his interests touching on all areas of North American ethnology, including linguistic and theoretical problems. He was largely responsible for developing modern techniques in historical anthropology. Among his major works are *Final Report of the United States DeSoto Expedition Commission* (1939); *Indians of the Southeastern United States* (1946); *The Indian Tribes of North America* (1952).

Elected a member of the National Academy of Sciences, Swanton was president of the American Anthropological Association (1932) and editor of the *American Anthropologist* (1911, 1921–23). In 1948 he was awarded the Viking Medal, the highest professional honour in U.S. anthropology. He died on May 2, 1958, in Newton, Mass.

BIBLIOGRAPHY.—*Essays in Historical Anthropology of North America* (1940), published in honour of Swanton by the Smithsonian Institution; W. N. Fenton, "John Reed Swanton," *Am. Anthrop.*, vol. 61 (Aug. 1959); National Academy of Sciences, *Biographical Memoirs*, p. 329–349 (1960). (M. W. St.)

**SWAT,** formerly (from 1926) a princely state in the Malakand agency of West Pakistan, was included as a district (with Chitral and Dir [*qq.v.*]) in the newly formed Malakand (*q.v.*) Division of West Pakistan as a result of a decision to that effect announced by the president of Pakistan on July 28, 1969. Area 2,934 sq.mi. (7,599 sq.km.). Pop. (1961) 614,395. Lying in a largely inaccessible region, Swat is reached by the Malakand, the Shah Kot, and other passes from the south. It is divided into two distinct parts: Swat Kohistan or mountain country, on the upper reaches of the Swat River and its affluents as far south as Ain; and Swat proper, which is further subdivided into upper and lower parts.

The Yusufzais (Afghans), who form the largest group of the population, are mainly concentrated in the lower valley, whereas Kohistan is peopled by Torwals and Garhwis. Fruit constitutes the chief export. Honey is also an important product, and the manufacture of curtains and woolen blankets is the principal cottage industry. Saidu, the capital, is 28 mi. (45 km.) NE of Malakand and is connected with it by a good road. It has a degree college, two high schools, and two hospitals. It is linked with Mingora, the chief commercial centre, by an asphalt road. Swat acceded to Pakistan soon after the partition of India. Constitutional reforms were granted to the people in 1954, and in the same year the administration of the adjacent territory of Kalam (pop. [1961] 10,304) was also entrusted to Swat.

Swat has great historical interest. It was one of the conquests of Alexander the Great and was also a remarkable stronghold of the Buddhist faith. Archaeological excavations at Butkara and Udegram near Saidu in the second half of the 20th century revealed an old civilization possibly dating back to the 5th century B.C.

SWAT RIVER, a river in West Pakistan, formed by the junction of the Gabral and Ushu rivers in Kohistan flows almost due south as far as Chakdarra and then turns to the southwest and west until it is joined by the Panjkora. The united stream sweeps in a great curve southwestward into the Peshawar Plain and joins the

Kabul at Nisatta after 400 mi. (650 km.). The river is utilized by canals to irrigate about 160,000 ac. (65,000 ha.). The valley, which is very narrow in the higher mountains, contains rich fertile tracts in Swat proper that are extensively cultivated.

(K. S. AD.)

**SWATOW** (SHAN-T'OU), a port city in eastern Kwangtung Province, People's Republic of China. Until it became a treaty port in 1869, Swatow had been a small fishing village 25 mi. (40 km.) downstream from the district capital at Ch'ao-chou (Ch'ao-an). Swatow is built on the tip of a rocky point on the north side of the channel leading to the T'o River but is not directly connected with the larger Han River on the north. Behind the city is a crowded rice delta of about 600 sq.mi. (1,554 sq.km.), marked by many rocky hills. This site makes the late summer typhoons especially severe, the most damaging being that of 1922 when 50,000 boatmen and townsfolk were drowned by the wind-driven waves. Aside from the railway to Ch'ao-an, only roads and the shallow Han River connect Swatow with the interior. The population in 1953 was 280,400.

**SWAZI,** Bantu-speaking agriculturalists and pastoralists, numbering about 410,000 and inhabiting Swaziland and part of the adjacent eastern Transvaal in the Republic of South Africa. Swazi culture is predominantly Nguni (*q.v.*), but the incorporation of original Sotho (*see* SUTO) occupants of the area has strongly influenced the political organization, rain ritual, and marriage regulations. Europeans did not defeat the Swazi by force, and much traditional culture persists within a modern framework.

The highest traditional powers (political, administrative, economic, and ritual) are shared between a hereditary male ruler (*Nggwenyama*) and his mother or a mother substitute (*Ndlovukati*). Marriage is by bridewealth (*q.v.*), and polygyny is the conservative ideal. The king's wives and children are settled in royal villages diplomatically dispersed throughout the territory. National officials are drawn from special clans, and a balance is maintained in local and central government between a well-defined aristocracy of birth and representatives of commoners. All important issues must be discussed by a central privy council (*liqoqo*) consisting mainly of royal clansmen, and a larger national council (*libandla*) attended by chiefs and headmen. The relationship of rulers and subjects is dramatically expressed in an annual ceremony, *Ncwala,* a ritualization of kingship. Cutting through local and kinship bonds are men's age classes, organized every five to seven years, for labour and other national services. Beliefs in magic and witchcraft interact within a highly organized ancestral cult. *See* also SWAZILAND.

BIBLIOGRAPHY.—B. A. Marwick, *The Swazi* (1940); H. Kuper, *An African Aristocracy* (1947), "The Swazi," *Ethnogr. Surv. Afr.*, pt. 1, "Southern Africa" (1952), *The Swazi, a South African Kingdom* (1963); D. Ziervogel, *Swazi Texts* (1957); J. F. Holleman (ed.), *Experiment in Swaziland* (1964). (H. KU.)

**SWAZILAND,** an independent kingdom in southern Africa, a member of the Commonwealth of Nations, is a compact country of 6,704 sq.mi. (17,363 sq.km.) surrounded on three sides by the Transvaal Province of the Republic of South Africa and on the east by Natal Province and Portuguese East Africa (Mozambique). The capital is Mbabane.

**Physical Features.**—Swaziland, lying on the eastern slopes of the great African plateau between the high veld and the coastal lowlands, falls naturally into four longitudinal regions. In the west the rugged edge of the high veld consists of steep quartzite ridges, ranging in altitude from 4,000 to 6,000 ft. (1,200 to 1,800 m.), and deep valleys cut in shales. A rainfall of 40–60 in. (1,000–1,500 mm.) occurs mainly in summer; the typical vegetation is temperate short grass. The middle veld, ranging from 1,500 to 4,000 ft. (450 to 1,200 m.), is rolling granite country with a rainfall of 25–40 in. (630–1,000 mm.) and a savanna vegetation of tall grass and scattered trees. Eastward, the granite hills dip gently beneath the younger sedimentary rocks of the low veld. This region is characterized by a relatively flat surface mostly 750–950 ft. (230–290 m.) above sea level; fertile soil; a low, highly variable rainfall (average about 20 in.) with a pronounced winter drought; and thorn-bush vegetation. In the east the volcanic Lubombo scarp rises abruptly from the Bushveld to form an undulating lava plateau averaging 1,500 ft. in altitude, with a moderate rainfall and a vegetation of short grass. The scarp is broken only by the deeply incised Mbuluzi, Usutu, and Ngwavuma rivers, which, with the Komati, drain eastward.

(P. ST.)

**History.**—According to the traditional account of the origin of the Swazi, when in the 16th century the main Bantu tribes were moving gradually southward along the coast of what is now Portuguese East Africa, a group diverged and crossed the Lubombo Range into the area that lies between the Pongola and Great Usutu rivers. Under pressure from the Zulus, the group moved northward to the Little Usutu River. Further attacks by the Zulus took place from time to time, and when King Sobhuza I died in 1836 his successor, Mswazi (Mswati) II, who reputedly gave his name to the tribe, moved farther north to the Pigg's Peak area. The Swazi now had a well-trained army and conquered the tribes to the north, but in 1846 their ruler ceded any claims that he had to the country north of the Crocodile River in favour of the Lydenburg Republic. It was at that time also that Mswazi was compelled to seek British aid against the Zulus.

During the 1880s large numbers of Europeans visited the Swazi king Mbandzeni in search of concessions. It may be said that these concessions were only intended to allow the concessionaires to share the use of the concession property with the Swazi.

In 1888 a charter of self-government was granted to the Europeans. Two years later, under a convention between the British government and the South African republic, a provisional government consisting of representatives of the two powers and a representative of the Swazi people was set up with the consent of the latter. In 1893 the British government signed a new convention permitting the South African republic to negotiate with the Swazi regent and her council for a proclamation allowing it to assume powers of jurisdiction, legislation, and administration, without incorporation in the republic. The Swazi refused to sign the proclamation, but in 1894 another convention was signed by the two powers, virtually giving effect to its terms. After the conquest of the Transvaal all rights and powers of the republic passed to Great Britain, and in June 1903 by an order in council under the Foreign Jurisdiction Act the governor of the Transvaal was empowered to administer Swaziland and to legislate by proclamation. In 1906 these powers were transferred to the high commissioner for Basutoland, Bechuanaland, and Swaziland. A commission was appointed in 1907 to deal with the problem of the concessions, and as a result of its report, land and grazing concessions were reduced by one-third. The regent did not accept this settlement and a deputation of protest was sent to London in 1908, but achieved little.

In 1963 the office of resident commissioner was replaced by that of Her Majesty's commissioner (equal in status to governor); in 1964 the office of high commissioner was abolished. A constitution providing limited self-government was promulgated in 1963. In 1967, under the new constitution of that year, the country became a protected state under the name of the Kingdom of Swaziland, and in the following year another and greater change took place when Swaziland became fully independent (*see* below).

**Population.**—At the 1966 census the population was 374,571 (not including 126 in transit), an increase of 58% over the 1956 figure. The African population was 362,367 (increase 57.7%), European population 7,987 (increase 34.9%), and other non-Africans 4,217 (increase just over 206%). The majority of the Europeans live in the towns of Mbabane, Manzini (formerly Bremersdorp), Stegi, Goedgegun, Hlatikulu, Mankaiana, Pigg's Peak, Emlembe (the Havelock Asbestos Mine area), Eranchi (the Swaziland Irrigation Scheme), Malkerns, Big Bend on the Great Usutu River, and Mhlambanyati (the Usutu Pulp Company and forest area).

The Swazi language (Siswati) is spoken by almost all Africans. The home language of 60% of Europeans is English and of 30% Afrikaans. English is spoken by 90% of the Coloureds.

In the 1956 census 60% of the African population was recorded as Christian, divided among 24 denominations, the remaining 40% adhering to indigenous religions. (*See* also SWAZI.)

**Administration and Social Conditions.**—*Government.*—In the United Kingdom responsibility for the administration of the territory rested, before 1967, with the Colonial Office; and Her Majesty's commissioner, resident in Swaziland, was the administrator, responsible directly to the Colonial Office. The constitution of 1963 provided for an Executive Council and a Legislative Council of elected and nominated members.

The 1967 constitution conferred internal self-government on Swaziland with the king as head of state. Two chambers of parliament were created, the Senate and the House of Assembly. Most of the provisions of this constitution were embodied in that of 1968, when Swaziland became fully independent. Elections to the 24 elected seats in the House of Assembly were held in 1967. The remaining six members of that House were appointed by the king. Six of the senators were similarly appointed by the king, the remaining six being elected by the House of Assembly.

The king appoints the prime minister; also the other ministers, acting on the prime minister's advice. The king, besides being a constitutional monarch, is also the *Nggwenyama,* that is, the head of the Swazi people and, as such, trustee of their land and of all minerals in Swaziland. The Swazi National Council continues to advise the king on all matters regulated by Swazi law and custom. Swaziland is a member of the Commonwealth of Nations, the UN, and the Organization of African Unity (OAU).

For administrative purposes Swaziland is divided into four districts (*see* Table).

*Area and Population of Swaziland by Districts*

| District | Area (sq. mi.)* | Population (1966) | Principal town |
|---|---|---|---|
| Hhohho . . . . . | 1,378 | 95,759 | Mbabane |
| Shiselweni . . . . . | 1,459 | 95,735 | Goedgegun |
| Manzini. . . . . | 1,571 | 101,277 | Manzini |
| Lubombo . . . . . | 2,296 | 81,800 | Stegi |

*1 sq. mi.=2.59 sq. km.

*Health.*—There were, in the late 1960s, 10 hospitals. The government also operates 17 clinics, while 24 are maintained by missions and 3 by the Swazi National Treasury. Several large industrial firms provide medical facilities for their employees. Tuberculosis, especially pulmonary, is one of the main health problems. Nutritional and deficiency diseases are also prominent, but malaria has been brought under control by a campaign of hut spraying.

*Justice.*—The head of the judiciary is the chief justice, who presides over the High Court of Swaziland. He is also a member of the Court of Appeal, but rarely sits in that capacity. There are in each district subordinate courts presided over by professional magistrates. There are also 14 Swazi courts, with 2 courts of appeal and a higher court of appeal. The Swazi courts have jurisdiction in all matters in which the parties are Africans, except for certain serious offenses. The right to prosecute in all courts rests in the attorney general. The chief justice, attorney general, judges, and magistrates are appointed by the independent Judicial Service Commission.

*Civil Service.*—The commissioner and deputy commissioner of police, government representatives abroad, and permanent secretaries are appointed on the advice of the prime minister, but all other officers are appointed by the independent Public Service Commission which is merely subject to the prime minister's general direction on matters of policy.

*Police.*—The police force was considerably expanded in the late 1960s to combine the functions of a civil police force and a para-military force. There is a police training college, one of the most modern in southern Africa.

*Education.*—In January 1963 a policy of school integration was adopted. After the mid-1950s, there was a striking increase in the enrollment of Swazi children; by the mid-1960s, about 52,000 were attending approximately 370 schools; under 3,000 of them were in secondary schools.

**The Economy.**—More than half of the area of territory is available for occupation by Africans, the rest being held by European landowners.

*Agriculture.*—Largely through the efforts of the agricultural college (opened in 1966) with courses for farmers, the research stations, and the agricultural demonstrators, there has been a great improvement in the agricultural methods of the Swazi farmer and consequently in crop yields. Livestock raising is important to the economy. Maize is the staple food of the Swazi and is the principal crop. The most important cash crop on unirrigated land is cotton. Sorghums are also grown, largely for beer making. Other crops are peanuts, tobacco, and beans. Rice is being grown on an increasing scale by European farmers and is an important export. In 1953 pineapple planting started on a fairly large scale, and a canning factory was set up. The tung oil industry has declined considerably because of the fall in world prices. Sugarcane is grown on a large scale in irrigated areas. There are plantings of citrus in the Malkerns area and in the low veld where soil and climate seem well suited for it.

Swaziland offers ample scope for irrigation from its large rivers. There are three important irrigation projects: Malkerns, controlling 10,000 ac. (4,000 ha.); Big Bend, 10,000 ac.; and the Swaziland Irrigation Scheme, 16,000 ac. (6,500 ha.).

*Forestry.*—Swaziland's forests are almost entirely man-made. By the late 1960s over 250,000 ac. were afforested, mainly with pine trees; the Commonwealth Development Corporation played a prominent part in this. The Usutu forests reached the production stage in 1961.

*Industry and Mining.*—By the late 1960s the Usutu Pulp Mill, designed to produce 100,000 short tons of pulp a year, was in full operation; Peak Timbers was producing sawn timber; two sugar mills were producing 160,000 short tons of sugar a year; and the pineapple industry was growing. Iron ore was being exported to Japan from the rich deposits at the Bomvu Ridge near Mbabane and through a railway line, constructed for the purpose, to the railhead on the border of Portuguese East Africa. A number of industries have been established at Matsapa (near Manzini) near the railway line, where an airfield is also in operation. The Havelock Mine is a large producer of asbestos, one of the territory's three most important exports. Other mineral production, including tin, gold, barite, and diaspore, is comparatively small, though there are extensive coal deposits in the eastern Bushveld.

*Finance.*—The main sources of ordinary revenue are income tax, customs and excise (under a customs union agreement signed in 1910 with the Republic of South Africa, Swaziland receives 0.5303% of the total collection of the republic), poll tax, base metal royalties (mainly from asbestos), and posts and telegraphs. Swaziland receives nearly one-quarter of its total revenue in grants from the Colonial Development and Welfare Fund. Chief items of expenditure are education, public works, administration, and land utilization. Currency is that of the Republic of South Africa (1 Rand = £0.587 = $1.40).

*Communications.*—In addition to the railway to Portuguese Africa, a £1,250,000 program of road improvement was begun in 1962. There are freight and passenger services by road. Swaziland has its own postal, telegraph, and telephone facilities.

Bibliography.—H. Kuper, *An African Aristocracy* (1947), *The Swazi* (1952); B. A. Marwick, *The Swazi* (1940); *Colonial Reports* and *A Year Book of the Commonwealth* (HMSO annually). (Jo. W. H.)

**SWEATING SICKNESS.** This disease, also known as the English sweat, appeared in England as an epidemic on six occasions—in 1485, 1506, 1517, 1528, 1551, and 1578. It was confined to England, except in 1528–29, when it spread to the continent, appearing in Hamburg, and passing northward to Scandinavia and eastward to Lithuania, Poland, and Russia; the Netherlands also were involved, but the disease did not spread to France or Italy.

Apart from the second outbreak, all the epidemics were severe, with a very high mortality rate. The disease was fully described by the distinguished physician John Caius, who was practising in Shrewsbury in 1551 when an outbreak of the sweating sickness occurred. His account, *A Boke or Counseill against the Disease commonly called the Sweate, or Sweatyng Sicknesse* (1552), is the main source of knowledge of this extraordinary disease.

The illness began with rigors, headache, giddiness, and severe prostration. After one to three hours, violent, drenching sweat came on, accompanied by severe headache, delirium, and rapid pulse. Death might occur from 3 to 18 hours after the first onset of symptoms; if the patient survived for 24 hours, recovery was usually complete. Occasionally there was a vesicular rash. Immunity was not conferred by an attack, and it was not unusual for patients to have several. Each epidemic lasted for only a few weeks in any particular locality.

Since 1578 the only outbreaks of a disease resembling the English sweat have been those of the Picardy sweat, which occurred frequently in France between 1718 and 1861. In this illness, however, there was invariably a rash, lasting for about a week, and the mortality rate was lower.

It is difficult to know what the sweating sickness really was. Caius attributed it to dirt and filth. All the epidemics occurred in late spring or summer, so it may very well have been spread by insects. The disease seemed to be more severe among the rich than among the poor, and the young and healthy were frequent victims. It is unlikely to have been a form of influenza or typhus.

R. Merliss (1952) identified it with relapsing fever, which is spread by lice and ticks and has many characteristics in common with sweating sickness. This explanation is certainly plausible. It is improbable that sweating sickness should appear as a well-defined disease and then vanish altogether.

Bibliography.—J. F K. Hecker, *The Epidemics of the Middle Ages*, Eng. trans. by B. G. Babington (1844; reprinting John Caius' *Boke or Counseill . . .* as an appendix); H. Senf, "Ein Kartographische Beitrag zur Geschichte des Englischen Schweisses," *Kyklos*, 3:273 (1930); R. Merliss, "The Sweating Sickness," *Med. Arts Sci.*, 6:445 (1952).

(O. G. E.)

**SWEATSHOP,** a term used to describe a workplace where conditions are oppressive and where there is unbridled exploitation of the workers. In England, the word "sweater" was used as early as 1850 to describe an employer or middleman who exacted monotonous work at very low wages. Charles Kingsley in his novel *Alton Locke* (1850) and in his political pamphlets directed attention to London "sweaters"; and the philanthropic London journalist Henry Mayhew in 1851 talked of "the sweating system." There were complaints of sweating in the United States also, beginning at the time of Civil War, when soldiers' wives were employed to make uniforms. It gained in intensity during the 1880s when immigrants from eastern and southern Europe provided a large source of cheap labour. In continental Europe the same conditions were present; and with the development of industrial production in Latin America and in Asia the problem emerged there also.

Certain conditions are necessary for sweating to be possible: (1) a mass of unskilled and unorganized labourers, often including women and children; (2) imperfect systems of management, which totally neglect the "human factor"; (3) ignorance of conditions or lack of will to intervene on the part of the state. Historically these conditions have been associated with the survival of home work and the development of contracting. Individual workers or groups of workers contract to do a certain job for a certain price. Sometimes they carry out this contract themselves; sometimes they let it out to subcontractors at lower prices. Contracting makes possible labour exploitation, often of women and children; and it produces erratic employment. When trade is brisk, extremely long hours are worked in seriously overcrowded workrooms or dwelling houses. When trade is slack, subcontractors, whose overhead costs are far lower than those of factory employers, dismiss workers without scruple. One of the earliest objectives of factory and minimum-wage legislation was to eliminate such exploitation.

Contracting and subcontracting are common in the garment manufacturing industry. In the 19th century, outwork existed in other industries, such as boot-and-shoe manufacture, soapmaking, cigar making, and the making of artificial flowers. Although legislation had by the middle of the 20th century either eliminated or carefully controlled sweating in most highly developed countries, the system was still operating in many countries in Asia, where larger numbers of people were engaged in home work than in industrial establishments.

Conditions tend to be worse in large cities, where sweatshops are hidden away in slum areas and are aggravated by influxes of cheap labour from outside. To the native poor engaged in tailoring in London in the 1880s, for example, was added a large immigrant labour force of unskilled foreigners. In the United States the tireless search for cheap labour encouraged such immigration until 1917.

The first large-scale official inquiry into the sweating system was carried out in England by a select committee of the House of Lords. Its report, published in 1890, described conditions in tailoring, bootmaking, furriery, shirt making, mantle making, cabinetmaking, cutlery and hardware manufacture, chainmaking and nail making, saddlery and harness making, military accoutrement establishments, and dock labour. It claimed that sweating involved: (1) a rate of wages inadequate in terms of work done or basic standard of living; (2) excessive hours of labour; and (3) insanitary conditions in the houses or domestic workshops in which the work was carried on.

The inquiry of the select committee did not bear fruit immediately. It was not until 1909 that the Trade Boards Act set up boards to fix minimum wages in specified industries such as machine-made lace manufacture and chainmaking. In 1918 the scope of the act was extended to cover any trade where the Ministry of Labour considered that machinery for the effective regulation of wages was inadequate. Government interference was important, chiefly because it permitted the development of collective bargaining. By 1939, though many workers still received low wages, there were no longer any sweated trades in Great Britain.

In the United States most of the pressure to eliminate sweating was applied by organized labour. A number of acts, culminating in 1882, prohibited Chinese immigration. In 1889 the tobacco workers in New York obtained the passage of a state statute forbidding all manufacture of tobacco in any tenement house; but this was held unconstitutional by the New York Court of Appeals and home work was prolonged for a number of years. Beginning with Massachusetts in 1912, a number of states passed laws creating wage boards or commissions. The U.S. Supreme Court, however, in *Adkins* v. *Children's Hospital* (1923) held that a U.S. statute authorizing a wage board in the District of Columbia to fix minimum wages of women and children violated the guarantees of the due process clause of the Fifth Amendment of the U.S. Constitution, since freedom to contract between the employer and the employee was impaired. The Adkins decision was reversed by the court in 1937 in the *West Coast Hotel Co.* v. *Parrish* decision. Many states were prepared to intervene in the labour market, and their action was supported not only by organized labour but by voluntary organizations, such as the National Consumers' League. By 1939 practically all states had limited the hours of labour for women, and several had introduced legislation prohibiting night work.

Four main factors contributed in other countries as well as in Great Britain and in the United States to the control of sweated industries: (1) social idealism; (2) the pressure of trade unions; (3) the extension of the franchise and the growth of labour parties; and (4) the growing economies of factory production and the increased interest in human relations in industry. In several countries there developed a tendency to let industries, in which both labour and management were strong, set their own standards. In unorganized and sometimes unorganizable industries the state intervened directly. The International Labour Organization was active in attempting to raise labour standards in countries where sweatshops were still common.

*See* also Clothing Manufacture: *Social and Historical Aspects.* (A. Bri.)

**SWEDEN** (Sverige), a kingdom of northern Europe, occupying the eastern and southernmost parts of the Scandinavian Peninsula and including the Baltic islands of Öland and Gotland (*qq.v.*). The length is about 1,000 mi. (1,610 km.), the extreme (mainland) breadth about 250 mi. (400 km.), and the total area, inclusive of inland waters, is 173,665 sq.mi. (449,793 sq.km.). Of this, 14,878 sq.mi. (38,535 sq.km.), or 8.6%, consists of about 100,000 lakes, of which the four largest are Vänern, Vättern, Mälaren (*qq.v.*), and Hjälmaren. The combined area of these four is

3,522 sq.mi. (9,121 sq.km.). The boundary length of Sweden is estimated at 6,100 mi. (9,817 km.), of which 4,724 mi. are coastal, 1,030 mi. common with Norway, and 347 mi. with Finland. The capital is Stockholm (*q.v.*).

This article contains the following sections and subsections:



## I. PHYSICAL GEOGRAPHY

**1. Structure and Relief.**—*The Baltic Shield and Caledonian Mountain Range.*—Almost the whole of Sweden forms part of the Baltic Shield with rock of Archean age. This extends to much of Norway and merges eastward, in Finland and the U.S.S.R., into the Russian Platform. The western edge of the shield experienced great folding and thrusting during the Caledonian orogeny, and thus Sweden shares many structural features with Norway. In particular, the highest mountain areas lie along the Norwegian frontier, forming the "keel" (*kölen*) of the peninsula. These are of Caledonian origin although they later experienced considerable denudation, and in places the older rocks are overlain by more recent sediments which are certainly post-Silurian and possibly of Rhaetic age. The highest individual peaks are in the central zone of this Caledonian Massif, known as the Seve Nappe. Kebnekaise, 6,965 ft. (2,123 m.), and Sarek, 6,857 ft. (2,090 m.), are the two highest. Both are in Norrbotten, north of the Arctic Circle.

*Norrland and the Bothnian Coastal Plain.*—Between the Caledonian mountains and the Baltic and roughly north of latitude 60° is the Norrland terrain of Archean rocks, mostly granites and gneisses, which gradually slope down from the high mountains toward the Baltic and form part of the Baltic Shield (*see* PRECAMBRIAN TIME: *Europe*). The northern half of this region consists largely of plains out of which rise isolated, rounded hills, but the southern half has an irregular relief of mountains or hills separated by fairly deep valleys. Norrland is flanked on the east, from Umeå northward to the Finnish border, by a narrow coastal plain, which because of isostatic readjustment is an area that has risen from beneath the waters of the Gulf of Bothnia, the northern arm of the Baltic Sea. This coastal stretch within the Archean zone is an area of depression in comparison with the Norrland area of elevation.

*The Central Lowlands.*—Southward from Söderhamn the coastal plain reappears and forms a second area of depression—central Sweden. The northern boundary of this area runs southwest from Söderhamn to west of Örebro, and then passes to the north of Lake Vänern. To the south, it is bounded by a line roughly following latitude 58°, north of Göteborg, through Lake Vättern and south of Norrköping. The rock types are still Archean granites and gneisses, but much of the area is covered by glacial deposits and includes Sweden's largest plains. To the northeast is the Uppsala plain, which merges southward into the gently undulating region of Södermanland with its numerous small rock outcrops and lakes of which Mälaren, with Stockholm at its eastern end, is the largest. Two other flat areas are the Västgöta plain, with Vänern (2,156 sq.mi. [5,585 sq.km.]), the largest lake in western Europe, in its centre, and the Östgöta plain, stretching from Lake Vättern to the Baltic. Between these three lowland areas, and bordering the Västgöta plain on its western side, are regions of low hills with considerable local relief, caused by faulting resulting in horsts (*see* FAULT).

*South Sweden.*—South Sweden consists largely of gneisses in the western half and granites in the eastern, but this geological distinction is scarcely reflected in the present relief. In fact, in contradistinction to the geology, this area is divided according to relief into two approximately equal halves by a line drawn roughly west-east. The more northerly of these halves comprises the South Swedish Highlands, rising to about 1,000 ft. (300 m.) above sea level especially near the southern end of Vättern, where Tomtabacken reaches 1,237 ft. (377 m.). This area slopes gently down to merge in the south into the very level south Småland Archean plain with an average elevation of about 500 ft., which on the east merges into a sub-Cambrian peneplain that in turn disappears beneath Cambrian rocks reaching to the Baltic coast; to the west are the narrow, complex areas of south Bohuslän, the Göteborg archipelago, and the small coastal plain of part of Halland.

*Skåne.*—This small area in the extreme south of Sweden is of great significance. It lies outside the Archean region and belongs geologically to Denmark and continental Europe, with their Cretaceous rocks. The fault, probably mainly of Variscan age, which divides it from the remainder of Sweden, could be considered to be one of the most important of European boundaries, separating the old rocks of Fennoscandia (almost all older than 300,000,000 years and most of them twice that age) from the much younger, 100,000,000-year-old, rocks to the southwest. This fault runs roughly northwest and southeast through the university town of Lund. As is always the case in such circumstances, however, it

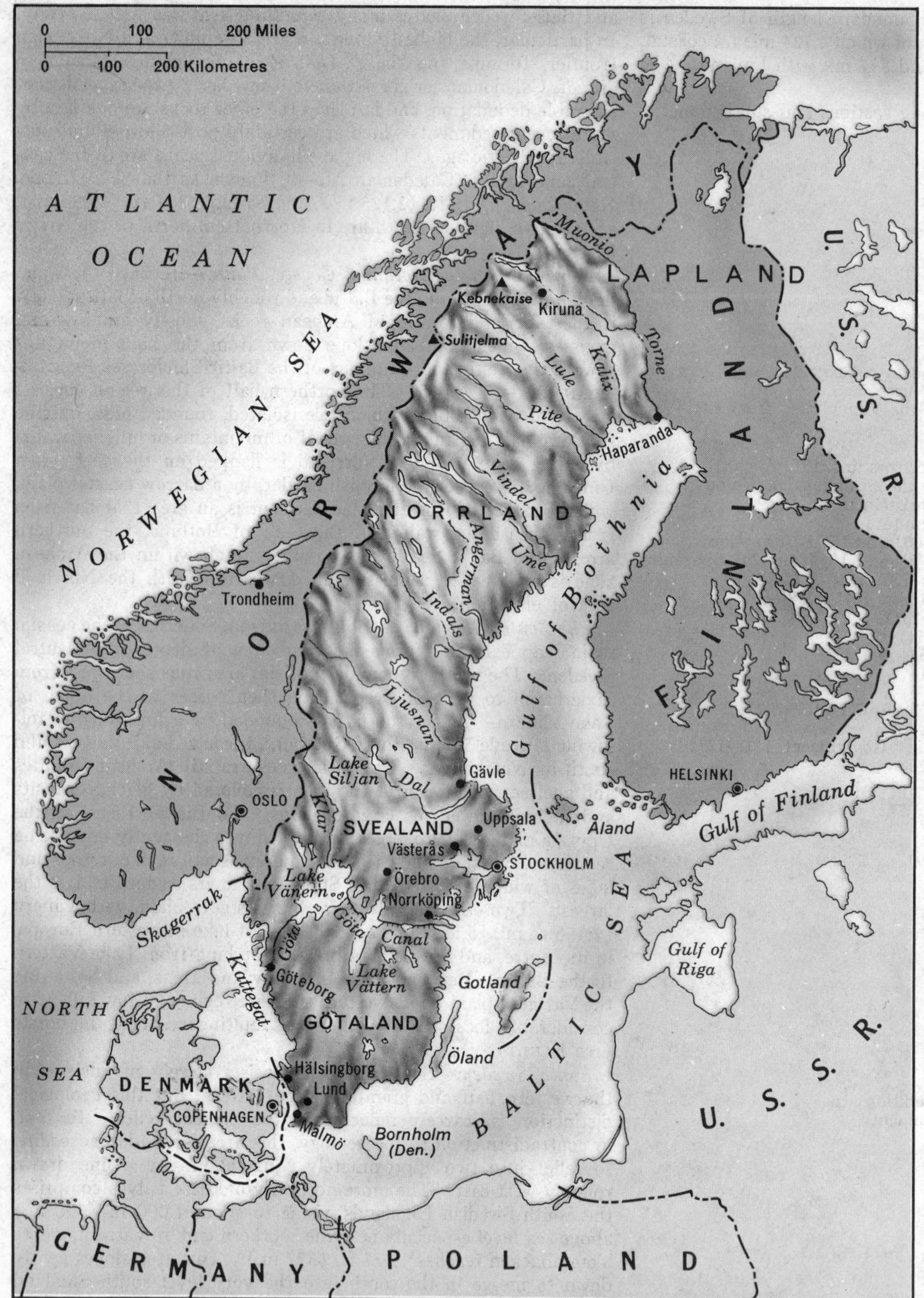


FIG. 1.—MAJOR PHYSICAL FEATURES OF SWEDEN

Great glacial troughs or U-shaped valleys, rock hollows now occupied by lakes, such as Torneträsk in northern Lapland (Lappland), and all the other features of intense glacial action in a highland region were produced in the mountains. In the highest of these, glaciers still exist; the most southerly is in Härjedalen, where the snowline is at 4,450 ft. (1,350 m.). In the far north of Sweden the snowline is at 2,900 ft. (880 m.) and the largest ice-field is Sulitelma, with an area of 8.5 sq.mi. (22 sq.km.).

In Central and South Sweden the most notable glacial features are concerned with deposition rather than with erosion, and probably 80% of the whole country is covered with morainic material. The most important is ground moraine left by the retreating ice sheets, and it is on this that almost all the agriculture of the country is located. Much of it was deposited beneath water, for at the time of the last major deglaciation what is now the Baltic reached to the ice margin. The end moraines of the same period derive their special characteristics from this, and the topography of the Uppsala region is unlike anything that can be seen elsewhere in Europe, for ground moraine deposited as lake (or sea) floor alternates with small end moraines. Here, too, are exceptionally large and long eskers (ridges of morainic material deposited by subglacial streams fed by ice meltwater). They reach 160 ft. (50 m.) in height and some are more than 60 mi. (100 km.) in length.

The great weight of the Scandinavian ice sheet was sufficient to depress that area of the earth's crust, and since it melted away the land has gradually been recovering its original level. It appears to have completely done so in southern Sweden, but in the Stockholm district it is still rising at the rate of 16 in. (40 cm.)

is in reality complex, so that to the northeast there is a parallel belt of fault-produced horst ridges, some 20 mi. (30 km.) in width. These are in Archean rocks, but the earth movements that produced them, although starting in Variscan times, continued to be active probably to Alpine times. In Skåne there is thus both the most recent solid rock in the country and also this unique boundary zone, producing a topography unique in Sweden.

**2. Glaciation.**—The present topography of Sweden owes much to the Ice Ages of the last half-million years. The Gulf of Bothnia was the main centre of European glaciation, and here the ice is considered to have reached a thickness of some 8,000 ft. (2,400 m.). At periods of maximum glaciation there was a slow outward movement of ice, but the more apparent modifications to the relief were made during lesser glaciations, when individual glaciers occupied the preglacial river valleys, radically altering their form.

and in the vicinity of Umeå by as much as 40 in. (1 m.) a century. This means a continual increase in land area, as more and more sea floor rises out of the water. The Stockholm archipelago is at a typical intermediate stage, only the shallower parts having so far become dry land.

**3. Climate.**—*Temperatures.*—The climate of Sweden is largely transitional between the maritime Atlantic coastland climate and the continental climate of farther east. It shows the variations to be expected in a country which spans $13\frac{1}{2}°$ of latitude, with $2\frac{1}{2}°$ within the Arctic Circle, and which is bounded on its western side for two-thirds of its length by mountains rising generally more than 5,000 ft. (1,500 m.) and in places reaching nearly 7,000 ft. (2,100 m.). The effect of the mountains is shown by comparing the temperatures of two places, one on either side of them. Haparanda is at the extreme northern end of the Gulf of Bothnia, and

Røst Island, in the Lofoten group off northwestern Norway, is some 130 mi. farther north and thus by latitude might be expected to be a little cooler. Both are very nearly at sea level. The mean temperature during January is −10.3° C (13° F) at Haparanda, as compared with 1.5° C (35° F) at Røst, a difference of nearly 12° (22°). Corresponding summer temperatures are 16.3° C (61° F) for Haparanda and 10.8° (51°) for Røst. The winter warming effect of the North Atlantic Drift and the summer cooling by North Atlantic waters, both important at Røst, are thus relatively absent at Haparanda, and the more extreme climate on the eastern side of the mountains is well demonstrated. The seasonal change from winter to summer is 27.2° C (49° F) at Haparanda, whereas in the milder, oceanic climate of Røst the difference is only 9.3° (17°). The annual precipitation, too, is strikingly different. Haparanda has less than 21 in. (530 mm.), while Røst has 28 in. (710 mm.); on the Norwegian coast within the influence of the mountains this figure rises to more than 160 in. (4,060 mm.).

These data contrast with those for two corresponding southerly stations, such as Esbjerg (Fanø) on the west coast of Denmark, and Växjö, at a height of 650 ft. (200 m.) in central South Sweden. Esbjerg has a January mean of 0.7° C (33° F) and Växjö −1.8° (29°); the July temperatures are respectively 15.7° (60°) and 16.5° (62°). The similarity of these figures for the two localities makes the effect of the absence of the intervening mountain range very clear. The two main centres of population, Stockholm and Göteborg, have mean temperatures of −2.5° C (28° F) and 0° (32°) respectively for January, with 16.9° (62°) and 17.1° (63°) for July.

Although the mountains on the west cut off most of the ameliorating effect of the southwesterly weather that would otherwise cross those areas into Sweden, the lowland has a much more equable climate than corresponding latitudes in the U.S.S.R., because of the drift of southwesterly air streams and pressure systems across the Skagerrak and Denmark, over southern Sweden, and northward. Nevertheless, the whole area is exposed to the approach of cool air from the northeast.

In the north, because of the long daylight hours, the summers are milder than might be expected. At Karesuando, on the Finnish border, at latitude 68°27′ N, there is the possibility of perpetual sunlight from May 26 to July 18, and the absence of night cooling has the effect of producing a considerable accumulation of warmth and a 24-hour growing period daily for vegetation. Correspondingly, there is permanent darkness in the winter months and a progressive cooling until the sun returns in the spring. These effects lessen toward the south. The low angle at which the sun sets at many times of the year also produces a long twilight, both in the evening and morning, and again the daylight is lengthened. The growing season, taken as the average period during which the mean temperature is above 3° C (37° F), is often longer than might be expected from the latitude. At Karesuando it lasts from May 18 to Sept. 24, at Haparanda from May 6 to Oct. 7, at Stockholm from April 11 to Nov. 6, and at Växjö from April 5 to Nov. 8.

*Precipitation.*—The annual precipitation for almost the whole of lowland Sweden south of Haparanda varies between 20 and 30 in. (500–750 mm.), with the western side wetter than the eastern; in a small area west of Växjö it reaches 40 in. There is precipitation in all months, but June, July, and August are the wettest. North of Haparanda the annual precipitation is less than 20 in. In these northern areas much of the precipitation is in the form of snow, and at Karesuando the ground is snow-covered on the average from the end of October to the end of May.

*Ice Conditions.*—The Gulf of Bothnia freezes in winter. Aided by the low salinity, ice begins to form along the shores of the northernmost part during November, closing the harbours of Luleå and similarly sited ports from mid-December to mid-May. Ice reaches the coast in the Gävle and Stockholm districts much later, generally not until January, and Gävle is closed to shipping from about mid-February to early April. Stockholm is not normally closed. The ice spreads seaward from the coast and covers the whole width of the gulf as far south as Sundsvall by about mid-February. There is often a complete bridge of ice across the neck of the gulf by the Åland Islands (Ahvenanmag Islands) by mid-February, but between this and the latitude of Sundsvall the central part of the gulf (between Sweden and Finland) remains covered only with broken ice. The extent, both in time and area, of the icing is extremely variable from year to year, and the above are averages for many winters. The usual thickness of ice along the coast of the gulf is about 30 in. (76 cm.), increasing to twice that in the far north. (R. K. Gr.)

**4. Vegetation.**—The Swedish vegetation can be divided into four regional groups.

The marine region comprises belts on the coasts and in the sea with an algae vegetation: the intertidal belt, with seaweeds and aquatic vascular plants (*Najas* and *Zostera*); the sublittoral belt, often reaching depths of 100 to 150 ft. (30–45 m.), with brown algae dominating in the upper and red in the lower parts; and the eulittoral belt with only scattered colonies of red algae.

The bare regions—maritime, continental, and alpine—are treeless. The maritime region consists of heaths with dwarf shrubs (*e.g.,* heather, bilberry, black crowberry); grass heaths with sheep's fescue and wavy hair grass; meadows, fens, and, on rocks and boulders, lichen communities. The continental, a steppe region, is found especially on Öland and Gotland and in eastern Skåne, and is conditioned by dry and warm summers; the steppes are rich in grasses, rockroses, *Anthericum,* and orchids, and their area has been increased by deforestation, burning, and heavy grazing. The alpine bare region comprises the areas above 2,000 ft. (about 600 m.) in northernmost Sweden and above 2,500–3,000 ft. in Dalarna. Its lower belt has shrublike willow, dwarf birch, blueberry and other *Vaccinium* species, *Cassiope, Dryas,* grasses, heath, and meadow vegetation; and in its upper belt, dwarf willow buttercup (*Ranunculus glacialis*), mosses, and lichens are characteristic; in its highest parts the soil is often entirely naked.

The coniferous forest regions cover the larger part of the country; the northern region reaches southward to about 61° N and has mostly spruce and Scots pine, with some birch, aspen, and rowan, or mountain ash; the southern reaches southward to the limit of the beech forests and has oak, beech, and birch; in both regions species of *Vaccinium,* moss, and lichen are characteristic and large areas, especially in the west, are occupied by raised bogs and fens.

The broad-leaved forest regions are the subalpine birch region and the beech region. The former holds a zone above the coniferous forests in the higher mountains with mountain birch dominating. The beech region comprises Skåne and parts of Blekinge and of the west coast; its other most important trees are pedunculate and sessile oaks, hornbeam, elm, ash, and maple. In acid soils the lower vegetation layers have heath character with *Vaccinium* species and wavy hair grass; in alkaline areas they are developed as meadows with anemone, yellow archangel, fumitory, ramson, and several grasses and sedges.

Although most of Sweden's plant species are postglacial immigrants from the south, some, for example, the spruce, have come from the east. Probably certain alpine species have survived at least the last glaciation in nunataks at the Norwegian coasts. In recent time the vegetation has been much changed by the planting of conifers in former broad-leaved forest areas, and by draining and cultivation of fens, etc. (A. H. W.)

**5. Animal Life.**—The mountain hare, various shrews, the ermine, weasel, red squirrel, fox, and elk are common to the entire country. The bear is protected and, with the wolf, wolverine, and lynx, is restricted to the northern forests. The wild reindeer is extinct, but there are large domesticated herds in Lapland. The elk is the most valuable game animal, but badger, otter, and the rare pine marten of the coniferous forests are hunted for their skins, as are the thriving wild descendants of escaped farm mink. The roe deer is scattered over the southern and central parts of the country with a tendency to spread northward. The Arctic fox and the lemming are confined to the northern highlands. The common porpoise is the only cetacean occurring in the Baltic, and with the gray seal it is held responsible for damage to fisheries.

Bird life is abundant, especially in spring and summer, several types such as the teal, snipe, golden plover, and wagtail being found throughout the country. In the northern mountains the ptarmigan is common; waterfowl frequent the lakes; the golden eagle, certain buzzards, owls, and the small Lapland bunting are found. In the coniferous forests, grouse, capercaillie, and woodcock, the principal game birds, are now less common; the crane lives in marshy clearings; birds of prey, as well as crows and many other passerines, range over a wide area. In the midlands, partridges and doves are fairly common. On the coast are large numbers of gulls and terns, also eider duck and the rare sea eagle. There are very few reptiles or amphibians, and the viper is the only poisonous snake. The rivers and lakes are generally well stocked with salmon, trout, char, pike, and perch. Off the west coast, cod, flatfish, mackerel, and herring, including sprat, are caught. In the brackish waters of the Baltic both salt- and freshwater forms are found, and a small herring called strömming is caught in great numbers. The crayfish occurs in many places in Central and South Sweden. Among the lower marine animals a few types of Arctic origin are found, not only in the Baltic but even in Lakes Vänern and Vättern, having survived the changes consequent on the separation of the Baltic Sea and the Arctic Ocean.

Insects are common, even in the north. In summer in the northern lowlands the gadfly drives the reindeer to the upper pastures and snowfields. (MA. BU.)

## II. THE PEOPLE

**1. Physical Types.**—The Swedes are a markedly homogeneous people, characterized to a certain extent by typically "Nordic" traits—long slim bodies, long oval faces, straight blond hair, and blue eyes. Another strain, of uncertain prehistoric origin, with heavy, short bodies, is noticeable, for example, in Dalarna. More recently assimilated were Finns, who colonized remote woodlands in Central Sweden in the 16–17th centuries, and Walloons brought in as ironworkers early in the 17th century. Some Finnish customs and folk beliefs and Walloon family names and physical traits remain as evidence of these immigrations. The many refugees, mainly Balts, who fled to Sweden after World War II seem to have been rapidly assimilated. In the far north there are small minorities of Lapps (*see* LAPLAND) in the mountain areas and of Finns on the Finnish border (together about 0.7% of the total population).

**2. Language.**—Modern Swedish derives from the common Norse language of the Viking age and is closely related to Danish and Norwegian, although having greater phonetic resemblance to the latter. The Lapp and Finnish minorities in the north have retained their own languages. (*See* further SWEDISH LANGUAGE.)

**3. Religion.**—Sweden was converted to Christianity during the 9th–11th centuries, mainly by English and German missionaries. The established church, to which 95% of the population belongs, is Lutheran, and is divided into 13 dioceses including the archbishopric of Uppsala (founded 1164). Much of the medieval ritual survived the enforcement of the Reformation by Gustav Vasa (Gustavus I), and the modern church presents a varied picture. Roughly, it may be said that in the north the Low Church dominates, in the southwest the High Church, and in Central Sweden the Free Churches, whose growth was encouraged by 19th-century revivalism. Constitutional religious freedom was extended by an act of 1952 which recognized the right of nonadherence to any church whatever. In 1965 there were about 345,000 Protestant dissenters, 35,500 Roman Catholics, and 13,000 Jews. Since 1958 women have been permitted to take holy orders in the established church.

**4. Customs and Culture.**—For long the Swedes were a nation of peasant farmers, and traditions of the old way of life have survived in the country districts. Southern and northern types of artifacts, social organization, customs, beliefs, and popular poetry reflect variations in natural conditions and in the intensity of farming and stock raising within Sweden's vast extent. In the south, however, differences between east and west are mainly the result of external cultural influences.

With the introduction of enclosures in the first half of the 19th century and the emergence of industrialism after 1870, the extremely conservative forces represented by the large villages and the self-sufficient farms disappeared, and at the same time improving communications and more extensive popular education made for uniformity. Traditions of a local character survived longest in certain parts of Härjedalen, in upper Dalarna, in southwest Småland, and in east Skåne. There is an interest, both artistic and historical, in preserving local traditions; extensive work in recording folklore has been carried out, and Sweden has numerous folklore museums, of which the largest is Nordiska Museet in Stockholm.

Increasing urbanization has not lessened the Swedes' enthusiasm for the great open spaces of their country. Outdoor activities play an important part in modern Swedish life, and much use is made of cabins in the mountains and forests and among the skerries. Favourite forms of organized sport are association football (soccer), skiing, skating, ice hockey and bandy, sailing, rifle shooting, and *orientering* (cross-country running with map and compass). (S. SV.)

## III. HISTORY

### A. FROM THE PREHISTORIC PERIOD TO *c.* A.D. 900

**1. Earliest Peoples and Cultures.**—The first migrations into Sweden probably occurred toward the close of the last glacial epoch (*c.* 12000 B.C.), when tribes of reindeer hunters roamed across the land bridge which joined Sweden with the continent. From the early postglacial period there are traces of occupation. Finds in the peat mosses of Skåne show a typical food-gathering culture, which later (*c.* 5000–3500 B.C.) spread throughout southern Sweden. New tribes, practising agriculture and cattle rearing, made their appearance about 2500 B.C., and soon afterward a peasant culture with good continental communications was flourishing in what are now the provinces of Skåne, Halland, Bohuslän, and Västergötland. The so-called Boat-Ax culture (an outlier of the European Battle-Ax cultures) arrived about 2000 B.C. and spread rapidly. During the Late Neolithic period southern and central Sweden display the aspects of a homogeneous culture, with central European trade links; in northern Sweden the hunting culture persisted throughout the Stone and Bronze ages.

The Early Bronze Age (from *c.* 1500 B.C.) was also characterized by strong continental trade links, notably with the Danube basin. Stone Age burial customs (skeleton sepulture, megalithic monuments) were gradually replaced by cremation. Rock carvings suggest a sun cult and fertility rites. Upheavals on the Continent, combined with Celtic expansion (*see* CELT) seem to have interrupted (*c.* 500 B.C.) bronze imports to Scandinavia, and a striking poverty of finds characterizes the next few centuries. The climate, comparatively mild since the Neolithic period, deteriorated, necessitating new farming methods. At this time iron reached the north.

For the Early Iron Age (*c.* 400 B.C.–*c.* A.D. 1) the finds are also relatively scanty, showing only sporadic contacts with the La Tène (*q.v.*) culture, but they become more abundant from the Roman Iron Age (*c.* A.D. 1–400) onward. The material from this period shows that Sweden had developed a culture of its own, although naturally reflecting external influences.

Trade links between the Roman Empire and Scandinavia gave Rome some knowledge of Sweden. The *Germania* (written A.D. 98) of Tacitus gives the first description of the *Sviones* (Swedes), stated to be powerful in men, weapons, and fleets. Other ancient writers who mention Scandinavia are Ptolemy, Jordanes, and Procopius.

(*See* further SCANDINAVIAN ARCHAEOLOGY.)

**2. Swedish Expansion and the Viking Era, from A.D. 400.**—At the beginning of this period a number of independent tribes were settled in what is now Sweden, and their districts are still partly indicated by the present divisions of the country. The Swedes were centred in Uppland, around Uppsala. Farther south the Goths lived in the agricultural lands of Östergötland and Västergötland. The absence of historical sources makes it impossible to trace the long process by which the Swedes gradually subjugated the remaining areas. This historical event is reflected darkly in the Anglo-Saxon epic poem *Beowulf* (*q.v.*), which gives the earliest-known version of the word *sveorice, svearike, sverige*

(Sweden), and also in the Old Norse epic *Ynglingatal* contained in the *Heimskringla* of Snorri Sturluson (*see* ICELANDIC LITERATURE: *Snorri Sturluson*).

REFOTO FROM RAPHO GUILLUMETTE

SIXTH-CENTURY BURIAL MOUNDS ON THE SITE OF OLD UPPSALA

As a result of Arab expansion in the Mediterranean area in the 8th and 9th centuries, the trade routes along the Russian rivers to the Baltic Sea acquired enhanced importance. In the second half of the 9th century Swedish peasant chieftains secured a firm foothold in what is now eastern Russia and ruthlessly exploited the Slav population (*see* RUSSIAN HISTORY).

From strongholds, which included the river towns of Novgorod and Kiev, they controlled the trade routes along the Dnieper to the Black Sea and Constantinople and along the Volga to the Caspian Sea and the East. Trade in slaves and furs was particularly lucrative, as the rich finds of Arab silver coins in Swedish soil demonstrate. Swedish Vikings also controlled trade across the Baltic; and it was for this activity that Birka, generally regarded as Sweden's oldest town, was founded (*c.* 800). Swedish Vikings overran (*c.* 900) the important Danish trading settlement of Hedeby, and they took some part in raids against Western Europe. (*See* further VIKING.) But from the 10th century control of the Russian market began to slip from Swedish hands into those of Frisian, German, and Gotland merchants.

### B. THE EARLY MIDDLE AGES

From about the 9th century, Sweden gradually became incorporated in the sphere of Western European culture. This is epitomized by the spread of Christianity there. A few Frankish missionaries had worked in Sweden for short periods as early as the 9th century, but no systematic evangelization took place until the 11th century. The new religion gained its first foothold in the Västergötland area, where King Olaf Skötkonung (d. *c.* 1022) was baptized. Olaf and his immediate successors, his sons Anund Jakob and Emund, and Emund's son-in-law Stenkil, had to fight against the adherents of the old heathenism, who had their main centre in Uppland, the famous temple at Uppsala (*q.v.*) being the chief religious shrine. In the succeeding reigns the struggle between adherents of the two faiths was intensified. The new cult steadily gained ground, nevertheless; some dioceses had come into existence by 1120, and under King Sverker (*c.* 1130–56) Cistercian monks were introduced. The establishment of Uppsala as an archbishopric in 1164 marked the final victory of Christianity, although Sweden was not formally constituted a province of the universal church until 1248. From 1210 onward the kings sought coronation at the hands of the church.

Royal power in Sweden, however, was still very weak in the early 13th century. The various territories remained largely independent, associated only in the form of a union under a common king. The king, after election by the Swedes, had to make an *eriksgata* (royal progress) through the central provinces to receive the homage of free men and their acclamation in the local assemblies (*ting*). The provinces were divided into smaller areas, *härad* (hundreds); these again were divided into parishes and towns. Each province had its own laws, mainly written down in the 13th or early 14th centuries, which perpetuated an archaic legal system.

At the close (*c.* 1050) of the Viking period the nobles were living as territorial lords on their own estates. But as church influence gradually destroyed slavery as an institution, the estates grew less remunerative and smallholdings were therefore leased to free or freed peasants. This led to much new cultivation. Meanwhile Swedish mining, centred round Västmanland and Dalarna, increased in importance, while a network of towns sprang up in the 13th century, very largely inhabited by German merchants.

During the first two centuries of Christianity, the political centre was the Götaland area. From this region came two dynasties, which from 1130 to 1249 alternated on the throne. One, associated with Östergötland, was founded by King Sverker; the other, from Västergötland, was descended from St. Eric (reigned *c.* 1160), whose historical role was obscure and insignificant but who after his death came to be regarded as Sweden's national saint. At this time the Valdemar kings of Denmark and the Danish nobility frequently intervened in Swedish dynastic feuds.

From the 12th century onward, the highest office of state in Sweden was that of *jarl* (earl). The *jarl,* an official in many ways comparable with the Frankish mayor of the palace (*q.v.*), was the leader of the traditional levy of armed men and ships (*ledung*). His power could often rival that of the king, and he was usually supported by the nobles. An aristocratic party, the Folkungar, developed and opposed the crown fairly successfully throughout the 13th century. At about the same time the practice of the king's consulting his leading subjects brought about the formation of the Council of State.

Despite their internal struggles the Swedes retained sufficient energy, using the *ledung* as an important weapon, to expand eastward toward the old trade routes originally exploited by the Vikings. Desire for conquest was combined with Christian missionary zeal and "crusades" were aimed at the Finns, Estonians, and Russians. The southwestern parts of Finland were subjugated no later than the mid-13th century, part of Karelia in about 1300, and the city of Vyborg was established as a trading centre and military base. The island of Gotland was also incorporated in the kingdom of Sweden. But of modern Sweden, Skåne (Scania), Blekinge, and Halland still belonged to Denmark and Bohuslän, Härjedalen, and Jämtland to Norway.

### C. THE LATER MIDDLE AGES

**1. Birger Jarl and His Successors to 1319.**—The dynasty of St. Eric came to an end with the death of Eric Ericsson (1222–49); the new elected king was his nephew Valdemar (1250–75), a minor whose father Birger, *jarl* since 1248, ruled until his death in 1266. Birger Jarl (*q.v.*) fought the aristocratic Folkung Party, severely defeating it in 1248 and 1251. He supported the church and enhanced the power of the crown by issuing the first Swedish national laws ordering the maintenance of peace in the church, the home, the *Ting* (assembly), and for women. Daughters as well as sons were granted inheritance rights. By granting privileges he encouraged the trade of the Lübeck merchants in Sweden.

Birger Jarl's policy was continued by his second son, Magnus Ladulås (1275–90), who after a revolt against his brother Valdemar was hailed as king. Magnus further strengthened his authority and reorganized the taxation system, replacing the obligation to take part in the *ledung* by fixed dues. He granted the church considerable freedom from taxation, however. By the Ordinance of Alsnö in 1280, those who performed military service were declared exempt from taxation; thus a privileged aristocracy was established, from which an army of knights could be raised. Collaboration between king and nobility was increased by the establishment of new offices of state, the *drots, marsk,* and *kansler,* corresponding roughly to those of lord high steward, marshal or constable, and chancellor. The office of *jarl* was now suppressed. The state council, of some importance since *c.* 1220, was in about 1280 extended and given a permanent status. Magnus' reign was characterized by closer relations with Denmark, expressed by the marriages of his daughter Ingeborg with King Eric VI Menved and of his son Birger with Eric's sister Märta.

During the minority of Birger Magnusson (1290–1318), the government was in the hands of the *marsk* Torgils Knutsson, who furthered the interests of the nobility at the expense of the church. He also extended Swedish power in Finland. On assuming personal power, Birger at first sought the *marsk*'s support against his two rebellious brothers, the dukes Eric and Valdemar. But the three brothers were reconciled in 1305, and Birger then had Torgils executed. However, the quarrel broke out afresh, and Birger was taken prisoner (1306) by the dukes. He was released on the intervention of Eric Menved, and in 1310 the country was partitioned among the three brothers, Duke Eric using a Norwegian marriage alliance with the daughter and heiress of Haakon V to combine western Sweden with adjoining portions of Denmark and Norway. But in 1317 King Birger managed to have his brothers seized and thrown into prison, where they died. The aristocracy now rose to avenge the dukes; Birger was driven into exile in Denmark, and in 1319 Duke Eric's three-year-old son Magnus (*q.v.*) was elected successor to the throne. He inherited the crown of Norway from his grandfather Haakon the same year. A regency was set up under the *drots* Mats Kettilmundsson.

**2. Magnus II Ericsson to the Scandinavian Union.**—The succeeding decades were peaceful, a time of cultural and economic progress. A colourful figure of the period was St. Bridget (*q.v.;* Birgitta). By a treaty (1323) with Novgorod, the frontier between Russia and Sweden through Finland was defined. Within Sweden itself the establishment (1347) of a common law, superseding the old provincial laws, did much to integrate the various provinces. However, the elective nature of the monarchy and the king's obligation to consult his council were reaffirmed. Although feudalism, as found in France and Germany, had never existed in Sweden, some characteristics of the system of chivalry appeared there in the 14th century. Swedish trade became dominated by the Hanseatic League (*q.v.*), which entirely controlled the export of iron, copper, hides, furs, and butter; in the towns the most powerful burghers were German merchants.

In the latter years of his reign King Magnus II (VI of Norway) Ericsson encountered increasing opposition. His taxation policy antagonized the church and the aristocracy, and unsuccessful wars with Russia and Denmark contributed to the discontent. The Danish king Valdemar IV seized the opportunity to recapture (1360) Skåne and Blekinge, which Sweden had won in 1332, and took Gotland (1361). Magnus made peace with King Valdemar (1363), marrying his son, Haakon, to Valdemar's daughter and heiress, Margaret. Haakon had since 1355 been king of Norway and his father's co-regent in Sweden. The Swedish nobles, alarmed at the prospect of Haakon's succession, rebelled; they called in Albert (Albrecht) of Mecklenburg, a nephew of King Magnus, who fought Magnus and Haakon and finally became king in 1364. He was forced, however, to buy aid by making substantial concessions to the aristocracy (1371). Sweden's real master at this time was its greatest and richest landowner, the *drots* Bo Jonsson Grip. After Bo Jonsson's death (1386) Albert tried to assert his authority, but the Swedish nobles now made an agreement with Margaret, who, since the death of her father, Valdemar (1375), and her husband, Haakon (1380), had been regent in Denmark and Norway. Albert was deposed (1389) and she became regent in Sweden also. There, by skilfully playing off different groups and interests, she strengthened the royal power and recovered many recently alienated crown estates. Tax reforms were introduced, and bailiffs subordinate to the regent were appointed to administer finances. Margaret's only son had died in childhood, so she designated as her successor Eric (*q.v.*) of Pomerania, her great-nephew. At a meeting of nobles from all over Scandinavia at Kalmar in June 1397, Eric was crowned king of the three kingdoms.

**3. Eric of Pomerania to Christian II.**—After Margaret's death (1412) Eric of Pomerania strove to weld the Scandinavian kingdoms into a centralized absolute monarchy and to extend the frontiers of Denmark southward. The former aim antagonized the Swedish Council of State, the latter led to a protracted war with Holstein. Eric's coinage policy and tax reorganizations aroused discontent among the peasants, and when the Hanseatic League, as part of the Holstein war, blockaded Eric's states, export of iron and copper was stopped. This outraged the miners of Västmanland and Dalarna, and a mine owner of the petty nobility, Engelbrekt Engelbrektsson (d. 1436), led a popular rebellion in 1434. Opposition was to royal absolutism rather than to the Scandinavian union. After some years' fighting Eric was deposed (1439 in Denmark and Sweden; 1442 in Norway). The council, led by the ambitious *marsk* Karl Knutsson Bonde, seized power, retaining its substance even after the election of a new union king, Christopher of Bavaria (1441–48). The council favoured aristocratic pretensions, but the part played by the common people in these struggles was constitutionally significant, for representatives of the peasantry began to attend state meetings. In this way the Swedish *Riksdag* (Parliament) came into being, with its four estates of nobles, clergy, burghers, and peasants.

On Christopher's death Karl Knutsson (*see* CHARLES VIII) was elected king of Sweden while Christian I (*q.v.*) of Oldenburg was hailed king in Denmark. In 1457 Charles was exiled by a faction of nobles under Archbishop Jöns Bengtsson Oxenstierna and Christian was elected king of Sweden (1457). A revolt against Christian breaking out (1464), Charles returned but held the crown for only six months, and again, with the help of the brothers Axelsson Tott, from 1467 until his death in 1470. Sten Sture the Elder (*see* STURE), a kinsman of the powerful Axelssons, was made state administrator in 1471. Christian was finally defeated at the battle of Brunkeberg (near Stockholm) in 1471. But despite Sten Sture's careful financial policy and the broad support he commanded from miners, burghers, and peasants, the Council of State desired to reestablish the union and hailed Christian's son Hans (Johannes) as king (*see* JOHN [Hans]) in 1497. They then found John's policies distasteful, and a revolt in 1501 led to the reappointment of Sten Sture as regent. Sten died in 1503 and was succeeded in office first by Svante (Nilsson) Sture (d. 1512) and then by Svante's son Sten Sture the Younger. Sten sought to establish a virtual dictatorship, but he was wounded in battle (1520) fighting against the Danish king Christian II (*q.v.*) and died soon afterward. Christian, crowned king of Sweden the following autumn, finally destroyed Sture's party in the so-called Stockholm blood bath in November 1520. (L. T. N.)

### D. The Early Vasa Kings, 1520–1611

**1. Gustavus I Vasa (1523–60) and the Reformation.**—The defeat of Sten Sture's party and the massacre of so many of its leaders left Gustavus I (*q.v.*) Vasa, who had fought in Sture's army, as the only prominent opponent of Christian II. His ability to continue the struggle, however, depended very largely on the aid of Lübeck, which feared Christian's plans for economic hegemony of the Baltic. With Lübeck's aid—perhaps on Lübeck's insistence—Gustavus was chosen king at Strängnäs in June 1523. He was forced to concede far-reaching economic privileges which gave Lübeck a dominant position in the Swedish economy. But he was not content to be Lübeck's puppet, and he resisted its demands throughout his reign. At first, however, he had no option but to extract money from his subjects, to meet Lübeck's demands; the resulting financial crisis led directly to the Reformation in Sweden.

The medieval Swedish church had escaped the Hussite or Wycliffite heresies. It had grown comparatively wealthy through tax exemptions, donations, and trade, and it probably owned something like a quarter of the land. But it was engaged in a costly struggle with the nobility for tax-exempted land; and a connection, through its leaders, with the higher aristocracy, which had supported the union, led to clashes with the Sture party. For the Stures had aimed increasingly at a strong monarchy, free of the constitutional checks which the aristocracy had traditionally supplied, and effectively in control of a national church. Their view that the church should contribute when the country was in need was not far removed from the notion that the wealth of the church is the wealth of the people, which became accepted doctrine when Lutheranism reached Sweden in the early 1520s. The pressure of Lübeck, the jealousy of the nobility, the traditional Sture policy that the king ought not to suffer "two lords in one land," and finally the refusal of the papacy to abandon clerics (such as Archbishop Gustavus Trolle) who had become politically impossible as partisans of Denmark—these were the factors that combined to produce the Reformation. The plunder of the church and the bribing of the nobility with church lands began after the Diet of Västerås in 1527 and continued throughout the reign of Gustavus. However, the spoils of the church made the crown, for the first time, really wealthy, and so gave strength and stability to monarchy and country.

Doctrinally the Swedish Reformation was Lutheran. Its most conspicuous leaders were the brothers Olaus and Laurentius Petri (*q.v.*), each of whom had great literary gifts; their writing did much to standardize the modern language of their country, as Luther's did in Germany. Except in Stockholm, Protestantism at first made slow progress. It was a religion to which the king had recourse for national ends, but not for a generation was it a national religion. Revolts in Västergötland (1529) and Dalarna (1531), and the great revolt of Nils Dacke in Småland (1542–43), bore witness to the unpopularity of the new services. Indeed, the decisive initial step at Västerås in 1527 had been forced through by the king only by a threat to abdicate. As consequences of this situation, considerable elements of the old faith were allowed to remain, there was a wide toleration of opinion, and doctrinally the position was kept remarkably vague. Gustavus himself was concerned only with the royal supremacy, and this led him, at the end of the 1530s, to a sharp quarrel with the reformers and an attempt to treat the church as a mere department of state.

The foreign policy of the reign was a reflection of these internal problems. Sweden was temporarily secure from any attempt to revive the union with Denmark, for Christian II had been driven from the Danish throne (1523) by his uncle, Frederick I, and until his death (1559) Frederick and his successor, Christian III, were linked to Gustavus by common fear of his restoration. This was seen clearly in the so-called Counts' War (1534–36), when Sweden and Denmark defeated an attempt by Lübeck and a coalition of German princes to restore Christian II, Gustavus taking the opportunity to break free from Lübeck's control. It appeared again in the Swedish-Danish alliance of Brömsebro (1541), which linked Gustavus at second hand to the League of Schmalkalden (his efforts to join the League itself having failed, but Denmark being a member) and brought Sweden into the French camp. But the country's situation prescribed caution in foreign affairs, and after 1535 Gustavus' only adventure was a brief war with Muscovy (1554–57). Gustavus' avoidance of risk was justified by the situation of the country and by results. When he died in 1560 the monarchy was strong and rich; it had acquired a considerable navy and had begun (since 1544) to form that army of conscript militiamen which was to be the instrument of Sweden's later greatness. Above all, by the Succession Pact of 1544 Gustavus had obtained the assent of his estates to the transformation of Sweden from an elective to a hereditary monarchy. On his death his eldest son, Eric XIV (*q.v.*), at once succeeded him.

**2. Eric XIV (1560–68), John III (1568–92), Sigismund (1592–99), and Charles IX (1607–11).**—On Eric's accession the latent struggle between the principles of popular despotism and aristocratic constitutionalism was renewed. It was heightened by the difficulties provoked by Gustavus' will, in which he had bequeathed to his younger sons large duchies, semi-independent of the crown. John, the eldest of Eric's half-brothers, had been made duke of Finland, where he attempted to carry on a private foreign policy at variance with that of the crown. Eric took strong measures. By the Articles of Arboga (1561) he forced a drastic curtailment in the franchises of the royal dukes, and in 1562 he imprisoned John. A specially constituted High Court became an instrument of tyranny against Eric's supposed enemies and particularly against members of the higher nobility.

Arbitrary, despotic, and proud, Eric had a high idea of his dignity. He attributed his failure to bring off a satisfactory foreign marriage to the ill will of his noble emissaries, and so intensified his vendetta against the aristocracy. His marriage with Karin Månsdotter, a girl of humble origin who had been his mistress, was at once a calculated insult to the aristocracy and a deliberate assertion of sovereign power. He took care, however, to cultivate the *Riksdag,* and when possible got it to endorse his actions; had he reigned longer, he might well have developed a real parliamentary despotism. In 1567, however, a sudden crisis of the morbid suspiciousness to which he was prone led him to murder Nils Sture and to order the slaughter of two other members of the influential Sture family. The deed temporarily unhinged him. He released his brother John from prison (1567) and after some weeks resumed the conduct of government. But John, with his younger brother Charles (later Charles IX), rose in revolt, deposed him, and in 1568 ascended the throne as John III (*q.v.*).

Eric's removal took place at a moment when Sweden was heavily engaged in war with Denmark and Poland. The collapse of the Livonian state ruled by the Knights of the Sword (a branch of the Teutonic Order), in the 1550s, had led to a scramble among their neighbours for the reversion to their territories. Eric, fearing that Denmark might make dangerous gains in this area, and hoping to secure control of the lucrative trade to Russia, had responded to an appeal from Reval (now Tallinn) for protection. A Swedish force went to Estonia, and the first stone in the later Swedish empire was laid. Eric, realizing that he must choose between the friendship of Russia and that of Poland, opted for Russia. But John had made a Polish marriage and hoped for gains of his own in Livonia. At the same time, Frederick II of Denmark, who aspired to recreate the old Scandinavian union, declared war on Sweden; and Sigismund II Augustus of Poland shortly joined him.

The Seven Years' War of the North (1563–70), in spite of brilliant successes by the Swedish navy, imposed a heavy strain on the country, which was almost blockaded from access from Western Europe. By the Peace of Stettin (December 1570) Sweden ceded its Estonian lands and had to pay a heavy indemnity to Denmark. John III contrived to evade compliance with the former provision, and for most of his reign he carried on a long and ultimately successful struggle with Russia. By the Peace of Täysinä (1595) Sweden established its occupation of most of Estonia, including the ports of Narva and Reval.

Meanwhile John III had been embarking on a religious policy of his own, designed to pave the way for a general reconciliation between the Protestant world and Rome. The policy broke down on Rome's refusal to make the concessions he considered indispensable, but in any case it had provoked strong reactions in Sweden. The country was now solidly Lutheran, and the Swedish Church was adopting precise doctrinal positions in the face of the imminence of a Roman Catholic successor; for Sigismund, John's heir, had taken the religion of his Polish mother. In 1587 Sigismund was elected king of Poland (Sigismund III; *q.v.*), and soon proved himself an ardent champion of the Counter-Reformation. For Sweden the dynastic union with Poland had obvious advantages for foreign policy, and an absentee monarch might well allow the higher aristocracy to regain the position they had lost since 1523. But the prospect of a return to Rome was nowhere popular. The accession of Sigismund in 1592 therefore inaugurated a period of domestic disturbance in which the cause of Protestantism offered a rallying cry to those who opposed the king. Foremost among these was Charles (*see* CHARLES IX), youngest son of Gustavus I, brother of John III, and uncle of Sigismund.

Charles rallied the church round him at Uppsala in 1593 in a kind of national covenant to defend the Lutheran cause. At the same time he persuaded the aristocratic council to unite with him in opposing the king's attempt to rule Sweden from Poland. The union was only temporary, however, and the council was not prepared to follow Charles into more or less open rebellion against the lawful sovereign, who was crowned in February 1594. By 1597 the solid national front of 1593 was dissolving: the council's members were seeking refuge in Poland, and Charles, supported mainly by the lower orders of the *Riksdag,* had passed from constitutional opposition to revolution. In 1598 Sigismund went to Sweden for the second time (his first visit was 1593–94), but his army was defeated at Stångebro. He failed to carry out the terms then agreed upon and so in 1599 was deposed by the *Riksdag*. The next year, at Linköping, Charles executed four of his leading noble opponents. He did not at once call himself king, however, and his coronation was deferred till 1607 because he had some scruples about the rights of John III's younger son, John. But from 1604, when young John renounced his claim and the *Riksdag* agreed to the Succession Pact of Norrköping, the crown was effectively transferred to the younger Vasa line.

The deposition of Sigismund led to a dynastic feud which lasted for nearly 60 years and which became linked with the old rivalry for the control of Estonia and Livonia and also with the struggle to preserve the Protestantism of the north. At first Poland had the advantage, and in 1605 Charles suffered at Kirkholm one of the most disastrous defeats of Swedish history. Thereafter, for some years, the duel was transferred to Russia, where Sigismund sought to establish himself or his son Wladyslaw as tsar (*see* RUSSIAN HISTORY). At the same time Charles's rash and provocative policy in the Baltic and the Arctic aroused the enmity of Denmark, where the young and ambitious king Christian IV hoped to re-establish the old Scandinavian union. When Charles died in 1611 he thus bequeathed to his son, Gustavus II (*q.v.*) Adolphus, wars with Denmark and Poland and in Russia. If the prospect in the field of foreign affairs was gloomy, the situation at home was no better. Charles's rule had alarmed and alienated the nobility; the country was exhausted by long wars; methods of administration were outdated, and the army and navy required drastic reform.

E. THE AGE OF SWEDISH GREATNESS, 1611–1718

**1. Gustavus II Adolphus (1611–32).**—On the accession of Gustavus Adolphus the nobility, led by Axel Gustafsson Oxenstierna (*q.v.*), extorted from the young king (who was not yet 17), as the price of his immediate assumption of government, a charter which was intended to guarantee the country against the excesses of Charles's parliamentary despotism and which might well have led to a long struggle between monarchy and aristocracy. That it did not do so was due to the restraint and wisdom of Gustavus and of Oxenstierna and to the reciprocal respect and affection which developed between them. Oxenstierna, created chancellor in 1612, retained that office, and the king's confidence, for the whole of the reign. Together they carried through a remarkable series of measures which make Gustavus' reign one of the great reforming epochs of Swedish history and which did much to make possible the emergence of Sweden for a time as a great power. These included reforms of the central and local government and of the judiciary, the systematic development and exploitation of the mineral resources of the country, the building up of an adequate armaments industry, the encouragement of foreign investment, the recruitment of foreign artisans and entrepreneurs, and the beginnings of the conversion of an increasing proportion of the old revenues in kind into revenues in cash. At the same time the navy was thoroughly overhauled and the army was trained in a new style of tactics which was to carry all before it on the battlefields of Germany. The reign was also a period of important educational progress, especially in regard to the expansion and endowment of the University of Uppsala.

In foreign affairs, although Gustavus was forced to accept a hard peace with Denmark in 1613, the first two decades of the reign saw the gradual emergence of Sweden, rather than Denmark, as the stronger Scandinavian power. The war in Russia was brought to a successful conclusion at Stolbova in 1617 by a peace which gave Sweden continuous territorial connection between Finland and Estonia and shut Russia off from access to the Baltic. The war with Poland went in Sweden's favour too. In 1629 Gustavus was able to conclude a six years' truce at Altmark which left him in possession of most of Livonia and permitted him to finance his coming war in Germany from the tolls at Prussian harbours.

Thus by 1630 Sweden had acquired a considerable Baltic empire and would have been in a strong position to settle old scores with Denmark. But the danger to Protestantism in Germany had provoked a strong sympathetic response in Sweden, and, further, Gustavus feared that an imperialist occupation of north Germany might be the prelude to an attempt to restore Sigismund to the Swedish throne. The expedition he took to Germany in 1630 (*see* THIRTY YEARS' WAR) was thus designed both to defend the cause of Protestantism and to protect Sweden's interests. Its brilliant success not merely changed the history of Germany but profoundly affected the history of Sweden. (MI. R.)

**2. Queen Christina (1644–54).**—The death of Gustavus Adolphus at the Battle of Lützen in November 1632 produced a crisis. His daughter Christina (*q.v.*), still a minor, was recognized as queen, and the regency was undertaken first by a Council of the Realm (*Riksråd*) and subsequently by five senators, in accordance with the *Form of Government* which, drawn up by Oxenstierna and approved by Gustavus shortly before his death, was approved by the *Riksdag* in 1634. By this constitution the five senators were also to be the leaders or presidents of five colleges or committees formed from a total council of 25, which was responsible for central government. Local government was to be in the hands of provincial governors.

During Christina's minority the government was controlled by Oxenstierna, who as chancellor was one of the five senators. He continued Gustavus' policy both at home and abroad. Although the treaty made with France in 1631 was renewed in April 1633, Sweden was severely defeated (autumn 1634) by imperial forces under Spanish command and its prestige was much damaged. As a result, Saxony made peace with the emperor in 1635 and Brandenburg followed in 1636; both then declared war on Sweden. Field Marshal Johan Banér (*q.v.*), however, won victories for Sweden at Wittstock (1636) and Chemnitz (1639). That won by Banér's successor, Lennart Torstensson (*q.v.*), was so decisive that Oxenstierna could now deploy the Swedish army against another enemy, Denmark. Torstensson invaded Jutland in 1643. The Danish king Christian IV was obliged to make peace at Brömsebro (Christianopel) in 1645, ceding to Sweden Jämtland and Härjedalen (Norway), Halland (Denmark), and the islands of Gotland and Ösel, and exempting from the Öresund tolls goods destined for Sweden and the Baltic provinces.

Christina had begun her personal rule in 1644. At first she clashed with Oxenstierna and was personally responsible for moves which contributed to the Peace of Westphalia, ending the Thirty Years' War in 1648. By this treaty Sweden acquired in Germany parts of Pomerania, the Baltic port of Wismar, the archbishopric of Bremen and the bishopric of Verden, and prize money for the Swedish soldiers. After 1650, however, she worked more closely with Oxenstierna. Although Christina encouraged trade and industry, she could not solve the desperate financial problems caused by prolonged war and aggravated by her own extravagance. In 1654 she became a Catholic and abdicated, having in 1649 declared as her successor her cousin Charles Gustavus (Charles X).

**3. Charles X Gustavus (1654–60).**—On the accession in 1654 of Charles X (*q.v.*) the costs of the court were cut down, and in the *Riksdag* of 1655 he imposed the so-called Reduction. By this law the nobles were obliged to restore to the crown certain endowed estates and a quarter of those granted since 1633. In future certain estates were to be given only temporarily, automatically reverting to the crown on the accession of a new monarch. The law was at once applied but ceased to operate during the years of war which followed.

Charles X's short reign was one of almost continual warfare, and Charles himself was a skilful general. The truce of Altmark, made with Poland in 1629, had been renewed in 1635, but because the Russians showed signs of attacking Poland, and therefore possibly encircling the trans-Baltic possessions of Sweden, Charles and the *Riksdag* decided to act first. He took Warsaw and Cracow (1655) and the Polish king, John Casimir, fled. But the successful defense of the monastery of Czestochowa late in 1655 revived Polish hopes. John Casimir returned to Poland, and two years of fruitless fighting ensued. In 1656 the Russians began an attack upon the Swedish Baltic provinces and Charles made an alliance with Frederick William, elector of Brandenburg. The emperor joined Sweden's enemies in the same year and Holland and Denmark followed. Brandenburg now deserted Sweden.

Fortunately for Sweden, these numerous enemies did not cooperate. Charles turned resolutely on Denmark, took Jutland, and led his troops over the ice to Fyn and then across the other islands to Sjaelland. Denmark was forced to make peace in February 1658 at Roskilde, ceding the Skåne provinces, the island of Bornholm, and Trondheim and Bohuslän in Norway. Both kingdoms were to cooperate to keep foreign fleets out of the Baltic. However, Dutch influence in Denmark remained strong, and Charles dared not turn to deal with problems in the east while there was any danger of the Dutch inciting Denmark to attack him. He therefore himself renewed the war in August 1658. But the Danes now put up a spirited resistance, and an attack on Copenhagen was repulsed (February 1659). Trondheim and Bornholm resisted

Swedish control. In this difficult situation, a *Riksdag* was summoned to Göteborg early in 1660, but Charles died (Feb. 13) during its session. (S. I. O.)

**4. The Regency (1660–75).**—Charles X was succeeded by his son Charles XI (*q.v.*), a child of four, and the antiroyalist leaders of the nobility therefore decided to reverse the trends of recent internal policy. On his death bed Charles X had tried to safeguard the power of the crown, so intimately bound up with the Reduction, by naming a regency pledged to carry on his reform plans. The antiroyalist party, however, prevailed upon the Estates to declare Charles X's will null and void, since it had been made without the Estates' consent. By making subsequent changes in the composition of the regency and the council, the high nobility secured control of the government. The *Riksdag* charged the new government with the continuation of the Reduction, but the qualifying clause "to be pursued with justice and moderation," inserted by the efforts of the nobility, was interpreted in such a way that the resumption of alienated crown land came to a virtual standstill.

The Estates also charged the government with procuring peace. With French help the status quo of 1648 was restored at the Peace of Oliva (April 1660) with the emperor Leopold I, Brandenburg, and Poland. Because of the critical illness of John Casimir of Poland, Sweden obtained two important advantages: the queen of Poland, anxious to gain support for the election of one of John Casimir's sons, agreed to renounce "eternally" both the Polish Vasa claim to the Swedish crown and the Polish claim on Swedish Livonia. At the Peace of Copenhagen (May 1660) Sweden restored to Denmark-Norway the province of Trondheim, with its access to the Atlantic, and the island of Bornholm. A third gain from the Roskilde Treaty of 1658 was also relinquished: the clause forbidding foreign navies to enter the Baltic was rescinded at the demand of England and the United Provinces. The Dutch, having supported Denmark-Norway, had already (November 1659) gained equality with Swedish subjects in respect of trade with the Swedish Baltic provinces. A double blow was thus struck at Sweden's hopes of dominating the Baltic politically and at its plans for commercial and maritime competition with the Dutch. The peace treaties of Oliva and Copenhagen, however, strengthened Sweden's hand in negotiations with Russia. In the Peace of Kardis (June 1661), Russia again recognized Swedish possession of Karelia, Ingria (Ingermanland), and Estonia.

Sweden now regarded itself as a satiated power; aggressive or preventive wars were no longer visualized as practical politics, and Sweden never exceeded these frontiers. Its population was now a little over 2,000,000, rising by the year 1700 to nearly 3,000,000, half of whom lived outside Sweden-Finland. The cohesion in the Swedish Empire was provided by Swedish political and economic policy and by Swedish civil and military administration.

What Swedish historians have labeled "the problem of the peace" remained: how to finance an army and a navy and erect fortifications to safeguard its great power position. On this problem there was no agreement. The non-noble Estates and many of the nobility (mainly of the lower and bureaucratic ranks) favoured a policy whereby the king should maintain the necessary forces by a resumption of alienated land more far-reaching than the one-quarter Reduction envisaged under Charles X, both in Sweden-Finland and in the Swedish Empire. The higher nobility, however, by securing control at the accession of Charles XI, were able to impose their solution: reliance on foreign subsidies, mainly from France, until expansion of trade and shipping (particularly the attempts at linking Russian and Polish trade with Europe via Swedish ports) should produce sufficient income in tolls and dues to pay for defense.

A distinction used to be drawn between the "pro-French" and "anti-French" regents and councilors of Sweden to explain changes in foreign policy. Modern historians, however, have focused attention more on the common aim of these men: a balancing policy between the European powers, perpetuating the peace of 1648 but allowing Sweden by its services as an armed mediator to reap advantages from existing tension between France and the Habsburg bloc, on the one hand, and between the two maritime powers, England and the United Provinces, on the other. Until 1675 the balancing policy was on the whole successful and brought various gains, chief of which was the formal installation (1664) of Sweden in the Holy Roman Empire (denied since 1648 by successive emperors) following a period of collaboration with the Habsburgs, both Spanish and Austrians, and with Brandenburg.

**5. The War of 1675.**—Charles XI was declared of age in 1672, but in reality the regents remained in control. Under the regency the Swedish Bank had been established in 1668 and the University of Lund founded in the same year. But the armed forces had been neglected in a period of great international tension; and, moreover, the regency had underestimated the danger of involving Sweden in a war not essential for its own defense when they signed a subsidy treaty with France in 1669. By the treaty Sweden undertook to prevent the emperor and other princes of the Holy Roman Empire from assisting the Dutch during the attack which Louis XIV and England were planning on the United Provinces. At most the Swedish government visualized its troops acting as an auxiliary corps while Sweden remained neutral. The real attraction of the treaty was embodied in secret articles; Sweden was by Louis XIV accorded that position of arbiter in the empire which it had long desired, and thought itself to have been made the arbiter also in western Europe by Louis's guarantee of the integrity of the southern Netherlands and his promise "not to ruin the Dutch."

Swedish calculations miscarried. After attacking the United Provinces in 1672 (*see* DUTCH WARS) Louis outmaneuvered the Swedish regents; by withholding money he was able to dictate the movements of the Swedish troops in Germany. The crossing of the Brandenburg frontier by Swedish troops from Swedish Pomerania in 1674 led to the Swedish defeat at Fehrbellin in June 1675 (partly explained by Sweden's desire to avoid a full-scale war), and Brandenburg and its allies, the United Provinces and the emperor, declared war on Sweden. This encouraged Denmark-Norway to invade Skåne.

The war for Skåne (1675–79) proved a tough one. The regents and most of the councilors were discredited by the poor state of the army and navy, and Charles XI himself and new men, prominent among them Johan Gyllenstierna (*q.v.*), took over the leadership both in the armed forces and in the administration. The Swedish victory at Lund (December 1676) marked a turning point, and by 1678 the Danish-Norwegian forces had been expelled and the guerrilla fighters of Skåne subdued. Peace was made at the Treaty of Lund (September 1679), and Denmark gave up hopes of reconquering Skåne. A joint future stand was agreed upon against Dutch commercial predominance in the Baltic, and the alliance was sealed by the marriage (arranged before the war) of Charles XI with Ulrika Eleanora, sister of Christian V of Denmark-Norway. Historians have often interpreted this treaty as an "alliance of equal partners," but recent research shows that Gyllenstierna and Charles envisaged Sweden as the dominant force.

During the war Sweden's German possessions had been overrun by the armies of the emperor, the elector of Brandenburg, and Denmark. Thanks to Louis XIV's diplomatic efforts, in the treaties of Nijmegen (*q.v.;* February 1679), St. Germain (June 1679), and Fontainebleau (September 1679), these were all restored except a small strip of Pomerania ceded to Brandenburg. However, the manner in which these treaties were concluded, with no consultation with the Swedish government, offended Charles XI. The Swedes also regretted that the Dutch were not deprived of their commercial advantages gained from Sweden in the 1650s.

**6. The Personal Rule of Charles XI (1679–97).**—The king and his new advisers were now determined to make Sweden independent of foreign subsidy treaties. "Reduction," the resumption of alienated crown land, or of land equivalent in value in respect of yearly income, was systematically pursued and continually widened from the one-quarter demanded by Charles X. At the end of the reign the crown, from having been in possession of less than one percent of all land in Sweden-Finland in 1679, once more held, as in the first quarter of the 16th century, over 30%. In the trans-Baltic provinces all land alienated during the period of Swedish rule had been resumed and the resumption of land alienated before that time had begun. Out of the total state income a fixed budget was set up which continued until 1809. This permitted a force of 25,000 hired troops for garrison duties, the payment of a civil administration embracing also church and education, and finally the maintenance of a national army of 40,000 men and a navy built to compete with the strength of Denmark-Norway and based at the new southern port, Karlskrona. During the work of reorganization, absolutism was introduced into Sweden and the Swedish Baltic provinces as a means to force through reform and to safeguard the crown against any future reversal of its achievements. In Sweden's German provinces, absolutism could not become the form of government since the constitutions of these possessions had been guaranteed by the Treaties of Westphalia (1648).

Charles XI's reign saw the encouragement of the arts, the growth of the capital, Stockholm, and the full incorporation into Sweden-Finland of the Danish and Norwegian provinces conquered under Charles X; the war of 1700–21 (*see* below) produced no guerrilla fighting in Skåne. In foreign affairs Charles XI and his advisers continued the "balancing policy." Sweden at first cooperated with the Dutch and the emperor (Treaty of The Hague, 1681) against Louis XIV, but the personal union of England and the United Provinces under William III in 1688 was considered as serious a threat to the balance of power as French expansion. For this reason Sweden remained uncommitted during the War of the Grand Alliance (*q.v.;* 1689–97), though Charles XI supplied the emperor with his quota of troops in respect of his duties as an imperial prince. An additional motive for neutrality was Sweden's desire to profit from the war in building up its commerce and shipping; its merchant fleet rose to 730 ships, the highest point ever reached in the great power period. Charles XI was made mediator at the Congress of Rijswijk (1697), but this remained an empty honour, Sweden gaining neither prestige nor advantage from its neutrality. During the war Sweden and Denmark-Norway intermittently cooperated in a policy of "armed neutrality" to protect common maritime and commercial interests, but at the same time Charles XI and his advisers, including Count Bengt Oxenstierna, contained Denmark from the south by a vigorous support of the duke of Holstein-Gottorp and the latter's possessions and rights in the ducal parts of Schleswig and Holstein. Before Charles XI's death (April 1697) he arranged for the dynastic ties with the house of Holstein-Gottorp to be continued by a marriage between his elder daughter, Hedvig Sophia, and his nephew Frederick Adolphus, duke of Holstein-Gottorp since 1694.

**7. Charles XII (1697–1718).**—Holstein-Gottorp issues loomed large in the early days of the reign of Charles XI's young son, Charles XII (*q.v.*). On Charles XI's death, Christian V of Denmark-Norway invaded the ducal parts of Schleswig-Holstein and razed the fortifications which Frederick Adolphus, with Swedish consent and help, was building there. The duke fled to Sweden. In an attempt to break Sweden's connection with Holstein-Gottorp, Christian V proposed to the regents of Charles XII a Danish dynastic alliance by the marriage of his daughter Sophia to Charles XII. The regents, however, had learned of Danish negotiations with Prussia and Russia for an anti-Swedish alliance, and the marriage offer was shelved. Charles XII, declared of age in November 1697, continued along traditional pro-Holstein-Gottorp lines; the marriage between Frederick Adolphus and Hedvig Sophia took place in 1698, and the Swedish army in Germany was reinforced to permit the ducal fortifications to be reerected. This Swedish defiance of Denmark-Norway accelerated Danish negotiations for an attack on Sweden. Those with Frederick Augustus I of Saxony (which the Swedish intelligence service did not discover) were completed in 1698 by Christian V and renewed in 1699 by his successor, Frederick IV; those with Tsar Peter of Russia bore fruit by 1700, and in February 1700 war broke out (*see* NORTHERN WAR).

Denmark-Norway and its allies had expected the Swedish nobility to rise against absolutism and the Reduction once Charles XII was attacked; but they remained loyal. The reorganized army and the newly built navy proved their worth, as did the young king himself, and the anti-Swedish coalition, reinforced by Prussia and Hanover in 1714, was kept at bay till Charles XII's death in November 1718 in spite of setbacks between 1709 and 1715.

Sweden, however, by 1718 was tired of absolutism and of war. The plague of 1710–11 (which cost many more lives than the war) and the loss of both civilian administrators and officers, imprisoned in Russia since 1709, had their effect. The loss of the Swedish Empire and the Russian occupation of Finland meant more. But in the last instance the intense dislike of the innovations in the financial and bureaucratic machinery which Charles XII had introduced in his attempt to mobilize the country's resources for the war effort unseated absolutism. Preparations for its overthrow had been made in the event of the king's death by those who resented the attempts at cabinet government, often with foreign helpers, and who contrasted it unfavourably with the "Swedish" bureaucratic absolutism of Charles XI's days.

F. THE GROWTH OF PARLIAMENTARY GOVERNMENT, 1718–1772

**1. Ulrika Eleonora (1718–20).**—Charles never married, and the absence of a direct heir facilitated the revolution, since those who favoured a return to constitutional government could play off two possible claimants, Charles XII's only surviving sister, Ulrika Eleonora, wife of Frederick of Hesse-Kassel, and the late king's nephew, Charles Frederick, duke of Holstein-Gottorp (the son of Hedvig Sophia and Frederick Adolphus). Ulrika Eleanora (*q.v.*) let herself be proclaimed hereditary ruler on the news of her brother's death; but the revolutionary forces in army and administration prevailed upon her by January 1719 to accept the crown from the Estates as an elected queen. She was crowned in May only after having sworn to honour a constitution to be formulated by the Estates. Even so, she proved to be too steeped in the absolutist tradition, and as her personal desire was for a joint rule with her husband this was cleverly used to engineer her abdication (1720) in favour of her husband, who became Frederick I (*q.v.*).

**2. Frederick I (1720–51).**—The crown, already weakened by the fact that Frederick I was an elected king, and circumscribed by the constitution of 1720, in which the king possessed only two votes in the council and could thus be outvoted, lost further prestige by the setbacks to Frederick's peace plans. European-wide support against Tsar Peter—which George I, elector of Hanover and king of England, had promised when Frederick agreed to cede Bremen and Verden to Hanover (November 1719) and most of Swedish Pomerania to Prussia (January 1720)—failed to materialize. Sweden was therefore forced to make peace with Russia at the Treaty of Nystad (Sept. 10, 1721), ceding Ingria, Estonia, and Livonia and also part of southeastern Finland. The crown mattered little in the ensuing struggles for power in Sweden, in which the bureaucratic and service nobility of Charles XI and Charles XII's reigns limited the privileges of the high nobility, and the Estates and the committees of the Estates (prominent among them the "secret committee") made inroads on the power of the council, still the preserve of the higher nobility. Throughout the reign there was a development toward parliamentary government with its demand that councilors should change according to success or failure of the parties which developed in the Estates. These parties were differentiated by their attitudes to dynastic problems and the issues of foreign policy. The Holstein party wanted to recognize Charles Frederick of Holstein-Gottorp (married to Anna Petrovna, daughter of Tsar Peter) as heir to the childless Ulrika and Frederick and thus to use him as a lever for the peaceful return of some of the lost Baltic provinces. The Hesse party opposed the Holstein candidature and sought support against it (in a rapprochement in 1727 with Great Britain) to work for a younger brother of Frederick I as heir to the throne.

When, after the death of Catherine I of Russia in 1727, Charles Frederick lost Russian support, party distinctions developed between the Hats (alluding to the cocked hats of the military), anxious to get back, if need be by force, part of the lost empire, and the Caps (alluding to nightcaps), intent on a pacific policy. At the *Riksdag* of 1738 the Hats emerged as a fully organized party, won election to important committees, and forced the resignation of Count Arvid Bernhard Horn (*q.v.*), the leading statesman of the 1720s and 1730s. The Hats remained in power until 1765, though from 1740 onward the two parties were evenly balanced in the *Riksdag*. The Hats' economic outlook was protectionist; they encouraged trade and manufactures and introduced reforms in the system of landholdings and the methods of agriculture. In their foreign policy they aimed to strengthen Sweden's armed forces and to demand a modification of the Treaty of Nystad. In 1741, in return for a promise of part of the former Swedish Baltic territories, Sweden gave support to Elizabeth, daughter of Peter the Great, in her successful coup against Tsar Ivan VI. The promise was not carried out, however; instead, in 1742 Elizabeth turned against Sweden.

The ensuing war was disastrous for Sweden, Finland being occupied by the Russians in 1742. The issue of the succession now became acute, Ulrika Eleonora having died in 1741. The most favoured candidates were the Danish crown prince, Frederick, and Peter Ulrich of Holstein-Gottorp, son of Charles Frederick and Anna Petrovna. Peter, however, was chosen by the Russian empress Elizabeth as her own heir, and at the Peace of Åbo (August 1743) Sweden, in return for the restitution of Finland, was forced to accept as crown prince a candidate picked by Russia, the prince-bishop Adolphus Frederick, also of the Holstein-Gottorp family. This peace made Sweden dependent on Russia. But temporary cooperation between the moderate Hats, led by Count Carl Gustaf Tessin (*q.v.*), and the Caps put an end to such dependence within a year. Friendly relations were reestablished with Denmark-Norway; the Russian troops on Swedish soil (there to prevent any intervention by Denmark on behalf of their crown prince) agreed to leave, and a bride (Louisa Ulrika, sister of Frederick the Great of Prussia) was found for the Russian-imposed Swedish heir from an anti-Russian court.

After 1744, however, strong party divisions reappeared, the Hats being supported by France and the Caps by a combination of Great Britain, Russia, and Denmark. The Hats had some success in their attempts to wean Denmark to their side; a treaty of friendship was signed between Sweden and Denmark in 1749, and in 1751 Gustavus (later Gustavus III), the son born to Adolphus Frederick and Louisa Ulrika in 1746, was betrothed to Sophia Magdalena, daughter of Frederick V of Denmark. The brilliant and ambitious Louisa Ulrika resented the Hats' enforcing this engagement, and she began to build a court party round her, dedicated to increasing the power of the crown once her husband should succeed Frederick I.

The intellectual life of the reign of Frederick I was lively, with a strong emphasis on the practical application of ideas. The compilation and modernization of the laws of Sweden (begun in the reign of Charles XII) was finished in 1734; newspapers and political pamphlets attracted writers of the calibre of Olof Dallin; Carolus Linnaeus (*q.v.*) undertook a tour of Sweden to suggest improvements in agriculture; the Academy of Science was founded in 1739 and the Statistical Office in 1749. (R. M. Ha.)

**3. Adolphus Frederick (1751–71).**—King Frederick died in 1751 and was succeeded by Adolphus Frederick (*q.v.*), who was under the influence of his stronger-minded wife. Tension between the king and council grew. In 1756 a rash effort at a *coup d'état* on behalf of Adolphus, instigated by his wife, failed. The royal couple were humiliated. They were threatened with dethronement in an act passed by the *Riksdag;* some of their friends were impeached and executed; and an autograph stamp was introduced in order to dispense with the king's personal intervention in government. Count Fredrik Axel von Fersen (*q.v.*), the foremost man in the Hat Party, was chosen in 1756 as *lantmarskalk* (speaker of the First Estate, the nobility).

Opposition grew therefore among the unprivileged classes against the nobility and the bureaucracy. The state's finances were in a serious condition, yet in spite of this, in 1757 Sweden was drawn into the Seven Years' War (*q.v.*), on the side of France and Austria, against Frederick II the Great of Prussia, largely because of French subsidies. The Swedish campaigns were badly managed, but peace was made with Prussia without loss of territory in May 1762. The Caps took office in the *Riksdag* of 1765–66. Russia and Prussia together decided to support the Swedish constitution, to prolong its general state of weakness, and at the same time to work against French influence. A Russo-Danish alliance was also formed with the purpose of maintaining the Swedish constitution. England was on the same side, and it is calculated that these powers spent 3,000,000 silver dalers to ensure the victory of the Caps, while France's contribution to the Hats was 2,000,000 dalers. Against the wishes of Adolphus and his wife, the crown prince Gustavus married the Danish princess Sophia Magdalena in October 1766.

The court had helped the Hats during the *Riksdag* of 1765–66. At the end of 1768, in order to overthrow the Caps, the king temporarily abdicated, thus forcing the council to call an extraordinary *Riksdag* which sat from 1769 till 1770. The Caps were now in a minority and their men were left out of the council, which was controlled by the Hats. The court had been promised that the king's power would be increased, but the Hats did not keep their word. Nor did the *Riksdag* succeed in solving the great financial problems.

In December 1769 Russia and Denmark came to an agreement that, should any change be made in the constitution of Sweden in the direction of increasing the king's power, they would uphold the existing constitution by force of arms. In February 1771 Adolphus Frederick died.

### G. Royal Reaction, 1772–1809

**1. Gustavus III (1771–92).**—The crown prince, who now became Gustavus III (*q.v.*), was in Paris when his father died. He returned home to meet the *Riksdag*. The Hats and the court party were receiving money from France, the Caps from Russia and England. The parties were of about equal strength. Gustavus now decided to precipitate a change of the constitution. Col. Jacob Magnus Sprengtporten crossed to Finland and succeeded in stirring up a rising. Johan Kristoffer Toll, a superintendent of forests, went to Skåne and won over the garrison at Kristianstad (Aug. 12, 1772). The council received news of the danger, however, so the king had to act speedily. On Aug. 19 he collected around him the officers of the guard and arrested the council in the royal castle at Stockholm. The Stockholm troops declared for him, and the people acclaimed him in the streets. On Aug. 21 a new constitution was approved. The king became again head of the government, with the right to appoint officials. Russia and Denmark were deterred from declaring war by France, which remained firm in its support of Gustavus.

Gustavus surrounded himself with capable men. Unusually gifted, but a visionary, he took an active interest in all spheres of government. Reforms were instituted in the administration and in judicial procedure; torture was forbidden; religious toleration was granted to dissenters, and from 1777 a comprehensive reform of the currency was carried out. To help the finances, distilling was decreed a royal monopoly and a number of distilleries were founded by the crown. This, however, created discontent among the peasantry and resulted in the growth of illicit distilling and a large increase in drunkenness. Another cause for dissatisfaction lay in the king's efforts to transform the nobility into a court nobility and to manage civil-service promotions so as to break the power of the old bureaucracy. In the *Riksdag* of 1786 Gustavus met with fierce opposition and most of his reforming policies were rejected.

Turkey's war with Russia in 1787 seemed to offer favourable conditions for foreign policy. Gustavus declared war on Russia in June 1788, taking command himself. A naval battle in July, off the island of Hogland, in the Gulf of Finland, was indecisive. In August a conspiracy, known as the Anjala League, was formed at Anjala, on the Russian-Finnish border, by a group of Swedish officers who opened peace negotiations with Catherine II of Russia. News now came that Denmark had entered the war as Russia's ally and had invaded Sweden. Gustavus hurried home and toured the country to rally support. Sweden was swept by a wave of patriotism. England and Prussia brought pressure to bear on Denmark and a truce was concluded between Denmark and Sweden.

By the beginning of 1789 Gustavus was strong enough to have the leaders of the Anjala League imprisoned. The *Riksdag,* called in February, proved to be stormy. The king, supported by the unprivileged Estates, drove through the Act of Union and Security (Feb. 21, 1789), which embodied far-reaching constitutional innovations: the council ceased to exist, the king acquired full powers over the administration of the state and the appointing of officials, and the *Riksdag* lost its initiative in legislation. Once again the authority of the king was dominant. The *Riksdag* became responsible for the national debts, the management of which was placed in the hands of a new department, the *Riksgäldskontor,* which was dependent on the *Riksdag* and which was given the right to take up new loans and to issue credit notes.

The Russian war on land became a war of exhaustion. During 1789–90 there were several naval battles, and at Svensksund (July 9–10, 1790) Sweden gained a great victory under the king's command. In August peace was concluded at Värälä without modification of frontiers. But Sweden's finances had been destroyed, and the internal strife now came to a head. One result was a conspiracy against the king's life. He died on March 29, 1792, after being attacked by an assassin.

**2. Gustavus IV (1792–1809).**—At the age of 13 Gustavus IV (*q.v.*) became king of Sweden with his uncle Charles, duke of Södermanland (later King Charles XIII), as regent. Duke Charles's closest associate was Baron Gustaf Adolf Reuterholm, a man of great powers of work but pedantic and of little intelligence. The regency brought order into the higher grades of government service and aimed to help agriculture. Reuterholm was not lacking in appreciation of the latest reforms: the limited freedom of the press, first instituted in 1766, was increased, but when the Terror of the French Revolution broke out (1792) it was restricted. The regency did not stand very high in repute. It wavered between a French and a Russian alliance. The king, the duke, and Reuterholm visited the Russian court in 1796 in order to arrange a marriage between the king and Alexandra, granddaughter of Catherine II, but the plan was abandoned when the king refused to give a guarantee for the princess to practise her Orthodox faith. On the basis of a treaty concluded with Denmark in 1794, the fleets of both Denmark and Sweden sought to protect neutral trade against privateers of England and other nations.

In 1796 Gustavus IV took the government into his own hands. He was scantily gifted but, combining obstinacy with passionate temper, he knew how to make himself felt. So bad were the state finances that the town of Wismar had to be mortgaged to Mecklenburg in 1801. In the course of a long journey in Germany in 1803–04 Gustavus came into touch with French *émigrés,* who inspired him with hatred of Napoleon. He joined the coalition of England, Russia, and Austria against France (1805–07) with the result that Pomerania and Stralsund, Sweden's last possessions in Germany, were lost. In the Treaty of Tilsit (July 1807) Napoleon and Alexander I of Russia agreed to attack Sweden unless it declared war against England, and they prevailed on Denmark to do the same. On Gustavus' refusing to break with England, Russia in February 1808 invaded Finland, where the army gave way. In the spring the Swedes marched again to the south of Finland and won several victories, afterward immortalized by the poet Johan Ludvig Runeberg (*q.v.*). The victories, however, were not decisive, and after the strong fortress of Sveaborg was treacherously surrendered (May) the Swedes again retreated and in December evacuated Finland. Gustavus became more and more difficult, annoying even England, his only ally. The feeling grew that the king must be dethroned. Gen. Georg Adlersparre started a revolutionary movement in Värmland (March 1809), but before he reached Stockholm Adj. Gen. Karl Johan Adlercreutz had seized the king (March 13, 1809), who was deposed and died in exile in 1837.

### H. The 19th Century

**1. Charles XIII (1809–18).**—The *Riksdag,* called together on May 1 by the provisional government under the regent Charles, duke of Södermanland, decided to draw up a new constitution and elect a king. The form of government which resulted was based on a division of power among the ministry, the representatives of the people, and the judicature. The king was to be advised by a ministry the members of which were to be appointed by him but to be answerable to the *Riksdag.* General legislation was to be the work of the king and the *Riksdag,* and the *Riksdag's* control over taxation was confirmed. As soon as this constitution had been adopted (June 6, 1809) the regent was recognized as King Charles XIII (*q.v.*). Charles was 61 years old and childless, and it was necessary to choose his successor. Public opinion in Sweden at this period was occupied with the possibility of a union of Norway and Sweden as a compensation for the loss of Finland. The *Riksdag* therefore chose as Charles's successor Prince Christian Augustus of Augustenburg, commander in chief in Norway, who declared that he could accept the offer only after a declaration of peace. During the late summer of 1809 the Russian war was extended to the north of Sweden and the Swedish forces met with two defeats. The Russians in the meantime had become weary of the war, and in September 1809 peace was concluded at Fredrikshamn (Hamina); Sweden lost Finland and Åland. Treaties of peace followed in 1810 with Denmark and France, which returned Swedish Pomerania to Sweden.

The heir to the throne, who had taken the name of Charles, died suddenly in 1810, and a *Riksdag* at Örebro had again to deal with the succession. Opinions were divided when a suggestion was made to elect one of Napoleon's marshals, Jean Bernadotte, prince of Pontecorvo. It seemed certain that Napoleon would approve, and Bernadotte was chosen. He assumed the name of Charles John. Charles XIII, though he had shown courage and patriotic feeling during Gustavus III's war with Russia, was not very intelligent and lacked strength of character. The crown prince therefore began to exert considerable influence, with beneficent results.

In 1812 Napoleon began his campaign against Russia. The crown prince perceived that Sweden could not possibly benefit from fighting with France against England and Russia; he seemed also to have thought out already his plans for conquest of Norway. In 1812 therefore he brought about a complete change in Swedish foreign policy. Napoleon's occupation of Swedish Pomerania (January 1812) facilitated the change, and Russia and England favoured the idea of Norway's passing to Sweden from Napoleon's ally Denmark. Sweden therefore concluded alliances with Russia (April 1812), Great Britain (March 1813), and Prussia (April 1813). After the defeat of the French armies in Russia, Charles John took part in the final campaigns as commander of the northern army, with Swedish as well as Prussian and Russian troops under him. With these the crown prince, after the battle of Leipzig (October 1813), turned against Denmark, which by the Peace of Kiel (January 1814) was forced to hand over Norway. By the Treaty of Vienna (1815), Swedish Pomerania was given to Prussia.

The Norwegians themselves, desiring independence, held an assembly at Eidsvoll (May 1814), where they framed a constitution and elected the Danish prince Christian Frederick as king; but a short war with Sweden forced them to surrender. Christian Frederick laid down his crown and a *Storting* (national legislative assembly) endorsed the union with Sweden. The act of union or *riksakt* was passed by the Parliaments of both countries in 1815; Norway retained its independence and its constitution, but remained united with Sweden. (K. Hl.; E. O. H. J.)

**2. Charles XIV (1818–44).**—In 1818 Bernadotte succeeded to the throne, as Charles XIV (*q.v.*) John, founder of a new dynasty. He was a strong personality, capable and lovable, but distrustful of new ideas and apprehensive of too great changes. A liberal opposition in the *Riksdag,* above all among the burghers, took a strong line against the government's repression of newspapers, against bureaucratic formalities, and against the king's tendency to disregard his ministers' advice. From the 1830s onward there was a question of reform in the matter of the representation of the people, and a great many bills were put forward without much success. In 1840 the state council was changed by the creation of special departments. In 1834 the currency was devalued. Much was done to develop the canal system; one section of the Göta

Canal was opened in 1822 and the rest in 1832. In 1842 compulsory elementary school education was established. In consequence of growing agrarian production (for instance of potatoes) and a reduction in the mortality rate, partly resulting from compulsory vaccination against smallpox, the population increased rapidly (from 2,500,000 in 1815 to 3,300,000 in 1845). This increase caused serious social problems in the countryside, where 90% of the people lived, particularly among the elderly working-class poor.

**3. Oscar I (1844–59).**—Charles XIV was succeeded in 1844 by his more liberal son Oscar I (*q.v.*). During Oscar's reign the industrial economic revolution began in Sweden. The expansion of the sawmill and iron industries was rapid, due partly to new machines and methods, and exports grew considerably. Restrictions on agriculture and commerce were relaxed; the guild system was done away with in 1846, and the old rules confining trade to the towns were removed. By decisions reached in the *Riksdag* for 1844–45 the right to suppress newspapers was definitely abrogated. In 1847 an important poor law system providing organized relief was introduced. One of the greatest questions of the period was that of communication: railways had to be built, but there were differences of opinion as to the laying down of the main lines through the sparsely inhabited land. In the *Riksdag* of 1853–54 it was decided that the main lines should be built by the state.

Friends of reform concentrated more and more on the demand for a thoroughgoing change in the formation of the *Riksdag,* and many proposals were submitted without any being accepted. The revolutionary movement which marked the year 1848 on the continent aroused feeling also in Sweden, and some street disturbances occurred in Stockholm. The government produced a new scheme of representation, which, however, was rejected by the *Riksdag* of 1850. A strong Scandinavian movement manifested itself (especially in Denmark and Sweden, although the Norwegians also took part in it); great meetings of students were held, but no program for the unity of the Scandinavian countries with any real life in it was ever framed.

When the Schleswig question led in 1848 to war between Denmark and the German states (*see* SCHLESWIG-HOLSTEIN QUESTION), a Swedish army was collected in Skåne and troops were carried over to the Danish island of Fyn, in case Jutland should be invaded; but they never had occasion to come into action. During the Crimean War (1854–56) Sweden and Norway maintained neutrality, and in November 1855 they reaped the benefit: a treaty (known as the November Treaty) was concluded with England and France by which the union states undertook not to cede any portion of their territories to Russia, while the two other powers undertook to prevent any Russian efforts in that direction. Side by side with the peace treaty in Paris ending the Crimean War (1856) there was concluded a separate agreement among Russia, France, and England in which Russia undertook not to fortify the Åland Islands.

The increasing consumption of spirits, as a result of the right to distill for household needs (legalized in 1787), led to a temperance movement conducted by persons such as Peter Wieselgren, a pastor. Private distilleries were forbidden by the *Riksdag* of 1853–54 and the distilling of spirits was regulated by the state.

**4. Charles XV (1859–72).**—The crown prince had already, because of his father's ill health, conducted the government for two years when in July 1859 he became king as Charles XV (*q.v.*). His liveliness of mind, personal friendliness, and artistic temperament won him great popularity, but he lacked thoroughness and perseverance and his extravagant imagination in certain situations was a danger. This became most noticeable in the German-Danish war of 1864 over Schleswig-Holstein, when he gave the Danes to understand that they could count on an alliance between Denmark and Sweden-Norway, an idea which had never had the sanction of the state councils of either of the union countries. A number of Swedes, however, did enter the Danish army as volunteers.

The social changes which had come about in the life of Sweden, including the decline in importance of the nobility and clergy in social and cultural life and the rise of commoners to high positions in the bureaucracy, necessitated a new form of electoral representation, and increasingly the general feeling was that the problem could be solved only by replacing the *Riksdag* of the four Estates by one with two chambers. The minister of justice, Louis de Geer, took the lead in the matter, and the government submitted a bill to this effect in the *Riksdag* of 1862–63. The new constitution was finally accepted by all four Estates in the *Riksdag* of 1865–66, and in January 1867 the first *Riksdag* of the new kind was assembled. The first chamber was composed solely of aristocrats, businessmen, and high officials and was elected by councils, which were themselves elected by a graded scale of voting, industrial and commercial companies and the rich having far more votes than the poor. The second chamber comprised members of the bourgeoisie and farmers and was elected by about 25% of the population, the right to vote being based on a property qualification too high to include the majority of the working class. It soon became evident that it was the peasants who had benefited most by the reform: within two years they dominated the second chamber and their party—the so-called Lantmanna Party—was a power to reckon with.

Through the influence of the finance minister, Baron J. A. Gripenstedt, Sweden was led more in the direction of free trade, and its treaty of commerce with France in 1865 was an important landmark in this development. All duties on grain were removed. In 1864 internal free trade had finally been established. Among other important reforms may be mentioned the criminal law of 1864 by which imprisonment became the main punishment for crime. The wars in progress on the continent caused the *Riksdag* to make some grants for armaments, but the government's proposal for a reorganization of the national defenses was rejected. The birth rate remained higher than the mortality rate, and from the 1850s part of the expanding population, especially those of the working class, began to move to the U.S. This emigration reached its first climax after the famine of 1867–68.

**5. Oscar II (1872–1907).**—After a prolonged illness Charles XV died in 1872 and was succeeded by his brother Oscar II (*q.v.*). The most noteworthy event in the latters' reign was the dissolution of the union with Norway. The position of the sovereign of the two countries had become extremely difficult, because modern parliamentarianism had progressed much farther in Norway than in Sweden and the power of the sovereign had consequently become much less extensive in Norway. On June 7, 1905, the Norwegian *Storting* declared the union with Sweden to be dissolved. The *Riksdag* finally agreed to the dissolution on certain conditions, and in October 1905 Oscar laid down the Norwegian crown (for details of the dissolution of the union *see* NORWAY: *History*).

During the first years of Oscar II's reign, the question of national defense had been the dominant one, the first chamber of the *Riksdag* contending for an improved system and the peasant members in the second chamber making demands for the abolition of the old land taxes and of the old army organization, which was very burdensome for the peasants. A number of army organization proposals were rejected, but in 1885 the *Riksdag* carried out a compromise: military service was increased from 30 to 42 days, and the state became responsible for part of the costs of the army organization and reduced the land taxes.

During the 1880s the question of customs duties caused bitter disputes. The increasing exportation of grain from the United States and Russia, together with the strong industrial competition among all countries, resulted in a protectionist movement in Germany and France which extended also to Sweden. The agrarian prices dropped sharply and emigration increased. The second chamber was protectionist and the first in favour of free trade; in 1887 the majority in the first chamber was so small that it would have been possible to bring about a protectionist system by the collective vote of the two chambers. The king then dissolved the second chamber, which returned with a majority in favour of free trade. But in the general election in the autumn of 1887 a technical mistake in the election of free trade candidates in Stockholm made their election invalid, with the result that the protectionists gained a small majority. The *Riksdag* of 1888 therefore accepted the customs system.

This issue had profound consequences both in the formation of parties in the second chamber and in other respects. New men came forward, the most conspicuous of whom was a Conservative, the landed proprietor E. G. Boström, premier from 1891 to 1900 and from 1902 to 1905. The question of the national defenses was provisionally settled by the *Riksdag's* decisions in the autumn of 1892 (at an extraordinary session), and then finally in 1901. In the latter year the *indelning* system was completely abolished; all males were now liable for military service and the training time was increased from 90 to 240 days in the infantry and a longer period in the case of the navy and special branches of the army. The land taxes were abolished in 1892.

At this period new legislation was necessitated by industrial development and the great increase in the number of industrial workers. New methods led to an enormous expansion of exports of paper pulp and iron ore. In 1900 Sweden had 5,150,000 inhabitants, of whom 22% lived in the towns. Between 1870 and 1900 the proportion of the population engaged in industry and commerce increased from 20% to 35%. In 1881 the conditions of labour for children in all factories were regulated and in 1889 a law was passed providing against injury while at work. The child labour law was amplified in 1900 by one dealing with the condition of industrial work for women and children. Trade unions were formed and collective agreements governing labour conditions were arranged between employers and workers.

In 1889 a Social Democratic Party was formed, and in the autumn of 1896 Karl Hjalmar Branting (*q.v.*) was elected to the second chamber as its first Social Democratic member. In 1900 the Liberal groups of the second chamber merged into one great party. The Liberals and Social Democrats demanded an extension of the suffrage for the election of the second chamber, but it was not until the severance of the union with Norway had given a strong impetus to a closer national union on new lines that the question came to be decided. The severance of the union led to the formation of the coalition ministry of Christian Lundeberg, a manufacturer, whose task it was to carry out the dissolution of the union. He was followed at the close of 1905 by a Liberal ministry with Karl Staaff as premier. The *Riksdag* of 1906 rejected his suffrage bill, and the ministry resigned. Rear Adm. Arvid Lindman succeeded, with a Conservative ministry; he found a way, in 1907, of solving the suffrage question on the basis of universal suffrage for men for the second chamber; the democratization of the graded scale of voting for the first chamber (no voter was allowed to have more than 40 votes); and proportional representation for both chambers. Among other important decisions may be mentioned the monopoly in the issuing of bank notes accorded to the Riksbank in 1897, the building (1898–1902) of a Swedish-Norwegian railway for the exportation of the Lapponian iron ore, the restriction of the right of companies to acquire land in northern Sweden (1906), and the part ownership of the state in the Lapland iron ore mines (1907).

(K. Hl.; S. C. O. C.)

### I. The 20th Century

When Oscar II died on Dec. 8, 1907, the crown fell to his eldest son, Gustav (Gustavus V; *q.v.*), who proved a capable king for a democratic epoch. Reforms were carried through, as, for instance, the law (1909) allowing peasants in Norrland to acquire land and leave it to heirs. In the autumn of 1911 the election for the second chamber of the *Riksdag* was held with a doubled electorate as a result of the reform bill of 1907, and the Lindman ministry resigned. Karl Staaff formed his second ministry. His government set aside the Lindman ministry's decision to build a warship of a new type, whereupon a movement to finance its construction by private subscription produced a sum of 18,100,000 kronor and the ship was built.

The Swedish people had been disquieted by the way in which the Russians were arming in Finland and by widespread Russian espionage in Sweden, and in February 1914, 30,000 peasants met in Stockholm to request the king that a comprehensive national defense plan be drawn up. When the king's answer was favourable, the Liberal ministry resigned. The king commanded the Conservative Hjalmar Hammarskjöld (*q.v.*) to form a ministry. K. A. Wallenberg became minister of foreign affairs.

**1. World War I.**—By the outbreak of World War I Sweden found itself more or less isolated from the armed blocs in Western Europe, from which it bought a large proportion of its food supplies, raw materials, and finished goods. Sweden declared itself a neutral power, measures for the reorganization of defense were passed, and Sweden succeeded in preserving its neutrality throughout the war despite external and even some internal pressure by activists favouring one or the other side. At first industry and commerce took an upward swing owing to large purchases by the belligerents; soon, however, this intensive buying exhausted stocks which could no longer be replenished, and the export of some goods was therefore made subject to licence. The state also confiscated sugar and other foodstuffs at fixed prices and distributed them by rationing and took over certain imports. At times there was an extreme shortage of some foodstuffs.

In 1917 the Hammarskjöld government resigned over the supply position. A Conservative ministry carried on for a short time until the general elections which brought considerable gains for the Social Democrats. A Liberal-Socialist coalition under Nils Edén took over, and Hjalmar Branting, Sweden's most famous Socialist, entered the government for the first time as minister of finance. The supply problem was solved by two agreements with Great Britain, the second one being the so-called *modus vivendi* agreement concluded in March 1918, providing for the limited import of vital goods in exchange for the loan of a large part of the Swedish merchant fleet and the substantial reduction of exports to Germany. The Russian and, following it, the German Revolution seriously affected Swedish thought and led to a revival of demands for democratization of the constitution. As a consequence, a special session (*urtima*) of the *Riksdag* passed a radical bill that included *inter alia* votes for women. One effect of the bill was to make the Social Democrats the strongest party in the *Riksdag;* the Conservatives were the second strongest. The Liberals, who lost some seats, split into two groups in 1923—the National Liberals (Folksfrisinnade) and the Liberals—thereby further weakening their position. A small Communist Party and a Farmers' Party were also formed.

Another consequence of the Russian Revolution, Finland's secession from the Russian empire, also affected Sweden. While the government recognized Finland's independence in January 1918, it did not dare grant military aid to the new nation lest this involve Sweden in the war. The government's policy adversely affected Finno-Swedish relations, and Finnish resentment was further increased by the dispatch of a Swedish naval expedition to the Åland Islands in February 1918, when the islands were threatened by a Russian landing. Finnish circles interpreted this action as an attempt to express practical sympathy with an earlier demand by the Ålanders to join the Swedish realm. Not until after Sweden's calm acceptance of the League of Nations' decision (1920) in favour of Finland's retention of the islands did this resentment gradually die down.

**2. The Interwar Period.**—The most striking development between World Wars I and II was the great advance of the Social Democratic Party. In 1920 the Liberal-Socialist coalition was followed by the first purely Social Democratic government under Branting, but the autumn elections resulted in a small setback for his party. A "business" ministry of a moderately Conservative character thereupon carried on until after the 1921 elections, when Branting again formed a government. This remained in office until 1923 and was followed by a number of short-term governments from the right or from the left, including a Liberal government under Carl Ekman which commanded only 33 votes from 231 seats but nevertheless carried on from June 1926 to the general elections in 1928. During this period the Social Democrats succeeded in passing a bill which greatly reduced armaments. In 1928 a Conservative government took office but was soon defeated. Another Liberal government, formed in 1930, resigned in 1932 after the autumn elections when the Social Democrats and the Farmers made considerable gains.

In October 1932 the Social Democrat Per Albin Hansson

(*q.v.*) formed his first ministry. Its program included strong measures to overcome the depression (*see* below) and aimed at financial expansion rather than economies. When the Social Democratic Party proved not strong enough to enforce these measures, an arrangement (the so-called *Kohandel*) with the Farmers was concluded (1933) and the opposition had to yield. Gradually developments in industry began to justify the government measures, and unemployment began to fall steeply. Apart from a few months in 1934, when the Farmers governed alone, the Social Democrats—either alone or in coalition with others—remained in office throughout the ensuing period, and in the elections in 1934 they nearly attained an overall majority. The feeling of security of tenure which their strong position gave them was reflected in the increasing calm that prevailed in labour relations and led to a standardization of the so-called collective agreements which by 1940 covered about 1,000,000 workmen.

ANTHONY HOWARTH—BLACK STAR

MODERN BUILDINGS IN THE SMALL IRON-MINING CENTRE OF KIRUNA, ABOUT 90 MI. FROM THE ARCTIC CIRCLE

The economic effects of the post-World War I crisis had affected Sweden. Early in 1922 unemployment rose to 160,000, but by the close of that year the nadir had been reached and Sweden's recovery kept step with that of the outside world. At the same time the democratization of the country increasingly affected the economic field. Labour had earlier been organized into trade unions and the cooperative movement flourished, but revolutionary ideas no longer prevailed; a policy of "progress by peaceful negotiation" was begun. The eight-hour day was introduced without wage reduction and, despite shorter working hours, production expanded. The merchant fleet was increased, pulp production was assisted by improved forestry, seed selection was introduced for the benefit of agriculture, and highly developed engineering works produced increasing quantities of goods for export. Sweden also became one of the countries which exported capital.

During the depression of the early 1930s a number of grave labour conflicts occurred; Sweden followed Great Britain in abandoning the gold standard, which relieved the position, although it improved only gradually. After World War I Sweden supported the League of Nations, prepared even to abandon in part its policy of neutrality. The gradual deterioration of the international situation, however, as well as the advent of the Nazis in Germany and the failure of the League to save Ethiopia, induced the government to reconsider the situation. Defense again became a primary consideration. After the German invasion of Austria (1938) Hansson promptly proposed increases in defense and Sweden advised the League that it proposed to resume its strict neutrality policy. The fall of Czechoslovakia (1939) further pointed the danger. Sweden declined Germany's offer of a nonaggression pact, but Swedish attempts to bring about closer inter-Scandinavian relations failed.

**3. World War II.**—On the outbreak of World War II the Social Democratic government strengthened defense and proclaimed the country's official neutrality. A comprehensive war trade agreement was concluded with Great Britain in December 1939, and after the outbreak of the Russo-Finnish War (November 1939) a coalition government of all parties was formed. The material aid given to Finland was of unparalleled generosity and endangered Sweden's own security, but Finnish requests for regular troops were refused although volunteers were helped and encouraged. Allied demands for the transit of British and French troops to Finland were rejected by Sweden as well as Norway.

The German invasion of Denmark and Norway (April 1940) isolated Sweden from the West. Despite heavy German pressure to allow the transit of troops and armaments, not until after the end of the war in Norway (June 1940) did Sweden enter into an agreement permitting German soldiers on leave, and goods, including war material, to pass over certain Swedish railways. On the outbreak of the second Russo-Finnish war (June 1941) Sweden was forced to a still greater concession. On June 25, 1941, permission for the transit of a whole armed division from Norway to Finland was granted. These agreements aroused bitterness and criticism in Sweden and brought sharp Allied protests. The traffic was ended in the late summer of 1943 after Germany's position had deteriorated and Sweden's military strength increased. Stringent reductions in Swedish exports to Germany were also made, and a comprehensive new war trade agreement was concluded with Britain and the United States.

All through the war Sweden was a shelter for refugees from German oppression, not only for Norwegians, Danes, and Finns but also for Balts and Jews of all nationalities. After the war, relief, largely in the form of credits, amounting to about $600,000,000 was extended mainly to Norway and Denmark, and medical supplies, food, and clothing were sent wherever needed. The Swedish Red Cross under Count Folke Bernadotte was actively engaged in aiding prisoners of war with the government's generous support.

**4. The Postwar Period.**—After World War II the Social Democrats dissolved the coalition and governed alone. The first postwar elections (1948) confirmed them as the strongest party, but the unexpectedly slow recovery of devastated Europe, the cumulative effect of unfavourable world trends, Europe's growing economic dependence on the United States, and the temporary elimination of Germany from world trade seriously affected Sweden's economy. Sweden had adopted a generous foreign credit policy to aid European revival; when the expected revival did not materialize, an economic crisis ensued. Large cuts had to be made in imports and expenditure was reduced, although this never affected expenditure on social welfare or defense.

King Gustav died in 1950, and his son Gustav VI Adolf (Gustavus VI; *q.v.*), who was 67, succeeded to the throne. In October 1946, after the death of Hansson, Tage Erlander became prime minister and in 1951 formed another coalition with the Farmers. Gradually the economic position improved, but the country blamed the coalition for high food prices and the 1952 elections resulted in slight losses for both government parties. The government continued to improve social services, and on Jan. 1, 1955, a compulsory health insurance scheme for the whole nation came into force. Rationing of alcohol was terminated on Oct. 1, 1955. The general elections in 1956 resulted in further losses for the coalition government, and the Social Democrats had to make important concessions to the Farmers to preserve the coalition. In October 1957 a national referendum took place on the subject of an additional national pension scheme, in which the plan advocated by the Social Democrats proved victorious. Thereupon the Farmers resigned from the government. On Oct. 31 Erlander formed a Social Democrat minority government. The new government had a slight ma-

J. ALLAN CASH—RAPHO GUILLUMETTE

HARBOUR AT STRÖMMEN, STOCKHOLM

jority in the first chamber but could not carry through bills in both chambers if the bourgeois parties united against it.

In the spring of 1958 this position became untenable when a bill dealing with improved old-age pensions was rejected in the second chamber; and on April 28 the *Riksdag* was dissolved. The elections on June 1, 1958, gave the following results for the lower chamber: Social Democrats 111, Centre Party (the new name of the Farmers' Party) 32, Conservatives 45, Liberals 38, Communists 5. The pensions bill was not submitted until the spring of 1959, when it was passed in the second chamber by the narrowest margin, 115 to 114. Another difficulty which faced the government was a deficit of over 100,000,000 kronor shown in 1959. Not until the government made the matter one of confidence was a "turnover tax" of 4% passed, and even that was made possible only because the Communists refrained from voting, thereby saving the government.

In June 1960, just prior to the general election, Erlander stated that his party would accept a mixed economy—*i.e.*, would accept different forms of ownership and not aim only at nationalization of industry. The elections, nevertheless, did not realize his hopes of an overall majority, nor did he achieve this at the 1964 elections, when the position in the lower chamber of the *Riksdag* was: Social Democrats 113, Liberals 42, Centre Party 35, Conservatives 32, Communists 8, Citizens Front 3. Thus the government continued to be dependent on the support of the Communists on all major issues. On June 1, 1965, after the resignation of Gunnar Heckscher, Yngve Holmberg was elected as new leader of the Conservative Party. In October 1957 the great Arctic Iron Ore Company, Luossavaara-Kirunavaara A.B., was nationalized.

On March 26, 1965, certain constitutional changes came into force in connection with the succession. In consequence, Crown Prince Carl Gustaf (born 1946), while immediately becoming titular head of state on the death of the monarch, would not be allowed to exercise his functions until his 25th birthday, his uncle, Prince Bertil, automatically becoming regent until the formal appointment of a regent. On May 17, 1968, a further reform in the constitution was approved, by which a unicameral system would be introduced in 1971 and the voting age reduced to 19 years starting with the 1970 elections; both these measures were confirmed by the *Riksdag* elected in September 1968. In the spring of 1966 a three-year agreement with wage adjustments totaling 6% was concluded, giving industry some breathing space. At the municipal elections on Sept. 18 the government party, the Social Democrats, lost heavily and in 1967 they began to fear that they might find themselves out of office after the 1968 elections. These forebodings were, however, not realized; on the contrary, the Social Democrats won a clear majority in the lower house (Sept. 15) while already controlling the upper house. The new *Riksdag*, which would remain in office only until elections in 1970 for the single-chamber *Riksdag*, showed the following picture in the lower house: Conservatives 32 (33), Centre Party 39 (36), Liberals 34 (43), Social Democrats 125 (113), Communists 3 (8). On Sept. 3, 1967, Sweden adopted the right-hand traffic system at a cost of about 600,000,000 kronor.

Sweden joined the United Nations in 1946, but the proposal for the North Atlantic Treaty Organization (NATO) led to much heart searching. When a Swedish proposal of a common defense pact with Denmark and Norway failed, the government decided not to join NATO. As a consequence, increasing amounts were spent on armaments. Sweden joined the Council of Europe, however, and actively participated in the work of O.E.E.C. and also joined the European Free Trade Association. Sweden steadfastly supported the United Nations, and on Aug. 12, 1963, signed the test ban agreement.

Sweden's relations with its Scandinavian neighbours continued very friendly and in March 1956 a Swedish-Norwegian agreement provided for greater facilities to Sweden for its transit traffic through Norwegian harbours in Trondheim Fjord, which would prove useful in time of war. Diplomatic relations with the U.S.S.R. and the Eastern European countries in 1955 and later years were affected by the discovery of cases of espionage in which members of foreign embassies were involved.

In June 1963 a former colonel of the Swedish Air Force, Stig Wennerström, was arrested for espionage on behalf of the Soviet Union. His activities had been going on for 15 years and had caused damage to Sweden's defense estimated at billions of kronor. Sweden's trade relations with the Soviet Union, on the other hand, improved during these years, especially as a result of Khrushchev's visit to Sweden in June 1964.

On July 28, 1967, Sweden made formal application to join the EEC as its government considered that the community was moving in the direction of putting emphasis on economic rather than political issues, thus enabling Sweden to adhere to its policy of neutrality. On Nov. 12, Sweden announced that it refused to recognize the new Rhodesian regime and would close its consulate in Salisbury; trade with Rhodesia was broken off on Nov. 22. On March 9, 1967, during a foreign affairs debate, the major parties agreed that the United States should stop bombing North Vietnam to enable peace negotiations to be started, and on April 18 it was announced that the government would not seek a new *agrément* for an ambassador in South Vietnam, although continuing to have an honorary consul there. On Aug. 21, 1968, the entire Foreign Affairs Committee backed the government in its condemnation of the invasion of Czechoslovakia, while the Communist leader, C. H. Hermansson, demanded the recall of the Swedish ambassador to the Soviet Union. (A. H. Hs.)

## IV. POPULATION

Population statistics have been recorded in Sweden since 1749, when the population was about 1,780,000. Between 1810 and 1850 there was a sudden sharp rise, from about 2,400,000 to about 3,500,000, attributed to "the peace, the vaccine against smallpox, and the potatoes." In 1965 (census) it was 7,772,506.

The birth rate is low (15.8 per 1,000 inhabitants in 1966) and so is the fertility rate. These factors, together with the declining death rate (10.1 per 1,000 in 1966), have led to an irregular age distribution and to an unfavourable ratio between the population of working age and the increasing number of old people.

The population is low in comparison with the area of the country, and is unevenly distributed, being much denser in the south than in the north. The table shows the distribution of population according to the 1965 census, and its density, by county (*län*), as well as the relation of the counties to the provinces (*landskap*). The latter are older territorial divisions which now have no administrative status, although their names remain in common use. Stockholm city, the capital, is a governorship (*överståthållarskap*) administratively separate from Stockholm *län*.

*Area and Population of Sweden*

| Province | Län | Area* (sq.mi.) | Population (1965) | Density (per sq. mi.)† |
|---|---|---|---|---|
| Norrland | | | | |
| Lappland, Norrbotten | Norrbotten | 40,879 | 259,579 | 6.3 |
| Lappland, Västerbotten | Västerbotten | 22,834 | 233,597 | 10.2 |
| Ångermanland, Medelpad | Västernorrland | 9,924 | 277,467 | 28.0 |
| Jämtland, Härjedalen | Jämtland | 19,903 | 130,848 | 6.6 |
| Hälsingland, Gästrikland | Gävleborg | 7,615 | 292,652 | 38.4 |
| Svealand | | | | |
| Dalarna (Dalecarlia) | Kopparberg | 11,724 | 281,923 | 24.0 |
| Värmland | Värmland | 7,497 | 287,097 | 38.3 |
| Närke | Örebro | 3,492 | 267,850 | 76.7 |
| Västmanland | Västmanland | 2,615 | 249,883 | 95.6 |
| Södermanland | Södermanland | 2,645 | 240,806 | 91.0 |
| Uppland | Uppsala | 2,084 | 184,701 | 88.6 |
| | Stockholm | 2,997 | 593,418 | 198.0 |
| | Stockholm (city) | 72 | 788,503 | 10,951.4 |
| Götaland | | | | |
| Östergötland | Östergötland | 4,278 | 365,754 | 85.5 |
| Västergötland | Skaraborg | 3,262 | 254,860 | 78.1 |
| Dalsland | Älvsborg | 4,928 | 389,843 | 79.1 |
| Bohuslän | Göteborg och Bohus | 1,986 | 665,728 | 335.2 |
| Halland | Halland | 1,904 | 179,905 | 94.5 |
| Småland (and Öland) | Jönköping | 4,436 | 296,119 | 66.8 |
| | Kronoberg | 3,827 | 164,288 | 42.9 |
| | Kalmar‡ | 4,487 | 235,598 | 52.5 |
| Blekinge | Blekinge | 1,173 | 149,482 | 127.4 |
| Skåne (Scania) | Kristianstad | 2,478 | 261,759 | 105.6 |
| | Malmöhus | 1,878 | 667,164 | 355.3 |
| Gotland | Gotland§ | 1,225 | 53,682 | 43.8 |
| Totals | | 173,665 | 7,772,506 | 44.8 |

*Source:* Statistical Abstract of Sweden (Statistisk årsbok) 1968, page 30.
*Including inland waters other than the four largest lakes, Vänern, Vättern, Mälaren, and Hjälmaren, whose combined area of 3,522 sq.mi. is, however, included in the total area. †Land area only. ‡Including the Island of Öland. §With adjacent islets.

In 1920, 55% of the population lived in villages or open country, in 1965 only 23%. The continuing urbanization has created serious social problems; e.g., in the rural areas a shortage of women and a decrease in the population of working age, and in urban areas a housing shortage. In 1967 there were 132 towns, of which 94 had over 10,000 inhabitants. After Stockholm, the largest were Göteborg (443,292) and Malmö (253,502).

With the spread of higher education, the proportion of young people gainfully employed has decreased. For boys aged 15 to 19 it was 54% in 1960 (74% in 1950). The proportion of married women gainfully employed increased from 14% to about one-third. By economic sectors the distribution of the gainfully employed showed a sharp decline in agriculture (from 20% in 1950 to 12.5% in the mid-1960s) and a rise in industry, commerce, and other service occupations.

The population is racially homogeneous. In the far north there is a minority (about 0.7% of the total population) of Finns and Lapps.

Since 1930 Sweden has changed from a country with net emigration to one with regular net immigration. Poverty and unsatisfactory social conditions caused emigration to increase from 1860, and more than a million Swedes in their best years emigrated to the United States from 1861 to 1910. Then U.S. immigration laws and a rising standard of living in Sweden after World War I caused a steep decline in emigration. After World War II the number of immigrants increased considerably. In the 1960s net immigration accounted for one-third of the total population increase with, in all, about 500,000 immigrants living in Sweden.

## V. ADMINISTRATION AND SOCIAL CONDITIONS

**1. Constitution and Government.**—*National Government.*—Sweden is a constitutional monarchy with male succession. The constitution rests primarily on the fundamental law of 1809. The executive power is vested in the King-in-Council; *i.e.,* in exercising his constitutional powers, the king must accept the advice of his ministers. Legislative authority is shared between the King-in-Council and the bicameral Parliament (*Riksdag*). Parliament alone has control of public finance, including the Bank of Sweden (*Riksbank*) and the National Debt Office. It also appoints two procurators general (*ombudsmän*) to supervise (1) military, and (2) all other branches of justice and administration.

Parliament is divided into two chambers of equal authority, an upper chamber (*första kammaren*) of 151 members, indirectly elected for eight years, and a lower chamber (*andra kammaren*) of 233 members, directly elected for four years. The seats are distributed in proportion to the constituency ballots of the parties.

A proposal for constitutional reform was accepted by the *Riksdag* in 1968, establishing—as from 1971—a unicameral parliament of 350 members, elected for three years. Simultaneously, a new electoral system will be introduced whereby parties will be represented in accordance with their national proportionality, certain percentage barriers counteracting the formation of small parties.

From 1921 suffrage was universal. The minimum voting age, after 1970, was 19.

As a rule, the king appoints the leader of the majority party as prime minister (*statsminister*) and asks him to form a government. The cabinet (*statsråd*) is composed of 18 members (the prime minister, the heads of the 11 ministries, and 6 ministers without portfolio). The king and cabinet meet merely to record and sign decisions made at the preliminary meetings of ministers.

There is a sharp formal division between the policy-making executive ministries, which are mainly secretariats for their respective heads, and the 100 or so purely administrative central boards and agencies, which are subordinated to the ministries in an organizational sense only. The central administration outside the ministries is largely independent of politics, which play little part in appointment to the public service. Swedish civil servants cannot be dismissed except in the case of default and after trial.

*Local Government.*—There are two overlapping systems: as representative of the national government, a crown-appointed governor (*landshövding*) heads an administrative board in each of the 24 counties; local self-government is run by popularly elected county councils and rural or urban district councils. The county administrative board holds supreme police authority within the county, and has some supervisory power over the local self-government bodies. Local councils are responsible for medical facilities, social welfare, education below university level, public services, and local taxes.

**2. Political Parties.**—The distribution of seats in Parliament (both chambers) after the 1968 election was: Social Democrats (Socialdemokraterna) 204, Liberal People's Party (Folkpartiet) 59, Conservatives (Högerpartiet) 57, Agrarian Centre Party (Centerpartiet) 60, Communists (Kommunisterna) 4. The Social Democrats have held office continuously since 1932, sometimes in coalition with the Centre Party. Foreign policy and the large-scale social reforms have usually received the unanimous backing of all parties except the Communists; more controversial issues have been taxation, budget economics, housing policy, and farm subsidies.

Since 1965 a state subsidy has been paid to every political party represented in the *Riksdag,* in proportion to the number of seats held.

**3. Taxation.**—Direct taxation is progressive, rising (in the late 1960s), for a married couple, from 30% of an annual income of 30,000 kronor (about $5,700), to about 40% of one of 60,000 kronor (about $11,400). In addition to an added value tax of 10%, indirect taxes are levied on alcoholic beverages, tobacco, coffee, gasoline, oil, electricity, etc. In 1968 a family with an income of 30,000 kronor paid an average of 46% in national and local direct taxes, indirect taxes, and contributions; the proportion on an income of 75,000 kronor (about $14,200) was 58%.

**4. Labour Unions.**—The Swedish labour market is characterized by the strong central organization of both workers and employees. The Confederation of Swedish Trade Unions (Landsorganisationen, abbreviated LO) represents 95% of all workers. A major factor contributing to peaceful labour-management relations is that LO is mainly composed not of craft unions but of unions organized on an industrial basis; *i.e.,* all workers in the same industry, irrespective of the type of work they do, belong to the same union. The Swedish Employers' Confederation (Svenska Arbetsgivareföreningen, or SAF) and LO collaborate closely on questions of mutual interest. Collective agreements on wages and conditions of employment play a dominant role in the labour market. Salaried employees also have strong central organizations. Unions, employers' organizations, consumers' and producers' cooperatives, and other popular organizations exert a considerable influence in Swedish political life.

**5. Living Conditions.**—The continuous rise during the 20th century in the Swedish standard of living can be attributed to a number of factors, not least to the uninterrupted peace the country has enjoyed since 1814. In spite of rising prices, full employment and increased productivity have led to a steady increase in real wages; for industrial workers, this was about 75% within the first 15 years after World War II. The normal income of an industrial worker in 1968 was between 20,000–25,000 kronor. A business executive earned an average of 50,000–60,000 kronor. Many families receive extra income from the wife's earnings or from secondary employment. Housing costs, including fuel and light, amount to 10–15% of the family budget and have remained fairly stable since before World War II, rents being controlled. In urban districts most people live in various types of multifamily dwellings, usually of good quality and well equipped with modern amenities though comparatively small, mostly with two or three living or bedrooms.

The high standard of living in Sweden is reflected in the consumption of goods and services, notably of the more dispensable items such as processed foods, ready-to-wear clothing, and foreign vacations, and also in increased leisure time. Industrial workers have a 42½-hour week, other employees a 42-hour week. Every employed Swede is entitled by law to four weeks' annual vacation with pay.

**6. Welfare Services.**—Sweden has an extensive system of social welfare, accounting for the largest item of expenditure in the state budget. It includes compulsory health insurance, maternity benefits, child allowances, retirement pensions, rent rebates to large families, free school lunches and school books, housing subsidies, unemployment benefits, etc. Most of these benefits are available to everybody, irrespective of personal income. The compulsory health insurance covers two-thirds of doctor's fees, hospital treatment, half the cost of medicine, and a tax-free cash sickness benefit.

Basic retirement pensions, adjusted to the cost of living, are paid to all citizens from the age of 67, regardless of income. Over and above this tax-financed, flat-rate national pension, a national supplementary pension, related to previous earned income and protected against inflation, was introduced in 1960; it is financed by employers. The two pensions together equal about two-thirds of the average yearly income earned during the 15 best years of gainful employment.

**7. Justice.**—The Swedish legal system derives ultimately from the medieval provincial laws. The first national code was introduced in the mid-14th century and was later replaced by that of 1734, on which subsequent development is based.

Both civil and criminal cases are tried in the first instance by the rural or municipal courts. The rural court (*häradsrätt*) consists of a trained lawyer as judge and from seven to nine elected laymen (*nämndemän*). If seven *nämndemän* are unanimously of a different opinion from the judge, they can overrule him. The municipal court (*rådhusrätt*) consists of the mayor (*borgmästare*), who is a permanent official and always a lawyer, and at least two other legally qualified persons (*rådmän*). The six Courts of Appeal (*hovrätter*) are next in rank; they sit in Umeå, Sundsvall, Stockholm, Göteborg, Jönköping, and Malmö. The highest tribunal is the Supreme Court of Justice (*högsta domstolen*) in Stockholm. Among special courts is the Labour Court for employer-worker disputes.

The guiding principle of amendments to the law has been to reform the offender and, by giving him vocational training, enable him to make a fresh start following his imprisonment. More than half of the existing prisons are run as open institutions. There is no death penalty.

**8. Education.**—Elementary education from the age of seven became free and compulsory in 1842. A far-reaching reform of the school system was initiated in 1962, after more than a decade of extensive experiment, with the introduction of a nine-year comprehensive school, without any concluding examination, which replaced existing primary and lower secondary schools. In the new schools compulsory schooling ends, at the age of 16, with form 9, which is divided into a number of branches: one for further theoretical studies in an advanced secondary school (*gymnasium*); others for general humanistic, technical, commercial, or social-economic studies; and one for preparatory vocational training. Teaching of foreign languages begins in the fourth grade with English; German or French is optional from grade 7. Pupils wishing to continue their studies after the ninth year (about 40% of the age group) have three choices: the three-year *gymnasium* which prepares for university entrance; the two-year, examination-free continuation school; and vocational schools with courses of up to four years.

Besides the two old universities in Uppsala (founded in 1477) and Lund (1668), there are universities in Stockholm, Göteborg, and Umeå. Various other institutions of technology, forestry, agriculture, commerce, dentistry, etc., have university status. A considerable expansion of the facilities at institutions of higher learning is in progress. Adult education activities are an outstanding feature of Swedish cultural life and are given substantial state support. People's high schools (*folkhögskolor*), run by county councils or by cultural, social, political, or religious organizations, aim at awakening interest in social and cultural questions among young people who have normally been gainfully employed for several years. Tuition is free in practically all of the schools as well as in the universities and colleges. Education is almost entirely the responsibility of the state.

**9. Defense.**—Sweden's policy of nonalignment in peacetime and neutrality in wartime is backed by a defense which is comparatively strong for a small nation and is the third largest item of state expenditure. The aim is total defense, *i.e.*, military defense supported by civil, economic, and psychological defense. A supreme commander coordinates activities of the services and directs military planning. Military service is compulsory for all males between ages 18 and 47. Training lasts ten months, followed by three one-month refresher periods.

A highly mechanized army of 700,000 men can be mobilized at short notice. The Home Guard, recruited voluntarily mainly from the age groups under 18 and over 47, is an integral part of the Army. The main object of the Royal Swedish Navy and the Royal Coast Artillery is to protect the long coast against invasion from the sea. Development in the Navy is toward a system of small mobile units operating from well-protected bases tunneled into solid rock. The Swedish Air Force, as befits its defensive role, is mainly composed of fighter and light bomber aircraft. Nearly all the equipment of the armed forces is produced within Sweden, *e.g.*, the advanced "S" tank, a throwaway anti-tank weapon, and supersonic fighters. During the 1960s an advanced multipurpose aircraft, the System 37 Viggen, was being developed for service at the end of the decade.

Every able-bodied Swedish citizen between 16 and 65 years of age who does not belong to the armed forces is liable to serve in the Civil Defense, the basic policy of which is mass evacuation and widespread provision of sub-rock and other shelters.

## VI. THE ECONOMY

The transition of the Swedish economy from a primarily agricultural to a primarily industrial basis began in the middle of the 19th century. It was linked with the development of the iron ore and forest industries and helped by the improvements in com-

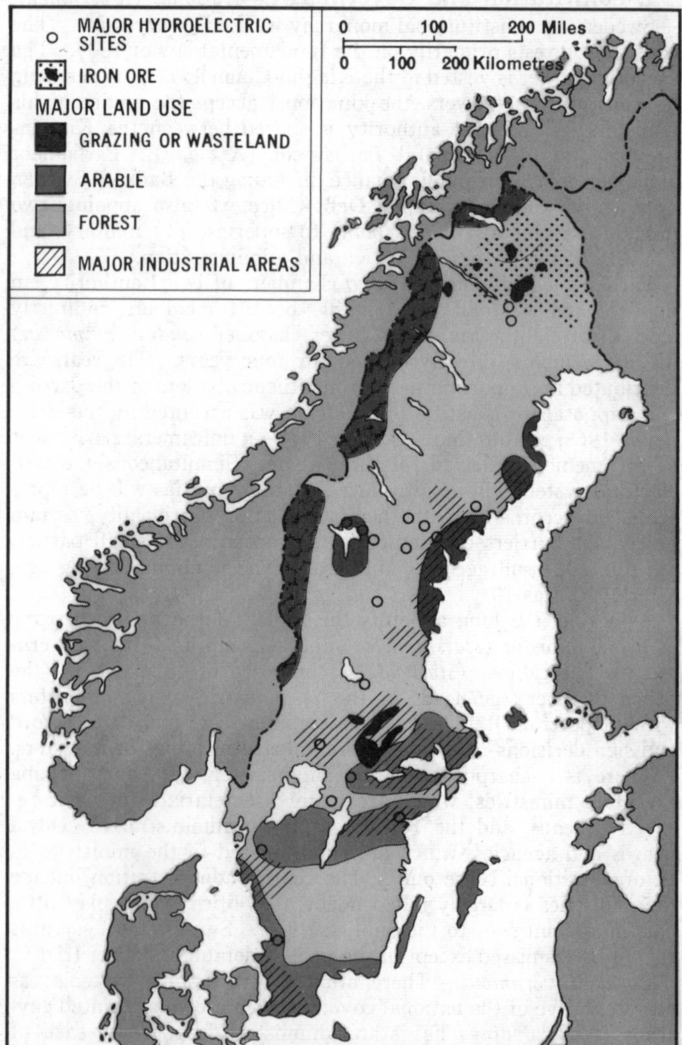


FIG. 2.—LAND USE AND MAJOR INDUSTRIAL AREAS OF SWEDEN

(LEFT) POLING LOGS TO A PAPER MILL (CENTRE) IN VÄRMLAND. (RIGHT) IRON ORE TRAIN LEAVING KIRUNA

munications brought about by the building of the railways and the spread of steam navigation. After World War II economic progress was rapid, total production increasing by two-thirds, and consumption by half, within 15 years. Of the gross national product in the 1960s, two-fifths was contributed by industry and one-fifth by distribution and communications; agriculture, forestry, and fishing together contributed less than one-tenth. Private enterprise accounted for three-quarters of the gross national product. The proportion of the total product devoted to investment rose from rather more than one-quarter to more than three-tenths.

### A. Production

**1. Agriculture.**—Only one-tenth of the whole area of Sweden is classed as arable or suitable for natural pasture. Of the agricultural land, nine-tenths is privately owned and about one-fifth is held on lease. After 1880 the number of people employed in agriculture steadily decreased, but output was maintained by mechanization. The country is practically self-sufficient in food. Agricultural prices are fixed and supported by Parliament with a view to establishing parity between agricultural and industrial incomes. By the late 1960s a government committee, considering future agricultural policy, proposed reduced production and a lower level of self-sufficiency. Farmers are encouraged to abandon small unprofitable farms so that these can be used for forestry or consolidated into larger units. Three-quarters of all holdings, however, are still under 15 ha. (37 ac.). Farmers do almost all their trading and processing through their own cooperatives.

The largest fertile districts are located in Skåne and around the lakes of Central Sweden. Of the arable land, two-fifths is used for grain (oats and barley, but also wheat and rye) and a similar area for fodder crops. Continuous plant research has produced improved varieties for Swedish conditions, and the yields in Skåne for barley and sugar beets are among the highest in the world. Meat and dairy products account for four-fifths of agricultural proceeds. Swine raising is important.

**2. Forestry.**—Forests, mainly of pine and spruce, cover about half the surface area of Sweden. The state owns one-quarter of the forests, private individuals one-half, and private companies the remainder. The estimated annual growth comfortably exceeds felling. Cutting and conservation are governed by law, and large-scale research is concentrated on increasing the yield and utilization of the wood.

**3. Fishing.**—The catch of fish by Swedish boats is adequate for domestic needs with a small surplus for export. More than half the catch is herring; cod is the next most important. On the west coast about two-thirds of all landings are in the province of Bohuslän, the centre of the canning industry. Freshwater fishing gives a much smaller catch, but its value is significant.

**4. Mining.**—Lapland contains some of the richest iron ore deposits in the world, estimated at 3,000,000,000 tons. The most important are at Kiruna, where the ore has a content of 60–70% iron and 1–2% phosphorus, and where underground mining has replaced open-cast operations. Other deposits of similar quality are at Gällivare and Svappavaara. Most of the Lapland ore is exported through the ice-free Norwegian port of Narvik (linked to Kiruna by rail in 1902), and some from Luleå.

The high-grade ores of Central Sweden have been worked since the 13th century. The domestic iron industry uses ore from the region of Bergslagen, but the deposits at Grängesberg, which have a high phosphorus content, are mainly for export. At Dannemora an ore with a low phosphorus content is mined. In the Skellefte region in North Sweden there are deposits of other ores, such as copper and lead. Uranium is found in Central Sweden.

**5. Fuel and Power.**—Sweden has extensive resources of water power but no worthwhile deposits of oil or coal. During the 1950s the contribution of coal and coke to total energy consumed fell from three-tenths to less than one-tenth, while that of oil rose from one-quarter to one-half; water power contributes one-third of all energy consumed, and Sweden is one of the few countries in which more than nine-tenths of electricity is supplied by water power. The water resources are of the low head type and are unevenly distributed. The resources in South and Central Sweden, near the main centres of demand, were developed early, but big rivers such as the Umeälv in North Sweden are now the most important sources. The transmission of large quantities of power to the southern part of the country is made possible by using a very high voltage system. Electricity production increased sixfold between 1939 and the early 1960s, when it was equivalent to nearly half the exploitable resources of water power. About three-fifths of the total output is used in industry. Underground installations account for half the total hydroelectric capacity.

A number of nuclear power stations are being established.

**6. Manufacturing Industries.**—Swedish industry is based on four major native resources—timber, iron ore, water power, and technical skill. There is a strong emphasis on quality. A characteristic feature of Swedish industry is the large number of small- and medium-sized units. Structural changes in the mid-1960s included numerous mergers and rapid Swedish industrial expansion abroad. Between 1938 and the early 1960s the volume of industrial production doubled, although the number of workers increased only slightly. This impressive increase in productivity was achieved by a large investment in plant and machinery, the training of a skilled labour force, and intensive research and development. A high proportion of the total industrial output is exported.

*Iron and Steel.*—Nearly all the pig iron produced is made with coke. Production of sponge iron (a Swedish development) increased after World War II until it was about one-tenth that of pig iron. Steel production expanded rapidly in the mid-1960s. Quality steels, largely produced in electric furnaces, but also by the Kaldo oxygen process, account for one-quarter of all ingot production.

*Engineering.*—The engineering industries form the largest industrial group. Their output is mainly of high quality specialized articles. Ball bearings are the most valuable single product. Automobile production expanded rapidly after World War II. Two firms dominate the electrical field; one specializes in heavy equipment for generation, transmission, and utilization of electrical power, the other in telecommunications equipment. Other Swedish products are compressors, munitions, office equipment, and automatic lighthouses. Shipbuilding is a major industry, and in the mid-1960s Sweden ranked third in world ship deliveries.

*Forest Industries.*—Timber and wood products were for long the major Swedish exports, but after World War II they took second place to the products of the mining and engineering industries. Vertical integration is characteristic of the forest industries and the production trend is toward higher added value. Log-floating is being replaced by a computerized truck and railway system. Pulp accounts for 30% of forest products, followed by paper (27%), sawn timber (22%), and wall board, prefabricated timber houses, furniture, etc. (21%). The exports of pulp and paper are 90% and 60% respectively of total production.

*Chemical Industries.*—Explosives and safety matches have been produced in Sweden since the 19th century. An electrochemical industry produces calcium carbide and ammonia. Ethyl alcohol, used to produce solvents and plastics, is a by-product of the sulfite pulp process. The china and glass industries are noted for their high standard of modern design. The food industries that form the second largest industrial category in terms of added value are directed toward the domestic market. The production of frozen foods is important.

### B. Trade and Finance

**1. Trade.**—Commerce is an important activity that employs about 500,000 people and accounts for one-eighth of the gross national product. Sweden is very dependent on foreign trade (exports are equivalent to about one-fifth of the gross national product) and the economy is therefore sensitive to fluctuations in world trade. After World War II foreign trade increased at twice the rate of domestic production and, since the terms of trade were increasingly favourable, made a dynamic contribution to the economy. Visible exports were usually rather less than imports, but the foreign earnings of the merchant navy are equivalent to about one-tenth of visible exports. About four-fifths of total trade is with Western European countries, particularly the Federal Republic of Germany, the United Kingdom, and other Scandinavian countries. Raw materials (mainly pulp, timber, and ore) sank from 44% of all exports to 25% during 1953–66, while semimanufactures (mainly paper and cardboard, iron and steel) rose from 20 to 25% and engineering products (mainly nonelectric machines, ships, and motor vehicles) from 26 to 39%. Sweden's share in the world export of forest products is 30% for pulp, 15% for sawn timber, and 11% for paper. Imports, consisting chiefly of raw materials and semifinished goods, machinery, motor vehicles, fuel, and consumer goods, increased rapidly in the 1960s and amounted to one-fifth of GNP in 1966.

There are close contacts between the Nordic countries in the economic field, at the official level through the Nordic Council, formed in 1952, and in the private sector through economic organizations and industrial enterprises. Within the European Free Trade Association (EFTA) of 1960, a common market for industrial products was established in Scandinavia, leading to a vigorous expansion of inter-Scandinavian trade, as exemplified by the tripling of Swedish exports to the other Scandinavian countries by the mid-1960s.

A special place in domestic distribution is occupied by Kooperativa Förbundet (KF), which started as a wholesale centre for the cooperative societies. KF is now engaged in both wholesale and retail trade, as well as production (*e.g.*, food processing, china, rubber goods), publishing, and insurance. In the early 1960s KF handled one-quarter of the nation's food trade.

**2. Currency and Banking.**—The unit of currency is the krona (plural kronor) of 100 öre (U.S. $1 = 5.17 kronor). The Bank of Sweden (1668), the oldest existing national bank in the world, is subject to Parliament and not to the government. Besides serving as a central bank for the commercial banks, it sets discount rates, controls the note circulation, and is generally responsible for monetary policy. Ordinary banking transactions are conducted by the 16 commercial banks; the five biggest, of which one is state-owned, control about four-fifths of the business. In the 1960s deposits in the 400 or so savings banks and in the Post Office Savings Bank exceeded slightly those in the commercial banks.

The role of the state in the Swedish economy has steadily expanded; whereas in 1938 the public sector accounted for less than one-sixth of the gross national product, by the mid-1960s the proportion had increased to one-quarter. Social welfare, education, and defense are the main items of government expenditure. Almost half the revenue is derived from direct taxes on income and capital at progressive rates (see *Taxation* above).

### C. Transport and Communications

Communications within Sweden have been difficult to develop because of the relatively long distances and the sparse population. The lakes and rivers, used widely from earliest times, were extended by canals in the 19th century, but the economic development of the country was closely linked with the building of the railways, in which the state took an active part from the beginning. An act of 1939 provided for the gradual nationalization of railways that were still privately owned. Since World War II passenger traffic has tended to decrease, and freight traffic to increase. All the main lines are electrified.

Between 1950 and 1960 the annual investment in roads almost doubled, and in the mid-1960s there was one car for every five inhabitants. Motorways were being constructed to link the main cities.

The merchant navy grew considerably in the 20th century and comprises about 840 ships, having a gross registered tonnage of more than 4,000,000. Roughly three-quarters of the tonnage is engaged in trade between foreign ports, making a significant contribution to the balance of payments.

In 1950 the commercial airlines of Denmark, Norway, and Sweden were merged to form the Scandinavian Airlines System (SAS), which operates a world network. Swedish domestic routes are operated by SAS and AB Linjeflyg, which is owned jointly by SAS and a consortium of Swedish newspaper companies. After World War II domestic passenger traffic expanded more rapidly than international traffic.

There are more telephones in relation to the size of the population in Sweden than in any other country in Europe. The Swedish broadcasting service is partly state-owned, offering three national radio programs and two television channels; there is no advertising.

Freedom of the press is guaranteed by the constitution. There are no great newspaper chains, some papers being privately owned and others subsidized by political parties. In all, there are about 110 newspapers and these are well supported in a country where every second inhabitant buys a daily paper. (L. O'C.)

Bibliography.—*Geography and General:* Axel Sømme (ed.), *The Geography of Norden* (1960); W. R. Mead, *An Economic Geography of the Scandinavian States and Finland* (1959); M. Zimmerman, *Les États scandinaves* (1933), vol. iii of *Géographie universelle,* ed. by P. Vidal de la Blanche and L. Gallois; C. A. M. Lindman, *Svensk Fanerogamflora,* 2nd ed. (1926); C.-E. Quensel, "Tendencies in Swedish Population Development," *Skandinaviska Banken, Quarterly Review,* vol. 38, no. 3 (1957); N. Andrén, *Modern Swedish Government* (1961);

E. Håstad, *The Parliament of Sweden* (1957); Swedish Board of Education, *The New School in Sweden* (1963); J. Orring, *The School System of General Education in Sweden* (1968); E. Westerlind and R. Beckman, *The Economy of Sweden: Structure and Tendencies* (1961); Swedish Central Bureau of Statistics, *Statistisk årsbok* (annual); Swedish Institute, *Fact Sheets on Sweden* and *Facts about Sweden.* Current history and statistics are summarized annually in *Britannica Book of the Year.*

*History:* For a selective bibliographical list *see* S. E. Bring, *Bibliografisk Handbok till Sveriges Historia* (1934). *See* also I. Andersson, *Sveriges Historia* (1943), Eng. trans. by C. Hannay, *A History of Sweden* (1956); R. Svanström and C. F. Palmstierna, *A Short History of Sweden* (1934); S. Carlsson and J. Rosén, *Svensk Historia,* 2 vol. (1961–62), vol. 2, 2nd ed. (1964); *The New Cambridge Modern History,* vol. v (1961), ch. xxii, "Scandinavia and the Baltic" by J. Rosén, and vol. vii (1961), ch. xv, by R. M. Hatton; *Svenska Arbetarklassens Historia* (1941– ); Royal Institute of International Affairs, *The Scandinavian States and Finland: a Political and Economic Survey,* compiled by G. M. Gathorne-Hardy and others (1951); *Survey of International Affairs, 1939–1946,* vol. 9, *The War and the Neutrals,* ed. by A. and V. M. Toynbee, with reference to the chapter on Sweden by A. H. Hicks (1956). Among the publications of the Swedish Institute in Stockholm, *see* S. Carlsson, *History of Modern Sweden* (1963); G. Hägglöf, *A Test of Neutrality, Sweden in the Second World War* (1961); K. E. Birnbaum, *Swedish Foreign Policy* (1962). N. Andrén, *Power-Balance and Non-Alignment* (1967); S. V. Anderson, *The Nordic Council: a Study of Scandinavian Regionalism* (1967); S. Oakley, *The Story of Sweden* (1966); *Suecana Extranca, Books About Sweden and Swedish Literature in Foreign Languages,* ed. by the Bibliographisk Institute of the Swedish Royal Library (1968); I. Wizelius (ed.), *Sweden in the Sixties* (1967); F. Schmidt, *The Law of Labour Relations in Sweden* (1962).

**SWEDENBORG, EMANUEL** (1688–1772), Swedish scientist, philosopher and theologian, one of the greatest and most learned men of his country, was born in Stockholm on Jan. 29, 1688, the second son of Jesper Swedberg, who was later appointed bishop of Skara. The family assumed the name of Swedenborg when it was ennobled in 1719. Emanuel was educated at Uppsala university; and after completing his course there he traveled abroad for five years (1710–14), visiting England, Holland, France and Germany in pursuit of scientific and mechanical knowledge. At that period his chief interests were mathematics and astronomy, and he was cordially received by John Flamsteed and by Edmund Halley. He was anxious to see and to hear Sir Isaac Newton, whose work he studied avidly, but there is no evidence that the two met. Swedenborg's inventive and mechanical genius flowered early, and his plans, practical and otherwise, ranged from a method of finding terrestrial longitude by the moon to new methods of constructing docks and even to tentative suggestions for the submarine and the airplane.

On returning home, Swedenborg began to publish a scientific periodical, *Daedalus hyperboreus* (Uppsala, 1716–18). Charles XII of Sweden was interested in the venture but would provide no funds, and after six issues the periodical was obliged to cease publication. Charles, however, in 1716 appointed Swedenborg assessor extraordinary to the Royal College of Mines, in which office, and later as assessor, he devoted himself for 30 years to the development and improvement of Sweden's metal-mining industry. But he continued to seek fresh knowledge in this and other spheres and from time to time traveled in Europe and in England in pursuit of learning in physics, chemistry, mechanics and philosophy. He had already published in 1718 the first work on algebra in the Swedish language; and in 1721 he published at Amsterdam his *Prodromus principiorum rerum naturalium* in which he offered a geometrical explanation of the phenomena of chemistry and physics. In 1734 he published his *Opera philosophica et mineralia,* 3 vol. (Leipzig), the first volume of which constitutes his *Principia rerum naturalium.* In this work, though without the facts that later scientists have demonstrated, he reached by inductive argument conclusions that are close to the theories of modern nuclear physicists. The first product of the infinite is conceived of as "pure motion" or conatus-to-create, and the subsequent creation is a complex of motion. The atom is composed of vortex particles, but these are compositions of motions more interior. The pattern strongly resembles the pattern of the atom as described in terms of nucleus and electrons. In the same work and from the same general principle Swedenborg suggested the nebular hypothesis to account for the formation of planets.

PORTRAIT BY PETER KRAFFT THE ELDER IN GRIPSHOLM CASTLE. BY COURTESY OF THE SVENSKA PORTRÄTTARKIVET

SWEDENBORG

During the next ten years Swedenborg was engaged in anatomical and physiological studies. As he had sought to find the "soul" of creation in pure motion, he now sought to understand the soul of man and to find it in its own kingdom, which is the body. He published *Oeconomia regni animalis,* 2 parts (London and Amsterdam, 1740–41), and *Regnum animale,* 3 parts (The Hague, 1744–45). Although in this field of study he made many experimental investigations, he used them only sparingly, because he recognized the danger of trusting too much to his own observations and of "originating a whole series of inductive arguments from my particular discovery alone. . . . I therefore laid aside my instruments . . . and determined rather to rely on the researches of others than to trust to my own" (introduction to *Oeconomia*). In both works he therefore begins each section with numerous quotations from the accepted experimental anatomists and then proceeds to reason upon them. Gustaf Retzius acknowledged that Swedenborg had been the first to indicate the real nature of the cerebrospinal fluid. In the *Oeconomia* Swedenborg also showed, long before any other physiologist, that the motion of the brain synchronizes with that of the lungs and not with that of the heart and circulatory system; and he discerned the relationship between various regions of the cerebral cortex and corresponding motor regions of the body.

It is, however, in the field of theology that the name of Swedenborg is chiefly known, and the circumstances in which he turned to theological studies have tended to obscure his reputation as a great scientist and philosopher. He asseverates that his entry upon this new study was in response to a divine vision and call; that his spiritual senses were opened so that he might be in the spiritual world as consciously as in this world; and that the long series of exegetical and theological works that proceeded from his pen constituted a revelation from God for a new age of truth and reason in religion. Furthermore, he held that this new revelation of the Lord was what was meant by the second advent. Because of his otherworld experiences Swedenborg has often been regarded as a spiritualist "medium," yet it may be observed that the normal idea of mediumship is reversed, the man being admitted into the spiritual world, not the spirits into the material world. Nor can he properly be classed among the mystics, for in his dry, matter-of-fact accounts of the spiritual world and in his acutely reasoned theology there is little in common with mysticism. His manner is still that of the scientific and philosophic investigator.

Philosophically he had consistently recognized the infinite as the indivisible power and life within all creation, and he had never wavered in his belief that this infinite was God. In his theology he maintains the absolute unity of God in essence and person. A trinity of persons in one God is, he says, an impossibility of thought, but since God is the Divine Man there is necessarily in Him, as in every person, a trinity of love, wisdom and activity; and in God these are infinite and divine. It was this God who came into the world as Jesus Christ for the redemption and salvation of men. The inmost soul of Jesus was the Divine itself, the one God; yet, in order that there might be an intimate contact of God with fallen man, the Divine assumed from Mary a human nature comprising all the planes of human life. But during the course of Jesus' life on earth, by resistance to every possible temptation and by living to their divine fullness the truths of the Word of God, all that was actually from Mary was expelled, and the planes of human nature were "glorified" from the indwelling Divine Soul and became the divine embodiment of that soul. The Trinity is therefore a Trinity in one Person, the Father being the originating Divine itself, the Son the embodiment of that Divine and the Holy Spirit the outflowing activity of the "Divine Human."

In rejecting tripersonalism Swedenborg necessarily rejects the orthodox conceptions of redemption. The redemption of mankind was a deliverance from the domination of evil. The hells, which are the communities of the spirits of evil men in the spiritual world, were aspiring to enforce themselves upon men's minds, destroying their freedom to discern between truth and falsity and therefore between good and evil. By admitting into Himself their temptations and by complete resistance to them, Jesus broke their power; and the inflowing of the Inmost Divine into the human plane thus perfected interposed an eternal and infinitely powerful barrier between the hells and men. The "Divine Human," to which belongs "all power in heaven and on earth," stands forever between man and the forcible imposition of themselves by the hells. Man is thus free to know and obey the truth. His salvation depends on acceptance of and response to divine truth.

Swedenborg, accepting that all creation has its origin in the divine love and wisdom, accepts that all created things are necessarily forms and effects of specific aspects of that love and wisdom and so "correspond," on the material plane, to spiritual realities. The material realm is one of effects whose causes are spiritual and whose purpose is divine. The Scriptures, he says, are written according to this principle of "correspondence," which becomes the key to unlock their spiritual teaching. In *Arcana coelestia,* 8 vol. (London, 1749–56), he presents a detailed interpretation of Genesis and Exodus according to the principle of correspondence; and in the posthumously published *Apocalypsis explicata,* 4 vol. (London, 1785–89), he does the same with the Book of Revelation and incidentally with many other parts of the Scriptures. The theological teaching in his works was collated as a systematic theology in *Vera Christiana Religio* (Amsterdam, 1771). The philosophy of the creation and maintenance of the universe is dealt with in *Sapientia angelica de Divino Amore et de Divina Sapientia* (Amsterdam, 1763) and *Sapientia angelica de Divina Providentia* (Amsterdam, 1764). Swedenborg's best-known work is probably *Heaven and Hell* (*De Coelo et ejus mirabilibus, et de inferno, London,* 1758).

Swedenborg died in London on March 29, 1772, and was buried in the Swedish church. In 1908 the Swedish government had his body removed to Uppsala cathedral.

Swedenborg neither preached nor founded a church. The New Jerusalem Church, founded by a few disciples about 1784, remains small but has branches throughout the world. The Swedenborg society was founded in London in 1810 to publish his works.

BIBLIOGRAPHY.—R. L. Tafel, *Documents Concerning the Life and Character of Emanuel Swedenborg,* 3 vol. (1875–77); G. Trobridge, *Swedenborg, Life and Teaching,* 4th ed. (1944); E. Swift, *Swedenborg, the Man and His Works* (1883; new ed., 1932); C. S. Sigstedt, *The Swedenborg Epic* (1953); also the *Transactions* of the International Swedenborg congress, 1910 (1911). (A. CM.)

## SWEDISH LANGUAGE.

**SWEDISH LANGUAGE.** Swedish, one of the Scandinavian languages (*q.v.*), is the national language of Sweden, where only certain minority groups speak other languages (*c.* 30,000 Finnish-speakers in northern Sweden, mostly in Tornedalen on the Finnish frontier, and *c.* 5,000 Lapp-speakers in Lapland). Historically, a distinction is made between East Scandinavian and West Scandinavian languages; Swedish and Danish belong to the former, Norwegian, Icelandic, and Faeroese to the latter. If, however, one considers the present-day relationship between the three continental languages, one is inclined to group Swedish and Norwegian together rather than Swedish and Danish; because Danish later began to diverge by itself, a modern Swede has more difficulty in understanding Danish than Norwegian. Swedish is spoken by about 8 million people, of whom 7½ million live in Sweden, 330,000 in Finland, and an ever-diminishing number in the United States and Canada. Up to World War II an old Swedish-speaking settlement of about 7,500 persons existed on the coast and nearby islands of Estonia. Most of these people now live in Sweden. In Finland, Swedish is officially recognized alongside Finnish.

**History.**—During the first six or seven centuries of the Christian era, practically the same Germanic language, Common Norse, was probably spoken over the whole of Scandinavia. By about 800, dialectal differences of such importance had appeared that the different Scandinavian languages could be distinguished. The history of the Swedish language is conventionally divided into two main periods: Old Swedish (O.Swed.; *c.* 800–1526) and New Swedish (after 1526).

**The Old Swedish Period.**—The history of the language up to *c.* 1225 is chiefly known from numerous runic inscriptions (*see* RUNE). After this, the Latin alphabet began to be used. Early Old Swedish (usually known as Runic Swedish) has a number of archaic traits: it preserves the old Germanic diphthongs, the four-case system in nominal declension, and almost complete conjugation of verbs according to person. It has not yet developed the indefinite article. The suffixed definite article (*e.g., -in* in O.Swed. *bokin* "the book," originally an enclitic demonstrative pronoun) came into use during this period. Further changes began to take place: *e.g.,* the old diphthongs *ai, au,* and *öy* were monophthongized (*ai* > *ei* > long *e; au* and *öy* > long *ö*). These changes occurred earlier in southern Sweden than in the more northern areas, where monophthongization probably did not occur until the 12th century. In certain peripheral dialects, in Gotland and in various areas of Finland and Norrland, these diphthongs are still preserved.

Especially during the 14th and 15th centuries, radical changes occurred in the language. Various vowel-shifts took place: for example, the long *a-, o-,* and *u*-sounds gradually changed to [o:] (at first written *aa* or *o,* but later with a new letter, *å*), [u:], and [ʉ:]. (For the phonetic symbols used in this article, *see* PHONETICS.) The voiceless dental fricative (originally written *þ,* later *th*) changed to *t.* (The corresponding voiced sound, also written *þ* in the earliest texts, but later *dh,* changed to a stop, *d,* but, on the whole, not until the New Swedish period.) The stops *g* and *k* were affricated before palatal vowels to *gj* and *kj.* The plosive element was later progressively weakened in favour of the fricative. The result of these changes, which were carried to their conclusion during the New Swedish period, is that older *g* and *k* before palatal vowels are now pronounced as [j] (*giva* [ji:va] "give") and [ç] (*kök* [çø:k] "kitchen") respectively. Older *tj* and *kj* have also become [ç] (*tjuv* [çʉ:v] "thief"), and the appearance of a new sound [ʃ] (also [ʂ], *see* below) for the combinations *sk* + palatal vowel, *skj, stj,* and *sj* (*sked* [ʃe:d] "spoon," *skjul* [ʃʉ:l] "shed," *stjäla* [ʃɛ:la] "steal," *sjö* [ʃø:] "lake"), is to be connected with these changes. Modern orthography, in the majority of cases, reflects a word's older phonology. All short syllables in stressed position were lengthened, and the accidence was simplified. A great number of Low German loanwords and derivative elements found their way into the language, especially during the later part of the medieval period, and, while the language of the oldest Swedish literature, written in the Latin alphabet (mainly codes of laws), is very pure Swedish, religious literature shows clear signs of Latin influence, particularly in the syntax.

**The New Swedish Period.**—New Swedish dates from 1526, when the New Testament was printed in Swedish. The written language attained such stability that widespread sound changes rarely occasioned alterations in spelling. Of such extensive changes, mention may be made of the following: in final position, old short *n* was lost (frequently with a change in the preceding vowel: *solen* > *sola* "the sun"). The combinations *rd, rt, rs, rn, rl* were assimilated to the alveolar sounds [ɖ], [ʈ], [ʂ], [ɳ], [ɭ]. Certain initial consonant-groups were also simplified: in the combinations *hj, lj, dj, hv* (*hjälpa* "to help," *ljus* "light," *djup* "deep," *hvad* "what") the first consonants were lost. In modern times, because of the influence of the written language on the spoken language, the older forms have occasionally been reintroduced, especially those that had survived in certain dialects. Thus, in the Swedish spoken by educated people, only the *-en* ending appears in forms such as *solen,* and not the *-a* ending as in *sola.* In the written language, most changes have occurred in vocabulary and syntax (*see* below).

**Phonology.**—Standard Swedish, as it is spoken in central Sweden, has 9 vowel-phonemes: /a, e, i, o, u, y, å, ä, ö/, and 18 consonant-phonemes: /p, t, k, b, d, g, f, s, ʃ, ç, v, j, m, n, ŋ, l, r, h/. In addition to [d], [t], [s], [n], [l], there is also a series of corresponding alveolar sounds which are phonemically distinct (cf. *bod* [bu:d] "shed" and *bord* [bu:ɖ] "table"; *vana* [vɑ:na] "custom" and *varna* [vɑ:ɳa] "to warn"). In phonemic descriptions of the language, however, these retroflex sounds are usually regarded as the phonetic result of the combination of the phoneme /r/ + a dental phoneme. Historically, they are the result of the assimilation of *r* + a dental. There are three more written letters in Swedish than in English: these are the vowels *å*, *ä*, and *ö*, which are placed at the end of the alphabet.

As regards the system of 9 vowel- and 18 consonant-phonemes, the following points are worth noting. As a rule, long vowels are qualitatively different from short vowels, most markedly in the case of /a/ and /u/, which, when long, are pronounced [ɑ:], [ʉ:], when short [a], [ɵ]. The vowel-phonemes /o, u, å/ can also differ qualitatively, viz. /o/: [u:], [u] (written *o*); /u/: [ʉ:], [ɵ] (written *u*); and /å/: [o:], [ɔ] (written *å* or *o*). Before alveolar consonants, /ä/ and /ö/ usually have a more open pronunciation: [æ], [œ]. The stops /p, t, k/ are aspirated immediately before a stressed vowel, except in the combinations *sp, st, sk*. The pronunciation of Swedish in Finland, however, totally lacks aspiration, undoubtedly as a result of influence from Finnish. In most of Sweden *r* has dental articulation; in southern Sweden, however, uvular *r* appears. In these areas (and in the pronunciation of Swedish in Finland) *r* + *d, t, s, n*, or *l* is usually pronounced as two separate sounds. As a variant of the normal lateral *l*, a "thick" *l* sometimes appears; this is often formed by a bow-shaped dropping of the tip of the tongue from the roof of the palate. It appears only in certain positions, especially after consonants, and more frequently after back vowels than front (*e.g.*, in *blod* "blood," and *tala* "to speak"). It never replaces lateral *l* when this latter is long, and does so only very exceptionally at the beginning of a word. This "thick" *l* is not found in some areas (for example, in southern Sweden and in Gotland), and is considered by many to be uncultivated pronunciation. The phoneme /ʃ/ can, in any position, appear as [ʂ], although [ʃ] is, perhaps, more usual before a stressed vowel, while [ʂ], appears in other positions.

A stressed syllable is always long, that is to say, it contains either a long vowel, or a short vowel followed either by a long consonant or by a number of consonants. When a stressed vowel loses its stress, it also loses its length: *e.g.*, [ˣkal:a] "to call," but [kalaˈhi:t] "to summon." The main stress is usually on the first syllable of a word, as is characteristic of Germanic languages. The numerous exceptions to this rule are mainly found in loanwords (*bakˈterier* "bacteria," *matemaˈtik* "mathematics"), in the many words formed with loaned suffixes (*läraˈrinna* "schoolmistress," *halˈvera* "to halve"), and also in certain words with prefixes (*beˈtala* "to pay," *förˈklara* "to explain"). Every Swedish word is pronounced with one of two different pitch accents, often known as "single tone" and "double tone." These tones can distinguish semantically between two words: *e.g.*, *anden* (single tone; definite form of *and*) "the duck," and ˣ*anden* (double tone; definite form of *ande*) "the spirit." The contrast between these two tones is different in different parts of the country. In central Sweden, disyllabic words with single tone have a rising-falling tone. The single tone is chiefly found in words which are, or were at an earlier stage of the language, monosyllabic: *e.g.*, ˈ*hus* "house," and *han* ˈ*sitter* < *sitr* "he sits." The double tone is found in native words which have, or had earlier, more than one syllable: *e.g.*, *han* ˣ*kallar* "he calls."

**Vocabulary.**—Although Swedish vocabulary is basically native, the language contains a great number of loanwords. Many everyday words are Low German loanwords (*språk* "language," *kort* "short," *fråga* "to ask"). With the Reformation in the 16th century and Sweden's political expansion in the 17th, a number of High German words were imported. From the middle of the 17th to the end of the 18th century, French had the greatest influence. During the 20th century most loanwords have been English. Ever since the 17th century there have been attempts to reduce the foreign element and to exploit native vocabulary. Recently, increasing attention has been paid to Norwegian and Danish, so as to avoid unnecessary divergences between these three languages. Swedish lends itself to extensive formation of new words by compounding, and occasionally the written language is overweighted by this practice.

**Morphology.**—Modern Standard Swedish does not formally differentiate between words originally masculine and originally feminine in gender. With regard to words for inanimate objects, a new *genus reale* has superseded masculine and feminine, and one pronoun (*den*) has been substituted for *han* "he" and *hon* "she." Masculine (*pojken, han* "the boy, he"), feminine (*flickan, hon* "the girl, she"), and *genus reale* (*stolen, den* "the stool, it") can be taken together as a *genus utrum*, in contrast to a *genus neutrum* (*huset, det* "the house, it"). However, in contrast to Standard Swedish, most Swedish dialects still have a three-gender system.

Apart from a special genitival form in *-s* (in both singular and plural), nouns and adjectives have no case inflection. Only personal pronouns have a special object form (cf. *jag* "I" and *mig* "me"). Most nouns form the plural with one of the following endings: *-or, -ar, -er, -n*. The majority of neuter nouns have the same form in the singular as in the plural. The definite form of a noun is formed by means of an ending: *e.g.*, *sol* "sun," *solen* "the sun," *solar* "suns," *solarna* "the suns"; *hus* "house" and "houses," *huset* "the house," *husen* "the houses." There is, however, an additional definite article, which is used when an adjective precedes a noun in the definite form: *e.g.*, *den lille pojken* "the little boy"; *de stora glasen* "the big glasses." The indefinite form of the adjective differs in ending from the definite form: *e.g.*, *ett stort hus* "a big house," but *det stora huset* "the big house."

As in all Germanic languages, verbs are either strong (*rida, red, ridit* "to ride," "rode," "ridden") or weak (*kalla, kallade, kallat* "to call," "called," "called"). In the spoken language, and normally in the written language, there is no inflection of the verb according to person, but in certain styles of the written language a special plural form is to be found, although this is falling out of use. Besides a compound passive, there is a passive form in *-s*; thus, present: *skräddaren lagar rocken* "the tailor repairs the coat," becomes *rocken lagas av skräddaren* "the coat is being repaired by the tailor"; and imperfect: *s. lagade r.* becomes *r. lagades av s.*

**Syntax.**—Because of the general lack of case inflection, the word order (subject–predicate–object) is fairly fixed. In principal clauses, inverted word order appears particularly in three cases: in interrogative sentences (*kommer du?* "are you coming?"), when a modification to the predicate precedes the predicate (*nu kommer han* "now he is coming"), and when a subordinate clause precedes the principal clause (*då jag kom, satt han vid bordet* "when I came, he was sitting at the table").

In contrast, for example, to German usage, the complement agrees with its subject in number and gender: *e.g.*, *pojken är stor* "the boy is big," *huset är stort* "the house is big," *pojkarna är stora* "the boys are big." The third person possessive pronoun is partly *hans* "his," *hennes* "her," *dess* "its," *deras* "their," and partly the reflexive *sin, sitt* (singular), and *sina* (plural). The first group is used when the possessive pronoun refers to a person or thing other than the subject, the second, reflexive, group when the pronoun refers back to the subject of the sentence.

To express future time, either the present tense of the verb is used, or a compound tense is formed with the auxiliary verb *skall* "shall," "will," or with the verb *komma* "to come": *e.g.*, *jag reser*, or *jag skall resa*, or *jag kommer att resa till England nästa år* "I shall go to England next year." A peculiar use of the imperfect appears in the spoken language: *e.g.*, looking at a beautiful flower, one might say: *Det var en vacker blomma* "what a beautiful flower!" (literally "that was a beautiful flower").

During the 20th century, the written language has been considerably influenced by the educated spoken language, especially in sentence structure, choice of words, and, to a certain extent, in inflection. A tendency to reduce the number of clauses in a sentence is to be observed. Of the three negations *icke, ej*, and *inte*, the written language earlier used chiefly *icke* and *ej*, while *inte*, practically the only form used in the spoken language, only appeared in writing in a looser style. By mid-century *inte* had become the prevailing form, even in the written language, while *icke* and *ej* steadily became less common. An example of the written language's inflectional approximation to the spoken language is to be seen in the tendency to drop the plural form of verbs. Certain features which tend to make the language more ponderous, however, have also appeared, such as the extensive habit of making the verb of the sentence into a noun and, instead, substituting a relatively meaningless verb to act as predicate (*e.g., Den 1 maj skall en sänkning av detaljpriserna äga rum,* literally "On May 1 a reduction of retail prices will take place," appears instead of *Den 1 maj skall detaljpriserna sänkas* "On May 1 retail prices will be reduced"). The facility with which passive forms can be formed by simply adding the ending *-s* has sometimes led to overuse of this form.

**Dialects.**—Swedish dialects are conventionally divided into the following groups: the South Swedish dialects (main province: Skåne); the Göta dialects (main province: Västergötland); the Svea dialects (main province: Uppland); the Norrland dialects (large parts of Norrland); the East Swedish dialects (Swedish as spoken in Finland and Estonia); the Gutnish dialects (Gotland). Particularly archaic features are to be found in the Norrland, East Swedish, and Gutnish dialects, as well as in the local dialects of the northern part of Dalarna. During recent decades, local peculiarities have been superseded more and more by the standard spoken language. The Svea dialects have played the greatest part in the formation of a "Received Standard," but the Göta dialects have also been important.

BIBLIOGRAPHY.—*History and Grammar:* A. Noreen, *Vårt språk: nysvensk grammatik,* 7 vol., incomplete (1903–24), *Altschwedische Grammatik mit Einschluss des Altgutnischen* (1904), and *Geschichte der nordischen Sprachen,* 3rd ed. (1913); I. Björkhagen, *Modern Swedish Grammar* (1944); N. Beckman, *Svensk språklära,* 9th ed. (1945); G. Bergman, *A Short History of the Swedish Language,* trans. by F. P. Magoun, Jr., and H. Kökeritz (1947); E. Wessén, *Våra folkmål* (a survey of Swedish dialects), 6th ed. (1960), and *Svensk språkhistoria,* 3 vol. (1956–62); B. Malmberg, *Svensk fonetik,* 2nd ed. (1956); R. J. McClean, *Teach Yourself Swedish: a Grammar of the Modern Language,* 3rd ed. (1950); A.-M. Beite *et al., Basic Swedish Grammar* (1963).

*Dictionaries: Ordbok över svenska språket,* ed. by Svenska Akademien, 23 vol. (by 1965 letters A–Sa had been covered) (1893– ); O. Östergren, *Nusvensk ordbok* (by 1965 A–U had been covered) (1919– ); W. E. Harlock and A. Gabrielson, *Svensk-engelsk ordbok* (covering A–R) (1936–51); E. Hellquist, *Svensk etymologisk ordbok,* 2 vol., 3rd ed. (1948); K. Kärre *et al., Engelsk-svensk ordbok,* 3rd ed. (1961); I. E. Gullberg, *Svensk-engelsk fackordbok (a Swedish-English Dictionary of Technical Terms . . .)* (1964). (S. C. E. F.)

## SWEDISH LITERATURE.

The first records of literature in Sweden are of more interest to the philologist than to the literary scholar, since the oldest form of Swedish writing is in runes. About 2,400 runic inscriptions survive from the earliest period of Old Swedish (*c.* A.D. 800–1200); most of them are found in Uppland (eastern Sweden) and date from the 11th and 12th centuries. Cut in stone, and often put into metrical form, they generally commemorate the genealogy and achievements of the dead. The most remarkable stone, the Rök Stone in Östergötland, dates from the 9th century and is unique in the length and interest of its inscriptions, written in seven different types of script (*see* RUNE: *Scandinavia*). Other notable inscriptions, in the so-called staffless script, have been discovered in the region of Hälsingland. Unfortunately, save for these runes, nothing of the earliest Swedish literature has survived, although it is likely that some kind of literary culture akin to that of Iceland existed (*see* ICELANDIC LITERATURE).

BY COURTESY OF THE ANTIKVARISK TOPOGRAFISKA ARKIVET, STOCKHOLM

THE RÖK STONE, ÖSTERGÖTLAND

**The Middle Ages (1200–1523).**—Swedish literature proper emerged slowly during the late Middle Ages. After a long period of linguistic change in Scandinavia (*see* SWEDISH LANGUAGE: *History*), Old Swedish established itself as a separate language, and the foundations of a native literature were laid in the early 13th century. At about the same time, however, the Christian Church defeated the old religion and introduced Latin as the language of the educated. The importance of Christianity in the cultural development of Sweden is immense, although the new religion prevailed only gradually, and pagan rites existed well into the Middle Ages and in remote districts much longer. Slowly, too, the primitive society of Viking times was replaced by a more complex organization, dominated by the nobility and clergy, patrons and providers of literature. Latin eclipsed the vernacular as a literary medium; and this helps explain the derivative nature of medieval Swedish literature. The most remarkable literary document of the period, the *Revelationes* (first published in 1492) of St. Bridget (*q.v.; c.* 1303–73), illustrates the relationship between the two languages: originally dictated by St. Bridget and written in Swedish, her revelations were immediately translated into Latin by her confessors—later to be retranslated into the vernacular. One more Latin writer of this period attained international recognition, the Dominican monk Petrus de Dacia (*c.* 1235–89), whose *Vita benedictae virginis Christi Christinae* offers a rare combination of psychological subtlety and mystic fervour.

The oldest extant manuscript in Old Swedish is *Västgötalagen* ("The Law of West Gotland"), part of a native legal code compiled in the 1220s. A number of such local codes survive: *e.g., Östgötalagen* and *Dalalagen,* records of provincial laws privately codified by a magistrate; and lawbooks like *Upplandslagen* (1296) and *Södermannalagen* (1327), compiled on official initiative and ratified by the king. These codes are forceful and full of concrete images; they often use alliteration and a solemn prose rhythm to make their pronouncements more memorable. They offer the happiest examples of the vernacular literature in their age and culminate in King Magnus Eriksson's *Landslag* (*c.* 1350) and in a similar work, *Um styrilsi kununga och hofdhinga* ("On the Conduct of Kings and Princes"), probably written *c.* 1330 for the guidance of the same ruler.

The poetry of chivalry reached Sweden *c.* 1300. *Eufemiavisorna* ("The Songs of Euphemia"), written in rhymed doggerel between 1303 and 1312, include a translation of Chrétien de Troyes's *Le Chevalier au lion* (*Yvain*) and a free adaptation of the story of *Floire et Blanchefleur* (*see* AUCASSIN AND NICOLETTE). The spirit of romance (*q.v.*) is also manifest in many of the anonymous ballads that, though not transcribed until much later, were probably composed in the 14th and 15th centuries. One of the best known, the ballad of *Ebbe Skammelsson,* is of Danish origin and tells a grim story of love and revenge mitigated by traces of chivalrous and Christian ideals. In some of the folk songs (as the ballads, inadequately, used to be called) the new ideals of courtly love (*q.v.*) are combined with pagan lore of elves, river-gods, and magic mountains, while others are inspired by historical events. Though heterogeneous in quality and style, and in most cases deriving from foreign sources, the ballads form the most accessible and enjoyable genre of Swedish medieval literature.

Apart from the ballads, the late 14th and the 15th centuries are bare of original literature, while translations and adaptations abound. These include versions of books of the Bible, a long doggerel romance of Alexander the Great (*Konung Alexander, c.* 1380), and a political allegory, the poem *Schacktavelslek* ("The Game of Chess"; *c.* 1465). In the rhymed chronicles, too—*e.g., Erikskrönikan, Karlskrönikan, Sturekrönikan,* and *Lilla rimkrönikan* (which, together with some minor chronicles, treats events up to 1520)—political interest prevails.

**Reformation and Stormaktstid (1523–1732).**—Two dates mark the beginning of modern Swedish history: 1523—the breach with Denmark and Gustavus I Vasa's accession; 1527—the breach with Rome and the establishment of a national Lutheran Church. The political revolution, which eventually brought Sweden to the position of a European power (*stormakt*), had no considerable effect on literature until a century later, but the Reformation wholly dominated Swedish letters during the 16th century.

The most important literary event of this period is the translation of the Bible (the New Testament, 1526, and the complete *Gustav Vasas bibel,* 1541), which inaugurated modern Swedish and provided an inexhaustible source of motifs, metaphors, and imagery for poets of subsequent times. Closely involved in the Bible translation were the apostles of the Swedish Reformation, Olaus Petri (1493–1552) and his brother Laurentius (1499–1573), as well as Laurentius Andreae (*c.* 1480–1552), at one time Gustavus' chancellor. Olaus Petri made other contributions to literature as well. After studying at Wittenberg, he returned to Sweden full of reforming zeal, which won him the king's favour; later his independence and critical spirit nearly cost him his life. His vigorous approach is revealed in his published sermons, hymn translations, catechism, and legal writings; it is shown, too, in *Een Swensk crönica* (published in 1818, in a collection of medieval historical documents), the first historical work in Sweden to be based on critical research. Olaus Petri may also have written the biblical *Tobie comedia* (1550), the first complete extant Swedish play. (*See* PETRI, OLAUS AND LAURENTIUS.)

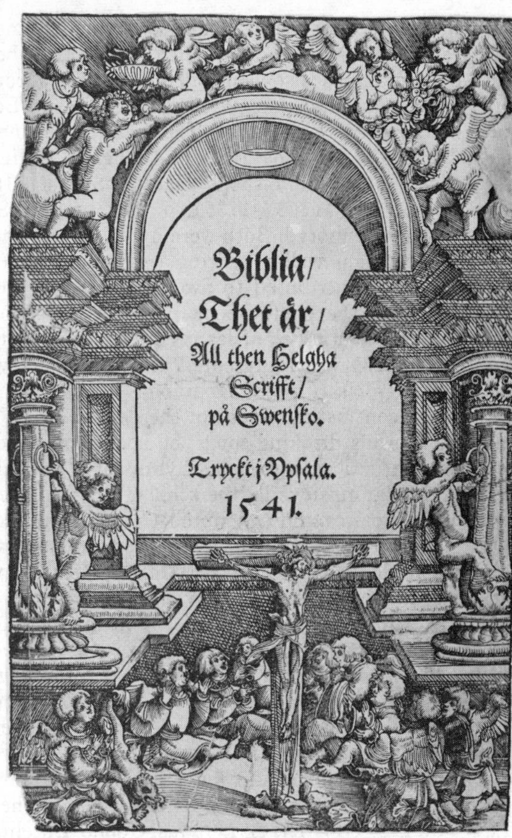


BOTH BY COURTESY OF THE TRUSTEES OF THE BRITISH MUSEUM; PHOTO; BY J. R. FREEMAN AND CO.

(ABOVE) WOODCUT PAGE FROM THE LATIN VERSION OF ST. BRIDGET'S "REVELATIONES," PUBLISHED AT LÜBECK IN 1492, SHOWING ST. BRIDGET AND HER CONFESSOR. (RIGHT) WOODCUT TITLE PAGE OF THE FIRST SWEDISH TRANSLATION OF THE BIBLE (1541)

As a consequence of the Reformation, two of Sweden's most distinguished scholars of the period were driven into exile. In his *Historia de omnibus gothorum sueonumque regibus* (1555), Johannes Magnus (1488–1544), Roman Catholic archbishop of Uppsala before the Reformation, provided Sweden with a number of valiant and glorious kings until then unknown to critical historians but readily accepted by the political ideologists of *stormaktstiden.* Johannes' brother Olaus Magnus (*q.v.;* 1490–1557) wrote the first geographical and ethnographical account of Scandinavia, *Historia de gentibus septentrionalibus* (1555), in which vivid description and accurate observation are mingled with nostalgic dreams of a hyperborean Atlantis.

Meanwhile academic learning was in decline. The University of Uppsala (founded 1477) closed in 1515 because of political unrest. It was not revived until late in the 16th century and became a focus of learning and letters only in the 17th century. Associated with it were Johannes Rudbeckius (1581–1646), one of the first Swedish educators, and Johannes Messenius (*c.* 1579–1636), who wrote several mythical-historical plays, such as *Disa* (1611) and *Signill* (1612). Although formless and crude, these plays enjoyed great popularity, as did Magnus Olai Asteropherus' *Tisbe* (performed 1610), the first nondidactic drama in Sweden.

In the first half of the 17th century, literature remained limited in scope and quantity. Some Latin poetry, the sermons of Rudbeckius, and a handful of plays are worth recording. A unique contribution, however, was made by the vagrant adventurer Lars Wivallius (*q.v.;* 1605–69), whose lyrics, many of them written in prison, reveal a feeling for nature new to Swedish poetry. With its intervention in the Thirty Years' War and the ensuing military triumphs, Sweden established itself as a European power. This led to a great development of national pride and culture, as is revealed in the literature of this epoch. The outstanding work is the allegorical epic *Hercules* (1658) by Georg Stiernhielm (*q.v.;* 1598–1672), written in vigorous hexameters and reflecting the social and political problems of the time, as well as the philosophical and religious views of its author. Stiernhielm was the greatest literary figure of the 17th century and was often in attendance at the court of Queen Christina (*q.v.*), an outstanding patroness of the arts. His followers included the two brothers Columbus, one of whom, Samuel (1642–79), wrote *Odae sueticae* (1674) and the prose *Mål-roo eller Roo-mål* (published in 1856), a charming collection of anecdotes that illumine Stiernhielm's character. A rival to Stiernhielm was the unidentified "Skogekär Bergbo," whose *Wenerid* (1680) is the first sonnet cycle in Swedish. Another unsolved problem of this period is the authorship of the epithalamium *Bröllopsbeswärs ihugkommelse* (first published in the early 19th century), a realistic poem long attributed to Stiernhielm. Several of Stiernhielm's admirers, including Urban Hiärne (1641–1724), formed a coterie at Uppsala in the 1660s. Hiärne led a troupe of student actors who in 1665 performed his play *Rosimunda* before the young Charles XI. He also wrote lyrics and the prose pastoral *Stratonice* (1666–68), the first "psychological" narrative in Swedish.

Stiernhielm aimed at an integration of Sweden's cultural heritage with the accepted ideals of continental classicism. His *Her-*

BY COURTESY OF THE KUNGL. BIBLIOTEKET, STOCKHOLM

FRONTISPIECE FROM THE FIRST EDITION OF "HERCULES," BY GEORG STIERNHIELM, 1658, ENGRAVED BY THE AUTHOR'S SON, GEORG OTTO STIERNHIELM *cules* is a hexameter epic, but it is rhymed, sometimes even alliterated, and full of old Swedish words that he was eager to revive. Columbus also demanded a more vigorous, flexible language for prose and poetry, as did "Skogekär Bergbo" in *Thet swenska språkets klagemål* ("The Lament of the Swedish Language"; 1658). National pride and religious feeling are combined in the works of the bishops Haqvin Spegel (1645–1714) and Jesper Swedberg (1653–1735), father of the Swedish mystic Emanuel Swedenborg. Both were hymn writers and ardent philologists. Spegel, as well as writing a religious epic (*Guds werk och hwila,* 1685), contributed to Swedberg's new hymnbook of 1695, which became the poetry book of the Swedish people and was like *Gustav Vasas bibel,* of lasting influence. Even Lasse Lucidor (*q.v.;* 1638–74) was represented in it. Lucidor, who called himself *den olycklige* ("the unhappy one"), gave intense lyric expression to the contrasting moods of the period: in his love songs and, above all, in his drinking songs, he is as pagan and reckless as he is repentant and devout in his hymns and funeral poems.

At Uppsala, meanwhile, the scholar Petrus Lagerlöf (1648–99) worked on poetics and attempted to impose purer classical standards, and Olaus Verelius (1618–82) edited and translated Icelandic sagas. Olaus Rudbeck (1630–1702), a man of vast energy and learning, became interested in Verelius' work and enthusiastically developed the theory that Sweden was the lost Atlantis and had been the cradle of Western civilization. These theories he launched in a massive work, *Atland eller Manhem* (1679–1702), deliberately written in Swedish to prove that the language was suited to scientific purposes. The work, translated into Latin as *Atlantica,* attained European fame.

Baroque and classicistic tendencies run parallel in late 17th-century Swedish literature. An exponent of the marinist style (*see* MARINO, GIAMBATTISTA) was Gunno Eurelius (ennobled as Dahlstierna; 1661–1709), whose elaborate epic *Kunga skald* was written for King Charles XI's funeral in 1697 in the manner of Marino's *Adone* (1623). Simpler in style is Johan Runius (1679–1713), who expresses a Christian stoicism of the kind found among the Swedish people during the disastrous early decades of the 18th century. Jacob Frese (1691–1729) is a gentler and more intimate poet; his lyrics and hymns contain some of the emotional pietism that became a feature of 18th-century thought.

**Classicism and Enlightenment (1732–1809).**—After the death of Charles XII (1718) and the collapse of his empire, a more utilitarian attitude to life and letters gradually developed. Olof von Dalin (*q.v.;* 1708–63) is the outstanding popularizer of the new ideas of the French and English Enlightenment. Educated at the University of Lund (founded 1668), he later went to Stockholm and began to publish, anonymously, *Then swänska Argus* (1732–34), the weekly periodical modeled on those of the English Joseph Addison and the Dutch Justus van Effen, and one of the first serious journalistic ventures in Sweden. Dalin's publication marks the beginning of a new era in Swedish letters: orthodoxy gives way to skepticism and enlightenment, Baroque ideals to classicism, and German influence to English and French; and the middle class begins, gradually, to take over the function of chief upholder of literature, though several of the poets of the period were noblemen. In *Argus* Dalin ridiculed the foibles of the capital in forceful, supple prose, and in *Sagan om hästen* ("The Story of the Horse"; 1740) he showed himself a master of allegorical satire. As a court poet and favourite, and as a member of Queen Lovisa's Vitterhetsakademi (Academy of Literature), he composed elegant occasional verses. He also wrote some pseudoclassical plays that, like many dramatic ventures of the early and mid-18th century, are academic and lifeless. An exception is *Swenska sprätthöken* ("The Swedish Fop"; 1740), the comedy by Count Carl Gyllenborg (1679–1746).

With the second phase of the Enlightenment, marked by the influence of Rousseau, are associated Hedvig Charlotta Nordenflycht (*q.v.;* 1718–63), Gustav Philip Creutz (*q.v.;* 1731–85), and Gustaf Fredrik Gyllenborg (*q.v.;* 1731–1808). In *Den sörgande turturdufvan* ("The Sorrowing Turtledove"; 1743), Fru Nordenflycht lamented the death of her husband in emotional and highly personal lyrics. Creutz was a more sophisticated personality. He wrote little, devoting his life after 1763 to diplomacy, but his few writings, of which the pastoral epyllion *Atis och Camilla* (1762) is the most important, reveal a mastery of form and versification. Creutz's view of life was Epicurean, while his friend Gyllenborg was a stern Stoic. Though lacking the formal elegance of Creutz's poetry, Gyllenborg's best poems, "Verldsföraktaren" (1762) and "Vinterkväde" (1759), have nobility and feeling for nature.

Then
Swänska
ARGUS,
N:o I.

Omne tulit punctum qui miscuit utile dulci, Horatius.

STOCKHOLM,
Tryckt hos Benjamin Gottlieb Schneider.

BY COURTESY OF THE TRUSTEES OF THE BRITISH MUSEUM; PHOTO, J. R. FREEMAN AND CO.

**TITLE PAGE OF THE FIRST NUMBER OF THE SATIRICAL REVIEW "THEN SWÄNSKA ARGUS," PUBLISHED ANONYMOUSLY BY OLOF VON DALIN, 1732–34**

Prose—particularly the novel—developed more slowly. The first genuine novel was *Adalrik och Giöthildas afwentyr* (1742–44), by Jacob Mörk (1714–63) and Anders Törngren (b. 1714), showing the influence of the Icelandic sagas and of Madeleine de Scudéry. But the raciest prose of this period is found in Jacob Wallenberg's *Min son på galejan* ("My Son on the Galleon"; 1781), a humorous, realistic diary of voyages on an East Indiaman. The only two 18th-century Swedish writers of European reputation were scientists: Carl von Linné (Linnaeus, *q.v.;* 1707–78) and the mystic Emanuel Swedenborg (*q.v.;* 1688–1772). Linné's work at Uppsala much enhanced the prestige of the university, and his travel books are remarkable for their understanding of nature and freshness of style.

The Gustavian period takes its name from the brilliant Gustavus III (1746–92), in all respects a royal patron of art and letters. At his court he collected the best writers of the time, and by founding the Swedish Academy (1786) he gave them official status. He was especially interested in drama and opera; thanks to his patronage, a proper theatrical tradition was begun, and the leading authors—often against their will—had to produce texts for performance. Gustavus himself sketched out some of these works, the best of which is the historic opera *Gustaf Vasa* (1786), the happy result of the collaboration between Johan Henric Kellgren (*q.v.;* 1751–95) and the composer J. G. Naumann. Kellgren was the great academic poet and the arbiter of taste, ruling that comedies should be modeled on those of the French, and that tragedies should be pseudoclassical. Beginning as a rationalist and satirist after the fashion of Voltaire, he reluctantly accepted pre-Romantic ideas in later life. In *Stockholmsposten,* the main organ of literary opinion in the capital, Kellgren used his polemical wit against Thomas Thorild (*q.v.;* 1759–1808), the truculent champion of individual genius, who wrote a long poem, *Passionerna* (1785), celebrating Ossian as the king of poets, but who is chiefly remembered for his polemical prose. After Kellgren's death the controversy was carried on by Carl Gustaf af Leopold (*q.v.;* 1756–1829), who still imposed pseudoclassical standards on the academy and applied them in his rhetorical odes and tragedies. Johan Gabriel Oxenstierna (1750–1818) did his most original work in 1770–74 while a diplomat in Vienna; *Skördarne* ("Harvests"; 1796) and *Ode till Camilla* (first published in the 19th century) reveal an elegiac, pre-Romantic feeling for the beauty of nature. Bengt Lidner (*q.v.;* 1757–93) was a follower of Thorild but showed much more poetic inspiration in his play *Erik XIV* (1782), his opera *Medea* (1784)—both lyrical rather than dramatic in tone—and in his most successful work, the ode *Grefvinnan Spastaras död* (1783). The influence of both Milton and the Bible may be traced in his use of language.

Carl Michael Bellman (*q.v.;* 1740–95) stands apart from the conflicting ideals of the time. A poet and musician, he fused his gifts in the lyrics of *Fredmans epistlar* (1790) and *Fredmans sånger* (1791). His combination of stylized realism with humour and the most delicate sense of language and rhythm is unique in

Swedish. He is the greatest Swedish lyricist of the 18th century.

The dissertation *Om upplysning* ("On Enlightenment"; 1793) by Nils von Rosenstein (1752–1824), the first secretary of the Swedish Academy, nobly expresses the highest ideals of the Gustavian epoch; and various memoirs, by G. J. Adlerbeth, G. J. Ehrensvärd, Count Fredrik Axel von Fersen, Duchess Hedvig Elizabeth Charlotte, and others, evoke the witty but artificial atmosphere of Gustavus III's court and illustrate the development of prose. Gustavus' son, Gustavus IV (1778–1837), did not encourage literature; however, the energetic Anna Maria Lenngren (*q.v.;* 1754–1817), wife of the editor of *Stockholmsposten,* wrote some of her best verse satires between 1795 and 1800, many of her anonymous shafts being aimed at aristocratic foibles. The sentimental idylls of Frans Mikael Franzén (*q.v.;* 1772–1847) also belong to these years; they are full of pre-Romantic idealism imbibed from German and English sources and later toned down under pressure from the academy.

**The Romantic Movement (1809–1830).**—The loss of Finland to Russia in 1809, the deposition of the king, and the new constitution of 1809 all greatly affected Swedish literature, for out of them an ardent national spirit emerged as one of the motifs of Swedish Romanticism. The teaching at Uppsala of Benjamin Höijer (1767–1812), admirer of Immanuel Kant and F. W. J. von Schelling, laid the basis for the idealism that soon became the core of Swedish Romanticism. The impact of Schiller, Goethe, and the German Romantics on the Swedish literature of the early 19th century was overwhelming, and Swedish Romanticism became as much dominated by German culture as the previous era had been by French. Student societies formed the focuses of the new movement, and the periodicals issued by them and their adherents—*e.g., Polyfem* (1809–12) and *Phosphoros* (1810–13)—attacked the academy. *Phosphoros,* from which the group called the Fosforister (Phosphorists) took their name, played an especially important initial role in the controversy between the old school and the new during 1810–20. Per Daniel Amadeus Atterbom (*q.v.;* 1790–1855), the most gifted of the Fosforister, first revealed his talents in his verse *Prolog* (1810) to *Phosphoros;* Vilhelm Fredrik Palmblad (1788–1852), publisher and prose writer, led the practical polemics at Uppsala; Lorenzo Hammarsköld (1785–1827), with Johan Christoffer Askelöf (1787–1848) and Clas Livijn (1781–1844), carried on the fray at Stockholm; while Johan David Valerius (1776–1852) and P. A. Wallmark (1777–1858) championed the old school, as for a time did Johan Olof Wallin (1779–1839), the greatest hymn writer of the century and the chief contributor to the new official hymnary of 1819.

Meanwhile another society, Götiska förbundet, had been founded in Stockholm in 1811, with the object of raising the moral tone of society by study of the heroic, "Gothic" past, as expressed in pre-Christian mythology (*see* GERMANIC MYTHOLOGY AND HEROIC LEGENDS). Erik Gustaf Geijer (*q.v.;* 1783–1847), one of the founders, suggested the publication of a periodical, and the first issue of *Iduna* (1811) consisted largely of his own poems; *e.g.,* "Vikingen" and "Odalbonden." Most of Geijer's poetry, including the first Swedish translation of Shakespeare's *Macbeth,* was written before 1816. Esaias Tegnér (*q.v.;* 1782–1846) also contributed to *Iduna,* though he refused to engage in literary controversy. It was Tegnér, however, who wrote the most popular poem of this period, *Frithiofs saga* (1825), an epic based on an old Norse theme. For Tegnér, as well as for Geijer, the poetic revival of the Gothic past was not only a matter of national feeling and moral concern. In the old Northern mythology they seemed to discern the same eternal patterns as in Greek mythology and Romantic metaphysics; religion, philosophy, and poetry appeared to be one and the same. In the poems "Skaldens morgonpsalm" and "Sång till solen," Tegnér pictures himself as a divinely inspired seer, and in the last canto of *Frithiofs saga,* written in the metre of Greek tragedy (the iamb), the myths of Christ and Balder (*q.v.*) are fused in the spirit of German idealism. However, clarity of thought and formal perfection were indispensable standards of criticism with Tegnér, and, hence, he often sided with the academicians in their struggle against Romantic obscurantism and formal innovations.

Several of the leading Romantics were learned men—Tegnér, Geijer, and Atterbom, for instance, were all university professors —and they often strove to embody a philosophical system, or an interpretation of history, in their poetic writings. The most ambitious attempt of this kind was Atterbom's *Lycksalighetens ö* ("The Isle of Bliss"; 1824–27), a somewhat shapeless verse drama dealing, on the literal level, with the love and adventures of the legendary Prince Astolf but, allegorically, with the history of poetry as an illustration of man's alienation from the Divine.

The greatest poet of the Romantic movement in Sweden is perhaps Erik Johan Stagnelius (*q.v.;* 1793–1823). Ugly, sickly, and, toward the end of his life, pitiably debauched, he held aloof from the schools and coteries of the day and created a poetic world of his own. The recurrent theme in *Liljor i Saron* (1821), a collection of "theosophical" poems, is the lament of Anima, the human soul, imprisoned in a world of darkness and sin. Stagnelius also wrote the only successful classical drama in Swedish, *Bacchanterna* (1822), celebrating the death and transfiguration of Orpheus.

A number of minor Romantic writers should be mentioned—*e.g.,* Adolf Törneros (1794–1839); Per Elgström (1781–1810); Samuel Hedborn (1783–1849), author of several attractive hymns and ballads and of an autobiography, *Minne och poesi* (1835); Arvid August Afzelius (1785–1871), collector of folk songs (*Svenska folkvisor från forntiden,* 1814–16); and Erik Sjöberg ("Vitalis," 1794–1828).

**The Coming of Realism (1830–1880).**—The most complex personality among the later Romantics was Carl Jonas Love Almqvist (*q.v.;* 1793–1866), who combined an extravagant imagination, as in his novel *Drottningens juvelsmycke* (1834), with the realism that is increasingly prominent in his works after 1836. Almqvist, a master of prose style, was at his best in the long short story, or *novell;* of his works in this genre, *Det går an* (1839), an outspoken attack on marriage, foreshadows Strindberg's method of raising problems for debate.

Meanwhile the realistic novel had advanced. Fredrik Cederborgh (1784–1835) wrote *Uno von Trasenberg* (1809–10) and *Ottar Tralling* (1810–18), lighthearted satires on life and manners. But the novel as an accepted genre was really established by Fredrika Bremer (*q.v.;* 1801–65), whose "sketches from ordinary life" appeared from 1828. Her novels, *e.g., Grannarne* (1837), have dated considerably but were formerly very popular in both Europe and the United States. Sophie von Knorring (1797–1848) wrote novels principally about aristocratic families, and the very popular Emilie Flygare-Carlén (1807–92) produced a long series of stories, including *Rosen på Tistelön* (1842), usually dealing with life on the Swedish west coast.

Realism, then, made only slow headway, in spite of the social consciousness of the liberal paper *Aftonbladet* and the example of the great Finnish-Swedish poet Johan Ludvig Runeberg (*q.v.;* 1804–77). The literature of the 1840s and 1850s is mainly an aftermath of Romanticism, though the critic Bernhard Elis Malmström (1816–65) was ostensibly an opponent of the movement—and even his work showed Romantic influence. His elegy *Angelica* (1840) has affinities with the graceful but insipid poetry of his contemporary Carl Vilhelm Böttiger (1807–78) and the older Karl August Nicander (1799–1839). There is a fresher feeling about Gunnar Wennerberg's *Gluntarne* (1849–51), songs about Uppsala student life in the 1840s, but there is nothing new in them. The movement known as Scandinavism produced a good deal of verse: Carl Vilhelm August Strandberg ("Talis Qualis," 1818–77), the fieriest poet of this type, later made excellent translations from Byron. Oskar Patrik Sturzen-Becker ("Orvar Odd," 1811–69) was a versatile writer with talents in verse and the short story. Popular reading was provided by August Blanche (1811–68), particularly in the successful *Bilder ur verkligheten* (1863–65), short stories depicting Stockholm life with humour and vivacity. He also wrote popular dramas. Frans Hedberg (1828–1908) held the stage at the Royal Theatre with pompous historical plays, such as *Bröllopet på Ulfåsa* (1865). The quasi-historical novels of Magnus Jacob Crusenstolpe (1795–1865) were much appreciated in their day.

Poetic realism became the official program of Signatur–poeterna (the "pseudonym poets"), a small group of the 1860s, including Carl David af Wirsén (1842–1912), Edvard Bäckström (1841–86), Pontus Wikner (1837–88), and Carl Snoilsky (*q.v.;* 1841–1903). However, only Snoilsky had the temperament and poetic gift needed to carry out the program. Some of his best work is found in *Dikter* (1869) and *Sonetter* (1871). Meanwhile Wirsén had established himself as the conservative literary critic, and from his post as secretary of the Swedish Academy he launched formidable opposition against all innovators, including Snoilsky. Viktor Rydberg (*q.v.;* 1828–95) exemplifies this rather uneasy transition from idealism to Naturalism even more patently than does Snoilsky. Novelist, poet, and critic, he began as a radical journalist and ended as a professor and author of philosophical poems (*Dikter,* 1882; *Nya dikter,* 1891). His most important early work was the ideological novel *Den siste athenaren* (1859), and his treatise *Bibelns lära om Kristus* (1862) had considerable influence through its attack on the narrow orthodoxy of the Swedish Church and prepared the way for scientific rationalism.

**Naturalism and Neoromanticism (1880–1900).**—Four influences combined to free Swedish literature from its petrifying conventions: English thought in the writings of Charles Darwin, Herbert Spencer, and J. S. Mill; French Naturalism as taught and practised by Émile Zola; the drama of the Norwegians Henrik Ibsen and B. Bjørnson; and the criticism of Georg Brandes. Modern Swedish literature begins with the work of August Strindberg (*q.v.;* 1849–1912), for the modern drama dates from his *Mäster Olof* (1872) and the modern novel from his *Röda rummet* (1879; *The Red Room*). By his originality, his mastery of prose and dialogue, his great energy, and the influence of his work and personality on Swedish, not to say European, literature, he is by far the greatest writer Sweden has produced.

Strindberg overshadows all other writers of the 1880s. Gustaf af Geijerstam (1858–1909), author of *Erik Grane* (1885) and of other novels and short stories, longed to lead his age but could not do so. Anne Charlotte Edgren-Leffler (1849–92) wrote a number of stories, collected in *Ur lifvet* ("From Life"; 1882–83), in which she satirized conventions adversely affecting women. The more gifted Victoria Benedictsson ("Ernst Ahlgren," 1850–88) died—by her own hand—before she had fulfilled her promise; she, too, but more boldly, was concerned with the position of women in society. Her stories (*Från Skåne,* 1884) have lasted better than her novels (*Pengar,* 1885, and *Fru Marianne,* 1887) and reveal how much regional characterization had entered into the new style of literature. With her was associated Axel Lundegård (1861–1930), who soon turned his talents to the historical novel. Regional poetry was written by Albert Ullrik Bååth (1853–1912) of Skåne, whose work was surpassed in beauty and originality by the work of another Skåne poet, Ola Hansson (*q.v.;* 1860–1925), also a novelist and critic. Hansson's early poems (*Notturno,* 1885) and his prose sketches (*Sensitiva amorosa,* 1887) reveal a boldness in imagery and the interest in psychological nuances more typical of the next decade.

The reaction against utilitarianism and Naturalism was begun in 1888 by Verner von Heidenstam (*q.v.;* 1859–1940) with his volume of verse *Vallfart och vandringsår* (1888). His later poetry and historical tales won him the Nobel Prize for literature in 1916. Although much of his work now seems precious and dated, his short contemplative lyrics are very fine. Oscar Levertin (1862–1906), stimulated by his friend Heidenstam's example, wrote poetry full of rich colours and the lore of the past, showing his affinity with the pre-Raphaelites, his knowledge of French Symbolism, and his awareness of his own Jewish heritage. His criticism, published in *Svenska dagbladet* and elsewhere, did much to mold contemporary taste. Gustaf Fröding (*q.v.;* 1860–1911), too, was encouraged by Heidenstam; the title of his first volume of verse, *Guitarr och dragharmonika* (1891; *Guitar and Concertina*), shows the two different strains in the poet, melancholy and gay, which constantly intermingle and out of which he wrested such original music. Despite the threat of madness, he managed to publish four more collections of poems before his reason finally gave way in 1898, by which time he had established himself as one of the greatest Swedish lyric poets. With Fröding, who was from Värmland, regionalism entered into Neoromantic poetry, and with the work of Erik Axel Karlfeldt (*q.v.;* 1864–1931) the province of Dalarna came into its own. Karlfeldt's mature poetry, such as *Fridolins visor* (1898) and *Hösthorn* (1927), reveals his individual strength and the richness of orchestration that he alone could give to Swedish and won him the Nobel Prize for literature in 1931.

Meanwhile Selma Lagerlöf (*q.v.;* 1858–1940) had developed the prose tale. Her long series of novels and short stories, beginning with *Gösta Berlings saga* (1891), reached an international public; she was, indeed, the first Swede to win the Nobel Prize for literature (1909). She often used old Värmland tales for material, though one of her best novels, *Jerusalem I* (1901), is set in Dalarna. Per Hallström (1866–1960) is a more skilful writer of short stories than of novels; like Lagerlöf, he did his significant work before 1910. Romantic, too, in his love for the skerries (rocky isles) was Albert Engström (1869–1940), storywriter, cartoonist, founder of the popular humorous paper *Strix,* and one of the most beloved of Swedish writers.

**The 20th Century.**—The *fin de siècle* and the early years of the 20th century were a period of decadence and pessimism in Swedish literature, as in European literature in general. Representative of this mood are Hjalmar Söderberg (*q.v.;* 1869–1941) and Bo Bergman (*q.v.;* 1869–1967). Both had links with the rationalism of the 1880s and the aestheticism of the 1890s, yet both stand apart from the Neoromantics. Both, like Strindberg, loved Stockholm, which perpetually recurs as the setting of their works. Söderberg's forte was the short story (*Historietter,* 1898), in which his psychological subtlety and irony are happily combined, and in which, as in his novels *Martin Bircks ungdom* (1901) and *Doktor Glas* (1905), he appears as a master of Swedish prose. Bergman also produced memorable short stories, but his real medium was the lyric; he developed and refined his talent in a series of collections from *Marionetterna* (1903) to *Riket* (1944).

From the beginning of the 20th century, industrialization, the growth of the press, and the spread of education increasingly influenced letters. The reading public continued to grow, and the volume of writing similarly increased, a marked feature being the development of the novel, with which are associated Gustaf Hellström (1882–1953), Ludvig Nordström (*q.v.;* 1882–1942), Elin Wägner (1882–1949), and Sigfrid Siwertz (1882– ). Hellström's work as journalist took him to other European countries and to the United States, and long residence in England greatly influenced him. His irony and careful realistic detail emerge in his best-known novel, *Snörmakar Lekholm får en idé* (1927; *Lacemaker Lekholm Has an Idea*), set in a small provincial town. Siwertz is a more elegant stylist—like so many Swedes he began as a lyricist—and a decisive influence upon him was the philosophy of Henri Bergson (*q.v.*), reflected in *En Flanör* (1914). His weightiest work is the family saga *Selambs* (1920; *Downstream*), a novel of Stockholm during World War I. Nordström came from Norrland, and his birthplace—Härnösand—is perpetuated in his work as "Öbacka." Overflowing with vitality and gifted with keen but grotesque humour, he did some of his best work in *Landsortsbohème* (1911) and *Planeten Markattan* (1937), but his most satisfying productions are the short stories in *Fiskare* (1907), *Öbackabor* (1921), etc. Elin Wägner was an ardent pacifist and feminist; her most powerful work is the peasant novel *Åsa-Hanna* (1918).

The outstanding novelist of the 1920s is Hjalmar Bergman (*q.v.;* 1883–1931). Gifted with a fantastically vivid imagination and restlessly energetic, Bergman wrote a long series of stories, many of which are set in "Wadköping" (his native Örebro) and its surroundings, others in Italy. In *Loewenhistorier* (1913), as in other works, Bergman depicts an irrational, impulsive, unsuccessful hero; in *Farmor och Vår Herre* (1921; *Thy Rod and Thy Staff*), he portrays one of the dominating female personalities who fascinate him. The satire *Markurells i Wadköping* (1919; *God's Orchid*) and *Swedenhielms* (1925), one of the few existing Swedish comedies, are his most widely known works.

Meanwhile the "proletarian" novel had been developed—not always by working-class writers—by Gustav Hedenvind-Eriksson

(1880– ), Martin Koch (1882–1940), and Ivar Lo-Johansson (1901– ), who is particularly concerned with the miseries of *statarens* ("farm labourer's") life. There is particularly harsh and telling criticism of working-class conditions in the Lars Hård series and other stories by Jan Fridegård (1897– ). Vilhelm Moberg (1898– ) wrote both realistic and historical novels of peasant life but achieved his greatest success with the broad prose epic about a group of Swedish emigrants to North America, *Utvandrarna* (1949; *The Emigrants*). Noteworthy contributions to the development of the Swedish autobiographical novel were made by two self-educated members of the proletariat: Eyvind Johnson (1900– ), with *Romanen om Olof* (1934–37), and Harry Martinson (*see* below), with *Nässlorna blomma* (1935) and *Vägen ut* (1936). The autobiographical element is evident, too, in the works of Agnes von Krusenstjerna (1894–1940). In her novel cycles, *e.g.*, the *Tony* trilogy (1922–26) and the Fröknarna von Pahlen series (1930–35), she describes her own aristocratic and upper-middle-class environment and analyzes a degenerate and perverted psychology.

The greatest Swedish writer of the 20th century is perhaps Pär Lagerkvist (*q.v.;* 1891– ), who won the Nobel Prize for literature in 1951. In his youth a bold formal innovator, he later developed an admirably pure prose style, as in the allegorical novel *Dvärgen* (1944; *The Dwarf*). Expressionistic in style are his collections of poems, *e.g.*, *Ångest* (1916), and his early plays, *e.g.*, *Himlens hemlighet* (1919), reflecting the dark years of World War I. Lagerkvist's writings during the 1920s include an autobiographical novel and love poetry, but the dominant theme throughout his work is a search for vital, often outspokenly religious, values.

Several of the best Swedish writers of the 20th century have been connected with the development of lyric poetry. Vilhelm Ekelund (1880–1949) found his ideals in the classical tradition, while Anders Österling (1884– ) was more of a poetic realist. The ballads of Dan Andersson (1888–1920) became very popular, as did the songs of *Fridas bok* (1922) by Birger Sjöberg (1885–1929). In Sjöberg's later work the formal disintegration characteristic of so much modern poetry becomes noticeable, though most of the poets of the 1920s and '30s were still traditionalists; *e.g.*, Karin Boye (*q.v.;* 1900–41), Bertil Malmberg (1889–1958), Johannes Edfelt (1904– ), and Hjalmar Gullberg (1898–1961). In Gullberg's later poetry, however, the light ironical style of his earlier works is replaced by a passionate upsurge not always capable of being expressed in traditional forms.

About 1930 a group of five "primitivistic" writers was formed, of whom Harry Martinson (1904– ) later developed into one of the finest and boldest lyricists of the century. Sensuous imagery and an intimate feeling for nature characterize much of his work. An attempt to revive the verse epic is his *Aniara* (1956), the symbolical story of a voyage of a spaceship, which was turned into an opera by K.-B. Blomdahl in 1959.

Among the forerunners of lyric modernism in Sweden were Lagerkvist and Sjöberg, but it was not until the early 1940s that formal experimentation became part of the program of a group of poets, the so-called generation of the '40s (*fyrtiotalisterna*). Influenced by the poetic technique of such writers as Ezra Pound and T. S. Eliot, Gunnar Ekelöf (1907–68), Erik Lindegren (1910– ), and Karl Vennberg (1910– ) were among the chief champions of lyric modernism. Lindegren's *Mannen utan väg* ("The Man Without a Way"; 1942) is typical of this generation's anguished search for a meaning in life. Ekelöf began as a Surrealist and then inclined toward Romanticism for a period, finally to find his own highly personal style in *Färjesång* (1941) and *Non serviam* (1945), which include some of the finest poems in the Swedish language. In his later works he turns against all the accepted ideas of poetic beauty and lyric expression, though the *Mölna-elegi* (1960) is still haunted by romantic echoes.

Bibliography.—*Anthologies:* C. W. Stork, *Anthology of Swedish Lyrics from 1750 to 1915* (1917); H. Schück *et al.*, *Sveriges nationallitteratur 1500–1920,* 30 vol. (1921–22); E. Gosse, "The Poetry of Sweden," in *The Oxford Book of Scandinavian Verse* (1925); S. Selander, *Levande svensk dikt från fem sekel,* 2 vol. (1928); R. Ahléen, *Swedish Poets of the Seventeenth Century* (1932); S. Selander, *Levande svensk litteratur från äldsta tider till våra dagar,* 24 vol. (1936–38); M. S. Allwood (ed.), *20th Century Scandinavian Poetry* (1951); *Swedish Fairy Tales,* trans. by I. Kaplan (1953); *Seven Swedish Poets* (Ekelöf, Gullberg, Lagerkvist, Lindegren, Malmberg, Martinson, and Södergran), ed. and trans. by F. Fleisher (1963).

*General Works:* E. N. Tigerstedt, *Svensk litteraturhistoria* (1948, 2nd ed. 1953); E. Bredsdorff, B. Mortensen, and R. Popperwell, *An Introduction to Scandinavian Literature* (1951); E. N. Tigerstedt (ed.), *Ny illustrerad svensk litteraturhistoria,* 5 vol. (1955–58, 2nd ed. 1966–67); I. Holm and M. von Platen, *La Littérature suédoise* (1957); A. Gustafson, *A History of Swedish Literature* (1961), with bibliographical appendix. *See* also *Vem är det?* (1912 *et seq.*); N. Bohman *et al.* (eds.), *Svenska män och kvinnor: biografisk uppslagsbok,* 8 vol. (1942–55); N. Afzelius, *Books in English on Sweden,* 3rd ed. (1951).

*Works on Particular Periods and Aspects:* V. Vedel, *Svensk Romantik* (1894); J. Mortensen, *Från Aftonbladet till Röda rummet: strömningar i svensk litteratur 1830–1879* (1905, 2nd ed. 1913); G. Castrén, *Stormaktstidens diktning* (1907); A. Blanck, *Den nordiska renässansen i sjuttonhundratalets litteratur* (1911); A. Nilsson, *Svensk romantik: den platonska strömningen* (1916); M. Lamm, *Upplysningstidens romantik,* 2 vol. (1918–20); B. Risberg, *Den svenska versens teori,* 2 vol. (1932–36); J. Nordström, *De yverbornes ö: sextonhundratalsstudier* (1934); R. Pipping, "Den fornsvenska litteraturen," in *Nordisk Kultur,* vol. viii:A (1943); K.-E. Lundevall, *Från åttital till nittital* (1953); G. Hilleström, *Theatre and Ballet in Sweden* (1953); Å. Runnquist, *Moderna svenska författare* (1959); S. B. F. Jansson, *The Runes of Sweden* (1962). (B. M. E. M.; St. Be.)

**SWEELINCK, JAN PIETERSZOON** (1562–1621), Dutch organist and composer, one of the principal figures in the development of organ music before J. S. Bach. Born in April 1562 in Amsterdam, he succeeded his father as organist of the Oude Kerk (Old Church), Amsterdam, about 1580, and remained in this post until his death. He married in 1590, and his wife bore him seven children. He seems never to have left the Low Countries and to have traveled only to Rotterdam and Antwerp. He died in Amsterdam on Oct. 16, 1621.

Although he composed much sacred and secular vocal music, including the *Chansons à 5,* the *Cantiones sacrae,* and settings of the Psalms, in the polyphonic traditions of France and the Netherlands, Sweelinck was chiefly known as an organist and keyboard composer. His keyboard music includes chorale variations, remarkable for their double and triple counterpoint; toccatas and fantasias showing the influence of the Venetian organ school; and sets of variations on secular tunes.

Sweelinck's fantasias are among the first works for organ to consist of contrapuntal variations on a single theme subjected to augmentation, diminution, and changes of rhythm. For his secular variations, Sweelinck drew upon popular tunes of several European countries. The set of variations on *Mein junges Leben hat ein End'* is perhaps his best-known work.

It is possible that Sweelinck met the English composers John Bull and Peter Philips during their visits to the Low Countries; Bull's "Fantasia on a Theme of Sweelinck" was the tribute of one keyboard virtuoso to another. Sweelinck's keyboard playing was widely known, and his organ pupils included the German composers Samuel Scheidt and Heinrich Scheidemann. Scheidemann's pupil J. A. Reinken was to hand on this tradition of organ playing to Dietrich Buxtehude. Sweelinck's works, edited by Max Seiffert, were published by the Vereeniging voor Nederlandse Muziekgeschiedenis in 12 volumes (1895–1903). The first volume, containing his instrumental works, was revised in 1943.

*See* H. Antcliffe, "J. P. Sweelinck," *Proceedings of the Musical Association,* vol. 61 (1934); R. L. Tusler, *The Organ Music of Jan Pieterszoon Sweelinck* (1958). (C. P. Co.)

**SWEET ALYSSUM** (*Lobularia maritima*), the ever-popular little white- or violet-flowered, fragrant, half-hardy perennial of the mustard family that is usually grown as an annual. It is widespreading on the ground, with branches rising 6 to 12 in., and numerous small flowers distributed in lengthening clusters. It occurs in both large and small forms, some with white-edged leaves and some with double flowers. It is an excellent edging plant that blooms over a long season. (J. M. Bl.)

**SWEETBREAD,** a popular term for certain glands of animals, particularly when used as food; these are usually the pancreas, called stomach sweetbread by butchers, and the thymus, or neck sweetbread. The term is also sometimes used to include the salivary and lymphatic glands. *See* Pancreas; Thymus.

**SWEET CLOVER** (MELILOT), a sweet-smelling weedy herb of the pea family (Leguminosae) grown for forage, soil improvement, and as a bee plant. The genus *Melilotus* comprises about 20 species, native to southeastern Europe and Asia Minor. They are annual or biennial erect herbs with three-parted leaves of usually small narrow leaflets and small yellow or white flowers borne in slender axillary clusters. Most of the species contain coumarin, resulting in a sweet odour and bitter taste.

Biennial white sweet clover, or Bokhara clover (*M. alba*); biennial yellow sweet clover (*M. officinalis*); and the bitter clover (*M. indica*), a winter annual adapted only to the southern and southwestern U.S., are of agricultural importance in the U.S. and Canada. The first two species have become widely naturalized throughout the U.S. and Canada, while bitter clover is widely scattered in the western U.S. *M. suaveolens,* a yellow-flowered species, is grown in a limited way in the southern prairies of Canada, and occasional plants of *M. altissima* have been collected in the eastern states. Several varieties have been developed such as Madrid for the corn belt, Erector for the Great Plains, and Willamette for the northwest.

*See* also GRASSLAND. (E. A. H.; N. TR.)

**SWEET GUM** (RED GUM), a North American deciduous tree (*Liquidambar styraciflua*) of the witch-hazel family (Hamamelidaceae), found usually in wet woods and bottomlands from Connecticut to southern Illinois and Oklahoma, south to Florida and eastern Texas. It recurs in northeastern Mexico and from central Mexico to Nicaragua. Sweet gum may grow up to 150 ft. tall and 5 ft. in diameter, but commonly is smaller. Its star-shaped leaves, which become brilliantly coloured in fall, are three- to seven-lobed and up to 7 in. across. Its inconspicuous unisexual flowers are without petals and are grouped into rounded heads: male heads are borne close to the twigs and in clusters; the female heads are solitary on long stalks. The fruit is spiny and consists of many capsules, each of which contains many sawdust-like abortive seeds but only one or two sound seeds, $\frac{1}{4}$ inch long, brown, and spread by wind.

From the wounded bark of sweet gum exudes a resin known as American storax, used in perfumes, soaps, and medicines. The wood, an important American hardwood, is used for boxes, furniture, millwork, veneer, and barrels. Sweet gum, a desirable ornamental tree, is most safely moved in spring and requires close pruning when transplanted. When planted north of its natural range, it should be placed in a well-drained, sheltered location. (J. W. TT.)

**SWEET PEA** (*Lathyrus odoratus*), a hardy annual climbing herb of the pea family (Leguminosae) commonly grown outdoors in the cool temperate regions of the world, especially North America and Europe. The sweet pea is a native of Italy, and hundreds of varieties have been developed under domestication. It is one of the most widely used commercial cut flowers because of its excellent durability and the ease with which the plants can be grown in greenhouses.

The fragrant flowers have an unusual colour range: from pure white through cream and various intermediate shades to deep orange; from pink to deep scarlet; and from blue shades to dark purple. In the home garden, sweet pea is often used as a climber in dense rows up to six feet tall or, especially in the dwarfed nonclimbing forms (var. *nanellus*), as a colourful compact border. The plants are frost-resistant. In mild climates, seeds may be planted in the late fall about one-half inch deep and two inches apart in rich garden soil for growth during the cool winter and for very early spring bloom. In less mild climates, seeds should be similarly planted in early spring after severe frosts are over and the soil can be properly worked.

These sun-loving plants are usually mulched to conserve soil moisture during their growth. (R. C. R.)

**SWEET POTATO,** a food plant of the morning-glory family (Convolvulaceae; *q.v.*), native to tropical America and widely cultivated in tropical and the warmer temperate climates. It is *Ipomoea batatas,* a tender perennial grown as an annual in regions where frost occurs. The stems are usually long and trailing, and bear entire to palmately lobed leaves of quite variable shape. The flowers, borne in clusters in the axils of the leaves, are funnel shaped, tinged with rose-violet or pink, and are similar in size and shape to those of the common bindweed. The edible part is the much enlarged tuberous root, varying in shape from fusiform to oblong or pointed oval. Root colours range from white through cream to orange, and occasionally purple inside, and from light buff to brown or rose, copper, and purplish red outside. The solids of the root consist largely of starch. The orange-fleshed varieties are high in carotene.

The sweet potato rarely produces flowers under common cultural conditions in latitudes higher than about 35°, and produces no seed above latitudes about 30° except under special cultural treatment. The seeds usually produce plants that are unlike the parent plant, therefore the sweet potato is propagated vegetatively by sprouts arising from the roots, or by cuttings of the vines. Seeds, however, are produced commonly in the field in the tropics. They have a very hard seed coat that may retard germination as much as a year, unless the seed coat is nicked or abraded, after which the seeds germinate promptly.

The sweet potato is now widely grown chiefly in the southern United States, in tropical America, the warmer islands of the Pacific, Japan, and the U.S.S.R. It is best adapted to light, friable soils such as sandy loams, since excessive vine growth and small yields or irregularly shaped roots are produced on very rich, heavy soils. At least four to five months of warm weather are required for large yields. In Japan the crop long has been grown for drying and for manufacture of starch and alcohol.

In the United States the sweet potato is propagated usually by bedding the roots close together in sand or light soil in a hotbed heated by manure, by flues or electricity, about four to five weeks before the frost-free date. The sprouts that emerge are pulled from the roots and transplanted to the field about 1 to $1\frac{1}{2}$ ft. apart on ridges 8 to 12 in. high, 3 ft. apart, after the weather and soil have become warm. The roots are harvested mostly about the time of the first frost in autumn, since cold soils cause them to deteriorate. The crop responds well to heavy applications of chemical fertilizers low to medium in nitrogen and high in phosphorus and potash. Heavy applications of animal manures or green manures often result in elongated, irregular roots and root surface injury by scurf, a fungus disease. Roots to be stored should be placed in the storage house immediately upon harvesting, at a temperature of 85° F. and a relative humidity of 85% to 90% for a week to ten days. Then the temperature is lowered to 50°–55° where it is kept as long as the roots are in storage. The "curing" period at high temperature and humidity is essential to hasten the healing of wounds caused in harvesting, thus reducing danger of loss from decay.

The eating quality—and also the market quality and storage life—are greatly improved by curing. If diseases are controlled, roots that are properly cured and stored remain in good edible condition six to seven months.

The sweet potato is very susceptible to several diseases, control of which requires great care in field and storehouse sanitation and management, seed-stock treatment with disinfectants, and crop rotation. (V. R. B.)

**SWEETSOP** (SUGAR APPLE), a small tree or shrub of the custard apple family (Annonaceae), known botanically as *Annona squamosa.* It has thin oblong-ovate leaves, solitary greenish flowers, and a yellowish-green fruit resembling a shortened pine cone. The tuberculate fruit, the fusion of many ripened ovaries and the receptacle, is 3–4 in. in diameter and contains a sweet creamy-yellow custardlike pulp. Native to the West Indies and tropical America, it has been widely introduced into the eastern hemisphere and is much prized as a fruit. *See* ANNONACEAE.

**SWEET WILLIAM** (*Dianthus barbatus*), an old-fashioned garden favourite of the pink family (Caryophyllaceae) and one of the most widely cultivated of the many species of *Dianthus* grown in gardens. A relative of the carnation (*q.v.*), it was first introduced into cultivation about 1575 and has since been grown throughout the temperate world. The original European plant and some modern forms are still grown as perennials, but nearly all the finest modern varieties are best treated as biennials. Some strains bloom from seed in a single season and are grown as annuals.

ROCHE

SWEET WILLIAM (DIANTHUS BARBATUS)

Sweet William, 12–20 in. high, has flat opposite leaves lanceolate to ovate-lanceolate in shape, and a stem slightly swollen at the joints. The flowers, borne in a profuse flattish cluster (corymb), have toothed petals that are red, white-dotted, or white-striped toward the slightly bearded base. The plant is variable as to colouring, especially in some modern varieties.

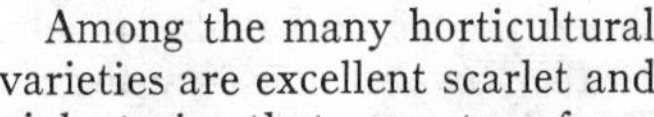

Among the many horticultural varieties are excellent scarlet and pink strains that come true from seed and double-flowered strains that usually do not seed true. Another sort, known as auricula-eyed, has white- or pale-centred flowers with a rim of contrasting colour on each petal.

Seeds of the biennial sort are best sown in June, then potted for carrying over the winter in a cold frame. Many biennials and all the perennials often persist from self-sown seed. (N. Tr.)

**SWELLENDAM,** a town of Cape of Good Hope Province, Republic of South Africa, in the valley of the Breede River, is 140 mi. (225 km.) E of Cape Town by road. Pop. (1960) 4,941, including 2,530 whites, 2,242 Cape Coloureds, and 169 Bantu. The town lies among the foothills of the coastal range, and a mountain stream runs down its length. It still has some buildings dating from the early days of South African history, the most notable being the Drostdy (1746), once the residence of the local governing official or *landdrost* and now a historical museum. Swellendam is the centre of a district that produces chiefly wool and wheat, but also apples, peaches, oranges, youngberries, and other fruit. One of the oldest roads into the interior passes through the town. Founded in 1745, Swellendam is one of the older Dutch settlements at the Cape, and was named after the Cape governor Hendrik Swellengrebel and his wife, whose maiden name was Ten Damme. In 1795 the burghers of Swellendam rose in revolt against the Dutch East India Company, expelled the *landdrost,* and set up the first of several local Boer republics in South Africa. (L. L. To.)

**SWETE, HENRY BARCLAY** (1835–1917), English biblical and patristic scholar, whose works on biblical texts are of great importance, was born at Bristol on March 14, 1835, and educated at King's College, London, and Caius College, Cambridge. He was ordained in 1858, and became dean of Caius College in 1865. In 1877 he accepted the college living of Ashdon, Essex, and in 1882 was made professor of pastoral theology at King's College, London. In 1890 he succeeded B. F. Westcott as regius professor of divinity at Cambridge, retiring in 1915. He died at Hitchin on May 10, 1917.

In 1887 Swete published the first volume of his edition of the Greek text of the Old Testament, completing the series in 1894; in 1898 the Greek text of the Gospel of St. Mark with notes and introduction; and in 1906 that of the Apocalypse of St. John. He was the editor of *Cambridge Theological Essays* (1905), *Cambridge Biblical Essays* (1909) and *Essays on the Early Church and Ministry* (posthumous, 1918). His historical and critical works include *The Apostles' Creed in Relation to Primitive Christianity* (1894); *Church Services and Service Books Before the Reformation* (1896); *Patristic Study* (1902); *The Appearances of our Lord After the Passion* (1907); and *The Last Discourse and Prayer of Our Lord* (1913).

**SWEYN I** (d. 1014), king of Denmark from *c.* 987 to 1014, son of Harald Bluetooth, the christianizer of Denmark. About 987 he rebelled against his father, who fled and died among the Slavs. This unhappy relationship of father and son formed the basis for statements found in the sagas that Sweyn was illegitimate. The history of the early part of his reign is obscure. The 11th-century historian Adam of Bremen alleges that a temporary conquest of Denmark by the Swedes took place at this time but there is no foundation for the story. A widely diffused tradition suggests that Sweyn was at some time captured by certain enemies (Slavs, Norwegians, or Swedes) and held for ransom. By 994, however, Sweyn felt strong enough to attempt foreign conquest, and, first ravaging the Isle of Man, he attacked England in alliance with Olaf Trygvesson, an exiled prince of the Norwegian house. The allies besieged London, which was fiercely defended, and harried widely both along the coast and inland. They made peace before the end of the year for a payment of 16,000 pounds. After being baptized, Olaf returned to Norway, where he established himself as king in 995. Sweyn no doubt returned to Denmark. The following years were marked by his increasing hostility toward Olaf, whom Sweyn, in alliance with Olaf Skötkonung, king of Sweden, and the exiled Norwegian Eric, earl of Hlathir, defeated at Swold in about 999. Olaf was never seen again after the battle, and a Danish rule of Norway through Eric and his brother Sweyn began. King Sweyn turned his attention to England again and led an expedition there in 1003. It ravaged widely, but though helped by treachery among the English, Sweyn suffered one severe defeat in East Anglia in 1004, and returned to Denmark in 1005, perhaps because there was a famine in England that made it impossible for him to feed his men. It is commonly believed that this expedition was a retaliation for the massacre of St. Brice's Day, Nov. 13, 1002, in which Gunhild, a sister of Sweyn, may have perished. Sweyn seems not to have personally accompanied the Danish invaders of 1006, and he certainly was not with the army of Thorkel, which was active in England from 1009 to 1012. One source suggests that Sweyn was disquieted by Thorkel's successes; in any event, he reappeared in England in 1013 and met with rapid success in a masterly campaign. By the end of the year he was master of the country and Aethelred II (*q.v.*) was in exile. He died practically in the moment of victory at Gainsborough on Feb. 3, 1014. He was buried at York, but some years later his bones were removed to Denmark and reinterred at Roskilde.

Little is known of Sweyn's policy apart from his opposition to the formation of a strong independent Norway, and his determination to conquer England. He seems at some time to have made an expedition into Schleswig, for what are apparently gravestones of two of his soldiers have been found at Hedeby (probably the modern Oldenburg). Sweyn was a Christian and personally appointed Gotebald as bishop of Skaane about 1000. His wife was a Slav princess, sister of king Boleslaw I of Poland, and widow of Eric the Victorious of Sweden. Her name is not known, but late Norse sources call her Gunhild.

*See* F. M. Stenton, *Anglo-Saxon England,* 2nd ed. (1947); *Encomium Emmæ reginæ,* ed. by A. Campbell (1949). (Al. C.)

**SWEYN II** (Sweyn Estrithson) (*c.* 1020–1074), king of Denmark from 1043 to 1074, was the son of Estrith, a sister of King Canute, and of Ulf, a Danish earl. His father fell into disfavour and was murdered by Canute's order about 1027, whereupon Estrith married Robert of Normandy and Sweyn fled to Sweden. After the death of Canute (1035), when Hardicanute was ruling in Denmark and Magnus in Norway, the young kings agreed that whichever lived the longer should succeed to the dominions of the other. Under this agreement Magnus became king of Denmark in 1042. Sweyn made approaches to him soon afterward and was made an earl and viceroy of Denmark. He used his position to acquire popularity and in 1043, while Magnus was involved with the Wends, he was received as king of Denmark. This embroiled Norway and Denmark in a protracted war during the reigns of Magnus (d. 1047) and Harald Hardraade. Sweyn was not a successful commander, and he suffered many defeats, despite support from the Swedes and from disgruntled Norwegians. Yet ultimately Harald, embarrassed by the power of Haakon Ivarsson, a descendant of the earls of Hlathir, acknowledged Sweyn as king of Denmark about 1064.

After Harald's death (1066), Sweyn was in a secure position. He intervened strongly in English affairs in 1069, sending troops and ships to support the rebels against William I, and in 1070 he himself joined the Danish fleet in the Humber. However, he withdrew under an agreement with William.

Sweyn encouraged the development of the church in Denmark, although he was on one occasion embroiled with the archbishop of Bremen, owing to an allegedly incestuous marriage.

Sweyn was a man of peculiarly retentive memory and personally communicated much detailed information to Adam of Bremen, who incorporated it in a history. Sweyn somewhat softened the inglorious story of his Norwegian war; he also claimed to have fitted out an expedition against England and to have secured acknowledgment by Edward the Confessor as his successor.

Sweyn died on April 28, 1074. He introduced a dynasty (the Valdemars) that ruled for 300 years. *See* DENMARK: *History*. (AL. C.)

**SWIDNICA** (Ger. SCHWEIDNITZ), a town in southwest Poland (Lower Silesia) in Wroclaw *wojewodztwo* (province). It lies on the Bystrzyca, a tributary of the Oder, in an agricultural area of the Sudeten foothills, 33 mi. (53 km.) SW of Wroclaw. Pop. (1960) 39,078. Two old routes meet there, and Swidnica was a fortress early in the 13th century. In 1291 it was incorporated in the Swidnica-Jawor independent Piast principality, passed to Bohemia in 1392, to the Habsburgs in the 16th century, and to Prussia in 1742. It returned to Poland in 1945.

In the Middle Ages Swidnica was an important commercial centre. Its beer was widely exported. In the 14th century it had hemp weaving, and in the 16th century paper was manufactured there. It is a railway junction on the Wroclaw-Walbrzych line, and has metal and electro-technical factories. Other developing industries include chemical, leather, timber, textile, food, and fireproof products. (T. K. W.)

**SWIFT, GUSTAVUS FRANKLIN** (1839–1903), U.S. pioneer in the meat-packing industry, whose promotion of the refrigerator car for railways was a significant step in the industry's development, was born June 24, 1839, at Sagamore (West Sandwich), Mass. When he was 14 he left school to take a position at a salary of $1 a week working for his brother, a butcher. By 1859, at the age of 20, he had gone into business for himself as a buyer and slaughterer of cattle on a small scale. In that year he opened his own butcher shop in Eastham and soon became the manager of a number of small shops, which he opened himself and placed in the charge of other men. In 1872 he became the partner of James A. Hathaway in the firm of Hathaway and Swift. Three years later Swift, who was the cattle buyer for the firm, transferred his headquarters to Chicago, where the centre of the cattle market had shifted. He soon determined that the meat-packing business would be substantially more profitable than the meat-selling business if some method were devised for shipping fresh meat from Chicago to the east, instead of sending live cattle to be slaughtered on arrival, as was the custom. He therefore hired an engineer to design a refrigerator car which would make this possible, and in 1877 he successfully shipped the first refrigerator carload of fresh meat to the east. In 1878 he formed a partnership with his brother and in 1885, with a capitalization of $300,000, the firm of Swift & Company came into being, with Swift as first president. At his death less than 20 years later, the capitalization had increased to $25,000,000, more than 80 times the original size. Swift was also a leader in the field of turning previously unused parts of slaughtered animals into valuable by-products. He died March 29, 1903, in Chicago.

*See* Louis F. Swift and Arthur Van Vlissingen, Jr., *Yankee of the Yards* (1927).

**SWIFT, JONATHAN** (1667–1745), Irish author, and from 1713 until his death, dean of St. Patrick's Cathedral, Dublin, the foremost prose satirist in the English language, and one of the great satiric masters of all time. His effectiveness results from his resourcefulness in devising satiric situations, the ingenuity and assurance of his execution, and an inimitable prose style: clear, direct, all bone-and-sinew. Although his position as a satirist has been acknowledged ever since his own time, in other respects he has always been a controversial figure, evoking widely disparate, and sometimes severe, judgments, of his work, his personality, and the significance of his fundamental satiric statement. Certain facts about him can be clearly stated. He was outstanding as a wit, a social personality, a clergyman, and a public figure. He wrote prose satires as widely different in theme and execution as *Gulliver's Travels, A Tale of a Tub,* and the *Modest Proposal;* he was a distinguished minor poet in an age of great minor poetry; and he was a master of political journalism.

THE GRANGER COLLECTION

JONATHAN SWIFT, PORTRAIT BY CHARLES JERVAS, ABOUT 1718

**Early Years.**—Swift was born in Dublin on Nov. 30, 1667. He was the son of Jonathan Swift the elder (1640–67) and grandson of the Rev. Thomas Swift, who had been vicar of Goodrich, Herefordshire, and was remembered for his unshakable loyalty to the Royalist cause during the Civil War. Swift's father, with three of his brothers, had settled in Ireland after the Restoration, and had become steward of the King's Inns, Dublin. In 1664 he had married Abigail Erick, who, though she may have been born in Ireland, was the daughter of an English clergyman who had been vicar of Thornton, Leicestershire. A daughter, Jane, was born in May 1666. In the spring of 1667, Jonathan the elder died suddenly, leaving his wife, baby daughter, and unborn son to the care of his brothers.

A posthumous child, and dependent on the generosity of his uncles, with no settled home, Swift may perhaps have suffered from a sense of insecurity. His education was not neglected, however. When he was six, he was sent to Kilkenny School—the best in Ireland—and in 1682, he entered Trinity College, Dublin. In a fragment of autobiography, written many years later, and first published as "Family of Swift" in 1755 (ed. by H. Davis, in *Miscellaneous and Autobiographical Pieces . . .*, 1962), he represents himself as having been so discouraged and sunk in his spirits by "the ill-treatment of his nearest relatives" that he neglected his studies, and so was only granted his B.A. degree (in February 1686) *speciali gratia* ("by special grace"). Actually, his career as an undergraduate seems to have been neither distinguished nor disgraceful, and the manner of his degree a device often used when a student's record failed in some minor respect to conform to the regulations, and not the "discreditable mark" against his name that he himself called it.

He continued in residence at Trinity as a candidate for his M.A. until February 1689, when the disorders that spread through Dublin after the Revolution of 1688 caused the college authorities to give permission for students to withdraw to safety. Swift sought security in England, and after visiting his mother (who had returned to Leicestershire at some date unknown), became a member of the household of Sir William Temple (*q.v.*), at Moor Park, Surrey.

**At Moor Park.**—Moor Park was to remain Swift's headquarters until Temple's death in January 1699, and it was there that he may be said to have achieved intellectual maturity. Temple, a man of wide culture, was engaged in writing his memoirs and preparing some of his essays for publication, and he needed someone to act as secretary. Swift's residence at Moor Park was interrupted; and the fact that he twice returned to Ireland (from May 1690 to December 1691 and from May 1694 to May 1696) points to some uneasiness about his prospects. His first return was in an attempt to obtain a post as secretary, and during his second he took orders, being ordained deacon in October 1694 and priest on Jan. 13, 1695, and at the end of the same month being preferred to the vicarage of Kilroot, near Belfast.

Much happened to Swift between 1689 and departure from Moor Park after Temple's death. He read widely in Temple's library. He met Esther Johnson (the future Stella), the stepdaughter of Temple's steward. She was a darkhaired child of eight when Swift first went to Moor Park, and his friendship with her began by his taking a share in her education. Probably in 1693 he went to Kensington on a mission for Temple, who had been asked for advice on a constitutional problem, and had a conference with William III. In 1692 he went to Oxford, where, after incorporation as a member of Hart Hall, he received an M.A. Also, between 1691 and 1694 he wrote a number of poems; of these six odes are extant.

His true genius did not find expression, however, until he turned from verse to prose satire, and wrote, mostly at Moor Park between 1696 and 1699, *A Tale of a Tub.* This, when published anonymously in 1704, was made up of three associated pieces: the *Tale* itself, a satire against "the numerous and gross corruptions in religion and learning"; the mock-heroic *Battle of the Books;* and the *Discourse Concerning the Mechanical Operation of the Spirit,* against the manner of worship and preaching of the Dissenters.

The *Battle* displays Swift's loyalty to Temple, whose *Essay upon the Ancient and Modern Learning* (1690) had been severely criticized by William Wotton, a defender of modern culture, and the distinguished scholar Richard Bentley (*q.v.; see* also ANCIENS ET DES MODERNES, QUERELLE DES). Swift allegorizes the attack on Temple, ridicules Wotton and Bentley, and in the famous episode of the bee and the spider with which the battle opens (in which the spider "feeding and engendering on itself . . . producing nothing at all, but Fly-bane and a Cobweb" is identified with the moderns; and the bee, which, by bringing home honey and wax, furnishes "Mankind with . . . Sweetness and Light" is equated with the ancients) expresses his own tenets concerning the right and universal standards in taste and literature. But it is the *Tale of a Tub* itself that is the most impressive of the three compositions, marked as it everywhere is by exuberance of satiric wit and energy, and by an incomparable command of stylistic effects, largely in the nature of parody. Swift saw the realm of culture and literature threatened by zealous pedantry, and religion—which for him meant rational Anglicanism—suffering attack from both Roman Catholicism and Dissent, and he proceeded to trace these dangers to a single source: the irrationalities which disturb what he regarded as man's highest faculties—reason and common sense.

**Vicar of Laracor.**—With Temple's sudden death in January 1699, Swift entered on a period of varied experience and considerable uncertainty. As nothing offered in England, in the summer he returned to Dublin as chaplain and secretary to the earl of Berkeley, then going to Ireland as a lord justice. During the next 12 years he was in England on four occasions, and won recognition in London for his personal charm and his wit as a writer. Otherwise his position remained unchanged. He had resigned his Kilroot vicarage while at Moor Park, but early in 1700 was preferred to several livings in the Irish Church, the principal being the vicarage of Laracor not far from Dublin. Often in Dublin, he was able to keep in touch with public affairs, both Irish and English. His *A Discourse of the Contests and Dissentions . . . between the Nobles and the Commons in Athens and Rome* (1701) is a forcible statement of his own Whig principles and an appeal to both political parties for moderation. *A Project for the Advancement of Religion, and the Reformation of Manners* (1709) is a reforming tract of a traditional kind. Of other writings of this period—publication of which was, however, delayed—the most notable are the *Sentiments of a Church-of-England Man,* and the *Argument against Abolishing Christianity* (both published in 1711, in his *Miscellanies*), the first a straightforward exposition, the second a masterpiece of ironic disputation against the Deists (*see* also DEISM).

In Ireland Swift remained the comparatively insignificant vicar of Laracor. He was, it is true, on friendly terms with Archbishop King of Dublin, and when in England he kept King informed of matters touching on the Irish Church; and during the longest of his sojourns in London, from November 1707 to June 1709, he was empowered by the Irish bishops to seek from the Whig administration an extension to Ireland of Queen Anne's Bounty, which had been recently granted to the Church of England. But in London he was increasingly well known. His religious and political essays, serious and ironic; the publication in 1704—anonymous but generally attributed to him—of *A Tale of a Tub;* certain *jeux d'esprit,* including the Bickerstaff pamphlets of 1708–09, which put an end to the career as a popular astrologer of John Partridge (whom he wished to discredit because of his attacks on the clergy) by first prophesying his death and then describing it with convincing detail; and a number of amusing pieces in the minor key, such as *A Description of the Morning,* printed by Steele in the *Tatler* in 1709—these brought him to the attention of the general public as well as to the circle of Whig writers presided over by Joseph Addison (*q.v.*). It is apparent, however, that he found much that gave him uneasiness, less in regard to personal affairs (though anything like adequate recognition in Ireland had escaped him) than in connection with the policies of the Whig administration. Swift was a Whig by birth and education, and the political principles that he had been setting forth in his writings were in the 17th-century Whig tradition. On the other hand, he was passionately loyal to the Established Church, and he came to view with apprehension the growing determination of the Whig administration to strengthen Dissent in Ireland at its expense. Increasingly he was aware of a conflict of loyalties.

Another and momentous period began for him when, on Sept. 7, 1710, he arrived in London. Events of great national importance were under way. A Tory ministry, headed by Robert Harley (later earl of Oxford) and Henry St. John (later Viscount Bolingbroke), was replacing the Whigs; the new administration was bent upon bringing hostilities with France to a conclusion. Also, a more protective attitude toward the Church of England was in prospect. Swift's reactions to this rapidly changing world are vividly recorded at the beginning of his famous *Journal to Stella,* the series of letters extending to 1713 which he addressed to Esther Johnson and her companion, Rebecca Dingley, who were now living in Dublin. The astute Harley, who had befriended Defoe and thereby gained the political services of a valuable writer, made overtures to Swift and, by assuring him that Queen Anne's Bounty would be extended to Ireland, won him over to the Tories. Swift had resolved his dilemma. But though he had placed Church above party, he did not renounce his deeply fixed and essentially Whiggish convictions regarding the nature of government. The old Tory theory of the divine right of kings had no claim upon him. The ultimate power, he insisted, derived from the people as a whole; in the English constitution it had come to be exercised jointly by king, lords, and commons, between whom it was of first importance that a balance be maintained, as a guarantee against all forms of tyranny. Swift sincerely believed that the new ministry reflected in its policies the desires of the whole nation, and was in this sense genuinely moderate. Of its communications with the Stuart Pretender he never knew.

Deceived though he was about the realities of Oxford-Bolingbroke politics, Swift made an important contribution to 18th-century Toryism by exposing it to his doctrine of rational freedom arising out of the whole of society. Quickly he became the ministry's chief political writer. By the end of October he had taken over the Tory journal, the *Examiner,* which he continued to write until June 14, 1711, when he turned to the preparation of a pamphlet in support of the Tory drive for peace. This, called *The Conduct of the Allies,* appeared on Nov. 27, 1711, some weeks before the motion in favour of peace was finally carried in Parliament. Both before this and in the months immediately afterward Swift was also turning out a stream of verse and prose, all politically inspired, whether serious, humorous, or vituperative. His services were not underrated by his friends in the ministry, and it was taken for granted that he would be rewarded by church preferment. But his reward was slow to come, and when it did—in April 1713—it proved to be the deanery of St. Patrick's Cathedral, Dublin, not the English bishopric he had hoped for. He left for Ireland in June 1713 but, early in September, was summoned back to London to heal, if possible, the rift between Oxford and Bolingbroke (*see* further OXFORD, ROBERT HARLEY, 1st Earl; BOLINGBROKE, HENRY ST. JOHN, 1st Viscount). His efforts were unsuccessful, and in the following spring he fled from the warring ministers, taking refuge in a friend's country parsonage in Berkshire, where the news of Queen Anne's death on Aug. 1, 1714, reached him. With the advent of George I the Tories were a ruined party, and Swift's career in England was at an end.

**Dean of St. Patrick's.**—He was to pass almost all the rest of his life in Ireland. On return to Dublin in the summer of 1714 he found himself the object of scorn and abuse on the part of the Anglo-Irish Whigs, and, bitter over the turn of events and emotionally exhausted, he retired to the seclusion of the deanery. He was, he felt, in a better position than anyone else to record the facts concerning the Oxford-Bolingbroke administration and the negotiations which had culminated, in 1713, in the Peace of Utrecht, and he had already finished several historical pieces, such as the *History of the Four Last Years of the Queen,* written in 1712–13, though not published until 1758. To supplement this he wrote an account of the circumstances attending the Tories' advent to power in 1710, and an *Enquiry into the Queen's Last Ministry*. Both remained unpublished until after his death.

Gradually he regained his full energy. He turned again to verse, which he continued to write throughout the 1720s and the early 1730s, to which period belong such impressive poems as *Death and Daphne, Verses on the Death of Dr. Swift* (in which he gives a striking self-portrait), *The Day of Judgment, An Epistle To a Lady,* and *On Poetry—A Rapsody*. By 1720 he was also showing a renewed interest in public affairs. In numerous Irish pamphlets he dealt with many aspects of Irish life. His tone and manner varied greatly, from direct presentation of economic and social facts to exhortation, humour, and irony. He was moved by his perception of the realities of the Irish situation, and by his desire to strike at Sir Robert Walpole and his Whig administration. Ireland's backward state he blamed chiefly on the blindness of the English government, but insistently he called attention to the things the Irish could themselves be doing to better their lot. Of the Irish writings the *Drapier's Letters* (1724–25) and the *Modest Proposal for preventing the children of poor people from being a burthen to their Parents or Country, and for making them beneficial to the Publick* (1729) are the best known, the first being a series purportedly written by M. B., a Dublin linen-draper, attacking the English government for its scheme to supply Ireland with copper halfpence and farthings, the latter a grimly ironic letter of advice in which a public-spirited citizen suggests that conditions could be alleviated were children to be used for food.

Certain events in Swift's private life must also be mentioned. Stella, who died on Jan. 26, 1728, had continued to live with Rebecca Dingley since moving to Ireland in 1700 or 1701. It has sometimes been asserted that Stella and Swift were secretly married in 1716, but that they did not live together: there is no evidence to support this story, however. It was friendship that Swift always expressed in speaking of Stella, not romantic love. The question may be asked, was this friendship strained as a result of the appearance in his life of "Vanessa" (Esther Vanhomrigh)? He had met Vanessa during his London visit of 1707–09, and in 1714 she had, despite all his admonitions, insisted on following him to Ireland. Her letters to Swift reveal her passion for him, though at the time of her death (June 2, 1723), she had apparently turned against him because he insisted on maintaining a distant attitude to her. We are still much in the dark concerning the precise relationships between these three people, and melodramatic theories that have been suggested rest upon no solid ground.

*Gulliver's Travels.*—When Stella died Swift had already enjoyed his greatest triumph as a satiric writer. It is uncertain when he began *Gulliver's Travels,* as the book published as *Travels into Several Remote Nations of the World . . . , by Lemuel Gulliver* came to be called. In origin it may perhaps date from the meetings of the Scriblerus Club, a group of Tory writers to which Pope, John Gay, Dr. John Arbuthnot, and Swift all belonged (*see* LITERATURE, SOCIETIES OF). It is known from Swift's correspondence that he was writing in earnest by 1721 and had finished the whole by August 1725. Since 1714 he had not been to England, but in 1726 he returned, carrying with him in manuscript the work designed, as he said in a letter to Pope (Sept. 29, 1725), to "vex the world rather than divert it." He visited Pope at Twickenham, where he was joined by other Scriblerians, and where he completed arrangements for its publication. *Gulliver's Travels* appeared on Oct. 28, after Swift had left for Dublin. Its success was immediate. Then, as ever since, it succeeded in "vexing" (as well as diverting) all classes of readers. To what extent is it a political allegory, hinting at the story of Oxford and Bolingbroke, their fall, and Walpole's policies? Is it essentially comic, or intended as misanthropic depreciation of mankind? How seriously are we meant to take Gulliver's utopian sketches? Its matter-of-fact style and its air of sober reality confer on it an ironic depth which defeats over-simple explanations.

Swift visited London once more, in the summer of 1727, to arrange for publication of *Miscellanies in Prose and Verse,* compiled with Pope, of which four volumes were eventually published (1727–32). He also seems to have hoped that an attempt might be made to break the Whig administration. But the death of George I in June 1727 brought the Tories no advantage, and Swift returned to Dublin for the last time in October.

*Later Years.*—The closing years of Swift's life have been the subject of some misrepresentation, and stories have been told of his ungovernable tempers and lack of self-control; it has been suggested that he was insane. From youth he had suffered from what is now known to have been Ménière's disease, an affliction of the semicircular canals of the ears causing periods of dizziness and nausea. But this in no way affected his mental powers, and he remained active throughout most of the 1730s, Dublin's foremost citizen and Ireland's great patriot dean. In the autumn of 1739, as he entered upon his 17th year of office as dean, a celebration was held in his honour. He had already begun to fail physically, and later suffered a paralytic stroke, with subsequent aphasia. In 1742 he was declared incapable of caring for himself, and guardians were appointed. He died on Oct. 19, 1745. He was buried in St. Patrick's Cathedral, next to Stella and beneath the Latin epitaph he had himself composed, which may be translated: "The body of Jonathan Swift, Doctor of Divinity, dean of this cathedral church, is buried here, where fierce indignation can no more lacerate his heart. Go, traveler, and imitate, if you can, one who strove with all his strength to champion liberty."

**Conclusion.**—Intellectually, Swift may be said to have his roots in the rationalism characteristic of later 17th-century England. It was this rationalism, with its strong moral bent, its emphasis on common sense, and its hatred of emotionalism, that gave him the standards by which he appraised human conduct and the norms which he defended in satiric terms. His principles—the positive core of all his work—are scarcely original; his originality is rather a matter of his satiric imagination and art. His tone varies from the humorous to the savage, but each of his satiric compositions is marked by concentrated power and directness of impact. His command of prose style—or rather, of a great variety of prose styles—is unfailing, as is his power of inventing episodes and all their accompanying details. His descriptive passages reflect the minds that are describing more than the things described. Rarely does Swift speak in his own person; almost always he works by ironic indirection through some imagined character like Lemuel Gulliver or the public-spirited citizen of the *Modest Proposal*. It is in his irony that craftsmanship and vision fuse. Swift's irony is operating everywhere: pulling in different directions, it creates the tensions characteristic of his writings. It reflects his vision of man's ambiguous position between bestiality and reasonableness.

BIBLIOGRAPHY.—*Editions, Correspondence, etc.: The Prose Works,* ed. by H. Davis, 14 vol. (1939– ); *The Prose Works,* ed. by Temple Scott, 12 vol. (1897–1908); *The Poems,* ed. by H. Williams, 3 vol. (1937; 2nd ed. 1958); *The Correspondence,* ed. by F. Elrington Ball, 6 vol. (1910–14), ed. by H. Williams, 5 vol. (1963–65); *Vanessa and Her Correspondence with Jonathan Swift,* ed. by A. M. Freeman (1921); *The Letters of Jonathan Swift to Charles Ford,* ed. by D. Nichol Smith (1935). Editions of separate works include *The Drapier's Letters,* ed. by H. Davis (1935); *Gulliver's Travels: the Text of the First Edition,* ed. by H. Williams (1926); *Journal to Stella,* ed. by H. Williams, 2 vol. (1948); *A Tale of a Tub . . . ,* ed. by A. C. Guthkelch and D. Nichol Smith (1920; 2nd ed. 1958). There is a bibliography in vol. xii of the Temple Scott *Prose Works. See* also H. Teerink, *A Bibliography of the Writings of Jonathan Swift* (1937; 2nd ed. revised and corrected by A. H. Scouten, 1963); L. A. Landa and J. E. Tobin, *Jonathan Swift: a List of Critical Studies . . . 1895 to 1945* (1945). Selections include *Selected Prose Works of Jonathan Swift,* ed. by J. Hayward (1949); *A Selection of Poems by Jonathan Swift,* ed. by J. Heath-Stubbs (1948); *Gulliver's Travels and Other*

*Writings,* ed. by R. Quintana (1958); *Gulliver's Travels and Other Writings,* ed. by L. A. Landa (1960); *Poetry and Prose of Jonathan Swift,* ed. by H. Davis (1964).

*Biography and Criticism:* C. Whibley, *Jonathan Swift* (1917); W. A. Eddy, *A Critical Study of Gulliver's Travels* (1923); E. Pons, *Les Années de jeunesse et le Conte du Tonneau* (1925); C. Van Doren, *Swift* (1930); W. D. Taylor, *Jonathan Swift, A Critical Essay* (1933); R. F. Jones, *Ancients and Moderns: a Study of the Background of the Battle of the Books* (1936; rev. ed. 1961); R. Quintana, *The Mind and Art of Jonathan Swift* (1936; reprinted with additions, 1953), and *Swift: an Introduction* (1955); D. M. Berwick, *The Reputation of Swift, 1781–1882* (1941); H. Davis, *Stella, A Gentlewoman of the 18th Century* (1942), *The Satire of Jonathan Swift* (1947), and *Jonathan Swift: Essays on His Satire and Other Studies* (1964); M. Johnson, *The Sin of Wit: Jonathan Swift as a Poet* (1950); M. K. Starkman, *Swift's Satire on Learning in A Tale of a Tub* (1950); H. Williams, *The Text of Gulliver's Travels* (1952); J. M. Bullitt, *Jonathan Swift and the Anatomy of Satire* (1953); M. Price, *Swift's Rhetorical Art* (1953); W. B. Ewald, *The Masks of Jonathan Swift* (1954); L. A. Landa, *Swift and the Church of Ireland* (1954); J. M. Murry, *Jonathan Swift, a Critical Biography* (1954); I. Ehrenpreis, *The Personality of Jonathan Swift* (1958), and *Swift: the Man, his Works, and the Age:* vol. i, *Mr. Swift and His Contemporaries* (1962); vol. ii, *Dr. Swift* (1967); K. Williams, *Jonathan Swift and the Age of Compromise* (1958); R. Paulson, *Theme and Structure in Swift's Tale of a Tub* (1960); J. P. Harth, *Swift and Anglican Rationalism: the Religious Background of A Tale of a Tub* (1961); E. W. Rosenheim, Jr., *Swift and the Satirist's Art* (1963); N. Dennis, *Jonathan Swift* (1964); M. Voigt, *Swift and the Twentieth Century* (1964); C. A. Beaumont, *Swift's Use of the Bible* (1965); J. G. Gilbert, *Jonathan Swift: Romantic and Cynic Moralist* (1966); R. Hunting, *Jonathan Swift* (1966); R. I. Cook, *Jonathan Swift as a Tory Pamphleteer* (1967).

*See* also J. J. Stathis, *Bibliography of Swift Studies, 1945–1965* (1967). (R. Qu.)

**SWIFT,** a bird of remarkable flight speed and maneuverability, any of the 76 species composing the family Apodidae (formerly Micropodidae). Although resembling swallows superficially, swifts are a nonpasserine group closely allied to hummingbirds. They are virtually cosmopolitan but are not found at higher latitudes and on some oceanic islands. Many species are migratory. Of small to medium size (3½–9 in.), they have compact bodies, small bills, large gapes, extremely short legs, and very small feet with a reversible first toe. The wings are long and pointed and the tail either short and truncate (sometimes spine-tipped) or very long and forked. The plumage is usually drab, blackish or bluish to gray-brown.

Swifts are the most aerial of birds, even mating and bathing on the wing. They subsist on insects captured in flight and rest only by clinging to vertical surfaces. The nests, of a salivary secretion or of plant fragments, etc., cemented together with the secretion, vary from simple wall-hugging brackets to long elaborate tubes. In parts of the Orient the hardened saliva nests of certain cave-dwelling swifts (*Collocalia*) are considered a delicacy when prepared as a soup.

Best known of American species is the chimney swift (*Chaetura pelagica*), a blackish, swallowlike bird that breeds throughout the eastern United States and winters in the upper Amazon drainage; during migration, these birds congregate in chimneys and hollow trees at dusk.

The closely related crested or tree swifts (family Hemiprocnidae) have crests, soft plumage, and strong legs adapted for perching. The three species are found in southeastern Asia and nearby islands. (E. R. Be.)

**SWIMMING,** the action of self-support and self-propulsion in the water as practised by man, is among man's most useful as well as pleasurable accomplishments.

Very important in the training of warriors in the days of early Greece and Rome, it gradually declined in popularity, according to some authorities because of the belief that epidemics sweeping throughout the Continent during the Middle Ages were caused by swimming or bathing out-of-doors.

Not until the second half of the 19th century was this prejudice sufficiently overcome for aquatic activity to be taken up widely again, first in Great Britain and later in other countries. The revived Olympic Games in Athens in 1896 accepted swimming as one of the international sports, to which diving was added in 1904. Women's swimming and diving became part of the international games in 1912.

## TEACHING SWIMMING

In many cases beginners have demonstrated some ability in swimming upon their first immersion in the water, but generally speaking it is a skill that must be acquired. With the increasing acceptance of swimming as a recreation has come increasing appreciation of its value in protecting life as well as in physical education, for it has gained recognition as one of the most beneficial of all forms of exercise. Many physical educators hold that there is no comparable physical activity that can contribute as much as swimming to a person's physical well-being.

Teaching of swimming was taken up by the schools; sectional and national learn-to-swim campaigns were conducted in most countries. During World War II nearly all belligerent nations included swimming as a part of the training of servicemen, and after the war the gains in swimming instruction and promotion were consolidated and furthered by national organizations such as the U.S. Council for National Cooperation in Aquatics. This organization, meeting annually, includes some 24 different organizations interested in furthering the cause of swimming because of its value as an all-around exercise. Among its more prominent members are the American Red Cross, the YMCA-YWCA, the Amateur Athletic Union (AAU), the National Collegiate Athletic Association (NCAA), the National Federation of State High School Athletic Associations, and the United States Office of Education.

**Methods.**—Many methods of swimming instruction have been tested as changes in strokes took place, but in the long run the great majority of teachers enrolled in one of two predominant schools: the European, whose protagonists believe the breaststroke should be taught first; and the U.S., whose followers assert that the crawl is mastered more readily than any other stroke. Both schools favour preliminary drills on land or in shallow water so that beginners may gain some knowledge of the required movement before attempting to swim.

The greatest handicaps in learning are failure to relax and haste in performing swimming movements. Fear of the water, or the mere nervousness experienced by most nonswimmers, generally causes muscle tension and leads to the feeling that it is necessary to thrash wildly with arms and legs in order to keep afloat. Every effort must be made to overcome these natural tendencies, for progress is dependent upon complete relaxation and unhurried movements. Instructors usually help pupils to become accustomed to immersion by having them play in shallow water, ducking the head and looking for objects on the bottom, before instruction starts.

In the military services, during World Wars I and II, when great numbers of men in their late 20s and early 30s had to be taught to swim, and speed in training was essential, a method of starting the pupil on his back was developed. In this position floating was facilitated, thus developing confidence in the water; normal breathing was utilized in contrast with the breathing difficulty in face-down strokes, and a very simple propulsive action was taught: a frog kick with a synchronous short arm stroke, the arms being underwater to prevent splash.

A newer approach to the teaching of swimming, called drown proofing, emphasizes breathing and complete relaxation. Developed by Fred R. Lanoue of the Georgia Institute of Technology, this system has been adopted by the U.S. Marine Corps and the Peace Corps, as well as by all trainees in the newly formed Outward Bound program. Eschewing the older techniques of learning in shallow water, swimmers are introduced immediately into water over their heads; by using breath control as well as natural buoyancy and a minimum of effort, they are able to stay afloat or propel themselves through the water slowly. Drown proofers with little instruction can stay afloat for hours. A part of the final test for drown proofers requires staying afloat with hands and feet tied.

Later innovations in teaching nonswimmers include the use of swim fins (which help teach leg drive), snorkels (which help the beginner to learn to breathe more easily), and swim buoys. Swim buoys (inflatable or solid) are attached firmly to the beginner's torso by means of straps, and supply the needed buoyancy for

SOME SWIMMING STROKES

(Above) Side stroke and scissors kick; (left) orthodox breaststroke and frog wedge kick; (below) butterfly stroke

RUSS KINNE

the beginner to remain afloat while mastering the various swimming strokes being taught.

**Floating.**—One of the most useful accomplishments of a swimmer is floating. It is largely a matter of buoyancy which varies considerably with individuals. Buoyancy cannot be taught, but body balance in the water can be acquired through knowledge. In learning to float, the beginner experiences difficulty in keeping the legs in the horizontal plane; this can be remedied by the counterbalance of extending the arms beyond the head, whether in face-down or back floating position. Some people are definitely "sinkers," unable to float in any position. For them, drown proofing is a worthwhile skill.

Motionless floating can be performed with proper breath control and body balance. Bending the knees to shorten the axis often improves balance in the water. Supine or back floating with a minimum of motion of the arms and legs is a valuable safety skill for the swimmer as well as for the novice.

## SWIMMING STROKES

Types of swimming strokes commonly used, and in the order of present popularity, are the crawl, sidestroke, backstroke, breaststroke, and butterfly. At earlier periods sidestroke and breaststroke were the most popular.

In the early years of competition, the standard racing style was sidestroke, in which the swimmer lay on his side with both arms continuously submerged. The first advance over this was made when swimmers conceived the idea of minimizing water resistance by bringing the upper arm above the surface when "recovering," which means bringing the arm, after it has completed a thrust, back into position to start a new thrust. This new stroke was called the single overarm. The double overarm followed, with both arms recovering above the surface and the body of the swimmer rolling from one side to the other. This stroke was made prominent in 1893 by an Englishman, J. Trudgen, who told of picking it up in South America. It took his name and served later to introduce the basic arm action of the crawl, the most efficient way of swimming developed up to that time.

The changes in the leg drive were marked by a consistent trend toward narrower and faster movements. Following the advent of the trudgen, the wide scissors kick of the sidestroke, originally performed with legs bent excessively, was reduced in scope and executed with the legs much straighter. With the introduction of the crawl, the legs began to whip up and down alternately in a gradually quickening thrash, speeding up by degrees from two to six proportionately smaller kicks to each cycle of the two arms.

**Breaststroke.**—Two styles of breaststroke have evolved, the ancient and orthodox, believed to be the oldest of all strokes, and the butterfly, a racing adaptation brought out in 1933 by Henry Myers of the United States. The orthodox breaststroke, used by the European school for teaching beginners, is a stroke of great practical value. It affords the means to assist a tired swimmer or support a drowning person with comparatively little effort; it enables the swimmer to advance safely through rough waters littered with flotsam or wreckage.

The breaststroke and the butterfly stroke are distinguished by different arm action. In the orthodox breaststroke the arms always remain under water. The two hands are extended together in front of the swimmer and start their pull about six to eight inches under the surface, with the arms pressing backward in a rounded and outward pattern of approximately 100°. When they reach their maximum spread, the hands are brought together under the breast, completing the circular pattern, and extended again quickly, palms down, to start another stroke.

The leg action for the breaststroke, known as the frog kick, is of two types, wedge kick or whip kick. The older wedge is characterized by a very wide kick in which the feet are drawn up, knees bent, and the kick produced by a vigorous rounded and outward sweep of the legs in a fully extended position until the feet come together again. The wedge kick is best described by what appears to be "squeezing" the water when the legs are at their widest spread. This widespread position creates considerably more drag than does the whip kick.

The more efficient whip type features a much narrower kick. The knees are kept much closer together, yet the feet reach out to engage the water by rotation of the upper thigh. The difference between the two types of kick is easily recognized. In the wedge the legs are fully extended while executing the squeezing action; in the whip, the legs never reach full extension until the kick is nearly complete. Experimental tests have indicated that the whip kick is superior in all respects.

**Butterfly.**—Regulations governing competition in the butterfly were revised in 1952 to permit a synchronous up-and-down action of the legs characterized by the term "fishtail" kick, or "dolphin." This new kick resulted in the separation of the breast- and butterfly strokes competitively. In the breaststroke it was ruled that the arms and legs must remain under the surface. In the butterfly stroke the leg kick could either be executed in the traditional breaststroke manner or in a simultaneous up-and-down movement of the legs and feet in the vertical plane. In the butterfly stroke the arms recover simultaneously above the surface, and in the propulsive phase press downward and backward under the body all the way to the thighs. The action of each arm is very similar to the pull in the crawl stroke.

Since the separation of the breast- and butterfly strokes there has been a constant study of the breaststroke technique in an endeavour to secure greater speed in competitive events. The body position is now flatter on the surface. The glide phase between the propulsive arm movements has been practically eliminated and the leg kick is narrower.

**Sidestroke.**—The sidestroke is valued chiefly for lifesaving purposes, as it is used in the most efficient carries devised for the rescue of the drowning. It is also the best stroke for carrying anything that must be kept dry while swimming. It is preferred by the average person for open-water pleasure swimming because it is faster than the breaststroke and the face remains constantly above water for ease in breathing. The body stays steadily on its side, as the name implies, and the arms propel alternately. The under arm starts from comfortable extension overhead and pulls below the body to the waist, then bends upward and pushes forward; the upper arm drives a little outside the body line, sweeping to the thigh, and recovers close to the surface. The legs open slowly for the scissors kick, the under leg moving backward, the upper leg forward, both knees bent a little, feet pointed, then the legs whip smartly together, the closing movement timed with the finish of the upper arm drive.

**Crawl Stroke.**—The crawl is the fastest of all known strokes, yet it requires little effort. Many of the greatest feats of endurance achieved by men and women stand to its credit, including crossing the English Channel and swimming the length of the Panama Canal. Its remarkable speed has made the crawl not only supreme in the competitive field (it is the universal choice in freestyle events) but also extremely valuable in saving drowning persons, in getting away from a sinking ship, and in battling strong tides or currents.

*History.*—There is evidence that the crawl was well known in some of the South Sea Islands long before Richard Cavill of Australia introduced it into England about 1900 and broadcast its merits by breaking the world record for 100 yd. with it. It was discovered that the stroke had been popular in the Solomons as far back as the oldest islanders could remember; and long before it was introduced in Australia, sportsmen in Honolulu frequently arranged swimming races at Waikiki Beach in which young Hawaiian swimmers used a stroke very similar to the one later demonstrated with such success by United States Olympic champion Duke Kahanamoku. The name "crawl" was coined as the result of a press account of the initial showing of the stroke, in which the writer stated that Cavill appeared literally to crawl over the water. Cavill performed two kicks per full stroke, and his action was adopted universally in Australia, so the leg drive remained unchanged until the stroke made its way to the United States.

The earliest knowledge of the crawl obtained in the U.S. was derived from hazy newspaper accounts and descriptions of Cavill's strokes. In attempting to imitate the action, U.S. swimmers unwittingly developed a faster leg drive, executing four scissoring kicks per stroke instead of the two performed by Cavill. The new leg drive was combined with the double overarm action of the trudgen, and the resulting stroke was called the four-beat crawl, to distinguish it from the two-beat variety.

Meanwhile, experiments had led to the belief that the four-beat leg thrash was more effective when composed of one comparatively wide and three very narrow scissoring motions. This style, termed the four-beat trudgen crawl or the four-beat single rhythm crawl, became the accepted racing stroke. The combination of movements was responsible for so notable an improvement in average performances that technical experts conceived the possibility of obtaining still greater speed from a six-beat drive set to a double rhythm—two major and four minor kicks—which would minimize resistance and afford more even distribution of propelling power. But coaches were unanimous in declaring that the swift thrash would prove entirely too laborious for distances longer than 100 yd., and the subject was dropped temporarily.

Late in 1917 two young swimmers of the New York Women's Swimming Association, Charlotte Boyle and Claire Galligan, determined to give the six-beat a trial, and by the summer of 1918 they broke records with it over the longer situation courses, 800 m. and one mile. So convincing was this demonstration that it caused a sudden change of mind among the coaches and competitors. The six-beat crawl immediately won favour in the U.S., as well as in other countries, and within a few years it had become the recognized stroke the world over, not only for racing but also for all-around purposes. A great many women and some men also used the eight-beat successfully in the early years of crawl swimming.

In spite of the fact that the six-beat crawl is the almost universal choice of sprinters, present-day distance swimmers use a variety of kicks, some six-beat, some four-beat, some scissors, some a combination of scissors and flutter, while some use their legs in a crossover kick as a balance against lateral movement, since it is well established that the arm stroke is the major propulsive force.

Debbie Meyer, 1968 Olympic champion (three gold medals), U.S. women's world record holder at all freestyle distances 200 yd. and over, and Mike Burton, 1968 Olympic champion, U.S. men's world record holder at 1,500 m., represent wide differences of leg action in their respective strokes. Miss Meyer represents the classic six-beat crawl, while Burton, particularly in distance racing, relies almost entirely on arm movements.

Developments in speed swimming after World War II were dramatic due largely to more and better facilities, both indoor and outdoor, more technical knowledge, better instruction, and better training methods. It becomes increasingly difficult to predict ultimate limits. In the men's 1,500-m. swim the 1956 men's Olympic record stood at 17:58.9 sec. The 1968 Olympic record for the same race stands at 16:38.9, a decrease of better than one minute.

*Method.*—The correct position of the body in crawl swimming is that of a streamlined whole, with the legs kept slightly under the surface. Raising the head high results in an exaggerated arch in the lower back, which increases body resistance. Lateral movements of the body should be avoided. The arms move alternately, so timed that one will start pulling just before the other

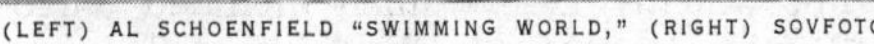
(LEFT) AL SCHOENFIELD "SWIMMING WORLD," (RIGHT) SOVFOTO

COMPETITIVE SWIMMING STROKES

(Left) Free-style competition in which, although any style may be employed, the crawl is preferred; (right) backstroke has finished its pull, thereby making propulsion continuous. Most crawl swimmers complete just about one-half of their arm pull before the recovering hand next enters the water. The hand enters the water with the elbow held high and slightly bent. Throughout the pull, the shoulder must always be over the elbow, and the elbow over the wrist and hand. The slight bend of the elbow affords greater strength in the action of the arm in pulling.

The power of the arm stroke can be thought of as pressing downward and backward during the first third of the stroke, pushing during the middle third and pushing through and backward but not upward during the final third of the action, completing an arc of roughly 180°. The direction of pull should be on a line from the shoulder moving under the body and out past the thigh on recovery.

On recovery the elbow is bent and carried high. The forearm circles quickly out and around until it points toward the place of entry. Then the elbow is extended, not fully, for the catch of the hand on a line with the shoulder.

The legs are held fairly straight but fully relaxed. The legs whip up and down alternately in an undulating action so that in both the up kick and down kick there will be a backward push against the water with the lower leg and more so with the foot. The scope of the thrash must vary somewhat according to the individual length of leg and the number of beats used per stroke.

Breathing is effected by turning the head to either side during recovery of the overwater arm, for the purpose of a quick inhalation, and then returning the head face downward, exhaling through the nose, or nose and mouth. Normally one breath is taken for each full cycle of the arms. In short distance sprinting, however, breathing may take place after two, three, or even four cycles of the arms. The skilled swimmer learns to breathe equally well on either side. It is not uncommon to see a skilled swimmer breathe once on the right side, then take his next breath on the left. This is called alternate breathing, or breathing every stroke and a half.

Crawl balance can be perfected only by hours and many miles of swimming under the watchful eye of a competent coach. The body should be straight and streamlined. The arm recovery is loose and relaxed, the elbows held high and hands relaxed before the catch. The legs should move in an easy relaxed up and down undulating pattern with the impetus coming from the hip muscles with little or no lateral movement. Lateral movement of the torso, as well as excessive arching of the back in an effort to ride high in the water not only affect proper balance in the water, but decrease speed and increase fatigue.

**Backstroke.**—The style of the backstroke in vogue prior to 1912 was aptly described as inverted breaststroke. That year Harry Hebner, the U.S. champion, amazed spectators in the Olympic race at Stockholm with his supine crawl featuring alternate arm pulls, never before seen in Europe, winning in record time. That exhibition soon drove the old stroke (double overarm on the back with a frog kick) into discard, for the back crawl is much faster, requires less effort, and is easier to learn.

In the back crawl the body position again remains as streamlined as possible. Due to the nature of the stroke and in order to get propulsion from the legs, a slight bend of the hips is necessary. If the bend at the hips is too pronounced, a "sitting" effect is created which produces too much drag to make the stroke effective. Each arm stretches above the head and enters the water at a point directly over the shoulder, the palm facing outward, the little finger entering the water first. After the hand enters the water the arm is pulled to the thigh. The pulling in the first third of the action is done with a straight arm, the middle third with a bent arm, and the last third with a final thrust of the arm to full extension. Authorities on the back crawl differ slightly on the extent of the elbow bend during the middle third of the pull as well as the degree to which the shoulders and body should roll. Most agree, however, that the body roll, while necessary for efficient backstroking, should not be more than 45°.

The legs execute an alternating up-and-down movement, similar to that of the crawl stroke, the emphasis being on the upbeat, kicking the water up and away. The head should remain still throughout the stroke. Breathing presents no problems, since the face is almost always out of water. Breathing, however, is cyclical as in all other strokes.

## COMPETITIVE SWIMMING

In 1869 the Amateur Swimming Association in England formulated standards for the sport. Other countries followed this leadership, the U.S. launching the Amateur Athletic Union in 1878 to cover swimming and other sports. Before many years all Western nations formed similar governing bodies which resulted in the revival of the Olympic Games in Athens in 1896.

Controlling national organizations met in London in 1908 at which time the International Amateur Swimming Federation (Fédération Internationale de Natation Amateur [FINA]) was formed, the purpose of which was to draft a code, supervise and register world records, and establish programs for the Olympic Games. Membership was permitted those countries that would subscribe to and abide by the code of rules laid down by FINA. From the handful of original subscribing countries, FINA grew to include an impressive number of 92 affiliated nations. Branches of aquatic sport over which FINA elected to assume authority are swimming, diving, and water polo. Synchronized swimming was formally added to the FINA program at the 1955 Pan-American Games.

Organizations operating under the FINA code in addition to the Olympic Games include the Pan-American Games, the Maccabiah Games, and the World Student Games (FISU).

**Freestyle.**—Freestyle (crawl) races, ever since Olympic competition restarted, have been more predominant than any other stroke. This also holds true for NCAA and interscholastic competition in the United States. Only in the 1960s did backstroke, breaststroke, butterfly stroke, and, particularly, individual medley races challenge the popularity of the crawl. Individual medley events demand the ability to swim all four strokes well in the same race.

The fact that large numbers of pools—either indoor or outdoor, short course (25 yd.) or long course (50 m.)—were constructed by municipalities, aquatic clubs, and high schools, as well as by universities and colleges after World War II, made a decided impact on the growth of the sport.

A study of the ten Olympics since 1920 reveals that excellence in performance follows no one pattern or nation, with Hungary, Denmark, Australia, Germany, France, Great Britain, Canada, Japan, and the United States becoming leaders at different times. Since 1920, however, with the exception of the 1932 and 1956 Olympics, the swimmers of the United States have won a large share of the Olympic honours.

The 1964 games at Tokyo featured the swimming of 17-year-old Don Schollander (U.S.), who was the first in aquatic history to win four gold medals. Australia's Dawn Fraser became the first woman swimmer to win a gold medal (100-m. freestyle) at three successive Olympics, while Galina Prozumenschikova's 200-m. breaststroke victory saw the Soviet Union on the winner's stand for the first time.

Mexico City, host of the XIX Olympic Games in 1968, featured world competition for the first time at an altitude (7,347 ft.) where the rarefied air presented problems to many of the competitors. Daniel Hanley, U.S. team physician, said in part that "athletes from sea-level countries performed below their best capabilities." The addition of several new events on both the men's and women's programs was favourable to U.S. swimmers. U.S. swimmers won 10 gold medals in men's swimming, while their women counterparts won 11. Mexico, however, celebrated its first gold medal in swimming when Felipe Muñoz surprised a strong field in the 200-m. breaststroke. Australia's Michael Wenden won two titles at 200-m. and 100-m. freestyle, both in Olympic record time. East Germany's Roland Matthes proved himself the world's premier backstroker, winning both dorsal races in Olympic record time. The only titles not won by U.S. women included Yugoslavia's first by Miss D. Bjedov at 100-m. breaststroke and a stunning win by Australia's Lynette McClements at 100-m. butterfly.

Even though the altitude adversely affected times in the longer events, Olympic swimming records were broken no fewer than 14 times, while five world records were established, considerably fewer than in 1964.

Many factors contributed to the U.S. rise to preeminence in swimming, the most important of which was the start of the Age Group Program. Conceived and founded in 1947 by Carl O. Bauer, athletic director at the Missouri Athletic Club, it is a program in which boys and girls can compete against local, sectional, and national records in age groups starting at 10 and under. Included also are racing programs in all competitive strokes for youngsters 10 and under, 11–12, 13–14, and 15–16. Attracting over a million youngsters annually, and administered by the Amateur Athletic Union, Age Group Swimming has produced national and Olympic champions in ever-increasing numbers since 1960. The AAU also sponsors the Junior Olympics, a program similar to Age Group for youngsters under 17. Other countries have instituted similar programs of their own. Help has come from coaches and editors of swimming news media such as *Swimming World* (U.S.) and *The Swimming Times* (London). The World Swimming Coaches Association, formed at the 1968 Olympic Games in Mexico City, has as one of its goals the exchange of technical information on swimming.

(LEFT) "FORT WORTH STAR TELEGRAM"-"SWIMMING WORLD," (TOP RIGHT) LYLE DRAVES, "SWIMMING WORLD," (BOTTOM RIGHT) RUSS KINNE

**DIVING**
**Some key attitudes shown in mid-dive: (left) inward, pike; (top right) backward, layout; (bottom right) forward, half twist**

All aspects of swimming are being continually explored. Out-of-water exercises, both in and out of season, body building, running, the use of both heavy and light weights to develop specific muscle groups, and isotonic and isometric exercises are some of an almost unlimited list of methods used to increase strength, muscle tone, and endurance.

Before interval training and repeat training came into prominence, swimmers trained mainly by swimming as much distance as they could in any given workout regardless of quality or speed.

Interval training, of which there are two types, slow and fast, consists of a series of repeat efforts with controlled rest periods. In slow interval training the rest period is always shorter in time than it takes to swim the prescribed distance. Fast interval training permits longer periods of rest with consequently greater recovery of the heartrate to normal. Slow interval training is primarily endurance work, while fast interval training becomes speed work, with endurance secondary. Repeat training is that type of swimming whereby rest periods between swims are long enough to permit almost complete recovery of the heart and respiratory rate. Almost all swimmers, Age Group to Olympic champions, use interval and repeat training methods.

## DIVING

The term diving is usually interpreted as fancy diving, a part of all aquatic meets, Age Group, scholastic, collegiate, national, and international. To dive, however, generally means to enter the water headfirst from a pool deck, a float, raised platform, or springboard. There are several methods of teaching beginners their first dives, the most popular of them being a progression of movements starting with a beginner sitting on the deck preparing to fall headfirst into the water. The next step is a one-knee takeoff, followed by a standing one-legged takeoff, then a fall-in from a solid stance. When these moves are mastered the dive can be enjoyed more fully by adding a spring from both feet. Throughout the progression pupils must be cautioned to keep the arms fully extended overhead with the hands firmly clasped together.

Even though diving became part of the Olympic program as early as 1904, it was in its infancy and involved little more than plain diving from 5-m. or 10-m. fixed platforms. Springboard diving, originally named variety diving and later changed to fancy diving, was included, which necessitated a method of judging the competitors. Divers were judged mainly on three qualities: elevation, execution, and entry.

The Olympic committee composed a table of dives permitted, listing a description of each, and a value for each dive based on the difficulty of performance. Early tables listed only 14 dives from the high (10-m.) platform and 20 from the springboard. Later platform tables came to list 58 different dives, while springboards listed 54. Additions to the diving tables are submitted to a 12-man international diving committee which approves proposed additions. Changes in diving, swimming, and water polo may not be altered during the 12 months preceding any Olympic Games.

RUSS KINNE

DEMONSTRATION OF RACING TURN. SWIMMER, UNDERWATER, PUSHING HIMSELF OFF THE POOL WALL TO BEGIN ANOTHER LAP

The report of the IV Olympics (1908) suggested elimination of the double somersault because it was believed too difficult to control and too likely to result in injury. By the 1960s, however, it was common among divers the world over, who combine complicated somersaulting and twisting movements with ease and incredible beauty.

**Groups of Competitive Dives.**—Competitive dives, both platform and springboard, are separated into different categories or groups: (1) Forward dives, in which the performer rotates ½ to 3½ turns before entering the water. (2) Backward dives, in which the performer stands with his back to the water and rotates ½ to 2½ turns. (3) Reverse dives, in which the performer changes direction from forward to backward after takeoff. The performer may make ½ to 2½ turns in this group. (4) Inward dives, in which the performer stands with his back to the water, and after the backward takeoff rotates inward ½ to 2½ turns toward the board. (5) Twisting dives, in which the performer turns laterally, twisting ½ to 3½ turns while rotating in a somersault motion. (6) Armstand dives (used in platform contests only), in which the performer must maintain a steady and perfectly balanced handstand at the edge of the platform before executing his dive.

The majority of dives included in the list of diving tables can be performed in three different positions: straight, pike, or tuck. In the straight position the body remains perfectly in line with no flexion at the hips or knees permitted. In the pike position, there must be a distinct flexion at the hips, but none at the knees. In the tuck position, the body is gathered into a ball with the hands grasping the shins tightly. In all three positions the toes must be pointed.

**Diving Equipment.**—Springboards at one metre or three metres from the water for competition must include movable fulcrums that enable the divers to adjust the flexibility to their own liking. Springboards of solid or laminated wood, and later covered with a fibre glass sheath, have been replaced by boards fabricated of extruded aluminum with a roughened nonslip surface built in. The aluminum board has been a standard fixture in all international contests since 1956.

Championship platform competition is held from a rigid (no spring) platform 10 m. high, 2 m. wide, not less than 6 m. long, and covered throughout with coconut matting. An intermediate platform at 6½ m. above the water can be used, the back and sides of which must be surrounded by a handrail, each level accessible by stairs. FINA rules that the platform must project at least 1.5 m. beyond the edge of the pool and the water must be 4.5 m. in depth.

## OPEN WATER SWIMMING

Long-distance swimmers have always been intrigued by the challenge of the English Channel. The first known attempt to cross was made by J. B. Johnson in August 1872. It was not until August 1875 that Capt. Matthew Webb completed the first successful crossing after he and others had failed. Swimming from Dover to Calais in 21 hr. 45 min., he created a sensation at the time. The Channel has been swum many times since, with the west to east crossing the more popular, the month of August being preferred because of favourable weather conditions. New York Women's Swimming Association and world record holder Gertrude Ederle captured the attention of the world when she became in 1926 the first woman to swim the treacherous Channel, and in so doing eclipsed the record time by almost two hours. Her record was made swimming crawl; Captain Webb chose the stroke of his time, breaststroke.

There is pleasure no matter where one swims, but swimming in salt water, lakes, rivers, or streams presents problems different from those of swimming pools. Among hazards to the swimmer are holes in streams or rivers, and at ocean beaches riptides, runouts, and undertow may exist. Swimming alone should always be avoided.

Riptides and undertow are peculiar to ocean and Great Lakes beach swimming. Local knowledge and safety skills can save many lives. Riptides are riverlike masses of water caused by a deep contour of the ocean bottom. These are bounded on both sides by eddies that swing more slowly back to shore. A swimmer should never attempt to swim directly against a riptide. The safest way is to swim parallel to the shore, even though being carried further out, until the edge of the riptide is reached. It is relatively easy then to swim to and gain footing on the shore.

Undertow is simply the receding portion of water that has been carried in by ocean breakers. Undertow water moves in two directions, the upper layer tending to move shoreward, the lower layer seaward. The wise swimmer can push from the bottom, level off on the surface, and make shore more safely.

No one should swim directly away from the shore at ocean or lakefront without an accompanying manned rowboat. Swimming parallel to the shoreline is much safer. With continually increasing activity in all allied water sports such as skin diving, snorkeling, SCUBA (self-contained underwater breathing apparatus) diving, spear fishing, water skiing, surfboarding, and sailing, it is important that participants not only be competent swimmers, but also be able to help prevent drownings; more particularly they should be aware of their own aquatic limitations.

BIBLIOGRAPHY.—The literature on the subject of swimming is considerable. The Swimming Hall of Fame at Fort Lauderdale, Fla., and the Bob Kiphuth Room in the Payne Whitney Gymnasium, at Yale University, are two sources of swimming information and memorabilia.

Two early books are Charles Steedman, *A Manual of Swimming* (1873) and Frank Sachs, *The Complete Swimmer* (1912). Other recommended works include: R. J. H. Kiphuth, *Swimming* (1942); Frances A. Greenwood, *Bibliography of Swimming* (1940); R. J. H. Kiphuth and H. M. Burke, *Basic Swimming* (1950); John A. Torney, Jr., *Swimming* (1950); D. A. Ambruster and others, *Swimming and Diving*, 5th ed. (1968); R. Dawson, *Age Group Swimming* (1961); F. Carlile, *On Swimming* (1963); B. Rajki, *The Technique of Competitive Swimming* (1963); J. M. Juba, ed., *Success at Swimming* (1958); G. Forsberg, *Modern Long Distance Swimming* (1963); E. Spears, *Beginning Synchronized Swimming;* Amateur Swimming Association, *Swimming to Win* (1963), *Survival Swimming, Swimming Instruction, Manual on Diving* (1964); Steve Clark, *Competitive Swimming As I See It* (1967); J. E. Counsilman, *The Science of Swimming* (1968); Fred R. Lanoue, *Drownproofing* (1963); Dan Rothenburg (ed.), *Swimming and Diving: the Official Coaching Book of the E.S.S.A.*, rev. ed. (1969).

Recommended publications include: *Handbook of the Amateur Swimming Association* (annually); *Amateur Athletic Union of the United States Official Swimming, Water Polo and Diving Rules* (annually); National Collegiate Athletic Association, *Official NCAA Swimming Guide* (annually); *Swimming Technique* (quarterly); *Swimming World* (monthly); *FINA Handbook* (quadrennial). *See* also *Britannica Book of the Year*. (K. B. ML.)

**SWINBURNE, ALGERNON CHARLES** (1837–1909), English poet and critic, outstanding for the boldness of his prosodic innovations and the brilliance and strangeness of his personality, was born in London on April 5, 1837. His childhood was spent partly on the Isle of Wight, where his father rented a house and part of the shore at Bonchurch, and partly at his grandfather's estate in Northumberland. The cliffs and crags of both places made a deep impression on him, and he early developed an intense love for the sea. Despite his later republican sympathies, Swinburne was proud of his aristocratic origins. His father was an admiral, his mother a daughter of the earl of Ashburnham, and his grandfather—who had been the friend of radicals and revolutionaries in France and had great influence over his grandson—was Sir John Swinburne, 6th Bart. Swinburne also liked to think that he was descended from the French house of de Polignac—a claim quite without foundation.

After being taught by his mother and then by a tutor, he went to Eton (1849–53), and, after private tuition, to Balliol College, Oxford. He left Oxford, without taking a degree, in 1860. While there he met Edward Burne-Jones, William Morris, and D. G. Rossetti and so became connected with the Pre-Raphaelites. After leaving Oxford he often visited Benjamin Jowett, his tutor. He shared a house in Chelsea with Rossetti and George Meredith (*qq.v.*) from 1862 to 1864, when he took lodgings which he occupied intermittently until 1879. An allowance from his father enabled him to follow a literary career. In 1861 he met Richard Monckton Milnes (later Lord Houghton, *q.v.*), who encouraged his poetry, fostered his reputation, and introduced him to the works of the marquis de Sade. In 1864 he traveled to Italy and met the aged Walter Savage Landor.

Literary success came with the publication in 1865 of *Atalanta in Calydon* (dedicated to Landor). The first series of *Poems and Ballads* followed in 1866. It was vehemently attacked for its "feverish carnality"—even *Punch* referred to the poet as "Mr. Swineborn." It was, however, enthusiastically welcomed by the younger generation, and the influential Ruskin acknowledged the arrival of a genius.

In 1867 Swinburne met Mazzini, and under his influence *Songs Before Sunrise* (1871) was principally concerned with the theme of political liberty. The second series of *Poems and Ballads*, less hectic and sensual than the first, appeared in 1878.

During this period Swinburne's health was being continually undermined by alcoholism and by the excesses resulting from his abnormal temperament and masochistic tendencies; he experienced periodic fits, from which, however, his remarkable powers of recuperation long enabled him to recover quickly. In 1879 he collapsed completely and was rescued and restored to health by his friend Walter Theodore Watts (later Watts-Dunton, *q.v.*). The last 30 years of his life were spent at The Pines, Putney, under the guardianship of Watts, who maintained a strict regimen and encouraged him to devote himself to writing. During these years he published 23 volumes of poetry, prose, and drama; five, written then, were published posthumously, and a mass of manuscripts remains unpublished. In 1909 he succumbed to pneumonia and died at Putney on April 10.

**Assessment.**—Swinburne is chiefly important as a lyric poet. His technical equipment and prosodic invention were extraordinary. The characteristic qualities of his verse are insistent alliteration, unflagging rhythmic energy, great variation of pace and stress, effortless expansion of a given theme, and evocative if rather imprecise use of imagery. His poetic manner is highly individual, and his command of word-colour and word-music remarkable. But too often the remorseless rhythms have, after a time, a narcotic effect, and a poem which begins by exciting the reader ends by fatiguing him. Swinburne has been accused of letting the sound take charge of the sense and of paying more attention to the melody of words than to their meaning.

Certainly, considering his voluminous output, he has surprisingly little to say. Although some subjects, in particular the sea, continued to call out the best in his genius, his most important works belong to the first half of his life. If Swinburne's poetry has a centre (which has been denied, notably by George Meredith), it is to be found in the idea of liberty. Emotionally this involved a departure from the usual modes of feeling; for Swinburne, pleasure was closely associated with pain, and in poems such as "Laus Veneris" (1866), "Anactoria," and "The Leper," he is clearly dealing with perverse forms of love. (It was this aspect of his work that appealed to the "decadent" writers of the 1890s.)

Swinburne was pagan in his sympathies and passionately antitheist: his denunciation of the Deity in *Atalanta*, where he refers to "the supreme evil, God," was erased from her copy by Christina Rossetti, and among his best-known lines is that from the "Hymn to Proserpine": "Thou hast conquered, O pale Galilean; the world has grown grey from thy breath." His nearest approach to a positive philosophy is to be found in his poem "Hertha." Politically, Swinburne, under the influence of Mazzini and Victor Hugo, was attached to the cause of national liberation and republicanism, though in later years he became markedly more conservative. His hero worship of these two men was typical of his tendency to extreme allegiances; in literature he was similarly devoted to Blake—on whom he wrote an important volume of criticism (1868)—to Shelley, to Landor, and to Baudelaire. His elegies on the two last are among his finest works.

BROWN BROTHERS

SWINBURNE

In *Atalanta in Calydon* and, less strikingly, if (with Jowett's assistance) more correctly, in *Erechtheus* (1876), Swinburne attempted to recreate in English the form and spirit of Greek tragedy; his understanding of the Greek tragic outlook, coupled with his lyrical powers at their finest, make *Atalanta* one of the most successful examples of its kind. His devotion to Shakespeare—his eloquent *Study of Shakespeare* appeared in 1880—and to the Elizabethan and Jacobean drama, of which he had an unrivaled knowledge, is reflected in the early play *Chastelard* (1865). This was the first of a trilogy on Mary, queen of Scots—a figure who had a peculiar fascination for Swinburne—and was followed by *Bothwell* (1874) and *Mary Stuart* (1881); these dramas are unactable, despite fine passages, and *Bothwell* in particular is inordinately long. Apart from *Atalanta*, which many consider Swinburne's masterpiece, his most successful long poem is *Tristram of Lyonesse* (published with other poems in 1882), which deals with Arthurian legend in a very un-Tennysonian way and in which the couplet is used with astonishing skill and variety. His novel, *Love's Cross-Currents*, first printed serially in 1877 as *A Year's Letters*, was published as a book in 1905; another novel, the unfinished *Lesbia Brandon*, appeared in 1952 (ed. by R. Hughes). Both are chiefly of interest for their autobiographical element and the light they throw on Swinburne's psychological abnormalities.

To those Victorians who did not regard Swinburne as blasphemous and depraved, he seemed, at the time of his early volumes, a poet to whom almost anything might be possible. His verse was intoxicating, both in its voluptuous vigour of movement and in its defiance of restraint and convention. Though his technical mastery remained, however, the promise was not fulfilled; Swinburne never, in any profound sense, matured. Whether it is correct to say, as Harold Nicolson has suggested (see *Bibliography*), that he early became impervious to outside impressions and so suffered from arrested development, or whether the abnormalities of his early manhood and the seclusion of his later years isolated him too much from normal human experience, it remains true that his genius did not develop and his understanding did not deepen with the years. Hence his achievement does not do justice to his gifts; but he remains important both as the symbol of mid-Victorian poetic revolt and, in his own right, as a lyric poet of unsurpassed virtuosity.

BIBLIOGRAPHY.—*Editions, Correspondence: Poems,* 6 vol. (1904; often reprinted); *Collected Poetical Works,* 2 vol. (1924); *Complete Works,* ed. by T. J. Wise and Sir E. Gosse, 20 vol. (1925–27; the Bonchurch edition), including bibliography by T. J. Wise (vol. xx). The most complete collection of the letters is the Yale edition, by C. Y. Lang, 6 vol. (1959–62); vol. 6 includes a previously unpublished account of Swinburne's abnormalities by Gosse. Selections include *The Best of Swinburne,* ed. by C. K. Hyder and L. Chase (1937); *Selected Poems,* ed. by E. Shanks (1950).

*Biography and Criticism:* Sir E. Gosse, *The Life of A. C. Swinburne*

(1917; revised as vol. xix of the Bonchurch edition); T. S. Eliot, in *The Sacred Wood* (1920); Sir Max Beerbohm, "No. 2 The Pines," in *And Even Now* (1920); T. E. Welby, *A Study of Swinburne* (1926); H. Nicolson, *Swinburne*, in the "English Men of Letters Series" (1926); G. Lafourcade, *La Jeunesse de Swinburne*, 2 vol. (1928) and *Swinburne: a Literary Biography* (1932); S. C. Chew, *Swinburne* (1929); C. K. Hyder, *Swinburne's Literary Career and Fame* (1933); H. Hare, *Swinburne: a Biographical Approach* (1940). (S. de R. W.)

**SWINDON,** a municipal borough and parliamentary division of north Wiltshire, England, 78 mi. (125 km.) W of London by road. Pop. (1961) 91,739. Area 9.5 sq.mi. (24.6 sq.km.). Until 1841 it was a small market town (now Old Swindon) with a population of less than 2,000, but after the Great Western Railway had built its main engineering works to the north, the population rapidly increased to 45,000, and in 1900 it received its charter. More than 21,000 persons are employed in the railway works; other industries include engineering, clothing, and tobacco. Under the Town Development Act, 1952, provisional approval was obtained from the Ministry of Housing and Local Government to accept overspill population and industry from the Greater London area. Planning approval was given to expand the population to 92,000 within the existing borough boundaries and a 75-ac. trading estate was developed close to the Swindon-Gloucester railway. In 1947 the first municipally owned arts centre in the country was opened, combining a small concert hall, a stage, and an art gallery.

**SWINE,** a name applied to the domestic pig, but also used to include its wild relatives. The animals constitute the family Suidae. Swine originated in the Old World. The typical genus *Sus* is exemplified by the domesticated pig and the wild boar. *See* Pig; Boar; Artiodactyl.

**SWINE FEVER** (Hog Cholera) is a devastating acute systemic infection of swine, caused by a virus, in which high fever and prostration are outstanding symptoms. The disease affects no other species of domestic livestock.

Natural infection results from immediate or mediate contagion. The disease may be acquired by healthy herds by the introduction of infected pigs. Exposure of swine in markets in infected areas is a common source of infection; so are vehicles and trucks in which pigs are conveyed from place to place; dealers, castrators who journey from farm to farm, and attendants may serve as agencies whereby contagion is conveyed. Outbreaks are likely to recur in premises where the disease has existed previously, as the virus appears to retain its vitality for fairly long periods outside the animal body.

Since the virus may persist in uncooked garbage, Canada, most of the states of the U.S., and Great Britain require that garbage fed to swine be sterilized by cooking.

After an incubation period (three to eight days after exposure) the disease is ushered in by fever, at which stage the seriousness of the disease may be underestimated or go unnoticed. Subsequent symptoms vary somewhat with the form the disease assumes. The animal has no appetite, is depressed, ill, and separates itself from its companions; the conjunctivas are reddened and congested and may secrete a mucopurulent discharge; vomiting is common, and constipation and diarrhea are both met with; sometimes the feces become dysenteric and the odour is peculiar and disagreeable.

In many cases a skin rash develops, the parts principally involved being the region of the ears, the axilla, the groin, and the skin covering the abdominal area. The mucous membrane lining the mouth, fauces, and pharynx may become inflamed; later ulcers form and become covered with a diphtheritic exudation. As a result the animal is unable to feed and respiration is difficult. The lungs may be the seat of pneumonic changes.

When this is the case the animal then has a short, dry, and paroxysmal cough; a nasal discharge, difficulty in respiration, and the other symptoms characteristic of acute lung infection. Gastritis and enteritis are common. The animal lies about and if compelled to move does so reluctantly and sometimes with a staggering gait and an arched back; later it is unable to rise and becomes comatose.

As in other acute septicemic diseases, a hyperacute form may develop and death supervene within a few days; or a less acute form may set in, with one or more groups of organs becoming involved. Outbreaks are often complicated by secondary infection, particularly of the *Salmonella* type. A chronic type is also encountered, in which life drags on over a considerable period; the animal becomes more debilitated and emaciated and it remains a possible source of infection to other pigs. Recovery from the various forms of swine fever occurs in some cases, the virulence and the mortality varying widely in different outbreaks.

Swine fever is widely distributed in Europe, North America, and Africa (*see* below). In countries where the disease must be reported, where infected animals are compulsorily slaughtered, and the premises quarantined, considerable control has been secured. In the U.S. the average loss from swine fever, including vaccination cost, was estimated in the 1960s to be about $25,000,000 a year. In England compensation paid by the Ministry of Agriculture during the first two-and-a-half years of the eradication scheme beginning March 1963 was estimated at £5,460,000 ($15,288,000). This covered full compensation for healthy animals and half value for pigs showing swine fever symptoms at the time of slaughter.

In the U.S. control is mainly by modified and killed vaccines, which are safer than the older method of simultaneous vaccination with a virulent swine fever virus and hyperimmune serum. In England and France vaccine is prepared from diluted defibrinated blood containing the swine fever virus inactivated with a solution of crystal violet in ethylene glycol. Pigs' blood is normally used but lapinized vaccine is popular in France. Crystal violet vaccine cannot be used on pigs incubating swine fever but will give immunity for about a year to healthy animals. Its use in England was discontinued in 1964 as part of the eradication scheme because it can mask swine fever symptoms in pigs carrying the disease.

**African Swine Fever.**—African swine fever is a highly contagious viral disease of swine. The symptoms and lesions are comparable to those of a severe hyperacute form of hog cholera but swine that are immune to hog cholera are susceptible to African swine fever virus. The African swine fever virus is carried by the African warthog *Phacochoerus aethiopicus*, and outbreaks of African swine fever in swine often follow contact with the African warthog. The incubation period is two to five days. Mortality is very high, and there is as yet no effective vaccine. The disease has been common in Africa and has been found in Western Europe. The high mortality, the lack of an effective vaccine, and the stability and infectivity of the virus make this disease a serious potential threat to swine industries everywhere.

(A. R. S.; Na. Br.; X.)

**SWINTON AND PENDLEBURY,** a municipal borough of Lancashire, England, 5 mi. (8 km.) NW of Manchester, contiguous with Salford. Pop. (1961) 40,470. Area 5.3 sq.mi. (13.7 sq. km.). A great part of the Clifton rural area was added in 1933. Cotton spinning and weaving, coal mining, the manufacture of electric batteries, and engineering are the chief industries. The town hall was opened in 1938. Anciently parts of Swinton were held by the Knights of the Order of the Hospital of St. John of Jerusalem. Swinton and Pendlebury, incorporated in 1934, forms with Eccles the Eccles parliamentary division of Lancashire, returning one member.

**SWISS LITERATURE.** In language and literature Switzerland has always been closely linked with its neighbours—Germany (and Austria), France, and Italy—because, of the four national languages, only the Raeto-Romance dialect, Romansh, is peculiar to Switzerland. There is also a substantial quantity of Swiss dialect literature. Chronologically, literature in Latin precedes all the others.

In the following survey all these literatures are considered, both on their own account and as parts of Swiss literature in an overall sense. Many of the writers mentioned have separate articles which provide biographical information and further critical comment; these may be found most conveniently by consulting the Index. The articles German Literature; French Literature; Italian Literature; and Raeto-Romance Dialects should also be consulted.

**Latin Swiss Literature.**—The oldest document relating to what is now Switzerland was not produced within its territory, for the first notable description of Helvetia and the Helvetii (*q.v.*) is to be found in the first book of Caesar's *Commentarii* (51 B.C.), commonly referred to as *Bellum Helveticum.* Among the Latin chronicles of the Middle Ages the *Casus Sancti Galli,* written by Ekkehard IV (d. 1060), a monk of St. Gallen (St. Gall), gives an impressive description of the highly developed culture of the Benedictine abbey of St. Gallen. Another chronicle, the *Johannis Vitodurani chronicon,* contains the world picture as seen by a Franciscan of Winterthur in the early 14th century. The Swiss humanists who expressed themselves in Latin devoted most of their prose and verse to description of their own country: *e.g.,* Albrecht von Bonstetten (*c.* 1442–*c.* 1504), dean of the abbey of Einsiedeln, in his *Superioris Germanie Confederationis descriptio* (1479), and Heinrich Loriti Glareanus (1488–1563), in his *Helvetiae descriptio* (1514). An important position in the history of general linguistics is taken by the Zürich polyhistor Konrad von Gesner (1516–65), who in his *Mithridates* (1555) undertook a survey of all languages known to him. For three centuries the two volumes *De Republica Helvetiorum* (1576) by the Zürich theologian Josias Simler (1530–76) remained the standard work on the constitutional law and politics of the Swiss Confederation.

The final phase of Swiss literature in Latin belongs to the 18th century and is largely connected with natural science. An outstanding example is *Uresiphoites helveticus, sive itinera alpina tria* (1708), the description of Switzerland given by the city physician of Zürich, J. J. Scheuchzer (1672–1733), a prolific writer of geographical and historical works.

**German Swiss Literature.**—In quantity, the most important literature of Switzerland is written in German. It first flourished in the age of the *Minnesinger* (*q.v.*), of whom more than 30, *i.e.,* practically one-fifth of those known, lived on what is now Swiss territory. The so-called Codex Manesse, the manuscript of *Minnesang,* or love lyrics, originated in Zürich, and was attributed to Rüdiger Manesse (1224–1304) and his son (d. 1297) by J. J. Bodmer, who was the first to have the Codex printed in 1758. Gottfried Keller made the Codex the subject of one of his *Züricher Novellen, Hadlaub* (1878). In this way the poetry of the *Minnesinger* has become part of the history of Swiss literature.

The first literary productions with national characteristics were popular ballads and chronicles. The ballads commemorate especially the great battles for freedom fought by the Swiss from the 13th to the 16th century. The most effective and influential of these is the ballad of William Tell (*q.v.*), which through its moral and political aspects maintained an important position as a narrative and as a play from the late 15th century onward. The chronicles, occasionally written for some local authority and often illustrated, flourished especially in Bern, Lucerne, and Zürich. The most famous chronicles, however, were those written by Johannes Stumpf (1500–?1578), and by Gilg (Aegidius) Tschudi (1505–72), a leading magistrate of Glarus. The content of Tschudi's *Chronicon helveticum,* which deals with the period 1000–1470, was widely known after its completion in the 16th century, although it was printed only in 1734–36.

The Reformation activities of Huldreich Zwingli (*q.v.*) had only an indirect influence on literature. Zwingli himself wrote mainly in Latin. The so-called Zürich Bible of 1529 was soon replaced by the Luther Bible, which, by way of Luther's powerful and authoritative use of the German language, made for a closer connection between the writings produced in Switzerland and Germany. One of the most important results of the work done by Zwingli was that the Protestant majority of German-speaking Switzerland established a permanent connection with the Protestant parts of western Switzerland, and with Protestant countries abroad. Thus one of the earliest Swiss accounts of England was produced (*c.* 1550) by the Zürich pastor and lexicographer Josua Maler (1529–99), and in the 18th century the first German translations of Shakespeare (by C. M. Wieland and J. J. Eschenburg) were published in Zürich.

The beginning of 18th-century literature in German-speaking Switzerland is marked by the works of a Bernese poet, and the end by those of a historian from Schaffhausen. The poetry of Albrecht von Haller (1708–77), especially "Die Alpen" (1732), helped to bring about a new poetic awareness in Germany, and belongs to the earliest specimens of German poetry appreciated in France. The most important work of Johannes von Müller (1752–1809), *Geschichten schweizerischer Eidgenossenschaft* (1786–1808), though a fragment, became the most representative piece of historical writing in German classicism and had a far-reaching influence on the style of historical writing. Between these two landmarks appears what is occasionally referred to as the Zürich school of criticism. Two members of this school, J. J. Bodmer (1698–1783) and J. J. Breitinger (1701–76), opposing the critical views of French rationalism and classicism, strongly promoted the appreciation of English literature (especially Milton's *Paradise Lost* and Thomas Percy's *Reliques*) in Germany. Their work started a revival of religious and national conceptions which had its special effect in the succeeding generations. Salomon Gessner (1730–88) had a European success with his revival of the idyll; for predominantly moral reasons J. C. Lavater (*q.v.;* 1741–1801) turned to physiognomy and became one of its innovators; J. K. Hirzel (1725–1803) surprised the reading public in 1761 with his description of the village Socrates, Kleinjogg. In importance, however, they were surpassed by J. H. Pestalozzi (1746–1827), who not only wrote the first village story in German, *Lienhard und Gertrud* (1781), but included in it the nucleus of his later meditations, covering the entire field of the nature and destiny of man.

In the 19th century international fame and critical estimate at home did not always concur. Thus *Der schweizerische Robinson* (*The Swiss Family Robinson*) (1812–27) by Johann David Wyss (1743–1818), and *Heidi* (1880–81) by Johanna Spyri (1827–1901) are examples of a worldwide success, though their purely literary merits were never considered very high in their native country. During the 19th century the significance of German Swiss literature gradually increased. Bern produced its greatest novelist in Jeremias Gotthelf (pseudonym of Albert Bitzius; 1797–1854), whose epic power was combined with a profound knowledge of human nature. The series of his great novels, most of which describe village life, opened with the *Bauernspiegel oder Lebensgeschichte des Jeremias Gotthelf* (1837) and ended in the year of his death with *Erlebnisse eines Schuldenbauers.* It was in fiction and poetry that the Zürich writers Gottfried Keller (1819–90) and Conrad Ferdinand Meyer (1825–98) achieved fame. Both realized their own possibilities and destinies comparatively late, a phenomenon frequently observed in the history of Swiss thought. Keller reached the first peak of his creative powers with *Der grüne Heinrich* in 1854, and Meyer with his verse epic *Huttens letzte Tage* in 1871. Meyer drew upon the mountains and the princely courts of the past, and as a writer of fiction he immersed himself in the life and culture of the Renaissance. Keller's prose and poetry are full of genial humour and exuberance matching the quality of his fundamentally human attitude, and his love for his country takes many different forms, from hymns of praise to pungent social criticism. The importance of this period is further emphasized by the writings of the Basel historian Jacob Burckhardt (1818–97), whose statements about the past, present, and future have become increasingly impressive and valid. His greatest disciple was Heinrich Wölfflin (1864–1945), who continued and completed that part of his master's work which was interrelated with the history of fine arts.

Many 20th-century authors, guided by the Swiss distrust of one-sided attitudes, believe that the values of tradition and emancipation are not necessarily irreconcilable. Thus, novelists such as Hans Albrecht Moser (1882–    ), Robert Faesi (1883–    ), Arnold Kübler (1890–    ), and Kurt Guggenheim (1896–    ), and poets such as Urs Martin Strub (1910–    ) aim at a sort of holism, an interpenetration of the forces of both the native country and the world at large. A similar universal humanism is an essential feature of the historical and literary essays of C. J. Burckhardt (1891–    ), J. R. von Salis (1901–    ), Fritz Ernst (1889–1958), Max Rychner (1897–1965), and Emil Staiger (1908–    ), and the cultural studies of Hans Zbinden (1893–    ). All are representative of a truly European Switzerland.

An appreciable minority holds to the values of rural contentment still current in the village and the small town. Heinrich Federer (1866–1928) and Alfred Huggenberger (1867–1960) are typical of this tradition. The playwright Cäsar von Arx (1895–1949), the novelist Meinrad Inglin (1893– ), and the Catholic poet Silja Walter (1919– ) likewise stress the conservative element in the new age of materialism and prosperity. Others furnish antidotes to the conventional order of things, and are alert to the stimulus of international thought. The anthroposophist Albert Steffen (1884–1963), for example, opened deeper vistas of the individual and of Far Eastern traditions. Marxist views have been expressed in the novels and short stories of Jakob Bührer (1882– ).

The last German Swiss poet of international repute was Carl Spitteler (1845–1924), who won the Nobel Prize in 1919 for his epics in verse and prose. Albin Zollinger (1895–1941) was the leading Swiss poet between World Wars I and II, and his bold use of intuitive imagery is a parallel to the new valuation of the unconscious by the Swiss psychologist C. G. Jung (*q.v.*). The two preeminent writers of the mid-20th century are Max Frisch (1911– ) and Friedrich Dürrenmatt (1921– ). Dürrenmatt's burlesque plays (*e.g., Romulus der Grosse,* 1949; *Die Physiker,* 1962 [*The Physicists,* 1964]), already widely known, are expressions of a revolt proclaiming uncompromising sincerity and greatness against the mass mediocrity of the age. Frisch has established himself both as a distinguished novelist (*Stiller,* 1954, *I'm Not Stiller,* 1958; *Homo Faber,* 1957, Eng. trans., 1959), and as a successful dramatist (*Andorra,* 1961); his main subject is the complicated, skeptical modern individual.

**French Swiss Literature.**—Though the French-speaking part of the Swiss population is only one-fifth of the total, the literature it has produced carries considerably more than its proportionate weight. This is partly because of the immigration of a number of talented Huguenot families, partly, though to a lesser degree, because writers born in the German-speaking part of the country occasionally decide to express themselves in French. This applies especially to the Bernese.

The beginnings of French Swiss literature proper coincide with the Reformation. Calvin, who settled in Geneva in 1541, exercised his influence on French literature through his diction, as well as through his theology, and although Geneva did not join the Swiss Confederation until 1815, the *"cité de Calvin"* was a constant influence on French Swiss literature. One of the first important studies of England in French was by the Bernese B.-L. de Muralt (1665–1749), whose stay in England in 1694 resulted in his *Lettres sur les Anglais et les Français* (1725). His work was admired by Rousseau, another European figure connected with Geneva, where he was born. For Rousseau the influences were mutual: he was not only a *citoyen d'un état libre* ("citizen of a free state"), as he described himself in the opening chapter of *The Social Contract,* but obviously shared the political and psychological conceptions of all Switzerland to such a degree that one is tempted to consider him its most brilliant publicity agent (*see,* for example, his *Considérations sur le gouvernement de Pologne*). Swiss subject matter was also dealt with by H. B. de Saussure (1740–99), one of the founders of modern geology, in his *Voyages dans les Alpes* (1779–96).

At the beginning of the 19th century French Swiss literature on the whole preferred international themes and was largely connected with the influential circle of Mme de Staël (*q.v.*), who in her manor house at Coppet, on the Lake of Geneva, entertained many of the leading intellectuals of Western Europe. Mme de Staël, like her friend Benjamin Constant, is generally associated with the literature of France; however, both were of Swiss extraction, and much of their work was inspired by their background. Another member of Mme de Staël's circle, the Genevan J. C. L. de Sismondi (1773–1842), made an important contribution to Italian history with his *Histoire des républiques italiennes du moyen âge* (1807–18). There was also K. V. von Bonstetten (1745–1832), whose outlook was fundamentally European, especially in *L'Homme du midi et l'homme du nord* (1824).

To a later development belong the humorous tales and sketches of Rodolphe Toepffer (1799–1846), depicting a more homely world (*La Bibliothèque de mon oncle,* 1832), while the poems of Juste Olivier (1807–76) testify to a pronounced patriotism (*Poèmes suisses,* 1830). The criticism of Alexandre Vinet (1797–1847), based on an essentially personal interpretation of Christianity, found an echo in both Switzerland and France. Toward the end of the 19th century a powerful international influence was exercised by the posthumous publication of the fragments of H. F. Amiel's *Journal intime* (1883–84), which caused Tolstoi to write a moving preface for its Russian translation. In his historical writings Philippe Monnier (1864–1911), in a manner reminiscent of Jacob Burckhardt, deals with Italy in the 15th and 18th centuries (*Le Quattrocento,* 1901; *Venise au XVIII^e^ siècle,* 1907). C. F. Ramuz (1878–1947) wrote strongly imaginative novels about life among vinegrowers and Alpine herdsmen. Gonzague de Reynold (1880– ) demonstrated the inward connection between German- and French-speaking Switzerland in the 18th century (see *Bibliography*), and depicted the whole of his country in his *Cités et pays suisses* (1914–48).

As much of 20th-century literary activity is centred on the city and canton of Geneva, contemporary French Swiss literature has a cosmopolitan air, and it is often difficult to distinguish what is peculiarly Swiss—as, for instance, in the prose of Henry Vallotton (1891– ) and the poetry of Gilbert Trolliet (1907– ). A typically European outlook is to be found in the essays of Denis de Rougemont (1906– ). More particularly Swiss themes are noticeable in the prose of Ramuz and Léon Savary (1895– ).

**Italian Swiss Literature.**—Only about 9% of Switzerland's total population use Italian as their native language. Their home is in the canton of Ticino and in some of the southern Grisons valleys. It is thus unlikely that the literature of such a small group could exist without a strong and permanent relation to Italian literature proper. Since the 18th century there have been a few nationally distinct features in what is often called the Swiss Italianità. As an exponent of the Age of Reason, Father Francesco Soave (1743–1806) of Lugano translated John Locke and Salomon Gessner into Italian, and, following the example of the latter, wrote his own *Novelle morali* (1782–84), which have appeared in hundreds of editions and have made the story of William Tell popular in Italy. A representative figure in the first half of the 19th century is Stefano Franscini (1796–1857), who helped to bring about the new unity of the Ticino and to connect it with the spirit of the Swiss Confederation. His main work, *La Svizzera italiana* (1837–38), bears as a motto a quotation from Albrecht von Haller: "Alpibus quidem ad Italiam spectantibus ego plurimum boni spero" ("The Alps looking toward Italy are my greatest hope"). His *Nuova statistica della Svizzera* (1847) proved to be a particularly effective description of Switzerland in that period.

The most outstanding poet and novelist of the Ticino is Francesco Chiesa (1871– ). A convinced regionalist, he combines a profound love of his country with an admiration for the great Lombard poets. His vast influence on his contemporaries has contributed toward keeping the Italianità of his region intact (*Calliope,* 1907; *I viali d'oro,* 1911; *Tempo di marzo,* 1925). One of his disciples, equally bent on exploring and interpreting his home country, was Giuseppe Zoppi (1896–1952) (*Leggende del Ticino,* 1928; *Presento il mio Ticino,* 1933). Italian-speaking Switzerland has also produced an eminent existentialist essayist and novelist in Felice Filippini (1917– ). Further contributions to Swiss literature include the scholarly essays of Piero Bianconi (1899– ) and Guido Calgari (1905– ), the fictional prose of Carlo Castelli (1909– ), and the poetry of Pericle Patocchi (1911– ), much of whose work is written in French.

**Raeto-Romance Literature.**—The Raeto-Romance dialect, Romansh, is used only in a few Grisons valleys. In 1776 a treatise by the Grisons historian and philologist Joseph Planta (1744–1827) was published in English by the Royal Society, making the existence of the language known to a wider public. Only in the 20th century, however, was it officially recognized: on Feb. 20, 1938, in a plebiscite of the whole country, Romansh, though represented by only 1% of the total population, was declared the fourth national language of the Swiss Confederation.

Raeto-Romance literature was in its origins predominantly ecclesiastical, and began in the Middle Ages. The Reformation gave it new life. In 1560 a fine translation of the New Testament was published; in 1679 the whole Bible was translated by J. A. Vulpius and J. Dorta. There is also a rich variety of popular songs, especially of the religious and political kind. Owing to its geographical distribution Raeto-Romance literature is essentially regional in character. Nevertheless, the anthologist Caspar Decurtins (1855–1916); the poets Peider Lansel (1863–1943), Jon Guidon (1892– ), and Artur Caflisch (1893– ); and the prose fiction writer Giachen Michel Nay (1860–1920) achieved decidedly more than a merely local fame in the 20th century.

**Swiss Dialect Literature.**—The fortunes of Swiss dialect literature vary according to the language situation in each section of the country. In the Ticino, dialect literature is produced with much devotion, but has been of little consequence. In the French-speaking part of the country the local dialects are on the wane. The important instances of dialect literature there belong to the past, such as the Genevan ballads commemorating the victory of the *escalade* in 1602. International fame was achieved by the various *ranz des vaches* (melodies sung, or played on the alphorn, by herdsmen).

Dialect literature flourishes mainly in the German-speaking part of the country, chiefly because there the people, regardless of social rank and education, consistently use dialect for everyday purposes. The existence of numerous local idioms might even produce an ever-increasing variety of dialect writings. This, however, would be at cross-purposes with the determination of writers and readers to remain on common ground with German literature as a whole. Some of the best poets express themselves both in High German and in their dialect. Thus Adolf Frey (1855–1920) published a volume of poems in the dialect of the Aargau (*Duss und underm Rafe,* 1891), and Meinrad Lienert (1865–1933) wrote several poems in the dialect of Schwyz. Almost every canton has its *Mundartdichter,* or local poet. There are vigorous novels in the Bernese dialect, by Rudolf von Tavel (1866–1934), and Simon Gfeller (1868–1943). Schaffhausen is represented in the novels of Albert Bächtold (1891– ); and Joseph Reinhart (1875–1957) wrote in the dialect of Solothurn.

**Patrimonium Helveticum.**—Without detriment to their connections with European civilization, many Swiss regard the existence of a manifold national literature with considerable satisfaction. Between the extremes of absolute diversity and absolute unity there is room for all aspects and expressions of thought and imagination. Since Switzerland has never had a representative cultural centre such as Florence once was for Italy and Paris still is for France—each group (and sometimes each individual writer) expresses itself according to its character and region. This may have its advantages, but it also has its dangers, which can only be overcome on the level of a vigorous national consciousness. So far this consciousness has proved adequate. A deteriorating structural change could occur only if the minorities were estranged from the confederate whole, or if the majority forces were tempted to exploit their position regardless of tradition.

Although the numerical relationship of the different languages is slightly shifting, there is no serious peril to the balance of the different cultures. On the contrary, because the underlying ideals are very much alive, they may produce further highlights of national integration. A development of more than 1,000 years is at the basis of Swiss literary life and will continue to shape what might be called an evergrowing *patrimonium Helveticum.*

(F. E.; H. Sn.; A. Bx.)

Bibliography.—*Anthologies:* R. Faesi, *Anthologia Helvetica* (1921), a collection of the six literatures mentioned. Anthologies based on each of the four national languages are: E. Korrodi, *Geisteserbe der Schweiz,* 2nd ed. (1943); C. Clerc, *Le Génie du lieu* (1929); A. Janner, *Scrittori della Svizzera italiana,* 2 vol. (1936); C. Decurtins, *Rätoromanische Chrestomathie,* 13 vol. (1888–1919). *See* also K. Bartsch, *Die Schweizer Minnesänger* (1886); L. Tobler, *Schweizerische Volkslieder,* 2 vol. (1882–84). For contemporary literature *see* B. Mariacher and F. Witz, *Bestand und Versuch* (1964); H. Leber, *Prosa junger Schweizer Autoren* (1964).

*General Histories:* G. de Reynold, *Histoire littéraire de la Suisse au XVIII<sup>e</sup> siècle,* 2 vol. (1909–12); H. E. Jenny and V. Rossel, *Geschichte der schweizerischen Literatur,* 2 vol. (1910); C. Clerc *et al., Panorama des littératures contemporaines de Suisse* (1938); G. Calgari, *Storia delle quattro letterature della Svizzera* (1958); H. Zbinden *et al., Schweizer Schriftsteller der Gegenwart* (1962). *See* also *Dictionnaire historique et biographique de la Suisse,* 8 vol. (1921–34).

*German Swiss Literature:* J. Bächtold, *Geschichte der deutschen Literatur in der Schweiz* (1892); J. Nadler, *Literaturgeschichte der deutschen Schweiz* (1932); E. Ermatinger, *Dichtung und Geistesleben der deutschen Schweiz* (1933); A. Bettex, *Die Literatur der deutschen Schweiz von heute* (1950). For Swiss German dialect literature *see* also O. von Greyerz, *Die Mundartdichtung der deutschen Schweiz* (1924).

*French Swiss Literature:* V. Rossel, *Histoire littéraire de la Suisse romande des origines à nos jours,* 2 vol. (1889–91); C. Clerc, "La Suisse romande," in J. Bédier and P. Hazard (eds.), *Histoire illustrée de la littérature française,* vol. ii, rev. ed. (1948–49); M. Weber-Perret, *Écrivains romands 1900–1950* (1951).

*Italian Swiss Literature:* G. Zoppi, introduction to *Scrittori della Svizzera Italiana* (1936); F. Filippini, *Una Corona di ricci* (1950).

*Raeto-Romance Literature:* *Dictionnaire historique et biographique de la Suisse,* vol. iii, pp. 622–626 (1926); P. Lansel, *Musa rumantscha: antologia poetica moderna* (1950). (A. Bx.)

**SWITHUN** (Swithin), **SAINT** (d. *c.* 862), Anglo-Saxon bishop of Winchester from about 852 to 861 or 862. Except for his profession to Ceolnoth, archbishop of Canterbury, and two attestations of genuine charters, nothing reliable is known of Swithun's life. In 971, on July 15, Aethelwold, bishop of Winchester, translated his body into the cathedral, after reports of miracles. Writers soon after this event, Wulfstan the precentor of Winchester, Lantfrith "the foreigner," and the homilist Aelfric, could find nothing about his life, hence it is unlikely that the accounts in later writers, such as William of Malmesbury, which make him tutor to King Aethelwulf and a miracle worker in his lifetime, have any basis of fact. They claim that he wished for burial outside the church, where, according to William, "he would be exposed to the feet of passers-by and the drops falling from above," a remark which some have tried to connect with the weather superstition linked to his day. After 971 his cult spread widely and his name displaced those of St. Peter and St. Paul in the dedication of the cathedral.

The origin of the superstition that rain on his day, July 15, means rain for 40 days, is obscure. The tale that he sent rain to prevent the removal of his body is a modern invention; the earliest writers make him appear in a vision to urge this translation. The first evidence for a weather prophecy seems to be a 13th- or 14th-century entry in a manuscript at Emmanuel College, Cambridge: "In the daye of Seynte Svythone: rane ginneth rininge/Forti dawes mid ywone: lestez such tithinge" (On St. Swithun's day it begins to rain; 40 days usually lasts such a happening). Here, however, it is connected with the day of his death, July 2, not of his translation, July 15.

Bibliography.—*Wulfstani cantoris narratio metrica de sancto Swithuno,* ed. by A. Campbell (1950); *Aelfric's Lives of Saints,* ed. by W. W. Skeat, no. xxi; J. Earle, *Legends of Saint Swithun* (1861); *Willelmi Malmesbiriensis monachi gesta pontificum,* ed. by N. E. S. A. Hamilton (1870); letter in *The Times* (London), July 31, 1963, from P. Clemoes, F. Stubbings, and G. Evans. (D. Wk.)

**SWITZERLAND** (German Schweiz; French Suisse; Italian Svizzera; the Latin Helvetia appears on the country's postage stamps) is a confederation or *Eidgenossenschaft* of 22 cantons (3 of which have half-cantons) with a republican and federal constitution. It is in Central Europe, bounded north by the Federal Republic of Germany, east by Austria and Liechtenstein (included since 1924 in the Swiss customs and monetary union), southeast and south by Italy, and southwest, west, and northwest by France. It forms an irregular-shaped mass with an area of 15,941 sq.mi. (41,288 sq.km.) of which the greatest length (west-southwest to east–northeast) is 226 mi. (364 km.), and the greatest breadth (north to south) is 137 mi. (220 km.). It has three major divisions: the Alps, the Mittelland (central plateau), and the Jura, which divide into numerous small regions, bound together as a political confederation, made originally for common defense. Of its area, 22.6% is unproductive (*i.e.,* steep slopes, bare rocks, areas of permanent snow and ice, lakes, etc.), 24.8% is forested, 24.3% is alpine pasture, and only 28.3% is improved farmland.

The neutrality of Switzerland, established by the Congress of Vienna (1815), has served Switzerland well geopolitically and economically. It has made possible the establishment in Geneva of headquarters for international good works (as the Red Cross), agencies, and organizations. The capital is Bern.

This article is divided into the following sections:



## I. PHYSICAL GEOGRAPHY

**1. Physiography.**—The country is drained by three great rivers, the Rhône, Rhine, and Aare, the first flowing west and the other two north from the central High Alps across the Mittelland. In addition, the southern canton of Ticino is drained by the Ticino from the St. Gotthard Massif southward to the Po, while in the extreme east a tongue of the canton of Graubünden (Grisons) drains northeast via the upper Inn Valley (Engadine) into the Danube. The Rhône and Rhine valleys are divided from that of the Aare by the great limestone ranges of the Bernese Alps (Oberland) and Tödi. The lower Aare Valley winds across the Mittelland to join the Rhine opposite Waldshut, but the upper Reuss, Rhine, and Rhône flow in wide glacially overdeepened trenches in the structural depression that separates the High Calcareous Alps from the Pennine Alps and the St. Gotthard Massif. The Pennine Alps provide the loftiest wholly Swiss summit (15,203 ft. [4,634 m.]) in the crowning Dufourspitze of Monte Rosa, though the Dom (14,911 ft. [4,545 m.]) in the Mischabelhörner, immediately north of Monte Rosa, is the highest entirely Swiss mountain mass. The Matterhorn (Italian Monte Cervino, French Mont Cervin, 14,688 ft. [4,477 m.]), one of the best-known Pennine peaks, is on the Swiss-Italian border near Zermatt. The highest summit in the northern parallel ridge is the Finsteraarhorn (14,022 ft. [4,274 m.] in the Bernese Oberland, while the lowest level within the Confederation is on Lake Maggiore (646 ft. [197 m.]).

The geological build of the Alps is exceedingly complex; the contorted, folded and overfolded sedimentary rocks have been fractured and eroded, exposing old crystalline cores at the surface; the Jura have a simple fold structure involving mainly Jurassic limestone. Much of the broken central plateau (Mittelland) is underlain by Oligocene and Miocene rocks, molasse outcrops in the Napf region. These Tertiary deposits are covered in many parts of the Mittelland by glacial and Recent deposits including moraines, sheets of boulder clay, fluvioglacial gravels, and peat.

The country drains to the North Sea (via the Rhine), the Mediterranean Sea (via the Rhône), the Adriatic (via the Ticino), and the Black Sea (via the Inn). Many rivers, because of their alpine regime, were once subject to seasonal floods which necessitated artificial embankment. The most important control scheme was that of Conrad Escher of Zürich (later Conrad Escher von der Linth) who in 1807–27 regulated the turbulent Linth above the Walensee, from which it emerges as the Limmat. An earlier (1714) successful work was the diversion of the torrential Kander into the Lake of Thun at Spiez, where it is now forming an extensive lake delta.

The Swiss lakes are numerous: the largest, Geneva (Lac Léman) and Constance (Bodensee), are on the French and German frontiers respectively and so are not wholly Swiss. Neuchâtel (83 sq.mi. [216 sq.km.]) is the largest all-Swiss lake. About one-fifth of Lake Maggiore (total area 82 sq.mi. [212 sq.km.]) at the northern end is Swiss; next in order of size are the lakes of Lucerne, Zürich, about half of the Swiss-Italian Lake of Lugano (19 sq.mi. [49 sq.km.]), the lakes of Thun, Brienz, Zug, Walensee, and Sempach; no others exceed 4 sq.mi. (10 sq.km.). Eleven of these lakes are in the Aare Basin; two (Maggiore and Lugano) are in the Po Basin, and the Lake of Geneva serves as a filter to the silt-laden Rhône as does the Lake of Constance to the Rhine. The beautiful chain of lakes in the upper Engadine includes the Sils (1.6 sq.mi. [4.1 sq.km.]), and the smaller, slightly lower lakes of Silvaplana and St. Moritz. Many small mountain lakes are of interest, such as the Riffelsee in which the Matterhorn is reflected; the picturesque Oeschinensee (5,190 ft. [1,582 m.] altitude) mirroring the snow-capped Blümlisalp; and the remarkable Märjelensee (7,749 ft. [2,362 m.] altitude), fed by glacial meltwater so that its level is variable, while on it float miniature icebergs from the Great Aletsch glacier.

Of the countless waterfalls in Switzerland, those of the Rhine (near Schaffhausen), under 100 ft. (30 m.) high, inclusive of rapids, and several hundred feet wide, are the grandest; but the most beautiful are of less volume and greater height, such as those of the Lauterbrunnen valley and particularly the Staubbach, a mere veil of water falling over the ledge of a rock bench with a drop of 984 ft. (300 m.).

*Glaciation.*—Switzerland contains many glaciers that are relics of the Pleistocene alpine glaciation; the number is estimated at more than 1,000 but no exact computations are possible because of numerous detached ice masses which may or may not rank as glaciers. Practically all of them are in retreat, a process that has become speeded up in recent years, notably exemplified by the Rhône glacier. They probably occupy 700 sq.mi. (1,800 sq.km.), unequally distributed; half the cantons possess no glaciers. The greatest area of permanent ice is found in the Valais (over half the total area), followed by Graubünden and Bern (about one-sixth each); then by Uri, Glarus, and the Ticino. Longest glacier in the Pennine Alps is the Gorner (under 10 mi. [16 km.]), but it is exceeded by the Great Aletsch (around 15 mi.) and by the Fiescher and the Unteraar (around 10 mi. each) which occupy the upper eastern valleys of the Bernese Oberland.

**2. Climate.**—In an area such as Switzerland which extends through less than two degrees of latitude, climate is influenced

FIG. 1.—MAJOR PHYSICAL FEATURES OF SWITZERLAND

more particularly by differences of altitude, aspect, and slope; these show wide and sudden variations; *e.g.*, snow-capped Monte Rosa (15,203 ft. [4,634 m.] high) is only 30 mi. (48 km.) distant in a straight line from Lake Maggiore, where subtropical vegetation flourishes along its shores which are only 646 ft. (197 m.) above sea level. Great heights are characterized by decreased pressure of the atmosphere. Monte Rosa summit records about half sea-level pressure; hence the possibility of mountain sickness. High insolation, brilliant sunshine, and dry air, particularly in winter, produce sunburn and ice dazzle which may cause temporary blindness. Among the Alps the average fall in temperature is about 0.7° C (1.3° F) on the south side and about 0.5° C (0.9° F) on the north side for each 330 ft. (100 m.) of ascent. The height of the alpine crests and their main direction also influence the winds. In addition to local winds at certain higher levels where they show a daily change of direction (downslope in the morning, and upslope in the evening), there are other characteristic winds that are less localized in their effects, such as the southerly Föhn (warm, dry, and oppressive) which affects especially Swiss valleys trending south to north (*e.g.*, the Reuss), particularly during spring and autumn; and the northerly Bise, a cold wind experienced in the Lake of Geneva region and in the north–south trending valleys. Switzerland's many local climates are important, not only in "Europe's playground" but also in the high level sanatoria such as Davos, Leysin, and Sierre-Montana. Hence, weather statistics have been carefully compiled for many stations.

January is the coldest month, the following means being recorded: Basel (Bâle) (909 ft. [277 m.] alt.) 0° C (32° F); Altdorf (1,480 ft. [451 m.]) 0.5° (32.9°); Davos (5,121 ft. [1,561 m.]) −7.2° (19°); St. Gotthard (6,877 ft. [2,096 m.]) −7.7° (18.1°); the Säntis (8,202 ft. [2,500 m.]) −9° (15.8°), while an unusually low average is at Bever (5,610 ft. [1,710 m.]) with −10° (14°). Annual precipitation (rain or snow) shows wide variations; *e.g.*, Basel has 32.5 in. (826 mm.); Altdorf, 49.0 in. (1,245 mm.); Davos, 35.7 in. (906 mm.); and the Säntis, 95.7 in. (2,430 mm.). On the Säntis the precipitation falls as snow from November to April inclusive, and only in July and August does rain predominate. Snow accumulates to a depth of 20 to 26 ft. (6–8 m.) at Bever and upward of 46 ft. (14 m.) on the Säntis. July is the hottest month, the average July records at Basel being 19° C (66.2° F), Altdorf 18° (64.4°), Davos 17° (62.6°), St. Gotthard 8° (46.4°), the Säntis 5° (41°), and Bever 12° (53.6°). The range of 22° C (40° F) at Bever tends to be extreme; the Säntis, though cold, is a more equable 14° (25°). The snow line, showing considerable local variations, lies at about 9,685 ft. (2,952 m.) on the western Alps which have heavy total precipitation and at about 10,500 ft. (3,200 m.) on the drier eastern Alps.

(*See* also ALPS.) (W. A. B. C.; A. F. A. M.)

**3. Vegetation.**—The remarkable variations in climate and altitude, together with differences of geological substructure and soil formation, made possible a rich and manifold flora, most of which established itself after the postglacial period. A few hours' climb takes one from the warm temperate zone vegetation of the mid-European lowlands to arctic types. On the south side of the Alps the vegetation subsides to the boundary of the Mediterranean region, or in the Central Alps to the forested areas of southeastern Europe. Natural woodland once covered the whole country up to the timberline but because of clearing and cultivation it now occupies only about a quarter of the total land area. In wooded districts the basic flora stock is of Euro-Siberian origin but Atlantic types immigrated from the west, Mediterranean from the south, and Pontic from the east. Flora in the alpine regions has a preglacial, indigenous basic stock, mingled with additions from the Arctic and sub-Arctic north, the mountains of Asia, and the Mediterranean area, all of which stem from the flora migrations in the Ice Age. There are about 2,600 phanerogamic and pteridophytic types, unevenly distributed. Particularly rich in interesting flora are the dry central alpine area, the southern foothills of the Alps and Jura, and the High Jura.

The widespread distribution of vegetation roughly follows the general climatic variations and the zones considerably overlap. The general distribution is as follows: (1) The low-lying districts by the Rhine and Lake of Geneva, the foothills of the Jura and the Alps, all of which have a mild climate. This belt supports mixed thermophilic deciduous trees (oak, hornbeam, elm, linden), vines, and walnut trees, good agricultural land, and parklands with ornamental trees from warmer areas. It extends from about 1,000 ft. to 1,600 ft. (300–500 m.) above sea level. (2) Immediately above this is a climax zone of beech and fir covering the main part of the Mittelland, the Jura, and the northern alpine valleys up to about 3,900 ft. (1,200 m.) with good arable and dairy farming land, and widespread plantations of spruce and pine. (3) A climatic zone comprising spruce forests with a moist, cool climate then reaches to the natural treeline which extends from the surrounding mountain chains toward the Central Alps at between roughly 5,250 and 6,250 ft. (1,600–1,900 m.). There, the matured soils are acid (podzolic brown soils or podzols) with acidophile flora, which becomes more and more stunted at higher levels of growth. Cultivation is negligible but there is well-developed cattle farming and lumbering. (4) Extending upward to about 7,000 ft. (2,100 m.) is the transition zone from the wooded levels to the alpine meadows. This lowest part of a treeless region is characterized by dwarf shrubs and extensive turf. On the acidic earths grow species of alpine rose (*Rhododendron ferrugineum*), blueberry (*Vaccinium*), and dwarf juniper; on the better soils and limestone grow many kinds of dwarf plants and shrubs, another alpine rose (*Rhododendron hirsutum*), the green alder (*Alnus viridis*), and the mountain pine (*Pinus mugo*), the last being particularly common in the east. (5) The alpine meadows and turfs rise to the grass limit, which lies near the climatic snow line and in the Northern Alps at about 8,200–9,500 ft. (2,500–2,900 m.). The area serves only for pasture or hay making. The alpine meadows are transformed into brilliant gardens between May and July and stay so for all the summer. Among the first to blossom are crocuses, soldanellas, anemones, gentians, primroses, narcissuses, and violets. These are followed by rhododendrons, big monkshood and gentians, the celebrated edelweiss, bellflowers, rampions, louseworts, crowfeet, groundsels, oxeye daisies and other composites, dryas, lilies, saxifrages, pinks, the beautiful alpine Papilionaceae, and other flowering plants. The rarer ones are now protected.

The southern foothills of the Alps have a warm, humid climate and the natural vegetation on the limestone soils is rich in thermophilic deciduous trees of sub-Mediterranean types such as flowering ash, hop hornbeam, and various oaks and elms. On the acid silicate soils there are oaks, sweet chestnuts, and birches. Vines, maize (corn), southern fruits (fig, apricot, peach, Japanese medlar, persimmon), and vegetables are cultivated. Rich gardens and parklands with southern trees and shrubs are found. There are many types of foreign conifers, also acacias, azaleas, camellias, magnolias, and camphor, eucalyptus, bamboo, and ginkgo trees.

This oak-chestnut belt, which ascends to about 3,300 ft. (1,000 m.) is followed by a beech- and then a spruce-belt. The latter is characterized by the occurrence of larches, which mostly form the timberline at about 6,250 ft. (1,900 m.).

Essentially different types of vegetation are found in the inner alpine valleys of Valais and Graubünden. The predominant woodland tree in the lowlands is the Scotch pine, the rest is mainly oak and spruce, with fir woods in shaded corners of some valleys and beech in scattered areas. There are steep slopes on the sun side with steppe turf, consisting mostly of *Festuca valesiaca, Stipa pennata,* and other steppe-grasses and many beautiful flowering herbs. Cultivation at 1,600–5,600 ft. (500–1,700 m.) is dependent on irrigation. Products include wine, cereals, and fruits. In the higher subalpine stage, the woods consist of larches, mountain pine and Arolla pine (*Pinus cembra*) with dwarf shrubs such as the *Rhododendron, Vaccinium,* willow, and spring heath. The timberline is high, in most places above 6,600 ft. (2,000 m.), and in the Engadine and in the southern side valleys of central Valais up to 7,500 ft. (2,300 m.). Upland cultivation at 4,300–5,000 ft. (1,300–1,500 m.) includes rye, barley, potatoes, and vegetables. The high alpine vegetation belts are similar to those in the Northern Alps but the flora is richer in rare species.

In addition to this climax vegetation there are plant associations which represent earlier stages in the development of localized vegetation. The woodlands, for example, are broken by a vegetation typical of marshes, moorlands, and meadows; in the high mountains there is vegetation typical of rocks and scree and many turf types different from the climax vegetation. This pioneer and transition vegetation is determined by local factors of climate and soil. It is widespread in the mountainous country, very diversified and rich in flowering species. If the soil matures and the climate is equalized, the vegetation changes to the climax and becomes much more monotonous in high regions. (WE. L.)

**4. Animal Life.**—Swiss fauna are mainly alpine but a mixture of species familiar to southern and north-central Europe is also found. Mammals include stoat, weasel, badger, otter, and fox. High in the mountains are the variable hare, marmot, and chamois. The alpine ibex, formerly a native but later hunted out of existence, has been reintroduced. Bears and wolves, once common, are no longer found. The once familiar lammergeier or bearded vulture (native but now exterminated) only occasionally enters the country. On the higher slopes are several game birds, including the rock partridge. The alpine chough is still common, but as elsewhere in the world it is being ousted by the jackdaw. The honeybee is domesticated in large numbers. (MA. BU.)

## II. THE PEOPLE

**1. Characteristics.**—Etruscans, Celts, Germans, and Raetians have left their mark on Switzerland in the course of its historical evolution. The contemporary population shows mainly traces of the Alpine (brachycephalic, high curved occiput, brown eyes, dark hair), the "Nordic" (mesocephalic, blue eyes, fair hair), and the Dinaric peoples (brachycephalic, planoccipitalic, brown eyes, brown hair). (*See* also EUROPE: *Anthropology.*)

**2. Languages.**—By the constitution of 1874, German, French, and Italian were recognized as national languages for the purposes of debates in the federal parliament and for the public notification of federal laws and decrees. On Feb. 20, 1938, Romansh (spoken mostly in Graubünden) was recognized as a fourth national language (*see* RAETO-ROMANCE DIALECTS). The two main language groups follow a general homogeneous pattern and border on France and Germany. The Ticino and parts of Graubünden are Italian-speaking. In 1960, 69.3% of the resident population spoke German, 18.9% French, 9.5% Italian, 0.9% Romansh, and 1.4% other languages. The percentages, counting only Swiss citizens, were 74.4, 20.2, 4.1, 1.0, and 0.3, respectively. Apart from regional accents, there are also numerous Swiss-German dialects, classed under the general term "Schwyzerdütsch" and used on official and formal occasions, as well as socially.

**3. Religion.**—The constitution of 1874, while recognizing no established Swiss church, guarantees full religious liberty and freedom of worship, as well as exemption from any compulsory church rates. It repeats the 1848 constitution in forbidding the settlement of Jesuits and their affiliated societies in Switzerland. According to the 1960 census, Protestants comprised 52.8% of the population, Roman Catholics 45.4%, Old Catholics 0.5%, Jews 0.4%, and others 0.9%. Protestants outnumber Catholics in 11 cantons, of which 9 are German-speaking and 2 (Vaud and Neuchâtel) French-speaking. The Catholics outnumber the Protestants in 14 cantons, including 10 German-speaking, 3 French-speaking (Genève, Fribourg and Valais), and the Italian-speaking Ticino.

The Roman Catholic priests, who outnumber the Protestant clergy, total more than 6,000 under five diocesan bishops: viz., those of Basel-Lugano (resident at Solothurn), of Lausanne-Geneva-Fribourg (resident at Fribourg), of Sankt Gallen, of Sion

(Sitten), and of Coire (Chur). The Protestant churches are federated as the Schweizerischer Evangelischer Kirchenbund (Fédération des Églises Protestantes de la Suisse) which was founded (1920) in Olten.

**4. Customs and Culture.**—The Swiss character has been influenced by the country's relatively healthful climate, poor mineral wealth, widespread soil infertility, and the barrier of the Alps, broken only by a few easily usable passes. Having to limit themselves geographically, the Swiss were forced to restraint, sober reasoning, the calculation of advantages and disadvantages, and to a realism reflected also in the works of their writers, musicians, and artists. Customs and traditions flourish particularly in the alpine region, showing mainly in dress, alpine festivals, and popular games and sports. The last two include flag-throwing, *Schwingen* (wrestling), shooting, *Kegeln* (bowling), *Hornussen* (throwing a stone with a string), and *Jassen* (card playing). Other facets are found in the music (played on drums, the *Hackbrett* [dulcimer], the zither, the accordion, and wind instruments including the clarinet and the alpine horn), popular songs (*Jauchzen, Jodeln* [yodeling]), and shepherds' ballads. Swiss handicrafts such as wood carving (in the Bernese Oberland), hand weaving (Graubünden, Ticino), embroidery (northeastern Switzerland), and straw plaiting (Aare region, Ticino) are world famous. There are many forms of social activity, including youth clubs, guilds, and societies associated with the survival of certain traditions such as the carnival (Basel), and the *Sechseläuten,* a spring festival celebrated annually in Zürich. (M. C. G.)

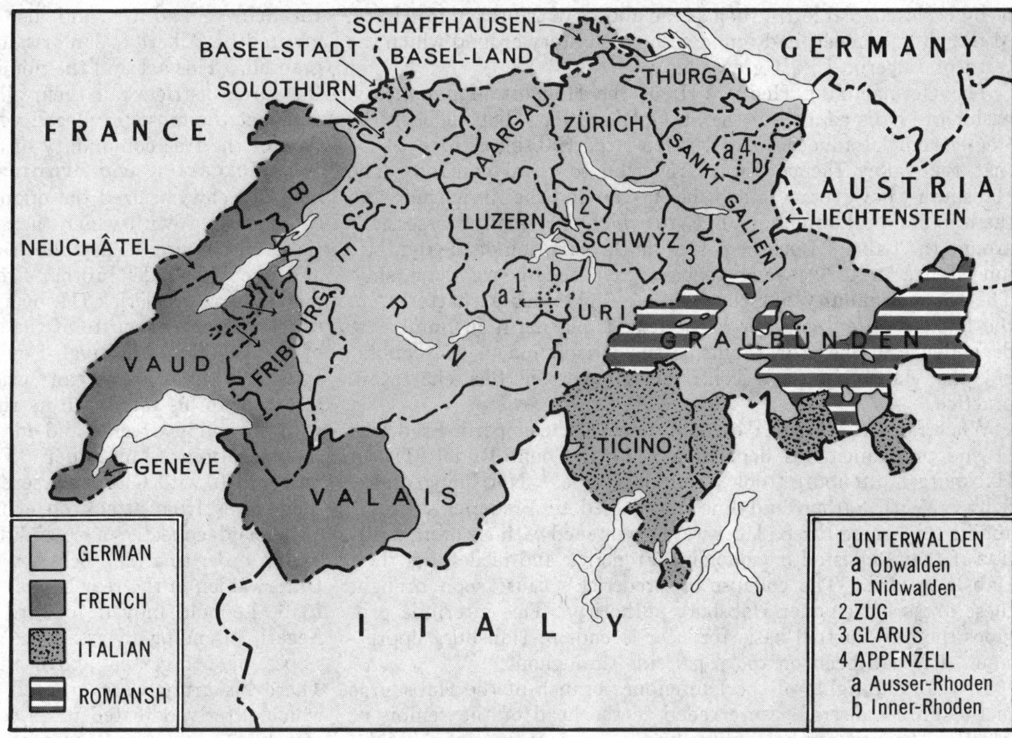


FIG. 2.—THE CANTONS AND MAJOR LANGUAGE AREAS OF SWITZERLAND

## III. HISTORY

The prehistoric culture of the Celts (*see* CELT) in what is now Switzerland is described in the article LA TÈNE. By the end of the 1st century A.D. both the territory of the Celtic Helvetii (*q.v.*) in the west and the Celticized Raetia (*q.v.*) in the east, together with the Vallis Poenina (*see* ALPS, ROMAN PROVINCES OF THE) and Vindelicia (north of Raetia), had been attached to the Roman Empire. The Great Migrations (*see* EUROPE: *History*) brought the Germanic Alamanni (*q.v.*) to the northern regions in the 5th century A.D., while the Burgundians (*see* BURGUNDY) were settled on the western borders. Conquest by the Franks and the subsequent partitions of the Frankish Empire eventually led to the division of the country north of the Alps between the Duchy of Swabia (*q.v.*), which was a constituent part of the German Kingdom, and the last Kingdom of Burgundy. The union of the Burgundian crown to the German crown of Conrad II, in 1032, theoretically consolidated all the present Switzerland in the Holy Roman Empire (*q.v.*).

Geographical realities, however, made the subjection of the Alpine highlands difficult for any of their overlords to enforce; and the same realities made Swiss history very intricate and local. The present article must be chiefly concerned to outline (1) the drawing together of the various localities into a Confederation; and (2) the process whereby the Confederation, originally a league of three districts—or, as they are now called, cantons—with later members allied to those three but not necessarily to each other, was transformed into a federal state. The history of the various cantons prior to their connection with the Swiss League must be left to the separate articles on them.

The Holy Roman Empire comprised German-speaking, French-speaking, and Italian-speaking peoples, and the linguistic frontiers of all three converge in Switzerland. It was among the German Swiss that the movement of confederation started—not as one for independence from the Empire, but for mutual protection against the local House of Habsburg (*q.v.*). Only later, when the Habsburgs had secured the Imperial dignity as a practically permanent possession, was the severance of the Swiss Confederation from the Empire gradually realized.

**1. The Forest Districts and the Habsburgs, to 1273.**—The founder members of the Swiss Confederation were Uri, Schwyz, and Unterwalden (*qq.v.*), the so-called Forest districts, or cantons.

In A.D. 853 Louis the German, ruler of the East Frankish Kingdom, or Germany, granted all his lands in the *pagellus Uroniae,* or subdistrict of Uri, to the Abbey of SS. Felix and Regula (the later Frauenmünster) in Zürich. Immediately dependent on the *Reich,* this abbey was not to be subject to the authority of the counts of the surrounding Zürichgau, but was to be protected by a *Vogt* (advocate), or special representative of the king. The lands in Uri which Louis granted to it comprised most of the valley of the Reuss between the present Devil's Bridge and the Lake of Lucerne (the upper valley, or Urseren, belonged to the Abbey of Disentis, on the headwaters of the Rhine); and the privileged position of the Zürich abbey's tenants gradually led the other men of the valley to "commend" themselves to it, that is to say, to acknowledge its lordship. The office of *Vogt,* having been given to one family after another, gradually became hereditary; and in 1218 it was acquired by the Habsburgs.

The Habsburgs, established in the Swiss Aargau from the early 11th century, had held the countship of the Zürichgau from 1173. In this capacity they ruled, as the German king's representatives, over two districts adjacent to Uri, namely Schwyz (to the north) and Unterwalden (to the west), in both of which they also owned lands in their own right. Schwyz, however, which is first mentioned in 972, had a community of free men settled at the foot of the Mythen in the area east of Steinen; over this community the counts had immediate authority, whereas west of Steinen the people were under local lords. For Unterwalden, on the other hand, there was no free community either in Obwalden (the upper valley, around Sarnen) or in Nidwalden (the lower valley, around Stans): all the land was held by lay lords, such as the Habsburgs, or by ecclesiastical lords, such as the abbots of Murbach in Alsace. Murbach, moreover, had founded the monastery around which the town of Lucerne (*q.v.*) grew up.

The German king Henry VII, of the Hohenstaufen dynasty, wishing to have control of the St. Gotthard Pass, bought back the *Vogtei* (official advocacy) of Uri from the Habsburgs in 1231, so that the valley thenceforward reverted to royal control. The Habsburgs, however, retained the Aargau and the Zürichgau; and their junior or Laufenburg line, to which the family possessions around the Lake of Lucerne passed on the partition of the dynastic inheritance in 1232, seems to have exercised its rights harshly. The free community of Schwyz in 1240 obtained a charter from the Hohenstaufen emperor Frederick II, placing it in immediate dependence of the crown, outside the jurisdiction of the counts; but the Habsburgs soon contrived to override this charter in practice.

When Pope Innocent IV excommunicated the emperor Frederick II and proclaimed his deposition (1245), Count Rudolf III of Habsburg-Laufenburg took the papal side. Not unnaturally, Schwyz, with Sarnen and Lucerne, rallied to Frederick's cause; and in 1247 these three places were threatened with excommunication if they persisted in upholding Frederick and in defying their Habsburg lord. The collapse of Frederick's cause soon brought these areas back under Habsburg authority. This interlude provides the only factual basis for later legends of Habsburg oppression. Uri had been on the papal side throughout.

In 1273 the rights of the Laufenburg branch of the Habsburgs in the Forest districts were ceded to the head of the senior, or Alsatian, branch of the family; and a few months later, in November, he was elected German king as Rudolf I (*q.v.*).

**2. The Everlasting League of 1291.**—Rudolf I, uniting in his person the characters of German king, count of the Zürichgau, landowner in the Forest districts, and head of the House of Habsburg, could be expected to exploit some of his functions in his personal interest. Though he recognized the privileges of Uri, he refused to acknowledge those of Schwyz. His royal grant of Austria and Steiermark (Styria) to his own sons (1282) did not immediately affect Switzerland, since the intervening countship of Tirol remained in the hands of its own counts; but on April 16, 1291, he precipitated a crisis by purchasing from the Abbey of Murbach (of which he was himself *Vogt*) all its rights in Lucerne and in Unterwalden for himself and his Habsburg heirs. This purchase threatened the communications of the Forest districts with the outer world by way of the Lake of Lucerne. On Aug. 1, 1291, a fortnight after Rudolf's death, when a struggle for the elective German crown was opening, the men of Uri, Schwyz, and Nidwalden formed the Everlasting League for self-defense against all who should attack or trouble them. This league, which was expressly stated to be a confirmation of an earlier one, was the foundation of the Swiss Confederation. Though Obwalden is not mentioned in the text of it, its name was later added to the appended seal of Nidwalden.

The League supported the anti-Habsburg candidates in the contest for the German royal succession. Uri and Schwyz allied themselves with Zürich on Oct. 16, 1291, and joined a general rising in Swabia against Rudolf's eldest son, Albert of Habsburg. Though the rising failed, Albert did not then obtain the German crown, which in 1292 went to Adolf of Nassau. In 1294 the first recorded meeting of the *Landsgemeinde* (legislative assembly) of Schwyz took place; and in 1297 King Adolf confirmed Frederick II's charter of 1240 not only for the free men of Schwyz but also for Uri.

In 1298 Adolf was overthrown by his Habsburg rival, who became German king himself as Albert I. Albert's rule was strict, but not oppressive: stories of his tyranny in the Forest districts date from two centuries later. Though he did not confirm the charters, he neither attacked Uri's ancient privileges nor abused his rights as king and count in Schwyz; and his appointment of a common administrator for Obwalden and Nidwalden (1304) was a step toward the unification of Unterwalden.

Albert's successor, the future emperor Henry VII, of the Luxembourg dynasty, on June 3, 1309, confirmed the charters of 1297 for Schwyz and Uri and also confirmed the liberties allegedly granted by Albert to Unterwalden, though in fact none had been granted. This act and the nomination of one bailiff to administer the three districts put them all in an identical political position, and that the most privileged yet given to any of them—the freedom of the free community of Schwyz.

**3. Morgarten and Brunnen.**—On Henry's death in 1313 the men of Schwyz seized the opportunity to attack the great Abbey of Einsiedeln, with which they had a long-standing quarrel as to rights of pasture. The abbot caused them to be excommunicated, and Leopold's elder brother Frederick of Habsburg (chosen German king, as Frederick III, by a minority of the electors), who was the hereditary advocate of the abbey, placed them under the ban of the Empire. His rival, Louis IV the Bavarian, to whom they appealed, removed the ban; whereupon Frederick issued a decree restoring to his family all its rights and possessions in "the three valleys" and in Urseren and entrusted Leopold I of Habsburg with the execution of this order. The Confederates hastily made arrangements with Glarus, Urseren, Arth, and Interlaken to protect themselves from attack on every side.

Leopold collected a splendid army at the Habsburg town of Zug in order to attack Schwyz, while a body of troops was to take Unterwalden in the rear by way of the Brünig Pass. On Nov. 15, 1315, Leopold moved forward along the shore of the Lake of Aegeri, intending to assail the town of Schwyz by climbing the slopes of Morgarten above the southeastern end of the lake. There his army were awaited by a force of the Confederates, which utterly defeated it. Leopold fled to Winterthur, and the attack by way of the Brünig was driven back by the men of Unterwalden.

On Dec. 9, 1315, representatives of the victorious highlanders met at Brunnen, on the Lake of Lucerne, and renewed the Ever-

THE BATTLE OF MORGARTEN, 1315. ILLUMINATION FROM THE "PRIVATE BERNER CHRONIK" BY DIEBOLD SCHILLING, 1484

lasting League. In their main lines the documents of 1291 and 1315 are very similar, the later one being chiefly an expansion of the earlier. That of 1315 is in German (whereas that of 1291 is in Latin) and has one or two striking clauses largely indebted to a decree issued by Zürich on July 24, 1291. None of the three districts or their dependents was to recognize a new lord without the consent and counsel of the rest. Strict obedience in all lawful matters was to be rendered to the rightful lord in each case, unless he attacked or wronged any of the Confederates, in which case they were to be free from all obligations. No negotiations, so long as the *Länder* (territories) had no lord, were to be entered on with outside powers, save by common agreement of all.

Louis the Bavarian solemnly recognized and confirmed the new league in 1316; and in 1318 a truce was concluded between the Confederates and the Habsburgs. The lands and subjoined rights belonging to the Habsburgs in the Forest districts were fully recognized as they had existed under Henry VII, and freedom of commerce was granted. But there was no word about the political rights of the Habsburgs as counts of the Zürichgau and of the Aargau.

The renown won at Morgarten by Schwyz, which had always been foremost in the struggle, led to the informal application of the name Sweicz (modern German Schweiz; *i.e.,* Switzerland) to the three Forest districts collectively as early as 1320. This name was extended to the Confederation as a whole, still informally, in 1352.

**4. Accessions to the League, 1332–64.**—In the aftermath of Morgarten, new members were admitted to the privileges of the original alliance of the Forest districts. The first to join was Lucerne, on Nov. 7, 1332, bringing a new, urban element into the association of pastoral communities and assuring its control of all the shores of the Lake of Lucerne. Next, on May 1, 1351, came the ancient town of Zürich (*q.v.*), when it was in fear of an attack by the Habsburgs. The League was thus advanced from the uplands to the plains; but the treaty of 1351 did not bind Zürich so closely as the other Confederates, so that later Zürich could occasionally incline to the Habsburgs in a fashion detrimental to its allies' interests.

The Habsburg Albert II of Austria began war against Zürich. This prompted the admission of Glarus and of Zug (*qq.v.*) to the League in 1352. Glarus, belonging to the Abbey of Säckingen (on the Rhine between Basel and Constance), refused to submit to the Habsburgs as *Vögte* of Säckingen and welcomed the aid sent by the Confederates; but its treaty of admission gave it an inferior status in the League, whose other members it was obliged to obey. Zug was abandoned by its Habsburg masters when the Confederates attacked it. Peace settlements, however, later in 1352 and, after a further crisis, in 1355, restored Glarus and Zug to the overlordship of the Habsburgs, who also regained their proprietary rights of 1291 in Lucerne.

These reverses were offset by the accession of Bern (*q.v.*) to the League on March 6, 1353, as the ally of the three Forest districts. Since the death of its founder, Berchtold V of Zähringen, in 1218, Bern had been an Imperial city, or free town of the *Reich.* Already in 1323 it had made a treaty with the Forest districts, but in 1352 had been forced to take part in the war against Zürich. Bern's membership was especially significant because it spread the League westward to the frontiers of Vaud, a Romance-speaking country then dominated by the House of Savoy (*q.v.*).

The Habsburgs in 1363 augmented their main seat of power, in Austria, by the acquisition of Tirol, which meant a very considerable advance into the Alpine region from the east. Despite this, the men of Schwyz, in 1364, by a bold stroke, won Zug for the League, of which it was thenceforward a permanent member. The Habsburgs acknowledged this conquest under a truce of 1368.

**5. Sempach and Näfels.**—Relations between the League and the Habsburgs soon deteriorated. The decisive conflict broke out in the time of Leopold III (1351–86), who under the partition of the Habsburg lands in 1379 received Steiermark, Kärnten (Carinthia), and Tirol and proceeded to reassert his family's authority over its western lands. Lucerne was particularly aggrieved at the demand for payment of customs to their bailiff at Rothenburg (a stronghold to the north of the town). The town refused to pay these dues and further irritated Leopold by granting citizenship to many of his own subjects, who could thus escape from his control. Finally the men of Lucerne attacked Rothenburg (1385); and this action, together with the grant of citizenship to the people of Sempach, provoked Leopold to war. With 6,000 men he advanced to crush Lucerne, which, with the Forest districts, raised about 1,600 men to oppose him. In the Battle of Sempach, on July 9, 1386, the Confederates were victorious, and Leopold himself was killed.

BY COURTESY OF THE BÜRGERBIBLIOTHEK, LUCERNE

**LUCERNE BECOMES THE FIRST TOWN TO JOIN THE EVERLASTING LEAGUE**

16th-century illumination from the *Amtliche Luzerner Chronik* shows citizens taking the oath on the Weinmarkt, 1332

In October 1386 a truce was made, but Glarus, which had risen in revolt against the Habsburgs after Sempach, continued fighting. Then Leopold III's elder brother, Albert III of Austria, led an army against Glarus. On April 9, 1388, the men of Glarus, with help from Schwyz, defeated him in the Battle of Näfels.

The seven-year Truce of Zürich, made in April 1389, secured the Confederates in all their conquests. After a period of tension in 1393, when the Zürich council adopted a policy of neutrality in case of war between other Confederates and the Habsburgs, the general truce was prolonged for 20 years on July 16, 1394, with various stipulations which consummated the success of the League. Glarus was released from Habsburg rule on payment of £200 annually (1394); Zug too was released; Schwyz got the *Vogtei* of Einsiedeln; Lucerne got the Entlebuch, Sempach, and Rothenburg; Bern and Solothurn (*q.v.*), which had been allied with Bern since 1295, were confirmed in all their conquests. Above all, the Confederation as a whole was relieved of Habsburg overlordship. The rights of the Habsburgs as landed proprietors, however, were expressly reserved: Bern and Zürich in fact were empowered to call on the other Confederates for armed support to maintain those rights.

By the end of the 14th century the League comprised Schwyz, Uri, Unterwalden, Lucerne, Zürich, Bern, Glarus, and Zug. However, the five latter members were allied, not with one another, but only with the three original members, the Forest districts.

**6. The First Italian Conquests and the Aargau.**—The treaty of 1394, though it was technically just a truce, freed the League from fear of the Habsburgs. Both it and its individual members could thus take the offensive to expand their territory. Uri perforce looked to the south, toward Italy. In 1403, therefore, Uri and Obwalden, in violation of the rights of the Duchy of Milan, together occupied the Val Leventina or Livinenthal, that is, the narrow valley of the upper Ticino River south of the commercially and strategically important St. Gotthard Pass; and in 1410 Uri finally annexed the Urseren Valley, thus obtaining complete command of the pass. Likewise in 1410, Uri and Obwalden, in dispute over pasturage with the local lords of the Val d'Ossola (Eschenthal) south of the Simplon Pass, appealed to the other members of the League for a joint occupation of that valley, which was achieved with the cooperation of all except Bern.

North of the Alps, Appenzell and the town of Sankt Gallen (*qq.v.*), after a decade of troubles, entered in treaties of *combourgeoisie* or reciprocal citizenship, with all the members of the League except Bern, in 1411 and 1412 respectively.

In 1412 the treaty of 1394 between the League and the Habsburgs was renewed for 50 years. Consequently, when the German king and future emperor Sigismund put Duke Frederick IV (1383–1439) of Tirol and Farther Austria under the ban of the Empire in 1415, the League hesitated to take action against Frederick till Sigismund declared that the treaty of 1412 did not release the Swiss from their obligations to the Empire. Then, in Sigismund's name, the several members of the League overran the extensive Habsburg possessions in the Aargau. The chief share fell to Bern, but certain districts (known as the *Freie Ämter* and the County of Baden) were joined together and governed as bailiwicks held in common by all members of the League (save Uri, busied in the south, and Bern, which had already secured the lion's share of the spoil for itself). This is the first case in which the League as a whole took up the position of rulers over districts which, though guaranteed in the enjoyment of their old rights, were politically unfree.

Meanwhile the Confederates had lost the Val d'Ossola to Savoy in 1414. They recovered it in 1416, thanks partly to alliance with the men of the Upper Valais (to the west of the Val d'Ossola; *see* VALAIS), who were then fighting for their own freedom. Next, in 1419, Uri and Obwalden bought from its lord the town and district of Bellinzona, at the end of the Val Leventina. This rapid advance, however, alarmed the duke of Milan, Filippo Maria Visconti; and the Confederates were not at one with regard to these southern conquests. Filippo Maria exploited the differences of the Confederates and reconquered Bellinzona and the valleys in 1422. Finally in 1426, by a large payment of money and the grant of certain commercial privileges, he obtained the formal retrocession of the Val Leventina, the Val d'Ossola, and Bellinzona.

**7. The Old Zürich War.**—Divergences of policy or of interest between the members of the League, largely the result of contrasting social conditions, had been accentuated not only with regard to the Italian conquests but also in the partition of the Aargau. They came to a head, in the so-called Old Zürich War, over the question of the Toggenburg succession.

Frederick VII, count of Toggenburg, the last great feudal lord in the area south of Lake Constance, possessed not only the Toggenburg or Upper Thur Valley but also Uznach (near the eastern end of the Lake of Zürich), Sargans and the upper valley of the Rhine from Sargans to the latitude of Feldkirch, the Prättigau (extending southeastward from the Rhine above Sargans), and the Davos Valley (at the farther end of the Prättigau). To protect this vast inheritance he had made treaties with members of the League; but on April 30, 1436, he died leaving no male heir.

Frederick's death was the signal for strife. While the Prättigau and the Davos Valley constituted themselves as the League of the Ten Jurisdictions, or Courts, Schwyz (supported by Glarus) and Zürich (backed by Frederick's widow) disputed the other territories. The other Confederates generally favoured Schwyz, to which some of them even sent military help; and Zürich, after two defeats, was forced in 1440 to make concessions. Zürich, however, was not resigned to this settlement and, in 1442, had recourse to alliance with Habsburg Austria, whose head, the future emperor Frederick III, had become German king in 1440.

Zürich's alliance with Austria, though it was permissible according to the terms of Zürich's accession to the League, infuriated the other Confederates. They all joined in war against Zürich, whose troops were completely defeated at St. Jakob an der Sihl, just outside the city (July 1443). Next year Zürich itself was besieged. Unable to get help elsewhere, King Frederick procured from France the dispatch of 30,000 mercenary troops—the so-called Armagnacs—under the dauphin Louis (*see* LOUIS XI). This ravaging army advanced across Alsace and then tried to capture Basel (*q.v.*), a free Imperial city which was allied to Bern and Solothurn. At St. Jakob an der Birs, outside Basel, a detachment of Confederate forces, not more than 1,500 strong, put up a desperate resistance to the Armagnacs (Aug. 26, 1444) before being completely defeated. Louis abandoned his enterprise soon afterward.

Hostilities between the Confederates on the one hand and Zürich and Austria on the other continued till 1450; then peace was made by arbitration. Zürich abandoned the Austrian alliance and recovered nearly all the lands which the Confederates had occupied.

(W. A. B. C.; H. Nz.; X.)

**8. Sigismund of Tirol and the Burgundian War.**—After the Zürich War members of the League made new agreements with the abbot of Sankt Gallen (1451), with Appenzell (1452), and with the citizens of Sankt Gallen (1454); and an alliance with the Imperial city of Schaffhausen was also concluded (1454). In 1458 a quarrel broke out with Sigismund of Tirol, the emperor Frederick's cousin, who had succeeded to the Habsburg lands on the upper Rhine and in Alsace on the death of his father, Duke Frederick IV, in 1439 (in the 1440s the German king had been acting as his guardian). Temporarily allayed in 1459, the quarrel was revived in 1460. The members of the League, except Bern, thereupon seized the Thurgau, which was ceded to them as a common lordship in 1461. Rottweil, an Imperial city in central Swabia, allied itself to the League in 1463; and Mulhouse, in the midst of the Sundgau (Habsburg Alsace), made an alliance with Bern in 1466. War between the League and Sigismund over Mulhouse and the Sundgau ensued in June 1468 but was ended in August by the Treaty of Waldshut. By this, Sigismund undertook to pay an indemnity of 10,000 gulden within a year, failing which he was to forfeit Waldshut (at the Rhine-Aare confluence) and his Black Forest possessions to the League.

Sigismund had no ready cash, and his efforts to obtain a loan led to a more serious war. By the Treaty of Saint-Omer, in 1469, Charles (*q.v.*) the Bold, duke of Burgundy, offered 50,000 gulden in cash against the pledge of Habsburg Upper Alsace, the countship of Ferrette, the Black Forest lands, and some Rhenish towns. Interpreting some permissive clauses of the treaty favourably to his own expansionist ambitions, Charles proceeded to occupy Upper Alsace. He appointed Peter von Hagenbach as his agent with instructions designed permanently to unite Alsace with the Burgundian territories. This threatened the Empire, and Frederick III declared the treaty void; it also greatly perturbed Bern, whose prospects of expansion were much reduced. Further, Charles the Bold was negotiating alliances with Savoy and with Milan and was also threatening to occupy Mulhouse.

One result was the formation of the Lower Union in 1473 by Basel, Colmar, Mulhouse, Sélestat, and Strasbourg, a defensive association against the Burgundians. Another result was the Perpetual Understanding of March 30, 1474, between Sigismund of Tirol and the Swiss, by which the former renounced any further territorial claims in Switzerland in return for promises of money to pay off his debts. This Perpetual Understanding was a definitive peace superseding the system of truces begun in 1389 and renewed in 1394 and in 1412.

Hagenbach was illegally arrested and executed in the spring of 1474—a deliberate act of defiance of Charles the Bold, who seemed to be fully occupied elsewhere. The Lower Union, supported by Bern, attacked Héricourt, beyond the southwestern frontier of Alsace, in November 1474; and Charles's great antagonist, Louis XI of France, promised cash subsidies while the war continued. Inspired by Niklaus von Diesbach, the Bernese advanced still farther in 1475, taking not only Blamont (southeast of Héricourt) but also a large number of places in Vaud and adjacent areas round Lake Neuchâtel, including Grandson, Orbe, Échallens, Jougne, Morat, Avenches, Estavayer, and Yverdon, most of which belonged to Savoy. The inhabitants of the Valais acted in collaboration with Bern to prevent any interference from the side of Milan.

Enraged and even a little alarmed, Charles the Bold came south in person in 1476, occupying Grandson at the end of February and hanging its Bernese garrison. Bern had gathered a considerable force from many states of the Confederation and from the Lower Union for the relief of the castle: too late to effect this, they offered battle on March 2 at Grandson. Charles's faulty generalship in the face of a disciplined force of pikemen, whom he despised as ignorant peasants, led to the rout, but not to the destruction, of the Burgundians. The duke regrouped his forces at Lausanne and again advanced against Bern in June. His way was blocked by the castle of Morat, held by Adrian von Bubenberg and 2,000 Bernese. The threat to this position was sufficient to bring 20,000 Swiss to its defense; and the Battle of Morat (June 22, 1476) ended in a complete Swiss victory.

Charles was defeated and killed at Nancy, in Lorraine, on Jan. 5, 1477. His inheritance was disputed between his daughter Mary and Louis XI of France. Savoy regained, with French help, much of Vaud.

**9. The Convention of Stans: Fribourg and Solothurn.**—Such unity as the Swiss had so far enjoyed had been based almost entirely on successful defense against external enemies, but their military prowess, nurtured by necessity, had made them potentially great: the latter part of the 15th century was the golden age of the mercenary soldier, and the Swiss had proved themselves the best available recruits. There was much money to be made by military service and, for the first time, prospects of lucrative employment opened to young men of valour. But the cessation of danger from outside and the lure of foreign gold were almost sufficient to turn friendly states into competitors. There was no constitution to hold them together, no common officers, seal, lawcourts, coinage, or flag; there was a growing divergence of interest between the cities and the mountain dwellers, as well as between east and west; there were numerous family feuds and endless local jealousies, culminating in disputes about the distribution of the booty taken in the Burgundian War and about the administration of the territories held in common, particularly the Thurgau.

Fribourg and Solothurn (*qq.v.*) were anxious to come within the circle of the Confederation, but neither Zürich nor Lucerne was very anxious for their support, while the rural members were anxious to maintain their numerical predominance over the cities. By 1481 differences had become so exacerbated that all common purpose seemed at an end and civil war threatened. It was averted by the intervention at Stans of the mysterious hermit (Nikolaus von der Flüe, or Bruder Klaus [1417–87]; beatified 1669 and canonized 1947), who arranged the compromise which held the Confederation together. By the Convention of Stans the full sovereignty of the component states was maintained and reasserted, but each agreed to abstain from attempts to foment internal discord or separatist activity among the subjects of any other state; the Confederate oath of union was to be renewed every five years; loot captured in war was to be divided proportionately among the participants in the campaign, but lands occupied were to be shared equally by the states involved. Ancient guarantees of mutual aid and assistance in war were renewed, and Fribourg and Solothurn were admitted as full sovereign members of the Confederation.

PAINTING BY AN ANONYMOUS 17TH-CENTURY MASTER, BY COURTESY OF THE SCHWEIZERISCHES LANDESMUSEUM, ZÜRICH

**PORTRAIT OF BRUDER KLAUS**

Bruder Klaus (Nikolaus von der Flüe) inspired the Convention of Stans (1481), which averted the disruption of the Swiss Confederation

**10. Waldmann's Zürich.**—Zürich had grown steadily in power and influence since the 1440s. Its textile manufactures had increased and with them the influence of the guilds, which shared effective authority in the city with the ancient aristocracy, the *Constafel*. Hans Waldmann (1436–89) was recruited to the guilds by apprenticeship and to the aristocracy by marriage; he took part in a number of campaigns, including the Battle of Morat, and was equally successful in war, business, diplomacy, and politics. Burgomaster in 1482, he became virtual dictator of the city, upholding the interests of the citizens against the peasants and turning the city itself into a community whose welfare, amusements, food, and clothing were subjected to regulation and supervision. In 1489, however, Waldmann had to face an armed peasants' revolt, which led to a constitutional revolution and to his execution. The aristocracy of birth and of labour joined hands, and the possibility of Zürich's dictatorship extending to the Confederation was averted. The struggle between the government and the peasants, however, was repeated with local variations in Schwyz, Unterwalden, Zug, Lucerne, and Sankt Gallen, although in no instance did the country people secure all their hopes.

**11. The Emperor Maximilian.**—The temporary eclipse of Zürich was followed by the last attack from the north. The emperor Maximilian I (*q.v.*), Frederick III's son, husband of Mary of Burgundy and also, from 1490, the successor of the retiring Sigismund of Tirol, sought to extend alike the Imperial prerogatives and the possessions of his House. In 1495 the Imperial Diet of Worms had put forth a revised constitution for the Empire ensuring internal peace and common taxation and setting up an Imperial Chamber (*Reichskammergericht*) as a final court of appeal. The Swiss communities were technically Imperial subjects and had reason to fear renewed Habsburg aggression. They were therefore anxious to renew the understanding with France—Charles VIII was opposing Maximilian in Italy and was ready to hire Swiss mercenaries—and unwilling to join the Habsburg-sponsored Swabian League for the maintenance of peace.

In the ancient Raetia to the southeast of the Confederation's territory there were many small communities, which had formed three leagues: the League of God's House (*Gotteshausbund*) of 1367; the Upper or Gray League of 1395, which eventually gave its name, in the form Graubünden (*q.v.*) or Grisons, to the whole area; and the League of the Ten Jurisdictions, or of the Ten Courts (*Zehngerichtenbund*), of 1436, mentioned above as arising from the Toggenburg succession. The last named was allied to the first from 1450 and to the second from 1471; and the Upper League and the League of God's House allied themselves to the Swiss Confederation in 1497 and 1498 respectively. In 1499 a boundary dispute between Tirol and the League of God's House had led to a Tirolese incursion into the Engadine and the Münstertal and thus to war with Maximilian: the Swiss came to the help of their ally, the emperor took up the implied challenge, and in the so-called Swabian War or Swiss War of 1499 there was fighting from Basel to Bormio. Battles raged at Hard, Bruderholz, Schwaderloh, Frastanz, and, most notably, against Maximilian himself at Dornach. Everywhere Maximilian, as usual, was unsuccessful; and the Peace of Basel, on Sept. 22, 1499, mediated by Ludovico Sforza (il Moro) of Milan, ended the war. In fact, although not in name, it was the recognition of Swiss independence.

**12. Basel, Schaffhausen, and Appenzell Admitted.**—Basel as a member of the Lower Union had taken part in the Burgundian War and had learned the value of Swiss cooperation: as an Imperial city it evaded with difficulty an obligation to support Maximilian in the Swabian War, while the Confederates obviously needed security in the northwest. The bishop of Basel was politically much less influential than he had formerly been; and on July 13, 1501, the state was admitted to the Confederation. It was a notable addition, for the city was well fortified, strong, relatively wealthy, a home of scholarship with an active university and with an industrious and busy population.

Schaffhausen, although smaller, was in much the same position: it had had much difficulty with local knightly landlords; it had sent men to help its Swiss neighbours since 1453 and been accepted by most as an ally; and it had firmly refused to join the Swabian

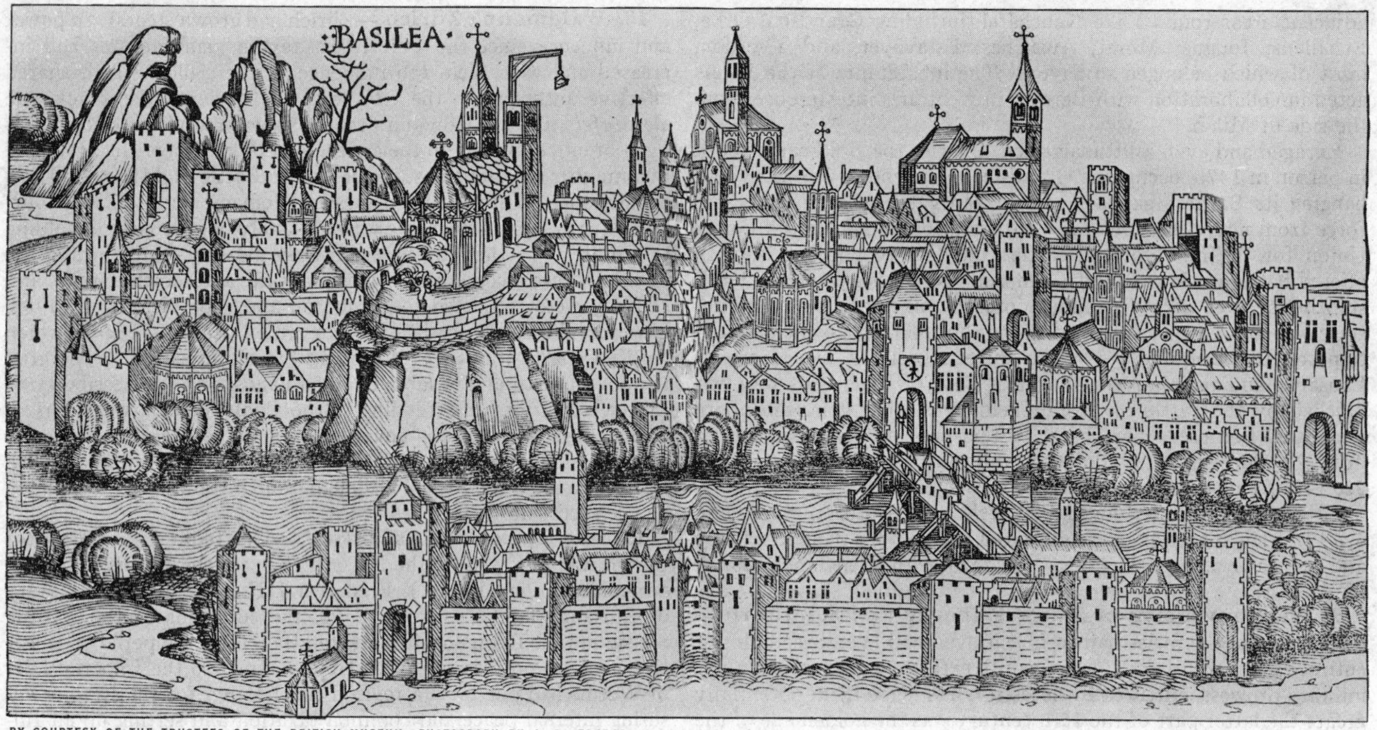


BY COURTESY OF THE TRUSTEES OF THE BRITISH MUSEUM; PHOTOGRAPH BY J. R. FREEMAN & CO., LTD.

VIEW OF BASEL AT THE END OF THE 15TH CENTURY, SHORTLY BEFORE IT JOINED THE CONFEDERATION IN 1501. WOODCUT FROM H. SCHEDEL'S "LIBER CHRONICARUM," NÜRNBERG, 1493

League. It received the reward of full admission to the Confederation on Aug. 10, 1501.

Finally, on Dec. 17, 1513, Appenzell, which had been an ally rather especially closely associated with the Confederation, was admitted to full membership and partnership. It was the last addition to the whole body, now 13 independent states, until the French Revolution, and it was accepted only because it helped to redress the balance of the "country" as against the "city" members.

**13. The Milanese Campaigns.**—The northern frontiers of the Italian states, especially Milan, were exceedingly ill defined. The southern route through Uri over the St. Gotthard was of growing importance for trade and much used by the mercenaries hired for service in Italy. The inhabitants of the Val Leventina, into which Uri had made a new incursion as early as 1440, had renounced their allegiance to Milan in 1475, during the Burgundian War; and they had been upheld in 1478 by armed men from Uri and other Swiss states, who then failed to take Bellinzona but defeated a much larger Milanese force at Giornico. Bern and the western Confederates on the other hand were not interested in this southward expansion and refused to support any further advances; and it was with some difficulty that in April 1503 Bellinzona and the Blenio valley were secured by Uri, Schwyz, and Nidwalden from Louis XII (*q.v.*) of France, as duke of Milan, in return for help against Ludovico il Moro. There was, however, growing resentment felt at the expenditure of Swiss lives in fighting on behalf of strangers, and opinion was markedly divided about the continued value of the French alliance, especially when France controlled Milan.

The greatest man in the Valais was Matthäus Schiner, bishop of Sion and a cardinal, who had turned against the French. In 1510 Schiner arranged for Swiss support of the Holy League formed by Pope Julius II for the expulsion of the foreigner from Italy. After the Battle of Ravenna in 1512 Swiss, papal, and Venetian forces in cooperation were able to secure the removal of the French from the plains of Lombardy. Massimiliano Sforza, son of Ludovico il Moro, returned as duke of Milan and acquiesced in the occupation of Locarno, Lugano, Mendrisio, and the Val d'Ossola by the Confederates, while the Graubünden secured the Valtellina, Bormio, and Chiavenna. At Novara (1513) a fresh French army was almost annihilated in a hard-fought battle. Another Swiss force penetrated into French Burgundy as far as Dijon but returned home when promised a substantial sum of money.

Francis I of France launched a new invasion of northern Italy in 1515. The division of interests between the eastern cantons (reluctant to leave the St. Gotthard route uncovered) and Bern (traditionally well disposed to France), together with a growing dislike of mercenary service and an equally strong distrust of Cardinal Schiner, led to a division of forces. Bern, Fribourg, Solothurn, and the Valais were bought off by the French in the Treaty of Gallarate; and a truncated Swiss army, with Milanese and papal support, was defeated on Sept. 14, 1515, at Marignano (*q.v.*) with heavy losses. Francis I agreed to easy terms in 1516, acknowledging all that the Confederates and the Graubünden had gained in the Bellinzona area except Domodossola and paying a considerable sum as well, while the Swiss promised not to serve in wars against the French king. This settlement is known as the Perpetual Peace.

**14. The Reformation: Zürich and Geneva.**—Five dioceses —Basel, Lausanne, Sion, Chur, and Constance—provided the framework for the ministrations of the Catholic Church to the Swiss people. Neither the institutions nor the men were suited to the changing needs of the 16th century. The bishops were sometimes nonresident, sometimes incompetent, often, as absentee landlords, disliked. The parish priests were frequently ignorant and sometimes lazy or immoral. While there were no territorial princes, as in Germany, to benefit by a redistribution of church property, the considerable monastic lands were coveted by certain cities. The humanism of the Renaissance (*q.v.*) could hardly impinge upon the lives and thoughts of peasant mountain dwellers, but contacts with Italy were easy and Basel became the home of Erasmus and Johann Froben's printing press.

All these things affected the career of Huldreich Zwingli (*q.v.;* 1484–1531), who became the most influential figure in the Swiss Reformation. A musical, intelligent boy of good peasant stock from the Toggenburg district, he had taught classics at the University of Basel and had been parish priest at Glarus (1506) and at Einsiedeln (1516) before becoming people's priest (*Leutpriest*) in the Zürich minster in 1518. He had, moreover, been to Rome and with Swiss armies in the field, had studied widely in the Fathers, and read the Bible in the original Hebrew and Greek. Experience had convinced him that mercenary service was harmful to his countrymen, and his Bible study and reading of the works of Erasmus had made him critical of the pope and opposed to indulgences.

In the all-important city of Zürich the pulpit, properly used, could be most influential, and on Jan. 2, 1519, Zwingli started a course of sermons on St. Matthew's Gospel such as had not been heard in the minster before: his teaching was inevitably called Lutheran although it was, in fact, the independent outcome of his own thought and studies. In the same year there was plague in Zürich, which caused a revivalist movement. Next, in 1520, Zwingli was denouncing the compulsory payment of tithe to the canons. The city council then permitted the public preaching of the "true divine Scriptures," and in 1522 Zwingli formally challenged ecclesiastical authority by eating meat (sausage) during Lent and by denouncing clerical celibacy. He set out his convictions and theological standpoint in 67 conclusions, which were publicly debated in Zürich in 1523. Appealing to the Bible, he convinced his hearers: the Great Minster was reformed, monks and nuns began to leave the cloister, the clergy to marry (Zwingli himself was publicly married in 1524), and the communion to be administered in both kinds, the income from church property being diverted to education or poor relief. Images were discountenanced, preaching encouraged, relics hidden or destroyed, monasteries dissolved, and finally, in April 1525, the Mass was superseded by a simple commemorative service. Zürich had thus by steady stages accepted the Reformation, and Zwingli was left almost as head of the state as well as religious leader. He published his doctrines in print, issued a vernacular translation of the Bible, rejected the teaching of the Anabaptists (who were proscribed), and secured a permanent majority of supporters in the city council.

The Catholic cantons made every effort to isolate the new teaching in Zürich and to prevent its extension even to the common lordships over which Zürich shared jurisdiction. It soon became apparent that religious and economic interests were likely to coincide: the strongly Catholic cantons were, generally, the rural mountainous areas, Uri, Schwyz, Zug, Unterwalden, Lucerne, Solothurn, and Fribourg, while the city-dominated communities, Basel, Bern, and Schaffhausen in particular, were lost to the old faith.

The coherence of the Confederation had been difficult to maintain in 1480: it proved almost impossible in 1529. Early in that year Lucerne, Uri, Schwyz, Unterwalden, and Zug, encouraged by Pope Clement VII and by the emperor Charles V, formed a separatist group known as the Christian Union; Zürich then tried to force the pace by an armed campaign in June, but the western states, particularly Bern, were not interested, and the antagonists were singularly loath to kill one another. The first armistice at Kappel (June 24) was followed by an agreement to dissolve the Christian Union, to allow freedom of worship in the common lordships, and to decline further foreign pensions. But neither side kept the spirit of the agreement. Then, in October, the efforts of Philip (*q.v.*) of Hesse to unite the Protestants by bringing Luther and Zwingli together at Marburg conspicuously failed.

By 1531, when an Italian adventurer attacked the Protestant Graubünden, the Forest cantons could refuse to come to the help of a non-Catholic state. They could also complain that the Evangelical faith was being forced on the Thurgau. Choosing time and place with great skill, the five Catholic cantons which had belonged to the Christian Union declared war on Zürich at Lucerne on Oct. 4, 1531, and sent a force north to Kappel, where they met a hurriedly raised detachment of volunteers from Zürich led by Jörg Göldli and with Zwingli in person among them. The Battle of Kappel (Oct. 11, 1531) resulted in a Catholic victory and in Zwingli's death.

Zürich thus lost the effective leadership of the Confederation, which devolved, not very satisfactorily, upon Bern; the Catholics regained an appreciable amount of ground, so that when the Jesuits came they were in a strong position. For almost three centuries after 1531 religion so divided the Swiss people that cooperation was hardly possible. The rare diets of the whole Confederation, necessary only for the administration of commonly owned territories, were brief and formal; the Protestant cities entered into cordial relations with England, Scotland, northern Germany, and Scandinavia; the Catholic states were the willing agents of France, Spain, and Austria on the rare occasions when these powers were found acting together. The wonder is that the Confederation survived at all.

Geneva (*q.v.*), which, it should be remembered, was not a member of the Confederation till 1815, occupied a strategically important position southwest of Vaud on the frontiers of lands more securely held by the House of Savoy. It had entered into a pact of co-citizenship with Bern and Fribourg in 1526 in order to throw off the rule of its bishop and to prevent its absorption by Savoy. The Protestant faith was brought into Vaud from France and preached by Guillaume Farel and Pierre Viret under the protection of Bern, which had already taken various parts of Vaud into a kind of protective custody. The Reformers were successful in 1535, after the usual public disputation, in inducing the independent city council of Geneva to forbid the public celebration of the Mass. Threatened by their former bishop and by Savoy, the Genevans appealed to Bern, and a Bernese force under Hans Franz Nägeli overran Vaud, occupied Lausanne, and brought temporary security to Geneva. At this juncture John Calvin (*q.v.*), who in 1536 had published at Basel his definitive *Christianae Religionis Institutio,* came to Geneva and, not without some setbacks, soon made that city the centre of an active and independent religious teaching. Calvinist doctrine was explicit and logical, the duties of the Christian household were clearly prescribed, attendance at church, particularly at sermons, was enforced, sumptuary laws were enacted by the city, an excellent system of schools was established, and ministers of religion were chosen with the greatest care for their character and capacity. By the Agreement of Zürich (*Consensus Tigurinus*), made with Heinrich Bullinger in 1549, Calvinism was free to infiltrate the whole of Protestant Switzerland.

The Catholic cantons would not agree to the inclusion of Geneva in the Confederation. Geneva therefore had to rely upon the alliance with Bern, upon the desire of the communities of the Valais that Savoyard aggression should be restrained, and upon the obvious interest of France in a friendly neutral at such a strategically important point. Savoy's attempt to capture Geneva by surprise in 1602 was a failure.

**15. The Counter-Reformation, the Valtellina, and the Thirty Years' War.**—The decrees of the Council of Trent (*q.v.*) inaugurated the Catholic Counter-Reformation. Their acceptance in Glarus, with the ultimate elimination of Zwinglianism there, was enforced to a large extent by well-managed campaigns collectively called the Tschudi War (1558–64) after their chief promoter the historian Gilg Tschudi (*q.v.*). From 1565 the work of reconverting the Swiss Protestants to Catholicism was actively sponsored by St. Charles Borromeo (*q.v.*), whose archdiocese of Milan included much of southern Switzerland. While he was ready to strain law and treaties in his zeal to stamp out the new beliefs, he set a personal example of piety, visited Einsiedeln, and founded the Collegio Elvetico, or Swiss College, in Milan, whence missionaries came north. The Jesuits also came and founded colleges of their own at Lucerne and at Fribourg; but the Inquisition found little support even in the Catholic cantons, and the Protestants who were expelled from Locarno took refuge in Zürich.

Lucerne, which was made the seat of a permanent papal nunciature in 1579, became the virtual capital of Catholic Switzerland. Its chief magistrate, Ludwig Pfyffer (d. 1594), who had served with Swiss mercenaries in France in the 1560s, conformed his policy to that of the French Holy League in the later Wars of Religion and made Lucerne the chief component of the Golden League (1586), which supported Philip II of Spain. Melchior Lussy (d. 1606) not only advanced the Golden League's cause by diplomacy, enriching himself in the process, but also won the pope's confidence and averted the threatened dissolution of the Confederation. Meanwhile Appenzell between 1579 and 1594 was subjected to a process of reconversion so intensive that the canton split into two zones, Äusser-Rhoden (Protestant) and Inner-Rhoden (Catholic).

The loosely united Graubünden and neighbouring leagues, two-thirds Reformed, one-third Catholic, controlled the important eastern passes, which were of interest alike to Milan and to Venice. Milan was under Spanish Habsburg control and jealous of its ancient commercial and territorial rival Venice, which in 1603 secured the friendship of the Graubünden. The Valtellina (*q.v.*)

was governed by the Graubünden and inhabited by Catholics; its roads formed the most convenient link between Milan and Austria, whose cooperation with one another was dangerous to France. A revolt in the Valtellina in 1620 led to Spanish support for the inhabitants against their northern masters and to successful Austrian intervention. France then took an interest in the affair; the Treaty of Monzón (1626) called in the pope as a third party; and further disputes, which led to further French intervention, were fomented by the local patriot Georg Jenatsch (*q.v.*), a pastor who eventually turned Catholic. By the settlement of 1639, the sovereignty of the Graubünden over the Valtellina was affirmed, with the rights of the Catholics there specially protected.

Meanwhile the revolt of Bohemia against the Austrian Habsburgs (1618) had inaugurated a conflict which grew to involve every great power of Europe: the Thirty Years' War (*q.v.*). All Switzerland was interested in the conflict, of which, indeed the affair of the Valtellina may be regarded as an aspect; but the religious division in the Confederation effectually prevented any corporate action. This was advantageous, for a Habsburg victory might have meant a renewal of Habsburg claims or an enforcement of the Edict of Restitution (whereby the Catholics recovered lost ecclesiastical lands), while a decisive Swedish triumph must have altered the balance of power in the Confederation decisively. Many Swiss soldiers were hired by either side, and much material was sold to the combatants at a profit, while the necessities of frontier defense caused all the 13 states to come to a rare agreement in the Defensionale of Wil (1647). The frontiers would be defended against any aggressor and a mixed council of war of Protestant and Catholics would direct a force recruited from all parts of the Confederation and its subjects and allies. The Defensionale was to be revised in 1668 and certain details were challenged later, but the acceptance of the principle of defense of neutrality was significant.

The negotiation of the Peace of Westphalia (1648) owed much to the indefatigable labours of Johann Rudolf Wettstein, burgomaster of Basel. It was appropriate that this European instrument should take notice of the explicit renunciation by the emperor Ferdinand III of all Imperial claims over Basel and the former Habsburg territories in Switzerland, an act followed by the abrogation of any claim by the Imperial Chamber to exercise appellate jurisdiction there.

**16. Economic Development from 1648.**—The soil of Switzerland, however carefully cultivated, could not support its growing population, and the temporary prosperity caused by the wars gave way to a depression in the latter part of the 17th century. Exports were necessary, and for this an industry was required which should use as little heat as possible and make the maximum use of human ingenuity and activity. Home industries were popular, partly because conditions in the valleys restricted outdoor work, particularly in the winter. Hence wood carving, spinning, frame-work knitting, and embroidery were popular; water power made textile manufacture (silk, cotton, and linen) profitable, particularly around the Lake of Zürich and in Sankt Gallen; and in western Switzerland the construction of clocks and watches and of musical instruments, at first luxury trades allied to the art of the goldsmith and the jeweler, centred in Geneva, spread to Neuchâtel, Olten, La Chaux de Fonds, and Le Locle. Basel was a commercial city, where stockings and silk ribbon and the preparation of tobacco and snuff occupied many; Bern remained primarily the capital of a great agricultural state, where the real or imaginary virtues of the peasant received an exaggerated recognition. Mercenary service, particularly with the French Army, was a popular form of employment, and returning soldiers brought news of foreign markets and fashions that was often valuable.

The government of a number of states, Bern, Lucerne, Fribourg, and Solothurn in particular, was in the hands of a patrician aristocracy, exclusive and splendid. Difficult economic conditions after the Thirty Years' War led to a rising in 1653 of the peasants of the Entlebuch against Lucerne. With the help of neighbouring governments it was suppressed, but it was followed by similar trouble in the Bernese Oberland and in the rural territories of Basel. The peasants seemed united, and the cities in alarm cooperated for the defense of their privileges, irrespective of religious differences. A battle at Herzogenbuchsee established the cities' superiority, and harsh punishments were meted out (followed by some belated reforms).

**17. The First Villmergen War.**—Zürich tried to make the Confederation more of a reality, but the attempt broke on the rock of religious prejudice. The Catholic states reinstituted the Golden League in 1655, and the expulsion of some Protestant families from Arth led to a split between Schwyz and Zürich which developed into civil war: Schwyz, Uri, Unterwalden, Zug, and Lucerne fought against Zürich and Bern. At Villmergen (Jan. 24, 1656) the Catholics under Christopher Pfyffer defeated their opponents and reasserted the favourable position secured at Kappel in 1531 and the complete individual sovereignty of the cantons.

**18. Relations with Louis XIV.**—In the age of Louis XIV the Swiss could hardly escape the all-pervading influence of France. If the Protestant states were not very eager to help the persecutor of the Huguenots, and the Catholic states looked to Spain for help, both could be influenced by the appeal of Jean de la Barde, the French ambassador, to renew the Perpetual Peace with France. In 1663 an embassy confirmed this renewal by a spectacular public oath in Notre Dame at Paris and for the next half century French influence was paramount in such external relations as the Confederation had.

Louis XIV's aggressive policy was in many respects at the expense of ancient Swiss interests. At the end of the 15th century Swiss influence had been almost paramount in the Franche-Comté and in Alsace, and these were exactly the areas against which Louis proceeded most successfully (*see* DUTCH WARS: *The Franco-Spanish War of Devolution* and *The War of 1672–78;* FRANCE: *History*). In 1668 the Habsburgs succeeded in recovering possession of the Franche-Comté, but the French threat to it alarmed the Confederates. Its final annexation to France in 1678 brought France to the Bernese frontier and caused fears for the future of French-speaking Vaud, and the French occupation of Strasbourg (1681) meant that Mulhouse and Rottweil could not hope to remain permanently linked with the Confederation. Basel, too, recognized how serious French pressure could be when a French battery at Hüningen confronted its defenses.

The Confederation remained discreetly neutral during the War of the Spanish Succession (*q.v.*), but politically its independence was the safer because of the outcome of that war, which checked French ambitions. During the war a particular setback to France occurred in Neuchâtel: on the extinction of the ruling family of Orléans-Longueville in 1707, a struggle ensued between the French candidate François Louis de Bourbon, prince of Conti, and the Prussian king Frederick I, in which the latter won the principality for the Hohenzollerns.

**19. The Second Villmergen War.**—The religious question in the common lordships, particularly the Thurgau and the Rheintal, was a delicate one, as the populations of both creeds were ruled by nominally cooperating states of similarly divergent faiths. Questions of mixed marriages and the education of children were urgent ones and roused strong feelings, which were accentuated by the attempt of the prince-abbot of Sankt Gallen to dictate to his mainly Protestant subjects in the Toggenburg district. A road entirely under Catholic control was being constructed from Schwyz into Imperial territory, and Abbot Leodegar Bürgisser was determined that the Toggenburgers should contribute labour and materials to its construction. They demurred and appealed successfully for support to Bern and to Zürich, and in 1712 an armed conflict broke out. The abbot had the support of the emperor Charles VI, which made France willing to mediate. Bern and Zürich cooperated well, while Lucerne was unable to coordinate effectively the forces of the Forest cantons. The abbot fled, the Protestants won a victory at Bremgarten, besieged Baden, and blockaded their enemies elsewhere. A final battle (July 25, 1712) at Villmergen settled the issue in their favour; and the Peace of Aarau (Aug. 11, 1712) established real equality of treatment for both sides in the common lordships, increased decisively the influence of Bern and Zürich in the Confederation, and entirely superseded the second Peace of Kappel.

**20. Domestic Affairs and Intellectual Life in the 18th Century.**—Every form of government existed side by side: a patrician aristocracy, proud, exclusive, and competent, ruled in Bern, Fribourg, Lucerne, and Solothurn; Zürich, Basel, and Schaffhausen were governed by their craft guilds and trading corporations; in the oldest states, Zug, Uri, Unterwalden, Schwyz, Glarus, and Appenzell, the primitive democracy of the *Landsgemeinde* assured the participation in the government of every adult male citizen; in Neuchâtel and Sankt Gallen autocratic princes were in power. Every state, individually or collectively, ruled subject territories; there was little sense of nationality and no common language, coinage, system of weights and measures, army, or lawcourts. There was a general air of contentment, prosperity, and industry.

A vigorous and varied intellectual life was evidenced by the work of Johann Jakob Bodmer, Johann Caspar Lavater, the Bernoulli family at Basel, Albrecht von Haller, and Johann Heinrich Pestalozzi (*qq.v.*), as well as the philosopher Isaac Iselin (1728–82). The country was increasingly visited by foreigners: Edward Gibbon wrote much of his *History of the Decline and Fall of the Roman Empire* in Lausanne; Voltaire was to be found on the frontier at Ferney. Jean Jacques Rousseau was proud to describe himself as a citizen of Geneva, and his thought was profoundly influenced by Swiss conditions.

The ideas of the Enlightenment (*q.v.*), rationalism, and general improvement which became widespread in 18th-century Europe were eagerly absorbed in Switzerland. The writings of Montesquieu, Voltaire, Diderot, D'Alembert, and the Encyclopaedists, as well as the almost homebred solvent thought of Rousseau, powerfully influenced the intellectual circles; many talked of liberty and equality in societies in which there was little practical application of either.

The general complacency was disturbed by several manifestations of discontent. Jean Daniel Davel attempted to free Lausanne and part of Vaud from the domination of Bern in 1723; he was unsuccessful and was executed. There was trouble in Appenzell raised by Lorenz Zellweger in 1733. Geneva unwillingly acquiesced in a greater degree of democratic government in 1738. A serious conspiracy against Bern headed by Samuel Henzi was suppressed in 1749. There were demonstrations against the authority of Uri in the Val Leventina in 1755 and armed opposition to the patricians of Fribourg in 1781; but neither these, nor somewhat similar explosions in Schwyz, Lucerne, and Geneva, presented any real challenge to constituted authority. A consciousness that something more than mere defense and self-interest held the Swiss states together was growing, and this found public expression in the formation of the Helvetic Society (Helvetische Gesellschaft) in 1761.

**21. The French Revolution and Napoleon.**—Some of the more advanced Swiss thinkers had found life more congenial in France than at home when the French Revolution started in 1789. In 1790 a "Club of Swiss Patriots" was founded in Paris by Jean Castellaz and supported by a number of Vaudois refugees, by Henri Monod, by Jean Jacques Cart, and, most notably, by Frédéric César de La Harpe (1754–1838), who from his post in St. Petersburg as tutor to the future Russian emperor Alexander I urged the French people to support the malcontents in Vaud and the Valais (his cousin Amédée Emmanuel de La Harpe was serving with the Revolutionary Army).

The conservatives in Switzerland were in strong opposition to French Jacobinism; yet when the War of the First Coalition against France broke out in 1792 (*see* French Revolutionary Wars) neither the French invasion of the lands of the bishop of Basel in April nor the massacre of Louis XVI's Swiss Guard in the Tuileries Palace on Aug. 10 provoked the Confederation into hostilities. The war party in Switzerland, led by Nikolaus von Steiger, was able to secure only an agreement that the Coalition might recruit Swiss mercenaries. There was, however, a good deal of anti-French activity in Switzerland.

The successful invasion of Italy by Napoleon Bonaparte (1796) and the Peace of Campo Formio (1797) were soon followed by the annexation to the French-sponsored Cisalpine Republic in northern Italy of the three provinces ruled by the Graubünden, namely the Valtellina, Chiavenna, and Bormio; and the Swiss could do nothing but accept the accomplished fact. In Paris, La Harpe and Peter Ochs (1752–1821) of Basel were urging a French invasion of Switzerland in the name of liberty, using the separatist movement in Vaud as an excuse of intervention. There were inspired riots in the Liestal near Basel and elsewhere, culminating in the proclamation of a "Lemanic Republic" in January 1798. The French Directory at once sent soldiers to the help of the insurgents: Bern resisted, but received no help from the Diet of the Confederation, which debated fruitlessly at Aarau. A French contingent was driven back at Neuenegg (March 5); but at the same time the main Bernese force capitulated at Grauholz, and the city of Bern was occupied. Great quantities of supplies and bullion were carried off to France by Bonaparte's agent Guillaume Brune.

Peter Ochs drafted a new constitution for a unitary Helvetic Republic. The cantons, whose number was increased to 23 by the emancipation of the subject and associated districts, were practically reduced to the status of prefectures; a bicameral legislature (Great Council and Senate), chosen indirectly by manhood suffrage, was to be responsible for lawmaking; and a Directory of five members was constituted the executive. The rights of the individual citizen were written into the constitution, including freedom of worship, of meeting, of petition, and of the press. A national militia was embodied, and local government was controlled by centrally appointed prefects. Geneva was annexed to France.

The new constitution was not imposed without resistance. In Nidwalden a revolt was savagely put down by Gen. Balthasar de Schauenbourg, but discontent continued to manifest itself in the east, especially when the country was marched over by opposing armies in the War of the Second Coalition. A compulsory alliance with France gave that country the right to use Swiss roads for military purposes, and the French guarantee of the Helvetic Republic offered easy opportunities for intervention. The Coalition regarded the Republic as a satellite of France, and in May 1799 Austrian and Russian forces under A. V. Suvorov met a French army under André Masséna near Zürich before making a classic retirement into the Vorarlberg. The campaign had devastated the countryside; the price of provisions rose alarmingly; and a bad harvest made the winter of 1800 one that was long to be remembered for misery and unemployment.

The cost of the new centralized government was relatively high, although the burden was more equally distributed, direct taxation being introduced for the first time and feudal dues, corvées, tithes, and ground rents abolished without compensation. Some money was spent on education, and an elaborate scheme of free or cheap public instruction (culminating in a national university as in France) was adumbrated, but little could be done in a short time. Pestalozzi, however, was given a free hand to proceed with his innovations, which attracted much notice, although his adventures in journalism, as editor of the *Helvetisches Volksblatt,* were less satisfactory.

The first constitution barely outlived the Directory in France. Then, after violent struggles between the protagonists of greater centralization and those who stood for more cantonal authority, the short-lived constitution of Malmaison was established in May 1801. Aloys Reding was chosen as *Landammann* or head of the state. He had to meet political and financial difficulties, culminating in a rebellion in Vaud and a kind of counterrevolutionary movement in the Aargau and in Bern. Napoleon promptly intervened to dictate the Act of Mediation from Saint-Cloud (Sept. 30, 1802; amplified on Feb. 19, 1803). This substituted a new Swiss Confederation for the Helvetic Republic. The cantons were again defined, with boundaries substantially as they have remained ever since. There resulted 19 cantons, namely the 13 of the pre-Revolutionary Confederation together with an enlarged Aargau, an enlarged Vaud (these two were created at Bern's expense), the Thurgau, an enlarged Sankt Gallen, Graubünden, and Ticino (*q.v.*). In the new cantons the representative democratic institutions were accepted; in the old *Landsgemeinde* cantons popular open-air voting continued but was limited to men of 20 years or more; and in the city cantons (Zürich, Bern, Fribourg, Solothurn, Basel, and Schaffhausen) the old aristocracy regained some of its

(TOP) HENRI CARTIER-BRESSON—MAGNUM; (BOTTOM LEFT) LOUIS RENAULT—PHOTO RESEARCHERS, INC.; (BOTTOM RIGHT) BURT GLINN—MAGNUM

SWISS CITIES

(Top) Lucerne: the old city wall is at left; in foreground is the Reuss River; (bottom left) Bern: the prison tower, centre, is a remnant of the medieval city walls; (bottom right) St. Moritz, famous for mineral baths and skiing

ancient influence under new forms. With Lucerne substituted for Schaffhausen, these latter became the directing cantons, having seniority in turn, the chief magistrate for the year having custody of the seal of the Republic and presiding over the assembly. The sovereign rights of the cantons, the issue of money, and control over customs, education, monasteries, and the posts were restored, but freedom before the law, of settlement, and of occupation was guaranteed to all citizens.

Napoleon was a relatively popular protector until war with Great Britain (*see* NAPOLEONIC WARS) obliged him to demand the 16,000 men promised him by the military convention which he had imposed on the new Confederation. British recruiting of mercenaries was stopped, and Switzerland was forced to participate in the Continental System, with great harm to its own commerce and industry, particularly in cotton. The Valais, which had been constituted as a separate republic outside the Swiss Confederation in 1802, was united with France as the *département* of the Simplon in 1810, nominally to put an end to anarchy; Ticino was occupied by French-commanded Italian troops to stop smuggling; and Neuchâtel was handed over to Marshal P. A. Berthier as a kind of feudal fief. Thousands of Swiss soldiers took part in Napoleon's invasion of Russia (1812); they fought well in the Battle of the Berezina during the retreat, but lost most of their effectives.

After the Battle of Leipzig (1813), when Napoleon's power was crumbling, the *Landammann* for the year, Hans Reinhard, called a special assembly at Zürich, which voted for armed neutrality. Metternich, the Austrian foreign minister, soon saw this policy to be on the whole to the advantage of France and therefore encouraged certain elements, who desired a restoration of pre-Revolutionary conditions, to apply for military help. An allied force marched through northern Switzerland on its way into France at the beginning of 1814, while the Napoleonic Act of Mediation was formally denounced.

**22. The Restoration.**—The Congress of Vienna (*q.v.*) devoted comparatively little time to the Swiss question, but certain of its decisions were nonetheless of far-reaching importance. It made as few boundary alterations as possible. Chiavenna, Bormio, and the Valtellina were annexed to Austria's new Kingdom of Lombardy-Venetia; but on the other hand, partly as a result of the efforts of Charles Pictet de Rochemont, Geneva was at last united to the Confederation with reasonable boundaries, as too was the Valais. Neuchâtel, over which the suzerainty of the king of Prussia was restored, was also admitted to the Confederation, and the independent existence of Vaud as a separate canton was accepted. Bern received the city of Biel and the former prince-bishopric of Basel. The whole Swiss state was declared neutral. The northern part of Savoy, belonging to Sardinia-Piedmont, was also neutralized.

The return of Napoleon to France for the Hundred Days in 1815 made no substantial difference: Swiss soldiers in the French service did not join him, and a Swiss contingent marched with the allies, who were allowed to cross Swiss territory, into France. A small modification of the frontier of Vaud and the creation of a customs-free zone in Gex and its neighbourhood were secured under the second Treaty of Paris (Nov. 20, 1815); and adjustments with Savoy followed under the Treaty of Turin (March 16, 1816).

The Swiss Confederation now consisted of 22 contiguous cantons. Its constitution, after a conservative patrician restoration in Bern and some rioting elsewhere, had been decided at the "Long Diet" of Zürich (April–September 1814), which produced the Federal Pact ratified in August 1815. Its keynote was the full restoration of the sovereignty of the cantons, almost the only federal institution being the Army, for the upkeep of which a special fund was voted. Each canton was equally represented in the Diet, Lucerne, Zürich, and Bern acting as chief city for two years in turn. The possessions of the monasteries were placed under federal protection, but the earlier general freedom of worship, as likewise that of settlement, was not retained. Each canton continued to collect its own customs, coin its own money, and manage its own affairs by the customary machinery. The franchise was everywhere limited so as to favour the old ruling families and the property owners, and any alteration of the federal *status quo* was made constitutionally impossible.

Military service with foreign powers again became possible: Louis XVIII of France gladly enlisted a number of Swiss. Reserving its neutrality, the Confederation declared its adhesion to the Holy Alliance in 1817, thereby pleasing the Russian emperor Alexander I; but political refugees in some numbers obtained asylum within its borders, so that Metternich complained that the country was a focus of revolutionary plots and in a state of anarchy. The Diet even agreed to place limitations on the freedom of the press and on the reception of aliens. Economically the country suffered from the rigid tariff restrictions of its neighbours (France and Austria in particular), from the decline in European purchasing power after the Napoleonic Wars, from successful British competition in world textile markets, and from its own constitutional inability to have any common policy on imports. Apart from some slight manifestations of embryonic nationalism and some rather more substantial signs of a religious revival, the Swiss states showed little activity in the 1820s.

News of the July Revolution in Paris in 1830 caused a good deal of excitement among the politically minded young men of certain Swiss cities. Clubs, societies, even athletic associations began to demand larger measures of cantonal democracy, more popular education, and some protection of women and children against industrial exploitation. A number of mass demonstrations led to the introduction of more liberal legislation in 11 of the larger cantons in 1831, implying acceptance of the principle of popular sovereignty and the expansion of the franchise. More schools and training colleges for teachers were opened and universities were founded at Zürich and Bern. There were, however, exceptions, and the surge forward was followed by a reaction. In Schwyz the opposition of reformers and conservatives was so violent that only the intervention of federal troops saved the state from civil war or self-partition. In Basel long-standing differences between the relatively wealthy city, with great external interests, and the predominantly agricultural countryside came to a head in 1831. The adoption of a democratic constitution for the state would give political preponderance to the country people, and this the citizens were determined to resist. After violent demonstrations in 1831 the canton was divided in 1833 into two halves, Basel-Stadt and Basel-Land, which have remained permanent.

Frederick William III of Prussia in 1831 most reluctantly abandoned a small part of his absolute rights in his principality of Neuchâtel (*e.g.*, that of nominating the whole of the cantonal council); but neither the republicans nor the monarchists there were long satisfied with the compromise, and clashes between them continued. One result of these differences was the formation in 1832 of the Siebnerkonkordat or Agreement of Seven (Zürich, Bern, Lucerne, Solothurn, Sankt Gallen, Aargau, and Thurgau), opposed by the conservatives united in the Sarnenbund or League of Sarnen (Basel-Stadt, Uri, Unterwalden, Schwyz, and Neuchâtel). None of these internal changes affected the traditional willingness of the country to shelter political refugees: Poles were welcomed in considerable numbers in the north, while the harbouring of Prince Louis Napoleon (particularly after his attempted coup at Strasbourg; *see* NAPOLEON III) and the notorious use of Swiss bases by the Italian revolutionary Giuseppe Mazzini almost brought about war.

**23. The Sonderbund War.**—The 1830s were years of considerable literary activity and of much thought about the future of the Confederation. Strictly constitutional revision was difficult, if not impossible, but the changing needs of the times and the general modification of opinion toward more liberal forms of government clearly suggested change. With a growth of national feeling went a growing conviction that there were certain minimum individual rights of the citizens that ought to be secured to all, and some were prepared to enforce this point of view; others were impressed by the expense and dislocation caused by each canton's having its own tariff and customs barriers. There were several local manifestations of discontent, but they remained localized and ineffective.

The bond which made concerted action feasible was found in religion. How was the principle of religious freedom to be enforced? The Articles of Baden (1834), condemned by Pope Gregory XVI but upheld by the liberal cantons, called for a general diminution of ecclesiastical privileges and exclusive claims. A mass demonstration against the appointment of the radically unorthodox D. F. Strauss to a chair of theology at Zürich in 1839 indicated the depth of passion aroused. Matters came to a head in Aargau. There in 1835 the monks of Muri had objected to taking an oath of loyalty, and in 1840 the Catholic minority demonstrated in arms against a liberal revision of the constitution. The cantonal government in 1841 dissolved the Aargau monasteries, which were held to have fomented the revolt. The Federal Pact of 1815, however, had expressly guaranteed the property of the monasteries against secularization, and the Aargau Catholics appealed to their friends in the south.

Lucerne, Uri, Schwyz, Unterwalden, Zug, and Fribourg, at a conference on Sept. 13, 1843, proposed to split themselves off from the cantons "disloyal" to the Federal Pact; and this alignment, to which Valais adhered in 1844, was to be the origin of the Sonderbund of 1845. The chief Catholic canton was Lucerne, and there Joseph Leu in 1844 secured the recall of the Jesuits, invited by Eutych Kopp, to undertake the teaching of theology and the control of the clerical seminary. This action was lawfully done and lay within the proper province of the canton, but was highly provocative. A demonstration against it in Lucerne itself was severely punished, and a general popular demand for the expulsion of the Jesuits from the Confederation was ignored. The radicals passed from argument to violence, and from most of the Protestant cantons bands of volunteers (*Freischärler*) marched on Lucerne under the command of Ulrich Ochsenbein, a Bernese staff officer. The expedition was mismanaged, and in a fight at Malters more than 100 men were killed and more than 1,800 made prisoner (April 1, 1845). On July 20, Joseph Leu was assassinated.

On Dec. 11, 1845, the Catholic cantons, Lucerne, Uri, Schwyz, Zug, Unterwalden, Fribourg, and Valais, formed themselves into a separatist confederation, the Sonderbund. The primary purpose was to prevent any alteration of the Federal Pact of 1815, even if this were the declared will of the majority of the people, and foreign alliances were welcomed to this end. Through 1846 opposition grew. Bern, Solothurn, Zürich, Vaud, and finally Geneva (under James Fazy) elected radical governments, determined to declare the Sonderbund an unlawful pact. In May 1847 Sankt Gallen joined the liberal cantons, and 12 votes out of 22 were certain. The Diet met in Bern in July 1847 under the presidency of Ochsenbein and by a majority declared the Sonderbund to be dissolved. A commission was appointed to draft a new Federal Pact, and the expulsion of the Jesuits from Lucerne, Fribourg, Schwyz, and Valais was ordered, together with their exclusion from the whole Confederation.

In the name of religion and of state rights the Sonderbund determined to resist by force. Its leader, Constantin Siegwart-Müller, purchased arms, collected an army under the command of Johann Ulrich von Salis-Soglio, and looked for support from France and Austria; but this support was slow in coming, partly because the British foreign secretary, Lord Palmerston, openly sympathized with the opposite side. The Sonderbund War was soon over. While at Lucerne there were divided counsels and uncertainty of purpose, the radical cantons entrusted their men and fortunes unreservedly to Guillaume Henri Dufour of Geneva, a somewhat conservative professional soldier, simple, upright, and unselfish. Dufour had more men than his opponents, and these better trained and equipped, with better guns and superior economic advantages. All these he used to decisive effect. Fribourg capitulated on Nov. 14, 1847, almost without fighting, and the ring closed relentlessly in on Lucerne. Zug surrendered on Nov. 21, and two days later the decisive battles were fought at Meierskappel and Gislikon. Lucerne was entered, officers, Jesuits, and nuns fleeing by steamer to Flüelen and then over the St. Gotthard to exile. Valais was the last canton to submit, on Nov. 28. Somewhat more than 100 men on both sides had been killed.

The costs of the war were charged to the losers, and Appenzell Inner-Rhoden and Neuchâtel had to pay fines for their neutrality. A collective note from the European powers, unsupported by Palmerston (who sent Stratford Canning with sympathetic instructions to Bern), could be and was ignored until the greater troubles of those powers in the revolutionary year 1848 left Switzerland free to work out its own destiny.

**24. The Federal Constitution of 1848.**—The revision commission had a new constitution ready for submission to the cantons in June 1848, and it was adopted with little change by 15½ cantons (1,897,887 votes) against 6½ (293,371 votes). The central authority was strengthened, particularly in regard to defense, law and order, and the promotion of the common welfare. There was to be a cabinet or Federal Council (*Bundesrat*) of seven, a supreme Federal Court (*Bundesgericht*), a Senate or Council of States (*Ständerat*) consisting of two representatives from each canton, and a National Council (*Nationalrat*) representing the country as a whole. Foreign affairs became the concern of the Federation only, although separate cantons might, with federal approval, make agreements not of a political nature with one another and with neighbouring countries. The posts, currency, weights and measures, and customs duties became the province of the Federation, which thus acquired an independent revenue, cantonal expenses being met by local levies, taxes on salt, an excise on wine, and stamp duties. Universal military service in a federal force was accepted; very small cantonal armies were approved, and the cantons controlled infantry training but not the cavalry or artillery. Service with foreign armies, military capitulations, and the acceptance of foreign pensions or decorations were prohibited. Freedom of the press, of worship, of association, and of settlement and equality before the law were secured to all, but these were somewhat narrowly interpreted in some cantons—the Jews remained under special disabilities and the Jesuits were excluded.

Bern became the seat of the government, Lausanne of the high court, and Zürich of the Federal Institute of Technology. It had been the hope of many that a great federal university at Zürich would unite the higher education of the country, the ordinary teaching of children being left to the cantons; but the existing academies at Geneva, Lausanne, and Neuchâtel and the universities of Bern and Basel were not prepared to accept this measure of academic unification, and in the end only technology was thus centralized. Similarly it was only after considerable differences of opinion that the French franc and the metric system of weights and measures were fully adopted.

**25. The Neuchâtel Crisis (1856–57).**—Neuchâtel, notwithstanding the rights of Frederick William IV of Prussia, had in 1848 adopted a republican form of constitution, which had been accepted as that of a federal canton. This was partly the work of the industrial region of Le Locle and La Chaux-de-Fonds and was resisted by the older ruling families, who proclaimed their loyalty to Frederick William. The last of several attempts at counterrevolution took place in September 1856, when the loyalists under Comte Frédéric de Pourtalès-Steiger gained possession of the castle of Neuchâtel and had to be ejected by force. Frederick William threatened to intervene on behalf of his "subjects" and mobilized his men; the Federal Army was placed on a war footing and sent to the northern frontier. British good offices and diplomatic pressure on Prussia by Lord Palmerston were followed by the mediation of Napoleon III, and in May 1857 the king gave way, renounced all sovereign rights, and secured an amnesty for his supporters.

**26. The Italian Question and Savoy (1859–60).**—Switzerland, like Great Britain, was a home for political exiles from many countries, in particular for Italian nationalists (*see* ITALY: *History*). In 1850 some measures were taken to prevent Switzerland from becoming too obvious a base for revolutionary propaganda, but the law on this subject was never very strictly enforced. In Ticino the sympathy of the population for Italian nationalism, combined with provocative anticlerical actions, led to Austrian reprisals in the form of the expulsion of Ticinese from Lombardy and of an economic boycott which caused much suffering. Perhaps only Austrian preoccupation elsewhere prevented matters from being pushed to extremities. When Sardinia-Piedmont, backed by France, began war against the Austrians in Lombardy in 1859 (*see* ITALIAN INDEPENDENCE, WARS OF), federal troops prevented Swiss sympathizers from crossing the frontier to join the Piedmontese and secured the internment of belligerents who fled north.

The war of 1859 was followed in 1860 by the cession of Savoy by Sardinia-Piedmont to France and the reopening of the question of the neutral zone of Chablais, Faucigny, and the Genevois. A federal councillor, Jacob Stämpfli, threatened to readjust matters by a Swiss occupation of this area—a threat impossible to carry into effect, as the easy repulse of a Genevan force that attacked Thonon in March 1860 clearly showed. In the end the neutral zone was enlarged a little, arrangements were made about the collection of customs, and the issue was shelved (until 1919 when full French sovereignty over the area was to be asserted and accepted). The war had further been responsible, indirectly, for the establishment of the International Red Cross Organization, a widely read pamphlet by the Swiss observer Jean Henri Dunant (*q.v.*) having drawn attention to the unnecessary sufferings of the wounded at the Battle of Solferino. In 1864, after much local activity, the Convention of Geneva regulated the care of wounded in war and arranged for the neutralization of the medical and ambulance services, distinguished by the federal cross in reverse colour.

**27. Railway Construction and Industrial Development.**—The Swiss people did not at first welcome the advent of the railway: it was believed to be aesthetically and technically unsuited to mountainous country and it threatened the prosperity of the roadside hotels. The interests of Basel and Zürich conflicted, and cantonal state rights were a serious obstacle. It was therefore not until 1847 that an experimental line was opened between Baden in Aargau and Zürich. After a report from the British engineer Robert Stephenson the Federal Council accepted the necessity for planned railway construction, and a conflict between Alfred Escher on the side of private enterprise and Jacob Stämpfli on that of state ownership and control resulted in the victory of the former. There was soon a mania for railway speculation, and lines were built with little or no coordination, sometimes in conscious rivalry. In 1853 the North Eastern Railway linked Zürich with the Rhine and the Lake of Constance, and in the same year the route Morges-Lausanne-Yverdon was opened; by 1859 the Central Railway joined Basel with Olten and thus to Lucerne on the east and to Solothurn, Bern, and Thun on the south.

Finance, politics, personalities, cantonal rivalries, and strategic considerations soon caused difficulties. The construction of a railway through the St. Gotthard Tunnel was not completed until 1882, after much negotiating with Germany and with Italy. Escher was chairman of the company responsible, the Confederation refusing to accept any financial obligations. The estimates proved inaccurate, and Escher was forced to resign, some part of the excess cost being borne by public funds. There were difficulties about gauge, locomotives, and differential rates, and in 1883 a suggestion of unification by public ownership was rejected by a small majority. A similar suggestion was rejected by a referendum in 1891; but in 1898 nationalization of certain main lines by purchase was accepted by a popular vote, and the principle was extended in 1903 and 1909. Better communications with the outside heightened the flow of the valued tourist traffic.

The existence of ample water power and an industrious population gave Swiss industry a good start, but the absence of coal made further developments difficult until the progress of hydroelectric schemes supplied an alternative source of heat and energy. Swiss textile manufactures, including cotton goods, largely held their own in a predominantly free-trade world but declined in face of growing protection and large-scale competition. Embroidery of good quality, however, was to maintain a wide market until about 1920, as did the Basel silk-ribbon industry. Dyeing led to a considerable development of the chemical industry; and the traditional localized watchmaking and clockmaking were supplemented by large-scale factory production, which met with considerable success and led to the making of a wide range of machines and locomotives.

The home production of grain decreased in the 1880s, when it became much cheaper to import foreign wheat; the farmers turned to stock breeding and dairy farming. Cheese making, the export of milk products of all kinds, and the chocolate industry became widespread.

**28. Constitutional Revision and Internal Politics to 1914.**—The German Kulturkampf of the 1870s against the Catholic Church (*see* GERMANY: *History*) had its repercussions in Switzerland. The issue of the *Syllabus errorum* by Pope Pius IX in 1864 had attracted a good deal of attention and helped to make the radicals also to some degree anticlerical, and the definition of papal infallibility by the Vatican Council in 1870 and the emergence of the Old Catholics in Germany, with many sympathizers in Switzerland, created difficulties. The Catholics of the diocese of Basel, in particular, refused to follow their bishop, Eugène Lachat, in accepting papal infallibility and declared him deposed. In this they were upheld by the cantonal governments, particularly Bern, but a majority of the clergy stood by their bishop, refused to accept his removal, and protested against the secularization of his property. Bern now required that parish priests should be chosen by their parishioners from among those who were approved by the government and had undergone a state examination. In Geneva the action of the pope in appointing Gaspard Mermillod to an apostolic vicariate there without any prior consultations led to Mermillod's being expelled from Switzerland (1873), to the recall of the nuncio, and to the prohibition of the activities of religious associations in schools.

The feeling thus aroused helped forward the growing demand for a general revision of the constitution of 1848. The introduction of the "initiative" (*i.e.*, the right of the people to propose legislation) into the canton of Zürich in 1865 was a victory of the left-wing democrats over Escher and his followers. The freedom of the press was extended, the principle of payments to councillors was accepted, and the example of Zürich was largely copied by Bern, Lucerne, and Solothurn. In 1866 the Jews, who had been denied freedom of settlement on commercial grounds, were admitted to full civic rights.

In 1874, partly as a result of the Franco-German War of 1870–71, a revision of the conditions of military service was generally demanded. The division between those demanding greater centralization and increased federal authority and those upholding the rights of the cantons was focused in the rivalry of Emil Welti of Aargau on the former side and Louis Ruchonnet of Vaud on the latter. The centralizing radicals were only partially successful; but a revised federal constitution was accepted by popular vote in April 1874. Direct popular control over the government was at the same time extended by the principle of the referendum, by which a national verdict on an issue could be sought if properly demanded by 30,000 votes or eight cantons. In 1891, moreover, it was agreed that a demand by 50,000 votes (the initiative) could bring similar machinery directly into operation.

Thanks to the reform of 1874, the Army was more directly centralized: discipline and military education, the provision of arms, and the collection of exemption-payments were to be federal matters, the force being based on the cantons (which also promoted some of the officers). Freedom of trade and choice of occupation within any canton was secured to all, and each canton was obliged to make provision for full primary education. Teaching was to be secular, civil marriages were made compulsory, and the foundation of new monasteries was forbidden. Certain other anticlerical regulations were made. The authority and appellate jurisdiction of the Federal Court at Lausanne was upheld and extended, and federal laws dealing with factories, bank notes, and the railways were made more comprehensive.

The opening of the St. Gotthard route attracted some attention to the Ticino: an increasing number of immigrants heightened party rivalries there, radicals and conservatives being almost precisely equally balanced. Religious feeling made matters worse; the conservatives were accused of manipulating the Ticinese elections so that they would remain permanently in power; and rioting in 1890 ended in the formation of a provisional government of Ticino. Armed federal intervention became necessary, a revised electoral law introduced proportional representation, and an increased electorate was followed by a radical and peaceable administration.

Growing industrialization and an increase in the size of the urban populations were accompanied by the spread of socialism in Switzerland. The Social Democratic Party, formed in 1870, avowedly existed to forward the claims of the manual workers and, under Otto Lang, began to demand social reforms and positive opposition to large-scale capitalist enterprise. A notable piece of practical socialism was the gradual nationalization of the railways.

Political refugees, their numbers increased by German antisocialist legislation, continued to be a source of difficulty. Anarchists were more difficult to control or eliminate. In 1898 the Austrian empress Elizabeth was assassinated in Geneva; and in 1902, after the murder (1900) of King Humbert of Italy, the Italian government demanded that action should be taken against Giulio Silvistrelli for provocative newspaper articles. A temporary breaking-off of diplomatic relations between Switzerland and Italy followed.

**29. World War I.**—When World War I broke out in 1914, public attention was soon transferred from the Swiss national exhibition to the needs of defense. The wisdom and the value of the policy of neutrality, imposed alike by public instruments, by national interest, and by tradition, was never in doubt. The citizen-army was rapidly mobilized and sent to guard the frontiers. There was a momentary controversy over the choice of a supreme commander, the parliamentary representatives voting for Theophil Sprecher von Bernegg, the Federal Council (supported by a decisive popular vote) choosing Ulrich Wille. A neutral Switzerland had certain advantages both for France and for Germany, and no attack upon its frontiers was ever seriously considered.

Universal military service, the rigours of campaign conditions without an enemy to fight, and the use of soldiers for public works were less resented than the economic conditions imposed on a country that could neither entirely feed itself nor supply all its own raw materials. The tourist traffic, which enthusiasm for mountaineering and allied pursuits had rendered especially active, came to an end; a run on the banks was with difficulty averted; and the large number of resident foreigners added certain difficulties. But it was soon apparent that Swiss services could be of value alike to both belligerent groups and a certain amount of trade became possible. For certain purposes Sète, on the French Mediterranean coast, became an open port for Switzerland. Heavy taxation and a good deal of borrowing were necessary.

The factory workers in the cities were discontented at the rapidly rising prices, and the Social Democratic Party became a vehicle for the teaching of Lenin, resident in Zürich until his transference to Russia by the Germans. The constitution, however, made political action slow and ineffective, and in November 1918 a general strike was called. The workers demanded a 48-hr. week, old-age pensions, national health insurance, female suffrage, the election of a new National Council by proportional representation, conscription of labour, and a capital levy. Prompt action by the administration, the hurried expulsion of the Soviet legation, the arrest of strike leaders, and the use of some show of military force ended the general strike quickly, after which a number of the demanded reforms were enacted. Concurrently with the general strike the serious influenza epidemic that affected so much of Europe wrought considerable havoc.

Swiss agencies, governmental and private, including the Red Cross, were much used by the belligerents, but the expression of Swiss opinion had little effect on the course of the war or on the peace negotiations in Paris. The collapse and partition of the Habsburg Empire decisively altered conditions on the Swiss eastern frontier, where the inhabitants of Vorarlberg (*q.v.*) wished to form themselves into a new canton of the Confederation. The decision about this rested with the Allies, who declined to detach the territory in question from the new Austrian state and ignored the principle of self-determination, so that the Treaty of Saint-Germain left the frontier there unchanged. Switzerland was affected in several ways by the Treaty of Versailles: the international control of shipping on the Rhine thereby became very much a concern of France; the agreement with Germany about the regulation of the St. Gotthard line was revised; and the neutralized "free" zone of Gex and northern Savoy became an undifferentiated part of the French republic.

**30. The League of Nations.**—The Covenant of the League of Nations, in spite of the flattering choice of Geneva as the headquarters of the organization, was not regarded with satisfaction in Switzerland. The guarantees for the maintenance of peace in Europe were less adequate than the Swiss project had suggested, and it was obviously difficult for a permanently neutral state to be associated with the enforcement of collective security and with active resistance to aggression. But Swiss idealism welcomed the general implications of the League, and outstanding difficulties were solved when, by the Declaration of London (Feb. 13, 1920), the Council of the League recognized the special position of Switzerland as permanently neutral and agreed that no military assistance, direct or indirect, could be required from it in the event of a breach of the Covenant, although "economic sanctions" would become applicable. The issue was long debated; the Federal Council advised entry into the League, which was accepted by the National Council by 115 votes to 50 and by the Council of States by 30 to 6. The necessary referendum on May 16, 1920, revealed even greater caution: 11½ cantons were for, 10½ against, and the final figures revealed a favourable majority of 90,000 in a total vote of 700,000.

On the social, economic, intellectual, industrial, and medical committees of the League of Nations Swiss help was prominent. The country readily accepted the Kellogg Pact abolishing war as an instrument of policy, and it advocated the early admission of Germany into the League. The passage of foreign armed forces across Switzerland, even on the most direct and manifest League missions, was strenuously and successfully resisted. Relations with the U.S.S.R., embittered by the murder of the Soviet representative V. V. Vorovski at Lausanne in 1923, remained unsatisfactory, and Switzerland opposed the admission of that country into the League in 1934. In 1935 trade relations with Italy were not broken off when Italian forces invaded Ethiopia, although an embargo was placed on the export of arms to both sides. The Chinese-Japanese War, the failure of the Disarmament Conference, the Spanish Civil War, and the successful *Anschluss* between Germany and Austria caused a national reaction, and in May 1938 Switzerland publicly refused to participate in future sanctions.

**31. World War II.**—Switzerland had foreseen the outbreak of a general conflict and was militarily prepared for World War II. On Aug. 30, 1939, Henri Guisan was elected general (commander in chief) by a large majority. The Army was mobilized, the frontiers guarded, and conscription of labour enacted. The tourist traffic and with it the hotel industry, already affected by European conditions, suffered greatly, and both imports and exports were exposed to severe and immediate limitations. With the fall of France in 1940 a large number of French and Polish troops crossed the frontier and were interned. Certain towns, notably Schaffhausen, were accidentally bombed. Defense measures were deliberately concentrated upon the mountainous interior, and these were not put to the test. War materials were supplied to both sides and conveyed by rail between Germany and Italy. A careful censorship was exercised over the press; incitement was avoided, as dislike for German National Socialist activities increased; and the Communist Party was proscribed. Home agriculture, grain-growing in particular, received all possible encouragement, and the country emerged from the war less impoverished than might have been expected.

**32. Switzerland from 1945.**—Diplomatic relations with the U.S.S.R. were reopened in 1946, but Switzerland remained solidly opposed to Communism. Every effort was made to cooperate with international organizations that was consistent with the maintenance of the increasingly difficult principle of permanent neutrality. Switzerland, therefore, did not join the United Nations, though it became a member of the five UN specialized nonpolitical agencies. It was not a member of the potentially federal European Economic Community, but in 1959 joined the much looser European Free Trade Association. In 1963 Switzerland joined the Council of Europe. Postwar prosperity was high (see *The Economy,* below).

On July 11, 1958, the government issued a statement in favour of arming the country with nuclear weapons. On April 1, 1962, a Socialist-sponsored proposal for a constitutional article prohibiting the manufacture, importation, transit, storage, or use of nuclear weapons in Switzerland was rejected in a national referendum. In 1963 Switzerland adhered to the Nuclear Test-Ban Treaty. By the mid-1960s there was, however, a fairly widespread dislike of the magnitude of the defense budget, representing about 33% of the total annual expenditure (but only 3.5% of the national income). In domestic affairs, agitation by French-speaking separatists in the Catholic Jura region of Bern Canton became an issue of some importance in the late 1960s, and federal troops had to be stationed there to protect property. A report commissioned by the federal government proposed in 1969 a "Jura statute" allowing considerable autonomy, followed by plebiscites in the various districts of the canton. (G. R. P.; X.)

## IV. POPULATION

The total population according to the 1960 census was 5,429,061, representing a 15% increase since 1950 (an average annual increase of 1.5%). The cantons registering the greatest gains were the industrial ones of Zürich, Zug, Basel, and Genève. The least densely populated cantons were the alpine ones; *e.g.*, Graubünden and Uri. The Jura cantons of Vaud and Neuchâtel were more thickly populated; the densest concentrations were in the cantons of Genève, Basel-Landschaft and Basel-Stadt, and Zürich (*see* Table). In 1960, 69.3% of the population spoke German, 18.9% French, 9.5% Italian, 0.9% Romansch, and 1.4% other languages. German is spoken by the majority of inhabitants in 19 of the 25 cantons, French in 5, and Italian in 1. Foreigners living in Switzerland (1960) numbered 584,739. The following

*Area and Population of Switzerland by Cantons*

| Cantons* | Area in sq. mi.† | Population (1967 est.) | Density per sq. mi. | Capital (city) |
|---|---|---|---|---|
| Aargau (Argovie; 1803) | 541.9 | 409,000 | 754.7 | Aarau |
| Appenzell Ausser-Rhoden‡ (Appenzell Rhodes Extérieures; 1513) | 93.7 | 50,500 | 538.9 | Herisau |
| Appenzell Inner-Rhoden‡ (Appenzell Rhodes Intérieures; 1513) | 66.6 | 13,500 | 202.7 | Appenzell |
| Basel-Landschaft (Bâle-Campagne; 1501)‡ | 165.3 | 188,100 | 1,137.9 | Liestal |
| Basel-Stadt (Bâle-Ville; 1501)‡ | 14.3 | 237,100 | 16,580.4 | Basel |
| Bern (Berne; 1353) | 2,659.0 | 984,000 | 370.0 | Bern |
| Fribourg (Freiburg; 1481) | 644.7 | 170,000 | 263.6 | Fribourg |
| Genève (Genf; 1815) | 109.0 | 310,800 | 2,851.3 | Geneva |
| Glarus (Glaris; 1352) | 264.2 | 42,000 | 158.9 | Glarus |
| Graubünden (Grisons; 1803) | 2,744.7 | 153,000 | 55.7 | Chur |
| Luzern (Lucerne; 1332) | 577.0 | 279,000 | 483.5 | Luzern |
| Neuchâtel (Neuenburg; 1815) | 307.6 | 164,000 | 533.1 | Neuchâtel |
| Nidwalden (Unterwald-le-Bas; 1291)‡ | 105.8 | 25,000 | 236.2 | Stans |
| Obwalden (Unterwald-le-Haut; 1291)‡ | 189.9 | 25,000 | 131.6 | Sarnen |
| Sankt Gallen (Saint-Gall; 1803) | 778.3 | 370,000 | 475.3 | Sankt Gallen |
| Schaffhausen (Schaffhouse; 1501) | 115.2 | 72,000 | 625.0 | Schaffhausen |
| Schwyz (1291) | 350.5 | 85,000 | 242.5 | Schwyz |
| Solothurn (Soleure; 1481) | 305.5 | 224,000 | 733.2 | Solothurn |
| Thurgau (Thurgovie; 1803) | 388.6 | 186,000 | 478.6 | Frauenfeld |
| Ticino (Tessin; 1803) | 1,085.3 | 232,000 | 213.7 | Bellinzona |
| Uri (1291) | 415.1 | 33,000 | 79.4 | Altdorf |
| Valais (Wallis; 1815) | 2,019.7 | 190,000 | 94.0 | Sion |
| Vaud (Waadt; 1803) | 1,239.7 | 495,000 | 399.2 | Lausanne |
| Zug (Zoug; 1352) | 92.2 | 64,000 | 694.1 | Zug |
| Zürich (1351) | 667.5 | 1,069,000 | 1,601.4 | Zürich |
| Total | 15,941.3 | 6,071,000 | 380.0 | |

*The local name (German or French) is given first with the year of entrance into the Confederation Ticino is Italian.
†1 sq. mi.=2.59 sq.km.
‡Half-canton (Nidwalden and Obwalden were formed from Unterwalden).

cities had populations exceeding 60,000: Zürich, Basel, Geneva, Bern, Lausanne, Winterthur, Sankt Gallen, Lucerne, and Biel. In 1967 the birthrate was 17.7 per 1,000 as compared with a deathrate of 9.1. (A. F. A. M.; X.)

## V. ADMINISTRATION AND SOCIAL CONDITIONS

**1. Government.**—The Confederation is composed of 22 cantons (often referred to as 25 federated states because three of them [Unterwalden, Basel, and Appenzell] are subdivided [*see* Table]). The cantons are built up of communes (nearly 3,000), which are usually grouped together to form districts (*Amtsbezirke*).

*Cantons.*—Each of the cantons and half-cantons has its own constitution, legislature, executive, and judiciary. Obwalden, Nidwalden, Glarus, Appenzell Inner-Rhoden, and Appenzell Ausser-Rhoden have preserved their ancient democratic assemblies (*Landsgemeinden*), in which all male citizens of full age meet annually (on the last Sunday of April or—in Glarus—on the first Sunday of May) in the open air for the purpose of legislation, taxation, and the election of an annual administrative council and of the members of the cantonal supreme court. In the remaining cantons the legislature (*Kantonsrat, Grosser Rat,* or *Grand Conseil*) is composed of representatives chosen by universal male suffrage (Vaud and Neuchâtel added female suffrage in 1959, Genève in 1960, Basel-Stadt in 1966, Basel-Landschaft in 1968, and Ticino in 1969) and usually by proportional representation. These councils deal with legislation and all questions not reserved to the federal government. They decide on cantonal taxes and appoint judges as well as cantonal representatives to the federal *Ständerat* (Council of States) unless the cantonal constitution demands public elections. The executive is elected by a popular vote. All cantons have the referendum and the popular initiative, the application of which varies.

*Communes.*—These are the real units, the actual seats of self-government. Their structure and functions vary according to past history (communes of burghers, communes of residents, political communes, parishes, etc.). The two principal types are the burgher communes (*communes bourgeoises* or *Bürgergemeinden*) and the political communes (municipalities or *Politische Gemeinden*). The burgher communes are now mainly of historical interest. Swiss citizens from cantons other than those in which they resided were, by the 1848 constitution, given voting rights there in cantonal and federal matters, but not in those relating exclusively to the commune. The 1874 constitution gave communal voting rights to all Swiss who could prove at least three months' residence.

Minor communes are controlled by a small council (*Gemeinderat*) chosen by a general assembly of all male (also female in the cantons of Genève, Vaud, Neuchâtel, Basel-Stadt, Basel-Landschaft, and Ticino—as well as in communes of the cantons of Bern and Zürich, which introduced female suffrage for communal affairs in 1968 and 1969 respectively) Swiss citizens over 20 years, of good conduct, and with three months' communal residence. In the larger communes a legislative body and an executive council are elected by universal suffrage. The executive council presided by a mayor has the management of all local affairs, including the enforcement of cantonal and federal laws or decrees, except matters relating to the burgher communes. Most communes take advantage of the referendum and initiative.

*Districts.*—These comprise a group of communes under a prefect (*Regierungsstatthalter*) who supervises the application of cantonal law and in certain cantons serves as first judge in minor administrative and police affairs.

*Constitution and the Confederation.*—On the cessation of the federal pact of 1815 a new constitution was accepted by general consent in 1848. A total revision was made in 1874 and this, with many modifications, is the one now in force. Any revision or amendment introduced by an initiative, on the demand of 50,000 franchised male citizens or by the federal parliament, needs a referendum decision with a majority of votes of the people and the cantons. In 1966 the Federal Assembly asked the Federal Council to study a total revision; the study will take several years.

Federal sovereignty is exercised by the Federal Assembly (*Bundesversammlung*—legislative) and by the Federal Council (*Bundesrat*—executive), both meeting at Bern. The Federal Assembly consists of two chambers of equal rights: the National Council (*Nationalrat*) and the Council of States (*Ständerat*).

The Swiss people are represented in the National Council by 200 deputies. Each canton and half-canton forms an electoral district and is guaranteed at least one representative. The deputies receive attendance pay and traveling expenses from federal funds; neither allowance is lavish. A general election of representatives to the National Council takes place every four years; voting is by proportional representation with universal male franchise for persons of 20 years of age or more, and any voter, other than a clergyman, may be elected a deputy. The Council of States consists of two members from each canton or one from each half-canton; *i.e.,* 44 in all. The mode of their election, term of membership, and rate of pay are cantonal matters and vary accordingly. Laws passed by the Federal Assembly can be vetoed by a majority-supported referendum based on popular demand by 30,000 enfranchised citizens.

The seven members of the Federal Council are elected for four years by the Federal Assembly and are responsible for the following departments: foreign affairs; interior; justice and police; defense; finance and customs; public economy; and transport, communications, and power. No canton may have more than one representative in the Federal Council; but according to custom the cantons of Zürich, Bern, and Vaud are represented; also the three main language groups are usually represented.

The president of the Federal Council (president of the Confederation) and the vice-president are elected for one year only (Jan. 1–Dec. 31) by the Federal Assembly and cannot be immediately reelected. The vice-president invariably becomes president the following year. Federal councillors cannot hold any other office and must not engage in any profession or trade. The federal government is being increasingly entrusted with matters formerly considered to be purely cantonal. Practising an open democratic political organization that respects minorities and easily changes federal and cantonal constitutions and laws, Switzerland has had no revolutionary movement of importance since 1918.

**2. Political Parties.**—There are nine parties represented in the National Council. No party—not even the Communist Partei der Arbeit (Labour Party: 5 seats)—is in permanent opposition. The principal parties are the Sozialdemokratische Partei der Schweiz (Swiss Social Democratic Party), the Radikal-Demokratische Partei (Radical Democratic Party), and the Konservativ-Christlichsoziale Volkspartei der Schweiz (Swiss Christian Conservative Party). At the 1967 election to the National Council these parties won 51, 49, and 45 seats respectively. Other parties include the Bauern, Gewerbe und Bürger Partei (Farmers', Traders', and Citizens' Party) (21 seats) and the Landesring der Unabhängigen (Independent Party) (16 seats). The Federal Council is composed of six members of the three larger parties (two from each) and one member of the Farmers', Traders', and Citizens' Party.

The Council of States at the close of the 1960s consisted of 18 Christian-Conservatives, 15 Radical-Democrats, 3 members of the Farmers', Traders', and Citizens' Party, 2 Social Democrats, 3 Liberal-Democrats, 2 Democrats, and one Independent.

**3. Taxation.**—Direct and indirect taxation, based upon federal and local laws accepted by general vote, are imposed differently by the communes, the cantons, and the Confederation. Up to 1915 the Confederation could levy only indirect taxes. A temporary constitutional amendment (approved in 1963 and in force from 1965 to 1974) gave a constitutional base for direct federal tax upon income and wealth. Rates of taxation in cantons and communes are fixed each year by decision of the voters or of the communal or cantonal parliament. Taxes are lowered for married people and further reduced if they have dependents under age 18.

**4. Living Conditions and Employment.**—The national income has been increasing constantly since 1945 and by the late 1960s exceeded 66,000,000,000 SFr. (U.S. $15,300,000,000) or 11,000 SFr. ($2,550) per capita. As extremely high individual incomes are rare, the repartition of the national income appears tolerably balanced. In spite of a growing inflation the average income of a Swiss worker showed an increase in buying power of more than 30% in the decade and a half after 1949. Postwar economic development caused a shortage in Swiss manpower and a strong influx of foreign labour, mostly from Italy and Spain, though this was curbed by restrictions in early 1965; 30% of the working population (which numbered about 2,700,000 in the mid-1960s) are non-Swiss citizens. Nearly one-half of the workers are employed in industry and handicrafts and about one-eighth in commerce, banking, and insurance. Agricultural workers have declined to about one-tenth. The population growth in general and especially in urban-industrial areas has provoked a housing shortage. There are no slums.

*Trade Unions.*—By the mid-1960s there were more than 30 unions with a combined membership of 782,000. The Schweizerischer Gewerkschaftsbund (Swiss Federation of Trade Unions) with 451,000 members had politically Social-Democratic tendencies. There were no Communist-dominated trade unions. Since the depression of the early 1930s trade unions have gradually denounced the use of strikes as economic or political weapons. Disputes are usually settled by arbitration.

**5. Welfare Services.**—The law stipulates that assistance to the poor is primarily the concern of the family. Public welfare services were developed in a typical federalistic way: first in communes, then in the cantons, and later in the Confederation. Social insurances that were introduced by amendments to the federal constitution already existed in some communities. The most important was the compulsory old-age insurance (introduced in 1948, extended in 1960 to cover invalidity) which provides annuities and rent allowances to all men over 65, all women over 62, widows, orphans, and invalids; it is financed by contributions from every worker under 65 and by smaller contributions from the cantons and the Confederation. The contributions (4.7% of incomes) are shared jointly with the employer and determine the amount of rent to a fixed maximum. The old-age subsidy does not cover the cost of living; communes, cantons, and the Confederation provide additional support for the destitute out of general revenues. Compensation for loss of earnings due to military service is similarly financed by contributions of 0.3% of incomes.

**6. Justice.**—Each canton elects and maintains its own magistracy for ordinary civil and criminal trials. Civil and penal laws are federal laws, but the laws of procedure and the execution of the penalties in criminal cases are left to the cantons. Capital punishment was abolished by the unified federal penal code of 1938, except under martial law, general mobilization, or war.

The Federal Supreme Court (*Bundesgericht*) sits at Lausanne. Its 26 members (plus the supplementary judges) are elected by the Federal Assembly to hold office for six years. The Federal Assembly also elects every two years the president and vice-president who cannot be immediately reelected. The original and final jurisdiction of the Federal Supreme Court extends to disputes between the Confederation, local governments, and private individuals, so far as these differences refer to federal matters and involve more than 8,000 SFr. in financial suits. It is a court of appeal against cantonal authorities in the application of federal laws and also against certain federal decisions. It is a court of trial for persons accused of treason or other offenses against the Confederation, and a court of cassation in criminal trials.

(W. E. Wh.; Er. M.)

*Police.*—Authority in general is exercised by the cantons but larger communes also maintain police forces. A small federal police corps enforces (mainly in collaboration with cantonal police) special federal laws concerning treason, forgery, etc.

**7. Education.**—The 1874 constitution stipulates that each canton or half-canton is sovereign in education, that elementary education is compulsory and free, that all public schools must be state directed, and that religious freedom be guaranteed. The Confederation financially assists public elementary schools, vocational training, and the cantonal universities, and by regulating examinations for the professions it also influences the curriculum of the higher middle schools. The only institutions of higher education maintained by the Confederation are the Eidgenössischen Technischen Hochschulen (Federal Institutes of Technology) at Zürich (founded 1855) and Lausanne (federalized 1969). The Interior Department in Bern administers education, and there is an education department in every canton.

Children attend primary schools between the ages of 6 and 15, but can enter secondary and lower middle schools that form a link with higher or vocational schools. Pupils enter higher schools between 11 and 13, remaining for two to five years, and are grouped in language-history and mathematics-science branches. Technical or vocational schools serve apprentices between 15 and 19. The higher middle schools either take pupils from the senior classes of primary schools or themselves provide the preparatory schooling. They prepare pupils for higher school certificate in three types of curriculums: classical (with compulsory Latin and Greek), modern language, and science. There are boys', girls', and coeducational institutions. By the mid-1960s the number of pupils at primary schools totaled about 600,000 (with 23,000 teachers); at secondary and lower middle schools 150,000 (with 6,000 teachers); and at technical and vocational schools 15,000 (with 400 teachers).

In addition to the Eidgenössischen Technischen Hochschulen, there are eight cantonal universities; viz., Basel (1460), Lausanne (1537), Geneva (1559), Zürich (1833), Bern (1834), Neuchâtel (1838), Fribourg (1889), and Sankt Gallen (1898). At Lausanne, Geneva, and Neuchâtel instruction is given in French; at Basel, Zürich, and Sankt Gallen in German. Swiss universities are lay (*laïques*), but all, except Fribourg, are in cantons of Protestant tradition. At Basel, Geneva, Lausanne, Neuchâtel, and Zürich the theological faculties are Protestant; at Bern there are Protestant and Christian-Catholic faculties; at Fribourg only a Catholic one. Of about 36,000 students in the late 1960s over 25% were foreigners.

**8. Defense.**—Being composed of militia, the Swiss Army contains no forces maintained permanently with the colours except a corps of 500 instructors—a system that is unique in Europe. The total number of men trained for military duty was approximately 500,000 in the late 1960s. Military service is compulsory and all male citizens from the age of 20 to 50 (officers to 55) are liable. Citizens unfit for duty must pay a military tax. Obligations of militiamen also include the maintenance of public order and security. After physical training for youths, provided by the cantons under the supervision of the federal government, the training is carried out under the defense department. Women between the ages of 20 and 40 years may volunteer for service in the unarmed women's auxiliary force (*Frauenhilfsdienst*).

The Army comprises a first line (*Auszug* or *Élite*) of men between 20 and 32, a *Landwehr* for men aged 33 to 42, and a *Landsturm* for those between 43 and 50. After 118 to 132 days of basic training members of the *Élite* undergo seven annual trainings of 20 days. Men in the *Landwehr* and in the *Landsturm* are called up for several refresher courses not exceeding 53 days in all. Officers are trained in cadet schools, courses lasting from 67 to 104 days, according to the arm of the service envisaged. As the militia keep their uniforms and small arms with ammunition in their homes, the whole Army can be rapidly mobilized.

The country has 4 Army corps and 12 divisions. There is a staff organization for the Army corps and a general Army headquarters in the National Alpine Redoubt. The 37 infantry regiments are equipped with automatic arms, mortars, and antitank weapons. The 17 artillery regiments are armed with 105-mm. guns and 105-mm. and 150-mm. howitzers. The Air Force in the mid-1960s comprised 21 squadrons and 400 first-line jet aircraft.

By the late 1960s annual military appropriations amounted to about 1,800,000,000 SFr. and modernization programs were underway.

In peacetime the Swiss Army has no commander in chief (general), commander of army corps (colonel) being the highest rank. If troops are mobilized on a large scale the Federal Assembly nominates a commander in chief, as it did in 1939 when Gen. Henri Guisan was appointed. There is a general staff under the Defense Department in Bern and a Military Defense Committee, with the defense councillor as chairman, and the chief of the general staff, the chief of instruction, the chief of armament, the army corps commanders, and the air force commander as members.

BY COURTESY OF (TOP RIGHT, BOTTOM LEFT, BOTTOM RIGHT) SWISS NATIONAL TOURIST OFFICE; PHOTOGRAPH, (TOP LEFT) CHARLES MAY—BLACK STAR

(TOP LEFT) WATERFRONT AT NEUCHÂTEL, CAPITAL OF THE CANTON OF NEUCHÂTEL; (TOP RIGHT) VINEYARDS NEAR CORTAILLOD ON THE LAKE OF NEUCHÂTEL; (BOTTOM LEFT) WHEELS OF CHEESE BEING STORED FOR RIPENING; (BOTTOM RIGHT) RHINE FALLS NEAR SCHAFFHAUSEN

The committee ceases to function when a commander in chief is appointed. Civil defense was declared a federal affair in 1959; proprietors and communes in places of certain significance and important facilities are responsible for building new shelters; civil defense training is compulsory for men. (K. Sm.; Er. M.)

## VI. THE ECONOMY

Landlocked, largely mountainous, with a damp climate and few useful mineral resources, Switzerland was endowed by nature with no more than the basis of a meagre pastoral economy. However, by skill and hard work the inhabitants have made it one of the most highly industrialized countries of Europe with a high standard of living. The economy supports not only the native population but also a sizable labour force from abroad.

Between 1800 and the mid-20th century the farming population fell from nine-tenths to about one-tenth of the total. Half the economically active population is now employed in manufacturing, building, and handicrafts. With its skilled labour force and intensive capital investment, Swiss industry can produce, largely from imported raw materials, items such as clocks and watches and precision instruments that can compete in distant markets by virtue of a high unit value relative to their weight.

An important consequence of continuing Swiss neutrality has been economic stability, at times in the midst of European chaos.

### A. Production

**Agriculture.**—Largely because of its mountainous character, little more than half the land is suitable for agriculture. Stock breeding and dairying are the mainstays of Swiss farming. There is over three times as much meadowland as arable (including orchards, market gardens, and vineyards), and the area of mountain pastures is almost as great as that of meadows. Despite natural handicaps farming is highly efficient, as shown by the high annual yields of the mid-1960s: wheat, 3.2 metric tons per hectare (1.3 per acre), and milk, 3,500 litres (924.6 U.S. gal.) per cow.

Most intensively worked are the "vine farms" and those equally small farms that specialize in the growing of vegetables, fruit, or tobacco. The vine farms, found particularly along the Lake of Geneva and in the Rhône Valley, supply about 40% of the country's wine requirements. There are pear and apricot plantations in the upper Valais, but fruit farming is subsidiary in the Mittelland where apples, pears, cherries, and plums are grown. About one-third of the grain requirements are supplied by the home crop, which accounts for most of the arable land, chiefly in the Mittelland. Potatoes and sugar beets are also important.

Animal husbandry accounts for nearly three-quarters of the total volume of agricultural production. The greatest concentration of cattle is in the northern foothills of the Alps, but cattle farming is important everywhere. Many cattle spend the summer on the mountain pastures. About one-quarter of the milk is used for cheeses (*e.g.*, Emmentaler, Gruyère, and Sbrinz), the principal agricultural export. Almost all the cattle are either of the Brown Swiss or Red-flecked Simmental breeds. Pigs are numerous but goats and sheep are declining.

Swiss farming is characterized by the owner-occupied family farm. Roughly half the farms are smaller than 12 ac. (5 ha.) and another quarter are between 10 and 25 ac. (4 and 10 ha.). Efficiency has been increased by a reduction in the number of farms and the growth of producing and marketing cooperatives. The interests of agriculture are represented by a central body, the Schweizerischer Bauernverband (Union Suisse des Paysans, or Swiss Farmers' Union).

**Forestry.**—Woodland covers nearly a quarter of the country's surface but its direct economic value is small, for the bulk of it serves to protect settlements and communication lines against climatic effects (*e.g.*, avalanches, rain floods, soil erosion) and is restricted in its exploitation. More than two-thirds consists of conifers, chiefly spruce and fir, the remainder being largely beech. About 70% of the forest belongs to the community and to public legal bodies; the rest is privately owned, mainly by farmers.

**Mining.**—There is a paucity of minerals, except for salt, which is mined at Bex (Valais), and Schweizerhralle and Ryburg (both near Basel). The mining of metal ores, of great importance up to the 19th century, is now confined to iron and manganese ore in the Jura Mountains and elsewhere. The meagre coal deposits are exploited only during fuel shortages. Limestone quarrying in the Alps and Jura is the basis of the cement industry.

**Power.**—Switzerland's shortage of solid fuel is largely counterbalanced by its great resources of waterpower which are harnessed by about 370 hydroelectric plants (installed capacity 7,750 MW). Since most of the power stations are of the "run-of-the-river" type, there is a summer production peak when the rivers have their maximum flow and electricity is exported. In winter, production is supplemented by high-pressure, reservoir-fed power stations in the High Alps, but winter imports of electricity are still necessary.

**Manufacturing Industries.**—There is a large and growing number of factories employing about two-fifths of the total labour force. Nearly one-third of the workers are employed in small concerns with less than 50 workers each. Characteristics of Swiss manufacturing are its high degree of specialization, its great dependence on imported raw materials or semifinished goods, and its reliance on foreign markets. More than two-thirds of the manufacturing labour force work in the four great export industries: textiles and clothing, metal goods, clocks and watches, and chemicals and pharmaceuticals.

Significant enterprises based wholly or largely on indigenous raw materials are the food industries; these include the production of condensed and powdered milk, chocolate, soup preparations, sugar, and beer, and the canning of fruit and vegetables. The cellulose and paper industry needs additional imports of timber. Salt and electric energy are inherent bases of the chemical industry, which has its greatest concentration around Basel. Electricity is also the basis for producing aluminum (about 69,000 metric tons in the late 1960s) mostly in Valais (from French bauxite). Production of pig iron and crude steel is insignificant.

The engineering industry has the largest share of the industrial labour force and exports two-thirds of its production. It is centred on Zürich Canton, where it arose to satisfy the needs of the textile industry. It expanded to include turbines and electrical equipment, and finally machine tools and precision instruments, now its most important branch. The textile industry, second in size of labour force and exporting nearly half its products, is still located in eastern Switzerland. The boot and shoe industry is largely based on Schönenwerd (in Solothurn). The most characteristic of Swiss industries is watch and clock making. In no other industry is the raw material cost so relatively small or production so much orientated toward export (more than 90%). The earliest site of the industry was Geneva, but the various places in the Jura (*e.g.*, La Chaux de Fonds, Le Locle, and Ste. Croix), taken together, are now more important.

Switzerland, with its spectacular alpine scenery, its lakes, resorts, and spas, has attracted tourists since the early 19th century and remains one of the principal tourist countries of Europe.

### B. Trade and Finance

**Foreign Trade.**—Imports exceed exports, for Switzerland must buy not only raw materials and fuel but also much of its food. However, earnings from year-round tourism cover over one-third the visible trade deficit, and other such items as receipts from insurance and banking services and transit companies reduce it further without, however, since 1961, being able to achieve a positive balance. Also the size of the monetary reserves (in gold and currency) held by the banks and credit establishments has helped the government to withstand the deficits in the balance of payments. Nearly two-fifths of exports comprise metallurgical and engineering goods, followed by chemicals, clocks and watches, and textiles. The Swiss have always keenly supported international moves to liberalize trade and in that spirit joined the European Free Trade Association. At the same time they hope eventually to form a multilateral association with the European Economic Community, which by the mid-1960s had become their chief trading source, with the Federal Republic of Germany as the principal partner.

**Finance.**—The unit of currency is the Swiss franc divided into 100 centimes with an exchange rate in the late 1960s of approximately SFr. 4.302 to U.S. $1 and SFr. 10.257 to £1 sterling. The central bank of issue is the Swiss National Bank (founded in 1905; opened in 1907). The currency has proved a strong one and has always been fully convertible. Thus in the first half of the 20th century Switzerland became one of the leading financial centres of Europe exporting capital for investment. In this respect Zürich is now more important than Basel and Geneva. The three largest banks are the Swiss Credit Bank, the Union Bank of Switzerland, and the Swiss Bank Corporation.

The central government's income is derived from the capital levy and customs and excise duties, together with half the yield from the military-exemption tax and stamp duties. By the late 1960s budget revenue (over SFr. 5,200,000,000) showed a moderate excess over expenditure. The gross national product was about SFr. 55,000,000,000.

### C. Transport and Communications

Control of the most important alpine passes and the ancient routeway through the Mittelland between the Rhône and Danube waterways give Switzerland a key position in European transit traffic. The main artery of European transalpine traffic, the St. Gotthard route, runs through Swiss territory. Historically, other routes, such as the Great St. Bernard and Simplon passes, were of earlier importance. (*See* Alps: *Principal Passes.*)

**Roads.**—The right to build roads was largely reserved by the cantons until 1958 when a federal plan was drawn up for a network of *Autobahnen* (motorways) and other national roads to be built. Of these the sections Geneva–Lausanne, Bern–Zürich, and short stretches near Lucerne and Lugano were largely completed by the end of the 1960s. Some mountain passes are impassable in winter, but at St. Gotthard, Simplon, and Lötschen, cars are ferried through tunnels by rail; there are motorway tunnels beneath the Great St. Bernard Pass and the San Bernardino (*see* Tunnel).

**Railways.**—For general traffic these cover more than 3,100 mi. (5,000 km.). There are also special rack and pinion (cogwheel) and funicular railways and aerial cableways. Switzerland's first railway line was inaugurated in 1847, and a federal railway system began operating in 1899, but many "private" companies (actually financed from municipal, cantonal, and state funds) remain. Because of availability of waterpower, electric traction was begun early; almost all railway lines are now electrified. Railway construction was expensive, for numerous bridges and tunnels had to be built; the Simplon Tunnel, more than 12 mi. (19 km.) long, is one of the longest in the world. Cogwheel and cable railways were pioneered in Switzerland, and the first Swiss funicular cable railway was built at Engelberg in 1927.

**Shipping.**—There are passenger shipping services on 12 lakes and on parts of the Aare and High Rhine. Canalization of the entire High Rhine is planned, to make Lake Constance the terminus of the Rhine navigation. Cargo shipping below Basel provides a direct link with the Lower Rhine ports and the sea. There is a small merchant navy (created by a government decree in 1941), of ocean-going vessels, comprising 30 ships which are registered at Basel. But the Rhine fleet has nearly 500 with a carriage capacity of about 450,000 tons.

**Civil Aviation.**—The airports of Zürich (Kloten) and Geneva (Cointrin) are important junctions of European air routes. Other international airports are at Basel and Bern. The national airline, Swissair, founded in 1931, is privately controlled with some state participation, and carried an average of 2,500,000 passengers a year by the late 1960s.

**Postal Service and Telecommunications.**—The unification of postal services on a federal basis took place with the Swiss constitution of 1848. The Universal Postal Union was founded in 1874 at Bern, where its secretariat remains. The Swiss telephone service is excellent and is integrated in a single dial system. There are national radio transmitters at Beromünster, Sottens, and Monte-Ceneri, and a shortwave centre at Schwarzenburg. Programs are conceded to the Schweizerische Radio-und-Fernsehgesellschaft (Société Suisse de Radiodiffusion et Télévision) at Bern, which also directs the television service inaugurated in 1958.

*See* also references under "Switzerland" in the Index.

(K. A. S.)

BIBLIOGRAPHY.—*General and Geography:* J. Russell, *Switzerland* (1962); J. Früh, *Géographie der Schweiz,* 3 vol. (1930–38); H. Gutersohn, *Géographie der Schweiz* (1950– ); E. Imhof (ed.), *Atlas der Schweiz* (1965– ).

*The People:* K. B. Mayer, *The Population of Switzerland* (1952); C. Bruschweiler, *Industrialisierung und Verstädterung in der Schweiz* (1952); P. Geiger and R. Weiss, *Atlas der schweizerischen Volkskunde* (1950– ); R. Weiss, *Volkskunde der Schweiz* (1946), *Häuser und Landschaften der Schweiz* (1959); M. Gschwend, *Schweizerische Bauernhäuser, Ber. d. dt. Arbeitskreises für Hausforschung* (1954).

*History:* H. Nabholz *et al., Geschichte der Schweiz,* 2 vol. (1932–38); W. Oechsli, *History of Switzerland, 1499–1914* (1922); E. Bonjour, H. S. Offler, and G. R. Potter, *Short History of Switzerland,* 2nd ed. (1955); Jacqueline Belin, *La Suisse et les Nations Unies* (1956); H. Kohn, *Nationalism and Liberty: the Swiss Example* (1956); H. Ammann and K. Schib (eds.), *Historischer Atlas der Schweiz* (1958); C. Gilliard, *A History of Switzerland* (1955); A. G. Imlah, *Britain and Switzerland, 1845–60* (1966); P. Gugolz, *Die Schweiz und der Krimkrieg, 1853–1856* (1965).

*Administration and Social Conditions:* C. Hughes (ed. and trans.), *The Federal Constitution of Switzerland* (1954), *The Parliament of Switzerland* (1962); W. E. Rappard, *La Constitution fédérale de la Suisse* (1948); Hans Tschäni, *Profil der Schweiz* (1966); G. A. Codding, *The Federal Government of Switzerland* (1961); *I. Williams* (trans.), *The Swiss Civil Code* (1925); A. Ernst, *Die Ordnung des militärischen Oberbefehls* (1948); Federal Department of Economics, *Législation Sociale de la Suisse* (annually); Association suisse de science politique, *Année Politique Suisse . . .* (annually).

*The Economy:* Federal Bureau of Statistics, *Statistisches Jahrbuch der Schweiz* (annually); Swiss Credit Bank, *The Swiss Economy* (annually); C. J. Allen, *Switzerland's Amazing Railways,* 3rd ed. (1965); W. Kaeser, *Géographie der Schweiz* (1965); OECD, *Switzerland* (economic surveys) (1965–67); Peter Tschopp, *Inflation et Politique Monétaire: Le cas de la Suisse* (1967).

Current history and statistics are summarized annually in *Britannica Book of the Year.*

**SWORD,** a hand weapon with a sharp metal blade that is longer than that of a dagger, though the distinction between sword and dagger is somewhat arbitrary. "Sword" is a general term that includes many special types of weapons, such as sabres, rapiers, scimitars, etc.

**Early History.**—It is possible that the earliest swords derived from the flint daggers of the Neolithic period, which may have been the models for the first hand weapons made of copper. Daggers with copper blades found in Mycenae have hilts attached to the blades by rivets. An important step in the construction of both sword and dagger was taken when the blade was continued in an extension, or tang, which became the core of the handle. The blade and hilt could thus not easily be broken apart by a blow. Most swords of the Bronze Age had leaf-shaped blades and small hilts. They have been excavated in large numbers throughout Europe. Swords of this kind (*ziphos; akinakes*) were used in the Homeric period, and are shown in paintings on Greek vases of the Hellenic period. Alternatively to the straight-edged, leaf-shaped sword was the so-called Bronze Age rapier, a sword with a long narrow blade for thrusting only.

In classical times the sword as a weapon was subsidiary to the spear. The Roman soldier's sword (*gladius*) was generally short, straight and broad, though a longer type of sword, known as the spatha, was also used. The word ensis was generally applied to swords of tribes outside the empire.

The Franks of the late Iron Age continued to use the long spatha, but as it was made of soft iron, the blade was easily bent. Some protection for the hands was given in early swords by the form of the hilt, but it was not until the early middle ages that the crossbar, or *quillon,* became fully developed for protective purposes.

By the 6th century Viking swords began to take the form that lasted for a thousand years. The sword had then acquired its four principal parts: (1) the pommel, a knob at the anterior end, which acted as a counterpoise to the blade; (2) the grip, covering the tang and grasped by the hands; (3) the crossbar or *quillon,* which protected the user's hand; and (4) the blade. (*See* figure.)

**The Middle Ages.**—It was the Vikings from Scandinavia who introduced the sword with the blade of carbonized iron. There has always been a mystery about the making of sword blades, hence the legends of Weyland the Smith, Siegfried's sword "Nothung" and King Arthur's "Excalibur." Modern science has discovered that some of these blades, which have patterns or "watering" inherent in them, were produced by what is called strip welding. Bundles of iron strips were bent over, hammered together, cut and bent again repeatedly, and the carbonization of metal, probably discovered accidentally, improved their strength and temper.

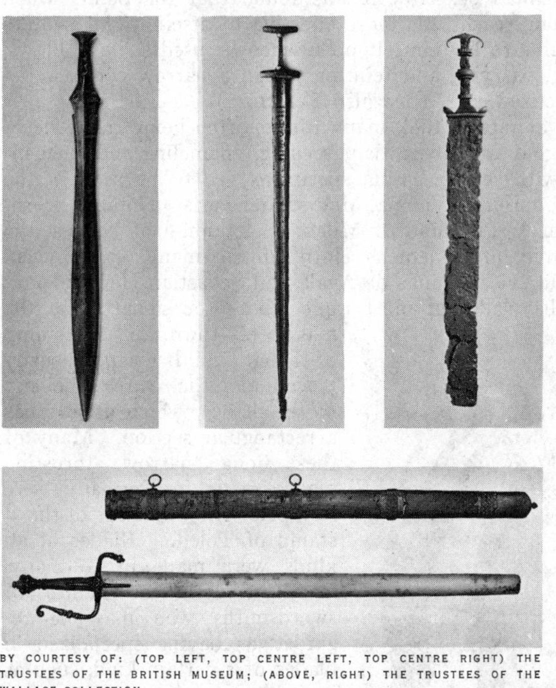

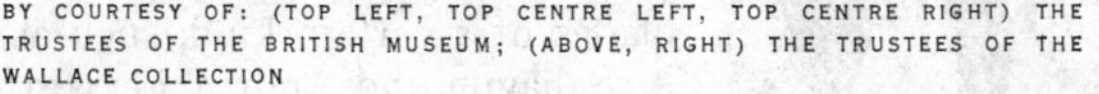

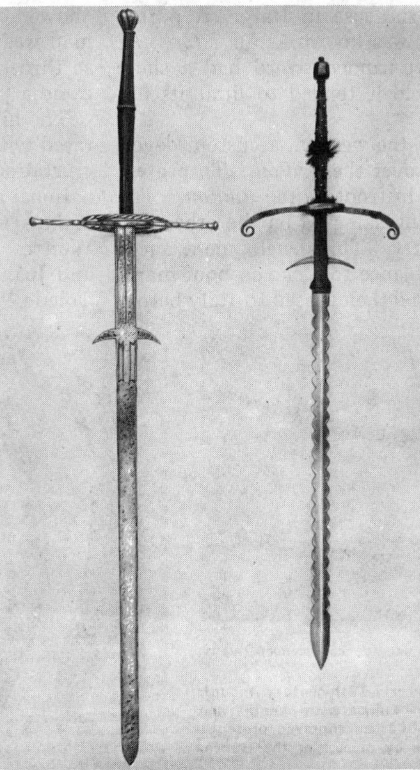



(Top left) Bronze Age sword; (top centre left) Viking sword; (top centre right) Roman sword in scabbard, A.D. 43–60; (right) two-handed German swords, about 1580; (above) heading sword with sheath, probably Hungarian, about 1620

The Viking sword, and its successor, the medieval knightly sword, usually had a straight blade, double-edged and pointed, with a shallow hollow down the centre, giving lightness with rigidity. The medieval sword was purely an offensive weapon; the user relied for bodily protection on his shield and defensive armour. The user's hand was protected by rigid *quillons,* either straight or with the ends curved toward the blade. The pommel was usually rounded, either as a sphere or a disk (so-called wheel pommel) and later fig-shaped.

In the course of years certain European centres of the craft were established, notably at Passau on the Danube, and later at Solingen in western Germany,

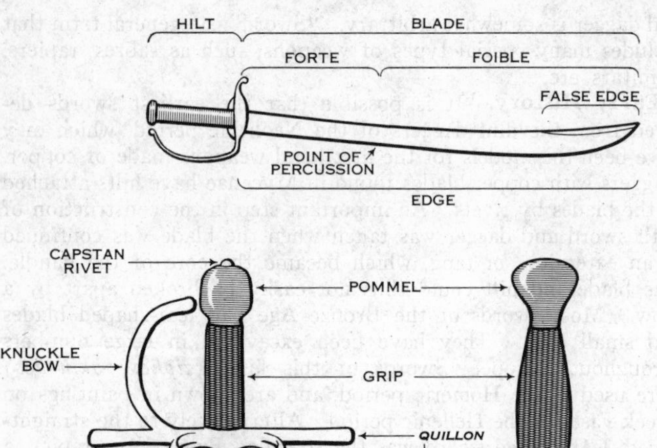


TECHNICAL NAMES OF THE PARTS OF A SWORD

where the craft was still active in the mid-20th century. Blades were exported from Solingen to all parts of Europe, often bearing the mark of a running wolf. Swords bearing distinctive names, denoting a common origin, were widely distributed in Europe, such as those inscribed Ulfbehrt and Ingelred. Other centres of the sword cutler's craft were places where the making of arms and armour in general had been established, notably in Milan in north Italy, and in the south German towns of Nürnberg and Augsburg. In Spain great skill was shown by the swordsmiths of Toledo. The names of many master craftsmen are known and are found engraved upon the blades themselves, which also carry the marks of the maker and often the city guild where they were proved.

In the late middle ages the knightly sword was sometimes lengthened, both in blade and hilt, and the latter so shaped that it could be grasped by both hands if necessary. In the 15th century the blades of straight-bladed swords were more usually double-edged and flat, sometimes stiffened by a sharp ridge down the centre. This was particularly the case in Italy. A purely thrusting sword, with a rigid blade, was known as an *estoc*. At the turn of the century the big two-handed sword had a short vogue, but the space needed to wield it tended to limit its advantages.

In order to have better control of the weapon, a custom developed of passing the right forefinger over the *quillon*. To protect it, a metal hook or ring was placed in front of the *quillon*. The next step was to place a corresponding half ring on the other side of the blade for the sake of symmetry. This development, nicknamed the *pas d'âne* from its resemblance to a cloven hoof mark, apparently developed first in Spain and then passed to Italy before the end of the 15th century. It is important as foreshadowing the development of the hilt whereby the hand was protected by a cagelike series of rings and bars forming part of the sword, instead of by a steel glove.

**The Later Sword.**—The sword underwent rapid changes in Europe during the first half of the 16th century, and proliferated in a variety of forms. These changes correspond with the period when defensive armour was beginning to fall into disuse, and special corps of soldiery were becoming components of national armies. The protection of the hand was carried a step farther by the provision of a knuckle bow; *i.e.*, a semicircular bar extending from the *quillon* toward the pommel. The next move was to add additional rings to guard the whole hand, both in the vertical and the horizontal planes. The old arming sword, which was wielded with a gauntleted hand, had been strictly cruciform. The 16th century saw the arrival of the rapier, with a long, narrow blade, and with the hand protected by a series of guards and counterguards.

The habit of carrying a sword with civilian dress had not been universal in the middle ages but it later became the custom for every gentleman to carry a rapier in civil life, and in consequence dueling increased. Previously, dueling had taken the form of judicial combats, conducted with strict formality. Dueling with a rapier rapidly encouraged the art of fencing. Schools conducted by masters of fence were set up to enable gentlemen to learn their skill at arms. The earliest known fencing book is a treatise, *Flos Duellatorum* or *Il Fior di Battaglia,* by Maestro Fiore dei Liberi (compiled in Italy in 1410). It demonstrated in a series of drawings combats with swords, sword and buckler, wrestling, etc. It was followed in the 15th century by a picture book by H. Talhofer, of which several manuscript versions exist. In the 16th century, books on fencing came from the printing presses, generally written by one of the masters of the schools of fencing, such as A. Marozzo and C. Agrippa in Italy, H. de St. Didier in France and George Silver, who was a stout defender of the rough-and-ready English fashion against his rival, "Signior" Rocco, an Italian who had set up his own school in London. The weapons used in dueling could be rapier and dagger (the latter held in the left hand and used for parrying), rapier and cloak, or two rapiers, but eventually fencing with the rapier or smallsword alone prevailed. At first both edge and point were used, but with the increase of manual dexterity it was found that the point, which allowed a long reach, was more effective by itself. The swordsman was liable to lay himself open when he used striking blows, so thrusting, parrying and feinting within a narrow compass became a practised art. (*See* also FENCING.)

The hilts of rapiers took many forms, often being richly decorated with gold and silver, damascening, enameling and even incrustation with jewels. Fine specimens are to be seen in the national armouries of Vienna, Madrid and Paris. Notable swordmakers were A. Piccinino of Milan, L. Palumbo of Naples, the Wundes family and Clemens Horn, among many, at Solingen, and Juan Martinez, Tomas de Ayala and Sebastian Hernandez at Toledo. The blades of most rapiers bear the signature of the maker, his town, and the stamp of the city guild, which is usually placed upon the *ricasso* (the base of the blade), which usually has a rectangular section. Many of these long, narrow, thrusting blades made in Germany were stamped with imitations of the ♀ stamp of Toledo. Blades of all kinds were made in Germany, inscribed with the names of swordsmiths who may be regarded as having specialized in blades of a certain kind, such as A. Sahagun and Andrea Ferrara. The last name is quite commonly found on the blades of broadswords of the 17th century and is

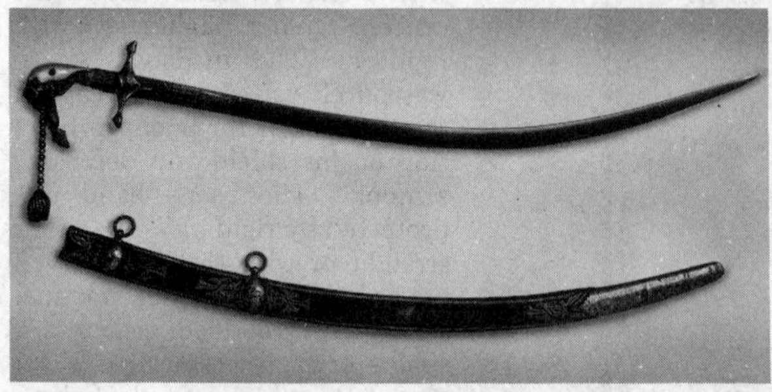

BY COURTESY OF: (ABOVE) THE TRUSTEES OF THE WALLACE COLLECTION; (RIGHT) THE IMPERIAL WAR MUSEUM

(Above) Persian scimitar and sheath with early-18th-century mounts and late-16th-century blade; (right) Gurkha kukris with sheaths and accompanying small blades: the kukri at right is an engraved presentation piece, given to Gen. Sir John Coleridge by officers of the Gurkha Rifles no indication of the actual maker. The blade is classified in two parts, the forte which is the anterior part, and the foible which is the forward part farthest from the hilt. In Spain a particularly elegant form of rapier hilt was developed in which the principal protection of the hand was a steel cup, often beautifully pierced with decorations. This developed at Toledo, but soon spread throughout much of western Europe. Generally speaking, those made in the south had deep cups while those produced in the Low Countries and England had shallower "dish" guards.

In the third quarter of the 17th century the rapier was reduced in size and simplified to what became known as the smallsword. This too was principally a civilian weapon, and the subject of much delicate and elaborate ornamentation. The blade of the smallsword was purely for thrusting, and usually had a hollow, triangular section. In other cases the blades were hexagonal, diamond-shaped or even elliptical in section.

New weapons produced their own writers on swordsmanship, notably the Scotsman, Sir William Hope, who wrote a number of manuals in the late 17th and early 18th centuries. H. Angelo's school of fencing in London is well known from his books illustrated by George Rowlandson.

Swords for specialized use and local types are legion, such as the straight broadsword with S-shaped *quillons* used by the German *Landsknechte* (professional infantry) in Germany and Switzerland in the 16th century. In the highlands of Scotland the two-handed sword lasted to the end of the 17th century in the form of the big *claidheammor* (great sword; whence "claymore") with drooping *quillons* ending in quatrefoils, and Scotland produced a characteristic variety of the basket-hilted broadsword.

The medieval arming sword had been replaced for war by the sword rapier, a heavier version of the civilian sword. Its successor was the cavalry broadsword, a simple and handy weapon on which the knuckles were protected by a single or basketlike guard, and the blade was flat and broad, sometimes double-edged and sometimes single, when it was called a backsword. Many broadswords of this type have come down from the time of the Civil War in England. Sometimes the solid guards of the hilts are chased with the heads of Charles I and his queen, and these are popularly called "mortuary" swords, referring to the execution of the king. The military form of the smallsword in the 18th century was more heavily built; further, it had a single knuckle bow and a pair of oval-shaped plaques in front of the *pas d'âne*.

**The Curved Sword and the East.**—The sabre is essentially a cutting weapon, with the blade sharpened on the convex edge only. It cuts well because only a small part of the arc first reaches the objective, and then bites into it.

Whereas the straight sword was the favourite in the west, the curved sword predominated in eastern Europe and Asia, although curved swords were not unknown in the west. In the middle ages there was the falchion, a sword with a cleaverlike blade, broadening toward the point and with a single curved cutting edge. That it was regarded as an oriental weapon is shown by the fact that in medieval manuscripts the sleeping guards at the Sepulchre are shown with falchions.

The Turkish invasion of Europe in the 16th century brought the west into close contact with the curved weapons of the east. The scimitar, which has a keen arc-shaped edge, derived from the Persian shamsheer. It was brought into Hungary and Poland, and western cavalry regiments in the late 18th and 19th centuries were armed with the curved sabre which derived directly from the east.

Turkish and Persian scimitars were often made with finely watered blades. These blades are often described as damascened, but Damascus was never a centre of the craft, only an entrepôt. Fine swords were made at Isfahan in Persia, at Constantinople, at Cairo under the Mamelukes and at Fez in north Africa. The north and middle European scimitar generally has a pistol-shape grip, which continues the curve of the blade in the opposite direction.

In India the scimitar is called a tulwar. Other Indian swords are the Maratha khanda and the gauntlet sword known as a pata, and in Burma the *dha*. The Gurkha kukri has a doubly curved blade, and can be used to decapitate an ox at one blow.

In Japan the sword has long been highly regarded. As early as the 13th–14th centuries great masters of the craft were making blades of remarkable quality, such as Yoshimitsu and Masamune. The possession of a sword is closely connected with the cult of ancestor worship, and swords were handed from one generation to another as objects of veneration. The Japanese sword has a long, slightly curved, single-edged blade and a two-handed grip in which the curve is extended in the same direction as that of the blade. The guards (tsubas), which are small and solid, are objects of special decoration; an owner might have as many as sixty different guards for his sword. Among the various kinds of Japanese swords are the *daisho*, a pair of swords, the larger being called a *katana* and the smaller a *wakizashi*. Swordsmanship was possibly an even greater cult in Japan than in the west, and expressed itself in formal and elaborate dueling.

**The Modern Sword.**—Since the middle of the 18th century the sabre has been predominant. Indeed, more than 80% of all European and American swords of the period fall within this category. The civilian small sword had virtually disappeared by 1800. Diplomats and some staff officers continued to wear small swords

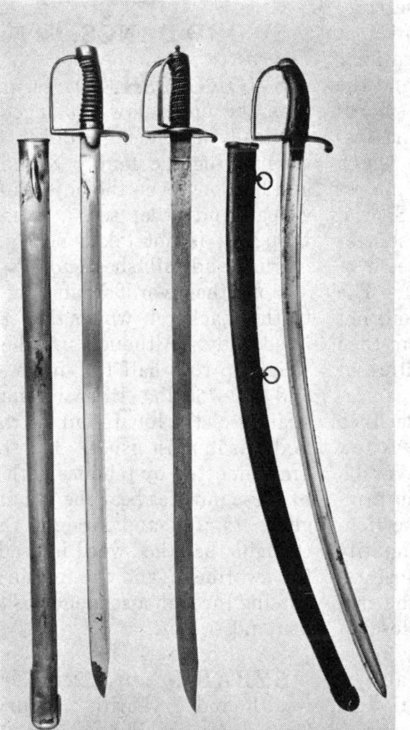

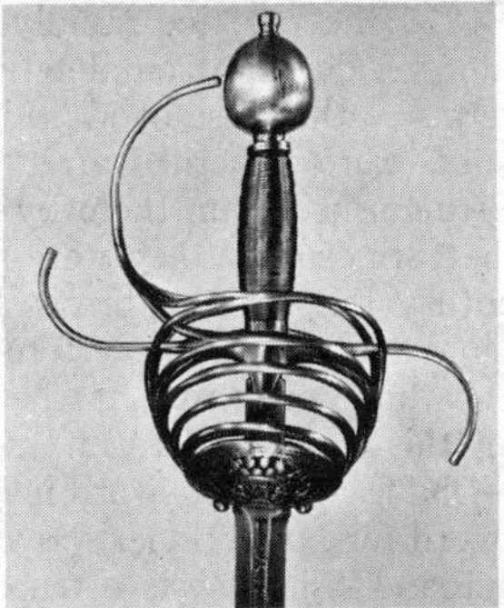

IN THE TOWER OF LONDON; BY COURTESY OF MINISTRY OF PUBLIC BUILDINGS AND WORKS

(Left) Three 19th-century English cavalry sabres: (top right) Spanish cup hilt rapier, mid-17th century, formerly in the collection of Frederick Augustus, duke of York (1763–1827); (centre) Italian rapier, late 16th century; (right) swept hilt rapier with Italian blade and, probably, German hilt, about 1590 of one type or another, but their numbers were few. Among the military sabres, those used by the cavalry were most important as weapons. The first sabres to be used by horsemen were usually straight or very slightly curved. Early in the 19th century the curve increased. Then, with the discovery that the point was used more often than the edge, the straight blade returned to favour. Another form of sabre, the naval cutlass, achieved its distinction during this era. It was a short weapon with a straight or slightly curved blade and a heavy guard suitable for fighting in close quarters and easily carried while climbing. It maintained its basic design until long-range naval actions of the twentieth century rendered it obsolete.

Officers and ranking noncommissioned officers of most arms and branches of service carried swords at some time during the 19th century. Indeed, the sword indicated rank and branch of service of the wearer. For this reason the swords of the last two hundred years are found in a greater variety of styles and forms than for any other comparable period.

As long as firearms were single-shot weapons and firepower was relatively low, the sword remained a vital weapon. During the American Revolution, cavalry leaders considered the sword the only true weapon of a trooper and scorned the use of firearms except for skirmish or picket duty. Infantry officers participated in charges with sword in hand or stood by with that weapon to help repel an enemy attack.

The adoption of repeating arms ended the sword's importance. As late as the U.S. Civil War cavalry still charged with sabre in hand, but the concept of the trooper as a mounted infantryman was developing. His revolver and his repeating carbine carried more weight than his sword. The last traditional cavalry charge by U.S. troops occurred on Luzon in 1906. There were some isolated actions by European cavalrymen during World War I and again on the eastern front in World War II, but these were anachronisms. The era of the sabre as a weapon had ended. As a symbol of rank and of arm of service, however, it is still in use, and it has been found to serve an important function from the standpoint of morale and the sense of tradition.

**Presentation and State Swords.**—A special category of swords comprises those used in state ceremonies and those presented to individuals as a mark of esteem or honour. The ceremonial or state swords have been used for many centuries at coronations, inaugurations and other solemn public occasions. Among them are the sword of justice, the sword of mercy and the sword of mourning. Usually they are huge two-handed swords richly mounted in precious metals, often set with gems, and frequently bearing the arms of the country, state or city to which they belong. Such swords have figured in the regalia of almost every European monarchy, and some are still in use. Special presentation swords or swords of honour have a much shorter history. The practice of giving a sword as a mark of esteem or as recognition for a heroic deed is as old as the sword itself. The manufacture of special swords for this purpose, however, did not achieve widespread popularity until the 18th century. From then until the third quarter of the 19th century huge quantities of them were made and presented by nations, states, cities, organizations and individuals. After 1875 the practice rapidly declined in popularity, although it has not yet died out completely. A few were presented to leading generals at the close of World War II. Usually these presentation swords were patterned after the principal swords of the day but distinguished from them by the richness of their mountings. In the 18th century they were primarily small swords; in the 19th century they were sabres. Most recently, however, there has been a tendency to revert to the medieval arming sword. Most of those presented at the close of World War II, in fact, were of this traditional form.

**The Headsman's Sword.**—One last class of sword may also be mentioned—the "heading" sword or executioner's sword. In many countries, both in Europe and Asia, it was often the practice to decapitate with the sword instead of the ax. Queen Anne Boleyn was beheaded with a sword at the Tower of London in 1536, and even in America at least one such execution is recorded in Massachusetts in 1644. In Asia the practice was still being used as late as World War II. The European "heading" sword traditionally had a long straight blade with a square "point." Asian swords tended to curved blades.

*See* also references under "Sword" in the Index.

BIBLIOGRAPHY.—*Prehistoric, Greek, Roman and Dark Ages:* J. Naue, *Die Vorrömischen Schwerter aus Kupfer, Bronze und Eisen* (1903); A. E. Remouchamps, *Griechische Dolch und Schwertformen* (1926); W. P. Brewis, "The Bronze Sword in England," *Archaeologia*, lxxiii (1924); P. Coussin, *Les Armes Romaines* (1926); W. Ginters, *Das Schwert der Scythen und Sarmaten* (1928); M. Jahn, *Die Bewaffnung der Germanen in der alteren Eisenzeit* (1916).

*Middle Ages and Renaissance:* J. Petersen, *De Norske Viking Sverd* (1919); G. F. Laking, *Record of European Armour and Arms through Seven Centuries,* 5 vol. (1920–23); E. de Beaumont, *La Fleur des Belles Epées* (1885); R. Forrer, *Die Schwerten und Schwertknaufe der Sammlung C. von Schwerzenbach* (1905); J. Schwietering, *Geschichte von Speer und Schwert im 12 Jahrhundert* (1912); A. Bruhn-Hoffmeyer, *Middelalderens Tveaeggede Svaerd,* i and ii (1954); R. E. Oakeshott, *The Archaeology of Weapons* (1960).

*17th–19th Centuries:* C. Welch, *History of the Cutlers' Company of London,* 2 vol. (1916, 1923); B. Dean, *Catalogue of European Court Swords and Hunting Swords* (1929); J. Drummond, *Ancient Scottish Weapons* (1881); J. D. Aylward, *The Smallsword in England* (1905); M. Bottet, *L'Arme Blanche de Guerre Française aux XVIII^e Siècle* (1910), *L'Arme Blanche des Armes Françaises 1789–1870, La Manufacture des Armes à Versailles* (1903); Z. Hartleb, *Szabla Polska* (1926); H. Seitz, *Svärdet och Värjan* (1955); C. J. ffoulkes, *Sword, Lance and Bayonet* (1938); H. T. Bosanquet, *The Naval Officer's Sword* (1955); War Office, *Text Book on Small Arms* (various dates); H. L. Peterson, *The American Sword, 1775–1945* (1954), *American Silver Mounted Swords 1700–1815* (1955).

*Oriental:* Lord Egerton of Tatton, *Indian and Oriental Armour,* 2nd ed. (1896); P. Holstein, *Armes Orientales* (1931); G. C. Stone, *A Glossary of . . . Arms and Armour* (1934); G. B. Gardner, *Keris and Other Malay Weapons* (1936); H. Joly and I. Hogitaro, *The Sword Book and the Same* (1913); Jungi Homma, *The Japanese Sword* (trans. 1939); Inami Hakusui, *Nippon-tô: the Japanese Sword* (1948); B. W. Robinson, *Primer of Japanese Sword Blades* (1956).

Information can be obtained from illustrated catalogues of public museums; *e.g.,* the Tower of London; Wallace Collection (3 parts, 1925–45); Victoria and Albert Museum; Metropolitan Museum, New York; Musée de l'Armée, Paris; Real Armeria, Madrid; Dresden (E. Haenel, *Kostbare Waffen*); Swiss National Museum, Zurich; Historical Museum, Bern; Waffensammlung, Vienna. *See* also articles on swords in *Zeitschrift für Historisches Waffenkunde* (1896–1945), and useful information in catalogues of auction sales of arms (full bibliography in the *Wallace Collection Catalogue of European Arms and Armour,* part iii, London, 1945). (J. G. MN.; HD. L. P.)

**SWORD DANCE:** *see* FOLK DANCE: *Ritual-Ceremonial Folk Dances.*

**SWORDFISH,** a large, dark-purplish fish of all warm seas, with the upper jaw prolonged far beyond the mouth to form a vertically flattened "sword." The single species, *Xiphias gladius,* constituting the family Xiphiidae, is a highly regarded foodfish, and has long been the object of commercial fishing in the Mediterranean and other seas. It is also highly prized as a gamefish, though it is not taken nearly so often by sportsmen as are the marlins and sailfishes (*qq.v.*).

Both the swordfish and the marlins are thought to be related to the mackerel, which they resemble in the beautifully streamlined body. Although swordfishes may grow to nearly 20 ft. and weigh up to a half ton, most specimens have a range of 6–10 ft. and 100–250 lb. In swimming, these fishes rely on the powerful beating of the lunate tail fin rather than on the undulations of the body, as in most fishes. The strong muscles of the very thick body are connected by tendons with the tail fin, so that the contractions of these muscles beat the tail fin back and forth while the stiff body glides rapidly and straight through the water. It is generally thought that the sword is used primarily to stun other fish, since the swordfish (and the marlin) swings its head back and forth in passing through a school of fish. The food consists chiefly of small fish and squids.

*See* also FISH. (C. L. HS.)

**SYBARIS,** an ancient Greek city in Italy, famous for the wealth and "sybaritic" luxury of its inhabitants, about whom largely apocryphal "Sybarite stories" of luxury and softness circulated in Greece for centuries. The city was situated on the Gulf of Tarentum, between the Crathis (Crati) and Sybaris (Coscile) rivers, which now meet about 4½ mi. (7 km.) inland but in ancient times may have had independent mouths. It was the oldest Greek colony in this region, founded about 720 B.C. by Achaeans and Troezenians. Placed in a very fertile area, and readily granting citizenship to new settlers, the city became great and rich, with a vast subject territory and daughter colonies even on the west coast, including Posidonia (Paestum) and Laus. The Sybarites were successful in a war against Siris, a few miles to the north. The rise of a tyrant, Telys, with popular support led to the exile and flight to Crotona of many members and supporters of the ousted oligarchy. War followed, and the victorious Crotoniates razed Sybaris and turned the waters of the Crathis over its ruins (510 B.C.).

The Sybarites fled to their colonies, but some apparently maintained their corporate identity in the early 5th century. In 452 they refounded Sybaris, but it was destroyed by the Crotoniates five years later. The Sybarites obtained Athenian support for a third foundation, but the Athenians soon expelled them from the city. They founded a fourth Sybaris farther south on the Traeis (Trionto) River, and the Athenians founded Thurii (*q.v.;* 444/443).

The modern place-name Sibari is only an approximation to the lost site of Sybaris. Some cemeteries, including the 4th-century Thurii cemetery, were uncovered in the 19th century. In 1949 the fourth Sybaris was identified at Castiglione di Paludi, where there are walls, tombs, and a Greek theatre; and in the 1960s geophysical prospecting and trial digging near the Crati located traces of 6th-century Greek occupation.

*See* T. J. Dunbabin, *The Western Greeks,* esp. ch. 2, 4, and 12 (1948); F. Rainey in *Illustrated London News* (Dec. 8 and 15, 1962).

**SYBEL, HEINRICH VON** (1817–1895), German historian and politician, a leading exponent of the Prussian, or political, school of historical writing, was born on Dec. 2, 1817, at Düsseldorf. While studying in Berlin (1834–38), he learned from Ranke (*q.v.*) the critical method of evaluating historical sources, and his first book, *Geschichte des ersten Kreuzzugs* (1841; Eng. trans. 1861) is among the most distinguished products of the Ranke school. His study of German kingship, *Entstehung des deutschen Königtums* (1844), belongs to the same group.

Sybel's political interests soon separated him, at least academically, from Ranke, whose detachment he grew to despise as soulless respectability. He held professorial chairs at Marburg (1846), Munich (1856), and Bonn (1861), saying of himself that he was four-sevenths politician and three-sevenths professor, and he came to believe passionately in the historian's vocation as teacher. His involvement in contemporary politics was consistent with these views. He sat in the Hessian Landtag (1848), the Erfurt Parliament (1850), the Prussian Landtag (1862–64; 1874–80), and the Prussian Constituent Assembly of 1867. A believer in Prussia's mission to lead Germany toward unification, he was an enemy of ultramontanism and feudalism; he rejected medieval imperial policy (*see* the pronouncements in his controversy with J. Fricker, ed. by F. Schneider, 1941). Until the war of 1866 Sybel opposed Bismarck over finance and the Polish and Danish questions. He later withdrew his opposition and as a National Liberal in the Constituent Assembly supported Bismarck in the *Kulturkampf.*

Sybel's political views are clear from his later books. His greatest work, *Geschichte der Revolutionszeit von 1789 bis 1795 (1789 bis 1800)* (5 vol., 1853–79), which was particularly valuable for its connection of French domestic events with the wider European scene, showed vigorous opposition to revolutionary ideals. A constant adversary of radicalism, he preferred a moderate degree of self-government combined with individual freedom. His last work, *Die Begründung des deutschen Reiches durch Wilhelm I.* (7 vol., 1889–94), for which Bismarck opened the state archives, is the first detailed account of the subject. It is somewhat marred, however, by a disregard of internal affairs and by excessive Prussianism.

In forming the *Historische Zeitschrift* in 1859 in Munich, Sybel provided the model for many other periodicals. In 1875 Bismarck appointed him director of the Prussian archives, and he began a great series of publications. Some of his articles and addresses have been collected in *Vorträge und Abhandlungen* (1897), which also contains a biography by C. Varrentrapp and a bibliography of Sybel's works. He died at Marburg on Aug. 1, 1895.

*See* G. P. Gooch, *History and Historians in the Nineteenth Century,* 2nd ed. (1952); H. Seier, "Die Staatsidee Heinrich von Sybels in den Wandlungen der Reichsgründungszeit 1862–71," *Historische Studien,* Heft 383 (1961).

**SYCAMORE,** the name applied to American species of plane trees (*Platanus*) and to a European species of maple (*q.v.*). The distinctive eastern sycamore (*P. occidentalis*), also known in certain localities as buttonwood or American plane, is probably the largest hardwood species in the eastern United States. Best development is attained on rich alluvial bottomlands, where it often reaches a height of 150 ft. and a diameter of 8 to 12 ft. It is occasionally found in pure groves, but is much more common as an occasional tree in association with other bottomland hardwood species such as river birch, red and silver maples, American elm, cottonwood, and willows. Sycamore features large, simple, shallowly three- to seven-palmately-lobed leaves, each with a long petiole or leafstalk swollen at the base and enclosing next year's bud. A pair of large leafy outgrowths or stipules at each node is another conspicuous feature.

The flowers are unisexual. Both sexes are borne in separate, solitary heads that appear in advance of the leaves. The fruit is a multiple head of obovoid achenes, each furnished at the base with a fringe of brown silken hairs.

Winter characters are also distinctive. The stout, brown, conspicuously zigzag twigs feature alternately disposed conical buds that are capped with a single scale and nearly surrounded by a leaf scar. Above each leaf scar is a prominent stipule scar which

(TOP) RUTHERFORD PLATT, (BOTTOM LEFT) J. HORACE MCFARLAND CO., (BOTTOM RIGHT) ROCHE

**SYCAMORE (PLATANUS OCCIDENTALIS) SHOWING (TOP) THE BROWN, OUTER LAYERS OF BARK WITH THE WHITE LAYERS BENEATH THEM, (BOTTOM LEFT) A LEAF AND (BOTTOM RIGHT) STAMINATE FLOWERS**

encircles the twig. The bark on small branches is creamy white; that on larger limbs and the trunk (except near the base of large trees) is characterized by the annual exfoliation of the brown outer layers to expose the lighter yellowish to white layers immediately below.

The Arizona sycamore (*P. wrightii*) is one of the most abundant hardwoods of southwestern United States. The tree features deeply five- to seven-lobed leaves and the multiple heads of achenes are borne in racemose clusters of from two to four. The California sycamore, *P. racemosa*, a medium-sized tree of the coast ranges and lower Sierra Nevada Mountains of California, features three- to five-lobed leaves, and fruit in racemose clusters of two to seven.

*See* also PLANE. (E. S. HR.; X.)

**SYDENHAM, THOMAS** (1624–1689), English physician who revolutionized clinical medicine by basing his treatment of diseases on detailed observations of the patients rather than upon Galenic dogma or other speculative hypotheses, was born at Wynford Eagle, Dorset, on Sept. 10, 1624. He entered Magdalen Hall, Oxford, in 1642 but left to serve the Parliamentary cause in the Civil War and did not graduate in medicine until 1648. He was elected a fellow of All Souls College the same year, but his studies were interrupted by the landing of Prince Charles in Scotland; in the subsequent campaign he was wounded while serving as a cavalry officer. He began to practise in Westminster, where he made the detailed study of London epidemics that formed the basis of his first book on the treatment of fevers (1666). Sydenham's book was greatly admired by John Locke, who (with John Mapletoft, professor of physic at Gresham College, London) helped him expand it into his major work, *Observationes medicae* (1676), which remained a standard medical textbook for two centuries.

Sydenham introduced tincture of laudanum (opium) into medical practice, was one of the first to use iron in the treatment of anemia, and helped popularize the use of quinine in the treatment of malaria. His most important therapeutic success was his management of smallpox by means of a cooling regimen quite contrary to the prevailing view. He was the first to describe scarlet fever and to explain the nature of hysteria and St. Vitus' dance (Sydenham's chorea). Among his clinical pupils were Thomas Dover, known for his powders, and Sir Hans Sloane, founder of the British Museum. Sydenham was a practical man with only a brief period of formal training, whereas most contemporary physicians were men of books. He was never elected to a fellowship of the Royal College of Physicians, as his views were regarded as unorthodox. He died in London on Dec. 29, 1689.

*See* J. F. Payne, *Thomas Sydenham* (1900); K. Dewhurst, *Dr. Thomas Sydenham* (1966). (K. DE.)

**SYDENHAM,** a residential area almost wholly in the borough of Lewisham (*q.v.*) but also extending into the Camberwell district of Southwark (*q.v.*), London, Eng. Its development dates from the reerection there (1854) of the Crystal Palace (burned down 1936); the first national recreation centre, built on the site with a main stadium and facilities for indoor sports, was opened in 1964. Sydenham Wells Park contains the site of medicinal springs popular in the 17th and 18th centuries. Former residents included the actress Sarah Siddons, the poet Thomas Campbell, and the colour printer George Baxter.

**SYDNEY,** the largest city of Australia and the capital, chief port, and industrial centre of the state of New South Wales, lies around the shores of Port Jackson in the southeastern part of the continent, on the eastern rim of a saucer-shaped depression known as the Cumberland or Sydney Basin. Pop. (1961 census): city, 172,202; metropolitan area, 2,183,388, an increase of 320,227 over the 1954 census. The Sydney coastline consists of a series of bold, scrub-covered headlands, alternating with crescent-shaped beaches. Other features of the coast include rock platforms, chains of shallow coastal lagoons, and sandpits and tombolos. The city has a temperate climate with a mean annual temperature of 17.6° C (64° F) and an annual average rainfall of 45 in. (1,140 mm.). More than 2,400 hours of sunshine are recorded annually; frosts are rare on the coast but may be severe inland. The prevailing winds are from the west and the northeast.

The excessive concentration of population around a few large cities is part of the overall population pattern of Australia. In the case of Sydney this concentration was due to the city's importance as the first settlement, and its consequent early development of harbour and storage facilities. As the main port Sydney naturally became the centre of government and also of the country's economic organization. Sydney proper lies on the southern shore of the harbour, and it is in that direction that the main commercial and industrial part of the city is to be found. Most of the city is hilly, the gradients, particularly in the harbourside suburbs, being short but steep. In the 1960s Sydney was growing rapidly both in area and population. Metropolitan Sydney covered an area of 671 sq.mi. (1,738 sq.km.). A notable feature of its continued outward sprawl was a shift of population, manufacturing, and retailing from the inner city to the suburbs.

Among Sydney's many fine buildings are the Town Hall (1889) on George Street, which houses the council chambers and a concert and assembly hall, and next to it St. Andrew's Cathedral (1888), whose original foundation stone was laid in 1819. Other notable churches are the Roman Catholic Cathedral—St. Mary's Basilica (1868)—and St. James' Church, the oldest church of any importance in the city. Opposite St. James' Church stands the Hyde Park Barracks, a fine example of Georgian architecture and a reminder of the city's origins, now used as a law court. The Old Mint Building (1811) is now also serving as a law court. The Australian Museum (1836) specializes in natural history, and the Public Library of New South Wales (1942) has a rich collection of books and manuscripts dealing with Australia, New Zealand, and the South Pacific. Other notable buildings and monuments include the State Parliament House (1811–17), the University of Sydney (1850), Captain Cook's Monument (1870), Macquarie Place, Vaucluse House (*c.* 1802–03), and the Sydney Hospital. The Sydney Harbour Bridge (1932), one of the largest steel-arch bridges in the world, has a central span 1,650 ft. (503 m.) long, which carries one footpath, eight lanes for motor vehicles, one bicycle track, and two lines of rail tracks. In 1964 the Gladesville Bridge, said to be the longest concrete-arch span bridge in the world, was opened. During the 1960s Sydney's skyline was changing rapidly as older structures were demolished and tall new office buildings took their place. A notable addition to the city's architectural achievements was the Opera House, which was under construction in the mid-1960s.

The inner city contains more than 830 ac. (335 ha.) of parklands. The largest parks are Centennial Park on the eastern boundary; Moore Park; Hyde Park, the site of the Archibald Memorial Fountain and the Anzac Memorial; the Domain, which houses the National Art Gallery (1871); and the Botanic Gardens, with a large collection of plants. To the west of the Botanic Gardens stands Government House (1837–45), the residence of the governor of New South Wales, and at the northern entrance to the gardens is the State Conservatorium of Music, designed by Francis Greenway in 1819. On the northern side of the harbour is the Taronga Zoological Park and Aquarium. Koala Park at West Pennant Hills, about 20 mi. from the city centre, is a wildlife sanctuary and a biological research station. In the suburbs there are more than 14,000 ac. (5,700 ha.) of parkland and two national reserves: Kuring-gai Chase (40,000 ac. [16,000 ha.]) to the north and the Royal National Park (36,900 ac. [14,900 ha.]) to the south.

The city is a great recreation centre; facilities are available for most varieties of sports, particularly outdoor games, and Sydney's fine playing fields include the cricket ground and the sports ground, lying to the southeast of the city centre. The magnificent ocean beaches (notably Bondi Beach) provide opportunities for swimming and surfing. There are also several swimming pools, notably at Victoria Park and Prince Alfred Park, and the Olympic Pool in north Sydney has a spectator capacity of 4,000. Amateur and professional musical theatrical groups flourish, including the Elizabethan Theatre Trust, a state-sponsored body that presents important works in all branches of entertainment. Each spring, during the first week of October, Sydney celebrates the "Waratah Spring Festival" with carnivals, parades, open-air concerts, operas, and dancing, which culminate in a grand procession of floats to honour the festival queen. Sydney is particularly noted for its many Asian restaurants.

There are many public and private hospitals, including four large teaching hospitals. The City Council, which administers an area of 11 sq.mi., meets once every two weeks and maintains four standing committees: finance, works, health and recreations, and city planning and improvements. Transport is provided by government-owned buses, trains, and ferries, and a few privately operated buses and ferries. Sydney has 156 route miles of electrified track, and the Central Railway Station (1906) coordinates the movements of more than 1,150 trains daily. There are about 6,700 mi. (10,780 km.) of streets in the metropolitan area, and four major roads link Sydney with Melbourne, Brisbane, and Bathurst. In the 1960s work was proceeding on multi-lane roads to facilitate the flow of traffic between the city and suburbs. Kingsford Smith Airport can accommodate the latest jet aircraft. The Australian Broadcasting Commission maintains one television and two radio stations in Sydney, and there are three television stations and six radio stations operated commercially.

The port of Sydney (Port Jackson) averages about 1 mi. in width and has a total area of 21 sq.mi. (54 sq.km.). The shoreline extends for more than 150 mi. (240 km.), and its 12 mi. of docks and 200 wharves handle a large proportion of the trade of New South Wales. The main exports are wool, wheat and flour, sheepskins, and frozen and preserved meats. The chief import from overseas is liquid fuels; inter- and intrastate imports include coal, timber, and sugar. Sydney is the largest primary wool market in the world, and about two-thirds of all wool sold in New South Wales is shipped through the city. The port is also a shipbuilding and repair centre, and the Captain Cook Graving Dock (1945) can accommodate large vessels.

Sydney's industrial supremacy in Australia is due partly to its accessibility to raw materials. The city accounts for about half of the factory output of New South Wales, mainly consumer goods, but there are also important industries associated with sawmilling, shipbuilding, engineering, chemicals, agricultural and earth-moving equipment, electrical equipment, and oil refining. In the mid-1960s Sydney had more than 15,000 factories, employing about 350,000; annual value of production was nearly £A800,000,000.

Port Jackson was first sighted by Capt. James Cook in 1770, and on Jan. 20, 1788, Gov. Arthur Phillip chose "the head of the cove, near the run of fresh water" as the site of the first Australian settlement. Phillip had originally intended to call the new settlement "Albion," but instead the name "Sydney" (from Sydney Cove) came into general use. Sydney Cove had been named by Capt. Cook after his benefactor Thomas Townshend, 1st Viscount Sydney. The population during the town's first years was just over 1,000, mostly convicts who were unskilled in the trades needed to establish a permanent settlement. In 1833 the administration of the town was put in the hands of three magistrates, and in 1842 it received a municipal council and became a self-governing corporation. Between 1830 and 1840, as the influx of convicts dwindled, the commercial life of Sydney developed. Secondary industries, limited at first to brickmaking and sawmilling, developed slowly, for the state policy of free trade discouraged the establishment of local industries. After federation (1901) the free trade policy was rejected, and the closer association between the states led to a rapid upsurge of interstate trade. World Wars I and II, which occasioned great industrial expansion, firmly established Sydney's preeminence in production.

Until 1820 Sydney covered only about one square mile, but the discovery of gold in New South Wales and Victoria boosted the population enormously. It rose from 10,815 in 1828 to 95,789 in 1861, to 383,333 in 1891, and to 1,235,267 in 1933. In 1901 Sydney was formally elevated to the rank of a city, the use of the title of lord mayor being created the following year. In 1948 the Sydney Corporation Act was repealed, and the city became subject to the control of the Department of Local Government, while still maintaining autonomy in government through its permanent administrative staff and elective council.

BIBLIOGRAPHY.—T. G. Taylor, *Sydneyside Scenery and How It Came About* (1958); Marjorie Barnard, *Sydney: the Story of a City* (1956); Council of the City of Sydney, *Sydney: Official Guide* (1958), *Facts About Sydney* (1959). (L. G. N.)

**SYDNEY,** a city of Nova Scotia, Can., is the commercial and industrial centre of Cape Breton County. Founded by Joseph Frederick Wallet des Barres in 1783 as a haven for United Empire Loyalists, and named after the colonial secretary, it was the capital of Cape Breton Island until 1820 when the island was united with Nova Scotia. The population was increased during the early 19th century by the immigration of Scottish Highlanders and later by the erection of a major steel plant. Sydney is a divisional terminus of the Canadian National Railways, and on the south arm of its harbour are excellent facilities for oceangoing vessels. It is the centre of a large coal-mining district with an urban population near 100,000. Glace Bay (*q.v.*), 14 mi. (23 km.) E, New Waterford, 14 mi. NE, and Sydney Mines on the north side of the harbour are the major mining centres. North Sydney, on the northwest arm of the harbour, is the terminus of the ferry to Port aux Basques, Nfd. Xavier Junior College (1952) is an affiliate of St. Francis Xavier University, Antigonish. Across the south arm of the harbour is an industrial park on the site of old Point Edward Naval Base. Pop. (1966) 32,767. (C. W. Rd.)

**SYENITE,** in petrology, the group name for a class of plutonic rocks composed essentially of an alkali feldspar and a ferromagnesian mineral. A special group of alkali syenites is characterized by the presence of a feldspathoid mineral (nephelite, or nepheline, leucite, analcite or sodalite).

The name was first used by Pliny for the rock occurring at Syene (Aswan) on the Nile River in Upper Egypt. This rock, extensively worked in ancient times for monumental structures, is a hornblende-granite with abundant quartz. A. G. Werner subsequently adopted the name for the class of rocks defined above, of which the type example is the hornblende-syenite of the Plauen'scher Grund, near Dresden, Ger. As essential constituents there occur soda orthoclase and green hornblende with subordinate amounts of oligoclase feldspar.

The texture of syenites is granular like that of the granites. Mineralogically these rocks differ from granites only by the absence or scarcity of quartz. The alkali feldspars include orthoclase, perthite, or albite, more rarely microcline, while the ferromagnesian mineral may be biotite, hornblende, or pyroxene. In the alkali syenites, the amphiboles or pyroxenes are frequently soda-bearing varieties. The more normal syenites are divisible into augite-, hornblende-, and biotite-syenites according to their prevalent dark-coloured mineral, but syenites are also divisible, as in the case of granites, into potash and soda syenites, according to the type of alkali feldspar. The accessory constituents include sphene, apatite, zircon, magnetite, and pyrites. Syenites are by no means common and are not of equal importance with granites and diorites from a geological standpoint.

Among the potash syenites are classed the original hornblende-syenite (Plauen) and the hornblende-syenite of Biella, Piedmont, Italy, of which analyses are given below.

The rocks known as nordmarkite and pulaskite are classed among the soda syenites. Nordmarkite originally described from the Oslo region (Norway) is built up of pink microperthite and subordinate aegirite and arfvedsonite together with some quartz, while the pulaskite syenites, first described from the Fourche Mountains, Ark., consist of soda orthoclase and alkali hornblende together with some biotite. Rocks transitional between syenites and diorites are known as monzonites.

The following analyses show the chemical composition of a few of the principal types of syenite. They are characterized by a

| | $SiO_2$ | $Al_2O_3$ | $Fe_2O_3$ | FeO | MgO | CaO | $Na_2O$ | $K_2O$ |
|---|---|---|---|---|---|---|---|---|
| 1 | 60.52 | 16.65 | 2.97 | 2.15 | 2.32 | 4.73 | 4.43 | 4.39 |
| 2 | 59.37 | 17.92 | 6.77 | 2.02 | 1.83 | 4.16 | 1.24 | 6.68 |
| 3 | 59.88 | 17.87 | 2.67 | 1.50 | 1.04 | 2.01 | 7.96 | 5.69 |
| 4 | 58.97 | 16.33 | 2.72 | 4.14 | 2.72 | 4.29 | 4.10 | 4.54 |

1. Hornblende-syenite, Plauen'scher Grund, Dresden, Ger.
2. Hornblende-syenite, Biella, Piedmont, Italy.
3. Nordmarkite, Oslo, Nor.
4. Syenite (mean of 12 analyses).

moderate amount of silica, relatively high alkalis, and alumina; while lime and magnesia are more variable but never in great amount. (C. E. T.)

**SYKES, SIR MARK,** 6TH BARONET (1879–1919), British traveler and politician, who represented the British government in the so-called Sykes-Picot negotiations (1915–16) between Great Britain and France, was born in London on March 16, 1879, the only son of Sir Tatton Sykes, 5th baronet. He was educated at Beaumont College and abroad, and at Jesus College, Cambridge. After serving in the South African War (1899–1902), he was secretary (1904–05) to George Wyndham, chief secretary in Ireland, and from 1904 to 1913 traveled extensively in Asiatic Turkey. He published vivid and valuable accounts of his travels in *Through Five Turkish Provinces* (1900), *Dar-ul-Islam* (1904), *Five Mansions of the House of Othman* (1909), and *The Caliph's Last Heritage* (1915). He was elected as member of Parliament for Central Hull, Yorkshire, in 1911 and succeeded as 6th baronet in 1913.

In 1914, just before the outbreak of World War I, he raised a battalion of the Yorkshire Regiment but did not accompany it to France; instead he was used on brief diplomatic missions in the Balkans and Turkey. Between 1915 and 1916 he was the chief British representative in the Sykes-Picot negotiations between France (represented by F. Georges Picot) and Great Britain to settle a basis of agreement on their claims, which were to be made good after the war, to those territories they hoped to detach from the Ottoman Empire. The resulting agreement, signed in May 1916 by Britain, France, and Russia (which was party to the talks), provided for the division of the area then covered by Syria and Iraq into spheres of French and British influence, and even direct administration, leaving Palestine to be subject to international control. These arrangements, which were secret, were publicized by the revolutionary Russian government in 1917; they were subsequently condemned by the Arabs and their supporters as improper, and inconsistent with promises of postwar independence made to the Arabs. The agreement, which Sykes later regretted, and in which his personal part is uncertain, never came into force.

Sykes remained active in Near Eastern missions for the Foreign Office between 1916 and 1918, and he keenly supported the movement for Arab freedom with which the agreement bearing his name had dealt so harshly. He revisited Syria in 1918, working (largely in vain) to smooth Anglo-French relations. He died suddenly in Paris on Feb. 16, 1919.

BIBLIOGRAPHY.—S. Leslie, *Mark Sykes: His Life and Letters* (1923); for the Sykes-Picot agreement *see* G. Antonius, *The Arab Awakening* (1938); S. H. Longrigg, *Syria and Lebanon Under French Mandate* (1958). (S. H. Lo.)

**SYLHET,** a town in the Chittagong division of East Pakistan and the headquarters of the district of the same name, lies on the right bank of the Surma River, 123 mi. (198 km.) NE of Dacca. Pop. (1961) 37,740. The town has three degree colleges affiliated to Dacca University. It is well known for its cane industry, and there are many tea factories. It has long been a centre of Islamic culture, and many holy men are buried there.

SYLHET DISTRICT has an area of 4,785 sq.mi. (12,393 sq.km.). Pop. (1961) 3,489,589. It comprises five-sixths of the former British Indian district of the same name, which formed part of Assam until the partition of India in 1947. It consists of the lower valley of the Surma River and is for the most part a uniform, well-cultivated plain, broken only by scattered clusters of sandy hillocks and intersected by a network of rivers and drainage canals. The low-lying swamps are a special feature of the district. Rainfall is heavy, reaching an annual average of 159 in. (4,040 mm.), of which more than 100 in. (2,540 mm.) fall between June and October. Rice is the chief crop. Tea cultivation flourishes in the southeastern hills. Lime is extensively quarried; other industries are boat building and the manufacture of fine reed mats, buttons from freshwater shells, ironwork inlaid with brass, and perfume. Search for oil in East Pakistan resulted in the discovery in 1955 of a gas field at Haripur, near Sylhet, that has estimated reserves of 280,000,000,000 cu.ft. More gas fields were subsequently discovered at Chhatak (1959), Rashidpur (1960), Kailas Tila (1962), and Habiganj (1963). (K. S. AD.)

**SYLLOGISM,** a two-premiss argument of any of several rather simple types distinguished by Aristotle or by those who followed in his tradition. Syllogisms are usually classified as categorical, hypothetical or disjunctive, depending upon the nature of their premisses. A categorical syllogism consists of three categorical statements (*i.e.*, statements of the forms "All *S* is *P*," "No *S* is *P*," "Some *S* is *P*," or "Some *S* is not *P*") which contain a total of at most three terms among them, each term occurring in at least two of the statements. A typical example would be:

No matadors are pirates.
Some Spaniards are matadors.
Therefore, some Spaniards are not pirates.

which is of the form (or mood) called *Ferio*:

No *M* is *P*.
Some *S* is *M*.
Therefore, some *S* is not *P*.

In the hypothetical syllogism one or both of the premisses are hypothetical in form (*i.e.*, have the form "If *p* then *q*"). Thus

If *p* then *q*.
If *q* then *r*.
Therefore, if *p* then *r*.

is one of the valid moods of the hypothetical syllogism. Similarly, a syllogism is disjunctive if one of its premisses is a disjunction. For example, every argument of the form:

Either *p* or *q*.
Not *p*.
Therefore, *q*.

is a valid disjunctive syllogism.

The term *syllogismos* ("syllogism") was used by Plato and occasionally by Aristotle simply with the sense of "argument." To this effect the latter gave his famous definition: "A syllogism is a discourse in which, certain things being posited, something else follows from them by necessity." In most cases, however, Aristotle used the term technically for the categorical syllogism. Later the meaning was extended by the Peripatetics to include hypothetical and disjunctive syllogisms. In Stoic usage the adjective *syllogisticos* ("syllogistic") was applied to any arguments of their five basic types.

*See* LOGIC and LOGIC, HISTORY OF. (B. Ms.)

**SYLT,** the largest and northernmost North Sea island of the German North Frisian group. Area 36 sq.mi. (93 sq.km.). Pop. (1961) 17,582. In the central section of the smooth west coast, cliffs of soft red sandstone rise to 135 ft. (41 m.). In the south the island is often only half a mile wide, but in the centre a beak-like peninsula extends 7 mi. (11 km.) E toward the Schleswig-Holstein coast. Road and rail connection with the mainland is carried by the Hindenburgdamm (causeway) for 7 mi. across the shallow tidal flats. There are a few small farmers, with dairy cattle and sheep, and scattered villages, such as Keitum; the principal settlement is the holiday resort of Westerland. (HA. T.)

**SYLVESTER, JAMES JOSEPH** (1814–1897), English mathematician who with his contemporary, Arthur Cayley (*q.v.*), founded the theory of algebraic invariants, was born in London on Sept. 3, 1814. In 1831 he entered St. John's college, Cambridge, where he gained high honours. In 1838 he was appointed professor of natural philosophy at University college, London. In 1841 he accepted the professorship of mathematics at the University of Virginia, but resigned after several months. Sylvester returned to London in 1845 where he obtained employment in actuarial work and took private pupils, one of whom was Florence Nightingale. In 1846 he entered the Inner Temple and in 1850 was called to the bar. About this time Sylvester and Cayley began an enthusiastic and profitable mathematical partnership. From 1855 to 1870 he was professor of mathematics at the Royal Military academy, Woolwich. It was not until 1876 that Sylvester got the first opportunity of his life commensurate with his talents, when he was appointed professor of mathematics at Johns Hopkins university, Baltimore, Md. In 1883 he returned to England to succeed Henry J. S. Smith as professor of geometry at Oxford. He died in London, March 15, 1897.

Sylvester was primarily an algebraist. With Cayley, he created the theory of algebraic forms. In the theory of numbers he did brilliant work, particularly in partitions and diophantine analysis. He worked by inspiration, and frequently it is difficult to detect a proof in what he confidently asserted. All his work is characterized by powerful imagination and inventiveness. While at Johns Hopkins, Sylvester founded (1878) the *American Journal of Mathematics*. *See* also MATRIX.

*See* E. T. Bell, *Men of Mathematics* (1937), "Invariant Twins, Cayley and Sylvester," in *The World of Mathematics,* ed. by J. R. Newman, vol. 1 (1956, 1962). (E. T. B.; X.)

**SYLVESTER, JOSUAH** (1563–1618), English poet-translator, best known as a translator of a popular biblical epic, was born in Kent and died on Sept. 28, 1618, at Middelburg in the Low Countries, where as secretary to the Merchant Adventurers he wound up a varied career. His chief production, the *Divine Weeks and Works,* translated from the French Protestant poet Guillaume du Bartas (1544–90), appeared in sections in 1592 and complete in 1608. This epic on the Creation, the fall of man, and other early parts of Genesis had high prestige in Europe generally and, in Sylvester's translation, was extremely popular in England in the first half of the 17th century. Its appeal was in its biblical matter, its reassuringly orthodox treatment of religion, nature as God's handiwork, science and cosmology, and in the grandiose, picturesque vigour of the writing—a quality only heightened in Sylvester's frequent extravagance of phrase, which Dryden, a youthful admirer, came to regard as "abominable fustian." Sylvester had some small influence on Milton and also had a share in the early development of the heroic couplet and the "poetic diction" which the Augustans were to refine.

The *Complete Works of Josuah Sylvester* were edited by A. B. Grosart in 2 vol. (1880).

BIBLIOGRAPHY.—P. Weller, *Joshuah Sylvesters englische Übersetzungen der religiösen Epen des Du Bartas* (1902); H. Ashton, *Du Bartas en Angleterre* (1908); A. H. Upham, *The French Influence in English Literature* (1908); G. C. Taylor, *Milton's Use of Du Bartas* (1934); G. Tillotson, *On the Poetry of Pope* (1938); J. Arthos, *The Language of Natural Description in Eighteenth-Century Poetry* (1949); V. L. Simonsen, "Josuah Sylvester's English Translation of Du Bartas' *La Première Semaine,*" *Orbis Litterarum,* viii, pp. 259–285 (1950).
(D. BH.)

**SYLVITE,** a mineral consisting of potassium chloride and the chief commercial source of potassium compounds, was first observed in 1823 as an incrustation on Vesuvius lava. Well-formed crystals were subsequently found in the salt deposits of Stassfurt, Ger., and Kaluszyn, Pol. It also occurs in the southern Harz region of Germany, in the nitrate deposits of Chile and Peru, and in the Permian salt basin of southeastern New Mexico and adjoining parts of Texas. Sylvite crystallizes in the cubic system with the form of cubes and cubo-octahedra and possesses perfect cleavages parallel to the faces of the cube. The composition is KCl and the crystal structure is similar to that of rock salt, NaCl. Crystals are colourless (sometimes bright blue) and transparent; the hardness is 2; specific gravity 1.99. Like salt, it is highly transparent to heat waves. The name sylvite is from the old pharmaceutical name, *sal digestivus sylvii.* (CL. F.; X.)

**SYLVIUS, FRANCISCUS** (FRANZ DE LE BOË, or DU BOIS) (1614–1672), German physician and anatomist, called the true founder of the iatrochemical school (*see* IATROCHEMISTRY), was born in Hanau on March 15, 1614. He studied at various universities, acquired a degree from Basel and became professor at the University of Leiden (1658), where his enthusiasm and original ideas attracted numerous students. An instance of pedagogical novelty, although not originality, was Sylvius' introduction of ward instruction in medical education.

Sylvius based his medical system upon such then recent developments in anatomy and physiology as the circulation of the blood and the recognition of the lymphatics, although still within the general framework of Galen's humoural physiology. At the same time, like his predecessor, J. B. van Helmont (*q.v.*), but omitting the mystical element so strong in the latter, he emphasized the chemical aspects of physiology. His study of salts led him to the belief that they were the result of the interaction of acids and bases, and he recognized their existence in living matter in his *Praxeos medicae idea nova* (1671–74).

According to Sylvius, digestion is a process of fermentation in which the saliva and pancreatic juice play the chief roles, the former determining digestion in the stomach and the latter directing the course of the digested food into blood or feces. The most important processes of normal and pathological life take place in the blood, and diseases are explained and treated chemically, the indications for treatment being based upon the presumed relationship between disease and drug.

In other aspects of medicine Sylvius distinguished between conglomerate and conglobate glands, and it is his name that is associated with the Sylvian aqueduct and Sylvian fissure, described in his *De spirituum animalium in cerebro cerebelloque confectione* (1660), although these structures appear to have been noted earlier by others. He also made some contribution to pediatrics through his posthumous *De morbis infantium* (1674), which, translated into English in 1682, gained favour perhaps more through its author's academic stature than through any singular importance of the contents.

Sylvius died in Leiden on Nov. 15, 1672.

BIBLIOGRAPHY.—M. Foster, *Lectures on the History of Physiology During the Sixteenth, Seventeenth and Eighteenth Centuries* (1924); S. E. Jelliffe, "Franciscus Sylvius," *Proceedings of the Charaka Club,* vol. iii (1910); K. E. Rothschuh, *Geschichte der Physiologie* (1953).
(C. D. O'M.)

**SYMBIOSIS** is the general term for the partnerships of dissimilar organisms; it denotes simply the living together of different kinds of organisms. Three major types of symbiosis may be recognized: (1) commensalism, in which food or space may be shared without evident benefit or harm to either organism or in which the benefit relation is one-sided, but without harm to the host; (2) mutualism, in which both host and guest (or the two partners) are obviously or apparently benefited; and (3) parasitism, in which the host is subject to varying degrees of injury while the parasite benefits. The term symbiosis has been widely used in the restricted sense of mutualism. The broader definition corresponds both to the original definition of symbiosis by Heinrich de Bary (1879) and to modern usage. Because of the great importance of parasitism to human life and economy, this subject is dealt with separately (*see* PARASITOLOGY).

**Commensalism.**—Pierre van Beneden (1876) referred to a commensal as an organism that "requires from his neighbour a simple place on board his vessel, and does not partake of his provisions. The messmate does not live at the expense of his host; all he desires is a home or his friend's superfluities." The arrangement represents a level of relationship a degree removed from that in aggregations of animals about a common food supply.

The commensal relation is often between individual larger host and individual smaller guest; the host organism is unmodified, whereas the commensal guest may show great structural adaptation consonant with its habits, as in the remoras (*q.v.*) that ride attached to sharks and other fishes, or no modification other than the habit of dependence on its host. The main types of dependence shown in commensalism are for shelter, support, locomotion (*i.e.,* distribution and spread), and food supply. These may be single or variously combined. Some of the more familiar household insects associated with man illustrate several of these relations—the house cricket, the common cockroach, etc. Only when the host-guest relation is recognizably specific, a particular guest species being regularly commensal with a particular host species, is commensalism sharply defined. The shelter relation is seen in the inhabitants of the tubes of marine worms, in the *Nomeus* fishes among the tentacles under Portuguese men-of-war, in the fierasfer fishes that occupy the cloaca of sea cucumbers, or in the insect inhabitants of field mouse nests. The support relation may involve plants sessile upon animals, as algae on turtle shell, or animals on plants, as bryozoans and hydroids on floating sargassum weed. Locomotion and food supply are combined in the remoras. Food supply is the main factor in the host of bacteria and protozoa that inhabit the gut of larger animals without apparent contribution to the digestive process of the host.

The opposite of commensalism is amensalism, in which one

(ABOVE) H. W. KITCHEN—PHOTO RESEARCHERS, INC.; (LEFT) UPI; (RIGHT) SYD GREENBERG—PHOTO RESEARCHERS, INC.

SYMBIOTIC RELATIONSHIPS

(Left) Commensalism (or in some cases mutualism) between a hermit crab, which has occupied a snail shell, and a sea anemone. (Above) Mutualism of white cattle egrets and elephants. (Right) Parasitism of wasp cocoons on a moth larva

population (the amensal) adversely affects another population. Man takes advantage of this type of relationship between colonies of the mold *Penicillium* and certain types of bacteria (*see* ANTIBIOTICS).

**Mutualism.**—Relationships in which there are benefits to both partners and in which both may be radically modified in adjustment to the mutualistic relation are widespread. They present diverse aspects. Mutualism may exist between plant and plant, between plant and animal and between animal and animal. The adjustments are both operational and evolutionary, and the mutualistic relation is one of the major types of co-operation in nature.

*Plant and Plant.*—In apparently mutualistic relations between plant and plant, the degree of benefit to one or the other partner may be obscure. One of the best known of such partnerships is that between fungi and algae to form lichens (*q.v.*), the discovery of which led to the coining of the term symbiosis. The support and protection supplied by the fungus, combined with the carbohydrate synthesis by the alga, makes possible the invasion of inhospitable rock surfaces and other adverse environments by lichens.

The relation of certain fungi with the roots of higher plants (mycorrhiza; *q.v.*) is extremely widespread and not, indeed, confined to the higher plants. Fungus mycelium (of various species) may form an enclosing feltlike mat around the roots of trees and other woody plants. In this case the benefit to the higher plant appears to lie in improved absorption of the food-bearing solution at the root surface. Even more intimate relations appear in the mycorrhiza of orchids, in which the fungus mycelium may be essential to normal germination and development. The fungus mat may be entirely external, or the fungus may send filaments throughout the host plant. In the latter case the filaments of mycelium on the roots replace the normal root hairs.

The combination of nitrogen-fixing bacteria with leguminous plants recalls the mycorrhizal relation in the obscurity of benefit to the bacteria, though in the legumes gall-like root nodules harbour the bacteria. The existence of the fixed association is the presumptive evidence of mutual benefit.

*Plant and Animal.*—The combination of green algae with various simple animals is made conspicuous by the resultant colouring of the animals. Various single-celled green algae, zoochlorellae, together with superficially similar yellow or brown flagellates, zooxanthellae, are regularly associated with protozoa, sponges, coelenterates, and flatworms. They are regularly present in the polyps of reef corals. In its life cycle the free-living marine flatworm *Convoluta roscoffensis* begins existence entirely free from zoochlorellae, acquires a dense intracellular population of the algae as it develops, whereupon it ceases active feeding, and finally loses the algae during senescence. In the similar association of algae with the fresh-water *Chlorohydra viridissimus* the supply of oxygen and carbohydrate food to the host animal and of carbon dioxide and nitrogenous food to the plant was experimentally examined and largely substantiated. In *Chlorohydra*, the transmission of the zoochlorellae to the egg cell takes place directly.

The habit of growing various fungi for food developed independently among beetles, termites, and ants. The fungi grown by various species of beetles of the families Ipidae and Platypodidae in burrows in tree trunks appear to be species-specific. The leaf-cutting ants commonly extend their destructive activities to horticultural plants and have thus been the focus of much study. The fungus-growing termites of the old world obviously developed this habit independently of ants and beetles. For all these insect gardeners some means of transmitting the fungus to a new nest is essential; in many forms remarkable special apparatus exists for this purpose.

An important mutualistic relation exists between larger animals like many ruminants (cow, goat, sheep, camel, etc.) and a series of bacteria that inhabit their alimentary tracts, for the bacteria aid in the digestion of cellulose or other food materials and synthesize certain vitamins. Enormous numbers of such bacteria may be harboured in special intestinal pouches (caeca) or elaborate divisions of the stomach.

Among the most interesting of the mutualistic plant-animal symbioses are those between insects and certain bacteria and fungi. In some instances the microorganisms (or symbiotes) live freely in the lumen of the alimentary tracts or in the associated caeca of their insect hosts. In other instances the symbiotes live within the tissue cells of the insect. In both instances the microorganisms appear to be highly specific and are transmitted from generation to generation by rather complicated mechanisms, usually via the eggs of the insect. In most instances the beneficial role played by the symbiotes is unknown, or only assumed; however, in many cases it has been shown that the insect cannot survive without the symbiotes and that the latter may produce certain essential vitamins or hormonelike substances. In aphids, for example, the symbiotes are believed by some to fix atmospheric nitrogen.

The insect-symbiote relationship is an intimate one since usually every individual of an insect species harbours the microorganism. The intracellular symbiotes live in cells called mycetocytes, which are frequently grouped into an organ or structure known as a mycetome. Some of the extracellular symbiotes occurring in the alimentary tracts of insects are known to take an active part in the digestive processes of the host (such as the bacteria found in the "fermentation pouches" of larvae of lamellicorn beetles). Certain bacteria are found in large numbers in the "gastric caeca" of higher Hemiptera. The arthropod hosts of the intracellular symbiotes occur in most of the principal orders of insects and numerous families of ticks and mites. Insects of both medical and agricultural importance are concerned, including such groups as cockroaches, lice, bedbugs, reduviid bugs, aphids, scale insects, beetles, and ants.

A vast series of plant-animal mutual benefit associations is supplied by the phenomenon of insect fertilization of flowers. These range from the most casual visitation of a flower by a wide variety of insects, in which there may be little or no modification for the accomplishment of pollination, to the most strict relation of a single species of flower with a single species of insect, in which both are modified for their mutual relations, as for example between the yucca plant and the yucca moth. Elaborate and complex flower mechanisms, in which exactness of fit of flower parts to a specific insect, and correspondingly elaborate insect structures that function solely in cross-fertilization of the appropriate plant, have been demonstrated (*see* POLLINATION).

*Animal and Animal.*—The mutualistic relations between animal and animal may begin at the simple level of the association of birds with large herbivorous mammals, as of the North American cowbird and the African tickbirds with domestic cattle, and the little white cattle egret, which associates itself with elephants and rhinoceroses as well as with domestic cattle throughout its range from North Africa to the East Indies.

The upsurge in skin diving led to the discovery that many marine organisms specialize in removing parasites from fishes. Smaller fishes and shrimps live by cleaning larger fishes, and the hosts thereby benefit; this mutualistic process has been termed cleaning symbiosis.

A more intimate level of such mutualism between diverse types of animals is found among marine animals. Hermit crabs of various species may beset their snail-shell house with hydroids (*e.g., Eupagurus constans* with *Hydractinia sodalis*) or with sea anemones (*Eupagurus prideauxi* with *Adamsia* species). Other crabs may regularly bear small sea anemones in their claws. Still others regularly have their shells grown over with various species of sponges. The advantage to the sessile animals is evidently that of locomotion, the advantage to the crustacean lies in protection or camouflage. Although some of these associations appear to be merely commensalistic, others approach mutualism, as shown especially by the hydroid *Hydractinia sodalis,* in which the basal layer that bears the polyps grows forward from the mouth of the snail shell inhabited by the hermit crab, thus making it unnecessary for the crab to undergo the hazard of changing its snail-shell house as it grows. The sea anemone *Adamsia* performs the same apparently essential function for its host. In addition many of these hydroids and sea anemones have long nematocyst-bearing filaments that serve as protection for themselves as well as for their hosts.

The cellulose-digesting mutualism of vertebrates and insects with bacteria is paralleled at the animal-animal level by a series of protozoa that accompany the bacteria in the alimentary tracts of various animals, ranging from harmless commensals to effective agents for cellulose digestion and to parasitism. The most sharply defined relation of this kind is represented by the association of primitive termites with characteristic and highly modified protozoans. It has been shown that the protozoans are characteristic of the species of termite inhabited.

The fungus gardens of the ants are matched by the relation between ants and aphids, and certain other insects. The ants give elaborate care to the aphids from which they obtain the secreted honeydew, protecting the aphids from adverse weather and moving them from one plant to another. Ants also protect aphids from certain of their natural enemies.

The series of nest inhabitants found regularly in the nests of both termites and ants exhibit the range from commensalism to a pseudomutualism of an elaborate and special form. Various families of insects, especially beetles, are associated with greatly modified ant and termite guests not found elsewhere. These forms produce special secretions, so much valued by the hosts that they treat them as normal and even favoured nest inhabitants.

The interrelations of commensalism, mutualism, and parasitism are extremely complex. It is evident that parasitism may evolve from either external or internal commensalism and that mutualism may commonly develop from the various types of commensalism. In the opposite direction, it is quite possible that mutualism may arise by complete adjustment of host and guest from an originally parasitic relation.

*See* also references under "Symbiosis" in the Index.

BIBLIOGRAPHY.—A. S. Pearse, *Animal Ecology,* 2nd ed. (1939); R. Hesse, W. C. Allee, and K. P. Schmidt, *Ecological Animal Geography,* 2nd ed. (1951); M. Caullery, *Parasitism and Symbiosis,* Eng. trans. by A. M. Lysaght (1952); P. S. Nutman and B. Morse, *Symbiotic Associations* (1963); C. Limbaugh, "Cleaning Symbiosis," *Scient. Am.* (August 1961).
(W. C. A.; K. P. S.; ED. A. ST.)

**SYMBOLIC LOGIC,** logic in which special signs or symbols are used for notation of the forms of sentences expressing propositions. *See* LOGIC; and LOGIC, HISTORY OF: *Modern Logic.*

**SYMBOLISTS, THE,** a group of French writers who considered themselves disciples of Stéphane Mallarmé and Paul Verlaine and who sought, between about 1885 and 1895, to react against Parnassian poetry (*see* PARNASSIANS), the Realist theatre, and the Naturalist novel in order to express by way of symbol the mystery of existence. Although writing in French, not all the Symbolists were of French birth: Jules Laforgue, Gustave Kahn, René Ghil, Albert Samain, and Henri de Régnier were French or of French parentage, but Albert Mockel, Maurice Maeterlinck, Georges Rodenbach, and Émile Verhaeren were Belgian; Jean Moréas was of Greek origin, and Francis Vielé-Griffin and Stuart Merrill were American by birth, although all three came to France in early youth.

The Symbolist manifesto was published by Moréas in *Le Figaro* on Sept. 18, 1886. There was no uniform doctrine, however, different theories being expounded in such reviews as *Lutèce* (1883), *La Revue wagnérienne* (1885), *La Vogue* (1886), *La Plume* (1889), and *Le Mercure de France* (1890). Verhaeren attempted a definition in *L'Art moderne* of April 24, 1887, but just how many dissident groups remained (Instrumentalists, Melodists, Verslibrists, etc.) is evident from Jules Huret's *Enquête sur l'évolution littéraire* (1891). Mallarmé's *Divagations* (1897), which incorporates ideas propounded at his Tuesday receptions attended by the younger generation, remains the most valuable statement of Symbolist aesthetics, just as his *L'Après-midi d'un faune* (1876) was the first masterpiece of Symbolist poetry, and also the greatest. Whatever their differences, the Symbolists were unanimous in acclaiming their precursor to be Baudelaire, whose theory of the *correspondances* between the senses they found applied by Arthur Rimbaud in his "Sonnet des Voyelles." They were also influenced by the poetics of Edgar Allan Poe and by the ideal to which Wagner aspired, of a synthesis of the arts. Schopenhauer's formula, "the world is my idea," and Eduard von Hartmann's theory of the unconscious likewise contributed to the Symbolist aesthetics.

All Symbolists retained the Parnassian concept of "art for art's sake" with its insistence on technical perfection, but they repudiated the descriptive imagery of the Parnassians. They aimed at an art more suggestive and more subtle, at poetic images projecting what Régnier called the poet's "inner dream." Poetry at this period assumed almost the status of a religion and, like religion, required to be shrouded in mystery. It was to have its own language, entirely distinct from that of prose. To this end, Mallarmé proceeded to create a "pure language" by using words in their etymological meaning, and to envelop poetry in a well-calculated hermetism. Interest in neologisms, already evident in Rimbaud and Laforgue, and in phonic values, inspired Ghil's *Traité du verbe* (1886) with its *Avant-dire* by Mallarmé. In order to "express the inexpressible," poets were urged in Teodor de Wyzewa's *L'Art wagnérien* (1886) to turn for guidance to the most suggestive of the arts, music, which by its nature reached deeper levels of the unconscious. They aimed at using in literature certain musical techniques of Wagnerian drama, the *Leitmotiv* (*q.v.*) for instance. Mallarmé and Verlaine considered the musical element in poetry to be fundamental, but Mallarmé remained more traditional in his versification and made abundant use of the *rime riche* advocated by Théodore de Banville, while Verlaine and his disciples experimented daringly with assonance, *vers impairs,* and metrical patterns borrowed from folk songs. To escape metrical rigidity, many writers, following the precedent of Mallarmé and Rimbaud, practised the prose poem; Laforgue, Vielé-Griffin, and Verhaeren, stimulated by the example of Walt Whitman, wrote free verse (*q.v.*), the chief exponent of which was Kahn in the preface to the second edition of his *Les Palais nomades* (1887). With this innovation, which Mallarmé deplored, many Symbolists claimed that French poetry had at last been freed from the bonds of classical prosody.

Mallarmé and Villiers de l'Isle-Adam envisaged the theatre as a temple for the enactment of a supreme ceremony. A. Antoine's productions of Ibsen revealed the possibilities of symbol on the stage; what the critic Édouard Schuré called "a theatre of the soul" was expressed in the productions of Paul Fort at his Théâtre d'Art (1890) and A. M. Lugné-Poe at his Théâtre de l'Oeuvre (1893). The most memorable examples of the Symbolist theatre, apart from Villiers de l'Isle-Adam's *Axël* (published 1890; produced 1894), were Maeterlinck's *Pelléas et Mélisande* (1893), with its dreamlike atmosphere, which was set to music by Debussy (1902); and Alfred Jarry's highly satirical *Ubu Roi* (1896), which caused an uproar. The Symbolist contribution to fiction was less significant, but J.-K. Huysmans' *À Rebours* (1884) drew public attention to Mallarmé, and Édouard Dujardin's *Les Lauriers sont coupés* (1888) influenced James Joyce. The Symbolists left their mark on world literature. Paul Valéry and Paul Claudel in France, Stefan George and Rainer Maria Rilke in Germany, Aleksandr Blok in Russia, and W. B. Yeats inherited from them an aristocratic conception of their art and a certain hermetism.

*See* also POETIC IMAGERY and articles on various writers mentioned.

BIBLIOGRAPHY.—E. Wilson, *Axel's Castle* (1931); A. G. Lehmann, *The Symbolist Aesthetic in France, 1885–1895* (1950); C. M. Bowra, *The Heritage of Symbolism* (1943); G. Michaud, *Message poétique du symbolisme*, 3 vol. (1947), *La Doctrine symboliste* (1947); M. Raymond, *From Baudelaire to Surrealism*, with a Reader's Guide by B. Karpel (1950). (E. M. So.)

**SYMMACHUS, SAINT** (d. 514), pope from 498 to 514, a native of Sardinia and apparently a convert from paganism, was in deacon's orders when he was elected as successor to Anastasius II and promptly consecrated, in the Lateran, on Nov. 22, 498. The election, however, was not unanimous: another candidate, Laurentius, having the support of a strong Byzantine party, was also consecrated, in Sta. Maria Maggiore, on the same day. A decision was obtained in favour of Symmachus from the Gothic (and Arian) king Theodoric; but peace was not established until 505 or 506, when Theodoric ordered the Laurentian party to surrender the churches of which they had taken possession. The schism was not fully healed till the reign of Hormisdas, Symmachus' successor. An important incident in the protracted controversy was the decision of the "Palmary Synod"—the fourth session of a council called by Theodoric at Rome in 502 to deal with the charges brought against Symmachus by the Laurentians—in favour of Symmachus; the bishops declared that there was no precedent for the pope's being judged by other bishops. The dispute gave rise to a body of spurious literature that was drawn on by later exponents of the doctrine *quod prima sedes non judicatur a quoquam* (*i.e.*, that no one can pass judgment on the pope).

Symmachus was a strong supporter of orthodoxy in the Acacian schism, and he burned the Manichaeans' books and expelled them from Rome. He was a friend of the poor and of the Catholics of Africa who were enduring persecution by the Arians. He erected or restored a number of Roman churches, an inscription on one of which (referring to the end of the Laurentian troubles) reads: "The biting of the wolves has ceased." Symmachus died on July 19, 514; the anniversary is his feast day. *See* also PAPACY.

**SYMMACHUS, QUINTUS AURELIUS** (*c.* A.D. 345–402), Roman consul in 391 and a distinguished author, was the son of a consular family of great distinction and wealth. His oratory brought him an illustrious official career culminating in the proconsulship of Africa in 373, the city prefecture at Rome in 384, and the consulship. When the emperor Gratian, influenced by the Christian bishop of Milan, St. Ambrose, ordered the statue of Victory to be removed from the Senate house at Rome in 382, Symmachus, who was an earnest pagan, was appointed by the Senate to go to Milan to plead with the emperor to cancel this antipagan measure; but the mission was a failure. After Gratian's murder in 383, Symmachus renewed his plea to Valentinian II to revoke Gratian's antipagan orders; but, largely owing to the opposition of St. Ambrose, he was again unsuccessful. Symmachus' oration *De ara Victoriae* was considered so brilliant that even after 19 years the poet Prudentius found it necessary to write a reply to it. The increasingly Christian character of Valentinian's court caused Symmachus to lose much of his influence; but when Magnus Maximus (*q.v.*) drove Valentinian from Italy in 387, Symmachus, who was regarded as the leader of the Senate, was appointed to offer the new emperor the Senate's congratulations on his elevation. When Theodosius I reconquered Italy, Symmachus was forgiven and appointed consul for 391. Under the pagan rule of Eugenius and Arbogast in 392–394 (*see* THEODOSIUS), he apparently regained some of his influence and survived under Honorius until 402. He owned three houses at Rome and no fewer than 15 estates in Italy, Sicily, and Mauretania.

Symmachus' extant works, of which the most important are the ten books of his *Letters*, have been edited by O. Seeck, in *Monumenta Germaniae Historica*, vol. vi, part 1 (1883). (E. A. T.)

**SYMONDS, JOHN ADDINGTON** (1840–1893), English man of letters, most widely known in his own day as the historian of the Italian Renaissance and now recognized as a pioneer in the study of homosexuality. Born at Bristol on Oct. 5, 1840, and educated at Harrow and Oxford, where in 1862 he was elected a fellow of Magdalen College, he developed early symptoms of pulmonary disease and after many journeys in search of health finally settled at Davos Platz in Switzerland, where most of his work was done, though with frequent journeys to Italy. In poetry particularly, Symonds found relief from grave emotional problems. The study of his own abnormal temperament resulted in *A Problem in Greek Ethics* (privately printed, 1883), an enquiry into sexual inversion, and this led to collaboration with Havelock Ellis (*q.v.*). Symond's most elaborate work, *Renaissance in Italy* (7 vol. 1875–86), is rather a series of extended essays than a systematic history. Fluent and picturesque, with the prejudices of its period, it was deeply indebted to such continental interpreters of the Renaissance as Jacob Burckhardt and Francesco De Sanctis. It was long useful and widely read, but it has been superseded.

Symonds also translated the sonnets of Michelangelo and Campanella (1878), and Cellini's autobiography (2 vol. 1888), and wrote a life of Michelangelo (2 vol. 1893). Essentially, he was an *homme des lettres*, diffusing his energies over English literature, Greek poetry, travel sketches, and a study of Walt Whitman (1893), of whom he was one of the first European admirers.

He died in Rome on April 19, 1893.

BIBLIOGRAPHY.—*Letters and Papers of John Addington Symonds*, ed. by H. R. F. Brown (1923); H. R. F. Brown, *John Addington Symonds: a Biography*, 2nd ed. (1903), based largely on the unpublished autobiography; P. M. Grosskurth, *John Addington Symonds* (U.S. title, *The Woeful Victorian;* 1964). (I. FL.)

**SYMOND'S YAT** (yat: gate, opening, pass), a low-lying neck of land, 12 mi. (19 km.) S of Ross-on-Wye, Herefordshire, Eng., between Huntsham Hill (475 ft.; 145 m.) to the north and the famous viewpoint Yat Rock (about 500 ft.) to the south, in the Carboniferous Limestone upland. It is bounded east and west by a meander of the River Wye which, in its 4-mi. (6.4-km.) course round Huntsham Hill, progresses westward only 600 yd. (550 m.); *i.e.*, the width of Symond's Yat. (AU. M.)

**SYMONS, ARTHUR WILLIAM** (1865–1945), the first English critic to advocate the importance of the French Symbolists (*q.v.*), was born at Milford Haven, Pembrokeshire, on Feb. 21, 1865. His schooling was irregular, but, determined to be a writer, he soon found a place in the London literary journalism of the 1890s. He joined the Rhymers' Club, contributed to the *Yellow Book*, and became editor of the *Savoy* (January–December 1896), with Aubrey Beardsley (*q.v.*) as art editor. Symons was versed in European literature, and his popularizing *Symbolist Movement in Literature* (1899) summed up a decade of interpretation and influenced both W. B. Yeats and T. S. Eliot. His criticism constitutes an ambitious attempt to create a general "aesthetic" from the unsystematized "impressionism" of Walter Pater (*q.v.*). Where Pater had isolated music as the type of all the arts, Symons' premise, in *Plays, Acting, and Music* (1903) and *Studies in Seven*

*Arts* (1906), was that "each art has its own laws, its own limits; these it is the business of the critic jealously to distinguish. Yet in the study of art as art, it should be his endeavour to master the universal science of beauty."

Symons' poetry is mainly *fin de siècle* in feeling, though it influenced Yeats in his middle period. *Silhouettes* (1892) and *London Nights* (1895) contain admirable impressionist lyrics, and at his best Symons is sensitive to the complex moods of urban life. His translations from Verlaine are notable, and he wrote elegant travel pieces.

In 1908 Symons suffered a severe mental breakdown, and, apart from *Confessions* (1930), which is a moving account of his illness, his career was virtually over. Other works included, in verse, *Images of Good and Evil* (1899), *The Fool of the World* (1906), and *Knave of Hearts: 1894–1908* (1913); and, in prose, the remarkable, partly autobiographical *Spiritual Adventures* (1905), and *Studies in the Elizabethan Drama* (1920). He died at Wittersham, Kent, on Jan. 22, 1945.

*See* his *Collected Works,* 9 vol. (1924; incomplete); R. Lhombreaud, *Arthur Symons* (1963). (I. Fl.)

**SYMPATHETIC SYSTEM:** *see* Nervous System: *Autonomic Nervous System.*

**SYMPHONIC POEM** (Tone Poem): *see* Program Music.

**SYMPHONY,** a musical term which since the middle of the 18th century has denoted a type of composition for orchestra; the classical symphony is in sonata form. The word is derived from the Greek *symphonia,* "concord." In Luke 15:25, *symphonia* is distinguished from *choroi,* and the two are translated as "music and dancing." The word has also been applied to two musical instruments, the sistrum in ancient times and the hurdy-gurdy in the Middle Ages.

In the 17th century the term was used, like "concerto," for certain vocal compositions accompanied by instruments; *e.g.,* the *Symphoniae sacrae* of Heinrich Schütz. The term is also found in Schütz's *Kleine geistliche Concerte,* where it is applied to the instrumental ritornello of a song.

**Origins.**—Since the middle of the 18th century the interpretation of the term symphony has become freer, but any work bearing this name requires close scrutiny. Preoccupation with vocal counterpoint until the 17th century ensured that musical designs remained essentially static. Tonality was a kind of anchor, and the music consisted of simply related harmonies. As instrumental techniques developed, greater freedom of line, harmony, and to some extent tonality became possible, though for a long time composers tended to regard instruments as if they were more agile and brilliant voices. This applies to Bach in the first half of the 18th century; Handel shows more sense of adventure in this respect, but his work is still basically polyphonic. In a prelude of Bach or a movement of a *concerto grosso* by Handel the treatment of key (tonality) is totally undramatic; the music swings from harmony to related harmony without more than a hint that it is ever likely to move out of an orbit centred on its original key. The harmonic scheme, in fact, is as calm and relaxed as that of a simple hymn tune whose successive chords are now spun out to accommodate elaborations of the texture, mainly of a contrapuntal nature. At the end of such a piece, no impression of movement is created. Violent changes of mood or texture are rare and real changes in tonality almost impossible. When Bach in the B minor Mass passes through mysteriously "foreign" harmony at the words *et expecto resurrectionem mortuorum* his purpose is expressive rather than structural; it is a way of drawing attention to the nature of the text at this point and of making a convincing transition between the F# minor of the *Confiteor* and the brilliant D major of the exultant movement, separately designed, which follows it. This is the process of modulation (*q.v.*), and real modulation in music before the early 18th century is usual only in such transitions between otherwise independent designs. It is scarcely ever found within the course of a homogeneous movement, where it would be disrupting to the calmly proportioned architecture.

The concept of modulation, however, is at the root of the sonata principle. While Bach was perfecting his polyphonic art, other composers (including his sons) were creating a kind of music that was entirely based on instrumental as opposed to vocal technique. Counterpoint is almost entirely dispensed with in these early examples, which aim at achieving maximum mobility in terms of simple chordal harmonies and rhythms. Their straightforward themes, often founded on triads, would have been utterly unsuitable as contrapuntal subjects. The use of simple harmony made it imperative to find a new means of contrast, and it was found that an increase of tension resulted from the music moving from one tonal region to another. The rhythmic impulse was at the same time sustained, or even intensified, so that there was no sense of discontinuity, but on the contrary a sweeping momentum hitherto unknown. When the new tonal region was reached, some kind of momentary relaxation was provided, leading perhaps to a new theme, possibly more ingratiating than the first. The so-called first and second subjects referred to in textbook analyses of sonata forms thus arose from a new attitude to tonality. To regard them merely as conveniently contrasting themes is to divest them of their underlying dynamic purpose. The second subject is not necessarily a "tune" at all; it begins at the moment when modulatory tension relaxes into a new channel—a new theme may or may not emerge. The essence of sonata music lies in its newfound ability, in the 18th century, to thrust a key away over the tonal horizon, so that a new vista is created. (*See* also Sonata.) This was the nature of the new dynamism in music. Composers of this new kind of music, if it was written for orchestra, called it symphony, and it originated in the theatrical or operatic overture, often termed *sinfonia* (*see* Overture). The fresh sense of movement permeated all kinds of music, but the word symphony thereafter was almost exclusively applied to orchestral works.

**Haydn, Mozart, and Beethoven.**—At first there was little to distinguish the early symphony from the divertimento or cassation (*qq.v.*) or even from the string quartet. The orchestra itself became more stabilized, with the strings as its basis, at first with the keyboard *continuo* to keep a "middle" going, but gradually doing away with this device as wind instruments were more extensively and skilfully used. Oboes and horns, in pairs, were used in many symphonies of the 1750s and 1760s. Flutes and bassoons were added, and trumpets and drums for special ceremonial occasions. The orchestra thus developed into a standardized unit, homogeneous as, say, the keyboard. As soon as the orchestral *tutti* became a norm, composers were free to explore its depths. Haydn, even in his earliest symphonies, thus had a ready-made instrument allowing him to compose unselfconsciously; and he owed this fact to G. M. Monn, G. B. Sammartini, and G. C. Wagenseil, even more than to J. W. Stamitz, founder of the Mannheim orchestra and the school of composers it inspired. Haydn was not the father of the symphony; he was its progeny. Nevertheless, it was due to him that the title "symphony" came to denote an orchestral work of the highest concentration, organization, and comprehensiveness.

The early operatic overture was often in three movements—an allegro, a slow movement, and a lively finale, often in fast triple or sextuple time, upon which the curtain rose. It is often supposed that the succession of movements in a classical symphony originated here, but contrasting movements became more necessary than ever when the explosive tensions of tonality were released. Everything that happens in such music is born of tonal tension, even the division into separate movements that had previously been no more than decorative. To the three movements a minuet was added. This served two purposes: first, to increase the sense of comprehensiveness by including a dance element, and second, to complement the brevity of the finale. So the four-movement symphony became a normal format that persisted almost unchallenged for 100 years and is still not discarded. Haydn and Mozart are the first complete masters of the symphony who were concerned with the felicitous interpenetration of certain prime elements—pure formal balance, concentration, variety of expression within the same work, and what may be called athleticism. With them, the symphony became a complete kind of orchestral music, and the term symphony has ever since been used to arouse the listener's highest musical faculties.

The greatest intensification of this challenge was made by

Beethoven. He did not surpass Haydn or Mozart in perfection of design, or even in sheer athleticism; in concentrated depth and variety of expression, however, mastered within the physically limited yet imaginatively vast confines of single works, no composer before or since has approached him. It was this attribute that made Brahms—one of his most masterly successors—fearful of composing symphonies at all. Beethoven, moreover, widened the scope of the orchestra itself, by increasing the number of instruments, adding an extra horn in No. 3 (*Eroica*), and trombones in No. 5, 6, and 9, sometimes also using piccolo, contrabassoon, and (in the Ninth) extra percussion. He also tended to place more weight on the finale of a symphony than did his precursors, especially in No. 5, 7, 8, and 9; in the latter, the last and greatest of the series, he took the unprecedented step of adding a chorus and vocal soloists to the finale.

**Later Developments.**—After Beethoven the Romantic movement of the 19th century was inclined to inflate the idea of symphony, expressive intensity arising from a high degree of subjectivity often being allowed to oust the more rigorous formal considerations; Beethoven's music cannot be held responsible for this, since no other composer, except possibly Bach, was so aware of structure, no matter how fierce or dramatic the expression. This gave his work an objectivity that is the reverse of Romantic. Some loosening of the discipline may be noticed in Schubert, though one should be careful not to confuse this element with positive new discoveries made by Schubert involving a more deliberate pace of thought. Nineteenth-century composers who showed resistance to the tendency to inflation and loose discipline—clearly followers of Beethoven and Schubert—are Schumann (whose great economy is often overlooked), Brahms, and Dvořák; they maintained classical traditions and classical energy while achieving complete individuality. Two early-19th-century symphonists of essentially 18th-century makeup were Mendelssohn and the Swedish composer F. A. Berwald, both of whom show less concern with the heroic than with elegance and balance.

The composers just mentioned may be said to represent one trend, perhaps the most faithful to the essential nature of the symphony as it had so far developed—not because of adherence to any rule book but because they strove to achieve a fine balance between the complexities of form and the more importunate demands of expression, on a scale comparable with that of the classical symphony. At the same time, the Romantic preoccupation with the emotional moment was inevitably slowing down the pace of music; it was becoming increasingly difficult to write a true allegro; Schubert's retardation of pace was a beginning, and Wagner's discovery of how to make musical structures large enough to encompass a whole act of a stage drama (and "large enough" means "slow enough") had an overwhelming effect upon other composers whose aims were unconnected with the theatre. The most notable of these was Bruckner, who, while creating music that has an individual grandeur—in spirit perhaps closer to Giovanni Gabrieli than to Wagner—constructed vast symphonies whose motion is for the most part of huge slowness, which would have been impossible without Wagner's influence. Wagner's sense of movement had also a deep effect on Mahler, who also wrote symphonies on an enormous scale, for enormous orchestras; here, however, subjective Romanticism sometimes intervenes at moments when structural demands might have been better met.

**The 20th Century.**—Mahler brings the history of the symphony up to the beginning of the 20th century. Parallel with German Romanticism, the Russian nationalists, particularly Borodin, M. A. Balakirev, and Tchaikovsky, were also producing an individual conception of the symphony. Tchaikovsky, however, proved to be less a nationalist than a subjective Romantic, whose violent emotional impulses frequently broke down discipline in a formal method derived largely from Schumann. Tchaikovsky's symphonies, like Mahler's, are basically programmatic in character, and to that extent only sporadically symphonic, for the expressive-illustrative elements sometimes ignore structural necessities. A movement such as the first of Tchaikovsky's Fourth Symphony, however, achieves a just balance, such as the Frenchman Berlioz (who greatly influenced him) more often found. The structural concentration of true symphony has not attracted French composers, and Berlioz (nearest in time to the classical symphonists—he began his *Symphonie fantastique* while Schubert was writing his great C major symphony) is still the finest French symphonic composer, whose best work is purer and more controlled than his reputation for Romantic illustrative extravagance would lead the casual listener to believe.

While German Romanticism was reaching the limits of inflation at the end of the 19th century, two Scandinavian masters were renewing the classical symphony by making fresh discoveries, Jean Sibelius with the concept of movement, and Carl Nielsen with that of tonality. Their reactions against the indiscipline of Romanticism are essentially complementary. The slowing down of musical movement mastered by Wagner had two serious effects on his successors: (1) many composers lost the power of classical movement, the ability to write the kind of allegro whose impetus is exemplified in Haydn and Beethoven; (2) tonality was no longer being used coherently, for the slowness meant that the conception of key as an "anchor" could no longer easily be sustained in such a time scale. Sibelius, for the first time, found a way to combine the vast slowness of the Wagnerian world with the athleticism of Beethoven, and his series of seven symphonies is a progressive mastering of this problem, culminating in the one-movement Seventh, in which transitions from one extreme to the other are made with astonishing skill and imaginative power. Sonata "form" no longer applies, but the disciplines are all derived from the phenomena that sonata music made possible, and the range of expression is comparable with that of the fully developed four-movement classical symphony.

This is true also of Nielsen's six symphonies, but here the discovery is tonal. The originality of this Danish composer lay in his clear understanding of the problem that was baffling the Romantics, whose dilemma was the result of a single great assumption—that tonality must be an "anchor." Arnold Schoenberg, who plunged into atonality and devised new serial disciplines to compensate for the loss, did so because he also shared this assumption, as is shown by his remark that "there is still a lot of good music to be written in C major." The operative phrase here is "in C major," with its suggestion of fixity. Nielsen discovered a structural way of making a symphony travel from one tonality—or sometimes a complex of warring tonalities—to another. The phenomenon is sometimes called progressive tonality, though emergent tonality would be a more accurate description. From it Nielsen was able to produce a new dynamism and music of great strength, as well as variety of character.

The reaction to the general slowing down of musical processes that came with the twilight of Romanticism has, in the 20th century, been more often negative than positive, and compositional methods have tended to produce totally static rather than dynamic results. Therefore valid symphonic music is rarer than in the past. Composers of the mid-20th century who have used the title have often done so loosely. It is no longer indicative of any particular method or format. Since, however, the term "symphony" has been the highest challenge in the field of orchestral music for many of the greatest composers of the last 175 years, it will no doubt continue to be applied to works in which the composer has essayed the widest range of expression and movement within the scope of a single work. The essence of symphony is disciplined inclusiveness; that is to say, the comprehensiveness of symphony will not exclude any natural resources of music—harmony, melody, rhythm, tonality, etc. Any avoidance of one such element, however concentrated, must necessarily bring about a sense of exclusiveness that will inevitably limit the music to less than the widest powers of the imagination. A symphony must be genuinely and consistently active if it is to rise to its proper level; it is by this standard, by which the greatest symphonists have survived, that it must stand or fall. Its actual form is no longer definable or predictable.

*See* also MUSIC: *The Evolution of Musical Style: Music in the 20th Century;* ORCHESTRATION; PROGRAM MUSIC. (RO. SI.)

**SYMPHYLA,** a class of small, many-legged arthropods (myriapods), the largest representatives being slightly less than one centimetre in length. The skin of these animals is thin, soft and colourless. They live under logs, leaves and stones, where their white bodies contrast sharply with the darker soil. Although symphylids occasionally devour dead insects, they usually subsist upon decaying vegetable matter and delicate rootlets and tissues of living plants. One species in particular, *Scutigerella immaculata,* is known to do extensive damage to such crops as celery, lettuce, asparagus and beets. This form is often spoken of as the "garden centipede," although the absence of poison jaws and other basic differences widely separate it from true centipedes (*q.v.*).

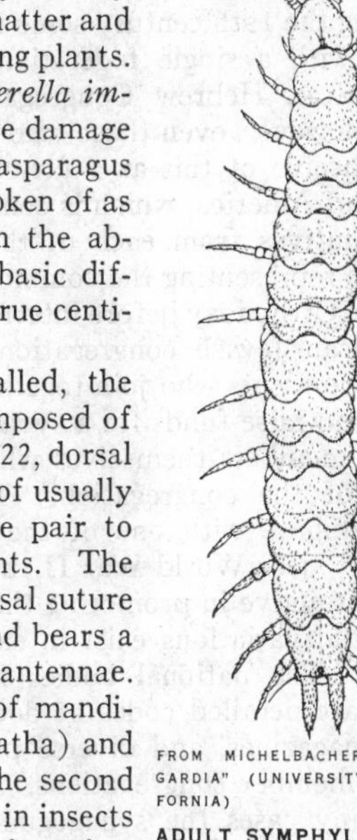

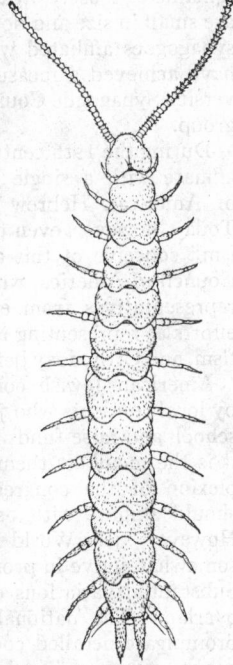

FROM MICHELBACHER IN "HILGARDIA" (UNIVERSITY OF CALIFORNIA)

ADULT SYMPHYLID (SCUTIGERELLA IMMACULATA)

As in other myriapods, so-called, the head is distinct. The body is composed of 14 segments, bearing 15, or rarely 22, dorsal plates, or tergites. Twelve pairs of usually five-jointed legs are present, one pair to each of the first twelve segments. The head, which bears a Y-shaped dorsal suture like that of insects, lacks eyes and bears a pair of long, many-segmented antennae. The mouthparts include a pair of mandibles, a pair of maxillulae (paragnatha) and two pairs of maxillae of which the second pair combine to form a labium as in insects and centipedes. Only one pair of respiratory spiracles are present; these open on the head near the bases of the antennae and allow air to all parts of the body via tubules called tracheae. The paired reproductive organs open by a single pore lying between the third and fourth pairs of legs, a characteristic placing them with millipedes and pauropods in the now widely recognized group Progoneata. The females lay their eggs in clusters in the ground. As with the millipedes, the young hatch out with three pairs of legs, the rest being developed later.

The symphylids have a world-wide distribution. Because of neglect by most collectors only about 100 species have so far been recognized. Formerly, they were placed in three families, two of which have been placed with the centipedes, the family Scutigerellidae remaining. The name Symphyla refers to the intermediate position of these animals, all of which show obviously connecting characters with other groups of tracheate arthropods, especially insects.

BIBLIOGRAPHY.—H. J. Hansen, "Genera and Species of the Symphyla," *Quart. J. Micr. Sci.*, vol. 53 (1901); Verhoeff in Bronn's *Klassen und Ordnungen des Tierreichs,* vol. 5 (1934); A. E. Michelbacher, "The Biology of the Garden Centipede *Scutigerella immaculata*," *Hilgardia*, vol. 11, pp. 55–148 (1938). (R. V. C.)

**SYNAGOGUE,** a Jewish house of worship. In Hellenistic Greek, *synagoge* was the term for assembly and later for the place where the assembly gathered, corresponding to the Hebrew *keneset* and *bet ha-keneset*. The phrase "meeting places of God" in Ps. 74:8 is generally assumed to be a reference to synagogues (and was so translated in the Authorized Version). Talmudic literature also uses the terms "house of the people" (based on Jer. 39:8) and "small sanctuary" (based on Ezek. 11:16) while Greek sources speak of "house of prayer" (*proseuche* or *proseukterion*) and occasionally "sabbath house." In modern times "temple" and *shul* (Yiddish, from the German *schule*) are common. United States usage often distinguishes between a temple, meaning a Reform Jewish synagogue, and a *shul,* an Orthodox Jewish house of worship.

### SYNAGOGUE HISTORY AND FUNCTIONS

**History.**—The beginnings of the synagogue are obscure. It most probably originated during the Babylonian Exile as an institution for public worship and instruction soon after the destruction of Solomon's Temple in 586 B.C. (*see* TEMPLE, JEWISH). After the return from the Babylonian Captivity, especially under Ezra and his successors, the synagogue developed side by side with the cult of the Temple in Jerusalem. Some scholars trace the origin of regular worship in the synagogue to the institution of Maamadoth, which formed part of the Temple worship; along with each of the 24 priestly divisions, certain towns would arrange for a two-week assembly of prayer and worship. The oldest dated evidence of a synagogue is the dedication of a house of worship to Ptolemy III (3rd century B.C.) inscribed on a marble slab discovered near Alexandria, Egy. Approximately 50 ancient synagogues were excavated in Palestine and the surrounding area during the 19th and 20th centuries, but they all date from the 2nd to the 6th century A.D. Philo and Josephus, as well as the New Testament and the early rabbinic sources, speak of the synagogue as an institution that had been in existence from early antiquity. The literature of the 1st century also refers to numerous synagogues not only in Palestine but in Rome and Greece as well as in various cities in Egypt and Babylonia and throughout Asia Minor. Toward the end of the second commonwealth (middle of 1st century A.D.) there were synagogues wherever there was a Jewish settlement of sufficient size to support organized congregational activity. The destruction of the Second Temple by Titus (A.D. 70) had no adverse effect on the synagogue, which had long been a well-established and independent institution. During the centuries following the fall of Jerusalem the synagogue gained in importance, becoming the centre of the corporate life of the Jewish community.

**Character.**—The character of the synagogue, often termed "the child of the dispersion," represented from its inception a radical departure from that of earlier places of worship. It was not restricted to any geographic locale that presumably possessed inherent sanctity; it had no sacrificial or sacramental ritual; it did not require the intermediacy of a special priesthood. Any group of Jews, regardless of place, may establish a synagogue and share the responsibility for the conduct of its affairs. Essentially democratic, the synagogue represents a fellowship of worshipers seeking God through prayer and study.

Certainly from the 1st century A.D., and probably much earlier, morning, afternoon, and evening services were conducted in the synagogue daily and on the sabbaths and festivals (*see* LITURGY, JEWISH). On special occasions, especially on the sabbath, the service included a sermonic exposition of the scriptural lesson as well as public lectures on various aspects of the law. The facilities of the synagogue, particularly the rooms adjoining the main prayer

WERNER BRAUN

PULPIT AND WOMEN'S GALLERY OF CONEGLIANO VENETO SYNAGOGUE, 1701, MOVED FROM VENICE TO JERUSALEM IN 1940 hall, were often employed for a variety of other purposes throughout the ages. They served as the meeting place for the leaders of the community and for popular assemblies, for publication of legal notices and decrees of the secular government (during the medieval period), for funerals of its leading members and rabbis, for weddings, circumcisions, and, at times, even for lodging of travelers. Above all, the facilities of the synagogue were used for the education of children. The modern synagogue provides regular public worship, a program of education for children, youth, and adults, and a variety of social, cultural, and philanthropic activities.

**Architecture.**—There is no typical synagogue architecture; the houses of worship were and are built in the prevailing architectural style. Numerous synagogues built after World War II are among the finest examples of advanced architectural design. The only prescriptions found in the Talmud are that the synagogue be built on the heights of a city and that it have windows ("light dwells with Him," Dan. 2:22; and of Daniel praying, "he had windows in his upper chamber open," Dan. 6:10), but even these few requirements are only theoretical. The modern synagogue usually contains an ark where the Scrolls of the Law are kept; a light above the ark called the eternal light or perpetual lamp; two candelabra; pews for the worshipers; and a raised platform, *bimah* (or *almemar*), from which the scriptural lesson is read and, often, services conducted. In the medieval synagogue, the *bimah* was usually located in the centre of the auditorium and a gallery was built in the back or on the sides of the auditorium for women worshipers. Also, a *mikvah,* a ritual bath, occasionally was included in the synagogue premises. Many Orthodox synagogues today retain all or several of these features. (*See* also RELIGIOUS ARCHITECTURE; JEWISH ART.) (E. MI.)

## SYNAGOGUE ORGANIZATIONS

**United States.**—Each Jewish congregation is an independent entity, governed in most cases by an elected board of directors. Nearly all describe themselves as Reform, Conservative, or Orthodox (*see* JUDAISM). No precise figures on the relative strength of the three are available, but it is believed that in the United States their numbers are approximately equal.

In the past, Orthodoxy was strongest in New York City and in the Middle Atlantic and New England areas. In smaller cities of the Midwest, South, and Far West the Reform temple was frequently the most prominent Jewish religious institution. Conservatism centred in some of the largest Jewish communities, though it was not especially prominent in New York. The evolution of American Jewry, however, changed this picture considerably. Thus, the movement of the Jews of New York City to the suburbs added strength to Reform and Conservatism; the growth of Los Angeles as a centre of Jewish population meant the strengthening of Conservatism and Orthodoxy in that area.

In regard to the constituency of each group, the most notable trend is the general decline in social-class differences. Many present-day Reform congregations, in contrast to those of an earlier period, include few if any persons who are members of the upper class. The constituency of Reform is now also overwhelmingly composed of persons descended from immigrants who originated in Eastern Europe rather than in Germany. While the Orthodox group is extremely variegated in composition, it still possesses the strongest links with the immigrant past. However, Orthodoxy increasingly utilizes American methods of organization, and in many Orthodox congregations English has replaced Yiddish as the language of common discourse.

National synagogue federations exist in the United States for each of the three groups: (1) the Union of American Hebrew Congregations for the Reform group; (2) the United Synagogue of America for the Conservative group; and (3) the Union of Orthodox Jewish Congregations of America for the Orthodox group. The Reform federation, founded in 1873, is the oldest and the best organized of the three. The Conservative federation, founded in 1913, was relatively inactive until the 1940s, becoming after that period, however, an important agency. The Union of Orthodox Jewish Congregations, although founded in 1898, has remained a loosely organized group. Most Orthodox congregations are small in size and do not have ties with any national body. The synagogues affiliated with the Young Israel movement, however, have achieved a measure of coordination, and the Yeshiva University Synagogue Council also has become a force in the Orthodox group.

During the 19th century some thought that all synagogues might affiliate with a single federation—hence names such as "Union of American Hebrew Congregations," or "United Synagogue." Today, however, even those who foresee a single "American Judaism" conceive of this as a far-off development. The Synagogue Council of America, which is composed of both rabbinical and lay representatives from each of the three groups, has confined its efforts to representing the common interests of Reform, Conservatism, and Orthodoxy before interreligious and governmental bodies.

American Jewish congregations have typically been organized by local residents who join together, hold services, start a religious school, and raise funds for a synagogue building. Initially at least it is the members themselves who shape the exact religious complexion of the congregation. They decide whether the group should affiliate with one of the national synagogue federations. However, after World War II the federations themselves became somewhat active in promoting the establishment of congregations. Substantial variations exist in each movement, and they tend to overlap. The national bodies have been generally hesitant to promulgate detailed codes of doctrine, though they publish textbooks, magazines, and diverse pronouncements for the guidance of their member congregations.

In many cases the synagogue has added an extensive list of activities to its traditional function of providing a place of worship and a centre for study by male adults of the sacred Jewish texts. Congregations increasingly become "synagogue centres" and sponsor club programs, athletic activities, and public lectures. They make their facilities available for a variety of Jewish and general communal purposes. Many congregations possess affiliated organizations, such as sisterhoods, men's clubs, and youth groups, which provide a varied program, generally with an emphasis on social activities. Sisterhoods, men's clubs, and youth groups are affiliated with federations sponsored by the national bodies.

The task of providing elementary Jewish education also has become a congregational rather than a communal responsibility. An important motivation for congregational affiliation is the desire to enroll children in the religious school of the institution.

The religious life of Canadian Jewry is essentially the same as that of the United States. Canadian synagogues belong to any one of the three U.S. congregational bodies. (M. SK.)

**Great Britain.**—In Great Britain synagogues are generally classified as Orthodox, Reform (similar to Conservative in the United States), or Liberal (similar to Reform in the U.S.). Most of these congregations are in Greater London, and the remainder are scattered in about 110 provincial communities. Historically, the oldest congregation is the small Orthodox Sephardic (Spanish and Portuguese) community, which dates from the Jewish Resettlement in 1656 and whose religious head is the *haham.* Its central synagogue in Bevis Marks in the City of London was built in 1701.

The largest religious body is the United Synagogue (Orthodox), established by act of Parliament in 1870, although its origins date back to the Ashkenazic settlers from Central and Eastern Europe at the end of the 17th century. This administers synagogues in the Greater London area. Its religious head is the chief rabbi of the United Hebrew Congregations of the British Commonwealth, whose general authority is also recognized by some of the other Orthodox synagogues in London, the provinces, and overseas. The congregations of the Federation of Synagogues (established 1887) and the Union of Orthodox Hebrew Congregations (established 1926) represent the more right wing of Orthodoxy; while the left wing is represented by the New London Synagogue, which separated from the United Synagogue in 1964.

Reform synagogues have grown from one in 1840 to about 24, and Liberal synagogues from one in 1902 to about 20. They are all affiliated to the World Union for Progressive Judaism. Members of different synagogal bodies unite in philanthropic, welfare, and cultural work; and the Board of Deputies includes representatives of all religious sections of British Jewry. (H. HA.)

BIBLIOGRAPHY.—For synagogue in general, *see* various articles under "Synagogue," "Liturgy," etc., in *Jewish Encyclopedia, Universal Jewish Encyclopedia,* Hastings' *Encyclopaedia of Religion and Ethics. See* also G. F. Moore, *Judaism,* vol. i, pp. 281–308 (1927); S. Krauss, *Synagogale Altertümer* (1922); S. Baron, *The Jewish Community* (1945) and *A Social and Religious History of the Jews,* 8 vol. (1952–58); Isaac Levy, *The Synagogue: Its History and Function* (1964). For architecture, *see* E. Mihaly, "Jewish Prayer and Synagogue Architecture," *Judaism,* vol. 7, no. 4, (1958); E. L. Sukenik, *Ancient Synagogues in Palestine and Greece* (1934); W. G. Tachau, "The Architecture of the Synagogue," *American Jewish Year Book,* vol. xxviii, pp. 155–234 (1926); R. Wischinitzer, *Synagogue Architecture in the United States* (1955), *The Architecture of the European Synagogue* (1964). For synagogue organizations in the U.S., see *American Jewish Year Book;* in Great Britain *The Jewish Year Book.* (E. MI.)

**SYNAPSE,** the functional conjunction between two neurons (nerve cells), making conduction of nervous impulses continuous from one to the other. Synapses occur between the axon terminations of one neuron and the cell body of an adjacent neuron (axosomatic synapse); or between axon terminations of one neuron and the dendrites of the next (axodendritic synapse). In some cases adjacent neurons are connected by both types of synapse; the term synaptic junction is used to describe this functional and anatomical relation. (*See* NERVE; NERVE CONDUCTION.) The term synapse is also used in embryology to denote the pairing and union of the homologous chromosomes of the male and female pronuclei. This process is also named syndesis.

(W. M. M.; X.)

**SYNCRETISM,** the act or system of blending or reconciling inharmonious elements. The correct etymology of the word is the punning one given by the ancient Greek author Plutarch, who explains in his *De fraterno amore* that the Cretans stopped their internecine strife and united when attacked by a common outside enemy; this they called *synkretismos* ("Con-Creting"). Later the term was used of tendencies or systems aiming at reconciling divergent philosophies or hostile theological factions. In this sense it was applied to the endeavours of John Cardinal Bessarion and others in the 15th and 16th centuries to harmonize the Aristotelian and Platonic philosophies, as well as to the attempts of the Lutheran theologian Georg Calixtus in the 17th century to bring together the warring factions—Lutheran, Reformed, and ultimately also Catholic—of the church. By that time the term had acquired a pejorative flavour; in the "syncretistic controversy" beween Calixtus and Abraham Calovius it appears as synonymous with "Samaritanism" (referring to the mixed Israelite-pagan religion practised, according to II Kings 17:24–41, by the foreign colonists settled in Samaria). The underlying idea of mixing heterogeneous elements expresses itself also in the later etymology of the term (since Erasmus); the real etymology having been forgotten, the word came to be derived from the Greek *synkerannymi,* "to mix."

In a narrower and almost technical sense the term denotes the religious development of antiquity during the Hellenistic period and more particularly toward the end of the Roman Empire. Religious syncretism is generally the result of the contact and interpenetration of different cultures, and the meeting between Orient and Occident, initiated by the conquests of Alexander the Great, produced the cultural phenomenon known as Hellenism (*see* HELLENISTIC AGE: *Hellenistic Civilization*). Hellenism found an even wider and more unified arena in the *oikoumene* ("inhabited world") of the Roman Empire. The blending of different cults and mythologies promoted by this contact mainly took the form of an increasing penetration of Oriental religions to the West. The coexistence, within the confines of the empire, of various cults and religious systems led to a process of identification. This was abetted by the basic tolerance of polytheism, whose monotheistic tendencies develop by way of inclusion and not (as for example in the Bible) by way of the exclusion and rejection of all other deities.

The growth of philosophical speculation, and in particular of Neoplatonism, allied itself to that process, since the weakening of individual gods facilitated their interpretation as symbols of one common cosmic denominator or divine principle (*e.g.,* the sun in the later Roman cult). The system of allegorical interpretation as developed in the schools of Alexandria admirably lent itself to syncretistic use and in the hands of the pagan apologists proved a useful weapon against Christian polemicists. Deities were identified with one another on the basis of a genuine identity (*e.g.,* Jupiter Capitolinus and Jupiter Latiaris), of superficial outward or phonetic resemblances (*e.g.,* Isis and Io, both being horned; Zeus Sabazius and the Jewish Sabaoth), or of functional or structural similarities (*e.g.,* Roman Jupiter, Greek Zeus, and Persian Mithra, or the Great Mother as Isis, Ceres, Demeter, Cybele). The devotees of a particular cult would consider all other deities as expressions, names, or representations of the particular deity that was the object of their worship. Popular ritual traditions, mythologies, the mystery cults, astrology, priestly cosmologies, philosophical speculation, and magic all contributed their share to a flourishing syncretism. In the hands of reflecting philosophers, it became a conscious and systematic effort. The progressive hellenization of the early Christian message also may fairly be described as a syncretistic process, though scholarly opinion concerning its extent and significance is divided.

As an unconscious, natural development syncretism occurs wherever cultures meet. The biblical record contains indications of much popular syncretism between Israelite and Canaanite religion. An example of conscious theological syncretism can be found in Gen. 14:22 where Abraham identifies his God with Melchizedek's El Elyon ("God Most High"). Christian missionary activity in many parts of the world has produced a great variety of syncretistic forms of religion combining native with Christian elements. (This syncretism is to be distinguished, however, from conscious adaptation by missionaries to the forms of indigenous cultures, such as the "accommodation" advocated by the Jesuit mission in Malabar and China.) Islam, Buddhism (particularly the Mahayana), and Hinduism too have known syncretistic developments. Thus Buddhism and Zoroastrianism mingled in the state religion of the Indo-Afghan kingdom of Kanishka (*q.v.*) in the 2nd century A.D., and Hindu-Buddhist syncretism is much in evidence in Ceylonese popular religion. In 19th-century India, the movement called Brahmo Samaj (*q.v.*) endeavoured to fuse Hindu and Christian values. Many modern religious systems and cults, whether sophisticated (*e.g.,* theosophy, the anthroposophy of Rudolph Steiner) or primitive (cargo cults; *q.v.*), are clearly syncretistic in character.

BIBLIOGRAPHY.—F. Cumont, *Les Religions orientales dans le paganisme romain,* 4th ed. (1929); J. Geffcken, *Der Ausgang des griechisch-römischen Heidentums* (1929); M. P. Nilsson, *Geschichte der griechischen Religion,* vol. 2, pp. 555–672 (1950); H. I. Bell, *Cults and Creeds in Graeco-Roman Egypt* (1953); F. C. Grant, *Hellenistic Religions: the Age of Syncretism* (1953). (R. J. Z. W.)

**SYNDICALISM,** an anticapitalist doctrine that stresses the autonomy of working groups and advocates direct industrial action to overthrow the capitalist order. Syndicalists thus differ from socialists, who advocate capturing the political state, whether by parliamentary or by revolutionary means, and enacting their programs. The syndicalists, like the anarchists, regard the state as inherently oppressive. For its control, they would substitute that of organized workers based on production units. The structure and administration of this proposed syndicalist community remain vague and utopian.

The syndicalist doctrine was first worked out by certain leaders of the French trade-union movement toward the end of the 19th century. The word *syndicalisme* means simply trade unionism; what is known in English as syndicalism the French call *syndicalisme révolutionnaire.* The movement flourished in France chiefly between 1900 and 1914 and had a considerable influence on other countries, especially Italy, Spain, and the Latin American nations.

It also had certain close resemblances to the direct action advocated in the United States at about the same time by the Industrial Workers of the World (*q.v.*). Like the French syndicalists, the IWW repudiated parliamentary action; but the IWW favoured strong, centralized unions rather than the typically small working units of the French syndicalists. There was also an analogous movement in Great Britain in the early decades of the 20th century called guild socialism (*q.v.*), but it was greatly modified both by the traditional parliamentarism of the British working class and by the nonrevolutionary character of the movement's intellectual proponents. Nevertheless certain British trade unions were permeated by syndicalist ideas between 1906 and 1914.

After World War I, syndicalism ceased to be a dynamic force, even in France. Its followers tended to be attracted either by revolutionary Communism, especially as represented by the U.S.S.R., or by the increasing possibilities in Western democracies for socioeconomic improvements through ordinary trade-union activity and parliamentary action. However, syndicalism remained an important residual force, at least during the interwar years, in many European countries. Left-wing trade-union agitations, usually called Trotskyite by the Communists, often resulted from old syndicalist influence. In Spain, in particular, an anarchist opposition to Communist Party discipline existed in the 1930s. During this same period, the Italian fascist dictatorship of Mussolini sought to use syndicalist sentiment, in perverted form, in recruiting support for his corporate state (*q.v.*). Syndicalist overtones were also discerned in some of the support, but not in the leadership, of the British general strike of 1926. The failure of this strike, which was hardly revolutionary, did much, especially in Britain, to turn workers toward parliamentary action instead of direct industrial action to achieve political ends.

Syndicalists often claimed that theirs was the most proletarian of all radical social theories and owed the least to middle-class theorists. This was true of its origin but hardly of its later development by Georges Sorel, whose exposition *Reflections on Violence* (1908) is the best-known syndicalist work. Sorel introduced into syndicalism the notion of social myths by which the workers could be irrationally stirred to revolutionary action. The general strike, advocacy of which the syndicalists had taken over from the anarchists, became in Sorel's hands a myth of this kind.

The syndicalist started from the assumptions common to most schools of socialist thought. He affirmed the inherent injustice of the wage system and the fundamental immorality of capitalist society, based, in his belief, on the exploitation of labour. He accepted and pushed to its logical conclusion the Marxian dogma of the class war; he therefore affirmed that solidarity of interests does not, and cannot, exist between capitalists and wage earners. From these premises he drew the usual socialist conclusion: that individual ownership of the instruments of production must be abolished and communal ownership and control substituted for it. But at this point syndicalism and socialism parted company. Whereas the socialist demanded ownership by the state and its dependent organs, such as the municipalities, the syndicalist demand was for direct ownership and control by the workers, acting through the organizations of their own creation—the trade unions and federations of unions.

State organization and control of industry are, in the syndicalist view, incompatible with true working-class emancipation. The state is, and must be, an instrument of class domination; it is, indeed, "the executive committee of the capitalist class." It exists to defend the interests of that class and is consequently as much the enemy of labour as capital itself.

The state is, moreover, hopelessly wedded to an uncreative bureaucracy, incapable of initiative and ignorant of industrial technique. Its control, even if it were benevolent (which the syndicalist denies it could be), would necessarily be despotic and inefficient; the spirit of routine would combine with inexperience to crush out the possibility of economic progress. Here the syndicalist endorsed the ordinary individualistic criticism of state socialism. Workers' control, exercised through the *syndicats*, would combine freedom with efficiency.

The form of social organization in which this ideal could be realized was ordinarily conceived somewhat as follows: The unit of organization would be the local *syndicat*. This would be brought into touch with other groups by means of the local *bourse du travail* ("labour exchange"), the established function of which was to act as an employment agency and a general centre for trade-union activities. When all the producers were thus linked together by the bourse, the administration of the latter would be able to estimate the economic capacities and necessities of the region, could coordinate production, and, being in touch through other bourses with the industrial system as a whole, could arrange for the necessary transfer of materials and commodities, inward and outward. A species of economic federation would thus replace the structure of capitalist industry, along with which the political and administrative machinery of the state would necessarily disappear.

Two features of this utopia need to be emphasized: consumers as such were excluded from any share in industrial control, and a localized system of industry was envisaged. This latter feature was a direct reflection of economic circumstances in France; both industry and trade unionism were much more local in range than in other and more highly developed countries. But the movement toward large-scale organization, which so profoundly affected every aspect of modern economic life, produced a corresponding modification in later syndicalist ideals.

Syndicalist theory starts from the idea of a class war, which must be waged relentlessly till a complete social transformation has been accomplished. The essential weapon in this struggle is the power of the organized workers. As the cause of the conflict is economic it must necessarily be fought out in the economic sphere. Syndicalist congresses thus persistently repudiated political action and pinned their faith to a general strike as the grand instrument of social revolution. This reliance upon industrial or direct methods of action flows necessarily from the fundamental notions of syndicalism as to the nature of the state, and also from strictly practical considerations.

Outside the mine or factory, workingmen hold divergent religious or political opinions that make effective mass action difficult, if not impossible. Inside, the nature of their employment gives them a sense of solidarity that overrides other differences and bands them together in the *syndicat* for common defense. To persuade them to pass from the defensive to the offensive is the syndicalist's task, and in the accomplishment of this, political labels and controversies would be a hindrance. The strike, therefore, is the characteristic syndicalist weapon. However limited in its scope and object, it is an educative experience. Successful, it inspires the workers with a sense of power; unsuccessful, it impresses upon them the servility of their lot and the necessity for better organization and wider aims. Thus, every strike is a preparation for the revolutionary day when the workers, or a fighting minority of them (for syndicalism repudiates as bourgeois the dogma of the sacredness of majority rule), shall seize the instruments of production by an expropriatory general strike. In the meantime, they are working out from day to day, in the ordinary course of their employment, the ethics and the jurisprudence of the new social order.

The syndicalist idea, as understood in France, may be said to have developed out of the strong anarchist and antiparliamentary traditions of the French working class, and to have been much influenced by the teachings of P. J. Proudhon and, on another side, by Louis Auguste Blanqui. A French delegate to the congress of the International Working Men's Association (known as the First International) held at Basel in 1869, for instance, prophesied that "the grouping of different trades in the city will form the commune of the future" when "government will be replaced by federated councils of *syndicats* and by a committee of their respective delegates regulating the relations of labour—this taking the place of politics."

These tendencies manifested themselves with increasing strength during the 1890s in the two main labour organizations of the period—the Confédération Générale du Travail (or CGT) and the Fédération des Bourses du Travail. The secretary of this latter organization, Fernand Pelloutier, did more perhaps than any other individual in his day to work out the characteristic doctrines of syndicalism and to spread them among his fellow workers. When these two bodies joined forces in 1902, trade unionism in general and syndicalism in particular received an immense accession of strength; and the syndicalist doctrine subsequently remained —in spite of the efforts of political socialists to capture the *syndicats* for their own purposes—the characteristic expression of

French revolutionary idealism until World War I. Thereafter, as noted above, it ceased to be a strong force. *See* FRANCE: *Administration and Social Conditions.* *See* also ANARCHISM; COMMUNISM; GENERAL STRIKE; GUILD SOCIALISM; INDUSTRIAL WORKERS OF THE WORLD; SABOTAGE; SOCIALISM; and references under "Syndicalism" in the Index.

BIBLIOGRAPHY.—H. Lagardelle, *Le Socialisme ouvrier* (1911); G. Sorel, *Réflexions sur la violence* (1908; Eng. trans. by T. Hulme, *Reflections on Violence,* 1914); J. G. Brooks, *American Syndicalism* (1913); L. Levine, *Syndicalism in France* (1914); G. D. H. Cole, *Self-Government in Industry,* 3rd ed. with appendix on syndicalism (1918), *Guild Socialism Restated* (1920); F. W. Coker, *Recent Political Thought,* ch. viii (1934); Paul F. Brissenden, *I. W. W.; A Study of American Syndicalism,* 2nd ed., 2nd ptg. (1957); R. Brecy, *Le Mouvement syndical en France: 1871–1921* (1963).

(G. D. H. C.; J. M. RE.; S. H.; L. D. E.)

**SYNGE, JOHN MILLINGTON** (1871–1909), Ireland's finest poetic dramatist, and a leading figure of the Irish literary renaissance, was born on April 16, 1871, at Rathfarnham, near Dublin. Educated at home and at private schools, he early showed the interest in nature that was to play a dynamic part in his drama. He studied languages at Trinity College, Dublin, 1888–92, and music at the Royal Irish Academy, and, deciding to become a musician, went to Germany in 1893. He spent much of the next four years there, in Italy, and in France. In 1897 he suffered the first stages of lymphatic sarcoma, from which he died.

BY COURTESY OF THE NATIONAL GALLERY OF IRELAND

SYNGE; DRAWING BY JOHN BUTLER YEATS, 1905

Yeats (whom he met in 1899 in Paris) gave Synge the best advice he ever received—to stop writing critical essays and go to the Aran Islands, where he would discover a life that had never found expression in dramatic terms. Synge had visited the islands in 1898, and until 1902 spent part of each year living among the people, observing how they faced life and death, learning their language. He recorded his impressions in the beautiful *The Aran Islands* (1907). His one-act plays—*The Shadow of the Glen* (1903) and *Riders to the Sea* (1904)—are based on stories heard from Islanders. His first three-act play, *The Well of the Saints,* was produced in 1905. In the same year he journeyed with the artist Jack B. Yeats through the Congested Districts of the western Irish seaboard, seeing the peasant life depicted with such irony, humour, and compassion in his most famous play *The Playboy of the Western World* (1907). It caused a riot at the Abbey Theatre (*q.v.*), so showing the penetration of his insight into human nature in general and the Irish character in particular.

Just before he died (in Dublin, March 24, 1909), Synge was working on an unfinished masterpiece, *Deirdre of the Sorrows* (published 1910), a vigorous, poetic dramatization of one of the great love stories of Irish mythology. In April a collection, *Poems and Translations,* was published. Synge would have been 39 years old at the time. His verse is impressive for its concentrated meaning and formal compactness. In November *The Tinker's Wedding* (published 1907) was produced in London.

Synge's career as dramatist was comparatively short but in that time he wrote seven plays, the seventh, unpublished until 1968, being *When the Moon Has Set,* thrice rejected by Yeats and Lady Gregory, his co-directors at the Abbey, but preserved by him in manuscript. All show an extremely sophisticated craftsman coping with primitive life. Alone among 20th-century dramatists, Synge uncompromisingly explores the primitive. He was convinced that:

> In Ireland, for a few years more, we have a popular imagination that is fiery and magnificent and tender; so that those of us who wish to write start with a chance that is not given to writers in places where the springtime of the local life has been forgotten, and the harvest is a memory only, and the straw has been turned into bricks . . . [and that] . . . all art is a collaboration; and there is little doubt that in the happy ages of literature, striking and beautiful phrases were as ready to the story-teller's or the playwright's hand, as the rich cloaks and dresses of his time. (Preface to *The Playboy of the Western World,* 1907.)

It was this conviction that drove him to record the colourful, outrageous sayings, flights of fancy, eloquent invective, bawdy witticisms, and earthy phrases of the peasantry from Kerry to Donegal. And, in dramatizing a primitive existence, he created a new, musical dramatic idiom, spoken in English but vitalized by Irish syntax, ways of thought, and imagery. It is an extremely accurate vehicle for the revelation of his dramatic vision, a vision that, though fundamentally tragic, also produced uproarious comedy. Synge has at once a tragic view of man as time's victim, pathetically powerless when pitted against the forces of a hostile universe; and an ebulliently comic view of man as a being who, because he is forced to realize his own inadequacy, creates a new and vital world in his imagination. In both tragedy and comedy Synge is obsessed by the transfiguring power of imagination: his characters seek refuge in it, are transformed by it, and are immortal because of it.

*See* also TRAGEDY.

BIBLIOGRAPHY.—*Works,* 4 vol. (1910; several reprints); *Collected Works,* 5 vol., general editor, R. Skelton: vol. i, *Poems and Translations,* ed. by Skelton (1962), ii, *Prose,* ed. by A. Price (1966), iii and iv, *Plays,* ed. by A. Saddlemyer (1968); *Plays and Poems,* ed. by T. R. Henn (1963); *Plays, Poems and Prose* (selections), Everyman's Library, 2nd ed. (1958), and *Four Plays and The Aran Islands,* World's Classics (1962), both ed. by Skelton. *See* also W. B. Yeats, *Synge and the Ireland of His Time* (1911), *The Death of Synge,* etc. (1928), and *Autobiographies* (1955); D. H. Greene and E. M. Stephens, *J. M. Synge, 1871–1909* (1959); A. Price, *Synge and Anglo-Irish Drama* (1961); E. Coxhead, *Synge and Lady Gregory* (1962). (B. KE.)

**SYNGE, RICHARD LAURENCE MILLINGTON** (1914– ), British biochemist, was awarded the 1952 Nobel Prize for Chemistry jointly with Archer John Porter Martin (*q.v.*) for their method of identifying and separating chemical elements by chromatography. He was born on Oct. 28, 1914, at Liverpool and educated at Winchester College and Trinity College, Cambridge. At Cambridge and in the Wool Industries Research Association's laboratories at Leeds he collaborated in chemical research with Martin. In 1943 he was appointed to the Lister Institute of Preventive Medicine, London, and from 1948 he worked at the Rowett Research Institute, Bucksburn, Aberdeenshire. He was elected fellow of the Royal Society in 1950. Partition chromatography (*q.v.*), devised by Martin and Synge, effected the partition of a substance between two liquids by very simple means instead of by a series of intricate chemical operations, and it became so widely used in chemical, biological, and medical research as to constitute almost a new scientific tool. In 1951 Synge, with four other scientists, formed a "science for peace" committee.

*See* E. Farber, *Nobel Prize Winners in Chemistry* . . . (1963).

(D. McK.)

**SYNOPTIC GOSPELS:** *see* GOSPELS.

**SYNOPTIC WEATHER CHART,** a term used peculiarly in meteorology for maps of any large or small portion of the globe, on which are plotted weather observations taken at various points over the area represented and at approximately the same time. In addition the data on the map are usually analyzed by means of conventional symbols, isolines, and shadings (*see* WEATHER FORECASTING).

The expression weather map or weather chart is essentially synonymous with synoptic chart. The adjective synoptic implies a brief or condensed means of presenting a combined or general view of something; but in meteorological parlance the word came to have the connotation of synchronous because, according to most schools of meteorology, only synchronous weather observations lend themselves to rational analysis for the purpose of preparing forecasts. The notable exception is in the U.S.S.R., where the official weather maps are not based on entirely synchronous observations but on observations made at the same local sun time.

Synoptic charts are published daily by the leading national weather services. A remarkable series of historical weather maps for the Northern Hemisphere, one a day from Jan. 1, 1899, to June 30, 1939, compiled and analyzed by a uniform technique, were published by the U.S. government (Weather Bureau) during World War II and were resumed in 1946. The earliest weather charts were made well before 1835 by collecting synchronous weather reports by mail. The first telegraphic collection of synoptic reports and mapping thereof for forecasting was accomplished by Urbain J. J. Leverrier following the Crimean War. From about 1870 the leading nations have published charts each day along with the official forecasts. The basic chart shows the synchronous observations at sea level or surface stations over a more or less extended area, generally at least a large part of a continent and often a whole hemisphere. For each weather station whose observations are taken at internationally standardized synoptic hours—one to four times a day—and received by radio or telegraph at the forecast offices, there are plotted in a model grouping around the circle representing the station on the map the values of or symbolic indications of a number of weather elements. For all stations at least the barometric pressure (usually reduced to sea level), the air temperature, the present weather, the wind direction and speed or force, and the sky cover will be reported. In some countries many stations also give visibility, dew point or relative humidity, forms, amounts and movements of clouds at different levels, net amount of pressure change during the last three hours, the characteristics or the tendency in the pressure during the last three hours, and the amount of precipitation after the last observation. In reports made by ships at sea, the water temperature, the state of sea, position and motion of the ship are also reported.

An innumerable variety of charts could be constructed from such reports; *e.g.*, charts to show the change in pressure and the change in temperature since the previous chart or in the last 12 hr. or 24 hr. are often made. The analysis of the basic surface chart consists usually of isobars, fronts (*q.v.*), and air mass (*q.v.*) designations, and shadings or symbols to show where precipitation and fog are present.

To obtain a three-dimensional synchronous view of the atmosphere, it is customary, in regions where upper-air soundings are regularly made, to construct synoptic charts for several levels in the free atmosphere. Plotted on them are the values of the elements given by the soundings at that level, usually only pressure, temperature, humidity, and wind. The levels selected may be surfaces of constant height, constant pressure, or constant entropy.

During the 1930s and World War II, after some experimentation with isentropic charts (*q.v.*), nearly all weather services gradually came to prefer constant-pressure charts; by 1945 they became practically internationally standard. The World Meteorological Organization recommended that analysis of the 700- and 500-millibar surfaces be made as a minimum. After World War II transmittal of sea-level and upper-air synoptic charts by means of facsimile (both telegraphic and radio) was developed, in the United States particularly.

To analyze much higher levels in the atmosphere some forecasters draw lines of equal wind speed (isotachs, isokinetics) on the constant-pressure charts for 500-, 300-, 200-millibar, and even higher surfaces, and prepare charts showing the topography of the tropopause.

For tropical regions isobaric and constant-pressure charts have not proved very helpful for forecasting, and experiments indicated that streamline charts would be more successful, though the technique is difficult and weather reporting stations are still too sparse over most of the tropics.

Prognostic charts represent the forecast patterns of pressure, height of pressure surfaces, or other elements (temperature, wind, etc.), for some future time. In forecasting for periods longer than one or two days, it is often necessary to construct mean synoptic charts to show averages of the elements over five days, a week, a month, or more.

Large areas of the oceans, and particularly of the polar regions and Southern Hemisphere, have few observing stations or ships and hence cannot be synoptically charted in the detail required by weather forecasters. Methods of extrapolation of soundings or map patterns to heights above those reached by many of the soundings have been found expedient under certain conditions.

For the principles of analysis and use of synoptic charts in forecasting *see* AIR MASS; FRONTS; ISALLOBAR; ISENTROPIC CHART; WEATHER FORECASTING.

BIBLIOGRAPHY.—S. Petterssen, *Weather Analysis and Forecasting* (1940); V. P. Starr, *Basic Principles of Weather Forecasting* (1942); H. C. Willett, *Descriptive Meteorology*, 2nd ed (1959). (R. G. SE.)

**SYPHILIS:** *see* VENEREAL DISEASES.

**SYRACUSE** (Italian SIRACUSA; ancient SYRACUSAE), a city of southeastern Sicily and capital of Siracusa Province, lies on the Ionian coast 33 mi. (53 km.) SSE of Catania and includes the small island of Ortigia (Ortygia). Pop. (1961) 89,717. It was the chief Greek city of ancient Sicily.

On the mainland the town's modern districts project in long straight lines among orchards, flower gardens, and the stone quarries (*latomie*) which contrast with the narrow winding streets of the older part on Ortigia. The Porto Grande occupies a natural harbour and is separated from Porto Piccolo by Ortigia. Signs of the various conquests (Byzantine, Norman, Saracen, Swabian, Aragonese, Spanish) were destroyed in the 1693 earthquake, and medieval buildings that remained were camouflaged in 18th-century Baroque style. Excavations have unearthed monuments, dating from the 2nd to the 8th century and interesting for their copious epigraphs (see *Archaeology* below). Tourism, based mainly on archaeological interest, is highly developed. The locality is noted for soft limestone used in ornamentation. Industries include wine making, vegetable oil refining, cement and soap manufacture, salt processing, and fishing (shellfish).

**Architecture.**—The Byzantine architectural style is visible in three churches: the small basilica of S. Pietro, with 16th-century modifications; the Duomo (cathedral), built in the 7th century on the site of a Doric temple; and the Church of Sta. Lucia (12th–13th centuries, with 17th-century modifications), erected on the spot where St. Lucy, the city's patron saint, was martyred. The apse of Sta. Lucia contains "The Burial of St. Lucy" ascribed to the painter Michelangelo da Caravaggio. The small church of Sta. Maria dei Miracoli bears traces of both Gothic and Aragonese influence. The Porta Marina is a 15th-century gateway with Gothic and Catalan niches. The most important medieval building is the Castello Maniace, built by Frederick II in the 13th century with a square base and round corner towers. The Palazzo Bellomo (from the same period with later renovations) houses the Medieval Museum and the Art Gallery which has an "Annunciation" by Antonello da Messina. The 14th-century Margulense-Macciotta, Montalto, Chiaramonte, and Abele palaces are rich in double- and triple-mullioned windows. The Lanza, Bellomo, Gargallo, and Banca d'Italia palaces represent 15th- and 16th-century Catalan and Gothic styles.

The influence of the Renaissance can be seen in the sculpture, the sarcophagi, and the stoups of the Gagini and Laurana schools. The Baroque element is visible in the Chapel of the Most Holy Sacrament, in the College Church, and in that of S. Benedetto; after the earthquake it showed itself in the Beneventano, Borgia, Bongiovanni, and Rizzo palaces, in the Archbishop's Palace, and in the facade of the cathedral (1728–57).

In the cathedral are impressive sculptures and paintings, candelabra, chandeliers, and ciboria chiseled by artists working in gold in the second half of the 18th century. Modern buildings include the Post Office, University, Banca d'Italia, Banco di Sicilia, and Government Palace. (M. T. A. N.)

**Archaeology.**—Ancient Syracuse had four districts: the island, Achradina (nearest the island), Tyche, and Neapolis. The island contains the remains of two Doric temples. The older, belonging probably to the early 6th century B.C., appears, from an inscription on the top step, to have been dedicated to Apollo, possibly also to Artemis. It was about 70 × 180 ft. (21 × 55 m.) and had 42 outer columns (6 columns along the ends and 17 along the sides), set close together and varying between 6 and 7 ft. wide at the base.

The other temple, which became the cathedral in A.D. 640 (it may have become a church even earlier), is to be dated after 480 B.C. It was of similar size (72 × 180 ft.) but had only 36 external columns (6 by 14). It is almost certainly the Temple of Athena. The site was previously occupied by buildings of the 7th and 6th centuries B.C., including a late 6th-century temple and a great sacrificial altar, which were destroyed to make room

LEONARD VON MATT

(TOP) THE REMAINS OF THE LARGEST GREEK THEATRE IN SICILY; (LEFT) WILD PAPYRUS PLANTS IN THE FOUNTAIN OF ARETHUSA NEAR THE WEST COAST OF SICILY; (RIGHT) SLAB OF PAINTED TERRA-COTTA (ABOUT 7TH–6TH CENTURY B.C.) SHOWING A GORGON WITH THE HORSE PEGASUS, FROM AN ARCHAIC TEMPLE WITHIN THE PRECINCTS OF THE TEMPLE OF ATHENA

for it. Their terra-cotta decorations were, however, carefully buried under the pavement of the space which surrounded it.

Near the west coast of the island is the famous spring of Arethusa (*q.v.*), where papyrus grows. According to the legend, the nymph Arethusa was changed into the spring by Artemis to deliver her from the pursuit of the river-god Alpheus (a river in the Peloponnese); and the spring, which was fresh until a medieval earthquake broke the barrier and let in the salt water, was supposed to be actually connected with the Alpheus. The large and well-arranged Museo Nazionale Archeologico contains important pre-Greek and Greek archaeological discoveries. On the landward side of the isthmus connecting the island with Achradina was the agora, in which remains of a colonnade of the Roman period have been found. To the west are the remains of the so-called "Roman gymnasium," probably a small theatre with a temple attached.

Both the island and Achradina had walls, but the most extensive defensive walls were those of Dionysius I, who built a wall about 12 mi. long around Epipolae, the plateau above Syracuse to the north. The southern wall of Epipolae, considerable remains of which exist, shows traces of different periods in its construction, and was probably often restored. It is built of rectangular blocks of limestone, generally quarried on the spot. Euryelus, the point where Epipolae narrows down to a ridge about 60 yd. wide, which is its only link with the hills to the west, still bears the ruins of a mighty fortress (Castello Eurialo), the most imposing, indeed, that has come down from the Greek period. There is no doubt that it was begun under Dionysius, although recent studies showed that the building belongs to more than one period; part of it may have been designed by Archimedes in the late 3rd century B.C. The total length of the works is about 440 yd. In front of the castle proper are three ditches, the innermost of which can be reached from the interior of the castle by a complicated system of underground passages. The front of the castle is formed by five massive towers; behind it are two walled courtyards, to the north of the easternmost of which is the well-guarded main entrance to the plateau of Epipolae (narrower minor entrances are to be seen on both the north and the south sides) connected by a long underground passage with the inner ditch in front of the castle proper. On the north side of Epipolae the cliffs are somewhat more abrupt; here the wall, similar to that on the south, is also traceable, but here it is apparently all of one period.

Remains of Greek and Roman private houses have been found, also several cemeteries, the most noteworthy being the Christian catacombs. Those near the church of Sta. Lucia are the most extensive (2nd century onward). Those near the 12th-century church of S. Giovanni are 4th–6th century, situated near an ancient temple, and contain the crypt of St. Marcianus; the catacombs of Vigna Cassia (3rd century onward) are also extensive.

In Neapolis, the western quarter, public buildings predominate. The Temple of Apollo Temenites has almost entirely disappeared, but the rock-cut Greek theatre is still to be seen. It is the largest in Sicily, being nearly 455 ft. (139 m.) in diameter and having originally 59 rows of seats; the 12 lower tiers were originally covered with marble. Each of the nine *cunei* or blocks of seats bore a name; the inscriptions of four of them are still preserved on the rock, in honour of Zeus, King Hieron II, his wife Philistis, and Nereis, who married his son Gelon in 238 B.C. Of the stage nothing but cuttings in the rock and foundations are visible. The theatre was altered again in Roman times. It commands a splendid view over the Great Harbour, and it is often used for classical performances. Not far off to the southeast is the Roman amphitheatre; it is partly rock-cut and partly built. It is exceeded in size only by the Colosseum and the amphitheatres of Capua and Verona, measuring about 460 × 390 ft. (140 × 119 m.) over all: the arena is 227 × 129 ft. (69 × 39 m.). West of the amphitheatre are the foundations of the great altar erected by Hieron II, 653 × 74 ft. (199 × 23 m.). To the northwest of the theatre a winding road ascends through the rock, with Byzantine tomb chambers on each side of it; in this district are hundreds of small niches cut in the rock, as a rule about 2 ft. square and a few inches deep, which contained inscriptions or reliefs relating to the cult of ancestors as heroes. In the cliffs below Epipolae are huge quarries, the famous Latomie of Syracuse; the Latomia del Paradiso contains the "Ear of Dionysius," a large artificial cave of unknown use and remarkable acoustic properties. Beginning about 1950, this whole quarter underwent thorough investigation and systematization.

Immediately outside Neapolis on the south the marshes of Lysimelia begin, which proved fatal to more than one besieging force. They are traversed by the Anapus (Anapo), with its tributary the Cyane (Ciane), the latter famous for the papyrus which grows wild in the stream. To the south of the Anapus is the hill Polichne, on which stood the Olympieum (Temple of Olympian Zeus), attributed to the early 6th century B.C. Its monolithic columns, of which two are still standing, are over 20 ft. high and 6 ft. in lower diameter: it is similar in plan to the Temple of Apollo but larger (about 73 × 203 ft.). The hill was frequently occupied in attacks on Syracuse by the besieging force. From Punta Caderini (ancient Dascon), south of the Olympieum, the shore of the Great Harbour begins to rise, until the rocky Penisola della Maddalena (ancient Plemmyrium) is reached.

(E. A. F.; T. A.; X.)

**History.**—Syracuse was founded from Corinth, according to Thucydides, in the year after the first Greek Sicilian colony, Naxos (*i.e., c.* 733 B.C.). It was an excellent site. The offshore island of Ortygia was easily defended, there was a large arable plain opposite (between the shore and the higher ground of Epipolae to the north), and Syracuse had the best harbour in Sicily (as well as a smaller harbour north of the island). Thucydides says that Archias, the Corinthian founder, drove out Sicels from Ortygia, and remains of their huts and tombs have been found; the archaeological evidence shows that at the same time the colonists also settled on the mainland.

Syracuse slowly reaped the advantages of its position. It became the natural port of distribution for Corinthian goods; it extended its territorial control by the establishment of small settlements at Acrae (*c.* 663), Casmenae (*c.* 643), and Camarina (*c.* 598). Many of the Sicels in its territory were reduced to serfdom and worked the land for Syracusan masters; a few independent villages remained. In the second half of the 6th century Ortygia was joined to the mainland by a mole, coinage was introduced, and buildings became more ambitious. But it was the Deinomenid tyranny that marked the decisive stage in Syracuse's development.

*Gelon and Hieron.*—Hippocrates, tyrant of Gela (498–491), threatened the independence of Syracuse and other cities, and Syracuse was saved only by the joint intervention of Corinth and Corcyra and the cession of Camarina (previously depopulated by the Syracusans). In 485 the *Gamoroi,* or landowners (*i.e.,* the descendants of the original settlers, who formed an aristocratic body), who had been expelled by the people and the Sicel serfs and had taken refuge at Casmenae, appealed to Hippocrates' successor Gelon (son of Deinomenes; hence "Deinomenid"), who took possession of Syracuse, without opposition, and made it the seat of his power. Gelon (*q.v.*) added to the population of Syracuse enfranchised mercenaries and the inhabitants of other cities conquered by him. His general rule was mild, and he won fame as the champion of the Greeks by his great victory over the Carthaginians at Himera (480). He is said to have been greeted as king; but he does not seem to have taken the title formally.

Gelon's brother and successor, Hieron (*q.v.;* 478–467/466), kept up the power of the city, and in 474 decisively defeated the Etruscans, who with the Carthaginians were the chief enemies of the western Greeks, at the Battle of Cumae. He won himself a name by his encouragement of poets, especially Aeschylus and Simonides, while his Pythian and Olympian victories inspired odes by Pindar and Bacchylides. But in his internal government he was suspicious, greedy, and cruel. After family disputes the power passed on his death to his brother Thrasybulus, who was driven out by a general rising (466). Syracuse thus became a democracy. Freedom was celebrated by a colossal statue and a yearly feast of Zeus Eleutherius. But when the mercenaries and other new settlers were debarred from office new struggles arose. The mercenaries held Ortygia and Achradina (the part of the mainland city nearest the island). The people therefore walled in the suburb of Tyche to the north of Achradina. The mercenaries were eventually expelled (*c.* 460). Although there were attempts to reestablish tyranny, and an institution called *petalism,* like the Athenian ostracism (*q.v.*), was devised to guard against such dangers, democracy was not seriously threatened for more than 50 years, during which Syracuse's hegemony over Greek Sicily was never successfully challenged. There were also naval expeditions to the Etruscan coast, Elba, and Corsica about 453 B.C., and Diodorus Siculus mentions great military and naval preparations of Syracuse in 439.

*The Defeat of Athens.*—There is little trace, however, of these preparations during the Peloponnesian War when the Athenians sent a small force to Sicily in 427 to support the Ionian cities against Syracuse. The Athenian force, only 20 triremes, was able to hold its own, and the Syracusan navy was small and ineffective, but when Athens in 424 sent reinforcements the Syracusan statesman Hermocrates was able to persuade the Sicilian cities to bury their differences at the Conference of Gela. The Athenians had to withdraw, but the grievances of Segesta and Leontini (the latter of which had been depopulated by the Syracusans in 422) gave them the opportunity to return with a much larger force in 415. Hermocrates had great difficulty in making Syracuse realize the danger, and had the Athenians moved directly on Syracuse the city might have fallen. But the Athenian command was divided and decided first to win over allies. This delay and the subsequent recall of Alcibiades, who had inspired the expedition, saved Syracuse. The defensive measures, however, were inadequate, and the Athenians gained control both of the harbour and of Epipolae, the plateau north of the city. Syracuse was near to surrender when the Spartan Gylippus slipped through the Athenian lines with a small relief force. Gylippus put new spirit into the defense, the Athenians were driven from Epipolae, lost control of Plemmyrium commanding the entrance to the harbour, and were confined to the harbour and its shores. Reinforcements arrived in 413 from Athens under Demosthenes and Eurymedon, but a bold night attack on Epipolae failed. Demosthenes urged immediate withdrawal, but Nicias hesitated and an eclipse of the moon made him delay further. In a fierce naval struggle in the harbour the Athenians were defeated, and when they attempted to retreat by land it was too late. The Athenians and allies who escaped the massacre were imprisoned in the quarries; Nicias and Demosthenes were executed.

*Dionysius I.*—In the enthusiasm following this overwhelming victory Syracuse sent a small squadron under Hermocrates to fight for Sparta against Athens in the Aegean. But in his absence his political opponents, led by Diocles, seized power and introduced a more radical form of democracy. Hermocrates was exiled in 409; in 408/407 he was killed in an attempt to enter the city. With him was wounded Dionysius, who soon (supported by some men of rank, among them the historian Philistus), by accusing the generals engaged at Acragas in the war against Carthage, obtaining the restoration of exiles, and confiscating the property of the rich at Gela, secured his own election as sole general with special powers. He next procured from a military assembly at Leontini a vote of a bodyguard; he hired mercenaries and in 405 came back to Syracuse as tyrant and kept his power till his death (367). But he was almost overthrown in 405. When he was obliged to evacuate Gela and Camarina, his enemies in the army reached Syracuse before him, plundered his house, and assaulted his wife. Dionysius arrived by night and killed or expelled his enemies, who established themselves at Etna. In 397 or 396 Syracuse was besieged by the Carthaginians under Himilco, who took up his quarters at the Olympieum, but his troops in the marshes below suffered from disease, and a masterly combined attack by land and sea by Dionysius ended in Himilco's defeat and withdrawal. Peace with the Carthaginians confirmed Dionysius in the possession of Syracuse, and left it the one great Greek city of Sicily, which, however enslaved at home, was at least independent of Carthage.

During the long tyranny of Dionysius the city grew greatly in size, population, and grandeur. Syracuse absorbed the populations of Greek cities in Sicily and Italy which had fallen to the Carthaginians or to Dionysius. The fortifications of Syracuse were extended. The island (Ortygia) had its own separate defenses; Dionysius drove out the old inhabitants and turned the place into a barracks, living himself in the citadel. He included in his new mainland walls the whole plateau of Epipolae, with a strong fortress at Euryelus, its apex on the west. Syracuse was now the most splendid and the best fortified of all Greek cities. Its naval power, too, was vastly increased; the docks were enlarged, and 200 new warships were built. The fleet of Dionysius was the most powerful in the Mediterranean. Doubtless fear and hatred of Carthage urged the Syracusans to acquiesce in the enormous expenditure involved. Much, too, was done for the beauty of the city; several new temples were built, and gymnasia erected outside the walls.

*Dionysius' Successors.*—Under his son Dionysius the younger a reaction set in among the restless citizens of Syracuse. His uncle Dion (*q.v.*) was for a time his trusted political adviser. Dion's idea seems to have been to make Dionysius something like a constitutional sovereign, and with this in view he invited Plato to Syracuse. But Philistus and other followers of Dionysius were opposed to any kind of liberal reform, and the result was the banishment of Dion from Sicily. In 357 Dion returned and besieged Dionysius in Ortygia; though he escaped, there was much bloodshed and destruction before Ortygia surrendered. Dion tried to establish aristocratic government but was assassinated in 354.

In the confusion that followed, Dionysius returned, and Sicily was again menaced by Carthage. Syracuse asked help from the mother-city, Corinth; and Timoleon (*q.v.*), who was sent out, drove Dionysius from Ortygia and recovered Syracuse. He then decisively defeated the Carthaginians and made a peace settlement in which they were confined to the smaller half of Sicily west of the Halycus (modern Platani) River. From 343 to 337 he was supreme at Syracuse, with the goodwill of the citizens. The tyrants' citadel on Ortygia was demolished. Syracuse, with an influx of many new colonists from Greece, Sicily, and Italy, prospered once more. Timoleon retired in 337 and soon died. After his death a splendid monument, with porticoes and gymnasia surrounding it, known as the Timoleonteum, was raised to honour his memory.

At some date before 317 another revolution at Syracuse apparently transferred the government to an oligarchy of 600 leading citizens. In 317 Agathocles (*q.v.*), with a force of Sicels from Morgantina and exiles from the Greek cities, backed up by the Carthaginian Hamilcar, became tyrant of the city. When he was hard pressed by the Carthaginians, he took the bold step of leading an expedition to Africa in 310. His campaign was at first successful and relieved the pressure on Syracuse, but his fortunes changed, and in the winter of 307/306 he was forced to withdraw finally. He was able, however, to secure an honourable peace with Carthage and to confirm Syracusan influence over eastern Sicily and parts of south Italy. Under his strong government Syracuse was free from faction, the fortifications were restored, and new public buildings erected. After his death in 289 came another period of revolution and despotism; and but for the brief intervention of Pyrrhus, king of Epirus, in 278–276, Syracuse, and all Sicily, would have fallen to the Carthaginians.

A better time began under Hieron II, who had fought under Pyrrhus and who rose from general to tyrant (king, as he soon came to be called). During his reign (*c.* 270–216/215) Syracuse seems to have grown greatly in wealth and population. Hieron's rule was kindly and enlightened, combining good order with a fair share of liberty and self-government. His financial legislation was careful and considerate; his regulations for the customs and the corn (grain) tithes were accepted and maintained under the Roman government. He encouraged the poet Theocritus and employed the mathematician and engineer Archimedes (*qq.v.*), both born in Syracuse. It was a time, too, for great public works. After a Roman attack on Syracuse (263) Hieron became a firm ally of Rome against Carthage (*see* PUNIC WARS).

*Capture by the Romans.*—Hieronymus, the grandson of Hieron, allied himself with Carthage, but he soon fell in a conspiracy (214). There was a fierce popular outbreak, and Hieron's family was murdered; the Carthaginian party finally got the upper hand. M. Claudius Marcellus was then in command of the Roman army in Sicily, and he threatened the Syracusans with attack unless they expelled Epicydes and Hippocrates, the leading anti-Romans. These two escaped from Leontini when Marcellus promptly stormed it. This sack roused the feeling of the Syracusans against any negotiations with the Roman general, and, electing Epicydes and Hippocrates generals, they closed their gates on him. Marcellus, after an unsuccessful attempt to negotiate, began the siege (213 B.C.), establishing a camp on Polichne, where the old Olympieum stood; but he made his chief assault on the northern wall by land and on Achradina by sea. The city was defended by a large garrison and by the ingenious contrivances of Archimedes, whose engines of war dealt havoc among the Roman ships and frustrated the attack on the fortifications on the northern slopes of Epipolae. Marcellus was obliged to besiege the city; at last, in 212, information was given him that the Syracusans were celebrating a great festival of Artemis. Making use of this opportunity, he forced the Hexapylon entrance (modern Scala Greca) by night and established himself on the heights of Epipolae and in Neapolis and Tyche. The strong fortress of Euryelus was isolated and soon had to surrender. Achradina and the island still held out; a Carthaginian fleet was moored off Achradina and Carthaginian troops were encamped near Polichne. But disease broke out in both armies. The Carthaginian ships sailed away; on their way back to Syracuse with supplies they were driven away by adverse winds and a Roman fleet. Achradina and the island still held out under the Syracusan mercenaries, till one of their officers, a Spaniard, betrayed them to the Romans (211). Marcellus gave the city up to plunder, and many of its art treasures were taken to Rome. Archimedes perished in the confusion of the sack.

(E. A. F.; T. A.; R. ME.)

Syracuse became the Roman governor's residence. Cicero has many references to it as a centre of Greek art and culture, and Augustus established a colony there. Frankish pirates plundered the city *c.* A.D. 280.

Legend attributed the beginning (certainly early) of Christianity at Syracuse to the three days St. Paul spent there on his way to Rome. The first bishop was said to have been Marcianus; Lucy, patron saint of Syracuse, was martyred *c.* 305 under Diocletian.

The Byzantine emperor Constans II attempted to make Syracuse his capital (663), but was assassinated there in 668. The Arabs took it in 878; Palermo became the leading city in Sicily, though Syracuse was always an important port. It was briefly regained for the Byzantine emperor by George Maniaces (1038–40), and it was the amir of Syracuse, Muhammad ibn Timnah, who encouraged the Normans to invade Sicily (1060). Under the Aragonese, Syracuse became the seat of the governor of the Camera Reginale, the domain of the queen of Sicily.

An unsuccessful revolt against the Bourbon government in 1837 led to Syracuse's demotion from provincial capital in favour of Noto (until 1865). During World War II it was heavily bombed by the Allies, particularly the port area.

*See* also SICILY: *History*. (X.)

SIRACUSA PROVINCE. The province (area 814 sq.mi. [2,109 sq.km.]; pop. [1961] 345,867) stretches across the hilly slopes of Monti Iblei and as far as the plains of Catania and Lentini. The economy is principally agricultural. The fertile land produces maize (corn), cereals, vegetables, vines, olives, citrus fruit, carobs, nuts, almonds, cotton, and fodder. There are small numbers of livestock. Commercial activities include food processing, canning, milling, salt extraction, the distillation of orange-blossom and aromatic herbs, and the production of olive oil and wine (muscatel). The province is crossed by the rail routes Catania-Syracuse-Pozzallo and Syracuse-Ragusa. Its most important towns are Augusta (military base and port), Avola, Floridia, Lentini, Noto, Pachino, and Palazzolo Acreide, the modern successor to ancient Akrae with its Greek and Roman ruins.

*See* also references under "Syracuse" in the Index.

(M. T. A. N.)

BIBLIOGRAPHY.—*Archaeology and Topography:* E. Mauceri, *Siracusa* (1930); G. E. Rizzo, *Il Teatro Greco di Siracusa* (1923); C. Anti, *Guida per il visitatore del teatro antico di Siracusa* (1948); L. Mauceri, *Il Castello Eurialo*, 2nd ed. (1956); M. Guido, *Syracuse* (1958).

(X.)

*Ancient History:* E. A. Freeman, *The History of Sicily*, 4 vol. (1891–94); J. Carcopino, *La loi de Hiéron et les romains* (1919); K. Fabricius, "Das antike Syrakus," *Klio* (Beiheft xxviii; 1932); T. J. Dunbabin, *The Western Greeks* (1948); A. G. Woodhead, *The Greeks in the West* (1962).

(R. ME.)

**SYRACUSE,** a city of New York, U.S., and the seat of Onondaga county, is midway between Albany and Buffalo, at the south end of Lake Onondaga (5 mi. long). It is the central city of the Syracuse standard metropolitan statistical area, which encompasses Madison, Onondaga and Oswego counties. Syracuse itself has lost population to the metropolitan area; in 1960 the population of the city was 216,038, as compared with 220,583 in 1950. The metropolitan area by contrast had a population of 563,781 in 1960, a 21.2% increase since 1950. The growth is spreading north to Liverpool, west to Auburn and east to Chittenango, reaching toward Oneida, Rome and Utica to form a single great central New York urbanized region. (For comparative population figures *see* table in NEW YORK: *Population.*)

**History.**—The site of Syracuse was the home of the Onondagas and the capital of the Iroquois federation called the Five (later Six) Nations, whose founding father was Hiawatha. Known also as "The Long House" or "People of Many Fires," the Iroquois formed a chain of nations, beginning with the Mohawks at the easternmost point and linking the Oneidas, Onondagas, Cayugas and Senecas on the west (*see* also IROQUOIS). The site was visited by the explorers Samuel de Champlain in 1615 and Pierre Esprit, sieur de Radisson, in 1651 (while a captive of the Mohawks) and by Simon Le Moyne, a Jesuit missionary, in 1654. At the site was a spring from which the Indians would not drink because they believed a demon lived in it, giving the water an evil smell; Le Moyne discovered that it was a fountain of salt brine. In 1655 a mission was founded by Fathers Joseph Chaumonot and Claude Dablon, and the next year a military post was founded near the present village of Liverpool (5 mi. NW of Syracuse); both were abandoned in 1658 because of the hostility of the Mohawks, but the mission was resumed in 1668 and continued through the century.

The first white settler at Syracuse was Ephraim Webster, who established a trading post there in 1786. In 1788 Asa Danforth, who came to be called "the father of Onondaga county," built a sawmill and a gristmill and organized the militia. Also in that year the state undertook by treaty with the Onondagas to manage the salt springs; in 1795 it acquired title to the springs and 10 sq.mi. of surrounding land in return for $1,000 in cash and promise of an annual rental of $700 and 150 bu. of salt. In 1797 the state began leasing the salt lands on a royalty basis. Three villages soon sprang up around the southern end of the lake: Webster's Landing and Salina in 1797 and Geddes (founded by James Geddes, the first manufacturer of salt on a large scale) in 1803. The landing was known by several names in succession until 1820, when a post office was established and the name of Syracuse was adopted, after the ancient Greek city in Sicily. Syracuse was incorporated as a village in 1825, became the county seat in 1827 and, absorbing Salina, was chartered as a city in 1847. From time to time various annexations of contiguous territory were made, including the village of Geddes in 1886. The Onondaga Indian reservation is located 6 mi. S of the city.

**Government.**—Syracuse has a mayor and council form of government. Because of the development of the metropolitan area, especially Onondaga county, local government is tending more toward a county or metropolitan form; for example, by 1950 it was evident that the supply of water then available was insufficient for further industrial development, and in that year the Onondaga County Water authority was created to attack the problem from an area standpoint. The city and county per capita costs of government are average for the cities and counties of upstate New York, as are the property tax rates. The city has a sales tax and is virtually debt free.

**Commerce, Industry and Transportation.**—The salt industry provided the original economic foundation of the city, as well as the source of its first private fortunes; Syracuse supplied most of the salt for the United States until 1870. Since then, however, the metropolitan area has developed into a manufacturing centre of considerable importance. The principal products are machinery, metal products, food, paper products and chinaware. It is the wholesale trade centre for the central New York region, rivaled only by Buffalo at one side of the state and Albany at the other. Syracuse is situated at the crossroads of central New York and is well served by highways and railroads. Hancock airport is supplemented by numerous other public and private airports. The State Barge canal is within easy reach; four oil pipelines complete the transportation system.

**Education and Cultural Activities.**—Syracuse is an outstanding educational centre, led by Syracuse University, a private coeducational institution founded in 1870 by the Methodist Church. Its colleges and schools offer facilities for graduate, professional and adult education; among them are the Maxwell Graduate School of Citizenship and Public Affairs, the College of Forestry (a unit of the State University of New York) and a branch college in Utica. Le Moyne, a Roman Catholic coeducational college, was founded in 1946. Nearby are two state university colleges of education, at Cortland and Oswego, and the Auburn Community College, a two-year institute. There are numerous musical and dramatic groups, including summer theatres at nearby Skaneateles and Fayetteville, the Everson Museum of Art, the Lowe Art Centre and the Barrows Art Gallery (Skaneateles). The Salt Museum near Syracuse and Rail City near Oswego feature the history of those industries. The fair grounds, where state fairs have been held since 1890, are at the western edge of the city.

**Recreation.**—The recreation opportunities of the city and area include many fine places for hunting, camping, boating, swimming and fishing; eight state parks in the Finger Lakes region; Lakes Ontario, Onondaga and Oneida; and the Adirondack Mountains.

(V. C. C.)

**SYR-DAR'YA** (ancient JAXARTES), a river of the U.S.S.R. and the longest river in Central Asia, which flows into the Aral Sea. It is formed by the confluence, in the eastern part of the Fergana Valley, of the Naryn and Tar (Kara-Dar'ya) rivers which have their source in the Tien Shan (Tyan' Shan') Mountains. The length of the Syr-Dar'ya is approximately 1,370 mi. (2,200 km.) from the confluence of the Naryn and Tar, and 1,800 mi. (2,900 km.) from the source of the Naryn. Its water capacity is slightly less than that of the Amu-Dar'ya (*q.v.*), and its total drainage area is 178,000 sq.mi. (462,000 sq.km.).

The Syr-Dar'ya waters the Fergana Valley through which it flows between mostly sandy banks. Until they reach that valley, the Naryn and Tar are mountain streams. The Syr-Dar'ya's main tributaries reach it in the Fergana Valley: on the right bank Kassansay, Gavasay, and Chada (Chadak-Say); on the left Isfayram, Shakhimardan, Sokh, Isfara, Khodzhabakyrgan, and Aksu. None of these bring any water to the main stream as they lose it in irrigation, soakage, and evaporation. On leaving the Fergana Valley the river cuts through the Farkhad Mountains, forming the Begovat Rapids, where the Farkhad hydroelectric station was completed in 1948. There, on the right bank, are the headworks of the Dal'verzin Irrigation System, and lower down, on the left bank, those of the north Golodnaya Steppe System. The river flows on through steep wooded banks, receiving on the right the tributaries Angren, Chirchik, and Keles, which feed a complex irrigation system. (*See* also FERGANA VALLEY.) The last important right-bank tributary is the Arys'. Below these tributaries the river crosses the eastern edge of the Kyzylkum Desert, where the banks and the bed of the river are formed from slightly indented loess-clay formations. The low steep banks are usually flooded at high water. The course here is meandering and indeterminate and often changes, forming creeks which may be lost in the sand. This is particularly so near and below the town of Kzyl-Orda. There the river is joined on the right bank by the large tributary Karaozek. Of the many lakes in the valley the largest, Birkazan and Klemzhaygan, contain fresh water. In its lower course the river passes over silt of its own creation and is thus raised above the surrounding country, causing frequent flooding in spring and summer. At its mouth it forms a small delta with several creeks, lakes, and marshes which are filled up at high water.

The Syr-Dar'ya derives most of its water from snow, and to a minor extent from ice and rain. The high-water period lasts for about five to six months, from March or April to August or September. The level is at its highest in June. The lower reaches of the river generally freeze in December, the ice breaking up in March; the middle reaches freeze only occasionally. In the upper course, in the Fergana Valley, the river freezes only in places for short periods. The Syr-Dar'ya is navigable within the limits of the Kzyl-Orda Oblast' of the Kazakh Soviet Socialist Republic, and above that in a few isolated sectors. The main towns on the river are Leninabad, Begovat, Kzyl-Orda, and Kazalinsk.

(G. E. Wr.)

**SYRIA** (As Suriyah). Modern Syria, known as the Syrian Arab Republic (Al Jumhuriyah al 'Arabiyah as Suriyah), is bordered on the north by Turkey, on the east and southeast by Iraq, on the south by Jordan and Israel, on the southwest by Lebanon, and on the northwest by the Mediterranean Sea. Area 71,498 sq.mi. (185,180 sq.km.). The present territory does not coincide with ancient Syria, which was the fertile strip between the eastern Mediterranean coast and the desert of northern Arabia. The modern Arab nationalist concept of Greater Syria extends this territory to the Euphrates, and thus includes Israel, Lebanon, and Jordan. Syria has been included in all the great empires of the eastern Mediterranean and southwest Asia—Egyptian, Hittite, Babylonian, Assyrian, Persian, Hellenistic, Roman, Arab, and Ottoman. After World War I, as part of the Levant States, it was included with Lebanon in the French Mandate from the League of Nations, and its present largely artificial boundaries were demarcated by 1925. In 1939 the sanjak of Alexandretta (Hatay) was ceded by France to Turkey. The Free French declared Syria independent in 1941, and the Syrian Republic was a founder member of the Arab League. French troops withdrew finally in 1946. A strip of Syrian territory along its border with Israel was occupied by the Israeli Army as a result of the Arab-Israeli war of 1967. The capital is Damascus.

This article is divided into the following sections and subsections:



## I. PHYSICAL GEOGRAPHY

**1. Geology.**—Syria comprises the northern fringe of the stable Archean platform of Arabia, generally overlain by younger sedimentaries. In the west the latter are faulted and folded along northeast-to-southwest and north-to-south axes, which continue the structural features found in Israel, Jordan, and Lebanon. In western Syria the exposed rocks are mainly of Jurassic and Cretaceous age, but they are locally overlain by Tertiary sediments, Pleistocene and Recent alluvium or lava flows. In the Hawran (Hauran) and Jabal al Duruz (Jabal Druze or Jebel Druse) there are extensive basalt outcrops with Recent volcanic craters. The centre and east of the country is mainly composed of thin sheets of Tertiary limestones and marls, overlying undisturbed Secondary rocks on the Archean platform. Jabal Ansariyah (Jebel Ansarieh) in the northwest is an anticline of Jurassic and Cretaceous rocks; to the east lies the partly downfaulted trough of Al Ghab. Along the Lebanese border Mt. Hermon (*q.v.;* Jabal ash Shaykh) and the Anti-Lebanon (Jabal al Sharqi) are similar upfolds of Jurassic and Cretaceous rocks. A series of minor folds extends northeastward across the Syrian Desert (Badiyat ash Sham) to Palmyra (Tadmor) and the Euphrates, beyond which their direction becomes west to east, parallel to the Anti-Taurus ranges in Turkey. In the extreme northwest there are some metamorphic rocks in the Kurd Dagh and Jabal Qusayr (Jebel Kuseir), a result of Cretaceous folding associated with the Anti-Taurus uplift and the Kyrenia Range of Cyprus.

**2. Relief and Drainage.**—The western folded region, together with the Jabal al Duruz, is mountainous. The remainder of the country is an upland plain sloping gently northward and eastward; to the south and east this plain is a stony, gravelly desert, but in the north and west it is a steppe region.

The coastal plain is narrow and interrupted by spurs of the Jabal Ansariyah, but south of Tartus it widens into the Plain of 'Akkar, through which runs the border with Lebanon. The coast is alternately one of sandy bays and rocky headlands with low cliffs. Jabal Ansariyah has an average width of 20 mi. (30 km.), and is highest in the north 5,125 ft. (1,562 m.). Its average height declines from 3,000 ft. (900 m.) to 2,000 ft. southward. Immediately east of Jabal Ansariyah is Al Ghab. This trough is about 40 mi. (65 km.) long, drained by the north-flowing Orontes River (Nahr al 'Asi) which has there created a large marsh due to a basalt sill impeding the river's flow. Between Homs and Hamah the Upper Orontes cuts a meandering gorge in the steppe plateau.

South of Homs the western border follows the crest of the Anti-Lebanon Range. The main ridge has a maximum height of 8,860 ft. (2,700 m.) near Zabadani, and its mean height is between 6,000–7,000 ft. (1,800 and 2,100 m.). Mt. Hermon (9,232 ft. [2,814 m.]) is a single whale-backed ridge. The two ridges are separated by a pass, the Zabadani Saddle, which carries the Damascus-Beirut road and railway.

The south-central section of the Syrian Desert, commonly called Al Hamad, is not featureless; three minor mountain ridges strike northeast from Damascus toward Palmyra. Similar ridges (*e.g.,* Jabal Bil 'as and Jabal al Bishri) continue to the Euphrates, and beyond (*e.g.,* Jabal 'Abd al 'Aziz). The lava region of the Hawran culminates in the extinct volcanic cone of Jabal al Duruz at 5,905 ft. (1,800 m.). Al Jazirah region stretches east of the Euphrates into Iraq, reaching the Tigris between Cizre and Fayshkabur (a width of about 25 mi.).

The Euphrates (*q.v.*), the largest river of Syria, rises in the highlands of eastern Turkey, enters Syria at Jarabulus (Jerablus) and flows south and then southeast to Abu Kamal near the Iraq border. Its only important left-bank tributaries, the Belikh and Khabur (Khabor or Habur), flow south from Turkey; its right bank tributaries (*wadis*) are seasonal. The Orontes (*q.v.*) rises

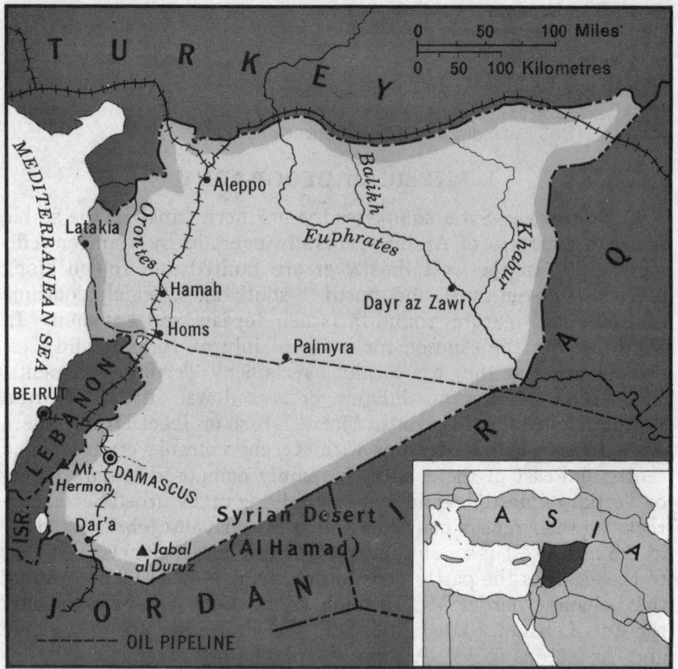


MAJOR TOWNS AND RAIL COMMUNICATIONS OF SYRIA

in Lebanon, drains the northern Bekaa (Al Biqa'), the western steppes, and Al Ghab before entering Turkey. The western Jabal al Duruz and the Hawran are drained by the Nahr al Yarmuk, a tributary of the Jordan River (Nahr al Urdunn). The Yarmuk Gorge forms the border in the southwest. The Zabadani Saddle and eastern Mt. Hermon are drained by the Barada (biblical Abana) and the A'waj (Pharpar), which water the fertile oasis of Damascus (Ghutah). The other rivers draining the mountains eastward are seasonal or lose their waters in salt marshes and mud flats in the desert. Several small perennial streams flow in steep gorges on the western slopes of Jabal Ansariyah to the Mediterranean; the largest of these are the northern and southern Nahr al Kabir (ancient Eleutherus).

**3. Climate.**—The coast and the western mountains have a Mediterranean climate with a long dry season from May to October. In the extreme northwest there is some light summer rain. On the coast, summers are hot, with mean daily maxima of 29° C (84° F), winters mild, with mean daily minima of 10° C (50° F). Only above 5,000 ft. (1,500 m.) is found relatively cool summer weather. Inland the climate becomes arid, with colder winters and hotter summers. Damascus and Aleppo have mean daily maxima of 35 to 38° C (95–100° F) in summer and mean daily minima of 1 to 3° (34–37°) in winter. In the desert, at Palmyra and Dayr az Zawr, mean daily maxima in summer reach 40.5 to 43° (105–109°) with extremes of up to 50° (122°). Snow is liable to occur each winter away from the coast, and frosts are common.

The coast and western mountains receive 30–50 in. (760 to 1,270 mm.) rainfall annually. The fall decreases rapidly eastward in lee of the mountains; the steppe, extending from the Hawran northward through Damascus, Homs, and Aleppo, and thence eastward to Al Jazirah, receives 10–20 in. (250 to 500 mm.) per year. The steppe region is widest in the Hawran and east of Homs, where gaps in the coastal ranges extend humid conditions farther east. Thus Jabal al Duruz receives more than 500 mm. In the desert, or Al Hamad, rainfall decreases to less than 130 mm. per year. Rainfall is variable from year to year, particularly in the spring and autumn months. This variability, combined with hot winds (khamsin) from east and southeast in early summer and autumn, makes cultivation without irrigation hazardous when there is less than 15 in. (380 mm.) mean annual rainfall and virtually impossible when it is less than 200 mm.

**4. Vegetation.**—There is much cultivation in the coastal plain and in Jabal Ansariyah, where the natural vegetation has been largely destroyed. *Garrigue*, degenerate Mediterranean scrub, and *maquis* cover many slopes. In the north there are some forests of Aleppo pine and isolated thin stands of Sessile and Syrian oak. Olive, carob, and fruit trees are common. The Anti-Lebanon and Mt. Hermon are mainly bare save for some scrub and ephemeral wild flowers, including alpine species; but the valleys bear poplar, willow, and alder. Much of the Hawran and the central and northern steppe in Al Jazirah have been cultivated, but a profusion of Mediterranean and Turanian shrubs and plants occur. Syria lies in the zone of contact between three major plant association regions—Mediterranean, Irano-Turanian, and Saharo-Sindian. The Jabal al Duruz bears kermes oak and *maquis*. Al Hamad supports only xerophytes and halophytes except along the Euphrates and its tributaries, where marsh vegetation and some trees grow.

**5. Animal Life.**—In the Anti-Lebanon and Jabal Ansariyah wolves are occasionally found; antelope and gazelle inhabit Al Hamad. Other mammals of the country include deer, wild cat, ichneumon, porcupine, hedgehog, squirrel, marten, ermine, otter, dormouse, rat, and hare. Vipers, lizards, and chameleons are common in the desert. Water fowl, including flamingoes and pelicans, abound in the lakes and marshes. Many migrating birds pause on their way north and south. Eagles, buzzards, kites, and falcons frequent the mountains. Among the insects, mosquitoes, sandflies, grasshoppers, and occasionally locusts are harmful.

(C. G. SM.)

## II. HISTORY

The earliest prehistoric remains of human habitation found in Syria and Palestine (stone implements, with bones of elephant and horse) are of the Middle Paleolithic period. In the next stage are remains of rhinoceros and of men who are classified as intermediate between Neanderthal and modern types. The Mesolithic Age is best represented by the Natufian culture, which is spread along, and some distance behind, the coast of the Levant. The Natufians supported life by fishing, hunting, and gathering the grains which, in their wild state, were indigenous to the country. This condition was gradually superseded by cultivation of crops, accompanied by the use of pottery, and to these was afterward added metal and metalworking, with manufacture of tools. Primitive pottery has been found in the north of Palestine and at Jericho, possibly dating from as early as *c.* 5000 B.C. The beginnings of metallurgy are later but may go back to about the mid-4th millennium. This art seems to have been introduced by a more northern race settling among a population of Mediterranean stock, who may have been the ancestors of the Semites. From this amalgam evolved the people who first built towns, which were characteristic of the Early Bronze Age. *See* further PALESTINE: *Archaeological Exploration* and *Prehistory and History*.

### A. EARLY HISTORY

History begins with the invention of writing, which took place in southern Babylonia perhaps *c.* 3000 B.C., the script being an original picture-character which developed later into cuneiform. An early Sumerian ruler of the city of Erech, named Lugalzaggesi, recorded his triumphal progress from the lower sea to the upper (the Mediterranean). Immediately after this, Syria appeared as the origin of a great migration of Semitic invaders into Babylonia by way of the Euphrates, the first of several such movements which are never traceable farther back than Syria. These first intruders have been given the name of Akkadians from their leader, Sargon (*q.v.*) of Agade or Akkad. According to legend, he was born obscurely on the upper Euphrates, launched on the river in a reed basket, and adopted in Babylonia, where he became the greatest conqueror and the most famous name in Babylonian history. From his new city of Agade he marched back up the Euphrates to the "cedar mountain" (the Amanus) and far beyond, if the various sources may be trusted.

It is probable that Sargon and his equally famous grandson Naramsin (*c.* 2275 B.C.) ruled effectively over the whole of Syria, to which they doubtless introduced the Sumerian writing that they had learned and adapted to their Semitic language in Babylonia. But the dynasty of Akkad was soon overthrown at its centre and superseded by the dynasties first of Guti and then of Ur. Nothing certain is known about the authority (if any) that the kings of Ur exercised in Syria, so far away from their capital. The end of their dynasty, however, was brought about chiefly by the pressure of a new Semitic migration from Syria, this time of the Amorites (*i.e.*, the westerners), as they were called in Babylonia. (*See* AMORITES.) Their invasion began before 2000 B.C., and before the 18th century B.C. they had covered both Syria and Mesopotamia with a multitude of small principalities and cities, mostly governed by rulers bearing some name characteristic of the Semitic dialect that the Amorites spoke. The period of Amorite ascendancy is vividly mirrored in the Mari letters, a great archive of royal correspondence found at the site of Mari, near the modern frontier with Iraq. They treat of the wars and general affairs of a multitude of states extending from northern Palestine to the upper Tigris. Among the principal figures mentioned are the celebrated lawgiver Hammurabi of Babylon (himself an Amorite) and a king of Aleppo of whom little is yet known. Part of his kingdom was the city of Alalakh, on the Orontes near what was later Antioch. This has yielded to excavation records both of the Amorite period and of a later age.

At about the same time (later in the 18th century B.C.) there began from Syria a movement of people in the opposite direction. This resulted in the Hyksos invasion of Egypt, which was subject to this foreign domination for about 150 years. The mixed multitude of the Hyksos certainly included Hurrians (*q.v.*), who, not being Aryans themselves, were under the rule and influence of Aryans and learned from them the use of light chariots and horses in warfare, which they introduced into Egypt, Syria, and Mesopotamia. The Hurrians established the kingdom of Mitanni, with its centre east of the Euphrates, and this was for long the dominant power in Syria, reaching its height in the 15th century B.C.

But other nations were growing at the same time, and in the 14th century Syria was the arena in which at least four great competitors contended. The Hurrians were first in possession, and they maintained friendly relations with Egypt, which, after expelling the Hyksos, had established a vast sphere of influence (it was scarcely an empire) in Palestine and Syria, under the kings of the 18th dynasty. Third of the powers disputing Syria in the 14th century were the Hittites (*q.v.*), who finally, under their greatest warrior, Suppiluliumas (*c.* 1350 B.C.), not only defeated the kingdom of Mitanni but established a firm dominion of their own in northern Syria with its principal centres at Aleppo and Carchemish. Fourth was the rising kingdom of Assyria, which became a serious contender in the reign of Ashur-uballit I. Indeed a fifth actor also appeared on the scene, the king of Babylon, but he was too distant and impotent to affect the issue.

This was the period of the Amarna letters (*see* TELL EL AMARNA), which vividly illustrate the decline of Egyptian influence in Syria, especially under Ikhnaton, the distress or duplicity of local governors, and the rivalry of the aforesaid powers. Egyptians and Hittites continued their struggle into the 13th century, but even the Battle of Kadesh, which Ramses II so boastfully claimed to have won (*c.* 1300 B.C.), led to no more than a treaty maintaining the equal balance. Assyria had already swept away the remains of Mitanni but itself soon fell into decline, and the Hittites were not long afterward driven from their centre in Asia Minor by the migration of "peoples of the sea," western invaders from the isles of the Aegean and from Europe (*see* SEA PEOPLES). These immigrants then marched down the coast of the Levant and threatened Egypt but were repulsed by Ramses III (*c.* 1190 B.C.).

While all the neighbouring states had failed to establish a lasting ascendancy in Syria, actual possession was assumed gradually by a people without sufficient cohesion to appear as a power at all. Various documents of the 14th century mention the Akhlame, who were forerunners of another vast movement of Semitic tribes called generically Aramaeans (*q.v.*). By the end of the 13th century these had covered with their small and loose principalities the whole of central and northern Syria. The Assyrians, however, were able to guard their homeland from this penetration, and henceforth much of the warfare of Assyrian kings was to be a mixture of aggression and defense aimed at the Aramaean states of Syria. At about the same time as the Aramaean invasion, the exodus of Israelite tribes from Egypt was proceeding. As the Israelites toward the end of the 11th century established a kingdom centred upon Jerusalem, the Aramaeans set up their principal kingdom at Damascus, and the wars between kings of Judah or of Israel and kings of Aram make up much of Old Testament history.

But the most formidable enemies of the Aramaeans and often of the Hebrews were the great military kings of the Assyrians. After a premature Assyrian incursion under Tiglath-pileser I early in the 11th century B.C., the real contest was reserved for the 9th and the 8th, during which the Assyrian empire was established over the west, though destined to be short-lived. At the Battle of Karkar in 853 B.C. Shalmaneser III of Assyria was opposed by Bar-Hadad I (Hebrew, Ben-Hadad; throne name, Hadadezer; Akkadian, Adad-idri) of Damascus, Ahab of Israel, and 12 vassal monarchs. In 732 Damascus, the Syrian capital, was at length captured by Tiglath-pileser III. But campaigns against the Aramaeans and Anatolians of northern Syria (called "Hatti-land") had to be undertaken by the Assyrians until almost the end of the Assyrian empire. Culturally, the most important achievement of the Aramaeans was the bringing of the alphabet into general use for public and private business.

Before the close of the 8th century B.C. began a massive southward movement of people, partly of Aryan stock, from the north and west. Pressure of these upon the Assyrian dominions and homeland became ever more severe, and they deeply affected Syria also; and in the 7th century came the invasion of the Cimmerians, followed by the Scythians. To these and to the Medes Assyria finally succumbed with the fall of Nineveh in 612 B.C. Nebuchadrezzar, when crown prince of Babylon, finally defeated the attempted rescue of Assyria by Necho II, king of Egypt, and annihilated his army at Carchemish in 605 B.C. In 597 he captured Jerusalem and carried its people into exile. Thereafter Syria was for half a century under the rule of Nebuchadrezzar's successors on the throne of Babylon.

But another and greater power, the Persians, then came to the fore. Under the leadership of Cyrus they subverted the rule of the Medes and assumed their empire, extending their conquests into Asia Minor, and then came to a final collision with Babylon, which Cyrus occupied in 539 B.C. He returned all the gods of Babylonia to their own places, and sent back the exiled Jewish community to Jerusalem, encouraging them to rebuild their Temple. In Darius I's great organization of the Persian dominions, Syria, with Palestine and Cyprus, was the fifth satrapy, bearing the name of "Across the River" (*i.e.*, the Euphrates), with tribute fixed at 350 talents of silver. Damascus and the Phoenician cities were still the chief centres of Syria under the Persians, and in Sidon was the core of the Phoenician revolt against Artaxerxes III, which ended with the destruction of that city in 345 B.C. But by this time the end of the Persian domination was at hand, and the Macedonians under Alexander III the Great were about to bring the whole Near East under Greek rule and influence.

Alexander invaded Asia Minor in 334 B.C., and his victory over the Persians at Issus in 333 was followed by the capture and enslavement of Tyre and Gaza. With the Battle of Gaugamela and the destruction of Persepolis the downfall of Persia was completed. *See* further PHOENICIA; PERSIAN HISTORY; DAMASCUS; BABYLONIA AND ASSYRIA: *History*. (C. J. G.)

### B. HELLENISTIC AND ROMAN PERIODS

**1. Hellenistic Age.**—After Alexander's death in 323 B.C. his marshals contended for control of the country, until after Ipsus (301) Seleucus I Nicator gained the northern part and Ptolemy I Lagus gained the southern (Coele-Syria). This partition between the Seleucids and Ptolemies was maintained for 100 years despite intermittent Syrian wars during the 3rd century (*see* SELEUCID DYNASTY). Their administrative methods varied. In the south the Ptolemies respected the existing autonomous cities, imposed a bureaucratic system on the rest of the country, and established no colonies. The Seleucids divided the north into four satrapies, which embraced the cities, and founded many cities and military colonies—among them Antioch, Seleucia Pieria, Apamea, and Laodicea (*qq.v.*)—drawing on European settlers. Republics replaced kings in the Phoenician coastal cities of Tyre (274 B.C.), Sidon, Byblus, and Aradus. Further political and cultural changes followed.

In 200 B.C. (or perhaps as late as 198) Antiochus III the Great defeated Ptolemy V at Panium and secured control of southern Syria, where he introduced the satrapal system. His subsequent defeat by the Romans at Magnesia (December 190 or January 189), however, resulted in the loss of both his territory in Asia Minor and his prestige, thereby fundamentally weakening the Seleucid empire, which ceased to be a Mediterranean power. Antiochus IV Epiphanes (175–163) stimulated the spread of Greek culture and political ideas in Syria by a policy of urbanization; increased city organization and municipal autonomy involved greater decentralization of his kingdom. His attempted hellenization of the Jews is well known.

Under the later Seleucid kings, with rival claimants to the throne and constant civil war, Syria disintegrated. In the north the Seleucids controlled little more than the areas of Antioch and Damascus; Commagene asserted its freedom, many of the cities claimed independence, and numerous petty chiefs established little principalities. Southern Syria was partitioned by three tribal dynasties, the Ituraeans, the Jews, and the Nabataeans. The country was seized later by Tigranes of Armenia (83) until his defeat by Pompey, who ended years of anarchy by making Syria a Roman province (64–63). (*See* also HELLENISTIC AGE.)

**2. Roman Provincial Organization.**—Pompey in the main accepted the status quo, but he reestablished a number of cities and reduced the kingdom of Judaea; ten cities of the interior formed a league, the Decapolis. The native client kingdoms of Commagene, Ituraea, Judaea and Nabataea were henceforth subjected to Roman Syria. Parthian invasions were thrown back in 51–50 and 40–39 B.C. and Mark Antony's extensive territorial gifts to Cleopatra (Ituraea, Damascus, Coele-Syria, etc.) involved only temporary adjustments.

Under the early empire Syria, which stretched northeast to the upper Euphrates and, until A.D. 73, included eastern Cilicia, became one of the most important provinces. Its governor, a consular legate, generally commanded four legions until A.D. 70. Administrative changes followed. Rome gradually annexed the client kingdoms. Ituraea was incorporated (*i.e.*, its territories were assigned to neighbouring cities) partly in 24 B.C., partly *c.* A.D. 93. Judaea became a separate province in A.D. 6, governed by procurators (apart from the shortlived control by Agrippa I, A.D. 41–44), until the destruction of Jerusalem in 70. Then the governor was a praetorian legate in command of a legion; next, under Hadrian, he was a consular with two legions, and the province was named Syria Palaestina. Commagene was annexed temporarily from A.D. 17 to 38 and permanently by Vespasian in 72. The caravan city of Palmyra came under Roman control, possibly during Tiberius' reign. Finally, Nabataea was made the province of Arabia in 105, governed by a praetorian legate with one legion.

Syria itself was later divided by Septimius Severus into two provinces—Syria Coele in the north with two legions, and Syria Phoenice with one. By the beginning of the 5th century it was subdivided into at least five provinces. The frontiers of Syria were guarded by a fortified *limes* (*q.v.*) system, which was thoroughly reorganized by Diocletian and his successors (particularly against cavalry attacks) and which endured until the Arab conquest; much knowledge of this system of "defense in depth" has been obtained with the aid of aerial photography.

**3. Economy and Culture.**—Syria's economic prosperity depended on its natural products (*e.g.*, wine, olives, vegetables, fruits, and nuts), on its industries (*e.g.*, purple-dyeing, glassmaking at Sidon, linen and wool weaving, and metalwork), and on its control and organization of trade passing by caravan from the east to the Mediterranean through such centres as Palmyra, Damascus, Bostra, and Petra. Further, Syrian merchants spread westward throughout the Latin provinces of the Roman Empire. The population of the country must have been larger than that of today. Though some cities were founded under the empire, these were not numerous, and Syria remained essentially rural. The urban upper and middle classes might be hellenized, but the lower classes still spoke Aramaic and other Semitic dialects in town as well as country. Roman influences were naturally weaker than Greek, though the army at first helped the spread of romanization, while Latin, not Greek, was the language of instruction in the famous law school at Berytus (Beirut) until *c.* A.D. 400.

The splendour of Syrian culture is seen in the magnificence of the cities (Antioch, ranking among the greatest cities of the empire, was the residence of the governor and later of the *comes Orientis*, who governed the diocese of the East), and in the luxury, gaiety, and versatility of the Syrians. This splendour is also evident in their schools of rhetoric, law, and medicine, in their art (the preeminence of Italian or Syrian elements in Syrian art is debated), in their literature and philosophy, and in the variety of their religions, both pagan and Christian.

**4. Byzantine Syria.**—During the three centuries Syria was administered from Constantinople, its cultural and economic life remained active, as names like Libanius, Ammianus Marcellinus, Procopius, and John Malalas (*qq.v.*) bear witness. Government became more bureaucratic but it was efficient. From the middle of the 5th century, by which time paganism had died out and monasticism was spreading, religious controversy took a political turn with the growth of the Monophysites (*q.v.*), in whom anti-imperial, nationalist, and secessionist sentiment found a rallying point. The repercussions of this heresy seriously weakened Syria and the Eastern Roman Empire. Nor were external dangers lacking. In the 4th century, during the campaigns of Constantius and Julian against Persia, Syria had again become a base of operations and at times endured Persian invasion; and the Huns had appeared before the end of that century. The Persian menace died down during the 5th century, but it blazed up again in the 6th, when Arabs also added to the danger. The Persian Khosrau I captured Antioch itself (540); and though he was outwitted by Belisarius and though Justinian's Persian wars ended in a "50 years' peace" (561 or 562), in 573 the Persians were back again. The invasion of Khosrau II, which began in 606, was later rolled back by the victories of Heraclius, but the peace of 628 brought no tranquillity to Syria. (H. H. SD.; X.)

### C. MEDIEVAL PERIOD

**1. Islamic Conquest.**—In the first half of the 7th century Syria was absorbed into the Muslim caliphate. Arab forces had appeared on the southern border even before the death of the Prophet Mohammed in 632, but the real invasion took place in 633–634, with Khalid ibn al-Walid as its most important leader. In 635 Damascus surrendered, its inhabitants being promised security for their lives, property, and churches, on payment of a poll tax. A counterattack by the emperor Heraclius was defeated at the Battle of the Yarmuk in 636; Jerusalem surrendered to the caliph Omar in 638; by 640 the conquest was virtually complete.

The new rulers divided Syria into four districts (*junds*): Damascus, Homs, Jordan, and Palestine (to which a fifth, Kinnasrin, was later added). The Arab garrisons were kept apart in camps and life went on much as before. Conversion to Islam had scarcely begun, apart from Arab tribes already settled in Syria; except for the tribe of Beni Ghassan, these all became Muslim. Christians and Jews were treated with toleration, and Nestorian and Jacobite Christians had better treatment than they had under Byzantium. The Byzantine form of administration remained but the new Muslim tax system was introduced. From 639 the governor of Syria was Mu'awiya (*q.v.*) of the Meccan house of the Omayyads. He used the country as a base for expeditions against the Byzantine Empire, for this purpose building the first Muslim navy in the Mediterranean. When civil war broke out in the Muslim Empire, as a result of the murder of Othman and the nomination of 'Ali as caliph, Syria stood firm behind Mu'awiya, who, after turning back an attack by the Iraqi Arabs at the Battle of Siffin (657), extended his authority over neighbouring provinces and was proclaimed caliph in 660, the first of the Omayyad line, which ruled the empire, with Syria as its core and Damascus its capital, for almost a century (*see* CALIPHATE).

**2. The Omayyads.**—The early Omayyad period was one of strength and expansion. The army, mainly Arab and largely

Syrian, extended the frontiers of Islam. It carried the war against Byzantium into Asia Minor and three times besieged Constantinople; eastward it penetrated into Khurasan, Turkistan, and northwestern India; and, spreading along the northern coast of Africa, it occupied much of Spain. This vast empire was given a regular administration which gradually acquired an Arab Muslim character. Syrians played an important part in it, and the country profited from the wealth pouring from the rich provinces to the empire's centre. The caliphs built splendid palaces and the first great monuments of Muslim religious architecture: the Dome of the Rock in Jerusalem and the Omayyad mosque in Damascus. The religious sciences of Islam began to develop, while Christian culture still flourished. Except under Omar II Christians were treated with favour; there were Christian officials at court, and the court poet of Mu'awiya, al-Akhtal, was a Christian.

Under the later Omayyads the strength of the central government declined. There were factions and feuds inside the ruling group: the Arabs of Iraq resented the domination of Syria; the non-Arab converts to Islam (*mawali*) resented the social gap between them and the Arabs; devout Muslims regarded the Omayyads as too worldly in their lives and policies; after the defeat and death of 'Ali's son Husain at the Battle of Karbala in 680, sentiment in favour of the family of 'Ali was still strong. The later Omayyads could not control these discontents. Their rule was finally overthrown and the family virtually destroyed by the new Abbasid caliphate in 750. (*See* also OMAYYADS.)

**3. The Abbasids.**—The end of the Omayyad dynasty meant a shift in power from Syria to Iraq. Syria became a dependent province of the caliphate. Its loyalty was suspect, for Omayyad sentiment lingered on, and the last pro-Omayyad revolt was not crushed until 905. The Christian population was treated with less favour; discriminatory legislation was applied to it under some caliphs, and the process of conversion to Islam went on. Closely connected with it was the gradual adoption of Arabic in place of Greek and Aramaic, although the latter survived in a few villages. (*See* also ABBASIDS.)

**4. From the 9th to the 12th Century.**—As the Abbasid caliphate disintegrated in its turn, Syria drifted out of the sphere of influence of Baghdad. In 877 it was annexed by the Tulunid dynasty of Egypt, and this began a political connection which was to last with intervals for more than six centuries. In northern Syria the Tulunids were succeeded by a local Arab dynasty, the Hamdanids of Aleppo, founded by Saif al-Daula (944–967); they engaged in war with Byzantium, in which their early successes were followed by the Greek recovery of Antioch (969). In central and southern Syria another Egyptian dynasty, the Ikhshidids, established themselves (941–969); their successors, the Fatimid caliphs of Cairo, later absorbed the whole country.

In spite of political disturbances, the 10th and 11th centuries were a period of flourishing culture. Around the court of the Hamdanids lived some of the greatest Arabic writers: the poets al-Mutanabbi and Abu-al-'Ala' al-Ma'arri, the philosopher al-Farabi, and the anthologist Abu-al-Faraj al-Isfahani (*qq.v.*). It was a period of ferment in Islamic thought, when the challenge to orthodox (Sunni) Islam from Shi'ism and its offshoots reached its height. The Fatimids were themselves Shi'is, although power moderated their beliefs. At the end of the 10th century Syria was threatened by the Karmatians, adherents of an extreme form of Shi'ism who had established a state in the Persian Gulf. The danger was beaten back, but it returned in a more insidious form as an esoteric doctrine spread by the Isma'ilis from their centre at Salamia (Selemiya) in northern Syria. In southern Lebanon another offshoot of Shi'ism took root: the Druze religion, preached by missionaries sent from Egypt by the Fatimid caliph al-Hakim. (*See* SHI'ISM; ISMA'ILISM; DRUZE.)

In the second half of the 11th century Syria fell into the hands of the Seljuk Turks, who had established a sultanate in Asia Minor (*see* SELJUKS). They occupied Aleppo and then Damascus, while Jerusalem remained in the hands of the Fatimids. But after the death of the sultan Malik Shah in 1092 the Seljuk Empire fell to pieces, and between 1098 and 1124 the crusaders occupied Antioch, Jerusalem, Karak in Transjordan, and the coast.

The crusaders organized their conquests into four states owing allegiance to the king of Jerusalem (*see* CRUSADES: *Organization of the Latin States*). Their situation was precarious. The crusaders were always a minority in their states, and they never penetrated far into the interior. They could maintain their position only so long as the Muslim states surrounding were weak and divided. Zangi, the Turkish ruler of Mosul, occupied Aleppo in 1128 and recovered Edessa from the crusaders in 1144. His son Nureddin united inner Syria and annexed Egypt. After his death, his kingdom was rebuilt and strengthened by his viceroy in Egypt, Salah al-Din (Saladin; *q.v.*), who ended the Fatimid caliphate, created a strong kingdom of Egypt and Syria, and defeated the crusaders at the great Battle of Hattin (1187). He recovered all Palestine and most of the inland strongholds of the crusaders. Soon afterward, however, the Third Crusade recaptured part of the coast, where European rule lingered for another century.

**5. The Ayyubids and Mamelukes.**—After Saladin's death his kingdom was split up among members of his family, the Ayyubids, who established principalities in Aleppo, Hamah (Hama), Homs, Damascus, Baalbek, and Transjordan and ruled them until 1260. The period of Nureddin, Saladin, and their successors was of great importance. Thanks largely to the establishment of Italian trading centres on the coast, and better security, economic life recovered and Syria reached a level of prosperity such as it had not enjoyed for centuries. The Ayyubid rulers stimulated culture and architecture. Following the Seljuks, they created a new land system based on the grant of rights over land in return for military service. They were champions of Islamic orthodoxy against the sects which had gained ground in the previous era. They supported orthodox theology and law and built colleges of a new type, the madrasahs, as centres of orthodox learning. Their efforts to stamp out heterodoxy were not completely successful. The Isma'ilis kept their strongholds in the Jabal Ansariyah, and their secret organization, the Assassins, had some political importance (*see* ASSASSIN). The Druze religion spread further.

Although strong internally the state was still in danger from the Bedouin tribes of the desert and from the Mongols, who invaded Syria for the first time in 1260 and sacked Aleppo. They were driven back not by the local rulers but by a new Egyptian military group, the Mamelukes (*see* MAMELUKE), a self-perpetuating élite of slaves and freedmen, mainly of Turkish and Caucasian origin, who had replaced the Ayyubids as rulers of Egypt in 1250. In 1260 they defeated the Mongols at the Battle of Ayn Jalut in Palestine; the victorious Mameluke general, Baybars, made himself sultan of a reunited kingdom of Syria and Egypt which he ruled until his death in 1277. This state continued to exist for over two centuries. In 1291 it won back Acre and other coastal towns from the crusaders, and a few years later it took the last crusading stronghold, the island of Ruad (Arwad). The Mamelukes reorganized the Ayyubid principalities as six provinces, of which Damascus was the largest and most important. Political power was in the hands of the Mameluke élite, who held land in virtual ownership in return for military service in the cavalry. But there was a local element in the government, the civil servants being drawn mainly from Syrian Arab families with their tradition of religious learning. Local rulers such as the Buhturids of Lebanon were recognized and absorbed into the "feudal" system.

Like the Ayyubids the Mamelukes were strictly orthodox in religion. Religious culture flourished and produced a number of great scholars such as the Hanbali jurist Ibn Taimiya. Alike for religious and political reasons the Mamelukes dealt severely with the religious minorities living in the coastal mountain ranges: Druze, Maronite Christians, Isma'ilis, and Alawites (or Nusairis; adherents of another creed derived from extreme Shi'ism and living in the Jabal Ansariyah). In the early Mameluke period Syria remained prosperous; the rulers constructed public works, and Venetian merchants carried on their coastal trade. But in 1401 came a blow to economic life: a new Mongol invader, Timur (Tamerlane), sacked Aleppo and Damascus. His empire did not long survive his death in 1405, but the damage had been done. The cities had been burnt, a large part of their population killed, and many craftsmen taken away to central Asia.

### D. Ottoman Period

**1. Ottoman Government, 16th–17th Centuries.**—Throughout the 15th century Mameluke Syria continued to decline, while a new power was growing to the north, that of the Ottoman Turkish sultanate in Asia Minor. Having occupied Constantinople and the Balkans it began to look southward. In 1516 Sultan Selim I defeated the Mamelukes at the Battle of Marj Dabiq and occupied the whole of Syria that year and Egypt the next. While Egypt later recovered some autonomy under the Mamelukes, Syria remained for 400 years an integral part of the Ottoman Empire. It was divided into provinces each under a governor: Damascus, Aleppo, and later Tripoli and Saida (Sidon, of which the administrative centre was later moved to Acre). Damascus, the largest, had special importance as the place from which the pilgrimage to Mecca was organized every year. The governor of Damascus led the pilgrimage when possible, and most of the revenues of the province were earmarked for its expenses.

The tax system continued in principle to be that of Muslim law—land tax, poll tax on Christians and Jews, and customs duties. But the Ottomans like their predecessors gave the right to collect and keep the land tax in return for military service and thus created a virtual landowning class. Later this system was allowed to decay, and tax collection was turned over to tax farmers (*multazims*), who themselves became in course of time a landowning class. Another official hierarchy, the religious hierarchy of judges, jurisconsults, and preachers, served as intermediary between government and subjects.

Within this framework of law, order, and taxation, the local communities were left to regulate their own lives. In the desert, the Bedouin tribes were controlled to some extent by gifts, the encouragement of factions, and occasional military expeditions, but otherwise were not interfered with. In the mountains, the Maronites and other Christians, Druze, and Shi'i Muslims of Lebanon, the Alawites, and Isma'ilis of Jabal Ansariyah, were watched by the Turkish governors of Tripoli, Sidon, and Damascus but were not interfered with so long as they paid their taxes. The Druze princes of Lebanon, first of the Ma'anid and then of the Shihabid family, were recognized as governors and chief tax collectors. In the Jabal Druze south of Damascus there grew up a community of Druze farmers under no control and paying no taxes. The authority of the Christian patriarchs over their communities was recognized, and in the corps of *'ulama'* (*q.v.*) most positions except the highest were held by members of local families with a tradition of religious learning, who continued to be, as under the Mamelukes, spokesmen and leaders of the Muslim citizens.

The early Ottoman governors paid much attention to agriculture, and their fiscal system was designed to encourage it. In parts at least of Syria it flourished during the 16th and 17th centuries, and, apart from cereals for local consumption, cotton and silk were produced for export. Aleppo and Damascus not only were important centres of handicrafts but also served as market towns for the desert and countryside and as stages on the desert routes to the Persian Gulf and Persia. Aleppo and Sidon were also important centres of trade with Europe; French and English had largely replaced Italian merchants, and there grew up also a class of Syrian Christian and Jewish merchants who developed contacts with Egypt, Italy, and France. Throughout the 17th and 18th centuries the position of the Christians indeed improved. Catholic missions, protected by France, enlarged the Catholic communities of both Latin and Eastern rites, founded schools, and spread the knowledge of European languages. The Oriental colleges at Rome produced an educated priesthood, and the Christian communities in Aleppo and Lebanon brought forth scholars such as the famous Joseph Assemani, Vatican librarian, and Arabic writers such as Germanos Farhat, Maronite archbishop of Aleppo. The traditional Muslim Arab culture could still produce a theologian of some originality in 'Abd al-Ghani al-Nabulsi and a systematic jurist in Ibrahim al-Halabi.

**2. Decline of Ottoman Authority.**—In spite of a widespread revolt in the early 17th century, Ottoman rule was in general stable and effective until the end of that century. After that it declined rapidly, in Syria as elsewhere. Control by the central government weakened; the standard of administration sank; the janizaries lost their discipline and became a menace to order. The result was a shrinkage of agricultural production as the villages suffered from the depredations of soldiery and tax collectors and from Bedouin incursions. This was a period of activity in the Syrian Desert, and tribes of the 'Anaza federation, moving northwest from Arabia, extended their control far into the settled land. In the towns also there was a decline. The desert routes were unsafe, and the European merchant colonies were shrinking. But there was still a vigorous commercial life, the standard of craftsmanship was high, and the great tradition of Islamic architecture continued.

Ottoman authority did reassert itself to some extent, but in a new form. For most of the 18th century Damascus was ruled by governors belonging to the 'Azm family, loyal to the sultan but with more independence than earlier sultans would have allowed. They controlled the janizaries, kept back the Bedouin, maintained security, and sometimes extended their authority to other provinces. In the province of Sidon power was held on similar terms by a ruthless and able Bosnian governor, Ahmad al-Jazzar (1775–1804), and his group of Mamelukes. Such rulers raised their own armies, but this involved further taxation and depressed further the condition of the peasants. Agriculture flourished only in the hilly districts which were virtually beyond Ottoman control, free from Bedouin attacks, and ruled by strong local rulers such as Dahir al-'Umar (1750–75), who protected agriculture and made Acre a prosperous centre of trade. In Lebanon too the production of silk flourished under the protection of the Shihabs and other great families.

**3. Early 19th Century.**—At the beginning of the 19th century, the population of Syria was perhaps 2,000,000. There were some islands of prosperity: Aleppo and Damascus (each with roughly 100,000 inhabitants), Mt. Lebanon, and certain other secluded districts. In general, however, the country was in decay, the small towns subsisting on local trade, the villagers receding in face of the Bedouin. The Ottoman hold on the country was at its weakest. At Acre, it is true, Jazzar maintained his strong rule and was able, with the help of a British fleet and the Turkish army, to hold Bonaparte back when he invaded Palestine in 1799. But in Damascus and Aleppo the governors were scarcely able to control the population of city or countryside. The prince of Lebanon, Bashir II (1788–1840), who had been installed by Jazzar and remained quiet while Jazzar was alive, gradually extended his control over districts beyond Lebanon. In 1810 the Wahhabis from central Arabia threatened Damascus.

**4. Egyptian Domination.**—In 1831 the ruler of Egypt, Mohammed Ali, sent his son Ibrahim Pasha (*q.v.*) at the head of his modern army into Palestine. Helped by Bashir and other local leaders, Ibrahim conquered the country and advanced into Asia Minor. He ruled Syria for almost ten years. The whole country was controlled from Damascus. There and in the provincial centres the governors were Egyptians, but they were assisted by councils representing the population. In political matters Ibrahim relied largely on Bashir, in financial concerns on a Syrian Christian adviser. New taxes were introduced and strictly collected, agriculture was encouraged, and the Bedouin were pushed back. After an abortive attempt to introduce trade monopolies, Ibrahim encouraged European traders by maintaining better security and creating special commercial courts. It was in this period that Beirut began to replace Sidon as an international port. The Christian and Jewish populations were treated with consideration.

After a time Ibrahim's rule became unpopular because his taxes were heavy and he disarmed and conscripted the population. The European powers (except France) also objected to Egyptian rule in Syria because it was a threat to the Ottoman Empire, the weakness or disintegration of which might cause a European crisis. In 1839 war broke out between Mohammed Ali and his suzerain, the sultan. Ibrahim defeated the Turkish army, but in 1840 the European powers intervened. After an ultimatum, a British, Turkish, and Austrian force landed on the Syrian coast; there was a local insurrection encouraged from outside, and the Egyptians were forced to withdraw from Syria, which reverted to the sultan's government.

**5. Ottoman Rule Restored.**—The next 20 years were a period of mounting crisis. Bashir II was deposed by the Ottomans because of his support of the Egyptians; his successor was soon deposed. Shihabid rule came to an end, and Lebanon became the scene of a struggle for power between Druzes and Maronites, with undertones of social conflict. In the rest of Syria, an attempt was made to apply the new Ottoman administrative system. The new system of taxation and conscription caused unrest. This situation was increased by the growth of European influence. The Muslim majority became aware of the weakness of the Islamic community, and the connection of France with the Catholics and of Russia with the Orthodox both encouraged the minorities to hope for a more favourable position, and focused on them the hostility of their Muslim compatriots. There was also economic unrest. From the 1820s European goods flooded the market and replaced the products of local craftsmen. This diminished the prosperity of the artisan class, largely Muslim, but increased that of the import merchants, mainly Christians and Jews.

The tension generated in these ways burst out in 1860, when a civil war of Druzes and Maronites in Lebanon touched off a massacre of Christians by the Muslim mob in Damascus. The Ottoman government sent a special commissioner to punish the guilty and suppress disorder. France sent an expeditionary force, and a European commission discussed the future of the country and decided that Lebanon (the mountain itself but not the coastal towns) should be an autonomous district (*mutasarrifiyah*), but no change should be made in the rest of Syria.

From then until the collapse of the empire Syria continued to be governed as a group of Ottoman provinces. From 1888 there were three: Damascus, Aleppo, and Beirut. The new administrative and legal system was more carefully applied, and a new type of educated official gradually raised its standards. The introduction of railways and telegraphs made possible a stricter control. A French-built railway linked Beirut and Damascus, with a later extension running north to Aleppo, and in 1908 the Hejaz railway was opened to take pilgrims from Damascus to Medina. Railways and better security encouraged agriculture. Transjordan and Al Jazirah, the district between the Upper Euphrates and Tigris, ceased to be wholly nomadic. In other parts, however, the growth of population outran the increase of production, and there began a large-scale emigration to North and South America. The trade of Beirut increased steadily: its modern harbour was built by a French company, and by 1914 its population had grown to about 150,000. Aleppo (pop. about 200,000) and Damascus (pop. about 250,000) both had a flourishing trade, but the crafts declined, and the desert routes had suffered from the opening of the Suez Canal.

In Beirut and other cities there was a considerable change in social life: the upper and middle classes adopted the clothes and social customs of Western Europe. Western-styled schools increased. The mission schools expanded: in 1866 the American Protestant Mission opened in Beirut the Syrian Protestant College (later the American University of Beirut), and in 1881 the French Jesuits opened the University of St. Joseph in the same town. The government opened schools, and young men of the great Arab families of the towns began to attend the higher schools in Constantinople and to go on to civil or military service.

Under Sultan Abdul-Hamid II (1876–1909) the Muslim Arabs of Syria were reasonably content. His emphasis on Islamic solidarity frightened the Christians, but the Muslims on the whole still regarded the Ottoman Empire as the political embodiment of Islam. Syrian Arabs played a leading part at the sultan's court.

After the Young Turk revolution of 1908 relations between Arabs and Turks grew worse. Power fell into the hands of a Turkish military group whose policy stimulated the growth of opposition. Arab nationalist feeling became more conscious, and political parties, both open and secret, were organized by Syrians in Cairo, Constantinople, and Paris as well as in Syria itself. Their explicit demand was for an improved status within the empire and some local autonomy, but there was a growing feeling in favour of independence and the establishment of a Syrian or Arab state. This was the aim of the secret Fatat Party founded in 1911. Many Christians, particularly Maronites and other Catholics, wanted an independent Lebanon with extended frontiers and under French protection. Among the nationalists were some who looked to England and France as allies in the struggle for independence, but others were conscious of danger from the outside. Foreign spheres of influence were growing: France had paramount influence on the Syrian coast and in Lebanon, while in Palestine all the powers competed for influence, and from the 1880s there had begun Jewish immigration from Russia and Eastern Europe with the aim of creating for the Jews a national home under international guarantee.

**6. World War I and After.**—When the Ottoman Empire entered World War I in 1914, Syria became a military base. In 1915 an Ottoman army under German command attacked the British position on the Suez Canal, and then from 1916 a British and Imperial force based on Egypt, with a French contingent, undertook the invasion of Palestine. By the end of 1917 Gen. Sir Edmund (later Field Marshal Viscount) Allenby had occupied Jerusalem and by November 1918 the rest of Syria. Most Christians and Jews welcomed the occupation; among the Muslims a large proportion had remained loyal to the empire, as being all that was left of the political independence of Islam, but the nationalist societies had made common cause with the ruler of the Hejaz, Sharif Husain, forming an alliance with Britain against their Turkish suzerain. An Arab army under the command of Husain's son Faisal, was formed in the Hejaz, with Syrian and other Arab officers and British help (*see* LAWRENCE, THOMAS EDWARD). It took part under Allenby's general command in the Syrian campaign, operating on the east flank in Transjordan and helping to capture Damascus.

When the war ended, Allenby installed an Arab military administration under Faisal in Damascus and the interior. The French took over the coast with Beirut as their centre, and the British took over Palestine. There followed four unsettled years while the fate of Syria was being decided. During the war the British government had made promises, to Husain and other Arab leaders, that the Arabs would be independent in those countries which they helped to liberate, subject to certain reservations of which the precise extent has never been clear. Then, in November 1918, Britain and France declared their intention of establishing in Syria and Iraq "national governments drawing their authority from the initiative and free choice of the native populations."

By the Sykes-Picot Agreement of 1916 (*see* SYKES, SIR MARK), France was to be free to establish its administration in Lebanon and on the coast, and to provide advice and assistance to whatever regime existed in the interior; Britain was to have similar rights in Transjordan and Iraq. Palestine was to be under international control, but France later agreed that it should be in the British sphere, while Britain had already, by the Balfour Declaration of November 1917, pledged conditional support for the establishment of a Jewish national home. It proved impossible to reconcile the various claims and pledges. In March 1920 a Syrian Congress meeting in Damascus elected Faisal king of a united Syria including Palestine; but in April the Allied Conference of San Remo decided that both should be placed under the new mandate system, and that France should have the mandate for Syria.

### E. MANDATE AND INDEPENDENCE

**1. The French Mandate.**—In June 1920 a French ultimatum demanding Syrian recognition of the mandate was followed by a French occupation and the expulsion in July of Faisal. In July 1922 the League of Nations approved the texts of the British Mandate for Palestine and Transjordan and of the French Mandate for Syria and Lebanon. Lebanon had already, in August 1920, been declared a separate state, with the addition of Beirut, Tripoli, and certain other districts, to the prewar autonomous province. Politically "Syria" henceforth acquired a narrower meaning; it referred to what was left of geographical Syria once Transjordan, Lebanon, and Palestine had been detached from it.

The mandate placed on France the responsibility of creating and controlling an administration, of developing the resources of the country, and of preparing it for self-government. A number of local governments were set up: one for the Jabal Ansariyah, where the majority belonged to the 'Alawi sect, one for the Jabal Druze where most of the inhabitants were Druzes, and one for the rest of Syria with its capital at Damascus.

The French mandatory administration carried out much constructive work. Roads were built; town planning was carried out, and urban amenities were improved; land tenure was reformed in some districts; and agriculture was encouraged, particularly in the fertile Al Jazirah. Some encouragement was given to industry. Foreign mission schools were protected and helped, but a system of state schools also was constructed, and the University of Damascus was established with its teaching being mainly in Arabic. Ancient sites were excavated and museums opened.

It was more difficult to prepare Syria for self-government because of the difference between French and Syrian conceptions of what was implied. Most French officials and statesmen thought in terms of a long period of control; the French army wanted strategic control of both Syria and Lebanon; French politicians hesitated to make concessions to Syria which might arouse expectations in North Africa. Further, they did not wish to hand over power to the Muslim majority in a way which might persuade their Christian protégés and clerical groups in France that they were giving up France's traditional policy of protecting the Christians of the Levant. In Syria, many members of the minorities and a smaller proportion of the majority wanted the French to remain as a help in constructing a modern society and government. The greater part of the urban population, however, and in particular the educated élite, wanted Syria to be independent and to include Lebanon, Palestine, and Transjordan if possible, and certainly the Druze and 'Alawi districts.

The first crisis in Franco-Syrian relations came in 1925, when a revolt in Jabal Druze, due to local grievances, led to an alliance between the Druze rebels under Sultan al-Atrash and the nationalists of Damascus, newly organized in the People's Party. For a time the rebels controlled much of the countryside. They penetrated into Lebanon and the orchards of Damascus. In October 1925 bands entered the city of Damascus itself, and this led to a two-day bombardment by the French. The revolt did not subside completely until 1927, but even before the end of 1925 the French had started a policy of conciliation. In 1928 elections were held for a Constituent Assembly. The nationalists won the election and took office in a new government. The assembly drafted a constitution, but their draft was not wholly acceptable to the high commissioner because it spoke of the unity of geographical Syria and did not explicitly safeguard the French position of control.

*Treaty of 1936.*—In May 1930 the high commissioner dissolved the assembly and enacted the constitution with certain changes. There followed unsuccessful negotiations for a Franco-Syrian treaty; but in 1936 the advent of the Popular Front government in France, the growing tension in the Mediterranean, and the grant by Britain of independence to Iraq (1932) and to Egypt changed the situation. Negotiations took place with the nationalists, now organized in the "National Bloc." A treaty was signed in September 1936. It provided for Syrian independence, Franco-Syrian consultation on foreign policy, French priority in advice and assistance, and the retention by France of two military bases. The Druze and 'Alawi districts were to be incorporated in Syria, but not Lebanon, with which France signed a similar treaty in November. A Parliament was elected; the leader of the Bloc, Hashim al-Atasi (*q.v.*) was chosen as president of the republic; and a nationalist government took office.

The Syrian government ratified the treaty before the end of 1936, but France never did so. When Turkey put forward claims to Alexandretta, where Turks were the largest element in the mixed population, France found it advisable, for strategic reasons, to yield to its demands. In 1937 the district (later given the Turkish name of Hatay) was granted an autonomous status; in 1939 it was incorporated into Turkey.

By the end of 1938 it was clear that the French government had no intention of ratifying the treaty. In July 1939 the president and government resigned, and the constitution was suspended.

**2. World War II and Independence.**—The outbreak of World War II ended political activity for the time. In June 1940, after the Franco-German armistice, the French high commissioner and commander in chief announced that they would cease hostilities against Germany and Italy and recognize the Vichy government. During the next year an Italian and then a German armistice commission were active. Political uncertainty and the growing scarcity of goods and rising prices caused unrest, which was led by one of the prominent nationalists, Shukri al-Kuwatli (*q.v.*). In May 1941 the Vichy government allowed German aircraft to land and refuel en route to Iraq, where hostilities had broken out between the British and a government favourable to Germany; and in June, British, Commonwealth, and Free French forces invaded Syria and Lebanon. French troops in Syria resisted for a month, but Damascus was occupied on June 21 and hostilities ceased at midnight on July 11–12.

From then until 1946 Syria was jointly occupied by British and French forces. At the moment of invasion, the Free French had proclaimed Syrian and Lebanese independence, and this was underwritten by the British government which recognized French predominance in Syria and Lebanon, provided France carried out its promise of independence.

Differences about policy soon arose. The Free French did not wish to grant independence until France was restored, and even then only in return for a treaty similar to that of 1936. The Syrian and Lebanese nationalists were unwilling to sign treaties, and wished to obtain independence before the British troops left. In the interests of its Arab policy, Britain used its position of strength to persuade the Free French to carry out their undertaking. Elections held in 1943 resulted in a nationalist victory, and Shukri al-Kuwatli became president of the republic.

There followed two years of disagreement about the transfer of authority from the French administration to the Syrian and Lebanese governments. The first crisis occurred in 1943 when an amendment of the Lebanese constitution in the direction of complete independence led to the arrest of the Lebanese government and their release after a British ultimatum; and the second in 1945, when the French refusal to transfer control of the local armed forces led to disorders, culminating in a French bombardment of Damascus and British intervention. After long negotiations and discussion in the UN Security Council, agreement was reached on simultaneous British and French withdrawal from Syria and Lebanon. Withdrawal from Syria was completed by April 1946. Syria had already become a founder member of the United Nations and of the Arab League.

**3. Post-1945 Developments.**—Since World War II the Syrian economy, despite uncertainty caused by the transition from *laissez-faire* capitalism to socialistic planning, has been remarkably resilient (see *The Economy,* below).

Political development has been less steady. The National Bloc, which had led the struggle for independence, held office until 1949, but gradually lost its popularity. In 1949 the army intervened: a *coup d'état* by Husni al-Za'im in March was followed by a second in August, led by Sami al-Hinnawi with the support of another nationalist group, the People's Party. Hashim al-Atasi became president, and negotiations took place for a union with Iraq. These were cut short by a third military coup, that of Adib al-Shishakli in December. For two years Shishakli ruled in combination with the politicians, but from 1951 to 1954 Shishakli ruled by himself. In foreign affairs he followed a policy more favourable to Egypt than to Iraq. He was dislodged by a further army revolt in February 1954, and constitutional rule was restored. Al-Atasi was restored to office, to be succeeded in 1955 by al-Kuwatli.

Elections in 1954 resulted in a Parliament of various groups, including the Baath Party, which combined radical Arab nationalism with a policy of social reform, and made a special appeal to the new educated classes. For the next few years there was a struggle for power. The Baath, allied with an army group led by 'Abd al-Hamid Serraj, outwitted the others. Their policy was for union with Egypt, and at the time of the Suez crisis (1956) they were responsible for blowing up the oil pipeline in Syria.

In 1957, however, they themselves seemed likely to be outbid by a combination of politicians and officers standing further to the left. Syrian policy and opinion seemed to be moving toward the U.S.S.R., with which an arms agreement (1956) and economic agreement (1957) were made. To check this development, the Baath persuaded Egypt to unite with Syria in the United Arab Republic (February 1958). The republic was to have an elected president, a central government including Syrian and Egyptian members, and regional governments. Later, a National Assembly was chosen, one-third of the members of which were Syrians.

*The Union with Egypt.*—At first the new state was ruled by a combination of the Egyptian military group with the Baath, held together by a common neutralist foreign policy and an empirical policy of social reform. But soon the balance of power tilted in favour of the central as against the regional governments, and in favour of Egyptians as against Syrians. In October 1959 the president, Gamal Abd-al-Nasser, appointed his closest associate, Field Marshal 'Abd al-Hakim Amer, as virtual governor of Syria, and in December the Baathist members of the ministry resigned. 'Abd al-Hamid Serraj, however, remained as minister of the interior, and in September 1960 was appointed head of the Syrian regional government. Dislike of Egyptian administrative control and a succession of bad harvests caused discontent, increased in 1961 by Egyptian measures of economic control and nationalization, and in September 1961 Syrian officers in the army carried out a *coup d'état*. Syria withdrew from the union, and as the "Syrian Arab Republic" reentered the Arab League and the UN.

*Syrian Arab Republic.*—A period of instability followed the secession. At first there was a constitutional government dominated by bourgeois nationalists, with Nazim al-Kudsi as president. A further *coup d'état* in March 1962 led to a suspension of constitutional rule. In 1963 another *coup d'état* installed a largely Baathist government with civilian and military elements; during 1963–64 power fell increasingly to the military. Lieut. Gen. Amin al-Hafez became chairman of the Presidential Council, premier, and *de facto* president.

In 1963 the Baathist government negotiated for union with Egypt and Iraq (which also had a Baathist government at the time); but the agreement reached in April 1963 was abortive, and later Hafez's government became increasingly hostile to Egypt, although common fear of Israeli expansion drew them together, and Syria took part in the regular Arab League's "summit" conferences to concert anti-Israeli action. Internally the government followed a policy of economic control. In 1964 it started to nationalize industry, commerce, and oil distribution; this caused some unrest. A provisional constitution was promulgated on April 25, 1964; in August 1965 a National Revolutionary Council was created to draft a permanent constitution.

In January 1966 a new 26-man cabinet headed by Salah al-Din Bitar, a moderate, replaced that of the Baathist extremists, led by Yussef Zayen, which had resigned the preceding month. In late February, however, left-wing elements of the Syrian Army and the Baath Party seized power, denouncing both Hafez and Bitar as reactionaries. The new regime nominated Nureddin al-Attassi as president and recalled Zayen as premier. On Sept. 6, 1966, Col. Selim Hatoum led an unsuccessful attempt to overthrow the Baathist regime. Thereafter, increasing tension between Syria and Jordan led Syria to seek closer relations with Egypt, and in November Zayen led a delegation to Cairo, where a defense agreement was concluded to run for five years with the option of renewal. Hostility between Syria and Jordan became increasingly open, and there were armed clashes on the frontier.

Syrian sabotage raids into Israel assumed more serious proportions in 1967 and culminated in heavy fighting on the border on April 7. Continuance of the raids led to reprisal threats from Israel, and Egypt, in pursuance of its mutual security pact with Syria, moved troops into the Sinai Peninsula. On May 16 a state of emergency was proclaimed in both Syria and Egypt. When war broke out between Israel and Egypt in the Sinai Peninsula on June 5, Syria was fully committed, and fighting started on the Syrian-Israeli border. On June 8, Syria accepted the UN cease-fire call, but hostilities were not ended until June 10. By then Israeli forces had seized the heights along the Syrian frontier, for a distance of 12 mi. into Syrian territory, and the Syrian garrison town of Kuneitra, 40 mi. from Damascus. Israel remained in occupation of these districts. Syria effectively boycotted the Arab summit conference at Khartoum, Sudan (August–September 1967), and maintained a more uncompromising attitude toward Israel, calling for a "war of popular liberation." During 1968–70 there were frequent armed clashes on Syria's border with Israel. The Syrian government strongly supported the right of Palestinian guerrillas to operate from Lebanese bases and denounced the cease-fire agreement that went into force on Aug. 7, 1970, between Egypt, Jordan, and Israel. During the civil war in Jordan in September 1970 a Syrian armoured force crossed the border into north Jordan in support of the guerrilla organizations, but withdrew after a heavy encounter with the Jordanian Army.

A series of political crises, within the framework of the ruling Baath Party, had resulted from a conflict between the "progressives," led by the head of state, Nureddin al-Attassi, who stood for close cooperation with the U.S.S.R. and the creation of a strongly Marxist economy, and the "nationalists," led by Gen. Hafez al-Assad, the minister of defense, who would have preferred to place emphasis on the war with Israel and the improvement of relations with Syria's Arab neighbours, and to see less dependence on the U.S.S.R. Assad was reported to have attempted to take over the government in February 1969; nevertheless, he remained in office in the new cabinet formed by Attassi. As a result of the continuing dissension within the Baath Party, Attassi resigned in October 1970, but later provisionally revoked his decision. A second attempt by Assad to overthrow Attassi was successful in November; Attassi was placed under house arrest and a more moderate Baathist regime was instituted. The new government was invited to join a proposed federation with Egypt, Libya, and Sudan.

*See* also LEBANON: *History;* EGYPT: *History;* ISRAEL: *History: The Arab-Israeli War, 1967;* UNITED ARAB REPUBLIC; ARAB LEAGUE. (A. H. H.; V. E. HI.; X.)

## III. POPULATION

The 1960 census gave a total population of 4,565,121. Populations of the major towns were: Damascus (capital, 529,963); Aleppo (425,467); Homs (137,217); Hamah (Hama; 97,390); Latakia (Al Laziqiyah; 67,604); and Dayr az Zawr (42,036). Palestinian refugees numbered more than 150,000 and lived on the outskirts of Damascus in camps maintained by the United Nations Relief and Welfare Agency. The nomadic Bedouin population, which has declined steadily since World War II, was estimated to be less than 200,000. The greatest population density is in the Hawran, Jabal Druze, and Hamah regions.

Most Syrians are of Semitic stock (primarily Arab) and speak Arabic, the official language. Kurds and Armenians are the principal minorities. The former live in Turkish border areas and in Damascus. The Armenian communities, both Orthodox and Catholic, number about 150,000 and live mainly in Damascus and Aleppo. The Assyrians, estimated at 20,000, often speaking the Syriac language (*q.v.*), live in villages along the Nahr al Khabur in the northeast, and on the western slopes of the Anti-Lebanon Mountains. Christians of various denominations, but mainly Orthodox, comprise less than 8% of the population; they have long been involved in commerce and are largely an urban middle-class community. There are more than 5,000 Jews.

Religious divisions are numerous and politically important, although less so than earlier in the 20th century. The main Muslim sects are orthodox Sunnis (the majority), Shi'a, Alawite (Alaouite or Nusairi), Isma'ili, and Druze. The Druze (160,000) and the Alawites (500,000) exert a disproportionate amount of influence. *See* also ARAB; KURDS; DRUZE; BEDOUIN.

## IV. ADMINISTRATION AND SOCIAL CONDITIONS

**1. Government.**—After the abrogation in 1966 of the 1964 interim constitution a provisional constitution was issued on May 1, 1969, following an extraordinary congress of the Baath Party. Under the new constitution the Baath was to be the only legal political party. The supreme power in the state was to be the People's Assembly, which would elect the head of state and ratify laws.

*Administrative Subdivisions of Syria*

| *Mohafazat* (Governorates)* | Area† (sq.mi.) | Population (1960 census) | Density (per sq.mi.) |
|---|---|---|---|
| Dar'a (Der'a) | 1,463 | 140,442 | 96.0 |
| Dayr az Zawr (Deir ez Zor) | 12,764 | 221,320 | 17.3 |
| Dimashq (Damascus) | 6,960 | 391,376 | 56.2 |
| Dimashq (Damascus), Municipality of | 39 | 529,963 | 13,588.7 |
| Halab (Aleppo) | 6,232 | 957,399 | 153.6 |
| Hamah | 3,421 | 324,627 | 94.9 |
| Haskah, Al (El Haseke) | 9,024 | 352,896 | 39.1 |
| Homs | 16,297 | 401,243 | 24.6 |
| Idlib (Idleb) | 2,291 | 322,778 | 145.2 |
| Laziqiyah, Al (Latakia) | 1,671 | 526,551 | 315.1 |
| Qunaytirah, Al | 699 | 108,590 | 155.3 |
| Raqqah, Ar (Rakka) | 8,494 | 178,417 | 21.0 |
| Suwayda, As (Es Suweida) | 2,143 | 99,519 | 46.4 |
| Total | 71,498 | 4,565,121 | 63.8 |

**Mohafazat* are named after their capital cities.
†1 sq.mi. = 2.59 sq.km.

Executive power was to be held by the president, who would act as supreme commander of the armed forces, appoint the prime minister, and have the power to dissolve the People's Assembly. The economy was to be planned along socialist lines. The Baath Party announced the formation of a nine-man "politburo," charged with the administration of Syria until elections could be held. These were later indefinitely postponed.

Administratively, the country is divided into 12 *mohafazat* (governorates) and a *madinat* (municipality) (*see* Table). These are subdivided into 42 *manatik* (subdistricts) which are further divided into 115 *nawaki* (counties). The smallest unit is the village. The Ministry of Interior appoints the *mohafaz* (governor) and other district officers.

*Political Organizations.*—From 1963 onward the Baath was the only legal political party in Syria, deriving its main support from the armed forces, which are drawn to no small degree from the religious minorities in Syria, particularly from the Alawis (a Shi'a sect). Conservative Muslim opinion tended to oppose the government through the 'Ulama, and the *Ikhwan al-Muslimin* (the Muslim Brotherhood). The Ba'ath al-'Arabi (the Arab Renaissance Party), founded in 1941 by Michel Aflaq and Salah al-Din Bitar, preached the doctrines of socialism and militant Arab unity. The Syrian Communist Party existed in the early 1970s but was officially banned in Syria. In 1968 a number of left-wing pro-Nasser elements banded together in exile to form the "National Progressive Front," and called for the overthrow of the Baathist regime. They included the Syrian Socialist Party, founded in 1952 by Akram al-Hourani.

**2. Justice.**—Judicial power is exercised by the People's Court, Courts of the Peace, and other courts and special tribunals. The People's Court at Damascus (established 1962) holds public trials of persons accused of crimes against the state. Religious courts, once a major source of justice in Muslim Syria, are now superseded by civil courts; they still, however, handle some questions involving personal status such as marriage and divorce.

**3. Taxation, Living Conditions, and Welfare Services.**—The guideline for tax reform under the Baath regime indicated that direct taxation would increase at the expense of indirect. The cost of living as measured by the Ministry of Planning's analysis of retail prices in five cities has slowly risen since 1955 at the average annual rate of less than 2%. The average annual increase in per capita income in the 1960s, after adjustments for inflated national income estimates, was less than 2%. The five-year plan (1960–65) sought a rate of 5%. Government housing programs were mainly restricted to Damascus.

The Labour Code of 1946 regulated conditions of work in industry, but did not apply to farm workers. Efforts to legislate agrarian reform met with little success because of opposition of the landowners, and it was not until September 1958 that measures, including regulations concerning landlord-tenant relationships, succeeded (see *Land Reform* below). In August 1959 a labour and social insurance code unifying the labour laws of Egypt and Syria came into force. It advocated an 8-hour day and a 48-hour week, plus health and accident insurance, and applied to both agriculture and industry. By decrees of March 1964 farm labourers were to receive 40% of the crop (10% more than the traditional share), depending on the services supplied; they could also negotiate an agreement (usually 35%) with consent of both parties. The average wage for unskilled farm labourers ranged from S£5 a day in the more populated areas to S£8 in Al Jazirah.

The social structure has undergone profound change since independence. Progress in health and education had by the 1960s been extended from towns to rural areas. In regions no longer dominated by landlords there was a marked change in the attitude of the peasants whose subservience to landlord rule began to give way to independent thought and action. Increased freedom encouraged migration, both rural and urban.

*Health.*—By the mid-1960s malaria was almost eliminated. Diseases such as tuberculosis, trachoma, and dysentery were on the decline because of improved water facilities and rural medical treatment through clinics built by the villagers and staffed by government employees. Shells of incomplete hospitals, however, are testimony to manpower deficiencies.

**4. Education.**—Primary education is free and compulsory. By the mid-1960s there were more than 3,800 primary schools with 600,000 pupils and 16,000 teachers. Secondary schools totaled about 600 with 120,000 students and 4,500 teachers. There were also 45 vocational schools and 9 teachers' training colleges. In 1967 private schools were brought under state control. The University of Damascus, founded in 1923, was in the mid-1960s considerably overcrowded with an enrollment of more than 30,000 full- and part-time students. Aleppo University (1960) with faculties of arts, science, engineering, law, Islamic law, education, dentistry, medicine, and business administration, had more than 6,000 students. In Damascus are the Arab Academy (1919), a higher polytechnic institute (1961), and institutes of music, agriculture, and social service.

**5. Defense.**—The Syrian Army, formed in 1946 after the departure of foreign troops, drew its first recruits from officers and men who had served in the *Troupes spéciales du Levant,* a force raised locally by the French under the mandate. But the Palestinian War of 1948 against Israel found it woefully undermanned and under-equipped. It expanded, however, during the various military regimes established after 1949, notably that of Adib ash-Shishakli who sent teams of officers to study abroad. Impatient with Western restrictions on arms supplies to the Middle East, Syria concluded an arms deal with the Czechs (in 1954) which set the pattern for subsequent contracts. Syria received substantial military aid from the Soviet bloc and from China. In the early 1970s the Syrian Army was said to total 50,000 men. There was also an irregular "Syrian People's Army." Syria had several military colleges—notably the school for officer cadets at Homs. Arab guerrilla organizations, such as al-Saiqa, operated from Syria and received training facilities, but these did not come under the control of the Syrian government. (V. E. Hı.)

## V. THE ECONOMY

The bulk of the population is engaged in agriculture which in the mid-1960s provided about one-third of the national income. Syria is not a major producer of crude oil. Following independence, Syrian economic development experienced two distinct phases influenced by political factors at home in the Arab world, and from the cold war. The first phase, the decade following World War II, was the period of laissez-faire capitalism which saw the development of the dry farming areas of Al Jazirah and the irrigation of lands adjoining the Euphrates and Khabur rivers. Reinvested war profits found a high return in grain and cotton farming. Crop production increased and the average per capita income growth was higher than for any other Arab country during the same period. However, by 1954 the growing power of the Socialists and their attempts to enact land reform plus the inclusion of a Communist in the cabinet caused the rate of investment in agriculture to decline considerably. The economy lost its sustaining force.

The second phase began after the September 1954 elections and continued in the mid-1960s. This period was politically marked by the union with Egypt (1958–61) and the beginning of the Baath Socialist regime in 1963. The union era was economically significant for its lack of expansion in all sectors. Potential investors remained cautious and the resulting uncertainty about the future encouraged the expatriation of profits. The new government wrote a ten-year plan, but by the time it was ready, Syria had seceded from the union.

By July 1965 the Baathist government had gained control of 95% of industrial production, 50% of the value of commercial transactions, and 15% of agricultural production as measured by land ownership. Imports and exports were nationalized and prices fixed for major agricultural products. Economic planning played an increasingly important role with the Five-Year Plan (1960–65) which envisaged an expenditure of S£2,720,000,000. However, because of political changes and lack of project studies this plan, frequently modified, was less than half fulfilled. A second plan (1965–70) called for total investments of S£2,780,000,000 of which local finances were to provide 55.6%, foreign borrowing and grants the remainder. Planning priorities in order of emphasis were: agriculture and irrigation; industry, mines, and oil; transport and communication; housing, health, education, and public administration.

**1. Agriculture.**—Although agriculture's share of the national income has declined at an average rate of 1% per year since 1955, it remained in the 1960s the basis of the Syrian economy. Wheat was the chief earner of foreign exchange until the early 1950s when medium staple cotton replaced it. The reasons for agricultural predominance lies in the relatively underpopulated nature of the country and mechanization which has brought increasing productivity per man and high net returns. Cultivable land—more than 30,000,000 ac. (12,000,000 ha.)—is Syria's prime national resource. Capital for the land development came from profits gained from supplying Vichy and Allied forces during World War II. The Baath government started a number of collective farms in the Ghutah and Hamah areas which were orchard and livestock operations confiscated under the Agrarian Reform decrees.

*Land Reform.*—A main effect of the Agrarian Reform decrees of 1958 was the withdrawal of capital and management and reduction of private investment. A secondary effect was the encouragement of peasant initiative. After amendment the law in June 1963 regulated the maximum area of ownership according to location and type of water available. Maximums for holdings varied from 37 ac. (15 ha.) in the densely populated Ghutah area around Damascus to 750 ac. (300 ha.) of nonirrigated land in Al Jazirah. More than 3,400,000 ac. (1,375,000 ha.) were confiscated from 2,770 owners. The sizes of lots distributed to new owners were chiefly conditioned by the size of the family but limited to a maximum of 75 ac. (30 ha.) of nonirrigated land or 20 ac. (8 ha.) of irrigated or tree-planted land. Confiscated but non-allocated land that otherwise would remain idle was rented to anyone who could farm it and liberal credit was granted by the nationalized banks to finance the purchase of farm materials. The authorities were totally unprepared during the drought years (1958–60) which placed a heavy burden on finances, but by the mid-1960s they began to make available improved seed and fertilizer, as well as undertaking the training of a small cadre of extension agents to improve cotton yields.

*Crops.*—The variable rainfall and temperature conditions produce a wide range of agricultural products. High quality medium staple cotton, the American coker wilt variety, is the nation's major and most reliable export. In years of good rainfall exportable surpluses of wheat can total more than 500,000 tons; domestic consumption is about 700,000 metric tons. Barley exports sometimes reach 400,000 tons; consumption is about 300,000 tons. Lentils, a major food crop often used in rotation with grains, are not exported. Sugar beets were introduced in the early 1950s, but because of poor prices and an arid climate which accelerated dryness they have not proved popular. Vegetables are grown for local consumption, but imports are still required from Lebanon. Increased security in the countryside has encouraged experienced farmers to invest in tree crops. Citrus has expanded sharply in the coastal region. Olives, grapes, and apples are more suited to higher altitudes and rocky soils. The Baathist government has attempted to revive the silkworm industry which thrived prior to the 20th century. The brocade factories now import silk from East Asia. The high-grade tobacco of Latakia meets domestic needs and has an export market; production exceeds 7,000 tons. The Tobacco Monopoly Board licenses cultivators.

*Irrigation.*—The area under irrigation in the mid-1960s, estimated at 1,500,000 ac. (600,000 ha.), has been extended by private pump installations for cotton growing. Extensive ground water and river supplies were being tapped. The chief government irrigation schemes are the drainage of Al Ghab Valley marshlands (begun by the French) to reclaim and irrigate 74,000 ac. (30,000

(TOP LEFT) HERBERT LAUKS FROM BLACK STAR; (TOP RIGHT) DIANE RAWSON—PHOTO RESEARCHERS, INC.; (BOTTOM LEFT) MARIE J. MATTSON—BLACK STAR; (BOTTOM RIGHT) BILL TRACY—PHOTO RESEARCHERS, INC.

**(TOP LEFT) THRESHING IN A SMALL FARMING VILLAGE; (TOP RIGHT) 12TH-CENTURY CITADEL AT ALEPPO; (BOTTOM LEFT) COVERED BAZAAR IN DAMASCUS, THE CAPITAL OF SYRIA; (BOTTOM RIGHT) COUNTRYSIDE NEAR DAMASCUS: IN CENTRE BACKGROUND IS MT. HERMON, THE HIGHEST PEAK IN THE ANTI-LEBANON RANGE**

ha.) and the Sind area of 25,000 ac. (10,000 ha.). The Sind went into operation in 1965. Five smaller schemes are projected. Although more than S£20,000,000 had been spent on the Euphrates Dam pilot studies and a contract awarded to the U.S.S.R., the government indefinitely postponed the project in 1965.

*Livestock.*—Sheep raising which declined with the cultivation of grazing areas has begun to increase. Water wells, initially dug in Al Jazirah to settle the Bedouin, are now utilized by herdsmen. Recurring droughts reduced herds as farmers sold sheep to buy subsistence needs, but by the mid-1960s the small farmers, with their increasing incomes, tended to buy animals if their income surpluses were not sufficient to buy land. The sheep population exceeded 5,000,000. There was an improvement in poultry production (with American varieties) and cattle breeding (with imported dairy herds from Denmark). All livestock except camels, have increased considerably since the prewar period.

*Forestry.*—The forest area, much reduced since Phoenician times, is less than 168,000 ac. (70,000 ha.) and is concentrated in the pine-covered mountains north of Latakia. There are reforestation programs for planting hillsides and goat raising has been outlawed to prevent damage to the seedlings. Poplar trees planted along irrigation ditches are harvested after 12 to 15 years and bring a good return at no cost since seedlings are free and the water would otherwise be lost through seepage. Poplars are used for building construction, though most of the nation's timber needs are imported.

**2. Fisheries.**—Although the country borders the Mediterranean, the coastal peoples prefer agriculture and especially fruit and tobacco growing to fishing. In the mid-1960s the imports of fish, crustaceans, and mollusks were 2,500 metric tons, three times the amount exported. The amount of local production is unknown. Lack of refrigerated transport and storage facilities have prevented the possible development of the large inland markets.

**3. Industry.**—Light industry has expanded due to high protective tariffs and the availability of cotton and food products which require processing. Traditional handicrafts, such as carpet weaving, leather making, glass blowing and the renowned silk embroidery and brocade (damask) work of Damascus were reviving in the city *suqs* (market places) in response to the tourist demand. In scattered villages domestic industries, particularly the making of camel and goat hair cloth, felt, and rope were declining. The main manufactured items are textiles, canned foods, sugar (Homs), plate glass (Aleppo), cement, oil products, and cigarettes. Output of electrical power in the mid-1960s exceeded 500,000,000 kw-hr. Ammonia, nitric acid, and nitrate dolomite plants were constructed in the 1960s by Italian, Soviet, and Czech contractors.

In December 1964 the government nationalized the largely undeveloped oil and mineral resources. This was followed in 1965 by widespread nationalization of industries and business properties. Virtually all concerns that employed more than 12 persons were confiscated; foreign owners were pledged a negotiated settlement.

*Minerals.*—There are widely distributed but undeveloped deposits of phosphates, lead, copper, antimony, nickel, chrome, and gypsum. Sodium chloride and bitumen deposits are being developed. However, petroleum, discovered in the mid-1960s, may have greater economic potential. Production from oil fields which border the Tigris River is expected to reach 3,000,000 tons by 1970, but the high sulfur content may deter foreign buyers.

The government-owned oil refinery with a capacity of 750,000 tons at Homs, built by a Czech firm, came into operation in 1959, and its output helps to cover Syrian requirements. (Domestic consumption of petroleum products in the 1960s averaged 1,000,000 metric tons annually). The refinery was being redesigned to double its output and to crack the high sulfur crude oil discovered in 1958 at Karachuk where reserves are estimated at 150,000,000 tons. A British consortium was building a pipeline to carry the crude oil to Homs. The Iraq Petroleum Company has constructed pipelines from Kirkuk (Iraq) to the ports of Baniyas and Tripoli (Lebanon). A pipeline from Saudia Arabia to the port of Sidon (Lebanon) also crosses southern Syria. Transit fees on pipeline oil represent a considerable source of foreign exchange.

**4. Foreign Trade.**—In the mid-1960s trade expanded as imports continued to outpace exports. There was a regular deficit which was largely corrected by oil transit royalties and emigrant remittances. Cotton usually accounted for nearly 50% of the value of exports even when grain harvests were good. The value of exports exceeded S£670,000,000 annually and imports (mainly industrial raw materials and manufactured articles) exceeded S£900,000,000. China was the largest importer after Lebanon. The Federal Republic of Germany, the United Kingdom, and the United States were the largest exporters.

**5. Finance.**—The unit of currency is the Syrian pound (S£) divided into 100 piastres, and stabilized (for official transactions) at S£3.56 (purchase) and S£3.58 (sale) to the $ U.S., and at S£10.75 to the £ sterling. The open market rate is approximately S£4.00 to $1.00. There are three budgets: an ordinary budget (revenue derived mainly from taxation and oil royalties, with expenditure mainly on education and defense); a development budget (earmarked for agricultural, irrigation, industrial, and transportation projects); and an autonomous budget (to handle increased costs of administering nationalized industries, universities, etc.). In the mid-1960s ordinary budget receipts exceeded S£700,000,000; about 20% came from direct taxes and about 30% from indirect while income from oil transit fees accounted for roughly 17%. By the mid-1960s international loans and aid agreements were increasingly significant. The banks, nationalized by the Union government in 1959, were renationalized in 1963 by the Syrian government. The Central Bank of Syria has assumed management of the commercial banks. The credit needs of large-scale agriculture are served by the Agricultural Co-operative Bank. Credit is paid mainly in kind in cooperation with the Grains Bureau.

**6. Transport and Communications.**—Communications are improving to meet modern demands. There are three railways, built under the Ottoman Empire. The Northern Line (the route of the "Taurus Express") leaves Syria northwest of Aleppo, passing northward into Turkey, where it follows the Turko-Syrian frontier before reentering Syria, crossing Al Jazirah region via Al Qamishli (Kamishli), and entering Iraq at Tall Kujak, to proceed to Mosul and Baghdad. The Hejaz Railway (narrow gauge) runs from Damascus to Ma'an in Jordan. The Damas, Hamah et Prolongements Railway (formerly French, now nationalized) runs on standard gauge from Aleppo to Hamah, Homs, and Tripoli, to continue south along the Lebanese coast. At Homs another line runs into Lebanon to Rayaq, where it connects with the little-used narrow-gauge line connecting Beirut with Damascus. Because of poor connections freight traffic has increased slowly, while passenger traffic has declined in favour of road and air transport.

Main roads are: (1) Damascus–Homs–Aleppo; (2) Damascus–Qunaytarah; (3) Damascus–Suwayda'–Dar'a and thence to Amman and Baghdad. All-weather roads connect Aleppo with Dayr az Zawr, Al Qamishli, and Ras al 'Ayn, and Damascus with Palmyra. The main desert road from Damascus to Baghdad, 540 mi. (870 km.), passes through the Iraqi frontier post of Ar Rutbah; it carries considerable passenger and freight transport.

There are three ports, Latakia, Baniyas, and Tartus; Baniyas is used only to ship oil from Iraq. Latakia, which has a deep-water harbour (completed 1959), handles the bulk of Syrian trade.

International airlines call mainly at Damascus Airport. Middle East Airlines serves Aleppo and Syrian Arab Airways provides internal and European services.

The Syrian Arab Republic Broadcasting Directorate in Damascus transmits in Arabic, French, and English, and includes Hebrew, Spanish, and Portuguese in its foreign programs. A television service was inaugurated in 1960.

*See* also references under "Syria" in the Index. (J. L. Si.)

BIBLIOGRAPHY.—*Physical Geography*.—L. Dubertret and J. Weulersse, *Manuel de Géographie, Syrie, Liban et Proche-Orient* (1940); R. Thoumin, *Géographie humaine de la Syrie Centrale* (1936); E. De Vaumas, "La Structure du Proche-Orient," *Bull. Soc. Geog. d'Egypte,* 22:265–320 (1950). (C. G. Sm.)

*Early History: Cambridge Ancient History,* vols. i and ii, 2nd ed. (1961– ), iii (1925), iv (1926), vi (1927); A. T. Olmstead, *History of Palestine and Syria to the Macedonian Conquest* (1931); P. K. Hitti, *History of Syria,* 2nd ed. (1957). (C. J. G.)

*Hellenistic and Roman Periods:* E. S. Bouchier, *Syria as a Roman Province* (1916); M. Rostovtzev, *The Social and Economic History of the Hellenistic World,* 3 vol. (1941), *The Social and Economic History of the Roman Empire,* 2nd ed. rev. by P. M. Fraser, 2 vol. (1957); A. H. M. Jones, *Cities of the Eastern Roman Provinces,* ch. 10 (1937); A. Poidebard, *La Trace de Rome dans le désert de Syrie* (1934); R. Mouterde and A. Poidebard, *Le Limes de Chalcis* (1945); F. M. Heichelheim, "Roman Syria" in T. Frank (ed.), *An Economic Survey of Ancient Rome,* vol. iv, pp. 121–257 (1938). (H. H. SD.)

*Medieval and Ottoman Periods:* P. K. Hitti, *History of Syria,* 2nd ed. (1957); S. R. Fedden, *Syria,* rev. ed. (1965); H. Lammens, *La Syrie,* 2 vol. (1921); A. H. Hourani, *Syria and Lebanon* (1946); J. Sauvaget, *Alep* (1941); C. Cahen, *La Syrie du Nord à l'époque des croisades* (1940); M. Gaudefroy-Demombynes, *La Syrie à l'époque des Mamelouks* (1923); O. L. Barkan (ed.), *Règlements Fiscaux Ottomans,* Fr. trans. by R. Mandtran and J. Sauvaget (1951); C. F. Volney, *Voyage en Syrie et en Egypte* (1787); J. L. Burckhardt, *Travels in Syria and the Holy Land* (1822); G. Antonius, *The Arab Awakening* (1938); G. Samné, *La Syrie* (1920).

*Mandate and Independence:* Z. N. Zeine, *The Struggle for Arab Independence* (1960); S. H. Longrigg, *Syria and Lebanon Under French Mandate* (1958); G. H. Torrey, *Syrian Politics and the Military* (1964); P. Seale, *The Struggle for Syria* (1965). (A. H. H.; V. E. HI.)

*The Economy:* Office Arabe de Presse et de Documentation, *L'Agriculture syrienne* (1964); Gabriel Abouhamid, *Les Budgets de la Syrie,* (1965); Centre d'Études et de Documentations, *L'Économiste arabe* (monthly); Royal Institute of International Affairs, *The Middle East* (1958); D. Warriner, *Land Reform and Development in the Middle East* (1957); International Bank for Reconstruction and Development, *The Economic Development of Syria* (1955); *Statistical Abstract of Syria* (annually); United Nations, *Economic Developments in the Middle East, 1956–57* (1958) and *1957–58* (1959).

Current history and statistics are summarized annually in *Britannica Book of the Year.* (J. L. SI.)

**SYRIAC LANGUAGE** belongs to the Eastern Aramaic group of the Semitic languages (*q.v.*). Since the name "Aramaic" came to mean "pagan," the Greek name "Syrian" or "Syriac" was adopted by the inhabitants of that region. It was the language of Edessa, present-day Urfa, in southeastern Turkey. Edessa became a centre of Christianity at the end of the 2nd century and the intellectual metropolis of the Christian Orient. As a result, the neighbouring Aramaic Christians adopted Syriac. Since the 5th century A.D., because of theological differences, Syriac-using Christians have been divided into Nestorians, or East Syrians, under the Persian sphere of influence, and Jacobite (Monophysites), or West Syrians, under the Byzantine sphere. The Nestorians were excluded from Edessa and settled in Nisibis in Persia.

These two groups became linguistically distinguished by certain differences of pronunciation, chiefly in the vowels. Thus, the Jacobites have *ō* instead of *ā*, *i* and *e* became confused into *i*, whereas *ō* and *ū* both became *ū*. The script likewise became differentiated.

**Writing.**—The earliest Syriac inscriptions (on stone) belong to the first half of the 1st century A.D. and to the second half of the 2nd century. The earliest extant documents not inscribed on stone date from A.D. 243 and come from Doura-Europos, Syria. The early Syriac script was an offshoot of a cursive Aramaic script. The script reads horizontally from right to left. The Syriac alphabet consists of 22 letters, all of them having consonantal values.

The order of the letters in the alphabet is the same as in Hebrew, but the names of some of them are slightly different; thus, *alaph* (Syriac), *aleph* (Hebrew); *gamal* (Syriac), *gimel* (Hebrew); *semkath* (Syriac), *samek̲* (Hebrew). The majority of the Syriac letters have different forms depending upon their position in a word, whether at the beginning, middle, or end, and whether they stand alone or joined to others. As in other Semitic languages, the consonants *'* (*alaph*), *w,* and *y* were originally employed to express vowel sounds.

A highly developed vocalic system was introduced in the beginning of the 8th century. Three main vowel systems developed using a combination of small Greek letters and of dots placed above and below the letters. The most important variety of the Syriac scripts is "estrangelo," derived probably from *satar angelo,* the "evangelic" writing. After the schism in the church, the Syriac language and script split into two branches. The western *serta* or *serto* ("linear") developed later into two varieties, the "Jacobite" and the "Melchite." The eastern branch, called Nestorian, had greater importance in the history of writing. When Arabic became the speech of daily life, it was sometimes written in Syriac script; the term for it is *karshuni* or *garshuni,* but its meaning is uncertain.

**Phonology.**—The consonant phonemes of Syriac are: labials *p, b, m, w;* dentals and sibilants *t, d, ṭ, š, s, z, ṣ;* liquids *l, n, r;* palatals and velars *k, g, q;* laryngeals *', h, ḥ, '*. The stops *b, p, d, t, g, k* become spirant *b̲, p̲, d̲, t̲, g̲, k̲* if they are preceded by a vowel. The vowels are *a, ā, e, ē, i, ī, o, ō, u, ū,* and a very short *ĕ*. The diphthongs are *aw, ay, āy* (Western Syrian *ōy*), *ēw, īw.* No syllable can begin with a vowel. All the consonants except *h, '* and *r* can be geminated (or long) in medial position. Gemination does not occur either initially or finally. There is no gemination in Western Syriac.

A few cases of partial and total assimilation as well as of metathesis occurring with the morpheme *t* of the reflexive-passive stem should be mentioned here. Metathesis occurs in the combination *tš, ts* becoming *št, st;* thus *'eštamlī* for *'etšamlī* "it was accomplished," *'estĕg̲ed̲* for *'etsĕg̲ed̲* "he was worshiped." Metathesis and partial assimilation occur in *tz, tṣ* becoming *zd, ṣṭ;* thus *'ezdĕqĕp̲* for *'etzeqep̲* "he was placed upright," *'eṣṭĕleb̲* for *'etṣĕleb̲* "he was crucified." Total assimilation occurs in the succession *t-'* becoming *tt* and *t-d* becoming *dd;* thus *'ettaqtal* for *'et 'aqtal* "he was killed," *'eṭṭašše* for *'etṭašše* "hide me," *neddak̲rak̲* for *netdak̲rak̲* "he remembers you." Likewise *n* as first radical of the root is assimilated to any consonant with which it is in contact: *'appeq* for *'anpeq* "he brought out."

**Morphology.**—Syriac has a set of independent personal pronouns used for the expression of the subject, and a set of shortened forms suffixed to the nouns and to the verbs. With the verb they express the direct complement, occasionally the indirect complement; with the noun, they express the possession. The forms of the nouns and of the verbs with the suffixed pronouns very often change their syllabic structure.

The noun has three states, an absolute, a construct, and an emphatic state. The absolute state is the pure stem and is used mainly for adjectival and participial predicates. The construct state has as a rule the same form as that of the absolute state and is used in the expression of possession (*mẹlẹk̲ 'ālmā* "the king of the world"). The emphatic state has the suffixed element *-ā* of the article, but lost its determined value so that *malkā,* originally "the king," came to mean "king."

There are two genders in Syriac, masculine and feminine. The mark of the feminine is the suffixed *-t*. Its form is *-at̲* with a noun in the construct state (*bīš-at*), *-ĕt̲ā* with a noun in the emphatic state (*bīš-ĕtā*), and *-ā* in the absolute state (*bīš-ā*). Several noun classes (animals, plants, parts of the body, utensils) are treated as feminine without having the feminine ending *-t*.

Syriac has two numbers, singular and plural. The forms of the plural are: for the masculine, absolute state *-īn* or *-ēn* (*bīš-īn*), construct state *-āy* (*bīš-āy*), emphatic state *-āy(y)ā,* mostly contracted into *-ē;* for the feminine the forms are, absolute *-ān,* construct *-āt,* emphatic *-ātā.*

*The Verb.*—There are biradical, triradical, and quadriradical verbs, the majority being triradicals. The basic stem of the regular triradical verb has the forms *qĕtal* (mostly transitive), and *qĕtel* (mostly intransitive). The verbs that have a first radical *w, y, n* or laryngeals as 1st, 2nd, or 3rd radical have different syllabic structures in the various tenses of the verb. The biradicals are of the types *qām, baz* (*z*), and *rĕmā,* whereas the quadriradicals have the form *qartel.* The derived stems are *qattel* (with geminated 2nd radical), serving mainly for the expression of the intensive (occasionally causative), and *'aqtel* (with the prefix *'a-*) for the causative. All these stems can form a passive-reflexive mood with the prefixed morpheme *'et̲,* the forms being *'et̲qtel* (from *qtal, qtel*), *'et̲qattal* (from *qattal*), and *'ettaqtal* (from *'aqtel*).

There is a considerable number of Syriac verbs having the prefix *ša-* (*šaqtel*) for the expression of the causative, and *qatqat* (that is, a repeated biradical root) for the expression of the frequentative.

The past is expressed by the "perfect," which is formed by suffixed morphemes (thus, **kĕtab̲* "he wrote," **kĕtabū* "they wrote"). Habitual or continuous action in the past is expressed by the active participle followed by the perfect of *hĕwā* "he was" (thus *dāḥel hĕwā* "he was fearing"). The future is expressed by the "imperfect" formed by prefixes or suffixes or both (thus, **nektūb* "he will write," *nektĕbūn* "they will write"). The present is expressed by the active participle followed by the personal pronoun, mostly in contracted form (thus **kāteb 'at* or **kātbat* "you write").

The expression for the 1st person is common for the masculine and feminine, whereas for the 2nd and 3rd persons there are special forms for the masculine and feminine. Note that the prefix of the imperfect 3rd person is *n,* against *y* of the other Aramaic dialects.

Like all the other Semitic languages Syriac has no verb "to have." The idea of possession is expressed by the verb *'īt̲* "there is, there are" followed by the indirect complement (thus *kĕmā laḥmīn 'īt̲ lĕk̲ūn* "how many loaves of bread do you have?" literally "how-many breads there-are to-you?").

The Syriac vocabulary is basically Semitic. Among the loanwords are some Hebrew words in the domain of religion and some Persian words from translations of Persian, but the great majority of loanwords are Greek. *See* also SYRIAC LITERATURE.

BIBLIOGRAPHY.—A. Ungnad, *Syrische Grammatik und Übungsbuch,* 2nd ed. (1932); T. H. Robinson, *Paradigms and Exercises in Syriac Grammar,* 4th ed. rev. by L. H. Brockington (1962); T. Nöldeke, *Kurzgefasste Syrische Grammatik,* trans. by James A. Crichton, *Compendious Syriac Grammar* (1904); L. Costaz, *Grammaire syriaque* (1955); C. Brockelmann, *Syrische Grammatik,* 7th ed. (1955).

(W. LU.)

## SYRIAC LITERATURE,

**SYRIAC LITERATURE,** literature written in Syriac by Syrian Christians until the language was finally superseded by Arabic in the 14th century A.D. Apart from its obvious interest to Semitic scholars, Syriac literature is of importance for the study of Syrian Christianity, for the fact that it preserves many translations of Greek Christian texts which have not survived in their original language, and for its role as an intermediary between ancient Greek learning and the Islamic world.

**Historical Survey.**—Syriac, one of several Aramaic dialects, was used in Edessa (*q.v.*) and Osrhoene (Osroene), its province, from about the 1st century B.C. (*see* SYRIAC LANGUAGE). The language was invigorated after the introduction of Christianity. The active Christian communities in Syria, Mesopotamia, and Persia instilled such life into the literary culture that Syriac literature surpassed all other Aramaic literatures in both its geographical extent and the variety of its character and historical significance. Its great range may be seen from inscriptions, which have been found as far south as India (also the so-called Indian crosses), as far east as China (the Chinese and Syriac inscription of Si-ngan-fu of 781), and as far north as Turkistan (monuments in the cemetery in Semirechye, Kazakh S.S.R.).

Literary creation in Syriac during the centuries was naturally influenced by the events of history. The christological controversy in the middle of the 5th century brought about the separation of the Syrian Christians from the Christians of the Byzantine Empire and the Western world who accepted the Council of Chalcedon in 451 (*see* COUNCIL). Also the Syrian Christians themselves became divided into the Monophysite West Syrians, called Jacobites (*see* ANTIOCH, SYRIAN ORTHODOX PATRIARCHATE OF), and the Nestorian East Syrians (*see* NESTORIANS). These events, so unhappy in their results for church history, did not cause retrogression from the point of view of literary creation. Indeed, they even brought incentives in the form of new themes.

Other great events which determined the fate of Christians in the Orient affected literary life also. The Arab conquest in the 7th century, which altered the political scene almost overnight, did not bring much change into the life of Christians under the Omayyad caliphs (660–750). Deeper changes were felt under the Abbasids from 750 onward. But when Arabic was made the current vernacular, an epoch was initiated which gradually and consistently began to affect the use of Syriac. Later there were Syrian authors who wrote in both Arabic and Syriac. The chaotic circumstances attending the disintegration of the caliphate toward the end of the 10th century were not favourable to literary creation. The invasion of the Mongols in the 14th century destroyed Syrian Christianity and brought Syriac literature to an end, except for an insignificant aftermath.

**Versions of the Bible.**—Proof of the Syrians' exceptional interest in and solicitous care for the preservation of the Bible lies in the fact that no other Christians in the ancient or medieval period produced so many different versions as they did. Besides the Diatessaron (*q.v.*) there were at least ten different versions of the Old and New Testaments. Besides these there is a tradition, unsupported by any surviving fragments, about a version of the Old Testament prepared by Catholicos Aba (d. 552).

Modern studies have led to new discoveries about the history of the biblical text. An observation made first by F. Perles, that the Old Testament Peshitta must have had some connection with the Targums, has found proper recognition by A. Baumstark, followed by C. Peters. Their studies show that the ancient Palestinian Targum was carried over into the East Aramaic language (*see* TARGUM). But the targumic substructure is far greater than that which has been found in the editions of the Peshitta text. New data have come to light which give a new perspective to the relation of the Peshitta to the Targums. The new material shows that superficially revised or even unrevised manuscripts continued to exist, and, as those codices were multiplied, the influence of the Palestinian Targum continued to be felt in the ancient Syriac Bible, particularly in the Pentateuch, the Prophets, and the Psalms, long after the revised version called the Peshitta was made.

The New Testament studies of D. Plooij and A. Baumstark strengthened the view that Tatian (*q.v.*) composed his Diatessaron in Syriac, not Greek. Therefore the earliest form of the Gospels in Syriac was the harmony, not the four separate Gospels. Entirely new and unexpected light has been shed upon the earliest history of the Gospel text. The new materials about the Old Syriac version of the Gospels necessitate a reorientation in the understanding of the history of the text. The Diatessaron was officially discouraged much earlier than was previously thought. The Peshitta is not, as was once believed, the work of Bishop Rabbula (*q.v.*). The remnants of his text that have come to light show that it was a type of the Old Syriac recension. Although the New Testament Peshitta originated before Rabbula, it gained ground very slowly. The Old Syriac text type was not a "library copy" but a text which in different forms continued to exercise its influence even centuries after Rabbula.

New light has also been shed on the version prepared by Thomas of Harcel in 615–616. The old controversy whether Thomas revised an earlier version prepared by Bishop Polycarp for Philoxenus (*q.v.*) of Mabbug or only copied Polycarp's version and furnished it with the textual critical apparatus has finally received a solution: portions of Polycarp's version identified in Philoxenus' commentary on John show that in the process of revision Thomas carried Polycarp's work farther.

New text materials have been published in A. Vööbus, *Peschitta und Targumim des Pentateuchs* (1958); *Studies in the History of the Gospel Text in Syriac* (1951); *Early Versions of the New Testament* (1954).

**Poetry.**—The earliest hymnographers of Syriac literature were the Gnostic Bardesanes (*q.v.;* 154–222) and Aswana (4th century), whose writings have not survived. The works of Ephraem Syrus (*q.v.;* 4th century) thus stand at the beginning of Syrian literature and were never surpassed by any later author. Two poetic forms were employed by him, the *mēmrā* and the *madrāšā.* The *mēmrā* is designed to touch the ear not as song but as spoken speech in metrical form, whether a narrative or didactic epic; it is in fact a metrical homily. A *madrāšā* is a more artful composition, composed in strophes and sung by a choir or double choir. Little has survived of the poetry of Qyrillona, a contemporary of Ephraem, or of Balai (d. after 432), whose themes and form show great variety. Some elegant poems ascribed to Balai found their way into liturgical books. The authenticity of many of the *mēmrē* ascribed to Isaac (*q.v.*) of Antioch (5th century) is uncertain. Among the West Syrians the place of honour belongs to Jacob (*q.v.*) of Serug, whose *mēmrē* on a variety of church and biblical subjects are superior to those that have come down under Isaac's name. Jacob's poetry was never surpassed by any later author.

At the beginning of Nestorian Christianity stands Narsai (d. *c.* 503), author of many *mēmrē* and the greatest poet of the East Syrians. The elegance of his poetry and the beauty of his style earned for him the reputation of the "harp of the Holy Spirit." The poetry of Elisha bar Quzbaye, Abraham of Bet Rabban, and Abraham bar Qardahe (all of the 6th century) is no longer extant. In the 13th century Giwargis Warda and Khamis bar Qardaha wrote hymns that were included in the liturgy. Abdisho bar Berikha (*see* ABHDISHO BAR BERIKHA) of Nisibis wrote "Paradise of Eden," a collection of 50 metrical homilies.

Editions and translations of Syriac poets are as follows: Balai, ed. by K. V. Zetterstéen with German translation (1902); Isaac of Antioch, edited by P. Bedjan (1903); Jacob of Serug, edited by P. Bedjan, 5 vol. (1905–10); Narsai, edited by A. Mingana, 2 vol. (1905); and Abdisho, "Paradise of Eden," partially ed. by H. Gismondi with Latin translation (1888).

**Translations from Greek.**—The Syrians began their literary activity by making Greek Christian writings available in Syriac. Almost all the important authors and documents of Christian Greek were translated by the Syrians, the resulting mass of material being so great that space forbids even the naming of selected works. Translating, which continued for centuries to be part of Syrian literary life, must have received an important incentive from the school of Edessa as early as its director Qyore in the first part of the 5th century (*see* EDESSA: *Edessene Christianity*). Its best-known translators were Hiba (Ibas; d. 457), known to tradition as "the translator," and his contemporaries Proba and Kumi. Such a lively centre of learning as Edessa remained until the closing of the school in 489 must certainly have provided stimuli for other educational centres, particularly those where former scholars of Edessa took up their residence. Teams of translators as well as individuals must have had their share in the work. Among later translators the best known are Paul of Callinicos (6th century), Paul of Edessa (7th century), the patriarch Athanasius II of Balad (d. 686), and Jacob (*q.v.*) of Edessa.

This Greco-Syrian translated literature is an essential source for works of Greek Christian literature that have not survived in their original language. An obvious example of this is the earliest dated Syriac manuscript (Ms. Brit. Mus. Add. 12,150), from the year 411. It includes four works originally written in Greek: Titus of Bostra's treatise against the Manichees, Eusebius (*q.v.*) of Caesarea's *Theophania*, the Pseudo-Clementine *Recognitions*, and Eusebius' account of the martyrs of Palestine. The first two of these survive in Syriac only, the third in a Latin translation also, and of the last only a part has survived in the original Greek.

The translators also put into Syriac most of the works of Aristotle and other ancient Greek philosophers, together with the writings of the chief medical and scientific authors of ancient Greece. These translations formed an important preparatory work for the rise of Islamic civilization. It was much easier to translate from Syriac into Arabic than directly from Greek into Arabic; thus, for instance, to take the works of Galen alone, 130 were translated into Arabic from Syriac and only nine directly from the Greek original into Arabic. For this reason many works of Greek learning exerted their influence on the Muslim world through the medium of Syriac.

**Biblical Commentaries.**—The earliest example of Syrian exegesis is the homilies of Aphraates (*q.v.*). The Syriac tradition of commentaries begins with Ephraem Syrus, who composed a series of them. Much of the exegetical work produced after the doctrinal separation is lost. Little remains of the commentaries by Philoxenus on the Gospels.

The great authors who carried on these traditions are connected with Edessa. Jacob of Edessa produced important scholia. In the mountains near Edessa in the 8th century, Lazar of Bet Qandasa compiled his commentary on the New Testament, based on earlier authors (Ms. Brit. Mus. Add. 14,683), and in 861 the monk Severus in the convent of St. Barbara completed an extensive commentary (Ms. Vatican syr. 103) based on Ephraem and Jacob of Edessa. Several centuries of sporadic exegesis were followed by the major commentaries on the Old Testament and the New Testament compiled in the 9th century by Moshe bar Kepha (Ms. Brit. Mus. Add. 17,274, Ms. Oxford Bodl. orient. 703, and Ms. Mardin 101/4 and 102/4), in the 12th century by Dionysius Bar-Salibi (*see* BAR-SALIBI, JACOB), and on the Old Testament in the 13th by the learned Bar-Hebraeus (*q.v.*).

Most of the exegetical works of the East Syrians are lost; only fragments survive from Mar Aba, John of Bet Rabban, Michael Badoqa, Henana, and Sabrisho bar Paulos. An idea of the extent of this work is given by an anonymous work written *c.* 900 (Ms. Birmingham Ming. syr. 553, Ms. Vatican syr. 578, and Ms. Chald. Patr. Baghdad 112 and 113) which is a repertory of the East Syrian exegetical tradition. The commentaries of Ishodad of Merv (9th century) are among the best produced by the Nestorians and had some influence on West Syrian exegesis. The most extensive of his Old Testament commentaries is that on Genesis; his commentary on the New Testament is also important. The *Gannat būssāmē* ("Garden of Delight"; Ms. Diyarbakir 29 and Ms. Berl. orient. quart. 870), a work of the 13th (?; according to J. M. Vosté of the 10th) century, is a rich source of extracts from the older exegetical tradition.

Editions and translations of Syriac biblical commentaries include: Aphraates, ed. by I. Parisot, *Patrologia Syriaca*, vol. I, 1–2 (1894–1907); Jacob of Edessa, ed. by G. Phillips with English translation (1864); commentaries on the Old and New Testaments compiled by Dionysius Bar-Salibi, ed. by I. Sedlaček, J. B. Chabot, and A. Vaschalde, with Latin translations, *Corpus Scriptorum Christianorum Orientalium: Series Syriaca* (referred to hereafter as *CSCO syr.*) II, 98–99, 101 (1906–40); Bar-Hebraeus on the Old Testament, ed. by W. E. W. Carr with English translation (1925); Ishodad of Merv, commentary on the Old Testament, ed. by J. M. Vosté and C. van den Eynde with French translation, *CSCO syr.* II, 67, 75, 80, 81, 96 (1950–63), and commentary on the New Testament, ed. by M. D. Gibson with English translation in *Horae Semiticae*, vol. 5–7, 10 (1911–16). Regarding the role of the school of Nisibis in hermeneutic literature, see A. Vööbus, *History of the School of Nisibis* (1965).

**Acts of the Martyrs and Lives of the Saints.**—Narratives form a large group in the Syrian literary creation. To cast into the mold of a tale the history of the saints was a favourite art of the Syrians. The earliest documentary evidence leads to Edessa, where in the late 4th century the acts of Sharbil and Barsamya, martyred under Decius, and of Gurya and Shamona, martyred under Diocletian, were composed. These were followed by a long series of similar documents about the martyrs persecuted in Persia under Shapur II in the 4th century and augmented by those about the victims of later persecutions. Among this material is a collection covering the period from Shapur II to Bahram IV and concluding with an epilogue explaining the structure and extent of this ancient source, which according to the intrinsic evidence must have been composed before 399. This work has been ascribed to Maruta, bishop of Maipherqat (Martyropolis), but this is pure speculation. Another collection, the Miles trilogy, is somewhat later.

When the persecutions ceased, the theme for narratives was found in the lives of ascetics, monks, and saints. The disciples of the monks in particular felt the need of paying homage to their monastic teachers by way of panegyrics, encomiums, and biographies. The annual commemoration in the monasteries also stimulated this kind of literary production. Among the many lives are some particularly valuable as historical sources. The earliest of these among the West Syrians is the biography of Bishop Rabbula of Edessa, written shortly after his death by one of his clergy.

The life of John bar Qursos (d. 538) was written by his disciple

Eliya after 542. The life story of John bar Aphtonya (d. 537), founder of the famous monastery of Qanneshre, is the work of an anonymous disciple. The biography of Maruta, metropolitan of Tagrit, was written by his successor, Denha (d. 660). Lives of the Eastern saints by John (*q.v.*) of Asia, bishop of Ephesus, written after 566, dealing with the monasteries and their inmates around Amida (modern Diyarbakir), is an excellent historical source.

Among the East Syrians outstanding examples are: the biography of Catholicos Aba written by an unknown admirer; another of Catholicos Sabrisho I (d. 604) by a monk Petros; an extensive life of Hormizd, the founder of a monastery at Alqosh which still survives, written by a monk Simeon; and the story of Ishosabran, martyred in 620, written by Ishoyahb III, who later became catholicos. Among the authors who produced this genre of writings the most eminent is Babai the Great (d. after 627), abbot of the Izla monastery, whose enormous literary production consisted in a great part of such works; biographies of the martyred monk Giwargis (d. 612) and the martyr Christina are the only examples that have survived. Much literature of this kind must have been in circulation, including many works that are purely legendary in content. Yet there survives a great bulk of documents whose authors with differing degrees of success exercised their first steps toward putting their eulogies into a framework of history, whether ecclesiastical or secular.

Editions and translations of works in this class of literature include: collection of acts of Persian martyrs attributed to Maruta, ed. by P. Bedjan, *Acta martyrum et sanctorum* (1890–97); biography of Rabbula, ed. by J. J. Overbeck, *S. Ephraemi Syri, etc., opera selecta* (1865), German translation by G. Bickell, *Bibliothek der Kirchenväter,* no. 103–104 (1874); Eliya's life of John bar Qursos, ed. by E. W. Brooks with Latin translation, *CSCO syr.* III 25 (1907); anonymous life of John bar Aphtonya, ed. by F. Nau with French translation (1902); Denha's biography of Maruta, ed. by F. Nau with French translation, *PO* 3 (1905); biographies of Aba and Sabrisho I, ed. by P. Bedjan (1895); Simeon's life of Hormizd, ed. by E. A. W. Budge with English translation (1894–1902); Ishoyahb III's story of Ishosabran, ed. by J. B. Chabot, *Nouvelles archives des missions scientifiques et littéraires,* 7 (1897); Babai's biographies of Giwargis and Christina, ed. by P. Bedjan (1894–95).

**Historical Works.**—The earliest Syriac historical work is the *Chronicle of Joshua,* written in 507 by an unknown monk in Edessa who described the events of the years 495–507 in Edessa, Amida, and Mesopotamia. It owes its survival to the fact that it was included much later in a historical compilation attributed to Dionysius of Tell Mahre (*see* below). The *Chronicle of Edessa,* written later in the 6th century, is a valuable source, although limited in extent. Its account, which at first is too lapidary but becomes somewhat fuller toward the end, covers 132 B.C.–A.D. 540. Among works produced during the following centuries, some stand out because of their extent and the wealth of their information. John of Ephesus (Asia) toward the end of his life completed a church history in three parts, of which only the last, covering the years 572–585, has survived. An anonymous work under the name of Zacharias Rhetor contains in books 3–6 a translation of a lost work written in Greek by Zacharias Rhetor; books 1–2 and 7–12 are a compilation of a monk in Amida.

The two earliest important chronicles produced during the Islamic period were those of Jacob of Edessa, preserved only partly, and an anonymous work, wrongly ascribed by J. S. Assemani to Dionysius of Tell Mahre, which *c.* 775 emanated from the monastery of Zuqnin (*see* DIONYSIUS TELMAHARENSIS). Dionysius did write a historical work, in 16 books covering 582–842, but only a fragment survives. However, it has survived in the following two great chronicles which mark the end of the West Syrian annalistic tradition. A monumental chronicle in 21 books by the patriarch Michael I (d. 1199) covers church history, secular history, and other events in three parallel columns, up to 1195. Michael's work, influenced by the chronicle of Jacob of Edessa, is valuable because it incorporates many historical sources and excerpts of documents—it is a veritable depository of lost documents. An anonymous chronicle later than, but independent of, Michael comprises a secular and an ecclesiastical part, the latter depending frequently on Dionysius of Tell Mahre; it was completed finally in 1233/34. Bar-Hebraeus wrote several historical works, including an ecclesiastical history and a chronography which is in fact a history of the world. His "Chronicle of Dynasties" belongs to Arabic literature.

East Syrian literature displays no parallel to this rich annalistic literature. The earliest chronicle is that by Meshihazekha, composed between 540–551 and known as the *Chronicle of Arbela.* Its information about the oldest period of Christianity in Adiabene is drawn from a still older but lost work, composed by Abel about the middle of the 5th century. A counterpart to the history of the metropolis of Adiabene is that of the metropolis of Bet Garmai, "History of Karka de Bet Selok and Its Martyrs," an anonymous work describing the history of the city, its bishops, and its martyrs under the Sasanian king Yazdegerd II; its last redaction belongs to the 6th century, but the original work was written earlier. The church history of Barhadbeshabba of Bet Arbaye belongs to the beginning of the 7th century.

There was little annalistic writing during the Islamic period. The "Various Narratives from Church and World History," by an anonymous monk who describes events from 590 to 680, provides data about the last period of the Sasanian dynasty. It used an earlier work. The church history by John bar Penkaye goes up to 686. The last historical work of the East Syrians is Eliya bar Shinaya's chronicle, written 1019, an important source which includes numerous chronological tables and lists of patriarchs.

The weakness of the East Syrians in this area is partly balanced by the variety of their historical interests, which cannot be paralleled in West Syrian literature. One branch particularly is eminent, created by the interest in the history of schools. Many works were devoted to education, only one of which has survived composed by Barhadbeshabba of Holwan (*c.* 600), giving an idea of this genre of literature. The East Syrians' historical interest was extended to the history of literature, and the catalogue of Abdisho bar Berikha is an invaluable source of information about Syrian authors and their works. A supplementary branch of study can be seen in the works on the history of monasteries, which also have no counterpart in the literature of the West Syrians. About 840 Thomas of Marga wrote the history of his own monastery of Bet Abe, the "Book of Governors." At about the same time Ishodenah of Basra, whose church history is lost, wrote a work on the founders of the monasteries and the ascetic authors.

Of Syriac historical writing, the following editions and translations are available: *Chronicle of Joshua,* ed. by W. Wright with English translation (1882); *Chronicle of Edessa,* ed. by I. Guidi with Latin translation, *CSCO syr.* III, 4 (1904); John of Asia's church history, ed. by E. W. Brooks with Latin translation, *CSCO syr.* III 3, (1935–36); Zacharias Rhetor, ed. by E. W. Brooks with Latin translation, *CSCO syr.* III, 5–6 (1919–24); Jacob of Edessa, ed. by E. W. Brooks with Latin translation, *CSCO syr.* III, 4 (1904–07); fourth part of the anonymous work ascribed to Dionysius of Tell Mahre, ed. by J. B. Chabot with French translation (1895); chronicle of Michael I, ed. by J. B. Chabot with French translation, 4 vol. (1899–1924); anonymous secular and ecclesiastical chronicle ed. by J. B. Chabot with Latin translation, *CSCO syr.* III, 14–15 (1917–37); Bar-Hebraeus' ecclesiastical history, ed. by I. B. Abbeloos and T. J. Lamy with Latin translation, 3 vol. (1872–77), and chronography, ed. by P. Bedjan (1890); *Chronicle of Arbela,* ed. by A. Mingana with French translation, *Sources syriaques,* vol. 1 (1907–08); "History of Karka de Bet Selok and Its Martyrs," ed. by P. Bedjan (1891); Barhadbeshabba of Bet Arbaye's church history, ed. by F. Nau with French translation, *PO* 9, 23 (1913–32); "Various Narratives from Church and World History," ed. by I. Guidi (1891), German translation by T. Nöldeke (1893); John bar Penkaye's church history, ed. by A. Mingana with French translation, *Sources syriaques,* vol. 1 (1907–08); Eliya bar Shinaya's chronicle, ed. by E. W. Brooks and J. B. Chabot with Latin translation, *CSCO syr.* III, 7–8 (1909–10); Barhadbeshabba of Holwan's work on education, ed. by A. Scher with French translation, *PO* 4 (1907); Ishodenah of Basra, ed. by J. B. Chabot with French translation in *Mélanges d'archéologie et d'histoire,* 16:222–293 (1896); catalogue of Abdisho, ed. by A. Vööbus with Latin translation, *CSCO Subsidia* (1966).

**Theology.**—The earliest theological works bear the names of Aphraates and Ephraem Syrus. The time of doctrinal conflict and storm opened new avenues and gave new themes in dogmatics. The man who laid the groundwork of Syriac dogmatics for followers of the doctrine of the one nature of Christ (*i.e.,* the Monophysites) was Philoxenus of Mabbug with his three books on the Trinity and incarnation and ten dissertations on the subject "One of the Trinity Has Become Flesh and Has Suffered." Among the many later theological works, some stand out as special achievements. Among these is the *Hexaemeron,* composed by Jacob of Edessa toward the end of his life, a continuation of a lost book on the question of theodicy entitled "The First Cause." The latter cannot be identified with a work bearing a similar title, the "Cause of Causes," a noteworthy treatise inspired by mysticism and by irenic endeavours toward other religions, presented in an attractive way, which from internal evidence must have been composed at least two centuries later.

In the 9th century the most noteworthy author was the patriarch Qyriaqos (d. 817), who wrote on various theological subjects (Ms. Jerusalem St. Mark's Mon. 129). John of Dara, a distinguished 9th-century theologian, wrote a work in four books about the resurrection of the body; another about the heavenly and earthly hierarchy (Ms. Vatican syr. 100), which is a commentary on Pseudo-Dionysius; a work in eight books about the soul, only partially preserved (Ms. Vatican syr. 147); four books on priesthood; and works on other subjects (Ms. Damascus Patr. 4/4 and 4/5). The prolific Moshe bar Kepha's (d. 903) incomplete work on predestination and free will was cast in at least four books (Ms. Brit. Mus. Add. 14,731), that on the soul in one book (Ms. Vatican syr. 147). His dissertation on paradise in three books was long known only through Arabic translations and a Latin translation made before the original manuscript was lost; this, as well as other works, was discovered in 1965 (Ms. Mardin 368 and 381). The most outstanding apologist was Nonnus of Nisibis (9th century), whose works include a treatise on trinitarian and christological problems. The last to cultivate this genre of literature was Bar-Hebraeus, whose "Candelabrum of the Sanctuary" (Ms. Vatican syr. 168) is a comprehensive exposition of Monophysite doctrine and whose "Book of [Sparkling] Rays" (Ms. Vatican syr. 169) is a more condensed exposé of the same material.

Among the East Syrians, dogmatic works occupy a more modest place. Among the treatises produced by Ishai, Henana, and Thomas of Edessa the most important is "About Union," dealing with the problem of divinity and humanity in Christ's person, a systematic presentation of the Nestorian theological position, written by Babai.

The "Book of Scholia," completed in 791/792 by Theodoros bar Koni in 11 books, is a mélange of exegetical, speculative, theological, and apologetic discussions. The last book is particularly valuable as it contains historical data on various early religious sects from sources now lost. The "Apology" of the catholicos Timothy I (d. 823) is in the form of a discussion with the Caliph al-Mahdi. There is no significant work in this area before Abdisho bar Berikha, of whose theological writings only the *Marganitha* ("Pearl"), the official exposition of the Nestorian doctrine in its last stages, survives.

Editions and translations of theological writings include: Philoxenus of Mabbug, ed. with Latin translation by A. Vaschalde, *CSCO syr.* II, 27 (1907), and by M. Brière, *PO* 15 (1920); Jacob of Edessa's *Hexaemeron,* ed. by J. B. Chabot and A. Vaschalde with Latin translation, *CSCO syr.* II, 56 (1928–32); the "Cause of Causes," ed. by C. Kayser (1889), German translation (1893); John of Dara's four books on priesthood, ed. by A. Hobeica (1911); Moshe bar Kepha's dissertation on paradise reprinted in J. P. Migne, *Patrologia Graeca,* vol. 111, col. 481–608 (1863); Nonnus of Nisibis, ed. by A. van Roey with Latin translation (1948); Bar-Hebraeus' "Candelabrum of the Sanctuary," first two parts ed. by J. Bakos, *PO* 22–24 (1930–33), third part by F. Graffin, *PO* 27 (1957); Babai's "About Union," ed. by A. Vaschalde with Latin translation, *CSCO syr.* II, 61 (1915); Theodoros bar Koni's "Book of Scholia," ed. by A. Scher, *CSCO syr.* II, 65–66 (1910–12); Timothy I's "Apology," ed. by A. Mingana with English translation, *Woodbrooke Studies,* vol. 2 (1928); Abdisho's *Marganitha,* ed. by A. Mai with Latin translation, *Scriptorum veterum nova collectio,* vol. 10 (1838).

**Ethics, Asceticism, and Mysticism.**—This genre also begins with Ephraem Syrus, whose whole literary creation is permeated with, and who devoted a series of writings especially to, the ascetic ideal. An anonymous "Book of Degrees," an extensive work in 30 chapters on Christian perfection which mistakenly has been connected with the Messalians (a sect that laid great stress on asceticism and on ceaseless prayer), also dates from the 4th century. A large collection of similar treatises which point to a certain Simeon were discovered by H. Dörries (see below, *Bibliography*).

An extensive mass of writings which centres on the name of John seems to contain also texts of Syriac provenance and not merely translations of writings of John of Lycopolis. Thus cultivation of this genre of literature had a great vogue before the separation of the Syrians, and continued after it.

The West Syrian tradition was greatly enriched by the important contribution of Philoxenus of Mabbug, the chief of whose numerous ascetic writings is his collection of 13 treatises on Christian perfection. His Edessene contemporary Stephanos bar Sudaile, in his "Book About the Hidden Secrets of the House of God," unfolds a mysticism influenced by Origen and pantheistic thinking. Later works in this field do not rise above mediocrity until the last great author, Bar-Hebraeus, who wrote a work on ethics and another on asceticism, "Book of the Dove."

The literature of the East Syrians shows how widely they cultivated asceticism and mysticism. Some of their writings in this field won respect far beyond their own confessional boundaries and even beyond the frontiers of the Syriac language. Babai's commentary on the *Centuries* of the Greek author Evagrius and Sahdona's "Book of the Perfection of Works" commanded wide esteem. Isaac of Ninive (7th century) is of special importance because his conception of mystical life became fundamental to East Syrian asceticism, but all that has survived from his extensive writings is his work in 82 chapters on Christian perfection. Nearly as high a reputation belonged to another 7th-century author, Joseph Hazzaya, whose many works show a wide literary variety (Ms. Birmingham Ming. syr. 601). John of Dalyata, who wrote both homilies and letters on monastic spirituality in the 8th century, was known as the "spiritual old one" (Ms. Cambridge Add. 1999). Other authors prolific in this field in the 7th and 8th centuries were Simeon Taibuteh, Abraham Bardashandad, and Dadisho of Bet Qatraye. Only a corpus of treatises and letters (Ms. Vatican syr. 185) survives from the learned Abdmeshiha of Hirta (9th century).

Editions of works in this genre include: "Book of Degrees," ed. by M. Kmosko with Latin translation, *Patrologia Syriaca,* I, 3 (1926); Philoxenus of Mabbug, ed. by E. A. W. Budge with English translation, 2 vol. (1894); Stephanos bar Sudaile, ed. by F. S. Marsh with English translation (1927); Bar-Hebraeus, ed. by P. Bedjan (1898), English translation by A. J. Wensinck (1919); Babai, ed. by W. Frankenberg with German translation (1912); Sahdona, ed. by A. de Halleux with French translation, *CSCO syr.* 86–87, 90–91, 110–113 (1960–65); Isaac of Ninive, ed. by P. Bedjan (1909), English translation by A. J. Wensinck (1923); about other sources, *see* A. Vööbus, *History of Asceticism in the Syrian Orient,* I–II (1958–60).

**Civil and Canon Law.**—Much of the canon law of the Greek church was translated into Syriac. The Syro-Roman lawbook, containing decrees of the Byzantine emperors Constantine I, Theodosius I, and Leo I in Syriac translation, was not part of Oriental canon law as practised but was a handbook for instruction. On the foundation of the Greek traditions the Syrians built the traditions produced by their own genius.

With regard to synodical canons the best traditions were kept by the Nestorians. The evidence for this lies in the corpus of synodical acts (*Synodicon orientale*), beginning with the synod held in 410 in Seleucia-Ctesiphon and ending with those of the year 775. The West Syrians had no corpus of equal extent, though there is a unique manuscript (Ms. Damascus Patr. 8/11) which among legislative documents has preserved a cycle of synodical acts otherwise unknown (Synodicon). Among the rich collections of canons that have survived, a special place is occupied by canons for monasticism. Ecclesiastical law is extant in many collections of canons set up by such West Syrian authorities as Rabbula, John bar Qursos, Jacob of Edessa, and Giwargis, bishop of the Arabs (d. 724), and by the patriarchs, such as John III (d. 873), Theodosius (d. 896), Qyriaqos (d. 817), and Dionysius of Tell Mahre (d. 845). Selected regulations were codified by Bar-Hebraeus in his *Nomocanon.*

Among the East Syrians there are the statutes of the school of Nisibis, the oldest of which date from the year 496. Many church leaders contributed to the canonical materials: Giwargis, metropolitan of Arbela (10th century), and heads of the church, such as Ishoyahb I (d. 596), Sabrisho II (d. 835), and John V bar Abgare (d. 905). Part of the lost collections of canons has been preserved in Arabic translation. Lawbooks were composed by the catholicos Mar Aba I, his later successors Henanisho I (d. 699), Timotheus I (d. 823), and Isho bar Nun (d. 828), and by two metropolitans of Rewardeshir, Simeon (7th century) and Ishobokht (8th century), who originally wrote in Persian, from which they were translated into Syriac. Selected material was incorporated into the *Nomocanon* of Abdisho.

Editions and translations of works of civil and canon law: Syriac translation of Syro-Roman lawbook, ed. by K. G. Bruns and E. Sachau with German translation (1880); *Synodicon orientale,* ed. by J. B. Chabot with French translation (1902); lawbooks by Mar Aba I and his successors, ed. by E. Sachau with German translation, 3 vol. (1912–14); monastic canons, ed. by A. Vööbus with English translation (1960); statutes of the school of Nisibis, ed. by A. Vööbus with English translation (1962); *Nomocanon* of Abdisho, ed. by A. Mai with Latin translation (1838); Bar-Hebraeus' *Nomocanon,* ed. by P. Bedjan (1898), Latin translation by J. A. Assemani (1838); *The Synodicon in the West Syrian Tradition,* ed. by A. Vööbus with English translation (1966).

**Philosophy.**—In philosophy, Sergius of Reshaina (d. 536) not only translated the works of Aristotle and Porphyry but also produced original works, the most important being on Aristotle's logic (Ms. Brit. Mus. Add. 14,658). Severus Sebokht (d. 667) wrote a dissertation on Aristotle's syllogisms (Ms. Brit. Mus. Add. 17,156) which has survived complete. Giwargis, bishop of the Arabs, cultivated peripatetic philosophy; his most important work is the commentary on the *Organon* and other works of Aristotle.

**Grammar.**—Grammatical studies, initiated by the translation of the Greek grammar of Dionysius Thrax (*q.v.*), were frequently treated. Among the West Syrians the work of Jacob of Edessa was an important stimulus; such writings culminated in the "Great Grammar" of Bar-Hebraeus. On the East Syrian side the studies of Hunain (d. 876) and others reached their climax in the work of John bar Zobi (13th century).

Bar-Hebraeus' "Great Grammar" was edited, with a German translation, by A. Moberg (1907–22).

**Science and Medicine.**—Encyclopaedias on the philosophical and natural sciences were written by Job of Edessa (9th century) and Jacob bar Shakko (d. 1241). In astronomical knowledge a classical representative is the West Syrian Severus Sebokht. In medicine the Syrians drew their knowledge from the Greeks, hundreds of Greek medical works being translated by Sergius of Reshaina, whose reputation was equally great among all the Syrians; by Hunain, who also corrected earlier translations; and by other authors who were less prominent. To this, original works were added by Sergius of Reshaina, Simeon Taibuteh, and Hunain.

Job of Edessa's work was edited by A. Mingana with English translation, *Woodbrooke Scientific Publications,* vol. 1 (1935).

BIBLIOGRAPHY.—W. Wright, *A Short History of Syriac Literature* (1894); R. Duval, *La littérature syriaque* (1907); A. Baumstark, *Geschichte der syrischen Literatur* (1922); J. B. Chabot, *Littérature syriaque* (1935); A. Baumstark, *Die syrische Literatur,* in *Handbuch der Orientalistik,* III, 2 (1954); I. Ortiz de Urbina, *Patrologia Syriaca* (1958). (AR. VÖ.)

**SYRINX,** the Greek name for the musical instrument more commonly known as the panpipes (*see* PANPIPE). In medicine and anatomy "syrinx" refers to: (1) a tubelike structure; (2) a fistula; and (3) a kind of secondary larynx found in birds.

**SYROS** (SYRA; modern Greek SÍROS), a Greek island in the centre of the Cyclades (length about 10 mi., breadth 6 mi.). Area 34 sq.mi. (88 sq.km.); pop. (1961) 19,750. Its importance in the Bronze Age is attested by Early Cycladic remains. In ancient times it was remarkably fertile, but the destruction of its forests led to loss of soil by erosion and left it a brown and barren rock with scanty aromatic scrub, pastured by sheep and goats. The Turks took it from the Venetians in 1537. During the War of Greek Independence (1821–29) Syros remained neutral; several thousand refugees, mostly from Chios and Psará, settled there under French protection (though the island was nominally Turkish until 1832) and helped make it the commercial centre of the archipelago in the 19th century. It later declined with the rise of Piraeus and Patras.

Hermoupolis (Greek Ermoúpolis; also called Síros), the chief town (pop. [1961] 14,402), and capital of the *nomos* of the Cyclades, stands on a bay on the east coast. Old Syros (Áno Síros), on a conical hill behind the port town, was built by the Venetians in the 13th century and still houses a large Roman Catholic settlement, mostly of Italian descent. Hermoupolis itself was founded by the refugees in the 1820s. The town is still of considerable industrial (tanneries, weaving, and loukoumi) and mercantile importance.

**SYZRAN,** a town of Kuybyshevskaya (Kuibyshev) Oblast' of the Russian Soviet Federated Socialist Republic, U.S.S.R., stands on the right bank of the Volga at its confluence with the Syzran River and just below its great loop around the Zhiguli hills. Pop. (1959) 148,866. The town was founded in 1683 as a stronghold at the eastern end of the Syzran defensive line. It is a significant river port and a major centre of the western part of the Second Baku oil field, and oil shales are mined near the town. Oil refining, glassmaking, engineering (agricultural machinery and hydroturbines), timber working, leather working, and food processing are the main industries. It is an important rail junction, with lines to Kuibyshev, Saratov, Penza, Saransk, and Ul'yanovsk. (R. A. F.)

**SZCZECIN** (German STETTIN), a town of northwest Poland and an important Baltic port, stands on Stettin Bay near the mouth of the Oder, 41 mi. (66 km.) from the sea. It is the administrative centre of Szczecin *wojewodztwo* (province). Pop. (1939) 268,915, almost entirely German and Protestant; (1960) 268,900, almost entirely Polish and Roman Catholic; (1964 est.) 303,000. The great shift in the population's composition resulted from the Potsdam Agreement of Aug. 2, 1945, which restored the town to Poland and transferred all German inhabitants who had not already fled to Germany.

Szczecin arose on the left bank of the Oder, in a valley surrounded on three sides by hills. The Old Town, with its fine Renaissance castle, still forms its heart. When the city walls were demolished in 1874 a new district was established, radiating from Grunwald Square. The neighbouring villages and hills were gradually incorporated, and residential districts were then built there. The industrial districts occupied the northern sector, along the Oder. The valley, there 4.3 mi. (7 km.) wide, is cut by tributary streams and canals, along which the port installations have been erected. Szczecin is one of the most picturesque towns in Poland, with lakes and parks and green spaces occupying nearly one-fifth of its area. The town has been rebuilt since World War II, when two-thirds of its buildings were destroyed or damaged.

The development of the port began in 1826, when regular navigation was started on the Oder. In 1926–27 the waterway to Swinoujscie (Swinemünde) was deepened. All port installations were demolished during World War II, and the canals were blocked by rolling stock and cranes; restoration was slow. The port's turnover increased by the mid-1960s to more than 11,000,000 tons. It has the largest turnover of all Polish ports and is the main coaling port. The cargoes handled are mainly coal, coke, and iron ore. Szczecin port constitutes an organic whole with the outport at Swinoujscie, which is also an independent junction for international sea lines and a harbour for deep-sea fishing fleets. The situation of both at the mouth of the Oder has led to the development of transit traffic with the German Democratic Republic, Czechoslovakia, and Hungary. Further deepening of the waterway has allowed still larger vessels to reach Szczecin.

The most highly developed industry of Szczecin is the building of ships, fishing boats, and yachts. Food-processing, chemical, and metal industries are also developing. There are an academy of medicine, a college of engineering, and a college of agriculture. The town also has four theatres, an opera house, a concert hall, and two museums.

A settlement was formed on the site of the present town about 2,500 years ago. A Slav Pomeranian fortress was erected there in the 9th century A.D., and the place became an important trade centre on the water and land routes. At the end of the 10th century it was incorporated in the Polish state by Mieszko I. The name of the town comes from *szczecina* (bristle), and it was known to the Danes as Børstaborg ("brush castle"). In 1243 Szczecin received municipal autonomy from Duke Barnim I, and it remained the capital of the originally Slavonic dukedom of Western Pomerania or Pomorze (*q.v.*) until 1637, when it passed to Brandenburg. It joined the Hanseatic League (*q.v.*) in 1360, and this contributed to its germanization. It was seized by the Swedes in 1648 and passed to Prussia in 1720. It was returned to Poland in 1945.

SZCZECIN *wojewodztwo* lies on the Baltic Sea bordering the German Democratic Republic and has a coastline of 53 mi. (85 km.). Pop. (1964 census) 838,000. The province was incorporated in Poland after World War II. It covers the western area of the Pomeranian lakelands, with varying moraine formations and numerous lakes. A deep layer of glacial formations covers Tertiary rocks with brown coal and Mesozoic rocks. The soils are mainly sandy and gray. Good chernozem soils are found only in the southern area of the province. About 32% of the population is employed in agriculture. The main crops are grain (rye, wheat, barley, and oats), potatoes, and sugar beet. Cattle breeding has not developed well, despite the meadows and pastureland. About 27% of the region is forested, and the timber economy of the province is at a high level.

Szczecin *wojewodztwo* is one of the least industrialized in Poland. Szczecin itself employs about 60% of those who work in industry. After shipping and shipbuilding, the principal industries are agriculture and timber. Fishing from Swinoujscie, Dziwnow, and Wolin is an important part of the economy. The best-known of the resorts along the coast are Miedzyzdroje and Swinoujscie. The main towns, after Szczecin, are Stargard Szczecinski, Swinoujscie, Soleniow, and Gryfice. (T. K. W.)

**SZÉCHENYI, ISTVÁN,** COUNT (1791–1860), Hungarian reformer and patriot whom his antagonist Lajos Kossuth called "the greatest of the Magyars." He was born in Vienna, capital of the Austrian Empire, on Sept. 21, 1791, of a Hungarian family with a tradition of national service. He served with distinction as a cavalry officer against the French in the Napoleonic Wars. When peace was concluded, he spent several years traveling and was deeply impressed by the economic development and political institutions of France and, still more, of England, which he contrasted with Hungary's backwardness. His first intervention in public affairs (1825) was to offer a year's income (60,000 florins) from his estates toward the foundation of a Hungarian National Academy of Sciences. Thereafter he launched a variety of projects: some were apparently rather frivolous, such as the promotion of horse racing and the foundation of an aristocratic club, the National Casino; others were of obvious utility, such as the introduction of a steamship service on the Danube.

Széchenyi put the case for far-reaching reforms in a series of books, including *Hitel* ("Credit," 1830), *Világ* ("Light," 1831), and *Stádium* (1833). His originality as a reformer lay in his iconoclastic attitude toward his nation's prejudices. While his fellow nobles believed all virtue to lie in the defense of the Hungarian constitution against Vienna, he declared boldly that the root of Hungary's evils lay in the antiquated nature of that constitution and, still more, in the laziness and complacency of its defenders: Hungary must reform its institutions and itself. His heart's inspiration was a love of his country and his people, but he put the case for all his reforms on realistic economic arguments: the nobles' exemption from taxation made it impossible to finance the modernization of the country; the inalienability of their estates meant that they could not raise credit on them for improvements; the servile condition of the peasants resulted in inefficient agriculture. The real purpose of his horse racing was to improve the breed of horses; that of the National Casino was to enable its members to read and to exchange ideas. So, too, he proposed to pay off the cost of a permanent bridge between Buda and Pest by a toll payable by all users, noble or not.

The effect of Széchenyi's activities was genuinely revolutionary. The traditionalist nobles were scandalized beyond measure, yet in a few years Széchenyi, almost single-handed, set the tide moving toward reform. By 1841, however, he was already a back number. His loyalty to the Austrian connection and his doctrines of self-criticism and self-help were distasteful to the younger generation; he in return feared that their chauvinism would drive Hungary into a conflict with Austria that must end in disaster. In his presidential address to the academy (1842), he protested against the attempt to Magyarize the non-Magyars of Hungary and was rewarded with a storm of abuse. He tortured himself with self-reproach for having opened an abyss and led Hungary to its verge. He joined forces with the Conservatives, for whom he took charge of the regulation of the Tisza River and the lower Danube. His *Fragments of a Political Programme* (1847) was an envenomed attack, political and personal, on Kossuth (*q.v.*).

Széchenyi took office in Lajos Batthyány's Cabinet of 1848 (*see* HUNGARY: *History*) as minister of communications and public works, but when conflict with Vienna broke out, his reason gave way; he was removed to an asylum at Döbling, a suburb of Vienna (Sept. 5). Even so, in 1859 he could publish a barbed polemic against Austrian absolutism in Hungary. Threatened with prosecution for sedition, he took his own life on April 8, 1860. Collected editions of his works appeared in 1884–96 and in 1922–30.

*See* A. Zichy, *Gróf Széchenyi István*, 2 vol. (1896–97). (C. A. M.)

**SZECHWAN** (SSU-CH'UAN SHENG), a province of southwest China, almost 220,000 sq.mi. (569,000 sq.km.) in area following the reaccession of Sikang (*q.v.*) in 1955. Pop. (1953) 65,685,063 (including Sikang); (1957 est.) 72,160,000. It contains four autonomous areas formed since 1952, inhabited predominantly by non-Han peoples (under 2% of total provincial population) living in the mountainous west and southwest: Ahpa (A-pa), Kantzu and Mu-li—all mainly Tibetan; and the Liang-shan area. Szechwan was once almost a separate country because of its size and population, as well as its self-sufficiency in resources.

**Geography.**—Topographically it is distinctive, with lofty mountains everywhere and tremendous rivers of unmeasured power potential. From cloud-ringed O-mei Shan, 9,900 ft. (3,020 m.) (famed for temples, monkeys and pines), southwest of Ch'eng-tu, to the infinite complexity of irrigated garden-patch farms, and the inspiring 1,000–2,000 ft. (300–600 m.) gorges of the Yangtze (*q.v.*), the marks of man's adjustment and transformation of the landscape are everywhere. The heart of the province is the Szechwan or Red basin that occupies a region that continued as a sea gulf well into the later Paleozoic period, and changed to a fresh-water lake during the Mesozoic with deposition of red sandstones and limestones that were later wrinkled into a northeast-southwest ridge and valley system. On the west are the young Great Snow mountains (Tahsüeh Shan) and the eastern plateau of Tibet, 13,000 ft. (4,000 m.) above sea level; to the north, the Tsinling Shan at 10,000 ft. runs into the Ta-pa Shan and Wu Shan on the east, while the south is marked by the Kweichow limestone plateau. The largest flat area is the Ch'eng-tu plain in the northwest of the basin. Szechwan means "four streams"; they are usually regarded as the Min, T'o, Chia-ling and the Ch'ien or Wu;

sometimes either the Yangtze or Fou Chiang is given instead of the Ch'ien. Most of the major streams flow south, cutting steep gorges through former Sikang, or widening their valley floors in the soft sediments of the Red basin to pour eventually into the Yangtze before it slices its precipitous gorge, 150 mi. due east, through the Wu Shan below Wan-hsien. Within the basin most of the rivers are navigable and provide the most common means of transportation. Inside the mountain ring, which provides a barrier against polar winds, a mild climate permits the growth of almost every crop and tree found in China. Precipitation averages 40 in. (1,000 mm.), and the growing season is 11 months; snow and freezing are rare although the foggy winters are penetrating. Because of the high humidity and constant cloud cover, the Chinese say that in Szechwan the dogs bark when they see the sun.

**Agriculture.**—Given favourable conditions for agriculture the large population has converted lowlands and terraced hillsides into intensive gardens everywhere. Rice, sweet potatoes, sugar cane, silk, tea, citrus, tobacco, cotton and tung oil are the primary products, with wheat, corn, soy beans, white potatoes and barley as secondary. Bamboo and palms on the lowlands are matched by conifers and alpine meadows on the high mountains. Szechwan is China's largest rice producer with surpluses for transport to deficit areas, along with outshipments of sugar, citrus, tung oil, spices and medicinal products. Liang-shan writing paper made from bamboo is prized by Chinese artists. The world's best natural bristle is plucked from the backs of Szechwan hogs; goats are also reared. Within high, secluded bamboo glades in the west live the rare giant panda bears.

**Industry.**—Minerals of industrial importance are increasingly exploited. Salt has long been pumped from natural brine wells, from 300 to more than 1,000 ft. deep, at Tze Kung, while bituminous coal outcrops are numerous around Chungking (*q.v.*). Iron ores are scattered; the largest deposit, estimated at 500,000,000 tons of about 40% iron content, is in the southeast of former Sikang province. Petroleum is reported extracted and refined on the middle Chia-ling river, less than 90 mi. N. of Chungking, while in the salt well area natural gas is also being converted into petroleum. Szechwan's first major hydroelectric station (48,000 kw.) was built northeast of Chungking. From the mountains in the west, small amounts of gold, silver, copper, lead, antimony and asbestos are produced. The pace of industrialization continues to increase. Chungking, the major industrial centre of southwest China, has an automatic thermoelectric power plant, iron and steel plants (open hearth and electric), textile mills, chemical works and lighter industries. Electric trolley buses run in the widened downtown streets, while cable cars have replaced many of the long flights of stone steps down to the rivers. In 1952 Szechwan's first railway, 313 mi., between Chungking and Ch'eng-tu, the provincial capital, was opened, followed in 1958 by the Pao-chi to Ch'eng-tu line, 400 mi. across the Tsinling Shan to the north. Two more lines are growing south, one from Chungking to Kuei-yang in Kweichow (190 mi.), by a bridge across the Yangtze; the other from Nei-chiang, the sugar centre, to K'unming in Yünnan (420 mi.). Ch'eng-tu is the terminus of the motor roads to the west. That change will continue is obvious, for there remains the challenge of damming the lower end of the great Yangtze gorges, a project first drafted during World War II and taken up again in China in the late 1950s; this would be one of the world's largest multipurpose river control projects, with 10,000,000 kw. power available for a 300-mi. area.

**History.**—In the past the keynote of Szechwan was isolation. Non-Han peoples related to the Thai stocks had their centres of the Shu and Pa states at Ch'eng-tu and Chungking respectively at least as early as the Chinese settlement in the Yellow river valley. They were conquered by the Ch'in from the north in 316 B.C., augmented by a large number of transported Chinese settlers who enlarged Ch'eng-tu's great irrigation system and built the walled city. A possible remnant of the pre-Chinese exists southwest of the Min Chiang in the Liang-shan autonomous area formed in 1952. During the Three Kingdoms period (A.D. 221–265), Ch'eng-tu formed part of the base of Chu-ko Liang, one of China's shrewdest and most admired historical strategists. At the end of the Ming dynasty widespread massacres left vacant land that was occupied in the 18th century by whole outside communities—most notably a large contingent from Kwangtung whose descendants around Ch'eng-tu still speak Cantonese. Since the main routes into Szechwan were over the Tsinling Shan, with the shift of Chinese power east and then south the province was somewhat forgotten except as a rice granary and control base against the non-Hans to the west. During the warlord days of the republic, the area was practically impregnable. After the start of the Chinese–Japanese war in 1937, industrial enterprises and millions of refugees from coastal provinces were evacuated to Szechwan which resulted in rapid economic development of the area. Chungking, former treaty port and the wartime capital of China, made Szechwan the political and economic centre and became the site of important military bases and headquarters installations for Chinese and allied forces.

Although the Japanese bombing of Szechwan cities, especially Chungking, was severe, the province was not entered by the invaders. However, in spite of other large cities like Ch'eng-tu, Luchow, Wan-hsien and I-pin (*qq.v.*), most of the population remains basically rural. (TE. H.)

**SZEGED,** a city in Hungary with *megye* (county) rights, lies just below the confluence of the Maros and Tisza rivers, geographically within Csongrád *megye,* 118 mi. (190 km.) SE of Budapest by rail. Pop. (1960) 99,061. A stronghold and trading entrepôt in the time of the Árpád kings (*c.* 890–1301), Szeged was sacked by the Tatars and Turks. The oldest building is the 16th-century Mátyás (Mathias) Church in the lower town (Alsóváros). The town developed in the 19th century as an important rail and road intersection point and river port, trading in Transylvanian timber, rock salt, and local farm produce. It became the economic centre of the Banat (a fertile region producing grain, paprika, tobacco, and hides) but lost this position after 1920 when most of the Banat was ceded to Rumania and Yugoslavia. Its university, founded in 1921, was originally a branch of the university at Cluj (Kolozsvár) in Rumania; there is a separate medical university. After World War II the textile industries were vigorously developed.

The town was rebuilt after the disastrous spring floods of 1879 with an encircling protective dike and two concentric arcs of boulevards. Apart from a conventional 19th-century town centre and the developing industrial quarters, a steppe village-town plan predominates, comprising low-built houses (with attached farmyards) that border wide streets. These sprawl out to the dike and beyond into the Great Alföld (plain), forming an extensive suburban area that was once part of the city but incorporated into Csongrád *megye* in 1950. (H. G. S.)

**SZÉKESFEHÉRVÁR** (German STUHLWEISSENBURG), the capital of Fejér *megye* (county) in west-central Hungary, lies 41 mi. (66 km.) SW of Budapest by rail. Pop. (1960) 55,934. The site of a Roman settlement, Alba Regia, it was chosen by Stephen I in the 10th century as capital of the early Hungarian kingdom, which it remained for 500 years. It became a strong fortress with a natural defense of marsh surround. In 1543 it was occupied by the Turks who sacked it before their withdrawal in 1686. The later 18th-century town was built largely from the ruins of the old one and contains a Baroque episcopal church and an episcopal palace in Empire style. Székesfehérvár was badly damaged (1944–45) during the fighting between German and Soviet troops. The town's traditional economic importance is as a market centre for local truck farmers, vine growers, and horse breeders, but it now has some light industries. Since the 19th century it has been a road and rail junction on the main routes from Budapest to the southwest. (H. G. S.)

**SZEKLERS** (Magyar SZÉKELY), a people inhabiting the upper valleys of the Mureș and Olt rivers in what was eastern Transylvania and is now Rumania. They were estimated to number very roughly about 400,000 in the 1960s and are officially recognized as a distinct minority group by the Rumanian government. Their origin has been much debated. According to their own tradition, repeated in Procopius' *De bello Gothico,* they were descended from Attila's Huns, while others have seen in them Black

Ugrians. It is, however, now generally accepted that they are true Magyars (or at least the descendants of a magyarized Turki people) transplanted there to guard the frontier, their name meaning simply "frontier guards."

Their ethnic identity as distinguished from other Rumanians is largely preserved by the continuing vitality of the Szekler (Szekel) language, a Magyar dialect (*see* HUNGARIAN LANGUAGE). Runes of ancient Turkic origin continue to be used as a written alphabet, the latinized Rumanian script being largely used for official and commercial communication, however. By the terms of the 1952 Rumanian constitution, the province of Mureș (with the highest concentration of Szekler population) was legally designated as the Magyar Autonomous Region (1964 pop. 819,429).

*See* also RUMANIA: *The People.*

*See* "Eastern Outposts of the Magyars: the so-called Szekelyek and Csangok," *Geographical Review,* vol. 31 (1941); Rumanian People's Republic, *Rumanian Statistical Pocket Book* (1965).

**SZENT-GYÖRGYI, ALBERT** (1893– ), Hungarian-U.S. biochemist, who was awarded the 1937 Nobel Prize for medicine and physiology "for his discoveries in connection with the biological combustion processes, with especial reference to vitamin C and the catalysis of fumaric acid," was born in Budapest on Sept. 16, 1893. His medical education at Budapest was interrupted by World War I, but he used an interval of leave after being wounded to complete his studies and graduate M.D. (1917). After the war he held posts at Pozsony (later Bratislava), Prague, Berlin, Hamburg, Leiden, and Groningen. In 1927 he transferred his laboratory to Cambridge, Eng., and subsequently spent a year in the United States. He returned to Hungary in 1932 and held the chairs of medical chemistry at Szeged and at Budapest. In 1947 he emigrated to the United States and became director of the Institute for Muscle Research at the Marine Biological Laboratory at Woods Hole, Mass. He became a citizen of the United States in 1955.

Szent-Györgyi's greatest achievement was the isolation from the adrenal glands and from various plant juices of hexuronic acid (ascorbic acid) and the provision of definite proof that this substance is identical with vitamin C. He was also the first to demonstrate the presence of flavin (riboflavin, or vitamin $B_2$) in animal tissues. With S. Ruznyak and others he investigated a substance, which he called vitamin P, that prevents abnormal capillary permeability in scurvy.

*See* also VITAMINS. (W. J. BP.)

**SZOLD, HENRIETTA** (1860–1945), founder of what became through her leadership the world's largest Zionist group, Hadassah (*q.v.*), the Women's Zionist Organization of America, was born in Baltimore, Md., Dec. 21, 1860. She pioneered in Americanization work after 1882, originating (1891) the night school for immigrant workers in Baltimore. A founder of the Jewish Publication Society of America (1888), she served until 1916 as the society's editor general, translator of Jewish classics and writer. In 1912, with 12 members, Miss Szold founded Hadassah. As its president she organized in 1916 a medical unit for Palestine comprising staff and equipment for hospitals, nurses' school, clinics and epidemiological and teaching services. The first woman elected to the World Zionist executive and member of the Palestine Jewish National Council, she held their portfolios of health, education and social welfare. She established Lemaan Hayeled (named after her death the Szold Foundation) for child welfare and research in juvenile problems. In 1933 she became director of Youth Aliyah, a worldwide movement to rescue and rehabilitate in Israel young victims of Nazi and other persecution. She worked also for Arab-Jewish *rapprochement* through common social and political planning. Miss Szold died in Jerusalem Feb. 13, 1945. She was recognized as the outstanding Jewish woman of her time, a pioneer in international social service, education and Zionist thinking.

*See* Marvin Lowenthal, *Henrietta Szold: Life and Letters* (1942); Rose Zeitlin, *Henrietta Szold* (1952). (T. DE S. P.)

**SZOLNOK,** a town of central Hungary and capital of Szolnok *megye* (county), lies 57 mi. (92 km.) ESE of Budapest at the confluence of the Tisza and Zagyva rivers. Pop. (1960) 45,553. Under the Árpád kings (*c.* 890–1301) it became a market and distributing centre for the rock salt of the Maramureș Basin. In the Middle Ages it was a noted strongpoint, fiercely contested by Magyars and Turks. In modern times it developed as a road and rail junction. The main road from Budapest to Debrecen passes through it, and railways with connections to Rumania, Yugoslavia, and the U.S.S.R. converge to cross the great bridge over the Tisza, completed after World War II. The town's activity is concerned mainly with the transit of goods rather than with industrial production, although several modern factories have sprung up on the right bank of the Tisza. One of Szolnok's assets is the subterranean supply of medicinal waters pumped from artesian wells, at a depth of more than 3,000 ft. (900 m.), to baths near the Tisza bridge. (H. G. S.)

**SZOMBATHELY** (German STEINAMANGER), the capital of Vas *megye* (county), Hung., lies near the Austrian-Hungarian frontier on the Gyöngyös River, a tributary of the Rába (Raab), 162 mi. (261 km.) W of Budapest. Pop. (1960) 54,465. The town is the successor of the nearby Roman settlement of Savaria (Sabaria), the capital of Pannonia (*q.v.*), and it was there in 193 that Septimius Severus was proclaimed emperor by his legions. St. Martin, bishop of Tours, was born there *c.* 330. The town was sacked by the Huns in the 5th century and declined in medieval times. In the 18th century Maria Theresa of Austria chose the city for the seat of a bishopric. The episcopal palace (Püspökvár) and the fine Baroque cathedral were built between 1781 and 1813. Szombathely grew in importance as a railway junction for the trunk lines from Vienna, Graz, Budapest, and Zagreb and developed as an agricultural centre, especially for local wines, fruit, honey, and spices, and for the manufacture of agricultural machinery. (H. G. S.)

**SZYMANOWSKI, KAROL MACIEJ** (1882–1937), Polish composer of orchestral music and the leading figure in the Polish musical revival, was born on Oct. 6 (new style; Sept. 24, old style), 1882, at Timoshovka, near Elisavetgrad in the Ukraine. He studied with his father and Gustav Heuhas and in 1901 with Z. Noskowski in Warsaw. His early piano works include preludes, studies, and the variations, op. 3. Though influenced by Scriabin and Richard Strauss, his style developed between 1909 and 1913 in his second symphony, second piano sonata, and the opera *Hagith* (Warsaw, 1922). During World War I he wrote his third symphony, showing oriental affinities; *Métopes* for piano; the *Mythes* for violin, including *The Fountain of Arethusa;* and the first violin concerto. Szymanowski's later works were remarkable for their lyrical inspiration and ornate craftsmanship. The best of his songs were written from 1915 onward and include the cycle *Slopiewnie.* His style reached maturity in the opera *Król Roger,* containing the well-known "Song of Roxana" (Warsaw, 1926). Folk-song elements were used in his ballet *Harnasie.* In his *Stabat Mater* and *Litania* he revived an archaic style. In 1926 he became director of the Warsaw Conservatory. His last compositions include the *Symphonie Concertante* and the second violin concerto. He died at Lausanne, Switz., on March 29, 1937.

*See* Stefania Lobaczewska, *Karol Szymanowski* (1950).

THIS letter corresponds to Semitic *tau* (meaning "mark"), the form of which on the Moabite stone (*see* MOAB) was X. In all Greek alphabets, as well as in the Lydian and the Latin, the form was T. Etruscan had a form T from which probably were derived the Umbrian form † and the Faliscan † and Y.

Latin cursive gives a form that leans to the right T. Carolingian T is based upon uncial T. Generally speaking, in medieval manuscripts the minuscule letter did not rise above the line and is sometimes difficult to distinguish from a minuscule *c*. In modern handwriting and printing, it is the custom to extend the vertical stroke above the horizontal.

The sound represented by the letter throughout its history has been the unvoiced dental stop. In English this has become more alveolar than dental, that is to say, it is pronounced by the tongue pressing upon the gums rather than the teeth. English unvoiced stops are probably also to be distinguished from the corresponding sounds in ancient Greek by the addition of a slight puff of breath following the sound, thus bringing the sound near

| NAME OF FORM | APPROXIMATE DATE | FORM OF LETTER |
|---|---|---|
| PHOENICIAN | 1200 B.C. | X |
| CRETAN | 600 | T |
| THERAEAN | 700–600 | T |
| ARCHAIC LATIN | 700–500 | T |
| ATTIC | 600 | T |
| CORINTHIAN | 600 | T |
| CHALCIDIAN | 600 | T |
| IONIC | 403 | T |
| ROMAN COLONIAL | PRECLASSICAL AND CLASSICAL TIMES | T T |
| URBAN ROMAN | | T |
| FALISCAN | | Y |
| OSCAN | | T T |
| UMBRIAN | | † † Y |
| CLASSICAL LATIN AND ONWARD | | T |

THE DEVELOPMENT OF THE LETTER "T" FROM THE PHOENICIAN THROUGH CLASSICAL LATIN TO THE PRESENT FORM

to being an aspirate. Greek would perhaps have transliterated the English unvoiced stops by the letters $\theta$, $\phi$, and $\chi$ rather than $\tau$, $\pi$, and $\kappa$. This tendency toward aspiration is carried to much farther lengths in the Irish dialects of English.

For an account of the Germanic consonant shifts involving the letter T, according to Grimm's Law, *see* GERMANIC LANGUAGES. *See* further ALPHABET. (B. F. C. A.; J. W. P.)

**TAAFFE, EDUARD,** GRAF VON (1833–1895), Austrian statesman whose tenure of office lasted longer than that of any other prime minister of the emperor Francis Joseph (*q.v.*). He was born in Vienna on Feb. 24, 1833, into a noble family of Irish origin. Brought up with Francis Joseph, he entered the public service in 1852 and was governor of Upper Austria in 1867. After being minister of the interior under F. F. von Beust (*q.v.*), he became minister of defense and public security on Dec. 30, 1867, in the "bourgeois ministry" of Prince Carlos Auersperg, whom he succeeded as prime minister of Austria on Sept. 24, 1868. Advocating concessions to the Czechs, against the majority of his colleagues, he resigned on Jan. 15, 1870, but was recalled to be minister of the interior under Alfred Potocki in April. When that cabinet fell (Feb. 4, 1871), he was appointed governor of Tirol.

Taaffe became minister of the interior again on Feb. 15, 1879, under Karl von Stremayr, and succeeded him as prime minister on Aug. 12. Professing himself devoted solely to his emperor, he relied mainly on the support of the Catholic Church and of the Slavs of the Austrian lands (Czechs and Poles) against the German nationalists (Liberals and others). His adroit opportunism, with the successes of his foreign minister G. S. Kalnóky (*q.v.*), recovered much of the prestige that Austria had lost since the 1850s (*see* AUSTRIA, EMPIRE OF), notwithstanding the scandal of the suicide of the crown prince Rudolf (*q.v.*) in 1889. His concessions to the Czechs, however, failed to satisfy the Young Czech Party (*see* BOHEMIA), and finally he tried to conciliate the Social Democrats with a bill for universal suffrage. When this was rejected by the *Reichsrat,* he resigned (Nov. 11, 1893). He died at Ellischau (Nalžovy), in Bohemia, on Nov. 29, 1895.

**TABARI, AL-** (ABU JA'FAR MUHAMMAD IBN JARIR AL-TABARI) (*c.* 838–923), Arab historian and theologian, was the author of a history of the world generally known as the *Annals.* Born at Amol in Tabaristan, he studied in Baghdad, Syria, and Egypt. Most of the rest of his life he spent in Baghdad, first as tutor to the vizier's son, then as a teacher of law and Tradition.

Originally a follower of the Shafi'ite school of law, he later established a school of his own; its influence was, however, short-lived. The *Annals* (*Ta'rikh al-Rusul wa al-Mulk,* "History of the Prophets and Kings") are a general history from the Creation to A.D. 915 and are famous for their detail and, in the later parts, their accuracy. His second great work, a commentary on the Koran (*Jami' al-Bayan* or *Tafsir*), is marked by a similar fullness of detail.

BIBLIOGRAPHY.—For the *Annals,* the text is ed. by M. J. de Goeje, 13 vol. (1879–1901); there is also a section trans. by E. Marin, *The Reign of al-Mu'tasim* (1951). For the *Jami' al-Bayan,* there is a Cairo edition in 30 parts (1902/03 and reissue 1905–12), with index by H. Haussleiter, *Register zum Qorankommentar des Tabari* (1912); another edition is by M. M. and A. M. Shakir, 3 vol. (1954– ). *See* D. S. Margoliouth, *Lectures on Arabic Historians* (1930); C. Brockelmann, *Geschichte der arabischen Litteratur,* vol. i, 2nd ed. p. 148 (1943), and supplement i, p. 217 (1937). (J. A. HD.)

**TABASCO,** a Gulf Coast state of southeast Mexico. Area 9,522 sq.mi. (24,661 sq.km.). Pop. (1960) 496,340. The surface is generally low and flat, largely covered with lagoons, watercourses, and swamps. In the south and southeast there is a higher area. Tabasco, a region of very heavy rainfall, is covered by dense forests that provide valuable fine woods and dyewoods. It is traversed by two large rivers, the Grijalva (also called Tabasco) and Usumacinta. The Usumacinta forms the boundary between Guatemala and Chiapas until the frontier of Tabasco is reached; it eventually flows into the Grijalva, the two rivers having a common outlet. There are few good roads, and the rivers are the principal means of transportation. There are also air and rail lines. The state capital is Villahermosa. The next most important town is Frontera, a port 3 mi. within the mouth of the Grijalva.

Juan de Grijalva explored the area in 1518, and in 1519 Cortés first clashed with the Indians, from whom he acquired his faithful ally, Malinche. Francisco de Montejo partially subdued them after constant uprisings in the 1530s and 1540s. Tabasco, an Indian name meaning "damp earth," became a state in 1824. The potential oil wealth of the area began to be exploited in the 1950s. Cattle, copra, bananas, cocoa, coffee, rice, sugarcane, rubber, vanilla, tropical fruits, and corn are the main agricultural products.

VILLAHERMOSA lies on the Grijalva River in an area of heavy rainfall. Pop. (1960) 52,262. It serves as a market centre for the cattle ranches and banana plantations of the surrounding countryside. In the mid-20th century Villahermosa became an important airline terminal. (J. A. Cw.)

**TABERNACLE** (Hebrew *mishkān*, literally "dwelling"), the name given in the English Bible to the portable sanctuary said to have been constructed by Moses in the wilderness as a place of worship for the Hebrew tribes (Ex. 25–31, 35–40). It is commonly held by scholars that this elaborate building, together with the complex ceremonies connected with it, is largely the product of a theoretical attempt to read back into the wilderness period the architecture and ceremonies of the later Jerusalem Temple.

The historical nucleus of this idealized structure is found in the ancient tradition that Israel's earliest sanctuary, before the building of a permanent Temple, was a simple tent—set up outside the tribal camp—within which God manifested his presence and communicated his will ("the tent of meeting," Ex. 33:7–11). The present biblical account of the building of the tabernacle is of exilic or postexilic date and is contained in the "Priestly" document of the Pentateuch (*see* PENTATEUCH), which reflects the theology of the Jerusalem priesthood. For them it was of transcendent importance that God should have a habitation where he might "dwell" among his people (Ex. 25:8; *cf.* I Kings 8:12 ff.; Ezek. 37:27). Characteristically, the Priestly writers transfer the portable sanctuary from outside the camp to its centre. As with the Solomonic Temple, the entire complex consisted of a large court surrounding a comparatively small building (the tabernacle proper). The court, to which alone the congregation was admitted, was enclosed by linen hangings and had the form of a rectangle composed of two squares. In the centre of the eastern square stood the altar of sacrifice (burnt offering), with a laver (a copper-bronze basin holding the water with which the priests performed their ritual ablutions) nearby; the corresponding position in the western square was occupied by the ark (*q.v.*), situated in the inner sanctuary of the tabernacle.

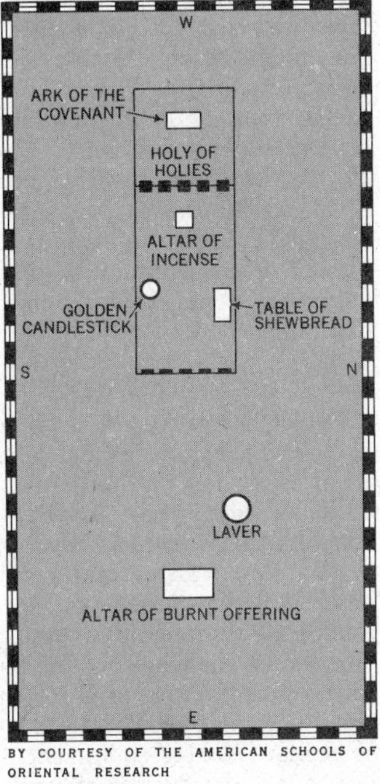


BY COURTESY OF THE AMERICAN SCHOOLS OF ORIENTAL RESEARCH

THE TABERNACLE AND ITS COURTS

The tabernacle itself was constructed of tapestry curtains, decorated with cherubim, spread over a framework of wood covered with gold. These delicate tapestries were protected by successive coverings of goat's hair cloth, tanned rams' skins, and goatskins. The entrance, at the east end, was closed by a "screen" (or portiere) hung from five pillars; the interior was divided into two rooms—"the holy place" and "the most holy place" ("holy of holies")—by a veil of the same material as the curtains of the walls and ceiling, hung on four pillars. The outer of these rooms (the holy place) contained the table on which the bread of the Presence (the shewbread) was placed, the altar of incense, and the seven-branched lampstand. The inner room (the most holy place), which was a perfect cube having just half the floor area of the outer, was conceived to be the actual dwelling place of the God of Israel, who sat invisibly enthroned above a solid slab of gold (the propitiatory or mercy seat) that lay upon the ark, a gold-covered wooden box containing "the testimony" (*i.e.*, the tablets of the Decalogue). At either end of the golden slab rose the golden figures of the cherubim. *See* also TEMPLE, JEWISH.

BIBLIOGRAPHY.—*See* articles on "Tabernacle" in Hastings' *Dictionary of the Bible, Jewish Encyclopedia,* and *Interpreter's Dictionary of the Bible; see* also A. H. McNeile, *The Book of Exodus,* pp. 73–92 (1908); S. R. Driver, *The Book of Exodus,* pp. 257 *et seq.* (1911); J. Morgenstern, *The Ark, the Ephod, and the "Tent of Meeting"* (1945); D. W. Gooding, *The Account of the Tabernacle* (1959). (R. C. DE.)

**TABERNACLES** (BOOTHS), **FEAST OF** (SUKKOTH): *see* JEWISH HOLIDAYS.

**TABES DORSALIS** (LOCOMOTOR ATAXIA) is a form of neurosyphilis characterized by chronic degeneration in the posterior columns of the spinal cord. The disease results in loss of muscular coordination. The first symptom, which occurs between about 15 and 25 years after infection, usually is a lessening or the loss of the ankle and knee reflex. As the disease progresses, the patient gradually loses his ability to walk and stand normally. Treatment is the same as for other forms of late syphilis. *See* also VENEREAL DISEASES: *Syphilis: Neurosyphilis.*

**TABLE,** a fundamental piece of furniture, in its simplest form is a flat slab supported on legs or pillars. From very early times the table was used for eating; in more advanced civilizations a great variety of designs were devised for other uses.

## EARLY TYPES

The table was known in a small and rudimentary form to the Egyptians, who used wood for its construction. The Assyrians had tables of metal and possibly other materials. Grecian tables were of bronze supported on three or four legs; in Roman villas the most favoured form was the tripod, but tables were also made with a single pillar or with four legs. The more costly examples were carved, inlaid, or otherwise ornamented. Cedar and other woods with a decorative figure were used in their construction. The legs, usually of bronze, were cast in the form of animals, sphinxes, or grotesque figures; examples found at Pompeii and Herculaneum are of graceful design and delicate workmanship. Most of the Greek and Roman tables were made for the use of persons who reclined on couches while eating and, therefore, were considerably lower than modern Western dining tables.

In early medieval times all furniture was very primitive, but some faint memory of the refinements of classical Roman civilization must have survived. Thus the emperor Charlemagne (d. 814) possessed three tables of silver and one of gold. (These were doubtless of wood covered with thin sheets of precious metal.) In the later Middle Ages long tables with rectangular tops were used in the great hall where the entire household assembled for meals, while smaller tables with circular or rectangular tops were set in the private chamber of the master of the house. In the hall the high table for the master and his guests stood on a dais, sometimes surmounted by a canopy, while at right angles to it down the length of the hall side tables were placed for the remainder of the company. Some medieval illuminated manuscripts show state banquets taking place at round tables with the guests seated on curved benches; a 15th-century example survives in Winchester Castle (Hampshire). The characteristic medieval table, consisting of massive boards of oak or elm resting upon trestles, could be dismantled and removed after meals.

Tables with attached legs, joined by heavy stretchers fixed close to the floor, appeared in the 15th century and became standard in the following century. These tables could not be dismantled and were not easily removable. In the early 16th century there was introduced an ingenious form of joined table, known as a "draw" table, which allowed for easy extension to double its normal length. The top was composed of three leaves, two of which were placed beneath the third. The two under leaves, supported on runners, could be drawn out, and when they were fully withdrawn the upper leaf fell into place between them. Such tables were commonly of oak, but walnut, elm, cherry, and other woods were also used. They remained in general use until well into the 18th century. The typical Elizabethan draw table was supported on four vase-shaped legs terminating in Ionic capitals at the top. In the 17th century the vases were often of vastly exaggerated proportions but became more modest as the century progressed. The illustrated inventory of the 25 tables of "Walnuttree and Markatre" and 14 of marble owned by Lord Lumley in 1590 shows a cosmopolitan taste; many are of Italianate style, with inlaid marble tops on a single baluster support. In Italy the Florentine artists in *pietra dura* (or coloured marbles) produced costly table tops overlaid with intarsia of semiprecious stones, which were exported widely.

### LATER TYPES

**The Folding Table.**—The most important innovation of the 17th century was the gate leg table, the distinctive feature of which was a top with one or more flaps supported on pivoted legs, each pair being joined at top and bottom by stretchers and so constituting a gate. Tables with folding tops were known in the 16th century, but their use did not become general until the 17th. The earlier examples had as a rule a single flap, but a triangular type with three flaps is known. By the mid-17th century two flaps were usually provided, producing an oval table large enough for dining, which took up very little space when the flaps were lowered and the gates folded into the frame. This construction has remained in use until the present day.

The smaller flap table with a single pivoting leg remained very popular in England throughout the 18th century, particularly for card tables. These were constructed in walnut, mahogany, or satinwood and when not in use were set against the walls as side tables. Excellent carving was lavished on the cabriole legs of these tables; on the finer examples the knees were carved with a shell or mask, and the feet ended in a claw and ball or a sensitively modeled volute. The folding table did not enjoy the same popularity in continental Europe as in England. Its appearance there—mostly in the west—was due to English influence, and its form varied little from the English prototype.

**The Side Table.**—A side table or serving table came to be an indispensable feature of the dining room, and in some instances it was fitted with shelves upon which the gilt plate of the house was displayed. The 18th-century side table was often intricately carved, either in gilded softwood or mahogany, and usually had a marble top. The weight of the marble necessitated a robust construction, but the elegance of the design with cabriole legs, carved frieze, and mask pendants gave an impression of lightness. Toward the end of the 18th century furniture makers began to pay more attention to convenience than to magnificence of effect, and the side table (which when used as a dining room serving table had provided no accommodation apart from its upper surface) developed into the true sideboard (*see* CABINET FURNITURE: *Neoclassicism*).

**The Console Table.**—This term is used to describe a type of table supported on brackets like consoles, or on two legs of similar form; it was designed to be placed against a wall and the back was usually screwed to the wall. The form originated in France or Italy in the latter part of the 17th century but soon became universal in noblemen's houses throughout Europe. The frames were elaborately carved and gilded, and the tops were made of coloured marble, or even semiprecious stones. Console tables were usually made in pairs or sets of four designed to stand between windows or on each side of doors and often had mirrors *en suite*. Their makers tended to borrow their designs from printed pattern books, and this has resulted in some uniformity of design, even in places geographically remote.

**The Silver Table.**—During the second half of the 17th century there appeared side or toilet tables with wooden frames completely covered with plaques of embossed and chased silver; such tables usually formed part of a suite consisting of table, looking glass, and a pair of candlestands. A number of late 17th-century examples survive in England (*e.g.*, in Windsor Castle), while some of the German palaces (Dresden or Hanover) have 18th-century suites of silver furniture. In England the silver table was replaced in the early 18th century by tables of similar design covered with gilt gesso, which was much less costly.

The term "silver table" is also applied to a light four-legged table of wood with a gallery around the edge. It was used to support the tea or coffee service, which might be of silver or of porcelain; the gallery prevented pieces from being knocked off.

**Writing and Toilet Tables.**—In the 18th century both English and French cabinetmakers showed great ingenuity in designing writing and toilet tables with numerous mechanical devices that could be folded into a small space. The pattern books of Thomas Sheraton (*q.v.*) show many such devices; the cabinetmaker David Roentgen, who worked in Germany and France, achieved fame throughout Europe as a constructor of toilet tables of this type.

**The Wine Table.**—Another invention of the latter years of the 18th century was the wine table, which was narrow and of semicircular or horseshoe form; the guests sat around the outer circumference. In the more elaborate versions the tables were fitted with a revolving wine carriage or bottle holder.

**The Gueridon.**—This is a small table designed to support a lamp or candelabrum. It originated in France toward the middle of the 17th century. Later examples, produced in Venice in the 18th and 19th centuries, were often supported by exotic figures.

**Other.**—The mahogany table with extra flaps, which could be inserted and supported on hinged legs to meet the varying needs of the company, had appeared in England in the 18th century and continued in vogue, with increasing heaviness, throughout the Victorian era. The elaborately carved and inlaid legs of the Victorian table were usually hidden beneath a voluminous tablecloth, but outstanding makers, such as Gillow or Holland, produced original designs that were carried out by craftsmen of unequaled skill. Apart from the low coffee table, no essentially new table forms have been devised in the 20th century. The architectural features of the table have, however, attracted architect-designers, such as Alvar Aalto. Space problems in modern apartments have encouraged experiments in convertibility. Such experiments as these have included adjustability of height, so that the dining table when not in use as such could be lowered to become a coffee or decorative table.

### THE ORIENT

Tables have occupied a far less important place in the Orient. In both Near and Far East the custom of sitting on the ground when eating has resulted either in very low tables or in no table at all for this purpose, and it is only in China, where chairs were adopted, that there has been any development analogous to that of the West. Large tables were never in favour, however, and large gatherings would sit at multiple tables; these were often round, the dishes being placed in the centre, and the radius conditioned by the length of the human arm. In both Near and Far East low tables were used for writing, and Indian miniature paintings show small tables placed by the side of couches for drinking vessels or smoking equipment. From the 18th century there has been a large production of small decorative tables in China, Japan, and the East Indies for export.

*See* FURNITURE DESIGN for illustrations and bibliography.

(J. F. H.)

**TABLE MOUNTAIN** (TAFELBERG) is the conspicuous flat-topped mountain lying to the south of Cape Town, South Africa, and towering above the city. The mountain forms the northern end of the high and rocky Cape Peninsula, which is composed of granite, Malmesbury shales, and, uppermost, the beds of the Table Mountain Series (Cape System), of which the Table Mountain Sandstone is the hardest and thickest rock. It is this sandstone, lying almost horizontal, which gives the mountain its characteristic tabular form, vigorous water and wind erosion having formed the precipitous two-mile-long northern face. The surface of the mountain is a plateau about 3,500 ft. (1,065 m.) high, backed by a lower plateau deeply dissected in places by stream erosion. The highest point (3,567 ft. [1,087 m.]) is Maclear's Beacon (near the northeastern face), set up by Sir Thomas Maclear in 1865. Detached from the main mountain by erosion are two subsidiary peaks: to the northeast the Devil's Peak (3,270 ft. [997 m.]), formerly called Windberg or Windy Mountain; and to the northwest Lion's Head (2,178 ft. [664 m.]), the lion's "back" declining northward to Signal Hill (often called the Lion's Rump).

The mountain is sometimes covered by the so-called "tablecloth," a more or less thick cloud, produced most often by southeasterly winds, the cloud or fog soaking the mountain top and the eastern slopes. Most of the annual rainfall is brought by the northwesterly winds in winter, the amounts varying between about 60 in. (1,525 mm.) at the top and 22 in. (560 mm.) in parts of Cape Town at the foot of the mountain. Five reservoirs on the mountain contribute to the water supply of Cape Town.

The flora of the mountain includes many proteas, heaths, and the very beautiful disa orchids which flourish in the very moist areas. The Compositae or daisy family of the Cape Peninsula number more than 60 native genera and 250 species, many of these being found on the mountain. On the drier western side of the mountain, succulents occur, including a few euphorbias and the stapelia or "carrion flower." Trees include the characteristic silver tree, together with the stinkwood, yellowwood, ironwood, and other trees also found in the Knysna Forest.

There are more than 300 classified routes up the mountain, varying greatly in difficulty. Access to the top was provided in 1929 by an aerial cableway, which transports 50,000 passengers annually to the summit.

*See* C. A. Lückhoff, *Table Mountain* (1951). (J. H. WN.)

**TABLE TENNIS,** an extremely fast indoor game, similar in principle to lawn tennis, was apparently derived from real or royal (indoor) tennis about 1880. It was known also under various trademarks ("Gossima," "Ping-Pong," etc.); in 1926 the present name was adopted by the International Table Tennis Federation (ITTF). Table tennis is a popular tournament sport in the Orient and Europe. There is limited interest in tournament competition in the United States, but it is a popular participant sport; tables and equipment are widely available at schools and public recreational facilities and in many private clubs and recreation rooms.

The ITTF, founded in Germany in January 1926, called a meeting that was attended by representatives of Austria, England, Germany, Hungary, and later that season of Czechoslovakia and Sweden. Thirteen congresses were held between the years 1926–27 and 1938–39 in European cities and in Cairo, Egypt. Suspended during World War II, it held its first postwar congress in Paris in March 1947. Congresses were later held (1948–57) in Europe, India, and Japan. The World Congress of 1957 was held in Stockholm, Swed., and thereafter it was held biennially beginning with the congress in Dortmund, Ger., in 1959.

International competition was dominated by European players through the 1930s. From 1927 through 1939 the men's singles was won by representatives of Hungary eight times, and of Austria and Czechoslovakia twice each; England's F. J. Perry won once, in 1929. When international competition was resumed after World War II, Czechoslovakia took the first men's singles title (1947), and then it went to England four times in a row, to J. Leach in 1949 and 1951, and to R. Bergmann (a naturalized English citizen who had won for Austria in 1937 and 1939) in 1948 and 1950. Thereafter, except for F. Sido's win for Hungary in 1953, the men's singles championships moved to the Far East, led by Japan (H. Satoh in 1952, and four in a row from 1954 through 1957), with Communist China coming on to win its first men's singles in 1959. The other events—men's doubles, women's singles and doubles, and mixed doubles, and the men's team (Swaythling Cup) and women's team (Marcel Corbillon Cup)—followed much the same pattern, although the United States, Yugoslavia, Rumania (especially in the women's and mixed doubles events in the 1950s), Germany, and Scotland managed to get in the winner's column on occasion.

For tables of World Championships *see* SPORTING RECORD.

**The Game.**—Table tennis is played by striking a pale, hollow celluloid ball ($4\frac{1}{2}$–$4\frac{3}{4}$ in. circumference, 37–39 g. weight, or 37–41 g. weight in the U.S.) with a racket (bat or, loosely, "paddle") over a net (6 in. high, 6 ft. long) fixed across a dark, nonreflecting table top (9 by 5 ft., 30 in. high). The blade of a typical racket is made of wood and is usually faced on both sides with stippled rubber to control the ball and to impart spin. The sponge-faced racket, which Japan used in winning a world championship in 1954, was banned under rules adopted by the ITTF in 1959.

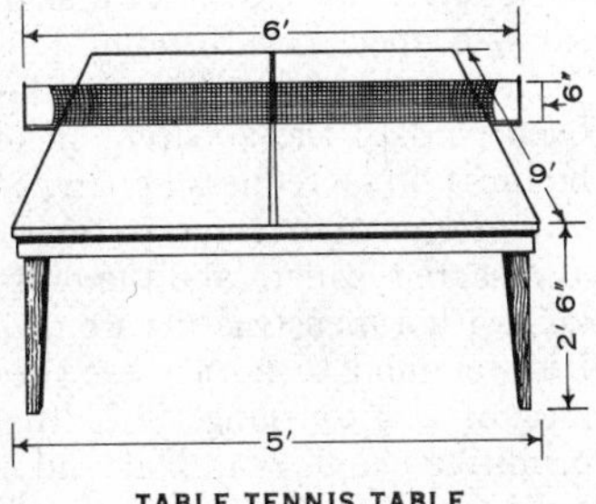

TABLE TENNIS TABLE

The server's racket hits the ball behind his end of the table so that it bounces first on his side of the table, then over the net on his opponent's side. In U.S. tournament play, the server cannot impart spin to the ball except by use of his racket. The ball is then struck to and fro directly over the net, after bouncing (volleying is illegal) until a point is scored by failure to make a good return. Service, after every 5 points, alternates and the winner is the player who first scores 21 points; but at score 20-all service alternates after each point. As in tennis, a game must be won by at least two points. In doubles, the ball must first touch the server's right half court and after passing over the net the receiver's right court; once in play, it may be placed anywhere on the table, as in singles, except that partners must alternate in returning the ball. One U.S. law prevents strictly defensive play.

The orthodox grip is assumed by "shaking hands" with the racket, as in lawn tennis, except that the table tennis racket or bat is not held at the end of the handle. The forefinger rests along the blade on the rear (backhand) side of the table tennis racket and the thumb on the forehand side. Slight variations from this grip are common. Many Asian players, including the Chinese and the Japanese, have used the "penholder" grip (handle held between forefinger and thumb, like a pen).

The basic shots are the push or half-volley, usually executed by meeting the ball with the racket in a near vertical position as the ball rises from the table; the forehand and backhand drives (characterized by topspin), executed by an upward stroke with the racket usually tilted toward the net; and the forehand and backhand chops (which impart underspin), executed by a downward stroke with the racket tilted away from the net and usually a defensive shot. There are many variations.

In the United States, the U.S. Table Tennis Association (USTTA) interprets the rules of the ITTF and publishes USTTA laws. There are comparable national organizations throughout the world. (P. W. R.; X.)

**TÁBOR,** a town in South Bohemia, Czech., lies on the Lužnice River, a tributary of the Vltava, 55 mi. (89 km.) S of Prague. Pop. (1961) 20,142. It was founded in 1420 as the regional centre of the militant Hussites (*q.v.*) by the more radical members of the movement, subsequently known as the Taborites, and led by Jan (John) Žižka. The Old Town is situated on a steep ridge rising from the right banks of the Lužnice; it is protected by ramparts and the large Jordan "pond" where the inhabitants once baptized their children. It has many important medieval buildings, including the town hall (1521), which houses the Hussite Museum. The town gate (*Bechyňská brana*) dates from 1420. In the central market place stands Žižka's statue. The square is fringed by crooked, narrow streets, planned to impede access by enemy intruders; underneath it extends a labyrinth of passages and cellars, also of tactical significance. Small-scale industry (agricultural machinery, textiles, and tobacco) has grown up at Tábor, which is a railway junction and nodal point in the road system. (H. G. S.)

**TABRIZ** (ancient TAURIS), the second largest city of Iran and capital of the Third ostan of East Azerbaijan Province, lies at an altitude of about 4,400 ft. (1,340 m.) at the northern foot of Kuh-e Sahand, about 330 mi. (530 km.) NW of Teheran. It is almost equidistant from the Turkish and Soviet frontiers and lies in the valley of Talkheh Rud (Aji Chai, "bitter water"), which flows westward to Lake Urmia. Pop. (1966) 404,855. The climate is continental: hot and dry in summer and severely cold in winter. It is surrounded by hot springs and is in an earthquake zone liable to frequent and severe shocks.

The most notable ancient buildings are the Blue Mosque or Masjid-i-Kabud (1465–66), built by Jahanshah, and the citadel or Arg. The mosque, renowned for the splendour of its blue tile decoration, had by the mid-1960s been extensively repaired. The citadel, built as a mosque before 1322, was adapted to its present use in 1809. It is remarkable for its simplicity, size, and the excellent condition of its brickwork.

The process of modernizing the town was accelerated after World War II. Streets were widened, buildings erected, and public gardens laid out with fountains and pools. The new buildings include a railway station, the largest in Iran, the Ustandari (office of the governor general), and Tabriz University with its faculties of arts, science, agriculture, medicine, and pharmacy. Just outside the city is a summer resort with the lake and pavilion of Shah Goli.

Tabriz is an important commercial centre with expanding industries. The principal product is carpets; others include soap, matches, paint, leather goods, cotton and wool textiles, and dried fruit and nuts. The city is a rail and road centre; it is linked by rail with Teheran and through Jolfa with the Soviet system. The extension of the railway from Tabriz to Turkey was under construction in the mid-1960s. An airfield lies east of the city.

The early history of Tabriz is unknown. The name is said to be derived from *Tap-riz* ("causing heat to flow"), a reference to the many thermal springs in the area. As Tauris, it was for a short time the capital of the Armenian king Tiridates III in the 3rd century A.D. It was rebuilt by Zubaida, wife of Harun al-Rashid, in 791, after being destroyed by an earthquake. Similar disasters followed, in 858, 1041, 1721, and 1780. In the 13th century Tabriz twice escaped being sacked by the Mongols by the payment of heavy ransoms; and on its final submission it was made the capital of Il-khan Ghazan (1295–1304) and his successor. In A.D. 1392 it was taken by Timur (Tamerlane), and was made a provincial capital by his son Miranshah. About 30 years later, the Kara-Koyunlu (Black Sheep) Turkmens made Tabriz their capital, and the Blue Mosque was built. It retained its position under the Safavid dynasty until 1548, when Shah Tahmasp I moved his capital westward to Kazvin (Qazvin), which was less exposed to Turkish attack. During the next 200 years Tabriz changed hands several times between Persia and Turkey. Under Nadir Shah (1736–47) it was the capital of northwestern Iran. In 1908 it became the centre of the Nationalist movement and has continued to play an important part in Iranian politics. Between 1900 and 1945 Tabriz was occupied five times by Russian troops. (M. V. S.-W.)

**TABU.** The basic meaning of the word tabu (taboo) in English is "forbidden," "prohibited," but it usually refers to actions barred by rules of manners or morals rather than of law; *i.e.*, by social convention in which there are nonrational elements. It has also been extended to apply to any ritual distinction of persons or things sacred or accursed.

**Origin and Scope.**—The term is of Polynesian origin. The form *tabu,* which Capt. James Cook noted when he first discovered its use at Tonga (Friendly Islands) in 1771, was later used by the Tongans when they adopted a written alphabet, but they later came to write the word as *tapu.* This is the most common Polynesian form with *kapu* as a variant, and various speculative etymologies have been given for the literal meaning; *e.g., ta,* "to mark," "strike," *pu,* "exceedingly." In Melanesia, corresponding terms in form and meaning are *dabung* (Busama) and *tambu* (generally). The term and the concept are not always equivalent even in Polynesia: in Samoa, the notion of "forbidden" is expressed by *sa* and some similar Oceanic words have different overt meanings. *Tabu* in the Trobriands is a kinship term applying among others to a female cross-cousin or other relative appropriate for marriage, while in Dobu it means a magic charm to cause disfigurement or disease. On the other hand, notions very similar to tabu are found widespread ethnographically and expressed by a great range of linguistic expressions, as for example in Rhodesia by *tonda* among the Ila and *bwanga* among the Bemba, or *haram* in the Arabic-speaking world.

The concept of tabu was soon adopted into European languages and, by its suggestion of mystery and of being related to primitive religious ideas, provoked an extensive literature. A major contribution was made by Sir James G. Frazer in his article on "Taboo" in the 9th edition of the *Encyclopædia Britannica* (1875–89) and in *The Golden Bough* (1890). He regarded tabu as a system of religious prohibitions, attaining its fullest development in Polynesia but traceable under different names in most other parts of the world; and, as something sacred, he contrasted it with the concept of *noa* (a Maori word meaning "profane"). He also regarded tabu as the negative aspect of magic, the rules of prohibition as contrasted with the positive aspect of magic, the charms and formulas for securing success. Frazer gave an elaborate classification of tabooed things and acts, and his work was valuable in bringing together a great mass of ethnographic information, in showing the range of the phenomena, and in stimulating enquiry into primitive religion; but his treatment was not sociological and many of his general ideas have not found modern support.

It should be emphasized that the meanings of tabu current in English and other western languages may be very different from those current in any one of the Polynesian or other communities in which the notion has been identified. Moreover, specific tabus are often not current for Polynesia as a whole. Frazer wrote that "the rule which forbids persons who have been in contact with the dead to touch food with their hands would seem to have been universal in Polynesia." But, while this rule was valid for many Polynesian societies, it did not apply, *e.g.,* to Tikopia, where it was quite proper for someone who had handled a corpse to prepare and partake of food, even without washing his hands. Again, tabu has been treated as if it represented an integral, closely knit system of prohibitions, but this is not so even in any single Polynesian society. The range of items and activities to which *tapu* may be applied need have no obvious general pattern, though the major items usually show consistency.

**Nature and Functions.**—One simple usage of *tapu* (in Tonga) is as a conventionalized expression of respect: at the beginning of a public address the speaker may say *Tapu mo hou 'eiki* ("My respects to the chiefs"). In conversation when something has been said which by Tongan ideas of propriety may perhaps be regarded as disrespectful or improper—such as a reference to a part of the human body or to an animal—the expression *Tapu mo koe* (equivalent to "If you will excuse my mentioning such a matter") is interpolated.

To modern Polynesians *tapu* may mean no more than a thing that must not be interfered with. So a Tikopia man may tell his child not to touch a visitor's camera or fountain pen, saying "It is *tapu,*" by which is meant not that the article in question has any particular quality of its own, but that interference with it is not allowed. Similarly in modern Melanesia a board set up on a tree with the word *tambu* on it may be simply a warning to people against going along a path or into an orchard, broadly equivalent to "trespassers will be prosecuted," or simply "keep off."

But the notion of tabu is usually much more complex. Generically it includes the idea that the object or action interdicted has some ritual quality, or that the sanction against a breach of the rule is extrahuman or supernatural. Very frequently this sanction is regarded as automatic in its action: a breach of tabu is followed logically and necessarily by some kind of trouble to the offender; *e.g.,* lack of success in fishing or hunting, sickness, death of a relative. In ordinary terms this would be regarded as accident or bad luck, but to the people concerned it is regarded as a punishment for breaking the tabu. A person meets with an accident or has no success in his pursuit and, in seeking for its cause, he or others infer that he has in some manner committed a breach of tabu.

With some tabus, however, the sanction is not automatic, but is invoked by the person controlling the tabu, and is believed to consist in the power of a god or spirit to punish the offender. From this point of view, Frazer's equation of tabu with negative magic is inadequate, according to his distinction between magic and religion, for this kind of tabu should come in the religious category. Another theoretical equation of tabu with negative mana (*q.v.*) by R. R. Marett, also fails. These two concepts in their Polynesian setting belong to different categories; standing for efficacy and power of a supranormal kind, mana is not necessarily connected with tabu.

In general, tabu has a dual significance. Much attention has been paid to the apparent inconsistency between the notions of holiness or sacredness apparent in many kinds of tabu (the head of a Polynesian chief is tabu as part of his general character as a sacred leader) and the notions of uncleanness in others (contact with a menstruating woman may be tabu in a defiling sense). But common to both these ideas is respect, associated with the idea of not touching. It is not found, as Frazer thought, that primitive peoples can make no moral distinction between the conceptions of holiness and of pollution, nor is it paradoxical that sacredness and prohibition should attach to the same object. Things that are sacred have some elements of prohibition attaching to them, but all things that are prohibited are not necessarily of sacred quality.

Tabus are often thought to be entirely irrational, even absurd, yet in some societies regular tabus have important social functions; *e.g.*, those against incest. Others have economic effects; *e.g.*, food tabus that restrict the diet of pregnant women or of totemic clans. Some kinds of tabu are not always in operation, but are set up for specific purposes; *e.g.*, those prohibiting fishing or picking fruit at certain seasons may be valuable in food conservation. Many tabu rules ritually symbolize important social relationships and may thus be a substitute for laws and form part of the moral code of the society.

**Theories.**—There have been many attempts at explanations of the origin of such beliefs and behaviour. One of the most ingenious was that of Sigmund Freud, who associated the concept of tabu with that of neurosis. He argued that tabus were generated in ambivalent social attitudes in which the social components largely replaced the sexual elements of the neurosis. The basis of tabu then is a forbidden action for which there exists a strong unconscious inclination. This may well hold for some (*e.g.*, incest tabus) but ignores the fact that an essential feature of tabu is the obedience of the individual to restrictions imposed by social tradition. Moreover, much of the desire to break through the prohibitions of the tabu may be quite conscious; *e.g.*, when tabus are placed upon food supplies.

Social anthropologists are not unanimous in their theoretical explanations, but there is broad agreement that the tabus current in any society tend to relate to objects and actions that are significant for the social order, and belong to the general system of social control. They may do this directly, as in emphasizing the status of chiefs and religious objects, or indirectly, as in the prohibitions on the killing or eating of totemic species which in themselves are of no particular significance but which, as indices of social units, form part of a symbolic framework for the society. It is often impossible to know why a particular action or article has been singled out for such respect behaviour. But a general assumption is that such ritualization of respect involves implicit recognition of danger in disturbing significant social relations.

*See* MORALITY, PRIMITIVE; PASSAGE RITES; PURIFICATION. *See* also references under "Tabu" in the Index.

BIBLIOGRAPHY.—J. G. Frazer, *The Golden Bough,* 3rd ed., 12 vol. (1907–15), especially vol. 2, *Taboo and the Perils of the Soul,* and abridged ed., pp. 19–22 and ch. xviii–xxii (1922); S. Freud, *Totem and Taboo* (1918); E. S. C. Handy, *Polynesian Religion* (1927); Raymond Firth, *(Primitive) Economics of the New Zealand Maori,* 2nd ed., pp. 246–262 (1959); F. R. Lehmann, *Die polynesischen Tabusitten* (1930); R. R. Marett, "Tabu," *Encyclopaedia of Religion and Ethics,* ed. by J. Hastings, vol. 12, pp. 181–185 (1921); M. Mead, "Tabu," *Encyclopaedia of the Social Sciences,* vol. vii, pp. 502–505 (1930–35); A. R. Radcliffe-Brown, *Taboo* (1939); H. Webster, *Taboo, a Sociological Study* (1942); W. Howells, *The Heathens,* ch. iii (1948); F. Steiner, *Taboo* (1956); W. A. Lessa and E. Z. Vogt (eds.), *Reader in Comparative Religion: an Anthropological Approach,* 2nd ed. (1965); F. J. Simoons, *Eat Not This Flesh: Food Avoidances in the Old World* (1961); A. Kiev (ed.), *Magic, Faith, and Healing: Studies in Primitive Psychiatry Today* (1964). (R. F.)

**TABULATING MACHINES:** *see* OFFICE MACHINES AND APPLIANCES.

**TACHEOMETRY,** a method used in surveying for quickly determining horizontal and vertical distances. The term is generally applied to operations in which distance is obtained by the measurement of a small angle lying opposite a short known base. Tacheometric instruments usually make use of a detached base; but, as in the case of the range finder (*q.v.*), the base line is sometimes an integral part of the instrument. Because of its size, the military range finder is not useful to the surveyor.

The instruments that make use of an external base may be divided into two groups: (1) those that make use of a fixed angle to measure an intercept on a distant staff, and (2) those that measure an angle subtended by a fixed base. In the latter case, the horizontal angle, subtended by a standard "subtense" bar of two metres and oriented at right angles to the line of sight, is measured on the circle of a theodolite (*q.v.*). In the former case, the theodolite is equipped with stadia wires that intercept a portion of the length of a graduated rod held vertically at the distant point by two rays that include the fixed angle. A double-image type of tacheometer causes a portion of the image to be displaced with respect to another and the linear displacement is read on a horizontal graduated staff. The tacheometric instruments are generally theodolites or transits modified by the addition of the optical distance measuring devices and implemented by various self-reducing devices for finding the horizontal and vertical components of the slope distance.

*See* RANGE FINDERS; SURVEYING. (K. S. Cs.)

**TACHINID FLY,** any species of the dipterous family Tachinidae (or Larvaevoridae), the larvae of which are internal parasites of other insects. As adults many tachinids superficially resemble house flies but are much more bristly, particularly on the abdomen; however, there is considerable diversity of form among the more than 5,000 known species. They range in size from 2 to 18 mm. Although most species are dull gray or black, some are marked with red, orange, or yellow, and a few are metallic green or blue.

Tachinids are of great importance in the control of destructive insects, particularly lepidopterous caterpillars and beetle larvae, and for this reason several species have been transported from one country to another to combat native or introduced pests. Outstanding examples include reduction of the sugarcane beetle borer in Hawaii by *Ceromasia sphenophori* from New Guinea, and control of the coconut moth in Fiji by a Malayan tachinid, *Ptychomyia remota. Centeter cinerea,* highly destructive of the Japanese beetle in Japan, has been brought to the United States to control that species. Caterpillars of the armyworm have been found locally to be 20 to 90% infested by larvae of red-tailed tachinids (*Winthemia*). *Compsilura concinnata,* introduced from Europe to control the gypsy moth and brown-tail moth, has been found to attack more than 200 species of caterpillars; in contrast, most tachinids are capable of parasitizing only a small number of hosts, often a closely related group of species; and a few have but one host. Some parasitize locusts, earwigs, squash bugs and related species, and a few other kinds of flies. Certain tachinids attack honeybees and silkworms, but these are not numerous. Many adult tachinids frequent blossoms to obtain nectar and thus serve as pollinators.

The means of entering the host has become highly evolved among Tachinidae. Some attach eggs to their victims, the larvae burrowing through the skin upon hatching. Others deposit living larvae, either directly upon the host or in situations allowing the larvae to attach to passing insects. Certain species lay their eggs on vegetation, which is eaten by caterpillars. Tachinid maggots usually breathe by an opening through the body wall of the host or by contact with its respiratory system. Larvae may remain within the host to pupate or may leave it. Most tachinids destroy their hosts, but others do not. (G. W. Bs.)

**TÁCHIRA,** a state in the Andean region of Venezuela bordering on Colombia. Area 4,286 sq.mi. (11,100 sq.km.). Pop. (1961) 399,163. Agriculture dominates the economy and coffee and sugar are leading commercial crops. Rural industry, closely related to agriculture, is to a considerable degree carried on in homes. San Cristóbal, the state capital and leading commercial centre, is on a trans-Andean highway about 34 mi. (55 km.) W of the border town of San Antonio. Relatively large deposits of coal are found at Labatera. La Alguitrana claims the distinction of having the first oil well (1878–79) in Venezuela.

Some inhabitants of Táchira belong to privileged groups who take great pride in the purity of their European ancestry.

(J. J. J.)

**TACHOMETER,** an instrument that indicates the speed of rotation of a shaft or machine element. The major types of tachometers are classed as (1) centrifugal, (2) electrical, (3) vibrating reed and (4) electronic.

Centrifugal tachometers employ a spindle driven by the shaft whose speed is to be measured. As the spindle turns, centrifugal force causes fly-weights that are attached to the spindle to be displaced away from the axis of rotation. These weights are restrained by springs. The position of the fly-weights and the rotational speed of the shaft are interrelated. Through a suitable linkage the position of the weights is calibrated in terms of rotational speed and is indicated by a pointer which is on the instrument scale.

One type of electrical tachometer uses a small permanent-magnet-field direct current generator driven by the shaft whose speed is to be measured. As the voltage output of the generator is proportional to the speed of the shaft, a voltmeter, which can be remotely located, is graduated to indicate speed. Another electrical type uses a small ammeter actuated by the current flowing in a circuit due to the charging and discharging of a condenser. The instrument spindle, which is driven by the shaft, in turn drives a switch to open and close the circuit. The current flowing is proportional to the number of "makes" and "breaks" of the switch and the ammeter is graduated in revolutions per minute.

The vibrating reed type of tachometer uses a series of thin steel reeds with natural frequencies ranging from low to high and corresponding to certain speeds. When an instrument of this type comes into contact with the machine one or more of the reeds will vibrate in sympathy with the machine and indicate the rate of speed. Such a tachometer is not driven by the shaft but responds to vibrations of the machine.

Electronic tachometers are of two types. The strobotac employs the persistency of human vision to detect the change in speed viewed under a flashing light. When the flashes are synchronized with the shaft's rotational speed, the shaft appears stationary. There is no need for mechanical contact with the shaft. This feature is important for devices of very small power output, for contact between spindle and shaft actually slows down such machines. The other electronic-type tachometer is basically a revolution counter that receives its impulse from a pickup (often magnetic), counts the revolutions in each second and displays the count directly as revolutions per minute. (R. A. O.)

**TACITUS, CORNELIUS** (*c.* 56–*c.* 120), historian whose accounts of 1st-century Roman history are still read for their vividness, irony, and stylistic brilliance.

**Family and Career.**—Tacitus has left the imprint of his personality upon his work but little evidence about his life, and here we are in debt to the letters of the younger Pliny (*q.v.*). Their connection may go back a generation. Pliny's uncle, the elder Pliny (*q.v.*), knew a Cornelius Tacitus, Roman knight and procurator (financial officer) of Gallia Belgica, who may have been the father or uncle of the historian. Tacitus belonged probably not to the old Cornelian aristocracy but to a rising family of Cisalpine Gaul or, more probably, Gallia Narbonensis, which had taken the Cornelian name on receiving Roman citizenship. The date of his birth was *c.* 56; his first name is given as Publius or Gaius. His family circumstances and his own ability opened the way to higher education, a good marriage, and an official career.

Tacitus studied rhetoric and took up advocacy under two leading orators, M. Aper and Julius Secundus. When he wrote the *Dialogus* he laid the scene in this period (74/75) and introduced them into the discussion. In 77 he was betrothed to the daughter of Agricola (*q v.*) and his marriage later in the year secured him influential support. Meanwhile he had entered on public office with the vigintivirate (one of 20 appointments to minor magistracies) and a military tribunate, followed by the quaestorship probably in 81. In 88 he became praetor and a member of the priestly college that kept the Sibylline Books. Then he held a provincial post for four years, possibly in command of a legion, and was away from home at Agricola's death in 93. On his return he experienced the last years of Domitian's oppression. In 97, under Nerva, he gained the consulship and delivered a funeral oration over Verginius Rufus, the famous soldier who had refused imperial power in 68–69. By now he was celebrated for his oratory and courted by aspiring advocates; but in 98 his personal feelings led him into literature: he wrote a biography of Agricola, followed by the *Germania,* an ethnographical study of topical significance. In 100, along with Pliny, he successfully prosecuted Marius Priscus for extortion in Africa. Then he wrote the *Dialogus,* and turned to political history with the *Histories*. This work was already published when he crowned his public career with the proconsulate of Asia in 112/113. Thereafter his life was devoted to the *Annals;* he died in the early years of Hadrian's reign (*c.* 120).

**Works.**—As a rhetorician Tacitus knew the various genres of literature, as well as oratory, and he applied the appropriate style to each of his works; but his historical instinct, trained by political experience, was always dominant. The *Agricola* (98) is a biography of his father-in-law, Gnaeus Julius Agricola, the famous governor of Britain (77 or 78–84) under Domitian. It is laudatory but systematic, and also describes the geography of Britain and the Roman conquest that culminated in Agricola's campaigns. Tacitus depicts him as a man of true Roman virtue, who defended the state without useless defiance or craven servility toward an evil emperor. He aimed at justifying moderate, efficient men like Agricola (and himself) against the criticism of those who were indulging their freedom under Nerva to glorify the martyrs of Domitian's reign.

The *Germania* (*de origine et situ Germanorum;* 98) describes the geography and customs and the various tribes of Germany in a regular ethnographical way. Tacitus relied upon written information, chiefly from the elder Pliny. He shows the simple virtue as well as the primitive vice of the Germans: here was something of the old Roman morality in contrast to the laxity of contemporary Rome. The Germans emerge as a formidable foe, weakened only by intertribal feuds. Against them the empire needed unity and strength. But, although Trajan was on the Rhine at this time, the *Germania* is hardly a political brochure either urging him to action or defending his caution.

The *Dialogus de Oratoribus,* although set in Tacitus' youth, was written after the reign of Domitian. Its Ciceronian style arises from its form and subject matter and does not point to an early stage of stylistic development. The discussion balances the practical case for oratory against the pleasure and virtue of a poet's life: in any event oratory has declined since republican days, owing to lower standards of morality and education. The political licence of the republic had encouraged true eloquence; the imperial peace destroyed its sources of inspiration. The work may be dated shortly after 98—perhaps in 102, if the dedication was to Fabius Justus as consul—and reflects Tacitus' mood at the time when he renounced oratory for history.

In the *Histories* (*Historiae*) Tacitus treated the period from Jan. 1, 69, with Galba in power, to the death of Domitian in 96. Only books i–iv and part of book v survive (for the years 69–70). They cover the fall of Galba and Piso before Otho (book i); Vespasian's position in the East and Otho's suicide, which makes way for Vitellius (book ii); the defeat of Vitellius by Vespasian's generals (book iii); and the beginning of Vespasian's reign (books iv–v). The original work contained 12 (or 14) books (it is only known that the *Histories* and *Annals,* both now incomplete, totaled 30 books). To judge from Pliny, several books were ready by 105, the writing well advanced by 107, and the work complete by 109. Then Tacitus proceeded not to the reigns of Nerva and Trajan (as he had lightly promised in the *Agricola*) but to the early principate.

The *Annals* (*ab excessu divi Augusti*), in traditional form, covered the period from the death of Augustus and accession of Tiberius in 14 to the end of Nero's reign in 68, thus linking up with the *Histories*. There survive only books i–iv, part of book v and most of book vi (these sections on Tiberius, from 14 to 29 and from 31 to 37), and books xi–xvi, incomplete at beginning and end (on Claudius from 47 to 51 and Nero from 51 to 66). The original work contained 18 (or 16) books. There is some evidence of groupings of six: books i–vi on Tiberius (subdivided into books i–iii on Tiberius and Germanicus, books iv–vi on Sejanus and Tiberius), and books vii–xii on Gaius (Caligula) and Claudius. To judge from his references to Parthian power, Tacitus had written most of books i–vi by 114 (Trajan's offensive against Parthia). If a reference in book ii, 61 to *mare rubrum* ("Red Sea") as the Roman frontier means the Persian Gulf, he was touching up these books in 116–117 (after Trajan's victory and before Hadrian's withdrawal); but the phrase refers rather to the Red Sea proper (after the annexation of Arabia in 105/106). In any event he probably completed the work early in Hadrian's reign.

**Sources.**—For the period from Tiberius to Vespasian Tacitus drew upon earlier annals and monographs, which contained material from public records, official reports, and contemporary knowledge, set out in chronological order. The work of Aufidius Bassus and its continuation by the elder Pliny covered these years; both historians also described the German wars. Among other sources may be noted Servilius Nonianus (on Tiberius), Cluvius Rufus and Fabius Rusticus (on Nero), and Vipstanus Messalla (on the year 69). They are only names to us, but much of their material will lie beneath Tacitus' narrative. He did more than combine his authorities: he consulted, where necessary, the senatorial records, the official journal, and such firsthand information as a speech of Claudius, the personal memoirs of the younger Agrippina, and the military memoirs of the general Corbulo. For Vespasian's later years and the reigns of Titus and Domitian he worked directly from official records and reports, using his own and his friends' personal knowledge.

**View of History.**—In studying Tacitus' historical attitude it is not enough to cite his personal reaction to Domitian's terrorism: his experience was more varied and constructive. While he condemned the maladministration and disorder of the republic, he had seen the corrupting effect of power upon Domitian and of powerlessness upon the Senate. He had lived through a double crisis of imperial policy when Nerva and Trajan came to the succession, and had witnessed the liberal Nerva at the mercy of the praetorian guard, and the benevolent Trajan regimenting the state. His own career had revealed to him, in court and administration, the play of power behind the facade of the principate. His experience intensified his temperamental pessimism. In the *Histories* he could describe, with overtones, how Galba's policy of adoption failed, where Nerva's was effective; how soldiers outside as well as inside Rome might make or unmake emperors; how Vespasian's restoration of order ominously degenerated into Domitian's tyranny. But, as he thought on the parallels, they stretched back to Augustus. Were they, then, symptomatic of a deep-rooted condition of the principate? It was historically logical to take up this problem in the *Annals*. The republic, he argues, had suffered under personal power but only at intervals in a course of freedom: it was Augustus who contrived permanent domination. The proof of this lay in direct transmission of power: hence the significance of Tiberius' accession in the *Annals*. Its effect was the corruption of public conduct between the extremes of despotism and servility. The loss of freedom cost Rome its virtue, and the history of the principate was a pattern of the consequences. Tacitus could claim impartiality because he was confident of his basic interpretation.

Tacitus' standards were those of traditional Roman behaviour, and he conceived history in personal terms. This attitude influenced his choice of material and dictated the emphasis of his description. His facts are generally accurate: only his arrangement distorts their impression; for he will make his view of a character explain every significant action. On the critical point of Tiberius' policy he had found a tradition—it is also in Dio Cassius—of the emperor as a man who applied his words and moods to all uses except the indication of his mind: Tacitus used this feature to illustrate his theme of Tiberius' universal hypocrisy. Similarly Claudius' weaknesses are total, Nero's instability is essentially evil. He heightens the contrast of characters: Tiberius and Germanicus, Claudius and his wives, Agrippina and Nero. Yet, when his composition is analyzed, he provides the evidence with which to modify the starkness of his interpretation. Even where he appears to neglect imperial administration and its benefits, this is not merely for lack of interest: routine efficiency, in his view, is subservient to degeneracy in high places. His political interpretation is on the human plane, following the example of Sallust: he leaves the individual free to choose good or ill and be judged accordingly at the bar of history. Though he refers to the anger of the gods and the malignity of fate, such expressions appear unsystematic and casual; for in these matters Tacitus was a conventional well-bred Roman. This is equally apparent in his attitude toward Jews and Christians, as far as he distinguished between them, both in his view objectionable for their un-Roman religion, the latter also for their "hatred of the human race" (*odium humani generis*).

**Method and Style.**—Roman historiography used the old "analistic" (yearly) form as a framework of chronology. This allowed the convenient entry of official data and had a traditional appeal through its ceremonial appearance. It also provided literary advantages. The formal arrangement enclosed elaborate episodes, and the contrast varied the tension of the narrative. This procedure is less marked in the *Histories*, where the extant books describe extensive operations during a short period; it is exploited fully in the *Annals*. Tacitus applied all the techniques of rhetoric that a historian had available: geographical surveys, ethnographical digressions, set battle pieces, public debates, character summaries, and characterizing speeches. But they became less conventional as he integrated his methods in the *Annals*, under a dramatic conception of history. Hellenistic historiography had given the Romans a technique of dramatic writing which set a scene and brought the actors before the mind's eye, with direct emotional impact, heightened by colourful, poetic language. It owed much to Roman epic, the ally of Roman history. An imaginative historian who interprets in terms of character and situation and who thinks visually will be, above all, dramatic. Tacitus was master of this art. But it was not art for art's sake. He fuses his portrayal of single episodes with his historical theme: his writing is the projection of his thought, especially in the *Annals*. The dramatic element is found in construction, when books end with catastrophes involving the death of notable persons. The Roman tradition of dignity limited the cheap use of sordid details, and Tacitus practises extreme concentration of effect. This often distorts his picture, especially when he has exaggerated his characterization. It also leads to the suppression of explanatory matter before and after his literary spotlight falls on the action. In military accounts, since he focuses attention upon the battle scene, neglecting the strategic situation, he is to this extent "unmilitary." But Tacitus seizes direct control of his reader's mind and imagination.

Above all, Tacitus shows his genius in his use of the Latin language, with its qualities of strength, colour and rhythm. His style is packed, it breaks the easy balance of sentences with striking asymmetry, and it plays on word order and variation of syntax. In this he owes a debt to Sallust. He writes in the grand style, helped by solemn and poetic vocabulary, and with the passion of a satirist. The historian lives in the writer, and his style displays its strongest features in the early books of the *Annals*, where his thought is most severe. As for his epigrams, which blast so many reputations, the brilliant trick of contemporary rhetoric has become the last word of a considered historical judgment: the Tacitean epigram is the lightning that flashes from the dark cloud under which he has placed the principate. One could mention Poppaea, who "had everything except honour" (*Annals*, xiii, 45; *huic mulieri cuncta alia fuere praeter honestum animum*), or Roman imperialism: "where they make desolation they call it peace" (*Agricola*, 30; *ubi solitudinem faciunt, pacem appellant*).

**Later Reputation.**—The immortality that Pliny prophesied for Tacitus remained in abeyance for two and a half centuries—unless the story that the emperor Claudius Tacitus (275–276) honoured and republished him is true—until Ammianus Marcellinus imitated his style in continuing his work. A thousand years later the Renaissance scholars resurrected him and studied his evidence for statecraft. The French welcomed his literary art, even before the Revolution made his history fashionable. Modern scholarship has probed his facts, examined his views, and analyzed his style, so that we may now set him critically among the immortals.

*See* also references under "Tacitus, Cornelius" in the Index.

BIBLIOGRAPHY.—*Texts:* C. D. Fisher and H. Furneaux, 3 vol. (1900–10); C. Halm and G. Andresen, rev. ed. by E. Köstermann, 3 vol., "Teubner Series," 8th–9th ed. (1960–62); W. Peterson *et al.*, in "Loeb Series" with Eng. trans. (1914–37).

*Commentaries: Agricola:* H. Furneaux, rev. ed. by J. G. C. Anderson (1922); *Germania:* J. G. C. Anderson (1938); *Dialogus:* W. Peterson (1893), A. Gudeman, 2nd ed. (1914); *Histories:* W. A. Spooner (1891), C. Halm and G. Andresen, 5th ed. (1916); *Annals:* Books i–vi, H. Furneaux (1896); books xi–xvi, H. Furneaux, rev. ed. by H. F. Pelham and C. D. Fisher (1907). *Translations:* A. J. Church and W. J. Brodribb, 3 vol. (1869–72); *Annals and Histories:* G. C. Ramsay, 2 vol. (1904–15); *Histories and Minor Works:* W. H. Fyfe, 2 vol. (1908–12).

*General:* G. Boissier, *Tacite* (1903; Eng. trans. 1906); F. Klingner, *Römische Geisteswelt,* 3rd ed. (1956); E. Löfstedt, *Roman Literary Portraits,* Eng. trans. by P. M. Fraser, ch. 7 and 8 (1958). *Literary discussion and bibliography:* A. H. McDonald in M. Platnauer (ed.), *Fifty Years (and Twelve) of Classical Scholarship,* 2nd ed. (1968). *On the historical material:* M. P. Charlesworth *et al.,* in *Cambridge Ancient History,* vol. x, ch. 19–25, pp. 871 ff. (1934). *See* also the monumental work of R. Syme, *Tacitus,* 2 vol. (1958). (A. H. McD.)

**TACLOBAN,** capital of Leyte Province, Republic of the Philippines. It is the largest city and distributing centre on the islands of Leyte and Samar and the only port east of Cebu with terminal facilities. Tacloban played an important role in World War II. On Oct. 20, 1944, U.S. Gen. Douglas MacArthur's forces landed at several points on the coastal plain along Leyte Gulf south of the city; from there the U.S. forces pushed rapidly northward to capture Tacloban on Oct. 21 and then westward to Ormoc, the largest Japanese stronghold and supply base on the west coast of Leyte. From the time of its capture until U.S. troops captured Manila, Tacloban was the temporary capital of the Philippine Commonwealth. Pop. (1960) 53,551. (An. C.)

**TACNA,** the southernmost department of Peru, is bounded on the southwest by the Pacific Ocean, on the north by Moquegua and Puno, on the east by Bolivia, and on the south by Chile. It has an area of 5,701 sq.mi. (14,766 sq.km.) and a population (1969 est.) of 90,600. The southwest portion of the department is a part of the Peruvian coastal desert, and settlement there is dependent on irrigation provided by the Río Sama and the Río Locumba. The eastern part of Tacna is in the high Andes. The one area of concentrated settlement is around the town of Tacna, the capital. On the irrigated lowlands sugarcane, cotton, grapes, fruit, and alfalfa are grown, while the few Indian inhabitants of the highlands produce wheat, barley, and potatoes and raise sheep and alpacas. Among the known but little exploited minerals of the department are silver, borax, gypsum, and sulfur. In 1956 the Peruvians began the development at Toquepala of what it was believed might prove to be the largest copper ore deposit in the world. The outlet for the copper would be through the port of Ilo.

The town of Tacna and its port of Arica, 48 mi. (77 km.) S and connected to the capital by rail, became famous during the long border dispute with Chile. *See* Pacific, War of the.

(P. E. J.)

**TACOMA,** a city in western Washington, U.S., a port of entry and the seat of Pierce County, lies on Commencement Bay, head of navigation on Puget Sound, at the mouth of the Puyallup River, 30 mi. S by water of Seattle. From Tacoma can be seen Mt. Rainier, 50 mi. (80 km.) E (*see* Mount Rainier National Park); via the Narrows Bridge the city has easy access to the Olympic National Park (*q.v.*).

From Commencement Bay in 1841 Lt. Charles Wilkes, commander of a U.S. exploring expedition, launched the first survey of the Pacific Northwest. Wilkes commented in his official journal upon the surrounding waterways: "Nothing can exceed the beauty of these waters, and their safety . . . I venture nothing in saying, there is no country in the world that possesses waters equal to these."

Except for the activities of the Hudson's Bay Company at Ft. Nisqually, there was little in the way of white settlement of the area before 1868. In that year, its original name—Commencement City, after the bay which Wilkes described—was changed to Tacoma, when Gen. Morton Matthew McCarver platted a new city in anticipation of its selection as the western terminus for the Northern Pacific Railway. The new name was a corruption of "Tahoma," the Indian name for Mt. Rainier.

Tacoma was incorporated as a city in 1875 under the laws of Washington Territory. It operates under a council-manager form of government in effect since 1953. Its population of 147,979 in 1960 was about 95% white; many of its citizens are of Scandinavian heritage, typical of the coastal cities of Washington. Tacoma is the central city of a standard metropolitan statistical area comprising Pierce County, with a population in 1960 of 321,590, a gain of 16.6% in the decade. (For comparative population figures *see* table in Washington: *Population.*)

Tacoma's principal manufactures include lumber and lumber products, aluminum, copper and copper by-products, ferroalloys, castings, and mineral wool. Electrochemical plants produce caustic and chlorine. Several candy manufacturers ship nationally and overseas, and men's wearing apparel is also a leading industry. Heavy cranes and logging equipment are manufactured to supply the needs of forest industry. Boatbuilding yards produce fishing boats and pleasure craft as well as watercraft to supply the armed services, marking Tacoma as one of the largest boatbuilding centres on the Pacific coast. Several major armed services installations, including Ft. Lewis, McChord Air Force Base and Madigan Army Hospital, were established nearby.

The University of Puget Sound (Methodist, founded 1888) and Pacific Lutheran University (established 1890) are located in the Tacoma area. The city also serves as headquarters for the Washington State Historical Society, whose five-floor museum overlooks Commencement Bay. The city maintains over 35 parks, composing a total of more than 1,700 ac.; the largest is Point Defiance Park, whose grounds contain a public yacht basin, a zoo, landscaped gardens, and also the restoration of old Ft. Nisqually.

(B. M. L.)

**TACONITE.** The name taconite was applied originally to an iron-bearing formation of supposedly Taconic age (Cambrian to Ordovician). Though this was an error the name was associated thereafter with iron-bearing rocks on the Mesabi Range in northern Minnesota consisting of chert (fine-grained quartz), magnetite, hematite, several silicates as minnesotaite, greenalite, stilpnomelane, and amphibole, and siderite. The rocks were originally chemical precipitates which now form beds of a maximum thickness of 750 ft. and a length of about 100 mi. along the strike. Their extent down the dip is unknown. In this taconite are found the high-grade iron-ore bodies which have supplied most of the iron of the U.S. As all taconite contains on an average 27% of chemically combined iron, it is considered the largest potential reserve of ore in the U.S. About 5,000,000,000 to 6,000,000,000 tons of it are near enough to the surface and contain sufficient amounts of magnetite so that its concentration to a high-grade product was in an advanced stage of development by the second half of the 20th century, and shipments of millions of tons of taconite concentrate and agglomerate were being made.

*See* also Minnesota: *Mining and Lumbering.*

*See* J. W. Gruner, *The Mineralogy and Geology of the Taconites and Iron Ores of the Mesabi Range, Minnesota* (1946). (Jn. W. G.)

**TACTICS** connotes the mechanics of fighting on land, sea, and in the air, both individually and collectively. From the Greek *taktika* ("matters of arrangement"), tactics are closely related to strategy (*q.v.*), which often dictates their employment; to weaponry, which frequently demands new tactics; to techniques, on which a given tactic often depends; and to principles of war, which both strategy and tactics must respect if victory is to result. For example, in the American Civil War, Gen. Robert E. Lee employed an offensive strategy by invading the North but, when confronted by Gen. George McClellan's army at Antietam, he employed defensive tactics. In 1941 England assumed a strategic defensive against Germany, but a tactical offensive against the Italians in Egypt. In the Pacific theatre of war in 1942, the U.S. chose a defensive strategy which hinged initially on a tactical offensive in the form of the assault and seizure of Guadalcanal. To achieve this, the U.S. Navy and Marine Corps employed amphibious tactics which, by utilizing carefully developed and rehearsed operational techniques, respected the established principles of war, including surprise with maximum concentration of force, thus opening the way to ultimate victory.

The 19th-century military theoretician Karl von Clausewitz defined tactics in his *On War* (Random House, Inc., New York, 1943) as "the formation and conduct of single combats in themselves" and strategy as "the combination of single combats with each other. . . . In other words, strategy forms the plan of the war, maps out the proposed course of the various campaigns which compose the war, and regulates the battles to be fought in each." His contemporary, Antoine Henri Jomini, deferred to space and time by defining tactics as the "maneuvers of an army on the battlefield, or combat maneuvers, and the various formations in which troops may be led to the attack." (C. Brinton, G. Craig, and F. Gilbert, "Jomini," ch. 4 in *Makers of Modern Strategy*, ed. by E. M. Earle, Princeton University Press, 1943.) Cyril Falls, the former Chichele professor of war history at Oxford University, defined tactics in *The Art of War* (Oxford University Press, 1961) as "the *art* of conducting a battle or section of a battle" while strategy "is the *art* of conducting a campaign." Another contemporary expert, Edward Earle, in his introduction to Falls' book, holds that strategy "is different from tactics—which is the art of handling forces in battle—in much the same way that an orchestra is different from its individual instruments." Most authorities differentiate between grand tactics, which are normally held to embrace all the tactical elements leading to battle, as opposed to minor tactics, which concern actual contact with the enemy.

This traditional view, which tends to subordinate tactics to strategy, has been disputed by, among other experts, the soldier-scholar Helmuth Karl Bernhard Moltke, who argued that strategy —"the practical adaptation of the means placed at a general's disposal to the attainment of the object in view"—is the bridge between the political element of war (purpose) and the tactical element (the actual mechanics of combat). While not disputing the importance of strategy, Moltke was careful to assign an independent position to tactics once battle was joined. Sound strategic preparation

> can limit the enemy's will if we are ready and determined to take the initiative, but we cannot break it by any other means than tactics, in other words, through battle. The material and moral consequences of any larger encounter are, however, so far-reaching that through them a completely different situation is created, which then becomes the basis for new measures. No plan of operations can look with any certainty beyond the first meeting with the major forces of the enemy. . . . The commander is compelled during the whole campaign to reach decisions on the basis of situations which cannot be predicted. All consecutive acts of war are, therefore, not executions of a premeditated plan, but spontaneous actions, directed by military tact. The problem is to grasp in innumerable special cases the actual situation which is covered by the mist of uncertainty, to appraise the facts correctly and to guess the unknown elements, to reach a decision quickly and then to carry it out forcefully and relentlessly. . . . It is obvious that theoretical knowledge will not suffice, but that here the qualities of mind and character come to a free, practical and artistic expression, although schooled by military training and led by experiences from military history or from life itself. (Earle, *op. cit.*)

For this reason the "great captains" of history have been supreme tacticians who followed fluid and flexible courses on the battlefield, and whose decisions were later subject to independent analysis and evaluation. These decisions, or tactics, have been weighed qualitatively and graded in the proportion that they have respected the material advantages or disadvantages of the time as applied to particular principles of war, such as security, mobility, surprise, and concentration of force, which singularly or collectively were necessary in a given circumstance to produce victory. They also have been treated quantitatively, first on land, later on the sea, and finally in the air. Throughout history various commanders have practised orthodox, unorthodox, offensive, defensive, aggressive, and delaying tactics. At first involving only primitive tribes armed with rude weapons and indulging the simple ambush usually followed by individual combats, these tactics eventually embraced highly trained and carefully organized forces whose arms grew increasingly complex through the ages.

Today's qualified ground commander must not only be skilled in general tactics applicable to land, amphibious, and airborne forces but also to those governing the use of supporting arms, for example artillery (including tactical nuclear weapons), armour, and aircraft; he must also master a host of special tactics compatible to orthodox and unorthodox and to nuclear and nonnuclear warfare in the jungle, desert, plains, and mountains. (*See* JUNGLE WARFARE.)

This article is divided into the following sections:



## I. TACTICS OF THE ANCIENT WORLD

In fighting the unending war for survival, prehistoric man employed tactics that from the first involved the three elements of firepower, movement, and protection. He employed missile weapons (stones, wooden spears, darts) and hand or side weapons (stone and flint knives and handaxes); he used terrain and flame as protection against both animals and the elements, and he also used fire as a weapon to force beasts from the protection of caves. His first military tactics were decidedly primitive—single encounters won by the strongest opponent. But as walled towns sprang up and armaments improved, as the wheel was invented and the horse domesticated, battle grew more sophisticated. Eventually tribes organized specific armies, trained and disciplined them, and developed metal weapons and armour.

**1. The Age of the Chariot.**—Around 1800 B.C. the Hyksos, migrating south from Asia, introduced the horse-drawn chariot as a tactical weapon in a series of battles that wrested most of the present Syria and Palestine from the Egyptians. These vehicles were small, usually holding one or two men armed with the bow. The front was protected. In battle, chariots preceded units of foot soldiers, a tactic that thoroughly disrupted the Egyptian formations.

The Egyptians quickly adopted the new tactics. Ahmose I and his successors developed a wider, lighter chariot and also introduced iron wheels with spokes, a notable improvement over the solid wooden wheels. In building a new empire, Thutmose employed a navy to establish forward supply bases that supported armies spearheaded by chariots and using two types of foot troops: heavy infantrymen who carried spears and long shields, and light infantrymen armed with spears, bows, battleaxes, and slings. The light, broad chariots generally carried specially trained bowmen. Thutmose's armies were probably formidable enough, but his continued prosperity seems to have hinged more upon a wise overall strategy, particularly in the political sphere, than upon any special ground tactics which in any event were doomed by the rise of the Assyrians.

**2. The Assyrians,** a fierce rạce who later conquered Egypt and by 671 B.C. dominated the eastern Mediterranean, made war their chief business. Employing weapons made of iron (taken from the Hittites), the Assyrians in open battle relied on both cavalry and heavy chariots backed by archers, spearmen, and shield bearers. They developed a chariot heavier than the Egyptians', and with protective felt coverings for the horses. They deployed both light archers, who often fought as skirmishers without protection, and heavy archers, who alternated with spearmen in the use of shield bearers. They began to use mounted bowmen and swordsmen independently, the first cavalry force. They also relied on terror for tactical purposes and were famed and feared for hard, fast actions.

To take cities, the Assyrians employed catapults and battering rams. The former, which some authorities believe the Assyrians invented in the 13th century B.C., were powered by ropes of hide, hair, or sinew (with their elasticity exploited in a way unknown today). One type of catapult was an ancient equivalent of the howitzer and mortar. It fired either arrows, weighing about a half-pound, or small metal balls, stones, or pebbles "coated in baked clay which shattering on impact prevented the enemy using them in his own machines." These "shells" weighed from 5 to 57 lb. and were thrown an estimated 400–800 yd. (A. Manucy, *Artillery Through the Ages,* U.S. Government Printing Office, 1949.)

Early battering rams were very simple—a large log manhandled to the task by a crew shielded from rocks or boiling oil with a carapace of interlocked shields (called the *testudo* or tortoise shell). The Assyrians, however, mounted the rams in "wooden towers, roofed and shielded in front with metal plates, and moved on six wheels. Under the roof was a platform for archers to pick off the defenders on the walls." (P. H. Stevens, *Artillery Through the Ages,* Franklin Watts, Inc., New York, 1965.) These machines grew very sophisticated, at times reaching 20 stories in height and manned by hundreds of soldiers—Josephus speaks of one that was pulled by 300 oxen and manhandled into position by 1,500 soldiers.

**3. The Persians.**—Assyrian tactics were adopted in part by the Persians who, commencing in about 553 B.C., rose to power under Cyrus. According to Herodotus' chronicle of these early wars, in the decisive Battle of Thymbra in 546 B.C., Cyrus' chariots were backed by infantry followed by javelin-equipped soldiers and archers with cavalry on the flanks and in the rear. According to Herodotus, Cyrus also employed the stratagem of bringing up his camels from his supply train and sending them mounted in advance of his force, "the reason being that the horse has a natural dread of the camel and cannot abide either the sight or smell of him." Cyrus indeed enjoyed a reputation for cunning. Frustrated in his later siege of Babylon, whose garrison had prepared for this eventuality and seemed unlikely to surrender, he posted armies "at the point where the Euphrates river enters the city, and another body at the back of the place where it issues forth." He then took a body of troops and diverted the Euphrates by a canal into a marsh; his troops entered the city through the river beds, taking the Babylonians by surprise and winning the city.

Expansion and consolidation continued under Cyrus' successors, most notably Darius (522–486 B.C.) and Xerxes (486–465 B.C.). Intent on protecting the empire in the east and west, Darius placed more emphasis on archers than on infantry and supported them with heavy chariots. To increase the shock value Darius attached scythes to the blades and wheels. A bit later, three curved blades were fastened to the pole, one straight forward, the others fanning out in front of the horses. These added to the terror of the attack.

The obvious vulnerability of the chariot lay in the horse which, despite considerable and sustained efforts, could not be adequately protected against a skilful archer. One answer was found in war elephants, which, though used for several centuries, were never very satisfactory because battle noises often confused them—indeed, the *mahout* carried a stake and mallet which on occasion he had to drive through the berserk animal's spinal cord to kill it.

Perhaps Darius' major contribution to military science was the reorganization of his ground force into divisions, each, of 10,000 men, organized into ten battalions, each battalion into ten companies, and each company into ten sections. James H. Breasted describes this organization as "one of the most remarkable achievements in the history of the ancient Orient, if not of the world." (*The Conquest of Civilization,* Harper & Bros., New York, 1926.)

After consolidating his eastern borders, Darius around 512 B.C. led his army north against the Scythians, a bloodthirsty race who, so Herodotus tells us, had "the contrivance whereby they make it impossible for the enemy who invades them to escape destruction, while they themselves are entirely out of his reach, unless it please them to engage with him. Having neither cities nor forts, and carrying their dwellings with them wherever they go; accustomed, moreover, one and all of them, to shoot from horseback; and living not by husbandry but on their cattle, their wagons the only houses that they possess, how can they fail of being unconquerable, and unassailable even?" By such tactics, including a scorched earth policy, the Scythians forced Darius to retreat "and as he did so they attacked his rearguard and captured his baggage train." Thus frustrated, Darius withdrew across the Bosporus, and prepared for war against Greece.

**4. The Greek Phalanx.**—The Greek city-states militarily emphasized the infantry phalanx, "the germ of all future European military development." Originally the phalanx was "a solid rectangle of heavily armored infantrymen carrying shield and spear and drawn up eight deep." It was more than a mere huddle of men, "for discipline and endurance were required to maintain cohesion and to prevent the opening of a dangerous gap in the front rank. . . . A battle between phalangite armies was a test of weight and stamina, with the two formations, locked closely together, contending until one side or the other broke ranks and fled. There was no place in warfare of this nature for generalship; once battle was joined, the individual was submerged in a mass of sweating bodies and, since reserves were unknown, there was no chance of outside assistance. . . . Victory in phalangial warfare was limited in extent, for the phalanx, by itself, was incapable of achieving a crushing success. It was too unwieldy and immobile to be adapted to pursuit. Casualties in early Greek warfare were light, and most hoplites lived to fight another day." (R. A. Preston, S. F. Wise, and H. O. Werner, *Men in Arms,* Thames and Hudson, London, 1962.)

In a major tactical refinement, an early Athenian ruler, Cleisthenes, reorganized his army into ten *taxes* or regiments of hoplites (citizens capable of buying themselves armour and weapons) with each *taxis* commanded by a strategos. The polemarch commanded the whole, but rotated tactical command among the strategoi. The core of the army consisted of heavy infantry that fought in a line phalanx from 8 to 25 ranks in depth. Hoplites made up the phalanx (in some cases physically backed by serfs to help them); conscripts were used for light infantry (generally unprotected) while wealthy citizens, who could afford horses in addition to arms and armour, comprised the cavalry.

The shock power of the Greek phalanx defeated the firepower of the Persians at Marathon in 490 B.C. To lure the Athenian army from Athens, which was to be won by internal revolt aided by another Persian force landing at Phaleron, the Persians landed a force in the Bay of Marathon. Commanded by Datis, this army numbered an estimated 15,000–25,000, mainly archers. To meet this force, Callimachus commanded an army estimated at 9,000–10,000 with tactical command rotated among ten strategoi, one of them Miltiades. After considerable vacillation, Callimachus was persuaded to attack the Persians. Miltiades is believed to have brought up the army in columns, which wheeled into line upon reaching the Plain of Marathon. The Persians presumably deployed in the sharply circumscribed area between the Charadra River on the right and a marsh on the left, and this terrain probably explains why Persian cavalry played no important role in the ensuing melee. To prevent the Persian flanks from overlapping his own, Miltiades reduced the centre of his phalanx to four ranks, strengthening each wing to eight. He then approached to within about 200 yd. of the Persians when, coming into range of the archers, he ordered an advance on the double, a move that brought his wings forward at a faster rate than his centre. As the centre began to give way, thus causing a concave formation, the Persian centre, pushing through, pulled the Persian lines into a convex formation. Quite unintentionally, Miltiades had won a double envelopment (a classic tactical maneuver). The Persian lines then broke into general retreat and, according to Herodotus, the Persians lost 6,400 killed and seven ships at a cost to the Athenians of only 192 killed. The Greeks quickly exploited the victory by marching on Athens and thus preventing the other Persian force from landing in accordance with the overall plan.

The phalanx, bulky and unwieldy though it was, remained with few modifications the standard Greek infantry formation for over a century. In the ensuing war with Persia (490–449 B.C.) followed by the Peloponnesian War (431–404 B.C.) the Greeks began to use cavalry and to employ bowmen. Early in the 4th century B.C. Iphicrates added light infantry, the peltasts. Some decades later another major advance was contributed by the master tactician, Epaminondas, who faced a Spartan army at Leuctra in 371 B.C. Like most of the Hellenes, the Spartans had not radically changed the shock tactic of the heavy, bulky phalanx (a shortcoming that Fuller logically attributes to the cult of the individual hero: "valor disdained inventiveness"). Most authorities give Epaminondas a force of 4,000 to 6,000, including unreliable allies, against some 10,000 Spartans. To compensate, Epaminondas, under cover of his cavalry, drew up his phalangeal formation in oblique order, putting his left forward and holding his right back, then placing reserves on the far left countering shock by super-shock and leaving enough reserve to go round the enemy's right wing—a tactical innovation that surprised and thoroughly defeated the Spartans.

**5. The Reforms of Macedonia.**—The reformation of the phalanx, however, was made by Philip of Macedon (382–336 B.C.) who built a truly professional and national army. Realizing that mobility is essential to successful tactics, Philip took the best of a number of parts to produce a tactically organized whole. He retained the phalanx, but instead of the Spartan version of the hoplite, whose personal gear weighed 72 lb. (each hoplite was assisted in battle by personal slaves), he crossed the hoplite with the more lightly armed and equipped peltast to gain a soldier armed with a longer and heavier spear, the sarissa. Philip's phalanx, numbering perhaps 8,000 troops, was organized in regiments of 1,536 men divided into battalions and companies, the smallest unit being the file or "squad" of 16 men.

The newly organized phalanx was a splendid defensive formation that could normally stop a chariot or cavalry charge. But, despite the music of flutes intended to keep the helots properly aligned, it was much too clumsy to pursue and destroy. Philip correctly reasoned that a mobile force must be organized and trained if victory were to be exploited. Using a proportion of one trooper to every six heavy foot soldiers, he developed three types of cavalry: light for reconnaissance and courier work, heavy armoured horse for the shock charge, and mounted infantry who could fight either on horse or on foot. He tied the heavy cavalry to the solid infantry phalanx with a force of light infantry called the Hypaspists, armed with bows, slings, and javelins. In Fuller's words, "the three together may be compared to a slow moving wall on the left, a fast moving door on the right, with a hinge in between." (J. F. C. Fuller, *A Military History of the Western World,* three vol., Funk and Wagnalls, Inc., New York, 1955.) While the phalanx held the enemy's centre, as at the Battle of Chaeronea in 338 B.C., the cavalry, commanded by Philip's 18-year-old son, Alexander, smashed the Theban-Athenian flank to rout the entire army.

Alexander only slightly modified the army bequeathed him. To Philip's small staff he added numerous specialists, including scientists; he reduced the "squad" from 16 to 8 men; and he broke down the siege engines, which Philip had imported from Sicily, into component parts so that they could be carried on the march and used in an attack, thus, as H. G. Wells suggests in his *Outline of History,* inventing "artillery preparation." In 334 B.C., with an estimated force of 30,000 foot and 5,000 horse, Alexander crossed the Hellespont. In 333 B.C. Darius brought an army across the mountains to cut Alexander's lines of communication, but Alexander defeated him decisively at Issus. While Alexander continued his march into Egypt, Darius rebuilt the Persian army and in 331 B.C. deployed it on the plain of Gaugameia in the vicinity of Nineveh. Hoping to entice Alexander into a set-piece battle under favourable odds, he had his engineers clear and level the field, the better to employ his awesome chariots. Although figures quoted by ancient historians are undoubtedly exaggerated, it appears that Darius commanded an army perhaps five times numerically superior to Alexander's force of 40,000 foot and 7,000 horse. In addition to the Persian infantry which, after the disastrous Battle of Issus, Darius had armed with swords and longer spears in answer to the sarissa, he deployed a vast host of cavalry, a large force of scythe-bearing chariots, and a few war elephants. After a careful reconnaissance of the battlefield, Alexander chose an echelon formation headed by his heavy cavalry, the Companions, with the light infantry, the phalanx, and the light Thessalian horse following. Divining the intention of Darius to charge with his chariots, Alexander fronted the Companions with a screen of light infantry. Behind the main formation he placed a reserve of two flying columns, composed of infantry and cavalry, posted "at an angle to the front—in order to take the enemy in flank should he attempt to sweep round the wings; or, if he did not, they were to wheel inwards to reinforce the front of the army." (Fuller, *op. cit.*)

As Alexander's force advanced toward the Persian lines, he inclined it obliquely to the right to lead the Persian chariots onto rough ground. Seeing Alexander's plan, Darius sought to counter with heavy cavalry attacks followed by a chariot charge, both of which were checked, though only after heavy fighting. Noting that Darius' front had been unmasked by his cavalry attacks, Alexander then led the Companions, along with four regiments of infantry on their left, directly at the Persian king. This penetration tactic collapsed the enemy front and forced Darius to flee the field. Meanwhile, however, Parmenio, Alexander's second in command with the Macedonian left, had become surrounded by Persian cavalry, a development that caused Alexander to break off the pursuit and lead his Companions to the charge. Having righted matters he again turned to a pursuit continued until midnight, but failed to capture Darius. Although estimates of casualties widely differ, one point is clear: at a slight cost in lives, Alexander defeated an army much stronger than his own and in doing so broke the power of Darius and laid claim to the Persian kingdom.

Ever adaptable, shortly before his death in 323 B.C. Alexander reorganized the phalanx, putting Persian light-armed troops together with the Macedonian hoplites.

**6. The Counterpoise of China.**—Until early in the 5th century B.C., Chinese armies conformed to the dynastic tradition of the West in that they "were invariably commanded by rulers, members of their families, powerful vassals, or trusted ministers" with war regarded "as a knightly contest" fought "to satisfy a whim, to revenge an insult, or to collect booty." (Sun Tzu, *The Art of War,* trans. by S. B. Griffith, Clarendon Press, Oxford, 1963.) The nobility was armed with the sophisticated reflex, or Tartar, bow—a much more powerful weapon than the Western single stave bow—and went to battle in chariots protected by retainers who carried spears and lacquered leather or varnished rhinoceros-hide shields and accompanied by footmen wearing only padded jackets for protection. Terrain suitable for chariot warfare restricted the development of tactics in short melees that usually were indecisive.

As states grew and in turn began to nibble at less powerful neighbours, China in the mid-5th century B.C. entered the Warring States period in which feudalism declined sharply and warfare became what one ancient Chinese nobleman termed a "fundamental occupation." Powerful rulers then formed standing armies commanded by professional officers who conducted important campaigns far from their home states. Technological changes, notably the invention of the crossbow (which did not appear in the West until the 11th century A.D.) and the introduction of iron weapons, began the decline of chariot warfare, although the chariot was still in use in the mid-4th century B.C., when the brilliant philosopher-general Sun Tzu is believed to have written his famous treatise on war. Otherwise, however, various Chinese armies had become generally sophisticated. Composed of swordsmen, archers, spearmen (or halberdiers), crossbowmen, and charioteers, these armies included highly trained, elite units able to maneuver independently and in coordination and controlled by bells, gongs, drums, flags, and banners. General staffs included such specialists as weather forecasters, map makers, commissary officers; engineers to plan tunnelling and mining operations; and experts in river crossing, amphibious operations, inundating, attack by fire, and the use of smoke. To provide security on the march, unit commanders employed flank and reconnaissance patrols to probe and test the enemy before combat. Sieges were conducted with scaling ladders, siege towers, and the protective testudo familiar to the Assyrians (but, because of the high cost in lives, they were disapproved of by Sun Tzu unless no other choice was possible). Such was the state of the military art that, in Sun Tzu's opening words, war had become "a matter of vital importance to the State; the province of life or death, the road to survival or ruin." (Sun Tzu, *op. cit.*)

Sun Tzu's treatise is an amazingly astute document which undoubtedly caused ancient war lord-emperors as much uneasiness as it later tended to arouse in the minds of 20th-century conventionally minded Western military commanders. It is essentially a demand for the indirect approach to war at the diplomatic, strategic, and tactical levels.

Having decided on battle, the able general pays the closest attention to such factors as terrain, weather, and the plans of the enemy, "for the crux of military operations lies in the pretence of accommodating one's self to the designs of the enemy. . . . And therefore I say: 'Know the enemy, know yourself; your victory will never be endangered. Know the ground, know the weather; your victory will then be total.' " Both strategy and tactics are fashioned with the knowledge that "all warfare is based on deception. . . . Therefore, when capable, feign incapacity; when active, inactivity. When near, make it appear that you are far away; when far away, that you are near." The able general must maneuver "to make the devious route the most direct and to turn misfortune to advantage." (Sun Tzu, *op. cit.*) The commander who understands the strategy of direct and indirect approach will win.

Having positioned his enemy by his own foresight, by control of his forces, by extreme mobility (aided by native scouts), and by careful terrain appreciation, the general next deployed two tactical elements: the *cheng,* or orthodox force, normally used to hold the enemy, and the *ch'i,* or unorthodox force, normally used to attack the enemy's flanks and rear. These two forces work together, interacting like interlocked rings. The one complements the other and if they are correctly used it is as if the commander holds a fully drawn crossbow which he can release at will.

That Sun Tzu's teachings stood the test of battle is suggested both by his own successful career and by those of the famous scholars who in succeeding Ch'in and Han empires commented on the work in detail. The *Art of War* not only anticipated Vegetius by 7 centuries, Machiavelli by 17 centuries, and Clausewitz by 21 centuries but it has stood the test of time far better than these later, more widely known classics in that, as Mao Tse-tung among others has proved, many of its precepts are valid today.

## II. THE ROMAN LEGIONS

Influenced by the Greeks and Etruscans, the early Romans employed a phalanx formation known as the legion, a combined force of foot soldiers and cavalry that with modifications served for several centuries. The decision to abandon the phalangeal legion probably stemmed from Roman defeats in the early 4th century B.C. at the hands of the invading Gauls, some of whose shock infantry tactics put the Romans to flight. Some authorities, however, trace the decision to the much later Second Samnite War (326–304 B.C.) when Roman leaders found the phalanx insufficiently mobile for mountain campaigns.

As it finally evolved, the new legion consisted of three major tactical components arranged in depth: the *hastati* or younger men, the *principes* or older men, and the *triarii* or veteran-reserves. Each component consisted of ten *maniples* (literally "handfuls," but akin to modern companies), the first two of 120 men each, the *triarii* of 60 men. The heavy infantryman wore a brass helmet and body armour, carried a shield, and was armed with a heavy broad-bladed thrusting sword (the *gladius*); in addition, the *hastatus* carried two seven-foot javelins (the *pilum*) while the *principium* and *triarius* carried a long spear (the *hasta*). The *maniples* were screened by skirmishers, called *velites* or light infantry, and by small cavalry units. One *maniple* from each division of heavy infantry, a *maniple* of *velites,* and a cavalry unit formed a cohort (battalion) of about 450 men. Ten cohorts constituted a legion, though apparently this figure was quite flexible and a legion often numbered considerably more.

In battle order the *maniples* deployed as on a checkerboard with an interval of one *maniple*—perhaps 60 ft.—between each in line; the second line, the *principes,* covered the intervals left in the first line, the *hastati;* and the third line, the *triarii,* composed of reserves and light infantry, covered both lines. This disposition meant that the second line could rush forward to join the first and present a solid front, or that the first could fall back on the second with a minimum of confusion, or that the first or second could shift to the right or left to create clear lanes for enemy war elephant or even cavalry charges. Normal offensive tactics called for the *hastati* to throw their javelins and attack on the double with the sword—thus anticipating the musket fire and bayonet charges of later centuries. If the first charge failed, the *principes* moved up, and if they failed the reserve could be utilized. As Fuller points out, "Tactically, these changes were radical. Close and distant fighting were combined; a reserve came into being, and the offensive and defensive were closely knit together." (Fuller, *op. cit.*) By replacing the single shock of phalanx fighting with a series of shocks induced by legion fighting, the Romans perforce relied on maneuver, and this meant continued drill and training probably to a height unprecedented in the world of that time. Further, the soldiers were turned to in fortifying encampments, if only for a single night, an arduous task but a practice that "allowed the Romans to combine the advantages of defensive and offensive war, and to decline or give battle according to circumstances, and in the latter case to fight under the ramparts of their camp just as under the walls of a fortress." (Fuller, *op. cit.*)

By coupling the inherent tactical advantages of the legion to a wise political strategy, Rome began its climb to domination of the Italian peninsula and then to the establishment of empire. In these centuries the legion underwent considerable modification. In the early years its two major weaknesses were the concept of rotating command and a lack of understanding of cavalry tactics, deficiencies underlined at Cannae.

**1. The Incursions of Hannibal.**—In 218 B.C. the young Carthaginian general Hannibal, after capturing the Roman city of Saguntum in Spain, marched into Gaul with an army of an estimated 90,000 infantry, 12,000 cavalry, and 37 war elephants—figures cited by Polybius, who possibly exaggerated. Though joined by dissident Gauls, Hannibal was forced to leave garrisons to protect his line of communications, and he also suffered from the guerrillalike tactics of the mountain tribes encountered when crossing the Alps. By the time he reached Cisalpine Gaul he commanded perhaps 20,000 infantry, 6,000 cavalry, and a few surviving elephants. In December 218 B.C. he encountered a numerically superior Roman army under Tiberius Sempronius at the Trebia River, persuaded it into battle while hiding his real strength, held its front by temporarily yielding his own infantry front, then loosed a surprise cavalry charge that routed the Romans.

Rome responded to this invasion by sending two armies to block the eastern and western approaches across the Apennines. Hannibal cunningly chose a middle route that, although forcing him to negotiate tortuous marsh terrain on the far side, allowed him to set an almost perfect ambush for Flaminius' legions in the hills surrounding Lake Trasimene. The result was annihilation of the Roman force. The road to Rome then stood open, but Hannibal, lacking siege engines (as opposed to Alexander), felt he could not march on the capital. Instead he chose to mark time, continuing to encourage the Roman cities to come over to him. Singularly unsuccessful with this strategy, in the spring of 216 B.C. he marched south, probably for forage purposes, toward the Adriatic coast, and captured a supply depot at Cannae where he encamped on the banks of the Aufidus River and where, in August, he was challenged by the largest Roman army ever fielded.

According to Polybius, Hannibal's army numbered 10,000 cavalry and 40,000 infantry, the war elephants having succumbed to disease. The Roman army numbered 80,000 infantry and 9,600 cavalry commanded by two consuls, G. Terentius Varro and L. Aemilius Paulus, who daily rotated command. Aemilius did not want battle in terrain that he felt was favourable to Hannibal's cavalry; but Varro, wanting to make a name for himself, insisted on it. As at the battle of the Trebia, Hannibal teased forward the Roman force in a day of skirmishing, then deployed his own forces in a crescent formation with the Spaniards and Gauls in the centre and with each wing flanked by cavalry. Against Varro's precipitous advance, Hannibal held with the Numidian light cavalry on his right and with his infantry in the centre while his heavy cavalry charged the Roman horse. The advancing Roman *maniples* soon forced Hannibal's centre back into a concave shape (as had happened to the Greeks at Marathon). But unlike Marathon, Hannibal now unleashed his African infantry, which fell on the Roman flanks while the cavalry chopped the Roman rear to pieces. This double envelopment—a tactical classic—virtually annihilated the Romans at a cost of perhaps 6,000 of Hannibal's men.

The road to Rome stood wide open, but again Hannibal refused to attack the capital, a decision bitterly remarked on by his cavalry general, Maharbal: "You know how to gain a victory, Hannibal; you know not how to use one."

**2. Scipio Africanus.**—In fact, Hannibal was momentarily stymied. None of the Roman cities had deserted; his single ally, Philip V of Macedon, had not yet launched his invasion of Italy. Nor were there to be further set-piece battles. The new Roman dictator, Quintus Fabius Maximus (called *Cunctator*, "Laggard"), ordered the army to refuse battle while constantly harassing the Carthaginian invaders. To counter what have become known as Fabian tactics, Hannibal marched south where he remained largely on the defensive while awaiting the "encirclement" of Italy by Macedon in the northeast and by Carthage in Spain and Sicily. His expectations were fulfilled only in Spain where a Carthaginian victory momentarily checked the Romans. But then a young officer, Scipio the Elder, veteran of Trebia and Cannae, was elected to the Spanish command and in 208 B.C. sent Hasdrubal's army in flight to Gaul and subsequently Italy, where it was destroyed a year later at the fateful Battle of the Metaurus, tactical surprise having been achieved by C. Claudius Nero. Scipio sent another Carthaginian army in flight to Morocco and by 206 B.C. claimed control of Spain. Appointed consul and transferred to Sicily, he trained an expeditionary force for the Carthage campaign. Landing in 204 B.C., he destroyed a large Carthaginian army, successfully besieged Utica, and in 202 B.C. broke the power of Carthage when he defeated Hannibal at the Battle of Zama.

Unlike most Roman commanders, Scipio was a student of warfare who was not above learning from the enemy. Tactically he made two important changes in the legion: he screened his reserves with a force of light infantry, enabling him to deploy them on the enemy flanks (as he had watched Hannibal do at Cannae), and he greatly increased the quantity and quality of his cavalry. Perhaps more important, he remained tactically flexible. In Carthage, after resorting to guile to hold the enemy's emissaries, he chose a night attack to defeat the Carthaginians; at Zama he shifted the *maniples* one behind the other to allow a passage for the enemy's elephants, which subsequently were thrown into ineffectual confusion by the blast of Roman horns and trumpets.

**3. The Professional Army.**—Scipio ushered in a century of expansion that caused extensive changes in the Roman army and ultimately in tactics. New wealth made military service increasingly unattractive to the property-owning burgesses. To replace them the consul-general, Gaius Marius, in about 107 B.C., began accepting volunteers from outside the propertied classes. These new men, as well as foreign auxiliaries, depended almost entirely on the individual commander's whim as to length of service, pay, and other rewards; thus Marius almost gave the army to its general rather than to the state.

Marius eliminated the old legion organization of *hastati, principes,* and *triarii* for the cohort, a basic tactical unit of 600 soldiers. Of the legion's ten cohorts, four served in the first line, and three each in the next two lines. These were supported by Numidian and Gaulish cavalry units, by Cretan and Numidian archers, and by Balearic slingers with two slings for short and long range. The traditional training and discipline was intensified and eventually standardized. As described in Vegetius' *De re militari,* for example, it was common practice in summer to march 20 mi. in five hours. To ensure a vigorous charge, recruits practised running, acquiring a speed that enabled them to get to an advantageous position with haste and thus prevent the enemy's reaching it. March security was constantly stressed, camps being carefully constructed for defensive purposes. The commander was aided by engineers and artillerymen who operated the *ballista,* which hurled stones up to 130 lb. and which were mounted on carriages drawn by mules (these may be seen today on Trajan's Column in Rome). They also used the onager (literally the "wild ass"), which fired stones up to 160 lb. over 2,000 ft., and catapults, which hurled missiles including heavy arrows, darts, bolts, or javelins in almost flat trajectory. Caesar's legions were probably each equipped with 60 catapults and 10 *ballistae.* Engineers employed a wide variety of complicated machines for sieges and were particularly skilled at constructing their own fortifications. In one campaign during the conquest of Gaul, as the eminent historian James A. Froude wrote, "Caesar, after feeling his way with his cavalry, found a rounded ridge projecting like a promontory into the plain where the Belgian host was lying. On this he advanced his Legions, protecting his flanks with continuous trenches and earthworks, on which were placed heavy cross-bows. Between these lines, if he attacked the enemy and failed, he had a secure retreat." Later, when Caesar had surrounded a force of 80,000 Gauls led by a young rebel, Vercingetorix, he was forced to add an exterior line of circumvallation against the threat from other Gaulish tribes. In an effort that involved moving an estimated 2,000,000 cu.m. of earth, "the legions set about creating a series of redoubts and barriers which would enable them, if needed, to fight off a simultaneous attack on front and rear. Dry and wet ditches, fronted by extensive abatis, a generous sprinkling of *cervi* [pronged instruments like the branching horns of a stag], a liberal sowing of *stimuli* [barbed spikes concealed beneath branches or lurking at the bottom of camouflaged pits deep enough to engulf horse and rider]—every lethal contrivance that ingenuity could devise and unremitting toil carry into execution, was employed to strengthen the defense against the coming trial of strength." (From Reginald Hargreaves, *Beyond the Rubicon,* The New American Library, Inc., New York, 1966.) When the Romans beat off an external attack by 250,000 Gauls, Vercingetorix surrendered—one of the greatest victories in Caesar's campaigns in Gaul where in a few years, as Plutarch tells us, he "had taken by storm above eight hundred towns, subdued three hundred States, and of the three millions of men, who made up the gross sum of those with whom at several times he engaged, he had killed one million and captured a second."

**4. The Decline.**—In the consolidation that followed the rule of the dictators, Augustus established a purely professional army of 28 legions supplemented by foreign auxiliaries and by a praetorian, or personal, guard of perhaps 10,000 men—in all, some 400,000 troops who swore allegiance to Augustus rather than to the new republic. For the most part these troops were stationed along some 10,000 mi. of frontier in permanent garrisons called *castella,* which supported a string of frontier outposts. Although fighting was frequent, it nominally consisted of punitive expeditions against revolting tribes and, because of superior Roman strength and armament, called for no particular tactical brilliance. In time a "garrison mentality" began to assert itself; a spiritual and physical lethargy increasingly pervaded the army, sometimes leading to horrendous disaster such as that suffered by Varus who, although on the march, was so burdened with trains and so lacking in ability that Arminius and his German barbarians succeeded in trapping and destroying three entire legions, or some 20,000 soldiers, in the Battle of Teutoburger Wald (A.D. 9).

A final reorganization of the army occurred under the later reigns of Diocletian and Constantine, who greatly expanded its numbers in order to field a mobile reserve force of infantry-cavalry that could quickly march to reinforce a threatened border area. By then, however, the legion as Caesar and Augustus knew it was rapidly becoming extinct. Soldiers no longer wore helmets and armour; the javelin was gone, replaced by pikes to defend against enemy horsemen; emphasis was increasingly given to heavy cavalry with both horse and rider protected by armour; the elaborate foot drills and infantry tactics, seemingly beyond the comprehension of barbarian recruits, had largely vanished.

These disruptive centuries had taught the barbarians something of war, for many of the tribes had fought both against and for the Romans, as for example the Goths who were admitted into the empire in the 4th century A.D. The Goth army, seemingly influenced by the Huns, traveled in large wagon trains that could rapidly be turned into wagon-forts, or *laagers,* what they called a "wagon city." Relying primarily on heavy cavalry for shock power, this army also employed infantry armed with pikes and with the long and short sword as well as battle-axes which could penetrate Roman armour and split the shield either when thrown or wielded. The Goths' major weakness lay in a lack of siege trains (Hannibal's chief failing) and so in A.D. 378 they failed to take Adrianople. In early August the Goths, led by Fritigern, were encamped a few miles away when attacked by a large Roman force. Hastily summoning his cavalry from a raid, Fritigern cunningly gained time first by parley, and next by firing the fields, which further delayed and confused the slowly deploying Roman legions. Fritigern's cavalry returned, routed the Roman horse, and then fell on the flanks of the massed legions. Meanwhile, volleys of missiles fired from within the *laager* had decimated the Roman ranks. Then Fritigern loosed his infantry to deliver the coup de grace which claimed an estimated 40,000 Roman-allied lives—an enormous defeat which finally opened the empire to outside invaders. Tactically, in Fuller's words, it introduced a new cycle in the art of war.

> Hitherto infantry normally had been the decisive arm, and when they relied upon shock weapons, they had little to fear from cavalry as long as they maintained their order. But the increasing use of missiles carried with it an unavoidable loosening and disordering of the ranks. The old shield-wall began to be replaced by a firing-line, and because archers and slingers cannot easily combine shield with bow or sling, and as the range of these weapons is strictly limited, and, further still, because they are all but useless in wet weather, opportunity for the cavalry charge steadily increased. The problem was how to combine missile-power with security against cavalry, a problem which was only partially solved by the introduction of the socket-bayonet in the late seventeenth century, and not finally until the percussion cap was invented during the early nineteenth, for it permitted the musket to be fired irrespective of the weather. (Fuller, *op. cit.*)

**5. The Rise of Byzantium.**—While the Western Empire dissolved into a sea of invading Germanic tribes, the Eastern Empire managed to survive by a judicious blending of city fortifications, of native armies, of privately controlled mercenary cavalry hosts, and of outright bribes to deflect such potential predators as the Huns and Ostrogoths. By the time of Justinian's reign (527–565) the mainstay of the army was the horse-archer supported by light cavalry and heavy infantry. As described by a historian of the time, Procopius, the mounted bowmen went "into battle wearing [mail] corselets and fitted out with greaves which extend up to the knee. From the right side hang their arrows, from the other the sword. . . . They are expert horsemen, and are able without difficulty to direct their bows to either side while riding at full speed, and to shoot an opponent whether in pursuit or flight. They draw the bowstring along by the forehead about opposite the right ear, thereby charging an arrow with such impetus as to kill whoever stands in the way, shield and corselet alike having no power to check its force." Justinian's great cavalry general, the young Belisarius, "found that the chief difference between the Goths and us was that our own Roman horse and our Hunnish *foederati* [mercenaries] are all expert horse bowmen, while the enemy has scarcely any knowledge at all of archery. For the Gothic knights use sword and lance alone, while their bowmen on foot are always drawn up to the rear. So their horsemen are no good till the battle comes to close quarters, and can easily be shot down while standing in battle array before the moment of contact arrives."

Belisarius did remarkably well to wrest North Africa from the Vandals and Italy from the Goths and Franks. Realizing that he could not cope with the numerically superior Goths, he used walled cities both to increase his strength and to wear down his enemies' in conducting sieges. His tactics were not static; for he sallied and raided from the walled cities, using superior archery power. Belisarius' rival and successor in Italy, Narses, used this missile power uniquely at the Battle of Taginae in A.D. 552. To counter the Gothic cavalry charge, Narses deployed some 8,000 troops in a solid pike-fronted phalanx winged on each flank by foot-archers backed by cavalry, so that, in Oman's words, "an enemy advancing against the center would find himself in an empty space, half encircled by the bowmen and exposed to a rain of arrows from both sides." (Charles Oman, *A History of the Art of War in the Middle Ages,* Houghton Mifflin Co., Boston, 1923.) In the event, Totila's horse was torn to shreds with the following infantry enveloped and decimated by Narses' horse—a great victory resulting from the first experiment combining pike and bow. Narses repeated this tactical innovation with equal success against Frankish foot-soldiers at the Battle of Casilinum (Capua) in A.D. 554.

Maurice (582–602) and his successors differed radically from the Western tradition in their approach to war. Though Hellenistic in outlook in many respects, they seem to have reverted to the Oriental thought of Sun Tzu in the sense of favouring diplomacy and deception (including bribery) to war, which, mainly because of limited human resources, should be fought only as a last resort. Since the almost constant incursions of the Slavs, Avars, Bulgarians, Persians, Saracens, Franks, Russians, and Turks meant a good many last resorts, the Eastern Empire attached the greatest importance to its armed forces, many details of which have been preserved in two treatises, the *Strategicon* attributed to Maurice and Leo VI's *Tactica.*

Maurice began a drastic reorganization of the army under which the standing army was reduced in size and restored to the control of the central government. The frontiers were fortified in depth, as Caesar had done, and defended in part with local militia, a system that evolved into decentralized defense with the empire divided into military districts or *themes,* each with a permanent army corps plus local militia, commanded by a *strategos,* who also headed the civil government. Around the hub of the empire, Constantinople, was a 60-ft. moat, within which were three walls, each with frequent towers, the innermost wall being 30 ft. high—a formidable defense further strengthened by a powerful fleet and by the secret and devastating weapon of "Greek fire," which was poured on ships or on scaling parties. The relatively small professional army was well ahead of its time. Although continuing to rely primarily on the mounted bowmen, it also included infantry and artillery, all of which were supported by engineers and quartermasters and by probably the first organized medical corps in history. Other innovations included sectionalized boats that, transported by mules, could be put together for fording purposes, and a series of military textbooks to instruct officers on diverse strategies and tactics, depending on who the enemy was.

This flexibility of thought and practice undoubtedly saved the empire on numerous occasions. In the 8th century, for example, when the Saracens swept up from the south in hordes of lightly armoured cavalry, the Byzantines developed the *theme* system of zonal defense; when the Saracens began protecting horse and rider in deference to the weight advantage of the imperial cataphract, the Byzantines developed new cavalry tactics that were similar to the old foot maniple-legion of the early Romans and far superior to the single line tactics of the enemy.

Despite the excellence of this army and of an equally fine navy, internal decay slowly took its toll.

## III. THE FEUDAL WEST

**1. Charlemagne and the Holy Roman Empire.**—The most durable of the Germanic tribes which had engulfed the Western

Empire was the Franks, which settled in Gaul. A simple political-military entity, each band of Franks paid allegiance to a single chief, and the bravest warriors constituted the chief's bodyguard, the *comitatus*. Unlike the Eastern barbarians, the Franks arrived as an infantry host armed with javelins and swords and adept in the use of the heavy battle-axe (*francisca*), which they threw with considerable accuracy. Slow to adapt to cavalry warfare, the Franks remained at a considerable tactical disadvantage as was shown by their defeat at Casilinum in A.D. 554 by Narses' Byzantine army, and by the Battle of Tours in A.D. 732 when the Frankish infantry under Charles Martel (714–741) barely held against the mounted Saracens.

Charles Martel began the necessary conversion to a cavalry force by extending the incipient feudalism of the Franks into a system of generous land grants, thus enabling nobles to raise and maintain mounted units that the king could call up for a certain period, eventually 40 days, each year. His grandson, Charlemagne (768–814), continued to develop heavy cavalry units, but also emphasized the importance of well-armed infantry and of siege and supply trains. In conquering what would become the Holy Roman Empire, Charlemagne relied primarily on feudal levies controlled by individual nobles who sprinkled the empire with fortified *burgs* or strongpoints from which their forces could contest the incursions of the Saracens, Magyars, and, later, the Vikings. Despite Charlemagne's many reforms, the armies of his successors were not highly regarded in Byzantium. Around 900 Emperor Leo VI instructed his generals when fighting the Franks: "You should take advantage of their indiscipline and disorder; whether fighting on foot or on horseback, they charge in dense, unwieldy masses which cannot maneuver because they have neither organization nor drill. . . . Hence they fall readily into confusion if suddenly attacked in front and rear—a thing easy to accomplish, since they are utterly careless and neglect the use of pickets and vedettes." (Oman, *op. cit.*)

**2. The Viking Raids.**—The unwieldy formations of the Franks could not readily cope with the hit-and-run Viking raids prevalent in the 9th century. Wearing mail armour and helmets and carrying swords and heavy double-bladed battle-axes that they wielded with both hands, the Norsemen swept down on enemy coasts in graceful, shield-studded long boats, attacked coastal and river settlements, rounded up horses, raided far inland, and escaped with their plunder—usually before the local feudal lord could react. These incursions were halted in the 10th century only by bribing the intruders with the gift of the rich province that bears their name, Normandy.

The Vikings enjoyed even greater military success in England and Ireland, more than half of which they occupied during 850–860. The English army consisted originally of unarmoured and ill-trained infantry called up from the tribal *fyrd*. King Alfred made some improvement to counter the almost constant Norse raids by dividing the *fyrd* into two parts, one for a set period, usually 40 days, and the other for peaceful occupations. Alfred also established a navy as an outer protective ring, supplemented with a sprinkling of stockaded forts called *burhs* in the countryside. In the 11th century King Canute established the system of *housecarles,* professional military bodyguards for nobility similar to the Frankish *comitatus;* subsequently a military elite developed, a quasi-nobility of *thanes* answering to the king. Although mounted, the *housecarles* and *thanes* fought on foot; they were protected by helmets and chain mail, carried elongated shields, and were armed with swords, spears, and the heavy Danish battle-axe; the less-well-armed infantry levies of the *fyrd* usually carried spears, javelins, and swords.

**3. The Battle of Hastings.**—The Saxon king Harold commanded just such a mixed force at the Battle of Hastings in 1066. Its exact size is not known, but it was not his normal strength since he had just been fighting the Norwegians at Stamford Bridge in Yorkshire and had hastened south upon learning of the Norman landing. It probably consisted of about 4,000 men drawn up on Senlac Hill, *housecarles* in phalanx formation in the centre and forward, his *fyrd* levies on either wing resting on fairly steep, protective slopes.

William landed with an estimated 5,000 men, his army consisting of armoured cavalry—knights armed with lance, sword, and mace—and infantry and archers armed either with the short Norman bow or the more powerful but ponderous crossbow that delivered a relatively slow rate of fire due to the elaborate arming process. William attacked first: a line of crossbowmen followed by infantry that made a passage of lines after the first discharge of arrows. According to William of Poitiers, the Norman left was easily repulsed and was pursued by Harold's right wing, the *fyrd,* acting against orders, who were badly cut up by William's cavalry as a result. Harold then re-formed his lines, which throughout the day withstood the charges of the Norman horse until the battle began to appear a standoff. The experienced Norman commander, William, presumably with the earlier action in mind, now employed a *ruse de guerre* by ordering his knights to simulate a rout. As he supposed, the Saxon *fyrd* followed, only to be cut to ribbons—a successful plan which, somewhat incredibly, worked twice. Having substantially weakened the Saxon flanks, William ordered his crossbowmen to deliver massed high-trajectory fire to be followed by a final all-out cavalry assault. One of these arrows struck Harold in the eye, a disaster that swept through the Saxon ranks and helped decide the battle for the Norman cavalry, which, charging the weakened wings, penetrated the phalanx to kill Harold and his closest bodyguards.

**4. The Age of the Knight.**—Hailed as an undeniable victory of cavalry over infantry, the Battle of Hastings heralded nearly three centuries of feudal warfare in which the mounted knight reigned supreme. Tactically it was a futile age. Although improvements appeared in fortifications, armour, and siege weapons, both the feudal structure and the church militated against advances in the art of war. In its desire to limit war and thus maintain the status quo, the church went so far as to forbid knightly tourneys and to proscribe from the battlefield such unchivalric weapons as the crossbow, "a weapon fateful to God and unfit for Christians"—neither ban proving particularly successful.

At home the conditions of feudal service hindered either king or noble from undertaking long campaigns. Knights were generally bound to 40 days of military service per year, and more than one nobleman was forced to lift a siege of a neighbouring castle when his vassals deserted at the end of this period; later, as mercenaries slowly came into service, the length of a campaign was often dictated by the size of the ruler's purse. Warring kings rarely possessed clear strategies—venality and vindictiveness ruled the day just as confusion ruled the battlefield. Battles when actually fought were short melees with the knights intent on unseating and capturing each other for ransom, while the accompanying ill-armed serfs or foot soldiers looted the battlefield. Armies lacked supply trains so that an army had to live off the land and could campaign only in fair weather months. The nobleman and his knights ruled the realm from castles that grew ever more elaborately fortified as returning veterans from the Crusades reported the defensive wonders of the castles in the Holy Land. (*See* CRUSADES.) The essentially defensive outlook was also expressed in armour which, with the change from mail to plate, became increasingly heavier and complicated until in the 13th century a dismounted knight, literally unable to raise himself, often fell easy victim to a serf-wielded club.

Although the polyglot forces comprising the First Crusade (1095–99) were voluntary and thus immune from the curse of limited service, they suffered greatly from a lack of cohesive command and organization. The Muslim armies at first proved no match for the heavy cavalry, but it did not take long for them to adapt by avoiding set battles in favour of harassment from foot bowmen whose fire outdistanced mounted bowmen. To compensate, the crusaders were forced to balance their armies with the addition of heavy infantry, a lesson that did not filter back to the continent and had to be relearned, often at great expense, in successive crusades. "Their tactical failing was that they did not appreciate the need for cooperation between infantry and cavalry. When they did, success was generally theirs; when not, frequently, unless the first charge succeeded, they were beaten." (Fuller, *op. cit.*)

**5. The Mongols.**—Toward the end of the 12th century, Genghis Khan (*q.v.;* 1167–1227) formed and trained an army that in 1215 captured Peking, capital of the Chin dynasty, and a few years later conquered the Kharismian empire (northern India-Turkistan-Persia), then marched north to defeat a Russian army on the Dnieper. His son, Ogadai, defeated the Chin Chinese to win northern China, invaded the lands of the Sung dynasty to the south, then led his army across Asia to invade Russia, sack Kiev, conquer most of Poland, and early in 1241 occupy Hungary.

The Mongol conquests represent a tremendous military achievement. Remarking on Subutai's campaigns in Poland and Hungary, J. B. Bury noted that these "were won by consummate strategy and were not due to a mere overwhelming superiority of numbers. . . . It was wonderful how punctually and effectually the arrangements of the commander were carried out. . . . Such a campaign was quite beyond the power of any European army of the time, and it was beyond the vision of any European commander."

The Mongol armies consisted primarily of horse-archers who, in the Eastern tradition, literally lived on horseback. Armed with bow, lance, and scimitar, the hardy, well-trained warriors used two varieties of bows and three "calibres" of arrows for various tactical situations. Some authorities believe that as early as 1218 Genghis Khan used guns and gunpowder for siege work in the conquest of Turkistan. According to Marco Polo, who visited Kublai Khan's empire, each warrior marched with 18 horses and mares in order to supply milk, blood, meat, and remounts. Subutai's armies marched in widely separated columns, the flanks ahead of the centre, with such mobility of the cavalry that the columns could converge upon plan after which they were tactically controlled in the Chinese fashion by a variety of signals. Tactically, Subutai's armies were not suitable for fighting in hilly wooded country, probably the reason he left Poland for the Hungarian plains. Later armies, particularly those of the Great Khan, grew increasingly sophisticated and included infantry and war elephants.

**6. Crécy, Poitiers, and Agincourt: The Decline of Feudal Warfare.**—Despite the monopoly of arms exercised by the mounted knight and the men-at-arms, the use of infantry never quite died out. On the continent serfs generally accompanied their noble masters into battle, and on occasion the knights themselves were forced to dismount and fight as infantry. As towns increased in size, they began to raise citizen armies that, because of lack of funds, remained primarily infantry levies. At Bouvines the infantry of Boulogne in 1214 showed great discipline and doggedness before they fell under repeated French cavalry attacks. In 1302 an army of knights under Robert of Artois suffered a serious defeat at Courtrai when, disdaining either reconnaissance or preparatory fire by Genoese bowmen, they attacked an infantry force of Flemish workers armed with pikes positioned on the far side of a marsh; with the horses quickly bogged down the knights were helpless and were slaughtered in wholesale numbers. The French nobility apparently ignored these indications of tactical vulnerability, a terrible mistake that was to cost them dearly in the so-called Hundred Years' War (*q.v.;* 1337–1453).

In England, William the Conqueror had carefully retained the infantry *fyrd* "partly as a defense against his own barons: a national levy of English infantrymen was employed to quell the baronial uprising in 1075." (Preston, *op. cit.*) Subsequent monarchs, finding the baronial control of feudal levies much too restrictive, began the involved practice of scutage, which enabled vassals to buy themselves out of their military obligations, the money being used to hire mercenary knights. This practice slowly evolved into the use of indentured companies of professional soldiers commanded by a nobleman who had contracted with the crown. Unlike their French counterparts, the English, particularly the mercenaries, were not above learning from the enemy, and as a result of their wars in South Wales they adopted the longbow, a six-foot vertical bow that effectively fired a three-foot arrow 250 yd. So superior was the longbow—a trained archer could fire six aimed shots a minute—that it became the national weapon of England, with villages required to hold weekly target practice. All men from 16 to 60 had by law to own and practise with the longbow; and were in danger of imprisonment if they skipped practice for such sports as handball, football, hockey, coursing, and cockfighting, or other such games.

The longbow was largely responsible for the victory of Edward I over the Scots at Falkirk in 1298; Edward II was defeated at Bannockburn in 1314 only because of his ill-advised cavalry charge that left his archers with no suitable targets and with no protection from the Scot cavalry. This and later battles in the north brought about a balance of forces between cavalry, dismounted men-at-arms, and archers, the last protected from cavalry charges by ditches and stakes driven into the ground as well as by the dismounted men-at-arms using spears and bills, the latter being a cutting and thrusting weapon with a hook-shaped blade on a six-foot shaft designed to unseat horsemen. This formation evolved into the one Edward III employed at the Battle of Crécy in 1346. Edward's numerically inferior army, perhaps 8,500 men, was drawn up in a defensive formation with two battles, or phalanxes, of dismounted men-at-arms forward, their inner and outer flanks continued by oblique lines of archers whose outer flanks rested on natural defenses and whose fronts were protected by ditches and stakes. Philip VI of France started the battle with an attack by Genoese crossbowmen, who were soon dispersed by the English longbowmen. Philip then ordered a series of cavalry attacks—15 in all—which were repulsed throughout the day to result in an English victory brought about by the coordination of the archers, the centre battles or phalanxes of dismounted men-at-arms, and the cavalry reserve which at a crucial point fell on the French flank.

The prince of Wales, known as the "Black Prince," who had fought at Crécy as a 16-year-old, employed a similar formation in 1356 at Poitiers where the French cavalry, then under John II of France, dismounted to attack and were again torn to shreds by the English.

These tactical victories held but slight strategic significance. Although the capture of King John at Poitiers threw France into a state of virtual anarchy, the English proved unable to meet the logistics problem—the supply of their forces for a period long enough to besiege successfully the numerous castles or strongpoints of the enemy. The stalemate allowed France to make a partial recovery under Charles V who chose the successful strategy of guerrilla warfare against the English forces. Using irregular bands called *routiers*, Bertrand du Guesclin eliminated most of the English holdings in France by harassment, surprises, ambushes, sudden assaults, and slow sieges. Unhappily for France this advantage was forfeited by the Armagnacs at the Battle of Agincourt in 1415, where once again the English yeomanry-soldiers decimated the attacking dismounted knights of Charles VI.

In Switzerland, meanwhile, warfare had undergone another radical change, also in favour of the infantry. Commencing in 1291 when the forest cantons formed the Swiss Confederation, the peasants and later the burghers rose against the feudal domination of Austria. Highly trained and motivated, the Swiss ground soldier became adept in the use of the halberd, a three-way weapon consisting of an eight-foot shaft holding a spear point, an axe blade, and a hook for pulling a rider from his mount. The rugged country favoured infantry tactics and an early major victory, the Battle of Morgarten in 1315, resulted from trapping an Austrian cavalry force in a mountain pass where the horses were unable to maneuver. When fighting cavalry in open terrain, the Swiss chose the old phalanx formation, in this case consisting of three-fifths halberds, one-fifth pikes, and one-fifth archers. In defensive warfare they turned the phalanx into a hedgehog bristling with the murderous 18-ft. pikes that were tipped with a 3-ft.-iron sleeve to prevent cutting by enemy swords. The Swiss preferred offensive warfare, and to gain the essential mobility the troops were protected only by helmet and cuirass; to retain combat readiness they "marched in battle-order of three columns in echelon" (Preston, *op. cit.*), attacking with a celerity and discipline that made them the scourge of the feudal battlefield. As was the case with the English, they continued to dominate the battlefield until the advent of field artillery.

## IV. THE INTRODUCTION OF GUNPOWDER

Whether the Arabs brought gunpowder from China to Europe or whether the Europeans invented it is still a hotly contested question among scholars. Certainly Europeans of the 13th century knew about gunpowder and by 1326 began manufacturing firearms. For an account of such primitive weapons as culverins and bombards, *see* ARTILLERY: *Origin and Early History*.

These early weapons were far from ideal. Casting deficiencies made cannon incredibly dangerous to fire; they were inaccurate at all but very close range and their bulk and weight made them difficult to deploy sufficiently close to a wall or tower. Early handguns could not even be aimed properly (*see* SMALL ARMS, MILITARY: *Historical Development to 1900: Early History*).

The more progressive armies nonetheless attempted to harness the potential of these new weapons. In fighting the Hussite Wars (1419–34; *see* HUSSITES) Jan Žižka of Bohemia first fully used artillery in Europe. In defending against cavalry charges, Žižka deployed armoured wagons, each sheltering infantry armed with handguns and crossbows, in a line called a *Wagenburg* or wagon fortress. Between the vehicles, he deployed four-wheeled carts holding cannon and protected by infantry armed with pikes. Behind each wing the cavalry waited in readiness to deliver a counterstroke or lead a pursuit. This formation thoroughly baffled the invading knights who unsuccessfully challenged it in more than 50 battles.

Cannon at first were used mainly for defensive purposes. In 1429 the defenses of Orléans, for example, included 71 large cannon and some smaller culverins while the besieging British employed cannon and mortars, though with little effect. Still, armies continued to cope with the problem of using artillery in the field. The French army, which in 1445 Charles VII had reorganized into a permanent professional force, used artillery trains developed by the Bureau brothers to force the British from their castles in Normandy and Guienne; in 1450 the French brought up two culverins at Formigny, where the British, deployed in the favoured *en herse* (harrow-like) infantry-archer formation, were blasted into defeat. The French repeated this success at Castillon in 1453, the year in which the Turks used immense cast-bronze bombards to batter down the walls of Constantinople. One of the bombards was 19 tons and fired a 600-lb. stone seven times daily. Some 60 oxen and 200 men were needed to move it.

Although the handgun and the cannon would continue to undergo enormous modifications into the second half of the 20th century, it was apparent to all of Europe that by the end of the 15th century explosive weapons were causing a revolution on the battlefield.

## V. THE AGE OF TRANSITION

**1. Changing Tactical Values.**—The introduction and successful application of gunpowder to warfare set off a technological-tactical competition between emergent nation-states sufficiently wealthy to wage almost incessant war in bids for dynastic supremacy at home and imperial supremacy abroad. By the end of the 15th century, war was becoming a serious if bloody profession. One of the first persons to respect the change was Machiavelli (1469–1527), who, in 1494, witnessed the French invasion of the Italian city-states. In his subsequent and often profound works he advised that "the foundation of states is a good military organization"—accordingly, "a Prince should therefore have no other aim or thought, nor take up any other thing for study, but war and its organization and discipline." Machiavelli, who was tactically a disciple of the Roman Vegetius, also offered considerable advice on tactics, most of it erroneous; but there is no doubt that he prompted a reappraisal of past strategic and tactical values.

Machiavelli's words were reinforced by almost constant weapon development. The arquebus with its primitive and unreliable matchlock ignition was eventually replaced by the wheel lock and then by the flintlock systems, though some commanders were reluctant to employ it without diluting the ranks of pikemen. Better casting methods were discovered for artillery and it was made more mobile and accurate by the development of the limber and trunnion. The wheel lock pistol was invented. Castles evolved into fortifications capable of withstanding prolonged artillery sieges. Each development changed tactical values from one decade to the next.

At Cerignola in 1503, when some 8,000 French soldiers and Swiss mercenaries met some 8,000 Spanish soldiers and German mercenaries, the disciplined fire of the Spanish arquebusiers won an immense victory over the French who suffered perhaps 4,000 killed in but one hour's fighting. In 1512 a Spanish army was decimated at Ravenna when the French surprised it with enfilade fire from 24 massed cannon. In 1515 a Spanish contingent of Swiss, whose phalanx formation still depended more on the "push of pike" than on firearms, was torn to shreds by French cannon combined with cavalry charges at Marignano. At Pavia in 1525 appeared the first skirmishers, 1,500 Spanish arquebusiers, who, as the contemporary Seigneur de Brantôme put it, "scattered by squads over the battlefield, turning, leaping from one place to another with great speed, and thus escaped the cavalry charge. By this new method of fighting, unusual, astonishing, cruel and unworthy, these arquebusiers greatly hampered the operations of the French cavalry, who were completely lost. For they, joined together and in mass, were brought to earth by these few brave and able arquebusiers."

This was an era of innovation, a time of trial and error, with each battle posing tactical challenges to commanders as diverse in ability as they were versatile in talent. By meeting and in some cases satisfying the new demands of the battlefield, these captains developed tactical systems that supplied the foundation for modern warfare.

**2. The Spanish Contribution: The Great Captain.**—To conquer the Moorish castle-strongholds in the Moorish Wars (1485–93), the Spanish rulers relied primarily on an army of infantry and artillery supported by engineers and a vast supply organization which allegedly included a train of 80,000 pack mules. Isabella's army also used a formation of field messengers as well as introducing what probably was the first field hospital in history.

The heretofore rudimentary Spanish tactics were greatly improved by continental volunteers and by Swiss mercenaries particularly adept in the use of the pike to thwart enemy cavalry, but it was a Spaniard, Gonzalo de Córdoba (1453–1515)—his troops called him el Gran Capitán—who tackled the essential tactical problem of melding the pike with the arquebus to form a phalanx balanced with heavy cavalry and artillery, the whole a well-trained, disciplined and mobile force which won a series of noteworthy victories against the French, Turks, and Arabs. In so doing, Gonzalo laid the foundations for an army which would claim tactical supremacy in Europe until its fall to the duc d'Enghien (later known as the Great Condé) at Rocroi in 1643.

To facilitate administration and march discipline, Gonzalo grouped his forces into companies varying from 100 to 250 men, with three companies forming an *escuadrone* commanded by a colonel. His successors expanded this organization into a basic tactical unit, the *tercio,* which consisted of about 3,000 troops broken into 12 companies of 250 men each and commanded by a colonel. By 1534 the fighting strength of the Spanish *tercio* was divided equally between pikemen and arquebusiers. Cavalry was one-twelfth of infantry strength, and there was one cannon to each 1,000 infantry. In battle the pikemen formed an oblong of some 25–30 ranks with the arquebusiers drawn up on the corners. As each rank fired, it retired to the rear where it was protected by the pike-phalanx while reloading. Once the firearms had done their work, the pikemen charged the battlefield, an effort often aided by a simultaneous cavalry attack on the flanks.

This rather cumbrous tactical formation, reflected in the French "regiment" created by Francis I, dominated the 16th-century battlefield while commanders continued to try various combinations of pike and arquebus. Effectiveness was heightened by the development of the musket, which appeared during the last half of the century, a more powerful and accurate weapon than the arquebus, but heavy and awkward, requiring 56 drill movements to reload. Accordingly, the phalanx remained ponderous and the problem of a satisfactory amalgamation of musketeers with pikemen was resolved only by the ultimate disappearance of the pike.

The commander faced other problems as the century wore on. The development of artillery had rendered the once formidable walls of the town and castle increasingly impractical. But now "low walls, shielded by a ditch and a glacis and backed by earth, became the rule. Italian mathematicians gave the lead in working out angles of fire; heavily gunned bastions gave a maximum cross fire. . . . The castle gave way to the fort." (Preston, *op. cit.*) No longer was field artillery able to blast into these bastions. Sieges grew more and more complicated, involving both engineering skill and considerable patience and sacrifice.

As the arquebus and musket became more effective, the role of cavalry had to be reexamined since the traditional charge *en haye* (full speed) was becoming much too costly. With the development of the wheel lock pistol, which could be fired from the saddle, the line charge was abandoned in favour of the elaborate *caracole*—an advance in columns with the lead troopers firing, then wheeling to the rear to reload.

The Spanish used these formations and tactics with considerable success in their early battles against the Dutch. To counter them, Maurice of Nassau turned to the Romans who centuries earlier had developed the more mobile maniple and cohort to defeat the Greek phalanx. This able commander formed infantry regiments consisting of ten companies of musketeers and pikemen in equal numbers—a total of 800 to 1,000 men. Supporting them with artillery and small but excellent bodies of cavalry, Maurice fought the Spaniards to a standstill in four campaigns. At the Battle of Nieuwpoort in 1600 he deployed his cohorts in chessboard fashion among the sand dunes; supported by light artillery, their fire broke the heavier Spanish formations, which were then attacked with cavalry.

**3. The Reforms of Gustavus Adolphus.**—This remarkable soldier-king, who ruled Sweden from 1611 to 1632, has been called the "father of modern tactics." Often compared to Philip of Macedon and to Alexander the Great, he undoubtedly would have proved the outstanding military genius of the century but for his premature death on the battlefield of Lützen during the Thirty Years' War (1618–48).

When Gustavus first campaigned at the age of 17, the armies of Europe were slavish imitations of the Spanish *tercios*. Seeing that they had grown helplessly cumbrous, the young king, as Maurice of Nassau had before him, set about to regain tactical mobility. He reorganized his infantry into brigades, each consisting of from two to four regiments. A regiment held two battalions, each of four companies. Gustavus increased the number of musketeers in each company to 75 and reduced the pikemen to 60 as well as shortening their pikes from 16 to 11 ft. and lightening their armour. The traditional deep formation was changed to one of six ranks that advanced in open order to close up to three ranks on the firing line, the first kneeling and the other two standing while firing a volley. The old musket was replaced with a lighter weapon that eliminated the awkward supporting yoke; eventually the wheel lock ignition was introduced as well as paper cartridges carried in bandoliers, innovations resulting in a more rapid rate of fire.

Gustavus also abandoned the Spanish *caracole* maneuver for heavy cavalry in favour of a return to shock tactics: the charge at full gallop with sword, the pistol for use in the following melee. He supplemented his cuirassiers with the first dragoons, or mounted infantry, which, armed with sabre and carbine, were deployed as cavalry in the attack and as infantry in the defense. In battle formation he placed his horse not only on the wings of the infantry, where they were protected by special companies of "commanded musketeers," but also behind infantry lines whence they could attack directly as ordered.

His improvements in artillery tactics were revolutionary. In addition to standardizing siege and field guns, his artillery commander, Lennart Torstensson, developed a cast-iron cannon, the famous "regimental" four-pounder weighing about 400 lb. (as compared to the usual half-ton or more); these were mounted on carriages manageable by either four men or two horses. This cannon, two to each regiment, fired ammunition carried in a thin wooden case holding a prepared powder charge wired to either the ball or to a "canister"—a metal can filled with scrap metal—an innovation enabling a good crew to fire eight rounds to every six shots fired by a musketeer. Backing the four-pounder was a nine-pounder, of which six guns were allocated per thousand troops.

Gustavus streamlined his army in other important respects. He established a special commissariat to deal with supply, which enabled him to reduce the number of baggage wagons per company. He stripped the infantry of most of its armour; he himself wore only a leather buff coat in battle. He virtually eliminated the traditional swarm of camp followers. He favoured younger commanders—in 1630 his general of artillery was 27 years old—and he promoted on seniority; he abolished flogging and paid considerable attention to the welfare needs of the troops. His magnetism on and off the battlefield instilled in both Swedes and foreign mercenaries the vital element of spirit that sometimes wins battles when all else fails.

The true test of the Gustavian reorganization and reforms came at Breitenfeld in 1631. There the great Austrian general Tilly opposed him with an army of perhaps 40,000 troops deployed in the standard Spanish fashion: "one or possibly two lines of *tercios;* 17 great squares of foot of 1,500 to 2,000 men each with heavy columns of cavalry on their right and left." (Fuller, *op. cit.*) Gustavus, commanding an army of perhaps 47,000, but including a large contingent of unreliable Saxons, deployed in checkerboard fashion with pikemen covering musketeers who filed between their ranks, fired in volley, and withdrew. Gustavus opened the battle with artillery fire from 100 cannon, which caused the Austrians to make a precipitate and unsuccessful series of cavalry charges. When later his left wing of Saxons gave way, Gustavus met the threat by a quick change of cavalry front backed with two infantry brigades. Not content with holding the Austrians, the infantry, supported by regimental cannon that answered the enemy as Gustavus later wrote, "with three shots for one," attacked; and while Tilly's right was thus engaged, Gustavus ordered a combined cavalry-infantry charge that drove in the Austrian left and ultimately won the field. The victory cost Gustavus about 3,000 killed, mostly from enemy cannon fire; the Austrians lost 7,000 killed, 6,000 wounded or captured, and all artillery and baggage trains.

This victory, in which mobility and firepower overcame numbers and pike, was repeated in 1632 at Lützen, where Gustavus faced the Austrians, under the veteran commander Wallenstein. At the height of this action, Gustavus, lost in the heavy mist, stumbled into a host of Austrian cavalry and was shot to death.

Although the map of Europe undoubtedly would have changed had Gustavus lived, his army nonetheless survived the next 15 years of incredibly brutal warfare which, finally ended by the Peace of Westphalia, raised Sweden to be the ranking Baltic power for nearly a century. Nor were his tactical lessons wasted. At the Battle of Rocroi, the Great Condé used them, along with battlefield boldness, to end the legend of the Spanish *tercio;* in England's Civil Wars Cromwell's New Model army relied on discipline, morale, and organization to defeat the dash of the Cavaliers, and later the tenacity of the Scots.

## VI. THE AGE OF LINEAR TACTICS

**1. The Reforms of Louis XIV.**—The French general Vicomte de Turenne (1611–75), who along with Condé bridged the interim years between the end of the Thirty Years' War and the reign of Louis XIV (1643–1715), "regarded battle as a last resort, to be accepted with caution and then only when conditions seemed favourable." (Preston, *op. cit.*) Instead of bloody confrontations he preferred to use maneuver and by surprise and deception force his enemy into a hopeless tactical situation while simultaneously protecting his own lines of communication.

Turenne's conservatism was compatible to the scientific spirit of the age which was soon to show in the administrative and tactical reforms made in the French military machine. Begun by Richelieu and his minister of war, Le Tellier, these were continued by Le Tellier's son, Louvois, who became minister of war to Louis XIV, and by Colbert and Vauban.

Largely responsible for centralizing army administration, Louvois, before he was finished, had put the French army into uniform, awarded medals for valour, provided for disabled soldiers, equipped the infantry with the socket bayonet (which Vauban had invented) and the flintlock musket (the *fusil*—thus the fusilier), established a quartermaster general's department that dotted the countryside with strategically located and defended magazines of food, forage, ammunition, and equipment, and introduced annual war games where new tactics could be tested.

A new tactical formation had been introduced with the help of Gen. Jean Martinet, the royal inspector of the army, whose precision drill was emulated throughout Europe to the extent that his name came to mean one who practises a rigorous, petty discipline. The replacement of the pike by the bayonet enabled Martinet to train his troops to deploy from column into line and advance in three ranks, pausing to fire platoon volleys on command, and finally to attack with the bayonet. The "line" was a geometrical formation—it was a prelude to the famed "square" of lines that provided ideal defense against cavalry charges—and the troops were trained to advance in unison, keeping step at a stately cadence of 80 paces per minute. Naturally, the enemy's artillery fire exacted a tremendous toll in these shoulder-to-shoulder ranks as did volleys of musket fire delivered at no more than 50 paces. Considering the overall shortage of recruits and the length of time required to train them in linear tactics, such slaughter was anathema, and prudent commanders increasingly grew leery of pitched battles. They were not difficult to avoid. Since the new tactical formation required open, level terrain, a commander not wishing to fight could retire to hilly, wooded country or to a defended strongpoint or city in order to spend the winter rebuilding his forces for a fresh campaign.

A natural result of this tactical prudence was the growth of siegecraft and fortification, a form of warfare in which the engineer Vauban excelled. Under Louis XIV's careful direction, Vauban modernized and strengthened forts throughout France, and as a result of Louis' various wars, Flanders and the approaches to the Low Countries. Vauban's basic design, his famous "first system," was traditional Italian as modified by the engineer De Pagan: "a polygon, usually regular, with bastions projecting from each angle, in such a manner as to subject the attacker to an effective crossfire. As it was perfected by the later Italian engineers this enceinte consisted of three main divisions: a thick low rampart, with parapet; a broad ditch; and an outer rampart, the glacis, which sloped gently down to the level of the surrounding countryside." (H. Guerlac, "Vauban," ch. 2 in *Makers of Modern Strategy,* ed. by E. M. Earle.) Later "systems" improved on this design by a number of technical refinements, including detaching the bastions to gain a defense in depth.

Vauban applied similar precision to siegecraft. As opposed to the costly assaults of the past, he worked out a methodical approach involving the leisurely construction of protected parallel and zigzag trenches by means of which cannon and trench mortars (the latter invented in 1673) could be brought to fire on the inner walls and bastions. As part of the final advance up the glacis, when troops were fired on by covered walks, Vauban employed soldiers armed with grenades. Because these troops were the tallest men in the army and because of the danger involved, they quickly became an elite arm known as the grenadiers. Vauban conducted nearly 50 of these sieges besides drawing plans for over 100 fortresses and harbour installations, some remains of which may still be seen today.

**2. Marlborough and the War of the Spanish Succession (1702–13).**—This decade of war which pitted the Grand Alliance—England, Holland, Austria, and parts of Germany—against France, Spain, and Bavaria, brought a decisive change in infantry tactics. When John Churchill, the earl of Marlborough, arrived in the Low Countries, he found a defensive mentality with generals, both allied and enemy, expecting "to dance the usual military minuet of limited maneuver, siege work, moderate objective, and few conflicts" (Paul Kendall, *The Story of Land Warfare,* Hamish Hamilton, London, 1957), a viewpoint compatible to the highly fortified nature of the terrain. Marlborough was an experienced general who as a young officer had fought under Turenne; he was also an accomplished diplomat and strategist who integrated sea power into his campaigns, and a supreme tactician who recognized that technological improvements, particularly the flintlock rifle and bayonet, favoured offensive warfare (a conclusion also reached by Charles XII, the young king of Sweden whose rapierlike tactics, combined with a reckless personality, defeated the Russians, Danes, Saxons, and Poles in the Great Northern War [1700–21]).

As the captain general of the coalition armies, Marlborough had no wish to be tied down in the fortified labyrinth of the Netherlands, particularly when strong French and Bavarian forces were poised on the upper Danube to strike at Vienna, largely undefended because of a revolt in Hungary. Overriding protests of Dutch-English politicians, Marlborough left an army of 70,000 to protect Holland in May 1704, boldly marched the rest of his forces to the Rhine and on to the Danube, some 250 mi., much of it across the face of a startled enemy, to join with the forces of Prince Eugene of Savoy and the margrave of Baden. Marlborough then pushed down the Danube, bypassed Marshal Marsin's position at Dillingen, but then came up against Donauwörth, hastily defended by Marsin with 14,000 troops who were busy fortifying the main terrain feature, a hill called the Schellenberg. Marlborough instantly attacked, a successful but brutal assault that cost him some 5,000 casualties, a contravention of conservatism that again startled the enemy. Marlborough next defied normal practices by ravaging Bavaria, a psychological move that he hoped would cause the elector to desert his French alliance, and a practical move in that he denied its resources to the enemy.

The French reacted by bringing three armies of some 60,000 troops together in the area of Blenheim, a village on the Danube. This maneuver, by threatening Marlborough's lines of communication to Germany, was intended to force him to retire. Instead, he joined with Prince Eugene's army and on Aug. 13 attacked—a complete strategic and tactical surprise from which the French, though fighting well, never recovered. To win the decisive Battle of Blenheim, Marlborough tied down the French left with Eugene's troops, which attacked early in the morning, then struck the flanks of Marshal Tallard's main defense, a move which caused the French commander to weaken his centre. In late afternoon Marlborough, who had exposed himself throughout the battle, ordered his carefully hoarded cavalry to advance against Tallard's centre; and two long lines trotted faster and faster until they met the French. The result was a rout with Tallard captured and thousands of French horse drowned in the Danube. Blenheim cost Marlborough some 5,000 killed and 7,000 wounded; the French lost more than 35,000 in a defeat that ended the Sun King's dreams of dominating Europe.

Blenheim established England as a major power and Marlborough as a supreme tactician, a reputation enhanced two years later by his victory over Marshal Villeroi's army at Ramillies. There, by a cunning feint, he caused Villeroi to weaken his right wing, which he attacked with infantry followed by cavalry brought behind the lines from his own right. At one point in the ensuing melee of 25,000 horses intermingled with thousands of infantry, Marlborough rushed to a crucial action only to be thrown from his horse and very nearly killed. He was rescued, however, and went on to claim a sweeping victory which he exploited throughout the summer by capturing fortress after fortress—in all, a brilliant campaign that pushed the French from the Spanish Netherlands. He pulled another tactical surprise at Oudenarde in 1708 where he pushed his advance guard into battle against Marshal Vendôme's army, then fed in units as they arrived on the battlefield—an "encounter" action defying traditional practice, which he exploited into victory by a final flanking cavalry attack. He followed this battle in 1709 with the expensive victory of Malplaquet and with two more seasons of successful campaigns in northern France, which forced the French to sign the Treaty of Utrecht early in 1713.

**3. Frederick the Great and Limited Warfare.**—The limited warfare of the latter half of the 18th century was characterized both by the conservatism of Turenne and Vauban and by the mobile-shock tactics of Marlborough and Charles XII. In quantity and ferocity there was nothing limited about the warfare of this period. What was limited was the objective: one gained a military decision in order to bargain diplomatically at an advantage. Warfare was confined to standing armies which included numerous mercenaries; campaigns did not generally affect the population as a whole. At the very least the people were spared the widespread devastation familiar either to the Thirty Years' War or to the modern wars of Napoleonic origin.

Maneuver was very popular, the usual goal being to cut the enemy's communications and force him to retire. The French officer Marshal de Saxe gave his opinion in his principal work, *Mes Rêveries* (1756–57): "I am not in favour of giving battle. . . . I am even convinced that a general can wage war all his life without being compelled to do so." This oft-quoted passage ignores the 1745 Battle of Fontenoy which De Saxe won by preparing redoubts from which his infantry took the English and Dutch under murderous enfilade fire. He was also greatly interested in firepower as is witnessed by his experiments with a unit that became the tactical ancestor of the division: he combined two brigades of infantry and one of cavalry with artillery to make a tactically self-sufficient force, yet one capable of concentrating with like units for battle.

This tactical dualism is also seen in the military career of the soldier-king Frederick the Great, who frequently relied on maneuver and evasion in his wars against the crowned heads of Europe, but who did not hesitate to fight numerous and costly battles that he felt necessary to sustain Prussia as a major European power. In *The Instructions of Frederick the Great for His Generals* (1747) he wrote: "In war the skin of a fox is at times as necessary as that of a lion, for cunning may succeed when force fails." But he also advised: "War is decided only by battles and it is not decided except by them." (Trans. by T. R. Phillips, The Stackpole Co., Harrisburg, Pa., 1944.) In a later judgment, Napoleon wrote: "What distinguishes Frederick the most is not his skill in maneuvering, but his audacity. He carried out things I never dared to do. He abandoned his line of operations, and often acted as if he had no knowledge whatever of the art of war."

Frederick held a very real knowledge of the art of war. He had been tutored extensively in military history and was raised in a military environment, including a brief campaign under the tutelage of Prince Eugene of Savoy. Assuming the throne in 1740, he took command of a splendid army which he enlarged to fight the First Silesian War against Austria. After a temporary setback by Austrian cavalry at Möllwitz in 1741, the young king made his heavy cavalry the finest in Europe. He continued to drill his army into magnificence: his infantry deployed with machinelike precision from column into line; its rate of musket fire was three times that of the opponent. He introduced horse-drawn artillery, not alone to bring the guns to the battlefield but to shift them during battle; he also relied on howitzers, heretofore used mainly for siegework, which eventually constituted one-third of his artillery strength. Stealing a page from the Greek general Epaminondas, he developed his famed oblique order of attack—in his words: "You refuse one wing to the enemy and strengthen the one which is to attack. With the latter you do your utmost against one wing of the enemy which you take in flank. An army of 100,000 men taken in flank may be beaten by 30,000 in a very short time. . . ." (R. R. Palmer, "Frederick the Great, Guibert, Bülow," ch. 3 in *Makers of Modern Strategy,* ed. by E. M. Earle.)

Rising above his tactics and various innovations was his own leadership, for he exercised a battlefield character in the tradition of Turenne and Marlborough. His discipline was indescribably harsh, and he was under no illusions concerning the loyalty of his soldiers—his commanders were not allowed to march at night or to camp near woods for fear of desertions. And yet these troops in campaign after campaign, where defeat often succeeded victory, followed him under the direst physical conditions and fought with frantic fury when Old Fritz, as they called him, was there to lead.

In Frederick's diverse battles he almost always was numerically inferior. To counter the larger but bulkier armies of his numerous enemies, he relied on mobility and firepower, which he often exploited both by strategic and tactical surprise, a combination devastatingly employed early in the Seven Years' War (1756–63) in which he faced the combined (but uncoordinated) might of France, Austria, Russia, Saxony, and Sweden.

In early November 1757, Frederick found himself in Saxony with a force of about 22,000 facing an enormous army of 60,000 to 80,000. The French general Soubise decided to cut Prussian communications by attacking in the manner of Frederick himself, that is, by ordering his columns to march around and strike the Prussian left and rear. Watching from the top of an inn in Rossbach, Frederick divined the plan in mid-afternoon and ordered his army to strike camp and deploy in a flanking position behind a screen of low hills. The French, marching without scouts, thought the Prussians were retreating. Suddenly the heavy Prussian cavalry smashed headlong into the van of enemy cavalry while Frederick's heavy cannon opened fire on the leading infantry columns. Finally, seven battalions of infantry poured from the hills to complete the carnage while his cavalry circled to strike the rear. Lasting scarcely an hour, this battle ended in a brilliant Prussian victory. At a cost of just over 500 casualties, Frederick claimed 3,000 enemy casualties, 5,000 prisoners including 8 generals and 300 officers, and 67 cannon.

Free to deal with the Austrian threat in Silesia, Frederick spent a week re-forming his army, then marched 170 mi. to Parchwitz. In early December he met Daun's Austrian army, an estimated 65,000 with 210 guns, sprawled in two lines five and a half miles on either side of Leuthen. Although Frederick's command numbered only 36,000 with 167 guns, he decided to attack. At the head of his own advance guard of 10 battalions and 60 squadrons, he pushed up the Breslau road at dawn, brushed aside an Austrian cavalry guard, and occupied the village of Borne, a height from which he could see the Austrian lines and which hid his approaching force. He then sent his cavalry in a feint at the Austrian right while ordering the four columns of his main force to form into two and wheel to the right behind the low rise. Fooled by Frederick's cavalry feint, Daun had already weakened his left and centre to support his right. At about noon the van of Frederick's main force, supported by artillery, debouched in echelon to strike Daun's left, which rapidly melted to expose his centre around Leuthen. After the fierce battle for Leuthen was lost, Daun attempted a final cavalry charge against Frederick's left, but now the Prussian reserve cavalry, heretofore hidden, charged onto the field, smashed this attempt, then circled to take the remaining Austrians in flank and rear. Frederick took some 6,000–7,000 casualties in this hard-fought battle, but the Austrians suffered probably 10,000 casualties with over 20,000 captured and the loss of 116 guns and some 4,000 baggage wagons. The defeat, moreover, opened the way to Breslau which surrendered its garrison of 17,000 two weeks later. In all, the Silesian campaign cost the Austrians between 40,000 and 50,000 with Prussia emerging as the most formidable military power in Europe. The key, of course, was the victory at Leuthen which Napoleon later described as "a masterpiece of movements, maneuvers, and resolution. . . ."

By the end of the Seven Years' War the preeminence of Prussian arms was unquestioned, with every commander in Europe attempting to emulate Frederick's organization and tactics. Such was the physical cost of these tactics, however, that Frederick—grown old, ill, and bitter—increasingly shied away from war, preferring fortresses, a standing army, and a full treasury to buttress his diplomacy. Perhaps he himself realized that as a dominant soldier-king he stood at the end of an era whose tocsin was to sound in 1775 far away from Prussia—in America.

## VII. NAPOLEON AND 19TH-CENTURY TACTICS

**1. The American Revolutionary War.**—In their almost incessant fighting, first against the Indians, then against themselves, the French and English colonists had long since discarded the formal tactics of the Old World in favour of Indian bush tactics, which stressed many of the features of guerrilla warfare, such as small units, loose formations, informal dress, swift movement, fire discipline, terror, the ambush, and surprise attack. The difference in the modes of warfare was clearly seen at the outbreak of the Seven Years' War in 1755 when Gen. Edward Braddock's force of 1,400 regulars and 600 provincials was ambushed and virtually eliminated in the forests of the Monongahela Valley by a combined force of French and Indians. The difference was further emphasized by the militia and by British regular forces which often used Indian scouts besides depending on irregular scouting units such as the famed, if overrated, Rogers Rangers.

Both terrain and temperament favoured this new form of warfare. The farmers and woodsmen who in 1775 voluntarily took up their muskets to defy British rule were accustomed to hunting small game at a time when laws against poaching and possessing firearms prevailed in Europe. The greenest American recruit took aim instinctively while his European opposite was trained only to point the piece at the enemy and fire on command—the volley fire of from 30 to 50 paces. At the Battle of Bunker Hill most of the British fire passed harmlessly over the Americans, who, possessing only a limited supply of ammunition, aimed "at the handsome waistcoats" and inflicted casualties estimated at 45% on them.

Although the militia soon gave way to a regular army commanded by George Washington, light infantry tactics flourished throughout the revolution. Other innovations also appeared. One was the long-barreled frontier rifle made famous by Daniel Morgan's sharpshooters. Although its grooved or rifled barrel, combined with a technique of wrapping the ball in greased cloth to make it fit more snugly, made it much more accurate and gave two to three times the range of the smoothbore musket, the piece lacked a bayonet and had a much slower rate of fire, which meant that riflemen needed protection by musketeers. Another feature of the Revolutionary War was the voluntary cooperation of the civil population, which, never far removed from the numerous campaigns, foreshadowed Napoleon's "nation in arms." Gen. John Burgoyne, for example, in his Saratoga campaign of 1777, was faced with something akin to a scorched earth policy as he marched from Montreal down to the Hudson. By the time he reached Saratoga, the New York and New England militias had concentrated in sufficient force to gain his surrender.

Some of these tactical differences rubbed off on the newly arrived Europeans. As early as 1757 a British officer, Lieut. Col. Thomas Gage, trained his men in forest fighting and formed the first light infantry regiment in the British Army. The Prussian General von Steuben, who arrived at Valley Forge in 1778 to teach Washington's soldiers linear tactics, recognized the difference in individual outlook and marksmanship ability between the farmer-woodsman and the European peasant and dispensed with the traditional precision deployment in order to exploit the more accurate American firepower. Lafayette and two of Napoleon's future marshals, Jean Jourdan and Louis Berthier, returned from service in this war with glowing accounts of new light infantry tactics. On the British side, Sir John Moore, who was to help shape the tactics of Wellington's armies, participated as a youthful subaltern. To these and other officers, it was evident that in North America a new kind of warfare had been fought.

**2. French Revolutionary Tactics.**—The French triumph at Valmy in 1792 owed more to the remnants of the royal army, particularly to its professional gunners and engineers, and to the confusion of Brunswick and the general weakness of the Prussians than to the soldiers of the new Republic. These were to emerge in their own right on the battlefield after the *levée en masse* of August 1793 called for a nation in arms—an "armed horde" to fight total war under the stimulus of Lazare Carnot, the brilliant minister of war who would fashion an organization suitable to the genius of Napoleon.

Carnot relied on numbers and revolutionary zeal. The Republican soldiers, the famed *sans-culottes,* gained a new mobility largely because they lacked either formal training or such traditional accoutrements as supply magazines, tents, and wagons. Bivouacking in fields and living off the land, they moved out rapidly to march overland at a quickstep of 120 paces per minute. Lacking time to train in the precision of linear tactics (as Steuben lacked time to train the Americans at Valley Forge), they spilled into battle in crooked lines of *tirailleurs,* stopping to fire at will from ditches or behind hedgerows. These vanguard skirmishers were followed by ragged "columns" which converged on a battlefield, as at Hondschoote in 1793.

As the army grew in size—by 1794 it had reached over 500,000—it developed in organization and skill. The ragged columns gradually turned into the "divisions" once called for by Marshal Saxe and later (1759) by the duke of Broglie and by the brilliant young nobleman Hippolyte de Guibert. While one division met and held the enemy, other divisions, marching on parallel roads, hastened to the battlefield or around an opposing flank to the extreme discomfiture of the enemy.

In embryo this was the national army practising the tactical mobility and flexibility demanded by Guibert who presciently wrote in 1772, in his famous *Essai de tactique générale:*

> But suppose there were to spring up in Europe a vigorous people, possessed of genius, power, and a favorable form of government; a people who combined with the virtues of austerity and a national soldiery a fixed plan of aggrandizement; who never lost sight of this system; who, knowing how to wage war at small cost and subsist by its victories, could not be reduced by financial considerations to laying down its arms. We should see this people subjugate its neighbors and overthrow our feeble constitutions, as the north wind bends the slender reeds.

**3. The Napoleonic Wars.**—In converting Guibert's words into a generation of aggression, Napoleon inherited a number of technical advantages introduced in the late 18th century. The artillery reforms of Jean Gribeauval, the building of roads and canals in France and Western Europe, the training of mathematicians and engineers, the resultant improvements in cartography—all combined with the new militant spirit and, after 1795, with Napoleon's leadership until, as it once had in Cromwell's days, professionalism and a patriotic cause joined to forge an invincible weapon.

Napoleon's military triumphs and disasters have been so exhaustively analyzed that repetition is only superfluous. That he was a consummate leader cannot be questioned, as he demonstrated in his early Italian campaigns when with a small, ragged army he pushed aside the Austrians and brought the Piedmontese to heel. The magic of his presence never vanished in subsequent campaigns, and when he left the field at Waterloo he left a permanent legend of personal leadership.

He was also a fine strategist and a capable tactician, but in neither field was he particularly original. Strategically he followed the ancient precept of "divide and conquer"; he was greatly indebted to a French officer, Pierre de Bourcet, who "had taught that an enemy could be misled by moves of different units which appeared to be disconnected but which were actually part of a connected plan. The aim was to compel the enemy to divide his forces, then to fall upon one part before it could be reinforced. This was the basis of Napoleon's strategy." (Preston, *op. cit.*) Tactically it meant reliance on maneuver, in which he early proved himself a master. He frequently emphasized its importance to his commanders, as witness his letter to the king of Naples in 1806: "The art of disposing of troops is the art of war. Distribute your troops in such a way that, whatever the enemy does, you will be able to unite your forces within a few days."

In achieving and maintaining such tactical flexibility, Napoleon relied on disciplined and streamlined infantry divisions, which eventually formed army corps. He also greatly strengthened his cavalry and artillery. Unlike Frederick the Great, he used his heavy cavalry for deep reconnaissance and also for pursuit in depth of a beaten enemy. Spurred by the teachings of Gribeauval and Jean Duteil, he made artillery a virtually independent tactical arm, one that grew increasingly stronger as the quality of his foot troops declined.

Once in contact with the enemy, Napoleon used his advance guard, normally an army corps, to fix and hold the enemy's front while his following corps deployed on the flanks and rear. For the holding action, Napoleon preferred a formation known as the *ordre mixte,* some battalions in line, others in column, the latter to exploit success, change direction in another front, or do anything else the turn of battle required. For assault, he preferred the *ordre profond,* three battalions of a regiment advancing behind each other with 100 muskets in front and nine ranks deep in each battalion. The assault was prepared by massed artillery fire, and was preceded by a line of skirmishers or *tirailleurs* whose fire held down the enemy while the French columns advanced.

Napoleon also liked to retain his heavy cavalry, the cuirassiers, to deliver the final charge.

These tactics were not particularly subtle, and in terms of lives they were very costly. One commentator estimates that battlefield disease and casualties cost the French Army 1,700,000 dead from 1793 to 1806. Napoleon during the First Empire conscripted nearly 3,000,000 men. He boasted that he could expend 30,000 troops a month.

His battles were to become ever more costly, his armies growing until they reached the 500,000 mark of his 1812 Russian expedition. In 1805 his great victory at Austerlitz cost him perhaps 7,000 casualties; in 1809 his victory at Wagram cost him some 23,000 killed and wounded; in 1812 the indecisive Battle of Borodino cost him 28,000 (and the Russians 45,000) casualties, the campaign itself spelling the demise of the Grand Army.

As his losses rose and as inexperienced recruits filled the ranks, Napoleon and his generals relied increasingly on mass tactics, on the shock power of columns of infantry, massed artillery fires (he reached a maximum of 200 guns at Borodino), and heavy cavalry charges. All these, however, became less effective as his continental enemies continued to grow in strength and to fight him with his own tactics, as in 1809 when Archduke Charles of Austria won a decision (some authorities say a victory) at Aspern-Essling. Even more prophetic, however, was the Peninsular War where a 39-year-old British officer, Lieut. Gen. Sir Arthur Wellesley (later the duke of Wellington), was fighting Napoleon's marshals with totally different tactics that in the end would prove decisive.

**4. Wellington's Tactics.**—To beat the French in a five-year war of attrition in Portugal and Spain, Wellington relied on a small, quite good British army, on Portuguese and Spanish armies of varying size and capabilities, on the British navy, on the judicious use of Portuguese and Spanish guerrillas (*see* GUERRILLA WARFARE), on French strategic and tactical weaknesses—and on his own brilliance as a master strategist and tactician.

As with Napoleon and with most generals, Wellington was the product of his environment. The American Revolution and the threat posed by the French in 1794 had resulted in some much needed British army reforms including that of conscription. Tactically, these reforms were largely the work of Sir John Moore, who had fought in America. In 1803, while training troops in a camp at Shorncliffe to meet an expected Napoleonic invasion, Moore reduced the standard three ranks to the two-rank line of the American war in order to bring additional firepower to bear; he also trained three regiments of riflemen for his light brigade, soon to become famous in Spain for its speed of march: on one occasion, using Moore's famous quick step of three paces at a walk, three at a run, Charles Craufurd marched 43 mi. in 22 hours.

In 1808 Wellington was an experienced campaigner familiar with these and other tactical innovations. Before sailing for Portugal he told a friend that the French "may overwhelm me but I don't think they will out-maneuver me. First, because I am not afraid of them, as everybody else seems to be; and secondly, because if what I hear of their system of maneuvers be true, I think it a false one as against steady troops."

After a slow start—he was recalled to England and was given overall command only after Moore's untimely death—Wellington cleared Portugal of the French and commenced a strategic offensive with a tactical defensive, an overall plan that often bent, as when the French drove him back into Portugal and invested Lisbon, but never broke. While willing to penetrate into Spain, Wellington could not afford to give battle except on his own terms. These were defined in two early victories in 1809, Vimiero and Talavera, which established Wellington's style, later to appear at Waterloo.

At Vimiero Wellington lined his troops on the hills, most of them away from the enemy, his solution to Napoleon's artillery barrage. Wellington countered the French attack columns with straight- and fast-shooting British riflemen fighting in line, thus gaining 100% firepower against the French 33%. Wellington also believed in fire economy. He held his fire almost until the point of contact. He then ordered a withering blast of fire which he followed with a limited bayonet counterattack.

The effect on the French was cataclysmic. The French Marshal Bugeaud, then a lieutenant colonel, later described a French attack against

> the red English line, still silent and motionless, even when we were only 300 yards away. . . . The English line would make a quarter-turn—the muskets going up to the "ready." An indefinable sensation nailed to the spot many of our men, who halted and opened a wavering fire. The enemy's return, a volley of simultaneous precision and deadly effect, crashed in upon us like a thunderbolt. Decimated by it we reeled together, staggering under the blow and trying to recover our equilibrium. Then three formidable *Hurrahs* terminated the long silence of our adversaries. With the third they were down upon us, pressing us into a disorderly retreat. But to our great surprise, they did not pursue the advantage for more than some hundred yards, and went back with calm to their former lines, to await another attack. We rarely failed to deliver it when our reinforcements came up—with the same want of success and heavier losses.

This tactical theme, with variations, Wellington played over and over. It was a victory of the line over the column. It scored time and again as did its principal variation, the infantry square, which the French cavalry failed to penetrate either at Almeida (1812) or at Waterloo (1815). In essence, it was a victory of infantry firepower and as such foreshadowed the bloody battlefields of future wars.

**5. The Post-Napoleonic Tactical Giants: Clausewitz and Jomini.**—In the lull that followed the Napoleonic Wars, two major attempts were made to codify their political, strategic, and tactical lessons. The first was *Vom Kriege* (*On War*), the ponderous work by von Clausewitz posthumously published in 1831. The second was *Précis de l'art de la guerre* (*Summary of the Art of War*) by Antoine Jomini (*q.v.*), published in 1837.

Each author was a professional soldier; and although Jomini attacked a good many of Clausewitz' tenets, he nonetheless often reached common ground with him. As Gen. J. D. Hittle later pointed out,

> The fundamental difference between Clausewitz and Jomini is that while the Prussian roamed in the psychological and philosophic domains of battle, peering into the metaphysical darkness whence come the intangible but nevertheless omnipresent components of combat, Jomini was more concerned with the more immediate character of war as it exists, and so dealt with the tangible, less with the philosophic. (J. D. Hittle, ed., *The Art of War,* The Stackpole Co., Harrisburg, Pa., 1947.)

Partly for this reason, and partly because of the segmental nature of Clausewitz' work (he died before completing it), Jomini gained a more immediate popularity. His early works had brought him to the attention of Napoleon. In the *Summary,* which was based on the study of strategy, tactics, and logistics of Napoleon's diversified campaigns, he attempted to establish basic principles of war, and he did so with a pedantry, including example and diagram, that laid the basis for the modern teaching of warfare—an accomplishment which, ironically, has earned him the censure of later commentators on the grounds that he attempted to return tactics to the geometric formality of the 18th century.

As Hittle correctly pointed out, however, the *Summary* was an immense contribution to the study of warfare. In writing on grand tactics, Jomini stressed the value of mobility and surprise in order to gain concentration of force to strike the enemy's decisive point. "In the course of his discussion he laid emphasis on such military conceptions as lines of operation and zones of operation, concentric and eccentric maneuver, and on interior as opposed to exterior lines of attack. He was the first military theorist to note the distinction between interior and exterior lines; and he regarded the former as being much the more likely to bring victory." (Hittle, *op. cit.*) In addition, he wrote knowingly on field operations such as river crossings, retreats, and pursuits, nor did he neglect supply and logistics. In Michael Howard's opinion, "It is doubtful whether a more methodical and comprehensive guide to the mechanics of military operations has ever been written." (Michael Howard, "Jomini and the Classical Tradition in Military Thought," ch. 1 of *The Theory and Practice of War,* Cassell & Co. Ltd., London, 1965.)

Jomini's influence on U.S. Army tactics was enormous. In the American Civil War most proper staff officers kept his work ready for instant reference. Many of its precepts are reflected in doctrines of the second half of the 20th century; and while some of its tactical discussion has been outdated by technological change, the work may still be read profitably by the professional officer.

Jomini's work complemented Clausewitz' more than it contradicted it. Although "discovered" at a much later date (Clausewitz was not translated into English until 1873), *On War* transcended the decades to lend itself to frequent quotation (and misquotation) by modern commentators. Where Jomini dealt mainly with specifics, the Prussian dealt far more with mystique, concerning himself primarily with the nature of war. Clausewitz denied that war could be fought by laws. Instead, the moral factor as well as fortune—what he called friction—were the omnipotent features of battle. More than Jomini he realized the violent impact of political revolution on war, and he thus bridged the century between Napoleonic warfare and the terrible total warfare of the 20th century.

**6. The Tactical Doldrums.**—Despite the esoteric writings of Clausewitz and Jomini, the 40 years following the Battle of Waterloo remained tactically unimaginative. Worn by 20 years of war, European rulers welcomed a political status quo maintained by regular standing armies whose autocratic leadership stultified any attempt to meet the organizational and tactical reforms suggested by either the Napoleonic Wars or by the technological progress inherent in the Industrial Revolution. Aside from occasional conventional campaigns, such as Field Marshal Radetzky's victory over the Piedmontese at Novara in 1849, the great powers, particularly England, confined themselves to waging colonial wars in which the "thin red line," the infantry square, the cavalry squadron, and the gunboats of the Royal Navy generally proved sufficient to cope with undisciplined native charges. In the United States a small regular army, sometimes buttressed with volunteers as during the Mexican War, fought British, French, Indians, and Mexicans in a series of small wars involving no particular strategic or tactical subtleties.

Simultaneously, however, the Industrial Revolution was greatly improving the weapons of war. The invention of the percussion cap and the cylindroconoidal or "long bullet" revolutionized infantry tactics. The former made the musket serviceable in all weathers, and vastly reduced misfires; the latter made the rifle the most deadly weapon of the century. As early as 1841 Prussia put into use a breech-loading rifle known as the "needle gun," a bolt-operated piece firing seven shots a minute, the great advantage of which was that one could fire from the semiprotective prone position. The revolver and repeating carbine opened new tactical vistas for the cavalry, whose mass charges would soon be discouraged by greatly improved artillery weapons. In 1846 an Italian officer designed a breech-loading artillery piece with a rifled barrel and shell. This was improved upon and, combined with better fuses, explosives, and casting methods, brought a more accurate and faster rate of fire. In 1862 the precursor of the machine gun, the Gatling gun, appeared.

The Industrial Revolution was also improving the means to wage total war. Inventions such as McCormick's reaper (1831) increased food production, which, in turn, increased national populations. Nicolas Appert's invention of canning meant that food could be preserved to support large armies in the field. The cotton gin, steam power, iron machinery, the sewing machine, the Bessemer and Gilchrist processes of steel manufacture, mass production methods—each helped to make possible the maintenance of large armies, just as the telegraph, railroad, and steamship, by offering controlled movement heretofore impossible, could not but influence strategy and tactics.

None of these developments immediately revolutionized conventional military structures or practices. The Crimean War (1854–56) may be described as the obscene child of obsolete tactics married to inept leadership. Yet by 1833 Germany was building a strategic rail network that in 1846 transported 12,000 Prussian troops with horses and guns to Cracow. In the U.S. more than 6,000 mi. of railroad track were laid between 1840 and 1850. At the Battle of Magenta in 1859 Napoleon III introduced rifled cannon, while "the shift of French strength from right to left flank carried out at an early stage of the campaign in Italy is possibly the first instance in war of what may be called a tactical employment of the railway." (Cyril Falls, *A Hundred Years of War,* Duckworth, London, 2nd ed., 1961.) It was across the sea, however, that the awesome influence of technology on war was first displayed.

**7. The American Civil War.**—Often termed the first modern war, in the sense that its prosecution demanded wholesale mobilization of peoples, industry, and transportation, this gargantuan conflict brought over 4,000,000 men to arms, of whom more than 600,000 died and nearly 400,000 were wounded.

The nearly 150 major battles brought significant tactical changes to warfare. Prominent among these were advance by fire and movement, the skilful employment of dismounted cavalry (particularly by Gen. Philip Sheridan), and the use of "massed" artillery fire. The importance of the railroad and telegraph to both strategy and tactics became clear almost from the beginning. Technical innovations included the extensive use of hasty field fortifications, bridge building, the railway gun, the Gatling gun (precursor of the machine gun), the Spencer repeating carbine, the land mine, wire entanglements, the observation balloon, and the hand grenade, not to mention numerous naval devices (*see* AMERICAN CIVIL WAR: *The Navies and the Blockade*).

Not all of the new weapons were employed, however. In 1861 the Union and Confederate armies used both the Springfield smoothbore musket and, to a greater extent, the muzzle-loading, percussion-capped rifle with an effective range of 500 yd. (compared to the musket's 50 to 100 yd.). The standard field artillery piece was a brass smoothbore 12-pounder with a range of approximately 1,500 yd.—a gun-howitzer called a "Napoleon," which at the time of its selection by the U.S. Army in 1857 the French Army already considered obsolete. The three-inch rifled Parrott gun was also in use.

Despite operational shortcomings of these weapons compared to improved European models, they nonetheless dictated a radical change in tactics. The increased range and accuracy of the rifle—whether muzzle- or breech-loading—automatically relegated cannon to a support role with the guns placed behind and protected by the infantry. As is usually the case when a missile weapon becomes technically superior, the rifle favoured the defense by an estimated three to one; that is, it would take three men in the attack to overcome one in defense. Protected by log-faced earthworks built by shovel and axe and supported by artillery, the defending riflemen made the assault a costly and often futile effort, but one that persisted until the end of the war.

Before the war, assault tactics "prescribed attacks with regiments of about a thousand men attacking on a narrow front of two companies in column." (Preston, *op. cit.*) This situation quickly changed to brigade attacks in line with a thousand or so troops attempting to leapfrog forward, thus anticipating later fire-and-movement tactics. Union and Confederate soldiers, however, displayed disparate styles. The former were trained to a battlefield formality particularly vulnerable to cannon and sharpshooter fire. The Confederates, undisciplined but intensely enthusiastic, fought more as independent skirmishers. As Fuller has noted, "the Federal soldier was semi-regular and the Confederate semi-guerrilla." (Fuller, *op. cit.*)

The action was generally furious. In the early phase of the Battle of Shiloh, "[Gen. Ulysses S.] Grant rode through the press, straightening out the sagging lines, directing artillery here, reorganizing a company of infantry there, the calmest man on the field. His horse was killed under him; he got another. A bullet took his hat off; he fought bareheaded; another went through his coat between arm and side, another tore the insignia from his shoulder; the 41st Illinois [regiment] cheered him when he shook still another from his pocket. Sherman saw trees whose leaves were utterly stripped by balls, the gully ran with blood, you could cross from one side to the other on the piled bodies, but Grant held the frayed lines firm." (Fletcher Pratt, *Ordeal by Fire,* published by William Sloane Associates, Inc., reprinted by permission of William Morrow and Co., Inc. © 1948 by Fletcher Pratt.). The battle at Spotsylvania was described by one participant:

"Nothing but piled-up logs separated the combatants. Our men would reach over the logs and fire into the faces of the enemy, would stab over with their bayonets; many were shot and stabbed through the crevices; men mounted the works, and with muskets handed them kept up a continual fire until they were shot down." (Pratt, *op. cit.*)

The cost in lives was enormous. At Shiloh each side suffered over 10,000 casualties; to win the Battle of Chickamauga the Confederates suffered 23,000 killed and wounded; 51,000 fell at Gettysburg. Although these numbers were appalling, commanders on neither side grasped the full significance of rifle firepower. Even the best tacticians continued to try frontal assaults: Gen. Ambrose E. Burnside at Fredericksburg, Gen. Robert E. Lee at Gettysburg; at Cold Harbor Grant lost 5,000 men in 10 minutes.

Tactical habits were nevertheless changing. As the war continued the bayonet was used less and less, some soldiers actually discarding it as a useless weapon. Cavalrymen also realized the futility of charging manned defenses. Instead, they increasingly functioned either as mounted infantry armed with the breech-loading carbine or independently as raiders deep inside enemy country.

The increased holding power of the defense was demonstrated in the first major battle of the war. At Bull Run in July 1861, Gen. T. J. "Stonewall" Jackson gained a lasting reputation by holding against Gen. Irvin McDowell's flank attack until the vanguard of Gen. Joseph Johnston's force arrived by rail. Lee repeatedly relied on the superiority of the defense when splitting his forces for the independent maneuvers that justly made him famous. At the Second Battle of Bull Run, Jackson contained more than double his own strength until Lee arrived the following day to deliver the decisive counterstroke. At Chancellorsville, half of the Confederate Army held under Lee while Jackson led the other half around the Union right in a surprise flank attack to win a victory against two-to-one numerical odds.

The major influence of the railroad on tactics was also demonstrated in the First Battle of Bull Run when part of Johnston's Confederate force reached Manassas by rail. Throughout the war both sides relied on rail transport which on occasion prevented tactical disaster. For example, after Gen. William S. Rosecrans' defeat at Chickamauga in September 1863, he was reinforced by 23,000 men with artillery who moved 1,200 mi. in seven days, an operation that would have taken three months by marching. Along with the telegraph, the railroad became a prime target for guerrillas, including the Confederate mounted raiders led by John Morgan and Bedford Forrest (*see* GUERRILLA WARFARE). Guerrilla warfare was frequently a major annoyance to Union commanders.

**8. Port Arthur: The Tactical Tocsin.**—The full impact of the American Civil War did not immediately strike European commanders. In the continental wars between Austria and Prussia (1866) and France and Prussia (1870), cavalrymen continued suicidal charges against redoubts manned by infantry armed in the case of France with the *chassepot,* a rifle that had a range of over 1,000 yd. and double the efficiency of the Prussian needle gun. Infantry columns on both sides maneuvered in close formations and suffered heavy losses from rifled artillery. Commanders persisted in ordering frontal attacks by infantry, which invariably failed with a heavy cost in lives.

Several reasons explain this obtuseness. One was the European superiority complex—when Count von Moltke, chief of the Prussian and German General Staff, was asked his views on the American war he replied that he was not interested in a struggle between two armed mobs. Another reason was the traditional failure of the professional officer to admit to the changing face of war. For every Moltke, who clearly saw the new power of the defense and the resultant need for flank envelopment, dozens of generals remained content with old customs and habits. Foreign observers of the American battles sent copious reports of various actions, but without noting the tactical significance. Still another reason was the spate of small colonial wars between 1850 and 1914, each calling for a variety of tactics and thus obfuscating the significance of technological advances and battlefield parity. It was all very well for the European officer to discuss the necessity of building up his firing line prior to an assault or the need to advance by fire and movement; but such tactics were unnecessary to the British fighting an Indian mutiny or to the Americans involved in bushwhacking operations in the Philippines (*see* GUERRILLA WARFARE; JUNGLE WARFARE). Many natives fought long and well, for instance the Zulu *impis* whose enveloping tactics cost the British dearly; but they lacked artillery and machine guns and generally relied on undisciplined, mass tactics. Surprisingly, the British infantry square was used in the colonies up to World War I.

The inventory of missile weapons was meanwhile growing. The Prussian needle rifle, a breech-loading weapon that helped win the Austro-Prussian War of 1866, gave way to the French *chassepot* in 1870. In 1885 Germany introduced the Mauser, a radically improved small-bore rifle fed by a metal magazine holding eight cartridges. A year later the French adopted the Lebel rifle, which fired a cartridge of smokeless powder. In 1888 the British adopted the magazine-fed Lee-Metford rifle—all pieces which would be used in World War I.

The dominance of the magazine-fed rifle was soon challenged by the machine gun and by improved artillery. In the Franco-Prussian War of 1870, France introduced Reffeye's 25-barreled mitrailleuse, the precursor of the Hotchkiss, Colt, and Maxim machine guns, the last appearing in 1884. Artillery improved to the extent that in the 1870 campaign Prince Kraft zu Hohenlohe smashed a French counterattack by "walking" his breech-loading cannon slowly from 1,700 down to 900 paces, an innovation in artillery tactics. By 1873 the Germans owned a field gun with a range up to 7,000 yd.; by 1880 a reasonably good howitzer for high-angle fire had appeared. Fixed fortifications were greatly improved by the development of heavy guns protected by steel cupolas that upon opening raised the gun to the firing position. By incorporating such weaponry in a ring system of forts, Gen. Henri Brialmont believed that he had made Liège impervious to attack (it held out for ten days in 1914). From 1870 to 1875 the French general Raymond de Rivières rebuilt a frontier left naked by the German seizure of Alsace-Lorraine—an expensive program resulting in a line of fortifications linked by the bastions of Belfort-Épinal-Toul-Verdun, a concept in many ways suggesting the later Maginot Line. Toward the end of the century the quick-firing field gun was in manufacture. By absorbing the recoil in a hydraulic cylinder, this gun could be mounted on a nonrecoiling, armoured carriage. At first it fired eight to ten rounds per minute; but in 1898 the French 75-mm. gun, made famous in World War I, provided an even faster rate of fire.

These weapons radically added to the potency of the defense as dramatically evidenced by the Boer War (1899–1902) and the Russo-Japanese War (1904–05). So formidable was the Boer line in the first or conventional phase of the war that on numerous occasions the defensive front was spread to an unheard of thinness. Yet the British attacks either failed to penetrate these fronts or, as at Spion Kop, penetrated only to be forced to yield, leaving their dead, as noted by an eyewitness, Deneys Reitz, "in swathes, and in places they were piled three deep." (Deneys Reitz, *Commando,* Faber and Faber, London, 1929.)

A more exact portent of World War I occurred across the world in Manchuria. In 1904 the Russians were defending Port Arthur, "a fortress held with magazine rifles, machine guns, and quick-firing artillery." (Fuller, *op. cit.*) The Japanese attacks could have been lifted from the later Western Front. Time and again Japanese infantry attempted to turn carefully defended Russian positions. Conducted at night, generally after extensive artillery preparation, these efforts turned the battlefield into a horror scene of searchlights and flares, of artillery shells exploding, and of the attackers falling before accurate machine gun and rifle fire. One series of night attacks cost the Russians some 3,000 casualties as opposed to 15,000 Japanese dead and wounded. A later series of assaults cost the Russians 400 killed, the Japanese some 11,000 killed and wounded. Total Japanese casualties in taking the citadel amounted to some 60,000. Taken with the rest of the war, this series of attacks indisputably established the superiority of defense—of men armed with rifles and machine guns firing from trenches protected by wire and supported by quick-firing artillery. Conversely it taught that such defenses could not be overwhelmed by frontal assault, but must be enveloped in attacks supported by wholesale numbers of heavy guns. As will be seen, the bulk of these lessons went unheeded, although Germany learned more than France or England.

## VIII. WORLD WAR I

**1. The First Battle of the Marne.**—In the autumn of 1914 Europe exploded "into a war releasing vast armies long trained to fight under complex plans long conceived to win." (R. B. Asprey, *The First Battle of the Marne,* J. B. Lippincott Co., New York, 1962.) In France, two weeks after the German invasion, over 2,000,000 soldiers were fighting along a 475-mi. front of mountains, valleys, hills, and plains, a war of maneuver that soon would turn to a war of attrition, and ultimately kill or wound 20,000,000 men.

The principals—Germany and Austria-Hungary on one side, France, England, and Russia on the other—had planned carefully, if erroneously, for the event. Germany envisaged a swift war of invasion under a general plan conceived by a former and brilliant chief of staff, Gen. Alfred von Schlieffen. The Schlieffen Plan called for a holding operation against Russia in the East; in the West it proposed a weak left wing, which would hold in the south while a strong right wing invaded France. The attack would be made through Holland and Belgium, each a neutral, and would encircle Paris—a hammer driving the French army to a border army anvil. Numerous commentators have suggested that Schlieffen sought to repeat the Battle of Cannae, but J. F. C. Fuller correctly points out that he sought to emulate Frederick the Great's success at Leuthen. The matter is somewhat academic in that his successor, Helmuth Moltke the Younger, drastically modified the plan primarily by strengthening the left at the expense of the right; in the event, he further weakened the right by transferring two of its corps to the Eastern Front.

Suffering the humiliation of its defeat by Prussia in 1870, France also held aggressive intentions. These were solidified in Plan XVII, a plan of concentration so developed that the commander-in-chief, Gen. Joseph Joffre, could advance to the attack on the German armies with all forces united. While the Russians invaded Prussia and Austria in the east, the French would fight a defensive action along the northeastern frontier until the 13th day of mobilization. Then all armies including the British Expeditionary Force on the left would assume the offensive. Plan XVII egregiously erred as to enemy capabilities. It not only greatly underestimated German strength, but completely ignored a possible German attack north of the Ardennes, which was the key move in the Schlieffen-Moltke plan.

Of the combatants, the Germans were incontestably stronger. Each of the 22 active corps consisted of two infantry divisions plus such corps troops as *Jäger* or light infantry, cavalry, heavy artillery, signal, medical, engineer, and supply and combat trains plus an air detachment of 12 planes. Germany's 14 reserve corps possessed neither corps artillery nor aircraft, but their state of training was sufficient to deploy them alongside active corps, one of the biggest surprises of the war to the Allies. To carry out the Schlieffen-Moltke plan, the German General Staff also relied on swift mobilization, including rail transfer of units to the demarcation point. Violation of Dutch and Belgian neutrality went without saying; to handle such static and imposing defenses as those at Liège (*see* above), which stood in the way of the drive to the Belgian plain north of the Ardennes, the Germans secretly developed enormous 420-mm. mortars—the first tactical surprise of the war to the Allies.

Armed with 1898 Mauser clip-fed, bolt-action rifles and dressed in field-gray uniforms, the German infantrymen stood well equipped in every item from waterproof cowhide packs to the famous spiked helmet that was light, cool, and waterproof and shaded the eyes and back of the neck. Backed by the 1908 water-cooled Maxim machine gun, the small unit was trained aggressively and so disciplined as to follow any order, but officers tempered primarily offensive tactics with an understanding of temporary emplacements including barbed wire and machine guns in the defense.

Similar in structure to the German corps, each of the 21 French active infantry corps counted 40,000 men; they lacked heavy artillery, but each division carried more field guns, of which the 75-mm. had no peer. Each corps maintained a reserve brigade of two infantry regiments as part of corps troops. But the French, unlike the Germans, did not integrate their 25 reserve divisions into the field armies, and at first preferred to fight their ten cavalry divisions as independent units rather than in formation.

Carrying a breech-loading 1886 Lebel rifle and wearing red trousers topped by a long, clumsy combination jacket-cloak of blue, the French infantryman carried a poncho, pack, entrenching tool, bulky mess gear, a cooking pot, and an extra pair of hobnail boots. The British "Tommy" carried the excellent if heavy Lee-Enfield clip-fed, bolt-action rifle, wore a light khaki uniform unsuitable for cold weather, and was trained for offense and defense, both his equipment and training having resulted from experience gained in the Boer War.

Deficiencies existed in each army. The German command system was far too inflexible, its top field commanders constantly quarreled, and its major ally, Austria-Hungary, was a dubious asset. The German infantry formations in no way respected the new defensive power of weapons, and the tendency to bunch for the final assault proved costly almost from the beginning, as in the battle against the British Expeditionary Force at Mons. Although German heavy artillery was first class, this advantage was partially offset by poor coordination between infantry and artillery, poor use of air-directed artillery fire, an inferior fuse that resulted in numerous duds and, along with other armies, failure of the gunners to provide adequate field protection for themselves and the guns, and finally a nearly disastrous underestimate of ammunition needs. Although the problem of supply in a mobile situation had received considerable attention—for example the provision of specially constructed field kitchens—supply in general suffered from the inadequacy of primarily horse-drawn field trains. The chief deficiency in the French Army stemmed from a mystical belief in the offensive, a doctrine of the *offensive à outrance* ("all-out offensive"): every traditional consideration governing tactics had to be subordinated to the spirit of the offense—terrain, security, supporting forces, artillery preparation, each became unimportant, indeed disastrous, if allowed to inhibit the infantry assault. Spirit and spirit alone ruled: "imprudence became a virtue." (Asprey, *op. cit.*)

This force in August 1914 precipitated a series of actions known as the Battle of the Frontiers. Everywhere along the line General Joffre's poilus moved forward and met the enemy in attacks frequently carried home with the deadly, thin, triangular bayonet. And everywhere along the line the enemy was ready, machine guns and artillery registered. The result was a tactical disaster for France. Keen but inept junior officers jumped to the attack without preparatory artillery fire, without guarding flanks, without building temporary emplacements behind them. No more did their generals set them right, or coordinate division and corps attacks, or lead in any sense of the word. Everywhere along the line the attacks were shredded by firepower so superior that in the brief Battle of Morhange over 10,000 Frenchmen fell.

By Aug. 24 Plan XVII had failed. In those few weeks the French lost perhaps 300,000 men including several thousand officers. The French armies stood in retreat along the line. On their left the British fought at Mons, lost heavily, and also began a retreat, one embittered by the belief that the French on their right had let them down. For Joffre, retreat was the order of the day—try to retain some cohesion, trade territory for time, try to scrape up a new mass of maneuver, try to attack again.

The situation was bleak, but not entirely one-sided. The British stand at Le Cateau, the French stand at Guise-Saint-Quentin—each a well-fought rearguard action that slowed and hurt the German right-wing armies, but that seemingly did not affect the overconfidence of the German commanders. Their reports, to Moltke, some 150 mi. away in Luxembourg, did not accurately assess their own or enemy strengths. Gen. Alexander von Kluck's and Gen. Karl von Bülow's vanguard divisions were miles ahead of their supply, rations were becoming short, men tired. The Germans assumed that the British were on the run, badly beaten; thinking they could now turn the French left, they began discussing a change in their line of advance. Instead of moving southwest around Paris, why not advance southeast and roll up the exposed French flank? On Aug. 31 Moltke approved this major change in the Schlieffen Plan.

The Germans failed to realize that Joffre, by use of a splendid rail network, had built a new army north of Paris; nor did they know that the British were not badly beaten but only temporarily demoralized. German failure spelled Allied survival. The turning movement proved fatal. Instead of taking the French in flank attack, Kluck found himself under flank attack from Joffre's new army north of Paris. Turning to meet this, he pulled away from von Bülow on his left—a gap dangerously filled with the British advancing from south of the Marne. Moltke now intervened in the guise of a relatively junior staff officer, Lieut. Col. Richard Hentsch. Armed with Moltke's authority, Hentsch visited the front, discussed the situation with various army commanders, then ordered the right-wing armies to withdraw to the line of the Aisne. On Sept. 9 the German withdrawal began—the Allies had won the Battle of the Marne.

**2. The Race to the Sea.**—The military failure on all sides to appreciate the tactical changes wrought by technology was voiced after the war by Sir John French:

> I cannot help wondering why none of us realized what the most modern rifle, the machine gun, motor traction, the airplane and wireless telegraphy would bring about. . . . I feel sure in my own mind that had we realized the true effect of modern appliances of war in August, 1914, there would have been no retreat from Mons, and that if, in September, the Germans had learnt their lesson, the Allies would never have driven them back to the Aisne. (Asprey, *op. cit.*)

By the end of the Marne campaign, neither side had yet fully realized the effect of modern weapons on the staying power of the defense in linear warfare. Without vastly superior numbers the sustained offensive was doomed to an "almost but not quite" status that would remain until development of the internal combustion engine offered a new mobility that, enhanced by the third dimension of air power, changed war of lines to war of areas.

Perhaps sensing this in 1914, the enemy made one more try. Scarcely had the German Army fallen back to the entrenched line of the Aisne, followed by the British and French in feckless pursuit, than Gen. Erich von Falkenhayn, who had replaced Moltke, began moving his divisions north in a desperate effort to outflank the Allied left. With Joffre matching each German power shift, this brief effort degenerated into "the race to the sea" until the battle line extended from the Alps to the English Channel, the soldiers on either side feverishly digging trenches and stringing wire. The tactical problem now was penetration—to choose a spot in the enemy line, blast through it with heavy guns, then attack with infantry. But the guns on neither side were in sufficient numbers, the guns available could not be fed: "before the war was a month old, because all belligerents had grossly underestimated the material demands of war, the supply of artillery ammunition began to fail." (J. F. C. Fuller, *The Conduct of War,* Rutgers University Press, New Brunswick, N.J., and Eyre & Spottiswoode, London, 1961.) By the end of November 1914, a stalemate had resulted—the war of mobility had turned to a war of attrition. German losses already approached 750,000, those of the Allies over 850,000—figures soon to seem mild.

**3. The Eastern Front.**—What Fuller has termed "the defensive trinity" of bullet, spade, and wire asserted its supremacy elsewhere than on the Western Front. In East Prussia the Germans screened one Russian army with a cavalry division backed by the fortress troops of Königsberg, then, shades of the American Civil War, moved the 8th Army by rail and forced march to the south to fight the Battle of Tannenberg. In the words of Hanson Baldwin, "a modern Cannae," it was a German tactical masterpiece that destroyed the entire Russian 2nd Army and blared the names of the German commanders, Generals Paul von Hindenburg and Erich Ludendorff, throughout the world.

The defense again asserted its power in the ensuing Battle of the Mazurian Lakes, where the Russian commander, Paul Rennenkampf, held against Hindenburg's frontal attacks and withdrew only when struck in the flank, a campaign grumbling to a halt by mid-September with the Russians removed from Prussian soil.

Similar events prevailed in the south and southwest. The Austrian columns that crossed the Sava and Drina rivers into Serbia were shredded into retreat—not until December did they take Belgrade, a campaign that cost Austria and Serbia each an estimated 100,000 casualties. The Austrians fared far worse in Galicia: by mid-September they had yielded this vast territory to the Russians, losing 250,000 killed and wounded and 100,000 prisoners in the process. German attempts to march over Poland subsequently were frustrated as were Russian efforts to overrun Silesia, all at a tremendous cost in men and arms. By the end of 1914 the Eastern Front was quiet.

**4. The Peripheral Fronts.**—The tactical failures of the Western and Eastern fronts in the autumn and winter of 1914 caused the Allied Powers to examine a peripheral strategy. To turn the German flank, Sir John French recommended a military-naval operation to capture Ostend and Zeebrugge; Lord Fisher, England's first sea lord, suggested a military-naval operation in Schleswig-Holstein; Lloyd George wanted to withdraw most of the BEF from France and land it in the Balkans; Winston Churchill proposed to attack Turkey through the Dardanelles. In January 1915, Britain decided in favour of Churchill's proposal, an operation that began with a local naval bombardment and grew to a full-scale combined operation for which neither the British army nor navy was in the remotest way tactically prepared.

The result was almost inevitable. The British, including Australian and New Zealand forces, landed at Gallipoli in the early spring of 1915. They gained a toehold on the peninsula but only at a terrible human toll. Reinforced with British and French units, they retained what amounted to little more than a beachhead but were unable to advance against prepared Turkish defenses. They were evacuated in January 1916. Of some 410,000 Allied soldiers involved, an estimated 252,000 were killed, wounded, missing, taken prisoner, or evacuated sick or died of disease.

Meanwhile another Allied excursion was taking place. In the autumn of 1915 France and England decided to attack the Balkans by landing an expeditionary force in Salonika. This hope quickly died. The official British war historian Brig. Gen. Sir James Edmonds later pointed out that for three years an Allied force totaling some 600,000 was contained "by half of the Bulgarian army with a little German stuffing." (Fuller, *op. cit.*)

**5. War in the Trenches.**—From 1915 on, the tactical problem of the Western Front was penetration. That autumn Allied offensives east of Artois and north of Champagne, although costing some 300,000 casualties, in no instance penetrated beyond the front line system of German trenches, a failure due partly to a defense in depth—in places the first line of trenches ran 3,000 yd. deep—and partly to the inability to sustain an infantry attack over ground cratered by shells and converted to quagmire by frequent rainfall. Failure unfortunately dissuaded neither side from suicidal tactics. Before the Allies could open a 1916 spring offensive, Germany decided to force France from the war by draining away its strength at Verdun.

To attack this bastion Germany trained special combat troops armed with flamethrowers and supported by mass artillery fire, the portent of a tactical reorganization that by 1918 would mature to foreshadow the battlefields of World War II. The offensive began in February. Making considerable progress at first, it slowed upon coming against the impressive outer and main forts and then it suddenly stopped: by mid-July this heartless operation, known colloquially as "the sausage grinder," resulted in a penetration of only five miles. Verdun itself, although hard pressed, was supplied by motor transport and continued to hold out: in all, a standoff action costing the Germans nearly 300,000 men, the French over 300,000.

Even worse, the battle for Verdun begat the Battle of the Somme, an Allied offensive begun in late June to help relieve pressure on Verdun. After an eight-day Allied bombardment which fired a total of 1,738,000 shells, the big guns "rolled" their fire forward, the British and the French advancing in the shadow of explosions—a tactical innovation along a 25-mi. front. By mid-November the attackers had made a maximum penetration of only 7 mi. Estimated casualties: 420,000 British, 195,000 French, 500,000 German.

These absurd offensives continued in 1917, the Allies attacking in Flanders and on the Aisne, the operations prepared by millions of shells, kicked off by vast armies, challenged by weather and fierce counteroffensives; battles fought in spring, summer, and autumn, sustained by hundreds of thousands dead and wounded, yielding a few miles of ground in either direction.

How to break the tactical stalemate?

As early as 1915 the Germans had tried gas, a cloud of greenish-yellow chlorine released from hundreds of cylinders brought to forward trenches. Although devastating to a surprised enemy, its physical influence was sharply circumscribed, and it was quickly countered by gas masks and respirators. In 1917 the Germans tried again, this time with a much more effective delivery system, artillery shells holding the more deadly phosgene and mustard gases. The Allies quickly replied in kind. Gas warfare became a hideous way of life until the end of the war.

The British attempted a different method of breakthrough, a "land ship," which would become known as a tank, to force a way for advancing infantrymen. Used first on the Somme in 1916, these crude machines quickly broke down on the rough, cratered ground, nor were they sufficiently numerous to exercise more than a local influence. Their potential, however, was shown just over a year later at Cambrai where nine battalions, 378 tanks, pushed off ahead of two infantry corps. In but one day this surprise attack against the strongest entrenched system on the Western Front gained 10,000 yd. Failure to exploit this fantastic penetration led to a counterattack and repulse, but the tactical lesson nonetheless was plain (if only to a few).

Similarly, the airplane began coming into its own. Used originally for reconnaissance—in August 1914 a British pilot reported the German change in direction of attack—these fragile machines, moving under 100 mph, gradually expanded in size and strength and mission; in early 1915 German zeppelins began raiding London and Paris, English bombers began raids on German railways. Tactical aircraft continued reconnaissance and photographic missions and in 1915 began spotting for artillery fire, a function heretofore provided by manned balloons. Since air superiority was essential to tactical surprise, air battles soon developed. At first pilots shot at each other with pistols and rifles, but these were soon replaced by machine guns synchronized to fire through a plane's propeller, a major development that by 1916 had fighter aircraft strafing ground targets. Planes continued to grow in size and power; rudimentary strategic bombing became a fact as did tactical air support: dogfights to gain control of tactical air space, the strafing of troops, gun positions, and convoys, reconnaissance, photography, and artillery spotting. As in the case of armour, the potential of the airplane in warfare, both strategically and tactically, was plain (if only to a few).

**6. The Tactical Breakthrough.**—To win the war in 1918, the German High Command decided "first to split the British and French armies, then destroy the British in detail." (R. B. Asprey, *At Belleau Wood,* G. P. Putnam's Sons, © 1965 by Robert Asprey.) Hindenburg and Ludendorff rested their hopes on a series of storm offensives undertaken by highly trained troops attacking by infiltration, tactics developed by Oskar von Hutier in his well-executed capture of Riga in September 1917. There surprise had been the keynote, the assault troops having been kept 70 mi. to the rear with approach marches begun only ten days before the attack. The attack was preceded by a mere five hours of artillery bombardment (the first two hours of gas only), the guns and mortars not having been registered previously in order to retain surprise.

Surprise was to remain the keynote of German plans for the Western Front. Three armies, of which the 18th Army under Hutier was the most important, were involved—in all, some 60 divisions consisting of men under 35 years of age, and secretly and rigorously trained behind both fronts throughout the winter.

The assault was to be tactically flexible. Training instructions, as later translated by the British war historian Edmonds, stressed that "the objective of the first day must be at least the enemy's artillery; the objective of the second day depends on what is achieved on the first; there must be no rigid adherence to plans made beforehand." Moreover, "the tactical breakthrough is not an objective in itself: its raison d'être is to give the opportunity to apply the strongest form of attack, envelopment." (J. E. Edmonds, *Military Operations, France and Belgium 1918,* Macmillan & Co. Ltd., London, 1935.)

As at Riga a surprise artillery barrage would launch the gigantic effort. This was to be a massive but carefully coordinated fire delivered along the entire attack front by nearly 6,500 guns and 3,500 trench mortars, which for the first two hours would fire gas shells. Great importance was attached to this display of firepower, and infantry commanders were instructed to exploit it by keeping their troops "close behind the barrage regardless of shell splinters. A single enemy machine gun which survives the bombardment does more harm than any number of our own shell splinters." (Edmonds, *op. cit.*)

After this initial disruption of enemy defenses, groups of *Sturmtruppen*—special teams armed with light machine guns, light trench mortars, and flame projectors—would then punch channels through enemy defenses to the immediate rear, thus disorganizing the defense before reserves could appear. The *Sturmtruppen* sometimes consisted of entire battalions, sometimes less, but they were to be kept up to strength by constant reinforcement. Their general instructions were to "push on, keep inside the divisional areas, do not trouble about what happens right or left." They were to allow enemy tanks "to pass through, to be dealt with by the artillery in the rear; but the infantry accompanying them was to be engaged." They would stop counterattacks with fire followed by bayonet attack. "Machine guns were never to retire." The assault units were also to bypass isolated centres of resistance, leaving them to be neutralized by battle units—small composite forces of infantry, machine guns, trench mortars, engineers, sections of field artillery, and ammunition carriers. Following closely, reserve troops were to enlarge the channels and consolidate gains against enemy counterattacks, but they "must be put in where the attack is prospering, not where it is held up." Specially trained artillery units would support the advance, but "the infantry must see what it can do for itself . . . [it] must be warned against too great dependence on the creeping barrage." Air power was also involved. In addition to its normal reconnaissance and artillery-spotting missions, special squadrons were to conduct low-level flights that were "always to cross the enemy front obliquely and then dive down and attack infantry, artillery, reserves and transport columns with machine gun fire and light bombs." (Edmonds, *op. cit.*)

This striking concept of the coordinated assault needed only dive-bombers and armour spearheads to become the famous *Blitzkrieg* of World War II. By beefing up the firepower of the battalion with trench mortars, flamethrowers, and a primitive version of close support artillery, the Germans made it the tactical unit of the assault—a brilliant innovation displaying a tactical genius hitherto unparalleled, but one demanding a complete turnabout from defensive to offensive warfare, not a simple matter with tired men and supply shortages.

Secret preparations for the attack continued throughout the winter. Beginning in March, ammunition for the massive opening barrage was brought forward at night to carefully camouflaged forward dumps. The most elaborate security precautions, including some ingenious deceptive measures, were invoked along the entire Western Front. The assault divisions and extra guns and mortars were kept in the rear for as long as possible, then at night were brought to forward assembly areas.

In late March 1918, the attack struck the surprised British along a 40-mi. front. In but three days the Germans penetrated British lines up to 14 mi. In six days they advanced in places up to 30 mi. But now the same lack of mobility that had neutralized earlier offensives worked its stultifying influence. The attacks slowed: "In some cases divisions stood miles ahead of their supply trains which lumbered with increasing difficulty over the pockmarked wasteland. Lacking ample reserves behind each front, Ludendorff had to move replacement units laterally, a slow task in view of the crowded conditions, then send them forward over the difficult terrain. The same terrain frequently prevented mobile artillery from keeping up with assault units. Disciplinary problems also existed. . . ." (Asprey, *op. cit.*) With each day these difficulties multiplied. The torn and tortured terrain, the old Somme battlefields, did not lend itself to mobility. By the end of March the infantry had little if any artillery support, ammunition was running low, some units had been without rations for 48 hours. The attack had failed. A German military writer later concluded that "the Somme desert had spoken its last inexorable and mighty word." (Edmonds, *op. cit.*)

With the first offensive halted, the Germans tried again, this time in the north. But now Marshal Ferdinand Foch, the newly appointed Allied commander in chief, was breathing fire into his troops; they were holding, and more divisions were coming rapidly forward by rail and road. In ten days the second offensive slowed and on April 29 halted. To lure the French from the Flanders front, the Germans next attacked in the south across the formidable Chemin-des-Dames against Pinon and Reims. Begun in late May, the diversion had an instant success that soon made it an end in itself, a breakthrough to the Marne with Paris a possible prize. But the same set of factors that had halted the earlier offensives was at work. The German divisions soon outran their supply. French and American divisions were rushed to the front by rail and truck. They met the enemy at Château-Thierry and Belleau Wood, held him, then drove him back. In early June the Germans tried again on the right; in mid-July on the Champagne front. With the failure of these offensives, Germany stood on the defensive.

The offensives had cost Germany mightily, but they had also cost the Allies, particularly the British. In compensation, the Allied failures had brought a unified command under Foch; their sacrifices had won time for the U.S. weight to arrive and be felt. In mid-July the French and Americans attacked the flank of the immense German salient at Soissons. Instead of a preliminary bombardment, the French commander, Gen. Charles Mangin, brought up troops by motor transport at night. Spearheaded by 350 tanks, they attacked at dawn, a tactical surprise yielding 30,000 German prisoners. In early August, 13 British divisions attacked the Amiens salient, another surprise supported by aircraft and 450 tanks, a battle later described by a German military historian as "the greatest defeat which the German Army suffered since the beginning of the war." (Fuller, *op. cit.*) In September the British struck in Flanders; ten days later an American army wiped out the Saint-Mihiel salient. With the elimination of the enemy salients, the final offensive began in late September 1918, in the Meuse-Argonne and along the French and British fronts. Although heavy fighting lay ahead, the end was at hand.

## IX. WORLD WAR II

**1. The Post-World War I Reaction.**—Nothing in the conflicts immediately following World War I, most notably the Russian Civil War, the Russian-Polish War, and the Turkish-Greek wars, suggested the change in tactics that would be wrought by the combination of increased firepower, improved communications, increased mobility of the tank and truck, and the third dimension opened by the airplane.

Nor was the postwar climate receptive to military study and experimentation, at least among the victor nations. Such was the widespread repugnance to war, and such the near bankruptcy of France and England that armies and navies were slashed in size and budget. Another world war, most people believed, simply could not happen: Germany was to be prevented from rearming by the Versailles Treaty; internal riots and famine in Germany and Austria further reduced the spectre. The European victors were far more interested in building protective leagues than new armies—the League of Nations, men believed, would by "collective security" prevent war. Preferring to let Europe treat its own problems, the U.S. quickly retreated into an isolation that disavowed anything more militarily serious than the banana wars of its own hemisphere.

To this feckless atmosphere must be added the traditional failure of the armed forces to learn from experience. Caution prevailed in the advanced curricula of the U.S., French, and English armies. Each chose to believe in the supremacy of the defense, the U.S. behind its oceans, Britain behind its channel, France behind its Maginot Line—a bristling belt of underground forts and tank traps extending from the Vosges westward to the Ardennes that the French believed was ample protection against invasion by the dreaded German *panzer* army.

Not everyone agreed with this defensive thinking. In 1921 an American marine, Lieut. Col. Earl Ellis, presciently forecast a war with Japan. Despite the British failure at Gallipoli, Ellis called for an American strategy in the Pacific that, once accepted, forced the Marine Corps away from land warfare in favour of developing amphibious tactics and techniques. Also in 1921 the Italian Giulio Douhet published a revolutionary work, *The Command of the Air,* in which he argued among other things that the bomber by attacking civil populations could break the will of the enemy. This theory attracted some important adherents—in the U.S., Billy Mitchell; in England, Hugh Montague Trenchard and Hugh Caswall Dowding—who expanded it to embrace strategic bombing of industrial targets and tactical dive-bombing of military targets on land and sea. The potential of the tank had already been foreseen by a few officers, among them J. F. C. Fuller who in 1918 wrote a remarkably prescient study, "The Attack by Paralyzation." Fuller called for armoured spearheads, "supported by aircraft, and later followed by the traditional arms," to punch through German defenses not so much in order to destroy enemy armies but rather to neutralize the command element, the division, corps, and army headquarters. The Allied commander, Ferdinand Foch, had made this tactical approach the basis of his 1919 offensive plans when the war ended. In the following decades armoured tactical theory received further study in England by Fuller, Sir Percy Hobart, and B. H. Liddell Hart; in France by Charles de Gaulle; in the United States by A. R. Chaffee, J. L. Devers, and George S. Patton, and these and other experts believed that taken with motor transport it would reintroduce mobility to the battlefield in favourable terrain.

The changing face of war was visibly suggested by the Japanese, Italian, and German aggressions of the 1930s and by the Spanish Civil War in which Italy and Germany (and to a lesser extent the U.S.S.R.) tested new tactics and equipment, including the dive-bomber, tank, and motor transport. Realizing belatedly that these nations had been building modern armies, the Western powers attempted to repair the neglect of nearly two decades, but they were unable to do so or even to realize the extent of the aggressors' war preparations.

**2. Early German Victories.**—On Sept. 1, 1939, Hitler loosed the full force of Germany's infantry-armour-air power against Poland, whose armed forces were so inadequate that Polish cavalrymen armed with lances were said to have charged German tanks. In less than a month the Wehrmacht overran this tragic country by a new type of warfare, the *Blitzkrieg* or lightning war, which was not fully comprehended in the West.

After a winter of quiet, Hitler struck again, this time overrunning Norway in order to gain naval and air bases. On May 10 Hitler invaded the West.

The German plan was largely the work of Erich von Manstein and Gerd von Rundstedt, although Hitler's own tactical influence was made clear during the actual fighting. In the first phase of the war, the Germans suffered no serious reverses. Their victories were gained with such swiftness, such precision, and economy of means that the *Blitzkrieg* was popularly accepted as a brilliant new tactical system. Actually it was the legitimate offspring of the infiltration tactics of 1918 mated with the greatly improved tank, better communications, motor transport, self-propelled artillery, and tactical aircraft. In the 1940 concept, the *Sturmtruppen* of 1918 were replaced with armoured task forces to form what Fuller accurately described as "an armor-headed battering ram which, under cover of fighter aircraft and bombers—operating as flying field artillery—could break through its enemy's continuous front at selected points." The breakthrough was to be followed by swift and deep penetration and exploited by motorized infantry and following infantry divisions. In many ways this tactical concept strongly resembled that worked out by the German High Command in 1918. The general idea was not to attempt to advance along the entire front, but rather to break through and expend reserve strength "where the attack is prospering, not where it is held up." The purpose of the breakthrough remained essentially the same: "to give the opportunity to apply the strongest form of attack, envelopment." (Edmonds, *op. cit.*)

The decision to invade France through the Ardennes gap—what the British war historian Major Ellis called "a secret tactical path" to Sedan—was a bold one in that the armour groups were compressed into three penetrations, each no wider than 2,000 yd., on a 12-mi. front. Preceded by Stuka dive-bombers which, in addition to terrifying forward French military units, caused enormous confusion and delay in rear areas by attacking columns of refugees to further disrupt road traffic, the *Kampfgruppen*, or battle groups, overran minimal resistance and pushed forward at top speed through the Ardennes to exploit a phenomenal tactical surprise. Hard on their treads came motorized infantry followed by regular infantry to form the "sides" to the "corridor" created by armour. As foreseen by Fuller in 1918, this armoured thrust, by cutting the defending forces in half, threw the "command" element off balance to the extent that it never recovered.

The impetus of armour was essential to this tactical concept, and it was only due to occasional insubordination by such commanders as Guderian that it was maintained. Also essential to the attack was air transport which early began supplying the armour columns with fuel; only six days after the attack started transport aircraft began flying in a forward armour repair shop base which eventually was manned by 2,000 skilled workers. Such technical proficiency proved the exception, however, since the army still depended largely on horse-drawn artillery and supply trains, and had the defenders properly deployed their forces and particularly their armour, which in numbers was superior to that of the Germans, and had the French Army not been in such a precarious state of morale, the results may well have proven disastrous to the Germans. As it turned out, however, the German mobility completely surprised and rapidly overwhelmed the French and British armies. By the time Gen. Maxime Weygand, hastily summoned from Syria, relieved the feckless Gen. Maurice Gamelin of command, the situation was beyond repair. Indeed, many authorities believe that the "miracle" of the British evacuation at Dunkerque occurred mainly because of command confusion in the German army, and not remaining Allied strength.

Although mimicking German tactics, the Italian performance was exceedingly poor. In North Africa and Greece, as in Ethiopia years before, Mussolini's armies moved haltingly, without confidence. Though vastly superior in numbers (two to one), arms, and equipment, they almost at once suffered a series of heavy reverses in Greece resulting in a precipitate and humiliating retreat—the unexpected victory of a patriotic people's army skilled in mountain warfare. Similarly, a British army of perhaps a quarter of the Italian strength pushed the enemy from Sidi Barrani and Tobruk in North Africa, capturing thousands of prisoners in the process.

German tactics in desert warfare came as a great surprise to the British in the early stages of the war. This was because the German *panzer* division was highly flexible in its use of arms, artillery being used in both defense and attack. For the British the antitank gun was a purely defensive weapon, and their use of powerful field artillery, which might have eliminated the German antitank gun, was inadequate. The Germans refused to commit themselves tank against tank, insisting that the armour action was coordinated with field artillery, antitank guns, and infantry.

The German Army was not yet finished with tactical surprises, though it faced a much different tactical environment in invading the U.S.S.R. Hitler's major goal, initially, was to eliminate the Red Army, a lightning campaign on one front, in order to free his hand for a war against England. Secondary goals were to win the food riches of the Ukraine and the oil of the Caucasus. In the event, these military and economic goals became inextricably mingled with political and ideological factors, with Hitler jumping at times frantically from one to the other.

To eliminate the Red Army Hitler relied on three army groups comprising 145 divisions of which about 20 were armour (a force buttressed by 12 second-rate Rumanian divisions as well as the considerable Finnish Army, about 250,000, attacking in the north). The number of armour divisions is deceptive, however, in that the number of actual tanks committed, some 3,500, was not appreciably greater than that used in France, but the High Command felt that the space factor would permit greater maneuverability, thus calling for more divisions with fewer tanks per division.

Each German army group was also supported by a tactical air force. The entire invasion force was greatly superior to the Russian defenders, who mustered some 150 divisions including 55 armour brigades, but who lacked modern arms and equipment. The overall strength of the Red Army was 2,500,000, but the divisions boasted few antitank guns while the air force flew mostly obsolescent planes. Moreover, Russian deployment was badly off-balance because of Stalin's primary fear of Japan.

Surprise and speed, the Germans believed, would result in envelopment before the Russian divisions could escape. At first the correct tactic indeed seemed to be for the armoured forces to thrust convergently while the infantry mopped up. Each army group literally charged forward, aided in some cases by air attacks on industrial centres and cities and by paratroopers dropping ahead to seize bridges and other vital points, a tactic that confused the Russians.

Each group captured hundred of thousands of Russians and thousands of tanks and guns, fabulous tactical victories that would have entranced the great captains of history and that are well described in Paul Carell's *Hitler's War on Russia* (1964) and in lesser detail in Edgar O'Ballance's *The Red Army* (1964; from which most of the figures below have been taken). To illustrate: Leeb's Army Group North, aimed at Leningrad, took 35,000 prisoners, 1,000 guns, and 400 tanks; Army Group Central under Bock and aimed at Moscow took 300,000 prisoners, 3,000 tanks, and 1,800 guns when Minsk fell; in July when taking Smolensk this group claimed another 300,000 prisoners, 3,000 guns, and 3,000 tanks. In late September Army Group South under Rundstedt took Kiev and 665,000 prisoners, 4,000 guns, and 1,000 tanks.

And yet, as Cyril Falls points out, the mopping up process attendant with these victories undoubtedly saved Moscow in that it prevented Hitler's armour vanguards from reaching the capital before cold weather and before substantial reinforcements had been brought from the east. Other critical factors, however, were also at work. One was Hitler's decision of late July to divert Guderian's armour from its drive on Moscow in favour of helping Army Group South to take Kiev. Guderian himself always claimed he could have taken Moscow at the time, but history is replete with generals bemoaning the "might-have-been" if left alone by mere politicians. Another factor was space for the surviving Russian remnants to fall back in and reorganize to fight another day. Their escape was due largely to the technical inability of the German columns to penetrate more deeply the Russian vastness. For technical limitations swiftly displayed themselves. By mid-November the German divisions were at half strength, there was a fuel shortage, and tanks and vehicles wanted maintenance. But the logistics system necessary to repair such deficiencies depended primarily on wheeled vehicles and horse-drawn transport, which simply could not cope with the trackless Russian wastes.

Thus time was consumed—that precious commodity which, in Napoleon's words, once sacrificed cannot be recovered. For now cold weather was closing fast. No winter clothing had been provided for the troops, no greatcoats, no antifreeze for the vehicles. As O'Ballance points out, German light and medium tanks could not operate in more than 18 in. of snow. German aircraft lacked ski undercarriages; neither were they furnished with electrical heating kits, which meant that a plane required one and a half hours to start in really cold weather. And then, also, Russian resistance began stiffening. Within six weeks of the invasion, the Kremlin had called up some 2,500,000 reservists. By the end of the year, although casualties were perhaps 1,000,000 killed and 2,500,000 captured, Stalin nonetheless fielded an army of 4,000,000 with about 200 divisions contacting the enemy.

Taken together, these factors spelled German failure. With the Kremlin spires literally in view, the German offensive stopped, the armies falling back on defensive positions usually consisting of fortified villages which formed all-round "hedgehog" protection.

Despite the German setback and subsequent defeats, the march into the U.S.S.R. was nonetheless a magnificent tactical achievement that neither top-level command confusion (caused primarily by Hitler's interference), equipment limitations, supply failures (in gasoline, antifreeze, and particularly winter clothing), nor political absurdities (the attempt to eliminate the Ukrainian population) can diminish.

**3. The Pacific War.**—On Dec. 7, 1941, Japanese bombers flying from a secret task force of aircraft carriers attacked Pearl Harbor, the major U.S. Pacific naval base. Within hours the bulk of the battleship fleet had been sunk. In the ensuing weeks and months Japanese ground, air, and sea forces seized Allied bases throughout the Pacific. By the spring of 1942 Japan was threatening Australia from nearby New Guinea and from the neighbouring Solomon Islands.

But the Japanese drive toward Australia-New Zealand was running out of steam, a process immensely aided by two important aircraft carrier battles which, as was the case with Germany in the Battle of Britain, cost planes and pilots not readily replaceable. Japan was next challenged on land, first in New Guinea by Australian-U.S. army units. At first making good progress, the Japanese thrust toward Port Moresby was subsequently thwarted by tortuous terrain coupled with supply failures. This slowing allowed time for a reorganization of the Allied forces, which fought and won the Battle of Buna-Gona—the prelude to the successful Allied offensive that pushed the enemy from New Guinea and went on to recapture the Philippines. Meanwhile, Japanese ambitions had been sharply frustrated on Guadalcanal and Tulagi by Gen. A. A. Vandegrift's 1st Marine Division which landed in August 1942.

This division was the result of a decade of planning for amphibious warfare. Long in manpower (before the war ended a reinforced amphibious division numbered over 21,000), it was short in training and because of a shortage of naval vessels it landed with greatly limited supply. The landing on Guadalcanal was uncontested, probably fortunate in view of the combat readiness of the regiments. On Tulagi resistance was determined but was overcome in a couple of days by the more highly trained raiders and parachutists. In short order the battle switched to Guadalcanal, the Japanese contesting its occupation not only by land but by sea and air from which they bombarded the Marine defensive perimeter for weeks on end.

Guadalcanal was not particularly exciting tactically. Psychologically the Marine defense exploded forever the myth of Japanese invincibility. Heretofore the Japanese Army had not really encountered a determined defense, excepting such isolated instances as Corregidor, which could not be reinforced. Where they had performed well in jungle country, as in Burma and the East Indies (*see* JUNGLE WARFARE), they now seemed at a loss for a cohesive tactical plan. Jealous services and commanders and poor leadership explain this in part. The net result was a series of uncoordinated ground attacks against the Marine perimeter. In a sense the Japanese were repeating the Allied-German errors of World War I, for they held no means of effecting a breakthrough—neither heavy artillery nor adequate coordination to obtain a substitute by naval gunfire or tactical air support. Although the Marines were defending with the advantage of compressed interior lines, shortages in everything from sandbags to barbed wire to aircraft made their task more difficult, particularly because of the high percentage of illness from malaria and dysentery. Nonetheless, despite repeated and very bloody attempts, the Japanese never accomplished more than a quickly repaired local penetration. By December 1942, when the Marines were relieved by U.S. soldiers, the Japanese had suffered incredible losses—thousands of dead compared to just over 700 Marine dead. The bulk of Marine losses stemmed from the several local offensives undertaken in order to extend the defensive perimeter. On Guadalcanal the Marines learned a lesson already grimly familiar to the French and British: a commander lacking control of the air and sea was not tactically free—on at least three occasions Vandegrift had to stop offensive tactics in order to protect his still thinly held perimeter.

The tactical importance of Guadalcanal lies not so much in the island fighting as in the means of bringing the Marines to the fight, that is, in hurriedly building enough transport shipping to carry hundreds of thousands of men and millions of tons of equipment many thousands of miles across dangerous oceans to land them on enemy-controlled territory. Although amphibious landings were scarcely novel to the U.S. Navy or Marines, the British experience at Gallipoli (*see* above) had dealt amphibious warfare a mortal blow in most military minds. Despite this attitude, since the late 1920s the Marines and Navy had been working on the problem of assaulting a fortified base from the sea. From 1934 on, the Marines, despite the antipathy of most senior naval officers, insisted on incorporating amphibious landings in annual maneuvers. A war was required, however, to produce the equipment essential to perfecting the art. The chief problem centred on getting men from the transports over the beaches as opposed to on the beaches, as had been the case at Gallipoli. Solving this problem required the closest coordination both between the landing force and the supporting naval and air forces, and in providing the landing force with sufficient mobility, speed, and firepower to propel it inland and support it until additional forces were landed.

This solution in turn posed problems in almost every field, but particularly in intelligence, communications, and supply. Tactically it meant trying to provide the landing force with protective amphibian vehicles that, besides riflemen, carried radiomen capable of calling for air and naval gunfire support.

The Guadalcanal experience, as well as later combat landings, brought significant changes in organization at both staff and command levels. The basic rifle squad was strengthened by reorganizing it into "fire teams" cored on automatic weapons and flamethrowers. To handle the immense supply problem, marine and naval officers were trained to "combat load" ships, and the shore party was formed to ensure the proper handling of cargo from the ship through the beachhead and ultimately to forward supply dumps. Consisting of engineers, pioneers, motor transport, and military police personnel under the command of a naval officer, the shore party functioned on the beaches where it often formed an integral part of the amphibious assault.

Following Guadalcanal, much new equipment also came into being, such as vastly improved armoured amphibian tractors to protect the Marines en route to and over the beaches; four-wheeled amphibian trucks called DUKWs, or ducks, which could operate in water and sand; tracked vehicles called weasels to carry supply or wounded over the roughest terrain; rocket launchers; simplified demolitions; improved flamethrowers; and better communications. The Navy introduced a host of new craft such as the LST (landing ship tank) and LSM (landing ship medium), seagoing vessels capable of transporting tanks and heavy equipment thousands of miles, and the rocket ship to provide last-minute fire support before the landing craft struck the beaches. Months of detailed planning and rehearsals preceded each operation. Transport shipping was "combat-loaded" so that tanks, trucks, artillery, fuel, rations, and water could be supplied to the landing force on a priority basis. Intricate plans controlled naval and aerial gunfire. Equally precise plans controlled small boat movement in order to observe the principle of concentration of force.

Despite later refinements, such as naval construction battalions—the famed Seabees, who often constructed roads and airfields within rifle range of the enemy—the basic concept of the amphibious assault remained valid. Within a year the outer barrier of Japan's island defenses was breached by U.S. ship-to-shore assaults. From 1943 to 1945 the U.S. Army employed amphibious tactics to work down the coast of New Guinea and finally to return to the Philippine Islands; the Marines, variously reinforced by Army troops, secured the Solomon Islands, then moved across the Central Pacific through the Gilberts, the Marshalls, the Carolines, the Marianas, and the Bonins to seize the major bastion of Okinawa. Marine and Army divisions were rehearsing plans for the invasion of the Japanese home islands when the war ended in 1945.

The amphibious offensive was not confined to the Pacific theatre. Landings in Morocco, Algeria, Sicily, and Italy were followed by the climactic Allied cross-channel operation of June 6, 1944, when 4,100 ships put ashore five divisions complete with tanks and artillery on the Normandy beaches. Such was the total record of tactical achievement that J. F. C. Fuller later described the amphibious landing as "in all probability . . . the most far-reaching tactical innovation of the war." (Fuller, *op. cit.*)

**4. World War II Tactics.**—The varied geographical and climatic conditions make it difficult to generalize about the tactics of a war in which a score of major campaigns were waged simultaneously in different parts of the world.

Fighting on the Soviet front, which in early 1942 ran from Leningrad to Rostov-on-Don—a 1,500-mi. battle line—was characterized by numerous offensives and counteroffensives that constituted some of the bloodiest fighting in the war.

Soviet tactics into late 1942 remained extremely primitive, with hastily trained and equipped divisions rushed into action in "armed horde" tactics at a fearful price in lives. So inadequate had been the Army's early performance that Stalin in late 1941 ruthlessly began weeding out incompetent commanders while simultaneously appealing to the patriotism of the troops to fight to save the mother country. After abolishing corps headquarters because of a lack of competent commanders, Stalin grouped divisions directly under armies, which in turn came under 12 "fronts" or army groups. Many of the divisions were little more than brigades of two infantry regiments, "about all some of the newly appointed commanders were capable of handling in action." (Edgar O'Ballance, *The Red Army,* Faber and Faber, Ltd., London, 1964.) Communications were dreadful—divisional commanders and their chiefs of staff quite routinely had to communicate by letter with their officers—and German air attacks raised havoc with both rail and horse-drawn supply.

Nonetheless, considerable progress was made. With the increase of tank production in factories east of the Urals and with the increasing flow of aid from England and the U.S., the Soviets formed armour regiments and brigades to provide close support for infantry. The new Soviet tanks were fitted with diesel engines to give them a greater operational radius; their heavy tanks carried a bigger (122-mm.) but not necessarily so accurate a gun as that of the German *panzer,* and they were also equipped with wider tracks for operations in mud and snow. Later in 1942 the Russians organized armour corps—actually division strength, or about 200 tanks—to operate independently, somewhat like German *panzer* armies. Similarly, with the Allies assuming responsibility for strategic bombing of Germany, the Soviets concentrated on producing tactical aircraft that formed "air armies," each consisting of several "air divisions" and placed under direct control of a front commander. The Russians also relied on large cavalry formations, which by the end of the war numbered 41 divisions or some 600,000 troopers. Each front deployed 2–3 divisions of cavalry to protect flanks and for operations in the spring thaw and autumn rains. Severe artillery shortages were also slowly repaired. In 1943 regiments of self-propelled guns appeared, and by the end of the year some 30 artillery divisions had been formed along with numerous rocket units.

The turning point on this front is conveniently marked by Germany's tactical defeat at Stalingrad, a major disaster precipitated by Hitler's refusal to allow his commanders a fluid defense. After Stalingrad the Germans never won another major battle. Indeed, by the summer of 1943 they were suffering enormous losses. For example, in the Kursk fighting they took 70,000 casualties and lost 3,000 tanks, 850 self-propelled guns, 1,000 other guns, 1,400 aircraft, and over 5,000 vehicles; they suffered comparable losses in the Orel and Kharkov fighting. Neither men nor equipment were replaceable. Yet Allied production simultaneously was mounting, lend-lease deliveries increasing. In 1944 the Soviets managed to launch ten separate offensives along a 2,000-mi. front.

Although Soviet tactics greatly improved from the early days, they still left much to be desired. The coordination of offensive arms never reached the high degree attained by the British and Americans (though the Soviet failure to use paratroopers effectively was often matched by the Allies). Numerous German and Austrian veterans have spoken of the inaccuracy of the gun on the famed T-34 tank, and they have also spoken graphically of the "human wave" suicidal tactics of the Soviets, practised right to the end. O'Ballance points out that the Soviet logistics system remained extremely primitive despite the use of Allied, largely U.S., vehicles (between 1942 and 1945 the U.S. sent this ally 385,000 trucks and over 50,000 jeeps); this to the extent that armour often had to carry the infantry. O'Ballance concludes, "It was often only Hitler's policy of static defense that enabled comparatively slow moving Red Army formations to make successful encircling movements." (O'Ballance, *op. cit.*)

The Soviet victory was nonetheless a noteworthy achievement of arms. But at what a price: an estimated 7,000,000 military dead, 10,000,000 civilian dead, 3,000,000 disabled.

Armoured columns in the desert warfare of North Africa achieved a mobility that makes the study of these intricate campaigns essential to the armour commander. Commanders on either side—Wavell, Sir Claude Auchinleck, and Bernard Montgomery on the British, Rommel on the German, Patton on the American—won noteworthy victories in a seesaw war whose outcome depended as much on supply as on any other factor. So long as Malta remained an operational British base, so long as planes could fly from this island to protect convoys crossing the Mediterranean, the British could afford offensive thrusts. With Malta practically neutralized, enemy convoys could steam from Italy to support Rommel's offensive strikes. Thus, in late 1941 and early 1942, Auchinleck won the impressive Battle of Sidi Rezegh, but could not exploit his victory because of increased pressure on Malta as well as a diversion of effort caused by the Japanese entering the war. In the summer of 1942 Rommel pushed the British back to El Alamein, but he could not exploit this gain because of a shortage of gasoline for his armour and because of the local superiority of British aircraft. Montgomery, who relieved Auchinleck as 8th Army commander, refused to attack until his divisions stood at full strength and supply was ensured. The result was impressive: on the night of Oct. 23 some 800 British guns fired a preliminary barrage while sappers probed through Rommel's protective minefields. The ensuing campaign, which pushed Rommel into Tunisia, cost him most of his tanks and the loss of about 30,000 prisoners. Coupled with the U.S.-British landings in North Africa in November, this action compressed the Axis forces into Tunisia where they were destroyed in detail, over 250,000 Germans surrendering on May 13, 1943.

The invasion of Sicily and Italy demanded tactics radically different from those of desert warfare. In either case they were a necessary prelude to the invasion of France. The landings in Sicily included extensive if not particularly effective paratroop drops besides a gigantic amphibious effort which Pres. Franklin D. Roosevelt described to the world: "The initial assault force . . . involved 3,000 ships which carried 160,000 men—Americans, British, Canadians, and French—together with 14,000 vehicles, 600 tanks, and 1,800 guns." Although this successful assault brought the fall of Mussolini's government, Hitler had no intention of evacuating Italy. Instead, Field Marshal Albert Kesselring fought an extremely capable rearguard action—at times static, at times fluid—that slowed and often stalemated Allied progress and that, despite Allied naval and air superiority, often exacted a disproportionate number of casualties for the limited gains involved. In a sense the conquest of Italy resembled the slugging matches of the later Pacific fighting on such islands as Saipan and Iwo Jima with gains often registered in hundreds of yards at a cost of thousands of casualties. The major difference, of course, was that both opponents were more easily supplied from rear area bases and not isolated, as was the case with the Japanese. As Allied air superiority asserted itself throughout Germany and Austria, however, the German supply problem often grew acute. Offsetting this was the Allied plan to land in France in the spring of 1944, a plan that drained units and equipment from the Mediterranean theatre. Attempts to speed the conquest were generally unsuccessful. One such involved an amphibious landing at Anzio, 50 mi. behind the German lines. On Jan. 22, 1944, a U.S. army corps including one British division landed against virtually no opposition, but after hesitation and delay, the subsequent battle cost the Americans nearly 24,000 casualties, the British nearly 10,000. Gen. Mark Clark's 5th Army, attacking up the western side of Italy, suffered in all about 80,000 casualties. By early June 1944, the enemy had counted 8,000 dead, 24,000 wounded, and 11,000 captured.

These earlier landings provided a fitting prelude for the final and very dramatic Normandy landings. Code-named Operation "Overlord," this action was of a scope difficult to comprehend:

Under the cover of vast air and sea armadas, and preceded by paratroopers dropping behind the major fortifications (and often suffering the most appalling casualties), 39 divisions, including French and Polish units, crossed the English Channel to land along 50 miles of the French coast. By end of D-day plus One, the fantastic naval effort had landed 176,000 troops and over 20,000 vehicles. Allied pilots flew 13,000 sorties and dropped over 10,000 tons of bombs on June 6 alone. (R. Asprey, *Semper Fidelis—the History of the Marines in World War II,* W. W. Norton & Co., New York, 1967.)

Everywhere the fighting was intense, often brutal. For example, when the Cherbourg Peninsula finally fell to the Americans on July 1, the U.S. VII Corps recorded 22,000 casualties including 2,800 killed while Rommel's forces had lost 39,000 soldiers in his determined defense of the peninsula.

Warfare on an even larger scale was simultaneously being fought on the Eastern Front, as witness the Soviet offensive against Field Marshal Busch's Army Group Center in the summer of 1944. There along a 350-mi. front Busch lost three armies in ten days—250,000 soldiers. In less than three weeks the Red armies drove 250 mi. through White Russia. In mid-July the Soviets attacked in the north and south, an all-out offensive continuing over 450 mi. to the Vistula to destroy over 500,000 German soldiers, over 2,700 tanks and self-propelled guns, 8,700 other guns, and 57,000 vehicles.

While the Russians were thus engaged, the Allied buildup continued in Normandy. On D plus 28 days the millionth Allied soldier was landed. Ten days later over 300,000 vehicles and a million tons of supplies were ashore. Within seven weeks 34 combat divisions were in France. With this buildup of force the Allies broke out of the Normandy beachheads to begin a sweep across western France and on into the heartland of Germany.

**5. Significant Developments.**—As World War I had furnished a host of lessons for the perspicacious military student, so did the multitudinous actions of World War II. Throughout the war in all theatres both quantity and quality of arms and equipment played an important, sometimes decisive, role. In the end quantity told—the immense Allied and particularly U.S. industrial production which accomplished delivery schedules in all fields formerly believed impossible of achievement. Tactically the most striking lesson was the need for coordination of arms at all levels. A classic example was the German *Blitzkrieg* which raised armour, used in mass and supported by tactical aircraft, self-propelled artillery, and mechanized infantry, to the arm of decision in suitable terrain. To open and support an offensive meant the control of air and sea, and where these were lacking, for example to the Americans on Guadalcanal or variously to the British and Germans in North Africa, the tactical commander was confined to a more or less static defense until viable supply lines were established. Where this did not happen, as with Rommel in North Africa, defeat was ultimately the result. In the case of the Germans in the U.S.S.R., where the enemy gained air superiority and where Soviet partisans constantly cut German supply lines, the local commanders were forced first to a defense made fatally static by Hitler's orders, and finally to rearguard actions which, lacking essential support, often resulted in tactical demolishment.

Allied air power influenced ground operations in two ways: an indirect, strategic effort designed to slow supply, cut enemy supply lines, and impede and ultimately halt enemy war production; a direct, tactical effort designed to gain and hold control of the air, and to support the local ground commander both by air strikes behind enemy lines and in close proximity to friendly front lines, and by visual reconnaissance and aerial photography. Close tactical air support played a secondary, but at times nonetheless important, role in the European theatre, perhaps the inevitable result of a virtually independent air force whose commanders were indissolubly married to the strategic air effort which, as in the case of heavy artillery in World War I, required a far greater number of machines and bomb tonnage to accomplish its mission than had been supposed—indeed, Douhet's hoped-for result of collapsing enemy will by civil bombings, not to mention the prediction of other airmen as to the disruptive and ultimately calamitous effect of industrial bombing on enemy production, fell far short of reality. Close air support was far more realistic in the Pacific theatre, particularly as offered by Marine fliers operating from both carrier and land bases and trained to support ground forces to the extent that they often bombed and strafed within 50 yd. of friendly front lines—but one should not forget that these tactical operations were designed in part to project the strategic air effort closer to the enemy home islands, the classic operations in this sense being Saipan-Tinian, Iwo Jima, and Okinawa. (*See* AIR POWER: *The Doctrine of Air Power: The Test in World War II.*)

The need for coordination of arms existed at the lowest tactical level. The "fire team" developed by the U.S. Marine Corps was matched by a variety of assault units in other services. Such was the variety of terrain and the quality of defense on all fronts that special units equipped for special tasks were employed. Infantry and armour remained the arms of decision, but commanders in all theatres increasingly organized task forces ranging in size from platoons to divisions, reinforced by tanks, artillery, rocket launchers, or other such support weapons dictated for a specific mission. Certain tailored combat teams became standardized as the war continued. The British commando units, composed of soldiers, sailors, and marines organized on a permanent basis, conducted raids throughout the war. In Burma the British commander, Brigadier Orde Wingate, developed special penetration groups of infantry which, supplied by air, operated with only mediocre success behind Japanese lines; a later American effort, Merrill's Marauders, met with more success, but the concept remains questionable even in the early 1970s. (*See* JUNGLE WARFARE.)

Both sides worked frantically to develop increased firepower. The potency of German armour was challenged first in Africa by the 2.36-in. rocket launcher, the "bazooka," and later by the 57-mm. and 75-mm. recoilless rifles. The VT (variable time) or proximity artillery fuse enabled a shell to be exploded automatically in electronic reaction to waves reflected from the target, a tremendous advance in both ground and antiaircraft fire. Rocket launchers capable of hurling thousands of explosive rockets were developed. Constant improvement was made in tactical air support, both in quantity and variety of armament, for example in the development of napalm, a flammable mixture that sticks to the target while burning.

Germany failed to maintain its original lead in arms and equipment, a failure resulting from a limited supply of raw materials, a fumbling and frightened bureaucracy, and finally from an industrial failure to produce in sufficient quantity such weapons as aircraft, tanks, artillery, and rockets—undoubtedly a failure attributable in large part to Hitler's desire for rapid and decisive victories that simply did not materialize. Although massive Allied bombing disrupted Germany's (and to a greater extent Japan's) industrial complex, its overall results stood far below those anticipated by strategic bombing proponents. The real failure was the enemy's inability to mass produce in order to repair enormous battlefield losses.

In a desperate attempt to regain weapon parity, Germany and its scientists developed the V-1 jet-propelled bomb, a random terror missile hurled against England. This weapon was replaced by the more formidable V-2 rocket, another random missile that despite intense local destruction failed in its intention of breaking British morale. The Japanese attempted to halt the American advance by the Kamikaze or suicide attack whereby a pilot dove his explosive-laden aircraft directly into American ships. Although this final effort caused severe fleet casualties, particularly at Okinawa, early warning, dispersion, and other evasive techniques reduced them to manageable if still costly proportions.

German scientists throughout the war attempted to develop the atom bomb, but were unsuccessful; the British-American effort succeeded only after the end of the European war. A U.S. B-29 bomber dropped the first atomic bomb on Hiroshima, Japan, on Aug. 6, 1945, the second a few days later on Nagasaki. Although these bombs were primitive objects, their annihilative power was only too evident, and Japan hastened to sue for peace.

Thus World War II ended—not with a whimper, but a blast. A blast and a question mark, for even the discovery of gunpowder did not represent a comparable turning point in warfare. With the advent of the atomic bomb, armies could no longer mass, landing forces were doomed, the historical basis of war itself was threatened—or so it seemed in 1945.

## X. THE NUCLEAR AGE

Despite the threat posed by Germany and Japan in World War II, relations between the U.S.S.R. and its Western allies were never warm. With the defeat of the Axis powers in 1945 this relationship quickly deteriorated into what became known as the Cold War (*q.v.*).

This state of affairs was characterized by two major Soviet political ambitions. The first, generally accomplished by 1950, consisted in establishing a protective insulation of Communist satellite border states stretching from the Baltic through the Balkans. The second, which did not have a similar success, consisted in fomenting the spread of Communism in certain war-torn countries and later in those countries which gained an independent status before their governmental machinery was sufficiently experienced to maintain it.

To this overall effort the West replied defensively by a series of political, economic, and military alliances. By 1950, despite Communist China's victory over the Nationalists, despite guerrilla wars being fought in such places as the Philippines and Greece, and despite a constant growth in the U.S.S.R.'s conventional military plant, U.S. armed forces, weak in numbers, were thinly spread in garrisons around the world. Some comfort derived from the fact that although the Soviet Union had developed an atom bomb, it stood a long way from nuclear parity with the U.S.—in other words, the U.S. atomic arsenal still spelled a considerable deterrent value. Unfortunately this conclusion applied only to Western Europe where the Soviets did not choose to make war. Instead, they chose Asia—an indirect strategy based on an ally's aggressive desires.

**1. War in Korea.**—Korea had been surrendered at the end of World War II by Japan and subsequently divided into two countries split by the 38th parallel. (For an account of the background and general conduct of the war, *see* KOREAN WAR.) A united Korea under Soviet aegis appealed to the Kremlin for a number of strategic reasons. It would act as a flanking buffer to China whose Communist leader, Mao Tse-tung, had shown an annoying independence of thought. It should have proved an easy acquisition: the United States was withdrawing occupation forces from South Korea and was paring down its strength in Japan. These moves, taken with public speeches by Gen. Douglas MacArthur, who commanded the American presence in the Far East, and by Pres. Harry S. Truman and Secretary of State Dean Acheson, seemed to indicate that Korea did not form an essential bastion to American strategy. Finally, an invasion would not require Soviet troops.

By June 1950, the North Korean Army had reached impressive strength, particularly when compared to that of South Korea, whose eight divisions had been equipped only cursorily by the U.S. On June 25, 1950, two North Korean armoured columns crossed the 38th parallel to invade South Korea. The United Nations, lacking a Soviet representative at the time, branded the aggression "a breach of the peace" and voted to intervene. From Tokyo, General MacArthur also recommended U.S. intervention. On July 1, U.S. ground troops, softened by years of easy occupation duty, began flying into South Korea where MacArthur wished to build a defensive perimeter north of Pusan. MacArthur's piecemeal commitment launched a series of delaying actions which forced the enemy to lose time in deployments and men in frontal attacks. In truth the enemy offensive was running out of steam. On July 19 MacArthur reported that the first phase of the campaign had ended and with it the North Korean chance for victory. The enemy continued to press toward his objective, however, not yielding the initiative until September.

MacArthur then pulled one of the most daring tactical moves in 20th-century warfare. Utilizing the amphibious capability perfected by the U.S. Marines in World War II, he ordered Gen. Oliver Smith to land the 1st Marine Division nearly 250 mi. north at Inch'on, a successful operation that almost immediately rewon the capital of Seoul. Simultaneously, Gen. Walton Walker's 8th Army attacked north from the Pusan perimeter. Within two weeks these actions completely reversed the tactical situation. UN troops were now probing north of the 38th parallel; the enemy front was not only dissolving but the North Korean Army verged on collapse. At a meeting between President Truman and MacArthur in mid-October 1950, "MacArthur assured Truman that the war was indeed in the final phase, that he anticipated an end to organized resistance by Thanksgiving and expected the 8th Army to celebrate Christmas in Japan." (S. B. Griffith, *The Chinese People's Liberation Army*, © 1967 by the Council on Foreign Relations, Inc. Used with permission of McGraw-Hill Book Company.)

MacArthur had reckoned without Chinese intervention. Shortly before mid-October, troops began filtering into North Korea. By the end of the month more than 200,000 Chinese soldiers, six armies and artillery units, were positioned to attack. The marches had been made at night in company and battalion size with the aid of North Korean guides and porters.

In many ways this was a primitive army. "The majority of the 'People's Volunteers' crossed the Yalu with 80 rounds of rifle ammunition and four or five 'potato masher' type grenades. In addition to his basic combat load, each soldier and officer carried a few extra clips for automatic rifles and 'burp' guns, loaded belts for machine guns, one or two mortar shells, or TNT for satchel charges. Each carried emergency rice, tea, and salt for five days, an 'iron ration' to be supplemented by food requisitioned from the natives. . . ." (Griffith, *op. cit.*) Communications as known to the West did not exist; below battalion level they consisted of signals by bugle calls, whistle, and shepherd horns.

Primitive, yes—but also an experienced army. Most of the senior officers had fought the Japanese either as members of Mao's or of Chiang's armies; many of the junior officers and noncommissioned officers had fought in the Civil War. "All were imbued with the tactical doctrine which the Communists had applied with such success against both enemies. This was based on mobility, deception, distraction, surprise, concentration of superior force at the vital point, a 'short attack,' and speedy disengagement." (Griffith, *op. cit.*)

The first clash occurred on Oct. 24 when the Chinese ambushed and destroyed a South Korean battalion maneuvering about 50 mi. from the Chinese border. In subsequent attacks against the parent regiment and the hastily committed U.S. 1st Cavalry Division, the Chinese units employed mortars before closing with Soviet "burp guns." This opening effort, what the Chinese called the First Phase Offensive, continued into November. A three weeks' lull followed as UN forces advanced to the north, then another Chinese offensive drove the UN forces some 70 mi. south of the 38th parallel. In late January 1951, the UN counterattacked and by the end of March reached the 38th parallel. In April and May the Chinese launched two massive attacks designed to push UN forces into the sea. Neither succeeded. In late May the UN again took the offensive. Within a month the Chinese armies were everywhere breaking. On June 23 the Russians proposed "cease-fire" talks. Henceforth the war became a static nightmare of elaborate patrols, raids, and battery and counter-battery fire.

In the fluid phase of the Korean War, the Chinese employed a variety of tactics that both deceived and surprised UN commanders. Their refusal to pursue the November 1950 offensive was completely misinterpreted by the U.S. high command, which believed that heavy casualties had forced the enemy to call quits.

Incredibly, MacArthur's intelligence people estimated 40,000–60,000 Chinese in Korea at this time; there were over 200,000, including 15 infantry divisions. What the U.S. high command held to be an offensive was in fact "primarily defensive: designed to slow the drive to the Yalu, to develop UN positions, to test UN capabilities, to measure UN command and leadership, and to try the mettle of UN forces." (Griffith, *op. cit.*)

From the beginning the Chinese claimed the night to fool the UN command regarding their actual strength, to protect themselves (along with excellent camouflage by day) from U.S. airpower, and finally to aid the attack. Chinese attacks, either by day or night, were intensely carried out in accordance with "the three fierce actions"—fierce fire, fierce assaults, and fierce pursuit: "first there came a series of probes by eight- to fifteen-men groups to feel out the defensive position, determine its outline, create confusion, and draw fire, particularly from automatic weapons. A brief lull succeeded these preliminaries. When the attack came in, 'superior numbers of troops' hit the front 'in coordination with strong enveloping tactics designed to fold the flanks of the defenders, 'to surround, isolate, and eventually destroy [them] piecemeal'. . . ." (Griffith, *op. cit.*)

Why did the Chinese fail?

The main answer lies in the weakness of their strengths. Primitive supply lines were a strength in that aerial interdiction could not impede seriously the forward flow of supply. But this supply was very light: the Chinese logistic requirement was based on 8–10 lb. of supply per day per front line soldier (as compared to 60 lb. for the American soldier). It was insufficient for cold weather warfare. In the winter of 1950–51 the Chinese 26th Army noted: "A shortage of transportation and escort personnel makes it impossible to accomplish the mission of supplying the troops. As a result, our soldiers frequently starve. . . ." (L. Montross, *U.S. Marine Operations in Korea 1950–53*, vol. 3, U.S. Government Printing Office, Washington, D.C., 1957.) During the winter campaigns, more than 90% of this army suffered frostbite. The Chinese 27th Army complained of 10,000 noncombat casualties alone out of a strength of four divisions. Despite the frequent ingenious repair of bombed bridges and railroads and the constant use of native porters, the supply was never sufficient to support a sustained offensive, nor were the primitive command communications between higher echelons sufficient to exploit local tactical successes. Even during the last two years, as Gen. Mark Clark pointed out, although the Chinese had repaired severe deficiencies such as a shortage of artillery and were "very strong" defensively, "offensively, they were not as strong. They couldn't maintain an attack for very long because of their difficulty with supply."

U.S. and UN tactics did not vary greatly from World War II. The decision not to use the atomic bomb, either in a strategic sense by attacking Peking or in a tactical sense by local attacks, was prompted by a political consideration reinforced by the tactical fact that the rugged terrain precluded profitable employment. Once the initial North Korean drive had been checked and a counteroffensive launched, UN mobility was hindered by poor roads, cumbersome supply "tails," guerrilla interference, and in some instances by tactical communication failures. Early Chinese attacks, particularly at night, proved unsettling, but commanders eventually discovered that these could be countered if tactical integrity was preserved.

UN fortunes visibly rose once Gen. Matthew Ridgway assumed command. Rolling with the punch until the Chinese effort slowed, he replied aggressively, at first with platoon-strength patrols, then with reinforced companies and battalions ordered "to find, fix and fight" the enemy. In late January 1951, he pushed two divisions forward to the line of the Han—"his tactics, careful and methodical, were designed to inflict maximum casualties with minimum loss. Infantry, air, armor, artillery, in almost perfectly coordinated actions, took a frightful toll. . . ." (Griffith, *op. cit.*) Marine tactics also impressed the enemy as this entry in the Chinese 26th Army records shows: "The coordination between the enemy infantry, tanks, artillery, and airplanes is surprisingly close. Besides using heavy weapons for the depth, the enemy carries with him automatic light firearms which, coordinated with rockets, launchers, and recoilless guns, are disposed at the front line. . . ." (Montross, *op. cit.*)

Although U.S. air power was prevented from bombing Chinese concentrations on the other side of the Yalu River, it is still doubtful if doing so would have radically changed the total effect. The difficult terrain, the Chinese habit of night marches and attacks, their relatively simple supply lines, their ability to circumvent bombed bridges and to repair railroads overnight—all softened the air campaign to the extent that Gen. Mark Clark later wrote: "The Air Force and the Navy carriers may have kept us from losing the war, but they were denied the opportunity of influencing the outcome decisively in our favor. . . . Our air power could not keep a steady stream of enemy supplies and reinforcements from reaching the battle line. Air could not isolate the front."

Another type of air power, however, proved invaluable: the helicopter, which had reached field forces in limited numbers shortly before the Korean War. Recognizing the tactical potential of this aircraft, the Marine Corps had conducted a series of tactical tests to see whether it could provide an answer to the tactical challenge posed by the atomic bomb. Primarily used for medical evacuation and resupply purposes in Korea, the "chopper" quickly won the unit commander's heart. One brigade commander found that in an active combat situation he could control units over 25 mi. apart. Other commanders learned that in a few hours a squadron of transport helicopters could move an infantry battalion over difficult terrain to influence decisively a tactical situation. On one occasion, when an infantry company was surrounded, six helicopters flew in ten tons of ammunition and evacuated casualties, thus enabling the troops to fight their way out.

The ground soldier and particularly the Marine were also aided by an elongated protective vest made from nylon pads and fiber glass. Weighing about nine pounds, this vest hindered or stopped penetration of pistol and machine-gun bullets and of most mortar or grenade fragments traveling less than 1,100 ft. per sec. Postwar studies concluded that these vests either eliminated from 60 to 70% of chest and abdominal wounds or reduced the severity of such wounds from 25 to 30%. Once the heavy and somewhat awkward vests had proved themselves, the effect on troop morale was extremely beneficial.

**2. Atomic versus Nonatomic War.**—The tactical pattern of the Korean War, which ended in truce followed by uneasy armistice, seemingly satisfied no one. In Asia and elsewhere the U.S.S.R. and China already had fomented guerrilla warfare—what the Chinese term "wars of national liberation"—and would continue to do so. (*See* GUERRILLA WARFARE; JUNGLE WARFARE.) Meanwhile, however, both the U.S.S.R. and the West were making impressive technological strides in what Herman Kahn has called "the Model T era" of atomic warfare. To many Western strategists, the development of the hydrogen bomb with its incredible kill potential spelled the end of conventional ground warfare. Despite the example of Korea, the next war, they reasoned, would be fought by the thermonuclear giants, the U.S. and the U.S.S.R. Such a holocaust could only be avoided by a strategy of nuclear deterrence. The primary delivery means for such weapons was the heavy bomber, and to retain its superiority in the atomic field the U.S. gave defense priority to building a massive bomber command, the Strategic Air Command or SAC. In the ensuing atomic era—Kahn calls this "the Model A era"—SAC has yielded in delivery importance to guided atomic missiles fired either from permanent silo-sites or from Polaris-type submarines.

The post-Korean conventional military reply to the atomic age varied with individual services. The keynote was dispersal of forces, which demanded increased mobility. In 1957 the U.S. Army, after considerable mental agony, adopted the pentomic division—partly a political decision in order to protect Army interests in nuclear weapon employment—a radical reorganization which replaced the three infantry regiments of the triangular division with five battle groups, each comprising about 1,400 officers and men. With splendid if somewhat questionable disregard of the kill potential of enemy nuclear weapons, the Marine Corps retained the heavy triangular division but concentrated on the "third dimension" of land warfare—troop delivery beyond the beachhead by means of the helicopter. The flexibility of the Navy-Marine "task force" concept, developed in World War II and employed in Korea, was stressed more than ever with emphasis on dispersal of ships en route to the target, limited concentration of shipping during landing, and troop dispersion in the target area. Command posts from corps to regimental and even battalion level were duplicated, and troops were intensively trained to protect themselves against atomic blast and radiation effects. Training exercises in all services were conducted in a tactical atomic bomb environment.

Meanwhile, however, the growth of nuclear parity between the U.S. and the U.S.S.R., the possibility of other nations producing atomic bombs, the worldwide abhorrence of the employment of such weapons, and the increasing reliance of the Communist nations on a far less technically sophisticated type of war—all seemed to be diminishing the prospect of an atomic war. This situation did not mean a return to conventional warfare as defined by the West. In 1959 dissident Communist guerrillas, possibly acting on instructions from the Communist government of North Vietnam, challenged the government of South Vietnam, an insurgency made the more successful because U.S. Army military advisers had trained the South Vietnamese Army in conventional tactics in order to oppose a Korean-like invasion from the north.

The growing nuclear stalemate and the Vietnam and other insurgencies caused the West and particularly the U.S. to begin broadening its primary policy of nuclear deterrence against aggression. Commencing with Pres. John F. Kennedy's administration, greater emphasis was placed on conventional armed forces with further emphasis on all-purpose flexibility including counterinsurgency forces. In 1961 the U.S. Army abandoned the pentomic division, which had proved too cumbersome and inflexible for use in "brushfire" wars involving limited forces and conventional weapons and yet lacked sufficient numbers and firepower to hold its own in a more conventional situation. It chose instead an "all-purpose" divisional base of three brigade headquarters consisting of varying numbers and types of combat battalions. This reorganization provided a division of about 16,000 troops whose organization and armament could be tailored to a specific mission.

To provide greater response capability, the Strategic Army Corps (STRAC), consisting of several standby, combat-ready units, was organized for rapid deployment and subsequent support by the Tactical Air Command (TAC) of the U.S. Air Force. This long-overdue reform resulted in a mobile striking force emulating the "task force" concept long practised by the U.S. Navy and Marine Corps. The latter's capabilities rested in two operational commands, the Fleet Marine Force, Atlantic, and the Fleet Marine Force, Pacific, which controlled three ground divisions and three air wings tactically organized, armed, and equipped for either nuclear or nonnuclear war. During this period the British Army also arranged to transport by air a substantial number of the conventional units stationed in the United Kingdom to any part of the world at short notice. These units comprised the Airborne Strategic Reserve.

**3. The War in Vietnam.**—The U.S. armed forces were relatively well organized for either a nuclear or a nonnuclear war when committed in strength to Vietnam commencing in 1965. Unfortunately, they were neither well organized, properly equipped, nor adequately trained to cope with insurgency warfare.

The background of the Vietnam war and of other insurgency-type wars as well as many of their tactical aspects, both friendly and enemy, are discussed elsewhere. (*See* VIETNAM; GUERRILLA WARFARE; JUNGLE WARFARE; INSURGENCY.) After the U.S. commitment, reciprocal escalation brought about four distinct wars: (1) the guerrilla or counter-insurgency war involving Viet Cong (VC) guerrillas organized into paramilitary and even regular military units; (2) the quasi-conventional ground war in the Central Highlands and south of the Demilitarized Zone (DMZ), which was being fought against VC units as well as against regular North Vietnamese Army units; (3) the naval war—"out-country" and "in-country" efforts, the latter called "riverine warfare" and involving coastal and inland waterway patrols to intercept supplies intended for the VC; (4) the air war—"out-country" war consisting of the aerial bombardment of selected military targets in North Vietnam, the "in-country" war of conventional heavy bombing and tactical air support. Each bred certain political, economic, and psychological problems which, taken together, constituted what was named the "other war": gaining and holding the support of an indigenous population who either willingly or under duress were helping the enemy. This goal has proved particularly elusive and attainment of it has been hindered by a divergence of opinion as to whether priority should be given to the civil or military effort. Most participants and interested observers agreed, however, that the civil problem was inextricably wedded to the military problem, and that the marriage had bred certain tactical problems answered only in part by limited departures from conventional warfare tactics.

U.S. strategy was dictated by Washington and implemented by General Westmoreland and his successor, Gen. Creighton Abrams. In view of the tendency of the top field commanders to criticize the restrictions imposed by Washington in prosecuting the war, it should be noted that this strategy was based in part, from the beginning of the U.S. involvement in the 1950s, on reports and recommendations made by ranking officers and civilians serving in Vietnam. Primarily it was an attrition strategy—a dependence on superior U.S. military manpower, firepower, and mobility to wear down and finally force the enemy from the war. In other words, it was a conventional strategy designed to gain a military decision. This strategy produced a variety of ground actions: patrols ranging from squad size to gigantic "sweeps" undertaken by divisions and even corps; conventional battles between companies, battalions, and regiments supported by artillery and in the case of the Americans, armour, naval gunfire, and tactical and strategic aircraft; defensive actions in both cities and country against VC raids and North Vietnamese Army "siege" operations. In addition, this strategy embraced extensive fleet shelling and massive strategic bombing that long ago surpassed the total Allied tonnage dropped in World War II, and an equally massive tactical air effort that in 1968 alone included 200,000 attack sorties dropping almost 1,000,000 tons of bombs in direct support of combat operations.

The basic U.S. tactic in fighting the ground war was that of "search"—originally to clear an area of VC and hold it secure and, when this proved impossible, to destroy that part of an area believed to be harbouring the enemy, or more simply: find the enemy, fix him, kill him. This was the conventional goal of conventionally organized units ranging from squad to division strength and supported in most cases by artillery (and in the case of the Marines by naval gunfire), by an awesome host of tactical aircraft, and by hordes of helicopters of varying size and function.

The prominence of the helicopter became an outstanding tactical feature of this ground war. The Marine Corps, a pioneer in helicopter battle tactics, employed helicopter squadrons integral to its air wings, an organizational concept that possesses maintenance and administrative advantages but one hindering ground reaction time to suitable enemy targets, often of a fleeting nature. The U.S. Army, which employed helicopter companies organic to the ground division, built two divisions around this machine. These "airmobile" divisions consist of approximately 16,000 troops equipped with 434 aircraft, mostly helicopters, and 1,600 land vehicles (compared to a normal Army division's 100 organic aircraft and over 3,000 ground vehicles). The dramatic increase in mobility and reaction time achieved by these divisions caused the secretary of defense, Robert S. McNamara, to describe the airmobile concept as "the beginning of a new era in land warfare." (F. Harvey, *Air War—Vietnam*, Bantam Books, Inc., New York, 1967.)

This optimistic judgment may prove premature even though the advantage in either a tactical or support role was enormous (for example, in World War II the U.S. Army claimed a "save" ratio of 71 out of 100 men wounded; in Vietnam the ratio is said to be 82 out of 100, an increase largely due to helicopter evacuation techniques. The Marine Corps pointed out that in Vietnam no wounded man "is more than 30 minutes . . . from a fully staffed and equipped hospital"). Tactically, however, limitations existed.

The mass employment of helicopters was not applicable to open areas defended by strong enemy forces, for example the plains of Western Europe. Further, an experienced if not particularly shrill voice speaking from Malayan and Vietnam service, Sir Robert Thompson, has pointed out that the helicopter, when misused, only aggravated the tactical impatience displayed by Americans in a situation demanding extreme patience.

While the increase in mobility cannot be contested, the division structure nonetheless held disadvantages. Not only had armour and armoured personnel carriers been sacrificed but all firepower heavier than the 105-mm. howitzer had vanished. And yet the logistic support requirement was enormous—up to 500 tons daily for a division in combat—and could be met by air transport delivery only at virtually prohibitive cost. In the winter of 1966–67 General Westmoreland asked for additional armour, a request repeated by General Abrams in mid-1968, presumably to help keep open essential road lines of communication to the Central Highlands where the original airmobile division was operating. Another disadvantage was the relatively high helicopter casualty rate from enemy fire despite overhead protection from other elaborately armed helicopters and tactical aircraft; this loss promised to increase once the enemy was equipped with shoulder-fired, heat-seeking missiles. Finally, in numerous instances the use of helicopters, particularly in small unit guerrilla situations, tended to forfeit tactical surprise although on occasion it could be preserved by the use of decoy techniques and low-level approaches. Noise limitation, however, combined with excellent enemy intelligence caused a veteran Marine officer to claim that "less than two percent of all U.S. offensive operations produce any contact whatsoever with the Viet-Cong." (W. Corson, *The Betrayal*, W. W. Norton & Co., Inc., New York, 1968.)

The helicopter was only one of a vast number of technological aids used by the U.S. in this war. Other innovations included rapid-firing rifles such as the M-14 and the one-time controversial M-16; lighter ammunition; more effective artillery shells such as the 105-mm. "Beehive," which upon detonation releases 8,000 steel flechettes; new types of machine guns, rockets, and grenade launchers; nauseous gases; improved tropical clothing, boots, and ancillary equipment; and better field rations. Combat troops also employed such sophisticated aids as electronic sensory devices known as "man sniffers," infrared sighting equipment, and short-range ground radars.

The air war involved a wide variety of aircraft including those devoted to defoliation (in 1967 "more than 4,000,000 gallons of herbicide and defoliation chemicals" were dropped in South Vietnam [Corson, *op. cit.*]) and to surveillance with the latest infrared photographic equipment. The riverine war in the Mekong Delta introduced a host of specially adapted craft ranging from aluminum-hulled patrol gunboats to jet-propelled river patrol boats and "unsinkable styrofoam and fiberglass swimmer support boats, Swift Boats, patrol air cushion vehicles (capable of speeds in excess of 65 knots, combat loaded, over land or water), and a bewildering list of modified amphibious craft, including monitors and armored troop carriers, sampans and junks." (U.S. Navy [History Division], *Riverine Warfare*, Washington, D.C., 1967.)

All of this equipment taken with, at one time, more than 500,000 U.S. troops on the scene plus tens of thousands more in direct support constituted an impressive military investment. Could it be justified? Some observers believed that it could have been had the VC been summarily defeated in a short time. (The student of insurgency warfare will instantly point out that this was impossible.) Not only had the VC not been defeated, some highly qualified critics point out, but by enlarging the war this massive effort had alienated further a significant portion of the Vietnamese rural and ethnic population, groups whose original partial alienation from (or lack of identification with) the Saigon government made them particularly suitable targets for persuasive Communist propaganda reinforced by various types of selected coercion. Further, the U.S. military effort, particularly aerial bombing, adversely affected a substantial portion of world opinion.

Some critics pointed out that the cart had been put before the horse, that U.S. strategy should have been politically and not militarily oriented—that the military effort should have confined itself to holding operations while emphasis went to strengthening the indigenous governmental structure, particularly the rural police forces and then the armed forces. Instead, the priority military effort had helped enlarge the scope of conflict, which in turn created new internal problems without solving the old ones. One oft-quoted example was the extensive defoliation program which, together with displaced labour forces, was said to have created a rice shortage in a country that once produced a healthy surplus. Search-and-destroy tactics, particularly in the earlier stages, brought a storm of criticism predicated on the misuse of judgment in attacking villages, including the misuse of air strikes and other supporting fires, all of which continued to swell already swollen casualty and refugee lists. One disillusioned Marine officer, Lieut. Col. William Corson, charged that "search-and-destroy tactics against VC-controlled areas have degenerated into savagery. The terrorism of the enemy has been equally matched by our own." (Corson, *op. cit.*) The My Lai incident of 1968, disclosed in 1969, gave credence to his charge. Some experts argued that conventional military weapons possessed no validity or effectiveness once an insurgency was well organized and under way. They could still kill, of course, but the problem was one of identification of an enemy and reversing the political orientation of a peasantry dominated by terror, if not conviction, to pro-Western attitudes. When weapons kill the innocent, they contribute positively to an insurgent cause, and when weapons are used in such abundance as in Vietnam, they will kill some of the innocent. Sixteen-inch naval shells, B-52 bombs, the weapons of an infantry battalion—if they hit a specific target accurately, cannot discriminate what political and ideological motivations may be there.

Such arguments are anathema to the proponents of the Vietnam effort who point out that nothing could equal the terrorism of the Viet Cong and the North Vietnamese, that aside from normal terrorist tactics—the killing, torture, kidnapping, and otherwise intimidating of the civil and particularly rural population—as one observer put it, "the enemy offensive during TET last February and in May [1968] resulted in 13,000 civilians killed, 27,000 wounded, 170,000 homes destroyed or damaged; and created 1,000,000 refugees with property damage estimated at $173,500,000." This aside, the prevailing military argument was that search-and-destroy was essentially a spoiling tactic. So long as the enemy enjoyed sanctuaries to the north and west, this tactic was necessary to bring on the quasi-conventional battles that, it was claimed, had hurt the North Vietnamese Army far more than the U.S. forces in addition to yielding large quantities of valuable intelligence and huge caches of food, weapons, ammunition, and medical supplies. Indeed, prominent official spokesmen in 1970, as on earlier occasions, expressed considerable optimism as to the war's ultimate outcome—statements unfortunately tarnished by unwarranted optimism so often expressed in past years. Ranking officers also pointed out that great care was taken in the selection of targets for air and artillery strikes, and that this and greatly improved coordination with South Vietnamese military and civil officials as well as better intelligence methods—for instance, computerized processing and the setting up of District Operational Intelligence Centers—had lowered the error ratio. Finally, it was argued, this was not the only tactic employed in waging what anyone must admit was a complex war of several dimensions.

A particularly successful combat tactic was the small, long-range patrol employed by both the Army and Marines. Consisting of a few highly trained men equipped to call in and adjust friendly air, artillery, or naval gunfire, a patrol slips into enemy territory either on foot or by helicopter. Operating normally for a five-day period, a patrol may confine itself to gathering information that the tactical commander may exploit by flying in additional forces; the patrol may also be disruptive, in which case it seeks out enemy supply trails and establishes appropriate ambushes. A "kill" patrol of the 101st Airborne Division carried weapons ranging from lightweight M-16 automatic rifles and M-60 machine guns to grenade launchers, hand grenades, and sharp-bladed Bowie knives. When possible, such patrols operated in the dark. Each soldier carried a can or two of meat rations and a five-day supply of rice—2½ lb. If a fire fight developed unfavourably, a patrol sought to extricate itself by helicopter call-in; one enterprising Marine lieutenant, when greatly outnumbered, ordered his people to don gas masks, then saturated the area with tear gas, which held the enemy until the helicopters arrived. This same officer, who led his patrol over a period of several months, obtained a final kill ratio of 226 confirmed VC dead to the loss of a few wounded Marines, a figure he believed would have been five times greater had an assault company, controlling its own helicopter transport, been instantly available to exploit numerous chances for really punishing the enemy. The reluctance of senior commanders, from the Pentagon to battalion level, to turn this war over to small unit commanders was a major tactical deficiency which showed few signs of improvement into 1970.

For some time the Marine Corps maintained a Kit Carson Scout Program that utilized former Viet Cong and North Vietnamese soldiers who had defected under the Chieu Hoi (Open Arms) Amnesty Program. After training, these people were normally assigned in pairs to an infantry battalion involved in seeking out and disclosing VC or NVA (North Vietnamese Army), detecting ambush sites and booby traps. The former enemy soldiers also acted as interpreters when needed. Such scouts were usually employed where they were familiar with the terrain, the people, and their former units. This program proved so successful that the Army also adopted it—by late 1968 nearly 1,000 such scouts were in U.S. service. The war also called into prominence such special tactical units as Army Special Forces which for years had operated with indigenous units both regular and irregular, sometimes far out in enemy territory; the Navy's sea-air-land or SEAL teams, which had extended the offensive aspect of river patrol operations inland; and the Navy-Army Mobile Riverine Force, an amphibious strike force of two army battalions designed to penetrate Viet Cong fortified areas in the Mekong Delta.

Small or large unit tactics were only one answer to the multifaceted challenge of the Vietnam war, and they provided no answer to its civil aspect. The function of the military in this respect was (and still is) a subject of contention between qualified experts, between civil and military officials, and between the U.S. Army and the Marine Corps, the latter situation being faintly reminiscent of 19th-century warfare when commanders, separated and out of touch, waged the type of campaign each deemed best. The Army held for the occupation of "liberated" areas by South Vietnamese Army units working in conjunction with the government's Revolutionary Development Program (the seventh such effort in as many years to win "the hearts and minds" of the people), a hopelessly inadequate solution in that these units had furnished neither adequate military security nor economic sustenance to the hamlets.

The Marines approached the problem differently. An attempt was made to carry out Revolutionary Development aims through a joint U.S.-South Vietnamese council composed of the senior military and civil officials of both governments, but the Marines also attacked the basic problem of providing local security to the hamlets. Taking a page from their campaigns in Nicaragua and Haiti during the "banana wars" of the 1920s, they evolved Combined Action Platoons—a small group of Marines working with South Vietnamese militia forces to provide village-hamlet security while helping civilians to a way of life free from the demands and brutality of the Viet Cong (but unfortunately not necessarily from either exorbitant taxes exacted by absentee landlords or graft collected by corrupt South Vietnamese Army and civil officials). The core of each CAP was a 13-man rifle squad that, augmented by a Navy medical corpsman, worked with a 35-man Popular Forces (militia) platoon—altogether 50 military personnel supported by Marine arms including air, artillery, and naval gunfire when necessary. The multi-mission of these platoons was to defeat VC attacks, deny the area to the VC for support, that is recruitment, food, or intelligence, gain essential intelligence concerning the enemy, and help the villagers help themselves—a difficult mission rarely accomplished in whole.

By mid-1968 the CAP program included nearly 2,000 Americans and nearly 2,700 Vietnamese militia in 100 different hamlets. The fact that this was a picayune effort, the result of priority combat requirements, was a major drawback. Another was the lukewarm cooperation of U.S. civilian aid agencies and the South Vietnamese Army including some of its U.S. Army advisers. Still another was the inability of a few Marines, linguistically inept, to overcome the fear of and in some cases the sympathy for the Viet Cong felt by large numbers of the peasantry.

Despite these disadvantages some observers believed that the CAP program, if properly expanded and supported, could have constituted a major breakthrough in fighting the "other war"—a war probably more important in the long run to national goals than the one waged by guns alone. The withdrawal of the Marines in 1970 saw the end of this particular program.

Bibliography.—K. von Clausewitz, *Vom Krieg,* the first three volumes of his *Hinterlassene Werke,* 10 vol. (1832–37; *On War,* Eng. trans in the Modern Library, 1943); E. M. Earle (ed.), *Makers of Modern Strategy* (1943), especially ch. 4, "Jomini" by C. Brinton, G. Craig, and F. Gilbert, ch. 5, "Clausewitz" by H. Rothfels, ch. 2, "Vauban: the Impact of Science on War" by H. Guerlac, ch. 3, "Frederick the Great, Guibert, Bülow: From Dynastic to National War" by R. Palmer, ch. 8, "Moltke and Schlieffen" by H. Holborn; C. Falls, *The Art of War* (1961), *A Hundred Years of War* (1953); R. A. Preston, S. F. Wise, and H. O. Werner, *Men in Arms* (1962); K. Toman, *A Book of Military Uniforms and Weapons* (1964); R. Bowood, *Soldiers Soldiers* (1965); J. F. C. Fuller, *A Military History of the Western World,* 3 vol. (1954–56), *The Conduct of War* (1961); A. Manucy, *Artillery Through the Ages* (1949); P. H. Stevens, *Artillery Through the Ages* (1965); P. Kendall, *The Story of Land Warfare* (1957); L. Montross, *War Through the Ages* (1946), *U.S. Marine Operations in Korea 1950–53,* 4 vol. (1957); Sun Tzu, *The Art of War,* Eng. trans. by Samuel B. Griffith (1963); R. Hargreaves, *Beyond the Rubicon* (1966); C. Oman, *A History of the Art of War in the Middle Ages,* 2 vol. (1923), *A History of the Peninsular War,* 6 vol. (1902); B. Lacroix, *Military and Religious Life in the Middle Ages and the Renaissance* (1874); E. Perroy, *The Hundred Years War* (1959); H. L. Blackmore, *Guns and Rifles of the World* (1965); C. Ardant du Picq, *Battle Studies,* Eng. trans. by J. N. Greely and R. C. Cotton (1946); W. S. Churchill, *Marlborough,* 2 vol. (1947); Frederick the Great, *Instructions for His Generals,* Eng. trans. by T. R. Phillips (1943); J. H. Preston, *A Short History of the American Revolution* (1933); C. Ward, *The War of the Revolution,* 2 vol. (1952); J. Laffin, *Links of Leadership* (1966); R. B. Asprey, "The Peninsular War," *Army Quarterly* (April 1959), *The First Battle of the Marne* (1962), *At Belleau Wood* (1965); "Hitler and Dunkirk," *Army Quarterly* (April 1952), *Semper Fidelis: the History of the Marines in World War II* (1967); J. Fortescue, *Wellington* (1925); H. Jomini, *Summary of the Art of War,* ed. by J. D. Hittle (1947); M. Howard (ed.), *The Theory and Practice of War* (1965), especially ch. 1, "Jomini and the Classical Tradition in Military Thought" by M. Howard; J. Coggins, *Arms and Equipment of the Civil War* (1962); F. Pratt, *A Short History of the Civil War* (1935); M. F. Steele, *American Campaigns,* 2 vol. (1931); D. Reitz, *Commando* (1929); H. Baldwin, *World War I* (1962); A. A. Vandegrift and R. B. Asprey, *Once a Marine* (1964); P. Young, *World War 1939–45* (1966); S. B. Griffith, *The Battle for Guadalcanal* (1965), *The Chinese People's Liberation Army* (1967); M. B. Ridgway, *The Korean War* (1967); R. D. Heinl, *Victory at High Tide* (1968); F. Harvey, *Air War—Vietnam* (1967); J. Weller, "The U.S. Army in Vietnam," *Army Quarterly* (Oct. 1967).

(R. B. As.)

**TADZHIK** (Tajik), the original Iranian population of Afghanistan and Turkistan. Tadzhik constitute a majority of the population of Soviet Tajikistan (*see* Tadzhik Soviet Socialist Republic); in the 1960s they numbered about 1,400,000 in the U.S.S.R., with more than 300,000 in Uzbekistan. They comprised about one-third of the population of Afghanistan, where their communities are numerous in the regions of Kabul and Herat, in Badakhshan, and in the western mountains.

Tadzhik were the heirs and transmitters of the central Asian sedentary culture that diffused in prehistoric times from the Iranian plateau into an area extending roughly from the Caspian Sea to the borders of China. Here were built villages of flat-roofed mud or stone houses along streams and rivers that irrigated fields of wheat, barley, and millet, and gardens famous for melons and a variety of fruits. Crafts were highly developed, and towns along the caravan routes linking Persia, China, and India were centres of trade.

Turks, and later Mongols, flowed westward into the area, and Pushtu speakers (Afghans) gradually pushed northward. As these nomadic peoples settled, they adopted Iranian culture, but in Turkistan many of the Iranians adopted Turkic speech.

The name Tadzhik refers to the traditionally settled Caucasoid people who speak a form of Persian called Tadzhik in the Soviet Union and *Farsi* or Persian in Afghanistan. In the high Pamirs a few thousand Mountain Tadzhik or Galcha speak the eastern Iranian languages, Yagnobi and Pamir.

*See* also AFGHANISTAN: *The People.*

BIBLIOGRAPHY.—D. N. Wilber *et al.*, *Afghanistan: Its People, Its Society, Its Culture* (1962); V. S. Rastorgueva, *A Short Sketch of Tajik Grammar* (1963); E. E. Bacon, *Central Asians Under Russian Rule* (1966). (EL. B.)

**TADZHIK SOVIET SOCIALIST REPUBLIC** (TADZHIKSKAYA SOVETSKAYA SOTSIALISTICHESKAYA RESPUBLIKA; TADZHIKISTAN, or TAJIKISTAN), a republic of the U.S.S.R. which achieved the status of a federal union republic on Dec. 5, 1929. Situated in the southeast of Soviet central Asia, the republic is bordered on the south by Afghanistan and on the east by the People's Republic of China. Area 55,251 sq.mi. (143,100 sq.km.). The capital is Dushanbe, which, from Dec. 1, 1929, to Nov. 11, 1961, was called Stalinabad.

**Physical Geography.**—In general the Tadzhik S.S.R. is high mountain terrain. Its whole eastern part covers the high-level valleys or *pamirs*. The country is traversed by many mountain ranges generally extending east-west, and including the Zeravshanski and Gissarski ranges in the west, and the Peter I (Petra Pervogo), Trans-Alai (Zaalaiski) and North and South Alichurski ranges in the Pamirs (*q.v.*). The north-south Sarykolski range forms the eastern frontier of the republic. Communism peak (formerly Pik Stalina; 24,590 ft. [7,495 m.]) and Lenin peak (Pik Lenina; 23,405 ft.) in the north of the Pamirs, and Karl Marx peak (22,067 ft.) in the south are the highest mountains in the Soviet Union.

South of Mt. Communism lies the 50-mi. Lednik Fedchenko, the longest continental ice stream in the world. With the exception of the Tadzhik section of the Syr-Darya (Jaxartes) in the Fergana valley; of the Zeravshan river, which loses itself in the Uzbek desert near Bukhara; and of the Markansu river, which flows into Sinkiang, all the glacier-fed streams are right-bank tributaries of the Amu-Darya (Amu-Dar'ya [*q.v.*]; or Oxus). The Amu-Darya rises in the Afghan Hindu Kush as the Vakhan-Darya and, as the Pyandzh (from Persian *panj*, meaning five; *i.e.*, the five streams which it collects on its way), it forms most of the frontier between Afghanistan and the Tadzhik S.S.R. It then receives the Vakhsh river, which rises in the Kirgiz S.S.R. and is called first Kyzyl-Su ("red water" in Uzbek), and lower down Surkh Ab ("red water" in Persian).

There are many lakes in the Pamirs formed either by glaciers or as a result of avalanches (produced by earthquakes) which dammed existing streams. The largest glacier-formed lake is Kara-Kul, 141 sq.mi. (364 sq.km.) and 780 ft. (238 m.) deep. Among lakes of such tectonic origin the largest and most recent is Sarezkoye Ozero, 38 mi. (61 km.) long and 1,657 ft. deep, formed in 1911.

The country has three types of climate. In the lowlands it is hot and dry, with a yearly rainfall averaging 10 in. and temperatures varying between 31° C. (88° F.) in July and 3° C. (38° F.) in January. In the foothills there is more rainfall and it is cooler. In the high mountains above 10,000 ft. there is only 3 in. of yearly precipitation and the yearly average temperature is below freezing point.

The northwestern lower slopes are well covered with forest. Many varieties of vegetation are represented, from saxaul scrub and jungle grass, through deciduous and coniferous forest to alpine pasture. Animal life is also varied. In the southern lowlands tigers, deer and many kinds of water birds are found. In the higher plateaus there are antelopes and huge lizards up to 4½ ft. long, and in the Pamirs there are bears and mouflons.

**History.**—The Tadzhik (*q.v.*) peoples are of Persian-speaking Iranian stock. They were included in the empires of Persia and of Alexander the Great of Macedonia. In the 8th century the Arabs crossed the Amu-Darya, conquered Sogdiana (*q.v.*; Transoxiana) which was inhabited by Tadzhiks, and called it Mavera un nahr ("land beyond the river"). Two centuries later the first Turkic invaders (from the northeast) seized Mavera un nahr, and in time, as both conquered and conquerors were Muslim, many Tadzhiks, especially those in the valleys of Syr-Darya and Amu-Darya, became turkicized.

Until mid-18th century the Tadzhiks were part of the amirate of Bukhara (*q.v.*), but then the Afghans conquered lands south and southwest of the Amu-Darya with their Tadzhik population, including the city of Balkh (*q.v.*), an ancient cultural Tadzhik centre. Another partition of the Tadzhik territory took place in 1895 when an Anglo-Russian commission fixed the northern frontier of Afghanistan on the Pyandzh river and separated the Russian and Indian empires by an Afghan corridor on the Vakhan-Darya extending to the Chinese frontier.

After the Russian Revolution of 1917 a considerable part of the Tadzhik people was included in the Turkistan Autonomous Soviet Socialist Republic established in April 1918. On Aug. 23, 1920, the revolution was extended to the khanate of Bukhara, which embraced most of the territory occupied by the modern Tadzhik S.S.R. In Oct. 1920 the Bukharan People's Soviet Republic was declared in being, and early in 1921 the Soviet army captured Dushanbe and Kulyab. From 1922 to the summer of 1923 Tadzhikistan was the scene of the Basmachi revolt, and rebel bands under Ibrahim Bek operated in Eastern Bukhara until 1926. In 1924 the Tadzhik A.S.S.R. was created as part of the Uzbek S.S.R.; in Jan. 1925 a Special Pamirs *oblast* was created out of the Kara-Kirgiz and Tadzhik parts of the Pamirs; and in Dec. 1925 this *oblast* was renamed the Gorno-Badakhshan Autonomous *oblast*. Tadzhikistan was thus composed of the following former administrative units: Eastern Bukhara, 7 volosts (rural districts) of the Samarkand *uyezd* (county), the 5 southern volosts of the Khodzhent (later Leninabad) *uyezd*, and 6 volosts of the Pamirs region. On Dec. 5, 1929, the status of the republic was raised to that of Soviet Socialist Republic.

Collectivization of agriculture was carried out in 1928 and 1929 in the face of considerable opposition. There were later periodical purges of the council of ministers and the party apparatus, including one in 1961.

**Population and Administration.**—According to the 1959 census the population was 1,979,897, including 1,051,164 Tadzhiks (53.1%), 454,433 Uzbeks (23%), 262,610 Russians (13.3%), 56,893 Tatars (2.9%), 26,921 Ukrainians (1.4%), 25,635 Kirgiz (1.3%), and 12,551 Kazakhs (0.6%). The density of population was 13.8 per sq.km. (about 36 per sq.mi.). The most thickly populated areas are the Leninabad district in the north of the republic and the Gissar and Vakhsh valleys. One-third of the population are town dwellers living in 14 towns and 31 "settlements of town type." The main towns are Dushanbe, Leninabad (*qq.v.*), Ura-Tyube, Kulyab and Kurgan-Tyube.

In the absence of any official statistics it can be assumed that all the inhabitants of the republic other than Russians and Ukrainians are actual or nominal adherents to the Muslim religion.

The government of the Tadzhik S.S.R. is the standard one for union republics. Control over every form of government, economic, social and cultural activity is exercised by the communist party. After the administrative reorganization carried out in 1962 the republic consisted of the Gorno-Badakhshan Autonomous *oblast* (*q.v.*) and a number of *raions* under direct republican administration. Leninabad *oblast* was abolished.

*Education and Culture.*—The culture of the Tadzhiks, who constitute a little over half of the population, is Iranian, their language closely resembling the Persian spoken in Iran and Afghanistan, although it has been written exclusively in Cyrillic (Russian) characters since 1940. About 27% of the population is made up of various Turkic elements, mainly Uzbek, and these, with the exception of a few small tribes in the south, stubbornly resist Iranization.

Several newspapers are published in the Uzbek language which is taught to Uzbeks attending school. During the Soviet period the Tadzhiks have laid claim to some of the principal Persian poets such as Rudaki and Omar Khayyam. Sa'di, Hafiz and Jami are described as "organically entering" the history of Tadzhik literature.

In the 1960s nearly 350,000 pupils were in school and 16,000 in kindergarten. Schools for young industrial and agricultural workers and "middle" special training establishments enrolled about 16,000 students, and more than 18,000 were in the seven higher educational establishments (including the Tadzhik State university, established 1948). A branch of the U.S.S.R. Academy of Sciences established in Dushanbe in 1941 became an independent academy in 1951. In Dushanbe there are radio and television transmitters broadcasting in Tadzhik, Russian and Uzbek languages.

**The Economy.**—The economy of Tadzhikistan is mainly concerned with the growing and processing of cotton. Industry is principally light and apart from cotton ginning and textile weaving it is connected chiefly with food processing. In agriculture the main crop is cotton, but fruit is grown extensively as well as food grains and technical crops. There is a considerable cattle-breeding industry.

Tadzhikistan has about 350 kolkhozes (collective farms) and 40 sovkhozes (state farms). About half of the total sown area is under irrigation. The main canals are the Vakhsh, the Great Gissar, the Great Fergana, and the Northern Fergana. A large area is under cotton, and the yields per acre are among the world's highest.

On the unirrigated lands, principally on the northern slopes of the Turkistan range and in the southeast of the republic, food grains (wheat, barley and millet) are grown and oil grains (mainly flax) are cultivated in the southeast. Stock breeding includes sheep, horned cattle, pigs, karakul sheep, angora goats, Lokai horses and yaks (in the eastern Pamir).

There are cotton-ginning factories in all the cotton-producing valleys, the principal ones being in Dushanbe, Regar and Kurgan-Tyube. Most of the textile weaving is carried on in the Dushanbe cotton *kombinat* (combine). Leninabad is an important centre of the silk-weaving industry. Large factories for the manufacture of carpets and woolen goods are at Ura-Tyube. Cotton-seed oil processing is allied to cotton ginning, the principal centres being Kanibadam, Leninabad, Kurgan-Tyube and Shaartuz.

There are fruit canneries at Kanibadam, Leninabad, Chkalovski and Regar and wineries at Dushanbe, Leninabad and Ura-Tyube. Minerals that are being exploited include lead and zinc (Kansai), fluorspar (Takob) and brown coal (Shurab); oil is produced at Kim and Nefteabad. In its hydroelectrical resources the Tadzhik S.S.R. occupies the second place in the U.S.S.R. (after the Russian S.F.S.R.), the main power stations being at Kairak-Kum on the Syr-Darya and at Perepadnaya on the Vakhsh canal. During the 1959–65 seven-year plan a gas pipeline from the Uzbek S.S.R. was planned and under construction.

*Communications.*—There are 160 mi. (258 km.) of standard- and 186 mi. (300 km.) of narrow-gauge railway lines. The main line, connecting the national network, is from Termez to Ordzhonikidzeabad. From Dushanbe to the Vakhsh valley and thence to Kulyab there is a narrow-gauge line. There are main highways between Dushanbe and Khorog, Khorog and Osh, Dushanbe and Ura-Tyube; Kurgan-Tyube and Kulyab also have road links with Dushanbe.

The Amu-Darya is navigable below Faizabadkala. Air transport is important and airlines join Dushanbe with Moscow, Tashkent, Baku and other towns. (G. E. Wr.; K. Sm.)

**TAFFETA** is a perfectly flat fabric in which the warp and weft threads are evenly interlaced so that equal numbers appear on the surface. There are two distinct types of silk taffeta, yarn-dyed and piece-dyed. Yarn-dyed taffeta has a stiff handle and a rustle known as "scroop" or "froufrou." It is used for evening dresses and for underskirts for couture dresses in chiffon or georgette. This type of taffeta is also used for academic hood linings. Piece-dyed taffeta, which is soft and washable, is a favourite fabric for linings. It is also used for electrical insulation and in a particularly strong form was much used for parachutes in World War II.

There are a large number of fancy taffetas, the best known being shot taffeta and taffeta chiné or warp-printed taffeta. Taffeta is also produced in yarns of wool, cotton, and man-made fibres. (D. M. Le.)

**TAFT, LORADO** (1860–1936), U.S. sculptor, lecturer, and teacher, was born at Elmwood, Ill., on April 29, 1860. He graduated from the University of Illinois, Urbana, where he first worked in sculpture, in 1879, and then studied at the École des Beaux-Arts in Paris, remaining in that city until 1885. Establishing himself in Chicago in 1886, he taught sculpture at the Art Institute and began his long career of public lecturer. He was elected to the National Academy in 1911. He participated actively in the formation of plans for public education in art, and served (1914–17) as director of the American Federation of Arts

Aside from many portraits, included among his works are: "Sleep of the Flowers" and "Awakening of the Flowers" for the Columbian Exposition (1893), "Despair" (1898), "Solitude of the Soul" (1900), the colossal "Black Hawk" near Oregon, Ill. (1911), Thatcher Memorial Fountain, Denver, Colo. (1918), and the "Fountain of Time" (1920), intended as part of a monumental complex of sculpture in Chicago.

In 1903 he published *The History of American Sculpture,* the first comprehensive work on the subject. His *Some Modern Tendencies in Sculpture* was published in 1920.

He died at Chicago on Oct. 30, 1936. (J. C. T.; A. T. G.)

**TAFT, ROBERT ALPHONSO** (1889–1953), U.S. senator and four times a candidate for the Republican presidential nomination, was one of the most influential political leaders of his generation. Born in Cincinnati, O., Sept. 8, 1889, he attended the public schools in that city and in Manila, Philippine Islands, where his father, William Howard Taft, 27th president and chief justice of the United States, served as governor-general; he later prepared for college at the Taft School in Watertown, Conn. Serious and scholarly from youth, he was graduated from Yale University in 1910 with highest honours and led his class at Harvard Law School, where he was editor of the *Harvard Law Review.* He passed the Ohio bar examination in 1913.

With his brother Charles and some friends he eventually organized the law partnership of Taft, Stettinius and Hollister. Taft was a brilliant lawyer, specializing in trust and utilities cases, and he also became a director of several successful business enterprises. During World War I he was turned down for military service because of impaired eyesight. He served as assistant counsel for the United States Food Administration, 1917–18, and as counsel for the American Relief Administration in 1919.

Although Taft grew up in politics, his formal apprenticeship as a politician did not begin until 1920 when he was elected to the Ohio House of Representatives. During his three terms in the House (1921–26) he took a keen interest in tax legislation and maintained a staunch party regularity. He served as Republican floor leader in 1925 and as speaker of the House in 1926. In 1930 he was elected to the Ohio Senate, but he was defeated for reelection in 1932. Six years later Taft won election to the U.S. Senate (1938). Entering it early in 1939, when the New Deal policies of Pres. Franklin D. Roosevelt were beginning to encounter strong opposition and the Republican Party was slowly reviving, he lost no time in establishing himself as a powerful influence. A tall, balding, and somewhat ungainly man who wore rimless spectacles and spoke in a harsh, flat voice, Senator Taft hammered away at the "vain, immoral, and dangerous" precepts of the New Deal, denouncing its "socialistic trends," and calling for economy, a balanced budget, and less centralization of power in Washington. Before the Japanese attack on Pearl Harbor he was an outspoken anti-interventionist; after the attack he threw his influence behind the war effort but was critical of Roosevelt's war policies on many occasions.

Taft was reelected to the Senate in 1944 by a narrow margin. But with the end of the war in 1945 and the election of a Republican majority in Congress in 1946, he entered a new phase of power and prestige. He was tireless in his role as chairman of the Republican Senate Policy Committee and well-informed on the legislation before Congress. He made himself the master of the 80th Congress, which Pres. Harry S. Truman denounced as the "worst Congress in history." Taft's most notable legislative achievement was the enactment of the Taft-Hartley Labor-Management Relations Act of 1947, which placed restrictions on organized labour, and, according to its sponsors, sought to balance the bargaining rights of management and labour. Taft retreated somewhat from the isolationism of his first years in the Senate, but he never became an internationalist. He sponsored social welfare measures in the areas of housing, health, and education, but continued to oppose increased centralization of power in the federal government.

Taft became a candidate for his party's presidential nomination in 1948. He had been Ohio's favourite son candidate at the convention of 1936 and a candidate of national influence in 1940. He came to the convention in 1948 with almost as much support as Thomas E. Dewey of New York, but was unable to prevent the well-organized Dewey group from capturing the nomination. It was a bitter defeat for Taft, who saw himself as the leader of resurgent Republicanism. He disliked the political views of Dewey and his followers, which were more liberal in domestic affairs and more internationalist than the orthodoxy that Taft represented. The election of Harry S. Truman in 1948 set the stage for what was probably the least productive period in Taft's public career, 1949–52. He attacked the Truman administration's China policy and talked of the "pro-Communist administration" and "the betrayal of America at Yalta." He endorsed the anti-Communist campaign of Sen. Joseph R. McCarthy of Wisconsin, but revealed his independence of mind when he said that he doubted whether a college professor should be fired just because he was a Communist.

In 1950 Taft was reelected to the Senate by an overwhelming majority, despite the opposition of organized labour, which condemned the Taft-Hartley Act. The next year Taft announced that he would once more seek the Republican presidential nomination. He campaigned vigorously and went to the convention with almost enough pledged delegates to win the nomination. But it was again denied him when the convention nominated Gen. Dwight D. Eisenhower. Always a strong party man, Taft supported Eisenhower and worked hard for his election.

After Eisenhower's victory, Taft became majority leader in the Senate. He was determined to work effectively with the new president and he quickly became Eisenhower's chief adviser in the Senate. His influence was apparent in many of Eisenhower's major decisions. Then, suddenly, in the late spring of 1953, Taft became seriously ill and on July 31, 1953, he died of cancer. His body lay in state in the rotunda of the Capitol on Aug. 2 and on the following day a national memorial service was held for him. In 1957 the Senate chose him as one of five outstanding senators of the past whose portraits were to be hung in the Senate reception room. The Robert A. Taft Memorial, a carillon tower near the U.S. Capitol, was dedicated in April 1959.

Taft was a superb parliamentarian with extraordinary ability to concentrate upon political and legislative problems. He became the symbol of his party in Congress and was often referred to as "Mr. Republican." His public personality inspired more confidence than affection, in part, it was said, because he tried to appeal to the logic rather than the emotions of his listeners. Walter Lippmann said, "The nation came to rely upon his character as something apart from his politics, and upon the quality of his mind rather than upon his political opinions." In 1914 Taft married Martha Wheaton Bowers, who had a flair for politics and assisted him in his campaigns. They had four sons, one of whom, ROBERT TAFT, JR. (1917–    ), also Republican, served in the Ohio legislature from 1955 to 1962, when he was elected to the U.S. House of Representatives. Defeated in his bid for the U.S. Senate in 1964, he was again elected to Congress in 1966 and 1968. He was successful in his second try for the U.S. Senate in 1970.

BIBLIOGRAPHY.—*Foundations of Democracy: a Series of Debates* by T. V. Smith, Robert A. Taft, *et al.* (1939); Robert A. Taft, *A Foreign Policy for Americans* (1951); William S. White, *The Taft Story* (1954); J. F. Kennedy, *Profiles in Courage* (1961). (D. W. GR.)

**TAFT, WILLIAM HOWARD** (1857–1930), 27th president and 10th chief justice of the United States, was born Sept. 15, 1857, in Cincinnati, O., the son of Alphonso and Louise Torrey Taft. His father was U.S. secretary of war and attorney general under Pres. Ulysses S. Grant and later served as minister to Austria-Hungary and Russia. The younger Taft entered Yale University at the age of 17, graduating with high honours in 1878.

**Early Political Career.**—After two years in the Cincinnati Law School and admission to the Ohio bar in 1880, Taft divided his time between legal practice and politics. In 1887 he was appointed a judge of the Superior Court of Ohio and three years later was named solicitor general of the United States. In that office he won varied and important cases before the U.S. Supreme Court. In 1892 he was named U.S. circuit judge for the sixth circuit, comprising Michigan, Ohio, Kentucky, and Tennessee.

Taft rapidly acquired a reputation for patience, courage, and mastery of jurisprudence. His opinions in various cases relating to disputes between labour and management aroused protests from labour leaders. Though his insistence upon the legal rights of the unions was advanced for his day, he stood firm in his emphasis upon the illegality of the secondary boycott and on the obligation of the courts to enforce their authority and to restrain violence through the power of injunction. That power, however, he utilized also to protect the effective operation of the antitrust laws.

In March 1900 Pres. William McKinley appointed Taft president of the Philippine Commission. To him this summons came as an unwelcome interruption of his judicial career; he accepted it more from a sense of patriotic obligation than because of pressure from Washington. His contribution to the pacification of the Philippines and the organization of their government ranks among the major accomplishments of his career. After rapidly achieving the end of military rule and the establishment of a civil government strong enough to maintain order, he gave attention to the development of the economic wealth of the Islands, construction of roads and harbours, and the education of the Filipinos toward limited self-government. He gained a spectacular success in the settlement of the delicate issue concerning the ownership of church lands taken over by the Filipinos from Roman Catholic friars.

On two occasions during his service in the Philippines, of which he became civil governor in July 1901, Taft was invited to become a justice of the United States Supreme Court. In declining, he sacrificed personal ambition to the claims of conscience in completing his mission in the Islands. In January 1904 Pres. Theodore Roosevelt recalled him to the U.S. to become secretary of war. Taft accepted the appointment with the stipulation that he would continue in close supervision of Philippine affairs.

As a member of the Cabinet he successfully undertook assignments far beyond the scope of routine duties. He became the troubleshooter of the administration, serving actually as executive assistant to the president, and earned a reputation both as conciliator and administrator. He was primarily responsible for the appointment of Maj. George W. Goethals as chief engineer of the Panama Canal and for the reorganization of the construction program that made possible its opening in 1914. Sent to Cuba in 1906 in the face of impending revolution, he effected a peaceful and successful settlement. During the same year he devised and supervised the measures taken to cope with the hardships that had resulted from the San Francisco earthquake and fire.

Such achievements gave Taft a preferred position as the Republican candidate to succeed Roosevelt as president when Roosevelt made clear his determination not to seek reelection in 1908. Taft's position was also strengthened because he was the president's choice. Taft had previously indicated a distaste for the presidency, but he was persuaded to change his mind by his wife and other supporters. At the Republican convention in June 1908, Taft was nominated on the first ballot and James S. Sherman of New York was nominated as his running mate. On Nov. 3 of that year he was elected president, gaining 321 electoral votes to Democrat William Jennings Bryan's 162 as well as a popular plurality of more than 1,000,000.

**President.**—Taft's triumph at the polls could not conceal or smooth away the difficulties that stemmed from a growing division within the Republican Party. He failed to recognize the rising power of the progressive, less conservative faction and included none of its members in his cabinet. Faithful to his platform promises, he determined to force a settlement of the tariff issue, and, with more honesty and courage than political acumen, he called a special session of Congress in an attempt to satisfy the popular demand for a reduction in duties. Congress, influenced by conservative Republican Sen. Nelson Aldrich, passed the Payne-Aldrich Tariff Act, which provided for only a limited reduction. Taft angered the Republican progressives by refusing to veto the bill.

THE GRANGER COLLECTION
WILLIAM HOWARD TAFT, PHOTOGRAPHED IN 1908

In spite of the disunity in Republican ranks and the growing strength of the Democrats, whose election victory in 1910 gave them control of the House of Representatives, the unspectacular achievements of Taft's administration served the cause of good government. The president sponsored federal economy and took steps toward the formation of an annual budget; he established the federal postal savings system; the impetus he gave to the conservation of natural resources was notable, although obscured by a controversy over public lands between Secretary of the Interior Richard Ballinger and forestry bureau chief Gifford Pinchot; his enforcement of the antitrust law was vigorous. Two of Taft's proposals in which he took special interest failed completely. The treaties of arbitration with Great Britain and France were so grossly amended by the Senate that he withdrew them; the tariff agreement with Canada, for which, with great difficulty, he won congressional approval, was ultimately rejected by Canada.

The last months of Taft's administration were clouded by a quarrel with Roosevelt that culminated in the disruption of the Republican Party. The president was shocked by the increasing radicalism of his predecessor. Roosevelt, impatient with what he regarded as Taft's inflexible conservatism, determined to contest the nomination for the presidency in 1912. On the first ballot the Republican convention gave a clear majority to Taft. Contending that the national committee had "stolen" sufficient votes to win in the convention, Roosevelt proceeded to organize his followers into the Progressive Party (also known as the Bull Moose Party) with himself as nominee. The Republican split guaranteed victory in November to the Democratic candidate, Woodrow Wilson, who received 435 votes in the electoral college, to 88 for Roosevelt, and 8 for Taft. The popular vote stood at Wilson, 6,293,454; Roosevelt, 4,119,538; Taft, 3,484,980. Taft's running mate, Sherman, died on Oct. 30, a few days before the election.

Taft found a satisfying harbour of retirement from the presidency in his appointment as Kent professor of law at Yale. In 1918 he was appointed to the National War Labor Board by President Wilson. He was a promoter of the League to Enforce Peace and a strong supporter of United States participation in the League of Nations. On the death of Chief Justice Edward White in 1921, Pres. Warren G. Harding appointed Taft to his place.

**Chief Justice.**—Taft officially assumed the functions of chief justice on Oct. 3, 1921. He found the court far behind in its work and promptly took steps to improve the efficiency of its judicial machinery. His influence was decisive in securing passage of the Judges Act of 1925, which enabled the Supreme Court to exercise wider discretion in its acceptance of cases and allowed it to give precedence to those of national importance. He worked incessantly and successfully to keep the court's docket clear.

The opinions of Taft as chief justice were popularly regarded, especially as they affected labour disputes, as bearing out his reputation for conservatism, but actually they illustrated his inclination to take a middle-of-the-road position. His approval of the use of court injunctions was limited by his insistence that injunctions not be employed to interfere with the right of workers to organize and strike. His constitutional opinions generally indicated his suspicion of innovations. In the Child-Labor case (1922), in which he was sustained by all but one of his colleagues, he made clear his conviction that to permit Congress to utilize its taxing power for the promotion of social reform, however desirable, would "completely wipe out the sovereignty of the states." In the Myers case (1926), however, he rendered an opinion greatly widening the power of the president to remove executive officers —an important contribution to constitutional law.

In the field of commerce Taft displayed tendencies less conservative than generally expected. He supported broad federal powers under the interstate commerce clause of the Constitution. His outstanding dissent placed him on the liberal side in opposition to the majority opinion that invalidated the law of 1918 fixing a minimum wage for women in the District of Columbia. The law in question, Taft insisted, dealt with the public interest in that sweatshop wages did as much to impair health and morals as did long hours; because of this the law in his judgment was constitutional.

Taft's service as chief justice brought him deep satisfaction, and he served in that office for almost nine years. His health, which had weakened after a heart attack in 1926, deteriorated rapidly early in 1930. On Feb. 3, he sent his resignation to Pres. Herbert Hoover. He died in Washington, March 8, 1930, and was buried in Arlington National Cemetery.

Taft was married June 19, 1886, to Helen Herron of Cincinnati. They had three children: Robert Alphonso Taft (*q.v.*), U.S. senator (1939–53); Helen Herron Taft (Mrs. Frederick J. Manning), dean and professor of history at Bryn Mawr College (1926–57); and Charles Phelps Taft, lawyer, author, and mayor of Cincinnati (1955–57).

Bibliography.—Henry F. Pringle, *The Life and Times of William Howard Taft,* 2 vol. (1939); Felix Frankfurter and J. M. Landis, *The Business of the Supreme Court* (1927); K. W. Hechler, *Insurgency: Personalities and Politics of the Taft Era* (1940); Frederick C. Hicks, *William Howard Taft, Yale Professor of Law* (1945); George E. Mowry, *The Era of Theodore Roosevelt: 1900–1912* (1958); A. E. Ragan, *Chief Justice Taft* (1938); Helen Herron Taft, *Recollections of Full Years* (1914).
(C. Sev.)

**TAGALOG,** the second largest ethnolinguistic group in the Philippines (after the Cebuano), numbered about 4,000,000 in the 1960s, and form the dominant population in the following areas: all provinces bordering Manila Bay except Pampanga; Nueva Ecija to the north; Batangas, Laguna, Marinduque, Mindoro, and Quezon to the south; and the city of Manila. The high Tagalog literacy rate is estimated at 70%; their Malayo-Polynesian language is closely related to Bisayan and Bikol (*q.v.*).

Next to English the most widely read and spoken tongue in the Philippines, Tagalog is by law the national language, and is a required school subject. However, English remains the language of government, business, instruction, and most of the press, sharing with Spanish and Tagalog the status of an official language.

Most Tagalog are farmers whose *sitios* (small hamlets) aggregate with surrounding farmland into barrios similar to U.S. townships. Most rice is grown in flooded, diked fields, but is produced dry in many upland areas. Almost all rice is locally consumed, but the other principal crops, sugar and coconut, are mainly for export. The importance of Manila has given the urban Tagalog leadership in local and overseas commerce, finance and manufacture, in the professions, and in clerical and service occupations, producing a most influential middle class. Because of Manila, the Tagalog served as primary mediators of more than 500 years of Chinese, Spanish, and U.S. influence, selecting from, interpreting, and adapting these foreign cultures to the basic Indo-Malayan social pattern. They have thus led in the modernization and westernization that has passed in varying degrees to all parts of the archipelago.

However, the Tagalog have sharply resisted alien economic and political control. They initiated the anti-Spanish propaganda movement of the 19th century and their generals led in armed revolts against Spain and the U.S. (1896–99). The principal national heroes of this period (José Rizal y Mercado, Andres Bonifacio, Apolinario Mabini, and Emilio Aguinaldo) were Tagalog. Tagalog were among the leaders in the subsequent achievement of Philippine independence by constitutional means (*see* PHILIPPINES, REPUBLIC OF THE: *History*).

More than 80% of the people in the Tagalog provinces are Roman Catholic; about 7% are members of the Philippine Independent (Aglipayan) Church, and about 3% are members of the several Protestant churches; Freemasonry is strong among them.

*See* C. Kaut, "Utang Na Loob: A System of Contractual Obligation Among the Tagalogs," *Swest. J. Anthrop.*, vol. 17 (1961); A. Rufino, *A Handbook of Tagalog Grammar* . . . (1963). (E. D. H.)

**TAGANROG,** a town and seaport of Rostovskaya (Rostov) Oblast' of the Russian Soviet Federated Socialist Republic, U.S.S.R., stands on the northern coast of Taganrogskiy Zaliv (Taganrog Gulf) of the Azovskoye More (Sea of Azov). Pop. (1959) 202,062. Founded in 1698 on an earlier site as a naval base and fortress, it developed in the 19th century as a major grain exporting port. Heavy industry is of importance. The author Anton Chekhov was born at Taganrog, and his house is preserved as a museum. (R. A. F.)

**TAGORE, DEBENDRANATH** (1817–1905), Indian philosopher and religious and social reformer, known as Maharshi, ("Great Sage" or "Seer"), combined intellectual aristocracy and saintly eminence with a practical zeal for educational reform, national liberation, and the reinstating of India's monotheistic religious traditions. He was born at Calcutta on May 15, 1817, the eldest son of Prince Dwarkanath Tagore (1794–1846). Dwarkanath Tagore, a rich landowner, had given financial support to Ram Mohun Roy's Brahmo Samaj (*q.v.*), and Debendranath Tagore succeeded Ram Mohun as leader of the movement, carrying on the founder's efforts to reform Hinduism and purify it of the excrescences it had accumulated over the many generations since the Vedic period. He emphasized the nondualistic aspect of Vedic philosophy, while stressing ethics and service as leading to direct experience of God.

Debendranath's formal education began when he was 9, at the Anglo-Indian School established by Ram Mohun, and was continued at Hindu College till he was about 17; his school years were merely a prelude to a long life of arduous self-education. He frequently visited pilgrimage places in the Himalayas, and he learned from the scholars of the northern as well as the southern regions of India. Among his achievements was the establishment of the Tattvabodhini Sabha ("Society" or "Meeting House for the Awakened Knowledge of Truth") and of the journal issued by this group. In 1886 he founded, as a retreat in rural Bengal, Santiniketan ("Abode of Peace"), later made famous by his son the poet Rabindranath Tagore (*q.v.*), who built there an educational centre, now an international university. Debendranath Tagore died at Calcutta on Jan. 19, 1905.

All of his publications were in Bengali except for a small book, *Vedantic Doctrines Vindicated* (1845), which contained English translations of some of his answers to critics of Indian thought. His scriptural anthology, *Brahmo-Dharma* ("The Religion of God"), incorporating Sanskrit texts mainly from the Vedas, the Upanishads, and the Bhagavad Gita, along with his Bengali translations and interpretive notes, was published in 1854.

BIBLIOGRAPHY.—*Autobiography of Maharshi Devendranath Tagore,* Eng. trans. (1909); Krishna Kripalani, *Rabindranath Tagore,* chapter on the poet's family background (1962); R. C. Majumdar and others, *An Advanced History of India* (1950). (AM. C.)

**TAGORE, RABINDRANATH** (1861–1941), Bengali poet and mystic, who won the Nobel Prize for Literature in 1913, was born in Calcutta on May 7, 1861. The youngest of the 14 children of the "Great Sage" (Maharshi) Debendranath Tagore (*q.v.*), he received his real education at home. He early began to write verses, and, after several books of songs in the 1880s, in 1890 published *Mānasī*, a collection that marks the maturing of his genius. It contains some of his most famous poems, including many in verse forms new to Bengali, among them the ode. It also contains his first social and political poems.

In 1891 he went to manage his father's estates in Shileida (Śilāidah) and Sayadpur. He lived there in close contact with village folk, and his sympathy for their poverty and backwardness was the keynote of much later writing. Stories "on humble lives and their small miseries" were collected in *Galpa Guccha* ("Bunches of Tales," 1912). He also became interested in political and social problems, and supported the *svadeśt* campaign, although never regarding independence as an end in itself. At Shileida too he came to love the Bengali countryside, most of all the River (the Ganges), perhaps his most oft-repeated image. During these years he published several collections—*Sonār Tarī* ("The Golden Boat," 1893), *Chitrā* (1896), *Chaitālī* ("Late Harvest," 1896), *Kalpanā* ("Dreams") and *Kṣaṇikā* (both 1900), *Naivedya* ("Offerings," 1901)—and two lyrical plays: *Chitrāṅgadā* (1892; Eng. trans. *Chitra,* 1913), in blank verse; and *Mālinī* (1895).

In 1901 Tagore founded a school at Santiniketan, near Bolpur; there he sought to blend the best in the Indian and Western traditions. Years of sadness (his wife and a son and daughter died between 1902 and 1907) inspired some of his best poetry. The English version of his most famous collection, *Gītāñjalī* (1910), won him the Nobel prize. He was awarded a knighthood in 1915, which he surrendered in 1919 as a protest against the Amritsar massacre (*see* INDIA-PAKISTAN, SUBCONTINENT OF: *History: British Imperial Administration*).

He continued to publish songs and poems: between 1916 and his death he published 21 collections. Much of his later life was spent in lecture tours in Europe, the Americas, China, Japan, Malaya, and Indonesia. Many of his works were translated into English, by himself and others, but the English versions fall far below the Bengali originals. His novels, although less outstanding than his poems and short stories, are worthy of attention; the most famous is *Gorā* (1910; Eng. trans., 1924).

In 1924 Tagore inaugurated the Visva-Bharati University at Santiniketan, as an all-India and international centre of culture. He died at Calcutta on Aug. 7, 1941.

*See* E. Thompson, *Rabindranath Tagore: Poet and Dramatist* (1926; rev. ed. 1948); K. Kripalani, *Rabindranath Tagore* (1962), with bibliography of works in English. (T. W. CL.)

**TAGUS** (Port. TEJO; Sp. TAJO), the longest river of the Iberian Peninsula (626 mi., 1,007 km.), rises about 100 mi. (161 km.) from the Mediterranean coast and flows out into the Atlantic Ocean at Lisbon. Its drainage basin of 31,159 sq.mi. (80,699 sq.km.) is only exceeded by that of the Ebro in the Iberian Peninsula. Compared with rivers of similar length, the Tagus has relatively few tributaries (59), although 16 are major ones; all the important tributaries come from the north and, rising on steep impervious mountain slopes of granites or schists, contribute greatly to frequent and violent floods. On Nov. 26, 1967, the worst natural disaster in Portugal since the Lisbon earthquake of 1755 occurred. After heavy rains, the lower Tagus rose suddenly and swept over about 275 mi. of roads and bridges, and more than 2,000 families were rendered homeless in the outskirts of Lisbon. In the flood of December 1876, the Tagus reached a flow of 15,850 cu.m. per sec., a record for all European rivers.

The Tagus rises in the Sierra de Albarracín at 5,250 ft. (1,600 m.) and near Ṭrillo it swings southwestward into its trough where it is joined by the Jarama at Aranjuez. From there the Tagus flows almost due west into Portugal, hugging close to the southern flank of the broad tectonic trough and in places (*e.g.,* Toledo) cutting through defiles on the edge of the Montes de Toledo. Joined by its longest tributary, the Alagón, at Alcántara, the river then enters a series of gorges along the frontier. In Portugal, it is joined at Constância by the powerful Zêzere, whose average flow is 460 cu.m. per sec., as compared with 50 for the Jarama. The Zêzere is fed by the heavy precipitation of the Serra da Estrela. After this confluence the Tagus swings southwest across the broad plains of Ribatejo, eventually reaching its tidal estuary at Lisbon, the Mar de Palha, which is up to seven miles wide. There, between the Lisbon suburb of Alcântara and the town of Almada on the south side, the Salazar Bridge—the longest suspension bridge in Europe and fifth largest in the world (*see* BRIDGES)—was built in 1966.

In the Spanish basin of the Tagus some 19 dams were completed in the 1960s on its tributaries, and the twin Entrepeñas-Buendía scheme on the upper Tagus and Guadiela was the largest in Spain.

This dual plant generates almost half of the total hydroelectric power of about 600,000 kw-hr. in the Tagus basin. Almost 70,000 ac. (28,327 ha.) were already irrigated, especially near Aranjuez and on the lower Jarama and Henares; eventually some 700,000 ac. were expected to be irrigated. In Portugal, small boats can reach Vila Velha de Ródão, but Santarém is the commercial limit of navigation. The Mar de Palha is an ideal shelter for the heavy traffic of the port of Lisbon. (J. M. Ho.)

**TAHA HUSAIN** (1889– ), Egyptian writer, stands at the forefront of his country's literary renaissance: his work, in Arabic, includes literary criticism, novels, short stories, history, social and political essays, educational studies, translations, and journalism. He was born at Maghaghah on Nov. 14, 1889, into a large family of modest means. At the age of two, he lost his eyesight. In 1902 he was sent to the Islamic University of al-Azhar, but he was soon at odds with its predominantly conservative authorities. He gravitated instead to modernist circles and to the Egyptian University, opened in 1908 and staffed partly by European scholars; in 1914 he became its first graduate. His first doctorate thesis, *Dhikra Abi l-'Ala'* (printed 1915), on al-Ma'arri, was the first all-round study in Arabic of a poet's background, life, and works. He was then sent to France at the state's expense, to study history; and after producing a second thesis, a study of Ibn Khaldun's social philosophy (in French, 1917) he secured a doctorate from the Sorbonne in 1918 and a *doctorat d'état* in 1919.

Taha Husain's career in the service of the Egyptian University and the Ministry of Education was often stormy, for his bold views enraged religious conservatives, and his fortunes varied with those of the political parties which, at different times, he supported. As minister of education in the last Wafdist government (1950–52), he vastly extended state education and abolished school fees.

Of the many polemics in which Taha Husain engaged, the fiercest was over his *Fi sh-Shi'r al-Jahili* (1926). In this book he contended that much reputedly pre-Islamic poetry has been forged by Muslims for various reasons, one being to give credence to Koranic "myths." For this he was declared an apostate.

In innumerable critiques, Taha Husain acquainted the public with both Arabic and French works; he also translated some Greek and French masterpieces.

Taha Husain's autobiography, *Al-Ayyam,* begun as a series of articles in 1926, was the first modern Arab literary work acclaimed in the West; it appeared in two volumes between 1927 and 1939 (Eng. trans., part i, *An Egyptian Childhood,* 1932, and part ii, *The Stream of Days,* 1943). He published a further book of memoirs, *Mudhakkirat,* in 1967. For his novels and shorter narratives he drew either on contemporary life or on early Islamic sources. In his later work he showed increasing sympathy with the plight of the poor, and therefore some leaning toward benevolent authoritarianism in government. A similar concern with the right relationship between the ruler and the ruled may be detected in his studies of the first four caliphs.

Prolific, versatile, and forceful, Taha Husain did much to mold a generation in which the literates were few and impressionable. He helped to clear intellectual deadwood and communicated his enthusiasm both for classical Arabic literature and for Western values. His style, combining linguistic purity with elegance and spontaneity, has been admired and imitated.

Bibliography.—Besides the works noted above, some further books by Taha Husain deserve special mention. There is a collection of his critical articles or "Wednesday discourses," *Hadith al-Arbi'a',* 3 vol. (1937–45). His narrative *Adib* (no date; *c.* 1935) is translated as *Adib ou l'Aventure occidentale* (1960); other narratives are *'Ala Hamish as-Sirah,* 3 vol. ("On the Margin of the [Prophet's] Life"; 1946–47), and *al-Mu'adhdhabuna fi l-Ard* ("Hell upon Earth"; 1949). *Al-Fitnah al-Kubra,* 2 vol. ("The Great Schism"; 1947–53), is historical. On education he wrote *Mustaqabal ath-Thaqafah fi Misr* (1938; Eng. trans. *The Future of Culture in Egypt,* 1954). *See* P. Cachia, *Taha Husayn* (1956); R. Francis, *Taha Hussein romancier* (1945); F. Gabrieli and others, *Taha Husein—omaggio degli arabisti italiani* (1964). (Pe. C.)

**TAHITI,** the largest and most important of the Windward Group and of the Society Islands, part of French Polynesia (*q.v.*), lies in the central South Pacific Ocean in latitude 17°40′ S and

FRED LYON—RAPHO GUILLUMETTE

BOATS TIED UP ALONG THE QUAY BORDERING THE MAIN STREET OF PAPEETE, CAPITAL AND CHIEF TOWN OF TAHITI

longitude 149°22′ W. It is of hour-glass shape, oriented northwest-southeast, with the larger portion called Tahiti Nui and the smaller Tahiti Iti, or Taiarapu; both portions are connected by the isthmus of Taravao. The island is about 33 mi. (53 km.) long and has an area of about 388 sq.mi. (1,005 sq.km.). Papeete (*q.v.*) is the capital and administrative centre of the island and of French Polynesia.

**Physical Geography.**—Tahiti consists of two ancient volcanic cones with secondary peaks, deeply dissected by valleys, and is surrounded by a coral reef lying from ½ to 2 mi. off shore. Orohena, the cone of Tahiti Nui, rises to 7,618 ft. (2,322 m.), with a lesser peak Aorai 6,788 ft. (2,069 m.); Roniu on Tahiti Iti is 4,341 ft. (1,323 m.). A narrow fertile plain surrounds the mountains, through which short, straight rivers, seasonally torrential, enter the lagoon. There is a high mountain lake, Vaihiria.

Lying in the easterly trade winds belt, Tahiti has clearly marked wet and dry sides with annual average rainfalls of 106.7 in. (2,710 mm.) and 72.3 in. (1,836 mm.); the greatest amount falls from December to March. Temperatures are high, varying from an average of 24° C (76° F) in July and August to 29° (84°) in January and February. Vegetation includes coconut palms, pandanus, lantana, hibiscus, and fruit trees.

**People and Population.**—The Tahitians are Polynesians who arrived from another of the Society Islands, Raiatea, a Polynesian cultural diffusion centre. On Tahiti they developed political districts, closely connected with a graded system of rank and authority, resting on the extended family organized around the temple. The high chiefs (*arii nui*) exercised considerable authority, supported by supernatural sanctions and a priesthood, but their relationship with lesser chiefs and people was reciprocal. This society disappeared under European impact, and intermarriage and the French policy of assimilation produced a people basically Polynesian, though with much admixture of other blood and deeply influenced by French culture (*see* also Polynesia).

The population, which declined after the first European contact, is increasing. The total population in 1962 was 45,430; of the total of 36,325 in 1956, 28,867 were French of Oceanic origin, 2,057 were French, 5,072 were Chinese (originally brought as labourers), and there were 329 others.

**History.**—The first European to discover Tahiti was Capt. Samuel Wallis in 1767; later visitors included L. A. de Bougainville (1767), Capt. James Cook (*q.v.;* 1769, 1773, 1777), and Lt. William Bligh (1788). The first permanent European settlers were members of the London Missionary Society who went to

Tahiti in 1797 to settle at the usual anchorage, Matavai Bay. Their influence, and that of European muskets supplied by other settlers and visitors, raised the prestige of the local chiefly family of Tu or Pomare, who aspired to achieve supreme power over the whole island. Pomare II (1803–24) embraced Christianity in 1812. Three years later, with the support of the Europeans, he triumphed over other Tahitian chiefs and established a "missionary" kingdom with a scriptural code of law. Under Pomare III (1824–27) and Queen Pomare IV (1827–77), a reaction by Tahitian rivals, the effects of disease, prostitution, and drunkenness, and the influence of European traders and beachcombers challenged the missionaries' hold. In 1836 French Roman Catholics attempted to open a mission in Tahiti, but Queen Pomare, on the advice of the English missionary and consul, had the two French priests deported. This brought a French frigate under the command of Abel Dupetit-Thouars in 1842 to demand reparations and to arrange a French protectorate; the protectorate became essentially a naval government of limited effect and weak finances and had virtually ceased to work by 1880, when Pomare V (Queen Pomare's son) abdicated and Tahiti was proclaimed a French colony.

**Administration and Social Conditions.**—Civil administration was set up by the Organic Decree of 1885. Tahiti was divided into districts, each under a chief and an advisory council, but authority really rested with the French and, very often, with the pastor of the Tahitian Protestant Church. After World War II, during which Tahiti adhered to the Free French movement of Gen. Charles de Gaulle, an elected representative or territorial assembly was set up in French Oceania, and in 1957 a council of government was added. All Tahitians (who had been French nationals since annexation) became French citizens in 1945. In 1958 Tahiti voted to remain within the French Community.

Education is shared by government and subsidized mission schools. Health conditions are generally good; there is no malaria, but mosquitoes carry elephantiasis. Tuberculosis is the main hazard. Government hospitals exist at Papeete and other centres, with dispensaries elsewhere. A French subsidy provides social services. (*See* also French Polynesia.)

**Economy.**—Agriculture is the main occupation, with copra as the chief export. Although copra does not provide sufficient trade, most Tahitians can support themselves easily on garden produce and on fish, which are plentiful. The livestock includes pigs, horses, cattle, and fowl. Retail trade and market gardening are dominated by the Chinese settlers.

There is a good coastal road around Tahiti, and interisland traffic is maintained by small vessels. Several shipping services on the Los Angeles–Sydney route call at Papeete. The island is also linked by air with Paris, Honolulu, and New Zealand.

Bibliography.—P. Loti, *Le mariage de Loti* (1881); E. Caillot, *Histoire de la Polynésie orientale* (1910); T. Henry, *Ancient Tahiti* (1928); J. C. Beaglehole, *Journals of Captain James Cook*, vol. i (1955); H. Deschamps, *Tahiti* (1957); P. O'Reilly and R. Teissier, *Tahitiens: Répertoire bio-bibliographique de la Polynésie Française* (1962); F. J. West, *Political Advancement in the South Pacific* (1961).
(F. J. Wt.)

**TAHMASP I** (1514–1576), Safavid shah of Persia from 1524 to 1576, was born in the village of Shahabad, near Isfahan, on March 3, 1514. He was the eldest son of Shah Ismail I (*q.v.*), whom he succeeded in 1524. The young monarch was for long a pawn in the hands of the Kizilbash tribal leaders, and his early years as shah were troubled by repeated incursions of the Uzbeks and by local uprisings. In 1534 the Ottoman Turks, under Suleiman I the Magnificent, attacked Persia, taking Tabriz, the Persian capital, and recovering territory in Mesopotamia that Shah Ismail had wrested from them. In 1538 the Turks again invaded Persia, taking Tabriz a second time. Driven from his country by a revolt, the Mughal emperor Humayun in 1542 took refuge at Tahmasp's court. Tahmasp later lent him troops for the recovery of his kingdom. Five years later a serious situation developed when Ilkhas Mirza, the shah's brother, rebelled and threw in his lot with the Turks. In the war which ensued Tabriz was once again lost; though it was soon regained, its vulnerability led Tahmasp to move his capital to Kazvin. Peace was concluded between Persia and Turkey in 1555. In 1561 the Englishman Anthony Jenkinson arrived at Tahmasp's court bearing a letter from Queen Elizabeth, his object being to establish trade between Persia and England across Russia. Tahmasp at first received him with courtesy, but bade him depart when he found that he was a Christian.

In Tahmasp's long reign the decorative arts became highly developed and the shah himself achieved some distinction as a painter and calligraphist. In his later years Tahmasp secluded himself in his palace, paying little attention to public affairs; he thus allowed the turbulent tribal leaders to increase their power, while the Uzbeks renewed their inroads on the northeastern provinces. When Tahmasp died (probably at Kazvin) in 1576 he left Persia appreciably weaker than it had been at his accession; on the other hand, he had succeeded in keeping the redoubtable Ottoman Turks in check. *See* also Persian History. (L. Lo.)

**TAHOE, LAKE,** a freshwater lake occupying a fault basin on the California-Nevada boundary in the northern Sierra Nevada, fed by numerous small streams and drained by the Truckee River to Pyramid Lake, Nevada. It measures 22 mi. (35 km.) north-south and 12 mi. east-west; its surface stands at 6,229 ft. (1,899 m.) above sea level and its maximum depth is 1,640 ft. (500 m.).

Numerous facilities cater to tourists attracted by the scenery (snowy peaks rising above coniferous forests), water sports, and trout fishing, and to winter sports enthusiasts. (R. F. Ln.)

**TAI CHEN** (Tai Tung-yüan) (1724–1777), Chinese historical geographer, philologist, and empirical philosopher, considered by many scholars to have been the greatest thinker of the Ch'ing period, leading figure in the movement called "Investigations Based on Evidence," was born at Hsiu-ning, Anhwei Province, on Jan. 19, 1724, of poor parents. He educated himself by reading borrowed books, and then, becoming acquainted with the scholar Chiang Yung, studied mathematics, philology, and the *Record of Rites* with him. Later he was invited by the emperor Ch'ien-lung (*q.v.*) to serve as one of the court compilers of the *Ssu-k'u ch'üan-shu*, the Imperial Manuscript Library. In this project Tai was exposed to many rare and otherwise inaccessible books.

Altogether Tai wrote, edited, and collated about 50 works, dealing mainly with mathematics, philology, ancient geography, and Confucian classics. In mathematics, he wrote the *Ts'e-suan*, a short discourse on Napier's rods (*see* Napier, John); and edited a collection of seven ancient mathematical works, the last of which is his own collation. In philology, he completed two works, the *Sheng-lei-piao*, a classification of ancient pronunciation; and *Sheng-yün-k'ao*, miscellaneous notes on phonology. Tai's collation of the 3rd-century-B.C. classic *Shui-ching-chu*, a study of 137 waterways in ancient China, which he prepared on the basis of a rare edition in the Imperial Manuscript Library, incited controversy during his life and after his death. Some scholars doubted whether he ever had access to the Imperial Manuscript Library edition, others charged him with plagiarizing a work produced earlier by Chao I-ch'ing. Most modern scholars agree with Hu Shi's conclusion that the work is unquestionably Tai's collation.

Perhaps Tai's greatest contribution to Chinese thought lies in the field of philosophy. Since the rise of neo-Confucianism during the Sung period, man had been believed to have a dual nature: a material one responsible for his passions, feelings, and desires, and a spiritual endowment which derives from Heaven-will and is therefore basically good (*see* Confucianism; Chinese Philosophy). Scholars before Tai Chen had attempted to refute this philosophy, but he was one of the very few who spoke out strongly against its futility, absurdity, and impracticability. He believed in the ever-presence of desires, feelings, emotions, and evil propensities; the only sure way to undermine their influence is an arduous quest for truth—truth attained by exactness, objectivity, and precision, whether it be literary, historical, philological, or philosophic. Meditation as practised by Sung philosophers is not pragmatic; search for incontestable evidence through textual criticism, on the other hand, is crucial.

Because he had no devoted followers, Tai's philosophy was not pursued during the first 100 and more years after his death, on July 1, 1777. Thanks to its closeness to Western thinking, however, his work began to be appreciated by returned students from abroad, and in 1924 the bicentennial of his birth was celebrated in Peking under the joint sponsorship of Hu Shih and Liang Ch'i-ch'ao. In 1936 the Chinese scholarly world paid tribute to Tai Chen with the publication of a complete and authoritative edition of his works, *Tai Tung-yüan hsien-sheng ch'üan-chi*.

No detailed study of Tai Chen is available in English. For general information, *see* Arthur W. Hummel, *Eminent Chinese of the Ch'ing Period,* vol. ii, pp. 695–700 (1944); for his philosophy, *see* Wing-tsit Chan, *A Source Book in Chinese Philosophy*, pp. 709–722 (1963). (Y. T. W.)

**TA'IF, AT,** a city and summer capital of Hejaz (*q.v.*), Saudi Arabia, lies at an altitude of over 5,000 ft. (1,520 m.), about 40 mi. (64 km.) ESE of Mecca with which it is linked by road. Pop. (1963 est.) 54,000. Once the seat of the pagan goddess Allat, it is revered now for the tomb of 'Abadullah ibn Abbas, cousin of the Prophet Mohammed, and for the graves of two infant sons of the Prophet. The royal palace and airport are at Al Hawiyah, 20 mi. N. (H. St. J. B. P.; X.)

**TAI LANGUAGES.** The Tai languages form an important branch of the Sino-Tibetan language family, which also includes Tibeto-Burman and Chinese (*see* Southeast Asian Languages). They are spoken by more than 30,000,000 people in a vast area stretching from south China through Laos and Thailand to the Malay Peninsula, and from Assam in India through the Shan States of Burma to the highlands of North Vietnam and to Hainan Island.

Tai languages are remarkably homogeneous. Although their mutual intelligibility is limited, many differences are merely dialectal. The best-known member of the group is the national language of Thailand, Central Thai or Siamese, which is based on the dialect of Bangkok and the central plain (*see* Thai Language). The major dialect areas of Thailand are central, northern (Yuan or Kammüang), northeastern (Lao), and peninsular. However, the dialects of Thailand are not easily classified in an absolute manner. Mutually exclusive sets of characteristics overlap the boundaries of subgroups in a complex way. Neither do dialectal and national boundaries coincide. The northeastern dialects of Thailand are to be classed with those spoken in the greater part of Laos. The northern dialects of Thailand have important characteristics in common with Shan and certain dialects of southern China and northern Laos such as Lü. The present-day position suggests that there has been a long history of population movement and contact, explained in part by the southward migrations of the Thai peoples.

Most of the Tai dialects of south China are classified by the Chinese linguist Fang-Kuei Li into two further groups on the basis of phonological and lexical criteria.

Tai languages have many Sinitic characteristics. They are isolating, monosyllabic, and noninflective. Syllabic structure is relatively simple, consisting of initial consonant(s) plus vowel with the possibility of syllable closure by a strictly limited range of continuant or stop consonants. Like Chinese, Tai languages are tonal in the sense that an important determinator of lexical meaning is the pitch or contour tone on which the word is pronounced. Among dialects, there are five to seven distinctive tones. Word order is an important grammatical feature.

Despite the Sinitic character of Tai, many of its speech-groups have come into contact with Indian civilizations, partly through the ancient Mon and Khmer empires (*see* below). Thai (Siamese) and Lao are particularly rich in borrowings from Mon-Khmer and Indic languages. The Indian Sanskrit and Pali, though genetically distinct from Tai, are recognized as classical languages by the Siamese and Lao peoples because of the deep-seated Hindu and Buddhist cultural influence among them. Neologistic Sanskrit derivatives are preferred to Western borrowings for modern technical vocabulary. The Indic connection has provided Siamese and Lao with many polysyllabic forms. Shan is heavily affected by borrowing from Burmese, and Black and White Tai by Vietnamese.

The script tradition is ultimately Indian. The earliest known writing systems are those of the period of the Sukhothai kingdom (13th–14th centuries A.D.). Sukhothai, in north-central Thailand, lay between the Indianized Mon and Khmer states, and the scripts of these peoples are the proximate origin of Sukhothai writing, from which have developed the scripts used in Thailand and Laos, and by Thai peoples in North Vietnam. Shan and certain other Tai languages of Burma and south China use scripts derived from Burmese, which is also Indian-based. Romanized scripts were introduced for some previously unwritten Tai dialects of southern China after 1949.

*See* also China: *The People: Ethnic and Language Groups: Chinese-Thai Languages;* Laos: *Population;* Shan Language; Shan State: *Race and Language;* Thailand: *The People;* Thai Peoples.

Bibliography.—H. L. Shorto, J. M. Jacob and E. H. S. Simmonds, *Bibliographies of Mon-Khmer and Tai Linguistics* (1963); Fang-Kuei Li, "A Tentative Classification of Tai Dialects," *Culture in History,* ed. by S. Diamond (1960); articles by W. J. Gedney, R. B. Jones, Fang-Kuei Li, and E. H. S. Simmonds, in *Indo-Pacific Linguistic Studies* (1965). (E. H. S. S.)

**TAILLE,** the direct tax from which the French kings of the *ancien régime* derived the major part of their revenue; it weighed intolerably upon those liable to it. Although essentially a royal tax, the taille was seigneurial in origin and retained that characteristic until the mid-14th century.

The earliest form of the taille was the request for goods, money, or labour services that the decline of slavery in the 10th century forced landlords to make of their tenants. From the 11th century, as an annual payment due from all the inhabitants of a seigniory except the clergy and the nobility, it was called *servitium, tallia, incisura* (the two latter words deriving from the notch or mark made on the collector's tally, or from the portion deducted from the wages of the taxpayer, or *focagium* [French, *fouage, feux,* the hearth]). The total sum required by the lord was apportioned among those liable according to their means; it was payable in installments. From the 13th century the amount due had sometimes become fixed by the custom of the manor; this was the *taille abonnée* or *taille jurée.*

The seigneurial taille which the king, like other landowners, raised from his demesne, developed as a result of the heavy expenses of the Hundred Years' War into the royal taille, levied throughout the land. For this reason its proceeds were thereafter classified as extraordinary revenue, as opposed to that derived from the royal demesne alone. At first levied (as in 1314) on their tenants by the ordinary landowners as an extra subsidy for the crown's benefit, this tax became in due course a genuinely royal taille, collected by the king's agents. The doctrine that this was a tax which the king alone could impose was first formulated in 1412; in 1439 both landlords and town authorities were forbidden to levy it without royal authorization. King Charles VII laid down the method and scales for its collection in a series of ordinances (1445–59) at the time when, along with the companies of mounted men-at-arms and the *francs archers* (*franc,* free, because exempt from the taille), the first standing armies were raised. Nevertheless the Estates General of 1484 denounced the taille as a wartime tax unjustifiably continued in time of peace.

From that time until the Revolution the taille was the subject of innumerable regulations designed to extract from it the maximum return and to establish more equitable assessment. The *taillon* or *crue de taille,* a supplement for the payment of troops, was added in 1549, and a repartition was carried out in the 17th century.

Taille was collected in two ways. In the districts of the *taille personnelle* (*i.e.,* the north of the kingdom), it was levied on an individual basis; in the districts of the *taille réelle* (*i.e.,* Guienne, Dauphiné, Languedoc, and Provence) it was levied on workers' land in the country districts and on businesses in the towns. In the first areas lists of those liable had to be drawn up; in the second the registers of land values had to be constantly revised. There was also another distinction. In the *pays d'élection* (districts without provincial estates and usually corresponding to the dioceses) taille was apportioned and collected by the *élus,* royal officials first established in the 14th century. But in the *pays d'état* (Brittany, Burgundy, Languedoc, Dauphiné, and Provence) the total amount was agreed upon by the estates of the respective provinces, under the fiction of a free gift. For the former the amounts required from each district were fixed and, at the parish level special assessors, appointed by the taxpayers, apportioned these amounts between the hearths or households.

Those exempt from taille in the 18th century included not only clergy and nobles who had never been subject to it, but also the inhabitants of most large towns. Exemptions (resulting, for instance, from the multiplication of ennobling offices in the judiciary and finance departments) increased steadily, leaving an even more intolerable burden on those who remained liable. The rate was also constantly raised, and it is estimated that the taille brought in 64,000,000 livres in 1780 and nearly 90,000,000 in 1789. It was abolished at the Revolution.

Bibliography.—N. L. J. Poullin de Viéville, *Nouveau code des tailles,* 3 vol. (1761); Auger, *Traité sur les tailles et les tribunaux qui connaissent de cette imposition,* 3 vol. (1788); J. J. Clamageran, *Histoire de l'impôt en France,* 3 vol. (1867–76); R. Stourm, *Les finances de l'ancien régime et de la révolution,* 2 vol. (1885); A. Vuitry, *Étude sur la régime financier de la France avant la révolution de 1789,* 3 vol. (1878–83); M. Marion, *Les impôts directs sous l'ancien régime* (1910); E. Esmonin, *La taille en Normandie au temps de Colbert* (1913); G. Dupont-Ferrier, *Études sur les institutions financières de la France à la fin du moyen âge,* 2 vol. (1930–32); C. Ambrosi, "Aperçus sur la répartition et la perception de la taille au XVIIIe siècle," *Revue d'histoire moderne et contemporaine,* vol. viii (1961). (Mi. F.)

**T'AI-NAN** (Japanese Tainan), a city on the southwest coast of Formosa (Taiwan). Pop. (1966) 414,826. It was an early settlement of Chinese emigrating from Kwangtung and Fukien provinces on the Asian mainland. From the early 17th century until 1885, T'ai-nan remained not only Formosa's largest town but also its political capital.

The city is the centre of a large rice-, sugar cane-, and peanut-producing area. Its manufactured goods include textile and rubber products, sugar, chemicals, plastics, aluminum products, small machinery, iron and steel products, and electrical appliances. T'ai-nan also is the centre of the salt industry along Formosa's southwestern coast, the headquarters of the Chia-nan irrigation system, and the service base for Civil Air Transport. It contains Cheng-kung University, one of Formosa's leading engineering schools. (N. S. G.)

**TAINE, HIPPOLYTE ADOLPHE** (1828–1893), French thinker, literary and art critic, and historian. Although he achieved fame over a very wide range of disciplines, Taine's deepest influence on his contemporaries was as an intellectual leader, as the embodiment of the 19th-century cult of science in its most devoted, high-minded, and often coldly rational form. His work represents, above all, a reaction against excessive emotionalism and spiritualist philosophy, and helped to provide a theoretical basis for the literary movement of Naturalism. The novel in particular, he urged, should be a "collection of experiments," a contribution to the scientific understanding of human nature, revealing the physical and psychological determinants of man's behaviour.

**Life and Works.**—When contrasted to the powerful unity of his work, the details of Taine's life are fairly banal. The son of a solicitor, he was born at Vouziers (Ardennes) on April 21, 1828, and was educated privately at home until his father's death in 1842, when he went with his mother to live in Paris; there he became an outstanding pupil at the Collège Bourbon, and in 1848 he entered the École Normale. He already held unorthodox views, having lost his Catholic faith, and his adherence to Spinozism led to his failure in 1851 in the *concours d'agrégation* in philosophy. Thereafter he taught for brief periods at Nevers and Poitiers, but in 1852 applied for leave of absence and, having returned to Paris, devoted himself to preparing his two doctoral dissertations: *De personis platonicis* and *Essai sur les Fables de La Fontaine* (1853; revised and published in 1861 as *La Fontaine et ses Fables*). He gained his doctor's degree in May 1853 and began an essay on Livy, *Essai sur Tite-Live* (1855), which, despite criticisms of its philosophical tendencies, was to win a prize from the Académie Française in 1855. In the same year he published his *Voyage aux eaux des Pyrénées* (entitled in later editions *Voyage aux Pyrénées*), a guidebook for which he had gathered material during a holiday necessitated by ill health in 1854.

Taine was now following the career of a man of letters, and he contributed frequent literary and historical articles to the *Revue de l'Instruction Publique,* the *Journal des Débats,* and the *Revue des deux Mondes.* These articles formed the basis for three books which greatly increased the reputation he had already won by his essays on La Fontaine and Livy. These were *Les Philosophes français du XIXe siècle* (1857), a polemical attack upon the eclectic philosophy of Victor Cousin and his school, dominant at that time in university circles, and also a lucid statement of his own theory of knowledge; a first volume of *Essais de critique et d'histoire* (1858); and his outstanding *Histoire de la littérature anglaise* (4 vol., 1863–64). In 1864 he followed Viollet-le-Duc, the architect, as professor of aesthetics and of the history of art at the École des Beaux-Arts in Paris, where he was to lecture for 20 years. His published courses include *Philosophie de l'art* (1865), *De l'Idéal dans l'art* (1867), and those devoted to the philosophy of art in Italy (1866), the Netherlands (1868), and Greece (1869). The 1860s were very productive and happy years. A second volume of essays, *Nouveaux Essais de critique et d'histoire* (1865), includes his justly admired articles on Balzac, Stendhal, and Racine; and in 1867 appeared perhaps the most personal of his works, *Notes sur Paris: vie et opinions de M. Frédéric-Thomas Graindorge*—to be followed by his well-observed, though partial, *Notes sur l'Angleterre* (1872), the result of two stays in England, in 1858 and 1871. In 1868 he married Mlle Denuelle, the daughter of a well-known architect and artist. In 1870 he published the two volumes of *De l'Intelligence,* a major work in yet another discipline, psychology, which had been one of his basic interests since his youth and underlies much of his writing on literature and art. In it he discusses the methodology of psychology and develops the theory of psychological determinism already stated in his literary works.

France's defeat by Germany in 1870–71 deeply affected Taine and led to a major reorientation of his work. The shift of his interests to politics is already seen in a brochure, *Du Suffrage universel et de la manière de voter* (1872). Above all he determined to seek the causes of the political instability which he held responsible for France's plight; he devoted the rest of his life to this end and to producing his great historical work, *Les Origines de la France contemporaine.* He even resigned his professorship after 1883 in order to be freer for this task, but he died (in Paris on March 5, 1893) before it was completed.

A first volume of his history, on *L'Ancien Régime,* appeared in 1876, followed by three volumes on the Revolution (1878–84). Only one volume of *Le Régime moderne* was published in his lifetime (1890); a second volume came out in November 1893. The entire work was reissued in 1899 in 11 volumes. There also appeared after his death his *Derniers Essais de critique et d'histoire* (1894), and an unfinished autobiographical and psychological novel, written *c.* 1861, *Étienne Mayran* (1910).

**Scientific Method and Assessment.**—Of a rationalist cast of mind even as a youth, Taine lost his Christian faith at the age of 15, and thereafter his ideas were formed in particular by his study of the "Idéologues" (especially Destutt de Tracy [*q.v.*]) and of Spinoza and Hegel. From the former group he took his positivism (*q.v.*)—his belief that all knowledge of reality must come from sense-experience; his emphasis on the collection of facts; and his rejection of all *a priori* knowledge. From the metaphysicians, on the other hand, he derived his lifelong aspiration to reach a synthetic explanation of the whole of life and the universe. According to Taine, the scientific method gives certainty, but it lacks completeness, because it is confined to the natural sciences. He argues that it can and should be applied not only in sociology, as his predecessor Auguste Comte (*q.v.*) had claimed, but also in the study of literature and art, in psychology, and above all in the realms of metaphysics and ethics; he even speaks of basing "a new religion" upon science.

The method Taine propounded for the study of literature (and also art) is well stated in the introduction to his history of English literature, perhaps his most celebrated piece of writing and a basic text for the understanding of his literary criticism. This introduction also contains his most notorious—and misunderstood—assertion that *"le vice et la vertu sont des produits comme le vitriol et le sucre"* ("vice and virtue are products like vitriol and sugar"). For Taine, the examination of literary "documents" leads to a closer understanding of the psychology of their author; this, complemented by scrutiny of the facts of his life and personality, makes it possible to discern the *"faculté maîtresse"*—the predominant characteristic—which determines his work; this, in turn, can then be "explained" by reference to three great conditioning facts, *"la race," "le milieu,"* and *"le moment"*—that is, roughly, his inherited personality, his social, political, and geographical background, and the historical situation in which he writes. The permanent impulsion of *"la race"* combines with the given environment (*"le milieu"*) to produce the "acquired speed" (*"vitesse acquise"*) at any given moment. It is evident that Taine's interest here is less in literature itself than in historical causation and psychology, and his method encouraged in his admirers an excessive preoccupation with biography and literary history at the expense of critical judgment. However, Taine's own abilities as a critic are revealed in his essays on Balzac and Stendhal (whose masterly psychological insight Taine was one of the first to acknowledge and admire), and in his lectures on painting.

Taine's scientific ambitions are most fully revealed in his psychological and philosophical writings. He stands alongside Théodule Ribot and Pierre Janet (*q.v.*) as a champion of scientific psychology, and though much of *De l'Intelligence* is outdated, it helped to modify contemporary methods of research by its emphasis on experiment, the search for causes, the physiological basis of personality, and the study of pathological cases. At the same time it intensified opposition to his ideas. He was angrily accused of holding a determinist and materialist view of man—not altogether unfairly, even though he himself claimed to reject materialism and argued that moral responsibility was compatible with determinism as he conceived it. In philosophy Taine seeks nothing less than to fuse positivism with German idealism, and to provide a method for a scientific metaphysic. He maintains that we can climb the pyramid of knowledge by a process of successively repeated abstractions and verifications, moving from the causes of particular phenomena to the causes of these causes, ultimately grasping the final causes of Life itself. And, as Taine contemplates this "hierarchy of necessities," which in his view comprises Nature, he yields to an exalted pantheism, inspired by Spinoza, in which he seeks to find a replacement for the Christian religion. Indeed, his personal philosophy, movingly expressed in essays on Iphigenia (contained in *Derniers Essais*) and Marcus Aurelius (in *Nouveaux Essais*), can be summarized as a fusion of pantheistic belief in the goodness of Nature with a stoic reconciliation to the individual's transitoriness and sufferings. Unfortunately, he fails to demonstrate the moral perfection he attributes to his impersonal "universal God," or to reconcile it with the existence of suffering and evil.

Taine's monumental work as a historian, *Les Origines de la France contemporaine*, is equally animated by scientific aims. Only by understanding the causes of France's situation would it be possible to legislate for its future development. His long analysis seeks to show that France's primary fault lies in excessive centralization, that this originated during the *ancien régime*, and that it was further intensified by the French Revolution, on which he shares and develops Burke's hostile view. Far from promoting liberty, as most Frenchmen believe, the Revolution merely transferred absolute power to even more illiberal hands. Undoubtedly his discussion is biased by the conservative and reactionary thesis he wishes to justify, and both the factual and the interpretative reliability of this work have been severely questioned, notably by Alphonse Aulard (see *Bibliography*). Here, as in much of his writing on literature and art, his primary merit lies less in the scientific objectivity he claimed than in his imaginative reconstruction of the past, and in his bold, stimulating generalizations, many of them not the dispassionate discoveries he believed them to be, but brilliant, intuitive hypotheses.

Émile Zola (*q.v.*), whose naturalist novels were particularly influenced by Taine's philosophy, once said that in Taine a poet and a rationalist were in conflict; one may sometimes think that the living interest of his works derives from the former rather than the latter. And although the nature of his literary criticism may seem brutal compared to the nuances of Sainte-Beuve's portraits, there is more subtlety to his determinism than at first appears. More generally, it is hard to deny that Taine promised more for the scientific method than it could achieve, and his overconfident trust in it provoked in the end either disillusionment (shared in part by Taine himself in his old age) or sharp reaction toward orthodox religion. Yet while later critics have justly shown the weaknesses of his thought, he still retains his power to stimulate and his representative stature as an outstanding scientific humanist of his age.

Bibliography.—There is no edition of Taine's collected works, but an authoritative biography and a selection of his correspondence has been edited by his widow under the title *H. Taine: sa vie et sa correspondance* (4 vol., 1902–07; *Life and Letters of H. Taine,* 3 vol., 1902–08). Most of Taine's works have been translated into English. Useful monographs include G. Barzellotti, *La Philosophie de H. Taine,* Fr. translation of Ital. original (1900); V. Giraud, *Essai sur Taine: son oeuvre et son influence* (1901; 6th ed., 1912); A. Aulard, *Taine, historien de la Révolution française* (1907); F. C. Roe, *Taine et l'Angleterre* (1923); D. D. Rosca, *L'Influence de Hegel sur Taine théoricien de la connaissance et de l'art* (1928); P. V. Rubow, *Hippolyte Taine: étapes de son oeuvre* (1930); A. Chevrillon, *Taine: Formation de sa pensée* (1932); M. Leroy, *Taine* (1933); A. Cresson, *Hippolyte Taine, sa vie, son oeuvre* (1951); S. J. Kahn, *Science and Aesthetic Judgment: a Study of Taine's Critical Method* (1953).

*See* also relevant chapters in P. Bourget, *Essais de psychologie contemporaine,* 4th ed. (1885); G. P. Gooch, *History and Historians in the Nineteenth Century,* 2nd ed. (1952); D. G. Charlton, *Positivist Thought in France, 1852–1870* (1959). (D. G. Ch.)

**T'AI-PEI** (Japanese Taihoku), one of the chief cities of Formosa (Taiwan). Founded in 1708, T'ai-pei after the middle of the 19th century became an important centre for overseas trade through its outport, Tan-shui. This trade was based upon tea and was dominated by British trading companies.

Situated in the centre of the largest agricultural basin in northern Formosa, T'ai-pei (population in 1964 was estimated to be 1,117,000) forms the nucleus of a major industrial area. The T'ai-pei industrial complex includes light and heavy industries within the urbanized area and also in several industrial suburbs, including Pan-ch'iao and Nan-chiang. Cotton and artificial fibre textiles, rubber goods, electrical appliances, alcoholic beverages, metal products, chemicals, coke, and printed materials are produced. T'ai-pei also is the island's major communications centre, containing the central workshops of the government-owned railway and Formosa's international airport. National Taiwan University and the Taiwan Provincial Normal University, as well as several professional and specialized training schools, are located in T'ai-pei. Because it contains more mainland Chinese than any other Formosan city, characteristic types of mainland entertainment, such as opera and fine regional restaurants, are found there.

Under Japanese rule (1895–1945) T'ai-pei was the seat of the Taiwan government-general; as a result it acquired the characteristics of an administrative centre, such as public buildings and extensive civil servant housing facilities. After the Communists took China in 1949, it became the capital-in-exile of the Nationalist government of the Republic of China, headed by Chiang Kaishek. (N. S. G.)

**T'AI P'ING REBELLION.** The T'ai P'ing rebellion of 1851–1864 in China was a great national religious-political upheaval. It inspired many other rebellions and revolutions in late 19th-century China, culminating in Sun Yat-sen's overthrow of the Manchu dynasty in 1911–12. Historical judgment of it has varied. The rebellion has been condemned as the work of "Cantonese bandits" or "long-haired bandits," and has been praised as a national agrarian and proletarian revolution. This great upheaval grew out of a complex background including political corruption of the Manchu regime, foreign aggression during and after the Opium War of 1839–42, agrarian distress, and severe famines that left many people homeless and ready to join the T'ai P'ings.

The titular leader of the rebellion was Hung Hsiu-ch'üan (1814–64), a Cantonese who had struggled in vain to gain office through government civil service examinations. After taking the metropolitan examination at Canton in 1836 he was given nine Christian tracts, which he read cursorily. His third attempt to pass the examination failed in 1837. He was so dismayed that he fell ill, suffered delirium, and had visions of an old man and a middle-aged man in heaven; the latter ordered him to kill demons on earth. After his vision, Hung continued to teach in a village school. Six years later, after his last examination failure in 1843, he decided to give up hope. His cousin then called his attention to the nine Christian tracts. Hung studied the booklets, which had the general title of "Good Words to Exhort the Age" (*Ch'üan-shih Liang-yen*), quotations and paraphrases mainly from the Old Testament, together with sermons. The compiler of the tracts, Liang A-fa (1789–1855), was the first Protestant convert in China. After reading the tracts Hung realized that the old man in his vision was God the Heavenly Father, the middle-aged man was Jesus Christ the Elder Brother, while he himself was the second son of God commissioned to destroy demons, and thus completing a new trinity. Hung and his cousin baptized each other and soon afterward organized the God Worshipers' society.

It was in 1850 that Hung ordered all God Worshipers in various places in mountainous Kwangsi province to resist government troops and to concentrate at Chin-t'ien. Their slogan—to share property in common—attracted many famine-stricken peasants, workers, miners and others. They took Yung-an in Kwangsi on Sept. 25, 1851, and Hung proclaimed himself the heavenly king of the T'ai-p'ing T'ien-kuo, or Heavenly Kingdom of Great Peace.

The T'ai P'ings thereupon sought to overthrow the Manchu dynasty, and advanced rapidly from Kwangsi through Hunan and Hupeh along the Yangtze valley. They formed themselves into separate battalions for men and women and behaved much better than the government troops. In March 1853 the T'ai P'ings established their "heavenly capital" at Nanking, and it lasted for 11 years. A northern expedition to take Peking failed but another expedition to reconquer the upper Yangtze valley scored many victories. Victory, however, was followed by a series of murders among the leaders of the rebellion in 1856. Two associate kings with hundreds of their followers were killed; an enormous army was taken away by the assistant king to southwest China.

Meanwhile, the inefficient government troops were replaced by a new force trained in Hunan by Tseng Kuo-fan (1811–1872). A Confucian scholar, Tseng employed his students as officers and created a Confucian army to combat the rebels. Tseng eventually managed to hem Hung's forces in Nanking. The T'ai P'ing attempts to take Shanghai in the 1860s then met with foreign intervention. Western volunteers organized the "Ever-Victorious army" under the command of F. T. Ward and then of C. G. Gordon (*q.v.*), who routed the T'ai P'ings in the greater Shanghai area. Nanking was taken by Tseng's force in July, 1864. By this time Hung Hsiu-ch'üan had committed suicide. Some T'ai P'ings fled to the southern coast and survived until 1866, and some, allied with the "Nien-fei" in North China, continued their anti-Manchu war until 1868. (*See* NIEN REBELLION.)

During their years of power the T'ai P'ings inaugurated many reforms. Their religion was a Chinese pseudo-Christianity. They knew only God the creator of the world, the Ten Commandments and baptism. They recognized the Sabbath and said grace before meals, but did not adopt the Lord's Supper and the Christian ideas of kindness, forgiveness and service to mankind. Their government system was a theocracy. The Heavenly King was both spiritual and temporal ruler, and his four associate kings and an assistant king were civil and military chiefs. All posts were hereditary. The legal code was severe. Organization of the army was elaborate, with strict rules governing soldiers in camp or on the march. The T'ai P'ings planned equal distribution of land according to a primitive form of communism, but did not put this system into practice. Families were graded in a co-ordinated system that took into account the exigencies both of peace and war. There was to be equality between men and women. Monogamy was the rule for the common people, but not for the kings. Prostitution, footbinding and slavery were prohibited, as well as opium smoking, adultery, witchcraft, gambling, and use of tobacco and wine. Chinese language simplification was practised. Westernization and industrialization were planned.

The T'ai P'ing rebellion failed because of poor leadership in military and civil administration, internal dissension, alienation of the Confucian literati, and the combined attack by Tseng's army and foreign-led forces. It ravaged 17 provinces and caused the loss of about 20,000,000 lives.

*See* also CHINA: *19th Century and Revolution.*

BIBLIOGRAPHY.—Ssu-yu Teng, *Historiography of the Taiping Rebellion* (1962); Eugene Boardman, *Christian Influence Upon the Ideology of the Taiping Rebellion, 1851–1864* (1952); Vincent Yu-chung Shih, "Interpretation of the Taiping T'ien-kuo by Non-Communist Chinese Writers," *Far Eastern Quarterly,* x, 2, pp. 248–257 (Feb. 1951); P. M. Yap, "The Mental Illness of Hung Hsiu-ch'üan," *Far Eastern Quarterly,* viii, 3, pp. 287–304 (May 1954); Kuo Ting-yee, "The Totalitarian Rule of the Taiping Heavenly Kingdom," *Annals of Academia Sinica,* no. 2, pt. 1, pp. 209–230 (May 1955); Franz Michael, "T'ai-p'ing T'ien-kuo," *The Journal of Asian Studies,* xvii, 1, pp. 67–76 (Nov. 1957); John S. Gregory, "British Intervention Against the Taiping Rebellion," *The Journal of Asian Studies,* xix, 1, pp. 11–24 (Nov. 1959); Yuan Chung Teng, "Reverend Issachar Jacox Roberts and the Taiping Rebellion," *The Journal of Asian Studies,* xxiii, 1, pp. 55–67 (Nov. 1963).

(S. Y. T.)

**TAIRA,** one of the most powerful groups of families, sometimes called clans, in Japan from the 10th through the 12th centuries. In the late 9th century the name Taira was conferred by the emperor upon several of his descendants who at that time were organized into four distinct but loosely related family groups. In the next few centuries the number of Taira branch families and clansmen increased appreciably. Providing troops for the Imperial Guards and performing military and police services in outlying districts on behalf of the imperial court, the Taira power and estates grew rapidly. When a dispute over imperial succession broke out in 1156, Taira forces, led by Kiyomori, made a bid for political power, ostensibly championing the interests of Emperor Goshirakawa. But after smashing the rival Minamoto clan, the Taira placed the defeated leader, Yoritomo, under the guardianship of the Hōjō (*q.v.*) and established themselves in the imperial capital at Kyōto.

The Taira domination of the imperial government lasted until 1180, during which time Kiyomori and his family secured appointment to numerous high offices and also acquired considerable wealth and lands. Taking advantage of the growing resentment against the Taira, Yoritomo, aided by the Hōjō, organized a revolt. This momentous struggle for power between the Taira and Minamoto houses, which inspired many legends and enduring tales of chivalry, is called the Gempei Wars in Japanese history. The Taira clan was decisively defeated by the Minamoto forces in 1185 at the great sea battle of Dannoura; the Taira never regained power after this disaster. (HN. KN.)

**TAISHŌ** (1879–1926), emperor of Japan from 1912 to 1926, was born in Tokyo on Aug. 31, 1879. The third son of Emperor Meiji, his personal name was YOSHIHITO. The emperor's two elder sons having died in infancy, Yoshihito was proclaimed crown prince on Nov. 3, 1889. He married a daughter of Prince Kujō in 1900 and had four sons: Hirohito (who succeeded him on the throne in December 1926), Yasuhito (Prince Chichibu), Nobuhito (Prince Takamatsu), and Takahito (Prince Sumi). Yoshihito ascended the throne on the death of his father on July 30, 1912. During his reign as the Taishō (Great Righteousness) emperor, Japan continued along the lines of modernization and Westernization begun in the Meiji period, and policies congenial to Western powers, especially Great Britain and the United States, prevailed. These included participation in World War I on the side of the Allied Powers, the anti-Bolshevik intervention in Siberia, and participation in the disarmament conference in Washington, D.C., while in domestic affairs there was increasing use of parliamentary procedures and broadening of the suffrage. However, the emperor played almost no political role. He became mentally ill in his later years. Hirohito was appointed prince regent in 1921, and the emperor lived in seclusion until his death, Dec. 25, 1926, at Hayama. (F. H. Co.)

**TAIT, ARCHIBALD CAMPBELL** (1811–1882), bishop of London and subsequently archbishop of Canterbury, who was a moderating influence during a period of tension in the Church of England, was born at Edinburgh on Dec. 21, 1811, the youngest child of Presbyterian parents. Educated at Edinburgh High

School, Edinburgh Academy, and Glasgow University, he proceeded to Balliol College, Oxford, where he joined the Church of England. After securing a first in classics (1833), he became fellow (1834) and tutor (1835) of Balliol. In 1836 he was made deacon and for five years combined the curacy of two villages near Oxford with his academic work. He early displayed a tendency to broad churchmanship and he resisted the exclusive teaching on the nature of the church upheld by the nascent Oxford Movement (*q.v.*). In March 1841 he was one of the four tutors who published a joint protest against Tract 90 (*see* NEWMAN, JOHN HENRY). In 1842 he succeeded Thomas Arnold as headmaster of Rugby, where he improved the prefectorial system. After his health had been weakened by a serious illness in 1848, he accepted the less exacting post of dean of Carlisle Cathedral. In 1850–52 he was a leading member of the royal commission which advised reform in Oxford University.

In 1856 Tait became bishop of London, where his avoidance of party issues meant that he faced opposition from both high churchmen and evangelicals. Ritualist controversies began to take place in those parishes where clergy introduced into their services ceremonial which was resented by those who believed that the Protestant Church of England was thereby being led astray into Roman Catholicism. Tait's acquiescence in the episcopal condemnation of the books *Essays and Reviews* (1860), which contained some advanced views on the higher criticism of the Bible, strained his close friendship with two of his former pupils, Frederick Temple and Benjamin Jowett, whose own contributions to the volume he had pronounced orthodox. Tait's later concurrence in the Privy Council's acquittal of two other contributors earned him some obloquy (1864). The diocese of London, however, prospered under Tait. He founded the Bishop of London's Fund to supply overgrown parishes with additional clergy, launched the Diocesan Home Mission, and supported evangelical campaigns to build more churches.

On becoming archbishop of Canterbury in 1868, Tait was faced with the bill disestablishing the Church of Ireland. His statesmanship largely accounted for its smooth passage and for the equitable treatment secured for the Irish clergy. He was bitterly opposed by high churchmen for his desire to dilute the damnatory clauses of the Athanasian Creed (1870–73) and for his support of the Burials Act (1880) legalizing non-Anglican burial services in churchyards. The passing of the Public Worship Regulation Act (1874)—admittedly much altered from what Tait had originally proposed—provided no useful solution to the ritualist controversies. He was more successful in his work on the royal commissions on ritual (1867) and ecclesiastical courts (1881) and in the esteem which he commanded in the House of Lords as a spokesman for the church. He died at Addington, Surrey, on Dec. 3, 1882.

*See* the *Life* by R. T. Davidson and W. Benham (1891).

(D. H. N.)

**TAIT, PETER GUTHRIE** (1831–1901), Scottish mathematician and physicist known for his work on thermodynamics, was born at Dalkeith on April 28, 1831. After attending the academy at Edinburgh and spending a session at the university, in 1848 he entered Peterhouse, Cambridge, graduating in 1852. As a fellow and lecturer of his college he remained in Cambridge until 1854 and then left to take up the professorship of mathematics at Queen's College, Belfast. There he joined Thomas Andrews in researches on the density of ozone and the action of the electric discharge on oxygen and other gases. From 1860 he served as professor of natural philosophy at Edinburgh until his death on July 4, 1901.

His earliest work was mainly mathematical, dealing especially with quaternions (*q.v.*). In 1864 he published the first of his important contributions to thermodynamics, working later on thermoelectricity and thermal conductivity. From 1879 to 1888 he was engaged in experimental investigations of deep-sea temperatures; these were extended to include the compressibility of water, glass, and mercury. Between 1886 and 1892 he published papers on the foundations of the kinetic theory of gases.

A selection from Tait's papers was published in two volumes (1898, 1900). With Lord Kelvin he collaborated in writing a *Treatise on Natural Philosophy* (1867), and with Balfour Stewart *The Unseen Universe* followed by *Paradoxical Philosophy* (1878).

*See* Edinburgh University, *University Portraits* (1958).

**T'AI-TSUNG** (597–649), the principal founder and second ruler of the T'ang dynasty in China. When only 20 years of age, he was instrumental in inducing his father, Li Yüan, who was governor of T'ai-yüan (Shansi), to make a bid for power in the anarchic conditions brought about by popular uprisings at the end of the Sui dynasty. T'ai-tsung's strategy was to move southwest and seize the western capital, Ch'ang-an, and to use the natural defences of Kuan-chung (Shensi) to provide a base from which to intervene in the struggles on the Yellow River plain to the east. Largely through his military genius, his forces had completely pacified the country by 624 and his father had become emperor of China. In 626, T'ai-tsung's father abdicated in his favour after a coup d'état in which T'ai-tsung's supporters killed his elder brother, the crown prince, who had been plotting against him.

After T'ai-tsung's accession to the throne, T'ang generals proceeded to carry the prestige of Chinese arms beyond the country's previous frontiers. By 630 the Northern Turkish empire in Mongolia had been destroyed, and after a series of campaigns Chinese power was established in Sinkiang and Chinese suzerainty recognized as far afield as Sogdiana and Afghanistan. On the other hand Koguryo in northern Korea resisted successfully, as it had done during the Sui dynasty. Internally, T'ai-tsung's reign was a period of conservative retrenchment during which the country recovered from the devastation of the civil wars. Though he was a military man capable of violent and autocratic actions, the picture he tried to create of himself was that of the perfect Confucian monarch, always open to frank criticism and advice from his ministers. The bureaucratic institutions established during his reign, largely based on those of the Sui era, were later considered to have been of unparalleled perfection. T'ai-tsung's reign, however, was marred by troubles over the succession to the throne. The crown prince was found guilty of treason and banished, and Kao-tsung, who eventually succeeded his father, was a weakling.

(E. G. PU.)

**TAIWAN:** *see* FORMOSA.

**T'AI-YÜAN** (formerly YANGKÜ OR YANG-CH'U), capital of Shansi Province, China, stands at the northern end of a heavily populated plain on the upper course of the Fen Ho. Ancient Mongol invasion routes lead from the north off the Mongolian plateau and from the south via Ta-t'ung. To the east through the T'ai-hang Shan is the old imperial highway from Peking via Shihmen to T'ai-yüan and then south and west to Sian. Both routes have railways and motor roads. Although the whole area lies within the brown, eroded loess highlands, the fertile T'ai-yüan plain produces an abundance of wheat, cotton and northern fruits and vegetables; sheep on the surrounding hills are raised for wool. There, too, are China's largest known reserves of high-grade bituminous coal. The city was known as the home of nationwide private banking, as a textile and leather centre (gold lacquered leather boxes and trays), and for metal production. Late in the 19th century an arsenal was built using the abundant local coal and iron ore; it was followed by an ironworks and by flour and textile mills. Under Japanese occupation, 1937–45, the city and its industries were vital for the control of north China despite the constant cutting of railway lines by Chinese guerrilla forces. Under the Chinese People's Republic (Communist) the population increased and T'ai-yüan expanded into a major centre for iron and steel, textiles, textile machinery, cement, and a phosphorus fertilizer plant (100,000-ton capacity). It has an institute of technology. Pop. (1953) 720,700; (1957 est.) 1,021,000.

(TE. H.)

**TAIZÉ COMMUNITY:** *see* GRANDCHAMP AND TAIZÉ COMMUNITIES.

**TA'IZZ,** a walled town and capital of Ta'izz *liwā'* (province) in southwest Yemen, lies in a fertile valley at the foot of Jabal Subr (9,863 ft. [3,006 m.]), 85 mi. (136 km.) NW of Aden. Pop. (1961 est.) 30,000. It was the capital of Yemen in the 12th century under Saladin's brother Turanshah. The town has five gates (three now blocked) and several main mosques, mostly founded by the Rasulids (13th–15th centuries) and rebuilt by the Turks in the 16th–17th centuries. The Rasulids and the Tahirids (1453–1516) also built schools, some of which still exist. Ta'izz is linked by unsurfaced but motorable roads with Aden and Al Hudaydah, and a hard-surfaced road to San'a' was under construction in the 1960s. A water supply to the town was installed by the United States. *See* also YEMEN. (W. H. Is.)

**TAJ MAHAL,** the mausoleum built on the south bank of the Jumna river, outside Agra in India, on the orders of the Mogul emperor Shah Jahan in memory of his beloved wife, Arjumand Banu Begum, called Mumtaz Mahal, "chosen one of the palace" (of which Taj Mahal is a corruption). She died in childbirth in the town of Burhanpur in 1631 after having been the emperor's inseparable companion since their marriage in 1612. The building was commenced in 1632, after plans had been prepared by a council of architects from India, Persia, central Asia and beyond; the credit for the final plan is given to one Ustad Isa, either Turkish or Persian, although the master builders, masons, inlayers and calligraphists, like the materials they worked with, came from all over India and central Asia. More than 20,000 workmen were employed daily to complete the mausoleum building itself by 1643, although the whole Taj complex took 22 years to complete, at a cost of 400 lakhs of rupees.

The complex consists of a rectangle measuring 634 yd. by 334 yd. aligned north and south. A central square garden area, 334 yd. on each side, leaves an oblong area at each end; that at the south consists of the sandstone entrance gateway with its attendant service buildings, while that at the north (river) end comprises the mausoleum itself, flanked on the west and east walls by two symmetrically identical buildings, the mosque and its jawab ("answer") respectively. All is enclosed within a high red sandstone boundary wall with octagonal pavilion turrets at the corners, while outside the enclosure at the south are ancillary buildings such as stables, outhouses and guard quarters. The whole complex is the begum's memorial; it was conceived and planned as an entity, since Mogul building practice allowed of no subsequent addition or amendment. Its northern end is the most significant architecturally, with mosque and jawab both facing the mausoleum itself. The mosque and jawab of red Sikri sandstone, with marble necked (not bulbous) domes and architraves and some restrained *pietra dura* surface decoration, contrast well with the mausoleum of pure white Makrana marble. This mausoleum, standing on a 312-ft.-square marble plinth 23 ft. high, is a square of 186 ft. with chamfered corners and with a massive arch in each face, rising to 108 ft.; over all is a bulbous double dome, supported on a tall drum, the pinnacle of which stands 243 ft. above garden level. The sky-line rhythm is enhanced by parapets over each arch, corner pinnacles and domed kiosks over each corner. At each corner of the plinth stands a three-storied minaret, 138 ft. high to the crowning kiosk; the countersunk face joints of the marble bricks provide textural contrast with the highly finished marble of the mausoleum, but unfortunately recall factory chimney construction to the sophisticated western beholder. Inside the mausoleum is the octagonal chamber, embellished with low-relief patterns and fine *pietra dura,* containing the cenotaphs of the begum and Shah Jahan. These, of marble decorated with superb *pietra dura,* are enclosed by an exquisite perforated marble screen studded with precious stones. A vault below, at garden level, contains the true sarcophagi.

The minarets lead the observer's eye from the mausoleum to its setting; this is now somewhat unsatisfactory, as trees obscure the view of other structures, and from the garden there is some feeling of restlessness; but from the river or from the fort the balance restores itself, and justifies H. R. Nevill's remark that "the Taj . . . is within more measurable distance of perfection than any other work of man" (*Agra Gazetteer,* 1921). Its design, successor in the indigenous tradition to the mausoleums of Humayun and the Khan-i-khanan at Delhi, has been criticized as "too feminine" —thus complimenting the designers' intentions. The Moguls are said to have "built like Titans and finished like goldsmiths"; certainly the Taj Mahal is their finest jewel. *See* ISLAMIC ARCHITECTURE.

BIBLIOGRAPHY.—Percy Brown, "Monuments of the Mughal Period," *Cambridge History of India,* vol. iv (1937), *Indian Architecture: the Islamic Period* (1942); for the controversy over the attribution of the design to a European, *see* V. A. Smith, *History of Fine Art in India and Ceylon,* pp. 182–185 (1930); E. B. Havell, *A Handbook to Agra and the Taj,* appendix i, new ed. (1924). (J. B.-P.)

**TAKIZAWA BAKIN** (1767–1848), Japanese novelist, regarded as the preeminent writer of Edo (now Tokyo), who deserves a place among the world's great storytellers, was born in Edo on July 4, 1767, the third son of a low-ranking samurai. Suffering, misery, and death filled his youth. His father and mother died before he matured, and, because of the famine and plague that struck Edo after 1780, Bakin alone lived to continue his family name. After much drifting, he relinquished samurai status, married a merchant's widow (for security, not love), and devoted over 50 years to writing. He died on Dec. 1, 1848.

With his more than 30 long novels—known as *yomihon,* "reading books"—Bakin created the historical romance in Japan. Court romances, military chronicles, nō plays, popular dramas, legends, and Chinese vernacular fiction all furnished him material. Although he borrowed from many sources, he added much that was original, and few authors have ever matched his tenacity and his devotion to craft. He freed the novel in Edo from subservience to actor, illustrator, and raconteur. Loyalty, filial piety, and restoration of once-great families comprised his main themes. His special attention to Chinese civilization, Buddhist philosophy, and national history was tempered by a concern for language and style, compassion for his fellow man, and a belief in human dignity. Still, the samurai tradition and his own innate stubbornness led him to support the established order and made him less an original thinker than an interpreter of his age. Although he himself irrevocably forsook his samurai status, he tried his utmost to preserve his son's samurai privileges. Among Bakin's *yomihon, Chinsetsu yumiharizuki* (1806–11; "Crescent Moon: the Adventures of Tametomo") and *Nansō Satomi hakkenden* (1814–42, "Satomi and the Eight 'Dogs' "), both on the theme of restoring a family's fortunes, are acclaimed as classics of Japanese literature. (L. M. Zo.)

**TAKLA MAKAN,** a desert in central Asia, the major central division of the Tarim basin. In general the Takla Makan is a region of drift sand and moving sand dunes, and is a waterless area except for the Khotan and Keriya rivers, which carry water northward into the desert. The sand dune desert is uninhabitable away from these rivers and from the Tarim river, which skirts the northern margins. The sand dunes occupy chiefly the south and southwest parts of the Takla Makan, where the full force of the northeast winds is felt. In this area there are two systems of dunes; one, of high chains, stretches from east to west, and the second, of transverse dunes, runs from north to south or northeast to southwest. The steeper sides of the dunes generally face toward the south, away from the direction of the prevailing winds, though there is local variation in alignment, facing and movement.

Between the lower Tarim river, in the northeast, and the Charchan desert, in the southeast, the surface generally is different from that of the rest of the Takla Makan. In this region the sand dunes are interrupted by tracts of level soil, or by areas of old channels, bare mesas and erosional remnants, swept clean by the wind. This is the zone in which the Tarim river and the lake, Lop Nor, have wandered repeatedly, so that in places there is fresh to brackish water available near the surface.

Vegetation and animal life are almost nonexistent in the dry heart of the Takla Makan, but along the permanent streams and locally in the eastern sector various steppe plants, reeds, tamarisks and poplars provide a thin scattering of plant life. On the lower Tarim river, and around Lop Nor, heavy reed growth does occur. The animal life of the region is concentrated at localities providing water and vegetation. Hares, rodents, foxes, wolves, wild pigs, a few antelope and, in a few places in the east, wild camels, are among the land animals. In general the animal population of the eastern sector is greater than that of the western zone. A variety of fish and birds are found along the lower Tarim river and throughout Lop Nor.

The climate of the Takla Makan is one of extremes. Winter temperatures as low as −23° or −24.5° C (−10° or −12° F) occur almost everywhere, and a temperature of −30° C (−22° F) has been observed in the southeast, where winter snowstorms sometimes occur. Temperatures as high as 30° C (86° F) have been recorded in late spring, but it is likely that higher temperatures occur in the interior dune areas in midsummer. Suffocating sandstorms occur, often enveloping the desert for days and producing an impenetrable dust haze.

*See* also SINKIANG; TARIM; LOP NOR. (J. E. SR.)

**TALAT PASHA, MEHMED** (1874–1921), a leader of the Young Turk revolution, was born in Edirne, Turkey, in 1874, the son of a minor Turkish official. After attending the Law School in Salonika (Thessaloniki), he returned to Edirne and worked in the local post office but was soon arrested for subversive political activity. Released two years later (1895), he became first a clerk, then chief clerk at the Salonika post office. In 1908 he was again dismissed, as being a member of the Society of Union and Progress, the organ of the Young Turk movement. After the Young Turk revolution in that year he became deputy for Edirne in the Turkish Parliament and was appointed minister of the interior (1909). He then became successively minister of the post office and president of the Society of Union and Progress. When World War I broke out he was again minister of the interior and in this capacity had to take responsibility for the ruthless transportation of the disaffected Armenians from the eastern vilayets to Syria and Mesopotamia, in the course of which the majority died of hunger, disease, and massacre. In 1917 he became grand vizier and held this post until the end of the war. When the armistice was signed in 1918 he escaped to Europe but was killed by an Armenian in Berlin on March 15, 1921. Although not well-educated, Mehmed Talat Pasha was intelligent and honest and was an idealist who loved and served his country well. Until the outbreak of World War I his influence was on the side of the Entente powers rather than on that of Germany. (M. P. P.)

**TALAVERA DE LA REINA,** a town of central Spain, in the province of Toledo, 70 mi. (113 km.) SW of Madrid. It lies on the right bank of the Tagus near its confluence with the Alberche. Pop. (1960) 31,900 (municipal). Historic monuments include the town walls, with 18 watchtowers dating from the 12th–13th centuries; the Gothic church of Santa María la Mayor; and the Mudejar church of Santiago. The town is on the Madrid–Cáceres railway. Agriculture is the main occupation, with tobacco and cotton crops forming the basis of much local industry, which also includes the manufacture of olive oil and agricultural machinery, and milk processing.

The town was of Roman origin and was conquered by Alfonso VI in 1083; Alfonso XI gave it to his queen, Maria of Portugal, whence the name "de la Reina." From the 16th century it was an important centre for woolen manufactures, but was even more noted for its silk and porcelain. In the 18th century the porcelain industry declined although it was revived to some extent after 1905. The royal silk factory, established in 1748, was closed in 1851. Economic recovery in the 20th century was largely due to the irrigation of land on the right bank of the Tagus which facilitated the cultivation of new crops.

In the Battle of Talavera (July 1809) during the Peninsular War (*q.v.*), the English under Sir Arthur Wellesley, in cooperation with Spanish troops, defeated the French, who were commanded by several generals including King Joseph Bonaparte. As a result of this victory Wellesley was made Viscount Wellington.

**TALBOT,** the name of one of the oldest families in the English nobility; it traces its descent from RICHARD TALBOT (d. 1174/75), who held Eccleswall and Linton, in Herefordshire, in the time of Henry II. Records mention several persons called Talbot living earlier in England, and in Normandy before 1066, among them Geoffrey Talbot (d. 1140), an opponent of King Stephen; but since Talbot was at first a nickname and not a hereditary surname, their relationship is obscure.

The descendants of Richard Talbot, with whom the proved pedigree begins, ranked for several generations among the lesser families of the Welsh border counties. GILBERT TALBOT (1276–1346) took part with other Marcher lords against Edward II's favourites, the Despensers, who had wrested estates from his daughter-in-law Elizabeth Comyn. With his son, Richard, he was taken prisoner by the royal forces at Boroughbridge (1322) but was later pardoned and restored to his estates. He was afterward king's chamberlain and justice of south Wales, and was summoned to parliament as a baron (1332). His son, RICHARD (*c.* 1305–56), 2nd lord, claimed extensive lands in Scotland in right of his wife, Elizabeth, daughter of John Comyn of Badenoch, and in 1332 he joined Edward Balliol in his invasion of Scotland, being present at the victory of Dupplin (Aug. 12). Captured by the Scots in Sept. 1334, he was released for a ransom of £2,000. His wife, also a coheiress of the Valence earls of Pembroke, brought him the manor of Painswick in Gloucestershire and the castle of Goodrich on the river Wye; their grandson later acquired in her right the Irish lordship of Wexford (1389). Richard afterward fought with the English armies in France at Morlaix (1342) and Crécy (1346). His son, GILBERT (*c.* 1332–87), served in France and also Spain. The family estates in Herefordshire, Gloucestershire, Oxfordshire and Kent were further increased by the marriage of Gilbert's son, RICHARD (*c.* 1361–96), to Ankaret, daughter and heiress of John, 4th Lord Strange of Blackmere, who brought him Whitchurch in Shropshire and other lands. His son, GILBERT (*c.* 1383–1418), 5th lord, campaigned in Wales against Owen Glendower, and, after proving himself one of Henry V's most vigorous captains in France, died during the siege of Rouen. On the death of his infant daughter and heir (1421), he was succeeded as 7th lord by his brother, JOHN (1384–1453), whose marriage to Maud, heiress of the lords Furnival, had brought him wide estates in Yorkshire, including Sheffield castle, which became a favourite family residence until 1618. In reward for his distinguished services in France he was created earl of Shrewsbury (1442) and earl of Waterford (1446).

The 1st earl's son, JOHN (*c.* 1413–60), was chancellor of Ireland during his father's lifetime and treasurer of England (1456–58). A strong Lancastrian, he was rewarded with grants from the forfeited Yorkist estates (1459–60) and was killed fighting for Henry VI at Northampton (July 1460). JOHN (1448–73), 3rd earl, at first shared his father's loyalties and was present in Henry VI's army at the second battle of St. Albans and at Towton (1461), but afterward made his peace with the new king, Edward IV, and was appointed chief justice of north Wales in 1471. His son, GEORGE (1468–1538), 4th earl, began a family tradition of devoted service to the Tudor kings. He fought at the battle of Stoke (1487), was steward of the household (1506–38), commanded the army which invaded France in 1513, and, as king's lieutenant in the north, crushed the rebels of the Pilgrimage of Grace (1536). FRANCIS TALBOT (1500–60), who succeeded his father as 5th earl, joined in the invasions of Scotland (1542 and 1544) and spent much of his life on the Scottish borders, being president of the council of the north from 1549 until his death. His son, GEORGE (*c.* 1522–90), 6th earl, who was styled Lord Talbot during his father's lifetime, was selected by Elizabeth I for the unenviable position of custodian of Mary Stuart, who spent the years 1569–84 in his castles at Sheffield and Tutbury or at Chatsworth house. His task was complicated by the limited funds allowed him by Elizabeth, and by the malicious attempts to discredit him of his second wife, Bess of Hardwick.

The 6th earl was succeeded in turn by two of his sons, but in 1618 the direct male line descended from the first earl ceased, and the title and estates passed to the head of a cadet branch of the family founded by SIR GILBERT TALBOT (d. 1517) of Grafton, Worcestershire, a younger son of the 2nd earl. This was GEORGE TALBOT (1566–1630), 9th earl, a Roman Catholic like nearly all his descendants until 1856, who had been ordained priest before he succeeded to the title. His great great nephew, CHARLES (1660–1718), 12th earl, was raised to the dignity of a duke for his services to William III (*see* SHREWSBURY, CHARLES TALBOT, Duke of), but as he left no son this title died with him and the earldom passed to his cousin, GILBERT (1673–1743), a Roman Catholic priest who never assumed the title. From this time the direct line of Sir Gilbert Talbot of Grafton began to fail. A nephew three times succeeded to an uncle, and the title then passed to a cousin, Bertram Arthur Talbot (1832–56), the 17th earl, who died unmarried. The lands were claimed under his will by Lord Edmund Howard, a younger son of the 14th duke of Norfolk and afterward Viscount Fitzalan, but the courts decided that the title and estates should remain together, and a successor to the earldom was found in Henry John Chetwynd-Talbot (1803–68), Earl Talbot, head of another line of the descendants of Sir Gilbert Talbot of Grafton, who became the 18th earl of Shrewsbury. The head of this family a century before had been William Talbot (d. 1730), successively bishop of Oxford, Salisbury and Durham. His son, Charles (1685–1737), lord chancellor (1733–37), was created Baron Talbot of Hensol in 1733. Charles's son, William (1710–82), was raised to the dignity of Earl Talbot in 1761, and William's nephew John Chetwynd (1750–93) added the title of Viscount Ingestre (1784), now usually borne by the earl of Shrewsbury's eldest son. All these titles have since been united in the line descended from the 18th earl. (C. D. R.)

**TALBOT, ARTHUR NEWELL** (1857–1942), U.S. engineer, one of the foremost authorities of his day on reinforced-concrete construction, was born in Cortland, Ill., Oct. 21, 1857. He was graduated from the University of Illinois and later served there as assistant professor of engineering and mathematics (1885–90) and professor of municipal and sanitary engineering, in charge of theoretical and applied mechanics (1890–1926).

Talbot was instrumental in establishing the engineering experiment station in 1904 at the University of Illinois, the first of its kind. His early investigations of concrete and reinforced concrete led to a number of important publications by the station, and he established in the United States the mechanical method of analysis of reinforced-concrete beams.

In 1914 Talbot began extensive studies on stresses in railroad tracks, which led to important findings for improvement of rails and roadbed. He also served as a consultant on problems concerning water purification and municipal sanitary works. Talbot died in Chicago on April 3, 1942. (S. C. Hr.)

**TALBOT, MARY ANNE** (1778–1808), English "Amazon" who served in the English army and navy disguised as a man, was born in London on Feb. 2, 1778. She believed herself to be the illegitimate child of William Talbot, 1st Earl Talbot. Seduced in January 1792 by a Capt. Essex Bowen, she accompanied him to Santo Domingo, in the Caribbean, disguised as his footboy and with the name John Taylor, and then to Flanders as a drummer. She was present at the capture of Valenciennes (July 1793), where Bowen was killed, and then deserted and joined a French lugger. Captured by the British in the English channel, she was transferred to the "Brunswick" and was wounded in Adm. R. Howe's victory of June 1, 1794. Soon at sea again, she was captured by the French and imprisoned for 18 months at Dunkirk. After a voyage to the United States in 1796, she returned to London in November 1796 and was seized by a press-gang, when her real identity was discovered. She later became a servant of Robert Kirby, a London publisher, who published her story in his *Wonderful and Scientific Museum*, vol. ii (1804) and in *The Life and Surprising Adventures of Mary Anne Talbot* (1809). She died in Shropshire on Feb. 4, 1808.

**TALBOT, WILLIAM HENRY FOX** (1800–1877), English photographer, contributed the basic process for photogravure (*see* Gravure: *History;* Photography: *History*). He was born at Melbury House, near Evershot, Dorset, on Feb. 11, 1800, and died there on Sept. 17, 1877. He was educated at Harrow and at Trinity College, Cambridge; for the 50-year period after he earned his M.A. (1825), he published many articles in physics, chemistry, mathematics, astronomy, and archaeology. Before L. J. M. Daguerre in 1839 exhibited pictures taken in sunlight, Talbot had obtained similar success, and as soon as Daguerre's discoveries became known he communicated the results of his experiments to the Royal Society. In 1841 he made known his invention of the calotype or Talbotype process and, after the development of the collodion process by F. S. Archer (1851), devised a method of instantaneous photography (*see* Camera Lucida and Camera Obscura). His antiquarian interests led him to become one of the earliest to decipher the cuneiform inscriptions from Nineveh (*q.v.*).

His works include *Pencil of Nature* (1844–46), of unusual interest because it was the first known book to be illustrated entirely with photographs; *Hermes, or Classical and Antiquarian Researches* (1838–39); *Illustrations of the Antiquity of the Book of Genesis* (1839); *English Etymologies* (1846).

*See* G. Grigson and C. H. Gibbs-Smith (eds.), *People . . .* (1954); B. Newhall, *The History of Photography . . .*, rev. and enlarged ed. (1964).

**TALBOT OF HENSOL, CHARLES TALBOT,** 1st Baron (1685–1737), English lawyer, lord chancellor of Great Britain from 1733 to 1737, was the eldest son of William Talbot (later bishop of Durham), a descendant of the 1st earl of Shrewsbury. Educated at Eton and at Oriel College, Oxford, he became a fellow of All Souls College in 1704. He was called to the bar in 1711 and in 1717 was appointed solicitor general to George, prince of Wales (later George II). He was a member of parliament for Tregony, Cornwall (1720–22) and for Durham (1722–33). He became solicitor general in 1726 and lord chancellor in 1733, when he was created Baron Talbot of Hensol. He died at his house in Lincoln's Inn Fields, London, on Feb. 14, 1737. Talbot, an efficient and scrupulous chancellor, enjoyed the reputation of a wit; he was a patron of the poet James Thomson, and Joseph Butler (later bishop of Durham) dedicated his *Analogy* (1736) to him.

*See* J. Campbell, *Lives of the Lord Chancellors,* vol. iv (1846).

**TALC** is the mineral name for the familiar hydrous magnesium silicate, a common mineral occurring as veins, foliated masses and as a constituent in certain rocks in metamorphic terranes. Talc is distinguished from almost all other minerals by its extreme softness. The hardness of 1 (easily scratched with the fingernail) imparts a soapy or greasy feel which accounts for the name soapstone or steatite for the compact aggregates of talc. Soapstones have been employed since ancient times for carvings, ornaments and utensils. Assyrian cylinder seals, Egyptian scarabs and Chinese figure carvings are notable examples. The resistance to attack from most reagents and to moderate heat makes soapstones especially suitable for sinks and countertops. Talc is also used for lubricants, leather dressings, toilet and dusting powders and certain marking pencils. The major industrial uses of talc and soapstone are in ceramics, paint, rubber, insecticides, roofing and paper.

The colour of talc is white, gray, yellow or various shades of green with a pearly or silvery lustre. Talc is usually found in foliated masses of thin, small, sometimes hexagonal plates. The individual plates easily separate along the perfect basal cleavages into thin flexible but inelastic lamellae (cleavage fragments of muscovite (*q.v.*) which can be confused with talc are elastic). Pyrophyllite (*q.v.*) can be distinguished from talc only by optical or chemical methods.

**Mode of Occurrence and Composition.**—Talc is found as a metamorphic mineral in the lower facies of metamorphism and is often associated with other minerals such as serpentine, tremolite (amphibole) (*qq.v.*) and forsterite (olivine; *q.v.*) and almost always associated with carbonate: calcite, dolomite or magnesite (*qq.v.*). Talc, $Mg_3Si_4O_{10}(OH)_2$, can occur as an alteration of a pre-existing mineral such as tremolite or forsterite as evidenced by preserving the crystal outlines of the pre-existing minerals. Talc also occurs as veins and masses formed at the expense of and replacing pre-existing mineral aggregates. Soapstones have two general types of occurrences: (1) a large group of soapstones are found intimately associated with metamorphosed carbonate rocks probably originally rich in magnesium. By the addition of water and silica and the removal of carbon dioxide, talc can be formed:

$$3MgCa(CO_3)_2 + 2H_2O + 5SiO_2 \rightarrow 2Mg_3Si_4O_{10}(OH)_2 + 3CaCO_3 + 3CO_2$$

(2) a large group of soapstones are found intimately associated with olivine- and/or pyroxene-rich igneous rocks which have been extensively altered by the addition of water and carbon dioxide or water and silica to form talc, for example:

$$\underset{\text{Forsterite}}{3Mg_2SiO_4} + 2H_2O + 5SiO_2 \rightarrow \underset{\text{Talc}}{2Mg_3Si_4O_{10}(OH)_2}$$

or the reaction may be as follows:

$$\underset{\text{Forsterite}}{4Mg_2SiO_4} + H_2O + 5CO_2 \rightarrow \underset{\text{Talc}}{Mg_3Si_4O_{10}(OH)_2} + \underset{\text{Magnesite}}{5MgCO_3}$$

A sequence of mineral formation ending in talc is very commonly observed: olivine plus pyroxene is altered to tremolite, which is altered to serpentine, which in turn is altered to talc plus carbonate. The alteration of serpentine by the addition of silica to form talc is common, with the result that serpentine-rich rocks and soapstones are usually found together. The conditions for the formation of talc apparently are often met in metamorphism—as evidenced by the world-wide occurrence of soapstones in many metamorphic terranes.

One of the remarkable features about talc is its simple, almost constant composition. Unlike other silicates, even closely related ones, talc appears to be unable to accept iron or aluminum into its structure and form solid solution series (*see* MINERALOGY: *The Nature of Minerals: Solid Solution*). This is especially curious because an iron analogue of talc is known, and the structurally related chlorite (*q.v.*) forms at least a partial solid solution series between the iron and magnesium end members.

**Crystal Structure.**—The crystal structure of talc, a phyllosilicate, accounts for its physical properties. The phyllosilicates are characterized by a hexagonal sheet structure arrangement of the $SiO_4$ tetrahedral groups formed by the sharing of three oxygen atoms from each $SiO_4$ tetrahedron with neighbouring $SiO_4$ tetrahedra with the silicon atoms arranged at the corners of hexagons. The fourth (unshared) oxygen atom of the tetrahedron is capable of forming chemical bonds with other metal atoms. (For description of this structure *see* AMPHIBOLE; PYROXENE.) In most phyllosilicates, talc included, the unshared oxygens are on the same side of the sheet. Two such sheets (oriented such that their unshared oxygens face each other) are bonded together by the magnesium atoms with the remaining charges balanced by OH groups (located at the centres of the hexagonal groups) also bonded to the magnesium atoms. This arrangement results in a double-sheet structure which completely satisfies the valence demands of the atoms. Therefore, these double-sheet units cannot be bonded to adjacent units by other metal atoms satisfying remaining charges. Consequently, the talc crystal is made up of stacks of these double-sheet units held together in the stack by the weakest of chemical bonds—the van der Waals' forces. Thus, this stacking can be disturbed by slight forces causing the slipping of the double-sheet units along this perfect cleavage direction.

(G. W. DEV.)

**TALCA,** a province of central Chile, spans coastal mountains, central valley, and the Andean cordillera. Separated in 1833 from Colchagua Province and then enlarged (1927–36) by the annexation of Curicó Province, Talca has an area of 3,915 sq.mi. (10,141 sq.km.). Pop. (1960) 206,154. Molina and Curepto are secondary administrative and trading centres. Grapes, wheat, edible legumes, and alfalfa are the major irrigated crops of the predominantly agricultural province. Sheep, particularly numerous in the coastal mountains, and cattle are the main livestock interests. Talca is served by the national north-south railway and paved highway, and by the railways to Constitución and Perquín. Tourist attractions include the Mondaca hot springs and sports fishing in Laguna del Maule and the Maule and Claro rivers.

TALCA CITY in the central valley, is the provincial capital. Founded in 1692, it is one of Chile's larger urban centres, with a population in 1960 of 68,148. Its wide streets and attractive central plaza give Talca a prosperous appearance. The city is a commercial and rail transportation centre. Its industrial products include matches, biscuits, candy, flour, tobacco, and clothing.

(J. T.)

**TALLADEGA,** a city of Alabama, U.S., the seat of Talladega County, is 57 mi. E of Birmingham in the foothills of the Blue Ridge Mountains. The city is in an agricultural and dairying region, with marble and limestone quarries and iron mines. The chief industrial products are cotton textiles, cottonseed oil, machine parts, pipe fittings, soil pipe, lumber, woolen worsted fabric, and yarn. Talladega College, a coeducational institution founded in 1867 by the American Missionary Association, and the Alabama School for the Deaf and Blind are located there. Nearby are Cheaha State Park and Talladega National Forest. The name Talladega, also applying to mountains south and east of the town, is Indian for "border town" as its site was on the edge of the Creek Indians' land. Andrew Jackson defeated a large force of Indians there in 1813. Talladega was settled in the 1830s and incorporated in 1835; the county was established in 1832. For comparative population figures *see* table in ALABAMA: *Population*.

(B. CR.)

**TALLAGE,** a term employed, while it was in ordinary usage, in the general sense of "tax," and applied to various seignorial, royal and municipal taxes (most of them also known by other names such as "aid"), but particularly to a tax imposed by the lord of an estate upon his unfree tenants. Tallage of this kind was already an established seignorial perquisite in England, as elsewhere in western Europe, in the 12th century. Its arbitrariness was generally greater than that of similar aids taken by lords from free tenants. Its frequency or its amount or both might be at the lord's will, though on many estates in the 13th century it had already become a fixed charge. In England from the reign of Henry II a lord sometimes required specific royal authority to take a tallage—when, for instance, the estate to be tallaged was a former royal estate.

In England at the end of the 12th century, "tallage" established itself as the name of a royal tax (developed by Henry II but not in principle novel) levied on estates in the king's hand and on boroughs. It was assessed by the king's itinerant justices, who had administrative as well as judicial duties, or by special commissioners. The assessors usually negotiated with the community of a borough or estate for a lump sum, but sometimes took the less popular course of tallaging individuals separately. Royal tallages were most frequent during John's reign; objection to them found expression in the Magna Carta. Under Henry III an interval of two to four years was usual and the average yield seemed no greater than before. At its highest, the yield of a tallage exceeded £5,000, and payment was prompt. London's contribution was by far the largest single item, sometimes exceeding a third of the whole. In the reign of Edward I, as the summons of representatives of boroughs to parliaments became more frequent, parliamentary taxation of boroughs and the king's estates was preferred to tallage. Edward I took a tallage in 1304 after a lapse of 36 years. It was last taken in 1312. An attempt to revive it in 1332 was abandoned in favour of a parliamentary grant.

(ER. S.)

**TALLAHASSEE,** a city of Florida, U.S., the capital of the state and the seat of Leon county, is in the northern part of the state 166 mi. W. of Jacksonville, 200 mi. E. of Pensacola and 20 mi. N. of the Gulf of Mexico. The city and the surrounding region are characterized by rolling hills, lakes, streams and giant magnolia and oak trees. Leon county and the 12 counties immediately to the west and east comprise the "big bend" of north central Florida, an agricultural area producing livestock, "shade-cured" (formerly called Spanish or Florida) tobacco, pecans, tung oil trees and diversified farm products. Among the industries of the city are lumber-planing mills, naval store refineries and pecan processing plants. It is a key wholesaling and distribution point for northwest Florida and southwest Georgia and is the seat of two coeducational universities, Florida State university and the Florida Agricultural and Mechanical university (*see* FLORIDA: *Education*). Among its stately homes are the Grove (completed in 1830), the Columns (1835), Goodwood (1843) and the governor's mansion (1957).

In 1539–40, Hernando De Soto and a Spanish expedition spent the winter in the vicinity, this incident leading to a local assumption that the first observance of Christmas in the present United States was conducted in or nearby the site at that time. Other Spaniards, while fighting the Apalachee Indians of the region, are supposed to have fortified a hill near the site in 1638. By 1675 seven Franciscan missions were established in the region, San Luis de Talimali, in the western section of the present city, being the most important. This mission, sometimes called Fort San Luis, was destroyed and the Apalachee Indians were dispersed by Gov. James Moore of South Carolina during Queen Anne's War (the War of the Spanish Succession, 1701–13), when he invaded Florida to punish the Spanish for having incited Indian attacks against white settlers in South Carolina. Tallahassee then acquired its name from a Creek Indian word meaning "abandoned village." From this time until Spain ceded Florida to the United States in 1821, Tallahassee remained quite insignificant.

When Florida became a U.S. territory it had two capitals, one in St. Augustine and one in Pensacola. The first territorial legislature met in Pensacola in 1822, the second in St. Augustine the next year. Tallahassee was named permanent capital in 1823 and the legislature first met there in 1824. Incorporated in 1825, it became the state capital when Florida entered the union in 1845.

Before the American Civil War Tallahassee became a trade centre for the rich cotton plantation country of middle Florida, partially because of its connection with the little port of St. Marks nearby. Negro slavery was more prevalent in Leon and adjoining counties than elsewhere in the state. During the war it was far removed from the significant battle areas. In the late 1800s and early 1900s, when south Florida entered its boom era, Tallahassee declined as a commercial and business centre. After 1940 it regained importance because of its position as the governmental centre of the state. The city has a council-manager form of government, in effect since 1920. The population (1960) was 48,174; standard metropolitan statistical area (Leon county), 74,225. For comparative population figures *see* table in FLORIDA: *Population*. (W. T. Jo.)

**TALLAPOOSA,** a river of northwestern Georgia and east central Alabama, U.S., rises in the piedmont area of western Georgia about 30 mi. WNW of Atlanta and flows southwest in an irregular, steplike course for about 268 mi., joining the larger Coosa River about 10 mi. N of Montgomery, Ala., to form the Alabama River. Its only large tributary is the Little Tallapoosa which joins it about midway in its course. All but the lower part of the drainage basin of about 4,500 sq.mi. lies in the Alabama-Georgia piedmont. Falls at Tallassee, Ala., chief city on the Tallapoosa, about 43 mi. upstream from its mouth, and a steep gradient above that prevented use of the river for navigation. Three private power dams (Martin, Yates, and Thurlow) above Tallassee created reservoirs such as Lake Martin (1,630,000 ac.ft.) for river control and recreation as well as power.

The name Tallapoosa is of Creek origin and many Indian villages were situated along the lower river before the 19th century. The Creek War Battle of Horseshoe Bend (1814) was fought in a river bend near what is now the northern end of Lake Martin, about 9 mi. N of Dadeville, Ala. (M. W. M.)

**TALLCHIEF, MARIA** (1925– ), U.S. ballet dancer noted for the crisp perfection of her technique, was born in Fairfax, Okla., Jan. 24, 1925, of American Indian descent. After studying with Bronislava Nijinska she joined the Ballet Russe de Monte Carlo in 1942 and soon became a leading dancer. In 1947 she was guest artist at the Paris Opéra, and in 1948, the year it was founded, she joined the New York City Ballet and was for a time its prima ballerina. She joined the American Ballet Theatre in 1960. Tallchief particularly excelled in the roles created for her by George Balanchine in *The Firebird, Orpheus,* and *The Nutcracker*. (LN. ME.)

**TALLEMANT DES RÉAUX, GÉDÉON** (1619–1692), French writer of informative and entertaining *Historiettes,* or short biographies. Born at La Rochelle on Oct. 2, 1619, of a rich Protestant family, Tallemant went early to Paris and began to frequent literary circles. In 1646 he married Elisabeth Rambouillet in the Protestant temple at Charenton. His later life was made miserable by family bankruptcy and by separation from his wife. She was received into the Catholic Church in 1665, he not until July 1685, about three months before the revocation of the Edict of Nantes. Tallemant died in Paris on Nov. 10, 1692.

Tallemant published nothing in his lifetime save a few poems in anthologies. His *Historiettes* were not published till 1834, from a folio manuscript that had appeared in a Paris auction. This contains a mass of particulars about leading men and women in Parisian society and French public life of the first half of the 17th century. Tallemant appears to have started writing in 1657 from data collected earlier. A good listener, he also took the trouble to seek out well-informed authorities for his lives (such as Boisrobert on Richelieu and Racan on Malherbe), with the aim of recording anything of interest that was not in the printed histories. His new, disturbing, and apparently chatty information about dignified persons was at first decried, but research has done much to establish its reliability. These acute jottings, often so near to the actual event, may be considered a firsthand source and have been useful as a corrective to later interpretations. There are modern editions by G. Mongrédien, 8 vol. (1932) and in the "Pléiade Series" by A. Adam (1960– ).

*See* E. Magne, *La Joyeuse Jeunesse . . .* (1921) and *La Fin troublée de Tallemant des Réaux* (1922); also E. Gosse, *Tallemant des Réaux or the Art of Miniature Biography* (1925). (W. G. ME.)

**TALLENSI,** a Negro tribe of about 40,000 sedentary cultivators densely settled in the open savanna zone of northern Ghana who speak a dialect (Talni) of the Gur language family allied to that of the Dagomba (*q.v.*). They are barely self-sufficient, growing millet and sorghum as staples, eked out with minor crops, small-scale husbandry of cattle, sheep, goats, and some poultry.

The normal domestic unit is the polygamous joint family of a man and his sons (and sometimes grandsons) with their wives and unmarried daughters. Married daughters live with their husbands in other communities, commonly nearby. Homesteads are scattered and settlements, which merge into one another, are the territory of exogamous, totemic, patrilineal clans or maximal lineages, segmented into a hierarchy of lesser lineages and held together primarily by the sanctions of common ancestor worship. Clans are politically autonomous, and jural authority is vested in clan elders. In one group of clans (Namoos, who claim to be of remote immigrant origin from the Mamprussi people) the senior elder is the chief; in the other group (Talis, who claim to be the aboriginal inhabitants) he is the ritual custodian of the earth; the two groups have affinal and cognatic ties.

Tenacious family and kinship bonds are buttressed by an elaborate ancestor cult that is expressed in a cycle of great festivals at sowing and harvest time in which the chiefs and earth custodians participate. Tallensi have shown considerable adaptability to change, accepting a federal native authority since 1937 and making good use of new schools, markets, and opportunities for labour migration. Under the republic the authority of chiefs and elders was replaced by official administrative agencies. Traditional values remained largely intact, but the expanding economy, education, and increasing Christian influence foreshadowed radical social change.

BIBLIOGRAPHY.—M. Fortes and E. Evans-Pritchard (eds.), "The Political System of the Tallensi," in *African Political Systems* (1940); Fortes, *The Web of Kinship Among the Tallensi* (1949); Fortes and G. Dieterlen (eds.), *African Systems of Thought* (1965); Fortes and D. Mayer, "Psychosis and Social Change Among the Tallensi," *Cahiers d'Etudes Africaines,* vol. 20 (1965). (M. Fs.)

**TALLEYRAND** (TALLEYRAND-PÉRIGORD), **CHARLES MAURICE DE,** PRINCE ET DUC DE BÉNÉVENT (1754–1838), French statesman and diplomat notable for his capacity for political survival, held high office during the French Revolution, under Napoleon, at the Restoration, and under Louis Philippe. As Louis XVIII's delegate to the Congress of Vienna, his skill in dividing the four allies who had defeated Napoleon won for France an effective voice in the settlement of Europe.

Talleyrand was born in Paris on Feb. 2, 1754, the son of Charles Daniel, comte de Talleyrand-Périgord, then colonel of the French grenadiers, and of Alexandrine de Damas d'Antigny. Both his parents came of old and aristocratic, but not wealthy, families. Charles Maurice was boarded out with a nurse in a Paris suburb, and when he was four years old he fell from a chest of drawers, dislocating his foot. This accident lamed him for life. His elder brother having died at the age of five, tradition would have decreed for Charles Maurice a military career; but because of his lameness his parents destined him for the church. From the age of 8 he was a pupil in the Collège d'Harcourt at Paris and at 15

THE GRANGER COLLECTION
TALLEYRAND, PORTRAIT BY PIERRE PRUD'HON

was sent as assistant to his uncle Alexandre, coadjutor to the archbishop of Reims, in the hope that some acquaintance with the activities and splendours of an episcopal palace might arouse in him an interest in his future career. In 1770 he entered the seminary of Saint-Sulpice at Paris; there he spent most of his time reading avidly, usually works such as those of Voltaire or Montesquieu which criticized existing institutions. A rebel by nature, and with no vocation to the priesthood, his behaviour was anything but edifying; and even while he was at the seminary he had a mistress, a young actress who lived nearby. Probably expelled (1775) for his scandalous conduct, Talleyrand nevertheless received minor orders at Paris on April 1, 1775; six months later he received from the king the Abbey of Saint-Denis at Reims. After two years' study at the Sorbonne, he took his degree in theology (March 2, 1778), and was ordained on Dec. 18, 1779. The following day his uncle Alexandre, now himself archbishop of Reims, named him his vicar-general.

Talleyrand did not allow his priesthood to debar him from any sort of worldly pleasure. He was a constant companion of the most fashionable wits and beauties of the day, men such as Louis, comte de Narbonne, Armand Louis de Gontaut, duc de Lauzun (later duc de Biron), Emmanuel Henri de Launay, comte d'Antraigues, and the Swiss banker Panchaud: and women like Louise de Rohan, daughter of prince Charles de Rohan-Montauban, comtesse de Brionne, and her daughter-in-law the princesse de Vaudémont, the comtesse de Brienne, and Adelaide Filleul, comtesse de Flahaut. By Adelaide he had a son, Auguste Charles de Flahaut, who became a general under Napoleon and an ambassador under Louis Philippe. In this society Talleyrand discussed secular rather than ecclesiastical affairs, particularly the current developments in revolutionary thought. Nevertheless, in 1780 he was appointed agent general of the clergy, a position which brought him into contact with the ministers of the crown and gave him an apprenticeship in state affairs. In this capacity he made proposals to improve the standard of living of the lower clergy. On Nov. 2, 1788, he was appointed bishop of Autun, and took possession of his diocese on March 15, 1789.

**The Revolution.**—No sooner had he arrived in his diocese than Talleyrand had to deal with elections for the forthcoming meeting of the States General. For his clergy he drew up a program of desired reforms, which they adopted, and for the country as a whole he demanded a constitution that would provide a genuine representative system, guarantees of liberty and property, and the ending of fiscal privilege. His clergy elected him as their deputy to the States General, which met at Versailles on May 5, 1789. During the earlier deliberations, Talleyrand showed himself in favour of the union of the three orders for voting purposes (*see* FRANCE: *History*); but he deplored mob rule and hoped that the reforms he had suggested would be carried through by the king, and not imposed upon him. There are doubts, however, of the truth of the story that on the night of July 16–17, 1789, Talleyrand, through the king's brother, the comte d'Artois, urged Louis XVI to use force against the Revolution, saying, when the king refused to do so: "then it only remains for each one of us to look out for himself."

Talleyrand's most important contribution to the work of the Constituent Assembly was his proposal (introduced Oct. 10, 1789, and carried Nov. 2) that church property should be appropriated by the state. He also took part in the debates on the constitution, and spoke (Aug. 4) in favour of the abolition of feudalism. He sponsored a draft law for introducing a uniform system of measures, and also laid before the assembly an important report on education. He notably associated himself with the Revolution when, as a bishop, he said Mass at an altar erected in the middle of the Champ-de-Mars, on the Fête de la Fédération (July 14, 1790). This proved, in fact, the last Mass he said publicly; that same evening he was in a gaming house and won large sums of money. Increasingly repudiating his identification with the church, he helped bring about passage of the Civil Constitution of the Clergy (July 1790), and was one of the first to take the prescribed oath (January 1791). A few days later, having been elected administrator of the *département* of Paris, he resigned as bishop of Autun. The fact that he no longer held a see did not, however, prevent him from joining two other "constitutional" bishops in the consecration (Feb. 24) of two new bishops who had been elected in accordance with the Civil Constitution. As a result, he was excommunicated by Pope Pius VI (April 13).

The death of Mirabeau (April 2, 1791) seems to have been a turning point in Talleyrand's career. Originally on bad terms, the two men had become more friendly since May 1789, and they frequented the same clubs and gambling houses. Talleyrand was never likely to exercise anything like Mirabeau's influence; but after Mirabeau's death he aspired to take his place as secret counselor of the king and he also replaced Mirabeau on the Directory (the controlling group) of the *département* of Paris. He was trying hard to establish himself among the political élite.

After the Constituent Assembly was dissolved (Sept. 30, 1791), Talleyrand began his diplomatic career. Sent to London by Valdec Delessart, the foreign minister, he had to persuade the English government not to join Austria, Russia, and Prussia, who were proposing to make war on France in order to restore the *ancien régime* there and to prevent the spread of revolution throughout Europe. Arriving in London (Jan. 24, 1792), Talleyrand was coldly received by the royal family, and wrote home that any hopes of an understanding with England were illusory. In meetings with William Pitt, the prime minister, and Lord Grenville, the foreign secretary, he proposed that both countries should guarantee to help defend the other's territories, France specifically recognizing British sovereignty in India and Ireland. Although the British government made no response, Talleyrand became convinced that Great Britain would not join France's enemies, provided that France did not attack the Dutch United Provinces. Returning to Paris (March 10), Talleyrand persuaded the new foreign minister, Charles Dumouriez, to appoint the young marquis de Chauvelin as plenipotentiary in London, and returned there (April 29) as Chauvelin's assistant. France had now declared war on Austria (which was allied to Prussia); Talleyrand managed to extract from the British government a declaration of neutrality (May 25), but events in France, especially the riots of June 20, when the crowds burst into the Tuileries Palace, made his position increasingly difficult and he left London on July 5. Although the fall of the monarchy (Aug. 10; *see* FRANCE: *History*) and the September massacres further alienated English sympathies, Talleyrand still sought to postpone Britain's entry into the war. He drew up for the provisional executive council a document designed for circulation to all European governments, which threw on Louis XVI all responsibility for the events of Aug. 10. Forbidden to continue his official mission in London, he was granted a passport to go there privately. Arriving on Sept. 18, he did all he could to avert war with Britain, but the invasion of Belgium by French troops and the opening of the Scheldt River to all shipping (November 1792), followed by the execution of the king (January 1793), made it inevitable. Talleyrand, who had been denounced (Dec. 5, 1792) by the Convention (evidence of his secret communication with the king having been found in the "iron box" in the Tuileries), and who was expelled from England early in 1794, tried unsuccessfully to reach Switzerland or Tuscany and eventually took ship for the United States (March 1794). He remained there for just over two years, profitably engaging in a variety of financial speculations.

**The Directory.**—After Robespierre's fall (July 27, 1794), events in France facilitated Talleyrand's return. On June 16, 1795, he petitioned the Convention to remove his name from the list of *émigrés,* as he had had full permission to leave France. His request was granted on Sept. 4, but he did not sail from Philadelphia until June 13, 1796; on July 31 he reached Hamburg, where he spent a month in the company of his friends Karl Friedrich, graf von Reinhard, and the comtesse de Genlis. Reaching Paris on Sept. 20, 1796, he immediately occupied at the Institut National (a reconstruction of Richelieu's Académie Française and other academies) the seat to which he had been elected the previous December. The paper which he read there (July 13, 1797) on the advantages France might derive from new colonies, showed that he again hoped to enter the political arena. Although all the members of the Directory, except Paul Barras, thought him despicable and dangerous, the reorganization of the ministry carried out in July 1797 enabled Barras, at the instance of Mme Germaine Necker de Staël-Holstein, to propose Talleyrand as foreign minister; and J. F. Reubell and L. M. de la Revellière-Lépeaux accepted him on condition that their nominees received other posts (July 18). Talleyrand's position was soon strengthened by the *coup d'état* of Sept. 4, 1797, which removed the two directors (L. N. M. Carnot and Charles Le Tourneur) who had voted against him. Talleyrand approved Bonaparte's conclusion of the Treaty of Campo Formio (Oct. 17–18, 1797) with Austria, thus winning the goodwill of the famous general. Like all the ministers under the Directory, Talleyrand had only limited power, effective control of foreign policy being exercised by Reubell. Talleyrand alone, however, was responsible for a breach between France and the United States, following the indignant withdrawal of the three American envoys from whom Talleyrand had demanded enormous bribes. He joined Bonaparte in urging on the Directory the Egyptian expedition. A year later (June 20, 1799) he tendered his resignation, probably believing that the unstable régime would not survive much longer. Meanwhile, by various means, chiefly the acceptance of large bribes, he had amassed a respectable fortune, and had deposited more than 3,000,000 francs abroad, in London and Hamburg.

Not long after Talleyrand's resignation, Napoleon returned from Egypt, carried through his *coup d'état* of Nov. 9–10, 1799, and established the Consulate. Talleyrand supported him, acting as intermediary to obtain the resignation of Barras, the last of the Directorate, and on Nov. 22 was reappointed foreign minister, an office he was now to hold until 1807.

**The Consulate and the Empire.**—Talleyrand's chief aim was the pacification of Europe, and he immediately began negotiations for peace with England. But they failed, and the first peace treaty (Lunéville, Feb. 9, 1801) was made with Austria. At home, Talleyrand used his influence to facilitate the return of *émigrés* and priests who had refused the oath, and urged the signing of the Concordat (July 1801) between Napoleon and Pope Pius VII. Later (March 10, 1802), at Napoleon's request, the pope signed a brief reconciling Talleyrand with the church and granting him lay status. Then, under pressure from Napoleon, Talleyrand regularized his position by marrying his current mistress, Mme Catherine Grand, the French divorced wife of an English employee of the Indian civil service.

Talleyrand took no direct part in the peace talks with England held at Amiens (1801–02), but he helped the First Consul establish French supremacy in Italy, Germany, and Switzerland. At the *consulta* of leading members of the Cisalpine (now to be called the Italian) Republic, convoked by Napoleon at Lyons (early 1802), Talleyrand engineered various changes in the republic's constitution and the election of Napoleon as its president. In Germany (much to his own profit) he helped to arrange the allocation of certain secularized church lands as compensation to those princes who had lost to France territory on the left bank of the Rhine.

Talleyrand tried hard to avert the renewal of war with England (May 1803) and, although he had helped Napoleon establish himself as "Consul for Life," he hoped to keep Napoleon's ambitions within bounds. His motives in counseling the abduction and execution of Louis Antoine Henri de Bourbon-Condé, duc d'Enghien, are, however, by no means clear. Whether he genuinely believed d'Enghien to be the leader of a plot to overthrow Napoleon, or merely invented the charge to suit his own plans, he was certainly responsible for telling Napoleon that d'Enghien was at Ettenheim in Baden, just across the Rhine. He urged d'Enghien's arrest on foreign soil, and then did his best, through diplomatic channels, to persuade the rest of Europe to condone the illegal seizure. He did nothing to prevent d'Enghien's execution, but later attempted to recover and destroy those documents in foreign archives which implicated him in the crime. When Napoleon became emperor (May 1804), he rewarded Talleyrand by appointing him Grand Chamberlain of the Empire, with an annual income of 500,000 francs. Later Talleyrand was also appointed to the sinecure office of vice-elector and was created (June 5, 1806) prince et duc de Bénévent (Benevento, a city in southern Italy formerly in the pope's possession). From his now vast incomes and the enormous bribes he received, he bought the magnificent château de Valençay, in Touraine.

Nevertheless, from 1805 onward, his influence with the emperor began to wane. He failed to persuade Napoleon, after the victory of Austerlitz to conciliate Austria, or to preserve the Holy Roman Empire, which was replaced (1806) by the Confederation of the Rhine and the Empire of Austria. Talleyrand was not given a free hand in the peace talks he conducted with England; they failed, as did negotiations with Russia, the latter because the tsar repudiated a treaty signed in Paris by his envoy Baron d'Oubril and Talleyrand. When France's war with Russia and Prussia was finally ended, by the Treaties of Tilsit (July 7 and 9, 1807), Talleyrand had no part in the negotiations. Alarmed by Napoleon's insatiable ambition, which he saw clearly could lead only to disaster, he resigned his office in August 1807. Napoleon, however, was already disillusioned with his minister. He had received innumerable complaints of Talleyrand's venality, and perhaps already doubted his loyalty. But he continued to consult him, and it seems clear (despite Talleyrand's later denials) that Talleyrand supported Napoleon's invasion of Spain. The deposed Ferdinand VII, with his brother and uncle (*see* SPAIN: *History*), were detained in Talleyrand's château de Valençay until 1814. In September 1808 Napoleon took Talleyrand to a gathering of European sovereigns at Erfurt. There Talleyrand had secret talks with Tsar Alexander I, urged him to oppose Napoleon, and thenceforward conducted a secret correspondence with both Russia and Austria. This treasonable activity did not, in fact, involve Talleyrand in any great risk, since it was approved by Joseph Fouché, minister of police, who shared Talleyrand's dismay at Napoleon's policies.

After the divorce of the empress Joséphine (1810), Talleyrand persuaded Napoleon to marry Marie Louise, daughter of the Austrian emperor Francis I, in the hope that alliance with the Habsburgs would provide a sense of achievement and thus modify Napoleon's ambition. But nothing, apparently, could accomplish that, and Talleyrand, hearing (1812) of Napoleon's proposed Russian campaign, declared that this was the beginning of the end. In January 1814 Napoleon asked Talleyrand to return to the foreign ministry in order to negotiate with the allies. Talleyrand, who was already planning to restore the Bourbons, refused, remaining unmoved despite violent abuse from Napoleon. When the allies entered Paris (March 31, 1814), the tsar stayed at Talleyrand's town house and was eventually convinced by him that only a Bourbon restoration would assure peace to Europe. Talleyrand persuaded the senate (only 63 out of 140 members of which were present) to constitute a provisional government of five members, one of whom was to be himself, and to declare Napoleon deposed. The new government immediately summoned Louis XVIII who, on May 13, 1814, appointed Talleyrand his foreign minister.

**The Restoration.**—As France's representative at the Congress of Vienna (1814–15), Talleyrand exhibited his diplomatic skill to the full. By stressing that European reorganization should be based on the principle of legitimacy, he contrived in effect to destroy the Treaty of Chaumont which had been made (March 9, 1814) between the four allies; drawing Austria and England into secret agreements designed to prevent Russia from annexing all Poland and Prussia all Saxony. This new triple alliance succeeded in reducing the territorial claims of the other great powers, and led to the agreement by which France was to retain its 1792 frontiers (after the Hundred Days, however, they were reduced to those of 1790). Nevertheless, the final settlement, by giving Prussia control of the east bank of the Rhine, ultimately constituted a serious danger for France.

Talleyrand remained at Vienna during the Hundred Days. On Louis XVIII's return to Paris (July 9, 1815), he was appointed president of the council (retaining the office of foreign minister). But the powerful Ultras (extreme royalists) were bitterly opposed to a ministry dominated by two former revolutionaries (Talleyrand and Fouché), and Talleyrand had forfeited the tsar's goodwill by his tactics at Vienna; under pressure, Louis XVIII was obliged to dismiss him (Sept. 24, 1815). Talleyrand then lived in retirement, writing his memoirs, until in 1829 his unerring political sense led him to ally with the Liberals in order to remove Charles X. He established contact with Louis Philippe, duc d'Orléans, and at the Revolution of July 1830 helped to make him king. As Louis Philippe's ambassador in London (September 1830–November 1834) he played a vital part in the negotiations between France and Britain which resulted in the creation of the kingdom of Belgium. The signature of an alliance between France, Great Britain, Spain, and Portugal (April 1834) crowned his diplomatic career.

Talleyrand died in Paris on May 17, 1838. He received the last sacraments, having signed, a few hours before his death, a document in which he declared himself reconciled with the church, and expressed regret for his former irregular conduct. He was buried at Valençay. He had separated from his wife in 1815, and left no legitimate issue.

Totally disregarding his vices, his treachery, and his venality, bourgeois liberals of the 19th century persisted in acclaiming Talleyrand as the great statesman who restored peace and order to Europe at the Congress of Vienna. But the verdict of modern historians, more remote from the conflicts of his period and the results of his work, must be more carefully weighed. His total lack of principle and overweening egoism leave a sense of distaste which neither his undoubted ability, nor his intelligence, nor the superb diplomatic skills, which he used almost always in the service of peace and liberalism, can totally dispel.

Bibliography.—Talleyrand's *Mémoires* were ed. by the duc de Broglie, 5 vol. (1891–92), Eng. trans. by A. Hall, 5 vol. (1891–92). Of his letters and dispatches, the following are the chief collections: G. Pallain, *La mission de Talleyrand à Londres en 1792* (1889), *Le ministère de Talleyrand sous le Directoire* (1891), *Correspondance inédite du prince de Talleyrand et du roi Louis XVIII pendant le congrès de Vienne* (1881), *Ambassade de Talleyrand à Londres, 1830–1834*, 2 vol. (1891); P. Bertrand, *Lettres inédites de Talleyrand à Napoléon, 1800–1809* (1889); M. Missoffe, "Talleyrand et Maret, duc de Bassano, lettres inédites," *Revue des deux mondes* (August 1954); H. Huth and W. J. Pugh, *Talleyrand in America as a Financial Promoter, 1794–1796*, 3 vol. (1942).

*Biographies:* The standard work is G. Lacour-Gayet, *Talleyrand, 1754–1838*, 4 vol. (1928–34). E. L. Dard, *Napoléon et Talleyrand* (1935; Eng. trans. by C. R. Turner, 1937), is based extensively on the Austrian archives. More recent but less original biographies are by A. Duff Cooper (1932; French trans. by H. and R. Alix, 1937); C. Crane Brinton (1937); the comte de Saint-Aulaire (1936); L. Madelin (1944); J. Bertaut (1945); R. Laforgue (1947); M. Missoffe (1956); E. Tarlé (1958). (J. Go.)

**TALL HALAF** (Tell Halaf), an ancient north Syrian city lying on the west bank of the Khabur River, 3 mi. NW of Ras-al-'Ain, not far from the Turkish border. Populous and important both in the prehistoric period and during the 1st millennium B.C., when it was an Aramaean centre (Bit-Bahiani), it was the Gozan of the Old Testament (II Kings 17:6), to which the Israelites were deported in 722 B.C. after the capture of Samaria by the Assyrians. The place was excavated by a number of German expeditions under the direction of Baron Max von Oppenheim between 1899 and 1927. At its fullest extent, in historic times, the city occupied about 150 ac. and was enclosed by lofty mud-brick walls which were protected by towers and bastions on three sides and by the river on the fourth.

The settlement was already flourishing in the 5th millennium B.C. and has yielded black and gray Neolithic monochrome pottery as well as a typical flint and obsidian blade industry and polished ground-stone celts. A series of typical north Syrian painted ceramic followed: the finest are vessels decorated in a lustrous paint on a shiny surface with geometric and animal designs. This attractively fashioned pottery has been named Tall Halaf ware from the primacy of its discovery on this site, although a greater range of it, properly stratified, was subsequently found at Arpachiyah near Nineveh. Seated figurines of a "mother goddess," also painted; models of cattle; designs of bucrania (ornamented ox skulls); and painted onagers were also characteristic. Evidence of the subsequent 'Ubaid Period has also been recovered from Halaf.

Although the site was no doubt continuously occupied, little is known about it in the long interval between the prehistoric period and the 9th century B.C. The first historic mention of the city (as Guzana) occurs in the reign of the Assyrian king Adad-nirari II, who exacted tribute from its ruler Abi-salamu; Ashurnasirpal II also marched against it, and in 808 B.C. Adad-nirari III sacked the city and reduced the district to a province of the Assyrian Empire.

The only known local ruler was an Aramaean prince named Kapara (*c.* 825 B.C.), who built a temple and a palace and caused his name to be inscribed on a series of basalt orthostats which adorned the walls of the temple-palace. The most notable architectural monument in Gozan was a *bit hilani* building—*i.e.*, one with a portico supported by pillars consisting of life-size caryatid stone figures of divinities mounted upon lions. A remarkable figure of a goddess carrying a bucket, with handle of Assyrian type, bears an inscription which proclaims that anyone defacing it shall be accursed by having his seven daughters indentured to Ishtar and his seven sons burned before the weather god. The city prospered in the 8th and 7th centuries B.C. when it was directly administered by resident Assyrian governors. Seleucid remains, including houses, baths, and graves, were found in the citadel. *See also* Aramaeans; Babylonia and Assyria: *Archaeology, Architecture and Art.*

Bibliography.—*Tell Halaf,* vol. i, ed. by Hubert Schmidt (1943), vol. ii, ed. by R. Naumann (1950), vol. iii, ed. by A. Moortgat (1955); M. von Oppenheim, *Der Tell Halaf, Eine neue Kultur im ältesten Mesopotamien* (1931), Eng. trans. by G. Wheeler (1933). (M. E. L. M.)

**TALLIEN, JEAN LAMBERT** (1767–1820), French revolutionary who became a leader of the moderates (Thermidorians) after he had helped to engineer the fall of Robespierre in 1794. He was born in Paris on Jan. 23, 1767. In 1789 he became secretary to a member of the Third Estate in the Estates-General, and then a foreman in the printing house that published the newspaper *Moniteur*. In August 1791 he brought out a wall newspaper, *L'Ami des Citoyens,* which was subsidized by the Jacobin Club. After taking part in the insurrection of Aug. 10, 1792 (*see* France: *History*), he became secretary to the Commune of Paris. This was the real beginning of his political career.

It is possible that he had some responsibility for the September massacres of 1792, which he later defended in his pamphlet "La Vérité sur les évènements du 2 septembre" (1792). Elected for the *département* of Seine-et-Oise to the National Convention, he sat with the Montagnards and opposed the Girondins (*q.v.*). During the trial of Louis XVI (December 1792–January 1793) he voted against a plebiscite and any postponement of the death penalty. He became a member of the Committee of General Security, and on March 9 was sent on a mission to organize recruiting for the army.

His most important mission was to the *départements* of the southwest, particularly to the Gironde. With Claude Ysabeau, he raised a revolutionary army and on Oct. 19, 1793, captured Bordeaux, which had rebelled during the federalist insurrection (*see* Vendée, Wars of the). Tallien immediately appointed a military commission to try those responsible, and levied a tax on the rich. But on 28 Brumaire year II (Nov. 18, 1793) he was denounced in the Committee of General Security for "his liaison with Madame Cabarrus, the divorced wife of the ex-noble Fontenay"; he had previously released her from prison in Bordeaux. Nevertheless at the end of December his mission was confirmed. Tallien was recalled to Paris in March 1794. He survived Robespierre's purge of the Jacobins on 23 Ventôse (March 13) and at first supported the Committee of Public Safety, approving the execution of Jacques Hébert and Georges Danton. But on 3 Prairial (May 22) the Committee ordered the arrest of Madame Cabarrus, who had followed Tallien to Paris, and he became its enemy. On

June 12 Robespierre denounced him. Feeling himself in danger, Tallien conspired with Paul Barras, Louis Fréron, Joseph Fouché, and others, and was one of the most active in Robespierre's fall on 9 Thermidor (July 27), when he prevented Louis Saint-Just from making his speech in defense of Robespierre.

From this time, Tallien was one of the important men in the Convention, and a leader of the so-called Thermidorian reaction. A member of the reconstructed Committee of Public Safety, he set Madame Cabarrus free on 25 Thermidor (Aug. 13) and married her on 6 Nivôse year III (Dec. 26). Tallien supported the attack on the members of the government Committees of 1793–94, who were tried and deported, and on 16 Germinal (April 5, 1795) decreed the arrest of all his enemies, the former Montagnards. After the abortive royalist rising of 13 Vendémiaire year IV (Oct. 5, 1795) he also denounced some of his colleagues for royalist sympathies. When the Directory was set up (November 1795) he became a member of the Five Hundred, but, suspected now by all parties, he no longer had any influence. He retained his seat until 1798 when he accompanied Bonaparte to Egypt. On his return (April 1801) he found his wife had finally left him; they were divorced in 1802. Supporting the first Restoration (1814) of Louis XVIII, then the Hundred Days, he was deprived of his pension at the second Restoration (1815) and lived in poverty. He died in Paris on Nov. 16, 1820. (A. So.)

**TALLINN** (German REVAL), a primary seaport and capital of the Estonian Soviet Socialist Republic, U.S.S.R., lies on the north coast and on the Gulf of Finland opposite Helsinki. The population (1959), including the suburbs of Nõmme and Pirita, numbers 281,714, a third of whom are Russians.

The foundation of Tallinn is ascribed to the Danish king Valdemar II, who in 1219 built a citadel on the site of a former Estonian stronghold. As merchants from the Baltic ports of Visby, Lübeck, and Bremen settled there in the 13th century, the town prospered and became a port and trading centre of the Hanseatic League (*q.v.*). Valdemar IV sold Tallinn to the Teutonic Knights in 1346, but on the dissolution of the Teutonic Order in 1561, the town surrendered to the Swedish king Eric XIV. Its trade was gradually destroyed, first by a great conflagration in 1433, then by a pestilence in 1532, and finally by a series of prolonged wars. The town was bombarded from the sea by the Danes in 1569 and was besieged by the Russians in 1570 and 1577. In 1710 Tallinn surrendered to Peter the Great, who later constructed a port there for his Baltic fleet. The town passed from Russian to Estonian rule in 1918, but fell under Soviet occupation in 1940, only to be taken by the Germans a year later. Tallinn suffered heavy bombardment by the Russians in March 1944, with almost a third of the homes destroyed, as well as the port and many ancient structures. On Sept. 22, 1944, Soviet troops took Tallinn.

After World War II the harbour was reconstructed as a port for the Soviet fleet. The town has become a major industrial and cultural centre. Its main industries include shipbuilding, engineering (radios, motors, and electrical and other machinery), cotton textiles, paper and pulp milling, and manufacture of cellulose and furniture. Though many new buildings dominate the town, the remains of the ancient citadel and the city wall with its many towers form a picturesque setting. An art museum houses a fine collection of modern Estonian painting and sculpture, and there are polytechnical and pedagogical institutes and schools for music and fine arts.

**TALLIS, THOMAS** (*c.* 1505–1585), the most important English composer of sacred music of the generation preceding that of William Byrd. Nothing is known of his education. In 1532, however, he held a post at Dover Priory and in 1537 at St. Mary-at-Hill, London; and his name appears in a list of persons who in 1540 received wages and rewards for services at the dissolution of Waltham Abbey in Essex. From Waltham he appears to have gone briefly to Canterbury and then to the Chapel Royal. In a petition to Queen Elizabeth I made jointly with William Byrd in 1577 he refers to having "served your Majestie and your Royall ancestors these fortie years," but his appointment as a gentleman of the Chapel Royal can hardly have been before 1542. The same document refers to one only previous instance of preferment and that, interestingly, from the hand of "your Majestie's late deare syster quene Marie." This was a 21-year lease of the manor of Minster in the Isle of Thanet (Kent) granted in 1557 to Tallis and Richard Bowyer, Master of the Children.

On Jan. 22, 1575, Queen Elizabeth granted Tallis and Byrd the monopoly for printing music and music paper in England. This gesture of royal favour to the two musicians, who were at this time joint organists of the Chapel Royal, did not at first operate to their advantage. The above-mentioned petition of 1577 seeks relief, in the form of an additional lease, for the loss of 200 marks incurred during the first two years. The lease was granted.

The first publication under their licence was a collection of 34 motets, 17 by Tallis and 17 by Byrd, entitled *Cantiones sacrae,* printed by T. Vautrollier in 1575. These Latin pieces, together with 5 anthems to English texts printed by John Day in his *Certaine Notes . . .* (1560–65), comprise all of his music that Tallis saw in print during his lifetime.

The latter years of his life were spent in Greenwich, where he died on Nov. 23, 1585. According to his epitaph Tallis was married "ful thre and thirty Yeres" (*i.e.,* in 1552) but had no children. His wife, Joan, who died in 1589, was buried in her husband's grave.

Tallis' long life spans a period that saw important changes in English music: changes of style between the generations of Taverner on the one hand and Byrd on the other, changes necessitated by the introduction of an English liturgy (which, however, did not entirely replace the Latin), and the development of an impressive school of keyboard composition. A substantial amount of Tallis' music remains, among which most of the forms of his day are represented. His Latin works include a modest, unnamed 4-part Mass; a 5-part Mass, *Salve intemerata,* skilfully derived from his antiphon of the same name; and a 7-part Mass, long known only from a number of sections and regretted as lost, which has now been entirely restored. There are also two settings of the *Magnificat,* one of 4 parts and one of 5, a comparison of which illustrates the contrast between the old and the new styles in Latin music which coexisted for a time in the mid-16th century. Tallis also made two settings of the *Lamentations of Jeremiah;* the first, especially, is among his finest works. An important part of Tallis' catalogue of works consists of two groups of compositions, one of Responsory settings, the other of Office hymns, forms in which his contribution is matched, among his contemporaries, most notably by the numerous similar settings by John Shepherd. Finally, among his Latin pieces, two in particular stand as demonstrations of Tallis' supreme mastery of the art of counterpoint: the 7-part *Miserere nostri,* an extraordinary feat of canonic writing, involving retrograde movement together with several degrees of augmentation; and the famous 40-part *Spem in alium,* a unique monument in British music, scarcely rivaled even by Robert Carver's 19-part *O bone Jesu.* Set out for eight 5-part choirs, *Spem in alium* is a remarkable demonstration of contrapuntal resource, a thoroughgoing example of imitative writing seemingly not at all limited by the scale of the work. What could have been Tallis' purpose in writing such a work, the performance of which would have been (and is) possible only under the most exceptional circumstances, is a mystery. But that it is a work of art, not merely a technical feat, is unquestionable.

Tallis, as a gentleman of the Chapel Royal at the time of the introduction of the Book of Common Prayer, was one of the first composers to provide settings of the English liturgy. He has left settings of the Preces and Responses, the Litany, and a complete Service "in the Dorian mode" which consists of the morning and evening canticles and the Communion Service, including the *Gloria,* which later ceased to be set. There are also three sets of psalms, several psalm tunes for Archbishop Matthew Parker's Psalter (printed in 1567 or 1568 but withheld from sale), and a number of anthems. Although some of these are adaptations to English texts of Latin compositions, several are found in 16th-century sources and therefore, perhaps, are the work of the composer himself or were at least sanctioned by him. Apart from adaptations, there exist also a number of original settings of English words.

Tallis' secular vocal music is negligible and his music for instrumental ensemble virtually so, but his keyboard music is substantial and significant. This includes both sacred and secular pieces, extended *cantus firmus* compositions, and arrangements of vocal works. Of his 23 extant keyboard pieces 18 occur in the mid-16th-century manuscript known as the Mulliner Book.

Tallis' Latin church music was published in *Tudor Church Music*, vol. vi (1928). His keyboard music is to be found in *Musica Britannica*, vol. i, "The Mulliner Book" (1951), and *Tallis: Complete Keyboard Works* (1953), both edited by Denis Stevens.

BIBLIOGRAPHY.—H. B. Collins, "Thomas Tallis," *Music and Letters*, x (1929); L. Ellinwood, "Tallis' Tunes and Tudor Psalmody," *Musica Disciplina*, ii (1948); D. Stevens, "The Keyboard Music of Thomas Tallis," *Musical Times*, xciii (July 1952). (Jo. D. B.)

**TALLY,** a primitive instrument of accountancy, consisting, in its developed form, of a narrow stick or strip of hard wood, notched along one edge or along two opposite edges, for about three-quarters or two-thirds of its total length, with notches representing quantities, and then split from one end through all the notches down to a transverse incision made halfway through it at about one-quarter or one-third of its length from the opposite end. The smaller, flat part thus detached is called the foil, or countertally; the larger part, with the unsplit end, is called the stock. Since the notches on stock and foil are complementary, the parties to a transaction, one of whom takes the stock and the other the foil, have a record which neither can vary without the other's agreement. Writing on the tally summarizes its notching and specifies its purpose. In the most primitive form, however, a notched stick serving merely to remind one of the progress of an account or "score" may be called a tally.

The chief interest of the tally centres on its official use in England, where, in the Middle Ages, it became the basis of government finance and one of the earliest negotiable instruments. Its official use in England is earlier even than the very early "exchequer" organization (*see* EXCHEQUER); soon after 1100 it was a settled system—a system, moreover, carefully differentiated from any private one and used for money only; and the tally continued to be the recognized form of receipt for payments into the Royal Treasury down to 1826. Though there were modifications of wording, the regular form of the Exchequer tally changed little save for a continually increasing length: the original 9 in. was extended in one extreme example (preserved at the Bank of England) to 8 ft. 6 in.

*See* H. Jenkinson, articles in *Archaeologia*, lxii and lxxiv (1911, 1924); A. Steel, *The Receipt of the Exchequer, 1377–1485* (1954). (H. JE.; X.)

**TALMA, FRANÇOIS JOSEPH** (1763–1826), French actor, a rebel in politics and in art, was born in Paris on Jan. 16, 1763. He made his debut at the Comédie Française on Nov. 21, 1787, as Seide in Voltaire's *Mahomet*. Influenced by his friend the painter David, Talma became one of the early advocates of historical costuming when he appeared in a Roman toga and headdress in the small role of Proculus in Voltaire's *Brutus*. He found his great opportunity in Joseph Chénier's antimonarchical *Charles IX*, which caused demonstrations in the theatre and aroused such dissension within the company that republican Talma established a rival troupe, known as the Théâtre de la République, on the site of the present Théâtre Français. There Talma developed realism in staging and costuming. When the two companies were reunited in 1799 at his theatre as the Comédie Française, Talma emerged as the supreme tragedian of the era. In both his scenic reforms and his acting, Talma was a leading precursor of 19th-century French romanticism and realism. His artistic credo was "grandeur without pomp, nature without triviality." Talma died in Paris on Oct. 19, 1826.

Talma wrote *Reflections on the Actor's Art* as a preface to the *Memoires de Lekain* (1825). (H. K. CY.)

**TALMUD** (Heb. "learning"), a compilation that was revered by the Jews as a sacred book from the time it was compiled down to the 18th century, the laws expounded therein being considered of divine origin on a par with those in the Torah (*q.v.*). After the emergence of the *Haskalah* (Enlightenment) movement in the 18th century, and later upon the rise of the Reform movement, many Jews ceased to think of it as divinely inspired, though they continued to regard it as of great value for the study of Jewish history, law, theology, folklore and ethics. A large segment of the Jewish population continues to regard the laws set forth in the Talmud as having been given by God, and the power of thought displayed in it by the Jewish sages of antiquity inspires profound respect in all students.

The Talmud comprises two main sections, the Mishna and the Gemara (the latter often called Talmud also), plus some additional laws called Baraitoth and passages from another collection called Tosefta. The Mishna ("repetition") is a lawbook, the work of the sages who lived in Palestine before the destruction of the Second Temple (A.D. 70) and a century and a half thereafter. The Gemara ("completion"), a commentary on the Mishna, is the work of later sages, the *amoraim*. The Talmud deals, in the main, with legal matters, and this part is called *halakha* (pl. *halakhoth*; "law"); the nonlegal part is called *haggada* ("saying," "narrative"). The *halakhoth*, the laws embodied in it, are based on Oral Law.

The Talmud is a storehouse of law, religion, history, ethics, metaphysical speculations, medical science, astronomy, and folklore. It is an encyclopaedia covering every phase of human activity, a mine of information for the study of religion, history and civilization not only of the Jews but of the peoples of the entire middle east. It is important for a proper understanding of the origin of Christianity, since this literature came from men who taught at the time when Jesus lived. It is essential for comprehension of the controversies over the law between the Pharisees and Jesus as recorded in the Synoptic Gospels.

For the Jews the Talmud was not merely a lawbook, regulating life; its discussions, being divinely inspired, were the purpose and essence of life itself. When the Jews were persecuted and driven from public life during the middle ages, they found consolation in the study of the Talmud. It stimulated and cultivated their minds, saving them from stagnation. By its study they were assured of a reward in the future world, and this conviction was a religious incentive to every Jew. In the middle ages, when the great majority of the European population was illiterate, the Jews were saved from total ignorance by their intense devotion to the study of the Talmud.

## ORAL LAW

**Traditional Laws.**—The Jewish people, like other peoples, in early times had unwritten as well as written laws. The written laws are those in the code called the Torah, the Pentateuch. But in the writings of the prophets as well as in the Hagiographa (*i.e.*, the Old Testament books exclusive of the Pentateuch and the Prophets) there are references to customs and laws that are not found in the Pentateuch. In the book of Jeremiah, for example, it is stated that when the prophet bought a field from Hanamel he wrote a deed in the presence of witnesses who affixed their signatures. There is no mention in the Pentateuch of the requirement of a deed and witnesses in the transfer of real property. In the book of Ruth it is said that Boaz told his kinsman that he would have to marry Ruth when he purchased the field from Naomi "in order to restore the name of the dead to his inheritance" (iv, 5). It is further stated that this was the custom "in former times in Israel concerning redeeming and exchanging: to confirm a transaction, the one drew off his sandal and gave it to the other, and this was the manner of attesting in Israel." This custom of transferring immovable property by the symbolic act of drawing off the shoe is not mentioned in the Pentateuch.

In ancient times, if a man did not pay his debts, his creditor had the right to take him into servitude; if he died and left the debt unpaid, the creditor could enslave his children. This is shown by a passage in II Kings (iv, 1) in which a woman cries to Elisha, "'Your servant my husband is dead; and you know that your servant feared the Lord, but the creditor has come to take my two children to be his slaves.'" This law is not mentioned in the Pentateuch.

It is evident from the book of Genesis that among the early Hebrews a man had to purchase his wife from her father. Jacob paid Laban in manual labour for the right to marry his daughters; David paid Saul 200 foreskins of the Philistines for the right to marry his daughter Michal. Yet the Pentateuch makes no reference to bride price. Nor is any writ in connection with marriage referred to in the Bible; nonetheless a custom of writing marriage documents prevailed among the early Hebrews. Such a document is recorded in the Elephantine papyri. Also, in the book of Tobit, it is said that when Raguel gave his daughter Sarah to Tobias he called her mother, "took a scroll and wrote out the contract; and they set their seals to it" (vii, 14).

The unwritten laws were as old as, and perhaps older than, some of those embodied in the Pentateuch. The sages of the Talmud recognized this when they said that thousands of laws or customs were forgotten during the time of mourning for Moses. Such nonpentateuchal laws came to be known as *halakhoth, torah shebe-al pe,* "Oral Law," while the laws of the Pentateuch were described as *torah shebikthab,* "written laws."

The unwritten law has been considered holy by all peoples. Sophocles made Antigone justify the burying of Polynices, against the order of King Creon, on the basis of "the immutable unwritten laws of god. They were not born today nor yesterday; they die not; and none knoweth whence they sprang." Aristotle spoke of written and unwritten laws, the latter of which were based upon nature and universally recognized. Philo, in his *Special Laws,* wrote, "For customs are unwritten laws, the decisions approved by men of old, not inscribed on monuments nor on leaves of paper which the moth destroys, but on the souls of those who are partners in the same citizenship." He differentiated between written and unwritten laws, stating, "Praise cannot be duly given to one who obeys the written laws, since he acts under admonition of restraint and the fear of punishment. But he who faithfully observes the unwritten deserves commendation, since the virtue which he displays is purely willed." Aristotle reflected a similar opinion in the *Rhetoric.*

**Pharisees and Sadducees.**—According to Josephus, who is upheld by the tannaitic literature, the Sadducees denied the authority of the Oral Law while the Pharisees adhered to it. But the Sadducees could not reject all the laws that were not mentioned in the Pentateuch, since no state can function without custom. The cleavage between the Pharisees and the Sadducees was due to the fact that the former maintained that the Oral Laws were as binding as the written laws and that transgressors of the unwritten laws should be punished as were those who transgressed the written laws. The Sadducees denied this, on the ground that the unwritten laws were less binding than the pentateuchal laws. The Pharisees also maintained that the pentateuchal laws must be amended and interpreted so as to conform to the changing culture and economic condition of the people; the Sadducees rejected such innovations. (*See* JEWISH SECTS DURING THE SECOND COMMONWEALTH: *Pharisees; Sadducees.*)

**Revisions and New Laws.**—In the course of time, however, all laws, written and unwritten, become outmoded. Some device or institution is needed to provide for amendment and interpretation in order to bring them into consonance with contemporary life. In the Jewish second commonwealth period such an institution was developed—the Sanhedrin (*q.v.*).

Before the Hasmonaean period the Jewish government was a theocracy. Religious authority was vested in the high priest, the representative of God. Theocracy was abolished after the establishment of the commonwealth, and nomocracy (the rule of the law) was instituted in its stead. A *bet din* ("court"), commonly known as Sanhedrin, was inaugurated in 141 B.C., with authority to interpret the pentateuchal laws and to enact the unwritten laws into statutory laws. Further, new laws were added by the *soferim,* "scribes," of the Sanhedrin (*see* SCRIBES). Rabbi Joshua said that certain new laws were introduced by the *soferim,* "and I cannot gainsay them" (*Tebul Yom* 4, 6). The *soferim* also modified the pentateuchal laws, holding that their modifications were in the tradition of the fathers. They amended, for example, the pentateuchal law concerning levitical purity. According to the Pentateuch, ritual cleansing could not be completed till after sunset. In later times this worked great hardship on the people, interfering with their daily lives. The sages therefore declared that the law applied only to priests in the matter of eating the sacred food. But the requisite of washing the whole body still worked hardship, so the sages reduced it to a mere washing of the hands before meals. Reference to this law is made in the Synoptic Gospels, where it is described as the "tradition of the elders."

It is stated in the Pentateuch that a Jew may not carry a burden on the sabbath, but Oral Law specified that things may be carried in the house. According to the Pentateuch cattle must be slaughtered before their flesh is eaten, but the method of slaughtering is not described; the Oral Law defines ritualistic slaughter as cutting the throat.

In some cases Oral Law took precedence over the written law or even nullified it. The Pentateuch states that the blood of a fowl should be covered with sand, but according to the Oral Law it may be covered with anything that happens to be at hand. The sages took cognizance of the fact that the Oral Law expresses the spirit of the law, namely that the blood be covered.

**Civil Law.**—Civil as well as religious laws in the Pentateuch are so ambiguous and narrow that no civilized society could have been governed without the Oral Law, which supplemented and interpreted the pentateuchal laws, making them adaptable to changing conditions and expressive of the evolving views of society. There are laws in the Pentateuch regarding damages and injury, but there are no specifications of gradations in torts, injuries and liabilities. No law is given regarding damages that are not discernible. For example, a person might mix another person's wheat with "sacred wheat," making it impossible for the second man to use it and thus causing a financial loss; yet the damage was not recognizable in pentateuchal law. According to the Oral Law, however, the person committing this act was obligated to pay for the damages he caused.

The laws of partnership, of the means of acquiring property and of personal agency are not dealt with in the Pentateuch but are based on Oral Law. The pentateuchal laws dealing with inheritance, for example, assumed the inalienability of bonded property from the possession of the tribe. When a person dies his estate is inherited by his sons; where there are no sons it passes to his daughters, and where there are no daughters it goes to the nearest kin. It must always remain in the family or the tribe. The idea of testament is not found in the Pentateuch for the simple reason that the Pentateuch does not recognize that property may be transferred to a stranger. The Oral Law took cognizance of changed social conditions and gave a person the right to write a will devising part of his property to anyone, even to a stranger. According to the Oral Law, man is immortal but the title to property is limitable by time. A man may stipulate that his will take effect after his death and the court is obligated to carry out his bequest.

No reference is made in the Pentateuch to writs, whether in connection with property transactions or loans. It is clear from papyri that as early as the 5th century B.C. a debtor gave his creditor a note in which he not only obligated himself to pay the debt but also gave the creditor the right to seize his property if the debt was not paid; if the debtor died before the loan was paid, his children had to pay it. The right of seizure of a debtor's property was based on the unwritten law, and the promissory note nullified the biblical laws that gave the creditor rights over the person of the debtor and his children.

Use of promissory notes also modified the pentateuchal law in connection with the sabbatical year. The Pentateuch clearly specifies that a debt that outlasts the sabbatical year can no longer be collected. To encourage loans to the needy, Hillel introduced the *prosbul* (derived from the Greek *pros boule,* "before the council"), in which the creditor deposited with the court a note stating that a debt owed him by A might be collected at any time the creditor chose. The creditor thus secured his debt against the provision of the pentateuchal law concerning the sabbatical year. A loan for which no note was given was forfeited if not paid before the year of release.

The Pentateuch refers twice to the *lex talionis,* an eye for an eye, a tooth for a tooth (Ex. xxi, 24; Lev. xxiv, 20), but injury and bodily mutilation as well as theft were considered private wrongs. It was not for the state to punish the offender; the matter was to be settled between the person who inflicted the injury and the one injured. The man who suffered the loss of an eye or any other member of his body could absolve entirely the man who caused the injury or could demand any satisfaction, even to taking out the eye of the man who caused the loss of his eye. *Talio* was the extreme satisfaction the plaintiff might demand, but it was not mandatory; the injured person could obtain satisfaction with money if he so wished. On the principle that two different persons could not have exactly the same members of the body, the sages enacted a law by which the injured man could not demand an eye from the person who caused the loss of his eye but that he could demand the value of his eye. In this way, the *lex talionis* was abolished.

**Shammaites and Hillelites.**—The sages of the commonwealth endeavoured not only to interpret the pentateuchal laws so as to bring them into consonance with contemporary life but also to incorporate some of the old *halakhoth* into statutory laws—in other words, to make them written laws in order that they might be used as a basis for deducing new laws in accord with the demands of the times. Two schools of thought arose in regard to the soundness and the validity of interpreting the pentateuchal laws and the *halakhoth*. One, the Shammaites, represented the conservative, the other, the Hillelites, the liberal point of view. They were named after the great sages Shammai and Hillel (*qq.v.*), the fifth and last of the *zugoth* ("pairs"), or joint heads of the Sanhedrin. Every sage enrolled himself as a Shammaite or as a Hillelite, and the two schools, which arose with the establishment of the commonwealth, continued until the time of the compilation of the Mishna.

To establish a legal system by which the pentateuchal laws could be interpreted, and to legalize the modification, Hillel applied three hermeneutic devices. These are (1) *kal wa-homer,* inference *a minori ad maius,* from the less important (law) to the more important (law); (2) *gezerah shawah,* inference by analogy of words; and (3) *hikish,* inference by analogy of subjects. These three principles were not introduced by Hillel, but it was he who organized them into a juristic discipline by which the entire pentateuchal law could be interpreted. Later the three were developed into seven, and Rabbi Ishmael, who lived after the destruction of the Second Temple, increased them to 13. In accepting the hermeneutics as a legal system the sages found it necessary to limit them in certain ways. In regard to penal law, for example, the inference from *minori ad maius* could not be applied; no penalty could be inflicted that was based upon an inference. Again, the principle of inference could not be made from a *halakha;* it was applicable only to the laws of Scriptures and to those *halakhoth* that had become statutory.

The method of interpretation of the pentateuchal laws was called Midrash Mikra and that of interpretation of the old *halakhoth* was called Midrash Halakhoth. The sages who interpreted the pentateuchal laws were called *darshanim,* "interpreters," and the place where they assembled was known as the Bet ha-Midrash.

The idea of intention as a legal principle was the great innovation introduced by Hillel. An act without intention, although willed, was not considered a legal act. For example, if a man gives a ring or money to a woman, this does not make her his wife. The consummation of a marriage requires intention. The man has to give the ring to the woman with the intention of marrying her by open declaration. Hence, according to talmudic law, marriages of minors and lunatics are invalid, since such persons cannot exercise intention. The principle of intention had a far-reaching influence on all Jewish laws, ritual, civil and criminal. Shammai and his school strongly opposed this innovation, but it became an integral part of the legal system of the Talmud.

***Rabbon* and *Tanna*.**—With the liberal views of Hillel prevailing among the sages, there came a change in the leadership of the Sanhedrin. Previously two men had headed this institution, the *nasi* and the *ab bet din.* The office of the latter was now abolished. Gamaliel (*q.v.*), grandson of Hillel, became the sole leader of the Sanhedrin, with the title *rabbon,* "our *nasi*" (*rabba* being the Aramaic form of *nasi*). The sages who interpreted the law were called *soferim,* "scribes," before the destruction of the Second Temple, and this term occurs in the Gospels; no title was appended to their names. After the destruction of the Temple the sages came to be called *tannaim,* and those who received authorization had the title rabbi.

The *tannaim* were jurists, as is exemplified in the *halakhoth* with regard to *jus in personam* and *jus in rem.* They held that the law was made for man and not man for the law. They maintained that society cannot be governed without law, and that the purpose of law is to prevent men from doing what is wrong and to punish violators. They held however that equity should be applied to decisions and leniency should take precedence over strictness in the application of the law. The *tannaim,* who were the spiritual leaders of the people, aimed to promote the general welfare by regulating the relations between man and God and between man and man.

## THE MISHNA

After the destruction of Jerusalem by the Romans in A.D. 70, Jabneh (modern Jamnia, located on the Judaean plain of western Israel), under the leadership of Johanan ben Zakkai, became the centre of Jewish learning. With the collapse in A.D. 135 of the Bar-Cochba revolt, which led to the virtual decimation of the Judaean population, the centre was moved to Usha in Galilee (near modern Haifa). (*See* YESHIVA.) During this momentous period in the history of the Jews the sages decided that the *halakhoth* should be assembled and codified. There was disagreement as to how the collection should be organized, one school holding that the *halakhoth* should be collected in the order of the biblical verses from which they were interpreted, the other maintaining that they should be arranged according to the subject matter. The view of the latter school prevailed, and the assembling of the *halakhoth* on this plan, begun by Rabbi Akiba ben Joseph, was continued by his disciples (especially Meir) and completed in the early part of the 3rd century A.D. by Rabbi Judah ha-Nasi, the Prince, known as rabbi par excellence. This collection of the *halakhoth* was called Mishna (Gr. Deuterosis), second to the Torah (the word is variously transliterated also as Mishne and Mishnah). Soon after its completion it became the standard work for further interpretations of the *halakhoth* and was revered as second only to the Bible. The halakhic decisions in the Mishna became binding.

**Orders of the Mishna.**—The Mishna is divided into six "orders" (*sedarim*), each order into tractates (*massekhtoth*), and each tractate into chapters (*perakim*). The *sedarim* are as follows:

1. *Zeraim* ("seeds"), 11 tractates. The first tractate, called *Berakhoth,* deals with worship and treats of benedictions and prayers and the time of the reading of the *shema.* In other tractates the biblical precepts are set forth relating to the rights of the poor, tithes given to the priests and the Levites, rules and regulations connected with agriculture and the laws connected with the sabbatical year.

2. *Moed* ("festivals"), 12 tractates. In this order the laws in connection with the sabbath and the festivals are set forth. One tractate is devoted to the laws connected with fasts. Another, *Shekalim,* treats of the half-shekel which every Jew had to contribute to the Temple.

3. *Nashim* ("women"), 7 tractates. This order deals with the laws of marriage and divorce and Levirate marriage and divorce. Also given are the regulations governing the relations between husband and wife and between the sexes in general. In this order the tractate *Nedarim* treats of vows and their annulment. Another tractate, *Nazir,* gives the laws concerning Nazirites.

4. *Nezikin* ("damages"), 10 tractates. The first tractate, called *Nezikin,* is divided into three parts: *Baba Kama* ("first gate"), in which the laws of damages and injuries and those regarding theft and robbery are set forth; *Baba Metzia* ("middle gate"), which treats of laws concerning found property, usury and hired labour; and *Baba Bathra* ("last gate"), which deals with *hazakah* (usucapion), the laws regarding the sale and purchase of immovable and movable property, and the laws of partnership and inheritance. *Sanhedrin* ("court") concerns the composition of the

court and trial procedure, with the different punishments for various offenses, with the principle of corpus delicti and with the laws of arbitration. *Makkoth* ("stripes") deals with the lashings to which a person is condemned by a court. *Shevuoth* ("oaths") treats of the different kinds of oaths, those made in private life and those administered in court. *Aboda Zara* ("idolatry") treats of the laws concerning idols and the relation to idol worshipers. Two other tractates that bear no relation to the main subjects are included in this order: *Eduioth* ("testimonies"), a collection of traditional laws; and *Pirke Aboth* ("sayings of the fathers"), or *Aboth,* a collection of ethical maxims of the sages.

5. *Kodashim* ("holy things"), 11 tractates. This order, devoted to the subject of sacrifices, contains the tractates *Tammid* ("daily sacrifice") and *Middoth* ("measurements"), which describe the daily sacrifices of the morning and of the evening, and of the area of the Temple, its courts, gates and the daily services of the priests and the Levites.

6. *Taharoth* ("purifications"), 12 tractates. It sets forth the laws of ritual cleanliness and uncleanliness, both in persons and in things, and the laws in connection with purifications. The tractate *Yadayim* ("hands") is devoted to the laws in connection with the ritual impurity of the hands, their defilement of the Holy Scriptures. In this tractate is related the controversy in regard to the canonicity of Ecclesiastes and the Song of Solomon.

**Character of the Mishna.**—The Mishna is a code of *halakhoth* consisting of religious laws and laws governing society. These *halakhoth* in general are not based on the Pentateuch; biblical texts are not quoted to substantiate the *halakhoth.* In *Baba Bathra,* which consists of ten chapters dealing with civil law, there is not a single reference to the Bible. References are made to biblical verses only in some chapters of a few tractates, and this practice can be traced to the Midrash form applied by many sages in interpretation of *halakhoth.*

Two orders—*Kodashim,* which treats of sacrifices, and *Taharoth,* which sets forth the laws of ritual cleanliness and uncleanliness—are concerned with matters that had become obsolete. They were included in the Mishna because, first, many of the tractates had already been compiled before Rabbi Judah's time, and, second, the Jews of the period had complete confidence that before long the Temple would be rebuilt and sacrifices restored.

Because the tractates were compiled at various different times, the Mishna shows a lack of consistency. The unevenness of the Hebrew language also can be attributed to the fact that it represents many periods of antiquity and of post-Hadrianic times. The sequence of many tractates within each order is of a later era and is mechanical. Rabbi Judah did not set the sequence.

The Mishna, being a code, does not contain *haggadoth,* legends such as occur in the tannaitic literature and in the Talmud (*see* below, *The Talmuds*). Messianic and eschatological ideas that were prevalent among the Jews of the time of its compilation are largely ignored. It is stated that those who do not believe in the Revelation and those who deny resurrection (spiritual) will not share in the future world. No mention is made of those who deny the coming of the Messiah. No reaction may be seen in the Mishna toward the Christians in general, or, with one exception, toward the Jewish Christians. In the tractate *Berakhoth* it is stated that, by law, when a Jew greets another Jew he should pronounce the Name, the Tetragrammaton, although pronouncing the name of God is prohibited in the Pentateuch (*e.g.,* Ex. xx, 7, "You shall not take the name of the Lord your God in vain"). Jewish Christians, on meeting their fellow Christians, greeted them, "Peace in the name of God and the Lord Jesus Christ." The sages, disregarding the injunction of the Pentateuch, introduced a law requiring pronunciation of the Tetragrammaton in order to signify that there is one Lord and that he is God, and that Jesus was not the Messiah; furthermore, this greeting would reveal believers in Jesus.

It may be asked, if the Mishna is a corpus juris, why does it contain divergent opinions in connection with the laws? The answer is that Rabbi Judah believed that the opinions of the minority as well as of the majority should be recorded, even though the decision of the law had to follow the majority opinion. The minority opinion was included so that if at some future time new laws were enacted the rabbis would be able to find support for their decisions in these minority opinions. When Judah thought that the decision of the law should follow the opinion of one particular sage he recorded his opinion anonymously or in the name of the sages; *i.e.,* he stated it as a majority opinion. Other principles were laid down regarding decisions of the law; for example, when there was a controversy between the schools of Shammai and Hillel, the law was decided in accordance with the latter.

The Mishna, though a code, cannot be compared to the Pentateuch, which was believed to be revealed by God to Moses and had to be administered by a high priest, a vicar of God. Nor can it be compared to the code of the Roman law: the sages did not derive their authority from secular rulers or magistrates; it was based rather on their profound knowledge of the law and ability to interpret it, and on the authorization received from their spiritual mentors, which, according to tradition, came down unbroken from Moses.

**Writing of the Mishna.**—A divergence of opinion exists with regard to the compilation of the Mishna. Many rabbis of the middle ages, particularly of Spain, followed by many modern scholars, maintained (and maintain) that neither the Mishna nor the *halakhoth* were committed to writing until the 6th century A.D. and that the Mishna was organized only orally by Rabbi Judah. On the other hand, many medieval rabbis, particularly of France and Germany, supported by many other modern scholars, were (and are) of the opinion that the Mishna was committed to writing by Judah. It can be deduced from internal evidence not only that the Mishna was written by Judah but that many *halakhoth* had been put in writing long before his time. The injunction against the writing of *torah shebe-al pe* (the unwritten law) refers only to the customs and the oral laws that had not yet been made statutory.

**Great *Tannaim*.**—Among the *tannaim* responsible for the shaping of the *halakhoth,* two disciples of Rabban Johanan ben Zakkai deserve particular mention: Rabbi Eliezer and Rabbi Joshua. Another sage was Rabban Gamaliel, the grandfather of Rabbi Judah ha-Nasi, the successor of Johanan ben Zakkai as head of the academy of Jabneh and chiefly responsible for the organization of the *halakhoth.* Rabbi Akiba by his great intellect and acumen had great influence in the shaping of the *halakhoth.* He introduced new methods of interpretation of the Bible for the purpose of enacting new laws. He laid the groundwork for the compilation of the Mishna that was accomplished later by Judah. His dialectic methods are recognized in the halakhic discussions of his disciples, particularly those of Simon, Judah, Jose and Meir. The last had the keenest legal mind. To this group must be added Rabbi Simon ben Gamaliel, the father of Judah ha-Nasi, who headed the academy at Usha. These are only a few of the *tannaim* who flourished after the destruction of the Second Temple. The tannaitic period ended with the compilation of the Mishna.

## THE TANNAITIC LITERATURE

**Midrash Mikrà.**—There are other collections of laws, the works of the sages who maintained that the *halakhoth* should be arranged according to the sequence of the pentateuchal passages. They are: (1) *Sifra* ("the book" par excellence), in which the *halakhoth* are arranged in the order of the passages in the book of Leviticus; and (2) *Sifre* ("the books"), in which the *halakhoth* are arranged in the order of the passages in the books of Exodus, Numbers and Deuteronomy. These collections are called Midrash Mikra. (*See* also MIDRASH.)

**Tosefta and Baraitoth.**—Rabbi Judah collected *halakhoth* that he felt should be recorded in the Mishna as a way of life for the Jews. He did not include those which at that time were out of date due to social and religious changes that had occurred in the life of the Jews. For example, the laws of impurity, held by the sages to be inapplicable to the pagans, had become obsolete after the destruction of the Second Temple, since pagans were now considered human beings like the Jews and the laws of impurity became applicable to them; likewise, the law that a woman can be among the seven called to the Torah was omitted, since at this time women were already segregated in the synagogues. Rabbi

Judah's disciple Rabbi Hiyya bar Abba made a collection, called Tosefta, of those *halakhoth* that were not recorded in the Mishna. The sequence and the arrangement of the orders of the tractates in the Tosefta are similar to those in the Mishna; three tractates—*Aboth, Middoth* and *Tammid*—were omitted since they did not contain *halakhoth.*

There are notable differences between the Mishna and the Tosefta. In the Mishna eschatological ideas are not recorded and there are no references to reward for the righteous and punishment for the wicked after death. The Tosefta, on the other hand, deals with these speculations, and it states that wicked Jews and wicked pagans will be judged in Gehenna for 12 months as a kind of purgatory. However the Jewish apostates and informers would never be released from punishment. Righteous pagans would share a portion in the future world, and thus were placed in the same category as Jews. None of this, not even the word Gehenna, is found in the Mishna.

During the second commonwealth the Pharisees were inimical toward the apocalyptists, who were occupied with esoteric doctrines and metaphysical ideas and believed in a supernatural Messiah and a physical resurrection. The apocalyptists became influential after the conquest of Jerusalem by the Romans; some accepted Christianity while others infiltrated the ranks of the Jewish people. The *tannaim,* heirs of the Pharisees, continued their opposition, which is revealed in a story related in the Tosefta: Four men—Simon ben Azzai, Simon ben Zoma, Elisha ben Abuya and Rabbi Akiba—went into *pardes* ("paradise") and steeped themselves in mystic and esoteric philosophy. Only Akiba emerged without impairment to his faith or detriment to his intellect. Simon ben Azzai met with an untimely death, Simon ben Zoma became demented, and Elisha ben Abuya turned apostate.

The opposition of the *tannaim* toward apocalyptic doctrines was unsuccessful; indeed some of the *tannaim* themselves resorted to such speculations. Their strictures against superstition did not deter some *amoraim* from adopting these beliefs. Under the stress of personal misfortune and national calamity, people tend to seek solace in superstition and mysticism, and such has been the inclination of many Jews throughout the ages. Medieval Cabala (*q.v.*) was an outgrowth of apocalyptism, and many rabbis of the middle ages regarded Cabala as a menace to true Judaism, as their predecessors, the *tannaim,* had regarded apocalyptism. (*See* also APOCALYPTIC LITERATURE.)

A story in the Tosefta illustrates the endeavours of the followers of Jesus to convert the Jews to belief in him as the true Messiah, and also the disposition of the *tannaim* toward the Jewish Christians. It concerns a nephew of Rabbi Ishmael, Eliezer, who was bitten by a serpent. A certain Jacob sought to heal him in the name of Jesus, son of Panthera. Rabbi Ishmael forbade Eliezer to accept the ministrations of Jacob, and though Eliezer died, yet Rabbi Ishmael exulted, because his nephew had not succumbed to the Christian faith. The story led the 3rd-century Christian writer Origen, in his treatise against the pagan Celsus, to accuse the Jews of spreading false tales regarding the genealogy of Jesus by maintaining that he was the son of Panthera.

A number of additional *halakhoth* not included in the Tosefta but found in the Talmud are laws of the tannaitic period called Baraitoth (sing. Baraita; from a word meaning "outside," thus *halakhoth* outside the Mishna). The Tosefta and the Baraitoth, since they contain *halakhoth* that were already obsolete at the time of compilation of the Mishna, as well as other *halakhoth* that arose afterward, are more important than the Mishna itself for the history of the religious and social life of the Jews. The use of Roman legal terms in the Tosefta and Baraitoth shows the influence of Roman law on the tannaitic halakhoth.

Both the Tosefta and the Baraitoth differ in some respects from the Mishna. The latter, since it is a code, presents the laws in a legal form. The others are more informal, and in the Tosefta some laws are illustrated by parables. For example, a law which states that the owner of a field must not throw stones from the field onto public property is illustrated in the Tosefta by a story that stresses the moral. Once a proprietor in clearing a field threw the stones onto the public road. A pious man, observing this, told the owner that he was really throwing stones onto his own property. Subsequently the owner, for economic reasons, was compelled to sell his field. Walking on the road where he had thrown the stones he stumbled on them and was injured.

## THE TALMUDS

The Mishna attained canonical authority soon after its completion. The sages and teachers who expounded it were called *amoraim,* and the work that resulted from their endeavours was the Gemara, known as the Talmud. The Gemara constitutes both a commentary on and an interpretation of the Mishna. There are two Gemaras—the Palestinian (*Talmud Yerushalmi*), written in Western Aramaic and replete with many Greek and Latin terms and expressions; and the Babylonian (*Talmud Babli*), written in the Eastern Aramaic dialect and sprinkled with Persian words. The Babylonian Talmud or Gemara is often called the Talmud.

**Contents.**—The Palestinian Gemara consists of 39 tractates: the entire orders of *Zeraim, Moed, Nashim* and *Nezikin* (with the exception of *Eduioth* and *Aboth*); and a section of the tractate *Niddah* of the order *Taharoth.* It contains none of the tractates of the order *Kodashim.*

The Babylonian Gemara consists of 37 tractates: one tractate, *Berakhoth,* of the order *Zeraim;* all of the order *Moed* except the tractate *Shekalim;* all of the order *Nashim;* all of *Nezikin* except *Eduioth* and *Aboth;* all of *Kodashim* except the tractates *Middoth* and *Kinnim;* none of the order *Taharoth* except *Niddah.*

The reason for the omissions is not known; perhaps they were lost. Although the Palestinian Talmud contains more tractates than the Babylonian, the latter is much fuller and larger.

**Talmudic Academies.**—The disciples of Judah ha-Nasi took up the study of the Mishna after his death. Tiberias became the centre of Jewish learning, but there were other *yeshivoth,* or academies, in Caesarea and Acco. The talmudic academies in Palestine soon fell into decay because of political and economic conditions. The Palestinian Jews at first were under the yoke of the Roman despotism. Later, when Christianity became the dominant religion of Rome, their condition worsened. They were not even allowed to communicate with their coreligionists in Babylonia and were compelled to employ a code to notify them of the intercalations of the year. By the end of the 4th century all of the academies in Palestine had ceased to exist and the compilation of the Palestinian Talmud came to an abrupt end.

Abba Arika, known as Rab, and Mar Samuel, disciples of Judah ha-Nasi, returned to Babylonia, their native land, after the death of their master, and Mar Samuel became the head of the *yeshiva* in Nehardea on the Euphrates. After that city was sacked by the Palmyrians a *yeshiva* was organized at Sura, headed by Rab (A.D. 219). Rab Judah ben Ezekiel, a disciple of Samuel, in mid-3rd century organized the great *yeshiva* in Pumbeditha which lasted more than seven centuries. These two *yeshivoth* became the leading centres of Jewish learning. The *yeshiva* of Pumbeditha was noted for the keen dialectics employed in the halakhic discussions, particularly prominent in which were Judah ben Ezekiel, Rabbah bar Nahmani and his nephew Abaye and his colleague Rabba. Their discourse at times soared into the realm of the incomprehensible.

In the *yeshivoth* the studies were designed for those persons, called *haberim,* who devoted their lives to research in the *halakhoth.* Sessions were also organized, however, to disseminate knowledge among laymen. There was a maxim among the *tannaim,* adhered to by the *amoraim,* that knowledge is superior to observance. These sessions were held in the spring in the month of Adar (March) and in the autumn in Elul (September), and the laity came to the *yeshivoth* and participated in talmudic discussions.

**Authors.**—All the *amoraim* contributed to the Talmuds, but the chief architect of the Palestinian Talmud (compilation of which ceased late in the 4th century) was Johanan bar Napakha, while the Babylonian Talmud was chiefly compiled by Rabbi Ashi (*q.v.*), the head of Sura academy in the early part of the 5th century A.D. It was completed by Rabina *c.* 499.

The *saboraim* ("those who reflect"), who flourished in the 6th and the first part of the 7th century, explained the terminology and interpreted many passages. They also established rules to help in the understanding of the Talmud. Their interpretations and explanations became a part of the work. While some of their interpretations help in the understanding of intricate passages, others lead to confusion. It is difficult to know which passages came from the *amoraim* and which were interpolated by the *saboraim,* since no early manuscripts exist. The work of the *saboraim* on the Talmud was later carried on by the *geonim* (*see* GAON).

The Babylonian Talmud became the standard text of Jewish law and religion. It was considered divine. The *halakhoth* in the Talmud were authoritative; no rabbi could differ from them, he could only interpret. However, the *geonim* conceded that *haggada* was not authoritative.

**Character of the Talmud.**—The Talmud consists of *halakha* and *haggada* (Aramaic *agada,* "legend" or "narrative"), the former being far more numerous. The *amoraim* used the same method in their interpretation of the Mishna as the *tannaim* had in their interpretation of the Holy Scriptures. They employed exegetical principles in elucidating the *halakhoth* and expressions in the Mishna. Where there was tautology of words or expressions, the *amoraim* used them as basis for the deduction of new *halakhoth.* When there was a clash between two tannaitic principles, the *amoraim,* in their endeavour to harmonize conflicting opinions, introduced a new law.

*Halakhoth.*—The *halakhoth* of the Babylonian Talmud are the production of sages who lived in the Diaspora. This is reflected in the many laws that had to be adjusted to the life of Jews who no longer had their own state and government. Mar Samuel in 219 introduced a law that was far reaching in the life of the Jews throughout the ages—that the civil laws of the country were binding on the Jews. Many *halakhoth* reveal the influence of the laws of the country in which the Jews lived: the Palestinian Talmud reveals a marked influence of the Roman law, whereas in the Babylonian Talmud there is evidence of the effect of Parthian customs. On the other hand, many *halakhoth* in both Talmuds are academic, showing no reflection of the prevailing laws nor of the life of the Jews of the time.

Some *halakhoth,* particularly those of an academic nature, are characterized by dialectics and sometimes by quibbling and hairsplitting. Only a few *amoraim* indulged in this sort of discussion, however; the Palestinian *amoraim* protested against it, and the majority of Babylonian *amoraim* also condemned it.

*Haggadoth.*—A considerable part of the Talmuds consists of *haggadoth* of varying types. Those whose purpose is biblical exegesis are homiletical and explain the Scriptures allegorically. Others are stories, legends and proverbs whose purpose is to convey a moral message. Some are theological, dealing with rewards and punishments in the future world, the messianic age and the resurrection. There are *haggadoth* dealing with mysticism, angelology, demonology, astrology, dreams and their interpretation. Others are political, describing in legendary form the lives of the Romans and the Persians. There are historical legends about the lives of biblical and postbiblical people and accounts of the sufferings endured by the Jews. There are also aphorisms and maxims, humour and gaiety.

The aphorisms often reveal psychological insight and a humanitarian spirit: "He who gives charity in secret is greater than Moses himself." "The house that does not open to the poor shall open to the physician." "Let the honour of your neighbour be to you like your own." "There are three crowns: of the Torah, the priesthood, the kingship; but the crown of the good name is greater than all." "Whoever runs after greatness, greatness runs away from him; he who runs from greatness, greatness follows him." "No man is to be made responsible for words he utters in his grief." "The soldiers fight and the kings are the heroes." "When the thief has no opportunity for stealing, he considers himself an honest man." "One eats, another says grace." "The thief invokes God while he breaks into the house."

*Superstition.*—Superstition figures prominently in the Talmuds particularly the Babylonian. Even the sages who deplored superstition were forced by public pressure to permit the wearing of amulets on the sabbath in order to avert the evil eye and protect the wearer from evil spirits. Dreams and their interpretation occupied the minds of men of the ancient world; references in the Bible to dreams and to those who had the wisdom to interpret them rightly are familiar. In the Talmud lengthy passages are devoted to dream interpretation, some sages believing that dreams are prophetic, others that they are of no significance. Belief in omens and astrology was widespread even among intellectuals, hence astrological speculations are found in the Talmud. Most *tannaim* and *amoraim,* however, condemned these beliefs as idolatrous. Other *amoraim,* regarded by the people as holy men capable of performing miracles, indulged in speculations in theosophy and mysticism. But mysticism was not integral to normative Judaism, and halakhists opposed it.

*Science.*—The sages of the Talmud were learned in geometry, astronomy and medicine, sciences that were of great importance in halakhic decisions: geometry in connection with the rules and matters of agriculture, astronomy in relation to the intercalation of the months and years, medicine in the matter of the laws of ritual purity and impurity.

*Other Religions.*—The attitude of the sages toward other religions was antagonistic. As monotheists, who maintained that God is universal—the God of the entire human race—they opposed idol worship. They forbade the partaking of bread and wine with pagans, since the pagans used wine in their libations to the idols and bread in their worship, and to the Jews the table was sacred. Their attitude toward non-Jews was analogous to that of the Hellenes toward non-Hellenes, but it was based not on belief in racial superiority but on religion, and the sages welcomed proselytes—one who accepted Judaism was regarded more highly than a native Jew (*see* PROSELYTE). No laws were directed against gentile Christians, but certain strictures were passed upon Jewish Christians, who were regarded as heretics and apostates and suspected besides of being informers to the Romans. The rabbis, since they considered the Jewish Christians to be the destroyers of Judaism, showed great animosity toward them. When Christianity became a gentile religion their animosity disappeared: Christianity was a different religion, one that brought the idea of the universality of God to the pagans. Passages about Jesus in the Babylonian Talmud show that the Babylonian *amoraim* had no conception of the historical Jesus and of the time when he lived; all they knew about him was compounded from hearsay. It is worthy of note that there is no mention of Christianity and its founders in the Palestinian Talmud. Either the rabbis were indifferent or they were afraid to speak candidly because at that time Christianity was the dominant religion of Rome; or, perhaps, passages concerning Jesus and Christianity have been deleted.

## CRITICISM AND COMMENTARY

**Attacks.**—The first attack against the Mishna was made by the Church Fathers, who construed it as a menace to Christianity. The Fathers interpreted biblical passages so as to support the truth of Christianity, while the *tannaim* employed the same passages to support their own tradition. There is no word in the Mishna about the founders of Christianity, hence the Church Fathers inferred that it denied the truth of Christianity. As a new, young religion, Christianity had to fight for its very existence, and the Mishna was regarded as a threat. Unable to read the Talmud in the original, church authorities relied occasionally on tendentious translations made by Jewish apostates. In the 6th century the emperor Justinian prohibited the reading of the Mishna.

Throughout the middle ages the Talmud continued to be attacked by Christians. A public disputation was held in Paris in the 13th century, and later there were disputations elsewhere. In the early part of the 16th century the apostate Johann Pfefferkorn wrote a bitter attack against the Talmud, on the basis of which the emperor Maximilian ordered it to be burned; the Christian humanist Johann Reuchlin (*q.v.*), however, defended the work against the accusations of the apostate, and the emperor rescinded his decree. The Talmud was, however, in fact frequently burned, and it is for this reason that so few early manuscripts survive. As late as the mid-18th century copies were burned in Poland, though after the middle ages the work was subject more to censorship than to destruction.

During the middle ages the Jewish Karaites, motivated chiefly by resentment against the exilarch and the *geonim,* attacked the Talmud as a compilation of casuistic arguments, myths and superstitions, denying also the divine origin of its laws (*see* KARAISM). During the period of decline in Jewish intellectual life during the late middle ages and Renaissance the Talmud came to occupy an exaggeratedly exalted position, being studied even to the exclusion of the Bible. The enlightenment that came in the 18th century, particularly as exemplified by Moses Mendelssohn, brought a reaction. Liberal Jews in modern days do not regard the Talmud as divinely inspired but as a portion of the sacred tradition and a monumental source of Jewish history. In modern *yeshivoth* it is still the major, sometimes the sole subject of study.

**Commentaries.**—The best commentary on the Babylonian Talmud was written by Rashi (*q.v.*), but there are numerous other commentaries and novellae compiled by rabbis throughout the ages. Among translations may be mentioned Herbert Danby's of the Mishna and the Soncino translation of the Talmud. However they are not perfect, and a critical edition of the Talmud is yet to be made. Many passages are corrupt, and the work was never well edited. While its language is chiefly Aramaic, it is a mixture of many dialects. It may be compared to a primeval, dense forest in which a person will lose his way without a skilful guide. (S. Z.)

**Source Criticism.**—The Talmud is not immune to the manifold problems besetting all ancient texts, particularly those that were orally transmitted (*see* TEXTUAL CRITICISM). Indeed textual criticism of the Talmud is as old as the Talmud itself, though not until modern times did it become a separate scholarly concern.

The rabbis of antiquity often emended rabbinic texts, inserting readings (*e.g., Talmud Babli, Berakhoth* 13b), substituting one reading for another (*e.g., T.B., Yebamoth* 41a) or rejecting outright Baraitoth (*e.g., T. B., Gittin* 73a) or statements of *amoraim* (*e.g., T.B., Pesahim* 11a) because they considered them to be hopelessly corrupt. Nor did later scholars of the Talmud desist from correcting one text on the basis of another that seemed to them to be more reliable. Sometimes they even emended a text without support from another text. Talmudic text criticism, unlike biblical criticism, which had to contend with a long and revered tradition, was always acceptable even to the religiously conservative scholar; it is more often than not the modern liberal scholar who protests against excessive emendation (even when sanctioned by tradition) on the ground that it is inconsonant with what is known about the natural development of texts in general.

That is not to say that the traditional attitude set no limits to talmudic textual criticism. A distinction was always drawn between a reading substantiated by internal evidence in the Talmud itself and a reading not so substantiated. The former was always taken to be valid, while the latter was acknowledged to have been open to the possibility of scribal error. With the advent of modern scholarship, this distinction ceased to be compelling.

Source criticism seeks to differentiate between the original statements as they were enunciated by their authors and the forms they took as a consequence of being orally transmitted; that is, between the sources and their later traditions. It is not to be confused with the kind of analysis—frequently carried out by the rabbis of the Talmud—which merely traces the historical sources of a given passage without judging whether or not the passage faithfully reflects these sources. Source criticism claims that the transmission of the Talmud was not, and perhaps could not have been, verbatim, and that the text became altered in transmission, with the result that many statements in the Talmud have not come down in their original form. Instead, what survives is the form assumed in the last phase of transmissional development. While such a study is pertinent to most ancient texts, it is particularly relevant to the Talmud, which primarily consists of quotations and their interpretations.

Traces of source criticism can be found in geonic literature, but credit for pioneering work belongs to the Galician-born scholar H. M. Pineles (1805–70), who in his *Darka Shel Torah* (1863) for the first time offered a systematic critical approach to the study of talmudic sources. J. N. Epstein (1879–1950), professor of Talmud at the Hebrew University, Jerusalem, made a major contribution to source criticism through his comprehensive *Introduction to the Mishna* (1948) and *Introduction to Tannaitic Literature* (1957).

*See* also references under "Talmud" in the Index. (D. WE.)

BIBLIOGRAPHY.—M. Mielziner, *Little Maxims and Fundamental Laws of the Civil and Criminal Code of the Talmud* (1898), *Introduction to the Talmud* (1915); Hermann L. Strack, *Introduction to the Talmud and Midrash* (1931); S. Krauss, *Talmudische Archäologie* (1910–12); W. Bacher, *Tradition und Tradenten in den Schulen Palästinas und Babyloniens* (1914), *Die Agada der Tannaiten* (1903); Max L. Margolis, *A Manual of the Aramaic Language of the Babylonian Talmud* (1910); J. Z. Lauterbach, *Midrash and Mishnah* (1916); S. Zeitlin, "The Halaka: Introduction to Tannaitic Jurisprudence," *The Jewish Quarterly Review* (1948), "Jesus in the Early Tannaitic Literature," *Abhandlung zur Erinnerung an Hirsch Perez Chajas* (1933), *The Rise and Fall of the Judaean State,* vol. i (1962). (S. Z.)

**TAM, JACOB BEN MEIR** (1100–1171), known also as RABBENU TAM, a grandson of Rashi (*q.v.*) and brother of Rashbam, was the most famous of the French glossators (*Tosafists*) on the text of the Talmud. He was born at Ramerupt, in northern France, in 1100. In 1147 he was attacked in his home and injured by a disorderly band who had attached themselves to the crusaders. He escaped to neighbouring Troyes, where about 1160 was held the first of the Jewish synods for which the Rhineland became celebrated. At this meeting it was laid down that disputes between Jew and Jew were not to be carried to a Christian court but were to be settled by fraternal arbitration. New conditions of life had arisen because of the closer terms on which Jews and Christians lived, and Jacob Tam was foremost in settling the terms which were to govern the relations, from the Jewish side. His practical ordinances (*takkanoth*), connected with marriage and divorce, trade, and proselytism, as well as with synagogue ritual, bear the stamp of enlightened independence within the limits of authoritative tradition and law. Of his legal work the most important was collected in his *Sefer ha-Yashar.* He was also a poet of considerable merit, composing both secular and liturgical poetry, and a grammarian. Rabbenu Tam died at Troyes June 9, 1171.

*See* H. Gross, *Gallia Judaica,* p. 230 ff. (1897); M. Schloessinger in *The Jewish Encyclopedia,* vol. vii, pp. 36–39. (I. A.)

**TAMALE,** the capital town of the Northern Region of Ghana, is 437 mi. (703 km.) NNE from Takoradi, Ghana's chief seaport on the Gulf of Guinea, and 406 mi. N from Accra, the capital of Ghana. Tamale lies 600 ft. (183 m.) above sea level in a plain between the White Volta to the west and the tributaries Taha Kulibong and Pagazaa to the east. Its nearest point to the White Volta is at Dalong, 22 mi. away. The climate is hot and wet. The town covers approximately 4.5 sq.mi. Pop. (1960) 40,443.

The official residence of the chief regional officer is in Tamale, and many government departments have their offices there. In addition to the regional education office, government educational establishments include a teachers' training college and a centre for instructing artisans in various trades. The vernacular literature bureau provides newspapers and literature for mass literacy campaigns in the region; personnel for these campaigns and for work in community development are trained at the rural training centre.

Tamale is an agricultural trading centre where the main occupation is farming and crop cultivation in particular. Yams, maize, guinea corn, millet, rice, peanuts, and cow peas are grown, and a small quantity of cotton is produced. There is some cotton milling, and the shea nut is processed. Commodities exported, but almost exclusively within Ghana, are rice, guinea corn, peanuts, cow peas, and shea butter. The principal imports are cotton prints, farm tools, hardware, salt, and kola nuts.

The main road, which runs northward from the coast roughly through the centre of the country, passes through Tamale; other roads enter it from the east and west. (J. S. KM.)

**TAMAR,** a river of England, rises within 4 mi. (6.4 km.) of the Bristol Channel and flows south across the southwestern peninsula to the English Channel at Plymouth. With its tributaries it drains 599 sq.mi. (1,551 sq.km.). Over the greater part of its length of 61 mi. (98 km.) it forms the boundary between Cornwall and Devon. For 30 mi. from its source at 720 ft. (219 m.), its valley (like those of its headstreams Deer and Claw and of its tributaries Ottery, Carey, Kensey, Thrushel, and Lyd which meet it near Launceston) is shallowly but clearly cut into low plateau lands on Carboniferous rocks. Farther downstream where it passes onto Devonian rocks and crosses an east-west, granite-defended ridge of higher land between Dartmoor and Bodmin Moor it exhibits impressive, incised meanders with steep wooded side slopes rising abruptly from a narrow, almost flat, valley floor. The meandering valley continues beyond tidehead (1 mi. below Gunnislake, formerly its lowest bridging point) through an important fruit and flower growing district. Its estuary, 19 mi. long to Plymouth Sound, up to 1 mi. wide and discontinuously fringed with salt marshes, is crossed by the railway at Saltash (I. K. Brunel's Royal Albert Bridge); like those of its lower tributaries, Tavy, Lynher, and Tiddy, the Tamar Estuary is a barrier to road traffic, carried by ferry at Torpoint and the Tamar road bridge upstream of Brunel's bridge. The sheltered deepwater estuary (−80 ft. Ordnance Datum at Saltash) is the site of Plymouth Naval Base and Devonport Dockyard. (R. S. W.)

**TAMARIND,** a tropical leguminous tree (*Tamarindus indica*) and its pod fruit. The tree, widely distributed in tropical countries, is generally considered to be native to eastern tropical Africa, from Ethiopia southward to the Zambezi river. The name (meaning in Arabic "Indian date") shows that it entered medieval commerce from India, where it is used not only for its pulp but also for its seeds, which are astringent; its leaves, which furnish a yellow or a red dye; and its timber. The tree attains a height of 70 to 80 ft. and bears elegant pinnate foliage and purplish or orange veined flowers arranged in terminal clusters.

The pods are filled with an acid juicy pulp containing sugar and various acids, such as citric and tartaric, in combination with potash. The acid pulp is used as a laxative, the pods being largely exported from the West Indies and Indonesia.

**TAMARISK,** a small group of shrubs or low trees of the genus *Tamarix,* constituting the family Tamaricaceae. The species of tamarisk and of an allied genus *Myricaria* (false tamarisk) grow in salt deserts, by the seashore or in other more or less sterile localities in warm-temperate, subtropical and tropical regions of the eastern hemisphere. Their long slender branches bear very numerous small appressed leaves, in which the transpiring surface is reduced to a minimum. The numerous small pinkish flowers, borne in long clusters at the ends of the branches or from the trunk, give the shrubs a feathery appearance. Each has four to five free sepals, and as many petals springing with the four to ten stamens from a fleshy disk. In *Tamarix* the stamens are free, while in *Myricaria* they are united into one parcel. The fruit is capsular and contains numerous seeds, each usually with a long tuft of hairs at one end. The value of these shrubs or trees lies in their ability to withstand the effects of drought and a saline soil; they grow where little else can flourish. On this account the common tamarisk (*T. gallica*) the salt cedar, or French tamarisk, is planted on seacoasts and affords shelter where none other could be provided. In Asia Minor *T. gallica* is one of the manna producers (*see* MANNA). The Athel tamarisk (*T. aphylla*), native to western Asia, has been introduced as a windbreak in desert areas in southern California. Several species are cultivated as ornamentals.

**TAMATAVE** (TOAMASINA), the chief port of Malagasy Republic (Madagascar) and capital of Tamatave Province, lies on the east (Indian Ocean) coast, 135 mi. (217 km.) NE of Antananarivo (Tananarive). Pop. (1963 est.) 50,500. It stretches along a sandy beach between two points prolonged by coral reefs. The southern coral reef forms the harbour, which is entered by two openings. Sandy or rocky bars have been cut to join the town with the Canal des Pangalanes, which links together the extensive lagoons of the east coast. The town was rebuilt and extended on modern lines after its destruction by hurricane in 1927. The remains of the old town are at the southern point. The modern town, to its north, centres around the treelined Avenue Poincaré. New construction includes the town hall, a sports stadium, a swimming pool, schools, and cinemas. The botanical garden of Ivoloina is 6 mi. (10 km.) N of the town.

Tamatave is the chief commercial centre of the republic and handles about 50% of its foreign trade. It exports the products of the east coast (coffee, vanilla, pepper, cloves, and graphite) and imports machinery, textiles, and foodstuffs. There are meat-preserving and canning factories; other industries are sugar refining and rum distilling. The town is the terminus of the railway from Tananarive (capital of the republic) and has an airfield with flights to the capital and to east coast towns.

Tamatave was first visited in the 17th century by the Portuguese, who founded a trade centre there. In 1811 it was occupied by the English and given to the French in 1814. In 1822 it was besieged by the Merina (Hova) kingdom and French occupation was finally consolidated in 1895.

TAMATAVE PROVINCE (area 27,765 sq.mi. [71,911 sq.km.]; pop. [1963 est.] 954,617) comprises the central part of the fertile east coast plain, which rises to dissected highlands in the west. It is drained in the south by the Mangoro River and in the north contains Lake Alaotra. The island of Sainte-Marie, just off the east coast, is part of Tamatave Province. (J. AR.)

**TAMAULIPAS** a northeastern state of Mexico. Area 30,822 sq.mi. (79,829 sq.km.). Pop. (1960) 1,024,182. The central and southern parts of the state are mountainous, but there are extensive fertile plains in the north. The coastal zone is sandy, much broken by lagoons, and sparsely inhabited. The foothills region back of this is usually well-wooded and fertile, and the low alluvial river valleys penetrate deeply into the Sierras. The climate is hot and humid on the coast, but is pleasant on the more elevated lands of the interior. Rainfall is abundant, especially on the mountain slopes of the south. Agriculture is the principal industry. Sugar, cereals, tobacco, cotton, and coffee are produced, and fruit is also grown successfully. Large tracts of farm land are irrigated. Stock raising receives some attention, and hides and cattle are exported. The preparation of istle fibre for export is becoming an important industry. Copper is mined and extensive deposits of petroleum and asphalt are being exploited. The state has excellent rail, air, and highway connections.

The capital of Tamaulipas is Ciudad Victoria (pop. [1960] 50,797), on the Monterrey and Tampico Railway, about 120 mi. (193 km.) from Tampico. The city was founded in 1750, and is on one of the trunk highways extending to Mexico City from the Texas border. Among other towns may be mentioned: Tampico (*q.v.;* 122,535), Ciudad Madero (53,628), Nuevo Laredo (92,627), Matamoros (*q.v.;* 92,327), and Reinosa (74,140), the latter three being on the U.S. border. Reinosa is the site of a large gas plant which has a daily production potential of 300,000,000 cu.ft. (8,500,000 cu.m.) of natural gas.

In 1957 a pipeline was opened to carry huge quantities of this gas into the United States. Many miles of new paved highways were completed in the state, bringing all of its towns within easy reach of each other. (J. A. CW.)

**TAMAYO Y BAUS, MANUEL** (1829–1898), Spanish dramatist, who, with Adelardo López de Ayala, dominated the Spanish stage from 1850 to 1870. He was born in Madrid Sept. 15, 1829, and died there June 20, 1898. He came of a theatrical family and was an accomplished man of the theatre. *Virginia* (1853) is an essay in classical tragedy. *La ricahembra* (1854) and *Locura de amor* (1855) are romantic historical dramas. Several "thesis" plays denounce, from a conventional conservative standpoint, moral evils in contemporary society: materialism (*Lo positivo,* 1862), dueling (*Lances de honor,* 1863), and tolerance of corruption in high places (*Los hombres de bien,* 1870). International fame came with *Un drama nuevo* (1867; English translation, *A New Drama,* 1915), a skilful and at times moving tragedy set in the Shakespearean theatre. His abandonment of verse reflects the movement away from Romantic extravagances toward greater naturalness, and his comfortable morality found ready acceptance with his comfortable audiences. (H. B. HL.)

**TAMBOV,** an *oblast* of the Russian Soviet Federated Socialist Republic, U.S.S.R., was formed in 1937. Area, 13,243 sq.mi. Pop. (1959) 1,549,001. It occupies the low, level Oka-Don plain on the watershed between the two river basins. Only in the east does the land rise slightly toward the Volga uplands. Drainage is north to the Oka by the Tsna and its tributaries and south to the Don by the Vorona and several smaller streams. The climate is continental, with a January average temperature of 11° C. (13° F.) and a July average of 20° C. (68° F.). The annual rainfall is 19 in., with a summer maximum. The natural vegetation is forest steppe, much of which has been cleared for agriculture since the soils are rich chernozems. There are large areas of pine forest on sandy soils only along the right bank of the Tsna and along the Vorona.

In 1959 only a small proportion, 408,210 or 26% of the population, was urban. These people live in seven towns and five urban districts, of which the largest are Tambov (172,171) and Michurinsk (80,653). Most of the industry is concentrated in these two towns, the other centres being engaged in processing local farm produce.

Agriculturally the *oblast* is important, with grains occupying first place. Winter rye, spring wheat, maize (corn), oats and millet are grown. Sunflowers are the chief industrial crop, but there is some sugar beet, hemp and tobacco. Potatoes, melons and other vegetables are widespread. Beef and dairy cattle and poultry are the main livestock.

Other principal towns are Morshansk, founded in the 17th century on the Tsna (manufactures of glass, cloth and makhorka tobacco); and Kirsanov (founded 18th century) on the Tambov-Saratov railway (smelting works). (R. A. F.)

**TAMERLANE:** *see* TIMUR.

**TAMIL,** a term used properly to designate a language of Dravidian (*q.v.*) origin of southern India, and derivatively to refer to the speakers of the language and their culture and literature (*see* TAMIL LANGUAGE; TAMIL LITERATURE). Numbering about 32,000,000 in the 1960s, the Tamils of varied social status and customs inhabit chiefly Tamil Nadu and parts of Kerala, Mysore, Andhra Pradesh, and northern and eastern Ceylon. Emigrant Tamils may be found in the Malagasy Republic, the Malay peninsula, Burma, Indochina, Thailand, south and east Africa, the Fiji and Mauritius islands, and the West Indies. The term Tamil was in very ancient times applied to the language and peoples of a wider area of south India, including those now speaking Malayalam.

Tamils live in a stratified society, predominantly patrilineal with patrilocal residence; in the kinship system of some peasant groups, however, matrilateral and affinal bonds are also found. Traditional marriage alliances are maintained between clanlike exogamous patrilineal subdivisions of endogamous groups. Among the lower strata divorce is permissible as is remarriage and widow remarriage, although these are disapproved in the higher strata.

The Tamil area in India is a centre of traditional Hinduism. It was from there that Shankara and Ramanuja established the *advaita* and *viśiṣṭādvaita* philosophies; *saiva siddhānta* philosophy is believed to be a distinctive contribution from and native to this area. Tamil schools of personal religious devotion (*bhakti*) have long been important in Hinduism, being enshrined in a rich literature dating back to the 6th century A.D. Buddhism and Jainism were widespread in the early Christian era and their literature predates the early *bhakti* literature. The *bhakti* movement is assumed to be a reaction against the puritanical demands of Jainism. Although the present-day Tamils are mostly Hindus, there are Christians, Muslims, and Jains among them. In the recent past, the Tamil area was also the home of the Dravidian movement which propagates desanskritization and debrahmanization of Tamil culture, language, and literature; it traces the cultural elements to pre-Aryan Tamil and Indus Valley civilization.

The Tamils have a long history of achievement; sea travel, city life, and commerce seem to have developed early. Tamil trade with Greeks and Romans is verified by literary, linguistic, and archaeological evidence. They have the oldest cultivated Dravidian language, and their rich literature reaches to the early Christian era. Chera, Chola, Pandya, and Pallava dynasties ruled over the Tamil area before the Vijayanagar empire extended its hegemony, and produced many a great king and kingdom. They had built great temples, irrigation tanks, dams, and roads. They played an important role in the spread of Indian culture in Southeast Asia. Cholas were known for their mighty naval power, and brought the Malay kingdom of Sri Vijaya under their suzerainty in A.D. 1025. This conflict was probably necessitated to maintain trade with China direct and unhampered. Though the Tamil area was integrated, culturally, with the rest of India for a long time, politically it was for most of the time a separate entity until the advent of the British in India. South Indian classical music and the classical dance Bharata Nātyam owe much to the Tamils, masters and teachers of these arts, and have long roots in Tamil culture.

BIBLIOGRAPHY.—K. A. Nilakanta Sastri, *The Culture and History of the Tamils* (1964), *Development of Religion in South India* (1963); T. V. Mahalingam, *South Indian Polity* (1955); N. Subramanian, *Sangam Polity* (1966); E. K. Gough, "Brahman Kinship in a Tamil Village," *American Anthropologist*, vol. 58 (1956); E. R. Leach (ed.), *Aspects of Caste in South India* (1960); E. I. Irschik, *Politics and Social Conflict in South India: the non-Brahman Movement and Tamil Separatism, 1916–1929* (1969); R. L. Hardgrave, *Dravidian Movement* (1965). (R. RA.)

**TAMIL LANGUAGE,** one of the principal Dravidian languages (*see* DRAVIDIAN), spoken in South India and perhaps the only example of an ancient classical tongue which has survived as a spoken language for more than 2,500 years with its basic structure almost unchanged. The official language of Madras (*q.v.*), it is one of the 14 major languages recognized by the constitution of India (1949). At the 1961 census, Tamil was the mother tongue of 30,465,442 persons, 7.4% of the population of India. It is also spoken in the north of Ceylon and by many settlers in South and East Africa, Mauritius, Malaya and Fiji.

The Tamil script can be traced to Grantha and Vaṭṭĕluttu epigraphical sources of the 3rd century A.D. onward (*see* TAMIL LITERATURE). That it had reached something akin to its present form by the 11th century may be seen from the inscription of Rājarāja Cola in the Great Temple in Thanjavur (Tanjore). Tamil script differs from others of South India mainly in excluding separate characters for the voiced velar, palatal, retroflex, dental and labial plosives, the voiced and voiceless aspirated plosives of these series, and the sibilants. However, the character of the palatal plosive *c* is realized as a dental or palatal sibilant in certain positions and is used to represent sibilants in loanwords. Also, Grantha characters are borrowed to represent the sibilants *s, sh,* the voiced plosive *j* and the voiced spirant *h*. Other plosives are represented by the corresponding voiceless unaspirated plosive.

Thus, the character for *k* represents also *kh, g* and *gh* in, for instance, Sankskrit loanwords. Moreover, the plosives are realized as voiced in certain positions according to fairly consistent rules, the principal being that a medial single plosive is realized as voiced, and a medial doubled plosive as voiceless with tense utterance. Tamil includes three consonants not found in the syllabaries of the Indo-Iranian languages of India and not now fully represented in other Dravidian languages: the trilled *r,* the alveolar nasal *n* and the retroflex fricative *l*.

Like other Dravidian languages, Tamil is regarded as agglutinative in formation. While its close affinity with other south Dravidian languages, especially Malayālam and Kanarese, is undisputed, the affiliations of the whole family have not been satisfactorily explained. The classical view, as stated by R. A. Caldwell, is that they are connected with the Scythian languages, but many of the similarities of structure and forms he cites may be accidental.

Tamil exhibits inflexional features also, wherein postpositional words are reduced to suffixes, sometimes monosyllabic. It agrees generally with other languages in broadly classifying words into verb roots, nouns and adjectives. In common with other languages of the same family, there is evidence, although vestigial, of a separate negative verbal conjugation and, in the sense of the Spanish *ser,* the verb for "to be" is unexpressed except in the negative. Case terminations are added to the plural noun-suffix and are unaffected by it, being identical with those used for the singular.

BIBLIOGRAPHY.—T. Burrow, *Dravidian Studies,* I–VI, in *Bulletin of the School of Oriental and African Studies* (1938–48), two papers in *Transactions of the Philological Society* (1945, 1946), and, with M. B. Emeneau, *A Dravidian Etymological Dictionary* (1961); R. A. Caldwell, *A Comparative Grammar of the Dravidian Languages,* 3rd ed.

(1913; reprinted 1956); T. P. Meenakshisundaram, "Tamil," in *Kalai Kkalanciyam,* vol. v (1958); K. V. Subrahmanya Ayyar, "The Earliest Monuments of the Pandya Country," in *Proceedings of the 3rd All-India Oriental Congress* (1924); A. Subbiah, "Voiced and Voiceless Stops in Tamil," in *Tamil Culture,* vol. v, no. 2 (April 1956) and "Tamil Language and Literature," in *The Languages of India* (1958).

(Jo. R. M.)

**TAMIL LITERATURE.** Tamil is perhaps the best-known of the Dravidian languages spoken in South India. Apart from Sanskrit, its literature is the oldest in India and, if epigraphical sources are included, may be said to commence in the 3rd century B.C. with some fragmentary cave graffiti found near Madurai. (*See* DRAVIDIAN; TAMIL; TAMIL LANGUAGE.)

**Period of the "Sangam".**—The earliest Tamil writings that may properly be termed literature are those of the *sangam,* or "literary academy." Tradition, much of it doubtless fanciful, tells of a *sangam* at Madurai which grew up during the middle ages, where a number of anthologies of secular court poetry were compiled—the Eight Anthologies, *Ĕṭṭuttŏkai,* and the Ten Songs, *Pattuppāṭṭu.* Possibly unique in early Indian literature, which is almost entirely religious, these poems are concerned with two main topics, love and the praise of kings and their deeds. Many, especially on the latter subject, display great freshness and vigour and are singularly free from the literary conceits of much of the other early and medieval literatures of India (*see* INDIAN LITERATURE).

Since they are secular, these poems are also free from the complex mythical allusions which are such an outstanding feature of most Indian art forms. *Sangam* poetry seems to be at least partly based on personal experience; in this respect it is curiously modern and unlike anything else to be found in India before the late 19th century. From references to trade with the west and other internal evidence, it seems likely that these poems belong to the first four centuries A.D., when trade with Rome via the middle east was still active.

*Paripāṭal,* possibly the last of these anthologies, marks the transition to the next, more formal, stereotyped style, for it includes both religious poetry, abounding in the usual allusions, and, still in the older vein, some fine descriptive poetry, which depicts the course of the Vaigai river, on which Madurai stands.

**Sixth to Ninth Centuries.**—To the 6th century and after belongs that great collection of Śaiva religious poetry (*see* HINDUISM: *Gods*) called, collectively, *Tirumuṟai.* Among its 12 books are the *Tevāram,* consisting of the hymns of Appar (Tirunāvukkaracu), Tiruñānacampantar and Cuntarar; and Māṇikkavācakar's mystical poem *Tīruvācakam* (Eng. trans. by G. U. Pope). The 12th book, the 12th-century *Pĕriyapurāṇam* of Cekkiḻār, describes the lives of the 63 Śaiva *nāyaṉmār* ("saints").

Of possibly the same period as the first few books of *Tirumuṟai* are the "Eighteen Minor Works." Largely didactic, these include the well-known collections of aphorisms, *Tirukkuṟal,* by Tiruvaḷḷuvar. This work is highly esteemed by the Tamilians, and there are several translations. Another similar work is the *Nālaṭiyār.*

Similar in subject matter to the *Tevāram,* though somewhat later in date, are the hymns of the *Nālāyirappirapantam,* which differ only in that they praise the god Viṣṇu (Vishnu). They are the work of the 12 Vaiṣṇava devotees or Āḻvārs, the most interesting of whom is, perhaps, Āṇṭāl, the girl-foundling reared by a Vaiṣṇava priest.

The epics *Cilappatikāram* and *Maṇimēkalai,* written by Iḷankovaṭikaḷ and Cāttanār respectively, may probably be assigned to the 6th or 7th century. The former tells of a merchant Kovalaṉ who neglects his wife Kaṇṇaki, lavishing his wealth on a courtesan called Mātavi. Later, impoverished as a result of his excesses, Kovalaṉ and his faithful wife travel to Madurai, where they try to start a new life, selling Kaṇṇaki's golden anklets to raise capital. Wrongfully accused of stealing these from the queen, Kovalaṉ is executed. Kaṇṇaki fully exonerates her husband before the king, who dies of remorse, and she herself, in her frenzied grief, tears off her left breast and curses the city, which is consumed by fire. She then makes her way to another royal city, Vañci, where she dies, and is received into heaven to join Kovalaṉ.

Though a Buddhist work, *Maṇimēkalai* is a sequel to the *Cilappatikāram* in that its heroine, Maṇimēkalai, is the daughter of Mātavi by Kovalaṉ. Mother and daughter have both become Buddhist nuns; the prince, Utayakumāraṉ, falls in love with Maṇimēkalai, and the pair finally realize that they were married in a former birth.

**Ninth to Twelfth Centuries.**—Three famous Tamil poets, Kampaṉ, Oṭṭakkūttaṉ and Pukaḻenti, belong to this period, but it is not possible to date them with any exactness. Kampaṉ was author of the principal Tamil version of the *Rāmāyaṇa.* In his version, given a South Indian setting, Rāma is regarded not only as hero of the story but as a god and incarnation of Viṣṇu—as is usually the case with vernacular *Rāmāyaṇas* in India. The work, begun by Kampaṉ, was completed by Oṭṭakkūttan.

Cayaṅkŏṇṭāṉ's *Kaliṅkattupparaṇi,* an 11th-century work, describes the victorious war waged by the Coḻa king against the neighbouring ruler of Kaliṅga. It opens with a grandiose genealogy of the Tamil king, and closes with a gruesome description of the carnage of battle and of the corpses being devoured by shedevils.

A number of commentators and grammarians belong to this period. Among the former may be mentioned Aṭiyārkkunallār, who wrote the commentary on *Cilappatikāram,* and Naccinārkkiṉiyar, who, in addition to commentaries on *Pattuppaṭṭu* and some of the *Eṭṭuttŏkai,* wrote one on part of the early "grammar" *Tŏlkāppiyam.*

**Twelfth to Sixteenth Centuries.**—Tamil literature became increasingly concerned with philosophical treatises and with creating *Purāṇas* (anthologies of religious legends), which, in this case, describe the myths about the various shrines of South India. Most important among the former are perhaps those (for example Mēykaṇṭatevar's *Civañāṇapotam*) which expound Śaiva-siddhānta philosophy.

Among the *Purāṇas* mention may be made of the *Tiruviḷaiyāṭaṟpurāṇam* of Parañcotimuṉivar, which recounts the 64 divine sports of the god Śiva (Shiva) in connection with the founding of the great temple at Madurai.

**European Influence and the Modern Period.**—After the collapse of the Vijayanagar empire in 1565, South India was split into a number of petty states, but some of these, such as Thanjavur (Tanjore), continued to patronize writers. Missionaries from the west were also active in the Tamil area. The earliest of these, apart possibly from St. Francis Xavier (*q.v.*), were Roberto de Nobili in the 17th century and another Italian Jesuit, Joseph Beschi, born near Mantua in 1680. Both lived as Hindu ascetics, and Beschi studied not only grammar but composition. He produced an epic, the *Tempāvaṇi,* which tells the story of St. Joseph and is based on an earlier model, *Cīvakacintāmaṇi.* In 1738 he produced a grammar of Tamil in Latin, probably the first to be written in a European language.

British Tamil studies were initiated by the manuscript collections of Col. Colin Mackenzie, who arrived in India in 1783. Later scholars of Tamil from the west included Robert Caldwell, whose *Comparative Grammar of the Dravidian . . . Languages* appeared in 1856; and the Rev. G. U. Pope who, besides writing a number of grammars, translated several Tamil works, including the *Tirukkuṟaḷ.*

In the 19th century, Tamil increasingly availed itself of western literary forms and ideas, and prose, hitherto reserved for inscriptions and commentaries, became accepted as a literary medium. The first novel was *Piratāpa Mutaliyār Carittiram,* by Vedanāyakam Piḷḷai. The most famous poet of modern times is C. Subrahmanya Bharati (d. 1922). Perhaps his most lasting work is *Kaṇṇan Pāṭṭu,* a touching and lyrical cycle on the god Kṛṣṇa (*see* VISHNUISM). His work combines the best of the techniques of east and west. More recent is *Pāratidācan* whose poems about children and the family are especially attractive.

Much modern Tamil writing is devoted to regional politics and can hardly be said to be of permanent value; however, such writers as Aṇṇātturai and Karuṇāniti proved their worth in other work; for example, in the writing of filmscripts, and their contribution to Tamil literature may become more lasting. A number of excellent literary journals, such as the humorous weekly *Āṉanta*

*Vikatan* and the magazine *Kalki,* afforded South Indian writers a medium and helped to foster good writing.

BIBLIOGRAPHY.—Translations into English, other than those mentioned in the text, include *The Lay of the Anklet,* trans. by V. R. Ramachandra Dikshitar (1939); *The Story of King Nala and Princess Damayanti,* trans. by M. Langton (1950); *The Ayodhya Canto of the Ramayana,* from Kampan's version, trans. by C. Rajagopalachari for the United Nations Educational, Scientific and Cultural Organization (1961). V. Cronin, *A Pearl to India: the Life of Roberto de Nobili* (1959); W. C. Mackenzie, *Colonel Colin Mackenzie* (1953); V. R. Ramachandra Dikshitar, *Studies in Tamil Literature and History* (1930). (Jo. R. M.)

**TAMM, IGOR EVGENYEVICH** (1895– ) Russian physicist, who was awarded the 1958 Nobel Prize for Physics jointly with P. A. Cerenkov and I. M. Frank "for the discovery and interpretation of the Cerenkov effect," was born in Vladivostok on July 8, 1895. This effect, which was first described by Cerenkov in 1934, is concerned with the emission of light waves by electrons moving at very high speeds and is of great importance for the study of nuclear physics (*see* CERENKOV RADIATION).

Tamm, a professor at Moscow University, and his co-worker Frank provided a theoretical explanation of the Cerenkov effect in 1937. He became one of the best-known Soviet physicists and a member of the Academy of Sciences of the U.S.S.R.

In 1946 Tamm shared the Stalin Prize with Cerenkov and Frank for their joint work on electron radiation. He worked on the quantum theory of diffused light in solid bodies, on the photoeffect on metals, and on methods for the control of thermonuclear reactions. His technique of interpreting the interaction of elementary nuclear particles is known as the Tamm method. He appeared on U.S. television in May 1963, appealing for international disarmament based on increasing trust among nations.

*See* T. N. Levitan, *Laureates: Jewish Winners of the Nobel Prize* (1960). (W. J. BP.)

**TAMMANN, GUSTAV HEINRICH JOHANN APOLLON** (1861–1938), German physical chemist whose researches into the states and reactions of matter, especially of metals, made him one of the founders of metallurgy, was born at Yamburg (Kingisepp), near St. Petersburg (Leningrad), on May 28, 1861. He studied at the University of Dorpat (Tartu) in Estonia, and in 1892 became professor and director of the Chemical Institute there. In 1903 he went to the University of Göttingen in Germany as a professor of inorganic chemistry and was head of the Institute of Physical Chemistry there from 1907 to 1930. He died at Göttingen on Dec. 17, 1938. Tammann made fundamental investigations of the changes in the condition of matter and their dependence on temperature and pressure and also studied the reactions of matter in a hard and brittle condition. Especially valuable were his introduction of thermal analysis in the construction of constitutional diagrams of metals, and his researches into the nature and structure of alloys.

Among Tammann's publications were *Lehrbuch der Metallographie* (1914; 4th ed., 1932); *Die chemischen und galvanischen Eigenschaften von Mischkristallreihen und ihre Atomverteilung* (1919). He was an editor of *Zeitschrift für anorganische und allgemeine Chemie.*

*See* W. E. Garner, "The Influence of Gustav Tammann," *Chemical Age,* vol. 66 (1952). (W. O. K.)

**TAMMANY HALL,** popular name of the executive committee of the Democratic Party of New York County, sometimes applied to the entire party structure in the county or in the city. From about 1800, with only occasional intermissions, as a political organization it was important in the city, and it exercised considerable influence in state administration and national affairs. Tammany societies patterned after the New York organization were formed in other states in the early 1800s but did not attain great importance.

**Origin.**—Before the American Revolution groups proclaiming fealty to King George III were organized in societies bearing the names of St. George, St. Andrew, and St. David. As a countermove, the revolutionists formed associations called the Sons of Liberty or the Sons of St. Tammany, the latter after Tamanend, a Delaware Indian chief (*fl.* 1682–1700) famed for wisdom, benevolence, and love of freedom, with the "saint" thrown in as a form of ridicule. After the achievement of American independence, these associations dissolved.

During the 1780s the leaders of the aristocratic and propertied elements of New York city and state successfully managed to limit the suffrage to freeholders and to strengthen the Society of the Cincinnati, a group of former officers of the Revolutionary Army with centralist and monarchial tendencies. To resist these influences, William Mooney, an upholsterer in New York City, founded the Society of St. Tammany or Columbian Order, on May 12, 1789, a few days after the inauguration of George Washington as the first president under the Constitution. His purpose was the creation of a national society that would be native in character and democratic in principle and action. Its officers were given Indian titles; the society's chief was grand sachem and his fellow chiefs, sachems.

For more than three decades after its organization, Tammany represented the middle-class opposition to the pretensions and power of the aristocratic party. Its "democracy" did not incorporate the aspirations of the lower economic groups. In that period it also lost its national and nonpolitical character and became intimately identified with politics in New York City.

Under the control of Aaron Burr until his political downfall after killing Alexander Hamilton in a duel in 1804, the society had an influential share in bringing about victories of the Republican (later called the Democratic) Party and was richly rewarded, particularly by Thomas Jefferson after he became president in 1801.

**Organization.**—Criticisms made by the opposition that a private society was engaging in politics resulted in a separation of the Hall's social and political functions. In 1805 the Society of St. Tammany obtained from the legislature a charter of incorporation as a benevolent and charitable body to give relief to members and others. Politically, the Democratic Party was organized as an apparently distinct body; in reality, however, the society's sachems controlled the political mechanism and prevented hostile factions from meeting in the society building, Tammany Hall.

The political organization initiated at that time consisted of general, nominating, corresponding, and ward committees. In the general committee was vested the power of convening the party's meetings and of making all necessary arrangements for elections. Composed originally of 30 members, three from each of the city's ten wards, this committee was gradually expanded until it had many thousands of members penetrating every section of the city. The real power consequently passed into the hands of the ward leaders, later organized as the executive committee of the party.

**Boss Rule.**—As early as 1806–07, revelations of widespread corruption of Tammany city officials resulted in the removal of the controller, the superintendent of the almshouse, the inspector of bread, and others. Despite such proved charges, many of the removed officials, including the society's founder, remained powerful Tammany sachems.

The bitterest opponents of Tammany were the Irish immigrants who were ineligible to be members of the "native-born patriots." As a protest against Tammany bigotry, hundreds of Irish migrants broke into a general committee meeting on the evening of April 24, 1817. Within a few years, the propertied leaders of Tammany were forced for their own preservation to take in the immigrants, naturalize and vote them, and join in the fight for manhood suffrage.

In the 1830s the pressures exerted by the Workingmen's Party and its successor, the Equal Rights Party, forced the general committee to oust the banking and merchant leaders. The election of its grand sachem, Martin Van Buren, as president of the United States in 1836 redounded to Tammany's prestige. Within a few years, however, the immigrant groups, organized into gangs, came under the control of the astute, unscrupulous, and engaging Fernando Wood, several times mayor of New York, who used them to break with and later control Tammany. Grand Sachem William M. Tweed (*q.v.*) initiated complete boss domination of the Hall in 1868. Corruption reached a climax under Tweed, when New York City was plundered of more than $200,000,000. Tweed died in jail but most of his confederates retained their wealth. Throughout the world, Tammany became synonymous with corruption and was the subject of some of Thomas Nast's most effective cartoons.

John Kelly, who succeeded Tweed, induced the leading reformers—Samuel J. Tilden, August Belmont, and Horatio Seymour—to serve as sachems. The real resuscitating factor, however, was the attachment of the tenement house masses to the district leaders, who could be counted on to help poor families in distress. The helping hand outweighed all of the denunciations. Richard Croker in 1886 and his successor in 1902, Charles F. Murphy, carried on the façade of making liberal avowals and supporting progressive candidates for the top of the ticket but failed to curb corruption within the administrative machinery.

**Reform.**—After Murphy's death in 1924, Judge George W. Olvany became county leader and with the assistance of Gov. Alfred E. Smith sought to alter the character of the Hall. On March 16, 1929, Judge Olvany resigned and was succeeded by a leader of the old school, John F. Curry. Revelations of corruption in Mayor James Walker's administration, as shown in the Seabury Report, discredited Curry but he remained in power until successive defeats of Tammany candidates led to his replacement by James J. Dooling in July 1934.

During the 12 years of Fiorello LaGuardia's reform administration, Tammany declined in power and was eclipsed by the more powerful Brooklyn and Bronx Democratic leaders. Many Democratic Party candidates repudiated Tammany. The organization found itself in dire financial condition and had to give up its headquarters in the building maintained by the Tammany Society. A succession of county leaders—Timothy J. Sullivan, Michael J. Kennedy, and Edward Loughlin—promised the elimination of corruption and pledged leadership for good government but failed to induce public confidence in the Hall. In the election of 1945, however, Tammany once more established its ability to turn out a sizable vote. The newly elected mayor, William O'Dwyer of Brooklyn, sought to control Tammany by ousting Loughlin and forcing the acceptance in March 1947 of Frank J. Sampson as county Democratic leader. Lacking the support of the district leaders, Sampson functioned as a figurehead and was soon replaced by Hugo Rogers, Manhattan's borough president. A bitter struggle between city hall and Tammany ensued, reflected in a series of district leadership fights in the 1949 primaries in which the regular organization defeated a group of insurgent reformers. Rogers, however, was ousted in favour of Carmine G. De Sapio.

Pressures from within and outside the organization brought about a reconciliation of Mayor O'Dwyer and the new Tammany leader but charges of underworld control of some district leaders and of others high in Tammany councils led to insistent demands for reform. Acting Mayor Vincent R. Impellitteri, who had been denied the regular nomination, ran as an independent, anti-Tammany candidate in the special election in 1950 and beat the organization decisively.

The Hall lost other important local and city elections to independent Democrats, moreover. De Sapio managed, however, to stave off threats to his leadership in the primary campaigns of 1951 and 1953. In 1953, he joined with Edward Flynn of the Bronx to support Manhattan Borough Pres. Robert F. Wagner, Jr., for the Democratic mayoralty nomination. After Flynn's death and Wagner's nomination and election, De Sapio was recognized as an important leader. He succeeded Flynn as Democratic national committeeman and also became secretary of state for New York. De Sapio's rule was criticized by reformers, including Mayor Wagner, who opposed his leadership in 1961 and won reelection that year. Four years later, John V. Lindsay, who had been elected to the U.S. Congress as a Republican, ran for mayor as a Republican-Liberal and defeated the regular Democratic candidate.

BIBLIOGRAPHY.—Gustavus Myers, *The History of Tammany Hall* (1917); M. R. Werner, *Tammany Hall* (1928); W. Riordon, *Plunkitt of Tammany Hall* (1948); A. Connable and E. Silberfarb, *Tigers of Tammany* (1967). (M. B. D.; M. R. W.)

**TAMMERFORS:** *see* TAMPERE.

**TAMMUZ,** Hebrew form of DUMUZI ("true-son"), a god of ancient Babylonia. In all periods of Sumerian and Akkadian literature, his name when written is prefixed by the sign for deity.

Dumuzi is first mentioned in a Sumerian list of divine names found at Shuruppak (modern Tell Fa'rah, in lower Iraq) and composed about the middle of the 3rd millennium B.C. Thereafter, he is named in texts found at Lagash, Umma, Drehem, and Ur. During the dynasty of Akkad (*c.* 2350–2230 B.C.) the Lagash calendar included a "month of the feast of Dumuzi." In a somewhat later account of the overthrow of the Guti (the dynasty that succeeded the Akkadian), their conqueror, Utukhegal, king of Uruk, says "Inanna is my support, Dumuzi, the *ama-ushumgal-an-na,* has declared my destiny." The Sumerian title which follows the name Dumuzi means "the heavenly dragon of the Mother" (*i.e.,* of Inanna; though a reference to "date clusters" is preferred by some scholars). *Ama-ushumgal* occurs as a personal name on some of the earliest Sumerian documents.

During the 3rd dynasty of Ur (end of the 3rd millennium B.C.), there was at Lagash a temple of Dumuzi, possessed of much property administered by officials, in which offerings were made to him. The 6th month at Lagash and the 12th month at Umma, neighbour of Lagash, were his festival months. By contrast, in contemporary tablets from Ur, the well-documented capital city of this dynasty, Dumuzi is not mentioned except in personal names derived from his name. No temple or offerings are recorded in his honour, and no festival month of Dumuzi occurs in the calendar used at Ur during the period in which most of the tablets are dated. It would appear therefore from the 3rd-millennium evidence that his cult was limited, for the most part, to Lagash and its neighbour Umma, and from this evidence nothing can be discovered about his relationship to the Sumerian deities or his place and function in popular story.

On these aspects, however, there is evidence from texts of the first half of the 2nd millennium B.C. Much of this evidence was not known to scholars before World War II. It lends no support to earlier constructions and interpretations of the Tammuz story or to alleged parallels with Adonis or Osiris.

Sinidinnam of Larsa states that he has "gratified the hearts of Shamash and Dumuzi." Larsa was the chief cult centre of Shamash (*q.v.;* Sumerian Utu), the sun-god, who is prominent in stories of Inanna and Dumuzi. On the other hand, Hammurabi (about 50 years later) does not name Dumuzi in the long list of deities in the prologue and epilogue of his code. A composite text of this period, the Sumerian king list, is authority for a tradition that Dumuzi was a king of ancient Sumer. The name is given both to a pre-diluvian king of Bad-tibira in the region of Uruk (biblical Erech), who reigned for 36,000 years, and to a post-diluvian king of Uruk, who reigned for 100 years. In the former entry he is described as a shepherd. In the latter he is a "SHU. PES. fisherman," of uncertain meaning. In both he is mortal.

The earliest evidence of the association of Dumuzi and Inanna (*see* ISHTAR) occurs in the quotation from Utukhegal quoted above. In a dialogue written in Sumerian and dating from the early 2nd millennium B.C., involving Enkimdu, the farmer, and Dumuzi, the shepherd, the sun-god Utu advises his sister Inanna to choose Dumuzi rather than Enkimdu for husband. This she does after hearing each recount the benefits he confers on mankind. In this dialogue, Dumuzi, "whose fat is good, whose milk is good," belongs with sheep, lambs, and kids. The dialogue probably reflects an older tradition and thus supplies something which is not discernible in the purely administrative texts and royal inscriptions of the Sumerian period. A text of the 1st Babylonian dynasty (*c.* 1800–*c.* 1600) represents Inanna in search of Dumuzi *ama-ushumgal-an-na.* She seeks "the shepherd" "in the sheepfold" and revives him with food, drink, and music.

An important feature in the story of Dumuzi is his presence in the underworld. A Sumerian version of Inanna's "Descent to the Underworld" appears to offer an explanation of this. It relates that on her return from the lower regions Inanna goes to the Sumerian city Kullab of which Dumuzi, her husband, is guardian. He receives her seated and wearing robes of state. Enraged by such *hauteur* Inanna bids the seven demons who have escorted her from below to "carry him off" to the underworld. This they presumably do, in spite of Dumuzi's tearful appeals to Utu. This suggests that the presence of Dumuzi in the underworld was thought of as a punishment and not as an incident in his search for Inanna. In later literature Erkallu, the underworld, is described as "the house of Tammuz," and he as "shepherd of the earth." The "earth" is another synonym for the underworld, called also Arallu, of which Dumuzi is named "lord." The myth of Adapa (*see* ADAPA) states that Tammuz and Gizzida disappeared from "the land," *matu,* a name also frequently employed to indicate the underworld. His disappearance is the theme of many laments, and there is no mention or celebration of a resurrection. He has disappeared to "the land of no return." There he is said to keep in check the demons who torment the sick. He is, however, rarely invoked in exorcisms. The Semitic version of Ishtar's "Descent" closes with a reference to a washing, anointing, and clothing of Dumuzi. This is probably a reference to an image of Dumuzi, possibly on the occasion of a lying-in-state, and to rites of the *taklimtu* ceremony at which such ritual washings, etc., were performed.

An explanation of the wailings for Dumuzi is given in the Epic of Gilgamesh (*see* GILGAMESH, EPIC OF). Ishtar smote Dumuzi "the shepherd" and "the lover of her youth," bruising his wing. For this reason he sits in the woods crying, "my wing, my wing." Ishtar ordains annual wailings for him. The majority of these laments are composed in the Sumerian language; some have an interlinear translation in Akkadian.

The city chiefly associated with Dumuzi is Uruk, the ancient Sumerian city, of which he together with Shamash and Gilgamesh was protector in the time of Utukhegal. Kullab, to which Inanna returned from the underworld, was part of Uruk. In northern Iraq there was a month of Dumuzi but little else to suggest that he was much honoured in Assyria. Mari, in southeastern Syria, also had this month in its calendar. In Palestine, there were wailings at Jerusalem: "and behold, there sat women weeping for Tammuz" (Ezek. 8:14). (The Masoretic text of Ezek. 8:1 gives the sixth month as the date of this wailing but the Septuagint gives the fifth.) The Jewish colony at Elephantine, an island opposite Aswan in Egypt, included the month of Tammuz in its calendar during the 5th century B.C. There is no evidence that Tammuz was honoured by the Hebrews before the time of Ezekiel, who, according to tradition, exercised his ministry in Babylonia, the early home of Tammuz cult.

For the context of the worship of Dumuzi, *see* BABYLONIA AND ASSYRIA: *Religion: Sumerian Pantheon: Herding Regions.*

BIBLIOGRAPHY.—A. Deimel, *Pantheon Babylonicum* (1914); M. Witzel, *Tammuz-Liturgien und Verwandtes* (1935); E. Douglas Van Buren, "Ancient Beliefs and Some Modern Interpretations," *Orientalia,* new series, vol. 18, pp. 494–501 (1949); S. N. Kramer (ed.), "Inanna's Descent to the Underworld," *Journal of Cuneiform Studies,* 5:1–17 (1951), *From the Tablets of Sumer,* ch. 19 (1956); F. R. Kraus, "Zur Moortgat 'Tammuz,'" *Wiener Zeitschrift für Kunde des Morgenlandes,* 52:36–80 (1953); O. R. Gurney, "Tammuz Reconsidered," *Journal of Semitic Studies,* 7:147–160 (1962); J. B. Pritchard (ed.), *Ancient Near Eastern Texts Relating to the Old Testament,* 2nd ed. (1955).

**TAMPA,** the seat of Hillsborough County, Fla., U.S., the principal manufacturing city and agricultural centre on the west coast of the state, lies at the mouth of the Hillsborough River as it enters an arm of Tampa Bay. The population in 1960 was 274,970, an increase of 120.5% in the decade; that of the Tampa-St. Petersburg standard metropolitan statistical area (Hillsborough and Pinellas counties) was 772,453, an increase of 88.8%. (For comparative population figures for both Tampa and St. Petersburg, *see* table in FLORIDA: *Population.*) (*See* also SAINT PETERSBURG.)

**History.**—Tampa was the name of an Indian settlement recorded by historians in the 16th century after Spanish explorers, including Hernando de Soto, and missionaries landed in its vicinity. In November 1823 Col. George M. Brooke was directed to establish a military post at Tampa Bay when the U.S. Army began the removal of Seminole Indians from north to south Florida, and Ft. Brooke was erected there in 1824. The fort was also active in the seven years of warfare (1835–42) brought on by attempts to remove the Indians to the west, and during the American Civil War it was bombarded and the port blockaded to prevent the shipment of cattle from Tampa to Cuba. Tampa was incorporated in 1855. In 1886 Vincente Martinez Ybor induced several cigar manufacturers to move there after they had been driven out of Havana, Cuba, by revolutionary disorders and from Key West because of labour disturbances and a disastrous fire. Tampa became a world leader in the production of clear Havana handmade cigars.

The greatest developer of Tampa was Henry B. Plant, who made it an international port and tourist resort. In the mid-1880s he connected the city by a standard-gauge railway with lines to the north; he also inaugurated steamship service to Key West and Havana. In 1891 Plant opened the Tampa Bay Hotel, a dark-red-brick castle of Moorish architecture topped by silvery domes and 13 minarets on which he had lavished $3,000,000. Five stories in height and extending over a six-acre tract on the Hillsborough River, the sprawling edifice became one of the popular luxury hotels of the world.

During the Spanish-American War, about 30,000 soldiers were camped in and near the city before embarking for Cuba. Cigar makers supported the Cuban independence movement, their aid being organized by the Cuban patriot José Marti; the cottage in Tampa where he made his headquarters is now a shrine.

The Latin quarter, known as Ybor City, which accounts for about 15% of the population, is the home of Spaniards and Cubans connected primarily with the cigar industry. They maintain their own imposing social clubs and hospitals. Their restaurants have an international reputation.

In the mid-1920s the man-made Davis Islands were created in the bay to provide sites for hotels, residences, apartments, a hospital and an airport. A landscaped six-mile boulevard bordering the crescent-shaped bay forms a scenic residential section.

**Commerce, Industry and Transportation.**—Tampa is a port of entry; after the opening of the Panama Canal in 1914 it became one of the most important ports on the Gulf of Mexico. The impact of the citrus industry is an important factor in the economy of Tampa. A large percentage of all phosphate mined in the U.S. is extracted from the adjoining county; much of it is shipped from Tampa. In addition to the numerous cigar factories there are more than 700 manufacturing plants. The tourist business is also important in the economy. The city is well served by rail and air lines as well as by harbour facilities.

**Education and Recreation.**—The University of Tampa, a private institution chartered in 1931, in 1933 was given a 99-year lease on the Tampa Bay Hotel building by the city. The state-supported University of South Florida was established in 1958 and opened in 1960. Features of the winter season in Tampa are the Gasparilla and Latin-American pageants and festivals, baseball, golf, tennis, and sailing.

**TAMPERE** (Swedish TAMMERFORS), the second largest town of Finland and the seat of a bishopric, is situated in Häme (Hämeen) *lääni* (county), 116 mi. (187 km.) NNW of Helsinki by rail. Pop. (1960 est.) 127,260. An important cultural, industrial, and communications centre, it occupies a narrow isthmus traversed by the Tammerkoski rapids which flow from Lake Näsijärvi to Lake Pyhäjärvi. It is a modern town with wide esplanades, parks, and gardens, and notable examples of 20th-century Finnish architecture and sculpture. The oldest building is the 15th-century stone church of Messukylä. The cathedral (Lars Sonck; 1907) is in the national-romantic style. Among works by prominent modern architects are the cemetery chapel (1960) by Viljo Revell (designer of the Toronto City Hall); the Finnish Institute of Social Sciences begun (1961) by Toivo Korhonen; and the open-air Pyynikki Summer Theatre, with a revolving auditorium (1959), the first of its kind in the world, by Jaakko Ieveskoski.

Tampere is a junction of railway lines from Helsinki and to the north and west; there are air connections with Helsinki Vaasa, Jyväskylä, Pori, Stockholm, and Copenhagen and passenger services on the lakes. The Tammerkoski provides power for Finland's biggest concentration of industry outside Helsinki, producing mainly textiles, machinery, and footwear. The first cotton mill was founded by a Scot, James Finlayson, in 1820, and industrial development was encouraged by fiscal privileges enjoyed by the town during 1821–1905. Tampere received its charter in 1779. It was the scene of an important battle in the Finnish War of Independence of 1918. (E.-S. Ku.)

**TAMPICO,** a city and leading port of Mexico, in the state of Tamaulipas, on the north bank of the Pánuco River, about 6 mi. from the Gulf of Mexico. In summer the climate is hot and humid, although a sea breeze modifies the temperature somewhat. In winter the temperature falls to freezing on occasional days when northers blow down along the Gulf Coast. Tampico is almost surrounded by swampy lands and lagoons.

The eastern and poorer part of the town stands on low ground only two or three feet above the river, and is subject to inundations. However, a modern sewer system, up-to-date street paving, and a better water supply, constructed after the beginning of the 20th century, greatly improved the sanitary conditions and reduced the death rate from epidemics. The western part rises about 150 ft., consists largely of residential districts and is provided with still better sanitary equipment. The business section is well built, largely of stone and brick, while many of the newer structures are of reinforced concrete and rise to six and seven stories. The city is well supplied with gas and electric light.

Tampico has excellent railway facilities, road connections with the Pan-American highway, and air services available to Mexico City, Veracruz, Brownsville, Tex., and other points. Although a bar exists at the mouth of the Pánuco River, jetties were built and the depth increased by dredging, so that vessels drawing up to 33 ft. can approach the waterfront of the city, while scows and other boats of light draft can navigate the river for more than 100 mi. upstream.

The Chijol Canal, begun in 1901, affords a waterway 6 ft. deep and 25 ft. wide for about 75 mi. southward through the oil fields to Túxpan. Modern port works, spacious enough to accommodate at the wharves 14 vessels at a time, steel sheds and warehouses, a union railway station within easy reach of the waterfront, and excellent equipment for loading oil tankers make Tampico the most up-to-date harbour in Mexico.

Tampico owes its importance to four of the most productive oil fields in the country (the Ebano, Pánuco, Huasteca, and Túxpan) which are situated within about 100 mi. of its site. Until 1901 it was a second-rate port, outlet of the fertile but relatively underdeveloped hinterland, with a reputation for unhealthful and unsanitary conditions. The rapid exploitation of petroleum resources resulted in a marked increase of population from about 10,000 in 1900 to 24,980 in 1921, to 82,475 in 1940, to 94,342 in 1950, and to 122,535 in 1960. For several years Tampico ranked as the greatest oil port in the world. Pipelines lead from the nearby fields, while fleets of scows bring oil from farther up the river. Pipelines and barges together are capable of transporting approximately 1,200,000 bbl. of oil daily from the fields to the port of Tampico.

Up river from the port agricultural activities were stimulated, fruits, vegetables, and grains being grown to supply the local food demands. Modern commercial establishments are stocked with U.S. and European goods. Hotels, clubs, restaurants, and places of amusement are numerous and well served. Because of high prevailing wage rates, the standard of living is generally higher than in most Mexican cities. Tampico is also noted as a vacation resort with excellent bathing, golfing, hunting, and fishing.

Besides those connected directly with the oil business, the industrial establishments of Tampico include many for the handling and repair of oil well machinery, yards for the building of river boats, an electric light and power plant, factories for making ice, clothing, and fruit preserves, sawmills, etc. In addition to petroleum, the exports include silver bullion (from San Luis Potosí, Aguascalientes, Torreón, and Monterrey), istle fibre, sugar, hides, live cattle, cottonseed cake, honey, fustic, sarsaparilla, coffee, and copper ores.

Tampico grew around a monastery which was founded in the ruins of an Aztec village by Andrés de Olmos, a Franciscan friar, in 1532. It was destroyed in 1683 by pirates and not reoccupied until 1823 when Gen. Lopéz de Santa Anna ordered that the site should be settled.

In 1829 a Spanish force under Isidro de Barredas was defeated at Tampico by Santa Anna. It was briefly occupied by U.S. forces during the Mexican War and again in 1862 by the French. The arrest of some American sailors in Tampico on April 9, 1914, led to the bombardment and occupation of Veracruz on April 22, 1914, by the U.S. Navy. (J. W. Mw.; R. B. McCk.)

**TAMWORTH,** a city of New South Wales, Austr., lies on the Peel River 1,279 ft. (390 m.) above sea level, 285 mi. (459 km.) N of Sydney by rail. Pop. (1961) 18,984. The city possesses several schools and a notable art gallery. The headquarters of Australia's only decentralized airline, it has regular air services with Sydney and Brisbane. It is the centre of an extensive agricultural district, and its industries include light engineering, flour and timber milling, egg processing, and the production of starch and gluten. Tamworth was the first Australian city to install electric street lighting (1888), an event celebrated by an annual "festival of light." (E. W. Wi.)

**TAMWORTH,** a market town and municipal borough in the Lichfield and Tamworth parliamentary division of Staffordshire, Eng., 15 mi. NE of Birmingham by road. Pop. (1961) 13,646. Area 4.2 sq.mi. It lies at the junction of the Tame and Anker rivers, in open country with wooded uplands. Offa, overlord of Mercia, built a palace there in the 8th century and surrounded the burgh by the great entrenchment known as Offa's dyke. During the 9th century Tamworth was destroyed by the Danes, but in A.D. 913 Aethelflaed, daughter of Alfred the Great, defeated them and built a timbered stockade at the junction of the rivers where the present castle stands. William the Conqueror bestowed the manor upon Robert de Marmion, who built the Norman castle, the walls and keep of which remain. It was largely restored in the Jacobean period. Tamworth, a borough since Saxon times, once possessed a royal mint, dating from Aethelstan's reign. Originally half the borough was in Staffordshire, the other half in Warwickshire, but in 1319 Edward III granted the Warwickshire half to the burgesses by letters patent. The town was incorporated by Elizabeth I in 1560 and a further charter was granted by Charles II in 1663. The whole borough was transferred to Staffordshire in 1889. The church of St. Editha (8th century) was rebuilt, after the Danes had burned it, by king Edgar who made it collegiate in A.D. 963. The existing Decorated building was erected after a fire in 1345. The grammar school, granted a charter by Elizabeth I in 1588, once formed part of the collegiate church. Guy's Almshouses (1678) were endowed by Thomas Guy, founder of Guy's Hospital, London, who also built the town hall over the open market in 1701. An ancient fair in honour of St. Swithun is still held (July 26). Two members of Parliament were returned by the borough from 1562 to 1885. Sir Robert Peel represented it during the first half of the 19th century. Tamworth, the centre of an agricultural and coal-mining area, specializes in agricultural engineering, textile weaving, paper making, the manufacture of asbestos and aluminum ware, and the making of terra cotta bricks from local clay.

**TANA, LAKE,** the largest lake of Ethiopia, lies in the northwest on a high plateau about 6,000 ft. (1,830 m.) above sea level. It forms a reservoir for the Blue Nile (known in Ethiopia as the Abbai), which drains from the southern extremity near Bahr Dar. The lake's surface covers 1,418 sq.mi. (3,673 sq.km.), with a surrounding drainage area of 4,500 sq.mi. (11,655 sq.km.). The alluvial plains of Dembea on the northern shore and Fogera on the east indicate that at one time the lake had been more extensive. Where the lake has been dammed by a lava barrier near Bahr Dar, the Abbai crosses the southern ledge, forming the spectacular Tis Esat Falls. The drop at this point has been harnessed for hydroelectric power. Though the source of the Abbai is popularly believed to be the Little Abbai River, to the south near Mt. Amedamit—the source identified by the British explorer James Bruce about 1770—the flow from the inlet of this stream to the outlet of the Abbai is probably part of a general flow toward the outlet at the southern end of a bay some 11 mi. long. Many narrow promontories (the largest, Gorgora, in the north) jut into the lake, separating small alluvial plains. Of the small islands fringing the shores, most notable are the two larger inhabited islands,

Dek and Dega, at the southern end; both contain historic churches famed for medieval manuscripts and paintings.

With abundant rainfall, the Lake Tana region produces grains, oilseeds, and coffee. There is also some cattle raising. A new road now connects Bahr Dar with Gorgora and there is regular motorboat service across the lake. The ancient *tanqua* (papyrus reed boat) is used for fishing. (G. C. L.)

**TANAGER,** the name for members of the songbird family Thraupidae (formerly Tanagridae) containing 197 species. They are small to medium-sized birds of rather generalized form, with medium-sized wings, feet and tails. The beak is heavy and somewhat similar to that of their nearest relatives, the sparrows. As a group tanagers are noted for the brilliancy of their plumage, though they have developed no ornamental tufts or plumes. Reds, yellows, greens, blues and blacks in solid colours are common and sometimes arranged in striking patterns. The sexes may be coloured similarly, or the female may be much duller than the male. In some species, however, both sexes are dull-coloured. No tanagers are notable songsters, but some have simple songs of pleasing quality.

HAL H. HARRISON FROM NATIONAL AUDUBON SOCIETY

MALE SUMMER TANAGER (PIRANGA RUBRA) AND YOUNG

The family is entirely confined to the new world, with its centre of abundance in the tropics. Only four species range north to the United States, and two regularly to Canada, and these are all migratory. Tanagers are arboreal birds, living in tree tops, undergrowth or shrubbery. Fruit is an important part of the diet of many species, and some feed almost entirely on mistletoe berries. Other species eat some insects.

The nest is a shallow, open structure. The eggs, two to four in number, may be white or bluish, immaculate or spotted. Monogamous pairing seems the rule and, in some species at least, while the female alone incubates, both sexes care for the young. In the tropics some species remain in pairs throughout the year.

When feathers were popular in millinery, brilliant tropical tanagers were often used as hat trimmings.

The best-known species are probably those of the United States, especially the scarlet tanager (*Piranga olivacea*), the male scarlet with black wings and tail, the female olive and yellowish; the summer tanager (*Piranga rubra*), with an all-red male; and the western tanager (*Piranga ludoviciana*), with the male yellow with reddish head and black wings and mantle. (A. L. Rd.)

**TANANARIVE:** *see* ANTANANARIVO.

**TANAQUIL,** the semilegendary Etruscan wife of Lucumo, who became Tarquinius Priscus (*see* TARQUIN), fifth king of Rome. She was a social climber, and because of her husband's lowly position in their own city (Tarquinii) she urged a move to Rome, where, by her prophetic powers, she foresaw that their fortunes would improve. There Lucumo adopted a Latin name Lucius Tarquinius, and she reportedly changed hers to Gaia Caecilia. On her husband's death, she made her son-in-law, Servius Tullius (*q.v.*), king. She was famous for her spinning and weaving, and there was a statue of her as Gaia Caecilia in the Temple of Semo Sancus, where her distaff and spindle were preserved as relics. A robe she had woven was similarly kept in the Temple of Fortune. Thus she became a model of virtue for Roman brides. Tanaquil and Gaia Caecilia are probably distinct personalities who somehow became associated at an early date.

*See* Livy, i, 34, 39, 41; Pliny, *Natural History*, viii, 74; Plutarch, *Roman Questions*, 30. (R. B. Ld.)

**TANA RIVER,** with a length of 440 mi. (708 km.), is the longest river of Kenya. Its numerous headwaters, among which the Sagana is considered to be the actual source of the river, rise in the high rainfall areas of the Aberdare Range and Mt. Kenya. These streams are collected and their water is carried northeastward along the ungraded section of the river containing Seven Forks, or Gtaru, Falls (440 ft. [134 m.]) into the semi-desert landscape through which the Tana flows in its middle course. Describing a wide arc, the river gradually assumes a southerly direction and opens out into the wide valley where it pursues an unstable and extremely sinuous course on a floodplain liable to widespread inundations. It reaches the Indian Ocean at Kipini, but a former outlet lies 20 mi. to the southwest. The river is navigable by launch, sometimes with difficulty, for 200 mi. (320 km.) upstream. In the upper Tana catchment Sasumua reservoir provides water for Nairobi; Kindaruma, at Seven Forks, is the site for a 40-megawatt hydroelectric scheme, and the Mwea-Tebere irrigation settlement has rice as its chief cash crop. On the forest-clad banks of the middle Tana the riverine Pokomo practise subsistence cultivation, and at Galole cotton is grown on a government irrigation scheme. (S. J. K. B.)

**TANBARK OAK** (*Lithocarpus densiflora*), an ornamental evergreen allied to the oaks, both of which belong to the beech family, Fagaceae. The tanbark oak, native to southern Oregon and northern California, is a tall tree of 75 to 100 ft., with alternate, leathery, toothed, more-or-less oblong three- to five-inch leaves covered on the underside with densely matted hairs that disappear in time.

The fruit is an acorn about one inch long. The tree is valued chiefly for its bark, which is an important source of tannin, but it is also an attractive ornamental. The waste bark of this tree and others is the tanbark used as a ground cover. (J. M. Bl.)

**TANCRED** (d. 1194), king of Sicily from 1190, of the Norman dynasty of Hauteville, was a natural son of King Roger II's son Roger, duke of Apulia (d. 1148), by a lady of the family of the counts of Lecce. During the reign of his uncle William I (from 1154) he conspired against the government, but eventually had to take refuge in Constantinople. Returning to the kingdom on William I's death (1166), he lived in concord with William II and obtained the countship of Lecce in 1169.

Short and ungainly, but quick-witted, Tancred showed ability as commander of the fleet in the expedition of 1185 against the Byzantines. When William II died (1189), a faction of the Norman nobility, reluctant to let the Sicilian crown go to Roger II's daughter Constance, wife of the Hohenstaufen German king Henry VI (*q.v.*), elected Tancred king. He was crowned at Palermo early in 1190, but his election split the anti-Hohenstaufen party, since some who had preferred a rival candidate (Roger of Andria) went over to Henry's side. In October, moreover, Richard I (*q.v.*) of England, brother of William II's widow Joan, seized the citadel of Messina: Tancred had to satisfy his heavy claims to money and treasure before Richard would depart (spring 1191).

Helped by the towns, to which he made concessions, Tancred suppressed rebellion in Apulia and Campania. In summer 1191 Henry gave up his siege of Naples. Henry was about to attack again when Tancred died, in Palermo, on Feb. 20, 1194, leaving his widow Sibyl (Sibylla) of Acerra as regent for his son William III. (E. Po.)

**TANCRED** (*c.* 1076–1112), Norman crusader from Sicily who was twice regent of Antioch (*see* CRUSADES), was a son of Marquis Odo and Emma, Robert Guiscard's daughter. He went with Bohemund I (*q.v.*) to Constantinople in 1096 but avoided taking the oath of allegiance which the other crusaders swore to the Byzantine emperor Alexius I. After Nicaea was taken, however, he paid homage to Alexius. He left the main crusading body after the capture of Heraclea-Cybistra and went south through the Cilician Gates to capture Tarsus, which Baldwin of Boulogne (later Baldwin I of Jerusalem), following with a stronger force, soon compelled him to relinquish. He then pressed on to take two other east Cilician cities held by the Armenians, Adana and Mamistra (Mopsuestia), where Baldwin again caught up with him, and there was a skirmish between the two crusading forces followed by a reconciliation. Tancred then took Alexandretta (Iskenderun) before rejoining the main crusading armies by now approaching Antioch (1097), which they took after siege in June 1098. Tancred played a leading part in the crusader conquest of Jerusalem in 1099, having previously taken Bethlehem. He then took Nablus, and was prominent in the crusaders' defeat of the Egyptians near Ascalon. He strengthened the position of Jerusalem by conquering Galilee, and took the title of prince of Galilee. After the death of Godfrey of Bouillon, crusader ruler of Jerusalem (1100), Tancred took Haifa, and supported Daimbert, the new Latin patriarch, in offering Jerusalem to Bohemund, but in fact Baldwin of Boulogne became his brother Godfrey's successor.

Tancred then went to Antioch as regent (Bohemund having been captured by the amir Danishmend) and gave up Galilee to Baldwin (1101). He recaptured the east Cilician cities, now in Byzantine hands, and then attacked the port of Latakia (Laodicea), also held by the Byzantines, having compelled Raymond IV of Toulouse to withdraw his troops from it and to give up all claims to north Syria. In early 1103, after nearly a year's siege, Tancred took Latakia. Shortly afterward Bohemund, now ransomed, took over his principality of Antioch from Tancred, who grudgingly relinquished also the cities he had captured as regent. However, the following year he was appointed regent of Edessa after Baldwin II of Edessa was taken prisoner in an unsuccessful crusader attack on Harran led also by Bohemund and Tancred. In 1104 the Byzantines recaptured the east Cilician cities and Latakia, and Bohemund went to Europe to seek reinforcements, leaving Tancred as his regent again in Antioch. Tancred won back from the Turks the city of Artah (1105), and then took Apamea (1106). In 1108 he retook Latakia and the east Cilician cities from the Byzantines, and refused to hand them back, regardless of the provisions of the Treaty of Devoll (1108) which Bohemund, his overlord, had signed after being defeated at Durazzo by Alexius. In the same year he unwillingly relinquished Edessa to Baldwin II, now released, and in 1109 was reconciled with him outside Tripoli, which the united crusaders then successfully besieged. Another reconciliation was required the following year, when Baldwin accused Tancred of treachery. Tancred carried out successful campaigns against the Turks of northern Syria before he fell ill and died at Antioch on Dec. 12, 1112.

The Tancred of Tasso's *Gerusalemme liberata* bears little resemblance to the historical character (*see* TASSO, TORQUATO).

*See* S. Runciman, *A History of the Crusades,* vol. 1–2 (1951–52).

**TANDY, JAMES NAPPER** (1740–1803), Irish politician, revolutionary, and popular hero, was born in Dublin. His family represented Trim and Athboy, County Meath, in the Irish Parliament for about 50 years from 1695. Starting as a small tradesman, he became a land agent and rent collector. He entered politics as a representative of the guild of merchants on the Dublin Common Council, where he made his mark by vehement denunciations of corruption. He joined the Irish Volunteer movement (*see* IRELAND: *History*) in the duke of Leinster's regiment, and when the independence of the Irish Parliament was announced in Dublin on May 27, 1782, his forces commanded the approaches to the parliament house. His influence waned after 1784 with the decline of the Volunteer movement.

A member of the Whig Club, he soon showed enthusiasm for the principles of the French Revolution, and he led the advanced Radical Party in Dublin city. In 1791 he helped Theobald Wolfe Tone and Thomas Russell to found a branch of the Society of United Irishmen in Dublin and became its first secretary. In February 1793, charged with having taken the oath of the Defenders' Society, he fled from Ireland and eventually arrived in Philadelphia, Pa., at the end of 1795. He went to Paris in 1798 and became jealous of Tone's success there. The French government appointed Tandy a general and sent him to Ireland to raise an Irish army. He landed at Rutland Island, off the coast of County Donegal, on Sept. 16, 1798, but learning of the failure of Gen. J. J. Humbert's landing in Connaught, he escaped by sea the same day.

Returning to France via Norway he was captured in Hamburg (November 1798). Under pressure from the English government, in September 1799 the Hamburg City Council handed him over to the British. Sentenced to death at his trial in Ireland (April 1800) he was eventually released unconditionally after Napoleon Bonaparte had demanded his extradition. He received a public ovation on arriving at Bordeaux (March 1802), and died there on Aug. 24, 1803. Tandy's name is remembered in the Irish ballad "The Wearing of the Green": "I met with Napper Tandy, and he took me by the hand, And he said 'How's poor old Ireland, and how does she stand?' " Though remembered for his picturesque adventures and his irresponsible exuberance as a politician, his career contained no real achievements. (D. G.)

**TANEEV, SERGEI IVANOVICH** (1856–1915), Russian composer and theorist, who as the principal practitioner of counterpoint was an influential figure in 19th-century Russian music, was born on Nov. 25 (new style; 13, old style), 1856. He studied composition with Tchaikovsky and piano with N. Rubinstein in Moscow. In 1878 he interrupted his career as a pianist in order to succeed Tchaikovsky at the Moscow Conservatory, where he served as director from 1885 to 1889, subsequently holding the post of professor of counterpoint and fugue. In 1895 his operatic trilogy *Oresteia* was produced in St. Petersburg. In 1905 he resigned his professorship in protest at measures against the threatened revolution and resumed his career as pianist and composer. In 1909 he completed his two-volume work on counterpoint in the strict style, on which he had worked for 20 years. His masterpiece, a setting of A. S. Khomyakov's "On the Reading of the Psalm," for chorus and orchestra, appeared shortly before his death in Moscow on June 19 (N.S.; 6, O.S.), 1915.

Taneev's compositions are relatively few but finely wrought; they are much more romantically beautiful than might have been expected of a composer who disliked all 19th-century music except that of Tchaikovsky (some of whose works he completed) and who regarded counterpoint as a branch of mathematics, reserving his highest admiration for Renaissance composers Okeghem and Josquin Després, Lassus, and Palestrina. Taneev was a great teacher and a great "character," a popular eccentric and a lifelong bachelor who for many years attracted without reciprocating the passionate love of the Countess Tolstoy. (G. AB.)

**TANEY, ROGER BROOKE** (1777–1864), fifth chief justice of the United States, whose decision in the Dred Scott case in 1857 became a centre of violent controversy, was born March 17, 1777, in Calvert County, Md. His father was a member of a family of planters, and he inherited the conservative tradition of the landed aristocracy of the South. His education in rural schools was supplemented by a family tutor and by three years of instruction at Dickinson College, from which he graduated in 1795. Since as a second son Taney would not inherit the family plantation, he was trained for a legal and political career. He studied law at Annapolis under Judge Jeremiah T. Chase of the Maryland General Court and was admitted to the bar in 1799.

**Early Career.**—In 1801 Taney settled in Frederick, Md., where he established himself as an able lawyer, achieved a position of prominence in political affairs, and raised a family. His marriage in 1806 to Anne Key, sister of Francis Scott Key, was a happy one and resulted in six daughters. Although his practice was demanding and his health frail, Taney found time for political activity, serving several terms in the Maryland legislature and gradually working his way into the leadership of the Federalist Party in the state.

When the War of 1812 split the Federalist Party (*q.v.*), Taney, a representative of inland agrarian interests, became the leader of the group, derisively referred to as "Coodies," which supported the conduct of the war. Although the former Federalists cooperated after the war on certain matters of state politics, the breakdown of the Federalist organization left Taney without party affiliation. In the 1820s he aligned himself with Andrew Jackson and thereafter was found in the ranks of the Democrats. This transition was not unnatural since Jackson, like Taney, was a slaveowner and a member of the landed aristocracy, and they shared many of the same views.

THE BETTMANN ARCHIVE
ROGER BROOKE TANEY

In 1823 Taney moved to Baltimore, where professional opportunities were greater, and was soon recognized as a leader of the Maryland bar. His extensive practice broadened his knowledge of the law and gave him wide acquaintance with the economic developments of his time. In 1827 he was appointed attorney general of Maryland, an appointment which honoured his legal attainment while allowing him to continue his private practice.

**The Bank War.**—Taney became a national figure as a result of his participation in the bank war of the 1830s. When Jackson reorganized his cabinet in 1831, Taney accepted an appointment as attorney general. At that time the Bank of the United States, chartered by Congress in 1816, had attained a dominant position in American finance and sought to exercise its influence in order to force immediately the renewal of its charter which was to expire in 1836. Although Taney had once regarded a national bank as a desirable instrument for regulating the currency, his experience with the activities of the Bank of the United States convinced him that the bank had abused its powers. When in 1832 Congress enacted a bill to renew the charter, Taney persuaded Jackson to veto it and wrote much of Jackson's veto message.

In the ensuing presidential campaign the Bank took an active part, financing its supporters and attempting to frighten its opponents by manipulating the credit structure. The revelation of these events after Jackson's re-election in 1832 led Taney and others to advise Jackson to withdraw government deposits from the Bank of the United States and place them in selected state banks. Jackson delayed action for a number of months but eventually in 1833 ordered William J. Duane, then secretary of the treasury, to remove the deposits. When Duane refused, Jackson dismissed him and gave Taney a recess appointment as secretary of the treasury. Taney's subsequent action in removing government deposits to a number of state banks was subjected to virulent partisan attack, much of which was undeserved since the bank had engaged in political and financial activities of questionable character. Nevertheless, Taney's attempt to improve and regulate the currency through a system of state banks proved ineffective, in part because Congress failed to enact implementing legislation. Although the Bank was not rechartered, opposition to Taney and his financial program was so strong that his appointment as secretary of the treasury was rejected by the senate when it was presented for confirmation. Three years of cabinet service, during nine months of which he held a recess appointment as secretary of the treasury, thus ended, and Taney returned to private life and attempted to rebuild his law practice.

**Chief Justice.**—In 1836, at the age of 59, Taney began the last and greatest phase of his career. As a reward for his political loyalty, Jackson appointed him Chief Justice of the United States to succeed the celebrated Federalist John Marshall. Despite Whig opposition, Taney was confirmed by the Senate and took the seat he was to hold for nearly three decades (1836–64). His appointment coincided with change and expansion in the personnel of the court, with the result that by 1837 all but two of the nine judges were appointees of Jackson or Van Buren. This change alarmed those who feared that property rights would be at the mercy of state legislatures. Although the Taney court did give greater scope to the exercise of state power than had the Marshall court, it was no less vigilant in maintaining federal supremacy until it foundered on the constitutional questions presented by Negro slavery.

*States' Rights.*—In his first great judicial utterance, *Charles River Bridge* v. *Warren Bridge,* 11 Pet. 420 (1837), Taney expressed his deeply held conviction that the powers conferred by corporate charters should be given a narrow interpretation in order to preserve the rights of the community. Speaking for a majority of the court, he rejected the claim of a bridge company that the subsequent grant by the state legislature of a charter to another bridge company impaired the obligation of contracts. The same emphasis on the rights of the community pervaded Taney's opinions dealing with the impact of the commerce clause on state regulatory legislation. He was unwilling to use the commerce clause as an instrument to defeat state regulation; *e.g., License Cases,* 5 How. 504 (1847), *Passenger Cases,* 7 How. 283 (1849), dissenting opinion. While he concurred in several opinions upholding state regulation on a police power rationale, his own view appears to have been that the states, in the absence of federal legislation, remained free to regulate commerce.

Despite his willingness to sustain state authority against constitutional attack, Taney's court cannot be characterized as interested only in "states' rights." Whenever state authorities threatened or interfered with the exertion of federal power, Taney was firm in upholding federal supremacy. His opinion in *Ableman* v. *Booth,* 21 How. 506 (1858), denying state power to obstruct the processes of the federal courts, remains a magnificent statement of constitutional federalism. Under Taney's leadership, federal judicial power was expanded over corporations; the admiralty jurisdiction was extended to inland waters; the federal government was held to have a paramount and exclusive authority over foreign relations; and congressional authority over U.S. property and territory was vigorously upheld.

*Dred Scott Decision.*—Until the mid-1850s the court avoided embroilment in the controversy over slavery which was constantly increasing in bitterness. As late as 1850, in *Strader* v. *Graham,* 10 How. 82, Taney succeeded in disposing of important constitutional questions relating to slavery on a narrow jurisdictional ground. However, by 1856 the prestige of the court was thought so great and the issue so momentous that the court was urged to settle the question whether Congress had power to restrict slavery in the territories. In the Dred Scott case, 19 How. 393 (1856), one of the great "self-inflicted wounds" of the Supreme Court, the court yielded to the temptation to solve this fundamental political controversy by constitutional decision. Taney, writing for a majority of the court, held that Negroes could not possess rights of citizenship entitling them to sue in federal courts; that the removal of a slave to a territory in which Congress, by the Missouri Compromise, had prohibited the holding and owning of slaves did not result in freedom because Congress lacked such power; and, finally, that the return of a Negro to a state recognizing him as a slave was conclusive as to his status. On the facts of the Dred Scott case, the third and narrowest ground was sufficient to dispose of the case. Taney's further holdings, that Congress had no power to exclude slavery from the territories and that Negroes could not be citizens, were disputed by vigorous dissenting opinions and were bitterly attacked by the Northern press. The decision became an issue in national politics and, with the victory of the Republicans in 1860, the prestige of the court reached the lowest point in its history. Taney's attachment for Southern culture thus resulted in an unsuccessful attempt to safeguard that culture from the legislative power of the Northern majority. (*See* also DRED SCOTT DECISION.)

**Final Years.**—Taney's last years were spent in futility and despair. His background led him to sympathize with the South, and he hoped that the South would be allowed to secede peacefully. During the war the court, though it continued to function as part of the government, was suspected of disloyalty. Taney, believing that war issues might come before the court, prepared in the privacy of his study a series of opinions in which he found various war measures unconstitutional. *Ex parte Merryman,* Fed. Cases no. 9,487 (1861), containing a vigorous defense of the rights of civilians in war time, is the only one of those opinions to be found in the reports. Taney's death in Washington on Oct. 12, 1864, went largely unnoticed and unregretted.

Taney's relations with his family and his associates were warm and pleasant. Not an effective platform speaker, he was at his best in personal association, where his warmth, kindness, and quiet charm quickly resulted in intimacy. He presided over the Supreme Court with dignity and courtesy, and his personal qualities, so his colleagues have testified, led to greater unity on the court than otherwise would have occurred. His legal abilities were of the highest order, as his concise, persuasive opinions indicate. Although a devout Roman Catholic, he refused to allow members of his faith to prosyletize among his wife and daughters, who with one exception were Protestants.

Any evaluation of Taney is complicated by the fact that his actions and attitudes affecting slavery and national unity are part of the tradition defeated in the Civil War. Yet his outstanding abilities had a lasting influence on the content and development of American constitutional law.

BIBLIOGRAPHY.—The leading biography is C. B. Swisher, *Roger B. Taney* (1935). *See* also Samuel Tyler, *Memoir of Roger Brooke Taney, LL.D.* (1872); B. C. Steiner, *Life of Roger Brooke Taney* (1922); Charles Warren, *The Supreme Court in United States History,* 2 vol., rev. ed. (1926); C. W. Smith, *Roger B. Taney: Jacksonian Jurist* (1936); Felix Frankfurter, *The Commerce Clause Under Marshall, Taney and Waite* (1964); Walter Lewis, *Without Fear or Favor: a Biography of Chief Justice Roger Brooke Taney* (1965). (R. C. C.)

**T'ANG,** the dynasty that ruled China from A.D. 618 to 907. The first emperor Li Yuan (or Kao-tsu, 618–626) was a member of the aristocracy of part-barbarian, part-Chinese origin, that had formed the governing class in the Northern Chou state, centred on Ch'ang-an in the 6th century, as well as in the Sui dynasty (A.D. 589–618). Li Yuan's success in obtaining the throne at the end of the Sui dynasty was largely due to his second son, Li Shih-min (or T'ai-tsung, 626–649), who succeeded him.

T'ai-tsung was succeeded by his son Kao-tsung (649–683), who soon fell under the domination of one of the most remarkable women in Chinese history, Wu Tse-t'ien or Empress Wu. She became the real power in the land even during her weak husband's lifetime. After his death she deposed her two sons in succession and ruled in her own name, a thing never achieved before or since in China. She changed the dynastic name to Chou but insured the eventual restoration of T'ang when invasions of the Khitans and Turks in the northeast necessitated an appeal to the people's loyalty.

During the reign of Kao-tsung the T'ang empire completed, at great cost, the conquest of northern Korea. But after *c.* 682 the northern Turks revolted, following 50 years of submission, and the Four Garrisons in Sinkiang were lost to the Tibetans. Also the Korean conquests were swallowed up by T'ang's erstwhile ally, the southern Korean state of Silla, which united the peninsula for the first time.

The aged empress's forced abdication in 705 was followed by an unstable period during which her two sons, Chung-tsung (705–710) and Jui-tsung (710–712), followed one another on the throne but were dominated by cliques centred around the empress of the former, surnamed Wei, and their sister, the T'ai-p'ing Princess. Successive *coups d'état* finally led to Jui-tsung's abdication in favour of his son, known as Ming Huang the Brilliant Emperor (alias Hsuan-tsung, 712–756). His reign, the longest in the dynasty, was also its high point of prosperity. With the help of able ministers he corrected administrative abuses that had grown up in the previous decade but efforts at fiscal reform, mainly carried out by special commissioners of aristocratic background, conflicted with the interests of the rising new landowning class. A political struggle ensued which resulted in the virtual dictatorship of the imperial kinsman Li Lin-fu, from 736 onward, after which the emperor withdrew into a life of pleasure.

Under Ming Huang the Chinese once more expanded on all fronts but at the cost of establishing large standing armies composed to a dangerous extent of non-Chinese troops. In the years 751–754 the Chinese suffered defeats in Manchuria; at the battle of Talas against the Arabs in central Asia; and especially against the state of Nan Chao in Yunnan. Real disaster struck in 755 with the revolt of the commander of the northeast sector of the frontier. This was An Lu-shan, of part-Sogdian and part-Turkish origin, who owed his promotion, like the barbarian generals in other sectors, to Li Lin-fu's fear of Chinese rivals.

The rebels captured the capital and drove the emperor to flight. The crown prince (Su-tsung, 756–762), who assumed the throne in the northwest succeeded, with the aid of a contingent of Uighur troops, in recapturing Ch'ang-an and Lo-yang. But the T'ang forces lacked strength to complete their victory and the war dragged on inconclusively until 762 when the last rebel pretender was killed. The northeastern provinces remained in control of former rebel generals who were acknowledged as T'ang governors; much of the rest of the country was in the hands of military leaders who were often as insubordinate as the former rebels. In the west the Tibetans, now at the height of their power, occupied large areas and in 763 they even briefly occupied Ch'ang-an. In the north, T'ang's allies, the Uighurs, were almost as oppressive as the Tibetans. The disruption of government by the rebellion led the emperors to place increasing reliance on their personal attendants, the palace eunuchs, who were given control of the palace armies.

During the reigns of Tai-tsung (762–779) and Te-tsung (779–805) the policy of the T'ang court was mainly a negative one of trying to control the militarists by diplomacy while the country slowly recovered from the effects of war. During the brief interlude of Shun-tsung's reign in 805 a reform party tried unsuccessfully to take the palace armies out of the hands of the eunuchs, who thereafter controlled the person of the sovereign, setting up and removing emperors as they pleased.

Under Hsien-tsung (805–820) some success was achieved in asserting central authority over the provinces but it was not lasting, and the northeast remained effectively autonomous to the end of the dynasty.

Hsien-tsung was murdered by eunuchs and the short reigns of Mu-tsung (820–824) and Ching-tsung (824–827) followed. Wen-tsung (827–840) plotted with his ministers to deprive the eunuchs of their military power but the plan misfired and resulted in the Sweet Dew incident of 833 in which three chief ministers and many other officials were slaughtered. Under Wu-tsung (840–846) the simultaneous decline of the Tibetan and Uighur empires eased the pressure on the northern and western frontiers. This was followed by the persecution of the Manichaean church in China, which had enjoyed Uighur protection, and this in turn led on to an unparalleled suppression of Buddhist monasteries and laicization of monks and nuns, a blow from which Chinese Buddhism never fully recovered.

The reign of Hsuan-tsung (846–859) was outwardly calm except for wars with Nan Chao in the south, but the demoralization of the central government and the lawlessness of the provincial armies and their leaders made the dynasty quite incapable of dealing with the disturbances, provoked to a large extent by maladministration and corruption, which broke out in an ever-rising crescendo under I-tsung (859–873) and Hsi-tsung (873–888). In 875 began the great peasant uprising known as the Huang Ch'ao rebellion, led by former salt smugglers. After roaming up and down the country for years the rebels occupied Ch'ang-an in 881. They were unable to organize the food supply of the capital and this, together with the intervention of Sha-t'o Turks, forced Huang Ch'ao to flee east in 883, where he was caught and killed.

From then on, while lawless bands terrorized the countryside, the T'ang court could only survive by playing off one military governor against another. In 903 Chu Ch'üan-chung, one of Huang Ch'ao's officers who had surrendered opportunely and obtained the governorship of the strategic region of K'ai-feng, gained control of the person of the T'ang emperor Chao-tsung (888–904). He settled the eunuch problem by a wholesale massacre. After his men had murdered Chao-tsung in 904 he placed on the throne a boy of thirteen (Chao-hsuan-ti), who was presently put through the motions of abdication. Chu Ch'üan-chung ruled over part of north China as T'ai-tsu of Later Liang (907–915). China fell apart into a number of independent kingdoms, and unity was not restored until after the founding of Sung (*q.v.*) in 906. (*See* also CHINA: *History.*)

**Social and Economic Life.**—During T'ang the economic centre of gravity of China shifted from the Yellow River plain to the Yangtze. The population of the latter region increased enormously, swollen by influxes of refugees from the north, especially after the rebellion of An Lu-shan. The canal system built by Yang-ti of Sui became the lifeline of the capital, especially after the efficiency of the transport system had been improved in the reign of Ming Huang and again under Tai-tsung. Trade, both internal and external, was stimulated by the unification of the country and its far-flung conquests. Much of this trade was in the hands of foreigners, particularly Iranians, who settled in large communities in the major cities. They came both by land through central Asia and by sea to Canton. Especially during the first half of the dynasty China was very receptive to foreign ideas. Foreign music and dancing were popular, and foreign types are common among the familiar T'ang pottery figurines.

Migration and economic development led to a breakdown in the system of state registration of population and distribution of land and to the growth of private estates. After the An Lu-shan rebellion the old system was finally abandoned and direct taxation was based on actual land under cultivation and on an assessment of the wealth of the household. The salt monopoly, introduced as an emergency war measure during the rebellion, became a major source of government revenue and continued into the 20th century. The increase in trade led to a need for coinage; as the government mints were unable to produce an adequate supply, counterfeiting was a chronic problem. The shortage of cash and the difficulty of transporting the bulky copper coins encouraged the development of credit instruments such as the so-called "flying money," a kind of bank draft. True paper money did not appear until the 10th century.

Society remained decidedly aristocratic but economic expansion led to the creation of a more broadly based landowning class. These new men began to push their way into the government by means of the examination system, which, although a development from earlier institutions, really began in Sui and T'ang. Empress Wu, especially, used it to undermine the position of the aristocratic clans. The competition between aristocratic privilege and the ideal of selection by merit continued throughout the dynasty.

**Religion and the Arts.**—The T'ang emperors officially supported Taoism because of their claim to be descended from Laotzu, but Buddhism continued to enjoy great favour through most of the period, especially under Empress Wu. The famous pilgrim, Hsuan-tsang, who went to India in 629 and returned in 645, was the most learned of Chinese monks and introduced new standards of exactness in his many translations from Sanskrit. In spite of such direct Indian influences through Indian teachers in China as well as Chinese pilgrims to India, the most significant development in T'ang was the growth of new indigenous schools which adapted Buddhism to Chinese ways of thinking. Most prominent were the syncretic T'ien-t'ai school which sought to embrace all other schools in a single hierarchical system, even reaching out to include Confucianism as well, and the radically antitextual, antimetaphysical Southern Ch'an (Zen) school which had strong roots in Taoism. The popular preaching of the salvationist Pure Land sect was also important. After the rebellion of An Lu-shan a nationalistic movement in favour of Confucianism appeared, merging with the efforts of T'ien-t'ai Buddhism to graft Buddhist metaphysics on to classical doctrine and lay the groundwork for the Neo-Confucianism of Sung.

In literature the greatest glory of the T'ang period was its poetry. By the 8th century poets had broken away from the artificial diction and matter of the court poetry of the Southern Dynasties and achieved a new directness and naturalism. The great flowering came in the reign of Ming Huang, the time of the great figures of Li Po (701–762), Wang Wei (698–759) and Tu Fu (713–770), besides a host of lesser names. The rebellion of An Lu-shan and his own bitter experiences in it brought a new note of social awareness into the later poetry of Tu Fu. This appears again in the work of Po Chü-i (772–846), who wrote verse in clear and simple language. Toward the end of the dynasty a new poetic form, the *tz'u,* in a less regular metre than the five-word and seven-word *shih,* and meant to be sung, made its appearance. The *ku-wen* or "ancient style" movement grew up after the rebellion of An Lu-shan, seeking to replace the euphuistic "parallel prose" then dominant. It was closely associated with the movement for a Confucian revival. The most prominent figures in it were Han Yü (768–824) and Liu Tsung-yuan (773–819). At the same time came the first serious attempts to write fiction, the so-called *ch'uan-ch'i* or "tales of marvels." Many of these T'ang stories later provided themes for the Chinese drama.

The patronage of the T'ang emperors and the general wealth and prosperity of the period encouraged the development of the visual arts. Though few T'ang buildings remain standing, contemporary descriptions give some idea of the magnificence of T'ang palaces and religious edifices and the houses of the wealthy. Buddhist sculpture shows a greater naturalism than in the previous period but there is some loss of spirituality. Few genuine originals survive to show the work of T'ang master painters such as Wu Taohsuan (*c.* 700–760) who worked at Ming-huang's court. As a landscape painter the poet Wang Wei was a forerunner of the *wenjen* or "literary man's" school of mystical nature painting of later times. The minor arts of T'ang, ceramics, metalwork, textiles, etc., give expression to the colour and vitality of the life of the period. Printing appeared for the first time during T'ang. Apparently invented to multiply Buddhist scriptures, it was being used, by the end of the dynasty, for such things as calendars, almanacs and dictionaries. The first printing of the Confucian classics came after the end of the dynasty in 932 in Szechwan.

*See* also references under "T'ang" in the Index.

BIBLIOGRAPHY.—C. P. Fitzgerald, *China: a Short Cultural History* (1935); K. S. Latourette, *The Chinese, Their History and Culture* (1946); A. Waley, *Life and Times of Po Chü-i* (1949); E. G. Pulleyblank, *The Background of the Rebellion of An Lu-shan* (1955); E. O. Reischauer, *Ennin's Travels in T'ang China* (1955). (E. G. PU.)

**TANGANYIKA, LAKE,** in East Africa, is the longest freshwater lake in the world (420 mi. [676 km.]) and the second deepest (4,708 ft. [1,435 m.]), but is comparatively narrow, varying in width from 30 to 45 mi. (48 to 72 km.). It covers about 12,700 sq.mi. (32,893 sq.km.) and forms the boundary between Tanzania and the Democratic Republic of the Congo. It occupies the southern end of the western arm of the Great Rift Valley, and for most of its length the land rises steeply from its shores. Although drinkable, its waters tend to be brackish.

The lake was first visited in 1858 by R. F. Burton and J. H. Speke, who reached Ujiji, the place where in 1871 H. M. Stanley "found" David Livingstone. The southern half was first circumnavigated by V. L. Cameron in 1874, when the Lukuga outlet was discovered, and the whole lake was surveyed by Stanley in 1876.

Though fed by a number of rivers, the lake is not the centre of an extensive drainage area. The largest river is the Malagarasi, which rises to the north of Kigoma and arcs eastward before discharging into the lake only about 50 mi. (80 km.) due south of its source. Others are the Ruzizi, which carries the overflow from Lake Kivu, and the Kalambo, having one of the highest waterfalls in the world (over 700 ft.; 213 m.).

The lake is situated on the dividing line between the floral regions of East and West Africa, and the oil palm, so characteristic of the latter, is found on its shores. Rice and subsistence crops are grown along the shores, and fishing is also of some significance. Hippopotamuses and crocodiles abound in the waters of the lake, and in places the rare West African sharp-snouted crocodile, *Crocodylus cataphractus,* occurs. The bird life is varied because of the lake's situation between the East and West African regions. The mountains north and south of Kigoma are the only places in Tanzania where the chimpanzee is found.

There had been considerable traffic across the lake before the arrival of the European, but this had nearly all been from west to east, so that many of the numerous tribes now living on its eastern borders trace their origins to areas in the Congo. They are predominantly Bantu, with traces of Hamitic (Tusi) influence in the north and of Ngoni in the south. The areas of both sides of the lake suffered heavily from the depredations of slave traders.

The chief towns on the lake are Bujumbura (Burundi); Uvira and Kalemi (Democratic Republic of the Congo); Kigoma, Ujiji, Karema, Mtakuja, and Kipili (Tanzania); and Mpulungu (Zambia). Steamers traverse the length of the lake in about four days, although navigation is impeded somewhat during the dry season by strong, shifty winds.

BIBLIOGRAPHY.—Accounts of the discovery and early exploration of Lake Tanganyika are to be found in the works of such explorers as Sir Richard Francis Burton, David Livingstone, V. L. Cameron, H. M. Stanley, E. C. Hore, and J. Thomson. (J. P. MT.; X.)

**TANGERINE,** a small thin-skinned variety of orange with a deep reddish-orange peel belonging to the mandarin orange species (*Citrus reticulata*). *See* ORANGE.

**TANGIER,** a port and chief town of the province of the same name in northern Morocco, lies on the Strait of Gibraltar, in a bay sheltered from the west wind by Tangier Point, and 36 mi. (58 km.) SW of Gibraltar. Pop. (1960) 141,714. With its surrounding suburbs, Tangier was an international zone from 1923 to 1956. In 1962 it became the summer royal residence.

The town is built on the slopes of a chalky limestone hill. The old town (medina), enclosed by the 15th-century Portuguese ramparts, descends toward the harbour; it is dominated on the northwest by a *kasbah* and the ancient sultan's palace (now a museum), and on the southeast by the Great Mosque. It is crossed by the Rue es Siaghine (des Siaghines), a busy street of money changers, jewelers, and banks, which runs from the Petit Socco (*souk*) to the Grand Socco at the southwestern gate of the medina, beyond which stretches the modern town. The Muslim population have quarters in the north of the medina, and the Jews and some Europeans are dispersed around the centre and the south. Newly built European quarters (mainly French) were developed south of Tangier, and others to the west on the Marchan Plateau and "the Mountain," where the houses are scattered among gardens.

Tangier developed into an important trade centre after it became an international zone (see *History*). Its prosperity resulted from its being a free money market. Although its trade declined during World War II, it continued to benefit from its special economic and financial status until 1960, when this status was abrogated, and it became a free port in 1962. The town has little industry except that of the building trades and tourism; there is some fishing. It is connected by rail and road with Fès, Meknès, Rabat, and Casablanca. There are regular shipping services to Europe via Gibraltar. The international airport at Bouhalf-Souahel lies 8 mi. (13 km.) S.

TANGIER PROVINCE stretches southeastward to the Er Rif Range. Area 141 sq.mi. (365 sq.km.). Pop. (1960) 164,246, of which two-thirds were Muslim; more than 40,000 Europeans, three-fourths of whom were Spanish; and about 15,000 Jews, mainly shopkeepers and merchants. The agricultural resources are low; the province produces vegetables only, though poultry breeding is a main occupation. (J.-J. Ds.)

### HISTORY

Few cities have had a more varied history than Tangier. Existing already in the 15th century B.C. as a Phoenician trading post, it later became Carthaginian, and the remains of a Carthaginian settlement are still to be seen near Cape Spartel. In 81 B.C. the Roman general Quintus Sertorius captured the city, then known as Tingis; it had previously belonged to the Mauretanian king Bocchus, a partisan of L. Cornelius Sulla in the Roman civil strife of the moment. In 38 B.C. it was taken on behalf of Octavian by a later King Bocchus from his brother King Bogud, who supported Mark Antony. Becoming a free city, in A.D. 42 it was made the capital of the Roman province of Mauretania Tingitana, with the name Tingis Colonia Julia Traducta; it remained important commercially after the political capital was removed to Volubilis.

After five centuries of Roman rule and a brief occupation by the Vandals, Tingis was captured by the Byzantines. When the Arabs arrived in the 7th century, however, Ceuta and not Tangier seems to have been their principal fortress. Uqba (Okba) ibn Nafi reached Tangier in 682 and from there raided deep into Morocco. In 707, when Musa ibn Nusayr was appointed governor of North Africa, he had to reconquer Tangier; the Berber Tarik ibn Ziyad was appointed as governor and in 711 raided Spain. In 951 Abdurrahman III of Córdoba annexed the city, and it remained under Muslim Spanish rule till the collapse of the Córdoban caliphate about 80 years later. Under the Almoravids Tangier became Moroccan again and remained so till captured by the Portuguese in 1471. In 1580 it passed, with Portugal itself, to Spain, returning to independent Portugal in 1656. In 1662 it was transferred to the English crown as part of the dowry of Catherine of Braganza. Great hopes were put on this new English possession; but though a fine mole was built and new fortifications erected, the expense of maintaining the city against Moroccan attacks, and the difficulties caused by Protestant suspicions of it as a centre of Catholicism, caused it to be abandoned again in 1684. Since then it has remained a portion of the Moroccan Empire.

**The 18th and 19th Centuries.**—Tangier began to play a significant role in history again at the end of the 18th and the beginning of the 19th century. At the end of the 18th century there was a British consul and over 100 British subjects there and in Tetuan. During the great siege of Gibraltar by the Spanish (1779–83), these were expelled by the sultan. During the 19th century Tangier became the diplomatic capital of Morocco. In 1840 the European consuls acting on behalf of the sultan were entrusted with forming a commission to supervise matters affecting public health in the city. This was the origin of the later Hygiene Commission; from 1893 this dealt not only with sanitation but also with the quarantine of shipping and pilgrims, the inspection of markets, street lighting, and fishing rights. The year 1844 marked the beginning of Sir John Drummond Hay's period of service as British representative in Morocco (1844–85); this was a period when British trade and political influence predominated.

In 1844 Tangier was bombarded by a French fleet as part of the French campaigns against Abd-el-Kader (*q.v.*) in Algeria. When the Spanish invaded Morocco in 1860, British policy, which was directed to preventing any continental power from se-

(LEFT) BURT GLINN—MAGNUM, (RIGHT) GEORGE DANIELL—PHOTO RESEARCHERS, INC.

(LEFT) MARKET SCENE IN TANGIER. (RIGHT) THE BAY OF TANGIER SEEN FROM THE SULTAN'S PALACE IN THE WALLED CITADEL, OR KASBAH curing control of the southern shore of the straits, led to the issue of a British warning that Britain would not permit a permanent Spanish occupation of Tangier or of the nearby Moroccan coast. About the same period, various foreign powers began to establish their own postal services. In 1857 the British Consulate General at Tangier opened a receiving agency for the Gibraltar Post Office; the Spanish followed suit in 1861, and the French about the same date. Just before World War I, the Germans also opened a Post Office, but it did not survive the war. On the establishment of the French protectorate in Morocco in 1912 the French Post Office was amalgamated with the Sharifian; but the British and Spanish Post Offices survived till after the end of the international regime in 1956. In 1864 a lighthouse was established at Cape Spartel; its neutrality was guaranteed by the sultan, but its maintenance was entrusted to the consuls.

**International Status.**—The result of these privileges was that Tangier received an international regime of its own when the rest of the country became a protectorate. Already in the proposed Franco-Spanish Agreement of 1902, the two powers declared themselves willing to see the eventual neutralization of the city; in the Anglo-French Agreement of 1904 it was laid down that Tangier should have a special status. This was confirmed at the Algeciras Conference (1906). With the establishment of the protectorate in 1912, a commission with French, Spanish, and British members was appointed; by 1914 it had with difficulty agreed on certain recommendations. Then came World War I; this necessitated fresh discussions so that a statute was not agreed upon until 1923. Five years later further modifications were introduced, Great Britain, France, Spain, the Netherlands, Belgium, Sweden, Portugal, and Italy being finally recognized as the administering powers. This statute remained operative until June 14, 1940, when Spain took advantage of the fall of France to occupy the zone in the name of the khalifa of Tetuan and to introduce a Spanish regime. After the war the victorious allies insisted on Spanish withdrawal, and on Oct. 11, 1945, the International Administration was reestablished, with the participation of the United States. Italy was readmitted later. An invitation was issued to the Soviet government, which, however, refused to come in so long as Franco's government took part. With some minor modifications the statute then remained in force until the independence of Morocco (1956).

**Administration Under the International Regime.**—During the international regime the representatives of the powers (with the exception of the U.S. minister) were no longer accredited to the sultan but occupied themselves with the administration of the city. Authority was vested in a Council of Control composed of the consuls general of the administering powers. Beneath this, there was a Legislative Assembly in which the European powers and the Moroccans were represented in fixed proportions (which were periodically adjusted to meet new conditions) and selected by such means as each government concerned thought fit. The sultan was represented by a *mendub,* who was in fact a nominee of the French authorities. The customs were manned by French officials. French influence was strong in the political and educational spheres. Economically and by population, however, the city, in so far as it was European, was predominantly Spanish, owing to the proximity of Spain, the presence of 17,000 Spanish residents, and the fact that it was surrounded by the Spanish-administered zone. The police were Moroccans under the command of French and Spanish officers with a Belgian commandant. Mixed courts administered justice. For many years the chief administrator was French; after World War II the post was reserved to members of smaller powers, such as the Netherlands or Portugal.

The international administration was often severely criticized for concerning itself chiefly with the balance of interest of the various European powers, particularly France and Spain, rather than with the welfare of the majority of the inhabitants. Certainly very little was done, except by private initiative, for the education, health, or labour conditions of the Moroccan population. Nevertheless, thanks to the security, the free money market, and the tourist attractions of the site, Tangier grew from a small seaport to a fine city of about 142,000, becoming an important residential and tourist centre, as well as a pole of attraction for adventurers of various types. It acquired an excellent port, and road and rail connections with the rest of the country.

**Integration with Morocco.**—After the recognition of Morocco's independence in 1956, the Moroccan members of Tangier's Legislative Assembly demanded that Tangier be integrated with Morocco. The powers concerned did not object, and on July 5, 1956, an interim agreement was reached (in the form of a protocol) for the transfer of control. On July 8 a Moroccan governor was appointed, and on Oct. 29, 1956, the Declaration of Fedala, signed by representatives of the powers concerned, finally abolished the statute and sanctioned the complete integration of Tangier into the rest of Morocco. A Royal Charter issued on Aug. 30, 1957, confirmed the special economic and financial status of Tangier as a free money market, subject to termination after six months' notice; such notice was in fact given in June 1959. In January 1962 a free zone was created in the port.

BIBLIOGRAPHY.—Rom Landau, *Portrait of Tangier* (1952); E. M. G. Routh, *Tangier: England's Lost Atlantic Outpost* (1912); G. H. Stuart, *The International City of Tangier,* 2nd ed. (1955). (N. BA.)

**TANIMBAR ISLANDS** (TIMORLAUT ISLANDS), a group of islands in the Malay Archipelago, southwest of the Aru Islands, between 6°20′ and 8°30′ S and 130°40′ and 132°5′ E. Politically, the islands belong to the Republic of Indonesia. They form part of the outermost alpine arc, which includes Timor and the Ewab Islands and recurves westward through Ceram (Seram) and Buru. The group lies outside the zone of the recent volcanic activity. There are about 30 islands, the largest being Jamdena, 70 mi. (113 km.) long and 28 mi. (45 km.) wide. Thickly wooded hills extend along the east coast; the west coast is lower where, opposite the island of Sera, a gulf extends far inland. In places there are precipitous cliffs, and a narrow foreshore is fringed with coconut palms and mangrove. There are many small islands off the western coast of Jamdena; off the northeastern coast is Larat, with a rocky coast and high cliffs and with thick vegetation along the foreshore. Off the southwestern coast is Selaru, which is 32 mi. (51 km.) long, rather flat, and has much grassland.

Though there are extensive swamps on many of the islands, there are practically no rivers, with a resulting lack of fresh water. The soil supports maize (corn), rice (in small stretches), coconut and sago palms, yams, plantains, mangoes, and papayas. The slight depth of soil prevents trees from attaining great height.

The vegetation includes sterculias and fig trees, leguminous trees and shrubs, myrtles, the scarlet hibiscus, pandanus, palms, a species of breadfruit tree, rare and lovely orchids of many kinds, crotons, dracaenas, and many varieties of ferns. The animal life shows Australian affinities and comprises wild buffalo, wild pig, the cuscus, flying fox, many snakes, lizards, and frogs. The birds include the scarlet lory, honey eater, ground thrush, and oriole. Butterflies are numerous and include *Papilio aberram,* and among the beetles is a gorgeous golden-coloured buprestid (*Cyphogastra splendens*).

The islands form part of the Maluku Tenggara (Southeast Moluccas) *kabupaten* (regency) in the province of the Moluccas. The capital of Jamdena is Saumlakki, at the southwestern end of the island, and of Larat, the town of the same name, on a narrow strait opposite Jamdena.

Though the Tanimbar group was discovered by the Dutch in 1629 and claimed by them in 1639 by right of discovery, Dutch rule was not established until about 1900. The isles were also visited by Capt. Owen Stanley in 1839 and became known to Banda traders in 1877.

The population in 1965 was approximately 50,000. The people are basically Oceanic Negroes of the Papuan variety, but there has been much mixture with Mongoloid strains, first of the Indonesian type and later, especially around the coast, with Malays. There are many pagans and a few Muslims. Christianity made some headway, and under Dutch rule cannibalism, piracy, slavery, headhunting, and intertribal fighting were suppressed. The men sometimes dye their hair a golden colour, and tattooing is known. Traces of totemism and of an age-group system survive. The houses of wood and *atap,* sometimes built in closely packed settlements, generally on piles and entered from underneath, have carved pillars and show much artistry of construction. The men are skilful boatbuilders, use the spear and bow and arrow (with which they are adept in shooting fish), hunt, search for trepang and turtle shell, keep pigs, and work in iron, copper, and gold. The women cultivate the fields after the men have prepared the ground, weave and dye sarongs, and plait.

(E. E. L.; B. A. L. C.; T. HER.; X.)

**TANIS** (biblical ZOAN), an ancient city in the Delta of Egypt, the capital of the 14th nome of Lower Egypt and, at one time, of the whole country; the ancient name, Djane, survives in the modern village San al Hajar ("San of the Stones"). Here, a few miles south of Lake Menzaleh (Manzilah), a huge mound of buried ruins rises from the salty flats caused by past erosion of the coast and invasion by the sea. The city owed its importance largely to its position as one of the nearest ports to the Asiatic seaboard, on the bridge between Asia and Africa.

The history of Tanis is imperfectly known. During 1884–85 Flinders Petrie found blocks of Pepi I (6th dynasty), and Pierre Montet also found blocks of Old Kingdom date, but many scholars suppose that these were removed from other sites, perhaps by Ramses II when he enlarged and beautified the city, or by some other pharaoh in search of easily quarried building stone. Among statues unearthed there were remarkable sphinxes in black granite found by Auguste Mariette in 1860 and once attributed to the Hyksos but now known to represent a 12th-dynasty pharaoh.

When the Hyksos (Shepherd Kings; *see* EGYPT: *History*) established their rule in Egypt *c.* 1720 B.C., their main stronghold was Avaris and their chief god Set (Setekh). Set was later the patron of San, judging by the monuments, and some think that Avaris (in Egyptian *Het-waret,* perhaps "the Castle on the Dunes") was in fact the earlier name of Tanis. The further identification with Pi-Ramesse or Per-Ramessu, the residence city of Ramses II, is even less certain, but the many colossal statues and blocks found in San bearing the name of Ramses II make it reasonable to suppose that Tanis was important in his reign.

About 1085 B.C. the 21st-dynasty pharaohs began their rule in the Delta. Tanis was their capital, and here in the precinct of the great temple they and at least some of their successors were interred. The tombs of Psusennes I and Amenemope, second and fourth kings of the 21st dynasty, and of Osorkon II and Sheshonk III of the 22nd were discovered by Pierre Montet; their silver coffins and stone sarcophagi, jewelry, and vessels are now in the Cairo Museum. The decline of Tanis was gradual but was accelerated by the rise of Pelusium, 20 mi. (32 km.) to the east, as a frontier city and entrepôt of trade.

BIBLIOGRAPHY.—W. M. F. Petrie, *Tanis,* 2 vol. (1885–88); Pierre Montet, *Les nouvelles Fouilles de Tanis, 1929–1932* (1933), *La Nécropole royale de Tanis,* 3 vol. (1947–60), *Les Énigmes de Tanis* (1952); J. von Beckerath, *Tanis und Theben* (1951). (M. S. DR.)

**TANIZAKI JUNICHIRŌ** (1886–1965), Japanese writer who, with Akutagawa Ryūnosuke (*q.v.*), was a prominent figure in Japanese literature in the years after World War I, was born in Tokyo on July 24, 1886. His career seems on the surface to have been one of violent change, from a complete rejection of Japanese tradition in his youth to an equally strong traditionalism in his middle years and after. Yet a single theme can be traced through the whole of his work: the quest for an ideal woman, symbol of an indispensable something that has been lost.

Tanizaki's earliest short stories, the first of which appeared in 1900, have affinities with Poe. They tend to be overwrought, and Tanizaki would probably not be thought an important writer had his career ended with its first, strongly pro-Western phase. After the great Tokyo earthquake of 1923, however, he moved to the more traditional Ōsaka region, which awakened him to traditional Japanese values. *Some Prefer Nettles* (1929), perhaps his finest novel, tells of marital unhappiness that is in fact a conflict between the new and the old. The implication is that the old will win.

During the 1930s Tanizaki produced a number of discursive lyrical works, part fiction and part essay, a return to the prose of the Heian period. The best of them is probably "The Story of Shunkin" (1933). He also undertook a rendition into modern Japanese of the greatest of Heian literary works, Lady Murasaki's *Tale of Genji.* During World War II, he occupied himself with *The Makioka Sisters* (published 1946–48), an affectionate, infinitely detailed evocation of prewar Ōsaka life. His writing after the war resembled the lyrical works of the '30s, with a strong mixture of eroticism that suggested a return to his youth. He died in Yugawara on July 30, 1965.

English translations of some of Tanizaki's works are available: *Some Prefer Nettles* (1955) and *The Makioka Sisters* (1957), both translated by Edward G. Seidensticker; and *The Key* (1961), *Seven Japanese Tales* (1963), including "The Story of Shunkin," and *The Diary of a Mad Old Man* (1965), all translated by Howard Hibbett. (E. G. SE.)

**TANK,** a heavily armoured, self-propelled combat vehicle embodying the basic military characteristics of firepower, mobility and crew protection. They are designed for many different purposes and may be used as part of large infantry units, as a separate striking force (such as an armoured division) or for reconnaissance. (For tactics and organization, *see* ARMOURED FORCES.)

### PREDECESSORS

The modern military tank is a direct outgrowth of World War I, but the idea underlying its development—protected, mobile striking power—had been used throughout the history of warfare. Many ancient peoples made use of war chariots to carry an attack to an enemy with speed and with some degree of protection. The armoured elephants of Hannibal and Kublai Khan were variations of the same idea. In the 15th century Leonardo da Vinci envisioned his covered chariots as a means of destroying the artillery just then being introduced to warfare. From time to time similar suggestions were advanced and occasionally devices of this kind were used in war. However, there is no evidence that such great military leaders as Condé, Turenne, Frederick the Great or Napoleon made any effort to revive the idea.

The invention of the "footed wheel" by R. L. Edgeworth in 1770 led to Thomas German's invention in 1801 of the jointed track. Neither of these was of any significance until a suitable engine was developed. Gottlieb Daimler's patent in 1886 of the high-speed internal-combustion engine opened the way for the first really practical self-propelled fighting vehicles. While interest in track-laying vehicles and improvements in their design continued in Britain and the United States during this period, the perfection of a reasonably efficient internal-combustion engine stimulated experiments with various types of armoured cars. F. R. Simms of Britain is credited with building in 1899 the first motor vehicle designed for combat purposes; it was a light four-wheeled motorcycle with an armoured shield and mounting a Maxim machine gun.

In the same year a U.S. army officer, R. P. Davidson, devised a three-wheeled automobile similarly armed and armoured. Davidson experimented also with steam-driven combat cars, as did the Russian engineer Lutski. Armoured steam-driven Fowler tractors with armoured trailers in train were used during the South African War in 1900 as supply vehicles and personnel carriers. Davidson's cars were followed in rapid succession by the Charron car in France in 1901 and the Simms war cars in Great Britain in 1902. The first turreted armoured cars were built by the firm of Charron, Girardot et Voigt in France in 1906 and purchased by Russia. These were followed by the Austro-Daimler cars in Austria-Hungary, which were the first four-wheel-drive automobiles. Several other British, French, Swiss and German cars appeared. Among them was the Armstrongs-Whitworth car designed by Walter G. Wilson, who later was prominent in design and production of British tanks during World War I. During this period the track-laying vehicle, as developed by Benjamin Holt, C. L. Best and others, was being adapted for farm machinery in the U.S.

During the years immediately prior to World War I, tacticians of the major powers which were to engage in that struggle did not seem to envision the part such a combat vehicle could play.

Lieut. Fleicz of the French army and Capt. (later Gen.) J. F. C. Fuller (*q.v.*) of the British army, as late as 1913 and 1914, respectively, predicted the machine gun would bring about static trench warfare, and suggested greater emphasis on means for overcoming it. But it was not until the soundness of their ideas was clearly demonstrated along the Aisne in 1914 that serious attention was given to armoured, trench-spanning vehicles.

### WORLD WAR I TANKS

The French, Belgians and Russians were quick to improvise armoured cars (*q.v.*) for fighting delaying actions against German advance cavalry. The tactics were informal but aggressive, depending on whatever the individual car commander decided. Winston Churchill, then first lord of the admiralty, quickly saw the natural affinity between aircraft and armoured vehicles. As a result, the royal naval air service under Capt. Murray Sueter improvised armoured car squadrons for protecting advanced air bases and rescuing pilots who crashed or were forced to bail out in enemy territory.

The war soon settled down to a practically continuous front because artillery and the machine gun dominated the battlefield. (*See* TACTICS and WORLD WARS: *World War I.*) There were no flanks. With position defense and frontal attacks the only basic tactics available to either side, defense became superior to offense. Even when salients developed which permitted a form of envelopment, the attacker's own flanks became exposed and attacks eventually ground to a standstill, with casualties reaching staggering proportions. The tremendous artillery fire preparation frequently destroyed the attacker's ability to sustain his own advance because his artillery could not be moved forward over the ground it had helped to make impassable.

**British Tanks.**—In Oct. 1914, Col. (later Gen.) Sir Ernest Swinton, having seen some American Holt caterpillar tractors used as heavy artillery tractors behind the lines, was struck with the desirability of arming and armouring such vehicles as an antidote to the German machine gun. He suggested the idea to the authorities but Churchill was the only member of the committee of imperial defense who was in favour of exploring it. At the end of Feb. 1915 the war office officially abandoned the Swinton proposals but Churchill immediately created a Landships committee under the chairmanship of Eustace (later Sir Eustace) Tennyson-d'Eyncourt, a prominent naval designer.

As a result of admiralty rather than war office sponsorship, certain naval terms came into use and persisted. Parts of armoured vehicles are still known by such naval terms as hull, turret, deck, sponson, barbette, superstructure, bow, hatch and compartment.

Various experimental machines were built, ending with a large vehicle having overhead tracks, mainly the product of W. G. Wilson and Sir William Tritton. Colonel Swinton learned of these and was authorized by the commander of the British forces in France to collaborate through the war office. In June 1915 the admiralty and war office joined hands. The abortive Dardanelles landing forced Churchill's resignation in July but the committee kept interest alive in spite of army apathy. In September, primary responsibility was turned over to the war office but the Landships committee continued to function with little change except in name.

The word "tank" was coined by Swinton. Originally, for secrecy, the hull and chassis of an experimental vehicle had been made in different shops. The hull was referred to as a water carrier for Mesopotamia and was called "that tank thing" by the workmen. The chassis was described as a demonstrational chassis for the royal marines. Swinton later recalled this and it led to his suggesting the adoption of the word "tank," which since has come into use in many languages.

The British decided to use the new tank corps to bolster a failing offensive on the Somme in spite of Swinton's arguments that it would be better to wait until more tanks were available. Out of 49 tanks, only 11 carried out the attack on Sept. 15, 1916. From then on, tanks were used in driblets and with little effect and often under unsuitable conditions because of military and political pressure. Yet their use raised Allied and lowered German morale. Not until the battle of Cambrai in Nov. 1917 were tanks used in mass. From then on they contributed greatly to reducing the previous heavy Allied casualties.

The first British tank, designated the Mark I, was produced in two types, a "male" weighing 31 tons and mounting two 6-pounders and four machine guns, and a "female" weighing 30 tons, mounting six machine guns. They were large, clumsy, and hard-riding and had limited radius, but they were well suited for trench warfare. Successive models incorporated improvements but their general appearance remained about the same throughout the war. All were about $26\frac{1}{2}$ ft. long, 14 ft. wide, and 8 ft. high; they were powered first by a 105-hp. Daimler water-cooled engine and later by a Ricardo 150-hp. engine. Their speed did not exceed $4\frac{1}{2}$ m.p.h. and fuel distance had reached only 24 mi. by the end of the war, while track life, because of a rigid suspension, was only about 50 mi. They could traverse obstacles $4\frac{1}{2}$ ft. high, span trenches $11\frac{1}{2}$ ft. wide, and climb a 22° slope. Armour thickness varied from 0.2 to 0.4 in. and was later increased to 0.47 in. In addition to combat tanks, supply, bridging, and salvage or recovery vehicles were built, sometimes by converting obsolete combat tanks.

During World War I the British also built a Medium Mark A or Whippet tank weighing 15.7 tons which carried a crew of only three men as compared with eight in the heavy tanks, and had greater speed and fuel distance than the heavy tanks. There later were a Medium B and a Medium C but these were available too late for combat.

**French Tanks.**—Though the British were the first to use tanks in battle, the French had actually preceded them in experimentation in this field. Much of this experimentation was civilian inspired. Instead of devices to defeat the German machine gun, effort initially was directed toward overcoming German barbed wire. Then, Col. (later Gen.) Eugene Estienne, like Colonel Swinton, saw an American Holt tractor, and conceived an armoured fighting vehicle. In collaboration with Eugène Brillié, a Schneider engineer who had been experimenting with small Holt tractors, the Schneider C. A. or *chat d'assaut* was successfully tested and placed in production.

Jules-Louis Breton, under-secretary of state for inventions, had been responsible for most of the earlier experiments. He succeeded in obtaining funds for proceeding with a larger vehicle designed by Col. Émile Rimailho of the St. Chamond firm and known as the *char St. Chamond.* Production was begun without consultation between the two groups. It was not until June 1916 that British developments in the new field were discovered. Premature British use of tanks on the Somme caused the French to rush pro-

BY COURTESY OF (ABOVE) U.S. SIGNAL CORPS, (RIGHT) IMPERIAL WAR MUSEUM

TANKS OF WORLD WAR I: (ABOVE) SMALL FRENCH RENAULT TANK; (RIGHT) LARGE BRITISH "MALE" MARK III duction and the first units of *l'artillerie d'assaut* began equipping in Dec. 1916.

The first French tank attack took place in April 1917 and ended in failure. Committees bickered, and a change in high command shifted emphasis to artillery production. Nevertheless, Estienne succeeded in getting the Renault firm to design and build a light two-man tank. Another shift in high command resulted in a decision to cease building all vehicles but the Renault model. The first of these was shipped to the United States. Production was slow and it was not until the French were frightened by the German Chemin des Dames offensive that industrial production was pushed.

Although the French made many of the same mistakes as the British and there was considerable confusion over the role these new weapons of war would play, a great deal was accomplished. Jealousies existed but over-all there was less vacillation, with cancellations and reinstatements of orders, than occurred in England. The small Renault tank was armed with either a machine gun or a 37-mm. gun. The Schneider and St. Chamond tanks were armed with a 75-mm. gun and two machine guns. Their respective weights were 7½ tons, 15 tons, and 25 tons, while their crews varied from two to nine men. Unlike the British tanks, French tanks used spring suspensions that produced a better ride and increased track life somewhat.

**German Tanks.**—Though the Germans had opportunities before and during World War I to take the lead in development of the tank, they failed to do so. It was not until the capture at Cambrai (Nov. 20, 1917) of a number of British tanks that the Germans possessed any serviceable armoured vehicles of this type. The captured tanks were assembled and repaired at Charleroi, where German experts studied them, but the idea of copying them was soon abandoned. Instead, reliance was placed on a model of German design which already was well along. A few of these were delivered in time to participate in the battle of St. Quentin on March 21, 1918, and in five additional actions before the Armistice in November. The Germans also used a few captured specimens in various actions, but they never had tanks in numbers at all comparable with those of the Allies.

The German model made during 1918 was built by the Daimler company. It was designed by Joseph Vollmer and known as the A-7V. It weighed 33 tons, was powered by two Mercedes-Daimler engines of 150 hp. each, had a crew of 18 men, mounted a small cannon and six machine guns and carried thick armour, which varied from 0.59 to 1.18 in., and was designed to be proof against 37-mm. gunfire.

**U.S. Tanks.**—Before the United States entered the war, both the Holt Tractor company and the C. L. Best company had built some experimental tanks. As early as 1915, Cleve Shaffer proposed armouring and arming Fageol orchard tractors. At about the same time, E. M. Wheelock of Pioneer Tractor company and Norman Leeds of Automatic Machine company offered tank designs to the British and A. C. Hamilton of Oakland Motors built an experimental tank for the British at their request.

Committees created by Gen. John J. Pershing decided to obtain British and French tanks but interest lagged until the battle of Cambrai and the signing of the Anglo-American tank treaty to build the Mark VIII tank. With tremendous optimism, high production rates were forecast. The Mark VIII program failed partly because of the failure of the American aviation program since the same engine was to be used in both. The light tank program was equally bad. Pershing was notified in Feb. 1918 that these tanks would start arriving in France in April, yet at that time only a handful of people were working on the project and a contract had not even been let. By June it was evident that no tanks would be available and so British and French vehicles were obtained. However, U.S. troops using British tanks had to serve in the British sector. Meanwhile, a Holt gas-electric, a Holt steam tank, an Endicott and Johnson steam tank, a Pioneer skeleton, a Ford one-man and a Ford Mark I three-man tank were being tested.

Efforts were finally concentrated on the copy of the Renault known as the 6-ton tank, on the Mark VIII and on the Ford one-man tank; but the first 6-ton tanks did not arrive in France until after the Armistice. At that time, 23,405 tanks were on order. The Ford one-man tank weighed three tons, carried a machine gun and was very cheap to produce since it used many of the standard Ford Model T passenger car components.

U.S. tank units saw action in both the British and U.S. sectors and were under the over-all command of Gen. S. D. Rockenbach. Tank training in the United States was in charge of Lieut. Col. (later General of the Army) Dwight D. Eisenhower.

### TANKS BETWEEN WORLD WARS I AND II

The plan for 1919, had the war continued, required a frontal assault by heavy tanks to achieve a breakthrough, with local exploitation by light tanks. This assault was to be followed by pouring fast medium tanks through the breaks, co-ordinated with aircraft attacks. This plan was conceived in part as a result of experiments showing that tank speeds could be considerably increased. The originator of the fast medium tank was Lieut. Col. Philip Johnson, whose first tank was designed to reach a speed of 20 m.p.h. Here was the real tactical lesson of World War I, but the victors retained only the memory of the war as it was fought with tanks and infantry in slow moving waves advancing under cover of a moving artillery barrage.

Voices were first raised in England against the accepted postwar tactics, principally by Col. (later Gen.) J. F. C. Fuller, author of the 1919 plan. He fostered the all-tank army and visualized land warfare resembling naval warfare. He was joined by Capt. B. H. Liddell Hart, who added the concepts of "tank marines"—tank-borne infantry co-operating with aircraft—and air-borne troops. They were joined by British Col. (later Gen.) G. LeQ. Martel, French Col. (later Gen.) Charles de Gaulle and German Col. (later Gen.) Heinz Guderian. However, the costs of the war and the quantities of tanks left over demanded economy, which influenced subsequent vehicle development and tactics as well.

Because track life was short, there was considerable interest in combination wheel and track tanks, several of which were designed by J. Walter Christie in the United States. But eventually, as rubber bogie tires were adopted and track life increased, these were abandoned. The increasing popularity of the civilian passenger car brought about other mechanical improvements, many of which were also translated into tank design. Speeds increased as did radius of operation or fuel distance, air-cooled and diesel engines came into use, better suspensions were devised, intercommunication systems for crew members were developed. The French produced the first welded and cast armour and Britain, in 1929, introduced short-wave radio for communication between tanks. Armament, however, remained light and seldom exceeded a 37-mm. gun or a heavy machine gun. Armour rather than armament was emphasized because it was visualized that tanks would fight infantry rather than tanks.

**United States.**—The National Defense act of 1920 eliminated the wartime tank corps and merged tanks with infantry. This action was of great influence tactically, as was peacetime economy. Interest in British tactical developments resulted in permission for the cavalry to work with "combat cars," a term coined to circumvent the law. A few experimental vehicles were developed which eventually resulted in an excellent and reliable light tank used by both infantry and cavalry, and a medium tank utilizing many light tank components was built for the infantry. Interest also was shown in the commercial Christie tanks, which could operate as wheeled vehicles by removing the tracks, but they were not considered sufficiently rugged for adoption especially since track life had reached 1,000 miles or more.

The M-2A4 light tank weighed 14 tons, had a crew of four and carried a 37-mm. gun and three machine guns. Its speed was 35 m.p.h. and its fuel distance was 100 miles. The M-2A1 medium tank weighed 23 tons and mounted a 37-mm. gun and light machine guns. The M-2A4 was of riveted construction; the M-2A1 medium tank was welded.

The German attack on Poland in 1939 caused a complete redesign of the M-2A1 medium tank and led to a large order for light tanks. Differences between infantry and cavalry finally were buried in the creation of an armoured force on July 10, 1940.

**Great Britain.**—The British royal tank corps, though its existence was in doubt for a period immediately after World War I, continued as a separate arm. A few hundred Vickers medium tanks were built, larger versions of the French Renault but embodying many improvements. Martel and Carden Lloyd tankettes, originally intended to utilize passenger car components, came into use. These vehicles were used in a series of developmental tactical organizations along the lines suggested by Fuller and Liddell Hart. Eventually there resulted four major British vehicle types: the tankette for machine gun and mortar transport, the light tank for reconnaissance, the cruiser tank for independent long range strikes and the infantry tank for close infantry co-operation.

The first group resulted in the famous Bren carrier, the second in the light Mark VI tanks—fast, lightly armoured two-man vehicles in the five-ton class. The cruiser tanks were in the 20-ton class with speeds up to 30 m.p.h. These vehicles were developments of the U.S. Christie tanks. The infantry tanks weighed about 26 tons and had thick armour. The Christie and the infantry types were armed with a 2-pounder gun and one or more machine guns.

With the beginning of the rearmament program in 1938, the royal tank corps was consolidated with British mechanized cavalry units as the royal armoured corps, and its expansion went forward concurrently with the design of additional new tanks.

**Germany.**—Germany was denied the use of tanks, aircraft and heavy artillery by the victors of World War I. Thus in later years the Germans had a distinct advantage in not being saddled with a great deal of obsolescent equipment as was the case with its former enemies. The 1919 plan was studied and modified in the light of the later writings of Fuller and Liddell Hart. Where the official British and U.S. doctrine was that tanks were to be used to exploit the advantage after an enemy line was broken, and the French doctrine was slow moving, crushing fire power, the Germans adopted the view that tanks were properly used to obtain the breakthrough itself and tactics were worked out with dummy vehicles. The mechanical details of tank design were secretly tested in the U.S.S.R. and after the Versailles treaty was abrogated, tanks were developed and openly displayed. The Germans concentrated on light and medium tanks of good design mounting slightly heavier armament than that used in other countries. Intervention in the Spanish Civil War worked out the details of German tactics and caused some modifications in design.

**France.**—The French experimented with a few tanks, and some modernization of wartime Renault tanks was undertaken after the war, but it was not until April 1926 that a new program for light, medium and heavy tanks was undertaken. Progress was slow until the Germans began to rearm in 1934. Even then, communist agitation and nationalization of war industries prevented as much progress as was intended. By 1939, nevertheless, approximately 3,000 modern tanks had been built. The French made notable progress in armour production; besides making considerable use of cast armour, they pioneered in work with welded armour. They were successful in combining thick, well-shaped armour with light suspension systems, thus holding down over-all weights. The French were among the first to use controlled differential steering, which permitted constant power to the track sprockets even when turning.

**U.S.S.R.**—The Russian automobile corps was formed late in 1914 and many foreign automobiles were armoured in Russia and used in combat even against German trenches. British and French troops sent to Russia after the Revolution were equipped with tanks. These were given to the White Russians when the troops were withdrawn and later became the first tanks in the soviet army. A few experimental vehicles were built which copied foreign designs. Later, foreign vehicles were imported, including British commercial tanks and tankettes and a U.S. Christie. With the start of the first five-year plan in 1928 the Russians began creating designs of their own.

Soviet intervention in the Spanish Civil War permitted field testing of designs, but more real experience was obtained in the war with the Japanese on the Manchurian frontier in 1938–39. The poor quality of Russian gasoline led to the adoption of diesel engines of German origin, and German torsion bar suspensions also were incorporated into Russian tanks. The Russo-Finnish War showed shortcomings in design although existing light and very heavy vehicle production could not be shut off immediately.

The Russians began World War II with a light T-26 tank copied from the British Vickers-Armstrongs 6-ton tank, small amphibious tanks, BT tanks developed from the U.S. Christie, several medium tank varieties and a few heavy tanks. The numbers were greater than those possessed by the Germans but the quality was not good and they were poorly handled. The T-26 tank existed in two models, one with a single turret mounting a 47-mm. gun. The other had twin turrets, each mounting a machine gun. The light amphibious tanks carried machine guns. The 11-ton BT tanks were armed with a 47-mm. gun. Both T-26 and BT varieties had been used in Spain. The T-28 and T-32 were medium and heavy types with multiple turrets mounting machine guns and short cannon either of 47-mm. or 76-mm. calibre.

**Other Nations.**—Most of the smaller nations purchased tanks from other countries, principally Great Britain, France, Sweden and Czechoslovakia. The first Swedish tanks were built from parts for German LKII light tanks shipped to Sweden after World War I and assembled under the direction of Joseph Vollmer, who had designed them originally. Spain built a few tanks of local design and the Czechs produced tanks for their own use as well as for export. The Japanese for some time used tanks purchased in Britain and France. In 1928, locally designed light, medium and amphibious tanks began to appear, some used by the army and some by the navy. Japanese tanks had considerable interchangeable parts, were thinly armoured and used diesel engines.

Poland, Austria, Australia, Belgium, Hungary, Canada and Italy produced some vehicles of their own design and others under license from other countries. Italy copied the French Renault near the end of World War I and built a few heavy tanks. The light Fiat copies of the Renault continued in use after the war. Later, British Carden Lloyd tankettes were built under license and evolved into a smaller vehicle. Experience gained in Ethiopia and in Spain in 1935–36 led to the design of medium tanks, lightly armed and armoured. Both were in use at the beginning of World War II.

## WORLD WAR II

The Spanish Civil War had demonstrated the deadliness of a concentrated attack sustained in depth on a narrow front. It was the method used by the Germans in attacking Poland in 1939. Tanks and dive bombers were given the primary role in achieving deep, fast-moving penetrations. Motorized infantry followed close behind. The campaign was a brief dress rehearsal for invasion of the Low Countries and France the following year. French and British tanks outnumbered the German tanks but were widely dispersed in accordance with the French principle of close infantry support. German tactics of punching in mass on narrow fronts made the most of the opportunity and the campaign was soon over.

From France, the war moved to North Africa. There the tactics were similar to the naval tactics originally envisioned by General Fuller. When Germany attacked Russia, its previous tactics were not as successful. The Germans used 2,400 tanks against the Russians' 24,000. Within three months the Russians had lost 17,500 tanks and the Germans 550, but the areas were great and the Russians traded land for time. The Germans had made an organizational change which weakened their thrusts. In 1939 there had been 300 tanks per armoured division. To attain what Hitler believed would be greater mechanized fire power, more armoured divisions were created with fewer tanks per division, but these units lacked punch.

The British and U.S. forces copied German organization and followed this change also. The Russians learned by experience. When they resumed the offensive at Stalingrad, the Russians had more tanks and aircraft and applied successfully the tactics the Germans had used in France. Differences in tactical concepts were reflected in the designs produced by different armies—the Germans particularly tending as the war went on to build more

BY COURTESY OF (LEFT) U.S. OFFICE OF WAR INFORMATION, (ABOVE) U.S. SIGNAL CORPS

TANKS OF WORLD WAR II: (LEFT) U.S. SHERMAN M-4 TANK UNDERGOING TESTS; (ABOVE) AMERICAN SOLDIERS EXAMINING A DISABLED GERMAN KING TIGER

heavily armed and armoured monsters, sometimes at the expense of mobility and mechanical reliability. The days when strategic surprise with large masses of armour was possible for one or another opponent gave way to fierce encounters between forces more equally matched in armour. Numbers, skill and daring were still to prove decisive in many actions, but the tank design race became one essentially between projectile and armour. In this the Germans always were in the lead.

Early in the war, tanks received a great deal of publicity. They were spectacular and many people in and out of military service became conditioned to their success. Later, in certain theatres where areas for maneuver were circumscribed, people jumped to the conclusion that tanks were obsolete. Yet right up to the end of the war the issues between the Germans and Russians were largely decided by tanks and self-propelled artillery. The tank served most usefully in World War II when employed in mass on suitable occasions by commanders who fully appreciated what it could and could not do. Again, it was most effective when used as a member of an integrated team including all the other ground arms and supported by suitable aircraft.

**Germany.**—After the Germans overran Czechoslovakia, they took over production of Czech TNH tanks, calling them 38 (t). German production was fairly well centralized and between 1939 and 1942 no overtime was worked. After the United States entered the war the first real attempt at economic mobilization was made, but it was not until 1944 that Albert Speer, then chief of production, was given power to forbid design changes which would interfere with production.

Hitler, either directly or indirectly, made many engineering decisions, sometimes on obscure details. In spite of the German totalitarian government, there was much extravagance in the number of vehicle types and in design complications, in addition to the tremendous use made of modified captured vehicles. Allied bombing caused some dislocation of production but, from 1940 to 1944, German tank production increased tenfold, then it fell, but only partly due to bombing. Other factors were oil shortage, use of slave labour, transportation difficulties and extravagance in man hours due to lack of knowledge of mass production methods.

Between 1939 and 1944, Germany produced 42,932 armoured vehicles. As the war forced the Germans more and more on the defensive, the trend was toward the armoured assault gun and huge tank destroyers rather than tanks because more of the former could be produced for the same effort. The Germans began the war with tanks mounting heavier armament than those of the Allies and during the war they constantly increased these calibres. Armour was also constantly thickened, it being a principle that the armour of a tank should be proof against the weapons it carried. Although many vehicle types were produced, the best of the German tanks probably was the Panther, which was developed after encountering the Russian T-34. The German vehicle was superior to the Russian except in mechanical reliability. The Panther had thick, well-sloped armour of welded construction. The main armament was a high velocity 75-mm. gun. This tank weighed 47 tons and had a speed of nearly 30 m.p.h. The Tiger, a heavier and somewhat slower tank, mounted an 88-mm. cannon. Late in the war, still heavier tanks mounting high velocity cannon up to 128 mm. were in use and even larger tank guns and new tanks were being tested.

**United States.**—After the German invasion of Poland, rearmament started in the U.S. but there was considerable confusion. The extent and need for arming were as vague as were the possible theatres of war should the United States become involved. Existing mobilization plans had to be scrapped, and lend-lease added to the confusion. After Pearl Harbor on Dec. 7, 1941, the president set up production goals so great that U.S. industry was aghast but willing to try to meet them. In spite of the president's demands that heavy tanks be produced and although the heavy M-6 tank design was available, the project was canceled because the new armoured force did not want a heavy tank and preferred to use available shipping space to ship twice as many medium tanks.

There was a great deal of bad blood between army service forces and the civilian War Production board but, in spite of the conflict between them, production was prodigious. There were 287,425 combat vehicles built during the war, together with enough spare parts to have built half again as many more.

The original M-3 medium tank had a 75-mm. gun mounted on the right front of the hull with machine guns in the bow and a 37-mm. gun and machine guns in the turret. This tank was known as the General Lee. When it was fitted with a more squat British turret, it was called the General Grant. It was produced with riveted, cast and welded armour and with different types of engines because of production limitations. Many of its limitations were overcome in a design which followed.

The M-4 medium tank, known as the General Sherman, with added armour and the 75-mm. gun in the turret, was in production by April 1942, and it reached Africa in time for the battle of El Alamein. Undergoing continual development during the war with 76-mm. guns or a 105-mm. howitzer on some models, the M-4 became by far the most widely used Allied tank in the war. A total of 49,234 was produced. Its components featured simplicity and ruggedness. Of particular interest were the volute spring bogie-type suspension, the highly developed V-8 engine and the rubber-block, rubber-jointed tracks. A life of 3,000 mi. was not unusual for these tracks, compared to about 600 mi. for the metal-jointed German tracks. Aside from the fact that the numbers of the Sherman tank supplied to Allied armies made possible the massing of superior tank forces in critical areas, its speed, maneuverability and capacity for sustained operation under severe conditions made the Sherman tank a vital factor in Allied victory.

Late in the war a compromise between the medium Sherman and the heavy M-6 was made in the 45-ton General Pershing. It mounted a 90-mm. gun, used torsion bar suspension and a torquematic stepless transmission. A few reached Europe before the war ended and some later also were landed on Okinawa. Light tanks went through a similar process of gun-calibre increase and the application of automatic transmissions adapted from motorcar design. The culmination of these was the M-24 or Chaffee 23-ton light tank, named after Maj. Gen. A. R. Chaffee.

The navy and marine corps had tested Christie amphibious tanks a few years after World War I. This led to a new concept in amphibious landings which received another impetus when the

Roebling rescue machine came to their attention in 1939. As the war went on, those vehicles were refined. Beginning with the marine corps landing on Betio (Tarawa), they were used more and more by the marine corps and eventually by the army. They were propelled in water by the motion of their tracks. Finally they were armoured and later turreted. Some were used as personnel carriers and some as accompanying artillery in landing operations. About 18,620 were built during the war.

**Great Britain.**—Immediately following the German invasion of Poland some members of the original World War I tank committee received permission to form a new committee at the ministry of supply. They produced a heavy gas-electric TOG tank, its initials representing "The Old Gang." The ministry meanwhile released for production a heavy Vauxhall tank. Disputes followed between Winston Churchill, then prime minister, and the committee with the result that the committee was dissolved and the Vauxhall tank became the 40-ton Churchill heavy tank.

Almost all existing tanks were lost at Dunkerque (Dunkirk). To catch up, vehicles were released for production with little testing. By the time the "bugs" were worked out, the tanks were obsolete. British tanks had a poor reputation because of this and because of lack of production inspection and control. Parliament investigated but was unable to fix responsibility. Meanwhile, production continued. Near the end of the war, British tank quality had improved and weapon calibres were more nearly the equal of the Germans.

Final models of the Churchill and Cromwell mounted 75-mm. guns. The faster and lighter Comets mounted 77-mm. guns. The Cromwell and Comet were in the cruiser class. In addition to combat tanks, the British devised several self-propelled guns and many special tanks such as the A.V.R.E. for throwing high explosive petards, "flails" for detonating land mines, carpet-laying tanks or "bobbins," flame throwers and others. About 24,000 tanks were produced, 3,600 were received from Canada and the United States furnished 25,600.

**U.S.S.R.**—The models laid down in 1938–39 and produced by 1940 revolutionized Soviet armour. The 26-ton T-34 medium was one of these. It was of the Christie type with wide (24 in.) tracks, had a low silhouette and a 30 m.p.h. speed provided by a good 500 h.p. liquid-cooled diesel V-12 engine. It was armed with a 76-mm. gun and later with an 85-mm. gun.

Another 1940 model was the KV heavy (named for Klementi Voroshilov, Soviet minister of defense), which weighed 52 tons and mounted a 76-mm. gun. The KV was much more heavily armoured than the T-34, which accounted for its greater weight, since in other respects it was much like the T-34. With these early wartime models the Soviets came into their own as designers, producers and users of fighting tanks. Before the war's end another heavy tank, the Joseph Stalin, was to appear. It was a logical step from the T-34 and the KV, in the progression toward thicker armour and more fire power, with the 51-ton JS-2 model mounting a 122-mm. gun.

In addition to Russian production of about 100,000 vehicles, the United States furnished Russia 13,303 combat vehicles (tanks, self-propelled weapons and scout cars) under lend-lease. The British furnished 4,260 and Canada 1,220 tanks in addition to huge numbers of Bren carriers from both. Figures for Russian tank losses in the war have never been released but are believed to have been in the neighbourhood of 100,000. Russian equipment was designed to do the job with the least possible expenditure of man-hours to produce, with simplicity and with absolutely no emphasis on finish or crew comfort.

**Other Countries.**—Czechoslovakia, Italy, Japan, Poland and Sweden produced some excellent light and medium tanks before and during World War II, and Argentina produced a few medium tanks resembling the U.S. Sherman. In the main these vehicles were lightly armed and armoured. The Japanese vehicles were distinguished by their use of common components as well as by their use of diesel engines that reduced the possibility of fire, an ever-present hazard in a tank. Czech and Swedish vehicles, and

BY COURTESY OF (ABOVE) EMBASSY FEDERAL REPUBLIC OF GERMANY, (RIGHT) U.S. ARMY, (BOTTOM LEFT) BRITISH INFORMATION SERVICE, (BOTTOM RIGHT) AKIRA TAKEVCHI

TANKS AFTER WORLD WAR II: (ABOVE) WEST GERMAN LEOPARD TANKS ON MANEUVERS; (RIGHT) U.S. M-60; (BOTTOM LEFT) BRITISH CHIEFTAIN; (BOTTOM RIGHT) JAPANESE STA-3

some Italian, were sold commercially to many smaller nations in the world.

### TANKS IN THE NUCLEAR ERA

During the postwar years the U.S.S.R. continued to emphasize tanks and increased the proportion of armoured units in the Red army. The Joseph Stalin (JS-3) tank, with sloping armour and dome-shaped turret, mounted a 122-mm. gun; the T-34 mounted an 85-mm. gun and weighed about 35 tons.

Both of these tanks were replaced by the T-10, which mounted a 122-mm. gun, and the T-54, which had a 100-mm. gun. The PT-76 amphibious tank of 1956 was followed by airborne, bridging and rocket projector tanks the next year.

Great Britain abandoned the basic distinction between cruiser and infantry tanks and instead adopted a single-purpose medium tank, the Centurion, later succeeded by the Chieftain. The latter had a multi-fuel engine and a remarkably low silhouette. The United States lacked a clear tank policy for a time after 1945 because of the overemphasis on nuclear weapons. Following the Korean War, during which tanks were used as artillery pieces, development of the hydrogen bomb and of tactical nuclear weapons led to a reappraisal and new designs. The M-60, with rounded cast armour, was adopted as the main battle tank of the U.S. army and went into quantity production in 1960. It mounted a British 105-mm. gun that became standard for all NATO tanks, was powered by a 750 hp. diesel engine, weighed 46 tons and carried a crew of four men.

France produced the light AMX13 and some excellent heavier vehicles. Sweden continued to manufacture and export tanks and in 1963 created the novel Bofors turretless tank. Japan resumed production of tanks for use by the Japan defense force. These tanks resembled U.S. medium tanks but had diesel engines and were scaled down somewhat to suit the Japanese soldiers.

Because tank *v.* tank warfare had not been visualized before World War II, armament had not been greatly emphasized, but the tank battles of World War II made guns the controlling factor in tank design. Postwar tanks, in fact, were identified in terms of their weapons rather than their weight. It was no longer customary to describe tanks as light, medium, or heavy but as light-gun, medium-gun, or heavy-gun tanks. The range of tank guns also increased. Most World War II tank fighting took place at distances of less than 1,000 yd. but after the war engagement at a range of 2,000 yd. or more was considered normal. In the 1960s the 120-mm. gun was considered the largest weapon that could be mounted on a tank with good effect. Such weapons required automatic loading devices, bore evacuators, electric primers, gyro-stabilizers, and highly developed range finders. For tank armour, light metals such as aluminum and magnesium were utilized, together with nylon and fibreglass components, so that armour protection could be provided with minimum weight. The fact that armour represented about one-third of the total weight of a tank indicated the importance of the use of lightweight materials.

With the advent of atomic missiles the concept of war underwent a complete change. Following a period of confused thinking, military concepts began to crystallize after 1950. Land warfare in the atomic age was believed most likely to take the form of thin screens of guerrillas or skirmishers capable of making sudden concentrations and attacks and equally quick dispersions.

Quick exploitation before an enemy recovers his balance after an atomic blast was considered to be of great importance. Tanks were thought to be well suited for use in atomic warfare because of the protection offered their crews from heat and flash. Their mobility would enable them to disperse and to reconcentrate rapidly as changes took place in a tactical situation either by the threat of or the use of nuclear missiles. Infantry on foot might be too slow and too vulnerable for such activity, and probably would be carried in armoured personnel carriers accompanying tank formations.

*See* also references under "Tank" in the Index.

BIBLIOGRAPHY.—R. J. Icks, *Tanks and Armored Vehicles* (1945); R. M. Ogorkiewicz, *Armour* (1962); M. M. Postan, *British War Production* (1952); British House of Commons, Report by Select Committee, *War Time Tank Production* (1953); C. M. Green, H. C. Thomson and P. J. Roots, *The Ordnance Department: Planning Munitions for War* (1955); H. C. Thomson and Lida Mayo, *The Ordnance Department: Procurement and Supply* (1960); F. O. Miksche, *Atomic Weapons and Armies* (1955); Royal Armoured Corps Centre, *Tank Museum Guide* (1951–61); articles in the U.S. periodicals, *Armor* and *Ordnance*.

(C. E. BR.; R. J. I.)

**TANKER,** a ship designed to carry liquid cargo in bulk. Its cargo is usually a petroleum product, either crude oil being carried from oil fields to refineries or gasoline being carried from refineries to distribution centres. The liquid is piped into the cargo space of the ship and is transported without use of barrels or other containers. Special tankers carry other liquids such as molasses, asphalt, wine, or liquefied petroleum gases, but the references in this article are all to oil tankers. Tankers differ from general-cargo ships in that they normally carry a full load of cargo in one direction and return without cargo.

Tankers vary in size from small coastwise vessels about 200 ft. long, carrying from 1,500 to 2,000 tons deadweight, up to huge vessels which are the largest ships afloat. In the early 1960s the first tankers of more than 100,000 tons deadweight appeared. By the late 1960s vessels of up to 300,000 tons had been laid down and the world tanker fleet amounted to more than 60,000,000 tons gross, accounting for one-third of world merchant shipping tonnage. The leading flags were Liberia (13,000,000 tons gross), Norway (10,000,000 tons), the British Commonwealth (9,000,000 tons), Japan (6,000,000 tons) and the United States (4,500,000 tons).

Experience with supertankers has shown that the direct cost of transporting oil goes down as the size of the tanker increases, apparently without limit; the limit on building larger tankers is the lack of suitable shore facilities for them. As more deepwater loading and unloading facilities are created, larger and larger tankers become economically feasible.

The speed of tankers has increased along with their size. In 1940 most tankers were powered with not more than 5,000 brake horsepower and made from 12 to 14 knots. In the 1960s most large tankers were given from 15,000 to 25,000 brake horsepower and made from 15 to 18 knots.

**Arrangement.**—Tankers almost invariably have their propelling machinery located in the stern. (*See* diagram.) The cargo-oil space occupies about 60% of the ship's length; usually there is a

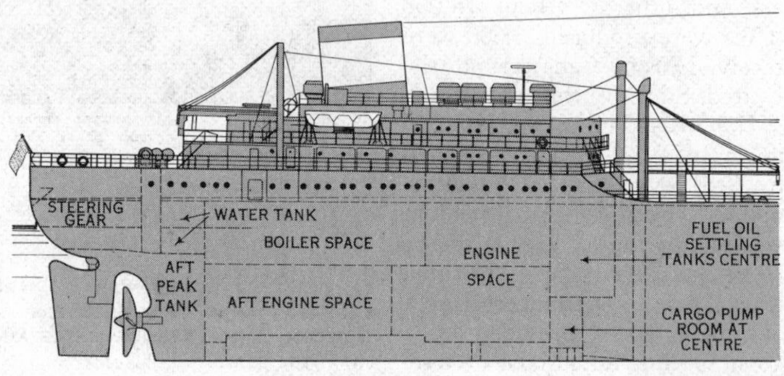


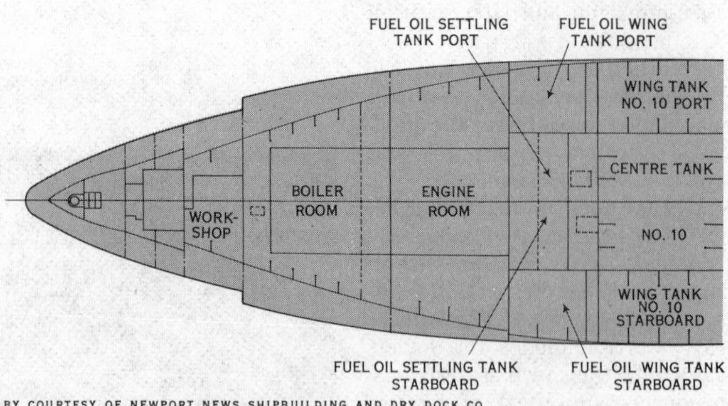


BY COURTESY OF NEWPORT NEWS SHIPBUILDING AND DRY DOCK CO.

BELOW-general-cargo hold in the bow, along with ballast or fuel tanks. The cargo space is isolated from the forward and after portions by cofferdams, watertight compartments which are kept empty. A pump room is located just forward of the machinery space, with sometimes an additional pump room forward or amidships. There is a "forecastle" (additional topside deck at the bow) and a house amidships, containing the pilothouse, other navigational spaces, and usually quarters for a few of the crew. A "poop" (additional topside deck at the stern) extends over the machinery space and, together with higher levels of deckhouses, quarters the rest of the crew. In the 1960s the practice began of building "all-aft" tankers, in which there are no amidships structures, the navigating bridge and all accommodations being incorporated in the poop, above the main machinery spaces. The cargo space is usually divided into two, three, or four rows of cargo tanks by longitudinal bulkheads; these are further divided into individual tanks (from 35 to 40 ft. long in large vessels) by transverse bulkheads. Access to the tanks is through oiltight hatches on the deck, cargo being loaded or discharged by means of the ship's own pumps, which may have a capacity in excess of 4,000 tons per hour.

Tanker crew accommodations are more livable than those of most vessels, because of the limited leave-time, which is often only about one day per passage. Single-person rooms, recreation lounges, and even swimming pools are fitted on the long-voyage tankers to enhance crew morale.

The density of the cargo carried by tankers varies from about 40 to more than 50 lb. per cu.ft. A tanker with enough capacity for a full deadweight cargo of light gasoline will have some empty tanks when carrying a full cargo of heavy crude oil.

Tankers are permitted by law to load more deeply, in proportion to their depth, than ordinary cargo ships. To be permitted this greater draft, they must provide special arrangements for fore-and-aft access for the crew in heavy weather, and for the quick freeing of the deck of seas which wash over it. The draft of tankers plying between the Arabian oil fields and Europe or the Atlantic coast of North America is limited by the Suez Canal to about 37 ft., although this depth is continually being extended by dredging. The extremely large tankers may be designed for drafts of 40 to 60 ft. but cannot use canals if fully loaded. A relatively high block coefficient is used to obtain maximum deadweight. The block coefficient is the ratio of submerged volume to the product of length, beam, and draft. The coefficient is frequently as high as 0.80, compared with about 0.60 to 0.70 for many passenger vessels and about 0.70 to 0.75 for most general-cargo ships.

BY COURTESY OF NEWPORT NEWS SHIPBUILDING AND DRY DOCK CO.

MEDIUM-SIZED OCEAN-GOING TANKER (27,000-TON DEADWEIGHT) OPERATING BETWEEN VENEZUELA AND NEW YORK

**Construction.**—The internal bulkheads, and the stiffening members, are usually entirely welded. The outside plating (shell and deck) is also welded but in large tankers a few fore-and-aft seams are riveted. It has been found that a riveted seam will usually stop a crack in the plating, thus preventing a minor crack from becoming a major fracture. Small tankers may be completely welded.

The upper deck and the bottom shell of tankers are invariably framed longitudinally; that is, the stiffening members that support the plating are run fore-and-aft instead of transversely as in other types of ships. In many tankers the side shell plating is also longitudinally framed. The thickness of the shell plating will vary from about $\frac{3}{4}$ in. for a small tanker to about $1\frac{1}{2}$ in. for a very large tanker.

Tankers are shorter lived than most steel ships because of the corrosive nature of their cargo. Crude-oil cargoes deposit corrosive sludges on the bottom and gasoline cargoes have a corrosive effect on the steel of the tanks. As a result, a tanker may last only 12 years instead of the 20-year life of a cargo ship, although protective coatings have been developed that help to withstand the corrosive effects of petroleum products.

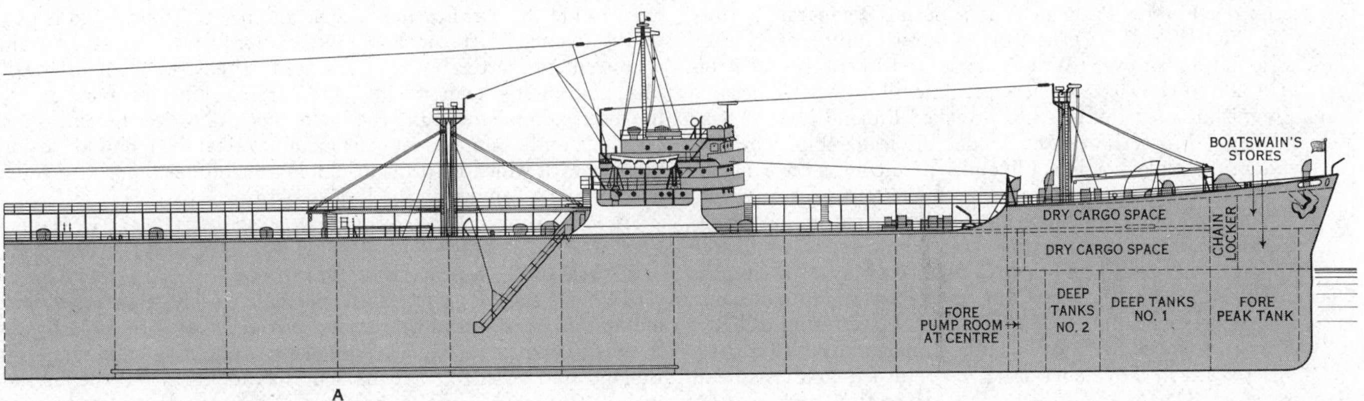

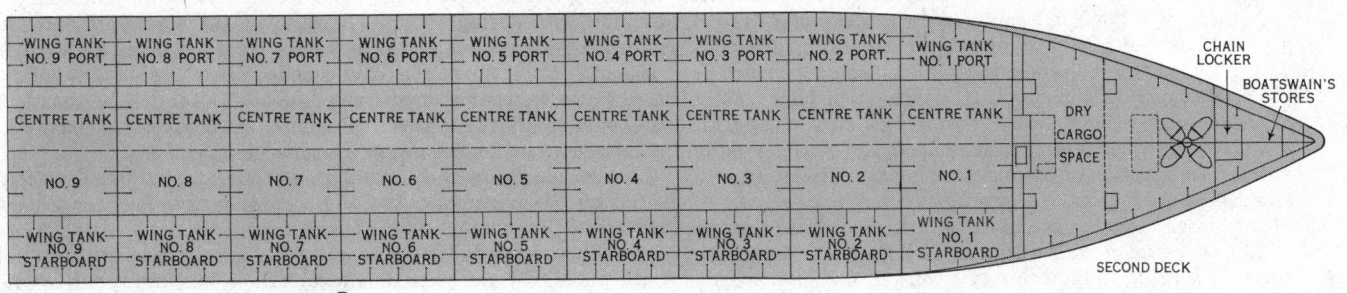

DECK ARRANGEMENT OF A TANKER: (A) PROFILE; (B) PLAN VIEW SHOWING CARGO TANKS

This deterioration takes place mainly in the cargo spaces, leaving the bow, the stern, and the machinery with years of useful life. It is, therefore, not unusual for an owner to scrap the cargo-tank portion of an old tanker and have a new one built and fitted into the old bow and stern. Since the new part is usually made larger than the discarded section, this procedure is sometimes called "jumboizing." Sometimes the vessel will be completely converted for the carriage of grain, iron ore, or other bulk cargoes.

When a tanker has discharged a cargo its tanks must be cleaned and freed of gas. This process is usually carried out on the ballast voyage back to the loading port. It is done by washing down with high-pressure steam. The resulting oil and water mixture must not be discharged into the ocean within 150 mi. of any coastline. The oil is then separated from the water by mechanical separators, the water being discharged overside and the oily sludge retained in tanks for later discharge to a shore installation.

Bibliography.—"History of Tankers," *Trans. Soc. Nav. Archit. Mar. Engrs, N.Y.*, p. 135 (1943), "Structural Design of Tankers," *ibid*, p. 444 (1949); G. A. B. King, *Tanker Practice* (1956); J. Bes, *Tanker Shipping* (1963). (J. P. Ck.; P. Df.)

**TANNER, HENRY OSSAWA** (1859–1937), U.S. Negro painter, whose style was naturalistic and whose subject matter was most often biblical, was born at Pittsburgh, Pa., on June 21, 1859. He was the son of Benjamin Tucker Tanner (1835–1923), bishop of the African Methodist Episcopal Church from 1888 to 1908 (when he retired at his own request) and author of a number of books, including *An Apology for African Methodism* (1867) and *The Negro's Origin* (1869). Henry Tanner was a pupil of Thomas Eakins, in Philadelphia, and of J. P. Laurens and Benjamin Constant in Paris, where he lived thereafter. He first exhibited at the Salon in 1895. Examples of his work may be seen at the Philadelphia (Pa.) Museum of Art; Los Angeles (Calif.) county museums; Art Institute of Chicago (Ill.); Metropolitan Museum of Art, New York City; and other public collections. He was a knight of the Legion of Honour and a member of several painters' societies. Tanner died in Paris on May 25, 1937.

**TANNER, VÄINÖ ALFRED** (1881–1966), Finnish statesman, an outstanding exponent of patriotic and democratic policies for his country's working class. He was born in Helsinki on March 12, 1881. Early associated with the cooperative movement, he entered the Finnish Parliament as a Social Democrat in 1907. After the Civil War (1918), he worked successfully to revive his party, orientating it toward Western-type parliamentarism. From Dec. 11, 1926, to Dec. 9, 1927, he was prime minister. He became foreign minister when the U.S.S.R. attacked Finland in 1939 (*see* World Wars: *World War II*). Under his leadership, working-class solidarity made possible Finland's heroic resistance in the "Winter War." After the peace of March 1940, he became minister of supply, but Soviet pressure forced his resignation in August. With the resumption of the war, he became minister of commerce and industry (July 1941) and then of finance (May 1942–August 1944). After the armistice, the Communists accused him of being one of those "responsible for the war." He was arrested on Nov. 6, 1945, and sentenced to 5½ years' imprisonment on Feb. 21, 1946. After his release in November 1948, he returned to Parliament. He was reelected chairman of the Social Democratic Party in 1957. He died in Helsinki on April 19, 1966. (E. K. I. J.; X.)

**TANNHÄUSER** (*c.* 1200–*c.* 1270), German lyric poet who became the hero of a popular legend. As a professional Minnesinger (*q.v.*) he served a number of noble patrons, and from his references to them it can be concluded that his career spanned the period *c.* 1230–*c.* 1270. Not much is known of his life, except that he traveled widely and almost certainly took part in the Crusade of 1228–29. There are six extant *Leiche* (lyric lays) by Tannhäuser, a few dance songs and love songs (the latter in a parodistic vein), and a group of *Sprüche* (gnomic poems).

The Tannhäuser legend is preserved in a popular ballad traceable to 1515; the origins of the legend itself probably lie in the 13th century. Enticed to the court of Venus, Tannhäuser lives a life of earthly pleasure, but soon, torn by remorse, he makes a pilgrimage to Rome to seek remission of his sins. The pope tells him that, as his pilgrim's staff will never put on leaf again, so his sins can never be forgiven. In despair Tannhäuser returns to the court of Venus. Shortly afterward his discarded staff begins to put forth green leaves. The pope sends messengers to search for Tannhäuser, but he is never seen again. The legend's most famous presentation is in Wagner's "music drama" *Tannhäuser* (first produced in 1845).

Bibliography.—G. Paris, *Légendes du moyen âge* (1904); W. Golther, *Zur deutschen Sage und Dichtung* (1911); P. S. Barto, *Tannhäuser and the Mountain of Venus* (1916); J. Siebert, *Der Dichter Tannhäuser: Leben, Gedichte, Sage* (1934); M. Lang, *Tannhäuser* (1936). *See* also L. Wolff in W. Stammler, *Die deutsche Literatur des Mittelalters: Verfasserlexikon*, vol. iv (1953). (Rd. J. T.; X.)

**TANNIN** (Tannic Acid), the generic name for a widely disseminated group of plant products, so named from their property of converting rawhide into leather (*q.v.*). They are soluble in water, and their solutions, which have an acid reaction and an astringent taste, are coloured dark blue or green by iron salts, a property utilized in the manufacture of ink (*q.v.*). Tannins occur normally in the roots, wood, bark, leaves, or fruit of many plants. They also occur to the extent of 45–65% in galls, pathological growths on species of oak and sumac resulting from the attack of an insect. (*See* also Tea; Gall, Plant.)

Tannins may be classified into two main groups: hydrolyzable tannins yield various water-soluble products, such as gallic acid $(HO)_3C_6H_2CO_2H$, protocatechuic acid $(HO)_2C_6H_3CO_2H$, and sugars; under similar treatment, condensed tannins, by far the larger group, form insoluble precipitates called tanners reds or phlobaphenes. Gallotannin or common tannic acid is the best known of the hydrolyzable tannins. It is obtained from Chinese or Aleppo galls by extraction with water or organic solvents. Tara, the pods from *Caesalpinia spinosa*, a plant indigenous to Peru, contains 40–55% of a gallotannin similar to that from galls and has become an important source for refined tannin and gallic acid. The European chestnut tree (principally *Castanea sativa*) and the American chestnut oak (*Quercus prinus*) yield hydrolyzable tannins important in leather manufacture. Among the important condensed tannins are the extracts from the wood or bark of quebracho, mangrove, and wattle.

**Uses.**—Besides their principal application in the manufacture of leather, tannins find use as a constituent to reduce the viscosity of drilling mud for oil wells, in boiler water to prevent scale formation, and in the clarification of wine and beer. Tannic acid is used in the dyeing of cotton and nylon. Because of its styptic and astringent properties, it has been used in the treatment of tonsillitis, pharyngitis, hemorrhoids, and various skin eruptions; it also has been administered internally to check diarrhea and intestinal bleeding, and as an antidote for metallic, alkaloidal, and glycosidic poisons with which it forms insoluble precipitates. *See* also references under "Tannin" in the Index.

*See* F. N. Howes, *Vegetable Tanning Materials* (1953); E. Haslam, *Chemistry of the Vegetable Tannins* (1966). (V. H. W.)

**TANNING:** *see* Leather; Tannin.

**TANTALUM,** a metallic element closely associated with niobium in ores and in properties, was discovered in 1802 by the Swedish chemist A. G. Ekeberg when examining minerals from Finland and Sweden. He named it tantalum after the mythological character Tantalus because of the tantalizing problem of dissolving the oxide of the new metal in acids. In 1801 C. Hatchett, an English chemist, also had discovered a new element that he named columbium. Because of the similarity of compounds of the two elements, they were regarded as being the same until in 1844 H. Rose, a German chemist, discovered both tantalum and a new element that he named niobium (for Niobe, daughter of Tantalus) in the mineral columbite. Later Rose realized that niobium and columbium were the same (*see* Niobium).

In 1866 niobium and tantalum compounds were actually separated by Swiss chemist J. C. G. de Marignac, thus permitting studies of the compounds of each element. Although some impure tantalum was produced by several early investigators, it was not until 1903 that the first ductile tantalum was produced by W. von Bolton in Germany. This ductile tantalum was used for incandescent lamp filaments until tungsten began to replace it in

1909. The first production of tantalum in the United States started in 1922. About this time C. W. Balke discovered that intentionally oxidized tantalum made an excellent rectifier of alternating current and its use in radio receiving sets and capacitors was established. Since then the use of tantalum in the electronics and chemical industries has grown steadily.

**Occurrence.**—Tantalum is a relatively rare metal. It ranks 54th in order of concentration of elements in the earth's crust and is found only in minerals which also contain niobium. The principal mineral is a ferrous manganese tantalate-niobate, (Fe, Mn) $(Ta,Nb)_2O_6$. If the tantalum oxide content exceeds the niobium oxide content, the mineral is called tantalite. If the niobium oxide content is greater, it is called columbite (*see* COLUMBITE [TANTALITE]). Tantalum also is found in other minerals, including pyrochlore, fergusonite, samarskite, euxenite, polycrase, and microlite, in each of which the niobium content generally exceeds the tantalum by a significant amount.

Tantalite and columbite usually are found in pegmatite dikes in quantities that rarely exceed a few pounds per ton. The chief sources are in Africa (Nigeria and Democratic Republic of the Congo), in eastern Brazil, and in Australia, generally as by-products of tin-mining operations. Tantalite minerals have been found in South Dakota and microlite in New Mexico.

**Production.**—Tantalum metal may be separated from the ore by several methods, each involving a series of chemical steps. In each process emphasis is placed on the separation of tantalum from niobium, since this is the most difficult step in the recovery process. In the classical method developed by Marignac in 1866, pulverized ore concentrates are fused with sodium hydroxide to form tantalates and niobates, which are leached with water and hydrochloric acid to remove most of the other metallic impurities and form insoluble tantalic and niobic acids. The mixed acids are dissolved in warm hydrofluoric acid to which is added a potassium compound so that a solution containing potassium fluotantalate, $K_2TaF_7$, and potassium niobium oxyfluoride, $K_2NbOF_6$, is formed. As this solution cools, the $K_2TaF_7$ precipitates, leaving the $K_2NbOF_6$ in solution. The $K_2TaF_7$ crystals are separated from the slurry by filtration and dried. They may then be reduced to obtain tantalum powder by electrolysis or sodium reduction.

A newer process based on work conducted at the U.S. Bureau of Mines in the early 1950s is now being widely used. Acid aqueous solutions of tantalum and niobium fluorides are placed in contact with methyl isobutyl ketone. At low acidity tantalum fluoride is extracted by the organic phase, and at high acidity the niobium fluoride is extracted. Once separated, the tantalum fluoride can be converted to $K_2TaF_7$ and reduced to tantalum metal.

Other methods of separating tantalum and niobium have been developed but are not used to any great extent. Tantalum metal is produced by powder metallurgy techniques (*see* POWDER METALLURGY: *Processes and Products: Refractory Metals*).

**Properties and Applications.**—Tantalum occupies the position in Group VA in the 6th period of the periodic table just below that of niobium. Its normal valence is 5, but in some compounds it can have the valence of 2, 3, or 4. A ductile metal having a silvery-gray colour, it is characterized by its high density, high melting point, and excellent resistance to attack by all acids except hydrofluoric and fuming sulfuric at ordinary temperature. The resistance to acids is related to the formation of a natural, thin, passive-oxide surface layer similar to that formed on stainless steel, titanium, and aluminum.

The applications for tantalum are based on its properties (high melting point, chemical inertness, and strength and ductility) and the dielectric properties of its oxide surface film. The most important uses for tantalum are in electrolytic capacitors and corrosion-resistant chemical equipment. Tantalum capacitors take advantage of the dielectric surface oxide film that can be formed on tantalum by anodizing. Tantalum capacitors have the highest capacitance per unit volume of any capacitors and are used extensively in miniaturized electrical circuitry. Chemical process equipment manufactured from tantalum is used for sulfuric acid concentrators, hydrochloric acid production, plating solutions, and a wide variety of processes requiring chemical inertness. Other uses include getters and components in electron tubes, rectifiers, and prosthetic devices.

*Some Physical Properties of Tantalum*

| | |
|---|---|
| Symbol | Ta |
| Atomic number | 73 |
| Atomic weight | 180.948 |
| Isotopes | 176, 177, 178, 179, 180, 181<br>182, 183, 184, 185, 186 |
| Crystal system | body-centered-cubic |
| Melting point (°C) | 2996 |
| Boiling point (°C) | $5425 \pm 100$ |
| Electrical resistivity at 25°C, microhm-cm | 12.45 |
| Thermal conductivity at 20°C, cal | 0.130 |
| Magnetic susceptibility, 25°C, cgs units | $0.827 \times 10^{-6}$ |
| Tensile strength (approx.) psi | 50,000 |
| Modulus of elasticity (approx.) psi | $27 \times 10^{6}$ |
| Specific heat, 25°C, cal/g | 0.034 |
| Latent heat of fusion, cal/g | 34.6 to 41.5 |
| Latent heat of vaporization, cal/g | 995 to 1021 |
| Superconducting transition temperature (°K) | 4.48 |
| Density (g/cc) at 20°C | 16.6 |
| Coefficient of linear expansion 27–2,900°C, per degree | $7.8 \times 10^{-6}$ |

Although tantalum has a very high melting point, it is not used as a high-temperature structural material to any great extent because of its rapid reaction with oxidizing environments. This high-temperature reactivity is in contrast to its chemical inertness at ambient temperatures and is related to the kinetics of oxidation at the different temperatures. At low temperatures a thin, tightly adherent uniform oxide film is formed, which resists chemical attack. At high temperatures the oxidation reaction proceeds very rapidly, forming a porous, nonadherent oxide scale which is easily penetrated by additional oxygen from the environment, causing the reaction to proceed very rapidly. At temperatures above about 1,400° C (about 2,550° F) the tantalum-oxygen reaction is so rapid that tantalum actually burns.

Several tantalum alloys have been developed that have useful structural properties at temperatures above about 1,090° C (2,000° F). Because of the high oxidation rate of tantalum and its alloys at these high temperatures, it is necessary to use protective coatings for use in air or other oxidizing environments. Typical protective coatings are silicides and aluminides formed by reacting the tantalum metal with an appropriate silicon or aluminum compound; these coatings are generally brittle and must be handled with care. In the absence of oxidizing environments, tantalum alloys may be used without protective coatings. An alloy containing 7.5% tungsten is used in some vacuum tubes for filament springs where retention of elasticity at high temperature is required. Tantalum is also used for high-temperature furnace components operating in vacuum or inert atmospheres.

**Tantalum Compounds.**—The most important tantalum compound is the carbide, TaC, which is used in the manufacture of some hard carbide tools for machining steels and other metals. Tantalum carbide may be made by the direct reaction of tantalum with carbon or the reaction of carbon with tantalum oxide. Tantalum oxide is used as an ingredient in some types of high refractive index optical glass. Many compounds of tantalum are known, but their uses are limited.

*See* also references under "Tantalum" in the Index.

BIBLIOGRAPHY.—G. L. Miller, *Tantalum and Niobium* (1959); A. G. Quarrell (ed.), *Niobium, Tantalum, Molybdenum and Tungsten* (1961); N. E. Promisel (ed.), *The Science and Technology of Tungsten, Tantalum, Molybdenum, Niobium and Their Alloys* (1964); T. E. Tietz and J. W. Wilson, *Behavior and Properties of Refractory Metals* (1965). (H. R. O.)

**TANTRISM** denotes a system of esoteric practices involving Yoga and meditation used in Hinduism and Buddhism for the fulfillment of worldly desires as well as the attainment of spiritual experience. The word tantrism is an anglicization derived from the Sanskrit word *tantra,* which designates a particular group of post-Vedic treatises (*see* SANSKRIT LITERATURE: *Purāṇas and Tantras*), heterogeneous in content, that deal with matters ranging from occult rituals to the control of psychological and physiological processes whereby the mind and the body may be made media for the realization of the ultimate truth. Tantrism is found in India, Nepal, Bhutan, Sikkim, and especially Tibet, the great seat of tantric Buddhism (*see* TIBETAN BUDDHISM; BUDDHISM: *Tibet*).

Tantric elements began to appear in Hindu and Buddhist works perhaps as early as the 6th century A.D.; yet, Tantrism is not viewed as orthodox teaching by every Hindu or Buddhist. Tantrism is associated with some unconventional practices. It upholds the efficacy of *yantra* (mystic diagrams) and of *mantra* (*q.v.;* mystic syllables or formulas). The *pancha-makara,* the five things whose names begin with the letter *m* (*madya, mansa, matsya, mudra,* and *maithuna,* respectively wine, meat, fish, parched grain, and sexual union), have been interpreted literally or as representing the five elements of the psychophysical Hatha Yoga (*see* YOGA). The lower tantras emphasize mundane rituals and occult powers; the higher tantras are devoted to meditation and psychosexual practices. In an attempt to achieve a state of transcendental ecstasy, the highest tantras advocate the methodical use of sexual union as a Yogic process, without the orgastic completion of the sex act. This practice is believed to create a state of bliss leading to the complete arrest of mental processes in a mystic sense of oneness with the true reality of the universe. Although Hindu Tantrism and Buddhist Tantrism share many elements in common, there are differences between them.

**Hindu Tantrism** is concerned mostly with practical techniques and lays little stress on theological theories, which it accepts from the main philosophical schools of Hinduism (*q.v.*). Basically it teaches that the nondual absolute reality has two aspects: Shiva (male) representing pure consciousness and transcendent passivity, and Shakti (female) representing energy and mental activity (*see* SHIVAISM; SHAKTISM). The truth regarding the union of Shiva and Shakti, as well as the nonduality of the absolute, is to be realized within the human body, which is believed to be a microcosm of the macrocosmic universe. Thus, the spinal cord represents the fabulous Mt. Meru, while the three main metaphysical veins (*ida, pingala,* and *sushumna*) running along the left, the right, and the middle of the spine, respectively, represent the three sacred rivers Ganges, Jumna, and Sarasvati; and the breathing process represents the course of time. Shakti, the female force, also called *kundalini,* lying serpentwise coiled and quiet at the lowest psychic centre (called a *cakra,* "wheel") of the body, is aroused and made to move upward through the higher psychic centres along the middle vein, so as to be united with Shiva, the male, residing at the *sahasrāra cakra,* which is described as a thousand-petaled lotus at the top of the head (*see* YOGA). This union of Shiva and Shakti brings about the transcendental realization of the absolute nonduality.

The psychosexual rituals of the tantras can be practised metaphysically within the yogi's own body, or physically between a yogi and a female partner. In the latter practice, the yogi is regarded as a manifestation of Shiva, and the female partner represents Shakti. Since the female aspect is considered to be the active power in the union, the Shakti is depicted in the active position in Hindu tantric iconography.

**Buddhist Tantrism** incorporates the basic elements of Yoga, meditation, *yantra, mantra,* and the metaphysical conception of the three main veins and the psychic centres. The major difference between Buddhist and Hindu Tantrism is the characterization of the male and female aspects. In Buddhist Tantrism the roles are reversed from those of Hindu Tantrism, thus the male is the active force and the female is the passive one. Although passive in nature, the female is depicted in the active position in Buddhist iconography, just as Shakti is in Hindu Tantrism. This situation has resulted in the Buddhist female aspect being erroneously designated Shakti in Western literature, the designation being incorrect because Shakti literally means "energy, activity," and the female aspect in Buddhist Tantrism represents "wisdom, passivity." The Buddhist tantric female aspect is called *prajna* ("wisdom").

Of the four classes of Buddhist tantra, the *anuttarayoga tantra* is the highest, and it is in this class that those tantras expounding the psychosexual practices are found. The male aspect is active and is equated with compassionate means; the female aspect is passive and is equated with wisdom. The Buddhist tantric yogi seeks to unite the male and female aspects through Yogic methods at the psychic centre in the genital region. This union produces the seed of enlightenment, called *bodhicitta,* which is not lost in orgastic emission but is made to ascend the metaphysical vein through the psychic centres until it reaches the cerebral centre that produces a state of transcendental ecstasy and a realization of the nonduality of absolute reality. This esoteric tantric practice is known in Tibetan Buddhism as the "shortcut" to enlightenment and is not to be performed by anyone not initiated into the proper method and the true meaning of the practice.

Tantrism is a practice common to the various sectarian schools of Tibetan Buddhism. In medieval times, the growing degeneration of tantric practices among those not properly initiated into them led to reform movements. These in turn resulted in the subsequent rejection of some tantras as being unorthodox Buddhist works. The reformed Yellow Hat sect, for example, accepts only four of the psychosexual tantras as orthodox, while the unreformed Rnying-ma-pa ("Old-ones") reject none of them.

Tantrism is reflected prominently in Tibetan art (*q.v.*), where wrathful forms of the serene Buddha are depicted with multiple heads and arms, equipped with macabre objects and weapons, and embracing a female in mystic union. Such images are called *Yab-Yum* ("Father-Mother") in Tibetan. *See* also BUDDHISM: *Regional Variations in Buddhism: Tantric Buddhism.*

BIBLIOGRAPHY.—Ferdinand Lessing and Alex Wayman, *Mkhas grub rje's Fundamentals of the Buddhist Tantras* (1968); David Snellgrove, *The Hevajra Tantra,* 2 vol. (1967); Sir John Woodroffe, *Principles of Tantra,* 2nd ed. (1952). (T. V. W.)

**TANZANIA, UNITED REPUBLIC OF.** An independent sovereign state of east central Africa, within the Commonwealth of Nations, consisting of the republics of Tanganyika and Zanzibar; the latter is composed of the two large islands Zanzibar and Pemba, with smaller islands. Pop. (1967) 12,313,469 (Tanganyika 11,958,754; Zanzibar 354,715). Of the total area of 364,943 sq.mi. (945,203 sq.km.), Tanganyika comprises 363,926 sq.mi. and Zanzibar 1,017 sq.mi. Zanzibar Island lies about 20 mi. (32 km.) off the coast of Tanganyika, Pemba Island about 25 mi. (40.2 km.). The capital is Dar es Salaam (*q.v.*).

This article is organized as follows:

## I. PHYSICAL GEOGRAPHY

### A. Tanganyika

**1. Relief and Drainage.**—The greater part of Tanganyika consists of an immense plateau varying in altitude from 3,500 to 4,500 ft. (1,000 to 1,400 m.). To the west it is bounded by steep escarpments of the western arm of the Great Rift Valley, which contains Lakes Tanganyika and Rukwa. The valley forks north of Lake Nyasa, and the eastern arm, which passes through the centre of Tanganyika, is less distinct; only the western wall is seen, as a cliff of varying height, until the troughlike characteristics of the Gregory Rift become noticeable near Kenya.

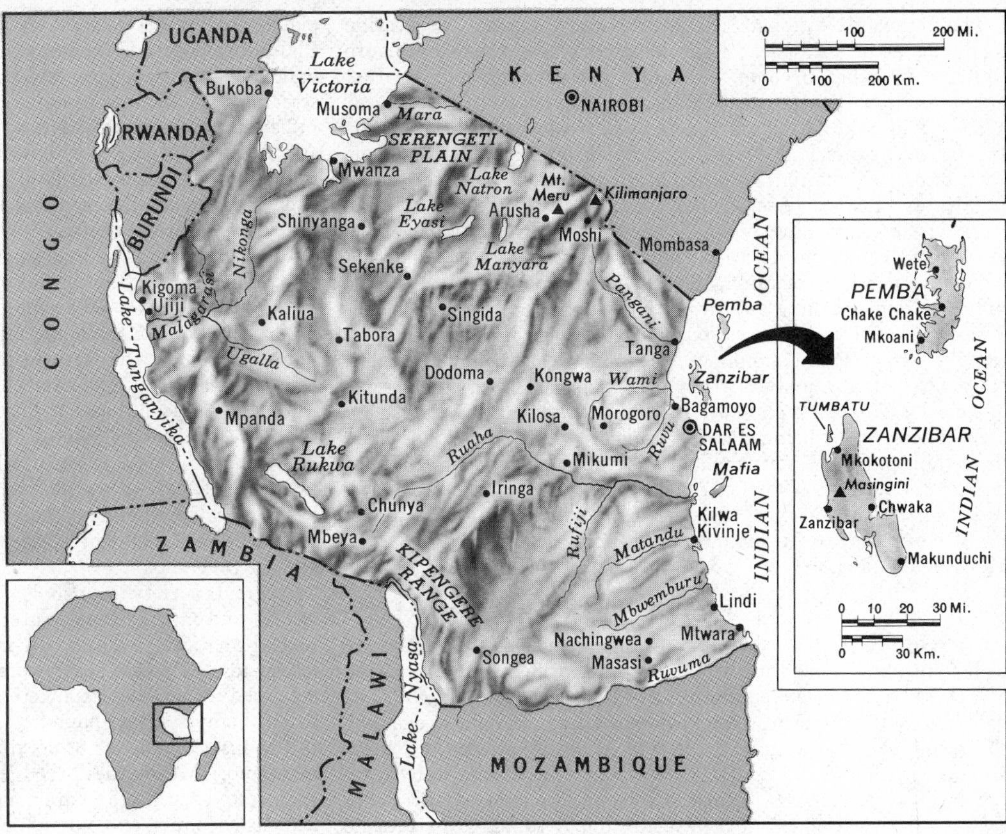

TANZANIA: MAJOR CITIES AND SURFACE FEATURES

The mountain systems are grouped in the northeast and southwest, with a ridge of highland between the two forming the eastern margin of the plateau. In the north are the volcanic peaks of Kilimanjaro (19,340 ft. [5,895 m.]) and Meru (14,979 ft. [4,566 m.]), and the Crater Highlands, with the famous game-filled Ngorongoro Crater. Running southeast from Kilimanjaro to the coast are the Pare and Usambara ranges. The Nguru and Uluguru mountains rise behind the coastal plain farther south. At the northern end of Lake Nyasa are the Livingstone Mountains, the Kipengere Range, the Poroto Mountains, Mt. Rungwe, and, farther west, the Ufipa Plateau.

Tanganyika has few permanent rivers, and most of the Central Plateau is devoid of running water throughout the dry season; only half the country is supplied with natural water throughout the year. The main rivers flowing to the Indian Ocean are the Pangani (Ruvu), which rises on Kilimanjaro; the Wami, whose tributary the Kinyasungwe-Mukondokwa has cut back into the plateau edge to capture some of the drainage of the interior; the Ruvu (Kingoni); the Rufiji, whose many tributaries include the Ruaha, which has also cut back through the plateau edge, the Kilombero, the Luwegu, and the Mbarangandu; and, farther south, the Matandu, Mbwemburu, Lukuledi, and the Ruvuma, which forms the southern boundary of the country.

The Mara, Kagera, and other rivers flow into Lake Victoria, the Malagarasi into Lake Tanganyika, and the Songwe and Ruhuhu into Lake Nyasa. Thus, Tanganyika forms the divide separating the headwaters of the three greatest rivers of Africa—the Nile, Congo, and Zambezi. About half of the great lakes Tanganyika and Victoria lie within the Tanganyikan borders. Lake Nyasa is wholly outside the country, though it forms part of the southwestern border (with Malawi).

**2. Climate.**—The climate is characterized by alternating wet and dry seasons. The small seasonal variation in temperature is much exceeded by the diurnal range, which is greatest over the Central Plateau, where it may be as much as 36° F (20° C), and least in coastal and lake regions, where it is about 14° F (8° C). Afternoon temperatures above 90° F (32° C) may prevail during the hottest months, from October to May. The equatorial climate is modified by lower temperatures on the high plateaus and mountains, giving a range of climates from the hot, humid coastal belt to regions of snow and ice on Kilimanjaro.

The rainy season is from November or December to April or May, when humidities may be uncomfortably high near the coast, with drought for the rest of the year. But the Kenya pattern of long and short rains prevails in northeastern Tanganyika, where the main rains are during March–May and the short rains in November–December. Much of the territory is semiarid, but very heavy rain falls at the northern end of Lake Nyasa (more than 100 in. [2,500 mm.]) and on the western shore of Lake Victoria (more than 80 in. [2,000 mm.]), where storms off the lake are concentrated by the prevailing winds. Annual variations are considerable, and because of unreliable rainfall extensive areas are suited only to pastoral development.

**3. Soils and Vegetation.**—Soil types include those of the plateaus, with a horizon of concretionary ironstone (murram), deep red earths, volcanic soils, calcareous black soils, sandy soils, and alluvial soils. With some exceptions, soils are poor, deficient in plant nutrients, and easily leached. Accelerated soil erosion is a serious problem. Miombo woodland (*Isoberlinia-Brachystegia*) occupies extensive areas in the west and south, and on open steppes grow scattered *Acacia* and myrrh trees (*Commiphora*). The baobab and *Euphorbia candelabra* are also characteristic. Evergreen forest, in which *Podocarpus* (yellowwood), *Chlorophora excelsa* (muvule, muule, or iroko), and various cedars are of economic value, occurs on mountain slopes. Above the forest may be found bamboo and open woodland with giant heathers. Higher still, Afro-alpine tree communities include giant species of *Senecio* (groundsel) and *Lobelia*. Coconut palms and casuarinas abound near the coast, as well as extensive mangrove swamps south from the Rufiji Delta.

**4. Animal Life.**—The country is unsurpassed in the number and variety of its wildlife: elephant, giraffe, zebra, rhinoceros, buffalo, together with lion, leopard, cheetah, hyena, and other carnivores; numerous varieties of antelope, including impala, gazelle, and wildebeest; snakes, lizards, chameleons, crocodiles, and other reptiles; and more than 1,000 varieties of birds, including game birds. Chimpanzees are found in the mountains east of Lake Tanganyika. The sitatunga is found in certain swamps, and the gerenuk (another rare antelope) in the Arusha, Kilimanjaro, and Tanga regions.

The Serengeti National Park is the most important reservation for plains game in Africa; it no longer includes the Ngorongoro Crater, which has become a separate conservation unit. Other smaller national parks include those of Ngurdoto Crater, near Arusha, and Lake Manyara. Of the game reservations the largest are the Selous and Rungwa River; smaller ones include the whole areas of Mt. Kilimanjaro and Mt. Meru and others at Lake Natron and Katavi Plain. (*See* further NATIONAL PARKS AND NATURE RESERVES.) The Rukwa Valley is one of the swarming areas of the locust, and game conservation there is administered by the Red Locust Research Association. Some of the game reservations have suffered from poaching and insufficient supervision, but at a conference on wildlife conservation held at Arusha in 1961 the Tanganyikan government announced a conservation policy more advanced than that adopted by any other African state. The tsetse fly (chiefly *Glossina morsitans*) infests wide areas, spreading sleeping sickness, but is being steadily eradicated by tree clearance and the establishment of permanent farms. Rainbow and brown trout were introduced into rivers of the northern and southern highlands, and Nile perch and tiger fish are caught in Lake Tanganyika. From November to March coastal big-game fishing is popular off Tanga and Mafia. (J. M. KE.)

B. ZANZIBAR

**1. Geology, Relief, and Soils.**—Both Zanzibar and Pemba are believed to have once formed part of the continent, the separation of Pemba having occurred during the Miocene Age, while Zanzibar dates from the Pliocene and Pleistocene ages. A deep channel, the result of rift faulting in the late Miocene, separates Pemba from the mainland and Zanzibar. Various types of limestone form the base of both islands. Raised sands and sandstones also occur together with varied residual deposits similar to alluvial strata on the adjacent mainland. Extensive weathering of the limestones combined with erosion and earth movements have resulted in a variety of soils, including red earths, loams, clays, and sands. Flat areas of coral limestone occur to the east, south, and north of Zanzibar and on the small islands to the west. Similar formations occur on the eastern seaboard of Pemba and on most of the islands. In places the coral is overlain by shallow red earth or alluvium.

The general impression of Zanzibar when approached from the mainland is of a long, low island with small ridges along its central north–south axis. Coconut palms and other vegetation cover the land surface. It is 52 mi. (84 km.) at its greatest length and 27 mi. (43 km.) wide. The highest point of the central ridge system is Masingini, 390 ft. (119 m.) above sea level. Higher ground is gently undulating and gives rise to a few small rivers, which flow west to the sea or disappear in the coral country. Two springs north of Zanzibar City provide an excellent water supply. Much of Pemba consists of small but steep undulating hills, and the western and southern coastline is deeply indented with creeks and bays.

**2. Climate.**—The climate is typically insular, tropical and humid. Rainfall is good, reliable, and well distributed. Northeast trade winds blow from December to March and southeast trade winds from May to October. Mean annual rainfall at Kizimbani (central Zanzibar Island) is 71 in. (1,800 mm.) and at Makunduchi (in the southeast) 63 in. (1,600 mm.). The "long rains" occur between March and May and the "short rains" during October–December. The two annual clove harvest periods are related to the seasonal rainfall pattern. From June to October is regarded as the "cool" season and November to March the "hot" season. Mean maximum temperature in Zanzibar City is 84° F (29° C) and mean minimum 77° F (24.8° C). The rainfall of Pemba is greater than that of Zanzibar, but the climate is otherwise similar. Figures for Wete, the capital, are: mean annual rainfall 77 in. (2,000 mm.), mean maximum temperature 86° F (30° C), mean minimum temperature 73° F (23° C).

**3. Vegetation.**—Small patches of indigenous forest and isolated large trees support the view that much of Zanzibar Island was originally covered by dense evergreen forest. The open coral outcrop country supports a dense thicket vegetation. The flat clay plains are grass covered. A noteworthy feature of the Chaani Plain in the north is the large number of palmyra palms. In damp valleys, papyrus, sedges, and tall grasses occur. In the few small streams and shallow swamps the giant aroid and, occasionally, raffia palms are found. Near the seashore the baobab, casuarina, and screw pine are characteristic trees, though many coconuts also occur on cultivated land above high-tide level. There have been many plant importations to Zanzibar over a long period of time. A feature of sheltered bays and creeks, especially in Pemba, is the dense stands of mangrove, two species of which yield bark rich in tannin, while others provide valuable timber.

**4. Animal Life.**—The major wild animals include leopard (a race peculiar to Zanzibar), civet cat, mongoose, two species of monkeys, lemur, the African pig, forest duiker, pygmy antelope, tree cony, squirrel, elephant shrew, and about 20 species of bats. Many of these animals are confined to the sparsely inhabited, bush-covered coral "Wanda" areas. Reptile life includes about 30 forms of snakes, five of which are poisonous, and the giant monitor. Frogs, toads, and tree frogs occur widely. Bird life is less varied and abundant than on the African mainland; excluding sea birds, 102 resident species have been recorded in Zanzibar and 73 in Pemba.

A great variety of fish is found both in the shallow coastal waters and in the deeper water of the Indian Ocean off the coral reef formations. Game fish include marlin, sailfish, tunny, and barracuda. Certain sea cucumbers found in shallow waters are collected, dried, and exported as bêche-de-mer (trepang). Shellfish of many species abound.

The insect fauna is not notably different from that of the nearby mainland. Mosquitoes breed freely during the rainy seasons. Insect pests such as the coreid bug (*Pseudotheraptus wayi*), which attacks coconuts, and animal pests and parasites, such as the tsetse fly and ticks (which transmit East Coast fever to cattle), have been the subject of research and control. Butterflies and moths, though common, do not offer the same variety as that in parts of the East African mainland. The Zanzibar Museum in Zanzibar City contains a first-class natural history section. (F. B. WI.)

## II. THE PEOPLE

A. TANGANYIKA

**1. Ethnography and Linguistics.**—Most of the peoples of Tanganyika are Bantu-speaking Negroes. They are among the northernmost Bantu peoples and were subjected to non-Bantu invasions from the north and to Arab contact from the coast. In the north and west are the southerly Interlacustrine Bantu kingdoms of Ha (numbering about 290,000), Haya (325,000), Fipa (80,000), and the smaller Kerewe, Zinza, Subi, and others. (*See* BANTU [INTERLACUSTRINE]; BANTU LANGUAGES.) There are about 120 different tribes, and several of the large ones have been affected by the Interlacustrine invasions, notably the Sukuma south of Lake Victoria (more than 1,000,000) and the Nyamwezi in west Tanganyika (363,000). In the south, tribes related to those of Zambia and Malawi include the Nyakyusa (*q.v.;* 220,000), Bena (196,000), and the Ngoni and Yao (*qq.v.*). In the centre and north, most Bantu tribes have been influenced culturally by the Masai (*q.v.*); they include the Gogo in the Dodoma region (299,000), Hehe (*q.v.; 220,000*), Arusha (68,000), Kuria (65,000), and Nyaturu (185,000). In the northeast dwell several tribes closely related to the Kikuyu and Kamba of Kenya, including the Chagga around Mt. Kilimanjaro (more than 300,000), Sambaa (194,000), and Pare (126,000). In the east and southeast are tribes that, unlike the others, reckon descent matrilineally and have been affected by Arab influence; among these are the Makonde of the Mtwara region (334,000), Luguru (202,000), Zaramo (183,000), Mwera (138,000), Zigua (134,000), Makua (123,000), and Rufiji (75,000).

The Great Rift Valley area in the north seems to have been a refuge for some non-Bantu tribes that were left unaffected by the many migrations of Bantu Negroes. The Hadzapi or Kindiga, hunters and gatherers reputedly akin to the Bushmen of southern Africa, live on the Lake Eyasi flats; the pastoral Sandawe are said to be related to the Hottentots. The Iraqw (134,000) and some small outlying groups are linguistically unrelated to any other known peoples; their language may have Cushitic affinities. There are also in the north about 50,000 Masai and 30,000 Barabaig, Nilo-Hamitic speakers, who migrated from Kenya and who, as warrior tribes, greatly influenced their neighbours.

Apart from the Hadzapi, Sandawe, Masai, and Barabaig, all the tribes are agriculturalists, traditionally growing corn (maize) and millets. Save for the few kingdoms or chiefdoms (Ha, Fipa, Chagga), these peoples lack centralized political authority; their density of population and political cohesion are low. Except on the coast and in some older inland towns, where Islam predominates, the African population generally follows traditional religion, although Christianity has made some headway. The slave trade, based at first on the coast, later on Zanzibar, had devastating effects throughout central and southern Tanganyika, much of which remains thinly populated.

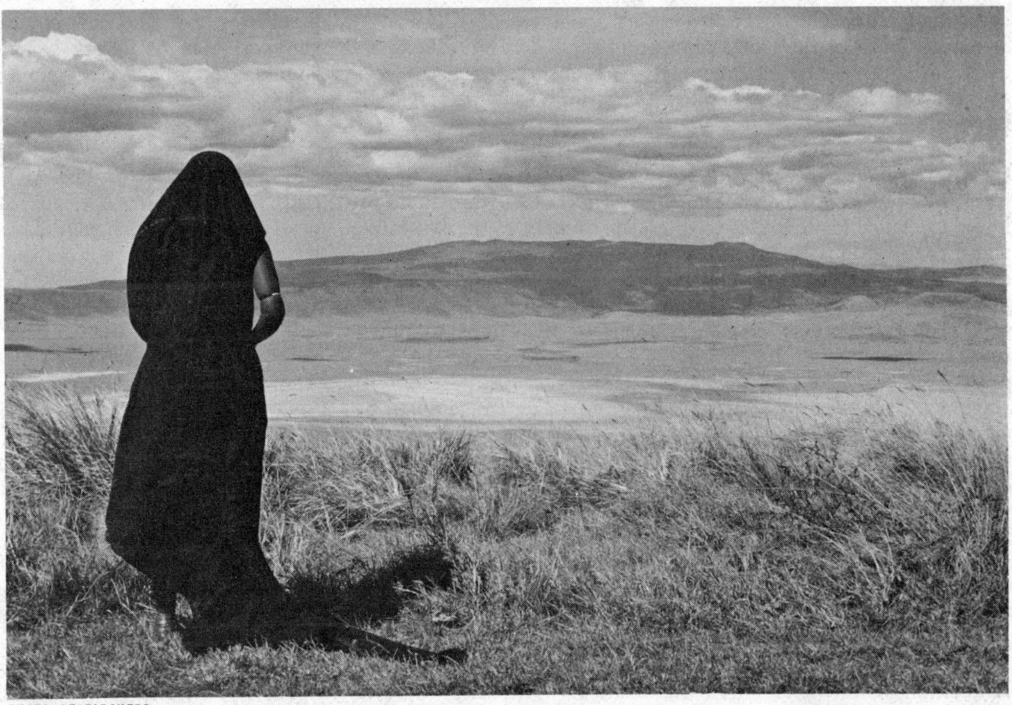

PHOTO RESEARCHERS

MASAI WOMAN ON THE RIM OF THE NGORONGORO CRATER, A MAJOR CONSERVATION AREA

(J. F. M. M.)

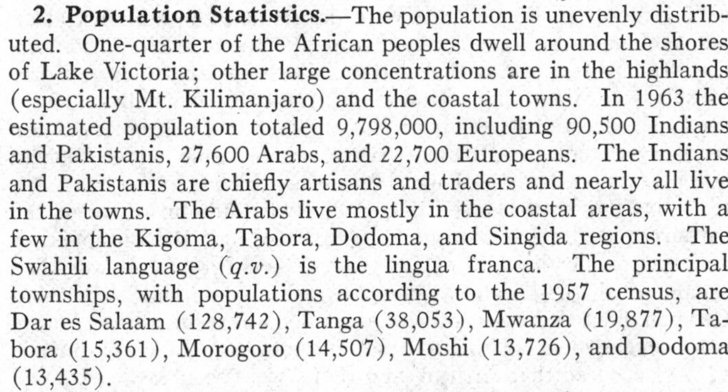

**2. Population Statistics.**—The population is unevenly distributed. One-quarter of the African peoples dwell around the shores of Lake Victoria; other large concentrations are in the highlands (especially Mt. Kilimanjaro) and the coastal towns. In 1963 the estimated population totaled 9,798,000, including 90,500 Indians and Pakistanis, 27,600 Arabs, and 22,700 Europeans. The Indians and Pakistanis are chiefly artisans and traders and nearly all live in the towns. The Arabs live mostly in the coastal areas, with a few in the Kigoma, Tabora, Dodoma, and Singida regions. The Swahili language (*q.v.*) is the lingua franca. The principal townships, with populations according to the 1957 census, are Dar es Salaam (128,742), Tanga (38,053), Mwanza (19,877), Tabora (15,361), Morogoro (14,507), Moshi (13,726), and Dodoma (13,435).

In the 1960s the African population was increasing at an average rate of nearly 2% annually, though in some of the highland tribes the increase was more rapid. The Asian communities had a higher rate of natural increase (about 2.5%).

(J. P. Mt.; J. M. Ke.)

B. Zanzibar

**1. Ethnography and Linguistics.**—The southern and eastern portions of Zanzibar Island are populated mainly by a Bantu-speaking people known as the Wahadimu (Hadimu); the northern portion of the island and adjacent Tumbatu are peopled by another Bantu-speaking people, the Watumbatu (Tumbatu). These two groups represent the earliest arrivals in Zanzibar. Throughout the 19th century, and after, they were expropriated from the western and more fertile parts of the island by later arrivals and still tend to keep aloof from the rest of the inhabitants. They are for the most part fishermen. Cattle raising was formerly one of their industries, but the herds have greatly diminished. Ropemaking (from coir) is carried on extensively by the Wahadimu women in the southern villages. The remainder of the population is of a very heterogeneous character, including Arabs, Europeans, Goans, Indians, and representatives of tribes from many parts of East Africa.

The aborigines of Pemba include the Watumbatu and Bantu-speaking Africans of mixed origins, who are known collectively and generically as Wapemba (Pemba). Pemba has evidence of 10th- to 16th-century Persian settlement, and the indigenous people claim Persian affinity, calling themselves Shirazis.

The language most widely spoken is a highly arabicized form of Swahili. Bantu languages are spoken by the indigenous Wahadimu, Watumbatu, and Wapemba. Among the Arabs, the language of the home is usually Swahili, and the use of pure Arabic is confined to scholars and recent arrivals from Arabia. Indian languages are spoken by the Asian communities, and English and Swahili are widely used and understood.

The majority of the Arabs and Africans are orthodox Sunni Muslims, though a few of the older Arab families, including that of the former royal family, are of the Ibadi sect (*see* Kharijites). There are a few hundred Christian Africans. Among the Asians, Muslims are the most numerous. There are minorities of Hindus, Parsees, Buddhists, and Christians.

**2. Population Statistics.**—The 1958 census showed the population of Zanzibar Island to be 165,253, that of Pemba 133,858. About 76% of the inhabitants were Africans, 16% Arabs, and 6% Asians. Zanzibar City had a population of 57,923. The main townships in Pemba are Wete (pop. 7,507), Chake Chake (7,167), and Mkoani (1,977).

(G. F. M. W.; X.)

## III. HISTORY

### A. Tanganyika

**1. Early History and Exploration.**—Most of the known history of Tanganyika before the 19th century concerns the coastal area, although the interior has a number of important prehistoric sites, including the Olduvai Gorge (*see* also the East African subsections of *History* and *Archaeology* in the article Africa). Trading contacts between Arabia and the East African coast existed by the 1st century A.D., and there are indications of connections with India. The coastal trading centres were mainly Arab settlements, and relations between the Arabs and their African neighbours appear to have been fairly friendly. After the arrival of the Portuguese in the late 15th century, the position of the Arabs was gradually undermined, but the Portuguese made little attempt to penetrate into the interior. They lost their foothold north of the Ruvuma (Rovuma) River early in the 18th century as a result of an alliance between the coastal Arabs and the ruler of Muscat (on the Arabian Peninsula). This link remained extremely tenuous, however, until French interest in the slave trade from the ancient town of Kilwa, on the Tanganyikan coast, revived the trade in 1776. Attention by the French also aroused the sultan of Muscat's interest in the economic possibilities of the East African coast, and a new Omani governor was appointed at Kilwa. For some time most of the slaves came from the Kilwa hinterland, and until the 19th century such contacts as existed between the coast and the interior were due mainly to African caravans from the interior.

In their constant search for slaves, Arab traders began to penetrate farther into the interior, more particularly in the southeast toward Lake Nyasa. Farther north two merchants from India followed the tribal trade routes to reach the country of the Nyamwezi about 1825. Along this route ivory appears to have been as great an attraction as slaves, and Sayyid Sa'id ibn Sultan himself (*see* below, *Zanzibar*), after the transfer of his capital from Muscat to Zanzibar gave every encouragement to the Arabs to pursue these trading possibilities. From the Nyamwezi country the Arabs pressed on to Lake Tanganyika in the early 1840s. Tabora (or Kazé, as it was then called) and Ujiji, on Lake Tanganyika, became important trading centres, and a number of Arabs made their homes there. They did not annex these territories but occasionally ejected hostile chieftains. Mirambo, an African chief who built for himself a temporary empire to the west of Tabora in the 1860s and 1870s, effectively blocked the Arab trade routes when they refused to pay him tribute. His empire was purely a personal one, however, and collapsed on his death in 1884.

The first Europeans to show an interest in Tanganyika in the 19th century were missionaries of the Church Missionary Society, J. L. Krapf and J. Rebmann, who in the late 1840s discovered Mt. Kilimanjaro. It was a fellow missionary, J. Erhardt, whose famous "slug" map (showing, on Arab information, a vast, shapeless, inland lake) helped stimulate the interest of the British explorers Richard (later Sir Richard) Burton and John Hanning Speke. They traveled from Bagamoyo to Lake Tanganyika in 1857–58, and Speke also saw Lake Victoria. This expedition was followed by Speke's second journey in 1860, in the company of J. A. Grant, to justify the former's claim that the Nile rose in Lake Victoria. These primarily geographical explorations were followed by the activities of David Livingstone, who in 1866 set out on his last journey for Lake Nyasa. Livingstone's object was to expose the horrors of the slave trade and, by opening up legitimate trade with the interior, to destroy the slave trade at its roots. Livingstone's journey led to the later expeditions of H. M. Stanley and V. L. Cameron. Spurred on by Livingstone's work and example, a number of missionary societies began to take an interest in East Africa after 1860.

**2. German Ascendancy.**—It was left to Germany, with its newly awakened interest in colonial expansion, to open up the country to European influences. The first agent of German imperialism was Karl Peters, who, with Count Joachim Pfeil and Karl Juhlke, evaded the sultan of Zanzibar late in 1884 to land on the mainland. He made a number of "contracts" in the Usambara area by which several chiefs were said to have surrendered their territory to him. Peters' activities were confirmed by Bismarck. By the Anglo-German Agreement of 1886 the sultan of Zanzibar's vaguely substantiated claims to dominion on the mainland were limited to a ten-mile-wide coastal strip, and Britain and Germany divided the hinterland between them as spheres of influence, Germany taking the region later known as Tanganyika. Following the example of the British to the north, the Germans obtained a lease of the coastal strip from the sultan in 1888, but their tactlessness, and fear of commercial competition, led to a Muslim rising in August 1888. The rebellion was put down only after the intervention of the imperial German government and with the assistance of the British Navy.

Recognizing the administrative inability of the German East Africa Company, which had hitherto ruled the country, the German government declared a protectorate over its sphere of influence in 1891 and over the coastal strip, where the company had bought out the sultan's rights. Germany was anxious to exploit the resources of its new dependency, but lack of communications at first restricted development to the coastal area. The introduction of sisal from Florida in 1892 by the German agronomist Richard Hindorff marked the beginning of the territory's most valuable industry, which was encouraged by the development of a railway from the new capital of Dar es Salaam to Lake Tanganyika. In 1896 work began on the construction of a railway running northwestward from Tanga to Moshi, which it reached in 1912. This successfully encouraged the pioneer coffee-growing activities on the slopes of Mt. Kilimanjaro. Wild rubber tapped by Africans, together with plantation-grown rubber, helped swell the country's economy. The government also supplied good-quality cotton seed free to African growers and sold it cheaply to European planters. The administration also tried to make good the lack of clerks and minor craftsmen by encouraging the development of schools, an activity in which various missionary societies were already engaged.

The enforcement of German overlordship was strongly resisted, but control was established by the beginning of the 20th century. Almost at once came a reaction to German methods of administration, the outbreak of the Maji Maji rising in 1905. Although there was little organization behind it, the rising spread over a considerable portion of southeastern Tanganyika and was not finally suppressed until 1907. It led to a reappraisal of German policy in East Africa. The imperial government had attempted to protect African land rights in 1895 but had failed in its objective in the Kilimanjaro area. Similarly, liberal labour legislation had not been properly implemented. The German government set up a separate Colonial Department in 1907, and more money was invested in East Africa. A more liberal form of administration rapidly replaced the previous semimilitary system.

World War I put an end to all German experiments. Blockaded by the British Navy, the country could neither export produce nor get help from Germany. The British advance into German territory continued steadily from 1916 until the whole country was eventually occupied. The effects of the war upon Germany's achievements in East Africa were disastrous; the administration and economy were completely disrupted. In these circumstances, the Africans reverted to their old social systems and their old form of subsistence farming. Under the Treaty of Versailles (1919) the U.K. received a League of Nations mandate to administer the territory except for Ruanda-Urundi, which came under Belgian administration, and the Kionga triangle, which went to Portugal.

**3. British Mandate.**—Sir Horace Byatt, administrator of the captured territory and, from 1920 to 1924, first British governor and commander in chief of Tanganyika Territory (as it was then renamed; all the territory under German control had been called German East Africa), enforced a period of recuperation before new development plans were set on foot. A Land Ordinance (1923) ensured that African land rights were secure. Sir Donald Cameron, governor from 1925 to 1931, infused new vigour into the country. He reorganized the system of native administration by the Native Authority Ordinance (1926) and the Native Courts Ordinance (1929). His object was to build up local government on the basis of traditional authorities, an aim that he pursued with doctrinaire enthusiasm and success. He attempted to silence the criticisms by Europeans that had been leveled against his predecessor by urging the creation of a Legislative Council in 1926 with a reasonable number of nonofficial members, both European and Asian. In his campaign to develop the country's economy, Cameron won a victory over opposition from Kenya by gaining the British government's approval for an extension of the Central Railway Line from Tabora to Mwanza (1928). His attitude toward European settlers was determined by their potential contribution to the country's economy. He was, therefore, surprised by the British government's reluctance to permit settlement in Tanganyika. The economic depression after 1929 resulted in the curtailment of many of Cameron's development proposals. In the 1930s, too, Tanganyika was hampered by fears that it might be handed back to Germany in response to Hitler's demands for overseas possessions.

At the outbreak of World War II Tanganyika's main task was to make itself as independent as possible of imported goods. Inevitably the retrenchment evident in the 1930s became still more severe, and, while prices for primary products soared, the value of money depreciated proportionately. Tanganyika's main objective after the war was to ensure that its program for economic recovery and development should go ahead. The continuing demand for primary produce strengthened the country's financial position. The chief item in the development program was a plan to devote 3,000,000 ac. (1,200,000 ha.) of land to the production of peanuts (the Groundnuts Scheme). The plan, which was to be financed by the British government, was to cost £25,000,000, and, in addition, a further £4,500,000 would be required for the construction of a railway in southern Tanganyika. It failed because of the lack of adequate preliminary investigations and was subsequently carried out on a greatly reduced scale.

**4. Constitutional Progress and Independence.**—Constitutionally, the most important immediate postwar development was the British government's decision to place Tanganyika under UN trusteeship (1947). Under the terms of the trusteeship agreement, Britain was called upon to develop the political life of the territory, which, however, only gradually began to take shape in the 1950s with the growth of the Tanganyika African National Union (TANU). The first two African members had been nominated to the Legislative Council in December 1945. This number was subsequently increased to four, with three Asian nonofficial members and four Europeans. An official majority was retained. In an important advance in 1955, the three races were given parity of representation on the unofficial side of the council with ten nominated members each, and for a time it seemed as if this basis would persist. The first elections to the unofficial side of the council, however, enabled TANU to show its strength, for even among the European and Asian candidates only those supported by TANU were elected.

A constitutional committee in 1959 unanimously recommended that after the elections, in 1960, a large majority of the members of both sides of the council should be Africans and that elected members should form the basis of the government. The approval of the British colonial secretary was obtained for these proposals in December 1959, and in September 1960 a predominantly TANU government took office. The emergence of this party and its triumph over the political apathy of the people were largely due to the leadership of Julius Nyerere (*q.v.*). Tanganyika became independent in December 1961, with Nyerere as its first prime minister. The November 1962 elections for the country's first president under a republican constitution resulted in an overwhelming victory for Nyerere. On Dec. 9, 1962, the anniversary of its independence, Tanganyika became a republic within the Commonwealth. (For later history see *Tanzania* below.)

### B. Zanzibar

The history of Zanzibar has been to a large extent shaped by the monsoons (prevailing trade winds); and by its proximity to the continent. The regular annual recurrence of the monsoons has made possible its close connection with India and the countries bordering the Red Sea and the Persian Gulf. Its proximity to the continent has made it a suitable jumping-off point for trading and exploring ventures not only along the coast but also into the interior.

**1. Early History and Portuguese and Omani Domination.**—Though the first references to Zanzibar occur only after the rise of Islam, there would appear to be little doubt that its close connection with southern Arabia and the countries bordering the Persian Gulf began before the Christian era. At the beginning of the 13th century, the Arab geographer Yakut recorded that the people of Lenguja (viz., Unguja, the Swahili name for Zanzibar) had taken refuge from their enemies on Tumbatu, the inhabitants of which were Muslims.

In 1498 Vasco da Gama visited Malindi, and in 1503 Zanzibar Island was attacked and made tributary by the Portuguese. It appears to have remained in that condition for about a quarter of a century. Thereafter the relations between the rulers of Zanzibar and the Portuguese seem to have been those of allies, the people of Zanzibar more than once cooperating with the Portuguese in attacks upon Mombasa. In 1571 the "king" of Zanzibar, in gratitude for Portuguese assistance in expelling certain African invaders, donated the island to his allies, but the donation was never implemented. A Portuguese trading factory and an Augustinian mission were established on the site of the modern city of Zanzibar, and a few Portuguese appear also to have settled as farmers in different parts of the island. The first English ship to visit Zanzibar (1591–92) was the "Edward Bonaventure" captained by Sir James Lancaster.

When the Arabs captured Mombasa in 1698 all these settlements were abandoned and (except for a brief Portuguese reoccupation in 1728) Zanzibar and Pemba came under the domination of the Arab rulers of Oman. For more than a century those rulers left the government of Zanzibar to local hakims (governors). The first sultan to take up residence in Zanzibar was Sayyid Sa'id ibn Sultan (*see* Sa'id ibn Sultan), who after several short visits settled there soon after 1830 and subsequently greatly extended his influence along the East African coast. On Sa'id's death in 1856 his son Majid succeeded to his African dominions, while another son, Thuwaini, succeeded to Oman (*see* also Muscat and Oman).

As the result of an award made in 1860 by Lord Canning, governor general of India, the former African dominions of Sa'id were declared to be independent of Oman. Majid died in 1870 and was succeeded by his brother Barghash (Burgash). Toward the end of the latter's reign his claims to dominion on the mainland were restricted by Britain, France, and Germany to a 10-mi. (16 km.)-wide coastal strip, the administration of which was subsequently shared by Germany and Britain (*see* above, *Tanganyika*). Barghash died in 1888. Both he and Majid had acted largely under the influence of Sir John Kirk (*q.v.*), who was British consular representative at Zanzibar from 1866 to 1887. It was by Kirk's efforts that Barghash consented in 1873 to a treaty for the suppression of the slave trade.

**2. British Protectorate.**—In 1890 what was left of the sultanate was proclaimed a British protectorate, and in 1891 a constitutional government was instituted under British auspices with Sir Lloyd Mathews as first minister. In August 1896, on the death of the ruling sultan, Hamad ibn Thuwaini, the royal palace at Zanzibar was seized by Khalid, a son of Sultan Barghash, who proclaimed himself sultan. The British government disapproved, and, as he refused to submit, the palace was bombarded by British warships. Khalid escaped and took refuge at the German consulate, whence he was conveyed to German East Africa. Hamud ibn Mohammed was then installed as sultan (Aug. 27, 1896). In 1897 the legal status of slavery was finally abolished. In 1913 the control of the protectorate passed from the Foreign Office to the Colonial Office, when the posts of consul general and first minister were merged into that of British resident. At the same time a Protectorate Council was constituted as an advisory body. In 1926 the advisory council was replaced by nominated executive and legislative councils.

Khalifa ibn Harub became sultan in 1911. He was the leading Muslim prince in East Africa, and his moderating influence did much to steady Muslim opinion in that part of Africa at times of political crisis, especially during the two world wars. He died on Oct. 9, 1960, and was succeeded by his eldest son, Sir Abdullah ibn Khalifa.

**3. Progress Toward Independence.**—In November 1960 the British Parliament approved a new constitution for Zanzibar. The first elections to the Legislative Council then established were held in January 1961 and ended in a deadlock. Further elections, held in June, were marked by serious rioting and heavy casualties. As a result of the elections ten seats were won by the Afro-Shirazi Party (ASP), representing mainly the African population; ten by the Zanzibar Nationalist Party (ZNP), representing mainly the Zanzibari Arabs; and three by the Zanzibar and Pemba People's Party (ZPPP), an offshoot of the ZNP. The ZNP and ZPPP combined to form a government with Mohammed Shamte Hamadi as chief minister.

A constitutional conference held in London in 1962 was unable to fix a date for the introduction of internal self-government or for independence because of failure to agree on franchise qualifications, the number of elected seats in the legislature, and the timing of the elections. However, an independent commission subsequently delimited new constituencies and recommended an increase in the numbers of the Legislative Council, which the council accepted, also agreeing to the introduction of universal adult suffrage. Internal self-government was established in June 1963, and elections held the following month resulted in a victory for the ZNP-ZPPP coalition, which won 18 seats, the ASP winning the remaining 13. Final arrangements for independence were made at a conference in London in September. In October it was agreed that the Kenya coastal strip—a territory that extended 10 mi. inland along the Kenya coast from the Tanganyika frontier to Kipini and that had long been administered by Kenya although nominally under the sovereignty of the sultans of Zanzibar—would become an integral part of Kenya on that country's attainment of independence.

On Dec. 10, 1963, Zanzibar achieved independence as a member of the Commonwealth. In January 1964 the Zanzibar government was overthrown by an internal revolution, Sayyid Jamshid ibn Abdullah (who had succeeded to the sultanate in July 1963 on his father's death) was deposed, and a republic was proclaimed.

Although the revolution was carried out by only about 600 armed men under the leadership of the Communist-trained "Field Marshal" John Okello, it won considerable support from the African population; this was demonstrated when Sheikh Abeid Amani Karume, leader of the Afro-Shirazi Party, was installed as president of the "People's Republic of Zanzibar and Pemba." Sheikh Abdulla Kassim Hanga was appointed prime minister, and Abdul Rahman Mohammed ("Babu"), leader of the new left-wing Umma ("The Masses") Party (formed by defectors from the ZNP), became minister for defense and external affairs. Pending the establishment of a new constitution, the cabinet and all government departments were placed under the control of a Revolutionary Council of 30 members, which was also vested with temporary legislative powers. Zanzibar was proclaimed a one-party state.

The revolution was marked by acts of violence against Arabs and Asians; members of these communities later left Zanzibar in considerable numbers. Measures taken by the new government included the nationalization of all land, with further powers to confiscate any immovable property without compensation except in cases of undue hardship. (For later history see *Tanzania* below.)

### C. Tanzania

By an act of union signed by their presidents, the Republic of Tanganyika and the People's Republic of Zanzibar became one state on April 27, 1964, at first called the Republic of Tanganyika and Zanzibar, renamed the United Republic of Tanzania on Oct. 29. Nyerere became president and Karume first vice-president. The cabinet included both Zanzibari and Tanganyikan ministers. The two countries, however, retained many of their individual characteristics, and Zanzibar did not take part in the first post-independence general elections, held in September 1965 on the basis of a new one-party constitution. Instead the members of the Revolutionary Council became members of the Tanzania National Assembly. Meanwhile in Tanganyika, to ensure a democratically elected government, voters in each constituency were able to choose between two TANU candidates. The efficacy of this method was evident when only six candidates were returned unopposed and several former ministers lost their seats. Nyerere was unanimously reelected president.

President Nyerere announced a five-year economic and social development plan in May 1964. In the economic field his aim was to make Tanzania less dependent upon foreign imports, and to do this numerous processing industries were developed, including seven textile mills, an oil refinery, and four factories for processing sisal. To help in these plans, loans were accepted from several countries, among them China, the U.S.S.R., the German Federal Republic, the German Democratic Republic, and Britain. This led to accusations from Western sources that Tanzania was becoming too closely associated with the Eastern powers, a view which was strengthened, though not justified, when Tanzania broke off diplomatic relations with Britain in December 1965 on Rhodesia's unilateral declaration of independence (*see* Rhodesia). Nyerere denied having pro-Communist sympathies and maintained that his country's role was one of nonalignment.

In February 1967 Nyerere announced the nationalization of all commercial banks, insurance companies, most of the flour milling industry, and the major wholesale trading companies. The government also took a majority share in seven other companies. All were promised full and fair compensation and employees were urged to stay on as civil servants.

## IV. ADMINISTRATION AND SOCIAL CONDITIONS

**1. Constitution and Government.**—The United Republic of Tanzania came into being as the result of an agreement between the presidents of Tanganyika and Zanzibar, which was later ratified by the legislatures of the two countries. Under the terms of the agreement a Constituent Assembly was to be summoned not later than April 26, 1965, until which time the united republic would adopt the constitution of Tanganyika modified to provide for a local legislature and executive in Zanzibar. Tanganyika at once ceased to have a separate government, but Zanzibar retained its Revolutionary Council and its own government. The meeting of the Constituent Assembly was delayed a further year pending the implementation of an interim constitution, which was approved on July 5, 1965. The summoning of the Constituent Assembly being indefinitely postponed, the interim constitution remained in force. It provided for a one-party state and envisaged the ultimate merger of the Tanganyikan TANU and Zanzibari ASP parties.

Under the constitution the president is the chief executive officer, holding office for five years. He is nominated by TANU and ASP acting together, and his nomination must be ratified by a plebiscite of the whole electorate of Tanganyika and Zanzibar at the time of elections to the National Assembly, though by a separate vote. Such a plebiscite took place in September 1965. The president is empowered to appoint two vice-presidents, who, together with a number of ministers, comprise the cabinet; this is presided over by the president himself. The assent of the president is required before any bill passed by the National Assembly becomes law. If he withholds his assent and the bill is again passed by the assembly with a two-thirds majority, he must give his assent within 21 days or dissolve the assembly. The dissolution of the assembly also involves a new election to the presidency. The assembly consists of a maximum of 204 members, of whom 55 may represent Zanzibar; the president may nominate ten members. Under the terms of the interim constitution, voters in each constituency may choose between two candidates selected by the National Executive Committee of the party; these are selected from among those party members who have submitted themselves for consideration with the support of 25 people from their constituency. The Tanganyika members of the National Assembly were elected in this way in September 1965. No elections to the assembly were held in Zanzibar, and the Zanzibar seats were held by the members of the Revolutionary Council.

By the beginning of 1967 the union between the two republics was far from complete. The original act of union provided for a local legislature and executive for Zanzibar dealing with internal affairs and having limited powers. In fact, the Revolutionary Council continued to deal with foreign governments and with many other aspects of government which might seem to fall pre-eminently within the scope of the union government. On May 11, 1965, the Revolutionary Council approved a new constitution for Zanzibar making the ASP the supreme authority and declaring all other parties illegal. A central committee of the ASP was set up, headed by the president of the party, and other committees were appointed to control education, finance, security, and other aspects of administration. The ministers were said to serve the party rather than the government, but the Revolutionary Council continued to exercise final power and to legislate by decree.

*Local Government.*—Tanganyika is divided into 17 regions under the direction of regional commissioners, political officers similar to junior ministers who sit in the National Assembly. This arrangement assists in the efficient operation of the National Development Corporation, established on Jan. 1, 1965, as the regional commissioners act as an interested link between the Ministry of Economic Affairs and Development on the one hand and the regional and area committee directly concerned with local developments on the other. Local government is concerned with such matters as primary education, agriculture, marketing, and health.

*Common Services.*—Tanzania is a member of the East African Common Services Organization, an interterritorial body, successor to the East Africa High Commission, administering certain common services including railways and harbour services, postal services, telecommunications, and customs, although each country is autonomous in fixing its customs duties. Under the terms of the Kampala Agreement signed by the three territories (Tanzania, Uganda, and Kenya) in April 1964 an attempt was made to eliminate the former imbalance of trade and to secure a more equitable distribution of industrial development.

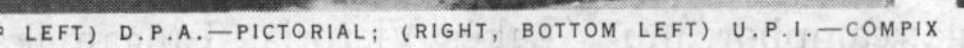

(TOP LEFT) D.P.A.—PICTORIAL; (RIGHT, BOTTOM LEFT) U.P.I.—COMPIX

VIEWS OF THE CITY OF ZANZIBAR: (TOP LEFT) PALACE OF THE FORMER SULTANS OVERLOOKS THE HARBOUR. (ABOVE RIGHT) NARROW THOROUGHFARE LINED WITH WHITEWASHED HOUSES. BARRED LOWER WINDOWS PROTECTED THE INHABITANTS FROM PIRATES PARADING THE STREETS AS LATE AS THE MID-19TH CENTURY. (ABOVE LEFT) A TOWER OF THE OLD ARAB FORT ON THE WATERFRONT, NOW USED AS A WOMEN'S CLUB

**2. Living Conditions.**—In the later 1960s the population was growing at the rate of approximately 2% yearly and over 40% of the population was under the age of 15. Almost 5,500,000 people were of working age and (in 1963) 366,000 were in paid employment, the rest being mainly engaged in cultivating tribal land. The number of paid employees fell between 1961 and 1963 owing, in part, to the introduction of minimum wage legislation in 1962. The average annual per capita income in 1963 was £24 ($67), near the average for East Africa; the cost of living, even in Dar es Salaam, remained fairly constant between 1960 and 1966. In 1964 trade unions in Tanganyika were dissolved by law and replaced by one National Union of Tanganyika Workers (NUTA). The general and deputy secretary of the union were appointed by the president, and the government planned, through the union, to link annual wage increases with productivity. In Zanzibar the Federation of Revolutionary Trade Unions was abolished in 1965 and its affairs were taken over by a special labour committee of the ASP. Farms and business concerns owned by non-Africans were nationalized, and an attempt was being made to introduce a national insurance scheme on the island.

**3. Health and Welfare.**—In the 1960s the government, missions, and local authorities maintained more than 800 maternity and child-health clinics in Tanganyika, together with about 250 hospitals with 15,000 beds, about 20 major leprosariums, and more than 1,000 outpatient dispensaries. The commonest diseases included malaria, sleeping sickness, smallpox, and leprosy. In Zanzibar medical services were nationalized and free.

**4. Justice.**—There is a High Court for the united republic with final jurisdiction in both criminal and civil cases, composed of a chief justice appointed by the president and of lesser judges appointed by the president after consultation with the chief justice. Subordinate courts have limited jurisdiction in each district. In November 1964 the Ministry of Justice was dissolved and its functions were transferred to the second vice-president. In Zanzibar a decree of Oct. 28, 1966, set up a secret court to try political offenders; it was suspended in December. The court would not have been bound by normal rules of criminal procedure.

**5. Education.**—Tanzania's five-year development plan (1964–69) included considerable provision for education, in the hope of making good the serious shortage of skilled and professional workers. About half the children of Tanganyika (500,000) attend the four-year course in the lower primary schools. Only one-sixth go on to the upper primary schools, and no more than 4% (20,000) enter the secondary schools or take craft courses. Trade courses are provided in residential government schools at Moshi and Ifunda and in a number of other voluntary centres. A technical college in Dar es Salaam provides advanced trade school courses and three-year courses for technicians. The University College of Dar es Salaam, part of the federal University of East Africa (founded 1963), has faculties of arts, science, law, and social sciences. In 1964–65 some 450 students from Tanzania were attending courses at the university, with many more in universities overseas. Considerable attention is paid to adult education, with literacy campaigns and courses for women in domestic economy and hygiene; more than 1,500 students attend evening classes at the technical college in Dar es Salaam. Several companies, including the Williamson Diamond Mines and the East African Railways and Harbours Board, run their own training projects. In the primary schools Swahili is the language of instruction, but English is introduced in the third year and becomes the normal teaching medium in middle schools. There are plans for expansion at all levels of education, but particularly in teacher training, by 1970. More than one-tenth of government expenditure, £4,000,000 ($11,200,000), is spent annually on education.

In Zanzibar schools have been nationalized and education is free, although very limited. Primary school places, only 3,000 in 1964, were increased to 7,500 in 1966, and agriculture and handicrafts were introduced into the curriculum. Secondary education is available only on a very limited scale, and the proportion of secondary to primary places is to remain static for the time being.

**6. Defense.**—A mutiny occurred in the Tanganyika army in January 1964; as a result, the two battalions of the Tanganyika Rifles were disbanded. Three completely new battalions, the Tanzanian People's Defense Force, were then raised, and it was planned that they should be organized on nontraditional lines.

About half the personnel would consist of volunteers from the National Youth Service combining two years' military duty with public works and village development projects. By a presidential decree of Oct. 5, 1964, the People's Liberation Army of Zanzibar was incorporated into the armed forces of the union republic as a further battalion of the Tanzanian People's Defense Force; it continued to act with a considerable degree of independence, however, and was trained by Chinese instructors. (K. I.)

## V. THE ECONOMY

### A. Tanganyika

Agriculture dominates the economy, accounting for about 80% of the exports by value. There is an important livestock industry, and mining production is considerable.

**1. Agriculture and Forestry.**—Sisal, introduced in 1892, is the most important product. By 1914 production reached 20,000 tons of fibre annually and by the mid-1960s was approaching 250,000 tons. Pyrethrum, tobacco, and wheat are grown in the upland areas; grains (maize [corn], millet, sorghum, rice), cotton, cocoa, pulses, peanuts, and oilseeds in the higher rainfall areas of the plains; and coconuts, cassava, cashew nuts, and citrus fruits in the coastal belt. The principal subsistence crops are rice, maize, cassava, sorghum, bananas, and pulses. Irrigation projects have been developed in central Tanganyika and in the Rufiji and Mbarali river basins. Sugar production near Moshi and in the Kilombero Valley was expanding; it reached 50,000 tons in the mid-1960s. In the drier plains pastoral tribes herd cattle, sheep, and goats, but tsetse infestation hinders the livestock industry. Meat production is increasing, however, and government cattle ranches have been developed. Areas of true forest are limited, but valuable timbers include muninga, camphor, muvule, and African mahoganies and blackwood. The cooperative movement is widespread, and the value of produce handled is about 25% of the total value of exports.

**2. Mining.**—Diamonds account for about two-thirds by value of Tanganyika's mineral output. Diamondiferous deposits around Shinyanga, south of Lake Victoria, were discovered in 1940 by J. T. Williamson, and by the mid-1960s the mine at Mwadui (in which the government acquired a half share) was producing more than 600,000 k. annually. Gold (about £1,200,000 annually), salt, silver, mica, and tin are among mining products. Immense deposits of iron ore and coal exist in the southwest near Lake Nyasa but are difficult of access. At least 190,000,000 tons of coal are estimated as minable. Production in the mid-1960s reached about 3,000 tons.

**3. Power and Industries.**—Electric power generation and supply are carried out by a company with an exclusive franchise. Major hydroelectric installations include one at Pangani Falls (17.5 megawatts) and the Hale Station on the Pangani River (21.5 Mw.). The latter, completed in 1964, has a transmission line to serve Dar es Salaam with virtually all its needs, and 33-kw. lines run east from Hale to Tanga and other coastal sites and west to Korogwe and Lushoto. Other main thermal power stations are at Tanga, Dar es Salaam, Arusha, Moshi, and Mwanza.

Manufacturing industries are mostly connected with agricultural and forest products (food, flour, and sisal processing, oil, and sawmilling) but include the production of textiles, clothing, cans, paint, and soap for local consumption, as well as soft drinks, beer, cigarettes, aluminum ware, bricks and tiles, coir and sisal matting, leather, cement, industrial gases, and shoes. By the 1960s manufacturing contributed about 4% of the gross domestic product.

**4. Trade.**—About 50% of Tanganyika's gross domestic product derives from agriculture, and the economy is therefore sensitive to changes in the prices of export products, notably sisal. Total exports (including those to Kenya and Uganda and re-exports) reached £65,000,000 ($182,000,000) in 1963, about one-quarter being taken by the U.K. and about one-fifth by other Commonwealth countries. Exports in order of value were sisal, cotton, coffee, diamonds, oilseeds, cashew nuts, meat and meat extracts, hides and skins, tea, gold, and pyrethrum. Imports (mainly textiles, vehicles and transport equipment, petroleum fuels, iron and steel, machinery, chemicals, and foodstuffs) included substantial quantities of local produce from Kenya and Uganda and totaled about £40,000,000 ($112,000,000) annually, more than one-third coming from the U.K.

**5. Finance.**—Most of Tanganyika's recurrent revenue is derived from income and personal taxes, local government rates, company taxes, customs and excise duties, and income from government properties. Among the main items of expenditure are education, communications, power, public works, police, agriculture, health, and labour. The currency is based on the East African shilling, which is legal tender for any amount and is subdivided into 100 cents. Tanzan Shs. 20 = Tanzan £1, the latter being at par with the U.K. pound sterling (= $2.80 U.S.). The Directorate of Development and Planning was set up to implement Tanzania's five-year development plan announced in 1964.

In February 1967 nationalization of foreign banks, insurance firms, leading trading companies, and sisal estates followed a declared aim of bringing principal means of production under government control.

**6. Transport and Communications.**—The railways form part of the East African Railways and Harbours System. There are three main lines, all of metre gauge. Tanganyika has about 21,500 mi. (34,500 km.) of roads, 3,900 mi. (6,200 km.) of which were classed as all-weather (1962). Main roads are from Dar es Salaam and Tanga inland and the north–south link from Nairobi in Kenya.

The East African Railways and Harbours Administration operates passenger and freight road services, and there are widespread local bus and truck services. More than 20 shipping lines operate services to Tanganyika, some calling at Tanga and Mtwara, as well as at Dar es Salaam. There are passenger and cargo services on Lakes Victoria, Tanganyika, and Nyasa. East African Airways Corporation operates internal scheduled flights and services to the U.K., South Africa, India, and Pakistan; other airlines maintain links with adjoining territories. There is the usual range of postal services but no house-to-house delivery by postmen, the box or private bag system being used. Scheduled air services are widely used for mail transport. There were 70 telephone exchanges in Tanganyika in 1966, 7 of which were fully automatic. Radio broadcasting is controlled by a corporation directed by a government-nominated board and emanates from Dar es Salaam, with a national program in Swahili and a second program in English and Asian languages. (J. P. Mt.; J. M. Ke.)

### B. Zanzibar

Prior to the development of East African mainland ports Zanzibar was the trade focus of this region and enjoyed an important entrepôt trade. The economy now depends on agriculture and fishing.

**1. Agriculture and Forestry.**—Considerable areas of fertile soil and a favourable climate make possible the production of a variety of tropical crops under plantation and peasant conditions. Following the revolution of 1964, land previously held by Arabs, Indians, and Africans was nationalized. Immigrant Africans still play an important part in plantation work.

The Zanzibari clove industry owes its development to Sa'id ibn Sultan. About 80,000 ac. are planted to cloves, and annual production averages about 11,000 tons (though there are great seasonal variations of crop), more than 75% from Pemba. The Clove Growers' Association was nationalized in October 1964.

Coconuts occupy about 160,000 ac., mostly on the island of Zanzibar. Copra, coconut oil, coir fibre, and rope are all important products of the industry, which also produces food, thatching, and basket materials. Other less important export crops are chilies, fresh fruits, tobacco, and kapok. The government has actively encouraged diversification of agriculture in order to reduce its dependence on cloves, and experiment and trial over many years have been conducted in the production of chilies, limes (for oil and juice), cacao, derris, and other crops.

Among local food crops, rice is the main cereal; cassava and sweet potatoes are widely grown; pulses and vegetables are minor crops. Tropical fruits grow exceptionally well (citrus, pineapple, mango, pawpaw).

The livestock industry is relatively small and is actively encouraged. Cattle are of the African humped zebu type, except for small herds of European-grade cattle kept in the town dairies.

Three small natural forests occur, and mangrove swamps contain species of economic importance. These are reserved and exploitation and replanting controlled. Most products are used locally, though there are exports of mangrove bark (for tannin) and timber from Jozani Forest in Zanzibar.

**2. Fisheries.**—Fish is an important part of the diet, and local fisheries employ about one-tenth of the population. Basket traps, seine, gill, and cast nets, and hand lines are used from local boats and canoes in the shallow waters round the islands. An East African Marine Fisheries Research unit is based in Zanzibar, and the fishing industry is actively encouraged to adopt modern equipment.

**3. Power and Industries.**—No exploitable mineral resources occur. A fine building lime is made by burning coral limestone, but this is strictly limited by local fuel supplies. Wood is the principal domestic fuel; a diesel plant supplies electricity to Zanzibar City. Small secondary industries have developed for processing agricultural products: a clove-oil distillery, coir extraction plants, and coconut oil and soap factories. Local handicrafts include mat and basket weaving, coir ropemaking, pottery making, and canoe and boat building. A few Indian silversmiths work in Zanzibar City.

**4. Trade.**—Internal trade is largely in the hands of Indian merchants and shopkeepers. Imports (more than half of which came from the U.K. and the Commonwealth) in the mid-1960s were valued at about £5,000,000, principally foodstuffs and textiles; domestic exports (chiefly to India and Indonesia) were £3,500,000, of which cloves and clove products made up more than 70%.

**5. Finance.**—The East African shilling (*see* above) replaced the Indian rupee as standard currency in 1936. Government revenue in the early 1960s was about £3,000,000 and expenditure was similar. Principal items of taxation are import duties, export duties on cloves and coconut products, and income tax. No poll or hut taxes exist.

**6. Transport and Communications.**—There is no railway. Of the 387 mi. (623 km.) of roads in Zanzibar, about 280 mi. (450 km.) were bitumen surfaced in the 1960s. Pemba had about 225 mi. (365 km.), of which 80 mi. (130 km.) were bitumenized. Frequent services link Zanzibar airport (one all-weather runway) with East African airports. There is also an all-weather runway at Pemba airport, near Chake Chake. Zanzibar port is served by British, other European, and U.S. shipping companies, and the government maintains a service with Pemba and the mainland. There are also passenger and cargo coasting vessels linking Zanzibar and the ports of Kenya and Tanganyika.

Normal postal services are maintained and savings-bank facilities provided. There is continuous service by direct cable, radio, and radiotelephone to East and southern Africa, Aden, Seychelles, and London. Internal telephone systems operate in both islands. The broadcasting station is at Marahubi Mlangoni from where Cable and Wireless, Ltd., operates the government's medium-wave and its own short-wave transmission services.

*See* also references under "Tanzania" in the Index.

(F. B. Wi.; J. M. Ke.)

Bibliography.—R. Coupland, *East Africa and Its Invaders from the Earliest Times to the Death of Seyyid Said in 1856* (1938); R. Oliver and G. Mathew (eds.), *History of East Africa,* vol. i (1963); V. Harlow, E. M. Chilver and A. Smith (eds.) *History of East Africa,* vol. ii (1965); K. Ingham, *A History of East Afrca* (1962); C. Leubuscher, *Tanganyika Territory: a Study of Economic Policy Under Mandate* (1944); J. C. Taylor, *The Political Development of Tanganyika* (1963); Department of Lands and Surveys, *Atlas of Tanganyika* (1956); Ministry of Mines and Commerce, *Summary of the Geology of Tanganyika* (1956); E. W. Russell (ed.), *The Natural Resources of East Africa* (1962); International Bank for Reconstruction and Development, *The Economic Development of Tanganyika* (1961); J. Listowel, *The Making of Tanganyika* (1965); A. M. O'Connor, *An Economic Geography of East Africa* (1966). For a full bibliography, *see* J. P. Moffett (ed.), *Handbook of Tanganyika,* 2nd ed. (1958).

W. H. Ingrams, *Zanzibar: Its History and Its People* (1931); Sir John Gray, *History of Zanzibar, from the Middle Ages to 1856* (1962); G. M. Stockley, *Report on the Geology of the Zanzibar Protectorate* (1928); R. O. Williams, *The Useful and Ornamental Plants in Zanzibar and Pemba* (1949); *A Guide to Zanzibar* (Zanzibar government, rev. ed.; 1961); M. F. Lofchie, *Zanzibar: Background to Revolution* (1965); P. Selwyn and T. Y. Watson, *Report on the Economic Development of the Zanzibar Protectorate* (1962); East African Statistical Department, *The Gross Domestic Product of Zanzibar 1957–1961* (1963). Current history and statistics of Tanzania are summarized annually in *Britannica Book of the Year.*

**T'AO CH'IEN** (T'ao Yuan-ming) (*c.* 365–427), Chinese poet, regarded by modern critics as the most important of his period, was born into a gentry family that had fallen on hard times. When he was about 20, he took a minor official post and for the next ten years was in the service of one or another of the ambitious generals who were threatening the moribund Chin dynasty. In 405, after a brief term as magistrate of P'engts'e, he retired from public life to make a precarious living as a farmer. On more than one occasion crop failure brought him and his family to the verge of starvation. On leaving his last post, he had written, "My instinct is all for freedom and will not brook discipline or restraint. Hunger and cold may be sharp, but this going against myself really sickens me. Whenever I have been involved in official life I was mortgaging myself to my mouth and belly." He had no more dealings with officialdom but stuck to the life of poverty and hardship, which he preferred to the rigours of respectability. At the time of his death he was known chiefly as a recluse and an eccentric.

T'ao Ch'ien's poetry was not much appreciated before the 8th century. The taste of his contemporaries was for an elaborate and artificial style, and his poetry is simple and straightforward, with a minimum of artifice. It deals with country pursuits and his essentially Taoist philosophy of life and death.

*T'ao the Hermit: Sixty Poems* was translated and annotated with an introduction by William Acker (1952); *Poems* was translated by Lily Pao-hu Chang and Marjorie Sinclair (1953). *See* also Chinese Literature: *The Six Dynasties and the Sui Period.*

*See* J. R. Hightower, "The *fu* of T'ao Ch'ien," *Harvard Journal of Asiatic Studies,* 17:169–230 (June 1954). (J. R. Hr.)

**TAOISM** has been an integral part of Chinese life and thought for 2,000 years. Like Confucianism (*q.v.*), it has influenced every aspect of Chinese culture, whether philosophy, religion, art, literature, or government. Throughout Chinese history, it has paralleled Confucianism, reinforcing, supplementing, and criticizing it, and it helped shape the development and transformation of Buddhism in China. In a true sense every Chinese is a Taoist. While Confucianism emphasizes social order and an active life, Taoism concentrates on individual life and tranquillity. Though this suggests that Taoism plays a secondary role, the fact is that in its advocacy of individuality, spiritual freedom, naturalness, simplicity, religious mysticism, *laissez faire* in government, and the transcendental ideal in art, it is as important as Confucianism in Chinese tradition.

The name "Taoist School" was not mentioned until the 1st century B.C., but the movement must have been developing for centuries before that. Tradition says that ancient philosophical schools emerged from government offices, and Taoism in particular from that of the historian. This theory may have been influenced by the fact that Lao-tzu, traditionally considered to be the founder of Taoism, was a curator of historical documents. The deeper meaning of the theory, however, is that Taoism arose in response to actual historical situations. In the 6th century B.C. feudalism in China was beginning to crumble. In the transition to a new age, society was beset with political disorder, economic chaos, and moral decay. For several centuries each of the "100 schools" of philosophy offered its own *tao* (literally, "way") as a solution. The *tao* offered by Lao-tzu and his followers was so unusual and so challenging that their movement alone came to be known as the Taoist School, *Tao-chia.*

Taoism is not a system of purely quiet contemplation or idle speculation. It is a philosophy offering a practical way of life. Later its teachings came to be utilized in the popular religion called *Tao-chiao.* In the Chinese tradition the two have been separate, but in the West they have often been confused under the name Taoism.

## PHILOSOPHICAL TAOISM

The origin of Taoism as a philosophy is obscure. The term *tao* can be traced to the earliest Chinese classics, and it is a basic term in all ancient Chinese philosophical schools, including Confucianism. But it was in Lao-tzu, Yang Chu, Chuang-tzu, the *Huai-nan-tzu,* the Neo-Taoists, and the *Lieh-tzu* that the Taoist philosophy developed.

**Lao-tzu.**—The fundamental doctrines of early Taoism are embodied in the *Lao-tzu,* also called the *Tao-te-ching.* Whether or not the book is an anthology of the 4th century B.C. (the point is disputed), its basic ideas and passages probably go back to Lao-tzu (*q.v.*), two centuries earlier. As the second title indicates, it is a classic on Tao and *te,* the "Way" and its "virtue." Previously the connotation of Tao had been social and moral; in the *Lao-tzu* it connotes for the first time the metaphysical. Tao "exists before heaven and earth." It is the "mother" and "ancestor" of all things. It is their "storehouse." It is at once their principle of being and their substance. "All things depend on it for life." It is One, everlasting, and unchangeable; it "operates everywhere and is free from danger." It is "invisible," "inaudible," "vague and elusive," but there is in it the "form" and the "essence." It is so absolute that it cannot be described; it "has no name." Furthermore, it is "nonbeing." The last idea, which appears to be nihilistic, simply means that Tao is prior to and above all things.

In its operation Tao is characterized by *wu-wei* (literally "no action"), which really means taking no unnatural action. It means spontaneity, noninterference, letting things take their own course. Tao "takes no action" but "supports all things in their natural state," and in this way "all things will transform spontaneously." As things arise, "Tao does not turn away from them." "It benefits all things but does not compete with them." "Tao invariably takes no action, and yet there is nothing left undone."

When man follows this natural way, he will abide with the one, the eternal, and the whole and will achieve a life of peace, harmony, and enlightenment. In dealing with things, he will "produce them but not take possession of them." In government he will adopt the policy of *laissez faire,* for "the best rulers are those whose existence is merely known by the people. . . . They complete their work. Nevertheless their people say that they simply follow Nature." Thus the natural way stands in direct opposition to all artificial regulation, organization, and ceremonies. This is the reason why the *Lao-tzu* vigorously attacks all formalities and artificialities. For the same reason it condemns war, taxation, punishment, superficial knowledge, and conventional morality.

The natural way is compared with the ways of water, the female, and the infant; that is, the ways of the weak. Along with weakness, the *Lao-tzu* also advocates humility, contentment, ignorance, submission, knowing where to stop, doing away with desires, accepting disgrace, and the like. This seemingly negative morality is deceptive. After all, "the greatest skill seems to be clumsy, and the greatest eloquence seems to stutter." "There is nothing softer and weaker than water, and yet there is nothing better for attacking hard and strong things."

While the weak seems to be glorified, the strongest stress really is on simplicity. A simple life is one of plainness in which profit is discarded, cleverness abandoned, selfishness eliminated, and desires reduced. It is the life of "perfection which seems to be incomplete" and of "fullness which seems to be empty." It is the life which is "as bright as light but does not dazzle." In short, it is the life of "superior virtue." This life requires all the important moral qualities taught in almost all ethical systems. To Lao-tzu, deep love, frugality, and not daring to be ahead of the world are "three treasures," and because of them one becomes courageous, generous, and a leader of the world. He urges us to love the earth in our dwelling, love what is profound in our hearts, love humanity in our associations, love faithfulness in our words, love order in government, love competence in handling affairs, and love timeliness in our activities. He wants us to maintain steadfast quietude and to be tranquil, enlightened, all-embracing, impartial, one with Nature, and in accord with Tao. He teaches us to "benefit all things," to "treat those who are good with goodness" and "also to treat those who are not good with goodness," and to "repay hatred with virtue." He admonishes us not to have ulterior motives, to show or justify ourselves, or to boast, to be proud, to hoard things, or to be extravagant. He advises us to know the subtle and the eternal, but when we do not know anything, to know that we do not know. Virtually all the ingredients of a virtuous life, including the Golden Rule, are included.

In short, the life of superior virtue is one of goodness, enlightenment, peace, and long life.

**Yang Chu.**—The note of life preservation is particularly strong in Yang Chu (*q.v.*), who may or may not have been an early Taoist. According to surviving isolated passages of his writings, he would not enter an endangered city, would not join an army, and would not care to exchange a single hair for the profits of the entire world. His main purpose in life was to "preserve life and keep the essence of his being intact." Mencius (*q.v.*) attacked him as an "egoist who denied the special relationship with the ruler." Whether Yang's doctrine actually degenerated to an irresponsible egoism or whether Mencius distorted it is a moot point. Yang Chu's teachings are certainly twisted in the "Yang Chu" chapter of the *Lieh-tzu* (see *Later Developments,* below), where his doctrine of self-preservation is coupled with pessimism on the one hand and hedonism on the other.

**Chuang-tzu.**—All the basic ideas in Lao-tzu are elaborated in the teachings of Chuang-tzu (*q.v.*). But his system is more than an elaboration; in it Taoism was extended to new dimensions and to a higher degree. To him, existence is not only spontaneity but the state of constant flux and incessant transformation. In Lao-tzu, the major notes are constancy and eternity; change is a minor one. In Chuang-tzu, change is the main theme. He conceives of the universe as a great current in which one state succeeds another in endless procession. No state can be retained, and time cannot be arrested. Life goes on "like a galloping horse." In these constant changes, things transform themselves by themselves, for this is the nature of things. There is no directing agency in this dynamic drama: "if there is a true director, there is no evidence of him."

In this process of rapid change, everything must follow its own nature. It is the nature of the eagle to fly high in the clouds, the nature of the dove to hop from tree to tree. A cypress will last for a thousand years, a mushroom for only a day. Each should live according to its nature. Similarly a man should be contented with his fate and "should not attempt to replace the way of heaven with the way of man." This is the true meaning of *wu-wei.* Though there is a much stronger element of fatalism in Chuang-tzu than in Lao-tzu, following Nature to him does not mean blind submission but rather a realistic recognition of one's own limits.

In the universe, then, there are these individual and continuous transformations, each in its own natural way. Such a universal process of rising and falling, of life and death, inevitably results in a world of differences and inequality, but all these are superficial, relative, often products of subjective points of view. Life and death cause each other, and neither right nor wrong is absolute. This and that, and possibility and impossibility, Chuang-tzu says, mutually produce each other. In reality, "all things are one," for Tao embraces all of them and combines them into a unity. A man of small knowledge will cut things up, discriminate, and make distinctions; a man of great knowledge will be comprehensive, impartial, and see Tao in all its unity. The ideal man will be a "companion with Nature" and a "friend of both life and death." He makes oneness his eternal abode. He abandons selfishness of all descriptions, be it fame, wealth, bias, or subjectivity. He knows his nature, nourishes it, and adapts it to the universal process of transformation. In this way he can "roam the universe" and be "emancipated." Having attained enlightenment through "the light of Nature," he moves in the realm of "great knowledge" and "profound virtue." He is then spiritually free. As the *Chuang-tzu* itself says of him,

> Alone he associates with heaven and earth and spirit, without abandoning or despising things of the world. He does not quarrel over right or wrong and mingles with conventional society. . . . Above, he roams with the Creator, and below he makes friends with those who transcend

AN ICONOGRAPHICAL REPRESENTATION OF SOME CONCEPTS OF TAO

BY COURTESY OF NELSON GALLERY OF ART, KANSAS CITY, MO.

"Fishing in a Mountain Stream," painting by Hsü Tao-ning, 11th century, ink on silk. Its sweeping view, comprising a number of well-harmonized elements, suggests the Taoist concept of the unity of the universe; the fewness and the smallness of the human figures convey the Taoist idea of man's relative role in the universal order

life and death and beginning and end. In regard to the essential, he is broad and comprehensive, profound and unrestrained. In regard to the fundamental, he may be said to have harmonized all things and penetrated the highest level. However, in his response to change and his understanding of things, his principle is inexhaustible, traceless, dark and obscure, and unfathomable.

In Chuang-tzu, Taoism reached the transcendental and mystical level, but its dynamism and realism became at the same time much stronger. Generally speaking, Chuang-tzu's universe is much more complex than that of Lao-tzu. It involves not only the states of being and nonbeing but also that of neither being nor nonbeing. Lao-tzu's way is directed chiefly to handling human affairs; that of Chuang-tzu aims chiefly at dealing with the universe. Lao-tzu's goal is social and political reform; that of Chuang-tzu is to "travel beyond the mundane world." Every passage of the *Lao-tzu* can be understood in terms of ordinary human experience, but what Chuang-tzu wants is pure experience—that is, identification with the universe. He speaks of "fasting of the mind," in which "the mind is empty to receive all things," and of "sitting down and forgetting everything," in which "the body is abandoned, the intelligence is discarded, one is separated from the body and free from knowledge, and one becomes identical with a great penetration." At the same time, in his emphasis on being true to one's own nature, his philosophy is much more individualistic than that of Lao-tzu. While the notes of mysticism, quietism, and fatalism are stronger, the ultimate goal is preservation of one's original nature and through it absolute spiritual freedom.

From the time of Chuang-tzu till the 2nd century B.C., the Taoist School remained influential. It was the chief rival of both Confucianism and Moism. Followers of Lao-tzu, Yang Chu, and Chuang-tzu probably traveled in slightly different directions, but the main tenets remained prominent and clear. Later they were synthesized in the *Huai-nan-tzu.*

**The *Huai-nan-tzu*.**—The *Huai-nan-tzu* is an anthology of treatises by Liu An (d. 122 B.C.), prince of Huai-nan, and scholars who gathered around him as his retainers. It represents a combination of Taoist teachings, and as such its originality is negligible. In it, however, the concept of Tao becomes more concrete. Using water as its analogy, the writer describes Tao as a concrete reality, all pervasive, the cause of all things, perfectly weak, taking no unnatural action, and yet bringing all things into completion. Furthermore, cosmogony becomes more elaborate and more definite. "There was a time before the time which was before the beginning," and "there was a time before the time which was before nonbeing." "Before heaven and earth took shape, there was only undifferentiated formlessness," which was called "the great beginning." In cosmological evolution, Tao originated from vacuity, and vacuity produced the universe, which in turn produced the material forces. The material forces of heaven and earth combined to form *yin* and *yang,* which in their turn give rise to the myriad things. In its broad outline this cosmogony has remained orthodox doctrine not only among Taoist philosophers but also among the later Confucianists.

In its attempt at synthesis, the *Huai-nan-tzu* combines certain non-Taoist elements, such as the Confucian emphasis on learning as a method of self-cultivation and the Legalist emphasis on law in government. In its discussion of the spirit, it even introduces such ideas as immortality on earth and the techniques of breathing, etc., to achieve it, thus paving the way for the later confusion of Taoist philosophy with Taoist popular religion. In spite of this fact, it maintained Taoism at a time when Confucianism had assumed the dominant role in government and thought. In addition, by approaching metaphysics and cosmology in an essentially rational spirit, it prepared for the emergence of rationalistic Neo-Taoism.

**Later Developments.**—In the 3rd and 4th centuries A.D., Taoism developed in three directions. The first was Neo-Taoism, the most important philosophical development in the history of Taoism, which finds expression in the commentaries on the *Lao-tzu* and the *Book of Changes* by Wang Pi (*q.v.*) and the commentary on the *Chuang-tzu* by Kuo Hsiang (d. 312), who probably appropriated ideas from Hsiang Hsiu (fl. 250). In them, nonbeing is no longer essentially in contrast to being but is the ultimate of all, or pure being (*pen-wu*), the One and the undifferentiated. According to Wang Pi, original nonbeing is beyond distinctions and descriptions. It is the pure being, original substance (*pen-t'i*), and the One in which substance and function are identified. It is always correct because it is in accord with principle. For Lao-tzu's destiny, Wang, anticipating Neo-Confucianism, substituted principle.

In the work of Kuo Hsiang, who carried Chuang-tzu's thought further, Nature (*tzu-jan*), not Tao, is the major concept. Things exist and transform themselves spontaneously, each according to its own principle. Compared with Wang Pi, Kuo Hsiang emphasizes being rather than nonbeing and the many rather than the one. To Wang Pi, principle transcends things; to Kuo Hsiang, it is immanent in them. To neither of them, however, is the sage one who withdraws into a hermit's life; he lives a life of social and political accomplishment, through taking no unnatural action. Significantly, the greatest sage to them was not Lao-tzu but Confucius.

The second movement was that of the "pure conversation," a way of life expressed in elegant, refined, and carefree conversation, devoid of the vulgarity of politics, earthly ambitions, and worldly values. It lasted from the middle of the 2nd century through the 6th, with Juan Chi (210–263), Hsi K'ang (223–262), and Hsiang Hsiu as outstanding representatives.

The third movement was fatalistic naturalism, represented by the *Lieh-tzu*, a product probably of the 3rd century. Its ideas are all original ingredients of Taoism, but the Taoist doctrine of taking no action has degenerated into complete abandonment of effort, spontaneity is confused with resignation, and having no desire is replaced by hedonism—all negative developments. On the positive side, Tao as the self-caused ultimate reality is much more strongly affirmed, and vacuity in the sense of eliminating desires and renouncing egoism is emphasized. In both of these the *Lieh-tzu* goes beyond Lao-tzu. In being indifferent to life and death and in ignoring the distinction of right and wrong, it pushes skepticism to the extreme; and in considering unceasing transformation as going in cycles according to fate, so that life and death, by their very nature, immediately succeed each other, it gives the doctrine of transformation a peculiar form. In these the *Lieh-tzu* goes beyond Chuang-tzu. In teaching that one should do away with the distinction between oneself and others, avoid a subjective state of mind, be vacuous, pure, and tranquil, and be in accord with Nature, it is essentially Taoistic and may well reflect, or even transmit, the teachings of Lieh-tzu, or Lieh Yü-k'ao (*c.* 450–375 B.C.), whose work had disappeared centuries before.

**Influence.**—As a philosophy Taoism declined after the 4th century, by which time Taoism and Buddhism had begun mutually to influence each other. In the 3rd and 4th centuries, Buddhist thinkers practised "matching the concepts" of Buddhism and Taoism, as a result of which Buddhists interpreted their philosophy in Taoist terminology while Taoism assimilated Buddhist ideas. Although Taoism eventually became a handmaid of Buddhism, it exercised far greater influence on Buddhist philosophy than vice versa. The major Taoist concepts of being and nonbeing were carried over to Buddhism. Some early Buddhist schools even called themselves "School of Original Nonbeing," "School of Nonbeing of Mind," etc. Like the Neo-Taoists, the Buddhists regarded ultimate reality as transcending all being, names, and forms, and as empty and quiet in Nature.

The greatest influence on Buddhism may be seen in the Chinese development of the Buddhist Meditation School (Ch'an or Zen; *see* ZEN). The Taoist tenets that Tao is everywhere, is indescribable, and can be discovered through enlightenment had a direct bearing on the development of Zen doctrines that the Buddha mind is everywhere, is indescribable by words and inconceivable in thought, and can be realized through enlightenment. The standard ways of Zen enlightenment are "absence of thought," "forgetting one's feelings," and "letting the mind take its own course," literal borrowings from Taoism, especially from Chuang-tzu. Many early Buddhist thinkers were experts in Taoist philosophy, and throughout history many Zen masters have been personal friends of Taoists.

Just as Taoism contributed to the development of Zen in the 7th and 8th centuries, so it contributed to the development of Neo-Confucianism in the 11th (*see* CHINESE PHILOSOPHY), but because of their "way of quietness and nonactivity," the Neo-Confucianists severely attacked the Taoists, and, as a result, Taoism ceased to be a vital philosophical system in the last millennium. As a way of life, however, it has never lost its hold on Chinese culture and society. Its spirit of harmony, simplicity, and peace has been eloquently expressed in Chinese landscape painting, landscape gardening, poetry, tea drinking, etc., and its spirit of naturalism, individualism, and freedom has strongly molded Chinese life. *See* also CHINESE PHILOSOPHY.

## RELIGIOUS TAOISM

**The Way of the Yellow Emperor.**—While the philosophy of Taoism was unfolding, a religious current, in progress from time immemorial, was developed by priest-magicians who offered divination and magic as means to inward power, restored youth, superhuman ability, and, most importantly, immortality on earth. Somehow this movement came to be known in the 1st century B.C. as the Way of the Yellow Emperor (Huang-ti) and Lao-tzu, and enjoyed an extensive following. In A.D. 143 Chang Ling (*q.v.*), also called Chang Tao Ling, a popular religious leader famous for healing the sick, formally organized the movement and required his many followers to donate five piculs (bushels) of rice (hence the name the Way of Five Piculs of Rice). His followers called him Heavenly Teacher, a title his direct descendants retained until the 1940s.

From the very beginning the Yellow Emperor–Lao-tzu movement was a conglomeration of sorcery, the arts of priest-magicians, and the philosophy of the Yin-Yang School, according to which all things are products of the cosmic negative and positive forces. Gradually it assimilated certain elements of Taoist philosophy. Wei Po-yang (fl. 147–167) combined all these in a coherent system and thus laid the philosophical foundation of the Taoist religion. In his *Ts'an-t'ung-ch'i* ("The Three Ways Unified and Harmonized"), he attempted to synthesize all these ideas for the sake of prolonging life through the practice of alchemy, whereby, it was believed, the two cosmic forces could be harmonized and the vital force (*ch'i*) of the universe concentrated in the human body. His book became the basis of the *Lung-hu* ("Dragon and Tiger") *Scripture* of unknown date, the *Huang-t'ing* ("Internal and External") *Scripture* (3rd century), and the *Yin-fu* ("Secret Accord") *Scripture* (8th century). Later, Ko Hung (253–333?), also called Pao-p'u-tzu, synthesized Taoist philosophy and Confucian ethics. His chief concern, however, was alchemy to prolong life, and he strongly defended the belief in immortals (*hsien*).

These two philosophers provided religious Taoism with a firm theoretical foundation and an elaborate system of practice. It was K'ou Ch'ien-chih (d. 432) who made it an organized religion, by regulating the ceremonies, fixing the names of deities, and formulating theology. His influence led to its being made a state cult in A.D. 440. State patronage reached its height in the T'ang dynasty (618–906), since when religious Taoism has existed primarily as a religion of the illiterate masses.

**Features.**—As a religion, Taoism is distinguished by several prominent features, outlined below.

*Multiplicity of Gods.*—Taoism has a god for almost everything—stars, animate and inanimate things, the whole and parts of the body, ancestors, famous historical beings, ideals, etc. Among these are the Jade Emperor, the Three Pure Ones (Heavenly Honoured Ones Without Form, With Form, and Brahma Form), the Dipper Star, the Great Unit, Gods of Literature, Wealth, Medicine, Kitchen, and Goddess of Mercy (from Buddhism). It worships numerous immortals, has 10 "Heavenly Grottoes," 36 subsidiary "Heavenly Grottoes," and 72 "Blessed Places," where immortals rule and await people to seek the "way." Besides, there are imitations of many Buddhist heavens and hells.

*Search for Blessings and Longevity.*—Popular Taoism is strongly characterized by piety and devotion, but its chief objectives are earthly blessings—happiness, health, wealth, the begetting of children, and, most of all, longevity. By the 7th century an elaborate system of practices was developed to achieve these blessings and to realize the Three Original Principles of Taoism, namely, Essence, Vital Force, and Spirit. These practices included breath control, baths, diet, mental concentration, sex hygiene, physical exercises, medicine, the use of charms, attempts at disappearance and change of bodily form, and alchemy, especially the effort to transmute mercury into gold. In their pseudoscientific alchemical experiments over the centuries, the Taoists made a number of scientific discoveries and perhaps contributed indirectly to the development of science in Europe.

*Superstitions.*—The Taoist religion is a rich reservoir of superstitions, including geomancy, fortune-telling, divination, and the use of charms. With modern reforms, these are fast disappearing but not entirely eliminated.

*Sects.*—Taoism is a wholesale imitation of Buddhism, notably in its clergy, temples, images, ceremonies, and canon. In organization it is generally classified under two schools, the Northern and the Southern. The Southern School, called the True Unity sect, prevailing south of the Yangtze, is traced to the so-called founder Chang Ling but more likely grew up in the 10th century. It emphasizes man's nature—that is, man's spirit or true self—and relies on charms and magic to preserve it. It depends on "self-power" and is idealistic and informal. Its priests are married, live at home, and regard as their head the Heavenly Teacher, who used to reside in the Dragon and Tiger Mountain in central China. He had no influence on the masses and should in no way be called a pope, as he sometimes has been in the West.

The Northern School, called the Complete Purity sect, probably founded in the 13th century, is centred at the White Cloud Temple in Peking. It emphasizes man's life—that is, man's vital force—and relies on medicine and diet to prolong it. It depends on "other-power" and is materialistic and formal. Its priests renounce the home, adopt vegetarianism, and live in temples.

*New Societies.*—The two schools have been declining since the last half of the 19th century. In their place new societies have grown up, such as the Tao Yuan (Society of the Way), founded about 1920. These are led by laymen, worship deities of all religions, shun superstition, reject the search for earthly immortality but promote charity and moral culture, and, like traditional Taoist sects, sometimes participate in political revolts.

*Ethical Teachings.*—To most followers, who also follow Confucianism and Buddhism, the Taoist religion is essentially a sanction of ethics. In the two most popular tracts, *The Treatise on Influence and Response* and *The Silent Way of Recompense,* which have been influential for centuries, Confucian moral values (filial piety, loyalty, love, righteousness, and good faith), Buddhist virtues (compassion, kindness to all creatures, and remonstration against all evil deeds), and Taoism's own ethics of patience, simplicity, contentment, and harmony are strongly advocated.

**Modern Status.**—As a religion of the masses, Taoism has been rapidly fading away, especially since the Communist government came to power in China. Without leadership, financial resources, or recruitment for priests, its future as an organized religion is dim, although private practice, including local temples and shrines in homes, will surely continue. Its superstitions, animism, and idolatry, however, have largely been replaced by social and economic reform activities. Although there is a National Taoist Association in Mainland China, practically all Taoist priests have returned to secular and productive life, and Taoist temples are being used for other purposes. But many elements of the Taoist religion—its fairy tales, magic, aesthetic imagination—are still rich in Chinese folk life, especially in festivals, while the virtuous life and spiritual serenity taught in its religious tracts will continue to influence the Chinese character for a long time to come.

*See* also references under "Taoism" in the Index.

Bibliography.—Karl L. Reichelt, *Religion in Chinese Garment* (1951); Wing-tsit Chan, *Religious Trends in Modern China* (1953), *A Source Book in Chinese Philosophy* (1963), and (trans.) *The Way of Lao Tzu* (1963). (W. C.)

**TAORMINA,** a town and tourist resort on the east coast of Sicily in the province of Messina, about 35 mi. (56 km.) from the towns of Messina and Catania, is on a hill that rises almost perpendicularly from the sea, near the foot of Mt. Etna. Pop. (1961) 8,903. The famous Greek theatre, rebuilt in Roman times, stands on the spur of Mt. Tauro, which affords a splendid view of Mt. Etna from summit to base on the southwest, and the mountains of Calabria across the sea to the north. There are remains of the Roman Odeon theatre, discovered during excavations in 1892, and of the so-called Naumachia (a reservoir), almost in the centre of the town. The Corvaia Palace, the Santo Stefano Palace (a splendid construction with fine paired windows), the Badia Vecchia, and the Ciampoli Palace belong to the medieval period. Taormina is connected by road and rail with Messina and Catania.

The town was the ancient Tauromenium, which took its name from Mt. Tauro, and was originally a settlement of the Siculi, resettled by Dionysius of Syracuse about 392 B.C. After receiving a further colony of refugees from Naxos in 358, it flourished under the mild rule of Andromachus, father of the historian Timaeus. Tauromenium was part of the kingdom of Hieron II from 263, and in about 210 it passed to the Romans as an allied city. Augustus made it a Roman colony, but it declined under Roman, and later Byzantine, rule. In A.D. 902 the city was taken by the Arabs, who destroyed it and massacred the population. Rebuilt by the Christians of Val Demone as New Taormina, it was again taken in 962 by the Arabs under the amir Ahmad, who renamed it Mu'izziyah. In 1078 it was taken by the Normans, under whom it had some prosperity, but it has remained a modest township. (A. R. T.)

**TAO-TE CHING:** *see* Lao-tzu.

**T'AO YUAN-MING:** *see* T'ao Ch'ien.

**TAPACOLO** (Tapaculo), the name given to a group of small to medium-sized birds comprising the passerine family Rhinocryptidae, peculiar to Central and South America. The 25 known species occur chiefly in the Andes, and are most numerous in Chile. A single species (*Scytalopus argentifrons*) occurs as far north as Costa Rica. The several types agree in having large, strong feet, rounded wings and rather short tails which are carried in an upright position. The bill may be either thin and awllike or decidedly thick. Certain modifications of the external nostrils are characteristic of the family. In coloration the plumage is mainly brownish or blackish and, in one form, spotted. The typical tapacolo (*Rhinocrypta lanceolata*), a native of Argentina, is crested and resembles a miniature domestic fowl. The widely distributed, wrenlike genus *Scytalopus* includes more than half of the known forms. All are notably furtive, have weak powers of flight and frequent bushes or undergrowth. Their varied calls are sometimes musical, but consist chiefly of harsh scolding notes.

Tapacolos feed on insects, larvae and related matter. Their nesting habits vary, some forms (*Scytalopus*) making nests on the ground and others in bushes. One species (*Teledromus fuscus*) digs a tunnel. Two white, unmarked eggs comprise a clutch. (E. R. Be.)

**TAP DANCE.** Tap dancing is a style of dance, which can be incorporated into any form of dance movement, in which more foot-to-floor contacts than normal are produced, in precise, rhythmical patterns. The taps are made audible by attaching small metal plates to the toe and heel of the dancing shoe.

All ethnic groups have retained some form of emphatic foot-to-floor contacts as part of their dance culture. The main sources of tap dancing, however, are the clog dancing of northern England, the reels and flings of Ireland and Scotland, and the rhythmic foot stamping of the African Negro; these basic elements came together in the dancing of the United States. The 19th-century performers in minstrel shows and showboats stylized and fused them into a form of dance and satire which rapidly became popular. Among the most noted of these performers were Ralph Keeler and Daniel Emmett and the dance team of Lynch and Diamond.

Near the end of the 19th century tap dancing acquired two specific techniques called "buck-and-wing," and "soft-shoe." The buck-and-wing was very active and fast, and was danced in wooden-soled shoes that made loud sounds. Soft-shoe was very relaxed and smooth and was danced in soft shoes. At the turn of the century, George Primrose was the most famous of the soft-shoe dancers, while Doyle and Dixon were exponents of the buck-and-wing.

Between 1910 and 1925 these two varieties of tap dancing merged and the modern metal tap made its appearance. The technique remained very much the same, consisting principally of: striking the ball of the foot on the floor with a brushing motion forward, sideward, or backward; stepping on the ball of the foot; dropping or scuffing the heel on the floor; scraping the foot over the floor; touching the toe of the foot to the floor; and making contact with any part of the shoe which would produce a sound. Handclaps and slapping of the body were also occasionally used. These steps were combined with a great variety of leg movements. Some of the tap dancers who began dancing during this period were Pat Rooney, George M. Cohan, the Four Fords, Johnny Boyle, Tom Patricola, and the great Bill Robinson, known as "Bojangles." In the 1930s tap was very popular for chorus dancing and in vaudeville.

Since 1940 tap dancing has added to its basic technique many of the movements of ballet and modern dance. The footwork has also developed so that an expert tap dancer can make about 64 taps in five seconds and, standing on one leg, can make 5 tap sounds with a single movement of the supporting leg.

As tap dancing became more visually interesting, it was widely used in motion pictures, outstanding performers including Fred Astaire, Gene Kelly, Ray Bolger, Ginger Rogers, Eleanor Powell. A *Concerto for Tap Dancer* was composed by Morton Gould, to be performed with orchestra. Paul Draper introduced tap dancing in the concert field with classical and jazz music. (P. Dr.)

**TAPE RECORDING, MAGNETIC.** The process of magnetic tape recording offers one of the most accurate and convenient methods of storing, and later reproducing, any type of information that can be converted into electrical signals. Sounds (*e.g.*, voice and music), electrical data from business machines and metering devices, video signals and the electrical impulses for the automatic control of machinery are examples of the material commonly stored on magnetic tape. Besides the accuracy and convenience of magnetic recording, the ability to erase the storage medium and reuse it many times gives a great economic advantage over other recording methods in many applications.

**History.**—The idea of storing electrical information by means of magnetized particles was expressed as early as 1888 by Oberlin Smith in an article in *The Electrical World*. However, Valdemar Poulsen, a Danish inventor, was the first to reduce the idea to practice with a recorder which stored the electrical signal on a wire of magnetic steel. He first applied for a Danish patent on this device on Dec. 1, 1898. A working model of the device created great interest at the Paris exposition in 1900, and many of the later applications of magnetic recording were envisioned at that time. Even with this enthusiasm, however, Poulsen could not find financial backers in Europe. In 1903, Poulsen and some American associates formed the American Telegraphone company for the manufacture and sale of an improved version of the device. The telegraphone would record continuously for 30 minutes on a length of piano-wire steel that moved at a speed of 84 in. per second. However, the device did not find wide application.

Following the failure of Poulsen's company, the general public heard little of magnetic recording for several years, but interest continued in many laboratories. W. L. Carlson and G. W. Carpenter of the U.S. Naval Research laboratory applied for a patent on alternating-current bias for magnetic recording in 1921, and in 1927 J. A. O'Neill received the first U.S. patent for a magnetic tape made by drying a liquid containing magnetic particles on the surface of a strip of paper. A German patent by Fritz Pfleumer of Dresden was issued in 1928 for a similar process. Until this time, the recording medium had been a wire or tape, entirely of or plated with magnetic metals.

During the 1920s Kurt Stille of Germany acquired a number of patents in this field through which he licensed others. One such licensee was Louis Blattner of England, who built a magnetic recording machine to record and synchronize sound with motion pictures. The "Blattnerphone" was used by the British Broadcasting corporation, and later it was bought by the Marconi company. Work on this method of recording progressed in Germany, England and the U.S. during the 1930s. In particular, the Magnetophon company of Germany succeeded in producing a magnetic, film-coated tape, based on Pfleumer's patent, that constituted a low-cost recording medium. During World War II the Magnetophon, using the coated tape, served the Nazi propaganda organizations well, and following the war its principles were copied and improved upon in many countries, with Germany, England and the U.S. the leaders in this work.

**Recording Media.**—Magnetic materials in almost every possible form are used in one magnetic recording application or another. Drums of nonmagnetic material have their surfaces coated with a magnetic material to record short bursts of information, such as those used in electronic computers and some types of data recording. Cylindrical surfaces of rubber or plastic, impregnated with magnetic particles, are used to record short messages in telephone answering and recording machines. Disks, coated or impregnated with magnetic material and recorded in parallel or spiral tracks, are used in such applications as office dictating machines and electronic computers.

Wire, the first magnetic recording medium, is still used for certain applications, such as portable recorders. Despite improvements in tape, drums, etc., more information can be stored in a given space on wire than on any other medium. However, the fidelity of reproduction, the signal-to-noise ratio, and cross talk (resulting from adjacent recorded layers being wound together on the same spool) are generally poorer than those of tape.

A variety of magnetic tapes have been developed. Some of the early machines used a solid metal tape of magnetic material. A magnetic stainless steel, Vicalloy, consisting of 52% cobalt, 11% vanadium and 37% iron, is particularly useful for both wire and tape. However, a paper or plastic tape coated with a magnetic powder proved to be the most useful form of magnetic recording material and far outstripped the others in variety of application as well as volume produced.

The magnetic material most often used in coating tape is the red form of iron oxide, $Fe_2O_3$. The way in which this powder is prepared, the impurities deliberately introduced or accidentally present, and the physical size and shape of the particles have much to do with the characteristics obtained. Red iron oxide particles, needle-shaped and roughly one micron ($\frac{1}{1,000,000}$ m.) in length, are widely used. The black oxide, $Fe_3O_4$, has also been used as a magnetic coating material; it produces a higher signal strength, but is more difficult to erase.

The magnetic powder is thoroughly mixed with a binder, the nature of the latter depending partly on the base material to which it will be applied. The polymeric vinyl chlorides, vinyl acetate, cellulose acetate and ethyl cellulose are commonly used. The solvent employed must not attack the base material or cause adjacent layers of tape to stick to each other when the tape is tightly wound and stored at relatively high temperatures. The object is to obtain a very thin but dense layer of iron oxide on the tape in a very uniform distribution. It must adhere tightly to the base tape, but not to an adjacent layer; it must be flexible, and preferably its characteristics should not change appreciably over many thousands of usages or many years of storage.

The base material may be paper or any one of several plastics. Paper is generally lower in cost and some papers are more stable than plastics in applications where relative humidity and temperature vary widely. However, paper tears easily under tension, and since any irregularity in the thickness of the magnetic layer results in unwanted variations and noise in the recording, even the smoothest paper has a serious disadvantage in performance as compared with plastic, which can be prepared with very smooth surfaces.

Cellulose acetate film can be manufactured at moderate cost with a smooth surface, and it has reasonably good tensile strength, tear resistance and dimensional stability. It is widely used for magnetic tape in thicknesses of about 0.0015 in. Mylar or Terylene (a polyester made from polyethylene terephthalate) is more expensive than cellulose acetate, but has superior characteristics. It is stronger, and more stable under high humidity and temperature conditions. It is also more stable with respect to time, making it possible to store recorded material for many years. It has sufficient strength and stability to be used in films as thin as 0.0005 in., thus greatly reducing the storage space required for a given length of tape. However, a smooth surface is somewhat more difficult to obtain on Mylar than on cellulose acetate.

A typical method of manufacturing tape begins with combining the iron oxide and the binder. The mixture is milled in a large rotating cylinder loaded with steel balls, a process that may require from one to several days. The resulting mixture is an extremely uniform, thick fluid resembling printer's ink. This is filtered to remove any lumps of more than about one micron in diameter.

The paper or plastic film is usually processed in webs up to 20 in. wide. The coating process is done in very clean rooms where only filtered air can enter. The web passes from its roll through a cleaning stage in which both surfaces are cleaned of every trace of dust, lint and other foreign matter; this is accomplished with vacuum suction action, assisted by static removal equipment. The web is then coated with a thin layer of solvent to make the surface receptive to the coating material. When this has had sufficient time to act on the surface, the magnetic coating is applied. This may be done in a fashion similar to engraved-roll printing, in which the amount of material to be applied is metered by the depth of the pattern engraved in the surface of a printing plate. The magnetic mix is applied to the engraved roll and the surface rubbed or scraped to remove the excess. The amount remaining in the engraved pattern is then transferred to the tape web by a rolling action, and the web continues through a drying chamber. When it is dry, the surface may receive a polishing, after which the tape web is ready to be slit and reeled.

The coating remaining on the web is 0.0001 to 0.0004 in. thick when dry, and tolerances of $\pm 0.000012$ in. may be held on the nominal thickness to assure proper performance. For tapes that are used for computers, automatic inspection devices detect any voids in the coating, since these could cause an omission in the stored information, resulting in a serious error.

The tape is slit and wound on reels varying from 3 to 14 in. or more in diameter, depending on the intended application. A 7-in. (outside diameter) reel is common in sound recording work and holds 1,200 to 1,800 ft. depending on the tape thickness.

A $10\frac{1}{2}$-in. reel (2,400 to 3,600 ft.) is widely used by the broadcast industry, and larger reels are frequently used in technical data recording and business-machine operations. Nominal tape widths most commonly used are $\frac{1}{4}$, $\frac{1}{2}$ and 1 in., with the $\frac{1}{4}$-in. size having the widest variety of applications.

**The Recording Process.**—The electrical signal to be recorded is usually applied to the tape by means of a "head" consisting of a coil wound around a core of magnetic iron which has a gap at the point where the tape moves across its surface. The current in the coil produces a magnetomotive force across the gap, magnetizing the particles in the tape. The strength and direction of final magnetization of a particular point on the tape will be determined by the strength and direction of the magnetic field at the moment that point crosses the gap. Thus the tape receives a magnetic record containing direction (north or south pole), amplitude, and linear dimension (along the tape) corresponding to the direction (plus or minus), amplitude and time of the original electrical signal. The exactness of this record depends on a variety of conditions, one of the most important being the original magnetic condition of the tape. There are two conditions which give predictable results. Either the tape should be completely demagnetized before recording, or it should be completely magnetized in one direction or the other. In early wire and tape recording, the latter condition was used. The tape was carried past a permanent magnet so arranged that it brought the magnetic particles to saturation, leaving the tape fully and uniformly magnetized in one direction. The recording head then had a direct-current component added to the signal; this direct-current bias was of the proper direction and amplitude to bring the tape just back to a neutral state. The signal, adding and subtracting from this bias, left the tape magnetized by an amount proportional to its own strength. This is called D.C.-biased recording, and gives comparatively low distortion and good amplitude. However, it has a higher inherent noise level and more distortion than A.C.-biased recording.

In A.C.-biased recording the tape is first completely demagnetized and comes to the recording head in a neutral state. There an alternating current is added to the signal current; it is much higher in amplitude than the signal current, and several times greater than the frequency of the highest-frequency signal to be recorded. In crossing the gap of the recording head the magnetic particles on the tape are subjected to many cycles of the bias current, and leave the head with a magnetization which is proportional to the signal. Very low distortion and high signal-to-noise ratios can be obtained with A.C.-biased recording. For sound and general signal recording, this type of tape recording gives performance superior to that of any other recording method.

For pulse recording, in electronic computers and other digital information devices, distortion is of no importance. It is simply desired to record and later detect the presence of a pulse. In most of these recorders the tape comes to the recording head in a neutral state.

In one system the head may normally carry a current that magnetizes the tape to saturation in one direction. A pulse then carries the current to the other extreme and back again, leaving a short area on the tape magnetized in the opposite direction. This is called two-level recording.

In the other commonly used system the head normally carries no current, and pulses may carry the magnetization of the tape to saturation in either a plus or minus direction. This is called three-level recording.

Losses are encountered in recording through eddy current and resistive and capacitive losses in the windings and core of the head. Space between the head and tape causes very high losses, particularly at high frequencies (short wave lengths). The gap must be very straight and true, and the surfaces in contact with the tape must be very smooth in order to obtain the best possible transfer of the signal pattern onto the tape. Optical polishing methods are commonly used for finishing the surfaces of the gaps and faces of the head that will be in contact with the tape. The gaps used in recording heads vary in length (direction of tape motion) from 0.0002 in., when used also as a reproducing head, to 0.010 in. or more for specialized applications. The tolerances on the trueness of the faces and edges of the gap are usually held to a few millionths of an inch. The width of the cores, and the resulting recorded tracks on the tape, vary from approximately 0.025 in. for certain types of data recording to 0.250 in. for professional audio recording.

**Reproduction.**—In reproduction, it is usually desired to use the recorded tape to reconstruct the signal, obtaining the same polarity, amplitude and time relationship that originally existed in the recorded signal. To accomplish this, the tape is passed over the same head used in recording, or one similar to it. To reproduce the signal in the proper time relationship, the tape speed must be identical during recording and reproduction.

The magnetized portions of the tape passing over the gap in the reproducing head cause the magnetic flux in the core to change, generating a voltage in the coil. This voltage is proportional to the speed of the tape and the amplitude and frequency of recorded signal. Assuming that the tape speed is constant and that a constant-amplitude signal has been recorded, the reproduced signal will have an amplitude proportional to the frequency of the reproduced signal. This gives a response which rises at the rate of 6 decibels per octave. However, as the lengths of the waves recorded on the tape become smaller, the gap in the reproducing head spans more and more of a wave length, and a loss in output is encountered which is known as "gap loss." At the frequency where the gap just spans one wave length of the recorded signal, the output is zero. In order to use the tape at as slow a speed as practical and still record high frequencies (short wave lengths of recorded signal), the reproducing head has a gap made as short as the technical progress of the art, and economics, will allow.

The amplifier that obtains its signal from the reproducing head must have a response curve which compensates for the special characteristic of that head, as well as for other losses in the heads and recording process. Some of these losses can be anticipated and compensated for in the recording amplifier. Thus it is necessary to have standards established before tapes can be freely exchanged from one recording machine to another reproducing machine. This has been done to some extent in the audio field, standards being established by industry committees.

In television and data recording and in machine control the frequency response problems are quite specialized and the tapes are usually recorded and reproduced on the same machine or a similar model. Few standards have been established since they are not seriously needed for tape interchanges. In business machine applications the problems are even more specialized. Here, it is not necessary to reproduce exactly what was recorded, but merely to detect and interpret each "bit" or pulse of recorded information. The reproduced signal generally does not resemble the recorded pulse, but does bear a definite relationship to it.

**Erasure.**—One of the features of magnetic recording which gives it an economic advantage over other recording methods is the ability to erase and reuse the recording medium thousands of times with little or no loss in the quality of recording. Erasure may be accomplished in either of two ways: (1) A reel of tape may be erased by subjecting the whole reel to a strong alternating magnetic field and slowly reducing the field to zero; this is called bulk erasing, and is similar to the method used by a jeweler when demagnetizing a watch, although the equipment must be of a different form to accommodate the large reels of tape. (2) The second method involves using a head, very similar to a recording head, to erase the tape just before it is recorded again; the tape passes over the gap in the head and is subjected to a powerful, high-frequency alternating field which diminishes as the tape passes away from the gap, leaving the tape in a demagnetized or neutral state. Professional sound-recording engineers frequently use both methods to make sure all the previous recording has been removed from a tape before it is used again.

**Tape Recording Machines.**—A wide variety of mechanisms has been devised to make use of tape recording in many different applications. Since only a small amount of power is required to move the light, flexible tape over the heads for recording or for playing back, it has been possible to make battery- and spring-driven portable mechanisms to record away from established power sources; the smaller ones are pocket-sized. The miniature machines, however, sacrifice some fidelity of reproduction to attain compactness. In particular, it is difficult to attain smooth motion and uniform speed, with the result that "flutter" and change of pitch can be noted in the playback of audio material. Larger portable units are available which give quite high fidelity and are often used for broadcast program recording in the field.

A large market developed in tape recorders for use in the home. These record and play tape at 1.87, 3.75 and 7.5 in. per second, usually on one-half of the width of the ¼-in. tape; this doubles the amount of tape available for recording or makes it possible to have two simultaneous channels for stereophonic recording. Prerecorded tapes are available, but the ease with which the amateur can produce acceptable recordings is a strong factor in the popularity of such recording devices. Some machines are designed to record four tracks on a ¼-in. tape, allowing even more intensive use of the tape with only a slight further sacrifice in the quality of reproduction.

Sound recorders for special applications are often quite complex. Those used for professional studio recording usually have three motors: one on the supply reel, one on the take-up reel and a third to drive the tape. Extreme care is taken to provide smooth and uniform drive so that reproduction of musical notes will remain in exact pitch with no discernible flutter. Another special application is voice-monitoring service, such as the monitoring of radio channels at an airport. Here, a 2-in. tape is used and a rotating head scans across the tape while the tape moves slowly forward. This makes possible a very long recording time on a comparatively short tape, and a particular passage may be returned to with a minimum of rewinding time.

The same principle, with much elaboration and much higher scanning speeds (1,500 in. per second), is in use for recording television broadcasts. The tape recorders used in data recording are similar to those used in professional audio recording. However, they may utilize wider tapes, and 10, 20 or more tracks may be provided by special multicore heads. In addition, the machines must be capable of starting and stopping the tape in very short intervals of time, and of driving the tape in either direction. The very low inertia of a short piece of tape makes it possible to attain speeds of 15, 30 or 60 in. per second in thousandths of a second. Various fast-acting capstans and brake systems are in use to start and stop the tape, and a slack loop is usually maintained between the reels and the working area by means of servomechanisms. *See* also PHONOGRAPH; and references under "Tape Recording, Magnetic" in the Index.

BIBLIOGRAPHY.—Joel Tall, *Techniques of Magnetic Recording* (1958); S. J. Begun, *Magnetic Recording* (1949); H. G. M. Spratt, *Magnetic Tape Recording* (1958); N. M. Haynes, *Elements of Magnetic Tape Recording* (1957); W. Earl Stewart, *Magnetic Recording Techniques* (1958). (W. E. ST.)

**TAPESTRY** is popularly assumed to be almost any heavy material, ordinarily wool, hand-woven, machine-woven, or even embroidered, used to cover furniture, walls, or floors; and this definition is justified in that it perpetuates the meaning of the Greek and Latin words from which the English word "tapestry" derives. Neither word defined the technique by which such articles were made.

This broad application of the term, which has resulted in much ambiguity in the interpretation of ancient documents, was to a large extent abandoned in the 18th and 19th centuries when the technical definition of a tapestry was narrowed to embrace only patterned or figured handwoven textiles, usually in the form of hangings, curtains, or upholstery, made either by the low-warp or high-warp method, and having a solid, weft-faced surface. Contemporary usage therefore brings the meaning of "tapestry" closer to the medieval "arras," which was still the current term in Shakespeare's time and beyond for this type of hanging.

Tapestry weaving differs from embroidery in that it is freely darned on a bare warp instead of being wrought upon an already woven material. The celebrated Bayeux Tapestry (*q.v.*) of the 11th century is therefore not a tapestry at all in the sense that the word has now acquired, since the design is embroidered upon the material and not woven into it. (*See* also WEAVING; RUG AND CARPET.)

## TECHNIQUE

**Characteristics of Tapestry Weaving.**—Tapestry differs from other forms of patterned weaving in that no wefts are carried the full width of the web, except by a very rare accident of design. Each unit of the pattern or the background is woven with a weft of the required colour, which is inserted back and forth only over the spot or section where that colour appears in the pattern. Typically, in plain-cloth technique, the weft passes over and under the warps alternately, and on the return shoot, under, where before it was over, and vice versa. The wefts, which are pushed tightly together by various devices (sword tip, reed, batten, or comb), so outnumber the warps as to conceal them completely; the latter appear only as more or less marked parallel ridges in the texture, according to their coarseness or fineness.

Where the margin of a colour area is straight and parallel to the warps, a slit is necessarily left, which may be treated in one of five different ways. First, it may simply be left open, as in the Chinese silk tapestries, which are called *k'ssu,* "cut silk," for that reason. Second, it may be left open on the loom, but sewed up afterward, as in European tapestries from the 14th to the 17th centuries, and also in some later types. Third, the weaver may dovetail his wefts, passing from one side, and from the other, in turn over a common warp. This may be either "comb" dovetailing—single wefts alternating—or "saw-tooth" dovetailing—clusters now from one side, now the other. Dovetailing has the double disadvantage of making the fabric heavier at that point and of blurring the outline. Persian weavers of the 16th century developed a successful variant in silk tapestry rugs, whereby a black outline weft was dovetailed over two warps—one of each of the adjacent colour areas—effectively hiding the coloured wefts in the compacting of the weave, and providing strong clear drawing. The same device is found several centuries earlier in Peru, but if there was a common source, examples from it have not yet been noted.

The fourth treatment—interlocking—was introduced in the Gobelins factory in the 18th century. Here wefts of juxtaposed colour-segments are looped through each other between the two warps which mark, respectively, the margin of each colour. This gives a continuous surface of even weight and was prized by the French weavers because the resultant effect more closely approximated that of painting.

Finally, one curious variant would, in strictest definition, fall outside tapestry, though it starts with the tapestry conception: between every two rows of tapestry-woven wefts is a cloth-woven, full-width shoot which makes the fabric solid. This type could be rigorously classified as a brocaded cloth, but the idea is that of tapestry, with the cloth structure subordinate and the problem solved being one in tapestry weave. The device, rare everywhere, is found in Japan in the 7th and 8th centuries, in east Persia in the 10th century (Moore Collection, Yale University), and in medieval Peru.

**High-Warp and Low-Warp.**—European tapestry may be woven on either of two types of looms, high-warp (*haute-lisse*) or low-warp (*basse-lisse*). In a primitive version of the former, the warps are attached to a beam at the top, and groups of warp threads are weighted at the bottom. The weft is beaten up toward the top. Such looms are pictured on Greek vases; the weaver shown is generally labeled Penelope and her fabled scheme of undoing the day's work at night becomes clear: she simply removed the weights and slipped the wefts off the warp threads. The more highly evolved vertical frame has heavy uprights (*bâti,* in French) holding a horizontal roller (*ensouple*) top and bottom, on which the warps are stretched. Each warp passes through a loop of cord (the *lisses*), and the loops encircling the warps which correspond to uneven numbers are fastened to one slender cylinder, those to the even, to a second cylinder, both being above the weaver but within reach so that he can pull forward with his left hand now one, now the other set of warps (*i.e.,* form the shed), in order to pass his bobbin (*broche*) behind them, this being a short, pointed, slim cylinder of polished wood on which his weft yarn is wound.

The low-warp loom, on the other hand, has the rollers on the same level at table height so that the warps stretched between them are horizontal, and the *lisses* are attached to two slats, each of which is connected with a treadle so that the weaver depresses the odd-numbered, or even-numbered series of warps to form his shed with movements of his feet, leaving both hands free to manipulate his bobbin. Production on this loom is nearly twice as fast as on the vertical loom, reducing cost proportionately. The cylinders in both instances serve to roll up the finished portion and unroll a further length of unwoven warps so that the section in process is always taut and in a convenient relation to the weaver. At both types of loom the weaver works from the back side and has a mirror into which he can look through the unwoven warps, and which is placed to reflect the portion in process; but while the high-warp weaver can examine his finished work directly by walking round to the other side of his loom, the low-warp worker has to tilt up his frame.

**Cartoons.**—The design is rendered first as a drawing on paper, the *petit patron;* then it is enlarged to the size which the tapestry is to be and is painted in exactly the correct colours on linen or, more recently, on paper. This is called the *grand patron.* Up into the early 16th century the *patron,* or cartoon, was sometimes called in French the *portrait* (or *pourtraict*). The artist specializing in designing (whether for execution in tapestry, or in other techniques and media such as embroidery, wood carving, and stained glass) was called a *portraitist.*

The full-size cartoon was sometimes itself hung as a substitute for tapestry; and large-scale paintings similarly rendered on great sheets of heavy but flexible linen, called *toiles peintes,* or "painted linens," were made expressly for this purpose. The most interesting collection of old *toiles peintes,* dating chiefly from the 16th century, belongs to the cathedral of Reims.

The high-warp weaver has the full-size cartoon which he is following hung beside him, but the low-warp worker has his laid under his warps, so he follows from immediately above his model. In both cases the main outlines are drawn with ink on the warps.

The design is executed, in all professional European work, at right angles on the loom so that in the finished hanging the warps run horizontally. This is aesthetically advantageous, since the warp ribbing tends to create a texture more or less reinforced by linear shadows, and if vertical, these sever the design, but if horizontal they bind it into continuity. Practically, however, horizontal warps are disadvantageous since they mean horizontal slits, with weight from the heavy wool fabric pulling on them as the tapestry hangs, and thus accelerating deterioration. That the aesthetic consideration should have prevailed over the practical is noteworthy.

The extra weft ends are left hanging loose on European tapestries, but they can be fixed with an additional twist and cut short, making a reversible fabric. This is a practice especially common in far eastern tapestry weaving, which is notably fine (*k'ssu* may count 60 warp threads per inch). All European tapestries are relatively coarse up to the 18th century with, in general, from 10 to 18 warps to the inch; transition from shade to shade is effected with irregular "comb-tooth" hatching.

**Twill Tapestries.**—Instead of the plain-cloth binding commonly found in tapestries, a twill can be used; *i.e.,* a weave in which the weft is floated over two or more warps, then under one or more warps, with this underpass shifted always one to the right or left making diagonal ribbing. Such a weave appears in tapestry for the first time, as far as can be determined, in Persia in a unique silk and metal-thread square, the design comprising a royal portrait, figure of angels, animals and plant motives; and from the 17th century on (Moore Collection, Yale University; Metropolitan Museum) it is used in goat's hair or wool, especially for shawls, in Khurasan and Kerman. The type is perpetuated in the well-known Kashmir shawls, and was probably introduced into Kashmir from Persia, along with other crafts, in the 16th century.

## EARLY HISTORY

**Early Examples.**—Early examples of tapestry weaving are so isolated and so fragmentary as to make it uncertain either when or where the art originated. The earliest known specimens of tapestry weaving of linen (datable between 1483 and 1411 B.C.) have been found in the favourable climate of Egypt. One bears the cartouche of Thutmose III, another of Amenhotep II, and the third, hieroglyphics; they were found in the tomb of Thutmose IV. The Amenhotep piece has the tablet bearing the king's name and titles upheld by uraei, set in a powdered pattern of lotus and papyrus flowers, with a narrow border on each side. Only the designs—in red, yellow, green, blue and brown—are tapestry-woven, the ground being plain cloth—in the tapestry areas the wefts are not kept straight, but curve to follow the drawing. A tapestry robe and part of a glove were also found in the tomb of Tutankhamen (d. *c.* 1350 B.C.).

At this period numerous Syrian ideas, techniques, and perhaps actual craftsmen were entering Egypt, and, since tapestry weaving does not occur again in Egypt in quantity until the 4th century A.D., it seems unlikely that the craft was indigenous.

Fragments of wool tapestries in graves on the Kerch Peninsula, of the 4th or 3rd century B.C., carry stag heads and ducks in the widely diffused Hellenistic style which was especially strong in

Syria, and about 200 to 500 years thereafter tapestry is represented again in a silk fragment, which though found at Loulan in central Turkistan has close Syrian connections. This is a band worked in seven colours (three browns, one evidently originally purple, two greens, light blue and crimson). In a central zone appears a scrolling stylized tree, in the crown of which appears a bird's head; the whole designed to present alternatively a conventional bird flanked by confronted griffins (composed of a crested bird with deer or horse feet) alternating with a symmetrical scroll. The border motive is a rosebud rendered as a heart in a deep calyx, and some of the multiple guard stripes are in continuously graduated polychromy. The bird nesting atop a cosmological tree, and the double image are both west Asiatic; fantastic griffin variations are a persistent feature of Syrian design; the heart-rose is the standard border theme on later Syrian textiles, where also compound borders with variant guard stripes are frequent, while the unusual graduated polychromy appears on approximately contemporary wool tapestries at both Palmyra and Dura-Europos. Thus this tattered strip represents the cultural linkage between the Mediterranean coast of Asia and its very heart.

The wool tapestry with graded polychromy found at Palmyra is ornamented only with groups of square dots, but that from Dura bears stylized lilies, and this figure, better drawn, appears also on wool tapestries found at Loulan which likewise may be assigned either to Syria or Persia. A closely related piece is known from south Russia. Tapestry weaving may well have been common in western Asia and especially in Syria at the start of the Christian Era; had climatic conditions been less unfavourable, a whole phase of the art now irretrievably lost might have survived.

**Egypt.**—Favourable conditions did exist, on the other hand, in Egypt, and consequently a mass of tapestry fragments has been recovered there, dating from the 4th to about the 10th century A.D.; these are especially numerous from the 5th to the 7th century and include some remarkable Coptic tapestries, exemplifying the Christian art of Egypt. These are mostly garment trimmings, woven into or (in inferior specimens) sewed onto tunics and cloaks. Tunic trimmings when complete consist of stripes over the shoulders (*clavi*) down front and back, varying in width from about 1 to 6 in., ranging in length from just below the belt to the very bottom; a neck piece; panels on the shoulders and near the knees which may be round (*orbiculus*) or rectangular (*tablion*); and cuffs. Parts of pillows also are quite common, wall hangings far less frequent, and when in solid tapestry weave—in contrast to tapestry motives inwoven in cloth—rare and proportionately important. A series of fragments formerly in Berlin representing dancers, in polychromy and silhouette, and some pillow panels, have naturalistic illustrations in a delayed Hellenistic style. Later examples are in the early Byzantine style (best examples, Dumbarton Oaks, Washington, D.C.).

The garment trimmings fall into two main classes: indigenous designs rendered either in polychromy, or more often in silhouette, most typically in some tone of purple (dyed with madder plus indigo); and designs copied, with more or less distortions, from Syrian shuttle-woven silk patterns (a distinction first established by Josef Strzygowski, and repeatedly noted by Oskar Wulff and Wolfgang Volbach). In the former, constantly recurring themes are the vine, or less often ivy; the amphora, frequently with the vine growing out of it; nude women, nude youth or boys, including dancers often armed; and animals, above all the lion and the hare—all explicable as descended from the Osiris cult and appropriate to burial robes because of their relevance to revival in a life after death. In the patterns copied from Syrian models, the styles of the different great textile-producing cities there can be recognized, and subjects from the local cults, so that, analyzed in their wider relations, they throw considerable light on the history of religion, as well as of art.

All types are woven with woolen wefts on linen warps, though a few with silk wefts have appeared, and cotton wefts are occasionally introduced to give a brighter white. Primarily in the 7th, and perhaps also the 8th century, the tapestry technique may be supplemented with embroidery, as in border margins, usually in split stitch. In a special variant, which is not true tapestry, the characteristic meanders or other geometric repeats are executed with a free bobbin, "free" because it follows the design without regard to consistency of weft direction, carrying a linen thread which stands out on a violet wool tapestry-woven (or repp) ground. The multiplicity of tones in polychrome pieces is noteworthy, especially from the 7th century on, and includes clear, delicate pastels.

Egyptian tapestry weaving deteriorated sharply from the 7th to about the 11th century, when it was somewhat improved within a very limited range. Into white (or dark green) linen garments were woven tapestry trimming bands in wool, or often in silk, occasionally with metal-thread enrichments, in groups ranging from a half-inch to a foot and more in width, with patterns of geometric enlacements, frequently enclosing small quadrupeds or birds (ducks) highly stylized, and inscriptions. Many of these merely simulate writing, but many are legible, in handsome angular Kufic scripts on earlier pieces, in cursive scripts later, giving religious phrases, or the names or titles of rulers, occasionally with the place name also (*tiraz*). A characteristic colour combination in silk is golden yellow and scarlet.

**Syria.**—From the 6th to the 8th century A.D., and doubtless from then on, striking wool tapestries were being made in Syria corresponding in style to the contemporary shuttle-woven silks, with animals or birds (commonly cocks) in energetic heraldic stylization, framed in roundels, almost always on a red ground. Later, from the 11th to the 13th century, silk and gold-thread tapestries were produced in Syria, highly distinctive in style, incorporating pagan motifs that were still being used in the old Phoenician cities when the crusaders took them over.

**Persia.**—Fewer specimens of Persian tapestries have survived, but one notable fragment (Moore Collection at Yale University) bears an ibex in the impressive Sasanian style, and a single piece from the Seljuk period (11th century) establishes the maintenance of the technique. This reappears in the 16th century (intermediate examples having all apparently been destroyed) as the medium for rich silk and metal-thread rugs of which only three are known still to exist (Moore Collection, N.Y.), though others are illustrated in Persian miniatures.

The modern descendants of these, occasionally silk but more often wool, in slit tapestry, with simpler patterns, are the familiar *kilims;* and the type extends, with variations in decorative style, through the Caucasus and Asia Minor into eastern Europe.

**Far East.**—Tapestry had long been in use in China, and there silk was the typical material, in a fine, light texture, the weave finished perfectly on both sides so that the panels are reversible. The warps are vertical in relation to the pattern. The "metal" thread, which is quite common, is the thinnest possible gold leaf applied to tough paper, cut in narrow strips and spirally wound on a silk core.

The earliest surviving examples, dating from the T'ang and early Sung periods (8th to 10th century), show only simple repeating patterns—flowerets, vine elements, ducks, lions—but are probably not representative of the full development of the time since they come only from remote desert stations of central Asia. Subsequent examples from the Ming period (1368–1622) are rare and exquisite. Abundant from the Ch'ing period (1644–1912), they show a severe artistic and technical decline. Especially plentiful are squares indicating rank, from official robes.

Tapestry technique traveled from China to Japan in the Ashikaga period (15th century), where it was used for characteristic motives, also in silk as a rule, and with vertical warps, but with a considerably coarser texture than Chinese work. The history of the art in Korea remains obscure, but rather coarse wool tapestry-woven rugs from there, with stylized motives, are well known in western markets.

**Western Hemisphere.**—How and when tapestry and a number of other complex Asiatic textile techniques were transmitted to the Americas is not known. Not all authorities agree that the connection took place. But examples of a fully established technique and style appear, perhaps as early as A.D. 600–700 in the Andean culture, while a vast amount of remains have come to light from the coastal cemetery sites of Peru, datable from about the 8th to the 12th century. In the Peruvian sites, bodies were buried characteristically in a squatting posture, fully dressed, indeed often wearing a multiplicity of garments hardly feasible in life, and padded and heavily wrapped into an approximate ovoid. The principal articles are: tunics, for men, varying in length and with or without sleeves; for women, full length, or in the Incaic period, a long skirt held under the arms with a sash; for both, enveloping mantles; breechcloths for men and boys; belts; and headbands. Besides tapestry, these Peruvian remains reveal the most varied techniques of weaving and needlework ever current in a single culture. (Excellent collections: Lima Museum; Brooklyn Museum; American Museum of Natural History, N.Y.; Textile Museum, Washington, D.C.)

The warps of the tapestries are of undyed cotton (the cotton of the region being naturally either white or brown), the wefts of wool—llama, guanaco, alpaca or vicuña—with cotton sometimes introduced for bright white. The range of available colours—made with natural dyes—is large, for the most part in saturated tones; the compositions are usually polychrome and powerful contrasts are preferred. Belted looms without heddles were used.

The patterns all derive from local cults: a feline divinity, in some presentations fantastically adorned; an anthropomorphic deity (or more likely several distinct personalities) ordinarily with an elaborate headdress and frequently carrying a staff; birds, including the eagle and the condor; and fish. Plant motives are comparatively rare. All are angularly conventionalized, with the rectangle and especially the diagonal as substructure, the style showing a marked preference for meanders and reciprocals. The latter range from the most rudimentary, the serration, with its section the Z or its magnification the chevron, to complex developments of overturned interlocking figures of naturalistic origin, notably condor heads.

In the later Middle Ages, the characteristic principles of conventionalization appear: elimination—as, omission of the mouth; fusion—as, nose and mouth merged into one spot; exaggeration—as, human profile reduced to a huge nose; and part-for-whole—as, the feline represented only by its claw. The application of these devices is unusually extreme.

Though a great advantage of tapestry is its flexibility which makes unnecessary repeating patterns, these strongly predominate in the Peruvian use of the technique in all periods. The organization of the repeats follows basic forms relevant to shuttle weaving: stripes; bands; and rectangular checks, implicit or explicit. Schemes unrelated to the fabric structure also are used: diagonal stripes, chevron stripes, lozenge checks. Within these, the succession whether of motives or of colour changes is often exceptionally complex. The usual unit is three, or its double, six—the latter a peculiarity of textile design in this region throughout its pre-Columbian history—and the permutations thereon are numerous, varied, and not infrequently remarkably ingenious.

After the Spanish conquest, European designs were supplied to highly skilled Inca weavers who executed them with their own modifications, producing an effective hybrid style (good examples, Boston Museum of Fine Arts).

Perhaps tapestry was also current in the other highly evolved pre-Columbian cultures of Central America and Mexico; but climatic conditions there have been destructive of textiles.

## EUROPEAN TAPESTRY

**Development of the Gothic Tapestry.**—References to the making of tapestries in western Europe occur throughout the Middle Ages, but the ambiguity of the term makes it impossible to be certain of the technique employed unless the object referred to has actually survived. Although the antiquity of Arras and Aubusson as tapestry-making centres is legendary, and a few rare tapestries, notably the series of panels in the cathedral of Halberstadt, Ger., are in a style that is pre-Gothic, it is only in the 14th century that the European tapestry tradition begins to emerge with any clarity. At this period the most sophisticated centres of production were in Paris and Flanders, and *tapissiers de la haute lisse* begin to be mentioned in both places in connection with the guilds. Large numbers of tapestries are recorded in inventories, and the more luxurious standards of living being adopted by the wealthy extended their use beyond the customary wall hangings to covers for items of furniture. Survivals are rare, however, and the outstanding example is the famous Angers Apocalypse (Angers Museum, Fr.), begun in Paris in 1377 for the duke of Anjou by Nicolas Bataille, and based on cartoons by Jean Bondol of Bruges. A slightly later series (*c.* 1385) showing the "Nine Heroes" and possibly from the same workshop was made for the duke of Berry, and is now in The Cloisters, in New York City.

**The Low Countries.**—Tapestry manufactories are first mentioned in Arras in 1313, and Flemish centres for tapestry weaving and tapestry dealing continued to multiply during the next two centuries, with Arras, Tournai, and, eventually, Brussels emerging as the most significant names. The decline of Paris as an art centre in the 15th century left Flanders with no serious competitor in the field, and extensive patronage by the dukes of Burgundy contributed to its prominence throughout the Gothic period. Tapestry themes covered a wide range, with romances of chivalry and history predominating over religious subjects.

Local marks did not become general until the 16th century and continual intercourse between the various centres, particularly Arras and Tournai, adds to the difficulty of determining where individual tapestries were made. Despite the prestige implied in the name of Arras, only one set of tapestries is inscribed with the actual name; they have been the basis for a large number of additional attributions. They show scenes from the lives of St. Piat and St. Eleutherius and were woven entirely in wool by Pierrot Feré in 1402 for the cathedral of Tournai, where large fragments still survive. The figure style relates to manuscript painting of the same period and shows considerable character in the faces. Several decades later the same centre was probably responsible for the distinguished series of scenes from the "Passion" in the cathedral of Saragossa, where some gold has been mixed with the wool.

Production in Tournai, which is first mentioned in connection with tapestry weaving in 1352, continued to expand throughout the 15th century, and it was from Tournai that Philip the Good, duke of Burgundy, commissioned the "History of Gideon," one of the most important tapestries of the period, for his new Order of the Golden Fleece. Like many of the tapestries mentioned in the records of the period, this series has not survived, but the abundance of documentary material and the numerous names involved gives some insight into the extent of the activity. In Arras a specially designed building was erected by Philip the Good to allow for the better conservation of his numerous tapestries.

A few familiar cycles tend to be repeated: of the histories, the Alexander tapestries in the Palazzo Doria at Rome and the history of Julius Caesar in the Historical Museum at Bern are outstanding; while among the numerous hunting and pastoral tapestries of the period, the Devonshire Hunting Tapestries (now in the Victoria and Albert Museum, London) provide a fine example from the second quarter of the 15th century. A feature of the Gothic period in general was the *menues verdures* (or garden tapestries), usually referred to in the modern market as *mille-fleurs* ("thousand flowers"). These have a dark-blue ground, strewn rather sparsely with flowering plants and bushes, and usually interspersed with animals and birds. At times they are combined with human figures or armorial bearings and may even supply a background for figure compositions, as in the highly decorative "Lady with the Unicorn" series of the early 16th century in the Cluny Museum, Paris, of which the origin is still uncertain, although it seems likely to be French rather than Flemish. *Grandes verdures* (or large garden tapestries) seem to have been introduced by the Poissonier family of Tournai *c.* 1500, and their exoticism was inspired by Vasco da Gama's trips to the Indies; an upper border treated as a bell-fringed valance is a recurring feature. Borders in general, which were to become so important at a later date, are rare on early Gothic tapestries.

The occupation of Arras by the French in 1477, and successive sieges of Tournai in the early 16th century, contributed to the rise of Brussels, which became the dominant tapestry-making centre of the Netherlands until the general decline of the craft in the late 18th century. From 1528 on it was obligatory to weave the Brussels city mark—an escutcheon flanked by B's—in the selvage, and the shopmark also was usually inserted. The patronage of the emperor Charles V and the skill of the Pannemaker family, the most accomplished weavers in Brussels throughout the greater part of the 16th century, combined to establish the reputation of Brussels. Fine tapestries from this centre are dispersed throughout the museums and collections of the world, the Austrian State collection (Kunsthistorisches Museum, Vienna) being particularly rich.

Two new trends became apparent at this period. The first, brought about by war and persecution in Flanders, resulted in the widespread diffusion of the Flemish art of tapestry weaving. Many Flemish artisans in the 16th century were forced to become refugees: some grouped together to live the life of traveling craftsmen; others attempted to reestablish their trade abroad. Flemish weavers were welcomed everywhere as carriers of a great tradition. Such itinerant masters established more or less enduring shops from England to Italy. The second important new trend emanated from Italy and reflected the superiority attached by the Italian Renaissance to the art of painting. The decisive step, which was to bring about the subordination of weaving to painting for more than 400 years in the art of tapestry, was taken when Pope Leo X commissioned Pieter van Aelst of Brussels to weave a series of tapestries illustrating the "Acts of the Apostles" from cartoons produced by Raphael between 1514 and 1516. Little or no concession had been made to the medium for which the cartoons were intended, but the tapestries were a great success, and numerous copies have subsequently been made.

Qualities introduced during the Renaissance were pushed even farther in the 17th century, when the dominant influence in the Brussels industry was Rubens (1577–1640). His most famous set was the "Triumph of the Eucharist," designed (1627–28) to the order of Archduchess Isabella of Spain, but imitations and adaptations of his style were legion. Heavy and elaborate columns were often substituted for side borders. On a more modest scale are the tapestry versions of genre paintings by Teniers, the younger (1610–90), where the border frequently simulated the actual picture frame.

**France.**—French tapestry weaving, after its eclipse in the 15th century, when nomadic weavers seem to have been more active than established shops, owes much of its eventual prestige to an unusual degree of royal patronage, resulting in the foundation of state shops, the names of which have now become household words. A prelude to this development was the factory established at Fontainebleau by Francis I in 1538. Although active for only 12 years and by no means an indigenous art in the first place (its masterpieces are by Flemish weavers from designs by the Italian painter Primaticcio), it provided a springboard for subsequent developments in Paris, where in 1551 Henry II established and endowed with special privileges the Hôpital de la Trinité workshop. Although workshops multiplied, results were at first disappointing. And it was due to the initiative of Henry IV, whose planning of his nation's economy emphasized the luxury production that has since been industrially important in France, that decisive steps forward were taken. In 1608 Henry IV gave official recognition to the French workshop (using the high-warp method) of Girard Laurent and Dubout by establishing them in the Louvre, and at the same time he encouraged the immigration of Flemish weavers practising the low-warp method, who would help Paris to compete with the flourishing industries of Brussels and Antwerp.

*Gobelins.*—At turn of the 16th–17th centuries, two Flemish weavers had been taken to France by government arrangement to establish *basse-lisse* looms (*de la marche*) in Paris: François de la Planche (or Franz van den Planken) and Marc Comans. Satisfactory working conditions were found for them in an old dye factory on the outskirts of the city which belonged to the Gobelin family, and so began the establishment commonly known by that name, which has lasted ever since. One of its first ambitious productions was an allegorical invention lauding Catherine de Médicis under the guise of Artemisia; for this the *petits patrons* were chiefly by Antoine Caron (*c.* 1515–1593); but the shop's most valuable asset was Rubens' "History of Constantine," and it was the verve and vitality of Rubens that brought new life to French designs at this period.

De la Planche died in 1627 and was succeeded by his son who broke with the Comans family and moved to the *faubourg* St. Germain-des-Près, leaving the Comans at the Gobelins. Competition became bitter, but both continued to produce a considerable quantity, as well as good quality, until they were superseded in 1662 by the royal factory, which purchased the Gobelins works as its seat.

Louis XIV's minister, Colbert, alert to profitable possibilities, recruited skilled personnel, not only from the de la Planche and Comans shops, but also from the old Louvre enterprise, and thus established ateliers of both horizontal and vertical looms. As director, he utilized Charles Le Brun (1619–1690), already experienced with tapestry in a brief-lived undertaking by Colbert's ill-fated predecessor, Nicolas Fouquet; the Gobelins shops were officially chartered as a royal factory in 1667. Le Brun designed the most important sets, the "Elements," the "Seasons," and above all, the "Life of Louis XIV," supplemented by the "Royal Residences," 37 large panels altogether. Le Brun's triumphant academicism dominated the work of Antoine and Charles Coypel (1661–1722, 1694–1752), and a half-dozen other designers who devoted themselves to classical and Biblical themes; a lighter spirit was introduced by Claude Audran the Younger (1637–1734), with his talent for decorative inventions, especially grotesques.

Louis XV (1710–1774), in his turn, was celebrated in a set of "Hunts" by Jean Baptiste Oudry (1686–1755). But the outstanding artist working for the factory during this reign was François Boucher (1703–1770), whose sophistication and polished elegance posed new problems for the weavers. Now indeed they must learn to paint with a bobbin, and to this end hundreds of new dyes were perfected for both wool and silk, until about 10,000 hues were available, to effect almost imperceptible tonal modulations; and interlocking of the wefts was introduced to render the transitions practically invisible, while the finest textures practical were used, from 20 to occasionally as many as 40 warps to the inch.

*Beauvais.*—Both Oudry and Boucher worked also for another major state-subsidized factory which had been carried on at Beauvais by two Flemings, Louis Hinart, for 20 years (1664–1684), and Philippe Béhagle for 27 more (1684–1711). Oudry made for it his famous "Fables de La Fontaine." Boucher in 1736 began to purvey Italian fêtes, Chinese scenes and various pastoral scenes with titillating overtones. The factory has been especially noted for furniture and screen panels. Beauvais tapestries were executed primarily by the low-warp method.

Two new types of decorative panels appear at the height of production, the architectural composition and the grotesque. The former usually shows a complex arcade with massive balustrade on which stand urns of flowers and perhaps a bird or two, as a peacock with trailing tail. In the latter, architectural tracery defines a complex of panels, framing a medley of festoons, scarves, vases, musical instruments, *putti,* masks and comedy actors. For the English taste, entire wall coverings were made at the Gobelins factory, much larger than, but stylistically like, these decorative panels.

By the end of the century, though technical standards were maintained, artistic deterioration set in.

*Aubusson.*—A third factory at the old-tapestry-making centre of Aubusson, which had operated as a modest private undertaking for a century and a half, was chartered as a royal factory in 1665, but practically all the output there was relatively coarse material for the open market. The most effective pieces are *chinoiseries.* Coarse, rather dull, verdures were made in quantities. Aubusson architectural panels either imitate those of the greater ateliers, often with more complex elements and the addition of animals, or depict a damasked wall hung with a painting or cluster of decorative objects, and garlands. The factory was especially successful in its production of carpets, with conventional or floral designs.

In all three shops the idea of tapestry as a woven picture was so predominant that the commonest border was a woven imitation of a carved and gilt frame.

"St. Michael," a panel from one of the pre-Gothic tapestries in cathedral of Halberstadt, Germany

"Horse and Lion," detail from a 6th-century Egyptian tapestry at Dumbarton Oaks, Washington, D.C.

Fragment of a polychrome portrait medallion, probably of Syrian origin

Detail of Coptic fragment showing a shepherd milking a goat, 3rd or 4th century A.D. The designs of the border (doves flanking vase of water of life holding vine) were derived from the immortality symbolism of the Osiris cult

# TAPESTRY

Panel depicting an angel showing the great harlot, symbol of idolatry and all abominations, to St. John, illustrating Rev. 17:1–2. One of the series of the Angers Apocalypse tapestry by Nicolas Bataille, begun 1377. 6 ft. 6¾ in. × 8 ft. 6¼ in. (2 m. × 2 m. 60 cm.)

"The Miraculous Draught of Fishes" from a cartoon by Raphael, drawn between 1514 and 1516. 16 ft. 3 in. × 14 ft. 5 in. (4 m. 95 cm. × 4 m. 39 cm.)

Detail from "The Bear Hunt," one of a series of Devonshire Hunting Tapestries made in Brussels and dating from the second quarter of the 15th century. In the Victoria and Albert Museum. The entire tapestry measures 13 ft. 5 in. × 33 ft. ¾ in. (4 m. 9 cm. × 10 m. 15 cm.)

BY COURTESY OF (TOP LEFT) THE VATICAN MUSEUMS; PHOTOGRAPHS, (TOP RIGHT) GIRAUDON, (BOTTOM) JOHN R. FREEMAN AND CO.

THE UNICORN IN CAPTIVITY

One of a series of Gothic tapestries showing the "Hunt of the Unicorn." French or Flemish. A date of about 1515 has been assigned to the series, but it has also been suggested that the set, or part of it, was prepared for the wedding of Anne of Brittany to Louis XII of France in 1499. In The Cloisters, New York city; a gift of John D. Rockefeller. 1937

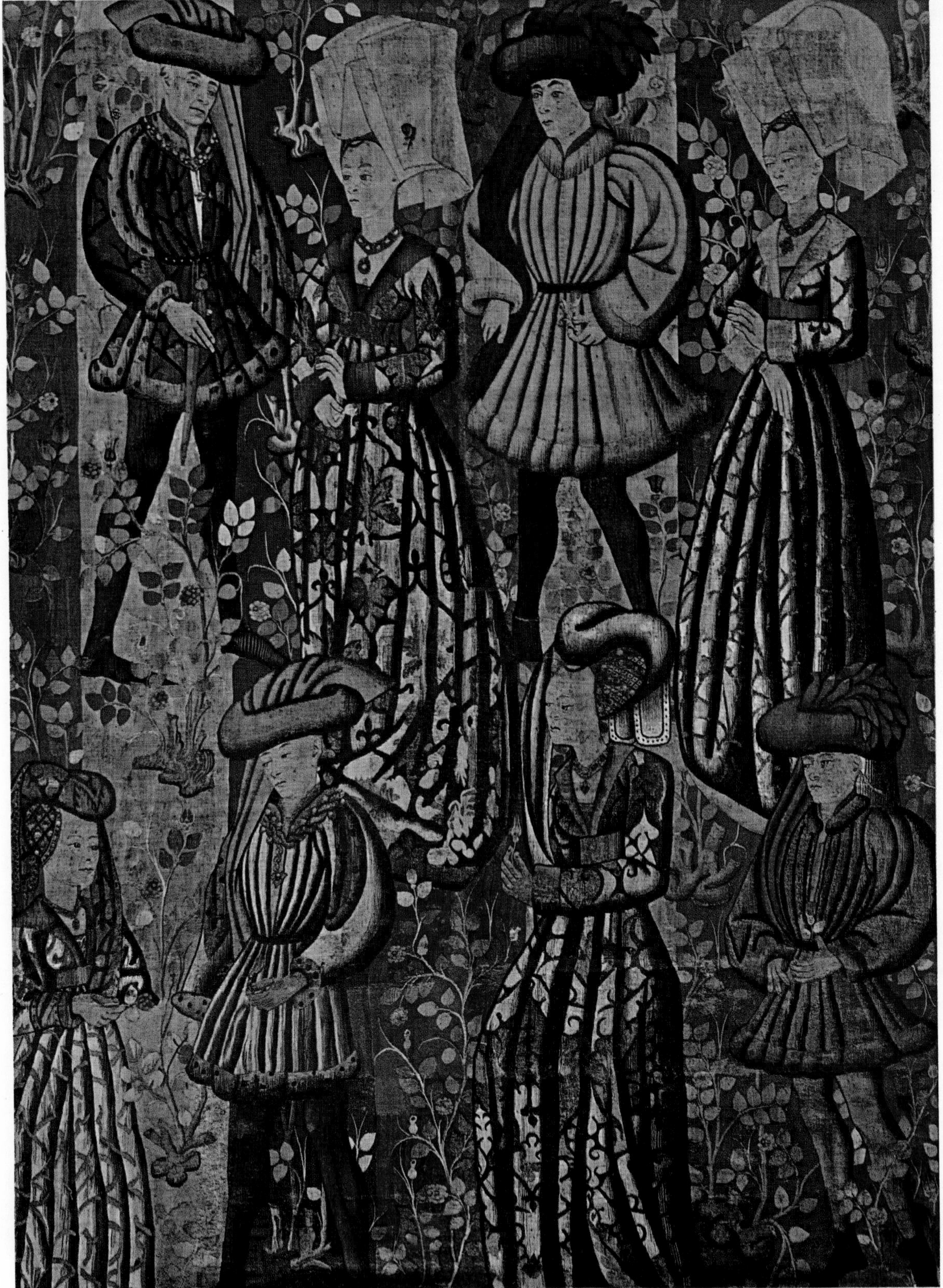

BY COURTESY OF THE METROPOLITAN MUSEUM OF ART, NEW YORK

## FRANCO-FLEMISH TAPESTRY

"Courtiers with Roses," the second of a set of three tapestries made towards the middle of the 15th century, perhaps at the order of Charles VII. It is woven of wool in a coarse texture of about 12 warps to the inch. The tapestry, which recalls the paintings of Jean Foucquet, has great decorative qualities. Since its exhibition at the Louvre in 1904 it has been recognized as one of the most important tapestries of its period. It was purchased in 1909 by the Metropolitan Museum of Art, New York

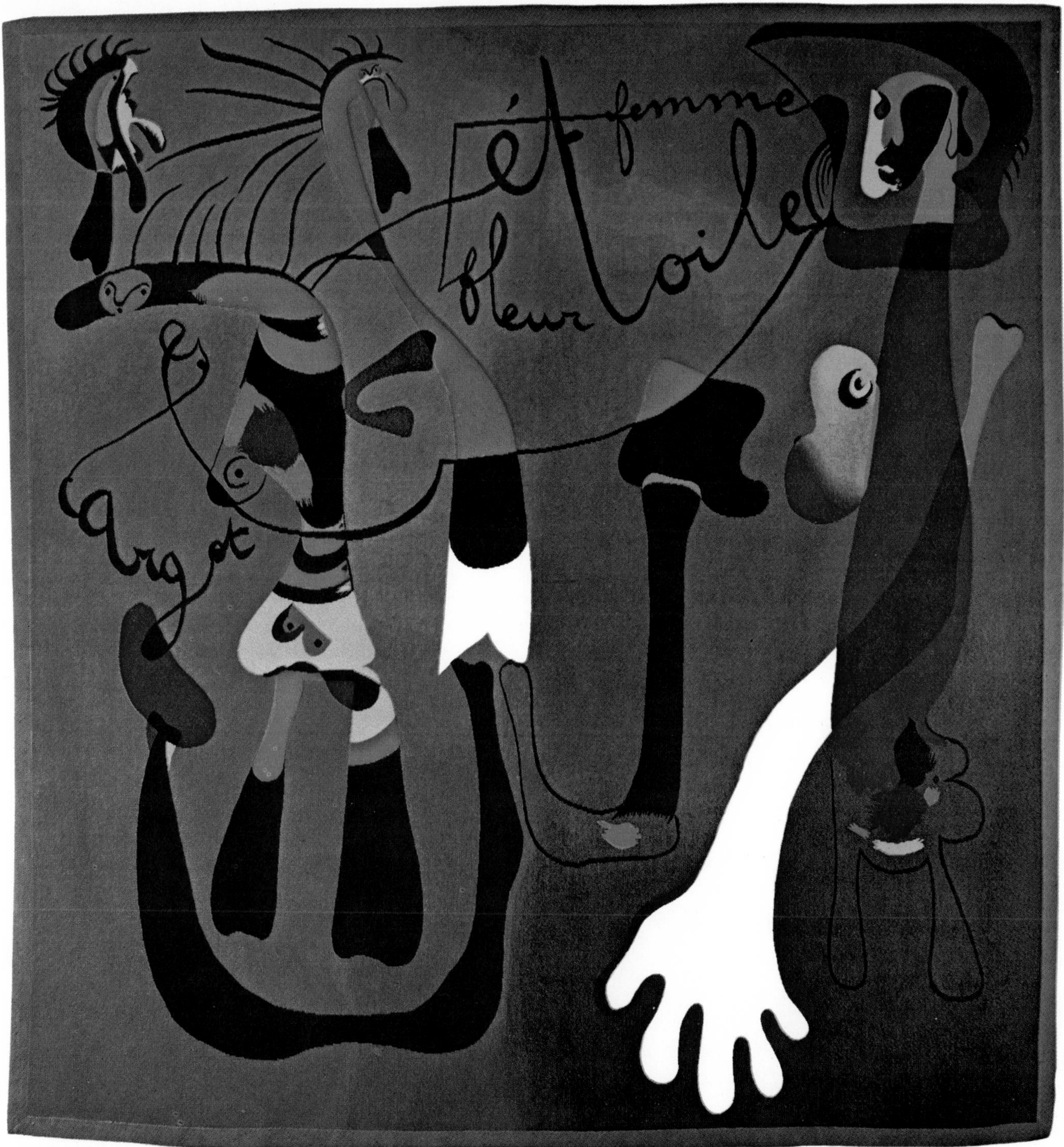


PHOTOGRAPH BY COURTESY OF SIDNEY JANIS GALLERY, NEW YORK

A 20TH-CENTURY TAPESTRY

"Femme, Fleur, Étoile" (Woman, Flower, Star) by Joan Miró (1893– ), Spanish. The tapestry, in the Seagram building, New York city, is a reproduction of a painting. The tapestry work was supervised by Marie Cuttoli, Paris. From the collection of Joseph E. Seagram & Sons

# TAPESTRY

"The Parade of the Buso" by István Ban, 1957. In the town hall of Mohács, Hungary. 10 ft. 10 in. × 15 ft. $9\frac{3}{4}$ in. (3 m. 30 cm. × 4 m. 82 cm.)

"The Five Wise and the Five Foolish Virgins," made in Romerike, Norway, in the mid-17th century. $77\frac{7}{10}$ × 61 in. (197 × 155 cm.)

"The Great Menace" from the series "The Song of the World" by Jean Lurçat, 1957. 14 ft. $5\frac{1}{4}$ in. × 29 ft. $6\frac{1}{4}$ in. (4 m. 40 cm. × 9 m.). "The Great Menace" depicts the bark of creation with man at the helm

BY COURTESY OF (TOP RIGHT) THE OSLO MUSEUM OF APPLIED ARTS; PHOTOGRAPHS, (TOP LEFT, BOTTOM) EDITA S. A., LAUSANNE

Apprentices in these factories, in order to attain the rank of master, had to produce a small specimen of their work with a difficult subject. Sometimes an elaborate vase of flowers was chosen, but often copies were made of paintings in the royal collection, and similar little pieces were made by the weavers in their own time to supplement their income.

**Italy.**—Itinerant Flemish and French weavers, setting up their looms in cities where there was temporary employment, brought tapestry weaving to Italy as early as the 15th century. First to establish a workshop was Leonello d'Este who brought Rinaldo di Gualtieri Boteram to Ferrara from Brussels. The second major factory, the Arazzeria Medici, was founded by Cosimo I in 1546. He began with two Flemish weavers from Ferrara, Nicholas Karcher and Jan Rost. The latter became the outstanding tapestry weaver in Italy. His signature on the tapestries is symbolized in a pun on his name—a chicken roasting on a spit. Well-known painters provided cartoons; *e.g.*, Bronzino, Alessandro Allori, Francesco Salviati. A noteworthy series of genre scenes was woven in 1639 from earlier designs by Francesco Ubertini. The Medici looms continued until the death of Giovan Gastone, the last Medici grand duke of Tuscany, in 1737.

**Spain.**—Flemish tapestries came in great quantity to the churches and palaces of Spain during the 15th century; to repair and care for them, Flemish weavers were brought in. Later, one of these, Frans Tons, established the factory of Pastrana during the reign of Philip IV. Another weaver, Jacob van der Goten, was commissioned by Philip V to start the factory of Santa Bárbara near Madrid in 1720. Long active, the great contribution of this factory was the production from 1776 to 1791 of 45 tapestries from brilliant cartoons by Goya. The factory was closed in 1835.

**Germany and Switzerland.**—Early Gothic tapestries were made in considerable numbers in southwest Germany, and hangings in a pre-Gothic style survive in the cathedrals of Halberstadt and Quedlinburg, but the craft remained closer to folk art than in Flanders or France. The tapestries are for the most part traditionally long, narrow strips, modest panels or cushion covers, coarse in texture, simple in shading, limited in palette, but with clear strong colours effectively contrasted. Doll-like figures, monsters half fairy tale and half heraldry, undulant banderoles with naïve explanations in bold Gothic lettering, scrolling foliation, and stiff flowerets often combined with patterned backgrounds to give a toyland charm.

This domestic type continued into the 17th century, but in addition, various shops were established for longer or shorter periods by wandering Flemings, who usually failed to equal the home-country style. A more sophisticated style eventually prevailed, when factories employing immigrant weavers were established in Berlin, Munich, Würzburg, and Dresden.

**Scandinavia.**—In Norway, fragments of tapestry with traces of human figures and trees have been found in the Oseborg Ship of the early 9th century. A more complete tapestry, found between two floors of the old church of Baldishol (Hedemark), can be dated around the end of the 12th century. Identifiable figures on it are two of the months of the year, April as a bird-catcher and May a mounted knight, each framed in an arch. The background had a decorative pattern; there is sharp, contrasting colour in the figures, and the colour areas are dovetailed.

Of the nearly 1,300 registered Norwegian tapestries, approximately 1,250 originated in the small rural communities; Norwegian tapestries may be considered a folk, or a provincial, art.

In Sweden there is no evidence of tapestry production before the middle of the 16th century when King Gustavus I introduced some Flemish weavers. The 18th century produced small coarsely woven panels, patterned with flowers and birds, attractive as a peasant craft.

**England.**—The major textile art in England was embroidery; when tapestries were needed, they were imported from Flanders. Their popularity can be judged, however, by the fact that inventories drawn up after the death of Henry VIII in 1547 show that the royal collection then comprised more than 2,000 tapestries, many of which had been confiscated by the crown on the dissolution of the monasteries.

Although references to Arras weavers in England occur off and on from the 13th century, and a few armorial tapestries have survived from the 15th century, it is not until the 16th century that tapestries from an established English manufactory can be securely identified. At this period tapestry workshops were set up by William Sheldon (d. 1570), producing mostly small panels and cushion covers. A later specialty of these shops was a series of topographic tapestries, woven in 1588 from contemporary maps of Midland counties, which featured bird's-eye views of hills, trees and towns, surrounded, according to the custom of the period, by Flemish-styled borders of architectural and figural ornament.

In 1619 a factory of tapestry weaving was established by royal charter at Mortlake near London. The director, Sir Francis Crane, enticed about 50 Flemings to settle in England with their families. Philip de Maecht came from Paris, where he had been a leading *tapissier*, to be overseer and master weaver. The Mortlake factory flourished under the patronage of James I and Charles I. Rubens supplied cartoons and suggested to Prince Charles the purchase of the Raphael cartoons of the "Acts of the Apostles"; Van Dyck designed new borders for these. But, under Charles II, the factory's last years showed sorry deterioration; it was finally closed in 1703.

From the end of the 17th century, the Poyntz brothers had a studio in Soho, where a number of former Mortlake artisans eventually produced a distinct style based on Chinese and Indian lacquerwork.

**Russia.**—Peter the Great, as part of his program of modernizing his country, established looms in his capital in 1716, with workers from the Gobelins. The most striking productions are portraits of Catherine the Great. (P. An.; D. W. Li.; X.)

### MODERN DESIGN IN TAPESTRY

During the main portion of the 19th century, in tapestry as in other luxury arts past styles were reproduced as closely as possible. The influence of industrialization was inescapable, of course, not only in tools, materials, and dyes, but in the new middle-class market and its demands. Machine-made tapestry, although an achievement in mechanical weaving, became a threat to the survival of the original craft.

In England programmatic designers saw the necessity for the revival and purification of craftsmanship; and in 1881 William Morris established a tapestry factory at Merton Abbey in Surrey. For about 15 years he and his associates had been designing not only for looms but also for pictorial wall decorations and stained glass windows; they were well prepared professionally to design tapestries. Morris and Walter Crane (1845–1915) contributed sketches, but most Merton tapestries were designed by the painter Sir Edward Burne-Jones (1833–98). More venturesome than any of the Merton Abbey products were the tapestry designs made in the 1880s by Arthur Heygate Mackmurdo (1851–1942), who in 1882 founded the Century Guild, the first of many groups of artists-craftsmen-designers to follow the teachings of William Morris. This tradition, influenced by more contemporary French developments, is continued in Scotland by the Edinburgh Tapestry Company and the Golden Targe Tapestry Studio, along with some others. The most ambitious 20th-century tapestry designed by a British artist, Graham Sutherland's enormous "Christ of the Apocalypse" (1962) for Coventry Cathedral, was, however, woven on Aubusson-Felletin looms in France (the largest tapestry ever to have been made there).

Elsewhere, from the late 19th century onward, there has been a resurgence of tapestry based on folk traditions. In Scandinavia this trend was already apparent in Norway shortly after 1890, when special efforts were made to base a modern tapestry art on native medieval weavings. The leaders were Gerhard Munthe (1849–1929), a well-known painter, and Frida Hansen (1855–1931), a weaver who studied the peasant craftsmanship of Norway and evolved an individual, light and open weave. More recent developments in Scandinavia have been made in Sweden and Finland. Marta Måås-Fjetterström (d. 1941) is the best-known Swedish tapestry artist, and her atelier continued to produce excellent works. In Finland a freer, more colourful art, more delicately scaled, has been practised by many; among the best-known are Martta Taipale, Laila Karttunen, and (for damask tapestry) Dora Jung. In Norway and to a lesser degree in Denmark similar work has been done. The church in the Scandinavian countries has been unusually receptive to this art. Traditional folk weaving has also been behind the revival of tapestry-making in Poland, Czechoslovakia, and Hungary since World War I; Poland especially has produced original designs executed in a remarkably free technique. In the Western Hemisphere folkcrafts, including Mexican tapestry weaving, have been revived throughout Latin America with varying degrees of success.

Germany, emulating Scandinavia, also began a revival of tapestry weaving around the turn of the century. A small tapestry industry set up at Scherrebek, near the Danish border of that day, from 1896 to 1903 was followed by similar enterprises at Kiel and Meldorf. The most significant development, however, was at the Bauhaus (*q.v.*) where a branch of modern tapestry design was developed during the 1920s and early 1930s, abstract in composition, and profoundly rooted in the loom technique and in the exploitation of fibres as strong textural elements. Anni Albers, long a resident and teacher in the United States, may be considered the chief practitioner of this kind of tapestry (more often restricted in size). She was the first weaver to receive the accolade of a one-man show at the Museum of Modern Art, New York, and like most modern tapestry weavers, she also designed for the textile industry.

Modern tapestry design was hindered during the greater part of the 19th century in France by the academic administration of the state factories, although progressive artists began to be affected by the English Arts and Crafts movement in the later 1880s. Gauguin (1848–1903), Émile Bernard (1868–1941), Paul Ranson (1862–1909), and the young Aristide Maillol (1861–1944) were among those who took an interest in and designed specially for tapestry weaving. But it was not until after World War I that French tapestry took the lead in a double way. The great modern painters of the day—Picasso, Braque, Matisse, Léger, Rouault, Miró, and others—permitted their works to be reproduced with extraordinary fidelity under the supervision of Mme Marie Cuttoli, a Paris connoisseur and promoter of exceptional taste. Aubusson, chosen for this important weaving, became once again a great tapestry centre. The direct translation of painting into tapestry, however, left little scope for the weaver, and it is the trend begun simultaneously by Jean Lurçat (1892–1966) that may be said to have truly inaugurated the 20th-century tapestry renaissance. Although he was experimenting since 1916, Lurçat's art did not become definitive until the 1930s, when under the impact of Gothic tapestry (particularly the Angers Apocalypse) and in collaboration with François Tabard, master-weaver at Aubusson, he formulated the principles that were to make tapestry once again a joint creation between artist and weaver, an art in its own right. No longer merely an imitation painting, tapestry once again exploits the coarser texture and the bolder but more limited range of colours that characterized the medieval work. Since World War II tapestries of Aubusson have become world-famous, and the enterprise has attracted many artists working primarily for this medium. They include Marcel Gromaire (b. 1892), Lucien Coutaud (b. 1904), and Jacques Lagrange (b. 1917).

*See* also references under "Tapestry" in the Index.

(Er. K.; D. W. Li.; X.)

Bibliography.—*I. General Works:* J. Guiffrey, E. Müntz, and A. Pinchart, *Histoire générale de la tapisserie,* 3 vol. (1878–1885); J. Guiffrey, *Histoire de la tapisserie depuis le moyen âge jusqu'à nos jours* (1886); G. L. Hunter, *Tapestries, Their Origin, History and Renaissance* (1912), *The Practical Book of Tapestries* (1925); L. von Baldass, *Wiener-Gobelin Sammlung* (1920); H. Schmitz, *Tapestries of the Vienna Imperial Court* (1922); B. Kurth, *Gotische Bildteppiche* (1923); G. J. Demotte, *La tapisserie gothique* (1921–24); W. G. Thomson, *A History of Tapestry: From the Earliest Times Until the Present Day* (1930); P. Ackerman, *Tapestry, the Mirror of Civilization* (1933); H. Göbel, *Wandteppiche,* 3 vol. (1923–34); J. Janneau, *L'évolution de la tapisserie* (1947); J. Lurçat, *Designing Tapestry* (1950); L. Guimbaud, *La Tapisserie de Haute et Basse Lisse* (1962); D. Heinz, *Europäische Wandteppiche* (1963); P. Verlet *et al., The Art of Tapestry* (1965).

*II. Europe.—Low Countries:* R. A. d'Hulst, *Tapisseries flamandes du XIV^e au XVIII^e siècle* (1960). *France:* M. Fenaille, *Tapisseries . . . des Gobelins* (1903); Jules Badin, *La Manufacture de tapisseries de Beauvais depuis ses origines jusqu'à nos jours* (1909); F. Salet, *La tapisserie française du moyen-âge à nos jours* (1946); Andre Lejard (ed.), *French Tapestry* (1946); R. Planchenault, *Les tapisseries d'Angers* (1955); Vercors (ed.), *Tapisseries de Jean Lurçat, 1939–1957* (1957); R. A. Weigert, *French Tapestry* (Eng. trans.) (1962). *Italy:* M. Viale Ferrero, *Arazzi italiani* (1961). *Spain:* A. F. Calvert, *Spanish Royal Tapestries* (1921). *Germany:* B. Kurth, *Die Deutschen Bildteppiche des Mittelalters* (1926); Marie Schuette, *Deutsche Wandteppiche* (1938). *Switzerland:* R. F. Burckhardt, *Gewirkte Bildteppiche . . . zu Basel* (1923). *Scandinavia:* Ornamo, Finland: Applied Art Association, Ornamo (1950–54), for articles on work of Dora Jung, Eva Anttila, Martta Taipale, and Laila Karttunen; Thor B. Kielland, *Norsk Billedvev, 1550–1800,* 3 vol. (1953–55), magnificently illustrated, English summary in each volume; "Scandinavian Design," *Craft Horizons,* March–April 1958. *England:* W. G. Thomson, *Tapestry Weaving in England* (1912); H. C. Marillier, *History of the Merton Abbey Tapestry Works* (1927), *English Tapestries of the 18th Century* (1930); E. A. Barnard and A. J. B. Wace, *The Sheldon Tapestry Weavers and Their Work* (1928).

*III. Other countries:* Lila M. O'Neale in collaboration with A. L. Kroeber, "Textile Periods in Ancient Peru," Univ. of Calif., *Publications in American Archaeology & Ethnology,* vol. 28 (1930); B. Vuilleumier, *Art of Silk Weaving in China* (1939); "Child Weavers of Egypt," *Craft Horizons,* Jan. 1958.

**TAPEWORM,** a parasitic flatworm lacking both a mouth and a digestive system; as an adult it clings to the intestinal wall of a variety of vertebrates, moves about in the intestinal contents, matures, mates, and produces eggs before it passes out of the host's body. Tapeworms constitute a class, Cestoidea or Cestoda, of the phylum Platyhelminthes. Their life cycles are complex and usually involve one or more intermediate hosts during the various larval stages. In a few cases the adult may be a single flattened individual, but in most species it consists of a ribbonlike body (strobila), usually white or yellowish, of many segments (proglottids) that are budded off behind an anterior holdfast organ called the scolex. The number of proglottids varies from three or four in some species to several hundred in others, and the length of the strobila from less than a millimetre ($\frac{1}{32}$ in.) to more than nine metres (about 30 ft.). With few exceptions each proglottid and unsegmented individual contains both male and female reproductive systems. In primitive tapeworms, as those of sharks, the proglottids detach from the strobila before the sex organs are mature; thus, each proglottid behaves as if it were an individual. In more highly evolved forms, as the tapeworms of man, this individuality is lost.

**Importance.**—In general, adult tapeworms are well-adjusted parasites, doing little obvious harm to their hosts. Even in heavy infestations, except for rare blockage of the intestine, there is no clear-cut evidence that serious damage is done. In Europe and the Americas, tapeworm infestations of man have been greatly reduced as a consequence of routine meat inspection. But where sanitation is poor and meat eaten undercooked, the incidence of the commoner tapeworms is high: in parts of Africa much of the population is infected with beef tapeworm (*Taenia saginata*); locally in the Baltic countries almost all of the population is infected with the broad fish tapeworm (*Diphyllobothrium latum,* or *Dibothriocephalus latus*); in parts of the southern United States up to 2% of the population may be infected with the dwarf tapeworm (*Hymenolepis nana*).

Larval stages can seriously damage the host. A certain larval stage (coenurus) of the gid parasite of sheep (*Multiceps multiceps*) usually lodges in the brain of sheep. Fluid-filled hydatid cysts of *Echinococcus* may occur almost anywhere in the body of sheep. Hydatids of the liver, brain, or lung of man are often fatal and have been most widely studied in Argentina, Australia, Chile, and Iceland. Infestation occurs only where man lives in close association with his dogs, and the dogs have access to infected sheep for food.

**General Form.**—A nonliving cuticle, which protects against the host's digestive enzymes, covers the tapeworm's body. It is secreted by the underlying cells of the subcuticula and is intimately associated with the dermal circular and longitudinal muscles. The internal organs lie in a spongy tissue (parenchyma), which in most species contains scattered chalk bodies (microscopic nodules of calcium and magnesium phosphates and carbonates). Both circu-

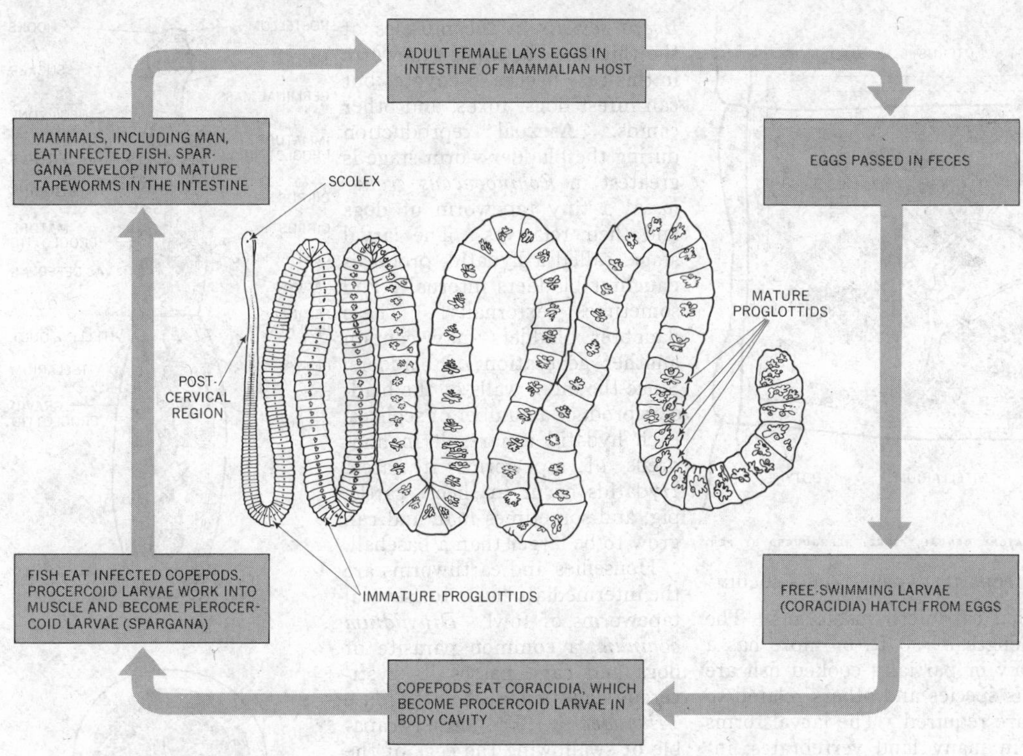
ADULT FEMALE LAYS EGGS IN INTESTINE OF MAMMALIAN HOST
EGGS PASSED IN FECES
FREE-SWIMMING LARVAE (CORACIDIA) HATCH FROM EGGS
COPEPODS EAT CORACIDIA, WHICH BECOME PROCERCOID LARVAE IN BODY CAVITY
FISH EAT INFECTED COPEPODS. PROCERCOID LARVAE WORK INTO MUSCLE AND BECOME PLEROCERCOID LARVAE (SPARGANA)
MAMMALS, INCLUDING MAN, EAT INFECTED FISH. SPARGANA DEVELOP INTO MATURE TAPEWORMS IN THE INTESTINE
SCOLEX
POST-CERVICAL REGION
MATURE PROGLOTTIDS
IMMATURE PROGLOTTIDS

FROM CRAIG AND FAUST, "CLINICAL PARASITOLOGY," 1964; REPRODUCED BY PERMISSION OF LEA & FEBIGER

FIG. 1.—LIFE CYCLE OF BROAD FISH TAPEWORM (DIPHYLLOBOTHRIUM LATUM)

lar and longitudinal muscles are present in bands, bundles, or sheets deep in the parenchyma.

The anterior headlike scolex of segmented forms serves as an organ of attachment; it is armed with suckers, phyllidia (leaflike projections), or bothria (sucking grooves), and may also bear hooks or spines on the attachment organs or on a muscular pad called a rostellum. Behind the scolex lies a region of cellular multiplication, the zone of growth, which buds off the proglottids. The cells of the parenchyma give rise to the organs as the proglottid is pushed away from the zone of growth by the new proglottids being formed; thus the proglottid farthest from the scolex is the oldest.

The nervous system in the scolex consists of a number of ganglia, commissures, and connectives from which arise the special nerves passing to the attachment organs and the two principal nerve cords of the strobila, which run a lateral course throughout the entire length of the worm. The two cords are bound together at the anterior end of each proglottid by a dorsal and ventral commissure arising from ganglia, and there is a nonganglionated commissure present at the posterior end of each proglottid. In addition, a nerve net in the subcuticula communicates with a dorsal and ventral nerve.

The excretory, or osmoregulatory, system is composed typically of two pairs (dorsal and ventral) of longitudinal canals, coursing through the strobila, with transverse vessels connecting the right and left trunks at the posterior end of each proglottid; a loop connects the dorsal and ventral vessel of each side in the scolex. Minute ducts lead from flagellated flame cells to the vessels.

The male reproductive organs usually mature first, and cross-fertilization of proglottids of the same or different individual is the rule, although it is possible for self-fertilization to occur (*i.e.,* within the proglottid). The male duct and the vagina may open side by side into a common atrium. There is considerable variation in the position of the openings. In unsegmented forms they may be terminal, subterminal, or ventral; while in segmented forms they may be ventral or lateral. The essential organs of the genital apparatus do not differ greatly from those of other groups of flatworms.

The oviduct leads from the ovary to the Mehlis' gland, where it may be met by an extension from the vagina prior to entering the gland or just after entering. A duct from the "yolk glands" (vitellaria) joins this fused duct, and the fertilized eggs enclosed in a shell leave the gland to be stored in the uterus. In some species the ripened eggs pass from the uterus into the proglottid, which eventually detaches as an egg packet; in some, the uterus has a separate opening, releasing eggs to the exterior directly.

**Life Cycle.**—The embryo develops within an eggshell, which in some species has a lid (operculum) that comes off at the time the egg hatches. In other forms, the shell must be digested away in the intestine of a host. The fertilized egg develops into a larva that bears hooks and is called an onchosphere. Eggs with opercula usually hatch in water, releasing the onchosphere, which in such cases is surrounded by a loose ciliated coat. This free-swimming larva (coracidium) cannot feed and thus is short lived; if, however, it is eaten by the proper intermediate host it continues its development.

Among the orders Pseudophyllidea and Trypanorhyncha, some species produce coracidia, but in most of the known life histories in these orders, and in the Tetraphyllidea, the eggs are not operculated and must be eaten by a crustacean. In either case, the onchosphere is released in the digestive tract of the host; with the aid of its hooks it pulls apart the cellular lining of the intestine wall and passes into the body cavity, where it grows as a procercoid. When the infected crustacean is eaten by the next host, the procercoid is released and, according to the species, either moves into the tissues or remains in the intestine of the second host. A cyst may form around the larva if it localizes in the tissues. The encysted larva then undergoes further growth and a loss of the larval hooks; the scolex forms and the larva is called a plerocercoid. In some species this is merely a growth stage that takes place in the intestine of the final (definitive) host.

The broad fish tapeworm of man has a uterine opening and eggs are shed continuously. These eggs hatch in water, and the coracidia are eaten by small crustaceans such as *Cyclops,* in which the procercoid develops. The plerocercoids are found in trout, perch,

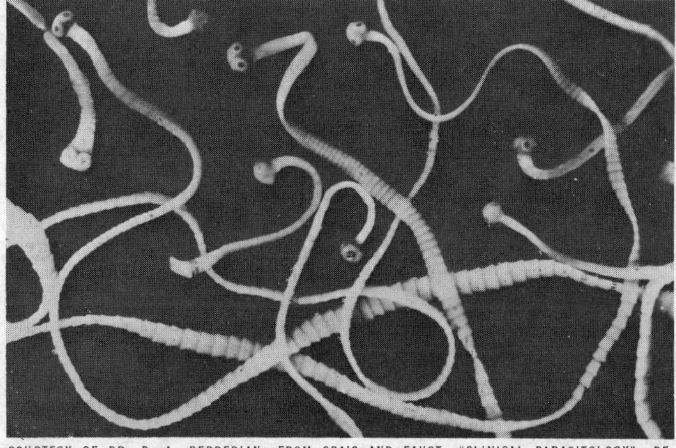

COURTESY OF DR. D. A. BERBERIAN, FROM CRAIG AND FAUST, "CLINICAL PARASITOLOGY"; REPRODUCED BY PERMISSION OF LEA & FEBIGER

FIG. 2.—BEEF TAPEWORM (TAENIA SAGINATA) RECOVERED FROM THE INTESTINE OF A MAN

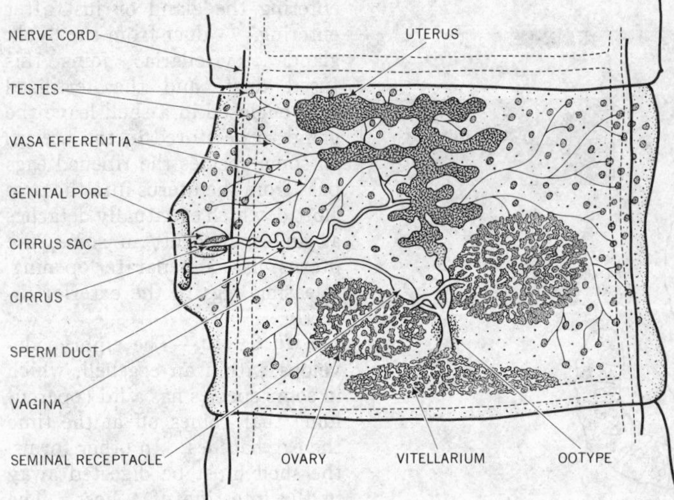


NOBLE AND NOBLE, "ANIMAL PARASITOLOGY LABORATORY MANUAL," 1962; REPRODUCED BY PERMISSION OF LEA & FEBIGER

FIG. 3.—A MATURE PROGLOTTID OF THE PORK TAPEWORM (TAENIA SOLIUM)

pike, and other freshwater fishes that eat microcrustaceans. The adult worm, which may attain a length of 30 ft. or more has a worldwide distribution wherever raw or partially cooked fish are eaten. For the development of this species and others related to it, two successive changes of host are required. The larval forms known as spargana, which occur in many land vertebrates, including man, have been shown to be the plerocercoids of pseudophyllidean worms of the genus *Spirometra,* which are primarily parasitic as adults in catlike carnivores and have a life history similar to *Diphyllobothrium.*

Cyclophyllidean life histories include two larval stages, *i.e.*, the onchosphere and the "bladder worm" (cysticercus). The latter is the infective or preadult stage. While arthropods (crustaceans, insects, mites, etc.) are the intermediate hosts for most species, the cyclophyllideans of carnivorous mammals, and also of man, usually utilize vertebrates for the intermediate host. Onchospheres of the beef tapeworm of man are released from the egg in the digestive tract of cattle. They migrate into the musculature, where each grows into a small bladder in whose wall a depression or invagination appears on the side opposite to the embryonic hooks. The scolex develops at the bottom of this invagination; once the suckers are fully formed, the cysticercus is infective. When raw or imperfectly cooked beef containing cysticerci is eaten by a human, the bladder is digested off, the scolex is evaginated, and the worm begins to produce proglottids from the region that originally connected the scolex to the bladder. Another human parasite, the pork tapeworm, has a similar development but has a rostellum armed with hooks and utilizes the pig as an intermediate host.

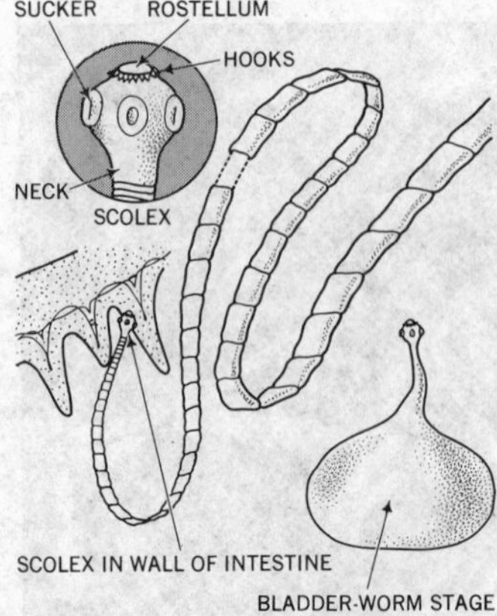


CLAUDE VILLEE, "GENERAL ZOOLOGY," SECOND EDITION; REPRODUCED BY PERMISSION OF W. B. SAUNDERS COMPANY

FIG. 4.—THE PORK TAPEWORM (TAENIA SOLIUM). INSET SHOWS THE HEAD

Other frequently encountered members of the genus *Taenia* are *T. pisiformis* of the dog, with the rabbit as the intermediate host, and *T. taeniaeformis* of the cat, with mice and rats as intermediate hosts. Asexual reproduction with the production of additional scolices occurs in some cyclophyllidean species. In the gid parasite of sheep the inner lining of the bladder produces a large number of scolices, each capable of developing into an adult worm if ingested by a dog or other suitable host. Such a larva is called a coenurus. Jackrabbits in Utah and Nevada frequently contain large numbers of coenuri of *Multiceps serialis* in the muscles of the thighs. The adult tapeworm in this case occurs in coyotes but can infest dogs, foxes, and other canids. Asexual reproduction during the bladder-worm stage is greatest in *Echinococcus granulosus,* a tiny tapeworm of dogs and their relatives. The larval stage, called a hydatid, produces daughter bladders internally and sometimes externally. These daughter bladders may contain another generation of bladders. Since the inner walls of the bladders produce a number of scolices, each hydatid can result in hundreds of tapeworms if eaten. Hydatids occur in sheep, cattle, pig, and sometimes man and can grow to be larger than a baseball.

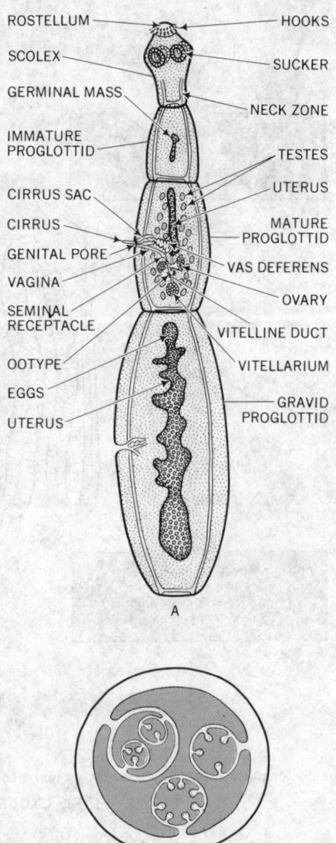


BROWN, "SELECTED INVERTEBRATE TYPES"; REPRODUCED BY PERMISSION OF JOHN WILEY & SONS INC.

FIG. 5.—HYDATID WORM (ECHINOCOCCUS GRANULOSUS): (A) WHOLE WORM; (B) CYST FROM LIVER OF MAN

Houseflies and earthworms are the intermediate hosts for several tapeworms of fowl. *Dipylidium caninum,* a common parasite of dogs and cats, passes its cysticercus stage in fleas or in the louse *Trichodectes.* The louse is capable of swallowing the eggs of the worm, but the adult flea cannot. Fleas become infected during their larval period, the eggs, when eaten, hatching in the intestine and the onchospheres migrating through the wall and into the body cavity. Development to the cysticercus stage does not occur until the flea metamorphoses as an adult. Man as well as dogs and cats can become infested if infected fleas are swallowed. Important cattle and sheep tapeworms such as *Moniezia expansa* pass the cysticercus stage in mites as do certain tapeworms of rabbits. *Hymenolepis nana,* the commonest tapeworm occurring in man, does not require an intermediate host though it can pass the cysticercus stage in beetles or fleas. If man becomes infected by swallowing eggs, the cysticercus stage occurs in the crypts of the wall of the small intestine, and the larva when mature evaginates, projecting into the intestine, and grows to adulthood.

**Classification.**—There are two subclasses: the Cestodaria, unsegmented parasites of the digestive tract and coelom of fishes with one species in the coelom of an Australian turtle; and the Cestoda. The latter group contains usually segmented species parasitic in the digestive tract; their larvae hatch from the egg and have six larval hooks instead of the ten found on cestodarian larvae.

One major group of the Cestoda has three larval stages and follicular vitellaria or a ventral vitellarium. It includes the following orders: Tetraphyllidea, primarily parasites of cold-blooded vertebrates, with scolex variably armed; Pseudophyllidea, parasites of warm- and cold-blooded vertebrates, with scolex usually armed with bothria; Trypanorhyncha, parasites of elasmobranch fishes, with scolex armed with bothria and four eversible proboscides, which are armed with hooks and spines.

A second group of the Cestoda has a compact dorsal vitellarium and two larval stages and consists of the order Cyclophyllidea, primarily parasites of warm-blooded vertebrates; scolex with four suckers, and frequently an armed rostellum. (N. W. R.)

**TAPIR,** a large, forest-dwelling, hoofed mammal that bears a strong likeness to a large pig, though there is no zoological relationship. There is only one genus, *Tapirus,* which constitutes the family Tapiridae, perissodactyl (*q.v.*) order. The geographical distribution of tapirs is peculiar: several species and subspecies are

YLLA FROM RAPHO-GUILLUMETTE

SOUTH AMERICAN TAPIR AND YOUNG

found in Central and South America, and one in southeast Asia. Fossil remains from Europe, China, and North America show that tapirs were once widespread; and that the extinction of intermediate forms has isolated the living species. The American species (*T. terrestris*, *T. roulini*, and *T. bairdi*) are all uniformly brownish, but the Asiatic, or Malayan, tapir (*T. indicus*) has black fore- and hindquarters and a whitish body; the young of all species are dark, with yellow and white stripes and spots, a pattern lost in six to eight months after birth.

The tapir's body, which can be 6 ft. (1.8 m.) long and weigh up to 600 lb. (272 kg.), is stout and barrel shaped; the tail short; and the nose and upper lip prolonged to form a short, highly mobile proboscis. The body is covered with short, harsh hair, which forms a short mane on the crest of the neck. The animal has four front and three hind toes.

There is no fixed mating season. In the American species a single young is born after a gestation of about 11 months; its life span is up to 30 years. Tapirs are exclusively vegetarian, eating leaves and water plants. In captivity they are generally very docile and friendly. They are on the whole solitary, and active at night. The flesh of tapirs is esteemed by the natives of the countries they inhabit. The Malayan species is in danger of extinction; the American species is still numerous. (L. H. M.)

**TAPS AND DIES:** *see* MACHINE TOOLS.

**TAPTI,** a river of western India. It rises in the Betul district of Madhya Pradesh and flows westward between two spurs of the Satpura Range, across the Khandesh Plateau in Maharashtra, and through the Plain of Surat in Gujarat to the Arabian Sea. It has a total length of about 436 mi. (702 km.) and drains an area of 25,200 sq.mi. (65,300 sq.km.). For the last 32 mi. (52 km.) past the port of Surat it is tidal, but is navigable only by small vessels. The port of Swally at its mouth, famous in Anglo-Portuguese history, is now deserted, having become silted up like the other ports in the Gulf of Cambay. The Tapti flows roughly parallel to the larger Narmada River to the north, from which it is separated by the main part of the Satpura Range. The two river valleys and the intervening range form the natural barrier between northern and peninsular India. (L. D. S.)

**TAR:** *see* COAL TAR; CREOSOTE; TARS, LOW-TEMPERATURE.

**TARA** (Old Irish TEMUIR), a low (*c.* 507 ft.) (155 m.) hill in County Meath, Ire., occupies an important place in Irish legend and history. Already in prehistoric times it was, probably, a cult centre, for the earliest remains so far identified there consist of a small passage grave (excavated 1955–59) dated to about 2100 B.C. It is known as *Dumha na nGiall* (Mound of the Hostages), a name that, like those applied to the other monuments on the hill, is derived from medieval topographical tracts. Numerous inserted Bronze Age burials were found in the earth mound that covered the grave. The mound lies just within the perimeter of a huge oval enclosure called *Ráth na Ríogh* (Rath of the Kings), near the centre of which are two conjoined earthworks: one called *Forradh* (Royal Seat), the other *Teach Cormaic* (Cormac's House). On the latter is a pillar stone, said to have stood formerly on the Mound of the Hostages and sometimes equated with the *Lia Fáil,* or inauguration stone of the kings of Tara. The other principal sites are a large ring fort known as *Ráth Laoghaire* (Laoghaire's Rath); two circular enclosures called *Claoin Fhearta* (Sloping Graves) and *Ráth Gráinne* (Gráinne's Rath); and a great rectangular earthwork, *c.* 750 ft. long, which is usually identified as the *Teach Miodhchuarta* (House of the Mead-circling) or banqueting hall referred to in ancient Irish literature. Of the remaining monuments, *Ráth na Seanad* (Rath of the Synods), excavated 1952–53, proved to be a ritual site that had undergone four successive enlargements between the 1st and 4th centuries A.D. The main earthworks on the hill are probably to be attributed to the first five centuries of the Christian era when Tara was the seat of a dynasty of Uí Néill kings who appear to have abandoned it in the 6th century. (A. T. Ls.)

**TARAFAH** ('AMR IBN AL-'ABD AL-BAKRI), Arab poet of the 6th century and author of one of the odes in the *Mu'allaqat* (*q.v.*). After a wild and dissipated youth spent in Bahrain, and after fighting in the war between the tribes of Bakr and Taghlib, he went with his uncle Mutalammis, who was also a poet, to the court of the king of Hira, 'Amr ibn Hind (d. 568–569), and there became companion to the king's brother. Having ridiculed the king in some verses, he was sent with a letter to the ruler of Bahrain and, in accordance with the instructions contained in the letter, was buried alive.

Tarafah's collected works were ed. by W. Ahlwardt in the *Divans of the Six Ancient Arab Poets* (1870). For a summary of his life and an Eng. trans. of his *mu'allaqah,* see A. J. Arberry, *The Seven Odes* (1957).

**TARANTELLA,** an Italian folk dance in rapid 6/8 time, danced in couples and characterized by light quick hops and tapping foot movements. Its origin is connected with tarantism, a disease or form of hysteria that appeared in Italy in the 15th–17th centuries and was obscurely associated with the bite of the tarantula spider: victims seemingly were cured by frenzied dancing. The name tarantella may be more directly derived from Taranto, a town located in the region where tarantism was especially prevalent. The tarantella appears in many ballets, including *Napoli, La Tarentule,* and *La Boutique Fantasque.* (LN. ME.)

**TARANTO** (ancient Greek TARAS; Latin TARENTUM), a port and important naval base of Puglia (Apulia), Italy, and chief town of Taranto Province, lies on the north inlet of the Gulf of Taranto, 50 mi. (80 km.) SSE of Bari. Pop. (1961) 200,974. The old part of the city (Città Vecchia) occupies a small island that almost entirely blocks the channel between the outer and inner harbours, Mare Grande and Mare Piccolo. It is joined to the newer sections on the mainland by two bridges, one of which, the Ponte Girevole, revolves to permit shipping to enter the Mare Piccolo. The mainland parts consist of the industrial Borgo (northwest), with the railway station, and the Città Nuova (southeast). The old city stands on the site of the Acropolis of Taras and contains the Aragonese Castle (rebuilt in 1480 and subsequently enlarged), the 11th-century Romanesque Cathedral of S. Cataldo (with a Baroque facade and early 15th-century campanile with mullioned windows), and the Church of S. Domenico Maggiore (1302), with a Romanesque-Gothic facade, an imposing portal, and a rose window. The Città Nuova contains the Arsenal (1803); the Banca d'Italia; the post office; the Government Palace (1896); the city library; the Meteorological and Geophysical Observatory (1905); the National Museum (with its 18th-century cloister of S. Pasquale), which houses an important archaeological collection covering Taranto and the rest of Apulia; the State Institute of Marine Biology (1931); and the Villas Garibaldi and Comunale Peripato. In the Mare Piccolo there is much oyster and mussel farming, and there is fishing with the ebb of the tide. Industries include canning and food processing, shipbuilding, and the manufacture of chemicals and bricks. Railways link the town with Brindisi, Metaponto, and Bari. (M. T. A. N.)

**History.**—At Scoglio del Tonno, northwest of Taranto, there are traces of Mycenaean Greek trade. In the 8th century B.C. (the traditional date is 706 B.C., but it may well have been earlier), Greek settlers from Sparta and Laconia conquered the Messapian village of Taras, on the river of the same name (modern Tara), and founded a new Taras on the peninsula (cut in 1480 by a canal) that lay between the Mare Piccolo and the Mare Grande. Taras soon became one of the leading cities of Magna Graecia, despite a catastrophic defeat by the native Iapygians *c.* 473; Callipolis (Gallipoli) and Hydrus (Otranto) were founded from Taras, as, in 433, was Heraclea (*q.v.*).

At the time of Archytas (*q.v.;* 4th century B.C.), the great philosopher and scientist, Taras reached its maximum splendour; it was then the chief city of the Italiote League, formed to protect the Greek cities scattered along the coast of the Ionian Sea from the recurrent attacks of the Lucanians and Iapygians. But with the death of Archytas, the league unfortunately lost its commander and eminent strategist (who, it is said, never lost a battle), and the Lucanians and Bruttii, assisted by Iapygians and Messapians, thereupon declared war on Taras itself, which turned first for help to Archidamus III, king of Sparta (killed 338), and then to Alexander the Molossian, king of Epirus (killed *c.* 330). But neither these nor subsequent hired defenders were effective, and the defeat of a Roman fleet off Taras in 282 led to war with the Romans; despite an appeal (281) to Pyrrhus (*q.v.*), king of Epirus, Taras finally submitted to them (272). During the Second Punic War most of Taras fell into the hands of Hannibal (213–212), but the consul Fabius Maximus recaptured and plundered it (209). The city, known under the Romans as Tarentum, although again confirmed as an allied city and obtaining a constitution with a senate and decurions, quadrumvirs, and aediles, never again held the right of minting coin. Some colonies, including Neptunia at Tarentum (123), were founded for discharged Roman legionaries, and many Roman families moved to Tarentum in search of a fortune. The town declined under the Roman Empire, despite attempts to repopulate it. (An. Mo.; C. Dr.; X.)

From the 6th to the 10th century, Tarentum changed hands repeatedly between Goths, Byzantines, Lombards, and Arabs. The Arabs destroyed the city and enslaved the inhabitants in 927; it was rebuilt in 967 by the Byzantine emperor Nicephorus II. Robert Guiscard captured it *c.* 1060, and it became part of the Norman territory in southern Italy; Bohemund (*q.v.*) I became prince of Taranto, and it served as a point of departure for Crusaders. (For its subsequent rulers, *see* NAPLES, KINGDOM OF.) It was fortified by Don John of Austria and during the late 16th and 17th centuries was repeatedly attacked by the Turks.

The French acquired Taranto by the Peace of Florence (1801); Napoleon created Marshal Macdonald duke of Taranto in 1809, and it was a French naval base during the Napoleonic Wars. After 1815 it was part of the Kingdom of the Two Sicilies.

After its union with Italy in 1860, Taranto became one of the most important strongholds of the Italian Navy. During World War I the British, French, and Italian fleets had bases at Taranto, and it was a meeting place for those divisions that fought at Salonika and in Macedonia and that effected the rescue of the Serbian Army. During World War II the naval base was heavily and effectively bombed (Nov. 11–12, 1940) by carrier-borne British planes; British landing forces were unopposed when they occupied the city on Sept. 9, 1943. (M. T. A. N.; X.)

**Ancient Remains.**—The Greek *polis* (which stood on the site of the present Città Nuova) was protected on the east by a ditch (the so-called *canalone*) and by solid walls of thick square blocks, remains of which were brought to light under the present Carmine farmhouse and in the Chiappari area on the Mare Grande.

Apparently the *polis* was separated from the Acropolis (also called the Rocca, corresponding roughly to the present Città Vecchia) by another wall; however, no trace of this was found during the construction of the present navigable canal. All these walls must have had fortified gates; ancient sources name several gates and streets, not all of which have been identified. The temples, of which there probably were many, remain undiscovered. Of the Temple of Apollo only a deposit of hundreds of statuettes of the god have been found, and two imposing Doric columns are all that remain of a temple presumably dedicated to Poseidon. There is little information regarding the civil buildings. Like Sparta, Taras rose from the union of small groups of houses, each with its own little cemetery; this explains the tombs of that period, which are scattered over the area of the ancient *polis*. These tombs yielded imported Greek vases (proto-Corinthian, Corinthian, proto-Attic, and black-figured Attic; also, very rare, red-figured Attic) and, from the beginning of the 4th century B.C., Italiote vases made by local craftsmen, imitations of figured Greek vases. There are interesting comic *phlyax* vases inspired by the popular theatre and the *vis comica,* characteristic of Tarentines of all periods. The magnificent gold and terra-cotta figurines surpass even those of Greece in delicacy and charm. Contrary to what written sources suggested, Taras unfortunately yielded very few statues. These are not all of Greek origin; some, the work of local artists or of Greeks adapting themselves to local requirements and temperament, seem animated by a clearly Italic realism. But, above all, the hundreds of reliefs in soft local stone are witness to the confident workmanship of skilled local craftsmen who, while conserving definite connections with the art of neighbouring Greece, present distinctive artistic tastes and tendencies.

Roman remains are better known. The remains of large public baths have been found along the Lungomare and near the church of S. Francesco. The ruins of an amphitheatre built of *opus reticulatum* (stone-faced concrete) lie beneath the present covered market; many scholars confuse this amphitheatre with the Greek theatre. Nothing is known of this theatre save that it was situated within view of the sea. Mosaic floors have been found in various places in the Città Nuova, and a whole house was discovered on the present site of the dry dock in the Arsenal. There are many cremation and burial tombs of the same period.

(An. Mo.; C. Dr.; X.)

TARANTO PROVINCE, created in 1923, was known as the Province of the Ionian Sea from 1936 to 1951. Pop. (1961) 465,395; area 941 sq.mi. (2,436 sq.km.). It is for the most part mountainous, with deep gulfs and a narrow coastal plain. Helped by a mild climate, agriculture (cereals, vegetables, olives, and fruit) and stockbreeding are widespread, and there is important trade in grapes and Apulian wine. The principal centres are Massafra, divided by the picturesque ravine of San Marco; Grottaglie, which has an airport and is famous for its ceramic ware; Castellaneta, with its striking cathedral (rebuilt in 1400) and its bell tower; and Martina Franca (1,414 ft. [431 m.] above sea level), a summer resort, notable for its Baroque buildings. (M. T. A. N.)

**TARANTULA,** strictly speaking, a large spider (*Lycosa tarantula*) with a body about one inch long which takes its name from the town of Taranto in southern Italy. Its bite was formerly believed to be the cause of a disease known as tarantism. In this malady the victim wept, skipped about and then went into a wild dance (*see* TARANTELLA). Unless assisted by special music or magic antidotes, the victim was expected to die. Investigations have shown that the bite of this spider is not dangerous to man and that the disease attributed to it must have had other causes.

*Lycosa tarantula* belongs to the wolf spider family (Lycosidae) and has numerous allies in various parts of the world. The tarantula spins no web and catches its prey by pursuit. It inhabits dry, well-drained ground where it digs deep burrows. In the winter, the opening of the burrow is covered with silk, and the spider becomes dormant. It lives for several years.

BY COURTESY OF THE ZOOLOGICAL SOCIETY OF LONDON

A EUROPEAN LYCOSID TARANTULA

The name tarantula is often applied indiscriminately to large, fearsome hairy spiders of the suborder Mygalomorphae but is usually reserved for members of the family Theraphosidae, which are found in the southwestern United States, Mexico, and tropical America. Most of these forms are harmless to man, except for their nonpoisonous bite. Many of these spiders tunnel into the soil, spending most of their life within this single burrow. They feed on large insects and occasionally on frogs, toads and mice.

In the southwestern United States, some tarantulas of the genus *Aphonopelma* attain a length of about 2 in. and a leg spread of from 4 to 5 in. These tarantulas are quite harmless and have been trained as pets; however, they can inflict painful wounds in self-defense. In South America, some tarantulas have a body length of more than 3 in. A few of these build huge webs and catch and kill large insects and even small birds for food.

*See* also SPIDER. (C. J. Go.; M. L. G.)

**TARAPACÁ,** the northernmost province of Chile, bounded north by Peru, east by Bolivia, south by Antofagasta and west by the Pacific. Area 22,422 sq.mi. (58,073 sq.km.). Pop. (1960) 123,070. It is part of the Atacama desert (*q.v.*) region of the Pacific coast of South America and is without water except at the base of the Andes, where streams flow down into the sands and are lost. In some of these places there is vegetation and water enough to support small settlements.

The wealth of Tarapacá is in its immense deposits of nitrate of soda (found on the Pampa de Tamarugal, a broad desert plateau between the coast range and the Andes, which has an elevation of about 3,000 ft. [915 m.]). The mining and preparation of nitrate of soda for export has provided an uncertain livelihood for the population of this province. Silver is mined near Iquique, the provincial capital. Unfavourable world markets for nitrate caused a decline in population after 1940. The principal ports of the province are Pisagua, Iquique and Arica (*q.v.*), from the first two of which "nitrate railways" run inland to the deposits.

Tarapacá was ceded to Chile by Peru after the war of 1879–83 and was organized as a province in 1884.

**TARASCO** (TARASCANS), the principal Indian group in the Mexican state of Michoacán, who term themselves and their language Purépecha. The expanding independent Tarascan nation at the time of the Spanish conquest dwindled until most Tarasco by the 20th century were confined to the pine- and oak-clad highlands dotted with volcanic cones and lakes west from Morelia and Lake Pátzcuaro and north from Uruapan and Parícutin volcano. Despite a culture that is more Old World than native, there is a marked retention of ethnic identity. During the 1960s there were approximately 60,000 persons of Purépecha speech, of whom perhaps one-fifth were monolingual. This language constitutes a linguistic family with no known relatives. Tarascan archaeology and history have been little studied, but artifacts and colonial accounts indicate that this group was the equal or superior of its Mexican contemporaries in the working of feathers, shell, wood, metal, and stone, and in military prowess; its architecture, however, was greatly inferior.

The Tarasco have no special tribal organization but participate in much the same political, economic, and religious organizations as do their neighbours of mixed ancestry. Agriculture is dominant; maize and wheat occupy most of the acreage, followed by pulses, cucurbits, barley, cabbage, and chili pepper. They also keep chickens, oxen, pigs, sheep, beehives, burros, and turkeys. In the mountain or sierra region forest products are quite important, and there the wooden house (*troje*) prevails. Among the leading cottage handicrafts are woodworking, pottery making, and weaving. Many Tarasco have gone as farm labourers (*braceros*) to the U.S., and most of the nearly 120 communities have at least one man who has lived in the U.S.

Among the leading communities are the Sierra capital Paracho, strongly Indian Cherán and Santa Fe, the Once Pueblos de la Cañada, and the sentimentally important former capitals Tzintzuntzan, Ihuatzio, and Pátzcuaro. In 1964–65 the Mexican government established a Tarascan regional coordinating centre in Cherán to develop schools, roads, hospitals, agriculture, and industry.

BIBLIOGRAPHY.—J. A. Mason, "The Native Languages of Middle America," in *The Maya and Their Neighbors* (1940); L. Mendieta y Núñez *et al.*, *Los Tarascos* (1940); D. D. Brand, "An Historical Sketch of Geography and Anthropology in the Tarascan Region," *New Mex. Anthrop.*, pp. 37–108 (June 1944); Smithsonian Institution, *Publications of the Institute of Social Anthropology,* no. 1, 2, 6, 7, 11 (1944–1951); Sociedad Mexicana de Antropología, *El Occidente de Mexico* (1948); G. Aguirre Beltrán, *Problemas de la Población Indígena de la Cuenca del Tepalcatepec* (1952); P. Carrasco Pizano, *Tarascan Folk Religion* (1952); J. Tudela, J. Corona Núñez, and P. Kirchhoff (eds.), *Relación de las ceremonias y ritos y población y gobierno de los indios de la Provincia de Michoacan (1541)* (1956); J. Corona Núñez, *Mitología Tarasca* (1957). (D. D. B.)

**TARASCON,** a town of southeastern France, in the *département* of Bouches-du-Rhône, 10½ mi. (17 km.) N of Arles. Pop. (1962) 6,475. It stands on the left bank of the Rhône opposite Beaucaire (*q.v.*), with which it is connected by railway and road bridges. Extensively damaged at the end of World War II, much of the town has been rebuilt, but the old quarters have kept their Provençal atmosphere with narrow streets, some still covered with inhabited archways. The Church of Sainte-Marthe is a historic monument. Of the Romanesque building (late 12th century) there remains chiefly the main porch flanked by richly ornamented columns. The church as a whole is Gothic (15th–16th centuries); its spire was destroyed in 1944 but was to be reconstructed. The crypt contains the tomb of St. Martha (the sister of Lazarus and the patron saint of the town) and that of Jean de Cossa (seneschal of Provence under King René), and the Chapel of Saint-Lazare, renovated by Louis II, count of Provence. The château, on a rock falling steeply into the Rhône from which Revolution prisoners were thrown into the river, was completed by René in the 15th century on the site of a Roman fortress. It has a courtyard, halls with painted *mélèze* (larchwood) ceilings, and two chapels, one above the other. Other buildings are the Hôtel de ville (1648), the Chapel of Notre Dame de Bonaventure (15th century), and the facade of the Benedictine Abbey (1358).

The town has manufactures of Provençal printed cloth and of paper pulp ("Rhône cellulose"), and a trade in fruit and early vegetables. In his novel *Tartarin de Tarascon* (1872), Alphonse Daudet satirized the life of the town and the southern character. The fête and procession are held on the last Sunday in June. The name of the town is associated with a legendary monster, La Tarasque, which was said to have ravaged the district and to have been tamed by St. Martha; its image figures in the town's coat of arms and in the procession. (JE. G.)

**TARBERT,** a fishing village and summer resort at the head of East Loch Tarbert, an inlet of the sea on the western shore of the mouth of Loch Fyne, Argyll County, Scot., 38 mi. (61 km.) SSW of Inveraray by road. Pop. (1961) 1,313. The name (met elsewhere in Scotland) denotes an isthmus, and the village is in fact on the neck of land joining Kintyre to the rest of Argyll. This isthmus is little more than 1 mi. wide, and boats used to be dragged across to the head of West Loch Tarbert, a narrow sea loch nearly 10 mi. (16 km.) long. There is a good harbour with a pier for passenger steamers about ¾ mi. from the village. The herring fishery, though declined, is the main industry together with some shipbuilding. Overlooking the harbour are the ruins of a castle built by Robert I, "the Bruce," in 1326.

**TARBES,** a town and the *préfecture* in the *département* of Hautes-Pyrénées, France, 98 mi. (158 km.) WSW of Toulouse by rail. Pop. (1962) 46,162. It lies in the centre of a fertile plain below the Pyrenees, and on the left bank of the Adour River, streams from which are conducted through the town. The domed cathedral of Notre-Dame de la Sède dates from the 12th–14th centuries, and the largely restored churches of Saint-Jean and Sainte-Thérèse from the 14th and 15th centuries. The birthplace of Marshal Ferdinand Foch (1851–1929) is kept as a museum, and a street named after him is the commercial centre. In the Jardin Massey, a park donated by King Louis Philippe's gardener, is a bust of the poet Théophile Gautier (1811–72), who was born at Tarbes, and a museum of paintings and antiquities. The town was replanned in the 18th century with the help of Antoine Megret d'Étigny, intendant of Auch.

Tarbes is mentioned in the 5th century A.D. as the capital of the ancient province of Bigorre and the seat of a bishop. It was taken by the English in the Hundred Years' War and suffered considerable damage (1569) during the Wars of Religion. In 1814 Wellington gained a victory over the French under Marshal Soult near Tarbes. Until the mid-19th century it was important only as a market and an administrative centre, but the construction of the railway from Morcenx in 1859 favoured the development of industry, and this was further encouraged by the establishment of an arsenal in 1872, after the Franco-German War. Between World Wars I and II the railways of the region were electrified, and important industries grew up near Tarbes, producing electrical and diesel equipment, and other machinery. Tarbes has also kept its importance as a market town for the surrounding agricultural district, and there is a stud for the breeding of Anglo-Arab horses. It is on the railway from Toulouse to Bayonne, and the airport 4 mi. (6½ km.) from the town serves Tarbes and Lourdes, which lies 12 mi. (19 km.) to the southwest. (Cl. B.)

**TARDE, GABRIEL** (1843–1904), one of the most versatile and productive of French social scientists of his day, was born on March 12, 1843, at Sarlat, Dordogne. He served as a provincial magistrate and as director of the Bureau of Criminal Statistics at the Ministry of Justice. In 1900 he was appointed professor of modern philosophy at the Collège de France. He died at Paris on May 13, 1904. The sequence of invention, repetition, conflict, and adaptation emphasized in Tarde's social philosophy seems to bear a close resemblance to Hegel's dialectic.

Tarde held that about one person in a hundred is inventive, yet that invention is the source of all progress. Inventions are imitated, but differ in degree and type of imitation, and this promotes opposition, both between varied imitations and between the new and the old in culture. The outcome of this opposition is an ultimate adaptation that then becomes in itself an invention.

He saw this sequence as an unending cycle constituting the process of history and social experience (*Social Laws,* 1898). He treated repetition in his most famous work, *The Laws of Imitation* (1890); opposition in *Universal Opposition* (1897); and adaptation in *Social Logic* (1895). In *Comparative Criminality* (1886) and other works on criminology he attacked the extreme biological theories of C. Lombroso and his school, pointing out the environmental influences on behaviour. He also contributed to the studies of law and political science, crowd psychology and economics. His *Economic Psychology,* 2 vol. (1902), later stimulated the institutional economics of J. A. Hobson in England and Thorstein Veblen and his followers in the United States.

*See* M. M. Davis, *Psychological Interpretations of Society* (1909). (H. E. Bar.)

**TARDIEU, ANDRÉ** (1876–1945), French statesman who attempted to carry on the policies of Georges Clemenceau in the aftermath of World War I. Born in Paris on Sept. 22, 1876, of an upper middle-class family, he studied at the École Normale Supérieure. After a period in the diplomatic service, he made his reputation as foreign editor of *Le Temps.* Elected to the Chamber of Deputies in 1914, he served with distinction in the Chasseurs-à-Pied during World War I till 1916. In 1917 he was sent on a special mission to the U.S. At the Conference of Paris (*q.v.*), he had a considerable part in drafting the Treaty of Versailles.

He was minister for the Liberated Areas (Alsace-Lorraine) in Clemenceau's government from November 1919 to January 1920. After Clemenceau's retirement he steadfastly refused to enter any government till 1926. In the Chamber and in the press he waged an uncompromising campaign against relaxation of the Treaty of Versailles. He lost his parliamentary seat in the elections of 1924 but recovered it in 1926. Then, to Clemenceau's chagrin, he accepted the ministry of public works and later the ministry of the interior under Raymond Poincaré. Leader of the right-centre in the Chamber, he was premier from Nov. 2, 1929, to Feb. 17, 1930, and again from March 2 to Dec. 5, 1930, advocating a policy of large national expenditure. He was minister of agriculture (1931–32) and of war (1932) in Pierre Laval's two cabinets before becoming premier for the third time on Feb. 20, 1932. Defeated in the general elections, he resigned on May 10, 1932. Finally, disgusted with the condition of public affairs, he retired from active politics in 1936. He died at Menton on Sept. 15, 1945.

Learned, witty, and self-assured, Tardieu wrote many books, including *La France et les alliances* (1908); *La Paix* (1921; English translation, *The Truth About the Treaty*); *Devant l'obstacle* (1927; English translation, *France and America*); and *La Révolution à refaire,* two volumes (1936–37), a denunciation of the French parliamentary system.

*See* G. Puaux *et al., André Tardieu* (1957). (J. C. de C.)

**TARDIGRADA,** a class of minute animals doubtfully placed among the arthropods (*q.v.*). The largest of the bear animalcules or water bears, as these animals have been commonly called, are not much more than 1 mm. in length, while most of them are very much smaller. They are free-living forms found in variable habitats, in damp moss, on flowering plants, in sand, fresh water and even in the sea; and in adaptation to this wide range of external conditions a large number of genera and species have been evolved.

The water bear has a well-developed head region and a short body composed of four fused segments, each represented externally by a pair of short, stout, unjointed limbs generally terminated by sharp claws, which seem to range in number from four to nine, but sometimes, as in *Batillipes,* ending in three pairs of racquet-shaped, digitiform outgrowths. The limbs of the last pair project backward from the posterior end of the body on each side of the anus. The cuticle, which is not chitinized, may be smooth or sculptured in various ways and is sometimes strengthened with segmentally arranged plates (as in *Echiniscus*) and sometimes provided with long paired hairlike cirri. An interesting feature of the structure of Tardigrada is the more or less fixed number of cells of which their body is composed. Thus the median dorsal strip of epidermis is composed of only 24 pairs of cells.

No special organs of circulation or respiration are known. The alimentary canal traverses the body from end to end. Within the fore gut is a pair of protrusible stylets, large glands that open into the esophagus, a muscular pharynx and large median and lateral glands that open into the intestine posteriorly. The nervous system, which is remarkably well-developed, consists of a bilobate cerebral ganglion, frequently provided with a pair of eye-spots, and of a ventral chain of five large ganglia connected by lateral commissures. The sexes are not distinct and the generative products are discharged either into the posterior end of the alimentary canal or directly to the exterior through a median pore in front of the anus. The eggs are large and in some cases at least are enclosed in the cuticle of the parent, which is cast to form a case for them. The young when hatched are about one-third the size of the parent, which they closely resemble except for the occasional absence of a pair of limbs that develop later.

FROM "CAMBRIDGE NATURAL HISTORY," BY PERMISSION OF THE MACMILLAN COMPANY, PUBLISHERS

ECHINISCUS SPINULOSUS, AFTER DOYÈRE

The Tardigrada are divided into two orders: (1) the Heterotardigrada, containing two families with nine genera (*Echiniscus, Batillipes,* etc.), in which the head is provided with two pairs of cirri in front, a pair of lateral cirri and a so-called *clava* or spatulate process, one on each side; and (2) the Eutardigrada, containing two families and three genera (*Macrobiotus, Hypsibius* and *Milnesium*), in which cephalic cirri are wanting.

The most remarkable feature of the tardigrades is their ability to withstand desiccation and low temperature. Under unfavourable conditions, tardigrades go into a state of suspended animation, or anabiosis. Specimens kept for eight days in a vacuum, transferred for three days into helium gas at room temperature, then exposed for several hours to a temperature of $-272°$ C came to life again when they were brought to normal room temperature; further, 60% of specimens kept for 21 months in liquid air at a temperature of $-190°$ C came to life. Specimens allowed to dry at room temperature and kept dry for 18 months returned to life in about two hours after having been transferred into water.

The Tardigrada cannot be assigned with complete confidence to the Arthropoda until it is proved that their oral stylets are modified appendages. Assuming that they belong to the Arthropoda, they must rank as a class by themselves. Some authors give Tardigrada phylum rank; a few scholars have suggested that the group is closer to Annelida.

BIBLIOGRAPHY.—E. Marcus, "Tardigrada," in Ward and Whipple's *Fresh-Water Biology,* 2nd ed. by W. T. Edmondson (1959) and "Tardigrada," in Bronn's *Klassen und Ordnungen* (1929); R. W. Pennak, "Tardigrada. Ecology of the Microscopic Metazoa, etc.," *Ecol. Monographs,* 10:572–579.

**TARENTUM:** *see* TARANTO.

**TARGUM.** The Targums are Aramaic translations—often interpretations or paraphrases—of the books of the Old Testament. In their earliest form they date from the time when Aramaic superseded Hebrew as the spoken language of large numbers of the Jews. (*See* HEBREW LANGUAGE; SEMITIC LANGUAGES.) In their origin they were designed to meet the needs of the unlearned among the people who had ceased to understand the Hebrew of the Old Testament. In the absence of any precise evidence on the point it is impossible to give more than a rough estimate as to the period at which Hebrew, as a spoken language, was generally displaced by Aramaic. It is certain, however, that Aramaic was firmly established in Palestine in the 1st century A.D., despite the fact that Hebrew still remained the learned and sacred tongue. Hence it may be reasonably inferred that the mass of the people had adopted Aramaic at a considerably earlier period, probably as early as the 2nd century B.C., and that the need of Aramaic translations of the sacred text made itself felt only a little later.

Just as the old Greek translation of the Pentateuch, the Septuagint (*q.v.*), came into being in Egypt about 200 B.C. to satisfy the needs of a Jewish population that increasingly favoured Greek over Hebrew as its vernacular, so, it appears, did the Targum on the Pentateuch appear at about the same time in western Asia—*i.e.,* Babylonia and Judaea—where Aramaic had become the commonest vernacular tongue. At first the Pentateuch alone was involved, apparently because only the Law was as yet canonized as Sacred Scripture. In time, however, in the case of both the Septuagint and the Targums, the books of the Prophets and of the Hagiographa (Psalms, Proverbs, Job, Ruth, Lamentations of Jeremiah, Song of Solomon, Ecclesiastes, Esther, I and II Chronicles; for Ezra, Nehemiah and Daniel, however, no Targums have been found) were turned into Greek and Aramaic.

The status and influence of the Targums became assured after the Temple was destroyed, when synagogues replaced the Temple as houses of worship. For it was in the synagogue that the practice of reading from the Law and from the Prophets became widely observed, along with the custom of providing these readings with a translation into Aramaic.

This role of the Aramaic Targum became so generally recognized that by the 2nd century A.D. the Mishna (codification of the oral tradition, incorporated in the Talmud) takes it for granted and merely inculcates certain regulations to be observed by the *Meturgeman* ("translator"), who had by this time acquired a definite status. The Mishna indicates that the *Meturgeman,* who was distinct from the reader, translated each verse of the Law into Aramaic as soon as it had been read in Hebrew; in the readings from the Prophets three verses might be read at a time (*cf.* Luke iv, 16 ff.; Acts xiii, 14 ff., 27; xv, 21).

The translator endeavoured to reproduce the original as closely as possible, but, inasmuch as his object was to give an intelligible rendering, a merely literal translation would sometimes be insufficient; hence the translators tended to take a more elastic view of their obligations. To prevent misconceptions, they expanded and explained what was obscure, adjusted the incidents of the past to the ideas of later times, emphasized the moral lessons to be learned from the national history and, finally, adapted the rules and regulations of the Holy Scriptures to the conditions and requirements of their own age. As time went on, the practice of introducing additional matter of an edifying character grew in popular favour and was gradually extended. The method by which the text was thus utilized as a vehicle for conveying homiletic discourses, traditional sayings, legends and allegories is abundantly illustrated by the later Targums, as opposed to the more literal translations of the earlier Targum of Onkelos (*see* below) and on the Prophets.

It would be incorrect to suppose, however, that the translation of the text was left entirely to the individual taste of the translator. The latter is rather to be regarded as the representative of a school of thought reflecting the spirit of the age in which he lived.

There can be little doubt that the Targums existed for a long time in oral form, and so long at least as the Targum tradition remained active there would be little temptation to commit it to writing. But it is highly probable that this procedure, in the case of the Targums, was mainly followed with respect to those parts of the Old Testament which were read in the synagogical services (*e.g.,* the Law and the Prophets) and that it was less rigidly observed in regard to the other portions of Scripture; a written translation of the latter would be of special value for the purpose of private study. Hence there is no need to reject the tradition as to the existence of a written Targum on Job in the time of Gamaliel I (1st century A.D.), especially as references to Targum manuscripts occur in the Mishna and elsewhere. But it was not these manuscripts but the living tradition of the learned that was recognized as authoritative throughout the period that closes with the compilation of the Talmud in the early centuries of the Christian era. The official recognition of a written Targum, and therefore the final fixing of its text, belongs to the post-Talmudic period, and is not to be placed earlier than the 5th century A.D.

## TARGUMS ON THE PENTATEUCH

**Onkelos.**—The so-called Targum of Onkelos owes its name to a mistaken reference in the Babylonian Talmud. In its original context, that of the Jerusalem Talmud, the passage refers to the Greek translation of Aquila the proselyte. Onkelos the proselyte was mistakenly identified with him and then credited with the Aramaic translation of the Pentateuch. With the exception of this one reference, the Targum is always introduced in the Babylonian Talmud by the phrase "as we translate" or "our Targum"; it is probable, therefore, that the name of the author, or authors, was unknown to the Babylonian Jews. It is first quoted under the title of the Targum of Onkelos by the gaon Sar Shalom (d. *c.* A.D. 859).

The Targum of Onkelos may be regarded as an official translation of the Law, in the Judaean Aramaic dialect, which was carried out in Babylon, probably about the 4th century A.D.; in its final form it cannot be earlier than the 5th century A.D. The translation, as a whole, is good, and adheres very closely to the Hebrew text.

Of all the extant Targums, that of Onkelos affords perhaps the most characteristic and consistent example of the exegetical methods employed in these works. Two principles may be said to have guided the translators. On the one hand, their primary object was to produce a faithful rendering of the original which at the same time would be intelligible to the people; for this purpose a purely literal translation would be insufficient. On the other hand, they regarded it as necessary to present the sacred text in such a manner as best to convey the particular form of interpretation then current. Later Jewish exegesis was especially concerned to eliminate everything in the sacred writings that might give rise to misconception with respect to God on the part of the unlearned.

Hence in the Targums various expedients were adopted for avoiding any reference to the Deity that might be misunderstood by the people or that involved apparent irreverence. Examples of this peculiarly Targumic method are: (1) the insertion of "word," "glory," or "presence" before the divine name, when God is referred to in his dealings with men; (2) the insertion of the preposition "before" when God is the object of any action; (3) the use of the passive for the active voice; (4) the use of periphrasis for the more pronounced anthropomorphisms, such as "to smell," "to taste"; (5) the use of different expressions or the insertion of a preposition before the divine name, when God is compared with man or the same action is predicated of God and man; (6) the use of distinctive terms "God" and "idol" where in the original the same characters are used to denote both God and heathen gods. Instances of this endeavour to maintain, as it were, a respectful distance in speaking of God occur on every page of the Targums;

at the same time, however, and by no means infrequently, less obviously physical human actions and passions are ascribed to God, a phenomenon that requires further study.

**Jerusalem Targums.**—Two other Targums to the Pentateuch are cited by Jewish authorities under the titles of the Targum Jerushalmi and the Targum of Jonathan ben Uzziel. Of these, the former contains only portions of the Pentateuch and is therefore usually designated the Fragmentary (Jerusalem) Targum.

The second Jerusalem Targum owes its ascription to Jonathan ben Uzziel to the incorrect solution (probably in the 14th century A.D.) of the abbreviated form by which it was frequently cited (viz., Targum Jerushalmi), hence the term "Pseudo-Jonathan" by which it often is designated. This Targum often represents a later and more successful attempt to correct and supplement the Targum of Onkelos by the aid of variants derived from an older source. It exhibits, also, that tendency to expand the text by additions of every kind that has been already noted as characteristic of the later stages of targumic composition. Homilies, legends, traditional sayings and explanations are utilized by the targumist, so that at times his works convey the impression more of a late exegetical work than of a translation.

It is not possible to determine the sources and dates of composition of these two Targums. It is generally agreed that, though the extant manuscripts are late, they preserve elements that go back to an early period. Most of these elements derive from the text tradition that gave rise to the Targum of Onkelos, yet others are independent of Onkelos.

We must assume that a tolerably fixed Targum tradition existed in Palestine from quite early times, and that the Targum of Onkelos was the main representative of this Targum tradition that existed among the Jews down to the 7th century A.D., the period to which the internal evidence compels us to assign the Targumim. (*Cf.* B. J. Roberts, *The Old Testament Text and Versions,* pp. 197–207 [1951].)

## TARGUMS ON THE PROPHETS

The official Targum on the Prophets is stated by the Babylonian Talmud to have been said by Jonathan ben Uzziel, the disciple of Hillel in Judaea, in the 1st century A.D., and is usually known, therefore, as the Targum Jonathan. Elsewhere in the Talmud, however, the quotations from this Targum are given under the name of Joseph bar Chijah, head of the school at Pumbeditha, in Babylonia, in the 4th century A.D. Both in language and style it closely resembles the Targum of Onkelos, and appears to have been modeled on that translation; in certain passages, indeed, it appears to have made use of it. Probably, like Onkelos, it did not assume its final form in Babylon before the 5th century A.D. It naturally follows from the character of the original that the rendering of this Targum is less literal than that of Onkelos, especially in the prophetic books, but, when due allowance is made for the difficulty of the Hebrew, it may be described on the whole as a faithful reproduction of the original text. Its peculiarities of rendering are a result of the same principles that were noted as underlying the translation of the Pentateuch.

Anthropomorphisms, as a rule, are avoided by means of the same expedients as those employed by Onkelos; expressions derogatory to the dignity of God, or of the heroes of the nation, are softened down; figurative language is either boldly transposed or its character clearly shown by introduction of the particle "as" or "like." There is, further, a tendency to interpret the prophetic utterances so as to make them applicable to the immediate enemies of the Jewish people. Lastly, in the obscurer passages the Haggadic method of interpretation (*i.e.,* employing legend, folklore, homiletics, etc.) is employed to its fullest extent, while the translation throughout shows a marked tendency to explanatory additions.

Of a Jerusalem Targum to the Prophets little is known, though it is probable that such a Targum existed, if only in oral form.

## TARGUMS ON THE HAGIOGRAPHA

These Targums are almost entirely the work of individuals, made in imitation of the older Targums.

**Psalms and Job.**—These Targums present certain features in common and may therefore be treated together. Like all the later Targums they exhibit a large amount of explanatory addition, chiefly Haggadic in character. At the same time the translation of the original is not neglected, and, when separated from the later accretions, this is found to follow the Hebrew fairly closely. Peculiar to these Targums are the double translations they give to many verses, one of which is usually Haggadic while the other is more literal. They cannot be earlier than the 7th century A.D. and possibly are of a considerably later date.

**Proverbs.**—This Targum stands apart because of the peculiarity of the language in which it is written. The influence of the Peshitta (Syriac) version of the Bible is so clearly marked that it has been described as a Jewish revision of that version. Setting aside the Syriasms due to the use of the Peshitta, however, the Targum shows affinity to the Targums on the Psalms and Job. The translation is literal and almost entirely free from Haggadic additions.

**Megilloth.**—The chief characteristic of the Targums to the Megilloth (*i.e.,* the latest books of the Hagiographa, namely the Song of Solomon, Ruth, Lamentations of Jeremiah, Ecclesiastes and Esther) is their exaggerated use of paraphrase. They mark the final stage in the development of Haggadic interpretation, in which the translation of the text has frequently disappeared in a mass of fanciful matter.

The Targum of Esther is known in three recensions: (1) that of the Antwerp Polyglot (late 16th century), almost a literal translation; (2) that of the London Polyglot (1657), which gives practically the same text with many additions of a Haggadic character; (3) the so-called second (*sheni*) Targum, a much larger work, containing a collection of later Midrashim ("explanatory commentaries") to this book.

The Targum on the Song of Solomon is of a similar character to that of the "second" Targum on Esther. These have been dated halfway between the Babylonian Targums (Onkelos and that to the Prophets) and the Jerusalem Targums on the Pentateuch and those on the greater Hagiographa.

**Chronicles.**—This Targum was first edited from an Erfurt manuscript in 1680–83; a more complete and accurate edition from a Cambridge manuscript was published in 1715. In the translation, which at times is fairly literal, use appears to have been made of the Jerusalem Targums on the Pentateuch and of the Targums on the books of Samuel and Kings. The text represented by the Erfurt manuscript is assigned to the 8th century, that of the Cambridge manuscript to the 9th century A.D.

BIBLIOGRAPHY.—W. Bacher, "Targum," *Jewish Encyclopedia,* vol. xii, pp. 57–63; B. J. Roberts, "The Aramaic Targumim," *The Old Testament Text and Versions,* ch. 14, with bibliography (1951); P. Churgin, *Targum Jonathan to the Prophets* (1927); *The Targum to Hagiographa,* in Hebrew (1945); F. Rosenthal, *Die aramäistische Forschung seit T. Nöldekes Veröffentlichungen* (1939); J. F. Stenning (ed.), *The Targum of Isaiah,* with a translation (1949); A. Sperber (ed.), *The Bible in Aramaic Based on Old Manuscripts and Printed Texts,* vol. i, *The Pentateuch According to Targum Onkelos* (1959).

(J. F. S.; H. M. O.)

**TARIFF,** a tax levied upon goods as they cross national boundaries, usually by the government of the importing country. The words tariff, duty, and customs are generally used interchangeably.

## NATURE AND FUNCTION OF TARIFFS

Tariffs may be levied either to raise revenue or to protect domestic industries, but a tariff designed primarily to raise revenue may exercise a strong protective influence and a tariff levied primarily for protection may yield revenue. Gottfried Haberler in his *Theory of International Trade* suggested that the best objective distinction between revenue duties and protective duties (disregarding the motives of the legislators) is to be found in their discriminatory effects as between domestic and foreign producers. If domestically produced goods bear the same taxation as similar imported goods, or if the goods subject to duty are not produced at home, even after the duty has been levied, and if there exist no home-produced substitutes toward which demand is diverted on account of the tariff, then the duty is not protective. A purely protective duty tends to shift production away from the export industries into the protected domestic industries and those industries producing substitutes for which demand is increased. On the other hand, a purely revenue duty will not cause resources to be invested in industries producing the taxed goods or close substitutes for such goods, but it will divert resources from the production of export goods to the production of those goods and services upon which the additional government receipts are spent. From the purely revenue standpoint, a country will select a relatively small number of articles of general consumption and subject them to low duties so that there will be no tendency to shift resources into industries producing such taxed goods (or substitutes for them). During the period when it was on a free-trade basis, Great Britain followed this practice, levying low duties on a few commodities of general consumption such as tea, sugar, tobacco, and coffee. If a country wishes to protect its home industries its list of protected commodities will be long and the tariff rates high.

Tariffs may be further classified into three groups—transit duties, export duties, and import duties.

**Transit Duties.**—This type of duty is levied on commodities that originate in one country, cross another, and are consigned to a third. As the name implies, transit duties are levied by the country through which the goods pass. Such duties are no longer important instruments of commercial policy but during the mercantilist period (17th and 18th centuries) and even up to the middle of the 19th century in some countries, they played a role in directing trade and controlling certain of its routes. The development of the German *Zollverein* (customs union) in the first half of the 19th century was partly the result of Prussia's exercise of its power to levy transit duties. The most direct and immediate effect of transit duties is to reduce the amount of commodities traded internationally and raise their cost to the importing country. In 1921, the Barcelona Statute on Freedom of Transit abolished all transit duties.

**Export Duties.**—Export duties are no longer used to a great extent, but they were common in the past and were significant elements of mercantilist trade policies. Their main function was to safeguard domestic supplies rather than to raise revenue. Export duties were first introduced in England by a statute of 1275 that imposed them on hides and wool. By the middle of the 17th century the list of commodities subject to export duties had increased to include more than 200 articles. With the growth of free trade in the 19th century, export duties became less appealing; they were abolished in England in 1842, in France in 1857, and in Prussia in 1865. At the beginning of the 20th century only a few countries levied export duties: Spain still levied them on coke and textile waste; Bolivia and Malaya on tin; Italy on objects of art; and Rumania on hides and forest products. Export duties are generally levied by raw-material-producing countries rather than by advanced industrial countries. The neo-mercantilist revival in the 1920s and 1930s brought about the reappearance of export duties, but only to a limited extent. In the United States export duties were specifically prohibited by the Constitution. This prohibition was incorporated in the Constitution mainly because of pressure from the South, which wanted no restriction on its freedom to export agricultural products.

If the primary objective of the export duty is revenue, rates are usually low, for in the last analysis the duty is borne by the domestic producer, who cannot charge prices higher than the world prices. In South and Central America practically all exported commodities are taxed, the duties ranging from 1% to 5%. Several countries depend upon export duties for a large part of their revenue. Chile, for example, at one time derived more than 75% of her total revenue from export duties.

To the extent that export duties raise the cost of raw materials to foreign manufacturers relative to the cost to manufacturers in the exporting country, export duties may act as a form of protection to domestic industries. As examples, Norwegian and Swedish duties on exports of forest products were levied chiefly to encourage milling, woodworking, and paper manufacturing at home. Similarly duties on the export from India of untanned hides after World War I were levied to stimulate the Indian tanning industry. In a number of cases, however, duties levied on exports from colonies were designed to protect the industries of the mother country and not those of the colony.

If the country imposing the export duty supplies only a small share of the world's exports and if competitive conditions prevail, the burden of an export duty will likely be borne by the domestic producer, who will receive the world price minus the duty and other charges. But if the country produces a significant fraction of the world output and if domestic supply is sensitive to lower net prices, then output will fall drastically and world prices may rise and as a consequence not only domestic producers but also foreign consumers will bear the export tax. How far a country can employ export duties to exploit its monopoly position in supplying certain raw materials depends upon the success other countries have in discovering substitutes or new sources of supply.

**Import Duties.**—Import duties are the most important and most common types of custom duties. As noted above, they may be levied either for revenue or protection or both, but tariffs are not a wholly satisfactory means of raising revenue, for tariff rates cannot be readily adjusted to current fiscal needs. In the United States, for example, revenues from import duties in 1808 amounted to twice the total of government expenditures, while in 1837 they were less than one third of such expenditures. Until near the end of the 19th century the customs receipts of the U.S. government made up about half of all its receipts. This share had fallen to about 6% of all receipts before the outbreak of World War II and by the 1960s was down to about 1½%.

A tariff may be either specific, ad valorem, or compound (*i.e.*, a combination of both). A specific duty is a levy of a given amount of money per unit of the import, such as $1 per yard or per pound. An ad valorem duty, on the other hand, is calculated as a percentage of the value of the import. Ad valorem rates furnish a constant degree of protection at all levels of price (if prices change at the same rate at home and abroad), while the real burden of specific rates varies inversely with changes in the prices of the imports. A specific duty, however, penalizes more severely the lower grades of an imported commodity. This difficulty can be partly avoided by an elaborate and detailed classification of imports on the basis of the stage of finishing, but such a procedure makes for extremely long and complicated tariff schedules. Specific duties are easier to administer than ad valorem rates, for the latter often raise difficult administrative issues with respect to the valuation of imported articles.

A list of all import duties is usually known as a tariff schedule. A single tariff schedule, such as that of the United States, applies to all imports regardless of the country of origin. This is to say that a single duty is listed in the column opposite the enumerated commodities. A double-columned or multi-columned tariff provides for different rates according to the country of origin, lower rates being granted to commodities coming from countries with which tariff agreements have been negotiated. Most trade agreements are based on the most-favoured-nation clause, which extends to all nations whatever concessions are granted to the most-favoured nation. (*See* MOST-FAVOURED-NATION TREATMENT.)

Every country has a free list that includes articles admitted without duty. By looking at the free list and the value of the goods imported into the United States under it one might be led to conclude that tariff protection is very limited, for more than half of all imports are exempt from duties. Such a conclusion, however, is not correct, for it ignores the fact that the higher the tariff, the less will be the quantity of dutiable imports. Attempts to measure the height of a tariff wall and make international comparisons of the degree of protection, based upon the ratio of tariff receipts to the total value of imports, are beset by difficulties and have little meaning. A better method of measuring the height of a tariff wall is to convert all duties into ad valorem figures and then estimate the weighted-average rate. The weight should reflect the relative importance of the different imports; a tariff on foodstuffs, for example, may be far more important than a tariff on luxuries consumed by a small group of people. A tariff index may be used to measure either the degree of protection afforded by a tariff schedule or the relative degree of import obstruction that it provides. If the amount of protection is under consideration, then it must be recognized that even a uniform ad valorem rate of duty will provide different protection to different countries, depending in part upon demand and cost differences between countries. The degree of obstruction to imports, on the other hand, would depend not only upon the height of the tariff but also upon the responsiveness of demand and supply, the changes of which are not considered in computing the tariff index. Consequently, it is misleading to construct only one tariff index for a given country. For each country a number of tariff indexes should be computed, one for each country from which it imports, for it often happens that a tariff severely restricts imports from certain countries but has little effect on imports from other countries.

## TARIFFS IN THE 20TH CENTURY

Viewing the development of tariffs and international trade since 1900, three broad periods can be distinguished: (1) from 1900 to World War I, (2) from 1919 to World War II, and (3) from World War II to the 1960s. During the first period tariffs were the main form of import control. They were moderate and relatively stable, and equality of competitive opportunity for imports from all countries was the rule, with exceptions found mainly in the trade relations between a few countries and their colonies.

The second period, from 1919 to 1939, was marked by frequent changes in duties, their rise to a higher level, the development of new control devices, and the negotiation of special trade agreements. There was some resurgence of protective tariffs immediately after World War I, caused in part by the strong national feelings aroused by the war and by difficult postwar economic adjustments. As political and economic conditions improved toward the middle of the 1920s the severity of trade restrictions was relaxed. In the late 1920s many governments negotiated commercial treaties that resulted in mutual reductions in duties. Soon after the beginning of the depression of the 1930s, however, this liberal trend was reversed. Import controls and higher tariffs were adopted by one country after another. Two outstanding examples of such legislation were the Smoot-Hawley Tariff (1930) in the United States and the British tariff of 1932 that ended nearly a century of virtual free trade for Great Britain. The world economic conference that convened in London in 1933 to deal with tariffs and international trade failed because it came too late to supersede the various national recovery programs that had already gained momentum in many countries, particularly the United States. Despite the moderating influence of the U.S. Reciprocal Trade Agreements Act (1934), which was designed to reduce tariffs and stimulate trade, the dominant trend in the trade policies of most countries during the 1930s was in the opposite direction; no effective methods of concerted action were devised for checking the deterioration of the economic relations among nations.

The third period, from World War II to the 1960s, brought radical changes in the nature and control of world trade. During the war the shortage of many types of goods for ordinary civilian use, and of the shipping to carry them, limited the volume of ordinary trade. Under these circumstances, tariffs and other means of control became subordinate to the decisions of the exporting countries as to whether the particular goods could be spared and as to whether transport was available to carry them. To a large extent, governments themselves participated in the procurement and distribution of many classes of goods. As the war progressed, the enlarged production programs of the Allies and of the countries friendly to them resulted in huge international movements of supplies. The problem of paying for these goods was virtually eliminated by the U.S. Lend-Lease Act, which authorized the president to make them available to friendly countries on a lend-lease basis, *i.e.*, without immediate compensation. A significant feature of the agreements concluded by the United States with more than 30 of the United Nations was the uniform pledge of all the contracting countries to collaborate after the war in a program designed to promote more liberal conditions for international trading and a more prosperous expanding world economy.

Soon after the war the United States and Canada, in order to facilitate the resumption of normal trade, relaxed their controls upon exports and extended loans to many other countries. Western European countries negotiated numerous trade agreements with each other. Unlike their predecessors of the prewar era, these agreements did not deal with changes in tariffs or other trade controls. The negotiations centred rather upon the lists of goods that each country was desirous of obtaining from the other and the delivery of which the other government agreed to facilitate. Generally speaking, even after the transitional period following World War II, the course of international trade was determined only to a small degree by the height of the tariff or by licensing systems. The main determinants were the needs of the war-torn areas for products essential to the rehabilitation of their economies.

By the close of 1947, new or tightened import restrictions had been brought into operation by various countries to prevent further loss of foreign exchange. These restrictions were directed chiefly against imports from the dollar countries of North and South America. To ease the settlement of uneven balances in the trade among the European countries themselves, a special intra-European payments plan was inaugurated in 1948. Under this arrangement portions of the dollar aid allocated through the Marshall Plan to European countries were made conditional upon the setting up by these countries of special accounts of equivalent value in their own currencies, against which members with whom they had an export surplus could draw to finance their deficits. This was later replaced by a flexible system for clearing balances, known as the European Payments Union.

The progressive improvement in production, monetary stability, and trade balance which many countries were making gave promise, by the beginning of 1950, of some trade normalization. Early in 1950 the western European countries that had received Marshall Plan aid agreed upon a series of steps for the liberalization of import quotas. Later, smaller groups of countries formed customs unions such as the Benelux customs union, the European Economic Community (Common Market), the European Free Trade Association (EFTA), and the Latin American Free Trade Association. (*See* EUROPEAN UNITY.) On the other hand, in the major countries of Asia, progress toward resumption of normal trade relations was largely dependent upon political developments. Among the factors hampering Asian trade were Communist control of China and continued disturbances in Southeast Asia. On the favourable side were the stabilization of the Japanese yen and the transfer of Japanese trade to private channels.

**General Agreement on Tariffs and Trade.**—The most important expression of the postwar desire of the nations of the world to liberalize and expand international trade was the General Agreement on Tariffs and Trade (GATT). It consisted of an integrated set of bilateral trade agreements (negotiated in five international conferences) aimed at the abolition of quantitative trade restrictions and the reduction of tariff duties among the contracting parties. GATT was concluded at Geneva, Switz., in 1947 and was originally considered as an interim measure pending the formation of a United Nations agency to supersede it. For this latter purpose the United Nations Economic and Social Council called an international conference on trade and employment that met in Havana, Cuba, from November 1947 to March 1948 to draw up the charter of an agency to be known as the International Trade Organization (ITO). The ITO was designed to support national policies for economic development and full employment and contribute to the gradual liberalization of world trade. Simultaneously the members of the preparatory committee of the ITO charter met in Geneva and negotiated the General Agreement on Tariffs and Trade. Of the 56 nations represented at Havana, 53 signed the proposed ITO charter, but only one subsequently ratified it, and plans for ITO were therefore abandoned. Since the ITO did not come into being, GATT was amplified and further enlarged at Annecy, Fr., in 1949, at Torquay, Eng., in 1951, and at Geneva in 1956 and 1961. A new conference for further negotiations, known as the "Kennedy round" (in honour of Pres. John F. Kennedy, during whose term the U.S. Trade Expansion Act of 1962 was passed), formally opened in Geneva in May 1964 and was continued in 1965.

GATT includes a long schedule of specific tariff concessions for each contracting party, representing tariff rates which each country has agreed to extend to others. In addition it includes a set of general rules for the conduct of international trade; these rules are, in effect, a code of commercial policy. They provide for unconditional most-favoured-nation clauses, elimination of quantitative trade restrictions, uniform customs regulations, and the obligation of each contracting party to negotiate for tariff cuts upon the request of another. The negotiating procedures followed under GATT agreements are essentially multilateral. The close contacts among the country representatives who attend the negotiating sessions, and the fact that each country is affected not only by its bilateral negotiations but also by the negotiations under way among other pairs of countries, make GATT negotiations in effect multilateral.

By 1965 the membership of GATT included 64 countries, which accounted for more than four-fifths of all world trade. Trade negotiations under GATT covered scores of thousands of commodities. Tariff concessions were granted on about two-thirds of the total imports of all GATT countries.

For current developments in tariff negotiations see *Britannica Book of the Year*. *See* also FREE TRADE; TRADE, INTERNATIONAL; and references under "Tariffs" in the Index.

BIBLIOGRAPHY.—F. W. Taussig, *Tariff History of the United States* (1931); Gottfried Haberler, *The Theory of International Trade with its Applications to Commercial Policy* (1936); Asher Isaacs, *International Trade* (1948); John M. Letiche, *Reciprocal Trade Agreements . . .* (1948); Lawrence Towle, *International Trade and Commercial Policy* (1956); Delbert Snider, *Introduction to International Economics* (1958); S. Enke and V. Salera, *International Economics* (1957); J. B. Condliffe, *The Commerce of Nations* (1950). (A. A. Ps.)

**TARIJA,** a department of southeastern Bolivia established in 1832 during the administration of Andrés de Santa Cruz. Area 14,526 sq.mi., pop. (1962 est.) 142,600. It is bounded south by Argentina, east by Paraguay, and west and north by the departments of Potosí and Chuquisaca. The plains provide excellent grazing lands for breeding horses, cattle, and sheep. Corn, wheat, fruits, and vegetables are grown. The eastern tropical region in the Chaco (*q.v.*) lowland produces tobacco, sugarcane, rice, bananas, cassava, and citrus. Mineral resources include petroleum, iron, and silver. Oil refineries are at Sanandita and Fortín Campero.

Tarija, the departmental capital (pop. [1962 est.] 20,851), in a small valley on the banks of the Río Grande de Tarija, was founded by Don Luis de Fuentes y Vargas in 1574. Its elevation, 6,250 ft., helps temper the climate. (J. L. TR.)

**TARIM,** the chief river of Sinkiang province, China, which gives its name to the great basin between the Tien Shan and Kunlun mountain systems of central Asia. It is 1,360 mi. (2,190 km.) long, and the area of the basin is approximately 300,000 sq.mi. (777,000 sq.km.), though another 50,000 sq.mi. (129,500 sq.km.) portion of the southwest Gobi desert sometimes is included with the Tarim basin.

The Tarim river is formed by the confluence of the Kizil (Kashgar) and the Yarkand rivers in the far west; it then flows for about 230 mi. (370 km.) NE, to be joined from the north by the Ak Su and shortly, from the south, by the Khotan, though the latter only reaches the Tarim for a period of about 40 days per year. Trending eastward, along the northern side of the Takla Makan desert, the Tarim divides repeatedly and has inter-dune lakes along its course. The Konche, issuing from the lake called Baghrash Köl, joins the Tarim just eastward of long. 88° E. The lower course of the Tarim is sluggish, diminishing in volume, and is aggrading its bed. In 1921 it broke out of its channel and returned to an old course followed before A.D. 330, also moving the marshy Lop Nor back to its classical location. The river is usually frozen from December through February. The March thaw causes inundations, followed by a great summer flood as the snows melt in the Tien Shan and the Kunlun.

The basin properly consists of three regional divisions, though sometimes five units are distinguished. The first division is the Takla Makan desert or central, waterless sand desert. The terminal depression of Lop Nor is the second division, which often is considered a part of the Takla Makan. Its salt-encrusted dry lake beds, old river channels and changeable marshy lake terminals of the Tarim seldom have permitted permanent occupancy. The third division comprises the belts of oases surrounding the Takla Makan on the south, west and north along the piedmont fringes north of the Kunlun, east of the Pamir and south of the Tien Shan. These oases lie between the gravel glacis of the upper piedmonts and the sands of the Takla Makan. The best-known oases on the south are Karghalik, Khotan, Keriya, Niya, Cherchen and Charkhlik. To the west are Yarkand and Kashgar. On the north are Wu-shih, Ak Su, Bai, Kuchche, Korlo and Karashahr. The southern oases have smaller water supplies and cultivable areas than those of the north, but the western oases are the largest. The two other regional units often included in the Tarim, for convenience, are: the Turfan depression, lying beyond the Kuruk Tagh to the northeast in the indeterminate zone between the Tarim basin and the Gobi country; and the Su-lo (Shuleh) basin at the western end of the Kansu corridor, north of the Nan Shan.

**Problems of Climatic History.**—The present-day climate of the Tarim basin is discussed in the article SINKIANG, but the problems of past climatic changes have been the subject of much study. In general the belief has increased that climate has not changed markedly since the end of the last glacial era, but that the water supplied by the melting of glacial ice left in the high mountains has been failing. The problem is connected with the supposed desiccation of central Asia. (*See* ASIA: *Exploration.*)

Regardless of cause, great changes have occurred in the Tarim basin during the last 2,500 years. Settlements away from the piedmont were abandoned, sometimes to be replaced by smaller settlements higher on the piedmont edge. Some localities formerly well watered and prosperous now are deserted and quite uninhabitable. Many streams no longer penetrate the desert fringe, and the Tarim has shifted its course repeatedly, to alter the route of the Silk road.

**Historical Geography.**—The chief old land route of contact between eastern and western Asia passed through the Tarim basin. A northern route along the southern foot of the Tien Shan connected the trans-Caspian lowlands, via Kashgar and the Pamir passes, with the Kansu corridor in the east; a southern route along the northern Kunlun piedmont made the same connections. The region was always essentially a corridor zone, since there never was sufficient moisture, widely distributed, to support extensive plant, animal or human life. This explains why the great nomadic tribes of Dzungaria, the Wu-sun, Sakas, Yue-chi, Huns, Turks and Mongols raided or made tributary the Tarim oases, but never permanently crossed the Tien Shan to occupy the basin. Yet the oases provided the resource for careful irrigation agriculture to small groups of people, and provided food, animals and water for small numbers of migrants, travelers and traders.

**Modern Conditions in the Tarim Basin.**—Basically, the Tarim is yet untouched by modern developments, either of mineral resources or of water conservation-irrigation systems. Chinese administration, in times of strong Chinese power, has kept the routes open and free from banditry, but during the 19th century such periods were short. The oases populations chiefly are Turkic peoples, unsympathetic to the Chinese, but neither sufficiently numerous nor united to develop their regional entity. The Chinese fear of foreign exploitation has prevented both full exploration of possibilities and the development of known resources. The lack of transport development has kept connections uncertain and movement both slow and costly. The Tarim has lain too far from the centre of any modern regional development to have shared in that growth. The Communist Chinese have plans for marked development of several localities of the basin, but the comparatively small opportunities make them of relatively low priority and, by the 1960s, little was achieved other than the political organization of the region and the settling of Chinese nuclei in most of the important oases. A few agricultural processing plants were established, and resource exploration begun.

Oasis agriculture remains the mainstay of the scattered settlements. Grains, cotton, silk, fruits and wool are the chief agricultural products, and Khotan jades are the only other important item. Little is exported from the basin, but local surpluses find a market among travelers passing through when conditions permit. *See* also SINKIANG; KASHGAR; KHOTAN; YARKAND RIVER; LOP NOR; GOBI; TAKLA MAKAN; DZUNGARIA. (J. E. SR.)

**TARKINGTON, (NEWTON) BOOTH** (1869–1946), U.S. novelist and dramatist whose satirical pictures of midwesterners represent his best work, was born in Indianapolis, Ind., July 29, 1869. He studied at Phillips Exeter Academy, Exeter, N.H., and at Purdue (West Lafayette, Ind.) and Princeton universities. In 1902–03 he was a Republican member of the Indiana legislature. A versatile and prolific writer, Tarkington won early recognition with the melodramatic novel *The Gentleman from Indiana* (1899). This was followed by the immensely popular romance *Monsieur Beaucaire* (1900), which he later adapted for the stage. *The Conquest of Canaan* (1905), a "problem" novel, was probably the most mature work of his early period. His humorous portrayals of boyhood and adolescence, *Penrod* (1914) and *Seventeen* (1916), became classics of their kind. He was equally successful with his portrayals of midwestern life and character: *The Turmoil* (1915), *The Magnificent Ambersons* (1918; Pulitzer Prize, fiction, 1919) and *The Midlander* (1924), combined as *Growth* (1927); and *The Plutocrat* (1927). *Alice Adams* (1921; Pulitzer Prize, fiction, 1922), a searching character study, is perhaps his most finished novel. He continued his celebrated delineations of feminine character in *Claire Ambler* (1928), *Mirthful Haven* (1930), and *Presenting Lily Mars* (1933), and wrote several domestic novels in his later years. His many plays include *The Man from Home* (1908), *Mister Antonio* (1916) and *Up from Nowhere* (1919), all with H. L. Wilson, and *Beauty and the Jacobin* (1912). He died on May 19, 1946, in Indianapolis.

Adopting William Dean Howells and Mark Twain as his literary models, Tarkington possessed an informal, charming style and a gift for characterization. However, sentiment often obscured his critical vision.

BIBLIOGRAPHY.—R. C. Holliday, *Booth Tarkington* (1918); James Woodress, *Booth Tarkington, Gentleman from Indiana* (1955); D. Russo and T. Sullivan, *A Bibliography of Booth Tarkington* (1949).

**TARLTON, RICHARD** (d. 1588), English actor and jester, the most famous comedian of the Elizabethan Age. One account of his early life states that, born at Condover, Shropshire, he was found "feeding his Father's Swine" by a servant of the earl of Leicester; another, that he was a London apprentice and innkeeper. First mentioned in 1570 for his didactic ballad on the "late great floods," by 1579 he was a well-known actor and the queen's favourite jester, the only one able to "undumpish" her when she was out of humour. In 1583 he became leading comic actor of the Queen's Men and groom of her majesty's chamber, being so described in his will, dated Sept. 3, 1588, the day of his death in Shoreditch. His plays, praised by contemporaries, are lost; but one, a farcical morality known as *The Seven Deadlie Sinns*, or *Five Plays in One*, was performed at court in 1585. Of later jestbooks published as Tarlton's, only one is authentic, but, like inn signs of him as late as 1798, they show how long his fame survived.

Tarlton's popularity and genius are undisputed. Thomas Nashe tells us that audiences began "exceedingly to laugh when he first peept out his head"; John Stow praises his "plentifull . . . extemporall wit"; Spenser mourns him as "our pleasant Willy . . . with whom all joy and jolly merriment/Is also deaded"; and in 1643 Sir Richard Baker says that "for the . . . Clown's part he never had his match, never will have." Though few of his parts are known, descriptions reveal his comic style. He tells us he is "flatnosed," with a squint; and sketches show him in country russet, holding pipe and tabor, and standing on one toe—a reminder that he introduced to London the rustic jig (a farce sung and danced to popular tunes) and was a skilled composer and performer of extempore ballads. But it is as creator of the stage yokel that he takes his place in theatrical history. Though Shakespeare refined Clown into Fool, the contrast between "witty fool" and "foolish wit" derives from Tarlton, as does the clowning of Bottom (and later country bumpkins)—a debt repaid by Shakespeare in Hamlet's "Alas, poor Yorick . . . a fellow of infinite jest, of most excellent fancy."

BIBLIOGRAPHY.—The scenario of *The Secounde Part of the Seven Deadlie Sinns* (MS at Dulwich College, London) is printed in W. W. Greg, *Elizabethan Dramatic Documents* (1931). *Tarlton's Jests* (?1592) was ed. by J. O. Halliwell-Phillipps (1844). *See* also L. B. Campbell, "Note on Tarlton," *Huntington Library Quarterly* (April 1941); E. K. Chambers, *The Elizabethan Stage* (1923); L. Hotson, *Shakespeare's Motley* (1952).

**TARN,** a *département* of southwestern France, formed in 1790 from the three dioceses of Albi, Castres, and Lavaur in the western part of Languedoc (*q.v.*). It is bounded north and northeast by Aveyron *département*, southeast by Hérault, south by Aude, southwest by Haute-Garonne, and northwest by Tarn-et-Garonne, and is included in the economic region of Midi-Pyrénées, established in 1964. Area 2,220 sq.mi. (5,751 sq.km.). Pop. (1962) 319,560. Extending northward from the Montagne Noire, it lies across the margin of the crystalline highlands and the lowlands of Aquitaine and is drained westward by tributaries of the Garonne River, including the Aveyron (which marks its northern limit), Tarn, and Agout. The granite country in the east forms exposed tracts of undulating plateau above 2,000 ft. (600 m.), with the highest parts, in the Montagne Noire, reaching 3,970 ft. (1,210 m.). The inclement climate and poor acid soils restrict farming. The traditional crops (rye and chestnut) have given way to grass and fodder crops; the highlands are concerned mainly with rearing cattle and sheep. Lead and zinc ores in the crystalline rocks are worked on a small scale at Peyrebrune. The lowlands and their valley extensions support a rich agriculture, with wheat, corn (maize), vineyards, orchards, and lush meadows on the valley floors. The sparkling wine of Gaillac is of high repute. At Castres and Mazamet, market towns at the foot of the Montagne Noire, old woolen industries survive. North of Albi (*q.v.*) is a small coalfield around Carmaux. Although there is an important post-World War II coking plant at Carmaux, much of the coal output is sent away, and for its industries (chiefly engineering and the manufacture of glass, cement, detergents, and man-made fibres) Albi relies mainly upon waterpower generated from the Tarn. Situated at an important crossing of the Tarn, Albi is the largest town and *préfecture* and is an old, established cathedral city, centre of an archbishopric. Its medieval brick bridge lies between the modern road and railway crossings of the Tarn. The fortified cathedral of Sainte-Cécile at Albi and the church of Saint-Alain at Lavaur are fine examples of southern Gothic architecture. The archiepiscopal fortress, Palais de la Berbie, houses the Toulouse-Lautrec Museum. The Goya Museum at Castres has a notable collection of Spanish art. Tarn is divided into two *arrondissements* centred upon Albi and Castres. It is under the jurisdiction of the Toulouse Court of Appeal and the *académie* there for administration of education. (AR. E. S.)

**TARN-ET-GARONNE,** a *département* of southwestern France, formed by a reorganization in 1808 of districts that before the Revolution had belonged to the historic regions of Guienne and Gascony (*qq.v.*), and the addition of a small portion of Languedoc. It is bounded north by Lot *département*, east by Aveyron and Tarn, south by Haute-Garonne, and west by Gers and Lot-et-Garonne, and is included in the economic region of Midi-Pyrénées, established in 1964. Area 1,435 sq.mi. (3,716 sq.km.). Pop. (1962) 175,847. It consists of lowland country in the clayey *molasse* tracts of the Aquitaine Basin, around the confluence of the Tarn and Aveyron rivers and of the joint stream with the Garonne. The mild climate and fertile soils make it a productive agricultural district, but it lacks mineral wealth and has little industry, though rubber manufacture has developed at Moissac. Wheat and corn (maize) are extensively grown, vineyards and orchards are also widespread, and cattle are fattened or kept for dairying. The lateral canal of the Garonne traverses the *département*, with a spur serving Montauban (*q.v.*). Montauban has a fine medieval brick bridge across the Tarn; it is the largest town and the *préfecture* and is the centre of the diocese that is coextensive with the *département*. Montauban and Castelsarrasin are the centres of the two *arrondissements* into which Tarn-et-Garonne is divided. The *département* comes under the jurisdiction of the Court of Appeal at Toulouse and under the *académie* there for the administration of education. (AR. E. S.)

**TARNOWSKI, JAN,** Count (1488–1561), Polish army commander, the mainstay of authority against the *szlachta,* or petty nobles. He was born at the Tarnow castle, of a magnate family. He fought well in southeastern Poland against Bogdan III of Moldavia (1509), at Wisniowiec against the Tatars (1512), and at Orsza against the Muscovites (1514). In 1517 he left Poland for travels in the Near East and in western Europe. In Portugal in 1520 he commanded an army against the Moors. Returning to Poland in 1521, he served against the Teutonic Knights.

In 1527 King Sigismund I appointed Tarnowski grand hetman (commander in chief of the army) and governor of the Lwow-Halicz province. Tarnowski won a great victory over the Moldavians at Obertyn in 1531 and commanded against Muscovy in 1535. He did much to bring immigrants to southeastern Poland. He was appointed governor of the Cracow province in 1535 and castellan of Cracow itself in 1536. He took the king's side during the "Poultry War" of 1536, a bloodless revolt of the *szlachta* against efforts to increase the royal power. Advocating a pro-Habsburg policy, Tarnowski in 1544 organized a private raid against Ochakov, a Turkish fortress on the Black Sea.

In 1548 Tarnowski sided with Sigismund II Augustus when the *szlachta* tried to annul the latter's marriage with Barbara Radziwill. A devout Catholic, he yet opposed the restoration of independent episcopal courts. He wrote *De bello cum . . . Turcis gerendo* (1552), for Charles V's projected war against the Turks, and *Consilium rationis bellicae* (1558), on traditional Polish methods of warfare. He died at Tarnow on May 16, 1561. (St. He.)

**TARN RIVER,** in southwestern France, 233 mi. (375 km.) long, enters the Garonne below Moissac. It rises above 5,000 ft. (1,500 m.) on the Lozère plateau in the Massif Central and flows west to enter its great gorge, between 1,300 and 1,700 ft. (400–500 m.) deep, across the limestone Causses plateaus between Florac and Millau. Its tributaries, the Jonte and Dourbie, flow in similar gorges between walls of white limestone. The gorges present an important tourist attraction. Below the small verdant basin of Millau, the Tarn is again trenched in the crystalline plateaus of the southwest part of the Massif Central, but near Albi the valley opens out in the fertile agricultural lowlands of Aquitaine. Below the confluence of the Agout, the Tarn turns northwest in a course nearly parallel with the Garonne but does not bend west toward that river until, some distance below Montauban, it has received an important tributary, the Aveyron. (Ar. E. S.)

**TARO** (*Colocasia antiquorum*), a coarse herbaceous plant of the arum family (Araceae; *q.v.*), called also eddo, probably native to southeastern Asia, whence it has spread to the Pacific Islands, where it is extensively cultivated for its large, spherical, underground tubers, rich in starch; these form an important article of food, especially in Hawaii. The Polynesian poi is a thin pasty mass of taro starch.

It is closely allied to the dasheen (*C. esculenta*), native to Indonesia, various cultivated forms of which are known as elephant's-ear. The dasheen tubers have a nutty flavour and contain more carbohydrates and proteins than the potato.

**TAROT,** a game of cards played in Germany (*tarok*) and central Europe and to some extent in France and Italy (*tarocchi*) (*see* Cards, Playing). The modern game uses 54 cards, comprising 32 suit cards, 21 tarots (permanent trumps), and a joker. Each suit includes 4 court cards, instead of 3 as in the 52-card French pack. The tarots, originally illuminated with individual designs of esoteric significance, now are usually printed only with the Roman numerals from I to XXI. The play of the game centres upon the manipulation of the tarots, each of which is privileged to win any suit card. Tarot includes many features that were borrowed by other games—competitive bidding, a scat or widow, melding of honour combinations, the sequence of matadors, the suitless or wild joker, the effort to capture specific counting cards in tricks, and extra score for the last trick.

**TARPEIA,** in Roman legend, daughter of the commander of the Capitol during the war with the Sabines caused by the rape of the Sabine women. According to the story, she offered to betray the citadel if the Sabines would give her what they wore on their left arms, meaning their bracelets; instead of this, keeping to the letter of their promise, they threw their shields upon her and crushed her to death. Simylus, a Greek elegiac poet, makes Tarpeia betray the Capitol to a king of the Gauls.

The story may be an attempt to account for the Tarpeian Rock, on the southwestern corner of the Capitoline Hill, being chosen as the place of execution of traitors. According to S. Reinach, however, the story had its origin in a rite—the taboo of military spoils, which led to their being heaped up on consecrated ground that they might not be touched. Tarpeia herself is a local divinity, the manner of whose death was suggested by the tumulus or shields on the spot devoted to her cult, a crime being invented to account for the supposed punishment. (R. B. Ld.)

**TARPON,** a marine fish closely allied to the herring, identified by a filamentous prolongation of the last dorsal fin ray, by the dorsal fin originating behind the ventrals, and by a bony plate on the throat between the two sides of the lower jaw. The body is covered with large, thick, silvery scales. Two species are known. The Atlantic tarpon (*Megalops atlantica*) occurs in tropical and subtropical parts of the western Atlantic from Brazil northward, occasionally as far as Nova Scotia; on the west coast of Africa; and, as a result of passage through the Panama Canal, on the Pacific side of Central America. It lives close inshore, often in semi-enclosed bodies of water, and in rivers sometimes 100 mi. or more from the sea. It evidently spawns in shallow water along shore during spring and summer. Tarpon have the habit of breaking the surface of the water and gulping air, the lunglike swim bladder functioning as an accessory respiratory organ. It is a favourite big game fish. The Indo-Pacific tarpon (*Megalops cyprinoides*) occurs around the shores of the Indian Ocean from as far south as Durban, South Africa, into the Pacific to Formosa and about as far east as the Society Islands. (L. A. Wd.)

**TARQUIN** (Tarquinius), the name of two kings of Rome.

Lucius Tarquinius Priscus, fifth king (traditionally 616–578 b.c.), was said to be the son of a Greek, Demaratus of Corinth, who came to live in Tarquinii in Etruria. The son in turn, originally named Lucumo, moved to Rome on the advice of his wife, the prophetess Tanaquil (*q.v.*). Changing his name to Lucius Tarquinius, he came to be appointed guardian to the sons of the king Ancus Marcius and finally supplanted them upon their father's death. Eventually he was assassinated at the instigation of Ancus' sons.

Tarquinius Priscus was said to have increased the Senate by the addition of 100 junior members and to have doubled the number of knights (*equites*). More authentic is his building program: he laid out the Circus Maximus, instituted the Roman Games (*Ludi Romani*), built the great sewer (*Cloaca Maxima*), and began construction of a wall around the city and the Temple of Jupiter Optimus Maximus on the Capitol. He carried on war successfully against the Sabines and subjugated Latium.

Lucius Tarquinius Superbus, seventh and last king (traditionally 534–510 b.c.), is in legend the son (or grandson) of Tarquinius Priscus and son-in-law of Servius Tullius (*q.v.*), the sixth king. He came to power by murdering his predecessor and set up an absolute despotism (hence his name Superbus, "the proud"). A reign of terror followed during which many senators were put to death. Eventually a revolt was instigated by the leading senators, immediate cause for which was the rape of Lucretia (*q.v.*) by Superbus' son Sextus. This resulted in the expulsion of the Tarquins and the end of the monarchy. Tarquinius' efforts to force his way back to the throne were in vain and he died in exile.

Although many of the details of their careers are clearly fictitious, they are probably both historical personages. Some modern authorities, however, believe that a single figure (or else a series of Etruscan kings) is behind the two legendary Tarquins. That they came from Etruria is confirmed by both Roman and Etruscan legend and has the strong support of archaeological evidence, for their presence in Rome coincides with a period of roughly 100 years of Etruscan influence in the city preceding the foundation of the republic.

That the monarchy was overthrown is historical fact, and the existence of at least one Tarquin cannot be questioned. Their successful wars with the Latins also must be regarded as fact. The text of a treaty between Tarquinius (Superbus?) and Gabii was preserved in the Temple of Semo Sancus in Rome as late as the time of Augustus. The foundation of the Temple of Jupiter on the Capitoline Hill, from both architectural and religious evidence, goes back to a time of strong Etruscan influence in Rome and would support the legendary account of its having been begun by Priscus and completed by Superbus. (R. B. Ld.)

**TARQUINIA** (ancient Tarquinii; medieval Corneto) a town in the province of Viterbo, Italy, about 4 mi. (7 km.) inland from the Tyrrhenian Sea and 11 mi. (18 km.) N of Civitavecchia. Pop. (1961) 11,691. Its Latin name Tarquinii came from the Etruscan Tarchuna or Tarchna. It was a member of the Etruscan 12-city league, in which it enjoyed a certain primacy, especially in religious affairs. According to popular tradition, the city was founded by Tarchon, son of the Etruscan eponymous hero Tyrrhenus. But this story, and the local legend of a divine priest Tages who taught the Etruscans religious rites, are later inventions aimed at justifying the city's position of leadership under the powerful Tarquin (*q.v.*) family.

The earliest archaeological remains at Tarquinia are 9th-century B.C. Villanovan well tombs (*tombe a pozzo*). The Etruscan tombs are mostly rock-cut chamber tombs dating from the 6th to the 4th century B.C., although in one such tomb was found a blue faience vase bearing the name of Bakenrenef (Bocchoris), an Egyptian pharaoh of the late 8th century. The main part of the necropolis is situated on the Monterozzi Hill, which comprises a ridge 3 mi. (5 km.) long to the SW of the ancient city, which occupies a position about 2 mi. (3 km.) NE of modern Tarquinia.

This necropolis contains the most important painted tombs in Etruria. The most famous of these is the "Fowling and Fishing Tomb," with its polychrome frescoes painted about 520 B.C. The "Tomb of the Lionesses" and "Tomb of the Leopards" show dancing and banquet scenes, as do the famous "Tomb of the Augurs" and the "Tomb of the Bacchants" (end of the 6th century B.C.). The "Tomb of the Triclinium" is the most outstanding 5th-century painted tomb, and the "Tomb of the Shields" is a masterpiece of 4th-century painting, while the polychrome frescoes of the "Tomb of Orcus and Polyphemus" also date from this century. A distinctive 2nd-century painting tradition, rare in Etruria, is found in the paintings of the "Tomb of the Cardinal."

The ancient city site was found on the hill La Civita by excavations carried out in 1934–38. Like other Etruscan cities, it was isolated and elevated. Remains of an imposing circle of walls have been uncovered, as well as the foundations of a great Etruscan temple known as the *Ara della Regina,* the decoration of which included a terra-cotta group of winged horses in Hellenistic style considered a masterpiece of Etruscan art. (*See* also Etruscans.)

Tradition places the first wars between Tarquinii and Rome in 394 and 388 B.C. These were followed by a long campaign between 358 and 351. Forty years of peace followed, terminated by a short war in 311 in which Tarquinii was overcome by Rome and became a *civitas foederata,* retaining its oligarchic institutions. The 4th and 3rd centuries were a period of great prosperity and Greek, later Roman, influence in art and culture. In 181 the first Roman colony was founded on its territory. In 90 B.C. Tarquinii received Roman citizenship and a government of *quattuorviri jure dicundo.*

Tarquinii was the seat of a bishopric in the 5th century A.D., but by this time malaria had depopulated the coastal areas of the province. It was probably shortly after the Lombard invasion in the 6th century that the old city site ceased to be inhabited and the population transferred to the lower-lying city known in medieval times as Corneto, from 1922 as Tarquinia. Tarquinia contains many Romanesque buildings, chief of which is the church of Sta. Maria in Castello begun in 1121. Medieval fortifications and towers are still extant, and there is a fine Gothic palace, Palazzo Vitelleschi (1439), now the archaeological museum. (Wm. C.)

**TARRAGONA,** a town in the region of Catalonia in northeastern Spain, and capital of Tarragona Province, is situated at the mouth of the Francolí River and on a hill (500 ft. [152 m.]) rising abruptly from the Mediterranean. Pop. (1960) 43,519. Located 60 mi. (96 km.) WSW of Barcelona, it is a flourishing seaport and serves as an important agricultural market; it is also the seat of an archbishop and has a provincial court of justice.

Tarragona (Tarraco) is basically a Roman city. Once capital of an Iberian tribe, it was captured in 218 B.C. by Gnaeus and Publius Scipio, who improved its harbours and enlarged its walls, transforming it into the earliest Roman stronghold in Spain. Julius Caesar initiated its period of splendour and called it Colonia Julia Victrix Triumphalis to commemorate his victories. A temple was built in honour of Augustus, who made Tarraco the capital of Hispania Tarraconensis, and the so-called Castle of Pilate is supposed to have been his imperial palace. Hadrian and Trajan endowed Tarraco with power and cultural prestige, while its flax trade and other industries made it one of the richest seaports of the empire. Its fertile plain and beautiful sunny shores were praised by Martial, and its famous wines extolled by Pliny. According to tradition, St. Paul, with the help of St. Thecla, founded the Christian Church in Spain at Tarraco in A.D. 60. The city was razed by the Moors in 714 and remained unimportant until the beginning of the 12th century, when it was recaptured by the Christians, and the archbishopric, founded early in the Christian era, was restored. After 1119 Tarragona resumed its new life as an important city of the Spanish kingdom of Aragon, and from it James I organized the conquest of Majorca (1229). Having inherited from Rome an imperial sense of unity, Tarragona has shown a stubborn loyalty to the kings of Spain and has always been a bulwark against invaders. In the War of Independence it desperately resisted the French Army of General Louis Gabriel Suchet, and, when taken (1811), it was ruthlessly sacked and its people massacred.

Tarragona lies on the coastal road and on the Barcelona-Valencia and Barcelona-Madrid railway lines. The old quarter, with many houses built partly of Roman masonry, is more than half surrounded by the Roman wall and square towers from the time of the empire. In this sense Tarragona is unique, and seen from the hills in the north at sunset it offers a superb view. Roman ruins include the theatre, amphitheatre, circus, forum, and necropolis, and nearby, an aqueduct, the so-called Tomb of the Scipios, and the Triumphal Arch of Bara. The cathedral (12th–13th century) is transitional between Romanesque and Gothic, with a very fine cloister. Many interesting buildings and patios of the Medieval and Baroque periods line the streets.

The most important avenues are the Rambla de San Carlos and the Rambla de San Juan, the streets of Apodaca and Union, and the beautiful palm-tree walk linking the two *ramblas.* Along with some fine parks and sports grounds, Tarragona has a Pontifical University, a school of arts and crafts, a large technical school specializing in industrial studies, a few important day and boarding schools, convents, libraries, museums, and a bullring.

Tarragona Province (area 2,426 sq.mi. [6,283 sq.km.]; pop. [1960] 362,679) contains mountains to the northwest and beautifully cultivated plains by the sea. It is known for its wines, hazelnuts, almonds, olive trees, wheat, tomatoes, fruit, and vegetables. Important towns in the province include Vendrell, Valls, Reus, and Tortosa. Important medieval monasteries are those of Poblet and Santas Creus, 25 and 15 mi. (40 and 24 km.) from Tarragona, respectively. Torredembarra, Cambrils, and San Carlos are pleasant fishing villages along the coast, and Salou (Vilaseca) is an excellent summer and winter resort. (E. Pu.)

**TARRASA,** a town in the province of Barcelona, Spain, 19 mi. (31 km.) NW of Barcelona city. Pop. (1960; mun.) 92,234. The successor of the Roman Egara, it became in 450 an important episcopal see with a cathedral, later destroyed. Existing historic churches include the 12th-century Romanesque Santa María and San Pedro, both of which have a 6th-century apse; the former church contains 9th-century primitive paintings. The baptistery of San Miguel probably dates from the 6th century. In the Santo Espíritu Church, begun in 1575, is an alabaster figure of Christ sculpted in 1544. The 12th-century castle (later a Carthusian monastery) has undergone reconstruction and houses the town museum. There is a museum of historic textiles, and a school for textile engineers which is unique in Spain. The town's main manufacture has for centuries been woolens; other products are nylon, cottons, carpets, mosaics, and glass. There are also mechanical and electrical concerns. Tarrasa has rail and road connections with Barcelona and Saragossa. (M. P. Ti.)

**TARS, LOW-TEMPERATURE,** the primary condensation products resulting from the carbonization of coal and such other organic substances as wood, peat and lignite at temperatures not exceeding 700° C. The term low-temperature tar usually refers to a low-temperature coal tar.

**Wood Tar.**—This tar is a by-product of the carbonization of wood. Two distinct types of wood tar are recognized: (1) hardwood tar and (2) resinous wood tar, the former derived from woods such as oak and beech, and the latter from resinous stumps and roots, particularly from pine wood.

*Hardwood Tars.*—The condensed volatile product of wood distillation is known as crude pyroligneous acid, which has the average composition: water 81%, methyl alcohol 3%–4%, acetic acid 6%–8%, tar 7%. After settling, the major portion of the tar separates from the aqueous acid although the latter always retains some tar in solution. The chemical constituents of wood tar form a complex mixture comprising the fatty acids, esters, ketones, alcohols, phenols (usually polyhydric) and their methyl ethers, together with waxes. The most important representatives of these groups present in the tar are formic and acetic acids, with their methyl esters, acetone, methyl and allyl alcohol, guaiacol, catechol, and esters of pyrogallol.

Beechwood tar is practically the only wood tar subjected to a complete straight distillation. Three fractions are usually collected, first the light oils and water containing acetic acid and methyl alcohol up to 180° C., then the heavy oils up to 240° C. and finally the pitch. The important fraction is the heavy oil from which beechwood creosote is obtained (*see* CREOSOTE).

The oils from wood tar are used as gum inhibitors in gasoline and as flotation oils; the pitch is used in briquetting (*see* FUELS).

*Resinous Wood Tars.*—These tars are represented by pinewood tar, which is commonly termed Stockholm or Archangel tar and is made extensively in the forests of the U.S.S.R., Finland and Sweden. It is an important commercial product and differs from hardwood tar in containing the pleasant smelling mixture of terpenes known as turpentine. Pine-wood tar is the residue left after the turpentine has been distilled, usually with the aid of steam. It is used widely in the manufacture of cordage, *e.g.*, tarred ropes and twine, and for impregnation of hemp fibre for oakum. It is used to a slight extent in pharmacy as a component of some ointments and antiseptics. Distillates of pine-wood tar, particularly the creosote fraction, are used in froth flotation processes (*see* METALLURGY).

**Peat Tar.**—A jet-black, semisolid oil, lighter than water, this can be dehydrated by heating at 100° C. On distillation up to 360° C. a hard pitch is obtained along with an oily distillate, the latter consisting of a neutral fraction, containing the solid waxes, phenols and only traces of basic compounds. The most striking characteristic of the neutral oils is their high degree of unsaturation as manifested by absorption of atmospheric oxygen. The waxes, which resemble the montan wax of lignite, melt at about 40° C. The acidic (phenolic) constituents of the tar consist of phenol and its homologues, the cresols and xylenols in small quantity, mixed with tar acids boiling at 250°–360° C. The latter show a carbolic acid coefficient of 31, *i.e.*, they are 31 times more powerful than phenol as bactericides. Among the phenolic constituents of peat tar, guaiacol, methylguaiacol and a methyl ether of pyrogallol have been identified. These ethers are absent from coal tar, but are found in wood-tar creosote, of which they form the major portion.

Peat tar may therefore be looked on as one of the transition steps from wood tar to coal tar. Although the products which can be isolated from peat tar are of undoubted value, the difficulty of winning and drying peat militates against the carbonization of this fuel on an industrial scale.

**Lignite and Brown Coal Tars.**—These tars resemble peat tar. They are usually black oils of rather buttery consistency owing to the presence of paraffin wax. Of an average density of 0.95, they retain a high percentage of water but solidify completely at 6°–8° C. In contradistinction to tars from bituminous coal, they are almost completely soluble in gasoline, a residue of only about 5% being usually left.

They are paraffinoid in nature, the wax content being as high as 10%. The crude wax melts at about 40° C. but from it a series of waxes with melting points from 46° to 73° C. has been obtained. The phenolic constituents resemble those of peat tar and are efficient bactericides. The basic components belong to the pyridine and quinoline series and are chiefly methylated derivatives. A distinctive characteristic of lignite tars is the presence of ketones in the neutral oils—a resemblance to the oils of wood tar. Lignite tars are of increasing importance as a source of fuels for internal-combustion engines, burning and lubricating oils and pitch (*see* LIGNITE).

**Low-Temperature Coal Tars.**—Vacuum tar has only been produced experimentally with the object of elucidating the composition of coal and the effect of heat upon this material. It is obtained when coal is carbonized at temperatures up to 450° C. under a pressure of 5–40 mm. Hg; the average yield is 14 gal. (6.5% by weight) per ton of coal. It is usually lighter than water (0.99 sp.gr.) and is especially interesting in that some of its constituents are identical with substances found in petroleum oils, and extractable from coal itself by solvents such as pyridine. It consists of 40%–45% paraffins and naphthenes, 40% ethylenic hydrocarbons richer in carbon than monoolefins, 7% aromatic hydrocarbons, chiefly homologues of naphthalene, and 10% phenols, mostly cresols and xylenols, with smaller amounts of tertiary alcohols and basic compounds. Naphthalene, anthracene, benzene and its homologues are all absent.

Among the more interesting constituents of vacuum tar are the naphthene, $C_{30}H_{60}$, called melene, which is also found in Galician petroleum and in the distillate of beeswax, and the hydrogenated phenols (alcohols) such as hexahydro-*p*-cresol and its homologues.

Low-temperature tar is produced by the carbonization of bituminous coals, containing 28%–35% volatile matter, at temperatures not exceeding 700° C., which is an optimum temperature for the production of gas, tar and smokeless fuel (*see* CARBONIZATION, LOW-TEMPERATURE). It is essentially a mixture of those volatile products of coal which are liquid at ordinary temperatures and which have not been subjected to the secondary thermal decomposition incidental to high-temperature carbonization in horizontal retorts. It is therefore regarded as a primary tar and has a widely varying composition.

Low-temperature tar is usually a brownish black oil, much less viscous than the tar made from the same coal at high temperatures. It is obtained in an average yield of 16–18 gal. per ton of coal carbonized, or 8%–9% by weight. This is approximately double the weight obtained by distilling the coal at 900°–1,200° C. Its specific gravity is 1.02–1.07, and owing to the low temperature at which it is formed, it is mainly paraffinoid in character, whereas high-temperature tar is almost wholly aromatic. The most distinctive characteristics of low-temperature tar are the almost entire absence of benzene and its homologues, naphthalene, anthracene and phenol; the unsaturated nature of the neutral oils, from which can be isolated solid paraffins; and the presence of solid, amorphous compounds, of either basic or phenolic nature.

The crude tar is a most unstable product and begins to decompose at about 200° C., finally yielding, when distilled to 360° C., an average of 65% oily distillate and 35% pitch. The amount of pitch formed on distilling low-temperature tar is therefore only half that obtained in a similar operation with high-temperature tar. The former, too, contains much less free carbon (*i.e.*, matter insoluble in benzene) than the latter, the average amount being 2%–4%. By modified extractions with caustic soda and sulfuric acid (*see* COAL TAR) the crude distillate can be divided into (1) neutral oils; (2) phenols; and (3) bases.

*Neutral Oils.*—These consist mostly of paraffins, naphthenes and olefins, with comparatively small amounts of methylated derivatives of naphthalene and anthracene. On treatment with concentrated sulfuric acid, the neutral oils are absorbed with the exception of some 12% consisting mainly of paraffins. Crude solid wax representing over 1% of the tar is obtained on cooling an acetone solution of the neutral oils. In the paraffin series, all the lower members have been identified, and in the higher ranges, the solid members from $C_{26}H_{54}$ to $C_{29}H_{60}$. The latter melt at 62° C. $\alpha$- and $\beta$-methylnaphthalenes have been isolated, but no naphthalene. Similarly $\beta$-methylanthracene occurs in a complex mixture of hydrocarbons crystallizing on cooling the high fractions of the distillates, but anthracene is absent. Neither fluorene nor carbazole has been identified in low-temperature tar; in addition to the hydrocarbons acenaphthene and diphenyl, there occur the fully hydrogenated products, perhydrofluorene, perhydroacenaphthene and dodecahydrodiphenyl.

*Phenols.*—The extraction of the phenolic constituents of the tar or its distillates is complicated by the fact that resinous and asphaltic substances accompany the phenols in solution in the alkali. These impurities, however, can be eliminated by agitation of the alkaline solution with organic solvents or by saturation with salt. The crude phenols (10%–20% of the tar) obtained on acidification as a black oil, can be further purified by extraction with light petroleum, followed by precipitation of the residue from an ethereal solution by fresh petroleum. The petroleum extract consists of low-boiling phenols including phenol itself, the cresols and 1,2,4-, 1,3,5-, 1,3,4-, and 1,4,2- xylenols. Catechol, $\beta$-naphthol and trimethylphenols have also been identified. The higher phenols of the tar are amorphous solids varying in colour from pale yellow to black.

*Bases.*—The crude bases, representing 2%–3% of the tar, are also composed of a low mobile fraction and a higher viscous fraction containing solid, amorphous substances of unknown constitution. The lower bases consist of pyridine and quinoline with their mono-, di- and tri- methyl derivatives. Only traces of primary bases are present in the tar. There have been identified pyridine, 2-methylpyridine, 3-methylpyridine, 4-methylpyridine, 2,5-dimethylpyridine, 3,4-dimethylpyridine, 2,4,5-trimethylpyridine, 2,3,4-trimethylpyridine, 2,4,6-trimethylpyridine, aniline, 2,3,5-trimethylpyridine, *p*-, *o*-, and *m*-toluidine, 2,3,4,5-tetramethylpyridine, quinoline, isoquinoline, and 2-methylquinoline.

*Utilization of Low-Temperature Tar Products.*—The commercial possibilities of low-temperature tar have not yet been fully developed, but its application in various directions has been demonstrated. The low-boiling distillates, owing to their unsaturated nature (*see* HYDROCARBON), form satisfactory fuel possessing certain antidetonating qualities. It has been claimed that the higher fractions of the neutral oils form an exceptionally good lubricant, while the so-called middle or dead oils are suitable for combustion in the diesel engine. Special characteristics are also claimed for low-temperature tar pitch, which can be used along with or in place of high-temperature tar pitch.

*See* H. H. Lowry, *Chemistry of Coal Utilization* (1945), supplementary vol. (1963). (D. D. P.; F. E. CI.)

**TARSIER,** a small primate of interest as an intermediate form between the lemur and the monkey. Tarsiers are represented today by one genus, *Tarsius,* and several species, constituting the suborder Tarsioidea (or Tarsiiformes). They inhabit several islands of southeast Asia, including the southern Philippines, Celebes, Borneo, and Sumatra. (For the tarsier mixture of advanced and primitive features and the evidence of its fossil remains, *see* PRIMATES.)

The spectral tarsier (*T. spectrum*), to which species all forms are sometimes referred by some authors, is rarely more than 16 cm. (about 6 in.) in body length, and the tail up to twice that length. Its silky fur ranges from buff to dark brown. The tarsier is well adapted to an arboreal life by the great elongation of its hind limbs (the ankle region, or tarsus, being especially affected—the feature to which the animal owes its name); the expansion of the tips of its digits into disklike adhesive pads; and the long, thin tail, tufted at the end, which serves as a balancer during flight and as a stabilizer and prop during climbing. Its rounded head, which can be rotated through 180°, has a shortened face with large goggling eyes, the most striking feature; the eyes face farther forward than those of lemurs. Its ears are large and membranous and almost constantly in motion, being furled or crinkled.

These are nocturnal and twilight-active animals. They prey mainly on insects for food but also take a little fruit. Except during the breeding season, tarsiers live alone. A single young is produced in a fairly well-developed state, well furred and with eyes open. (W. C. O. H.)

**TARSUS,** in southern Turkey, the birthplace of St. Paul (Acts 22:3), is a very ancient city on the Cydnus River (Tarsus Çay) in the alluvial plain of Cilicia in the Ichel *il.* Pop. (1965) 57,035. Excavations carried out under the guidance of Hetty Goldman before and immediately after World War II at Gözlü Kule on the southwestern periphery of the modern town show that, with some interruptions, settlements existed there from the Neolithic to the Islamic period.

Tarsus' prosperity over more than a millennium, between the 5th century B.C. and the Arab invasions in the 7th century A.D., was primarily due to the fertility of its soil and its commanding position at the southern end of the road from Anatolia to Syria by way of the Cilician Gates, the only major pass in the Taurus Range. Through the gates Xenophon and, later, Alexander III the Great (*qq.v.*) both passed with their armies. A third factor was the excellent and sheltered harbour of Rhégma, whereby Tarsus established strong maritime connections with the Levant and consequently absorbed many Semitic characteristics.

With less justification than many another Cilician city, Tarsus claimed a Hellenic origin, with Perseus and Heracles numbered among its mythical founders. In fact, the first authenticated appearance of the city in history is the record on a clay tablet of the rebuilding of Tarsus and Anchiale by the Assyrian king Sennacherib (705–681 B.C.) after an unsuccessful rebellion in Kue (Cilicia). After the decline of Assyrian power, Tarsus was ruled by native princes with the probably hereditary name or style of Syennesis. This local autonomy even continued under the Persian Empire, but in the 4th century the city was regularly administered by a satrap, and a series of coins was issued with legends in Aramaic. During the Macedonian occupation, the territory of Cilicia was disputed between the Seleucids and Ptolemies, and for a short time Tarsus was named Antioch-on-the Cydnus, apparently in honour of Antiochus Epiphanes. Thereafter it enjoyed an autonomy not far removed from anarchy until, with the crushing of the Cilician pirates by Pompey in 67 B.C., it was absorbed into the new Roman province of Cilicia. The city found favour with both Caesar and Mark Antony, and the royal progress of Cleopatra's sumptuous barge up the Cydnus to Tarsus, where the queen had an assignation with Antony, is one of the most memorable though not one of the most important events in the city's history. More important was the establishment of the university, where a flourishing school of Greek philosophy turned out such outstanding men as Athenodorus Cananites (*q.v.*), the teacher of Augustus.

During the Roman and early Byzantine periods, Tarsus was one of the leading cities of the Eastern Empire, its prosperity assured by its agriculture and an important linen industry. It styled itself "first, greatest, and most beautiful," "metropolis of the three provinces of Cilicia, Isauria, and Lycaonia." Its rivalry with Anazarbus (*q.v.*) was resolved when the province was divided in early Byzantine times into Cilicia Prima, with Tarsus as metropolis, and Cilicia Secunda, under the primacy of Anazarbus.

With the Arab onslaught on Cilicia soon after A.D. 660, Tarsus was laid in ruins, though a tenuous continuity of its greatness may be seen in the consecration of Theodore, an *émigré* Tarsiot, as archbishop of Canterbury in 668. More than a century later, in A.D. 787, the Abbasid caliph Harun al-Rashid rebuilt the city and transformed it into a military base for the Arab raiders who year after year invaded Byzantine territory by way of the Cilician Gates. The city's northern gate was consequently known as the Gate of the Holy War. The only surviving gate, the western, is still sometimes wrongly described as the Gate of St. Paul. In 965 all Cilicia was won back from the Muslims by the Byzantine emperor Nicephorus II Phocas, Tarsus surrendering after a siege. In 1097 the city was taken by the crusaders, but much more important was its absorption in the 12th century into the Christian kingdom of Little Armenia, of which it remained part until it was captured by the Mamelukes in 1359. A century and a half later it had passed into the hands of the Ottomans.

Apart from the objects, now housed at Adana (about 25 mi. [40 km.] E of Tarsus), that were discovered at Gözlü Kule, little is known of the ruins of ancient Tarsus. A large concrete mass, known as the Frozen Stone (*Donuk Taş*), still to be seen above the surface, is almost certainly the substructure of a Roman public building. Chance finds of sculpture, mosaic, and sarcophagi are also made by workmen digging the foundations of new buildings.

Modern Tarsus is a wealthy commercial centre. Its climate much improved after the draining of the swamps that formerly made the city a hotbed of malaria. In the 6th century Justinian diverted the course of the Cydnus to drain off surplus water in time of flood; but as the old channel was later neglected for centuries, the river and its harbour were gradually silted up and became stagnant marshes. These were drained in the early days of the Turkish republic by the planting of a eucalyptus forest, and the river now flows through the eastern extremity of Tarsus.

Bibliography.—W. Ramsay, *Cities of St. Paul* (1907); G. Le Strange, *The Lands of the Eastern Caliphate* (1930); A. H. M. Jones, *Cities of the Eastern Roman Provinces* (1937); H. Goldman (ed.), *Excavation at Gözlü Kule, Tarsus,* 3 vol. (1950–63); G. F. Hill, *Catalogue of the Greek Coins of Lycaonia, Isauria, and Cilicia* (1900). (M. R. E. G.)

**TARTAGLIA** (Tartalea), **NICCOLÒ FONTANA** (1499–1559), Italian mathematician, originated the science of ballistics and contributed a method for solving cubic equations. He was born at Brescia, where he was brought up in poverty by his mother. During the sack of Brescia by the French Army (1512) the boy received sabre cuts on the head; the ensuing speech difficulties caused the nickname Tartaglia, the stutterer, which he adopted. In 1534 he settled in Venice as a teacher of mathematics. In 1535 he was challenged to a problem-solving contest by Antonio Maria Fiore, a pupil of Scipione del Ferro, professor of mathematics at Bologna. Del Ferro had discovered the solution to the cubic equation, but kept it secret; upon his death it passed to Fiore. All problems proposed by Fiore led to cubic equations and when Tartaglia rediscovered the solution his victory was assured.

In 1537 appeared Tartaglia's first work, *Nova Scientia,* a treatise on gunnery, important as a pioneer attempt to establish the laws of falling bodies. Shortly afterward Tartaglia was approached by Girolamo Cardano (*q.v.*), physician and lecturer in Milan, requesting that Tartaglia publish his solution of the cubic or let Cardano include it in his forthcoming book. This Tartaglia refused, but on a later visit to Milan, hoping to become adviser on artillery to the Spanish Army, he confided the solution to Cardano under promise of secrecy. In 1545 appeared Cardano's *Ars Magna,* giving the solution to the cubic as well as the quartic, the latter discovered by his pupil, Lodovico Ferrari. Tartaglia responded in *Questioni et inventioni diverse* (1546), a collection of problems proposed to him by prominent men and dedicated to Henry VIII. He berated Cardano for his breach of faith; this led to a sequence of six printed cartels and countercartels between Ferrari and Tartaglia. The feud culminated in a public dispute in Milan, Aug. 10, 1548, which Ferrari apparently won. Tartaglia lost his position as public lecturer at Brescia and returned to Venice. His troubles in Brescia are described in the *Travagliata inventione* (1551). Best known is his *Trattato di numeri et misure,* three volumes (1556–60), an encyclopaedic work on elementary mathematics. Tartaglia also published translations of Euclid and Archimedes. He died in Venice, Dec. 13, 1559. His works were published as *Opere del famosissimo Nicola Tartaglia* (1606). (O. Oe.)

**TARTAN** is a cross-checkered repeating pattern, or "sett," of differently coloured bands, stripes, or lines of definite width and sequence, woven into woolen cloth (sometimes with silk added). Such patterns have existed for centuries in various countries and may be found in a Japanese print or in a primitive Sienese painting but nowadays have come to be regarded as peculiarly Scottish and, throughout the English-speaking world, as being a quasi-heraldic Scottish family device. Tartans were often used for the old Highland "belted plaid," a rectangular piece of cloth confined by a belt round the wearer's waist, below which it fell in rough pleats (sometimes sewn). The upper, larger portion was brought up to form a kind of cloak around the shoulders. From this garment the smaller kilt appears to have originated in the earlier part of the 17th century.

**History.**—Great significance and antiquity have long been claimed for many Scottish family or clan tartans; but the meagre references to "tartan" that can be gleaned from 15th- and 16th-century writings are somewhat overworked. Confusion and rash assumptions may well have arisen from the variety of spellings encountered therein and from the meanings of old words.

Proof of the antiquity of a tartan as a family or clan badge can only be satisfactory in the form of a specimen of the material, accompanied by contemporary evidence as to its significance; for example, the documentation afforded by at least two portraits of members of the same family or clan wearing the same tartan. From the earliest known painted representation of the Highland dress, J. Michael Wright's "Highland Chieftain," in the Scottish National Portrait Gallery, Edinburgh, all that can be learned is that a small cross-check or "tartan" pattern was adapted to use in kilt, plaid, and hose about 1660. The chieftain is believed to be a Campbell, but no stretch of imagination will relate the pattern that he wears to that of any "Campbell" tartan (or any other established tartan) of today. The 18th century, however, provides a substantial number of portraits forming a reliable pictorial record of some tartans. But the pleasantly naïve painter Richard Waitt, practising in the first quarter of the century, seems to prove by his collection of portraits of members of the Grant clan, all in plaids of different tartan, that these can have no clan or family significance. The Swiss David Morier, military painter to King George II, provides evidence, in his exciting "An Incident in the Rebellion of 1745" (at Windsor Castle), that an individual clansman in Prince Charles's army might wear coat, waistcoat, plaid or kilt, and hose, each of different tartan. Some of the patterns resemble those of today: B. du Pan's "Children of the Prince of Wales" (1746, also at Windsor) shows the eldest, Prince George (later George III), in dress of the Royal Company of Archers of a design remarkably close to that of the modern Royal Stewart tartan. It seems very odd that a Hanoverian prince should be wearing a pattern of such significance at the date of this picture (1746). But there is little doubt that portraits dating from the latter half of the 18th century show the Highland gentleman wearing such tartan as pleased him in colour and design, including different garments of unrelated tartans. (It must of course be recognized that in particular localities of the somewhat primitive Highlands, weavers would be tenacious of preferences and traditions in design; and that local dyes might be prevalent.)

Highland dress and the tartan were proscribed after the Jacobite rising of 1745 (*i.e.,* from 1746 to 1782). However, the Highland regiments of the latter 18th century wore tartan; therefore, uniform military tartans came to be designed. A number of these, mostly based on the earliest, that of the 42nd Regiment of Foot or "Black Watch" (which was frequently termed "government" tartan), have survived as approved "clan" tartans. The result of permitting military tartans may well have been to modify the effects of the proscription. There is little doubt that much of the present interest in, and affection for, the tartan can be attributed to its official military employment and to the honours won by the Highland regiments. This led during the first half of the 20th century, however, to the introduction (deplored by many) of "fancy" tartans with no military traditions to support their adoption.

The largely military revival of tartan from the late decades of the 18th century seems to have reached a high peak during the state visit of George IV to Edinburgh in 1822. The following three decades saw undiminished interest and produced an imaginative and systematic recording of "clan tartans" (rather lacking in integrity, perhaps) by authors and artists, creating what has been called "The Great Tartan Myth." Intermittent efforts to explode this in the interest of historic truth have failed: 150 years of the combined efforts of artists, writers, publishers, manufacturers, and tailors had created a tradition and firmly established tartan as a Scottish clan badge. (A. E. H. M.)

**Current Practice.**—Most clans have but one tartan, though, where this is bright, a muted pattern called a hunting sett is used for everyday wear on the moors and mountains. The "dress tartan," a modern conception, has sometimes been represented in the market by white-based tartans, which do not look well on men and were not meant for them. White-based tartans were known originally as "arisaid setts" and were worn by women, on whom they do look well. The gray-based setts (quite a different matter) are often the groundwork of a true hunting tartan. Women's tartan dress (with varying local corsages) continued to be worn in the glens and has latterly enjoyed some revival. The uniforms of certain Scottish regiments provided for trousers, or "trews," of tartan and for riding breeches of tartan.

The antecedents of modern tartan dress, as has been said above, emerge from the mists of antiquity—though portraits of chieftains, their pipers, and other officers of their households in more recent times are an important source of evidence of dress detail and, latterly, of clan tartan. This evidence is sounder than that of the tartan books that began to be issued in the 19th century. Another, though limited, source is the Public Register of All Arms and Bearings in Scotland where, in the few cases in which verbal armorial blazon on parchment is accompanied by a miniature emblazonment, the latter can be made up into a kilt-size sett. Discretion is necessary in working such emblazonments out into setts, but they can be taken to show the general hue and special characters of quite a number of tartans. Such sources are considered by Lyon Court (presided over by Lord Lyon King of Arms) through which tartans are authorized and registered; and the chiefs of clans are consulted too. About 1950 a tartan committee was set up by Lord Lyon. The committee considers matters remitted to it by Lyon Court, from the standpoint of reporting on historical and practical aspects of setts which Lyon Court is being asked to use in this or that application. Its observations are considered and sanctioned by Lord Lyon King of Arms (where necessary in consultation also with the Standing Council of Scottish Chiefs) and become a guide and instruction for tartan weavers and outfitters. The result is that a number of tartans have been given statutory certainty from their inclusion in duly registered armorial bearings. This has regularized the commercial manufacture and sale of tartans, so that registered tartans are correctly reproduced—even though commercial pseudo-tartans and checks have continued to increase, and though an individual cannot be prevented from inventing a sett and having it made up to order.

The Scottish Tartan Centre, founded at Stirling in the mid-1960s, makes an intensive study of tartans. Its collections (including those of the early 19th-century weavers Wilson's of Bannockburn) supplement the earlier collections of Moy Hall (the Inverness-shire seat of the Mackintosh) and of the Highland Society of London, and are of growing use in clarifying the history and details of tartans and Highland dress and in providing valuable evidence when required for consideration in Lyon Court.

To the frequent modern question: "What is my tartan?" the answer is: "The one applicable to your surname"—if it be the name of any clan, sept, or great family. Name-spelling is usually immaterial, because it was chaotic until the mid-19th century. If of no clan or sept a person of Scottish connection may find there is a "district tartan" applicable to his ancestors' "habitat." Several "Scottish" general tartans are also available. (T. I.)

BIBLIOGRAPHY.—J. Logan, *The Scottish Gael . . . .* 2 vol. (1831); J. S. Stuart (ed.), *Vestiarium Scoticum* (1842); J. S. Stolberg and C. E. Stuart, *The Costume of the Clans . . .* (1845); R. R. M'Ian and J. Logan, *The Clans of the Scottish Highlands,* 2 vol. (1845–47); H. F. McClintock, F. Shaw, and J. Telfer Dunbar, *Old Irish and Highland Dress . . . .*, 2nd ed. (1950); D. C. Stewart, *The Setts of the Scottish Tartans* (1950); C. Hesketh, *Tartans* (1961); J. Telfer Dunbar, *History of Highland Dress* (1962). For colour diagrams, *see* R. Bain, *The Clans and Tartans of Scotland* (1938; 2nd ed. by M. O. MacDougall, 1954); F. Adam, *The Clans, Septs, and Regiments of the Scottish Highlands,* 4th ed. rev. by Sir Thomas Innes of Learney (1952). *See* also A. E. Haswell Miller, "The Truth About the Tartan," *Scotland's Magazine* (Edinburgh, Nov. 1947). The Scottish National Portrait Gallery, Edinburgh, contains a unique collection of photographs, manuscript notes, and drawings of contemporary portraits recording Highland dress. (A. E. H. M.)

**TARTAR:** *see* TARTARIC ACID.

**TARTARIC ACID** is one of the most important of the organic acids. Its sparingly soluble acid salt was known to the Greeks and Romans as a deposit in wine casks or vats during the fermentation of grape juice to wine. This crude crystalline crust of argol, which contains about 75% potassium acid tartrate (bitartrate), can be partly purified by recrystallization to tartar. When further purified, it becomes cream of tartar. K. W. Scheele first isolated tartaric acid in 1769 by boiling tartar with chalk and decomposing the product with sulfuric acid. Tartaric acid crystallizes from water in colourless monoclinic prisms. At ordinary temperatures these crystals are free of water of crystallization, have the composition $C_4H_6O_6$ and melt at 169°–170° C. Tartaric acid, assigned the structural formula $HO_2CCHOHCHOHCO_2H$, belongs to the hydroxy polycarboxylic acids.

**Manufacture.**—The by-products of wine fermentation, press cakes from grape juice, lees (dried slimy sediments) and argols constitute the raw materials from which tartaric acid, cream of tartar and Rochelle salt (potassium sodium tartrate) are made. The raw materials containing impurities are subjected either to steam autoclaving at 50–60 lb. pressure or dry roasting at 150°–160° C. The crude tartar is indirectly heated in the dry state, suspended in water, then neutralized with calcium hydroxide; the precipitated calcium tartrate is filtered. The filtrate is evaporated for recovery of potassium sulfate, and the cake is treated with sulfuric acid. Sparingly soluble calcium sulfate remains largely undissolved, whereas the tartaric acid passes into solution. The dilute liquor is concentrated to the crystallizing point in vacuum pans and cooled. The crude product is redissolved in water, treated with chemicals to remove impurities and decolorized by heating with charcoal. The filtered colourless solution is concentrated and allowed to crystallize. After the granular material is removed by centrifugation and dried in a rotary drier, the pure tartaric acid meets the requirements specified in the *United States Pharmacopeia.* Rochelle salt is prepared from argols blended to contain 75%–85% potassium bitartrate and less than 6% calcium tartrate. The roasted product is neutralized with sodium carbonate, clarified and evaporated to crystallize the Rochelle salt. Cream of tartar (potassium hydrogen tartrate) is usually produced by mixing filtrates from the manufacture of tartaric acid, Rochelle salt and potassium sulfate. After purification and decolorization with carbon, the material is allowed to precipitate under acid conditions. Tartar emetic (antimony potassium tartrate) is prepared by heating in water, 3.4 parts of antimony oxide and 4.3 parts of potassium bitartrate. The product separates in colourless transparent crystals which gradually lose water of crystallization, becoming opaque.

**Applications.**—Tartaric acid is widely used in carbonated drinks, effervescent tablets and powders and as an acidulent in gelatin, dessert and fruit jellies. It has many industrial applications; *e.g.,* in the cleaning and polishing of metals, in calico printing for controlling the liberation of chlorine from bleaching powder, as a mordant in wool dyeing, in certain photographic processes for printing and developing, and as ferric tartrate in blueprinting. Rochelle salt is used extensively in the silvering of mirrors, as a component of crystal-controlled electronic oscillators, in the processing of cheese and as a mild cathartic in drug preparations. Cream of tartar is employed in baking powders, in hard candies, and taffies for its ability to invert cane sugar, as a cleaner of brass, in the electrolytic tinning of iron and steel and in gold and silver coating of metals. Tartar emetic is used extensively in therapeutics for nauseant, expectorant and emetic effects. In tropical infections such as trypanosomiasis and kala azar, it is administered intravenously. Tartar emetic finds use in other varied fields; *e.g.,* in the control of insects on farms and as a mordant in fixing basic colours on cotton, leather and fur.

**Chemical Reactions.**—Tartaric acid is oxidized by hydrogen peroxide in the presence of ferrous salts to dihydroxymaleic acid. Reduction with hydrogen iodide forms first *d*-malic and finally succinic acids. Heating forms pyruvic and pyrotartaric acids and finally a black residue. Ammoniacal silver solution is reduced with the formation of a silver mirror. Tartaric acid has the ability to form complex metal ions with aluminum, iron, copper and lead, and prevents their precipitation on the addition of bases.

*Stereoisomeric Tartaric Acids.*—Four varieties of tartaric acid are recognized: (1) the ordinary dextrorotatory tartaric acid

STEWART
Official tartan of the royal family

BLACK WATCH
A regimental tartan of the British army

BUCHANAN

ROB ROY

GORDON (Dress)

MACLEOD OF LEWIS

MACDONALD (Ancient)

MACPHERSON (Dress)

SCOTTISH CLAN AND REGIMENTAL TARTANS

# TARTAN

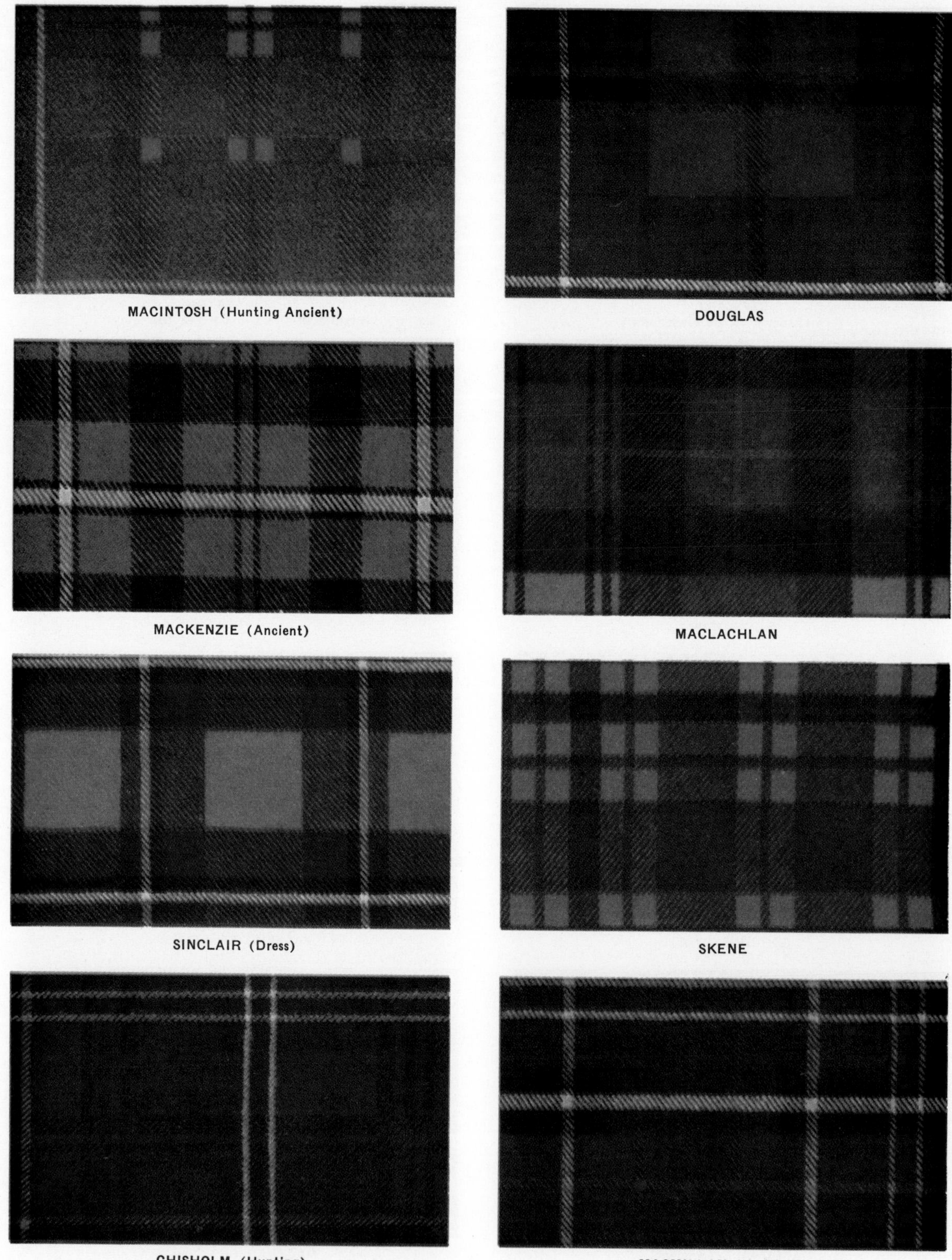

MACINTOSH (Hunting Ancient)

DOUGLAS

MACKENZIE (Ancient)

MACLACHLAN

SINCLAIR (Dress)

SKENE

CHISHOLM (Hunting)

MACMILLAN (Hunting)

TARTANS OF SOME SCOTTISH CLANS

found either free or as potassium and calcium tartrates in the juices of tamarinds, mulberries, pineapples, unripe beetroot and especially in grapes; (2) levorotatory tartaric acid, which occurs naturally in the fruit and leaves of *Bauhinia reticulata*, a native tree of the Mali Republic, but which originally was obtained by the resolutions of the salts of racemic acid. Except as regards its interactions with other optically active substances, its chemical properties are identical with those of the dextro-acid and in all its physical properties it resembles this acid except that it turns the plane of polarization of light to the left and its crystalline salts show hemihedral faces like those of the dextro-acid, but oppositely situated, as object to mirror image; (3) racemic acid, $(C_4H_6O_6)_2{\cdot}2H_2O$, which is obtained from the tartar mother liquor and dried at 110° C. to the anhydrous form, melts at 206° C. It is produced synthetically by oxidation of fumaric acid, by hydroxylation of fumaric or maleic acids, or by mixing molecular proportions of the *d*- and *l*- acids; (4) mesotartaric acid is obtained when cinchonine tartrate or *d*-tartaric acid or its alkali salts are heated for prolonged periods at 170° C. The anhydrous form of the acid melts at 159–160° C. The meso form can be synthesized by hydroxylation of fumaric or maleic acids. It is inactive like racemic acid but rather for the reason that the molecule has a plane of symmetry. Unlike the racemic mixture, it is not resolvable into optically active varieties. The chemical study of the optical properties of these four tartaric acids by Louis Pasteur forms the foundation of modern conceptions of stereoisomerism. *See* STEREOCHEMISTRY. (P. P. R.)

**TARTARS:** *see* TATAR.

**TARTINI, GIUSEPPE** (1692–1770), Italian violinist, composer, and theorist who helped establish the modern style of violin bowing and who formulated principles of ornamentation and harmony. Born at Pirano, Istria, on April 8, 1692, he studied divinity and law at Padua and at the same time established a reputation in fencing. Before the age of 20 he secretly married a protégée of the archbishop of Padua, resulting eventually in his arrest. Disguised as a monk, he fled from Padua and took refuge in a monastery at Assisi. There his violin playing attracted attention and ultimately influenced the archbishop in his decision to allow Tartini to return to his wife at Padua. In 1716 he went to Venice, where he rivaled the reputation of F. M. Veracini. Later he was at Ancona and eventually returned to Padua, where he was appointed principal violinist at the Church of S. Antonio in 1721. From 1723 to 1725 he directed the orchestra of the chancellor of Bohemia in Prague. In 1726 he returned to Padua, where, two years later, he founded a school of violin playing and composition. He made only one concert tour of Italy, in 1740. He died at Padua on Feb. 26, 1770.

Tartini's playing was said to be remarkable for its combination of technical and poetic qualities, and his bowing became a model for later schools of violinists. P. Nardini, G. Pugnani, and A. N. Pagin were among his pupils. His works include about 200 violin concertos and the same number of violin sonatas, though only a small number of them were published. The sonata entitled "Trillo del Diavolo" (Devil's Trill), written after 1735, was discovered by P. M. F. Baillol and was first published in J. B. Cartier's *L'Art du Violon* (1798). Tartini also wrote quartets, trios, symphonies, and, toward the end of his life, religious works, including a five-part *Miserere* and a four-part *Salve Regina.*

He contributed to the science of acoustics by his discovery that when any two notes are produced steadily and with intensity, a third note, known as the "difference tone," is heard. This discovery was of help in allowing violinists to play in time more reliably. Accordingly Tartini held that double stopping on the violin was not in tune unless the player could hear this difference tone. He also devised a theory of harmony based on affinities with algebra and geometry. He made these observations the basis of a theoretical system that he set forth in his *Trattato di musica* (1754), expanded into *Dissertazione dei principi dell'armonia musicale* (1767). An English translation of this work, an "Account of Tartini's Treatise on Music" by B. Stillingsfleet, is contained in *Principles and Power of Harmony* (1771). Tartini's theoretical works also include *Trattato delle appogiature,* a treatise on ornamentation. *Delle ragioni e delle proporzioni,* long attributed to Tartini, is by the mathematician Don A. Colombo and contains a list of Tartini's theoretical writings. A letter on violin playing, addressed to his pupil M. Lombardini, was translated into English by Charles Burney (1771).

*See* M. Dounias, *Die Violinkonzerte G. Tartinis* (1935); A. Capri, *G. Tartini* (1945). (Cs. CH.)

**TARTU** (German DORPAT), an old university town of the Estonian Soviet Socialist Republic, U.S.S.R., is on the Emajõgi River in the east-central part of the republic. Pop. (1959) 74,263. The principal section of the town lies south of the river, and the more important buildings are clustered around the ruins of a 13th-century cathedral.

The town's history dates back to 1030, when the Russian prince Yaroslav I erected a fort on a site called Yur'yev. From about 1224, when it was seized by the Teutonic Knights, until it was captured by the Russians about 1558, the town enjoyed great prosperity. Then for more than a century Tartu was held alternately by the Swedes, the Poles, and the Russians until, in 1704, it was annexed to the Russian Empire, and four years later the bulk of Tartu's population was deported to the interior of Russia. Following a devastating fire about 1777, the town was almost entirely rebuilt and its fortifications transformed into tree-lined promenades. The town passed to Estonian rule in 1918, but in 1940 it fell under Soviet occupation. Tartu was severely damaged during World War II under the Germans (1941–44) but later, as a part of the Soviet Union, became important for production of agricultural machinery, footwear, foodstuffs, and lumber.

The University of Tartu, chartered by Gustavus II Adolphus of Sweden in 1632, was evacuated to Parnu on the advance of the Russians in 1699. In 1710, when Parnu was also besieged, the university was closed until, in 1802, it was reopened at Tartu. German influence predominated in the university until the russification of the 1890s. Though in 1919 the institution reflected Estonia's independence as the Estonian University, Soviet influence has predominated. The university is noted for its observatory, art museum, botanical garden, and its library of more than 2,250,000 volumes. In 1951 another higher educational institution, the Academy of Agriculture, was established in Tartu.

**TARXIEN:** *see* MALTA: *Archaeology;* PAOLA-TARXIEN.

**TASHKENT,** an *oblast* of the Uzbek Soviet Socialist Republic, U.S.S.R., was founded in 1938. It adjoins the Kazakh, Kirgiz, and Tadzhik S.S.R.'s and has an area of 6,023 sq.mi. (15,600 sq.km.). It is divided into 13 *rayons* and has 9 towns and 14 "settlements of town type." The *oblast* is situated at the northwestern edge of the Tien Shan (Tyan' Shan') Mountains in the basin of the middle course of the Syr-Dar'ya. Most of its territory consists of a plain intersected by the Syr-Dar'ya, Angren, and Chirchik rivers. The northeast is mountainous (Kuraminskiy, Ugamskiy, and Pskemskiy ranges), with peaks rising to 14,000 ft. (4,250 m.); the Golodnaya Step' (Hungry Steppe) occupies the southwestern part. The climate is continental, with a mild winter and a long, hot, dry summer. Rainfall varies from 10 in. (250 mm.) in the plains to 20 in. (500 mm.) in the foothills and mountains.

In 1959 the population was 2,260,881 (58% urban), of whom about 40% were Uzbeks and 29% Russians, the majority of the latter living in Tashkent. The rest are Kazakhs, Tatars, Ukrainians, Tadzhiks, and Koreans (about 3%). The towns are Tashkent, Chirchik, Angren, Almalyk, Yangi-Yul', Begovat, Mirzachul', Yangi-Abad, Yangi-Yer.

Industrially, the *oblast* is highly developed and includes about 3,000 factories. The geographical position has promoted industry connected with metal processing, machine construction, and other enterprises working on imported raw materials. There are agricultural machinery works, railway workshops, cotton textile and paper mills, and clothing and shoe factories. Food industries include meat-packing, flour milling, and fruit and vegetable canning. Brown coal is mined at Angren. Large electric power stations at Farkhad, Chirchik, Nizhne-Bozsu, and Ordzhonikidze provide 90% of the power used. The main crop is cotton, which provides more than 20% of Uzbekistan's total output. Of the total sown area of 155,000 ha. (about 380,000 ac.), more than two-thirds is devoted to cotton. Jute and oleiferous plants (such as flax and sesame) and vegetables and melons are grown. Livestock breeding includes pedigree cattle centres in the Chinaz and Mirzachul' *rayons.*

The main Moscow-Tashkent-Krasnovodsk railway traverses the *oblast,* with Ursat'yevskaya the junction for the Fergana Valley railway. From Tashkent branch lines run to Chirchik and Angren. Of the extensive network of roads, the principal are the Tashkent-Termez and Tashkent-Dushanbe routes.

There are in the *oblast* more than 20 professional schools and 40 "middle" special training establishments, including mining, industrial, electromechanical, and cotton-ginning *tekhnikums.* There were 18 higher educational establishments (including the Tashkent V. I. Lenin University). (G. E. Wr.)

**TASHKENT,** the capital of Tashkentskaya (Tashkent) Oblast', and also capital of the Uzbek Soviet Socialist Republic, U.S.S.R., from 1930. Pop. (1959) 911,930. Though it is one of the oldest and largest cities of Central Asia, about half the population is composed of Russians and other non-Asians.

Probably founded in the 6th or 7th century, Tashkent was taken by the Arabs early in the 8th century A.D. It was important economically until the beginning of the 13th century, when it was destroyed by the khan of East Turkistan, Kuchlük. Rebuilt in the middle of the 13th century, it became part of the Timurid Empire until the end of the 15th, when it resumed a partly independent economic existence. From the beginning of the 19th century it was part of the Kokand khanate and was captured by the Russians in 1865, when it became the commercial, cultural, and administrative centre of Russian Turkistan. The new city, built under the tsarist regime, was greatly developed after the Revolution, but much of the old city with its 12 gates still remains. It is the headquarters of the Turkistan Military District.

Tashkent has many major heavy-industry enterprises, including textile, agricultural, and building machinery, and electrical and mining equipment. The most important light industry is the Tashkent textile *kombinat.* Abrasives, china and pottery, paper, furniture, and food and chemical products are also produced. Apart from the Tashkent V. I. Lenin University, the Uzbek Academy of Sciences, and 16 higher educational establishments, Tashkent contains many technical training establishments. Theatres include the Alisher Navoy Opera and Ballet Theatre and a puppet theatre. There are also a concert hall, circus, cinemas, and a cinema studio, and 11 parks and 4 stadiums. Many newspapers are published in the Uzbek, Tadzhik, and Russian languages, and there are radio and television broadcasting stations.

(G. E. Wr.)

**TASMAN, ABEL JANSZOON** (*c.* 1603–*c.* 1659), the greatest of Dutch navigators and explorers, the discoverer of Tasmania, New Zealand, the Tonga and the Fiji Islands, was born at Lutjegast in Groningen, probably in 1603. He entered the service of the Dutch East India company in 1632 or 1633. His first exploring voyage was to Ceram as captain of the "Mocha" in 1634. He sailed in 1639 under Matthew Quast on an expedition in search of the "islands of gold and silver" in the seas east of Japan. After a series of trading voyages to Japan, Formosa, Cambodia and Palembang, he was chosen by the governor general of the Dutch East Indies, Antonio van Diemen, to command in 1642 the most ambitious of all Dutch voyages for the exploration of the southern hemisphere.

**Tasman's Voyage 1642–43.**—By 1642 Dutch navigators had discovered discontinuous stretches of the western coast of Australia, but whether these coasts were continental and connected with the hypothetical southern continent of the Pacific remained unknown. Tasman was to answer this problem, following instructions based on a memoir by Frans Jacobszoon Visscher, his chief pilot. He was to explore the Indian ocean from west to east, south of the ordinary trade route, and, proceeding eastward into the Pacific (if this proved possible), to investigate the practicability of a sea passage eastward to Chile, to rediscover the Solomon Islands of the Spaniards and to explore New Guinea.

Leaving Batavia on Aug. 14, 1642, with two ships, the "Heemskerk" and "Zeehaen," Tasman sailed to Mauritius (Sept. 5–Oct. 8), then southward and eastward, reaching his most southerly latitude of 49° S. in about 94° E. Turning north he discovered land on Nov. 24 in 42° 20′ S. and he skirted its southern shores, naming it Van Diemen's Land (now Tasmania). A council of officers on Dec. 5 decided against further investigation, so he missed the opportunity of discovering Bass strait. Continuing eastward, he sighted on Dec. 13, in 42° 10′ S., the coast of South Island, New Zealand, and explored it northward, entering the strait between North Island and South Island but supposing it to be a bay. He left New Zealand on Jan. 4, 1643, at North cape under the impression that he had probably discovered the west coast of the southern continent, which might be connected with the "Staten Landt" discovered by W. C. Schouten and J. Le Maire south of South America: hence the name of "Staten Landt" which Tasman gave to his discovery in honour of the states-general.

Convinced by the swell that the passage to Chile existed, Tasman now turned northeast and on Jan. 21 he discovered Tonga and on Feb. 6 the Fiji Islands. Turning northwest, the ships reached New Guinea waters on April 1 and Batavia on June 15, 1643, completing a ten months' voyage on which only 10 men had died from illness. Tasman had circumnavigated Australia without seeing it, separating it from the hypothetical southern continent.

The council of the company decided, however, that he had been negligent in his investigation of the lands discovered and of the passage to Chile. They sent him on a new expedition to the "South Land" in 1644.

**Tasman's Voyage 1644.**—Tasman's instructions ordered him to establish the relationships of New Guinea, the "great known South Land" (western Australia), Van Diemen's Land and the "unknown South Land." He sailed from Batavia on Feb. 29, steering southeast into Torres strait, which he mistook for a shallow bay, coasting the Gulf of Carpentaria and then following the coast of Australia to 22° S.

Although he was rewarded with the rank of commander and was made a member of the Council of Justice of Batavia, his second voyage was also a disappointment to the company because it had failed to reveal lands of potential wealth. In 1647 Tasman commanded a trading fleet to Siam, and in 1648 a war fleet against the Spaniards in the Philippines. He had left the company's service by 1653 and died probably before Oct. 22, 1659, and certainly before Feb. 5, 1661.

Bibliography.—The standard authorities are J. E. Heeres (ed.), *Abel Janszoon Tasman's Journal* (1898); R. Posthumus Meyjes (ed.), *De Reizen van Abel Janszoon Tasman en Franchoys Jacobszoon Visscher* (1919). *See* also R. H. Major, *Early Voyages to Terra Australis,* Hakluyt Soc. (1859); J. B. Walker, *Abel Janszoon Tasman; his life and voyages* (1896); J. C. Beaglehole, *The Discovery of New Zealand* (1939); G. C. Henderson, *The Discoverers of the Fiji Islands,* pp. 3–99 (1933). The first published account in England of Tasman's voyage of 1642–43 (a translation from the Dutch of Arnoldus Montanus, 1671) appeared in John Ogilby's *America,* pp. 653–661 (1671). In 1682 Robert Hooke published in his *Philosophical Collections,* no. 6, pp. 179–186, the first English translation of D. R. van Nierop's *Eenige oefeningen* (1674), comprising extracts from a journal of the voyage.

(H. M. Ws.)

**TASMANIA,** the smallest state of the Commonwealth of Australia, comprises the large island of Tasmania and numerous smaller islands lying to the south of the southeastern edge of the continental mainland. Tasmania, which is separated from the mainland by the Bass Strait, a 150-mi. (240 km.)-wide stretch of shallow sea (30–40 fathoms), is a shield-shaped island with a maximum length of 180 mi. (290 km.), a maximum width of 190 mi. (306 km.), and an area of 25,050 sq.mi. (64,879 sq.km.) including Macquarie Island, about 90 sq.mi. (233 sq.km.). The total area of the state, including King Island and the Furneaux Group in the Bass Strait, and Bruny, about 1,333 mi. (2,145 km.) SE of Tasmania, is 26,383 sq.mi. (68,332 sq.km.), or less than 1% of the area of Australia. The state capital is Hobart. (X.)

## PHYSICAL GEOGRAPHY

**Physical Features.**—Western and northern Tasmania are surfaced by Precarboniferous rocks and dominated by Paleozoic fold structures. The oldest Precambrian strata, comprising quartzite,

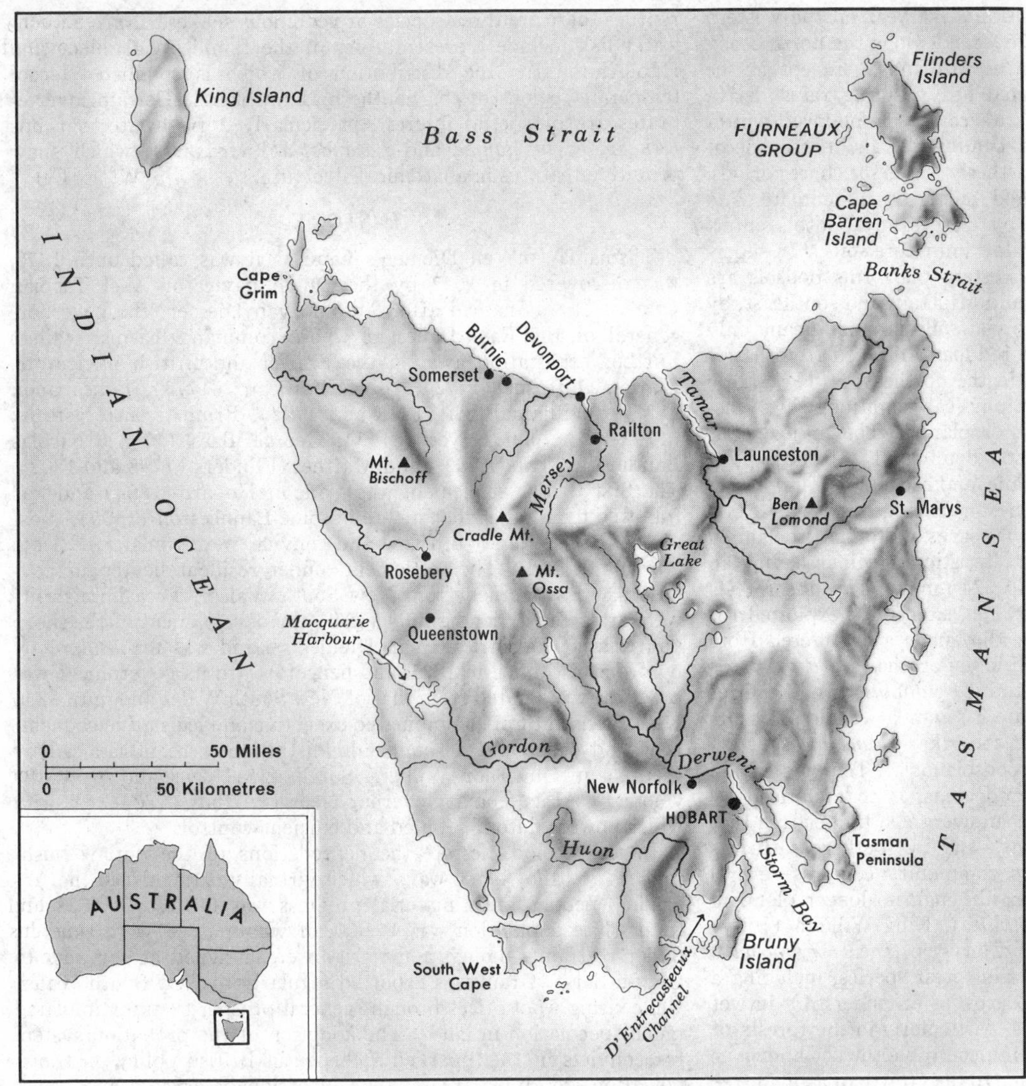

MAJOR CITIES AND PHYSICAL FEATURES OF TASMANIA

tained lakes that quickly filled with sediment. Many river systems, notably the Derwent, may have originated from the linking of these lakes, while extensive lowlands, notably southwest of Launceston, derive from the lake sediments. Tertiary faulting also resulted in the formation of Bass Strait and in extensive basaltic lava flows. The central and western highlands were glaciated in the Pleistocene when Bass Strait was largely drained by a retreat of the sea. A postglacial rise in sea level submerged not only the strait but also river estuaries.

Tasmania may therefore be described as an island of plateaus, platforms, and rugged ranges, exhibiting the most spectacular mountain scenery in Australia.

Along the west coast are remarkably even, deeply incised platforms up to 1,500 ft. (460 m.) in height, upon which stand isolated monadnocks. Detached portions are King Island and the Furneaux Group. Eastward lie discontinuous rugged ranges of Paleozoic fold structures rising above 4,000 ft. (1,200 m.), and in the northwest a basalt plateau sloping northward from 2,000 ft. to a cliff coast. The northeastern platforms are generally below 500 ft., but to the south lie the geologically complex and maturely dissected northeastern highlands (4,600 ft. [1,400 m.]). The southwestern portion is the Ben Lomond block, a flat-topped dolerite mesa (more than 4,000 ft.)

schist, gneiss, and other metamorphic rocks, outcrop in an axial belt from around Cradle Mountain southward to South West Cape. Younger unmetamorphosed Precambrian rocks outcrop in the northwest. Between these two occurrences and bordering the axial belt both along the west coast and inland are Cambrian, Ordovician, Silurian, and Devonian rocks, the latter also occupying extensive areas of the northeast. The metamorphism and folding of the Precarboniferous strata took place mainly in the earth movements of the Devonian period, which resulted in the intrusion of granites and the injection of metallic lodes. Precambrian rocks are the hosts of major tin deposits at Mt. Bischoff and Renison Bell and of scheelite on King Island. But the most important ore deposits occur in the Cambrian rocks, especially in schisted volcanic areas. In Carboniferous and Permian times much of Tasmania was glaciated, as evidenced by striated surfaces and tillite deposits.

By contrast, central and southeastern Tasmania are characterized by unfolded Permo-Triassic sediments intruded by Jurassic dolerite, the major lineaments being determined by Tertiary faulting. In the west and the north these rocks, which once covered most of the fold structures unconformably, have been almost entirely removed and exist largely where preserved by downfaulting. In the centre and the southeast, where the rainfall is much lower, the horizontal Mesozoic cover has been preserved and the resistant dolerite, also horizontal, dominates the landscape. Peneplanation in the late Mesozoic followed by early Pliocene faulting resulted in the uplift of the Ben Lomond block, the central plateau, and the highland blocks of the south and the southwest. Intervening rift valleys trending north-northwesterly originally con-

with residual tors (up to 5,010 ft. [1,527 m.]). Westward lies the Midland rift valley, floored partly by soft Miocene lake sediments and drained by mature meandering rivers. In the centre stands the high, relatively undissected, dolerite central plateau, bounded northeast by a fault scarp, west by glacial troughs, and sloping southward from 4,000 to 2,000 ft. Its surface includes 5,000 small rock-basin lakes of glacial origin in the west and a few large, very shallow lakes of unknown origin in the east. To the west and south lies the high dissected western edge of the dolerite sills, with the highest point in Tasmania (Mt. Ossa, 5,305 ft. [1,617 m.]), and, in the Ducane Range, the only extensive area of glaciated alpine scenery in Australia. Southeastern Tasmania comprises low dissected dolerite sills with fault-determined basins, ranges, and troughs.

The coastline owes much to faulting and postglacial drowning. Silt deposition and the growth of sandpits and tidal marshes, aided by a recent emergence of about 70 ft., are widespread, but particularly marked in the north. The southeast, with its deep Huon and Derwent rias and drowned interfluve summits tied together into peninsulas, is one of the finest drowned coastlines in the world.

**Climate.**—Tasmania lies in the westerly wind belt of the mid-latitudes. Local surface-controlled winds, gusty and variable in direction, give clear skies, abundant sunshine, and a wide daily temperature range. Except in upland areas, monthly temperatures range from 15.6° to 18.3° C (60° to 65° F) in summer and from 7.2° to 10° C (45° to 50° F) in winter, the east coast being about 2° C warmer than the west coast because of modifying warm (north) and cool (south) sea currents, respectively. In general, rainfall derives from southern maritime air masses and decreases eastward. It exceeds 100 in. (2,540 mm.) a year on the western ranges, averages 50–30 in. (1,270–762 mm.) along the north coast, and 30–20 in. (762–508 mm.) in the Midlands. Except in the east and southeast, where occasional heavy spring rains derive from northern maritime air masses, there is a pronounced winter maximum. In summer, northern continental air masses occasionally bring Tasmania hot, dry northerly winds for short periods.

**Soils.**—Tasmania, with its rugged relief, humid climate, and forest vegetation, is characterized by gray, sandy podsols, interspersed with extensive tracts of shallow immature soils. In superhumid highland areas and on the western platforms podsols are replaced by peats, and in the subhumid Midlands and southeast, by brown earths and black soils. Alluvial soils are significant only along the middle Derwent. Fertile red loams derived from basalt occur in the northwest and locally in the northeast. (P. St.)

**Vegetation.**—The wide range in physical conditions gives Tasmania a great variety of habitats for plants. The major plant communities are sclerophyll forest (dominated by eucalypts), temperate rain forest, austral montane, and sedge moor and heath. Areas of these and of coastal stretches are included in about 1,000 sq.mi. (2,590 sq.km.) of eight national parks and other proclaimed reserves. Sclerophyll forest is characteristic of regions having an annual rainfall of less than 60 in. (1,524 mm.). The fine forests in the 30–60 in.-rainfall areas have been extensively exploited for timber and for the paper industry; they have also suffered from destructive fires. Species of economic importance are *Eucalyptus regnans, E. obliqua, E. gigantea,* and *E. globulus.* In the drier central and eastern parts of the state a savanna woodland occurs in which *E. pauciflora* is dominant; she-oaks (*Casuarina* species) and wattles (*Acacia* species) are conspicuous. Temperate rain forest, which develops in superhumid areas, is characterized by myrtle (*Nothofagus cunninghamii*), an evergreen timber tree that grows to a height of 100 ft. (30 m.), and by southern sassafras (*Atherosperma moschatum*). This community contains several endemic conifers valuable as timber although no longer plentiful —the Huon pine (*Dacrydium franklinii*), King William (Billy) pine (*Athrotaxis selaginoides*), and celery-top pine (*Phyllocladus aspleniifolius*). Myrtle and other rain-forest species, including a tree fern, *Dicksonia antarctica,* also grow as an understory in wet sclerophyll forests. In certain areas, particularly in the forests of the south and southwest, an almost impenetrable thicket known as horizontal scrub develops. This is due to the growth of a small tree called horizontal (*Anodopetalum biglandulosum*). The slender trunk of the tree falls over under its own weight, and from it branches arise that behave in the same way. In both sclerophyll and rain-forest regions large areas of acid, waterlogged soil support a sedge moor characterized by button grass (*Gymnoschoenus sphaerocephalus*). In the wettest sections this sedge forms large tussocks 2–6 ft. high, but elsewhere other members of the family Cyperaceae and of the Restionaceae are dominant. On the mountain plateaus are found many plants having subantarctic affinities. These include *Nothofagus gunnii,* Tasmania's only deciduous tree or shrub, and certain cushion plants. The latter are perennial evergreen dicotyledons with numerous branches bearing small stiff leaves closely overlapped; a cushion plant forms a firm mound often 3 ft. (1 m.) or more in diameter.

**Animal Life.**—Native mammals comprise 2 species of monotremes and 19 species of marsupials. Of the latter, 7, including the Tasmanian devil, the thylacine or wolf, and wombat, are endemic. Nearly half of the Tasmanian marsupials are carnivores or omnivores (whereas in mainland Australia herbivores preponderate). Several species are locally abundant and 2, Bennett's wallaby and the pademelon, are exploited for fur and meat. The 2 monotremes, or egg-laying mammals, which are wholly protected, are widespread; they are the echidna, or spiny anteater, and platypus. The latter occurs in many freshwater lakes and streams. Birds characteristic of the open forest include the honeyeaters and wattlebirds (family Meliphagidae), and also parrots and cockatoos. The fairy penguin nests along the coasts. The Tasmanian mutton bird is of economic importance. This migratory bird travels between southeastern Australia and the Aleutian Islands; its large breeding grounds are on the islands of Bass Strait. Among the reptiles there are three species of venomous snakes. Native freshwater fish include representatives of the families Galaxiidae and Haplochitonidae, the distribution of which is confined to cool temperate regions of the Southern Hemisphere. Certain invertebrates are of special interest, particularly 2 freshwater shrimps (*Anaspides tasmaniae* and *Paranaspides lacustris*), which show primitive features in anatomical structure. (W. M. C.)

## HISTORY

Tasmania, or Van Diemen's Land as it was called until 1856, was discovered in 1642 by the Dutch navigator Abel Tasman (*q.v.*). It was named after Antonio van Diemen, the governor-general of the East Indies at whose command Tasman sailed. Further exploration awaited the French and British navigators, Marion Dufresne (1772), Tobias Furneaux (1773), James Cook (1777), William Bligh (1788 and 1792), Bruni d'Entrecasteaux (1792–93), John Hayes (1793), George Bass (1798), Nicolas Baudin (1800 and 1802), and Matthew Flinders (1798 and 1802). The first British settlement was made at Hobart (1804) and was followed by another that was to become Launceston (1806); most of the first settlers, both free and convict, were transferred from Norfolk Island. The settlement, under resident lieutenant governors, was governed from New South Wales. Free immigrants were attracted by land grants and by the development of the sheep and whaling industries. Van Diemen's Land was made a colony by order in council in 1825, and henceforward its government was practically separated from that of New South Wales and until 1850 was exercised through nominated executive and legislative councils. Law and order and a sound administration were introduced by Lieutenant Governor William Sorell (1817–24) and were developed by Lieutenant Governor George Arthur (1824–36), with wider powers, into a detailed and efficient control.

In this period, despite the depredations of the outlaw bushrangers and the "black war," which virtually extinguished the Aboriginal people, great material progress was made. In 1828 the total white population was 17,000, of whom 7,500 were convicts under restraint, though a majority were assigned as servants to free settlers. Grain was exported regularly to New South Wales, while rising wool prices brought general prosperity and stimulated much speculation in land. The adoption of the probation system for convicts in 1840 marked a change in British policy on transportation, depriving free settlers of assigned servants and transforming the colony into a penal settlement. The influx of population was rapid until 1847, growing to 70,000, but the ratio of free to unfree was reversed. In the late 1840s the boom gave way to an economic depression, and the colonial government faced a deficit, which local opinion attributed to the cost of police and jails. Belatedly, the home authorities offered some relief but not before public opinion was roused to demand representative institutions and the cessation of transportation of British convicts. Representatives were first elected to the Legislative Council in 1851, and the transportation policy ceased in 1853.

The constitution was settled more definitely in 1856 with the election of a two-chamber Parliament and with the appointment of the first responsible ministry. From 1856, the colony was known as Tasmania.

The gold discoveries in Victoria in 1851 caused inflation and labour shortage in Tasmania, and the economy was unable to support the strain. The whaling industry declined and with it shipbuilding. The adoption of a protectionist policy by Victoria injured Tasmanian manufactures. After 1857 a prolonged depression, lasting 25 years, was marked by deficits, reduction in services, opposition to all forms of taxation, political feuds, and frequent changes in ministries. Under competition from continental Australia, wheat production declined to its present insignificance.

After 1880 economic conditions improved, largely because mining industries were opened up in the west and northeast. The hardwood forests were exploited, and fruit growing in the south became the basis of small manufacturing and export industries. Railways, roads, and harbour facilities were developed, while relative political stability was achieved, particularly during the Fysh ministry (1887–92). After the recession following on the failure of the Bank of Van Diemen's Land in 1891, there was from 1894 to 1899 a slow recovery during Sir Edward Braddon's ministry. In the 1890s a majority of Tasmanians supported the movement that ended in 1901 with Australian federation (*see* AUSTRALIA, COMMONWEALTH OF: *History*).

Economic development slowed down after 1910 as the mining boom passed, and during the next 25 years Tasmania was relatively depressed, the worst years being 1922–26 and 1931–35. Population grew slowly, the birth rate fell, and the exodus of the young and more vigorous people was resumed.

State politics entered a new phase with the founding of the Labor Party in 1903. Labor first took office in 1909 and was again returned to power in 1914. From that time both the Labor and the Liberal (Nationalist) parties sponsored social and industrial legislation. All the administrations faced financial difficulties, which were not resolved until in 1933 the Commonwealth government set up the Grants Commission, through which special financial assistance is given to the state. This enabled Tasmania to bring the level of its social services up to the national average. After 1942 uniform taxation throughout the Commonwealth and virtual Commonwealth control of the main sources of revenue, together with the provision of reimbursement grants to the states, favoured Tasmania, which received more *per capita* in such grants than any other state. With increasing revenue, supported by loan funds backed by the Commonwealth, Tasmania has invested since 1950 in a large capital works program, especially in the development of hydroelectric power, which in turn has stimulated the growth of much secondary industry.

A Labor government was formed in 1934 and won eight successive elections, continuing without a break to govern the state until the 1969 election when it was replaced by a Liberal-Centre Party coalition. (W. A. TY.)

## POPULATION

For more than a century Tasmania experienced a steady drift of population to the mainland, and only two periods of net immigration have been recorded: from 1875 to 1905 during the mining boom and from 1947 to 1961. The population increased from 115,705 at the 1881 census to 172,475 in 1901, to 213,780 in 1921. In 1947 it was 257,078; in 1961, 350,340; and in 1966, 371,416. Since 1962 Tasmania's traditionally high rate of natural increase has tended to decline; in 1962 the crude birthrate was 25.01 and in 1966, 19.93.

At the 1966 census Hobart was the eighth largest city in Australia, with a metropolitan population of 119,469. Launceston had a metropolitan population of 60,456. Other towns with a population of more than 5,000 were Burnie-Somerset (18,042), Devonport (14,874), Ulverstone (6,842), and New Norfolk (5,770).

## ADMINISTRATION AND SOCIAL CONDITIONS

**Administration.**—The state of Tasmania is administered by a governor, who is the direct representative of the British sovereign, and by a Parliament comprising a Legislative Council and a House of Assembly. Election is by the Hare-Clark System of a single transferable vote and with the obligation to record at least three preferences. The state is also represented in the Senate and House of Representatives of the Commonwealth Parliament. Local government is by 3 city councils (Hobart, Launceston, and Glenorchy), 2 government commissions (Clarence and Kingsborough), and 44 municipal councils.

**Education.**—The state Education Department controls almost 300 schools comprising infant, primary, and—in country towns—area schools, high schools (including comprehensive high schools), and district schools. Attendance is compulsory between the ages of 6 and 16. Special provision has been made for mentally retarded children and for those with physical handicaps. Nonstate, fee-charging schools total more than 60 and contain only one-sixth of all children attending school. Most of the nonstate schools are affiliated with religious denominations; since 1967 they have received state assistance on the basis of pupil numbers. Teacher training is provided by teachers' colleges in Launceston and Hobart and by the faculty of education at the University of Tasmania. The university (founded 1890) had in the late 1960s a teaching staff of about 150, with 2,500 students, and awarded degrees in arts, commerce, law, science, engineering, agriculture, and medicine.

**Health.**—Hospital services are provided by the state, as well as by private (but subsidized) institutions maintained by religious denominations and public bodies. Public hospital services include general hospitals at Hobart, Launceston, Latrobe, and Burnie, maternity hospitals at Hobart and Launceston, 16 district hospitals, and 25 district nursing centres. In addition, Hobart and Launceston have special institutions for the care of crippled children, tuberculosis patients, and the aged and invalid (also at Wynyard); New Norfolk has a mental hospital. State medical officers are provided in 12 municipalities that cannot support a private practitioner. The state also provides a child welfare service (for expectant mothers and infants under two years) and school medical and dental services. Annual X-ray examinations for adults are compulsory by law.

**Social Services.**—Various social service benefits are payable under Commonwealth legislation, notably child endowment (family allowances), maternity allowances, unemployment and sickness benefits, invalid pensions, allowances for wives and children of invalid pensioners, and age and widows' pensions. Except for maternity allowances and child endowment, benefits are subject to residential qualifications and a means test.

**Living Conditions.**—There are no great extremes of wealth or poverty in Tasmania; the more prosperous sections of the community comprise ranchers, professional workers, and retailers. Home ownership is a fundamental feature of Tasmanian life. The numerical importance of small and medium property owners is reflected in the relatively conservative tendency of both political parties. The work force of the larger industrial, mining, and public utility undertakings is organized in well-established labour unions. The minimum wages and conditions of Tasmanian employees are regulated either by awards of the Commonwealth Arbitration Court or by state wages boards.

## THE ECONOMY

**Agriculture.**—Agriculture is restricted by rugged relief and a superhumid climate to a belt through the north and east. Level, cultivable land is nowhere extensive. To overcome the disabilities of small-scale production and distance from markets, farmers tend to diversify farm enterprises, to concentrate on such specialties as fruit, hops, stud stock, and superfine wool, and to intensify their methods. Specialized dairying for butter manufacture occurs only in the far northwest and far northeast. Elsewhere in the north, mixed dairying (for butter) and vegetable growing (chiefly potatoes and peas) are dominant. Apples and pears are grown in the Tamar and Mersey valleys. Sheep farming, with some subsidiary beef-cattle raising and cereal cultivation (mostly oats but also soft wheat and barley), typifies the Midlands, but toward the north and south fat lambs increase in importance relative to wool. The central plateau is used for summer grazing. In the southeast hops are a specialty of the irrigated alluvial terraces of the middle Derwent, small fruits of the hills west of the lower Derwent, and stone fruits east of the lower Derwent.

**Fisheries.**—Productivity is limited by a narrow continental shelf and by the low plankton content of the subtropical east Australian current. Fishing is mostly confined to the north and east coasts. The principal species caught are barracouta and crayfish, but snapper or school shark and gummy shark are also taken, primarily for their liver oil. Scallops are dredged chiefly from the d'Entrecasteaux Channel, and whitebait is taken in many Tasmanian rivers. Salmon and some mackerel, flounder, and mullet are also caught. Tuna is increasing in importance. Like agriculture, fisheries rely on export markets, chiefly Melbourne and Sydney.

**Mining.**—Tasmania produces a variety of minerals including, since 1967, iron ore. Savage River ore (38% iron) is mined by opencut southwest of Mt. Bischoff, concentrated to 67% iron, converted to slurry, piped to Port Latta near Stanley, pelletized, and shipped (2,000,000 to 3,000,000 tons a year) to Japan. Other minerals produced are copper (about 15,000 tons), zinc (50,000 tons), lead (16,000 tons), tin (1,500 tons), and tungsten (1,800 tons: 1,300 scheelite, 500 wolfram). Copper is derived largely from the West Lyell opencut mine near Queenstown. At Rosebery the underground Rosebery and Hercules mines furnish mainly zinc, but also lead and copper. Tin is mined at Renison Bell and Mt. Cleveland in the west and at Rossarden, Gladstone, and South Mt. Cameron in the northeast. Scheelite deposits are worked on King Island and wolfram derives mainly from the northeastern tin mines. Subbituminous Triassic coal is mined (less than 100,000 tons a year), chiefly near St. Marys. Limestone is quarried (about 350,000 tons a year) for cement production at Railton, and for metallurgical purposes, carbide manufacture, and agricultural lime.

**Manufacturing Industries and Power Supply.**—Secondary industry, like agriculture, is handicapped by the absence of a large local market and by shipping difficulties, but has the advantage over the rest of Australia of cheaper power (wholly hydroelectric; some to be thermal from 1971). The state has therefore concentrated on electrometallurgical and electrochemical specialties and on processing its own primary products. With only 3.2% of Australia's population, Tasmania produces more than one-tenth of the electricity generated in Australia and one-fifth of the electricity used in industry. Although development, which is undertaken by the state-owned Hydroelectric Commission, has hitherto been largely confined to the central plateau, current expansion involves the Mersey, Forth, and Wilmot rivers in the northwest, and the Gordon River in the southwest. Industries using bulk power supplies include the electrolytic zinc refinery at Risdon, which treats zinc concentrates from Broken Hill and Rosebery, the aluminum reduction works and ferromanganese plant at Bell Bay near George Town, the pulp and paper mills at Boyer near New Norfolk and at Burnie, the pulp mills at Port Huon, and the carbide works at Electrona south of Hobart. Other important industries include the manufacture of woolen yarn (Launceston), other textile goods (Launceston and Devonport), chocolate (Claremont, near Hobart), hardboard (Burnie), plywood (Somerset), and titanium pigments (near Burnie).

**External Trade.**—Tasmania lies within the Australian customs area. Interstate trade, of which one-eighth of the exports and one-tenth of the imports are carried by air, accounts for nearly three-quarters of Tasmania's exports and four-fifths of its imports. Of total exports, primary products, such as greasy wool, fresh fruit, potatoes, mineral concentrates, hides and skins, peas, hops, and fish, furnish more than one-third. Secondary products include zinc ingots, newsprint and writing papers, woolen manufactures, scoured wool, sawn timber, copper, canned fruit and vegetables, silver-lead, butter, tungsten, tin, jam, carbide, and confections. Apart from raw wool (grades not produced in Tasmania), imports are mainly producers' materials and manufactured consumers' goods, principally machinery, motor vehicles, petroleum products, hardware, textiles, clothing, and foodstuffs. Hobart handles nearly twice as much sea trade as Launceston; Launceston handles nearly twice as much air trade as Hobart.

**Finance.**—Tasmania has benefited considerably from federal grants paid annually in accordance with the recommendations of the Commonwealth Grants Commission and from substantial tax reimbursement grants paid by the Commonwealth government on condition that no taxation is levied by the state on incomes received by persons or companies. These grants have reduced the adverse effects of Tasmania's relative disadvantage in taxable capacity and have made possible somewhat higher standards, especially in education and health services.

**Transportation and Communications.**—Internal transport is coordinated by the Transport Commission, which operates most of the 570 route miles (917 km.) of railway (3 ft. 6 in. gauge) (1.07 m.) and licenses and operates road-passenger and road-freighting services. Two-thirds of the main road mileage has been paved. Radio and television stations, both national and commercial, serve the main cities. Transportation to the Australian mainland is provided by cargo and passenger ships, by "drive-on" ferries (for motor vehicles), and by frequent air services.

*See* also references under "Tasmania" in the Index. (P. St.)

Bibliography.—L. Rodway, *The Tasmanian Flora* (1903); W. M. Curtis, *The Student's Flora of Tasmania,* part I (1956), part II (1963); W. M. Curtis and J. Somerville, "The Vegetation (of Tasmania)" in *A.N.Z.A.A.S. Handbook of Tasmania* (1949); E. Le G. Troughton, *Furred Animals of Australia* (1941); M. Sharland, *Tasmanian Birds* (1958); E. R. Guiler, *Marsupials of Tasmania* (1960); A. H. Spry and M. R. Banks (ed.), "Geology of Tasmania," *J. Geol. Soc. Aust.* (1962); B. Beatty, *Tasmania—Isle of Splendor* (1968).

R. W. Giblin, *Early History of Tasmania,* 2 vol. (1928–39); W. D. Forsyth, *Governor Arthur's Convict System: Van Diemen's Land 1824–36* (1935); K. E. Fitzpatrick, *Sir John Franklin in Tasmania, 1837–1843* (1949); W. A. Townsley, *The Struggle for Self-Government in Tasmania, 1842–1856* (1951); also articles in *Historical Studies, Australia and New Zealand,* vol. 1, no. 1; vol. 3, no. 12; vol. 4, no. 15; and vol. 5, no. 17 (1940 *et seq.*); R. M. Hartwell, *The Economic Development of Van Diemen's Land, 1820–1850* (1954); L. L. Robson, *The Convict Settlers of Australia* (1965); H. L. Roth, *Aborigines of Tasmania* (1966); Tasmanian Historical Research Association, *Papers and Proceedings* (1951– ).

R. M. H. Garvie, *A Million Horses: Tasmania's Power in the Mountains* (1962); Lands and Surveys Department, *Atlas of Tasmania* (1965); Commonwealth Statistician (Canberra), *Statistics for the State of Tasmania, Pocket Year Book of Tasmania, Monthly Review of Business Statistics* (Tasmania); also *Year Book of the Commonwealth of Australia.*

L. F. Giblin, *Federation and Finance,* Report of the Australian and New Zealand Association for the Advancement of Science, vol. xviii (1926); *Report of Committee on Tasmanian Disabilities Under Federation* (1925); *Reports of Commonwealth Grants Commission* (1936); H. P. Brown, "Some Aspects of Federal-State Financial Relations" in G. Sawer (ed.), *Federalism in Australia* (1949).

**TASMANIAN DEVIL** (*Sarcophilus harrisii*), a pouched mammal, or marsupial (*q.v.*), of the family Dasyuridae. It is now restricted to Tasmania but is in no danger of extermination. The condition of skulls and other bones found in Victoria suggests that this animal inhabited the Australian mainland until recently. It is terrestrial and heavily built, resembling a small bear or badger (hence the specific name of *ursinus,* or bearlike, given it when first observed). From nose to tail-tip it measures about 3½ ft. (about 107 cm.). The general colour is black tinged with brown; chest, shoulder, and rump patches are white. Its fierce expression, strength, and harsh, husky cough or snarl have earned the animal its name of devil or native devil and its exaggerated reputation for ferocity. The mating season is in March and April, the young being born in May. Their variable diet consists of small mammals, birds, lizards, and carrion. (Jo. E. H.)

**TASMANIANS,** an extinct Negritoid people once found in Tasmania (*q.v.*). Male average height was about 5 ft. 6 in. (1.7 m.); they had flat noses and wide nostrils (the nasal index being the highest on record), shorter and broader heads than mainland Australian Aboriginals, full, fleshy lips, bushy beards, and very curly to woolly hair.

Two main theories of their origin are held: (1) They formed the original population of eastern coastal Australia; then, yielding to Australoid immigrants, they crossed into Tasmania. (This view implies a land corridor [available 7,000 years ago] or shorter stretches of ocean and also winds and currents in the opposite direction to those now prevailing.) (2) They drifted to Tasmania in canoes or rafts from the New Hebrides region where there are similar Negritoid types; winds and currents favour such voyages as well as possible landings on the Queensland coast.

The most reliable assessment of Tasmanian population before European settlement in 1803 is 2,000 or less; the last full blood is recorded as having died in 1876. This peaceful people became fearful and resentful when faced with dispossession and with cruelty on the part of some European convicts and settlers. By 1826 the clash was officially recognized; by 1831 (to prevent their extermination by the settlers) they were removed first to Gun Carriage Island and then to Flinders Island, where, in spite of care, they languished and died out.

The Tasmanians were organized as five tribes, each with its own dialect or language. They usually traveled in small groups, gathering food and hunting with sticks and clubs; they had neither spear-thrower nor boomerang. They held corroborees, cremated the dead, scarred and red-ochred their bodies, and engraved lines and circles on rocks. *See* also Australian Aboriginals.

Bibliography.—H. Ling Roth, *The Aborigines of Tasmania* (1890); J. Bonwick, *The Daily Life and Origin of the Tasmanians* (1870); J. B.

Walker, *Early Tasmania* (1914); C. Turnbull, *Black War* (1948); W. Schmidt, *Die tasmanischen Sprachen* (1952); A. Capell, *A New Approach to Australian Linguistics*, pt. 1 (1956); J. B. Birdsell, "The Racial Origin of the Extinct Tasmanians" (pp. 105–122), N. W. G. Macintosh, "A Survey of Possible Sea Routes Available to the Tasmanian Aborigines" (pp. 123–144), and A. L. Meston, "The Tasmanians—a Summary" (pp. 145–150), in *Rec. Queen Vict. Mus.*, vol. ii, no. 3 (1949); R. Ruggles Gates, "Racial Elements in the Aborigines of Queensland, Australia," *Zeitschrift für Morphologie und Anthropologie*, Bd. 50, pp. 150–166 (1960); N. W. G. Macintosh and B. C. W. Barker, *The Osteology of Aboriginal Man in Tasmania*, Oceania Monograph No. 12 (1965). (A. P. E.)

**TASSO, TORQUATO** (1544–1595), the greatest Italian poet of the late Renaissance and author of the epic *Gerusalemme liberata*, was born in Sorrento on March 11, 1544, the son of Bernardo, also a poet and author of the long and romantic *Amadigi* (1560), and Porzia de' Rossi. His childhood was overshadowed by family misfortunes and when, in 1552, Bernardo was banned from the kingdom of Naples, Torquato followed him into exile. Four years later, while father and son were staying in Rome, his mother died. His father's exile and the somewhat mysterious death of his mother struck the imagination of the young Torquato. In 1557 he went with his father to Pesaro and Urbino and there he had his first experience of court life. In 1559 they were in Venice and in 1560 Torquato went to Padua to study law, philosophy and rhetoric, a study which he continued in Bologna between 1563 and 1564, and then again in Padua until 1565. In Padua he met the philosopher Sperone Speroni and became aware of the subtleties of the classicist theory of poetry. He became a friend of Scipione Gonzaga, the future cardinal, and entered the Academy of the Eterei which Gonzaga had founded. In Padua he also composed his first epic, the *Rinaldo* (publ. 1562), and his lyrical poems to Lucrezia Bendidio and Laura Peperara.

Toward the end of 1565 Tasso entered the service of Luigi Cardinal d'Este and went to live in Ferrara, where, as a young poet admired by the court, he passed the happiest period of his life. In the Ferrarese academy he expounded his *Conclusioni d'Amore* (publ. 1581) according to the Renaissance tradition of love treatises. From Paris, where he went with the cardinal in 1570, he wrote an interesting letter which shows him as a subtle political observer. In this period he composed his complimentary verses for the duke's sisters, Lucrezia and Leonora d'Este, and his love lyrics for Laura Peperara and Eleonora Sanvitale. He associated with men of letters such as Guarini and Giambattista Pigna, and participated in the life of the court—his pastoral drama *Aminta* (publ. 1580) was performed on the island of Belvedere in the summer of 1573. In 1574 he began his tragedy *Galealto re di Norvegia* and in April 1575 he completed the *Gerusalemme liberata* which he had begun a few years earlier. In Jan. 1572 he had entered the service of Duke Alfonso II, with a high salary and without heavy duties.

During the last months of 1575, however, this happy period of his life began to be overshadowed by the psychological disturbances which tormented him for the rest of his life. Before publishing the *Gerusalemme*, he asked many people for advice, including Gonzaga, the theologian Silvio Antoniano, Speroni and the versifier Pietro Angeli da Barga. The critical observations for which he had asked humiliated and irritated him, and he was deeply concerned with most of the moral and poetical problems raised by his advisers. At this time Tasso developed an acute egotism accompanied by a persecution mania, which showed itself in such episodes as his throwing a knife at a servant whom he suspected of spying on him, and in his frequent, restless travels. From Sorrento, where he stayed with his sister in 1577, he went to Rome, and thence, in April 1578, again to Ferrara. At the beginning of July he moved to Mantua, and then to Padua, Venice, Pesaro and, finally, to Turin, as a guest of the marquis Filippo d'Este. In Feb. 1579 he returned to Ferrara during the festivities for the wedding of the duke with Margherita Gonzaga and, thinking himself neglected, he flew into a rage. The duke had him arrested, chained and imprisoned in the Ospedale di Sant'Anna, where he remained for seven years. That this was due to his alleged love for Leonora, the duke's sister, must be considered a legend. It is more likely that the real cause of the duke's severity was the danger Tasso represented to the Este court, where, even after the exile of the duke's mother, Renée of France, a sympathizer of Calvin, there survived sympathy for Calvinistic reform. Accusations of heresy by Tasso could have helped the pope in his anti-Este policy.

BY COURTESY OF L. LOCATELLI-MILESI-TOMBINI, BERGAMO
TASSO; PORTRAIT BY F. ZUCCHERI, 1594

During his seclusion in Sant'Anna the poet remained in touch with the outside world through his correspondence and the many occasional poems which he wrote, and he also composed most of his *Dialoghi* and the *Apologia* in defense of his epic. Finally, in July 1586, thanks to the intervention of Father Angelio Grillo and of Vincenzo Gonzaga, prince of Mantua, Tasso was allowed to leave Sant'Anna.

In Mantua, where he received a warm welcome, he finished his tragedy *Galealto* under the new title *Torrismondo* (publ. 1587). In Oct. 1587 he fled from Mantua and took refuge in Rome, where he spent most of his last years as the guest of Cardinal Gonzaga and then of the cardinals Pietro and Cinzio Aldobrandini, to whom he dedicated in 1593 his recast epic *Gerusalemme conquistata*. He went for short periods to Florence in 1590, to Mantua in 1591 and to Naples, where he hoped to recover his mother's dowry, in 1588, 1592 and 1594. In Naples he was the guest of G. B. Manso who eventually became the author of one of the first biographies of Tasso, and there he wrote his religious poems, the *Monte Oliveto* (publ. 1605) and the *Sette giornate del mondo creato* (publ. 1600–05), besides a fragment of the *Vita di San Benedetto* and his last dialogues. In Rome he composed *Le lagrime di Maria Vergine* (1593) and *Le lagrime di Gesù Cristo* (1593). During his last years his illness and discontent continued, despite the fact that he was then receiving many honours and proofs of friendship—in 1594, plans were being made for his poetical coronation in Rome. By then he was tired and no longer interested in fame. In March 1595 he fell ill and asked to be transferred to the convent of Sant'Onofrio in Rome, where he died on April 25, 1595.

**Tasso's Works.**—When Tasso composed his epic *Rinaldo* (publ. 1562), relating the youth of the hero in 12 cantos *in ottave*, he paid little attention to the Aristotelian rules: the poem reveals his technical ability, but not as yet his poetical genius. In comparison the *Aminta*, composed ten years later, is already a masterpiece. This pastoral drama reflects the ephemeral period of happiness which Tasso enjoyed at the Ferrarese court. Technically it stands halfway between the eclogue in dialogue form and the melodrama, and is full of literary reminiscences of Theocritus, Moschus, Achilles Tatius, Virgil, Ovid, Propertius, Claudian and Nemesianus, as well as of Petrarch, Politian, Jacopo Sannazzaro, Ariosto, Pietro Bembo and others. The allusions to the court are of great delicacy and the result is a work of extreme literary preciosity. The *Aminta* has been defined as the idealization of court life. The inspiration of the poet is lyrical rather than dramatic and in this respect the work ranks with his sonnets, *canzoni* and madrigals.

The *Rinaldo*, the *Aminta* and the *Rime* (publ. 1581–87) are a prelude to the composition of the *Gerusalemme liberata*. The idea of an epic poem on the conquest of Jerusalem arose in Tasso's mind at a very early date (the first drafts belong to his Venetian and Paduan period), and grew during his stay at Ferrara; the work was completed in 1575. The subject and structure of the poem offered him the possibility of expressing his complex nature, while responding to a taste that was typical of his time. The *Liberata* resumes and develops a Renaissance literary tradition: the desire to renew the classical epic and to reconcile it with the new trends of the Counter-Reformation. While engaged in composing the

*Liberata,* Tasso wrote his *Discorsi dell'arte poetica* (rewritten later as *Discorsi del poema eroico,* publ. 1594), in which he expounded his qualified acceptance of the Aristotelian rules (for instance, unity of action was not to exclude a variety of episodes) while in fact upholding the rights of poetry. In the *Liberata,* Tasso narrates the actions of the Christian army led by Geoffrey of Bouillon during the last months of the first crusade, culminating in the conquest of Jerusalem and the battle of Ascalon. To the principal action he adds a number of episodes, including (in deference to the d'Este family) the story of Rinaldo d'Este, his rebellion, his love for the pagan Armida and his repentance and decisive participation in the final battle. Tasso also adds the story of the love of the Italian Tancred for the beautiful Saracen Clorinda, whom Tancred kills without recognizing her; the secret passion of Erminia, princess of Antioch, for Tancred; and the intervention of supernatural forces in favour of Aladino, king of Jerusalem. These episodes give him the opportunity of expressing the different aspects of his inspiration but his lyricism predominates even in his epic work. The language is lyrical in the Petrarchan tradition, and lyrical, too, is the rhythm of his hendecasyllables and of his *ottave.*

The poetical novelty of the *Liberata* aroused violent criticism, to which Tasso replied in 1585 with his *Apologia.* Tasso's prose works (*Dialoghi* and *Lettere*) show his ability as a stylist who, while following classical models, achieves a modern form in which classical and popular patterns are admirably blended. The works of his last years have no poetical significance: the *Conquistata,* in which he tries to rewrite his epic according to strict moral and rhetorical preconceptions, is a document of the poet's decline, while the tragedy *Torrismondo* shows passages of real poetry only where the poet allows his lyrical inspiration to express itself.

Tasso's life soon became the subject of a legend concerning his alleged love for the princess Leonora and his mysterious madness. The latter is described as simulated in Alessandro Guarini's *Farnetico savio* (1610), while Tasso's love affairs are narrated in the early biographies by G. P. D'Alessandro (1604) and G. B. Manso (1621). This legendary tradition lasted until the 19th century, in spite of the doubts already expressed in the 18th century by G. Tiraboschi and P. A. Serassi. During the romantic period Tasso's life became a symbol of the poet's life and the subject of novels and dramas (of which the most famous is Goethe's *Torquato Tasso,* 1790). Later criticism, while rejecting legendary details of Tasso's life, concentrated on determining the pathological background of his genius and on underlining the moral weakness of the man. Twentieth-century criticism tends to see him as the tragic result of the civilization of the Renaissance.

Standard editions of Tasso's works are: *Le Rime,* ed. by A. Solerti (1898–1902); *La Gerusalemme liberata,* ed. by A. Solerti (1895–96), L. Caretti (1958); *Aminta,* ed. by B. T. Sozzi (1957); *La Gerusalemme Conquistata,* ed. by L. Bonfigli, 2 vol. (1934); *Dialoghi,* crit. ed. by E. Raimondi (1958); *Le Lettere* (1852–55) and *Prose diverse* (1875) ed. by C. Guasti; and *Appendice alle opere in prosa,* ed. by A. Solerti (1892). English editions include *Godfrey of Bulloigne, or the Recoverie of Hierusalem,* trans. by E. Fairfax (1600); *Jerusalem Delivered,* trans. by J. K. James, 2 vol. (1884); L. E. Lord, *A Translation of the Orpheus of A. Politian and the Aminta of T. Tasso* (1931).

Bibliography.—For a full bibliography *see* A. Tortoreto and J. G. Fucilla, *Bibliografia analitica tassiana, 1896–1930* (1935); A. Tortoreto, "Nuovi studi su T. Tasso (Bibliografia analitica: 1931–1945)," in *Aevum,* XX, pp. 14–72 (1946); and more recent, Tortoreto's annual contributions in the periodical *Studi Tassiani. See* also A. Solerti, *Vita di T. Tasso,* 3 vol. (1895); E. Donadoni, *T. Tasso: Saggio critico,* 2 vol. (1921); W. Boulting, *Tasso and his Times* (1907). (G. A.)

**TASTE:** *see* Smell and Taste.

**TATA,** a Parsee priestly family, originally from the former Baroda state, India, that produced several distinguished merchants, industrialists and philanthropists. Founder of its greatness was Jamsetji Nasarwanji Tata (1839–1904), educated at Elphinstone college, Bombay. Joining his father's trading firm in 1858 and aided by a powerful imagination, he entered on an outstanding career which contributed massively to India's industrial development. He organized cotton mills in Bombay and Nagpur; founded the Tata Iron and Steel company, one of the largest integrated steelworks in the world; and planned the use of hydroelectric energy resulting in the formation, after his death, of the Tata Power companies, which supply electricity to Bombay city and the surrounding areas. He introduced sericulture into India; founded the Indian Institute of Science in Bangalore; applied the findings of science to the cultivation of cotton and other crops; built the Taj Mahal hotel; and established an endowment for the advanced professional and technical training of Indians abroad. A man of high social ideals, he was a pioneer in his attitude to labour, and devoted an overwhelming proportion of his firm's profits to practical philanthropy.

His sons, Sir Dorabji J. Tata (1859–1932) and Sir Ratanji Tata (1871–1918), inherited both his fortune and his traditions. Under their guidance the firm expanded into a group of associated companies, covering basic industries. Sir Ratanji founded a department of social science and administration at the London School of Economics, and financed certain social studies at the University of London. Sir Dorabji established a trust for international research into leukemia and endowed a hospital for cancer research in Bombay.

In 1932 on the death of Sir Dorabji, Sir Naoroji Saklatvala, one of the founder's nephews, became chairman of the group. On his death in 1938, J. R. D. Tata (1904– ), whose father R. D. Tata was a cousin and partner of the founder, became chairman. By the late 1950s the group controlled the largest single aggregation of Indian industry, including among its interests not only textiles, steel and electric power, but also agricultural equipment, locomotives, diesel trucks, chemicals, cement, vegetable oils, soap and toilet products, insurance, radios and industrial investment. Eighty-five per cent of the capital of the parent company, Tata Sons Private Limited, was held by the various charitable trusts endowed by the family. (B. Sh. S.)

**TATABÁNYA,** a town of northwest Hungary in Komárom *megye* (county), 35 mi. (56 km.) W of Budapest by road. Pop. (1960) 52,044. The town grew considerably after World War II and became the main settlement in the lignite basin between the Vértes Hills to the south and the Gerecse Mountains to the north. Much of Tatabánya's industry also derives from the bauxite resources of this part of Hungary, as the town marks the northeastern extremity of the mining region. The manufacture of aluminum and the chemical industries are well established, and there are two large thermoelectric stations. Tatabánya ranks with Székesfehérvár as one of the most vigorous urban centres of northwest Hungary. (H. G. S.)

**TATAR** (Tartar), a member of a Turkic-speaking people whose main seat is in the U.S.S.R. along the central course of the Volga River and its tributary the Kama, thence east to the Ural Mountains. They are also settled widely in eastern and southeastern European U.S.S.R. and in southern Siberia. They numbered about 5,000,000 in the 1960s (comprising the largest ethnic minority in the Russian Soviet Federated Socialist Republic). Linguistically, they belong to the northwestern or Kipchak (*q.v.*) branch of the Turkic languages (*q.v.*). The ancient name Tatar has been attributed to many groups with little or no relationship to the people identified here. The name was sometimes given to single tribes or to all nomads of the Asian steppes and deserts, including Mongols and Turks generally (early Chinese and Russian sources). The term likewise was applied to peoples and states of the Mongol Empire (13th–14th centuries A.D.): Crimean Tatars, Siberian Tatars, Kazan Tatars, Kasimov Tatars.

Among elements entering into the composition of the Tatars of the Volga were Turkic nomads of the south Russian steppe (Kipchak and others) dating from the first millennium A.D. Ancient Bulgaria (not to be confused with modern Bulgaria) covered in part the territory of modern Tataria (*see* Bulgaria [on the Volga]). Other elements were added by the establishment of the Mongol Empire in Russia and by the defeat of Kazan (*q.v.*) by Ivan the Terrible in 1552. Neighbouring peoples were absorbed, including some Chuvash and Mordvin (*q.v.*), as late as the 19th century.

A distinct group on the Oka River near Kasimov, their former capital, are the Kasimov Tatars (reported since the 15th century), who still preserve their identity even when they live among the Volga Tatars. Mishar Tatars also live in the territory; grouped with them are the Meshcheryak Tatars under the cultural influence of the Bashkir (*q.v.*), although preserving Tatar speech; Teptyar Tatars also have settled among the Bashkir. Karagash are a small Tatar group near the city of Astrakhan (*q.v.*). Kryashen Tatars are a large Christian group who live among the Muslim majority of Tatars; the Nagaybak Tatars near Chelyabinsk are a much smaller Christian group descended from the Kryashen.

From the 9th to 15th centuries Tatar economy was based on mixed farming and herding, nomadic peoples being absorbed during the Middle Ages. Having long been sedentary, they continue to farm and to breed livestock and have an ancient tradition of craftsmanship in wood, ceramics, leather, cloth, and metal. The Tatars have long been famous as traders; during the 18th and 19th centuries they earned a favoured position within the expanding Russian Empire as commercial and political agents, teachers, and administrators of newly won Central Asian territories.

As a medieval power, the Tatars had a complex social organization; the nobility preserved its civil and military leadership into Russian times, following the conquest of Kazan; distinct classes of commoners were merchants and tillers of the soil. At the head of government stood the khan of the Tatar state, part of whose family joined the Russian nobility by direct agreement in the 16th century. This stratification continued until the Russian Revolution.

The Tatars were converted to Islam in the 14th century and, as Sunnites, were instrumental in bringing the faith to Turkistan. Still surviving, however, are such pre-Islamic practices as folk beliefs in spirits of the forest, of the water, and of the household.

*See* also TATAR AUTONOMOUS SOVIET SOCIALIST REPUBLIC; TURKIC PEOPLES; and references under "Tatar" in the Index.

BIBLIOGRAPHY.—S. A. Tokarev, *Etnografiya Narodov SSSR* (1958); B. Ischboldin, *Essays on Tatar History* (1963); N. N. Poppe, *Tatar Manual* (1963); U.S.S.R., *Narodnoe Khozyaystvo* (1965). (L. K.)

**TATAR AUTONOMOUS SOVIET SOCIALIST REPUBLIC** (TATARSKAYA AVTONOMNAYA SOVETSKAYA SOTSIALISTICHESKAYA RESPUBLIKA), in the Russian Soviet Federated Socialist Republic, U.S.S.R., lies in the middle Volga Basin around the confluence of the Volga and Kama rivers. It was formed in 1920 and covers an area of 26,255 sq.mi. (67,600 sq.km.). The Volga flows north-south across the western end of the republic, while the Kama, its largest tributary, forms a roughly east-west axis through the greater part. Within the republic the Kama is joined by its two major tributaries, the Vyatka and the Belaya. Generally, the relief is that of a low, rolling plain. The area west of the Volga is higher and rises to 771 ft. (235 m.), representing the extreme northern end of the Volga Uplands, which form a high right bank of the river. The land also rises in the east of the republic toward the Urals Foreland. The southeast is occupied by the Bugul'ma-Belebey Upland, which reaches a height of 1,220 ft. (371 m.). The climate is markedly continental, with prolonged, severe winters and hot summers. At Kazan the January average temperature is −13.8° C (7° F) and the July average 20° C (68° F). Annual rainfall is about 15–16 in. (380–405 mm.), with a summer maximum. Snow cover may be up to 24 in. thick.

The greater part of the republic lies in the forest-steppe zone on degraded or podzolized chernozems (black earths). The northwestern part is in the area of broad-leaved forest, chiefly oak and lime on gray forest-earth soils, but centuries of clearing have greatly reduced the forest area. Regions of poor, sandy soil are typically under pinewood. Along the rivers are broad, floodplain meadows, although those on the Volga and lower Kama have disappeared under the waters of the Kuybyshev (Kuibyshev) Reservoir, which extends up the Volga through the whole republic and up the Kama to Bondyuzhskiy. Altogether more than 1,100 sq.mi. (2,850 sq.km.) of the republic have been flooded by the reservoir.

The Tatars are a Turkic people (*see* TATAR; TURKIC PEOPLES) and the descendants of the Mongols of the Golden Horde, who established themselves in this area in the mid-13th century, largely replacing or absorbing the previous Bulgar population. As the Golden Horde declined in power in the 15th century, it split into separate groups, of which the Kazan khanate was the most northerly. The khanate was for long engaged with Muscovy in a struggle that was finally resolved in 1552 when Ivan IV, the Terrible, besieged and captured Kazan. Several revolts followed, but they were severely crushed. Attempts to convert the Tatars forcibly to Orthodoxy led to their participation in the Pugachev revolt of 1773–74. After the Russian conquest of Kazan, colonization began, and fortified lines were established in the Trans-Kama to protect the newly won lands. (*See* also KAZAN.)

The population in 1959 was 2,850,417 (1969 est. 3,139,000), of which about 47% was Tatar, the remainder being Russian, with small numbers of Chuvash, Udmurt, Mordva, and Bashkir. (The Tatars in 1959 numbered 4,967,700 in the U.S.S.R. as a whole.) Of the Tatar Republic, 42% of the population was urban. There are 14 towns and 22 urban settlements. The largest of the towns are Kazan (646,806), the capital, Bugul'ma (60,980), Zelënodol'sk (60,472), and Al'met'yevsk (48,611).

An important factor facilitating the growth of industry in the Tatar A.S.S.R. since the Revolution is its location between the core region of the U.S.S.R. around Moscow, the Urals industrial area, and the Second Baku oil field, while the Volga and Kama rivers, with the navigable Vyatka and Belaya, form major routeways linking all three areas. The Bugul'ma-Belebey Upland in the southeast forms part of the Second Baku oil field. The first well was drilled in 1943, and subsequent development was very rapid. Al'met'yevsk, one of the main oil towns, was a village in 1939. Other centres are Bugul'ma, Leninogorsk, Aznakayevo, and Bavly. Pipelines run from Al'met'yevsk west to Gorki and east to Sverdlovsk. Together with petroleum, natural gas is obtained, the chief centre being at Minnibayevo, which has a gas pipeline to Kazan. The petroleum, with the salts of the upper Kama, has encouraged the growth of the chemical industry, chiefly at Kazan and Bondyuzhskiy. Engineering works are concentrated largely in the towns along the Volga and Kama, notably at Kazan, Zelënodol'sk, and Chistopol'. Timber working is widespread and includes the production of crates and boxes, prefabricated houses, furniture, and veneer. Paper and pulp are made at Mamadysh and at a group of neighbouring towns on the Kama. Also widespread is the processing of leather and furs, particularly for making shoes and felt boots. The manufacture of soap and other fat products is important in Kazan. Some linen and cotton cloth is made.

Agriculture is also important, and 57% of the republic is arable. Dredge corn (rye and oats together) is widely grown, but spring wheat, maize (corn), millet, and buckwheat are also significant. A large area is sown with legumes, especially peas and lentils. Potatoes, sugar beet, hemp, and sunflowers are valuable industrial crops, while tobacco is grown in the Volga right-bank area. Around Kazan market gardening is developed, and the Volga villages are noted for their apple orchards. Cattle, especially dairy cows, are kept in considerable numbers, as are sheep and goats. Before the Revolution the Tatars rarely kept pigs, but the number of pigs is steadily increasing.

There is heavy freight traffic along the rivers, with rafted timber forming the largest commodity (around 2,500,000 tons a year). Regular passenger services also connect the river ports of the republic to Moscow and all parts of the Volga Basin. The republic is less well served internally by railways, although two main lines between Moscow and the Urals cross the northwest and southeast corners. Work was in progress in the 1960s to link these main lines by a meridional railway from Agryz to Bugul'ma. Another line runs north-south through the Volga right-bank area.

(R. A. F.)

**TATE, (JOHN ORLEY) ALLEN** (1899– ), U.S. poet, critic, biographer, and novelist, was born in Winchester, Ky., on Nov. 19, 1899. He entered Vanderbilt University, Nashville, Tenn., in 1918, where he helped found *The Fugitive*, a poetry magazine (1922–25) which became internationally famous. Other prominent members of the group were Merrill Moore, Robert Penn Warren, John Crowe Ransom, and Donald Davidson. The "Fugitives" were neither a movement nor a clique, and probably the only common ground in their poetry was a faith in both tradition and experiment, a faith which paralleled, whether or not it reflected, their background of Southern social tradition and pioneer energy. A similar mixture of conservatism and radicalism characterized the Southern Agrarian Movement for which Tate, Ransom, Davidson, and Warren were leading spokesmen between 1930 and 1936. Basically Agrarianism, which began in the Great Depression and ended during World War II, opposed the abstraction, dehumanization, and cultural deprivation implicit in industrialism. The weakness of the movement was that its proponents could only offer the alternative of subsistence farming. But Tate never abandoned his Agrarian beliefs. They form one of the supporting timbers of his work.

From 1924 to 1934 Tate lived as a free-lance writer in New York, Europe, and Clarksville, Tenn. During this period he published biographies of "Stonewall" Jackson (1928) and Jefferson Davis (1929) as well as three books of poetry. In 1934 he began his teaching career at Southwestern College in Memphis, Tenn., followed by appointments at the Woman's College of the University of North Carolina, Princeton University, and the University of Minnesota (1951–68). Under his editorship (1944–46) *The Sewanee Review* acquired worldwide importance.

Throughout Tate's poetry runs a consistent pattern of searching for wholeness. His earlier work frequently dramatized a subjective impotence to bring feeling and knowledge together, as in his best-known poem, "Ode to the Confederate Dead." The poems written from about 1930 to 1939 broaden this apprehension of imbalance to include society, as in the brilliant and sadly ironical "The Mediterranean" (1932). In his fine later poems Tate consolidated his earlier approaches by positing that only through the subjective wholeness of the individual can society itself be whole. This view emerged tentatively in "Seasons of the Soul" (1943) and confidently in "The Buried Lake" (1953), both devotional poems. In 1956 Tate was awarded the Bollingen Prize for Poetry.

As an essayist Tate, with Socratic patience, has turned one of the century's finest dialectical minds on important aesthetic, cultural, and societal controversies, wherein he invariably flushes a villain named "positivism." The excellence of Tate's novel *The Fathers,* published in 1938 and reissued in 1960 with critical acclaim, adds a final dimension to a career of startling diversity, made all the more startling by the fact that in two of the dimensions, poetry and criticism, he must be reckoned a master. Tate's poems are contained in *Poems* (1960); his essays in *Essays of Four Decades* (1969).

*See* also R. K. Meiners, *The Last Alternatives: a Study of the Works of Allen Tate* (1963). (J. R. Ss.)

**TATE, NAHUM** (1652–1715), English poet laureate and playwright, adapter of other men's plays, collaborator with Nicholas Brady (*q.v.*) in the famous *New Version of the Psalms* (1696). He was born in Dublin, Ire., graduated from Trinity College there and moved to London. Tate wrote some plays of his own but he is best known for his adaptation of the Elizabethans. His version of Shakespeare's *King Lear,* to which he gave a happy ending in which Cordelia married Edgar, held the stage well into the 19th century.

Tate also wrote the libretto for Purcell's *Dido and Aeneas* (*c.* 1689). Some of his hymns found a lasting place in Protestant worship—"While shepherds watched"; "Through all the changing scenes of life"; and "As pants the hart for cooling streams."

Tate was commissioned by Dryden to write the second part of *Absalom and Achitophel* (1682), although Dryden added the finishing touches (probably including the portraits of Elkanah Settle and Thomas Shadwell) himself.

The best of Tate's own poems is *Panacea, a Poem on Tea* (1700). He succeeded Shadwell as poet laureate in 1692 and died in London on July 30, 1715. The belief that Tate lived until 1716 long caused it to be thought that he was superseded as poet laureate during his lifetime.

**TATIAN** (TATIANUS) (2nd century A.D.), Christian apologist, missionary and heretic, and editor of the *Diatessaron* (*i.e.,* the four Gospels in a continuous narrative). He was born in Mesopotamia of Syrian parentage and educated in Greek learning, in which he became proficient. He was initiated into the mysteries, though into which is not known, but after this became acquainted with the Old Testament and was converted to Christianity. Tatian then went to Rome, where he was a hearer of Justin Martyr.

After the death of Justin, Tatian became a heretic. Among his pupils were Rhodon, and, perhaps, Apelles and Clement of Alexandria. He made a missionary journey to the east and worked in Cilicia and Pisidia, using Antioch in Syria as the centre of his efforts.

The heresy that Tatian either founded or adopted was the Gnostic heresy of the Encratites. Their main doctrines were the evil nature of matter, an absolute forbidding of marriage, abstinence from wine and perhaps from meat. It would also seem that Tatian believed in the existence of aeons, one of whom was the Demiurge of the world. He denied the salvation of Adam. It is also stated that in his celebration of the mysteries (*i.e.,* the Eucharist) he used only water.

According to Eusebius, Tatian wrote many books; of these the names of the following survived: *On Animals, On Demons, Address to the Greeks, Book of Problems* (an attempt to deal with contradictions found in the Bible), *Against Those Who Have Discussed Divine Things, On Perfection According to the Saviour,* the *Diatessaron,* and a recension of the Pauline epistles. Of these books only two—the *Diatessaron* and the *Address to the Greeks* —are extant. The *Address to the Greeks* belongs to Tatian's Catholic period. He has the double purpose in view of exposing the weakness of the pagan view of the universe and of commending the Christian explanation. The omissions in the *Address* are even more remarkable than its statements. There is at the most not more than an allusion to Christ, who is never mentioned by name, and though there are frequent allusions to the regaining of life, which is accomplished by union with the Logos, there is no reference to the doctrines of the incarnation or of the atonement.

Editions of the *Address to the Greeks* are found in O. von Gebhardt and A. Harnack, *Texte und Untersuchungen zur Geschichte der altchristlichen Literatur,* vol. iv (1888), and E. J. Goodspeed, *Die ältesten Apologeten,* pp. 266–305 (1914); an English translation by B. P. Pratten was published in the "Ante-Nicene Christian Library," vol. iii, pp. 3–48 (1867).

*See* also DIATESSARON.

BIBLIOGRAPHY.—Johannes Quasten, *Patrology,* vol. i, pp. 220–228, with full bibliography (1950); Robert M. Grant, "The Date of Tatian's Oration," *Harvard Theological Review,* 46:99–101 (1953), and "The Heresy of Tatian," *Journal of Theological Studies,* N.S., 5:62–68 (1954); Arthur Vööbus, *History of Asceticism in the Syrian Orient,* vol. i, pp. 31–45 (1958). (B. M. M.)

**TATRA MOUNTAINS** (HIGH TATRA), the highest range of the central Carpathians, rise steeply from a high plateau (2,600 ft. [793 m.]) along the Polish-Czech border, varying in width toward Czechoslovakia from 9 to 15 mi. (14–24 km.) and running from west to east about 40 mi. (64 km.).

**TATTOOING** is the introduction of pigment through ruptures in the skin. Sometimes the term is loosely applied also to scarification (*see* MUTILATIONS AND DEFORMATIONS; BRANDING). Tattooing proper has a nearly world-wide distribution, except that it is rare among populations with the darkest skin colour, and was absent from most of China (at least in recent centuries). Among various peoples tattooed designs are thought to provide magical protection against sickness or misfortune, or serve to identify the wearer's rank, status or membership in a group. Decoration is perhaps the commonest motive for tattooing.

Tattooing occurs on Egyptian mummies dating from about 2000 B.C., and is mentioned by classical authors for the Thracians, Greeks, Gauls, ancient Germans and ancient Britons; the Romans tattooed criminals and slaves. After the advent of Christianity tattooing was forbidden in Europe, but persisted in the near east and in other parts of the world.

In the Americas many Indian tribes customarily tattooed the body or the face, or both. The usual technique was simple pricking, but some California tribes introduced colour into scratches, and many tribes of the arctic and subarctic, most Eskimos and some peoples of eastern Siberia, made needle punctures through which a thread coated with pigment (usually soot) was drawn underneath the skin. In Polynesia, Micronesia and parts of Malaysia pigment was pricked into the skin by tapping on an implement shaped like a miniature rake. In moko, a type of Maori (*q.v.*) tattooing, shallow coloured grooves in complex curvilinear designs were produced on the face by striking a miniature bone adze into the skin. In Japan needles set in a wooden handle are used to tattoo very elaborate multicoloured designs often covering much of the body. Burmese tattooing is done with a brass penlike implement with a slit point and a weight on the upper end. Sometimes pigment is rubbed into knife slashes (*e.g.,* in Tunisia, among the Ainu of Japan, Ibo of Nigeria and Chontal Indians of Mexico); or the skin is punctured with thorns (Pima Indians of Arizona and Senoi of Malaya) or other simple needlelike implements.

Tattooing was rediscovered by Europeans when the age of exploration brought them into contact with American Indians and Polynesians. The word tattoo itself was introduced into English and other European languages from Tahiti, where it was first recorded by James Cook's expedition in 1769. Tattooed Indians and Polynesians, and later Europeans tattooed abroad, attracted much interest at exhibits, fairs and circuses in Europe and the U.S. during the 18th and 19th centuries. Stimulated by Polynesian and Japanese examples, tattooing "parlours" where specialized "professors" applied designs on Euroamerican sailors sprang up in port cities all over the world. The first electric tattooing implement was patented in the U.S. in 1891. The U.S. became a centre of influence in tattoo designs, especially with the spread of U.S. tattooers' pattern sheets. The nautical, military, patriotic, romantic and religious motifs are now similar in style and subject matter throughout the world; characteristic national styles of the early 20th century have disappeared.

In the 19th century released U.S. convicts and British army deserters were identified by tattoos, and later the inmates of Siberian prisons and Nazi concentration camps were similarly marked. Tattooing has long been especially characteristic of European and U.S. sailors. Before World War I tattooed symbols of other occupations were very common in continental Europe and sometimes occurred in England. Members of criminal gangs still frequently identify themselves with a simple tattooed device. During the late 19th century tattooing had a short vogue among both sexes in the English upper classes. Except for Euroamerican and Japanese types, and for special medical applications, tattooing is moribund or extinct in most parts of the world.

There are sometimes religious objections to the practice ("You shall not make any cuttings in your flesh on account of the dead or tattoo any marks upon you . . . ," Lev. xix, 28). Tattooing has been implicated in such disorders as skin cancer, and in 1961 the practice was sharply restricted by the New York city government because of the role of contaminated tattooing equipment in spreading hepatitis (*see* GALL BLADDER, BILIARY TRACT AND LIVER, DISEASES OF).

BIBLIOGRAPHY.—W. D. Hambly, *The History of Tattooing and Its Significance* (1927); H. Ebenstein, *Pierced Hearts and True Love, an Illustrated History of the Origin and Development of European Tattooing and a Survey of Its Present State* (1953). (W. C. ST.)

**TATUM, EDWARD LAWRIE** (1909– ), U.S. biochemist, who shared the 1958 Nobel Prize for Medicine and Physiology with George W. Beadle and Joshua Lederberg (*qq.v.*) for research in genetics, was born in Boulder, Colo., on Dec. 14, 1909. He was educated at the University of Chicago and the University of Wisconsin (A.B., 1931; Ph.D., 1934). His doctoral thesis dealt with the nutrition and biochemistry of bacteria. Following a year of postdoctoral study in The Netherlands, Tatum went to Stanford University where he collaborated with Beadle on research into the biochemical aspects of heredity. This work was carried out on the common fruit fly, *Drosophila,* and especially the red bread mold, *Neurospora,* but the principles derived from it are of wide application in biology. One application was to the study of the genetics of bacteria—a field of research opened to modern techniques by Tatum and Lederberg at Yale University in 1946. In 1957 Tatum went to the Rockefeller Institute as a member and professor. (N. H. H.)

**TAUFIQ AL-HAKIM** (1902– ), Egyptian writer, is generally considered the most outstanding Arabic dramatist yet to appear. He was born in Alexandria on Oct. 9, 1902, and studied law at Cairo University, graduating in 1925. He then went to Paris to continue his legal studies, but devoted much time to the theatre, in which he had become interested in Cairo. Returning to Egypt in 1930, he worked as a legal officer in rural areas and later in the ministries of Justice and of Social Affairs in Cairo. In 1943 he resigned, to devote himself entirely to writing.

After some early efforts, Taufiq al-Hakim won fame as a dramatist with *Ahl al-Khaf* ("The People of the Cave," 1933), based on the story of the Seven Sleepers of Ephesus. The real subject of the play, however, is man's fight against time. This began a series of "dramas of ideas," or of "symbolism." They include *Shahrazad* (1934), based on the *Thousand and One Nights* (*q.v.*); *al-Malik Udib* ("King Oedipus," 1939); *Pijmaliyyun* ("Pygmalion," 1942); and *Sulaiman al-Hakim* ("Solomon the Wise," 1943). His output of more than 50 plays—some one-act, some full-length—also includes many on Egyptian social themes. *Sirr al-Muntahira* ("The Secret of the Suicide Girl," 1937) shows an aging doctor obsessed by his success with women finally brought to his senses by his wife's stratagem. *Rasasa fi l-Qalb* ("A Bullet in the Heart," 1944) contrasts woman's fickleness with man's idealism in friendship. Taufiq al-Hakim's boldest drama was the extremely long *Muhammad* (1936), based on the life of the Prophet—not, however, intended for acting.

Taufiq al-Hakim made drama a respected Arabic literary genre. Prose plays had been primarily lightweight comedy or farce, while verse had been used for heroic drama. Ahmad Shauqi (*q.v.*) had excelled in the latter and had been perhaps the only Arabic dramatist of genius before Taufiq al-Hakim. The latter writes only in prose—a flexible prose of high quality yet not old-fashioned, interspersed with colloquial Arabic where appropriate (especially in social drama). His characters are types, and there is sometimes insufficient action. But his plays stimulate thought, in much the same way as do those of George Bernard Shaw (*q.v.*).

Among Taufiq al-Hakim's other works is his novel, *Yaumiyyat Na'ib fi l-Aryaf* ("Diary of a Provincial Legal Officer," 1937; Eng. trans., *The Maze of Justice,* 1947), a highly amusing satire on Egyptian officialdom, autobiographical in form.

BIBLIOGRAPHY.—There are French translations of many of Taufiq al-Hakim's plays, notably by A. Khédry (*La Caverne des songes,* 1939; *Tewfik al-Hakim: Théâtre arabe,* 1950; and *Tewfik al-Hakim: Théâtre multicolore,* 1954). *See* J. M. Landau, *Studies in the Arab Theater and Cinema* (1958); and the introduction to R. Rubinacci's translation of *Ahl al-Kahf* (*Quei della caverna,* 1959). (J. A. HD.)

**TAULER, JOHANN** (*c.* 1300–1361), German Dominican, together with Meister Eckhart and Heinrich Suso (*qq.v.*) one of the Rhineland mystics, was born in Strasbourg. Educated at the Dominican convent at Strasbourg and the *studium generale* at Cologne, he later became a lector at Strasbourg. During a period of exile, Tauler preached and lectured in Basel, returning again in 1347–48 to Strasbourg, where he died on June 16, 1361. He was greatly influenced by Eckhart, though his teaching, based on Thomas Aquinas, stresses practical rather than speculative mystical theology. References to the "Friends of God" (*Gottesfreunde*) appear in his sermons (written in Middle High German and valued highly by Martin Luther), alluding to a circle of like-minded devout Rhinelanders much influenced by Tauler, Eckhart, and Suso.

BIBLIOGRAPHY.—Sermons ed. by F. Vetter (1910), Eng. trans. by Walter Elliott (1910). *See* also P. Strauch, "Zu Taulers Predigten," *Beiträge zur Geschichte der deutschen Sprache und Literatur,* 44:1–26 (1920); J. M. Clark, *The Great German Mystics* (1949).

**TAUNTON,** a market town and municipal borough (1877) and the county town of Somerset, Eng., in the Taunton parliamentary division, 48 mi. (77 km.) SW of Bath by road. Pop. (1961) 35,192. Area 3.8 sq.mi. (10 sq.km.). It lies on the River Tone in the Vale of Taunton Deane, sheltered on three sides by the Quantock, Blackdown, and Brendon hills. The town was founded by the Saxon king Ine, who built the first castle there about A.D. 710. The bishops of Winchester, who owned the manor, obtained their first charter from Edward the Elder in 904. Bishop Giffard of Winchester built the second castle early in the 12th century and founded a priory of Augustinian canons in 1127. During the English Civil War the castle was thrice besieged by royalists, before Sir Thomas Fairfax relieved the town in 1645, and at the Restoration Charles II deprived Taunton of its charter of incorporation. The castle was dismantled, apart from its gateway and the great hall where Judge Jeffrey's "Bloody Assize" took place after the failure of the Monmouth rebellion at the Battle of Sedgemoor in 1685.

Taunton, in the diocese of Bath and Wells, is the seat of a suffragan bishopric. The churches of St. Mary Magdalene and St. James are Perpendicular in style. Huish's Grammar School shares in the endowment of Robert Huish, who died in 1615; Taunton, King's College, Queen's College, and Wellington are local public schools; in the town are a technical college and the Somerset College of Art. In Taunton is the Somerset County Cricket Club ground. There are hunting and fishing in the district.

The Saturday market, dating from before the Conquest, has become one of the largest livestock and produce markets in the southwest. Shirts and collars and agricultural machinery are manufactured.

**TAUNTON,** a city of Massachusetts, U.S., and seat of Bristol County, is 35 mi. (56 km.) S of Boston at the head of navigation on the Taunton River, 14 mi. (23 km.) above Fall River. The centre of Taunton, the "Green," is about one mile from the Weir, the port of the city. Taunton was settled after purchase of land from the Indians and in 1639 became a town with representatives in the general court of Plymouth colony. The name was derived from the English home of many of the settlers. In the 18th century six towns were detached from the original grant.

Taunton was a base of operations during King Philip's War (1675–76). In 1687 a town meeting declined to meet a tax levy by Sir Edmund Andros "without their own assent in an assembly." A Liberty pole with a flag inscribed "Liberty and Union" was raised on the "Green" in 1774 to express opposition to the Boston Port Bill. During Shays's Rebellion in 1786–87 the courthouse was twice besieged by insurgents who were dispersed each time by a judge, Gen. David Cobb.

Ironworks, established in 1656, were operated successfully until 1876; iron bars were sometimes used as a medium of exchange. Brickmaking and shipbuilding were other early industries. Silverware production, begun in 1824, remains important. Modern industries also include jewelry, plastics, and electronics.

The nearby Dighton rock has inscriptions long attributed to the Norse, but believed now to be the work of Indians or of a Portuguese explorer. Taunton became a city in 1864. For comparative population figures *see* table in MASSACHUSETTS: *Population.* (CA. M. C.)

**TAUNUS,** a wooded highland of West Germany, extending over parts of the *Länder* (states) of Hesse and Rhineland-Palatinate, Federal Republic of Germany. It lies to the east of the Rhine with the Main on the south and the Lahn on the north and is about 50 mi. (80 km.) long. Its southern edge stands 5–10 mi. (8–16 km.) back from the Main but slopes steeply to the Rhine, and from Bingen downstream forms precipitous crags. The average elevation is 1,500 ft. (460 m.), with a higher ridge above the Rheingau (the slopes to the Rhine between Biebrich and Bingen). The highest points occur in the east, where the Grosser Feldberg (2,887 ft.; 880 m.), Kleiner Feldberg (2,710 ft.; 826 m.), and Altkönig (2,618 ft.; 798 m.) dominate the Wetterau and the valley of the Main. The geological core of the system consists of (?Archean) argillaceous schists, capped by quartzite (Devonian) and broken through in places by basalt. On the northern side, which sinks on the whole gently toward the Lahn, the higher graywacke formation (Devonian) is considerably developed. The hills are generally well wooded with beech, with some pine plantations; large areas of forest were cleared for cultivation in the Middle Ages. The lower slopes are, where possible, planted with vineyards, orchards, and chestnut and almond groves. The Rheingaugebirge, in the Rhine gorge, has vineyards that yield famous wines. The Taunus is also famous for its mineral springs and health resorts; *e.g.*, Wiesbaden, Königstein, Bad Homburg.

Among numerous ancient ruins are the castle of Falkenstein; the fortress of Königstein; a Cistercian abbey at Eberbach; and two concentric lines of pre-Roman fortifications at Altkönig. The chief historical monument, however, is the Saalburg, a Roman fort serving as a centre of communications along the *limes* (*q.v.*), or fortified frontier line drawn from Rhine to Main by Domitian.

At Niederwald above Rüdesheim stands the gigantic "Germania" statue commemorating the war of 1870–71. The steep crags of the western end of the Taunus, where they abut upon the Rhine, are rich in the romantic associations of the great river. There are the rock of the siren Lorelei, the old castles of Stahleck and Pfalz, and the quaint medieval towns of Lorch, Kaub, and St. Goarshausen. (R. E. DI.)

**TAURI,** the earliest known inhabitants of the mountainous south coast of the Crimea, called after them in ancient times the Tauric Chersonese. Nothing is certain as to their affinities. They were not Scythians and are not likely to have been Celts. They were famous in the ancient world for their virgin goddess, identified by the Greeks with Artemis Tauropolos or with Iphigenia (*q.v.*). The Tauric custom of sacrificing shipwrecked strangers to the goddess was the ground of the story of Iphigenia and Orestes among the Tauri, which is the subject of plays by Euripides (*Iphigeneia in Tauris*) and Goethe (*Iphigenie auf Tauris*). The Tauri were given to piracy on the Black Sea. Toward the end of the 2nd century B.C. they were dependent allies of the Scythian king Scilurus, who from their harbour of Symbolon (Balaklava) harassed Chersonese (*see* CHERSONESE, TAURIC). Their later history is unknown. (E. H. M.; X.)

**TAURUS** ("the Bull"), in astronomy, the second sign of the zodiac. It is a constellation of very great antiquity, the Pleiades and Hyades (*qq.v.*), two of its constituent star clusters, being possibly referred to in the Old Testament; Aldebaran, its brightest star, is mentioned by Hesiod and Homer. The Greeks fabled this constellation to be the bull which bore Europa across the seas to Crete and was afterward raised to the heavens by Jupiter. Aldebaran is the principal object in the Hyades. Many of the Hyades (but not including Aldebaran) form an associated group of stars with a common motion. The measurement of the motions of these stars permits an accurate determination of their distance; these measurements show that they are situated at approximately 130 light years from the sun.

Aldebaran itself is a reddish giant star, located at a distance of about 80 light years from the sun. The constellation contains the "Crab nebula," a gaseous mass which has been shown fairly conclusively to have originated in the outburst of the new star, or nova, of A.D. 1054. Photographs indicate that the nebula is expanding in size from year to year. The structure of the Milky Way in Taurus is complex, with dark, almost starless lanes and bright nebulosity.

**TAUSEN, HANS** (1494–1561), the protagonist of the Danish Reformation, called "the Danish Luther," was born at Birkende on the island of Fyn. He joined the order of the Knights Hospitalers at Antvorskov, near Slagelse, and after studying and teaching at Rostock (1516–21) and Copenhagen (1521–22), he visited the University of Louvain (1522), where he made the acquaintance of the Flemish humanists. He became a good linguist, understanding both Greek and Hebrew. In 1523 he went to Wittenberg, where he studied for a year and a half before being recalled to Antvorskov. Most of the Danish reformers were influenced by the Reformation in south Germany and Switzerland, but Tausen was more directly inspired by Luther himself, and the victory of the Lutheran type of Reformation in Denmark was largely due to him. In consequence of his doctrines he may have been imprisoned at Antvorskov; in 1525 he was confined in his order's priory at Viborg in Jutland, where he preached from his prison to the people assembled outside, till his prior lent him the pulpit of the priory church.

After revolts against the youthful bishop Jörgen Friis on the part of young burghers who had studied in Germany, Tausen left the Hospitalers in order to preach in the town under the burghers' protection. They prevented his arrest by the bishop, and in October 1526 he was made an official Lutheran chaplain by King Frederick I. Tausen found a fellow worker in Jörgen Jensen Sadolin, whose sister he married. He probably was the first Danish priest to marry; he also was the first to use Danish instead of Latin in the church services, and the manuals he published were of great importance not only for the Lutheran congregation in Viborg but also for creating a Reformed liturgy in Denmark.

In 1529 Tausen was transferred to Copenhagen, and there he continued his work with great success. But after the death of the king he was accused of blasphemy by Bishop Joachim Rönnow (1533) and condemned to expulsion from the dioceses of Sjaelland and Skane. The people then rose in arms against the bishop, who might have been murdered but for Tausen's intervention. Rönnow then permitted him to preach everywhere in the diocese on condition that he moderate his tone. In 1535 he published a translation of the Pentateuch from the Hebrew. On the final triumph of the Reformation (1536) Tausen was made a lecturer of Hebrew in the reorganized University of Copenhagen (1537), and in 1542 he became bishop of Ribe, an office that gave him many difficulties, especially with the nobility of Jutland. He died at Ribe on Nov. 11, 1561.

See *Dansk Biografisk Leksikon,* vol. xxiii, pp. 367–379 (1942); N. K. Andersen, *Confessio Hafniensis* (1954). (P. G. L.)

**TAUTOLOGY,** from a Greek word meaning "saying the same thing," is a word used technically in logic in a sense somewhat different from that in which it is used, pejoratively, in grammar. In the latter, a tautology is a needless repetition of a single idea in several words, as if more than one idea were being expressed (*see* FIGURES OF SPEECH).

In logic, the notion of a tautology in the propositional calculus is due to C. S. Peirce (1885). For this notion, and for the symbols used in this article, *see* LOGIC: *The Propositional Calculus.* The name tautology, however, was introduced in 1921 by Ludwig Wittgenstein, whose philosophical use of the notion, outlined in the article LOGICAL POSITIVISM, requires its extension from the propositional calculus to the full theory of types, including the functional calculi of first and higher orders. This extended notion, which was explained somewhat cryptically by Wittgenstein, and more satisfactorily by F. P. Ramsey in 1926, is, in fact, a less precise forerunner of what is now more usually called "validity" (*see* LOGIC: *The Metatheory of the Pure Functional Calculus of First Order*). Later logical positivists, especially Rudolf Carnap, amended Wittgenstein's doctrine in the light of the distinction that there is an effective test of tautology in the propositional calculus but no such test of validity even in first-order functional calculus.

As an example of a tautology in the extended sense of Wittgenstein-Ramsey, consider the formula $p \supset_x F(x) \supset \bullet\, p \supset (x)\, F(x)$ which is a theorem (in fact an axiom) of the pure functional calculus of first order. Suppose that there is available a list, possibly infinite, of names for all the individuals, say: $i_1, i_2, i_3, \ldots$. Then replace the two universal quantifiers that occur in the formula, each by a corresponding conjunction, so that we have:

$$[p \supset F(i_1)]\ [p \supset F(i_2)]\ [p \supset F(i_3)]\ \ldots \supset \bullet\, p \supset F(i_1)\, F(i_2)\, F(i_3) \ldots$$

This last may not be properly a formula, that is to say, it may be infinite in length, so that it is impossible actually to write it out. Nevertheless, we may abstractly consider such quasi-formulas; and in the same abstract way we may consider truth-table computations (or better, quasi-computations) applied to them, which may be infinite in width and length but are otherwise just like the finite truth-table computations that were explained in the article LOGIC in connection with propositional calculus. Moreover, in the case of the particular quasi-formula in question, it is clear that it is a tautology in the sense that, for every assignment of truth-values to its elementary parts $p$, $F(i_1)$, $F(i_2)$, . . . , the truth-table computation assigns to the whole quasi-formula the value truth. The analogy to the notion of tautology in the propositional calculus fails in only one respect: because the truth-table computation may be infinite, effectiveness is lost. Wittgenstein and Ramsey characterized logic by the property that its theorems are tautologies in this extended sense. (Ao. C.)

**TAUTOMERISM,** in chemistry, is one basis upon which pure chemical compounds can behave as if they possess two or more distinct structures. In those instances in which the structures in question correspond to identical, or nearly identical, relative positions in space of all constituent atoms (*see* STEREOCHEMISTRY), the phenomenon is at present considered to find its explanation in the theory of resonance (*see* RESONANCE). In those other instances, however, in which the structures in question correspond to widely different relative positions of at least one atom, the phenomenon is explained in a different manner, and the term "tautomerism" has been coined for its description. The present article is concerned only with tautomerism in this sense, and no further mention of resonance will be made here. (For a description of a widely useful compound with tautomeric characteristics, *see* ACETOACETIC ESTER.)

It is commonly believed that any compound which exhibits tautomerism is an equilibrium mixture of two or more substances, and that these substances have the structures indicated by the behaviour of the mixture. A tautomeric mixture then must exhibit the reactions to be expected of all structures involved since all the corresponding substances are actually present. On this view, the reason that a tautomeric mixture appears to be a single pure substance is that its various components (or tautomerides, as they are often called) are capable of rapid interconversion; consequently, they are separable from one another only with considerable difficulty, if at all. Moreover, it usually happens that only one of the tautomerides is present to an appreciable extent in the equilibrium mixture.

An alternative explanation of tautomerism, which may be correct in some instances, is that all the molecules present have the same structure but are able to react in two or more different ways.

A typical example of tautomerism is provided by acetaldehyde, which behaves in most respects as if it has the stable, so-called keto structure I, but in other respects as if it has instead the unstable, so-called enol structure II. This compound has never been separated into its two assumed components,

$$\underset{\text{I}}{CH_3-CH=O} \qquad \underset{\text{II}}{CH_2=CH-OH}$$

and all attempts to prepare a substance (vinyl alcohol) with the structure II have led instead to ordinary acetaldehyde. The belief is universally held that acetaldehyde is essentially pure keto (I), and that only minute traces of the enol form (II) are present in equilibrium. For this reason, acetaldehyde is usually said to possess structure I. In methyl ethyl ketone, similarly, traces of the two enol forms IV and V are supposed to be present in addition to the stable keto form III.

$$\underset{\text{III}}{CH_3-\overset{\overset{\displaystyle O}{\|}}{C}-CH_2CH_3} \qquad \underset{\text{IV}}{CH_2=\overset{\overset{\displaystyle OH}{|}}{C}-CH_2CH_3} \qquad \underset{\text{V}}{CH_3-\overset{\overset{\displaystyle OH}{|}}{C}=CH-CH_3}$$

The above interpretation of tautomerism would seem highly arbitrary and not at all convincing if no tautomeric compounds were known which can actually be separated into the tautomerides. Fortunately, a few such compounds have been discovered. Of these, the one which has received the most careful study is doubtless acetoacetic ester (ethyl acetoacetate). On the one hand, this substance appears to be a typical ketone, as in VI, since it forms an oxime with hydroxylamine, a hydrazone with hydrazine, and a cyanohydrin with hydrogen cyanide (*see* ALDEHYDES AND KETONES).

$$\underset{\text{VI}}{CH_3-\overset{\overset{\displaystyle O}{\|}}{C}-CH_2-CO_2C_2H_5} \qquad \underset{\text{VII}}{CH_3-\overset{\overset{\displaystyle O}{\|}}{C}-C(CH_3)_2-CO_2C_2H_5}$$

Moreover, when treated with an excess of both sodium ethoxide and methyl iodide in alcoholic solution, it is transformed into a dimethyl derivative to which the structure VII can be definitely assigned. On the other hand, it appears to be a typical unsaturated alcohol, as in VIII, since it absorbs bromine very rapidly, gives a colour with ferric chloride, and has a pronounced acidic character. Moreover, when treated with diazomethane,

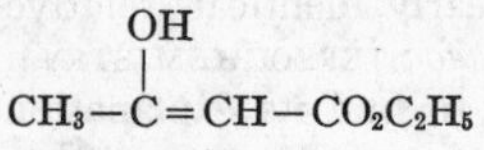

$$CH_3-\overset{OH}{\overset{|}{C}}=CH-CO_2C_2H_5 \quad \text{VIII} \qquad CH_3-\overset{OCH_3}{\overset{|}{C}}=CH-CO_2C_2H_5 \quad \text{IX}$$

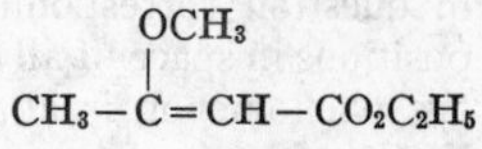

$CH_2N_2$, it is transformed into a methyl derivative to which the structure IX can be definitely assigned.

That this compound really is a mixture of two different substances with the structures under discussion was demonstrated in 1911 by L. Knorr, who found that the two components could be separated at −78° C., at which temperature their rate of interconversion is slow. At ordinary temperatures, the equilibrium mixture has been shown (K. H. Meyer, 1911) to consist of about 92.6% keto and 7.4% enol (in the pure liquid ester); these figures were obtained from a titration of the ester with bromine, with which the enol, but not the keto, form reacts rapidly.

A more complicated example of keto-enol tautomerism is presented by diacetylsuccinic ester, which has been obtained as the diketo form X, the keto-enol form XI, and the dienol form XII. (Actually, altogether five different forms of this ester are reported

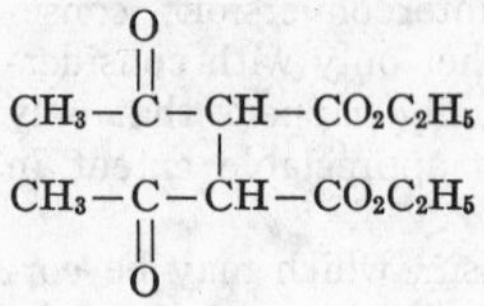

$$\begin{array}{l} CH_3-\overset{O}{\overset{\|}{C}}-CH-CO_2C_2H_5 \\ \qquad\quad | \\ CH_3-\underset{O}{\underset{\|}{C}}-CH-CO_2C_2H_5 \end{array} \quad \text{X} \qquad \begin{array}{l} CH_3-\overset{OH}{\overset{|}{C}}=C-CO_2C_2H_5 \\ \qquad\quad | \\ CH_3-\underset{O}{\underset{\|}{C}}-CH-CO_2C_2H_5 \end{array} \quad \text{XI}$$

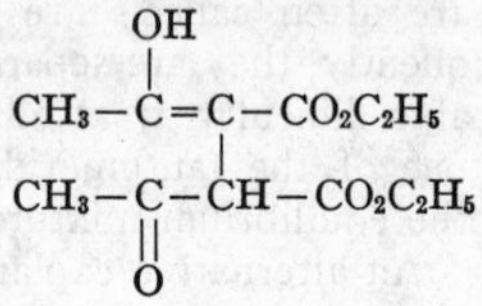

$$\begin{array}{l} CH_3-\overset{OH}{\overset{|}{C}}=C-CO_2C_2H_5 \\ \qquad\quad | \\ CH_3-\underset{OH}{\underset{|}{C}}=C-CO_2C_2H_5 \end{array} \quad \text{XII}$$

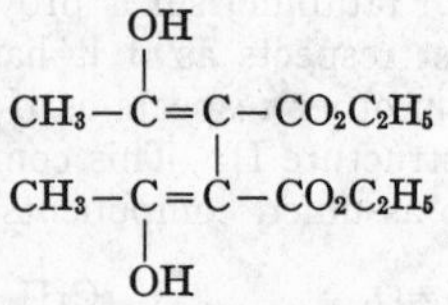

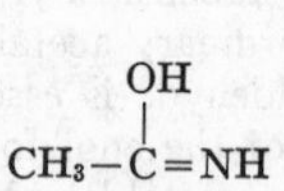

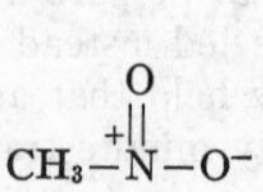

to have been isolated; two of these are apparently stereoisomers of other forms.)

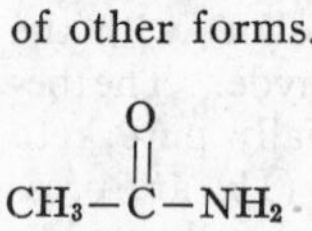

$$CH_3-\overset{O}{\overset{\|}{C}}-NH_2 \ \text{XIII} \qquad CH_3-\overset{OH}{\overset{|}{C}}=NH \ \text{XIV} \qquad CH_3-\overset{O}{\overset{\|}{\overset{+}{N}}}-O^- \ \text{XV} \qquad CH_2=\overset{OH}{\overset{|}{\overset{+}{N}}}-O^- \ \text{XVI}$$

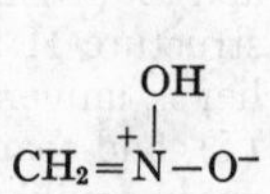

In addition to the above keto-enol tautomerism, a number of other types of tautomerism are also well known. For example, the amides of carboxylic acids (*see* AMIDES) exhibit the so-called lactam-lactim tautomerism. Thus, with acetamide, it is considered that the lactam form XIII predominates, but that the lactim form XIV may be present also in traces. Similarly, with a primary or secondary nitro compound (*see* NITRO COMPOUNDS), the nitro form, as in the structure XV of nitromethane, is considered to predominate greatly over the aci nitro form, as in XVI. A rather different type of tautomerism is illustrated by the fact that the same product results from the action of hydroxylamine upon benzoquinone as from the action of nitrous acid upon phenol.

From its first method of preparation, this substance should be the monoxime (*see* OXIMES) of benzoquinone with the structure XVII, whereas, from its second method of preparation, it should

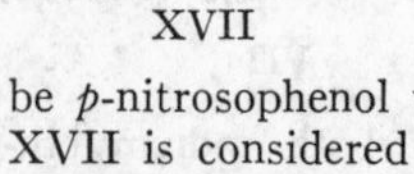

$$HO-N=\langle\quad\rangle=O \quad \text{XVII} \qquad O=N-\langle\quad\rangle-OH \quad \text{XVIII}$$

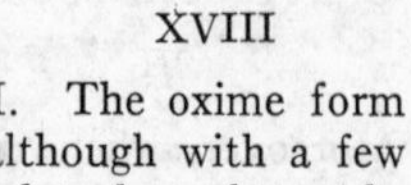

be *p*-nitrosophenol with the structure XVIII. The oxime form XVII is considered to be the more stable, although with a few analogous compounds both forms are reported to have been obtained.

**Prototropy and Anionotropy.**—In the various types of tautomerism mentioned so far, the tautomeric structures differ in the position of a hydrogen atom (and also in the arrangement of the valence bonds). Most types of tautomerism, of which only a few have been described here, belong to this class; such tautomerism is sometimes designated by the special name of "prototropy" (from "proton," the nucleus of the hydrogen atom, plus the Greek *trepein*, to turn). A few examples are known, however, in which the structures differ in the position of some other atom or group of atoms (as well as in the arrangement of the valence bonds). Thus, the two unsaturated chlorides XIX and XX, and the corresponding alcohols XXI and XXII, are rather

$$CH_3-CH=CH-CH_2Cl \quad \text{XIX} \qquad CH_3-\underset{Cl}{\underset{|}{CH}}-CH=CH_2 \quad \text{XX}$$

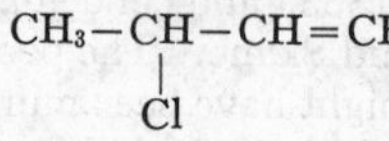

$$CH_3-CH=CH-CH_2OH \quad \text{XXI} \qquad CH_3-\underset{OH}{\underset{|}{CH}}-CH=CH_2 \quad \text{XXII}$$

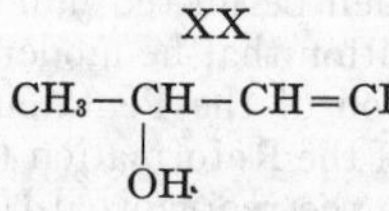

easily interconverted. The action of hydrogen chloride upon either alcohol gives a mixture of the two chlorides, and either chloride readily undergoes a partial spontaneous rearrangement into an equilibrium mixture of the two. Such tautomerism is sometimes referred to as "anionotropy" since the structures differ in the position of an atom or radical that is capable of forming a stable anion.

**Ring-Chain Tautomerism.**—A further important type of tautomerism can be illustrated with the example of 5-hydroxypentanal, which reacts with phenylhydrazine to give the phenylhydrazone XXIII, but with methyl alcoholic hydrogen chloride to give the cyclic product XXIV. In the first of these reactions,

$$HO-CH_2-CH_2-CH_2-CH_2-CH=N-NH-C_6H_5 \quad \text{XXIII}$$

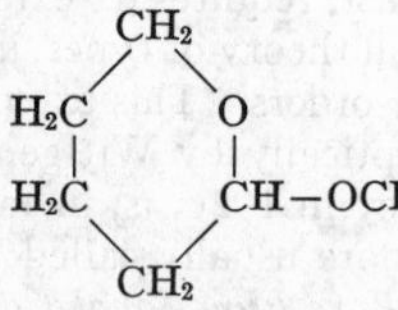

$$\text{XXIV: six-membered ring } CH_2,\ H_2C,\ H_2C,\ CH_2,\ CH-OCH_3,\ O$$

the original compound appears to have the structure XXV, but in the second it appears to have the structure XXVI instead. This type of tautomerism occurs with those hydroxy aldehydes and ketones with which the cyclic form would have either a five-

$$HO-CH_2-CH_2-CH_2-CH_2-CH=O \quad \text{XXV}$$

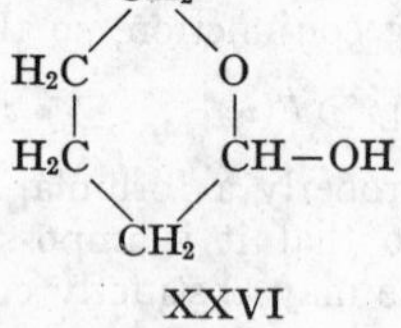

$$\text{XXVI: six-membered ring } CH_2,\ H_2C,\ H_2C,\ CH_2,\ CH-OH,\ O$$

or six-membered ring, and it is especially important in the sugar series. *See* CARBOHYDRATES.

*See* L. Pauling, ***The Nature of the Chemical Bond,*** 3rd ed. (1960).

(G. W. WD.)

**TAVERNER, JOHN** (*c.* 1495–1545), English composer whose work represents the culmination of the tradition of elaborate polyphony practised in England in the first half of the 16th century. His name first appears in a visitation record as a clerk-fellow of the collegiate church of Tattershall in Lincolnshire in 1525. In October 1526 a letter from Bishop Longland of Lincoln to Cardinal Wolsey represents Taverner as being reluctant to give up his living at Tattershall "and the prospect of a good marriage which he would lose by removal"; nevertheless a month later he took up his duties as *informator* or master of the choir in the chapel of Wolsey's Cardinal College (later Christ Church), Oxford. In 1528 Taverner was accused of heresy and imprisoned on the charge that he had concealed heretical books. John Foxe records that "the Cardinal for his musick excused him, saying, that he was but a musitian, and so he escaped." In 1530 he left Oxford, at which time his musical career may be considered to have terminated.

He appears to have been an agent of Thomas Cromwell in the suppression of monastic establishments. He lived out his life in Boston, Lincolnshire, where in 1537 he was elected a member, and in 1541 a steward, of the Guild of Corpus Christi. He died at Boston on Oct. 25, 1545.

Taverner's Latin church music, which includes six complete Masses, demonstrates a variety and skill, a range and a power that comes as the climax of pre-Reformation English music. In the field of instrumental music, an adaptation of the section of the *Benedictus* of his Mass *Gloria tibi Trinitas* associated with the words *In nomine Domine* became the prototype of a large number of instrumental compositions known as *In nomine* or *Gloria tibi Trinitas* during the succeeding century and a half.

See *Tudor Church Music,* vols. i and iii (1923, 1924); H. B. Collins, "John Taverner's Masses," in *Music and Letters,* vol. v (1924).

(Jo. D. B.)

**TAVOY,** a town and district in the Tenasserim division of Burma. The town lies on the left bank of the river of the same name, 30 mi. (48 km.) from the Andaman Sea and 150 mi. (241 km.) S of Moulmein. Pop. (1953) 40,312. A considerable coasting trade was developed with other ports of Burma and with Singapore, which received the bulk of the tin ore for which the district became important.

Tavoy District has an area of 5,404 sq.mi. (14,000 sq.km.) and a population (1962 est.) of 297,871. It lies between lower Thailand and the Andaman Sea of the Bay of Bengal, enclosed by mountains on three sides, viz., the main chain of the Bilauktaung on the east, rising in places to 5,000 ft. (1,500 m.), which, with its densely wooded spurs, forms an almost impassable barrier between Burmese and Thai territory. The railway southward from Moulmein to Ye is continued by a road to Tavoy, but main access is still by sea. The Tavoy River is navigable for vessels of considerable size. It is interspersed with many islands and, with its numerous smaller tributaries, affords easy and rapid communication. In this southern part of Burma the climate is almost equatorial. The annual rainfall averages more than 200 in. (5,000 mm.). The staple crop is rice. Forests cover an area of nearly 5,000 sq.mi. (13,000 sq.km.).

Tavoy, with the rest of Tenasserim, was handed over to the British at the end of the first Burmese War in 1826. *See* further Burma. (L. D. S.)

**TAWNEY, RICHARD HENRY** (1880–1962), English economic historian and an outstanding social critic of his time, was born in Calcutta, India, on Nov. 30, 1880, and died in London on Jan. 16, 1962. He was educated at Rugby School and at Balliol College, Oxford. After social work in London at Toynbee Hall (*q.v.*), he became an active member in Rochdale of the Workers' Educational Association (WEA) and played an important part in its development, teaching tutorial classes at Oxford University (*see* Adult Education) and eventually becoming president of the WEA (1928–44). While at Oxford he wrote his first major work, *The Agrarian Problem in the Sixteenth Century* (1912). Appointed to the London School of Economics in 1913, he became reader there in 1919 and was professor of economic history from 1931 to 1949, when he was made professor emeritus.

Tawney was an influential member of many economic boards and committees and became a valued governmental adviser. But his greatest contribution was to the work of the Labour Party (he was several times an unsuccessful Labour candidate). He urged greater state social investment, and many of his projects—raising the school-leaving age, extension of workers' education, and fixing of minimum wages—were effected. An ardent Christian and Socialist, he insisted that the basis of socialism was humanism. A good society could be built only by good men and not by dogmas or by merely changing the machinery of government. He condemned the acquisitiveness of capitalist society, which corrupted both rich and poor, as a morally wrong motivating principle. Tawney held that men want and need work not only for the income it provides but because they want to be creative and make a contribution to society. They can achieve a sense of fulfillment in their work only if they are convinced that it is important and serves some useful purpose. In capitalist societies, work was deprived of its inherent value, and, seen solely as a means to something else, it became drudgery.

Many of Tawney's books have become classics, notably *The Acquisitive Society* (1921), *Equality* (1931), and *Religion and the Rise of Capitalism* (1926), a study of the relation between Protestant thought and economic behaviour in the 16th and 17th centuries.

**TAXATION.** Taxes are compulsory levies for general governmental purposes. They include income taxes, excise taxes, tariffs, and a great variety of other types; they do not include governmental receipts from borrowing, gifts, reparations, or various direct charges for special services.

Clear-cut lines among the various types of public revenue are hard to draw, and each type shades into adjacent classes. For example, in a twilight zone between taxation and borrowing are the compulsory loans levied by Canada, Great Britain, and the United States during World War II (in the form of refundable income taxes) and by Denmark and Israel in the 1950s. Also difficult to classify are social insurance contributions (not generally designated by law as taxes, except in the United States); they progressively take on the character of taxes as the relationship between the amount of the individual's contributions and the amount of his benefits is weakened by legislative action. Though generally thought of as a means of raising revenue, taxes are recognized also as a major instrument of national economic policy. In war or time of emergency, governments increase taxes to restrain inflation, and in time of depression they reduce taxes to stimulate the economy. When government spending equals one-fourth to one-third of the gross national product, as in Western Europe and North America, taxes play a crucial role not only as a source of revenue but as a balance wheel in the economy.

This article deals with taxation only in a broad, general sense and does not attempt to describe specific taxes in detail. (For special forms of taxes *see* the section on taxation in various country articles and also Corporation Tax; Excess-Profits Tax; Excise Tax; Income Tax; Local Government: *Finance and Local Freedom;* and Tariff.)

**History.**—Only late in human history did governments come to rely on taxes for the bulk of their revenue, especially on taxes levied equitably and with the consent of the governed. For centuries, the public domain was the chief source of public revenue, and taxation consisted largely of excises on domestic consumption and customs duties on foreign trade. It was the duty of the unprivileged classes—slaves, vassals, peasants, colonists, and conquered peoples—to support the ruling classes, whether they were the free citizens of Athens and Rome, the lords and nobles of the feudal barony, or the courtiers of Louis XIV. Taxes as a badge of freedom rather than a mark of bondage are a modern phenomenon.

In ancient Greece and Rome, income from mines, tribute from subjugated countries, gifts from wealthy citizens, and taxes on trade and consumption filled virtually all revenue needs. Except for Rome's famed inheritance and capitation taxes (both foreshadowed by ancient Egyptian taxes) and certain emergency levies in Greece, direct taxes on income and wealth were unknown.

Taxes of any kind had little place in the agrarian feudal system of the Middle Ages. The king, the duke, the count, the baron—each in turn derived income from the land he held directly and levied rentlike dues on those who held land at his pleasure, *i.e.,* on those beneath him in the feudal hierarchy. From the 14th century on, as the feudal system was gradually broken up by dissipation of the public domain, by growth of industry and commerce, and by centralization of government, these patrimonial revenues slowly gave way to taxes.

Land, as the primary source of wealth, also became the primary source of taxation during this period. Both local and central governments in England turned to land taxes, basing them at first on area (the old *hidage* and *carucage*) but later on annual rental value. The French counterpart was the arbitrary annual *taille* on estimated farm income. The early American colonies broadened the British type of land tax into a property tax whose base included land, houses, personal property, and faculty (the rated earning capacity of one's trade or profession). With the great growth of foreign and domestic commerce between the 14th and 19th centuries, import and export duties and internal excises became important, especially in France, Spain, and other commercial centres. Poll taxes (levied at so much per head) and such levies as the hearth tax and window tax (both designed as rough measures of the taxpayer's wealth) also flourished in this period.

Rebellion against arbitrary and oppressive taxation played a major role in modern history. Such milestones in British constitutional history as the Magna Carta (1215) and the Bill of Rights (1689) helped establish the principle of consent and representation in taxation. Failure to apply this principle to the colonies played no little part in the American Revolution. Much of the desperation that exploded in the French Revolution grew out of France's tax system—one of the most oppressive and inequitable tax systems of all time. The French government, as well as many others, followed the practice of turning over the collection of taxes to contractors known as tax farmers, who often employed harsh measures and aroused the hatred of the people. At the time of the Revolution the system was abolished, and many of the tax farmers were executed.

The establishment of representative democratic government, the advent of the industrial revolution, and the development of modern ideals of social justice and equality left their imprint on both the principles and the forms of taxation. The 19th century saw expediency and oppression in taxation gradually make way for equity and uniformity. With the unfolding of new forms and differentiated sources of wealth, taxes on incomes and inheritances were adopted and refined, and property taxes were broadened.

Great Britain adopted an income tax in 1799 and a death transfer tax in 1796, broadened both measures (after setting the income tax aside from 1816 to 1842) midway through the 19th century, and brought them to something like their modern form near the turn of the century. Although customs and excises continued to be an important source of revenue, the central government during the first half of the 20th century greatly intensified its use of direct taxes on income and estates. "Local rates" on real estate continued to be the mainstay of local tax systems.

The United States did not make effective use of income and inheritance taxes until about the time of World War I. Before that time, tariffs, excises on liquor and tobacco, and sales of land furnished the bulk of federal revenues. The peculiarly American general property tax provided most of the revenues needed at the state and local levels. But during World War I and in the interwar period, the federal government adopted an estate tax, developed its corporate and individual income taxes, expanded its excises, and introduced social security payroll levies. The states meanwhile tapped such new sources as gasoline taxes, retail sales taxes, motor vehicle levies, and net income taxes, largely abandoning the property tax to the local units.

Under the pressure of World War II, central government taxes everywhere were brought to new peaks, both in their severity and in their adaptation to such nonrevenue ends as curbing of inflation and prevention of war profiteering. After the war, most belligerents granted only modest tax reductions in the face of large debts, continued inflation, and deteriorating relations between the major world powers. The outbreak of the Korean War in 1950 touched off a new wave of tax increases, but within three or four years, such countries as Australia, New Zealand, the United States, Canada, Great Britain, the Netherlands, and Germany were again reducing tax rates. In 1964 the U.S. Congress approved a substantial reduction in income and excise taxes, justified in part as a necessary stimulant for the economy.

**Modern Forms.**—As modern economic society progressively exposed new facets of wealth, income, and transactions, tax planners and legislators responded with a bewildering array of levies. The production and receipt of income, the ownership and transfer of wealth, the sale and use of commodities and services, the carrying on of a business, and a host of other economic factors all became bases or objects of taxation.

The versatility of income as a tax base can be visualized by observing the gantlet of taxes it may have to run as it flows into, through, and out of a corporation. At the point of entry, income may be subject to (1) taxes on gross receipts or gross income (often classed as consumption taxes because they are largely passed on to consumers in higher prices); (2) taxes on the net profits remaining after all expenses are deducted; (3) taxes on excessive profits, especially in wartime. Once inside the corporate walls, net income which is not distributed to stockholders may encounter taxes on undistributed profits. At the point of exit, income paid out as dividends may encounter a distributed profits tax like the post-World War II British tax of 30%. As it reaches the stockholder, dividend income may be subject to (1) a progressive personal income tax applying a uniform schedule of rates to net income regardless of source; (2) a schedular income tax applying different rates to different sources of income; (3) a special tax or surtax on investment income; (4) special credits or allowances under the regular income tax. To this galaxy of income taxes should perhaps be added the low-rate levies on business payrolls and individual wages used to finance social security programs.

Property remains the principal local tax base in the English-speaking world. Broadest of all property taxes is the general property tax in the United States, an impersonal levy by local governments on both real estate and personal property, measured by exchange value and levied against owners. Narrower and more personal is the British system of local rates, confined to real estate, measured by annual rental value, and in part levied as a tax on occupants. Even narrower are the rural land taxes of Asia, the Middle East, and much of Europe.

Most personal of the taxes on property ownership are the progressive taxes on personal net worth (assets minus liabilities) levied in the form of (1) annual net worth taxes, as in Scandinavia, Germany, and the Netherlands; and (2) one-time capital levies, as in many European countries in the wake of both World Wars I and II. In the United States, constitutional barriers stand in the way of a national net worth tax.

Transfers of wealth by death are taxed in most Western countries under both estate taxes (levied on the decedent's estate as a whole) and inheritance, succession, or legacy taxes (levied on the heirs' distributive shares). Comparable taxes apply to transfers by gift.

Another major group includes consumption taxes, those which are generally passed on to consumers in the form of higher prices even though initially levied on producers or distributors. The term hidden taxes ordinarily refers to this group of levies. In their more general forms, they are levied as turnover, gross income, or value-added taxes at several stages of production; as sales or purchase taxes at the manufacturing, wholesale or retail stages; as use taxes on the consumer; and as tariffs or customs duties on imports and exports. In their more limited forms, they appear as selective excises on liquor, tobacco, gasoline, luxuries, and many other commodities and services; or as profits from government monopolies of salt, liquor, matches, tobacco, and the like.

Business taxes, in the broadest sense of the term, refer to all taxes arising out of the ownership and operation of businesses. More narrowly and usefully, the term refers to a separate category of taxes applicable only to business entities as such and bearing no relation to the personal status of the owners or operators of the business. In this sense, it includes on one hand such general privilege taxes as incorporation fees, capital stock taxes, the occupational taxes popular in the southern United States, the German *Gewerbesteuer*, and the French *patente*. On the other hand, it covers levies which single out certain types of business for special taxation, *e.g.*, in the United States the state taxes on insurance companies, usually measured by gross premiums, and on public utilities, measured by gross earnings or property. Corporate income and profits taxes are also often labelled business taxes.

**General Classifications.**—Tax literature and usage abound with general classifications. Apart from groupings by tax base or source, one of the most useful classifications is by type of effective rate structure, *i.e.*, progressive, proportional, and regressive types. The distinction depends upon the ratio of tax liability to net income (or net worth). If the ratio rises as income rises—*i.e.*, if the tax takes a greater percentage of a person's income, the larger that income—the tax is progressive. If the ratio is constant, the tax is proportional. If it declines as income rises, the tax is regressive. The terms are applied both to particular taxes and to tax systems as a whole. Among specific taxes, the personal net income, net worth, and death and gift taxes are almost universally progressive. Most property, sales, and excise taxes are levied at proportional rates but are regressive in effect; for example, a 5% sales tax takes a larger percentage of a small income than of a large income because the taxed items represent a larger percentage of the small-income than of the large-income budget.

Another widely used distinction is that between direct and indirect taxes. A direct tax is one that tends to be borne by the persons upon whom the government levies it. An indirect tax is one that tends to be shifted, *i.e.*, passed on to others in the form of higher prices received or lower prices paid by the taxpayer. Since it is difficult to determine precisely who bears the final burden of a given tax, the line between the two is not easy to draw. Customarily classed as direct taxes are net income, net worth, death, gift, and land taxes. Consumption taxes, many business taxes, payroll taxes, and taxes on realty other than land are ordinarily considered to be indirect. Relative emphasis on direct versus indirect taxes as thus classified varies greatly from country to country.

Another useful distinction, encountered particularly in discussions of custom duties, is that between specific and ad valorem taxes. A tax or duty is specific when it is based on some physical measurement or quantity, *e.g.*, so much per pound, per yard, or per gallon. It is ad valorem when it is based on value and levied as a percentage of that value, *e.g.*, 15 mills per dollar (1.5%) of property value.

**Objectives and Criteria.**—The pervading objective of taxation, in concert with other government policies, is to promote the general welfare. Taxes contribute to this end by providing the financial foundation for the substantive functions of government and at the same time serving as an engine of social and economic betterment which nations can call upon to reduce excessive inequalities of wealth, to check inflation and war profiteering, and to promote economic stability.

How can the broad welfare objectives of taxation be translated into guideposts for tax policy? In the search for an answer, the maxims propounded by Adam Smith in his *Wealth of Nations* in 1776 provide a traditional point of departure. He set forth the tests of equity, certainty, convenience and economy as follows:

I. The subjects of every state ought to contribute towards the support of the government, as nearly as possible, in proportion to their respective abilities; that is, in proportion to the revenue which they respectively enjoy under the protection of the state.
II. The tax which each individual is bound to pay ought to be certain, and not arbitrary. The time of payment, the manner of payment, the quantity to be paid, ought all to be clear and plain to the contributor, and to every other person.
III. Every tax ought to be levied at the time, or in the manner, in which it is most likely to be convenient for the contributor to pay it.
IV. Every tax ought to be so contrived as both to take out and to keep out of the pockets of the people as little as possible, over and above what it brings into the public treasury of the state.

Appropriate as they were in his day, both as standards and as reform slogans in taxation, Smith's canons depend for their present day validity largely on what is read into them. For example, Smith directed his maxim of certainty against the evil of lodging power over the amount and terms of taxes in the "tax-gatherer, who can either aggravate the tax upon any obnoxious contributor, or extort, by the terror of such aggravation, some present or perquisite to himself." In its modern context, the demand for certainty is usually a protest against too frequent changes in tax laws, regulations and court decisions. Moreover, the unfolding of the principle of progression in taxation has infused new meaning into Smith's maxim of equity. Even with modernized content, however, his canons furnish little more than three common-sense rules of tax administration and one basic principle, that of equity, for the distribution of tax burdens.

That this set of guides is no longer adequate is hardly surprising in view of the sweeping economic, social and political developments since Smith's day. Concepts of justice have changed profoundly. Methods of measuring economic strength have been refined. Democratic control of taxation has been won. Tax administration has vastly improved. Economic systems have become enormously more complex and interdependent. The sense of social responsibility and, with it, the role of government have steadily grown. In response to these changes, it was inevitable that the functions of taxation should be broadened and its standards recast. As adapted to modern circumstances, the canons may be re-examined under four major headings: (1) social justice; (2) consistency with economic goals; (3) ease of administration and compliance; and (4) revenue adequacy.

*Social Justice.*—That taxes should be just is a self-evident first principle of taxation. But in taxation, as in other fields, justice is a product not of scientific analysis but of a people's value judgments. As reflected in contemporary tax systems, the value decisions modern societies have made regarding social justice appear to require: (1) that taxes be impartial in their application—the "equity" test; and (2) that taxes, on balance, be designed to reduce economic inequalities—the "equality" test. Unfortunately the precise meaning and the practical dictates of these tests are not readily definable and have, in fact, been the subject of extended controversy.

It is, to be sure, widely agreed that equity in taxation requires impartial (not identical) treatment, *i.e.*, equal taxes on persons in like circumstances and reasonably differentiated taxes on persons in unlike circumstances. Thus, the equity criterion sets up the presumption that even when taxation is asked to serve such external ends as redistribution of income or recapture of excessive war profits, the internal structure of the taxes levied should adhere to the principle of reasonable classification and impartial treatment. But the nub of the problem is: What is reasonable classification in taxation—what characteristics of a person identify him with or differentiate him from other persons for taxing purposes? And once acceptable criteria have been developed for classifying people, what relative tax burdens should the different classes bear?

For a limited group of levies on the border line of taxation, it has been deemed equitable to classify people and tax them according to the quantity of benefits received from government. Where such benefits can be identified and measured, at least roughly, and the social interest does not demand a subsidy to the individual or group benefited, it is reasonable to apply the benefit principle. Gasoline taxes and social security employment levies are commonly justified on the ground that special benefits—the use of the highways and protection against insecurity—accrue to the taxpayer in direct proportion to the amount of tax he pays.

But the difficulty of measuring most government benefits and the desirability of providing many services on the basis of need narrowly limit the application of the benefit principle. And the day when "taxation according to benefits received" was a battle cry in the struggle to shift the yoke of taxation from the overburdened masses to the exempt nobility has long since passed.

Accordingly, the principle of ability to pay is generally invoked as a basis for classifying and differentiating among people for tax purposes. Deceptively simple in appearance, this concept involves many difficulties of application. At the outset, one notes that ability to pay as such is subjective, an attribute of persons, not things. Yet its measure for tax purposes is necessarily objective, an external quantity such as income or wealth. An individual's ability may be gauged by his flow of income or spendings over a certain unit of time or his stock of wealth at any given time. Net income is widely recognized as the best index. But the amount of net income is only one element in the measurement of ability. Individual income tax laws also take into account (1) family obligations, recognized in marital and dependency exemptions, and (2) less universally, the source of the income, recognized in differential treatment favouring "earned" over "unearned" income. Even after this yardstick, properly calibrated, ranks individuals according to their income, the question remains as to how much more a person of high rank should pay than one of lower rank.

Except for one or two fleeting references to progression, Adam Smith answered that taxes should be proportional to income. Nearly 75 years later, the Scottish economist John R. McCulloch still held, "The moment you abandon . . . the cardinal principle [of proportion], you are at sea without rudder or compass, and there is no amount of injustice and folly you may not commit." Expressing the predominant modern view, F. W. Taussig replied that only through progression could democratic ideals of justice in taxation be achieved. As to the lack of precise standards for determining the degree of progression, E. R. A. Seligman added that it is better to approximate justice than to be clearly unjust.

While progression is, in practice, essentially a 20th-century phenomenon, it is interesting to note that the Indian sage Manu recognized the principle more than 3,000 years ago in these words:

"To make the burden of taxes equal . . . is not effected by a mere numerical proportion. The man who is taxed to the amount of one-tenth . . . of an income of 100 rupees per annum, is taxed far more severely than the man who is taxed an equal proportion of an income of 1,000 rupees, and to a prodigious bigness more severely than the man who is taxed an equal proportion of 10,000 rupees per annum."

In the development of ability-to-pay theories of progressive taxation, the "sacrifice" doctrines have played a major role. An offshoot of hedonistic or utilitarian economics, these doctrines find their most refined expression in A. C. Pigou's least-sacrifice theory. It holds that progression is necessary to minimize the aggregate direct burden of taxes on individuals. The theory stands or falls on the validity of its assumptions (1) that different people are about equally efficient as "pleasure machines," *i.e.,* that they have similar capacities for satisfaction, and (2) that the marginal utility of money diminishes as income increases, *i.e.,* that as an individual's income rises, the want-satisfying value of each additional unit of it falls. If these assumptions are valid, it follows from (2) that the larger the income, the smaller the sacrifice in giving up a unit of it in taxes, and from (1) that the relation between income and sacrifice is similar for different people. Minimum sacrifice thus calls for progressive taxes which bear heavily on the less important units at the margin of large incomes and lightly on the more important units at the margin of small incomes.

Modern welfare economists question the stated assumptions, pointing out that they cannot be verified until a way is found not only to measure satisfactions but to compare them among different people. They are therefore disinclined to accept a defense of progression which is based on sacrifice doctrines.

Not satisfied with attenuated translations of "ability to pay" into "progression," many noted thinkers have rested their case for progressive taxation simply on a desire to reduce inequalities in wealth and income. Adolph Wagner argued in *Finanzwissenschaft* (1880) that defenses of progression on the basis of ability to pay become meaningful only in terms of greater economic equality. In his view, reducing inequality of incomes increases the general welfare by enabling more urgent needs to be satisfied at the expense of less urgent needs. Taussig's later use of the equality criterion was based mainly on his interpretation of the democratic consensus that ". . . such great degrees of inequality as the modern world shows are regarded as not consonant with canons of justice." Henry C. Simons, writing in the 1930s, stated also that the case for sharp progression must rest on the ethical judgment that the prevailing degree (and/or kind) of inequality in wealth and income is "distinctly evil and unlovely."

*Consistency with Economic Goals.*—The importance of harmonizing the economic overtones of taxation with the economic goals of the community—seen as efficient allocation and full employment of resources, rising living standards and economic stability—has long been recognized. But the concept of using taxes actively to promote a stable economy and full use of resources gained currency only toward mid-20th century, largely through Lord Keynes and his followers. Every tax became recognized as affecting the spending power and propensity of taxpayers as consumers and producers and their incentives to exert effort and initiative as workers, managers and investors. The ideal tax structure thus is one which (1) restricts private spending during inflation and expands it during depression and (2) interferes least with, or perhaps even stimulates, effort and risk taking.

The health and growth of a modern industrialized economy depend upon an adequate volume of demand for the goods and services it is capable of producing when fully employed. Whether that demand will be forthcoming depends on the aggregate spending of consumers, businesses, and governments. When income is withdrawn from the spending stream by individuals who neither spend it nor invest it (or by businesses which neither distribute it nor spend it on inventories, plant, and equipment), the net result is to dry up demand and employment. Alternatively, when individuals and businesses as a whole run deficits and augment their spending by borrowing money or drawing on assets, the result is to inflate demand and employment. Left to itself, the private economy will experience cyclical slumps and booms. In this setting, it is desirable that central governments use taxes as part of a coordinated fiscal-monetary policy to stabilize the economy.

Tax policy in this context has to concern itself, first of all, with the cyclical stability of total spending. Flexible taxes serve as one means of resisting or correcting its instability, of restricting total spending in a boom period and expanding it in a slump. This approach calls for a tax system and a tax policy which increase tax collections relative to expenditures in booms and decrease them in depressions. It applauds progressive income taxes, whose revenues automatically expand and contract more than in proportion to the ups and downs of national income; current collection and withholding magnify this stabilizing impact by making tax revenues respond instantly to changes in income. Contracyclical tax policy also enlists short-term changes in tax rates to impound or free purchasing power. The British White Paper on Employment Policy (1944) stated that "the ideal to be aimed at is some corrective influence which comes into play automatically—on the analogy of a thermostatic control . . ." and suggested "variation of rates of taxation and the incorporation of some system of deferred credits (repayable in bad times) as a permanent feature of national taxation." In accord with this suggestion, the government adopted a "tax regulator" law under which it could move the rates of certain payroll and consumption taxes up and down against the grain of the business cycle.

Unless contracyclical tax measures are already imbedded in the law, tax increases to combat inflation and tax decreases to counter deflation may be unduly delayed in the legislative and administrative process. This is especially likely in the U.S., where tax proposals by the executive do not have the thrust provided by parliamentary systems under which the government in power stands or falls on the acceptance or rejection of its program.

Under the U.S. system, the executive proposes but the congress disposes—often slowly and only after successive modifications by the house of representatives through its ways and means committee, by the senate finance committee, by the senate itself, and finally by the joint conference committee. Nonetheless, in severe economic fluctuations, it may be necessary to reinforce automatic variations in revenues with discretionary changes in tax rates to generate the required anti-inflationary surpluses or expansionary deficits. To overcome the possible delay inherent in the U.S. system, the president in 1962 recommended to the Congress enactment of "stand-by authority" to permit a quick temporary across-the-board reduction in individual income tax rates to cope with recessions. Congress did not respond to this recommendation, and in 1965 a far milder presidential proposal urging Congress to ensure "that its procedures will permit rapid action on temporary income tax cuts if recession threatens" got no immediate congressional response.

In contrast with the wide area of agreement among economists on the broad principles of anticyclical tax policy, there is no consensus on whether tax systems should be biased toward stimulating or damping down total spending in the long run. For the classical economists of an earlier age, this was no problem. Full employment was largely taken for granted, and savings were seen as the key to progress, as an unmixed blessing to be disturbed as little as possible by taxes, especially progressive taxes. But the great depression of the 1930s raised the spectre of the mature or stagnant economy, beset with persistent unemployment, weak markets, redundant savings, and lagging investment. It suggested to Keynes's followers that tax policy coupled with government expenditure should seek to activate dormant purchasing power and increase the flow of spending. This would call for taxes which bear heavily on the private incomes least likely to be spent and lightly on those most likely to be spent. To the extent that high incomes are less likely, and low incomes more likely, to be spent by their recipients, progressive taxes would be welcomed under these circumstances.

Under the impact of World War II, the feared circumstances did not materialize. In fact, the economic record of the first decade after the war suggested that, at least under conditions of armed peace, the problem of containing chronic inflation might replace the problem of sustaining aggregate demand. In the second decade after World War II the picture changed again. In the United States, the slow rate of economic growth in the late 1950s, the unsatisfactory recoveries after the 1957–58 and 1960–61 recessions, and the persistence of substantial unemployment pointed to the desirability of comprehensive tax reduction and reform to spur the economy's advance. After considerable delay in the legislative process, a huge tax cut was enacted in 1964. Together with the 1962 measures, this action reduced both individual and corporate income taxes by nearly 20%. Excise taxes were sharply reduced in 1965. All told, the 1961–65 actions reduced tax liabilities by more than $20,000,000,000 in a successful effort to remove the "fiscal over-burden" which had been retarding the advance of the U.S. economy. The success of the tax cut in stimulating the economy to new heights led to a new acceptance and understanding of fiscal policy in the United States.

Taxation is often called upon to serve economic ends other than those concerned with aggregate spending and saving. Taxes are employed to subsidize the production of certain items, *e.g.*, protective tariffs, and to penalize the production of others, *e.g.*, the heavy taxes levied by dairying states on oleomargarine. In World War II, high excises were imposed on automobiles and radios to divert resources from their production into war production. The elimination of unwarranted economic gain from war has been a primary objective of excess profits taxes (*q.v.*). Taxation has thus come to be widely used as an instrument of indirect economic control.

A novel provision for stimulating investment in new machinery and equipment was enacted by the U.S. Congress in 1962. It granted business a 7% tax credit for investment in certain depreciable property. The purpose was to reduce the risk and increase the profitability of new investment and improve business liquidity, which is of particular importance for new and smaller firms.

*Ease of Administration and Compliance.*—The exacting requirements of social justice and economic harmony in taxation are necessarily tempered by considerations of administrative efficiency and taxpayer convenience. Unless a tax can be administered at a reasonable cost to both government and taxpayers and without large-scale evasion by illegal means and avoidance through legal loopholes and subterfuges, it becomes unworkable no matter how laudable its economic and social objectives. The sense of equity is as surely violated by a tax which applies unequally to taxpayers in identical circumstances because of lax administration as it is by a tax which is basically unfair in its statutory provisions. From the standpoint of administration and compliance alone, taxes should be simple to compute and easy to understand (understanding being a matter of the concepts and tax returns which confront the taxpayer), assessed on an obvious base easily arrived at, levied at moderate rates, and payable in a convenient manner.

But the degree of simplicity required or of complexity permissible is not an absolute. Much depends on the nature of the tax; for example, the minimum complexity required to bring about tolerable equity in an excess profits tax is much greater than that required in a tobacco tax. Much also depends on the scope of the tax—how widely it applies and how deeply it cuts. The demands for ease and simplicity of the United States individual income tax were far less pressing at the end of the 1930s, when it applied at moderate rates to 4,000,000 persons, than during World War II or in the mid-1950s, when it applied at heavy rates to more than 50,000,000. Factors external to a given tax must also be taken into account. The lack of coordination of federal, state, and local tax systems, for example, imposes costs and irritations arising not out of a particular tax but out of the conflict and duplication among taxes and taxing jurisdictions. Even more important are the factors external to the tax system as a whole. The general level and standards of the civil service establish a boundary beyond which taxes cannot go in the direction of refinement and complexity. Administrative techniques and competence, in turn, depend in good part on the stage of development of society. A country that is sparsely settled and industrially undeveloped is likely to have very simple administrative machinery and therefore to rely heavily on taxes with an easily discoverable base, *e.g.*, land taxes and taxes on imports and exports. In more advanced countries, the machinery and the economic data on which it depends are better geared to direct, personal taxes, such as those on incomes. Level of public education, attitudes toward government, and concepts of tax justice are likewise vital in determining how complicated a tax may be without jeopardizing its success.

*Revenue Adequacy.*—The receipts of government must be sufficient to commandeer for the state that part of society's real resources which social and economic policy wishes to devote to collective use. Traditionally, it was demanded that taxes alone free the necessary resources for collective use each year, *i.e.*, balance the budget annually. This position was later modified to permit deficits in bad years, provided they were offset by tax surpluses in good years, *i.e.*, provided the budget were balanced cyclically. Many modern economists have abandoned the idea of a balanced central government budget as an end in itself. Their goal is a balanced economic budget for the nation, sufficient total spending to balance and sustain the income flowing from production and employment. After World War II, the British, Canadian, and, to a lesser extent, the United States government budgets were presented in the perspective of the national economic budget.

In this conception, taxes are not levied for revenue alone. The test of adequate yield as applied to the tax system is not that it cover a predetermined level of government expenditure but rather that, together with borrowing if necessary, it raise the required funds in the manner best calculated to further the end of full and stable employment. The quantitative role of taxation becomes interlocked with its qualitative role.

This reasoning applies primarily to central governments. Their fiscal policies may appropriately be designed to offset tendencies toward economic instability in the private sector of the economy. But for local governments, more closely analogous to private persons, taxation remains primarily a means of raising revenue. In the United States, for example, local governments differ from the central government in that they lack money and central banking powers, their debts are held externally, and they have neither the ability nor the responsibility to maintain high levels of employment. In this context, the traditional aims of stable tax yields and at least cyclically balanced budgets remain valid.

**Shifting, Incidence, and Effects.**—To know only who bears the impact of a tax, *i.e.*, who turns the money over to the government or its agents, is to know very little indeed about the social and economic consequences of that tax. The tax may set loose forces which enable the original payer to obtain higher prices for the goods or services he sells or pay lower prices for those he buys, thus giving him relief through shifting. The tax may also affect both private and governmental consumption and investment and hence the national income. To pass final judgment on a tax, one needs to know how it affects the distribution of real income available for private use, called its incidence, and what repercussions it has on the level of national income, called its effects.

Unfortunately, the way in which a tax affects the distribution and level of income cannot be isolated for precise statistical study. Since conclusions must perforce be reached largely through deductive processes combining reasonable assumptions with analysis of economic forces, the theory of incidence and effects is heavily dependent on the economic theory of price and income determination. A fairly general consensus on the incidence of the major taxes has been tentatively reached along the lines indicated above in the classification of taxes into direct and indirect.

**Comparative Revenues and Burdens.**—Valid international comparisons of tax burdens or tax rates are difficult to make. Comparisons of tax rates or per capita taxes are especially likely to be misleading because of differences in purchasing power of money (not reflected in exchange ratios), in standards of living, in distribution of income, etc. Even the ratios of taxes to national income or product—most widely accepted as a reliable index of comparative burdens—do not tell (1) whether taxes equaled, exceeded, or fell short of government spending and (2) whether the governments spent the proceeds wisely in terms of efficiency and honesty of administration and effectiveness in gauging and following the preferences of the body politic.

*See* also references under "Taxation" in the Index.

BIBLIOGRAPHY.—Harold M. Groves, *Financing Government,* 6th ed. (1964); Roy Blough, *The Federal Taxing Process* (1952); Richard Goode, *The Corporation Income Tax* (1951), *The Individual Income Tax* (1964); Ursula K. Hicks, *Public Finance,* 2nd ed. (1955); J. M. Keynes, *How to Pay for the War* (1940); A. C. Pigou, *A Study in Public Finance,* 3rd rev. ed. (1949); Henry C. Simons, *Personal Income Taxation* (1938); Josiah Stamp, *The Fundamental Principles of Taxation* (1936); Nicholas Kaldor, *An Expenditure Tax* (1955); Randolph E. Paul, *Taxation in the United States* (1954); American Economic Association, *Readings in the Economics of Taxation* (1959); Richard A. Musgrave, *The Theory of Public Finance* (1959); R. A. Musgrave and A. T. Peacock (eds.), *Classics in the Theory of Public Finance* (1958); J. F. Due, *Government Finance,* 3rd ed. (1963), includes sections on Canada; Otto Eckstein, *Public Finance* (1964); J. A. Maxwell, *Financing State and Local Governments* (1965); Joint Economic Committee, U.S. Congress, *The Federal Tax System: Facts and Problems* (1964). (W. W. HR.)

**TAXODIACEAE,** a small but very important family of cone-bearing plants, including some of the largest trees known. The California redwood and the other American and Oriental genera are important timber trees. Many species are planted for ornament.

The genera customarily recognized are: *Sciadopitys* (umbrella pine), *Sequoiadendron* (big tree), *Sequoia* (coast redwood), *Metasequoia* (dawn redwood), *Taxodium* (bald cypress), *Glyptostrobus, Cryptomeria* (Japanese cedar or redwood), *Athrotaxis, Taiwania,* and *Cunninghamia.* All occur in the Northern Hemisphere in America, Asia, or both, except the genus *Athrotaxis* from Tasmania. The trees have scale-like or needlelike leaves, often in frondlike branchlets.

ADAPTED FROM G. LAWRENCE, "TAXONOMY OF VASCULAR PLANTS," 1951, THE MACMILLAN COMPANY, NEW YORK

REPRESENTATIVE SPECIES OF THE FAMILY TAXODIACEAE

The staminate, or pollen-bearing, cones are solitary (terminal or axillary) or clustered; their spirally arranged scales bear three to nine pollen cases, or sporangia. The ovulate, or seed-bearing, cones are solitary and terminal on a branch and are composed of many spirally arranged scales fused more or less completely with the bract, which becomes thick and woody; their two to nine seeds are erect in some genera and inverted in others. Embryogeny in the family ranges from the extreme type of cleavage polyembryony in *Sciadopitys* to the rather advanced form in *Sequoia.* The number of seed leaves, or cotyledons, varies from two to eight. For details on structure and life cycles, *see* CONIFERS. (R. W. H.)

**TAXONOMY,** the science of classification in a broad sense, is usually restricted to biological classification and specifically to the classification of plants and animals. The term is derived from the Greek *taxis* ("arrangement") and *nomos* ("law"). Taxonomy is, therefore, the methodology and principles of systematic botany and zoology, and sets up arrangements of the kinds of plants and animals in hierarchies of superior and subordinate groups.

## CLASSIFICATION

**Taxonomic Categories.**—The major taxonomic categories, or taxa (sing. taxon), are the kingdoms Plantae and Animalia; however, some authors propose a third kingdom, Protista, for those organisms not clearly plant or animal under arbitrary criteria, such as bacteria, protozoa, slime molds, etc. (For the characters commonly used to distinguish plants from animals, *see* ANIMAL; and introductory paragraphs of PLANTS AND PLANT SCIENCE.) Main subordinate groups are successively the phylum (or division for plants), class, order, family, genus, and species.

In the following table the scientific "credentials" of a paramecium, a pine and a dog illustrate the seven basic (obligatory) taxonomic categories used to identify and classify organisms. Each lower taxon is part of the larger taxon that precedes it.

| | | | |
|---|---|---|---|
| Kingdom | Protista | Plantae | Animalia |
| Phylum | Protozoa | Tracheophyta | Chordata |
| Class | Ciliata | Pteropsida | Mammalia |
| Order | Holotricha | Coniferales | Carnivora |
| Family | Parameciidae | Pinaceae | Canidae |
| Genus | *Paramecium* | *Pinus* | *Canis* |
| Species | *Paramecium caudatum* (paramecium) | *Pinus nigra* (black or Austrian pine) | *Canis familiaris* (any breed of dog) |

In many cases need has arisen for a more precise definition of the taxonomic position of an organism to express a finer degree of relationship of the component groups. Traditionally, this has been effected by splitting the original taxa and then inserting a newly formed category; *e.g.,* it has been found necessary to insert super- or sub-categories, such as the subclass Gymnospermidae (or Gymnospermae) between Pteropsida and Coniferales in the plant column above, and the subphylum Vertebrata between Chordata and Mammalia in the animal column.

Here are expanded lists of the taxa that specialists in animal or plant systematics might use (together with the standard suffixes required or recommended for certain of them by the respective codes of nomenclature). Some of the ranks (including the "sub-" and "infra-" ones) are not required, and supplementary ones may be introduced if they do not create confusion or alter the sequence of the basic seven ranks (*see* above).

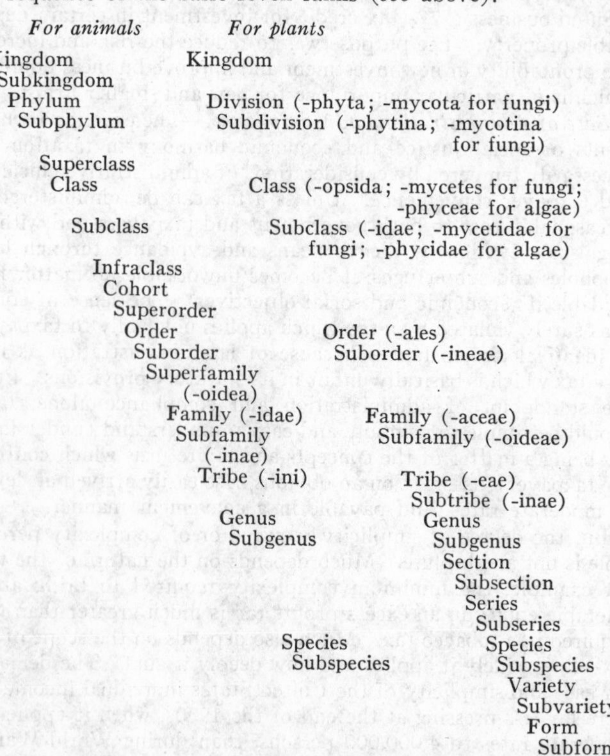

| *For animals* | *For plants* |
|---|---|
| Kingdom | Kingdom |
| Subkingdom | |
| Phylum | Division (-phyta; -mycota for fungi) |
| Subphylum | Subdivision (-phytina; -mycotina for fungi) |
| Superclass | |
| Class | Class (-opsida; -mycetes for fungi; -phyceae for algae) |
| Subclass | Subclass (-idae; -mycetidae for fungi; -phycidae for algae) |
| Infraclass | |
| Cohort | |
| Superorder | |
| Order | Order (-ales) |
| Suborder | Suborder (-ineae) |
| Superfamily (-oidea) | |
| Family (-idae) | Family (-aceae) |
| Subfamily (-inae) | Subfamily (-oideae) |
| Tribe (-ini) | Tribe (-eae) |
| | Subtribe (-inae) |
| Genus | Genus |
| Subgenus | Subgenus |
| | Section |
| | Subsection |
| | Series |
| | Subseries |
| Species | Species |
| Subspecies | Subspecies |
| | Variety |
| | Subvariety |
| | Form |
| | Subform |

Thus, a complete taxonomic identification of the dog would be:

Kingdom Animalia
Subkingdom Metazoa
Phylum Chordata
Subphylum Vertebrata
Superclass Tetrapoda
Class Mammalia
Subclass Theria
Infraclass Eutheria
Cohort Ferungulata
Superorder Ferae
Order Carnivora
Suborder Fissipeda
Superfamily Canoidea
Family Canidae
Subfamily Caninae
Tribe (none)
Genus *Canis*
Subgenus (none)
Species *Canis familiaris*
Subspecies (none)

In addition, breeders would add further breed designations, not considered true taxa, such as "collie," "German shepherd," and "cocker spaniel." (In some cases certain taxa are not used. In classifying the dog, for example, there is no need for tribe, subgenus, and subspecies designations; however, subkingdom and infraclass designations have been inserted.)

**Importance.**—The purpose of taxonomy is to develop a convenient and precise method of classifying knowledge that conforms to fundamental principles of biology. The role, then, of taxonomy, or systematics, is to rank categories in a hierarchical system. The function of nomenclature is merely to determine what an organism is to be called, what its scientific label should be. The need for naming the categories (many of which are recognized in common speech) produces an intimate relation between taxonomy and zoological and botanical nomenclature. The taxonomic name provides an index symbol to the biological literature containing all recorded information about the species or group.

Taxonomy depends on descriptive biology for most of its materials, but descriptions of plants and animals, and most alterations of the system of classification, are now made within the framework set up by the taxonomists of the past. This framework is the slow growth of two centuries of proposal and critique. Some taxonomic problems are subject to experiment, and taxonomy does not rest upon descriptive morphology alone. Structure, however, is an indication of subtle genetic, physiologic and growth processes, so much progress depends upon correlations of structural differences and similarities. In the pre-Darwinian era, the categories of the classificatory system (especially the species and genus) were thought of as reflecting some mystical relation to the ideas of the Creator. In the light of evolutionary theory (*see* EVOLUTION, ORGANIC), the classification of organisms tends toward a more and more exact reflection of their natural relations; *i.e.*, of their phylogeny (*see* ANIMALS, PHYLOGENY OF).

Modern taxonomy depends upon the reproduction of basic genetic homology (*see* HOMOLOGY) through evolutionary time together with modification by means of genetic mutation, recombination, reproductive isolation and natural selection. All life, so far as is known, is interrelated and genetically continuous in the past, and all life has undergone adaptive evolution and branching of taxonomic groups in geologic time. A few living species have not changed sufficiently to require taxonomic reassignment since Mesozoic times (ending more than 70,000,000 years ago), and several living genera are recognized from fossils in Triassic deposits (over 160,000,000 years old). One living genus of brachiopods (*Lingula*) is known from fossil shells of Ordovician age (about 350,000,000 years old).

**Method.**—The basic method of taxonomy is to compare and weigh the characteristics of the structure of plants and animals by the methods of comparative anatomy, and to interpret the major subdivisions in the light of comparative genetics, biochemistry, physiology, embryology, behaviour, ecology and geography. Systems of classification based upon a single set of characters, or drawn up from a single viewpoint, must be reinterpreted by the study of all available knowledge of the forms concerned.

Classification may begin purely as a matter of convenience, as was the case with early botanical classifications, which developed in association with the use of herbs and plant products in medicine. Such classification based on the more superficial distinctions rather than on the more fundamental similarities and differences is termed artificial. The distinction between an artificial and a natural classification was necessarily obscure in the century before Darwin.

The basic units of the classificatory system are readily recognizable kinds or species (*see* SPECIES: *Biological Species*). Some of these are distinguished in common knowledge, like the horse and the ass, or white oak and red oak. These instances also illustrate the first step in the process of classification, the grouping together of the various single-hoofed animals related to the horse (horse, ass and zebra) as the horse genus, *Equus*, and similarly the grouping of acorn-bearing trees into the oak genus, *Quercus*. By the simple device of combining the name of the genus with that of the species, the resulting names indicate the relationships and allow for additional species to be included when discovered. The technical scheme of generic and specific names in Latin, established by Linnaeus in the mid-18th century, has proved satisfactory and has in fact greatly stimulated the exploration of the world for the distinguishable kinds of plants and animals.

The merit of the Linnaean system lies in its suitability for continued correction, as well as expansion, in the light of increasing knowledge, without loss of its essential character. A large proportion of our knowledge of plants and animals comes to be correlated with the system of classification. The amplification and correction of the classification is a continuing active function of taxonomic research.

**Species and Genera Concepts.**—Definition of species as "an evolved (and probably evolving), genetically distinctive, reproductively isolated, natural population" is analytical, practical and understandable in the light of biological theory. Different species populations, whether sexual or asexual, have different genetic characters that may be detected by quantitative incidence of genes, qualitatively different genes, polygenic characters, or chromosomal changes in arrangement and numbers, all of which are reflected in the structure or the living activity of the component individuals.

It is estimated that more than 300,000 plant species and more than 1,000,000 animal species have been named. Descriptions of newly discovered species add between 15,000 and 20,000 each year. Over half of the known species of plants and animals are insects (class Insecta), and about one-third of all known species of animals are beetles (order Coleoptera). There is probably no single species of living or extinct plant or animal that is of no importance to man, either economically or for his basic understanding of organic nature.

As the knowledge about the variability of species increased, and when species began to be studied as populations, it was realized that the collecting of specimens constitutes only a method of sampling. A subordinate category, the subspecies, was established for series of organisms only partially reproductively isolated and often connected by transitional (or intergrading) populations.

Geographic gradients of variation, either uniform or separated by "steps," as topographic, climatic or other barriers reduce genetic exchange, form an important aspect of variation within species. Such gradients of variation are termed clines, and those in which there are interruptions or irregularities are referred to as step-clines. To distinguish as named subspecies the segments of a uniform variation gradient (particularly of a single character) appears to be fallacious. The segments of a sloping step-cline, however, may correspond exactly to a series of subspecies defined on other grounds.

The subspecies of zoological systematics is defined most often on a geographic and ecologic basis, and is derived from the Linnaean concept of variety subordinate to the species. Botanists have generally used "variety" in the same sense as zoologists use "subspecies," although the International Code of Botanical Nomenclature (*see* below) provides for usage of both subspecies and variety (*varietas*), a refinement many botanists find useful in the analysis of variations and evolutionary process. The Botanical Code also governs names of forms (*formae*), usually more or less sporadic but distinctive phases of a species (or subspecies, or variety) that occur without distinct geographic distribution.

Turning again to the species level, a most important clarification of the concept lies in the recognition that purely morphological definition must be subordinated to the concept that the species is composed of populations in which variability is inherent. The "closet naturalist" (without experience with living populations in their natural habitat) was exposed to the fallacy of describing variant individuals as species. Much of modern taxonomic investigation is occupied in the re-evaluation of the work of earlier taxonomists by means of more adequate collections, anatomical study, and concepts from the fields of genetics, embryology, physiology, biochemistry, ecology, psychology and geography.

Re-examination on the basis of larger collections (*i.e.*, a representative sample) may unite a whole series of supposedly distinct forms into one, or may separate distinct forms that had long been included in a single variable species. A few species have now been subjected to comprehensive genetic analysis, especially among the fruit flies of the genus *Drosophila,* and such analysis throws much light on taxonomic problems.

The morphological characteristics distinguishing genera are ordinarily (but not necessarily) more sharply defined than those distinguishing species, and the distinctions between genera are regarded as having an origin more remote in time than those between their included species. Thus the concept of the genus comes to have especial importance in paleontology (*q.v.*). The genetic and biochemical reality of the genus or other more inclusive taxonomic category is attested by instances in which one species of parasite, symbiote or predator is associated exclusively with several species within a single genus, or several genera within a single family.

So many genera are familiar in ordinary thought and language, like the oaks (*Quercus*), the maples (*Acer*), the cats (*Felis*), some of the squirrels (*Sciurus*), etc., that there should be no difficulty in the wider application of the concept of the genus as a natural group of related species. Definition of genera by means of characters thought to be of generic value may lead to an arbitrary and unnatural assortment of species. The synthetic assortment of known species into their evident groups, as if they were building blocks, thus becomes an extremely important check on generic classification. It has been discovered that characteristics suitable for the definition of genera in one group may be useful only in the distinction of species in another. When the number of species of a genus is large, these may fall into subordinate groups, which are referred to as subgenera. When a single species has a number of sharply distinctive characters separating it from a related group of species within a genus, it may be placed in a monotypic genus by itself.

Study of fossil remains of both plants and animals obviously introduces the dimension of time into variation, and this affects all of the categories, and would complicate the distinction of the groups of lower rank even more were it not for the fact that the interruptions in the paleontological record supply convenient gaps between species and genera. As paleontological data accumulate, important modifications of the classification of the higher groups become necessary (*see* below).

Geographic series of subspecies, connected by intergradation where they meet, or similar series with overlapping variation (as on chains of islands), are matched by series of geographically representative but fully distinct species. Ecological differences in the habitats of the component members of such series has led to local adaptation. When former geographically separated species have been brought together by a breakdown of the barriers between them, the two species may form a hybrid population, one species may eliminate its competing relative, or each may occupy different ecological niches in the same region. Ernst Mayr clarifies this problem by the distinction of species as sympatric, if their areas of distribution overlap, and allopatric, if their geographic ranges are distinct.

**Higher Categories.**—Just as well-known sharply defined species and readily recognizable genera serve to introduce the words "species" and "genus" in the more precise sense of taxonomy, common knowledge is reflected in the language for some of the larger divisions at the other end of the system of classification. The primary division, into the plant and animal kingdoms, appears in various languages. A few groups, like the sponges, mollusks, insects, birds and ferns, correspond rather precisely with the more exact zoological and botanical categories.

The taxonomy of the higher groups may be pursued analytically, beginning at the top and searching for the successive subdivisions of the kingdoms, or it may be studied by the synthetic method, beginning with the more factually defined groups nearer the bottom of the scale, and especially with the genera. The arrangement of the groups above the species level has been improved by additional information from many sources, particularly from paleontology, comparative anatomy, embryology and ecology. Related taxonomic groups of whatever rank may be presumed to share varying degrees of genetic identity by means of descent from common ancestry, and the ranking of taxonomic categories is at least roughly correlated with the comparative number and complexity of shared homologous characters.

The difference between an artificial and a natural classification of the higher groups rests primarily on the distinction between analogy and homology. The discernment of both homology and analogy in the structures of animals closely or remotely related forms the contribution of comparative anatomy to taxonomy. Because homologues and analogues may be associated in the same structure, the practical distinction may be far from simple. As wings, the wings of a bird and of a bat are analogous and not homologous; *i.e.,* they must be presumed to have arisen independently and not one from the other. As fore-limbs, the wings of a bird and those of a bat are plainly homologous, as they are also with the arm of man or the foreleg of an elephant, and support other evidence as to the relation of these several forms within the subphylum Vertebrata. In a broad sense, homology may be of quite a different type, like the correspondence between the alternating generations of ferns and flowering plants so brilliantly demonstrated by W. F. Hofmeister.

Homology of structures predicates the common inheritance of the characters under consideration, while independently derived analogous structures that resemble each other are said to be convergent (*i.e.,* the wings of birds and insects). Independently derived functional adaptive evolution of a basically homologous character (*i.e.,* the stiff tail feathers of woodpeckers and creepers), or independently evolved vestiges of a formerly adapted homologous structure (*i.e.,* the reduced eyes of cave fishes and cave salamanders), are often referred to as examples of parallel evolution.

The successive subordination of the series of groups, with steadily increasing number of the lower categories in most types (not in all) is reflected in the familiar comparison with a branching tree, with its trunk, main branches, smaller branches and finally twigs. Actually when the major groups are traced backward in the light of paleontology, the origins prove to be remote in time and apparently close together, and one is tempted to write of a phylogenetic "selaginella" or "fernclump" rather than of a "tree." Thus all of the main groups of living mammals trace back to the Early Tertiary or Late Cretaceous, and most of the principal groups of animals, the phyla, appear in the earliest known fossil-bearing strata of Cambrian age approximately 550,000,000 years old.

The exact relations of branch to branch or of branch to trunk are often unknown, being for the most part lost in the imperfections of the paleontological record. There are accordingly numerous groups at every level in the classification that are regarded as equivalent, and much effort has been expended to make them reasonably so. It may be pointed out that much difference of opinion over taxonomic groups in general applies to their rank in the hierarchy rather than to their validity as definable groups.

Many of the intermediate categories, especially the orders and families, are essentially the resultant of evolutionary specialization in a single direction (like the orders for the ichthyosaurs or whales, or the family of sea snakes). A different type of order or family is represented by a group that retains (or reacquires) the capacity for divergence into several major types of environment (*i.e.*, terrestrial, subterranean, arboreal and aquatic), and whose members thus compete with a wide variety of other animal types for specific ecological niches. Examples are supplied by the order Rodentia, the Saurischian dinosaurs, or the weasel family, the Mustelidae. Thus the adaptable or pliant group is often sharply distinguished from the specialized or end group. This involves a generalization as to the "irreversibility of evolution." Complex identical genetic patterns never originate twice nor, if lost, ever appear again in evolutionary history. Parallel mutations of genes and chromosomes may be repeated, but almost all taxonomic characters are genetically far more complex. Still another example of nonequivalent categories is evident in the difference between the grades "order" and "family" in an ancestral group like the Reptilia, and a derived group such as the Mammalia.

A major problem is introduced by paleontology in groups in which the evidence of ancestral approximation (at the point of divergence of the branches of the phylogenetic tree) has been discovered. The various genera close to the point of origin may either be associated with their later derived and more distinctive descendants, in a vertical classification, or with the primitive forms of the other branches to which they may be more closely similar in actual morphology, in a horizontal classification. This antithesis of phylogenetic and morphological definition of groups is notably exemplified by the Early Tertiary ancestry of horses, rhinoceroses and tapirs. In both types of classification, the more inclusive taxonomic categories are monophyletic and are presumed to have originated from a single ancestral species.

The tendency to give equal importance to all comparative characters of organisms often leads to bias and to errors of judgment. Because the order of taxonomic classification is based upon homology through descent, principles of evolution are both substantiated by taxonomic data and, in turn, may be used for taxonomic interpretation. For example, it is possible to distinguish homology from analogy and both from fortuitous resemblance, strongly adaptive from weakly adaptive or nonadaptive characters, primitive from derivative characters, rapidly evolving from slowly evolving characters, persistent conservative characters from labile changing characters, qualitative from quantitative characters, progressively functional characters from regressed vestiges, relatively complex from relatively simple characters, and individually acquired characters from hereditary characters.

**Relationship to Other Sciences.**—Since some classification is essential for the establishment of scientific botany and zoology, taxonomy in its origins is one of the most elementary of disciplines. The record-keeping function of taxonomy affords an essential continuing service to all of the biological sciences. As these have grown to maturity, they have returned to draw problems and insights from the parent science, and the parent taxonomy has been infused with new interest from the light thrown upon its material and its categories by comparative genetics, embryology, biochemistry, physiology, ecology, biogeography and behaviour. The synthetic science of ecology, growing out of the older less critical natural history, depends implicitly on sound development of systematic botany and zoology.

Two promising approaches to classification are chemical and numerical taxonomy. Although both approaches derive from long-standing observations, recent technological advances have generated renewed interest in them. Chemical taxonomy has been revitalized by the development of refined biochemical methodology and instrumentation. It attempts to establish relationships on the basis of chemical similarities among organisms. Numerical taxonomy ("taximetrics") is the numerical evaluation of the degrees of likeness of characters among organisms and the consigning of types to taxonomic categories on the basis of the data. Computers programmed with information regarding chemical and physical analysis, observable characters, and other data can provide estimations of the degree of relatedness of organisms. The technique is of course only as valid as the program devised by taxonomists.

Future taxonomic progress may be expected by the discovery of new species, both living and fossil; relating taxonomic data to investigations in other biological sciences; further understanding of evolutionary processes; development of new analytical techniques in mathematics, morphology and basic life processes; and also by verifying the facts and interpretations of past taxonomists as well as weeding out past errors of fact and theory. Basic research in taxonomy continues to have important effects in the applied sciences of medicine and agriculture. (K. P. S.; A. E. E.)

## NOMENCLATURE

Nomenclature plays an important but restricted role in taxonomy, as an essentially legalistic system for the application of scientific names to categories recognized in taxonomic classifications. It is distinct from taxonomic judgment as to what the entities are and how they should be classified (*see* above); and it is distinct from identification, or the association of an organism with a recognized taxonomic entity.

No binding rules can be established for such matters as the delimitation of a species or the evaluation of a given characteristic. But internationally accepted rules do exist for the application of names, once the taxonomic judgment has been made. A taxonomist often has a problem deciding the rank (level in the taxonomic hierarchy) or diagnostic limits (circumscription) of a recognized entity. The differing opinions among biologists, depending upon their personal beliefs, are thus often reflected in differing names for the same organisms. Codes of nomenclature have been devised by popular consent among biologists to specify the accepted hierarchy of categories and to state how, when an organism is classified in a particular way, certain regulations apply in selecting (or providing) the proper scientific name for it.

**Codes.**—There are three principal codes of nomenclature, adopted by international biological congresses. They are abbreviated in this article as follows: ICBN, *International Code of Botanical Nomenclature* (*The International Code of Nomenclature for Cultivated Plants* supplements the ICBN with provisions for names, not in Latin form, for cultivated varieties of plants ["cultivars"]); ICNB, *International Code of Nomenclature of Bacteria;* ICZN, *International Code of Zoological Nomenclature.*

Most of the detailed articles and recommendations of the codes amplify and elucidate four basic principles regarding scientific names: (1) The name of a species—the basic unit of classification—must conform to the binomial ("binary" of the ICBN and the ICNB; "binominal" of the ICZN) system (*see* below) of nomenclature—the practice, first consistently and extensively used by Linnaeus, of designating a species by a two-word scientific name. (2) The name must have been properly published, with a description of the organism. (3) The name must have priority; *i.e.*, the same name must not previously have been used for another organism in the same kingdom (or, in the case of bacteria, for algae, fungi, protozoans, or viruses), and it must be (with certain limitations) the first name applied to the organism. (4) The name must be standardized in its application by a particular sample, or type, with which the name is permanently associated.

*The Binomial System.*—The name of a species consists of the name of the genus plus a specific epithet (ICBN, ICNB) or specific name (ICZN). Names of species not published in accord with this system, or published in works in which this system is not consistently employed, are ruled inacceptable. Names of genera and species may be derived from any source or may be arbitrarily composed; they may not be rejected merely because they are inappropriate.

*Publication.*—All nomenclatural codes require publication of new names by acceptable methods of printing intended for permanent record and accessible to scientists. Distribution of microfilms, specimen labels, or certain other materials, especially ephemeral ones, does not constitute publication by present rules. In establishing priority (*see* below), the date of publication is the actual date of availability or distribution—not necessarily the date printed in a work, if there is evidence that actual publication was on a different date. Various conditions are specified in the codes to validate publication; chief among these for botanists is the requirement that names of new taxa of plants (not including bacteria and fossils) must (since certain dates) be accompanied by a description or diagnosis in Latin (or by a reference to a previously published Latin description or diagnosis). A diagnosis is a brief description emphasizing the distinguishing or distinctive characters of a taxon. The description of a new species or lower taxon of fossil plants or algae must be accompanied by an illustration or figure. New names for animals and bacteria need at present be accompanied only by a description (in any language) or reference to a previously published description.

*Priority.*—The principle of priority does not apply above the rank of family in any of the codes. The ICZN and the ICNB do not formally recognize any rank below that of subspecies, while the ICBN recognizes variety and form as categories of lower rank. Priority is a simple means of insuring that each taxon bears a unique name. If two or more taxa (described as separate species, varieties, genera, etc.) are considered by a taxonomist to be the same, he uses the oldest of the pertinent names. If different parts, or sexes, or stages in the life history of an organism have received different names before recognition that they belonged to the same taxon, the oldest name is to be used. In actual application, many refinements in priority have proved desirable.

In addition to the requirements for proper publication of a name, a number of other restrictions on absolute priority exist, principally the following.

Starting points: No name is acceptable if the date of its publication was earlier than that of certain specified works. For most plants and bacteria, the starting point is Linnaeus' *Species Plantarum* (first ed., 1753); later works are designated for some algae, fungi, and mosses, and for all fossils. For animals, nomenclature begins with Linnaeus' *Systema Naturae* (10th ed., 1758).

Tautonyms: The ICBN and the ICNB do not allow tautonyms, names in which the specific epithet is identical with the generic name (*e.g., Linaria linaria*).

Conservation: The codes provide for action to retain ("conserve") certain names as exceptions to otherwise strict application of the rules. Botanists may refer names of families or genera (not species) to appropriate committees for possible recommendation for conservation to an International Botanical Congress. Bacteriologists may refer any name for conservation or rejection to a Judicial Commission for provisional action pending decision by an International Congress for Microbiology. Zoologists may refer any name to the International Commission on Zoological Nomenclature, which is empowered to suspend almost any provision of the ICZN and to annul or validate names in the interests of stability, subject to review by an International Congress of Zoology; a name that has been unused for more than 50 years (but is discovered to be an older synonym) is to be referred to the Commission and not resurrected unless the Commission so directs.

Rank: The ICBN provides that a name has priority only within its rank. In contrast, the ICZN makes no distinction for purposes of priority between names published for species or subspecies; for genera or subgenera; or for tribes, subfamilies, families, or superfamilies.

*The Type Method.*—One of the more recent achievements of the codes has been universal acceptance of the type method. A nomenclatural type is that constituent element of a taxon to which the name of the taxon is permanently attached. The nomenclatural type of a species (or lower taxon) is a specimen; the nomenclatural type of a genus is a species; for a family, it is a genus; etc. A name cannot be used in a sense that would exclude its type. Thus, the name of a species applies to its type specimen, plus all other individuals deemed to be of the same species; a family always includes its type genus, plus all other genera deemed to belong to that family; and so forth. The nomenclatural type of a family (or subfamily, etc.) is the genus upon which its name is based (*e.g., Hesperia* is the type genus of the subfamily Hesperiinae of the family Hesperiidae).

The concept of "type" is strictly a nomenclatural device, and the adjective "typical" in this connection does not have any necessary reference to what is the common or most representative element of a taxon. The usefulness of this device in taxonomic practice is considerable: for example, if two or more described taxa are deemed to be the same, it is basically because their types are deemed to be the same—and the law of priority requires use of the oldest name. If a described taxon is deemed to consist of two or more elements, the name remains with that element that includes its type, and the newly segregated elements require new names. If one is in doubt as to the application of a name, the type is the ultimate authority; the name applies at least to that entity. The ICZN requires that the type species be stated when a new name for a genus is published. The ICBN requires designation of the type for any taxon of the rank of family or below. The ICNB provides for designation of a type strain (or living culture) for a species or subspecies.

Requirements for designation of types are comparatively recent, and in much of the older literature types are not clearly designated. The codes provide for selection of types when the original author did not specify them. Under certain conditions, a type may be a description or figure. A typical or "nominate" (ICZN) subdivision of a genus or species bears the same name unaltered; *e.g.,* the subgenus of *Oenothera* that includes the type species of the genus is subgenus *Oenothera;* the variety of *Bromus inermis* that includes the type specimen of the species is *Bromus inermis* var. *inermis.* (Botanists now require that the ultimate rank must be stated, whether subspecies, variety, or form; *"Bromus inermis inermis"* is not proper style.) It is not good practice to contrast a subspecies or variety with "the species," for that is actually contrasting a part with the whole; one may, however, contrast a segregate with the typical or nominate element.

**Stabilization.**—An oft-stated aim of nomenclature is to arrive at stability and universality in scientific names. Changes in names often result from application of the codes, as prior names are discovered in the literature, as the type method is applied, or as names are conserved. Ideally, ultimate stability would eventually be reached if codes did not change. However, changes in name also result from changes in taxonomic opinion, about which the codes can say nothing. The ICBN authorizes the use of eight family names, sanctioned by long usage, as alternatives to names for those families based on the name of a type genus and ending in *-aceae* (*e.g.,* Labiatae or Lamiaceae for the mints, Gramineae or Poaceae for the grasses). With this stated exception, a taxon can have only one correct scientific name—in a given position, rank, and circumscription. The correct name of the crab apple is *Malus prunifolia,* unless one believes it to belong to the same genus as the pear, in which case the correct name is *Pyrus prunifolia.* Whether apples and pears belong to the same genus is a question of circumscription at the generic level, which affects the position of the species involved. Whether a taxon should be considered a variety or subspecies of another species, or a "good" species in its own right, is a question of rank. Taxonomic judgments such as these cannot be legislated by any code. No biologist is required to accept the judgment of another as to the classification of a taxon if he is otherwise convinced by the evidence. Listing of synonyms (different names for the same organism) may not always be agreed upon. As more is learned about classification, more changes in names will occur, reflecting improved taxonomic understanding. There can never, for this reason if for no other, be permanent stability in all names without permanent sterility in taxonomic research.

**Style and Conventions.**—Scientific names are always treated as if they were Latin regardless of their actual origin. Specific epithets must, if adjectival in form, agree in gender with the generic name, which is a substantive (noun) in the nominative singular (*e.g., Rosa alba*). When the form is not adjectival, such words are either genitives (possessives, as *Papilio bairdii*) or substantives in apposition with the name of the genus (*e.g., Verbascum thapsus*). The name of the genus always begins with a capital letter (much popular newspaper usage notwithstanding). The second component of a species name begins with a lower-case letter. The ICBN does permit—but does not recommend—beginning specific epithets with a capital letter if they are derived from the name of a person or are vernacular or old generic names (*e.g., Verbascum Thapsus*), but the ICZN and the ICNB require that the specific epithet be lower cased. Names of genera and lower categories are customarily printed in italic type, and may be followed (in Roman type) by the name (or abbreviation) of the author who first validly described the taxon; his name is placed in parentheses if the rank (ICBN and ICNB) or position has been changed, and the ICBN and ICNB require (and ICZN permits) adding the name of the author responsible for the change, as a bibliographic aid. All codes include rules and recommendations on such matters as spelling, endings, correction of errors, and latinization, in efforts to promote uniformity and simplicity without doing too much violence to classical principles.

**Literature.**—The worker in nomenclature requires extensive library facilities, covering over two centuries of biological literature, to determine the usage of names, the citation of previous works, the possible mention of types, the validity of publication and availability of names, and so forth. Some use has been made of computers to sort and retrieve nomenclatural information, and such methods will doubtless increase in the preparation of synonymies and the detection of homonyms (identical names applied to different organisms), as the literature becomes increasingly vast. While computers cannot make judgments on such matters as taxonomic synonymy or validity of publication, they can aid in indexing and rapid manipulation of the data given them by the taxonomist. (E. G. V.)

BIBLIOGRAPHY.—*Classification:* R. E. Alston and B. L. Turner, *Biochemical Systematics* (1963); L. D. Benson, *Plant Classification* (1957) and *Plant Taxonomy: Methods and Principles* (1962); R. E. Blackwelder, *Classification of the Animal Kingdom* (1963) and *Taxonomy* (1967); P. H. Davis and V. H. Heywood, *Principles of Angiosperm Taxonomy* (1963); O. Hedberg (ed.), *Systematics of To-day* (1958); V. H. Heywood, *Plant Taxonomy* (1967); V. H. Heywood and J. McNeill (eds.), *Phenetic and Phylogenetic Classification* (1964); E. Mayr, E. G. Linsley, and R. L. Usinger, *Methods and Principles of Systematic Zoology* (1953); Lord Rothschild, *A Classification of Living Animals* (1961); E. T. Schenk and others, *Procedure in Taxonomy* (1956); G. G. Simpson, *Principles of Animal Taxonomy* (1961); R. R. Sokal and P. H. A. Sneath, *Principles of Numerical Taxonomy* (1963).

*Nomenclature: International Code of Botanical Nomenclature* adopted by the Tenth International Botanical Congress Edinburgh, August 1964 (1966—currently revised and published at 5-year intervals); *International Code of Nomenclature for Cultivated Plants 1961* (1961); "International Code of Nomenclature of Bacteria," *Internatl. Jour. Syst. Bact.*, 16:459–490 (1966); *International Code of Zoological Nomenclature* adopted by the XV International Congress of Zoology (ed. 2, 1964); L. H. Bailey, *How Plants Get Their Names* (1933; reprinted 1963); W. I. Follett, "New Precepts of Zoological Nomenclature," *AIBS Bull.* 13 (3): 14–18 (1963); F. Raymond Fosberg, "Subspecies and Variety," *Rhodora*, 44:153–157 (1942); Theodore Savory, *Naming the Living World* (1962).

**TAY,** the longest river in Scotland, has a catchment area of 2,400 sq.mi. (6,216 sq.km.) covering nearly all Perth and parts of Angus and Argyll. Its discharge is among the highest in the United Kingdom. The headwaters are at about 2,500 ft. (762 m.) on the north side of Ben Lui, east of Dalmally. Several small streams gather to form the Fillan Water, which, after passing through Lochs Dochart and Iubhair, is known as the River Dochart. The river then assumes a northeasterly direction for many miles among Highland hills of 2,000–4,000 ft.; it then enters the head of Loch Tay along with the River Lochay. On leaving Loch Tay, the largest lake in Perth, it receives the River Lyon, and about 5 mi. (8 km.) downstream of Aberfeldy it curves eastward to Logierait, where there enters, as a left-bank tributary, the flow from the great Garry-Tummel System, a main stream receiving the Rannoch-Tummel. The joint stream flows south-southeast to Dunkeld, receives the Highland River Bran on the right bank, and turns east-southeast through the gap between Birnam Hill and Newtyle Hill into fertile lowlands. It turns southwest at the great elbow at the Isla junction near Cargill and southeast once more near the junction with the Almond. After flowing through a gap in the low hills continuing the line of the Sidlaws, on which the city of Perth stands, the river turns east to enter the Firth of Tay at the confluence with the Earn. From Newburgh in Fife, the firth runs northeast past Dundee to open out into the North Sea off Buddon Ness in Angus.

The firth broadens gently to 3 mi. upstream of Dundee, narrows to 1 mi. between Broughty Ferry and Tayport, and finally broadens to 3 mi. near its mouth, 120 mi. (193 km.) from the headwaters of Ben Lui. Dundee is accessible to shipping at all stages of the tide. Small vessels can reach Newburgh and even Perth, but navigation is impeded by shifting sandbanks. (A. T. A. L.)

**TAY, LOCH,** the largest lake in Perth, Scot., in Breadalbane, is approximately in the middle of the county. It is a glacially excavated ribbon lake about 355 ft. (108 m.) above mean sea level and generally from 90 to 600 ft. in depth. It is 14½ mi. (23 km.) long from Killin—where the Rivers Lochay and Dochart converge at the head—to Kenmore, where the River Tay takes egress at the foot. The breadth is from just under half a mile to just over 1 mi. The spring salmon fishing is well known. Near Kenmore a small wooded islet contains the tumbled ruins of a priory founded in 1121 by Alexander I in memory of his queen, Sibylla, who was buried there. (A. T. A. L.)

**TAYLOR, (JAMES) BAYARD** (1825–1878), U.S. author known primarily for his lively travel narratives and for his translation into English of Goethe's *Faust*, was born in Chester County, Pa., Jan. 11, 1825. He was a restless student at Bolmar's Academy in West Chester, Pa., and the academy at Unionville, Pa., before he was apprenticed to a printer at the age of 17. In 1844 his first book, a volume of verse, *Ximena*, was published. He then made an arrangement with the *Saturday Evening Post* and the *United States Gazette* to finance a trip abroad in return for publication rights to letters describing his travels. His experiences in Europe resulted in the extremely popular *Views Afoot* (1846). In 1847 he settled in New York and began a lucrative career in journalism. *Eldorado* (1850) recounted his trials as a *Tribune* correspondent in the 1849 California gold rush. He continued his trips to remote parts of the world—to the Orient, to Africa, to Russia—and became renowned as something of a modern Marco Polo. In 1862 he became secretary of the U.S. legation at St. Petersburg, and in 1878, shortly before his death, became U.S. minister to Germany. He died on Dec. 19, 1878.

Some works of this later period were *The Poet's Journal* (1862); the novels *Hannah Thurston* (1863), *John Godfrey's Fortunes* (1864), and *The Story of Kennett* (1866); and the translation of *Faust* (1870–71), which remains his best-known work. Although greatly lauded in his day, Taylor was undistinguished as a novelist and poet, being at his best in his travel narratives and in an occasional richly textured poem, such as those in *Poems of the Orient* (1855). Collected editions of Taylor's poetical and dramatic works appeared in 1880.

BIBLIOGRAPHY.—M. H. Taylor and H. E. Scudder, *Life and Letters of Bayard Taylor* (1884); A. H. Smythe, *Bayard Taylor* (1896); Richard Cary, *Genteel Circle: Bayard Taylor and His New York Friends* (1952).

**TAYLOR, BROOK** (1685–1731), English mathematician, noted for his contributions to the development of the calculus, was born at Edmonton in Middlesex on Aug. 18, 1685. He was educated at St. John's College, Cambridge, and studied mathematics under John Machin and John Keill. He obtained in 1708 a remarkable solution of the problem of the centre of oscillation, which, however, remained unpublished until May 1714, when his claim to priority was disputed by Johann (Jean) Bernoulli.

Taylor's *Methodus incrementorum directa et inversa* (1715) added a new branch to the higher mathematics, now designated the calculus of finite differences. Among other ingenious applications, he used it to determine the form of movement of a vibrating string, by him first successfully reduced to mechanical principles. The same work contained the celebrated formula known as Taylor's theorem, the importance of which remained unrecognized until 1772, when J. L. Lagrange realized its powers and termed it the basic principle of differential calculus.

In his essay on *Linear Perspective* (1715) Taylor set forth the basic principles of the art in an original and more general form than any of his predecessors; but the work suffered from the brevity and obscurity that affected most of his writings.

Taylor was elected a fellow of the Royal Society early in 1712, sat in the same year on the committee for adjudicating the claims of Newton and Leibniz, and acted as secretary to the society from 1714 to 1718. From 1715 his studies took a philosophical and religious bent. Taylor died on Dec. 29, 1731, at Somerset House, London, and was buried at St. Ann's, Soho. *See* also TAYLOR'S THEOREM.

**TAYLOR, DAVID WATSON** (1864–1940), U.S. marine architect, built the first ship-model testing establishment in the

United States, at the Washington (D.C.) navy yard, and formulated certain basic principles of ship design. Born in Louisa County, Va., March 4, 1864, he graduated from the U.S. Naval Academy in Annapolis, Md., and the Royal Naval College, Greenwich, Eng., with the highest grades made until then at those institutions.

Beginning in 1899, Taylor undertook the first studies to find what characteristics of a ship hull governed its water resistance. By a methodical series of extensive proportions, internationally known since 1910 as the Taylor Standard series, he determined the actual effect of changing those characteristics and thus made it possible to estimate in advance the resistance of a ship of given proportions. His *The Speed and Power of Ships* (1910), which sets forth this knowledge, is still an informative publication in its field.

From 1915 until 1921, Rear Admiral Taylor was responsible for the design and construction of surface and submarine vessels and of aircraft for the U.S. Navy, including the first plane to fly the Atlantic. He made many other contributions to aeronautics in 15 years of service on the National Advisory Committee for Aeronautics. (H. E. Ss.)

**TAYLOR, EDWARD** (*c.* 1645–1729), now generally considered the foremost poet in colonial America (his poems having remained in manuscript until 1939), was born in Leicestershire, Eng., in or near Coventry, probably of a dissenting family. Unwilling to subscribe to the required oath of conformity because of his staunch adherence to Congregational principles, he gave up schoolteaching, emigrated to New England, and was immediately admitted by Pres. Increase Mather as a sophomore at Harvard College. After his graduation in 1671, he was settled as minister in the frontier village of Westfield, Mass., where he remained until his death. Small in stature, he was remembered by his contemporaries for his intensity of nature and his personal charm. He married twice and became the father of 13 children, most of whom he outlived. His grandson Ezra Stiles, president of Yale College during the American Revolution, inherited most of his manuscripts and the greater part of his 200-vol. library.

By his express desire, Taylor's 400-page quarto manuscript "Poetical Works" was not published by his heirs. It came into the possession of Yale in 1883 by the gift of a descendant, and the best of Taylor's verse was published in 1939. The important poems fall into two broad divisions. "God's Determinations Touching His Elect" is an extended verse sequence thematically setting forth the grace and majesty of God as a drama of sin and redemption. The "Sacramental Meditations," about 200 in number, were written over a period of 44 years, from 1682 to 1725. Taylor described them as "Preparatory Meditations Before My Approach to the Lord's Supper."

The achievement of Taylor is his adroitness in fusing an ecstatic religious vision with earthly realities by means of homely diction and imagery drawn from the daily round of Puritan life. Central to all his poems is the typical metaphysical mode: the extravagant trope and the association of image and idea that is intended by its tension to draw poetic sparks.

*The Poetical Works of Edward Taylor* (1939), edited by T. H. Johnson, is a selection of poems, together with a biographical sketch, critical introduction, and notes. *The Poems of Edward Taylor* (1960), edited by Donald E. Stanford, is a comprehensive edition, including the complete text of the "Meditations."

(T. H. Jn.)

**TAYLOR, FREDERICK WINSLOW** (1856–1915), U.S. engineer who laid the foundation for scientific industrial management, was born March 20, 1856, at Germantown, Pa. In 1875 he was apprenticed as patternmaker and machinist in a small Philadelphia firm. In 1880 or 1881, while employed as a gang boss at the Midvale Steel Company, he became convinced that a standard day's work on any operation should be measured. This conviction led him to undertake a series of careful experiments resulting in important achievements in two fields: in mechanical engineering, the discovery with Maunsel White of a new method of tempering tool steel, permitting metal-cutting operations at high speed (1898); and in the field of management, perfection of that system of shop management that later came to be known as scientific management. He introduced time-and-motion studies, as well as systems of incentive pay for labour. From 1893 to 1901, as consulting engineer in management for many industrial plants, Taylor forwarded the principles of scientific management. (*See* MANAGEMENT SCIENCES.) He died March 21, 1915, in Philadelphia.

Taylor's writings include *Notes on Belting* (1893); *The Adjustment of Wages to Efficiency* (1896); *Shop Management* (1903); *On the Art of Cutting Metals* (1906); and *The Principles of Scientific Management* (1911), reprinted in *Scientific Management* (1947).

*See* F. B. Copley, *Frederick W. Taylor, Father of Scientific Management* (1923); C. B. Thompson, *The Taylor System of Scientific Management* (1917).

**TAYLOR, JEREMY** (1613–1667), English clergyman and writer, represents the best of the religion and culture of the Anglican royalists during the period of the English Civil War, and his ornate prose is among the glories of the English language. He was baptized on Aug. 15, 1613, at Holy Trinity church, Cambridge, the son of Nathaniel Taylor, a barber. He was educated at the Perse school, made a sizar of Gonville and Caius college in 1626, given a junior fellowship in 1633, and ordained in the same year. When he was deputizing for his friend Thomas Risden as lecturer at St. Paul's in 1633, his eloquence and good looks made a sensation, and brought him to the notice of Archbishop Laud, who was greatly impressed, but considered him too young for immediate preferment. Two years later, by a stretch of authority, he presented Taylor to a fellowship at All Souls college, Oxford. A friendship with Francis a Santa Clara (Christopher Davenport), a learned Franciscan, led to an often repeated and always vigorously repudiated accusation that Taylor had a leaning toward the Church of Rome. In March 1638, William Juxon, bishop of London, presented him to the living of Uppingham, where he married Phoebe Langsdale on May 27. In the following November Taylor returned to Oxford to preach the annual Gunpowder plot sermon, the first of his published works. It is, in the main, a conventional attack on the recusants but some passages give promise of future greatness. In Nov. 1642 Taylor had left Uppingham and was with the king at Oxford, where he published his first important work, *Of the Sacred Order, and Offices of Episcopacy.* In it he assembles with persuasive skill most of the arguments then in circulation in favour of episcopacy, but adds little new. In 1643 he was made D.D. by royal decree and given the small living of Overstone, which he never visited. He next appears in Wales where he was taken prisoner with the royalist forces at Cardigan castle in 1645. On his release he joined the grammarian William Nicholson in setting up a school at Newton hall in Carmarthenshire, near Lord Carbery's seat at Golden Grove where he served as chaplain.

BY COURTESY OF THE WARDEN OF ALL SOULS COLLEGE, OXFORD. PHOTO, THOMAS-PHOTOS

JEREMY TAYLOR: DETAIL OF PORTRAIT IN THE COLLECTION OF ALL SOULS COLLEGE

The next ten years were the happiest, and the most fruitful, of Taylor's life. His literary genius was at its height. *The Liberty of Prophesying* (1647) is a noble plea for religious liberty to be granted to all whose principles would not lead to the overthrow of the state or destroy the foundations of the Christian faith. After the Restoration, the breadth of toleration pleaded for in the book caused Taylor some embarrassment and he is said to have made an effort to suppress it, but there is little doubt that it expressed his real beliefs though he was not always able to practise them. *The Great Exemplar* (1649) consists of discourses, meditations and prayers on "the life and death of the ever blessed

Jesus Christ." It is the earliest of his devotional works and must have shown him the direction in which his gifts could best be exercised. *The Rule and Exercises of Holy Living* (1650) and *The Rule and Exercises of Holy Dying* (1651) so clearly supplement each other that they are usually regarded as one book. They were written to help members of the Church of England who were deprived of a regular ministry by the disturbances of the Civil War, but their wisdom and beauty have made them popular with all denominations. *Holy Living* contains encouragement to the life of prayer, general directions for godly living and prayers and meditations suited to both these subjects. With illustrations drawn from the classical moralists and a wide range of other reading, as well as from Christian teaching, Taylor inculcates moderation, cheerfulness, contentment and reliance upon the divine goodness. By 1651 when he wrote *Holy Dying,* he had lost both his wife and his patroness, Lady Frances Carbery. He had been her spiritual director and close friend, and the oration which he delivered at her funeral is one of the finest in the English language. The first chapter of *Holy Dying* exhibits the full glory of Taylor's prose. The beauty of his language, the richness and variety of his fancy, match the nobility of his theme. Death is presented as an inevitable good for those who live and die as Christians. John Wesley owed much to these two books.

*Twenty-eight Sermons* (1651) and *Twenty-five Sermons* (1653) *Preached at Golden Grove* make up *Eniautos, a Course of Sermons for all the Sundaies of the Year* (1653). They are full of beautiful cadences and delicately wrought images. *The Real Presence and Spirituall of Christ in the Blessed Sacrament* (1654) attacked the doctrine of transubstantiation. *Unum Necessarium* (1655), a study of repentance intended as prolegomena to a work of casuistry which he had long been meditating, contained a repudiation of Calvinistic doctrines of original sin and predestination which plunged him into controversy with high churchmen and Presbyterians alike. *The Golden Grove* (1655), a manual of instruction and prayers, contained also *Festival Hymns,* a collection of not very successful poems in irregular verse.

Taylor had by this time become the spiritual counselor of the diarist, John Evelyn, who helped him with gifts of money. After two short imprisonments for his religious principles (1655), he left Golden Grove and lived at Mandinam, an estate in Wales belonging to Joanna Bridges whom he had recently married. Later he moved to London and ministered to scattered congregations of Anglican royalists, frequently visiting great houses in the country. *A Discourse of Friendship* (1657), written at the request of Mrs. Katherine Philips ("the Matchless Orinda"), is his only secular work. *A Collection of Offices* (1658), intended as a substitute for the proscribed Book of Common Prayer, shows his wide acquaintance with eastern liturgies. Taylor had become intimate with Edward, 3rd Viscount Conway, who offered him a chaplaincy on his large estates in Ulster. He went there in June 1658 and for the next two years was mainly occupied with *Ductor Dubitantium—a Great Instrument for the Determination of Cases of Conscience* (1660), dedicated to Charles II. It is vast both in bulk and learning, a maze of illustration and digression, but remains of value for its profound scholarship and as the first complete work of casuistry in English.

Taylor's reputation for unorthodoxy militated against an English appointment, which he would have much preferred, and he was made bishop of Down and Connor (1660), to which was added, in 1661, the administration of the diocese of Dromore. He was also made a member of the Irish privy council and vice-chancellor of Trinity college, Dublin. There he was instrumental in reconstituting the university after the disorders of the Civil War. In his diocese he worked equally hard, but was not happy. The Scots who had colonized Ulster were followed over by Presbyterian ministers who were resolutely hostile to episcopacy. Thirty-six of them were in possession of church livings, and these Taylor deprived after they had refused all his advances. He filled their places with men from England or of English extraction. At his first visitation (1661) he preached on *The Minister's Duty in Life and Doctrine,* the best of his post-Restoration sermons, in a style less elaborate than his earlier work. At the request of his brother bishops he wrote a *Dissuasive From Popery* (part i, 1664; part ii, 1667). Both are marred by overstatement and inaccurate quotation. *Chrisis Teleiotike* ("The Unction Which Perfecteth"; 1664) is the best study of confirmation to appear before the 19th century. Taylor died on Aug. 13, 1667, in Lisburn, of a fever caught while visiting a sick man. He was buried on Sept. 3 in Dromore cathedral, which he had himself rebuilt.

*The Whole Works of Jeremy Taylor* were edited, with a life, by Reginald Heber, 15 vol. (1822); there was a revised edition by C. Page Eden, 10 vol. (1847–54). *The Golden Grove, Selected Passages From the Sermons and Writings,* was edited by Logan Pearsall Smith, with a bibliography by R. Gathorne-Hardy (1930).

Humane, generous, impulsive, handsome, of great personal charm, Taylor was among the most lovable of men. His prose is filled with a joyous prodigality of beauty; in it he gave his genius full rein so that the sentences run on and on, gathering new beauty as they go, with complete indifference to orderliness or structure. In a learned age Taylor was one of the most learned and he poured all the wealth of his wide reading into his books, drawing perhaps most often upon the moralists of Greece and Rome. He was a close observer of nature and could describe with an inspired rapture the sheen on the breast of a dove, the groping tendrils of a vine or the petals of a newly opened rose. In spite of the vicissitudes of his life, his religious faith was of singular serenity and it is this which constitutes much of the charm of his devotional writings. He never threatens, but draws his reader to holiness by his own love of it. He has been accused of borrowing from other writers in his devotional books, but they are in fact entirely original. In controversy he was never at his best and in much of his other work he was apt to spoil his effects by overaccumulation of detail and superfluous argument.

As a theologian Taylor shared the Laudian love of beauty and order and respect for antiquity, but he was also influenced considerably by his contemporaries William Chillingworth and Henry More.

Bibliography.—The earliest authority on Taylor's life is *A Funeral Sermon Preached at the Obsequies of . . . Jeremy Lord Bishop of Down by George Rust,* which can be relied on. Anthony à Wood's *Athenae Oxonienses* (1691) and *State Papers, Charles II, Domestic and Irish,* add details of interest. F. R. Bolton, *The Caroline Tradition of the Church of Ireland* (1958), supplies some details of Taylor's Irish period. E. Gosse, *Jeremy Taylor* (1903), has useful comments on Taylor as a writer but must be used with caution as to fact. Coleridge admired Taylor greatly and references to him are scattered throughout his prose works, especially in *Notes on the English Divines,* ed. by Derwent Coleridge (1853), and *Literary Remains,* vol. 3 (1838). *See* also C. J. Stranks, *The Life and Writings of Jeremy Taylor* (1952).

(C. J. Ss.)

**TAYLOR, JOHN** (1578–1653), English pamphleteer and journalist, commonly called "the Water-Poet," was born at Gloucester, Aug. 24, 1578. He was sent to a grammar school but became, as he said, "mired in Latin accidence" and was apprenticed to a Thames waterman. He served in the Navy and saw action at Cadiz (1596) and Flores (1597). Returning to London, he worked as a waterman, held a semiofficial post at the Tower for some years and was an active member of the Watermen's Company. He increased his income and his fame by dedicating verses to noble patrons and by a series of extraordinary journeys, which he described entertainingly in oddly-titled pamphlets. With a companion as light-hearted as himself, he went from London to Queenborough, Kent, in a paper boat with two stockfish tied to canes for oars. He amused the court and the public, especially in his verbal battles with another eccentric traveler Thomas Coryate. *The Pennyles Pilgrimage . . . of John Taylor . . . on foot from London to Edenborough* (1618) describes a journey perhaps suggested by Ben Jonson's similar undertaking, though Taylor denied any suggestion of burlesque. He reached Braemar and, returning through Leith, met Jonson, who good-naturedly gave him 22 shillings to drink his health in England. He undertook a journey to Prague—where he was entertained by the queen of Bohemia (1620)—for a wager, as he did the travels described in *A Verry Merry, Wherry-Ferry-Voyage, or Yorke for my money* (1622) and *A New Discovery by Sea, With a Wherry From London to Salisbury* (1623). When the Civil War began, Taylor, who took a public house in Oxford (where he stayed, in Oriel College, during the plague of 1625) wrote royalist pamphlets, but when the city surrendered (1645) he returned to London and kept "The Crown" (later "The Poet's Head") off Long Acre until his death in Dec. 1653.

Editions include: *All the Workes . . . beeing 63 in Number* (1630), reprinted, 3 pt. (1868–69); *Works . . . Not Included in the Folio Volume of 1630,* 5 pt. (1870–78); C. Hindley (ed.), *Works,* a selection (1872) and *Miscellanea Antiqua Anglicana,* vol. ii and iii (1873).

*See* R. B. Dow, "John Taylor" in *Harvard Summaries of Theses* (1931).

**TAYLOR, JOSEPH** (*c.* 1586–1652), English actor mentioned in the folio Shakespeare of 1623 as one of the 26 who took principal parts in all of those plays. He was with the Duke of York's Company in 1610 but involved himself in a lawsuit with John Heminge, by leaving it to join the Lady Elizabeth's in the next year. Taylor appeared in the actor list of the latter company in *The Honest Man's Fortune* (1613) and *The Coxcomb* (1613). From 1616 he was one of the Prince's Company and from 1619 was with the King's Men, where he remained until he retired, playing several of Burbage's parts, including Ferdinand in *The Duchess of Malfi* and Hamlet. There is a legend that he was trained by Shakespeare to play Hamlet. In many of Beaumont and Fletcher's plays he had a leading role, and he is one of the ten actors who signed the dedication of the first folio of those dramatists (1647). Taylor led the King's Men, with J. Lowin, after Heminge and H. Condell, and in 1630, after Heminge's death, obtained two shares in the Globe Theatre, and one in the Blackfriars. In 1639 he was appointed yeoman of the revels. He died at Richmond, where he was buried on Nov. 4, 1652.

**TAYLOR, MAXWELL DAVENPORT** (1901– ), U.S. Army officer, a pioneer in airborne warfare, was born at Keytesville, Mo., Aug. 26, 1901, and graduated from the United States Military Academy in 1922. Taylor assisted in the organization of the U.S. Army's first airborne division, the 82nd, early in World War II. At great personal risk, he passed through enemy lines 24 hours before the Allied invasion of Italy in 1943 to confer with Italian leaders in Rome concerning possible airborne seizure of Roman airfields. Later he led the 101st Airborne Division in the assaults in Normandy and the Netherlands, and his division gained wide fame for its defense of Bastogne during the "Battle of the Bulge" in 1944. As commanding general of the 8th Army in 1953 Taylor directed UN forces in Korea during the closing phases of the Korean War. He then served as Army chief of staff (1955–59) and three years later was appointed chairman of the joint chiefs of staff. In 1964 he became U.S. ambassador to the Republic of Vietnam, which was being given increasing military support by the U.S. He resigned this post in July 1965. (W. Sı.)

**TAYLOR, WILLIAM** (1821–1902), U.S. Methodist missionary, whose indefatigable zeal carried him all over the world in a missionary career that lasted nearly 50 years, was born in Rockbridge County, Va., on May 2, 1821, of Scotch-Irish and English parentage. On March 15, 1843, he was admitted on trial in the Baltimore Conference of the Methodist Episcopal Church and in 1847 was ordained elder. Taylor was sent to California in 1849 by the Missionary Society, arriving in San Francisco, via Cape Horn, when it was still a city of tents. Standing on a box or a whisky barrel in the plaza, he made his powerful voice heard by as many as 20,000 people and converted many.

Taylor's evangelistic tours, taken more or less independently of the church authorities, took him throughout the United States and Canada (1856–61), and to England (1862), Australia (1863), the West Indies (1864), India (1870–75), South America (1877–78, 1880, 1883–84), and South Africa (1866, 1884). On his first South American visit (1877–78) he organized a system of self-supporting schools on the west coast. Elected missionary bishop for Africa in 1884, he established a chain of missionary stations in the Congo and self-supporting missions in Liberia. His steadfast belief that "God had taken William Taylor into a peculiar partnership" filled him with self-confidence and courage and also made him impatient with official direction and supervision. For years he was a thorn in the flesh to bishops and board secretaries. In 1896 he was retired by the general conference, and he died on May 18, 1902.

Taylor wrote 14 or more books, including *Seven Years' Street Preaching in San Francisco* (1856); *Christian Adventures in South Africa* (1867); and *Story of My Life* (1896).

*See* Wade Crawford Barclay, *History of Methodist Missions,* vol. iii, pp. 179 ff. (1949–57); Oscar MacMillan Buck, "William Taylor" in *Dictionary of American Biography,* vol. xviii, pp. 345–346. (W. C. B.)

**TAYLOR, ZACHARY** (1784–1850), 12th president of the U.S., was born in Orange County, Virginia, Nov. 24, 1784. Within the year his father, Richard Taylor, an officer in the American Revolution, made a new home for his family in Kentucky, where he was appointed collector of the port of Louisville, then on the border where Spaniards and Indians were still a menace. In this environment Zachary Taylor spent his youth. He gained what little schooling he was to enjoy from Elisha Ayres, a New England tutor, who was employed by the elder Taylor. In 1806 young Taylor volunteered during the difficulties caused by Aaron Burr's southwestern schemes and saw brief military service. Two years later, through the instrumentality of his relative James Madison and others, Taylor was given a commission by President Jefferson as first lieutenant in the 7th Infantry.

THE BETTMANN ARCHIVE

ZACHARY TAYLOR; DAGUERREOTYPE PORTRAIT, 1849–50

**Military Career.**—As captain and major he served through Harrison's Indian campaign and the War of 1812 in the Northwest Territory and at the close of the war temporarily left the Army because reduction to peacetime strength had lowered his rank. In 1816 President Madison reappointed him to his old rank, and there ensued 20 years of garrison life at various posts, varied in 1832 by an expedition against Black Hawk. At the outbreak of the Seminole War (1835) he was an infantry colonel in the Northwest; soon orders came for him to take his command to the Everglades. In this bewildering warfare he spent three years and was promoted to the rank of brigadier general by brevet for his service in the Battle of Lake Okeechobee. He was able to make little headway against the Indians and in 1840 asked to be relieved. He was assigned to duty in Louisiana and while there established a home in Baton Rouge and acquired a large plantation in Mississippi. In 1841 he was given command of the Second Department of the Western Division of the Army, with headquarters at Ft. Smith, Ark.

When Texas was acquired in 1845, Taylor was ordered by the War Department to take up a position along the southern border of Texas; by the spring of 1846 he had moved down to the mouth of the Rio Grande with a force of over 3,000 men and established Ft. Brown. A strong Mexican force was stationed at Matamoras, and soon there were border skirmishes that resulted in war. Even before war was declared on May 13, Taylor had defeated the Mexicans at Palo Alto (*q.v.*) and Resaca de la Palma on May 8 and 9. The news of these victories and of the occupation of Matamoras on May 18 was received with great appreciation throughout the country, and various persons, including Whig politicians and editors, began to look upon Taylor as a possible presidential candidate. After months of waiting for wagons and boats, Taylor moved to the head of navigation on the Rio Grande, established a depot at Camargo, and set out for Monterrey, which he captured on Sept. 21 after a hard-fought three-day battle. When President Polk disapproved the eight week's armistice granted by Taylor upon the surrender of Monterrey, and Secretary of War Marcy began to make suggestions as to the movements of his subordinates, Taylor became convinced that the administration was trying to discredit him for political purposes. His letter of Nov. 5 to Gen. E. P. Gaines criticizing Polk and Marcy found its way into the press, called forth a rebuke from the secretary of war, and increased the friction between Taylor and Washington authorities. When his superior, Gen. Winfield Scott, preparing an expedition against Veracruz and Mexico City, ordered most of Taylor's seasoned troops to join him, Taylor was further incensed. Although instructed to concentrate his remaining troops at Monterrey and remain on the defensive, he crossed the mountains to Saltillo and on Feb. 22, 1847, engaged the army of Santa Anna in battle at Buena Vista (*q.v.*). Although outnumbered 4 to 1, the Americans, inspired by the leadership of "Old Rough and Ready" and aided by skilful artillery fire, won a brilliant victory and saved the north of Mexico. At home the feeling was general that Taylor had been treated unfairly by an administration that was jealous of his growing popularity.

**Political Career.**—Shrewd Whig politicians had become increasingly convinced of Taylor's potentialities as a candidate. Very early in the war, Thurlow Weed of New York began pushing him, and popular enthusiasm made his task easier. Taylor's correspondence was skilfully handled; he was reluctant, he maintained, and with truth, to be a seeker for the office; he had never voted and, though a Whig in sympathy, was not an avowed partisan. As a slaveholder he was certain to gain votes in the South, where there was a good deal of suspicion that Northern influences dominated the Whig managers. These advantages were sufficient to ensure success, and in the Whig convention, on the 4th ballot, Taylor won the nomination from Clay, Webster, and Scott. An opportune split in the Democratic Party ensured his victory, and on March 5, 1849, he was inaugurated.

Few presidents have entered office with less knowledge of what was expected of them. The new executive expected to be a nonpartisan president, leaving to Congress all legislative matters and confining himself to executing the laws. With Colonel Bliss, his son-in-law, to phrase his thoughts, he, at first, was more or less influenced in his policies by Vice-President Fillmore, but it was not long before the superior astuteness of Senator Seward, Fillmore's rival in New York State, accomplished results. After the new president became convinced that it was his duty to build up the Whig Party by means of clever patronage, deserving Whigs began to come into their own.

With these preliminary lessons learned, Taylor found his most perplexing problem to be the status of the newly acquired territory. As a soldier he was eager to see stable government established, and for this purpose he authorized Congressman King of Georgia to go to California and urge an application for statehood. When Congress met in December 1849, the president had the pleasure of reporting that California was ready to become a state and that New Mexico would be ready soon. He recommended the admission of California and expressed the hope that the slave issue would not be injected into the situation. When Southern representatives objected because California had prohibited slavery, he resented their protests. He declared himself willing to accept any law providing for admission and warned Southern leaders that he would take the field if necessary to carry out such a law and hang any who resisted. He was not in favour of conciliating those opposed to his policy and referred contemptuously to the Compromise of 1850 (*q.v.*) as the "Omnibus Bill." In other respects his administration was running into trouble; charges were made against his secretary of war, Crawford, to the effect that he had used his official position to pursue a claim successfully before the secretary of the treasury by which he benefited financially. This charge deeply mortified Taylor, who prided himself on scrupulous honesty, and he determined to reorganize his Cabinet. Then came the fatal July 4, 1850, when exposure to heat at the Washington Monument ceremonies and injudicious eating combined with worry brought on a serious intestinal disturbance that resulted in Taylor's death five days later. The doctors diagnosed his illness as cholera, but it seems to have been acute gastroenteritis. He was succeeded by his vice-president, Millard Fillmore (*q.v.*).

A combination of honesty, simplicity, determination, and common sense had brought Taylor successfully through a variety of difficult situations and by a strange turn of the wheel carried him to the White House. In 1810 Taylor had married Margaret Smith (1788–1852), who bore him six children, three of whom survived him. One daughter, Sarah Knox Taylor, married a young subaltern, Jefferson Davis, in 1835, surviving the marriage but three months. His only son, Richard Taylor (1826–79), graduated from Yale in 1845 and, after a short service in his father's camp, became a sugar planter and politician in Louisiana. At the outbreak of the Civil War he entered the Confederate Army and eventually became a lieutenant general. His memoirs, *Destruction and Reconstruction* (1879), earned high praise from military historians.

*See* also references under "Taylor, Zachary," in the Index.

BIBLIOGRAPHY.—E. J. Nichols, *Zach Taylor's Little Army* (1963); Brainerd Dyer, *Zachary Taylor* (1946); Holman Hamilton, *Zachary Taylor, Soldier of the Republic* (1941), *Zachary Taylor, Soldier in the White House* (1951); William K. Bixby, *Letters from the Battlefields of the Mexican War* (1908); Justin H. Smith, *War with Mexico*, 2 vol. (1919). (R. F. N.; B. Dy.)

**TAYLOR'S THEOREM,** the statement of an important mathematical formula discovered by Brook Taylor (*q.v.*) in 1712 and published three years later in his *Methodus incrementorum directa et inversa* (1715). The theorem later was recognized as a basic principle in differential calculus; the first rigorous proof was given by A. L. Cauchy (*q.v.*).

It may be written in the form of an infinite series:

$$f(x+h) = f(x) + hf'(x) + \frac{h^2}{2!}f''(x) + \cdots \qquad (1)$$

and under suitable conditions it makes possible the computation of the value of $f(x+h)$ to any desired accuracy when the value of $f(x)$ and its derivatives $f'(x)$, $f''(x)$, . . . , for a particular fixed value $x$ are known; *e.g.*, with $x = 1$,

$$\log_e (1+h) = 0 + h - \frac{h^2}{2} + \frac{h^3}{3} - \frac{h^4}{4} + \cdots$$

Taylor's formula with remainder may be written as a finite sum:

$$f(x+h) = f(x) + hf'(x) + \cdots + \frac{h^{(n-1)}}{(n-1)!}f^{(n-1)}(x) + R_n \qquad (2)$$

where

$$R_n = \frac{h^n}{n!}\, f^{(n)}(x + \theta h)$$

and $\theta$ is a fraction between 0 and 1. Several other formulas have been devised for $R_n$. Sometimes one of these may be used to check on the accuracy obtained by using a given number of terms of (1). Moreover, formula (2) is valid in some cases when formula (1) is not. The binomial series is a special case of Taylor's series (*see* BINOMIAL THEOREM).

*See* also FUNCTION; SERIES. (L. M. G.)

**TAYMYR NATIONAL OKRUG** (or DOLGANO-NENETSKIY NATIONAL OKRUG), created in 1930, forms the northern part of Krasnoyarskiy Kray, U.S.S.R. Area 339,498 sq.mi. (879,300 sq.km.); pop. (1965 est.) 36,000. The *okrug* occupies the hilly Taymyr Peninsula, the most northerly part of the Eurasian continent, which terminates in Cape Chelyuskin (77°45′ N). From the Taymyr hills it extends southward across the north Siberian Lowland, drained chiefly by the Khatanga and its tributaries, across the steep, north-facing scarp of the central Siberian Plateau and includes the northern part of the plateau, known as the Putoran Mountains. In the west, the *okrug* includes the lowest part of the course of the Yenisey River. The northerly latitude brings an extremely severe climate, with prolonged, cold winters and brief, cool summers. Tundra conditions are found almost everywhere, with a scanty moss and lichen vegetation and areas of sphagnum bog. Only in the south does sparse, stunted forest appear. Included in the *okrug* is the Severnaya Zemlya (*q.v.*) Archipelago in the high Arctic.

The unfavourable conditions and remoteness (Dudinka, the administrative centre on the Yenisey, is 1,256 mi. [2,021 km.] from Krasnoyarsk) account for the sparse population (0.1 per sq.mi.). In Dudinka and two urban settlements there were 20,206 people in 1959, mostly Russians. The rural inhabitants are mostly seminomadic Nentsy (Samoyeds), who live by reindeer herding, fishing, and hunting. The chief wealth lies in the mining of the Putoran

Mountains, centred on Noril'sk, but that town is outside the *okrug's* jurisdiction. Dudinka, with 16,332 people in 1959, has rail connection to Noril'sk and serves as its outport. Ust'-Port, on the Yenisey, has a fish cannery. Dikson, at the mouth of the Yenisey (Yeniseyskiy) Gulf, and Nordvik, on the Khatanga (Khatangskiy) Gulf, where salt is obtained, are small ports on the northern sea route. (R. A. F.)

**TBILISI** (Tiflis), the capital town of the Georgian (Gruzinskaya) Soviet Socialist Republic, U.S.S.R., stands on the Kura River. Pop. (1966 est.) 823,000. It has an attractive appearance, laid out on hilly ground and cut through by the river, partly in a steep-sided and picturesque gorge. Its streets are tree lined, and there are many gardens and parks, including a botanical garden (1845). The modern architecture in general relies heavily on traditional Georgian and Armenian styles. Among architectural survivals of the town's long history are the Sion Cathedral, begun in the 5th century, although frequently rebuilt at later periods, and the Metekhi Palace of the Georgian kings. The many cultural and educational establishments, mainly on the right bank of the Kura, include the Georgian Academy of Sciences, a university, polytechnic and agricultural institutes, other higher educational institutes, more than 75 research foundations, a theatre of opera and ballet, and Russian and Georgian dramatic theatres. It is a centre of the film industry and of printing and publishing.

Besides the Georgian Military Highway across the Caucasus, Tbilisi has roads and railways to Sukhumi on the Black Sea, to Baku on the Caspian, and to Yerevan and Turkey. A branch railway runs to Telavi in the Alazani Valley. First in its wide range of industries is engineering, especially machine tools, agricultural equipment, and electrical products. Electric locomotives are made, and there are locomotive repair yards.

The textile industry is well developed and produces natural and artificial silk, cotton goods, and worsted. Plastics, leather goods and footwear, furniture and veneer, bricks, and chinaware are made, and brewing, wine making, and food processing (especially tea, margarine, and chocolate) are important. Power for industry is derived from the Ortachalskaya hydroelectric plant in the town itself and from the Zemo-Avchala and the two Samgora plants nearby.

The town is of ancient origin, founded in A.D. 458 (in some sources, 455), when the capital of the old Georgian kingdom was transferred there from Mtskheta. Its strategic importance in controlling the passage between western and eastern Transcaucasia gave the town a stormy history. It was captured and sacked on many occasions and knew many masters: Persians in the 6th century, the Byzantine Empire and the Arabs in the 7th. In 1122 King David II ("the Builder") of Georgia captured Tbilisi and made it his capital. In 1234 it fell to the Mongols, and in 1386 it was sacked by Timur. The Turks captured the town on several occasions, and in 1795 it was burned to the ground by the Persians. Its final capture was by the Russians in 1801, when it was a town of 20,000 inhabitants. The Russians constructed the Georgian Military Highway across the Caucasus to Tbilisi from Vladikavkaz (now Ordzhonikidze). (R. A. F.)

**TCHAIKOVSKY, PETR ILICH** (1840–1893), the most renowned of all Russian composers during the first half of the 20th century, was born at Votkinsk in the Vyatka Government on May 7 (new style; April 25, old style), 1840. He was greatly attached to his mother, and the tender feminine atmosphere of his early years was rudely broken when he was sent to school in St. Petersburg at the age of eight. In 1852 he entered the School of Jurisprudence, which he left in 1859 to join the Ministry of Justice as a senior clerk. In the meantime he had become an amateur musician and made some attempts at composition. In 1861 he began to study harmony, and the following year he entered the St. Petersburg Conservatory. At the end of his course he was appointed professor of harmony at the newly opened Moscow Conservatory. The composition of his First Symphony in 1866 produced acute nervous disorders that, together with hallucinations, were to affect him continuously. In 1868 he visited St. Petersburg, where he met Dargomyzhski, Balakirev, Rimski-Korsakov, and others. Surprisingly, he was received with more understanding by these nationalists than by the conservatory-trained Moscow composers, and Balakirev in particular gave him invaluable help and advice. In 1869 his first opera, *The Voyevoda,* was produced in Moscow with mixed success, and later that year he composed the first version of his masterpiece, the *Romeo and Juliet Overture,* the subject of which had been suggested to him by Balakirev. The main compositions of the next few years were the First String Quartet (containing the well-known andante cantabile movement), the Second Symphony, and, in 1875, the First Piano Concerto and the Third Symphony. The concerto was written for his friend Nikolai Rubinstein, who, however, not only refused to play it but criticized it so mercilessly that Tchaikovsky rededicated it to Hans von Bülow. In 1876 he wrote *Francesca da Rimini* and his first ballet, *Swan Lake,* and his fourth opera, *Vakula the Smith,* was produced.

**Later Life and Works.**—The year 1877 was one of critical importance. It marked the beginning of his extraordinary association with his benefactress, Nadejda von Meck, a wealthy widow who, attracted both by Tchaikovsky's music and by his personality, provided him with financial independence for 13 years in the form of a generous annual allowance. By mutual agreement they never met, a fact that resulted in a voluminous intimate correspondence, throwing much light on Tchaikovsky's character. Another significant event was his disastrous marriage in July of the same year with Antonina Milyukova, a former music student. She had become infatuated with him in much the same way as Tatyana was infatuated with Eugene Onegin in the Pushkin opera on which Tchaikovsky was working at that time. Not being able to behave with Onegin's heartlessness, and hoping perhaps that marriage would conceal knowledge of his homosexual inclinations, Tchaikovsky married her on the understanding that, though physical love with a woman was denied to him, he would remain her friend. The resulting tension drove him to an attempt at suicide, and they were legally separated in October 1877.

Yet during this period he wrote some of his finest works. While working on *Eugene Onegin* he also wrote the Fourth Symphony, both completed abroad while he was recovering from his state of nervous depression. This rest did indeed help him forget the horrors of the past months, but both his compositions and his letters show that whatever happiness he was to enjoy during the remainder of his life would be increasingly modified by a tendency to melancholy and morbid introspection, which had always been ingrained in his nature. Soon after returning to Russia, Tchaikovsky abandoned his irksome conservatory duties and in 1881 declined the directorship of the conservatory. Between 1878 and 1881 he produced the *Violin Concerto,* the Second Piano Concerto, the *Italian Capriccio, 1812 Overture,* and the *Serenade for Strings.* Of his operas, the *Maid of Orleans* was a failure in 1881, but in 1884 *Onegin,* which had hitherto only achieved a *succès d'estime* in Moscow, enjoyed great popularity in St. Petersburg, largely due to the tsar's personal admiration for it. The third and best of his four orchestral suites also dates from 1884, and the following year he wrote his *Manfred* Symphony, again to a plan suggested by Balakirev. He began to spend more and more time traveling in Russia and abroad, and in 1888 he successfully undertook his first international tour as a conductor, visiting Leipzig, Berlin, Prague, Hamburg, Paris, and London. On his return to Russia he moved to Frolovskoye, where in 1888 he wrote his Fifth Symphony and the *Hamlet Overture.* After a second tour the following year he composed *The Sleeping Beauty* ballet, and in 1890 his second Pushkin opera, the *Queen of Spades.* An event embittering the remaining years of his life occurred in the autumn of 1890 when Madame von Meck discontinued her allowance under the false impression that she was near bankruptcy. Their epistolary friendship was thus brought to an end. In 1891 Tchaikovsky visited the United States, where he conducted concerts in New York, Baltimore, and Philadelphia. His two last works for the stage, the one-act opera *Iolantha* (1891) and the *Nutcracker* ballet (1892), were first performed together in December 1892 with only moderate success, although the famous ballet suite had already won favour. In 1892 Tchaikovsky moved to a house at Klin (later established as the Tchaikovsky Museum), where he wrote his Sixth Symphony

(*Pathétique;* 1893), which he rightly believed to be a masterpiece. He lived only to hear the first performance, indifferently received; ten days later, on Nov. 6 (N.S.; Oct. 25, O.S.), 1893, he died suddenly in St. Petersburg from cholera caused by drinking unboiled water. Whether this action entailed an element of suicide—which he had often contemplated and once attempted—has never been established.

**Evaluation.**—Since Tchaikovsky's death no composer has suffered more from changes of fashion or from the extremes of over- and undervaluation. On the one hand he achieved an enormous popularity with a very wide audience (particularly adolescents), largely through his more emotional works; on the other, the almost hypnotic effect that he was able to induce led to serious questioning of his true musical quality. It seems probable that time will add to, rather than diminish, his stature, if only because performances, recordings, and publications have disclosed that there are fine works of Tchaikovsky still to be discovered. He is certainly the greatest master of the classical ballet, demonstrated by *Swan Lake* and the symphonically conceived *Sleeping Beauty.* The six symphonies may lack formal unity but all contain delightful music. The last three are deservedly famous, though to these should be added the neglected *Manfred* Symphony. On a somewhat lower plane the First Piano Concerto and the *Violin Concerto* nevertheless deserve a higher reputation than vehicles for virtuosity. Notable among his other orchestral works are the early *Romeo and Juliet Overture* and the exquisite *Serenade for Strings.* Although his operas contain many fine pages, Tchaikovsky was never a true operatic composer. *Eugene Onegin* is, however, a masterpiece, while the dramatically effective *Queen of Spades* has perhaps obscured the claims of *The Little Slippers*—his revised version of *Vakula the Smith.* The chamber and piano music is largely undistinguished, but his numerous songs include several fine examples.

Though unequal, his music shows a wealth of melodic inspiration and imagination, and a wonderful flair for orchestration. It also shows lapses of taste, partly redeemed, however, by his enormous technical efficiency. Though his work may be said to illustrate cosmopolitan tendencies of Russian music, its underlying sentiment and character are as distinctively Russian as that of the Russian nationalist composers. His success in bridging the gulf between the musician and the general public partly accounted for the exalted position he enjoyed toward the middle of the 20th century in the U.S.S.R.

Bibliography.—G. Abraham, *Tchaikovsky* (1944); G. Abraham (ed.), *Tchaikovsky: a Symposium* (1946); H. Weinstock, *Tchaikovsky* (1943); P. I. Tchaikovsky, *Diaries,* Eng. trans. by V. Lakond (1945).
(D. M. L.-J.)

**TCHEREPNIN, NIKOLAI NIKOLAEVICH** (1873–1945), Russian composer of ballets, songs, and piano music, was born in St. Petersburg on May 14 (new style; 2, old style), 1873. After studying law at the university, he entered the St. Petersburg Conservatory as Rimski-Korsakov's pupil for composition (1895–98). He became conductor of the Belyaev symphony concerts and of the imperial opera and from 1908 to 1914 conducted Diaghilev's opera and ballet productions in western Europe. From 1918 to 1921 he was director of the Tiflis Conservatory. He then settled in Paris, where he directed a Russian conservatory. He died at Issy-les-Moulineaux, near Paris, on June 26, 1945. Tcherepnin was a gifted but not a strikingly individual composer. The best of his ballet scores was the first, *Le Pavillon d'Armide* (1907). The most successful of the others were *Narcisse et Echo* (1911), *The Masque of the Red Death* (1916), and *Romance of a Mummy* (1925). Among his other works are symphonic poems, piano pieces (including *Esquisses sur les images d'un alphabet russe*), and songs.

Aleksandr Nikolaevich Tcherepnin (1899– ), pianist and composer of operas, ballets, orchestral works, chamber music, and piano works, son of the preceding, was born in St. Petersburg on Jan. 21 (N.S.; 9, O.S.), 1899. He studied first at Tiflis and later at the Paris Conservatoire. In 1918 he married the Chinese pianist Lee Hsien-ming. Between 1934 and 1937 he visited China and Japan and established a firm in Tokyo for the publication of works by Japanese and Chinese composers. He experimented with a nine-note scale and with novel conceptions of rhythm. In 1948 Tcherepnin was on the faculty of the San Francisco Music and Art Institute. From 1949 to 1964 he taught piano and composition at DePaul University in Chicago. (G. Ab.)

**TCZEW,** a town and district capital in Gdansk (Danzig) *wojewodztwo* (province), Poland, on the left bank of the Vistula about 19 mi. (31 km.) above its mouth and 20 mi. (32 km.) SSE of Danzig. It is a railway junction for Warsaw, Danzig, Bydgoszcz, and Chojnice. Pop. (1960 est.) 33,696. It developed as an important river port on the main trade route to Danzig. After World War I it was a frontier town between Poland and the Free City of Danzig and handled the export trade in coal before the building of the port of Gdynia. It has a river shipyard, railway workshops, and a gasometer factory.

Tczew is mentioned in historical documents of the end of the 12th century. It was given to Poland in 1282 by the will and testament of the last duke of Danzig and Eastern Pomerania (Pomorze) but was occupied by the Teutonic Knights from 1308 until 1466. Seized by Prussia after the First Partition of Poland, in 1772, it was returned to Poland by the Treaty of Versailles in 1919. (T. K. W.)

**TEA,** a beverage made from the dried leaves of the tea plant, an evergreen shrub or small tree (*Camellia sinensis*) of the family Theaceae. Tea is consumed as either a hot or a cold beverage by about one-half of the world's population, yet it is second to coffee in commercial importance, largely because a significant portion of the world's tea crop is consumed in the growing regions. Of less importance are the medicinal properties of tea. Composed chemically of caffeine and tannin, tea is used as a stimulant and as an astringent, while the seeds of the tea plant are a source of a volatile oil.

The word "tea" comes from a Chinese ideogram pronounced "chah" in Cantonese and "tay" in the dialect of Amoy. As "chah," the word traveled to Japan, India, Persia, and Russia, but the English "tea" was derived from the "tay" form, which was brought by the Dutch to Europe by way of Java. In the known references to tea in English during the years 1650–59, the word appears in its earlier form of "tee" but was pronounced "tay." It was first spelled "tea" in 1660 but was pronounced "tay" until the mid-18th century.

**History.**—The origin of the use of tea as a beverage, though lost in antiquity, is rich in legend. Japanese mythology credits the origin of tea in China to the plight of Bodhidharma, the Buddhist saint, who is said to have remained seated before a wall in meditation for nine years. During one of his meditations the saint fell asleep, and, upon awakening, he was so chagrined that he cut off his eyelids to assure no recurrence of his sin. Cast to the ground, the severed eyelids took root and grew as the tea plant, whose leaves, when infused in hot water, produced a beverage that was capable of banishing sleep.

A Chinese legend places the introduction of tea as a beverage in the reign of the mythical emperor Shen Nung, about 2737 B.C.

THE BETTMANN ARCHIVE

TEA PROCESSING IN CHINA; ENGRAVING FROM A 19TH-CENTURY ENGLISH BOOK

However, the earliest mention to which modern scholars give credence is found in the *Erh Ya*, an ancient Chinese dictionary, about 350 B.C. It is believed that tea cultivation began in the interior province of Szechwan in China, gradually extending down the Yangtze Valley to the seaboard provinces.

In the *Ch'a Ching*, a handbook of tea written by Lu Yu about A.D. 780, the product is described as a type of cake made from leaves that had been steamed, crushed, and molded. The cake was fired and toasted or shredded and then steeped in salted boiling water.

Tea cultivation was introduced into Japan, along with Chinese civilization, around the last decade of the 6th century. However, there is no record of successful tea cultivation in Japan until early in the 8th century, and not until the 13th century did tea become a popular Japanese beverage.

The Japanese variety of tea was introduced into Java in 1684 by Andreas Cleyer, a German naturalist and doctor of medicine. In 1827 a young Dutch tea taster, J. I. L. L. Jacobson, risked his life to penetrate China's forbidden tea gardens and bring back tea seeds and labourers in order to cultivate the tea plant in the Dutch East Indies. He is generally recognized as the founder of Indonesia's tea industry.

Tea was first mentioned in European literature in 1559 as *chai catai* (tea of China) in *Navigationi e Viaggi* ("Voyages and Travels") by Gian Battista Ramusio, a noted Venetian author. The first reference to tea by an Englishman, in 1615, is credited to R. L. Wickham, who was in charge of the English East India Company's agency at Firando, Jap.

England was the greatest coffee-drinking country in the world when tea was first publicly sold at Garway's Coffee House in London in 1657. Advertised as "That Excellent and by all Physitians approved China drink," tea gained in popularity, and, within a few years, metal or leather trade coins, used in lieu of small change and known as tea and coffee tokens, were generally accepted as currency in London's 2,000 coffeehouses. The world's greatest tea monopoly, the English East India Company, which flourished from 1600 to 1858, played a major role in the introduction of China and India teas into England and colonial America and in popularizing the beverage. In an effort to perpetuate this monopoly, the British Parliament passed the Tea Act of 1773, which precipitated the Boston Tea Party and which was a contributory cause of the American Revolution. The colonists' resentment of the role played by tea in their bickerings with the mother country created an unfavourable image of the beverage, an image from which it never fully recovered. By mid-20th century, Englishmen were consuming about 5 times as many pounds of tea as coffee, while Americans were consuming about 25 times as many pounds of coffee as tea.

The use of tea as a beverage was well established in Holland by the mid-17th century, and the afternoon tea custom spread across the Atlantic to New Amsterdam (now New York City). With tea also came the teaboards, teapots, silver spoons, strainers, and other tea table items that were the pride of Dutch housewives. Milk was not used at first, but the socially correct ladies of New Amsterdam offered sugar and sometimes saffron and peach leaves as flavouring agents for tea. Their guests would either nibble a lump of sugar or stir powdered sugar into their tea; hence tea tables were provided with partitioned "bite and stir" boxes.

The custom of serving afternoon tea and cakes was originated by Anna, wife of the 7th duke of Bedford, around 1840. Since at that time people ate prodigious breakfasts and no other meal until dinner was served at 8 o'clock, the duchess instituted a new meal, with tea and cakes at 5 o'clock.

The founding of India's tea industry stems from the appointment of a committee by Gov. Gen. Lord William Henry Cavendish Bentinck, in 1834, to formulate a plan for tea cultivation. However, indigenous tea had already been discovered in northern India (upper Assam) by Maj. Robert Bruce and an Indian, Moneram Dewan, in 1823.

One of the most picturesque eras in maritime history was that of the clipper ships, which transported tea from China to England and North America. Its most celebrated chapter was perhaps that of the Great Tea Race of 1866, which started at Foochow, China, and ended 99 days later at London after covering 16,000 mi. Of the 11 competing clipper ships, "Taeping" was the winner at the London dock, and "Ariel" the winner at The Downs, ten minutes ahead of her rival.

**Botany.**—While the tea plant was originally designated by Linnaeus as *Thea sinensis,* it is now known botanically as *Camellia sinensis,* which emphasizes its close relationship to the cultivated camellia, *C. japonica.* Many varieties of tea have been described and named, but there is no general agreement among botanists or horticulturists as to varietal limits. A part of the difficulty is that early authors had wholly inadequate collections of reference material and that the tea plant in cultivation, like all cultivated plants, varies in character, depending on local conditions and on the special qualities for which various strains were selected and propagated.

BY COURTESY OF THE LIPTON TEA COMPANY
TEA STEM WITH FLOWERS

While the accepted scientific name stems from Linnaeus' description, the species was well known to earlier European botanical authors, for Linnaeus gives no less than ten references to earlier botanical literature.

The tea plant is an evergreen shrub, which in its natural state grows to a height of 15 to 30 ft., but the tea planter keeps it pruned down to a height of 3 to 5 ft. In its general appearance and the elliptic form of its two- to five-inch-long leaf, it resembles the myrtle. The five petaled blossoms are white, with yellow anthers, and suggest the wild rose; the fruit is a woody capsule containing three seeds. The plant grows well in the monsoon climate of the tropics, from sea level up to 6,000 ft., doing best in the higher altitudes; in more temperate zones, where there is danger of frost, it is grown at low elevations. The commercial tea belt of the world is largely confined to a ring of mountains around or near the Equator, within 42° N and 33° S.

**Diseases and Pests.**—The tea bush is subject to attack by a wide variety of pests and blights, but the greater number of them are comparatively harmless. Generally speaking, it is the neglected, undernourished, or otherwise weakened tea bushes that become prey to the attacks of blights. Among the leaf diseases that may be mentioned are: blister blight, gray, brown, and copper blight, bird's-eye spot, *Cercosporella theae,* rim blight, sooty mold, *Phoma theicola, Phaeospharella theae,* and scabbed leaves.

Diseases that attack both leaf and stem include: blister blight, red rust, bacterial leaf and stem diseases, black rot, and horsehair blight. Stem diseases include: two varieties of branch canker, pink diseases, three varieties of dieback, *Massaria theicola,* stump rot, galls on plucked shoots, burrs, and callous outgrowths. Control of many of these diseases is effected by pruning and then burning the affected parts; spraying with Bordeaux or Burgundy mixture, or lime-sulfur solution; or more intensive cultivation.

Root diseases, which seldom ascend to the stem and branches, usually result in the death of the affected bushes. Certain diagnosis includes examination of the roots for threadlike fungus mycelium.

A serious insect menace is the helopeltis bug, the so-called tea mosquito, which thrives on the sap of young tea leaves. This pest is common in Java and parts of India.

Other enemies of tea are the leaf-rolling caterpillar of the tea tortrix moth, which enmeshes the tea leaves in its web, and the shot-hole borer *Xyleborus fornicatus,* a beetle that roams over the stems and branches, drilling holes that render the plants useless as tea producers. The latter pest is especially prevalent in Ceylon. Mites in chromatic profusion (red spider, orange mite, pink mite, yellow mite, etc.) attack tea leaves during a period of drought, turning them yellow and black, and ultimately causing them to fall off the bush. However, a good rain so stimulates growth that the bushes produce new vigorous shoots and usually survive the attack. Certain species of termites and nematodes are pests locally.

In some cases insect attack actually produces higher quality teas; *e.g.*, in India's premier hill districts of Darjeeling green fly attacks result in stunted leaves that provide some of the world's best teas.

**Cultivation.**—On large plantations, where tea is usually grown from seed in nursery beds, the young plants are transplanted to prepared tea fields when they are six to eight inches high, usually in six months' time. They are set out in rows, three to six feet apart. In two years, when they reach a height of four to six feet, they are cut down to less than a foot. By the end of the third year they are ready for plucking. Chinese, Japanese, and Formosan tea growers working mostly small family gardens do not set out nurseries but cultivate the shrub either by planting the seeds directly where they are to be grown or by layering; *i.e.*, transplanting. Weeding, cultivation between the rows, and pruning continue regularly for 25 to 50 years, the average life of a tea bush. When in full bearing—about the 10th year—a plant yields as much as ¼ lb. of leaf in its several flushes (growths of new shoots) during the season.

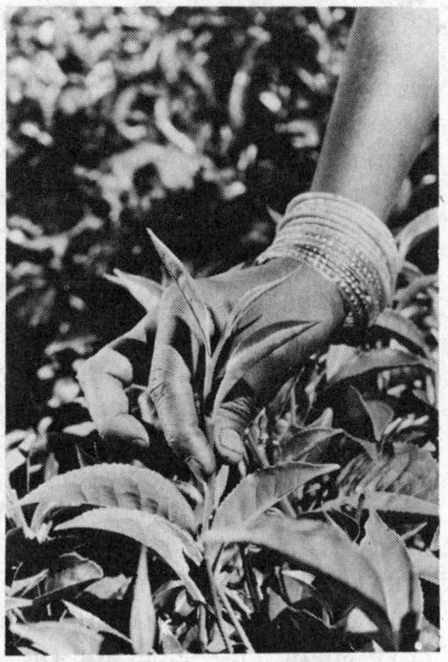

CEYLON TEA CENTRE

PICKING THE MOST TENDER LEAVES OF THE TEA PLANT WHICH YIELD THE BEST GRADES OF TEA

Tea leaves are plucked either by hand or with special shears. In the tropical areas of southern India, Ceylon, and Indonesia, harvest continues throughout the year, but in the subtropical regions of northern India and China and in Japan and Formosa, the harvests are seasonal. The flavour and quality of the tea leaves vary with the climate, soil, age of the leaf, time of harvest (even from season to season), and method of preparation.

**Manufacture.**—Teas may be divided into three classes: (1) fermented, or black tea; (2) unfermented, or green tea; and (3) semifermented, or oolong tea. These classes result from different processes applied to the same kind of leaf, or even to leaves from the same plant, though various regions generally specialize in one type.

Most stages of processing are generally common to the three types of tea. First, the fresh leaves are withered by exposure to the sun or by heating in trays until pliable (usually 18–24 hours). Next the leaves are rolled by hand or machine in order to break the leaf cells and liberate the juices and enzymes. This rolling process may last up to three hours. Finally, the leaves are completely dried either by further exposure to the sun, over fires, or in a current of hot air, usually for 30–40 minutes.

In making black tea, the leaves, after being rolled, are fermented in baskets or on glass shelves or cement floors under damp cloths, usually for ½ to 4½ hours, followed by the usual drying process until the leaves are black and crisp. The process of fermentation, or oxidation, reduces the astringency of the leaf and changes its colour and flavour.

Green tea is made by steaming without fermentation in a perforated cylinder or boiler, thus retaining some of the green colour. The leaves are lightly rolled before drying.

Oolong teas, which have some of the characteristics of both black and green teas, are partially fermented before drying.

After drying, teas are graded by cutting, sifting, and sorting machines before being packaged. The principal grades are broken orange pekoe (terminal buds and the finest leaves); pekoe, pekoe souchong, and congou (successively coarser leaves); and pekoe dust (fine, broken tea).

Black teas are made in Communist China (the north China congou, or black leaf, from Hankow and the south China congou, or red leaf, from Foochow), India, Ceylon, Java, Malawi, Kenya, Japan, and Formosa. Green teas are produced in Communist China, Japan, India, and Indonesia, while oolong teas are obtained from Formosa and Foochow.

**Production.**—*India.*—India, the world's largest producer of tea (mostly black teas), supplied about one-third of the total in the mid-1960s and also led the world in tea exports. Tonnage in both categories increased substantially after World War II. More than 60% of India's exports were shipped to the United Kingdom, while most of the balance went to the U.S.S.R., Egypt (U.A.R.), the U.S., the Republic of Ireland, and Canada.

The principal tea-growing districts of northern India are in the Assam Valley and Cachar, in the contiguous districts of Darjeeling and Jalpaiguri (more commonly known as the Duars), and in Terai in West Bengal. In southern India tea is grown in the elevated region overlooking the Malabar Coast in Kerala and in the Nilgiris hills. It is also cultivated on a much smaller scale in northwest India in the Kangra and Dehra Dun districts of Punjab.

Other than the teas sold under contract, those of northern India are sold at tea auctions in Calcutta or London, while those of southern India are auctioned in Cochin and London. Both Calcutta and Cochin are important shipping centres.

The Tea Board of India, established by the Tea Act of 1953, consists of a chairman and 38 members representing the central and state governments and all interests connected with the industry. It has extensive functions and responsibilities under the direction of the central government.

*Ceylon.*—Ceylon's production and exports of tea have also made rapid strides since World War II, holding second place to India. Though approximately 40% of Ceylon's exports go to the United Kingdom, large amounts are also exported to Australia, the U.S., South Africa, Egypt, Iraq, Canada, New Zealand, several minor European markets, and others.

The principal tea-growing districts of Ceylon are in the Central Province and Uva, but there are also extensive districts in the southwest, notably in the Kelani Valley. Known generally as Ceylons, these teas, though all black teas, are classified as high grown, medium grown, and low grown and by their district names. They are known specifically by their garden marks, of which there are more than 2,000. A tea land is said to produce high-grown tea if its mean elevation is 4,000 ft. or more above sea level; medium-grown tea between 2,000 and 4,000 ft.; and low-grown tea at elevations below 2,000 ft.

Colombo is the only local market and the principal shipping point. Weekly auctions are held there throughout the year, and the remainder of the crop is either sold by private contract or shipped to London for auction.

*Communist China.*—There are few tea plantations in China proper, but most of the tea is grown by farmers around their homes in the mountainous regions. For this reason a large portion of the tea-producing districts in eastern China remained intact despite eight years of Japanese occupation in the late 1930s and early 1940s. Although no statistics have ever been available as to acreage and production, authorities believe that China was the world's largest tea producer prior to 1936, but in the mid-1960s it was estimated that China placed third in both world production and export.

Prior to World War II, China's principal exports went to the U.S.S.R., followed by Africa, the United Kingdom, and the U.S. No official figures have been available since 1949, and importing countries' statistics exclude shipments of tea from Communist China to the U.S.S.R. and Eastern Europe. Shipments to these areas are judged to be sufficiently large to strip all other information of much of its significance. However, the United Kingdom, the Netherlands, Hong Kong, Egypt, and Australia have imported large quantities of Communist China's teas.

*Japan.*—Though Japan ranked fourth in world tea production in the mid-1960s, most of the tea was sold for domestic consumption. Green tea accounts for more than 80% of Japan's tea exports, with the largest portion going to North Africa, particularly to Algeria and Morocco. The United Kingdom and the U.S. also purchased some teas from Japan. The chief producing district is in the environs of Shizuoka, the centre of Japan's export tea trade. Almost the entire export is shipped through the port of Shimizu, eight miles away.

*Indonesia.*—Indonesia was the fourth largest producer of tea prior to the Japanese invasion in 1942, but during World War II and the postwar era tea production was reduced to a comparatively insignificant amount. By the mid-1960s production had begun to increase, and Indonesia stood in fifth place in world production. Until 1958, the Netherlands had been the largest importer of Indonesian tea, sometimes taking about 50% of the shipments. In that year the United Kingdom became the largest purchaser of Indonesian teas, followed by the Netherlands, Belgium, Australia, the U.S., and Germany. About 75 to 80% of the tea is grown in Java and the remainder in Sumatra. The principal tea-growing districts in Java are in the Bogor and Preanger areas in the western part of the island, but tea is grown almost throughout the island. In Sumatra, the chief tea-growing district is in the highlands south of Medan. Mainly black teas are exported.

Jakarta, on the northwest coast of Java, is the centre of the tea trade in Indonesia, its port being Tandjungpriok. Prior to World War II, the auction at Jakarta played a large part in the distribution of Indonesian teas, and these auctions, or tenders, were resumed in 1948. Tea also may be shipped to an outmarket against specific orders received from buyers, or it may be shipped to Antwerp or London for auction. Sumatra's tea export trade is centred in Medan and shipped from Belawan, 16 mi. away.

*Pakistan.*—Pakistan has made substantial gains as a tea producer since its establishment as an independent country in 1947. The United Kingdom, the largest customer for Pakistani tea, imports more than 75% of the total. The principal tea-growing region in Pakistan is in the district of Sylhet. Pakistani teas are generally black and are known as Sylhets and Chittagongs. Chittagong is the centre of the country's tea trade, and all teas are shipped through its port.

*Formosa.*—The tea industry of Formosa (Taiwan) has recovered well from the extensive damage it suffered during World War II. Its largest customers are the U.S., Morocco, the United Kingdom, the Netherlands, and Hong Kong. The tea districts are generally confined to the northern part of the island around T'ai-pei and Hsin-chu. T'ai-pei is the centre of Formosa's tea trade, and all teas are shipped from the port of Chi-lung, about 18 mi. away. About half of Formosa's teas are black; the remainder is either green or semifermented.

*Other Countries.*—Tea is grown in the U.S.S.R., principally in the Georgian S.S.R. and to some extent in the Azerbaijan S.S.R. Most of the tea plantations in this area of Transcaucasia are located on the southern slopes of the Adjar hills near the eastern shore of the Black Sea. This is the farthest north that tea is cultivated anywhere. There are no reliable statistics for tea production in the U.S.S.R. after 1945, but it is generally believed that production has increased tremendously since World War II. Considerable scientific attention is given to the cultivation and manufacture of tea, as well as mechanical picking. Besides consuming its own production, the U.S.S.R. imports tea from Communist China, India, and Ceylon.

Several African countries have become important as growers and exporters of tea. Outstanding among these are Kenya, Malawi, Uganda, and Tanzania (Tanganyika). The United Kingdom, the U.S., and Canada are among the leading importers of African teas.

A small quantity of tea is also produced commercially in Argentina and Brazil.

**Consumption.**—The people of Great Britain and Ireland are generally considered the world's greatest tea drinkers, consuming about ten pounds per person annually. Blends of India, Ceylon, Java, and China teas are the long-term favourites of the English and Irish people, and Indias and Ceylons are also drunk unblended to some extent. In the United Kingdom, the destination of about half of the world's tea exports, the afternoon tea is the most characteristic of British institutions.

British people find little difficulty in satisfying their appetite for tea. It is served at tearooms, tea caravans, tea gardens, restaurants, and in railway cars, offices, and factories. Even the farmer's tea is brought to him while he is working in the fields. The right of English dock workers to an adequate tea was upheld in court following a strike that lasted several days.

In few countries is tea more popular than in Australia and New Zealand, where annual per capita consumption varies from seven to eight pounds. Blends of India, Ceylon, and Java teas are the most popular. In many homes and in most hotels, tea is served seven times a day, from before breakfast to immediately before retiring. Most large business establishments serve tea to their employees in the morning and afternoon. The tin "billy" can in which the bushman makes his tea is frequently referred to as a "Matilda" and is celebrated under this sobriquet in Australia's near-national song, entitled "Waltzing Matilda."

Canada is the foremost tea-drinking country of the Western Hemisphere, with an annual per capita consumption of almost three pounds. The demand is chiefly for Indias and Ceylons. The people of the Netherlands lead the nations of continental Europe as tea drinkers, with an annual per capita consumption of about two pounds.

Per capita consumption of tea in the United States is about ½ lb. annually. Consumption is heaviest in New England and the Middle Atlantic region, and otherwise among those people who have strong ties to countries where tea drinking prevails. Also, some sections of the country are seasonal consumers, as the Southern states, where little hot tea is consumed in winter, but where there is liberal consumption of iced tea in summer. In the West and Midwest little tea is consumed at any time of the year. More than 90% of the tea consumed in the United States is composed of blends of Indias, Ceylons, and Indonesias, but Americans are generally indifferent to the cup quality of tea and have slight knowledge of the differences in types of tea. It is purchased by proprietary names owned by packers, retailers, or wholesalers.

Such merchandising innovations as iced tea, the tea bag, and instant tea have served to popularize tea in the U.S. and to americanize the beverage to some extent. Iced tea was first introduced —it would not be incorrect to say "invented"—at the St. Louis World's Fair in 1904. In the summer months iced tea competes favourably with leading soft drinks for public demand. Some form of tea bag or tea ball was known at the beginning of this century, and it replaced loose or bulk tea as the most popular form during the 1950s. Soluble, or instant, tea was first distributed widely around 1960. Its use has been primarily for iced tea, since it eliminated the need for boiling water in preparing the beverage.

As the most popular beverage in the U.S.S.R., tea is consumed at all meals and at all times of the day. It is usually served in a glass rather than in a cup, and it is flavoured with lemon or jam rather than milk or cream.

The Chinese, originators of tea drinking, do not use teapots as a rule but simply infuse the tea with water much below the boiling point in the cups from which it is drunk, without milk, sugar, or lemon. Although no statistical data is obtainable, many authorities believe that the Chinese are the world's greatest tea consumers. Certainly in no other country except Japan does tea drinking appear to be more universal. Tea is drunk in China by people of all ages, in all classes, on all occasions, and at all times of day or night. It is served on receiving visits, making purchases, transacting business, and at all ceremonies. It is invariably offered on entering a Chinese house, and a covered, handleless cup, with freshly infused tea, is placed before each guest. The request to take more is generally construed as a polite hint that the interview or visit should end. In the cities, teahouses (*kwans*) flourish. They are the equivalent of the continental cafes and are the only convenient places of public resort. At a teahouse, the practice is to use two cups—a large one for brewing that will hold about ½ pt., and a thimble cup, smaller than a demitasse, from which the beverage is drunk.

Like the Chinese, the Japanese are great tea drinkers. They

have a worshipful regard for it and refer to it as *O Cha*, meaning "Honorable Tea." It is the custom in the home, upon arising, to offer tea to one's ancestors by placing it before the altar and to offer it to one's parents before partaking oneself. Every woman of good family is schooled in the etiquette of the ancient Tea Ceremony (*q.v.*) as part of her classical education; at least three years of instruction and practice are considered necessary to acquire proficiency.

**Chemistry and Brewing of Tea.**—The principal chemical constituents of tea are caffeine, tannin, and essential oil. The first supplies the stimulating quality, which, because of its purity, is without harmful reaction; the second, the strength of body; and the third, the flavour and aroma, chief factors in determining cup value in a trade sense.

The ideal preparation of tea is one that extracts a maximum of caffeine and not an excessive amount of tannin. Such a preparation also conserves the aroma and flavour. From the chemist's point of view the two main essentials in tea brewing are fresh water, freshly boiled, and a three- to five-minute infusion. Since tea infuses more readily in soft water than in hard water, small, thick, full teas are required for soft water, while brisk, full, flavoury teas should be used with hard water. Generally speaking, a five-minute infusion is best for fully fermented teas, like those of India, Ceylon, or Indonesia.

*See* also references under "Tea" in the Index.

Bibliography.—Kakuzo Okakura, *The Book of Tea,* 14th ed. (1928); F. W. F. Staveacre, *Tea and Tea Dealing* (1929); H. J. Moppet, *Tea Manufacture: Its Theory and Practice in Ceylon,* 2nd ed. (1931); E. C. Elliott and F. J. Whitehead, *Tea Planting in Ceylon* (1931); H. K. Rutherford, *Planters' Note Book,* 8th ed. (1931); Agnes Repplier, *To Think of Tea!* (1932); C. R. Harler, *The Culture and Marketing of Tea,* 3rd ed. (1964), *Tea Manufacture* (1963), *Tea Growing* (1966); W. H. Ukers, *All About Tea* (1935), *The Romance of Tea* (1936); E. A. Houghton Roberts, "Chemistry of Tea Fermentation," *Advances in Enzymology,* vol. ii, p. 113 (1942); V. D. Wickizer, *Coffee, Tea and Cocoa* (1951), *Tea Under International Regulation* (1944); Commonwealth Economic Committee, *Plantation Crops* (1950); Ernest Hainsworth, *Tea Pests and Diseases and Their Control* (1952); R. D. Morrison (International Tea Committee), *Tea: Memorandum Relating to the Tea Industry and Tea Trade of the World* (1945); E. A. Curtler, *The Cultivation and Manufacture of Tea in Ceylon and India* (1932); International Tea Committee, *Bulletin of Statistics* (1953); Morris B. Jacobs (ed.), *The Chemistry and Technology of Food and Food Products,* vol. ii, pp. 1683–1705, 2nd ed. (1951); D. M. Forrest, *Hundred Years of Ceylon Tea, 1867–1967* (1967). (J. P. Q.)

**TEA CEREMONY,** a time-honoured institution in Japan, is rooted in the principle of Zen Buddhism and is founded upon the adoration of the beautiful in the daily routine of life, such as preparing a meal and tea, cleaning the house and garden, etc. The Japanese word for the ceremony, *cha-no-yu* (literally "hot water tea"), means an aesthetic way of entertaining guests, who, after they have been served a meal, are served thick, weak tea made of pulverized tea leaf stirred in hot water. Everything is done according to the established rules of etiquette. The entertaining takes place in the tea room (*chaseki*), usually a small building constructed to suggest refined poverty, with great forethought given to the choice of material and the construction. The room is usually about nine feet square, or smaller. It contains an alcove for ornaments and a small sunken fireplace, which is used for heating the kettle during winter; in summer a brazier with a charcoal fire is used. Each guest enters the room in humility by crawling through a small opening less than three feet square.

The founders of the Tea Ceremony emphasized the following four qualities: (1) harmony among guests and utensils; (2) respect, not only among the participants but also for the utensils; (3) cleanliness, derived from Shinto, the ancestral religion of Japan, which requires each participant, before entering the *chaseki,* to wash his hands and rinse his mouth as symbolic gestures of cleansing himself externally and internally; and finally, (4) tranquillity, which suggests the indescribable quality of mellowness which is given to the article by long and fond use.

Bibliography.—E. S. Morse, *Japanese Homes and Their Surroundings* (1885; new ed. 1961); F. F. Brinkley, *Japan—Its History, Arts and Literature* (1901); Kakuzo Okakura, *The Book of Tea* (1925); A. L. Sadler, *Cha-No-Yu: the Japanese Tea Ceremony* (1963). (J. Har.)

**TEACH** (Thatch), **EDWARD** (d. 1718), English pirate, popularly known as Blackbeard, is believed to have been born at Bristol and to have gone to the West Indies during the War of the Spanish Succession (1701–13). He is first heard of as a pirate at the end of 1716. In 1717 he captured a large French merchantman, renamed her "Queen Anne's Revenge," and converted her into a warship of 40 guns. His outrages in the Caribbean Sea, and on the coasts of Carolina and Virginia, quickly earned him an infamous notoriety. In 1718 he made his base in an inlet in North Carolina, making an arrangement with the governor, Charles Eden, with whom he shared his prizes. The planters of that state finally requested help from the governor of Virginia, Alexander Spotswood, who sent two sloops under Lieut. Robert Maynard. On Nov. 22, 1718, Maynard boarded Teach's ship and, after a hard fight in the James River, shot the pirate dead.

*See* C. Johnson, *A General History of the Robberies and Murders of the Most Notorious Pyrates* (1724); P. Gosse, *The Pirates' Who's Who* (1924). (C. C. L.)

**TEACHER TRAINING** is generally concerned with preparation in subject matter and professional education, including psychology, methods, and practice teaching. This article covers principally teacher training for public elementary and secondary schools and continuing education related to that training.

## HISTORY

France and Germany began teacher education as early as the 17th century and continued to be influential in shaping patterns of training in other countries. With the secularization of schools in Germany, work in teacher education was greatly extended through the influence of Wilhelm von Humboldt (*q.v.*), who became minister of education in 1809. He helped establish a planned educational program, set up regular standards and examinations for teachers, and encouraged the development of pedagogical seminaries. In 1826 a year of trial teaching was established as a requirement of all candidates for teaching positions. In 1831 examinations in pedagogy, as well as in the main subjects of the higher school course, were made requirements for secondary school teachers.

Teacher education in the United States gained acceptance largely between 1820 and 1865. In the northeast the normal school (the original name for teacher-training schools) took root. The common school with equal opportunity for people of all classes led inevitably to support of a normal school to train teachers; the widening range of ability of students attending school brought an emphasis on teaching methods. Because of widespread establishment of common schools, Samuel R. Hall opened his private normal school at Concord, Vt., in 1823. In 1839 the first of the public normal schools was established by the state of Massachusetts. Traditionally, however, the training of teachers had been one of purely liberal education, and the effort to professionalize teacher education started a continuing controversy. The Yale College catalog of 1829–30 required completion of a liberal education appropriate for all before the beginning of any professional training. Thomas Jefferson at the University of Virginia and George Ticknor at Harvard experimented in elective programs with subjects of utilitarian value for preprofessional work, and this influence helped the new normal schools to establish themselves. (*See* also Normal School.)

The training of teachers in England dates from early in the 19th century, when the National Society for Promoting the Education of the Poor in the Principles of the Established Church and its Nonconformist rival, the British and Foreign School Society, first attacked the problem of elementary education on a national scale. Both societies adopted the "monitorial system," in which older scholars learned their lessons from the adult teacher in charge of the school and then taught them to the younger children. Some training was found to be necessary and training schools were accordingly set up. One of these developed into the Borough Road Training College, which is still in existence. About 1840 James Kay (afterward Sir James Kay-Shuttleworth), to whom, more than to any other single man, the English educational system is due, began the movement that replaced the monitors by "pupil-teachers;" *i.e.* boys and girls who were regularly apprenticed for a period of five years from the age of 13 and both learned the art of teaching and continued their education under the head teacher of an elementary school. Kay's scheme also involved training colleges where professional and academic education could be carried to a higher stage after the apprenticeship was completed. He himself founded the college which, as St. John's College, Battersea, London, was taken over by the National Society and furnished a model widely imitated.

These early patterns of teacher education had their beginnings at a time when educational responsibility rested primarily with the church. When governments began to assume civil responsibility for establishing and maintaining schools, they also began to determine the preparation and qualification of teachers. As the percentage of children enrolled in school in the United States increased, and higher numbers continued into the secondary schools, standards of certification were raised and collegiate study was increasingly expected of elementary as well as secondary school teachers. The period from 1920 to 1930 has been described as that in which normal schools became teachers colleges in answer to this expectation. The period of 1950–65 saw the teachers colleges broaden their curricula and become universities. In England the first major development toward increasing educational opportunity came in 1918, but it was not until the Education Act of 1944 creating the modern and technical secondary schools that reform assumed significant proportions.

## IMPACT OF UNIVERSAL EDUCATION

In the 20th century, as the privileges of education were extended throughout the world, the International Bureau of Education and later the United Nations Educational, Scientific, and Cultural Organization (UNESCO) actively promoted international exchange of information and the systematic gathering of educational data.

The predominant institution for the education of elementary teachers was a normal school following completion of the elementary school. These institutions gave courses in both general and professional education. A few countries offered education for elementary teachers at the level of higher education, either through the university or through higher schools of education. Still other countries offered a combination of work beginning at the secondary level and extending into the higher education level.

The preparation of secondary school teachers was both academic and professional. Academic preparation was provided for (1) through work at the regular universities; (2) through work at special institutions providing both academic and professional training; (3) by bringing in persons with special proficiency (engineers, for example, might teach mathematics; or pharmacists, chemistry); (4) in special schools for music, physical education, or art; (5) in countries with no higher educational institutions, by sending teachers abroad for training. Professional training was provided in a variety of ways.

**Courses and Requirements.**—The professional courses for secondary teacher training fall under three general headings: education, psychology, and practice teaching. Prevalent among education courses are those which deal with teaching methods and general orientation to education. The psychology courses provide for general psychological orientation and child or adolescent psychology. Practice teaching is uniformly provided but differs in length of time and type of work done by the student. In Austria a year of probationary service under the guidance of experienced teachers is provided. In the Federal Republic of Germany practice teaching includes two years of preparatory service following academic studies with two four-week periods of practical work in a school during vacations.

The subjects taught in primary-teacher-training establishments reflect the following persistent requirements in general education: mother tongue, a second language, history, mathematics, sciences, and geography. Professional subjects closely approximate the course offerings indicated in the requirements for preparation of secondary teachers. More specialized provision is made for the study of child development, together with more emphasis on methods. Persistent offerings in special subjects include physical culture, drawing, penmanship, music, handwork, domestic economy, agriculture and rural studies, health, and arts and crafts. These subjects reflect a trend to train teachers in areas that will enable them to contribute to national needs in agriculture, health, and domestic patterns. Furthermore, they indicate that primary education universally deals with a wider variety of cultural emphases than reading and writing alone, and that these subjects are of sufficient significance for recognition in the curricula of teacher education.

A comparative study of teacher training for primary schools in the U.S.S.R. and the U.S. revealed many similarities between the four-year course in pedagogical schools for the training of primary school teachers in the U.S.S.R. (1955–56) and the four-year course of the State Teachers College at Oneonta, N.Y. (now State University of New York College at Oneonta). The fundamental difference in the two programs was that the Soviet program gave emphasis to teaching methods in direct relation to subjects, while the Oneonta course gave separate consideration to the child and his curriculum in a two-year integrated methods course.

Just as the beginnings of teacher education took place almost simultaneously in the various countries of Western Europe, so following World War II there was a nearly universal review of the adequacy of education in an effort to extend opportunity to a larger number of people in various countries. (*See* ILLITERACY: *Reduction of Illiteracy;* SECONDARY EDUCATION.)

The United Nations Universal Declaration of Human Rights (adopted in 1948), which states that everyone has a right to education, made its influence felt in recognizing throughout the world the need to extend compulsory education. The effect of these developments on teacher education was direct. Extension of teacher education was needed because of the extension of compulsory education, the increases in population of school age, and the extension of the years of schooling. In Costa Rica, for example, there were 3,500 students in secondary schools in 1948 and more than 45,000 in the late 1960s. Enrollment in primary schools of Iraq was 90,000 in 1944 and 1,000,000 by the late 1960s. Similar increases in primary and secondary school enrollments were experienced in country after country, with consequent attempts to expand teacher-training institutions and programs to keep pace. The World Survey of Education revealed that in 1930–34, the number of students specializing in education in institutions of higher education represented 1% of the total enrollment. In 1955–59, they accounted for 2%, an annual increase of 38% over the 1930–34 figure.

The International Bureau of Education has, since 1931, conducted a yearly International Conference on Public Education (after 1945 in cooperation with UNESCO). As early as 1935 pressures were felt on teacher education programs, and the conference that year was devoted to problems of primary teacher training. In 1953 and 1954 the problems of primary teacher education and problems and issues in preparing secondary school teachers were the subjects of conferences. Reports from various countries and the recommendations of those attending reflected practice and also served as guideposts to ministries of education in formulating programs in teacher education. They revealed discernible trends in the 1960s that were not readily identifiable earlier:

1. Longer preparation for elementary teachers and greater specialization for secondary teachers. No doubt the worldwide stress on newer programs in science and mathematics influenced this development.

2. Elimination of barriers between training of elementary and secondary teachers. In England and Wales, the McNair Report (1944) and the Robbins Report (1961) made recommendations which, in effect, made teacher-training institutions an organic part of the universities. In 1965–66, universities in England, Scotland, and Canada introduced a bachelor of education degree, although it had marked differences as defined by various universities.

3. Technology. Countries as widely separated geographically as Sweden, Thailand, and Hungary reported the use of television with practice teachers to permit viewing of actual classes with-

out disruption of classrooms. Videotape was used in many institutions to permit students to observe their own work and improve it. Computer-assisted instruction began to appear in the late 1960s. Techniques for using such devices were included in programs.

4. Student-teacher relationships. The expansion of schools to include wider segments of the population increases the importance of the teacher-student relationship. This was reflected in the use of sensitivity training, group dynamics, micro-teaching, interaction analysis, simulation games, and emphasis on self-concept as it affects learning. There was also an influence on the design of courses, such as the section of the required training in Belgium that attempts to focus curriculum, spirit, and methods on man and society and their relationship.

5. Advanced training centres. The U.S.S.R. Academy of Pedagogical Sciences is designed to train pedagogical scientists in research, in pedagogical theory, and in development of new discoveries and hypotheses which form the basis of school practices. Turkey's five-year plan of reform provided for the training of 3,000 university teachers and research workers. India developed 97 secondary extension service centres, 45 primary extension service centres, and 1 research centre to serve teachers colleges. The federally funded Research and Development Laboratories and Regional Educational Laboratories also reached beyond existing programs of teacher education. The U.S. Higher Education Act (1965) and the Education Professions Development Act (1967) were also designed to provide training opportunities for graduate students and college and university personnel.

6. Special education. There is almost universal expansion of training for special education teachers. Examples include the University of Warsaw chair of special pedagogy and Yugoslavia's Education Law of 1958.

7. Nursery school teachers. Educational opportunity is being extended to preschool children in increasing numbers. The Head Start Program in the United States was one example. Nurseries for children of working mothers were being developed in many newly industrialized countries. This expansion brought about an extension of training for nursery school teachers as well.

**Quality of Teacher Education.**—A threat to the quality of training has arisen from the shortage of teachers. At the same time that attention was being given to improving quality and extending time for programs of teacher training in a majority of countries, those same countries were forced to set up emergency training measures. Many countries provided increased living allowances for students in training, in order to encourage more people to enter the profession. Others temporarily shortened the training periods. Appointments were made with required part-time study to bring the emergency teacher up to standards.

A recurring problem in providing qualified teachers is that of reaching the rural areas. By the late 1960s, 15 countries had established national or regional institutes or centres to bring training to rural areas. Nepal developed Mobile Normal School Teams to conduct nine-month training courses for youth. By rotating each year, all of Nepal could be covered in three or four years. In the United States the Teacher Corps was created (1965) to recruit and train able people to teach in low-income areas, both rural and urban. In England, the Plowden Report (1967) recommended establishing a relationship between training colleges and "priority" schools—priority in terms of need. Teacher aides were being used in many countries to help meet problems of overloaded classrooms. Training courses for aides were being developed.

The National Council for the Accreditation of Teacher Education in the United States worked on such problems as setting up criteria for selection of candidates in teacher education, the balance between general and professional courses, adequate supervision of practical teaching, selection of laboratory experiences, and the encouragement of research to determine the effectiveness of applied criteria.

A review of the status of teacher education would not be complete without noting that 1965 marked the beginning of a period of renewed efforts to pursue research which would serve as a basis for improving teacher education and a period of extensive experimentation in the pattern of teacher education. This experimentation was generally directed toward reducing the multiplicity of formal courses in favour of closely supervised teaching experience. Students became members of teaching teams; more time was spent on tutorials and related clinical experience.

**Supplementary Education and Training.**—As in other professions, newer methods and new developments in the fields of knowledge necessitated further education for teachers with experience. In many countries seminars or institutes were conducted by the government. The content reflected the major concern of the governmental agency. For example, in Czechoslovakia, Belorussia, and elsewhere in the U.S.S.R. a summer training course was required to prepare for greater emphasis on practical and polytechnic training in the secondary curriculum. In India in 1966, the National Council for Educational Research and Training set up conferences on science education in 20 university centres. Bulgaria arranged 120 conferences within one year to help teachers relate the practical and theoretical aspects of new developments. Materials centres either in a central place or in a bookmobile were used to bring new ideas to teachers on the job.

In the U.S., local school systems frequently sponsored in-service training courses, and the universities conducted extensive summer programs for teachers. The National Science Foundation conducted training programs for teachers and equipped traveling science laboratories to serve the purpose of educating both children and teachers in contemporary science. The Continental Classroom television program was another effort to bring current information to teachers. The National Defense Education Act (1958) and the Elementary and Secondary Education Act (1965) provided loans and fellowships for students planning to teach in various fields, and for teacher-training institutes and other aids for graduate education.

Even before education became a civil responsibility, members of the profession met to share ways of improving their work. They cooperated with governments and institutions of higher learning in modern efforts. They worked with the Area Training Organizations in England, and they developed significant and influential plans for educational improvement in Ireland, Scotland, Australia, and Canada. In Ontario, for example, they conducted summer workshops for teachers and developed a permanent training centre. The National Education Association of the United States, with its various affiliates, conducted continuous research for the improvement of the profession. The World Confederation of Organizations of the Teaching Profession conducts an annual conference and stresses in-service education in its program of action. (*See* also EDUCATION, SOCIETIES OF.)

Other significant developments in further education included research centres. In Brazil, for example, the Brazilian Centre of Educational Research was established in 1955. The purposes of its centres are: (1) to study cultural and educational conditions and trends in the development of Brazil's regions and society as a whole, with a view to gradually formulating a national education policy; (2) to make plans, recommendations, and suggestions for the reform of Brazilian education; (3) to prepare reference works, textbooks, and other educational materials and to conduct special studies on school administration, curricula, educational psychology and philosophy, the training of teachers and other matters connected with the improvement of teacher training; (4) to arrange training and supplementary courses for school administrators, those responsible for educational guidance, educationists and primary teachers in teacher training and primary schools.

The 20th century has seen the wide use of international exchange in the training of teachers. The technical assistance programs of UNESCO, the Agency for International Development (AID), and the Fulbright Scholarship programs in the United States, the British Council, the Ford and Rockefeller foundations, the American Friends Service Committee, the Alliance Française, and the Southeast Asian Board of Scholarships and Exchange of Professors made international exchange significant in the training of teachers throughout the world (*see* also STUDENT AID). These exchanges helped to establish certain common directions in teacher education, but they also emphasized the fact that teacher education must be rooted in the culture and expectations of the particular country in which it functions.

*See* also EDUCATION, HISTORY OF; EDUCATIONAL PSYCHOLOGY; HIGHER EDUCATION: *Teacher Training;* ELEMENTARY EDUCATION; PRE-ELEMENTARY EDUCATION; SECONDARY EDUCATION; and references under "Teacher Training" in the Index.

BIBLIOGRAPHY.—U.S. Department of Health, Education, and Welfare, Division of International Education, *Education in the U.S.S.R.*, bulletin no. 14 (1957); I. L. Kandel, *New Era in Education* (1955); B. Holmes, "Teacher Education in a Changing World," *Yearbook of Education* (1963); W. A. D. Lloyd, *The Old and the New Schoolmaster* (1960); G. D. Robbins, *Teacher Education and Professional Standards in England and Wales* (1963); Merle D. Borrowman, *The Liberal and Technical in Teacher Education* (1956); C. A. Richardson, H. Brule, and H. Snyder, *Education of Teachers in England, France, and the U.S.A.* (1953); A. M. Kazamias and B. G. Massialas, *Tradition and Change in Education: a Comparative Study* (1965); E. King, *Other Schools and Ours,* 3rd ed. (1967); I. N. Thut and D. Adams, *Educational Patterns in Contemporary Societies* (1964); Government of India, *Education and National Development,* Report of the Education Commission (1964–66); World Confederation of Organizations of the Teaching Profession, *Annual Reports* (1965–69), *Soviet Education,* Dec. 1968, vol. xi, no. 2, May 1969, vol. xi, no. 7; *Encyclopedia of Educational Research,* 4th ed. (1969); UNESCO, *World Survey of Education, ii:* "Primary Education" (1959), *iii:* "Secondary Education" (1962), *iv:* "Higher Education" (1966); UNESCO, International Bureau of Education, "Training of Primary Teacher Training Staffs," no. 182 (1957), "In-service Training for Primary Teachers," no. 240 (1962), "Teachers Abroad," no. 290 (1966), *International Yearbook of Education,* vol. 29 (1967), *International Review of Education,* vol. xiv (1968), no. 4 and vol. xv (1969); *London Times Educational Supplement* (1967 and 1968); D. C. Scanlon and J. Shields (eds.), *Problems and Prospects in International Education* (1968). (T. D. R.)

**TEACHING METHODS:** *see* AUDIO-VISUAL EDUCATION; EDUCATION, HISTORY OF; EDUCATIONAL PSYCHOLOGY; ELEMENTARY EDUCATION; EXAMINATIONS; LEARNING; MONTESSORI SYSTEM; PRE-ELEMENTARY EDUCATION; PROGRAMMED LEARNING; SECONDARY EDUCATION. *See* also EDUCATION (ARTICLES ON).

**TEAK** is one of the most valuable world timbers. Known from ancient times—the Sanskrit name is *saka*—teak has been widely used in India for more than 2,000 years. The generic name *Tectona* is from the Malayan word *tekku.* Teak is a large deciduous tree of the verbena family (Verbenaceae), with a straight but often buttressed stem, a spreading crown and four-sided branchlets with large quadrangular pith.

The leaves are opposite, or sometimes whorled in very young specimens, 1 to 2 ft. (0.3 to 0.6 m.) long and 6 to 12 in. (15 to 30 cm.) wide. On sucker shoots and seedlings the leaves are much larger, often from two to three feet long. In shape they somewhat resemble those of the tobacco plant, but their substance is hard and the surface rough. Small white flowers, very numerous, in large, erect, cross-branched panicles, terminate the branches. The fruit is a drupe, two-thirds of an inch in diameter. The bark of the stem is about one-half an inch thick, gray or brownish-gray, the sapwood white; the unseasoned heartwood has a pleasant and strong aromatic fragrance and a beautiful golden-yellow colour, which on seasoning soon darkens into brown, mottled with darker streaks. The timber retains its aromatic fragrance to a great age.

FOOD AND AGRICULTURE ORGANIZATION OF THE UNITED NATIONS

**AGED TEAK LOG SECTIONED TO SHOW ITS SEASONED DARK HEARTWOOD**

Teak thrives best in districts with a mean annual rainfall of more than 50 in. (1,270 mm.) and a mean annual temperature between 75° and 81° F (24° to 27° C). It is native to India, Burma and Thailand; its natural northern limit of growth in these areas is about the 25th parallel, although plantations have been established as far north as the 32nd parallel in the Punjab. The tree is not found near the coast; the most valuable forests are on low hills up to 3,000 ft. (914 m.). Stands are also found in the Philippines, in Java and elsewhere in the Malay archipelago, although there is no record of its being native in those places. Teak grows on a great variety of soils, but there is one indispensable condition—perfect drainage or a dry subsoil. On level ground, with deep alluvial soil, teak does not always form regularly shaped stems, probably because the subsoil drainage is imperfect.

During the dry season the tree is leafless; in hot localities the leaves fall in January, but in moist places the tree remains green until March. At the end of the dry season, when the first monsoon rains fall, the new foliage emerges.

The principal value of teak timber for use in warm countries is its extraordinary durability. In India and in Burma beams of the wood in good preservation are often found in buildings several centuries old, and instances are known of teak beams having lasted more than 1,000 years. In one of the oldest buildings among the ruins of the old city of Vijayanagar, on the banks of the Tungabhadra in southern India, the superstructure is supported by planks of teakwood 1½ in. thick. These planks, examined in 1881, had been in the building for 500 years and were still in a good state of preservation and showed the peculiar structure of teak timber in a very marked manner. In the wall of a palace of the Persian kings near Baghdad, which was pillaged in the 7th century, two archaeologists in 1811 found pieces of Indian teak which were perfectly sound. In the old cave temples of Salsette and elsewhere in western India, pieces of teak which must have been more than 2,000 years old have been found in good preservation. The timber is practically imperishable under cover.

Teak is used for shipbuilding, fine furniture, door and window frames, wharves, bridges, cooling tower louvres, flooring, paneling, railway cars and venetian blinds. An important property of teak which affects utilization is its extremely good dimensional stability. It is of medium weight (45 lb. per cubic foot), strong and of average hardness. Termites eat the sapwood but rarely attack the heartwood; it is not, however, completely resistant to marine borers. Although the tree flowers freely, few seeds are produced as many of the flowers are sterile. Spread by self-sown seed is impeded by the forest fires of the dry season, which in India generally occur in March and April, after the seeds have ripened and have partly fallen. Although germination is slow, in its youth the tree grows with extreme rapidity. Two-year-old seedlings on good soil are five to ten feet high, and instances of more rapid growth are not uncommon. In Burmese plantations teak trees on good soil have attained an average height of 60 ft. in 15 years, with a girth, breast high, of 19 in. In these plantations it is estimated that the tree under favourable circumstances will attain a diameter of 24 in. (girth 6 ft.) at the age of 80. Normal exploitable girth limits are 7 ft. 6 in. for good forests, and 6 ft. 6 in. for poor teak forests. In the natural forests of Burma and India, teak timber with a diameter of 24 in. is never less than 100 and often more than 200 years old. Mature trees are generally not more than 100 to 150 ft. high.

Although the largest volume of teakwood produced is used in India and Burma, Ceylon and the east, much of the best quality is exported. Burma produces most of the world's teak supply. India, Thailand, Java and Ceylon rank next in production.

Burma teak comes mainly from the Pegu Yomas and Chindwin drainage areas, and is floated down the Sittang and Irrawaddy rivers to Rangoon. The most important teak forests in India are found in Madhya Pradesh, Mysore, Madras, Coorg, Bombay and Kerala. Practically all Indian teak is utilized within the country, and the supply falls short of actual requirements. Thailand teak is shipped from Bangkok mainly to European markets. Teak has been cropped in Central America and elsewhere in the new world, but it has never been commercially successful.

*See* United Nations Food and Agricultural Organization, *Country Reports on Teak* (1956). (W. L. S.)

**TEASDALE, SARA** (1884–1933), U.S. poet whose work, personal and confessional in nature, is noted for its classical simplicity and lyric intensity. She was born in St. Louis, Mo., on

Aug. 8, 1884, and was privately educated there. Upon her marriage in 1914 she moved to New York, where she continued to make her home after being divorced in 1929. She died in New York City on Jan. 29, 1933.

Encouraged by her family, Sara Teasdale began writing at an early age and published her first book, *Sonnets to Duse and Other Poems,* in 1907. From the beginning her work was well received; with *Rivers to the Sea* (1915) she was established as a popular poet; for *Love Songs* (1917) she won the Pulitzer Prize for poetry in 1918. These early poems, some of which became for a time standard anthology pieces, typically express a variation of the theme of feminine love, employ the simplest of lyric forms, and give the impression of spontaneous and liquid movement. Gradually, however, her poetry developed gravity and dignity, and her later books—especially *Dark of the Moon* (1926)—include poems that display great purity of form and technical brilliance. Her work is narrow in range and written in a distinctly minor key, but on occasion it rises to excellence.

Her *Collected Poems* appeared in 1937.

**TEBESSA** (the Roman THEVESTE), a town of Algeria, lies on a plateau 146 mi. (235 km.) S of Annaba and 12 mi. (19 km.) W of the Tunisian frontier. Pop. (1960) 26,622. The hub of the town is Kasbah square and there is a modern church built from the ancient ruins.

The central feature of the triangular-shaped town is the walled Byzantine citadel, a square with 12 towers and 4 gateways. Solomon's gate, on the east, was named after the Byzantine general who built the ramparts in 530; and on the north is the splendid Roman quadrifrontal arch of Caracalla (214), each side of which is flanked by a pair of monolithic columns. The temple of Minerva, built in 211, is now a museum containing remarkable mosaics and sculptured oil lamps. The most beautiful historic building is the Christian basilica, 1 mi. N from the town centre and restored in the 1930s. It has traces of three successive constructions: the subterranean church and its catacombs (1st century); the first basilica (315–350), one of the strongholds of the Donatist heresy; and the upper basilica (after 350). Together with gardens and the remains of a 6th-century Byzantine military establishment, it makes one of the loveliest sights of Algeria. Outside Solomon's gate are the ruins of a Roman amphitheatre, and to the south of the town hot baths were uncovered.

A prehistoric site, Tebessa was an outpost of Carthage in the 7th century B.C. and in 146 B.C., a Roman garrison. At its height in A.D. 200, it declined in the 5th century under Vandal dominion and in the 6th century was occupied by Byzantines and later by Berbers. With the Arab invasion of the 7th century it disappeared from history. The Turks stationed a small garrison of janizaries there in the 16th century, but after French rule began in 1840 Tebessa was developed as the easternmost of the Algerian gateways to the south.

Tebessa is linked by rail to Annaba and is also a road junction, and its airport ($\frac{1}{2}$ mi. away) is served by French airways. In addition to working the important phosphate mines of Kouif (northeast of Tebessa and linked by rail), the people live by trade, especially in sheep, esparto and grain, and there is a thriving handicraft production of carpets. (R. GU.)

**TEBU** (TIBBU, TUBU), a Muslim Negro-Berber people of the eastern and central Sahara (*q.v.*) who were estimated to number about 35,000 in the 1960s. Living either as nomadic herdsmen or as farmers (*e.g.,* near oases), they have two major tribal divisions: the Daza and the Teda. Dates are a staple; a variety of grains, legumes, and root crops are cultivated; cattle, goats, donkeys, camels, and sheep are kept; and caravan trade is an important factor in the economy. Sedentary Tebu villagers typically have palm-thatched, rectangular mud houses (Daza) or cylindrical huts of mud or stone with conical thatch (Teda). They are patrilineal, pay bridewealth (*q.v.;* usually livestock), and first-cousin marriage is tabu; polygyny is not uncommon. Commoners are distinguished from nobles, and the Teda tribe have a so-called sultan, but real power typically rests with local headmen who inherit their offices.

*See* also BORKU; CHAD, REPUBLIC OF; FRENCH EQUATORIAL AFRICA; NIGER, REPUBLIC OF THE.

BIBLIOGRAPHY.—W. Cline, *The Teda of Tibesti, Borku, and Kawar in the Eastern Sahara,* "Gen. Ser. Anthrop.," vol. 12 (1950); P. Fuchs, "Ueber die Tubbu von Tibesti," *Arch. Völkerk.,* vol. 11 (1956); G. P. Murdock, *Africa: Its Peoples and Their Culture History* (1959); L. C. Briggs, *Tribes of the Sahara* (1960).

**TECHNETIUM,** element 43, was the first example of the creation of a hitherto unknown element by artificial means. The name, from the Greek word meaning artificial, commemorates this fact and has been accepted by the International Union of Chemistry. It is the homologue of manganese (25) and rhenium (75) in the periodic system. Formerly known as masurium, it follows molybdenum (42) and precedes ruthenium (44). The chemical symbol is Tc, and the atomic weight (mass number) of its best-known isotope is given as 99.

This element has been extensively sought in natural ores, notably by I. Noddack and W. Noddack, who in 1925 claimed to have detected its X-ray spectrum in the same series of experiments that led to the discovery of rhenium. However, the findings of the Noddacks were not confirmed by other experimenters. It is now known that its natural existence is most improbable because it would contradict well-established rules of nuclear stability. However the fission of uranium does yield extremely small amounts of radioactive isotopes of technetium.

In 1937 E. Segrè and C. Perrier found several radioactive isotopes of element 43 in molybdenum targets that had been bombarded with deuterons in the cyclotron. Using the methods of radiochemistry, they gave positive evidence that some of the radioactivity was produced by element 43. At the same time they established several chemical properties of the new element.

Technetium can be produced by several types of nuclear bombardment, such as neutrons on molybdenum or deuterons on molybdenum, and is also a product of the fission of uranium (O. Hahn and F. Strassmann, E. Segrè and C. S. Wu). The latter nuclear reaction promised to supply the largest amounts of the element. If it existed in ores, its geochemistry would probably be similar to that of rhenium.

The element is metallic in its properties; it is isomorphous with rhenium; and $Tc^{99}$ has a density of 11.49 g./cm.$^3$ Metallic technetium becomes a superconductor at 7.75° K. In the course of a chemical analysis technetium would separate in the second group (sulfides insoluble in acid solution) and would usually appear with rhenium, although it can be separated from this element by a distillation at 180° C. in a current of hydrogen chloride. Its separation from molybdenum, which is often of practical importance, can be obtained by precipitating the molybdenum from an acetic acid solution with 8-hydroxyquinoline. Technetium stays in solution.

Among the technetium compounds are the oxides $TcO_2$, $Tc_2O_7$, the sulfide $Tc_2S_7$ and the important ion $TcO_4$ which gives pertechnetates similar to permanganates and perrhenates.

More than 15 isotopes of technetium were known in the 1960s, ranging in mass number from 92 upward (*see* NUCLEUS: *Chart of Properties of the Nuclides*). They are all radioactive, some emitting electrons, some decaying by orbital electron capture and some undergoing isomeric transitions. Following these isomeric transitions, the characteristic X-ray emission of technetium is observed; this provided an early opportunity for the spectroscopic observation of the K X-ray lines of this element before macroscopic amounts of it were available.

Beginning in 1944, substantial progress in the study of technetium was made in the laboratories of the atomic energy agencies of several countries. Since $Tc^{99}$ has a beta-decay period of about 200,000 years, it was possible to isolate many grams of it. This isotope is obtained either as a fission product or by neutron capture of molybdenum followed by a beta decay.

If the technetium formed in nuclear reactors in existence in the 1960s were extracted, there would be an annual production of several hundreds of kilograms, quite comparable to the annual production of some of the rarer natural elements. Thus the possibility of practical applications for this element is not excluded. In this connection it is interesting to note that it has been reported that technetium compounds and alloys are very effective in the prevention of corrosion.

The availability of relatively large amounts of technetium permitted study of it through the ordinary methods of chemistry and physics, without taking advantage of its radioactive properties. Investigations were conducted on its X-ray spectrum by external excitation, the crystal structures of the element and of its compounds, and the optical spectral lines. Also several chemical compounds were prepared in pure form and studied thermodynamically and otherwise, confirming the general analogy with rhenium.

In 1952 it was reported by Paul W. Merrill that spectra of stars of the S type show strong technetium lines. The astrophysical reason for this remarkable fact is not known.

BIBLIOGRAPHY.—C. Perrier and E. Segrè, "Some Chemical Properties of Element 43," *J. Chem. Phys.*, vol. 5 (1937); G. Friedlander and J. W. Kennedy, *Nuclear and Radiochemistry*, 2nd ed. (1964); R. Colton, *The Chemistry of Rhenium and Technetium* (1965).

(Eo. S.)

**TECHNICAL EDUCATION** is concerned with teaching applied sciences, special training in applied science, technical procedures, and skills required for the practice of trades or professions, especially those involving the use of machinery or scientific equipment. Technical education emphasizes the understanding and practical application of basic principles of mathematics and science rather than the attainment of proficiency in manual skills. It has as objectives the preparation of graduates for occupations between the skilled crafts and the engineering or scientific occupations. Technical schools or institutes usually offer instruction to students beyond school age, although many variations exist. In most countries the basis, at least, of technical training is offered at the secondary level, often in special schools, as the technical secondary schools of Great Britain, and some countries include technical education in the elementary curriculum. At the other end of the scale, it is usually considered to be below the professional level, but there is no clear dividing line. The picture is further complicated by the fact that many institutions that are designated colleges offer work below the college level, and some that are designated technical institutes or polytechnics offer advanced scientific and professional work, as, for example, the Massachusetts Institute of Technology.

For this article, the following definition has been used: Technical education is that education offered in post-high school curricula that generally are one to three years in length, are terminal in nature and not designed to lead to a baccalaureate degree, and are offered in a wide variety of institutions, such as technical institutes, junior colleges, night schools, extension divisions of colleges and universities, and proprietary schools. Variations from this are indicated.

Under this definition technical education may be distinguished from vocational education, which places major emphasis upon imparting manual skills to an individual to prepare him for a single occupation or trade. Vocational education is generally offered in vocational, or trade, schools or comprehensive high schools. Technical education may also be distinguished from professional education, which places major emphasis upon the theories, understanding, and principles of a wide body of subject matter designed to equip the graduate to practise in such fields as medicine, law, and engineering. Professional education necessitates the completion of at least four years of college and generally requires a significant amount of graduate work beyond the baccalaureate degree. (For programs at the secondary level, *see* VOCATIONAL EDUCATION. For technical education at the college level, *see* HIGHER EDUCATION; ENGINEERING EDUCATION.)

Graduates of technical curricula may be roughly classified as follows: (1) engineering and science aides, such as draftsmen, designers, laboratory technicians; (2) technical supervisors, such as foremen, chief inspectors, production supervisors; (3) technical specialists, such as time study men, methods analysts, quality control men; (4) technical salesmen.

A narrower definition of technical education normally implies those curricula that are engineering related, but the term is also sometimes more broadly and loosely used to embrace nonengineering related curricula from one to three years in length in agriculture, applied and graphic arts, business, education, and health services.

## UNITED STATES

The need for technical education evolved as a result of the Industrial Revolution, and, beginning early in the 19th century, a movement for the education of the workingman took place in both England and the United States. A number of mechanics' institutes were founded, whose purpose it was to impart technical information and skills to farmers and mechanics. Some of the early mechanics' institutes that sprang up in the larger industrial centres were The General Society of Mechanics and Tradesmen, founded in New York in 1820; the Maryland Institute in Baltimore, 1825; Franklin Institute in Philadelphia, 1824; and Ohio Mechanics Institute in Cincinnati, 1828. Most of these institutions flourished briefly and then closed. Ohio Mechanics Institute (now called Ohio College of Applied Science) is the only survivor still in existence that has a continuous history of offering training for technical occupations.

A significant early impetus given to technical education in the United States was the passage of the Morrill Act in 1862, which granted large blocks of land to the several states for the support of public colleges of agriculture and mechanic arts. With this assistance many of the states established land-grant colleges, and most of these institutions in the early years offered much education that was technical in content and level (*see* LAND-GRANT COLLEGES AND UNIVERSITIES).

Numerous private institutions founded in the years preceding and following the Civil War functioned largely as technical institutes but have since become more conventional four-year engineering and science schools. These include Pratt Institute, founded in 1887; the Rochester Institute of Technology, which traces its history back through the merger in 1891 of the Rochester Athenaeum, 1829, and Mechanics Institute, 1885; the Polytechnic Institute of Brooklyn, founded 1854; Cooper Union, 1859; Drexel Institute, 1891; and Carnegie Institute of Technology, 1900.

### STATUS OF TECHNICAL EDUCATION

The identification of "technical education" as having a level and content of its own was initially stimulated by a report, "A Study of Technical Institutes," published by the Society for the Promotion of Engineering Education (SPEE) in 1931. Although the report dealt with the technical institute as a type of educational institution, it also identified this level of education as "occupying an area beween the skilled crafts and the highly scientific occupations."

The years since this report have witnessed a more rapid growth of technical education than the previous century. This has been due in part to: (1) The 1931 SPEE study of technical institutes. (2) The rapid development of scientific and engineering industries, which have created a need for trained technicians. (3) The tremendous need of the armed forces for technicians. (4) The accreditation of technical-terminal curricula by the Engineers Council for Professional Development. (5) The growing body of literature devoted to this type of education. (6) The granting of the associate's degree for technical-terminal programs, giving status to this level and type of education. (7) The report of the National Survey of Technical Institute Education (published in 1959) conducted for the American Society of Engineering Education under a grant from the Carnegie Corporation.

Surveys of U.S. technical education reveal that the engineering-related curricula enrolling the largest numbers of students were electrical technology, mechanical technology, and architectural and civil technology. The largest enrollments in nonengineering curricula were business, health services, and education. In these surveys slightly more than three-fifths of the students were enrolled on a full-time basis, and more than three-fifths were in publicly controlled institutions. (L. F. SH.)

## UNITED KINGDOM

**England and Wales.**—Technical education in the modern sense did not develop in England on any substantial scale until the last decade of the 19th century. The mechanics' institutes, founded in great numbers from 1823 to about 1860, were intended to instruct workingmen "in the scientific principles of arts and manufactures," but for the most part they quickly became diverted to social and literary rather than industrial education. The Great Exhibition at the Crystal Palace in 1851, which confirmed fears that Great Britain's industrial primacy was being threatened, led the government to establish a science and art department, but the grants that it distributed did little beyond developing an arid examination system.

The 1867 international exhibition at Paris shook British complacency. It led to the founding, in 1880, of the City and Guilds of London Institute to promote the teaching of applied science. In 1883 the institute opened the Finsbury Technical College for the training of artisans and in 1884 the Central Training College at South Kensington to train technical teachers and the higher ranks of industry. Meanwhile, quite independently, Quintin Hogg opened in 1882 the Polytechnic in Regent Street, London.

The Technical Instruction Act, 1889, empowered the newly created county councils and the county borough councils to give limited aid to technical education out of public funds. In 1891 the Local Taxation (Customs and Excise) Act unexpectedly made further large sums of money (popularly called "whiskey money") available for this purpose. Consequently, the decade 1889–99 saw great activity in the provision of buildings for the teaching of applied science and technology. In addition to public effort, funds provided by the City of London Parochial Charities Act, 1883, aided the building in London of more polytechnics.

In 1899 the Board of Education Act created a single national department charged with the supervision of public education throughout England and Wales. The Education Act, 1902, similarly made the county and county borough councils general purpose education authorities, responsible for supplying or aiding the supply of secondary and technical as well as elementary education. The preoccupation of the board of education and the local education authorities with the development of the newly established secondary system considerably slowed down provision for technical education for more than ten years. Nevertheless, about 1905 trade schools for boys and girls leaving elementary schools began to be established in London, Middlesex, and elsewhere; and in 1913 these schools were made eligible for grant as "junior technical schools."

The first decades of the 20th century were marked by development of technical education by local education authorities, but also by continuing prejudice against it on the part of the public at large, who supposed that it qualified students only for menial work. As a result, the secondary technical schools, though vigorously championed by certain enthusiasts, appeared unlikely ever to match the grammar schools in numbers or reputation. But World Wars I and II, and the demand in each for skilled personnel, brought a gradual recognition that technical education was vital to an industrial society. Technical studies began to be taken up in secondary schools of all types; and the growing preoccupation of the universities with them added to their prestige. By the 1960s a distinct pattern of strictly technical institutions could be seen. There were about 300 local technical colleges (besides 7,600 local evening institutes), and about 160 area and 25 regional colleges offering increasingly advanced work. The Council for National Academic Awards, formed in 1964 and empowered to grant its own degrees, promised increasing status for technical studies at the higher levels. Outside the state system there was a flourishing body of private correspondence colleges offering a wide variety of technical courses.

**Scotland.**—Modern technical education in Scotland began with the founding by George Birkbeck in 1800 of a class for instructing Glasgow operatives in "mechanical and chemical philosophy." In 1823 this class broke away from the Andersonian Institute, to which it was attached, to form the first mechanics' institution. Two years previously there was opened in Edinburgh the School of Arts, claimed to be the first institution in Great Britain founded expressly to give scientific instruction to workingmen.

Until 1897 the English science and art department covered Scotland as well, and consequently statutory development of technical education was broadly parallel with that in England, except that under the Educational Endowments (Scotland) Act, 1882, money was provided for establishing and maintaining technical schools. The Andersonian Institute and the Glasgow Mechanics' Institution were merged in what became the Royal Technical College, Glasgow, and the School of Arts in the Heriot-Watt College. The former, since 1956 called the Royal College of Science and Technology, Glasgow, in 1964 was chartered as the University of Strathclyde.

Codes of regulations in 1899 and 1901 organized elementary technical instruction in "continuation classes." To encourage advanced work the 1901 code provided that outstandingly good and well-equipped technical colleges could be exempted from its regulations and grant aided on special terms. The Education (Scotland) Act, 1908, recognized 11 of these "central institutions," as they became known.

In the 1960s technical education was being provided in 16 central institutions, including agricultural and veterinary colleges, and in over 1,100 "continuation class centres."

**Northern Ireland.**—Before 1922 education throughout Ireland was regulated from England. In the 19th century, despite the nonindustrial character of the country, technical education developed remarkably. It received an added stimulus in 1899 when a Department of Agriculture and Technical Instruction was created. In 1922, 39 technical schools managed by local authorities were handed over to the Northern Ireland government. They included the Belfast College of Technology, one of the largest and best in the British Isles.

The Education (Northern Ireland) Act, 1923, further stimulated technical education by abolishing the restriction on expenditure to a *2d.* rate and merging it in the general expenditure of the local authorities. Junior technical and commercial schools expanded, especially in the provision of day classes.

The Belfast College of Technology prepares students for degrees in engineering and related subjects offered by the Queen's University. Among its students are also trades scholars, who are apprentices granted scholarships by the Ministry of Education for extended courses. Each of the counties is well equipped with technical schools, County Down, for instance, having 8, with 25 subsidiary centres.

### REPUBLIC OF IRELAND

The Department of Education set up in 1924 took over the functions of the Technical Instruction Branch of the Department of Agriculture and Technical Instruction established by the Agricultural Technical Instruction (Ireland) Act, 1899. Following the report of the Commission on Technical Education, issued in 1927, which noted especially the lack of technical instruction in rural areas, a system of rural continuation schools was developed, offering full- and part-time classes to meet the needs of their localities. Technical colleges and schools maintained by local authorities were established in all cities and large towns.

### BRITISH COMMONWEALTH

**Australia.**—With increasing industrialization, much attention was paid to technical education, especially after 1940. In all states there are technical secondary schools or courses, and part-time training schemes, from three to five years in duration, for apprentices.

The University of Queensland runs correspondence courses in technical education up to degree standard. Altogether, by the 1960s, Australia had more than 200 technical schools and colleges.

**New Zealand.**—At the secondary level there are technical high schools in the large towns; in the smaller ones consolidated schools offer technical courses. There is a Technical Correspondence School in Wellington.

(*See* also NEW ZEALAND: *Administration and Social Conditions: Education.*)

**Canada.**—In both English and French educational systems there are technical high schools and trade schools at the secondary level. Post-secondary technical institutes numbered more than 30 in the 1960s and had an enrollment of 12,000 students. The Nova Scotia Technical College and the agricultural, pharmacy, and veterinary colleges in Ontario are of university status, as is Macdonald College, the agricultural faculty of McGill University, Montreal, Que.

The western universities and New Brunswick have schools of engineering and agriculture. Newfoundland has a technical college at St. John's for the fishing industry. (*See* also CANADA: *Administration and Social Conditions: Education.*)

**India.**—In many elementary and some secondary schools instruction in handicrafts was made compulsory during the 1950s. Further technical education was provided in universities and technical institutions at four levels: vocational training; diploma courses; first degree courses; postgraduate courses.

The responsibility for education was assumed by the states, but the central government, through the All-India Council for Technical Education, coordinated and improved facilities. It maintained the Delhi Polytechnic and established the Institute of Technology at Kharagpur in West Bengal (1951) and those at Bombay (1958), Madras (1959), and Kanpur (1960). The number of institutions awarding various grades of diploma in engineering and technology had risen by the 1960s to more than 350.

**Pakistan.**—At the time of partition in 1947 Pakistan had three engineering colleges and some industrial institutes. The Council of Technical Education prepared a national development plan. In 1951 the first of six technical secondary schools was opened at Karachi and the establishment of the Karachi Polytechnic (assisted by the Ford Foundation) begun. Engineering colleges were established in the Punjab and the North-West Frontier Province in the 1950s. A polytechnic institute was founded at Dacca, East Pakistan, in 1955, and another at Chittagong in 1962. In 1961, schools of engineering and technology were founded in East Pakistan and West Pakistan. The Swedish Pakistani Institute of Technology, Karachi, was established in 1958. Some Pakistanis were training abroad under the United Nations Program of Technical Assistance and the Technical Co-operation Scheme of the Colombo Plan. By 1964 East and West Pakistan each had a directorate of technical education, and polytechnic evening classes had been begun for practising craftsmen, who were also to be assisted by mobile workshops. The polytechnics also were training technical teachers, and training colleges for polytechnic and engineering college teachers were being set up in both East and West Pakistan.

**Other Commonwealth Countries.**—After World War II much effort was made, by governments, UNESCO, and other agencies, to overcome the difficulties for technical education in developing countries resulting from insufficiency of general primary and secondary skills among pupils and lack of buildings, equipment, and staff. In the 1960s training for African technicians was being provided in the United Kingdom under the Special Commonwealth Assistance Plan for Africa (SCAPA). Great Britain also provided specialist advisers and teachers by means of the Commonwealth Educational Co-operation Scheme; and under the Overseas Service Aid Scheme trained technical staffs could be retained by governments until enough local staff had been trained. By the 1960s more than 5,000 technicians were training in the United Kingdom under the Colombo Plan for Co-operative Economic Development in South and South-East Asia.

*African Countries.*—By the 1960s Ghana had a technical university (the Kwame Nkrumah University of Science and Technology, founded 1961) and 9 technical institutes. Nigeria had more than 20 trade training institutes, as well as technical colleges in Lagos and Ibadan. Scientific and technical studies figured large in the programs of the universities of Ahmadu Bello (1962), Ibadan (1962), Ife (1961), Lagos (1962), and Nigeria (1960). Sierra Leone had 2 technical institutes, at Freetown and Kenema. Uganda had one technical college and numerous centres for rural trades and homecraft. Kenya had a polytechnical college and a technical institute in Nairobi. Malawi had a college of commerce.

## CONTINENTAL EUROPE

Technical education is highly organized throughout the continent of Europe. France, West Germany, Italy, and the U.S.S.R. may be taken as examples.

**France.**—Technical education was brought under state control in 1892 and codified by the *Loi Astier* of 1919. Provisions were made for three main levels: apprenticeship, intermediate, and higher. The first and second were usually entered from the elementary school; the third was open only to students possessing the baccalauréat awarded at the end of a secondary course.

In the 1960s pupils 13–18 years of age could obtain three-year courses in *collèges d'enseignement technique;* and five-year courses in *lycées techniques* or in the technical departments of other secondary schools. A sizable minority of the *collèges* and *lycées* was private. Higher technical instruction is given at national schools, such as the École Polytechnique, the École Centrale des Arts et Manufactures, whose aim is to produce future industrial leaders, and the Écoles Nationales d'Agriculture at Grignon, Montpellier, and Rennes. There are similar national schools for horticulture, veterinary science, aviation, and mining.

**German Federal Republic.**—During the 19th and early 20th centuries Germany built up a comprehensive national system of vocational training for workers of all grades. The Hitler regime perverted this, and the collapse of Germany in 1945 temporarily laid it in ruins. It was later built up again on similar lines, at varying rates in the different *Länder*.

In the 1960s apprentices and other young people were receiving theoretical technical training in the *Berufsschulen.* These were post-elementary vocational schools giving obligatory courses lasting three years or until the end of apprenticeship, when an examination was taken. Next came the *Berufsfachschulen,* which offered full-time diploma courses lasting from one to several years, mostly to girls leaving elementary school, with particular stress upon domestic subjects, office routine, training in fine handicrafts, and artistic training. The *Fachschulen* provided higher technical education for those with practical experience, the course varying in length from six months only to eight six-month periods. The universities had technical faculties, and several of the technical colleges had university status.

**Italy.**—During the 1960s the number of technical training institutions in Italy greatly increased. Pupils being transferred from elementary to secondary school at 11 years of age could choose a program with a technical-scientific bias; and for pupils more than 14 years old there were industrial schools, vocational training institutes with special schools attached, and technical institutes. There were about 1,500 vocational and technical industries. Students holding vocational and technical diplomas could enter the universities, where students of science and engineering were beginning to outnumber others, a trend encouraged by the government. The government-maintained polytechnics of Milan and Turin had university status.

**U.S.S.R.**—The first technical institutes in Russia were founded in the 18th century. A system of lower and secondary technical schools was created by Alexander II (reigned 1855–81), in three grades: crafts and industry schools for workmen; lower technical schools for foremen; and middle technical schools for assistant engineers.

*Soviet Period.*—With much increased industrialization the need for technicians was acutely felt. The Soviet government created in 1920 a State Committee of Vocational Education, which built up a network of technical schools. In 1929 these were transferred to the State Council for Economy and subsequently to commissariats of industry and transport. The government established secondary *technicums* side by side with factory schools for the training of skilled workmen. With the establishment of the Federal Ministry of Higher Education, all technical institutes throughout the U.S.S.R. were classified to teach: (1) technology; (2) light industry; (3) construction and architecture; (4) mining and metallurgy; (5) transport; (6) agriculture and forestry.

By mid-20th century, technical education was being given, without charge, to young people 14–17 years old in 1- to 3-year courses in urban and rural vocational training schools; to workers following 6-month vocational courses in their factories; and to more advanced and older students in a network of secondary special and higher educational establishments throughout the U.S.S.R., and through evening or correspondence courses. A majority of students received state allowances, the best receiving larger stipends.

Vocational training pupils (who in the 1960s numbered more than 1,500,000) were given uniforms, and hostel accommodation with board, and were paid for factory work done as part of their training. They were guaranteed posts in their speciality on qualifying. Students at secondary technical schools (both men and women) were enrolled between 14 and 30 years of age and had to have a minimum of 8 years' schooling, their technical course being in this case of from 3 to 4 years. For students with a secondary school background the course is from 1½ to 3 years. There is no age limit for the evening and correspondence courses. Higher technical students take 5- to 6-year courses in polytechnical and other special establishments; at the engineering faculties of certain universities; and at colleges connected with industrial enterprises. Workers qualifying through evening or correspondence courses receive extra paid leave of absence for periods from 20 days to 5 months to enable them to prepare for examinations or present their diploma theses. (*See* also UNION OF SOVIET SOCIALIST REPUBLICS: *Administration and Social Conditions: Education.*)

### MIDDLE EAST AND NON-COMMONWEALTH AFRICA

Much of the technical training in the Middle Eastern countries has been provided by oil companies and other commercial interests. Nevertheless, government systems were developing in the 1960s. Syria had more than 40 technical schools, and its University of Damascus included faculties of engineering and agriculture. Lebanon's trade schools included one in hotelkeeping. Tunisia had 66 technical schools. The United Arab Republic opened an Institute of Technology at Helwan in 1963 and trained semiskilled workers at about 50 vocational training centres. Vocational studies were prominent in the schools of Iraq and Israel. The Israel Institute of Technology in Haifa had a staff of more than 600. In Saudi Arabia the Higher Institute of Technology at Riyadh, founded in 1962 through the UN Special Fund, was training 1,000 engineering students, some of them as teachers; an Arabic technical terminology also was being composed there. Turkey had trade schools, technical schools, and evening classes. In Istanbul there was a technical university. The Middle East Technical University, at Ankara, was founded in 1956. (*See* also TURKEY: *Administration and Social Conditions: Education.*)

Among the more important African institutions may be mentioned the faculty of science and technology at the University of Madagascar at Tananarive (founded in 1961); the Centre d'Apprentissage and Lycée Technique at Dakar in the Republic of Senegal; the École Industrielle at Mogadishu in the Somali Republic; the Collège Technique and Lycée Technique d'État at Brazzaville, Congo (Republic); the Lovanium University's faculties of engineering and agriculture and the telecommunications school (founded in 1962), both at Léopoldville, Democratic Republic of the Congo.

In the Republic of South Africa the Department of Education, Arts and Science was responsible by the 1960s for technical colleges, technical and commercial high schools, and vocational schools for whites, in the principal cities; and a technical college for Indians at Durban. Technical studies could be pursued by whites at the universities; Indian students could take commercial subjects at the university college founded for them at Durban in 1960. The Department of Bantu Education assisted the development of the Bantu homelands by offering two-year courses at more than 50 vocational training schools for Bantu. Further schools were founded in 1961 in the Transkei, Ciskei, Northern Transvaal, and Zululand. The total of trainees was more than 2,000.

(H. C. D.; L. R. BU.; X.)

### CHINA AND JAPAN

Technical education in Communist China has received the highest priority because it is considered essential to the goal of economic development through industrialization. Its characteristics include strict planning by the state, in accordance with the needs of economic development, and phenomenal expansion in the number of schools and proliferation of fields of specialization.

Many different types of technical schools have been established on the secondary level for increasing numbers of students in the 15–18 age group. On the mass level, thousands of so-called Red and Expert colleges and spare-time schools in rural areas were opened to serve the dual purpose of eradicating illiteracy and providing fundamental technical training in industrial and agricultural undertakings. Thus, technical education in China covers a wide range, from the training of technologists in such fields as electronics to the dissemination of information concerning the simplest labour-saving techniques.

Ideological considerations and shortage of teaching staff and facilities have compelled the Communist state to adopt the principle of "combining education with productive labour," by which students on higher and secondary levels are required to receive their practical training in industrial plants where they engage in productive labour, while industrial workers are given formal technical education in schools. The scene in technical education is one of total mobilization of trained personnel and existing facilities.

Technical education in Japan differs significantly from that of China, due principally to the advanced level of Japanese education as a whole, its high level of industrial development, and its free access to Western technical knowledge. These factors have been responsible for the exceptional rate of economic growth in postwar Japan and are reflected in the character of its technical education.

Based on an industrial system that already compares favourably with advanced Western countries, Japan's technical education aims at the application of modern science and technology to all aspects of economic life; the educational program carried on by the Future Farmers of Japan is an example of this effort in the field of agriculture. Another major objective is the introduction of more and newer technical subjects into elementary and secondary schools. Curriculum revisions along this line were completed for elementary schools and for lower secondary schools in the early 1960s, thus covering the entire period of compulsory education. Technological education also is provided both on the upper secondary school level and the junior college level as a part of the endeavour to extend the benefits of technical education, through their students, to all aspects of Japanese life.

*See* also ADULT EDUCATION; EDUCATION, HISTORY OF; and references under "Technical Education" in the Index. (C. T. HU.)

BIBLIOGRAPHY.—*United States:* George Ross Henninger, *The Technical Institute in America* (1959); Leo F. Smith and Laurence Lipsett, *The Technical Institute* (1956); William E. Wickenden and Robert H. Spahr, *A Study of Technical Institutes* (1931); *A Facsimile Reprint from the Report of Benjamin Franklin Greene, Director of Rensselaer Polytechnic Institute, 1846–1858* (1949). (L. F. SH.)

*United Kingdom:* K. H. R. Edwards, *The Secondary Technical School* (1960); Ministry of Education, *Better Opportunities in Technical Education* (Parliamentary Papers: Cmnd. 1254, 1961); Scottish Education Department, *Technical Education in Scotland* (1961); Central Office of Information, *Technical Education in Britain,* 3rd ed. (1962); A. MacLennan, *Technical Teaching and Instruction* (1963); M. Jahoda, *The Education of Technologists* (1963); British Association for Commercial and Industrial Education (BACIE), *Journal* (quarterly; 1963– ); M. Argles, *South Kensington to Robbins: an Account of English Technical and Scientific Education Since 1851* (1964); H. C. Dent (ed.), *Year Book of Technical Education and Careers in Industry* (annually).

*British Colonies and Commonwealth:* City and Guilds of London Institute for the Advancement of Technical Education, *Commonwealth Technical Training Week Bulletin* (1960– ); Department of Technical Co-operation, *Review of Colonial Research 1940–60* (1964), *Compendium of Training Courses in Britain for Overseas Students* (1964); *Colombo Plan Technical Co-operation Scheme, 1963–64* (1964); Canadian Department of Labour Information Branch, *Education, Training and Employment* (1961); A. E. Snead, *Survey of Technical Training Needs and Facilities in the Gambia* (1964); R. Kilby, "Technical Education in Nigeria," *Bulletin of the Oxford University Institute of Economics and Statistics,* vol. 26, no. 2 (May, 1964); A. B. Graham *et al., Technical Education in Pakistan* (1961).

*Europe: France:* British Association for Commercial and Industrial Education, *Education and Training in France* (1961); A. Léon, *Histoire de l'éducation technique* (1961); H. Buisson, "L'Enseignement technique," *Avenirs,* no. 113–114, IV, *La Formation des techniciens* (monthly, Oct. 1960); *École normale supérieure de l'enseignement technique, Paris* (50th anniversary commemoration, 1912–62, 1962).

*Germany:* H. Arntz (ed.), *Germany Reports: Science and Education* (1961); H. Lehmann, *Jugenderziehung in der Welt der Arbeit* (1961); H. Klein, *Polytechnische Bildung und Erziehung in der DDR* (1962); M. Keilhacker, *Pädagogische Grundprobleme in der gegenwärtigen industriellen Gesellschaft* (1964); G. Kerschensteiner, *Begriff der Arbeitsschule* (1964).

*Italy:* London and Home Counties Regional Advisory Council for Technological Education, *Technical Education in Northern Italy* (1964); G. Martinoli, *L'università nello sviluppo economico italiano* (1962).

*U.S.S.R.:* M. Anstett, *La formation de la main-d'oeuvre qualifiée en Union Soviétique de 1917 à 1954* (1958); K. G. Nozhko, *Methods of Estimating the Demand for Specialists and for Planning Specialized Training Within the U.S.S.R.* (1964).

*Other Countries: Israel:* Israeli Ministry for Foreign Affairs: Department for International Co-operation, *Israel's Programme for Training Opportunities, 1964–1965* (1964). *Arab States:* United Nations, *Technical Education in the Arab States* (1965).

*General:* London and Home Counties Regional Advisory Council for Technological Education, *Learning from Europe* (France, German Federal Republic, Netherlands, Sweden, Switzerland, 1963); Organization for Economic Cooperation and Development, *Inventory of Training Possibilities in Europe* (1965); International Vocational Training Information and Research Centre, Geneva, *Training for Progress in Europe and the World* (quarterly, 1961– ); UNESCO, *Technical and Vocational Education and Training* (1964); British Council Fellowships Department, *Training in Britain: Schedule of Special Courses Designed for Overseas Candidates 1964–65* (1963); A. Maddison, *The Use of Foreign Training and Skills in Developing Economies* (1964).

(H. C. D.; L. R. Bu.; X.)

**TECHNICAL SCHOOL** (Great Britain): *see* Secondary Education; Education, History of.

**TECHNOLOGY, HISTORY OF.** The history of technology is the story of man's long and painful efforts to control his material environment for his own benefit. Man has been able to do this, as no other creature has, by two means: first, the use of tools; and second, the application of reason to the properties of matter and energy. For many thousands of years, however, his progress in technology was made by trial and error, *i.e.*, by empirical advance, which nonetheless made possible impressive achievements. It was only toward the end of the 18th century that technology began to become applied science, with results in the 19th and 20th centuries that have had enormous influence.

There has always been a close interaction between the form of man's society and the technology which it produces. The political, social, economic, and even religious organization of a culture influences the kind of problems and goals that are set before the engineer and the importance and magnitude of the undertakings with which he is concerned. The technology of a culture is also strongly influenced by the geography of the area in which it arises and by the materials available for engineering work.

By the study, in these broad terms, of the technology of earlier times, often quite different from our own in geography and physiography and in political, social, and economic organization, we can better understand the interaction of modern man's efforts to control both his material and his human environment in order to give himself the kind of life that he believes to be worth having. (*See* Civilization and Culture.)

Up to the 18th century the technology of all cultures had been based upon craft skills, patience, much labour, and remarkable ingenuity. These societies may be termed the "Craft" Societies. Since the 18th century our technology has developed the use of machines, power, precision, iron, and applied science into an entirely new place in a society which has also changed in very important and fundamental ways. This new way of life may be designated the "Industrial" Society.

What we are concerned with, then, is the story of man's rise as a tool-using and reasoning animal, from the first true man with a stick or stone in his hand up to a modern man controlling the means of man's production and man's destruction.

This article is organized as follows:

## I. PREHISTORIC TECHNOLOGY

**1. Paleolithic.**—The material wants of prehistoric man were clearly less complex than those of civilized man. He therefore needed much simpler technical equipment to control his material environment to his own benefit. He used wood, stone, bone, leather, reeds, vines, clay, and, much later on, metals. All these materials required the use of tools, except for reeds, vines, and clay, which could be worked by hand. Significantly, these same materials remained the basic materials of technology until the last few centuries. During this prehistoric period technical progress was very slow, yet some very important discoveries and inventions were made.

The earliest evidence of man's use of tools comes from the remains of stone tools, from which this age takes its name—Paleolithic (*q.v.*), or Old Stone Age (*see* also ARCHAEOLOGY: *Prehistory*). But he also used tools of wood, bone, and other materials, most of which have perished.

Paleolithic man had certain other important technological innovations. Evidence of the use of fire has been found in the oldest known remains of man. Later he built fireplaces, some of which were designed to provide good draft. He had considerable knowledge of foods—he knew which were edible and which poisonous. He lived in caves for some time and then devised crude shelters, in some areas made of skins. Remains of stone scraping tools and excellent bone needles show that he made clothing out of animal skins.

Paleolithic man caught fish with spears and with hook and line. He caught animals with ingenious traps and used the spear-thrower and the bow and arrow to extend the range of his hand and arm.

In addition to his technological achievements, early man made social and cultural advances. Family, clan, and tribal organizations existed, and there was division of labour, at least among the sexes. Clay figurines have been found which show an interaction of art and magic. The existence of burial rites and other ceremonies indicate religious development and probably a priesthood—the first group to be freed, at least partially, from the responsibility for its own protection and food supply.

The most important technical contribution of the Paleolithic is the development of tools. The use of stone tools probably began with the recognition that stones cracked and split by nature could serve useful purposes better than wood and bone tools. By about 100,000 years ago man was clearly making stone tools for his own use (*see* further FLINT AND OTHER STONE TOOLS). This was a most important transition, for while a few other animals use tools, only man makes them for his own use. Flint tools predominated because this material could be worked by hammering with stone, wood, or bone to strike off coarse chips of flint or to force off smaller chips by pressure. Skills gradually developed until by the end of the Paleolithic the tools show delicacy of workmanship, sometimes are even decorated, and many have handles worked on them. By this time man was also drilling bone, shell, and even stone. He then had a fairly complete set of carpenter's tools—axes, adzes, gouges, and drills. Modern tests using actual Paleolithic tools have shown them to be quite efficient.

**2. Neolithic.**—About 10,000 B.C. a series of technological and social changes, which we call the Neolithic (*q.v.*), or New Stone Age, began in various parts of the world. Cultures technologically Neolithic were to arise later in many other parts of the world, *e.g.*, those of the North American Indians when they were first discovered. These cultures were enormously richer than those of the Paleolithic.

The basic distinction between the Neolithic and the Paleolithic was the development of animal husbandry and agriculture. Man learned to domesticate sheep, goats, cattle, and pigs for food. Farming appeared, as well as fishing, hunting, and collecting wild seeds and berries for food. Neolithic man discovered that wild seeds could be planted and then cultivated, thereby providing greater convenience and a much greater yield, with much less labour. He found also that irrigation was beneficial and that certain plants such as wheat, rice, millet, corn, yams, and squash were most satisfactory for agriculture. He even discovered the merits of crop rotation and fertilization.

The results of this agricultural revolution were far-reaching. The food surplus thus produced called for special buildings for storage. Changes took place in the way in which man prepared his food: the saddle quern appeared for grinding grain, and bread-making involved the use of yeast and a primitive oven. Fermented liquors were produced and beer was definitely known by 3000 B.C.

HIRMER FOTOARCHIV, MÜNCHEN

EGYPTIAN LIMESTONE STATUETTE, FROM ABOUT 2500 B.C., IN THE CAIRO MUSEUM, SHOWS A SERVANT GIRL OF ESTATE OWNER UR-IR-EN USING A SADDLE QUERN FOR GRINDING GRAIN

This greater food supply led to an overall increase in population and in the size of the social unit. The helter-skelter arrangement of the Paleolithic village was replaced by houses arranged in patterns along definite streets, with buildings constructed of mud, reeds, logs, stone, or clay. Protection was improved by stockades and ditches. Spinning thread and weaving cloth also began in Neolithic times, and clay was formed into vessels and then heated to make a firm, hard pottery.

**3. The Bronze Age.**—The Bronze Age (*q.v.*), which began about 4000 B.C. in the Near East, was remarkably fertile in fruitful inventions and discoveries, for its achievements made possible a basic economic and social reorganization of society which can be styled the Urban Revolution. Among its technical contributions were at least six of great importance: (1) the copper and bronze from which the Age takes its name and which involved the whole art of casting and metallurgy; (2) harnessing of animal power (the ox, the ass, and the horse); (3) wheeled vehicles, with their greater efficiency in moving heavy loads; (4) the sailboat, which provided better water transportation and was the first use of wind power on a large scale; (5) the potter's wheel, with its greater possibilities for pottery; and (6) bricks, which came into use for building as early as 4500 B.C. (*See* also ARCHAEOLOGY: *Neolithic and Bronze Ages in Europe*.)

Copper and then bronze were found to be malleable, *i.e.*, they could be hammered into shape, beaten into sheets, and cut into pieces. Man next made one of the most important discoveries: these metals could be formed into sharpened tools. Unlike his other materials, copper and bronze could be melted and cast to form almost any desired shape and size. They were also more durable than wood or stone, especially for tools, which could be easily resharpened by rehammering or grinding.

But to utilize the advantages inherent in copper and bronze required a complex of ingenious inventions. A furnace capable of high temperatures from an air blast was needed for melting the metals for casting and for reducing them from their ores, and crucibles and molds had to be designed. The practical metallurgy of separating the metal from its ores was also developed.

Once these techniques had been worked out for copper and bronze, it was not too difficult to use silver, lead, and tin in a similar way. Iron was a more difficult problem, because much higher temperatures were required. But it was soon possible to produce nonferrous alloys of importance, though brass did not appear until much later.

This metallurgical activity—casting, reduction, and alloying—involved a technology far more abstruse and demanding than that of the potter, weaver, or boat builder, to say nothing of the farmer or herdsman. Metallurgical processes also seemed mysterious and magical, even to the metallurgists. It is not surprising that in these early societies, as among many contemporary primitive people, metallurgists and miners were more than craftsmen, more than specialists, and somewhat set apart. Very early, therefore, they had a special status and were the first class after the priest-magicians to be withdrawn from direct food production to engage in a full-time occupation considered to be socially worthwhile. They were, in fact, the first engineers, and their skills were of great importance to Bronze Age culture.

By 3000 B.C. the wooden plow was being pulled by oxen. The ox was used for this purpose before the horse because his broad shoulders permitted an easy attachment to a simple harness. The ox-drawn plow was of great importance, for plot cultivation was replaced by field cultivation. Agriculture was then wedded to stock raising, and it became necessary to raise food for these animals as well as for humans. The animals also provided fertilizer for the fields. Handling the ox and the heavy plow required a man's strength, so that agriculture came to be principally men's work rather than women's.

A 12TH-CENTURY DRAWING OF A HEAVY-WHEELED PLOW WITH A TEAM OF OXEN HARNESSED BY A YOKE ENTIRELY UNSUITED FOR HORSES. FROM HERRAD VON LANDSPERG, "HORTUS DELICIARIUM"

In using draft animals a basic discovery had been made—that man could control and use to his own advantage a motive power other than his own muscles. Oxen could also be used to pull a sledge, and horses and asses could carry loads. Along with this use of animal power went one of the most critical inventions of all time. How, when, and where they first appeared is not known, but two- and four-wheeled vehicles were in use in the Tigris-Euphrates culture prior to 3000 B.C. (*see* further WHEEL). By that time oxen, horses, and asses were used in combination with either the sledge, the wagon, or the chariot to provide motive power for land transportation in a form not to be superseded in its basic features until the Middle Ages in Europe.

Boats driven by sails appeared in Egypt prior to 3000 B.C. Sailed, rowed, paddled, or hauled boats became available to transport heavy and bulk loads economically by water. This revolution in transportation led to a great expansion of trade, especially in the import of raw materials and the export of craft goods, which in turn spurred the growth of the new classes of traders and artisan-craftsmen.

One craft influenced by the demand for export goods was that of the potter. Hand-formed pottery had been made for a long time, principally by women, but with the invention of the potter's wheel this work was taken over by the men, who served a long apprenticeship to develop the necessary skill. Thus a new full-time craft was born.

The potter's craft is another example of the trend toward increased specialization, changes in the economic relations of the sexes, and profound changes in the organization of society from one based on agriculture to one based on trade and craft manufacture. The power of the king, the war chief, and the priest was threatened and gradually replaced by the power of capital, that is, the power of wealth not founded upon land. It was this profound change in technological, social, economic, and political life that constituted the Urban Revolution. It was this accumulation of wealth, improvement of technical knowledge, increasing specialization of craft skill, and expanding trade that made civilization possible and so provided a basis for large-scale engineering projects in the great river cultures of the Tigris-Euphrates and the Nile.

## II. THE URBAN REVOLUTION IN THE TIGRIS-EUPHRATES AND THE NILE VALLEYS

The first appearance of large units of organized society in the Old World occurred in the valleys of the Tigris-Euphrates and the Nile. Although the actual areas and populations concerned were not great, these social units were most important because they produced a buildup of technical potential and its synthesis in the Urban Revolution, an entirely new form of society which we call civilization.

Civilization first appeared at these particular places at this time because of a number of elements, the most important being the presence of a river that could be used for transportation and irrigation. There was also a valley of alluvial soil in which agriculture was relatively easy and very productive. Moreover, the important advances of the Bronze Age formed some of the technical foundations of these civilizations.

The Urban Revolution led to the appearance of cities based on specialization, a craft economy, trade, and the new economic and social organizations to which these factors gave rise. Without the Urban Revolution the new technical devices would have been just conveniences, the new materials only luxuries, and the new crafts could not have flourished.

### A. THE TIGRIS-EUPHRATES VALLEY

In the Tigris-Euphrates Valley the river flows down to the Persian Gulf, bringing with it rich soil that forms extensive alluvial deposits. The area flooded periodically, but with proper flood control, drainage, and irrigation, a substantial surplus of food was produced. These river-control measures marked the beginning of civil engineering.

Although the valley lacked stone or flint for tools and stone or wood suitable for building, there was an ample supply of clay for bricks and a good supply of copper. The people built wheeled vehicles for land transportation and small boats for navigating their difficult river, marking the beginnings of naval architecture

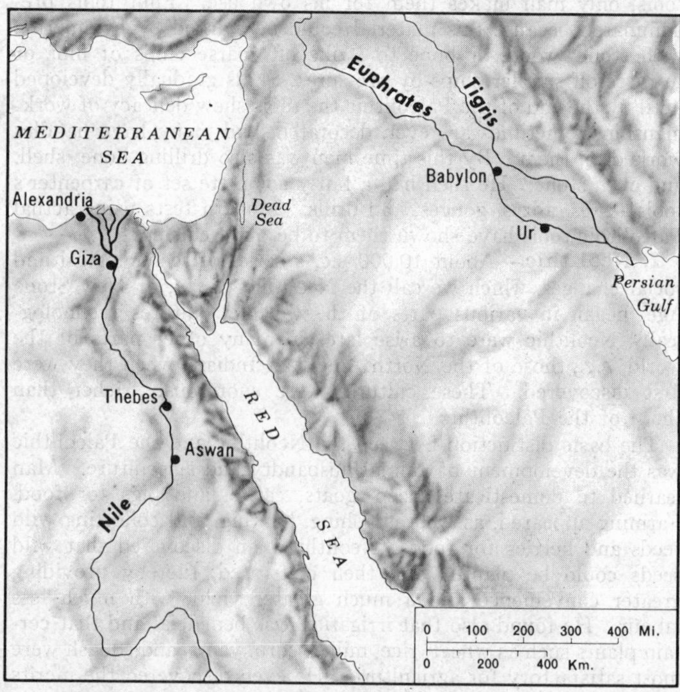


THE REGIONS OF THE TIGRIS-EUPHRATES AND NILE VALLEYS

and mechanical engineering. Architectural engineering originated in their need for construction of large buildings, granaries, workshops, and temples, and for building their great city walls for defense.

**1. The Social Evolution.**—In exploiting the resources of their valley, these people evolved a society in which the temple priests played a most important part in both their economy and their technology. The agricultural organization, together with its flood control and irrigation systems, was managed largely by engineer-priests who also supervised the construction of the great temples and ziggurats (*see* below). Other technical priests supervised the specialized craft shops of bakers, brewers, smiths, wool washers, carders, spinners, weavers, and so on. Tools, wagons, boats, plows, plow animals, and stud bulls were owned by the temple. This collectivistic organization ensured a rational exploitation of the land, systematic maintenance of canals and irrigation systems, and the production of an agricultural surplus for trade.

The traders and merchants were independent of the temple priests because by 3000 B.C. certain imports such as copper, bronze, timber, and stones had become necessities, and the extent and volume of trade in those commodities were considerable.

Although the Tigris-Euphrates Valley forms a natural geographic and economic unit, it was seldom politically so united. Throughout most of its history a number of its powerful cities were engaged in constant warfare. The wars produced a labour force of slaves, a demand for metal weapons, and a need for elaborate city walls for defense.

This complex society had to invent writing to maintain records of taxes, shares due and paid in, and so on. It also required a standard system of weights and measures and a balance for weighing. While farmers needed a calendar and a system of time reckoning, engineers needed surveying tools and methods for laying out canals, irrigation systems, temples, and defensive walls. The engineer also had to have a mathematics capable of calculating volumes, areas, and angles. This led to the beginnings of pure science.

There was also a high level of craftsmanship. Goldsmiths could solder, and they worked in gold ribbon or wire, producing fragile chains and delicate filagree work. The coppersmiths could hammer, cast, and make specialized tools such as axes, adzes, chisels, gouges, drills, knives, saws, nails, clamps, and needles. Their jewelers could drill the hardest stones and engrave them for seals, and sculptors worked in as difficult a stone as basalt. The carpenters constructed boats, chariots, wagons, and even harps and lyres of the highest quality, and potters produced coloured glazes, some of which were exported.

In the Tigris-Euphrates culture, three things were of special technological interest: the ziggurats, large pyramidlike structures dominating the cities; the enormous defense walls, which reflected the political instability of the valley; and the extensive systems of irrigation and flood control, which formed the basis of an agricultural economy.

**2. Ziggurats.**—The ziggurat was a religious structure, always associated with a temple. Although other peoples built similar structures in other parts of the world, there were important differences among them. The Egyptian pyramid was made of stone, with inside chambers, and its purpose was to preserve an embalmed body; it was a tomb, nothing more. The Maya-Aztec culture in Central America also constructed large brick or stone pyramids that sometimes had chambers, but they were intended to serve as religious altars. The ziggurat was always made of brick and had no internal chambers. It too served as a kind of altar, but its primary purpose was to provide a suitable home for a god whose original home had been on a mountain. The ziggurat was, then, a kind of artificial holy hill, and each city of this culture had its own. Its sloping sides and terraces were landscaped with trees and shrubs (hence the Hanging Gardens of Babylon).

The ziggurats and temples were constructed with a core of sun-dried brick set in mud. The outer faces were consolidated by hammering into the wet brickwork thousands of pottery goblets or by a facing of baked brick set in bitumen. The ziggurat had a series of steps leading to the upper terraces and finally to the summit, where there was a small temple of whitewashed brick and imported timber, adorned in silver, lead, copper, and lapis lazuli.

The great ziggurat of Ur, with a tower about 800 ft. (240 m.) high, may have inspired the legend of the Tower of Babel. The lower stages were black, representing the underworld; the top stage was red, representing the hospitable earth; the shrine itself was covered with blue-glazed tile, representing the heavens; and the roof was gilded, representing the sun. This architectural masterpiece had a number of constructional refinements: the vertical lines were slightly convex to offset an optical illusion by which they would otherwise appear concave, and the floor plan had slightly convex sides for the same purpose. The Tigris-Euphrates culture used this principle 20 centuries before the Greeks, to whom it has been commonly attributed. (*See* further UR; PRE-HELLENIC ARCHITECTURE: *Mesopotamia.*)

A ZIGGURAT (AS RESTORED)

**3. City Walls.**—All the cities of the Tigris-Euphrates culture had city walls from their beginnings and continued to maintain and add to them. Some built walls of incredible size and strength, such as the famous walls of Babylon, built during the reign of Nebuchadrezzar (605 to 562 B.C.). Today they are in ruins, having been used as brick quarries in both ancient and modern times. Many of the irrigation dams across the Euphrates today are built entirely of bricks taken from these walls.

Originally there was an outer and an inner wall surrounding the entire city. The outer wall was double, its outer part 24 ft. (7.3 m.) thick and built of burned bricks 13 by 13 by 3 in. (33 by 33 by 8 cm.) laid in bitumen. The inner part was of unburned brick, 36 ft. (11 m.) from the outer, with the space in between filled with dirt to produce an elevated road on which several chariots could ride abreast. The inner part was also 24 ft. (7 m.) wide and had towers every 150 ft. (46 m.). The total outer wall was then about 84 ft. (26 m.) thick. Its height is not known, but it was at least double the thickness, or about 175 ft. (63 m.) high. The inside wall was also double, and its entire width was 55 ft. (17 m.), and its height probably 120 ft. (37 m.).

These walls were only the defenses of the city itself. Nebuchadrezzar's palace had additional walls: the first wall, of burned brick, was 20 ft. (6 m.) thick and 60 ft. (18 m.) high; the second, third, fourth, and fifth were each higher than the others and had defense towers . The sixth wall was as high as some of the tallest modern buildings. The Ishtar gateway leading to the palace was covered with blue-glazed brick and large reliefs showing bulls, lions, and dragons in white, blue, yellow, and black. The royal records also speak of great bronze gates.

**4. Irrigation and Flood Control.**—Although there was a need for a centrally planned irrigation system in the Tigris-Euphrates Valley, there were so many small city-states constantly at war that there was no centrally built, maintained, and controlled system of irrigation canals and basins. Nonetheless, irrigation was extensive and on the whole effective.

There was a main canal conducting the waters of the Tigris through the plains to Ur on the lower Euphrates. Another went to the north of the Tigris and was carried by an aqueduct over a smaller river. A great dam was built on the Euphrates to irrigate the area around Babylon. The characteristics of the Tigris and Euphrates produced a system of irrigation different from that possible on the Nile, and one that was more difficult. Both the Tigris and the Euphrates rise suddenly and irregularly between April and June and bring down in their headlong rush a tremendous amount of silt. Because this water came too late for winter crops and too early for spring crops, it was necessary to expend a tremendous amount of labour to build storage basins and to keep them and the feeder canals free of silt, but the water once stored could be used when desired. These people could thus harvest three crops every two years. Additional heavy labour was required for works to control destructive floods.

In the Tigris-Euphrates cultures the engineer was able to undertake large-scale works because there was a wealthy, strong central government sanctioning expenditure of a substantial economic surplus on defense, on religious structures, and on irrigation and flood control. The engineer himself was a priest or a palace official and so had access to power and the necessary capital. Good engineering is evident in the extensive use he made of local material, and his construction methods also made effective use of cheap slave labour. Although little refinement or skill was required in this construction, there were impressive achievements.

### B. The Nile Valley

The ancient Egyptians inhabited an area different in many important respects from that of the Tigris-Euphrates. Consequently the technologies that arose in these two places were very different. The Nile Valley stretches in a long narrow strip, in some places only a few miles wide, and in no place, except in the delta, much more than 30 mi. (48 km.) wide. Because this area was extremely fertile, it attracted people from very early times. Geographically it was well protected, and very little external defense was needed.

The Nile created no overwhelming engineering problems. It flooded gently, regularly, and predictably from August to October, just in time for seeding winter or spring crops. Although it brought down from the mountains a rich silt adequate for renewing the land, there was not so much as to silt up irrigation canals quickly. Only dikes and basins were needed to spread the water over the fields while its rich silt settled out. The water could then be drained off by opening dikes lower down the river.

About 2000 B.C. the Egyptians added to this basin irrigation a system of canals, dams, and reservoirs, which permitted irrigation of areas not amenable to the basin system and which also made possible year-round irrigation. While irrigation was necessary to Egypt and involved much labour, it was far easier than that required in the Tigris-Euphrates Valley.

The Nile flows peacefully and slowly from the First Cataract at Aswan to the Mediterranean and provides a broad channel for easy transportation. The flooding of the Nile also was the means by which the Egyptians could easily transport heavy weights, such as building stones, because these could be moved onto barges when the Nile was low and carried down to their destination at the flood, and the cargo could be removed when the river receded.

The Nile Valley was also favourably endowed with raw materials. Egypt was far less dependent on imports than were the Tigris-Euphrates cultures. There was a local supply of good flint; stone tools were therefore used by Egyptian farmers long after the Tigris-Euphrates people used bronze. Except for timber, Egyptian imports were almost entirely luxury items. Limestone was quarried at Tura and Masara, and the whole area had an abundance of good building stone, such as granite, basalt, diorite, and quartzite. Furthermore, all these materials were either on the surface or could be worked by tunneling into the cliff faces, and all were available for easy transportation by river.

**1. Egyptian Civilization.**—Almost from the beginning of the Urban Revolution the Nile Valley formed a more natural economic unit than did the Tigris-Euphrates Valley. A centralized government appeared very early, and power came under the control of the palace rather than the temple, so that the accumulation of economic surplus was in the hands of the monarch and not the priests.

Egyptian religious beliefs generated much of their engineering activity. Their religion was strongly materialistic, yet the Egyptian gods were believed to sit in moral judgment on the soul of the individual after death. The Egyptian believed that the body would literally rise again from the grave. In addition, the many souls of the Egyptian had to return to the body at intervals. It was thus essential for the body to be preserved, not only because it would be necessary for the resurrection but also for the peace of the souls until the final resurrection should come. These beliefs accounted for embalming, pyramids, and cliff tombs.

The engineer held a high position in Egyptian society. He was commonly an army officer, a priest, or a member of the nobility, and sometimes even a member of the royal family.

Industry was rather limited, but there was an enormous agricultural surplus. Egyptian commerce included a substantial Nile trade, as well as trade with Crete, India, and with the Tigris-Euphrates Valley. Much of the commerce was in precious materials, but it also included other items, such as timber.

Much of this trade was carried by private merchant ships, which were protected by the navy. Though similar to merchant ships in construction, with hulls built of small pieces of wood jointed together and given lateral rigidity by thwarts and longitudinal strength by means of a hogging frame (there was no internal rib frame), navy ships were not as high in the ends and had wooden bulwarks to protect the rowers and raised platforms for the archers and grapnels. Ramses II (*c.* 1304–1237 B.C.) had 400 vessels on the Arabian Gulf, some having an overall length of 488 ft. (149 m.). Fleets of this sort need not surprise us, because as early as 3500 B.C. the Egyptians had sailboats and other boats built of planks, and by 3000 B.C. Egyptian sailing ships were freely navigating the eastern Mediterranean.

The Egyptian economy was based upon agriculture. The fertile soil of the delta needed only to be scratched, the seeds sown, and the harvest was bountiful. Thus the plow received little development in ancient Egypt. The upper lands were tilled with a simple wooden plow having metal points, two handles, and a pole attached to a yoke of oxen. No reins were used; usually a man other than the plower guided the oxen with a short stick.

The arts and crafts of the Egyptian economy were nonetheless important, particularly for local supply. They were carried on almost entirely in small shops, much as they are today. Weaving at a high level was done, and even the finest modern weaving is not as perfect as the best of the Egyptians. Rich cloth was embroidered in gold thread, and patterned weaving was also done. Excellent leather work was common. The cabinetmakers produced the finest furniture, much of it inlaid with ebony and ivory. The jewelers worked in gold inlaid with precious stones; silver and gold services were produced, and their vases were the artistic equal of any the Greeks produced later. Metalworking was outstanding, principally in copper and bronze. The Egyptian craftsman knew smelting, forging, soldering, alloying, inlaying, engraving, and gilding. The metalworkers were, for instance, able to produce good copper pipe, 1,300 ft. (396 m.) of which was found in one of the temples.

The wheel was used by the potters, who had good clay to work with. They also glazed their pottery in blue, green, yellow, and red, and even were able to glaze cut stone and to glaze over writing. The Egyptians did beautiful enameling, particularly on gold. They worked in glass, producing mosaics, bottles, and beads with writing on them. The gemworker worked on quartz, using a jeweled or flint point because bronze was not hard enough. Alabaster vases survive which were cut out with tubular drills of copper, with sand or perhaps emery as the cutting medium. Imitation pearls, amethysts, and emeralds made by the sophisticated Egyptians fooled the rather gullible Greek tourists of later times.

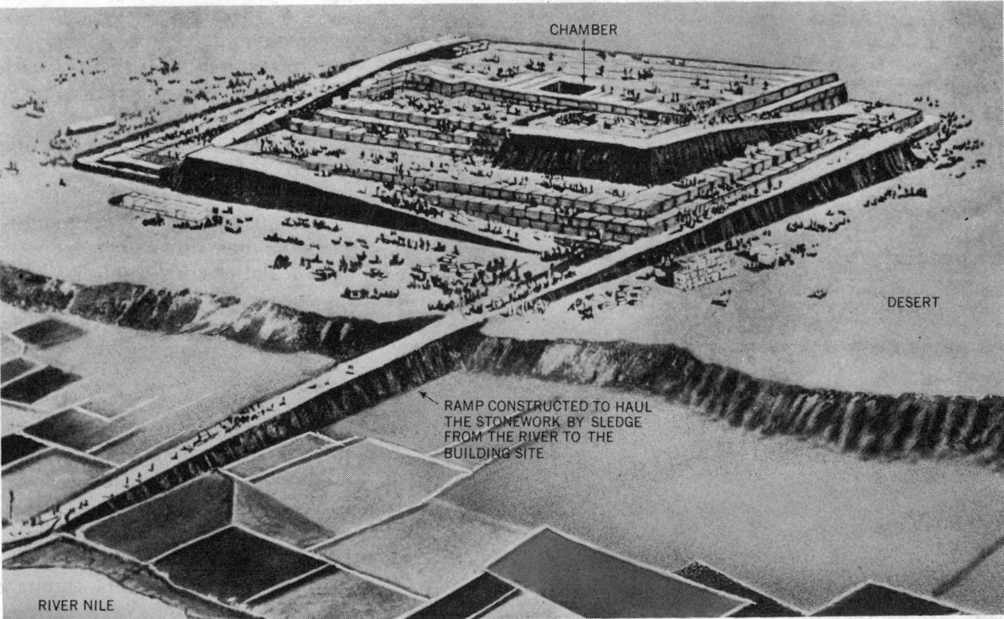


THIS DRAWING SHOWS HOW THE GREAT PYRAMID OF KHUFU (CHEOPS) AT GIZA MAY HAVE BEEN CONSTRUCTED WITHOUT CRANES, PULLEYS, OR MECHANICAL TACKLE. THE STONES FOR THE PROJECT TOTALED 2,300,000 AND AVERAGED 2.5 TONS EACH

Thus the Egyptian material culture was that of a highly refined people, skilled in the arts of peaceful living yet able to defend themselves. The army was used in peace principally as a skilled engineering labour force, though there was also a considerable supply of unskilled (usually nonslave) labour available for irrigation projects and construction of temples, pyramids, tombs, and obelisks. The Egyptians had no need for great walls, bridges, or river embankments, although they had far better materials to work with than did the Mesopotamians.

**2. Pyramids.**—Though from early times the Egyptians had had buildings of rough stone blocks and had cut and dressed the hardest rocks, the most outstanding feature of their pyramids and temples is the sudden perfection of stone masonry—a measure of the rise of Egyptian culture under the influence of the Urban Revolution. When the Egyptians found the suitable form of the pyramid and temple and the easily worked stone of their quarries, there was a rapid development. In fact, from the combination of the art form and these techniques grew what was to be the basic nature of Egyptian engineering construction: gigantic buildings, designed to be durable and characterized by grandeur and extreme accuracy of work, in at least some of their features (*see* further EGYPTIAN ARCHITECTURE).

The rocks from which these buildings were constructed, principally limestone and sandstone, were quarried systematically, utilizing only tools of copper and bronze. The extremely heavy stones were generally transported from the quarries to the site of the pyramid by boat, utilizing the Nile. Hatshepsut's barge, for example, carried two obelisks 97.5 ft. (30 m.) long and weighing 350 tons each.

The Egyptians handled stone blocks without any lifting tackle, and recent studies conclude that they did not use rollers either. The basic tools were the lever and the ramp, plus high concentrations of unskilled labour. The temples and pyramids were probably built stage by stage, the stones, according to most authoritative opinion, being hauled up along dirt ramps, probably on sledges, and slid into place.

The pyramid was built of a core of blocks of nummulitic limestone fitted rather loosely into place, and this core was covered by an outer casing of blocks of fine limestone fitted very precisely one to the other. Close joints, less than $\frac{1}{50}$ of an inch, were made by fitting the blocks together before they were put in place, the dressing being done very carefully to get an exact fit. The outer faces of the pyramid were dressed after the pyramid was completed.

The magnitude of these finished structures and the precision with which they were constructed is impressive. The Great Pyramid at Giza contains approximately 89,000,000 cu.ft. (2,518,000 cu.m.) of stone, and the area of the base is about 13 ac. (5 ha.). When the casing blocks were in place the base was 752 ft. (230 m.) square, and the pyramid was probably just under 500 ft. (150 m.) in height. It consisted of about 2,300,000 blocks, each weighing an average of about $2\frac{1}{2}$ tons and arranged in some 210 layers, the total weight being just under 5,000,000 tons. The base is an exact plane very nearly horizontal, but tilted slightly from the northwest to the southeast corner by about half an inch. The dimensions of the sides are very closely equal; the difference is only 1 part in 5,000. The corners are right angles to within a maximum error of 3.5′, and the sides are oriented north, east, south, and west to within a maximum error of 5.5′. (*See* PYRAMID.)

HISTORICAL PICTURES SERVICE

BARGE TRANSPORTATION OF QUEEN HATSHEPSUT'S OBELISKS DOWN THE NILE RIVER. THIS SCENE IS RESTORED FROM A RELIEF ON THE WALL OF THE QUEEN'S TEMPLE AT THEBES

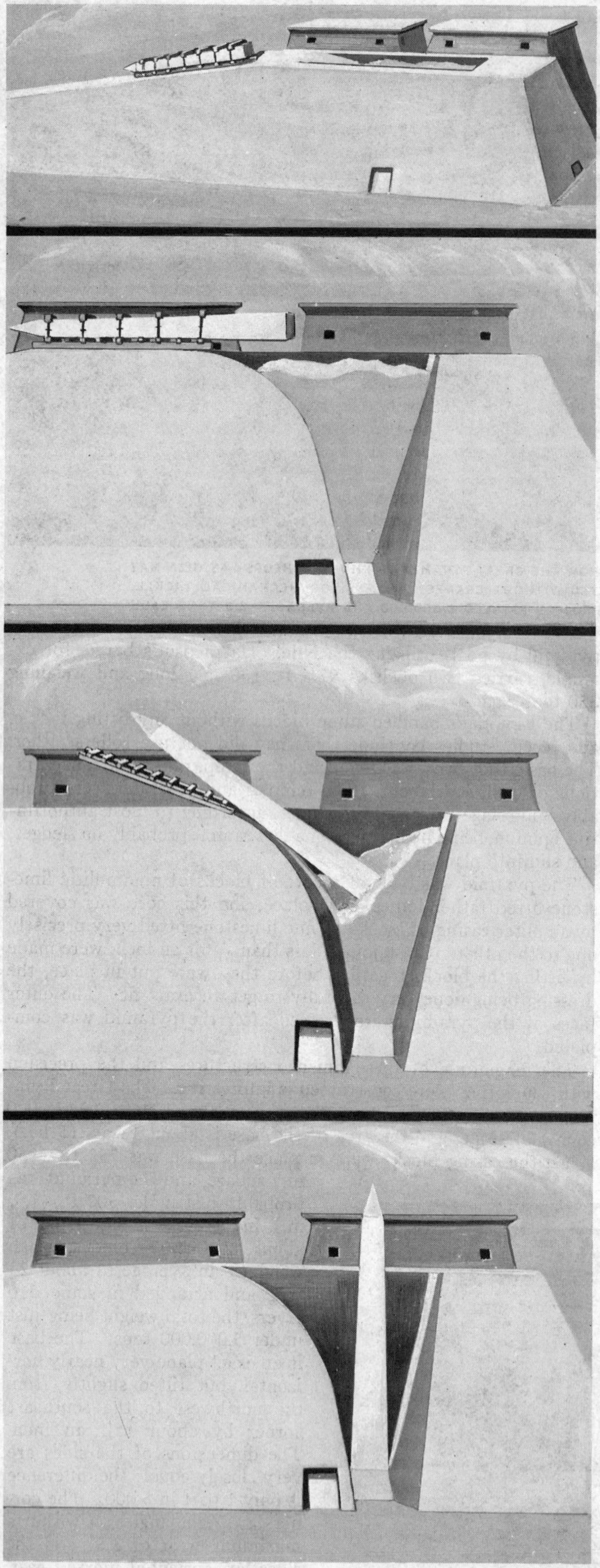

**3. Obelisks.**—Egyptian obelisks were large slender stones erected as religious symbols within the courtyards of the temples. Great numbers of these of various sizes appeared throughout later Egyptian history. Still in place in a quarry at Aswan is an obelisk that was intended to be 137 ft. (42 m.) tall, with a base 13.75 ft. (4.19 m.) square, and tapering slightly to the pyramidion at the top. Made of hard red Aswan granite, the obelisk weighs about 1,168 tons. The Egyptians could probably have gotten it out of the quarry in about six months, but work was abandoned when a crack was discovered. The available evidence and engineering calculations indicate that obelisks were erected using ramps, a sledge, and a brick-lined hole filled with dry sand which was carefully removed to let the obelisk down exactly onto the prepared base. *See* OBELISK.

ERECTION OF AN OBELISK: (TOP TO BOTTOM) OBELISK HAULED UP RAMP BY SLEDGE; PARTIAL REMOVAL OF SLEDGE WITH ALL LASHINGS REMOVED; OBELISK EASED INTO SURROUNDING SAND; OBELISK DRAWN UPRIGHT ON ITS PEDESTAL

## III. GREEK AND HELLENISTIC CULTURES

The mainland of Greece is broken into a number of small valleys by a series of steep mountains. It was in these valleys and in a few fertile plains that classical civilization grew. For geographical reasons alone it was impossible for any Greek city-state to attain the wealth, power, or centralization possible in the Nile Valley.

**1. Early Greek Technology.**—The Greek states remained relatively small units throughout their history, and their economic capacities were extremely limited. Although iron tools

HISTORICAL PICTURES SERVICE

ANCIENT GREEK SHIPS. PADDLE-SHAPED RUDDER, HELD TO THE SHIP'S SIDE, WAS WORKED BY A THWARTSHIP TILLER

were available, as well as a supply of excellent raw materials, such as limestone, marble, and good wood for building, Greek society looked upon the man who worked with his hands as somewhat inferior and not far above the status of a high-class slave. Thus labour was in relatively limited supply, and most of it was slave.

The religion of the Greeks led them to construct temples which were also public buildings. In contrast to Egyptian beliefs, Greek ideas of life after death were vague, and there was little concern for tombs.

Many of the small cities were far from a water supply, and it was necessary to construct rather primitive aqueducts. Certain city-states, of which the most outstanding were Corinth and Athens, undertook commerce and overseas trade, but this was generally of a coastal nature. Their principal peacetime engineering efforts were then in building temples, aqueducts, and ships. Greek engineering was always on a small scale, and since it did not involve complex problems, primitive methods were usually satisfactory. From an engineering standpoint, the classical Greeks were not impressive.

Greek technology involved the working, in a primitive way, of iron, a metal that had been very scarce in earlier periods. The Greeks had a number of technical devices, such as the wine press, based upon such simple devices as the lever. Weaving was known to them, but it was distinctly inferior to Egyptian work. Although the states were almost continuously at war with one another, this did not result in major defensive works for their cities.

**2. Greek Ships and Buildings.**—Because of their need for defensive sea power, the early Greeks did contribute to the development of ships. The Homeric ship had a keel, a sternpost, a stempost, ribs, and outside planking fastened with treenails. It was carvel-built (*i.e.*, the planks were flush at the seams) as compared with the clinker-built (overlapping) construction of the northern Vikings, and the keel was fully developed to give longitudinal strength. This type of construction was unknown in Egypt and northern Europe for many centuries. The Homeric ship was a long narrow vessel, whereas the Egyptian ship was quite broad and much larger. Estimated to have been not more than 125 ft. (38 m.) long and with a capacity of about 50 men, the Homeric ships had a forecastle partly decked over, a ram bow, and apparently a small poop with a high curving sternpost. A raised gangway ran the entire length. The construction was probably quite light, because the ships often broke up upon ramming. As in Egyptian ships the mast was lowered by a forestay, but the Homeric ships had shrouds and a square sail that permitted them to sail before the wind. A most important contribution of Homeric shipbuilders was the keel; the Egyptians had only the hogging frame. The Homeric ships were also low in the waist, since they had to be rowed, except before the wind. Later there were oar holes and built-up sides, with one man to an oar. By 250 B.C. some of the Greek ships had lead sheathing.

Despite their artistic achievements as architects, the classical Greeks were not remarkable structural engineers. The Greek builder, working with soft stone and iron tools, used rectangular blocks of a size easily lifted into place by a gang of men, without attempting to get a precise fit, since he set them in mortar. Like the Babylonians and the Egyptians, the Greeks were acquainted with the arch, but they too used it only rarely. Their principal form of construction was the temple, which consisted only of walls, columns, and a simple roof. Because the Greeks had substantial timber available, it was possible for their roofs to span a considerable distance, but these roofs transmitted both a downward and an outward thrust upon the supporting walls or columns. As a result the Greeks needed heavy walls and colonnades to take up the side thrust.

Although the effects of their contributions to engineering were not felt for a long time, the development of mathematics and the science of mechanics by the Greeks laid the foundation for the beginning of engineering as an applied science.

**3. Hellenistic (Alexandrian) Engineers.**—With the death of Alexander the Great (323 B.C.), his vast empire collapsed, and there arose in the eastern Mediterranean a number of cultures that were at least partial inheritors of the world of classical Greece. One of the most interesting was that centred around the city of Alexandria. This Hellenistic society flourished from approximately 300 B.C. to A.D. 300 and was of considerable technological importance. (*See* HELLENISTIC AGE.) It was a mixture of various peoples and cultures, polyglot in religion, in language, and in social and economic customs, but united by trading and manufacturing cities of great wealth. There was, however, no strong central government to control the wealth and no priesthood to control the economic surplus. It was therefore not possible to undertake large-scale engineering operations. Despite these limitations this society made important contributions to the advance of technology. Their engineers confined themselves to small-scale devices, but had the advantage of the classical Greek development of, and interest in, the theory of mechanics.

HISTORICAL PICTURES SERVICE

A WELL SWEEP, USING THE PRINCIPLE OF THE LEVER TO RAISE WATER

A NORIA USED TO RAISE WATER TO A HIGHER LEVEL

From this period survive the earliest names of engineers and books about technology. Four men especially worthy of mention are: Hero of Alexandria, Ctesibius, Philo of Byzantium, and Vitruvius. Vitruvius was, to be sure, a Roman, but he based most of his celebrated treatise, *De architectura,* upon Alexandrian sources. These men, who lived between 300 B.C. and the early years of the Christian era, used a number of mechanical devices. The lever had been used in its simplest form for prying by both the Egyptians and the Tigris-Euphrates peoples. It was used in a

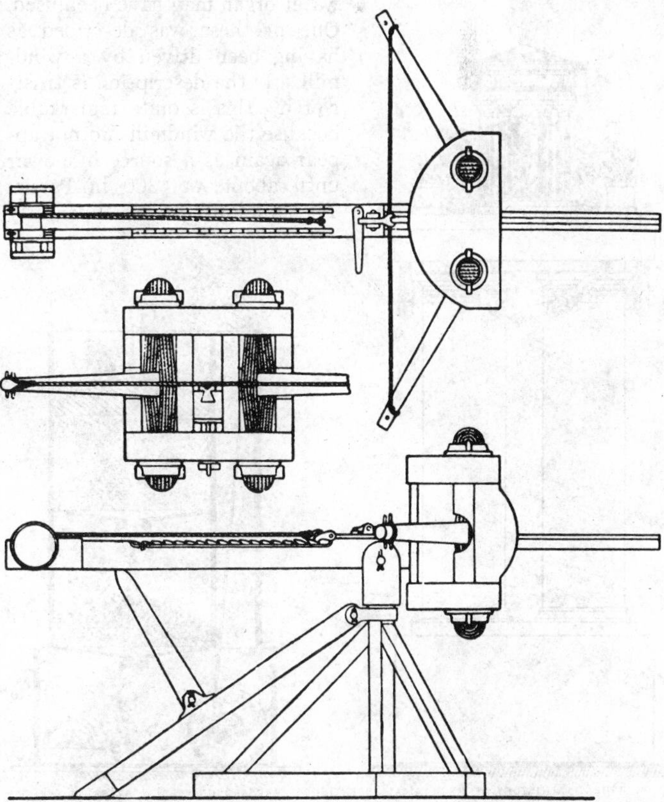



HERO'S CROSSBOW

water-raising device, called the well sweep, in Egypt as early as 1500 B.C., and it is still so used in this area. The lever may also have been used in warfare to lift men over walls, and legend has it that Archimedes used it to lift ships at the siege of Syracuse. There is no evidence of the use of the pulley and windlass in the Tigris-Euphrates Valley, Egypt, or Greece, but they were in use at Alexandria by the beginning of the Christian era. Wedges and inclined planes were known from the very earliest times, but the screw made its appearance in the Hellenistic world for oil and wine presses and as a water screw. There were also cranes having from one to four masts, which combined the principles of the lever, the pulley, and the windlass. Descriptions survive of pulley blocks, and there were directions on how to calculate the mechanical advantage of different types of windlasses. These mechanisms were sometimes operated from the power of a treadmill.

Alexandrian engineers used mechanical equipment for raising water. The water screw, traditionally ascribed to Archimedes, may have been invented in Egypt, but Vitruvius wrote that it was used to clear mines, to pump out the holds of ships, and for irrigation. The noria, described by Vitruvius, was also used to raise water. This was an undershot waterwheel having pots for lifting water on its circumference. It might have been as much as 30 or 40 ft. (9 or 12 m.) in diameter. In theory, the noria was driven by the current of the stream, but sometimes it had to be assisted by a treadmill.

Alexandrian engineers were skilled in constructing mechanisms for warfare. The bow and the sling had developed in Neolithic times; of the two the bow is more important technologically. To increase its strength, mechanisms were developed to draw and hold it in readiness. Extra flexion was obtained by separating the single bow into two arms. Hero described extensions of this crossbow principle to throw a very long arrow and heavy balls. This device, the ballista, was probably invented about 400 B.C. and improved by Ctesibius. It had a range of about 300–400 yd. (270–370 m.).

Ctesibius and Philo both described the force pump, which served as a domestic water pump and as a fire engine. The Alexandrian engineers also pumped air, and as early as the 2nd century B.C. a water organ may have been used. One of these was described as having been driven by a windmill. If the description is trustworthy, this is quite remarkable because the windmill did not appear again as a source of power until about A.D. 300 in Persia. The windmill organ apparently had a trip-hammer action, a device which was not to appear again until the Middle Ages.

BROWN BROTHERS

**RECONSTRUCTION OF A WATER CLOCK FROM VITRUVIUS' DESCRIPTION**

The most generally exploited sources of power were slaves. Although animals supplied a further source, they were used rather inefficiently. The high cost of feed in a relatively dry climate also served to discourage the use of animal power. Since human muscular power was adequate for most purposes, Alexandrian engineers directed their talents in other directions, especially in the development of instruments of precision and curious little amusement devices.

**4. Mechanical and Precision Devices.**—Ingenious mechanisms, intended to produce motion while using a minimum of power, were nearly all weight driven. For example, there were puppet theatres in which a fire was lighted, girl figures came out and danced, the Bacchus inside turned and poured libations, a winged Victory turned on the top, and the entire display ran up and down a track. Power was provided by a lead weight falling under the control of a quantity of millet or mustard seed escaping slowly through a hole. There were also lamps with automatic feed of the wick and oil; these involved clever gearing and an understanding of pneumatics and hydraulics.

These small devices provided Alexandrian engineers with invaluable experience with mechanical elements, especially lever systems, gears, and pulleys.

The Alexandrian engineers also concentrated on instruments of precision for measuring angles and time. These instruments played an important part in the history of mechanical devices and were early examples of precision instruments that were to become critical appendages in the development of astronomy and modern engineering. Most important of those for measuring time were water clocks (*see* CLEPSYDRA). Later editors of Vitruvius' works added to their books illustrations upon Renaissance designs, but scholars have reconstructed a water clock to fit Vitruvius' description. In the water clock two critical problems were solved: (1) how to get uniform flow of water; and (2) how to convert a uniform time motion into the solar time then in use.

The Alexandrians used the cyclometer to measure distances for surveying. This was one of the earliest applications of a chain of gears, but gears also used to move heavy weights were described by Hero. Vitruvius described a flour mill employing gearing—unique because gearing was generally used for transmission of motion, not for transmission of power.

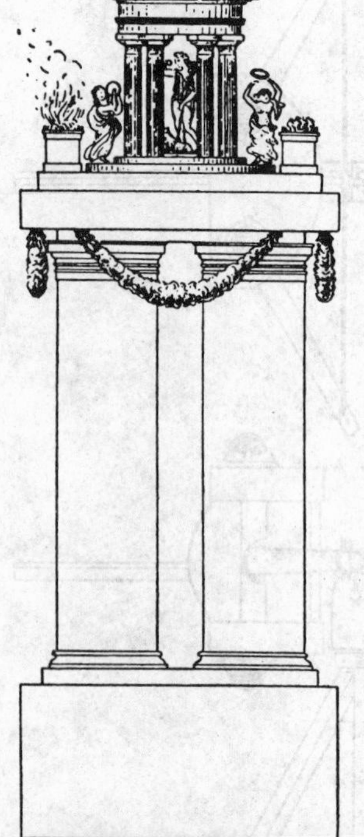

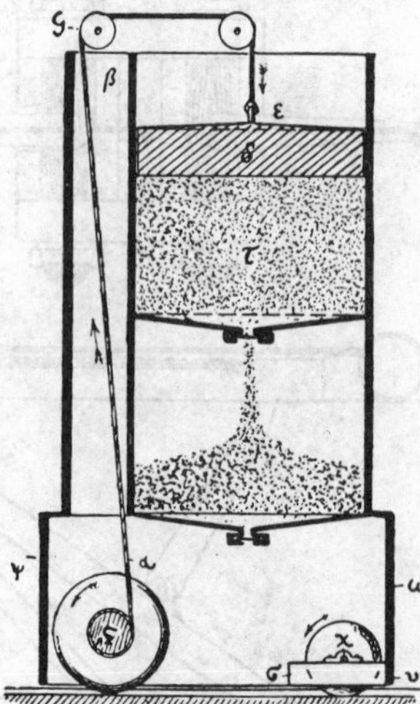

A. P. USHER, "A HISTORY OF MECHANICAL INVENTIONS"; HARVARD UNIVERSITY PRESS, COPYRIGHT 1929, 1954 BY THE PRESIDENT AND FELLOWS OF HARVARD COLLEGE

**TEMPLE MECHANISM: (LEFT) PUPPET THEATRE; (RIGHT) DRIVING MECHANISM FOR THEATRE**

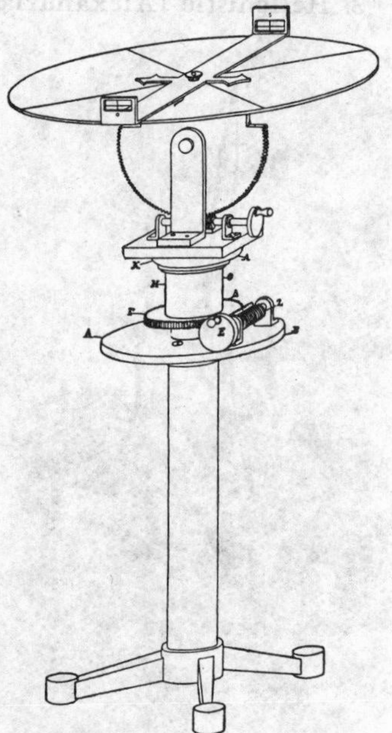

A. P. USHER, "A HISTORY OF MECHANICAL INVENTIONS"; HARVARD UNIVERSITY PRESS, COPYRIGHT 1929, 1954 BY THE PRESIDENT AND FELLOWS OF HARVARD COLLEGE

**THE DIOPTRA**

One instrument, the dioptra, was developed by Hero into a precision instrument for surveying. Originally an astronomical instrument, Hero converted it into a transit, and from this invention he advanced a new theory of surveying. Little is known of earlier Egyptian surveying techniques, except that the results were accurate. The Greeks measured horizontal angles at 90° with the groma, or surveying star, and measured slope fairly well by the chorobates, a crude device about 20 ft. (6 m.) long with plumb bobs and a water level. These devices had been used as early as the 7th century B.C. in tunneling from both ends for a distance of 550 yd. (500 m.). Hero's dioptra, however, was a major step forward, for, except for a telescope and compass, it had all the features of the modern transit. He gave a full description of it and its use in his treatise on surveying.

**5. Milling Grain.**—A number of other appliances that appeared for the first time in this era were not mentioned in engineering treatises, probably because they were considered too commonplace or because the authors, under the influence of classical theories of mechanics, did not consider them machines. One was a device for milling grain. Early methods had been simply to pound with pestle and mortar or to use the saddle quern, but, with the increase in weight of the implements, the work of grinding grain ceased being women's work and instead became the work of male slaves. The earliest certain reference to the quern was made by Cato (234–149 B.C.), who described a rotary mill turned by two asses, but wrote that it was also sometimes turned by two male slaves. Great querns, turned by men or horses, have been found in large numbers in Pompeii. The weight of the upper stone was carried by a spindle fitted in the lower stone. There were holes through which the grain passed down, and the stone was turned by wooden bars. The use of asses in turning these querns was probably one of the earliest applications of animal power to industrial work.

BY COURTESY OF (TOP) UNIVERSITY OF MINNESOTA PRESS, COPYRIGHT 1952 BY THE UNIVERSITY OF MINNESOTA; PHOTOGRAPH (RIGHT) BROWN BROTHERS

(ABOVE) DETAIL FROM A MILLER'S SHOP SIGN IN POMPEII SHOWING QUERNS IN USE; (RIGHT) GREAT QUERNS EXCAVATED FROM POMPEII

**6. The Impact of Hellenistic Technology.**—The concern of Hellenistic engineers with the study and control of motion, both in theory and in sophisticated mechanisms, proved most significant, and the fundamental theories worked out for them proved adequate for many centuries. They included the theory of mechanical advantage of the five simple machines (the lever, the wheel and axle, the pulley, the wedge, and the screw), as well as the theory of the elementary principles of hydrostatics. Furthermore, the Alexandrian engineers had all the elementary motion chains: the screw, the wheel, the cam, the ratchet, the pulley, and the gear. The crank was known, but not the crank chain which we call the treadle. The development of animal and nonmuscular power, which was to come later, arose out of the change in scale in engineering work rather than in new principles.

The Alexandrian period was therefore highly important in the history of technology. Its actual engineering achievements seem meagre in comparison with those of the Tigris-Euphrates and Egyptian cultures and with those of the Roman culture, which was partially contemporaneous with it, but it marks an important transition from the engineering of cultures based upon man and his hand tools to cultures exploiting animals and mechanisms. The achievements of the Hellenistic engineers marked the beginning of a technical revolution that was eventually fulfilled during the Middle Ages in the West.

## IV. ROMAN CULTURE AND TECHNOLOGY

The Roman political, social, and economic organization required a different kind of technology. Even though the Romans had a strong central state with great political and financial power, there was considerable autonomy of local government. The Romans undertook a regulated and orderly expansion of the public services required by the rise of cities and their high population density. Though calculating and materialistic, the Romans had a broad tolerance of many religious groups. In the architectural and building arts their aim was primarily utilitarian. They were not greatly concerned with the construction of great temples, monumental graves, or even walls for defense. Instead they built palaces, baths, amphitheatres, granaries, bridges, roads, aqueducts, and drainage canals. Public institutions and buildings had a political function and were an integral part of the Roman political organization. The practical means by which the Romans maintained their power were prosperity, law, the army, order, and the display of prestige and power.

The needs of government required a number of contributions from engineering. Because communication was necessary to maintain the strong bureaucratic centralization of this vast and far-flung empire, roads, writing, and the Latin language had to be spread abroad. Efficient utilization of labour and building materials, especially stone and concrete, was needed to construct great aqueducts supplying water to the large populations in the cities and to build the great public buildings, the most magnificent of the world of antiquity.

Roman organizational skill was especially important in the use of labour in extensive engineering projects. Workmen's associations, united by religious and economic bonds but sharply distinguished by trade, guarded the construction traditions passed from generation to generation and from experienced workmen to apprentices. Similarly, organizations of architects and engineers provided training and status. Although aristocrats were taken into these training schools, men from the ranks were accepted as well. In addition to these associations there was another group of professional corporations, the contractors. In large undertakings such as masonry construction, this group controlled the mass of unskilled labour for the state and undertook the planning, execution, and responsibility for the project.

This organization of labour and skill produced a sharp division between the crafts, so that they became almost independent of one another. For example, one association constructed the solid brick or concrete walls, another applied the marble facing. This specialization, however, did not prevent a slow but sure advance of engineering knowledge gained by empirical means.

**1. Architecture and Engineering.**—The separation of the craftsman and the architect from the building engineer meant that connection between the aesthetic elements and the constructional elements in Roman architecture was lost. Compared with the organic nature of Greek, Egyptian, and Babylonian architecture, Roman architecture had a certain inherent contradiction. The result was an independent evolution of the technical building methods, as opposed to their architectural and decorative features, which were derived from Alexandrian Greece. As an art that had completed its cycle, Alexandrian architecture was not rejuvenated by the Romans. Hybrid and lacking in constructive spirit, its rapid decay climaxed in excessive ornateness and poor execution.

At the same time, however, the technical aspect of Roman building made progress. The construction associations valued cumulative experience and progressive improvement made primarily by practical discoveries. While most of their techniques were jealously guarded and handed down in symbolic written form, these groups were prepared to take advantage of new discoveries. The result was that the 3rd and 4th centuries A.D. saw both decadence in Roman architecture as an art form, *e.g.*, in marble ornamentation, and, at the same time, some of the empire's greatest triumphs in building construction, as in the extension of the principles and techniques of the arch and the vault to the dome. The building art was still full of constructive spirit toward the end of the empire, but it declined because political uncertainty caused the collapse of public and private prosperity, and no further building on a large or costly scale could be undertaken. Thus today many Roman buildings, because they have lost their marble ornamentation, are better architecturally than they were in Roman times. Building construction preserved the simplicity, dignity, and strength of the republic, while Roman art and architecture showed the influence of the luxury, decadence, and weakness of the empire.

Since the goals of building construction were to represent the importance, the impressiveness, and the grandeur of Rome, the organic feature of this architecture was vast, covered, and open spaces in harmony with each other. The principal constructional problem faced by the Roman engineer was how to span large enclosed spaces far too great for the wooden construction of the Greeks and for the stone construction of the Egyptians. The solution was twofold: (1) an entirely new structural form, or at least an entirely new development of a structural form, the arch and the vault; and (2) the development and use of materials, especially brick and concrete, in new ways.

The arch had been timidly attempted by the Egyptians and the Babylonians and it was known to the classical Greeks. It was used systematically, though on a rather small scale, in Etruscan bridges and tombs from the 7th century B.C. From this Etruscan origin the arch and the vault were improved slowly but steadily to greater and greater size until their constructional possibilities were highly developed by the Romans.

When the arch was used to span great distances, as the Romans did, new problems arose. Other peoples had spanned great widths within the limits of available timber, as did the Greeks; or they had found it necessary to divide the rooms by intermediate columns in the Egyptian manner. The Roman engineer had to face two very difficult problems: first, the efficient construction of walls, arches, and vaults (a problem for the mason); second, and, far more difficult, the design of arches and vaults in combinations so that the lateral thrusts would be balanced against each other insofar as possible and any residual thrusts carried to the ground. Both problems were, however, closely bound together in producing a building architecturally able to span wide spaces yet with good illumination and proper balance, while constructionally providing a highly stable building that would be able to defy time with a minimum of upkeep.

**2. Building Construction.**—*Walls.*—The Romans used widely divergent methods of constructing building walls at different times and places, but everywhere they based their building on the advantageous use of local materials and skills. In the East, in Greece, and in Asia Minor, Syria, and North Africa, where there were skilled masons and good supplies of stone suitable for squaring, the Romans used substantial blocks of cut stone. In central Italy they continued the Etruscan type of squared masonry stone, with the stone used either as solid masonry or as a facing. The typical Roman edifice or structural wall was, however, a sort of concrete set in molds that were sometimes temporary or sometimes an integral part of the wall.

In walls of cut stone the courses were of uniform thickness. The blocks were parallelepiped in shape, with the width equal to the height and both equal to either one-half or one-third of the length. (All the dimensions were multiples of linear units of measurement.) In ashlar (facing and core) the stones for facing the outside wall were alternately either headers or stretchers. In every case the stones were bonded; that is, the square end of some were laid to the front face so that the stones of the face were bonded back into the core. The headers, which served to bond the facing to the core, sometimes had curves at their inner end

A CONSTRUCTION VIEW OF A ROMAN WALL, SHOWING THE PLACEMENT OF THE STRETCHERS (PARALLEL TO FACE OF WALL) AND THE METHOD OF BONDING THE HEADERS TO THE CORE

to reinforce the hold of the bond. In walls of this sort the core was either concrete or layers of tamped random rubble.

Walls of concrete masonry were most characteristic of Roman methods, particularly in Italy and in the western regions of the empire. They usually consisted of a facing, commonly of burned brick, which served as a mold and was put into place by skilled masons. Then the *caementum* was put into place by unskilled labour overseen by the masons. This was not usually of concrete in the ordinary sense, but was constructed of alternate layers of stone and gravel mixed in place with a very thin cement. The facing bricks, of uniform sizes, were laid with mortar joints of less than one-third of an inch. In the course of time there was a gradual increase in the thickness of Roman bricks to approximately 2 in. (5 cm.), and in joints there was some slow increase in size. These variations in no way were detrimental to the solidity of Roman cement-brick wall. This was due to the excellent quality of the cements and to the close union between the facing and the core through the use of bonding.

Roman methods of wall building survived long into the Middle Ages and were used by Byzantine and Western builders. Though they built good solid walls for their great public buildings, this was not always true in private dwellings. At the time of the republic, Rome was built largely of unburned brick, although burned bricks were also used. Augustus' boast that he found Rome a city of brick and left it a city of stone is clearly an exaggeration, but he had a point. In the empire these unburned bricks were used for private or everyday uses in much the same way that they had been used in Egypt, Greece, and Babylonia.

*Arches.*—To make possible the Roman goal in building construction, the Romans used the arch, the vault, and the dome. The full true arch was used widely, *e.g.*, over doors, for bridges, and for sewers. Sometimes it was the free arch, full or segmental, and sometimes it was the arch bonded to the materials above it. Thus the characteristic form of Roman building construction was rows of arches supported on piers, and arches which supported the vault or dome structure above them.

Arches were made of a number of different kinds of material, one of the most important being concrete-brick, in which the brick was commonly embedded in concrete work. When exceptional size or great resisting power was called for, the Romans frequently used double or even triple ribs of bricks to form their arch. Usually the arch was constructed of large bricks about 2 ft. square to form ribs filled later with concrete. Sometimes the arch of brick showed in the outside facework; at other times these ribs were inside the concrete. These ribs had several functions: first, to control internal stresses in the concrete; second, to determine the line of thrust; and third, to prevent deflection. Relieving arches were sometimes built into walls in order to give them stability and sometimes to locate stresses at given points on foundations provided only at these points. (*See* ARCH AND VAULT.)

*Vaults and Domes.*—Growing out of the arch, in order to span large enclosed spaces, was the vault. This basic characteristic of Roman building, and a Roman invention, occurred in three principal forms: the barrel vault over a rectangular area; the groined or cross vault, *i.e.,* the intersection of two vaults; and the dome set over a circular or polygonal base. The typical Roman vault construction was of concrete, formed by centring to give a complete semicircle. As with the arch, brick ribs distributed the main stresses. This method of construction was both rapid and economical, but it required centring to sustain the tremendous weight until the concrete set, although the brick ribs put in place first could take much of the load.

Any sinking or inequality in the foundations would result in undistributed stresses and cracking. One solution was to use elaborate foundations, which were far more substantial than those deemed necessary today. Another was to distribute the load of vaults through ribs and piers to the foundation. This principle was long the basis of Romanesque and Gothic vaulting. The basic principle, then, was not to use massive brick or concrete arches but rather a kind of hollow brick caisson penetrated by cast concrete.

*The Internal Balance of Forces.*—The most important characteristic of the Roman vaulted buildings, and the greatest contribution of the Romans to building methods, was the organic structure of the whole. All the elements—the wall, the arch, the simple or groined vault, and the dome—were manifestations of a single idea. The Roman vaulted building achieved a perfect balance of all its parts, in both construction and design, in an arrangement that provided for counterbalancing the thrusts of the heavy superstructure. This principle, which was strictly Roman, represented an enormous advance over anything that had previously been done in building construction. It was even a greater contribution to the building art than either the arch or the vault. In effect it consisted of equilibrium based upon the elimination of the thrusts by mutual oppositions and by transferring all the residual thrusts to the outside walls. The question then was how to take up the final thrust. Sometimes this was done with external buttresses, which were later used extensively in Gothic architecture, but more commonly internal buttresses were used. Sometimes an internal buttress on a lower portion became an external buttress for an upper portion. This system, which became the basic principle of later church construction, could be very complex, as seen in the Baths of Diocletian, one of the most magnificent ancient buildings and one of the best engineering designs. It is also apparent in the Baths of Constantine and the Temple of Minerva, where the side portions serve as buttresses for the main portion. From these Roman forms also came the basic structure of Byzantine architecture, particularly the dome.

*Construction Tools and Techniques.*—Centring was common and inclined planes were used. The Romans had no particular problems of lifting, for the blocks of stone were relatively small and the pulley and the multiple purchase were available. They sometimes used cranes—in fact, cranes of the same type were used in parts of France and Italy as late as 1900. Rapid construction was one of the most typical, most important, and perhaps the most fully developed of the Roman technological achievements.

**3. Aqueducts.**—The Roman aqueduct was one of the most characteristic of all Roman structures (*see* AQUEDUCT). It was used to carry large quantities of water to the great cities of the Roman Empire for drinking, public and private baths, fountains, and irrigation, and it even supplied some country villas along the way. The aim was to collect the water from springs and rivers and to convey it partly by tunnels and partly by channels supported on walls and arches to a reservoir outside of the city, from which it was distributed. With few exceptions, the great aqueduct was an open channel (*i.e.,* without pressure). Since it depended on gravity flow, it had to avoid an adverse slope and sudden changes of gradient that would produce too sudden a change of speed. The entire channel, therefore, had to be kept above the level of the reservoir at some height across the plains that commonly surrounded the Roman cities. Thus Roman engineers often had to take long detours to get a favourable gradient. This was sometimes done with great precision, but often crudely.

Roman aqueducts were better building structures than they were hydraulic systems. The tunnels were sometimes 2 mi. (3 km.) long. When channels were set on top of long masonry structures that crossed over valleys and plains, one aqueduct was sometimes superimposed on another to save masonry. The Romans apparently had difficulty in making the channel permanently watertight, for it required continual repair and reconstruction. This problem was described in detail by Sextus Julius Frontinus in his book *De aquis urbis Romae* when he was superintendent of aqueducts in A.D. 97. The problem was considerable, for in those times the city of Rome had a supply of about 38,000,000 gal. per day. Rome's water was supplied by about 9 aqueducts, whereas in the Middle Ages the city simply used the waters of the Tiber.

The Romans on rare occasions used a siphon system with adverse gradients. The pipes were of terra cotta or wood, sometimes of metal or lead, and usually embedded in masonry. This type of aqueduct was not often used near Rome because of its small capacity, but it was used elsewhere. However, the principal use of hydraulic flow in pressure tubes was in distribution from the reservoirs. This was accomplished by lead pipes and a system of taps and valves.

The reservoirs were connected directly to the aqueduct systems. Some reservoirs were as large as 21,600 sq.ft. (2,000 sq.m.), but their construction was quite simple. No large arches or vaults were used; instead, a rectangular space was divided at regular intervals by a series of light arcades that supported the covers. These arcades were commonly connected by barrel vaults, and doors were provided for shutting off parts of the reservoir for cleaning. The outside walls, which were subjected to lateral pressure, were usually supported by earth embankments or sometimes by external masonry buttresses. The inside walls were covered with cement.

DEUTSCHEN MUSEUMS, MÜNCHEN

PAINTING BY ZENO DIEMER OF A NETWORK OF ROMAN AQUEDUCTS, SHOWING SECTION UNDERGOING REPAIRS

**4. Roads.**—Roman roads comprised the most extensive and durable highway system known to the ancient world (*see* further ROADS AND HIGHWAYS: *Roman Roads*). They radiated from Rome in all directions. As a means of consolidating the empire, they provided rapid transportation of the Roman legions and enabled a relatively small army to maintain law and order over a vast territory. The roads were also a means for transmitting the emperor's orders, making possible a highly centralized government in Rome. They were also the route by which taxes and plunder were returned to enrich the capital.

By modern standards they were built with a tremendous waste of materials and labour, but their construction was based upon different principles. The modern principle is to support, on a subgrade soil, a pavement that is only a wearing surface and a roof. Roman roads were of masonry construction, of a depth and solidity intended to last and to be maintenance free. Their cost was reduced by this durability and the fact that many of them were built in peacetime by the legions.

In general the Romans had little regard for topography; they tended to build their roads in straight lines, undaunted by natural obstacles. Thus they cut through mountains, filled in valleys, and bridged marshes. Not even the seas stopped them. In some places the roads run right down to the water's edge and then come up on the other side—for instance, on the coast of France, where the road ran from Reims to the channel, then up on the other side and on to Scotland. On the great route to the East, the Via Appia ran down the heel of Italy, then across to Macedonia, and over to the Hellespont, Palestine, Suez, Egypt, and Africa.

There were a number of different types of Roman roads, which again shows the genius of the Roman engineer. In constructing these roads he admirably suited his construction to the purpose of the road and to the available local materials. Romans usually built gravel roads early in their history, but in marshy areas log roads were built. Later, construction was often improved as the need arose. The typical Roman road became the paved road, which was relatively narrow, never more than 65½ ft. (20 m.) wide, and this only at the entrance to Rome. The average width was about 33 ft. (10 m.), but sometimes as little as 13 or 16½ ft. (4 or 5 m.). This included both the main roadway and the two paved strips that nearly always ran alongside.

In construction the soil was first removed to a solid foundation, and if necessary the bottom of the excavation was shaped, leveled, and rammed or rolled. If this was not sufficiently solid, piles were driven in, then a layer of sand 4–6 in. (10–15 cm.) in thickness, or sometimes a layer of mortar 1 in. (2.54 cm.) thick was put down. On top of this was masonry: first, flat stones were laid on their face in hard cement or clay. This was usually about 1 ft. (0.3 m.) thick, but on poor foundations it was sometimes as much as 2 ft. (0.6 m.). This was covered with a course of concrete about 10 in. (25 cm.) deep, made up of pebbles, rock, broken brick, and mortar or clay tamped firmly into place. Then 12–20 in. (30–50 cm.) of gravel and coarse sand concrete was rolled on in thin layers. On top of this was the wearing surface with a very marked crown. The crown was obtained when the stone was set into this last freshly laid layer of finer concrete. The wearing surface was 8–12 in. (20–30 cm.) in depth, and the material depended upon the local supply. In some cases hard silex was used, or even basalt. These top stones were irregular polygons of pentagonal or hexagonal shape set in mortar; they were 2–3 ft. (0.6–0.9 m.) in diameter and sometimes as little as 6 in. (15 cm.) thick. Only their upper faces were finished. Their adjoining sides were fitted so closely that no mortar was required in between. The total result was a very solid and rigid masonry structure about 3¼–5 ft. (1–1½ m.) thick. Occasionally the order varied, and on minor roads this basic plan was much simplified. The Roman highway engineer, however, always took great pains to provide proper drainage, to build a solid heavy structure, and to provide a solid bond of courses one to the other and, where gravel was used, to take great care in tamping.

Because the layout was as straight as possible and because the Romans preferred the heights and avoided the cuts and valleys for drainage and military reasons, the gradings of the Roman roads seem excessive. Sometimes there was as much as 15–20% not only in the mountains but on plains, and at bridge approaches 10–12% was common. The result was that when the roads were used for troops and light horse rigs, they were reasonably satisfactory, but when later they came to be used for commercial loads, the grades proved to be too great.

**5. Summary of Roman Engineering.**—Roman accomplishments extended to many other construction projects, such as embankments, dikes, viaducts, open cuts, and tunnels. Their military architecture was also notable, as seen in remains of their fortifications, walls, towers, and field entrenchments. Their other achievements included harbours, lighthouses, quays, timber structures (such as military bridges), and methods of supplying river water to houses and heating systems for the baths.

Their greatest contributions, however, were: first, the arch, perhaps not originated but certainly developed by the Romans to a higher degree than ever before, and with it the vault and the dome; second, the internal balance of forces in building; third, the development of brick and concrete structures; fourth, the Roman road; and fifth, the Roman aqueduct. Their other significant contributions were: organizing power and a systematic use of labour to achieve great ends; a vast and complex store of empirical technical knowledge; careful adaptation of means, men, and materials to a clearly seen purpose; high excellence in their workmanship; and the stability and enduring power of most of their works. Perhaps most important of all was the immense progress in the development of constructional means. While conserving what was found to be good, constant improvements were made. The technique of the Roman engineer was empirical and without foundation in science, but his methods were fundamental in the West until well into the 18th century.

## V. TECHNOLOGY AND SOCIETY IN THE MIDDLE AGES

From the 4th through the 14th centuries, major technological advances were made, and the concept of this era as "dark" or static is not valid for the historian of technology. Invention and development were especially fruitful from the 12th through the 14th centuries.

By the 10th century the barbarians, who had overrun the Roman Empire and established themselves in northwestern Europe and Britain, had developed a civilization from the heritage of the past and by their own creative efforts. Having built their society on the ruins of the Roman world, the barbarians assimilated many Roman techniques.

The Byzantine world also served to transmit the technology of the Islamic Near East and that of the Far East to Western Europe. Another route by which technology came to the West was Muslim Spain. Trade with the Muslim world and with Byzantium brought contacts with India and China, where technology was generally more advanced than in the West. Thus many important processes and devices, such as silk-working machinery, iron casting, gunpowder, paper and various printing processes, and the fore-and-aft rig for sailing ships may have been transmitted to the West, although the possibility of separate Western invention cannot be entirely ruled out.

The one-time barbarians, who should be identified as Europeans by the 12th century, made several significant technological contributions, including the use of soap for cleansing; the making of barrels and tubs; the cultivation of rye, oats, and hops; the heavy plow; and the easily heated compact house. Before 1100 they had also introduced the horseshoe, an improved method of harnessing the work horse, and a three-field system of crop rotation.

**1. Developments in Agriculture.**—The improved harness and the invention of the horseshoe increased the drawing power of the plow horse three or four times. The older harness, which had a yoke resting on the withers of a pair of animals and two straps about each animal from both ends of the yoke, was satisfactory for oxen but not for horses. The strap or girth passing around the neck of the animal from the yoke pressed upon its trachea, and when the animal strained the yoke cut its air supply. The new harness consisted of the padded horse collar resting against the animal's shoulders.

More efficient exploitation of animal power and the use of the improved and heavier wheeled plow played a major role in determining the character of the manorial system. The increased use of four- and eight-animal teams to draw the sturdy plows probably encouraged communal agriculture as a means of pooling the limited animal power and equipment of the serfs working the manorial lands.

The three-field system of cultivation, another important invention on the manor of northern Europe, provided more land under cultivation and also a greater harvest. However, it allowed less time for the fallow field to recover its fertility, and it necessitated the use of more manure. Urban communities mushrooming in the 12th century helped meet this need, as the sewage could be used on neighbouring fields.

**2. Development of Power Sources.**—The introduction and widespread use of natural and animal power sources by medieval man influenced the development of agriculture and the economy in general. Not only were the effects of the increased exploitation of power potential discernable at the time, but Europeans were gaining a familiarity with techniques which would later contribute to the dramatic industrial transformation of Britain and then Europe during the 18th and 19th centuries. Furthermore, the introduction of wind and water power during the Middle Ages was already relieving man from some of the most grinding physical labour.

Besides human muscles, three power sources were used in the Middle Ages: animal, water, and wind. These sources were exploited through wheels and the mechanisms by which the power was transmitted and the force-time-distance relationship of the power altered. The combination of power source, wheel, and transmission mechanism, which often included gearing, was usually designated as a mill. A mill could be further identified by the type of work done.

*Water Mills.*—Of the three distinct types of water mills, the simplest and probably the earliest was a vertical wheel with paddles on which the force of the stream acted. Next was the horizontal wheel used for driving a millstone through a vertical shaft attached directly to the wheel. Third was the geared mill driven by a vertical waterwheel with a horizontal shaft. This required more knowledge and engineering skill than the first two, but it had much greater potential. Vertical waterwheels were also distinguished by the location of water contact with the wheel; first, the undershot wheel; second, the breast wheel; and third, the overshot wheel. These waterwheels generally used the energy of moving streams, but tidal mills also appeared in the 11th century (*see* TIDAL POWER).

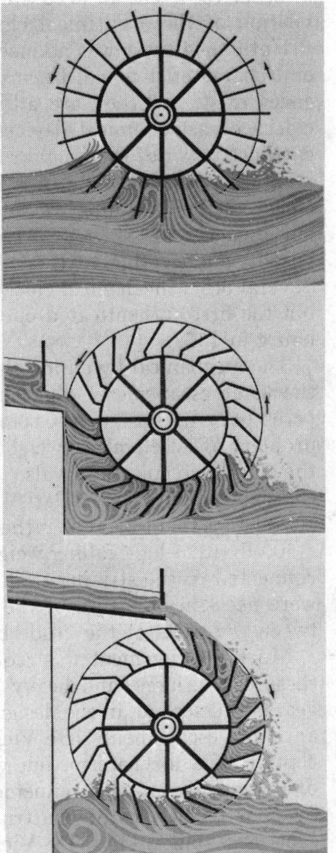

TYPES OF WATERWHEELS

(Top) Undershot waterwheel; (centre) the breast waterwheel; (bottom) overshot waterwheel

Each type of mill had its particular advantages and disadvantages. Since relatively little is known of their development before the Middle Ages, we shall simply note the characteristics that suggest an order of appearance within the context of the complexity of construction and the possibilities for utilization.

The simple vertical wheel required little extra structure, but the force and rate of power take-off were dependent upon stream characteristics and wheel diameter. Since change of power direction was not involved, this wheel proved most useful in raising water, utilizing, for instance, a string of pots worked by a chain drive.

The horizontal-wheel mill (sometimes called a Norse or Greek mill) also required little auxiliary construction, but it was suited for grinding because the upper millstone was fixed upon the vertical shaft. The mill, however, could only be used where the current flow was suitable for grinding.

The geared vertical-wheel mill was more versatile. Construction was relatively simple if the wheel were of the undershot kind, for the wheel paddles could be simply dipped in the stream flow, whether it was river, tide, or man-built millrace. A millwright could choose his gear ratio to match power utilization with rate of stream flow, and the wheel could be mounted in a bridge arch or on a barge anchored in midstream. Vitruvius described the first geared vertical wheel for which we have good evidence. This mill is also of major significance because it was the first application of gearing to utilize other than muscle power. This mill had an undershot wheel and, unlike the breast or overshot wheels, did not make use of the weight of falling water.

Mills with geared breast and overshot wheels required more auxiliary construction, but they allowed the most generalized exploitation of available water power. A major construction problem was locating a mill where the fall of water would be suited to the desired diameter of the wheel. Either a long millrace from upstream or a dam could be used.

We know little of the details of geared-mill development between the time of Vitruvius and the 12th century. An outstanding installation was the grain mill at Barbegal, near Arles, France, which had 16 cascaded overshot wheels, each 7 ft. (2 m.) in diameter, with wooden gearing. It is estimated that this mill could meet the needs of a population of 80,000.

Even though the highly adaptable, geared mill, with its widely diversified stream-flow conditions, was used in the Roman Empire, historical evidence suggests that its most dramatic industrial consequences occurred during the Middle Ages in Western Europe. After the 13th century the overshot waterwheel appears to have become more common than the undershot wheel.

The geared mill of the Middle Ages was actually a general mechanism for the utilization of power. The power from a horse or cattle mill was small compared to that from overshot waterwheels, which usually generated 2–5 hp., but droughts or freezing conditions did not stop the animal mill, and it could be used where water power was not available.

*Windmills.*—By the mid-13th century technologists were beginning to generalize the concept of mechanical power. Under such circumstances it is not surprising that the geared mill was also utilized on a wide scale to tap wind power.

The windmill (*q.v.*), which appeared later in Western history than the water mill, was a more complicated geared mill, and the circumstances of its invention are obscure. Even though the windmill was used in the Middle East in the 10th century, those which first appeared in Europe in the 12th century were probably independently developed. The Middle East mills had a simpler vertical shaft and a horizontal sail plane analogous to the horizontal waterwheel.

The complexity of the Western horizontal-shaft-geared windmill arose from the necessity of turning the sails into the wind. The post mill was the first solution. In this case, the miller and his assistants could turn a heavy mill housing on the great post upon which the housing rested and turned. By the late 14th century turret (sometimes called tower) mills were also used. Since only the upper portion of these mills turned, a more heavily constructed mill housing was possible.

Windmills became familiar features of the landscape of northwestern Europe in the 13th century; there were 120 windmills in the vicinity of Ypres alone. With the passage of time, the mechanism of both types became more sophisticated. Brakes were introduced to limit the speed of grinding stones, and the sail beam was placed at a slight angle for more power from the passage of the wind across the sails. Wood shutters were also substituted for the wood-framed canvas sails of the first mills.

By the end of the Middle Ages both the windmill and the water mill embodied the primary characteristics of the modern mill. The mill had found numerous applications, many of which required new devices and mechanisms for specialized power transmission. These adaptations were often as complex as the basic mill design. By the 16th century printed books with woodcuts showed many such machine elements that could be traced back to the Middle Ages. Among these were the cam and tappet, the windlass, gear trains, the crank, the bow spring, the treadle, and the flywheel.

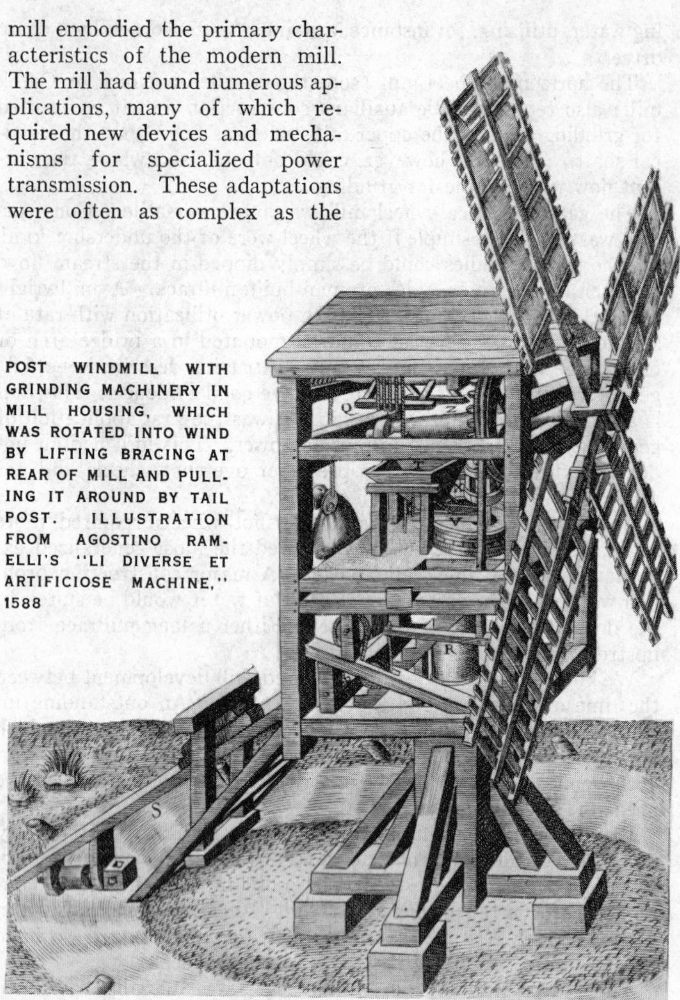

POST WINDMILL WITH GRINDING MACHINERY IN MILL HOUSING, WHICH WAS ROTATED INTO WIND BY LIFTING BRACING AT REAR OF MILL AND PULLING IT AROUND BY TAIL POST. ILLUSTRATION FROM AGOSTINO RAMELLI'S "LI DIVERSE ET ARTIFICIOSE MACHINE," 1588

*Applications of Mill Power.*—The mill was most widely used for grinding grain, but its utilization for other tasks had a considerable impact upon society.

One important application was the use of water mills for fulling cloth, a finishing process that provides more body and greater resistance to wear by compressing, shrinking, and binding the fibres more closely together. Before the 13th century, cloth to be fulled was immersed in a tub or trough of water, and fuller's earth was added as a degreasing agent. Then the cloth was pressed or trampled by foot or hand. But the water mill for fulling consisted of a trough and two wooden hammers that worked alternately by tappets or cams on a drum fixed to the shaft of a waterwheel. Fulling mills, which were also used for felting unwoven fibres, enjoyed widespread use in Britain and resulted in a shift of the textile trade from the urban centres of the eastern lowlands to the country districts of the north and west where there were fast-running streams suitable for water power.

The water mill replaced human muscle power in other endeavours. During the first decades of the 13th century waterwheels were used at the silver mines in the Alpine region of Trent and the South Tirol, and in the 14th century the water mill became fairly common in all Alpine regions. The mill then spread into the copper and silver mining districts of Germany. The great waterwheel powered the hammers used for crushing the ore and for forging the wrought iron, and it moved the bellows supplying the blast to raise furnace temperatures. In the 16th century waterwheels were used extensively to raise water by pumps from flooded mine shafts.

From the 12th century water power came to be used by malt mills, wood-turning mills, mills for grinding pigments, grinding mills for cutlery, paper mills, and silk-twisting mills.

**3. Clocks.**—The invention and perfection of the mechanical clock introduced new elements of first importance for an industrial technology: the refinement of mechanical design; an impressive facility in the use of geared wheels and other precision mechanisms; and development of the principles of applied mechanisms. The water clock, known in ancient Egypt, was further developed by the Alexandrian engineers of the early Christian era. Its basic principles remained essentially the same until the 13th century, but the complexity of its mechanisms increased. Along with the water clock, the sun dial and the sand glass were used for measuring time. All three of these devices lasted long after the appearance of the mechanical clock, surviving through the 18th century in a modified form because they were cheaper, reasonably accurate, and easier to repair.

The Alexandrian engineers designed water clocks in combination with various puppet devices in which the hours were sounded by a reed and trumpet or by a ball falling on a bronze gong. The puppet show was sometimes quite complex and involved devices for showing the phases of various heavenly bodies. A few of these water-clock puppet shows were apparently built in Europe, but most were sent as gifts to various Christian monarchs from the Muslim world, an example of the diffusion of technology from the Muslims to the Christian world during the Middle Ages.

The time-measuring device of the water clock was water that was allowed to flow out at a controlled rate through a small orifice. The motion was transmitted from a float by means of weights, cords, rollers, and pulleys, which in turn controlled and moved a bewildering variety of symbols and figures giving astronomical data, the hours of the day, and ingenious displays.

Both falling weights and gears—two fundamental elements of a mechanical clock—were used in the puppet shows of Alexandria, but the problem of obtaining regular weight-fall had to be solved in order to invent an accurate mechanical clock. The critical invention of the mechanical clock, therefore, was the escapement.

Until 1344 there was no mechanical clock movement whose general characteristics can be analyzed in detail. Many early references exist, but they are all doubtful or clearly refer to water clocks or astronomical devices. A clock erected in 1344 at the entrance tower of the Carrara Palace in Padua by either Jacopo de' Dondi or his son Giovanni is the first identifiable mechanical clock. It had a falling weight as the source of power, a mechanical escapement and a balance wheel to control the fall of this weight, and gearing to transmit the motion to signal the hours. Several other mechanical clocks were built about this time in Italy, but the first authenticated one outside of Italy appeared in Strasbourg in 1352.

The mechanical invention that controlled the falling weight was the verge escapement, which included a balance wheel or a foliot (crossbar) balance (*see* CLOCK). These escapements solved the problem of accelerating weight-fall by stopping the movement of the clock at regular intervals. The escapement of a clock built for the Palais de Justice in Paris by Henri de Vick between 1364 and 1370 had a foliot balance rather than a balance wheel. It also had a 500-lb. (225 kg.) falling weight and a 1,500-lb. (680 kg.) weight connected to the striking-train mechanism. These heavy weights were necessary because of the great friction and interference between the parts of the crude blacksmith-forged mechanism.

Much improvement was required in the mechanical clock from these crude, large, and heavy devices: first, in the design of the gears; and second, in the design and construction of the foliot balance and escapement. De Vick, for example, had a brilliant conception of a mechanism, but what was necessary was refinement of design. Even with refinement, the clockmaker was held back by poor techniques of construction and by the lack of precision tools and skill. Thus, De Vick's clock stood at the close of the primary development of the mechanical clock, yet at the beginning of a long process of refinement in mechanical concepts. No changes in the basic mechanism were to occur until the introduction of the pendulum in the second half of the 17th century.

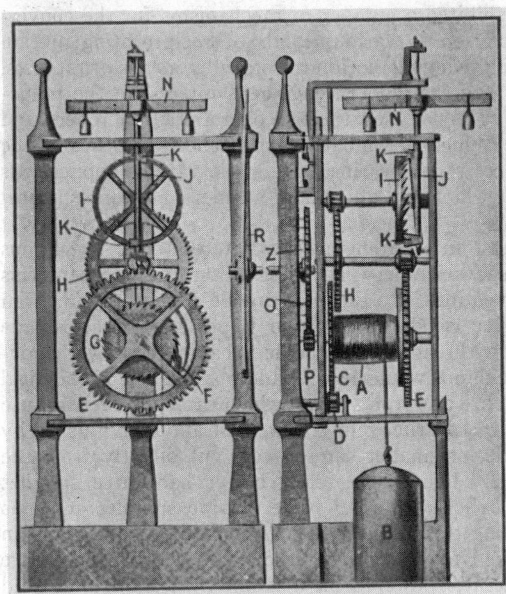

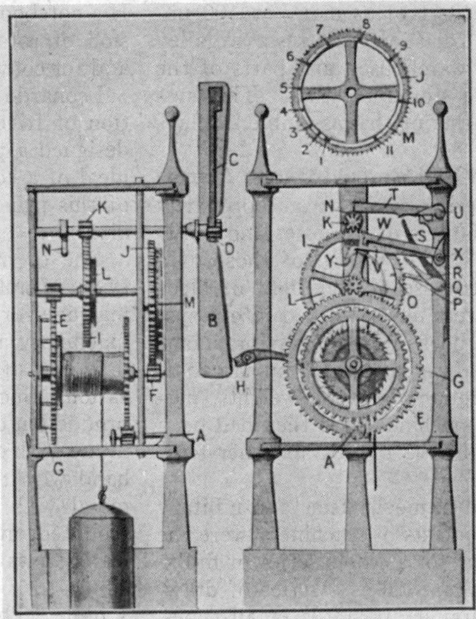

HENRI DE VICK'S CLOCK BUILT FOR THE PALAIS DE JUSTICE, PARIS. (LEFT) THE GOING TRAIN; (RIGHT) THE STRIKING TRAIN

## VI. THE FLOWERING OF EUROPEAN TECHNOLOGY

Since the Middle Ages Western man has thought of nature as a great complex of energy and matter to be utilized for his own benefit. In fact there has been a cumulative character and a continuity of development in the West extending from the Roman era —a continuity defying division into eras and epochs. Of particular importance in this respect were the outstanding inventions and achievements of the Italian architect-engineers, the German metallurgists and printers, and the Dutch construction engineers from the 15th to the early 17th century.

**1. Canal Construction.**—Bertola da Novate (*c.* 1410–75), one of Europe's outstanding civil-hydraulic engineers, proposed new and improved canals to strengthen Milan economically. First he improved the existing canal system to the northwest, which had carried the cathedral stones to Milan from the quarries near Lake Maggiore and which had become known as the Naviglio Grande. Bertola then built a canal from Abbiate, on the Naviglio Grande, to Bereguardo, a village to the southwest near the Ticino River, where it became navigable for boats destined for the important trading centre of Pavia and the Po River. The Bereguardo Canal, completed in 1458, was about 12 mi. (15 km.) long and had the first complete set of canal locks—one of the major inventions in civil engineering history.

The mitred canal gate, which improved the San Marco lock in the northeastern part of Milan, was probably invented by Leonardo da Vinci. The lock made possible the interconnection, formerly prevented by their different levels, of the Martesana Canal and the Naviglio Grande. Earlier canal lock gates had been vertical lift gates raised by a windlass (similar to the portcullis of the medieval castle) or single gates swinging on vertical axes. Leonardo's San Marco lock (*c.* 1500) was of masonry. Its gates of wood were reinforced by iron straps at the joints and by iron hinges. A pair of gates swung together at a mitred joint to prevent water leakage. The twin-mitred gates angled into the downward force of the stream, and thus the force had a component carrying the strain into the masonry wall. Because the gates could not be opened against a head of water, small hinged doors or wickets near the bottom admitted water into a lock before the gate was opened. Thus the pressure on each side of the gate was equalized before chains pulled the gates against the side walls of the lock.

The San Marco lock survived into the 20th century much as Leonardo designed it.

**2. Improved Production Techniques.**—Upon completion of the canal systems, Milan's industry and trade flourished. Entrepreneurs and craftsmen increased production by introducing ingenious techniques for mass production, some of which were described by Vannoccio Biringuccio (1480–*c.* 1539), author of the influential work on metallurgy, *Pirotechnia.* He observed that one brass foundry in Milan could furnish all of Italy with its products. It employed eight masters and helpers in one room who did nothing but form molds in loam for the object manufactured on that particular day. Among the objects made at the shop were harness buckles, cups, belt buckles, chain links, bells, window fastenings, and thimbles. Other craftsmen specialized in hammering brass tinsel, filing thimbles, and turning candlesticks. This system made possible the extensive marketing of brass objects through lower production costs.

Milan's neighbouring city-state, Venice, had another remarkable industrial enterprise, the naval arsenal, where galleys were constructed and armed. In the 15th century the arsenal used effective production techniques and an assembly line to make the famous Venetian galleys that maintained the Mediterranean trade of the city. Because in both the 15th and 16th centuries the Turks challenged the naval power of the Venetians, a large fleet of military galleys was of critical importance.

A typical Mediterranean galley of 1500 was about 120 ft. (37 m.) long and had a 15-ft. (5-m.) beam. Construction was of wood, with planking laid over the keel and ribs carvel fashion (edge to edge). The galley carried about 150 oarsmen, each with a great 120-lb. oar, but with a favourable wind a lateen, or triangular sail, could be used. Forward was a cannon and small gun and a ramp that could be used for boarding after contact with an enemy vessel.

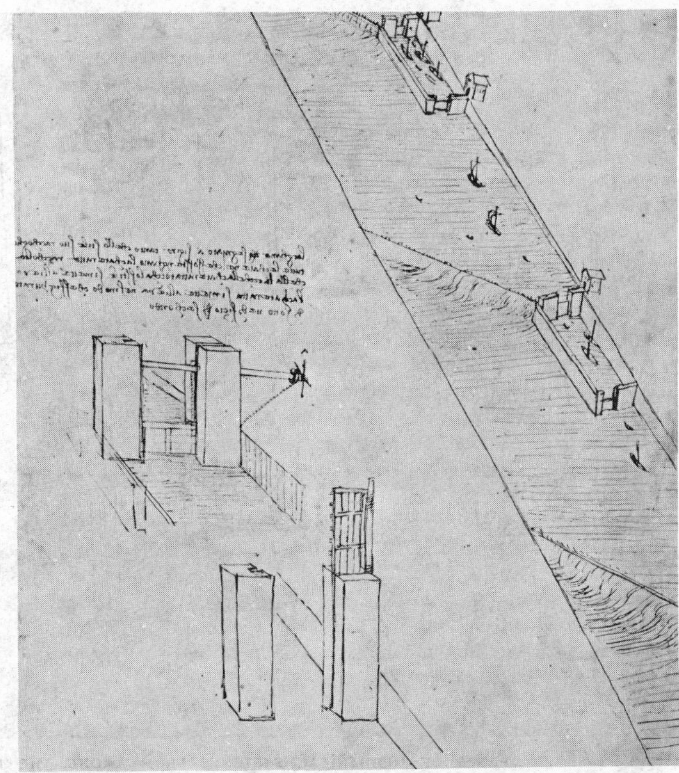

LEONARDO DA VINCI'S SKETCHES FOR HIS CANAL AND LOCK SYSTEM

The arsenal maintained a reserve fleet of as many as 100 unassembled galleys. The numbered parts of each reserve galley were stored in the arsenal yard and warehouses, and parts of the same type for different galleys were stored together. This system saved space and avoided the weathering that assembled galleys would have suffered.

**3. The Work of Leonardo da Vinci and Albrecht Dürer.** —In considering Leonardo's engineering work, we are primarily concerned with the extensive compilations of his notes and drawings. His notebooks, begun in 1488, were typical of those of a practising engineer. Except for a treatise on the flight of birds and one on hydraulics, these notes were never worked into a systematic treatise. The rest of the notebooks were roughly organized material for treatises that could have been written on human anatomy, the anatomy of the horse, motion, impacts, weights, moments of force, and the elements of machinery. If they had been systematically organized, they would have rivaled all other treatises of the 16th century.

Leonardo was especially interested in mechanisms and military engineering, although his notes on elements of machinery were the most complete. There were drawings for a whole series of mills: water, wind, horse, tread, and crank, as well as a series of drawings concerned with pumps and hydraulic apparatus of all types, many of them clearly designed to be driven by power. The sketches showed not only general features but also the details of the parts. There were also fairly detailed sets of drawings on textile machinery, on the manufacture of metallic parts, and on artillery. Some of the sketches were those of existing equipment; others were attempts to apply known principles to the solution of problems. Still others were clearly original ideas. Among his original ideas were industrial appliances invented for profit (his needle-polishing machine) or for fame (his flying machine).

Leonardo took the most important step of separating the study of mechanisms from the general study of machinery. Earlier engineers and many of Leonardo's successors considered every machine as unique and consisting of parts peculiar to it. They had no concept of a mechanism: a mill was a mill; a stamp was a stamp. Thus generalized concepts were lacking, and the approach was empirical. But Leonardo's works manifested generalized concepts, *e.g.,* his means for transmitting and converting the form of motion. His notebooks exhibited a number of mechanisms for the conversion of rotary motion to various kinds of reciprocating motion and for converting swinging motion to rotary by means of ratchets.

Leonardo also had the modern engineer's interest in the reduction of friction. He sketched the use of antifriction rollers and designed a pulley block in which he approached more nearly the ideal of a complete roller bearing. He made various applications of this principle, which he called the "wonder of the mechanical art."

One of his most intense engineering interests was in various types of automatic machinery, an outstanding example being his machine for cutting files. In this machine he applied to industrial machinery a falling weight as a source of power. He also made drawings of screw-thread cutting devices having practical application. Such machines would have made possible the economical production of bronze and iron screws, which came into general use in the 16th century. Earlier screws were cast and then finished by hand with the file, or smaller screws were cut directly from the metal with a file. Leonardo's screw cutter had three spindles mounted on the machine frame. The outside spindles acted as lead screws moving the frame through which they passed and in which they worked in nuts. The screw was cut on the centre spindle. The operator powered the machine by a crank and could change drive gears to vary the pitch of the screw being cut.

Leonardo made many drawings of metalworking devices, including a series for shaping iron by rolls and drawing frames. These had been known since the 12th century for light work, but Leonardo was the first to propose their use in heavy work and to drive them by power. Actually not until the 18th century were rolling mills extensively used, because there were problems of power, details of heavy construction, and unknown properties of the metals at various temperatures.

Albrecht Dürer (1471–1528), the Leonardo of the north, wanted to do for Germany what the Italian architect-engineers had done for their homeland. Dürer planned an ideal town, considering social conveniences as well as problems of defense. The foundries were situated in the southern corner so that prevailing winds carried noxious fumes away from the town castle. Another section was the site of church activities. The town hall, together with its square and fountain, and the nearby marketplace formed a communal centre. The coppersmiths, molders, and turners lived near the foundry, and bakers, butchers, and brewers occupied the food quarter. Some streets were reserved entirely for craftsmen.

**4. German Metallurgy.**— The Fugger family of Augsburg was heavily involved in silver and copper extraction and processing in Hungary and in the Alpine province of the Tirol. Jakob Fugger, "the Rich," became head of the family enterprises in the 1490s and formed a partnership with the mining engineer Johannes Thurzo, who agreed to improve mines and smelters in return for a part of the resulting savings. The Fugger-Thurzo Trading Company's silver and copper mines, smelters, and mills in Hungary, in combination with the growing investment in copper and silver properties in the Tirol, allowed the family to dominate the European market. In 1495 Thurzo built a large smelter at Neusohl in Upper Hungary to smelt the area's silver-rich copper ore. The copper was mar-

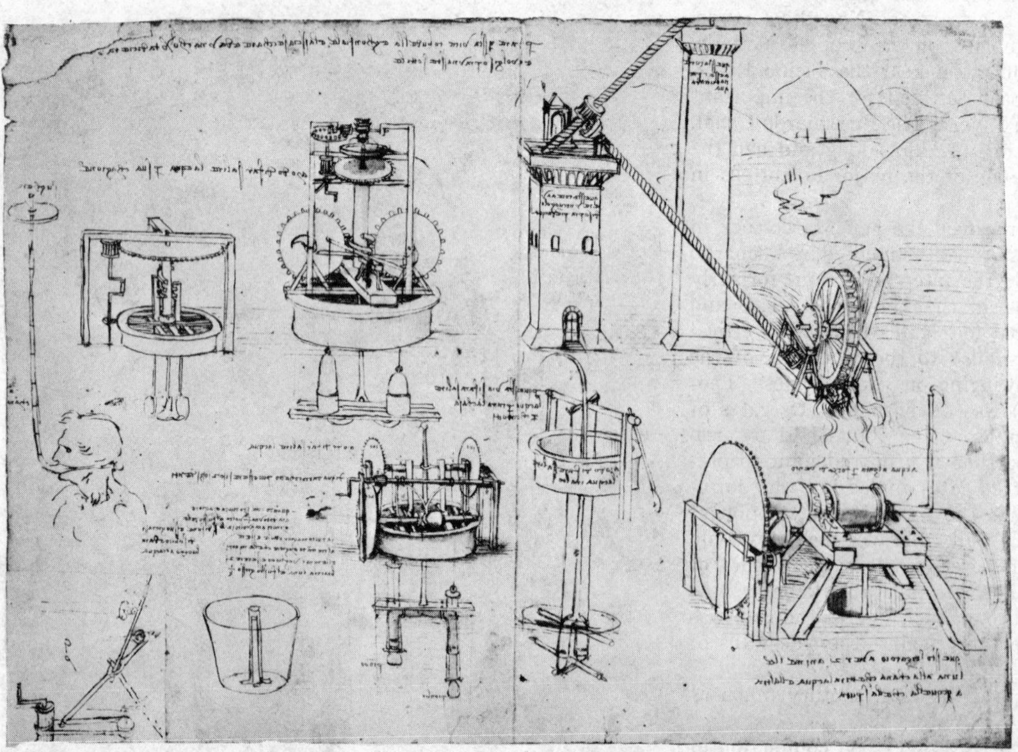

PAGES OF MECHANICAL SKETCHES FROM AMONG THE MANY SCIENTIFIC STUDIES CONTAINED IN LEONARDO DA VINCI'S NOTEBOOKS keted as sheets, plates, and other forms, while much of the silver went into government mints.

The newly invented liquation method was used to extract silver from copper ore. In the process, crude argentiferous copper was melted with lead in a small blast furnace and cast in cakes in copper molds. In the next step, the liquation process itself, the cakes of copper-lead-silver were heated on the hearth with charcoal at a temperature above the melting point of lead and below that of copper, thus allowing the more fusible lead to be drained off, carrying with it the silver, which was chemically attracted to the lead. The copper (the spent liquation cake) was then further refined for marketing, but the liquated lead and silver had to be separated. Using cupellation (a process known from antiquity), the lead-silver was melted on the hearth with charcoal and bone ash, and an air blast was directed on the surface of the melt to oxidize the lead. The lead oxide (litharge) was run over the rim of the furnace; that remaining was combined with the bone ash deposited on the hearth, and the silver was collected in a pocket at the bottom of the hearth.

Improved chemical techniques, along with the utilization of natural power and machines, increased the output of nonferrous metals. Fast-flowing mountain streams powered the heavy waterwheels that drove the furnace bellows and activated the heavy trip-hammers at the forge. Waterwheels also powered crushing machines and operated pumps that drained the mines and made possible deeper shafts. *De re metallica,* a treatise on mining by the German engineer Georgius Agricola (1494–1555), has remarkably descriptive woodcuts showing the various machines at work. Specific machine elements included gear trains, flywheels, windlasses, cranks, fans, bellows, cams and tappets, treadles, chain-and-ball pumps, bucket pumps, and suction pumps. Impressive mechanical systems included water mill hoists, crushing mills, and windmill-powered ventilation fans.

A WOODCUT ILLUSTRATION SHOWING 16TH-CENTURY MINING OPERATION; FROM "DE RE METALLICA" BY GEORGIUS AGRICOLA

The technique of casting, especially in bronze, had been known to antiquity, and by the 16th century casting in both brass and bronze was common. Molds for large bronze and brass casting were of loam, while lead and tin for pewter were commonly cast in molds of soft stone, metal, and sand or clay. Sheet lead was cast for roofing and for the siding of ships by pouring lead down an inclined sanded plane. Not until about 1615 were lead sheets rolled for these purposes. Precious metals were also cast and then die stamped for coins.

**5. Assaying.**—In the 16th century no field of metallurgy was more advanced than that of assaying. It was the technical means by which certain economic and financial questions could be answered before the capitalist invested in a mining or metallurgical enterprise. The assayer also determined the quality of coinage, which had long troubled the economy.

The complex assay technique involved special furnaces, utensils, weights, balances, and fluxes. Though the basic concern of the assayer was quantitative analyses of ores and metals, he also resorted to qualitative assaying by observing the colour of the flame and smoke and by use of the bead test (using glass rather than borax). His principal handicap was lack of precise furnace control and means of measuring temperature.

The empirical knowledge of the 16th-century assayer remains impressive against a 20th-century background. Assayers knew, for example, of the depression of the melting point in alloys and of the proportions for minimum melting point in alloys. Knowing that certain molten metals did not mix, they were able to separate two liquid metals, as in liquation. They recognized the existence of terminal and intermediate solid solutions, the formation of intermetallic compounds, the process of hardening by cold working and of annealing to produce softening, and the changes in properties resulting from transformation or from solubility changes. They also knew of different affinities of metals for each other and for nonmetals (this was in fact the principal means of assaying and refining). They were aware of metals replacing each other from solutions of their salts and of diffusion in the solid state of metals (this was used in making steel, cementing gold, and blanching silver). The relationships between the structure and the properties of metals, as well as fracture tests, were used to determine quality and as a guide for composition and for heat treatment.

An important step taken during the 17th century was the application, made in 1664 by Henry Power, of the microscope to the study of fracture structure. It was also discovered that sparks struck from steel would provide a rough gauge of its properties. Density measurements had been made as early as the 11th and 12th centuries, and in the 17th century lists of densities of metals and alloys became extensive and even systematic. The limited information obtained from tests of metal strength may have been of some use to engineers, but assaying techniques were not used in an organized way to serve the engineer and builder until the 18th century.

No general theory of metals was really possible until the second quarter of the 19th century, when chemical theory, atomic theory, and the theory of crystalline structure were being formulated. However, the economically important and technically refined practice of assaying produced factual information and accurate numerical data from which the scientist later formulated hypotheses and generalizations. Fortunately the assayers were literate men as a result of their responsibility for keeping accounts of precious metals and their close contacts with highly placed persons in state and private enterprise. Thus they were able to organize and record their empirical information about copper, lead, and precious metals. This was not the case with the ironmaster dealing in a comparatively crude bulk product. Not until the 18th century was there a study devoted exclusively to iron by R. A. F. de Réaumur.

HISTORICAL PICTURES SERVICE

A 16TH-CENTURY ASSAYING ROOM, AS ILLUSTRATED BY LAZARUS ERCKER

The outstanding 16th-century books on metallurgy by Vannoccio Biringuccio, Georgius Agricola, and Lazarus Ercker all discussed assaying in addition to a general discussion of metallurgy.

The lag in scientific treatment of metallurgical data did not prevent the assayer from proving his worth to the miner and smelter as well as to the master of the mint. Ercker wrote in the dedication of his treatise that he intended it to be useful in developing the rich metal and mineral resources of the Holy Roman Empire by both imperial and private enterprise. Ercker believed that God had put metals and minerals in the earth to be obtained, converted, and employed by man in his labours. Therefore, with the help of God and through complete information (supplied by Ercker), he believed these resources would be further developed and long maintained.

**6. Printing.**—The invention of printing with movable cast type is an outstanding example of the increased sophistication, complexity, and precision of technology in the early modern era. Its history throws light upon the actual process of complex inventions.

The invention of printing is also an example of the epoch-making effect of technical change on the diffusion of knowledge, particularly technical knowledge. Once the fundamental breakthrough occurred in printing, improvement and refinement followed rapidly. In a decade, printing developed from the crude type forms of the earliest text printed between 1444 and 1447 (the "Fragment of the World Judgement") to the masterly printed 42-line Bible of about 1453.

The invention of printing is of interest as one of the first instances of substitution of mechanical devices for hand work in order to obtain accuracy and refinement of execution, as well as reduced cost. Furthermore, printing was one of the first examples of mass production of a standardized product. Also noteworthy is the fact that the print shop from the beginning was characterized by capitalistic methods; it was from the outset a factory rather than a craft shop.

Printing with movable cast type was not a simple invention; it was the bringing together of a number of earlier inventions. The invention of paper was an absolute prerequisite to printing, since parchment and papyrus were completely unsuitable. Parchment was difficult to handle, irregular in thickness, costly, and in limited supply; papyrus was hard and brittle. Linen paper, which was suitable, had been invented in central China at the close of the 1st century A.D. It spread rapidly in China, reaching the West in the mid-12th century through the Islamic world.

Other prerequisites were ink and the press. Early wood-block printers used thin distempers, which were soon replaced by boiled oil. The cloth and wine press was modified for printing by applying a quick-acting screw, by the means of holding the paper and type to prevent twisting, and by devices to give uniform pressure of the plate.

Another prerequisite was a metal suitable for type casting. In the 17th century lead-based alloys were common, but the first type of the 15th century was probably a tin-based alloy of the kind used by pewterers.

The printing problems of the 15th century centred around engraving and casting. They required for their solution a number of minor inventions to which two distinct crafts, the wood engraver and the goldsmith, contributed. The goldsmith had already become familiar with dies, punches, and delicate methods of casting in connection with the manufacture of coins and jewelry. The wood engraver had a long history as a printer, using single-block illustrations. Although the historical order of occurrence is uncertain, it is clear that wood-engraved prints were known in 1418, wood-engraved prints with engraved text by 1437, and wood-engraved books with printed text and illustrations about 1440.

*The Role of Gutenberg.*—Johann Gutenberg (*c.* 1398–1468) is generally credited with the next great step forward. The more moderate Gutenberg supporters accept the passage in the *Chronicle of Cologne* of 1499 naming Gutenberg as the inventor of printing at Mainz but allow a "prefiguration" in Holland of printing with movable type. Gutenberg's more dogmatic followers insist that the Dutch books were all block-printed pages and not from movable type. Probably the Dutch technique anticipated the German (Gutenberg) method and even inspired it, but it is equally clear that the German work later surpassed it.

The city records of Avignon, France, for the years 1444–46 refer to Procopius Waldvoghel (Waldfogel) of Prague who registered agreements to teach the art of the goldsmith and of writing mechanically. In July 1444 he agreed to deliver "2 alphabets of steel, 2 iron forms, a vise or screw, 48 forms of tin, and various other items pertaining to the art of writing." Another contract refers to "27 Hebrew characters, 48 letters engraved on iron, and

HISTORICAL PICTURES SERVICE

A PRINTING PRESS OF 1520, FROM A CONTEMPORARY WOODCUT ILLUSTRATION instruments for writing mechanically in Latin." Here, then, is evidence of hard metal punches and type molds. There is, by contrast, no evidence for the use of hard metal punches by the Dutch or by the Germans this early. No evidence of printing survives at Avignon, however. Thus it is clear that various lines of development were leading toward perfecting printing with movable type through wood engraving, metal engraving, and metal founding.

Gutenberg, Johann Fust, and Peter Schoeffer were associated in an enterprise connected with printing in Mainz from 1450 to 1455. One of them, or the group, made important contributions to the printing process. It is fairly certain that Fust was the financier. Possibly the technical genius was Schoeffer, because there was a marked improvement in a psalter printed by Fust and Schoeffer after they had separated from Gutenberg. However, the outstanding products of the Mainz group can be dated by an almanac of about 1448 and the famous 42-line Bible of about 1453. Gutenberg, then, was associated with an effort that produced the most impressive early works in modern printing.

The precise chronology of invention of printing cannot be developed on the basis of historical evidence, but logic provides a list of problems solved in the invention of a system of printing with movable cast type. These were the selection of a suitable metal for casting, the design of an adjustable metal type mold, and stamping with a hard punch the letter-forming matrix.

The first type cast by Gutenberg was probably of pewterer's metal and in a metal mold. (The first molds were not adjustable, but a distinct mold was used for each different size matrix, *e.g.*, *m* and *w*; *o* and *s*; *i* and *j*; and so on.) A steel punch, like those used by the goldsmith or coin minter, probably impressed the matrix with the letter form. The type in final form was a slender rod of rectangular cross section usually about an inch long, with the letter formed at one end. The typesetter fixed the type in page forms that made up the face of the press. From 2 to 16 pages were placed in the press to be printed on a single sheet of paper. The critical invention that made type available in quantity and also permitted technical excellence in printing was the adjustable type mold with a lead or copper matrix.

The resulting 42-line Bible was far ahead of the best manuscripts in quality, and the best books became objects of luxury, not simply cheap substitutions for manuscripts. As a matter of fact, cheap books were not available for some time. There were many professional copiers who, at low pay and for years after the development of printing, could turn out manuscript copies of small books less expensively than the printer. (*See* further PRINTING.)

**7. Dutch Dikes, Drainage, and Windmills.**—Much as German printing and metallurgy were outstanding during the 16th century, when Germany enjoyed an era of economic and political prominence, Dutch engineering was impressive in the late 16th and early 17th centuries, when the northern Netherlands won independence and commercial power. The Dutch engineers were especially noted, then as now, for winning land from the ocean and inland seas.

The skill and heroic achievements of the Dutch engineers have long inspired admiration, for between 1540 and 1690 they reclaimed about 440,000 ac. (178,000 ha.) from the ocean and inland seas. By the end of the 15th century the Dutch had developed effective diking techniques. In Friesland, where the sea was strong, they used earth cores plastered with clay that was strengthened by seaweed or straw, along with palisades of piles. Centralized administration of large projects furthered the activity.

More complex was the reclaiming of rich lands from great inland marshes and seas. This activity in the formation of polders (enclaves of reclaimed land) involved surrounding drowned land by a ring dike, digging a network of drainage ditches or canals within the polder, erecting drainage pumps, and constructing exterior sluices to carry the pumped water off to main drainage canals or rivers.

During the 16th century the windmill-driven scoop wheel for drainage became common. These mills lifted the water up and out of the polder. There were also windmill-driven screw pumps. Simon Stevin (1548–1620), one of Europe's great engineers, described drainage mills of advanced designs in an outstanding treatise on the principles and practice of drainage-mill use and construction.

## VII. ORIGINS OF THE BRITISH INDUSTRIAL REVOLUTION

### A. Iron, Coal, and Steam

In the 17th and 18th centuries iron, coal, and steam played increasingly significant roles and contributed greatly to the transformation of society through an industrial revolution (*q.v.*).

**1. Increased Iron Consumption.**—During the Middle Ages the price of iron had remained fairly stable despite the steady rise of wages and the price of raw materials, but in the 16th century, even with technical improvements such as larger smelting units and better machines for producing the furnace blast by water power, the increased cost of labour and particularly of fuel led to higher prices for iron. However, the consumption of iron rose steadily. In the early 16th century about 60,000 tons per year were produced in western Europe, approximately half of it in Germany and about a fifth in France. Frequent wars, mechanization of the armament industry, increasing use of iron castings, the use of cast iron in the production of wrought iron, and the need for kitchenware and simple tools and utensils contributed to increased demand.

Changing standards for heavy artillery produced new requirements in the quantity and size of iron castings. For larger cannon, as many as four blast furnaces had to be used. Musket balls were cast, but Biringuccio stated that the best were forged in dies. Iron cannon balls were cast in split molds.

**2. Smelting Improvements.**—The market demand and fuel shortages brought responses from inventors and engineers, especially in Britain. One solution was an increase in furnace size, which, along with an increased air supply, led to higher furnace temperatures, higher yield, and higher efficiency. Thus, while in 1600 an average blast furnace could produce about $1\frac{1}{2}$ tons of pig iron a day, by 1700 about $2\frac{1}{2}$ tons of pig iron per day were produced from less than 3 tons of charcoal.

The medieval furnaces had been less than 10 ft. (3 m.) high and used natural draft or foot-operated bellows. Since the furnace temperatures were not high enough to melt the reduced iron, it dropped as a spongy mass to the bottom of the furnace. This "bloom" of iron was removed from the furnace, leaving nonferrous matter as slag. The bloom was then reheated and hammered to remove the slag.

During the 14th century the furnace for smelting iron underwent fundamental changes. The *stückofen*, a German invention, may have resulted from increased furnace heights (as high as 30 ft.) and stronger air blasts (bellows driven by a waterwheel). Early in the century it was found that iron collecting at the bottom of the furnace was liquid and that the liquid could be run free for casting. The hotter furnace melted the iron, and it also kept the descending iron longer in contact with glowing charcoal. This increased the carbon content of the iron, lowered its melting point, and further facilitated the production of liquid, rather than bloom, iron.

The liquid iron was cast into molds near the furnace tap as "pigs." If the cast pigs were to be made into wrought iron, they were carried to the forge, which was often equipped with waterwheel-powered bellow furnaces and hammers. In the furnaces the excess carbon was burned off and the metal heated for forging. By the 17th century waterwheel-operated rollers shaped large cross-section blooms from the forge into bars.

As the blast furnace spread throughout Europe in the 15th century, the availability of cast iron increased its consumption. There was also an increase in iron production resulting from the development of a continuous process in which ore and fuel were added at the top of the furnace and the iron tapped at the bottom. A longer operating cycle was also possible before it was necessary to reline and repair the furnace. In 1400 in England the smelting process could not be continued longer than 6 days; by 1600 in Germany it lasted as long as 24 days; and by 1700 in England the blast furnace could be operated continuously for about 40 weeks.

Mechanization became common in working iron. Power-driven tilt hammers appeared in the 16th century, as did power wire drawing, rolling, and slitting mills. The furnaces, however, were usually fed by men or animals without the help of machinery.

As the use of the blast furnace and cast iron increased in the 16th and 17th centuries, a number of problems developed. A bewildering variety of iron came from the furnaces, and its behaviour varied accordingly. Variations in ferrous materials were thought to be due to variations in furnace conditions, and not until the 18th century was the role of carbon in iron recognized, since slight modifications in temperature could produce substantial variations in the amount and state of carbon content.

The next 150 years were to make iron and steel the most important engineering materials. This did not occur, however, until the pressing problem of fuel shortage was solved by the substitution of coal for charcoal.

**3. Increased Consumption of Coal.**—In late medieval Europe, coal in the Low Countries was mined on a limited scale. In the first half of the 16th century the output of these mines increased three to four times to provide fuel for the growing manufacture of iron and other metals along the Meuse River. But the greatest development occurred in Great Britain, where by 1675 more than 2,000,000 tons of coal per year were produced, amounting to five times the production of the rest of the world.

This shift from a wood-burning to a coal-burning economy raised problems in three important areas: first, in the industrial use of coal, especially in smelting iron; second, in mining coal; and third, in transportation.

By 1603 the price of wood from Britain's depleted forests was so high as to be prohibitive for many industries. Some industries, such as wine, alum, or brick manufacturing, easily shifted from wood or charcoal to coal. But for other industries a shift of this sort required the invention of new methods. For instance, the glassmakers found that, in switching from charcoal to coal, the coal fumes darkened the glass.

The problem of charcoal shortage led the iron industry to move nearer the surviving forests, but this also meant farther away from markets and sometimes from the ore. The problem of replacing charcoal had to be solved in several of the ironmasters' processes: smelting iron from ore in the furnace; the production of wrought iron from pig iron at the forge; and in working wrought iron into manufactured goods. In each instance the products of coal combustion could damage the material.

Smelting was the most difficult problem because the iron ore had to remain at high temperatures in order to be reduced and carbonized into cast iron. The solution came from a remote field: the production of beer. In drying malt for beer, charcoal had been used, but in order to reduce the price some brewmaster decided to use coal. The effect of the fumes on the taste of the beer was abominable. The idea occurred to someone that the more noxious fumes could be driven from coal by heating it, *i.e.*, by converting it to coke. After a number of attempts from 1640–50, the British brewmasters eventually succeeded in substituting coke for charcoal. Yet it was not until 1709 that Abraham Darby successfully applied coke to blast-furnace smelting.

Abraham Darby I (1677–1717) and his son established an ironmaking dynasty, and their works at Coalbrookdale became the leading centre of metallurgical progress. Darby also introduced a coal-fired reverberatory furnace for remelting cast, or pig, iron; and his son contributed a system, involving careful ore selection, which allowed refining coke-smelted cast iron into bar, or wrought, iron at the forge furnaces. As a result of the Darbys' work the market for cast-iron products (pots, kettles, furnaces, and so on) increased, especially after a technique for thin casting in dry sand molds was developed by the father.

The Darbys pioneered in other metallurgical techniques as well. In order to use coke economically, the furnaces at Coalbrookdale had to be enlarged so that the iron ore could remain in contact with the coke longer, and the temperature had to be increased by a more powerful air blast.

Although Henry Cort (1740–1800) is credited with the invention of the puddling technique for making wrought iron without charcoal, he is better remembered as the inventor of a system of converting pig or cast iron into wrought iron without charcoal and in quantity. Cort's puddling process, described in his patents of 1783–84, utilized a coal-burning reverberatory furnace and a rolling mill. It involved heating the pig iron in the hearth of the furnace, where the fuel did not come in contact with the iron, but the heat passed from the furnace and over the adjacent hearth. With a chimney supplying an air draft, no bellows were used. The carbon in the most exposed melt combined with oxygen from the air, and the relatively carbon-free portions of iron, whose melting point rose as a result, became stiffer and were removed by the ironworker in large globs. Impurities were then hammered out, and the wrought iron blooms were shaped under the forge hammer.

Cort completed his system by passing his forged bars or plates through V-grooved rolls that not only further shaped (elongated) the wrought iron into rods but also pressed out earthy particles, cinder, and impurities. The good quality and quantity of malleable iron made possible by Cort's system strengthened the British economy on the eve of the French Revolutionary and the Napoleonic Wars. Malleable iron found use where cast iron could not function, *e.g.*, in anchors and many ship fittings.

The increased demand for coal, which began in the 16th century and intensified in the 18th, raised problems of finance and of mechanization and power, of draining the mines as miners moved deeper after exhausting surface veins. The value of coal was too low to allow the use of horse mills, which were economical in mining gold and silver. Since water power was not always available, there was a need not only for improved pumps but also for a new source of power to drive them. The solution was found in the steam engine, the history of which began with the need for pumps.

**4. Development of Pumps and Power Sources.**—Agricola illustrated his 16th-century *De re metallica* with many examples of pumps. Among these was a chain of dippers powered by a man through reduction gears, or by animal and water mills. Agricola also depicted suction pumps, force pumps, and a "rag and chain" system used in central European mines. Each type had limitations: nature restricted the suction pumps; the force pumps overstressed the pipes, which were usually wooden; and the "rag and chain" system put a heavy load on the power source. These pumps could remove water from depths of several hundred feet, but this required an elaborate mechanical system involving overly large waterwheels or a series of pumps at different levels, with the accompanying problem of power transmission or location. Limited underground space discouraged the use of pumps in relays.

The increase in size of towns also produced a greater demand for centralized water supply and for pumping units. Though the Roman solution had been to use aqueducts with gravity feed, European cities in the 16th and 17th centuries used pumps operated by waterwheels or windmills (the English city of Gloucester had such a windmill water supply in 1542). By 1526 Toledo, Spain, had a complex apparatus built by an Italian engineer, Juanelo Turriano, and in 1548 Augsburg had a water supply provided by mechanical power. Other German towns soon followed suit. In 1582 London pumped its water supply, as did Paris in 1608. Throughout the 17th century, city waterworks became common. Since great volumes of water were moved, large but inefficient sets of pumps and waterwheels were used.

Other circumstances defined the need for new power sources. Windmills and water mills not only were large for the delivered horsepower but they had limitations imposed by geography and climate. The locations of towns and heavy industry before the steam age demonstrated their dependence upon the fall line of rivers. While in freezing weather these towns and industries would lose this valuable power source, summer might bring a paralyzing drought. Some ironworks were limited to less than two months of operation because of climatic conditions. Labour problems and high capital costs per unit resulted from idle machinery. Prevailing winds made windmills economical in some areas, but without potential in others. Nevertheless, areas with water and wind power were frequently the cradles of economic development. The

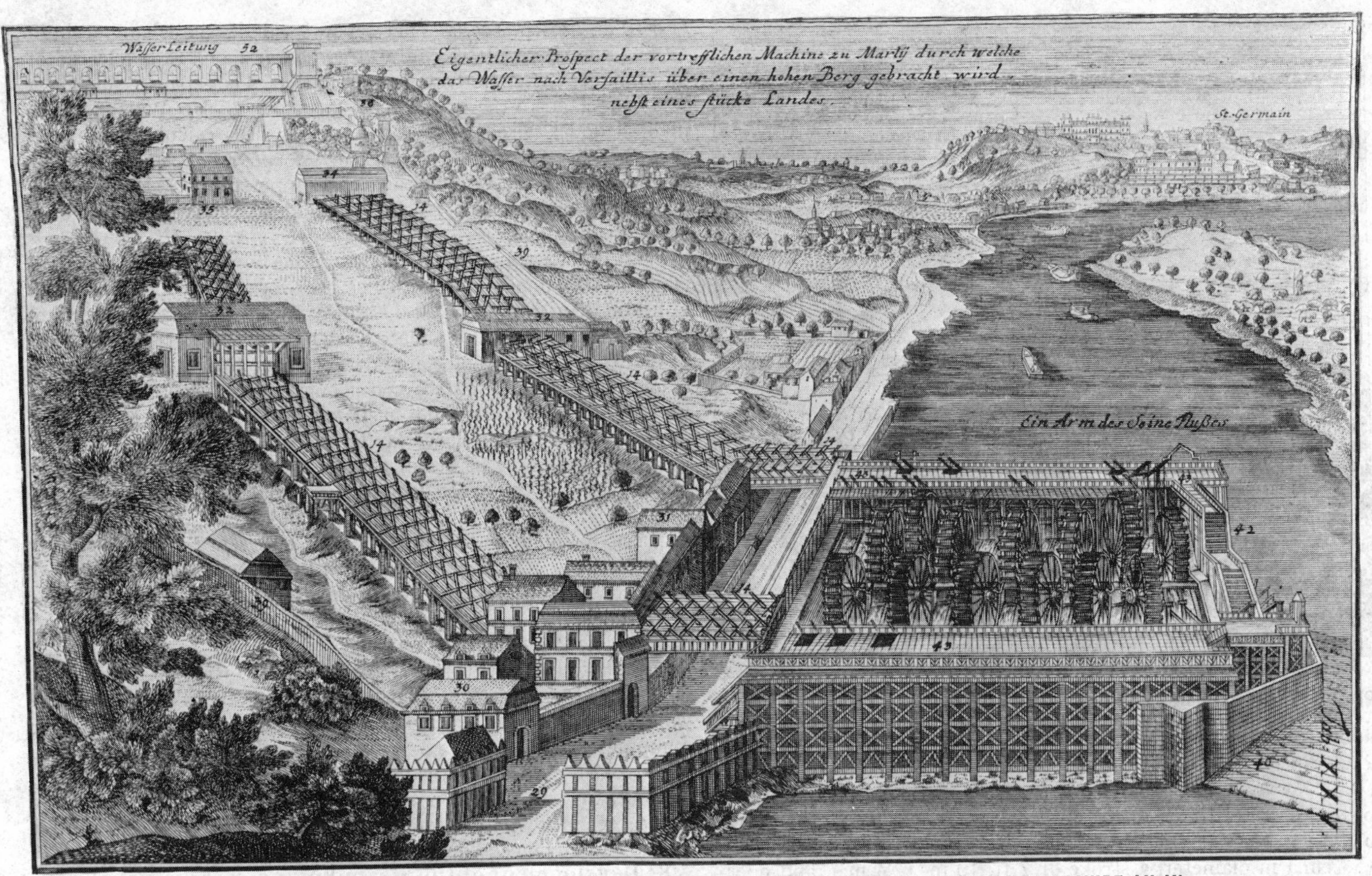


WATERWHEELS DRIVEN BY THE FORCE OF THE RIVER CURRENT ACTIVATE A SYSTEM OF PUMPS TO PROVIDE AN INLAND WATER SUPPLY. FROM JACOB LEUPOLD'S "THEATRUM MACHINARUM HYDRAULICARUM," 1724–25

need for a reliable, low-cost, concentrated, and widely available source of power for industry was obvious, but the drainage of mines was the most pressing problem and was the immediate cause of the development of the steam engine.

**5. Early Steam Engines.**—The earliest steam prime movers, which functioned without the pistons and cylinders of later engines, used air pressure working against a vacuum, and some used the force of steam pressure as well (*see* STEAM). Edward Somerset, 2nd marquess of Worcester (1601–67), built what was probably the first steam device capable of economically significant work. Though the design of his water-commanding engine is uncertain, it probably resembled that of Thomas Savery, patented in 1698.

Savery's engine had a vessel with stopcocks for admitting steam from a boiler. A stopcock-controlled supply of cooling water from a tank above was directed over the hot surface of the steam vessel. Self-regulating valves admitted water from below to the steam vessel or out of the vessel to a higher discharge level. In operation, the hand-controlled stopcock was opened to admit steam into the steam vessel, then this was closed, and the stopcock controlling the cooling water from the elevated tank was opened to run over the steam vessel, condensing the steam and creating a vacuum. A valve in the pump pipe then opened automatically as atmospheric pressure at the base of the pump pipe forced water into the vacuum. Next, the steam was admitted again into the nearly water-filled vessel to force the water up through pipe outlets.

Savery's engine found application in at least one mine and several water-supply installations. He clearly demonstrated the possibility of using air and steam pressure in a pump, but his device had to be located within 20 ft. (6 m.) of the water level at the bottom of the mine. This meant that the draft from the fire helped to ventilate the mine, but if the pumping device failed and the mine flooded there would be no means of clearing it. Furthermore, the device could not push water up to the top of a deep mine because the permissible boiler pressure was limited to less than 8–10 atm. The device had no safety valve to prevent explosions, and it required about 20 times more coal than a modern engine.

The next major innovation in steam-engine design was the introduction of the piston and cylinder. Otto von Guericke (1602–86) had shown the potential of air pressure moving a piston against a vacuum, and Christiaan Huygens (1629–95), the Dutch scientist, and his assistant Denis Papin (1647–*c.* 1712) had experimented with gunpowder explosions and steam to create a vacuum beneath a piston. Papin recognized the economic significance of the atmospheric engine, but it was an Englishman, Thomas Newcomen, who invented the first industrially significant piston-and-cylinder steam engine.

**6. Newcomen's Atmospheric Engine.**—Little is known of Newcomen's career, though his letters to Robert Hooke of the Royal Society indicated an interest in developing pump pistons. Sometime after Savery's patent of 1698, Newcomen, Savery, and John Cawley joined forces. The first working atmospheric engine of Newcomen and his associates was built at Wolverhampton, Eng., in 1712. At first Newcomen used surface condensation on his engines, but faulty operation suggested the advantages of internal jet condensation.

In Newcomen's engine the piston was lifted by a counterweight on the pump side, and steam flowed into the piston cylinder under very low pressure. When the steam was condensed by the cooling water to form a vacuum, the piston was pushed down by atmospheric pressure working against this vacuum. Since the steam had only enough pressure to flow in and clear the cylinder of the water of condensation, no work was done by steam pressure.

A challenging problem was to design a mechanism to operate the various cocks and valves automatically. An engraving of 1719 shows the solution: a plug tree for operating the cocks and valves. This was Newcomen's invention, despite anecdotes of his lazy and ingenious "tap boy" Humphrey Potter conceiving of the device to save his manual efforts.

In the larger Newcomen engines it was necessary to use large

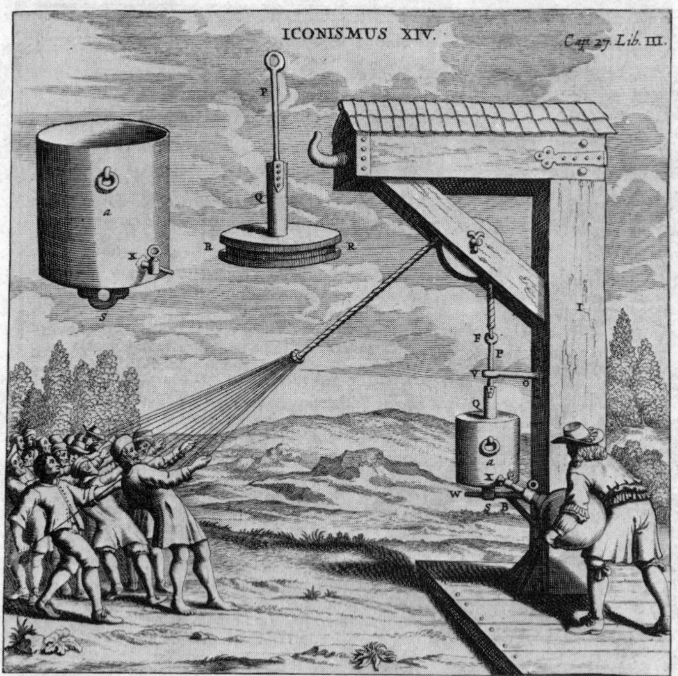


OTTO VON GUERICKE'S DRAMATIC DEMONSTRATION OF THE PRESSURE OF THE ATMOSPHERE MOVING A PISTON INTO A VACUUM. THE MAN AT THE RIGHT HAS EXHAUSTED THE CYLINDER WITH GUERICKE'S AIR PUMP. FROM OTTO VON GUERICKE, "EXPERIMENTA NOVA," 1672

piston diameters in order to get the required power with the safety of low pressures. One engine, for instance, had a cylinder 21 in. (53 cm.) in diameter, a stroke of 7 ft. 10 in. (2.4 m.), and operated at 12 strokes per minute. The actual water raised showed that its effective horsepower was about 5½. Thus the smallest Newcomen engines were about equal to the smaller windmills in capacity, but the larger engines were much greater in power than any unit of the earlier prime movers. The Newcomen engine, then, marks the effective beginning of the utilization of a new source of power. With changes introduced by John Smeaton (1724–92), the Newcomen engine held its place for about 75 years, being used almost entirely for raising water.

Though Newcomen's invention satisfied the need for a cheap, constant source of power that could be located anywhere, it had major faults. Besides wasting steam, it was not possible to get rotary motion directly from its walking beam and chain with available crank motions because only the downstroke was a power stroke. The engine could, however, pump water to a reservoir to power a waterwheel supplying rotary motion. The Newcomen engine used neither steam pressure nor the expansive power of steam. These faults were attacked by James Watt, whose work on the steam engine was basically a scientific and critical revision of the Newcomen engine.

**7. James Watt's Experiment: The Separate Condenser.**—In 1763 Watt was given the job of repairing a model of the Newcomen engine used for instruction at the University of Glasgow. This engine, which had a 2-in.- (5-cm.-) diameter piston and a 6-in. (15-cm.) stroke, would run for a few strokes and then stop, yet the boiler seemed to be capable of supplying adequate steam. Watt analyzed the heat losses and the character of steam in imaginative quantitative experiments. He noted that loss of heat through cooling and reheating the walls of the cylinder was considerable and that this was probably the reason why the engine stopped. The idea occurred to him to keep the cylinder as hot as the steam that entered it to avoid useless condensation. There were two possibilities: a steam jacket on the cylinder to keep it warm, and a separate condenser and an air pump to avoid the alternate cooling and reheating of the cylinder. Thus the cylinder would be kept hot and the separate condensing chamber cool. His experimental piston-and-cylinder apparatus of 1765 consisted of a brass cylinder made from a syringe 1¾ in. (4½ cm.) in diameter and 10 in. (25 cm.) long. The separate condensing chamber, built of tin and submerged in cold water, was designed to be cleared of air and water by a hand condensate pump. The separate condenser was connected to the cylinder by cocks or valves. Watt's experimental model raised an 18-lb. weight, and his calculation showed that the effective pressure was 13.6 psi (pounds per square inch) as compared to the 14.7 psi theoretically possible. This, of course, was considerably more efficient than the effective 7–8 psi of a Newcomen engine.

Watt demonstrated the soundness of his hypothesis by the engine efficiency obtained. In his device the work was done not by the atmosphere working against a steam-created vacuum but by steam working against a steam-created vacuum.

Watt's patent of 1769 claimed: first, jacketing the cylinder with insulation and/or steam to keep it hot; second, the use of a separate condenser kept as cool as possible; third, the use of an air pump to clear the condenser and cylinder; and fourth, the use of the expansive force of steam (although this was not embodied in his early engines). Watt demonstrated that the steam engine was a heat engine by striving for a maximum temperature differential between cylinder and condenser. In one sense, he was simply modifying the Newcomen engine, yet he added so many important inventions and innovations—and created the engine so nearly as it is today—that, by comparison with the usefulness of other engines, his engine was the strategic invention.

The design for Watt's early engine had certain disadvantages, however. It retained the chain acting on an arc at the end of the walking beam, and the engine was therefore still only good for pumping. The engine was single-acting (steam acting only on one stroke), and steam was still admitted during the whole stroke without any cutoff. Nonetheless, the design was based upon a sound, scientific perception of the properties of steam, and it marked an advanced concept that was to be carried much further.

**8. Development of the Steam Engine.**—The transition from Watt's concept of 1769 to engines in practical operation involved a number of technical and business problems, as well as long delays. First, Watt's ideal design outran the existing facilities for building engines. Though financial support was received from John Roebuck, a Scottish chemical and iron manufacturer, the high cost of developing the steam engine, along with his other engagements, forced Roebuck into bankruptcy. In a sense this was

CULVER PICTURES, INC.

THE ATMOSPHERIC ENGINE OF THOMAS NEWCOMEN

THE BETTMANN ARCHIVE

JAMES WATT'S STEAM ENGINE

fortunate for Watt, because in the liquidation of Roebuck's affairs Matthew Boulton, the great Birmingham manufacturer and entrepreneur, became interested and in 1773 took over Roebuck's share in Watt's patent. Boulton's contributions considerably hastened the production of Watt's engine. He provided a large engineering shop in which parts of Watt's engine were built in 1774, and he supplied the necessary resources, business experience, and technical knowledge to manage the firm successfully.

The demand for the early Boulton and Watt pumping engines was small, except in the Cornish tin mines, where coal was dear and the fuel economy critical (the Cornish owners contracted to pay for the Watt engines out of fuel savings). In other mines, where coal was plentiful, the Newcomen engine was reasonably satisfactory. When it became apparent that their huge enterprise required greater output than the demand called for, Boulton and Watt saw the need for developing an engine of more general industrial use.

The resulting double-acting engine and its power-transmission linkage were described in Watt's patents of 1781–82. In this engine steam was cut off before the cylinder was entirely filled, and the engine operated by the subsequent expansion of steam. These elements, which were essential to the general utility of the engine, marked the climax of Watt's work. They also marked a turning point in assuring the prosperity of the firm.

After 1784 Watt rated his engines in horsepower, having defined this as 33,000 ft-lb. per minute. The first double-acting engine was capable of only 10 hp., but later engines developed 20 hp., and a few were rated at 40, 50, and even 80 hp.

The real advantage in Watt's work, however, was the increase in efficiency, which reduced the cost of operation and gave the engine a wider market. For a 40 hp. engine, an atmospheric engine required about 16 lb. of coal per horsepower hour, while Watt's double-acting engine required only about $8\frac{1}{2}$ lb. of coal per horsepower hour. The double-acting engine with cutoff and an expansion of $1\frac{1}{2}$ times required only slightly more than $6\frac{1}{4}$ lb. of coal per horsepower hour. The Cornish tin mines recorded an actual reduction in coal consumption after the introduction of these engines to about one-third of what it had been with Newcomen engines.

The full exploitation of the steam engine developed in two directions: first, in higher pressures; and second, in the investigation of the thermodynamics of steam and its properties. With higher pressure more economical results could be obtained, and the steam engine could be applied to locomotion because of the consequent reduction of engine weight per horsepower unit and the possibility of dispensing with the condenser. Denis Papin had been on the verge of this development, and Jacob Leupold published a sketch of a high-pressure engine in the 1720s. Why then did it not appear earlier? The limiting factor was not the concept or a matter of design, since all the valves and the piston motions were much the same as those of the low-pressure engine. The cause of delay in going to higher pressures was that neither boilers nor cylinders were then available with the required strength and accuracy. Watt's fear of higher pressures discouraged other English engineers for a generation or more. In 1784 William Murdock, one of Watt's workmen, undertook a high-pressure locomotive action, but Watt discouraged it. It only became possible to go to higher pressures through improvements made from 1775 to 1800 in the manufacture of iron and in the working of metal. The first really significant high-pressure results were obtained by Oliver Evans of the United States and Richard Trevithick of Britain between 1800 and 1801.

### B. Textiles

The mechanization of a basic consumer goods industry was a necessary preliminary to the British Industrial Revolution. The mechanized cotton factory, which became the most characteristic feature of the Industrial Revolution, is an excellent example of a continuing historical process of major significance.

**1. Beginnings of Mechanization.**—In earliest times fibres could be spun (twisted and drawn out) into yarn or thread without the use of tools. The bundle of fibres, after carding (combing) with thistle or teasel heads, was spun between one hand and leg, while the other hand drew out the yarn. The loom had warp, or lengthwise, threads. The weaver passed the weft, or crosswise, thread by means of a shuttle through the shed, or opening, made by raising simple heddle frames to which alternate warps were fastened. These simple movements of the carder, spinner, and weaver, however, proved subtle and complicated to the many inventors who tried to imitate them mechanically.

BY COURTESY OF THE METROPOLITAN MUSEUM OF ART, FLETCHER FUND, 1931

WEAVING OF WOOL ON A VERTICAL LOOM—DETAIL OF A PAINTING ON AN ATHENIAN SCENT BOTTLE, ABOUT 560 B.C.

Thousands of years before Christ, spinners began to use the free spindle for twisting the fibres. An early model was a wooden stick about half an inch in diameter and less than a foot in length. Near the bottom end of the spindle was a stone or clay disk, called the whorl, which gave momentum to the rotating spindle in the manner of a flywheel. While drawing out the fibres with one hand, the spinner would use the other hand to turn the spindle, which twisted the drawn fibres into yarn. As late as the 19th century, hand spinning with the spindle over a bowl of water to give the proper humidity was common in India, and cotton for the finest muslins was spun in this way.

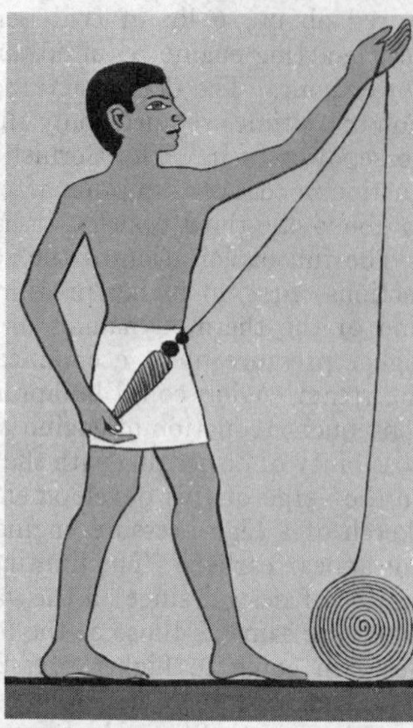

REDRAWN FROM SINGER, HOLMYARD & HALL. "A HISTORY OF TECHNOLOGY" AFTER F. CAILLIAUD. RECHERCHES SUR LES ARTS ET MÉTIERS DE L'ÉGYPTE, ETC.," PL. XVII, PARIS, 1831

AN EGYPTIAN SPINNER USING A FREE SPINDLE: FROM THE TOMB OF KHETY, BENI HASAN, EGYPT, ABOUT 1900 B.C.

Records and remains that would allow precise dating of innovations in textile production before the Middle Ages are scarce. In the 4th or 5th century A.D., unknown inventors in Europe introduced suspended heddles, which were rectangular frames hung above the horizontal loom frame. By means of cords attached to the heddle and to the warp yarn the shed was opened for the passage of the shuttle. With more than two heddles it was possible to weave fancy fabrics. Before the late Middle Ages, the suspended reed frame had been introduced for beating-in the weft of the horizontal loom to a tight fit. (*See* also SPINNING and WEAVING.)

**2. Mechanization of Spinning.**—The winding, or quilling, wheel probably came to the West from the Orient during the Roman domination of the Near East. In one of the earliest uses of continuous rotary motion, this wheel wound yarn from the spindle onto the quill, or bobbin, that was incorporated in the shuttle. The quilling wheel may have stimulated the invention of a wheel to drive the spindle, thereby creating a spindle-wheel. The spinning-wheel, which appeared in the 13th century, was essentially the hand spindle with its whorl modified to make a pulley, and driven by a rope belt from a large wheel. The rigid spindle mounting, the momentum of the large wheel, and the speed ratio between the large wheel and the spindle pulley allowed greater output. Apparently the quality of this yarn was limited, for a drapers' guild of Speyer, Ger., in 1298 permitted wheel-spun yarn to be used in the weft but not in the warp, where a yarn of greater tensile strength was necessary. A major disadvantage of the spinning-wheel was the reversal of wheel motion between spinning and winding. After the twisting cycle, the wheel had to be rotated in the opposite direction for the yarn to be wound on the spindle.

SPINNING WHEEL WITH SEPARATE BELTS TO DRIVE THE FLYER AND BOBBIN AT DIFFERENT RATES, IN CONTRAST TO THE OPERATION OF THE OLDER SPINDLE WHEEL; FROM "DAS MITTELALTERLICHE HAUSBACH," 1480

The incorporation of a U-shaped flyer upon the spindle, a step taken in Europe during the mid-15th century, made it possible to spin and wind fibres simultaneously. The great wheel of the spindle-wheel, essentially a flywheel, carried two rope drives: one to turn the spindle and one for the flyer. Different speeds followed from the different sizes of the spindle and flyer pulley wheels. The U-shaped flyer turning around the bobbin twisted the yarn while the smaller pulley wheel turned the bobbin faster, causing it to draw out and wind the spun yarn. Even with the flyer, bobbin, and wheel drive, the spinner had to draw out the strand of fibres from the distaff and move the yarn from one flyer hook to another to wind the spool evenly. Later a building motion caused the spool gradually to rise or fall on the spindle shaft in order to wind evenly.

The output of yarn greatly increased with the use of the spinning wheel, but it rose even further when by 1524 a crank, connecting rod, and foot treadle had been added.

**3. Developments in the British Textile Industry.**—The efforts of inventors and industrialists to replace human and animal muscles with mechanisms intensified in the middle decades of the 18th century in Britain. Because there existed a considerable disparity between the amount of capital available for investment in the textile industry and the available labour supply, the need for labour-saving mechanisms was great, and ingenious men found a more hospitable environment for their clever mechanical devices than formerly. The knitting machine invented in 1589 by William Lee, a curate of Calverton in Nottinghamshire, previewed in its effects the impact of the famous 18th-century inventions of John Kay, James Hargreaves, Richard Arkwright, Samuel Crompton, and Edmund Cartwright. John Kay's machine, patented in 1733, contained a shuttle that rode on the lower horizontal member of his loom's rectangular reed frame. Kay propelled his flying shuttle by use of a driver, or picker, at each end of the raceway. By jerking an attached cord in the direction in which the shuttle was to go, the shuttle impelled by the picker was sent flying across to the other picker. With the flying shuttle, the weaver greatly increased his output.

Mechanization of the loom was accompanied by mechanization elsewhere in the textile industry. Lewis Paul patented in 1738 a spinning mechanism that drew out fibres of wool (and later cotton) by a sequence of rollers. In his system of roller drafting, each successive pair of rollers revolved faster than the preceding pair, thus drawing out the loose sliver of carded wool in preparation for spinning. He also attempted to speed up another step in textile production with his carding machines of 1738 and 1748. Another machine patented in 1758 included a flyer and bobbin to spin the yarn.

Richard Arkwright improved upon Paul's roller-spinning system and brought it into widespread use. He supplied his wooden water frame (so named because shortly after its invention it was water powered) with four bobbins of roving (sliver drawn out from wool and slightly twisted). The four strands of roving, nearly $\frac{1}{2}$ in. in diameter, fed into a series of pairs of rollers and were drawn out. Four flyers twisted the yarn, and the spinning attendant wound the yarn evenly on the bobbin, using the notches on the flyer, as was done on the 15th-century spinning wheel. The coarse, strong, well-twisted yarn of the water frame, or throstle, proved most suitable for the warp of the loom, and weavers were to use the yarn of other inventions—the spinning jenny and the spinning mule—for the weft well into the 19th century.

The spinning jenny, invented by James Hargreaves about 1764, resembled the spinning wheel even more closely and has been called a multiple spinning wheel. By the time Hargreaves had perfected and patented his machine in 1770, the flying shuttle had come into general use, and the rate of production from the loom dictated further mechanization of spinning.

The spinning jenny imitated the hand movements of drawing out, but it drew out eight strands simultaneously. It was a multiple spindle wheel with a bar clamp holding eight strands in a parallel and horizontal row. A single wheel with a crank drove the yarn spindles, and a belt drive transmitted power from the crank to a beam, or large-diameter shaft, which in turn drove the separate yarn spindles by individual rope drives. The operator moved a carriage back and forth on the two longer top members of the frame with his left hand as he turned the crank with his right—one direction for spinning and the other for winding, as with the spindle wheel. Lower centre, across the short span of the frame, was a row of bobbins (eight in the original jenny). At the beginning of the spinning cycle, roving extended from the roving bobbins up to the moving carriage, under the bar clamp, and on to the yarn bobbins. The operator clamped the roving with the carriage bar when he had the desired length of roving between yarn bobbins and carriage. Then he pulled back on the carriage, drawing out the span of roving and simultaneously turning the spindles to unwind enough yarn to impart a twist to, and make yarn of, the roving. When drawing out was complete, a final spin gave the yarn a temporary excess of twist that was subsequently imparted to the contiguous roving. Then the direction of the wheel reversed to wind the new yarn. The operator released the carriage bar clamp and moved the carriage forward to take a new bite of roving when roving again spanned the distance from roving to yarn bobbins.

Samuel Crompton, who became annoyed with the malfunctionings of the jenny, devoted his modest income and considerable ingenuity between 1774 and 1779 to improving the design; ultimately he combined the rollers of Arkwright and Paul with the basic spinning-winding principle of the jenny. He aptly named his cross of the water frame and the jenny a mule. Mule spinning proved suitable for the weft, while the water frame produced a coarse, strong cotton yarn suitable for the warp.

In the 1770s Richard Arkwright combined many of these mechanical inventions into a factory system of production. The early mills or factories usually concentrated upon cotton production, partially because cotton could withstand the strains of the mechanized process better than wool.

**4. Mechanization of the Loom.**—Kay's flying shuttle had mechanized the shuttle throw, and, since the 13th century, foot treadles had lifted the warp to make the shed. Besides Kay's invention the other major 18th-century improvements were the mechanization of the plain loom and drawloom.

A plain loom could weave patterns if the number of heddles to raise the warp selectively was increased, but it then became rather cumbersome. The answer was the drawloom, which had long been used in the East for weaving silk. Essentially the drawloom substituted a figure harness for the large number of heddles that would be necessary for figured designs. The figure harness was simpler to operate, and with the aid of an attendant, or drawboy, cords were worked to raise the warp threads, which were gathered into groups as required by the pattern.

In the 18th century French inventors strove to replace the drawboy with a mechanism. Because France was famous for figured silk cloth, the pressure for a labour-saving draw mechanism was greater there than in Britain or other nations, where relatively plain woollens or cottons predominated. Basile Bouchon, his associate Falcon, and Jacques de Vaucanson (1709–82) designed imperfect devices, but Joseph Marie Jacquard, drawing upon their prior experience, built a practical automatic drawing mechanism.

Born in Lyons, a centre of the silk industry, Jacquard invented a device which was a forerunner of 20th-century punch-card controls, but the Jacquard control was mechanical rather than electronic. A punched card for each throw of the shuttle determined the selection of warp threads lifted to form the shed. A master designer punched the cards, and even pictorial representations could be woven by a card sequence. The cards replaced the drawboy, and a set of cards once punched could be repeated as often as the market demanded. By 1833 Lyons alone had 60,000 persons employed in the manufacture of figured goods with Jacquard looms.

Early Jacquard looms were not power looms. Whether a drawloom with Jacquard attachment or plain, the loom proved difficult for adaptation to steam or water power. Edmund Cartwright (1743–1823) became aware of the need for power weaving to keep pace with the potential of high-output spinning machines. Despite his lack of mechanical experience, Cartwright invented a power loom, which he patented in 1785. His loom was a crude affair that never achieved commercial success, although it incorporated the basic features of an automatic power-driven sequence of operations. The model that emerged as the most practical was that of Richard Roberts (1789–1864), a machine maker of Manchester. His loom of the 1820s involved an automatic sequence for driving the batten, raising the warp to create the shed, throwing the shuttle, and winding the woven cloth.

**5. The Cotton Gin.**—The mechanization of spinning not only stimulated development of improved looms but it also created an enormous demand for cotton fibre. The soil and climate of the southern United States were particularly well suited for growing cotton of the short-staple, green-seed variety. Existing methods for removing seeds from the raw cotton required it to be done slowly by slave hand labour.

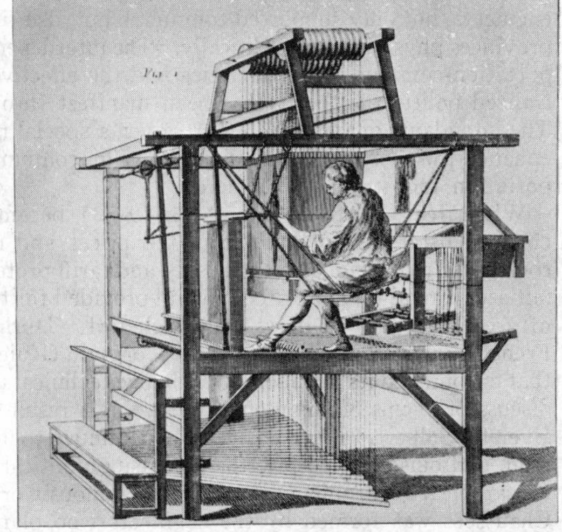

HISTORICAL PICTURES SERVICE

EIGHTEENTH-CENTURY LOOMS AS SHOWN IN DIDEROT'S "ENCYCLOPÉDIE"

Eli Whitney (*q.v.;* 1765–1825) designed and built a cotton-seed cleaning machine, the cotton gin, during the winter of 1792–93. His gin was a simple machine which, depending upon its size, could be powered by man, animal, or water. It received raw cotton from a hopper, caught the cotton on the wire teeth of a revolving cylinder, and drew the fibre but not the seeds between narrow iron slots of a breastwork. Revolving brushes cleared the clean fibre from the cylinder teeth.

Though he was granted a patent in 1794, Whitney did not profit greatly from his invention, since infringements of the patent were common. The gin, however, brought widespread cultivation of cotton in the South, and the Southern planters exported to Liverpool and other cotton ports, as well as to the young textile industry of New England. What had once been a relatively minor agricultural crop, painstakingly prepared by hand, rapidly became a mainstay of the economy.

C. Transportation

Development of an international cotton industry and the creation of a factory system of production would have been frustrated if it had not been for the development of a transportation system allowing the economical flow of trade from raw material, through manufacturer, to market. Especially important in the early years of industrialization were the inland canals and ocean navigation. Adam Smith (1723–90), writing in *The Wealth of Nations* on the eve of the canal era, foresaw the impact that an improved system of inland communication would have upon the economy. He observed that historically industry had generally flourished in those areas where water transportation was possible.

During the 18th century Britain drew upon the Continent for civil engineering knowledge to build her own transportation network. Skilled and experienced Dutch engineers were utilized to execute drainage works, build harbours, and make rivers navigable. But during the 19th century, when British engineering achieved new heights, the flow of technical knowledge reversed. Samuel Smiles, writing in 1861, observed "after the lapse of a century, we find the state of things has become entirely reversed. Instead of borrowing engineers from abroad, we now send them to all parts of the world." This dramatic reversal had taken place during the Industrial Revolution.

**1. French Engineering Accomplishments.**—The 17th and 18th centuries had been distinguished by triumphs of French engineering. Sébastien Le Prestre de Vauban (1633–1707), Bernard Forest de Belidor (*c.* 1693–1761), Jean Rodolphe Perronet (1708–94), and Jacques Gabriel (1667–1742) built bridges, harbour works, and roads during an era when the state stimulated and regulated the economy to further national interests.

The emphasis upon engineering during the reign of Louis XIV demonstrated the dependence of a would-be centralized regime upon the civil engineer. The network of roads, bridges, canals, and navigable river channels, constructed by the government corps of engineers, not only supported commerce but also tied together the provinces physically and politically. The interdependence of transportation-communication facilities and the effectiveness of a centralized political authority has been manifest throughout history. The intendants of Louis XIV were given a special responsibility to enhance this power through promotion of communication, transportation, industry, and commerce.

When Jean Baptiste Colbert (1619–83) became Louis XIV's chief minister, he not only regulated prices and quality but encouraged French industry by subsidy and tariff protection. He also initiated a road-building program and provided for the construction of great harbours at Brest and Rochefort. During his ministry French civil engineers organized the Corps du Génie, an association that encouraged its members to exchange technical information and discuss problems of common interest. As a result of the stimulus given by Colbert, French engineering continued to flourish after the reign of Louis XIV despite the increasing political debility of the monarchical government. In 1716 the famous Corps des Ponts et Chaussées was formed by the engineers who planned the roads, bridges, and canals of France, and in 1747 the École Nationale des Ponts et Chaussées became the modern world's first school of engineering.

Colbert provided for the construction of one of Europe's great engineering works, the Canal du Midi, or Languedoc Canal, which joined the Mediterranean and the Atlantic. The canal, begun in 1666, was opened in 1681 and perfected by 1692, giving passage across southernmost France and making unnecessary the voyage around Spain via Gibraltar for ships of suitable draft. Pierre-Paul Riquet (1604–80), an organizing genius with the conceptual power of a great engineer and the valuable support of Colbert, was appointed contractor for the canal, and by 1669 he commanded a work force of 8,000 men.

The Canal du Midi has been considered by some 20th-century engineers the greatest civil engineering feat in Europe from Roman times to the 19th century. Shipping utilized the navigable portion of the Garonne River from its mouth, near Bordeaux, to Toulouse. The canal rose 206 ft. (63 m.) by means of 26 locks in the 32 mi. (52 km.) from Toulouse to the summit level. The summit level of the canal extended for 3 mi. (5 km.), and then the canal dropped 620 ft. (190 m.) by means of 74 locks in the 115 mi. (185 km.) to the Mediterranean near Sète.

A major problem for a canal with a high rise was supplying water at the summit level for feeding the locks in the two descents. Riquet suggested a supply from mountain rivers and streams near the summit level and the use of a storage reservoir for dry seasons. His concept proved conspicuously successful. Other solutions devised by Riquet and his staff of engineers included construction of the Malpas Tunnel, through which the canal passed for 180 yd. (165 m.); major aqueducts, which carried the canal over intervening rivers; and culverts, which carried numerous streams under the canal.

This great engineering achievement, along with other engineering accomplishments in Europe prior to the Industrial Revolution in Britain, made available to the British a vast accumulation of technical knowledge through contemporary descriptive literature. The *Philosophical Transactions* of London's Royal Society, for example, carried detailed accounts of the Canal du Midi, and there were authoritative works on engineering, such as C. A. de Coulomb's *Essai. . . à quelques problèmes de statique. . .* (1776), in which he introduced the use of calculus in engineering theory. Thus the written word, firsthand observation, and oral reports served to diffuse the French civil engineering experience to a nation needing communication and transportation facilities, especially such waterways as canals.

**2. British Civil Engineering.**—Generally, the economy of a canal as compared to other available means of inland transportation could be demonstrated by the load a horse could draw or carry: a pack horse could carry $\frac{1}{8}$ ton; a horse drawing a wagon, about 1 ton; a horse pulling a wagon on rails, 8 tons; and a horse drawing a canal barge, 50 tons. If the transportation demand were heavy, the capital expenditure would be offset, then, by the mechanical efficiency of the canal system.

LATHE DESIGNED IN 1843 BY SIR JOSEPH WHITWORTH

The first British canal of major economic significance was begun by James Brindley (1716–72), with the financial support of the Duke of Bridgwater. The duke needed a canal for transporting coal from his mines at Worsley to the textile manufacturing centre at Manchester, a distance of 10 mi. (16 km.). Since the price of transporting the coal was halved after the canal was built, the duke believed that further benefits would accrue if the canal were extended from Manchester to Liverpool, an additional 30 mi. (48 km.).

After Parliament enacted a bill authorizing his engineering project, the duke employed Brindley, an unschooled millwright, who had won a reputation in the district, to carry out the project. Brindley encountered major engineering problems and responded with solutions characterized by bold conception, organizational genius, patience, and perseverance. His equal facilities in mechanical and civil engineering were revealed by the transportation-drainage system he provided in the Worsley mines and which he integrated with the canal system. A subterranean channel hewn out of rock extended from the barge basin at the head of the canal into the workings of the mines; this channel acted as a mine drain, as a feeder for the main canal at the summit level, and as a small barge-carrying canal. Within the mines Brindley used railways to move coal from the subterranean vein to the channel, and at Manchester he erected a waterwheel-driven hoist to lift the coal from the barges up to the populated area. Thus he had planned a mechanized transportation system by which the coal moved from the face of the coal in the duke's mines to the consumer at Manchester or Liverpool. The canal system from Worsley to Manchester cost £220,000, but the annual income rose from £12,500 in 1776 to £80,000 in 1792.

Several other civil engineers of Brindley's time deserve mention. John Smeaton (1724–92), of whom James Watt said, "his example and precepts have made us all engineers," numbered among his triumphs the historic lighthouse on Eddystone reef off the Cornwall coast near Plymouth. This structure, built under the most trying circumstances, was designed of interlocking stone blocks dovetailed to the reef to withstand the fury of the sea. Smeaton also improved the efficiency of the Newcomen engine, and he planned the Forth and Clyde Canal, which in 1790 joined Scotland's east and west coasts.

Thomas Telford (1757–1834), whose great engineering works included a magnificent suspension bridge across the Menai Straits, was one of the outstanding engineers of the Industrial Revolution. Like John Metcalf and J. L. McAdam, Telford was self-taught, but all three men gained fame as prominent road builders.

The transportation facilities built by these engineers considerably stimulated the revolutionary pace of industrial growth in Britain after 1770. For example, by cutting a waterway from Liverpool to Manchester and through the counties of Chester, Stafford, and Warwick, Bridgwater and Brindley opened the way for the industrialization of northwestern England—now England's most densely populated area—and for the creation in Manchester of the world's greatest cotton-manufacturing district.

## VIII. THE WATER TURBINE

The development of the steam engine proved the basis for a general use of power in industry. While it overcame serious limitations of waterwheels and windmills, and it produced large amounts of power in any location where fuel was available, there were certain limitations, since coal supplies were often inadequate at established industrial centres where power was being applied. However, there were many sources of water power available in areas without coal. Because many of these sources were not suited to either the undershot or the overshot wheel, especially of the size possible of construction at the beginning of the 19th century, there was a demand for a new type of hydraulic motor. There were many attempts to utilize these sources of power more completely, but, until the turbine appeared in the 1830s, they met with little practical success.

**1. Steps Leading to the Invention of the Turbine.**—The water turbine operates on a principle quite different from that of the waterwheel. In the overshot wheel, power is obtained from falling water, while in the undershot wheel, power is obtained from the impact of rapidly flowing water. But in these waterwheels there is no motion of the water relative to the buckets of the wheel doing work. In the turbine, however, power is derived from impulses set up between the fast-flowing water and the curved passages in which it is contained. This means that the water must be confined either in tubes or in channels set up between vanes in a close-fitting case, and there must always be movement of water relative to the vanes.

The first evidence of the transition from the horizontal waterwheel to the turbine appeared in one of Leonardo da Vinci's sketches. His device showed curved vanes set at an angle to the axis of rotation, but it had no casing. Bernard Forest de Belidor in 1737 described a device similar to Leonardo's in which the wheel was raised above the tailrace level. It therefore operated as a water turbine with partial emission of the water, since it had no casing. Wheels of this sort came into common use by the second half of the 18th century in southern France and Italy. Jacques Besson in 1579 provided one of the earliest drawings of a water turbine. This was the pit or tub wheel, a cone-shaped wheel with vanes that was fitted into a masonry pit. Although water acted on these vanes by both impact and weight, the gap between the wheel and the masonry pit resulted in a large escape of water. By the beginning of the 18th century the clearance had been improved and there was more economy in the turbine's operation. A wheel built at Toulouse early in the 18th century was more nearly a turbine. The river water was guided into a masonry sluiceway and aimed at the vanes of a Belidor-type horizontal wheel. Though the vanes had been transformed in shape and were joined by a casing, it was not a full turbine because there was a substantial gap between the wheel and the casing and therefore considerable escape of water. However, the wheel was completely submerged.

By the second half of the 18th century much practical empirical success had been achieved. Further development followed: (1) a critical revision of the various horizontal water turbines commonly used in southern Europe from the 15th to the 16th century, and (2) the development of the science of hydraulics by experimental and mathematical analysis. A simple reaction wheel produced in 1750 by John Andreas von Segner was studied by Leonhard Euler, who analyzed its problems in scientific terms and was thereby led to the development of a crude turbine in which a fixed upper portion formed a cylindrical reservoir. Small tubes inclined at a calculated angle delivered water to an annular trough of the lower portion, which turned clockwise on an axis. From the bottom of the trough 20 tubes diverged as they descended to horizontal ends, ejecting the water to the air. This turbine was purely experimental, and though it may have had some commercial use, its real significance was that it represented the initial invention of the reaction turbine, based upon scientific analysis. Claude Burdin tried to improve the efficiency of these wheels and to develop the Euler reaction turbine further. In 1822 he produced an original design in which the wheel was completely submerged and the water was guided to the rotating vanes by a stationary inner case having guide-vane compartments. There were important defects, however, in Burdin's design; the inner surfaces of the moving vanes were too flat to get the full effects from the impulse and the reaction that were necessary for significant operation, yielding insufficient power for efficient use.

**2. Invention and Development.**—Benoît Fourneyron, a student of Burdin, became interested in the problems of the reaction wheel and began active work on the turbine in 1823. By 1827 he had developed a small turbine of about 6 hp., for which he won a prize from the Society for the Encouragement of National Industry. Fourneyron's invention received further support from F. Caron, a forgemaster, who ordered a 10-hp. turbine for his blowers and later ordered a 50-hp. turbine for his forge hammers. In 1832 Fourneyron produced and patented a 50-hp. wheel that also won a prize. The wheel consisted of a stationary inner part with gates that could control the water. The moving portion was the outer wheel in which there were two annular iron plates supporting 30 curved vanes. Actually this combined both impulse and reaction, but it is significant that it could operate with a head of only 4.59 ft. (1.4 m.). However, Fourneyron's next turbine, which produced 40 hp., operated with a head of 354 ft. (108 m.). No previous hydraulic motor could utilize such varied sources of water power and give so much power.

The development of the turbine from 1832 to 1855 was characterized by much variety in design. Although both reaction and impulse turbines were tried, the impulse turbine was better adapted to streams of varying flow and to high heads of water of small volume. The crucial invention for the impulse type of turbine was the work of Pierre Simon Girard, who in 1855 invented a device for "ventilating" the vanes by providing air spaces at their inner bend so that the water would not completely fill the interval between the vanes.

Variations in flow methods also led to a number of different types. Fourneyron's reaction turbine operated with radial flow outward, but in the U.S. James Thomson about 1851 and James B. Francis in 1855 produced reaction turbines with radial flow inward, and this became the predominant American type. The French inventor Jonval in 1841 produced reaction turbines with axial flow, some up and some down. There were also many combinations of radial and axial flow in reaction turbines. Girard's turbine with axial flow either upward or downward became the commonest impulse type.

The wheel of the simple impulse turbine originally had fixed, flat vanes around its circumference. An improved form, developed about 1854, had spoon-shaped buckets fitted to the rim of the wheel to which a jet of water was applied tangentially. A wheel designed in the 1880s by Lester Allen Pelton resulted in much higher speeds and considerably less splashing. Pelton's wheel used a centre ridge in each bucket to split the water jet so that it would glide smoothly over the two halves. This type of wheel has found application in many modern installations.

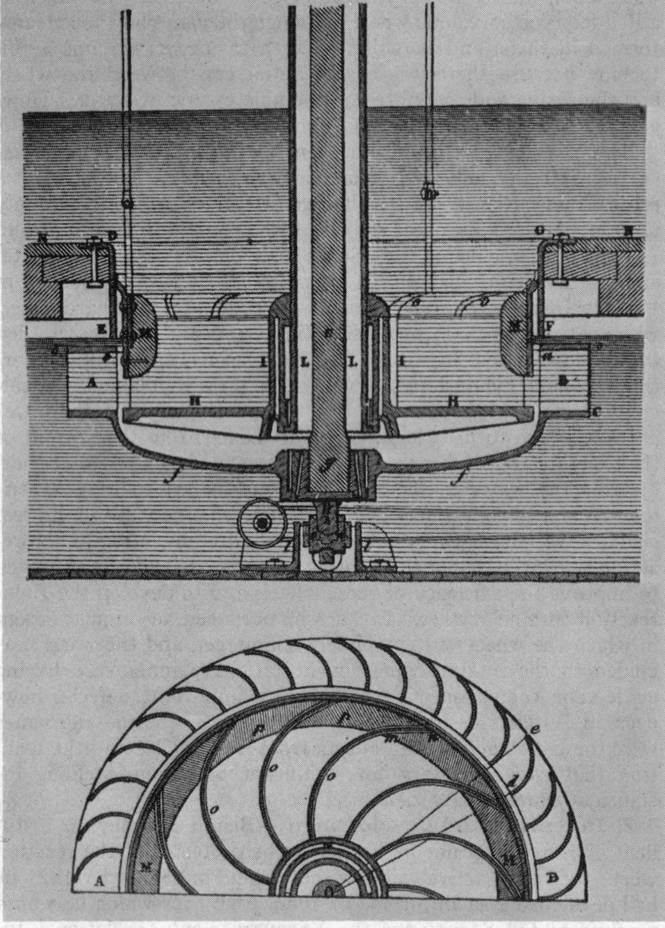

BROWN BROTHERS

THE 50-HP. FOURNEYRON TURBINE, 1832

Another important step was taken in 1910 by Forrest Nagler, who produced a much lighter and simpler type of runner for reaction turbines. His work went back to that of Jonval, who had developed a reaction turbine in which the flow was purely axial. The runner of Jonval's turbine consisted of a narrow row of blades on a large disk. Nagler replaced Jonval's design with one in which there were a few stationary flat blades at the end of a cylindrical casing, the openings between the blades being governed by movable gates, or wickets. This runner, which in effect was a propeller similar to that on a large ship, permitted high speeds with a low head of water. By 1940 Nagler runners had come into extensive use.

Nagler's propeller turbine operates at maximum efficiency with a constant head and with a constant volume of water. Furthermore, any variation in the power load required causes a decrease in efficiency. A propeller patented by Victor Kaplan in 1920 enabled the turbine to give increased efficiency at heads greater or less than normal and therefore an increase in output under unfavourable conditions. In order to match more accurately the correct angle for a given flow of water, Kaplan provided fixed gates but adjustable runner blades.

## IX. DEVELOPMENT OF THE RECIPROCATING STEAM ENGINE

**1. Improvements by Watt's Successors.**—Many improvements were made in the design and construction of the reciprocating steam engine in the century following James Watt's work, but no alteration in principle was introduced until the appearance of the steam turbine in the 1880s.

Since Watt never used boiler pressures greater than 10 psi, he found no advantage in cutoff of the steam earlier than one-fifth of the stroke or in the need for more than one cylinder. However, with the work of Jonathan Hornblower, one of Watt's contemporaries, there was the first appearance of the compound engine in which the steam passed successively through two cylinders. In 1781 Hornblower actually tried out an engine of this sort, but the courts decided that it was an infringement of Watt's patents. Arthur Woolf in 1804 built the first high-pressure compound engine, which expanded the steam to several times its original volume and was therefore much more efficient than Watt's engine. Woolf did not run into patent difficulties because Watt's patents had expired in 1800.

Actually the very extensive provisions of Watt's patents held back the development of the reciprocating steam engine in England. Also, the commercial success of the firm of Boulton & Watt led any innovators to have serious doubts about trying any other type of engine. However, William Murdock in 1785 built a high-pressure engine with a vertical oscillating cylinder. This engine, which was single acting and had a piston that acted directly on a crank, also used the D-slide valve for the first time.

From 1800 to 1860 the general design of pumping engines remained nearly constant, even though some of the details were altered and simplified. However, the engine for driving machinery underwent considerable development. The walking beam typical of the Watt and the Newcomen engine was a cumbersome device. With the invention of the planing machine by Richard Roberts by 1830, it was possible to replace this awkward piece of machinery by a crosshead and a connecting rod acting directly on a crankshaft and carrying a flywheel.

Watt's engines were expensive to run, for they burned about $9\frac{1}{2}$ lb. of coal per horsepower hour, and, with low pressures of 5–10 psi, they required both a condenser and an air pump. The solution was sought in higher pressures. In the United States this was tried by Jacob Perkins, Oliver Evans, and John Stevens, and in England by Richard Trevithick. All of these men went immediately to pressures of 50–70 psi, but the work of Oliver Evans was by far the most influential. He established the high-pressure engine in the United States, and by 1860 pressures of 60-80 psi were common, whereas in England engines at this date were all working with less than 60 psi.

**2. Greater Efficiency.**—The increasing size of reciprocating steam engines in the 19th century meant that central in their development was a struggle for higher efficiency. This took two forms: (1) the study of devices for admission and control of the steam, which eventually permitted a more effective steam cycle; and (2) the development of a theoretical analysis of exactly what happens inside the steam cylinder, which finally permitted a scientific design of the action of the engine.

*Devices for Controlling the Steam.*—Murdock's D-slide valve was replaced by the short D-valve on small engines and by the long D-valve on larger units, although both had certain disadvantages. The D-valve could not cut off the steam earlier than one-half the stroke without throttling or "drawing" the steam as it entered the cylinder. The long D-valve provided a shorter passage for the steam, but its longer travel and larger rubbing surface produced great friction, especially with higher pressures. Later the double-ported valve reduced both friction and throttling. The Meyer expansion valve, which was introduced to give a sharp and variable cutoff without changing the exhaust, consisted of two slide valves, one mounted on top of the other and each driven by a separate eccentric. The lower of these was an ordinary slide valve with its ports passing right through it. The upper valve consisted essentially of two blocks on one rod that had right- and left-hand threads. These blocks covered and uncovered the openings in the lower valve, but by rotating the rod the blocks could be brought closer together or farther apart, thereby regulating the cutoff and the expansion of the steam.

The cylindrical valve was in use before 1840. It consisted of two pistons on a rod operated by an eccentric. The valve chest was usually mounted alongside the cylinder, and the pistons were made tight by metallic rings. The cylindrical valve had many advantages: it was easy to achieve steam-tight contact with the valve chamber; the rubbing surfaces were small; and, since the steam could be admitted between the two pistons, it produced a balance of the pistons and little pressure on the bearing surfaces. The packing of the gland of the piston rod had the advantage that it was subjected only to exhaust pressures and not to the full boiler pressure. The small amount of friction meant not only that there was little wear but that little power was required to operate the valve itself. The cylindrical valve was expensive to make, yet it was effective, especially with increases in steam pressure. It is still commonly used on the high-pressure side of compound engines, but it is not easy to vary the cutoff and therefore is not adapted to governor control.

As the steam engine came to be used more and more for driving machinery, it was essential to secure uniform speed of operation. This led to the use of the flywheel, which served as a reservoir, alternately storing and restoring excess energy resulting from the variations of turning action of the connecting rod in relation to the crank. It also to some extent prevented sudden changes of speed from variations in load.

A governor was also needed to maintain constant speed. This had been introduced by Watt in order to prevent variations in speed greater than a certain amount when the load was altered. Watt's method had been to use the governor to vary the amount of steam fed to the cylinder by opening or closing the throttle valve. Governors of this sort persisted well into the 20th century. With the Wilson Hartnell governor (1885), which controlled the speed to within a variation of 1.25%, it was simpler to alter the cutoff and so regulate the steam entering the cylinder at the latest possible moment rather than to control a throttle valve.

The famous Corliss valve gear, patented in 1849, had four valves, one admission and one exhaust at each end of the cylinder. The four valves were cylindrical and turned through a small angle, and all were operated by a single eccentric. Drop valves of the balanced type were also introduced to overcome the limitations of sliding and rotating valves. The most prevalent type of valve for larger stationary engines was the Meyer expansion valve, controlled by a Hartnell governor. Typical practice in the U.S. in 1876 for engines up to 250 hp. was, however, to use a D-slide valve, with a governor acting on the throttle.

In 1876 condensers were not in general use in the U.S., though they were quite common in England and on the Continent. Pressures of 80–100 psi were common in the U.S., but European pressures were seldom more than 75 psi. Thus the concern with improved efficiency had lead to a number of different types of valves and valve gears, but few of the many devices introduced from 1800–60 actually persisted.

*Theoretical Analysis.*—Engineers in this period were obsessed with the economy to be obtained through the expansion of steam, but there was a limit to what could be secured from improved valve design. It took some time to recognize the losses incurred by contact of the steam with the cooler surfaces, even though Watt had noted that the reduction of these losses would improve the efficiency of the engine. The U.S. engineers first recognized the importance of short stroke and high speed in order to produce a condition in which the steam was in contact with the smaller area of the cylinder wall for a shorter time, thereby reducing the initial condensation as well as the loss of heat through both piston and cylinder walls, both of which were then cooled by the exhaust steam of the previous stroke. These observations became clear as a result of theoretical studies and experimental research on the properties of steam, as well as the application of scientific analysis to the steam engine.

The theory of the steam engine in Watt's day was very limited. Boyle's law of gases was known, but it was not until 1801 that Charles's law was announced. Joseph Black at Glasgow, who was Watt's friend, had measured the latent heat of steam. Watt repeated this for himself and determined the temperature of steam at various pressures. From about 1800 onward, however, there were two lines of important development: the determination of the actual properties of steam; and an understanding of the relationship of heat and work.

In 1825 the French government sponsored a determination of the temperatures of water vapour under pressures as high as 350 psi, and in 1843 the United States government initiated a similar project. The investigations begun in 1847 on the properties of steam by Henri Regnault proved to be the most accurate and the most comprehensive up to that time. It became clear that first, the latent heat of steam varies; second, the total heat increases by 0.305 units for each degree of increase in the liquid boiling point; third, the specific heat of superheated steam is equal to 0.4805; fourth, steam does not obey Boyle's law, which is true only for perfect gases; and fifth, steam is not a gas but a vapour. The concept of saturated steam was also introduced. Regnault pointed out that superheated steam does not condense on cooling until its temperature has fallen to the boiling point of water at that pressure.

These results were of tremendous importance in providing engineers with data for the study and design of steam engines, and they remained standard for nearly 50 years. Between 1915 and 1924 H. L. Callendar collected, critically examined, and tested the whole body of knowledge about the properties of steam, and the result was the compilation of the first genuine set of tables on steam. These were replaced in 1936 by the tables of Joseph H. Keenan and Frederick G. Keyes, who provided new accuracy and data relating to higher temperatures and pressures.

Along with the growing knowledge of the properties of steam, there developed a fundamental knowledge of thermodynamics. While in charge of the boring of cannon in the arsenal in Bavaria, Benjamin Thompson, Count von Rumford, in 1798 noted the tremendous amount of heat that was produced. Careful measurement of the work done and the heat produced led finally to a value of the mechanical equivalent of heat of 783.2, an error of only 1%. Moreover, the caloric theory of Antoine Lavoisier and his predecessors was replaced by the dynamic, or kinetic, theory of heat.

Little attention was paid to Rumford's work at the time, though he is known today as the founder of thermodynamics. But during the next 50 years considerable advance was made. In 1824 Sadi Carnot showed that since heat only does work as it falls from a higher to a lower temperature, the efficiency of the ideal heat engine is independent of the working substances and depends only on the initial and final temperatures. Carnot's theory was gradually modified and adapted, and it remains one of the most important elements in the theory of the steam engine, as well as a cornerstone of thermodynamics.

The dynamic theory of heat was not fully accepted until more accurate and comprehensive experimental evidence was available. In fact it was not until the work of James Joule, between 1840 and 1850 that the kinetic theory of heat was definitely established.

All this theoretical work was expressed in abstract and mathematical form far beyond the capacity of most engineers, and before 1850 it had little, if any, direct influence on the design of the steam engine. Application of these theories came about as a result of the work begun by William J. M. Rankine in 1849, in which he showed that condensation must take place in expansion. His results were corroborated by Gustave Adolphe Hirn, who in utilizing a glass cylinder observed the actual formation of the mist. Rankine's work was incorporated (1859) in a classic of technology, *A Manual of the Steam Engine and Other Prime Movers,* which gave the first systematic account of steam power. Rankine showed that if the cylinders and pistons behaved as nonconductors of heat, the volume of steam consumed per stroke would be equal to the volume of the cylinder up to the point of cutoff. But these surfaces are not nonconductors. Since they are cooled by the exhaust steam of the previous stroke, they cause some condensation of the entering steam and therefore require an increase in the volume of the steam. The water thus condensed is reevaporated during expansion, resulting in a loss of heat energy. Rankine showed that this loss may be considerable and that it could seriously affect the design of the engine.

By 1860, then, a genuine theory of the steam engine clearly indicated that, if high efficiency were to be obtained, the essential elements would comprise: first, high boiler pressures; second, high initial temperature in the cylinder; third, a relatively short stroke to diminish admission condensation; fourth, expansive working; and fifth, low condenser temperatures. To incorporate these principles in the actual design of an engine required a combination of British and American practices and even higher pressures than those in use in the U.S. The greatest possible efficiency in the condenser and the air pump, a development that came later, was more closely connected with the development of the steam turbine.

**3. From 1870 to 1900.**—The development of the steam engine from 1870 to 1900 was characterized by high pressures, high speeds, and high efficiency. These goals could not be achieved by the development of theory and the accumulation of experimental data alone. They also required new materials, new workshop processes, and new demands for power. The demand for larger engines and more economy became greater as the mills and workshops increased in size.

In 1854 John Elder successfully launched a ship having a compound engine, and this led to land use of similar engines, particularly since they reduced coal consumption from 4 to $2\frac{1}{4}$ lb. per horsepower hour. However, the demand for larger units on land did not become significant until the late 1800s, by which time steamships were using triple-expansion engines. Large land installations were usually only compound engines, but with their application to electric power stations there was a tendency to follow marine practice until large, vertical, triple-expansion reciprocating steam engines became standard. Within a dozen years, the steam turbine drove them out of existence, and within 25 years the diesel engine produced serious competition for the turbine.

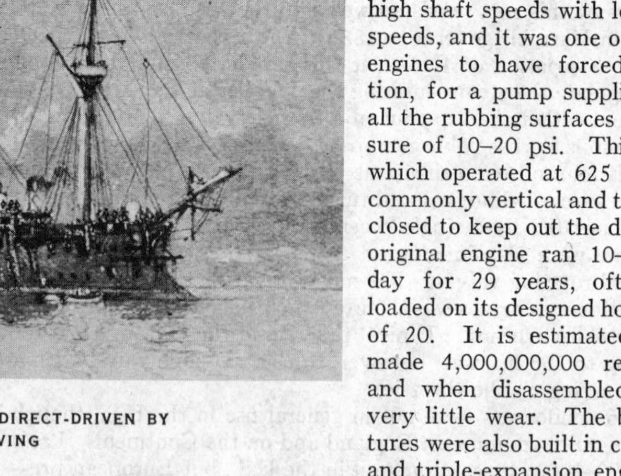

HISTORICAL PICTURES SERVICE

THE "RICHELIEU," EQUIPPED WITH THE FIRST DYNAMO DIRECT-DRIVEN BY A RECIPROCATING STEAM ENGINE; FROM AN 1887 ENGRAVING

In the further development of the reciprocating steam engine there were at least four landmarks: the Brotherhood engine of 1871; the Willans central-valve engine of 1885; the Belliss and Morcom quick-revolution engine of 1890; and the uniflow engine, first designed in 1885 but finally successful in 1908.

Peter Brotherhood patented an engine in 1871 that had three cylinders arranged radially about a crank, with steam admitted through a rotary valve. It was intended to drive high-speed machines directly, without gears or belts. Brotherhood engines were built in sizes from 7 to 35 hp. and used pressures of 40 psi. The largest engine operated at 225 rpm, which was about twice the speed of ordinary reciprocating steam engines of the 1870s. These engines were used on the French warship "Richelieu" in 1875 to drive the first direct-driven dynamo, as well as the ship's centrifugal circulating pumps. In 1878 the first self-propelled torpedo to sink a warship in action had a Brotherhood-type engine. By 1895 about 7,500 of these engines had been built, and they continue to be made today.

The central-valve engine of P. W. Willans, originally designed in 1874, was perfected in 1885. Engines of this type were commonly compound or triple expansion, except for the smallest sizes, the cylinders being arranged vertically in tandem and the pistons mounted on a common connecting rod that was tubular and had ports. Steam was admitted at the upper end of the tube, and the cylindrical valves inside the piston rods were on a long rod that covered and uncovered the ports, the central valve being operated by an eccentric on a crankpin. The work cycle of this engine is of some interest, because the work was done by difference in pressure on two sides of each piston on the downstroke. On the upstroke the pressures were the same on both sides. This engine also had an air buffer by which compressed air compensated for the inertia of the parts on the upstroke, so that there was no reversal of load on the bearings on the connecting rod or on the crankshaft main bearings. The result was very quiet operation and little wear. For 20 years engines of this sort were used largely for driving dynamos, and a great number of them were built. They had very low steam consumption, but the power-to-weight ratio was rather low, and the mechanical efficiency was less than 90%, even for a double-acting engine.

The Belliss and Morcom quick-revolution engine of 1890 was lighter and less expensive than the Willans engine. It operated at higher speeds and therefore permitted smaller and less expensive generators to give the same output. It had a short stroke and high shaft speeds with low piston speeds, and it was one of the first engines to have forced lubrication, for a pump supplied oil to all the rubbing surfaces at a pressure of 10–20 psi. This engine, which operated at 625 rpm, was commonly vertical and totally enclosed to keep out the dust. The original engine ran 10–12 hr. a day for 29 years, often overloaded on its designed horsepower of 20. It is estimated that it made 4,000,000,000 revolutions and when disassembled showed very little wear. The basic features were also built in compound and triple-expansion engines, the latter having three cranks 120° apart to give a uniform turning effect. The use of higher pressures in superheated steam would have been impossible without the features of this engine, especially its use of metallic packing and mineral oil for lubrication.

The uniflow engine developed in 1885 by T. J. Todd had exhaust ports in the centre of the cylinder. These were opened and closed by a very long piston, thereby avoiding the alternate heating and cooling of the cylinder ends by the exhaust steam. The steam entered only at each end and then discharged in the centre. Todd's engine attracted very little attention until 1908, when J. Stumpf designed more suitable valve gears for it. The engine then came into rapid use, and by 1914 several hundred were being used to drive generators, fans, rolling mills, colliery winding gears, ships, and locomotives. This engine occupies less floor space than any other horizontal engine of equal power and can be as efficient as a triple-expansion engine, with the additional advantage that its efficiency varies little with the load.

With the uniflow engine and the triple-expansion high-speed vertical engine, the story of the reciprocating steam engine ends. Further progress was to be made with steam power but through the use of the steam turbine rather than with the reciprocating steam engine, although there are many conditions to which the reciprocating steam engine is still peculiarly adapted.

## X. EVOLUTION OF THE STEAM TURBINE AND THE STEAM BOILER

### A. The Steam Turbine

**1. De Laval's Turbine.**—The basic principle of the steam turbine was not new. About the 1st century A.D. Hero of Alexandria described a device that was essentially a reaction turbine, and Giovanni Branca experimented with an impulse turbine about 1629. But the work of these men did not have any commercial importance, and it was not until the latter part of the 19th century that any significant contributions were made. Carl G. P. de Laval of Sweden, one of several pioneers in the development of the steam turbine, built a small 42,000-rpm reaction turbine in the early 1880s. But he is better known for his work in developing the single-stage impulse steam turbine.

The basic principle of De Laval's impulse turbine was to have one or more steam jets directed upon a number of radial blades fixed at an angle around a single disk. With this arrangement of blades and jets, if the steam enters the atmosphere abruptly from one or more small nozzles its velocity is very low. But if the nozzle is designed to produce expansion of the steam, there is an enormous increase in velocity. In fact, if the steam is expanded into a vacuum from a properly designed nozzle, the steam velocity can be of the order of 3,000–4,000 ft. per second. Despite the fact that the mass of the steam is relatively small, its high velocity permits considerable work to be done. The problem of nozzle design to ensure maximum expansion of the steam and therefore maximum increase in velocity was not actually solved by De Laval until 1888. Nonetheless he was able to design an effective impulse turbine without having nozzles of ideal design. His main problem was the centrifugal stresses set up at the high peripheral speeds demanded for an efficient turbine. The actual turbine disk had to be made of high-tensile steel, and it had to be in perfect balance. Since the centrifugal force increases as the square of the velocity, any inequalities that were negligible in the disk at slow speeds become enormous at high speeds. There was a further problem in adapting the impulse turbine to the actual drive of mechanisms. Because the speed of the turbine was too high for direct drive even of electric generators, De Laval had to use high-speed reduction gears. For satisfactory operation it was necessary to have wheels with wide but small teeth that were cut in helices in order that more continuous and uniform force could be exerted by the driver.

Though De Laval's first impulse turbine of 1882 was a triumph of scientific knowledge and mechanical ingenuity, it had certain limitations: the practical difficulty in utilizing the high speeds necessary for its efficiency; and the fact that the single-wheel impulse turbine could not at this time be made in large sizes; it was limited to about 450 hp. If the turbine were to rotate at slower than ideal speeds, energy would be wasted. Nonetheless, the De Laval turbine had the advantage of simplicity in construction; it was lightweight; and its steam consumption was low. Within its range it was as efficient as any other steam engine, and it was used fairly extensively for driving fans, pumps, and electric generators.

**2. Parsons' Turbine.**—The reaction turbine built by Charles Parsons in England in 1884 proved to be of more general industrial significance than De Laval's, but it was not a greater achievement. Parsons was the first to solve the problems, on a practical scale, of the utilization of the properties of steam and the theory of motions of fluids in the reaction turbine. The first unit built by Parsons developed 10 hp. and utilized steam at 80 psi. This turbine rotated at 18,000 rpm and was coupled directly to a dynamo. The shaft had 15 gunmetal rings, each having radial slots around its outer edge and set at an angle of 45° to the face. Between these rings were 15 half-rings fitted to upper and lower halves of the casing, and these had similar slots on their internal edges. Steam admitted in the middle flowed through the slots toward each end, where it was exhausted to the atmosphere. Toward the ends of the shaft the slots were deeper and the blades between them longer because there was a gradual decrease in pressure from the middle to the ends. The blades themselves were flat and only thinned at the edges. These fixed and moving blades admitted the steam through fixed guide blades to all the blades of each ring.

PARSONS' ORIGINAL STEAM TURBINE, 1884, SHOWN DRIVING AN ELECTRIC GENERATOR

The Parsons turbine called for scientific knowledge and mechanical ingenuity of a high order. Because of its high speed of rotation, Parsons found it necessary to provide special bearings. Recognizing that the chief loss of energy was in leakage of the steam past the blades, he focused his attention on the best form for the blades, using blades with curved faces in his turbine of 1888. The double parallel flow from the middle to the ends was retained, and he provided an increase in diameter of the drums toward the ends. The efficiency of his turbine was therefore improved. The earlier turbine had required 125 lb. of steam per kilowatt-hour, whereas the later unit consumed only 58 lb. per kilowatt-hour. In 1889 four 75-kw. Parsons units that operated at 4,800 rpm became the first steam turbines to be installed in a public power station.

In 1889 Parsons left his old firm and struck out for himself. Since the firm retained the patents on the parallel-flow turbine, Parsons worked out a new type of turbine having a radial flow outward. This type was demonstrated in 1897 on the famous "Turbinia," a ship about the size of a modern torpedo boat. Using three shafts, each capable of developing 700 hp., the ship traveled at a record speed of 34½ knots. In the same year Parsons installed a 150-kw. set in an electric power station at Plymouth, Eng. The early turbines had been noncondensing (*i.e.*, the steam was not condensed but was exhausted to the atmosphere), but, as their size began to increase and economy became more important, they came to be of the condensing type. It was extremely important to pass the steam to the condenser with as little delay or restriction as possible, and in 1899 Parsons patented a form in which the turbine and the condenser formed a single unit.

As it became increasingly evident that it would be advantageous to make the turbine larger, Parsons built tandem units with the high pressure and the low pressure on the same shaft but enclosed in separate casings.

**3. Refinements in Design.**—The Parsons patents gave his company nearly a monopoly, and many engineers turned to removing the limitations of the De Laval single-stage impulse turbine, which involved high-velocity steam expanding in nozzles at one step from the full pressure of the supply to the pressure of the exhaust. It also involved centrifugal stresses set up in the wheels and blades by the high speed necessary for maximum efficiency. Charles G. Curtis of the U.S. introduced his velocity-compounding turbine in 1898. He avoided the limitations of the De Laval turbine by adding rows of moving blades with fixed guide blades to direct the steam on the driving blades. In the Curtis turbine the blades were so designed that the velocity of steam was reduced by stages. This made it possible to use essentially the impulse principle but to work with high efficiency while operating at lower revolutions per minute. In 1896 C. E. A. Rateau of France combined the impulse with the pressure-compounding principle of Parsons and produced a number of impulse, or velocity, wheels on a shaft separated by sets of blades which in fact were nozzles in which there was a limited drop in pressure. The Rateau turbine reduced considerably the high speed required for a single-wheel impulse turbine.

It was not until 1915 that research was applied to the design of condensers. The old steam condenser usually had been a tank provided with a number of water tubes to provide the largest possible cooling surface. Real efficiency was only the result of chance, and there was no consideration given to the flow of steam over the tubes or to the separation of air at the lowest temperature and separation of water at the highest temperature. The first man to undertake a more scientific design of a condenser was Delas. He arranged the tubes in a series of V's across the condenser, which facilitated the access of the exhaust steam and air to the cooling surface. Because the steam passed from the top to the bottom of the condenser and crossed only relatively narrow bands of tubes, there was only a small drop in pressure. The Delas tubes were also arranged in a diamond pattern, with the long diameter of the diamond at an angle to the vertical so that no tube was directly above another. Thus the drip from the upper tube ran around only a portion of the circumference of the tube just below it, and the area of wetted surface was reduced. There was therefore an increase in heat transfer, since there was no insulating film of water. It was known that small condensers of the older types were on the whole reasonably satisfactory, but larger condensers built on the same design proved much less efficient. In determining the reason for this inefficiency, a group of engineers of the Vickers firm showed that there was a difference in pressure between the top and the bottom of the condenser, and that the way to improve efficiency was to increase the area of approach to the tubes and decrease the length of steam passage between the tubes. In the Vickers condenser the steam enters at the top, flows around the entire circumference, and then flows radially to the centre. The steam condenses on the outer rows of tubes, collects at the bottom of the shell, and is drawn off by a pump. This represents a major improvement over earlier arrangements.

**4. Advantages over the Reciprocating Steam Engine.**—Thomas Edison, in developing the first large dynamos, found that they required steam engines operating at 1,000–1,500 rpm, but these speeds were impossible for the larger horsepower units with reciprocating pistons. However, the opposite was true of turbines. As size increased, it was possible to design turbines for lower and lower speeds, and from this fact the steam turbine was quite early married to the dynamo. The reciprocating steam engine, particularly in the larger sizes, vibrated considerably, but turbine vibration was practically nonexistent. In size, the reciprocating steam engine proved to be limited; units of 6,500–7,800 hp. for marine use were about the maximum. But in the space of 30 years the turbine grew from a crude machine of 10 hp. to one embodying hundreds of refinements of design and producing as much as 60,000 hp. in a single unit. It was applied in enormous units to the propulsion of ships and to the production of electric power. Furthermore, its more efficient use of heat energy permitted an economy not possible with the reciprocating steam engine. With the use of superheated steam, higher pressures, and the scientifically designed condenser, the steam turbine assumed essentially the form that it has at the present time.

### B. The Steam Boiler

The development of steam boilers closely paralleled that of steam engines. The steam engines of Watt's day were supplied from a wagon-type boiler. The boiler was set in brickwork with a fire grate underneath, and the hot gases ran in flues along the outside. In the first quarter of the 19th century a variety of boiler types appeared: some were made of copper, some of wrought iron. However, metals of more than ¼-in. thickness could be handled by only a few machines and not at all by hand, so that boiler construction limited the pressures which were possible.

The first step forward from these early boilers was the fire-tube boiler with an internal fire grate. One common fire-tube type was the Cornish boiler, which consisted of a long cylindrical shell with a single fire flue passing down its middle, the flue being about one-half the diameter of the boiler itself. Another important type was the locomotive boiler, invented simultaneously in 1829 by Marc Séguin in France and George Stephenson in England. This boiler employed a large number of smaller fire tubes passing through a cylinder filled with water and steam.

**1. Pressure Gauges.**—The earliest pressure gauges usually consisted of mercury in a U-tube that was connected at one end to the boiler, with the other end left open to the atmosphere. However, most of the early engineers depended upon a lift safety valve to blow off at the desired pressure.

The first reliable gauges, still in use today, date from the mid-19th century. In 1849 Eugène Bourdon invented a curved metal tube of elliptical cross section with the free end closed and the fixed end open to the pressure inlet. Since internal pressures greater than external pressures tend to straighten out the tube, this motion passing through a linkage allows the pressure to be read on a dial. In 1851 Schaffer utilized a circular corrugated plate, the movement of the centre of which passed through a linkage and so registered the pressure on a dial.

**2. Feed Water Heaters.**—The drive to increase efficiency led also to the feed water heater, sometimes called the "economizer." If feed water at an initial temperature of 50° F (10° C) was preheated to 100° F (38° C), there was a fuel saving of 6%, and, preheated to 180° F (82° C), there was a fuel saving of as much as 11%. Economizers were widely adopted after 1880 since they were inexpensive, efficient, and particularly useful where fuel was expensive or the installation large.

**3. Stokers.**—In order to produce steam uniformly, a regular and skilful supply of fuel was necessary. The increased size of boilers and increased rates of steam, however, meant not only that the labour of stoking was heavy but the fire grates became so large that the men simply could not throw the coal that far. Automatic stokers were introduced about 1880. Some had a hopper and chamber just outside the fire opening, and a ram pushed forward each delivery of coal from the hopper; some used a vertical ram from below; still others had fire bars on an endless chain that ran on rollers, the fuel being fed from a hopper.

**4. Superheat.**—After the work of Rankine, the advantages of superheat and of dry steam became apparent. Wet steam, the steam taken directly from a boiler, always contains small drops of water. These drops of water do no work; in fact, they actually absorb heat, and in the steam supply for a turbine these drops can have a disastrous effect.

Various attempts were made to dry the steam. A number of early steam dryers had varying degrees of success, but none of them was sufficient for the large steam turbine. Instead, the process of superheating the steam proved to be the most efficient and economical means of securing dry steam. The principle was to superheat the steam on its way from the boiler to the engine by passing the steam through narrow coils of tubing in the flue uptakes of the boiler. As a result the drops of water evaporate, the temperature increases without change in pressure, and therefore a smaller weight of steam fills the cylinder up to the point of cutoff. Initial condensation is thus eliminated, and for turbines it reduces friction caused by the water drops on the blade and parts of the turbine.

Tentative experiments begun in 1850 used superheat at about 100° F (38° C) above the temperature of the steam in the boiler, but the amount of superheat soon rose to 300–400° F (150–200° C). It was found that steam consumption was about 10% less for each 100° F of superheat. By 1895 it was in general use, and modern installations often have a special superheating boiler for supplying turbines. *See* further Boiler.

## XI. THE PRODUCTION OF METALS AND ALLOYS

By the 18th century steel was being made by heating wrought iron in a furnace with charcoal, then bending, heating, and rolling several times to produce what was called shear steel. Because this process was expensive and possible only on a small scale, steel continued to be used only for knives, weapons, and tools. In 1740 Benjamin Huntsman of Sheffield, Eng., produced cast steel by heating a pure Swedish iron in a crucible with charcoal. Though Huntsman's crucible-cast steel proved that steel parts could be made in many copies without the labour of wrought iron, its main significance was that its exceptional hardness made it suitable for metalworking tools.

In 1850, then, cast iron, wrought iron, and cast steel were available, but only to a limited extent for engineering purposes. The revolution in steel processing over the next 50 years brought about a tremendous increase in the capacity and speed of production, in the cheapness and ease of manufacture, and, perhaps most important of all, in the control by which these materials were available in known and certain characteristics.

**1. The Hot Blast Furnace.**—One very important improvement remained to be made for the blast furnace—the invention of the hot blast. In 1825 it was generally thought that the colder the air in the blast of the furnace, the more efficient it was. Incredible as it may seem, men went to some trouble to cool this air, passing it over cold water or through pipes encased in ice. In 1828 J. B. Neilson of Scotland developed a method of preheating the air blast before its entry into the furnace, and in 1829 it was tried at the Clyde Ironworks. With the air blast heated to 300° F (150° C), the coal required to produce a ton of iron dropped from 8 to 5 tons.

By 1833 Neilson was using air blasts 600° F (315° C), with a further reduction to 2¼ tons of coal required per ton of iron. Using a tubular cast-iron oven to preheat the air to his blast furnace, Neilson's process won immediate acceptance.

The heat, as Neilson used it, was supplied directly by solid fuel, but Faber du Faur suggested using the waste gases of the blast furnace itself. In 1860 this hot blast was improved by E. A. Cowper, who used a regenerator, a wrought cylinder 60 ft. in height and 28 ft. in diameter, that had a circular flue extending from the bottom to the top. The rest of the interior was filled with loose firebrick; after 1875 these bricks were arranged in rows, with alternate bricks projecting along vertical channels. Combustion of the air and the waste gases of the blast furnace, which enter at the bottom, heats the bricks red hot as the exhaust goes out the chimney. The inlet and exhaust valves are then closed, and the cold air is admitted as the hot blast goes to the furnace via the hot blast valve. Since continuous hot-air blasts are needed for the blast furnace, there are usually two or four of these regenerators per furnace.

The Cowper stove (*q.v.*) produced two important results. First, with the hot blast, iron ores could be utilized that were not possible with the cold blast. This proved to be the foundation of the Scottish iron industry. Second, anthracite coal could be used, and this was the foundation of the Pennsylvania iron industry.

**2. Bessemer's Converter Steel.**—The blast furnace could now turn out good pig iron rapidly and cheaply from almost any ore and with almost any fuel. But the brittleness of cast iron limited its use. Wrought iron and steel were being produced, but the process was slow, costly, and uncertain. The problem was how to produce steel from cast iron easily and cheaply. A solution occurred to Henry Bessemer of England. He used an air blast blown through molten pig iron to burn out all the silicon and carbon. At first he tried a mixture of air and steam, then air alone. He discovered that the combustion of the impurities in the iron produced a temperature high enough to make the steel as liquid as water and that in half an hour he could convert cast iron into a wrought iron of better quality than any then available. In Bessemer's fixed vertical converter of 1855, there was loss of heat while the molten metal was run into and discharged from the converter. A newer type patented in 1860 contained about 49 ½-in. holes in the base through which air was blown. Iron melted in a furnace above the level of the converter was run into the converter while it was in a nearly horizontal position. The converter was slowly returned to a vertical position by hydraulic means, and an air blast of 15 psi was turned on. When all the impurities were burned out, the blast was shut off and the converter was returned to its horizontal position. Bessemer could then add definite quantities of cast iron of known composition. The converter, then brought upright, had the blast continued until all the additives were thoroughly mixed in. The converter was again brought horizontal, the blast shut off, and the steel run out through a wrought iron trough into molds.

Chemically the carbon and silicon in the pig iron were oxidized at the increased temperature, with the air blast supplying the agitation and the oxygen. After about 20 min. all the carbon was burned up and the iron itself was beginning to oxidize. Iron oxide, silica, and earthly substances formed a fusible slag, but the liquid iron could be run out at the tap hole. In theory, if the draft were stopped at the correct point, iron of any desired carbon content could be made, but in practice this was impossible, and so the run was burned to completion and the desired carbon added in the amounts specified.

Bessemer's process at first proved troublesome. Having sold his process rights to a number of ironmasters who tried it out and found the results variable and often unsatisfactory, Bessemer was much abused. In a subsequent investigation he determined that the trouble was in the variations of pig iron used by the various firms. Chemical tests showed that Bessemer had by sheer luck used a pig iron low in phosphorus and sulfur but that the other iron men had used a pig iron high in these materials. Bessemer persuaded the disappointed ironmasters to sell their rights back to him, a move that was the basis of Bessemer's later enormous fortune. Upon further examination Bessemer found that the original ore from which these pig irons had come was low in phosphorus. The ques-

THE BETTMANN ARCHIVE

MANUFACTURE OF STEEL, USING BESSEMER CONVERTERS; FROM AN 1875 ENGRAVING tion was how did it get into the pig iron? Since the iron makers had used a kind of cinders as a flux in a puddling furnace, Bessemer tried to get pig iron from the same ores without the use of this flux, and the result was a pig iron low in phosphorus that is still known as Bessemer iron. Now the results were satisfactory, especially after Robert Mushet had suggested the use of spiegeleisen, a pig iron containing about 20% manganese. With his partners Bessemer then set up the firm of Henry Bessemer & Company in Sheffield, Eng. The demand for a metal harder than wrought iron and less brittle than cast iron was enormous, and, in the 24 years that the partnership existed, the owners had a return of 81 times their original investment. Bessemer almost immediately undersold his competitors by 40 to 50%. Bessemer steel replaced wrought iron for the ever-expanding railroads and for construction work because of its higher tensile strength. It was soon used for boilers, piston rods, connecting rods, and crankshafts. It was a new and stimulating factor in engineering practice. Bessemer had, in fact, laid the foundations for two most important advances: first, for the provision of steel of known and uniform characteristics; and second, for the use of alloy steels and the heat treatment made possible by the use of these alloys. The importance of Bessemer's work is given by these figures: in 1855, the year of Bessemer's invention, approximately 50,000 tons of steel were produced; in 1898, the year that Bessemer died, 4,660,000 tons of steel were produced. Bessemer's success attracted many men to the problem of steel production. Among the few who succeeded were the Siemens brothers, whose process ultimately supplanted the Bessemer process as the leading method of steel manufacture.

**3. The Siemens Process.**—The German-born Siemens brothers belonged to a family famous for its scientists and inventors. William Siemens and his brother Friedrich became interested in the new theories and applications of heat and energy. In 1856 Friedrich Siemens applied the regenerative heating principle to the furnace. The two brothers designed a number of furnaces on this principle, but as the furnaces increased in size they encountered more and more difficulties. Finally they designed a system in which the fuel was converted into a gas before it was burned. In 1861 William Siemens was issued a patent for that principle and in the same year constructed a furnace having separate gas producers and firebrick regenerators. Neither principle nor the gas furnace was new, but the Siemens brothers were the first to make it commercially successful. An important advance occurred when Émile and Pierre Martin of France used a furnace of this type in 1864 to produce steel from pig iron and steel scrap.

The advantages of the Siemens process were most important. It proved to be very efficient, for the heat loss was very small, but more importantly, the flame could be kept perfectly steady for any length of time. Furthermore, the flame could easily be made to oxidize, or reduce, or remain neutral. In short, the Siemens brothers not only increased the efficiency but, what was more important, introduced control.

The use of the regenerator principle to manufacture steel made possible the Siemens open-hearth method (1861), in which pig or cast iron and scrap are melted in an open-hearth furnace to produce molten steel. The hearth is a basin-like bottom of a reverberatory furnace, 40 ft. long by 15 ft. wide and about 2 ft. deep ($12 \times 4.5 \times 0.6$ m.), which is lined with heat-resisting materials. Natural gas or sprayed oil is mixed with air for combustion, and the gas fuel is preheated by the regenerator. When a high temperature is reached, the carbon goes off as an oxide, and the steel looks as though it is boiling. The silicon, phosphorus, and sulfur oxidize and combine with limestone or spiegeleisen to form a slag that rises and can be removed from the surface. The Siemens process proceeds much more slowly than the Bessemer process, and it permits testing for the desired carbon content. It can thus be stopped at any desired point, and the molten metal can be run into molds or ladles.

Though the Bessemer process had the advantage that no fuel was required to produce the steel from pig iron, the Siemens process permitted better control and produced a larger and more uniform yield from a given weight of pig iron. Bessemer steel is still used for steel rails, but Siemens, or open-hearth, steel has a much wider application (*e.g.*, bridges, general construction, plates for ships, etc.).

**4. The Basic Process.**—The third important process in the era of cheap steel is the basic, or Gilchrist-Thomas, process. Bessemer had used a siliceous lining in his converters that had produced an acid slag and therefore did not remove the phosphorus in the original pig iron. The ultimate solution was the work of Percy C. Gilchrist, a chemist, and his cousin Sidney G. Thomas, a metallurgist. Their solution was to replace the acid lining of the furnace with a basic, or alkaline, lining for both the Bessemer and the Siemens process and then during the operation to add quicklime. Though Thomas announced the method in 1878, it attracted very little attention, until in the following year it was publicly demonstrated.

This method was adopted even more rapidly than had been the Bessemer process. The results of the basic process were most important. First, the phosphorus-bearing ores, the most widespread and the most plentiful of all the ores, became usable. Second, the open-hearth process generally replaced the Bessemer process for basic-steel manufacture.

With these three steel processes in use, steel was abundant and easily available from pig iron. Steel production was cheap and rapid, and pig iron from almost any ore was usable. With adequate means of control, it was possible to make steel not only of any carbon content, but of almost any desired alloy.

**5. Alloy Steels.**—Alloy steels go back to 1871 with the work of Robert Mushet and his tool steel, in which chromium and tungsten were added to steel to produce a material that attained its maximum hardness if cooled in the air. After 1880 steels containing nickel, chromium, or both were used, but until 1910 they were used almost exclusively for guns and armour plate.

The first commercial departure in alloy steels from guns and armour was made with tool steel. In 1880 there began 26 years of research on cutting metals by Frederick W. Taylor and Maunsel White of the Midvale Steel Corporation. They produced high-speed cutting steel that was immensely superior to the carbon steels then in use. Previously Mushet's tungsten steel had been hardened for tool steel by heating to about 1,500 to 1,550° F (815 to 845° C). Taylor and White, however, found that if this tool steel were heated to a point just below where it would crumble if it were touched, that is, 1,900 to 2,012° F (1,040 to 1,100° C), and if it were allowed to cool steadily, there was a great increase in toughness and hardness. This process marked the beginning of a new era in tool steel. Later, tool steel was made from other alloys, such as cobalt, molybdenum, and vanadium, and some tool steels were not really steels at all, *e.g.*, Stellite, in wide use from 1900 to 1925, composed of 55% cobalt, 15 to 25% tungsten, and 15 to 25% chromium.

Since 1910 alloy steels have had a variety of uses, *e.g.*, engines and machinery, automobiles, bridges, and locomotives. By the use of alloys it has become possible to control or increase the tensile strength of steel, as well as its hardness, toughness, and its resistance to corrosion. Of course, heat treatment has added another dimension to steel processing.

**6. Nonferrous Metals and Alloys.**—For many centuries copper, zinc, tin, and lead were known as metals. Bronze, an alloy of copper and tin, was produced in ancient times, as was brass, an alloy of copper and zinc. Gunmetal, a hard bronze of eight parts of copper and one of tin, was used before steel for cannon and is still in wide use. Antimony, which was also known from early times, taken together with lead and tin was used in type metal; it was also used in Babbitt and other antifriction metals.

Though aluminum is one of the most widely distributed of the metallic ores, it was not until 1825 that Hans Christian Oersted isolated the metal by working with potassium. From 1827 to 1852 a few chemists obtained a small amount of aluminum in the form of a gray powder, principally by the action of pure sodium on sodium aluminum chloride, a very expensive process. Then almost simultaneously in 1886 Charles Martin Hall, in the United States, and Paul L. T. Héroult, in France, utilizing the electric furnace and a solution of aluminum oxide in fused aluminum sodium fluoride, were able to obtain pure aluminum. Its properties permit it to be cast, wrought, extruded, drawn into thin wire, rolled into thin sheets, welded, and even soldered for a remarkable variety of uses. It can also be alloyed with copper, silicon, zinc, manganese, nickel, and magnesium for most industrial applications.

**7. Metallurgy Becomes a Science.**—Prior to 1860 most metallurgical processes were looked upon as a complete mystery, and the practical man depended upon his rule of thumb. The result was varieties of cast iron that appeared gray, white, and mottled. Steel alloys and a host of nonferrous alloys were produced by mechanical or heat treatment but they had been produced largely by accident or by trial and error in the first place.

The development of a scientific theory of metallurgy began effectively with H. C. Sorby in 1861. Sorby, a geologist, was familiar with the technique of grinding down thin slices of rocks and examining their structure under a microscope. Applying this to metals, he polished a thin piece and then either etched it with an acid or other reagent or permitted it to oxidize by air. Sorby found that the metals had a pattern and a structure and that some of the parts were attacked while others were not. He also discovered that the patterns of their structure were characteristic of the metal. Sorby worked only on iron and steel, but produced some of the most beautiful photomicrographs that have ever been seen. However, his work attracted very little attention. Only about 1880 did metallurgists in France, Germany, and England begin to take up his work. By combining Sorby's methods of examination with chemical analysis, particularly of alloys, they further extended the correlation of microscopic structure with the mechanical and physical properties of the metal. This resulted in a tremendous accumulation of information, such as rates of cooling from the molten condition, rates of expansion, rates of electrical conductivity over wide ranges of temperature, etc.

A genuine theory and science of metals and their alloys developed rapidly with the application of J. Willard Gibbs's phase rule (1876), which enabled a clearer understanding of the formation of the various components of alloys, and, after 1912, with the work of William H. Bragg and his son William Lawrence Bragg, who developed an X-ray analysis technique for the study of crystals.

After 1890 the theories of hundreds of alloys of nonferrous metals were worked out and the foundations laid for heat treatment of nonferrous metals, the aim being usually formation and fixation of particular compounds or solid solutions or altering the sizes of the grain. Hardness and strength of both iron and steel and the nonferrous metals usually are associated with a fine-grained structure, but consideration must also be given to properties desirable for rolling or drawing and for resistance to high temperatures and to corrosion. Since 1900 metallurgists have solved problems of increasing importance, such as high stresses and high temperature, to meet the demands of industry and research. These problems became increasingly important with the introduction of jet-powered aircraft, nuclear power, space exploration, and deep-sea research, all of which depend upon the metallurgist for a variety of new and reliable materials.

## XII. DEVELOPMENT OF THE INTERNAL-COMBUSTION ENGINE

Though the advance of steam power led to installations of greater and greater horsepower, there was also a need for engines of less horsepower. Many factory operations were too light for steam power, and the steam engine was too costly. There was also a need for engines of greater flexibility and lighter weight, especially for land and air transportation. The result was the development of the internal-combustion engine, which became most significant with the discovery of petroleum in quantity in 1859. *See* INTERNAL-COMBUSTION ENGINE.

### A. GAS ENGINES

**1. Early Inventions.**—The first attempt to derive power from an internal-combustion principle had been made in 1680 by Christiaan Huygens and again in 1690 by Denis Papin. Both men exploded a small amount of gunpowder in a large cylinder, expelling the air through check valves. When the resulting gases were cooled, a partial vacuum was created so that atmospheric pressure pushed down on the piston and did work. Significantly enough, both men utilized atmospheric pressure pressing against a vacuum created by the condensation of gases, a principle that paralleled the development of the steam engine in its early stages, as in the work of James Watt.

The first real internal-combustion engine was used by Robert Street in 1794 to raise water. In the motor cylinder Street used a lever to connect the piston to a pump. Building a fire at the base of the cylinder, he evaporated a few drops of turpentine. The piston was drawn up, and air was admitted and mixed with the vapour. Then a flame was inserted in a touchhole and the mixture exploded. This pushed the motor piston up, forcing the piston of the pump down.

In 1820 William Cecil experimented in England with a heavy piston and a cylinder, the piston being lifted by the explosion of a mixture of hydrogen and air. Then the piston fell under atmospheric pressure and did work. With 60 rpm, regular explosions consumed 17.6 cu.ft. of hydrogen per hour. The device proved to be very noisy, but Cecil is of importance because he was the first to measure the pressures produced inside the cylinder.

By 1823 Samuel Brown had produced the first practical engine operated from gas. He also used a gas explosion to obtain a vacuum. A flame in the cylinder was used to drive out the air, and the flame then was extinguished by a water jet. Brown had in fact several cylinders operating on a crank shaft, and by 1826 his engine was successfully applied to a carriage. In 1827 one of his engines drove a 36-ft. boat that traveled at 7 knots, and in 1832 another engine was installed at Croydon, Eng., for raising water.

W. L. Wright in 1833 was the first to apply the explosion of the air-and-gas mixture to the piston on the working stroke, and his double-acting engine gave an impulse every half revolution of a crank shaft. The gas and air were supplied from two reservoirs by separate pumps at low pressure, and the mixture entered spherical chambers at each end of the motor cylinder. An explosion was produced by inserting a flame through a touchhole, and the combustion products were ejected through exhaust valves. Both cylinders and piston in Wright's engine were surrounded by a cooling water jacket.

In 1838 William Barnett invented the compression system that continues to be used in internal-combustion engines. Its basic principle was to compress the explosive mixture before ignition either by using pumps in separate receivers and then letting the gas mixture, controlled by a piston valve, flow into the cylinder or by drawing the mixture of gas and air into the cylinder by means of pumps and using the mixture to displace the exhaust gases. Compression, then, was partly by pumps and partly by the cylinder piston. In both types of engine, however, ignition took place at dead centre, and the piston therefore got the full impulse of the whole working stroke.

Barnett is also significant for an ingenious ignition device, called the "Barnett Lighting Cock," which he introduced as early as 1832 and which remained in use until 1892. This was most important for the development of the gas engine until an electrical firing system could be adequately developed.

After Barnett, progress with gas engines slowed down until 1859 when two Italian engineers, Eugenio Barsanti and Felice Matteucci, introduced a gas engine of some importance. It embodied a tall cylinder and a heavy piston. The gas-air mixture was admitted and fired by an electric spark, and the resulting explosion forced the piston up. The piston rod was a rack that engaged a pinion at the end of the stroke. A partial vacuum plus the weight of the heavy piston actually did the work. This engine required a heavy flywheel for continuous application of full power. It was noisy and mechanically an outrage, but it had certain theoretical advantages: first, a very wide range of expansion; second, low gas consumption.

The early experimenters with the gas engine found a rather limited fuel supply for their engines. Since gas was needed in quantity, hydrogen and turpentine clearly would not do, and the only other fuel available was town-lighting gas. In the 1790s, however, William Murdock introduced the coal gas process, and after 1820 the considerable development in England of gas for lighting permitted some experimental advance in the internal-combustion engine. However, the production of petroleum in quantity after 1859 provided what was to become the basic fuel for the internal-combustion engine, and the time was ripe for development of an engine of real commercial value.

The first commercially significant internal-combustion engine, produced in 1860 by J. J. E. Lenoir, resembled externally an ordinary high-pressure steam engine, except that the valve systems admitted both gas and air and discharged the products of combustion. Lenoir's first engine, of 3 hp., had a flywheel that impelled the piston on the first part of the stroke. This drew in a mixture of gas and air at atmospheric pressure, and cutoff occurred. When the electric spark fired, the resulting explosion propelled the piston to the end of the stroke. Lenoir made extravagant claims for the efficiency of his engine, stating that an engine of 1 hp. could operate for 12 hr. on 100 cu.ft. of coal gas. Had that been true, it would have operated at about one-half the cost of similar power from a steam engine. Actually the Lenoir engine required about three times this amount of fuel and was really uneconomical as far as fuel consumption was concerned. But the Lenoir engine worked well, and it was sound from an engineering point of view; it was smooth in action, with no shock of explosion, and the cost of construction was favourable as compared with steam engines of the same power. By 1865, 400 Lenoir engines were in use in France, and soon 1,000 were in operation in Great Britain. They were widely used for low-power jobs, pumping, printing, etc. They proved to be quite durable; some were in perfect condition after 20 years of continuous operation. The Lenoir engine was also successfully applied to an experimental road carriage and to a boat, both of which used a hydrocarbon similar to gasoline.

**2. Theoretical Development.**—The theoretical development of the internal-combustion engine began with vague and often incorrect notions of gaseous explosions. Lenoir believed that the power was provided in a sudden blow, resulting from a rapid rise in pressure followed by an equally rapid fall and that therefore better economy could be achieved if the explosion could be slowed down. He therefore tried to inject sprays of steam or water to avoid explosion and produce burning. R. W. Bunsen showed that actually the opposite was true and that the explosion of gas and air was really a kind of continuous combustion. G. A. Hirn showed that the heat evolved in the explosion was only a fraction of the total heat produced and that the rest was produced during the expansion of gases. Thus expansion was not to be avoided but induced.

The next step was to study the advantages of a preliminary compression of the gas-air mixture. In 1861 G. Schmidt undertook the study of economy in the gas engine. He found that if he compressed the gas-air mixture to three atmospheres before it entered the cylinder, there was a great expansion and transformation of heat, and so he provided in his experimental engine compression pumps that were worked by the engine itself. In the same year François Million in France went further and provided separate pumps for compression of the air and the gas in a reservoir. The motion of his piston drew in a charge of the mixture under pressure, and electric-spark ignition followed. Thus the whole of the piston stroke could be powered by explosion, rather than only part of it. With the work of these two men the advantages of compression were firmly established.

Further parallelism of the development of the internal-combustion engine with that of the reciprocating steam engine occurred when Alphonse Beau de Rochas studied the influence of two factors on the economy of the gas engine using compression: first, the volume of the hot gases employed; and second, the extent of the surfaces exposed. The results of his studies, published in 1862, were very similar to Rankine's theoretical and experimental studies of the steam engine in 1859. De Rochas found that certain conditions must be at a maximum for economy: first, maximum cylinder volume for the least possible cooling surface; second, maximum rapidity of expansion; third, maximum amount of expansion; and fourth, maximum pressure at the beginning of expansion.

De Rochas was also responsible for the four-stroke cycle, which has since formed the basis of gas- and oil-engine practice. But it was 14 years before his theoretical results were fully accepted. From the introduction of his theories in 1862 until the appearance of an effective Otto engine in 1876, De Rochas' own designs had ignition difficulties, as did most engines of the time. Lenoir had also experienced trouble with his electrical ignition, but he significantly suggested that the gas-air mixture could be ignited by a higher temperature produced by compressing the mixture to one-fourth of its volume. This was essentially the principle used later by Rudolf Diesel. Although De Rochas never built an engine, he laid the theoretical basis for the work of the German engineer Nikolaus A. Otto, who in 1877 patented his famous "silent gas engine." Otto's engine, based upon his independent invention of the De Rochas compression cycle, was superior in workmanship and detail to all previous engines, and it also embodied an efficient ignition system. Otto did for the four-stroke-cycle principle what Lenoir had done for his predecessors, that is, he embodied all that had gone before in a practical precision engine. The Otto engine was quite economical, operating on 20 cu.ft. of gas per horsepower hour. Although the engine was a great engineering success, Otto himself was rather weak on theory. He accepted Lenoir's idea that engine economy was due to slow expansion of the gases in the cylinder, and he associated this with the curious phenomenon called "stratification." Actually its efficiency was due to compression, which Otto himself thought was of no significance. Nonetheless, the Otto engine was as great a landmark in the history of the internal-combustion engine as was Watt's double-acting engine in the history of the reciprocating steam engine, for it proved to be the basis of all later development. The small horsepower engine brought about a revolution in road transportation, and it also assisted the growth of the small factory, in which the use of more powerful engines was not economical.

**3. Mechanical Improvements.**—In 1879 an important development occurred with the appearance of the two-cycle engine, which could produce more power for a given size of engine and could give more uniform speed because there was a working stroke for every revolution of the crank. Introduced by Dugald Clerk, the two-stroke engine used a pump at the side of the main cylinder to deliver the explosive mixture when the piston reached the end of the backward stroke, and exhaust ports at the front end of the cylinder opened as the piston reached the end of the forward stroke. However, it did not give twice the power of the four-cycle engine, as one might expect, because the admission valve was open for a shorter portion of the stroke and therefore the charge was smaller. A few engines were made, but the two-stroke engine did not come into use largely because the demand for the large gas engine had not arrived, and it was 20 years before Körting revived the Clerk cycle for large powers. However, in 1891 Day substituted an enclosed crankcase for the charging pump in the small two-stroke engine. Day built several types of gas engines: one, a two-port engine, had a single valve; and another, a three-port engine, had no valve, all of the ports being opened and closed by the action of the piston. This latter type is not used in modern gas engines but it does appear in oil or gasoline engines. The two-port type is found in the Bollinder marine oil engine, commonly used in British trawlers.

After 1912 there was little change in gas engines smaller than 400–500 hp. The larger sizes became standardized rather early and were made by mass production. Many of the larger sizes came to be made by combining smaller units of the vertical type into multicylinder engines.

**4. Fuel Supplies.**—New sources of fuel supply for gas engines became available after 1860. Siemens, needing gas for his open-hearth steel furnaces because no solid fuel could give the required temperature, developed producer gas by burning coke in a limited supply of air. In 1878 Dowson developed a plant for making this gas, and by 1881 producer gas was used to drive a 3-hp. Otto gas engine. The water-gas process, by which steam was passed over red-hot coke to produce carbon monoxide and hydrogen, was an intermittent process because the steam cooled down the coke and air had to be admitted at intervals, but by 1889 Ludwig Mond introduced the method of admitting air and steam to the hot coke so that the result was a continuous process producing a mixture of producer and water gas. However, it soon became apparent that if coal scraps were used instead of coke, the by-products of tar and ammonia would reduce the cost, since the ammonia could be converted into ammonium sulfate, which is useful as a fertilizer. Supplies of gas such as this enormously enlarged the possibilities of the gas engine, and its size rose from 100 hp. to as much as 500–600 hp.

There were also improvements in the ordinary gas producers. Instead of drawing in air by a fan or blowing in air and steam, the producer was hooked directly to an industrial gas engine, and the engine sucked in gas from the producer as fast as it was required. There was therefore a pressure inside the producer less than atmospheric and hence less danger of carbon monoxide in the air of the producer house. This method not only reduced the cost of gas production but it also made possible the use of almost any combustible material for the fuel bed (*e.g.*, wood waste, sawdust, bark, coir dust, coconut shells, sugar cane refuse, cottonseeds, or rice husks). This meant, then, that the gas engine could be used to provide power for preliminary manufacturing processes on farms, plantations, forests, and mines, and in places where cheap coal was not available. This had enormous economic and social consequences.

A still further supply of gas became available in the waste gases from the blast furnace. In 1892 B. H. Thwaite suggested that these waste gases, which had previously simply been burned, could be used. In 1895 the Glasgow Iron Company adopted this method, and its use spread rapidly in Germany and the United States.

The increase in size of the gas engine made possible by cheaper fuels led to two new mechanical problems. It proved difficult to construct the large cylinders free from strain because of unequal cooling in the mold, and the cylinders were therefore not capable of withstanding the stresses set up by large temperature gradients in the material when the engine was in operation. Also, it was difficult to keep the piston cool. For small engines the water jacket was effective, but for larger engines it was necessary to design a hollow piston cooled by the internal flow of water that was supplied by a jointed tube, one end of which could follow the motion of the piston.

### B. Gasoline Engines

The success of the gas engine led to many attempts to utilize other fuels. In 1884 Gottlieb Daimler passed a current of warm air through a definite thickness of gasoline to produce a mixture of gasoline vapour and air, which was ignited in the cylinder by a hot platinum tube. His engine, which had a four-stroke cycle and an enclosed crankcase, used splash lubrication. The admission valve was opened by suction, the exhaust valves by a cam. Previously, internal-combustion engines had been of slow speed, usually less than 200 rpm, and of heavy construction, about 1,000 lb. per horsepower hour. But by 1886 Daimler had been able to construct a gasoline engine operating at 800 rpm and having a weight-to-horsepower ratio of only 88 lb. per horsepower. Though both the speed and the lightness of the engine were important, the use of a liquid fuel was the crucial solution to the difficulty of applying the internal-combustion engine to road transportation.

Daimler, too, had difficulties with fuel. Gasoline was then a laboratory material, and there were wide variations in the available fuel. Furthermore, his surface-type carburetor tended to evaporate the lighter fractions before the heavier fractions, and therefore the composition of the fuel changed as the engine ran. By 1893, however, Wilhelm Maybach had produced a carburetor that utilized a needle valve and a float. The gasoline passing through a nozzle under the suction of the engine and mixing with the air through a fine gauze at increased velocity produced an excellent mixture.

Daimler applied his engine only to boats and canal barges. Later others applied them to automobiles and aircraft. These engines were nearly always of the vertical type, although some V and radial types were produced quite early. The cylinders were at first air-cooled, but later they were nearly always water-cooled, either through natural circulation or by means of pumps.

In the late 1890s and the early 1900s the gasoline engine profited from several improvements. The ignition system was improved first with the use of the induction coil and the dry battery and then with the introduction of the magneto. A number of different valves were tried—the rotary valve of the Corliss type, the piston valve, poppet valves, etc. Fuels such as benzene and kerosene were tried, but gasoline predominated, especially after 1914 through the development of various cracking processes. The main development, however, was further advance in lightness through the use of aluminum and its alloys. Next was greater reliability through improved design, materials, and workmanship, and third was cheaper engines made possible by mass production.

### C. Oil Engines

**1. Priestman and Stuart Engines.**—The medium oil engine used a fuel with a specific gravity of about 0.8 that was similar to kerosene. This development began with Priestman in 1884. In his engine, oil was sprayed by air pressure into a vaporizer that was heated by a lamp. The resulting fuel was drawn into a cylinder mixed with air, compressed, and fired by a hot tube. Once the engine was running, the lamp could be removed since the vaporizer was adequately heated by the hot exhaust gases.

There were a number of oil-engine inventors after Priestman, the most important being Akroyd Stuart. In his engine, called the Hornsby-Akroyd engine, no separate vaporizer or ignition was required. To start the engine a portion of the cylinder was heated with a blowtorch. Air was drawn into the cylinder by suction, and oil was sprayed in by a small force pump. The return stroke of the piston forced the air into the hot end of the cylinder, and ignition took place by the heat of compression. The heat of combustion kept the cylinder end at the proper temperature, and no blowtorch was required after starting. This engine had no coils, dry batteries, accumulators, magnetos, or spark plugs, and so was quite simple. Fuel consumption in the early engines was about one pint of kerosene per horsepower hour, but this was soon improved to about half a pint.

**2. The Diesel Engine.**—Although Rudolf Diesel patented his engine in 1892, he was unable to construct an engine until 1897, and it was some years before a commercially successful model was developed. Unlike the Hornsby-Akroyd engine, this four-stroke-cycle engine did not vaporize the fuel; the air, but not the fuel, was compressed by the piston to pressures of about 500–600 psi. This compression of the air resulted in temperatures of about 1,000° F (538° C). The fuel was fed in at a rate such that combustion took place at nearly constant pressure. The diesel engine was usually vertical and of rather heavy construction. It used rather heavy fuel with a specific gravity of from about 0.83 to as much as 1.1. Originally the fuel was forced in by air at 1,000 psi. It was, however, costly to compress the air, and a method of solid injection was invented by James McKechnie in 1910. In this the fuel was admitted through a needle valve at pressures of about 4,000 to 7,000 psi produced by a small pump.

From the beginning the greatest advantage of the diesel engine was its efficiency. At first it was built in small sizes, but by 1912 single vertical engines of 50, 80, or 120 hp. of the four-stroke cycle were built, and these units were combined to give 750 hp. However, some of the same difficulties experienced by the large gas engine had to be overcome; in fact, these difficulties were greater because of the higher temperatures and pressures in the diesel engine. Smoother operation was made possible in the four-stroke engine because of multiple cylinders, and greater power was obtained by introducing double action with enclosed cylinders, and two-stroke engines. Both of these, however, required cooling the piston with either water or oil. Some double-acting, four-stroke engines were built before 1915, and they became well established after 1925. The two-stroke diesel engine was similar to the two-stroke gas engine, and it worked equally well in either direction. It could be reversed by letting the engine nearly stop and then admitting compressed air before the piston reached the end of the stroke.

**3. The Semidiesel Engine.**—The economy and reliability of the diesel engine led to efforts to combine its principles with those of the Hornsby-Akroyd engine to produce a lighter engine of lower cost, with equally high efficiency. The result was the semi-diesel engine, which could use a fuel similar to that of the diesel engine. Both horizontal and vertical types were built, usually of less than 600 hp.

### D. The Gas Turbine

The gas turbine was an attempt to achieve the advantages of the internal-combustion engine without the complications associated with reciprocating motion. It operates by directing a continuous stream of hot gases against the blading of a turbine rotor.

The success of the steam turbine led to attempts to apply its principles to a gas turbine in the early 1900s. R. Armengaud and C. Lemale of France built the first successful unit in 1903. It consisted of a three-cylinder multistage compressor and a combustion chamber in which liquid fuel and air from the compressor were burned. The products of combustion, cooled somewhat by water injection, were then expanded through an impulse turbine wheel. Though its efficiency was only about 3%, it was a significant achievement.

In 1908 M. Karavodine built a 2-hp., 10,000-rpm unit with four combustion chambers that directed their hot gaseous products in sequence against a simple De Laval impulse turbine wheel. A gas turbine was also developed by Hans Holzwarth of Germany, who began a series of tests in 1905. He used a constant-volume combustion chamber in which fuel and air were introduced under pressure. After ignition, the pressure was increased about 4½ times, causing a valve to open for passage of the hot gases into nozzles directed against the turbine blading.

The modern constant-pressure combustion gas turbine is the work of many individuals. Perhaps the most prominent was Sir Frank Whittle of England, who in 1930 developed a jet-propulsion engine with a blower-type compressor that was operated by a gas turbine. Further development during World War II brought about a new era in air transportation.

## XIII. ELECTRICAL ENGINEERING AND ELECTRONICS

**1. Beginnings.**—Until the last quarter of the 19th century technology was dominated by the mechanical and the civil engineer, but from about 1870 electrical engineering came to have greater and greater importance, and after 1925 electronics became the leading field of technological advance.

The growth of electrical engineering was in marked contrast to that of mechanical and civil engineering, which had a long history of practical achievement based largely upon empirical methods derived from accumulated experience and with only limited applications of the results of pure scientific research. But electrical engineering was made possible only by the purely scientific studies of Franklin, Faraday, Ampere, Ohm, Oersted, and Henry. The basic principles of electricity discovered and formulated by these men excited the imaginations of inventors the world over, though electrical engineering, too, went through a brief period of empirical advance. For example, Thomas Davenport, of Vermont, in 1834 devised the first practical electric motor, with an efficient design based upon a rotating armature, and Henry's strong electromagnets found practical application in an ironworks in New York in 1831. In 1860 Antonio Pacinotti invented the basic direct-current dynamo. Ten years later Zénobe Théophile Gramme of Belgium had in operation the first commercial dynamo, thereby launching the age of electric power.

Yet when Nikola Tesla, in the United States in 1887, produced his "polyphase motor" to make possible the widespread use of alternating current, empiricism was not enough, and he had to apply the scientific principles of electricity to solve his technical problems.

**2. Rise of Electrical Power.**—The first phase of the electrical industry centred on sources of limited electrical power—dry cells, accumulators, and wet batteries. These were adequate for certain purposes, such as Samuel F. B. Morse's telegraph of 1837 and Alexander Graham Bell's telephone of 1875. Both inventions grew out of a long preceding series of experiments, and both were made almost simultaneously by other men, but Morse and Bell provided the basic forms that have continued to the present day.

Electrical engineering would have been of only secondary importance if it had had to depend only on these limited sources of power. Crucial to its development were the inventions of the electric dynamo, the electric motor, and the electric transmission line. These produced a revolution in the use of power, for they led ultimately to great hydraulic and steam turbines capable of producing hundreds of thousands of kilowatts of electrical power. The steam turbine, with its far greater efficiency in the use of oil, coal, and now atomic energy, produced so much power that it could not possibly be used at the site—only electric transmission lines and electric motors of any desired size could literally electrify industry.

But all this did not come about at once. In 1831 Faraday had discovered the basic principle of the dynamo. In 1832 Hippolyte Pixii applied Faraday's results to a working dynamo that produced alternating current. In the following year he was able to generate direct current using brushes and a commutator. But these devices were only experimental and depended on the limited capacity of permanent magnets. In 1845 Charles Wheatstone showed that electromagnets could be used to open up possibilities of enormous expansion in the use of dynamos. By 1870 many inventors had tried their hand at the dynamo and had worked out the primary

BROWN BROTHERS

THOMAS A. EDISON WITH HIS ORIGINAL ELECTRIC LAMP AND A LATER IMPROVED VERSION

variations of winding its coils. But these machines produced variable currents useful only for some electroplating and a few arc-lighting systems. Most electric current in commercial use was still furnished by batteries.

The decisive steps were taken from 1865 to 1870. Pacinotti's improved methods of winding produced a steady current but attracted little notice. Here again the strategically important invention was a critical revision of an existing machine, for Gramme, in 1870, utilizing the same principles and a ring armature, produced what was to be a commercially successful source of power.

In 1873 at the Vienna Exhibition occurred one of the great accidental discoveries: it was found that Gramme's dynamo was reversible and could also be used as a motor. There followed a rapid advance of the electrical industry, so that by 1880 the primary accomplishments in lighting, traction, and production of power were realized in practice.

The first important use of electrical power available in greater quantities was for incandescent lighting systems. Warren de la Rue in 1820 and Joseph Wilson Swan in 1878 had tried to replace the arc lamp with an incandescent electric lamp, with only experimental success. Beginning in the fall of 1877 Thomas Edison made a long series of trials and finally recognized that the solution lay in the broader problem of the general design of a lighting circuit. He then devised the parallel circuit and worked out with great originality all the primary details of mains, house circuits, and connections with the dynamos. This redefined the problem of the lamp itself, for no adequate illumination could be obtained unless the resistance of the lamp was much greater than anything previously tried. By the fall of 1879 Edison turned to carbonized filaments. Problems of detail, especially the evacuation of the glass bulb, were gradually solved, and a successful demonstration was made on Oct. 21, 1879. Electric lighting for the world was born.

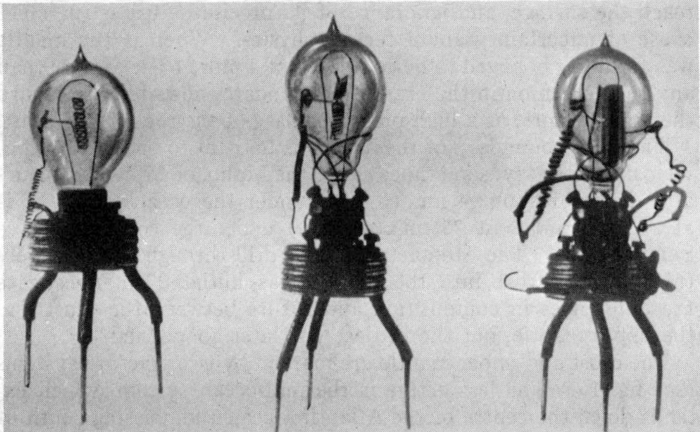

BROWN BROTHERS

THE FIRST THERMIONIC ELECTRON TUBES INVENTED BY J. A. FLEMING FOR RECTIFYING HIGH-FREQUENCY OSCILLATIONS

Edison's concept was wider than just electric light. His essential achievement was a combination of many electrical devices in a comprehensive system for the production and distribution of electricity. In addition to the electric light and the dynamo, Edison solved problems of wiring, meters, and fixtures, and he even made improvements in the reciprocating steam engine to give more regular and efficient operation at the central power station.

The building and equipment of a central station and its distribution system required a large outlay of capital. Since the demand for electric light was only for six or seven hours a day, even then requiring only about 10% of plant capacity for efficient operation, there was a powerful incentive to encourage wider uses of electricity, both domestic and industrial. Such an extension of electricity required: (1) improvement of prime movers of greater efficiency and capacity, *e.g.*, the steam or water turbine; (2) new techniques of long-distance transmission of electrical power; and (3) further development of flexible and efficient electric motors in sizes and types suited to a wide variety of uses.

The key to the transmission problem lay in use of high-voltage alternating current. Edison had advocated low-voltage direct current for safety reasons, and Marcel Deprez actually tried this method (1880–90), but after 1885 advances in the technical problems of production and transmission of alternating current, plus the special problems of transformer design and the production of suitable alternating-current motors, led to new possibilities.

A power house was begun at Niagara Falls in 1891. By 1907–08 ten turbines of 5,000 hp. each were in operation driving alternating-current generators to supply large quantities of electricity, not only to local plants built especially to use it but also to an area of more than several hundred square miles. Thus a new stage in the production of power had been reached. Power plants of this sort grew rapidly in size and numbers throughout the world. All that remained was to connect them into power networks to make possible wide electrification of areas without other sources of power, as well as to change the entire character of factories using electric motors as their primary source of power.

**3. Electronics.**—The telegraph and the telephone had made communication quick, cheap, and easy over vast distances, but inventions growing out of two areas of pure science were to change communications even more profoundly. This resulted from discovery of the "Edison effect" in 1883 and the experiments of Heinrich Hertz in 1886. Still later, in 1904, John Ambrose Fleming, with his invention of the first thermionic electron tube, was to take up the properties of electron discharge in a way to make wondrous things possible. Also, the scientific work of Maxwell, Henry, Kelvin, Kirchoff, Heaviside, and Helmholtz was waiting practical application.

The first man to explore the practical possibilities of electromagnetic waves was Guglielmo Marconi, who in 1899 achieved practical success in transmitting radio (then called "wireless") signals, utilizing high voltage across a spark gap as the transmitter and a coherer as the receiver. From his first limited success with very simple circuits, Marconi applied the concept of tuning, which made possible much greater ranges. The next step was to find a better detector of the radio waves than the coherer, and in 1902 Marconi invented the magnetic detector. This was soon followed by electrolytic and crystal detectors, the latter using materials such as silicon or galena, the ancestors of the modern transistor. By 1901 Marconi had initiated transatlantic radio communications, and by 1910 most ships had regular wireless communication available.

In 1906 Lee De Forest improved the experimental diode of Fleming by adding an intervening grid to the hot filament and plate. This grid made it possible to control the flow of electrons from the filament to the plate. De Forest's triode made possible enormous amplification of the feeble radio currents, both as a detector and as an amplifier. Though De Forest recognized the triode's amplifying properties in a suitable circuit, it remained for Edwin Howard Armstrong to study the characteristic curves of this thermionic valve and to show how it could be used for simultaneous rectification and amplification. In 1913 the feedback circuit, produced simultaneously by several men, was introduced to increase the amplification, and Armstrong's superheterodyne circuit of 1919 provided the capstone.

THE BETTMANN ARCHIVE

LEE DE FOREST AND HIS TRIODE TUBE, 1906

The age of electronics had dawned and was publicly recognized when radio broadcasting began in the 1920s. Intensified work in applied research, *e.g.*, in improvements in vacuum tubes, made television experimentally possible in 1927 and contributed to a host of other applications, such as the electron microscope, electronic controls of machinery, and computers, which followed at bewildering speed.

Meanwhile, the principle of the old crystal detector was to come into its own after A. H. Wilson's 1930 exposition on semiconductors and J. Bardeen, W. Shockley, and W. H. Brattain's first practical transistor of 1948. The transistor (*q.v.*), along with developments in the 1960s in integrated circuitry, created thousands of new uses for electronics, in industry, in the home, and in outer space.

BIBLIOGRAPHY. *General Works:* Walter H. G. Armytage, *A Social History of Engineering* (1961); K. Derry and T. I. Williams, *A Short History of Technology* (1960); James Kip Finch, *The Story of Engineering* (1960), *Engineering and Western Civilization* (1951); R. J. Forbes, *Man the Maker: a History of Technology and Engineering* (1958); Richard S. Kirby, Sidney Withington, Arthur B. Darling, and Frederick G. Kilgour, *Engineering in History* (1956); Friedrich Klemm, *A History of Western Technology* (1959); Joachim Leithauser, *Inventors of Our World* (1958); S. Lilley, *Men, Machines and History* (1948); Lewis Mumford, *Technics and Civilization* (1934; reissued 1963); Charles Singer, J. Holmyard, A. R. Hall, and Trevor I. Williams, *A History of Technology,* 5 vol. (1954–58); Abbott Payson Usher, *A History of Mechanical Inventions* (1954).

*Periodicals: Technology and Culture: the International Quarterly of the Society for the History of Technology* (1959– ); *Transactions: the Newcomen Society for the Study of the History of Engineering and Technology* (1920– ). (R. S. Wo.)

**TECTONOPHYSICS,** a word coined in 1939 by N. L. Bowen, embraces the application of geophysical methods to the study of the physical forces involved in the formation and deformation of the earth's crust. These physical aspects, together with their geological and chemical counterparts, provide a complete description of the structure of the earth's crust and of the changes affecting it. The physical processes chiefly find expression in faulting, folding, and mountain-building episodes (orogenies, diastrophism) by which the crust has been built up. The chief concern of this article is the mechanism of mountain building and its sources of energy. (For crustal movements and deformation, *see* FAULT; FOLD; EARTHQUAKE. *See* also GEOLOGY: *Structural Geology.*)

**The Earth's Interior.**—The causes of mountain building lie in the earth's interior. Seismic waves from earthquakes and explosions show this to be divided into three chief layers: a liquid central core, 2,170 mi. (3,492 km.) in radius; a surrounding mantle, 1,800 mi. (2,900 km.) in thickness, of solid, dense rock; and a thin crust. It is in the mantle that the causes of mountain building must be sought.

The crust is about 3 mi. thick under the oceans and 20 to 45 mi. (32 to 72 km.) thick under continents and mountains, the thickness varying with elevation. The oceanic crust is generally thought to consist of basalt and serpentinite beneath a thin layer of sediments, while the continental crust consists chiefly of granite (or gneissic, in a structural sense) rocks and rocks of sedimentary origin. Basalt may extend beneath them to form a continuous layer about the earth.

It is not certain whether any unaltered samples of the mantle reach the surface, and ignorance of its precise nature is the chief cause of uncertainty about tectonophysics. Whereas the mantle was formerly believed to be composed of a more basic silicate than any rock common in the crust, some modern views tend to regard the upper mantle as a high-pressure phase of the rock in the crust.

The upper boundary of the mantle is thought to be the Mohorovicic discontinuity, sometimes called the Moho, or M, which occurs at a depth of about 4 mi. (6 km.) under the oceans, while it is at a depth of about 25 mi. (40 km.) under the continents (*see* SEISMOLOGY). The Mohole project to drill through the relatively thin oceanic crust into the mantle was initiated to investigate the differences in composition and nature between the crust and the upper mantle, but the project was later abandoned.

The crust and upper mantle are marked by two fracture systems (*see* fig. 1). The less active is the mid-ocean system, which extends down the centre of the Atlantic Ocean and, passing south of Africa and Australia, crosses the Indian and Pacific oceans. It is a wide, rifted, submarine ridge along which occur shallow earthquakes and occasional volcanic islands of basalt, like the Azores.

The more active continental system consists of those belts of young mountains and island arcs that rim the Pacific Ocean and form the Alpine and Himalayan mountains. Along it lie the highest mountains, the deepest ocean trenches, all deep-focus earthquakes (from 45 to 450 mi. deep), and most volcanoes (*see* EARTHQUAKE; VOLCANO).

The lava, steam, and other gases erupted by volcanoes arise from the mantle in such quantities and of such compositions that the whole of the continents, oceans, and atmosphere, respectively, may have grown by their additions during geological time. That this growth did occur is indicated by the zoned structure of continents, with the present, active mountains generally on the margins and successively older mountains and roots of mountains ranged around a few very old continental nuclei. The basaltic

FIG. 1.—CONTINENTAL AND OCEANIC FRACTURE SYSTEMS

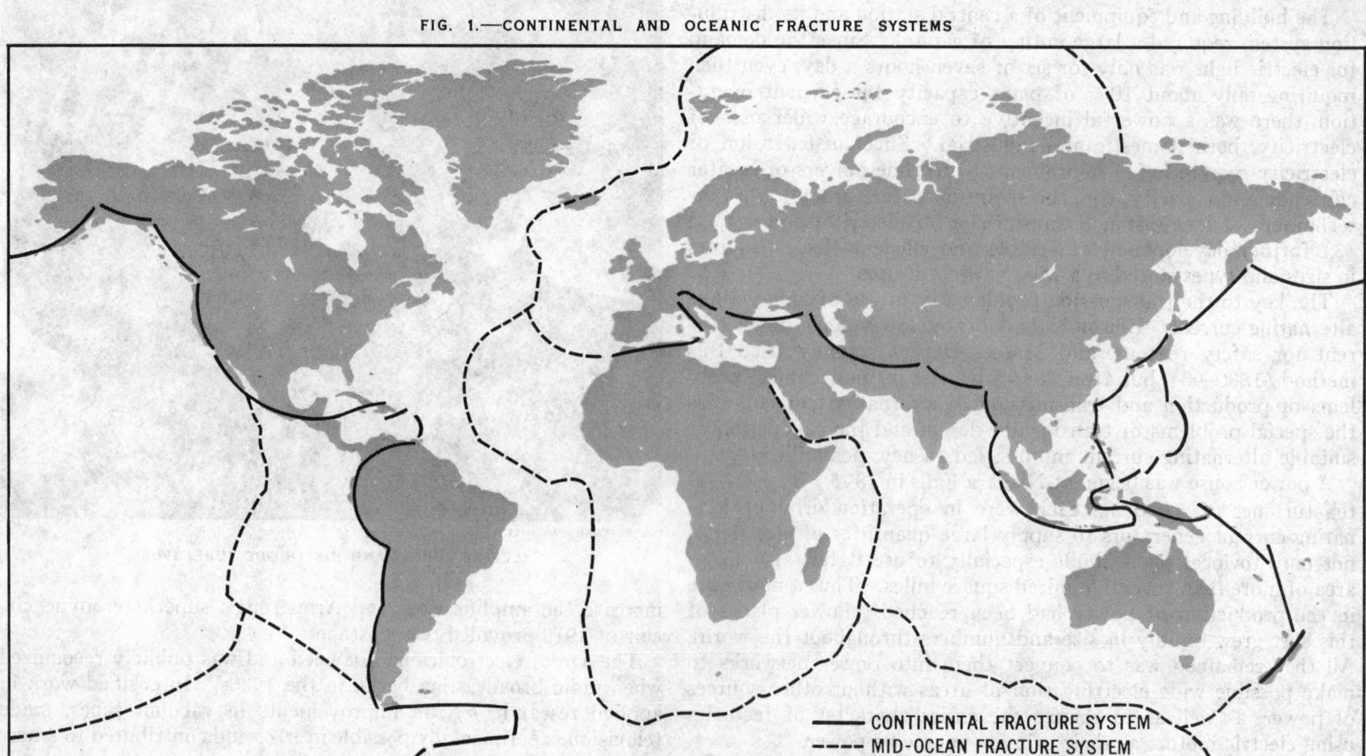

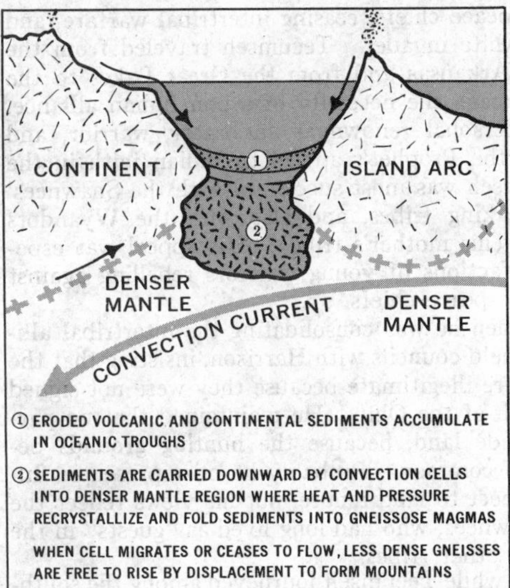


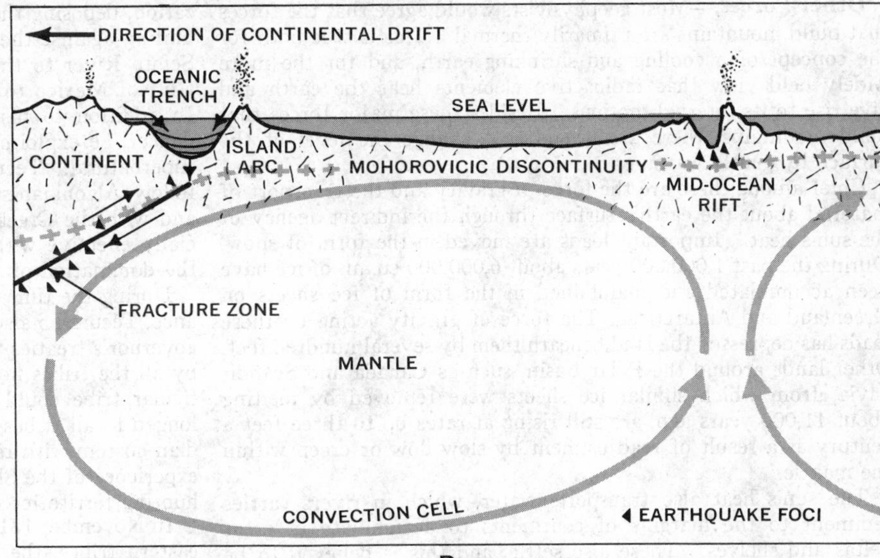


FIG. 2.—(A) MECHANISM FOR MOUNTAIN BUILDING; (B) MECHANISM FOR CONTINENTAL DRIFT

lavas erupted by volcanoes in the course of geologic time could have been converted, by erosion and subsequent recrystallization, to the gneissic rocks of the present landscape.

Fundamental to an understanding of tectonophysics is the question of the strength of the earth and whether it fails by flow or by fracture. The answer is not simple nor is there complete agreement on the following hypothesis. The earth's reaction to tides and to earthquakes indicates a rigidity greater than that of steel, but flow is suggested by the precise adjustment of the earth's oblate shape to its speed of rotation and by the slow rise of those lands, like Canada and Scandinavia, that were depressed by the weight of former ice sheets. (*See* also GEODESY; ISOSTASY.)

The apparent contradiction has been resolved by assuming that the earth is brittle to quick motions but capable of slow plastic flow. When it is realized that all but the outer few miles of the solid mantle of the earth is at a temperature of thousands of degrees and that, if exposed, it would appear white-hot, it is easier to believe that creep at rates of about an inch a year may be taking place within the solid earth.

**Theory.**—An early theory of mountain building was the contraction hypothesis, according to which the earth was formed from the sun and has been cooling ever since. Thermal contraction was considered to have pushed up mountains like wrinkles.

The discovery of radioactive elements in 1896 and the realization that their decay generates heat made it uncertain whether the interior of the earth is cooling or not. Some believe that the amounts of uranium, thorium, and potassium are small and that the earth, at least to a depth of several hundred miles, is cooling. In 1929 Sir Harold Jeffreys enunciated the general physical principles of the contraction hypothesis, and 20 years later A. E. Scheidegger showed that mountains formed by horizontal compression might be expected to have the arcuate forms and some other features observed in mountains and island arcs, but no explanation depending upon contraction has been offered for mid-ocean ridges.

Others believe that more heat is generated than can be carried out by conduction, and Arthur Holmes and F. A. Vening Meinesz suggested the convection current hypothesis, according to which the earth's mantle is very slowly turning over in gigantic convection cells that bring heat to the surface and raise mountains. If this is so, the currents probably rise beneath the mid-ocean fracture system (*see* fig. 2) and sink beneath the continental fracture system.

About 1910 F. B. Taylor and A. Wegener pointed out that the similarities in shapes and geology of several adjacent coasts, and especially the Atlantic shores of Africa and South America, suggest that they were formerly united and that the continents have moved apart, pushing up the Andes and the Alps in their advances. They offered no adequate explanation for this theory of continental drift (*see* CONTINENT).

Recent measurements of the direction of magnetization prevailing when certain old rocks were formed have supported the idea of polar wandering—that the poles and axis of rotation have moved relative to the crust. According to some interpretations, there is evidence of independent movements of the continents also. (*See* GEOMAGNETISM.)

In 1937 P. A. M. Dirac stated that there is no proof that the attraction due to gravity has remained constant and proposed that its slow weakening causes the observed expansion of the universe. S. W. Carey and B. C. Heezen have tried to explain tectonophysics by a theory of an expanding earth.

Finally various suggestions have been advanced to explain the earth's surface features as a result of the birth of the moon from the Pacific Ocean or of the impact of large meteorites, but these theories are hard to reconcile with geological evidence.

Limited knowledge prevents a final decision, but information gained since 1946, when the extensive exploration of the ocean floors began, suggests that a compromise solution may be possible. J. D. Bernal, R. S. Dietz, and H. H. Hess hold that convection cells move in the mantle at the rate of about an inch a year. These currents rise and separate under the mid-ocean ridges, uplifting them, producing the observed rifts, and providing the measured high flows of heat. Such currents rising under the mid-Atlantic ridge could have formed the South Atlantic Ocean and separated Africa and South America during the past 200,000,000 years in accordance with geological evidence. These currents are considered to sink along the continental fracture system, producing its compressional features.

According to this view, the blocks of continental material do not drift through the mantle but are borne along in random motion on its currents, sometimes splitting and moving apart, as across the Atlantic, and sometimes amalgamating to form composite continents like Asia. The margins of the continents also grow by the accumulation of lavas and sediments. Thus, the gneisses of the continents are considered to be rafts of material exuded from the interior, accumulated, and altered, but the oceanic crust is chiefly a hydrated phase of the top of the mantle. The distribution of former mountain systems can be explained by migration of convection cell currents from time to time.

This theory of tectonophysics thus combines part of several older theories, including convection, drift, growth, and compression. Even slow expansion of the earth is not entirely excluded and may indeed be necessary to provide space in the ocean basins for the ascension of volcanic waters that would otherwise have drowned the continental platforms. (*See* also EARTHQUAKE: *Theory and Research*.)

**Other Forces.**—Most geophysicists would agree that the forces that build mountains are primarily thermal. This is true both for the concept of a cooling and shrinking earth, and for the more widely held view that radioactive elements heat the earth and give rise to its internal motions. Besides these major forces that build mountains, there are others that change the level of the surface by gentle warping.

Chief among these are the force of gravity and the transport of material about the earth's surface through the indirect agency of the sun's heat. Important loads are moved in the form of snow. During the past 1,000,000 years about 6,000,000 cu.mi. of ice have been accumulated and maintained in the form of ice sheets on Greenland and Antarctica. The force of gravity acting on these loads has depressed the land beneath them by several hundred feet. Other lands around the Polar Basin, such as Canada and Scandinavia, from which similar ice sheets were removed by melting about 11,000 years ago, are still rising at rates up to three feet a century as a result of readjustment by slow flow or creep within the mantle.

The sun's heat also transports water, which in rivers carries sediment to the margins of continents to accumulate in great deltas and shelves. These also settle, and this is believed to be the reason why most of the Atlantic coast of North America is sinking relative to sea level at a rate of 1–2 ft. per century. Holland, at the mouth of the Rhine, is sinking even faster, and places from which the sediment is derived rise. A minor cause of disturbances that has recently been recognized is the impact of large meteorites. The largest crater recognized definitely to be so formed is the Vredfort Ring in South America, which is a semicircular ring of hills with a diameter of 30 mi.

*See* also GEOLOGY: *Physical Geology.*

*See* J. A. Jacobs, R. D. Russell, and J. Tuzo Wilson, *Physics and Geology* (1959); H. H. Hess, "The Evolution of Ocean Basins" in *The Sea,* ed. by M. N. Hill (1962–63). (J. T. WI.)

**TECUMSEH** (TECUMTHE) (*c.* 1768–1813), a Shawnee who attempted to create a pan-Indian alliance to revitalize tribal culture and preserve tribal lands. Born in present-day Ohio, he was acquainted from boyhood with border warfare. As an adolescent he participated in the campaigns of the Shawnee and their neighbours against the Kentuckians who were beginning to cross the Ohio River. His father and two elder brothers were killed in the struggle against white encroachment, which culminated in the defeat of the Indians at Fallen Timbers (1794). At the ensuing Treaty of Greenville (1795) the Indians made a substantial cession of land north of the Ohio. Refusing to attend the treaty council, Tecumseh broke with the reigning Shawnee chiefs and gathered a following of dissident warriors. Never recognized as a chief by an official council, Tecumseh was called by his followers "Chief of the Beautiful River."

Tecumseh found his principal white opponent in Gov. William Henry Harrison (*q.v.*) of the Indiana Territory. Between 1802 and 1809, Harrison secured the cession of 33,000,000 ac. of Indian land north of the Ohio. Tecumseh angrily ascribed the loss to the corruption of the "peace" chiefs who had signed the treaties. He found an ally in his brother Laulewasikau (or Tenskwatawa), known as "the Prophet," who in 1805 temporarily assumed leadership of the revitalization movement. Armed with his declaration that he had been taken up to the spirit world and was now bearing a revelation from the "Master of Life," the Prophet announced that the Indians could recover their lands and their integrity by abstaining from alcohol and the other perversions of white civilization, deposing the peace chiefs, ceasing intertribal warfare, and uniting against the white invader. Tecumseh traveled from the Scioto River to the Arkansas and from the Great Lakes to the Gulf of Mexico to preach the necessity of a pan-Indian alliance. In addition to his personal renown as an orator, warrior, and dancer, he exploited the Prophet's appeal to Indian faith in the supernatural. Tecumseh was most successful with the Shawnees' fellow Algonkian-speaking tribes, and also with the Wyandots and with the Creeks (his mother's tribe). His appeal was especially effective with factions of young warriors rebelling against the domination of the peace chiefs.

BY COURTESY OF THE CHICAGO NATURAL HISTORY MUSEUM

**19TH-CENTURY PORTRAIT BELIEVED TO BE OF TECUMSEH**

During the time when he was consolidating the intertribal alliance, Tecumseh also held councils with Harrison, insisting that the governor's treaties were illegitimate because they were not signed by all the tribes north of the Ohio. He maintained that no particular tribe could cede land, because the hunting grounds belonged to all tribes in common. Probably he misrepresented Indian custom with respect to land tenure, but his views reflect the experience of the Shawnees, who had long lived as "guests" in the hunting territories of other tribes.

In November 1811, while Tecumseh journeyed among the southeastern tribes, the Prophet's warriors attacked an expeditionary force under Harrison and were defeated at the Battle of Tippecanoe. Discredited, the Prophet fled to British Canada.

The Shawnees had fought on the British side during the American Revolution, and Tecumseh long hoped for British aid against the Americans. The British, however, refused him official encouragement until the outbreak of war between the United States and Britain in June 1812. At that point, Tecumseh and his followers allied with the British forces at Ft. Malden. They fought several successful campaigns along the Canadian border, but U.S. Capt. Oliver Hazard Perry's naval victory at Put-In-Bay cut their supply lines and forced them to withdraw. During the retreat across Ontario from Ft. Malden, Tecumseh persuaded the British commander to make a stand at the Thames River. In the Battle of the Thames, Tecumseh was killed (1813). With him perished the project of a pan-Indian alliance.

BIBLIOGRAPHY.—J. M. Oskison, *Tecumseh and His Times* (1938); G. Tucker, *Tecumseh: Vision of Glory* (1956); A. F. C. Wallace, "Political Organization and Land Tenure Among the Northeastern Indians, 1600–1830," *SWest. J. Anthrop.,* 13:301–321 (1957). (M. E. YO.)

**TEDDER, ARTHUR WILLIAM TEDDER,** 1ST BARON (1890–1967), British air marshal, who had a large share in the success of the Allied landings in Normandy in World War II, was born at Glenguin, Scot., in 1890 and educated at Whitgift School and Magdalene College, Cambridge. He was commissioned in the army in 1913 and served in France in World War I, being attached to the Royal Flying Corps in 1916. He was granted a permanent commission in the Royal Air Force in 1919.

In 1934, after service in a number of training establishments, he was appointed director of training. From 1936 to 1938 he was air officer commanding the Far East Command. He then returned to the Air Ministry as director of research and development. Early in World War II he became deputy air member for development and production at the Ministry of Supply. In 1941 he was appointed air officer commanding in chief in the middle east, and subsequently he took command of all the Allied air forces in that area. During his command the air force played a notable part in expelling the enemy from North Africa. In 1944 he was deputy commander of the Allied Expeditionary Force under Gen. Dwight D. Eisenhower and played a large part in planning and controlling the Allied landings in Europe. Much of his success was due to the efficient manner in which he cooperated with other Allied forces. Between 1946 and 1950 Lord Tedder was the first peacetime chief of the air staff and senior member of the air council. He was created knight grand cross of the Order of the Bath in 1942 and elevated to the peerage in 1946. He died in Surrey, Eng., on June 3, 1967. (E. B. BN.)

**TEDDINGTON,** a part of Twickenham in the borough of Richmond upon Thames (*q.v.*), London, Eng., mainly residential, lies on the river close to Bushy Park and Hampton Court Palace. Teddington Lock is the biggest on the Thames. The National Physical Laboratory, the National Chemical Laboratory, and the

Teddington Laboratory are scientific establishments in the locality. Eminent residents have included Peg Woffington, the actress, who died there in 1760 (*see* WOFFINGTON, PEG); Robert Dudley, earl of Leicester; William Penn, the Quaker; Richard Doddridge Blackmore, the author of *Lorna Doone,* who also died there; and Noel Coward, the playwright and actor, who was born there. (W. H. Jo.)

**TEES,** a river of England that rises on the east side of Cross Fell in the northern Pennines and flows 70 mi. (113 km.) SE and E to the North Sea, draining an area of more than 700 sq.mi. (1,800 sq.km.).

Its upper course forms the boundary between the counties of Durham and Westmorland. From its source to below Middleton it flows in a typical Pennine dale through an attenuated ribbonlike strip of farmland flanked by high, bleak, and peaty tracts of moorland. At Caldron Snout and again at High Force there are attractive waterfalls where the river crosses the hard dolerite outcrop of the Whin Sill. From Caldron Snout, right to its mouth, the river forms the boundary between the counties of Durham and Yorkshire. Below Middleton the valley opens, and its farmlands become more extensive. The river flows past Egglestone Abbey, Rokeby Hall, and Barnard Castle—well known through Sir Walter Scott's poems—and receives important right-bank tributaries, the Lune, Balder, and Greta, from subsidiary dales to the west. The last-named carries an important route, crossing the Pennines by the saddle of Stainmore. Below Barnard Castle the Tees meanders across a fertile clay plain to its estuary below Middlesbrough, where, until the 19th century, it entered the sea by shifting channels among extensive mud flats. The tortuous channel below Stockton-on-Tees has been straightened by artificial cuts, and, since 1854, the channel through the estuary has been concentrated and trained by the Tees Conservancy Commission. Extensive areas along the estuary shores have been reclaimed by dumping slag.

The river is tidal to Worsall, but the historic crossings carrying the main south-north lines of communication lie upstream—in Roman times at Piercebridge and later near Darlington. In its lower course the chief tributaries are the Skerne, entering by Darlington from south Durham, and the Leven from the Cleveland Hills, entering below Yarm. An old river port, Yarm lost trade to Stockton-on-Tees, and the latter in turn to Middlesbrough, when the railway was extended there in 1830; but most of the trade is now handled directly for the great chemical and iron and steel works of the estuary shores at their own jetties, and, since 1950, Teesport has been developed as an oil terminal. Until the 20th century Stockton-on-Tees was the lowest bridge point, but there are now bridges at Middlesbrough. Middlesbrough and Stockton-on-Tees (*qq.v.*) are the main centres of a great industrial conurbation that has developed since 1825 along the Tees between the Durham coalfield and the Cleveland ironstone field. The estuary area itself is underlain by important deposits of salt and anhydrite that are among the bases of its chemical industry. (AR. E. S.)

**TEESSIDE,** a county borough of England situated on both the north and south sides of the River Tees, extending inland 12 mi. (19 km.) from its mouth, created under the provisions of the Local Government Act, 1958.

From April 1, 1968, it took over local government powers and functions covering the county borough of Middlesbrough; the boroughs of Redcar, Stockton-on-Tees, and Thornaby-on-Tees; the urban districts of Billingham (save a small part) and Eston, and parts of the urban districts of Guisborough and Saltburn; and of the rural districts of Stockton and Stokesley. Pop. (1968 est.) 392,990. Area 77 sq.mi. (199 sq.km.). Teesside includes the whole of the parliamentary constituencies of Middlesbrough East, Middlesbrough West, and Stockton-on-Tees, and parts of the Cleveland, Richmond (Yorkshire), and Sedgefield constituencies. The area north of the River Tees is in the geographical county of Durham, and that to the south is in the North Riding of Yorkshire but for certain purposes (*i.e.,* commissions of assize and of the peace, lord lieutenancy, sheriffs) the whole area is deemed to form part of the North Riding. The former county borough of Middlesbrough had been incorporated in 1853 and the boroughs of Redcar, Stockton-on-Tees, and Thornaby-on-Tees in 1922, 1852, and 1892, respectively, and the urban districts of Billingham and Eston created in 1923 and 1894. Middlesbrough is a Roman Catholic episcopal see.

While Teesside is an industrial area well known for its steel and chemical industries, within its boundaries are seashore and fine sandy beaches (at Redcar), and it is in close proximity to moorland and national parks. All parts of the area can claim links with the past. Billingham's name is Saxon in origin and the area remained an agricultural village throughout the Middle Ages. In the Eston area, there are traces of a camp, or fort, covering three acres and probably built during the Early Bronze Age; at the time of Domesday the manor was in the possession of the count of Morrain. In Middlesbrough a cell was consecrated in 686 by St. Cuthbert at the request of St. Hilda as abbess of Whitby and was later, until the dissolution of the monasteries, maintained by a small colony of Benedictine monks; part of the former borough known as Acklam was also listed in the Domesday Book. The abbeys of Rievaulx and Fountains held land in Redcar, spelled in 1170 as "Redker." The Saxons built a settlement at Norton, part of Stockton, which grew up around the manor and later castle of the bishops of Durham, to whom the town belonged, and it is said that King John granted a charter to the town in 1214. Thornaby was in the 8th century called Thormodby by the Danes; in Domesday Book it appears as Tormozby.

The rapid change to a pattern of industrial growth began at the turn of the 19th century with the development of the river to export coal from the Durham coalfields. The population of Stockton rose from 3,700 in 1801 to 7,800 in 1831. In 1825 the Stockton and Darlington Railway was opened mainly to transport coal, but the line was also the first passenger railway in the world. This line was extended in 1830 to Middlesbrough, which by 1840 had grown to 5,000. This railway was extended to Redcar in 1846. The shipbuilding industry also developed at this time.

The decline in coal exporting in the mid-19th century was compensated for by the discovery of iron ore in the Eston and Cleveland hills in 1851. Throughout the area of Teesside, but particularly on the south side of the river, the era of iron, and later steel, manufacture began. All parts experienced further rapid growth; *e.g.,* Middlesbrough's population grew from 7,631 in 1853 to almost 40,000 in 1872. Several first steps in the production of iron and steel were initiated in the area, and large sums of money were invested in new developments after World War II.

In the early 1920s the chemical industry began at Billingham, manufacturing fertilizers in particular. It grew rapidly in the years preceding World War II and even more extensively afterward, especially at Wilton on the south side of the river, with the introduction of processes making basic synthetic products for materials used by manufacturers of clothing, fabrics, household goods, and builders' materials, etc.

From the 1950s the river near the estuary was further dredged and new deepwater docks and oil berths were constructed capable of taking ships of 100,000 tons. In 1968 the port dealt with 16,730,000 tons of cargo. This fostered the establishment of petrochemical and allied industries; the construction of a large iron ore terminal capable of handling 10,000,000 tons per annum awaited government approval at the beginning of 1970. Most of this development took place on reclaimed land that was previously tidal. While the steel manufacturing and processing industry (including shipbuilding, heavy engineering, and bridge-building all over the world) and the chemical industry predominate, light industries were also well established. (E. C. P.)

**TEETH** are hard white structures found in the mouth in man and many animals and used variously for mastication of food, seizing and holding objects, combat, cutting, chiseling, and other incidental purposes. Each tooth consists of a crown and one or more roots. The crown is the functional part that is visible above the gum. The root is the unseen portion that supports and fastens the tooth in the jawbone. The shapes of the crowns and the root characteristics vary in the different parts of the mouth and from one animal to another.

The different modern dentitions have been attained under the pressures of biological laws of evolution (see *Evolution and Comparative Anatomy,* below). Some dentitions are very restrictive and adapted to a particular diet. Carnivores cannot chew the fresh grass or hay that makes up the diet of a horse, nor can sheep handle a meat diet. Other dentitions, like that of man and the great apes, are very general (omnivorous) and can prepare both flesh and vegetable foods. Modern man's dentition is highly variable and shows signs of general reduction in size and form, as compared with the dentition of fossil man.

Occasionally the statement is made that man gradually is losing all his teeth. This is based on the observation that certain teeth fail to develop in some individuals and are of a reduced form in others. To conclude that the trend must continue is a fallacy. The future survival and selection pressures of evolutionary laws will determine the fate of man's dentition, not the fact that the present shift is in a given direction.

**Human Dental Anatomy.**—Man has two sets of teeth during his lifetime. The first set is acquired gradually between the ages of six months and two years. As the jaws grow and expand, these teeth are replaced one by one by the teeth of the second set. The first set is known as the milk, deciduous, or primary dentition. The second set is called the permanent, or secondary, dentition. The permanent molar teeth are not replacements but additions and increase the capacity of the dentition as the jaws increase in size.

The right side of a dentition is, except for minor variations, a mirror image of the left. The upper teeth differ from the lower and are complementary to them; the relationship is in some respects similar to that of a mortar and pestle. There are 5 deciduous teeth and 8 permanent teeth in each quarter of the mouth, making a total of 32 permanent teeth to succeed the 20 deciduous ones. Each quadrant has four specific types of teeth, which have different shapes and uses. These are the incisors, the canines (or cuspids), the bicuspids (or premolars), and the molars (*see* fig. 1).

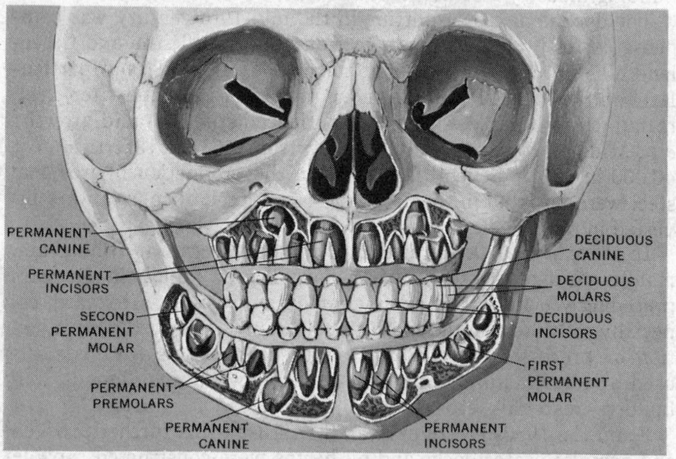


FIG. 1.—SKULL OF A FOUR-YEAR-OLD CHILD, SECTIONED TO SHOW ROOTS OF THE DECIDUOUS TEETH AND TOOTH GERMS OF THE PERMANENT TEETH

*Incisors.*—The permanent incisors, of which there are two in each quarter of the mouth (total number eight), are used principally for biting and cutting. The upper ones have a delicate tactile sense that enables them to be used for identifying objects in the mouth by nibbling. The biting portion is wide and thin, making a chisel-shaped cutting edge. The upper central incisor is the largest. The lateral incisor, next in line, is smaller and sometimes irregular in form. The lower ones are much smaller and are very similar to each other. They bite against the upper incisors, either edge to edge or slightly inward on the tongue side. An edge-to-edge biting position is acquired as the teeth wear down, particularly among peoples whose main foods are coarse or gritty.

*Cuspids.*—Next to the incisors is the canine, or cuspid (total number four). It is at the corner of the mouth, the third tooth from the midline. It frequently is pointed and rather peglike in shape. The cuspid is absent in many mammals that have developed protective horns; in some other animals it is a great defensive weapon by virtue of its size. In man the cuspid tooth has the function of cutting and tearing. Its length and position are such that it does not normally protrude beyond the level of the other teeth, and this permits a side-to-side chewing motion that is not possible in the other primates, which have long canines. The upper cuspid in man is popularly called the eyetooth, from its position under the eye.

*Bicuspids.*—The two bicuspids, or premolars (total number eight), are next in line. They replace the baby molars but have a somewhat different function. Each has two cusps (tapering projections on the crown), although the lower second bicuspid frequently has a small third one. The first lower bicuspid often has a compressed appearance, as though it had been squeezed on the sides. This gives a prominence or sharpness to the forward sloping edge that is reminiscent of the scissors action against the long upper cuspid of man's remote ancestors. The roots of the bicuspids are reduced forms compared with those of fossil and modern anthropoids. The upper first bicuspid generally has two roots, sometimes one; the second generally has one root, sometimes two; the lower bicuspids have one root each. Occasionally they are found divided in two.

*Molars.*—The three molars (in each quadrant; total number 12) are the teeth farthest back in the mouth. They are used exclusively for grinding. The upper molars have four (sometimes three) cusps, whereas the lowers have five (sometimes four). The number and position of the cusps and the character of the grooves between them differ among individuals. Generally the upper molars have three roots and the lowers two.

In persons of European origin the first molar usually is large, the second smaller, and the third the smallest. In some other groups the third molar is larger than the second, though smaller than the first.

*Deciduous and Permanent.*—In the milk, or deciduous, dentition there are only 20 teeth, 10 in each jaw, 5 in each right and left segment. They include, in each quadrant, 2 incisors, 1 cuspid and 2 molars. The molars are replaced by the permanent premolars, or bicuspids. The incisors and cuspids are replaced by the permanent incisors and cuspids. In the deciduous dentition there are no predecessors to the three permanent molars. The deciduous dentition differs from the permanent in its smaller size, whiter colour, greater constriction of the necks of the teeth, and in the fact that the roots of the molars are widely spread to give a wider base and an accommodation for the developing permanent tooth germs.

*Eruption.*—This term refers to the emergence of teeth through the gums in living persons; in the study of fossil or recent skeletal remains it means emergence above the level of the jawbone. Eruption is variable among individuals both as to timing and as to order. In the deciduous dentition the lower first, or central, incisor comes in first, between the sixth and ninth month. This is followed by the upper central and lateral incisors. The other teeth erupt at four- to six-month intervals, the dentition being completed by two years of age. The sequence of permanent-tooth emergence follows different patterns in different individuals. In some, the lower first molar is the first permanent tooth to appear; in others it is the lower central incisor. This occurs about the sixth year.

From this time on there is a succession of loss of deciduous teeth and emergence of permanent teeth in the presence of jawbone growth, expansion, and change. This process continues intermittently with rest periods until about age 12, when the second molars arrive. The third molars, or wisdom teeth, usually do not come in until about age 18 or 20. Occasionally a deciduous tooth is retained into adulthood when its successional tooth fails to develop or when the permanent tooth is in an abnormal position. This follows a genetic pattern, along with other phenomena of the dentition.

**Histology.**—Teeth are composed of several tissues (fig. 2).

*Dentin.*—The main bulk or core of each tooth is dentin, a calcified tissue made up of approximately 30% organic matter and water and 70% inorganic matter, principally calcium and phosphorus. Dentin is a highly sensitive tissue with a circulation of lymph in its tubules. The tubules extend from the inner pulp cavity to the periphery, more or less perpendicularly to these surfaces. The dentin extends almost the entire length of the tooth, being covered by enamel on the crown portion and by cementum on the roots.

*Enamel.*—Enamel is the hardest tissue in the body, consisting of 96% inorganic material and 4% organic matter and water. This tissue receives its nourishment, slight as it is, from the dentin that it covers. Some circulation of fluids in enamel has been shown by use of radioisotope tracer materials. The enamel has no nerve supply. Microscopically, it is seen to be composed of fine, hexagonal prisms arranged at right angles to the outer surface of the tooth and extending to the underlying dentin.

*Cementum.*—Cementum is another calcified tissue. It affords a thin covering to the root of the tooth and has the appearance of a modified type of bone. In a few instances, as in horses and rabbits, where the enamel is folded, the cementum extends beyond the confines of the root surface and fills these folds, thus serving as a substantial part of the functional chewing surface. It serves normally as a medium for attachment of the fibres that hold the tooth to the surrounding tissues (periodontal membrane).

*Pulp.*—Nerves, lymph, blood vessels, and fibrous tissue make up a structure generally known as the pulp or "nerve," occupying a cavity located in the centre of the tooth. The pulp canal is long and narrow with an enlargement, the pulp chamber, in the coronal end. The canal extends for about four-fifths the length of the tooth, with communication to the general nutritional and nervous systems through the apical foramina (holes) at the end of the roots. Lining the entire wall of the pulp cavity are the resting odontoblasts (columnar mesodermal cells) that originally functioned to produce the tubules of the dentin. Upon stimulation from decay or other external contact to the dentin proper, the odontoblasts may again resume activity and produce another layer of so-called secondary dentin. This differs somewhat from the first dentin; it is less well organized and in certain respects resembles bone. Secondary dentin is a protective mechanism, designed to counter the losses from the advancing carious (decay) or wear processes.

**Embryology.**—Teeth are produced by specialized tissues in-

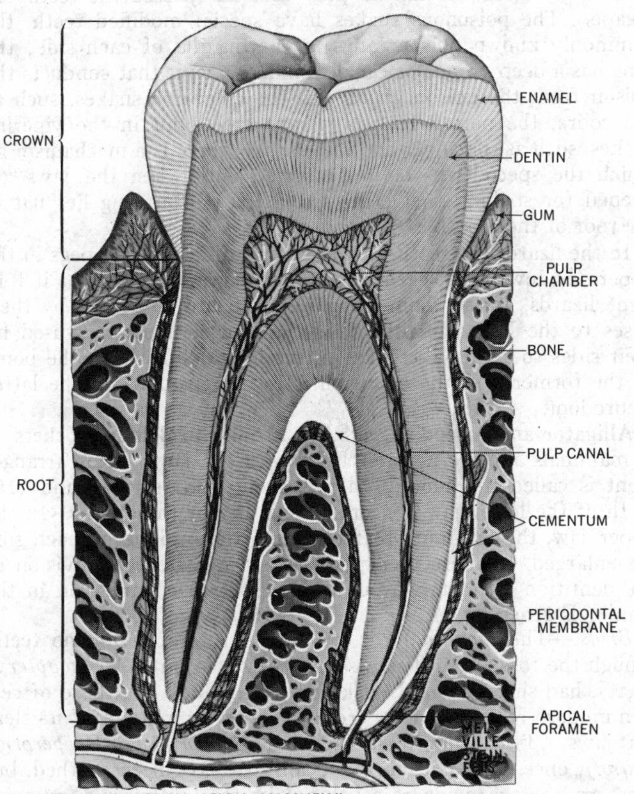


BY COURTESY OF AMERICAN DENTAL ASSOCIATION

FIG. 2.—CROSS-SECTION OF A HUMAN MOLAR

duced and organized from simple elements of the ectodermic and mesodermic layers of the embryo. During the seventh to tenth week of fetal life, ten distinct and separate thickenings of certain cell groups develop in the epithelial covering of each jaw. Each of these so-called enamel organs stimulates some of the underlying mesodermic cell elements to transform their character for the specialized function of producing a protoplasmic substance in the form of tubules, which later calcify and form the dentin.

At the same time the cells of the thickened epithelial layer also differentiate into enamel rod producers. The sum total is a tooth germ in which the process of enamel and dentin production goes on simultaneously from a common starting lineup of cells, the enamel cells (ameloblasts) proceeding outward and the dentin cells (odontoblasts) inward (fig. 3). Thus, the enamel and dentin

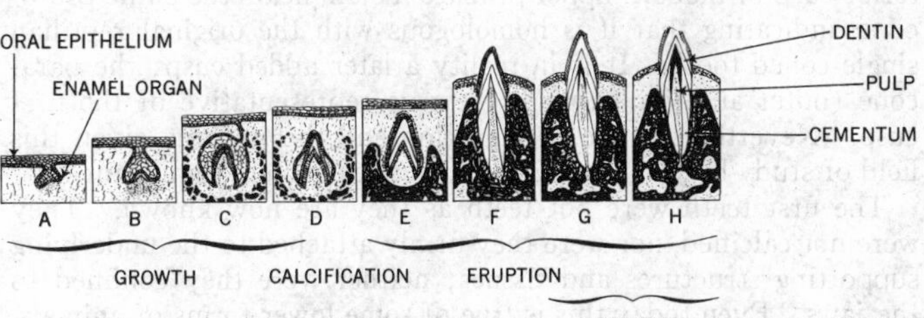


FROM BALINT J. ORBAN, "ORAL HISTOLOGY AND EMBRYOLOGY," 4TH ED. (1957), THE C. V. MOSBY COMPANY

FIG. 3.—DIAGRAMMATIC ILLUSTRATION OF THE LIFE CYCLE OF THE TOOTH

(A) Initiation (bud stage); (B) proliferation (cap stage); (C) histodifferentiation (bell stage) and active morphodifferentiation; (D) apposition; (E) intraosseous; (F) eruption into oral cavity; (G,H) attrition

are developed in direct contact with each other. The tissues soon are calcified by deposition of calcium salts in the matrices of processes and tubules. The ameloblasts remain on the surface after enamel formation is completed. After eruption of the tooth they frequently are a source of annoyance by their affinity for stains and surface discoloration. At the termination of dentin production, the odontoblasts remain as a lining of the pulp chamber, ready to resume function by formation of the secondary dentin upon the proper stimuli (see *Pulp*, above).

**Evolution and Comparative Anatomy.**—Teeth and bone have figured conspicuously in evolutionary studies and theory; they constitute major evidence in prehistoric studies. The teeth, particularly, persist through time by virtue of their calcified structure and their resistance to erosion and the various conditions of burial. With a few exceptions, the history of the evolution of tooth form and structure is complete. Comparison of the many modern dentitions with their predecessors reveals their origins and transition. Modern man's dentition differs from that of his fossil forebears in the size of teeth and in the proportionate development or modification of structural parts. Similar points of difference are found between man and the other anthropoids. The differences between tooth forms and combinations in the animal classifications are striking.

Various theories have been proposed to explain the evolution in form from the simple conelike tooth of the early reptiles to the complicated patterns of human molars. In early discussions of the subject disputes over some sequences and stages were common. The fossil record, however, now indicates more clearly the pathway of these changes. The theory of trituberculy, developed largely by the U.S. paleontologists E. D. Cope and H. F. Osborn, has had the greatest influence. According to this theory, the simple peglike tooth, originally derived from the placoid scales, developed two additional smaller pegs or cones, one in front of (paracone) and one behind (metacone) the original main cone (protocone). This is known as the triconodont stage and is represented by fossils of extinct mammals. The two added structures were supposed then to have moved externally in the upper teeth and internally in the lower, to form a triangle. Specimens are known that show that these cusps evolved in this triangular position and did not migrate. This tritubercled tooth is considered the basic ancestral form from which all modern mammalian dentitions were derived, by addition and subtraction as well as by modification of

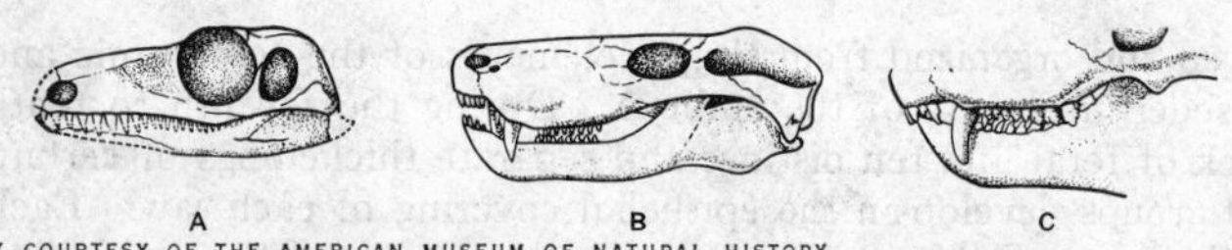


BY COURTESY OF THE AMERICAN MUSEUM OF NATURAL HISTORY

FIG. 4.—THREE MAJOR STAGES IN THE EVOLUTION OF TEETH

(A) Homodont stage in which all the teeth have the same form; (B) pre- and post-canine stage in which the dentition has been divided into anterior and posterior parts by the elongation of the canines; (C) heterodont stage in which the teeth have taken on specialized forms and functions, differing in the various locations of the dental arcade

cusps. The names of the cusps as developed in the Cope-Osborn system still are used in the literature, although later evidence shows a few discrepancies in the plan. As an example, the internal anterior cusp of modern upper primate molars bears the name protocone, indicating that it is homologous with the original reptilian single-coned tooth. It is in reality a later added cusp; the paracone (outer anterior cusp) is the true representative of the first cusp. Nevertheless, the organization and the impetus given this field of study by Cope and Osborn were extremely significant.

The first teeth were not teeth as they are now known. They were not calcified, nor were they firmly attached to the underlying supporting structures and tissues; neither were they confined to the jaws. Even today this is true of some lower forms of animals.

Fish display the earliest trends in the evolution of teeth. In some, the scales at the edge of the mouth are used as teeth and are replaced by the ones next in line as they are needed. Some fish have calcified structures as in the higher animal forms, generally confined, however, to a single cone shape. These are constantly formed in the jaw and erupt from time to time to succeed their predecessors as they are worn out or lost.

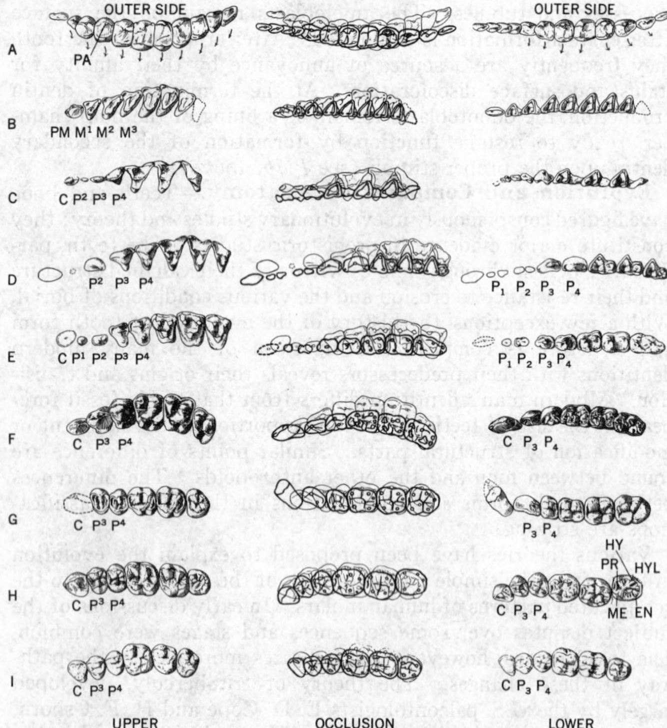


BY COURTESY OF THE AMERICAN MUSEUM OF NATURAL HISTORY

FIG. 5.—NINE STRUCTURAL STAGES IN THE EVOLUTION OF TEETH FROM THE SIMPLE HOMODONT STATE (A) TO THE COMPLEX HOMINOID HETERODONT STAGE (I)

Key: PA = paracone; P = premolar; M = molar; C = canine or cuspid; PR = protoconid; HY = hypoconid; HYL = hypoconulid; ME = metaconid; EN = entoconid

A brief description of the teeth of the members of the main vertebrate groups follows.

*Cyclostomes.*—In the lampreys and hags the teeth are horny cones.

*Elasmobranchs.*—These include the cartilaginous fishes, such as sharks and rays, in which the teeth are arranged in several rows. The hind ones move forward as those in the front row fall out. In some of these fishes the teeth are set in positions like flat pavement blocks; in the rays they are like flat plates that crush against each other. This flatness gives them the appearance of the molars of man. Except for the saw of the sawfish, elasmobranch teeth are not embedded in sockets. The body of the tooth, called the osteodentin, resembles bone and has no pulp cavity; it is therefore unlike the dentin of the higher vertebrates.

*Bony Fishes.*—Both primitive and advanced bony fishes show great variability in teeth. In the sturgeon there are no teeth at all, while in other fishes each of the several bones bounding the mouth, including the branchial arches, bears teeth. The pike's mouth and pharynx are completely armoured with teeth. The pike and hake have hinged teeth that bend to allow food and prey to pass down the throat, but become erect and bar exit of anything that has gone by. The hinge is a soft-tissue attachment with elastic ligaments. Most of the bony fishes have osteodentin, but the hake and a few others have vasodentin, which has many blood vessels running through it.

*Amphibians.*—These include the frog, toad, and salamander, among others. Although the teeth are less numerous than in the first three classes, they do occur regularly on the palate as well as on bones and make up the lower and upper jaws proper. The toad has no teeth, and the frog has none in the lower jaw. The extinct stegocephalid amphibians, ancestral to the reptiles, are of particular interest because of their complex convoluted type of dentin, known as labyrinthian. They are called labyrinthodonts.

*Reptiles.*—These have considerable variety in the dentition. The first separation of anterior from posterior teeth by the specialized elongation of the canine tooth occurred in this class.

Turtles have no teeth, although the ectodermal ingrowth (dental band) from which teeth develop in other animals is present in the turtle embryo. The place of the teeth in these reptiles is taken by horny jaw cases.

Among the snakes the nonpoisonous varieties have two rows of teeth in the upper jaw, one on the maxilla and another on the palatine and pterygoid bones, while in the lower jaw there is only one row. These teeth are sharp pegs ankylosed to the bones and so strongly recurved that no prey that has passed the teeth can escape. The poisonous snakes have special modified teeth, the commonly known poison fangs in the maxilla of each side; the fang has a deep groove or canal running down it that conducts the poison from the poison gland. In the colubrine snakes, such as the cobra, the poison fang is always erect, but in the viperine snakes, such as the adder and rattlesnake, there is a mechanism by which the specialized tooth is erected only when the jaws are opened for striking. At other times the poison fang lies flat in the roof of the mouth.

In the lizards the teeth usually consist of a series of pegs in the upper and lower jaw, each resembling the one in front of it. In some lizards, as the chameleon, the teeth are ankylosed by their bases to the bone; in others, as the iguana, they are fused by their sides to a wall-like ridge on the lateral surface of the bone. In the former case the dentition is called acrodont, in the latter pleurodont.

Alligator and crocodile teeth are fitted into definite sockets as in mammals and are not ankylosed with the jaws. This arrangement is called thecodont. In this group the 1st, 4th, and 11th teeth of the lower jaw are larger than any of the others. In the upper jaw, the 3rd and 9th teeth from the midline on each side are enlarged. This regularity suggests the pattern of division of the dentition into the various tooth groups that are seen in the mammals generally.

*Birds.*—The modern birds are distinctive in having no teeth, though the fossil record shows that the dawn bird, *Archaeopteryx* (*q.v.*), had sharp-pointed, socketed teeth, much like those of certain modern reptiles, arising from the anterior margins of its slender jaws. Two other fossil birds, *Ichthyornis* and *Hesperornis* (*qq.v.*), once were said unequivocably to have been toothed, but most ornithologists now reject this claim for *Ichthyornis* and point to the ambiguous nature of the evidence in the case of *Hesperornis*.

Many birds do, however, have bony plates or serrations on the bill to enable them to grasp or filter their food. The so-called egg tooth possessed by hatchlings of most species of modern birds (and of oviparous reptiles) is not a true tooth but a horny process on the tip of the upper mandible, used to break the eggshell from within; it soon disappears.

In these first six groups of vertebrates the dentitions are quite simple in form, being in the main of the cone type, except for particular specializations. Also in most of these classes there is a continuous succession of teeth, so that replacements for lost teeth are always at hand. This arrangement for continual succession of teeth is called polyphyodont.

*Mammals.*—Among the mammals may be found a very wide variety of dentitions and specializations. This class has the heterodont type (many shaped) as opposed to the homodont (single shaped) dentition that is found among the other classes. In the mammals the polyphyodont dentition, or continuous succession of teeth, is reduced to a diphyodont dentition; *i.e.*, there is only one replacement of the first set. In the marsupials the reduction is carried still further, for only one premolar in each segment of the jaw is replaced, while in the toothed whales there is no succession at all. When one set has to do duty throughout life the dentition is called monophyodont.

Some of the specializations among the mammals are extreme. The rodents, for example, have incisors that continuously grow throughout life. The horses and other hoofed animals have large teeth that are folded and have very long roots. These long, heavily ridged teeth are practically as efficient as the continuously growing variety. Cats, dogs, and other carnivores likewise have teeth that evolved from the tritubercled form as well as the other orders; however, the dentition of these animals developed in a direction that would serve in cutting, grasping, and shearing rather than grinding. Some mammals lost parts of their dentition rather than added to them. Some, though only a few, of the so-called edentates have lost all their teeth, but even the toothless members have vestiges of teeth in the early developmental stages.

All the primates have similar dentitions. The main differences between them are in the emphasis of expression of parts, in the relative sizes of parts, in the overall size of the dentition, and in the actual number of the types of teeth. The lemurs exhibit a certain coarseness on the surface of the teeth, in contrast with human teeth. They also tend to vary in the number of premolars, from two to four in each of the four quadrants. The aye-aye has even lost all the canines; it retains only the upper and lower central incisor, one upper premolar, and none of its lower premolars. The anthropoids (monkeys, apes, and man) follow a rather consistent formula as to number of teeth; the main exception is that the platyrrhine (New World) monkeys have three premolars in each quadrant, whereas the catarrhine (Old World) forms have two. Some platyrrhines have two rather than the usual three molars.

**Variations in Man.**—Although following a basic pattern throughout, modern man's dentition does show considerable variation from one population to another. The main differentiating characteristics are those in the tongue side of the upper incisor teeth (absence or presence of shovel shape), in the expression of the areas near the gum margin of the posterior teeth (ridges, cusps, and grooves), in the general wrinkling or smoothness of the occluding surfaces, and in the overall size of the dentition.

Failure of certain teeth to erupt has been reported among populations. Absence of one or more third molars, or wisdom teeth, has been reported in 19% of the white populations of central Europe; absence of upper lateral incisors is reported in from 2 to 3% in most groups. Reductions in the form or pattern of certain teeth and modification or absence of certain cusps are also frequently noted. These variations follow a regular pattern, with the third molars, lateral incisors, and second premolars being the teeth most commonly affected.

Differences in the frequencies of these occurrences have been used in anthropological studies to describe the dentition of various population groups. One population may be distinguished from another by comparing the different frequencies of these features. The frequencies reflect the characteristics of the genetic composition of populations.

**Dental Formulas.**—It is convenient to indicate the number of each kind of tooth in one side of the upper and lower jaw in the various mammalian orders by the use of dental formulas. The order and number are indicated from left to right, as in the case of man's formula: incisors $\frac{2}{2}$, cuspids $\frac{1}{1}$, premolars $\frac{2}{2}$, molars $\frac{3}{3}$. This is condensed into $\frac{2.1.2.3}{2.1.2.3}$. Some typical formulas are:

| | |
|---|---|
| Primitive mammalian | $\frac{3.1.4.3}{3.1.4.3}$ |
| Typical marsupial | $\frac{5.1.3.4}{4.1.3.4}$ |
| Anthropoidea: | |
| Platyrrhina | $\frac{2.1.(2–3).(2–3)}{2.1.(2–3).(2–3)}$ |
| Catarrhina | $\frac{2.1.2.3}{2.1.2.3}$ |

For additional information on dentitions (fossil and modern), *see* articles on particular animal groups. *See* also references under "Teeth" in the Index.

BIBLIOGRAPHY.—P. M. Butler, "Studies of the Mammalian Dentition," *Proc. Zool. Soc. Lond.*, series B 109 (1939); A. A. Dahlberg, *The Dentition of the American Indian* (1949); W. K. Gregory, *Evolution Emerging* (1951), "A Half Century of Trituberculy," *Proc. Am. Phil. Soc.*, vol. lxxiii (1934); C. F. A. Moorrees, *The Aleut Dentition* (1957); B. Orban, *Oral Histology and Embryology* (1944); P. O. Pedersen, *The East Greenland Eskimo Dentition, Numerical Variations and Anatomy* (1949); J. T. Robinson, "The Dentition of the Australopithecinae," *Transv. Mus. Mem.*, 9 (1956); G. G. Simpson, *Tempo and Mode in Evolution* (1944). (A. A. DG.)

**TEETH, ARTIFICIAL.** The replacement of missing natural teeth with substitutes of various kinds has been practised from ancient times, when human and animal teeth and wood were used. In the last quarter of the 18th century one-piece restorations of porcelain began to be used, and at the beginning of the 19th century Giuseppangelo Fonzi, an Italian dentist practising in Paris, introduced individual porcelain teeth mounted on gold or platinum bases. Porcelain teeth were introduced into the United States about 1817, reputedly by Anthony A. Plantou. Early in the 19th century, through the efforts of J. Leon Williams, the appearance of artificial teeth was much improved by designing the teeth to harmonize with the shape of the face. Teeth were made in three typical facial forms: square, tapering, and ovoid. At the same time the effectiveness of the chewing surfaces of the back teeth was improved by the anatomical designs of Alfred Gysi of Switzerland.

In modern times porcelain and plastic teeth are made in such a great variety of shapes, sizes, and colours that almost any natural teeth can be closely matched. Modern artificial teeth are usually fastened to plastic bases that resemble the natural gums. The combination of teeth and base is an artificial denture, commonly called a set of false teeth or a dental plate. Artificial teeth are also used in dental bridges, which are cemented to natural teeth.

Dental porcelain is prepared by fusing a mixture of feldspar (orthoclase), flint (silica), and clay (kaolin) at about 2,400° F (1,300° C). The high-melting flint and clay are fused together in a vitreous mass formed by the relatively low-melting feldspar. Much of the fusion is done under a partial vacuum to reduce porosity and increase strength. Suitable opacities and colours are obtained by adding small amounts of metallic oxides, such as those of titanium, chromium, nickel, cobalt, iron, and uranium. The uranium oxide causes artificial teeth to glow (fluoresce) in ultraviolet light in much the same manner as natural teeth.

The manufacture of porcelain teeth begins with the carving of the desired shapes and sizes out of plaster of paris or other suitable material. These models are made one-fifth larger than the finished product to allow for shrinkage during fusion. In one common process, split metal molds are made from the models. Starch, powdered porcelain of varied composition, and water are mixed to a thick paste and packed into the molds. The packing is done in stages: the porcelain mixture (resembling in composition the translucent enamel covering of natural teeth) is packed into the appropriate position in the mold, and a more opaque porcelain (resembling the dentin core of natural teeth) is placed in another part of the mold. The molds are closed and heated to bake the porcelain to a hard state so that the teeth can be removed for a final fusing. Other methods employ flexible rubber molds into which the porcelain paste is vibrated until it is condensed sufficiently to be removed from the mold for final fusing. Bridge teeth are frequently made by fusing a dental porcelain to a precious-metal casting or by veneering the casting with a plastic.

Approximately 30% of all modern artificial teeth are made of plastics, consisting principally of polymethyl methacrylate. By comparison with porcelain teeth, plastic teeth are less brittle, are easier to grind and polish, make a firmer union with the plastic base, and make less noise when being used. However, porcelain teeth are generally preferred because of their chewing efficiency and longer wear.

Artificial teeth are shipped from the factory inserted in wax on plastic cards or blocks. A card usually contains a set of six front teeth (two cuspids and four incisors of either the upper or lower jaw) or a set of eight back teeth (four bicuspids and four molars of either jaw). However, the dentist or dental laboratory may purchase teeth singly or in any combination desired. The normal number of natural teeth is 32, but the four third molars (wisdom teeth) are not supplied in artificial sets because there is usually not room for them in an artificial denture.

*See* also PROSTHODONTICS. (G. B. D.; G. C. PR.)

**TEFILLIN:** *see* PHYLACTERY.

**TEGERNSEE,** a lake of West Germany in Upper Bavaria, Federal Republic of Germany, lies at 2,380 ft. (725 m.) above sea level among wooded mountains on the fringe of the Bavarian Alps, its northern end (Gmund) being about 30 mi. (48 km.) S of Munich by road or rail. The lake is about 3.9 mi. (6.2 km.) long, 0.9 mi. (1.5 km.) broad, and 3½ sq.mi. (9 sq.km.) in area, with a maximum depth of 237 ft. (72 m.). Its waters discharge through the Mangfall into the Inn. It is a much frequented summer and winter resort, with facilities for yachting and other water sports and for winter sports. Main centres are Tegernsee on the eastern shore, with the castle of the Bavarian king Maximilian I (until 1803 a Benedictine abbey, founded in the 8th century); Bad Wiessee on the western shore, a spa with iodine and sulfur springs; and Rottach-Egern on the southern shore at the foot of the Wallberg (5,650 ft. [1,722 m.]), from whose summit are views across the Mangfall Range to the Hohe Tauern, and of the Zugspitze to the southwest. About 3 mi. up the Rottach Valley is a picturesque waterfall, the Rottachfälle. (R. E. DI.)

**TEGNÉR, ESAIAS** (1782–1846), the greatest Swedish poet of his age. Born at Kyrkerud in Värmland, on Nov. 13, 1782, he was thrown on his own resources by his father's death in 1792. He entered Lund University in 1799, graduated in 1802, and in 1812 was appointed professor of Greek. He continued to lecture at Lund until 1824, when he became bishop of Växjö.

Tegnér first won literary fame with his patriotic poem *Svea,* which was awarded the highest prize of the Swedish Academy in 1811. In 1812 he joined Götiska Förbundet, a romantic, nationalist league founded by Erik Gustaf Geijer and others, and between 1812 and 1813 published some of his finest poems in its periodical, *Iduna.* The solemn "Skaldens morgonpsalm" and "Sång till solen" were particularly notable. His topical poems—*e.g.,* "Hjälten," a tribute to Napoleon—are also remarkable. He was originally associated with the Romantic movement, but later reacted against its emotional and mystical aspect, *fosforismen,* so-called from its periodical *Phosphoros,* and represented by the work of Atterbom. "Strength and clarity" were what he demanded of poetry in the famous *Epilog vid magisterpromotionen i Lund 1820.* He had entered the Swedish Academy in 1819. His greatest poetic achievement was *Frithiofs saga,* a cycle based on an Old Icelandic saga; it became a national poem and was translated into most European languages. Other outstanding poems of this period were *Nattvardsbarnen* (1820) and the verse narrative *Axel* (1822; Eng. trans. by R. G. Latham, 1837), modeled on Byron.

The year of the publication of *Frithiofs saga* (1825) marked not only a peak in Tegnér's development as a poet but also a turning point in his life. From then on he was a sick man, and an unhappy love affair added to his suffering. He describes his state of mind in the mid-1820s in a moving poem, *Mjältsjukan* ("Melancholia"). After 1826 his duties as bishop left him little time for poetry, and yet some of his famous poems, such as "Sång den 5 april 1836" (commemorating the 50th anniversary of the founding of the Swedish Academy) and "Den döde," a love poem dedicated to a young married woman in Växjö, date from this period. He devoted special attention to education in his diocese, and his addresses at the end of the school year are of great interest. As bishop he was automatically a member of the *riksdag* and had to spend long irksome periods in Stockholm. Originally a liberal, he became increasingly conservative and entered into controversies with the successful liberal spokesmen of the time in parliament and press. These disputes and his ill-health led to embitterment. Following a stroke in 1840 he showed signs of mental disorder. During a period of convalescence he wrote "Kronbruden," an idyll in hexameters, which is his last important poem. He died at Östrabo, near Växjö, on Nov. 2, 1846.

Tegnér's poetic reputation has been confirmed by posterity. He is also regarded as Sweden's most brilliant orator and wittiest letter writer. His letters did not become widely known until his posthumous works were published by his grandson in 1873–74, at a time when the public was becoming weary of lyrical romanticism and ready to appreciate Tegnér's realistic prose style, distinguished by sparkling wit and pregnancy of expression.

An edition of Tegnér's works, by E. Wrangel and F. Böök, was published in 10 vol. (1918–25). A complete edition of his letters was begun by the Tegnér Society (1953).

BIBLIOGRAPHY.—G. Brandes, *Esaias Tegnér* (1878); F. Böök, *Esaias Tegnér,* 2 vol. (1946); E. Wrangel, *Tegnér i Lund,* 2 vol. (1932); A. Werin, *Esaias Tegnér. Från det eviga till Mjältsjukan* (1934).

(AT. WN.)

**TEGUCIGALPA,** the capital of Honduras, was founded about 1579 on the slopes of Mt. Picacho as a gold and silver mining centre. Pop. (1961) 134,075. It alternated with Comayagua (35 mi. [56 km.] NW) as capital from 1824 to 1880, when it was made the permanent capital of the republic. In 1938 Tegucigalpa was combined with the city of Comayagüela, across the Choluteca River to the south, to form part of the Central District. The city is located on hilly terrain hemmed in by mountains at an altitude of 3,200 ft. (975 m.), with average daily temperature ranging from 65° F (18° C) in January to 75° F (24° C) in June. The dry season extends from November through April, sometimes causing severe water shortages before the rains begin, and the rainy season lasts from May through October.

One of the few capitals in the world without a railroad, Tegucigalpa depends largely on the international airport at Toncontín. Freight can be trucked in over the all-weather South Highway from the Pacific or from the adjoining republics of El Salvador and Nicaragua, but goods coming from the north must be brought by ship to Puerto Cortés, then by rail or dry-weather road to Potrerillos, and finally by all-weather road to Tegucigalpa.

The city's principal public buildings include the presidential palace, Central Bank of Honduras, legislative palace, and National University, all near the Mallol Bridge, and the cathedral, facing Morazán Park, named for the country's greatest hero. Industrial production is small and mostly for local consumption; products include textiles, sugar, and cigarettes. (M. D. M.)

**TEHERAN** (TEHRAN), the capital city of Iran, lies on the southern slopes of the Elburz (Alborz) Mountains at a mean altitude of 3,800 ft. (1,158 m.) above sea level, and at a direct distance of 62 mi. (100 km.) from the Caspian Sea. It is enclosed by two rivers, the Karaj and the Jajrud, which flow from the Elburz Mountains. Pop. (1966) 2,695,283.

Teheran has a typically continental climate with warm summers and relatively cool winters, but the Elburz Mountains, often rising to more than 13,000 ft. (4,000 m.), provide the region with excellent resorts and add to the attractions of a beautiful capital. During the summer, especially on national holidays, most of the urban population go to the high mountain resorts in the Shemiran and Lavasan districts to escape the hot weather. In the winter skiing is popular on the Lashkarak Hills and on the heights of Abe Ali, 19 and 38 mi. (30 and 60 km.) from Teheran respectively. In Teheran itself, winter weather is mostly sunny and invigorating.

The Karaj (or Amir-Kabir) dam provides electric power for the city and, together with the Latian (or Farah Naz Pahlavi) dam, also provides its water supply.

Modern Teheran has an area of 109 sq.mi. (280 sq.km.). To the northeast, at a distance of 44 mi. (71 km.), the snow-covered and inactive volcano peak of Demavend (*q.v.*, 18,625 ft. [5,678 m.]) can be seen quite distinctly. Firdausi Square, at the junction of Shahreza Avenue and Firdausi Street, forms the city's new centre, which was formerly Sepah Square (Maidan-i-Sipah), but the population centre is still Sepah Square with the bazaar located on its southern side.

The centre of Teheran's modern buildings lies to the north of Shahreza Street, which is the fashionable part of the town. The growth of the city can also be observed along the two roads connecting it with Shemiran, the summer resort of the capital. Modern villas, attractive buildings, and the private houses along the highways in Tajrish, Darband, Gholhak, and Niavaran, surrounded by ancient trees, complete the scene.

Teheran, in contrast with the other cities of Iran, is almost wholly lacking in historic buildings, but the Iran Bastan Museum in the southeast corner of Firdausi Square contains a fine collection of antiquities excavated from historical and prehistoric monuments and sites. There are also several holy sites such as the shrine of Sayyid Nasruddin in Khayam Avenue, the shrine of Imam Zadeh Yahya in Udlajan and, even more popular, the shrines of Hazrat Hamzeh ibn Musa al-Qasim and of Hazrat Abdul Azim in the old city of Ray, both with gold domes and huge minarets. These are places of pilgrimage for Shiʿite Muslims; together with the fire temple known as Takht i-Rustam, not far from Teheran and dating back to the Sassanid period, these are classified as historical monuments. To these may be added two mosques, the Masjid-i-Shah in the bazaar quarter and the Masjid-i-Sepahsalar in Baharistan Square, which are considered artistic masterpieces with especially fine tile-work.

The early 19th-century Gulistan Palace, with its marble and museum halls containing valuable historic treasures such as the jewel-studded Nadiri throne and the peacock throne (*takht-i-tavus*), is one of the world's most celebrated palaces. Here, in October 1967, the coronation took place of the shahanshah Mohammed Reza Pahlavi Aryamehr and Queen Farah, the shahbanu of Iran. Second only to the Gulistan Palace is the Marmar Palace, the façade of which is covered with marble work. A fine dome with glazed tiles towers over this palace. Here the shahanshah receives foreign delegates.

The Saad-Abad and Shahvand palaces on the heights of Tajrish and Darband accommodate the offices of the Ministry of the Royal Court.

The Parliament (*Majlis*) building is in Baharistan Square and the Senate House is near the Marmar Palace. There are three universities: the Teheran University, the Arya Mehr Technical University, and the National University. The stadiums named after Mohammed Reza Shah Pahlavi and the Amjadieh stadium are centres for sport and recreation. Another stadium with a capacity for 100,000 people was under construction in the late 1960s. There are in addition several athletic clubs. A fine opera house was opened in October 1967.

The official religion of Teheran, as of Iran, is Islam, but there are churches of the Christian, Jewish, and Zoroastrian faiths.

The city possesses a number of attractive parks, squares, and boulevards. The best known of these are the Elizabeth II Boulevard, Shahanshahi Shahyad Square, Valiahd Square, Sepah Square with the equestrian statue of the late shah, Reza Shah the Great, Firdausi Square, with the statue of the poet Firdausi (*q.v.*), Valiahd Park, and the City Park.

**Communications and Industries.**—Teheran is connected by air with the interior of the country as well as with foreign countries. The international Mehrabad airport lies 6 mi. (10 km.) W of Firdausi Square. Another large airport at the end of the 26-mi. (42 km.) Teheran–Karaj motorway was under construction in the late 1960s. The Iranian state railway traverses Teheran from all directions and the railway line from Teheran to Turkey and Europe was due for completion. The Teheran–Rasht–Pahlavi highway, the Teheran–Turkey highway, and the highway connecting the Caspian Sea with the Persian Gulf via Teheran made the capital a centre of considerable commercial and social importance in the late 1960s.

Teheran has four television transmitters and four radio broadcasting stations. Its industrial enterprises include the Peykan car manufacturing company, the Fiat Assembly Company, the Iran National Jeep and Rambler Company, cement factories, sugar refineries, textile factories, and armament and ammunition factories.

**History.**—Teheran is a successor of Iran's ancient capital Ray (*q.v.*), which was destroyed by the Mongols in A.D. 1220. There are still traces of this city about 3.7 mi. (6 km.) S of Teheran. There, near the shrine of Hazrat Abdul Azim, stands the tomb of Reza Shah the Great, the founder of modern Iran. Geographers believe that Teheran was one of the suburbs of Ray in the 4th century A.D. Teheran's expansion began during the reign of Shah Tahmasp I (1524–76) of the Safavid dynasty. Agha Mohammed Shah Qajar (reigned 1794–97) made it his capital and Teheran has since remained the capital of Iran. Reza Shah the Great (reigned 1925–41) took further steps to expand the city and the reign of the shahanshah Mohammed Reza Pahlavi has been a period of rapid and ever increasing modernization. The shahanshah has entrusted Queen Farah, with her interest in architecture, with the formation of plans for building a greater Teheran to house 5,500,000 people.

(M. A. Ma.)

**TEHUANTEPEC, ISTHMUS OF** (Istmo de Tehuantepec), lies between the gulfs of Campeche and Tehuantepec, with the Mexican states of Tabasco and Chiapas on the east and Veracruz and Oaxaca on the west. It includes a part of Mexico lying between the 94th and 96th meridians of longitude west. The isthmus is 137 mi. (220 km.) across at its narrowest part from gulf to gulf, and 120 mi. (193 km.) from the Gulf of Campeche to the head of Laguna Superior, an inlet of the Gulf of Tehuantepec. The Sierra Madre breaks down in the isthmus into a broad, plateaulike ridge, whose elevation, at the highest point reached by the Tehuantepec railway (Chivela pass), is 781 ft. (238 m.). The northern side of the isthmus is swampy and densely covered with jungle. The whole region is hot and malarial except on the open elevations where Pacific winds render it comparatively cool and healthful. The annual rainfall on the Atlantic or northern slope is 48 in. (1,219 mm.) and the maximum temperature about 35° C (95° F) in the shade. The Pacific slope has a drier climate.

Since the days of Hernán Cortés, the Tehuantepec isthmus has been considered a favourable route, first for an interoceanic canal and later for an interoceanic railway. Its proximity to the axis of international trade gave it some advantage over the Panama route, which was counterbalanced by the narrower width of Panama. When the great cost of a canal across the isthmus compelled engineers and capitalists to give it up as impracticable, numerous projects for the construction of a railway were initiated. The railway was finally opened to traffic in 1907; it is 192 mi. long, extending from Puerto México on the Gulf of Campeche to Salina Cruz on the Gulf of Tehuantepec. There are rail connections to Veracruz, Mexico City, and the Guatemalan border. Salina Cruz is a free port with large dry docks. The town of Tehuantepec is the centre of the distinctive Tehuanas, whose social organization is matriarchic. The Tehuana women are noted for their beauty and for their colourful fiesta dress.

(J. A. Cw.)

**TEHUELCHE,** an effectively extinct Indian tribe once occupying the plains of Patagonia (*q.v.*) from the Río Negro to the Strait of Magellan. Their great stature and physical vigour created a giant tradition in European literature. Since the arid, windswept nature of Patagonia made agriculture unprofitable, the

Tehuelche were nomadic hunters. Before the 16th century they lived much as did their kinsmen the Ona (*q.v.*) in Tierra del Fuego, but the introduction of horses by Europeans greatly enlarged their sphere of action and culture. By the 1960s their survivals were largely linguistic.

*See* T. Caillet-Boys, "Extinction of the Tehuelche Indians," *Geogrl J.*, vol. 103 (1944); J. H. Steward (ed.), *Handbook of South American Indians*, 7 vol. (1946–59).

**TEILHARD DE CHARDIN, PIERRE** (1881–1955), French Jesuit paleontologist and thinker whose originality of aim and method invites comparison with that of such devout pioneers as Pico della Mirandola, Ramon Llull, or even Origen, was born on May 1, 1881, at Sarcenat, near Orcines, Puy-de-Dôme. Having acquired from his father a habit of keen observation and an interest in geology, he was sent in 1892 to the Jesuit College of Mongré, at Villefranche-sur-Saône. In 1899 he joined the Jesuit noviceship at Aix-en-Provence. Because of the expulsion of the Jesuits from France, his subsequent studies were carried out in Jersey (1901–05) and finally, after an interval of teaching in Cairo (1905–08; during which time he carried out his first explorations in the Fayum), at Hastings in England, where he was ordained priest in 1911. He then studied paleontology under Marcellin Boule at Paris (1912–14). He served during World War I as a regimental stretcher-bearer (battles of Ypres, Verdun, Chemin des Dames and the Marne) with the rank of corporal, though he was offered the post of chaplain with the rank of captain. He taught at the Institut Catholique in Paris for some years but soon began his visits to China, where in December 1929 he was concerned in the discovery of an exemplary specimen of Peking man (*Sinanthropus*). Further travels took him to the Gobi Desert, Sinkiang, Kashmir, Java, and Burma. He spent 1939–46 at Peking in near-captivity. After World War II he returned to Paris. In 1951, however, making a detour by way of South Africa, he went to the United States to spend the rest of his life with research teams there (apart from another visit to South Africa in 1953). He died in New York on April 10, 1955.

TEILHARD DE CHARDIN

Most of Teilhard's writings were scientific, and especially concerned with mammalian paleontology. His philosophical books were the product of long meditation: *Le Milieu divin* appeared in 1926–27 (Eng. trans. 1960); *Le Phénomène humain* in 1938–40 (Eng. trans. *The Phenomenon of Man*, 1959). His *Lettres de voyage* (1923–39) and *Nouvelles lettres de voyage* (1939–55), collections of correspondence and reminiscences, were published in English as *Letters from a Traveller* (1962). The letters he wrote to his cousin Marguérite during his 4½ years in the army were collected as *The Making of a Mind* (1965). *L'Apparition de l'homme* (1956; *The Appearance of Man*, 1965), *La Vision du passé* (1957; *The Vision of the Past*, 1966), and *Science et Christ* (1965) consist of essays put together for the collected edition of Teilhard's works. Officials of his order regarded Teilhard's later intellectual musings as exceeding the bounds of priestly reflection and banned their publication during his lifetime. He aimed at a metaphysic of evolution, holding (against Bergson) that it was a process converging toward a final unity (Teilhard's "omega point").

The Aristotelian idea that material objects tend to seek their natural places fell victim to the astronomy of Galileo, and the bifurcation of nature (duality of body and spirit) introduced by Descartes banished intrinsic finality completely from the material world. Teilhard shows that what is of permanent value in traditional thinking can be maintained and even integrated with a modern scientific outlook if one accepts that the tendencies of material things are directed, either wholly or in part, beyond the things themselves toward the production of more complex, more perfectly unified beings that can rightly be called higher. In place of the Darwinian-Spencerian "survival of the fittest" Teilhard espouses "survival of the more complex." He regards basic trends in matter—gravitation, inertia, electromagnetism and the like—as being ordered toward the production of increasingly complex, higher types of aggregate.

To Teilhard, living things are directed by two tendencies simultaneously: inwardly toward self-perfection (called radial energy), and outwardly—away from the individual and its species—toward biological evolution (called tangential energy). Both types of energy he regards as "psychic," though admitting that between the tendencies of nonliving and of living things there is not identity but only analogy. He uses analogy again to compare the first appearance of life on earth (still a great mystery) with the appearance of man. While some evolutionists regard man simply as a prolongation of the Pliocene world—an animal more successful than the rat or the elephant—Teilhard argues that the appearance of man brought an added dimension into the world. This he defines as the birth of reflection: animals know, but man *knows* that he knows; he has "knowledge to the square."

Another great "mutation" in Teilhard's scheme of evolution is the socialization of man. This is not the triumph of herd instinct but a cultural convergence of humanity toward a single society. Love in this scheme is the highest radial energy; it makes a man more of a person (and so more perfect) because and not in spite of the fact that it binds him more closely to his fellows: union differentiates. Evolution has gone about as far as it can to perfect man physically: its next step will be social. Such evolution is currently in progress. Between peoples—in economics, in politics, and in habits of thought—more and more links are being established in something like a geometric progression. What may look like servitude, leveling, and ugliness hides growth in complexity and reflection. Man is approaching his final development; there is a convergence.

Theologically, Teilhard sees concurrent convergence toward an omega point in organic evolution (a final state, at present hypothetical) and a true omega point in Christian revelation, usually described as the Parousia, or second coming of Christ. Christianity is "a phylum of love within the world of nature"; it unites men into a mystical body that is more than a social or moral union; "Christ has attributes universal and cosmic, and these constitute him the personal omega point that is hypothetically invoked by the metaphysics of evolution." Teilhard's thought was Christocentric, following that of his teachers Léonce de Grandmaison and Joseph Huby. His ideas of cosmic redemption revived what the Early Christian Father Irenaeus had written on the recapitulation of all things in Christ. From the medieval philosopher Duns Scotus, Teilhard took the idea that the work of Christ is primarily to lead creation to fulfillment and to be its own crown, while the conquest of evil is only secondary to his purpose. Although claiming a pre-established harmony between the evolutionary tide as observed by science and the teaching of the Christian revelation, Teilhard shows the complete gratuity of the latter and thus avoids falling into pantheism.

Evil is represented by Teilhard as growing pains within the cosmic process: the disorder that is implied by order in process of realization. This does not take account of sin as a failure of love, and has been criticized as the blind spot in Teilhard's thinking. Looking at death in the light of Christ's resurrection, Teilhard calls it a mutation that frees the individual from entropy and allows him growth in radial energy without a corresponding expenditure on tangential energy. It might appear that Teilhard never fully worked out the relation of this mutation (death)—which is in store for each individual—to the mutation from individual life to corporate life, a jump that appears to be imminent for humanity as a whole.

BIBLIOGRAPHY.—C. Cuénot, *Pierre Teilhard de Chardin . . .* (1958); N. Corte, *Pierre Teilhard de Chardin*, Eng. trans. (1960); Paul Grenet, *Teilhard de Chardin*, Eng. trans. (1965); C. E. Raven, *Teilhard de Chardin: Scientist and Seer* (1962); H. de Terra, *Memories of Teilhard de Chardin* (1965); C. F. Mooney, *Teilhard de Chardin and the Mys-*

*tery of Christ* (1966). Books and articles about Teilhard are listed annually in *Archivum historicum Societatis Iesu.* (J. H. Cn.)

**TEISSERENC DE BORT, LEON PHILIPPE** (1855–1913), French meteorologist, noted for his discovery of the stratosphere, was born in Paris on Nov. 5, 1855, the son of an engineer. He began his scientific career in 1880, when he entered the meteorological department of the Central Bureau of Meteorology in Paris under E. E. N. Mascart. In 1883, 1885, and 1887 he made journeys to North Africa to study geology and terrestrial magnetism, and during that period published some important charts of the distribution of barometric pressure at a height of 4,000 m. In 1892 he became chief meteorologist to the bureau but resigned in 1896 and founded a private meteorological observatory at Trappes, near Versailles, where he carried out investigations on clouds and the problems of the upper air. In 1898 he published an important paper in *Comptes Rendus* detailing his researches by means of balloons into the constitution of the atmosphere. His discovery of the so-called isothermal layer, or stratosphere, will always stand out as one of the most important events in the study of the upper atmosphere. (*See* also BALLOON FLIGHT.) He also carried out investigations in Sweden and over the Zuider Zee, the Mediterranean, and the tropical region of the Atlantic. He died at Cannes on Jan. 2, 1913.

**TEITA** (TAITA), a Bantu-speaking people numbering 60,000 (1960s) mainly in the Teita Hills of southeastern Kenya (*q.v.*). These agriculturalists call themselves and their language Dabida. Their chief crop is maize, but they also grow vegetables and bananas for market in Mombasa by irrigating through furrows and pipes of banana stems. Cattle, goats, and sheep are valued for exchange and sacrifice. Many Teita work in Mombasa; others are found as labourers throughout east Africa. The tribe is grouped into seven patrilineal dispersed clans (*vichuku*). A clan segment, a lineage (*kivalo*) of about four generations, is the basic social unit. These lineages are formed into districts, the major modern administrative units. Men initiated together form an age set (*q.v.*); elders of senior sets are members of councils, presided over by district headmen. There has been a relatively recent development of tribal associations, some of which have been strongly nationalistic and politically active. Worship is directed toward propitiation of ancestral and community powers; in tribal crisis, the skulls of the forebears are offered a sacrifice of sheep, oxen, and beer (women are excluded from this ritual; in others they can be priestesses).

See A. H. J. Prins, *The Coastal Tribes of the North-Eastern Bantu* (1952). (J. F. M. M.)

**TEKAKWITHA** (TEGAKWITHA, TEGAKOUITA), **KATERI** (1656–1680), the first North American Indian ever presented to Rome for sainthood was born probably at Ossernenon (Auriesville), N.Y., in 1656. Her father, a pagan Mohawk chief, her mother, a Christian Algonkian, and her brother died of smallpox when she was four. The disease left her with pitted skin, poor eyesight, and damaged health. Staying with her anti-Christian uncle, she was deeply impressed at the age of 11 by the lives and words of three passing Jesuits, the first Christians she had spoken to. For years she refused marriage proposals and virtuously performed drudgeries common to squaws. At 20 she was instructed in religion and baptized Katherine by the Jesuit Jacques de Lamberville, who had been astonished at her knowledge and practice of Christian ideals. In her home village she was jeered, stoned, calumniated, and threatened with torture. She narrowly escaped death by fleeing 200 mi. through forests to the Christian Indian mission of St. Francis Xavier at Sault St. Louis near Montreal. There in summer she toiled in the fields and during the winter hunts she carried heavy loads. Practising her faith heroically in suffering, prayer and kindness, she merited the title "Lily of the Mohawks." She died at the age of 24, on April 17, 1680. Her practice of heroic virtue was recognized by the Sacred Congregation of Rites in 1943.

See *Positio of the Historical Section of the Sacred Congregation of Rites on the Introduction of the Cause for Beatification and Canonization and on the Virtues of the Servant of God, Katherine Tekakwitha, the Lily of the Mohawks* (1940). (J. V. J.)

**TEKIRDAG,** a town and capital of the *il* (province) of the same name in European Turkey, lies on the Sea of Marmara, 78 mi. (126 km.) W of Istanbul. Pop. (1965) 27,069. It is an important market centre for agricultural products. A main road links the town with the Istanbul-Uzunkopru railway at Muratli.

A Greek settlement founded probably in the 7th century B.C., the town was originally called Rhaedestus or Bisanthe, and later Rodosto. Since 1923 it has been officially known under its Turkish name of Tekirdag ("prince's hill"). Rodosto was for centuries the port of the Adrianople (Edirne) area, but its trade suffered when Alexandroupolis (Dedeagatch), on the Aegean Sea, became the terminus of the railway up the Maritsa River. The town was conquered by the Turks in 1360; it was occupied successively by the Russians (1877–78), the Bulgars (1912), and the Greeks (1920–22). The Greek church of Panagia Rheumatocratissa contains the graves, with Latin inscriptions, of Hungarians banished from their country early in the 18th century by the German captors of Buda. The population of Tekirdag in 1914 was estimated at 25,000, half of it Greek. In 1927, after the Greek-Turkish exchange of populations, Tekirdag had only 14,569 inhabitants. (N. Tu.; S. Er.; E. Tu.)

**TEKTITE,** the name given by F. E. Suess (from the Greek *tektos*, "melted"), for the natural glass objects found in various parts of the world and thought to be either meteorites or the result of impact on earth by meteorites, asteroids or comets. They range in weight from less than a gram to about eight kilograms and are of varied colour, shape and surface sculpture. Most are black, some are green, a few are yellow. Some are lustrous and some have a delicate sheen from minute alternating ridges and furrows which swirl over the entire surface, following the contorted internal structure. The younger, less-corroded tektites include spherical, elliptical, lenticular, teardrop, dumbbell, disk and button forms. They have been used as charms or amulets; and in folklore were regarded as an index of the richness of alluvial gold and tin deposits in which they are often found.

Tektites came to rest in groups at widely different times in the earth's history, with none arriving in between. Potassium-argon age dating suggests ages ranging from about 700,000 years old (Pleistocene tektites of Australia and southeast Asia) to about 34,000,000 years old (Texas tektites of the Eocene age). Stratigraphic evidence suggests that Australian tektites may be much younger than 700,000 years, and the Texas tektites may be as old as 45,000,000 years. They are known on every continent except Antarctica and South America and are usually given distinctive names according to where they are found. Among these names are moldavites (Bohemia), australites, billitonites and javanites (Indonesia), indochinites, philippinites, bediasites (Texas), Darwin glass (Tasmania) and Libyan desert glass. They are known from the Ivory Coast and Georgia (U.S.). The americanites from Colombia and Peru, originally believed to be tektites, are now known to be volcanic glass. The button form of australite, showing two periods of melting, furnishes strong evidence that tektites came from outside the atmosphere. Such a form can be explained only if a sphere of glass plunged into our atmosphere. It would melt on the forward side, the area of greatest friction, but as the fragment slowed, some melt would flow toward the lee and curl to form a flange. There is equally strong evidence that most tektites formed from soil and sedimentary rocks like those on earth. Sand-size glass particles in tektites, identified by Virgil E. Barnes as lechatelierite (fused quartz), have a consistent earthly counterpart only in the quartz of sandy and shaly sedimentary rocks and soil (*see* SILICA: *The Silica Minerals*). Chemically, tektites are more closely related to sandy and shaly sedimentary rocks than to any other rock group. Because of this G. Linck believed tektites came from another planet blanketed by sedimentary rocks.

In 1962 it was found that puddlelike deposits of layered indochinites in Southeast Asia are related in their gross chemical aspects both to the associated soil and underlying sedimentary rock, and to splash-form indochinites. A growing volume of isotopic and other chemical data also support the origin of tektites mostly from soil. Detrital quartz grains, identical in size and shape to those in the soil and sedimentary rock on which tektites rest, have been identified in layered tektites from Thailand. Some of these quartz grains were altered to coesite, one of the high-density forms of silica produced by high pressure. Coesite (*q.v.*) is found in association with meteorite impact craters.

L. J. Spencer thought tektites might be formed from meteorite impacts on earth. Harold C. Urey in 1955 suggested that the impacting bodies might be asteroids, but in 1957 proposed that shock waves from comets might be a more logical means for their formation. If the button form was produced by impact or shock waves, then molten glass must have been ejected beyond the atmosphere to solidify, before plunging back into the atmosphere.

*See* also METEORITES: *Glass Meteorites;* GEOCHEMISTRY: *Meteorites and Geochemistry.* (V. E. B.)

**TEL AVIV-JAFFA,** a twin city of Israel on the Mediterranean Sea, 47 mi. (76 km.) NW of Jerusalem by road, is the communications and commercial centre of the country and also a principal cultural centre. Jaffa (Yafo, Japho, Joppa, [*q.v.*]) is an ancient port, dating back possibly to 2000 B.C.; Tel Aviv is a new creation founded in 1909 by Zionist settlers on the sand dunes north of Jaffa. In the British mandate period (1923–48) there were two municipalities, but in 1950 Jaffa was incorporated with Tel Aviv. The combined population (1969 est.) was more than 400,000. The municipalities of Ramat Gan, Holon, and Bnei Brak are satellite towns; the total population is more than 750,000.

The principal streets of Tel Aviv are Allenby Road (1918), running from the city centre toward the shore, and a series running south to north parallel with the shore, the chief being Yarkon, Eliezer Ben-Yehuda, Dizengoff, and the Rothschild Boulevard. The town has constantly extended northward and nearly half the municipal area is now north of the Yarkon River, which in the mandate period was the boundary. In Arab Jaffa the main streets were Butros (Peter), close to the seashore, and King George V Avenue (now Jerusalem Boulevard), laid out in 1927 to link the suburbs of the two towns. Important buildings in Jaffa are the municipality and the district government offices, damaged in the War of Independence, the Russian Orthodox Church, St. Peter's Monastery (Franciscan), and the English church. In Tel Aviv the Great Synagogue, the chief banks and commercial buildings are in Allenby Street. There are more than 400 synagogues (many are just rooms) in the municipal area.

The original nucleus of Tel Aviv was the Herzlia *Gymnasium,* the Hebrew secondary school. The original Museum of Art was the house of Meir Dizengoff, the first mayor. Beside it a new art gallery, bearing the donor's name, Helena Rubinstein, was dedicated in 1959 in the civic centre, which also includes a concert hall; the Temple of Culture, built in 1957; and the Habima (*q.v.*) Theatre, home of the national dramatic company, opened in 1945. The Mograbi Cinema was formerly the principal auditorium for operas and concerts. In a northern suburb rises a vast pile, the offices of the Labour Federation (Histadrut). Near it are the centre of the Zionist Organization of America and a journalists' and writers' club. Most of the country's daily newspapers and periodicals are published in the town. The parks are small since, before the establishment of the state, Tel Aviv was congested because of the great cost of land. A school of law and economics, established with municipal help in the Mandate period, in 1959 became a branch of the Hebrew University of Jerusalem, to be eventually transferred to the University of Tel Aviv. The university has opened its own faculties of law and the social sciences as well as of the humanities and science, medicine and the Fine Arts. It is growing rapidly and by the early 1970s had more than 9,000 undergraduate students. The Labour Federation is active in promoting adult education, and maintains two residential colleges and an Afro-Asian institute with courses in economic and social sciences for students from Africa and Asia. There are also an academy of music, teachers' training colleges, and a broadcasting and television station.

The main urban and interurban transport service is provided by buses run by cooperative societies. Service taxis (Sherut), in which the passenger pays for a seat, ply along the main thoroughfares and also between the towns. There are two railway stations: one in the northern outskirts for the line to Haifa; the other near the commercial centre, connecting with Lydda (Lod) and Jerusalem. Tel Aviv is the centre of the road system of the whole country. The combined port of Jaffa and Tel Aviv, formed after the state was established, was closed in 1965, except for fishing vessels. The main industry since the establishment of the state has been construction. There are no heavy industries, but light industries of many kinds flourish—textile, furniture, foodstuffs, pharmaceutical. Tel Aviv is the principal banking and insurance centre of Israel. Citrus fruit from the southern region is the main export, but most of the fruit is exported through Haifa.

For the history of the city, *see* JOPPA. (No. B.)

**TELEGRAPH** (Gr. *tele,* "far"; *graphein,* "to write"), a system of communication at a distance through the medium of electromagnetic phenomena, in which the information transmitted is in (or may signify) written, printed or pictorial form.

The evolution of telegraphy may be traced from the signaling methods and codes of the ancient and primitive peoples to the visual system of Claude Chappe and thence with the growth of scientific knowledge to the first commercial application of electricity and magnetism to the "electric telegraph." Development in the mid-19th century provided the public with the only rapid means of communication until the advent of the telephone, which led to a continuous decline of public telegraph traffic within national boundaries during the 20th century. However, the continued development of telegraph technique evinced particularly in the teleprinter and improved transmission methods has enabled operation to be delegated to its users in certain fields. Public exchange service that gives direct printing communication between subscribers nationally and internationally is increasing rapidly. Many organizations—commercial, transportation, press and government—operate private networks for their internal business traffic. The high information density that can be carried telegraphically and the overwhelming value of the printed record provide a service that cannot be given by the telephone. *See* also FACSIMILE TRANSMISSION.

This article, which traces the development of telegraphy, is divided into the following sections:

I. Historic Telegraphs
II. Direct-Current Transmission Circuits
III. Telegraph Codes
IV. Machine Telegraphs; Exploitation of Circuit Capability
V. Printing Telegraphs
VI. Line Plant
VII. Transmission Theory
VIII. Telegraph Switching
IX. Submarine Telegraphy
X. Radio

## I. HISTORIC TELEGRAPHS

**Pith Ball and Spark.**—Sir William Watson in England demonstrated in 1747 that an electric current could be transmitted through a considerable length of wire using the earth for the completion of the circuit. In 1753 the first suggestion for an electrical telegraph was made in Scotland by an anonymous writer to *Scots Magazine,* signing himself C. M., who advised using an insulated wire for each letter of the alphabet. At the receiving end of each wire a pith ball was to be suspended above a piece of paper marked with an alphabetical letter. As a charge was sent along a given wire, the ball would attract the paper beneath it, and thus words could be spelled out. He further suggested that bells might be substituted for the papers, which could be struck in turn by a ball as a charge was sent along a wire. The idea was carried out by Georges Louis Lesage in Geneva in 1774, and similar telegraph systems were suggested by Bétancourt and Lomond in 1787. Then followed other suggestions using a separate wire for each letter, by Reusser, or Reisser, in 1794, and by Francisco Salvá in 1798; each of them proposed a system of visual telegraphy by causing a spark to appear at a gap at the receiving end of each wire as desired.

Sir Francis Ronalds worked a telegraph in England in 1816 with transmitting and receiving apparatus consisting of circular plates, on which were inscribed letters and figures. In front of each plate was a disk with an aperture which allowed one letter and its corresponding figure to be visible. The plates were rotated by clockwork regulated so that the same letter was displayed simultaneously at both ends. A crude electric machine charged the line when the sender desired, and the divergence of a pair of pith balls at the receiving end indicated to the operator that the letter or figure appearing at that moment was to be recorded.

Toward the end of the 18th century, Luigi Galvani and Alessandro Volta conducted experiments which revolutionized preconceived ideas of electricity and its effects. In 1786 Galvani accidentally discovered that it was possible to cause a direct or continuous flow of current along an electrical conductor by bringing two dissimilar metals into contact with a moist substance. In 1800 Volta introduced an electric battery which became known as the voltaic pile, the principles of which became embodied in the modern battery, and in that year Salvá demonstrated that voltaic currents could be used for transmitting signals.

**Electrolytic Telegraphs.**—An immediate result of the introduction of the voltaic pile was the discovery by William Nicholson and Sir Anthony Carlisle in 1800 that the passage of an electric current caused decomposition of liquids into their constituent elements.

Based on this principle Salvá in 1805 and Samuel Thomas von Soemmerring in 1809 introduced apparatus in which a voltaic pile was used for sending signals whose presence was indicated at the receiving end by the liberation of hydrogen. Later researches by Sir Humphry Davy on the decomposition of chemical compounds by electric current were applied in the United States to another type of telegraph by John Redman Coxe in 1816 and Harrison Gray Dyar in 1828. Both Coxe and Dyar operated a telegraph using the electric current to produce electrical decomposition at the end of the conductors. Dyar operated his telegraph line over 8 mi. on Long Island, using a single wire with ground return circuit to mark coded signals on a moving strip of litmus paper by discoloration from the received electric current.

**Electromagnetic Needle.**—At the beginning of the 19th century, a new set of ideas followed the introduction of the electromagnet. In 1819 Hans Christian Oersted discovered that a magnetic needle could be deflected from its normal position by passing a current through an adjacent wire and that the deflection was to the right or left, according to the direction of current. A year later Johann Salomo Christoph Schweigger found that the deflection of the needle could be increased by surrounding it with a number of turns of wire, and in 1825 William Sturgeon in England produced and named the electromagnet.

The action of the electric current on a magnet was first applied to telegraphy by André Marie Ampère in 1820, at the suggestion of Pierre Simon Laplace that the deflections of small magnets placed at the receiving ends of 26 wires could be used to indicate the letters of the alphabet. Ampère's apparatus was the pioneer of many needle instruments which came into existence between 1829 and 1841. The names of Carl Friedrich Gauss and Wilhelm Weber, Sir William Fothergill Cooke and Sir Charles Wheatstone, and the brothers Highton (Henry and Edward) are associated with some of the more important needle instruments.

In 1831 Joseph Henry (*q.v.*) constructed and successfully operated an electromagnetic signaling apparatus which consisted of a magnetized steel bar supported on a pivot in a horizontal position, which could be attracted by a magnet. When the magnet was energized by current the extremity of the bar was caused to strike a bell, and intelligence was conveyed by coded sound combinations.

Gauss and Weber conducted important experiments in 1833 on line conductors in which they demonstrated that the line conductor need not be insulated over its entire length. They used a single-needle telegraph to communicate with each other and proved that, by proper combination, five signs are sufficient for communication. In the early experiments of Cooke and Wheatstone, five wires and five needles were employed but later were reduced to one of each. In the single-needle instruments a magnetic needle was pivoted in the centre of a wire coil and intelligence was transmitted by deflecting it in accordance with a prearranged code.

The name of Samuel F. B. Morse, a U.S. artist and later professor of natural science at Yale university, is universally associated with the telegraph as result of his invention of the code bearing his name. From 1850 to the 1920s Morse was the code most generally used and, in its cable code form, is still in use. He is often credited with the invention of the telegraph on his return to the United States from a trip to Europe in 1832, during which he became acquainted with the works of Michael Faraday, but he definitely produced a telegraph instrument that was exhibited in 1837. The transmitter comprised a comb (or "portrule") with "teeth" spaced at intervals in conformity with a code. The comb was passed beneath a contact lever so that it made and broke an electric circuit. The pulses of current passed through an electromagnet, causing it to deflect a lever carrying a pencil, thus producing an undulating line on a paper tape moved by clockwork to record the signals received.

In a practical application of these ideas Alfred Vail, an associate of Morse, discarded the "portrule" in favour of a simple hand-operated contact lever or key, and it was later found that the signals could be reliably interpreted by ear from the sound of the movements of the electromagnet armature. Recording was also discarded, not to be revived until much later. After initial government support a full-scale demonstration between Washington, D.C., and Baltimore, Md., was given in 1844, but when this support was withdrawn other sources were enlisted to form a company in 1845.

In England public interest in Cooke's and Wheatstone's developments was growing in the same period, and the Electric Telegraph company was formed in 1845.

BY COURTESY OF (LEFT) EXCHANGE TELEGRAPH COMPANY, (RIGHT) SMITHSONIAN INSTITUTION

(LEFT) EARLY STOCK-MARKET TELEGRAPH PRINTER, 1873; (RIGHT) MORSE TELEGRAPH INSTRUMENT, 1837

## II. DIRECT-CURRENT TRANSMISSION CIRCUITS

**Simplex.**—The elementary telegraph circuit consists of a contact device (a "key," if hand operated) that makes and breaks the connection between a source of current (*e.g.*, a battery) and the line, according to the signaling code, and the pulses of current passing to the distant end of the line actuate the receiving device; *e.g.*, a "sounder" if aural reception is required. Alternate transmission of messages in both directions along the line may be made by suitable connections of instruments, and intermediate stations may be connected.

Two general schemes have been employed: in one, during the idle condition, no current flows in the line (fig. 1[A]); in the other, the closed-loop system, current flows in the line (fig. 1[B]). In the latter, as shown, a send-receive switch must be operated before sending can take place, but an alternative connection can be used in which the free contact of the transmitter can serve this purpose automatically.

Instead of single-current (on and off), double-current (current reversal) signaling may be used with definite advantage (fig. 2). Although it requires a polarized receiver (one sensitive to current direction rather than current strength), variations in line characteristics have less effect and entail less frequent adjustment of the receiver. At terminal stations a double battery

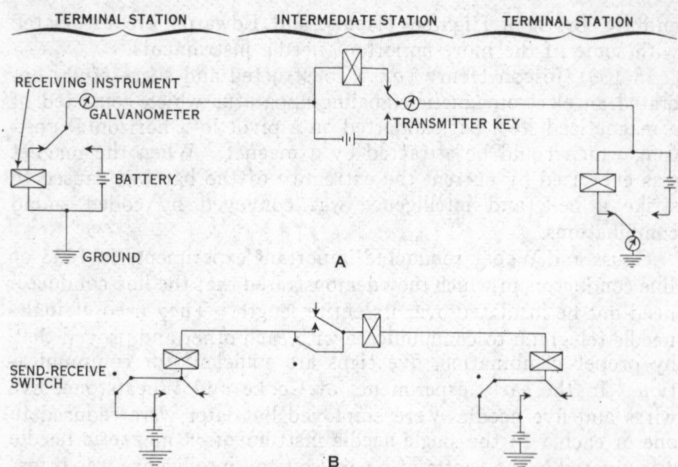


FIG. 1.—TWO SIMPLEX TRANSMISSION SCHEMES IN IDLE CONDITION: (A) SINGLE-CURRENT CIRCUIT, IN WHICH NO CURRENT IS FLOWING; (B) CLOSED-LOOP SYSTEM, IN WHICH CURRENT IS FLOWING

is usual, but at intermediate stations a single battery with a commutating key would be used.

**Duplex.**—The duplex scheme, permitting simultaneous transmission in both directions between two terminal stations, was first proposed in 1853 by Wilhelm Gintl. The principle is the interconnection of the transmitting and receiving devices with the line and a balancing network, so that the receiver is unaffected by the sending current from its own station but responds to the operation of the distant transmitter. It is usual for double-current signaling to be employed. The differential form (fig. 3)

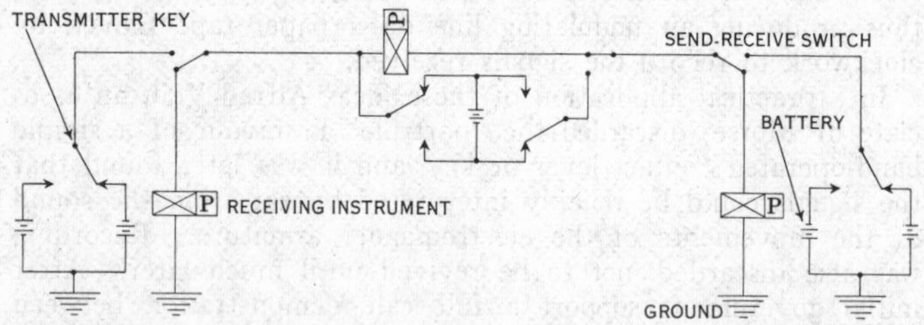


FIG. 2.—SIMPLEX CIRCUIT FOR DOUBLE-CURRENT (CURRENT-REVERSAL) SIGNALING

uses a receiver or relay with two identical windings connected so that the current from the transmitter divides to produce opposing magnetic effects, part flowing into the line and part into the balance or artificial line, which is adjusted so that the magnetic effects of the currents in the two paths balance to produce no resultant effect on the receiver. The changes in line current due to the action of the distant transmitter produce an unbalanced effect in the windings of the receiver, which responds accordingly. Bridge duplex (fig. 4) utilizes a receiver or relay with a single

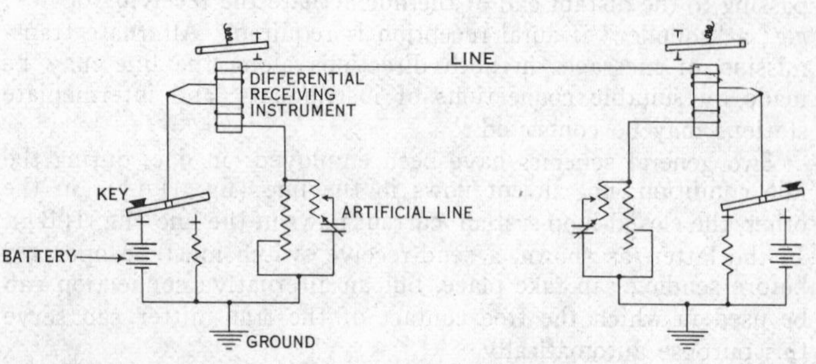


FIG. 3.—DIFFERENTIAL DUPLEX CIRCUIT

winding connected across one diagonal of a Wheatstone bridge circuit formed by two equal impedances, the line and the artificial line. When the artificial line is accurately adjusted to simulate the electrical characteristics of the line, the operation of the transmitter, which is in the other diagonal of the bridge, produces no change in electrical potential across the receiver and hence no response.

**Quadruplex.**—To increase further the message capacity of a

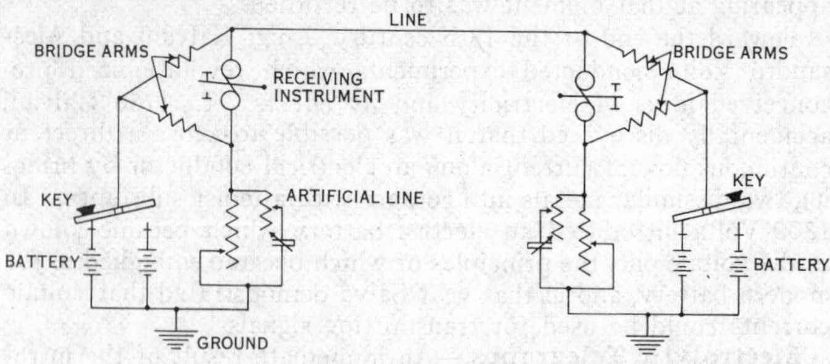


FIG. 4.—BRIDGE DUPLEX CIRCUIT

single telegraph circuit, Thomas A. Edison produced a combination of double-current and modified single-current duplex, providing for the transmission of two messages in each direction simultaneously. Two receiving devices are used, one polarized and responding to the direction of current, the other nonpolarized and responding to change in current magnitude irrespective of direction. With the development of other transmission methods, this system was discarded.

In modern practice, except for submarine cable usage, direct-current transmission is employed usually only over distances up to 100 mi. Both single- and double-current simplex methods are used in different areas of the world. With the single-current method, the closed-loop system, without send-receive switches and using a return conductor in place of earth, with one current source in the loop, is general. In the double-current method, the simple arrangement of two lines, one for each direction of transmission to avoid switching of transmitters and receivers and with no intermediate stations, is usual.

**Derived Circuits.**—Direct-current telegraph circuits may be derived from, and worked simultaneously with, telephone circuits by superposition. Superposing permits one ground-return telegraph circuit to be operated over the two wires forming a metallic-return telephone circuit. In a common form (fig. 5) a repeating coil or transformer is interposed at each terminal between the telephone apparatus and the line. The transformer winding which is connected to the line wires has a centre tap connected to the telegraph apparatus. By this arrangement the telegraph currents are divided, half passing over each wire; no effect is produced upon the telephone apparatus because, in dividing equally, the two halves neutralize each other's magnetic effect. The alternating currents of the speech transmission so traverse the line windings of the transformer as to cause the maximum magnetic effect and are thus repeated to the telephone apparatus.

**Telegraph Repeaters.**—With increasing length of a telegraph line, the received current becomes weakened so that eventually it will not operate the receiving device reliably. It was first appreciated by Edward Davy that a relay could be used to repeat signals from one line to another, the armature of an electromagnet operating contacts to send the signals anew with the original current strength. Hence by dividing a line into sections and inserting repeaters between each section, the signals can be re-

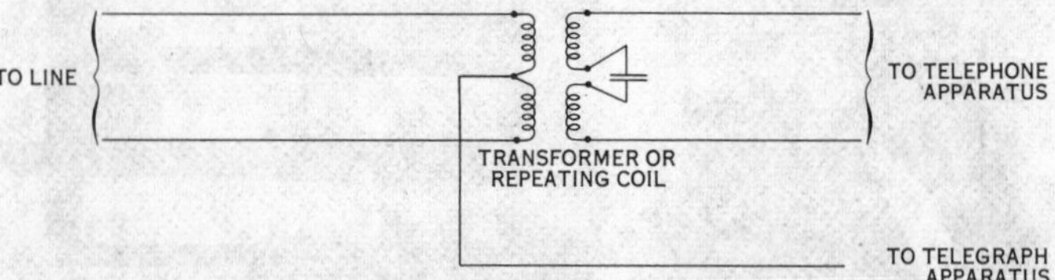


FIG. 5.—SIMPLEX CIRCUIT FOR TELEGRAPH TRANSMISSION ON TELEPHONE LINES

newed in magnitude before they deteriorate to an unusable level. In the direct-current transmission circuits described above, repeaters can be formed by making the receiving device a relay and connecting the armature or tongue to the adjacent line in place of the transmitter, the transmitting battery being connected appropriately. In the case of the closed-loop circuit, additional relays must be used in connections to prevent signals from being fed back into the line from which they were received.

Distortion of signals takes place in transmission such that, although they can be restored in magnitude by a relay, the relative timing of the signal elements is disturbed and retransmission over a further section would render them liable to faulty interpretation. In machine telegraph transmission at a regular speed, regenerative repeaters can be employed to receive and retransmit the signals with all the elements restored to a perfect time relationship. This is done by automatically examining the instantaneous condition of the incoming signal at unit element intervals in correct phase and maintaining this condition on the outgoing line until the next instant of examination.

## III. TELEGRAPH CODES

The best-known code is the Morse Code (fig. 6). It was the most generally used until about the mid-1920s and is still used in a modified form on some submarine cable systems and radiotelegraph circuits and in some situations where mobile stations with simple apparatus are required. The code comprises combinations of dots and dashes of one line condition (*e.g.*, current on) separated by periods of the other line condition (*e.g.*, current off); the duration of a dot is taken as one unit, that of a dash three units; the space between character components is one unit, between characters three units and between words six units (five for automatic transmission).

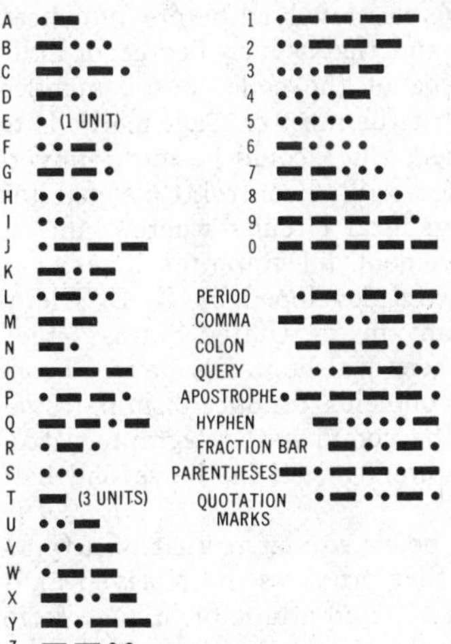

FIG. 6.—INTERNATIONAL MORSE CODE

Early machine telegraphs used an obvious code on the basis of one pulse for A, two for B and so on, but with the development of more sophisticated systems, the advantage of codes in which all character signals are of equal length became apparent, and J. M. E. Baudot applied the idea of Gauss and Weber of a five-unit code. This, with variations in the character allocations, became the most widely adopted by mid-20th century. Five units with two-condition signaling provide 32 permutations, sufficient for the Roman alphabet and (by using two permutations as case-shift signals) figures, punctuation signs and the control of certain essential mechanical functions of a printing receiver. For certain special applications, a six-unit code that avoids the use of case-shift signals is used.

Since all permutations of the five-unit code are significant, an error in the reception of any signal element will result in a wrong character being recorded. So that faulty reception can be detected, particularly after transmission over circuits liable to severe disturbance (*e.g.*, long-distance high-frequency radio), a seven-unit code was devised by J. B. Moore which permitted the detection of mutilation. In a modified form proposed by H. C. A. Van Duuren, its use rapidly spread (fig. 7). Seven units provide 128 permutations, only 35 of which are used to signify characters. Reception of any of the others indicates mutilation in transit. The 35 permutations possess the common characteristic of having three elements of one kind and four of the other.

## IV. MACHINE TELEGRAPHS; EXPLOITATION OF CIRCUIT CAPABILITY

With the commercial development of the telegraph in the late 1840s it became obvious that the manual sending methods of forming the code signals directly were unable to exploit the full capabilities of the transmission lines, and attention of many inventors was turned to increasing the speed of signaling and providing more convenient means of generating and recording signals.

**Wheatstone System.**—The Wheatstone system (1858) employed perforated tape to operate the transmitting mechanism, which was driven by clockwork and later by electric motor. The Morse signals were received by an "inker" in which an inked wheel marked the dots and dashes on a moving tape. When first brought into use in the 1860s the system was capable of about 70 words per minute, but by the early 1900s it had been developed to 300–400 words per minute.

| FIGURES | LETTERS | INTERNATIONAL TELEGRAPH ALPHABET NO.2 | | | | | VAN DUUREN 7-UNIT CODE | | | | | | |
|---|---|---|---|---|---|---|---|---|---|---|---|---|---|
| | | I | II | III | IV | V | I | II | III | IV | V | VI | VII |
| – | A | ● | ● | | | | | | ● | ● | | ● | |
| ? | B | ● | | | ● | ● | | | ● | ● | | | ● |
| : | C | | ● | ● | ● | | ● | | | ● | ● | | |
| W.R.U. | D | ● | | | ● | | | | ● | ● | ● | | |
| 3 | E | ● | | | | | | ● | ● | ● | | | |
| % | F | ● | | ● | ● | | | | ● | | | ● | ● |
| @ | G | | ● | | ● | ● | ● | ● | | | | | ● |
| £ | H | | | ● | | ● | ● | | ● | | | ● | |
| 8 | I | | ● | ● | | | ● | ● | ● | | | | |
| BELL | J | ● | ● | | ● | | | ● | | | | ● | ● |
| ( | K | ● | ● | ● | ● | | | | | ● | | ● | ● |
| ) | L | | ● | | | ● | ● | ● | | | | ● | |
| . | M | | | ● | ● | ● | ● | | ● | | | | ● |
| , | N | | | ● | ● | | ● | | ● | | ● | | |
| 9 | O | | | | ● | ● | ● | | | | ● | ● | |
| ϕ | P | | ● | ● | | ● | ● | | | ● | | ● | |
| 1 | Q | ● | ● | ● | | ● | | | | ● | ● | | ● |
| 4 | R | | ● | | ● | | ● | ● | | | ● | | |
| ' | S | ● | | ● | | | | ● | | ● | | ● | |
| 5 | T | | | | | ● | ● | | | | ● | | ● |
| 7 | U | ● | ● | ● | | | | ● | ● | | | ● | |
| = | V | | ● | ● | ● | ● | ● | | | ● | | | ● |
| 2 | W | ● | ● | | | ● | | ● | | | ● | | ● |
| / | X | ● | | ● | ● | ● | | | ● | | ● | ● | |
| 6 | Y | ● | | ● | | ● | | | ● | | ● | | ● |
| + | Z | ● | | | | ● | | ● | ● | | | | ● |
| CARR. RET. | | | | | ● | | ● | | | | | ● | ● |
| LINE FEED | | | ● | | | | ● | | ● | ● | | | |
| FIG. SHIFT | | ● | ● | | ● | ● | | ● | | | ● | ● | |
| LET. SHIFT | | ● | ● | ● | ● | ● | | | | ● | ● | ● | |
| SPACE | | | | ● | | | ● | ● | | ● | | | |
| UNP. TAPE | | | | | | | | | | | ● | ● | ● |
| SPECIAL COMBINATIONS | | | | | | | | | | | | | |
| RQ | | | | | | | | ● | ● | | ● | | |
| IDLE α (C.S.) | | | | | | | | ● | | ● | | | ● |
| IDLE β (C.M.) | | | | | | | | ● | | ● | ● | | |

FIG. 7.—FIVE-UNIT CODE AND SEVEN-UNIT ERROR-DETECTING CODE

Initially a knowledge of Morse code was necessary for the preparation of the transmitter tape, but later keyboard perforators were devised that perforated all the holes corresponding to a character on depression of the appropriate key. Further improvements to the system included receiving reperforators that reproduced the original tape, facilitating retransmission, and the Creed printer which translated from the perforated tape to printed characters. The system required groups of operators at each end to keep it fully loaded and was supplanted by more convenient multiplex systems. Nevertheless the system had a considerable life, even persisting on some radio circuits.

**Multiplex (Time Division).**—The alternative to a single high-speed communication is the division of the capability of the circuit among several operators, allocating a channel to each. This can be effected by allotting connection to the transmission line cyclically to each operator for a given period; *e.g.*, one character (character interlacing) or one element (element interlacing). At the receiving end of the circuit the individual receiving devices are similarly connected in cyclic order so that they record the appropriate signals.

Systems on this principle had been proposed by Wheatstone and Moses G. Farmer. A certain amount of development was done by A. J. Meyer and P. B. Delaney, but J. M. E. Baudot produced the first successful system using a five-unit code and printing receivers. The principle is illustrated in fig. 8. The "clock" determining the period and sequence per channel and code element comprises a mechanical distributor in which an arm rotating with uniform speed connects the line sequentially to segments of a conducting ring that are connected to a battery through keys set to the code permutation.

After the transmission of one character, the permutation is changed in time for the next revolution, while the other channels are being dealt with. A similar distributor at the receiving station connects the receiving devices synchronously in similar sequence but with an appropriate time lag according to the signal propagation time. Special devices are used for maintaining accurate synchronism and correct phase between sending and receiving distributors. In the original system the code keys were operated directly, but in later usage perforated tape and automatic tape readers were introduced. Speeds of up to 6 × 40 words per minute were achieved.

Systems based on the Baudot were used extensively on land lines until the late 1930s and are still used on submarine cables. They are also used on radiotelegraph links because synchronous operation affords a protective feature to transmission accuracy. Later developments in this field are leading to the obsolescence

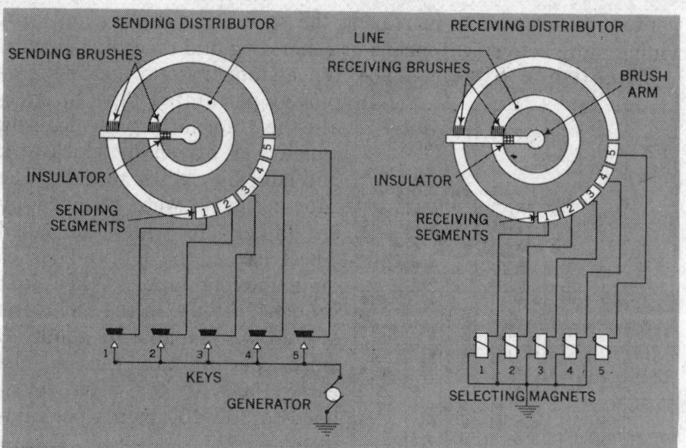


FIG. 8.—DISTRIBUTOR SYSTEM (BAUDOT) FOR MULTIPLEX TRANSMISSION

of the electromechanical distributor; electronic oscillators and pulse distributors, with no moving parts, provide the clock system for the sequential interconnection of the circuit elements.

**Multichannel Carrier Systems (Spectrum-Division Multiplex).**—Toward the end of the 19th century proposals were made to use tones of different frequency or pitch to carry telegraph code signals. Experimental systems by E. Gray and E. J. P. Mercadier proved unsatisfactory and it was not until further developments, particularly the thermionic valve, that practical systems were evolved toward the end of the 1920s. The principle of a carrier system is that, in place of a direct current, an alternating current is used to carry the code signals. This may be done by varying the amplitude of the carrier (*e.g.*, switching on and off), changing the frequency (frequency modulation, FM) or changing the phase of the carrier (PM). Each of a number of different frequencies can carry a separate telegraph signal, the spacing of the frequencies depending upon the required speed of transmission. Each channel is controlled by an independent transmitter, and the outputs are connected to the common transmission line through electrical filters to prevent mutual interference. At the receiving station each channel is filtered out separately, and an amplifier-detector terminating in a relay reproduces a D.C. code signal for the operation of the receiving instrument.

The spacing of channels is standardized at 120 cycles per second (c.p.s.) for 66 words per minute teleprinter operation, and systems of 12, 18 and 24 channels are usual. In the United States 150- and 170-c.p.s. spacings are used and the speed is generally 60 words per minute, but later systems are capable of 100 words per minute; the number of channels varies up to 16. The range of frequencies is usually restricted to those of speech, and telephone circuits or carrier channels (on line or microwave radio) are used as the transmission path.

In Europe the majority of systems use amplitude modulation, while in the United States some of the original AM systems have been replaced by FM systems. The use of phase modulation involves some technical complexities and is not generally used.

Voice-frequency multichannel transmission by mid-20th century had become the most widely used method of providing main telegraph links and was extending into the field of intercontinental line communications. Multichannel systems are also applied to radiotelegraph routes. These are generally of the frequency-shift variety of modulation, which is less susceptible to the effects of noise and fading encountered on long-distance radio circuits.

## V. PRINTING TELEGRAPHS

The earliest printing telegraphs were worked on the step-by-step principle in which a type wheel with characters evenly spaced around its circumference is advanced by an electromagnet and ratchet one character for each current impulse received from the line. Trains of impulses caused the type head to rotate from one character to the next one; on cessation of the pulses a paper tape was brought into contact with the inked type at the printing position. This was a development from the Wheatstone ABC in which the characters were only indicated on a dial. Such systems were used for many years for stock exchange quotation telegraphs. The major drawback was the liability of the type head to get "out of step" due to interfering currents in the line, and means had to be provided to rotate the type wheel to a known position periodically.

An improvement on this system was produced by D. E. Hughes. The type head rotated continuously in synchronism with a distributor at the sending end, and operation of a piano-type keyboard caused a current impulse to be emitted at a point in the revolution corresponding to the chosen character. This, at the receiver, caused a paper strip to be brought momentarily in contact with the type wheel as the corresponding type passed the printing point. Speeds of up to 60 words per minute could be achieved by skilled operators, and this system persisted on some European circuits until the 1930s.

The Baudot multiplex system used printing receivers working with a five-unit code. Five levers, set in alternative positions by electromagnets, respond to the element signals and, when these coincide with a series of notches in a disk carried by the continuously rotating type-head shaft, a printing hammer automatically brings paper tape in contact with the inked type.

**Teleprinters.**—Until the 1920s the successful printing telegraph systems involved at some point in the system continuous synchronism of sending and receiving apparatus, which meant that a skilled setting-up procedure was involved before full-speed communication could take place and that a high degree of skill, including in some cases knowledge of the code, was demanded of operators. This restricted use of the most efficient methods to main lines. Methods were pursued which could be more universally applied and would demand less skilled control, thus enabling printing telegraphs to be used on local circuits where traffic is intermittent. To meet this requirement, telegraph machines (*i.e.*, teleprinters or teletypewriters) were developed by E. E. Kleinschmidt and the Morkrum company in the United States, Creed and company in England and Siemens-Halske in Germany. From the mid-1940s other European countries produced similar machines. The teleprinter became the commonest telegraph instrument, and hundreds of thousands were in use in the second half of the 20th century.

The teleprinter comprises a keyboard similar to that of a typewriter and a printing mechanism that produces the received message either as a continuous line of type on a tape or in page form on a continuous roll of paper. The motive power is provided by an electric motor running at a controlled speed, but the mechanisms are coupled to it by clutches that are brought into operation automatically only when required.

The depression of a key of the keyboard causes each of a set of five bars to take up one of two positions according to the five-unit code permutation representing the character and also engages the clutch of the transmitting mechanism for the period of trans-

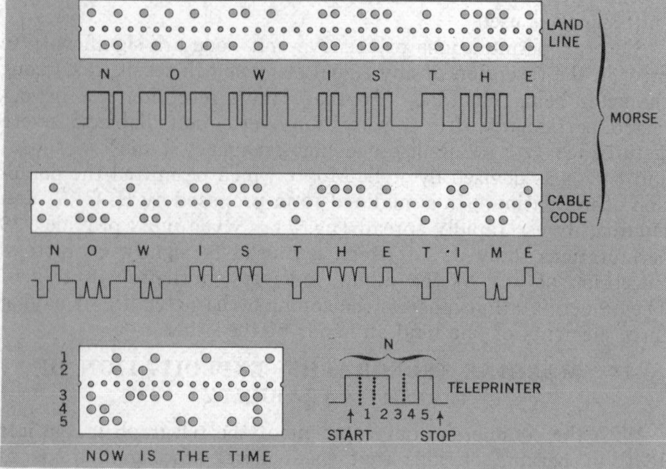


FIG. 9.—PERFORATED TAPES FOR AUTOMATIC TRANSMISSION AND SIGNAL CURRENT WAVE FORMS

mission of the individual character. A cam assembly permits a contact or contacts to be operated at discrete intervals in accordance with the setting of the permutation bars to form the code signal transmitted to line. The five-unit code signal is always preceded by a start element and succeeded by a minimum period of the rest condition (1–1½ units in duration), hence this code is often termed a seven-unit start-stop code.

The received signals operate the teleprinter via an electromagnet. The first motion of the electromagnet armature engages the clutch of the mechanism, and at the mid-instants of the code elements the position of the armature is recorded by mechanical store elements, which are linked to the printing mechanism in one of several possible ways.

In one way, latches are selected to halt a rotating type head at the appropriate position; in others the positioning of slotted combination bars enable individual type bars, as in a typewriter, to be brought into action, or a rectangular type box is displaced according to the mechanical addition of the displacements of the storage elements. Since the receiver is started for the reception of each character, slight speed differences from the transmitter do not produce an accumulative phase error leading to malreception.

Teleprinters are capable of speeds of 60–100 words per minute and can be operated by competent typists. Where the utmost use of the line capability is desired, an automatic tape transmitter can be used in place of the keyboard. Receiving reperforators may be used, with or without printing, where retransmission over another circuit is necessary, to avoid rekeying the message.

## VI. LINE PLANT

Bare wires were used as line conductors as early as 1816. In that year, Francis Ronalds demonstrated a telegraph system that employed a bare wire covered with glass tubing impregnated with pitch and buried in the ground. However, for reasons of economy, the early commercial telegraphs were operated with bare wires supported overhead on poles. This open-wire pole-line construction was generally used thereafter, and even after the middle of the 20th century still constituted a large portion of outside telegraph plant. Cables, which are groups of insulated wire held together by a common cover or sheath, were introduced early in the century to a limited extent, and their utilization, both aerially suspended and underground, greatly increased thereafter. Open-wire pole-line construction and suspended aerial cable are commonly used in open country, but as telegraph lines approach congested areas, underground cables are generally used. Underground cable is also used almost exclusively for local distribution within a congested area.

**Overhead Lines.**—Poles used for supporting wires and cables are usually of wood, although steel and concrete poles are sometimes used. In open-wire construction the bare line wires are supported on insulators, usually of glass or rubber, mounted on pins set vertically in wooden crossarms. In general, bare copper wires are used, ordinarily about 0.114 in. in diameter, weighing 210 lb. per mile, or 0.104 in. in diameter, weighing 172 lb. per mile. Other sizes are employed to a limited extent, and wires of galvanized iron, bronze and other materials have been used with considerable success. Cables, when placed on poles, are supported by suspension strands, consisting of high-strength stranded wires. The weight of the cable to be supported determines the strength of suspension strands used, the heavier cables requiring strands having a strength exceeding 18,000 lb. Cables are fastened to the suspension strands by various means, and the suspension strands are fastened to the poles by small metal clamps.

Conductors in cables designed for telegraph service are of soft drawn copper varying in diameter from 0.036 in. to 0.102 in. Ordinarily, cable conductors are separated and insulated by paper wrapped spirally about them, although cables having rubber-insulated conductors are often used for short distances. The insulated conductors are arranged in pairs which consist of two conductors twisted together or in quads consisting of two pairs twisted together, or four wires in spiral form. These pairs and quads are arranged compactly in layers. Paper insulated conductors are enclosed in a lead sheath, while rubber-covered conductors may be enclosed in lead or a covering of heavy braid. The number of conductors provided in telegraph cables varies, the largest in common use in the early 1960s being 404 pairs. The outside diameter of this cable is 2⅝ in. and the weight 7¾ lb. per foot.

**Underground Construction.**—Where cables are placed underground within a city, some form of conduit with independent duct space for each cable is usually employed to permit the cables to be readily installed and removed. The ducts are usually of hollow tile, creosoted wood or fibre. Iron pipe may be used in special situations. All ducts are three inches or more in diameter, and the conduit is buried at least two feet deep. As the length of cable which can be pulled through a duct is limited, splicing chambers or manholes are provided at intervals of about 500 ft. These manholes are at least 3 ft. wide, 5 ft. long and 4½ ft. deep, and in many cases considerably larger sizes are required. They are usually constructed of brick or concrete with a removable cover.

Cable is pulled into conduits one length at a time, and the ends are spliced together. In splicing paper-insulated cables, a foot or more of sheath is removed from the end and a few inches of the insulation is removed from the conductors. Conductors are then joined by twisting, soldering or other means, and the joints are insulated with small paper or impregnated cotton tubes. After all conductors are joined, the splice is wrapped with strips of muslin and a lead sleeve slipped over it. This sleeve is held at each end to the cable sheath by means of wiped soldered joints.

Where cables are laid underground in open country, it is feasible to bury such cables directly in the ground without conduit protection. Large machines prepare a trench, lay the cable and cover the trench in a single operation.

**Submarine Cable.**—In submarine cable the conductor is made of copper, stranded or having a central wire surrounded by strips wound spirally. Over this is molded the insulation. Formerly gutta percha was almost universally employed for the insulator, but deproteinized rubber, both natural and synthetic, later competed successfully with gutta percha, while polyethylene bid fair to supplant both of them. Continuous inductance loading in the form of a thin ribbon or thread of highly permeable nickel-iron alloy wound around the conductor greatly increased the speed at which the later cables could be worked. To protect the insulation at depths where marine borers are found a brass tape is wound around it. Next comes a cushion of jute yarns upon which the spirally wound armour, or sheathing wires, rests. In the deeper portions of the ocean galvanized high-tensile steel wires are used, sometimes individually covered by tarred cotton tape or braid. As the depth decreases these are replaced by galvanized wrought-iron wires of larger size, and the armour gradually is increased in size and weight until, near the shore, a double layer is used. The added protection is necessary to prevent damage from anchors, trawler fishing gear, chafing against rocks and, in northern latitudes, ice. An outer double wrapping of tarred jute yarn or jute tape steeped in a compound of tar and pitch further preserves the armour from corrosion. The outside diameter of the ordinary deep-sea type of cable is about one inch, and the weight in air about two tons per nautical mile. The shore-end types run as large as 3½ in. in diameter and weigh as much as 30 tons per nautical mile.

## VII. TRANSMISSION THEORY

In a direct-current telegraph circuit the transmitted signal can be considered as a sequence of similar rectangular pulses of potential applied at time intervals that are multiples of the duration of the shortest code element, as in the example in fig. 10(A). Analysis of the elementary pulse wave form into sine wave components by Fourier's method shows that it contains a band of frequencies ranging from zero to infinity; the relative magnitudes are indicated in fig. 10 (B). If the duration of the element pulse is $T$ seconds ($T$ might be 0.02 sec. in teleprinter operation), there will be no components at precisely $\frac{1}{T}$, $\frac{2}{T}$, $\frac{3}{T}$, c.p.s. When a particular pattern of pulses of duration $nT$ seconds is continuously repeated, the components become concentrated at frequencies that are multiples of $\frac{1}{nT}$, but the relative magnitudes are still bounded by the fundamental curve. As an example, if the signal is a repeated train of Morse dots, $n = 2$ and the component frequencies are $\frac{1}{2T}, \frac{3}{2T}, \frac{5}{2T}, \ldots$ c.p.s.; *i.e.*, the fundamental plus the odd harmonics of the dot frequency (fig. 10[C]).

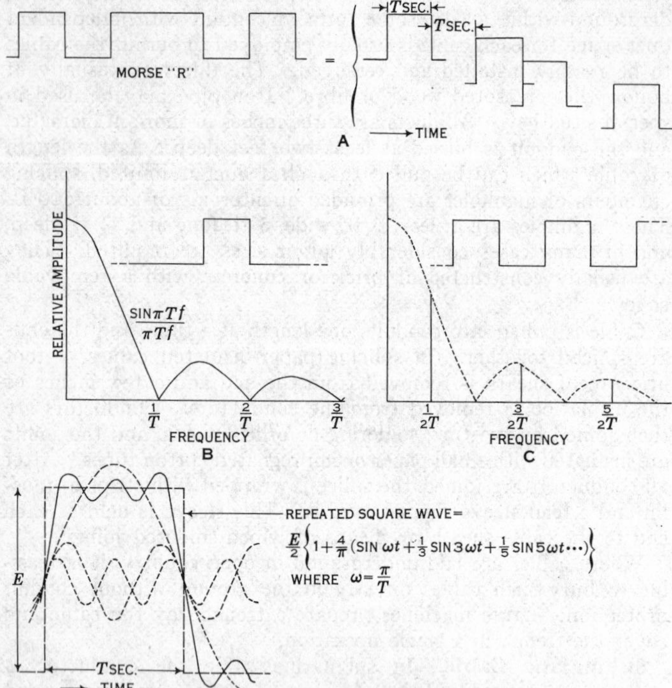


FIG. 10.—EXAMPLES OF TELEGRAPH TRANSMISSION WAVE FORMS (*see* TEXT). ($E$ = VOLTAGE)

This may be more readily appreciated by reference to fig. 10(D), which illustrates how the combination of the first three components begins to approximate to the rectangular wave form.

To reproduce the signal wave form completely at the receiver, it would be necessary for the telegraph line to transmit all the frequency components without change of relative amplitude and phase, but in practice this is unnecessary. The energy conveying the essential message is concentrated in the lower part of the frequency spectrum, and the higher-frequency components may be discarded without destroying the message. Excellent operation can be obtained when the circuit reduces frequencies corresponding to $\frac{0.8}{T}$ c.p.s. to one-half of their original amplitude relative to the fundamental component and the response at frequencies of $\frac{3}{2T}$ c.p.s. is negligible. However, on local lines where the transmission capability is more than adequate, it is usual to transmit a frequency range including $\frac{3}{2T}$ c.p.s., to permit less critical adjustment of apparatus.

In carrier transmission, there is a similar distribution of signal energy with respect to frequency in side bands symmetrically located about the carrier frequency, the lower side band being a mirror image of the upper one. Hence the frequency band width required is double that for direct-current transmission.

The energy of the signal is dissipated in transmission to an extent dependent on the resistance, capacitance, inductance and leakance of the line. The effects of capacitance and inductance increase with frequency but have some opposing characteristics. The inherent characteristics of telegraph cables are such that the resistance and capacitance preponderate, so by artificially increasing the inductance (*i.e.*, "loading" the cable), by the insertion of inductor coils at uniform distances or by wrapping the conductor with magnetic material, the dissipation of the higher frequencies can be reduced and a higher speed of operation obtained. Even with this, the relative magnitudes of the various frequency components have to be modified to the correct proportions by inserting at the sending or receiving end (or both) of the line correcting devices or equalizers with frequency responses that compensate for those of the line.

The transmission path may be subject to interfering currents from various sources; *e.g.*, induction from other telegraph systems, power supply systems, stray currents from traction systems or varying earth potentials due to changes in the earth's field. The magnitude of interfering currents limits the speed of operation on a long cable because the higher frequencies required are severely reduced in magnitude and the signals become too deformed to be interpreted correctly.

**Telegraph Distortion.**—The perfect telegraph signal changes its condition according to the code at predetermined intervals of time. In the course of transmission it is restricted in frequency range, either purposely to prevent the higher frequencies from interfering with other channels in a multichannel system or incidentally by the line characteristics, so that the transitions from one condition to the other are not abrupt but occur in a finite time. The receiving instrument or relay is operated from one condition to the other when the received current attains certain values. If there are no interfering currents, the transmitting path is conveying the currents of various frequencies in the correct relationships and the relay is adjusted to the correct operating values, the signal will be perfectly reproduced (assuming a perfect transmitter) with the transitions taking place at the prescribed intervals. But if interference is present these currents will increase, or decrease, the signal received and the relay operating currents will be attained at other instants. Similar displacements in time of the relay operations will ensue if the relay is maladjusted or the line is incapable of transmitting the required range of frequencies in their proper relationship. If the telegraph distortion (time aberration of the signal) is too great, the margin (maximum acceptable distortion) of the receiver will be exceeded and confusion with other code signals will ensue.

## VIII. TELEGRAPH SWITCHING

Communication between a large number of stations requires either direct lines from each to every other one or means of transferring messages from one line to another at central points. Stations can be grouped around different centres and distant traffic concentrated to use intercentre lines at higher efficiency. In the early days of telegraphy, the only means of handling messages between widely separated points was to record them at intermediate points and retransmit them on the next stage of the route. About the beginning of the 20th century exchanges were brought into use in large cities for the manual interconnection by means of switchboards of local lines using hand-speed Morse, but the diversity of methods and speeds used on long-distance lines dictated the continuance of the employment of operators at long-distance centres, which persisted at places dealing with international traffic to the late 1950s.

The successful introduction of telegraph exchanges awaited the development of a standardized telegraph machine and cheaper telegraph circuits, which eventuated as the teleprinter and multichannel carrier systems.

**Teleprinter Manual Switching.**—In the early 1930s a few European countries introduced subscriber exchange service, Telex, for teleprinters, using single-channel voice-frequency signaling, over the public telephone networks. In the second part of the decade this service was extended internationally. During World War II the development of teleprinter communication proceeded rapidly on both sides; large manually switched networks were put into operation using separate telegraph circuits comprising multichannel systems on main routes and direct-current signaling on local circuits. In the United States the extensive exchange system (TWX) was based on a line system using derived direct-current circuits and multichannel carrier.

The switchboard closely resembles a telephone manual switchboard in which lines terminate in jacks (sockets) that are interconnected as desired by flexible conductor cords terminating in plugs. The operator, of course, communicates with the subscribers by teleprinter.

**Teleprinter Automatic Switching.**—The desire for further reduction of human intervention in telegraphs led to automatic switching on principles similar to those for telephony. Systems were designed during the mid-1930s and in fact introduced to a limited extent in Germany before World War II. Introduction elsewhere in Europe was delayed until the late 1940s and '50s. In some countries the operator is provided with a dial, like that of an automatic telephone, for setting up a connection; in others the called number is sent from the keyboard, and apparatus at the exchange converts the signals to pulses for operating the switches. Special signals are sent back for indications of "engaged," "line out of order," "number unobtainable," etc., to be printed. On receipt of a call the teleprinter is automatically started and sends its own number automatically to confirm the connection to the caller.

**Reperforator Switching.**—The systems of switching so far mentioned provide both-way communication (but not necessarily simultaneously) by direct line connection between two stations. However, flexibility in message handling can be achieved by semiautomatic or automatic means in which the message is received as perforated tape in the exchange and then retransmitted over an appropriate outgoing line to the recipient or the next switching centre en route. The idea of tape relay systems led in the late 1930s to the development of the printing reperforator by which the message is simultaneously typed on the tape as it is perforated. In the first systems, operators read the address from the tape which was torn off on completion of the message and transferred it to the appropriate position in the office, where it was sent onward with an automatic transmitter. This system was further developed so that the receiving operator could place the message tape in one of an adjacent group of autotransmitters and connect that automatically to the required outgoing line by pressing the appropriate one of a group of buttons controlling relay switching apparatus. By the mid-1950s fully automatic tape relay was achieved. In this, the originating operator sends route code letters at the head of the message. The code letters are sensed automatically following reperforation and interpreted by a director that automatically sets up connections through the exchange and causes the message to be retransmitted at high speed to a reperforator and associated retransmitter, from where it is sent out on the next section of its route. If lines are busy at any stage in the process, the message is kept stored in the perforated tape.

**Applications.**—In the early 1960s the use of switching systems was extensive and extending rapidly to reduce the labour costs of human handling. Europe generally appeared to favour the line-switching technique for the public services, both Telex and ordinary telegrams, and automation proceeded. Private networks operated by public utilities and business concerns for communication between head and branch offices and factories, etc., employed various of the systems described.

United States practice followed two distinct patterns. The subscriber service (TWX) was, necessarily, a line-switching system, but the public telegraph service (Western Union Telegraph Company) developed on a message-switching basis, due largely to the economic relationship between costs of station apparatus and transmission channels where great interurban distances are involved. There were also many large private networks.

Military organizations of nations with overseas bases operated world-wide systems in which message switching was employed. Trunk circuits were carried by cable and radio.

## IX. SUBMARINE TELEGRAPHY

Except for a few river and harbour cables, the first submarine cable was that laid in 1850 between England and France. It was broken shortly after communication had been established but was successfully followed the next year by another, between Dover and Calais. The first transatlantic attempt in 1857 was a failure when the cable broke at 2,000 fathoms' depth during laying and could not be recovered. However, the Atlantic was spanned in 1858 between Ireland and Newfoundland. After a few weeks the cable's insulation failed, and it had to be abandoned. It was 1866 before the first permanently successful transatlantic cable was laid. In the same year another cable, partially laid in 1865, was also completed. These two, with which the U.S. financier Cyrus Field and the British scientist Lord Kelvin were closely associated, were the only transatlantic cables until 1869, when the French laid a cable. In the following 60 years, the earth-encircling telegraph cable network became fully established, and no new long-distance routes were established afterward.

The principle of inductive loading proposed by Oliver Heaviside in 1887 was applied to some short cables at the turn of the century, but it was not until the 1920s, when improved magnetic alloys became available, that it could be applied economically to very long cables. Even so, only a few long telegraph cables (across the Atlantic and Pacific oceans) are of this type. Advances in utilization were chiefly due to improvements in the cable apparatus.

**Sending.**—Originally, except for the attempt to use printing telegraphs on the first cross-channel cable, hand-speed Morse operation was used. Due to the lack of knowledge about methods of equalizing the transmission of the various frequency components of signals in the early days, the long and short elements of the code suffered appreciable distortion, and the cable-code method which uses equal length pulses of opposite polarity for dots and dashes was used. It was also found advantageous to apply short reversed periods of opposite polarity following each code element ("curbing"). Except for relatively short cables, it was not found satisfactory to use five-unit code until it was introduced by the U.S. companies on transatlantic loaded cables. Other operators maintained the use of cable code chiefly because of large investment in extensive systems of chains of interconnected cables.

Hand sending with the double key in cable code was superseded by the automatic transmitter modified from the Wheatstone machine by two French engineers, Belz and Brahic, in 1879, which used a perforated tape. Later, as techniques for reception improved and higher speeds became possible, multiplex operation was introduced.

**Receiving.**—Due to the characteristics of long submarine cables and the requirement to extract the greatest speed from an expensive channel of communication, the received currents are very feeble, often effectively only of the order of ten microamperes. This necessitates much more sensitive apparatus than that employed on land lines. The earliest specialized instrument was the mirror galvanometer of W. Thomson (later Lord Kelvin) by which the signals were read as deflections of a reflected spot of light on a scale; this was used on the first Atlantic cable. In 1867 Thomson produced the siphon recorder, in which an ink siphon is harnessed to the moving coil of the galvanometer so that the signals are recorded as an undulating line on paper tape. With the development of sensitive relays more robust recording instruments could be employed and receiving reperforators appeared about 1900. This greatly facilitated retransmission at intermediate stations. In the early 1920s the invention of the Creed Morse printer provided the next step of translation from the perforated tape. About ten years later a direct printer which could cope with the various-length cable-code signals completed the development of cable-code operation.

The higher speeds made possible by the loaded cable led to the use of five-unit code on certain routes to facilitate repetition of signals from land-line multiplex systems. The higher capability of the cable was difficult to realize reliably with the existing electromagnetic relays which decrease in sensitivity as they are adjusted for higher speed, and so thermionic valve terminal amplifiers were introduced to amplify the signals for use with more robust high-speed relays to feed the multiplex apparatus.

**Transmission and Repeaters.**—Simplex operation was used in the early days of submarine cables, but the desirability of duplexing was immediately felt. Early attempts were not very successful, because the weak received signals made it imperative to achieve accurate and stable artificial lines for balancing the cable, since the residual unbalance introduced interference from the sent signals at the same end. Improvements in the manufacture and adjustment of artificial cables made duplex operation usual on unloaded cables, but no generally satisfactory means of producing a balance for loaded cables was found. However, one special cable, laid in 1928 between Nova Scotia and the Azores, had graded loading that tapered to zero at the ends and was successfully duplexed.

The possible speed of operation of a given type of cable terminating at a particular station will be inversely proportional to the square of its length, so where convenient it is desirable to split long routes into sections, locating repeater stations on islands on transoceanic routes where the signals can be completely regenerated. The ultimate limit in speed is determined by the interference induced by natural phenomena, such as changes in the magnetic and electric fields of the earth and electric storms. These effects are manifested in shallow water near the shore, so if the signal can be amplified before it reaches this area, it can be raised above the interference level and faster operation obtained. The technique of the submerged telegraph repeater was first employed by the Western Union Telegraph company in 1950. The repeater consisted of a valve amplifier with equalizing networks, contained in a watertight steel case, the necessary power for its operation being supplied from the shore via the cable. Such repeaters may be located 60–300 mi. from shore at depths of 250–1,250 fathoms. Such a repeatered cable can be operated only in the simplex fashion, but the speed may be increased three- or four-fold over unrepeatered duplex. This method is best employed on routes where there are at least two cables to provide both-way communication, but repeaters can be inserted in both ends and be switched in or out of circuit from the shore to reverse the direction of working.

Submerged telegraph repeaters have been applied to many of the transatlantic telegraph cables by U.S. companies and to a few in the British commonwealth cable system.

Typical speeds of operation of long-distance unloaded cables range from 250 to 600 characters per minute duplex. Loaded cables about 2,000 mi. long are capable of 2,500 characters per minute simplex, and repeatered unloaded cables attain similar speeds.

### X. RADIO

Radiotelegraphy is essentially carrier telegraphy at relatively high frequency. The radio carrier may be directly modulated by the telegraph signal in any of the usual modes (*i.e.,* amplitude or frequency) or by a subcarrier system of one or more channels (*i.e.,* the telegraph signals may be borne over a line to the radio transmitting station by a voice-frequency carrier that is then sent by a radiotelephony transmitter). Radio propagation over long distances is subject to severe disturbances that cause the signal to fade and introduce interference by atmospheric noise, which results in distortion and sometimes mutilation of the signal. To minimize these effects, diversity reception may be employed. Diversity can be of several forms: time diversity in which the message is repeated twice and the most likely version of the message accepted in the case of disagreement; space diversity in which two receiving aerials separated by a considerable distance feed a special receiver that selects the stronger signal; or frequency diversity in which the telegraph signal is sent simultaneously on two different frequencies.

Teleprinter transmission can be more seriously impaired than synchronous transmission, because if the start or stop elements of character signals are incorrectly received, the mechanism is likely to become out of step and successive characters to be incorrectly printed. Therefore, on regular fixed traffic routes, synchronous time-division multiplex is often employed and as a further protection a seven-unit error-detecting code may be adopted. When a return channel is available a system of automatic error-correction devised by Van Duuren is used. In this, the detection of an error causes a special signal to be sent back to the transmitting office to request the automatic repetition of the previous three characters of the message, which are automatically stored in the apparatus; meanwhile, the output of the receiving apparatus is blocked until the originally faulty signal has been received again. If this is then apparently correct, through transmission is resumed; if not, the automatic repetition cycle is repeated. In practice, the error rate in the printed message may be reduced by a factor in the order of 100. Such systems can be connected in teleprinter networks; the teleprinter signal is received at the sending terminal station on a reperforator, and the tape from this is accepted by the multiplex apparatus, which automatically translates it into the special seven-unit code. At the receiving end of the multiplex the signals, after being checked for conformity, are automatically translated back into teleprinter code signals.

In some countries, particularly where interurban distances are great and the terrain rugged, microwave radio-relay systems are being introduced as more economical than long-distance carrier telephone cable, and channels in such systems can be used to bear multichannel telegraph systems. *See* also references under "Telegraph" in the Index.

Bibliography.—C. Bright, *The Story of the Atlantic Cable* (1903); F. J. Brown, *Cable and Wireless Communications of the World,* 2nd ed. rev. (1930); D. H. Cameron, *Submarine Telegraphy* (1927); J. A. Fleming, *Propagation of Electric Currents in Telephone and Telegraph Conductors,* 4th ed. rev. (1927); H. H. Harrison, *Printing Telegraph Systems and Mechanisms* (1923); T. E. Herbert, *Telegraphy,* 5th ed. rev. (1930); H. W. Malcolm, *The Theory of the Submarine Telegraph and Telephone Cable* (1917); D. McNicol, *American Telegraph Practice* (1913); J. Z. Millar, "Preview of the Western Union System Radio Beam Telegraphy," *J. Franklin Inst.,* pt. 1, 241:316–326; pt. 2, 242: 23–40 (1946); H. W. Pendry, *Baudot Printing Telegraph System,* 2nd ed. rev. (1920); Edward Lind Morse (ed.), *Samuel F. B. Morse, His Letters and Journals,* 2 vol. (1914); G. A. Schreiner, *Cables and Wireless and Their Role in the Foreign Relations of the United States* (1924); T. P. Shaffner, *The Telegraph Manual* (1859); H. G. Sellars, "A Brief Chronology for Students of Telegraphs, Telephones and Posts," *Teleg. Teleph. J.* (Nov. 1927 *et seq.*); W. D. Weaver, *Catalogue of the Wheeler Gift of Books, Pamphlets and Periodicals in the Library of the American Institute of Electrical Engineers* (1909); Western Union Committee on Technical Publications, *American Telegraphy After 100 Years* (1944); R. Appleyard, *Pioneers of Electrical Communication* (1930); A. F. Harlow, *Old Wires and New Waves* (1936); W. T. Perkins, *Modern Telegraph Systems and Equipment* (1946); R. L. Thompson, *Wiring a Continent* (1947). *See* also Western Union Engineering Department textbooks, prepared for the American School of Correspondence, Chicago; Federal Communications Commission *Annual Reports; Bell System Technical Journal; Post Office Electrical Engineers' Journal;* The Institute of Electrical and Electronics Engineers, *Proceedings of the IEEE, IEEE Spectrum; Western Union Technical Review;* J. W. Freebody, *Telegraphy* (1959); K. Henney (ed.), *Radio Engineering Handbook,* 5th ed. (1959); H. Fülling, *Fernschreib-Übertragungstechnik* (1957); E. Rossberg and H. Korta, *Fernschreib-Vermittlungstechnik* (1959); R. Roquet, *Théorie et technique de la transmission télégraphique* (1954); D. Faugeras, *Appareils et installations télégraphiques* (1955); F. Schiweck, *Fernschreib-Technik,* 2nd ed. (1944). (W. P. Ma.; L. K. W.)

**TELEKI, PÁL,** Count (1879–1941), Hungarian scholar and prime minister, was born in Budapest on Nov. 1, 1879, of a famous Transylvanian family. He entered Parliament as early as 1905 but found time to travel widely and to acquire international distinction in his favourite field, geography. He was premier from July 19, 1920, to April 14, 1921, but then withdrew from party politics, in which he never greatly believed, holding the true functions of government to be educative and moral. He held a chair of geography at Budapest University and was also head of the Cartographic Institute and president of the Boy Scouts Association. He returned to office as minister of education on May 14, 1938, and became premier again on Feb. 15, 1939. Passionately convinced of the justice of Hungary's claim for a revision of the Treaty of Trianon (*q.v.*), he nevertheless struggled to avoid any dependence on Germany. During World War II he concluded a treaty of eternal friendship with Yugoslavia (December 1940). After the Yugoslav *coup d'état* of March 1941, however, Germany demanded Hungary's help against Yugoslavia, while Great Britain threatened dire consequences if Hungary gave it; and in the night of April 2–3, 1941, Teleki took his own life.

*See* C. A. Macartney, *October Fifteenth,* 2nd ed. (1961).

(C. A. M.)

**TELEMANN, GEORG PHILIPP** (1681–1767), the most highly regarded German composer of his time, was born at Magdeburg on March 14, 1681. Self-taught as a musician, he entered the University of Leipzig in 1701, intending to study law. He soon abandoned his studies for a musical career, however. He founded the Collegium Musicum (students' orchestra), undertook the direction of the Leipzig Opera, and, in 1704, was appointed organist at the Neue Kirche. In 1705 he left Leipzig, and, after some years as court composer at Sorau and Eisenach and as musical director at

Frankfurt-am-Main, he finally settled in Hamburg in 1721. In 1722 he was offered the post of organist at the Thomaskirche, Leipzig. He declined the position, which was then given to J. S. Bach. In 1737–38 he traveled for eight months in France.

As a composer Telemann was amazingly productive. In Hamburg he provided five churches with music; he conducted the opera and gave frequent concerts with the Hamburg Collegium Musicum (which he had formed). In addition to these activities, he regularly supplied music for several courts and for the city of Frankfurt. Within the space of 15 years no less than 44 of his works were published—some engraved by himself—among them several complete sets of cantatas for the church year, the large instrumental collection *Musique de Table,* and the first music periodical, *Der Getreue Music-Meister* (which alone contains 70 of his compositions).

Telemann was on friendly terms with J. S. Bach, to whose son Carl Philipp Emanuel he became godfather; Handel sent him rare plants for his garden; and Johann Mattheson was enthusiastic in his praise. Both Bach and Handel copied and arranged several of his works for their own use. He was twice married and had eight sons and two daughters, but of his family only one grandson, Georg Michael Telemann, became a musician. Telemann died in Hamburg on June 25, 1767.

In his lifetime Telemann was most admired for his church compositions. These vary from small cantatas, suitable for domestic use or for use in churches with limited means, to large-scale works for soloists, chorus, and orchestra.

Telemann's secular vocal music also has a wide range, from simple strophic songs to the dramatic cantata *Ino,* written at the age of 84. Of his operas the comic ones were the most successful, particularly *Pimpinone,* based on the same plot as Pergolesi's *La serva padrona,* which it preceded by eight years. His orchestral works consist of suites (called *ouvertures*), *concerti grossi,* and concertos. His chamber works are remarkable not only for their quantity but for the great variety of instrumental combinations and the expert writing for each instrument. Representative of his instrumental output is the collection *Musique de Table,* containing orchestral suites, concertos, and chamber music.

Telemann's compositions combine the principal styles and forms of his time—Italian, French, and German, with some excursions into Polish and English territory. His music is notable for its expressive melodies, surprising harmonies, buoyant rhythms, masterly instrumentation, its wit, and its variety.

An edition comprising a selection of Telemann's works was published by Bärenreiter (1953– ). (W. G. Be.)

**TELEMARK,** a *fylke* (county) of southern Norway. Area 5,919 sq.mi. (15,329 sq.km.). Pop. (1960) 146,634. From the coast of the Skagerrak it extends 112 mi. (180 km.) northwestward, covering uplands and mountains carved by many branched valleys. Gausta (6,178 ft.; 1,883 m.), near Rjukan, is the highest point. Numerous lakes include Tinnsjø, Møsvatnet, Totak, Fyresvatn, Nisser, Bandak, Heddalsvatnet, and Norsjø. Norsjø is connected by canals with Bandak and Heddalsvatnet, giving access from the ports of Skien and Porsgrunn to Dalen and Notodden. The county is crossed in the north by a highway between eastern and western Norway, and in the south by the Oslo-Stavanger railway, with branches to the coastal towns of Brevik and Kragerø. Huge waterfalls at Rjukan and Notodden provide power for electrochemical works. The power potential of the Tokke River beyond Lake Bandak was being developed during the 1960s to provide an important addition to the public supply of southeastern Norway. The county town, Skien (pop. [1960] 15,251), one of the oldest towns in Norway and the seat of a court of appeal, is an important centre of the pulp and paper industry. Porsgrunn (10,423) is known for its porcelain factory. Kragerø (9,686) is a picturesque summer resort and yachting centre. (L. H. Hg.)

**TELEMETRY** is that branch of electronic engineering concerned with the measurement of physical signals at a remote location. It encompasses measurement of the variable at the source, separation of the relevant information, and its transmission to a desired location where it is displayed.

The most advanced technical developments of telemetry are utilized in the space program. An unmanned orbiting vehicle is the site of measurements of surface temperatures, magnetic fields, ambient radiation intensity, and other variables necessary in the scientific investigation of space and the development of improved vehicles. In a manned vehicle, additional instrumentation monitors such signals as the astronaut's pulse rate, blood pressure, and respiration rate. Success of the mission and control during the flight require that the results of these measurements be transmitted as frequently as possible to earth receiving stations. (*See* also Space Exploration.)

Telemetry is also utilized in the control of gas flow through long-distance pipelines. Telemetry equipment measures pressure and flow along the line and transmits the information to control stations where pumps and valves are adjusted to ensure constant pressure for all users. Other applications include systems for the automated computer control of industrial processes (*e.g.,* factories) and equipment for basic research in biology, particularly for studies involving observation of physiological signals from animals inaccessible in normal activities.

The telemetry system ordinarily includes: (1) measurement devices; (2) data-processing equipment at or near the point of measurement; (3) electronic communication equipment to transmit the information (*e.g.,* by wire or radio) to the desired site; (4) data-processing equipment at the receiving station; and (5) display devices (cathode-ray tubes, loudspeakers, or tape recorders). Items (2) and (4) are the system elements unique to telemetry.

Efficient design of the telemetry system commonly requires that the data-processing equipment collect information from many (*e.g.,* 30) measurement devices and combine the data in such a way that a single electrical signal can be transmitted that will convey the measured variables simultaneously. The desired economy of communication equipment and channel capacity is achieved by a combination of time and frequency multiplexing—the distinguishing characteristic of electronic telemetry systems.

Time multiplexing is the process of time sharing among distinct signals. Any physical signal can be decomposed into a sum of sinusoidal signals of various frequencies (*e.g.,* speech consists primarily of sinusoidal signals of frequencies from 100 to 4,000 cps [cycles per second]). The fundamental sampling theorem of communication theory states that all the information in a signal can be represented by a sequence of samples of the signal, with the samples taken at a rate at least twice the maximum frequency of the signal (*e.g.,* speech can be represented by 8,000 samples per second, even though each sample may be only one-millionth of a second in duration).

Thus, time multiplexing is accomplished by iteratively sampling each of the set of signals. If the 20 signals A, B, C, . . . , T are to be transmitted and each must be sampled ten times per second, the data-processing equipment samples signal A for $\frac{1}{200}$ sec., then B for the next $\frac{1}{200}$ sec., and so forth through the sequence. After $\frac{20}{200}$ sec. ($\frac{1}{10}$ sec.), the second sample of signal A is taken. The single, composite signal to be transmitted to the receiving station then includes the information on all 20 physical measurements. The time sampling can be accomplished by electronic circuitry automatically switching among the 20 signals or by a rotating electric switch that connects the output electrical circuit successively to each of the measurement instruments for $\frac{1}{200}$ sec.

Frequency multiplexing is accomplished by simultaneously transmitting over a common path signals from several sources, each signal being assigned a distinctive reference frequency or band of frequencies. For example, long-distance telephone equipment (underground cable or microwave relay) permits transmission of signals from 100 cps to more than $10^6$ cps; if separate speech signals are modulated (or shifted in frequency), 250 signals each of 4,000 cps bandwidth can be transmitted simultaneously over one system. The modulation process is accomplished with electronic equipment analogous to that utilized in commercial radio and television broadcasting (*see* Broadcasting).

The transmitted signals are received by electronic equipment where demodulation devices separate the individual signals for operating the distinct display and recording instruments or provide input data for a digital computer used to interpret the measured data. (J. G. Tl.)

**TELEOLOGY** means explanation by reference to some purpose or end (Greek *telos,* "end"; *teleios,* "complete"); also described as final causation, in contrast with explanation by reference to efficient causes only. Human conduct, insofar as it is considered rational, is generally explained with reference to ends pursued or alleged to be pursued; and human thought tends to explain the behaviour of other things in nature on this analogy, either as of themselves pursuing ends, or as designed to fulfil a purpose devised by a Mind external to nature. The most celebrated account of final causation was given by Aristotle when he laid down that for a full explanation of anything it was necessary to take account not only of the "material," the "formal," and the "efficient" causes, but also of the purpose for which the thing existed or was produced, namely its "final" cause.

With the rise of modern science in the 16th and 17th centuries, interest was directed to mechanistic explanations of natural phenomena with reference to efficient causes; if teleological explanations were used they took the form, not (as in Aristotelian teleology) of saying that things develop toward the realization of ends internal to their own natures, but of looking even on biological organisms as machines ingeniously devised by an Intelligent Being. William Paley gave classical expression to this kind of teleology (*Natural Theology, or Evidences of the Existence and Attributes of the Deity Collected From the Appearance of Nature,* London, 1802).

In the 19th century controversy centred on whether the phenomena of growth, regeneration, and reproduction characteristic of living organisms could be explained in purely mechanistic terms. The "vitalism" of Hans Driesch (1867–1941), according to which some entelechy (*q.v.*) must be postulated in an organism, found little support after his death. There remains, however, the question whether biological processes can be explained purely in physicochemical terms ("mechanistic" explanation), or whether the problems of structure, function, and organization necessitate some kind of teleology.

*See* C. D. Broad, *The Mind and Its Place in Nature* (1925); J. Woodger, *Biological Principles* (1929). (D. M. E.)

**TELEOST,** any typically bony fish belonging to the group Teleostei. In the classification issued in 1846 by Johannes Müller, the geologically modern bony fishes were arranged in three subclasses, Dipneusti, Ganoidei, and Teleostei, the last including the great majority of the fishes, all those with a homocercal tail fin. Subsequent work, especially on fossil fishes, has shown that the ganoids are not a natural group, some being related to very primitive fishes, others, namely the Holostei, which include the recent bowfin and gars, *Amia calva* and *Lepidosteus,* approaching the teleosts.

The extinct Pholidophoridae and Oligopleuridae are exactly intermediate in structure between the Holostei and Teleostei, and have been included by some authorities in the one group, by others in the other. This led C. T. Regan to combine the Holostei and Teleostei to form one subclass, termed Neopterygii. *See* Fish.

**TELEPHONE.** The term telephone (from the Greek roots, *tele,* "far," and *phoné,* "sound") was first used to describe any apparatus for conveying sounds to a distant point. Specifically, the word was applied as early as 1796 to a megaphone, and not long afterward to a speaking tube. Subsequently the name string telephone was given to the device invented long before by Robert Hooke (1667), in which vibrations in a diaphragm caused by voice or sound waves are transmitted mechanically along a string or wire to a similar diaphragm which reproduces the sound. Still later, devices employing electric currents to reproduce at a distance the mere pitch of musical sounds were called telephones. Nowadays, however, this name is assigned almost exclusively to apparatus for reproducing articulate speech and other sounds at a distance through the medium of electric waves. The term telephony covers the entire art and practice of electrical speech transmission, including the many systems, accessories and operating methods used for this purpose.

This article is divided as follows:



## I. INVENTION

Like most inventions, the telephone drew heavily upon previous work and had scarcely appeared before notable improvements were made. Among the pioneer contributors in this field, the most outstanding was Alexander Graham Bell, who invented, and patented

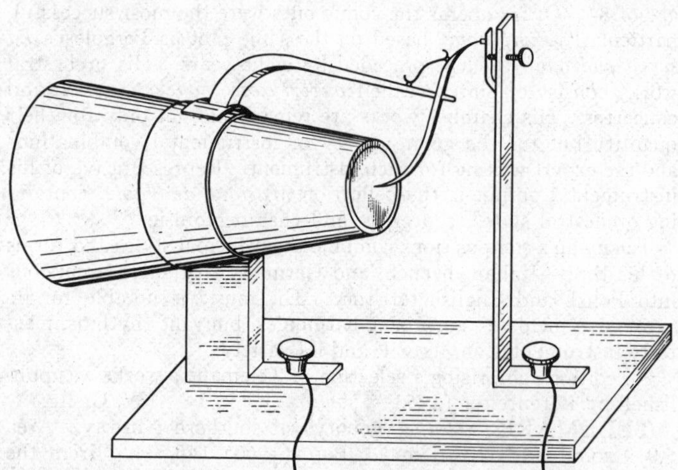

BY COURTESY OF BELL TELEPHONE LABORATORIES, INC.

FIG. 1.—TRANSMITTER OF JOHANN PHILIPP REIS, 1861 OR 1862

in 1876, the first telephone capable of practical use. As early as 1874 he had conceived the correct principle of telephone transmission, which he later stated as follows: "If I could make a current of electricity vary in intensity precisely as the air varies in density during the production of sound, I should be able to transmit speech telegraphically."

This conception of an undulatory current corresponding to a speech wave formed the foundation for the entire telephonic art. Earlier workers, notably C. G. Page in the United States (1837) and Charles Bourseul in France (1854), had devised methods employing the make-and-break principle of the telegraph for transmitting the pitch of sounds, but not articulate speech, to a distant point.

J. P. Reis came closer. Working at Frankfurt, Ger., in 1860 and subsequent years, he devised an apparatus using at the transmitting end a diaphragm structure something like that of the human ear to control an electric current (fig. 1). At the other end of the circuit this produced audible tones by controlling the magnetization of a needle whose changes of length, in accordance with the magnetostrictive effect discovered by Page, vibrated a sounding board. Later, an electromagnet was substituted for the needle. Reis's mechanism, like others before and after, included the important feature of deriving the electrical power for transmitting sound by making the sound power control the current from a battery.

Reis had some comprehension of the requirement for electrical transmission of speech, for he noted in his memoir on telephony the need "to set up vibrations whose curves are like those of any given tone or combination of tones" (S. P. Thompson translation). Though his apparatus served primarily to reproduce tones by the make-and-break scheme, he did, by extremely delicate adjustment, succeed in reproducing articulate sounds quite imperfectly. Reis seems not to have realized, however, that this success resulted because his apparatus could, over a very narrow range of speech volume, operate on the principle of changing an electric current in accordance with the voice wave by varying a loose contact, in this case a spring contact between platinum electrodes. His understanding of his own apparatus is indicated by his statement that "each sound vibration effects an opening and a closing of the current." About 20 years later, the German patent office after careful investigation decided that Reis's instrument was not a "speaking telephone."

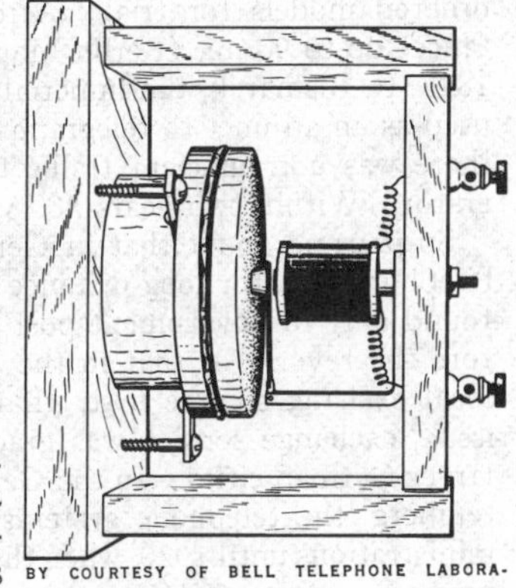

BY COURTESY OF BELL TELEPHONE LABORATORIES, INC.

FIG. 2.—"GALLOWS FRAME" TRANSMITTER OF ALEXANDER GRAHAM BELL, JUNE 3, 1875

In the following years attempts were made by other workers (*e.g.*, the Italians A. Meucci and I. Manzetti) but without full realization of the requirements for articulate speech.

Bell's approach was different. In the summer of 1874 the idea of the "electric speaking telephone" became complete in his mind. He described to his father a form of apparatus consisting of a strip of iron attached to a membrane which, when actuated by the voice, would vibrate in front of an electromagnet, thus inducing an undulatory electric current theoretically capable of transmitting speech. At the receiving end a similar device could be used in reverse to reproduce the voice. But Bell doubted that the current generated by the voice would be strong enough to be useful, and for almost a year he made no attempt to construct the apparatus. On June 2, 1875, while working in Boston on multiplex telegraph apparatus, Bell heard over an electric wire a sound corresponding to the twang of a steel spring at the other end. Recognizing this as a manifestation of the undulatory current principle, he gave his assistant, Thomas A. Watson, instructions for embodying it in a model (fig. 2) of a telephone. The transmitter and receiver were of the electromagnetic type described a year before, and in between was a circuit which included an electric battery. This apparatus transmitted speech sounds the next day, June 3. Bell filed his application for a U.S. patent on Feb. 14, 1876 (fig. 3). Further experiments produced an instrument which on March 10, 1876, transmitted the first complete sentence: "Mr. Watson, come here; I want you."

A few hours after Bell filed his application for patent, Elisha Gray filed a caveat (*i.e.*, a notice of intent to perfect his ideas and file a patent application within three months) for an electric telephone. Gray described a "liquid transmitter," somewhat similar to one patented by Thomas A. Edison for telegraphy in 1873. In Gray's transmitter a

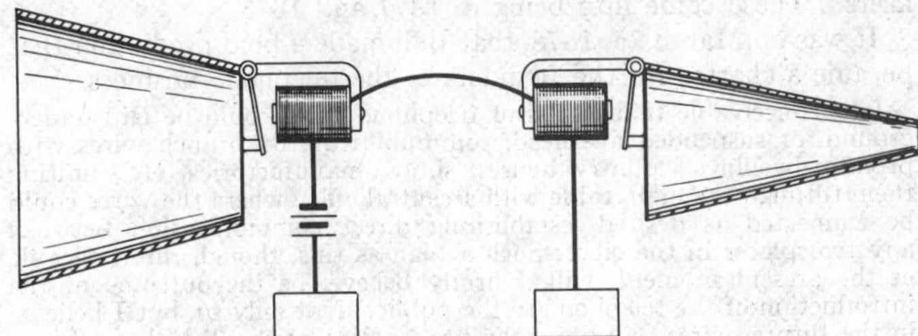

BY COURTESY OF BELL TELEPHONE LABORATORIES, INC.

FIG. 3.—ELECTROMAGNETIC TRANSMITTER (LEFT) AND RECEIVER (RIGHT) ILLUSTRATED IN BELL'S FIRST TELEPHONE PATENT, FILED FEB. 14, 1876

voice-actuated diaphragm varied the electrical resistance, and hence the current, by changing the depth of immersion of a rod in water. Bell in his application mentioned the possibility of a similar liquid transmitter, and later used it for his historic summons to Watson. The variable-resistance principle, which subsequently, in the form of a variable carbon contact, proved vital to telephone transmission, makes it possible to obtain an electric wave which is an amplified copy of the sound wave. Like Bell's receiver, Gray's was of the electromagnetic type, similar to one he had patented in Great Britain in July 1874 and in the U.S. in July 1875.

In view of Bell's prior filing of a patent application, the patent for the telephone was issued to him on March 7, 1876. Gray's status as to the invention of the telephone is best set forth in his own words, written to Bell on March 5, 1877: "I do not claim even the credit of inventing it." The claims of Gray, Daniel Drawbaugh and others were subsequently threshed out in prolonged litigation, involving about 600 separate suits, which finally resulted in Bell's patent's being upheld in a divided vote by the supreme court of the United States.

Bell's first transmitter employing electromagnetic induction, while valid enough in theory, delivered such feeble electrical currents as to be inadequate for general application. The liquid transmitter afforded considerable improvement, but this too had drawbacks. The final essential element for a satisfactory working telephone was the variable-contact carbon transmitter, due in large measure to Thomas A. Edison, as discussed below.

## II. INTRODUCTION AND GROWTH

**1. United States.**—The development of the telephone business in the United States was undertaken by a group of Bell's backers, under the leadership of Thomas Sanders and Gardiner G. Hubbard. They began by renting or lending telephones in pairs to individuals for local communication. The instruments were extremely crude. Connection between them was made by a circuit consisting of a single iron wire with ground return; transmission, which was uncertain and poor at best, was possible for only a few miles. Initially there were no switchboards to interconnect a number of

BY COURTESY OF THE BELL TELEPHONE SYSTEM

(Left) First telephone to transmit human voice, 1876; (centre left) first telephone with two wooden transmitter-receivers, 1878; (centre right) upright desk telephone, 1897; (right) Alexander Graham Bell opening the New York–Chicago long-distance line, 1892 users. These came into being in 1877 and 1878.

It was on March 25, 1878, that Bell made a bold prediction that became a charter for the founders of the telephone business:

> It is conceivable that cables of telephone wires could be laid underground, or suspended overhead, communicating by branch wires with private dwellings, country houses, shops, manufactories, etc., uniting them through the main cable with a central office where the wires could be connected as desired, establishing direct communication between any two places in the city. Such a plan as this, though impracticable at the present moment, will, I firmly believe, be the outcome of the introduction of the telephone to the public. Not only so, but I believe, in the future, wires will unite the head offices of the Telephone Company in different cities, and a man in one part of the country may communicate by word of mouth with another in a distant place.
>
> I am aware that such ideas may appear to you Utopian. . . . Believing, however, as I do that such a scheme will be the ultimate result of the telephone to the public, I will impress upon you all the advisability of keeping this end in view, that all present arrangements of the telephone may be eventually realized in this grand system. . . .

The owners of the telephone patent early incorporated their business, and funds were raised for its progressive development, under the leadership of Theodore N. Vail, who became general manager in 1878. It was recognized that telephone performance is a matter of mutual concern to users, and the practice was established of leasing telephones instead of selling them.

Within ten years after the issuance of the Bell patent, the organization of the Bell Telephone system had assumed something close to its present form. The local systems were gradually brought together into regional companies operating throughout a state or several states. The systems of these regional companies were linked together by long-distance circuits operated by the American Telephone and Telegraph company. This company, through ownership of stock in the regional companies, became the parent company of the Bell system.

The Western Electric company was acquired in 1882 as chief manufacturer and supplier for the Bell system, as well as to conduct research and development. In 1925 the Bell Telephone laboratories was organized to take over the expanding research and development activities for the system. In the 1960s the American Telephone and Telegraph company had more than 2,400,000 stockholders, constituting the largest number of public owners for any one corporation in the world.

After the expiration of the basic telephone patents, many independent telephone companies sprang up all over the country. Competition became so intense that in many localities there were two companies sharing the business. As this became an increasing source of inconvenience and expense to the public, the service was unified through acquisitions and mergers so as to leave a single company, either Bell or non-Bell, operating in each area. Provision was made for interconnecting the facilities of non-Bell companies with those of the Bell system, thus making possible the interconnection of nearly all telephones in the United States, as well as connections to the rest of the world. Service and rates are regulated by state utility commissions and the Federal Communications commission.

In the decade after 1954, the number of telephones in the world almost doubled—from about 90,000,000 to more than 170,000,000, divided about equally between the U.S. and other countries.

**2. Great Britain.**—Bell visited England and Scotland on his wedding trip in 1878 in the hope of developing a demand for the telephone. Despite the able support of Lord Kelvin, Sir William Preece and others, he aroused little public interest. He did, however, demonstrate his invention to Queen Victoria, who asked to purchase a pair of telephones and instead was presented with two instruments done in ivory. Interest was stimulated by this royal recognition, and the first telephone exchange was opened in London in 1879 with seven or eight subscribers. Several telephone companies were organized in various parts of Great Britain, but in 1880 the British courts held that the telephone system was legally a telegraph system under an antecedent law which made the telegraph a government monopoly under the postmaster general. The government officials, reluctant to assume the risks involved in developing this new form of communication, issued licences on a royalty basis to several private companies, which were later consolidated into a single company. A few municipal telephone systems were also established under licence.

As the potentialities of telephone communication began to be appreciated, the government gradually took over the service. In 1896 the post office purchased the long-distance lines, and in 1902 it began establishing in London its own local telephone exchanges which were interconnected with those of the privately owned company. Finally, on Jan. 1, 1912, the post office acquired all the private telephone properties. Since then the post office has operated practically all telephones in Great Britain. When the Irish Free State was established, the British post office transferred to the Free State government its telephone system in southern Ireland. The British post office maintains a large research and development organization. Telephone apparatus is supplied by private companies that manufacture to post-office specifications.

**3. Germany.**—In Germany the telephone was a government monopoly from the beginning. Heinrich von Stephan, postmaster general and manager of the imperial telegraphs, when he learned about Bell's invention from an article in the *Scientific American,* ordered models for trial. After successful experiments at distances up to 90 mi. (Berlin-Magdeburg), he suggested on Nov. 9, 1877, to Bismarck, the imperial chancellor, that the telephone be used as an adjunct to telegraph service in rural post offices where there was not sufficient traffic to justify a trained telegraph operator. Within two years 800 villages were thus connected.

So it came about that in Germany the first public use of the telephone was for long-distance communication, telephones being found only in government post offices. The situation was therefore the reverse of that in the United States and Britain, where local exchanges came first. Later, as public demand forced the issue, exchange service was gradually introduced, starting in the larger German cities. In the German states of Bavaria and Württemberg, the telephone systems were operated by the state administrations until 1920, when they were transferred to the German post office.

**4. France.**—In France the telephone was first exhibited at the Paris exhibition in 1878, where it attracted little interest. The next year, however, the French telegraph officials, unwilling themselves to pioneer in this new field, granted concessions to several private companies which later consolidated into the Soeiété Générale des Téléphones. This company initiated public telephone service in Paris in 1881 and subsequently in other cities. Starting in 1883, the French government established exchanges in various centres. In 1889 the government took over the entire private system, and after that time operated the telephone service.

**5. Switzerland.**—In Switzerland a privately owned telephone system was established under government concession in Zürich in 1880, while the government itself opened exchanges in Bern and Basel in 1881. Thereafter the government proceeded rapidly to establish new exchanges, and in 1886 purchased the Zürich system. After that time the Swiss government operated all telephones.

**6. Scandinavia.**—The Scandinavian countries have achieved a high degree of telephone development. In Sweden, the International Bell Telephone company of New York opened exchanges in Stockholm and Göteborg in 1880, and not long after in Malmö and elsewhere. In 1883 a competing telephone company was set up in Stockholm under the enterprising leadership of H. T. Cedergren. Co-operative telephone associations were established in Göteborg and in many rural communities. After a strongly competitive phase, in which the government participated, virtually all telephones were taken over by the state during the period 1890–1923.

The Swedish administration not only maintains a development organization, as do most other countries in Europe, but is unique among European telephone administrations in possessing factories for production of telephone equipment.

In Norway the International Bell Telephone company in 1880 secured franchises for Oslo and Drammen. The next year local companies established exchanges in several cities and a competing system in Oslo. Within ten years, largely through local enterprise, the telephone came to hold much the same place in Norwegian rural life that it does in the sparsely settled districts of the U.S. Ultimately the state acquired the more important local systems, and by the 1960s about 94% of the country's telephones were government operated.

In Denmark, likewise, the telephone was introduced by private enterprise, the government interposing no serious difficulties. Gradually numerous small systems were consolidated into several relatively large organizations. The principal one is the Copenhagen Telephone company, a stock company in which the government owns a controlling interest.

**7. Belgium and the Netherlands.**—In Belgium telephone exchanges were first established in various cities by private concessionaires. In 1896, however, the telephone system became a complete government monopoly, and has remained so. Private grants formed the initial pattern in the Netherlands also. As competition with the government telegraphs became apparent, the private telephone systems were integrated into a single government system.

**8. Austria, Italy and Spain.**—Austria followed the typical European course, starting with private companies which later were bought in so as to create a government monopoly.

In Italy the story is somewhat different. To begin with, concessions were granted to private companies, and in a number of important cities competitive situations arose. As the disadvantages of competition manifested themselves, consolidation was effected either voluntarily or by the dictates of local authorities. Partly as a result of onerous regulations, telephone development failed to keep pace with that in other European countries. In 1925 the structure of Italian telephone service assumed essentially the form that obtains today. Five concessionary companies operate local and toll service, each within one of the five zones into which Italy has been divided for this purpose. These companies are privately operated, although the government participates in the ownership. The government operates long-distance interconnecting service as well as the land-line portion of international service.

In 1924 Spain granted a concession to a subsidiary of the International Telephone and Telegraph company of New York to provide a nation-wide telephone system to supersede the previous government-owned and privately owned systems, a limited development. There were operating difficulties during the Spanish civil war, and in 1945 the government purchased the International Telephone and Telegraph operating interest.

**9. Canada.**—Canada, divided by natural barriers and with most of its population concentrated near the long southern border, nevertheless followed the U.S. in the rapid growth of telephone service. In the 1960s almost every home had a telephone, and Canadians led the world as its most frequent users. Most of the telephones in Canada are administered by seven private companies, which were banded together as the Trans-Canada system to furnish through service.

**10. Latin America.**—Early development of telephony in Latin America was slow for various reasons. In many cases foreign capital was obtained through private concessions, but certain countries where this was done followed the European plan of subsequent transfer to government ownership.

In the 1960s Argentina led the Latin-American countries in telephone development, followed by Brazil. Telephone systems of some size in Latin America were operated by subsidiaries of certain companies located in foreign countries, as follows: International Telephone and Telegraph corporation, in Brazil, Chile, Peru and Puerto Rico; the L. M. Ericsson company, in Argentina and Peru; Cable and Wireless, Ltd., in Peru. Mexico's largest system was owned jointly by the IT&T corporation and the L. M. Ericsson company.

**11. Other Countries.**—Telephone development in the rest of the world may be summarized with the statement that while some sort of telephone service is to be found almost everywhere, systems of substantial size include those of Japan (second only to the U.S.), the U.S.S.R., Australia, Czechoslovakia, Poland, South Africa, and New Zealand.

**12. ITU and CCIF.**—Much of the progress in international telephone communication may be attributed to the work of international co-ordinating bodies. This work now centres in the Union Internationale des Télécommunications (UIT), called in English the International Telecommunication union, abbreviated ITU. This organization, now an agency of the United Nations, was founded in 1865 as the Union Télégraphique Internationale. The purposes of this organization as set forth in its charter are: "To maintain and extend international co-operation for the improvement and rational use of telecommunication; to promote the development of technical facilities and their most efficient operation, in order to improve the efficiency of telecommunication services, increase their usefulness, and make them, as far as possible, generally available; to harmonize the actions of nations in the attainment of those common ends." The ITU has a membership in about 90 countries and territories. The activities of the

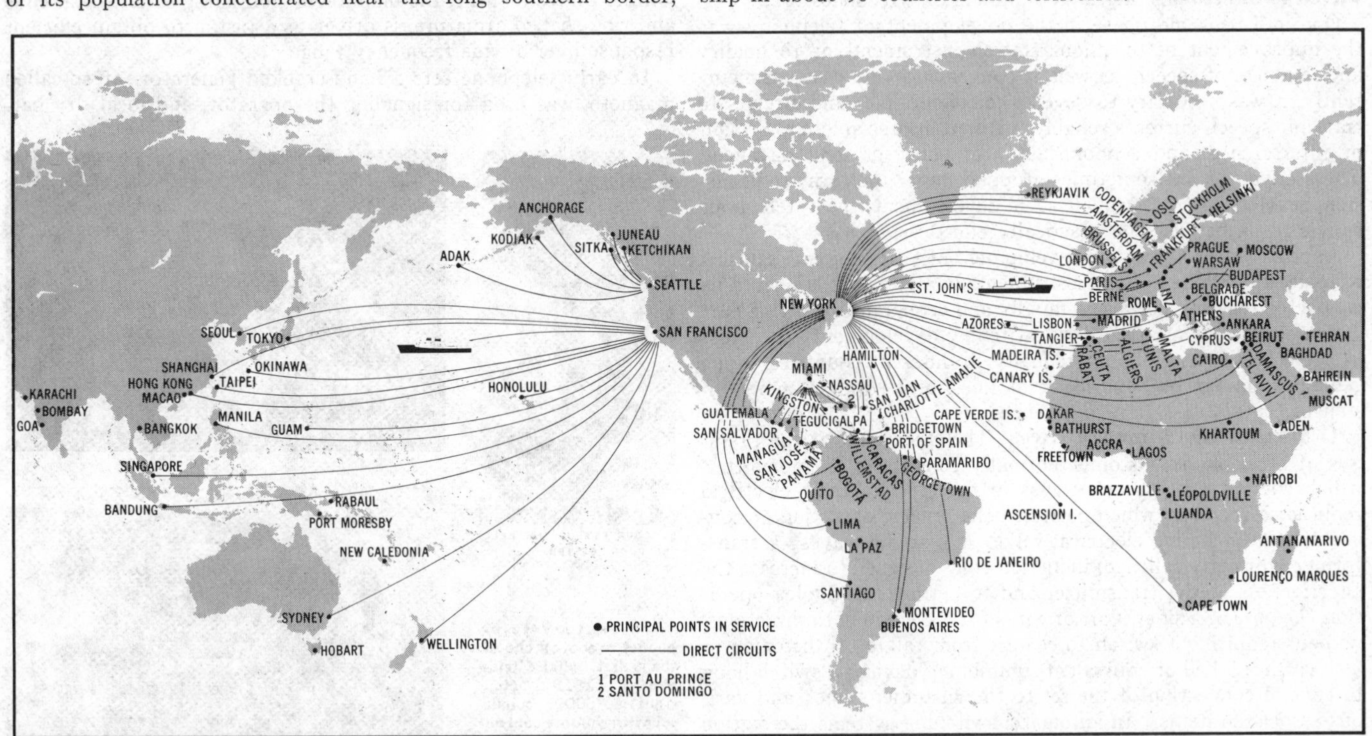


BY COURTESY OF BELL TELEPHONE LABORATORIES, INC.

FIG. 4.—U.S. OVERSEAS TELEPHONE CIRCUITS

ITU and its constituent bodies are financed by contributions from member governments.

For many years there were three permanent and essentially autonomous organs of the ITU: (1) the Comité Consultatif International Téléphonique (International Telephone Consultative committee), abbreviated CCIF, founded in 1924; (2) the Comité Consultatif International Télégraphique (International Telegraph Consultative committee), abbreviated CCIT, founded in 1925; and (3) the Comité Consultatif International des Radio Communications (International Radio Consultative committee), abbreviated CCIR, founded in 1927.

For implementing its work, each of these international consultative committees organized a number of study groups covering different phases of activity. A plenary assembly distributes questions to be investigated by the study groups. These work by correspondence or by meeting and submit their findings to the succeeding plenary assembly, which studies and discusses them and makes recommendations. Ordinarily the recommendations take the form of directives or rules which, without being mandatory, are usually observed by the technical and operating services of the government administrations and private operating agencies of the countries belonging to the union. The director of the consultative committee co-ordinates the work of the study groups, of the plenary assembly and of the committee as a whole.

The work of these committees has emphasized the importance of good engineering and transmission standards to world-wide communication service and has gone far in bringing about the introduction of such standards. In particular, exhaustive consideration has been given to problems of transmission and interference, frequency bands and allocations, standards of telephone performance and questions of suitable rates and classes of service, all of which has contributed to effective international long-distance telephony. On Jan. 1, 1957, the CCIF and CCIT were merged into a single committee known as the CCITT (Comité Consultatif International Téléphonique et Télégraphique).

## III. TECHNICAL DEVELOPMENT

The first telephones were extremely crude; it was barely possible to talk over them. The problems of transmitting speech for substantial distances were not understood, or even visualized. Nor was there the slightest comprehension of the complications involved in interconnecting large numbers of telephones.

One indispensable phase in the development of telephony was the improvement of telephone station instruments as to quality and loudness of speech, as well as convenience and cost. Concurrently, it was necessary to develop telephone lines and circuits to transmit speech currents reliably, without appreciable impairment or interference, and economically, for short or long distances. These advances are sometimes grouped under the term transmission development. Through such development, most telephone conversation has become practically effortless.

Another essential was the development of switching mechanisms whereby any two telephone instruments in a large system could be connected together certainly, rapidly and economically. This part of the advance is referred to as switching development. Progress in these areas came about gradually in different countries, along generally similar but not identical lines, and with, in many instances, substantial time differences.

**1. Station Instrumentalities.**—The station set at the premises of a telephone customer normally consists of a transmitter, which converts the speech waves in the air into their electrical replicas; a receiver, which performs the reverse operation of converting the incoming electrical waves into sound waves; a transformer (formerly called an induction coil) designed to increase the effectiveness of the transmitter and to permit full duplex operation (*i.e.,* use of a single pair of wires for speech in both directions, without requiring a switch to change from talking to listening or vice versa); a bell or equivalent summoning device; a switch hook to control connection of the set to the customer's line; and various associated items. In automatic switching systems the station set also includes a device, such as a dial, for generating signals to actuate the switching mechanism.

Bell's original electromagnetic transmitter served also as the receiver, the same instrument being held alternately to the mouth and the ear. An important forward step was the invention by Émile Berliner in 1877, and by Thomas A. Edison later in the same year, of different forms of transmitters utilizing variable-contact resistance between two solid electrodes connected in a battery circuit. Berliner employed metallic electrodes, while Edison used semiconducting materials, particularly plumbago (*i.e.,* graphite). Berliner also introduced the induction coil into the transmitter circuit in 1877.

The principle of the microphone contact (*see* MICROPHONE), which underlay both the Berliner and Edison transmitters, was elucidated by David E. Hughes in England in 1878. By virtue of this principle, energy from a battery is controlled by the voice waves so that the telephone transmitter acts as an amplifier as well as a converter of sound waves. The first recorded recognition of amplification through a microphonic contact seems to be found in a German patent of Robert Lüdtge, issued Jan. 12, 1878.

A transmitter in which granular carbon was used for the variable contact was invented in 1878 by Henry Hunnings, an English clergyman. Edison invented a transmitter whose carbon granules were obtained from anthracite coal, and Anthony C. White in 1890 invented the solid back transmitter, using a "button" of granular carbon placed between a fixed electrode and a diaphragm-actuated movable one. White's transmitter incorporated all the basic features of the modern telephone transmitter, though great improvements in efficiency (up to a thousandfold amplification of speech sounds), naturalness, resistance to aging and other features have resulted from continuing research and development. Extensive studies of the properties of speech and hearing have contributed to this result.

Modern telephone receivers utilize the same basic principles as those found in Bell's original instrument. Fundamentally, the receiver consists of a permanent magnet having pole pieces wound with coils of insulated fine wire, and a diaphragm driven by magnetic material which is supported near the pole pieces. Speech currents passing through the coils vary the attraction of the permanent magnet for the diaphragm, causing it to vibrate and produce sound waves. Through the years the design of the electromagnetic system has been continuously improved to provide better talking qualities. In a later type of receiver, introduced in the United States in 1951, the diaphragm, consisting of a central cone and ring-shaped armature, is driven as a piston to obtain efficient response over a wide frequency range.

In early telephone sets a hand-cranked generator, or so-called magneto, was used for signaling the operator, and local dry bat-

BY COURTESY OF THE BELL TELEPHONE SYSTEM

20th-century telephones: (above) one of the first dial telephones, 1919; (top right) "500" colour set with volume control for bell, 1954; (bottom right) pushbutton telephone teries supplied power to the transmitter. A centralized battery arrangement for signaling was invented in 1880 and one for both talking and signaling in 1886. With the gradual introduction of this common battery system, magneto telephone sets were largely superseded.

The first suggestions for mounting a telephone transmitter and receiver on a common handle, thus forming what is now known as a handset, were made by two Englishmen, C. A. McEvoy and G. E. Pritchett, in 1877. Starting in 1878, a type of handset devised by Robert G. Brown was used by boy operators in the Gold and Stock telephone exchange in New York city. Handsets for customers' use were introduced in France about 1882 and spread quickly in Europe. Initial difficulties in meeting satisfactory transmission standards with the handset arrangement were gradually overcome, and most modern instruments are of this type.

Methods of connecting the transmitter and receiver to the line likewise have been gradually improved. Starting with work by George A. Campbell, arrangements known as antiside-tone circuits have been developed whereby most of the electrical energy generated in the transmitter is directed toward the distant station, with a minimum entering the speaker's receiver.

Apart from the basic telephone instrument, special customer equipment and arrangements are provided to meet individual requirements of various kinds. Telephone sets are available which permit the user to hold a conversation without lifting the receiver, a small microphone being used to pick up the voice and a small loud-speaker to reproduce the incoming speech. There are loud gongs or other signaling devices for noisy locations, amplifiers for persons with subnormal hearing, automatic answering devices, arrangements for recording conversations, loud-speakers, etc.

Telephone pay stations installed in public or semipublic locations provide a coin telephone set which includes, in addition to the usual station equipment, a coin collector having one or more slots designed to accept legitimate coins and reject slugs or spurious coins. The coins, in passing down their respective slots, strike distinctive gongs whose tones permit an operator to supervise the deposits. Many coin collectors are arranged to hold the coins in suspension in a hopper, with means provided whereby the suspended coins can be collected or refunded, depending on whether or not the desired connection is completed.

Key telephone systems, affording greater flexibility of telephone usage than a single station set, are frequently used in business offices and residences. Combinations of push-button, turn-button or lever-type keys, installed on a desk or table or mounted integrally in the base of a telephone set, can be arranged to perform a variety of functions, particularly where two or more lines and a number of stations are involved. Thus a telephone may be connected to any of several lines, a call may be held on one line while conversation proceeds on another, etc.

**2. Telephone Lines.**—Telephone circuits are furnished principally by wire lines, although radio is used to a considerable extent. Telephone lines comprise a network of wires which interconnect individual telephone stations, central offices and communities. These wire lines are of two forms—cable and open wire. The usual type of cable consists of insulated copper wires, twisted together and usually covered with a protecting sheath. Open-wire lines consist of bare wires, generally of copper, fastened to insulators which are supported on poles at some distance above ground, commonly on pins in crossarms.

Following previous telegraph practice, the first telephone circuits utilized a single overhead wire, usually iron, with ground return. An important early improvement was the development by Thomas B. Doolittle in 1877 of hard-drawn copper wire that gave good tensile strength together with improved electrical conductivity. The advantages of a two-wire or so-called metallic circuit in reducing noise and interference were soon realized. It was found also that by transposing the wires (*i.e.,* interchanging their positions) a number of circuits could be carried on a single pole line without excessive interaction which would permit the conversation on one circuit to be heard on another. These several features made possible a successful open-wire telephone line between Boston and New York in 1885.

Early in telephone history, as the number of open-wire circuits strung on poles and rooftops in the large cities began to reach the point of impracticability, methods of compacting the lines in overhead or underground cable were tried. At first the wires were placed in pipes and sealed against moisture with oil, paraffin or asphaltum. Means were soon developed whereby lead, heated to plasticity, could be extruded over a core of conductors. The introduction of dry paper as insulation for the conductors completed the foundation for the modern telephone cable.

Research and development covering many materials and processes made it possible to increase the number of pairs in a full-sized local cable from a maximum of 50 in the year 1888 to more than 2,000 in the second half of the 20th century. This increase was accomplished largely by reducing the size of the copper wires, from 25 lb. per wire mile in 1888 to 4 lb. Following World War II, new types of cable sheath were developed in order to reduce cost and lessen dependence on lead supply. One form uses thin layers of aluminum and steel covered with polyethylene.

In a typical urban or suburban installation, insulated wires from each customer's premises extend to a distribution cable which in turn connects to a feeder cable leading to the central office. In densely built areas the feeders are generally placed in underground ducts; elsewhere, overhead. Circuits between central offices, known as trunks, are provided in trunk cables which usually employ larger wires than those leading to customer stations.

The network of lines which interconnect approximately 75,000 communities in the U.S. include approximately 35,000,000 mi. of wire on 260,000 mi. of route. More than 90% of the wires are in cable, the remainder open wire. For the rest of the world, the percentage of long-distance facilities furnished by cable ranges from nearly 100% in a few countries to a very low figure in the less populated regions. Since cable is virtually stormproof, it affords much greater reliability than does open wire.

A type of long-distance cable common in the U.S. employs conductors 36 mils in diameter, weighing 20 lb. to the mile (no. 19 AWG gauge). In making this cable, two paper-insulated wires are first twisted together to form a pair; then a quad is formed by twisting two pairs together. This twisting aids in the prevention of cross talk (*i.e.,* overhearing) between different pairs. In European toll cables, four conductors are usually twisted together to form a spiral four or star quad. In either case the quads are grouped together and enclosed by the sheath. Such a cable may be supported aerially or placed in an underground duct, or, with a suitable protective covering of jute or steel tape, may be buried in the ground. A special type of cable used for coaxial systems is discussed under *Carrier Systems* below.

**3. Phantoms.**—Around 1900 the principle of "phantoming" two pairs of wires was introduced. The original idea of phantoming was devised by Frank Jacob in 1882 and the present method by John J. Carty in 1886. The phantom arrangement makes it possible to derive from two pairs of wires a total of three telephone circuits. The additional circuit, called the phantom, is obtained by using the two wires of each pair in parallel as a side of the phantom. To render this scheme practical, efficient balanced transformers were needed for the end connections, and transposition arrangements were required to keep the cross talk between the three circuits within tolerable bounds. The phantom principle came to play an important part in both open-wire and cable plant. Because the presence of phantoms makes high-frequency transmission difficult, the advent of carrier systems greatly curtailed the use of phantoms for long-distance circuits.

**4. Loading.**—As speech currents pass along a line their strength decreases (a process referred to as attenuation), so that after some distance they become too weak to actuate a receiver properly. Studies by A. Vaschy (1889) and Oliver Heaviside (1893) developed the theoretical possibility of improving the transmission efficiency of telephone lines by artificially increasing their inductance. Various investigators speculated on the practicability of approximating the beneficial effect of an increase in uniformly distributed inductance by introducing in the line concentrated or lumped inductance in the form of low-resistance loading coils. Finally, in 1899, Michael I. Pupin and George A. Campbell (working independently, Pupin having a slight priority) discovered that the key to the problem was the spacing of the loading coils. By providing at least pi (*i.e.,* about 3.14) loading coils per wavelength at the highest frequency to be transmitted, a substantial reduction in the attenuation of the speech waves is obtained. Thus a cable circuit may, by means of coil loading, be made to transmit telephonic currents as efficiently as a nonloaded one whose conductors weigh many times as much.

Another way of adding inductance to a cable circuit was proposed by Carl Emil Krarup of Copenhagen, his idea being to wind helically along the copper conductor a fine wire of soft iron. A cable with this continuous loading was placed between Elsinore and Helsingborg in 1902. While continuously loaded cables have proved of some importance for submarine applications, coil loading has been almost universally preferred for loaded land cables.

By 1913 coil loading made it possible to extend the useful range of open-wire circuits to approximately 2,000 mi., and to employ underground cable to connect Washington, D.C., and Boston via New York city. After electron tube amplifiers became available, open-wire loading was largely abandoned, but loading is still extensively applied on cable circuits used for voice frequencies, and especially on local trunk circuits.

Satisfactory loading requires that the loading coils have very low energy losses in their magnetic cores and copper windings. The toroidal-shaped cores of modern loading coils make use of a powdered magnetic alloy whose particles are individually insulated, compressed under high pressure and then usually heat treated to develop optimum magnetic properties. Progressive improvement of magnetic core materials has brought about large reductions in the size and cost of loading coils, as well as improved performance. A core material commonly used in the U.S. consists of an alloy of nickel, iron and molybdenum known as molybdenum permalloy, discovered by Gustav W. Elmen. In Europe powdered iron cores of somewhat larger size are employed.

**5. Electron Tubes and Repeaters.**—For years the range of telephony was severely limited by loss of energy due to dissipation along wire lines, or to spreading in the case of radio waves. The idea of inserting one or more repeaters in a telephone line for the purpose of reinforcing or amplifying the telephonic currents from some local source of energy is almost as old as the telephone itself, but many years elapsed before the quest for a satisfactory repeater achieved success. In a so-called mechanical repeater, tried in 1904, inertia of the moving parts was found to present inherent limitations. Subsequently H. E. Shreeve developed a repeater employing carbon-contact amplification which was capable of practical use. The real solution to the amplification problem, however, was found in the device invented by Lee De Forest in 1906, which he called the audion, and which is now known as a three-electrode vacuum tube or electron tube, or in England as a valve. In its original form as used in radiotelegraphy, this tube was unsuited for telephone purposes (*see* ELECTRON TUBE; AMPLIFIERS). Research by Harold D. Arnold, Irving Langmuir and others showed that a major requirement for adequate performance in an amplifier was the creation of a high degree of vacuum inside the tube envelope. By 1914 satisfactory high vacuum tubes were produced. Using telephone repeaters with amplification supplied by vacuum tubes, telephone service between New York and San Francisco was inaugurated in 1915.

Continuing development work brought about many improvements in vacuum tube repeaters. Efficient circuits and auxiliary equipment were devised for utilizing the amplifier element and associating it with the line circuits. The life of the repeater tube most commonly used in 1917 was about 1,000 hours, whereas standard tubes of a type introduced in 1935 have a life of about 90,000 hours, equivalent to more than ten years of continuous operation. In addition, the power required to heat the tube filaments was reduced to one-tenth that required in 1917.

With repeaters available, transmission defects of different kinds became increasingly apparent. The lines, particularly if loaded, were found to introduce severe distortion by reason of differences in the transmission efficiency and transmission velocity at different frequencies. Furthermore, large variations in transmission loss resulted from changes in the electrical resistance of cable conductors with temperature, or from changes in the leakage of open-wire conductors. Extensive developments in the field of network theory made it possible to design equalizers with frequency characteristics that compensate accurately for the line distortion. Variations in line loss are automatically counteracted by transmission regulators. Devices known as companders, in which the amplitude of speech syllables serves to compress the range of speech volumes at the transmitting end and to introduce a corresponding expansion at the receiving end, have proved beneficial in reducing the effect of line noise on both wire and radio circuits.

Another unwanted effect on telephone circuits is the presence of electrical echoes due to discontinuities in the line. These, when converted into sound, may disturb both talker and listener. The echoes become more annoying the longer they are delayed and hence are of greatest concern on long circuits. They are controlled by restricting their occurrence, by reducing the line delay or by applying devices called echo suppressors to prevent their reaching the telephone users.

The vacuum tube provided for the first time the means for precise measurement of these and other transmission effects, and thus made it possible to establish a firm foundation for the transmission art. Vacuum tubes connected as generators of electric oscillations supply the range of frequencies needed for communication measurement. Other vacuum tubes amplify the extremely weak currents involved in telephone transmission to a level at which they can be conveniently measured.

Following the three-element tube, many different types of vacuum tubes were developed for various applications. These include tubes with four or five elements for providing high and stable amplification, klystrons and traveling wave tubes for operation at extremely high frequencies, phototubes responsive to light, etc. Millions of cold-cathode, gas-filled electron tubes are used in telephone handsets attached to multiparty lines to permit ringing only the desired one out of four or more stations on a line. The normal life of such tubes is estimated to be hundreds of years.

**6. Carrier Systems.**—It is common practice on long-distance routes to multiply the circuit capacity by the application of carrier telephone systems. These are called carrier systems because of the underlying principle, known as modulation, whereby the voice frequencies modulate a higher frequency current which "carries" the voice currents. A voice wave is composed of undulations with a frequency of occurrence ranging from about 200 to 3,000 per second or, as it is commonly expressed, from 200 to 3,000 cycles per second (c.p.s.). In the modulation process these frequencies are transposed to a higher frequency range (*e.g.,* 10,200 to 13,000 c.p.s.) for transmission over the line. By using different carrier frequency bands a number of conversations can be sent simultaneously over one transmission path. At the receiving end the carrier frequency bands are separated by electric networks called filters (invented by G. A. Campbell in 1915), and the original voice frequencies are recovered by an inverse process known as demodulation. Carrier systems make extensive use of vacuum tubes—as amplifiers, as oscillators for generating carrier frequencies and sometimes as modulators for shifting bands of frequencies from one range to another.

The art of multiplex carrier telephony grew out of the harmonic telegraph systems associated with the names of Gray, Bell, E. Mercadier and others. The extension of the carrier principle to telephony, together with the use of electrical resonance instead of mechanical resonance for selecting the carrier frequencies, was accomplished in 1891 by two Frenchmen, Maurice Hutin and Maurice Leblanc. During the period 1908–11, demonstrations of carrier techniques were conducted by Ernst Ruhmer in Germany and Maj. Gen. George O. Squier in the U.S.

Following experiments between Toledo, O., and South Bend, Ind., in 1917, the first commercial application of the carrier principle was made in 1918 on an open-wire line between Baltimore, Md., and Pittsburgh, Pa., giving four additional telephone circuits on a pair of wires. With modern carrier techniques, as many as 16 telephone circuits are derived from a single open-wire pair. Beginning in 1934 in Germany, a system which yielded one extra telephone channel on a lightly loaded cable pair was extensively applied in Europe.

Application of substantial numbers of carrier channels to cables necessitates many more repeaters because of the higher attenuation of the cable pairs, so that minor imperfections in each amplifier become quite serious. The solution to this problem was provided by Harold S. Black when he invented the negative feedback amplifier in 1927. The complete development of the underlying theory came in subsequent work by Harry Nyquist. Though difficult in theory, the idea itself is quite simple. A part of the amplifier output is fed back to the input in such a way as to give practically distortionless amplification, together with almost complete absence of variation in amplification as a result of power supply variation and tube aging. The improvement thus obtained may be a thousandfold or more.

The negative feedback principle is now applied almost universally to amplifiers used for any purpose. This principle formed the basis for the introduction in 1937, between Toledo and South Bend, of a 12-channel carrier system operating on nonloaded cable pairs. Today carrier systems are quite generally used on long-distance cable routes, yielding circuits with excellent transmission properties for distances up to thousands of miles. Important in this connection has been continued progress in the control of cross talk and noise. Cable carrier systems in the U.S. are arranged to derive 12 to 24 telephone circuits from two nonloaded 19-gauge pairs. Similar systems, some of them providing much larger numbers of channels, are used in Europe and elsewhere.

With the aid of a special type of cable conductor, called a coaxial unit or merely a coaxial, carrier techniques have been greatly expanded. A coaxial consists essentially of a copper tube, commonly about the size of a lead pencil, with a wire centrally supported inside. A full-size cable may contain as many as eight such coaxials, plus a number of conventional pairs of wire. By applying amplifiers at close intervals, four to eight miles, a very wide band of frequencies can be transmitted over a single coaxial.

The transmission properties of a coaxial circuit were considered by various 19th-century workers, especially Lord Kelvin and Alexander Russell. But it was a far journey from these studies to a wide-band transmission system suitable for long-distance multichannel telephony and television. The first such coaxial systems were applied in 1936 between New York city and Philadelphia and between Berlin and Leipzig. More highly developed systems are now widely used in both the U.S. and Europe.

A type of coaxial system introduced between Minneapolis, Minn., and Stevens Point, Wis., in 1939 utilizes a frequency band nearly three megacycles (*i.e.,* 3,000,000 cycles) wide, with two coaxials giving either 600 two-way telephone channels or a television circuit in each direction. Techniques were further augmented in a system, first applied in 1952, which provides a frequency band nearly eight megacycles wide, so that two coaxials can provide either (1) 1,800 telephone channels; or (2) 600 telephone channels plus a 4.2-mc. television circuit in each direction. Since a long coaxial system may have 1,000 or more repeaters connected in tandem, each one providing a ten-thousandfold amplification, the utmost perfection is necessary in the performance of each repeater.

The minimum distance for which carrier systems prove economical depends on the cost of the terminal apparatus. In recent types of systems the economical distance has been greatly reduced, so that carrier can be used for short-haul toll circuits, interoffice trunks and rural circuits.

**7. Radio.**—Radio, originally employed for telegraphy, has become an important instrument for telephone purposes. Both the theoretical and the utilitarian aspects of radio transmission are treated elsewhere (*see* BROADCASTING; RADIO).

The same basic principle of modulation used in carrier systems is required to shift the telephone signals to the desired radio frequency. There are several different kinds of modulation that may be used in either radio or wire systems. Simplest of these is amplitude modulation, in which the amplitude of a modulating wave (*e.g.,* a speech wave) controls the amplitude of a sine wave carrier. The first complete analysis of amplitude modulation was made by John R. Carson, who showed that in order to convey the intelligence only one of the bands of frequencies generated in the process need be transmitted. Because of its efficient use of frequency space, Carson's single side band method is widely employed.

Another common form is frequency modulation, wherein the instantaneous frequency of a sine wave carrier is varied in proportion to the amplitude of the modulating wave. This method makes it possible by sacrificing frequency space to gain an advantage in the ratio of signal to noise.

Still another form is pulse modulation, in which the carrier consists, not of a sine wave, but of a series of pulses whose amplitude, duration, position or mere presence may be controlled so as to convey the message. In pulse code modulation, originated by A. H. Reeves in 1939, successive quantized samples of the modulating wave produce corresponding code patterns of pulses. This provides, at the expense of band width, low vulnerability to noise and interference and adaptability to repeated regeneration of the signals without distortion. For multichannel transmission, the pulses corresponding to different channels are interleaved.

The advantages of being able to telephone without a wire connection were obvious from the beginnings of radio. Many early radio experimenters, notably R. A. Fessenden and De Forest in America and Quirino Majorana, Giuseppe Vanni and V. Poulsen in Europe, succeeded in transmitting speech over distances of a few miles. Several essentials for practical application were lacking, however—a practicable generator of continuous high-frequency waves, a means for modulating these waves in accordance with speech and a receiving amplifier for revivifying the waves after enfeeblement in transit. In the main, it was the vacuum tube that provided the solution for all these problems.

In 1915, the same year that telephone service across the U.S. was begun, intelligible speech was experimentally transmitted by radio from Arlington, Va., to Hawaii and to Paris. In 1927 the first commercial overseas radiotelephone circuit was opened between the U.S. and England. Service from Berlin to Buenos Aires, Arg., was begun in 1928, from England to South America and Australia in 1930, and service between the U.S. and South America, Central America, the Hawaiian Islands, the Philippine Islands, the Netherlands Indies and Japan during the years 1930 to 1934. In the 1960s radiotelephone service was available between all principal countries not connected by wire and in addition was used in many instances to supplement wire facilities. Most of the overseas radiotelephone circuits were in the short-wave range from 3 to 30 mc., where long-distance transmission is accomplished by reflecting the waves from the ionosphere. The performance of the radio circuits, although fairly satisfactory, was subject to some difficulty due to atmospheric disturbances.

Radio systems that make use of scattering from the tropospheric layer in the atmosphere can transmit wide frequency bands capable of handling a number of telephone channels to distances "beyond the horizon." A system of this type was placed in service between Miami and Havana in 1957.

Starting with service to the steamship "Leviathan" in 1929, radiotelephone service has been extended to many large oceangoing ships. Thousands of smaller ships in coastal waters, on lakes, in harbours and on rivers are equipped for connection to shore telephone stations by radio. Commercial radiotelephone service between the public telephone system and motor vehicles in cities and on highways began in the U.S. in 1946. Other vehicles were provided with radiotelephone sets for private services, such as those of airlines, police, taxicabs, etc., and there were mobile radio stations for public service on trains and airplanes. Radio systems were used also for bridging short water gaps and crossing other difficult terrain. Portable radiotelephone equipment was employed in emergencies such as floods or hurricanes to bridge gaps in the regular toll circuits until normal service could be restored. Radio paging systems were available in which a small receiving set carried on the person was used to summon an individual to the nearest telephone in order to receive a call.

Repeatered radio systems for obtaining substantial numbers of long-distance telephone circuits, as well as broad frequency bands for television transmission, are used in many parts of the world.

These commonly transmit radio waves of thousands of megacycles, known as microwaves, over line-of-sight paths. As early as 1934 a microwave radio system developed by A. G. Clavier and others was employed for transmission across the English channel. The large-scale development during World War II of microwave techniques for radar use provided a powerful stimulus in the postwar development of microwave communication systems. A microwave radio-relay (*i.e.*, repeatered) system was placed in service between New York city and Boston in 1947, and one across the United States in 1951. This latter system provides six radio channels in each direction, and each radio channel affords either 600 telephone circuits or a single television circuit.

Concentration of large numbers of circuits on a single route by means of carrier systems, coaxial systems or radio-relay systems yields large economic advantages through sharing common elements of cost including right of way, line conductors, installation, line maintenance, radio towers, power supply, etc. Combining the requirements for both telephony and television on a common route affords further economy.

**8. Submarine Telephony.**—Submarine cables for transmitting telegraph signals antedated the invention of the telephone. Many years went by, however, before long submarine cables suitable for telephony became practical. As early as 1891 a cable containing four wires was laid under the English channel, between St. Margaret's bay, Eng., and Sangatte, Fr. During the next five years several cables of similar construction, suitable only for shallow water and relatively short distances, were placed under the channel.

When cable is laid in deep water, the high pressure necessitates a different type of cable, the usual construction for deepwater telephone cables consisting of a central conductor surrounded by insulation around which is a return conductor. The first such cables were laid in 1921 between Key West, Fla., and Havana, Cuba, a distance of more than 100 mi. Each of these cables provided a single voice circuit and four telegraph circuits. Two years later the first long submarine cables adapted for carrier telephone transmission were placed across the 40-mi. stretch between the California coast and Santa Catalina Island.

For spanning greater distances with the wide frequency band required to accommodate a number of telephone channels, intermediate repeaters are needed. The first submerged telephone repeaters were applied between Anglesey, Wales, and the Isle of Man in 1943 and between Lowestoft, Eng., and Borkum, Ger., in 1946. These repeaters were adapted only for shallow-water operation. Repeaters designed for deepwater use were included in a pair of cables placed in 1950 between Key West and Havana, the two cables giving a total of 24 telephone circuits.

To handle the expanding requirements for transatlantic telephone service, the first transoceanic telephone cable system, between Clarenville, Nfd., and Oban, Scot., with an extension from Newfoundland to Nova Scotia and a radio-relay link to Portland, Me., was placed in service in 1956. This was a joint project of the American Telephone and Telegraph company, the British post office and the Canadian Overseas Telecommunication corporation. The two cables on the main crossing had submerged repeaters at approximately 40-mi. intervals to provide a total of 36 telephone circuits. The vacuum tube repeaters were designed to operate continuously and flawlessly with no attention for at least 20 years, at depths up to 2,000 fathoms. Similar submarine systems between Port Angeles, Wash., and Ketchikan, Alaska, and between California and Hawaii are in service. The first cable (5,300 nautical miles) between Hawaii and Japan (1964) provided 128 voice circuits, the same number provided in 1965 by a cable linking New Jersey with France.

**9. Information Theory.**—Progress in telephony and allied arts was greatly furthered by the formulation of a comprehensive theory underlying the communication of information. This theory, variously referred to as information theory (*q.v.*) or communication theory, resulted from studies by Claude E. Shannon, Norbert Wiener and others, following earlier work by R. V. L. Hartley. It states in essence that information of the kind contained in messages transmitted over communication systems is measurable; as a consequence, the loss of information caused by unpredictable perturbations (noise) introduced during transmission can be evaluated. The basic unit of measure is a "yes-or-no" choice, which is called a bit (short for *bi*nary digi*t*). All information can for communication purposes be expressed as, or encoded into, sequences of on-or-off (*i.e.*, binary) pulses. The development of the basic mathematical theory made it possible to treat transmission factors such as band width, noise, distortion and the like, and the relations among them, in quantitative terms. This facilitated the comparison of different transmission systems—for example, systems using different forms of modulation, different coding, etc. The theory also established upper limits for the rate at which information can be transmitted over systems of different kinds.

**10. Switching.**—Establishing a connection between any two telephones out of a large group is a complicated process. Even in the simplest situation, where both telephones are served by the same switchboard, it is necessary to: (1) observe that a customer wishes to make a call; (2) connect the operator (or switching mechanism) to his line; (3) determine what telephone he wishes to be connected with; (4) select a speech path between them which is not already in use; (5) determine whether the wanted telephone is idle or busy; (6) if idle, ring the bell, or if busy, inform the calling customer; (7) determine when the call has ended; and (8) restore all equipment to its quiescent state, in readiness for other calls. If the telephones are served by different switchboards, perhaps in widely separated cities, it is also necessary to determine what switchboard serves the wanted telephone and how it may be reached.

From the beginning, the importance of the switching function in telephony was recognized, but the means initially employed were

BY COURTESY OF THE BELL TELEPHONE SYSTEM

CENTRAL-OFFICE SWITCHING SYSTEMS

(Left) Step-by-step switches; (centre) crossbar switches; (right) logic units for electronic switching primitive. The first telephone switching arrangement was provided by the Holmes Electric company at Boston in 1877, by using for telephone connections in the daytime the line wires and plug-and-block connectors employed for a burglar alarm system at night. A commercial telephone switchboard placed in operation at New Haven, Conn., in 1878 served 21 stations on eight grounded lines. In contrast, a modern central office may serve as many as 100,000 telephones on 50,000 lines.

The New Haven exchange, and other primitive ones, provided a separate switch for each combination of lines that might have to be connected together. For eight lines this required only 28 switches; but the number of switches increased much more rapidly than the number of customers and quickly became impracticable. With 100 lines, for example, 4,950 switches would have been required. To get around this difficulty, the cord circuit was introduced in 1880. Each line was terminated on the switchboard in a socket (called a jack), and a number of short flexible circuits (called cords) with a plug on each end were also provided. Two lines could thus be interconnected by inserting the two ends of a cord in the appropriate jacks. This was an efficient system as long as the number of calls passing through a switchboard could be handled by a single operator.

Another early invention, which permitted much larger volumes of traffic to be handled efficiently on a manual basis, was the multiple system devised by Leroy B. Firman in 1878. With this, each customer's line is connected to a number of jacks, placed at suitable intervals along the switchboard, so that one is within the reach of every operator.

With the introduction of the multiple system, it became necessary to develop a busy test to determine whether or not a line with which connection was desired was already in use through a connection made at some other part of the switchboard. In a manual switchboard the operator performs this test by touching the tip of a connecting plug to a conducting sleeve forming part of the jack of the desired line. If the line is busy, a click is heard in the operator's receiver.

In 1895 the magnetically operated drop signals which informed the operator of a customer's desire for service were first replaced by incandescent lamps. These were more reliable and smaller than the drop signals and permitted a much more compact arrangement of the subscriber's jacks.

There was continuous improvement to adapt manual switchboards to the growing volume and complexity of telephone traffic and to modern standards of workers' comfort and of customers' convenience. There also were improvements in the associated circuits. But the design of all subsequent manual switchboards was based upon the plug-ended cord, the multiple, the busy test and lamp signals.

The idea of fully automatic switching also appeared quite early. In fact the first patent for an automatic switching system was issued to Daniel Connolly, T. A. Connolly and T. J. McTighe in 1879, only two years after the first primitive switchboard in Boston. This system never achieved commercial success. In 1889 Almon B. Strowger invented an automatic system which was installed at La Porte, Ind., in 1892, the first commercial automatic exchange in the world. The system was subsequently developed by Alexander E. Keith and other engineers of the Automatic Electric company into a form which is still extensively used throughout the world under the names step-by-step or Strowger system. In this system the switching mechanisms are operated directly by pulses generated at the customer's instrument. Originally the customer operated a push button to produce the switching pulses, but this and other types of calling devices gradually gave way to the dial mechanism now in general use. This was invented in 1896 by A. E. Keith, C. J. Erickson and John Erickson of the Automatic Electric company.

The basic mechanism around which the Strowger system is built is the Strowger switch, which is sometimes called a connector and sometimes a selector according to the use to which it is put. In complete form this consists essentially of two parts: a ten-by-ten array of terminals (the bank) arranged in a cylindrical arc; and a movable switch (the brush) which is translated along the axis of the cylinder by one ratchet mechanism and rotated about it by another, so that it can be brought to the position of any one of the 100 terminals. Each ratchet mechanism is driven by an electromagnet, which can respond to the pulses produced by a telephone dial.

Many other switching systems have been invented, notably in the United States, Germany and Sweden, and a number of them have been put into successful commercial operation. Some of these have operated on the step-by-step principle but have used different types of apparatus. Others have operated on the principle of common control, in which pulses are stored for a short time in a device which then controls the switches either directly or through some intermediate mechanism.

The distinguishing feature of such systems is that the common-control mechanisms (known as registers, senders, translators, directors, markers, etc.) are not assigned to the customer for the duration of his call but are used only as long as they are needed and are then free to serve other customers. Thus each serves many calls per hour, and few are required; it is therefore practicable to provide complicated devices which can perform a variety of useful functions but which would be too expensive to assign for the duration of the call. Systems using common control have great flexibility and efficiency in the use of trunk groups, and are especially advantageous for large exchanges and for automatic routing of long-distance calls.

The earliest common-control systems were developed by the Western Electric company, primarily to meet the needs of large metropolitan centres. In a program beginning in 1906, two systems were developed alongside one another, and both proved to be successful. One, called the rotary system, was first put into commercial service in England in 1914. The other, called the panel system, went into commercial use at Newark, N.J., in January of the following year. Common-control principles were also applied to the step-by-step switch by the Automatic Electric company, and the resulting system was adopted by the British post office in 1922 for use in London. The more recent common-control systems have been crossbar systems, of which several commercial types have been developed by the Bell system in the United States, by the Swedish Telecommunication administration and the L. M. Ericsson company in Sweden and by subsidiary companies of the International Telephone and Telegraph company in Belgium and Germany.

The most important concepts in the evolution of the modern types of crossbar exchange were probably translation, the sender, the marker, the crossbar switch and the principle of call-back operation. Translation, invented by E. C. Molina of the American Telephone and Telegraph company in 1906, makes it possible to convert incoming dial pulses from decimal to nondecimal form and thus affords flexibility and efficiency in the use of trunk groups. The sender, first used in the rotary system, is essentially an automatic mechanism which generates new dialing signals, either in the code given by the translator or in other appropriate codes.

The basic function of the marker is to make a preliminary test of several alternative paths to a wanted destination through an array of switches, before any of the switches is closed, so as to avoid the possibility of encountering a busy switch after part of the switching operation has been performed. It was invented by N. G. Palmgren and G. A. Betulander of Sweden in 1912 and was first used commercially in a system manufactured by the Relay Automatic company of England from 1915 to 1920. As used in crossbar systems of the Bell system, it has been developed into a complex assemblage which serves as the basic control element for the entire switching operation. Among other things, it tests the circuits before connections are established; it seeks out alternate paths when needed; and it reports trouble conditions which may be encountered in its preliminary tests. Since it can examine a large number of trunk circuits practically simultaneously, it uses them with great efficiency.

The crossbar switch is essentially a multiple relay structure affording fast operation and reliable contacts of precious metal. Unlike other switches mentioned above, the moving parts have little inertia and move through small distances. It was first conceived in America by Homer J. Roberts of Automatic Electric company in 1901, and later patented in separate forms by John G. Roberts and John N. Reynolds, both of Western Electric company. The first satisfactory mechanical design, worked out by Palmgren and Betulander in Sweden in 1919, was used by the Swedish telephone authorities in a commercial exchanger in 1926. Aside from a small-scale trial installation in Stockholm in 1919, which was subsequently abandoned, this was the first public use of the crossbar switch. The system in which it was used, however, and all other crossbar exchanges in Sweden until about the middle of the century, operated on step-by-step principles. Most of the crossbar switches used in America and other countries follow the Swedish design.

Call back is a principle of operation, invented by Edson L. Erwin in 1938, which has been effectively used in crossbar systems. When a customer originates a call, the register stores not only the wanted number but also the identity of the calling telephone, which is determined automatically. The connection with the calling subscriber is then disconnected, and an entirely new connection established, from a favourable point within the exchange, to both the calling and wanted telephones.

All the automatic switching systems described were built around the electromagnetic relay and other electromagnetically operated devices. The relay employs magnetic attraction produced by an electric current to move a magnetic armature and thus open or close electrical contacts so as to perform switching or other operations. This device dates back to the early part of the 19th century, and in a form much cruder than the present was the basis for the development of telegraphy. The name relay results from the early use of the device to pass along telegraph signals after enfeeblement in transmission. As switching systems developed, relays came to be employed for a wide variety of purposes, including multiple contacts, slow or fast operation or release, marginal operation, etc. Modern switching systems require approximately 1,000 relay operations to establish a single telephone connection, and some systems have as many as ten relays per subscriber. Hence, reliability in relays is extremely important. Less than one failure in 40 years of service is a normal criterion for satisfactory operation.

As automatic switching systems were improved, their application was extended until, by the 1960s, more than 90% of the world's telephones were automatic, as compared with 15% only a generation earlier. This metamorphosis occurred not only because automatic operation is faster, more accurate and more economical than manual service, but more basically because in many areas the enormous number of operators necessary to support the rapid telephone growth would have far exceeded the possible supply.

In America the crossbar system, designed originally for metropolitan areas, presented so many advantages as compared with earlier automatic systems that its basic principles were soon applied in other fields. Crossbar tandem equipment, for example, is the modern version of the tandem principle developed originally for manual systems. Through the tandem scheme, traffic between offices on opposite sides of a large metropolitan area is handled through one or more intermediate (tandem) offices which act as clearinghouses for these relatively small amounts of traffic, handling them more efficiently than if direct paths were provided and thus reducing the number of trunk circuits required.

Another type of crossbar system is specially adapted to the automatic switching of long-distance circuits. With this, connections are made on a two-path or four-wire basis, a separate path being used for each direction of transmission so as to obtain superior transmission performance on connections comprising a number of circuit links in tandem.

The first crossbar switching system in the long-distance field, introduced in Philadelphia in 1943, enabled operators but not customers to dial long-distance calls. This advance was followed by another which permitted direct dialing by customers without the aid of an operator. The switching mechanism selects the route to the distant telephone. Should it find all direct circuits busy, it explores in succession as many as five alternate routes, and establishes the connection along the least circuitous one available. All this is done automatically. Necessary information regarding direct and alternate routes to the destination is permanently available in a translator, which supplies it to the control circuits as required.

Arrangements for customer dialing of at least some intercity calls were provided in all the principal countries of the world by the mid-1950s. In North America a complete program was worked out for eventually handling substantially all calls in this way. The initial installation of equipment to permit nation-wide dialing by customers was placed in service at Englewood, N.J., in 1951. With this equipment, customers were able to dial directly about 11,000,000 other customers in selected areas as far away as San Francisco. They dial a three-digit area code followed by the digits of the directory listing of the called number. By the mid-1960s this type of service had been extended to more than 83% of the Bell system telephones.

Closely related to automatic switching is the automatic recording of data for preparing the customer's bill. The simplest means for this purpose, used in either manual or automatic offices, is an electromechanical counter, known as a message register, which records the number of calls made by a customer. In a more elaborate arrangement, referred to as multiunit registration, the register can be operated more than once for a single call, the number of operations depending on the distance and duration of the call. Each customer is billed on a bulk basis for all of the "message units" totaled on his register. This plan is widely used in America and almost universally elsewhere. Another method of charging is "automatic ticketing," first introduced in Belgium. With this method, automatic equipment prints for each call a ticket similar to one that might be prepared by an operator.

In the U.S., where distances are great and the tariff structure complicated, a highly versatile type of message registration system, called automatic message accounting (usually abbreviated to AMA), was developed. In this system the information needed for billing calls is recorded in the form of coded holes in paper tape. Automatic processing of the tapes in an accounting centre yields bills with any desired amount of detail. The AMA system is extensively used in association with direct distance dialing.

A big step in the improvement of telephone service in outlying areas resulted from automatizing the telephone switching in very small communities. Community dial offices, either of the step-by-step or all-relay type, were provided in many localities. These function with no attendance except for occasional maintenance visits.

Another phase of telephone switching is found in switchboards, known as private branch exchanges, which are located on the customer's premises. The private branch exchange (abbreviated PBX) serves both for interconnecting the station sets of the customer's establishment and for connection over trunk lines to the central office. The smaller PBX's can be placed on a desk and operated by a person who may perform other duties as well. Large PBX's resemble central office switchboards and may be of either the manual or automatic type.

Exploratory developments are well under way in the principal communications laboratories of many countries with the ultimate objective of replacing electromechanical switching systems with electronic ones. A small beginning had been made in some units that are partly electronic and partly electromechanical. Among these may be mentioned the mechanoelectric system developed by the International Telephone and Telegraph company in Belgium and first installed at Ski, Nor., in 1954. By the mid-1960s fully electronic switching systems had been introduced in the U.S.

**11. Associated Services.**—Much of the plant required for telephone service is well adapted to the provision of other types of communication service, so that economies usually can be effected by designing the plant to handle the combined requirements of different services. The earliest of such associations was with the telegraph. Direct-current telegraph channels superposed on the telephone wires were leased to private customers and to the companies furnishing message telegraph service, and were employed also for telephone line maintenance. The introduction of carrier transmission methods made it possible to derive as many as 18 telegraph channels from one telephone circuit. Such channels serve both for teletypewriter exchange service, which is a switched service analogous to telephone service, and also for private-line teletypewriter service.

Satisfactory picture transmission requires a frequency band of about the same width as that for telephone conversation. Special networks are provided for picture service, and occasional use is made of regular telephone circuits for this purpose. Telephone circuits are employed also to render facsimile and other services. High-speed transmission of information in the form of pulses is being increasingly applied for both commercial and military purposes. Generally speaking, the chain networks used for the radio broadcasting of either sound or television programs are provided in conjunction with the telephone plant. For good quality of music reproduction, a frequency band somewhat wider than that adequate for speech is required. Television broadcasting necessitates a very wide frequency band, equivalent to that required for about 1,000 telephone circuits.

Television circuits are derived, commonly in association with large numbers of telephone channels, from coaxial or microwave systems. Wire broadcasting systems, in which sound programs are conveyed by wire directly to the customers' premises, are in limited use.

**12. Later Advances.**—Foremost in the area of new art in the industry is the transistor (*q.v.*), invented by W. H. Brattain and John Bardeen and first announced in 1948. This is a three-electrode amplifying device employing a semiconductor such as germanium or silicon. An improved form, known as the junction transistor, was invented later by William Shockley. The transistor can perform many of the functions previously assigned to vacuum tubes but is far more efficient because it requires no power to heat a cathode. Furthermore, it operates with much lower electrode voltages and is much smaller than a vacuum tube. Because of the transistor's low power dissipation and low voltage requirements, other electronic components associated with it can be miniaturized. The overall result is that the size, weight and power consumption of apparatus employing transistors usually can be reduced to a small fraction of that for equivalent apparatus using vacuum tubes.

Transistors therefore find large and varied applications in almost every field of electronics, and particularly in telephony and associated services, including not only places where vacuum tubes were previously used but many new situations as well. Thus transistors promised economies through more extensive use of amplification and carrier techniques in the local telephone plant.

In contrast with relays and other electromagnetic devices which require a minimum of several thousandths of a second to operate, electronic devices such as the transistor may be used to perform switching operations with a speed of the order of a few millionths of a second. Besides being faster, the electronic devices also are capable of performing more complex operations involving choices based on conditions existing at the instant. This means that no longer must a large complement of apparatus be set aside to serve a customer during the entire period of his call, or even a large part of it. The extremely high speed was expected to afford substantial economies in new switching systems through centralizing of functions and time sharing of the apparatus used for establishing connections. The common apparatus would serve a large number of customers in such rapid succession that each one received the equivalent of continuous and exclusive service. Reduction of space and power requirements would yield further economy. Altogether, the new art of solid-state electronics provided the basis for a revolution in both switching and transmission technology.

Research on the use of hollow wave-guide conductors as transmission lines promised new long-distance systems that would transmit extremely wide bands of frequencies, of the order of thousands of megacycles, to provide a great multiplicity of communication channels. Intercontinental submarine cables with amplifiers capable of handling large numbers of telephone channels promised to be of increasing importance to world communication. Radio communication via artificial satellites, such as the commercial service inaugurated by the Early Bird satellite in 1965, offers potentialities for providing wide transmission bands for communication across oceans. Such bands might be used for television or other visual presentations, or for telephone or data communication. There might be (1) a number of relatively low-altitude satellites (2,000–3,000 mi. high) each serving as a passive reflector, or (2) one or more satellites equipped for use as an active relay station. There is special interest in an active satellite placed about 22,300 mi. above the equator with an orbital velocity enabling it to remain above the same spot on Earth. (*See* further SPACE EXPLORATION: *Space Programs: Applications Satellites.*)

As to telephone service in general, there are no indications of saturation in demand, even in highly developed areas. Substantial further growth in number of telephones and their utilization is therefore in prospect. Large expansion could also be envisioned in services associated with telephony—such as those provided by video telephones (opened in limited commercial service in the U.S. in 1964).

*See* also references under "Telephone" in the Index.

BIBLIOGRAPHY.—For an account of Elisha Gray's invention *see* Lloyd W. Taylor, "The Untold Story of the Telephone," *Am. Phys. Teach.*, 5:243–251 (1937). General references are as follows: Count T. A. L. du Moncel, *The Telephone, Microphone and Phonograph* (1879); S. P. Thompson, *Philipp Reis: Inventor of the Telephone* (1883); G. B. Prescott, *Bell's Electric Speaking Telephone* (1884); H. N. Casson, *The History of the Telephone* (1910); F. L. Rhodes, *The Beginnings of Telephony* (1929); William Aitken, *Who Invented the Telephone?* (1939); A. W. Page, *The Bell Telephone System* (1941); A. B. Clark, "The Development of Telephony in the United States," *Trans. Amer. Inst. Elect. Engrs.*, vol. 71, p. 348 (1952); F. E. Terman, *Electronic and Radio Engineering*, 4th ed. (1955); M. J. Kelly, Sir Gordon Radley, G. W. Gilman and R. J. Halsey, "A Transatlantic Telephone Cable," *Communs Electron., Lond.*, vol. 17, p. 124 (March 1955); R. L. Peek, Jr., and H. N. Wagar, *Switching Relay Design* (1955); A. A. McKenzie, "New Era in Telephony: Electronic Switching," *Electronics*, 37:71–86 (October 1964). (E. I. G.)

**TELESCOPE,** an optical instrument employed to view distant objects (Gr. *tele*, "far," *skopein*, "to see").

**Early History.**—The telescope was invented in Holland about 1608. The credit has been attributed variously to three individuals, Hans Lippershey and Zacharias Janssen, spectacle makers in Middelburg, and James Metius of Alkmaar (brother of Adrian Metius, the mathematician). The traditional story is that Lippershey, happening while holding a spectacle lens in either hand to direct them toward the steeple of a neighbouring church, was astonished on looking through the nearer lens to find that the weathercock appeared nearer. Accordingly he fitted the lenses in a tube to preserve their relative distance and thus constructed the first telescope.

Telescopes were made in considerable numbers and found their way over Europe soon after their invention. Galileo states that, happening to be in Venice about May 1609, he heard that a Belgian had invented a perspective instrument for making objects appear nearer and larger. The day after his return to Padua he made his first telescope by fitting a convex lens in one end of a leaden tube and a concave lens in the other end (*see* LENS). A few days afterward, having succeeded in making a better telescope, he took it to Venice, where he communicated the details to the public and presented the instrument itself to the doge Leonardo Donato. The senate, in return, settled him for life in his lectureship at Padua and doubled his salary, which previously had been 500 florins. Galileo devoted much of his time to improving the telescope. He conquered the difficulties of grinding and polishing the lenses, and soon succeeded in producing telescopes of greatly increased power. His first telescope magnified 3 diameters; he soon made instruments magnifying 8 diameters, and finally one magnifying 33 diameters.

With this last instrument Galileo discovered in 1610 the satellites of Jupiter, and soon afterward the spots on the sun, the phases of Venus, and the hills and valleys on the moon. He demonstrated the revolution of the satellites of Jupiter round the planet, and gave rough predictions of their configurations, proved the rotation of the sun on its axis, established the general truth of the Copernican system as compared with that of Ptolemy, and fairly routed the fanciful dogmas of the philosophers. These brilliant achievements, together with the immense improvement of the instrument under the hands of Galileo, overshadowed in a great degree the credit due to the original discoverer, and led to the universal adoption of the name of Galilean telescope for the form of instrument invented by Lippershey.

In the Galilean telescope the object glass is a convex lens and the eyepiece concave (*see* fig. 1). Johannes Kepler was the first to explain the theory and some of the practical advantages of a convex eyepiece (*see* fig. 2) in his *Dioptrice* (1611). The first person who actually constructed a telescope of this form was the Jesuit Christoph Scheiner, who gives a description of it in his *Rosa Ursina* (1630). William Gascoigne pointed out one great advantage of the form of telescope suggested by Kepler, viz., the visibility of the image of a distant object simultaneously with that of a small material object placed in the common focus of the two lenses. This led to his invention of the micrometer and his application of telescopic sights to astronomical instruments of precision. It was not till about the middle of the 17th century, however, that Kepler's telescope came into general use, and then, not so much because of the advantages pointed out by Gascoigne, but because its field of view was much larger than that of the Galilean telescope. The first powerful telescopes of this construction were made by Christiaan Huygens, after much labour, assisted by his brother. With one of these, of 12-ft. focal length, he discovered the brightest of Saturn's satellites (Titan) in 1655, and in 1659 he published his *Systema Saturnium,* in which was given for the first time a true explanation of Saturn's ring, founded on observations made with the same instrument. Because of the imperfections of the single objective lens it became essential to increase the focal length when high magnifying power was required. G. D. Cassini discovered Saturn's fifth satellite (Rhea) in 1672 with a telescope of 35 ft. and the third and fourth satellites in 1684 with telescopes made by M. Campani of 100- and 136-ft. focal length. Huygens states that he and his brother made object glasses of 170- and 210-ft. focal length, and he presented one of 123 ft. to the Royal Society of London. Adrien Auzout (d. 1691) and others are said to have made telescopes of from 300- to 600-ft. focus, but it does not appear that they were ever able to use them in practical observations. James Bradley, on Dec. 27, 1722, measured the diameter of Venus with a telescope whose object glass had a focal length of 212¼ ft. In these very long telescopes no tube was employed. They were termed aerial telescopes.

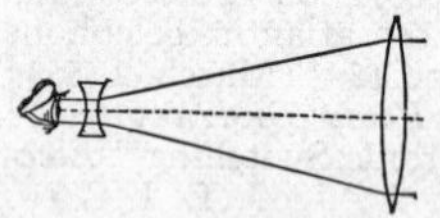

FIG. 1.—DIAGRAM SHOWING COURSE OF RAYS WHEN THE EYE LENS IS CONCAVE (OR NEGATIVE)

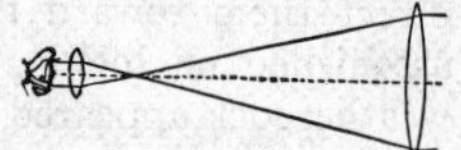

FIG. 2.—DIAGRAM SHOWING COURSE OF RAYS WHEN THE EYE LENS IS CONVEX (OR POSITIVE)

**Early Reflecting Telescopes.**—It was not until mid-18th century that these unwieldy instruments were supplanted by the achromatic telescope. Meanwhile the refracting type of telescope had a rival in the reflecting telescope invented by Sir Isaac Newton. It was, in fact, Newton who discovered what was the trouble with the refractor which led to the need for excessive length. It had been supposed that the only imperfection in the image arose from the error known as spherical aberration, and the efforts of opticians were concentrated on devising lenses of suitable forms of curvature to correct this. In 1666 Newton discovered the different refrangibility of light of different colours, and he soon perceived that the fault of the refracting telescope was that the light of different colours followed different paths; so that if, for example, the telescope was focused sharply for blue light—the green image would be altogether out of focus and blurred. He overhastily concluded from rough experiments (*Optics,* book i, part ii, proposition 3) "that all refracting substances diverge the prismatic colours in a constant proportion to their mean refraction." If this were true no combination of refracting substances could bend the path of the light without introducing colour, and therefore no improvement could be expected in the refracting telescope. He therefore turned his attention to the construction of reflectors. The form later known as the Gregorian reflector had been proposed by James Gregory in 1663; but he had not succeeded in constructing the instrument practically.

Newton, after much experiment, selected an alloy of tin and copper for his specula, and he devised means for grinding and polishing them. He did not attempt the formation of a parabolic figure on account of the probable mechanical difficulties, and he had besides satisfied himself that the chromatic and not the spherical aberration formed the chief fault of previous telescopes. Newton's first telescope so far realized his expectations that he could see with its aid the satellites of Jupiter and the horns of Venus. Encouraged by this success, he made a second telescope of 6⅓-in. focal length, with a magnifying power of 38 diameters, which he presented to the Royal society in Dec. 1671. A third form of reflecting telescope was devised in 1672 by N. Cassegrain. No further practical advance appears to have been made in the design or construction of the instrument till the year 1723, when John Hadley (best known as the inventor of the sextant) presented to the Royal society a reflecting telescope of the Newtonian construction, with a metallic speculum of 6-in. aperture and 62⅝-in. focal length, having eyepieces magnifying up to 230 diameters. The instrument was examined by James Pound and Bradley, the former of whom reported upon it in *Philosophical Transactions,* 1723.

Bradley and Samuel Molyneux, having been instructed by Hadley in his methods of polishing specula, succeeded in producing some telescopes of considerable power, one of which had a focal length of eight feet; and, Molyneux having communicated these methods to Scarlet and Hearn, two London opticians, the manufacture of telescopes as a matter of business was commenced by them. However, it was reserved for James Short of Edinburgh to give practical effect to Gregory's original idea. Born at Edinburgh in 1710 and originally educated for the church, Short attracted the attention of Colin Maclaurin, professor of mathematics at the university, who permitted him about 1732 to make use of his rooms in the college buildings for experiments in the construction of telescopes. In Short's first telescopes the specula were of glass, as suggested by Gregory, but he afterward used metallic specula only, and succeeded in giving to them true parabolic and elliptic figures.

**Achromatic Telescopes.**—The historical sequence of events now brings us to the discovery of the achromatic telescope. The first person who succeeded in making achromatic refracting telescopes seems to have been Chester Moor Hall, of Essex, Eng. He argued that the different humours of the human eye so refract rays of light as to produce an image on the retina which is free from colour, and he reasonably concluded that it might be possible to produce a like result by combining lenses composed of different refracting media. After devoting some time to the inquiry he found that by combining lenses formed of different kinds of glass the effect of the unequal refrangibility of light was corrected, and in 1733 he succeeded in constructing telescopes which exhibited objects free from colour. The principal development of the achromatic refractor is due to John Dollond who invented it independently (*Phil. Trans.,* 1758). In principle his object glasses were of the pattern mainly used at the present day, viz., convex lens of crown glass combined with a concave lens of flint glass. The concave lens is of less power than the convex, so that the combination converges the light as a single convex lens would do; but the flint glass, having much wider difference of refractive index for light of different colours, is able to correct the colour dispersion introduced by the more powerful crown lens. A triple objective, consisting of two convex lenses of crown glass with a concave lens of flint glass between them, was introduced in 1765 by Peter, son of John Dollond. This type is also employed in some modern telescopes. The difficulty of making large transparent and homogenous disks of glass at first limited the use of these achromatic lenses to small telescopes for terrestrial use.

**Later Improvements.**—Late in the 18th century William Herschel greatly advanced the art of making mirrors of speculum metal, a hard brittle alloy having a composition of one part tin and two parts copper and a reflectivity of about 60%. Herschel's telescopes were much in demand for they were of better quality and larger than any previously made. His two most famous telescopes were the 20-ft. of 19-in. aperture and the great 40-ft. of 48-in. aperture completed in 1789. The next step in the improvement of the reflector was made by Lord Rosse who built a series of telescopes culminating in the Parsonstown reflector of 72-in. aperture in 1845. The refracting telescope was brought back into favour in the first quarter of the 19th century after Joseph von Fraunhofer, who had learned from the younger Guinand how to make glass, succeeded in casting several disks of glass of excellent quality and in making lenses from them, computing the curves himself. The desire for greater magnification and light-gathering power led to the construction of lenses of larger and larger aperture. The U.S. optician Alvan Clark was especially successful in figuring large lenses and produced a long series of instruments culminating in the 36-in. of the Lick observatory and the 40-in. of the Yerkes observatory, which was completed in 1897. Disks of optical glass of so great a size, free from strain, striations, veins and bubbles and other troublesome defects, are extremely difficult to cast and anneal. The great thickness of glass required for these large lenses absorbs an appreciable fraction of the light and reduces their effectiveness as light collectors. These and other reasons resulting from the shift in observing techniques discussed below caused a change back to reflectors early in the 20th century.

COURTESY OF (TOP LEFT) YERKES OBSERVATORY, (TOP RIGHT) LICK OBSERVATORY, (BOTTOM LEFT) SIR HOWARD GRUBB PARSONS AND CO., LTD., (BOTTOM RIGHT) DOMINION ASTROPHYSICAL OBSERVATORY

**(Top left) 82-in. reflector, McDonald Observatory, Texas; (top right) 120-in. reflector, Lick Observatory, California; (bottom left) 74-in. reflector, Astrophysical Observatory, France; (bottom right) 72-in. reflector, Dominion Astrophysical Observatory, Victoria, B.C.**

In the meantime many of the disadvantages of the speculum metal mirrors had been eliminated by the development of the silver-on-glass mirror. The discovery of a simple process by which a thin film of silver could be deposited on a glass surface was made by Justus von Liebig; the application of this discovery to glass mirrors and the methods of making and testing such mirrors was carried out by Jean Foucault in the 1860s. A freshly prepared silver film has a high reflectivity exceeding 90% throughout the visual spectrum. For wave lengths shorter than the blue the reflectivity falls at first slowly and then rapidly to a value of about 4% in the ultraviolet at 3,200 Å.

In the 1930s a process was developed by John Strong for coating glass mirrors with a film of aluminum by a vacuum distillation process. On exposure to the air the surface of the aluminum film rapidly oxidizes, giving a hard and durable reflecting layer. The reflectivity of the aluminum film is nearly as high as that of a freshly deposited silver film in the visual and does not have the large drop in reflectivity in the ultraviolet. The aluminum film deteriorates much less rapidly than the silver, requiring replacement every five or ten years while the silver must be renewed every few months. With these advantages aluminum almost completely replaced silver for coating large astronomical mirrors.

In order that the mirror shall not bend under its own weight and destroy the precision of the optical surface the glass disk must be very thick, usually about one-eighth of its diameter. Furthermore, to reduce the distortion of the mirror by changes in temperature, the present practice is to use mirrors of fused quartz or of a glass, such as Pyrex, that has a low coefficient of thermal expansion. The disk is ground to the rough shape required and then figured to the exact paraboloid or other surface specified. Since the final figure must not depart from the theoretical surface by more than a very few millionths of an inch this is a long slow process; short periods of polishing being interspersed with careful optical tests to determine where the next polishing should be done and how much glass should be removed at each point.

After a precise surface has been achieved a layer of silver or aluminum is deposited to complete the mirror. The layer of metal is so thin that it does not affect the accuracy of the surface. When the surface tarnishes, the old film can be removed chemically and a new film deposited without injuring the figure of the glass.

(D. Gi.; A. S. E.; H. S. Js.; A. B. Ml.; I. S. B.)

## THEORY OF THE TELESCOPE

**Magnifying Power.**—The telescope consists essentially of two parts, the objective and the eyepiece. The light first passes the objective which forms an image, similar to that appearing on the ground glass of a camera. In small terrestrial telescopes the objective is an achromatic lens; in astronomical telescopes it may be either a lens or a concave mirror. The eyepiece is a short focus lens, like a small hand magnifier, which is used to look at and magnify the image formed by the objective. The magnifying power of a telescope is equal to the focal length of the objective divided by that of the eyepiece.

**Image Brightness.**—In addition to the magnifying power other factors that determine the performance of a telescope are image brightness, resolving power and field of view. In general a beam of light whose diameter is equal to that of the objective enters the telescope. The diameter of the beam leaving the telescope and entering the eye is equal to the objective diameter divided by the magnification. If the diameter of this beam, or emergent pencil as it is called, is greater than the diameter of the pupil of the eye, part of the light fails to enter the eye and is wasted. On the other hand, if the emergent pencil is much smaller than the pupil of the eye the apparent brightness of the image will be much lower than that of the object and the image will appear dark and indistinct.

The diameter of the pupil of the eye, however, varies through a large range depending on the illumination. Thus in full daylight the diameter of the pupil is 1.5 to 2 mm. while in darkness it expands to 8 or 10 mm. It is for this reason that telescopes designed primarily for nighttime observations have an exit pupil of at least 7 mm.; *e.g.*, the 50-mm., 7-power binocular used widely by the U.S. navy. An objective aperture of about one-fourth this would be adequate for daytime observation with the same power. In many general-purpose binoculars, however, a compromise emergent pencil of 3 to 5 mm. diameter is used as in the case of the 6- or 8-power glass with a 25- or 30-mm. objective.

**Resolving Power.**—The resolving power of a telescope is defined as the inverse of the smallest angle by which two points must be separated in order that they appear double in the telescope. From the wave theory of light it can easily be proved that the resolving power is proportional to the aperture of the telescope divided by the wave length of the light. If the magnification is increased to too high a value relative to the aperture of the objective the object appears blurred and no additional details can be detected. In general, no gain in observable detail is achieved by pushing magnification appreciably higher than the aperture of the objective expressed in millimetres.

**Field of View.**—The field of view of a telescope is defined as the angular diameter of an object that just fills the field that can be seen at one time. The apparent field of view is the angle subtended by the image of this object at the eye and is equal to the field of view times the magnification. The size of this apparent field of view is fixed primarily by the design of the eyepiece. The negative lens used as an eyepiece in the Galilean telescope gives a very small apparent field, ranging from 30° in a low-power opera glass to 5° in a telescope of high power. For this reason this type of eyepiece is used only in very low-power opera glasses and in cheap field glasses. The eyepiece consisting of a single positive lens suggested by Kepler yields a larger field but the definition is poor except at the centre of the field.

The first important improvement in eyepieces was made by Huygens, who introduced a design having two lenses separated by a distance equal to the average focal length of the component lenses. The Huygenian eyepiece, which gives an apparent field of about 45°, is still used, especially for the lower powers. The best instruments of the 20th century use the orthoscopic eyepiece, which consists of four lenses cemented in two groups and which yields critical definition even in the higher powers over an apparent field of 40° to 50°. Wide-field binoculars and some military instruments use the Erfle eyepiece, which consists of up to six glass elements and yields an apparent field of 65° to 70°.

**Erectness of the Image.**—For terrestrial observations the question of the erectness of the image must be considered. The negative eyepiece of the Galilean telescope yields an erect image. All of the other eyepieces mentioned above give inverted images if used alone with the objective. Erection of the image may be attained for the other types of eyepiece by the introduction of a third lens system between the objective and the eyepiece. This is the procedure used in the common draw tube telescope, although the introduction of the additional lens limits somewhat the field of good definition. The best instruments erect the image with two erecting prisms commonly of the Porro type (*see* BINOCULAR INSTRUMENT). This type permits the effective use of even the wide-angle Erfle eyepiece mentioned above.

## ASTRONOMICAL TELESCOPES

**Photographic and Photoelectric Observation.**—By the end of the 19th century the photographic plate had been developed to the point that it had many advantages over the eye for astronomical observations. The first of these is greater sensitivity for the study of faint objects such as nebulae or galaxies. Thus the photographic plate records fainter and fainter objects the longer it is exposed, while the eye sees nothing additional after the first glance. A few minutes exposure of the plate records everything the eye can see with the same instrument but the exposure may be continued for hours. No eye has ever seen the detail recorded on most astronomical photographs of nebulae, galaxies and other faint objects.

A second advantage of the photograph is the permanent record which it provides and which may be studied at leisure in the laboratory. The information recorded on a single plate may require months of measurement to evaluate. Such a photograph is often of value years later to determine the initial state of a star that afterward explodes into a nova, or to locate the position of a planet that later calculations show passed the region covered by the plate at the time of its exposure.

Finally, modern photographic plates are sensitive to a much wider range of wave lengths than the eye.

Many other astronomical problems require the precise measurement of the brightness of an object with a photoelectric photometer or the analysis of its light with a spectrograph. For this purpose the objective of the telescope is used like a condensing lens or burning glass to concentrate the light of a star or other object on the aperture of the photometer or slit of the spectrograph.

Because of these developments visual observations are practically never made with the large modern telescopes used for fundamental research in astronomy. Strictly speaking these instruments are not telescopes at all but cameras or light-condensing systems. Most such telescopes have provision for the insertion of an eyepiece in place of the plateholder and this is occasionally done to view the field and make certain the telescope is pointed at the desired object before starting a long exposure. Another eyepiece is often mounted beside the plateholder to observe a guide star just outside the field being photographed. This is checked from time to time during the exposure and the position of the telescope adjusted to compensate for slight errors in the telescope drive. However, since practically all actual observations are made photographically or photoelectrically the telescopes are designed to give them maximum effectiveness as cameras or light condensers rather than as visual telescopes.

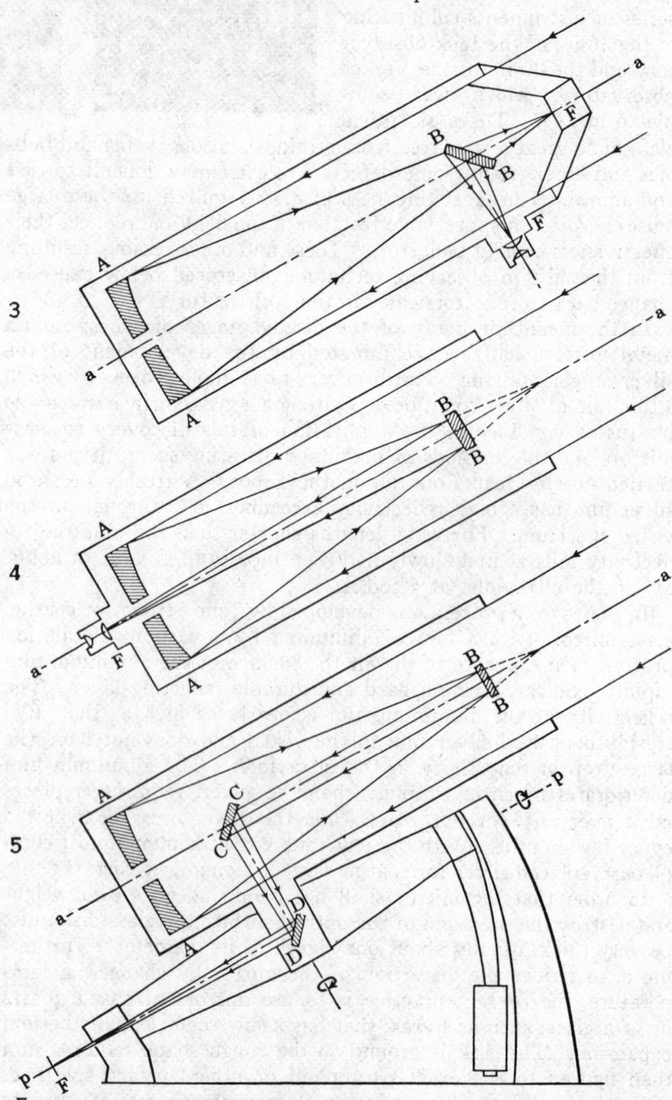


FIG. 3–5.—(3) PRIME FOCUS AND NEWTONIAN TELESCOPE; (4) CASSEGRAIN TELESCOPE; (5) COUDÉ TELESCOPE

(*See* PHOTOGRAPHY, CELESTIAL; PHOTOMETRY, ASTRONOMICAL; SPECTROSCOPY, ASTRONOMICAL.)

**Change in Design.**—This shift in the method of observation early in the 20th century resulted in a radical change in telescope design. The photography of very faint objects requires an objective of great speed, that is, one with a large ratio of aperture to focal length, *f*. Many problems require achromatism for the full range of plate sensitivity from the ultraviolet to the infrared. The two-lens objective of the 19th-century telescope with its lack of achromatism except for a narrow range of wave lengths in the visual and its aperture of *f*/15 to *f*/20 is quite inadequate for this method of observation. The concave paraboloidal mirror, however, is completely achromatic and gives critical definition at apertures as large as *f*/3. As a result practically all large telescopes constructed after 1900 were of the reflector type using concave mirrors with apertures between *f*/3 and *f*/6. (*See* fig. 3–5.)

The reflecting telescope introduced several new problems of design. Thus a concave mirror (AA in fig. 3–5) focuses the image at a point (F) in the centre of the incoming beam of light (prime focus). Except in the largest telescopes an observer placed at this focus to load plates and manipulate the telescope would obstruct too much incoming light. Most reflecting telescopes, therefore, have a small 45° plane mirror (BB in fig. 3) mounted a short distance inside the focus to reflect the image to a point just outside the incoming beam. Since this arrangement was first proposed by Newton, this is known as the Newtonian focus.

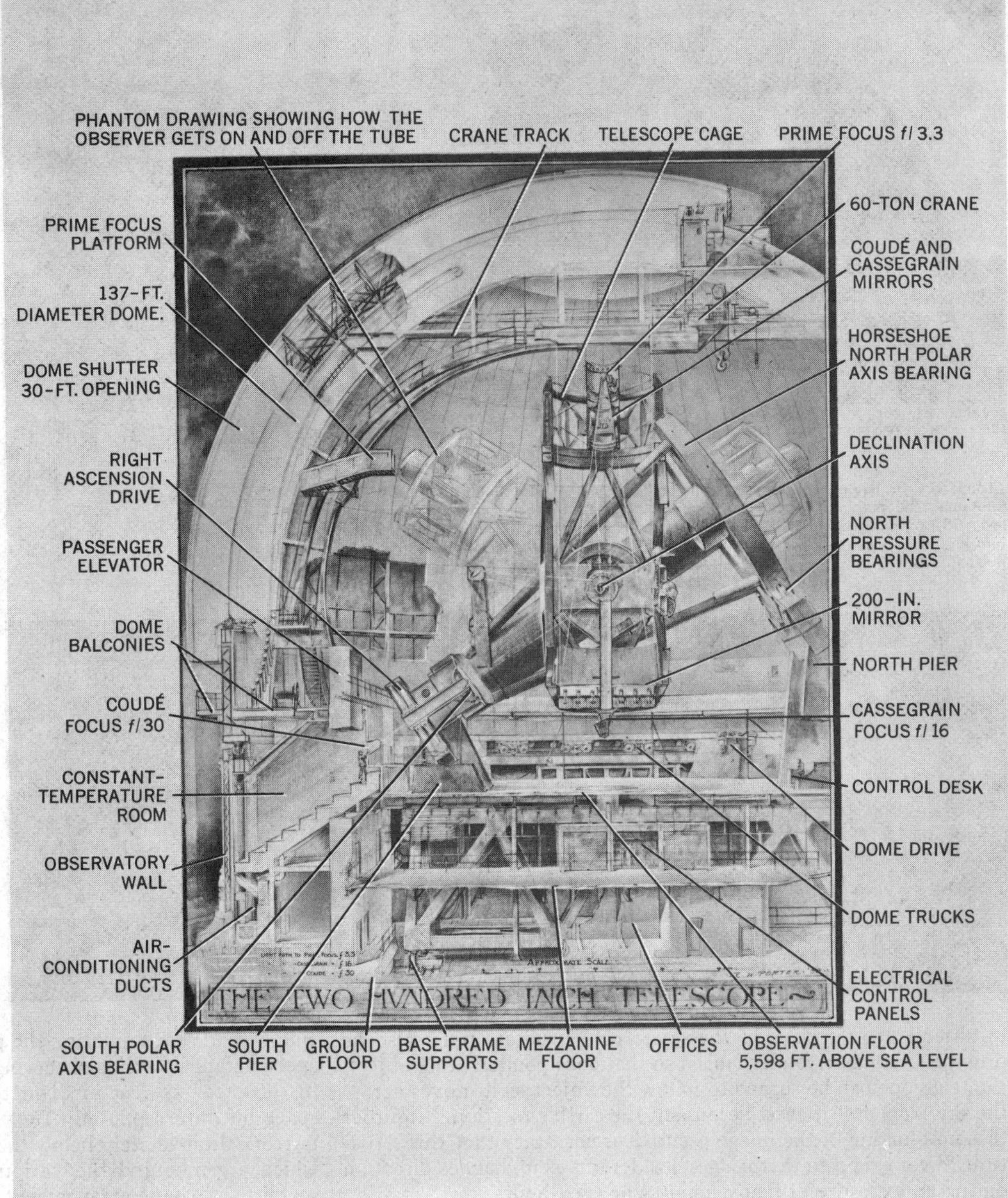

COURTESY OF R. W. PORTER AND THE CALIFORNIA INSTITUTE OF TECHNOLOGY

SECTIONAL DRAWING OF THE 200-IN. HALE TELESCOPE SHOWS THE TELESCOPE CUT AWAY ALONG A VERTICAL PLANE THROUGH THE POLAR AXIS

For some purposes a longer focal length and therefore smaller ratio of aperture to focal length may be desirable. This is obtained by placing slightly inside the focus a convex mirror (BB in fig. 4) which reflects the light back through a hole in the centre of the main mirror and forms the image just behind this mirror. Because of the telephoto effect of this convex mirror, the focal length is increased by a factor of 3 to 8, and the ratio of aperture to focal length is decreased by the same factor. From the inventor of this arrangement the focus is known as the Cassegrain focus.

Finally in the coudé (French, "elbow") arrangement the light from a Cassegrain mirror is reflected down the polar axis by one or more plane mirrors (BB, CC and DD in fig. 5). In this case the focus, usually a short distance below the south polar bearing, remains fixed as the telescope is turned toward various parts of the sky. This arrangement can therefore be used to condense light on the slit of a spectrograph or other instrument too large to be mounted on the telescope.

**Wide-Field Cameras.**—For many investigations it is necessary to photograph large areas of the sky at one exposure. This requires a field of good definition much larger than that provided by the simple achromat of the refracting telescope or by the paraboloidal reflector, especially when this is used at the low focal ratios needed for the photography of faint objects. For these studies complicated three- or four-lens systems, very similar to the anastigmat lenses for ordinary photography, were originally designed. These have been constructed with apertures up to 20 in.

In 1931 Bernhard Schmidt of the Hamburg observatory, Bergedorf, Ger., invented an entirely new optical system for use as a wide-angle camera. It consists of a concave spherical mirror and a thin correcting plate placed at the centre of curvature of the mirror. The very superior corrections of this system compared with that of any lens system made it possible to construct wide-angle cameras operating at apertures greater than *f*/1. Others have been constructed with an aperture as great as 53 in. The chief problem in the manufacture of the Schmidt camera is the corrector plate that has to be hand figured to a complicated fourth degree curve which is much more difficult than the spherical surfaces of the ordinary lens.

**Mounting.**—The mirror and photographic plate, spectrograph or photometer must be mounted on a structure that can be pointed

COURTESY OF (TOP, RIGHT) MT. WILSON AND PALOMAR OBSERVATORIES, (BOTTOM LEFT) LICK OBSERVATORY, (BOTTOM RIGHT) U.S. NAVY

(Top) 200-in. Hale reflector telescope and (right) 48-in. Schmidt telescope, Palomar and Mt. Wilson observatories, California; (bottom left) 20-in. astrographic telescope, Lick Observatory, California; (bottom right) 26-in. refractor telescope, U.S. Naval Observatory, Washington, D.C.

to objects at any place in the sky. This structure must also be provided with a drive mechanism so that once pointed at an object, the telescope can be turned to follow the object as it moves across the sky from east to west because of the earth's rotation. In order that no blurring of the image occurs it is necessary that this structure be very rigid so that it does not deform as it changes direction during an exposure of many minutes or even hours.

In typical mountings designed for modern telescopes, the main mirror is mounted at the lower end of the structure while for direct photography the plate is placed at either the prime or Newtonian focus near the upper end. In the Cassegrain or coudé arrangements the convex mirror is at the upper end.

In general, a structure can be pointed in all directions if two mutually perpendicular axes of rotation are provided. In very small visual telescopes these axes are often made vertical and horizontal in what is known as an altazimuth mount. For telescopes that are to be driven to follow the object across the sky, the equatorial mount is used. In this mount one of the axes, known as the polar axis, is made accurately parallel to the axis of the earth. The axis perpendicular to this is known as the declination axis. This type of mounting has the great advantage that any object can be followed from east to west by driving the polar axis at the uniform rate of one revolution in 24 hours.

Three different types of equatorial mounting were developed. (1) The English off-axis mount in which the polar axis is a relatively small tube with two bearings, one at the north and the other at the south. The telescope tube is mounted on one side with a counterweight on the other side of this polar axis. (2) The fork type has the telescope mounted between the tines of a fork projecting out from the two polar axis bearings both of which are at the south. (3) The yoke mounting holds the telescope tube symmetrically in a yoke, the polar axis bearings of which are at the north and south. This type provides the most rigid support for the telescope and is therefore used for the largest instruments. Its disadvantage is that either the telescope cannot be pointed to the north pole or the north bearing must be made so large that the telescope can be turned down into it.

**The Hale 200-in. Telescope at Palomar Observatory.**—As of the 1960s the largest telescope constructed was the 200-in. Hale reflector on Palomar mountain in California. The main mirror is 200 in. in diameter and 24 in. thick and is ground and figured to give a focal length of 55 ft. To reduce thermal distortion during temperature changes it was cast from Pyrex glass with a ribbed structure and when finished weighed 14½ tons. In order to avoid flexure as the mirror is turned into different directions it is floated on 36 elaborate lever support systems each of which applies a force to the mirror just sufficient to compensate for the pull of gravity on the section of the mirror assigned to it. The mirror and its support system are mounted at the bottom of the telescope tube which is a rigid girder structure about 60 ft. long and with the mirror weighs 140 tons. At the centre of the upper end of the telescope tube is the prime focus cage in which provision is made for mounting the plateholder, photometers and small spectrographs. While observing at this focus the astronomer rides in the cage, six feet in diameter, which provides ample working space but intercepts only 13% of the light approaching the main mirror. Immediately below the observer's cage is a second cage in which are mounted the various secondary mirrors for the Cassegrain and coudé arrangements. When needed these mirrors are tipped forward into operating position by remote control.

The telescope tube is mounted between the arms of a yoke on declination bearings which permit the telescope to turn in a north-south direction. The yoke in turn is supported at both the north and south ends on the polar axis bearings which allow rotation of both telescope tube and yoke about an axis parallel to the earth's axis. The north polar bearing is made in the shape of an open horseshoe, the outer bearing surface having a diameter of 46 ft. This allows the upper end of the telescope tube to turn down to the centre of the bearing and thereby point at the north pole. The total weight of the telescope tube and yoke which turns about the polar axis is over 500 tons. North and south bearings are pressure-oil-pad types and have so low a friction that a $\frac{1}{12}$-h.p. motor is sufficient to drive the telescope when following a star.

At the Cassegrain focus the focal length is 267 ft. and at the coudé focus it is 500 ft. In addition to the photoelectric photometers and small dispersion spectrograph for use at the prime focus, a large spectrograph is available for use at the coudé focus. This has a collimator of 30-ft. focal length and five Schmidt cameras of aperture 12 in. and focal lengths from 8 in. to 12 ft.

The telescope is housed in a dome 135 ft. high and 137 ft. in diameter. The dome is rotated with a drive which automatically keeps the shutter opening in the dome lined up with the telescope at all times. The rotating part of the dome weighs 1,000 tons. (*See* also OBSERVATORY [ASTRONOMICAL].)

**Large Telescopes.**—The largest telescopes in operation in the mid-1960s are listed in the table. They are all reflectors, since no refractor with an aperture greater than 30 in. was built after the 19th century.

*Large Telescopes*

| Name | Location | Aperture (in inches) | Focal length of primary | Date completed |
|---|---|---|---|---|
| Hale . . . | Palomar Mtn., Calif. | 200 | 660 | 1948 |
| Lick . . . | Mt. Hamilton, Calif. | 120 | 600 | 1959 |
| Crimean . . . | Crimea, U.S.S.R. | 102 | 395 | 1960 |
| Hooker. . . | Mt. Wilson, Calif. | 100 | 508 | 1917 |
| Kitt Peak . . | Kitt Peak, Ariz. | 84 | 220 | 1963 |
| McDonald . . | Mt. Locke, Tex. | 82 | 324 | 1939 |
| Haute Provence . | St. Michel, France | 74 | 385 | 1958 |

*See* also Binocular Instrument; Telescope, Radio; Transit Circle and Zenith Telescope for treatment of special types, and references under "Telescope" in the Index.

Bibliography.—H. C. King, *The History of the Telescope* (1955); for construction details and theory: G. R. Miczaika and W. M. Sinton, *The Tools of the Astronomer* (1961); G. P. Kuiper and B. M. Middlehurst (eds.), *Telescopes* (1960). Specific telescopes are described in the publications of the observatories operating them. (I. S. B.)

**TELESCOPE, RADIO.** Radio waves arriving at the earth from the solar system, the galaxy, and the extragalactic nebulae are a source of remarkable information about the universe (*see* Radio Astronomy). No less remarkable are the huge and delicate radio telescopes invented to extract this information from the minute quantities of energy that these distant objects send us.

**Steerable Paraboloids.**—Observations in radio astronomy are carried out with various kinds of radio telescope, of which the best known resemble the 250-ft. (76-m.) diameter reflector erected at Jodrell Bank, Eng. Grote Reber made the first radio maps of our galaxy in 1942 with such a reflector. This kind of radio telescope, the steerable paraboloid, functions as shown in fig. 1. Radio waves from a distant astronomical source S fall on the curved surface, which, being made of a good electrical conductor, causes the waves to be reflected in accordance with Snell's law; thus the ray incident at R is reflected in the direction RF. If the reflecting surface is correctly curved, all the reflected rays can be made to arrive at the same focus F. The curve that accomplishes this is the parabola; consequently, the correct shape for the reflecting surface is a paraboloid. The downcoming energy is spread thinly over the extensive circular aperture, but the focusing property causes it to converge on the radio receiver; it is detected at the receiver if the amount of energy passing through the circle C that forms the rim of the reflector is sufficiently large to be detectable.

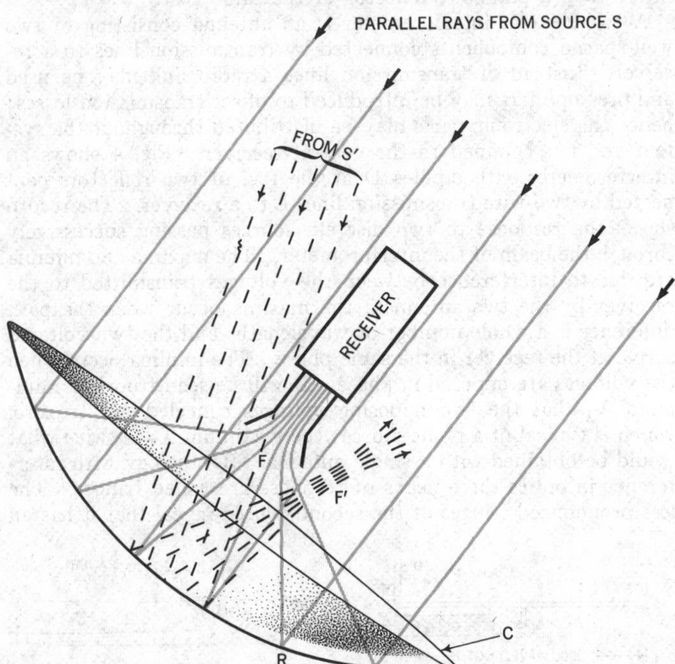


FIG. 1.—STEERABLE PARABOLOID

At the focus F is placed an electromagnetic horn that "swallows" the converging energy and pipes it through a hollow wave guide to the receiver. At lower frequencies dipoles connected to electrical transmission lines are used in place of horns. For successful action the aperture of the horn must be about equal in extent to the radio wavelength, because that is the least compass into which the converging waves can be condensed.

A source S′, not in exactly the same direction as the source S, sends its energy toward a point F′, which is off to the side of the collecting horn; if it is too far to the side, it fails to be collected and passes back into space. The paraboloid antenna thus has the ability to receive from a narrow cone of directions around S and to ignore other directions. This property of directivity is important in discriminating one source from another and in discerning fine detail in such sources as the sun, where it is necessary to be able to examine small areas around sunspots without intercepting radiation from other parts of the sun. It is customary to describe this property of the antenna by its beamwidth, which is the angle between directions from which only half the full power is received. Bearing in mind that the size of the focal area increases as the wavelength increases, it will be seen from fig. 1 that the larger the antenna the narrower the beamwidth, provided the wavelength remains fixed, and conversely that if the size of the antenna is kept fixed, then the shorter the wavelength the narrower the beamwidth. Beamwidths for some representative sizes of antennas are listed in Table I. The beamwidth, which is shown in degrees and minutes of arc, refers to an ideal antenna that is precisely of paraboloidal shape.

Table I.—*Beamwidths of Various Antenna Sizes*

| Diameter of antenna | Wavelengths | | | |
|---|---|---|---|---|
| | 3 cm. | 10 cm. | 30 cm. | 3 m. |
| 60 ft. . . . | 7′ | 23′ | 1°10′ | 11°40′ |
| 140 ft. . . . | 3′ | 10′ | 30′ | 5° |
| 210 ft. . . . | 2′ | 7′ | 20′ | 3°20′ |

In practice, however, the surface will depart from the true paraboloid for such reasons as manufacturing tolerances, the force of the wind, uneven expansion and contraction of the structure, and sagging of the parts under their own weight. As a consequence, an actual antenna does not focus as well as a true paraboloid would; some of the focused energy thus fails to be collected by the horn. The ability of the antenna to receive energy is expressed in terms of its effective area, which equals the area of a perfect absorber intercepting as much energy as is collected at the focus of the actual antenna and delivered to the receiver. The effective area is typically about 60% of the actual aperture. Each antenna has a wavelength limit beyond which its performance is seriously impaired by imperfect focusing.

The way in which the effective area $A$ deteriorates as the wavelength decreases is expressed by the equation

$$A = \frac{\mathcal{D}\lambda^2}{\lambda^2 + 2\pi\mathcal{D}Q} \times \pi R^2$$

where $R$ is the radius of the circular rim of the paraboloid, $\mathcal{D}$ is the factor by which the effective area would fall below the physical area $\pi R^2$ even if the reflector were perfectly paraboloidal, and $\lambda$ is the wavelength. The quantity $Q$ measures the imperfection of shape. If we suppose that waves are radiated by the antenna from a source at the focus, then the wave fronts emerging from the aperture are plane, but if there is a bump on the reflector, then there will be a bump, almost twice as high, on the emerging wave front; $Q$ is the mean square departure of this wave front from the plane of best fit.

Not all radio telescopes have a parabolic reflector, and, indeed, any type of radio antenna is usable. Every radio telescope, however, comprises an antenna, a receiver, an output indicator, and a means of pointing the beam in known directions (fig. 2).

The receiver may assume various forms; for example, it may consist simply of an amplifier, a detector, a direct-current amplifier, and a filter for smoothing the fluctuations. The output indicator is essentially a meter, usually a recording milliammeter giving a permanent record on a paper chart. In addition, how-

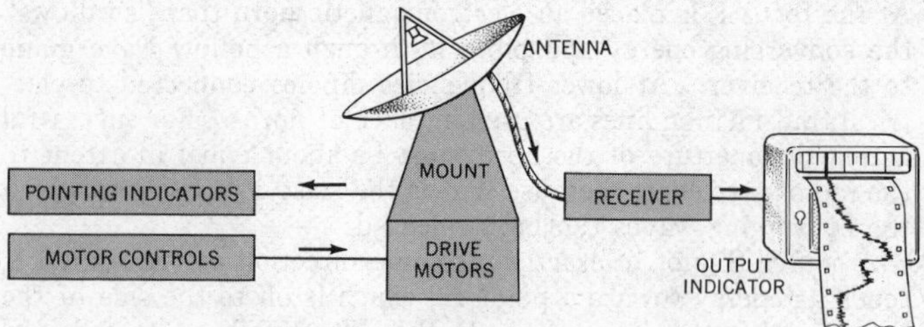


FIG. 2.—BASIC COMPONENTS OF A RADIO TELESCOPE

ever, the observational results will be recorded on punched cards or magnetic tape if they are to be fed to a computer for numerical analysis, or typed out on an automatic typewriter if the output is in final form suitable for publication.

To point the beam of a radio telescope, one simply mounts the antenna suitably and with the aid of drive motors and position indicators drives the antenna to the desired position. In sizes up to about 100 ft. it is convenient to use an equatorial mount, in which one axis of rotation is parallel to the earth's axis; then in order to follow a radio source as it moves across the sky, it is sufficient to compensate for the earth's rotation by driving the antenna westward about its own polar axis. The larger antennas use altazimuth mounts, which are cheaper to build to the requisite strength, and it is necessary to drive such antennas both in altitude and azimuth to follow a source. Since the drive motors are called on to vary their speed in a precisely defined way, a computer is required to control an altazimuth drive system.

Mechanically steered paraboloids, such as those described above, represent only one type of radio telescope. Typical examples of such steerable paraboloids are listed in Table II.

TABLE II.—*Some Mechanically Steered Paraboloids*

| Diameter (ft.) | Location | Mount | Wavelength limit |
|---|---|---|---|
| 250 | Jodrell Bank, Eng. | altazimuth | 21 cm. |
| 210 | Parkes, New South Wales, Austr. | altazimuth | 5 cm. |
| 150 | Stanford, Calif. | altazimuth | 50 cm. |
| 140 | Green Bank, W.Va. | equatorial | 2 cm. |
| 120 | Haystack Hill, Mass. | altazimuth | 2 cm. |

For many purposes the large steerable paraboloids have not been large enough, and various more sophisticated antennas have been developed. To understand why the demand for greater effective area cannot be met by enlarging the simple steerable paraboloid, imagine an antenna 500 ft. in diameter all of whose dimensions are precisely twice those of a certain 250-ft. antenna. The larger antenna will require eight times as much steel but will provide only four times as much collecting area. Moreover, under the increased weight, the structural members, which must be twice as long as in the 250-ft. antenna, will sag away from the true paraboloid by four times as much as before, so that even more steel will have to be added to stiffen the structure. It is clear that the cost per square metre of collecting area is higher for the larger antenna. This explains why radio astronomers have often been able to accomplish more for a given capital outlay by adopting other antenna designs.

**Fixed Reflectors.**—Much more effective area can be obtained for the same cost if the reflector does not have to be movable. An example is furnished by the 1,000-ft. spherical reflector built by W. E. Gordon of Cornell University at Arecibo, P.R. (fig. 3A). Each zone of a spherical reflector possesses a focus; for example, the outermost zone AB has its focus at R, and the zone CD has its focus at Q. The energy coming from the source S directly overhead converges on the line PR, where a special collector can be placed. If this collector is rotated about the centre of the sphere to position P′R′ as in fig. 3B, it is in the correct position to receive energy from the source S′. Thus the beam of the antenna has been pointed away from the zenith without the reflector having been moved.

Another example of a fixed reflector is the 600- × 400-ft. parabolic cylinder constructed by G. W. Swenson at the Vermilion River Observatory in Illinois (fig. 3C). Downcoming energy comes to a line focus FG, which is occupied by a large number of small antennas connected by transmission lines to a receiver. This radio telescope receives signals only from sources on the meridian, but the altitude of the beam can be varied by adjusting the electrical phase of each focal antenna.

In still another design (J. D. Kraus of Ohio State University) a tiltable flat reflector T (fig. 3D) reflects incoming rays from directly overhead into the horizontal direction toward a fixed reflector R, which is a zone of a paraboloid with its focus at F. A similar large radio telescope was built by J. F. Denisse at Nançay, France.

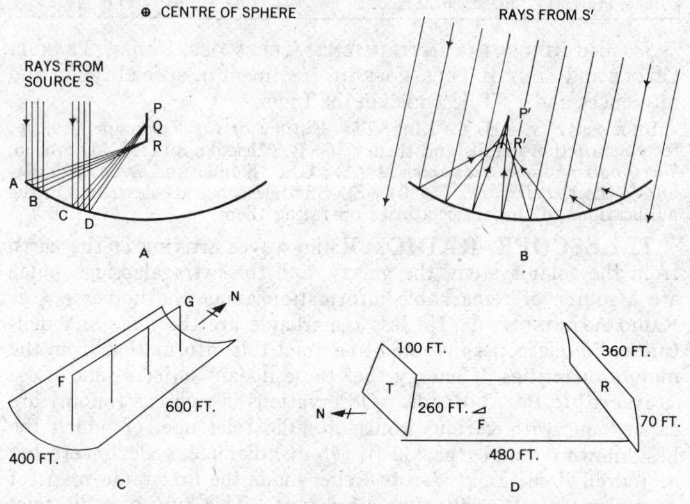


FIG. 3.—FIXED REFLECTORS

(A) Spherical reflector. (B) Spherical reflector with collector rotated to receive energy from a different source than shown at left. (C) Parabolic cylinder reflector. (D) Tiltable flat reflector

**Interferometers.**—The most pressing problem at the time of the discovery of the radio sources was to ascertain the precise locations of the sources and their angular diameters. Had very large parabolic reflectors been available, they would have accomplished this aim; because they were not, the answers were obtained with modest antennas deployed as interferometers. In the subsequent development of radio telescopes, interferometers have maintained their important role, especially in new discoveries, essentially because of their ability to furnish better angular resolution than a parabolic reflector of the same cost.

A two-element interferometer is an antenna consisting of two well-spaced components connected by transmission lines to a receiver. Instead of transmission lines a radio link may be used and preamplifiers may be introduced to offset transmission losses; hence the electronic parts may be distributed throughout the system and not confined to the central receiver. Fig. 4 shows an interferometer with dipoles D at the foci of two reflectors connected by two-wire transmission lines L to a receiver. The record shows the response to two discrete sources passing successively through the beam of the interferometer. The maxima and minima are due to interference between the voltages transmitted to the receiver by the two antennas; the maxima occur when the path difference is a whole number of wavelengths and the two voltages arrive at the receiver in the same phase. The minima occur when the voltages are opposed in phase. It will be seen from the minimum $N_1$ that the two opposing voltages canceled out to zero, which is typical of a point source; the maximum $X_1$ is twice what would be obtained with a single antenna. By analogy with interference in optics these peaks of response are called fringes. The less pronounced fringes of the second source reveal that it has an

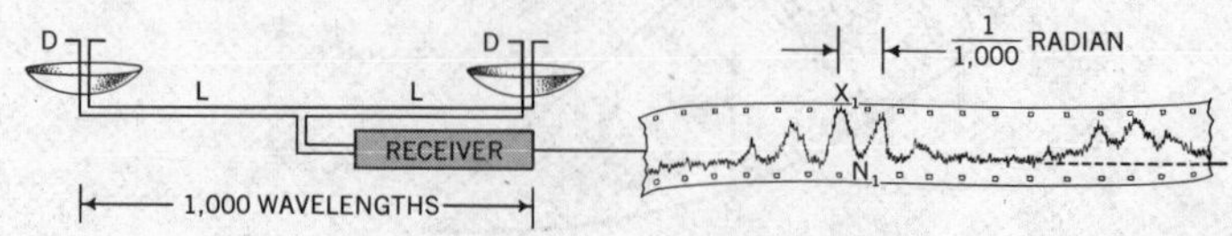


FIG. 4.—INTERFEROMETER

BY COURTESY OF R. N. BRACEWELL

FIG. 5.—CROSS ANTENNA, STANFORD, CALIF.

angular extent that is an appreciable fraction of the angle between fringes, because when the radiation from the centre of the source cancels out at the receiver, the radiation from the edges does not cancel out.

When the antennas are *n* wavelengths apart on an east-west line and are pointed at the meridian, the fringe separation is one *n*th of a radian; *e.g.*, with a spacing of 1,000 wavelengths the fringe separation is 0.001 radians or 0.057°. Such an instrument allows source diameters of about one minute of arc to be determined, which would be well beyond the capability of the component antennas taken singly. This interferometer also permits the source position to be pinpointed to about a minute of arc in right ascension.

To do as well with a single antenna would require one about 1,000 wavelengths long, which would be much more costly. The extra cost would, however, buy a larger effective area, which, under most circumstances, would be highly valuable.

The mapping of complex sources can also be accomplished by interferometry. For this purpose observations must be made with a range of antenna spacings. One plan, which has been highly developed in England by M. Ryle, is to move the antennas bodily; another is to construct several antennas in fixed locations; *e.g.*, in a cross.

**Cross Antennas.**—An example of a cross is shown in fig. 5, where two arrays of equatorially mounted antennas, all driven in unison, are shown arranged in a cross. The cross arrangement was first demonstrated by B. Y. Mills in Sydney, Austr., with long fixed arrays of metre-wave dipoles, but the cross in fig. 5 is an adaptation to steerable microwave reflectors. The voltages, delivered to the centre by the two arms, are multiplied together, and the product, which is instantaneously printed by an automatic typewriter, gives the brightness temperature of the sun. The fine beam of the instrument is able to single out a patch of the sun amounting to only 1% of the surface at a time and is capable of scanning the entire sun to build up a meteorological map by means of isotherms.

Crosses may be very large. The Mills cross of the University of Sydney, for example, has arms one mile long, and similar instruments constructed in the Soviet Union by V. V. Vitkevich and in Italy by M. Ceccarelli have arms one kilometer long. Details of some of these instruments are shown in Table III.

TABLE III.—*Cross Antennas*

| Length (ft.) | Location | Wavelength (cm.) | Beamwidth (minutes of arc) |
|---|---|---|---|
| 375 | Stanford, Calif. | 9.1 | 3.1 |
| 1,800 | Fleurs, New South Wales, Austr. | 21 | 3 |
| 5,200 | Hoskinstown, New South Wales, Austr. | 73<br>269 | 2.8<br>10 |
| 3,281 | Bologna, Italy | 92 | 4 |
| 3,281 | Serpukhov, U.S.S.R. | 200 | 15 |

*See* also RADIO ASTRONOMY; TELESCOPE.

BIBLIOGRAPHY.—Complete issues of the following periodicals are devoted largely to radio telescopes: *Proceedings of the Institute of Radio Engineers*, vol. 46 (Jan. 1958); *IRE Transactions on Antennas and Propagation*, vol. AP-9 (Jan. 1961); *Proceedings of the Institution of Radio Engineers Australia*, vol. 24 (Feb. 1963). For photographs and technical discussions, *see* J. L. Steinberg and J. Lequeux, *Radio Astronomy* (1963) and R. N. Bracewell, "Radio Astronomy Techniques" in *Encyclopaedia of Physics*, vol. 54 (1961). (R. N. BL.)

**TELESIO, BERNARDINO** (1509–1588), Italian philosopher and scientist, inaugurated empiricist reaction against the authority of abstract reason as represented by scholastic Aristotelianism. He was born of noble parentage at Cosenza, in the Kingdom of Naples, where he was later to add lustre to the circle of thinkers known as the Accademia Cosentina. After studies (1518–35) in Milan, Rome, and Padua, he spent about nine years in a monastery. Thereafter he lived mainly in Naples (1545–52 and 1563–87) or at Cosenza, where he died.

The first two books of Telesio's *De rerum natura iuxta propria principia* ("On the Nature of Things According to Their Own Principles") appeared in 1565, the complete work, in nine books, in 1586 (modern edition by V. Spampanato, 1910–23). He also published three subsidiary essays on physical science in 1570 and left others, some of which were printed in 1590. Contemporary popes had encouraged him, and he saw nothing anti-Catholic in his doctrine; but from 1596 to 1900 the *De rerum natura* and two minor works were on the Index "pending correction."

Discarding Aristotelian physics, Telesio proposed an inquiry into the data of the senses, from which he held all human knowledge to be derived. He argued for two incorporeal first principles, heat and cold, acting on the inert matter of the earth: from the varying degrees of this action's intensity all the diverse types of existence result. In his psychology and ethics, there is no clear qualitative distinction between animal and human faculties, nor between the physiological and the spiritual. Defects in his system were pointed out by his pupil Francesco Patrizzi, whose objections he tried to meet; but he set the example of independent investigation that Tommaso Campanella and others were soon to follow.

*See* N. C. Van Deusen, *Telesio, the First of the Moderns* (1932); N. Abbagnano, *Bernardino Telesio* (1941); G. Soleri, *Telesio* (1944).

**TELESPHORUS, SAINT,** pope from *c.* 125 to *c.* 136, is said to have been a Greek. St. Irenaeus calls him a glorious martyr. His feast day is Jan. 5. (J. V. HN.)

**TELEVISION,** the electrical transmission of pictures in motion and the simultaneous electrical transmission of the accompanying sounds. A discussion of the theories upon which such transmission is based will be found in the articles RADIO and RADIO RECEIVER; the electrical transmission of still photographs is discussed in FACSIMILE TRANSMISSION.

This article is divided into the following parts:

## I. INTRODUCTION

The purpose of a television system is to extend the senses of vision and hearing beyond their natural limits. Television systems are designed, therefore, to embrace the essential capabilities of these senses, with appropriate compromises between the quality of the reproduction and the costs involved. The aspects of natural vision which must be considered in a television system include the ability of the human eye to distinguish the brightnesses, colours, details, sizes, shapes and positions of the objects in the scene before it. The aspects of hearing include the ability of the ear to distinguish the pitch, loudness and distribution of sounds. The television system must also be designed to override, within reasonable limits, the effects of interference and to minimize visual and aural distortions in the transmission and reproduction processes. The particular compromises adopted for public television service, *i.e.,* by broadcast means, are embodied in the television standards adopted and enforced by the responsible government agency in each country.

Television technology must deal with the fact that human vision employs many hundreds of thousands of separate electrical circuits, in the optic nerve from the retina to the brain, to convey simultaneously in two dimensions the whole content of the scene on which the eye is focused, whereas in electrical communications it is feasible to employ only one such circuit (*i.e.,* the broadcast channel) to connect the transmitter and the receiver. This fundamental disparity is overcome in television by a process of image analysis and synthesis, whereby the scene to be televised is first translated into an electrical image, and the latter is then broken up into an orderly sequence of electrical impulses which are sent over the channel one after the other. At the receiver the impulses are translated back into a corresponding sequence of lights and shadows and these are reassembled in their correct positions on the viewing screen.

This sequential reproduction of visual images is feasible only because the visual sense displays persistence; that is, the brain retains the impression of illumination for about 0.1 sec. after the source of light is removed from the eye. If, therefore, the process of image synthesis occurs within less than 0.1 sec., the eye is unaware that the picture is being reassembled piecemeal, and the viewing screen appears as if its whole surface were continuously illuminated. By the same token, it is then possible to re-create more than ten complete pictures per second and to simulate thereby the motion of the scene so that it appears to be continuous.

In practice, to depict rapid motion smoothly, it is customary to transmit from 25 to 30 complete pictures per second. To provide detail sufficient to accommodate a wide range of subject matter, it is customary to analyze each picture into 100,000 or more elementary details. This analysis implies that the rate at which these details are transmitted over the television system exceeds 2,000,000 details per second. In order to provide a system suitable for public use and yet one that is capable of such speed has required the full resources of modern electronic technology.

## II. HISTORY OF TELEVISION

Perhaps the beginning was in 1839 when Alexandre Edmond Becquerel discovered the electrochemical effects of light: he observed that when two electrodes are immersed in a suitable electrolyte and illuminated by a beam of light, an electromotive force is generated between the electrodes. Then in 1845 M. Faraday discovered a connection between light and electricity, namely, the rotation of the plane of polarization of a light beam under the influence of a magnetic field. About 30 years later John Kerr of Glasgow observed the birefringence of certain materials under electrostatic stress. This led to the light-modulating device known as the Kerr cell.

Early ideas for the realization of television assumed the transmission of every picture element simultaneously, each over a separate circuit (as, for example, a system suggested by George Carey of Boston in 1875); but in about 1880 the important principle—subsequently adopted in all forms of television—of rapidly scanning each element in the picture in succession, line by line and frame by frame, with reliance on persistence of human vision, was proposed, notably by W. E. Sawyer in the U.S. and Maurice Leblanc in France. This established the possibility of using only a single wire or channel for transmission.

In 1817 J. J. Berzelius had isolated the element selenium and in 1873 came the discovery of its photoconductive properties, first noticed by L. May and published in London by Willoughby Smith. This appeared to provide an important clue to the secret of practical television and led to a proposal by Paul Nipkow. Nipkow in 1884 patented in Germany a complete system, an original feature of which was the spirally apertured rotating disk that provided, at both sending and receiving ends, a simple and effective method of image scanning. Until the advent of electronic scanning all workable television systems depended on some form or variation (*e.g.,* mirror drums, lensed disks, etc.) of the mechanical sequential scanning method exemplified by the Nipkow disk. It deserves an important place in the history of television and the mode of operation is briefly explained below.

As illustrated in fig. 1, the image to be televised is focused on a rotating disk having square apertures arranged in a spiral. As the disk rotates, the outermost aperture traces out a line across the top of the image, and the light passing through the aperture varies in direct proportion to the light and shade (*i.e.,* brightness values) of that line of the image as it is traversed by the aperture. When the outermost aperture has passed over the image, the next inner aperture traces out another line, parallel to and immediately below the line just traced. The changes in the light passing through the second aperture represent, in sequence, the brightness values present in the image along this second line. As the disk continues to rotate, successive lines are traced out, one beneath the other, until the whole area of the image has been explored, one line at a time, whereupon the process is repeated with each rotation of the disk; of course, the more apertures, and hence lines, the greater the detail that can be analyzed.

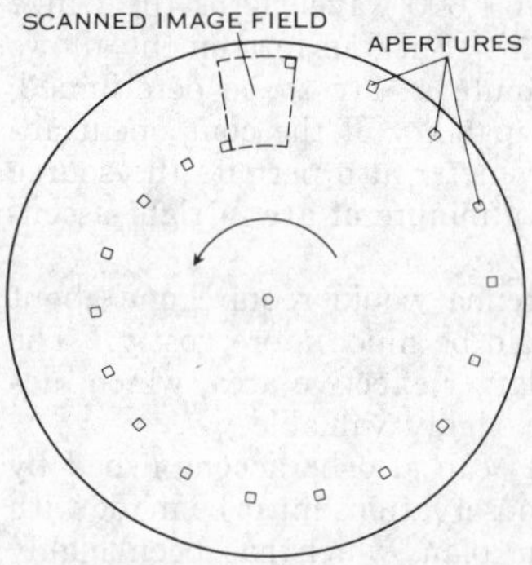

SCANNED IMAGE FIELD
APERTURES

FIG. 1.—NIPKOW DISK FOR AN 18-LINE PICTURE

In this way the detail of the whole image is sequentially explored in an orderly manner. The light passing through the apertures enters a photoelectric cell that translates the sequence of light values into a corresponding sequence of electric values. These are transmitted over a single circuit to the receiver where the electrical impulses cause light to be produced by a lamp (such as a gas-discharge lamp) capable of reproducing the sequence of light values. The light from the lamp is projected onto the surface of a disk similar to that at the transmitter. This disk must rotate in precise synchronism, and by a scanning process reciprocating that already described, the brightness values are reassembled in their proper positions, and the original image is reproduced. Provided the rotation is at sufficient speed, persistence of vision enables the eye to see the image as a whole rather than as a series of moving points. The need for exact synchronism between camera and receiver scanning speeds is fundamental not only to the mechanical system which has been described above but to every television system.

The slow response of selenium to changes of light was, however, a serious handicap. Therefore, the researches in Germany of first W. Hallwachs in 1888 and later J. Elster and H. Geitel (who produced by 1913 a potassium-hydride coated cell with both an improved sensitivity and the ability to follow rapid changes of light) for the first time rendered possible any practical working system. This cell made use of the photoemissive—as distinct from photoconductive—effect.

In 1897, following the earlier researches of Sir William Crookes and J. J. Thomson, K. F. Braun in Germany introduced a cathode-ray tube with fluorescent screen. The Russian, Boris Rosing, in 1907 was the first to suggest its use in the receiver of a television system which, at the camera end, made use of mirror-drum scanning. He succeeded in transmitting and reproducing some crude geometrical patterns, and so ranks as an important pioneer.

In 1904 J. A. Fleming invented the two-electrode valve; Lee De Forest added the grid in 1906 and made amplification possible, another essential step toward practical television.

In 1908 came a most remarkable contribution by A. A. Campbell Swinton, who outlined a method which, in all essentials, is the basis of modern television. Lack of amplifiers and other difficulties confined this to what Swinton called "an idea only," but he clarified and elaborated it before the Röntgen Society of London in 1911. He proposed, in essence, the use of cathode-ray tubes, magnetically deflected, at both camera and receiver. In the former was a mosaic screen of photoelectric elements; the image of the scene to be transmitted was focused onto this screen, the back of which was then discharged by a cathode-ray beam tracing out a line-by-line scanning sequence. Swinton's brilliant ideas were too advanced for early application and it was left to others to put them into practice many years later.

Meanwhile, experimenters in Europe and the U.S. were trying to make a less ambitious beginning. The neon gas-discharge lamp, produced by D. M. Moore of General Electric in 1917, offered a simple means of electrical modulation of light at the receiver. It was adopted by J. L. Baird in England and C. F. Jenkins in the U.S., who in 1923 began experimenting with mechanical methods using the Nipkow principle. In 1926 Baird gave the first demonstration of true television, by electrically transmitting moving pictures in halftones. These pictures were formed of only 30 lines, repeating approximately 10 times per second. The results, though inevitably crude—flickering badly and with a dim receiver screen a few inches high—nevertheless became the start of television as a practical technology and did much to stimulate further research, while also forming the basis of some experimental broadcasting in England between 1929 and 1935.

Mechanical systems lacked sensitivity, as became progressively manifest with attempts to increase the number of lines, and thus the possible definition of the pictures. Swinton and others had pointed out that television pictures, for good quality and definition on a screen of reasonable size, would need to be analyzed into at least 100,000 and preferably 200,000 elements. Since the number of elements is approximately equal to the square of the number of lines, it can be seen that any system using 30 or even 100 lines would be inadequate—300 being more nearly the minimum. Although mechanical systems were with difficulty made to operate on 200 and more lines, thought increasingly turned toward the greater potential of electronic methods. Hence a most important landmark was V. K. Zworykin's patent, first filed in 1923, for the iconoscope camera tube. Later, he constructed such a tube; and by 1932 the Radio Corporation of America (RCA), with an improved cathode-ray tube for the receiver, was able to demonstrate all-electronic television (initially on 120 lines), so proving the soundness of Swinton's theoretical ideas. The compactness and convenience of the electronic camera were remarkable, and its sensitivity, greatly aided by the unique "storage" feature of the iconoscope, was comparable with ciné cameras of the time.

Continuing work on electronic systems was greatly stimulated. In the U.S. the development was mainly carried out in the RCA laboratories: very soon the number of scanning lines was increased to 343 and other improvements followed fast. Germany was also active, especially in the development of hard-vacuum cathode-ray tubes by Manfred von Ardenne. Indeed, by 1935 a regular broadcasting service had begun there, though with medium definition only—namely 180 lines. In the Netherlands, too, the Philips laboratories took up television research.

In Great Britain, Electric and Musical industries (E.M.I.) set up in 1931 a television research group under Isaac (later Sir Isaac) Shoenberg, a dynamic and farsighted man of long experience in the radio transmission field in both Russia and England. He fostered the evolution of a complete and practical system based on: (a) a camera tube known as the Emitron—an advanced version of the iconoscope—and (b) an improved hard-vacuum cathode-ray tube for the receiver. The team produced by 1935 a complete and practical system, including all the complex electronics surrounding the camera and receiver tubes, as well as the intervening control and amplifying circuits. Shoenberg saw the need to establish a system that would endure for many years, since any subsequent changes in basic standards—particularly the number of scanning lines and their repetition rate—could give rise to severe technical or economic problems. He therefore proposed the use of 405 lines with 50 frames per second, and interlaced scanning to give 25 pictures per second without flicker—ambitious for those days but fully justified by events. The government authorized the British Broadcasting corporation to adopt these standards, as well as the complete E.M.I. system, from the outset of the world's first public high-definition service that was launched in London in 1936. So adequate were they that until 1964 they formed the sole basis of the British service, then being gradually superseded by the international 625-line standard. Initially, and for a short time only, the system was under comparison with alternate broadcasts from a 240-line, 25-picture system developed by the Baird company. The latter employed mechanical scanning methods in the camera and suffered gravely from lack of sensitivity as well as other practical limitations.

By the mid-1930s electronic television was fast advancing in all its aspects. Important questions were the settling of basic standards (number of lines and frames per second) before the introduction of public broadcasting services in the U.S. and elsewhere, though these questions were not everywhere fully resolved until about 1951. The U.S. soon adopted a picture repetition rate of 30 per second while in Europe it became 25 (*see* section III, below). These two standards have been perpetuated and all the countries of the world use one or the other, though technical advances have now obviated the need for disparity. The arguments in relation to the number of lines were based on the need for an effective compromise between, on the one hand, adequate picture definition, and, on the other, a frequency bandwidth that could be technically and economically acceptable. Unfortunately world standardization has never been achieved, though for new television services all countries are adopting one of only two standards, namely, 525 lines per picture at 30 pictures per second—the U.S. standard—and 625 lines at 25 pictures per second, usually known as the European standard. Complications arise when programs are transmitted between countries using different standards.

The U.S. began regular television broadcasting in 1941, but most other countries, apart from Great Britain, were not ready to begin services until the 1950s when television was widely introduced throughout the world. When wartime restrictions governing the manufacture of receivers were removed in 1946, the stage was set in the U.S. for a rapid growth of the television broadcasting industry. By 1949 there were 1,000,000 receivers in use; the 10,000,000 mark was passed in 1951 and the 50,000,000 mark eight years later. About half that number were in use in the 50 other nations which by then had established regular program services.

By the late 1960s receivers in use throughout the world totaled about 225,000,000; about 83,000,000 were in the U.S., 15,600,000 in the U.K., and 6,100,000 in Canada; Japan and the U.S.S.R. had about 20,000,000 sets in each country.

Technical advances have been continuous, particularly the great improvements in camera tubes (*e.g.*, the image orthicon and the Vidicon, which latter was at last able effectively to exploit the photoconductivity principle) that were made from 1945 onward (*see* section III, B, below). By the early 1950s technology had progressed so far, and television had become so widely established, that the time was ripe to tackle in earnest the problem of creating television images in natural colours.

Colour television was by no means a new idea, since its attraction and possibility early engaged the imagination of inventors. A German patent in 1904 contained the earliest proposal, while in 1925 Zworykin filed a patent disclosure for an all-electronic colour television system using registered Paget-type colour filter screens. The screens were placed in planes optically conjugate to the photo-

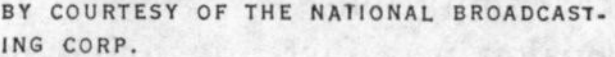

BY COURTESY OF THE NATIONAL BROADCASTING CORP.

(Above) The first U.S. commercial television antenna, built atop the Empire State Building, New York City, 1938; (top right) Franklin D. Roosevelt, the first U.S. president to appear on television, photographed as he went before the cameras, 1939; (right) V. K. Zworykin, inventor of the iconoscope, by an early experimental set with a 5-in. screen, c. 1938

sensitive target of the camera tube and to the fluorescent screen of the viewing tube. The first practical demonstration of television in colour was given by Baird in 1928: he used mechanical scanning with a Nipkow disk having 3 spirals of 30 apertures, one spiral for each primary colour in sequence. The light source at the receiver comprised two gas-discharge tubes, one of mercury vapour and helium for the green and blue colours, and a neon tube for red. In 1929 H. E. Ives and colleagues in the Bell Telephone laboratories transmitted 50-line colour television images between New York and Washington, D.C.: this also was a mechanical method, but one which sent simultaneously the three primary colour signals over three separate circuits. In the same year Frank Gray, also of Bell laboratories, applied for a patent that described a method of transmitting two or more signals over a single channel; this introduced important new principles that were to be the foundation of modern (compatible) colour television as it was developed about 20 years later.

In the course of serious researches toward the realization of colour television, it began to emerge that two basic approaches were possible. One was the frame-by-frame sequential transmission of signals corresponding to each of the three primary colours. This method was in most respects relatively simple to achieve but involved an increased rate of scanning in order to avoid colour flicker, with resulting transmission difficulties from both the higher bandwidth and the inability to use existing black-and-white receivers to reproduce any pictures originated in colour. This kind of system is therefore usually described as non-compatible. The alternative approach—practically much more difficult, even daunting at first—recognized the advantage to be derived from a colour transmission system in which signals representing the three primary colours were transmitted simultaneously, and which could also be compatible with existing black-and-white transmissions. Such a system would mean that any pictures originated in colour could still be receivable (in black and white) on a black-and-white receiver.

In 1938 G. Valensi in France brilliantly pioneered the path to compatible colour television when he patented a method which enabled "the output from a single transmitter to be received not only by television receivers provided with the necessary equipment but also by the ordinary type of receiver which is more numerous and less expensive and which reproduces the pictures in black and white." Although Valensi's proposals—which are too intricate to describe here—have not been precisely adopted in practice, they were influential in later approaches to the problem of compatibility.

Experimental work on colour (on high-definition standards) was taken up in both Great Britain and the U.S. during the late 1930s. Similar methods were explored by Baird in Great Britain and Peter Goldmark of the Columbia Broadcasting system (CBS) in the U.S., who both demonstrated sequential systems using rotating colour filters on the cameras and the receivers. The CBS method was used for some experimental broadcasts before World War II, and these were resumed in 1951 as a service authorized by the Federal Communications commission (FCC). However, public interest was small, and after only a few months the broadcasts were abandoned.

Serious attention was then given by the National Television Systems committee (NTSC) in the U.S. to the development of a fully compatible simultaneous system. Its work led to brilliant achievement, and in 1953 a system capable of operating within the current black-and-white standards was accepted by the FCC. The essentials of this system, known as the NTSC system, have formed the basis of colour systems throughout the world. The basic principle is the combination of two image transmissions: one carrying information about the brightness, including the finest details of the televised scene, to which black-and-white receivers respond; the other, of coarser structure, carrying the colour information. This second component has no appreciable effect on black-and-white sets, while colour receivers use a combination of the two image transmissions. Since the ability of the human eye to perceive detail is most acute when viewing white light, the brightness component of the colour images carries the impression of fine detail, and the superimposed coarse colour information does not substantially alter the sharpness of the resulting colour picture.

In the U.S., public broadcasting using the NTSC system began in 1954. The same system was adopted by Japan, where it came into service in 1960. Other countries favoured modifications of the NTSC system. One such was devised by W. Bruch of the German Telefunken company; known as PAL (phase alternation line), this comprised a small but subtle variant of the NTSC method. The other, SECAM (*système électronique couleur avec mémoire*), differing rather more radically, had been put forward earlier by Henri de France in Paris. Both alternatives aimed at reducing the sensitivity of the colour system to certain forms of distortion encountered in transmission and broadcasting, and had special application to European conditions. Countries were divided in their preferences: in 1967 Great Britain and the Federal Republic of Germany began colour broadcasting using the PAL system, while in the same year France and the U.S.S.R. also introduced colour, adopting the SECAM system. One or other of these three systems was being adopted by all countries.

Colour television is technically much more complex than black and white. In the late 1960s most cameras embodied either three or four pick-up tubes, while in the receiver a shadow-mask, three-gun, cathode-ray tube, first demonstrated by A. N. Goldsmith and A. C. Shroeder of RCA in 1950, formed a successful and widely adopted type of display device for domestic purposes (*see* section IV, B, below). Widespread purchase of colour receivers began about 1964 in the U.S., and by the early 1970s over 20,000,000 colour sets were in use there. (T. H. B.)

## III. FUNDAMENTALS OF PICTURE TRANSMISSION AND RECEPTION

The quality and quantity of television service are limited fundamentally by the rate at which it is feasible to transmit the picture information over the television channel. As already noted, in modern practice the televised image must be capable of being dissected, within a few hundredths of a second, into more than 100,000 picture elements. This implies that the electrical impulses corresponding to the picture elements must pass through the channel at a rate as high as several million per second. Moreover, since the picture content may vary from simple close-up shots having little fine detail to comprehensive distant scenes in which the limiting detail of the system comes into play, the actual rate of transmitting the picture information varies from time to time, from a few impulses per second to several million per second. The television channel must be capable, therefore, of handling information over a continuous band of frequencies several million cycles wide. This is testimony to the extraordinary comprehension of the sense of sight. Hearing is comparatively crude. The ear is satisfied by impulses which can be carried over a channel only 10,000 cycles wide.

In the United States, the television channel occupies a width of 6 mc. (6,000,000 cycles per second) in the radio spectrum. This is 600 times as wide as the channel used by each standard sound broadcasting station. In fact, each television station uses nearly six times as much spectrum space as all the commercial sound broadcasting channels combined. Since each television station must occupy so much spectrum space, few channels are available in a given locality. Moreover, the quantity of service is in conflict with the quality of reproduction. If the detail of the television image is to be increased, other parameters of the transmission being unchanged, the channel width must be increased proportionately, and this decreases the number of channels which can be accommodated in the spectrum. This fundamental conflict between quality of transmission and number of available channels dictates that the quality of reproduction shall just satisfy the typical viewer under the normal viewing conditions of the home. Any excess of performance beyond this would ultimately result in a restriction of program choice.

The first requirement to be met in image analysis is that the reproduced picture shall not flicker, since flicker induces severe visual fatigue. Flicker becomes more evident as the brightness of the picture increases. If flicker is to be unobjectionable at brightnesses suitable for home viewing during daylight as well as evening hours (25 to 100 foot-lamberts), the successive illuminations of the picture screen should occur not less than 50 times per second. This is approximately twice the rate of picture repetition needed for smooth reproduction of motion. To avoid flicker, therefore, twice as much channel space is needed as would suffice to depict motion. The same disparity occurs in motion-picture practice, in which satisfactory performance with respect to flicker would require twice as much film as would be necessary for smooth simulation of motion.

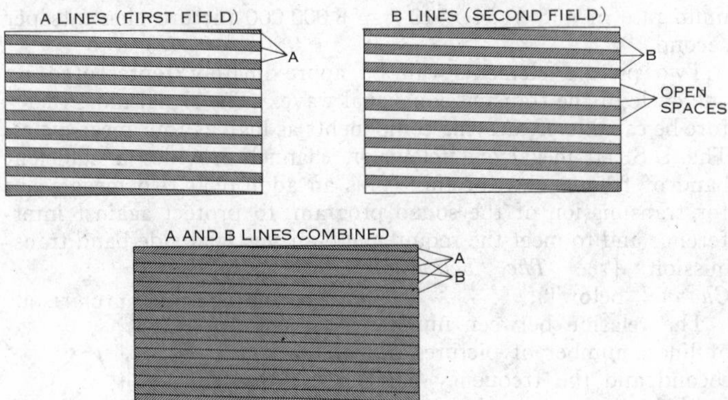


FIG. 2.—COMBINATION OF TWO SEPARATE SCANNING CYCLES (FIELDS) DURING EACH TRANSMISSION PERIOD PRODUCES COMPLETE PICTURE

A way around this difficulty has been found, in motion pictures as well as in television, by projecting each picture twice. In motion pictures, the projector interposes a shutter briefly between film and lens while a single frame of the film is being projected. In television, each image is analyzed and synthesized in two sets of spaced lines, one of which fits successively within the spaces of the other (fig. 2). Thus the picture area is illuminated twice during each complete picture transmission although each line in the image is present only once during that time. This technique is feasible because the eye is comparatively insensitive to flicker when the variation of light is confined to a small part of the field of view. Hence flicker of the individual lines is not evident. If the eye did not have this fortunate property, many towns possessing two television channels would have only one.

It is thus possible to avoid flicker and simulate rapid motion by a picture rate of about 25 per second, with two screen illuminations per picture. The precise value of the picture-repetition rate used in a given region has been chosen by reference to the electric power frequency which predominates in that region. In Europe, where 50-cycle power is the rule, the television picture rate is 25 per second (50 screen illuminations per second). In North America, the picture rate is 30 per second (60 screen illuminations per second) to match the 60-cycle power which predominates there.

The higher picture-transmission rate of North America allows the pictures there to be about five times as bright as those in Europe for the same susceptibility to flicker, but this advantage is offset by a 20% reduction in picture detail for equal utilization of the channel.

The second aspect of performance to be met in a television system is the detailed structure of the image. A printed halftone engraving may possess several million halftone dots per square foot of area. Such reproductions are intended for minute inspection and the dot structure must not be apparent to the unaided eye even at close range. Such fine detail would be a costly waste in television, since the television picture is viewed at comparatively long range (5 to 15 ft. in the typical home setting) and the picture area is not greater than 2 sq.ft. Under these conditions, a picture structure of about 200,000 halftone elements is a suitable compromise. This detail is about equal to that which is provided by 16-mm. home motion pictures and substantially exceeds that of the 8-mm. film widely used for amateur cinematography.

The physiological basis of this compromise lies in the fact that the normal eye, under conditions typical of television viewing, can resolve pictorial details if the angle they subtend at the eye is not less than two minutes of arc. This implies that the structure of 200,000 elements in a picture one foot high can just be resolved at a distance of about ten feet. The structure of the picture may be objectionably evident at short range, *e.g.*, while tuning the receiver, but it is inappropriate to require the system to assume the heavy costs of transmitting detail which would be used by a small part of the audience for a small part of the viewing time.

The third item to be selected in image analysis is the shape of the picture. This has been standardized universally as a rectangle whose width is one-third longer than its height. This 4 by 3 ratio (aspect ratio) was originally chosen to match the dimensions of standard 35-mm. motion-picture film (prior to the advent of the wide-screen cinema) in the interest of televising film without waste of frame area. The width of the screen rectangle is greater than its height, as in the proscenium of a theatre, to accommodate the horizontal motion which predominates in virtually all televised events.

The fourth determination in image analysis is the path over which the image structure is explored at the camera and reconstituted on the receiver screen. In the original Nipkow disk, this path was a series of arcs of circles (fig. 1). In modern television, the pattern is a series of parallel straight lines, each progressing from left to right, the lines following in sequence from top to bottom of the picture frame. The exploration of the image structure proceeds at a constant speed along each line, since this provides uniform loading of the transmission channel under the demands of a given structural detail, no matter where in the frame the detail lies. The line-by-line, left-to-right, top-to-bottom dissection and reconstitution of television images is known as scanning, from its similarity to the progression of the line of vision in reading a page of printed matter. The agent which disassembles or reassembles the light values along each line is called the scanning spot, and the path it follows is the scanning pattern or raster.

The geometry of the modern scanning pattern is shown in fig. 2.

It consists of two sets of lines. One set, marked A, is scanned first and the lines are so laid down that an equal empty space is maintained between lines. The second set, marked B, is laid down after the first, and is so positioned that its lines fall precisely in the empty spaces of set A. The area of the image is thus scanned twice, but each point in the area is passed over once. This is known as interlaced scanning, and is used in all the television broadcast services of the world. Each set of alternate lines is known as a scanning field; the two sets together, comprising the

*Television Systems of the World*

| Region or country | Number of lines per frame | Number of pictures per second | Maximum detail (picture elements per frame) | Available picture band width (mc.) | Channel band width (mc.) |
|---|---|---|---|---|---|
| United Kingdom . . | 405/625 | 25 | 130,000/ 210,000 | 3/5 | 5/7 |
| North America, South America, Japan . . | 525 | 30 | 150,000 | 4 | 6 |
| Europe, Australia, Africa, Eurasia . . | 625 | 25 | 210,000 | 5* | 7* |
| France and French dependencies . . | 819/625 | 25 | 440,000/ 210,000 | 10.4 | 14 |

*Six and eight megacycles respectively in some countries.

whole scanning pattern, are known as a scanning frame. The repetition rate of field scanning is standardized in accordance with the frequency of electric power, as noted above, at either 50 fields per second or 60 fields per second. The corresponding rates of frame scanning are 25 and 30 frames per second. The localities in which various scanning standards are used are listed in the table.

The total number of lines in the scanning pattern has been set to provide a maximum pictorial detail of the order of 200,000 picture elements. Since the frame area is 4 units wide by 3 units high, this figure implies a pattern of about 520 picture elements in its width (along each line) and 390 elements in its height (across the lines). This latter figure would imply a scanning pattern of about 400 lines, were it not for the fact that many of the picture details, falling in random positions on the scanning pattern, lie partly on two lines and hence require two lines for accurate reproduction. Scanning patterns are designed, therefore, to possess about 40% more lines than the number of picture elements to be reproduced in the vertical direction. Actual values in use in television broadcasting in various regions are 405 lines, 525 lines, 625 lines and 819 lines per frame, as listed in the table. These values have been chosen to suit the frequency band of the channel actually assigned in the respective geographical regions.

The scanning spot is made to follow the paths shown in fig. 2 by imparting two repetitive motions to the spot simultaneously (fig. 3). One is a horizontally directed back-and-forth motion. The spot is moved at constant speed from left to right and then returned as rapidly as possible, while extinguished and inactive, from right to left.

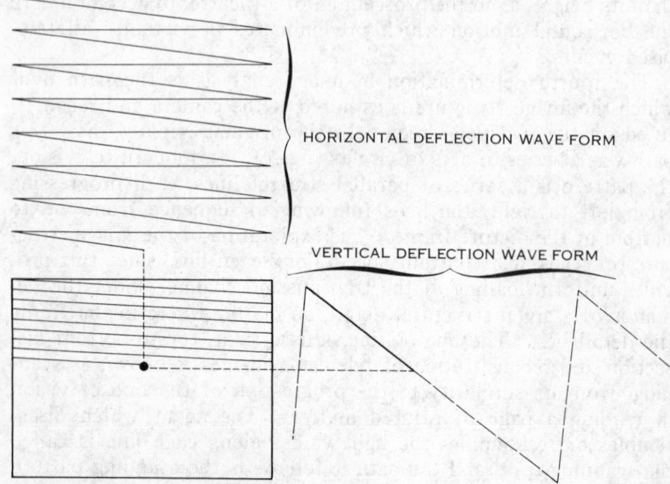


FIG. 3.—SCANNING PATTERN AND WAVE FORMS FOR HORIZONTAL AND VERTICAL DEFLECTION IN SEQUENTIAL PARALLEL-LINE SCANNING

Simultaneously, a vertical motion is imparted to the spot, moving it comparatively slowly from top to bottom of the frame. This motion spreads out the more rapid left-to-right scans, forming the first field scan of alternate lines and empty spaces. When the bottom of the frame is reached, the spot moves vertically upward as rapidly as possible, while extinguished and inactive. The next top-to-bottom motion then spreads out the horizontal line scans so that they fall in the empty spaces of the previously scanned field. Precise interlacing of the successive field scans is facilitated if the total number of lines in the frame is an odd number. All the numbers of lines used in ordinary transmissions (*see* table) were so chosen.

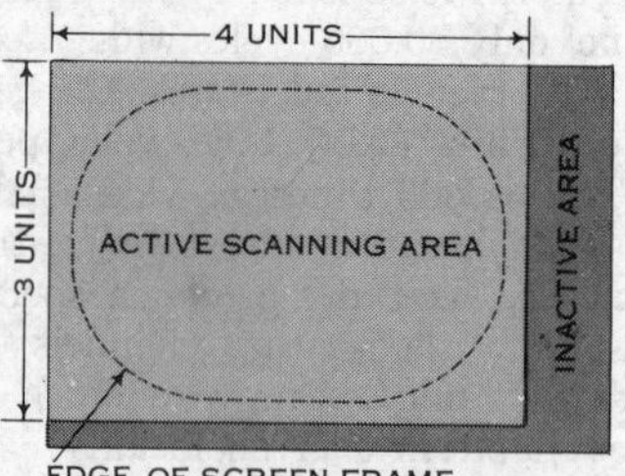


FIG. 4.—ACTIVE AND INACTIVE PORTIONS OF SCANNING PATTERN

The return of the scanning spot from right to left and from bottom to top of the frame, during which it is inactive, consumes time which cannot be devoted to transmitting picture information. This time is used to transmit synchronizing control signals which keep the scanning process at the receiver in step with that at the transmitter. The time lost during retracing of the spot proportionately reduces the actual number of picture elements which can be reproduced. In the 525-line scanning pattern used in the U.S., about 15% of each line is lost in the return motion and about 35 out of the 525 lines are blanked out while the spot returns from bottom to top of two successive fields. The scanning area actually in use for reproduction of the picture contains a maximum of about 435 picture elements along each line and has 490 active lines, capable of reproducing 350 picture elements in the vertical direction. The frame can accommodate at maximum, therefore, about $350 \times 435$ or 152,000 picture elements. The detail-transmission capacity of the scanning patterns of other systems is listed in the table.

The time taken by the scanning spot to move over the active portion of each scanning line is of the order of .00005 sec. (50 microseconds or $\mu$ sec.). In the U.S. system, 525 lines are transmitted in $\frac{1}{30}$ sec., which is equivalent to about 64 $\mu$ sec. per line. Up to 15% of this time is consumed in the horizontal retrace motion of the spot, leaving 54 $\mu$ sec. for active reproduction of as many as 435 picture elements in each line. This represents a maximum rate of $435 \div 54 \times 10^{-6} \cong 8{,}000{,}000$ picture elements per second.

Two picture elements can be approximately represented by one cycle of the transmission signal wave. The signal must therefore be capable of carrying components as high as four megacycles. The U.S. six-megacycle television channel provides a sufficient band of frequencies for this (plus an additional two megacycles for transmission of the sound program, to protect against interference and to meet the requirements of vestigial side-band transmission [see *The Television Channel*, below]).

The relation between number of lines, number of pictures per second and the frequency band needed to transmit the picture information is

$$F = \tfrac{1}{2}R = KL^2P$$

where $F$ is the frequency band in cycles per second which must be transmitted, $R$ is the rate of scanning picture elements per second, $L$ is the number of lines per picture, $P$ the number of pictures per second and $K$ a factor (approximately 0.5) which takes into account the spot retrace losses,

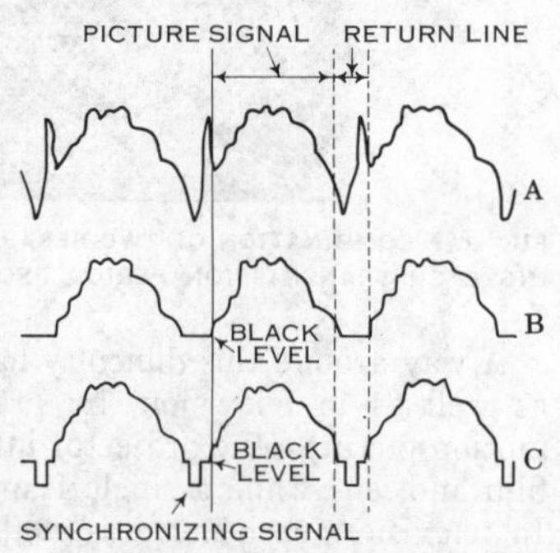


FIG. 5.—VIDEO SIGNAL

(A) Signal as obtained from pickup; (B) after blanking out return-line signal and inserting black level; (C) after adding synchronizing signal

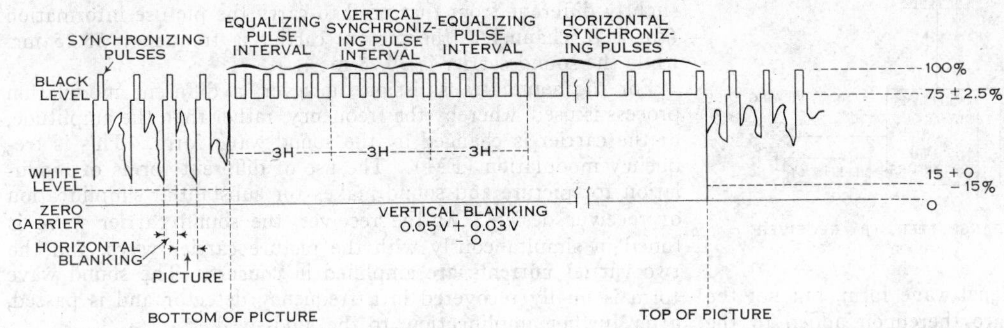


FIG. 6.—WAVE FORM OF SYNCHRONIZING SIGNAL: H, LINE-SCANNING PERIOD; V, FIELD-SCANNING PERIOD

the aspect ratio and vertical resolution losses due to line straddling.

The relationship between the ideal and actual scanning patterns is shown in fig. 4. The part shown as darker is lost during the spot retraces. The remaining area of the pattern is actively employed in analyzing and synthesizing the picture information and is adjusted to have the 4 by 3 dimensions of the standard aspect ratio. In practice, some of the active area may also be hidden behind the decorative mask which surrounds the picture tube of the receiver, as shown by the dashed line.

### A. The Television Picture Signal

The translation of the televised scene into its electrical counterpart results in a sequence of electrical impulses known as the television picture signal. This can be represented graphically as a signal wave form in which the electrical values (voltage or current) are plotted vertically against time, plotted horizontally. Corresponding to the electrical values and time, respectively, are the brightness of the image at each point on the scanning line and the position on the line of the point in question. These quantities are shown in fig. 5.

The television signal wave form is a continuous sequence of electrical values, corresponding with the brightnesses along each line, interspersed with blank periods representing the times during which the inactive scanning spot retraces from the end of one line to the beginning of the next. A blank interval also occurs when the scanning spot, having reached the bottom of the frame, retraces to the top.

Superimposed on the blank intervals are additional impulses, known as synchronization signals. The horizontal synchronization signal is a small impulse which occurs shortly after the completion of each scanning line. Its purpose is to cause the scanning spots at the transmitter and receiver to retrace to the next line at precisely the same instant. The vertical synchronization signal is a serrated series of impulses (fig. 6) which occurs shortly after the scanning spot has reached the bottom of the frame, causing the receiver and transmitter spots to retrace to the top in synchronism.

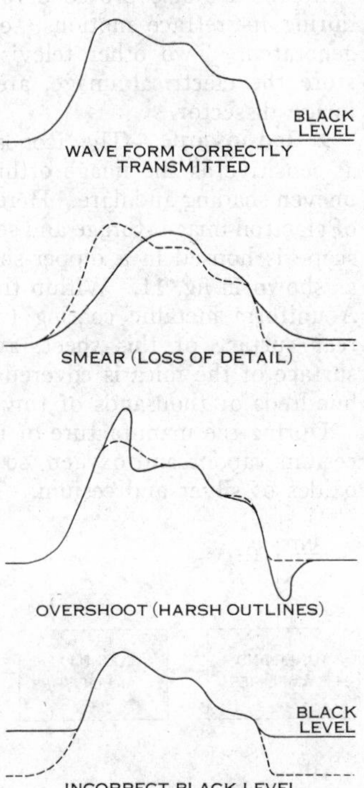


FIG. 7.—TRANSMISSION DEFECTS IN PICTURE SIGNAL WAVE FORMS

Since the signal wave form embodies all the picture information to be transmitted from camera to receiver screen, the television system must deliver the wave form to the picture tube of each receiver as accurately and as free from blemishes as possible. Unfortunately, virtually every item of equipment in the system (amplifiers, cables, transmitter, the transmitting antenna, the radio wave in space, the receiving antenna and the receiver circuits) conspires to distort the wave form or permits it to be contaminated by "noise" or interference.

Among the possible distortions (fig. 7) are: (1) failure to maintain the rapidity with which the wave form rises or falls as the scanning spot crosses a sharp boundary between light and dark areas of the image, producing a loss of detail or smear in the reproduced image; (2) the introduction of overshoots which cause excessively harsh outlines; and (3) failure to maintain the average value of the wave form over extended periods, which causes the image as a whole to be too bright or too dark.

Throughout the system, amplifiers must be used to keep the television signal strong relative to the random electrical currents (noise) which are everywhere present. These random currents, caused by thermally induced motions of electrons in the circuits, cause interference having a speckled appearance, known as "snow." Pictures received from distant stations are subject to this form of interference, since the radio wave is then so weak that it cannot override the random currents in the receiving antenna. Interference of a striated type may be caused by the signals of stations other than that to which the receiver is tuned. Care in the design of the receiver tuner and amplifier circuits is necessary to minimize such interference, and channels must be allocated to neighbouring communities at sufficient geographical separations and frequency intervals to protect the local service.

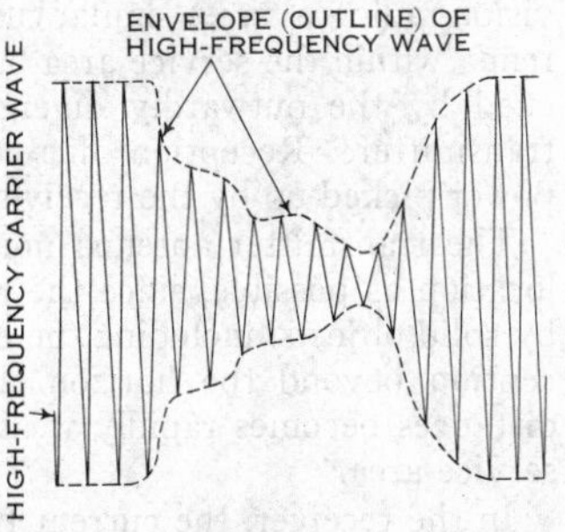

ENVELOPE (OUTLINE) OF HIGH-FREQUENCY WAVE

HIGH-FREQUENCY CARRIER WAVE

FIG. 8.—TRANSMISSION OF PICTURE SIGNAL BY AMPLITUDE MODULATION OF A HIGH-FREQUENCY CARRIER WAVE; ENVELOPE (BROKEN LINE) HAS SHAPE OF PICTURE SIGNAL WAVE FORM

The television signal wave form can be conveyed within transmitting and receiving apparatus, and over short distances of wires and cable, in the form shown in fig. 5. For transmission over greater distances, however, as in network connections and over the air, the signal wave form must be imposed on a high-frequency carrier wave. The broadcast transmitter, for example, is actually a generator of very-high-frequency or ultrahigh-frequency alternating current; *i.e.*, current which reverses its direction several tens or hundreds of millions of times per second. When such a current (known as the carrier current) is passed through the transmitting antenna, it produces a radio wave of the same frequency which travels through space and induces a weaker, but otherwise identical, current in the receiving antenna.

At the transmitter the picture signal wave form changes the strength, or amplitude, of the high-frequency carrier current by a process known as amplitude modulation. The alternations of the carrier current are thus constrained to take on a succession of amplitudes which match the shape of the signal wave form, as is revealed in the outline or envelope of the carrier current (fig. 8).

The functions of the television system which generate, transmit and utilize the television signal wave form are shown in fig. 9. The scene to be televised is focused by a lens on a camera tube, within the camera. A scanning spot within the camera tube is passed over the image in the scanning pattern of fig. 3, its motion being controlled by the synchronization generator. The latter equipment also renders the scanning spot inactive during its retrace motions and generates the synchronization signals mentioned

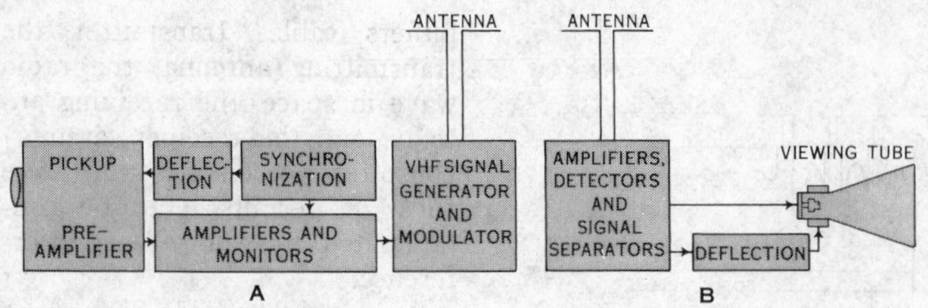


FIG. 9.—BLOCK DIAGRAM OF (A) TRANSMITTER, (B) RECEIVER

above. The camera produces the signal wave form, but not the synchronizing signals. The latter are thereupon added to the signal and the complete signal wave form (fig. 5 and 6) is established. The signal is then amplified as required, by amplifiers capable of operating over the wide band of frequencies (from a few cycles per second to 4,000,000 or 5,000,000 cycles per second) necessary to preserve the precise shape of the wave form. In a transcontinental network, the signal may pass through more than 100 such amplifiers in tandem before it finally reaches the transmitter. There the wave form is amplified to a high power level. Concurrently, the carrier current is generated by other circuits of the transmitter. The signal wave form and carrier current are then combined in the modulator, which imposes the wave form on the carrier (fig. 8). The modulated carrier current may then be further amplified (typically to 10,000 or more watts) and finally passed through the transmitter antenna, which radiates the television radio wave. A similar current is induced in any receiving antenna within the service area but the current is enormously weakened by the outwardly diverging travel of the wave from the transmitter. Reception of excellent quality is possible when the power picked up by the receiving antenna is only 0.00000001 w.

The transmitter antenna must be as high and in as exposed a location as possible, since the radio waves tend to be intercepted by solid objects, including the earth's surface at the horizon. Reception beyond the horizon is possible, but the signal at such distances becomes rapidly weaker as it passes to the limit of the service area.

In the receiver, the current from the antenna is passed through a tuner, which separates it from other currents of different carrier frequencies which may be present from other stations. The desired current is then amplified in several successive amplifier stages, while still in the amplitude-modulated form. Passage through a detector follows. The picture signal wave form is thereby recovered and is passed through still another amplifier before being sent to the picture tube. The picture screen displays a scanning spot whose brightness is controlled by the picture signal. Simultaneously, the signal is applied to synchronizing circuits which abstract from it the synchronizing signals. These are used to control the motion of the scanning spot so that it traces out the scanning pattern in precise synchronism with the motion of the scanning spot in the camera.

Transmission and reception of the accompanying sound program are accomplished by the apparatus shown in fig. 10. The microphone produces a signal wave form which represents the sound pressure changes impinging on it. This wave form is amplified, transmitted over the network and finally fed to the sound transmitter. The latter, like the picture transmitter, is a generator of high-frequency carrier current, but of a frequency slightly different from that used to carry the picture information (for U.S. channel 2, the picture carrier is frequency 55.25 mc. while the sound carrier is 59.75 mc.).

For the sound transmission, however, a different modulation process is used, whereby the frequency, rather than the amplitude, of the carrier is changed by the sound wave form. This is frequency modulation (FM). The use of different forms of modulation for picture and sound makes for substantial simplification of receiver design. At the receiver, the sound carrier wave is tuned in simultaneously with the picture carrier wave, and the two carrier currents are amplified in concert. The sound wave form is finally recovered in a frequency detector and is passed, after further amplification, to the loud-speaker.

The amount of amplification conferred on the picture and sound currents by a typical television receiver is extremely large. When tuned to a station at a distance of 50 mi., the power picked up by the antenna is typically $10^{-11}$ w., whereas the signals fed to picture tube and loud-speaker, after amplification, are of the order of 1 w. That is, the receiver produces a faithful amplification of the order of 100,000,000,000 times.

### B. Television Camera Tubes

The television camera tube is an electronic device which converts an optical image into a sequence of electrical impulses; *i.e.,* it produces the television picture signal. Three types of television camera tube are in wide use: the image orthicon, the orthicon and the Vidicon. These devices differ in detail but have in common the following elements: (1) a photosensitive surface, on which the scene to be televised is focused by a lens, which converts each light value into a corresponding value of electric charge and forms thereby an electrical image; (2) a means of storing the electrical image, that is, causing the charge to accumulate during the interval of several hundredths of a second between successive scannings of each line in the image; (3) an electron beam, formed in an electron gun and deflected over the electrical image, following the scanning pattern of fig. 2; and (4) a mechanism for producing an electrical current or voltage which is proportional at every instant to the electric charge accumulated at the point passed over by the electron beam at that instant. The latter is the picture signal represented in the wave form of fig. 5.

Means are also provided for extinguishing the scanning beam during its retrace motions, so that no television signal is then generated. Two other television pickup devices, which do not store the electrical image, are the flying spot scanner and the image dissector.

**1. Iconoscope.**—The iconoscope is obsolete, since it is not as sensitive as the image orthicon and its images are subject to uneven shading and flare. Here it serves to introduce the concepts of electron image storage and scanning in simple form. The iconoscope is housed in a dipper-shaped vacuum-tight glass envelope, as shown in fig. 11. Within the wide end is a flat sheet of mica. A uniform metallic coating (the signal plate) is placed on the rear surface of this sheet, away from the image. The front surface of the mica is covered with a mosaic comprised of many hundreds of thousands of tiny globules of silver.

During the manufacture of the tube the mosaic is treated with cesium vapour and oxygen, so each globule has a surface of the oxides of silver and cesium. This combination of elements pos-

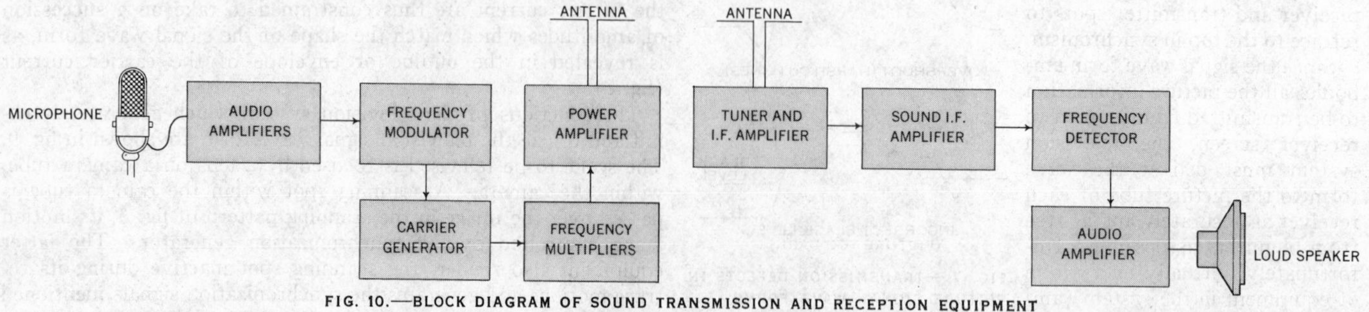


FIG. 10.—BLOCK DIAGRAM OF SOUND TRANSMISSION AND RECEPTION EQUIPMENT

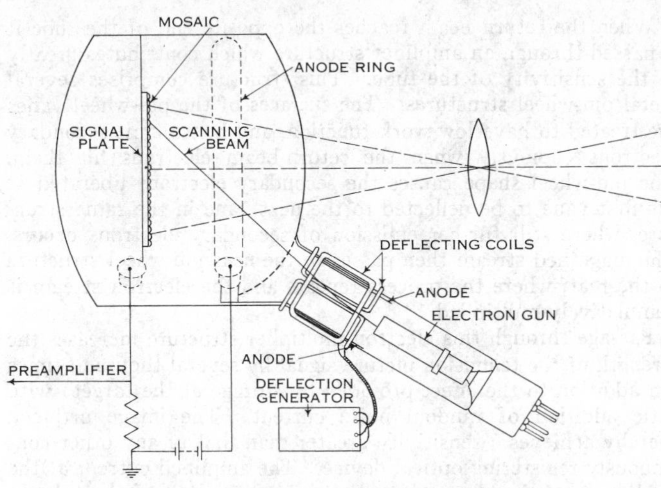


FIG. 11.—ICONOSCOPE CAMERA TUBE

sesses a low electronic work function, that is, electrons are readily liberated, by the photoelectric effect, when light falls on the surface. Since the globules are insulated from each other and from the signal plate by the mica, the loss of electrons under illumination causes the globules to assume and hold a positive charge, the charge on each globule being proportional to the strength of the illumination falling on it and to the time it has been illuminated.

When an optical image is focused on the mosaic, the whole surface assumes a distribution of positive charge which matches the distribution of light in the image, and the amount of charge at each point steadily increases until the scanning spot passes over the globule at that point.

The scanning spot of the iconoscope is formed by a narrow beam of electrons, shot out of an electron gun in the side arm of the tube. On its way to the mosaic this beam passes within two sets of electromagnet coils. Currents like those of fig. 3 are passed through these coils, causing the beam to be deflected horizontally at a rapid rate and vertically at a slower rate. The extent of the horizontal motion is adjusted from top to bottom of the mosaic, so that the pattern traced out by the electron beam on the mosaic is a rectangular pattern like that in fig. 2.

The electrons in the beam are accelerated to a relatively high velocity (the accelerating potential in the electron gun is of the order of 1,000 v.). When the beam hits a globule, therefore, it transfers a substantial amount of energy to the atoms of the globule and the globule surface gives off electrons (additional to those freed by the optical image) by virtue of the impact. This effect is known as secondary electron emission.

The number of secondary electrons thus liberated depends on the electrical potential which the globule in question has assumed under the prior influence of the light falling on it. As each globule is passed over by the beam, therefore, it undergoes a sudden change in electrical potential, the amount of the change being proportional to the light falling on it. The change in potential of the globule is transferred through the mica support to the signal plate behind it, the globule and plate forming in effect the plates of an electrical capacitor. Thus, as the beam passes in succession over the globules lying along a given scanning line, the signal plate assumes a succession of voltages (the picture signal) which match the corresponding succession of light values along that line. The signal plate is connected to an amplifier, external to the iconoscope, which increases the strength of the picture signal.

The secondary electrons liberated by the impact of the scanning beam are in large part collected by a positively charged anode ring (fig. 11), but some of the electrons fall back on the mosaic in a random pattern, thus destroying to some degree the charge pattern produced by the optical image. This produces uneven shading and flare in the reproduced image, as previously mentioned.

The phenomenon of charge storage, by which the magnitude of the electrical image is continually increased between successive scannings of each line, is of the utmost significance in television technology. The Nipkow disk (and other nonstorage television pickup devices) employs only the light which is present at a given point in the image at the instant the scanning spot passes over that point. Since in modern television the area of the scanning spot is only about $\frac{1}{200{,}000}$ of the area of the scanning pattern, only this small fraction of the light of the image can be used. But when the image charge is stored in increasing amount for the full interval between successive scannings of a given point, the accumulated charge is then theoretically about 200,000 times that which can be accumulated during the time the beam moves through its own width.

**2. Orthicon.**—The orthicon camera tube was the first successor to the iconoscope. A refined version (the CPS Emitron described below) is used in England for studio work. This tube (fig. 12) is housed in a cylindrical glass structure, on one end of which the optical image is focused on a mosaic. This mosaic is similar to that of the iconoscope, but is made up of a precise array of squares of photosensitive material, forming by evaporation on a transparent support. A transparent metal coating on the reverse side serves as the signal plate.

The optical image is focused on the signal plate, passing through it and the support to the mosaic, where it creates and stores a positive electrical charge image, in the manner of the iconoscope. The electron beam is formed in an electron gun at the other end of the tube and is directed toward the mosaic and deflected by electromagnet coils surrounding the tube so that it passes over the mosaic in the standard interlaced scanning pattern. The electrons are accelerated by a low voltage, so that they do not liberate any substantial number of secondary electrons. Instead, the negative electrons in the beam land on the mosaic squares, neutralizing the stored positive charge and ultimately building up a negative charge. The electrons in the beam are then repelled and return to the opposite end of the tube where they are removed by a positive collecting electrode which surrounds the electron gun. The change in electrical potential, undergone by each mosaic element as its charge is neutralized, is transferred by capacitive action, as in the iconoscope, to the signal plate. The latter thereby undergoes a succession of voltage changes which constitute the picture signal and which are passed to amplifier stages external to the tube.

The orthicon is unstable if subjected to high light levels. The CPS Emitron minimizes this difficulty by care in the design of the mosaic structure, but the tube operates best under closely controlled illumination and hence is used primarily in studios rather than in outdoor situations.

**3. Image Orthicon.**—The image orthicon is, by common consent, the most highly developed of the television camera tubes and is perhaps the most remarkable electronic device in existence. In its most refined form, its sensitivity to light is phenomenally great. It can respond to light levels far below those capable of exposing motion-picture film or affecting the eye itself (the "film speed" rating of such tubes is of the order of ASA 10,000). Less sensitive image orthicon tubes are used in broadcasting practice; they serve to produce satisfactory image quality under any light levels likely to be encountered in studio and outdoor scenes.

The image orthicon is similar to the orthicon but includes an additional electrical-imaging process and contains a high-gain amplifier based on the phenomenon of electron multiplication. It is the principal camera tube used for live-scene telecasting.

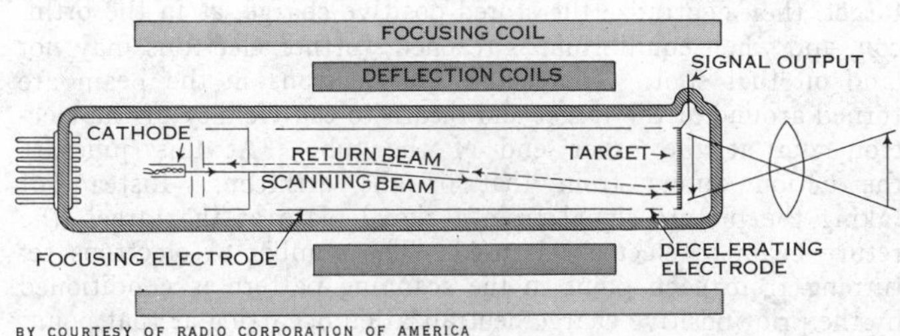


BY COURTESY OF RADIO CORPORATION OF AMERICA

FIG. 12.—ORTHICON CAMERA TUBE

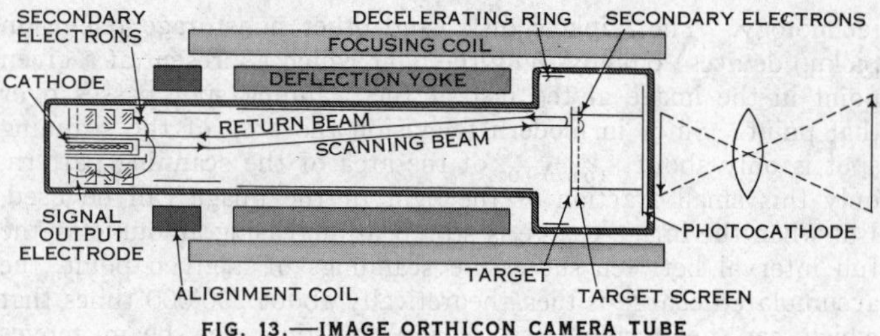

FIG. 13.—IMAGE ORTHICON CAMERA TUBE

The image orthicon (fig. 13) is housed in a cylindrical glass envelope having an enlarged section on one end, which is closed by an optically flat glass plate on the inside of which is deposited a continuous photosensitive coating (photocathode). The optical image is focused through the glass support onto the coating, where it liberates electrons by photoelectric emission, the emission at each point matching the amount of light in the image at that point.

The liberated electrons stream away from the photosensitive surface, through the enlarged cylindrical portion of the tube, until they encounter the target electrode. This is a piece of very thin glass of uniform thickness. The streams of electrons induce secondary emission of electrons from the surface of the glass, and the latter are collected by a fine mesh screen (500 or more meshes to the inch). This lies parallel and close to the glass target; the streams of image electrons pass through it on their way to the target.

Since the glass target is very thin, its longitudinal electrical resistance, through its thickness, is small (resistance varies directly with the length of the conducting path). The changes in electrical potential induced by secondary emission are transferred through this low resistance to the opposite face of the target, where they are scanned by the electron beam. Conversely, the lateral resistance, across the face of the thin glass target, is very great (since electrical resistance varies inversely with the cross section of the conduction path). Consequently any tendency of the charge pattern to dissipate itself laterally is arrested, and the fine structure of the electrical image is preserved throughout the scanning interval. Moreover, as the streams of electrons from the photocathode continue to fall on the target glass, the intensity of the electrical image continually increases; that is, storage of charge occurs.

Both the photocathode and the target are continuous surfaces and in themselves contribute no structural limit to the detail of the image. The fine mesh screen which collects the secondary electrons from the target imposes the limit on detail, and consequently the holes in the screen must be substantially smaller than the scanning spot. Actually, the screen possesses nearly 1,000,000 holes in an area of 1.5 sq.in., compared with the roughly 200,000 picture elements into which the image is dissected.

The stored charge image on the reverse side of the target is scanned by an electron beam, which, like that of the orthicon, is accelerated at lower voltage and is actually decelerated before hitting the target, so that the scanning electrons have a velocity corresponding to voltage from zero to a few volts. Consequently, the secondary emission caused by scanning produces no deleterious effects.

The electron beam is deflected in the standard interlaced scanning pattern over the electrical image by magnetic fields produced by coils external to the tube. When the beam electrons hit the target, they neutralize the stored positive charge, as in the orthicon, and when equilibrium is reached, further electrons may not land on that spot. Thereafter, the electrons in the beam are turned around at the target and return to the vicinity of the electron gun at the other end of the tube. At this juncture the action differs from that of the orthicon. Instead of taking the picture signal from a signal plate at the target, the return beam of electrons is used. The number of electrons returning from each point in the scanning pattern is conditioned by the prior positive charge neutralization occurring at that point. Consequently the return beam constitutes a picture signal current.

When the return beam reaches the opposite end of the tube it is passed through an amplifier structure which contributes greatly to the sensitivity of the tube. This structure comprises several metal pin-wheel structures. The surfaces of the pin-wheel vanes are treated to have low work function, and hence emit secondary electrons copiously when the return-beam electrons hit them. The pin-wheel shape causes the secondary electrons liberated at the first vane to be deflected to the next vane in the same structure, where still further emission of secondary electrons occurs. The magnified stream then passes to the next pin-wheel structure to the rear, where the process repeats and the electron stream is cumulatively multiplied.

Passage through this electron multiplier structure increases the strength of the television picture signal by several thousand times (in addition to the effect provided by storage at the target) with little addition of random noise current. The image orthicon thereby achieves a sensitivity greater than that of any other continuously registering optical device. The amplified current at the final stage of the electron multiplier is passed out of the tube to a conventional vacuum-tube or transistor amplifier.

**4. Vidicon.**—The Vidicon camera tube, first used in the early 1950s, was the first camera device to employ the phenomenon of photoconductivity. In its early form it was sluggish (objects in motion were reproduced with noticeable smear) and hence it was limited to industrial applications. Later versions were free of this defect and the Vidicon came to enjoy wide use in broadcasting, in monochrome and colour service. The tube elements (fig. 14) are contained in a cylindrical glass envelope, substantially smaller than the image orthicon and hence more adaptable to portable cameras. At one end, a transparent metallic coating serves as a signal plate. Deposited directly on the signal plate is a photoconductive material (a complex compound of selenium) whose electrical resistance is high in the dark but progressively lowers as the amount of light increases.

The optical image is focused on the end of the tube and passes through the signal plate to the photoconductive layer, where the light induces a pattern of varying conductivity which matches the distribution of brightness in the optical image. The conduction paths through the layer allow positive charge from the signal plate (which is maintained at a positive voltage) to pass through the layer, and this current continues to flow during the interval between scans. Charge storage thus occurs, and an electrical charge image is built up on the rear surface of the photoconductor.

At the other end of the tube an electron beam is formed and passed through magnetic fields which deflect it, in the standard interlaced scanning pattern, over the rear surface of the photoconducting layer. The beam electrons neutralize the positive charge on each point in the electrical image and the resulting change in potential is transferred by capacitive action to the signal plate, from which the television signal is derived. There is no structural limit within the photoconductive layer itself, that is, the electron beam scanning spot imposes the only limit on the image detail.

It is possible, therefore, to derive an image of broadcast quality (200,000 picture elements) from a photosensitive area no larger than 0.2 sq.in. This permits the use of small and comparatively inexpensive lenses, with correspondingly large depth of focus for a

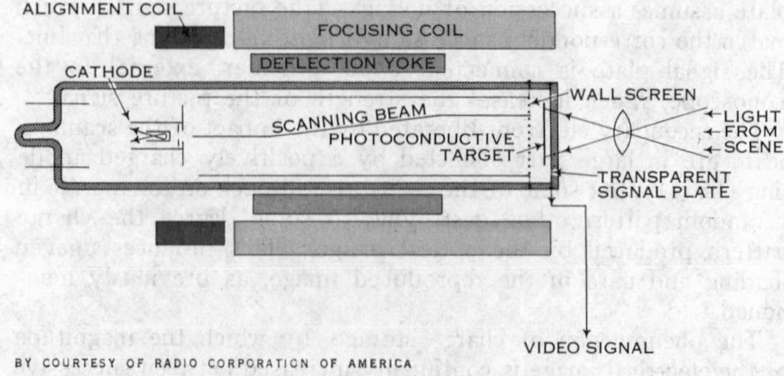

BY COURTESY OF RADIO CORPORATION OF AMERICA
FIG. 14.—VIDICON CAMERA TUBE

given lens opening. The internal structure of the tube is very simple and this, with its small size, makes it adaptable to a wide range of camera arrangements in broadcasting, industrial and military applications.

**5. Flying Spot Scanner.**—Another form of television pickup device, used in televising film transparencies, is the flying spot scanner (fig. 15). The light source is a cathode-ray tube in which a beam of electrons, deflected in the standard scanning pattern, impinges on a fluorescent phosphor surface. The beam produces thereby a spot of light which moves in the scanning pattern. The

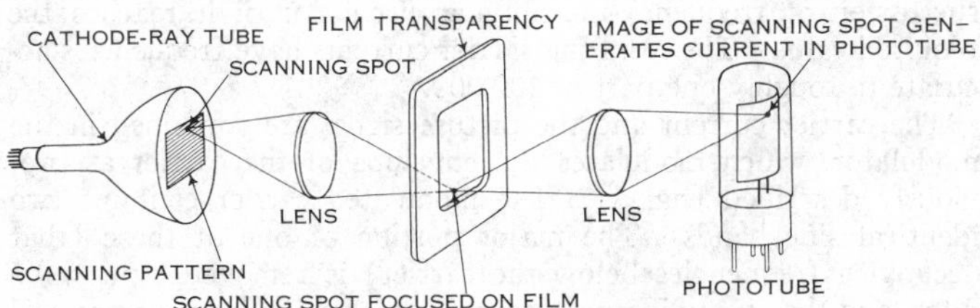


FIG. 15.—FLYING SPOT CAMERA SYSTEM

light from this spot is focused optically on the surface of the photographic film transparency to be televised. As the image of the spot moves, it traces out a scanning line across the film, and the amount of light emerging from the other side of the film at each point is determined by the transparency of the film at that point. The emerging light is collected and caused to enter a photoelectric cell which produces a current proportional to the light entering it.

This current thus takes on a succession of values proportional to the successive values of transparency along each line in the scanning pattern, that is, it is the picture signal current. No storage action occurs, so the light from the cathode-ray tube must be very intense and the optical design very efficient to secure noise-free reproduction. The flying spot system may be used with motion-picture film if an optical immobilizer is used. (See *Television Recording,* below.)

### C. Video Amplification

The picture signal wave form produced by the television camera is initially very weak, of the order of a few hundredths of a volt, and is therefore ready prey to the random currents (noise) present in the succeeding transmission circuits. Immediately upon leaving the camera, therefore, the signal must be strengthened, and this process must be repeated at intervals throughout the transmission to the picture tube at the receiver. The strengthening process, known as video amplification, occurs in electron tubes or transistors. The picture signal is applied to the control electrode of the tube or transistor, which governs the passage of charge carriers from the input to the output. Since the carriers complete this passage in a few thousandths of a millionth of a second, the control electrode is able to exercise control over the output current several hundred million times per second, that is, at rates considerably higher than the upper frequency limit of the video signal. The video amplifier must, however, provide uniform amplification throughout the band of frequencies from a lower limit near zero cycles per second (c.p.s.) to many millions of c.p.s. The amount of amplification tends to fall off near the upper frequency limit, since it takes a finite time for the output current of the amplifier to charge the electrical capacitance present at the tube or transistor output electrode. This effect may be counteracted by inserting a small inductance coil in the output circuit which resonates with the capacitance at a frequency above the upper limit of the video signal spectrum.

At the other end of the spectrum, near zero frequency, the amplification also tends to fall off as a result of incomplete coupling between successive amplifier stages. This effect may be counteracted by care in proportioning the resistive and capacitive elements in the coupling connections, which makes possible uniform amplification down to about 30 c.p.s. However, it is impractical to reach zero frequency (direct current), since a succession of direct-current coupled amplifiers displays unmanageable instability. This difficulty is circumvented by arranging for the envelope of the broadcast carrier current to have a fixed amplitude at a level corresponding to black (absence of light in the televised scene). In this way the average brightness of the image may be preserved and recovered.

Video amplifiers, both of the tube and transistor varieties, can be designed to cover a remarkably comprehensive range, amplifying a picture signal comprising any combination of frequency components lying between 30 c.p.s. and as high as 10,000,000 c.p.s. This implies not merely that the amplitudes of all such components are uniformly increased, but that their relative times of occurrence are strictly preserved. Only if these requirements are met can the fine structure, as well as the gross outline, of the picture signal wave form be preserved from the camera to the receiver picture tube.

### D. The Television Channel

When the band of frequencies in the picture signal is imposed on the high-frequency broadcast carrier current in the modulator of the transmitter, as previously described (fig. 8), two bands of frequencies are produced above and below the carrier frequency. Thus, if the picture signal occupies a band of frequencies extending to four megacycles, two side bands are produced which extend four megacycles downward and four megacycles upward from the carrier frequency. The side bands are identical in frequency content, that is, both carry the complete picture signal information. One of the side bands is superfluous and, if transmitted, would wastefully consume space in the broadcast spectrum. Therefore, the major portion of one of the side bands is removed, and the other is transmitted in full. Complete removal of the superfluous side band is possible, but this would complicate receiver design. Hence, a vestige of the unwanted side band is retained to serve the over-all economy of the system. This technique is known as vestigial side-band transmission. It is now universally employed in all the television broadcast systems of the world.

The television channel contains the picture carrier frequency, one complete picture side band and a vestigial portion of the other picture side band. In addition, the carrier for the sound transmission and its side bands is included within the channel. Since the band of frequencies needed to convey the sound is very much narrower than that needed for the picture, it is feasible to include both sound-carrier side bands. To avoid mutual interference between sound and picture, the picture and sound side bands must not overlap. Moreover, some space must be allowed at the edge of the channel to avoid interference with the transmissions of stations occupying the adjacent channels.

These requirements are met in the television channel shown in fig. 16. Each contains the following bands: 4.5 mc. for the fully transmitted picture side band, 1.25 mc. for the vestige of the other picture side band, 0.15 mc. for the sound carrier and its two side bands and the remaining 0.1 mc. to guard against overlap between picture and sound and between channels. In compatible colour transmissions an additional colour-information signal, known as the chrominance subcarrier, is included within the fully transmitted picture side band (fig. 22). A special technique (frequency interlacing, described under *Compatible Colour Television,* below) avoids interference between the two signals which then occupy a portion of the channel in common.

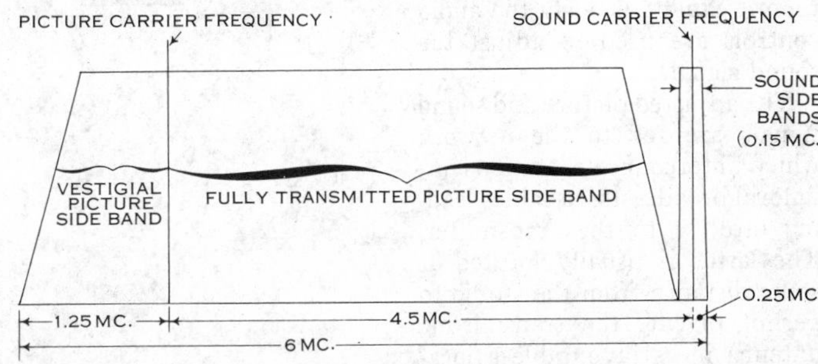


FIG. 16.—ALLOCATION OF TELEVISION CHANNEL FOR MONOCHROME BROADCASTING IN THE U.S.

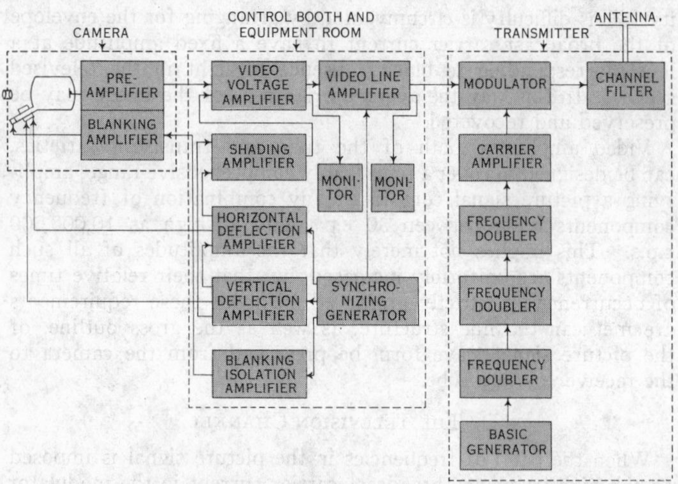


FIG. 17.—DETAILED BLOCK DIAGRAM OF MONOCHROME TRANSMITTER

The television channels of the U.S. are assigned in the following segments of the spectrum: VHF channels 2, 3 and 4, 54–72 mc.; 5 and 6, 76–88 mc.; 7 through 13, 174–216 mc.; and the UHF channels, 14 through 83, 470–890 mc. These channels are allocated to communities according to a master plan established and administered by the Federal Communications commission. No more than seven VHF channels are provided in any one area (this number is allocated only to New York and Los Angeles). Many smaller cities must be content with one or two channels.

### E. The Television Transmitter

The task of the television transmitter is to produce the picture and sound carriers, and their side bands, in conformity with the arrangement of the channel assigned to it. The electronic equipment which performs these functions is shown in fig. 17. The central element is the synchronizing generator, which controls the timing of the scanning of the camera and which produces the synchronizing impulses. It applies three control functions to the camera: timing for horizontal (line-by-line) deflection of the scanning beam; timing for vertical deflection (field-by-field); and the blanking impulses which extinguish the scanning spot during its retrace motions. The camera, under the control of the synchronizing generator, produces the picture signal without the synchronizing impulses. The picture signal is passed first through a preamplifier within the camera housing and then through additional amplifiers in the control room of the studio. In one of these amplifiers, the synchronizing impulses from the synchronizing generator are added to the picture signal. At this point, it is customary to inspect the quality of the reproduced image by feeding the signal to a monitor which displays the image on a picture tube. The monitor screen is viewed by the program director and operating personnel. Any shortcomings are corrected by instructions telephoned to the camera operator or by adjustment of video controls in the control room. Simultaneously the audio controls are used to adjust the sound signal.

The adjusted picture and sound signals are fed to the network which interconnects stations or, in local broadcasts, to cables leading directly to the transmitter. The latter is usually located at some distance from the studio to permit placing the transmitting antenna in as favourable a location as possible with respect to the intended service area.

The transmitter performs two functions: generation of the carrier currents for picture and sound, and imposition of the sound and picture signals on the respective carrier currents. Precautions are taken to assure that the frequencies of the carrier waves have precisely the values assigned to the channel in use. Small wafers of quartz, which vibrate under electrical forces by virtue of the piezoelectric effect, are used as the basic sources of the carrier currents.

The frequency at which quartz can vibrate is lower than that of the intended radio waves, so the current is passed through a succession of frequency-multiplying circuits until it reaches the required value. The resulting carrier currents have frequencies accurate to roughly one part in 200,000.

The carrier current and the picture signal are combined in the modulator, which modulates the envelope of the carrier as previously described (fig. 8). The modulated carrier contains two identical side bands. The major portion of one of these (that occupying frequencies below the carrier) is removed by a wave filter, and the remaining part, plus the picture carrier current and the fully transmitted side-band currents, are passed to the transmitting antenna. A similar arrangement (carrier-current generator, frequency multipliers and frequency modulator) produces the sound carrier current and its side bands. These are also fed to the transmitting antenna, which is designed to direct the radiated waves toward the surface of the earth and to minimize radiation toward the sky.

### F. The Television Receiver

At the receiver (fig. 18), the sound and picture carrier waves pass through the rods of the receiving antenna, inducing currents which are identical in form to those flowing in the transmitter aerial, but much weaker. The carrier currents and their side bands are conducted from the antenna to the receiver by a lead-in transmission line, typically a $\frac{1}{2}$-in. ribbon of polyethylene plastic in which are embedded two parallel copper wires. This form of transmission line is capable of passing the carrier currents to the receiver, without relative discrimination between frequencies, on all the channels to which the receiver may be tuned.

At the antenna terminals of the receiver, the picture and sound signals are at their weakest, so particular care must be taken to control noise at this point. The first circuit in the receiver is a radio-frequency amplifier, particularly designed for low-noise amplification. The channel-switching mechanism (tuner) of the receiver connects one of several individual circuits to this amplifier, each tuned to its respective channel. This amplifier magnifies the voltages of the incoming picture and sound carriers and side bands in the desired channel by about ten times and it discriminates by a like amount against the transmissions of stations on other channels.

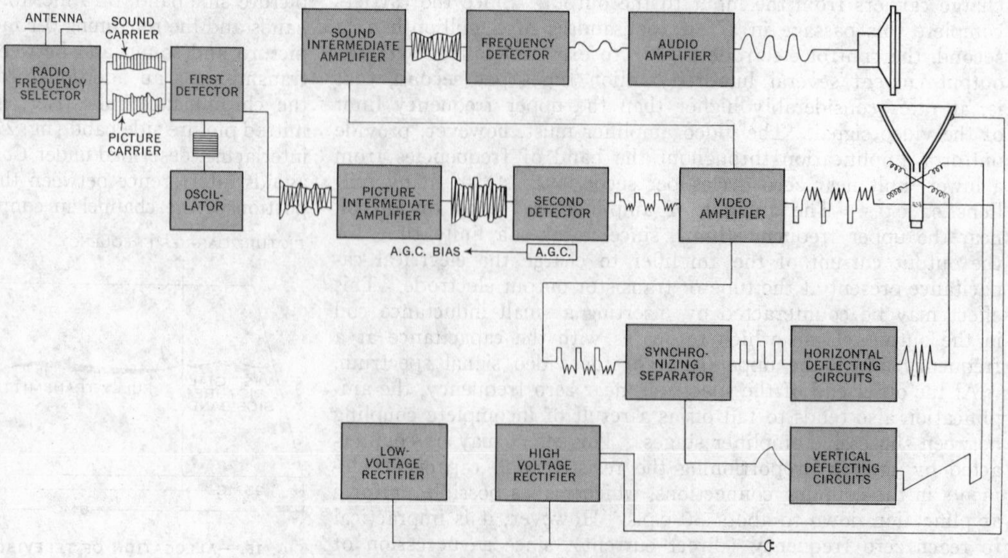


FIG. 18.—BLOCK DIAGRAM OF MONOCHROME RECEIVER, SHOWING WAVE FORMS BETWEEN COMPONENTS

From the radio-frequency amplifier, the signals are passed to the superheterodyne mixer, also a part of the tuning mechanism. This is a circuit that transposes the frequencies of the sound and picture carriers to values better suited to the subsequent amplification processes. The transposed frequencies (intermediate frequencies) remain the same, no matter what channel the receiver is tuned to. In typical receivers they are located in the band from 41 to 47 mc.

Since the tuning of the subsequent amplifiers (intermediate-frequency amplifiers) need not be changed as the channel is switched, they can be adjusted for maximum performance in the 41–47-mc. range. Two to four stages of such amplification are used in tandem, increasing the voltage of the picture and sound carriers by a maximum of 25 to 35 times per stage, representing an over-all maximum amplification of the order of 10,000 times. The amplification of these intermediate-frequency stages is automatically adjusted by a process known as automatic gain control in accordance with the strength of the signal, full amplification being accorded to a weak signal, less to a strong signal. After passage through the intermediate amplifiers, the sound and picture carriers and their side bands reach a relatively fixed level of about one volt, whereas the signal levels applied to the antenna terminals may vary, depending on the distance of the station and other factors, from a few millionths to a few tenths of a volt.

From the last intermediate amplifier stage, the carriers and side bands are passed to another circuit, known as the video detector. This removes one-half of each alternation of the signal currents, converting the alternating current into pulsating direct current. An averaging circuit or filter then forms, from the direct-current pulsations (1) a picture signal, which is a close replica of the picture signal produced by the camera and synchronizing generator in the transmitter, and (2) a frequency-modulated sound signal whose variations in frequency match the variations in sound pressure which impinged on the studio microphone. Thus far, the picture and sound signals are handled simultaneously in each amplifier and detector circuit. Both may also be passed through a video amplifier which increases their voltage by about ten times.

At this point the picture and sound signals separate. Another video amplifier passes the picture signal to the picture tube, where it controls the brightness of the scanning spot. Simultaneously, the picture signal wave form is passed to a circuit (the synchronizing signal separator) which selects the blank periods in the wave form (fig. 5 and 6) and the superimposed synchronizing signals.

Finally, the sound signal is passed through a sound intermediate amplifier and frequency detector (discriminator or ratio detector) which converts the frequency modulations into pulsations representative of the sound pressure variations. This current is passed through one or two additional audio-frequency amplifier stages to the loud-speaker, which reproduces the sound waves in conformity to those in the studio.

Meanwhile, back at the synchronizing signal separator, the synchronizing signals are passed through filters which separate the horizontal synchronizing impulses (fig. 5) from the serrated vertical synchronizing impulses (fig. 6). The synchronizing impulses are then passed, respectively, to the horizontal and vertical deflection generators. These produce the currents that flow through the electromagnet deflection coils, causing the scanning spot of the picture tube to be deflected across the viewing screen in the standard scanning pattern.

The synchronizing signals control the timing of these currents, causing the scanning spot of the receiver to move synchronously with that of the camera. Pains are taken in the synchronizing action of the receiver to prevent the scanning motion from being disturbed by interference, since such disturbances would displace the picture elements from their correct positions in the pattern. It is one of the achievements of the modern television system that the scanning pattern is stably reproduced even when the picture signal is so infested with noise that the picture elements themselves are barely recognizable. This fact is of particular significance in colour transmissions.

In addition to the amplifiers, detectors and deflection generators described above, the receiver contains two power-converting circuits. One of these (the low-voltage power supply) converts the alternating current from the power line into the direct current needed for the tube or transistor circuits; the other (high-voltage power supply) produces the high voltage, typically 15,000 to 18,000 v., needed to create the scanning spot in the picture tube.

The receiver controls commonly provided for adjustment by the viewer are: (1) the channel switch, which connects the required circuits to the radio-frequency amplifier and superheterodyne mixer to amplify and convert the sound and picture carriers of the desired channel; (2) a fine tuning control which precisely adjusts the superheterodyne mixer so that the response of the tuner is exactly centred on the channel in use; (3) a contrast control which adjusts the voltage level reached by the picture signal in the video amplifiers, producing a picture having more or less contrast (greater or less range between the blacks and whites of the image); (4) a brightness control which adjusts the average amount of current taken by the picture tube from the high-voltage power supply, thus varying the over-all brightness of the picture; (5) a horizontal-hold control, which adjusts the horizontal deflection generator so that it conforms exactly to the control of the horizontal synchronizing impulses; and (6) a vertical-hold control, which performs the same function for the vertical deflection generator. Additional adjustments provided for the serviceman include adjustments for the height and width of the picture (magnitudes of the deflection currents) and adjustments (linearity controls) to secure precisely uniform rates of horizontal and vertical scanning so as to avoid distortion of the shapes of the objects in the picture.

### G. Television Picture Tubes

The television picture tube is illustrated in fig. 19. The tube is a highly evacuated, funnel-shaped structure. The viewing screen is located inside the tube face, a curved glass plate which closes the wide end of the funnel. The screen itself is composed of fluorescent materials, a mixture of two complex chemical compounds such as silver-activated zinc sulfide and silver-activated zinc cadmium sulfide. These materials, known as phosphors, glow with blue and yellow light, respectively, under the impact of high-speed electrons. The phosphors are mixed, in a fine dispersion, in such proportion that the combination of yellow and blue light produces white light of slightly bluish cast. A water suspension of these materials is settled on the inside of the face plate of the tube during manufacture, and this coating is overlaid with a film of aluminum sufficiently thin to permit the bombarding electrons to pass without hindrance. The aluminum provides a mirror surface which prevents the backward-emitted light from being lost in the interior of the tube and reflects it forward to the viewer.

At the opposite end of the tube is the electron gun (fig. 20), a cylindrical metal structure which generates and directs a stream of free electrons, the electron beam. At the rear of the electron gun is the cathode, a flat metal support covered with oxides of barium and strontium. These oxides have a low electronic work

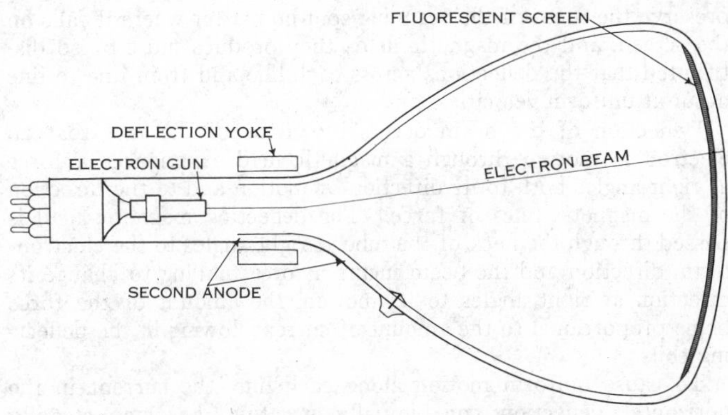

FIG. 19.—BASIC ELEMENTS OF MONOCHROME PICTURE TUBE

function; when heated by the heater coil behind the metal support they liberate electrons. In the absence of electric attraction, the free electrons form a cloud immediately in front of the oxide surface.

Directly in front of the cathode is the cylindrical sleeve of the gun, which is made electrically positive with respect to the cathode. The positively charged sleeve (first anode) draws the negative electrons away from the cloud and they move down the sleeve toward the viewing screen at the opposite end of the tube. They are intercepted, however, by a flat disk (the control electrode) having a small circular aperture at its centre. Some of the moving electrons pass through the aperture; others are held back.

The television picture signal is applied, from the video amplifier previously mentioned, between the control electrode and the cathode. During those portions of the picture signal wave form which make the potential of the control electrode less negative, more electrons are permitted to pass through the control aperture, whereas during the more negative portions of the wave, fewer electrons pass. The brightness control applies a steady (but adjustable) voltage between control electrode and cathode. This voltage determines the average number of electrons passing through the aperture, whereas the picture signal causes the number of electrons passing the aperture to vary from the average.

From the aperture, the controlled stream of electrons passes down the anode sleeve into the glass neck of the tube. Inside the latter is a graphite coating, which extends throughout the funnel

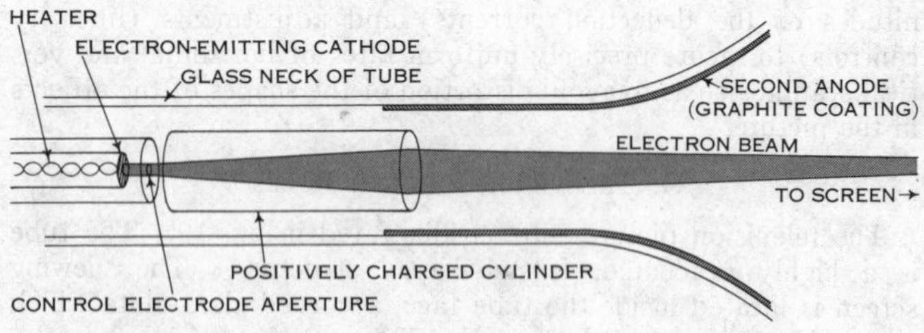


FIG. 20.—ELEMENTS OF PICTURE TUBE ELECTRON GUN

of the tube and connects to the aluminum back coating of the phosphor screen. The full value of positive high voltage (typically 15,000 v.) is applied to this coating and it therefore attracts the electrons from the sleeve along the neck into the funnel and toward the screen of the tube. As the electrons emerge from the sleeve and come under the influence of the graphite coating, each electron experiences a force which directs it toward the centre of the viewing screen. The electron beam is thus brought to focus on the screen and the light there produced is the scanning spot. Additional focusing forces may also be provided by an adjustable permanent magnet surrounding the neck of the tube, which introduces magnetic lines of force parallel to the direction of the electron beam. The scanning spot must be intrinsically very brilliant since (by virtue of the integrating property of the eye) the light in the spot is effectively spread out over the whole area of the screen during scanning.

Scanning is accomplished, as previously outlined, by two sets of electromagnet coils. These coils must be precisely designed to preserve the focus of the scanning spot no matter where it falls on the screen, and the magnetic fields they produce must be so distributed that the deflections across each line and from line to line occur at uniform velocities.

Deflection of the beam occurs by virtue of the fact that an electron in motion through a magnetic field experiences a force at right angles both to its direction of motion and to the direction of the magnetic lines of force. The deflecting magnetic field is passed through the neck of the tube at right angles to the electron-beam direction and the beam incurs a force tending to change its direction at right angles to its motion, the amount of the force being proportional to the amount of current flowing in the deflecting coils.

To cause uniform motion along each line, the current in the horizontal deflection coil, initially negative, becomes steadily smaller, reaching zero when the spot passes the centre of the line and then increasing in the positive direction until the end of the line is reached. The current is then reversed and very rapidly goes through the reverse sequence of values, bringing the scanning spot to the beginning of the next line. The rapid rate of change of current during the retrace motions causes pulses of a high voltage to appear across the circuit feeding current to the coil, and the succession of these pulses, smoothed into direct current by a rectifier tube, serves as the high-voltage power supply.

A similar action in the vertical deflection coils produces the vertical scanning motion. The two sets of deflection coils are combined in a structure known as the deflection yoke which surrounds the neck of the picture tube, directly at the junction of the neck with the funnel section.

Picture tubes vary in screen size and measurements are made diagonally across the tube face. Tubes having diagonals as small as 4 in. are used in transistor-portable receivers, whereas tubes measuring from 17 to 27 in. are used in table and console model receivers. The design trend has called for greater angles of deflection, with correspondingly wider funnel sections and shallower over-all depth from electron gun to viewing screen. The increase in deflection angle from 55° in the first (1946) models to 114° in models produced in the 1960s required corresponding refinement of the deflection system because of the higher deflection currents required and the greater tendency of the scanning spot to go out of focus at the edges of the screen.

## IV. COMPATIBLE COLOUR TELEVISION

The technique of compatible colour television comprises two transmissions. One of these, the luminance transmission, employs methods essentially identical to those of the monochrome television system. The second, the chrominance transmission, has virtually no effect on monochrome receivers. When used with the luminance transmission in a colour receiver, however, it produces an image in full colour.

The luminance-chrominance method of representing colour values is one of several alternative ways in which coloured light may be analyzed and synthesized. This method is particularly appropriate in a television system since it produces a compatible signal which can serve both black-and-white and colour receivers by one and the same broadcast.

Historically, compatibility was of great importance because it allowed colour transmissions to be introduced without obsolescence of the many millions of monochrome receivers in use. In a larger sense, the luminance-chrominance method of colour transmission is advantageous because it utilizes the limited channels of the radio spectrum more efficiently than other colour transmission methods.

To create the luminance-chrominance values, it is necessary (in the present state of the art) first to analyze each colour in the scene into primary colours. Coloured light may thus be analyzed by passing the light through three coloured filters, typically red, green and blue. The amounts of light passing through each filter, plus a description of the colour transmission properties of the filters, serve uniquely to characterize the coloured light.

The fact that virtually the whole range of colours may be synthesized from only three primary colours is essentially a description of the process by which the eye and mind of the observer recognize and distinguish colours. This process, like visual persistence, is a very fortunate property of vision, since it permits a simple three-part specification to represent any of the 10,000 or more colours and brightnesses which may be distinguished by human vision. If vision were dependent on the energy versus wave length relationship (the physical method of specification), it is doubtful if colour reproduction could be incorporated in any mass-communication system.

By transforming the primary-colour values, it is possible to specify any coloured light by three other numbers: (1) its luminance (brightness or "brilliance"); (2) its hue (the redness, orangeness, blueness or greenness, etc., of the light); and (3) its saturation (its vivid *v.* pastel quality). If the intended luminance value of each point in the scanning pattern is transmitted by the methods of the monochrome television system, it is only necessary

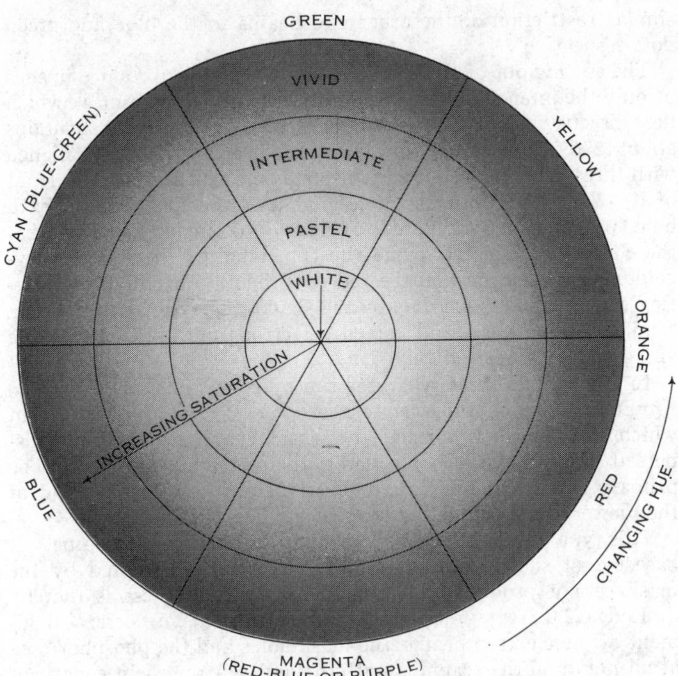


FIG. 21—HUE AND SATURATION (CHROMINANCE) VALUES ARRANGED IN POLAR CO-ORDINATES

to transmit, via an additional two-valued signal, supplementary information giving the hue and saturation of the intended colour at the respective points in the scanning pattern.

Chrominance, defined as that part of the colour specification remaining when the luminance is removed, represents two independent quantities, hue and saturation. These may be represented graphically in polar co-ordinates (fig. 21) with saturation as the radius and hue as the angle. The centre of the diagram represents white light (the colour of zero saturation). Points on the outermost circle represent the most saturated colours, arranged counterclockwise in the order in which they appear in the spectrum from red to blue. Points on any radius of the diagram represent all colours of the same hue, the saturation becoming less (the colour less vivid or more pastel) as the point approaches the central "white point." A diagram of this type is the basis of the international standard system of colour specification.

In the colour television system of the U.S., the chrominance signal is an alternating current of precisely specified frequency (3.579545 ± 0.000010 mc.), the precision permitting its accurate recovery at the receiver even in the presence of severe noise or interference. Any change in the amplitude of its alternations at any instant corresponds to a change in the saturation of the colours being passed over by the scanning spot at that instant, whereas a shift in time of its alternations (a change in the phase angle of the alternations) similarly corresponds to a shift in the hue.

As the different saturations and hues along each scanning line are successively uncovered by scanning in the camera, the amplitude and phase, respectively, of the chrominance signal change accordingly. The chrominance signal is thereby simultaneously modulated in amplitude and in phase. This doubly modulated signal is imposed on the picture signal carrier current, along with the luminance signal.

The television channel, when occupied by such a compatible colour transmission, appears as shown in fig. 22 (compare this with the channel when occupied by a black-and-white transmission, fig. 16). The chrominance signal takes the form of a subcarrier located precisely 3.579545 mc. from the picture carrier frequency.

The picture carrier is thus simultaneously amplitude modulated by the luminance signal to represent changes in the intended luminance, and by the chrominance subcarrier which, in turn, is amplitude modulated to represent changes in the intended saturation and phase modulated to represent changes in the intended hue.

When compatible colour transmissions are received on a monochrome receiver, the receiver treats the chrominance subcarrier as though it were a part of the intended monochrome transmission. If steps were not taken to prevent it, the subcarrier would produce interference in the form of a fine dot pattern; that is, the subcarrier would change the brightness of the scanning spot 3,580,000 times per second, or about 190 times during the 0.000053 sec. consumed by the active scanning of each line. The dot pattern, fortunately, can be rendered almost invisible in monochrome reception by deriving the timing of the scanning motions directly from the source that establishes the chrominance subcarrier itself. The dot pattern of interference from the chrominance signal therefore can be made to have opposite effects on successive scannings of the pattern; that is, a point brightened by the dot interference on one line scan is darkened an equal amount on the next scan of that line, and the net effect of the interference, integrated in the eye over successive scans, is virtually zero. Thus, the monochrome receiver in effect ignores the chrominance component of the transmission. It deals with the luminance signal in the conventional manner, producing from it a monochrome image. This monochrome rendition, incidentally, is not a compromise; it is essentially identical to the image that would be produced by a monochrome television system viewing the same scene.

The channel for colour transmissions (fig. 22), when used by colour receivers, would appear to be affected by mutual interference between the luminance and chrominance components, since these occupy a portion of the channel in common. Such interference is avoided by the fact that the chrominance subcarrier component is rigidly timed to the scanning motions. The luminance signal, as it occupies the channel, is actually concentrated in a multitude of small spectrum segments, by virtue of the periodicities associated with the scanning process. Between these segments are empty channel spaces of approximately equal size. The chrominance signal, arising from the same scanning process, is similarly concentrated. Hence it is possible to place the chrominance channel segments within the empty spaces between the luminance segments, provided that the two sets of segments have a precisely fixed frequency relationship. The necessary relationship is provided by the direct control by the subcarrier of the timing of the scanning motions. This intersegmentation is known as frequency interlacing. It is one of the fundamentals of the compatible colour system, and without it the superposition of colour information on a channel originally devised for monochrome transmissions would not be feasible.

When a colour receiver is tuned to the transmission represented in fig. 22, the picture signal is recovered in a video detector in the usual manner. An amplifier stage, tuned to the 3.58 mc. chrominance frequency, then selects the chrominance from the picture signal and passes it to a synchronous detector which recovers independently the amplitude-modulated and phase-modulated components. The synchronous detection process recovers the phase-modulated component by measuring the signal alternations against a reference timing signal transmitted during a part of the retrace motion between scanning lines. The detector is also simultaneously responsive to the amplitude-modulated com-

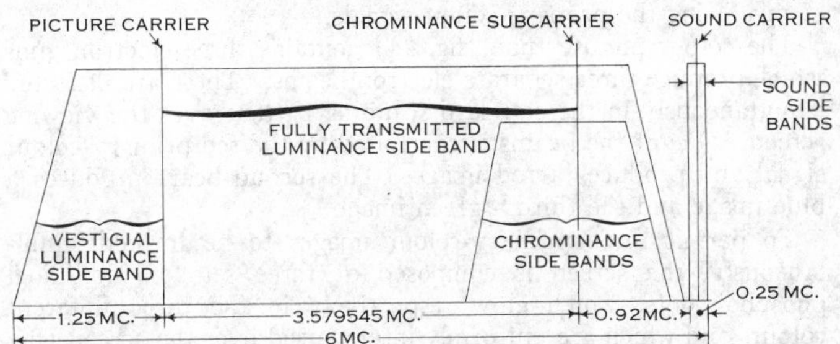


FIG. 22.—ALLOCATION OF TELEVISION CHANNEL FOR COMPATIBLE COLOUR TRANSMISSION IN THE U.S.

ponents, in the manner of the video detector in monochrome reception.

### A. Colour Camera and Picture Tube

The terminals of the colour television system, the camera and picture tube, analyze and synthesize, respectively, the colour quantities present at each point in the scanning pattern. The television camera in its current state of development does not produce the luminance, hue and saturation values directly. Rather it produces three picture signals, representative of the amounts of three primary colours present at each point in the image pattern. From these signals the luminance and chrominance components are then derived by manipulation in electronic circuits.

The typical colour television camera (fig. 23) contains three image orthicon tubes, with an optical system which casts an identical image on the sensitive surface of each tube. The optics comprise a lens and four mirrors which reflect the image rays from the lens onto the three camera tubes, as shown. Two of the

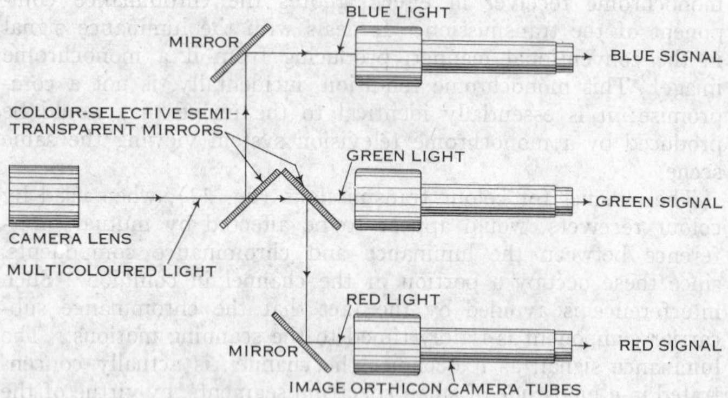


FIG. 23.—SCHEMATIC DIAGRAM SHOWING SELECTIVE SEPARATION OF LIGHT IN COLOUR CAMERA

mirrors are of a colour-selective type (dichroic mirror) which reflects light of one colour and transmits the remaining colours. The mirrors, plus colour filters which perfect their colour-selective action, direct a blue image to the first tube, a green image to the second tube and a red image to the third tube.

The deflection systems of the three camera tubes are arranged to produce essentially identical scanning patterns in each tube, so the picture signals developed by the respective tubes represent images of the same geometrical shape, differing only in colour. The respective primary-colour signals are passed through video preamplifiers associated with each camera tube and emerge from the camera as separate entities. If compatibility were not required, and if sufficient space were available in the radio spectrum, the three signals might be transmitted to the receiver over separate channels. Actually, as mentioned above, the primary-colour signals are recast into luminance and chrominance components; at the receiver the latter are converted back into primary-colour signals before application to the colour picture tube. In the mid-1960s, colour cameras employing four camera tubes were introduced, particularly for studio work. The fourth tube is exposed directly to the scene without an intervening mirror or filter and thus produces a luminance signal of high quality. The three remaining tubes are then confined to the less demanding functions of producing the primary-colour signals.

The colour picture tube (fig. 24) contains three electron guns which produce three separate electron beams. These are deflected simultaneously in the standard scanning pattern over the viewing screen. One of the beams is controlled by the red primary-colour signal and produces a red image. The second beam produces a blue image and the third a green image.

To permit three primary-colour images to be formed simultaneously, the screen is composed of three sets of individual phosphor dots, which glow respectively in the three different colours and which are uniformly interspersed over the screen (fig. 24). The "red" beam impinges only on the red-glowing phosphor dots, being prevented from hitting the other two colours, with similar restriction of the other two beams to the blue and green dots respectively.

The sorting out of the three beams so that they produce images of only the intended primary colour is performed by a mask which lies directly behind the phosphor screen. This mask contains about 200,000 precisely located holes, each accurately aligned with three different coloured phosphor dots on the screen in front of it. Electrons from the three guns pass together through each hole, but at slightly different angles. The angles are such that the electrons arising from the gun controlled by the red primary-colour signal fall only on the red dots, being prevented from hitting the blue and green dots by the shadowing action of the mask. Similarly, the "blue" and "green" electrons fall only on the blue and green dots, respectively.

In this manner three separate primary-colour images are formed simultaneously, as the scanning proceeds. The colour dots of which each image is formed are so small and so uniformly dispersed that the eye does not detect their separate presence. The primary colours in the three images thereby mix in the mind of the viewer and a full-colour rendition of the image results.

This type of colour tube is known as the shadow-mask tube. It has several shortcomings: (1) the electrons intercepted by the mask cannot produce light and the image brightness is thereby limited; (2) great precision is needed to achieve correct alignment of the electron beams, the mask holes and the phosphor dots at all points in the scanning pattern; and (3) precisely congruent scanning patterns, as among the three beams, must be produced. In the late 1960s a different type of colour tube, the Trinitron, was introduced in Japan. In this tube the shadow-mask is replaced by a metal grille having vertical slits extending from the top to the bottom of the screen. The three electron beams pass through the slits to the coloured phosphors, which are in the form of vertical stripes aligned with the slits. The grille directs the majority of the electrons through the slits, few of the electrons are intercepted by the grille, and a brighter picture results.

### B. Colour Transmitter and Receiver

Fig. 25 shows the essential elements of the colour transmitter, as they differ from the monochrome transmitter shown in fig. 17. Immediately following the colour camera is the colour coder which converts the primary-colour signals into the luminance and chrominance signals. The luminance signal is formed simply by applying the primary-colour signals to an electronic addition circuit which adds the values of the three signals at each point along the respective picture signal wave form. Since white light results from the addition, in appropriate proportions, of the primary colours, the resulting sum signal represents the black-and-white (luminance) version of the colour image. The luminance signal thus formed is subtracted individually, in three electronic sub-

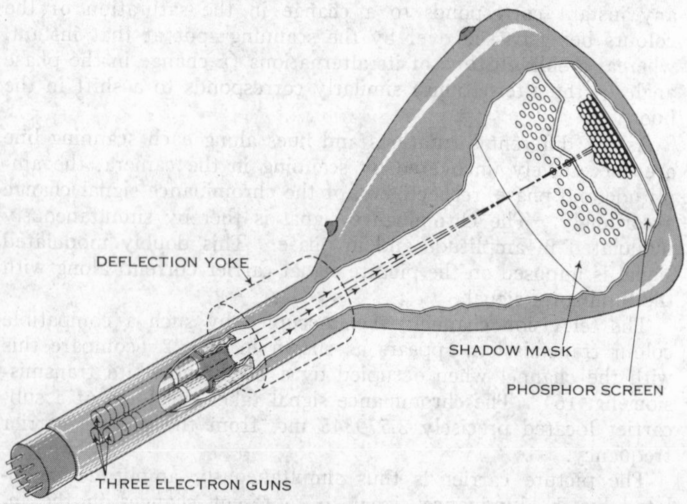


BY COURTESY OF RADIO CORPORATION OF AMERICA

FIG. 24.—COLOUR PICTURE TUBE EMPLOYING THE SHADOW-MASK PRINCIPLE traction circuits, from the original primary-colour signals, and the colour-difference signals are then further combined to produce two signals, which represent points on the orange-cyan and green-magenta axes of the chrominance diagram (fig. 21). These signals are then applied simultaneously to a modulator, where they are mixed with the chrominance subcarrier signal. The latter is thereby amplitude modulated in accordance with the saturation values and phase modulated in accordance with the hues. The luminance and chrominance components are then combined to form the over-all colour picture signal (fig. 26), which is then carried to the transmitter over the network or studio-transmitter link.

The chrominance subcarrier is generated in a precise electronic oscillator at the standard value of 3.579545 mc. Samples of this subcarrier are injected into the signal wave form during the blank period between line scans just after the horizontal synchronizing pulses. These samples are employed in the receiver to control the synchronous detector, mentioned above. Finally, the horizontal and vertical deflection currents, which produce the scanning in the three camera tubes, are formed in a scanning generator whose timing is controlled by the chrominance subcarrier. This common timing of deflection and chrominance transmission produces the dot-interference cancellation in monochrome reception, noted above.

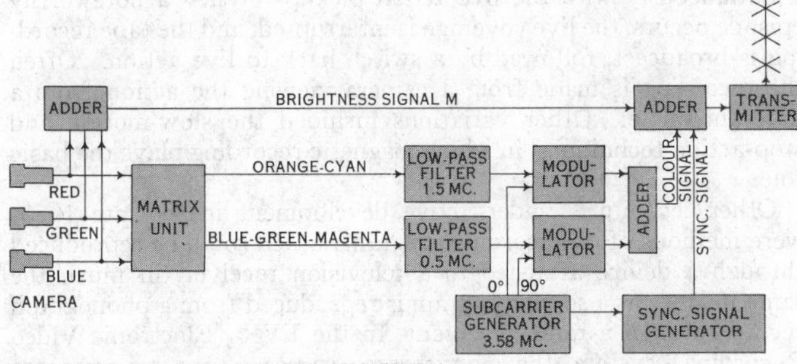


BY COURTESY OF RADIO CORPORATION OF AMERICA

FIG. 25.—BLOCK DIAGRAM OF COLOUR TRANSMITTER

At this stage, the colour picture signal can be handled in the same manner as the monochrome signal, except that throughout the network and in the transmitter special precautions must be taken to transmit the chrominance subcarrier at its correct amplitude, with its amplitude and phase modulations preserved against incidental distortions.

The colour receiver (fig. 27) contains a tuner and intermediate-frequency amplifiers similar to those used in monochrome receivers, but specially designed to preserve the chrominance subcarrier during its passage through these stages. The colour receiver also has power supplies, sound reception circuits and synchronization and deflection current generators similar to those used in monochrome reception.

The colour reproduction processes are divided into the luminance and chrominance functions. A video detector develops the luminance component and applies it through video amplifiers simultaneously to all three electron guns of the picture tube. This part of the signal thereby activates all three primary-colour images, simultaneously and identically, in the fixed proportion needed to produce white light. When tuned to monochrome broadcasts, the colour receiver produces a monochrome image by means of this mechanism, the chrominance component then being absent.

When the receiver is tuned to a colour broadcast, the chrominance subcarrier component appears in the output of the video detector and it is thereupon operated on in circuits which ultimately recover the primary-colour signals originally produced by the colour camera. The recovery starts in the synchronous detector. This is followed by circuits which perform the inverse operations of the addition and subtraction circuits at the transmitter. The end result of this manipulation is the production of three colour-difference signals which represent, respectively, the

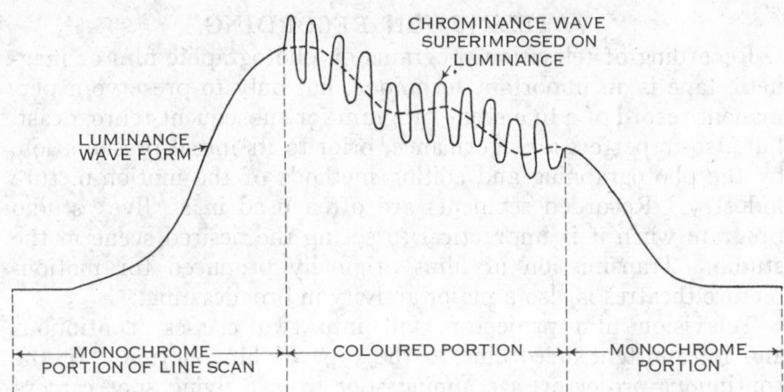


FIG. 26.—PICTURE SIGNAL WAVE FORM FOR COLOUR TRANSMISSION

difference between the luminance signal, already applied to all three electron guns of the picture tube, and the primary-colour signals.

The three colour-difference signals are applied separately to the respective electron guns, where each reduces the strength of the corresponding electron beam to change the white light, which would otherwise be produced, to the intended colour for each point in the scanning line. The net control signal applied to each electron gun bears a direct correspondence to the primary colour signal derived from the respective camera tube at the studio. In this manner, the three primary-colour signals are transmitted as though three separate channels had been used.

The colour receiver controls to be adjusted by the viewer (in addition to the tuning, brightness, contrast and synchronizing controls present in monochrome receivers) are the hue control and the saturation control. The hue control adjusts the timing of the synchronous detector. It sets the reference phase against which the phase modulation of the chrominance subcarrier is measured, and hence shifts all the hues in the reproduced image. The hue control is usually adjusted by reference to the colour of the flesh of the performers, since unnatural flesh tone is readily recognized even if the viewer has no knowledge of the intended hues in other parts of the scene. The saturation control adjusts the magnitudes of the colour-difference signals applied to the electron guns of the picture tube. If these magnitudes are reduced to zero, by turning the saturation control to the "off" position, no colour difference action occurs and the reproduction occurs in monochrome. As the saturation control is advanced, the colour differences become more accentuated, and the colours become progressively more vivid. This control is adjusted to suit the personal preference of the viewer. Natural appearance of flesh tone is an appropriate index. In the late 1960s, the more elaborate colour television receivers began to employ a system known as "automatic hue control." In this system the viewer makes an initial manual adjustment of the hue control to produce a rendition of flesh tones to suit his preference. Thereafter, the hue control circuit automatically maintains the preselected ratio of the primary colours corresponding to the viewer's choice. Thus the most critical aspect of the colour rendition, the appearance of the faces of the performers, is prevented from changing when cameras are switched from scene to scene, or when tuning from one broadcast to another.

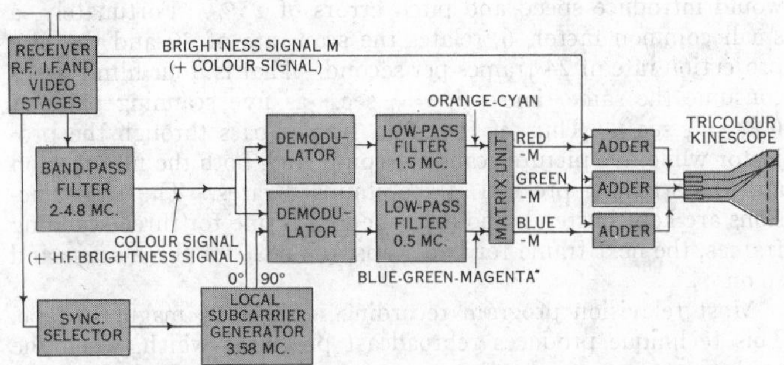


BY COURTESY OF RADIO CORPORATION OF AMERICA

FIG. 27.—BLOCK DIAGRAM OF COLOUR RECEIVER

### V. TELEVISION RECORDING

Recording of television programs on photographic film or magnetic tape is an important technique, not only to preserve a permanent record of a live-scene program for subsequent rebroadcast, but also to perfect a performance, prior to its initial presentation, by the photographing and editing methods of the motion-picture industry. Recorded segments are often used in a "live" studio program when it is impractical to set up the desired scene in the studio. Transmission of films originally produced for motion-picture theatres is also a major activity in broadcasting.

Television film projectors fall into two classes, continuous and intermittent, according to the type of film motion. In the continuous projector, a scanning spot from a flying spot camera tube is passed through a rotating optical system, known as an immobilizer, which focuses the scanning spot on the motion-picture film. As the film moves continuously through the projector, the immobilizer causes the scanning pattern as a whole to follow the motion of the film frame, so that there is no relative motion between pattern and frame. The light passes through the film to a phototube where the light, modified by the transmissibility of the film at each point, produces the picture signal. As one film frame moves out of the range of the immobilizer, the next moves into range and there is a condition of overlap between successive scanning patterns.

The optics are so arranged that the amount of light in the spot focused on the film is constant at all times and in all positions. This constancy permits the film to be moved at any desired speed, while the pattern scans at the standard rate of 25 or 30 pictures per second. The film is actually moved at the standard rate for motion pictures, 24 frames per second, so the speed of objects and pitch of the accompanying sounds (picked up from the sound track by conventional methods) are reproduced at the intended values.

In the intermittent projector, which more nearly resembles the type used in theatre projection, each frame of film is momentarily held stationary in the projector while a brief flash of light is passed through it. The light (which passes simultaneously through all parts of the film frame) is focused on the sensitive surface of a storage-type camera, such as the Vidicon. The light flashes are timed to occur during the intervals between successive field scans, that is, while the extinguished scanning spot is moving from bottom to top of the frame. The light is strong enough to produce an intense electrical image in the tube during this brief period. The electrical image is stored and is scanned during the next scanning field, producing the picture signal for that field. Light is again admitted between fields and the stored image scanned thereupon by the second field. When one film frame has been thus scanned, it is pulled down by a claw mechanism and the next frame takes its place.

In Europe and other areas where the television scanning rate is 25 picture scans per second, the custom is to operate intermittent projectors also at 25 frames per second, or about 4% faster than the intended film projection rate of 24 frames per second. The corresponding increases in speed of motion and sound pitch are not so great as to introduce unacceptable degradations of the performance. In the U.S. and other areas where television scanning occurs at 30 frames per second, it is not feasible to run the film projector at 30 film frames per second, since this would introduce speed and pitch errors of 25%. Fortunately, a small common factor, 6, relates the scan rate of 30 and the film projection rate of 24 frames per second. That is, four film frames consume the same time ($\frac{4}{24} = \frac{1}{6}$ sec.) as five scanning patterns ($\frac{5}{30} = \frac{1}{6}$ sec.). Thus, if four film frames pass through the projector while five picture scans are completed, both the film motion and the scanning proceed at the standard rates. The two functions are kept in step by holding one film frame for three scanning frames, the next frame for two scans, the next for three scans and so on.

Most television program recording is done on magnetic tape. This technique produces rebroadcast programs which, when the equipment is in good adjustment, are virtually indistinguishable from the original broadcast. The magnetic tape, 2 in. wide, is moved at 15 in. per second past a magnetic recording head which rotates across the width of the tape, imposing on it a series of crosswise magnetic line patterns which correspond to the lines of the scanning pattern. To keep the pickup and tape motions closely identical during recording and playback, index signals are imposed during recording and these are used to control the drive motors during playback. The television signal is recorded by frequency modulation on a carrier signal, thus avoiding the difficult problem of direct recording at the extremely low frequencies (30 c.p.s. and less) present in the picture signal itself.

Magnetic video recording is widely used in broadcast operations, not only because of its high quality but because it is immediately available (without subsequent processing) for playback. In the U.S. many of the network programs broadcast in and west of Chicago are derived from magnetic recordings, stored for an hour or more after their release along the eastern seaboard to allow for the difference in time in western cities. Recording of colour programs is also a common practice on magnetic tape, but in the 1960s it was subject to somewhat lower quality than black-and-white recording, since the necessary precision of tape transport and pickup rotation is greater in the colour system.

Many variations of the basic techniques of recording television program material were introduced in the late 1960s and widely used in sports telecasting. The first to be developed was the "instant replay" method, in which a video tape recording is made simultaneously with the live-action pickup. When a noteworthy episode occurs, the live coverage is interrupted, and the tape recording is broadcast, followed by a switch back to live action. Often the recording is made from a camera viewing the action from a different angle. Other variations included the slow-motion and stop-action techniques, in which magnetic recording plays the basic role.

Other techniques under active development in the late 1960s were methods of prerecording programs which could be reproduced through a device attached to a television receiver, in much the same manner as a sound program is reproduced from a phonograph record through a radio receiver. In the EVR (Electronic Video Recording) system, the monochrome values of the program are carried by a plastic film, similar in principle to motion picture film; the same film carries the colour information in coded form. The EVR playback device, through which the film runs, combines the monochrome and colour values into a signal suitable for operating a standard colour receiver. The SV (SelectaVision) system was under development to produce the same result using somewhat different principles of operation. *See* also TAPE RECORDING, MAGNETIC.

### VI. TELEVISION BROADCASTING

The methods and equipment employed in television broadcasting follow the basic principles outlined above, but differ in detail according to the nature of the program source; *i.e.,* the studio, film or a point remote from the studio.

**1. Studio Programs.**—Television studios, like those for sound broadcasting, are designed with acoustical properties which produce a "live" sound without noticeable reverberation. The studio must also possess a comprehensive system of lighting, capable of creating uniform illumination of several hundred to a thousand foot-candles for monochrome productions.

For colour programs, a substantially greater level of light is required to overcome the losses in the mirrors and filters within the camera. In addition to general lighting, localized lighting fixtures ("scoops" and spotlights) are used to emphasize the centre of interest, for modeling of facial contours and the like. A ventilating system capable of removing the heat generated by the lighting system without noise must be provided and air conditioning may be needed if the lighting system is to be used for extended periods in the summer months.

The cameras and microphones are mounted so that they can follow the action on the set. The camera usually is carried on a dolly equipped with smooth-rolling wheels and is mounted on an elevating and training stand which permits the camera operator to achieve the desired angle and position relative to the action.

BY COURTESY OF (ABOVE) WNBQ, NATIONAL BROADCASTING COMPANY, CHICAGO, (TOP RIGHT) NATIONAL BROADCASTING COMPANY, NEW YORK, (BOTTOM RIGHT) COLUMBIA BROADCASTING SYSTEM

**TELEVISION BROADCASTING:** (Above) A film camera chain that adapts photographic film for television transmission. It consists of 16- and 35-mm. projectors, a slide projector, a multiplexer for transmitting the three kinds of film in combination, and a monitor. (Top right) A television program in production. The centre camera is mounted on a crane dolly for vertical movement. (Bottom right) A television studio monitoring booth. The program director, technical director, and lighting director oversee the on-the-air picture on the large monitor and preview the pictures to follow on the smaller monitors

The microphone is mounted on a boom or long arm which can position the microphone above the action, just out of view of the camera. The floor crew (camera operator, a man to assist the operator in moving the camera dolly, the microphone boom operator and the director's floor assistant) are equipped with earphones through which instructions are relayed from the control room.

Studio scenery for television productions is generally simpler than that used in motion-picture production. Since the production occurs in "real time" the cameras must be strictly co-ordinated with the action and must move from one set to another, on the floor of a single studio, as the presentation proceeds. In live broadcasts, retakes cannot be made, and close co-ordination of camera and microphone action with the script must be achieved in rehearsal.

Control of the camera is achieved in part by telephoned instructions from the control room, but the main reliance for correct composition and focus is placed on the cameraman, who views the picture picked up by his camera on an electronic view finder. This is a compact picture monitor connected to the camera tube. The camera is usually equipped with a lens turret containing as many as four lenses of different focal lengths. The turret is rotated by the camera operator (while the camera is not in action) to bring into play the lens having the focal length appropriate for the desired area of the set. The lenses are similar to those used in 35-mm. professional motion-picture cameras, with maximum apertures of the order of $f/4.5$ to $f/3.5$. Small apertures are used wherever possible to secure the necessary depth of focus.

**2. Film Broadcasting.**—To permit uninterrupted programming, two film projectors are needed, one of which is being readied for the next reel while the other is on the air. A single camera tube may accept images from either of the projectors by use of a mirror set at 45° to the respective optic axes (fig. 28). The picture and sound signals produced by film equipment are viewed and auditioned on monitors and are adjusted by video- and audio-control operators, as in studio productions. When an iconoscope camera tube is used, the video-control operator must adjust special controls to minimize the flare and uneven shading to which this type of tube is subject.

Televising colour film requires that the coloured image be broken up into three primary-colour images, as in the studio camera for colour productions (fig. 23). Vidicon camera tubes or flying spot cameras are used.

**3. Outside Broadcasts.**—To televise sporting events and other programs at locations remote from the studio, portable equipment is used. This includes cameras, microphones and several units which house the control and switching system, monitors and the synchronization generator. The portable synchronization unit, which performs all the functions of the more elaborate generators permanently installed in the studio building, must meet rigid standards since it must correctly control the scanning of millions of receivers and is often dependent on uncertain power sources at remote locations.

Remote broadcast signals may be fed directly into a network connection, but more usually they are transmitted to the associated station by a microwave radio system. This comprises a low-power transmitter operating at a frequency in the vicinity of 2,000 or 7,000 mc., using frequency modulation for the picture transmission and a receiver at the studio or transmitting station. At these extremely high frequencies, a highly directive radio beam may be produced by reflecting the radio waves from a paraboloid surface ("dish" antenna) of modest size. The radio energy is thereby so concentrated that a transmitter power of less than one watt is capable of covering distances of 10 to 20 mi. so long as the path from transmitter to receiver is unobstructed.

**4. Networks.**—National distribution of major television programs is achieved through a comprehensive common-carrier network system. Three types of facilities are used. Within a given city, special telephone lines ("video pair" circuits) are provided; these are specially equalized to provide uniform transmission over the wide band of frequencies occupied by the picture signal.

For intercity connections, coaxial cables were once widely used, although these were largely replaced by the microwave relay system. The coaxial cable consists of two electrical conductors, a hollow sheath and a wire located concentrically within it. This configuration of conductors is capable of transmitting a wide band of frequencies without discrimination over a distance of several miles. At intervals of about eight miles, video amplifier repeaters restore the signal energy lost in the preceding section of cable. The early coaxial cable network in the U.S. was limited to a maxi-

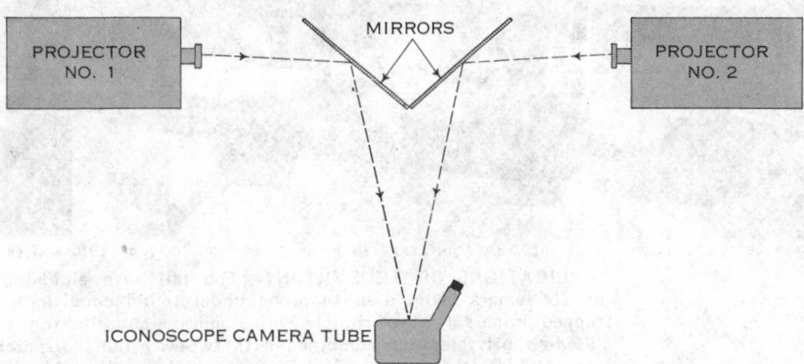


FIG. 28.—ARRANGEMENT FOR USING EITHER OF TWO FILM PROJECTORS WITH ONE CAMERA TUBE

mum frequency range of about 2.7 mc., substantially less than the 4-mc. maximum actually present in the picture signal. Later coaxial cable installations, with repeater amplifiers every four miles, could handle a maximum frequency range of nearly 8 mc.

Major reliance for television network transmission in the U.S. is placed on the microwave relay system. This consists of a large number of relay stations (over 100 are needed to span the country) operating in the vicinity of 4,000 mc. Highly directive transmitting and receiving antennas, mounted on towers in exposed locations at intervals of about 25 mi., receive and retransmit to the next relay station a frequency-modulated picture signal.

**5. Transoceanic Broadcasts.**—The initial attempt to interconnect the television networks of Europe and North America came in 1962, when the American Telephone and Telegraph company used its artificial satellite, called Telstar, to relay television signals between Andover, Me., Goonhilly Downs, Cornwall, Eng., and Pleumeur-Bodou, Brittany, France. The first transmission, of a purely experimental nature, originated in the U.S. on July 10, 1962, and this was followed the next day by transmissions to the U.S. from France and England; the first colour transmission occurred on July 16. Reception was limited to about 15 min., the period during which the satellite was within sight of the sending and receiving stations. To maintain continous transmissions, the planners of the system proposed using a series of satellites, so that at least one would always be in position to relay signals. An alternate proposal called for a single relay satellite in a "stationary" orbit, so adjusted that it would remain always above the same point on the surface of the Earth. The first public demonstration of this system was on Oct. 10, 1964, when television coverage of the opening ceremonies of the Olympic games was relayed from Tokyo to North America via a Syncom satellite positioned above the Pacific ocean. *See* also BROADCASTING.

**6. Community Antenna Television (CATV) Systems.**—During the 1960s, a new method of providing television service to the home was introduced and rapidly gained acceptance in many communities. This involves setting up a "community antenna" in a high and exposed location, where excellent reception is obtainable, and retransmitting the signals via a local coaxial cable system to homes in the vicinity. The CATV system is particularly advantageous in towns surrounded by hills or other obstructions which prevent high quality reception by individual antennas at each home. Another, more recent, application has occurred in major metropolitan areas where local reception is degraded by the reflection of signals from tall buildings ("multipath interference") which produce one or more "ghost" images displaced on the screen from the desired picture. The CATV service is provided, after an initial installation charge of $15–$35, at a monthly charge of about $5. Since the service provided by CATV systems is superior to local reception at homes in the majority of such poor reception areas, and the costs are moderate, this method of reception has become a large factor in television broadcasting practice. By the end of the 1960s there were nearly 5,000,000 subscribers served by more than 2,300 CATV systems in the United States.

## VII. CLOSED-CIRCUIT TELEVISION

The term closed-circuit television, which originally meant a local system consisting of a camera and several monitor receivers connected by a coaxial cable, came to refer to any system, however extensive, in which the televised subject matter is intended for the organization that owns or has hired the system for its exclusive use, as against broadcasting or other general use by the public. Such systems are widely used in industry and commerce and for educational purposes. They range from a single camera and monitor installed in a steam plant to monitor flame condition or water level to a nationwide network hired on a single-occasion basic (*e.g.*, by an automobile manufacturer to present information on new models to dealers assembled in theatres having projection television equipment). Coaxial cable is used in local installations, but microwave relay systems identical to those used in broadcasting may be employed for large closed-circuit hookups.

Since a closed-circuit system is entirely under the control of its proprietor and is not intended to serve the general public, it is possible to employ scanning standards which differ from those used in broadcasting. Advantage of this freedom in system design is taken in the so-called slow-scan closed-circuit system, which is used to transmit signature records and balances in banks, for example.

In the typical slow-scan system, the pictures may be scanned at a rate as slow as one picture every three seconds, with a scanning pattern of 180 lines per picture. The maximum frequency in the picture signal then reaches only 8,000 c.p.s., which can be transmitted inexpensively; *i.e.*, over ordinary telephone lines. In the majority of closed-circuit systems for industry, education and theatre projection, however, the

(TOP LEFT, RIGHT) MOTOROLA INC., (BOTTOM LEFT) BOARD OF EDUCATION, CITY OF CHICAGO, (BOTTOM RIGHT) RADIO CORPORATION OF AMERICA

APPLICATIONS OF TELEVISION: (Top left) An eight-inch-diameter transistorized camera being used to probe underground conditions to aid in rescuing trapped miners. (Top right) Police officers coordinating traffic by means of closed-circuit television combined with two-way radio dispatch facilities. (Bottom left) Closed-circuit television makes it possible for the special skills of teachers to be shared by larger audiences of students. (Bottom right) An experimental camera designed to transmit picture of astronauts en route to the moon image-quality requirements are essentially identical to those of broadcasting, so the broadcast standards are used.

**1. Equipment.**—Equipment for closed-circuit television is similar to but generally less elaborate than that used for broadcast purposes. The Vidicon camera tube is used in industrial television almost to the exclusion of other types, since it is less expensive than the other types and more suitable for compact cameras. In educational television, however, image orthicon tubes and associated equipment very similar to broadcast-station units are widely used. Since closed-circuit installations in industry are seldom operated by television specialists, care must be taken in equipment design to make operation and maintenance simple. An important industrial use is in viewing remote or hazardous events in which it is inconvenient or unsafe to have an operator directly in attendance at the camera. For such purposes, controls for remote operation of the camera, including adjustment of lens aperture and focus, are provided.

**2. Applications in Education.**—Educational television is often conducted on a public-broadcast basis in cities where a channel is available for this purpose and where the expense of the transmitting station can be borne. The simpler and less costly closed-circuit system found increasing favour with educators, however, particularly in larger institutions and in medical schools, where the whole installation can be confined to one building or a few neighbouring buildings.

In education, television's most impressive use is extending the range of a gifted teacher beyond a single classroom. When a broadcast system is available, pupils in many schools may be taught simultaneously by a particularly able teacher prior to a more personal instruction and discussion of the subject matter in individual classes with a local teacher in attendance. While motion pictures may also be used in this way, the televised image commands the pupils' attention to a far greater extent than does film projection. Even when film is used as a program source, the psychological impression on the student is heightened.

Television is also an important teaching aid in bringing to a number of students simultaneously the details of an experiment or operation which otherwise could be viewed only by a single person or small group. Examples include viewing through a microscope and bringing medical students directly into visual contact with operating procedures without interfering with those performing the operation. Use of closed-circuit television for instruction in surgical procedures is widespread; elaborate colour-television installations have been made in medical schools and hospitals, colour being an important adjunct in delineating diagnosis and procedure. An important advantage of television in such instruction is that the final outcome is not known as the demonstration proceeds and this lends an air of expectancy which is lacking when colour motion pictures are used for the same purpose.

**3. Industrial Applications.**—One of the first uses of closed-circuit television in industry was an installation of boilerwater-level monitors at the Hell Gate electric generating station in New York, made directly after World War II. This application later was extended to the monitoring of flames in burners and smoke issuing from stacks. Here the justification for television, as against photographic methods, is the need for immediate information without the delay of film processing. Other applications involve the safe handling of nuclear materials, jet fuels and other hazardous substances. A stereoscopic form of television, comprising two complete systems which present two images separately to the two eyes of the operator, has been used in conjunction with precise remote-handling equipment for packing radioactive substances, disposing of radioactive wastes and the like. The ability of the television camera to operate in situations unfriendly to human observers (as outside the fuselage of an airplane in flight, to observe operation of landing gear during engineering tests) also accounts for increasing usage in industry.

The radiation hazard brought industrial television into play in X-ray technology. A fluoroscope or other device for translating X-ray intensities into visible light is viewed by a sensitive television camera and the image brought out at a safe distance from the exposure site. Here, again, motion-picture photography might be used, but the television system permits immediate observation without processing delays and avoids the cost of film and processing which might, in the course of a year, outweigh the cost of a simple television system.

Television systems may also be used for surveillance, particularly to assist guards in patrolling restricted areas. Another surveillance application is in reading numbers on freight cars in railway switchyards to aid the yardmaster in making up trains.

**4. Commercial Applications.**—The primary application of closed-circuit television in commerce, as contrasted with industry, is remote inspection of records in banks and other institutions. In one installation, four branches of a bank were connected with 12 mi. of coaxial cable to permit any teller to call for the signature card or the current balance of any depositor from a central bookkeeping department. Although the initial and maintenance costs of such a system were substantial, the speed and accuracy with which doubtful accounts may be checked justified the use of the system. Extension of this technique to remote reading of blueprints and other records depended upon lowering the cost of interconnecting cables and increasing the detail of images so that, for example, a full 8½ by 11-in. page of typewritten material could be read on a monitor without error.

Techniques akin to those of television are finding increased use in other commercial and industrial fields. One application is a scanning technique whereby printed characters are "read" and identified by comparing the character with each of a series of standard templates or matrices. This may be done by storing the video signal arising from scanning in a memory array in the form of voltages which may be compared with a similar array of voltages in a matrix corresponding to each letter or number to be recognized. Either mechanical or electronic scanning may be used in this technique. *See* also references under "Television" in the Index. (D. G. F.)

Bibliography.—G. R. M. Garrett and A. H. Mumford, "The History of Television," *Proc. Instn Elect. Engrs,* 99:25–42 (April–May 1952); H. A. Chinn, *Television Broadcasting* (1953); R. Bretz, *Techniques of Television Production,* 2nd ed. (1962); D. G. Fink, *Television Engineering,* 2nd ed. (1952), (ed.), *Television Engineering Handbook* (1957); J. W. Wentworth, *Color Television Engineering* (1955); V. K. Zworykin and G. A. Morton, *Television: the Electronics of Image Transmission,* 2nd ed. (1954); D. G. Fink and D. M. Lutyens, *The Physics of Television* (1960); W. H. Buchsbaum, *Fundamentals of Television* (1964); B. Grob, *Basic Television,* 3rd ed. (1964). (D. G. F.; T. H. B.)

**TELFORD, THOMAS** (1757–1834), Scottish architect and civil engineer renowned for his building of roads and bridges, was born near Westerkirk in Eskdale, Dumfriesshire, on Aug. 9, 1757, the son of a shepherd. After apprenticeship to a stonemason in Langholm, he worked as a journeyman mason in Eskdale and Edinburgh until 1782, when he traveled to London and was employed in building Somerset house under Sir William Chambers. At this time his ambition was to become an architect and his self-education was directed to this end. After a brief period of employment at Portsmouth his patron, William Pulteney, obtained for him the post of surveyor of Shropshire in 1786. While so engaged, Telford built churches at Bridgnorth and Madeley, rebuilt the county jail, excavated the ruins of Uriconium (mod. Wroxeter) and constructed many bridges, including three over the river Severn at Montford, Buildwas and Bewdley, the second being of iron.

In 1793 Telford was appointed agent and engineer to the Ellesmere Canal company and forsook architecture for engineering. His two great aqueducts which carry this canal over the Ceiriog and Dee valleys at Chirk and Pont Cysylltau showed him to be a master of the structural use of cast iron and brought him national fame. In 1803 he was employed by the government on a development scheme for the Scottish Highlands, where he was responsible for the Caledonian canal, harbour works at Aberdeen, Dundee and elsewhere and the building of over 900 mi. of roads, including many bridges. Telford was next engaged on the improvement of the roads from Chester and Shrewsbury to Holyhead in the course of which he built his two famous suspension bridges over the river Conway and the Menai straits. The threat of railway competition induced canal companies to employ him to carry out improvement works which included a new tunnel at Harecastle, Staffordshire, on the Trent and Mersey canal, the improvement of the Birmingham canal and the construction of a new canal from Wolverhampton to Nantwich. Among Telford's other works were the Göta canal in Sweden, St. Katherine's dock, London, roads in the Scottish lowlands and the bridges over the Severn at Tewkesbury and Gloucester. On the invitation of the founders, Telford became first president of the Institution of Civil Engineers. He died in London on Sept. 2, 1834.

BIBLIOGRAPHY.—*Life of Thomas Telford, Written by Himself . . . With a Folio Atlas* (1838); S. Smiles, *Life of Thomas Telford* (1867); A. Gibb, *The Story of Telford: the Rise of Civil Engineering* (1935); L. T. C. Rolt, *Thomas Telford* (1958). (L. T. C. R.)

**TELL, WILLIAM,** Swiss hero who, like Robin Hood, symbolizes the struggle for political and individual freedom. Historically, the existence of Tell is disputed, at least since the 19th century; but as a legendary figure he has always enjoyed enormous popularity.

According to popular legend, Tell was a peasant from Bürglen, a small village in the canton of Uri, where he lived in the 13th and early 14th centuries. One day he came with his son to Altdorf, to find that the Austrian governor (Gessler) had had a hat placed on a stake in the main square as a symbol of Austria's sovereign power. Each passerby was expected to bow in front of this hat, but Tell was too proud to do so, and as a penalty he was compelled by Gessler to test his marksmanship by shooting with his crossbow an apple from his little son's head. To Gessler's amazement, Tell succeeded, but as he had threatened the governor—saying that his second arrow was destined for Gessler's heart—he was arrested and put on a boat to be taken to Gessler's castle at the northern end of Lake Lucerne. During the journey a great storm arose, and, as Tell was an expert helmsman, he was freed so that he might steer the boat to safety. But when the boat came near the shore, he seized his bow and escaped by a bold leap ashore. As a final act of defiance and revenge, he later killed Gessler from an ambush in the "Hohle Gasse" ("Hollow Way"), near Küssnacht. This deed, together with other events (such as the signing of the secret covenant of the confederates in the meadow of Rütli, in 1291), was the signal for the rise of the people against Austrian rule (*see* SWITZERLAND: *History*).

The origins of this legend are obscure, and early chronicles, which deal with the misdeeds of the Austrian governors, fail to mention Tell. The first evidential basis for the Tell story is contained in two 15th-century texts: a song of *c.* 1477 (containing a fragment of an older "Tellenlied" no longer extant), and a chronicle of *c.* 1470 (in the so-called *Weisse Buch von Sarnen*). The song gives a mutilated account of the apple scene, only hints at the rest of the story, and extols Tell as the first Swiss confederate; one feature of the song—that Tell is threatened with death if he misses his target—is missing from the chronicle. The chronicle tells of the cruel deeds of the governors and links "Tall," as he is called here, with the Rütli covenanters. Subsequent versions are all combinations or elaborations of these two texts. With the 16th-century chronicle *Chronicon Helveticum* (published 1734–36) of Gilg Tschudi (*q.v.*)—which generally rounds off the tale, giving, for example, November 1307 as the date of Tell's deeds and New Year 1308 as the date of Switzerland's liberation—the story finds its classic form. Tschudi's account was for a long time definitive and was the main source of Schiller's *Wilhelm Tell* (1804), the stirring play that gave the tale worldwide renown.

It is evident from the transmission of the Tell story that its rise and development are popular rather than historical. But, although 19th-century historians (*e.g.,* J. E. Kopp) and later critics have shown that many so-called historical chronicles—including the *Weisse Buch* and especially Tschudi's—are defective and unreliable, there is still no conclusive evidence for or against Tell's existence, and it may simply be that some of the deeds attributed to him have been culled from other heroic figures or mythical sources. Because marksmanship is a central feature, not only of the extant texts of the Tell legend but also of other legends, scholars have been led to perceive relationships. For instance, William Cloudesley in Britain, Egill (or Eigil) in Scandinavia, and Henning Wulff (or Wulffen) in Germany are all found to share similarities with Tell. It is thought that they may all derive from a 10th-century Norwegian prototype. Nearest to the Swiss tradition—especially the "Tellenlied"—is the story of the marksman Toko, as told in the Danish chronicle of Saxo Grammaticus (*c.* 1200). However, it is not clear how the saga may have reached Switzerland. Perhaps it was introduced by 15th-century Humanists in an attempt to find a story for the origins of the Confederation that would appeal to the growing Swiss national consciousness; certainly the contemporary fanciful chronicle *Vom Herkommen der Schwyzer und Oberhasler* points in a similar direction by giving the confederates Swedish and Frisian ancestry.

Whatever its origin and authenticity, the legend of William Tell has been a constant and powerful source of artistic inspiration. The theme of Tell has been treated by composers (*e.g.,* André Grétry and Rossini) and artists (*e.g.,* J. H. Füssli [Henry Fuseli] and Ferdinand Hodler), as well as poets and dramatists. It plays an important part also in the Swiss popular theatre, from the time of the Uri play (the so-called *Urner Tellenspiel*) of *c.* 1512 to the 20th-century productions at Altdorf and Interlaken. The myth is still vital, and there has been a continued popularization of the tale both in the cinema and in television.

In the course of time the figure of Tell has taken on various forms and meanings: 15th-century Humanists, for example, regarded him as the Swiss Brutus, a national hero who embodied the principles of moral freedom; in 18th-century France he became the much-cited champion of the rights of man and an idol of the Revolution. At all events, Tell's significance—in Switzerland and beyond—lies less in a disputed historical fact than in the mighty power that he represents as an exponent of the age-old passion for freedom.

BIBLIOGRAPHY.—*Texts: Das Weisse Buch von Sarnen* (ed. by H. G. Wirz) and *Das Lied von der Entstehung der Eidgenossenschaft* and *Das Urner Tellenspiel* (both ed. by M. Wehrli) are contained in *Quellenwerk zur Entstehung der schweizerischen Eidgenossenschaft,* Abt. III, Bd. 1 and 2 (1947–52).

*History and Tradition:* R. Meszlény, *Tell-Probleme* (1910); K. Meyer, *Die Urschweizer Befreiungstradition* (1927); F. Gropengiesser, *W. Tell in der Schweizer Geschichtsschreibung* (1940); R. Labhardt, "Wilhelm Tell als Patriot und Revolutionär, 1700–1800," *Basler Beiträge zur Geschichtswissenschaft,* vol. 27 (1947); B. Meyer, "Weisses Buch und Wilhelm Tell," *Der Geschichtsfreund,* vol. 112 (1959); H. G. Wackernagel, "Bemerkungen zur älteren schweizerischen Geschichte in volkskundlicher Sicht," *Beiträge zur Volkskunde der Universität Basel dargebracht* (1960).

*Treatment in the Arts:* P. Lang, *Die schweizerischen Tellspiele* (1924); E. Merz, *Tell im Drama vor und nach Schiller* (1925); F. Müller-Guggenbühl, *Wilhelm Tell im Spiegel der modernen Dichtung* (1950). *See* especially F. Heinemann, *Tell-Ikonographie* (1902), *Tell-Bibliographie* (1907). (M. WE.)

**TELL EL AMARNA** (TALL AL AMARNA), the modern name given to the collection of ruins and rock tombs in upper Egypt, on the east bank of the Nile, 58 mi. (93 km.) by river below Asyut and 190 mi. above Cairo. The ruins are those of Akhetaton, the city built about 1375 B.C. by Ikhnaton (Amenhotep IV) as the new capital of his kingdom (in place of Thebes) when he abandoned the worship of Amon and devoted himself to that of the Aton; *i.e.,* the solar disk. Shortly after Ikhnaton's death the court returned to Thebes, and the city, after an existence of hardly more than 15 years, was abandoned (*see* IKHNATON).

Tell el Amarna is of great interest not only because of its association with the revolutionary Pharaoh Ikhnaton but also because it is one of the few city sites of ancient Egypt that has been carefully excavated. The first scientific clearing of the site was undertaken by Sir Flinders Petrie in 1891–92, and in succeeding years both British and German archaeologists unearthed the ruins of the city, which extended along the Nile for a distance of five miles. Because Ikhnaton chose a virgin site for his capital and because of the relatively short duration of its occupancy the excavators could reconstruct an accurate picture of the layout of the city.

When Ikhnaton ordered the founding of the city in the fourth year of his reign, he had stelae (inscribed tablets) carved in the cliffs at the end of the desert to demarcate the city limits. Although the city as a whole displays little in the way of town planning, the major official quarters at its centre were carefully organized. Running north and south throughout the entire length of Akhetaton was the Royal road, on either side of which were the principal buildings. The largest of these was the Great temple of the Aton, the enclosure wall of which was nearly ½ mi. long and 300 yd. broad. The temple consisted primarily of a series of walled courts separated by towered gateways leading eastward to the main sanctuary, which was completely in the open air. An elevated platform in the centre of this final court served as the high altar to the sun-god. Throughout the length of the temple and also outside its walls were numerous offering tables of stone and mud brick. The open character of the cult of the Aton stood in contrast to that of the Theban Amon, whose worship had been carried on in the dimly lighted innermost chambers of his temple.

South of the Great temple were situated the buildings for Ikhnaton's use. On the east side of the Royal road was the commodious residence of the royal family, provided with terraced gardens, while directly across the road was the official palace, where the affairs of state were carried on. Both these buildings, as indeed most of the dwellings at Tell el Amarna, were constructed principally of mud brick, baked in the sun. Stone was sparingly used for such architectural elements as columns and doorways. Many of the rooms of these complex royal buildings had walls, floors and ceilings painted in a lively naturalistic style. Such scenes as those depicting the intimate family life of Ikhnaton from his living quarters are among the masterpieces of Egyptian art. A bridge, spanning the Royal road, joined the two buildings and provided a place where the king might appear publicly to reward his nobles with gifts of gold. A second smaller temple to the Aton, similar in plan to the Great temple, lay immediately to the south of the king's residence.

Two other buildings from the central city are important as sources of major archaeological finds. In the house of the sculptor Thutmose were discovered many of the masterworks of Amarna sculpture, notably the portraits of Queen Nefertiti. In 1887 the chance diggings of a peasant woman in the records office brought to light a store of approximately 350 clay tablets inscribed in the cuneiform script. From these tablets, written by the vassal princes of the Egyptian empire in Syria and Palestine, as well as by the kings of Babylonia, Assyria and Mitanni, to Amenhotep III and his son Ikhnaton, it is possible to trace the decline of the Egyptian empire of the 18th dynasty. Ikhnaton, who was deeply preoccupied with religious matters at Akhetaton, had a corresponding lack of interest in foreign affairs.

Unlike Thebes, where crowded conditions had forced the construction of multistoried houses, the dwellings at Akhetaton had only one floor. The nobles possessed spacious villas with landscaped gardens. A small shrine open to the sky for the worship of the Aton was one of the distinctive features of such an estate. Generally the bedrooms and other rooms surrounded a central living room, the roof of which was higher than that of the rest of the house, thus permitting clerestory lighting and ventilation. The workers were lodged in simple cottages lined next to one another in rows.

Toward the end of Ikhnaton's reign there is evidence of his desire to seek a possible reconciliation with the old priestly hierarchy of Thebes. At about the same time a rift between Ikhnaton and his wife, Queen Nefertiti, developed; the queen retired to the north part of Tell el Amarna, where a special palace was constructed for her use. The archaeological evidence from this quarter suggests that she was an ardent supporter of the Aton religion.

In the desert hills to the east were hewn the tombs of the important officials. These tombs resemble those at Thebes in having an exterior forecourt, an entrance hall sometimes provided with columns, and a second hall at the rear of which was a small room containing a statue of the tomb owner. These chambers were accessible for the funerary cult; the burial shaft generally descends from the floor of the first hall, but in none of the tombs has any burial been discovered. Although the work in decorating the tomb chapels was often hastily and incompletely carried out, the painted reliefs of these tombs have been a major source of information regarding the daily life and religion of Akhetaton. The representations of various buildings of Tell el Amarna that appear on the walls have been valuable aids to the excavators in interpreting the often meagre architectural traces surviving in the actual city, particularly of the Great temple, which was razed to the ground by the opponents of the Aton religion after Ikhnaton's death. In these tombs the emphasis is upon the activities of the owner in Akhetaton rather than the life after death. In a number of the tombs have been found versions of the hymn to the Aton, in which is described the universality of the sun-god as creator and sustainer of all life. The reliefs are in an unconventional, often exaggerated style, tending to reflect a momentary and emotional aspect rather than the static mood that had characterized Egyptian art previously. The tomb of Ikhnaton and his family is situated in the side of a dry watercourse about 4 mi. E. of the city. It contains an unprecedented scene of the royal family in mourning over the death of the princess Meketaton, who was buried in a section of the tomb. There is no certain evidence, however, that either Ikhnaton or his wife was ever interred there.

The return of the court to Thebes in Tutankhamen's reign must have been rather sudden, since houses under construction in the northern sector of the city were abandoned before completion. The reform in religion and art that Ikhnaton had sought to effect ended in failure, for the number of faithful adherents was relatively small. Even at Tell el Amarna itself in the homes of the workers were discovered figures and names of the gods of the older tradition. After the Pharaoh died, a number of his retainers found it more convenient to adapt themselves to life at Thebes rather than support a lost cause at Akhetaton. *See* also references under "Tell el Amarna" in the Index.

BIBLIOGRAPHY.—J. D. S. Pendlebury, *Tell el-Amarna* (1935); J. D. S. Pendlebury *et al., The City of Akhenaten,* 2 vol., part iii (1951); N. de G. Davies, *The Rock Tombs of El Amarna,* 6 vol. (1903 *et seq.*); C. F. Pfeiffer, *Tell el Amarna and the Bible* (1963).

(E. F. W.)

**TELLICHERRY,** a town and seaport in the Cannanore District of Kerala, India, lies 42 mi. (68 km.) N of Kozhikode (Calicut). Pop. (1961) 44,763. On a group of low wooded hills running out to the sea, it is protected by a natural breakwater of basalt rocks. To the north of the town is a small river (14 mi. [23 km.] long), which is, however, navigable only for 3 mi. Tellicherry is the seat of Brennen College (founded 1862), with about 700 students. There is also a flourishing furniture industry. It is the chief outlet for pepper grown in the surrounding region, for coffee and sandalwood from the Western Ghats, and for coconuts grown all along the Malabar Coast. In 1683 the British East India Company established a factory at Tellicherry on a site formerly occupied by a French mud fort. It was the company's first major trading post on the Malabar Coast, and it became important as an entrepôt for pepper. (G. KN.)

**TELLURIUM** is a brittle, silvery-white metallic chemical element closely allied in physical and chemical properties with selenium. The symbol of tellurium is Te; atomic number 52; atomic weight 127.60. There are 24 known isotopes, with mass numbers ranging from 107 to 135 (*see* ISOTOPE; NUCLEUS: *Chart of Properties of the Nuclides*).

In 1782 F. J. Müller von Reichenstein, in examining Transylvanian gold minerals, suspected the presence of a new element and called it *metallum problematicum* or *aurum paradoxum.* In 1798 M. H. Klaproth extracted tellurium from white gold ore, named it, and established its identity as differing from antimony, with which it had been confused. It was not until 1832 that J. J. Berzelius made a careful study of the chemistry of the element.

**Occurrence.**—Although widely distributed, tellurium has an estimated percentage in the earth's crust of only $10^{-9}$. Rarely found as native tellurium, it commonly occurs as tellurides of copper, lead, silver, gold, iron, and bismuth. Typical minerals are sylvanite, $(Au,Ag)Te_2$; calaverite, $AuTe_2$; muthmannite, $(AuAg)Te$; krennerite, $(AuTe_2)$; petzite, $(Ag_3AuTe_2)$; tetradymite, $Bi_2Te_2S$; rickardite, $Cu_4Te_3$; melonite, $NiTe_2$; and altaite, PbTe. Tellurium minerals are found in the United States, Canada, Mexico, South America, Sweden, central Europe, Zambia, the U.S.S.R., Japan, New Zealand, and Western Australia. The chief sources of tellurium are the slimes from copper and lead refineries and flue dusts from processing of telluride gold ores.

**Uses.**—Although comparatively large supplies of tellurium are available, no single use has been developed that creates a large demand for this element. Small concentrations of tellurium in aluminum alloys increase ductility, in tin alloys increase the hardness and tensile strength, and in stainless steels increase the machinability. Appreciable increase in the depth of chill in iron (*see* CAST IRON) can be obtained by addition of minute amounts of tellurium. The addition of 0.05% Te to lead increases its resistance to corrosion. In manganese-magnesium alloys tellurium increases resistance to corrosion. Tellurium has been used as a brightener in certain plating baths. A beryllium-copper-tellurium alloy has been reported. Selenium and tellurium in copper or copper-rich alloys improve machinability without producing so-called hot-shortness. Both are used in preference to sulfur.

In alloys like Babbitt metal addition of tellurium refines the grain structure, aids casting, and improves physical properties at high temperatures. Tellurium in hydrogenation and cracking catalysts used for conversion of heavy oils to motor fuels reduces carbon formation. The addition of 0.1 to 2% tellurium in rubber compounding improves resistance to heat, oxidation, and abrasion and increases resiliency. Tellurium diethyldithiocarbamate is the fastest known accelerator for butyl rubber. Some organic tellurium compounds have germicidal properties, and diethyl telluride possesses antiknock characteristics. This latter use has not been important, since it is accompanied by a disagreeable odour. Zinc tellurite has been patented as an antifouling paint. Tellurium has been used to a limited extent in colouring glass or porcelain, large colloidal particles giving a blue colour, small particles a brown colour, and telluride a red to red-violet colour. Acid solutions of dioxide have been used as a dip for silver ornaments, giving a "platinum finish" to the metal. Soluble tellurium compounds are used in toning baths in photography. As little as one micromole of tellurium taken into the human body gives the breath a penetrating garliclike odour, which may appear in less than half an hour after ingestion; it is reported that 2 g. of tellurium as sodium tellurite may be a lethal dose.

Bismuth telluride, $Bi_2Te_3$, is a semiconducting material from which can be made *p-n* junctions that have a high thermoelectric power and a low ratio of thermal to electric conductivity. When electric current is passed in the proper direction through such a junction, the junction is cooled (the Peltier effect). Useful cooling can be achieved with a temperature differential of greater than 40° C, but at present the efficiency of such devices is too low for economical use in large-scale refrigeration. Bismuth telluride is *n*-type when it contains a slight excess of tellurium; it is *p*-type when it contains a slight excess of bismuth. The crystalline compound has a rhombohedral structure and melts at 580° C. Another semiconductor, lead telluride (PbTe) is used as a thin-film infrared photoconductor.

**Methods of Production.**—The crude copper anodes used in the electrolytic refining of copper contain a high percentage of selenium and tellurium that was present in the ore. Upon electrolysis of the copper, the selenium and tellurium and other valuable elements (gold and silver) settle in the electrolyte as anode mud. Although procedures for the recovery of tellurium are not identical in this and other types of residues, the general principles include fusion with sodium carbonate and nitrate or extraction with sodium hydroxide, neutralization of the water solution of sodium tellurite to form precipitated tellurium dioxide, and, finally, dry reduction of the tellurium dioxide by means of a mixture of flour and borax to form molten tellurium. An alternative method includes solution of the dioxide in hydrochloric acid and reduction with sulfur dioxide to form precipitated tellurium. Tellurium appears on the market in the form of bars, as ground crystalline tellurium, or as dry precipitated powder. Some tellurium has been redissolved in nitric acid (specific gravity 1.2) and crystallized as basic nitrate.

**Properties.**—Tellurium has a density of 6.25; it melts at 449.8° C and boils at 1,390° C; its hardness is 2.3 (Mohs). Its heat of fusion is 4.27 kcal. per gram atom. It crystallizes in hexagonal-rhombohedral prisms and is isomorphous with the stable gray modification of selenium. The brown, so-called "amorphous" tellurium (produced when aqueous tellurous acid is reduced) has been shown by x-ray diffraction to be very finely divided crystalline (hexagonal) tellurium. Colloidal preparations are easily made by reducing dilute solutions of telluric acid with hydrazine or sulfurous acid, with or without protective colloids. Elementary tellurium is not very metallic in character; it is a poor conductor of heat and a semiconductor. The photoelectric effect is only about 0.01% as strong as that of gray selenium. The electrical properties of tellurium are better understood than those of selenium, primarily because it is easier to prepare tellurium single crystals. Alpha-particle bombardment of tellurium produces $^{133}Xe$. The vapour of tellurium at the boiling point is diatomic $Te_2$. Tellurium-vapour lamps also containing mercury provide almost a continuous spectrum that approaches the characteristics of daylight.

Tellurium occurs in Group VI of the periodic system with oxygen, sulfur, and selenium. In the second long series of 18 elements, it lies between antimony and iodine. Although strongly electronegative, tellurium is less so than selenium, sulfur, or oxygen. Tellurium exhibits oxidation states of $-2$, $+2$, $+4$, and $+6$. These are illustrated by ($-2$) hydrogen telluride and the tellurides; ($+2$) tellurium dichloride; ($+4$) tellurium dioxide, tellurous acid, the tellurites, and the tetrahalides; ($+6$) tellurium trioxide, telluric acid, the tellurates, and hexafluoride. The chemical behaviour of elementary tellurium is similar to that of selenium. It burns in air or oxygen with a blue-green flame, forming the dioxide. Freshly precipitated tellurium oxidizes slowly in air at room temperature. It is unaffected by hydrochloric acid, but both nitric acid and aqua regia oxidize it to tellurous acid. Halogens react to form halides. Tellurium reacts with most metals at elevated temperatures to form tellurides.

**Compounds.**—Hydrogen telluride ($H_2Te$) is a colourless, foul-smelling, toxic gas which is prepared by the action of hydrochloric acid on aluminum or magnesium telluride or by action of water on aluminum telluride ($Al_2Te_3$). Hydrogen telluride is less stable than $H_2Se$; the heat of formation is $+23.8$ kcal. per mole. Its melting and boiling points are $-51°$ C and $-2.3°$ C, respectively. Its solubility in water is at least 0.09 moles per litre at atmospheric pressure. Hydrogen telluride is both a stronger reducing agent and a stronger acid than either hydrogen sulfide or hydrogen selenide. Its aqueous ionization constants are $K_1 = 2.3 \times 10^{-3}$ and $K_2 = ca\ 10^{-11}$. Sodium telluride ($Na_2Te$) is prepared by a direct combination of sodium and tellurium in liquid ammonia; an appropriate excess of tellurium dissolves the precipitated $Na_2Te$ and yields a polytelluride (*e.g.*, $Na_2Te_2$ or $Na_2Te_6$). Hydrogen telluride may be added to aqueous solutions of sodium hydroxide to form NaHTe or $Na_2Te$. Air or oxygen must be excluded, since oxidation will cause complete precipitation of tellurium. The $+2$ oxidation state is illustrated by tellurium dichloride, $TeCl_2$, and the dibromide, $TeBr_2$. The dichloride is a black solid, melting at 208° C and boiling at 328° C; the dibromide is a chocolate-brown solid whose melting and boiling points cannot be measured because of thermal disproportionation to tellurium and tellurium tetrabromide. The dihalides react rapidly with water according to the following type of reaction: $2TeCl_2 + 2H_2O \rightarrow Te + TeO_2 + 4H^+ + 4Cl^-$. The tetrahalides, $TeF_4$ (melting point 129.6° C), $TeCl_4$ (melting point 224° C), $TeBr_4$ (melting point 363° C), and $TeI_4$ (melting point 280° C), are hygroscopic solids which undergo hydrolysis to yield $TeO_2$. Tellurium dioxide is essentially insoluble in water, giving solutions (*ca* $10^{-5}$ molar) of "tellurous acid." Ionization constants reported for tellurous acid are: $K_1 = 2 \times 10^{-3}$ and $K_2 = 10^{-8}$. Dissolved in strong acids, $TeO_2$ forms the positive ion $(TeOOH)^+$; in basic solutions $TeO_2$ dissolves to form tellurites. The alkali tellurites are subject to air oxidation at elevated temperatures. Tellurium dioxide can be prepared by heating the trioxide above its melting point but is most commonly prepared by the ignition or neutralization of tellurium basic nitrate, $2TeO_2HNO_3$.

Hexafluoride, telluric acid, and the tellurates illustrate the $+6$ valence for tellurium. Contrasted with the other halides, hexafluoride has a much lower melting and boiling point, $-37.8°$ and $-38.9°$ C, respectively. Orthotelluric acid ($H_6TeO_6$) is easily prepared by the chromic acid oxidation of tellurium basic nitrate or the hydrogen peroxide oxidation of an acid solution of tellurium dioxide. A solubility curve for telluric acid shows $H_2TeO_4 \cdot 6H_2O$ to be the stable form below 10° C and $H_2TeO_4 \cdot 2H_2O$ to be the form crystallized above 10° C.

Salts of the hypothetical acids pyrotelluric, $H_2Te_2O_7$, and tetratelluric, $H_2Te_4O_{13}$, are known. Orthotelluric acid loses water at 100°–200° to form polymetatelluric acid $(H_2TeO_4)_n$, where *n* is about 10. Conversion to tellurium trioxide, $TeO_3$, is complete at 300° to 360° C.

Organic compounds vary in complexity from the relatively simple alkyl tellurides to the more complex cyclic compounds that contain tellurium in the ring.

There are simple aliphatic compounds of the types, $R_2TeX_2$, $R_3TeX$, and $RTeX_3$. Among the aromatic derivatives there are types $R_2Te$, $R_2Te_2$, $RTeR'$.

**Analytical.**—Like selenium, tellurium is easily precipitated from dilute hydrochloric acid solutions by reducing agents, such as sulfur dioxide or hydrazine hydrochloride. Two common reactions are used for the separation of tellurium from selenium. (1) Red selenium is precipitated from strong hydrochloric acid solutions by sulfur dioxide; tellurium is not. Upon separation of the selenium by filtration, the solution is diluted and the tellurium precipitated by further addition of sulfur dioxide. (2) The fusion of selenium and tellurium with potassium cyanide forms potassium selenocyanate, KSeCN, and potassium telluride, $K_2Te$. Bubbling air through a water solution of this mixture precipitates elemental tellurium. The addition of potassium iodide to a dilute acid solution of tellurium precipitates tellurium tetraiodide, $TeI_4$, which is soluble in an excess of potassium iodide, forming $K_2TeI_6$. Tellurium is commonly weighed as the element. Tellurous acid may be oxidized to tellurate by potassium permanganate. Tellurates are reduced quantitatively by titanous chloride.

Bibliography.—K. W. Bagnall, *The Chemistry of Selenium, Tellurium, and Polonium* (1966); F. A. Cotton and G. Wilkinson, *Advanced Inorganic Chemistry*, 2nd ed. (1966); M. Sneed *et al.*, *Comprehensive Inorganic Chemistry*, vol. 8, 2nd ed. (1954); N. D. Sindeeva, *Mineralogy and Types of Deposits of Selenium and Tellurium* (1964).
(W. L. Jo.)

**TELUGU,** one of the four literary languages of the Dravidian family, is spoken by about 38,000,000 persons. It is the language of that part of Andhra Pradesh, India, beginning north of Madras city and extending northwest to Bellary, where Telugu meets Kanarese, and northeast to Orissa. It is an independent language of the family, with numerous peculiar features. Its literature dates from the 11th century, its inscriptions from the 7th. *See* Dravidian. (M. B. E.)

**TELUGU LITERATURE.** Telugu, like the other languages of south India, is of the Dravidian family (*see* further Telugu; Dravidian).

**Early Period.**—The oldest extant examples of Telugu are in inscriptions of Cālūkya kings, dating from the 9th century onward; the earliest literary work to survive is the 10th-century *Kumārasaṃbhavam* by Nannecoḍa, a lengthy poem based on a Puranic legend. Nannaya's version of the *Mahābhārata* (*q.v.*), written between A.D. 1022 and 1063, an abridgment of the Sanskrit epic, was completed by two later writers.

The well-known Indian literary form the *Śataka* ("century of verses") was particularly popular in Telugu; in the 12th century Vemana wrote a number of *Śatakas* on moral topics.

Two 15th-century poets should be mentioned: Śrīnātha (1365–1440) and Potana (1400–75). The former wrote, among many other works, a version of the Nala and Damayantī story, an episode in the *Mahābhārata,* while the latter's masterpiece was the Telugu version of the *Bhāgavatapurāṇa,* which tells of the incarnations of the god Viṣṇu (*see* Vishnuism).

**The 16th Century.**—The Vijayanagar Empire, whose court language was Telugu, was at its most powerful in the Deccan under Kṛṣṇadevarāya, who reigned from 1509 to 1530, and this period was the golden age of Telugu literature. The king himself was a poet and composed an epic, *Āmuktamālyadā,* completed in 1520. It tells the story of a girl devotee of Viṣṇu, a foundling reared by a priest in the god's service, who had been the god's consort in a former birth. So much did she love Viṣṇu that she used secretly to wear the garlands with which her adoptive father was later to adorn his image. When separated from him, she pined away, and he finally consented to her becoming his bride.

Two of the most famous poets at Kṛṣṇadevarāya's court were Peddanna and Timmanna. Peddanna wrote an epic called *Manucaritram,* and Timmanna one called *Pārijātāpaharaṇamu* ("Rape of the Night-Queen Flower"). This recounts an episode in the life of Kṛṣṇa (Krishna; *q.v.*), in which the god increases the jealousy between his two consorts, Rukmiṇī and Satyabhāmā, by presenting to Rukmiṇī a flower from the Night-Queen tree, which grows only in heaven, ruled by the god Indra. Satyabhāmā first upbraids and finally kicks her husband, who in the end agrees to uproot the tree to pacify her, a promise that involves a journey to heaven and a fight with Indra.

Another poet of about the same time is Suranna, who composed the *Kalāpūrṇodayamu* in 1585. The story is of a comedy of errors: a heavenly maiden, Rambhā, and Nalakūbara, her lover, are tricked into falling in love with another pair of lovers, Kalābhūṣiṇī and Maṇikaṃdhara, who impersonate them. False and real lovers meet in a maze of errors, but the pretenders are eventually found out.

Tenāli Rāmakṛṣṇa is sometimes thought to have been jester to Kṛṣṇadevarāya, though this seems doubtful. Many stories have been attributed to him; of these, some describe his pranks (many at the expense of Tatācāri, a protagonist of Vaiṣṇavism), and some are in more serious vein.

**The 16th to the 19th Century.**—After the collapse of the Vijayanagar Empire in 1565, Telugu literature in the northern Deccan went through a period of stagnation and decadence. It flourished, however, at the courts farther south, where political conditions were more settled. Thanjavur (Tanjore) and Madurai attracted a number of Telugu writers between 1650 and 1830. Perhaps best known among these are the songwriters, especially Kṣetrayya, Tyāgarāja, and Śyāmā Śāstri. Tyāgarāja (1767–1847) was the greatest of the three. He wrote a number of songs in praise of Rāma (*q.v.*) in simple, direct Telugu, and these *Kīrtanas* ("songs of praise") are still sung. Such was the influence exerted by Tyāgarāja and others that Telugu came to be regarded as *par excellence* the language of music.

**Modern Period.**—The advent of the British brought Telugu into contact with Western literary forms and ideas, and some Europeans took an interest in Telugu. Chief among them was C. P. Brown, whose dictionaries, English-Telugu and Telugu-English, appeared in 1852.

The father of modern Telugu literature was K. Viresalingam Pantulu (1848–1919). He was quick to appreciate the possibilities of such Western forms as the novel and the drama. The first Telugu novel, *Rājaśekharacaritramu,* was his adaptation of Oliver Goldsmith's *Vicar of Wakefield.* Under the influence of Rabindranath Tagore (*q.v.*), a new school of poetry attempted to convey direct personal experience, which would formerly have been considered in bad taste. The short story has been favourably received; Guruzada Appa Rao was the first short-story writer and Adivi Bapirazu a worthy successor.

Bibliography.—A. S. Panchapakesa Ayyar, *Royal Jester: or, Tenali Rama,* 2nd ed. (1943); P. T. Raju, *Telugu Literature: Andhra Literature* (1944); G. V. Sitapati, "Telugu," in *Indian Literature,* ed. by Dr. Nagendra (1959).
(Jo. R. M.)

**TELUKBETUNG,** a port in South Sumatra Province, Indonesia, capital of Lampung *Kabupaten* (residency), lies on the southern coast of Sumatra on Teluk (bay) Lampung, about 224 mi. SSE of Palembang by rail. Pop. (1961) 133,901. The immediate vicinity is mountainous, with Gunung (Mt.) Betung and Gunung Ratai to the west. The hinterland is low lying and was one of the earliest areas of transmigration from Java. The eruption of Krakatau (*q.v.*) in 1883 virtually destroyed the town. Between 1905, when immigration began, and the mid-1960s, the proportion of Javanese and Sudanese in the district rose to about one-third. Telukbetung is the chief port for the area, with services to Merak in Java.

**TEMA,** a port of Ghana, West Africa, formally opened in 1962, lies on the coast 18 mi. (29 km.) E of Accra, the capital.

Pop. (1960) 14,937. The choice of this site was due to its suitability for development into a deepwater harbour, enclosing 500 ac. (200 ha.), to serve the Volta Basin area and the eastern part of the country, Accra itself being unsuitable because of silting. The government acquired 64 sq.mi. (166 sq.km.) of land, north of the harbour and largely on the savanna, and entrusted its development to the Tema Development Corporation, established in 1952. The port now has three miles of breakwaters, ten deepwater berths, an oil tanker berth, a dockyard, warehouses, and transit sheds. A separate fishing harbour with cold-storage and marketing facilities is east of the lee breakwater. A "New Town" was planned to serve the harbour and provide industrial and residential facilities, the plan envisaging seven communities with a total potential population of 85,000 by 1970 and full modern amenities. Water supply, main drainage, and electricity are provided, and there are rail and road links with the country's main systems. About 800 ac. (325 ha.) were set aside for allocation to private industrial enterprise, and various industries have been established there, including chemical and aluminum works and an automobile assembly plant. (G. J. D. R.)

**TEMIR-TAU** (SAMARKANDSKI until 1945), a town in the Karagandinskaya (Karaganda) Oblast' of the Kazakh Soviet Socialist Republic, U.S.S.R., about 17 mi. (28 km.) N of Karaganda on the Samarkandski Reservoir (formed by the Nura River), is the terminus of a short branch railway from Solonichki Station on the Tselinograd-Karaganda line, a few miles east. Pop. (1959) 76,725. The town, which was once a small sawmilling settlement, developed rapidly during World War II with the establishment of a hydroelectric power plant and a steel mill. There are various technological institutes and a medical training school. There is also a synthetic rubber plant, and at Solonichki is the Karaganda metallurgical factory ("Kazakhstanskaya Magnitka"), completed in 1960. (G. E. WR.)

**TEMNE** (TIMNE), a Negroid people occupying approximately 11,000 sq.mi. (4,450 ha.) in northwest Sierra Leone (*q.v.*). They number more than 500,000 and are divided by dialect into a northern and a southern group. Temne is a semi-Bantu language of the Niger-Congo family (*see* AFRICAN LANGUAGES). The Temne resemble the Mende (*q.v.*) in their pattern of settlement and live mainly by growing rice; women also fish. Rice, cattle, and goats are important for exchange and sacrifice. Land rights are based on descent from original settlers or conquerors, or on length of settlement. The Temne are divided into patrilineal, eponymously descended clans (*abuna*) that generally are not localized. The chief's office is partly religious, and he is sometimes a member of the Ragbenle and Poro secret societies. One or the other society conducts his installation ceremonies, during which he and some of his officials go into sacred seclusion. The women's Bundu society mainly prepares girls for marriage. Polygyny, levirate (*qq.v.*), and widow inheritance are practised; women attain some independence through trade and are sometimes influential in family affairs. Religion is concerned less with high gods than with prayers and sacrifices to nature and ancestral spirits. These beliefs are in decline through migration and industrialization, and the traditional activities of the secret societies are generally hidden except in more rural places.

BIBLIOGRAPHY.—H. Langley, "The Temne," *Sierra Leone Stud.*, vol. 22 (1939); V. Dorjahn, "The Changing Political System of the Temne," *Africa*, vol. 30 (1960); M. McCulloch, *Peoples of Sierra Leone Protectorate* (1950); J. Littlejohn, "Temne Space," *Anthrop. Q.*, vol. 36 (1963), "The Temne House," and "The Temne Ansasa," *Sierra Leone Stud.* (Dec. 1962). (K. L. LI.)

**TEMPERA** is a kind of painting executed with paints that consist of pigment ground in a medium that is miscible with water; a few moments after application the paint is sufficiently resistant to water to allow overpainting with more colour. Thin, translucent layers of paint produce a clear, luminous effect and the colour tones of the successive brushstrokes blend optically. When the paint is skillfully built up, it will retain its luminosity, as well as the effect of its undercoats, as an opaque or semiopaque coating. Tempera is distinguished from the other aqueous paints which are either transparent (*see* WATER-COLOUR PAINTING) or solidly opaque (gouache, casein [*qq.v.*], poster colours). Tempera may be applied in thin, transparent washes or in heavy, opaque touches when required, but these are not typical of the work as a whole.

Tempera paints have their distinctive properties because they are emulsions. An emulsion is a stable mixture of an oily ingredient (oils, fats, resins, waxes) and a thick, gummy or gluelike (colloidal) aqueous ingredient. The proverbial rule that oil and water do not mix does not apply when the oil is of an emulsifiable type and there is a good emulsifier in the water solution. The oily ingredient of an emulsion is dispersed in the aqueous solution in myriads of tiny round droplets. The binding ingredients in water colour, gouache and poster colours are not emulsions; they are simple gluey solutions.

The word tempera originally came from the verb "temper," *i.e.*, to bring to a desired consistency; dry pigments were made usable by "tempering" them with a fluid binding and adhesive vehicle. The Italians distinguished such painting from fresco painting (*q.v.*), the colours for which contained no binder. The artist was said to "temper" his colours with egg or with oil. Eventually, after the rise of oil painting, the use of the word tempera became confined to its present meaning. In some circles, especially among artists who work solely for reproduction, "tempera" has been indiscriminately used to denote any opaque water medium and the labels on some aqueous colours in tubes and jars bear this name, but this usage is incorrect and confusing.

### TECHNIQUE

The standard tempera vehicle is a natural emulsion, egg yolk, thinned with water. The yolk of hen's eggs contains a fatty substance (egg oil) emulsified with a gummy substance (albumen) and a few minor ingredients, chief among which is lecithin, a powerful emulsifier and stabilizer. The man-made emulsions of more recent origin are variants of the original egg vehicle. Their purpose is to create some special property of manipulation or some effect for an individual requirement; they aim at duplicating or closely resembling the good properties of straight egg-yolk tempera, such as its tough, leathery permanent paint film.

In preparing the paint, the yolk is separated from the white and is dried by being rolled on a paper towel, and its sac is punctured; a pure yolk is thus obtained, without any white. The ingredients of pure egg yolk and their proportions govern the whole technique of egg tempera—its behaviour, its effects and its longevity. Egg white was never used in easel painting; it is a relatively weak and impermanent paint binder. The yellow colour of the yolk is imperceptible when pigmented; moreover, it is a fugitive colouring matter (carotene) which soon disappears on exposure. The pigments (the same as those used in water colour) are ground to paste consistency with water and kept in screw cap jars. Prior to each day's work the artist mixes with egg yolk as much of a colour as he needs. He paints with fine red sable water-colour brushes; a skilled technique of brushwork is gained from experience. The three basic points of control are the amount of water used, the loading of the brush and the manner of stroking. It is a deliberate, controlled method, adaptable to carefully planned work rather than to spontaneous painting. A finished drawing (cartoon), in which all the artist's creative problems are worked out, is made first; this is traced on the ground. The artist's efforts can then be devoted to the technique and the development of colour and painterly effects. The special ground for tempera painting is a rigid wood or wallboard panel coated with gesso, which is a brilliant white, ivory smooth, fully absorbent preparation made of precipitated chalk and rabbitskin glue.

Variants of the pure egg-yolk vehicle have been developed to widen its use among contemporary artists, although earlier painters chose to develop a superlative skill in the handling of a somewhat difficult and intractible material rather than to make the material itself amenable to a more easily acquired skill. Among the man-made emulsions a popular one is prepared by shaking or homogenizing whole egg with linseed oil; this vehicle is preferred by many painters to that of pure yolk. Another is gum tempera, the standard recipe for which contains gum arabic or cherry gum emulsified with a blend of dammar varnish and stand oil. This vehicle is also well-liked by numerous painters; it can produce an

"The Presentation in the Temple" by an unknown 15th-century Byzantine painter. $17\frac{1}{2} \times 16\frac{5}{8}$ in. ($44\frac{1}{2} \times 42\frac{1}{4}$ cm.)

"Madonna and Child" by Giotto (Giotto di Bondone)

## EARLY DEVELOPMENTS IN TEMPERA PAINTING

The earliest European tempera paintings were done by Byzantine artists who followed circumscribed traditions. Duccio (*c.* 1255–*c.* 1319) developed from this Byzantine tradition, but achieved a wider and more subtle range of colour with a standard, controlled egg tempera technique for painting on wood panels (left). A parallel colouristic development can be seen in late Byzantine painting (above). Giotto (1266/67?–1337), whose great fresco paintings are in a style heralding the Renaissance, introduced the same monumentality into his tempera paintings (top left)

"The Calling of the Apostles Peter and Andrew" by Duccio (Duccio di Buoninsegna)

BY COURTESY OF (TOP LEFT, BOTTOM LEFT) NATIONAL GALLERY OF ART, WASHINGTON, D.C., SAMUEL H. KRESS COLLECTION, (TOP RIGHT) THE METROPOLITAN MUSEUM OF ART, NEW YORK CITY, BEQUEST OF LIZZIE P. BLISS, 1931

# TEMPERA

"The Crucifixion" by Carlo Crivelli, *c.* 1490. 29⅝ × 21¾ in. (75¼ × 55¼ cm.)

"An Apostle" (St. John or St. Simon) by Piero della Francesca

"Portrait of a Doge" by Gentile Bellini. 21½ × 17 in. (54⅗ × 43⅕ cm.)

## LATER DEVELOPMENTS IN TEMPERA PAINTING

The works of the 15th-century Italian artist Sandro Botticelli (opposite, Plate III) and his contemporary Carlo Crivelli (top left) represent the highest possible degree of skill and refinement using pure egg tempera. Since tempera is a meticulous medium, best suited to a deliberate and largely linear style, only the addition of oil could produce tempera works of greater flexibility and flow. Thus, all the paintings on Plates II and III, except "The Crucifixion" and "Mars and Venus," though primarily tempera, probably employ some oil, either in the form of infinitely refined glazes (as in the painting at left) or mixed in some way with the aqueous tempera itself (above and at the top of Plate III). With the development of oil painting, tempera became a neglected medium. It was revived in the 20th century in England, Germany, and the U.S.A. Ben Shahn and Andrew Wyeth (Plate IV) are notable American practitioners

"St. Francis in Ecstasy" by Giovanni Bellini. 48½ × 55 in. (123⅕ × 139¾ cm.)

BELLINI AND BOTTICELLI

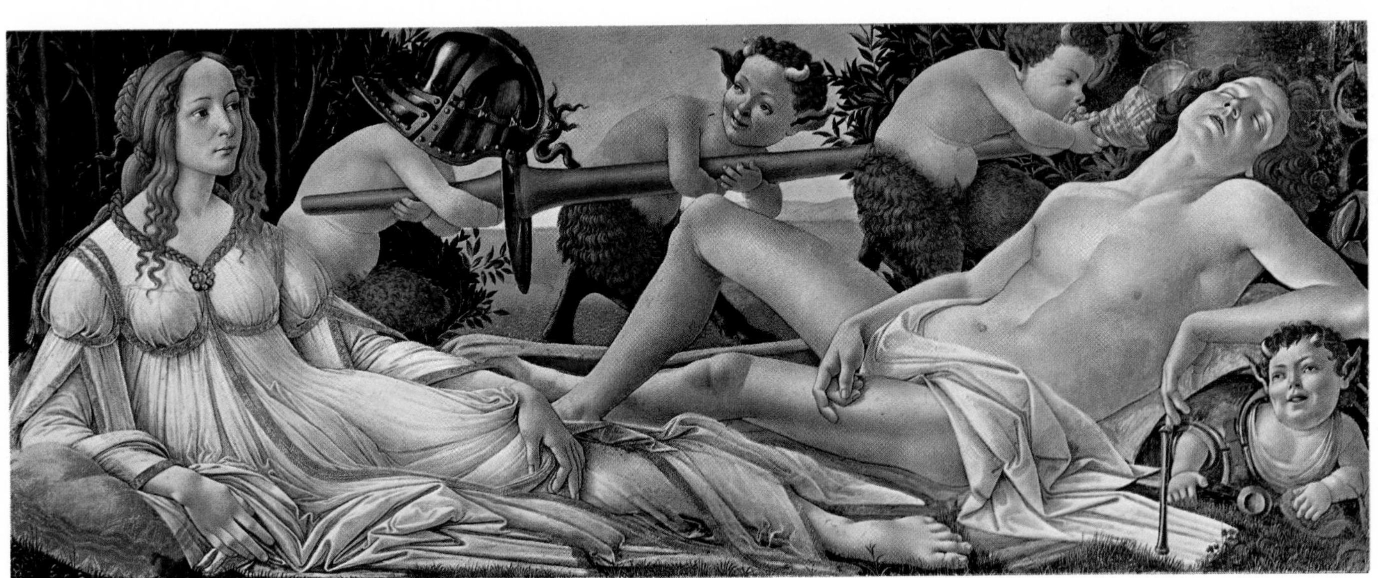

"Mars and Venus" by Sandro Botticelli, *c.* 1485. 27¼ x 68¼ in. ( 69 x 173½ cm.)

# TEMPERA

"Mine Disaster" by Ben Shahn, 1948. 24 × 30 in. ($60\frac{9}{10}$ × $76\frac{1}{4}$ cm.)

"Christina's World" by Andrew Wyeth, 1948. $32\frac{1}{4}$ × $47\frac{3}{4}$ in. ($81\frac{9}{10}$ × $121\frac{1}{4}$ cm.)

BY COURTESY OF (TOP) THE ART INSTITUTE OF CHICAGO, GIFT OF THE SOCIETY FOR CONTEMPORARY AMERICAN ART, (BOTTOM) THE MUSEUM OF MODERN ART (NEW YORK CITY), PURCHASE FUND, 1949 almost impasto effect when desired. Wax temperas are made from a group of experimental recipes and have the reputation of producing delicate, sensitive effects. Casein colours are opaque water paints, not correctly classified as tempera. Modern tempera paintings are sometimes varnished or overpainted with thin, transparent oil glazes to produce full, deep-toned results, or they are left unglazed for blond effects. Unvarnished tempera paintings, especially the pure egg-yolk variety, will assume a pleasing, satiny sheen when polished with cotton wool.

### CASEIN PAINTING

For more robust, solid or spontaneous effects than are obtainable with tempera, artists have used colours ground in a solution of casein (*q.v.*). In the form of homemade curd made from soured skim milk, it has been a traditional adhesive and binder for more than eight centuries. Refined, pure, powdered casein which can be dissolved with ammonia has been used by artists for easel and mural paintings since the latter 19th and early 20th centuries. More recently, ready-made casein paints in tubes have come into very wide use to create effects that approach those of oil paintings. Casein painting permits the use of bristle brushes and a moderate impasto, like oil painting, but not the fusion of tones. It is preferred by some because of speedy drying and mat effects. When dry, the paint becomes water-resistant to a considerable degree. Casein paintings may be varnished to further resemble oil paintings, and they are frequently glazed or overpainted with oil colours. Proper technique calls for the use of rigid boards or panels; casein is too brittle for canvas.

### HISTORY

No positive date is assigned to the first use of egg yolk as a binder of colours; it is so readily available that it may have served the most primitive cultures. The earliest European forerunners of a controlled egg-tempera medium are found among the religious paintings of the Byzantine era. By the 13th century a well-developed, standard technique on wood panels emerged in Italy; the works of Duccio (*c.* 1255–1319) in Siena and Cimabue (*c.* 1240–*c.* 1302) in Florence are outstanding examples. The medium served well when panel painting moved to a higher plane of artistic and technical sophistication as in the tempera paintings of Giotto (1267?–1337) and the Lorenzettis of 14th century Siena. Anonymity and routine following of symbolism gave way to a more individual, personal or inventive manner; the madonnas and saints were depicted as actual people. The Italian schools thereafter developed until their style of painting culminated in a refinement and perfection which it is not possible to excel with pure egg tempera. A number of painters exhibit this high stage of development; examples are the Venetian Carlo Crivelli (*c.* 1430/35–*c.* 1493/95) and, perhaps the most accomplished of all, the Florentine Sandro Botticelli (1444/5–1510).

With the changing demands of the times, art forms evolved from the generally dry and deliberate linear styles that were admirably served by tempera, to a more flowing, intensely coloured, spontaneous and juicier kind of painting, with smooth blending of colours and tones. Artists necessarily turned to the use of oily materials.

The earliest examples usually cited in historical accounts of oil painting are actually tempera paintings with thin, transparent oil glazes; such pictures are perhaps more accurately classified as tempera painting in its ultimate form. But before oil painting supplanted it, tempera was used for a group of paintings that constituted a transitional stage; the medium was still aqueous tempera, but with properties that could scarcely have been duplicated by strict adherence to the pure egg-yolk technique as used from Giotto to Botticelli. In the paintings of this transitional group there was fusion of tones and a choice of scenes and subjects that challenged the potential of egg yolk and presaged oil-painting technique. Perhaps a little oily ingredient was incorporated into the paint in some manner; it seems to require some such alteration to duplicate the effects of Carpaccio (*c.* 1460–1525/26) for instance, or of Giovanni Bellini (*c.* 1430–1516), who eventually did employ oil paint. Use of old techniques continued long after the introduction of new ones, so the rapidly changing practices of the 15th century cannot be attributed to specific dates.

In the following centuries tempera was practised sporadically; it never became a totally defunct technique. In the mid-19th century its literature was studied intensively, although academically for the most part, for its relationship to oil painting. Egg tempera is completely and satisfactorily documented and the technique can be easily reconstructed from writings and from hundreds of examples that have survived in fine condition. One prominent source of information is *The Book of the Arts or Treatise on Painting,* written in the late 14th or early 15th century by Cennino Cennini; it is a complete treatise on artists' techniques of the Gothic and early Renaissance periods. Cennini's idol was Giotto, and the book stems directly from Giotto's studio. Besides tempera it covers fresco, oil paints for decorative work and a number of studio practices. It also contains observations on painting, the proper personal behaviour and decorum of artists, the minutiae of artists' materials and procedures (*e.g.,* "the yolk of a town hen's egg is paler than those of country hens").

Artists in Europe and the United States in the latter part of the 19th and the early part of the 20th centuries found both pure and oil-glazed tempera techniques, such as those used by the early Italian and Flemish masters, very appropriate for their own work, particularly for blond effects. A strong revival of tempera followed, elevating it to a significant position among standard 20th-century techniques.

*See* also PAINTING.

BIBLIOGRAPHY.—Cennino Cennini, *Il libro dell' Arte,* a 15th-century manuscript, 3 vol.: vol. i, Italian text (1932–33), vol. ii, Eng. trans. by D. V. Thompson, *The Craftsman's Handbook* (1932–33, 1954), vol. iii, D. V. Thompson (ed.), *The Practice of Tempera Painting* (1936); Ralph Mayer, *The Painter's Craft* (1948), and *The Artist's Handbook of Materials and Techniques,* rev. ed. with extensive bibliography (1957). (RH. M.)

**TEMPERAMENT,** in psychology, refers to that aspect of personality concerned with emotional dispositions and reactions, and their speed and intensity; the term often is used to refer to the prevailing mood of a person. Historically, the notion of temperament in this sense originated with Galen (*q.v.*), who developed it from an earlier physiological theory based on the assumption of four basic body fluids (humours): blood, phlegm, black bile, and yellow bile. According to their relative predominance in the individual, they were supposed to produce, respectively, a sanguine, phlegmatic, melancholic, or choleric temperament (Lat. *temperare,* "to combine or mingle in due proportion"). This theory constitutes the first of many attempts to group human beings into types, and its stress on the physiological determination of temperament is echoed in modern theories emphasizing the action of the endocrine glands; *e.g.,* an increase in the secretion of adrenaline produces heightened emotional reactivity (*see* EMOTION). Modern psychology attributes primary importance to the activity of the autonomic nervous system (*see* NERVOUS SYSTEM), and particularly its sympathetic branch, in accounting for emotional reactivity: autonomic over-responsiveness is intimately linked with neurotic dispositions, but such responses can easily be conditioned (*see* CONDITIONING), and consequently individual differences in ease of conditioning (also probably innate) likewise play their part in determining temperament.

External physical characteristics have often been supposed to permit positive identification of different temperaments, but empirical studies have almost universally yielded relatively low correlations. Very thin, lean people tend to be introverted and to develop symptoms of anxiety and depression when suffering from neurotic disorders; very broad, fat people tend to be extroverted and to develop symptoms of hysteria and psychopathy when suffering from neurotic disorders. But these relationships are slight and of little help in prognosis or treatment.

Modern investigations have left little of Galen's original theory standing and involve such methods as the experimental measurement of a person's emotional reactions in standardized stressful situations and detailed statistical analysis of the relationships observed. The resulting picture is highly complex, revealing, among other things, a tendency for individuals to respond consistently to stress with only one of the many parts of the body controlled by the autonomic system, and it is this part that is most vulnerable in neurotic breakdown. *See* also PERSONALITY; HYSTERIA. (H. J. EY.)

**TEMPERAMENT, MUSICAL,** a term applied principally to systems for tuning instruments of fixed pitch, such as the keyboard instruments. These systems were designed to produce, by means of tempering (*i.e.,* a slight mistuning), a maximum number of intervals (especially major thirds) both melodically and harmonically acceptable to the ear.

**Just Intonation.**—When two notes are sounded together, they are pleasing to the ear when their wavelengths or frequencies bear a simple numerical ratio to each other (or very nearly so). Unisons have a frequency ratio of 1:1 and octaves 2:1. These intervals are so fundamental that they are accepted in all systems and need not be tempered. The next most harmonious interval is the perfect fifth, with the ratio 3:2 (its complement being the perfect fourth, with the ratio 4:3).

To add intervals together, the frequency ratios have to be multiplied together. Now, if fifths are added together, a new note is formed each time. For instance, in just intonation (*i.e.,* in mathematically exact intervals), starting with C and G, one then obtains D such that D and C have the ratio 9:4 or, bringing the D down an octave, the ratio 9:8. This interval is a major tone and is still reasonably concordant. If the process is repeated, one obtains an E giving with C an interval of two major tones with the ratio of 81:64, which is unbearably discordant. This may explain why in early medieval music, dominated by the theory of the pure fifth, the tone, fourth, fifth and seventh were regarded as concordant but the major third as discordant. If, however, a natural major third is sung, the frequency ratio will be 5:4, *i.e.;* 80:64.

The difference between the pure major third and the one obtained from four pure fifths is an interval with the ratio of 81:80 and is known as the comma of Didymus. The reason for this is that just as $3 \times 3 \times 3 \times 3 = 81$ is a different number from $5 \times 16 = 80$, so the two E's are actually different notes. The problem lies in the fact that musical notation recognizes only one E and musicians similarly want only one E. The question then arises as to what extent this duplication applies to other notes or to, say, a whole major scale.

At this stage it becomes difficult to visualize ratios of large numbers and an additive numerical measure for intervals becomes necessary. This is easily obtained by taking logarithms of the frequency ratios; by convention, the octave is divided into 1,200 cents. Thus:

$$\text{No. of cents} = \frac{1{,}200}{\log 2} \times \log \text{ of frequency ratio}$$

The ratios and cents of the two independent basic intervals are: perfect fifth = 3:2, 701.955; and major third = 5:4, 386.314. As all musical intervals are derived from ratios of products of the prime numbers 2, 3 and 5 only, cents of all the other intervals can be obtained by addition and subtraction of these two intervals. (Trumpets and horns produce "harmonics" that include other notes based on the numbers 7, 11, 13 and 17, but the player is expected to modify these in performance.) Thus the following intervals are obtained: perfect fourth (4:3, 1,200 − 701.955 = 498.045); major tone (9:8, 701.955 − 498.045 = 203.910); diatonic semitone or minor second (16:15, 498.045 − 386.314 = 111.731); minor sixth (8:5, 1,200 − 386.314 = 813.686); minor third (6:5, 701.955 − 386.314 = 315.641); major sixth (5:3, 498.045 + 386.314 = 884.359); chromatic semitone or augmented unison (25:24, 386.314 − 315.641 = 70.673); and the difference between a diatonic semitone and a chromatic semitone = 41.058 cents. Also, the comma of Didymus = 4 × 701.955 − 2 × 1,200 − 386.314 = 21.506. This interval is consequently more than one-fifth of an equal-tempered semitone.

In the C major scale the relative frequencies and cents to the nearest whole number from the first note are: C (24, 0); D (27, 204); E (30, 386); F (32, 498); G (36, 702); A (40, 884); B (45, 1,088); C (48, 1,200). All the possible intervals in the octave can be checked by subtracting the cents. They all come out right except D − A = 680 is not a fifth and D − F = 294 is not a minor third. As they are both too narrow by 22 cents (the comma of Didymus), the solution might appear to be to alter D to 182 cents. This makes D − A and D − F right but then D − G and D − B would be too wide by a comma. Further, the note B♭ would have to be 996 to be a fourth above F or 1,018 to be a minor third above G, again differing by a comma.

If adjacent notes in the scale are subtracted the result is the following intervals: 204, 182, 112, 204, 182, 204, 112. In other words, an octave consists of two diatonic semitones of 112 cents, three major tones of 204 cents and two minor tones of 182.404 cents (ratio 10:9). As music recognizes only one type of tone, one requirement for a practical scale is to standardize on some compromise size of tone.

**Tempered Scales.**—*Mean Tone Temperament.*—It has been shown that if the fifths are kept pure by making all tones of 204 cents, the major thirds are unbearably sharp by a whole comma. If all the tones are minor, neither fifths nor thirds are right. If, however, one takes an average, or mean tone, of 193.157 cents, the major thirds will be pure and the fifths will be only a quarter of a comma flat. The semitones will have to be equal to half the difference between the octave and five mean tones, or (1,200 − 5 × 193.157) ÷ 2 = 117.107; *i.e.,* one-quarter comma sharp. The chromatic semitone will then be tempered to 193.157 − 117.107 = 76.050, also a quarter comma sharp. The fifth will be 3 × 193.157 + 117.107 = 696.578. In the mean-tone system the difference between a minor second and an augmented unison, *e.g.,* C♯ to D♭, is still 41 cents, or just over two-fifths of an equal-tempered semitone. Consequently, on keyboard instruments, if there are only five accidental keys within the octave it is necessary to decide which are the most useful five. The usual choice is C♯, E♭, F♯, G♯ and B♭. If an A♭ is needed (*e.g.,* to use with E♭) and G♯ is used instead, the interval is 772.628 − 310.264 = 462.-364, which is 35.681 cents out for a pure fourth and produces a howling sound known as the "wolf."

*Equal Temperaments.*—There is a second criterion for tempering a practical scale: fretted instruments, such as guitars, lutes and viols, that have strings tuned to any interval other than unisons or octaves need a cyclic division of the octave so that pure octaves can be obtained from all appropriate combinations of two strings and two frets. The only way to do this is to divide the octave into a certain number of exactly equal intervals. As a scale consists of five tones and two semitones, the octave must be divided into $5x + 2y$ parts where $x{:}y$ is approximately 193:112, or 1.7:1.

(1) The 12-note system. The simplest case is when $x = 2$ and $y = 1$. The octave is then divided exactly into 12 and this gives the normal equal temperament. All semitones and minor seconds are tempered to 100 cents each and the tone becomes 200 cents, etc. The same note has to serve both for C♯ and for D♭ (although music does require two different notes) and F has to be used for E♯, and so on. The major third is 14 cents too sharp and is just on the limit of pleasantness. The overriding merit of this system is its simplicity.

(2) The 19- and 31-note systems. If $x = 3$ and $y = 2$, the octave is divided into 19 equal intervals of 63 cents. The notes are in the order: C, C♯, D♭, D, etc., with a note between E and F for both E♯ and F♭. If $x = 5$ and $y = 3$, the octave is divided into 31 equal intervals of 38.7 cents. The order of notes is then C, D♭♭, C♯, D♭, C$\chi$, D, . . . E, F♭, E♯, F, . . . . This system is remarkably close to mean-tone tuning (and to just intonation), as can be seen in the table of comparisons below. A harpsichord built in 1606 by Vito Trasuntino has 31 keys to the octave; it could be tuned exactly according to this system.

| | Just | Mean Tone | 12-note system | 19-note system | 31-note system |
|---|---|---|---|---|---|
| Chromatic semitone . . | 71 | 76 | 100 | 63 | 77 |
| Diatonic semitone . . | 112 | 117 | 100 | 126 | 116 |
| Tone . . . . . | 182 or 204 | 193 | 200 | 190 | 194 |
| Minor third . . . | 316 | 310 | 300 | 316 | 310 |
| Major third . . . | 386 | 386 | 400 | 379 | 387 |
| Fifth . . . . . | 702 | 697 | 700 | 695 | 697 |

**History.**—During the late medieval and Renaissance periods the 12-note equal temperament must have been familiar, as is shown by (1) the extensive use of fretted instruments such as the lute and viol; (2) organists' instructions to tune by fifths, tempering them just sufficiently to make the thirds usable; and (3) a few keyboard and viol fantasias that modulate enharmonically through all the possible keys. The equal-tempered major third, especially on keyboard instruments, is, however, offensively sharp to sensitive ears and toward the end of the Renaissance theorists were experimenting with other systems of tuning that produced better thirds.

The baroque era brought the decline of the lute and viol and the rise of wind instruments whose fingering favoured purer thirds, and this encouraged the introduction of mean-tone tuning. This system, however, allows little modulation and no enharmonic modulation.

Accordingly, as the technique of composition developed in the 18th century, despite attempts at duplication of accidentals on organs, the change to equal temperament was advocated by J. S. Bach and others. It should be remembered that an infinite range of intermediate tunings between mean tone and equal temperament is possible; such intermediate tunings were probably much used in earlier centuries. (G. F. Ol.)

**TEMPERANCE.** The word temperance, which strictly means moderation, acquired a particular meaning in connection with intoxicating liquor and is here used in that sense.

**History.**—Ever since man in some distant age first discovered the process of fermentation by which sugar is converted into alcohol and carbonic acid, and experienced the intoxicating effects of the liquor so produced, there has been a temperance problem. The records of the ancient oriental civilization contain many references to it and from very remote times efforts were made by priests, sages and lawgivers in India, Persia, China, Palestine, Egypt, Greece and Carthage to combat the injury of drunkenness to the individual and society. But the evil appears never to have been so great or the object of so much attention in the ancient world as it came to be in western countries, especially in modern times. (*See* Alcoholism.)

The intoxicating drinks consumed by ancients were wines obtained from grapes or other fruits and beers made from various kinds of grain. These products were not confined to the east, but were also known to the ancient civilizations of Mexico and Peru and to other peoples who used the sugar-containing juices and other substances indigenous to their countries. In the time of the Romans the people of northern Europe used fermented liquors made from honey (mead), barley (beer) and apples (cider) in place of grape wine. All such drinks produce intoxication if taken in sufficient quantity, but their action is much slower and less violent than that of distilled spirits. This difference is a result of the greater concentration of alcohol in distilled spirits, which leads to a more rapid absorption of the alcohol into the blood stream and to a higher concentration of alcohol in the blood.

Potable distilled spirits were apparently not known until the 13th century. The distilled essence of wine or aqua vitae (brandy) is mentioned then as a new discovery by Arnaldus de Villa Nova, a chemist and physician, who regarded it, from the chemical or medical point of view, as a divine product. It probably came into use gradually, but once the art of distillation (*q.v.*) had been mastered it extended to other alcoholic products in countries where wine was not produced. (*See* also Alcoholic Beverages, Distilled.)

The concentrated form of alcohol thus evolved long carried with it the prestige of a divine essence given to it in the middle ages. It had potent properties and was held to possess great virtue, a view embodied in the name "water of life," and at one time almost universally held. Ardent spirits seemed particularly desirable to the people of the cold and damp regions of northern Europe, where people took to it with avidity when it became cheap and easily accessible. That happened in England in the early part of the 18th century, and from the ensuing bad results there eventually arose the modern temperance movement. The legislature had been busy with the liquor traffic for more than two centuries previously, but its task had been the repression of disorder: drunkenness was a nuisance and had to be checked in the interests of public order. It is significant that though drunkenness had been prevalent from the earliest times, necessity for attempts at legislative control did not arise until after the introduction of distilled spirits.

Intemperance was one of many problems which arose during the latter half of the 18th century to become the subject matter of social reform in the 19th century. A breach had been made in the unthinking traditional belief in the virtue of alcoholic liquor, and medical thought, as soon as it began to be concerned with health as distinguished from the treatment of disease, took up the matter. In 1804 Thomas Trotter of Edinburgh, Scot., published a book on the subject, an expansion of his academic thesis written in 1788. Benjamin Rush of Philadelphia, who had studied in Edinburgh and London, wrote a striking paper on the subject in the same year; and soon after this the organized temperance movement got under way in the United States.

**Temperance and Prohibition Organizations.**—In 1808 a temperance society was founded at Saratoga, N.Y., and in 1813 the Massachusetts Society for the Suppression of Intemperance made its appearance. These seem to have been the earliest organizations, though the device of a pledge of abstinence had been introduced in 1800. The movement made rapid progress, mainly under the influence of the churches. In 1826 the American Society for the Promotion of Temperance was founded in Boston, Mass., and by 1833 there were 6,000 local societies in several states with more than 1,000,000 members. The campaign was directed primarily against the use of distilled spirits only, and the proposal to include all alcoholic drinks in the pledge of total abstinence, though adopted by a few societies, was rejected in 1833 by the American society, but accepted in 1836 and retained thereafter.

In Europe the earliest organizations were formed in Ireland. A temperance club is said to have been started at Skibbereen in 1818, and others followed; but it was in 1829 that the organized movement began to make effective progress with the formation of the Ulster Temperance society. By the end of that year there were 25 societies in Ireland and 2 or 3 in Scotland. In 1830 the movement spread to Yorkshire and Lancashire, and supported a newspaper called the *Temperance Societies' Record,* according to which there were then 127 societies with 23,000 paying members and 60,000 associated abstainers. In 1831 the British and Foreign Temperance society was founded in London with the bishop of London (Charles Blomfield) for president and Archbishop John Sumner for one of the vice-presidents. This important society, of which Queen Victoria became patron on her accession in 1837, came to an end in 1850, when the cause was under an eclipse.

The most remarkable episode in the temperance campaign at this period was the mission of the Rev. Theobald Mathew of Cork, commonly known as Father Mathew, greatest of all temperance missionaries. He traveled through Ireland in the years 1838–42 and everywhere excited intense enthusiasm. People flocked to hear him and took the pledge in crowds. In 1841 the number of abstainers in Ireland was estimated to be 4,647,000; in three years the consumption of spirits fell from 10,815,000 to 5,290,000 gal. This was not all due to Father Mathew, because great depression and distress prevailed at the same time, but he exercised an extraordinary influence. In 1843 he went to England, where he had less (though still great) success, and in 1849 to America. He died in 1856, by which time the cause had fallen into a depressed state in both countries. In the United States a flash of enthusiasm of a similar but smaller character, known as the Washingtonian movement, had appeared. In 1845 a law prohibiting the public sale of liquor was passed in New York state but repealed in 1847; in 1851 Maine adopted prohibition.

The Church of England Temperance society, much the largest at mid-20th century, was founded in 1862 and reconstituted in 1873. It was incorporated in 1907, reconstituted again in 1911 and 1921, and recognized by the church assembly in 1923. It carries on an extensive publication department and educational courses, police court and prison gate missions to seamen, traveling vans and inebriate homes.

The United Kingdom alliance, founded in 1853, became the chief political organization. Its object was prohibition of the drink trade, but it adopted the policy of local prohibition by means of local option. It began publication of the "national drink bill," a calculation of the national expenditure on alcoholic liquors. Other legislative organizations in Britain are the National Temperance league, the British Temperance league, the National United Temperance council, the National Temperance federation, the Temperance Legislation league and others in Scotland, Ireland and Wales. There is also a Royal Army Temperance association and a Royal Naval Temperance society. International societies enumerated are the World League Against Alcoholism, the World Prohibitive federation, the International Orders of Good Templars and the World's Woman's Christian Temperance union.

Thus temperance and total abstinence became the objects of the united efforts of education and legislation in many regions. This union was probably promoted in part by the fact that once a person has become an alcoholic recovery usually requires total abstinence. In later years the organized movement in many countries embraced both voluntary and compulsory abstinence and combined the inculcation of individual abstinence with the promotion of legislation for the reduction or suppression of the alcoholic liquor traffic. On the whole the latter predominated, particularly in the United States, where organized agitation made temperance or prohibition partly a political question and produced various experiments in legislation. (*See* PROHIBITION.) Besides combining the moral and the political elements the modern movements were characterized by the following features: (1) international organization; (2) organized co-operation of women; (3) juvenile temperance; (4) teaching of temperance in schools and elsewhere; (5) scientific study of alcohol and inebriety.

*International Organization.*—The first international temperance organization appears to have been the Order of Good Templars, formed in 1851 at Utica, N.Y. It spread over the United States and Canada, and in 1868 was introduced into Great Britain. Several years later it was extended to Scandinavia, where it became very strong. Temperance societies had previously existed in Norway from 1836 and in Sweden from 1837; these seem to be the earliest examples on the continent of Europe. The Good Templars organization also spread to several other European countries, to Australasia, India, south and west Africa and South America. Several other international societies were founded, and international congresses were held, the first in 1885 at Antwerp, Belg. A World's Prohibition conference was held in London in 1909, attended by about 300 delegates from temperance societies in nearly all parts of the world. This conference resulted in the foundation of an International Prohibition federation, embracing every country in Europe with three or four minor exceptions, the United States, Mexico, Argentina, much of the British commonwealth, China, Japan, Israel, Tunisia and Hawaii.

*Alcoholics Anonymous.*—This is an organization of alcoholics and recovered alcoholics who have become total abstainers. It is an international organization, started in the United States but gradually extended to other countries. Its primary object is to aid alcoholics to recover from their addiction.

*W.C.T.U.*—The organization of women, which has become international, dates from 1874, when the National Woman's Christian Temperance union was founded at Cleveland, O. It employs educational and social as well as political means in promoting legislation. About 1883 Frances Willard, who had been the moving spirit of the union, carried this organization of women into other lands and formed the World's Woman's Christian Temperance union, which by the 1960s had branches in about 50 countries.

*Juvenile Groups.*—The inclusion of children in temperance organization goes back to 1847, when a society of juvenile abstainers who had taken the pledge was formed at Leeds; it took the name of Band of Hope. The practice spread, and in 1851 a Band of Hope union was formed. Within the next century a number of such unions were established in Scotland, Ireland and separate counties in England; the Bands of Hope were said to number about 15,000 in all.

*School Programs.*—The teaching of temperance in schools, a feature of social education and moral propaganda, was begun by private effort in 1852 when John Hope inaugurated a regular weekly visitation of day schools in Edinburgh. In 1875, at the invitation of the National Temperance league, Sir Benjamin Richardson wrote his *Temperance Lesson Book,* which was adopted by many schools as a primer. In 1889 school teaching by traveling lecturers was taken up by the U.K. Band of Hope union, and the example was followed by many other societies which spent large sums on itinerant lecturers. The Church of England Temperance society carried on similar work. In 1906 the board of education in Ireland made hygiene and temperance a compulsory subject in the public schools; in 1909 the English board of education issued a syllabus of temperance teaching; in Scotland courses in hygiene and temperance were adopted by many local educational authorities.

The question of temperance teaching in the United States was first taken up by the Woman's Christian Temperance union in 1879; it was believed that by teaching the physiological effects of alcohol to all children the problem of intemperance would be effectually solved, and a systematic political campaign was planned and carried out for the purpose of obtaining compulsory legislation to give effect to this idea. The campaign was successful in New York in 1884, in Pennsylvania in 1885 and subsequently in other states. Laws were passed in every state making antialcohol teaching part of the curriculum in the public schools. Teaching of temperance became compulsory in Canada except in Quebec and Prince Edward Island; in France in 1902; in Sweden in 1892; and in Ireland. It became optional in Australia, South Africa, some parts of India, Belgium, Finland, Denmark, Norway, Germany and Switzerland. *See* also LOCAL OPTION; LIQUOR LAW.

(A. SL.; A. J. CN.)

**TEMPERATURE:** *see* CALORIMETRY; HEAT; INVERSION OF TEMPERATURE; METEOROLOGY; SEASONS; THERMOMETRY.

**TEMPERATURE, BODY:** *see* ANIMAL HEAT; FEVER.

**TEMPERING:** *see* HEAT-TREATMENT.

**TEMPLARS.** The Knights Templars or Poor Knights of Christ and of the Temple of Solomon was one of the three great orders of knighthood founded at the time of the Crusades (*see* KNIGHTHOOD, CHIVALRY AND ORDERS). It was founded during the early years of the Kingdom of Jerusalem (*see* CRUSADES), when the crusaders controlled only a few strongholds, and pilgrims to the Holy Places were often molested by marauding Muslim bands. Pitying the plight of such pilgrims, eight or nine knights, led by Hugues de Payns, a native of Champagne, vowed (late 1119 or early 1120) to devote themselves to their protection and to form a religious community for that purpose. They swore obedience to the patriarch of Jerusalem and took vows of poverty and chastity, adopting the rule of the Augustinian canons. Baldwin II, king of Jerusalem, gave them quarters in a wing of the royal palace, next to the al-Aqsa Mosque in the area of the former Jewish Temple; and from this circumstance they derived their name.

Their numbers increased rapidly; many knights who had gone on crusade or pilgrimage, even those with considerable territorial possessions, joined the order. Hugues de Payns, who returned to the West (1127) to gain recognition for the order, also collected recruits. At the Council of Troyes (1128) the rules and customs of the knights were carefully studied and were supplemented by further precepts, derived from the Benedictine rule and probably drawn up by St. Bernard of Clairvaux. The order had its early troubles, nevertheless. A letter from Hugues to his knights (discovered by Dom J. Leclercq, *see* bibliography) shows that when Hugues returned to Jerusalem, he found that many of them had difficulty in reconciling a religious vocation with the bearing of arms and were leaving or were tempted to leave in order to join more traditional orders. This probably explains why Hugues asked St. Bernard (whose uncle André de Montbard joined the order and afterward became grand master) to write a vindication of the order's aims. In his treatise *De laude novae militiae* (*c.* 1130–35) St. Bernard emphasized the importance of the Templars' mission, contrasting the pure and disciplined life of the "poor knights" with the dissolute behaviour of those who remained in the world. He called especially on those excommunicated for sins of violence and who had undertaken a pilgrimage to the Holy Places in order to obtain absolution, to ensure a real amendment in their lives by joining the order.

Hugues de Payns died in 1136. His successor as grand master, Robert de Craon, obtained from Pope Innocent II confirmation of the order's rule and customs and was granted certain important privileges. By Innocent's bull (*Omne datum optimum,* 1139) the Templars were exempted from paying tithes and were allowed to maintain their own chapels, served by priests of their own choice. The order was also exempted from the jurisdiction of any bishop in whose diocese it might have property. This privilege changed the whole character of the order; released from obedience to the patriarch of Jerusalem, it was able to diversify its activities and rapidly became much more than a confraternity of knights serving the Holy Sepulchre.

**The Rule and Customs of the Templars.**—The *regula pauperum commilitonum Christi* was drawn up in Latin at the time of the Council of Troyes and revised (*c.* 1130) by the patriarch of Jerusalem, Étienne de Chartres. The earliest extant version dates from *c.* 1131. A French version, expanded to include various provisions (the *retrais et establissemens*) made by successive general chapters of the order, was made *c.* 1188. When the Teutonic Knights were established as a military order in 1198, their rule was based on that of the Templars.

The Templars were divided into four classes: knights, sergeants, chaplains, and servants. Only the knights who were of noble birth wore the distinctive white surcoat adopted in 1130 and marked (after 1148) with a red cross. The order was controlled by the grand master, but he could make no important decisions without the assent of the general chapter. For the election of a grand master the chapter met in special session. It first chose 2 brothers; these 2 co-opted 2 others, the 4 another 2, and so on until a college of 12 had been formed. Of these, 8 were knights, and 4 sergeants. The 12 men chose one of the chaplains to act with them (he was supposed to represent Christ amidst his apostles), and these 13 elected a new grand master. Each house (Temple) of the order was ruled by a commander, who, like all the other brothers, owed obedience to the grand master. If the Templars owned more than one establishment in a particular country, the commanders there were subordinated to a grand commander (sometimes cálled the visitor or preceptor).

The fighting force consisted of the knights and the sergeants (the latter being of non-noble birth). All were bound to accept combat at odds of one against three. Their equipment, although sound and serviceable, was never to be rich, and the personal poverty to which each individual Templar was vowed was indicated by their seal, which portrayed two knights mounted upon one charger. Besides the knights who took perpetual vows, the Templars also received temporary members, whose vows covered only a specific period of time.

**History of the Templars in the Levant.**—Once free (1139) from obedience to the patriarch of Jerusalem, the Templars rapidly diversified their activities. They continued to escort pilgrims, but with the firm establishment of the Latin States routes in the Holy Land had become much safer. Meanwhile a steady flow of recruits meant that the Templars could put in the field an army of several hundred knights; they also acquired considerable wealth. Thus the Knights became a vital element in the defense of the Latin States, garrisoning every town of any size. They also sent contingents to fight for the king of Jerusalem or the ruler of any other of the Latin principalities in any war against the Muslims.

At first the Templars possessed no real fortresses of their own; the earliest they came to hold were probably in Spain, where they took part in the Reconquest. But from the mid-12th century they followed the Hospitallers (*see* SAINT JOHN OF JERUSALEM, ORDER OF THE HOSPITAL OF) in receiving grants of castles and territory in the Latin States. When, in 1150, King Baldwin III of Jerusalem refortified Gaza in order to blockade the Egyptians in Ascalon, he entrusted its defense to the Templars, who alone had sufficient knights adequately to garrison it. At about the same time they were also given custody of Safita (Chastel-Blanc) and Tortosa in the county of Tripoli, and Baghras and other fortresses in the principality of Antioch. In these castles and the lands depending on them, the Templars very soon became completely independent of the king or any other territorial ruler.

Furthermore, the order soon acquired such weight that the grand masters aspired to treat on equal terms with temporal sovereigns. At the siege of Ascalon (1153), when a breach had been made in the town walls, the grand master Bernard de Tremelay (who was subsequently killed in the action) presumed to restrict to the Templars the honour of fighting their way in. When King Amalric I sought to punish (*c.* 1173) a Templar, Walter de Mesnil, who had ambushed Assassin envoys traveling under the king's safe conduct, the grand master Eudes de Saint-Amand refused to hand Walter over. Amalric, who had to kidnap Walter in order to bring him to justice, decided to ask for the suppression of the order but died before he could do so. Gerard of Ridefort (grand master by 1186) engaged unashamedly in power politics in order to further a private vendetta. In vengeance against Count Raymond III of Tripoli, who before Gerard had joined the order had prevented his marriage with a rich heiress, Gerard, on the death (1186) of the child king Baldwin V, procured the coronation of Baldwin's mother Sibyl and of her husband the weak Guy of Lusignan, although the will of Baldwin IV (d. 1185) had left the regency to Raymond until such time as the pope and the Western rulers should settle the succession (*see* CRUSADES). A little later, when he and the grand master of the Hospitallers were leading an embassy to Raymond, Gerard urged his companions to attack a vastly greater Muslim force near Nazareth and was almost the sole Christian survivor from the disaster (May 1187). When Saladin invaded the Latin States (May 1187) and besieged a castle in the town of Tiberias, King Guy had to raise a large army to repel him; to help with this, Gerard gave Guy all the Templars' bullion. But it was on Gerard's insistence that Guy marched directly across the waterless hills in an attempt to relieve Tiberias. As a result the exhausted Frankish Army was destroyed (Battle of the Horns of Hattin, July 4). Of the captured Templars only Gerard escaped execution; released in 1188, he was killed (October 1189) during the siege of Acre.

Gerard's successor as grand master, Robert de Sablé, gave steady support both to King Guy and to the English king Richard I, from whom he bought the island of Cyprus. But the Templars' arrogant treatment of the Greek townsmen there soon provoked a revolt, which was put down severely (1191). Robert then returned Cyprus to King Richard, who transferred it to King Guy. The Templars, however, kept various strongholds on the island. As time went on, generous donations enabled them to increase the number of their castles in the Holy Land. In 1217 they built the great Chastel-Pèlerin, south of Acre; the fortress of Safed in Galilee, which they had held before 1187, was rebuilt in 1240. The Temple in Acre was almost a city in itself, one entire building (*la voûte,* the vault) being used as a storehouse. In the 13th century the importance of the order still further increased because, as the Latin States declined, so they came more and more to depend on the manpower and material resources that the Templars and Hospitallers could draw from the West.

From the moment when the emperor Frederick II arrived in the Holy Land (Sixth Crusade), the Templars displayed open hostility to him, and he retaliated by confiscating their possessions in Sicily. Some years later, when Richard, earl of Cornwall, visited the Holy Land (1240), he found the Templars on the verge of war with the Hospitallers; the former favoured an alliance of the Christians with the kings of Damascus, the latter one with the sultans of Egypt. Although contingents from both orders, each about 300 strong, fought side by side at Gaza (1244), where they were wiped out by an army of Khwarizmian Turks in Egyptian pay, relations between the two orders continued more than strained.

The Templars took part in all the 13th-century wars against the Muslims, notably in the Seventh Crusade (that of Louis IX), in which the grand master William of Sonnac was killed in the Battle of al Mansurah (1250). Their territorial possession continued to grow because impoverished lords sold them their seigniories and castles; in this way they acquired Sidon and Beaufort (1260). But soon some of their strongholds fell to Baybars, Mameluke sultan of Egypt. By the treason of a Syrian messenger, Baybars gained possession of their castle of Safed in 1266; all the brothers taken in the fortress refused to renounce their faith and were martyred. As a result of Baybars' capture of Antioch (1268), the Templars lost Baghras and all their other castles in the principality, and in 1271 Baybars took Safita (Chastel-Blanc) near Tripoli. Despite these disasters and dangers, the Templars continued to ferment discord among the Christian princes of the Levant; they quarreled (1277) with Bohemund VII of Tripoli; and the grand master William of Beaujeu supported the claims of Charles I, king of Naples and Sicily, to be king of Jerusalem instead of King Hugh III of Cyprus. As a result, Hugh destroyed their castle of La Castrie on Cyprus.

During the last months (1291) of the Latin States, when stronghold after stronghold fell to the sultan Qalawun, the Templars put up a magnificent resistance. William of Beaujeu was killed fighting in the streets of Acre, where the Temple held out for several days after the town had fallen to the Muslims. Its last defenders, along with many of the assailants, were killed when a wall was mined and collapsed (May 1291). The Temple at Sidon was abandoned in July, its defenders retreating to Tortosa; but this fortress in its turn was evacuated (early August), the Templars finally taking refuge in Cyprus, which appeared a good base for any possible future campaigns against the Muslim powers.

**History of the Templars in Western Europe.**—Although the Templars did their fighting in the Levant (and also, to some extent, in Spain), it was, nevertheless, from the West that they drew their riches and their recruits. Alfonso I (d. 1134), king of Aragon, bequeathed his kingdom to the Templars and the Hospitallers; the former were later able to cede their claim to Alfonso's successors in return for a number of castles and seigniories in Aragon. Other sovereigns, such as King Louis VII of France and King Stephen of England, gave lordships and estates to the order, as did innumerable less important men. On each of its estates the order quartered several of its members to see to the management and collect the revenues. Bullion was collected at various central houses, such as the Paris Temple, and was eventually escorted to the Levant by knights of the order and carried on ships owned by themselves. The existence of this chain of treasure houses, and of so efficient an organization for the transport of bullion, caused the Templars to be used as bankers. Many pilgrims to the Holy Land entrusted their estates to their care, and the Templars transmitted the revenues to the owners while they were in the Levant. The Templars' honesty was recognized by Muslims as well as by Christians, and important clients, including sovereigns, had recourse to their services. The kings of France, in particular, habitually borrowed from the Templars and used the Paris Temple as a safe deposit. In this way the order, with its vast resources spread throughout every country in Christendom, grew to wield great financial power.

**Suppression of the Templars.**—With the aim of coordinating all resources for the increasingly difficult task of defending the Holy Land against Muslim attack, and in order to end the scandalous quarrels between Templars and Hospitallers, the Council of Lyons (1274) proposed to merge the two orders into one. The scheme was, however, never carried out, although it formed part of various plans for later crusades and was taken up by King Philip IV of France, who, in 1308 when he had already launched his attack on the Templars, proposed to Pope Clement V that the two orders should be dissolved and their members transferred into a new order of Knights of Jerusalem, of which one of Philip's sons should be grand master.

King Philip was ostensibly on good terms with the Templars. Jacques de Molay (*q.v.*), the grand master, was godfather to one of the king's children, and Hugues de Pairaud, the order's visitor general in France, had supported Philip in his quarrel with Pope Boniface VIII. Although Philip had withdrawn his treasure from the custody of the Templars in 1295, he restored it to their keeping in 1303, and in 1304 he granted the order a general permission to hold in mortmain all the estates they had recently acquired. In 1306 he took refuge in the Paris Temple during a riot. Nevertheless, he was probably alarmed at the power of the order, and its riches were bound to excite the covetousness of a ruler chronically short of ready money, one, moreover, who had already almost bled white both the Jews and the Lombards in his realm.

Meanwhile, unfortunate rumours were circulating to the discredit of the Templars. A certain Esquiu de Floyran, from Beziers, was reputed to have revealed "the secrets of the Templars" to King James II of Aragon in 1304 or 1305. But James seems to have given little credence to Esquiu's revelations, and so Esquiu went to France, where he was better received. Philip suggested to the pope that he should investigate the matter, but he did not wait for papal action, introducing his own spies into the order to collect evidence. Clement V had already summoned the grand master from Cyprus to Avignon to discuss projects for a new crusade; he now mentioned to Molay the accusations made against the Templars, and Molay agreed (August 1307) that an enquiry should be held.

However, before any papal proceedings could be started, Philip's spies had denounced the Templars to the grand inquisitor of France, William of Paris. William, as was customary, asked the help of the secular arm in dealing with these alleged heretics, and as a result of secret messages sent to every royal bailiff and seneschal throughout the country, all the Templars in France, including the grand master, were arrested on the night of Oct. 13, 1307. They were imprisoned and their property sequestrated, nominally to be administered for the benefit of the Holy See but in fact for that of the king of France. The prisoners were interrogated by royal officials on the charges that had been made against them; under torture one after another confessed himself guilty. The main accusation concerned the ceremonies for the admission of knights to the order; it was alleged that candidates were required specifically to deny Christ and to spit upon a crucifix. Even Molay agreed that he had done this. Other accusations were of alleged sodomy in the order, and charges that the knights had made secret treaties with the Muslims.

The pope became worried at the turn the French enquiry was taking, especially because Philip was inviting other rulers to follow his example and to arrest and question the Templars in their realms. But unfortunately Clement, the first Avignonese pope, was in a very weak position vis-à-vis the French king; moreover, Philip could always hold over him the threat to revive the charge that Clement's predecessor, Boniface VIII, had been an intruder in the Holy See (*see* PHILIP IV). However, Clement tried to assume direction of the case; he suspended the authority of the grand inquisitor of France (Oct. 27, 1307), himself ordering the arrest of Templars in every country (Nov. 22). As a result, arrests were made in England on Jan. 10, 1308; in Sicily on Jan. 24; and in Cyprus on May 27. But in Spain the knights resisted arrest and had to be besieged in their strongholds; that of Monzon fell on May 17, but Castellat held out until Nov. 2, 1308.

Meanwhile the pope and the king of France had made a compromise agreement (May 1308), by which papal commissioners were to assume responsibility for the safe custody of the Templars and of their possessions. The enquiries were to be continued by diocesan bishops (July 1308), the pope reserving for himself the right to interrogate the grand master, the visitor general of France, and the grand preceptors of Normandy, Aquitaine, and Cyprus. It was agreed that the fate of the order should be settled at a council to be held at Vienne. In interviews with the new interrogators, most of the Templars now retracted their previous confessions, saying that they had made them only under duress; as a result, King Philip ordered these men to be burned as relapsed heretics, and by judgment of a provincial council held at Sens (May 1310), 54 died at the stake.

The Council of Vienne met in October 1311. In March 1312 Philip himself went to Vienne to put pressure on the pope. As a result, the order was finally suppressed (March 22, 1312) by a decision taken not openly in the council but in the papal consistory. A papal bull dated May 2, 1312, decreed that all its property should be transferred to the Hospitallers. This decision was not, however, carried out in Spain or in Portugal, where the property was divided among other knightly orders, which by maintaining the Templars' tradition virtually ensured the order's continuation, although under other names.

The dignitaries and other members of the order had all this while remained in prison. Molay, who had retracted his original statements, became fearful after the burning of the 54 at Sens and again pleaded guilty to the various charges. Despite two appeals (November 1309 and March 1310), he never managed to be heard by the pope in person and was eventually, with the other dignitaries of the order, condemned to perpetual imprisonment by a commission of three cardinals (March 18 or 19, 1314). On hearing the sentence, Molay and others again retracted, proclaiming their innocence before a vast crowd of people. They were burned as relapsed heretics by Philip's officers that same afternoon. In other countries the fate of individual knights varied with the disposition of the rulers toward the order. All in Aragon declared themselves innocent of the charges and were officially cleared by the national council. In Portugal the knights formed a new order. In England and in Castile some confessed themselves guilty and were condemned to perpetual imprisonment (there were no executions). But in Cyprus, where the order had given support to the usurper Amalric of Tyre, King Henry II treated the knights with great cruelty, and most of them died in prison in the castle of Kyrenia.

The question of whether or not the Templars were really guilty has been, from the time of the Reformation, a matter of passionate dispute among historians. Some, following Joseph von Hammer-Purgstall (*Mysterium Baphometis revelatum,* 1818), have maintained that the order, or at any rate some of its members, held gnostic beliefs, and they attributed to the Templars the use of mysterious symbols, including the representation of Baphomet, a gnostic idol. Others have suggested that side by side with the official rule there existed in the order a secret one, and a secret ritual practised only by some initiates. The Templars have also been put forward as the true ancestors of various sects or groups, notably the Freemasons, in which rites of initiation are important; and an "Order of the Temple" that existed in England and in Germany in the 18th century specifically claimed derivation from the knights. The theory that the knights had a secret rule has not won much support, however, and the suggestion of Hans Prutz (*Entwicklung und Untergang des Tempelherrenordens,* 1888) that the obligation to deny Christ and spit on the crucifix was sometimes imposed to test the absolute obedience of the knights to their superiors is also much disputed. In fact, most historians adjudge the Templars to have been innocent of the charges made against them.

*See* also references under "Templars" in the Index.

BIBLIOGRAPHY.—For the considerable literature on the Templars, *see* M. Dessubré, *Bibliographie de l'ordre des Templiers* (1928). An account of the origin of the order is given by the chronicler William of Tyre, *Historia rerum in partibus transmarinis gestarum,* book xii, ch. 7; *see* also J. Leclercq, "Un document sur les débuts des Templiers," *Revue d'histoire ecclésiastique,* vol. lii, no. 1 (1957); G. de Valous, "Quelques observations sur la toute primitive observance des Templiers et la regula pauperum commilitonum Christi," and P. Cousin, "Les débuts de l'ordre des Templiers et saint Bernard," in *Mélanges Saint Bernard* (1954). On the Templars' rule *see* G. Schnürer, *Die ursprüngliche Templerregel* (1903); E. H. Parent de Curzon, *La règle du Temple* (1886); C. H. Maillard de Chambure, *Règle et statuts secrets des Templiers* (1840). On the Templars' properties *see* the marquis d'Albon, *Cartulaire général de l'Ordre du Temple, 1119?–1150,* 2 vol. (1913–22) and the other documents as manuscripts no. 1–71 of the New Latin Acquisitions of the Bibliothèque Nationale, Paris. *See* also J. Michelet, *Procès des Templiers,* 2 vol. (1841–51); G. Lizerand, *Le dossier de l'affaire des Templiers* (1923); H. Finke, *Papsttum und Untergang des Templerordens,* 2 vol. (1907); G. G. Addison, *The History of the Knights Templars, the Temple Church, and the Temple* (1842; 3rd ed., 1852); M. Merville, *La vie des Templiers* (1951).

(J. B. R.)

**TEMPLE, FREDERICK** (1821–1902), archbishop of Canterbury and educational reformer, was born on Nov. 30, 1821, in Leukas, one of the Ionian islands off Greece, where his father was resident for the British lord high commissioner. The family moved to Corfu in 1828 and returned to England in 1830. Educated first by his mother, Temple went to Blundell's School, Devonshire, in the year his father died, leaving the family impoverished (1834). In 1839 he won a closed scholarship to Balliol College, Oxford, where he took a double first in mathematics and classics (1842). Although impressed with the teaching of the Oxford Movement, he came to prefer the liberal churchmanship of his friends A. P. Stanley and Benjamin Jowett. Appointed lecturer and subsequently fellow of Balliol, Temple was ordained priest in 1847 but left Oxford in 1848 for the Education Office. From 1850 to 1855 he was principal of Kneller Hall, a training college for workhouse schoolteachers, and from 1855 to 1857 an inspector of education.

In 1857 he was appointed headmaster of Rugby, having been recommended by Matthew Arnold as a man closely resembling his father, Thomas Arnold, the reformer of Rugby, in both capacity and ideals. Temple's headmastership justified Arnold's claim. He widened the curriculum, notably in the teaching of history, music, and science; he erected new buildings; above all, he commanded an exceptional influence for good over both boys and staff through his sermons and the example of his strong and invigorating personality. He achieved fame as an educational reformer in his work for the Schools Enquiry Commission of 1864–67 (*see* EDUCATION, HISTORY OF). He also won undeserved notoriety for his contribution ("The Education of the World") to *Essays and Reviews* (1860), a controversial volume censured by convocation in 1864 for its advanced views on religious matters. Consequently, the announcement of his appointment as bishop of Exeter in 1869 provoked much protest and some opposition. Temple acted with dignity and restraint and only after his consecration agreed to withdraw his essay from future editions of the volume.

His episcopate was marked by indefatigable energy in his encouragement of secondary education, splitting of the diocese to create the new see of Truro, and promotion of the cause of temperance. In 1885 he was appointed bishop of London, where he played a leading role in convocation and became the chief adviser of his close friend E. W. Benson, archbishop of Canterbury. When Benson died in 1896, Temple succeeded him, despite growing blindness and advanced age. Together with W. Maclagan, archbishop of York, he issued an official reply to Pope Leo XIII's bull that denied the validity of Anglican orders. He worked for unity within the Church of England and always tried to achieve a peaceful settlement of ritualistic controversies. In 1899 both archbishops pronounced that processional lights and the liturgical use of incense were illegal. Temple died on Dec. 23, 1902, in London.

Temple's rugged appearance, harsh voice, and terse manner sometimes repelled those whose acquaintance with him was slight. He lived simply, spoke plainly, and acted honourably. He personified exactly the Victorian concept of manliness. His younger son, William Temple (*q.v.*), also became archbishop of Canterbury.

*See* E. G. Sandford (ed.), *Memoir of Archbishop Temple,* 2 vol. (1906); F. D. How, *Six Great Schoolmasters* (1904). (D. H. N.)

**TEMPLE, RICHARD GRENVILLE-TEMPLE,** 1ST EARL (1711–1779), English statesman, the brother-in-law of William Pitt, was born in London on Sept. 26, 1711, the eldest son of Richard Grenville (d. 1727) of Wotton, Buckinghamshire. His mother was Hester (*c.* 1690–1752), daughter, and ultimately heiress, of Sir Richard Temple, Bart. (1634–97), of Stowe, Buckinghamshire, and sister of Richard Temple, Viscount Cobham, whose title she inherited in 1749; in the same year, her husband having been long dead, she was created Countess Temple. Her son, Richard Grenville, was educated at Eton. He was member of Parliament for Buckingham Borough (1734–41 and 1747–52) and for Buckinghamshire (1741–47). In 1752 he inherited his mother's titles together with the estates of Stowe and Wotton and took the name of Temple in addition to his own surname of Grenville. From the time of the marriage in 1754 of his sister Hester with William Pitt, afterward earl of Chatham, Temple's career was linked with that of his new brother-in-law.

In November 1756 Temple became first lord of the admiralty in the ministry of the duke of Devonshire and Pitt. He was disliked by George II, who dismissed both him and Pitt from office in April 1757. But when the coalition Cabinet of the duke of Newcastle and Pitt was formed in June of the same year, Temple received the office of keeper of the privy seal. He alone in the Cabinet supported Pitt's proposal to declare war with Spain in 1761, and they resigned together in October. From this time Temple became one of the most violent and factious of politicians, and it is difficult to account for the influence that he exerted over his brother-in-law. He was at variance with his younger brother, George Grenville, when the latter became first lord of the treasury in April 1763, and he had no place in that ministry; but the brothers were reconciled before June 1765, when Temple refused to join his brother's government and persuaded Pitt to refuse likewise.

By 1765, however, the old friendship between the brothers-in-law was dissolving; and when at last in June 1766 Pitt consented to form a government, Temple refused to join, being bitterly offended because, although offered the head of the Treasury, he was not to be allowed an equal share with Pitt in nominating to other offices. Temple then began to inspire the most virulent libels against Pitt; and with his brother George he concentrated the whole Grenville connection against the government. After George Grenville's death in 1770 Temple retired almost completely from public life. He died at Stowe, on Sept. 12, 1779.

Bibliography.—*The Grenville Papers,* ed. with notes by W. J. Smith, 4 vol. (1852–53), a considerable portion of which consists of Earl Temple's correspondence; H. Walpole, *Memoirs of the Reign of King George the Second,* ed. by Lord Holland, 3 vol. (1846), *Memoirs of the Reign of King George the Third,* ed. by G. F. R. Barker, 4 vol. (1894); Sir L. Namier, *The Structure of Politics at the Accession of George III,* 2nd ed. (1957), *England in the Age of the American Revolution* (1930); J. Brooke, *The Chatham Administration, 1766–1768* (1956). (A. Al.)

**TEMPLE, SIR WILLIAM,** Bart. (1628–1699), English statesman, diplomat, and writer whose thought and prose style had a considerable influence on many 18th-century writers, including Jonathan Swift. He was born on April 25, 1628, at Blackfriars, London, the eldest son of Sir John Temple, later master of the rolls in Ireland. Educated at Emmanuel College, Cambridge, he traveled abroad from 1648 to 1652, visiting France, Germany, and the Netherlands. While passing through the Isle of Wight he met Dorothy Osborne (*q.v.*), with whom he was to conduct a long and famous correspondence, and whom he married on Christmas Day, 1654. For the next eight years Temple resided mainly in Ireland, becoming member for Carlow Borough in the Irish Convention (1660) and for Carlow County in the Parliament elected in 1661. After the prorogation of the Irish Parliament in May 1663, however, he moved to England, settled at Sheen, near Richmond, Surrey, and, attaching himself to Henry Bennett (later earl of Arlington), the secretary of state, embarked on a diplomatic career. In 1665 he was appointed minister resident to the Spanish court at Brussels, and in January 1666 he was created a baronet.

The outbreak of the War of Devolution (1667–68) and the French invasion of the Spanish Netherlands confronted him with the twin problems of ending the existing conflict between England and the Dutch Republic and checking French aggression in an area where English interests were vitally concerned. The first problem was solved by the Treaty of Breda of July 1667, in the negotiation of which he took little part; the second by the Triple Alliance of January 1668, between England, the United Provinces, and Sweden, recognized as his most brilliant achievement. Unfortunately, Charles II and Arlington remained faithful to the policy of the Triple Alliance for little more than a year, concluding in May 1670 the secret Treaty of Dover, by which England became pledged to wage war on the United Provinces in alliance with France. Thus, Temple received no more substantial reward than appointment (July 1668) as ambassador at The Hague, where he made the acquaintance of the young prince of Orange, afterward King William III; and on his return to England in September 1670 he met with a cold welcome and practical relegation to obscurity.

With the failure of the Anglo-French attack on the Dutch (1672–74), however, he came again into favour, the more so as the minister upon whom Charles II was beginning to rely, Sir Thomas Osborne, earl of Danby, was a cousin of Temple's wife and an old acquaintance. After negotiating the Treaty of Westminster with the Dutch in February 1674, Temple was made ambassador at The Hague in May 1674, dispatched to the peace conference at Nijmegen in July 1676, allowed to cooperate with Danby in bringing about the marriage of William of Orange and Princess Mary in November 1677, sent back to The Hague to arrange a fresh treaty with the Dutch in July 1678, and required to pay a last visit to Nijmegen, where a general peace was signed at the beginning of 1679. Danby wanted to make him secretary of state, but repeated pressure from king and minister failed to induce him to accept. In February 1679, in the midst of the panic produced by the revelations of Titus Oates (*q.v.*), Temple was summoned home but again refused office.

It was thus, rather strangely, only after Danby's fall (April) that Temple agreed to play any part in the domestic affairs of his own country. On April 21, 1679, the Privy Council was remodeled; its numbers, exclusive of certain supernumeraries, were reduced to 30, of whom half were to be great officials and half noblemen or gentlemen of wealth and distinction without office. Temple was allowed to claim the credit of having suggested the change and accepted membership in the new body. For a time, indeed, he shared with the marquis of Halifax, the earl of Sunderland, and the earl of Essex considerable influence within it and, to strengthen his position, secured return as member for Cambridge University to the Parliament of 1680–81. By 1680, however, Temple found that the new council was little more than a screen behind which the king was pursuing a policy of which he could not approve; thereafter his attendance became irregular. On Jan. 24, 1681, he was struck off the council and went into permanent retirement. In 1686 Temple bought a small estate, which he named Moor Park, near Farnham in Surrey. His last years were clouded by failing health and personal sorrow. His only surviving child, John, was appointed secretary at war by William III in 1689, but within a week he made the costly mistake of advising the king to trust a man who proved a traitor, and committed suicide through remorse. In 1695 Lady Temple died. Temple died at Moor Park on Jan. 27, 1699.

Jonathan Swift, who joined his household as a kind of secretary in 1689 and (with a break from 1694 to 1696) continued to live at Moor Park as Temple's assistant and protégé until his patron's death, observed: "he was a person of the greatest wisdom, justice, liberality, politeness, eloquence, of his age and nation; the truest lover of his country, and one that deserved more from it by his eminent public services, than any man before or since: besides his great deserving of the commonwealth of learning; having been universally esteemed the most accomplished writer of his age." In his edition of Temple's *Letters* (1700) Swift wrote, "this author has advanced our tongue to as great a perfection as it can bear," and Dr. Johnson praised Temple as "the first writer who gave cadence to English prose." Temple's works enjoyed a considerable popularity in the 18th century, and eight editions of his collected works appeared between 1720 and 1770. His influence on Swift, who copied out most of his patron's writings during his decade of service, is difficult to calculate but was almost certainly considerable. The easy, graceful, lucid conversational style, particularly of the later essays, formed an admirable model for Swift, and much of Temple's political and philosophical thinking can be traced in Swift's works.

Of Temple's earlier and more seriously formal works, the most notable are the *Essay on the Origin and Nature of Government* (*c.* 1672, published 1680 in *Miscellanea I*), which anticipates many modern views of society and politics; the *Observations upon the United Provinces* (1673), for which he has been hailed as a pioneer in the sympathetic interpretation of one people to another; and the perceptive essay *Of Popular Discontents* (written 1684–85, published 1701 in *Miscellanea III*).

The majority of his most celebrated essays, however, were written at Moor Park and were collected by Swift and himself in *Miscellanea, the Second Part* (1690) and the posthumous *Third Part* (1701). These later essays display most of Temple's essential characteristics: his charm and tolerant humanity, his interest in other people and places, his mixture of skepticism and freethinking with conventional Christianity, and his high-minded neo-Epicureanism. In *Miscellanea II*, the essay *Upon the Gardens of Epicurus; or, Of Gardening, in the Year 1685* is typical in its informal movement from philosophical discussion and a learned survey of the history of gardens to practical advice on figs and apricots, and a disquisition on Chinese ideas of beauty. Another in that collection, *Of Poetry*, reveals Temple's grasp of literary history and, in its willingness to explore such unfamiliar areas as Scandinavian literature, is unusually suggestive; it has been rightly called one of the most pleasant, original, and "modern" pieces of 17th-century literary criticism. In the *Essay upon the Ancient and Modern Learning* (also in *Miscellanea II*), however, Temple, in his desire to attack what he somewhat ignorantly regarded as the presumptions of the modern scientific movement, allied himself too wholeheartedly with the "ancients" and precipitated the controversy known as the Battle of the Books, wherein he was vigorously defended by Swift against the attacks of William Wotton and Richard Bentley (*q.v.*; *see* also ANCIENS ET DES MODERNES, QUERELLE DES). His praise of "old wood to burn, old wine to drink, old friends to converse with, and old books to read" is felicitously phrased, but the essay as a whole is intellectually obtuse and does less than justice to the modernity of Temple's mind. Finer and more characteristic are the long essay *Of Heroic Virtue* (in *Miscellanea II*), which, better than anywhere else, shows Temple's view of history, and the delightful *Of Health and Long Life* (in *Miscellanea III*).

BIBLIOGRAPHY.—*Editions: The Early Essays and Romances of Sir William Temple* (1930; includes *The Life and Character of . . . Temple* by his sister Lady Giffard, first published in abbreviated form in 1728), ed. by G. C. Moore Smith; *Essays on Ancient and Modern Learning and on Poetry* (1909), ed. by J. E. Spingarn; *Essays of Sir William Temple* (1911), ed. by J. A. Nicklin; *Five Miscellaneous Essays by Sir William Temple* (1963), ed. with an introduction by S. H. Monk.

*Life:* T. P. Courtenay, *Memoirs of the Life, Works and Correspondence of Sir William Temple*, 2 vol. (1836); C. Marburg, *Sir William Temple* (1929), H. E. Woodbridge, *Sir William Temple, the Man and His Work* (1940); R. F. Jones, *Ancients and Moderns*, 2nd ed. rev. (1961). (A. BG.; R. P. C. M.)

**TEMPLE, WILLIAM** (1881–1944), archbishop of Canterbury, whose intellectual equipment and range of contemporary interests, coupled with goodness and gaiety of spirit, made him the most influential English ecclesiastic since J. H. Newman. Born at Exeter, Devonshire, on Oct. 15, 1881, the second son of Frederick Temple (*q.v.*), he was educated at Rugby and Balliol College, Oxford, where he was a president of the Oxford Union. From 1904 to 1910 he was fellow and lecturer in philosophy at the Queen's College, Oxford, being ordained in 1909.

After being headmaster of Repton School (1910–14) and rector of St. James's, Piccadilly, London (1914–17), Temple became the leader of the Life and Liberty Movement (*see* ENGLAND, CHURCH OF: *20th-Century History and Development: Constitutional Changes*). Thereafter he was successively a canon of Westminster (1919–21), bishop of Manchester (1921–29), archbishop of York (1929–42), and archbishop of Canterbury (1942–44). He helped start and then became editor of the *Challenge* (1915–18) and edited a new religious quarterly, the *Pilgrim* (1920–27). He died at Westgate-on-Sea, Kent, on Oct. 26, 1944.

Temple's literary output was varied and continuous throughout his life. His unusual powers of concentration enabled him, for example, to write parts of his Gifford Lectures, *Nature, Man and God* (1934), at odd moments as he went about his diocese and to finish his largest philosophical work, *Mens creatrix* (1917), the night before his marriage. His other works include *Christian Faith and Life* (1931, mission addresses at Oxford University); *Readings in St. John's Gospel*, 2 vol. (1939–40); and *Christianity and Social Order* (1942). His last book to be published, *The Church Looks Forward* (1944), illustrates the range and quality of his speaking. He had a retentive memory and a capacity to think while he spoke; he produced terse, well-shaped, closely reasoned speeches, often without a note, not emotional in their matter or manner, yet persuasive by their sincerity and the clarity of their intellectual argument.

He cared for people. He wrote an amazing number of letters in his own hand to persons seeking his guidance and was generous to the fault of allowing many to impose on him too easily and of accepting them often at their own valuation. In conference and committee, by his unruffled temper and humour he could resolve personal tensions, and he had a flair for finding forms of words and for reshaping policies on which general agreement could be achieved.

Though he never professed to be an administrator, he embodied and set in motion a fruitful policy of development within the Church of England, in its relations with other churches, and in the relations of church and society. He was chairman of the Commission on Doctrine in the Church from 1925 to 1938.

He was an Anglican delegate to the ecumenical conference on Faith and Order at Lausanne (1927) and chairman of the Edinburgh Conference (1937), and he was the leading influence and guiding mind in the initiatives that led to the formation of the British Council of Churches and the World Council of Churches (*see* ECUMENICAL MOVEMENT).

His human sympathies and sense of social justice made him quick to join with others in the application of Christian principles to social ethics. In this field his influence on thought and practice was conspicuous, and he had the courage of his convictions. For some time he was a member of the Labour Party (1918–25), and he always had a strong sympathy with the Labour movement. From 1908 to 1924 he was president of the Workers' Educational Association. He was chairman of a carefully planned international and interdenominational Conference on Christian Politics, Economics and Citizenship (1924). His influence inside and outside Parliament brought the various churches of the country to support the Education Act of 1944. (L. S. HU.)

**His Thought.**—For many years Temple believed that the best account of Jesus would be given not in terms of traditional metaphysical concepts, such as substance, but by matching a Christ, whose glory was revealed in a Johannine vision, with the insights and concepts associated with absolute idealism. This meant inevitably a certain unease in Temple's treatment of creation and of evil and sin, but it made possible a cosmic perspective for the Christian faith.

It was from such a perspective that Temple's social theories developed. Within this Hegelian idealism there were links between the communities of church and state, and the establishment enabled the church to follow its high calling to permeate society. Further, as Christian principles fulfilled natural law, there could be authoritative Christian pronouncements on social problems and economic policies.

Of major importance was Temple's view of revelation, which in some ways links him with Albrecht Ritschl and liberal theologians. On this view, while every occurrence is in its own degree a revelation of God, a special revelation is given only in a person. Christian revelation has thus to be understood as a personal encountering rather than as the deliverance of revealed truths.

Reference is often made to a change discernible in Temple's later thought, but its significance can be exaggerated. As his preface to the report on *Doctrine in the Church of England* (1938) shows, he had for some time been moving away from a vision of the glory of Christ and an incarnational theology based on an idealist metaphysics. What came to Temple with a decisive impact in the catastrophe of World War II was a dominant sense of Christ as redeemer, and without denying the importance of a Christocentric metaphysics he had now a greater conviction of its difficulties and limitations. But central to Temple's thought from first to last was "the fact of Christ" and the eventual possibility of some Christian map of life. (I. T. R.)

*See* F. A. Iremonger, *William Temple* (1948).

**TEMPLE, JEWISH,** the national shrine of ancient Jewry, on Mt. Zion in Jerusalem, believed to be located on the spot where Abraham built the altar for the sacrifice of Isaac (Gen. 22; *see* MORIAH). The Temple was the place of sacrificial worship, the seat of the Great Sanhedrin, and the centre for festival pilgrimages; only the ritually pure could enter. Its predecessor was the tabernacle (*q.v.*). In existence, with one interruption, from the mid-10th century B.C. to A.D. 70, the Temple had two phases: Solomon's Temple and the Second Temple (including that rebuilt by Herod).

The entire religious and political history of Judaism is tied in with the Temple. In the Bible it is represented as the dwelling place of the Divine Presence (Shekinah; *q.v.*). Prophets saw their visions there. Prayers were directed to it, even from a distance. In the period of the Second Commonwealth, nearly all the central institutions of Judaism were concentrated in the Temple. Josephus and Philo saw a cosmic symbolism in it: the Temple hill was the centre of the world. Much of the Talmud deals with its ritual; a "sanctuary that is above" was believed to correspond to the "sanctuary that is below" (*Zebahim* 62a). In the biblical era the Temple was called the House of Yahweh, or the Place. In the postbiblical period it was known simply as the House (*Bayit*) or the Chosen House (*Bet ha-Behira*).

The original Temple, as related in II Samuel and I Chronicles, was conceived by David, who selected Jerusalem as the capital city of the united kingdom of Israel and Judah and brought the ark there (*see* DAVID). It was erected by his son and successor Solomon (reigned *c.* 974–*c.* 934 B.C.). Solomon's Temple was destroyed by the Babylonians under Nebuchadrezzar in 586 B.C. (or, according to some scholars, 587 or 588), and the Jews were deported to Babylonia. In 537, with the authorization of Cyrus, conqueror of Babylonia, the Jews started to return to their home. Urged on by Haggai and Zechariah, they began the reconstruction of the Temple *c.* 520 B.C. under Darius, and the Second Temple was consecrated in 516 (*see* also HAGGAI, BOOK OF). The Second Temple was rebuilt by Herod the Great in 20 B.C., though this structure was never quite finished and work on it continued till A.D. 70, when it was destroyed by the Romans. Thereafter the sacrificial rites were discontinued, and the synagogues, houses of prayer and study, took the place of the Temple. Not until the modern period did the Jewish people cease to hope for the restoration of the Holy Temple and for the return of the Divine Presence to it. In the Orthodox prayer book this hope for the restoration of the Temple and of the sacrifices is still affirmed; Reform and Conservative prayer books do not express hope for the restoration of the sacrifices. (X.)

**Temple of Solomon.**—Although Solomon's Temple is perhaps the most famous shrine in world history, it is impossible to describe it accurately. The descriptions in I Kings 6, II Chron. 3, and Ezek. 41 are not sufficiently clear, and, moreover, they make use of obscure technical terms that cannot always be translated correctly. While archaeological discoveries have resolved some of the difficulties and provided important collateral information, the fact remains that no building quite like the Temple has ever been excavated. Through arrangements with King Hiram of Tyre, Solomon secured Phoenician (called Sidonian) architects, craftsmen, and materials; thus the Temple must have represented Phoenician architecture. No Phoenician temples of the 10th century have been found, but a small temple unearthed at Tall Tainat in Syria and dated at 1000 B.C. follows the plan of Solomon's Temple: a vestibule, a hall, a holy of holies, all of the same width and arranged in one long rectangular structure.

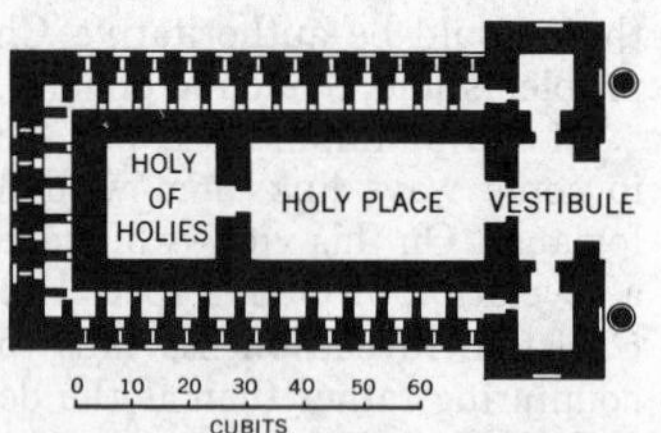


FROM VINCENT AND STEVE, "JERUSALEM DE L'ANCIEN TESTAMENT"

FIG. 1.—GROUND PLAN OF SOLOMON'S TEMPLE BASED ON RECONSTRUCTION BY L. H. VINCENT AND A. M. STEVE

The courtyard before the Temple contained the altar and the "sea." Animal sacrifices were offered to God on the altar, which measured 30 ft. (9 m.) square and was 15 ft. high (II Chron. 4:1). (Measurements given here are converted from the biblical "cubit," a unit of measure equal to a little more than ½ yd., or, more nearly, ½ m.). The "sea" was a bronze basin 15 ft. in diameter and 7½ ft. high (I Kings 7:23–26), used by the priests for their ritual ablutions (II Chron. 4:6). The Temple building proper was embellished by two free-standing bronze columns 18 ft. in circumference and 27 ft. high; their height was enhanced by large capitals (I Kings 7:15–22). Roland de Vaux points out that Phoenician temples provide analogies for these columns, and he refers also to the two pillars of Heliopolis mentioned by Lucian in his *de Dea Syra* (28), Herodotus' comment on the two steles of Hercules' temple at Tyre, and the two pillars found on a relief from the neighbourhood of Tyre (*Ancient Israel*, p. 314; McGraw-Hill Book Company, 1961).

One entered a vestibule (*ulam*) before coming into the main hall (Holy Place, *Hekal*), which was 60 ft. long. Beyond, at the far end of the structure, was the Holy of Holies (*Debir*), a 30-ft. cubical chamber in which the Shekinah was thought to dwell and where the high priest performed the service on the Day of Atonement. Of the furnishings of the Temple, mention should be made of the ark (*q.v.*) of the covenant; the mercy seat (*q.v.*), above the ark, overshadowed by the wings of two golden cherubim (*see* ANGEL); the menorah, a seven-branched candelabrum; the Urim and Thummim (*q.v.*); the table on which shewbreads were placed (*see* SHEWBREAD); and the small altar for the burning of incense.

Solomon's empire became so wealthy through conquest and trade that the king was impelled to embark on a spectacular building program, especially in the capital. The Temple, which took seven years to complete (I Kings 6:38), seems to have been subordinated to the palace, which required 13 years (7:1); thus the Temple may have been conceived as the king's sanctuary. It is worth noting that Jeroboam, when he rebelled successfully against King Rehoboam, established two competing temples, his own "king's sanctuary" at Bethel and another at Dan (I Kings 12:25–33). Attempts at reconstructing models of Solomon's Temple continue to be made. (C. H. Go.)

**Second Temple.**—The Second Temple was built during the reign of Zerubbabel and with the encouragement of Darius (Ezra 5:2; 6:13 ff.). The description of the Temple in Ezek. 40 ff. is assumed to be not merely a vision of the future but based on exact measurements for rebuilding. Architecturally, it resembled Solomon's Temple, but it did not contain the ark of the covenant, the Urim and Thummim, or the cherubim, since these had disappeared; and, according to Haggai (2:3), it was "as nothing" in comparison with the splendour of Solomon's Temple. Its prestige, however, was exceptional; the Book of Tobit relates how Jews in the Diaspora appeared zealously for the annual festivals. The Temple service is partially described in Sirach (Ecclesiasticus), and the Letter of Aristeas pictures its environs. The important sections of the Temple were the *Azaroth:* Court of Women, Court of Men, Court of Priests, and Holy of Holies. The service was most complicated and necessitated special instruction for the priesthood.

In 168 B.C. the hellenizing king of Syria Antiochus IV Epiphanes desecrated the Temple by sacrificing to Zeus there, touching off the Hasmonaean revolt. Three years later the Temple was cleansed and rededicated by Judas Maccabaeus in Kislev (December) 165, an event celebrated annually at Hanukkah (*see* MACCABEES). In 63 B.C. Pompey entered the Temple, and in 54 Crassus plundered its treasury.

Beginning in 20 B.C., Herod the Great, an enthusiastic builder, enlarged the site and rebuilt the Temple in grandeur. A golden eagle set over its gate, signifying Roman dominion, infuriated some of the Zealots, and several young scholars who dared to shatter this symbol of Roman power were executed at the command of Herod (Josephus, *Antiquities of the Jews*, xvii, 149). Jesus, according to the Gospels (*e.g.*, Matt. 21:12), drove the money changers from the stalls in the outer courtyard; their function was to exchange the many different coins of the pilgrims into Palestinian currency for purchase of the sacrificial animals. Jesus foresaw the destruction of the Temple (Matt. 24:1–2), as, according to the Talmud, also did Rabban Johanan ben Zakkai (*Yoma* 39b). The disaster of A.D. 70 is commemorated annually in the fast of the 9th of Ab.

The Jews hoped to rebuild the Temple in A.D. 130 when Hadrian ordered the rebuilding of Jerusalem, but they were thwarted. This may have led to the Bar-Cochba revolt.

Descriptions of the environs, services, and destruction of the Temple are recorded in Josephus (especially *Antiquities*, xv, 11; *Jewish War*, v, 5; and *Against Apion*, i, 22) and the Talmud (tractates *Middoth*, *Shekalim*, and *Yoma*); also in Tacitus and the Apocrypha (books of Tobit, Judith, Baruch, Maccabees, and Ecclesiasticus). Some of its sacred vessels are portrayed on the Arch

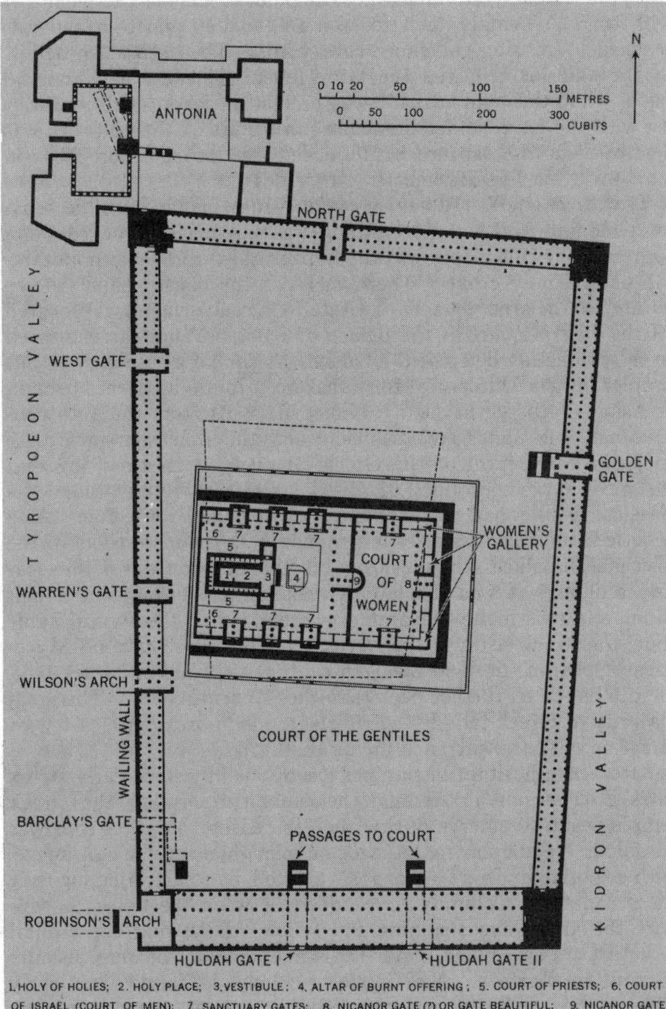


FROM VINCENT AND STEVE, "JERUSALEM DE L'ANCIEN TESTAMENT"

**FIG. 2.—GROUND PLAN OF HEROD'S TEMPLE AND OUTER COURTS BASED ON RECONSTRUCTION OF L. H. VINCENT AND A. M. STEVE**

The Antonia was a fortress, earlier called Baris, renamed in honour of Mark Antony in Herodian times; probably the "barracks" or "castle" referred to in Acts 21–23. Warren's Gate, Wilson's Arch, Barclay's Gate, and Robinson's Arch are existing structures, in varying states of preservation, named for the persons who first observed them. The Huldah Gates are mentioned by this name (that of a prophetess who used to preach there) in the Talmud

of Titus, in Rome. The wall surrounding the Temple grounds was 1,550 m. (5,085 ft.) long; a small portion of it, known as the Wailing Wall (*q.v.*), was long the last shrine of world Jewry, the one remnant and reminder of ancient grandeur.

The site of the Temple today is occupied by the Muslim shrine the Dome of the Rock (Qubbat al-Sakhra), erected by the caliph 'Abd al-Malik in A.D. 688–691. (S. B. Ho.)

Bibliography.—G. Ernest Wright, *Biblical Archaeology*, pp. 136–145 (1957); Cyrus H. Gordon, *The World of the Old Testament*, pp. 181–189 (1958); F. J. Hollis, *The Archaeology of Herod's Temple* (1934); K. Möhlenbrink, *Der Tempel Salomos* (1932); W. F. Albright, *Archaeology and the Religion of Israel* (1942); W. Novack, *Lehrbuch der hebräischen Archäologie*, vol. ii, pp. 25–53 and 71–83 (1894); *The Jewish Encyclopedia*, vol. xii, pp. 81–101; R. H. Pfeiffer, *History of New Testament Times* (1949); S. Zeitlin, *The Rise and Fall of the Judean State*, pp. 256 ff. (1962); P. L. Garber and E. G. Howland, *Solomon's Temple: a Reconstruction* (1957); L. H. Vincent and A. M. Steve, *Jérusalem de l'Ancien Testament*, 3 vol. (1954–56); W. F. Stinespring in *The Interpreter's Dictionary of the Bible*, vol. iv, pp. 534–560 (1962).

**TEMPLE ARCHITECTURE.** The word "temple," from the Latin word *templum*, originally signified any holy enclosure or building screened from the eyes of the profane. It is the dwelling place of the god; it serves the purpose of housing his image; and it is the architectural frame of the liturgy and cult of the god. The architectural forms of temples are manifold; they are primarily conditioned by the requirements of the cults, which in their turn reflect different religious beliefs. In later times "temple" came to signify, in a broader sense, any shrine of any denomination or even of fraternal orders. (*See* also Religious Architecture.)

**Hypaethral Temples.**—This form of temple, often called a temenos, is generally dedicated to a nature deity thought to promote the fertility of the soil, of animals and of men. This being a common idea in primitive religious thought, the geographical and chronological spread of open-air temples is very wide. Their architectural form is vague and insignificant. A wall or hedge fenced in the holy place; an altar was built for the offerings, and a grove of holy trees or a spring was the seat of the deity. During the Bronze Age in Crete and Greece this form of temple was a common feature, to judge from the many representations of related cult scenes found on ring stones and seals. The best known examples are in Cyprus: Idalium (4th–3rd century B.C.), Tamassus (6th–5th century B.C.) and Ajia Irini (10th–7th century B.C.). In Gaul and Great Britain the druid temples were of similar type, and Nordic sagas testify to their existence in the Scandinavian countries in pre-Christian times. Mountain peaks and hilltops were often chosen for hypaethral temples. They are found in Greece (Mount Ida [Psiloriti], Parnassus, Olympus) and are particularly common in Asia Minor. The Hittite temples of Yazilikaya, with famous rock reliefs, and Qareh Dagh serve as early examples; while Phrygian sites, like Midas City south of modern Eskisehir, belong to a later period, as does Nimrud Dagh in eastern Anatolia. Such temples seem to have been dedicated mostly to rain-producing weather gods or astral deities, divine incarnations of the celestial bodies.

**Cave Temples.**—Natural or artificial caves were also used as temples in different regions. In the Mediterranean area such temples are found on the island of Malta where they date back to the middle of the 2nd millennium B.C. A typical example is the hypogeum of Hal Saflieni, an elaborate system of communicating caves of a very articulate architectural form, with finely cut door jambs and lintels, carved altar stones and wall decorations in relief or painting. The Kamares cave and the Zeus grotto, both on the slopes of Mount Ida in Crete, are basically of the same type but of less elaborate shape. Much more developed in form is the cave temple at Abu Simbel in upper Egypt, dating from the 13th century B.C., and the great temple caves in India and China. The latter should be considered as translations into rock carving of real temple architecture; they have lost the character of caves.

**Egypt.**—The Egyptians erected monumental temples in stone, and their generic form, later to be enlarged and further developed, emerged as early as the Old Kingdom (the 3rd millennium B.C.) in the shape of Pharaonic mortuary temples connected with the pyramids at Saqqarah (Sakkara) and Giza (*see* Pyramid). The mortuary temples were dedicated to the divine Pharaoh, and it can be deduced that they in essential parts duplicated the salient features of the royal palace. Through a long entrance corridor a large forecourt was reached and from there an inner court, facing the temple proper. To reach the holy of holies, poorly lit corridors and a series of small rooms were passed until the central cella of the temple was entered. Access to that part was reserved for the priest, just as audiences to the living Pharaoh were granted only to his highest officials. What in his lifetime served the divine Pharaoh as a ceremonial court residence fulfilled a similar purpose for his cult after his death. The mortuary temple was the only type of temple existing prior to the New Kingdom (18th–20th dynasties, 1580–1100 B.C.), and the earliest preserved regular temple, dedicated to a god, was that built by Queen Hatshepsut at Dayr al Bahri close to Thebes (*c.* 1500 B.C.). What in the mortuary temples was grouped according to a more concentrated and entangled plan was stretched out along a common central axis, but the architectural elements were the same: entrance ramp, forecourt, gate, colonnaded inner court and the temple cella proper, surrounded by smaller rooms used for storing votive offerings and the like. The actual sanctuary was the innermost part of the whole complex and was strikingly small in comparison with the preceding courtyards and halls. This was true also for the fully developed temples of the 19th dynasty (1350–1205 B.C.), such as the great temples at Luxor and Karnak which may well stand as typical examples of Egyptian temple architecture. The entire holy area was walled in and a gate, flanked by two upward tapering towers (the outer pylon), led into the first courtyard. A second pylon led to a colonnaded room (the hypostyle hall), lit by small clerestory windows; from here the inner courtyard was reached through two other pylons and a series of rooms. At the far end of the courtyard was the temple itself, dwarfed by all the preceding structures. The layout was monumental and displayed along a common axis which marked the ceremonial way of the holy processions, typical to Egyptian liturgy. This type of temple building, once firmly established in the Ramesside period, continued essentially unchanged through the entire period of Egyptian ancient history. One of the best preserved examples is the Ptolemaic temple of Horus at Edfu (3rd century B.C.). (*See* EGYPTIAN ARCHITECTURE.)

**Western Asia.**—In comparison with Egyptian temple architecture the Sumerian, Babylonian and Assyrian temples followed a less rigid pattern. The plans lacked axiality and the enclosed area contained, in addition to various rooms for the priests and storerooms for temple treasures and archives, a relatively small temple building, generally without a cult image. The principal feature of the temple complex was the ziggurat (*q.v.*) or stepped pyramid, with stairs or an inclined plane leading to the terraces and the summit. The basic religious ideas governing the temple form were the same as those expressed in the hypaethral temples on mountain peaks. The deities worshipped were conceived as astral gods, incarnated in the heavenly bodies. In some cases, at least, each step of the ziggurat was dedicated to a separate divinity, as in the famous example at Babylon, in which each of the seven stages was dedicated to a separate planet.

The Hittite temples at Bogazköy in Asia Minor (*c.* 1400 B.C.) displayed a different plan: a central rectangular courtyard, on all sides surrounded by a series of rooms, one of which was the shrine proper with the cult image and the altar. It was so placed that it seems to have been the architect's intention rather to hide it from the worshipper than to make it the focus of his attention.

**The Jewish Temple.**—The temple used by the Jews during their migration from Egypt to the Promised Land is known as the Tabernacle. It is described in the Bible (Ex. xxv–xxvii; xxxvi–xxxvii) and was, in accordance with the nomadic way of life of the Jews of the period, a tent shrine. The tent, made of brightly colored linen and woolen material, contained a small inner room, the holy of holies, and a larger outer room, both surrounded by a verandalike structure. The total size was about 30 by 60 ft., and it was placed in a closed court measuring 150 by 75 ft. In the holy of holies stood the ark of the covenant, and the outer room contained an altar, the table for the shewbread and the seven-branched candlestick.

This simple transportable tent shrine became the model for the great Temple of Solomon, probably erected in the years 959–952 B.C. and destroyed by Nebuchadrezzar in 586 B.C. It is described in all its splendour in the Bible (I Kings vi–vii), but as nothing of the building exists and the description is far from clear, it remains problematic. Two courtyards lay in front of the shrine after Egyptian fashion, and the interior of the temple was lighted by latticed clerestory windows as in Karnak. These seem to be the only egyptianizing features of the temple, and more significant stylistic parallels must be sought at Phoenicia whose King Hiram of Tyre assisted Solomon in planning the building.

When the Babylonian captivity came to an end, the re-erection of the temple began. It was preceded by the prophetic vision of Ezekiel (Ezek. xl–xliii) which may have influenced the architect of this so-called Second Temple and certainly meant much for the planning of Herod's Temple. The former was an attempt to reproduce the fabulous Solomonic building in a time of poverty and distress, while the latter, built between 20 and 9 B.C. must have been one of the more important monuments of the early Roman empire in the near east. The outer courtyard, the Court of the Gentiles, with a colonnaded perimeter of about 4140 ft., rested on mighty retaining walls, at points reaching the height of 140 ft. The Temple itself rose on an elevated platform and was reached by passing two more courtyards. The decorative details of the exterior reflected the late Hellenistic and early imperial taste, while the temple itself was erected in traditional conformity with the ritual and religious requirements of the cult. It was destroyed at the capture of Jerusalem by the emperor Titus in A.D. 70. (*See* PRE-HELLENIC ARCHITECTURE.)

**The Aegean World and Greece.**—In Minoan Crete the separate, monumental temple building was unknown. The common form of their cult places was the hypaethral shrine on a mountaintop or in a holy grove. There was also the house chapel, incorporated in the great palaces of Crete. One such chapel was located off the central court of the palace of Knossos, and was dedicated to the protecting deity of the palace. A similar house chapel, but simpler in its architectural form, has been found in Greece proper, at Asine (14th century B.C.). Since Knossos from the 15th century B.C. was under Achaean rule and the Achaeans in Greece spoke an early form of the Greek language, it is surprising that the most typical product of Greek architectural creativity, the classical temple, had no forerunners during the Bronze Age. As a generic form it had features in common with the main room of the Mycenaean palaces, the megaron, but the megaron was not a separate building, as was the later Greek temple, nor was it a cult room, and it is highly debatable whether it had the typical gable roof so characteristic of the Greek temple. Moreover, no Mycenaean megaron survived the 12th century B.C., and no Greek temple can be traced further back than the 8th century B.C. The great majority of Greek temples were oriented in approximate east-west direction with the entrance facing east.

After some hesitant beginnings exemplified by some early structures at Thermon in Aetolia, the canonical form of the Greek temple began to emerge during the 7th century B.C. Its core was an oblong rectangular room (naos or cella) housing the cult image, with a porch in front (pronaos) created by the projecting side walls (antae). Columns were added between the antae to support the architrave spanning the porch. Balancing the frontal structure was a similar porch (opisthodome) at the rear, usually without an entrance. A peristyle or colonnade, found at an early stage in most of the important Greek temples, surrounded the building and added to the impression of quadrilateral completeness, so characteristic of the classical Greek peripteral temple. The entire building rested on a low stepped platform (stylobate) which lifted it above the surrounding ground level and at the same time made the shaded colonnade accessible from all sides. The roof was a slightly sloping gable roof with projecting eaves. The altar stood outside the temple, usually in front of the entrance at the east end. Altar, temple and surrounding area were enclosed and formed the holy precinct (hieron) often with additional smaller buildings. On the more important temple sites, such as Olympia and Delphi, the different Greek city states built their own buildings, called treasuries, serving as repositories for their votive gifts and as meeting points during the festivals. All over the hieron votive statuary was erected. Other votive gifts were placed in the naos itself and sometimes, as in the Parthenon at Athens, the rear part of the temple served as a special treasury. The exterior of the temple (the peristyle, the pronaos and the triangular gable fields of the roof) gave ample opportunity for applying sculptural decorations, in form of friezes and pedimental groups. Many of these decorations were brightly painted in red, blue, purple and brown. The interior was windowless and lit only from the door. In the dim twilight of the naos the great cult image dominated the room.

The temples of classical Greece were built in stone or marble and the masonry was laid with admirable precision. The earliest temples were of simpler construction and the materials were sun-

Parthenon, a 5th century B.C. Doric temple. Athens, Greece

Rock-cut temple of Rameses II at Abu Simbel, Egypt. Nineteenth dynasty (about 1270 B.C.)

Greek Doric temple, 5th century B.C., at Segesta, Sicily

Interior, showing part of the dome of the Pantheon; Roman, A.D. 110–125

Temple of Fortuna Virilis; Roman, 1st century B.C.

## EGYPTIAN, GREEK AND ROMAN TEMPLES

BY COURTESY OF (TOP RIGHT) UNITED ARAB REPUBLIC TOURIST OFFICE, (CENTRE LEFT) E.N.I.T., ROME; PHOTOGRAPHS, (TOP LEFT) ALISON FRANTZ, (BOTTOM LEFT) FOTOTECA UNIONE, ROME, (BOTTOM RIGHT) ALINARI

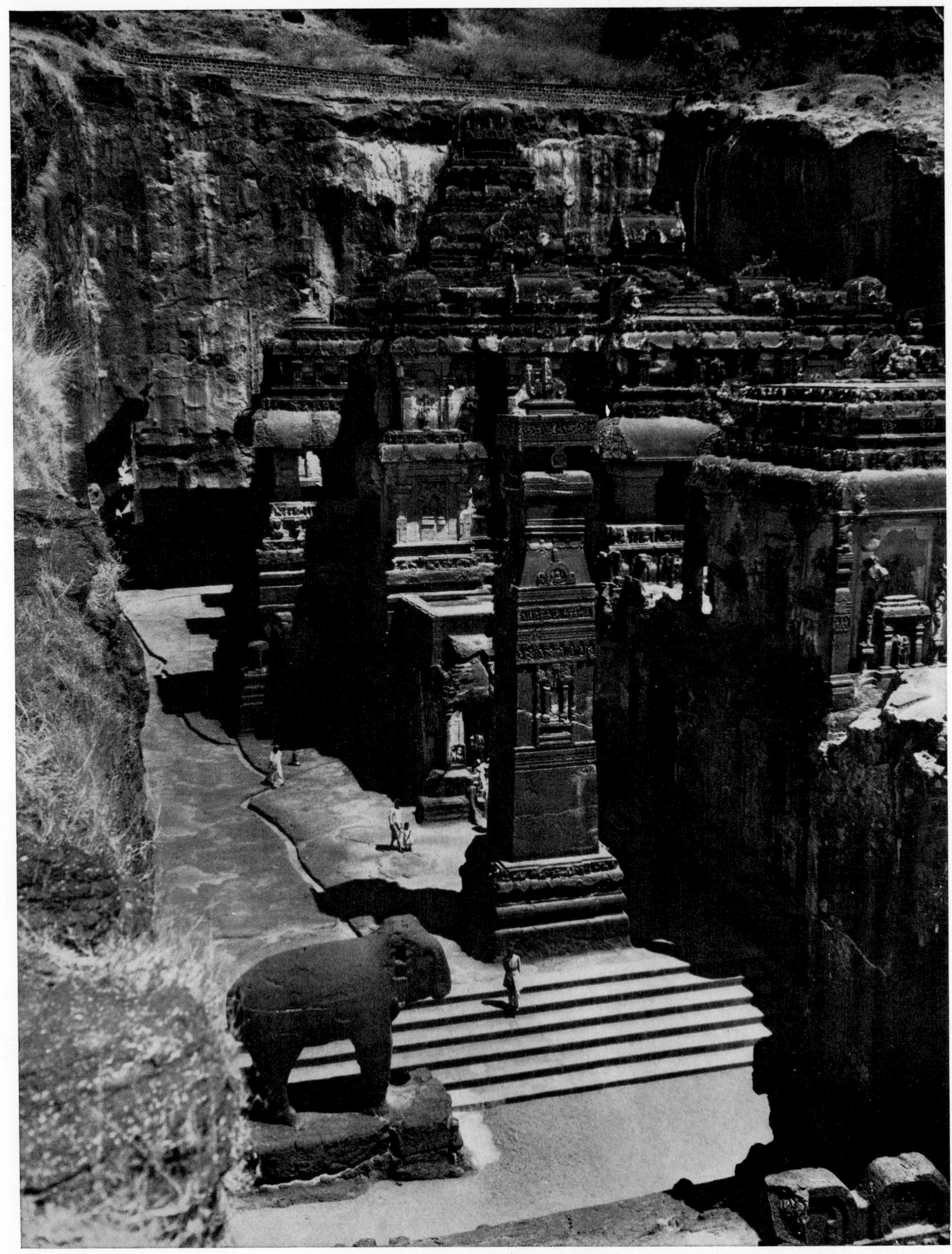

**INDIAN ROCK-CUT CAVE TEMPLE**

Kailasanatha, Ellora, India, an unusual rock-cut monolith with all sides exposed. Dravidian style, 8th to 10th centuries

Yashamon gate of the tomb shrine of Iyemitsu, Nikko, Japan. Tokugawa style, middle of 17th century

Hall of Annual Prayers, Temple of Heaven complex, Peking, China; Ming dynasty, reconstructed in the 19th century

Lama temple, Peking, characteristic of northern Chinese tradition; 18th century

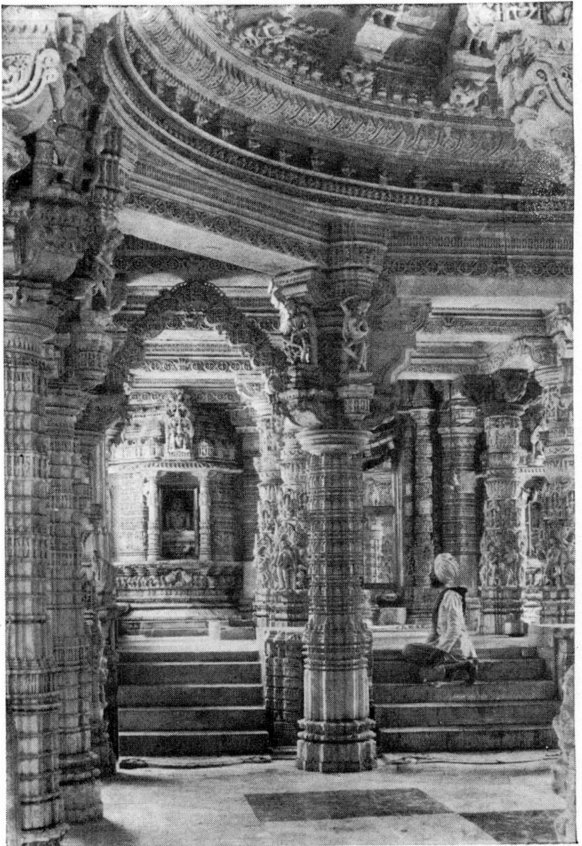

Dilwara temple, Mt. Abu, India. Jaina style, 11th century

Subramanya shrine in the temple of the great pagoda at Tanjore, India. Dravidian style, Chola period, *c.* 907–1053

EAST ASIAN TEMPLES

PHOTOGRAPHS, (TOP LEFT) DE COU FROM EWING GALLOWAY, (TOP RIGHT, CENTRE RIGHT, BOTTOM RIGHT) EWING GALLOWAY, (BOTTOM LEFT) HERBERT G. PONTING

# TEMPLE ARCHITECTURE

Small stupas on a terrace of the great temple at Borobudur, Java (*c.* 7th and 8th centuries)

Stupas at the base of the Shwe Dagon pagoda at Rangoon, Burma

## BUDDHIST TEMPLES OF SOUTHEAST ASIA

PHOTOGRAPHS, (TOP) LOUIS FREDERIC—RAPHO, (BOTTOM) W. SUSCHITZKY dried brick on stone foundations and timber for columns and superstructure (entablature). Many of the decorative elements of the classical temple reveal their origin from wooden or terracotta forms, as the Doric frieze and the different types of column capitals.

Greek temples were spread over the entire Greek world and the great majority of them were of the so-called Doric order. Early examples are the temple of Apollo at Corinth, the temple of Hera at Olympia and many well-preserved temples in Sicily and south Italy, such as those in Syracuse, Selinus, Segesta, Agrigentum (Agrigento) and Paestum. The outstanding examples of Doric temples of the 5th century B.C. are the temple of Hephaestus (*c.* 450–440 B.C., formerly known as the Theseum) and the Parthenon (447–432 B.C.), both in Athens.

In the east Greek provinces of Asia Minor, the Ionian order was commonly used and the temples displayed not only different decorative principles but also a more complicated plan, as the temple of Apollo at Didyma, south of Miletus. Characteristic of many Ionian temples is their great size, the most famous ones being the temples of Artemis in Ephesus and Sardis.

A specific form, rare in Greece, is the round temple with a circular naos surrounded by an annular peristyle. Such a temple is called a tholos and examples exist in Delphi (5th century B.C.) and in Epidaurus and Olympia (4th century B.C.). (*See* GREEK ARCHITECTURE; ORDER.)

**Central Italy and Rome.**—Material remains of early Etrusco-Italic temples are few and insufficiently known. Most of them were built of perishable material, such as sun-dried brick and wood, and what remains is mainly fragments of the painted terracotta revetments that adorned them. From these it can be concluded that Greece and the east Greek provinces of Ionia were the main sources of inspiration for the decorative details. In plan these temples differed in some essential respects from the normal Greek temple. The peristyle was missing and so was the stylobate. Thereby the frontal and axial approach to the building was stressed in a new way. The Roman architect Vitruvius gave an elaborate description of a specific type of Etruscan temple with three cellas. Actually, the three-cella temple was rare, and its use was limited to instances when three deities (a triad) were worshipped in one temple, as in the temple on the Capitoline hill in Rome, which was built during the period of Etruscan influence and dedicated to Jupiter, Juno and Minerva. Etruscan usage had a direct impact on the formation of the later Roman temple. The deep pronaos and the wide intercolumniations are two other features of the Roman temple derived from Etruscan forms. The frontality and axiality inherent in the Etruscan plan was in Roman republican times further emphasized by placing the temple on a high podium, accessible by a flight of steps at the front side. The ritual orientation of the Greek temple and its free placement in an open hieron did not occur on Italic soil. Roman republican temples of the 3rd and 2nd centuries B.C. often had a forecourt, symmetrically laid out in front of the temple. The temple formed therefore the monumental backdrop of the forecourt, with a distinct front façade. (*See* ETRUSCANS.)

In decorative details the Roman temples followed Greek and Hellenistic patterns and developed them further. The Corinthian order was favoured over the Ionic, and the Doric was rarely used. Both the outside and the inside of the cella walls were richly decorated with marble incrustations, pilasters and half columns; and the buildings became more and more luxurious. A typical Roman form was the so-called pseudoperipteral temple with half columns decorating the exterior cella walls so as to give the false effect to a peripteral temple. Outstanding examples of this kind are the temple of Fortuna Virilis in Rome (first half of 1st century B.C.) and the so-called Maison Carrée at Nîmes (1st century A.D.).

In imperial times the court in front of the temple grew out to an entire colonnaded forum dominated by the temple placed close to its rear end. The forum of Caesar (47 B.C.) was thus dominated by the temple of Venus Genetrix, that of Augustus by the temple of Mars Ultor, and that of Domitian and Nerva by the temple of Minerva. The great temple of Jupiter at Heliopolis, Syria (now Baalbek, Lebanon) illustrates the end of this development (begun during the reign of Hadrian and completed early in the 3rd century A.D.). The giant temple towers over a vast courtyard which is preceded by a hexagonal forecourt with a triple entrance gate. The temple itself has a colonnade on all sides, a feature which came into fashion again in the times of the emperor Hadrian. Thus the temple of Venus and Roma, built under his reign, and the so-called Hadrianeum, both in Rome, were peripteral temples.

The round temple with annular peristyle is common: the temple of Vesta in Forum Romanum (originating in the 6th century B.C.); and those temples at Tivoli (1st century B.C.); in Forum Boarium at Rome (1st century A.D.) and at Baalbek (3rd century A.D.). The most magnificent of them all is the Pantheon (*q.v.*), a vast domed building erected under the reign of Hadrian. *See* ROMAN ARCHITECTURE. (EK. S.)

**India.**—Indian temples show clearly the development from sacred cave to free-standing structure. The earliest existing monumental temples are all rock cut and developed with caves. The earlier temples, such as those at Bihar, and at Karli, near Bombay, show a great cave interior, divided by piers or columns into nave and aisles, with a small stupa, or solid masonry curve-topped structure enclosing a relic of Buddha, and a façade cut in the face of the rock. A second common type of rock-cut temple consists of those in which, in addition to the shrine proper, there are great courtyards surrounded by cells for monks. The most remarkable groups of cave temples are those at Ajanta and Ellora. The dates vary from the 2nd century B.C. to the 6th and 7th centuries A.D. The Dravidian- and Jain-constructed temples both show a power and heaviness of general mass with an amazing intricacy of carved detail that is more typical of rock-cut than free-standing structures, and the characteristic pyramidal towers, with their strongly marked horizontal mouldings and vertical projections have almost the character of artificial mountains and cliffs. The part played by figure sculpture in its lavishness, its multitude of figures and their bold relief, is unlike that played in any other structural style, and without doubt owes much, also, to rock-cut prototypes. The plan type shows usually a vast rectangular enclosure entered through several monumental gateways, crowned with enormous, solid towers. Near the centre is the shrine proper, containing the cult statue, sometimes approached by vast, colonnaded halls, and every exposed surface of the great towers and the interior columns and walls is covered with a rich network of sculpture and ornament. (*See* INDIAN ARCHITECTURE.)

**East Indies.**—Indian influence is marked in the temple ruins found in scattered places through Cambodia, Burma, Java and nearby islands. All of the great temples are elaborations of the stupa idea and consist in essence of one or more stupas on raised terraces. Thus in the Shwe Dagon pagoda at Rangoon are a multitude of small stupas crowned with high, spirelike finials, surrounding a central stupa that rises to a height of over 350 ft., and the whole surface is heavily gilded. At Borobudur, Java, the great Buddhist temple (*c.* 7th or 8th century A.D.) consists of a series of terraces around a hill 150 ft. high, at the top of which is a large stupa surrounded by 16 smaller ones. All of the stone lining of the terrace walls is covered with exquisite relief sculpture, not only illustrating the life of Buddha, but also containing many pictures of ordinary, everyday events. The most remarkable of these eastern Buddhist temples is Angkor Wat at Angkor in Cambodia (attributed to the first half of the 12th century and apparently originally intended as a Brahman temple, being converted to Buddhist uses later). This consists of three great symmetrical terraces with elaborate stairs, corner towers, porticos and colonnaded halls, with a great stupalike tower as the climax in the centre. The sculpture and ornament, although typically Khmer, show distinct traces of Hindu influence. The extremely classic character of some of the pier and column capitals is noteworthy.

**China.**—Farther east an entirely contradictory tradition governed temple design, that of the wooden-columned prayer halls of China. As all Chinese monumental buildings, the Chinese temple structure had a wooden framework of horizontal beams and vertical columnar supports which was raised on a stone platform and crowned by a large ornamental roof with overhanging eaves. Since the entire weight of the roof was directed upon the columnar supports through a system of complicated bracket capitals, the Chinese architect was free to use curtain walls and light screen windows throughout the building for decorative purposes. The planning of a temple complex, whether Confucian, Buddhist or Taoist, also followed that of an imperial palace or a great residential home, with three identical buildings grouped on the three sides of an open court, which was entered from its fourth side, directly opposite the central structure, through a gatehouse. Additional buildings or gateway structures could be laid along the main axis in a similar manner, with or without connecting corridors or verandas between them. In Buddhist temples, often there was on either side of the main axis in the outer court a small tower, one containing a drum and the other a bell. Aesthetically, the architectural character varied with the locality. Those in the north were full of monumental grandeur, as in the temple of Confucius or such monasteries in the western hills as that of Wo-fu-szu (both rebuilt in the Ming and the Ch'ing dynasties). Those in the Yangtze valley were more picturesque, with exaggeratedly curved roofs and slimmer supports, as in the 18th century Sheng-yin-szu in the West Lake in Hangchow. (*See* CHINESE ARCHITECTURE.)

**Japan.**—In Japan the elaborate formality of the typical Chinese temple is absent. In fact, the native Shintō temples were based upon very primitive house ideas; they were simple, rectangular buildings with heavily thatched roofs. Architectural effect was gained, however, through the monumental torii or gateways which crossed the main entrance paths. Many votive stone lanterns also decorated the grounds. In the Buddhist temples the halls themselves were based entirely on Chinese prototypes, but the detail was typically Japanese in its composition and its mannered realism. Outstanding examples include the temples of the magnificent group at Nikko, largely of the 17th century, and the Honganji temple at Kyōto. The genius for placing temples is well seen in the island temples that dot the Inland sea, especially those of the sacred island of Itsuku-shima, near Hiroshima. *See* also JAPANESE ARCHITECTURE, and references under "Temple Architecture" in the Index. (WE. F.)

**TEMUCO,** capital of Cautín province, Chile, situated in the heart of Araucania (*q.v.*). Pop. (1960) 72,132 (112,065 mun.). It was founded in 1881 as a frontier outpost on a strategic crossing point of the Cautín River. The land was ceded in a Chilean-Araucanian compact ending the Indian wars, drawn up on adjacent Cerro Ñielol. This forested hill, preserved as a natural park, affords vistas of the central valley and of the volcano-studded Andean cordillera, appropriate to this lake-country gateway. Temuco is an agricultural, livestock, and forest products centre. Of special interest is the Araucanian Indian market. (J. T.)

**TENASSERIM** is the regional name commonly applied to the long narrow strip of southern Burma lying between the border with Thailand (in general the mountain ridge, reaching in places 5,000 ft. [1,500 m.]) on the east and the Andaman Sea on the west. It was conquered by the British from Burma in 1826 and was for many years known as the Tenasserim Province. Later, when Burma was a province of British India, it was constituted a division, with the commissioner's headquarters at Moulmein, and was divided into the six districts of Toungoo, Salween, Thaton, Amherst, Tavoy, and Mergui, though geographically Toungoo and Thaton were north of Tenasserim proper. When Burma became independent in 1948, Salween District formed the core of the new Karen State (*q.v.*), and the Tenasserim Division was reduced in the north to a narrow strip between the Karen State and the Gulf of Martaban. The 1962 estimate of population was 1,543,393, with an area of 21,297 sq.mi. (55,160 sq.km.). The important town and port of Moulmein lies on the south bank near the mouth of the Salween River; opposite is the smaller town of Martaban. Amherst, south of Moulmein, was planned as its main port but was superseded by improvements to Moulmein itself. The district to the south, Tavoy (*q.v.*), is the main source of Burma's tin and wolfram. *See* also BURMA. (L. D. S.)

**TENCIN, ALEXANDRINE CLAUDE DE GUÉRIN DE** (1682–1749), prominent French social figure, patroness of writers and herself a writer, was born at Grenoble, France, on April 27, 1682. She became a nun early in life, but soon abandoned her vows in obscure circumstances around which many legends grew. After the death of Louis XIV she sought fortune at court and became the mistress of Cardinal Dubois, of the regent and of many other personalities. To one of her lovers, the Chevalier Destouches, she gave a son who became the philosopher D'Alembert. Imprisoned in the Bastille in 1726 on a false though plausible charge of murder, she was released after an intervention by her brother Pierre, then an archbishop, later a cardinal. Thereafter she sought less scandalous distinction, as a hostess. Bernard de Fontenelle, Montesquieu (whom she twice assisted in the publication of his works), Pierre de Marivaux and Jean Marmontel frequented her salon. She was esteemed by Pope Benedict XIV. Her best-known work is an autobiographically inspired novel, *Mémoires du comte de Comminges* (1735). She died on Dec. 4, 1749.

*See* P. M. Masson, *Madame de Tencin* (1909). (RT. S.)

**TEN COMMANDMENTS:** *see* DECALOGUE.

**TENERIFE** (TENERIFFE), the largest of the Canary Islands, is located in the Atlantic Ocean opposite the northwest coast of Africa. Area 795 sq.mi. (2,058 sq.km.); pop. (1960) 387,767. Of irregular shape, it is the main island of the Spanish province of Santa Cruz de Tenerife. Its relief is mountainous and volcanic (mainly of trachyte, a light-coloured volcanic rock). The narrower northeastern part rises sharply to a jagged mountain ridge, except near La Laguna, where a corridorlike depression forms the island's only extensive lowland. The remaining two-thirds of Tenerife appears as a vast composite dome surmounted by the famous peak, Pico de Teide. The main crater is imperfect, but southeast of the peak is an undulating plain of pumice and lava at 6,500 to 7,500 ft. (1,981 to 2,286 m.), with a strong outer rim that attains nearly 9,000 ft. (2,717 m.) at Guájara. The northern and western parts of the master crater have been obliterated by the newer volcanic outbursts that have built up the central cone, which here slopes unbrokenly to the coast. The central cone has a double top, a lower summit (Chahorra; 10,180 ft. [3,103 m.]) being connected by a short narrow ridge to the higher, steep-sided cone of El Pitón (12,172 ft.; 3,710 m.). Each summit has a small crater with a floor perforated by blowholes, some of which emit sulfurous vapours.

Though there is no record of an eruption from either summit orifice, recent eruptions pierced the lower flanks of the volcano, at about 6,000 ft. (1,828 m.) in the northwestern part of the island and considerably nearer sea level in the east. In 1705 a lava stream on the northwest flank buried much of Garachico, nearly filling its harbour. In 1795 lava poured from three vents on the eastern flank and from a crater near Güimar. In 1798 a moderate flow occurred on the northwest slopes, and in 1909 a minor eruption yielded a three-mile stream of brittle, black lava in the same area. During 1933 some volcanic activity occurred on the ocean floor off Tenerife.

The climatic and vegetation zones up the Pico de Teide are of exceptional interest (*see* CANARY ISLANDS). Nearly all the inhabitants of Tenerife live on the lower slopes below 4,500 ft. (1,370 m.) and within a few miles of the sea. Almost half the population is in or near Santa Cruz, the capital, and La Laguna, the former capital. Most of the other inhabitants live on the intensively cultivated slopes near the north coast, where the chief towns are La Orotava, Icod, and Puerto de La Cruz. Near the south coast, where the climate is drier and camels are common beasts of burden, there are many small villages, but Güimar is the only town. All the main settlements are linked by good roads, one of which traverses the lava and pumice plains of the master crater (Las Cañadas). There is an airport at Los Rodeos.

*See* O. M. Stone, *Tenerife and Its Six Satellites* (1889); L. Diego Cuscoy, *The Book of Teneriffe* (1957). (R. P. BE.)

**TENGGERESE,** a Proto-Malayan people perhaps with Veddoid strains (*see* VEDDA), numbering about 10,000 (1960s), and living in the isolated mountain districts of East Java (Republic of Indonesia). Their pagan religious beliefs indicate some influence from the Indo-Javanese and Islamic cultures of the lowlands. They live in small mountainside villages, make clearings in the jungle and raise dry-land rice. *See* also MALAY ARCHIPELAGO: *Anthropology*.

**TENG HSIAO-P'ING** (*c.* 1902– ), Chinese revolutionist and a major Communist Party leader, was born in the southwestern Chinese province of Szechwan. After study in France and the Soviet Union in the early and mid-1920s, he returned to China, where he became a leading organizer of Communist guerrilla units in the south. He joined the forces of Mao Tse-tung and Chu Teh in south-central China, fought with them in campaigns against the Nationalists, and participated in the Communist retreat to the northwest known as the Long March (1934–35). During the Sino-Japanese War (1937–45) Teng was a political officer with one of the Communists' major fighting units. In the successful civil war against the Nationalists (1946–49), he continued as a political officer and was among the conquerors of central and southwest China.

In the early years of the Communist Chinese regime, established in 1949, Teng served as the party's top official in his native southwest China. He was brought to Peking in 1952 to become a vice-premier, but his major endeavours were within the party organization and by the mid-1950s he was considered one of the half-dozen most powerful men in the nation. He became secretary-general of the party in 1954 (redesignated general secretary in 1956) and a Politburo member in 1955. After the mid-1950s he also was among the leading officials who worked with Communist parties of other countries, specializing in liaison with the party in the Soviet Union. In the 1960s Teng was in the forefront of China's ideological dispute with the Soviet Union; in July 1963 he led a Chinese delegation in Moscow in negotiations that were largely abortive and became a major turning point in the deterioration of Sino-Soviet relations. As a consequence of the "great proletarian cultural revolution" in 1966, Teng seemed to have lost some of his prestige and power in the Communist hierarchy. Nonetheless, he continued, at least nominally, as a major figure in his capacity as general secretary and as head of the party's secretariat. (D. W. Kl.)

**TENIERS,** the name of a family of Flemish artists who flourished at Antwerp and Brussels during the 17th century; their most famous member was David Teniers, the younger, prolific painter of genre scenes of peasant life and of paintings of art historical importance showing the collections of the regent of the Netherlands.

David Teniers, the elder (1582–1649), worked in Antwerp, where he apparently began his career as a pupil of his brother Juliaen; he is also said to have studied in Italy under Elsheimer and Rubens. He became a master in the Antwerp guild in 1606–07, and in the 1630s is recorded as an art dealer. A number of paintings in the style of his more famous son used to be attributed to him, but in fact almost nothing is known about his work except that he seems to have been mainly a painter of religious subjects.

David Teniers, the younger (1610–1690), the son and pupil of the foregoing, was born in Antwerp, where he was baptized on Dec. 15, 1610, becoming a master in the guild there in 1632–33 and dean in 1645. In 1637 he married Anna, daughter of the painter Jan Brueghel. As an artist he was prolific and painted almost every kind of picture, but chiefly genre scenes of peasant life. His early works in this vein show the influence of Adriaen Brouwer (example in Munich, Bayerische Staatsgemäldesammlungen), but he soon modified the harshness of Brouwer with a blander, sweeter idiom, which he may partly have learned from the Dutch. He was brilliant at handling crowd scenes in an open landscape and adept at characterizing his figures with a warm, human, and often humorous touch. His landscape settings are beautifully atmospheric, and his still-life details attractive and precise. Examples of his work in this manner, the best of which seem to date from the decade 1640–50, are to be found in all the major galleries, since they were extremely popular in the 19th century, especially in England. A typical example is the "Village Fête," signed and dated 1643 (National Gallery, London). In the same decade he also painted a number of monumental processions, such as the "Procession of the Civic Guards of Antwerp" (1643, Leningrad).

Although he continued to paint peasant scenes until nearly the end of his life, latterly with much help from assistants, Teniers developed a second career from 1651 onward, when he became court painter and keeper of the art collections to the regent of the Netherlands, the archduke Leopold Wilhelm, in Brussels. In his capacity as keeper he painted several views of the archduke's picture gallery showing the originals, most of which are now in Vienna, clearly enough for them to be recognized. He also made many small-scale individual copies of these pictures, 244 of which were engraved in 1660 under the title "Theatrum Pictorium." As a pictorial inventory of a great 17th-century collection, this book of engravings was unique in its time and still constitutes an invaluable source for the art historian. Teniers was also court painter to Don John of Austria, who succeeded the archduke as regent in 1656, and was the main founder of the Antwerp Academy, opened in 1665. He died in Brussels on April 25, 1690.

Tenier's son, also named David (1638–1685), often imitated his father's work.

*See* the excellent short account in H. Gerson and E. H. ter Kuile, *Art and Architecture in Belgium, 1600 to 1800* (1960), pp. 144–47, with further bibliography. (M. W. L. K.)

**TENNANT, FREDERICK ROBERT** (1866–1957), English philosophical theologian who essayed a harmony of science and religion within an empirical approach to theology, was born at Burslem, Staffordshire, on Sept. 1, 1866. He read science at Caius College, Cambridge, and was ordained while teaching science at Newcastle-under-Lyme High School (1891–94), becoming lecturer in theology and fellow of Trinity College, Cambridge, in 1913. He died in Cambridge on Sept. 9, 1957.

In four early books Tennant discussed the concepts of sin (1902, 1912), the fall (1903), and miracle (1925). His articles for the 14th edition of *Encyclopædia Britannica* (1929) included those on "Deism," "Faith," and "Sin." In the first volume (1928) of his chief work, *Philosophical Theology,* he explicitly acknowledges his debt to James Ward (*q.v.*). In chapter 12 Tennant shows himself temperamentally and philosophically unsympathetic to mysticism and argues that to justify the claims of religious experience to reveal God needs an independently established theism, derived by a "laborious ascent" from such knowledge about the self and the world as is supplied by epistemology, psychology, and the natural sciences. Volume ii (1930) describes this ascent and gives Tennant's version of the argument from design: that a broad survey of human life and experience shows the need for the concept of purposiveness in many fields, and such considerations, while inconclusive if taken alone, lead collectively to a cumulative argument for God based on a "cosmic teleology." His bold endeavour to combine scientific and theological thinking was, however, overtaken by developments within both empirical philosophy and theology, where, on different grounds, claims for the reasonableness of Christianity were soon to be condemned. But at a time when religious thought was being challenged more by scientific methods and attitudes than by scientific conclusions, Tennant was a powerful apologist. He brought to his task an acute mind, a wide range of interests, and the ability to develop an argument with a robust thoroughness and notable honesty.

*See* D. L. Scudder, *Tennant's Philosophical Theology* (1940), with list of his works; and the memoir by C. D. Broad, *Proceedings of the British Academy,* 44:241–252 (1958). (I. T. R.)

**TENNENT,** the name of three prominent American Presbyterian clergymen, father and sons.

William Tennent (*c.* 1673–1745), whose chief contribution to Presbyterianism and to American colonial life was as a teacher of ministers, was born perhaps in the north of Ireland and graduated from the University of Edinburgh in 1695. He began as a Presbyterian but in 1704 and 1706 took orders in the Anglican Church in Ireland. On Sept. 6, 1718, he landed at Philadelphia and ten days later joined the Presbyterian Church. For two years he served in East Chester, N.Y., and several years at Bedford, N.Y., settling later along Neshaminy Creek just north of Philadelphia. There he served as pastor and began in 1736 a small school, called derisively the "Log College." During his career Tennent educated about 21 of the most useful and gifted ministers of the colonial Presbyterian Church, among them his sons Gilbert and William, Samuel Blair, Charles Beatty, John Rodgers, Samuel Finley, and John Redman. They became known as the New Side, opposed to the more rigidly orthodox Old Side of the Scotch-Irish majority.

Tennent welcomed the English evangelist George Whitefield (*q.v.*) to Philadelphia and persuaded him to assist the New Side in its revival effort, known as the Great Awakening. Tennent and the New Side enlisted also the active support of such men as Jonathan Dickinson and Ebenezer Pemberton, thus assuring that colonial Presbyterianism would be predominantly New School. Indirectly, Tennent's Log College was a forerunner of Princeton University, inasmuch as his example inspired the New Side to found Nassau Hall. Tennent died May 6, 1745.

GILBERT TENNENT (1703–1764), a popular evangelist second only to Whitefield, and the eldest son of William Tennent, was born in County Armagh, Ire., on Feb. 5, 1703, and educated by his father, with perhaps a year at Yale College. He entered the Presbyterian ministry in Delaware in 1725, and the year after settled at New Brunswick, N.J. Under the influence of his father and of a Dutch pastor, T. J. Frelinghuysen, he soon became a rousing preacher and evangelist. Very quickly he emerged as the natural leader of the "Log College men" and the dominant figure in the Great Awakening. When Whitefield was persuaded by William Tennent to aid the New Side, he found a like spirit in Gilbert, whom he persuaded to follow him up in his evangelistic tour of New England. As a "Sun of Thunder" Tennent did so and became a most controversial figure throughout the colonies. When the Presbyterian Church broke up (1741) into New Side and Old Side, Tennent and Jonathan Dickinson became the two leaders of the New Side. In 1743 Tennent took over Whitefield's tabernacle in Philadelphia and made of it the Second Presbyterian Church. Ten years later he and Samuel Davies raised over £4,000 on a trip through England and Scotland for the building of Nassau Hall. He was a leader in the move that reunited the New Side and the Old Side in 1758. Tennent died July 23, 1764.

WILLIAM TENNENT (1705–1777), the second son of the elder William, was born in County Armagh on June 3, 1705. For nearly 44 years he was pastor of the Presbyterian Church at Freehold, N.J. Noted as an eccentric, he was sympathetic with his brother Gilbert's revivalistic views. He died March 8, 1777.

The elder Tennent's younger sons, John and Charles, were also Presbyterian clergymen.

BIBLIOGRAPHY.—L. J. Trinterud, *Forming of an American Tradition: a Re-examination of Colonial Presbyterianism* (1949); T. C. Pears, Jr., and Guy S. Klett, "William Tennent and the Log College," *Journal of the Presbyterian Historical Society*, 28:37–64, 105–128, 167–204 (1950); W. B. Sprague, *Annals of the American Pulpit*, vol. iii (1858); C. H. Maxson, *Great Awakening in the Middle Colonies*, ch. 3 (1920); E. S. Gaustad, *Great Awakening in New England*, pp. 32–37 (1957); Elias Boudinot, *Memoirs of the Life of the Rev. William Tennent* (1807; many later editions), a biography of the younger William but dealing also with other members of the family. (L. J. T.)

**TENNESSEE,** a south-central state of the United States, is bounded on the north by Kentucky and Virginia; on the east by North Carolina along the line of the crest of the Unaka mountains to within 26 mi. (42 km.) of Georgia, where the boundary turns due south; on the south by Georgia, Alabama and Mississippi along the 35th parallel of north latitude; on the west by the Mississippi river, which separates it from Arkansas and Missouri. The extreme length of the state from east to west is 432 mi. (695 km.) and the extreme breadth is 112 mi. (180 km.), its area being 42,244 sq.mi. (109,412 sq.km.) of which 482 are water surface. The name "Volunteer state" was given to Tennessee because of its remarkable record in furnishing volunteers in the War of 1812 and in the Mexican War. It is the 34th state of the union in size. The capital is Nashville and the state entered the union June 1, 1796, as the 16th state. The iris is the state's official flower, the tulip poplar its official tree, and the mockingbird its official bird. The state flag consists of a red field upon the centre of which is depicted a blue circle edged with white and which contains three white five-pointed stars. At the fly end of the flag is a blue stripe separated from the red field by a narrow white stripe. The name "Tennessee," is of Indian origin and is generally believed to be derived from the name of an ancient Cherokee capital.

## PHYSICAL GEOGRAPHY

**Physical Features.**—The state lies between the extremes of approximately 35° and 36° 41′ N. and 81° 40′ and 90° 18′ W. It is popularly divided into three large divisions known as east, middle and west Tennessee. The first extends from the heights of the Unaka ridges along the North Carolina border, across the valley of the Tennessee river to the heights of the Cumberland plateau. The middle section includes a part of the Cumberland plateau, all the Highland rim plateau and the Central basin, and extends westward to the Tennessee river. The western division includes the plateau region from the Tennessee river to the steep slope which overlooks the Mississippi flood plain; also a narrow strip of lowland which extends to the Mississippi river. From a maximum elevation of 6,642 ft. at Clingmans Dome near the North Carolina border, in Sevier county, the surface descends to 182 ft. on the Mississippi river in Shelby county. The Unaka mountains, which occupy a belt 8 mi. wide along the state's eastern border, are a series of somewhat irregular ridges developed on complexly folded and faulted crystalline rocks. Sixteen peaks exceed 6,000 ft. in height and maximum elevation reaches 6,285 ft. That part of the Great Appalachian valley which traverses Tennessee is known as the valley of east Tennessee. It consists of parallel ridges and valleys developed by erosion on folded sandstones, shales and limestones, the valley quality predominating because the weak limestones were of great thickness. The valley areas vary in height from 600 ft. in the southwest to 1,600 ft. in the northeast. The northeast ridges are more numerous and higher than the southwest.

Along the southwest border of the valley a steep escarpment, known as Walden's ridge, rises to the Cumberland plateau. This plateau has a mean elevation of about 1,800 ft. and a rolling topography, the northern portion sloping toward the northwest.

The western edge of the plateau is much broken by deep indentations of stream valleys, and drops suddenly downward about 1,000 ft. to the Highland rim plateau, so named from the scarp which forms an encircling rim around the Central basin. It is fairly level except where it is cut by river valleys. The Central basin lies for the most part 400 to 600 ft. below the rim; a few hills or ridges rise to the level of the rim. The basin is elliptical in form, extending nearly across the state from northeast to southwest with an extreme width of about 60 mi.; near its centre is the city of Murfreesboro, and Nashville lies in the northwest.

Between the Central basin and the lower Tennessee river is the western Highland rim. Westward from the lower Tennessee river the surface rises rapidly to the summit of a broken cuesta or ridge and then descends gently and terminates abruptly in a bluff overlooking the Mississippi flood plain. This is called the plateau slope of west Tennessee, which is part of the east Gulf coastal plain. The bluff, 150 to 200 ft. in height, traverses the state in a rather straight course; between it and the meandering Mississippi, except at a few points where that river touches it, lie low bottom lands varying in width according to the bends of the river and containing numerous swamps and ponds. In the northern portion, principally in Lake county, is Reelfoot lake, which occupies a depression formed by an earthquake in 1811. It is 18 mi. long and has a maximum width of 3 mi.

The whole of the Appalachian province of Tennessee and the southern portions of the Cumberland plateau, the Highland rim, and the Central basin are drained southward and westward by the Tennessee river and its tributaries. The valley of the lower Tennessee is drained northward by the same river. The northern portions of the Cumberland plateau, Highland rim and Central basin are drained northward and westward by the Cumberland river and its tributaries. The western slope of the east Gulf plains is drained directly into the Mississippi by several small streams.

**Climate.**—The mean summer temperature varies according to elevation from 62° F. (17° C.) on the Unaka mountains to 72° (22° C.) on the Cumberland plateau, or 75° in the valley of east Tennessee and on the Highland rim, 77° in the Central basin and about 78° on the east Gulf plains of west Tennessee. The mean winter temperature for each of these divisions varies little from 38°, and the mean annual temperature ranges only from 57° in east Tennessee to 58° in middle Tennessee and to 60° in west Tennessee. Killing frosts are rare between the third week in April and the middle of October, especially in the southern and western parts of the state. An average annual precipitation of about 50 in.

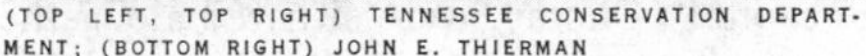
(TOP LEFT, TOP RIGHT) TENNESSEE CONSERVATION DEPARTMENT; (BOTTOM RIGHT) JOHN E. THIERMAN

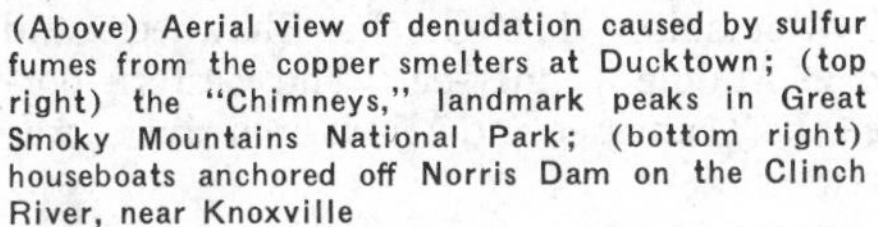
(Above) Aerial view of denudation caused by sulfur fumes from the copper smelters at Ducktown; (top right) the "Chimneys," landmark peaks in Great Smoky Mountains National Park; (bottom right) houseboats anchored off Norris Dam on the Clinch River, near Knoxville

(1,270 mm.) is quite equally distributed over the state, and a little more than one-half of it is well distributed through the spring and summer months. The average annual snowfall is about 8 in. The warm, moisture-bearing winds blow low from the south or southwest with a free sweep across the state in a direction nearly parallel with the trend of the mountains. The commingling of these winds with upper cold currents from the north gives rise frequently to westerly and occasionally to easterly winds.

**Soil.**—The Central basin, the less elevated parts of the valley of east Tennessee, and parts of the outer portion of the Highland rim have a fertile soil of limestone origin. There are narrow strips of rich alluvium along many of the rivers. The soils on the mountains, on the ridges of the valley of east Tennessee and on the eastern slope of the east Gulf plains vary greatly, according to the rocks from which they are derived. In the Cumberland plateau, in the inner portion of the Highland rim and in the higher parts of the western slope of the east Gulf plains, the soil for the most part is sandy and thin.

**Plants and Animals.**—At one time the greater part of the state was covered with forests, but less than 10% of the virgin forest remains. There are some great stands of oak, elm and beech that are original growth. Common throughout the state are sycamore, basswood, cherry, walnut, hickory, locust, poplar and maple trees. Hemlock, pine, spruce and balsam are found in abundance in eastern Tennessee. The swampy sections of western Tennessee are similar to the deep south in their vegetation. Cypress, pecan, tupelo, cotton gum and chinquapin grow there. Altogether, more than 150 types of trees are found within the state's borders. Redbud, dogwood, wild grape, passionflower and trailing arbutus are the most widely seen flowering shrubs and vines. Types of wildflowers include violets, daisies, black-eyed Susans, goldenrod, asters, gentians and Jerusalem artichokes. In the mountain regions, the commonest flower is the rhododendron; others frequently seen are many types of trillium, azalea, wild honeysuckle and mountain laurel. The state flower, the iris, is most commonly found in middle Tennessee, as is yellow jasmine. In western Tennessee lilies and orchids abound in the west woodlands.

During pioneer days, bison, elk, Virginia deer, black bears, wolves, panthers and lynxes were common in Tennessee. Virginia deer are still fairly numerous and there are bears and lynxes in the mountainous and wooded parts of the state. Fox, skunks and opossums are probably the best known of the fur-bearing animals found in the state. Others include raccoons, minks, muskrats, rabbits, squirrels, weasels, woodchucks and chipmunks. The Russian wild boar is infrequently seen in the wooded parts of eastern Tennessee. Many birds once common to the region have become extinct there. These include the passenger pigeon, the Carolina parakeet and the prairie chicken. The bald eagle is found in the wilds of the Cumberland plateau, and on rare occasions golden eagles are seen in the Great Smokies. The great blue heron, the green heron and nearly all of the other types of wading and swimming birds are numerous along the state's waterways. Common birds include the mockingbird, robin, bluebird, killdeer, meadowlark, cardinal, towhee, screech owl, hawk, chickadee, whippoorwill, flicker, woodpecker and wren. The largest game bird is the wild turkey. Other game birds are grouse, quail, ring-necked pheasant, bobwhite and dove. Of the many kinds of fish found in Tennessee's streams and lakes, particularly numerous are catfish, buffalo fish, drum, bass, pike, jack salmon, crappie, perch and bream. Of the reptiles found in the state, the rattlesnake, copperhead and cottonmouth moccasin are poisonous.

**State and National Parks, Historic Sites.**—The state parks of Tennessee comprise more than 250,000 ac. (102,000 ha.) of land. Practically all of the parks have lakes and streams and all of them are wildlife refuges. The largest, Natchez Trace State park, is in western Tennessee and contains 42,000 ac. (17,000 ha.). It is named for the famous early road that connected Nashville and Natchez, Miss. Fall Creek Falls State park (15,777 ac.) contains Fall Creek falls, whose height of 256 ft. make it the highest falls in the eastern United States. David Crockett State park (1,000 ac.) is immediately west of Lawrenceburg, where Crockett lived. Other state parks include Big Ridge, Booker T. Washington, Cedars of Lebanon, Chickasaw, Montgomery Bell, Norris Dam, Pickett, Shelby Forest and Standing Stone. The western half of the Great Smoky Mountains National park is situated on the eastern boundary of Tennessee—the other portion of the park is in North Carolina. The park comprises about 800 sq.mi., with approximately 238,000 ac. in Tennessee. In the park are mountain peaks more than 6,000 ft. in height. Part of the Appalachian trail runs through the park area. Considered one of the most beautiful of the national parks, in part because of the unique, deep blue haze that overhangs the mountains, it was dedicated in 1940.

Tennessee is also rich in historic sites. Eight historical areas are administered by the National Park service. The Andrew Johnson National monument, at Greeneville, contains the home of the 17th president, the tailor shop in which he worked as a young man, and the cemetery in which he is buried. Cumberland Gap National Historic park includes portions of Tennessee, Kentucky and Virginia, and contains the Gap through which the early pioneers passed in the settlement of Kentucky, Tennessee and other states of the Old Southwest. Cades Cove, part of the Great Smoky Mountains National park, is a preserved mountain community of the early 19th century. Chickamauga and Chattanooga National Military park is partly in Tennessee and partly in Georgia. The Tennessee portion of the park contains the battlefield of Lookout mountain, and Orchard Knob, Missionary ridge and Signal point on Signal mountain. The park commemorates two of the most famous military engagements of the Civil War. Stones River National Military park, near Murfreesboro, is the site of one of the hardest fought Civil War battles, a three day engagement in Dec. 1862–Jan. 1863. Fort Donelson National Military park commemorates the 1862 battle which opened the Tennessee river to Union troops and gunboats and first brought General Ulysses S. Grant to prominence. Shiloh National Military park is the battlefield on which was fought the first major battle of the western campaigns of the Civil War, in 1862. Near Hohenwald, southwest of Nashville, is the grave and monument to the explorer Meriwether Lewis (*q.v.*).

There are also a number of state and privately owned historic sites of great importance. Rocky Mount, near Johnson City, was capitol of the Southwest Territory from 1790 to 1792, and is the oldest surviving territorial capitol in the United States. The William Blount mansion, in Knoxville, became the residence of the territorial governor in 1792 and continued until Tennessee attained statehood in 1796. Ft. Loudoun, near Madisonville on the Little Tennessee river, is an exact reconstruction of a British fort constructed in 1756–57 (see *History,* below). Oaklands, in Murfreesboro, is a Civil War site of local significance. The Sam Davis home, between Nashville and Murfreesboro, commemorates a young Civil War scout who chose to be hanged rather than betray his behind-the-lines informant. Cragfont, east of Gallatin, is the restored home of a Revolutionary War and War of 1812 military leader and one of the most impressive pioneer structures in the state.

The best-known site in the state is the Hermitage, the beautiful home of Andrew Jackson, the seventh U.S. president. Also in Nashville are Ft. Nashborough, replica of the first stockaded fort in the area; Traveler's Rest, the restored home of John Overton, early jurist and Andrew Jackson's close friend and advisor; the state capitol, a classic Greek structure designed by William Strickland; the Parthenon, an exact reproduction of the famed Greek temple; and Belle Meade, the mansion house and outbuildings of one of the most famous southern plantations and a world famous thoroughbred horse nursery and stud farm. South of Nashville at Franklin is the Carter house, a structure that stood in the middle of the Civil War battlefield of Franklin. Farther south, at Columbia, is a museum house commemorating James K. Polk, the 11th U.S. president. In Jackson the city maintains the home of Casey Jones, the legendary railroad engineer, as a historic site and railroad museum. In Memphis the Fontaine house is a superb example of Victorian architecture. South of Memphis, near the Mississippi river, is Chucalissa Prehistoric Indian town, an archaeological reconstruction of an Indian village which may have been visited by the explorer Hernando de Soto in 1541.

## HISTORY

**Exploration and Settlement.**—Southeastern Tennessee was the home of the Cherokee Indians when white men first entered the area. Believed to have been one of the tribes of the Iroquois, originally, the Cherokees were probably the most civilized of all North American Indians. Many of them were in Georgia and South Carolina, but the strongest towns and villages of the Cherokee nation, including the capital (Chota), were situated along the river valleys of the Great Smoky mountains. From these villages the Cherokees sent hunting expeditions into Middle Tennessee, to which they claimed ownership. The Creeks, Shawnees, and Chickasaws also hunted in Middle Tennessee. The western portion of the state, between the Tennessee and Mississippi rivers, was claimed by the Chickasaws.

The first white man known to have visited Tennessee was the Spanish explorer, Hernando de Soto, who in 1540 entered briefly the southeastern portion of the state. Some historians believe De Soto traversed the entire southern portion of the state, crossing the Mississippi river from a point near the present site of Memphis; the generally accepted theory, however, is that he followed a more southerly course through northern Alabama and Mississippi.

PHOTOS (TOP LEFT, TOP RIGHT, BOTTOM LEFT) BRUCE ROBERTS FROM RAPHO GUILLUMETTE PICTURES; (BOTTOM RIGHT) TENNESSEE CONSERVATION DEPARTMENT

HISTORIC SITES IN TENNESSEE (TOP LEFT) RECONSTRUCTION OF FT. NASHBOROUGH (ORIGINAL NAME OF NASHVILLE) ON THE CUMBERLAND RIVER. THE SETTLEMENT WAS FOUNDED IN 1779; (TOP RIGHT) THE HERMITAGE, RESIDENCE OF ANDREW JACKSON, NORTHEAST OF NASHVILLE, WAS COMPLETED IN 1835. (BOTTOM LEFT) RECONSTRUCTED 18TH-CENTURY PIONEER HOMESTEAD IN GREAT SMOKY MOUNTAINS NATIONAL PARK. (BOTTOM RIGHT) CHATTANOOGA AND THE TENNESSEE RIVER FROM LOOKOUT MOUNTAIN, SITE OF THE CIVIL WAR "BATTLE ABOVE THE CLOUDS" NOV. 24–25, 1863

Père Marquette, the French missionary and explorer, in his voyage down the Mississippi in 1673, camped upon the western border of the state and eight years later Robert Cavelier, sieur de La Salle, and his companions left Canada to complete the exploration of the river. La Salle built Ft. Prud'homme in 1682 upon a Chickasaw bluff, near the present site of Memphis, but it was soon abandoned. Later the French built Ft. Assumption, where Memphis now stands, and kept a garrison there, but made no attempt at colonization. The territory was a part of the English grant to Sir Walter Ralegh in 1584, and of the later Stuart grants, including that in 1663 to the proprietors of Carolina. James Adair of South Carolina, a fur trader and explorer, is supposed to have been the first to go from the English colonies into Tennessee. A party of Virginians led by Thomas Walker (1715–94) in 1750 reached the Cumberland river and Cumberland mountains and named them in honour of the royal duke. In 1756–57 Ft. Loudoun, named in honour of John Campbell, earl of Loudoun, was built on the Little Tennessee river, about 30 mi. S. of the present site of Knoxville, as an outpost against the French who were then active in the whole Mississippi valley, and was garrisoned by royal troops. The fort surrendered to the Cherokee Indians Aug. 8, 1760. The settlers in the region were massacred, as was the garrison (Aug. 9) while retreating to Ft. Prince George.

The first permanent white settler in Tennessee was William Bean, who in 1768 built a cabin along the Watauga river in the northeastern portion of the state. Within the next few years settlements were established near Bean's cabin and also along the Holston and Nolichucky rivers. Hundreds of additional settlers arrived after the defeat of the Regulator insurrection, a popular uprising against excessive taxes, in North Carolina in 1771. These settlers negotiated a ten-year lease with the Cherokees for the land they occupied, and then drew up a compact of government called the Watauga association, mutually binding themselves to observe a body of law. A general committee of 13 was elected to exercise legislative powers and this committee elected 5 of its number to exercise executive and judicial functions. In 1775 the land was purchased from the Cherokees as a part of the negotiations by which Richard Henderson made his famous purchase (*see* also KENTUCKY: *History*).

**Part of North Carolina.**—With the approach of the American Revolution, the idea of becoming a colony with a royal governor was abandoned, and on petition of the inhabitants the territory was designated by North Carolina in 1776 as the Washington district, which in 1777 became Washington county, with the Mississippi river as the western boundary. The population increased rapidly and soon several new counties were created.

During the American Revolution the Watauga and Holston settlers joined to defeat decisively the British forces under Maj. Patrick Ferguson. Though warned by Ferguson to cease aiding the Colonial forces, the mountaineers under John Sevier, Isaac Shelby and William Campbell, nevertheless crossed the mountains to attack Ferguson on Oct. 7, 1780, caught up with him at King's mountain, S.C., and aided by some North Carolina troops, killed or captured his entire force. In 1779 James Robertson (1742–1814) led an overland expedition that planted a settlement on the Cumberland river in middle Tennessee. The women and children of Robertson's party arrived at the settlement in the spring of 1780 after a harrowing four-month voyage down the Tennessee river and then up the Ohio and Cumberland rivers, under the command of John Donelson. The infant settlement of Nashborough, named after Gen. Francis Nash of North Carolina, was self-governed after the fashion of its sister settlement in east Tennessee. The Cumberland compact, which contained the first provision for recall of elected officials in the history of the United States, remained in force until 1783, when North Carolina made the renamed town of Nashville the county seat of the newly created Davidson county.

**The State of Franklin.**—After the American Revolution the legislature of North Carolina offered in 1784 to cede its western territory to the general government, provided the cession be accepted within two years. The Watauga settlers, indignant at this transfer without their consent, and fearing to be left without any form of government whatever, assembled in convention at Jonesboro on Aug. 23, 1784, and chose delegates to a later convention to form a new state. Meanwhile North Carolina repealed the act of cession and created the western counties into a new judicial district. A second convention of the Watauga settlers broke up in confusion without accomplishing anything; but a third adopted a constitution, which was submitted to the people, and ordered the election of a legislature. This body met early in 1785, elected Sevier governor of the new state of Franklin, filled a number of offices and passed several laws in anticipation of an autonomous existence.

In May 1785 William Cocke presented to the federal congress a memorial requesting recognition of Franklin as a state. Congress refused to accede to this request, however, and subsequently North Carolina renewed its efforts to effect a return of the "Franklinites" to the allegiance of the mother state. For a time two sets of officials claimed authority in Franklin; but North Carolina finally prevailed after remitting taxes unpaid since 1784. In 1788 Sevier's term as governor of Franklin expired, and, no successor being elected, the state of Franklin came to an end. Sevier was arrested on a charge of treason, but was allowed to escape, and soon afterward was again appointed brigadier general of militia.

**The State of Tennessee.**—On Dec. 12, 1789, North Carolina again ceded the territory to the United States government, stipulating that all the general provisions of the ordinance of 1787 should apply except that forbidding slavery. Congress accepted the cession and, on May 26, 1790, passed an act for the government of the "Territory south of the River Ohio." William Blount was appointed the first governor, and in 1792 Knoxville became the seat of government. The chief events of Blount's administration were the contests with the Indians, the purchase of their lands and the struggle against Spanish influence.

A census ordered by the territorial legislature in 1795 showed more than 60,000 free inhabitants (the number prescribed before the territory could become a state), and accordingly a convention to draft a state constitution met in Knoxville on Jan. 11, 1796. The instrument, which closely followed the constitution of North Carolina, was proclaimed without submission to popular vote. Sevier was elected governor, and Blount and Cocke United States senators. In spite of the opposition of the Federalist party the state of Tennessee was admitted to the union on June 1, 1796.

With the subsequent rapid increase of population, the dread of Indians and Spaniards declined. Churches and schools were built, and soon many of the comforts and some of the luxuries of life made their appearance. The question of a circulating medium of exchange was acute during the first half of the 19th century, and state banks were organized, but they suspended specie payments in times of financial stringency. The bank of Tennessee, organized in 1838, had behind it the credit of the state, and it was hoped that money for education and for internal improvements might be secured from its profits. The management became a question of party politics, and later, during the American Civil War, its funds were used to advance the Confederate cause.

The development of west Tennessee along the Mississippi was rapid after the beginning of the 19th century. This section was purchased from the Chickasaw Indians in 1818, and in the following year Tennessee's most populous county, Shelby, was created with its county seat at Chickasaw Bluffs (now Memphis).

The peculiar topographical conditions made the three sections of the state almost separate commonwealths, and demand for better means of communication was insistent. The policy of state aid to internal improvements found advocates very early, but a definite program was not begun until 1829 when commissioners for internal improvements were appointed and an expenditure of $150,000 was authorized. In 1835 the state agreed to subscribe one-third to the capital stock of companies organized to lay out turnpikes, railways, etc., and four years later the proportion became one-half. The general policy was continued, and in 1861 more than $17,000,000 of the state debt was due to these subscriptions, from which there was little return.

Andrew Jackson was the dominant figure in Tennessee politics during the second quarter of the 19th century. The state's first representative in congress and one of its first superior court judges, Jackson's career had gone into virtual eclipse until his well-earned fame in the War of 1812 revived it. His nomination for president in 1824 ushered in a period during which he literally dictated his party's policies, but his attempt to dictate the election of Martin Van Buren as his successor in 1836 brought about a revolt against him in his own state. Sen. Hugh Lawson White received Tennessee's electoral votes that year and his followers became the leaders of the newly formed Whig party. During the next 20 years that party carried every presidential election in Tennessee, including even that of 1844 when a native son, James K. Polk, was the Democratic candidate for president.

**The American Civil War.**—When the Whig party split nationally on the slavery issue Tennessee became nominally Democratic. Proslavery sentiment was strong in middle and west

Tennessee, but less strong in east Tennessee; loyalty to the Union, however, was strong in all sections of the state. The lack of a strong secessionist sentiment among the people of the state helped prevent the adoption of extreme measures when the representatives of nine southern states met in Nashville in 1850 to consider the sectional issues confronting the country. In 1860 Tennesseans again demonstrated their loyalty by voting for the Constitutional Union party's candidates, John Bell and Edward Everett, in the presidential elections. As late as Feb. 9, 1861, voters defeated a proposal to hold a convention for the consideration of seceding from the Union.

This pro-Union sentiment changed almost overnight when Pres. Abraham Lincoln called on Tennessee to provide troops to help put down the southern rebellion. On May 7, 1861, the state entered into a "military league" with the Confederacy, and on June 8 the people of middle and west Tennessee voted overwhelmingly to sever their ties with the Union; by an equally overwhelming majority east Tennessee voted to remain in the Union. Thus, when Gov. Isham G. Harris proclaimed that Tennessee had declared its independence of the union, Andrew Johnson of east Tennessee refused to resign his seat in the United States senate and was upheld in that action by the people of his section. East Tennessee remained Unionist throughout the Civil War, and has been strongly Republican in its politics ever since.

Next to Virginia, the state was the chief battleground during the Civil War. In Feb. 1862 Gen. U. S. Grant and Commodore A. H. Foote captured Ft. Henry on the Tennessee river and Ft. Donelson on the Cumberland. The Confederate line of defense was broken and Gen. D. C. Buell occupied Nashville. Grant next ascended the Tennessee river to Pittsburg Landing, with the intention of capturing the Memphis and Charleston railway, and on April 6 and 7 defeated the Confederates in the battle of Shiloh. The capture of Island No. 10 in the Mississippi on April 7 opened the river as far south as Memphis, which was captured in June. During Dec. 31–Jan. 2 Gen. William S. Rosecrans (Federal) fought with Gen. Braxton Bragg (Confederate) the bloody but indecisive battle of Stones River (Murfreesboro). In June 1863 Rosecrans forced Bragg to evacuate Chattanooga. Bragg, however, turned upon his pursuer, and on Sept. 19 and 20 in one of the bloodiest battles of the war, defeated Rosecrans at Chickamauga. General Grant then assumed command, and on Nov. 24–25 defeated Bragg at Chattanooga, thus opening the way into east Tennessee. There Gen. A. E. Burnside at first met with success, but was shut up in Knoxville by Confederate Gen. James Longstreet, who was not able, however, to capture the city, and on the approach of Gen. W. T. Sherman retired into Virginia. Almost the whole state was now held by Federal troops, and no considerable military movement occurred until after the fall of Atlanta in Sept. 1864. Then Gen. J. B. Hood moved into Tennessee, expecting Sherman to follow him. Sherman, however, sent reinforcements to Thomas and continued his march to the sea. Hood fought with Gen. John M. Schofield at Franklin, and on Dec. 15–16 was utterly defeated by Gen. George H. Thomas at Nashville, the Federals thus securing virtually undisputed control of the state. (*See* AMERICAN CIVIL WAR).

**Reconstruction.**—After the occupation of the state by the Federal armies in 1862, Andrew Johnson was appointed military governor by the president (confirmed March 3, 1862), and held the office until he was inaugurated vice-president of the U.S. on March 4, 1865. Republican electors attempted to cast the vote of the state in the national election of 1864, but were not recognized by congress.

Tennessee was the first of the Confederate states to be readmitted to the union (July 24, 1866) after ratifying the 13th and 14th amendments to the United States constitution. Tennessee freed its slaves by an amendment to the state constitution ratified by a vote of the people on Feb. 22, 1865, but suffrage was not conferred upon the Negro until two years later (Feb. 25, 1867). The state escaped "carpet bag" government, but the native whites in control, under the leadership of William G. Brownlow, exhibited almost every phase of the Reconstruction policy. All persons who had either directly or indirectly taken part in the war against the union or had given aid to the Confederacy were denied the right of suffrage. In the election of 1869, the acting governor, D. W. C. Senter, ordered the election commissioners to issue to all actual citizens of the state permits to vote. The Democrats united with the conservative Republicans and Senter was easily elected. At the same time a Democratic and conservative legislature was elected, thus placing the state government again in the control of officers elected by the majority of the people. The Ku Klux Klan, originating in 1865 at Pulaski, Tenn., spread over the state and the entire south, and in 1869 nine counties in the middle and western section were placed under martial law because of the Klan's activities against the Loyal (or Union) league, an organization supporting the union, and the Negroes.

A constitutional convention met in Jan. 1870 and revised the old constitution, which was ratified by the people in May. In 1873 a school law was passed which provided for state and county superintendents, separate schools for white and Negro children, and a state tax to aid in paying the expenses of these schools. A progressive step was the final compounding of the old state debt at 50 cents on the dollar by an act of the legislature in 1883.

In 1904 the Adams law, which prohibited the sale of intoxicating liquors in towns of 5,000 inhabitants or less, was passed. Successive laws concerning prohibition were passed in 1910, 1913, 1915 and 1917; nevertheless, Tennessee voted for repeal of national prohibition in 1933. In 1915 a law was passed providing for mothers' pensions. In 1917 the letting of prison labour to private contractors was prohibited, and an act was passed forbidding the limiting of the output of coal in order to increase the price. In the same year a state budget commission was created. On Aug. 18, 1920, the state ratified the proposed amendment to the federal constitution, providing for woman suffrage. As the 36th state to ratify, Tennessee brought the number to the requisite three-fourths.

After World War I Tennessee became a major industrial state, largely as a result of the Tennessee Valley authority (*q.v.*). This giant network of navigation-flood control-hydroelectric power dams on the Tennessee river and its tributaries began with the construction of Wilson dam at Muscle Shoals, Ala., in 1916. This dam, intended originally for the production of nitrates and left unfinished at the end of the war, became the focus of the controversy in the 1920s between private power interests and those who advocated governmental development of the hydroelectric potential of the Tennessee river. The dedication of Sen. George W. Norris of Nebraska to the development of public power facilities which could be used as a "yardstick" against which to measure the rates of private power companies reached fruition in 1933 when the TVA was created as a part of Pres. Franklin D. Roosevelt's New Deal program. The subsequent building of dams which provided cheap electric power to the area, and the later development of giant steam plants which provided additional power both for industry and for atomic power installations in Tennessee and Kentucky did much to improve Tennessee's economy.

**Modern Politics and Issues.**—Except for the years 1881–83, 1911–15 and 1921–23, the Democratic party has controlled the executive office since 1870. In 1920 and again in 1928 the state gave its electoral votes to the Republican presidential candidate. Tennessee returned to the Democratic fold in 1932, but in 1952, 1956 (despite the fact that in that year Tennessean Estes Kefauver was the Democratic nominee for vice-president), 1960 and 1968 the Republican party won the state's electoral votes. Tennessee remained firmly Democratic in state elections and in the election of senators until 1968, when the Democrats held five of the nine representative seats. The Democratic presidential candidate, Lyndon B. Johnson, carried Tennessee in the 1964 election and Republican Richard M. Nixon won its vote in 1968. The first Republican elected to the U.S. senate from Tennessee by popular vote was Howard H. Baker, Jr., in 1966.

## GOVERNMENT

Tennessee's constitution has been amended only once (in 1953) since its adoption in 1870. The constitution's cumbersome amending process, though somewhat liberalized at that time, still requires that a proposed amendment pass both houses of two consecutive general assemblies, the first time by a majority of the total membership of each house and the second time by a two-thirds vote of the total membership, after which it must be ratified by a majority of all citizens of the state voting in the gubernatorial election. Amendments may also be proposed by a constitutional convention and ratified in like manner by the people, but the legislature must first propose the holding of such a convention and this proposal must be approved by a majority of those who vote on it at a governor's election. Other changes made included the lengthening of the governor's term of office from two to four years with the provision that he could not succeed himself; the granting to the governor of the power of veto over individual items in appropriations bills; the consolidation of certain city and county functions; the raising of legislator's salaries; the granting of a certain amount of home rule to localities; and the repeal of the poll tax, which, in fact, had not been regularly collected.

State elections are held in even-numbered years on the first Tuesday after the first Monday in November, but local and county elections are held the first Thursday of August, which, in even-numbered years, is also the date for statewide primary elections.

**Legislative.**—The governor is the state's only popularly elected executive officer. He is elected for a term of four years and is not eligible to succeed himself. The speaker of the state senate is, by virtue of that office, lieutenant governor and succeeds the governor in the event of his death or removal from office. The treasurer, comptroller of the treasury and secretary of state are elected by joint ballot of both houses of the general assembly. The secretary of state's term is four years; the others are two-year terms. The attorney general is appointed by the members of the supreme court for an eight-year term. The heads of the major departments of the state government are appointed by and serve at the pleasure of the governor. These departments are agriculture, conservation and commerce, corrections, education, employment security, revenue, finance and administration, highways and public works, insurance and banking, labour, mental health, public health, public welfare and safety.

Following the historic U.S. supreme court decision in *Baker* v. *Carr* on March 26, 1962, that Tennessee's legislative apportionment was a proper subject for review by federal courts, a special session of the legislature adopted reapportionment legislation for the first time since 1901; this gave greater representation to urban areas but was found by a federal court still to be inadequate. The court set a 1966 deadline for the legislature to remedy the inequity.

In May 1966 the general assembly reapportioned the legislature on a one-man one-vote basis, subdividing the urban counties into senatorial districts despite state constitutional prohibitions. The reapportionment was upheld by federal courts, but the matter of subdivision of urban counties under the state constitution was left to state courts. A constitutional amendment that, in effect, made the apportionment conform to the constitution was adopted in 1966. Other amendments adopted established four-year terms of office for senators, as compared with two-year terms for house members; required legislators to live in the district they represented; extended the allowable time for legislative sessions; provided for split sessions of the assembly; and authorized the payment of an annual salary to legislators. Constitutional provisions retained were: membership to be 99 in the house and 33 in the senate; origin of bills in either house, but passage only by majority vote of the full membership of each house; overriding of a governor's veto by majority vote of the full membership of each house; and the prohibition against the holding of legislative membership by ministers, priests, or rabbis.

**Judiciary.**—The administration of justice is vested in a supreme court, a court of appeals, chancery courts, circuit courts, criminal courts, courts of general sessions, county courts, justice of the peace courts and recorders' courts. The supreme court, which has appellate jurisdiction only, consists of five judges elected by the state at large for a term of eight years, one for each of the three grand divisions (east, middle and west) and two for the state at large. The judges designate one of their number to preside as chief justice. The court of appeals is composed of nine judges, three from each grand division of the state, elected for a term of eight years. This court has jurisdiction of appeals in all equity cases, with a few exceptions, and it may transfer any case to the supreme court. The state is divided into 15 chancery divisions. Chancellors are elected for terms of eight years, and a court of chancery is held in every county seat in each division. Many of the divisions have more than one chancellor.

The state is divided into 21 circuits, in each of which a circuit judge is elected for a term of eight years, and a circuit is held in every county seat. Some circuits have more than one judge. There are also 15 criminal judges, principally in the most heavily populated areas, who are elected for eight-year terms.

Each county is divided into civil districts, varying in number according to population or other factors, and each district elects at least two justices of the peace for a term of six years; each county town or incorporated town also elects one justice of the peace. A recorder has concurrent jurisdiction with a justice of the peace. In several of the counties the county court is composed of a county judge, elected for a term of eight years, together with the justices of the peace. In other counties the court is composed of the justices of the peace alone who elect one of their number as chairman. The government of each county is vested principally in the county court. A county trustee, whose duty it is to collect state and county taxes, and a sheriff are elected by the people of the county for a term of two years; a clerk of the county court and a registrar are also elected by the voters of the county for a term of four years.

**Finance.**—Educational appropriations consume the largest portion of the total expenditure of state funds, with highways second and public welfare third. Chief sources of revenue are general sales tax, motor vehicle licences, general property tax, gasoline tax, tax on insurance companies, sales tax on tobacco and alcoholic beverages, an excise tax and an inheritance tax. Various other licences, fines and forfeitures help to augment the state's revenue funds.

Total state revenues in the second half of the 20th century were more than $800,000,000 annually; total expenditures were about $760,000,000 of which about 34% was for education, more than 28% was for highways, more than 11% for welfare and more than 11% for cities and local governments. The gross debt was about $176,000,000. Though personal income was up considerably since World War II, the state's per capita income remained among the lowest in the nation.

## POPULATION

The population of Tennessee in 1800, four years after it obtained statehood, was 105,602. Its population ranked 15th among the 22 states and territories that then composed the union, and was classified as 100% rural. The period from the first census in 1790 to 1800 was the one of the most rapid growth in the state's history—the population increased by nearly 196% during that time. Immediately before the Civil War, in 1860, the state had a population of 1,258,520 of whom about 275,000 were Negro slaves. It had advanced to the 8th most populous state, and was about 96% rural in character. At the beginning of the 20th century, the state had slipped to 14th in rank of population with a total of 2,020,616 persons by the 1900 census. It was still largely rural in character: about 84% of the people were classified as nonurban dwellers. The decade between 1910 and 1920 was the period of the slowest growth in the state's history. In 1920 the population was only 7% greater than it had been in 1910. Since 1920 the Negro population has been steadily rising, but its proportion of the total population has been declining since 1880. The 1950 population showed a total of 3,291,718 persons living within the state, making Tennessee the 16th in size of population among the states. The rural population had declined to 55.9% of the total at that time. There were four standard metropolitan areas in 1960. They were Chattanooga (Hamilton County in Tennessee and Walker County in Georgia); Knoxville (Anderson, Blount and Knox counties); Memphis (Shelby County in Tennessee, to which Crittenden County in Arkansas was added in 1963); and Nashville (Davidson

*Tennessee: Places of 5,000 or More Population (1960 Census)**

| Place | Population | | | | |
|---|---|---|---|---|---|
| | 1960 | 1950 | 1940 | 1920 | 1900 |
| Total state | 3,567,089 | 3,291,718 | 2,915,841 | 2,337,885 | 2,020,616 |
| Alcoa | 6,395 | 6,355 | 5,131 | 3,358 | — |
| Athens | 12,103 | 8,618 | 6,930 | 2,580 | 1,849 |
| Bristol | 17,582 | 16,771 | 14,004 | 8,047 | 5,271 |
| Brownsville | 5,424 | 4,711 | 4,012 | 3,062 | 2,645 |
| Chattanooga | 130,009 | 131,041 | 128,163 | 57,895 | 30,154 |
| Clarksville | 22,021 | 16,246 | 11,831 | 8,110 | 9,431 |
| Cleveland | 16,196 | 12,605 | 11,351 | 6,522 | 3,858 |
| Columbia | 17,624 | 10,911 | 10,579 | 5,526 | 6,052 |
| Cookeville | 7,805 | 6,924 | 4,364 | 2,395 | — |
| Covington | 5,298 | 4,379 | 3,513 | 3,410 | 2,787 |
| Dickson | 5,028 | 3,348 | 3,504 | 2,263 | 1,363 |
| Donelson | 17,195 | 1,765 | — | — | — |
| Dyersburg | 12,499 | 10,885 | 10,034 | 6,444 | 3,647 |
| Eagleton Village | 5,068 | — | — | — | — |
| East Ridge | 19,570 | 9,645 | 2,939 | — | — |
| Elizabethton | 10,896 | 10,754 | 8,516 | 2,749 | — |
| Fayetteville | 6,804 | 5,447 | 4,684 | 3,629 | 2,708 |
| Fountain City | 10,365 | — | — | — | — |
| Franklin | 6,977 | 5,475 | 4,120 | 3,123 | 2,180 |
| Gallatin | 7,901 | 5,107 | 4,829 | 2,757 | 2,409 |
| Greeneville | 11,759 | 8,721 | 6,784 | 3,775 | 1,817 |
| Harriman | 5,931 | 6,389 | 5,620 | 4,019 | 3,442 |
| Humboldt | 8,482 | 7,426 | 5,160 | 3,913 | 2,866 |
| Inglewood | 26,527 | — | — | — | — |
| Jackson | 33,849 | 30,207 | 24,332 | 18,860 | 14,511 |
| Johnson City | 29,892 | 27,864 | 25,332 | 12,442 | 4,645 |
| Kingsport | 26,314 | 19,571 | 14,404 | 5,692 | — |
| Knoxville | 111,827 | 124,769 | 111,580 | 77,818 | 32,637 |
| La Follette | 6,204 | 5,797 | 4,010 | 3,056 | 366 |
| Lawrenceburg | 8,042 | 5,442 | 3,807 | 2,461 | 823 |
| Lebanon | 10,512 | 7,913 | 5,950 | 4,084 | 1,956 |
| Lewisburg | 6,338 | 5,164 | 3,582 | 2,711 | 1,421 |
| Lynn Gardens | 5,261 | — | — | — | — |
| McMinnville | 9,013 | 7,577 | 4,649 | 2,814 | 1,980 |
| Madison | 13,583 | — | — | — | — |
| Maryville | 10,348 | 7,742 | 5,609 | 3,739 | — |
| Memphis | 497,524 | 396,000 | 292,942 | 162,351 | 102,320 |
| Milan | 5,208 | 4,938 | 3,035 | 2,057 | 1,682 |
| Millington | 6,059 | 4,696 | 730 | 657 | — |
| Morristown | 21,267 | 13,019 | 8,050 | 5,875 | 2,973 |
| Murfreesboro | 18,991 | 13,052 | 9,495 | 5,367 | 3,999 |
| Nashville | 170,874 | 174,307 | 167,402 | 118,342 | 80,865 |
| Newport | 6,448 | 3,892 | 3,575 | 2,753 | 1,630 |
| Oak Ridge | 27,169 | 30,229 | — | — | — |
| Paris | 9,325 | 8,826 | 6,395 | 4,730 | 2,018 |
| Pulaski | 6,616 | 5,762 | 5,314 | 2,780 | 2,838 |
| Red Bank-White Oak | 10,777 | — | — | — | — |
| Rockwood | 5,345 | 4,272 | 3,981 | 4,652 | 2,899 |
| Shelbyville | 10,466 | 9,456 | 6,537 | 2,912 | 2,236 |
| Springfield | 9,221 | 6,506 | 6,668 | 3,860 | 1,732 |
| Tullahoma | 12,242 | 7,562 | 4,549 | 3,479 | 2,684 |
| Union City | 8,837 | 7,665 | 7,256 | 4,412 | 3,407 |
| Whitehaven | 13,894 | 1,311 | — | — | — |
| Woodbine-Radnor-Glencliff | 14,485 | — | — | — | — |
| Woodmont-Green Hills-Glendale | 23,161 | — | — | — | — |

*Populations are reported as constituted at date of each census.
Note: Dash indicates place did not exist during reported census, or data not available.

County to which Sumner and Wilson counties were added in 1963; *see* NASHVILLE). In 1960, 47.6% of the state's population lived in these metropolitan areas.

In 1960 Tennessee had a population of 3,567,089, an increase of 275,371 or 8.4% over 1950. The state ranked 17th in size of population. The population per square mile in 1960 was 84.4 (326.0 per square kilometer), as compared with 49.6 for the U.S. as a whole. The 1960 urban population was 1,864,828 or 52.3% of the total, continuing the trend toward increasing urban residence. Distribution by race and nativity, according to the 1960 census was as follows: 83.5% native white; 0.4% foreign-born white and 16.5% nonwhite, practically all Negro. In line with the rest of the U.S. the percentage of persons 65 years old or over was increasing, being 8.7% in 1960. The percentage of the population 14 years old and over that was in the labour force was 52.6 in 1960.

## EDUCATION

The first steps toward the creation of a common school system for Tennessee were taken in 1823, when an act was passed setting aside for school purposes the revenue and taxes accruing from public lands. From that beginning until the adoption of a uniform school code in 1925, more than 1,000 different acts were passed pertaining to the educational system.

Under the new code the administration is vested in a state commissioner of education; a state board of education, consisting of the commissioner, the governor and nine other members; a county superintendent and a county board in each county; and in cities, city boards of education.

The commissioner and the other members of the state board are appointed by the governor. The county superintendent is elected biennially by either the county court or by popular ballot. The county board consists of seven members (unless otherwise provided), elected by the county court or by popular ballot, for a term of seven years, one retiring annually.

The state board of education prescribes the rules and regulations for the operation of the school program, and prescribes standards and requirements for curriculum, teacher certification, school buildings, grading and instructional materials. It also maintains and controls the five state colleges and Tennessee Agricultural and Industrial state university.

The quarterly county court has power to issue bonds, levy taxes and provide funds for buildings for the county schools. The court is under obligation to maintain at least one four-year high school within the county.

Public schools are free to all persons above six years of age. Attendance is compulsory between the ages of 7 and 16 unless high school standing has been attained. A state that had a history of segregated schools for whites and Negroes, Tennessee began to desegregate them after the U.S. supreme court decision in 1954 declared such schools unconstitutional.

**Universities and Colleges.**—The largest institution of higher learning provided by the state is the University of Tennessee, at Knoxville. Chartered by the legislature of the Southwest Territory in 1794 under the name of Blount college, it became East Tennessee college in 1807 and East Tennessee university in 1840. It was incorporated as Agricultural and Mechanical college in 1869 and took its present name in 1879. The main campus remains at Knoxville, but the graduate school; school of biological sciences; colleges of medicine, dentistry and pharmacy; school of nursing; and division of public health are at Memphis. The agricultural extension branch office and the school of social work are at Nashville; substations of the agricultural experiment station are at Jackson, Columbia, Greeneville, Crossville, Springfield and Lewisburg; and there is a branch of the university at Martin. Other state-controlled schools include Memphis State university (1909); East Tennessee State university at Johnson City (1911); Middle Tennessee State university at Murfreesboro (1909); Tennessee Technical university at Cookeville (1915); Austin Peay State university at Clarksville (1927); and Tennessee Agricultural and Industrial State university at Nashville (1912).

Privately controlled institutions of higher learning include Bethel college, McKenzie (Presbyterian, 1842); Carson-Newman college, Jefferson City (Baptist, 1851); Fisk university, Nashville (American Missionary association affiliate, 1867), originally established by the Freedmen's bureau as a school for Negroes; George Peabody College for Teachers, Nashville (nonsectarian, 1785); Lincoln Memorial university, Harrogate (nonsectarian, 1897); Maryville college, Maryville (United Presbyterian, 1819); Southwestern at Memphis, Memphis (Presbyterian, 1848); Tennessee Wesleyan college, Athens (Methodist, 1857); Tusculum college, Greeneville (United Presbyterian, 1794); Union university, Jackson (Baptist, 1825); University of the South, Sewanee (Protestant Episcopal, 1857); and Vanderbilt university, Nashville (nonsectarian, 1873), one of the best-known schools in the south and endowed by Cornelius Vanderbilt.

## HEALTH, WELFARE AND CORRECTIONS

The state department of public health, headed by a commissioner of cabinet rank, is made up of 11 divisions which have jurisdiction over central administration, local health service, crippled children's service, dental health, laboratories, preventable diseases, sanitary engineering, tuberculosis control, vital statistics, hospital survey and construction, medical care and industrial hygiene. A department of mental health provides psychological, nursing, statistical, fiscal and personnel service, as well as directing work in forensic psychiatry, mental health education, psychiatric social work, nutrition and the engineering and planning of mental health installations. There are state mental hospitals at Knoxville, Nashville and Bolivar; a psychiatric hospital in Memphis; a home for the mentally defective in Donelson; and community mental health centres in various parts of the state.

The department of correction has its main penitentiary at Nashville. A branch known as Brushy Mountain prison is located at Petros in east Tennessee. There the prisoners work principally in the state coal mines and on a farm. Fort Pillow state farm in west Tennessee is primarily for first offenders.

The department of public welfare administers programs of public assistance to the aged, the blind, the disabled and to dependent children. It also aids in rehabilitation and training of sightless persons; regulates public and private child care agencies; oversees adoptions and placing of dependent children in foster homes.

### THE ECONOMY

Tennessee was primarily an agricultural state until the second quarter of the 20th century, when manufacturing became the major source of the state's wealth. Pre-Civil War Tennessee, especially the middle and western portions, belonged to the "king cotton" complex of southern states; however, the state's economy was never as completely geared to cotton as that of the states of the deep south. Tobacco has almost always been the state's second most valuable crop, with corn, hay and wheat also ranking high in value of production. Since World War II Tennessee's already diversified farming has been affected by two major trends: emphasis on livestock production and the mechanization of farm operations. The breeding of show cattle (particularly Jersey, Angus and Hereford breeds) has become important in the state's rapidly growing livestock and dairy industry. Tennessee walking horses are bred almost solely for show. The once comfortable and utilitarian plantation horse with its "rocking chair ride" became less a riding horse, though its exaggerated gaits are much admired.

**Agriculture.**—The number of acres of farmland remained fairly constant in the second half of the 20th century, but with more intensive cultivation there had been a constant decline in acres of cropland harvested. By the 1960s there were about 1,400,000 ac. less than in 1925. Much former cropland had been turned into pasture needed for the growing livestock industry in Tennessee. During this same period the size of the average farm increased from 70.8 to about 100 ac. and the average value of land and buildings from about $3,000 to about $13,000. The number of farm operators declined from more than 250,000 to slightly more than 200,000, of whom approximately 120,000 were full owners, 30,000 part owners and 50,000 tenants; there were about 400 managers. Of the farm operators about 10% were nonwhites, most of them Negroes. Tennessee farmers averaged total cash receipts from farming of more than $475,000,000 annually, about evenly divided between livestock and their products and crops. Livestock income was chiefly from dairy products, cattle and hogs. Leading crops were tobacco, soybeans, hay, corn and cotton.

**Forests.**—In the late 1960s Tennessee's forest lands totaled about 14,000,000 ac. and contributed a large portion of the state's agricultural and industrial income through lumber and wood products, furniture and pulp paper industries.

**Minerals.**—Tennessee ranks about 27th among the states in the value of its mineral products. The principal minerals are coal, cement, stone, phosphate rock, zinc and sand and gravel. Other mineral products of economic value were clays, lime, manganese, lead, gold, silver, barite, petroleum, natural gas and celestite. Production of copper, with the gold and silver by-products of the smelting process, is largely confined to Polk county in the southeastern portion of the state. The coal-producing area is in the Cumberland plateau; building marble, for which Tennessee is famous, comes from the eastern part of the state; and phosphate deposits are localized in middle Tennessee.

**Manufacturing.**—Tennessee experienced a rapid industrial development in the second half of the 20th century. From the early 1930s to 1960s the number of manufacturing establishments and their employees approximately tripled. Chief industries in the late 1960s included chemicals, food and kindred products, textiles, electrical machinery, lumber and wood products, pulp and paper, printing and publishing, and primary metals. Among large industrial installations were the aluminum plant at Alcoa, chemical plants at Kingsport and Old Hickory, and newsprint mills at Calhoun.

**Transportation.**—Railway mileage in Tennessee, 4,078 mi. in 1920, decreased to less than 3,500 mi. in the second half of the 20th century. Paralleling the decline of railway mileage was a steady growth of the highway system which totaled more than 75,000 mi. by the late 1960s, of which about 8,500 mi. were state roads. Much freight formerly handled by railroads had been taken over by highway trucking firms; much additional freight was being carried by barges on the Tennessee and Cumberland rivers, where huge dams and locks constructed by the Tennessee Valley authority and by the U.S. army corps of engineers had made possible massive barge tows and extremely low shipping charges.

*See* also references under "Tennessee" in the Index.

BIBLIOGRAPHY.—W. T. Alderson and Robert H. White, *A Guide to the Study and Reading of Tennessee History* (1959). *History—General:* Cartter Patten, *A Tennessee Chronicle* (1953); Philip M. Hamer (ed.), *Tennessee; a History,* 4 vol. (1933); Joseph H. Parks and Stanley J. Folmsbee, *The Story of Tennessee,* 4th ed. (1963); Stanley J. Folmsbee *et al., History of Tennessee* (1960); Mary U. Rothrock, *This Is Tennessee* (1963); Robert H. White, *Tennessee: Its Growth and Progress* (1936); Tennessee Historical Commission, *Tennessee Old and New,* 2 vol. (1946); W. T. Alderson and Hulan Glyn Thomas, *Historic Sites in Tennessee* (1967); W. T. Alderson and R. M. McBride, *Landmarks of Tennessee History* (1965); W. T. Alderson, *Tennessee: a Student's Guide to Localized History* (1966).

*History—Various phases:* Donald Davidson, *The Tennessee,* 2 vol. (1946–48); Robert L. Kincaid, *The Wilderness Road* (1947); Laura Thornborough, *The Great Smoky Mountains* (1937); Tennessee Secretary of State, *Tennessee Blue Book* (1890– ); Stanley F. Horn, *The Army of Tennessee* (1953), *The Decisive Battle of Nashville* (1956); T. M. N. Lewis and Madeline Kneberg, *Tribes That Slumber* (1958); Samuel C. Williams, *Dawn of Tennessee Valley and Tennessee History* (1937), *Early Travels in the Tennessee Country, 1540–1800* (1928), *History of the Lost State of Franklin* (1933), *Tennessee During the Revolutionary War* (1944), *Beginnings of West Tennessee, in the Land of the Chickasaws* (1930); Thomas P. Abernethy, *From Frontier to Plantation in Tennessee* (1932); Lyman C. Draper, *King's Mountain and Its Heroes* (1954); Blanche Henry Clark, *The Tennessee Yeoman, 1840–1860* (1942); Claude A. Campbell, *The Development of Banking in Tennessee* (1932); Henry T. Malone, *Cherokees of the Old South* (1956); Robert S. Cotterill, *The Southern Indians* (1954); Stanley J. Folmsbee, *Sectionalism and Internal Improvements in Tennessee, 1796–1845* (1939); Robert H. White, *Development of the Tennessee State Educational Organization* (1929); Chase C. Mooney, *Slavery in Tennessee* (1957); Robert S. Henry, *First With the Most Forrest* (1944); James W. Patton, *Unionism and Reconstruction in Tennessee, 1860–1869* (1934); Thomas B. Alexander, *Political Reconstruction in Tennessee* (1950); Daniel M. Robison, *Bob Taylor and the Agrarian Revolt in Tennessee* (1935); Harriette Arnow, *Seedtime on the Cumberland* (1960), *Flowering of the Cumberland* (1963); John Anthony Caruso, *The Appalachian Frontier* (1959). *See* also Robert H. White, *Messages of the Governors of Tennessee,* 7 vol. (1952–67).

Current statistics on production, employment, industry, etc., may be obtained from the pertinent state departments; the principal figures are summarized annually in the *Britannica Book of the Year.* (W. T. A.)

**TENNESSEE RIVER,** the largest tributary of the Ohio river, U.S., is formed by the confluence of the Holston and the French Broad rivers 4.5 mi. (7.2 km.) above Knoxville, Tenn. The upstream tributaries of the Tennessee drain the southern part of the Appalachian mountains, and the highest part, the Great Smokies, has the largest total rainfall in the eastern half of the U.S. The Holston, the Clinch and their tributaries rise on the mountain slopes that flank the valleys in western Virginia; the French Broad, the Little Tennessee and their tributaries rise in the high mountains of western North Carolina; the Hiwassee and its tributaries rise in the mountains of western North Carolina and northern Georgia.

The Tennessee flows south-southwest to Chattanooga, turns west through the Cumberland plateau into northeast Alabama, continues west across the northern part of Alabama, turns north on the boundary between Alabama and Mississippi and, continuing north across Tennessee and Kentucky, unites with the Ohio at Paducah, Ky. The drainage basin includes parts of seven states.

The Tennessee itself is 652 mi. (1,049 km.) long, and with the Holston and the North fork of the Holston forms a channel about 900 mi. (1,450 km.) long. Its drainage basin covers about 39,000 sq.mi. (99,800 sq.km.).

**History.**—The name of the river, like that of the state, may have come from a village of the Cherokee Indians, located on the Little Tennessee, and named "Tanase" or "Tennassee."

Detailed exploration of the Tennessee river took place during the period of rivalry between the French and the English for the territory west of the Appalachians. A few small forts and posts had been established by each rival. Previous to this, other early explorers and fur traders had entered the lower river from the Ohio.

The lands along the upper (Holston and Watauga) valley began to receive American settlers by the 1770s and 1780s. These had crossed the Appalachians from North Carolina or had arrived by way of the Appalachian valley routes (such as the Shenandoah) from Virginia and Pennsylvania. The first house in Knoxville, at the head of the Tennessee, was built in 1786; the townsite was soon surveyed. By this time it became possible for the river itself to serve as a route for further movement southwestward. Many settlers continued downstream on flatboats to the lands between Knoxville and Chattanooga, or into what is now northern Alabama. However, more westward settlements resulted from travel on overland routes through the Cumberland gap (60 mi. northeast of Knoxville) or on roads westward across the Cumberlands. The role of the Tennessee as a westward passage was negligible as compared to the Ohio.

Originally the Tennessee was navigated with difficulty, and only by shallow-draft boats. The upper course was shallow where mountain ridges were broached, filled with short rapids which hindered navigation except at high water and the river was subject to seasonal fluctuations. The rapid run-off from mountainous upstream tributaries, followed by periods of lower flow, resulted in both downstream floods and periods of insufficient water for safe navigation. The middle course of the Tennessee, through the Cumberlands, was tortuous, contained whirlpools and was interrupted by the famous Muscle Shoals (*q.v.*). Only the lower course, north-flowing in western Tennessee, was easily navigated.

The Tennessee furnished an early but circuitous route to eastern markets for flour, bacon, whisky and other products of the pioneers. Flatboats made the downstream journey to the Ohio, and thence to the Mississippi and to New Orleans. From there shipments went by sea to Atlantic coast markets. Upstream traffic, via keelboats, was not important. Steamboat operation on the river dates mainly from the 1820s. The advent of railroads in the valley, after the 1840s, kept river traffic from assuming the significance it had on other western, more easily navigated rivers.

Only two cities of considerable size are on the Tennessee: Knoxville at the head of navigation, and Chattanooga at an important river crossing and route centre. Traffic westward from Chattanooga focuses through the "gorge" of the river, cut through the Cumberland plateau. In early settlement days the site of Chattanooga was an important "landing." Cities of moderate size on the river (all in Alabama) are Guntersville, Decatur, Florence and Tuscumbia; these date from early settlement. Sheffield, also on the river, was not founded until the 1880s. Savannah, in western Tennessee, is the largest town on the lower course. Many of the early "landings" and "ferries" were by the second half of the 20th century only hamlets or were in ruins.

The northward-flowing lower course of the Tennessee was of utmost importance during the Civil War. It and its valley offered an invasion route into the western Confederacy. The very downstream part of the course is paralleled by the Cumberland river (*q.v.*). Confederate Ft. Henry was on the Tennessee; Ft. Donelson was 12 mi. away on the Cumberland. The army of General Grant, accompanied by federal gunboats, struck southward in the valley in February 1862. The Confederate armies fell back to Corinth, Miss., and the Union armies moved almost to the southern boundary of Tennessee. Here was fought the battle called either Pittsburgh Landing or Shiloh. With the eventual capture of the middle and western valley by Union forces, and the fall of Chattanooga, the entire Tennessee valley fell to Union forces. The upper valley in mountainous east Tennessee saw little fighting except at Knoxville; in fact, many upper east Tennesseans remained loyal to the Union.

River traffic on the Tennessee remained of only moderate importance into the early 1900s. Interestingly, for a time, marble from the Knoxville and other quarries was actually shipped to eastern building projects via the circuitous river route. The development of the river system to a higher place among the inland waterways of the United States came during the 20th century (*see* TENNESSEE VALLEY AUTHORITY).

The Tennessee is today a series of reservoirs, called lakes, each impounded by a dam. The nine mainstream dams are Kentucky, in Kentucky; Pickwick Landing, in Tennessee; Wilson, Wheeler and Guntersville, in Alabama; and Hales Bar, Chickamauga, Watts Bar, and Ft. Loudoun (which impounds the water to Knoxville at the confluence of Holston and French Broad), in Tennessee. The impoundments are extensively used for recreation. (L. DD.)

**TENNESSEE VALLEY AUTHORITY,** a U.S. government agency established in 1933 to control floods, improve navigation and produce electrical power along the Tennessee river and its tributaries. The jurisdiction of the Tennessee Valley authority (TVA) is generally limited to the drainage basin of the Tennessee river, but some of its activities extend beyond the region.

The drainage basin, an area of almost 39,000 sq.mi. (99,800 sq.km.) covers parts of seven states: Alabama, Georgia, Kentucky, Mississippi, North Carolina, Tennessee and Virginia. Its 1965 population was approximately 3,500,000.

The Tennessee, fifth largest among U.S. rivers in volume of stream flow, provided a means of westward travel by American frontiersmen as early as 1800. Travel on the river was interrupted, however, at Muscle Shoals, Ala., where the river dropped approximately 100 ft. in the course of 20 mi. Early efforts by state and private interests to cope with the shoals met with failure or with only limited success. It was not until World War I that national attention was drawn to the Tennessee. At that time the U.S. government determined to erect two nitrate manufacturing plants at Muscle Shoals for the manufacture of munitions: these plants were to free the nation from dependence on Germany and Chile for nitrates. The government also determined to construct a dam on the river to supply hydroelectric power to run the nitrate plants, along with a steam-electric plant to provide additional power. None of these undertakings had been finished by the end of the war, when it was decided to suspend construction work, though Wilson dam was later completed. The government's investment in the Muscle Shoals properties up to 1918 was somewhat more than $100,000,000.

In the next 15 years there were as many as half a dozen serious proposals for liquidating the government's investment at Muscle Shoals. Some failed to reach the action stage and congress refused to approve others. Two bills providing for government development of the properties were approved by congress, but were vetoed by the president. In 1933, two unusual circumstances combined to produce a decision on the question: (1) in that year the country was in the depths of a great depression; (2) Pres. Franklin D. Roosevelt strongly favoured a course regarding the Muscle Shoals properties that would put idle men to work and stimulate the economy of the region. These circumstances, placed against the background of a long history of frustration and delay, were sufficient to cause congress to pass a bill introduced jointly by Sen. George W. Norris of Nebraska and Rep. Lister Hill of Alabama to establish the Tennessee Valley authority. The bill was signed by President Roosevelt on May 18, 1933.

The act established the TVA as a regional agency of the U.S. government. In legal form the authority was a public corporation; though it was a governmental agency it had many of the attributes of a private corporation. The TVA established its administrative headquarters at Knoxville, Tenn. It was governed by a board of three directors appointed by the president by and with the advice and consent of the senate. The TVA normally employed somewhat more than 15,000 people. The greatest concentrations of TVA personnel were in Knoxville and Chattanooga, Tenn., and at Muscle Shoals, Ala.

**The TVA Program.**—Those who drafted the TVA act visualized that agency as something approaching a federal department of natural resources for the Tennessee valley. The program outlined for the new agency did not contemplate for it any new or startling powers; for most of the things it was to do were already being done, in the Tennessee valley and elsewhere, by a host of governmental agencies. What was new about the TVA was that its activities were to be focused on a river drainage basin, and that they were to be brought together in the hands of a single agency. The TVA, then, represented a new approach to

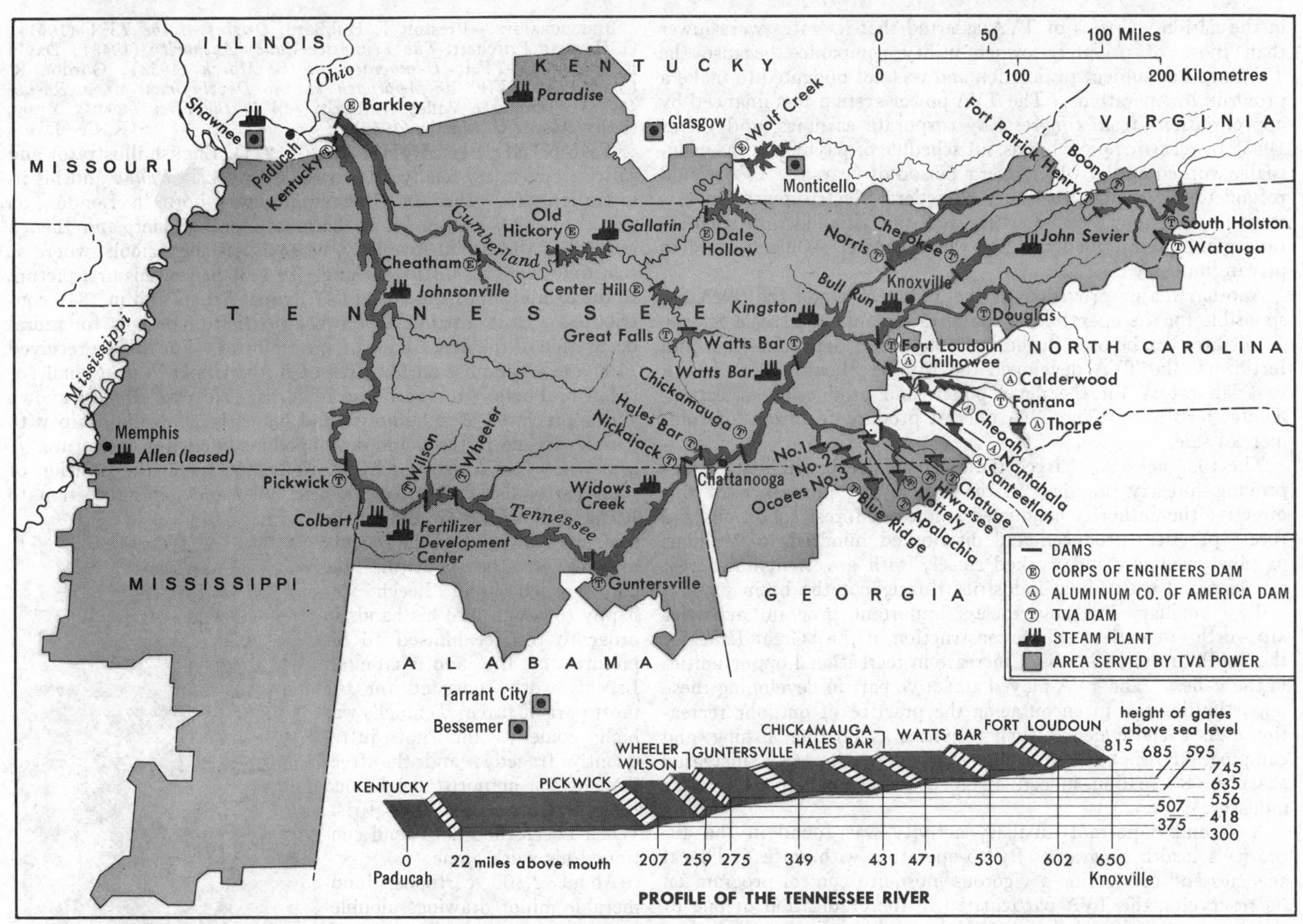

AREA SERVED BY THE TENNESSEE VALLEY AUTHORITY

the administration of natural resources in the United States.

The 1933 act, recognizing water as a basic natural resource, gave the TVA three broad, basic powers over the Tennessee river: (1) it was directed to take such action as might prove necessary to control floods on the river; (2) it was required to develop navigation on the river; (3) it was instructed to produce and market electric power "so far as [may prove] consistent with such purposes." The constitutionality of the TVA was immediately challenged but was upheld by the supreme court in the case of *Ashwander* v. *TVA* (1936) and in later decisions.

The TVA eventually operated 32 major dams, 9 of them on the main stream of the Tennessee and 23 on its tributaries. Of this total the TVA built 21; it purchased a few from a private power company; and a few, originally built and owned by a private industry, were operated by the authority as part of its river control system. (The TVA also marketed electric power from five dams constructed by the U.S. army corps of engineers on the Cumberland river, but since these are in another drainage basin they are not considered here.) All dams in the system were managed as a unit, with emphasis first of all on flood control. It was, of course, not possible to avoid all floods, for that would have required complete control of every minor tributary stream, which was not economically practicable. Large floods, however, were prevented; no major flood damage occurred on the Tennessee river after the system of dams was completed.

Navigation, the second major responsibility of the TVA, increased markedly after 1933. In that year the river carried little commercial traffic: mainly short-haul bulk items such as sand and gravel. The TVA built navigation locks into each of its nine main dams, deepened and otherwise improved the channel, and encouraged both local governments and private businesses to develop port facilities along the river. As a result, river traffic increased from 33,000,000 ton-miles in 1933 to 600,000,000 in 1950 and more than 2,000,000,000 in the 1960s.

A third major activity named in the 1933 act, the production and sale of electric power, was a highly controversial issue and was resisted by privately owned power companies. At first it was confined to the output of the turbines installed in the big dams. In carrying out this function, the TVA entered into contracts with municipalities and co-operatives to supply wholesale power for distribution and joined with them in purchasing the facilities of privately-owned electric utility companies in the region. These purchases established an integrated power service area in which the TVA was the sole supplier of power. To the end of World War II, and for several years thereafter, hydroelectric plants supplied most of the power. The continuing growth of power requirements for homes, farms and industry, together with a vast expansion in power requirements for defense plants such as those of the Atomic Energy commission, made necessary the extensive construction of steam plants. In 1950, 90% of the power produced by the TVA system came from the big dams, but by 1962 this had shrunk to about 25%. The decrease in the percentage of hydroelectric power was accounted for by the big new steam-electric plants built after 1950. One of these plants was the largest of its kind in the United States and another was the second largest. They consumed a total of about 18,000,000 tons of coal a year.

In the 1960s the TVA power system, which included 48 dams and several steam plants, possessed a generating capacity of nearly 12,000,000 kw. TVA sold its power in bulk, almost half of it to federal agencies, principally the Atomic Energy commission; of the remaining half, about one-third went to large industries, which were served directly, and about two-thirds to 155 locally-owned municipal and co-operative distribution systems. Electric rates in the Tennessee valley, reflecting the economies resulting from the authority's emphasis on mass markets, were among the lowest in the nation. Critics of TVA asserted that its rates were lower than those of privately owned utility companies because the TVA was not subject to taxation and was not obligated to make a profit on its operations. The TVA power system was financed by appropriations from congress, by corporate earnings, and (after 1960) by electric power bonds. A schedule of payments was eventually worked out by which over a period of years the TVA would refund to the national treasury all federal electric power investment in the valley. Some critics were not satisfied with such arrangements and argued that the whole project should be sold to private industry.

Another major provision of the 1933 act made the TVA responsible for the operation of the nitrate plants at Muscle Shoals. As nitrates can be used in the manufacture of both munitions and fertilizers, the TVA developed the Muscle Shoals plants into a vast laboratory for the development and production of experimental fertilizers. The TVA did not produce fertilizer for commercial sale.

The 1933 act also charged the TVA with responsibility for improving forestry practices in the region. In pursuance of this directive the authority conducted studies of forest conditions and forest practice, produced and distributed hundreds of millions of pine seedlings, and worked closely with governmental forest agencies and with forest industries throughout the basin.

Two auxiliary but nevertheless important program activities are worthy of notice. First, construction of the "Great Lakes of the South" resulted in a vast increase in recreational opportunities in the valley. The TVA played an active part in developing these opportunities and in encouraging the practice of outdoor recreation. As a consequence, such activities as boating, fishing, and camping, known only in rudimentary form in 1933, increased sharply. Recreation, indeed, assumed the proportions of a major industry.

A second important auxiliary activity was found in the authority's health program. By co-operating with state and local agencies and conducting a vigorous mosquito control program on its reservoirs, the TVA participated in the eradication of one of the area's most dread diseases. In a region where malaria had been endemic, no case of malaria traceable to the river was reported after 1948.

**Methods of Work.**—Two outstanding features characterized TVA's approach to the regional administration of natural resources. First was application of the principle of multiple use throughout the watershed. It is possible to develop a river for the single purpose of preventing flooding, or of promoting navigation, or of producing electric power; but it is also possible to develop it for all three purposes simultaneously, and for other subsidiary purposes as well. In 1933 there were very few multiple-use water installations in the United States, and there was no river basin to which the multiple-use principle was applied in its entirety. In this respect the TVA was a unique institution in U.S. river basin development.

TVA's operating methods were unique in yet a second important respect. Instead of building the agency into a regional supergovernment, the TVA board of directors decided to work, to the maximum degree possible, through the valley's existing governments—the states, counties and municipalities. This made for an intricate network of agreements and contracts among the governments of the basin covering a wide variety of activities, such as health, forestry, agriculture, parks and other recreational facilities, navigation and electric power. The TVA thus became one of the foremost practitioners of co-operative administration to be found in the United States.

The TVA is held in high esteem in other countries. Some 3,000 foreign visitors, many of them high government officials, visit the valley each year to see for themselves how the TVA operates and what it has achieved. It has been the inspiration for similar projects in other lands—in India, for example, with its Damodar valley development, and in Colombia with its Cauca river project. The TVA inspired no similar river valley developments in the United States, though a number of principles that it developed were put into operation in various river basins.

Bibliography.—Preston J. Hubbard, *Origins of the TVA* (1961); C. Herman Pritchett, *The Tennessee Valley Authority* (1943); David E. Lilienthal, *TVA: Democracy on the March* (1953); Gordon R. Clapp, *The TVA: an Approach to the Development of a Region* (1955); Tennessee Valley Authority, *TVA: the First Twenty Years,* ed. by Roscoe C. Martin (1956). (R. C. Ma.)

**TENNIEL, SIR JOHN** (1820–1914), English illustrator and satirical artist, especially known for his work in *Punch* and his illustrations for *Alice in Wonderland,* was born in London on Feb. 28, 1820. Although he became a probationer, and then a student of the Royal Academy, he soon left the schools, where at that time there was little teaching. In 1836 he sent his first picture to the exhibition of the Society of British Artists and in 1845 contributed a 16-ft. cartoon to the competition of designs for mural decoration of the new Palace of Westminster. For this he received £100 and a commission for a fresco in the Upper Waiting hall (or "Hall of Poets") in the house of lords. He was already known and appreciated as a humorist and his early companionship with Charles Keene fostered and developed his talent for caricature.

In 1850 he was invited by Mark Lemon to fill the position of joint cartoonist (with John Leech) on *Punch,* in succession to Richard Doyle. Gradually he took over altogether the weekly drawing of the political "big cut," which John Leech was happy to resign into his hands in order to restrict himself to his pictures of life and character. Leech's work consisted for the most part of farce; Tenniel's was high comedy and not infrequently tragedy; and the freedom of the humorist heightened the severe beauties of the satirist. When Leech died his friend continued his work alone.

About 2,300 cartoons, innumerable minor drawings, double-page cartoons for *Punch's Almanac* and other special numbers and 250 designs for *Punch's Pocket-books* comprise the sum of Sir John Tenniel's work for the periodical in the service of which he spent the greater portion of his life. His most famous cartoon was probably "Dropping the Pilot" (1890), on the subject of Bismarck's resignation.

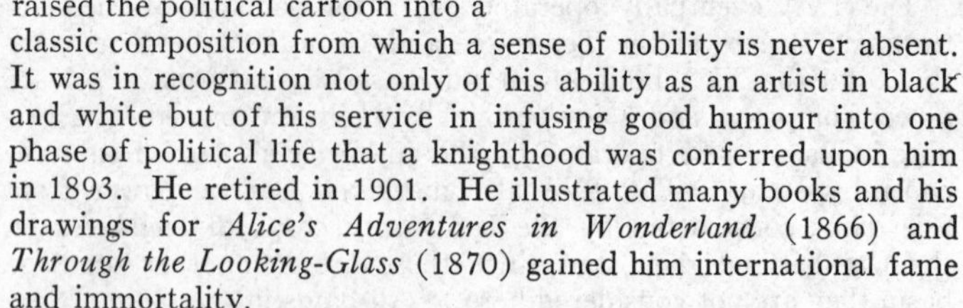

PHOTOGRAPHED FROM A WOODCUT IN THE BRITISH MUSEUM BY JOHN R. FREEMAN AND CO.

**"DROPPING THE PILOT," CARTOON BY TENNIEL COMMENTING ON THE FORCED RESIGNATION OF OTTO VON BISMARCK FROM THE GOVERNMENT OF KAISER WILLIAM II OF GERMANY**

In his drawings for *Punch* he raised the political cartoon into a classic composition from which a sense of nobility is never absent. It was in recognition not only of his ability as an artist in black and white but of his service in infusing good humour into one phase of political life that a knighthood was conferred upon him in 1893. He retired in 1901. He illustrated many books and his drawings for *Alice's Adventures in Wonderland* (1866) and *Through the Looking-Glass* (1870) gained him international fame and immortality.

See *Cartoons by Sir John Tenniel* (1901); and M. H. Spielmann, *History of Punch* (1895). (H. Es.)

**TENNIS.** Two games bearing the name tennis are closely connected by origins but are widely different. One, "lawn tennis," may be regarded as the descendant of the other, which is sometimes termed "royal tennis," "real tennis" or simply "tennis" in England but is called "court tennis" in the U.S. Lawn tennis, generally called tennis in the U.S., is the more popular and will be considered first.

## LAWN TENNIS

As an independent member of the family of ball games of which the parent root probably developed in Egypt or Persia, 500 years before the Christian era, lawn tennis is relatively modern and it had its beginning in England. It is played by men and women, at night as well as day, indoors as well as outdoors, on various surfaces—dirt, grass, clay, concrete, asphalt, wood and composition.

In 1874 an Englishman, Maj. Walter C. Wingfield, devised and applied for a patent for a "new and improved portable court for playing the ancient game of tennis." Wingfield's court was wider at the base lines than at the net and so often referred to as the hourglass court, and the game was introduced as Sphairistiké, shortened to Stické, or as its enemies liked to call it, "Sticky." The court was set up outdoors, on the grass, and under the new name tennis-on-the-lawn or lawn tennis its popularity quickly grew. About this time the All England Croquet club, located in Wimbledon, a suburb of London, discovered that its exchequer was empty, or almost so, and added the term "Lawn Tennis" to its title and several grass courts to its facilities. The first championship was held on these Wimbledon courts in June 1877, on a rectangular surface measuring 78 ft. long and 27 ft. wide, with a net 3 ft. 3 in. high at the centre. There were 22 competitors, of whom the majority were either court tennis or rackets players. The winner, Spencer W. Gore, was a former rackets star and a native of London.

It is interesting to note that the dimensions of the lawn tennis singles court remained unchanged after that time. In 1878 the height of the net was set at 4 ft. 9 in. at the posts, and 3 ft. at the centre. In 1880 the net was lowered to 4 ft. at the posts, and in 1884 to 3 ft. 6 in.

From the start until 1907, the championships at Wimbledon were won by natives of the British Isles. The early Wimbledon, however, with its bleacherless courts and general air of calm, bore little resemblance to its successors. Yet from the start the All England club had a decisive influence on the game. The Lawn Tennis association (English) was founded in 1886, the International Lawn Tennis federation not until 1912. In the interim, the game had spread to other continents.

Lawn tennis was said to have been introduced into the United States by Miss Mary E. Outerbridge, who spent the winter of 1874 in Bermuda and there saw the game played by British officers of the garrison. She returned with a lawn tennis net, some rackets and balls, obtained from the regimental stores through the courtesy of the colonel. One of her brothers, A. Emilius Outerbridge, helped her lay out a court on the grounds of the Staten Island Cricket and Baseball club. James Dwight and F. R. Sears, Jr., of Boston, Mass., obtained a tennis set from England and laid out a court at Nahant, a seaside resort in Boston harbour, a little later. The first tournament in the United States, a handicap event, was played at Nahant in Aug. 1876. The first official championships of the United States, playing under English rules and with English balls, was held at the Casino, Newport, R.I., on Aug. 31, 1881. There were 25 competitors entered in the singles and 13 pairs in the doubles. The singles was won by Richard D. Sears of Boston, who held the title every year until 1888. In 1881, the United States National Lawn Tennis association, with Gen. R. S. Oliver of the Albany Tennis club as president, was formed.

This period might be called the age of innocence of lawn tennis. In both England and the United States, the players were amateurs and sportsmen, the tournaments few in number, and watched by small galleries. In the United States, from the time of Sears until 1900, most U.S. champions were volleyers, Oliver S. Campbell and Robert D. Wrenn, who held between them seven singles titles in the 1880s and 1890s, especially so. During this period the game was played chiefly along the eastern seaboard. In 1900 a cup was donated by Dwight F. Davis, then an undergraduate at Harvard, for international competition. (From the start, all Davis Cup competitions consisted of four singles and one doubles match.) The first contest was played in Longwood, near Boston, on Aug. 8, 9 and 10, 1900, and was won by the United States, three matches to none. (One was not played, and one left unfinished.)

In 1907, Norman E. Brookes of Australia became the first overseas player to win the Wimbledon men's title. Meanwhile in the United States there was a swing away from the net game. Both William A. Larned, who held the U.S. title from 1907 to 1912, and William T. Tilden, who dominated world tennis from 1920 to 1925, were able to play the net and play it well. Yet both won the majority of their titles from the base line. In 1912 a new influence was felt in the game. For the first time in U.S. tennis the champion did not come from the eastern seaboard. That year the title was won by Maurice E. McLoughlin, a Californian trained on courts of asphalt. He introduced the cannon ball service, a weapon used by every U.S. star since then.

PHOTOGRAPHS, (LEFT) WIDE WORLD, (RIGHT) UNITED PRESS INTERNATIONAL

(LEFT) WILLIAM TILDEN, U.S., WHO DOMINATED WORLD TENNIS FROM 1920 TO 1925, IN PLAY AT THE 1930 U.S. SINGLES MATCHES AT FOREST HILLS. (RIGHT) HELEN WILLS MOODY ROARK, U.S., ONE OF THE MOST NOTEWORTHY WOMEN PLAYERS IN TENNIS HISTORY, SMASHES A HIGH ONE IN HER DEFEAT OF HELEN JACOBS, U.S., IN 1938 FOR THE ALL-ENGLAND WOMEN'S TITLE AT WIMBLEDON

By this time tennis may be said to have come of age. In 1915 the national championships of the United States were removed from the tranquillity of the Casino at Newport, R.I., to the urban setting of the West Side Tennis club at Forest Hills, Long Island. Attracted by the spectacular playing of McLoughlin, crowds turned out for the matches. At the same period, interest grew in the Davis Cup matches. In 1903, when it had been captured by the Doherty brothers, R. F. and H. L., for Great Britain at the Longwood Cricket club, in Brookline, Mass., only two nations were represented, and hardly 2,000 spectators saw the contests each afternoon. In 1914, seven nations from three continents competed, and the challenge round played at Forest Hills just after World War I broke out was witnessed by 10,000 people. Australia with the left-handed veteran Brookes, and Capt. Anthony Wilding (killed in action in Flanders in 1915) met McLoughlin and R. Norris Williams, an undergraduate at Harvard. There have perhaps been greater matches in tennis history; but few so dramatic, so grim or so spectacular. The speed of shots on both sides was tremendous. The rallies were few. It was a different style from the tennis played by the Dohertys which was based on accuracy rather than sheer speed. Tennis had changed as the world was changing.

Tilden won the title at Wimbledon in 1920, the first but not the last male American to do so. He repeated the next year, and in 1923 the first Californian, William M. Johnston, won the men's singles. In 1920 Tilden and Johnston beat the Australians at Auckland, N.Z., taking the Davis Cup back to the United States. With Williams and Vincent Richards they formed the best balanced team ever to appear on a court in an international match, and through their efforts Australian, Japanese and French challengers for the trophy were regularly defeated until 1927. The U.S. influence on sport at this period was visible in many ways. Money was now an important factor in competitive tennis. Huge crowds attended national championships and Davis Cup matches in every land. As an example, the old grounds seating several thousand spectators under wooden roofs at the Worple road, Wimbledon, were abandoned in 1921 for a new, modern, concrete tennis stadium, one mile away, seating 15,000. This stadium which was opened by King George V on June 22, 1922, attracted players from Spain, France, the United States, Italy, Ireland, Scotland, Sweden, Holland, South Africa, Belgium, Rumania, Denmark, Greece, New Zealand, Australia and England that summer. It cost £140,000, and was probably paid for in a few years. Likewise in 1923 the wooden stands of the West Side Tennis club at Forest Hills were replaced by a concrete stadium seating more than 13,-000. The first Wightman Cup matches inaugurated the stadium.

UNITED PRESS INTERNATIONAL

DON BUDGE, U.S., WINNER OF FOUR MAJOR SINGLES CHAMPIONSHIPS IN 1938, PLAYS A FOREHAND DRIVE

By this time young Frenchmen were advancing in the technique of the game, and a French team composed of J. R. Lacoste, J. Borotra, H. Cochet and J. Brugnon (the "Four Musketeers") reached the challenge round of the Davis Cup for the first time in 1925. Two years later they were the survivors of 25 nations, and crossing the ocean found themselves for the third time challenging the holders, the United States, at Philadelphia, Pa. This time they discovered that age had stemmed the power of the two great U.S. stars, Tilden and Johnston. They carried the cup back to France. This was the first of six years of French successes in tennis.

In 1933, a total of 32 different countries challenged France for the Davis Cup. The trophy was finally won by Great Britain, who defeated the French in the challenge round at Paris. For the first time in 20 years this international sporting cup was returned to the land which gave the game birth.

With its young stars Fred Perry and "Bunny" Austin, Great Britain was in the driver's seat until the arrival of another star from California, J. Donald Budge. Perry had won three successive championships at Wimbledon (1934–36) and three times at Forest Hills (1933, 1934 and 1936).

Budge not only succeeded Perry as Wimbledon and U.S. champion but set a new record when in one year (1938) he won the four major singles championships of the world—Australia, France, Great Britain and the United States. One of Budge's most noted victories was his defeat of Baron Gottfried von Cramm, German star, in the deciding match of the Davis Cup Interzone final at Wimbledon in 1937. Tilden declared afterward that it was one of the finest matches he had even seen. Von Cramm won the first two sets and Budge evened the score. Then the German took a commanding 4–1 lead in the final set, but Budge again pulled even and finally, after having had five match points in the 14th game, he won it for the set and match. Budge again defeated Von Cramm in the 1937 final at Forest Hills to win his first U.S. championship.

The loss of Budge to the professional game in 1938 after he had repeated his Wimbledon, Forest Hills and Davis Cup victories proved to be a severe blow to U.S. Davis Cup play. In 1939 Robert L. Riggs, who had won at Wimbledon and was to become U.S. champion about ten days later, and Frank Parker, who had two years of challenge round experience, lost the cup after they had led Australia 2–0 in the challenge round tie at Merion Cricket club, Haverford, Pa.

So again, as in 1914, Australia captured the Davis Cup as World War II halted international competition, this time for six years. Bombs damaged the Wimbledon grounds and other clubs throughout Europe. In the United States, the U.S. Lawn Tennis association helped keep tennis alive during the war. The development of junior tennis, a major activity of the USLTA, was emphasized and a nationwide program provided opportunities for thousands of boys and girls under 18 years of age to learn the game.

The USLTA championships were held during the war period. Most of the leading players were in the armed forces but a few on furlough or stationed near Forest Hills competed with the younger players. The wartime champions included: (in U.S. navy) Lt. Donald McNeill; Seaman Robert L. Riggs; Lt. Frederick R. Schroeder, Jr.; and Lt. Joseph R. Hunt (killed in a plane accident); and Sgt. Frank A. Parker (U.S. army).

After the war interest in the game revived quickly throughout the world. In 1946, 20 nations challenged for the Davis Cup which had been held since 1939 without competition by Australia. The Americans won 5–0 in Melbourne and retained the cup for the next three years at Forest Hills. John A. ("Jack") Kramer, Frederick R. ("Ted") Schroeder, Frank A. Parker and Richard A. ("Pancho") Gonzales were the outstanding Americans during these four years and none of them lost a singles match in these challenge rounds.

The public, so long starved of the glamour of top tennis entertainment, flocked to the major championships. At Wimbledon the first winner was the tall Frenchman Yvon Petra, but the U.S. provided the next five winners, all of whom were players of great character and individuality of style. Kramer, later to amass the greatest fortune ever made from the game as a professional player and promoter, was the "power-player" par excellence; the tall Robert Falkenburg relied on service speed and volleying the return; Schroeder based his game on a superb net attack and an invulnerable backhand, coupled with remarkable stamina; J. Edward ("Budge") Patty possessed an immaculate touch, while Richard Savitt put his trust in service power and heavily hit ground strokes. Another great American of this era was Gonzales, who won his national title at Forest Hills in 1948 and 1949. He turned professional at the then unusually young age of 21 and maturing in his new status became the world's greatest player of the 1950s, and, in the view of many, the greatest player yet seen.

In 1950 the balance of power swung back to Australia. The fine athletic physique and speed play of Frank A. Sedgman and his doubles partner, Kenneth B. McGregor, won back the Davis Cup for Australia and this partnership retained the trophy in 1951 and 1952, in which latter year Sedgman had already won at Wimbledon. In 1951 this partnership won all four of the major doubles championships—an achievement without precedent.

Despite the loss of two such fine players to the professional ranks in Jan. 1953, the Australians were able to replace them by the 18-year-olds Lewis A. Hoad and Kenneth R. Rosewall from Sydney. Much of the credit for Australia's extraordinary feat of continuing to hold the Davis Cup in these circumstances went to the shrewd captaincy of Harry Hopman.

The more mature and experienced Americans E. Victor Seixas and M. Anthony Trabert, who had won Wimbledon and the U.S. title respectively in 1953, recaptured the Davis Cup in 1954 at Sydney in front of a world record crowd of 25,600 on the opening day. But only eight months later the Australians, tuned to concert pitch by Hopman, beat the same American team at Forest Hills by 5–0. Australian domination was consistent except for the successful American raid at Brisbane in Dec. 1958 when Alejandro Olmedo, a Peruvian by birth, succeeded in beating the Australians Ashley J. Cooper and Malcolm J. Anderson, and, in partnership with Hamilton F. Richardson, Anderson and Neale A. Fraser in the doubles.

The U.S.–Australian monopoly of the top honours was first breached during the 1950s by Jaroslav Drobny, exiled from Czechoslovakia, whose amazing repertoire of strokes, including his remarkable left-handed flexibility overhead, won him the French title in 1951 and 1952 and the Wimbledon crown in 1954 in a memorable final of a record number of 58 games against Rosewall.

After Drobny followed other Europeans in Sven Davidson (Sweden), Kurt Neilsen (Denmark), Nicola Pietrangeli (Italy) and Manuel Santana (Spain), all of whom appeared as winners or finalists in the major championship finals.

In 1955 Trabert won three of the major championships and then turned professional and the following year Hoad repeated this feat but was defeated in the U.S. final by his compatriot, Rosewall. After their successful Davis Cup defense in 1956 Rosewall turned professional and Hoad followed him into the paid ranks immediately after becoming the first postwar player to retain a Wimbledon men's singles title.

This left another young Australian, Ashley Cooper, as the world's leading amateur player and in 1958 he won the Australian, Wimbledon and U.S. championships, leaving only the French title to his elder and left-handed compatriot, Mervyn Rose.

For the next two seasons major honours were shared by Pietrangeli, Olmedo and the left-handed Neale Fraser. Two new stars emerged in 1960 from Queensland, Rodney G. Laver and Roy Emerson. In 1962 Laver achieved the elusive "grand slam" of all four major championships which had been captured only by Donald Budge in 1938, as already noted.

Laver turned professional after Australia's successful defense of the Davis Cup in 1962 to pit his maturing skill against Rosewall, who had inherited the mantle of Gonzales as the world's leading exponent. In 1963 Charles R. (Chuck) McKinley captured the Wimbledon title for the United States for the first time in eight years and, teamed with Dennis Ralston, went on to take the Davis Cup from the Australians, 3–2, at Adelaide in December 1963. Australia regained the Davis Cup in September 1964, at Cleveland, O., with Emerson and Fred Stolle over McKinley and Ralston, 3–2.

A feature of the 1950s and 1960s was the advance of the Latin-American countries. The Peruvian Alex Olmedo was the first player from his continent to win a major singles championship when he won the Australian title in 1959 and followed this by capturing the Wimbledon crown. He was followed in 1963 by Rafael Osuna of Mexico, who won the U.S. championship and had been a member of his country's Davis Cup team, which upset all tradition by beating the United States in 1962, and reached the challenge round against Australia. In 1965 Santana became the first Spanish player to win the U.S. championship, and the first continental European since Henri Cochet of France in 1928. And in Davis Cup play, Spain, represented by Santana, Juan Gisbert, Luis Arilla and Juan Couder, won the European Zone for the first time in history and went on to defeat the U.S., American Zone winner, and India, Eastern Zone victor, but lost the challenge round against Australia. In 1966 Brazil upset the U.S. to win the American Zone but was defeated by India, which in turn lost to Australia.

Individual honours were divided in 1966. Emerson won his fifth Australian singles title, another Australian, Tony Roche, captured the French championship, Santana succeeded Emerson as Wimbledon champion and Fred Stolle (Australia) won the United States title at Forest Hills. Australian players also dominated play in 1967, Emerson winning championships in Australia and France, and John Newcombe winning the U.S. and Wimbledon titles. Ralston and Stolle, leading amateurs, joined the professionals, which were dominated by Rosewall and Laver.

One of the biggest upsets in all Davis Cup competition occurred in 1967 when Ecuador, with newcomers Francisco Guzman and Miguel Olvera, beat the U.S. in the American Zone final. Australia retained the Cup, defeating Spain in the challenge round.

In 1968 open tennis was sanctioned by the International Lawn Tennis federation for a limited number of tournaments, and the first open Wimbledon was won by Laver.

In Davis Cup competition, U.S. Negro player Arthur Ashe, ranking as the world's top amateur after winning the U.S. Amateur and the U.S. Open championships, led his teammates Clark Graebner and doubles players Stan Smith and Bob Lutz to a 4–1 U.S. victory over Australia in the 1968 challenge round—only to be himself upset in the final match by once doubtful starter Bill Bowrey. Following the 1968 competition the heads of tennis associations from Australia, France, Great Britain, and the United States recommended that the Davis Cup be made an open competition as soon as feasible.

**Women Players.**—Tennis was played by women from the start; but their entry into competitive tournaments was delayed, and it was not until 1884, seven years after the championships began, that Maud Watson became the first woman's champion at Wimbledon by winning from an entry of 13 players. In the United States a tournament for women was held at the Philadelphia Cricket club, and was won by Ellen Hansell in 1887. This tournament was held again in 1888 and it became the first official cham-

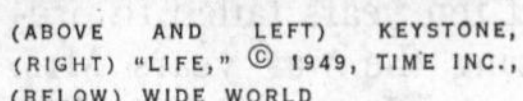

(ABOVE AND LEFT) KEYSTONE, (RIGHT) "LIFE," © 1949, TIME INC., (BELOW) WIDE WORLD

(Above) Lewis Hoad, Australia, stretches to make a forehand return. (Right) Jack Kramer, U.S., serves, his racket meeting the ball high above his head. (Left) Tony Trabert, U.S., makes an overhead smash as partner Victor Seixas ducks out of the way. (Below) Ann Haydon, England, uses backhand to stroke the ball just over the net

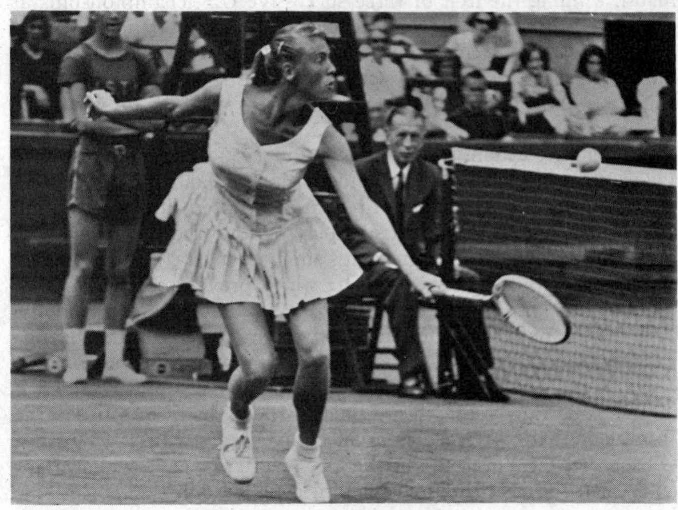

pionship for women in 1889. It was won by Bertha Townsend. Elisabeth Moore, later singles champion, described the costumes of the period in this way: "The girls were wearing lawn dresses with leg of mutton sleeves, sailor hats, and ornamental tennis shoes. My dresses, which were of white lawn, swept just clear of the grass on ordinary shots; but brushed it when I stooped."

In those days the game was played chiefly from the base line. In England the standard of play was and remained for some time much higher than in the United States, yet women still served underhand. In 1904 a new star appeared, May Sutton, a girl of 16 and the first of a long line of Californian champions who revolutionized U.S. and world tennis. She was gifted with a strong constitution and a heavily topped forehand drive which enabled her to win the American title that year, and also to defeat Miss D. K. Douglass (afterward Mrs. Lambert Chambers) at Wimbledon in 1905, thus becoming the first American ever to capture an English title. She again defeated her rival to win the championships in 1907, and 22 years later she returned to Wimbledon and reached the quarter finals of the singles in a strong field.

An important influence on the game for women was Suzanne Lenglen, a French girl who first appeared at Wimbledon in 1919. Born at Compiègne, France, in 1899, she won her first championship at St. Cloud in 1914. Between 1919 and 1926 she dominated the game, winning at Wimbledon six times.

The next leading player was Helen Wills, later Helen Wills Moody Roark. She played Mlle Lenglen only once, at Cannes in 1926, when she was a young girl, losing 6–3, 8–6. Like her rival she had every stroke, supported by a more powerful forehand drive, the weapon of every champion. She had a matchless record in competitive tennis, winning the first of her seven American titles in 1923 and the first of her eight Wimbledon titles four years later.

Another great woman player, also an American and a Californian, was Alice Marble. Despite illnesses which would have discouraged most players, she ended as Wimbledon and U.S. titleholder in 1939. She was the first woman champion to develop a really hard service and possessed an all-round game to which she added unusual severity at the net and overhead.

Miss Marble won her fourth and last U.S. championship in 1940, defeating for the third time the resolute Helen Jacobs, who had succeeded Mrs. Moody as U.S. titleholder in 1932 and as Wimbledon champion four years later. The next ten years failed to produce any great woman champion. During the war years Mrs. Sarah Palfrey Cooke, an easterner, and Pauline Betz, a Californian, led the field, Mrs. Cooke winning her second championship in 1945 and Miss Betz her fourth in 1946, after which they turned professional and Margaret Osborne duPont, Louise Brough, Doris Hart and Shirley Fry, sometimes referred to as "the big four," dominated the game at Forest Hills, Wimbledon and in other countries wherever they competed, including France, England, South Africa and Australia. Then in 1951 Maureen ("Little Mo") Connolly from California, like Miss Sutton in 1904, took complete command, winning the first of three successive U.S. championships at Forest Hills before she had reached her 17th birthday. Miss Connolly was the second youngest player to capture the title. Miss Sutton was only a few days younger when she won the championship in 1904 and Miss Wills was almost a year older when she captured her first U.S. title in 1923.

On her first attempt at Wimbledon in 1952 Miss Connolly won the crown and successfully defended it in 1953 and 1954. In 1953 she also won the Australian, French and United States titles and so this mistress of ground stroke play became the first woman to hold the four major championships simultaneously. She sustained a leg injury while horseback riding which prevented her from defending her United States title in 1954. Later Miss Connolly, perhaps the only player of the postwar era to rank with Suzanne Lenglen and Helen Wills Moody Roark, became a professional.

Doris Hart won the U.S. championship in 1954 and retained it in the following year when Louise Brough had recaptured the Wimbledon title after an interval of five years. In 1956 Althea Gibson of New York became the first Negro player to win a major title when she won the premier hard court title in the world—the French championship—at Paris. She was the dominating player for the next two seasons, notably by reason of her service power, winning both the Wimbledon and U.S. championships. The U.S. strength in depth weakened at this time and the British trio of Angela Mortimer (1955), Shirley Bloomer (1957) and Christine Truman (1959) won the French championship, as did the Hungarian Suzy Kormoczy in 1958.

The first player to break the 13-year-old postwar U.S. monopoly of the Wimbledon and U.S. championship titles was Maria Bueno, a superb stylist from Brazil. She won both these championships in 1959 with artistic ease and retained her Wimbledon title in 1960. She, however, lost her American title to her doubles partner, Darlene R. Hard of California. Miss Hard had already won the French championship that year, and went on to retain her U.S. title in 1961 following the severe illness of Miss Bueno.

In the season of 1961 two British players won major championships: Ann Haydon took the French title and Angela Mortimer became the first British singles winner at Wimbledon for 24 years.

Margaret Smith, a player of rare physique and power, won the Australian championship in 1966 for the seventh consecutive time. In 1962 Miss Smith took the French and United States championships but Karen Susman (U.S.) won at Wimbledon. In 1963 Miss Smith lost her French title to her compatriot, Lesley Turner; became the first Australian woman ever to win Wimbledon; but lost her U.S. championship to Miss Bueno, who won both at Forest Hills and Wimbledon in 1964, when Miss Smith won in Italy and France. In 1965 Miss Smith won at Wimbledon and Forest Hills; Miss Bueno in Italy.

Mrs. Billie Jean King captured Miss Smith's Wimbledon title in 1966. Miss Smith, who retired temporarily at the end of 1966, did not defend her U.S. title which was captured by Miss Bueno for the fourth time as she defeated Nancy Richey in a two-set final. For the first time two women players shared the no. 1 ranking in the United States when the honour was divided between Mrs. King and Miss Richey. The latter won the Australian title in 1967 and the French crown in 1968. In 1967 Mrs. King won at Wimbledon and became U.S. champion for the first time. Having turned professional, she won at Wimbledon again in 1968, its first open play, but was defeated in the final of the U.S. Open championship by Virginia Wade of Great Britain.

**Wightman Cup.**—In 1923 a cup was donated by Mrs. George Wightman, the former Hazel Hotchkiss of California and herself national singles champion of the United States in 1909, 1910 and 1911 and winner of some 47 other U.S. titles, for competition between teams of women players from the United States and England. The Wightman Cup was first contested at Forest Hills, Long Island, on Aug. 11 and 13, 1923. The annual contest is held alternately in the two countries, with five singles and two doubles matches. The first contest was won by the United States. By 1930 each side had won on four occasions: but then the United States' team won for the next nine years until the competition was abandoned in 1940 owing to the war. After the war the United States' dominance was even more pronounced, producing a string of 12 more consecutive victories, and never losing more than two of the seven rubbers. The British girls, with Christine Truman contributing to three wins, succeeded for the first time in 28 years at Wimbledon in 1958 by the minimum margin of 4–3 and repeated this performance in 1960. In 1961 the U.S. recaptured the cup and held it through the mid-1960s. In 1966 at Wimbledon Great Britain had a commanding lead of 3 to 1 but the U.S. girls won the next three matches for the victory. In 1967 they won, 6 to 1, but Great Britain recaptured the cup in 1968.

**The Federation Cup.**—A new international competition for the women's team tennis championship of the world was inaugurated with the Federation Cup by the ILTF in honour of its 50th anniversary in 1962. The first competition for the cup, held at the Queen's club, London, in 1963 was won by the U.S. team when Billie Jean Moffitt and Darlene Hard beat the top-seeded Australians Margaret Smith and Lesley Turner in the finals. In 1964 Australia defeated the U.S. at Philadelphia, 2 to 1, and repeated their victory the next year at Melbourne. The U.S. recaptured the cup at Turin, Italy, in 1966, defeating West Germany, and won again in 1967 over Great Britain, but lost to France in the quarter-final round in 1968. At Athens, Greece, in May 1969 the U.S. regained the cup by defeating Australia, the defending champions. *See* SPORTING RECORD: *Tennis.*

(J. R. TU.; E. S. BR.; R. MCW.)

## STANDARD GRIPS AND STROKES

Many outstanding players and coaches have written books and manuals on how to play tennis, a few of which are listed in the *Bibliography,* below. The following descriptions of the standard grips and strokes originally were prepared by Tilden, one of the all-time great players, for the United States Lawn Tennis association's *Official Tennis Guide,* 1942 (*Official Tennis Guide with the Official Rules, 1942,* copyright 1942 by A. S. Barnes and Co.). Tilden's instructions have been revised only to comply with subsequent changes in the rules (see *Rules of Lawn Tennis,* below). (X.)

**Forehand Ground Stroke Grip.**—Hold the racket as if it were standing on the edge of the frame, the handle pointing toward you, the short strings perpendicular to the ground, the long strings parallel to it. Then "shake hands" with it—literally. The handle settles comfortably into your palm. Close your fingers tightly around the handle. The racket is then, or should be, part of the straight line of your arm. There should be no angle at your wrist. The hand rests along the outside, or right side, of the handle, the thumb and fingers wrapped around the handle, naturally and comfortably. The racket thus becomes an extension of the arm that can be moved as easily as if it belonged there.

**Backhand Ground Stroke Grip.**—Obviously, the forehand grip, as described in the foregoing paragraph, is impossible for a backhand shot, since it would be swung against the back of the hand itself. Therefore, a change is necessary. Move the hand one-quarter of a circle on the handle, backward, so that the hand rests directly on top of the handle, the knuckles of the hand pointing to the sky. Grip the handle tightly. If it is more comfortable to run the thumb up the handle, do so. If not, wrap it around as in the forehand grip. The shot off the backhand travels directly across the wrist with this grip. Swing freely from the shoulder with both these grips and keep the wrist stiff and locked on all drives. The grip is about the same for a volley.

**Service Grip.**—The grip for service is just midway between the forehand and the backhand grip. Take your forehand grip and then turn the hand half way back to the backhand position.

On all grips, hold the racket tight at the moment of impact with the ball. Loosen your grip between shots so as not to cramp the hand from too great a strain.

**Forehand Drive.**—The forehand drive is one continuous swing, which is considered in three sections:

The speed of the shot is decided by the length of the swing behind the body. The farther back you start your swing the faster the racket will move forward, and the speedier your shot will be.

The direction of your stroke, whether it is hit straight or cross court, is determined by that portion of the swing in front; that is, alongside your body. In other words, as you face off court, it is the space within the lines from your hips. If you meet the ball back near your right hip, the shot goes toward the right; if you meet it directly in front of the belt buckle, it goes on a straight line; and if you meet it up in front of your left hip, the shot goes cross court to your left.

When awaiting the ball, face your opponent across the net. As soon as you see the ball coming toward you, decide which side, fore or backhand, you will play it. Then change your body position accordingly so that you face off the side line, while your shoulders are along the line of the shot you are going to make. As the ball reaches you, drop your weight to your back foot and commence your swing well behind your body, meeting the ball with the racket in its forward flight just in front of your body and follow through to the end of your swing.

This brings us to the third portion of the swing, the portion beyond or nearer the net than the body, which is called the follow-through. This determines the spin or twist on the shot and is the factor that holds the ball in court. For the drive the racket meets the ball flat and passes up and over the top of the ball, thus spinning the ball away from you and downward. It is the same spin as a pitcher's drop in baseball. The racket passing under the ball, making it float or drag, is the "chop" or "slice" stroke (*see* below).

The swing, as described, is in three parts, but is made in one free movement that carries the whole body along with it. It is as essential in tennis to follow through from the beginning of your swing to the extreme end of your reach as it is in golf or baseball. It gives direction and control of length.

There is a certain height at which to hit a tennis ball correctly. There are other heights at which one should never hit it unless caught out of position. The drive should be hit at a height never lower than your knees or higher than your shoulders. If the ball must be met at either of these heights, do not drive. Merely defend it and put it back and wait for another chance to drive. The height at which a tennis ball may be driven hardest is about waist high and at a distance about three feet from your body.

In making the drive, first be certain your form is correct. See to it that your feet are correctly placed so that you are sideways to the net. Next make sure your racket face meets the ball flat and that your racket passes up, over and slightly outside the ball, thus pulling it toward you. Do not try to hit hard until you have learned to hit correctly. Speed will come later, but correct form can be learned only before you have formed bad habits in stroking that are almost impossible to break.

**Backhand Drive.**—The laws of footwork are exactly the reverse of those applying to the forehand drive. The back foot is now the left, while the front foot is the right. The swing is from well behind the body, as in the forehand shot. The grip, as previously explained, is changed one-fourth on the handle, so that the hand is on top of the handle, while the shot travels across the wrist, which is locked and stiff. The racket head should be slightly in advance of the hand when it meets the ball, and the face of the racket is flat. The ball travels across the short strings. There is less top spin to this stroke than the forehand, because the follow-through is less. Use your left hand as a balance, well behind your body, and be sure to keep your body well away from the ball, so as not to cramp your swing. Bend to meet the ball with the racket head slightly on the side away from you and pull it toward you cross court.

**Service.**—Service is the "opening gun" in tennis. It is putting the ball in play, and every man should learn a service that will be a distinct advantage. Service has made many players famous. Maurice E. McLoughlin, the "California Comet," was world renowned for his service. Robert Lindley Murray, Elia Fottrell, Harold Throckmorton, S. Howard Voshell and many other players were noted for their services. All these men hit their deliveries hard, but they never sacrificed accuracy to mere speed. They were always careful to put the ball in court. They served very few double faults.

Foot faults should be avoided. The easiest way to serve legally is to remember that one foot must be on the ground behind the line and the other foot must not touch inside the court until your racket has struck the ball. Stand at least six inches behind the base line and you will not foot fault.

**Slice Service.**—This is the most common form of service. It requires the least effort and has the greatest chance of going in court.

To hit this service, stand behind the base line with your feet at an angle of about 45° to the line. Drop your weight back on your right foot. Toss the ball well above your head and slightly to the right in advance of it. Swing your racket up and forward with one rhythmic movement, at the same time shifting the weight forward toward the left foot. Meet the ball as high above your head as you can comfortably reach. The racket face is outside, or on the right side of the ball, and slightly over it. It travels from right to left. Swing directly through this, imparting a twist to the ball to spin it from left to right. This tends to hold the ball in court.

*American Twist Service.*—The stand and grip for this service are the same as for the slice. The ball is thrown slightly to the left of the head and almost directly above it. If anything, it may be slightly behind. The body is bent backward and the ball hit at a point more to the left than in the slice. The racket travels up and over the ball which is below and inside the strings. The ball is really between your face, turned upward to watch it, and the face of your racket which is travelling from left to right away from your body. This service carries extreme twist and a high bound, but with not so much speed as a slice or flat service. There is more wrist turn to this service than in the slice. The body movement causes a distinct pull on the stomach muscles and those along the right side. The slice service is hit with the shoulder and arm muscles.

*Reverse Twist.*—This delivery is a totally different style of service and is not one for regular use. The server, to deliver this service, should stand facing the net with both toes on a line with the base line. The ball is thrown about shoulder high. The ball is caught and carried on the strings for a short space. The racket passes up and over the ball, which is outside the racket face from the server. This service carries extreme twist but little speed or control. The hitting plane is about shoulder high instead of over the head. The weight control is faulty. In fact, it is not a service for a beginner to learn.

**Volley: Forehand and Backhand.**—The volley is the shot made by taking the ball in the air before it has struck the ground. It is "hitting it on the fly," as the common expression goes. The laws of footwork and body position are the same for volleys as for ground strokes, the body always sideways to the net and weight moving forward.

The ground stroke or drive is made from the back of the court. The volley is made from the front of the court or net position. Volleys should not be made from behind the service line if it is possible to drive.

The drive has a distinct follow-through and a long swing. The volley has little or no follow-through and a very short swing. All volleys should be blocked or undercut and not stroked or topped.

The shot is made with a short swing from behind the body. The racket face meets the ball flat or, if the shot must be made from below the top of the net and lifted, slightly under the ball. The wrist is stiff and locked. The angle of the shot is determined by the angle made by the flight of the ball coming to you and the racket face. The racket moves forward, meets the ball and stops completely. It does not follow through. It blocks the ball, which rebounds by its own speed plus the body weight behind the racket.

**Smash.**—The overhead smash is the stroke killing the ball in the air when it is lobbed over your head. This shot should be modeled as nearly after your service as you can do it, except that it is hit with less twist and more speed. (W. T. T.)

## RULES OF LAWN TENNIS

Tennis is one of the few games that are played around the world under the same rules. The official rules are promulgated by the ILTF and are widely available in the publications of the various affiliated national tennis associations and other organizations interested in promoting the sport.

### The Singles Game

**The Court, Net and Fixtures.**—The size, shape and markings on the court as determined by the rules are shown in fig. 1. The net is 3 ft. high at the centre, where it is held down taut by a strap not more than 2 in. wide, and the cord or wire (maximum diameter one-third of an inch) from which it is suspended is attached to or passes over the tops of the posts, which are 3 ft. 6 in. high.

A band covers the cord or wire for not less than 2 in. nor more than $2\frac{1}{2}$ in. in depth on each side. The spaces behind the base lines and at the sides indicated on the diagram are required in Davis Cup and other official ILTF championships. The centre line is 2 in. wide; all other lines are not less than 1 in. nor more than 2 in. wide, except the base line, which may be 4 in. wide. The centre mark is 4 in. long and 2 in. wide.

The permanent fixtures of the court include the posts and the net with its cord or wire, strap and band, and also any back or side stops, the umpire, linesmen and spectators and their chairs or stands, and all other objects around and above the court.

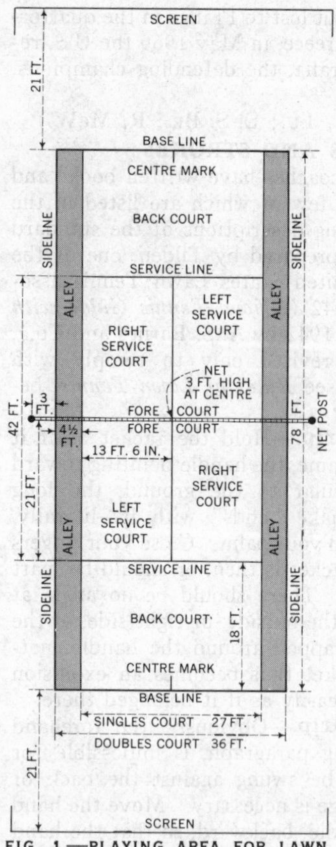

FIG. 1.—PLAYING AREA FOR LAWN TENNIS. THE ALLEYS ARE USED ONLY IN DOUBLES PLAY

**The Ball.**—The tennis ball has a uniform outer surface, any seams being stitchless. It must be more than $2\frac{1}{2}$ in. and less than $2\frac{5}{8}$ in. in diameter, and more than 2 oz. and less than $2\frac{1}{16}$ oz. in weight.

**Play.**—The choice of sides and the right to serve or receive in the first game of a series is decided by toss (spinning or throwing up a racket). The winner may choose, or require his opponent to choose: (1) the right to be server (serve first) or receiver, in which case the other player chooses the side; or (2) the side, in which case the other player chooses the right to be server or receiver.

The service is delivered alternately from behind the right and left courts, beginning with the right. Immediately before commencing to serve, the server stands with both feet at rest behind the base line, and within imaginary continuations of the centre mark and the sideline. The receiver may stand wherever he pleases on his own side of the net and the server must not serve until the receiver is ready. The server then tosses the ball into the air and before it hits the ground strikes it with his racket. The delivery is completed (the ball is in play) at the moment of impact. There is no restriction regarding the kind of service that may be used.

The server throughout the delivery may not materially change his position (location) by walking or running, and must not touch inside the court with either foot until his racket has struck the ball (see *Standard Grips and Strokes: Service,* above). The ball served must pass over the net and hit the ground within or upon any line bounding the diagonally opposite service court. In the absence of a linesman and umpire it is customary for the receiver to determine whether the service is good. The server continues to serve until he wins or loses one game, when the service passes to his opponent. The players change sides at the end of the first, third and every subsequent alternate game.

If the service lands outside the proper service court, it is a fault. It also is a fault if the player breaks any of the above rules, if he misses the ball when he swings, or if the ball touches a permanent fixture (other than the net, strap or band) before it lands in the proper court. After a fault, another ball is served from behind the same half of the court. If this, too, is a fault, the server is charged with a double fault and loses the point.

A let is called when a ball breaks or is obstructed as specified in the rules, or to provide for an interruption of play. When a let is called for a service, that one service is replayed; when called under any other circumstance, the point is replayed. The service is a let if the ball touches the net, strap or band but either falls within the proper court or touches the receiver or anything he wears or carries, or if the receiver is not ready.

The receiver must return a good service by hitting the ball on the first bounce so that it goes over the net to fall anywhere within his opponent's side of the court, after which the players alternately hit the ball back and forth across the net until one of them fails to make a good return and a point is scored. After the service either player may volley the ball, that is, hit it before it touches the ground.

When the ball is in play, a player fails to make a good return and loses a point if the ball bounces on the ground twice before he returns it; if his return lands outside any of the lines bounding his opponent's court; if he touches the ball with his racket more than once in making a return or if the ball touches him or anything he wears or carries, except his racket; if he or his racket or anything he wears or carries touches the net, posts, cord or wire, strap or band, or the ground within his opponent's court; or if he volleys the ball before it has passed the net.

**Scoring.**—The receiver scores a point if the server delivers a double fault. After the service, either player or side scores a point if the opposition fails to make a good return of the ball. A game is won by one side scoring at least four points; the first point is 15, the second is 30, the third is 40 and the fourth is game point.

A game must be won by at least two points, so that after a tie score at three points, or 40–40 (deuce), one side must score two consecutive points to win. The first point scored after deuce is called vantage, advantage or simply "ad." If the other side wins the next point the score returns to deuce. A score of zero is called love; *e.g.,* 30–love is 30–0.

A set consists of one side winning at least six games. A tie score at five games is a deuce set, after which one side must win two consecutive games to win the set.

In major tournament play (*i.e.,* championships and Davis Cup tournaments), a match consists of three out of five sets for men; two out of three for women.

### The Doubles Game

**The Court.**—As shown in fig. 1, the doubles court is 36 ft. wide, 4½ ft. wider on each side than the singles court. Those portions of the singles side lines that lie between the service lines are called the service side lines (those portions of the singles side lines between service lines and the base lines may be omitted if desired). The server may stand anywhere behind the base line between the centre mark and the doubles side line.

**Order of Serving and Receiving.**—The pair who will serve in the first game of each set decide which partner will do so, and the opposing pair decide similarly for the second game. The partner of the player who served in the first game serves in the third; and the partner of the player who served in the second game serves in the fourth. The players continue throughout the set to serve in that order. Similarly, each pair decide which shall receive the first service by the opponents, the other receiving the second, and they continue in that order.

**Play.**—The rules applying to the play of the singles game apply also to doubles. A fault is incurred as in singles, and also if the ball served touches the server's partner or anything he wears or carries; but, if the service is not a let, and touches the receiver's partner or anything he wears or carries before it hits the ground, the server wins the point.

After the service, either partner of the opposing pairs may return any shot, but if his partner should touch the ball with his racket their opponents win the point. (E. S. Br.)

## ROYAL OR COURT TENNIS

**History.**—Court tennis may well be called a royal game, having been popular with various kings of England and France. In the ball games of the Greeks and Romans may be seen the rudiments of the French *jeu de paume,* which is the ancestor of modern tennis in a direct line. The origin of the name is quite obscure. The most probable derivation is from the word *Tenez!* (Take it! Play!), especially in view of the large number of French terms that adhere to the game; *e.g.,* grille, tambour (drum, from the sound on the board that formed the face of that buttress) and *dedans.* Further, a poem dealing with the game, written in Latin elegiacs by R. Frissart, makes the striker cry *"Excipe!"* (Take it!) before each stroke; this seems to correspond with the custom which enjoins the rackets marker to call "play" whenever a legitimate stroke has been made.

In the *Alexiad* of Anna Comnena (about A.D. 1120) is a reference to a game played on horseback in which a staff, curved at the end and strung with strings of plaited gut was used. This game was played in a court called "a court for goff" (*sic;* according to the Lexicon of *Alexandrine Greek*) and some similar game, corrupted through *tchangan* into *chicane,* was played in France. Good authorities also find a more ancient derivation of the game in Egypt, in Persia and among the Arabs before Charlemagne. In A.D. 1300 the game was also known as *La Boude.* Throughout the century indeed it was played in France and by the highest in the land. Louis X died from a chill contracted after playing, and Charles V was devoted to the game. In England the game, or some form of it, was known, Chaucer alluding to it in the words "But canstow playen racket to and fro."

THE BETTMANN ARCHIVE INC.

FIG. 2.—COPPER ENGRAVING OF EARLY COURT TENNIS, 1612. AT THIS DATE THE RACQUET WAS IN USE BUT THE NET HAD NOT YET REPLACED THE FRINGED OR TASSELED ROPE STRETCHED ACROSS THE COURT. NOTE LE PETIT TROU AND LA LUNE, "WINNING OPENINGS" ON THE FAR END WALL

The 16th century was the golden age of court tennis in France. Francis I built a magnificent court at the Louvre, where his son Henry II, one of the best players of his day, built a second and larger court. Charles IX was a keen player and granted a royal charter to the Corporation of Tennis professionals. Henry IV was equally keen and in 1596 there were said to be 250 courts in Paris alone. An English visitor in 1598 wrote "There be more tennis players in France than ale-drinkers or malt-wormes (as they call them) with us." Louis XIII and Louis XIV both played tennis but by 1657 the number of courts in Paris had declined to 114. The Royal tennis court at Versailles was the scene of the famous tennis court oath of June 20, 1789, which marked the start of the French Revolution.

In England, too, court tennis was in its heyday in the 16th century. Henry VII was a good player and played on courts in Woodstock, Wycombe, Westminster, Sheen and Windsor. At Windsor in 1506 he entertained the king of Castile who played a tennis match against the marquis of Dorset. Henry VIII was an outstanding tennis player and in 1530 built the court at Hampton Court palace which is still in use. He also built four courts at Whitehall and one at St. James's palace. Elizabeth I was a keen spectator. Charles I and Charles II were both good tennis players. Charles II built a magnificent new court at Whitehall and Pepys made several allusions to the king playing tennis. A print of 1641 shows James II as a boy in a tennis court. Tennis in England declined in the 18th century and in the second half of the 20th century there were 15 courts in play. In Scotland a most interesting open-air court at Falkland Palace, built in 1539, is still in occasional use.

In the late 19th century courts were built in Australia at Hobart (1854) and Melbourne (1882) which are still in play.

Court tennis was introduced to the U.S. in Boston in 1876. The first court in New York was opened at the Racquet and Tennis club in 1890, and today there are two courts there in its later premises on Park avenue. Other courts are still in play at Boston, Mass., Philadelphia, Pa., Tuxedo Park, N.Y., Greentree, Long Island, and Aiken, S.C.

It is possible to trace a world's open championship of court tennis back to the early 19th century and holders of this title have been: 1816, Marchisio (Italy); 1819, Philip Cox (Great Britain); 1829, J. E. Barre (France); 1862, E. Tompkins (Great Britain); 1871, G. Lambert (Great Britain); 1885, Tom Pettitt (United States); 1896, P. Latham (Great Britain); 1905, C. Fairs (Great Britain); 1907, P. Latham (Great Britain); 1908, C. Fairs (Great Britain); 1912, G. F. Covey (Great Britain); 1914, J. Gould (United States); 1922, G. F. Covey (Great Britain); 1928, P. Etchebaster (France); 1955, J. Dear (Great Britain); 1957, A. Johnson (Great Britain); 1959, N. R. Knox (U.S.); 1969, G. H. Bostwick (U.S.).

Peter Latham had the distinction of being world champion of rackets also. Gould, Bostwick and Knox are the only amateurs ever to have won the world championship. Pierre Etchebaster, a French Basque and professional at the New York Racquet and Tennis club, held the title for 27 years until he retired at the age of 60 undefeated, and was undoubtedly the outstanding player of the modern era.

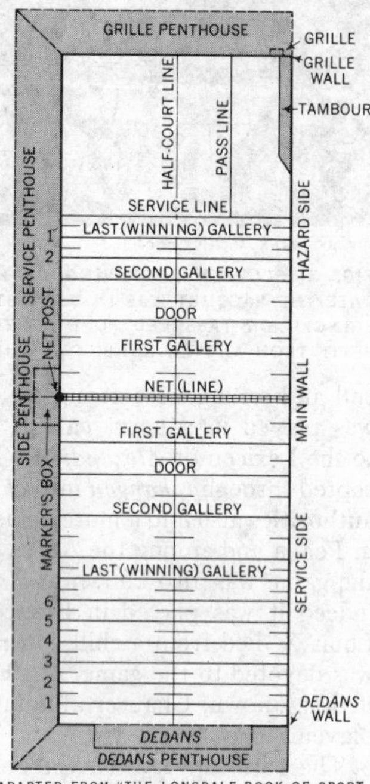


ADAPTED FROM "THE LONSDALE BOOK OF SPORTING RECORDS," SEELEY, SERVICE AND CO., LTD., LONDON

FIG. 3.—PLAYING AREA FOR COURT TENNIS

**General Description of Game.**—Court tennis is played on a four-walled indoor court somewhat larger than a lawn tennis court (*see* fig. 3). Although there is no standard size, the following dimensions may be regarded as suitable: the space enclosed by the walls, 110 ft. by 38 ft. 8 in.; the floor however, measuring but 96 ft. by 31 ft. 8 in., the difference being the width of a roofed corridor (the "penthouse") which runs along the two end walls and one of the side walls. Across the middle of the court a net is stretched and the first object of the game is to strike the ball over this with a racket. The net is 5 ft. high at the ends, 3 ft. at the middle, and divides the floor into two equal parts—the "service" side and the "hazard" side. The cement floor and walls should be smooth but not polished.

The height of the court to the tie beam is 30 ft. The height of the play line, above which the ball must not go, is 18 ft. at the sides and 23 ft. at the ends. The roof of the penthouse slopes downward toward the court, the lower edge being 7 ft. 1½ in. from the floor, the upper edge 10 ft. 7 in., the width 7 ft. The *dedans* is an open gallery in the wall at the service end of the court, under the penthouse. It is 21 ft. 8 in. in width; the upper edge is 6 ft. 10 in. from the floor, the lower edge 3 ft. 3 in. Looking from the *dedans,* the right-hand or main wall has one peculiarity, the tambour, a sloping buttress toward the far end, to form which the wall is built inward, reducing the breadth of that part of the court to 30 ft. 2 in. In the right-hand corner of the hazard side end wall (as viewed from the *dedans*) is the grille, an opening 3 ft. 1 in. square. The left-hand wall, along which runs the penthouse, is not continuous, being broken by a long opening between the floor and the penthouse similar to the *dedans,* and at the same height from the ground. The low walls under this opening and the *dedans* are called the batteries. There is no wall in front of the marker's box, through which the court is entered on either side of the net post. This long opening in the left-hand wall is divided into galleries and doors, the latter situated where the entrances to the court used to be in early courts. The galleries are marked by posts, which also serve to support the penthouse. The galleries, *dedans* and grille are known as the openings; three of these—the grille, *dedans* and winning gallery—are winning openings, for if a ball in play is struck into one of these, the striker scores a point. In the earlier French courts there were other winning openings such as: *l'ais* (the board), an upright board 9 ft. by 1 ft. in the left-hand corner of the *dedans* wall; *le petit trou* or *le trou,* a hole 16 in. square at the bottom of the other side of the wall; and *la lune,* a round opening high up by the play line, one at each end of the court. The court has certain lines painted on the floor which are also continued perpendicularly on the walls. On the hazard side is the half-court line, the pass line and the service line. The first is required in doubles or in certain forms of handicap game. The pass line is drawn 7 ft. 8 in. from the main wall, the service line 21 ft. 1 in. from the grille wall. The rectangle contained by the pass and service lines forms the service court. The other lines, both on the hazard side and service side, mark the chases, which will be explained below.

**Equipment.**—The balls vary in the three countries where the game is chiefly played—England, United States and France. In England balls weigh approximately 2½ oz. and are 2¼ in. in diameter. They are made of strips of cloth wound tightly together, tied with twine and covered with white melton cloth. The French ball is harder and faster than the English; and the American ball lies somewhere between the two. The racket is usually about 27 in. long and weighs about 16 oz. The head is about 9 in. long and 6 in. broad, but there are no restrictions as to size or weight. The head is somewhat pear-shaped, but its centre line does not correspond with the centre line of the handle, since the head is curved upward. Some of the early rackets were strung diagonally (*i.e.,* in diamonds); later, vertical-horizontal stringing was universally adopted; then followed knotting at the points of intersection, a practice which later disappeared.

**Scoring.**—A match in England and the U.S. consists ordinarily of the best of three or the best of five sets, a set being scored by the player who gets six games first. Sets of "eight games," *i.e.,* the set won by the player who gets eight games first, are generally played in France.

Occasionally vantage sets are played; *i.e.,* when each player has scored five games or seven games as the case may be, the set continues until one player gets an advantage of two games. In these conditions sets sometimes continue for a very long time, and sets where over 60 games have been played are recorded. In matches for the world's championship the best of 13 sets of six games are generally played on three different days with an interval between them. Scoring is as in lawn tennis. The score of the player who won the last stroke or made the last chase is called first.

**The Game.**—The players decide who shall serve by spinning a racket on its head. One spins and the other calls "rough" or "smooth," the rough side of the head of the racket showing the knots of some of the lower strings. The winner takes the service side, service being an advantage. In four-handed games the winners of the spin often take the hazard side, since by doing so they can decide which of their opponent's service each one will elect to take. He serves from any part of the court and in any way he thinks best, and the ball must go over the net, strike the side penthouse, and fall into the service court. His opponent ("striker-out") tries to return the ball over the net before it has touched the ground a second time; he may volley or half-volley (strike the ball as soon as it touches the court) his return. For a stroke to be good, it must be made before the second bounce of the ball, and the ball must go over the net (even if it touches it), and must not strike the wall above the play line, nor touch the roof or rafters.

**The Chase.**—The chase is an ancient and somewhat complicated device which gives some advantage to skill over brute force. In most games a player has to return the ball either on the volley or after it has bounced once; a ball that bounces twice is called "not up." In court tennis this is not so and a ball that is "not up" makes a chase at the point where it strikes the ground on its second bounce. Neither player scores a point when a chase is made; the point goes into cold storage until it is played off, either when one player has reached 40 or when there are two chases in cold storage in the same game. When this happens the players change ends and play off the chase or chases. The nearer the chase is to the back wall, the better it is and the more difficult it is to beat. This is where skill is at a premium. The player who allowed the ball to bounce a second time and make a chase now has to make a better chase to win the point. If any stroke he makes in the course of the rally is going to make a worse chase, his opponent can leave it and thereby win the point.

The marker standing by the net is responsible for calling out the score and for naming the chases. To enable him to mark the chases the floor of the court is ruled off in transverse lines. On the service side these start at one-yard intervals from the back wall and are numbered from one to six. From chase six to the net further lines are ruled, corresponding to the centre of the galleries which line the side wall and called by the name of the gallery to which they refer, *i.e.,* last gallery, second gallery, door, first gallery and line. A ball entering directly into one of these galleries makes a chase in exactly the same way as when the ball bounces twice. On the hazard side there are no chase lines at the back of the court and a ball "not up" in this area loses a point as in other games. The galleries are the same as on the service side except that the equivalent of the last gallery is called the winning gallery and a ball entering it rings a bell and wins a point outright. Under the winning gallery there are two chase lines marked one and two. (AB.)

BIBLIOGRAPHY.—A. Wallis Myers, *Fifty Years of Wimbledon, 1877 to 1926* (1926); U.S. Lawn Tennis Association, *Fifty Years of Lawn Tennis in the United States* (1931); *Spalding's Tennis Annual* (1912 *et seq.*); S. Wallis Merrihew, *The Quest of the Davis Cup* (1928); J. R. Lacoste, *Lacoste on Tennis* (1928); Helen Jacobs, *Tennis* (1941); William T. Tilden, *How to Play Better Tennis* (1957); L. Budge, *Tennis Made Easy* (1945); Maureen Connolly, *Power Tennis* (1954); Maurice Brady, *Encyclopaedia of Lawn Tennis* (1958); Lord Aberdare, *The Story of Tennis* (1959); *Sports Illustrated Book of Tennis* (1961); *International Lawn Tennis Almanac* (annual); U.S. Lawn Tennis Association, *Official Handbook* (annual); W. M. Fischer Lawn Tennis Library, New York University, New York, N.Y. (E. S. BR.; AB.)

**TENNYSON, ALFRED TENNYSON,** 1ST BARON (1809–1892), often regarded as the chief representative of the Victorian Age in English poetry, was born at Somersby, Lincolnshire, on Aug. 6, 1809. The Tennysons were an old Lincolnshire family whose prosperity had been established by the poet's grandfather, George Clayton Tennyson of Bayons Manor. George Clayton the elder preferred his second son, Charles, to his eldest, George Clayton the younger (1778–1831), whom he disinherited, and who took orders, married Elizabeth Fytche (1781–1865), and was presented to the rectory of Somersby.

Alfred, the fourth of his 12 children, was sent in 1815 to Louth Grammar School—where he was unhappy—with two of his brothers, Frederick and Charles. He left in 1820, but, though home conditions were difficult, his father managed to give him a wide literary education. Alfred was precocious and before his teens had composed in the styles of Thomson, Pope, Scott, and Milton. To his youth also belongs *The Devil and the Lady* (first published in 1930), which shows an astonishing understanding of Elizabethan dramatic verse. Byron was a dominant influence; at the news of his death (1824) he flung himself on the ground in a passion of grief and carved on sandstone "Byron is dead."

At the lonely rectory the children were thrown upon their own resources. All writers on Tennyson emphasize the influence of the Lincolnshire countryside on his poetry, the Wolds, the plain, the sea about his home, "the sand-built ridge of heaped hills that mound the sea," "the waste enormous marsh."

In 1824 the health of Tennyson's father began to break down, and he took refuge in drink. Alfred, though depressed by unhappiness at home, continued to write, collaborating with Frederick and Charles in *Poems by Two Brothers* (1826; dated 1827). His contributions (more than half the volume) are mostly in fashionable styles of the day.

In 1827 Alfred and Charles joined Frederick at Trinity College, Cambridge. There Alfred made friends with Arthur Hallam, the gifted son of the historian Henry Hallam. This was the deepest friendship of Tennyson's life. The friends became members of "The Apostles," an exclusive undergraduate club of earnest intellectual interests. Tennyson's reputation as a poet increased at Cambridge. In 1829 he won the Chancellor's Gold Medal with a poem called *Timbuctoo.* In 1830 *Poems, Chiefly Lyrical* was published, and in the same year Tennyson, Hallam, and other Apostles went to Spain to help in the unsuccessful revolution against Ferdinand VII. Tennyson took away many vivid memories, especially of the scenery of the Pyrenees. In the meantime Hallam had become attached to Tennyson's sister Emily but was forbidden by his father to correspond with her for a year.

THE GRANGER COLLECTION

TENNYSON, PHOTOGRAPHED ABOUT 1861

In 1831 Tennyson's father died. Alfred's misery was increased by his grandfather's discovery of his debts. He left Cambridge without taking a degree, and his grandfather made financial arrangements for the family. In the same year Hallam published a eulogistic article on *Poems, Chiefly Lyrical* in the *Englishman's Magazine.* He went to Somersby in 1832 as the accepted lover of Emily.

In 1832 Tennyson published another installment of his poems (dated 1833), including "The Lotos-Eaters," "The Palace of Art," and "The Lady of Shalott." Among them was a satirical epigram on the critic "Christopher North" (John Wilson; *q.v.*), who had attacked *Poems, Chiefly Lyrical* in *Blackwood's Magazine.* Tennyson's sally prompted a scathing attack on his new volume in the *Quarterly.* The attacks distressed Tennyson, but he continued to revise his old poems and compose new ones.

In 1833 Hallam's engagement was recognized by his family, but while on a visit to Vienna he died suddenly (Sept. 15). The shock to Tennyson was severe. It came at a depressing time; three of his brothers, Edward, Charles, and Septimus, were suffering from mental illness, and the bad reception of his own work added to the gloom. Recent research has shown that his frustrated courtship of Rose Baring and his attachment to Sophy Rawnsley increased his psychological difficulties. Yet it was in this period that he wrote some of his most characteristic work, "The Two Voices" (of which the original title, significantly, was "Thoughts of a Suicide"), "Ulysses," "St. Simeon Stylites," and, probably, the first draft of "Morte d'Arthur." To this period also belong some of the poems that became constituent parts of *In Memoriam,* and lyrics later worked into *Maud.*

In May 1836 his brother Charles married Louisa Sellwood of Horncastle, and at the wedding Alfred fell in love with her sister Emily. For some years the lovers corresponded, but Emily's father disapproved of Tennyson because of his bohemianism, addiction to port and tobacco, and latitudinarian religious views, and in 1840 he forbade the correspondence. Meanwhile the Tennysons had left Somersby and were living a rather wandering life nearer London. It was in this period that Tennyson made friends with many famous men, including Gladstone, Landor, and Carlyle. Carlyle, writing to Emerson in 1842, described him as

> a man solitary and sad, dwelling in an element of gloom, carrying a bit of Chaos about him, which he is manufacturing into Cosmos . . . One of the finest-looking men in the world. A great shock of rough, dusky, dark hair; bright, laughing hazel eyes; massive aquiline face, most massive yet most delicate; of sallow brown complexion, almost Indian looking, clothes cynically loose, free-and-easy, smokes infinite tobacco. His voice is musically loose, fit for loud laughter and piercing wail, and all that may lie between; speech and speculation free and plenteous; I do not meet in these last decades such company over a pipe!

Edward FitzGerald, another friend, at this time felt, despite the poet's "humours and grumpiness," "a sense of depression . . . at the overshadowing of a so much more lofty intellect than my own."

In 1840 Tennyson invested his patrimony in a project for woodcarving by machinery. Its failure plunged him into financial difficulty; and family worries, besides his ill health and nervous instability, brought him near to a breakdown. But the then fashionable "water cure," which he took several times during the

1840s, seems to have done him good, for we hear of his resuming his port-and-tobacco regime.

In 1842 he published *Poems,* in two volumes, one containing a revised selection from the volumes of 1830 and 1832, the other new poems. The new poems included "Morte d'Arthur," "The Two Voices," "Locksley Hall," and "The Vision of Sin," and other poems that reveal a strange naïveté, such as "The May Queen," "Lady Clara Vere de Vere," and "The Lord of Burleigh." The new volume was not on the whole well received. But the grant to him at this time, by Sir Robert Peel, of a pension of £200 helped to alleviate his financial worries.

To this period belongs the strange poem *The Princess,* a serio-comic fantasy on the higher education of women, which appeared in 1847, to the usual accompaniment of unfavourable reviews. It sold well, however, and this encouraged Tennyson to take up an old project of writing an Arthurian epic.

The year 1850 marked a turning point. Tennyson resumed his correspondence with Emily Sellwood, and their engagement was renewed and followed by marriage. Meanwhile Edward Moxon offered to publish the elegies on Hallam that Tennyson had been composing over the years. They appeared, at first anonymously, as *In Memoriam,* which had a great success with both reviewers and the public, won him the friendship of Queen Victoria, and helped bring about, in the same year, his appointment as laureate.

After his marriage, which was happy, Tennyson's life became more secure and outwardly uneventful. There were two sons: Hallam (1852–1928) and Lionel (1854–86). The times of wandering and unsettlement ended in 1853, when the Tennysons took a house, Farringford, in the Isle of Wight. Tennyson was to spend most of the rest of his life there, and at Aldworth, near Haslemere, Surrey, which he built as a summer home in 1868.

His position as the national poet was confirmed by his ode on the death of Wellington (1852)—though the critics at first thought it disappointing—and the famous poem on the charge of the Light Brigade at Balaclava, published in 1855, first in the press and then in the *Maud* volume. *Maud* itself, a turbid and unsatisfactory "monodrama," provoked a storm of protest; many of the poet's admirers were shocked by the morbidity, hysteria, and bellicosity of the hero. Yet *Maud* was Tennyson's favourite.

His Arthurian project at last issued in *Idylls of the King* (1859), which had an immediate success. Tennyson, who loathed publicity, had now acquired a sometimes embarrassing public fame. The *Enoch Arden* volume of 1864 perhaps represents the peak of his popularity. New Arthurian *Idylls* were published in *The Holy Grail, and Other Poems* in 1869 (dated 1870). These were again well received, though some readers were beginning to show discomfort at the "Victorian" moral feeling that Tennyson had imported into his source material from Sir Thomas Malory.

In 1874 Tennyson decided to try his hand at poetic drama. *Queen Mary* appeared in 1875, and an abridged version was produced at the Lyceum in 1876 with only moderate success. It was followed by *Harold* (1876; dated 1877), *Becket* (not published in full until 1884), and the "village tragedy," *The Promise of May,* which proved a failure at the Globe in November 1882. This—his only prose work—shows Tennyson's growing despondency and resentment at the religious, moral, and political tendencies of the age. He had already caused some sensation by publishing a poem called "Despair" in the *Nineteenth Century* (November 1881). It evoked a parody by Swinburne, who had already laughed at the muzzy metaphysics of the laureate's "Higher Pantheism"; and a stream of pamphlets, lectures, and sermons. A more positive indication of Tennyson's later beliefs appears in "The Ancient Sage," published in *Tiresias and Other Poems* (1885). Here the poet records his intimations of a life before and beyond this life.

Tennyson accepted a peerage (after some hesitation) in 1884. In 1886 he published a new volume containing "Locksley Hall Sixty Years After," consisting mainly of imprecations against modern decadence and retracting the earlier poem's belief in inevitable human progress. This challenge to the Liberal thought of the day prompted Gladstone to write a protesting article in the *Nineteenth Century* for January 1887.

In 1889 Tennyson wrote the famous short poem "Crossing the Bar," during the crossing to the Isle of Wight. In the same year he published *Demeter and Other Poems,* which contains the charming retrospective "To Mary Boyle," introducing "The Progress of Spring," a fine lyric written much earlier and rediscovered, and "Merlin and the Gleam," an allegorical summing-up of his poetic career. In 1892 his play *The Foresters* was successfully produced in New York. Despite ill health, he was able to correct the proofs of his last volume, *The Death of Oenone . . . and Other Poems.* He died at Aldworth on Oct. 6, 1892.

**Assessment.**—Tennyson was revered by most Victorians as the greatest poet of his time, both for his mastery of verse technique and his "message." He was also admired for his accurate depictions of nature. In the 20th century, however, many readers have become less enamoured of his verse technique, which they have found, though sometimes exquisite, very limited; they feel that Tennyson does not realize anything like the full strength of the English language, and the famous Tennysonian "music" has come to seem too much a matter of removing *s*'s and mouthing out hollow *o*'s and *a*'s. As for the "message," it is sometimes thought obscure, and more often vague, trite, or "dated," while the poet's passion for botanical detail has become wearisome.

Adverse critics have tended to accept the intuitions of FitzGerald and Carlyle that Tennyson did not put enough of himself into his poetry. They remark on the contrast between the mellifluous, polished, Victorian-Hellenistic verse and the poet who wrote it, the unconventional recluse with the manners of a Lincolnshire peasant-farmer. Henry James, who met Tennyson in old age, made the discovery that "Tennyson was not Tennysonian." His art seemed to be too much one of exclusion. This point was made by Ezra Pound, who quoted Walter Bagehot's rhetorical question, "Is it credible that Tennyson's whole mind should be made up of fine sentiments?" and continued:

> Of course it wasn't. It was that lady-like attitude toward the printed page that did it—that something, that ineffable "something," which kept Tennyson out of his works. When he began to write for Viccy's ignorant ear he immediately ceased to be the "Tennyson so muzzy that he tried to go out through the fireplace," the Tennyson with the broad North accent, the old man with the worst manners in England (except Carlyle's), the Tennyson whom "it took the whole combined efforts of his family and his publishers to keep respectable." (*The Literary Essays of Ezra Pound,* ed. by T. S. Eliot. All rights reserved. Reprinted by permission of New Directions Publishing Corp., U.S.; A. V. Moore, U.K. and Commonwealth).

Much more sympathetic criticism, however, can also be found among post-Victorian writers on Tennyson. G. K. Chesterton, in *The Victorian Age in Literature* (1913), admirably suggests the pleasures to be savoured in Tennyson's "magical luck or skill in the mere choice of words—'Wet sands marbled with moon or cloud'—'Flits by the sea-blue bird of March'—'Leafless ribs and iron horns'—'When the long dun wolds are ribbed with snow'—in all these cases," says Chesterton, "one word is the keystone of an arch which would fall into ruin without it." Chesterton also speaks of strong phrases that suggest Virgil: "Tears from the depth of some divine despair"—"There is fallen a splendid tear from the passion-flower at the gate"—"Was a great water; and the moon was full"; lines which "do not depend on a word but on an idea." Chesterton considers, surely rightly, that Tennyson was "first and last a lyric poet."

A more influential critique is T. S. Eliot's essay on *In Memoriam* (in *Essays Ancient and Modern,* 1936). Eliot considers Tennyson a great poet because of his "abundance, variety and complete competence." He stresses Tennyson's metrical accomplishment: "without making the mistake of trying to write Latin verse in English, he knew everything about Latin versification that an English poet could use." Eliot agrees with earlier critics that Tennyson is not a master of the long poem; *Maud* and *In Memoriam* "are each a series of poems," *The Princess* is "an idyll that is too long," the *Idylls of the King* "are no different in kind from some of his early poems"; these poems are descriptive and picturesque rather than narrative. Eliot finds that "The fury of *Maud* is shrill rather than deep, though one feels in every passage the exquisite adaptation of metre to the mood. . . ." He places *In Memoriam* highest among Tennyson's major works.

While Eliot praises generously the range of Tennyson's technical accomplishment, he is perhaps unfair to the didactic content of *In Memoriam.* He accuses Tennyson of confusing the Christian hope of eternal life with belief in the inevitable progress of humanity. But it is part of the Christian faith to believe in the ultimate transformation of earth into paradise; and Tennyson's own belief that life is morally meaningless without hope of personal survival is reiterated in the poem. Eliot apparently objects to the lack of firm dogma in Tennyson's assertion of his hopes and admission of his doubts and fears; we may think that Tennyson here shows an unusual sensitiveness and honesty, when we reflect on the temptation to simplify experience in order to bring his poem to a more unequivocally comforting conclusion.

Persuasive as Eliot's essay is, it is still not easy to arrive at a satisfactory judgment on Tennyson's achievement as a whole and to determine where its centre lies. Tennyson lacks the interesting "prose" side that, in their different ways, Matthew Arnold, Gerard Manley Hopkins, and Hardy all have. Apart from some penetrating critical remarks in notes and memoirs, he can be judged only on his poetry, and it is not clear how much of this can be regarded as of intrinsic, as well as of historical, interest. Much of the praise of his contemporaries can be discounted; Tennyson flattered them, as they flattered him, with the conviction that theirs was a great age and he was its great poet. His least satisfactory work is often to be found on this "public" level. The Wellington ode is an impressive public utterance, but a good deal of it is continuous with a rather shallow cult, in other poems, of the "great broad-shouldered Englishman," which, if it contains an element of sincere simplicity, also permits simple-mindedness and, worse, some boasting and conceit. Tennyson's political poetry has not worn well. Then—again in the "popular" range of his work—there is, besides genuine naïveté, a certain false simplicity, which appears in "Dora" and in the (admittedly much better) *Enoch Arden.* The simplicity in these poems is too studied and artificial. Finally, the sentimentality of poems like "The May Queen," which was noted in Tennyson's own day, has not become more bearable with the years. Tennysonian pathos, even at its best (as in the late poem "Rizpah"), has a dangerously self-conscious note, and the sentimental strain in it can become so gross as to assimilate it to the melodramatic falsetto of "Locksley Hall" and the worst parts of *The Palace of Art* or *Maud.* Sometimes, too, this strained indulgence in the pathetic is associated with a mawkishness and silliness that are common in Tennyson's early work and to which his early reviewers did ample justice.

In considering the "classical" element in Tennyson's work we reach more satisfactory ground for praise. Tennyson's lifelong devotion to classical poetry, especially Virgil, produced many memorable lines and phrases, and his poems afford several instances of the successful "symbolic" treatment of classical subjects; "Ulysses" is perhaps the finest, but "Tithonus" and the later "Lucretius" have fine moments. Yet Tennysonian classicism is not altogether satisfying. It is too often merely a question of manner, of a skilful recalling of ancient poetry and a taste for picturesque decoration. The substance of his "classical" poetry is limited in a way analogous to the limitation of that "fine ear" that the poet so carefully cultivated.

Some modern admirers have laid stress on the realistic and comic aspects of Tennyson's work. About the latter, it may be felt that FitzGerald was right when he said "Alfred cannot trifle." The realism, especially in the Lincolnshire dialect poems, is a more solid achievement, but we may doubt whether it is truly central in Tennyson's work as a whole.

Tennyson's mysticism, on the other hand, has received less attention, but is important. Tennyson was not gifted as a religious or philosophical thinker, and the strictly argumentative part of *In Memoriam* cannot engage most of us as it did the poet's contemporaries. But the mystical feeling for the past, together with an awed sense of the mystery of life, represents something profound in Tennyson, and without this capacity for wonder we should not have had "Crossing the Bar" or "Flower in the crannied wall."

A complete judgment of Tennyson cannot be reached without considering the Romantic tradition of which he was the consolidator, and which laid such stress on the specialized poetic region called "the soul." We should also, perhaps, have to know more than is at present known about his life during the 1830s and '40s. Some readers may be content to regard him solely as the poet of such poems as "The Bugle Song," in which he so exquisitely renders a human emotion through a rendering of the sights and sounds of nature. It is understandable that we should wish to see a greater poet than that in Tennyson, but we are then faced by the difficulty implied in his own admission that he had "nothing to say." Perhaps the Tennyson who had nothing to say is Tennyson after 1850, when the process of "pulling himself together" seems to have cut him off from the deepest sources of his poetic inspiration. Yet even in the earlier poems it seems significant that among the most admired are "Mariana" and "The Lady of Shalott," where the evocation of visual images and care for the management of sound are what most remain in the memory. It is in the most poignant passages of *In Memoriam,* in the most personally felt parts of *Maud,* in some of the lyrics he added in 1850 to *The Princess,* and in the unforgettable "Break, break, break," that Tennyson achieves his most distinctively personal poetry; these things are among the most sensitive expressions in English of the emotions of nostalgia, trouble, and grief. But they do not make him a poet on the grand scale. Where he tries to be one, where he is most consciously the spokesman of "the age," he strains his voice and coarsens his art. We may not agree wholly with FitzGerald that the 1842 poems are all that matter, but few of us now suppose that Tennyson had the resources to write the modern epic after which he hankered; the *Idylls* as a whole do not fulfill the promise of the early "Morte d'Arthur" and survive, like *The Princess,* only in short passages. Perhaps the most attractive work outside the dream-world poems and the poignant lyrics may be found in the vein of mellow personal poetry revealed in "The Daisy" and a few later poems. But these successes are somewhat marginal; and our conclusion may be that time will reduce the voluminous Victorian laureate to a place in our literature as modest—but as secure—as that of Thomas Gray.

Bibliography.—The standard collected edition is published by Macmillan in 1 vol. (1894; frequently reprinted); there is also a 1-vol. edition in the "Oxford Standard Authors Series" (1953). To these should be added *Poems by Two Brothers* (1826, dated 1827; reprinted with additions, 1893); *Suppressed Poems . . . 1830–62,* ed. by J. C. Thomson (1904); and *The Devil and the Lady* (1930) and *Unpublished Early Poems* (1931), both ed. by C. B. L. Tennyson.

*Biography and Criticism:* Hallam Tennyson, *Alfred Lord Tennyson: a Memoir by His Son,* 2 vol. (1897); Sir Charles Tennyson (the poet's grandson), *Alfred Tennyson* (1949); H. Nicolson, *Tennyson: Aspects of His Life, Character and Poetry* (1923; 2nd ed. 1925; reprinted 1960); P. F. Baum, *Tennyson Sixty Years After* (1948); J. H. Buckley, *Tennyson: the Growth of a Poet* (1960); J. Killham (ed.), *Critical Essays on the Poetry of Tennyson* (1960); J. Richardson, *The Pre-eminent Victorian* (1962); V. Pitt, *Tennyson Laureate* (1962); R. W. Rader, *Tennyson's Maud: the Biographical Genesis* (1963). Important critical essays are A. C. Bradley, "The Reaction Against Tennyson" (1917; reprinted in *A Miscellany,* 1929); W. H. Auden's introduction to *Selections from Tennyson* (1946); and B. Willey, in *More 19th-Century Studies* (1956). (W. W. Ro.)

**TENREC** (Tendrac), an insect-eating mammal of the family Tenrecidae, confined to Madagascar. They are among the largest members of the order Insectivora, ranging in length from 12 to 16 in. The coat consists chiefly of bristles and hairs, with some flexible spines. The general hue is brown tinged with yellow. From 12 to 16 or even 20 young are produced at birth.

In habits tenrecs are nocturnal; they live in the brush in the mountain regions, and in the dry season they hibernate in deep burrows. The long flexible snout is used to root up worms and grubs, and ground insects form part of its nourishment. When fat before hibernation, tenrecs are much valued as food by natives. *See* Insectivore.

**TENSOR ALGEBRA.** Tensors were invented to express geometric entities arising in the study of manifolds (*see* Manifolds; Tensor Analysis). Since manifolds were originally considered only in the small in terms of co-ordinate systems, tensors were expressed in terms of functions involving many indices which obey certain transformation laws when the co-ordinate system is changed. Subsequently, a global study of manifolds resulted in an invariant treatment of tensors and their algebraic analysis. This is the subject of tensor or multilinear algebra.

**Tensors and Vector Spaces.**—Technically, a tensor of type $(s,r)$ is an element of a vector space $V_{s,r}$ associated with a given vector space $V$ of dimension $d$. Any basis of $V$ induces a basis of $V_{s,r}$ in terms of which every tensor $T$ in $V_{s,r}$ can be represented by its components

$$T^{j_1 j_2, \ldots, j_s}_{i_1 i_2, \ldots, i_r}, i_1, \ldots, i_r, j_1, \ldots, j_s = 1, \ldots, d$$

The vector space $V_{s,r}$ can be constructed from $V$ in the following way: Let $V^*$ denote the dual space of $V$; that is, the vector space of linear functions of $V$. Then $V_{s,r}$ is the collection of scalar-valued functions of $r + s$ variables, $r$ of them in $V^*$ and $s$ of them in $V$, which are linear in each variable when the others are left fixed. Thus each $T$ in $V_{s,r}$ gives the scalar value $T(v^1, \ldots, v^s, \alpha_1, \ldots, \alpha_r)$ for every $v^1, \ldots, v^s$ in $V$ and $\alpha_1, \ldots, \alpha_r$ in $V^*$. If $e^1, \ldots e^d$ is a basis of $V$, let $\phi_1, \ldots, \phi_d$ be the basis of $V^*$ which is dual to $e^1, \ldots, e^d$ so that $\phi_i(e^j) = 0$ if $i \neq j$ and $\phi_i(e^i) = 1$. Because $T$ is linear in each variable separately, $T$ is completely determined by its values

$$T(e^{j_1}, \ldots, e^{j_s}, \phi_{i_1}, \ldots, \phi_{i_r}) = T^{j_1, \ldots, j_s}_{i_1, \ldots, i_r}$$

If $\phi_{i_1} \otimes \ldots \otimes \phi_{i_s} \otimes e^{i_1} \otimes \ldots \otimes e^{i_r}$ is the tensor which gives the value 1 on $(e^{j_1}, \ldots, e^{j_s}, \phi_{i_1}, \ldots, \phi_{i_r})$ and 0 for any other choice of basis vectors, then

$$T = \sum_{i,j=1}^{d} T^{j_1, \ldots, j_s}_{i_1, \ldots, i_r} \phi_{i_1} \otimes \ldots \otimes \phi_{i_s} \otimes e^{i_1} \otimes \ldots \otimes e^{i_r}$$

Suppose a different basis $f^1, \ldots, f^d$ of $V$ had been chosen and suppose $f^i = \sum_{k=1}^{d} a^i_k e^k$. Then the dual basis of $f^1, \ldots, f^d$ is the set of linear functions $\Psi_1, \ldots, \Psi_d$, where $\Psi_i = \sum_{l=1}^{d} b^l_i \phi_l$ and $(b^l_i)$ is the inverse of the nonsingular matrix $(a^i_k)$. In terms of the new basis, $T$ is represented by its components

$$T(f^{j_1}, \ldots, f^{j_s}, \Psi_{i_1}, \ldots, \Psi_{i_r}) =$$

$$\sum_{k,l=1}^{d} a^{j_1}_{k_1} a^{j_2}_{k_2} \ldots a^{j_s}_{k_s} b^{l_1}_{i_1} b^{l_2}_{i_2} b^{l_r}_{i_r} T^{k_1, \ldots, k_s}_{l_1, \ldots, l_r}$$

Thus a tensor of type $(s,r)$ can be described as a function of $r + s$ indices depending upon a basis which obeys the transformation law in the last formula when the basis is changed. The advantage of the invariant definition of $V_{s,r}$ (*i.e.*, independent of a basis) is that it is applicable to the case where the scalars form only a ring and also to infinite-dimensional vector spaces. It is also aesthetically more pleasing. The description of $T$ in terms of its components $T^{j_1, \ldots, j_s}_{i_1, \ldots, i_r}$ is useful in explicit computations.

**Construction and Properties of Tensor Algebra.**—Two tensors can be multiplied to give another tensor. If $T$ is a tensor of type $(s,r)$ and $\bar{T}$ is a tensor of type $(\bar{s},\bar{r})$, then $T\bar{T}$ is a tensor of type $(s + \bar{s}, r + \bar{r})$, where

$$T\bar{T}(v^1, \ldots, v^s, v^{s+1}, \ldots, v^{s+\bar{s}}, \alpha_1, \ldots, \alpha_r, \alpha_{r+1}, \ldots, \alpha_{r+\bar{r}}) =$$

$$T(v^1, \ldots, v^s, \alpha_1, \ldots, \alpha_r) \cdot \bar{T}(v^{s+1}, \ldots, v^{s+\bar{s}}, \alpha_{r+1}, \ldots, \alpha_{r+\bar{r}})$$

In terms of a basis the components of $T\bar{T}$ are

$$T^{j_1, \ldots, j_s}_{i_1, \ldots, i_r} \bar{T}^{j_{s+1}, \ldots, j_{s+\bar{s}}}_{i_{r+1}, \ldots, i_{r+\bar{r}}}$$

From this multiplication an associative algebra called the tensor algebra $\mathcal{T}$ can be constructed over the vector space $V$. The elements of $\mathcal{T}$ are the scalars together with the sum of all the spaces $V_{0,r}$ for $r = 1,2,3,\ldots$. Two tensors of type $(0,r)$ and $(0,\bar{r})$ can be multiplied by the rule above to give a tensor of type $(0, r + \bar{r})$. This rule together with the distributive law determines the multiplication in $\mathcal{T}$. The tensor algebra $\mathcal{T}$ has these properties, which characterize it completely:

1. It contains $V = (V_{0,1})$ and a unity element, the scalar 1. The smallest algebra in $\mathcal{T}$ containing $V$ and 1 is $\mathcal{T}$.

2. If $\mathcal{R}$ is any associative algebra with unity, any linear mapping of $V$ into $\mathcal{R}$ can be extended to a map of $\mathcal{T}$ into $\mathcal{R}$ which preserves multiplication.

**Tensor Product of Vector Spaces.**—The multiplication of two tensors is a special case of the tensor product of vector spaces. If $V_1, \ldots, V_k$ are $k$ vector spaces, their tensor product $V \otimes \ldots \otimes V_k$ is the vector space of scalar-valued functions in $k$ variables in $V_1^*, \ldots, V_k^*$ respectively which are linear in each variable separately. If $v^i$ lie in $V_i$, $i = 1, \ldots, k$, then their tensor product $v^1 \otimes \ldots \otimes v^k$ has the value $v^1(\alpha_1)v^2(\alpha_2) \ldots v^k(\alpha_k)$ on $(\alpha_1, \ldots, \alpha_k)$ in $V_1^*, \ldots, V_k^*$ respectively. The space $V_{s,r}$ is the tensor product of $V^*$ taken $s$ times and $V$ taken $r$ times.

**Tensor Fields.**—The tensors which arise in the study of manifolds are obtained by attaching to each point of a smooth $d$-dimensional manifold a $d$-dimensional vector space, its tangent space or space of directional derivatives. The tensors considered are those associated with each tangent space. A tensor field of type $(s,r)$ on a manifold is a function which assigns to each point of the manifold a tensor of type $(s,r)$ associated with the tangent space at that point. If a co-ordinate system with co-ordinate functions $x_1, \ldots, x_d$ is chosen about some point $m$ of the manifold, then the directional derivatives $\frac{\partial}{\partial x_1}, \ldots, \frac{\partial}{\partial x_d}$ form a basis of the tangent spaces of points near $m$. In terms of this basis, a tensor field of type $(s,r)$ has components $T^{j_1, \ldots, j_s}_{i_1, \ldots, i_r}$ which are functions of the co-ordinates $x_1, \ldots, x_d$. On the whole, tensor analysis studies the analytical properties of tensor fields, while tensor algebra deals only with the algebraic properties of tensors associated with a fixed vector space.

**Associated Algebras.**—Closely related to the tensor algebra $\mathcal{T}$ over a vector space $V$ are several other algebras, the most important for geometric and topological applications being the Grassman or exterior algebra over $V$. In this algebra, the elements to be multiplied are skew-symmetric tensors. A tensor $T$ of type $(0,r)$ is skew-symmetric if $T(\alpha_{\pi(1)}, \alpha_{\pi(2)}, \ldots, \alpha_{\pi(r)}) = \epsilon(\pi) T(\alpha_1, \alpha_2, \ldots, \alpha_r)$; $\epsilon(\pi)$ is $+1$ or $-1$ depending upon whether the permutation $\pi$ of the integers $1,2,\ldots,r$ is even or odd. Any tensor $T$ of type $(0,r)$ can be made skew-symmetric by alternating it; *i.e.*, $\text{ALT}_r(T)$ is skew-symmetric, where $\text{ALT}_r(T)(\alpha_1, \ldots, \alpha_r) = \frac{1}{r!} \sum \epsilon(\pi) T(\alpha_{\pi(1)}, \ldots, \alpha_{\pi(r)})$, summed over all permutations $\pi$ of the integers $1, \ldots, r$. The exterior algebra $\mathcal{G}$ over $V$ is the space of skew-symmetric tensors in $\mathcal{T}$ where the multiplication is the product of two tensors made skew-symmetric. Thus if $T$ and $\bar{T}$ are skew-symmetric tensors of type $(0,r)$ and $(0,\bar{r})$ respectively, $T \wedge \bar{T} = \text{ALT}_{r+\bar{r}}(T\bar{T})$ is a skew-symmetric tensor of type $(0, r + \bar{r})$. Under this multiplication $\mathcal{G}$ becomes an associative algebra with unity of dimension $2^d$ which contains $V = (V_{0,1})$ and in which $v \wedge v = 0$ for each $v$ in $V$.

An algebra with the symmetric tensors can be formed in a similar manner. A tensor $T$ of type $(0,r)$ is symmetric if $T(\alpha_{\pi(1)}, \ldots, \alpha_{\pi(r)}) = T(\alpha_1, \ldots, \alpha_r)$ for every permutation $\pi$ of the integers $1, \ldots, r$. Any tensor of type $(0,r)$ can be made symmetric, *i.e.*, $\text{SYM}_r(T)$ is a symmetric tensor of type $(0,r)$ where $\text{SYM}_r(T)(\alpha_1, \ldots, \alpha_r) = \frac{1}{r!} \sum T(\alpha_{\pi(1)}, \ldots, \alpha_{\pi(r)})$, the sum taken over all permutations $\pi$ of the integers $1, \ldots, r$. The polynomial algebra over $V$ is the space of symmetric tensors in $\mathcal{T}$ where the multiplication is the product of two tensors made symmetric. Thus if $T$ and $\bar{T}$ are symmetric tensors of type $(0,r)$ and $(0,\bar{r})$ respectively, then $T \times \bar{T} = \text{SYM}_{r+\bar{r}}(T\bar{T})$.

A generalization of Grassman algebras called Clifford algebras is important for the study of certain representations of orthogonal groups. If $B$ is a symmetric tensor of type (2,0) over $V$, the orthogonal group of $B$ is the group of nonsingular linear transformations $l$ on $V$ for which $B(l(v), l(v)) = B(v,v)$ for all $v$ in $V$. The Clifford algebra of $B$, which contains $V$ and in which $v \cdot v = B(v,v)1$, is useful for studying the spin representations of this group. The Clifford algebra of $B$ is constructed from $\mathcal{T}$ in the following way: Let $\mathcal{I}_B$ denote the ideal in $\mathcal{T}$ generated by all elements of the form $v^2 - B(v,v)1$ for $v$ in $V$; *i.e.*, $\mathcal{I}_B$ is the set of all linear combinations of elements of $\mathcal{T}$ of the form $T(v^2 - B(v,v)1)$ or $(v^2 - B(v,v)1)T$. The Clifford algebra of $B$ is the algebra $\mathcal{T}/\mathcal{I}_B$; *i.e.*, $\mathcal{T}$ with the elements $\mathcal{I}_B$ set equal to zero. If the field of scalars is not of characteristic two, and if $e^1, \ldots, e^d$ is a basis of $V$, then $e^{i_1} \cdot e^{i_2} \cdot e^{i_3} \cdots e^{i_k}$ $(i_1 < i_2 < \ldots < i_k)$ is a basis of the Clifford algebra, so that the Clifford algebra has dimension $2^d$. If $B$ is identically zero, the Clifford algebra is the previously constructed Grassman algebra. *See* also DIFFERENTIAL GEOMETRY.

BIBLIOGRAPHY.—C. Chevalley, *The Construction and Study of Certain Important Algebras* (1955); N. Bourbaki, *Algèbre Multilinéaire* (1948); A. I. Borisenko and I. E. Tarapov, *Vector Analysis and Tensor Calculus* (1963). (I. M. S.)

**TENSOR ANALYSIS.** The concept of tensors and the knowledge of some of their properties can be traced back to C. F. Gauss, G. F. B. Riemann, and E. B. Christoffel; their algebra and analysis were shaped into a systematic method by C. G. Ricci and T. Levi-Civita, who coined for this powerful branch of mathematics the name of absolute differential calculus.

Its chief aim is to construct and discuss relations or laws generally covariant; such, that is, as remain valid in passing from one to any other system of coordinates. This makes the subject of prime importance for differential geometry. It became the object of widespread interest after the advent of general relativity theory, in which a principal requirement is precisely such unrestricted covariance of physical laws. There are interesting applications of tensor analysis—both finite and infinite dimensional—to classical mechanics, quantum mechanics, fluid mechanics, elasticity, aeronautics, and rheology (*q.v.*).

**Definitions; Algebra of Tensors.**—Consider a continuous $n$-dimensional manifold or space $S_n$ (*see* MANIFOLDS), whose element or point $P(x_\iota)$, is determined by assigning the values of $n$ real independent variables or coordinates $x_\iota$. Let $Q(x_\iota + dx_\iota)$ be another point of $S_n$. Then the ordered point-pair $P,Q$ or the set of differentials $dx_\iota$ is called a vector. (To begin with, the idea of size or length is foreign to this concept, $S_n$ being thus far a nonmetrical manifold.) Let the $x_\iota$ be transformed into any other system of $n$ coordinates $x'_\iota$, the former being continuous functions of the latter with continuous derivatives $\partial x_\iota / \partial x'_\kappa$ and nonvanishing, finite Jacobian $J = \left|\frac{\partial x_\iota}{\partial x'_\kappa}\right|$; then $dx_\iota$ are transformed into

$$dx'_\iota = \frac{\partial x'_\iota}{\partial x_\alpha} dx_\alpha$$

to be summed over $\alpha = 1$ to $n$, and vice versa, $dx_\iota = (\partial x_\iota / \partial x'_\alpha) dx'_\alpha$. (The convention will be adopted that every term in which an index occurs twice, is to be summed over all its values.) Any set of $n$ magnitudes $A^\iota$, functions of the $x$, that are transformed by this rule, *i.e.*, into

$$A'_\iota = \frac{\partial x'_\iota}{\partial x_\alpha} A^\alpha$$

form a contravariant tensor of rank 1, the $A^\iota$ being its $n$ components. For contravariant tensors upper indices are used, an exception being made for $dx_\iota$, the prototype of all such tensors. Next, any $n$ magnitudes $A_\iota$ that are transformed as the differentiators $\partial / \partial x_\iota$, *i.e.*, into

$$A'_\iota = \frac{\partial x_\alpha}{\partial x'_\iota} A_\alpha$$

form a covariant tensor of rank 1, lower indices being used for such tensors. These two kinds of tensors, of rank 1, are also termed vectors; *e.g.*, three-vectors, four-vectors (such as the relativistic four-velocity or four-potential, in space-time, $S_4$), and so on, according as $n = 3, 4, \ldots$. Similarly, any $n^2$ magnitudes $A_{\iota\kappa}$ transformable into

$$A'_{\iota\kappa} = \frac{\partial x_\alpha}{\partial x'_\iota} \frac{\partial x_\beta}{\partial x'_\kappa} A_{\alpha\beta}$$

form a covariant, and any $A^\iota$ transformable into

$$A'_{\iota\kappa} = \frac{\partial x'_\iota}{\partial x_\alpha} \frac{\partial x'_\kappa}{\partial x_\beta} A_{\alpha\beta}$$

form a contravariant tensor of rank 2. Again, $n^2$ magnitudes $A_\iota{}^\kappa$ transformable into

$$A'_\iota{}^\kappa = \frac{\partial x_\alpha}{\partial x'_\iota} \frac{\partial x'_\kappa}{\partial x_\beta} A^\beta{}_\alpha$$

are said to form a mixed tensor of rank 2, covariant in $\iota$ and contravariant in $\kappa$. The extension to any rank is obvious. Any $n^{r_1 + r_2}$ magnitudes $A^{ik\cdots}_{\iota\kappa\cdots}$, with $r_1$ lower and $r_2$ upper indices, which are transformed according to the rule

$$\left(A^{ik\cdots}_{\iota\kappa\cdots}\right)' = \frac{\partial x_\alpha}{\partial x'_\iota} \frac{\partial x_\beta}{\partial x'_\kappa} \cdots \frac{\partial x'_\iota}{\partial x_a} \frac{\partial x'_\kappa}{\partial x_b} \cdots A^{ab\cdots}_{\alpha\beta\cdots} \qquad (1)$$

form a mixed tensor of rank $r = r_1 + r_2$. This is the most general concept of a tensor.

A tensor of rank zero, called also a scalar, is a single function of the $x$, invariant with respect to any transformations of coordinates, $f' = f$. $A_{\iota\kappa}$ is symmetrical if $A_{\iota\kappa} = A_{\kappa\iota}$, and antisymmetrical or a skew tensor if $A_{\iota\kappa} = -A_{\kappa\iota}$, implying $A_{\iota\iota} = 0$. Similarly for $A^{\iota\kappa}$. Analogous definitions hold for mixed tensors, and for higher ranks. Symmetry and antisymmetry are invariant properties.

The transformed tensor components being linear homogeneous functions of the original ones, the sums of corresponding components of tensors of same rank and kind form again a tensor. Thus, $A_\iota, B_\iota$ being covariant vectors, so is $A_\iota + B_\iota = C_\iota$. Similarly, $A_{\iota\kappa} + B_{\iota\kappa} = C_{\iota\kappa}$, and so on. The addends, functions of $x_\iota$, must be taken at the same point of $S_n$. If a tensor vanishes in one coordinate system, it will vanish also in any other. Consequently, any tensor equation, if valid in one, holds also in any other coordinate system. This is the chief reason of the importance of tensors in pure geometry and physics.

The outer product of two tensors of ranks $r$ and $s$ (*i.e.*, the array of $n^{r+s}$ products of their components) is again a tensor, of rank $r + s$. Thus, $A_\iota B_\kappa = C_{\iota\kappa}$, $A_{\iota\kappa} B_\lambda = C_{\iota\kappa\lambda}$, $A_{\iota\kappa} B^\lambda = C^\lambda{}_{\iota\kappa}$. The contraction, an operation of almost magical efficiency, applicable to any mixed tensor, consists in equating one of its $r_1$ lower to one of its $r_2$ upper indices and summing over it from 1 to $n$. The result is again a tensor, with $r_1 - 1$ covariant and $r_2 - 1$ contravariant indices; *e.g.*, a contraction of $A^\lambda{}_{\iota\kappa}$ gives $A^\kappa{}_{\iota\kappa} = A_\iota$, a vector; $B^{\lambda\mu}_{\iota\kappa}$ contracted once becomes $B^{\lambda\kappa}{}_{\iota\kappa} = B^\lambda{}_\iota$, and this yields $B^\iota{}_\iota = B$, a scalar.

The inner product is the outer product (supposed mixed) contracted once or more. Thus, the inner product of $A_\iota$, $B^\kappa$ is $A_\kappa B^\kappa$, a scalar; that of $A_{\iota\kappa}$, $B^{\lambda\mu}$ gives $A_{\iota\kappa} B^{\lambda\kappa} = C^\lambda{}_\iota$, a mixed tensor, and after a second contraction, $A_{\iota\kappa} B^{\iota\kappa} = C^\iota{}_\iota = C$, a scalar. Unlike $A_\kappa B^\kappa$, $A_\kappa B_\kappa$ is not invariant; it has no tensor character, and likewise for $A^\kappa B^\kappa$. Conversely, if $A_\kappa B^\kappa$ is a scalar for any covariant vector $A_\kappa$, $B^\kappa$ is a contravariant vector. Similarly, if $A_{\iota\kappa} B^{\iota\kappa}$ is a scalar for any covariant $A_{\iota\kappa}$, $B^{\iota\kappa}$ is contravariant. This is an efficient method of establishing the tensor character of a set of $n, n^2, \ldots$ magnitudes. (*See* also TENSOR ALGEBRA.)

**Differentiation.**—The differentiation of tensors with respect to the coordinates yields, in certain circumstances, further tensors. If $f$ is a scalar function of the $x$, or scalar field, $\partial f / \partial x_\iota = f_\iota$ is a covariant vector, the gradient of $f$ (but $\partial^2 f / \partial x_\iota \partial x_\kappa$ is not a tensor; again, if $du$ be an invariant, $dx_\iota / du$ is, but $d^2 x_\iota / du^2$ is not a vector). Further, if $A_\iota$ be a vector, $B_{\iota\kappa} = \partial A_\iota / \partial x_\kappa - \partial A_\kappa / \partial x_\iota$ is a skew tensor, the rotation of $A_\iota$. Finally, if $A_{\iota\kappa}$ be antisymmetric, $B_{\iota\kappa\lambda} = \partial A_{\iota\kappa} / \partial x_\lambda + \partial A_{\kappa\lambda} / \partial x_\iota + \partial A_{\lambda\iota} / \partial x_\kappa$ is again such a tensor, the expansion of $A_{\iota\kappa}$.

In what precedes only such properties of tensors were treated as are independent of any metrical considerations, the space $S_n$

being thus far a nonmetrical, amorphous manifold. Let now its metrics be fixed by laying down the line element, a quadratic differential form with coefficients $g_{\iota\kappa} = g_{\kappa\iota}$, prescribed functions of the $x$,

$$ds^2 = g_{\iota\kappa}dx_\iota dx_\kappa \tag{2}$$

to be considered as invariant and to serve as the measure of the (squared) size or length of the vector $dx_\iota$. Then, $dx_\iota$ being contravariant, $g_{\iota\kappa}$ will be covariant. Equivalently it may be said that a certain symmetrical tensor $g_{\iota\kappa}$ is being impressed upon $S_n$ as the fundamental or metrical tensor, converting it into a metrical manifold, a Riemannian space.

The minors $g^{\iota\kappa}$ of $g = |g_{\iota\kappa}|$, divided by $g$, form again a symmetrical tensor, the contravariant metrical tensor, to be used along with $g_{\iota\kappa}$. The outer product and contraction can be used in raising and lowering tensor indices. Thus $g^{\iota\kappa}A_\kappa = A^\iota$ and $g_{\iota\kappa}B^\kappa = B_\iota$.

The angle $\theta$ between two (copunctal) vectors $A^\iota$ and $B^\iota$ is defined by the invariant $\cos\theta = g_{\iota\kappa}A^\iota B^\kappa/AB$; $A,B$ being their sizes. The unit vector $\dot{x}_\iota = dx_\iota/ds$ determines, locally, a direction in $S_n$. The angle between two directions $\dot{x}_\iota$, $\dot{y}_\iota$ is given by $\cos\theta = g_{\iota\kappa}\dot{x}_\iota\dot{y}_\kappa$.

**Integrals.**—The integral $\int dx_1, \ldots, dx_n$, briefly $\int dx$, extended over a region of $S_n$, is transformed into $\int Jdx'$, and the determinant $g$ into $g' = J^2g$. Consequently, $\int\sqrt{g}dx$ is an invariant metrically impressed upon that region, its size or volume (area, if $n = 2$). This concept is readily extended to any submanifold of $S_n$ characterized by $x_\iota$ as functions of $m < n$ parameters $p_a$, the role of metrical tensor being taken over by

$$h_{ab} = g_{\iota\kappa}(\partial x_\iota/\partial p_a)(\partial x_\kappa/\partial p_b)$$

If, by a proper choice of the coordinate system, all components $g_{\iota\kappa}$ are reducible to constants, the metrical space $S_n$ is Euclidean or homaloidal (flat). This is but a very special case of a Riemannian space. In general such a reduction is not possible, and $S_n$ is non-Euclidean.

Differentiation of tensors, aided by metrics, yields an unlimited number of new tensors. The oldest of such is Riemann's set of four-index symbols of 1861. The simplest metrically differential tensor, however, was discovered in 1869 by Christoffel. This is the covariant derivative of a vector $A_\iota$,

$$A_{\iota,\kappa} = \frac{\partial A_\iota}{\partial x_\kappa} - \{\iota\kappa, \lambda\}A_\lambda \tag{3}$$

where $\{\iota\kappa, \lambda\} = g^{\lambda\mu}[\iota\kappa, \mu] = \{\kappa\iota, \lambda\}$ and

$$[\iota\kappa, \mu] = \tfrac{1}{2}(\partial g_{\mu\iota}/\partial x_\kappa + \partial g_{\kappa\mu}/\partial x_\iota - \partial g_{\iota\kappa}/\partial x_\mu)$$

are Christoffel's symbols (not forming a tensor). Again,

$$B^\lambda{}_{,\kappa} = \partial B^\iota/\partial x_\kappa + \{\alpha\kappa, \iota\}B^\alpha$$

is a mixed tensor.

$$C_{,\lambda}^{\iota\kappa} = \partial C^{\iota\kappa}/\partial x^\lambda + \{\lambda\alpha, \iota\}C^{\alpha\kappa} + \{\lambda\alpha, \kappa\}C^{\iota\alpha}, \tag{4}$$

$$C_{\iota\kappa,\lambda} = \partial C_{\iota\kappa}/\partial x^\lambda - \{\iota\lambda, \alpha\}C_{\alpha\kappa} - \{\kappa\lambda, \alpha\}C_{\iota\alpha} \tag{5}$$

are the covariant derivatives of $C^{\iota\kappa}$ and $C_{\iota\kappa}$. The covariant derivative of $g_{\iota\kappa}$ itself vanishes identically. Noteworthy for their applications are

$$A^\iota = \mathrm{Div}(A^{\iota\kappa}) \equiv \frac{1}{\sqrt{g}}\frac{\partial}{\partial x_\kappa}(\sqrt{g}A^{\iota\kappa}) \text{ and } \mathrm{div}(A^\kappa) \equiv \frac{1}{\sqrt{g}}\frac{\partial}{\partial x_\kappa}(\sqrt{g}A^\kappa),$$

the vector divergence of a skew $A^{\iota\kappa}$ and the scalar divergence of $A^\kappa$; *e.g.*, one group of James Clerk Maxwell's equations is represented by $\mathrm{Div}(F^{\iota\kappa}) = C^\iota$, where $C^\iota$ is the four-current and $F^{\iota\kappa}$ the electromagnetic skew tensor (six vector); the second group being expressed by equating to zero the expansion of $F_{\iota\kappa} = g_{\iota\alpha}g_{\kappa\beta}F^{\alpha\beta}$.

**Geodesics, Null Lines.**—The most characteristic curves of the metrical $S_n$ are its null or minimal lines, $ds = 0$, and "shortest" curves or geodesics defined by $\delta\int ds = 0$, with fixed terminals. The equations of a geodesic are

$$\ddot{x}_\iota + \{\alpha\beta, \iota\}\dot{x}_\alpha\,\dot{x}_\beta = 0 \tag{6}$$

where $\dot{x} = dx/ds$. They determine, *e.g.*, in the case of space-time, the motion of a free particle in the metrical, and gravitational, field $g_{\iota\kappa}$. The null lines are imaginary or real according as equation (2) is a definite or nondefinite form. The former is the case of spaces proper as contemplated by the pure geometer, and the latter that of space-time with one positive and three negative $g_{\kappa\kappa}$. The null lines of space-time represent light propagation. The definiteness or nondefiniteness of the quadratic form and its index of inertia (number of negative $g_{\kappa\kappa}$ terms) are invariant properties.

**Parallel Displacement of Vectors.**—A fruitful contribution to tensor analysis due to Levi-Civita is the concept of parallel displacement of a vector with respect to a curve. The metrical $S_n$ can in general be imagined as imbedded locally in a Euclidean space $E$ of $\frac{1}{2}n(n+1)$ dimensions. Levi-Civita defined parallel displacement in $S_n$ as a consequence of a parallel displacement in $E$. In spite of the ultraspatial construction, parallelism is intrinsic, expressible by the $S_n$ metrics alone.

If $x_\iota = f_\iota(s)$ are the parametric equations of any chosen curve $C$, then the differential equations along $C$

$$\frac{dA^\iota}{ds} + \{\alpha\beta, \iota\}A^\alpha\dot{x}^\beta = 0 \tag{7}$$

with the initial vector $A^\iota(s_o) = A_o^\iota$ determine uniquely a contravariant vector $A^\iota$ at each point of the curve. The vector $A^\iota$ at the point corresponding to $s = s$ is said to be obtained by a parallel displacement of the vector $A_o^\iota$ with respect to the given curve $C$, and is said to be parallel to $A_o^\iota$. Any two vectors generated as above, one at each point, are parallel with respect to $C$.

Let it be required to construct a curve whose tangents follow from each other by parallel displacement along the curve itself. This gives the equations (6), so that the curve is a geodesic. The latter is thus throughout "parallel to itself"—an interesting generalization of the property of Euclidean straights. Accordingly, a vector transferred along a geodesic remains equally inclined to it.

If a vector $X^\iota$ be carried by parallel displacement along two different paths $a,b$ from $O$ to $O'$, the two vectors at $O'$, equal in size, generally differ in direction. One is parallel to $X^\iota$ via $a$, the other via $b$. In short, parallelism depends on the route of transfer or is nonintegrable (unless $S_n$ is essentially Euclidean). Thus also, if the vector be carried around a circuit, it returns at $O$ with its direction changed.

The covariant derivative of the vector is the tensor $X_{\iota,\alpha}$. Its covariant derivative $X_{\iota\ \alpha,\beta}$ is not symmetric in $\alpha$ and $\beta$. A straightforward calculation shows that

$$X_{\iota,\beta,\alpha} - X_{\iota,\alpha,\beta} = R^\kappa_{\iota\alpha\beta}X_\kappa \tag{8}$$

where

$$R^\kappa{}_{\iota\alpha\beta} = \frac{\partial}{\partial x_\alpha}\{\iota\beta, \kappa\} - \frac{\partial}{\partial x_\beta}\{\iota\alpha, \kappa\} + \{\alpha\gamma, \kappa\}\{\iota\beta, \gamma\} - \{\beta\gamma, \kappa\}\{\iota\alpha, \gamma\} \tag{9}$$

This is the Riemann-Christoffel or curvature tensor whose vanishing is the necessary and sufficient condition for the reducibility of $g_{\iota\kappa}$ to a constant tensor, or the criterion of a homaloidal (Euclidean) space.

**Riemann's Four-index Symbols and Curvature.**—Riemann's own set of four-index symbols is the covariant tensor $(\iota\mu, \lambda\kappa) \equiv R_{\iota\mu\lambda\kappa} = g_{\mu\alpha}R^\alpha_{\iota\kappa\lambda}$. Conversely, $R^\alpha{}_{\iota\kappa\lambda} = g^{\mu\alpha}(\iota\mu, \lambda\kappa)$. Like equation (9), the symbols are antisymmetric in $\kappa$, $\lambda$. Three more linear relations hold between them. This reduces the number of independent symbols to $\frac{1}{12}n^2(n^2-1)$; *e.g.*, six for a three-space, twenty for an $S_4$, and but one for a surface, say (12, 12). This symbol divided by $g$ is a scalar of the surface, its Gaussian curvature $K$. If a vector undergoes parallel displacement around a circuit on a surface, it returns with its direction changed by an amount equal to $\int Kd\sigma$, the Gaussian curvature of the surface integrated over the surface area enclosed by the circuit. As a consequence, the excess (over $\pi$) of the angle sum in any geodesic triangle is $\int Kd\sigma$, a famous theorem due to Gauss. (*See* also DIFFERENTIAL GEOMETRY.)

In the case of three or more dimensions the curvature properties can no longer be expressed by a single magnitude, but require for their description the knowledge of the whole curvature tensor or the associated Riemann symbols. The concept of Gaussian curvature is now replaced by that of Riemannian curvature; *i.e.*, at any point $O(x)$ of $S_n$, the set of Gaussian curvatures $K$ of geodesic surfaces of all possible orientations laid through $O$. If $h_{\alpha\beta}$ be the metrical tensor of such a surface as submanifold, then $K = \frac{1}{h}(12, 12)_k$, the symbol to be calculated with $h_{\alpha\beta}$. This and the determinant $h$ can be expressed in terms of the tensor $g_{\iota\kappa}$ of the manifold and the vector pair, $\xi^\iota$, $\eta^\iota$, fixing the orientation. The result is

$$K = \frac{(\iota\kappa, \lambda\mu)\xi^\iota\eta^\kappa\xi^\lambda\eta^\mu}{(g_{\iota\lambda}g_{\kappa\mu} - g_{\iota\mu}g_{\kappa\lambda})\xi^\iota\eta^\kappa\xi^\lambda\eta^\mu} \tag{10}$$

In general, $K$ will depend on position and on orientation. In other words, with regard to curvature, $S_n$ may be nonhomogeneous as well as anisotropic (*e.g.*, space-time within or around matter); but if $K$ is everywhere isotropic, it is also constant throughout $S_n$ (Schur's theorem). By equation (10) the necessary and sufficient condition for isotropy of Riemannian curvature becomes $({}_\iota\lambda, \kappa\mu) = K(g_{\iota\kappa}g_{\lambda\mu} - g_{\iota\mu}g_{\lambda\mu})$ or $R^\alpha{}_{\iota\kappa\lambda} = K(\delta^\alpha{}_\kappa g_{\iota\lambda} - \delta^\alpha{}_\lambda g_{\iota\kappa})$ with constant $K$. *See* also RIEMANNIAN GEOMETRY.

BIBLIOGRAPHY.—H. D. Block, *Introduction to Tensor Analysis* (1962); D. F. Lawden, *Introduction to Tensor Calculus and Relativity* (1962); I. S. Sokolnikoff, *Tensor Analysis,* 2nd ed. (1964); L. Brillouin, *Tensors in Mechanics and Elasticity,* trans. by R. O. Brennan (1964). (L. SN.; A. D. ML.; X.)

**TENTERDEN, CHARLES ABBOTT,** 1ST BARON (1762–1832), lord chief justice of England, was born at Canterbury on Oct. 7, 1762, the son of a hairdresser. He was educated at King's School, Canterbury, and Corpus Christi College, Oxford, and entered the Middle Temple in 1787. For several years he practised as a special pleader under the bar, and was finally called at the Inner Temple in 1796. He joined the Oxford circuit and made rapid headway. In 1801 he was appointed recorder of Oxford. In 1802 his influential *Law Relative to Merchant Ships and Seamen* appeared. In 1808 he refused a seat on the bench; this, however, he accepted in 1816, being made a judge of the court of common pleas.

On the resignation of Lord Ellenborough in 1818 he was promoted to the chief justiceship of the king's bench, and presided over several important state trials, notably that of Arthur Thistlewood (*q.v.*) and the Cato Street conspirators (1820). He was raised to the peerage in 1827 as Baron Tenterden of Hendon. Never a great lawyer, Tenterden made his way by steady hard work. He was an uncompromising Tory and had no sympathy with the reform of the criminal law carried out by Sir Samuel Romilly. He strongly opposed the Catholic Relief Bill and the Reform Bill. Tenterden died on Nov. 4, 1832.

*See* E. Foss, *The Judges of England* (1870).

**TENTERDEN,** a municipal borough in the Ashford parliamentary division of Kent, Eng., 19 mi. (31 km.) SSE of Maidstone. Pop. (1961) 4,948. An agricultural centre, it lies on a hill above the Newmill Channel, a tributary of the Rother, whose fertile valley (Rother levels) was once an estuary; in the 18th century the sea was within two miles of Tenterden, which was a limb of the Cinque Port of Rye. St. Mildred's Church is mainly Early English, and its Perpendicular tower is associated with the legend of Goodwin Sands, which tells how the abbot of St. Augustine's, Canterbury, diverted funds for repairing the sea wall protecting Earl Godwin's island in order to build the steeple; in 1099 an inundation took place, and "Tenterden steeple was the cause of the Goodwin Sands." The nearby church of High Halden has an octagonal wooden tower with a belfry of wooden tiles (shingles). In 1449 Tenterden was incorporated with Rye and granted a charter which did not function until 1463. In 1600 it was reincorporated under the "Mayor, Jurats and Commons" as the town and hundred of Tenterden, the members of the corporation ranking as barons of the Cinque Ports.

**TENURE, JUDICIAL,** refers to the length and conditions of office for judges. Essential to the maintenance of an independent judiciary is a tenure of office adequate to ensure freedom from political and economic pressure. The truth of this proposition was recognized by the authors of the Constitution of the United States, and all judges of federal courts created pursuant to art. iii hold office during "good behaviour"; *i.e.*, for life. Most other federal judges are granted similar tenure by statute. Thus, though a federal judge is eligible to retire at full salary after a given number of years of service, he may not be compelled to surrender his office except for misbehaviour. Similar constitutional and statutory protection is afforded judicial compensation, which may not be reduced during the tenure of an incumbent. Both the federal and English judicial systems have demonstrated the value of and necessity for such extended tenure of office, even at the occasional price of retaining a superannuated or less competent judge. A federal judge's tenure can be involuntarily terminated only by impeachment and conviction as prescribed in art. ii, sec. 4 of the U.S. Constitution.

The state court systems in the U.S. have lagged far behind, with the result that political influence is rife in the administration of justice in the states. Few states provide for life tenure. The terms of judges in other state courts vary from 2 to 21 years. Life tenure is usually associated with a judiciary appointed by the executive, as in the federal and English systems. Where the judiciary is elected, terms of office have been severely restricted as part of the Jacksonian notion of democratic control of the courts.

Most reform movements do not, however, recommend life tenure. They seek a system whereby an incumbent is required to run for reelection on the basis of his record, giving the electorate a choice of retention or rejection. This method of tenure, generally known as the Missouri plan, has the support of the American Bar Association, among others, although there is no evidence to show that the Missouri plan has any advantages over the life tenure system of the federal courts.

Beginning in the 1950s the states turned to commissions and special courts with powers to remove judges from office, thus reducing even further the independence of their judges. In some states, however, notably in California, the commissions had a chastening effect on judicial behaviour. (P. B. K.)

**England.**—Until the end of the 17th century most judges were appointed *durante bene placito* ("during the royal pleasure"); and there were many instances of judges being dismissed. When the Act of Settlement, 1701, s. 3, came into force in 1714, judges were appointed *quamdiu se bene gesserint* ("during good behaviour"), and they were removable (and probably removable only) upon an address by both houses of parliament. The Judicature act, 1925, s. 12, preserves this position, which applies to all judges of the high court and court of appeal; and by ss. 13–15 their salaries and pensions were established and charged on the consolidated fund, so that they are not subject to the annual vote of parliament. However, these provisions are subject to the omnipotence of parliament, and statute has reduced and, more recently, increased the salaries and pensions. All judges appointed since the Judicial Pensions act, 1959, must retire when they become 75 years old. A county court judge is removable by the lord chancellor for "inability or misbehaviour," and he must retire when he is 72 years old; subject to a possible extension to 75 (County Courts act, 1959, s. 8). The lord chancellor similarly has power to remove any justice of the peace, and many other lower judicial officers. The independence of English judges is thus secured less by formal provisions of law than by the public opposition likely to be aroused by any improper attempt to coerce them. (R. E. MY.)

**TENZING NORGAY** (?1914– ), Sherpa mountaineer, the first man, with Sir Edmund Hillary, to set foot on the summit of Everest (29,028 ft.), was born in 1914 (he believes), in Solo Khumbu, the district south of Everest which is inhabited by the Sherpas. He was named Namgyal Wangdi. At the age of 18 he migrated to Darjeeling, where he lived by carrying loads, and in 1935 and 1936 went as porter on Everest expeditions. In 1938 he carried to Camp VI (27,200 ft.). After World War II he set up as sirdar, or organizer of porters, and accompanied a number of expeditions. In 1952 the Swiss made two attempts on the southern route up Everest, on both of which Tenzing was sirdar. He went as sirdar of the British expedition in 1953 and formed the second summit pair with Hillary. From a tent at 27,900 ft. on the southeastern ridge they reached the summit at 11:30 A.M. on May 29. After this achievement Tenzing received many honours and was regarded with religious awe by many Nepalese and Indians.

*See* Tenzing Norgay, *Man of Everest,* as told to James Ramsey Ullman (1955). (C. W. F. N.)

**TEPEXPAN MAN** is one of the most important skeletal remains of early American Indians because of the good data concerning its geological position and contemporary faunal remains. It was found in 1947 by Helmut de Terra and associates near the village of Tepexpan in the Valley of Mexico. The skeleton, once identified as male, seems to be that of a female no older than 30 years when she died, and about 1.5 m. (not quite 5 ft.) tall. The skull is large, with an endocranial capacity of 1,540 cc. The cranial index is 79.89 (breadth/length $\times$ 100).

Most other crania of early American Indians, such as those found at Lagoa Santa, Braz., Punín, Ecuador, and Midland, Tex., have been narrower, with an index below 75. There is always some variation within a group, and this relatively broader-headed individual could easily have been a member of a group whose mean cranial index was much less. Some early skeletal remains found later at Tehuacán Valley come close to Tepexpan chronological estimates.

The skeleton lay face down and flexed in silt deposits of the El Risco sand, a lake facies of the Upper Becerra formation. This silt suggests a moist period and was overlain by caliche deposits suggesting a dry climatic period. Geologically these deposits permitted an estimate of 11,000 to 12,000 years ago for the silt. A radiocarbon age of 11,003 $\pm$ 500 years was derived from a peat specimen belonging to the same level as that of the skeleton.

A number of fossil elephant remains and an obsidian flake were found in related deposits. These, and bones of horse, bison, pocket gopher, and deer indicate a habitat with more luxuriant vegetation than in modern times and suggest that this man may have been a big-game hunter.

Bibliography.—H. de Terra, J. Romero and T. D. Stewart, *Tepexpan Man* (1949); H. M. Wormington, *Ancient Man in North America* (1957); R. F. Heizer and S. F. Cook, "New Evidence of Antiquity of Tepexpan . . . ," *Southwestern Journal of Anthropology,* vol. 15 (1959); S. Genovés, "Revaluation of Age, Stature and Sex of the Tepexpan Remains, Mexico," *American Journal of Physical Anthropology,* vol. 18 (1960). (W. S. Ln.)

**TEPLICE,** a town of the North Bohemian region of Czechoslovakia, known for its hot springs, lies on a rocky spur below the Ore Mountains (Erzgebirge), 56 mi. (90 km.) NNW of Prague. Pop. (1966 est.) 51,614. At Milešovka Mountain (southeast) is the important observatory maintained by the Czechoslovak Academy of Sciences. Teplice is a rail and road junction.

Archaeological evidence suggests that the springs were known to the Romans, and they are mentioned in Bohemian legend (8th century). In 1156 a convent was founded there by Judith, queen of Bohemia; two ancient towers in the grounds of the 18th-century Clary-Aldringen Palace are thought to be remains of this foundation. The belief that gunshot wounds could be alleviated by the Teplice waters led to the Austrian, Prussian, and Saxon authorities maintaining their own spa establishments in the 19th century for disabled men.

The proximity of lignite deposits caused industrial development in and around Teplice in the 19th century (mining, glass, pottery, timber, and engineering). In 1879 flooding of the lignite mines by the underground springs damaged industrial and spa activities alike, and later, Teplice was overshadowed by Karlovy Vary (formerly Carlsbad) and other spas in West Bohemia. After World War II it prospered again both industrially and as a cure resort. (H. G. S.)

**TEQUILA,** a variety of mescal (*q.v.*), the Mexican brandy, distinguished by its place of production: the states of Guanajuato and Jalisco, especially around the town of Tequila. The roasted crowns of several species of *Agave* provide the mash for fermentation and distillation. *Tequila almendrado* is almond flavoured. (L. Ka.)

**TERAI** (Tarai) (*i.e.,* "moist land"), the name given to the strip of formerly marshy land stretching parallel to the lower ranges of the Himalayas in northern India. It extends roughly from the Jumna (Yamuna) River on the west to the Brahmaputra on the east, and a large portion of it lies within Nepal. The name is also used officially for a subdivision of Nainital District in Uttar Pradesh. At its northern edge, where the often riverless forest tract of the bhabar (coarse gravel deposits) ends, a series of springs burst from the surface, and these, increasing and uniting in their progress, form the numerous streams that intersect the Terai and were responsible for its marshy character. The Gogra (Ghaghara) is the great river of the Terai proper and is navigable from the Himalayan foothills.

For long the Terai was the haunt of elephants, tigers, leopards, and many other wild animals. It was notoriously unhealthy and only sparsely inhabited by tribes seemingly immune to malaria. Gradually agriculturalists from the adjoining plains to the south penetrated the Terai, draining it, training the streams, and cultivating the land so that comparatively little of the Terai now remains. The Terai is known in Bengal (both West Bengal and the northern part of East Pakistan) as *duars.* (L. D. S.)

**TERAMO,** chief town of Teramo Province, Abruzzi Region, Italy, and the seat of a bishop, lies between the Tordino and Vezzola rivers 15 mi. (24 km.) from the Adriatic and from the Gran Sasso d'Italia. Pop. (1965 est.) 43,795. Remains include the ruined Roman amphitheatre; a 12th–14th-century cathedral, with a square campanile, in which is a portal of 1332; and the Church of S. Agostino, containing a 15th-century polyptych. There is an astronomical observatory 2 mi. (3 km.) from the town. Teramo is linked to the coastal resort of Giulianova on the Milan–Brindisi railway. Agriculture, mainly cereal production, and ceramics are the main occupations. The town is the successor of Interamnia (Interamna) of the tribe of the Praetuttii. Invaded by the Goths and Lombards, and rebuilt by Bishop Guido (1155), it followed the fortunes of the kingdom of Naples.

Teramo Province, with an area of 752 sq.mi. (1,949 sq.km.) and a population (1965 est.) of 262,468, is mainly engaged in agriculture. Traditional occupations are the making of majolica and terra-cotta, with an art school at Castelli. There is a Gothic cathedral at Atri, a 12th-century Franciscan shrine at Isola del Gran Sasso d'Italia, and a Bourbon fortress at Civitella del Tronto. (M. T. A. N.)

**TERAPHIM,** a Hebrew word, found only in the plural, of uncertain etymology, referring apparently to some sort of idol. In Gen. 31, which tells the story of Rachel's stealing her father's teraphim (variously translated "images," "household gods," "gods" in English Bibles), they are clearly plural, small, and portable, but details as to their precise configuration, etc., are lacking. From I Sam. 19, which describes Michal's use of the teraphim to save David from Saul, it appears that the teraphim was singular and man-sized. The passage further suggests that in the early monarchical period (late 11th century B.C.) a regular place in every household was still reserved for the teraphim; while in the 8th century, Hosea (3:4) speaks of "ephod and teraphim" as essential elements in the national worship. Later the teraphim, like other pre-Israelite religious elements, were banned by the prophets. The meaning of the story in Gen. 35:2–4 ("strange gods" or "foreign gods" in English Bibles) clearly is that the employment of teraphim was given up by Israel in order that Yahweh alone might be served at Bethel. In Judges and Hosea the teraphim are closely associated with the ephod (*q.v.*); both are mentioned in connection with divination (*cf.* II Kings 23:24; Ezek. 21:21; Zech. 10:2). In view of Ezek. 21:21 and Hosea 3:4, it is difficult to suppose that the teraphim were purely household idols.

**TERATOLOGY,** the study of abnormalities and monstrosities in plants and animals. *See* Monster.

**TERBIUM** (symbol Tb) is a silver-white metallic element of the rare-earth group, atomic number 65 and atomic weight 158.924. The only isotope occurring in ores is $Tb^{159}$ which is stable; radioactive $Tb^{160}$ (half-life 73 days) is used as an indicator in the study of coprecipitation processes. The element was discovered by C. G. Mosander in 1843 in a heavy rare-earth fraction called yttria, but its existence was not confirmed for at least 30 years and pure compounds were not prepared until 1905. The name terbium was derived from the town of Ytterby in Sweden. Terbium occurs in many rare-earth minerals such as gadolinite, xenotime, euxenite, and samarskite; it is also found in the products of nuclear fission. However, it is usually obtained as a by-product from the monazite sands, a source of thorium. Ion-exchange techniques are utilized for commercial production.

Terbium is one of three rare earths that have an oxidation state of plus four (*see* CERIUM; PRASEODYMIUM). The brown oxide prepared by air ignition has the approximate formula $Tb_4O_7$; $TbO_2$ is obtained by a more drastic oxidation procedure; and $TbF_4$ is prepared by use of elemental fluorine. In all other salts and in solution terbium is trivalent with an ionic radius of 0.923Å and behaves as a typical rare earth. The thermal neutron cross section is 55 barns. Its solutions are colourless and have discrete absorption lines in the ultraviolet region of the spectrum which are of use for quantitative analysis. Because of unpaired 4f electrons, the trivalent terbium ion is very strongly paramagnetic. The metal is prepared in a highly pure form by thermoreduction of the anhydrous fluoride with calcium metal. It is slowly oxidized by air at room temperatures and by cold water. The melting point of the metal is 1,356° C, its density is 8.253 g. per $cm^3$ for the hexagonal close-packed structure; it is ferromagnetic below −68° C (*see* also RARE EARTHS). (LD. B. A.)

**TERBORCH** (TER BORCH), **GERARD** (1617–1681), Dutch painter, who developed his own distinctive type of interior genre, in which he depicted with grace and fidelity the atmosphere of well-to-do middle-class life, was born at Zwolle. His father had been an artist and had visited Rome, but from 1621 was employed as a tax collector. Surviving drawings made by the young Terborch in 1625 and 1626 are proudly inscribed and dated by his father. In 1632 Gerard was in Amsterdam and in 1634 he was a pupil of Pieter Molyn (Molijn) in Haarlem. He visited England in 1635, Rome in 1640, and from 1646 spent two or three years in Münster, Westphalia, where the peace congress was in session. The masterpiece of this period is the "Peace of Münster" (National Gallery, London), of 1648, which portrays the delegates of Holland and of Spain assembled to sign the peace treaty. After a stay in Madrid he had finally returned to his own country by the end of 1650. In 1654 he was married in Deventer, where he settled for the remainder of his life, dying there on Dec. 8, 1681.

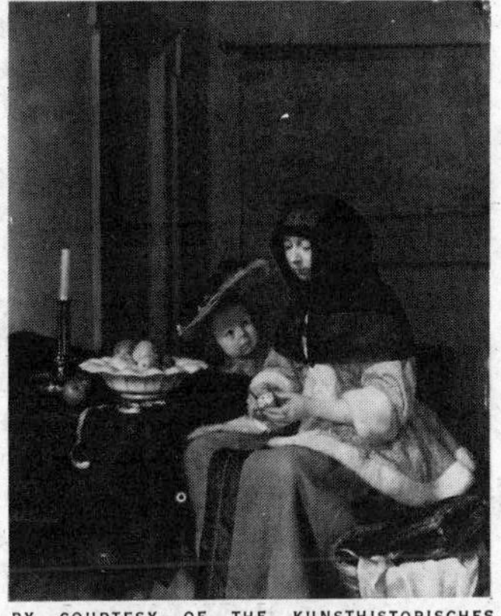

BY COURTESY OF THE KUNSTHISTORISCHES MUSEUM, VIENNA

"WOMAN PEELING APPLES" BY GERARD TERBORCH, 1661

Terborch's works consist almost equally of portraits and genre pieces. His characteristically delicate technique can be appreciated in the portraits, which are painted on a small, almost miniature scale, though many of them are full-lengths. In colour they tend to be subdued, due largely to the sober costume of the times, but by subtlety of tonal gradations and mastery in rendering diverse surface textures he was able to achieve an extraordinary richness of effect. His superb colour sense appears to greater advantage in genre subjects, though always employed with masterly restraint. In his earlier years he painted many guardroom subjects in the manner of Pieter Codde and Willem Duyster, but later, from about the time when he finally settled in Holland, he painted calm, exquisitely drawn groups, posed easily and naturally against shadowy backgrounds, and imbued with an almost aristocratic elegance that is unique among Dutch painters of his time. Among many fine examples of Terborch's art may be mentioned "The Letter" (Buckingham Palace, London), "The Concert" (Berlin), "Fatherly Advice" (Amsterdam), and "Woman Peeling Apples" (Vienna).

*See* E. Plietzsch, *Gerard Ter Borch* (1944). (R. E. W. J.)

**TERCEIRA,** an island in the Atlantic Ocean, belonging to Portugal and forming part of the Azores (*q.v.*) archipelago. Pop. (1960) 72,485; area 153 sq.mi. (397 sq.km.). Terceira ("the third") was so called because it was the third island of the archipelago to be discovered by the Portuguese. The commercial importance of Angra do Heroísmo, the chief town and port, has much increased owing to the NATO military air base at Lajes, maintained by the Portuguese Air Force. Since World War II the United States Air Force has used it as a military transport station. Praia da Vitória, with its wide bay protected by a breakwater, handles military supplies for the air base. (J. Ao.)

**TEREDO,** a genus of highly specialized wormlike bivalve mollusks (*q.v.*) belonging to the family Teredinidae, commonly known as shipworms, pileworms, teredos, or teredines. They are related to the piddocks (*q.v.*) and to the soft-shelled clam, *Mya*. There are about 10 genera, the best known being *Teredo* and *Bankia*, and perhaps 100 species. They are worldwide in distribution, generally living in marine or brackish water, though a few species are found in fresh water. They can be extremely destructive to wooden vessels or waterfront installations and have been of great concern to maritime peoples since earliest times. They have been called "termites of the sea" because the damage they do is not readily seen; the outer surface of the wood may look undamaged and yet the interior may be completely riddled.

Teredos are known to have existed as far back as the Jurassic period. Before the advent of man, they lived in fallen trees that were carried into the sea by rivers or that had fallen along the shores; they were thus important in the reduction of the wood to the elements. It was only when man began building wooden ships and wharves that teredos became pests.

**General Features.**—Teredos may be compared to a soft-shelled clam, the body of which has been stretched out so that the highly modified shell covers only a very small portion of the anterior end of the animal. The body is wormlike and, unlike other bivalves, most of the vital organs are posterior to the posterior adductor muscle. The separate siphons, used in feeding and respiration, are relatively short and protrude from the minute opening of the burrow into the water. The incurrent siphon carries water and food in; the excurrent carries wastes out. The valves of the shell are nearly hemispherical, with a deep right-angled notch in the ventral half of the anterior margin. Parallel with the edges of the notch, the outer surface of each valve is marked with fine ridges that when magnified appear as rows of minute teeth like those of a file. The large muscular foot, which protrudes through the anterior gape, acts as a suction disc to hold the valves tightly against the anterior end of the burrow when the teredo is actively boring. As in the piddocks, the anterior adductor muscle has migrated to the outside of the shell. Posteriorly, a large lobe or auricle is produced for the attachment of the powerful posterior adductor muscle. At the umbos (prominences at the hinges) and on the ventral margins of the valves opposite to them are large rounded knobs or condyles on which the valves rock. The large foot muscles are attached to the apophyses, two calcareous "arms" that protrude from under the umbos. The large posterior adductor muscle supplies the force for boring, and the shell is the tool with which it works. When actively boring, the teredo contracts the anterior adductor muscle, bringing the anterior end of the valves together and spreading the posterior end. The foot is firmly attached to the end of the burrow and the foot muscles contracted, drawing the valves forward and bringing the denticles hard against the wood. Then, the forceful contraction of the posterior adductor muscle spreads the valves anteriorly and the filelike denticles scrape against the wood, rasping off fine particles. The rhythmic contraction and relaxation of the anterior and posterior adductor muscles may be repeated many times before the animal rests. The surface of the foot and the margins of the mantle are covered with cilia that carry the fine particles of wood into the mantle cavity and to the mouth.

At the posterior end of the stomach is a large sac or caecum usually filled with wood particles. Digestive enzymes in the stomach and caecum can reduce the wood sugars to a usable form, and provides some of the food of the teredo. Teredos also feed on microscopic plants and animals carried into the mantle cavity through the incurrent siphon.

When shipworms are undisturbed, the siphons can be seen extending from the minute opening at the surface of the wood and

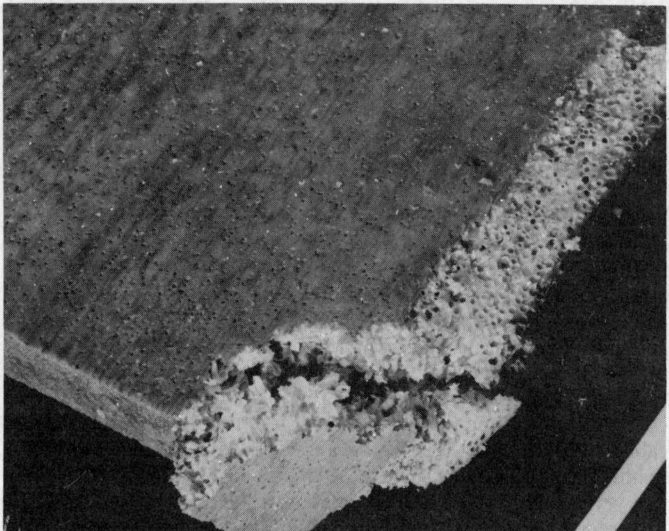

(ABOVE) CHARLES E. LANE, (BELOW) A. J. MCQUIRE

(Above) A one-inch plank infested by shipworms. The larvae bore into the wood through tiny holes on the surface (the broken edge shows the internal damage inflicted); (below) *Bankia australis,* photographed by X ray, inside a board submerged for six months

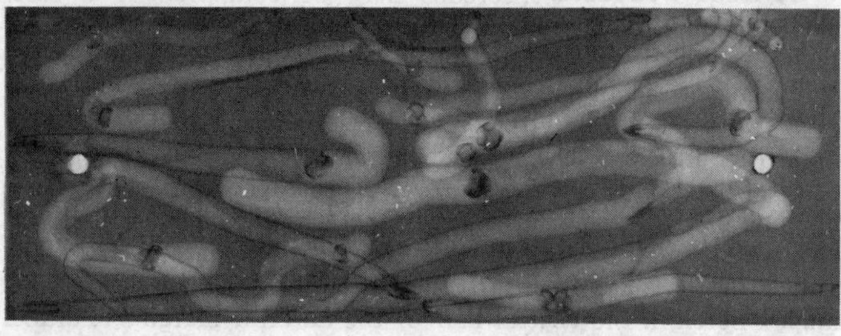

waving about gently in the water. If they are disturbed, however, or conditions become adverse, the siphons are drawn into the burrow and the opening is plugged by a pair of paddle-shaped plates (pallets). The pallets effectively protect the animal against predators as well as adverse conditions such as reduced salinity, pollution, or silting. Inactive shipworms may remain for extended periods of time with the siphons retracted.

The breeding habits of the various members of the family vary considerably. In some species, the eggs and sperm are emitted into the water, where fertilization takes place. In others, fertilization is internal, but the eggs are extruded into the water at an early stage in development. In still others, the gills serve as a brood pouch where the young are held until development is nearly complete. All species have a free swimming period, and it is by this means that new timber is invaded. Eventually, the embryo shipworm must settle on wood or die. It first attaches itself by a single byssus thread; then, with the edges of its valves, it scrapes together loose wood fibres with which it makes a small cone to protect itself during the period of change from a typical embryonic bivalve to a highly specialized boring animal. The shell changes radically in shape, and the apophyses and pallets develop at this time. Once these changes are complete, active boring begins. As the animal grows, the burrow is lengthened and gradually widened. Although the entrance hole remains nearly microscopic, the anterior end of the burrow may reach an inch or more in diameter as the animal grows. In temperate seas teredos usually attain only a few inches in length, but in tropical seas some species may reach six feet. Growth is usually rapid; the young at the time of attachment are about .25 mm. but they may reach over 100 mm. in length within a month.

**Control Measures.**—The ships of Archimedes of Syracuse were protected by a sheathing of lead. Copper sheathing was first used by the British in 1758. Although it was expensive, because it wore thin and had to be constantly replaced, copper gave complete protection both from borers and fouling organisms such as barnacles. In the days of the clipper ships, nearly all vessels sailing in tropical seas were sheathed with copper, but it was found necessary to insulate the copper from the rudder iron since these two elements tend to react corrosively. With the advent of metal ships the problem of teredos ended so far as commercial shipping was concerned, but it is still a problem for the smaller fishing or pleasure boats and specialized ships such as mine sweepers, which are made of wood.

So far as waterfront installations are concerned, teredos are still a significant though decreasing problem as more and more wharves and piers are being constructed of steel and concrete. The Dutch were the first to be greatly concerned with the depredations of *zeeworms,* for the very existence of much of their country depended on the maintenance of a series of dikes partly constructed of wood. As a result of a severe infestation of the dikes, there appeared in 1733 an important book on teredos written by Godfrey Sellius. (It was he who showed that shipworms were mollusks rather than worms.) Of the more recent attacks, the most famous was the invasion of shipworms in San Francisco Bay during 1917–21, when destruction of wharves and jetties was estimated to have cost over $25,000,000.

Since that time there has been an almost continuous series of investigations into the teredo problem. Numerous techniques have been developed for the protection of wood against teredo. Some are quite effective; however, many are far too involved and too expensive to be practicable on a large scale. An old but still most practical method of protection is to treat wooden wharves with coal tar creosote solution. If a high quality creosote is properly applied and allowed to impregnate the piling, the wood will give long service. The effect seems to be largely mechanical: the creosote clogs the denticles of the young teredo and renders the rasping tool ineffective. As the creosote leaches from the outer surface of the pile it is replaced by that within.

The owner of a wooden boat has a choice of a large number of available paints and coatings. However, successful and lasting protection can only be achieved if the coating is kept intact. The slightest abrasion or wearing off of the paint will allow the teredos to enter, and once inside, destruction is rapid. The most effective paints are soft and have a copper base giving protection against both boring and fouling organisms. Fibre glass coatings are used to some extent on small boats and the glue used in making marine plywood has been developed as a deterrent to borers.

Despite all the advances made in teredo control, there is still no permanent protection against them, and constant checks must be made on any wood in contact with seawater.

BIBLIOGRAPHY.—W. G. Atwood *et al., Marine Structures, Their Deterioration and Preservation,* National Research Council (1924); W. J. Clench and R. D. Turner, "The Genus *Bankia* in the Western Atlantic," *Johnsonia* 2, pp. 1–28 (1946); C. L. Hill and C. A. Kofoid (eds.), *Marine Borers and Their Relations to Marine Construction on the Pacific Coast,* Final Report on the San Francisco Bay Marine Piling Committee (1927) which has a fine section on the biology of the Teredinidae; Woods Hole Oceanographic Institution, *Marine Fouling and Its Prevention,* U.S. Naval Institute (1952); W. F. Clapp and R. Kenk, *Marine Borers, an Annotated Bibliography,* Office of Naval Research, Dept. of Navy (1963); R. D. Turner, *A Survey and Illustrated Catalogue of the Teredinidae* (1966). (R. D. T.)

**TEREK,** a river of the U.S.S.R., one of the main streams draining northward from the Caucasus. It is 373 mi. (600 km.) long and drains a basin of 16,873 sq.mi. (43,700 sq.km.). It rises from the glaciers of Gora (Mt.) Kazbek in the main Caucasus range and cuts its way northward through the series of ranges in spectacular gorges, between which are mountain basins. Emerging from the foothills, it turns eastward between the Caucasus and the Nogay steppe and enters the Caspian Sea by a complex delta. Its chief tributaries are the Ardon, Urukh, and Malka on the left and the Sunzha on the right. The average annual discharge is 12,360 cu.ft. (350 cu.m.) per sec., but much water is drawn off for irrigation. Freezing takes place only in the most severe winters. For much of the 19th century the Terek represented the frontier of Russian settlement in the Caucasus, and the Cossack fortified villages then established on its northern bank formed the setting of Tolstoi's novel *The Cossacks.* (R. A. F.)

**TERENCE** (Publius Terentius Afer) (*c.* 185?–*c.* 159 B.C.), was, after Plautus, the greatest Roman writer of comedy. Information concerning his life comes from the account by Suetonius (fl. 2nd century A.D.), prefaced to Aelius Donatus' 4th-century commentary, which quotes the (often conflicting) statements of earlier writers. It relates that he was born in Carthage and came to Rome as a slave in the house of Terentius Lucanus, a senator, by whom he was educated and set free. He won the friendship of certain noble Romans; the prevailing view included among these the younger Scipio and Laelius, who were even said to have helped him in his work. His first play was the *Andria,* which at the order of the aediles he read to the elderly comic dramatist Caecilius (who died 168 B.C.). After the production of the last of his plays, in his 25th year, he went to the east; from this voyage he did not return.

This account is partly contradictory and wholly unreliable. That Terence had noble friends is indeed clear from his own prologues. From the *didascaliae* (prefaces to the plays), confused as they are, it appears that his six plays were produced between 166 and 160 B.C. Their order is uncertain; but it is agreed that the first was the *Andria* ("Woman from Andros"), translated from the *Andria* of Menander.

The scene, as in all Terence's plays, is in Athens. Simo wishes his son Pamphilus to marry Philumena, daughter of their neighbour Chremes. But Pamphilus has secretly formed a liaison with Glycerium, a poor but modest girl who has recently come to Athens from Andros with her supposed sister Chrysis, now dead. The lovers are saved by the discovery that Glycerium is herself the long-lost daughter of Chremes. Terence, in translating Menander's play, made certain alterations (attested by Donatus); he changed the opening monologue into a dialogue, and he added two characters, Charinus, who is in love with Philumena, and his servant Byrria. The fact that he had made alterations became known to a rival of Terence, an elderly dramatist named Luscius Lanuvinus. He protested that a translator had no right to "spoil" (*contaminare*) his original. To defend himself, Terence was forced to write a prologue, in which he asserted that all he had done was to borrow suitable material from a very similar play by Menander, the *Perinthia* ("Woman from Perinthus"). He further claimed that he had merely followed the example of his predecessors, Naevius, Plautus and Ennius, whose "carelessness" he would rather imitate than the *obscura diligentia* of his critic. It seems reasonable to suppose that Terence is not here defending himself merely against the charge of borrowing material from a second Greek source; that is in fact the procedure of which he boasts, and which he intends to repeat. His enemy seems to have retorted "In that case you have spoiled not *one* Greek play but *two*"; a charge to which he replies in the prologue to the *Heautontimorumenos* ("Self-Tormentor"). He repeated this procedure in the *Eunuchus,* adding (he says) to Menander's *Eunuchus* two characters from the *Colax* ("Flatterer") also by Menander. Again in the *Adelphi* ("Brothers") he says that he has inserted a scene from the *Synapothnescontes* ("Dying Together") of Diphilus, "carelessly" omitted by Plautus in the *Commorientes,* his translation of that play. These changes he would not himself, of course, have described as "spoiling"; that is the unpleasant word used by his critic. What he omits to mention is that he made other changes which were not borrowing but original invention. Through a misunderstanding of these passages, "contaminate" has come in textual criticism to mean "combine"; but it cannot be shown that the word ever had this sense in Latin.

Terence's second play was perhaps the *Hecyra* ("Mother-in-law"); but this play failed twice (as the two prologues explain) before it was finally produced in 160 B.C. The *Phormio,* one of his liveliest plays, was translated from Apollodorus' *Epidicazomenos* ("Litigant"). His masterpiece, the *Adelphi,* was produced at the funeral games of Aemilius Paulus (father of the younger Scipio) in 160 B.C.

It is noteworthy that Terence uses the prologue no longer to explain the plot but (after the manner of the Aristophanic *parabasis*) to reply to his critics (*Andr.* 5–7). In using his Greek models, apart from "borrowing" from a second original, Terence permits himself various liberties. Names are altered, Greek allusions toned down, characters slightly changed, individual scenes remodeled (*e.g., Eunuchus* 539 ff. is turned from a monologue into a dialogue of considerable power by Terence's addition of a character, Antipho). These and other changes are attested by Donatus; they show beyond doubt that Terence was not content to be a mere translator, but tried by delicate changes to improve on Menander himself.

The central interest in Terence's plays is character. In almost every play there is at least one pair in like circumstances who behave differently; *quam uterquest similis sui!* (*Phor.* 501): "how like each is to himself!" The charm of Terence's Latin and his lack of comic power are referred to by Julius Caesar, whose judgment seems to have been generally endorsed in antiquity.

**Influence.**—The simplicity of Terence's Latinity and his moralizing tone made him a favourite author in the middle ages. He was not, however, moral enough for Hrosvitha, the nun of Gandersheim, who in the 10th century wrote six Christian comedies modeled on Terence but portraying the victory of chastity over lust; there is a farcical element. One of the first Italian comedies, Ariosto's *I Suppositi* (1509), owes something to the *Eunuchus,* and was itself the model for George Gascoigne's *The Supposes,* the first prose comedy of English literature (1566). In the early 16th century Dutch schoolmasters developed what is known as the education-drama, or the "Christian Terence." Molière based his *L'École des maris* (1661) on the *Adelphi* and his *Les Fourberies de Scapin* (1671) on the *Phormio.* The *Phormio* was performed by the boys of St. Paul's school in 1528. George Chapman's *All Fools* (acted 1599) is based on the *Heautontimorumenos,* with borrowings from the *Adelphi.* Charles Sedley's *Bellamira* (1687) is adapted from the *Eunuchus;* Thomas Shadwell's *The Squire of Alsatia* (1688) from the *Adelphi.* The *Andria* is imitated in Steele's *The Conscious Lovers* (1722), the *Adelphi* in Fielding's *The Fathers, or The Good-Natured Man* (posthumously published 1778). Thornton Wilder's novel, *The Woman of Andros* (1930), is partly based on the *Andria.*

Bibliography.—The *editio princeps* appeared in 1470. Other editions: R. Bentley (1726); A. Fleckeisen, "Teubner Series" (1898); R. Kauer and W. M. Lindsay, Oxford Classical Texts (1926); J. Marouzeau, 3 vol. with French trans., in the "Budé Series" (1942–49); S. Prete (1954); *cf.* G. E. Duckworth, *The Nature of Roman Comedy* (1952); W. Beare, *The Roman Stage,* 2nd ed. (1955); E. Paratore, *Storia del teatro latino* (1957). (Wm. Be.)

**TERESA, SAINT,** of Ávila (or de Jesús; Teresa de Cepeda y Ahumada) (1515–1582), Spanish mystic, originator of the Carmelite Reform, and author of spiritual classics. Great as was her accomplishment in active life, to which the Discalced Carmelite houses still stand witness, it was the beauty of her interior life, as it is revealed in her writings, that causes her to be looked upon as one of the world's greatest religious women. Her spiritual works are read as widely today as they ever were: a list of Spanish books in print dated 1964 shows no fewer than nine editions of her *Obras completas* to be available.

Teresa de Cepeda was born in Ávila, in central Spain, on March 28, 1515, the daughter of a well-to-do *hidalgo.* In her *Life* she describes her father as "a man of prayer, charitable to the poor, and fond of reading good books," and her mother, "devoted to us children, remarkably beautiful, and gifted with common sense." Teresa's seven brothers became colonial officials in South America; her two sisters married and lived in Spain. When Teresa was 14 her mother died; two years later her father sent his vivacious daughter to a boarding school. Illness forced her to leave after a year and a half, and while convalescing she began to give serious thought to her vocation in life.

Despite her father's opposition, Teresa went to the Carmelite Convent of the Incarnation in Ávila (probably in 1535) and became a novice for the religious life. Within 2 years her health collapsed, and she was an invalid for 3 years. While recuperating at her uncle's country home, the young nun, through the reading of religious classics, developed a great love for mental prayer, which she later defined as "friendly conversation with Him Who we know loves us." After her recovery, however, the young sister at Incarnation became spiritually tepid; although observing the community exercises, she had, she later wrote, "ceased to pray."

For 15 years Teresa continued in a state that she describes thus: "On the one side God was calling me; on the other, I was following the spirit of the world. It was as if I wished to reconcile two contradictories. So distressful was the conflict that I do not know how I endured it." One day in 1555, while praying before a representation of the thorn-crowned Christ, her heart was touched, and she made her complete surrender to Christ; a new life of prayerful union began, but not without a heroic struggle with herself and hostility from many of her associates. Frequently during her life, this very intelligent, matter-of-fact, and humble woman calmly relates, Christ conversed with her and directed her activities. Among her spiritual directors were the celebrated Dominican theologian Domingo Bañez and two saints: the Jesuit Francis Borgia and the Franciscan Peter of Alcántara.

**Carmelite Reform.**—In 1558, after 22 years in the convent, Teresa began to consider, for those who would aspire to it, the restoration of Carmelite life to its original observance of austerity. It required complete separation from the world in order that the nuns could more intently meditate on the law of the Lord and, through a prayerful life of penance, exercise what Teresa termed "our vocation of reparation" for the sins of mankind. Such a life was enjoined by what is known as the Primitive Rule of Carmel, as approved by Innocent IV in 1247 for the Carmelite friars (the nuns did not come into existence until 1452). It reflects the tradition of prayer and penance that goes back, it is said, to the prophet Elias (Elijah) and his spiritual descendants of the Christian era, the hermits of Mt. Carmel. (*See* CARMELITES.) But in the 14th and 15th centuries the religious orders had relaxed their observance. By the standards of the Primitive Rule, Incarnation Convent was patently lax. Not, indeed, morally lax—Teresa herself assures us of this and extols the lives of many of her sisters. But separation from the world, dedicated contemplation, uniform evangelical poverty, and penitential observance lived more in pious esteem than in daily practice.

In 1562, after prolonged prayer and consultation, Teresa with the authorization of Pope Pius IV and the encouragement of the bishop of Ávila opened the first convent of the Carmelite Reform, with four women as its first subjects, in an old building she named in honour of St. Joseph. From municipal as well as religious personages came a storm of hostility that took on tornado proportions, especially because the convent would exist without endowment; but Teresa, undaunted, insisted on poverty and subsistence only through the alms of the people. Five years later the Carmelite general came from Rome and not only approved the Reform but directed Teresa to establish more convents. Before he left Spain, he gave her another mandate: to endeavour to establish monasteries of men who would observe the Primitive Rule. In 1567, while at Medina del Campo, where she had founded her second convent, Teresa met a young Carmelite priest, Juan de Yepes, later to be canonized as St. John (*q.v.*) of the Cross. In this brilliant friar, Teresa knew that she had the man to initiate the Carmelite Reform for men. A year later John with two other friars opened the first monastery of the Reform at Duruelo; before her death, Teresa saw 12 such monasteries founded.

Although she desired nothing more than to live in the prayerful quiet of the cloister—she describes her first five years at St. Joseph's as "the most peaceful years of my life"—Teresa, obedient to the will of her religious superiors, spent most of her last two decades of life in the arduous work of establishing and nurturing more convents of the Reform. After the Ávila foundation, Teresa, in spite of frail health and great difficulties, founded 16 more convents, from Seville in the south of Spain to Burgos in the north, "without so much as a penny to buy one."

In 1575, while Teresa was at the Seville convent, a controversy erupted in the Carmelite family that almost obliterated the Reform. It was primarily a jurisdictional dispute between the observants of the Mitigated Rule, called the Calced ("Shod"), and the friars of the restored Primitive Rule, known as the Discalced (*i.e.,* wearers of sandals). Teresa had foreseen the trouble and had endeavoured to prevent it, but her efforts were of no avail. As mother of the Reform, she naturally became the centre of the acrimonious quarrel. She was ordered by the Carmelite general, to whom she had been grossly misrepresented, to go to a convent in Castile, remain in obscurity, and desist from founding more convents. Four years later, mostly because of the efforts of the Spanish king Philip II, who knew and admired Teresa, and the papal nuncio, a solution was effected whereby the Carmelites, nuns and friars, of the Primitive Rule were made independent in jurisdiction; this was confirmed by a rescript of Pope Gregory XIII in 1580.

At the age of 64, broken in health but with a spirit vibrant as ever, Teresa was directed to resume the work of the Reform. In journeys that covered hundreds of miles, she took up her exhausting mission of visitations, settling administrative problems, and establishing five more convents. The greatness of this very human as well as holy woman—among whose many gifts was a sparkling sense of humour—does not lie so much in her visible achievements as in her interior life of prayer, heroic obedience, and deep humility. En route to Ávila from Burgos, Teresa was stricken at her Alba de Tormes convent with a cerebral hemorrhage and repeated heart attacks. She died there on Oct. 4, 1582; 40 years after her death, she was canonized by Pope Gregory XV, and her feast is celebrated on Oct. 15.

**Writings.**—Through four centuries the writings of St. Teresa have been acknowledged spiritual classics. Her most celebrated work is the *Life,* written under obedience to her directors, which she never intended for the general public; it is not only the story of her life but, like the *Confessions* of St. Augustine, the history of a great soul. *The Book of the Foundations* describes the establishment of her convents and is interspersed with salutary exhortations. Her writings on the progress of the Christian soul toward God are recognized masterpieces: *The Way of Perfection, The Interior Castle, Spiritual Relations, Exclamations of the Soul to God,* and *Conceptions on the Love of God.* Thirty-one of her poems and 458 of her letters are extant.

In the history of Christian mysticism and spirituality, these writings occupy a special place because of their distinctive combination of great ardour and utter candour. Always reluctant to claim any spiritual prerogatives for herself on the basis of the mystical experiences granted to her, Teresa felt constrained, in spite of her diffidence, to acknowledge these experiences as the gift of God and to praise him for them. Interpreters of prayer and of the mystical life, such as Friedrich von Hügel and Friedrich Heiler, have therefore drawn upon her writings for much of their documentation, and believers in search of inspiration and spiritual strength have likewise found them here. As Heiler has said, "St. Teresa, with her masterly analysis from which every modern psychologist may learn, stands unsurpassed among all the mystics and one might call her the woman psychologist among the saints. Yet in her the simplicity and intensity of her experience are not injured by the psychological self-analysis. Her achievement has been to experience and at the same time to observe the experience" (*Prayer,* Oxford University Press, New York and London, 1932).

The first collected edition of St. Teresa's works was published at Salamanca in 1588; several revised editions were produced subsequently, including that by P. Silverio, *Obras de S. Teresa de Jesús* (1924). The manuscript of the *Life,* in the saint's handwriting, is in the Escorial, near Madrid; original manuscripts of her other writings are in various libraries and convents in Spain. The first English translation of the *Life* appeared in 1611; another in 1870 by David Lewis, reedited in 1910 by Benedict Zimmerman. The Benedictines of Stanbrook Abbey, England, have made notable translations of her works. An English version of her writings is by E. Allison Peers, *The Complete Works of St. Teresa* (1946), and, by the same translator, *The Letters of St. Teresa* (1949).

BIBLIOGRAPHY.—W. T. Walsh, *Saint Teresa of Ávila* (1943); E. Allison Peers, *Mother of Carmel* (1946); P. Silverio, *Saint Teresa of Jesus* (1947); W. J. Doheny, *Selected Writings of St. Teresa* (1950); M. Auclair, *Saint Teresa of Avila,* Eng. trans. by K. Pond (1953); J. P. Kelly, *Meet Saint Teresa* (1958); F. von Hügel, *The Mystical Element of Religion,* 2 vol., rev. ed. (1961); F. Heiler, *Prayer: a Study in the History and Psychology of Religion,* Eng. trans. by S. McComb (1932).

(J. P. KE.; X.)

**TERESINA,** chief city and capital of the state of Piauí, Brazil, is located on the right bank of the Parnaíba River about 220 mi. (354 km.) from the port of Parnaíba and about 200 mi. (322 km.) from São Luís in Maranhão. Pop. (1960) 100,006.

The city was founded in 1852 as the new capital of Piauí, and since then it has become the chief commercial centre of the middle Parnaíba valley. It has textile factories, sugar refineries, distilleries, soap factories, and sawmills. It ships out cattle, hides, goat skins (from the *caatinga* or uplands of eastern Piauí), maize, rice, cotton, and manioc. It is reached from Parnaíba by shallow-draft river steamers; a railroad which terminates at Timon (Maranhão), on the left bank of the river opposite Teresina, connects with São Luís and carries much of the commerce of the middle Parnaíba valley. An all-weather highway connects with Fortaleza in Ceará; and there are air services to all parts of Brazil. Formerly called Therezina, the city was named after the empress Teresa Cristina Maria of Brazil. (P. E. J.)

**TERHUNE, ALBERT PAYSON** (1872–1942), U.S. novelist and short-story writer, famous for his popular stories about dogs, was born in Newark, N.J., on Dec. 21, 1872, the son of a Presbyterian clergyman, Edward Payson Terhune (1830–1907) and Mary Virginia Hawes Terhune (1830–1922), herself popular for romantic novels and books on household management written under the pen name of Marion Harland. He received his first schooling in Paris and Geneva, Switz., while his father was serving as chaplain of the American churches of Rome and Paris. Terhune graduated from Columbia University, New York City, in 1893, traveled in Egypt and Syria, and returned to New York, joining the staff of the *New York Evening World* in 1894. His first book was *Syria from the Saddle* (1896); his first novel, *Dr. Dale* (1900), was written in collaboration with his mother. He wrote assiduously in his spare time to free himself from journalism and published more than 12 books before he left the *Evening World* in 1916.

In 1919 appeared the first of his popular dog stories, *Lad, a Dog*. He had moved to a farm near Pompton Lakes, N.J., which he named "Sunnybank," and there for the rest of his life he wrote, bred prize collies, fished, and hunted. He wrote more than 25 books after 1919, nearly all of them novels in which dogs played conspicuous parts, including *Bruce* (1920), *The Heart of a Dog* (1924), *Lad of Sunnybank* (1928), and *A Book of Famous Dogs* (1937). He also wrote two autobiographical books, *Now That I'm Fifty* (1925) and *To the Best of My Memory* (1930). He died at Sunnybank on Feb. 18, 1942.

**TERM.** In traditional logic (*see* LOGIC: *Traditional Logic*) a term is properly the subject or predicate of a categorical proposition. Aristotle so used the Greek word *horos* (limit), apparently by an analogy between the terms of a proportion (*see* below) and those of a syllogism. *Terminus* is the Latin translation of this, used for example by Boëthius. Hence in medieval logic the word came to be used also for common and proper names generally (*see* NAME [IN LOGIC]); and even for what were called syncategorematic terms—words such as *and, if, not, some, only, except,* which are incapable of being used for the subject or predicate of a proposition (*see* MEANING). In everyday English, the meaning of term has been broadened still further, to that of an item of terminology, any word or phrase with a particular meaning.

In mathematics, the terms of a fraction (*see* FRACTION) are the numerator and denominator. The terms of a proportion are the four numbers which enter into the proportion (*see* ALGEBRA) or the corresponding numerical expressions that denote such numbers. Similarly the terms of a sum are the numbers which are added together to constitute the sum, or the numerical expressions denoting them. In this sense an infinite series (*see* SERIES) is thought of as a sum of an infinite number of terms; and a polynomial (*q.v.*) is a sum of a finite number of monomials which are the terms of the polynomial. (Ao. C.)

**TERMAN, LEWIS MADISON** (1877–1956), U.S. psychologist, specialized in intelligence testing and in the research study of gifted children. He was born on a farm in Johnson County, Ind., on Jan. 15, 1877. He took his graduate training at Clark University, Worcester, Mass., and from 1910 until his retirement in 1943 was professor of psychology and education at Stanford University. Terman published the first important and widely used individual intelligence test in the U.S., the Stanford-Binet, which he described in *The Measurement of Intelligence* (1916). In connection with this test, he employed the term IQ (intelligence quotient), signifying a score on an intelligence test that takes account of both chronological age and mental age in such a way that the average child of any age has an IQ of 100. Working with a group of other psychologists during World War I, he was largely responsible, also, for the first notable group intelligence tests, the Army Alpha and Army Beta (*see* further PSYCHOLOGICAL TESTS AND MEASUREMENTS).

Terman recognized the great importance to society of identifying intellectually gifted children and of providing them early in their lives with exceptional educational opportunities. In 1921 he selected 1,500 California children whose IQ's were over 140 (about 0.5% of the population) and began to study their development. He continued this research until his death 35 years later, by which time he had obtained definitive evidence that gifted children tended to be healthier and more stable emotionally than the average child and that they retained their high ability in adulthood. Terman's last progress report on this continuing study was *The Gifted Child Grows Up* (1947). He died at Palo Alto, Calif., on Dec. 21, 1956.

*See* also GIFTED CHILDREN.

*See* E. G. Boring, "Lewis Madison Terman," in National Academy of Sciences, *Biographical Memoirs* (1959). (R. R. S.)

**TERMEZ,** a town and capital of Surkhan-Dar'inskaya (Surkhan-Darya) Oblast' of the Uzbek Soviet Socialist Republic, U.S.S.R., lies on the right bank of the Amu Dar'ya (Amu-Darya) and on the Karshi-Dushanbe (Stalinabad) railway. Pop. (1959) 22,063. With a maximum temperature of 50° C (122° F), it is one of the hottest towns in the U.S.S.R. It has occupied two previous sites: the earlier, on the Amu Dar'ya, flourished as a trading centre from the 10th century, but was destroyed by the Mongols in 1220; the later was on the Surkhandar'ya. The older site is preserved as a state monument and contains a 9th-century mausoleum. Termez has a cotton ginning factory and other light industries. (G. E. WR.)

**TERMINI IMERESE,** a town in the province of Palermo, northern Sicily, 20 mi. (32 km.) ESE of the town of Palermo. Pop. (1961) 23,171. At the centre of the Gulf of Termini Imerese, it lies on two levels connected by steps and the Serpents' Road. The Church of the Annunziata has a superb 16th-century cupola. The town's well-known thermal saline springs were praised by Pindar. The town is on the coastal road and railway from Palermo to Messina. There is intensive cultivation of citrus fruits, vines, and olives, and a flourishing hotel industry.

The ancient Thermae Himerenses was founded by the Carthaginians in 408 B.C. after the destruction of the nearby Himera. The tyrant Agathocles was born there in 361 B.C. (M. T. A. N.)

**TERMINUS** (Lat. "boundary stone"), originally, in Roman cult, a stone or post set up in the ground with the following religious ceremonies. A hole was dug and a fire lighted; a victim was sacrificed and its blood poured into the hole, together with incense, fruits, honey, wine, and the ashes of the sacrifice. Then the boundary stone, which had been previously anointed and crowned with garlands, was placed upon the hot ashes and fixed in the ground. Anyone who removed a boundary stone was accursed (*sacer*) and might be slain with impunity; a fine was afterward substituted for the death penalty. From this sacred object evolved the god Terminus. On Feb. 23 (the end of the old Roman year) the festival called Terminalia was held. The owners of adjacent lands assembled at the common boundary stone and each garlanded his own side of the stone. An altar was set up and offerings of cakes, grain, honey, and wine were made. Later a lamb or a suckling pig was sacrificed. The proceedings closed with songs to the god and general merrymaking in which all the members of the family and the servants took part.

A similar festival was held at the old boundary of the Roman territory between the fifth and sixth milestones on the road to Laurentum. When the Capitoline temple was to be built the auguries forbade the removal of one of these *termini* (a boundary mark of some old precinct?) and it was enclosed within the walls of the new sanctuary, an indication of the immovability of such stones and of the permanence of the Roman territory.

BIBLIOGRAPHY.—G. Wissowa, *Religion und Kultus,* 2nd ed., p. 136 (1912); W. W. Fowler, *Roman Festivals,* p. 324 (1899); J. G. Frazer, *Fasti of Ovid,* vol. ii, pp. 481 ff. (1929); E. Marbach in Pauly-Wissowa, *Real-Encyclopädie der classischen Altertumswissenschaft,* s.v.

(X.; R. B. LD.)

**TERMITE,** the name for usually pale-coloured, soft-bodied insects of the order Isoptera (*see* INSECT). They all live in large social colonies. Termites cause severe economic damage to wooden structures and wood products, particularly in the tropics and warm temperate regions. An account of termite biology and social life is given in the article SOCIAL INSECTS.

**General Features.**—The wingless nymphs and workers are frequently whitish, a characteristic that has resulted in the misnomer "white ants." Worker termites have thick waists and can be readily distinguished from worker ants which have wasplike constrictions of the abdomen. Furthermore, flying termites have four membranous wings of almost equal size whereas flying ants have smaller hindwings. Termites, unlike ants, have a basal crack or suture in each wing by means of which the wings are shed in a fraction of a second following the colonizing flight.

JOHN H. GERARD

TERMITES EATING YELLOW PINE. GREATLY MAGNIFIED

Termites are found in greater numbers of species and individuals in the tropics than in the colder regions. From temperate North America, 45 species are recorded; from temperate Eurasia and North Africa, 40 species are known.

Grass, leaves and dead wood form the principal diet of termites, although some tropical species eat the organic humus of soils, a few eat fungi and some eat living woody plants.

**Control Measures.**—Methods to control termites are often necessary throughout the United States and occasionally in southern Ontario and British Columbia in Canada. Damage in Eurasia extends northward to a line through southern France, the Balkan countries, the southern U.S.S.R., southern and coastal China, Korea and Japan. Although termites are not spreading northward in their natural habitat, a few species have been introduced and established in heated buildings in many northern cities. Because most termites are soft-bodied and easily injured by arid conditions, they cannot live long after being exposed to dry air. The sterile workers and soldiers are blind and have a neutral reaction to light if the humidity is high enough. The majority of species in the fairly advanced family Rhinotermitidae and in the most advanced family Termitidae are dependent upon soil moisture for their existence. The species in one fairly primitive family, Kalotermitidae, are called dry-wood termites. These excavate their nests and chambers in dry or damp wood above ground.

*Dry-Wood Termites.*—Dry-wood termites are seldom found north of the Gulf states, New Mexico and Arizona, or east of the northwestern Pacific states. *Kalotermes flavicollis* causes damage in the Mediterranean countries, and some other species cause economic damage as far north as southern Japan. One largely tropical genus, *Cryptotermes,* can live in the dry wood of furniture. The dry-wood termites show no external indications of their presence but they may be detected by the characteristically hollow sound heard on tapping the wood near their galleries. When their chambers are exposed, accumulated masses of dry pellets of excrement may pour out.

Infestation may be prevented by inspection of lumber prior to its use, by placing screens (20 meshes per inch) over openings in the building, by using wood that has been treated chemically in commercial plants, by dipping wood in a solution of pentachlorophenol (5%, in a light petroleum oil) for three minutes and by covering exterior woodwork with heavy coats of paint around holes and cracks.

Liquid insecticides (trichlorobenzene; 2% chlordane in oil; 5% pentachlorophenol in oil; 6% DDT in oil; and benzene hexachloride) sprayed into the inhabited termite galleries often give satisfactory results. Poison dusts (smelter dust, white arsenic, paris green and 50% DDT) blown upon the termites in the galleries may effectively kill the entire colony within a few weeks.

*Subterranean Termites.*—Most control measures against the subterranean termites are designed to prevent their gaining entry into wooden structures which are in close contact with the soil. It is much easier to build relatively resistant structures than it is to eradicate termites after infestation. Precautions include cement foundations, a distance of at least 18 in. between the ground and any untreated wood, and ventilation under houses without basements. Cement grout, coal-tar plastic cement or coal-tar pitch should be used to seal off all holes around pipes in foundations below the ground level. Copper or zinc metal shields may be placed between woodwork and the top of cement foundations. All joints in the metal should be tightly sealed and the outer edges should be at least three or four inches wide beyond the sill and bent downward at an angle.

Subterranean termites that have already gained access to a building will die if their contact with soil moisture is broken. Soil poisons around the foundations are effective for several years. The poison is placed in a deep trench or in holes bored with a soil auger 18 in. apart. Heptachlor, aldrin, dieldrin, lindane and chlordane are the poisons usually used.

*See* also references under "Termite" in the Index.

BIBLIOGRAPHY.—A. Mallis, *Handbook of Pest Control,* 4th ed. (1964); U.S. Department of Agriculture, "Insects," *1952 Yearbook of Agriculture* (1952); C. L. Metcalf and W. P. Flint, *Destructive and Useful Insects,* 3rd ed. (1951); in the U.S. bulletins on termite control are available from Superintendent of Documents, Government Printing Office, Washington, D.C.

(A. E. E.)

**TERMS, DISTRIBUTION OF.** In logic a term is said to be distributed in a proposition when explicit reference is made to its whole extent or extension. Otherwise (that is, not only when reference is made explicitly to a part only of the extension of the term, but when explicit reference is simply not made to its whole extension) it is said to be undistributed. Thus, in a proposition of the form *No S is P* both the subject and the predicate are distributed. In the form *Some S is P,* neither *S* nor *P* is distributed. In *All S is P, S* is distributed, but *P* is not. Lastly, in *Some S is not P, S* is not distributed, but *P* is. Briefly, only universal propositions distribute the subject term (*S*), and only negative propositions distribute their predicate (*P*). Naturally, singular terms (including proper names used as singular terms) are always distributed, for they only refer to one object, and cannot refer to less.

The importance of the distribution of terms arises from the fact that it is a principle of formal inference that no term may be distributed in the conclusion unless it was distributed in the premisses. That is why, *e.g., All S is P* can only be converted into *Some P is S* (not into *All P is S*), and *Some S is not P* cannot be converted at all.

**TERN,** a gull-like aquatic or marine bird, often called a sea swallow because of its trim shape and buoyant flight. Terns constitute the subfamily Sterninae of the family Laridae. They are nearly worldwide in distribution, many of them ranging far during migration, the most notable long-distance migrant being the Arctic tern (*Sterna paradisaea*) (*see* MIGRATION, BIRD). In length, terns range from about 8 to 22 in., and, as compared with gulls, they are more slender, longer-winged, and shorter-legged. Many species are mainly gray and white; others range from almost black to pure white.

They may be grouped broadly as follows. Noddy terns (*Anous* species), dark-coloured, and the white fairy tern (*Gygis alba*) are mainly tropical and subtropical. Inca tern (*Larosterna inca*), dark-coloured, with white plumes on side of head, are found in

Peru and northern Chile. Capped and crested terns, many mainly pearl gray above, paler (to white) below, with a black cap or smallish black crest, are arctic circumpolar species. Marsh terns, largely dark-coloured; little terns (length 8–10 in.), which have partial black cap; and the large-billed tern (*Phaetusa simplex*) are South American.

Terns are colonial breeders, with no nest to a well-formed one, on the ground. The fairy tern lays one egg, on a horizontal tree limb. Most terns lay two eggs. One brood a year is the rule but the sooty tern (*Sterna fuscata*), also known as wideawake, breeds at about nine-month intervals. The majority obtain their food by diving from the air. They eat a variety of aquatic life, such as invertebrates and small fishes, and terrestrial insects that are blown into the water. They seldom eat larval lobsters or any significant amount of commercially important fish. In some parts of the world, the eggs, especially of the sooty and noddy terns, are gathered in great quantity for human food. (R. S. Pr.)

**TERNATE,** a volcanic island of Indonesia in the *kabupaten* (regency) of Maluku Utara (North Moluccas). It is the northernmost of the line of islands off the western coast of Halmahera, Indon., which stretch southward to the Batjan Archipelago, and lies 18 mi. (29 km.) west of the Halmahera coast. It is 6 mi. wide and has an area of 41 sq.mi. (106 sq.km.). Pop. (1957 est.) 33,964. The island consists mainly of a conical volcano 5,627 ft. (1,715 m.) in height, with three peaks (Arfat, Madina, and Kekan), its curious formation being due to many extremely destructive eruptions. In the last four centuries there has been constant volcanic activity on Ternate, the worst being the eruption in 1763. An eruption in 1840 destroyed nearly every house in the town of Ternate. The northern half of the island suffered most from volcanic activity. On the southern and eastern coasts are forests and luxuriant vegetation, with a good deal of cultivated land on the flat strip by the shore; vegetation extends even far up the mountainside. Rice and maize (corn) are grown, also sage, coffee, pepper, nutmegs, and fruit.

The local inhabitants are of very mixed blood, probably Malay predominating, but with Papuan elements. They have a language of their own, written in the Arabic character, and are Muslim by religion; there are some Christians also.

Ternate Town, with an estimated (1957) population of 23,500, lies on the southeast coast of the island, at the foot of the mountain. It is a picturesque settlement, the houses interspersed among a wealth of trees, with the volcano for a background. The port on the bay between Ternate and Tidore (to the south) is a regular place of call for interisland vessels. Ternate was once a leading centre of clove cultivation. Although it is the headquarters of the regency of Maluku Utara, it has only the shadow of its former importance. Its small trade is made up chiefly of copra and nutmeg.

In the 12th century, Javanese controlled the clove trade, later to be joined by Malaccan and Indian merchants. In the century before the advent of the Europeans, Ternate became the seat of a Muslim sultanate. The first Western visitor was the Portuguese Francesco Serra (1512). Soon thereafter Portuguese ships from Malacca began to visit Ternate to load cloves. Fearing Spanish competition upon the arrival in 1521 of the ship "Victoria" (of the Magellan expedition), the Portuguese obtained a treaty from the sultan whereby they secured (on paper at least) the monopoly of the spice trade and the right to establish a fort on Ternate (1522).

Commercial and religious conflicts caused the expulsion of the Portuguese in 1574. In 1579 Sir Francis Drake called at the island, but the visit was never followed up by English trading vessels. In 1599 Jacob van Neck established Dutch relations with Ternate. After an attack by a Spanish fleet in 1606 the sultan placed himself under Dutch protection and gave them the spice monopoly in his territories. To maintain the monopoly and maintain high prices, the Dutch East India Company restricted production by cutting down clove trees. The serious decline in welfare led to a popular revolt in 1650. It was sternly suppressed and ended in a new agreement with the sultan; cultivation of cloves was henceforth forbidden in Ternate and other islands of the northern Moluccas. Another revolt in 1683, this time led by the then ruling sultan, was also put down and the sultan reinstated as a mere vassal of the company. Executive power was gradually gathered in Dutch hands until the Japanese occupation during World War II and the subsequent independence of Indonesia in 1949. (E. E. L.; J. O. M. B.)

**TERNI,** chief town of Terni Province in Umbria, central Italy, and the seat of a bishop, lies 62 mi. (100 km.) NNE of Rome by road on the Nera River. Pop. (1966 est.) 103,240. Its important remains are a Neolithic village, cemeteries of the Villanovan period, an amphitheatre, and Roman walls. The cathedral, originally built in 550, was reconstructed in the mid-17th century. The Romanesque Church of S. Salvatore was erected over a Roman building, possibly a temple of the Sun; the 9th-century Church of S. Alò belonged to the Knights of Malta. Churches of the 13th century are S. Lorenzo, S. Pietro, S. Cristoforo, and S. Francesco (1265) with a fine bell tower added in 1345. In the Paradisi Chapel is a fresco of the Last Judgment (Giotto School). Nonreligious architecture includes the Torre Barbarasa (13th century); the Palazzo Mazzancolli (14th century); and the Renaissance Palazzo Spada, the last work of Antonio Picconi da Sangallo who died at Terni in 1546.

The chief attraction near Terni is the Cascata delle Marmore (4 mi. [6 km.]). These falls were created by the consul Manius Curius Dentatus by deflecting the waters of the Velino River into the Nera River below; they are now used for manufacturing hydroelectric power.

Manufactures include iron and steel, arms, machinery, textiles, sugar, soap, and *pasta* products. There are electrochemical plants, distilling, and tanning. Vegetable and fruit growing on irrigated land is intensive.

Terni is on the site of the ancient Interamna Nahars, which was occupied by Sulla. In the 14th century it became a dominion of the church. Half of the town was destroyed in World War II but it reemerged larger and more active with modern industrial plants.

Terni Province is watered by the Tiber and the Nera and is hilly and well irrigated. Area 819 sq.mi. (2,122 sq.km.); pop. (1965 est.) 226,279. Important towns are Narni (birthplace of the emperor Nerva), with light industries; Nera Montoro, with a chemical industry; Piediluco, which has a picturesque lake; and Orvieto, famed for its Romanesque-Gothic cathedral. Acquasparta and San Gemini are thermal spas. Wine is exported and ceramics and wrought iron are produced. (M. T. A. N.)

**TERNIFINE FOSSILS,** so-called after the local name for part of the Eghriss plain south of Mascara (*q.v.*), Alg.; excavations for a new village, in 1870, revealed there (on the west side of a Muslim cemetery, used as a sand pit, and consisting of silt that filled a Pleistocene lake that existed about 450,000 years ago) a wealth of fossil mammal bones and Abbevillian-Acheulian stone tools. The cemetery barred excavation except in the sand pit, which became flooded after 1888 when diggers tapped an artesian spring. Between 1954 and 1956 the French paleontologist Camille Arambourg and co-workers pumped out the water to find considerable remains of extinct African fauna and a great quantity of primitive artifacts of European mid-Pleistocene type.

Three human jawbones and a fragment of skull from the pit (closely resembling *Pithecanthropus* and *Sinanthropus; qq.v.*) were identified as belonging to a being whom they named *Atlanthropus mauritanicus*. The discovery shed light on the nature of the Abbevillian-Acheulian toolmakers, concerning whom speculation continued despite the abundance of their products throughout the Old World.

*See* also Archaeology: *Prehistory: Culture History of the Pleistocene;* Man, Evolution of: *Homo Erectus*.

Bibliography.—M. Boule and H. V. Vallois, *Fossil Men* (1957); C. B. M. McBurney, *The Stone Age of Northern Africa* (1960); C. Arambourg and R. Hoffstetter, *Le Gisement de Ternifine* (1963).
(Ca. A.)

**TERNOPOL',** a town and administrative centre of Ternopol' Oblast' in the Ukrainian Soviet Socialist Republic, U.S.S.R., stands on the left bank of the upper Seret, 75 mi. (121 km.) ESE of

L'vov (Lvov). Pop. (1959) 52,245. Originally belonging to the princes of Galicia (*q.v.*), Ternopol' later passed to Poland and, in the first partition of Poland in 1772, to Austria. After World War I Ternopol' was returned to Poland, but was annexed by the U.S.S.R. in 1939. During World War II the town suffered almost total destruction. Its present importance is as a regional centre and railway junction. Five lines (from L'vov, Drogobych, Chernovtsy, Khmel'nitskiy [Khmelnitski], and Korosten') converge on Ternopol', linking it to all parts of western Ukraine. It has relatively small-scale light industries, chiefly processing foodstuffs. Natural and artificial leather working and the manufacture of footwear are important. Reinforced concrete items are also produced.

TERNOPOL' OBLAST' was formed in 1939 from territory annexed from Poland. Area 5,367 sq.mi. (13,900 sq.km.); pop. (1959) 1,085,586. The *oblast* lies athwart the Volyno-Podol'skaya Upland, with its southern boundary along the Dniester River, to which the greater part drains. The rolling, loess-covered hills of the upland are cut up by river valleys, notably that of the Seret. Intensive agriculture, even on slopes, has led to the widespread development of erosion gullies. The whole *oblast* is in the forest-steppe zone, but only small patches of oakwood survive. Soils are fertile chernozems, slightly podzolized in the west.

Of the 1959 population only 17% were urban, living in 14 towns and 12 urban settlements. The towns are all small local centres engaged in sugar refining and the processing of other farm products. A little lignite is mined. The economy is overwhelmingly agricultural, and the density of the rural population is one of the highest in European Russia. Grains, mainly rye, wheat, and maize (corn), occupy over half the arable land. Sugar beet leads the industrial crops, especially in the east. Sunflowers are grown in the west and some tobacco in the south, while hops are generally important. The widespread potato crops are used for human and animal consumption and for distilling. (R. A. F.)

**TERPANDER** (fl. *c.* 675 B.C.), of Antissa in Lesbos, Greek poet and musician, is said to have won a prize in Sparta at the feast of Apollo Karneios in the 26th Olympiad (676/2). He is alleged to have founded the first "establishment" (Gr. *katastasis*) of music at Sparta before the Second Messenian War, and to have "invented" the seven-stringed *kithara* (which was already known in Minoan times). He was proverbially famous as a singer to the *kithara* (*see* LYRE), and is credited with important developments in the songs (Gr. *nomoi*) for that instrument, but the authenticity of the few surviving literary fragments ascribed to him is at best doubtful. It is probable that when Sappho spoke of the primacy of the Lesbian singer she was thinking of the fame won by Terpander.

For fragments and allusions, *see* J. M. Edmonds, *Lyra Graeca,* vol. 1, 2nd ed. (1928) in the "Loeb Series"; *see* also *Poetae melici Graeci,* ed. by D. L. Page, pp. 362–363 (1962). (JN. A. D.)

**TERPENES** are members of a class of naturally occurring hydrocarbons (*q.v.*) of the general formula $(C_5H_8)_n$, the name being derived from turpentine, which is a mixture of terpenes. Terpenes occur in the essential oils of many plants and in the gummy exudates (oleoresins) of many trees and shrubs. The term terpenes is frequently used in a broader sense to include compounds which contain oxygen and may be regarded as being derived from the terpene hydrocarbons.

The terpenes and their derivatives are broadly classified according to the number of $C_5H_8$ units which they contain, and range in molecular size from volatile oils of molecular formula $C_{10}H_{16}$ to giant molecules such as that of natural rubber containing about 4,000 $C_5H_8$ units. The classes are: monoterpenes, $C_{10}H_{16}$; sesquiterpenes, $C_{15}H_{24}$; diterpenes, $C_{20}H_{32}$; triterpenes, $C_{30}H_{48}$; tetraterpenes, $C_{40}H_{64}$; polyterpenes, $(C_5H_8)_n$. Nearly all of the terpenes possess carbon skeletons that may be regarded as being built up from isoprene units $(\overset{1}{C}-\underset{\displaystyle C}{\overset{2}{C}}-\overset{3}{C}-\overset{4}{C})$ in various combinations and the early recognition of this common structural feature (O. Wallach, Isoprene Rule, 1887) was of great help in the elucidation of their structures. The isoprene units may be linked in a variety of ways leading to acyclic, monocyclic and polycyclic subclasses within the broad classes of terpenes, depending upon the number of carbon atom rings that result. Myrcene (I), an acyclic monoterpene; limonene (II), a monocyclic monoterpene; $\alpha$-pinene (III), a bicyclic monoterpene; and vitamin A (IV), an oxygenated, monocyclic diterpene, exemplify this further classification and the dotted lines indicate the division of the carbon skeletons into isoprene units.

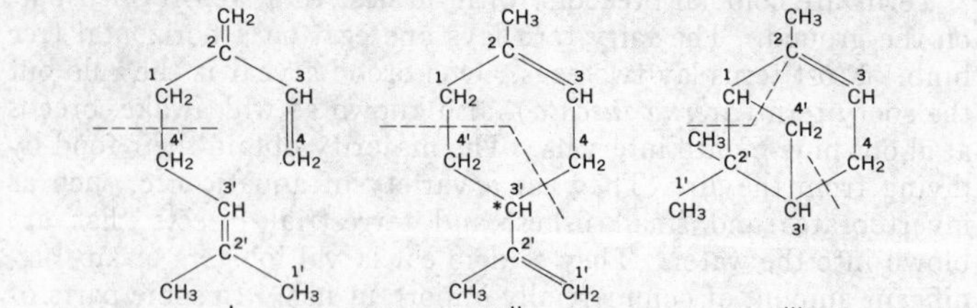

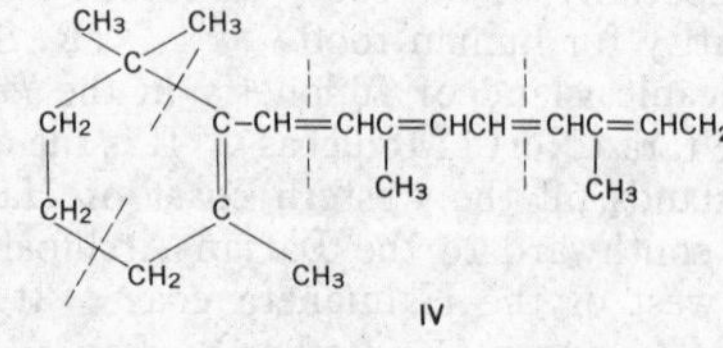

The problems in molecular structure presented by the terpenes have challenged the imagination and skill of organic chemists since the latter part of the 19th century. The first investigations were mainly concerned with the structures of the monoterpenes $(C_{10}H_{16})$ but as those structural patterns became familiar and techniques for investigation were developed, attention was turned increasingly toward the terpenes containing 15 to 40 carbon atoms.

Typically the establishment of the structure of a terpene follows the sequence: isolation; purification; degradation by oxidation to simpler compounds of known structure; postulation of a structure based on the results of the degradation; and validation of the structure by unambiguous synthesis.

## MONOTERPENES

The monoterpenes are isolated from their natural sources by distillation of the plant matter with steam. They are volatile oils, less dense than water, and have normal boiling points in the range 150°–185° C. Purification is usually achieved by fractional distillation at reduced pressures or by regeneration from a crystalline derivative. Acyclic monoterpene hydrocarbons are few in number and it is their oxygenated derivatives which are more widespread in nature and of greater importance. Important oxygenated acyclic monoterpene derivatives include the terpene alcohol citronellol (V) and the corresponding aldehyde citronellal (VI), both of which occur in oil of citronella, as well as citral (VII), found in lemon-grass oil, and geraniol (VIII), which occurs in Turkish geranium oil.

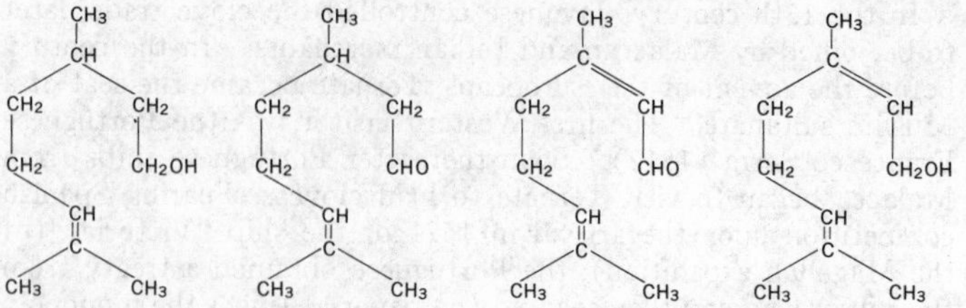

Citronellal is converted by treatment with acid into the monocyclic monoterpene alcohol isopulegol from which a mixture of stereoisomeric menthols (IX) is produced on catalytic hydrogenation. The process is used commercially to supplement the natural sources of menthol (oil of peppermint), widely used as a flavouring and in medicinal preparations. Citral (VII), upon reduction with sodium amalgam, yields geraniol (VIII), an important component of rose perfumes. Citral may be condensed with acetone to

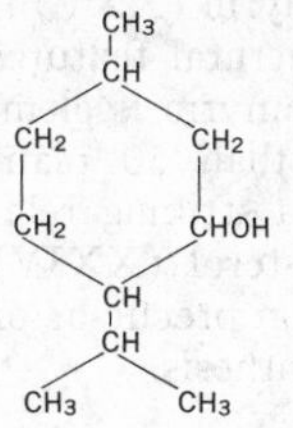

IX 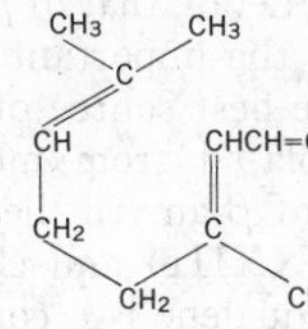 X 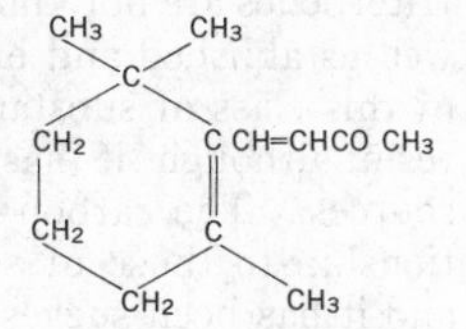 XI

yield the important intermediate ψ-ionone (X) from which β-ionone (XI) results on cyclization with acid. Although β-ionone cannot be regarded as a terpene, it is of great importance as a starting material for the synthesis of vitamin A (IV) and as a component of violet-scented perfumes.

Limonene (II), an oil of normal boiling point 177° C., is a major component of orange and lemon oils and is typical of the monocyclic monoterpene hydrocarbons. Others of this class are terpinolene, α- and β-phellandrene and α-, β- and γ-terpinene, all of which have the same carbon skeleton as limonene and differ only in the location of the two carbon-to-carbon double bonds. Limonene is optically active as are most of the terpenes and their derivatives which contain an asymmetric carbon atom, starred in the formula of limonene (II) (*see* STEREOCHEMISTRY). The racemic form of limonene is known as dipentene, and results from the dimerization of isoprene, $CH_2{=}C(CH_3)CH{=}CH_2$. Limonene is converted to isoprene by contact with a heated metallic filament. Few commercial uses, other than as flavourings, exist for the monocyclic monoterpene hydrocarbons. Menthol (IX), which has already been mentioned, and the oxygenated derivatives

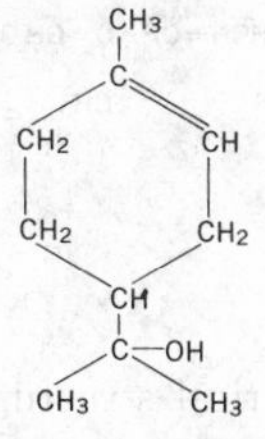

XII 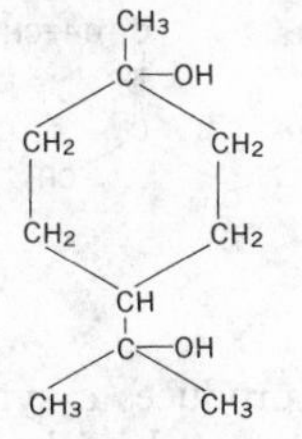 XIII

α-terpineol (XII) and 1,8-terpin (terpin hydrate) (XIII) are chemicals of commerce. Mixtures of 1,8-terpin, α-terpineol, terpinolene and the terpinenes result from the treatment of α-pinene (III) with acid, and the mixture finds use as "pine oil," an inexpensive disinfectant, deodorant and wetting agent.

Of normal boiling point 156°, α-pinene (III) is representative of the bicyclic monoterpenes, and the most abundant and important monoterpene. It is the major component of ordinary turpentine which is prepared from pine trees or stumps either by extraction followed by rectification or by distillation with steam. It is a major component of "sulfate turpentine," a by-product of the manufacture of paper, and is important as a component of paints and varnishes and as a raw material for the production of a wide

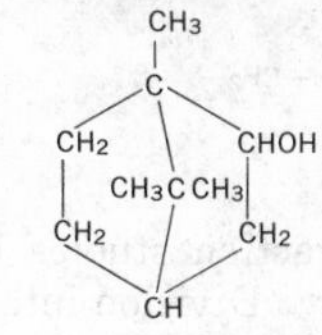

XIV 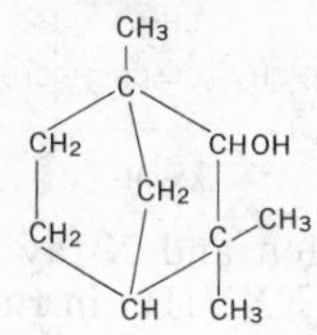 XV 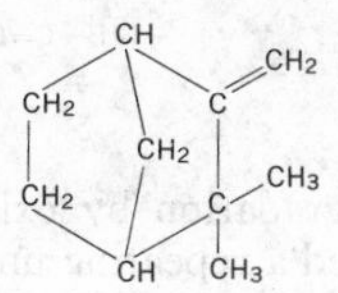 XVI

variety of products employed in chemical industry.

Its use in coating materials depends upon its good properties as a solvent and upon its conversion by air oxidation into a polymeric, resinous film. Its function as a starting material for conversion to more useful products results from its abundance and its structure, which has a high degree of chemical reactivity. The chemical reactions of α-pinene have been studied more thoroughly than those of any other terpene and the study has contributed greatly to the understanding of molecular rearrangements (*q.v.*) in organic chemistry.

Treatment of α-pinene with acids under various conditions leads to a host of products among which are terpinolene, the terpinenes, α-terpineol (XII) and terpin (XIII) previously mentioned, and in addition borneol (XIV), fenchyl alcohol (XV) and the hydrocarbon camphene (XVI).

The formation of the latter three compounds involves molecular rearrangement and advantage has been taken of the structural changes to provide a commercial synthesis of the important bicyclic terpene ketone, camphor (*q.v.*).

## SESQUITERPENES

Sesquiterpenes, $C_{15}H_{24}$, are isolated from their natural sources by distillation with steam or by extraction since they are of lower volatility than the monoterpenes. They are purified by fractional distillation *in vacuo* or by chromatography. The sesquiterpenes demonstrate an even greater complexity of structure than the monoterpenes, and oxygenated sesquiterpenes are commonly encountered.

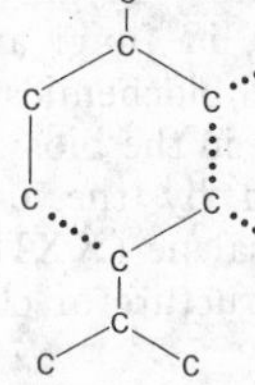

XVII 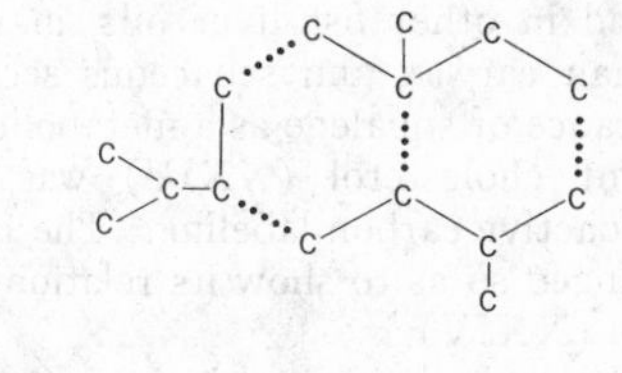 XVIII

Two arrangements of isoprene units are found in bicyclic sesquiterpenes, the cadalene (XVII) and the eudalene (XVIII) types, and the carbon skeleton of a sesquiterpene may frequently be determined by heating it with sulfur or selenium to effect dehydrogenation to the corresponding naphthalenic hydrocarbons: cadalene, 4-isopropyl-1,6-dimethylnaphthalene; or eudalene, 7-isopropyl-1-methylnaphthalene. In those cases where sulfur dehydrogenation fails to yield information about the carbon skeleton of a sesquiterpene a systematic degradation by oxidation to compounds of known structure is necessary.

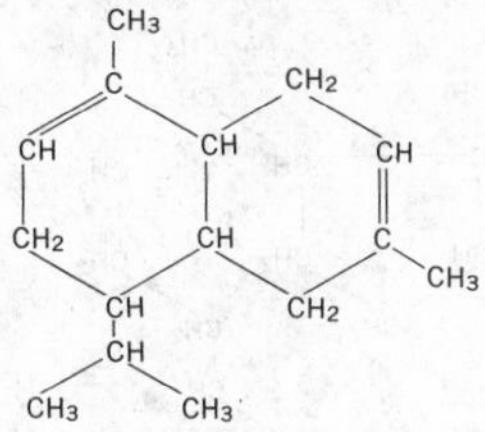

XIX 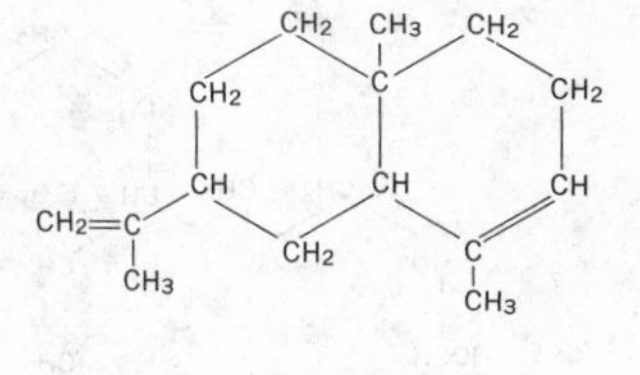 XX

Cadinene (XIX), the principal component of oil of cubeb, is a typical sesquiterpene of the cadalene type. It is an optically active oil of normal boiling point 275° C. Selinene (XX), present in celery oil, is typical of the eudalene type.

## DITERPENES

Phytol (XXI), an oxygenated acyclic diterpene, is an important building block of the chlorophyll molecule from which it is obtained on saponification. The arrangement

$$\underset{\underset{CH_3}{|}}{CH_3CH}CH_2CH_2CH_2\underset{\underset{CH_3}{|}}{CH}CH_2CH_2CH_2\underset{\underset{CH_3}{|}}{CH}CH_2CH_2CH_2\underset{\underset{CH_3}{|}}{C}{=}CHCH_2OH$$

XXI

of isoprene units in phytol is identical with that in vitamin A (IV), a monocyclic diterpene derivative, and is typical of the head-to-tail arrangement of isoprene units found in most terpenes.

The commercial importance of the bicyclic monoterpene α-pinene is paralleled in the diterpenes by abietic acid (XXII), a tricyclic carboxylic acid which constitutes the major portion of rosin. Rosin is the nonvolatile portion of the oleoresin of members of the pine family and is the residue left after the isolation of turpentine. Rosin is used as such in the production of varnish and coating materials and, in the form of its sodium salt, for sizing

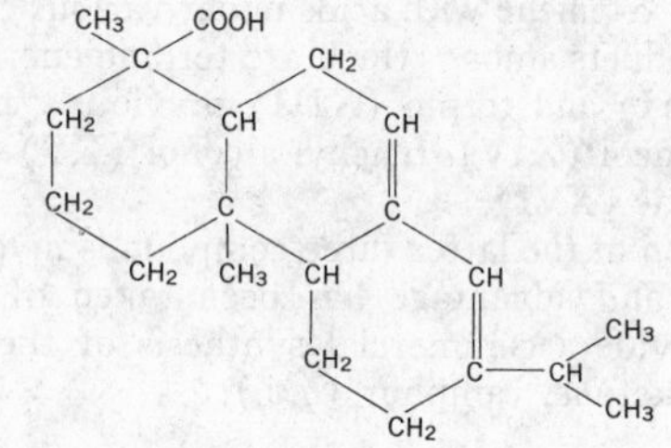

XXII

paper, as an emulsifying agent in producing synthetic rubber and in yellow laundry soap. It is among the cheapest organic acids.

## TRITERPENES

The acyclic triterpene hydrocarbon squalene (XXIII) constitutes more than half of the liver oil of certain species of sharks and is otherwise rather widely distributed in nature. It has been found in other fish-liver oils, in vegetable oils, in fungi and in human earwax and sebaceous secretions. The biochemical importance of squalene as a metabolic intermediate in the biosynthesis of cholesterol (XXIV) was demonstrated by the use of radioactive carbon labeling. The formula of squalene (XXIII) is arranged so as to show its relationship to the structure of cholesterol (XXIV).

Although cholesterol is not a terpene, the demonstration that it has a terpene as precursor in metabolism represented a major

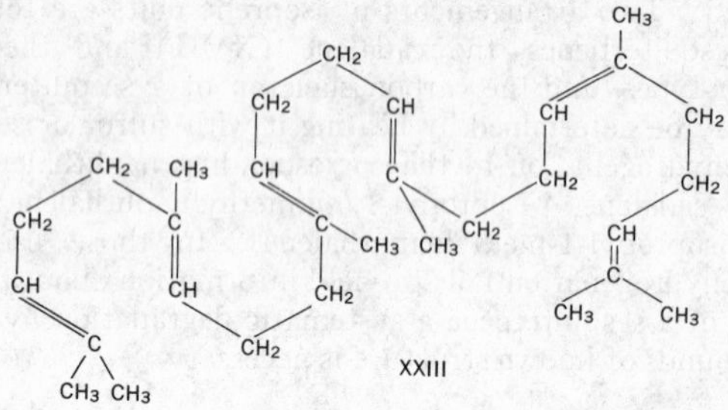

XXIII

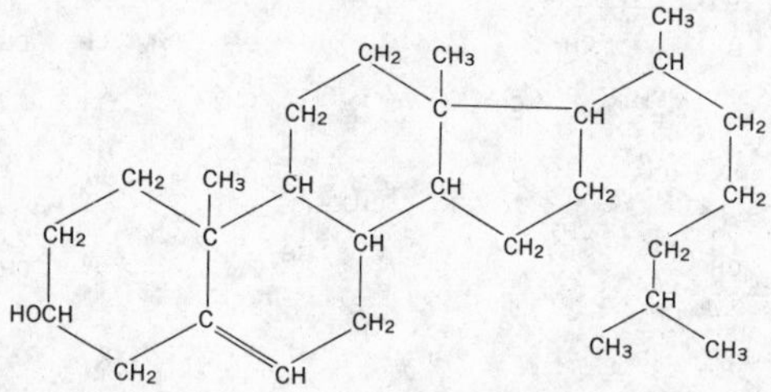

XXIV

advance in understanding the biochemical relationship between the two important classes of compounds involved.

Although tri- and tetracyclic triterpenes are known, by far the most abundant triterpenes found in nature are those having five

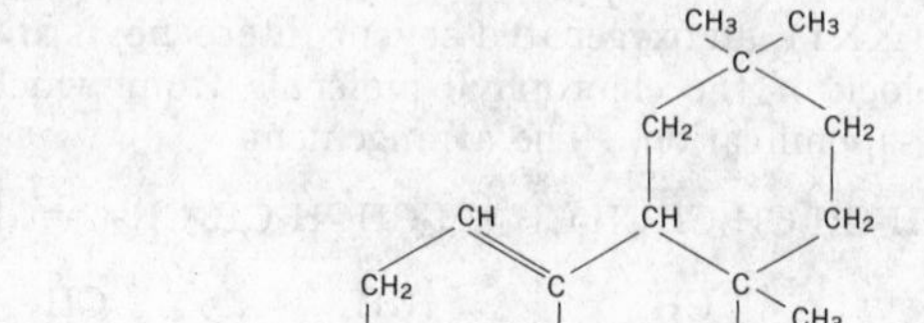

XXV

carbon rings. The pentacyclic triterpenes, either free or combined with sugars in glycosides (saponins), occur in all parts of many plants. Although the structures of many of the pentacyclic triterpenes are not known in full detail, that of β-amyrin (XXV) is well established and exemplifies the important structural features of this class of substances. The best source of β-amyrin is elemi resin although it has been isolated from more than 50 plant sources. The carbon skeleton of β-amyrin bears a striking relationship to those of squalene (XXIII) and cholesterol (XXIV) and it has been suggested that squalene is a common precursor of the pentacyclic triterpenes and the sterols in biosynthesis.

## TETRATERPENES

The large class of yellow, orange or red, fat-soluble plant and animal pigments known as carotenoids are classed as tetraterpenes although they have in general the molecular formula $C_{40}H_{56}$ rather than $C_{40}H_{64}$ as required by $(C_5H_8)_8$. The fact that their structures can be built up from isoprene units justifies their classification as terpenes. The carotenoids are isolated from their natural sources by solvent extraction and purified by chromatography. Lycopene (XXVI), the red pigment of the ripe tomato, exempli-

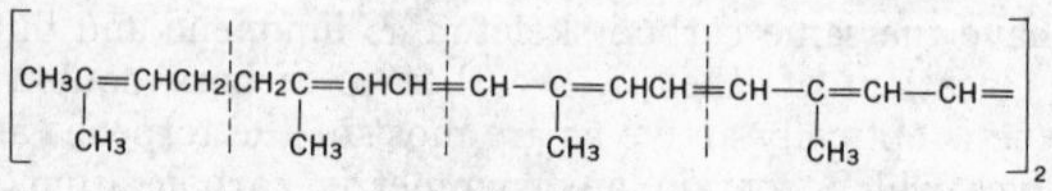

XXVI

fies the class of acyclic tetraterpenes. The dotted lines in the formula show the division into isoprene units, and it is to be noted that the usual head-to-tail attachment of isoprene units is interrupted in the centre of the molecule with a single tail-to-tail

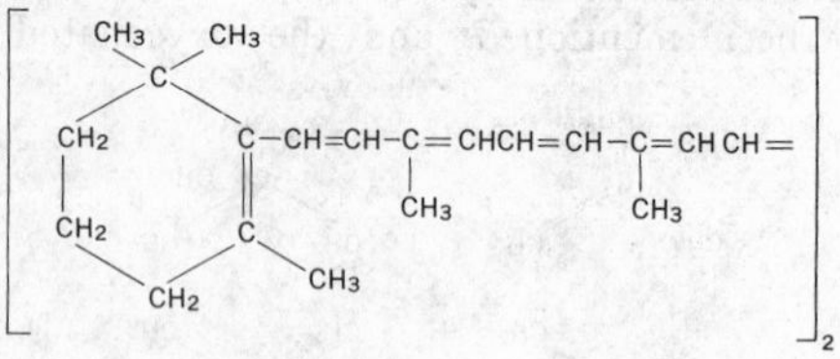

XXVII

attachment that produces a symmetrical structure. This feature is generally encountered in the tetraterpenes, as is the long series of alternating single and double, carbon-to-carbon bonds (conjugated system) which is responsible for the absorption of light and hence the bright colours of the compounds.

The most important and abundant tetraterpene is β-carotene (XXVII), the principal yellow pigment of the carrot; β-carotene is of nutritional importance since the animal organism is apparently able to cleave the molecule at the point of symmetry with the production of vitamin A (IV). The role of vitamin A and structurally related terpenoid molecules in the synthesis of the pigments in the eye necessary for vision has been demonstrated.

## POLYTERPENES

Rubber, which occurs in the latex of the rubber tree, is a polyterpene hydrocarbon, $(C_5H_8)_n$ where $n$ is 4,000–5,000. Chemi-

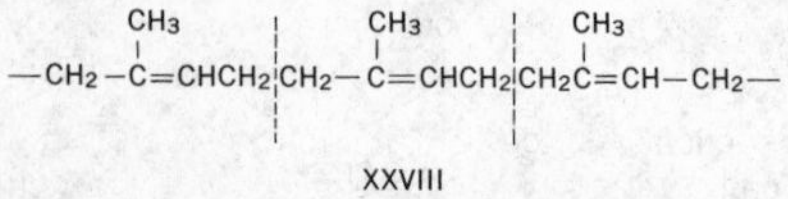

XXVIII

cal degradation by oxidation and X-ray diffraction studies have revealed a repeating unit (XXVIII) in rubber. Division into isoprene units is indicated. The vulcanization of rubber involves the establishment of cross linking between the chains through sulfur atoms. Gutta-percha differs from rubber in the way in which the methyl ($CH_3$) groups are arranged; in gutta-percha they are on opposite sides (trans arrangement) of the chain and in rubber they are on the same side (cis arrangement).

BIBLIOGRAPHY.—E. Guenther *et al.*, *The Essential Oils*, vol. 1 (1948); J. L. Simonsen *et al.*, *The Terpenes*, 5 vol. (1947–57); L. Ruzicka, "Biogenesis of Terpenes," *Experientia*, vol. 9 (1953); H. Gilman *et al.* (eds.), *Organic Chemistry*, vol. 4 (1953); G. Ourisson *et al.*, *Tetracyclic Triterpenes* (1964, 1965). (R. H. EN.)

**TERRACINA,** a town and port of Latina Province in central Italy, between the Ausonian Mountains and the Tyrrhenian Sea, is 64 mi. (103 km.) SE of Rome. Pop. (1961) 28,590.

The town was occupied by the Volscians, who called it Anxur, and about 400 B.C. it passed under Roman domination, under whom it was known as Tarracina, becoming an important city on the Appian Way from Rome to Capua and Brundisium. Between the end of the republic and the first two centuries of the empire, the city assumed great importance, as witnessed by the remains of the forum; the sumptuous temples, baths, and theatres; and the remains of the villas of the emperors Tiberius, Galba, and Vitellius.

The new town lies close to the sea, with the old town on the slopes above. There are municipal parks, a town hall (1958), and a museum. Though the town was damaged during World War II, many ancient structures remain. Dominating the town are the ruins of the Temple of Jupiter Anxur and the ancient Anxur wall. The cathedral of S. Cesareo (1074) stands over the ancient temple of Roma and Augustus, the remains of which can be seen in the outer walls.

Fishing, food preserving, floor surfacings, and electrical appliances are the major industries, and muscatel grapes are exported.

**TERRA COTTA,** generally considered, may apply to all kinds of fired clay, but has come to refer chiefly to a fairly coarse, porous type which when fired assumes a colour ranging from dull ochre to red and is most frequently left unglazed.

Baked clay, because it can be easily manipulated before it is fired and is relatively durable, has been used throughout the world since earliest times for pottery and sculpture and for many architectural purposes. While clays vary widely in composition in different areas, all are subject to fusion by heat into a hard substance varying in colour, porosity and strength in accordance with its content and the temperature to which it has been subjected. (*See* CLAY AND CLAY MINERALS.)

The most characteristic feature of objects in terra cotta is their obvious dependence on the plasticity of the material before it is hardened by fire. The clay when wet can be pressed or poured into molds; it may be cut, incised and folded; and it is responsive to the slightest pressure of the hand. Because of this, early artists sometimes attempted bolder designs in terra cotta than in more resistant materials. The coarser clays, however, do not readily lend themselves to sharp edges and precise definition of forms. Early works in terra cotta illustrate both the advantages and limitations of these material qualifications. For this reason there is often a superficial similarity between simply made terra-cotta works so far divided by time and distance as early Greece and the more modern cultures of Latin America.

Not only do the varied characteristics of the material, especially in primitive cultures, influence the form terra-cotta works are likely to take, but technical considerations in the procedure of firing also play a part. It is necessary that an object modeled in clay be thoroughly dry before being subjected to the intense heat of the kiln. In drying, and again in firing, the clay shrinks, and if one part dries much more rapidly than the rest it may crack and break away. It is necessary, therefore, to maintain a nearly equal thickness and avoid solid masses of clay of which the outer layers, drying more quickly, would shrink and crack. While this presents little difficulty in the making of pottery and low reliefs, it forces the sculptor to adopt complex methods for work in the round.

It was early found that very small figures could be fired successfully when solid, but larger works had to be rendered hollow before firing. There are three general methods by which this can be done: by pressing thin layers of clay into a mold (or pouring the clay in liquid form, called slip, into the mold and pouring off the residue after a thin shell has set); by hollowing out the heavier portions of the work; or by building up the work from the beginning with hollow forms. Throughout the history of terra cotta the first method has been the most popular. Not only does it permit evenness of drying and therefore successful firing, but it affords the possibility of multiplying the image indefinitely once the mold is made. The exploitation of this technique can be seen in the architectural decoration of the Etruscans, the figurines from Tanagra with their variously assembled parts, the repeated figures in Chinese tomb sculpture and the elaborate ornamentation of the Certosa at Pavia. But for a figure to be produced in an uncomplicated mold, deep undercutting must be avoided. As a result the surfaces are likely to be relatively unbroken, depending for contrast on incised pattern or applied colour.

Of importance particularly for the other methods of achieving a hollow form is the fact that an object to be fired can have no interior framework of a foreign substance. Since clay in a moist state will support little weight unassisted, constant attention must be paid to the relative size of the supporting members. The effect of this consideration may be seen in much modern terra-cotta sculpture built up from hollow forms. While it may place some limitations on the artist, it often imparts to the work a formal unity of a character peculiar to this use of the medium.

Colour has been used extensively in terra cotta ranging from the mat colours of applied slip (fine clay suspended in water) to the brilliant glazes of which the earliest examples come from Egypt and the near east. Since often the colour was not fired and thus fused with the surface, many once colourful objects have lost much of their original effect and appear in misleading simplicity to the modern eye. Few past cultures seem to have prized, as do modern sculptors, the native texture and colour of terra cotta.

Much of the use of terra cotta has been of a purely utilitarian kind since it is a relatively cheap, durable product of versatile nature. In places such as Mesopotamia and parts of Italy where stone has not always been easily accessible, it has served in architecture both for structure and ornament. In the 19th century, with the growth of iron construction, terra cotta commercially produced in the form of tile and sculptured ornament again became popular. It was light, adaptable to the many styles of ornament in demand and, as was discovered late in the century, could form a fireproof case for the vulnerable iron structure. *See* AEGEAN CIVILIZATION; CHINESE SCULPTURE; POTTERY AND PORCELAIN; TILE. (J. C. T.)

## GREEK, ETRUSCAN AND ROMAN

Good clay was abundant throughout Greece and Italy and was used in ancient times for pottery, sculpture and in architecture. (*See* also GREEK ART; ROMAN ART; ETRUSCANS.)

**Literary Sources.**—Pliny in his *Natural History* gives an account of the art of terra-cotta sculpture (*plastice*), which contains much useful information. The most significant statements are the following: (1) Boutades of Sikyon invented the art of making portraits in terra cotta and antefixes in the form of human beings (xxxv, 151); (2) Rhoikos and Theodoros of Samos invented the technique of clay modeling long before the Bacchiades were exiled from Corinth; *i.e.,* before about 657 B.C. (xxxv, 152); (3) Eucheir, Diopos and Eugrammos of Corinth introduced the art of clay modeling into Italy in the 7th century B.C. (xxxv, 152); (4) Damophilos and Gorgasos decorated the temple of Ceres in Rome, which was dedicated in 493 B.C. (xxxv, 154); (5) Vulca was called from Veii to Rome at the time of Tarquinius Priscus (616–578 B.C.) to make the cult statue of the temple of Jupiter Capitolinus, which was dedicated after the flight of Tarquinius Superbus in 510 B.C. (xxxv, 157). Pliny (xxxv, 158) and Plutarch (*Publicola,* xiii, 1–2) both speak of Etruscan terra-cotta sculpture with wonder and admiration; Vitruvius (iii, 3, 5) refers to terra-cotta pedimental sculptures as an "Etruscan fashion."

Some of these statements square with the facts as archaeology has revealed them, others do not. The tradition that the art of clay modeling was practised in Greece in early times is borne out by discoveries of small terra-cotta figures dating back to the early Bronze Age and of larger ones from the 7th century B.C. That this art was introduced into Italy by Greek artists and flourished there especially in the late Archaic period—when the temples of Ceres and Jupiter Capitolinus were dedicated—is substantiated by discoveries of a large number of terra-cotta statues and reliefs of that epoch in Etruria showing strong Greek influence. Moreover, that some of these Etruscan and Greek sculptors worked also in Rome is suggested by the fragments of important terra-cotta sculptures of that period that have been found there. On the other hand Pliny (perhaps quoting Varro) evidently confused some of his dates. Excavations at Samos have shown that Rhoikos and Theodoros were active in the 6th not the 7th century B.C., and if Vulca worked on the cult statue of the temple of Jupiter Capitolinus, which was dedicated after 510 B.C., Tarquinius Superbus rather than Tarquinius Priscus must have given the commission.

The terra-cotta sculptures of Greece, Etruria and Rome consist of statues, statuettes and reliefs.

**Statues.**—Terra-cotta statues were particularly popular in Italy, where marble was scarce until the opening of the Carrara quarries in the 1st century B.C., and in Cyprus. Discoveries at Kalydon, Thermos, Olympia and the Agora of Athens, however, show that terra-cotta sculptures must have been commoner in Greece than was once thought. Practically all served as decorations of temples.

That Pliny's and Plutarch's admiration of Etruscan terra-cotta statues was justified is borne out by the discoveries of such statues, large and small, throughout Etruria and etruscanized Latium. The life-sized statues of Apollo, Herakles and Hermes from Veii rank, both artistically and technically, among the greatest achievements of this kind. They once adorned the ridge pole of a temple, as shown by the terra-cotta bases found with them. Many other examples, both single figures and groups (some partly in relief), served as acroteria and antefixes of temples or came from pediments. Excellent specimens, chiefly of the Archaic period, a few of the later 5th and the 4th century B.C. and many of the Hellenistic epoch have been found at Caere (Cerveteri), Satricum (Conca), Falerii (Civita Castellana), Lanuvium (Lanuvio), Veii (Veio), etc.

Another common use for statues in terra cotta among the Etruscans was for figures placed on the lids of sarcophagi. Life-size archaic examples from Caere are in the Louvre and in the Villa Giulia museum, later ones in the British museum, the Archaeological museum in Florence and elsewhere. A large number of terra-cotta urns for holding the ashes of the dead, in the form of miniature sarcophagi, also have reclining figures on the lid. They date from the 3rd and 2nd centuries B.C. and often portray the deceased with great realism.

The style of these Etruscan sculptures, like that of Etruscan paintings, at times shows strong Greek influence, but it mostly has a marked local flavour. The spirit is sometimes gayer, at other times more morose or fiercer than in the Greek counterparts.

With the extended use of marble for sculpture in Italy in the 1st century B.C. terra-cotta statues became scarce. Relatively few have come to light in Pompeii and elsewhere in the Roman domains.

*Technique.*—Etruscan and Greek terra-cotta statues were not molded but modeled, from the bottom up, with coils and wads of clay, in thick walls. The clay was mixed with sand and grog to provide porosity, diminish the shrinkage and avoid distortion; and over this a coating of finer clay was generally added. Before firing the surface was painted, the prevalent colours being white, brownish red and black. The firing of such large statues as the Apollo of Veii and the warriors in New York required great care. The kiln must have been built round them, as they could hardly have been moved in the green state. The temperature has been computed to have been about 960° C., approximately the same as that used in firing Greek pottery. In the sanctuaries of Asclepius at Epidaurus and Corinth, as well as in Italy, there have been found life-size votive figures consisting generally of heads or of parts of the body that had been diseased and subsequently cured. They date mostly from the 4th to the 1st century B.C. and are made in molds in well-levigated clay.

**Statuettes.**—The commonest use of terra cotta was for small figures not over six or seven inches in height. They have been found in tombs and sanctuaries, on many different sites in Greece, Cyprus, Rhodes, Asia Minor, north Africa, Italy and Sicily, and range from the Bronze Age to the Roman period. Among the earliest are primitive figures from Cyprus, with planklike bodies or birdlike features. The painted and glazed statuettes of the Minoan period from Crete are more sophisticated in their modern-looking costumes, with full skirts, bare breasts and narrow waists. The Mycenaean and geometric figures, though schematic, are often in lively, lifelike poses. Women, horsemen, children and animals are favourite subjects. Particularly interesting are groups from Cyprus and elsewhere, consisting of men in chariots, dancers, warriors, in the so-called snow-man technique, modeled with great freedom.

From the 7th and 6th centuries B.C., all over the Mediterranean, the Greek terra-cotta statuettes reflect the changing styles in sculpture. Those of the 7th century show close contact with the orient both in subjects and renderings. In the 6th century the standing and seated female figure is favoured, the latter being generally shown holding a flower or other offering in one hand or with a child on her lap. Quantities of such statuettes have been found in votive deposits near the temples of Paestum (Poseidonia), the Heraion of Foce del Sele and other sites. The nude male standing figure, the so-called *kouros* type, is comparatively rare; only isolated examples have been found; *e.g.,* at Perachora and Veii. Among the most attractive statuettes of the late Archaic period are figures of women engaged in household tasks, horsemen, barbers and animals, found mostly in Boeotia. Though summarily modeled, they have vivacity and style.

Fifth-century terra-cotta statuettes continued the types prevalent in the preceding times, especially of seated and standing women, but with more freedom in the rendering of features and drapery. They are not as common as in the preceding or succeeding periods, but some are worthy products of their epoch and show the repose and serenity of the contemporary marble sculptures. A common type of the first half of the 5th century is a female mask or bust, generally hollow at the back, which is found both in central Greece and Rhodes.

From the late 4th century B.C. the types are more numerous. They represent no longer always divinities or votaries, but mostly the people of their time. Women are particularly popular. They are shown in graceful poses—standing, leaning against a pillar, walking or sitting, doing their hair, carrying a child or playing games. Comparatively few young men or children or animals appear, but an old nurse with a child in her arms, or a teacher with his pupil and particularly actors in their characteristic outfit are not uncommon. Since many of such statuettes were first found at Tanagra, in Boeotia, during the 1880s, they are still commonly called Tanagra figurines, though similar examples later came to light in other parts of Greece.

In the Hellenistic period the centres of manufacture in terra-cotta statuettes, as well as in marble and bronze sculpture, shifted from Greece proper to Asia Minor. In the little town of Myrina extensive discoveries were made in 1880–82 and other sites later yielded rich harvests. The new spirit of Hellenistic art is reflected in these statuettes. Instead of the quiet, gentle women, youths and children prevalent during the preceding periods, there are people in lively attitudes with draperies rendered in multiple folds going in different directions. Mythological subjects, especially flying Victory and Eros, as well as caricatures occur. Many Hellenistic terra-cotta statuettes from Italy and Sicily formed part of the grandiose vases then prevalent; *e.g.,* the Canosa and Centuripe wares. Those from Egypt are naturally influenced by the beliefs there current, representations of Horus, Bes and an orientalized Aphrodite being popular.

The same Hellenistic types continue throughout the Roman age, as extensive discoveries at Pompeii and throughout the Roman empire, including Gaul, Belgium and Britain, indicate. The Roman terra cottas from Egypt again stand apart, being of brown, local terra cotta and representing Egyptian deities in a Greco-Egyptian style. Of special interest are the large statuettes that reproduce famous sculptural works, *e.g.,* Polyclitus' "Diadumenus," found in Asia Minor and elsewhere.

*Technique.*—The technique of terra-cotta statuettes is of course different from that of statues. They are made of well-levigated clay and molded; comparatively few are modeled by hand. A mold was first made and baked to considerable hardness; moist clay was then pressed into it, of the thickness required, and allowed to dry; the resultant shrinkage made it easily removable from the mold. The back was made in another piece, sometimes summarily by hand, with a venthole for evaporation. Often heads and arms were

Mexican statue of the god Xipe Totec dressed in human skin, from Coatlinchan, Valley of Mexico; Mazapan culture, A.D. 1400–1500

Ancient Chinese tomb sculpture; Wei dynasty, 6th century A.D. *Left,* seated dancing girl of buff clay with traces of polychromy; *right,* dancing girl of unglazed clay

Lydian revetment of painted terra cotta from Sardis; 6th century B.C.

Peruvian portrait vase decorated with the head of a bat

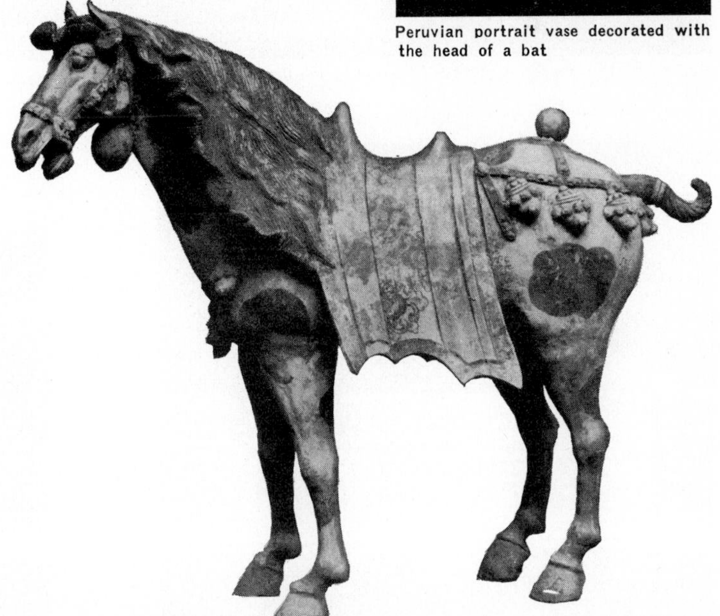

Chinese sepulchral figurine of a horse; T'ang dynasty, A.D. 618–906. Funerary pottery is the only remaining evidence of the advanced techniques of T'ang craftsmen

Cretan painted terra-cotta statuette of a woman in a swing; Middle Minoan period, 1600 B.C.

ANCIENT AMERICAN, ASIAN AND MEDITERRANEAN TERRA COTTA

BY COURTESY OF (TOP LEFT, CENTRE RIGHT) THE AMERICAN MUSEUM OF NATURAL HISTORY, (OTHERS) THE METROPOLITAN MUSEUM OF ART, FROM (TOP CENTRE AND RIGHT) FLETCHER FUND, 1928, (BOTTOM RIGHT) ROGERS FUND, 1925, AND (CENTRE) GIFT OF V. EVERIT MACY, 1911

# TERRA COTTA

Cretan painted terra-cotta vases exemplifying the informal floral and marine designs characteristic of Middle and Late Minoan ceramic art; 1600–1500 B.C.

Etruscan painted terra-cotta head of a statue of Hermes from Veii; *c.* 500 B.C.

Relief depicting the Greek myth of Bellerophon and the Chimera; found on the island of Melos, 5th century B.C.

Etruscan head of the statue of Apollo from Veii; late 6th century B.C.

Etruscan urn with a statue of a reclining woman on the lid and a battle scene on the front; 3rd–2nd century B.C.

Etruscan funerary statues of a husband and wife on lid of sarcophagus from Caere (Cerveteri); dating from 500 B.C.

## ETRUSCAN AND MEDITERRANEAN TERRA COTTA

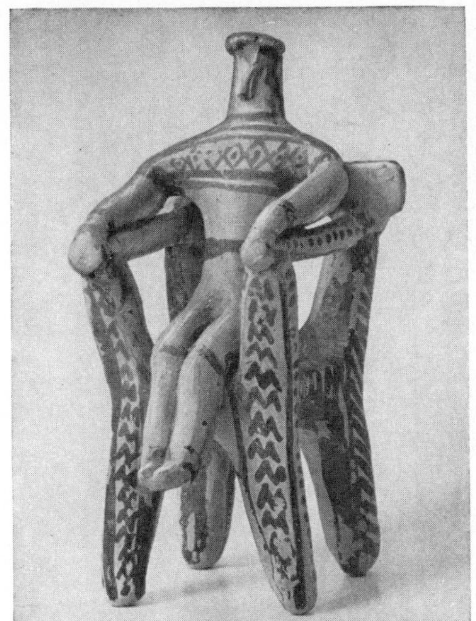

Seated Greek terra-cotta statuettes showing evolution in style: *left,* painted male figure seated in an armchair, 8th century B.C.; *centre,* seated goddess, Archaic period, 6th century B.C.; *right,* female Tanagra figurine seated in a chair, 4th–3rd century B.C.

Roman mural relief depicting the myth of Oenomaüs and his unfaithful charioteer, Myrtilus; Augustan period, 27 B.C.–A.D. 14

Greek terra-cotta head of a statue of Zeus from Olympia; early 5th century B.C.

Greek head of a kore broken from a statue; Archaic period, 6th century B.C.

Greek statuette of a flying Victory; Hellenistic period, Asia Minor type, 3rd–2nd century B.C.

## GREEK AND ROMAN TERRA COTTA

BY COURTESY OF (BOTTOM LEFT) THE MUSEUM OLYMPIA, (OTHERS) THE METROPOLITAN MUSEUM OF ART, FROM (TOP LEFT) FLETCHER FUND, 1931, (CENTRE LEFT) FLETCHER FUND, 1926, (TOP CENTRE) ROGERS FUND, 1906, (BOTTOM CENTRE) ROGERS FUND, 1947, (RIGHT) ROGERS FUND, 1906, 1909, AND (TOP RIGHT) GIFT OF J. PIERPONT MORGAN, 1917

# TERRA COTTA

**TERRA-COTTA SCULPTURE, 14TH–20TH CENTURIES**

*Top left:* "Madonna and Child," statuette in glazed terra cotta by Donatello (*c.* 1386–1466), Italian

*Top right:* "Nativity Group," glazed terra-cotta figurines by Antonio Rossellino (1427–*c.* 1479), Italian

*Right:* "Kneeling Angel," by Giovanni Lorenzo Bernini (1598–1680), Italian

*Bottom left:* "Seated Figure," terra-cotta figurine by Aristide Maillol (1861–1944), French

*Bottom centre:* "Female Satyr Carrying Two Putti," terra-cotta statuette by Claude Michel (Clodion) (1738–1814), French

*Bottom right:* "Song of the Vowels," by Jacques Lipchitz (1891– ), Latvian-French

BY COURTESY OF (TOP LEFT, TOP RIGHT) THE METROPOLITAN MUSEUM OF ART, NEW YORK, (RIGHT) THE FOGG ART MUSEUM, HARVARD UNIVERSITY, (BOTTOM LEFT) THE MUSEUM OF MODERN ART, NEW YORK, GIFT OF MRS. SAIDIE A. MAY, (BOTTOM CENTRE) THE WALTERS ART GALLERY, BALTIMORE, (BOTTOM RIGHT) THE MUSEUM OF MODERN ART, NEW YORK, GIFT OF THE SCULPTOR; PHOTOGRAPHS, (BOTTOM LEFT, BOTTOM RIGHT) SOICHI SUNAMI also made separately, in different molds and variously combined, so that in spite of a limited number of molds there is great diversity. In the words of E. Pottier, "there are many sisters, but few twins." An engobe or slip of white clay was added (while the clay was still leather hard) and when bone dry the figures were fired to a moderate heat. Finally colours were added in tempera—blue, red, pink, yellow, brown, violet and rarely green for the garments, brownish for the skin of men and boys, pink for the cheeks of women, auburn for hair, red for lips and brown or blue for eyes. Gilt sometimes occurs for details, such as jewelry, or as an all-over covering; also sometimes black. Few figures now retain their original colours; in most only the drab terra cotta remains.

After the extensive discoveries at Tanagra had come to a stop toward the end of the 19th century, the popular demand for the charming figurines naturally persisted and as a result many forgeries were made which found ready acceptance with the public. Among them are mythological groups and single figures in affected attitudes that can easily be distinguished from the Greek originals. Sometimes, however, the figures were made from molds taken from ancient statuettes, and then only the somewhat blurred surface, or the addition of inappropriate details or mistakes in the application of the colours betray the hand of the forger.

**Reliefs.**—In addition to terra-cotta statues and statuettes, reliefs played a large part in Greek, Etruscan and Roman art. They served as decorations of temples and other buildings, especially in those countries where a wood and clay construction instead of stone was in use. Many examples of all periods have come to light in Italy and Asia Minor, mostly of the Archaic and Hellenistic periods, some of the 5th and 4th centuries B.C. They are decorated with floral designs, preferably palmettes, scrolls, rosettes, meanders and spirals, combined in effective patterns, or they have figured representations, such as chariot races or banquets or mythological subjects. Revetments of this kind have been found at Larisa (Larissa) in Asia Minor, Sardis in Lydia, southern Italy and throughout etruscanized central Italy. Many simas and antefixes have decorative features in relief consisting of lions' masks, female heads and other motives.

Besides architectural reliefs, votive ones are common. Two classes call for special mention—the Tarentine and the Locrian. At Tarentum many examples have been found which range from Archaic to Hellenistic times and apparently served as votive offerings to nether deities. They represent local divinities and heroes and are made in local clay in a broad, smooth style. Dionysus and his cycle were especially popular. The Locrian reliefs are generally small and meticulously executed. Again local cults dictated the subjects. The majority were offerings to Persephone and relate to the cult of the dead. They, too, were a local product, made of local clay. The period of production was relatively short; almost all extant examples belong to the first half of the 5th century B.C.

The Melian reliefs, so called because many have been found in the island of Melos, were apparently not votive but served for the decorations of chests. They are often of fine quality and may be assigned to the second quarter and the middle of the 5th century. Mythological subjects predominate, but scenes from daily life also occur. There were of course many other uses for terra-cotta reliefs. They served as decorations of small altars and of all sorts of utensils, and even of furniture. The Etruscan urns of the 3rd and 2nd centuries above mentioned generally have reliefs on their sides depicting scenes from Greek mythology, such as the combat of Eteocles and Polyneices, in Hellenistic Greek style. Applied reliefs appear on vases from Centuripe and other Hellenistic wares. Necklaces and other jewelry were sometimes made in terra cotta and gilded, chiefly for sepulchral use.

The Romans used terra-cotta reliefs on both the interior and exterior of buildings. Cicero speaks of fixing such reliefs (*typoi*) on the corner of his little atrium. Circular holes served for fastening them by means of plugs to the walls. The subjects are mostly mythological. Dionysus and his satyrs and maenads are especially popular. Occasionally Roman subjects occur. Lamps were generally made of terra cotta in antiquity and the Roman ones are regularly decorated with reliefs on their upper surface.

*Technique.*—The majority of these reliefs—Greek, Etruscan and Roman—were made in molds, and there are many repeats. Sometimes a mold was taken from an existing relief and was then naturally smaller in size because of the two successive shrinkages. Like the statues and statuettes these reliefs were all gaily coloured, but much of the polychromy has disappeared.

**Use in Buildings.**—Lastly, terra cotta served purely utilitarian purposes, especially on the roofs of buildings. Roof tiles—both flat ones and curved, covering ones—were often made of terra cotta; also the covering slabs along the raking cornice of the pediment, the cornice itself, the gutters and parts of the pediment. Many such plain terra-cotta slabs have been found in ancient sanctuaries that had terra-cotta roofs and revetments. Sometimes terra-cotta slabs were decorated with paintings. From a temple of the 7th century B.C. at Thermon in Acarnania slabs that served as metopes have been preserved, some with their painted decoration still visible. At Klazomenai terra-cotta sarcophagi of the Archaic Greek period with painted scenes have come to light, and terra-cotta slabs with painted decoration have been found lining walls of Etruscan tombs. Bricks in wall construction were much used; they were not always fired, but merely sun-dried.

**Collections.**—The most representative collections of Greek terra cottas are in the British museum, the Louvre and the museums of Berlin, Naples, Paestum, Syracuse, Athens, Olympia, Boston and New York. The Etruscan ones may best be studied in the museums of Florence, Perugia, the Villa Giulia museum in Rome, the British museum, the Ny-Carlsberg Glyptotek in Copenhagen and the Metropolitan museum in New York. Most of the Roman examples are in Rome, Naples, Pompeii and in the provincial museums of France, England and Germany. (G. M. A. R.)

## MODERN EUROPE

Neither for architectural decoration nor for free sculpture was terra cotta a frequently used medium between the end of the Roman empire and the 14th century, although the simple technical procedures were kept alive in the making of pottery. By the 15th century, however, a notable revival was in full progress particularly in Italy but also in Germany. Terra cotta was then used in architecture in two distinctive ways. For brick architecture terra cotta, similar in colour and substance to the building material, formed the ideal decorative element and, molded or carved, served in its natural colour for elaborate friezes, window and door moldings and inset medallions. The church of St. Catherine, Brandenburg, is a highly decorated example of the German usage. In Italy fine examples are to be found throughout the north; indicative of the variety are the upper windows of the Municipal palace at Piacenza (begun 1281), the buildings of Biagio Rossetti (14?–1516) in Ferrara and the Ospedale Maggiore (after 1456) in Milan. For contrast terra cotta was sometimes combined effectively with stucco or stone as in the apse of Santa Maria delle Grazie in Milan.

The second new use of terra cotta was in that of the highly glazed and coloured sculpture introduced in Florence early in the 15th century by the Della Robbias (*q.v.*). This work could be used more effectively in combination with marble and stone than could unglazed ornament, and it added a freshness of accent quite unparalleled. The effect was imitated both in France and Spain and the use of terra cotta, glazed and unglazed, spread throughout Europe. As a novelty Francis I had the entire façade of the little château of Madrid, which once stood in the Bois de Boulogne, richly decorated with enameled terra cotta by Girolamo della Robbia. But by the end of the 16th century terra cotta had once more fallen from popularity for architectural decoration, not to become a significant material again until the 19th century.

Free sculpture in terra cotta, too, found its revival in 15th-century Italy. Jacopo della Quercia, Donatello, Verrocchio and almost every other prominent sculptor left works in the material. Of particular interest, aside from the work of the Della Robbias, are the lifelike, coloured figure groups in Modena by Guido Mazzoni (1450–1518), who worked also in France, and the more sophisticated compositions of Antonio Begarelli (1498?–1565) in the same city. Sometimes terra-cotta sculpture was painted in natural colours, sometimes in imitation of marble or bronze, but despite this and the skilful complexity of modeling, the characteristics of form identifiable with terra cotta are usually evident.

Aside from the completed works in terra cotta, not many in number, remaining from the 17th century, there exist many figures intended, as were those of Bernini, as studies or models for work in marble. Many of the 17th- and 18th-century portrait busts in terra cotta also were used for this purpose, but they are made striking by a faithfulness in the rendering of personal characteristics less frequently found in other media and exhibit a quality of immediacy not transferable to the sterner material. Among the most descriptive are the busts created in France during the 18th century by such sculptors as Jean Baptiste Lemoyne, Jean Jacques Caffiéri and Jean Antoine Houdon.

It was also during the 18th century in France that small, freely modeled allegorical and mythological groups in fine terra cotta, less delicate than the contemporary porcelains but more robust in form and action, were produced in large numbers at Sèvres and met with great popular favour. Foremost among the creators of these fantasies was Claude Michel, called Clodion (1738–1814). Portrait statuettes of historical figures and famous contemporaries were also produced in profusion toward the end of the century but seem to have had a less universal appeal. The factories at Sèvres, closed during the French Revolution, were reopened under Napoleon but produced little more terra cotta.

**19th and 20th Centuries.**—While terra cotta was used by sculptors in the 19th century, especially by those working usually in bronze, it had little character of its own. When used commercially to reproduce figures for the popular market it was regularly disguised. Not until the early years of the 20th century, when the artist, taking a fresh interest in the properties of his medium, began to choose materials in which he could work directly, did it again assume positive character in art. Its use was linked to the revived interest in pottery, and many artists experimented with mixtures and glazes to produce effects of colour and texture. In architecture it was first revived by architects such as Karl Friedrich Schinkel (1781–1841), who became interested in earlier design in brick, and it served various historical styles and structural purposes throughout the century. The Architecture academy (1832–35) in Berlin by Schinkel and the Natural History museum (1873–80) at South Kensington, London, by Alfred Waterhouse are two very different examples. But the concern of modern architects and sculptors for the structural and aesthetic properties of their material has gained for terra cotta, along with other mediums, a new place in architectural ornament free from past usages and styles. (J. C. T.)

*See* also references under "Terra Cotta" in the Index.

Bibliography.—*Statues:* W. Deonna, *Les Statues de terre cuite dans l'antiquité* (1906); G. Q. Giglioli, *L'Arte Etrusca* (1935); G. M. A. Richter and C. F. Binns, "Etruscan Terracotta Warriors in the Museum," *The Metropolitan Museum of Art Papers,* no. 6 (1937); E. Kunze, *Neue Meisterwerke griechischer Kunst aus Olympia* (1948); M. Santangelo, "Veio, Sanctuario di Apollo, Scavi fra il 1944 e il 1949," *Bollettino d'Arte,* pp. 147 ff. (1952). *Statuettes:* E. Pottier and S. Reinach, *La nécropole de Myrina* (1887); F. Winter, *Die Typen der figürlichen Terracotten* (1903); D. Burr, *Terracottas From Myrina in the Museum of Fine Arts, Boston* (1934); G. Kleiner, "Tanagrafiguren, Untersuchungen zur hellenistischen Kunst und Geschichte," *15tes Ergänzungsheft des Jahrbuchs des Deutschen Archäologischen Instituts* (1942); T. B. L. Webster, *Greek Terracottas* (1950). *Reliefs:* E. D. van Buren, *Figurative Terra-cotta Revetments in Etruria and Latium* (1921), *Archaic Fictile Revetments in Sicily and Magna Graecia* (1923), *Greek Fictile Revetments in the Archaic Period* (1926); H. von Rhoden, *Die Terracotten von Pompeji* (1880); H. von Rhoden and H. Winnefeld, *Architektonische römische Tonreliefs der Kaiserzeit* (1911); L. Kjellberg, *Larisa am Hermos,* ii, *Die architektonischen Terrakotten* (1902–1934); T. L. Shear "The Architectural Terracottas," *Sardis,* xi (1926); P. Jacobsthal, *Die Melischen Reliefs* (1931); P. Wuilleumier, *Tarente* (1939). *Catalogues, etc., comprising all three categories:* A. Levi, *Le terrecotte figurate del Museo Nazionale di Napoli* (1926); Heidenreich, "Terrakotten," in Pauly-Wissowa, *Real-Encyclopädie der classischen Altertumswissenschaft,* 2nd series, ix, col. 808–820 (1934); H. Goldman (ed.), *Excavations at Gözlü Kule, Tarsus,* i (1950); R. A. Higgins, *Catalogue of Terracottas in the British Museum,* vol. i (from 730 to 330 B.C.) (1954). (G. M. A. R.)

**TERRARIUM,** a transparent container, of glass or plastic panels or sides, with an adjustable lid, in which plants are grown usually in a naturalistic arrangement. It is actually a miniature greenhouse providing conditions of soil moisture, humidity, warmth, and light required for the successful growth and cultivation of small plants.

Terrariums, also called Wardian cases, bottle gardens, glass gardens, and crystal gardens, are available in a wide variety of shapes and sizes; any suitable container can be used: an aquarium tank, candy jar, fish bowl, bottle, or homemade enclosure. When both plants and small animals are maintained together in such containers, the resulting microcosm is usually called a vivarium. Fernery, desertarium, and other terms are descriptive of the main type of plant life of a terrarium.

**History and Uses.**—The idea of raising plants in portable glass containers first occurred to early collectors who constructed crude glass-paneled boxes to carry exotic plants over long distances. Credit for perfecting the terrarium is usually given to Nathaniel B. Ward, an English botanist. His Wardian case, a popular feature in fashionable Victorian houses, was the precursor of the modern terrarium.

Terrariums can be both decorative and instructive. In modern heated apartments and houses, terrariums afford a degree of humidity, which can be fairly consistently maintained, required by many small tropical foliage plants, woodland plants, and orchids. Artistically designed terrariums are often displayed at flower shows, in classrooms, and in offices. Florists have spurred interest in glass gardening and often offer for sale established terrariums. A carefully planned and properly maintained terrarium or vivarium is an attractive way of illustrating the natural history of certain organisms and affords a controlled means of scientific observation and plant propagation.

**Preparation and Care.**—Woodland and jungle plants are easiest to maintain in the terrarium because of the constant humidity in the receptacle. Cacti and the other succulents can also be easily maintained if given slightly different conditions.

The most popular container is the rectangular aquarium, since the large opening permits the free use of both hands in arranging and planting a miniature woodland or desert. Next in favour is the drum-shaped aquarium, which, owing to the much smaller opening, requires some measure of patience and dexterous manipulation to create a picturesque effect.

Proper drainage is of utmost importance in the growing of plants in the terrarium, particularly for desert plants. This can be established by the use of porous soil and a bed of gravel or sand at the bottom of the container to the thickness of at least an inch. The incorporation of powdered or granulated charcoal in the soil is beneficial in preventing sourness or acidification. Since soil does not show attractively through the glass, it is recommended to line the walls with sphagnum or other woodland moss, face down, to the depth of the intended soil level, so that a green mat is presented to the outside.

The best soil for glass gardens is a mixture of sand, well-rotted leaf mold, and regular garden loam. The soil should be packed against the mossy lining and the objects placed in position, more soil being applied as the work progresses. Generally, soil in the terrarium should not exceed three inches in depth; of course this will depend materially on the size and shape of the container.

Plants should not be crowded together, as they will soon spread out and quickly spoil the naturalistic effect desired; it is better to use plants that grow slowly. If a desert garden is decided upon, suitable dwarf cacti should be chosen. Such a garden will give pleasure for many years if properly cared for. Other succulents adaptable to a desertarium are the small, rosette-forming *Haworthias,* seedling *Gasterias, Aloes,* stapelias (which look very "cactusy" despite their thornless appearance), and euphorbias. The sprawly *Kalanchoes* and *Bryophyllums* are less desirable and tend to become "leggy" and push their way up to the opening; they are not recommended unless they can be kept small by frequent pruning or pinching back the tips. Most temperate zone woodland plants, including tiny ferns, lichens, mosses, partridgeberry, native violets, holly, dwarf English ivy, and seedling evergreens do best in a cool room or sun porch (not in direct sunlight). For a warm room it is better to choose tropical plants such as African violet, small-leaved begonias, crotons, peperomia, selaginella (a mosslike creeper), dwarf palms, bromelias, and seedling aroids like philodendrons and Chinese evergreens (*Aglaonema*).

When all the plants have been pressed into the soil, fine gravel or broken bits of rock should be sprinkled over the soil surface in desertariums and fir bark or wood chips in woodland terrariums. Such soil covers guard against any rot diseases that might creep in unexpectedly and at the same time prevent the soil from splattering over the plants and against glass sides when water is applied. Rocks, accessories, or novelty objects are often used to complete a picturesque scene, but care should be taken to avoid cluttering up the terrarium with meaningless and space-consuming bric-a-brac.

Particles of soil or gravel adhering to the plants should be removed with a small brush. In the woodland or jungle garden, water can be applied immediately after the terrarium has been planted to settle the soil and keep the roots moist; however, in the desert garden, water should be withheld for a few days so that any delicate root systems that have been injured or bruised in transplanting would be sufficiently healed. Thereafter, water need only be given in sparing quantities. During the summer months occasional "sweating" (allowing moisture to condense on the glass) will prove highly beneficial to desert plants, and for other plants the sweating process can be encouraged regularly throughout the year. Often the sweat bath will suffice as the only means of supplying moisture to the plants. The sweating process requires the placing of a piece of glass or lid over the opening of the terrarium and leaving it closed for several hours until condensation takes place.

Light and fresh air are two important factors in the successful management of terrariums. The woodland case will require less direct light and therefore can be placed in more sheltered places within the home, but a desertarium demands as much light as possible.

Ventilation can be regulated by adjusting the cover over the opening. Except when the sweating process is desired, the lid should be placed to allow about an inch or two of space for air to pass freely. If the terrarium always shows too much condensation and there is possibility of rot or fungus damage, the cover should be removed to permit the soil to dry out considerably. Terrariums require very little care when once established and should last for a number of years. Occasionally a plant may be lost and require replacement.

Glass gardening is one of the most fascinating hobbies that can be indulged by both adults and children. It is a worthwhile project for shut-ins, for children interested in nature subjects, and for the homemaker who wishes to ornament the home with a bit of the outdoors.

*See* M. Gilbert, *Starting a Terrarium* (1961). (L. Cu.)

**TERRE HAUTE,** a city of western Indiana, U.S., on the Wabash river, 73 mi. W.S.W. of Indianapolis, is the seat of Vigo county and one of the oldest cities in the state. The site was once a point of rendezvous for Indian tribes; nearby Fort Harrison was the scene of a battle between forces of Capt. Zachary Taylor and Tecumseh in 1812.

Terre Haute is on a plateau 50 ft. above the river, and the French name, meaning "high ground," was adopted by members of a small land company who platted the town in 1816. It became a key point on the National road (1835), the Wabash and Erie canal (1849) and the Richmond railroad (1852). When it was incorporated as a town in 1832 Terre Haute had a population of less than 1,000; by 1853, when it was chartered as a city, the population was almost 7,000.

The discovery of bituminous coal and other minerals paved the way for industrial development; by 1875 Terre Haute was one of the chief manufacturing centres in the midwest, producing steel and other commodities from resources available in the immediate area. Through World War I expansion of the city continued at a phenomenal rate.

After 1920 the rate of growth slowed, but Terre Haute's industrial output of chemicals, pharmaceuticals, plastics, clay and foundry materials, glass, clothing, foodstuffs and other products places it as one of the principal manufacturing cities of the state. Pop. (1960) 72,500; standard metropolitan statistical area (SMSA; Vigo county) 108,458. In 1963 Clay, Sullivan and Vermillion counties were added to the SMSA, increasing its area from 415 to 1,499 sq.mi. and the population (1960 figures) to 172,069. (For comparative population figures *see* table in INDIANA: *Population.*)

Located in or near Terre Haute are: St. Mary-of-the-Woods, a Roman Catholic college for women organized in 1840; Indiana State Teachers college, established in 1870 as a normal school; and Rose Polytechnic institute, for men, founded in 1874 and named for Chauncey Rose, a local entrepreneur.

The city is the birthplace of Eugene V. Debs, labour and Socialist leader; the author Theodore Dreiser and his brother, the composer Paul Dresser (who changed the spelling of the family surname), were born nearby. Four miles from the city is a federal penitentiary. (V. M. B.)

**TERRISS, WILLIAM** (WILLIAM CHARLES JAMES LEWIN) (1847–1897), a leading English actor of later Victorian days, was born in London on Feb. 20, 1847. After trying the merchant navy, sheep farming in the Falkland Islands and horse breeding in Kentucky, he went on the stage. He was immediately successful and appeared at the principal London theatres from 1868 until his death.

Terriss joined Henry Irving at the Lyceum theatre in 1880, playing such parts as Cassio, Mercutio and Henry VIII. He then became the leading man at the Adelphi theatre, where, as the hero of melodramas he became the idol of the public, his fine voice and appearance and breezy manner making a great appeal. His last appearance was made at the Adelphi in *Secret Service* under tragic circumstances. He was stabbed to death by a madman, Richard Prince, while entering the theatre on Dec. 16, 1897.

Terriss married Isabel Lewis, and their daughter Ellaline Terriss became a great popular favourite in both straight and musical plays, appearing with her husband, Sir Seymour Hicks. She was leading lady at the Gaiety, the Vaudeville, the Globe (then the Hicks), the Aldwych and many other London theatres, and also toured much of the world with great success.

*See* A. J. Smythe, *The Life of William Terriss* (1898). (W. J. M.-P.)

**TERRITORIAL SYSTEM (U.S.)** From its inception as a nation, the United States has had land areas designated as territories, including western continental lands in the early years and overseas dependencies and trusteeships in more recent times. The federal Constitution in 1787 delegated to Congress the responsibility of establishing territorial governments and since that time four general types have developed: (1) organized or incorporated territories; (2) unorganized or unincorporated territories; (3) dependencies; and (4) trusteeships.

**Organized Territories.**—The pattern for organized territories was first established by the Ordinance of 1787, better known as the Northwest Ordinance. This act, perhaps the most important law enacted under the Articles of Confederation, instituted a plan of government for the region north of the Ohio River from Pennsylvania to the Mississippi River. This important ordinance, the model for the creation of other territorial governments, guaranteed basic civil and political rights in the territories. It also provided a three-stage plan by which all the territories could advance from the status of unorganized territory to organized territory to eventual statehood. By 1912 all contiguous territories had qualified for statehood.

The problem of territorial government became more involved with the purchase of Alaska in 1867, the annexation of Hawaii and the gaining of the Philippines, Guam, and Puerto Rico as an aftermath of the Spanish-American War in 1898, the purchase of the Virgin Islands in 1917, and the annexation of other small islands. The idea that all territories should eventually become states was discarded in favour of the view that some dependencies should retain a subordinate position.

The Supreme Court of the United States in the 1901 Insular Cases made a distinction between incorporated and unincorporated territories and held that Congress was restricted in its legislation regarding incorporated territories by constitutional limitations while unincorporated territories were only partially protected by the constitution. With the admission of Alaska and Hawaii as the 49th and 50th U.S. states in 1959, the last of the existing organized territories disappeared.

**Unorganized Territories.**—The unorganized or unincorporated territories, under the jurisdiction of the Department of the Interior, had varying degrees of local self-government ranging from some autonomy to commonwealth status. By the 1960s all unincorporated territories had considerable voice in local matters. American Samoa was the only unincorporated territory whose residents were not granted U.S. citizenship. Its residents were still classed as nationals. Samoa had a locally elected legislature with a governor and a secretary appointed by the Department of the Interior.

The residents of Guam and the Virgin Islands were U.S. citizens and had control of legislative and judicial affairs, but their governors were appointed by the president of the United States. The policy of promoting self-government for these territories was furthered by filling territorial civil offices with native-born residents whenever practicable.

Both the Philippine Islands and Puerto Rico emerged from an unincorporated status to that of commonwealth status, and the Philippines gained complete independence in 1946. From the beginning of civil government in the Philippines the question of eventual independence had been raised and the way was prepared in 1935 with the creation of the Philippine Commonwealth. As a commonwealth, the Philippines had control of its domestic affairs but not of its foreign relations.

The residents of Puerto Rico were granted United States citizenship in 1917. By an act of Congress in 1952 the island became a self-governing commonwealth "closely associated with the United States," which remained responsible for the island's foreign affairs.

**Dependencies.**—Following World War II, the Pacific island dependencies, Midway, Wake, and several smaller ones, remained under the jurisdiction of the Navy Department and were not self-governing. The Panama Canal Zone was under the control of the Department of the Army, which appointed the governor who administered the civil government and headed the Panama Canal Company.

**Trust Territories.**—The Pacific island groups, the Carolines, the Marshalls, and the Marianas, all of which had been Japanese mandates under the League of Nations, were placed under the jurisdiction of the United States as Trust Territories by the United Nations in 1947.

The Marianas, with the exception of Rota, were administered by the Navy Department. The Carolines and the Marshalls and the island of Rota became the responsibility of the Department of the Interior. They were governed by a high commissioner who was responsible for their economic and social development and for their training in self-government. (H. B. Me.)

**TERRY, DAME ELLEN** (1847–1928), English actress, became most celebrated during her long partnership (1878–1902) with Sir Henry Irving (*see* Irving). Although trained in the traditional techniques of the English theatre by her parents, provincial "strolling players" at the time of her birth, she was essentially a personality actress whose beauty, charm, vivacity, and immediate, sincere command of sentiment and pathos on the stage endeared her to audiences both in Britain and in North America. Although she survived Irving by more than 20 years, and her career became desultory after his death, she never lost her hold on the public imagination and continued to be loved and admired, more for herself than for her relatively infrequent performances.

Ellen Terry was born in Coventry, Warwickshire, on Feb. 27, 1847. (The records there show her name as "Alice Ellen Terry." All her life she believed the year of her birth to have been 1848, and she so gives it in her memoirs.) The second surviving daughter in a large family of which several were to become well known on the stage—among them Kate (1844–1924), Marion (1852–1930), Florence (Floss; 1854–96), and Fred (1863–1933)—she had no formal schooling, but, like Kate, rapidly developed into a celebrated child (later, adolescent) actress. She made her debut at the age of nine in the child's part of Mamillius in *The Winter's Tale,* which Charles Kean, son of Edmund Kean (*q.v.*), produced in London in April 1856; she remained in Kean's company until 1859; later, along with Kate, she joined the stock company playing at the Theatre Royal, Bristol, where she played leading parts in Shakespeare and in stock.

In 1864, aged 16, she left the stage to marry the painter G. F. Watts (*q.v.*), to whom she had sat as model. Watts was a melancholic man almost three times her age; although he made many fine portraits and sketches of her, the marriage survived a bare ten months. His patroness, Mrs. Thoby Prinsep, was determined that Ellen should go. In her despair, she could scarcely be induced to return to the stage, but eventually did so, though playing with little of her former distinction. It was in 1867 that she first appeared, by chance, with Irving, playing Katherine to his Petruchio in Garrick's version of *The Taming of the Shrew.*

ELLEN TERRY, ABOUT 1878

The following year she left the stage abruptly to live for six years in Hertfordshire with the architect and theatrical designer Edward Godwin (1833–86), whom she had met in Bristol, and who became the father of her children, Edith (1869–1947) and Edward Gordon Craig (1872–1966; *q.v.*). When her association with Godwin began to fail, it was the author, dramatist, and producer Charles Reade who found her and brought her back to the stage. She returned reluctantly, to earn money to keep her children and to help her lover, and as Portia showed new maturity in the Bancrofts' striking production of *The Merchant of Venice* (1875), designed by Godwin. On parting from Godwin (who married in 1876), she became responsible for maintaining their children. Before joining Irving at the Lyceum in 1878, she completed a successful season with John Hare, actor-manager at the Court Theatre. In 1876 she received a divorce from Watts and married an undistinguished actor, Charles Kelly, mainly to give her children a "name." They soon separated; and Kelly died in 1885.

When she joined Irving, Ellen Terry was 31 and Irving 40. She was now for the first time to work in close association with a man of genius whose life and resources were to be dedicated to the theatre, and who was to make the Lyceum a centre for new, striking interpretations of Shakespeare in particular. His approach to sponsorship of new plays was that of a great stage visualizer and star actor who required a scenarist (such as his favourite, the facile dramatist and adapter W. G. Wills, 1828–91) to assemble a script that would give him a framework for compelling performance and spectacular stage effects. As part of his *mise-en-scène* he needed a beautiful woman to lend her own glamour to his productions. Ellen Terry responded to his needs with selfless dedication, playing many great Shakespearean parts—Portia (1879), Juliet and Beatrice (1882), Lady Macbeth (1888), Queen Katharine (1892), Imogen (1896), Volumnia (1901), Ophelia (1878), Desdemona (1881), and Cordelia (1892). She willingly undertook such humble roles as Rosamund in Tennyson's *Becket* (1893), in which all the limelight shone upon the master.

Whether in London or on arduous provincial tours, in New York or on exhausting excursions across North America, Ellen Terry acted as Irving's leading lady until she had grown too old for most of the parts in his repertory. They severed their partnership only in 1902, three years before his death. Their relationship was as close in private as in public life, and it was only when his affection began to wane in the 1890s that she entered into her famous "paper courtship" with Bernard Shaw (*q.v.*). This correspondence is one of the most brilliant in the history of English letter writing. In 1907 she married the American actor

James Carew, some 30 years her junior; although they soon parted, he remained her friend.

It was in comedy and in plays of tender sentiment, as well as in Shakespeare, that Ellen Terry shone. She wept real tears as the Queen in Wills's *Charles I* (1879) and as Margaret in his *Faust* (1885); and laughed real, gay laughter as the washerwoman in *Madame Sans-Gêne* (1897). When she left Irving it was to play Mrs. Page with Beerbohm Tree and Mrs. (Madge) Kendal, in *The Merry Wives of Windsor* (1902); and Shaw eventually persuaded her to appear as Lady Cecily Waynflete in *Captain Brassbound's Conversion* (1905), one of several parts he wrote with her in mind. When she celebrated her golden jubilee in 1906 at the Theatre Royal, Drury Lane, all the theatrical personalities of the day shared the stage with her.

In her later years, although reasonably well endowed (Irving had paid her £200 a working week for most of 20 years), she still had to earn her living. She worked spasmodically in the theatre (last appearing on stage in 1925, in Walter de la Mare's *Crossings*); in films; and as a Shakespearean lecturer-recitalist, reinterpreting her successes on tours in the U.S., Britain, and Australia. Her warm, generous personality made her a favourite wherever she went, but eyesight and memory began to fail. Belatedly, in 1925, she was made a Dame Grand Cross of the British Empire. She died on July 21, 1928, at her cottage, Smallhythe, Kent, which became the Ellen Terry Memorial Museum and in 1939 was given to the National Trust by her daughter Edith Craig.

BIBLIOGRAPHY: *See* her *The Story of My Life* (1908; as *Ellen Terry's Memoirs,* with preface, notes, and additional biographical chapter by E. Craig and C. St. John, 1932); also her *Four Lectures on Shakespeare* (1932). The correspondence with Shaw was edited by C. St. John (1931; 2nd ed. as *Ellen Terry and Bernard Shaw: a Correspondence,* 1949). *See* also Edward Gordon Craig, *Ellen Terry and her Secret Self* (1931); Roger Manvell, *Ellen Terry* (1968).

(R. MA.)

**TERTIARIES,** associations of lay men and women in connection with the Roman Catholic mendicant (*q.v.*) orders. The institution of tertiaries arose out of the Franciscan movement. When the immediate disciples of St. Francis had become an order bound by the religious vows, it became necessary to provide for the great body of laity who could not leave the world but who desired to carry out in their lives the spirit and teaching of the Franciscan movement. St. Francis therefore drew up a rule for those of his followers who were debarred from being members of the order of Friars Minor. At first they were called Brothers and Sisters of the Order of Penance; later, when the friars were called the First Order and the nuns the Second Order, the Order of Penance became the Third Order of St. Francis—whence the name tertiaries. (*See* FRANCISCANS: *Third Order.*)

In time a tendency set in for members of the Third Order to live together in community, and in this way congregations were formed who took the usual religious vows and lived a fully organized religious life based on the rule of the Third Order with supplementary regulations. These congregations are the regular tertiaries as distinguished from the secular tertiaries, who live in the world, according to the original idea. There are many congregations of regular tertiaries, both men and women. In 1883 Leo XIII caused the rule to be recast and made more suitable for modern times. In 1957 Pius XII issued a general constitution for the Third Order of St. Francis which not only stressed the spiritual life of the tertiaries but also placed emphasis on the importance of apostolic works.

At an early date the other mendicant orders formed third orders on the same lines as the Franciscan, and so Dominican, Carmelite, Augustinian, Servite, and Premonstratensian tertiaries, together with a large number of others, began. (J. C. WE.)

**TERTIARY,** in geology, the time interval next after the Cretaceous period and before the Pleistocene. Currently it is considered as a period of the Cenozoic era (*q.v.*) as indicated on the accompanying geologic time chart, but in the past it has usually been given the rank of an era.

The name Tertiary (from the Latin *tertiarius,* "belonging to the third part") was first used and defined by Giovanni Arduino in the 18th century in a letter to Antonio Vallisnieri, professor in the University of Padua, Italy. Subsequently the term was used by G. Cuvier and A. Brongniart in 1801 for deposits in the Paris basin. The early geologists perceived that the much faulted and folded beds of rock bearing comparatively few fossils, which they observed in some localities, were much older than the largely undeformed and fairly abundantly fossilized beds found elsewhere. Therefore they classified the deformed rocks, the oldest that had been observed, as Primary; and the younger rocks that in places overlay the Primary as Secondary. A third group that overlay the Secondary sequence was distinguished, and this became the Tertiary. As indicated above, the Tertiary was ranked as an era until the most recent deposits, dating from the beginning of the Pleistocene epoch, or Ice age, and including much glacial till and unconsolidated alluvium, were distinguished as the Quaternary, and both were designated periods of the Cenozoic (recent-life) era. The Secondary rocks were assigned to the Mesozoic (middle-life) era and the Primary rocks to the Paleozoic (ancient-life) era; and the oldest rocks, those older than the Paleozoic, were designated as belonging to Precambrian time.

This article deals with the evolution of life and with geologic conditions during the Tertiary and discusses the history of the study of the period and its division into epochs and stages. For general information on the place of the Tertiary in geologic time *see* GEOLOGY: *Historical Geology.* For more detailed information about the epochs included in this period *see* PLIOCENE; MIOCENE; OLIGOCENE; EOCENE AND PALEOCENE.

*Geologic Time Chart*

| System and Period | Series and Epoch | Distinctive Records of Life | Began (Millions of Years Ago) |
|---|---|---|---|
| CENOZOIC ERA | | | |
| Quaternary | Recent (last 11,000 years) | | |
| | Pleistocene | Early man | 2+ |
| Tertiary | Pliocene | Large carnivores | 10 |
| | Miocene | Whales, apes, grazing forms | 27 |
| | Oligocene | Large browsing mammals | 38 |
| | Eocene | Rise of flowering plants | 55 |
| | Paleocene | First placental mammals | 65–70 |
| MESOZOIC ERA | | | |
| Cretaceous | | Extinction of dinosaurs | 130 |
| Jurassic | | Dinosaurs' zenith, primitive birds, first small mammals | 180 |
| Triassic | | Appearance of dinosaurs | 225 |
| PALEOZOIC ERA | | | |
| Permian | | Reptiles developed, conifers abundant | 260 |
| Carboniferous | | | |
| Upper (Pennsylvanian) | | First reptiles, coal forests | 300 |
| Lower (Mississippian) | | Sharks abundant | 340 |
| Devonian | | Amphibians appeared, fishes abundant | 405 |
| Silurian | | Earliest land plants and animals | 435 |
| Ordovician | | First primitive fishes | 480 |
| Cambrian | | Marine invertebrates | 550–570 |
| PRECAMBRIAN TIME | | | |
| | | Few fossils | more than 3,490 |

**Life in the Tertiary.**—Of the various organisms whose fossil remains are preserved in Tertiary rocks the mammals are most notable. During this period mammals evolved from small primitive creatures which survived the reign of dinosaurs to become the dominant vertebrates. The modifications which took place in various mammalian lines during Tertiary time are astounding, and as a result mammalian stages of evolution often provide the easiest means for world-wide correlation of Tertiary deposits.

The Paleocene was characterized by a variety of generally small primitive mammals only remotely related to modern types, but with the beginning of the Eocene many of the more modern stems appear. Concurrently, extinction of aberrant or unsuited phyla such as uintatheres, creodonts, titanotheres and oreodonts occurred at various times and many lines of development did not survive the Tertiary.

The diverse Tertiary fishes, both fresh water and marine, were already broadly differentiated by Cretaceous time, and subsequent development was little more than speciation. Of the various amphibians, only frogs, salamanders and the wormlike caecilians survive the period. Lizards, snakes, crocodiles and turtles are the few reptiles which survived the age of dinosaurs. Birds are sparsely represented but the known fossils show an early diversi-

TABLE I.—*Some Different Regional Standards and Suggested Correlations*

| European | |
|---|---|
| Epoch | Stage |
| PLIOCENE | Calabrian |
| | Astian |
| | Plaisancian |
| MIOCENE | Pontian |
| | Sarmatian |
| | Tortonian |
| | Helvetian |
| | Burdigalian |
| | Aquitanian |
| OLIGOCENE | Chattian |
| | Rupelian |
| | Tongrian |
| EOCENE | Ludian |
| | Bartonian |
| | Auversian |
| | Lutetian |
| | Cuisian |
| | Ypresian |
| PALEOCENE | Thanetian |
| | Montian |

| North America terrestrial vertebrates | |
|---|---|
| Epoch | Age |
| PLIOCENE | Blancan |
| | Hemphillian |
| MIOCENE | Clarendonian |
| | Barstovian |
| | Hemingfordian |
| | Arikareean |
| OLIGOCENE | Whitneyan |
| | Orellan |
| | Chadronian |
| EOCENE | Duchesnean |
| | Uintan |
| | Bridgerian |
| | Wasatchian |
| PALEOCENE | Clarkforkian |
| | Tiffanian |
| | Torrejonian |
| | Dragonian |
| | Puercan |

| West America marine megafaunal | |
|---|---|
| Epoch | "Stage" |
| PLIOCENE | San Joaquin |
| | Etchegoin |
| | Jacalitos |
| MIOCENE | Neroly |
| | Cierbo |
| | Briones |
| | Temblor |
| | Vaqueros |
| | Blakeley |
| OLIGOCENE | Blakeley |
| | Lincoln |
| | Keasey |
| EOCENE | Keasey |
| | Tejon |
| | "Transition" |
| | Domengine |
| | Capay |
| PALEOCENE | Meganos |
| | Martinez |

LOCAL EQUIVALENTS

| California marine foraminiferal | |
|---|---|
| Epoch | Stage |
| PLIO-PLEIST. | Wheelerian |
| PLIOCENE | Venturian |
| | Repettian |
| MIO-PLIOCENE | Delmontian |
| MIOCENE | Mohnian |
| | Luisian |
| | Relizian |
| OLIGO-MIOCENE | Saucesian |
| | Zemorrian |
| OLIG. | Refugian |
| EOCENE | Narizian |
| | Ulatisian |
| | Penutian |
| PALEOCENE | Bulitan |
| | Ynezian |

Table I.—*Some Different Regional Standards and Suggested Correlations* (*Continued*)

**Indonesia (East Indies) marine**

| Epoch | Stage | |
|---|---|---|
| Pliocene | h | 2 |
| | | 1 |
| Mio-Pliocene | g | |
| Miocene | f | 3 |
| | | 2 |
| | | 1 |
| | e | 5 |
| | | 4 |
| | | 3 |
| – – – | | |
| Oligocene | | 2 |
| | | 1 |
| | d | |
| | c | |
| Eocene | b | |
| | a | 2 |
| | | 1 |
| Paleocene | ? | |

**New Zealand marine**

| Epoch | Stage | |
|---|---|---|
| Pliocene | Castlecliffian | |
| | Barwoonian | Nukumaruan |
| | | Waitotaran |
| | | Opoitian |
| Miocene | Tara-nak-ian | Urenuian |
| | | Tongapo-turuan |
| | Awamoan | |
| | Hutchinsonian | |
| Oligocene | Waitakian | |
| | Duntroonian | |
| | Ototaran | Whaingaroan |
| | | Kaiatean |
| Eocene | Waimatean | Tahuian |
| | | Bortonian |
| | ? | |
| Paleocene | ? | |

**South America terrestrial vertebrates**

| Epoch | Age |
|---|---|
| Pliocene | Chapadmalalan |
| | Montehermosan |
| | Tunuyanian |
| | Huayquerian |
| Miocene | Mesopotamian |
| | Chasicoan |
| | Friasian |
| | Santacrucian |
| Oligocene | Colhuehuapian |
| | ? |
| | Deseadan |
| Eocene | ? |
| | Mustersan |
| | ? |
| | Casamayoran |
| Paleocene | Riochican |
| | ? (Salamancan?) |

fication into modern types, presumably in the late Mesozoic and early Tertiary eras.

Marine invertebrate faunas of the Tertiary include a variety of pelecypods and gastropods, and abundant large and small foraminifera; echinoids are highly diversified, with the Clypeasroida ("sand dollars," etc.) being characteristic of the Cenozoic. The ammonites, so conspicuous previously, did not continue into the Tertiary.

In the plant world, the greatest advances were among the flowering plants (angiosperms). Specialization of structures adapted to insect pollination, and fructifications suitable for dissemination by birds and other animals accompanied the general progress of animal evolution. *See* also Paleobotany; Paleontology.

**Conditions During the Tertiary.**—The end of the Cretaceous was marked in most areas by a great regression of the sea and by a shifting of the basins of deposition, generally toward the present margins of the continents. New marine transgressions were initiated in the Paleocene and lower Eocene in many parts of the world. During the Eocene, these transgressions advanced notably in most places. Tethys, the seaway extending from the western Mediterranean across to India, was finally broken up about the beginning of the Miocene. Marine transgressions during the Miocene were often as extensive as those of the Eocene, but in general the seas encroached less and less on the land in the later Tertiary.

The great mountain ranges of the western hemisphere, such as the Rocky mountains and the Andes, were established by the beginning of Tertiary time, but they had periodic rejuvenations during the period. Alpine orogeny, however, appears to have been mid-Tertiary in its expression. The coast ranges of western United States, although representing a zone diastrophically active during most of Tertiary time, assumed their present shape during the late Tertiary and Pleistocene, a history more or less applicable to other mountain chains in the great seismic belts.

Continental or terrestrial deposits of Tertiary age accumulated on all the land masses which were emergent during the period. These deposits occur in many places, but those of western United States, Argentina,

TABLE II.—*Some Divergent Tertiary Classifications*

<table>
<tr><th>European stages</th><th colspan="2">A common usage, North America, Europe</th><th colspan="2">North America pre-1924, some European usages</th><th colspan="2">North America vertebrate paleontologists, some European</th><th>Some micropaleontologists</th></tr>
<tr><td>Calabrian</td><td>Pleistocene</td><td rowspan="3">Pliocene</td><td rowspan="3">Pliocene</td><td rowspan="5">Pliocene</td><td>Pleistocene</td><td rowspan="5">Pliocene</td><td rowspan="2">Plio-Pleistocene</td></tr>
<tr><td>Astian</td><td rowspan="2">Pliocene</td><td rowspan="4">Pliocene</td></tr>
<tr><td>Plaisancian</td><td>Pliocene</td></tr>
<tr><td>Pontian</td><td colspan="2" rowspan="6">Miocene</td><td rowspan="5">Miocene</td><td rowspan="2">Mio-Pliocene</td></tr>
<tr><td>Sarmatian</td></tr>
<tr><td>Tortonian</td><td rowspan="3">Miocene</td><td colspan="2" rowspan="4">Miocene</td><td rowspan="3">Miocene</td></tr>
<tr><td>Helvetian</td></tr>
<tr><td>Burdigalian</td></tr>
<tr><td>Aquitanian</td><td colspan="2" rowspan="4">Oligocene</td><td rowspan="3">Oligo-Miocene</td></tr>
<tr><td>Chattian</td><td colspan="2" rowspan="3">Oligocene</td><td colspan="2" rowspan="3">Oligocene</td></tr>
<tr><td>Rupelian</td></tr>
<tr><td>Tongrian</td><td>Oligocene</td></tr>
<tr><td>Ludian</td><td colspan="2" rowspan="6">Eocene</td><td rowspan="8">Eocene</td><td rowspan="6">Eocene</td><td colspan="2" rowspan="6">Eocene</td><td>Eo-Oligocene</td></tr>
<tr><td>Bartonian</td><td rowspan="5">Eocene</td></tr>
<tr><td>Auversian</td></tr>
<tr><td>Lutetian</td></tr>
<tr><td>Cuisian</td></tr>
<tr><td>Ypresian</td></tr>
<tr><td>Thanetian</td><td colspan="2" rowspan="2">Paleocene</td><td rowspan="2">Paleocene</td><td colspan="2" rowspan="2">Paleocene</td><td rowspan="2">Paleocene</td></tr>
<tr><td>Montian</td></tr>
</table>

western Europe, Egypt, India and northern China are perhaps the best known and have furnished most of the known terrestrial fossils of this age.

In the early Tertiary, tropical climates extended to much higher latitudes than at present (for instance, to 50° N. or more along the western coast of North America). Subsequently the isotherms gradually retreated toward the equator, culminating in the Pleistocene ice age. The present-day narrow tropical belt is abnormal and during much of geologic time the tropics were as widespread as in the early Tertiary.

**Epochs and Stages of the Tertiary.**—The Tertiary faunas of western Europe consist, for the most part, of mollusca of modern aspect, and in 1830 Gérard Paul Deshayes determined the percentages of living species found at several horizons.. With the aid of Deshayes' percentages, the work of J. J. d'Omalius d'Halloy in Belgium, and of Thomas Webster and William Buckland in England, Sir Charles Lyell in 1833 divided the Tertiary into three main epochs, viz., Eocene with 3½%, Miocene with 17% and Pliocene with 35% to 50% of recent species. In 1854 Heinrich Ernst von Beyrich in Germany introduced the term Oligocene for the time interval represented by deposits transitional between Eocene and Miocene. A fifth division, called the Paleocene, was proposed by Wilhelm Philipp Schimper, also in Germany, in 1874 for the earliest part of the Tertiary on the basis of paleobotanical evidence.

At present the five epochs of the Tertiary are recognized not on the percentage of living species, as first defined by Lyell, but on the general character and comparative stage of development of the faunas, or on stratigraphic relationships.

Some geologists group the epochs of the Tertiary into two primary divisions, as follows:

Later Tertiary or Neogene { Pliocene, Miocene

Earlier Tertiary or Eogene (or Paleogene or Nummulitic) { Oligocene, Eocene, Paleocene

During the Tertiary, the marine faunas became increasingly more provincial and in consequence there is much difficulty in making intercontinental correlations. Because of this, local standards have been established, notably in North and South America, Indonesia (East Indies), New Zealand and Australia. In some areas, as in the western United States there are as many as three different standards used, each primarily utilizing a different group of organisms for recognition of the intervals. As a result there are divergent correlations of the same local sequence with those of Europe (*see* Table I).

As proposed by Lyell, Beyrich and Schimper, the five epochs are not definitely bounded, and inasmuch as their types are found in different basins and there are certain intervals (such as the Pontian and Sarmatian) not clearly included in any epoch, a number of discrepancies have arisen in their usage and significance (*see* Table II).

In addition to the epoch subdivisions of the Tertiary, there early arose a series of time-stratigraphic units, or stages. This concept was first proposed by Alcide d'Orbigny in 1840 and 1842 and subsequently formed the basis for most regional correlation in Europe. Because the types of these stages are not always in the type areas of the epochs and because of the uncertain boundaries of the epochs, there is disagreement with regard to the placement of some stages. *See* also references under "Tertiary" in the Index.

BIBLIOGRAPHY.—M. G. Wilmarth, "Geologic Time Classification of United States Geological Survey Compared with Other Classifications," *Bull. U.S. Geol. Surv.*, 769:1–138 (1925); A. M. Davies, *Tertiary Faunas,* vol. 2 (1934); A. Papp and E. Thenius, *Tertiär* (2 vol.), in F. Lotze, *Handbuch der Stratigraphischen Geologie* (1959); W. Harland, A. Smith, B. Wilcock (eds.), *The Phanerozoic Time Scale* (1964); W. Harland *et al.* (eds.), *The Fossil Record* (1967). (J. W. D.)

**TERTULLIAN** (QUINTUS SEPTIMIUS FLORENS TERTULLIANUS) (*c.* 155–after 220), one of the greatest of the early Christian writers of the west, was born of pagan parents in Carthage. His education gave him a fair knowledge of philosophy and Greek and Latin literature and he was further trained in the law. In his youth deeply involved with the literary social life of the day, he remained for the whole of his life under the spell of the word, but his legal training left an even greater impress on his personality and his writings. He became an expert in law, though it is most unlikely that he is to be identified with the jurist Tertullianus, of whose writings the *Corpus iuris civilis* gives a few excerpts.

In mature manhood Tertullian became a Christian (*c.* 193). He does not give the reasons for his conversion, which took place in Rome or Carthage, but the heroism of Christians in times of persecution impressed him deeply and personal experience is probably reflected in his famous words *semen est sanguis Christianorum* ("the seed is the blood of Christians," *Apologeticum* 50). After his conversion he devoted himself to the study of Scripture and of Christian literature, and by using his knowledge of law, literature and philosophy he became the great defender of the Christian faith against the pagan state, against the Jews and against several heretic sects. According to Jerome he became a priest of the church of Carthage. His clerical status is denied by several modern scholars, but his preponderant role of teacher and the catechetical character of several of his treatises which apparently summarize sermons seem to confirm the information of Jerome, who concerning Tertullian draws on reliable tradition.

Tertullian carried on his literary activity between the years 195 and 220. His works show an ever-growing rigorism which led him to sympathize with Montanism (*q.v.*), and about 207 he openly went over to this sect. But soon he broke off from it to become the head of a small group, the so-called Tertullianists, who survived at Carthage up to the time of St. Augustine. Nevertheless Montanism did not prevent him from remaining dogmatically orthodox in most respects. His doctrine of the Trinity finds its best expression in the late work *Adversus Praxean* (after 213), and it is in this doctrine and in Christology that he made his greatest contribution to theology. In his latest works there is a growing violence and then, after 220, his literary activity ceases altogether. Having done battle with pagans, Jews, Marcionites, Gnostics, Monarchians and Catholics he died in Carthage, according to Jerome at a great age.

The works of Tertullian, most of which cannot be exactly dated with certainty, fall into three classes: the apologetic (defending Christianity against paganism and Judaism), the polemical-dogmatic (refuting heresies and heretics) and the disciplinary, moral and ascetic works (among which those of the extreme Montanist period form a special group, already marked as such by Jerome).

**Apologetics.**—The *Ad nationes* and the *Apologeticum,* which are related to each other, both seem to have been written in 197 and both defend Christianity against paganism. The first is a mere collection of material drawn from the Greek apologists; the *Apologeticum,* directed to the governors of the Roman provinces, is a very personal work in finished form. The argumentation shows clearly the influence of the author's juridical training. It is the most famous of all Tertullian's works and it has a textual tradition of its own. In the *De testimonio animae,* written soon after the *Apologeticum,* Tertullian discusses the *testimonium animae naturaliter Christianae:* the awareness of the creator in the soul, by nature Christian, as derived immediately from the universe and as evidenced in the ordinary language of men. *Ad Scapulam* (212), an admonition to the persecuting proconsul of Africa, anticipates a topic elaborated later by Lactantius. *Adversus Iudaeos* deals with the problem of Jewish tradition and particularly with that of the Old Testament. Its main source is Justin's dialogue with Trypho. According to Tertullian the Law is abolished because the giver of the New Covenant has already appeared. Henceforth the Old Testament must be interpreted spiritually. Ch. 9–14 are merely excerpts, made by a compiler, from book iii of Tertullian's *Adversus Marcionem.*

**Polemical-Dogmatic Works.**—In *De praescriptione haereticorum* (*c.* 200) Tertullian again makes the most of his knowledge of law. His aim was to end the controversy between Catholics and all heretics by advancing the technical argument of the *praescriptio,* a legal objection leading to rejection of a cause. According to Tertullian the heretics cannot use Scripture because it is not theirs; the gospel is the possession of the church, handed down to it by apostolic tradition. Other treatises deal with single heresies. In *Adversus Marcionem,* the major source for knowledge of the heresy of Marcion, Tertullian draws on Justin, Irenaeus and probably on a treatise by Theophilus of Antioch. *Adversus Hermogenem,* directed against the doctrine of Hermogenes, a painter living in Carthage according to whom God had created the universe out of preexisting matter, gives an explanation of the Christian teaching on creation. *Adversus Valentinianos,* dealing with the Gnostic sect of the Valentinians, depends on the first book of Irenaeus' great work against heretics. The *Scorpiace* is a defense of martyrdom against the Gnostics, who are compared to scorpions.

*De carne Christi* and *De resurrectione carnis* are closely connected: both deal with the resurrection of the body, which was denied by pagans, Sadducees and heretics. In *De carne Christi* Tertullian proves, against Docetism, that Christ was really born, that he truly lived, died in human flesh and rose from the dead. He defends the Virgin's true and real motherhood and stresses the human nature of Christ by maintaining that he was ugly. This treatise paves the way to *De resurrectione carnis,* which refutes those who denied the resurrection of the flesh. The *Adversus Praxean* (213), already mentioned, is directed against the Trinitarian doctrine of Praxeas. In it the term *trinitas* occurs for the first time. It is the most important contribution to the doctrine of the Trinity in the ante-Nicene period, though it is not free from subordinationism. *De anima* (*c.* 213) is a refutation of heretical doctrines about the soul, which leads Tertullian into controversy with pagan philosophy. It contains not a well-thought-out system of psychology but a series of theories of polemical intentions. Tertullian's chief thesis is the corporeality of the soul; he also advocates traducianism (*see* CREATIONISM AND TRADUCIANISM). His chief source was the pagan physician Soranus.

**Disciplinary, Moral and Ascetic Works.**—*Ad martyras,* a short address to a number of Christians (or catechumens) who were in prison awaiting martyrdom, dates probably from 197; that the famous martyrs Perpetua and Felicitas belonged to the group cannot be proved, and it is also uncertain whether Tertullian is the editor of their *Passio.* The *De spectaculis* (197 or 202) is a condemnation of all public games. In *De cultu feminarum* (between 197 and 201), Christian women are warned not to be dominated by pagan fashion. Three treatises, *De baptismo, De oratione* and *De paenitentia,* written between 200 and 206, all of them addressed to catechumens and similar in composition and tone, can be considered as a trilogy. The first, particularly important for the history of the baptismal rite, is the only ante-Nicene treatise on any of the sacraments. *De oratione,* which gives the earliest exposition of the Lord's Prayer in any language, deals with the interior and exterior discipline of prayer. *De paenitentia* is important for the history of ecclesiastical penance. *De patientia,* of the same period, sheds light on Tertullian's personality.

*Ad uxorem,* composed between 200 and 206, gives suggestions which his wife is to follow after his death. In the first book he admonishes her to remain a widow, in the second he discusses the possibility of remarriage: if she wishes to remarry it must be to a Christian. In *De exhortatione castitatis,* written some years later, he again takes up the problem of second marriage, which he now rejects as contrary to the will of God. In *De virginibus velandis* (*c.* 208) he returns to the idea which he had already formulated that women, whether married or unmarried, should be veiled. *De corona* (211), written in defense of a soldier who refused to wear a wreath, discusses a far more important problem: that of the participation of Christians in military service. The same problem, but in a larger framework, that of the behaviour of Christians in the pagan world, is discussed in *De idololatria* (211); the Christian must abstain from everything that is in any way connected with idolatry.

Tertullian's last works are characterized by Jerome as a sort of libel in which he discusses the controversies which brought about his rupture with the church. To this group belong *De monogamia, De fuga, De ieiunio* and *De pudicitia.* In *De monogamia* (213) the third of Tertullian's treatises on marriage, he regards second marriage as illicit and almost adulterous. In *De fuga* (212) he holds—in opposition to his previous views—that to take refuge in flight during persecution is against the will of God. *De ieiunio* is a fierce attack on the Catholic rejection of the Montanist practices of fasting. In *De pudicitia* he attacks the church again, this time in the field of penitential discipline, dealing particularly with the power of the keys. The *De pallio* is a small and bizarre tract, full of wit and sarcasm, in which Tertullian explains why in everyday life he substituted the mantle (*pallium*), the traditional garb of philosophers, for the Roman toga. The work is a sort of literary tour de force and the reader wonders if it is to be taken seriously. The change of dress coincides either with Tertullian's conversion or with his separation from the Catholic Church.

**Style and Influence.**—Tertullian was the first Christian theologian to leave behind an extensive collection of works written in Latin. With him early Christian Latin literature made a magnificent start. Though he was certainly not the creator of early Christian Latin, a distinction which has erroneously been claimed for him, he was the first to introduce the special idiom of Latin-speaking Christians into literature. In style he is inspired by the Asianic manner, the fashionable "modern" style of his day, which preferred short paratactical sentences, adorned with all sorts of play on sounds and words, to the long classical periods. His style is highly personal, often pregnant and terse and not free from obscurity, though at the same time powerful and passionate.

Tertullian never even tried to create a theological system, but he often found formulas and definitions which were clear and precise, particularly in his doctrine of the Trinity. Some of his formulas are identical with those of the Council of Nicaea (325), and in his Christology he anticipates the Chalcedonian definition (451). All his works bear the stamp of his juridical training, not only in language and style, but even more in his way of thinking. His juridical training supplied him his major argument against heresy, the *praescriptio;* the way in which he deals with the relation of God and man is equally inspired by his juridical training, words such as debt, satisfaction, guilt, compensation, occurring regularly. Law also inspired his defense of the Christians against the state. He exercised great influence on Christian thought, particularly (in the view of many, though not all, scholars) through Cyprian, who sifted the thoughts he had given, rounded them off and turned them into current coin, always aware of his dependence on Tertullian, whom he designated as his master.

*See* also references under "Tertullian" in the Index.

Bibliography.—Works in J. P. Migne, *Patrologia Latina,* vol. 1–2 (1879); incomplete critical editions in *Corpus scriptorum ecclesiasticorum Latinorum,* vol. 19 (1890), ed. by A. Reifferscheid and G. Wissowa, vol. 47 (1906), ed. by A. Kroyman, vol. 69 (1939), ed. by H. Hoppe and A. Kroymann, vol. 76 (1957), ed. by V. Bulhart and P. Borleffs; and *Corpus Christianorum, series Latina,* vol. 1, ed. by E. Dekkers (1953–54), vol. 2 (1954), ed. by A. Gerlo. For editions of separate works to date see *Corpus Christianorum,* vol. 1; Eng. trans. by P. Holmes and S. Thelwall in *Ante-Nicene Christian Library,* vol. 7 (1868), 11 (1869), 15 (1870), 18 (1870). *See* also long bibliography in J. H. Waszink's edition of *De anima* (1947); J. Quasten, *Patrology,* vol. 2 (1953); B. Altaner, *Patrology* (1960). (Ch. Mo.)

**TERUEL,** a town in northeastern Spain, and capital of the province of the same name, is on the left bank of the Guadalaviar River at its confluence with the Alfambra, and on the Calatayud-Sagunto railway, about 70 mi. (113 km.) NW of Valencia. Pop. (1960) 19,776 (mun.). The older part of Teruel has remains of its old walls and the towers which fortified them, narrow streets and crumbling medieval houses, but modern suburbs have been built outside the walls. In the cloisters of San Pedro lie the remains of the celebrated "lovers of Teruel," Diego Juan Martínez de Marcilla and Isabel de Segura (13th century). Their story is the subject of works by Tirso de Molina, Juan Pérez de Montalbán, Juan Eugenio Hartzenbusch, and—in an Italian setting—by Boccaccio. Structures from the 16th century include the cathedral and an aqueduct built by Pierre Bedel. Teruel was the scene of fierce fighting in the Civil War (1936–39).

Teruel Province (area 5,715 sq.mi. [14,803 sq.km.]; pop. [1960] 215,183). Three-quarters of the province is covered by mountains, mainly Cretaceous, belonging to the Iberian System, the highest ranges being the Sierra de Albarracín and the Montes Universales, both in the southwest near the border of the province of Cuenca. Heavy snow falls in the mountainous region every winter, and most of the waters flow into the Ebro River. In the northeast, where a plain runs northward into the province of Zaragoza, a Catalan dialect is spoken.

Alcañiz (pop. [1960] 10,035) is the second largest town in the province, most of the others containing less than a quarter of its population. Some of the festivals in the smaller towns are of great antiquity. At Castellote, a festival called the Romería del Llovedor, or Rain Procession, is celebrated by the men in May and by the women on Whit Monday. At Híjar hooded penitents wander round the streets beating drums from Thursday to Saturday in Holy Week.

Marble and chalk are quarried, and the chief products include corn, wine, oil, cheese, fruits, timber, flax, hemp, silk, and wool. (C. D. L.)

**TERZAGHI, KARL** (1883–1963), U.S. civil engineer who established soil mechanics (*q.v.*) as one of the basic subjects of civil engineering science, was born in Prague, Czech., on Oct. 2, 1883. He served in the Air Corps of the Austrian Army during World War I and then joined the staff of Robert College (American), in Istanbul, Turk. Although much work on foundations, earth pressure, and stability of slopes had been done earlier, Terzaghi, as a result of research during the period 1919–25, provided the unifying concepts that made soil mechanics a science. These were published in *Erdbaumechanik* (1925). Following this he spent four years in the United States, where he obtained widespread recognition as a teacher, research worker, and consulting engineer. From 1929 to 1938 he held the newly created chair in soil mechanics at the University of Technology in Vienna and then served as professor of civil engineering at Harvard University from 1946 until his retirement in 1956, though he served there as consultant and lecturer until his death. Terzaghi was president of the International Conference of Soil Mechanics and Foundation Engineering from its inception in 1936 until 1957. His consulting practice was worldwide, and he wrote more than 200 scientific papers. He died in Winchester, Mass., on Oct. 25, 1963. (A. W. Sk.)

**TESCHEN** (Polish Cieszyn, Czech Tesin), a province divided between Poland and Czechoslovakia in 1920, which had been originally one of the Polish Silesian principalities. It became part of the Bohemian crown in 1335, passing with that crown to the Austrian Habsburgs in 1526; after the death of the last Piast prince of Cieszyn in 1625, the principality was administered in an Austrian *Kronland.*

On the eve of World War I Teschen Silesia covered 881 sq.mi. (2,283 sq.km.). According to the Austrian census, its population rose between 1880 and 1910 from 262,412 to 426,667. The latter total comprised 233,850 Poles (54.8%), 115,604 Czechs (27.1%), and 76,916 Germans (18.1%). The increase in population was explained by rapid industrialization, the area being particularly rich in coking coal.

Soon after the collapse of Austria-Hungary, the two regional political organizations, the Polish National Council and the Czech National Committee, established on Nov. 5, 1918, a frontier on an ethnic basis. The Prague government refused to recognize the agreement, claiming the whole of Teschen Silesia on historic grounds. On Jan. 23, 1919, Czech troops attacked the small Polish garrisons and occupied the major part of the disputed territory.

On Feb. 5 an armistice was concluded, cutting the area in two almost equal parts. On Sept. 27 the Allied Supreme Council decided to hold a plebiscite, which, however, was never held because of Czech opposition. In July 1920, when the Russo-Polish War (*q.v.*) took an unfavourable turn for Poland, Wladyslaw Grabski, the Polish prime minister, was forced at Spa, on July 10, to agree to a partition of Teschen Silesia by the Allies without a plebiscite. Partition was determined by the Paris Conference of Ambassadors on July 28, with Czechoslovakia obtaining 491 sq.mi. (1,272 sq.km.). While the Czech part, which comprised the industrial basin, included about 140,000 Poles, there were practically no Czechs in the Polish part.

In September 1938, at the time of the Munich Conference, the Polish government asked the Czechoslovak government for treatment of the Polish population in the Czech part of Teschen Silesia on the same terms as the other national minorities within Czechoslovakia. President Edvard Benes of Czechoslovakia accepted on Sept. 22 "the principle of frontier rectification." On Oct. 1 a new Polish-Czechoslovak frontier, practically identical to that of Nov. 5, 1918, was established.

After World War II Wladyslaw Gomulka, Polish deputy premier, declared in Moscow on June 26, 1945, that Teschen Silesia was "historically and ethnically Polish," but Poland would accept a territorial settlement with Czechoslovakia based on the principle of self-determination. Zdenek Fierlinger, the Czechoslovak premier, refused to discuss any cession of the territory attributed to Czechoslovakia on July 28, 1920. Under Soviet pressure that frontier line was restored. (For the town of the same name *see* CIESZYN.)

*See* R. Fitzgibbon Young, "The Teschen Question," in H. W. V. Temperley's *History of the Peace Conference of Paris,* vol. iv (1921); B. Kożusznik, *The Problem of Cieszyn Silesia* (1943). (K. SM.)

**TESIN:** *see* CIESZYN.

**TESLA, NIKOLA** (1856–1943), U.S. inventor of electrical devices and equipment who introduced the first practical applications of alternating current, was born July 9, 1856, at Smiljan, Croatia (Yugoslavia). He attended the polytechnic school at Graz, specializing in physics and mathematics, and finished his studies at the University of Prague in 1880. Four years later he went to the United States and for a time was with Thomas Edison's company. He then established the Tesla laboratory in New York city and devoted his efforts to research.

Tesla conceived the rotating magnetic field principle as an effective method of utilizing alternating current for power. He patented the induction, synchronous and split-phase motors, and new forms of generators and transformers; this equipment formed the system for the generation and use of power from Niagara falls. By means of lectures in Europe and the United States beginning in 1891, he announced discoveries and applications of high-frequency alternating current, including the high-frequency resonant transformer, or "Tesla coil." Tesla died in New York city, Jan. 7, 1943.

The 100th anniversary of his birth was commemorated by scientific institutions throughout the world, and the unit of magnetic flux density in the MKS system was named the "tesla" in his honour.

BIBLIOGRAPHY.—John J. O'Neill, *Prodigal Genius: the Life of Nikola Tesla* (1944); The Nikola Tesla Museum, *Centenary of the Birth of Nikola Tesla, 1856–1943,* vol. 1, *Lectures, Patents, Articles* (1956), vol. 2, *Articles, Letters, Documents* (1961); Inez Hunt and Wanetta W. Draper, *Lightning in His Hand: the Life Story of Nikola Tesla* (1964). (L. I. A.)

**TESO** (ITESO), a Nilo-Hamitic people of central Uganda, numbered about 525,000 in the 1960s; they are closely related to the Kumam of Uganda (62,000), and also to members of the Karamojong tribal cluster of eastern Uganda.

Unlike most Nilo-Hamites (*q.v.*), the Teso are sedentary cultivators, keeping some cattle; they grow much cotton and are counted among the most progressive farmers of Uganda. Much of their traditional culture and organization was lost through suppression by the conquering Ganda (*q.v.*) under Kakunguru at the end of the 19th century. The age set (*q.v.*) and the clan lost their importance, and much of the indigenous territorial organization was destroyed. The basic local group is the *etem,* a small settlement that may comprise several hamlets; today the term is applied to the subcounty, an administrative subunit of one of the six counties.

The homesteads of a hamlet are usually those of the men of an extended family based on a three- or four-generation patrilineal descent group. Genealogical ties are rarely reckoned beyond this range. There are also vaguely defined patrilineal clans dispersed throughout Teso.

Although age sets no longer function as groups, it is known that they were generally arranged in a permanent recurrent cycle of seven or eight names. Almost all indigenous religion has been replaced by Christianity; previous to their conversion, the Teso believed in an omnipotent but remote god, Akuj, and in a god of calamity, Edeke.

*See* J. C. D. Lawrance, *The Iteso* (1957); P. Gulliver and P. H. Gulliver, *The Central Nilo-Hamites* (1953). (J. F. M. M.)

**TESSIN, CARL GUSTAF,** COUNT (1695–1770), Swedish court official, statesman, collector and writer, helped to create a modern Swedish prose style, and his poems and fables can still be admired. He was born in Stockholm on Sept. 5, 1695, the son of the great architect Nicodemus Tessin the Younger (1654–1728). After studies in France and Italy he was employed on his first diplomatic missions before succeeding, in 1728, to his father's post of superintendent of the court and to the task of completing the new Stockholm castle according to his father's design. This he did with help from Carl Hårleman and from foreign artists (mostly French), who also helped him to set up a Swedish Academy of the Fine Arts.

Though he stood for aristocratic government against royal absolutism, Tessin admired Charles XII and became a founder of the Hat party in the hope that its policy would regain some of the provinces lost in the Great Northern War (*see* SWEDEN: *History*). He was elected *lantmarskalk* in 1738 by a large majority but failed to prevent his party from starting war against Russia in 1741 without guarantees of foreign aid. After the peace of Åbo (1743), however, he cleverly extricated Sweden from "the Russian bear-hug." Adolphus Frederick (*q.v.*), Russia's nominee as heir to the Swedish throne, was married to the imperious Prussian princess Louisa Ulrica in 1744; Tessin formed a strong friendship with her, and they finally induced Adolphus Frederick to conciliate Denmark by renouncing his hereditary interest in Schleswig-Holstein. Tessin was appointed tutor to the prince Gustavus (born in 1746) and head of the chancellery, but he lost Louisa Ulrica's friendship by insisting on a marriage contract (1751) between Gustavus and a Danish princess instead of her Prussian niece. His letters of advice to Gustavus were printed at the expense of the diet (1751 and 1753) during its struggle against the crown and won European fame as models of educational writing, but he had to resign the chancellery in 1752 and the tutorship in 1754.

When he withdrew from public affairs (1761), he found himself desperately short of money in his retirement at Åkerö, and the books and the works of art on which he had spent his personal fortune were sold. Later he was formally reconciled to the royal couple, thanks to Gustavus. He died at Åkerö, on Jan. 7, 1770. He left voluminous diaries, and many of his private letters survive.

**TEST ACTS,** in England, Scotland, and Ireland, provided that none but those who professed the established religion were to be eligible for public office. In England discrimination against Roman Catholics and Nonconformists did not take this particular form until the reign of Charles II, chiefly because, until this comparatively tolerant period, the severity of the laws against recusants, whether Catholic or Nonconformist, precluded the possibility of their being so employed. In Scotland legislation followed soon after the Reformation, while in Ireland the support given to James II until his defeat at the Battle of the Boyne in 1690 led to the introduction of tests designed to exclude dissenters from almost all branches of public life.

The form that the test took in England was to make the receiving of Holy Communion according to the rites of the Church of England a condition precedent to the holding of public office. It was first embodied in legislation in the Corporation Act of 1661 (one of the acts in the so-called Clarendon Code) which enacted that, in addition to taking the oaths of allegiance and supremacy and subscribing a declaration against the Solemn League and Covenant, all members of town corporations were within one year before election to receive the sacrament of the Lord's Supper according to the rites of the Church of England. The immediate occasion of the extension of this principle to all public offices was the king's declaration of indulgence (March 1672) dispensing with the laws inflicting disabilities on all Nonconformists or recusants: Parliament reacted by passing the first Test Act, of 1673, to which Charles was compelled to consent. This act provided that all persons holding any office, civil or military, were to take the oaths of supremacy and allegiance and to subscribe a declaration against transubstantiation, and were, in addition, to receive the sacrament within three months after admittance to office. This act, which did not apply to peers, was followed by a second Test Act in 1678, to the effect that all peers and members of the House of Commons should make a declaration against transubstantiation, invocation of saints, and the sacrifice of the Mass; an exception being made in favour of the heir presumptive, James, duke of York.

Both Charles II and James II circumvented this legislation by use of the dispensing power, afterward abolished by the Bill of Rights (1689). Throughout the 18th century there were amendments to, and partial repeals of, the Test Acts, and a number of acts of indemnity to relieve those who had committed breaches of them from the consequences, but repeal had to wait until the 19th century. An act of 1828 removed the necessity of taking the sacrament as a qualification for office, and the Roman Catholic Emancipation Act of 1829 abolished the requirement of oaths and declarations against transubstantiation. Formal repeal of the Corporation Act and the Test Acts of 1673 and 1678 followed in acts of 1871, 1863, and 1866, respectively, while in 1871 religious tests were abolished in the universities except for degrees and professorships in divinity and certain kindred subjects.

In Scotland, the form of the legislation was different in that the taking of communion formed no part of the test. An act of 1567 made profession of the reformed faith a condition of public office, and a further Test Act was passed in 1681 but abolished in 1690; and in the 18th century the legal disabilities were confined to those engaged in education. All tests were abolished in 1889.

In Ireland, on the other hand, the principle of using the sacrament as a test was adopted by an act of 1704, which followed earlier legislation exacting oaths of allegiance and declarations against Roman Catholic beliefs and practises from peers, members of the House of Commons, bishops, and members of both branches of the legal profession; English legislation on oaths and declarations was adopted by Yelverton's act in 1782. All these provisions were abolished by the Promissory Oaths Act (1871).

Article VI of the Constitution of the United States prescribes that "no religious test shall ever be required as a qualification to any office or public trust under the United States." A similar provision is included in most state constitutions. (W. T. Ws.)

**TESTAMENTUM DOMINI** (Testament of Our Lord), one of a series of writings, claiming to embody the fundamental rules of the early Christian Church, others of which were the *Apostolic Constitutions* and the *Apostolic Tradition* of Hippolytus (*see* Constitutions, Apostolic; Hippolytus, Canons of Saint). It falls into three distinct parts: an apocalyptic introduction (book i, ch. 1–18; the division into books, however, was clearly not original); a church order proper (i, 19–ii, 24); and a conclusion (ii, 25–27) of the same apocalyptic character as the introduction.

The testament has several distinctive characteristics. First and foremost is its ascription to the Lord himself, an attempt to claim the highest possible sanction, higher than that claimed by the various compilations styled "apostolic." This fact alone indicates the preexistence of certain of the latter. Again, the whole tone is one of highly strung asceticism, and the regulations, by their severity, point to a small and strictly organized body. They are "the wise," "the perfect," "sons of light"; but this somewhat Gnostic terminology is not accompanied by any signs of Gnostic doctrine, and the work as a whole is orthodox in tone. They are set in the midst of "wolves," despised and slighted by the careless and worldly: there is frequent mention of "the persecuted" and of the duty of "bearing the cross." Charismata, and above all exorcisms, occupy a very important place. There is a vivid realization of the ministry of angels, and the angelic hierarchy is very complete. Great stress is laid upon virginity (although there is no sign of monasticism), fasting, and regular attendance of the whole clerical body and the "more perfect" of the laity at the hours of prayer.

The testament was originally written in Greek, probably in the 4th–5th century; it survives only in a 7th-century Syriac translation (*editio princeps* by Ignatius Ephraem II Rahmani, 1899, with Latin translation).

*See* James Cooper and A. J. Maclean, *The Testament of Our Lord,* Eng. trans., with introduction and notes (1902); and *Dictionnaire de théologie catholique,* vol. xv, col. 194–200 (1946). (W. E. Co.; X.)

**TETANUS** (Lockjaw) is an acute infectious disease caused by a bacillus and the poison it elaborates in human tissues. It is characterized by muscular rigidity and spasms. The almost constant involvement of the muscles of the jaw accounts for the popular name of the disease.

**History.**—Although a comparatively rare disease, tetanus has been recognized for centuries, as is shown by the picturesque descriptions of the disease by Hippocrates (5th–4th century B.C.), Aretaeus (2nd century A.D.), and John of Arderne (14th century); the observation of its occurrence from such trivial injuries as the bite of a tame sparrow, noted by G. B. Morgagni (18th century); and the concern of Joseph Lister (19th century) over tetanus among hospital patients. Landmarks of tetanus research in modern times included the recognition of the infectious nature of the disease, by A. Carle and G. Rattone, A. Nicolaier, and others, 1884–88; isolation of the bacillus and its toxin by S. Kitasato, T. Weyl, and A. Nicolaier, 1889–92; animal experiments on both active and passive immunization by S. Kitasato, E. von Behring, W. Schütz, and L. Vaillard, 1890–92, and the application of experimental results to veterinary and human medical practice by many workers; crystallization of the neurotoxin (*see* below) by L. Pillemer and K. C. Robbins, 1949; and the development of improved methods of treatment by L. Eckmann, 1960.

**Cause.**—The bacillus of tetanus, *Clostridium tetani,* is a slender rod visible with the conventional microscope. It occurs in the dormant (spore) and vegetative, toxin-producing forms. Conversion of the spore into the vegetative form occurs under conditions of oxygen deprivation; *i.e.,* various levels of the anaerobic state. Although ten different strains of *Clostridium tetani* have been identified, it is fortunate that the neurotoxins of all ten strains can be completely neutralized by a single antitoxic serum.

The vegetative forms, which elaborate the poison, are destroyed as easily as the vegetative forms of other bacteria. The spores, however, show variable degrees of resistance to thermal and chemical agents; *e.g.,* they are killed in 1 hour by dry heat but in 5 minutes by live steam (autoclaving), or in 12 to 15 hours by 5% carbolic acid but in 2 to 3 hours by 1% bichloride of mercury. Animal experiments by A. A. Anwar and T. B. Turner (1956) indicated that penicillin and the tetracycline compounds (principally terramycin) are lethal for the bacillus, mainly in the vegetative forms; not all authorities are willing to rely solely on antibiotics as preventive agents against tetanus.

Protected from sunlight and other adverse environmental conditions, the spores may survive for a number of years—possibly almost indefinitely. The spores are distributed widely in nature, mainly in the superficial layers of the soil. In general, the degree of soil pollution parallels the amount of fecal contamination from natural or artificial manuring or from human excreta.

The most important predisposing cause of tetanus is a wound which permits entrance of spores of *Cl. tetani* into tissue of a susceptible host. The wound may be trivial or severe, varying from simple superficial abrasions to severe lacerations. Not infrequently the source of infection may be obscure (cryptogenic tetanus).

Both the occurrence and the severity of tetanus are governed by the amount of poison elaborated by the organism and absorbed by the body, and the resistance of the host. Although a definite spectrum of resistance to the neurotoxin among lower animals is documented, natural immunity does not occur in human beings. Hence, in the absence of artificially acquired protection (*see* below, *Control*), conditions favourable to implantation and growth of *Cl. tetani* determine the occurrence and course of the disease, which can be rendered less severe by artificially induced immunity or by nonspecific treatment; *i.e.*, antibiotic medication, sedative drugs, general care, and miscellaneous measures. Race, geographical location, sex, age, occupation, and the like are significant only insofar as they are related to environmental conditions which either facilitate or impede the development of tetanus.

Tetanospasmin, the neurotoxic component of the toxin elaborated by *Cl. tetani,* is one of the deadliest poisons known to man. It is transported from the local focus of infection (portal of entry) to the ganglion cells of the anterior horns of the spinal cord, which are then stimulated. The neurotoxin is believed to act on the synthesis and liberation of acetylcholine, a substance having a key role in the synaptic transmission of nerve impulses throughout the body. The clinical expression of central nervous system stimulation consists of fairly constant rigidity, local or generalized, frequently and unpredictably punctuated by tonic spasms. The muscles most intensively activated are those that oppose gravity; *i.e.*, the extensor groups of the limbs and neck and the masseters, which close the jaw. Local tetanus, confined approximately to the zone of injury, may occur as a precursor to generalized tetanus or as an isolated manifestation of the disease.

The period of incubation (interval between the entrance of spores and the appearance of clinical tetanus) is related to the rate of release of toxin from the portal of entry. In about 20% of civilian hospital cases the incubation period is 2 to 5 days, in 60% it is 6 to 15 days, and in the remainder it is 16 to 85 days. The region of a wound has no proved relationship to the incubation period. The prophylactic use of antitoxin may prolong the period. Statistically, the length of the incubation period is inversely related to the fatality rate; *i.e.*, the longer the period the more likely the recovery. Moreover, the speed with which the disease becomes generalized in the individual patient is important in the ultimate outcome: the slower the onset of generalized symptoms, the better the outlook.

**Symptoms and Course.**—Tetanus may be local or general; when general, it may be mild, moderate, or severe. In local tetanus the stiffness and spasms may be restricted to the muscles near the wound. When the injury occurs in the head or neck (cephalic tetanus), one or more cranial nerves may be paralyzed. If the patient survives, the paralysis gradually disappears. When tetanus is general it is usually symmetrical (involving both sides of the body in equal degree). Sometimes, however, this pattern of symmetry is violated (unilateral, abdominothoracic, or limb tetanus), with spasticity limited or more pronounced on one whole side of the body, in the muscles of the abdomen or thorax, or in one or more limbs, and occasionally without stiffness of the jaw.

Early complaints may be difficult to evaluate by examination; but when the disease process becomes more pronounced, alterations in physical behaviour, ranging from mild to severe, are encountered. In general, the main symptoms of tetanus are quite characteristic. They are:

1. Rigidity of the body musculature. This is expressed by stiffness of the jaw (trismus), a fixed spastic sardonic smile (risus sardonicus), difficulty in swallowing, backache, rigid abdominal wall, tight thorax (with the volume at its maximum—a fact of basic importance in treatment), fixed extremities, rigid neck (sometimes with a backward retraction), and spasms of the muscles of the bladder and bowel, causing retention of the urine and constipation.

2. Muscular spasms. These occur at unpredictable intervals, in various degrees of severity from mild contractions to alarming episodes associated with excruciating pain, fractures of the spinal vertebrae, brain hemorrhages, and even sudden death of the patient.

Accessory signs and symptoms are profuse drenching perspiration and overactive tendon reflexes. The mind remains clear and the temperature normal (in the absence of certain complications).

Complications include pneumonia, collapse of one or more lung lobes, suffocation from severe muscular spasms, brain hemorrhages, injuries to the teeth, tongue, or mouth from convulsions, starvation, dehydration, fractures of the spine, fever of varied origin, pulmonary embolus with sudden death, perforated peptic ulcer, and undesirable effects from therapy; *e.g.*, serum sickness (early or delayed; *see* SERUM THERAPY), and coma from the intensive use of sedative drugs designed to prevent convulsions and suffering.

The onset and course of tetanus is sometimes erratic. For example, the classical stiff jaw may be late in appearance or even absent. Likewise, marked modifications, with associated difficulties in diagnosis, may reflect the attenuating effect of antecedent or immediate immunization measures (serum or vaccine).

**Treatment.**—Tetanus treatment employs antitoxic serum (preferably of human origin in order to avoid the serious hazards of serum sickness), sedative and relaxant drugs, compounds to control secondary infections (penicillin, tetracyclines, and allied medication), surgical procedures as required to avoid suffocation from laryngeal obstruction (tracheotomy), conservative but adequate care of wounds, measures to prevent water and chemical imbalance (dehydration and acidosis), maintenance of adequate caloric balance to avoid malnutrition, and continuous expert medical and nursing care. The creation of special tetanus treatment centres has been recognized as a critical step in the direction of minimizing the case fatality rate.

A definite statistical reduction of mortality followed the introduction of serum treatment of tetanus: from 90 to 70% among patients with short incubation periods (1–5 days) and from 70 to 29% among patients with longer incubation periods (5–10 days) (H. Zinsser, 1960). The importance of sedation and nursing care is reflected in the low death rate of 23% among a group of patients treated without tetanus antitoxin (J. Bryant and H. D. Fairman, 1940). Treatment combining drug-induced paralysis with the use of a respirator has lowered the death rate to 9% (L. Eckmann, 1960). In general, however, the mortality from tetanus is estimated at 40–50%. Danger of death is much higher in tetanus of the newborn, approaching 100% in some parts of the world.

The outlook in individual cases is best where the patient is in good health, is free of severe convulsions or complications (especially all forms of serum sickness), has only slight difficulty in swallowing, has a mild form of the disease (as evidenced by a long incubation period and slow generalization of symptoms), is neither very young nor aged (the periods when mortality is highest), has mild wounds, and obtains expert treatment. In the average case two or more weeks are required for recovery. Sometimes sudden and unexpected death occurs during apparently healthy convalescence. Occasionally the disease lasts for months or several years. With the exception of certain complications, *e.g.*, compression fractures of the vertebrae, recovery from tetanus is complete. No matter how seriously ill the patient may have been, the mind is perfectly clear after the disease has run its course. Unfortunately, tetanus may occur more than once in the same individual; therefore active immunization with tetanus toxoid must be instituted at an appropriate time interval following recovery. An attack of tetanus never of itself confers immunity.

**Control.**—The three basic factors in the control of tetanus are: (1) control of the environment to reduce opportunities for infection; (2) proper treatment of wounds; and (3) protection with tetanus antitoxin or tetanus toxoid, or both.

Environmental control has definite but limited possibilities. Accident control among children and adults, proper obstetrical procedures and care of the newborn, careful supervision in the manufacture of suture material (especially catgut) and therapeutic serums, avoidance of airtight dressings over smallpox vaccinations, and avoidance of the hazards of firecrackers, blank cartridges, bullets, and burns have significantly reduced the incidence of tetanus.

Proper treatment of wounds is essential to avoid local infection, death of tissue, and the associated formation of anaerobic environments in the body—factors favourable to the development of tetanus. Adequate cleansing, removal of devitalized tissue and foreign bodies, avoidance of injury to both healthy and disturbed structures, proper use of available antibacterial agents (penicillin and the tetracycline compounds), and immobilization of injured parts constitute a five-point program for the prevention of tetanus.

Tetanus antitoxin (antitetanic serum) for rapid protection is available throughout the world. For widespread use it is prepared from the blood serum of horses or cows that have been inoculated with tetanus toxoid or tetanus toxin, or both, and have become immune. On a limited scale, tetanus antitoxin of human origin (human tetanus-immune globulin) is available for special indications, such as allergy to animal serums; its universal use would result in a minimal incidence of all forms of serum sickness. The serum is concentrated and standardized in terms of an arbitrary unit. It must pass routine tests for safety before it is released for clinical use.

Tetanus toxoid, which stimulates active immunity in the person receiving the injection, is available either alone or combined with a variety of vaccines (diphtheria, whooping cough, typhoid, poliomyelitis, etc.). It is prepared by chemical alteration of the toxin, followed by tests to ensure absence of toxicity and to determine its potency.

Passive protection with tetanus antitoxin is desirable in all cases of injuries considered likely to be contaminated with spores of *Cl. tetani.* Active protection with tetanus toxoid is a relatively slow process which requires weeks or sometimes months for optimal development. Everyone should be actively protected against tetanus. This is especially true because a significant number of tetanus cases occur under conditions which are not controllable by routine serum (antitoxin) prophylaxis. Moreover, active protection of women in the childbearing period of life would result in temporary passive protection of newborn infants. Institution of this procedure on a large scale among primitive peoples would minimize the incidence of the highly fatal tetanus of the newborn.

Although tetanus respects no age, sex, economic status, or occupation, certain groups are considered more in need of routine active immunization than are others. They include the armed forces, civilian populations in danger of military attack, allergic individuals, farmers, industrial workers, childbearing women in localities with high incidence of tetanus of the newborn, and infants and children.

When tetanus antitoxin of animal origin (equine or bovine) is used, a detailed list of precautions against serum sickness must be obeyed. With the use of tetanus antitoxin of human origin these precautions may be largely ignored. The dose of antitoxin must be adequate: recognition of the inadequacy of time-honored doses has led to the recommendation of at least 5 to 15 times the amount used in World War I. Of vital importance is awareness of the enhanced protection conferred by antitoxin of human origin, one unit of which is estimated as equivalent to 100 units of foreign (bovine or equine) serum (J. C. Suri and S. D. Rubbo, 1961).

Tetanus toxoid is employed to build active immunity against future exposure to the disease. It does not confer immediate protection after the manner of tetanus antitoxin. Tetanus toxoid is injected in a series of two, and preferably three, doses, with appropriate intervals between the inoculations. Ordinarily, adequate protection emerges within a week after the second or third injection. At almost any time after completion of the original series of injections, very minute doses of toxoid can evoke very rapid, high, and prolonged elevations of antitoxin in the patient's body. Allergic reactions to tetanus toxoid are rare.

In patients not previously protected with tetanus toxoid, antitoxin must be employed to afford immediate protection. If the smaller doses of antitoxin (up to 5,000 units) are used, the first toxoid injection may be started at the time of the antitoxin inoculation, but at another site; subsequent doses of the toxoid are given according to routine schedule. With larger doses of antitoxin, however, the first dose of toxoid must be timed to coincide with maximal elimination of antitoxin, since large amounts of antitoxin neutralize the effects of toxoid. The higher the dose of antitoxin, the longer the interval for the initial dose of toxoid. When tetanus antitoxin of human origin is given in the small amounts needed for protection, toxoid may be injected simultaneously, at the customary distant separate site.

In civilian practice a reliable history of toxoid inoculation validates the routine use of tetanus toxoid in the event of injuries considered possibly conducive to the development of tetanus. In military practice, however, certain evidence indicates the possible need for combined toxoid-antitoxin prophylaxis, although the reliability of tetanus toxoid alone has also been documented. In civilian practice the sole established indication for supplementary antitoxin is the factor of delay in administration of a booster dose of toxoid. The length of the delay is governed by the nature and severity of the wound.

The value of tetanus antitoxin was first demonstrated in World War I, following the introduction of prophylactic passive immunization in the British Army toward the end of 1914. The reliability of tetanus toxoid in veterinary medicine was proved in France, where the active immunization of horses began in 1925. In human medicine, conclusive evidence of the prophylactic value of tetanus toxoid was obtained during World War II. In addition, the value of selectively prescribed tetanus antitoxin was reflected in the lowered mortality when the antitoxin was given in addition to toxoid at the time of injury; and the attenuating, if not preventive, effect of toxoid was indicated by the absence of deaths among cases given four or five injections before the onset of clinical tetanus.

The remarkable reduction of morbidity and mortality from tetanus during the later stages of World War I and during World War II focused attention on the sad statistics of other major wars. The comparative incidence of tetanus per 1,000 wounded has been tabulated as follows: Crimean War 2.0, American Civil War 2.07, Franco-Prussian War 3.5, Peninsular War (Wellington's campaign against Napoleon) 12.5.

**Incidence.**—Despite the worldwide distribution of the bacillus, comparatively few injured persons develop tetanus. In the U.S. the reported number of cases of tetanus decreased from 1,472 in 1920 and 560 in 1940 to less than 300 in the 1960s. Tetanus of the newborn has become relatively uncommon in the U.S. but persists in many other parts of the world. Tetanus in all age periods still appears with discouraging frequency in countries of high population density and low economic advantage. Postoperative tetanus, formerly attributable to contaminated catgut, is now rare. Adequate preventive measures have been credited with the reduced incidence of tetanus from wounds such as compound fractures, lacerations, and firecracker burns.

Bibliography.—L. Eckmann, *Tetanus, Prophylaxe und Therapie* (1960); H. Zinsser, *Microbiology,* 12th ed. by D. T. Smith *et al.* (1960); W. W. C. Topley and G. S. Wilson, *Principles of Bacteriology and Immunity,* 4th ed. by G. S. Wilson and A. A. Miles (1955).

(R. Sh.)

**TETENS, JOHANN NIKOLAUS** (1736–1807), German philosopher, mathematician, and economist, the most prominent representative of the Enlightenment (*q.v.*) philosophy in Germany, was born at Tetenbüll, South Schleswig, on Sept. 16, 1736. He was educated at the universities of Rostock and Copenhagen. He became professor of physics at Bützow University in 1763 and director of the *Pädagogium* (academy) there in 1765. In 1776 he was appointed professor of philosophy at Kiel University, where he later held the chair of mathematics. In 1777 he published his major work, *Philosophische Versuche über die menschliche Natur* ("Essays on Human Nature"; new ed. by W. Uebele, Berlin, 1913 *et seq.*). He gave up teaching and theoretical work in 1789 in order to enter public service, becoming assessor and then councilor of state and deputy in the Danish Ministry of Finance in Copenhagen, where he died on Aug. 15 (19?), 1807.

Tetens' *Philosophische Versuche* was the most important philosophical work written in Germany in the period immediately preceding Kant's *Critique;* it clearly shows the influence of the latter's *Dissertation* of 1770. In the preface to the *Philosophische Versuche* Tetens states, "metaphysical analysis . . . must be preceded by psychological analysis"; and further, "however far we proceed in metaphysical psychology, the authenticity of its propositions must always be tested by empirical knowledge." In this emphasis on the necessity of proceeding by way of construction in philosophy and on the importance of empirical foundations, Tetens approaches very close to the spirit of Kant, who valued his work highly and always kept a copy of the *Philosophische Versuche* on his writing table. Tetens was the only important German thinker to embrace, with some modifications, the empirical psychology in vogue in Great Britain and France during the 18th century; he calls the faculty of forming and combining ideas "understanding." In his threefold division of consciousness into feeling, will, and understanding he influenced Kant, to whose theory of knowledge these concepts are fundamental.

BIBLIOGRAPHY.—M. Schinz, *Die Moralphilosophie von Tetens* (1906); W. Uebele, *J. N. Tetens, nach seiner Gesamtentwicklung betrachtet, besonderer Berücksichtigung des Verhaltnisses zu Kant* (1911); A. Seidel, *Tetens Einfluss auf die kritische Philosophie Kants* (1932).

**TETRAGRAMMATON,** the four consonants, YHWH, of the name of the Hebrew God. *See* YAHWEH.

**TETRAHEDRITE,** a mineral consisting typically of copper sulfantimonide, but often of complex composition. It is an important ore of copper, in the pure form containing 57.5% of this metal; it is also largely worked as an ore of silver, of which it sometimes contains as much as 30%. The formula of tetrahedrite is $Cu_3SbS_3$ but copper is usually isomorphously replaced by variable amounts of silver, iron, zinc, mercury, lead, or cobalt, and the antimony by arsenic or bismuth. Numerous special names have been applied to varieties differing in chemical composition; the arsenic compound, $Cu_3AsS_3$, is known as tennantite (after the English chemist Smithson Tennant). The old German name *Fahlerz* includes both tetrahedrite and tennantite.

Well-developed crystals are of frequent occurrence; they belong to the tetrahedral class of the cubic system and their tetrahedral form is a characteristic feature of the mineral. In the accompanying figure (A) shows a combination of a tetrahedron and a trigonal tristetrahedron, and (B) a tetrahedron with the rhombic dodecahedron.

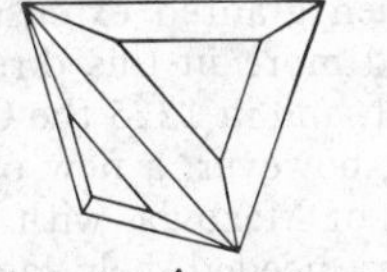
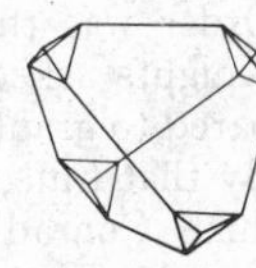
CHARACTERISTIC CRYSTALS OF TETRAHEDRITE

The colour of the mineral is steel gray to iron black, and the lustre is metallic and brilliant. The streak is usually black; sometimes, however, it is dark cherry red, and very thin splinters of the mineral then transmit a small amount of blood-red light. The hardness is 4.5, and the specific gravity varies with the composition from 4.4 to 5.1. There is no cleavage and the fracture is conchoidal.

Tetrahedrite occurs in metalliferous veins, associated with chalcopyrite and other sulfides. Fine groups of crystals, coated on their surface with brassy or brilliantly tarnished chalcopyrite, were formerly found at Herodsfoot Mine, near Liskeard in Cornwall, Eng.

Tennantite occurred as small crystals of cubic or dodecahedral habit in many Cornish copper mines, especially in the neighbourhood of Redruth. It is also found as small, brilliant crystals very rich in faces in the white crystalline dolomite of the Binnenthal in the Valais, Switz., and under the name binnite was long considered as a distinct species. It occurs in the Harz Mountains of Germany, in Freiberg, Saxony, the silver mines of Mexico, Bolivia, and Peru, and in the United States in silver and copper mines in Arizona, Colorado, Montana, Nevada, and Utah.

(CL. F.; L. J. S.; X.)

**TETRAPODA,** the term for the backboned animals with four limbs, the land vertebrates, including amphibians, reptiles, birds, and mammals. It is now primarily a term of convenience, but in some classifications it has taxonomic validity as a superclass collateral with the superclass Pisces (fishes) under the subphylum Vertebrata. *See* VERTEBRATE.

**TETRARCHY,** literally "rule of a quarter," is applied by the contemporary orator Demosthenes to the four governmental divisions into which Thessaly was divided (342 B.C.) by Philip II of Macedonia. Under the Roman Empire the term was loosely used of any small principality in the eastern provinces, notably in Galatia, Syria, and Palestine. Herod the Great and his brother Phasael were made tetrarchs of Judaea by Mark Antony in 41 B.C. As king of Judaea, Herod had his brother Pheroras made tetrarch of Peraea by Augustus in 20 B.C. After Herod's death (4 B.C.) two of his sons were made tetrarchs: Antipas of Galilee and Peraea, Philip of Batanaea, Auranitis, and Trachonitis; his eldest son, Archelaus, who ruled Samaria, Judaea, and Idumaea, was given the higher title of ethnarch. In modern times the term tetrarchy is applied to the rule of four emperors under Diocletian and his colleagues between A.D. 293 and 305. (A. H. M. J.)

**TETRICUS** (GAIUS PIUS ESUVIUS TETRICUS), rival Roman emperor in Gaul A.D. 270–273, was a Gallic noble, related to Victoria and her son, the emperor Victorinus, under whom he was governor of Aquitania. On Victorinus' murder he was proclaimed emperor, apparently backed by the influence and money of Victoria. His very numerous coins mark the height of the 3rd-century inflation. It was apparently in his reign that Gaul experienced the worst incidence of the German invasions, and he was threatened by successive mutinies. When the emperor Aurelian appeared in Gaul with an army, Tetricus, after private treaty with his opponent, deserted to him in the course of the battle. Aurelian pardoned him, and appointed him governor of southern Italy.

(JN. R. M.)

**TETSCHEN:** *see* DECIN.

**TETUÁN** (TETOUAN), the chief town of Tetuán Province and Jabalah (Djéblé) region, Morocco, is 10 mi. (16 km.) from the sea, at the point where the Wadi (Oued) Martin crosses the limestone of Er Rif range at a height of 2,500–4,000 ft. (800–1,200 m.). Pop. (1960) 101,352. It is built on a rocky plateau, detached from the southern flank of the Jebel Dersa. The Roman Tamuda stood immediately above it. In the 14th century the Marinid sultans built a fortress there which became a corsair stronghold, provoking the Spanish expedition that led to its destruction. In the 16th century Tetuán was populated by Muslim refugees from Spain. Spanish troops first occupied it in 1860 and again in 1913; it then became the residence of the Spanish high commissioner and of the sultan's khalifa. The old town is still surrounded by ramparts on three sides, enclosing the suqs (market places) and the mellah (Jewish quarter). Apart from the well-developed handicraft trades, commercial activities include livestock, fruit and farm products, fish canning, and the manufacture of textiles, soap, matches, and building materials.

Tetuán Province comprises the western Rif, except the hinterland of Tangier. Cereals are grown on the fertile plains and hills where the principal rural markets (Alcázarquivir, Larache, and Arcila) are found. (G. L. M.)

**TETZEL** (TEZEL), **JOHANN** (*c.* 1465–1519), German Dominican preacher of indulgences and first public antagonist of Martin Luther, was born at Pirna in Meissen about 1465. After studying at Leipzig he entered the Dominican order, being appointed inquisitor for Poland (1509), and later for Saxony. Between 1503 and 1510 he was in constant demand as a preacher of indulgences. He became a preacher for the indulgence attached to the contributions to the construction of St. Peter's, Rome, in the diocese of Meissen (1516), and those of Magdeburg and Halberstadt (1517).

Tetzel's preaching at Jüterbog, near Wittenberg, in the spring of 1517 was the occasion for the publication of Luther's 95 theses at Wittenberg on Oct. 31, 1517, which provoked an uncompromising reply, published under Tetzel's name but really written by Konrad Wimpina. Tetzel grasped the explosive character of Luther's thought and saw that the main issue involved the very basis of the Catholic theory of the church, on whose authority he published 50 theses in May 1518. At the end of 1518 he withdrew to Leipzig priory, where he died on Aug. 11, 1519.

Tetzel was by no means a profound theologian and was far from orthodox in his teaching on indulgences for the dead. His view that a mere gift sufficed to secure this indulgence, together with the financial transactions surrounding the preaching of it, gave rise to the grave abuses which helped to bring about the Reformation. In a sense the harm done by Tetzel was increased by his ability and appeal as a preacher. His style can be judged by specimen sermons he issued for the parochial clergy. For portrait, *see* article REFORMATION.

*See* N. Paulus, *Johann Tetzel der Ablassprediger* (1899). (I. HP.)

**TEUTOBURG FOREST, BATTLE OF THE.** In the late summer of A.D. 9 three legions with auxiliary troops under the Roman commander P. Quinctilius Varus were ambushed beyond the Rhine and destroyed by Arminius (*q.v.*), a chief of the Cherusci, allied with certain other German tribes. The circumstances of this battle, including its topography and even its precise date, have been the subject of a vast literature, since it has been generally believed that but for Varus' disaster Germany between the Rhine and the Elbe would have been romanized.

Tacitus (*Annals,* i, 60) indicated that the *Teutoburgiensis saltus* was near the country between the Ems and Lippe rivers; the modern name Teutoburger Wald for the range of hills southeast of Bielefeld was a 16th-century guess at his meaning. The identification is by no means certain, but it cannot be far wrong. Varus was moving from his summer camp just west of the Weser to a fort named Aliso on the Lippe (variously identified at points as far apart as Haltern and Paderborn) but had been deflected into difficult country to put down a supposed rising of which Arminius had deliberately given him news. Although Cassius Dio (3rd century A.D.) speaks of hills surrounding the army's route, Velleius Paterculus (a contemporary) and Tacitus emphasize the marshy terrain. If *saltus* meant "forest" rather than "mountain defile," the site might be west or northwest of the Wald, but this does not greatly alter the distance from the Roman bases on the Rhine.

As to the claims of Arminius to be *liberator Germaniae* (Tacitus, *Annals,* ii, 88), it must certainly be emphasized that in his day there was no united Germany and that Roman influence among the discordant tribes beyond the Rhine continued powerful for a long time to come. But in recent times it has also been denied that Augustus ever had any intention of annexing Germany east of the Rhine. Contemporary testimony (*e.g.,* Augustus' *Res Gestae,* 26, ". . . I pacified Germany . . . up to the mouth of the Elbe"; Velleius, ii, 97) is equivocal; there is no adequate archaeological evidence of occupation; and literary authorities say little or nothing about roadmaking, the construction of permanent camps and settlements, and the normal accompaniments of Roman rule. Yet the occupation was at most limited to 20 years, and aerial photography may still have something to reveal. The silence of Velleius, given the inexpert and prejudiced character of his military history, is not surprising, and Cassius Dio's full narrative is missing for the period 6 B.C. to A.D. 4. Accounts of Varus' activities in Germany up to A.D. 9 are certainly rhetorical, but all are agreed that he was imposing taxation and doing the judicial work associated with a Roman governor. If the period between the death of Drusus (9 B.C.; *see* DRUSUS, NERO CLAUDIUS) and the organization of a regular tribute-paying province seems long, the history of Moesia (*q.v.*) in the same period provides some parallel. It still seems likely that the loss of these three legions at a time of manpower shortage brought a drastic modification of Roman plans.

BIBLIOGRAPHY.—R. Syme in *Cambridge Ancient History,* vol. x, ch. 12 (1934), and A. Franke in Pauly-Wissowa, *Real-Encyclopädie der classischen Altertumswissenschaft,* 2nd series, vol. v, 1166–71 (1934), provide summaries of the more important earlier work; *see* also W. John in Pauly-Wissowa, *op. cit.,* vol. xxiv, 907–984 (1963). On the site and date *see* T. Rice Holmes, *The Architect of the Roman Empire,* vol. ii, pp. 164–176 (1931). (G. E. F. C.)

**TEUTONIC ORDER, KNIGHTS OF THE** (German DEUTSCHER ORDEN or DEUTSCHER RITTERORDEN, that is, German Order of Knights of St. Mary the Virgin), a religious body which played a major role in Eastern Europe in the later Middle Ages.

**Origin.**—In 1189, when crusading forces were besieging Acre in Palestine (*see* CRUSADES), some German merchants from Bremen and Lübeck formed a fraternity to nurse the sick there. After the capture of Acre (1191) this fraternity took over a hospital in the town and began to describe itself as the Hospital of St. Mary of the German House in Jerusalem. Pope Clement III approved it, and it adopted a rule like that of the original Hospital of St. John of Jerusalem. The death of the Hohenstaufen emperor Henry VI in 1197, when he was planning a great expedition to Palestine, caused an important change: a number of German crusaders who had arrived in Palestine decided to return home; to fill the gap the German princes and bishops, together with King Amalric II of Jerusalem, in 1198 militarized the fraternity, making it a religious Order of Knights.

The new Order was put under a monastic and military rule like that of the Templars (*q.v.*). It received privileges from Popes Celestine III and Innocent III and extensive grants of land, not only in the Kingdom of Jerusalem but also in Germany and in the Italian possessions of the Hohenstaufen German kings. It had a stronghold in Acre, but Montfort, in the hinterland northeast of Acre, became its main castle and was long the residence of its high master (*Hochmeister,* sometimes translated as grand master).

**Hermann von Salza.**—The Frankish states in Palestine and Syria, under pressure from the Muslims and torn by dissensions among their own rulers, offered only limited possibilities of successful establishment to the German nobles who joined the Order. The man who saw that clearly and found the solution to the problem was Hermann von Salza. Coming from the lower nobility of Thuringia, Hermann by sheer ability had made his way to the office of high master of the Order in 1210. He saw that the various motives behind the crusading movement were not strong enough to enlarge the Frankish outpost in the Near East; but meanwhile the rate of increase of Western Europe's population was still sufficient for an expansion of Christendom into Eastern Europe. Hermann therefore committed the Order to the German *Drang nach Osten,* or "Drive to the East" (*see* further GERMANY: *History*).

The Order's first European enterprise started in Hungary in 1211, when King Andrew II invited a group of the Knights to protect his Transylvanian borderland against the Kumans (*q.v.*) by colonizing it and by converting its people to Christianity. The Order was then granted extensive rights of autonomy; but the Knights asked more in this direction than their hosts were prepared to grant, and in 1225 the Order was expelled from Hungary. By that time, however, a new opportunity was opening: a Polish duke, Conrad of Mazovia, with lands on the lower reaches of the Vistula River, needed help against the pagan Prussians (*see* PRUSSIA).

Earlier in the 13th century the Cistercian monk Christian of Oliva, who was probably of Polish origin, had begun to preach Christianity to the Prussians. Pope Innocent III consecrated him bishop of Prussia in 1215; but soon afterward a pagan reaction forced Bishop Christian to seek political and military backing from Conrad of Mazovia. Conrad granted castles and lands around Chelmno (Ger. Kulm), on the right bank of the Vistula, to the bishop; but the latter was unsuccessful in organizing crusades from this Kulmerland, which the Prussians overran. Conrad then invited the Teutonic Order to take control (1225 or 1226).

Hermann proceeded very carefully, in order to avoid a repetition of what the Order had experienced in Transylvania. He already enjoyed the confidence of the Hohenstaufen emperor Frederick II, whom he had served as a diplomat. So, when Conrad made his offer, Hermann in 1226 obtained from Frederick the so-called Golden Bull of Rimini as a legal basis for the settlement. By this charter, Frederick confirmed to Hermann and to the Order, not only the lands to be granted by Conrad, but also those which the Knights were to conquer from the Prussians. Whereas previously the Papacy had enunciated a principle of liberty for the converted Balts and had represented political and military intervention as a transitory necessity, the text of Frederick's charter emphasized that the subjection of the pagan peoples was no less important than the conversion of them to Christianity; and Frederick endowed the high master of the Order with the same administrative and jurisdictional rights as were exercised by the princes of the Empire. Identity of territorial functions, however, did not make the high masters princes of the Empire themselves: princes were immediate vassals of the emperor (*see* FEUDALISM; PRINCE), and the Golden Bull of Rimini made no mention of any feudal link between high master and emperor. Obviously Hermann did not intend to break the custom, developed since Pope Gregory VII's time, that no ecclesiastic, except bishops and those Benedictine abbots who had been "members" or princes of the Empire for centuries, should become the vassal of a secular ruler.

Hermann's intention of keeping his relations with the Papacy intact is illustrated by his obtaining a new privilege from Pope Gregory IX in 1234, which can be regarded as the second foundation charter of the Order's Prussian state. When Conrad of Mazovia had formally granted the Kulmerland and had effectively ceded a base on the left bank of the Vistula to the Order (1230) and when Bishop Christian had fallen into the hands of the Prussians (1233), the Papacy was ready to accept the Order's present and future conquests as the property of the Holy See and to grant them back to the Order in perpetual tenure.

In 1230 Hermann von Salza sent Hermann Balk to be land master (*Landmeister* or provincial head) of the Order's new territory. A series of well-prepared campaigns began with the invasion of the Kulmerland in 1231; and in 1233 a general crusade for the conquest of Prussia was launched. The Knights themselves formed only a skeleton force, directing operations and consolidating their results. The main bulk of the armies was to consist of crusading laymen, volunteers for a definite term of service. This supply of volunteers, however, was not left to chance. Hermann von Salza, who moreover had increased the Order's possessions around Halle in central Germany, made contact with the lands under the archbishop of Magdeburg and concluded an alliance with the House of Wettin (*q.v.*), which was already powerful on the middle Elbe River. Also he got help from Silesia and from Bohemia. Finally, transport problems were largely solved through Hermann von Salza's understanding with Lübeck, whose citizens were pioneers of long-distance shipping in the Baltic.

Hermann von Salza died at Salerno, in Italy, on March 20, 1239.

**The Knights of the Sword.**—In 1237, less than two years before Hermann von Salza's death, the Order of the Brothers of the Sword (*Schwertbrüderorden*), also known as the Knights of the Sword or the Livonian Order, which had been founded in 1202 to help the bishops of Riga to christianize the lands at the eastern end of the Baltic, was made a branch of the Teutonic Order, its head becoming land master of Livonia (*q.v.*). The Teutonic Order, however, never established such effective control over these northern provinces as it did over Prussia: its authority there was sharply contested by various bishoprics (Riga became an archbishopric in 1245); northern Estonia was under Danish suzerainty till 1346; an attack by the Knights on the neighbouring Russian state of Novgorod led to their defeat by Alexander (*q.v.*) Nevski on Lake Peipus in 1242; and Courland (*q.v.*), the southern part of the Livonian land master's province, was connected with Prussia only by a very narrow strip of coastland, since Samogitia, the hinterland, remained in the possession of hostile Lithuania (*q.v.*) except for the brief period 1398–1411. For further details on the Knights of the Sword, *see* ESTONIA: *History;* LATVIA: *History.*

**The Colonization of Prussia.**—With the help of the volunteer crusaders, the Teutonic Order pushed its Prussian conquests farther and farther toward the lower Neman (Niemen, Nemunas). By 1260 it was already in possession of Samland, the country north of the Pregel estuary. Castles were built to form a network of military and administrative centres (there were 23 of them by the end of the 13th century), the more important ones being the seats of commanders of districts, each with his convent of knights-brethren. The architecture was of a uniform type: a bulky square of brick walls round a courtyard, with a defensive system of deep ditches.

Apart from the members of the Order, who were of course celibate, lay members of the knightly class who had come as volunteer crusaders might receive lands for themselves and their families to hold as fiefs from the Order, in return for military service. Up to the 1260s these grants of land might be very large, and during this period only about 100 families were thus settled.

The Order also proceeded to found German towns: marketplaces with a German population were established—probably in localities where the indigenous Prussians had traded with their western neighbours before the Order's arrival. A charter known as the *Kulmer Handfeste* (1233) granted liberty of river traffic and local jurisdiction to Kulm and to Thorn (Torun); and towns which grew up later, including Königsberg (originally a military stronghold; *see* KALININGRAD), received privileges on the same model. Before the end of the 13th century, moreover, the Order was controlling the production of grain in its territory and taking charge of the export of grain oversea.

At first the settlement of German peasants was on a comparatively small scale. In 1261, however, a great insurrection of the subject Prussians broke out, and for 12 years the Order's survival in Prussia was threatened. A further decade of violent fighting restored the Order's supremacy. A new land policy was adopted in the 1280s: many of the larger holdings of the German vassals were reduced in order to provide land for more settlers, whose number subsequently rose to about 500 families, and a strong influx of German peasants was organized. Cultivation spread gradually from the lower Vistula and the Baltic coast to the southern and southeastern borderland, which had previously been left wild. Immigration continued till 1410, notwithstanding the decline of Europe's population and economic stagnation in the second half of the 14th century. (*See* further PRUSSIA.)

Montfort, behind Acre, fell to the Muslims in 1271, and Acre itself fell in 1291. The high master Konrad von Feuchtwangen then moved his seat to Venice; but in 1309, when Philip IV of France was destroying the Order of the Templars (*q.v.*), the Teutonic high master Siegfried von Feuchtwangen took the precaution of transferring his residence to Marienburg (Pol. Malbork), on the easternmost bank of the Vistula delta. Thenceforward successive high masters were themselves land masters of Prussia, while the Order's possessions in Germany were under a *Deutschmeister* or "German master" and Livonia remained under a land master of its own. In Marienburg the high master held court in a great brick building in the North German type of the Gothic style; his permanent council, comprising the other grand officers of the Order, became something like the ministry of a modern state.

**Polish and Lithuanian Relations.**—From the end of the 13th century the Order's foreign policy was determined by the need to reduce the isolation of Prussia. When the succession to Pomerelia, that is, to the easternmost part of Pomorze (*q.v.*), was in dispute between Poland, Brandenburg, and the Teutonic Order, the Knights took Danzig (Gdansk) in 1308 and obtained Brandenburg's assent to their annexing most of the rest of Pomerelia in 1309. They thus won a territorial link with the lands on the Oder River, feudally dependent on the German kingdom; but in so doing they cut Poland off from access to the Baltic. In the east, however, the Lithuanians still resisted the Order's attempts to widen the corridor between Prussia and Courland.

Poland and Lithuania were inevitably antagonized by the Order's expansion. The Lithuanian Gediminas (*q.v.*) and Wladyslaw I (*q.v.*) of Poland fought against it; and though Wladyslaw I's successor Casimir III (*q.v.*) made the Peace of Kalisz (1343) with the Order, the anti-German reaction continued to grow in strength among the Eastern European peoples. Moreover, the death of the Holy Roman emperor Charles IV (1378) was followed by the disintegration of the great block of territory which his dynasty, the House of Luxembourg, had built up on the Elbe and Oder Rivers; and this meant that the prospect of efficient support for the Order from the Empire was seriously reduced. The Lithuanian prince Jogaila (Jagiello) promised to cede Samogitia to the Order in 1382; but his marriage to the Polish queen Jadwiga, in 1386, radically changed the situation. Becoming king of Poland, as Wladyslaw II (*q.v.*), and accepting Christianity for himself and for his people, he could threaten the Order with a powerful coalition along its southern and eastern borders at the same time as he deprived it of all pretext for a crusade.

Vytautas (*q.v.*) of Lithuania, temporarily estranged from Poland, ceded Samogitia to the Order in 1398; but in 1401 Wladyslaw II and Vytautas were reconciled. Rebellion against the

Order in Samogitia began in 1408, the high master Ulrich von Jungingen attacked Poland in 1409, and the Poles and Lithuanians defeated the Knights in the Battle of Grunwald (*q.v.*) in 1410, at which Ulrich was killed. Heinrich Reuss von Plauen successfully defended the Marienburg, but had to renounce Samogitia to Lithuania and the Dobrzyn Land (southeast of the Kulmerland) to Poland at the First Peace of Torun in 1411, which also imposed a heavy ransom for captives.

A general collapse of the Order's moral and political authority ensued. Wartime devastation, coupled with a recession in the Baltic trade, ruined the economy, and Poland did not relax pressure. Heinrich Reuss von Plauen, elected high master in 1411, was deposed in 1413 by a faction hoping vainly to conciliate the Poles. Moreover, the secular nobles in Prussia, regarding the Order's political status as an anachronism, saw no treason in cooperating with Poland. In 1440 the nobles and the towns formed the Prussian League to assert themselves against the Order; and in 1454 Casimir IV of Poland responded to their appeal for military help. After a long war, during which the high master Ludwig von Erlichshausen had to move his residence to Königsberg (1457), the Second Peace of Torun (1466) was concluded: the Order ceded Pomerelia and the left and right banks of the Vistula, together with the bishopric of Warmia (Ermland), to Poland. The rest of Prussia was left to the high master as a subject of the Polish crown.

**The End of the Knights.**—The Teutonic Order's rule in Prussia came to an end in 1525, when the high master Albert (*q.v.*), under Lutheran influence, dissolved the Order there and accepted its territory as a secular duchy for himself under Polish suzerainty (*see* also HOHENZOLLERN; PRUSSIA). The land master of Livonia held his province for his Order till 1558; then most of its territory was partitioned between Russia, Sweden, and Poland-Lithuania, and in 1561 the land master Gotthard Kettler became secular duke of Courland, as a vassal of the Polish king. Meanwhile, in 1530, the emperor Charles V had made the still Catholic *Deutschmeister* a prince of the Holy Roman Empire; the latter's successors, with their seat at Mergentheim on the Tauber River, controlled the Order's lands in central and southern Germany till 1809, when Napoleon, at war against Austria, declared the Order to be dissolved and distributed its lands among other principalities. The Austrians reestablished the Order in Vienna, as an ecclesiastical institution, in 1834.

*See* also references under "Teutonic Order, Knights of the" in the Index.

BIBLIOGRAPHY.—J. Voigt, *Geschichte des Deutschen Ritterordens*, 2 vol. (1857–59); H. von Treitschke, "Das deutsche Ordensland Preussen" (1862; reprinted in his *Historische und politische Aufsätze*); E. Caspar, *Hermann von Salza . . .* (1924); C. Krollmann, *Politische Geschichte der Deutschen Ordens . . .* (1932) and *The Teutonic Order in Prussia* (1938); E. Joachim and W. Hubatsch (editors), *Regesta historico-diplomatica Ordinis S. Mariae Theutonicorum*, 2 parts (1948–50); F. L. Carsten, *The Origins of Prussia* (1954). (H. Lz.)

**TEUTONIC PEOPLES:** *see* GERMANIC PEOPLES.

**TEVFIK PASHA, AHMED** (AHMET TEVFIK PASA) (1845–1936), the last Ottoman Turkish grand vizier, was born in Istanbul on Feb. 11, 1845. His father, Ferik Ismail Hakki Pasha, was the commander of the Danube region. Ahmed Tevfik was of Crimean descent. He graduated from the military cadet school as a lieutenant in 1862. Four years later he resigned his commission and joined the foreign service to become in 1871 second secretary to the embassy in Florence. He served in various embassies and was appointed chargé d'affaires to St. Petersburg in 1877. On the declaration of war with Russia he returned to Istanbul and was appointed political adviser to Abdul-Kerim Pasha, commander of the region with headquarters at Sumnu in Bulgaria.

In 1895, after 10 years as ambassador in Berlin, Tevfik Pasha returned to Istanbul to become foreign minister, a post he held for 14 years. After the Young Turk Revolution of 1909 he was made grand vizier. When Abdul-Hamid II was forced to abdicate, Mehmed V (1909–18) kept him as grand vizier, but he resigned and became ambassador in London. There he remained until World War I. During the war he served as member of the Senate. He became grand vizier again after the armistice (1918), but following the occupation by the Allies he resigned and again became a member of the Senate. In 1919 he was head of the first delegation to the Paris peace conference, but he was ill received by Clemenceau and had to return. He went there again in May 1920 but refused to sign the Sèvres peace treaty because he considered it incompatible with Turkish sovereignty. In 1920 he became grand vizier for the third time and headed the Turkish delegation to the London peace conference in February 1921. There he openly declared his support for the Turkish representatives from Ankara. When the Sublime Porte government came to an end in November 1922, he was still grand vizier. He died in Nisantasi, Istanbul, in 1936. (M. P. P.)

**TEVIOT,** a river of Scotland, flowing near the southern border. Teviotdale comprises a large part of Roxburgh. The headstreams rise at about 1,500 ft. (460 m.) in the watershed between Teviotdale and Eskdale around Wisp Hill (1,950 ft. [594 m.]) on the Dumfries boundary. The river flows northeast for about 37 mi. (60 km.), past the town of Hawick, and joins the Tweed (*q.v.*) at Kelso. It is joined on the right by the Slitrig, the Rule, and the Jed, on the left by the Borthwick and the Ale. All of them are trout streams, and the Teviot also has some salmon fishing. The Teviot is a fairly rapid and shallow stream winding between terraces (haughs) across a flat-floored valley with steep bluffs, at first narrow in hill country, then about a half mile wide in a broader dale, then widening out among the rolling ground-moraine hummocks of the main lower basin of the Tweed. (A. T. A. L.)

**TEWFIK PASHA, MOHAMMED** (MUHAMMAD TAWFIQ PASHA) (1852–1892), khedive of Egypt, eldest son of the khedive Ismail, was born in Cairo on April 30, 1852. He had a difficult upbringing; his father, mistaking his mildness for stupidity, neglected his education. Nevertheless, he was for a few weeks president of the Council of Ministers during the crisis which precipitated Ismail's deposition on June 26, 1879. Summoned by Sultan Abdul-Hamid II to succeed his father, he adopted a cooperative, if passive, attitude toward Anglo-French control of Egyptian state finances. Nationalist opposition to foreign influence increased from September 1881 when he was faced by a military mutiny. In February 1882 he was forced to accept a Nationalist ministry with Arabi Pasha (*q.v.*) as minister of war. Tewfik Pasha's position in the capital having become intolerable, he retired to Alexandria where he stayed during the disorders and British naval bombardment in July. On Sept. 25, after the collapse of the Nationalist revolt, he returned to Cairo under the protection of the British army. Relying solely on the advice of Sir Evelyn Baring (later earl of Cromer), the British representative, he acquiesced in the British occupation and in 1884 reluctantly agreed to the British request for Egyptian withdrawal from the Sudan. Tewfik Pasha took a special interest in irrigation, education, and justice. He showed little desire to keep up the unapproachable state of an Oriental ruler, and in many ways his manners were less Oriental than European. He was a strong advocate of monogamy. He died at Hulwan on Jan. 7, 1892, and was succeeded by his son, Abbas Hilmi Pasha.

*See* Earl of Cromer, *Modern Egypt*, 2 vol., 2nd ed. (1911). (R. L. HL.)

**TEWKESBURY,** an ancient market town and municipal borough in the Cirencester and Tewkesbury parliamentary division of Gloucestershire, Eng., stands near the confluence of the River Severn (which forms the parish boundary for some miles) and the Warwickshire Avon, 11 mi. (18 km.) N of Gloucester and 9 mi. (14 km.) NW of Cheltenham. Over the Avon is the medieval King John's Bridge. Pop. (1961) 5,822.

The town's most striking feature is the abbey church of St. Mary, founded by Robert Fitz Hamon and consecrated in 1123. It occupies the site of a Saxon hermitage, built by the monk Theoc (Theuk), from whom the place is said to have derived its name, and that of a small Benedictine abbey (founded in 715). The tower and nave were finished in 1150, and after the church had been largely destroyed by fire in 1178 important rebuilding took place. In the 15th century the Despenser family was responsible for considerable additions including the clerestory of the choir and several of the chantry chapels. The abbey was relinquished in 1539/40 but the choir, transepts, and central tower were purchased by the people of Tewkesbury for £453, while practically all the conventual building was destroyed. The impressive square Norman tower (148 ft. [45 m.] from ground to pinnacles and 46 ft. [14 m.] wide) affords extensive views over the low-lying countryside. The nave has seven Norman pillars on each side, more than 30 ft. (9 m.) high and 6 ft. (2 m.) in diameter. The 14th-century groined vaulting of the roof has a fine series of carved bosses; the west arch and window can be seen to advantage from outside. The window dates from 1686, the earlier one having been destroyed by a storm in 1661. There are interesting early tombs, particularly those of the Despensers. Restoration work was started in 1875 by Sir George Gilbert Scott.

The earls of Gloucester made Tewkesbury a free borough in the 12th century; the charter of liberties granted by William III in 1698 still remains in force.

There are many fine old houses ranging from half-timbered Tudor and Jacobean, with overhanging upper stories, to attractive red-brick buildings of the Queen Anne and Georgian periods. A quaint watermill is near the abbey and notable and picturesque inns include the Hop Pole, mentioned in *Pickwick Papers,* and the Bell, featured in the novel, *John Halifax, Gentleman,* by Mrs. Craik (Dinah Maria Mulock). The Black Bear, dating from 1308, is perhaps the oldest inn in Gloucestershire. The Tudor House Hotel in the High Street was formerly the old Academy founded in 1712 by the Rev. Samuel Jones of Pennsylvania. At the Cross is held the town's annual October fair, the site of the ancient Barton Market. Tewkesbury, reputedly famous for mustard in Shakespeare's day, is a centre for boating and angling, particularly on the slow-flowing Avon; its main industries are flour milling, engineering, and boat building. (B. C. F.)

**Battle of Tewkesbury.**—In this battle (May 4, 1471) of the Wars of the Roses (*q.v.*) Edward IV finally defeated his Lancastrian opponents. Queen Margaret, wife of the imprisoned Henry VI, had landed at Weymouth from France with her son, Prince Edward, on April 14, the day of the Yorkist victory at Barnet. She was subsequently joined by Edmund Beaufort, duke of Somerset, his younger brother John, and John Courtenay, earl of Devon, who persuaded her that Lancastrian strength in the west was still unbroken; accordingly, after a halt at Exeter, the army struck inland toward the Welsh border. Edward IV, having reorganized his troops, marched from Windsor on April 19 to intercept the Lancastrians. On May 2 the armies made contact at Chipping Sodbury, but the Lancastrians slipped away toward Gloucester, where they hoped to cross the Severn. Refused admission to the town, they hurried north, and on the afternoon of May 3 entrenched themselves just south of Tewkesbury. The Yorkists, coming from Cheltenham, camped just a little farther south. Battle was joined the next morning, each side being about 3,000 strong. The duke of Somerset commanded the Lancastrian right, Prince Edward the centre, and the earl of Devon the left. Richard, duke of Gloucester, led the Yorkist left, King Edward the centre, and Lord Hastings the right. The Lancastrians had a useful defensive position, but Somerset sought to turn the Yorkist left by a surprise attack through the wooded ground on his own flank. This attempt miscarried, the Yorkists broke the main Lancastrian position, and the Lancastrian centre collapsed. Some, fleeing toward the river, were slain in Bloody Meadow, others by the abbey mill. About 1,000 perished, including Prince Edward, Devon, and Somerset's brother John. Somerset, dragged from the abbey, was executed on May 6; Queen Margaret was taken from hiding on May 7. The murder of Henry VI in the Tower completed the Lancastrian ruin.

*See* W. Bazeley, "The Battle of Tewkesbury," *Transactions of the Bristol and Gloucestershire Archaeological Society,* vol. xxvi (1903); A. H. Burne, *The Battlefields of England,* 2nd ed. (1951). (Gy. T.; X.)

**TEXARKANA,** an urban community on the boundary line of Texas and Arkansas, U.S., 165 mi. NE of Dallas. First settled in 1874, Texarkana, Tex. (Bowie County), was incorporated in 1875; Texarkana, Ark. (seat of Miller County), in 1881. The two cities have separate municipal governments but are integrated economically. A railroad and bus centre, the community has many manufacturing plants. Ordnance plants of the U.S. Army are located nearby. Pop. (1960) community, 50,006 (Texarkana, Tex., 30,218; Texarkana, Ark., 19,788); standard metropolitan statistical area (Bowie County, Tex., and Miller County, Ark.), 91,657. For comparative population figures *see* table in ARKANSAS: *Population* and in TEXAS: *Population.* (N. McG.)

**TEXAS,** popularly known as the "Lone Star State" for the single star in its flag, a west south-central state of the United States, won independence from Mexico in 1836, was a republic until 1845, and was then annexed by the U.S., becoming the 28th state. Bounded on the southwest by Mexico, on the west (but north of its Trans-Pecos region) by New Mexico, on the north by Oklahoma, on the northeast by Arkansas, on the east by Louisiana, and on the southeast by the Gulf of Mexico, its total boundary is 2,845.3 mi. (4,579 km.), including major bends of rivers and seacoast. Its area in 1964, after the Chamizal settlement transferring 437 ac. to Mexico, was reduced to 267,338 sq.mi. (692,402 sq.km.)—262,839 sq.mi. (680,750 sq.km.) of land and 4,499 sq.mi. (11,652 sq.km.) of water surface. In size it ranks second only to Alaska. The state flower is the bluebonnet, the bird the mockingbird, the tree the pecan, the song "Texas, Our Texas." The state flag consists of a blue perpendicular stripe (next to the staff) on which is placed a single white star; and two horizontal stripes, the upper white, the lower red. The capital is Austin (*q.v.*).

Obscured by a mist of myths conceived by others and by fictions maintained by its own, Texas has been extravagantly praised and deplored from its beginning. An early example of censure was a 16-page pamphlet written in 1845 by Edward Everett Hale: *How to Conquer Texas, Before Texas Conquers Us.* The tone of the censure had not changed much a century later. Never less than sixth of the U.S. states in population in every federal census from 1900 to 1960, second largest in area, and first in its capacity for illusion, Texas is one of the few states to have been an independent nation (1836–45) before joining the Union. More than any other member of the former Confederate States of America (1861–65), Texas escaped the economic and social penalties of being a unit of the American South after 1900; beginning notably in the 1940s petroleum and later petrochemicals were its stimulants.

So great are its area and diversity, which are causes of problems peculiar to it, that Texas is easier to comprehend as a region than as a state. Indeed, it is unique in having the right to divide itself into more states, an event even less likely of realization than the transformation of Texans into a taciturn people. The joint resolution on the state's annexation to the U.S. says: "New States of convenient size, not exceeding four in number, in addition to the said State of Texas . . . may hereafter, by the consent of said State, be formed . . . ." Any definition of the state's character is imperfect, a result of its vast area and diversity. The culture of the Rio Grande Valley is foreign to that of the Great Plains area, hundreds of miles to the north. The concerns of the El Paso region are seldom those of the Texas that touches Louisiana, nearly 800 mi. (1,290 km.) to the east. Dalhart, in the Texas Panhandle, is nearer to the capitals of New Mexico, Kansas, Colorado, Oklahoma, and Nebraska than to the capital of Texas. The state's area is as much an obstacle as an advantage.

Texas is almost exactly midway between the Atlantic and Pacific. Its 624-mi. (1,000-km.) seacoast (tidewater) is the third longest of the conterminous states. It has a border touching a foreign nation whose civilization, language, and dominant religion differ from its own, longer than all the rest of the states together. It is a land of extremes, and of such almost inconceivable variety that it cannot be compared with any other state, not even with any other equal land area in the nation. Its mineral wealth is its fortune: since the 1930s it has been first among the states in the value of its mineral production, mainly oil and natural gas.

The historian Walter Prescott Webb has shown that by accident "Texas stands in the physical path of a special destiny." The accident is a cultural triangle in which three natural environments, three molds of separate cultures, meet and oppose each other in Texas: the woodlands, the plains, and the desert. There is also a fourth, the sea.

Texas is the only state to retain ownership of its public lands, a circumstance of large importance in financing education. The republic of Texas claimed a public domain of more than 225,000,000 ac. (91,057,500 ha.). By the Compromise of 1850, 72,892,000 ac. (29,499,400 ha.) of this land were transferred to the U.S. for $10,000,000 and, in 1855, an additional $2,750,000. The transferred land eventually formed parts of the states of New Mexico, Kansas, Colorado, and Wyoming. Nearly 52,000,000 ac. (21,044,400 ha.), or roughly 30% of the state's total area, were given to benefit public education, later endowed by land sales, rents, mineral leases, and royalties.

More important are the distinctive contributions of Texas to Western civilization: the union of the common and the civil law that produced the doctrines of community property and homestead exemption, the abolition of special pleading, and the blending of law and equity in a single court. These innovations, growing out of the Texas revolution, have spread not only throughout the U.S. but to some extent throughout the English-speaking world.

## PHYSICAL GEOGRAPHY

**Physical Features.**—Texas (lying between longitude 93°31′ and 106°38′ W and latitude 25°50′ and 36°30′ N) tilts to the southeast, as if propped up against the western mountains. Thus the streams flow from the northwest to the southeast, almost parallel with each other. Eight of them (Sabine [*q.v.*], Neches, Trinity, Brazos, Colorado, Guadalupe-San Antonio, Nueces, and Rio Grande [*q.v.*]), empty into the Gulf of Mexico. The Rio Grande, longest of the rivers, forms the southwestern boundary of Texas. The Red River (*q.v.*), second longest and the only one of importance not bearing a Spanish name, is part of the northern boundary, and the Sabine is part of the eastern boundary.

The Balcones fault is a natural partition having an extraordinary effect on the state's history, culture, and economy. Cutting Texas in two in an irregular line, the fault extends east from the Rio Grande, near Del Rio, to San Antonio, northeast to Austin, and, after bulging to the west, northeast to the Red River east of Wichita Falls. East of the fault lies roughly 40% of the state's area, all of its most populous cities except El Paso, far to the west, and most of its wealth and rainfall. The region east of the line is humid and buoyant; that west of it is dry and comparatively hard up except where it has been sweetened by irrigation or the discovery of oil.

Texas is divided by the four North American physiographic regions that extend into it: the Gulf coastal plain, entering from the east; the central lowlands, from the north; the Great Plains, from the northwest; and the eastern ranges of the Rocky Mountains, which cross the Texas Trans-Pecos region (the western part of the state between the Rio Grande and the southern boundary of New Mexico), also from the northwest.

*Gulf Coastal Plain.*—The Gulf coastal plain covers the favoured 40% of Texas east of the Balcones fault. The region, rising from sea level to an elevation of 800 ft. (245 m.), is divided into five fairly distinct areas. The coastal prairies, extending 75 to 100 mi. (120–160 km.) inland between Corpus Christi and Port Arthur, comprise one of the richest agricultural and mineral areas of the state, yet also the most urban and industrial. This is the economic heartland of Texas. Entering the state from the east and extending 100 mi. westward are the southern yellow pine forests. West of the pine belt is one of secondary forest growth, popularly known as the post-oak belt. Adjacent to the post-oak belt are the fertile blackland prairies, which extend in a long, narrow V-shape from the Red River on the north to the fifth area, the Rio Grande Plain, on the southwest. The last, south and southwest of San Antonio, is popularly known as the brush country, or Chaparral, but it also includes in southernmost Texas the lower Rio Grande Valley. The valley is a small but important area, with a year-round growing season, that is rich in irrigated citrus and winter vegetable production.

*Central Lowlands.*—Flanked by the coastal plain on the east and by the Great Plains on the west and south are the central lowlands, reaching into Texas from the north in a belt nearly 200 mi. wide. Sloping upward from an elevation of 800 ft. on its eastern edge to 2,500 ft. at the cap rock escarpment separating the central lowlands from the Great Plains province on the west, the region is divided into three areas. On the east, extending north and south from the Red River into central Texas, is the Grand Prairie, a sharply rolling country. On the eastern and western edges of the Grand Prairie are minor forest areas known as the Cross Timbers; the larger West Cross Timbers is a hilly area spotted with post-oak woodlands and prairies. West of it are the rolling prairies, largely covered with mesquite, which extend to the Great Plains region on the west.

*Great Plains.*—The Great Plains (*q.v.*) region in Texas, a vast L-shaped province west and south of the central lowlands and west of the Gulf coastal plain, extends to the eastern slopes of the Rocky Mountains. The region rises abruptly from an elevation of 2,500 ft. (760 m.) at the well-defined cap rock escarpment on the east and very gradually slopes upward to an elevation of 4,600 ft. (1,400 m.) at the New Mexico boundary. The generally flat area is broken on the north by several canyons, notably the Palo Duro Canyon of the Red River. The region may be divided into three areas (but two of them, the Edwards Plateau and the central Texas Basin, are often classed as parts of the central lowlands, with which in some ways they are more in character). The larger area to the north is the Staked Plains, or Llano Estacado (*q.v.*), itself divided into the North and South plains. The Edwards Plateau, forming more than half of the bottom of the L, extends eastward to the Balcones fault. A rugged limestone tableland comprising nearly an eighth of the state's area, it is almost as flat as the Staked Plains. Between the plateau on the south and the central lowlands on the north is the central Texas Basin, itself divided into the Texas hill country, a resort and vacation area, and the Burnet-Llano Basin on the north. The hilly central Texas Basin is in an intermediate stage of erosion between the youth of the Edwards Plateau and the old age of the central lowlands. Many exceptions must be made, however, when the Edwards Plateau and the central Texas Basin are included in the Great Plains region. As the eastern edges of both are on the Balcones fault (elevation 800 ft.), they are exceptions to the Great Plains' elevation range of 2,500 to 4,600 ft.

*Rocky Mountains.*—The Rocky Mountain region that crosses Trans-Pecos Texas from northwest to southeast is the most barren but in many ways the most interesting of the state's four physiographic regions. It includes desert lands, the highest mountains in Texas, and the strange beauties and contrasts of the Big Bend National Park. Its lowest elevation is 2,000 ft. (610 m.) at the eastern edge of the Stockton Plateau and elsewhere; its highest elevation is Guadalupe Peak, 8,751 ft. (2,667 m.). Sparsely populated except for El Paso in the westernmost tip of Texas, the region is divided into five areas. They are, from east to west, the Stockton Plateau, a rolling plain that is a Trans-Pecos extension of the Edwards Plateau; the Big Bend National Park; the Davis Mountains, which reach an elevation of 8,382 ft. (2,550 m.) in Mt. Livermore; the Diablo Plateau, a high plateau that includes Guadalupe Peak; and the upper Rio Grande Valley at the western tip of Texas, chiefly a mountain and desert area except for a narrow, irrigated alluvial strip, 100 mi. long and important for its cotton production, along the Rio Grande.

*Popular Division.*—The people of Texas more commonly think of the state as being divided into seven geographic regions. Under other circumstances of history these regions might reasonably have become separate states. Each has distinctive physical features as well as to some extent an economy and culture of its own. In the mind's eye of most Texans these regions are virtually provinces whose names are proper nouns: (1) east Texas, spared the mildew of William Faulkner's Deep South by its oil; (2) the Gulf Coast, a golden littoral of energy and cities; (3) the Rio Grande Valley, the almost-tropics, with its chain of small cities that together are the fourth largest city in Texas; (4) the Border, indelibly Mexico and the valley's cast-off kin; (5) west Texas and the Trans-Pecos, the last the desert, the first the Old West of romantic fiction, side by side and sharing drought's poverty of purse and spirit; (6) the Panhandle, with nothing to rest the eye on, not even a tree, except the surprise of cities rising from the Great

Plains; and finally (7) central Texas, the vast middle region, pragmatic and more stable than the others. Here in the centre the other six regions merge and lose their identities in what, in the small towns, is fancied to be the heart of Texas—rural civilization.

The extraordinary diversity of the state's climate, soil, vegetation, and animal life is caused in part by its location but to a larger extent by its enormous area, a fact so obvious as to be neglected when Texas is compared with any other state. This land area, a twelfth of the area of conterminous U.S., must be always held in mind to give proportion to superlatives of the state's physical geography and in some cases to understand that the superlatives are not so exceptional as they may at first seem. (Even more must the state's area be held in mind in evaluating its leading position in many categories of agricultural and mineral production, later subjects.) The land area of Texas is larger than that of France, the largest country in Europe; it is larger than the combined area of many states. To make statistical comparisons of Texas with other states is often unrealistic. For instance, the state does not produce more cotton than any other state because its growers are more efficient or its land more fertile or because it produces more cotton per acre (it does not) but because it has so many acres on which to grow cotton.

**Climate.**—Texas lies almost wholly in the belt of medium (mesothermal) temperatures, and the state has been variously divided into climatic regions (usually 12) of temperature and rainfall. Of all aspects of the state's physical geography, however, climate is revealed the least by scientific or technical exposition. It may be that the excesses of Texas weather provided Texans' earliest impetus toward exaggeration—the gasconade and flamboyance that have become characteristic.

In late autumn, winter, and early spring, cold winds blow down across the top of Texas, pushing rapidly across most of the state, sometimes reaching as far as the lower Rio Grande Valley in southernmost Texas. Texans call the cold waves "northers," blue northers, wet northers, or dry northers. The chief characteristic of a norther that distinguishes it from what other people call a cold wave is the sudden, dramatic fall in temperature. Such a decline may amount to 20° or 30° F (11° to 17° C) in two or three hours, but temperatures fall below 32° F (0° C) only for short periods. Texas weather is often violent: July to September is the season of greatest hurricane activity, and tornadoes strike through a wide east-west band of the state. A study by the U.S. Weather Bureau in 1961 showed that Texas averaged 28 tornadoes a year between 1916 and 1961. This average held true in subsequent years. In 1953, the most destructive year for tornadoes in the state's history, four twisters killed 142 people, injured 781, and damaged or destroyed more than $44,000,000 worth of property.

All Texas is sometimes cold in the winter, and all of it is hot nearly every day in the summer. Mean annual temperatures range from 55° F (13° C) at the top of the Panhandle to 74° F (23° C) on the lower Rio Grande, the temperatures rising in roughly parallel east-west belts. Rainfall averages more than 55 in. (1,397 mm.) annually in the small easternmost section of the state, decreasing gradually, in north-south belts, to the west until it is less than 10 in. (254 mm.) annually at El Paso. Snow averages 20 in. (508 mm.) annually in the northern Staked Plains and in some of the mountain areas, but otherwise snow is not a factor in Texas weather.

**Soil.**—Roughly 130 soil series, divided into more than 500 soil types, have been identified in Texas. The state's surface has been divided into 14 land resource areas (broad areas of more or less uniform soil, topography, climate, and vegetation), but its soils may be grouped into six general classes. These are the heavy coastal clays, including the river bottoms extending into the interior of the state; the sandy and sandy clay soils of the east Texas timber belt; the limestone soils of the blackland prairies, Grand Prairie, Edwards Plateau, and parts of the Trans-Pecos area; the mottled red and gray loam soils of north central Texas; the sandy and sandy loam soils of the high plains; and the rough stony lands of the Trans-Pecos and large areas of southwest Texas.

**Vegetation.**—Natural life in North America has been more profoundly affected by fencing than by any other of man's devices, the naturalist Roy Bedichek has written, and "Texas is certainly the most fence-conscious state in the Union . . . ." For all its injury to nature, however, the fence has created a cultural resource of significance. Rights-of-way for rail and automobile traffic were securely fenced with natural growths still intact, preserving what Bedichek calls elongated "relic areas" that include nearly all the species present when Western man first occupied the country.

It may be that no other part of the world of comparable size equals Texas in its variety of native plant life. The state has virtually the whole range of plant life possible within the moisture limits of its latitude. Its shape even more than its great area causes this exceptional diversity through the broad range of natural conditions made possible by its peninsulalike extensions: the Panhandle, the Trans-Pecos, and the southward-pointing V-shape made by the meeting of the Rio Grande and the Gulf shoreline. Other causes of this variety are the climatic effects of the state's elevation range, its geographic position on the continent with respect to the Gulf of Mexico, the Mississippi Valley, and the Rocky Mountains, and one of the most complex and varied geologic systems in the nation, creating a wide variety of surface soils.

Various authorities have divided the state into different areas of native vegetation, but a division of 14 such areas is common. Almost 24,000,000 ac. (9,712,800 ha.) are classified as forest land, of which nearly 12,000,000 ac. (4,856,000 ha.) grow commercial timber. Texas has about 225 tree types, but the most valuable commercially are the shortleaf, longleaf, and loblolly pines. The state has four national forests, with a gross area of more than 1,700,000 ac. (687,990 ha.) in the heart of the east Texas timber belt. In the Trans-Pecos Mountains are small growths of Douglas fir, piñon pine, Rocky Mountain white pine, and some varieties of western oak. Texas is the only state having native growths of both eastern and western pines and oaks. Desert vegetation of southwest Texas and the Trans-Pecos area includes the yucca, ocotillo, lechuguilla, candelilla, guayule, maguey, creosote bush, and several hundred varieties of native cacti. Some rare species of juniper grow in the Chisos Mountains. The 570 species of grasses found in Texas include nearly half of the varieties growing in the U.S., and the state has more than 4,000 different species of native wild flowers, some of which grow only in Texas. One of these is the bluebonnet, the state flower.

The area of chief botanical interest is the Big Thicket, an ill-defined area in the southern part of the east Texas forest region. The Big Thicket, largely unknown even to most Texans, is a giant wild garden, in some places almost impenetrable because of its junglelike growth, whose importance as a great botanical and wild life preserve is slowly being effaced by lumber and oil production. Covering about 2,000,000 ac. (809,400 ha.) of southern Polk and Tyler counties and northern Hardin and Liberty counties, the Big Thicket is a swampy land of mystery and myth. For more than a century it was a sanctuary for criminals, army deserters, and conscientious objectors of the American Civil War and World War I, but its considerable and unheralded significance is as a living botanical museum. The only remaining tribe of Texas Indians, the Alabama-Coushatta, lives on a reservation on the northern edge of the Big Thicket.

**Animal Life.**—The list of birds found in Texas includes nearly two-thirds of all species found in North America north of Mexico and many more than are found in any other state. It includes all species ever listed in the rest of conterminous U.S. between the Atlantic seaboard and the Rocky Mountains with the exception of about 20% of those found in Florida and the same percentage of those occurring along the Canadian border. The great flyways of North American birds lie between the Appalachian and the Rocky mountains and except for one considerable leak near the mouth of the Mississippi, the low-flying, easily winded species are herded through Texas in their migrations. Of the more than 800 kinds of birds found in Texas, 42 are permanent residents, 225 are winter residents, and 70 are summer residents. The others are transients that stay only long enough to rest during migrations.

The lowlands of the Texas coast are unrivaled in the U.S. for bird scenery, not only for bewildering variety but also for abundance. This is notably true of the town of Rockport, near Corpus

Christi and the centre of the Aransas National Wildlife Sanctuary. The attention of the Western world has been drawn to the tragic circumstance of the whooping crane, which is making its last stand in the Aransas Sanctuary. But a famous game bird, the prairie chicken, is also on the verge of extinction only a few miles inland. The prairie chicken has been endangered by the gradual assumption of its habitat for rice farming, and by poison sprays used to kill the boll weevil, important in the bird's diet. Besides the Aransas preserve, Texas has four other national wildlife refuges, several state refuges, and six Audubon Society preserves, including South Bird Island in the Laguna Madre, one of the two U.S. winter havens for the white pelican.

Nearly half of the nation's wild turkeys, the state's most prized game bird, occur in Texas, and fossil evidence indicates that it is one of the state's oldest inhabitants. Ducks, geese, and quail are the other game birds of importance.

Native mammals of importance to Texas for various reasons are several species of deer (especially the white-tailed, or Virginia, deer), the chief game animal; several furbearing animals of commercial value; and four species of coyote, destructive but much maligned predators and subjects of considerable folklore. Virtually curiosities in the 20th century are three mammals whose extinction in Texas has been slowed by belated conservation procedures. The American bison, or buffalo, largest of native North American mammals, once lived on the Texas plains in tremendous numbers; long before the second half of the 20th century the only bison in Texas, outside zoos, were bred on a few ranches as a hobby. Texas bighorn sheep and the pronghorn antelope were once common in the state, as was the prairie dog, one animal that is not conserved. More than 400,000,000 prairie dogs once lived in a single colony in west Texas and hundreds of millions lived throughout the region, but by the 1960s their numbers had dwindled to only a few hundred in widely scattered areas. The prairie dog was systematically poisoned by the federal wildlife service and by ranchers because of its destruction of range grasses, its principal food.

All four of the poisonous snakes of the U.S. (copperhead, water moccasin, rattlesnake, and coral snake) and perhaps a third of the nation's harmless snakes are found in Texas. The alligator is fairly common in east Texas rivers and lakes.

A small lizard, the horned toad, is a commonplace of Texas that is a subject of myth and folklore. Some other subjects of folklore are a bird, the chaparral, also called paisano and roadrunner; a mammal, the nine-banded armadillo; and a poisonous arachnid, the vinegarroon, or vinegarone, a whip scorpion found in southwest Texas, whose power to injure is much less than that attributed to it by border legends.

The Texas coastal waters produce the Atlantic and Gulf South's greatest harvest of shrimp, which constituted about half of the entire Texas Gulf marine crop. Although the state's oyster crop has declined, it continues to be of importance as a marketable food commodity and of even more importance as a source of shells, providing lime for the petrochemical industry. Saltwater fishes of commercial value are red snapper, redfish, saltwater trout, drum, grouper, whiting, flounder, and mackerel. Between 200 and 250 species of fish are found in the bays and offshore coastal waters of Texas and about 200 species of freshwater fish are found in the state.

**State and National Parks.**—The Big Bend National Park takes its name from the huge U-turn made by the Rio Grande 200 mi. (322 km.) SE of El Paso. Natural life ranges from subtropical cacti in its arid basins to Douglas fir trees on its 8,000-ft. (2,440-m.) Chisos, or Phantom, mountain range. In the deserts live peccaries and rare hummingbirds; in the mountains are lynx and eagles. The park (788,682 ac. [319,180 ha.] owned by the U.S.) was established in 1943 and includes desert, foothills, mountains, and river valley. The three precipitous canyons of the Rio Grande are the Boquillas, Mariscal, and, the deepest, Santa Elena, 1,500 ft. (457 m.). Emory Peak, of the Chisos Range, is the highest elevation in the park (7,835 ft. [2,388 m.]).

Development of the Guadalupe Mountains National Park is under way as a result of federal and state legislation in 1966–67. The 77,518-ac. (31,372 ha.) park, in far west Texas, includes Guadalupe Peak, the state's tallest, and McKittrick Canyon.

Padre Island National Seashore was established by the National Park Service in 1963. It comprises 80 mi. (130 km.) of barrier beach between Corpus Christi and Port Isabel.

The Mission San José de San Miguel de Aguayo (Mission San José), at San Antonio, is one of two national historic sites in Texas. Mission San José is owned by the state and is also a state park. Texas had 61 recreational and historical state parks in various stages of development in the late 1960s. Compared with the state's vast area, however, the number and extent of its parks are not great. Scenically the most rewarding are Davis Mountains in the Trans-Pecos region, and Palo Duro Canyon in the Panhandle.

Of larger interest and importance are the Spanish missions of San Antonio, El Paso, and Goliad, some of them state parks. One of these, in midtown San Antonio, is the most famous monument of Texas: the Alamo, which means "cottonwood" in Spanish; it was the church for Mission San Antonio de Valero. The present structure, the second on the site, was begun in 1758 but never completed. Following the meandering course of the San Antonio River southward from the city is Mission Road leading to four Spanish missions founded at the city in the early 18th century.

The four are the missions Nuestra Señora de la Purísima Concepción de Acuña (Mission Concepción), San José, San Juan Capistrano, and San Francisco de la Espada. By far the most important is the Mission San José. The present church, begun in 1768, is the finest of Texas missions, and even in the 18th century the Spaniards called San José "the queen of missions." In time it became the largest and the most prosperous, and the intricate, baroque beauty of its facade and baptistry window, carved by the Spaniard Pedro Huizar in two periods totaling 18 years, makes it one of the chief architectural treasures of the U.S.

The Mission Concepción (*c.* 1735), 2 mi. (3.2 km.) N of San José, is the best preserved Texas mission. Ninety miles southeast of San Antonio, at Goliad, is the modern restoration of the Mission Nuestra Señora del Espíritu Santo de Zúñiga and, more important, the chapel of the Presidio Nuestra Señora de Loreto de la Bahía (La Bahía). The presidio chapel is original and ranks architecturally with the missions of San Antonio. La Bahía has the additional advantage of a commanding site on a hill that overlooks a cultivated valley. Other missions, including earlier ones near El Paso, are mainly modern reproductions or restorations.

The Spanish Governor's Palace in downtown San Antonio, completed in 1749, is also a modern restoration but a superb and important one. The palace was not the official residence of the governor of the Province of Texas but the residence of the presidial captain, who was, in the absence of the governor, the ranking representative of the king of Spain. It became known as the Governor's Palace long after it was built. Another restoration in midtown San Antonio is La Villita (the Little Village), a sharp contrast to the elegance of the Governor's Palace. The little adobe houses were occupied in the 18th century by soldiers and their families of the Presidio San Antonio de Bexar.

## HISTORY

Man has been traced through 15,000 years of the state's prehistory, but historically—the time in which people of European origin have known the land that became Texas—the state's history began early in the 16th century.

**Exploration and Settlement.**—The Spaniard Alvar Núñez Cabeza de Vaca opened this period when he and three companions, sole survivors of a wrecked ship, washed up on the Gulf Coast in 1528. Years later he wrote an account of this adventure, the first written record of the land. Within two decades Francisco Vázquez de Coronado and the followers of Hernando de Soto, searching for mythical cities of gold and gems, explored parts of Texas. The first settlement in Texas was made in the extreme western part of the state, near El Paso, in 1682, an accident of fate for which the Indians of New Mexico, revolting against Spanish rule, were responsible (*see* El Paso). The next settlements were made in the extreme eastern part of Texas, in 1690, when French designs on the land aroused the Spanish to establish missions there.

In 1685 René Robert Cavelier, sieur de La Salle, explorer of the Mississippi, sailed from France with a small fleet to establish a colony at the mouth of the Mississippi. He missed the mouth of the river, perhaps deliberately, and with remnants of his unlucky expedition managed to establish a small colony near Matagorda Bay on the Texas Gulf Coast. Within two years La Salle had been slain by his own men and most of the members of his colony had perished. Before the century closed the Spanish missions in east Texas were hard put to cope with the increasing hostility of the Indians, and the missions were abandoned. For a brief time most of Texas then remained virtually unoccupied. Indeed, the Spanish were remarkably complacent about their claim to Texas throughout the 18th century, though an incident in 1714 briefly spurred them again and for the most part ended the influence of French aspirations on Texas. That was the appearance in Texas of the French explorer Louis Juchereau de Saint Denis, causing the Spanish to establish what proved to be permanent settlements at San Antonio, Nacogdoches, and Goliad. By 1800, when the three places were the only ones in Texas that could be called towns, the number of settlers in the future state was perhaps 7,000 but probably less. The events of Texas history, however, were to proceed swiftly after the early 1800s.

**Revolution and Republic.**—For three centuries after Cabeza de Vaca the land belonged to the Spaniards, then to the Mexicans for a brief interval (1821–36), and afterward to Americans. Mexico, of which Texas was a part, won its independence from Spain in 1821. Late that year 300 American families, led by Stephen F. Austin, 28-year-old heir to the dreams of his father, Moses Austin, began colonizing land granted by Mexico. Other groups followed until perhaps 30,000 Americans, four times the number of Mexicans, were living in Texas by 1836. The Mexican government, though suspicious of the burgeoning American population in Texas, was unable to cope with it while contending with its own spasms of revolution and a rapid succession of administrations. The American colonists got their land from Mexico, but their different language and culture caused them to shun the republic. Mexico tried in vain to discipline the colonists. It abolished slavery, it levied duties, it established military garrisons, and at last it declared martial law and tried to disarm the Texans. Inevitably, fighting erupted at several points, notably at Gonzales on Oct. 2, 1835, when the Mexicans were repulsed in the first battle of the Texas revolution.

Meeting at San Felipe on Nov. 3, Texans formed a provisional government but could neither agree to declare their independence nor on much else; this want of unity was to continue with tragic consequences. In December San Antonio was captured from the Mexicans, who agreed to withdraw to Mexico. That was the Texans' last victory until the final battle more than three months later. On March 2, 1836, when the Mexican dictator Antonio López de Santa Anna (*q.v.*) had recaptured San Antonio and was closing in on the Alamo's few defenders, Texans meeting at Washington-on-the-Brazos declared their independence, established the Republic of Texas, and elected David G. Burnet provisional president. Command of the army was given to Sam Houston (*q.v.*), formerly a U.S. congressman and governor of Tennessee, who is the most remarkable figure in Texas history.

It would be hard to conceive of a more tragic or more heroic beginning for a new nation than the Battle of the Alamo. When the siege began on Feb. 23, the Alamo (*q.v.*) was defended by about 150 men, including David Crockett, James Bowie (*qq.v.*), and Col. William B. Travis, the commander. On March 1 a reinforcement of 32 men succeeded in slipping through Santa Anna's lines, but further help was prevented by confusion and dissension in the provisional government. By March 4 the Texans were besieged by about 4,000 Mexicans. Defying Santa Anna's demands for surrender, the Texans fought their hopeless battle until March 6, when Santa Anna assaulted the Alamo on all sides and overwhelmed the defenders. The last Texans perished in hand-to-hand fighting inside the Alamo. Subduing the defenders (estimated at 182 to 187) cost the Mexicans between 1,000 and 1,600 lives.

After the Alamo fell, Col. James W. Fannin, commanding 300 men at Goliad, was ordered to retreat. He was finally able to do so on March 19 but was overtaken by the Mexicans that afternoon. Greatly outnumbered, he surrendered after a hopeless battle, and the Texans were returned to Goliad. On March 27, at Santa Anna's order, Fannin's entire force was slaughtered in cold blood. The battle of the Alamo and the Goliad massacre gave the Texans a battle cry when the two forces met for the last time: "Remember the Alamo, remember Goliad!" The Battle of San Jacinto, a brief, bizarre climax to the revolution, was fought on April 21 on the San Jacinto River, near the site of what was to be the city of Houston. After days of retreat, General Houston defeated the larger force in a surprise attack during the Mexicans' siesta. Six hundred Mexicans were killed and 200 wounded during the 20-minute battle. Santa Anna (later freed) and 700 others were captured in 24 hours. Fewer than a dozen Mexicans escaped. Of the 800 Texans in the battle, nine were killed and 30 wounded.

The historian Andrew Forest Muir has shown that most of the Texans who were killed at the Alamo, murdered at Goliad, or fought at San Jacinto had never been in Texas before the first weeks of 1836, and that most of the men who had lived in Texas before the revolution chose not to join the army. Few of the exact details of the whole revolutionary campaign are generally agreed upon, and even more are the details of the last, decisive battle disputed or unknown. The Battle of San Jacinto, Muir wrote, "is the most controversial event in all of Texas history."

**Annexation.**—The new nation endured perilously for a period of almost ten years. After Texas was annexed by the U.S., technically on Dec. 29, 1845, but in fact on Feb. 19, 1846, a war with Mexico ended the contest for the land. It had been a melancholy contest.

Time and again the U.S. had spurned the land. Aaron Burr (*q.v.*) was the first to go after it. But Thomas Jefferson, embittered by Burr's rivalry for the presidency in 1800 and head of a nation rich in the new lands of the Louisiana Purchase, was little concerned whether the nation's western boundary was the Sabine or the Rio Grande. Between the rivers was Texas, claimed but not

THE BETTMANN ARCHIVE

VOLUNTEERS!

**Men of the Granite State!**

**Men of Old Rockingham!! the strawberry-bed of patriotism, renowned for bravery and devotion to Country, rally at this call. Santa Anna, reeking with the generous confidence and magnanimity of your countrymen, is in arms, eager to plunge his traitor-dagger in their bosoms. To arms, then, and rush to the standard of the fearless and gallant CUSHING---put to the blush the dastardly meanness and rank toryism of Massachusetts. Let the half civilized Mexicans hear the crack of the unerring New Hampshire rifleman, and illustrate on the plains of San Luis Potosi, the fierce, determined, and undaunted bravery that has always characterized her sons.**

**Col. THEODORE F. ROWE, at No. 31 Daniel-street, is authorized and will enlist men this week for the Massachusetts Regiment of Volunteers. The compensation is $10 per month---$30 in advance. Congress will grant a handsome bounty in money and ONE HUNDRED AND SIXTY ACRES OF LAND.**

**Portsmouth, Feb. 2, 1847.**

War with Mexico: (left) the Alamo, an 18th-century mission chapel in San Antonio, defended to the death by Texans against vastly superior Mexican forces, Feb. 23–March 6, 1836; (right) 1847 poster urging New Hampshire volunteers to fight in the Mexican War quite secured by Spain, and there Burr dreamed of creating a new American frontier. His dream came a cropper when he was betrayed by a cohort and ruined by Jefferson. A decade later the land was again rebuffed when James Monroe, trading for title to Florida, relinquished to Spain America's claim to Texas. Next Andrew Jackson schemed with his friend Sam Houston to get the land for the U.S., and gradually Texas became one of the great political issues of the time. Opposing Pres. John Tyler's hope of taking Texas into the nation, Daniel Webster resigned as secretary of state. The issue was not so much Texas as slavery: Texas would be another slave state. Sam Houston hurried toward his goal of annexation by pretending to deal with Great Britain. The British, though they had no wish to acquire Texas, opposed annexation by the U.S. and at one time thought of using force to prevent it. The U.S. Congress, fearing Britain's motives, narrowly approved annexation in 1845.

The slavery issue caused the rise of virulent antipathy toward Texas. Typical were the publications, in the early 1840s, of the Anti-Texass Legion, whose name was so spelled for reasons of abuse. Hale's pamphlet (*see* above) cited six dangers of admitting Texas to the union, two of which were not unheard of a century later. Admit Texas to the union, Hale wrote, and the U.S. would have "The introduction into the union of an unprincipled population of adventurers, with all the privileges of a State of naturalized citizens," and "The creation of an enormous State, in time to become the real Empire State of the country."

Frederick Law Olmsted, in *A Journey Through Texas,* the second volume of his southern trilogy of the 1850s, opposed the charge, common at the time, that the U.S. got Texas through guile: "We saw the land lying idle; we took it. . . . When the history [of the state's rebellion, independence and annexation] is candidly reread, the story that the whole movement was the development of a deliberate and treacherous plot for the conquest of Texas, appears a needless exaggeration of influences that really played a secondary part. . . . The land was fertile; that was the kernel of the matter." (Olmsted was one of the first to take notice of a Texan trait that was to become better known, and more objectionable to others, in the next century: "So anxious is every one in Texas to give all strangers a favourable impression, that all statements as to the extreme profit and healthfulness of lands must be taken with a grain of allowance. We found it very difficult, without impertinent persistence, to obtain any unfavourable facts.")

**Confederacy.**—Sam Houston, hero of the revolution, twice president of the republic, loved and loathed by the people, who divided for and against this expert at controversy, was elected to the U.S. Senate soon after Texas was admitted to the Union. He was replaced in 1859, after nearly 14 years in the Senate, when the Texas legislature took revenge for his belief that the Union should be preserved and refused to reelect him. ("I make no distinction between southern rights and northern rights," Houston said late in 1858. "Our rights are rights common to the whole Union.") In an astonishing proof of his powers, he was then elected governor without silencing his appeals for unity before an electorate that yearned for secession. His unfinished term as governor was to be a dismal end to his career. A little more than a year later, after the people of Texas spurned his pleas for national unity by voting to secede from the U.S., Houston was deposed. He retired to his farm and died two years later.

**Reconstruction and After.**—The state's role in the Confederacy and the Civil War was not important except as a supplier of men, material, and services. But it paid a large price during the excesses of Reconstruction. Texas was the ninth state in the nation in per capita wealth in 1860; in 1880, seven years after Reconstruction ended in Texas, it was 36th. Texas was one of the last Confederate states to be readmitted to the Union (1870), but radicals controlled the state until 1873. Livestock and railroad interests dominated the state between Reconstruction and the end of the century. In 1901, when the Spindletop oil gusher blew in at Beaumont, oil began more than half a century of dominance.

The great governor of modern Texas history was James Stephen Hogg, a progressive, who was elected in 1890 on a platform promising regulation of corporations but especially of railroads, which he had disciplined earlier as attorney general. The most important reform of his two terms was the creation of the Texas Railroad Commission. The commission later became the most influential state regulatory body in the U.S. when control of oil production was added to its powers. A large man in character and physique, Hogg's altruistic influence was effective for nearly 20 years. Three other but very different political figures abused and for long periods influenced the state during the first half of the 20th century: James E. Ferguson, impeached as governor in 1917; his wife Miriam A. Ferguson, afterward twice governor; and W. Lee O'Daniel, twice governor and twice U.S. senator. The flamboyance and rural demagoguery of this trio gave an additional dimension to the state's reputation for eccentricity. Texas's first Republican senator since Reconstruction, John G. Tower, won a special election in 1961 and was elected to a full term in 1966.

In and out of the state, the chief interests of Texas history are the years of Spanish-Mexican and Anglo-American colonization, the revolution of 1836, and the decade of independence.

## GOVERNMENT

The Texas constitution, adopted in 1876, is one of the longest and least efficient of the state constitutions, and it may be the most frequently amended. A charter of over 50,000 words, including, in the late 1960s, 180 amendments, it contains much statutory material, a contradiction of the principles of constitutional law. Both the state's constitution and statutes have long been the subjects of reform movements.

**Legislature.**—The constitution, which makes the legislative branch of government far more powerful than the executive and judicial branches, reflects the suspicion and fears of radical domination during Reconstruction. Texas government is believed to be more dominated by its legislature than that of any other state. The legislature, composed of 31 senators and 150 representatives, convenes biennially in odd-numbered years. Special sessions may be called by the governor.

**Executive.**—A governor and a lieutenant governor head the executive branch. The chief power of the governor, whose veto can be overruled by a two-thirds vote of both houses of the legislature, is appointive, an influence gradually and formidably enlarged throughout the first half of the 20th century. The governor appoints certain individual officers and commissioners of state government and the members of most of the 175 state boards and commissions. The elective officers of state government are the governor, lieutenant governor, attorney general, comptroller of public accounts, treasurer, commissioner of the general land office and commissioner of agriculture, each selected for a two-year term, and the three members of the Texas Railroad Commission, elected for six-year overlapping terms.

**Judiciary.**—The entire Texas judiciary, which is divided into three levels, is elective. At the top are, in effect, two supreme courts. One (nine members) is so called and has jurisdiction in civil law. The other (three members and an appointed commission of two) is the court of criminal appeals and has jurisdiction in criminal law. Texas and Oklahoma are the only states with separate "supreme" courts for civil and criminal cases. The second level of the judiciary are the 13 courts of civil appeals (three members each). The 150-odd district judges comprise the third level.

**Finance.**—Although Texas has no income or corporation taxes, the state in 1961 levied a 2% general sales tax, increased to 3% in 1968; with a 1% general sales tax levied by about 300 municipalities, the total general sales tax was 4% in most of the state. Other substantial revenues are derived from taxes on the state's enormous production of oil and natural gas plus a heavy sales tax on cigarettes and gasoline. A report made in 1950 by the Texas Legislative Council, the research agency of the legislature, showed that 36% of the state government's annual revenue came from direct taxes on petroleum and its products and from such other petroleum sources as royalties, leases, and bonuses. An amendment to the state constitution approved in 1942 gives the comptroller the power to veto, in effect, any appropriation of the legislature that exceeds anticipated revenues.

**POPULATION**

The population of the area that was to become the state of Texas seems to have been between 6,000 and 7,000, few of whom were Anglo-Americans, at the opening of the 19th century. Figures on the growth of the population in the first half of the century are questionable, but by 1850, the date of the first federal census, the population was 212,592, ranking 25th among the states. In the following decade the population made its greatest proportional increase (184.2%) to 604,215 in 1860. The growth of the population was slowed by the American Civil War and Reconstruction, but in the 1870s the population made its next greatest proportional increase (94.5%) to 1,591,749 in 1880. In 1900 the population was 3,048,710, ranking sixth among the states. The census figures, and the percentages of increase over the preceding census, for the first half of the century were: 1910, 3,896,542 (27.8%); 1920, 4,663,228 (19.7%); 1930, 5,824,715 (24.9%); 1940, 6,414,824

*Texas: Places of 5,000 or More Population (1960 Census)**

| Place | Population | | | | |
|---|---|---|---|---|---|
| | 1960 | 1950 | 1940 | 1920 | 1900 |
| Total state | 9,579,677 | 7,711,194 | 6,414,824 | 4,663,228 | 3,048,710 |
| Abilene | 90,368 | 45,570 | 26,612 | 10,274 | 3,411 |
| Alamo Heights | 7,552 | 8,000 | 5,700 | — | — |
| Alice | 20,861 | 16,449 | 7,792 | 1,880 | — |
| Alvin | 5,643 | 3,701 | 3,087 | 1,519 | 986 |
| Amarillo | 137,969 | 74,246 | 51,686 | 15,494 | 1,442 |
| Andrews | 11,135 | 3,294 | 611 | — | — |
| Angleton | 7,312 | 3,399 | 1,763 | 1,043 | — |
| Aransas Pass | 6,956 | 5,396 | 4,095 | 1,569 | — |
| Arlington | 44,775 | 7,692 | 4,240 | 3,031 | 1,079 |
| Athens | 7,086 | 5,194 | 4,765 | 3,176 | — |
| Austin | 186,545 | 132,459 | 87,930 | 34,876 | 22,258 |
| Balch Springs | 6,821 | — | — | — | — |
| Ballinger | 5,043 | 5,302 | 4,472 | 2,767 | 1,128 |
| Bay City | 11,656 | 9,427 | 6,594 | 3,454 | — |
| Baytown | 28,159 | 22,983 | — | — | — |
| Beaumont | 119,175 | 94,014 | 59,061 | 40,422 | 9,427 |
| Beeville | 13,811 | 9,348 | 6,789 | 3,063 | — |
| Bellaire | 19,872 | 10,173 | 1,124 | — | — |
| Bellmead | 5,127 | — | — | — | — |
| Belton | 8,163 | 6,246 | 3,572 | 5,098 | 3,700 |
| Big Spring | 31,230 | 17,286 | 12,604 | 4,273 | — |
| Bonham | 7,357 | 7,049 | 6,349 | 6,008 | 5,042 |
| Borger | 20,911 | 18,059 | 10,018 | — | — |
| Brady | 5,338 | 5,944 | 5,002 | 2,197 | — |
| Breckenridge | 6,273 | 6,610 | 5,826 | 1,846 | — |
| Brenham | 7,740 | 6,941 | 6,435 | 5,066 | 5,968 |
| Brownfield | 10,286 | 6,161 | 4,009 | — | — |
| Brownsville | 48,040 | 36,066 | 22,083 | 11,791 | 6,305 |
| Brownwood | 16,974 | 20,181 | 13,398 | 8,223 | 3,965 |
| Bryan | 27,542 | 18,102 | 11,842 | 6,307 | 3,589 |
| Burkburnett | 7,621 | 4,555 | 2,814 | 5,300 | — |
| Cameron | 5,640 | 5,052 | 5,040 | 4,298 | 3,341 |
| Canyon | 5,864 | 4,364 | 2,622 | 1,618 | — |
| Carrizo Springs | 5,699 | 4,316 | 2,494 | 954 | — |
| Carthage | 5,262 | 4,750 | 2,178 | 1,366 | — |
| Childress | 6,399 | 7,619 | 6,464 | 5,003 | 692 |
| Cleburne | 15,381 | 12,905 | 10,558 | 12,820 | 7,493 |
| Cleveland | 5,838 | 5,183 | 1,783 | — | — |
| Coleman | 6,371 | 6,530 | 6,054 | 2,868 | 1,362 |
| College Station | 11,396 | 7,925 | 2,184 | — | — |
| Colorado City | 6,457 | 6,774 | 5,213 | 1,766 | — |
| Commerce | 5,789 | 5,889 | 4,699 | 3,842 | 1,800 |
| Conroe | 9,192 | 7,298 | 4,624 | 1,858 | — |
| Corpus Christi | 167,690 | 108,287 | 57,301 | 10,522 | 4,703 |
| Corsicana | 20,344 | 19,211 | 15,232 | 11,356 | 9,313 |
| Crockett | 5,356 | 5,932 | 4,536 | 3,061 | 2,612 |
| Crystal City | 9,101 | 7,198 | 6,529 | — | — |
| Cuero | 7,338 | 7,498 | 5,474 | 3,671 | 3,422 |
| Dalhart | 5,160 | 5,918 | 4,682 | 2,676 | — |
| Dallas | 679,684 | 434,462 | 294,734 | 158,976 | 42,638 |
| Del Rio | 18,612 | 14,211 | 13,343 | 10,589 | — |
| Denison | 22,748 | 17,504 | 15,581 | 17,065 | 11,807 |
| Denton | 26,844 | 21,372 | 11,192 | 7,626 | 4,187 |
| Donna | 7,522 | 7,171 | 4,712 | 1,579 | — |
| Dumas | 8,477 | 6,127 | 2,117 | — | — |
| Eagle Pass | 12,094 | 7,276 | 6,459 | 5,765 | — |
| Edinburg | 18,706 | 12,383 | 8,718 | 1,406 | — |
| Edna | 5,038 | 3,855 | 2,724 | — | — |
| El Campo | 7,700 | 6,237 | 3,906 | 1,766 | — |
| El Paso | 276,687 | 130,485 | 96,810 | 77,560 | 15,906 |
| Ennis | 9,347 | 7,815 | 7,087 | 7,224 | 4,919 |
| Falfurrias | 6,515 | 6,712 | — | — | — |
| Farmers Branch | 13,441 | 915 | — | — | — |
| Fort Stockton | 6,373 | 4,444 | 3,294 | 1,297 | — |
| Fort Worth | 356,268 | 278,778 | 177,662 | 106,482 | 26,688 |
| Freeport | 11,619 | 6,012 | 2,579 | 1,798 | — |
| Gainesville | 13,083 | 11,246 | 9,651 | 8,648 | 7,874 |
| Galena Park | 10,852 | 7,186 | 1,562 | — | — |
| Galveston | 67,175 | 66,568 | 60,862 | 44,255 | 37,789 |
| Garland | 38,501 | 10,571 | 2,233 | 1,421 | 819 |
| Georgetown | 5,218 | 4,951 | 3,682 | 2,871 | 2,790 |
| Gladewater | 5,742 | 5,305 | 4,454 | — | — |
| Gonzales | 5,829 | 5,659 | 4,722 | 3,128 | 4,297 |
| Graham | 8,505 | 6,742 | 5,175 | 2,544 | 878 |
| Grand Prairie | 30,386 | 14,594 | 1,595 | 1,263 | — |
| Greenville | 19,087 | 14,727 | 13,995 | 12,384 | 6,860 |
| Groves | 17,304 | — | — | — | — |
| Haltom City | 23,133 | 5,760 | — | — | — |
| Harlingen | 41,207 | 23,229 | 13,306 | 1,784 | — |
| Hearne | 5,072 | 4,872 | 3,511 | 2,741 | 2,129 |
| Henderson | 9,666 | 6,833 | 6,437 | 2,273 | — |
| Hereford | 7,652 | 5,207 | 2,584 | 1,696 | — |
| Highland Park | 10,411 | 11,405 | 10,288 | 2,321 | — |
| Hillsboro | 7,402 | 8,363 | 7,799 | 6,952 | 5,346 |
| Hitchcock | 5,216 | 1,105 | — | — | — |
| Houston | 938,219 | 596,163 | 384,514 | 138,276 | 44,633 |
| Huntsville | 11,999 | 9,820 | 5,108 | 4,689 | 2,485 |
| Hurst | 10,165 | — | — | — | — |
| Irving | 45,985 | 2,621 | 1,089 | 357 | — |
| Jacinto City | 9,547 | 6,856 | — | — | — |
| Jacksonville | 9,590 | 8,607 | 7,213 | 3,723 | 1,568 |
| Kermit | 10,465 | 6,912 | 2,584 | — | — |
| Kerrville | 8,901 | 7,691 | 5,572 | 2,353 | 1,423 |
| Kilgore | 10,092 | 9,638 | 6,708 | — | — |
| Killeen | 23,377 | 7,045 | 1,263 | 1,298 | 780 |
| Kingsville | 25,297 | 16,898 | 7,782 | 4,770 | — |
| Lake Jackson | 9,651 | 2,897 | — | — | — |
| La Marque | 13,969 | 7,359 | — | — | — |
| Lamesa | 12,438 | 10,704 | 6,038 | 1,188 | — |
| Lampasas | 5,061 | 4,869 | 3,426 | 2,107 | 2,107 |
| Lancaster | 7,501 | 2,632 | 1,151 | 1,190 | 1,045 |
| Laredo | 60,678 | 51,910 | 39,274 | 22,710 | 13,429 |
| Levelland | 10,153 | 8,264 | 3,091 | — | — |
| Liberty | 6,127 | 4,163 | 3,087 | 1,117 | 865 |
| Littlefield | 7,236 | 6,540 | 3,817 | — | — |
| Lockhart | 6,084 | 5,573 | 5,018 | 3,731 | 2,306 |
| Longview | 40,050 | 24,502 | 13,758 | 5,713 | 3,591 |
| Lubbock | 128,691 | 71,747 | 31,853 | 4,051 | — |
| Lufkin | 17,641 | 15,135 | 9,567 | 4,878 | 1,527 |
| McAllen | 32,728 | 20,067 | 11,877 | 5,331 | — |
| McKinney | 13,763 | 10,560 | 8,555 | 6,677 | 4,342 |
| Marlin | 6,918 | 7,099 | 6,542 | 4,310 | 3,092 |
| Marshall | 23,846 | 22,327 | 18,410 | 14,271 | 7,855 |
| Mathis | 6,075 | 4,050 | 1,950 | — | — |
| Mercedes | 10,943 | 10,081 | 7,624 | 3,414 | — |
| Mesquite | 27,526 | 1,696 | 1,045 | 674 | 406 |
| Mexia | 6,121 | 6,627 | 6,410 | 3,482 | 2,393 |
| Midland | 62,625 | 21,713 | 9,352 | 1,795 | — |
| Mineral Wells | 11,053 | 7,801 | 6,303 | 7,890 | 2,048 |
| Mission | 14,081 | 10,765 | 5,982 | 3,847 | — |
| Monahans | 8,567 | 6,311 | 3,944 | — | — |
| Mount Pleasant | 8,027 | 6,342 | 4,528 | 4,009 | — |
| Nacogdoches | 12,674 | 12,327 | 7,538 | 3,546 | 1,827 |
| Nederland | 12,036 | 3,805 | — | — | — |
| New Braunfels | 15,631 | 12,210 | 6,976 | 3,590 | 2,097 |
| North Richland Hills | 8,662 | — | — | — | — |
| Odessa | 80,338 | 29,495 | 9,573 | — | — |
| Orange | 25,605 | 21,174 | 7,472 | 9,212 | 3,835 |
| Palestine | 13,974 | 12,503 | 12,144 | 11,039 | 8,297 |
| Pampa | 24,664 | 16,583 | 12,895 | 987 | — |
| Paris | 20,977 | 21,643 | 18,678 | 15,040 | 9,358 |
| Pasadena | 58,737 | 22,483 | 3,436 | — | — |
| Pecos | 12,728 | 8,054 | 4,855 | 1,445 | 639 |
| Perryton | 7,903 | 4,417 | 2,325 | — | — |
| Pharr | 14,106 | 8,690 | 4,784 | 1,565 | — |
| Plainview | 18,735 | 14,044 | 8,263 | 3,989 | — |
| Port Arthur | 66,676 | 57,530 | 46,140 | 22,251 | 900 |
| Port Lavaca | 8,864 | 5,599 | 2,069 | 1,213 | — |
| Port Neches | 8,696 | 5,448 | 2,487 | — | — |
| Raymondville | 9,385 | 9,136 | 4,050 | — | — |
| Richardson | 16,810 | 1,289 | 720 | — | — |
| Richland Hills | 7,804 | — | — | — | — |
| Rio Grande City | 5,835 | 3,992 | — | — | — |
| River Oaks | 8,444 | 7,097 | — | — | — |
| Robstown | 10,266 | 7,278 | 6,780 | 948 | — |
| Rosenberg | 9,698 | 6,210 | 3,457 | 1,279 | — |
| San Angelo | 58,815 | 52,093 | 25,802 | 10,050 | — |
| San Antonio | 587,718 | 408,442 | 253,854 | 161,379 | 53,321 |
| San Benito | 16,422 | 13,271 | 9,501 | 5,070 | — |
| San Marcos | 12,713 | 9,980 | 6,006 | 4,527 | 2,292 |
| San Pedro | 7,634 | 8,127 | — | — | — |
| Seguin | 14,299 | 9,733 | 7,006 | 3,631 | 2,421 |
| Seminole | 5,737 | 3,479 | 1,761 | — | — |
| Sherman | 24,988 | 20,150 | 17,156 | 15,031 | 10,243 |
| Silsbee | 6,277 | 3,179 | 2,525 | — | — |
| Sinton | 6,008 | 4,254 | 3,770 | 1,058 | — |
| Slaton | 6,568 | 5,036 | 3,587 | 1,525 | — |
| Snyder | 13,850 | 12,010 | 3,815 | 2,179 | — |
| South Houston | 7,523 | 4,126 | 982 | — | — |
| Stamford | 5,259 | 5,819 | 4,810 | 3,704 | — |
| Stephenville | 7,359 | 7,155 | 4,768 | 3,891 | 1,902 |
| Sulphur Springs | 9,160 | 8,991 | 6,742 | 5,558 | 3,635 |
| Sweetwater | 13,914 | 13,619 | 10,367 | 4,307 | 670 |
| Taylor | 9,434 | 9,071 | 7,875 | 5,965 | 4,211 |
| Temple | 30,419 | 25,467 | 15,344 | 11,033 | 7,065 |
| Terrell | 13,803 | 11,544 | 10,481 | 8,349 | 6,330 |
| Terrell Hills | 5,572 | 2,708 | 1,236 | — | — |
| Texarkana | 30,218 | 24,753 | 17,019 | 11,480† | 5,256 |
| Texas City | 32,065 | 16,620 | 5,748 | 2,509 | — |
| Tyler | 51,230 | 38,968 | 28,279 | 12,085 | 8,069 |
| University Park | 23,202 | 24,275 | 14,458 | — | — |
| Uvalde | 10,293 | 8,674 | 6,679 | 3,885 | 1,889 |
| Vernon | 12,141 | 12,651 | 9,277 | 5,142 | 1,993 |
| Victoria | 33,047 | 16,126 | 11,566 | 5,957 | 4,010 |
| Waco | 97,808 | 84,706 | 55,982 | 38,500 | 20,686 |
| Waxahachie | 12,749 | 11,204 | 8,655 | 7,958 | 4,215 |
| Weatherford | 9,759 | 8,093 | 5,924 | 6,203 | 4,786 |
| Weslaco | 15,649 | 7,514 | 6,883 | — | — |
| West University Place | 14,628 | 17,074 | 9,221 | — | — |
| Wharton | 5,734 | 4,450 | 4,386 | 2,346 | — |
| White Settlement | 11,513 | 10,827 | — | — | — |
| Wichita Falls | 101,724 | 68,042 | 45,112 | 40,079 | 2,480 |
| Yoakum | 5,761 | 5,231 | 4,733 | 6,184 | 3,499 |

*Populations are reported as constituted at date of each census. †Combined population of Texarkana city in Miller County, Ark., and Bowie County, Tex.
Note: Dash indicates place did not exist during reported census period, or data not available.

(10.1%); 1950, 7,711,194 (20.2%); 1960, 9,579,677 (24.2%). A 1967 estimate by the Bureau of the Census placed Texas fifth in population (10,873,000), ahead of Ohio. Population density was 36.4 persons per square mile in 1960, far below the population density (50.5) of the U.S.

By the middle of the 20th century the character of the population was undergoing a quick metamorphosis that created a formidable contention within the state: in the ten years between 1940 and 1950 Texas changed from a predominantly rural to a predominantly urban state, bringing about a shift in character, attitudes, and aspirations that continued through the 1960s. Though the rural-urban conflict is old to most American states, it arose suddenly in Texas and with more effect than in many states.

People moving into Texas moved to the cities, which was to be expected. What multiplied the cities' peril was that masses of people from the state's rural areas also moved to the cities in the decades of the 1940s and 1950s. This population shift caused the burgeoning cities to have the majority of votes by the late 1940s but the comparatively deserted rural areas had the majority where it counted—in the legislature, though this was altered to some extent through redistricting of congressional and state legislative districts in 1967. The exodus from rural areas is a national phenomenon with common causes, but in Texas it was also impelled in other ways. The long drought ending in 1957 and the decline in cotton cultivation caused by the loss of foreign markets were large influences in forcing the state's farm tenants into the cities.

In 1956, 87% of the state's surface was farm and ranch land with a population estimated at 950,000. The remaining 13% of the surface was urban, its population estimated at 7,707,000. The state's 23 metropolitan areas (more than those of any other state but by no means all of urban Texas) composed of only 39 of the state's 254 counties, contained 8 of every 10 Texans in the 1960s. The speed of the state's population shift concealed some of its dangers in the more gradual national trend. In 1934, 40% of the state's population was on the farm; 20 years later the figure had shrunk to 13%. From 1930 to 1954 the state's farm population declined by 52%, nearly twice as much as the national decline of 28%. In the decade following 1945 Texas lost farm population more than twice as fast as did the nation (28% to 12%). Between the federal censuses of 1940 and 1950, 108 Texas counties gained population, but 146 counties lost. In that decade the state's urban population jumped 66%, and by 1950 Texas was 62.7% urban compared with 64% for the nation; by the 1960 census the figure was 75%, compared with the national 69.9%.

In 1960 the white population of Texas was 8,374,831; the nonwhite population was 1,204,846, of whom 1,187,125 were Negroes. In every census from 1870 to 1960 the population showed a decline in the percentage of Negroes, who were 14.4% of the population in 1940 and 12.4 in 1960. The Latin-American (Mexican) population in 1960 was 1,417,811, or 14.8% of the total.

Texas was fancied to be filling with newcomers from the north after World War II, recalling Edward Everett Hale's plea, in 1845, for "the North (to) pour down its hordes" upon Texas. But through 1960 the surge in the state's population did not come from outside the state. Texas has always been at least three-quarters full of Texans. The state's increasing population was due to a high proportion of births over deaths and even more to Texans' reluctance to leave Texas. The population increased by 1,868,483 between 1950 and 1960, but only 113,831, or about 6% of the total increase, were added by the excess of newcomers over people who left the state. In 1960, 76% of the population was born in Texas.

Texas was thought to be filling with northerners when oil and industry overtook agriculture's economic dominance. Such thinking had some substance in the larger cities, but for Texas as a whole it was a delusion at the time of the 1950 census, when most newcomers were from next-door states. The 1950 census showed that more newcomers came from Oklahoma than from any other state, followed by Louisiana and Arkansas. For nearly a century the mutual concern for cotton attracted southerners to the state; it was the South that poured down its hordes upon Texas. Although the 1950 census showed that natives of all northern states nearly equaled those of the South in Texas, by the 1960 census the southerners outnumbered the northerners by three to two.

Despite the extravagance of newspaper and magazine reports about the state after World War II, Texans are similar to newer-model Americans anywhere. Until the 1950s and 1960s, however, there was the difference that broader opportunity had enlarged those traits common to areas of new chances and new methods. The traits are characteristic of frontiers, where goals are often personal rather than civic—the acquisition of wealth and identity to the exclusion of aesthetics and reforms. A frontier in spirit need not have the rusticity of a Wild West movie; it can have skyscrapers and symphony orchestras. But by the 1960s the frontier spirit was much diminished as a characteristic of the state's population.

## EDUCATION

Both the republic and the state of Texas set aside public lands for the support of state institutions. The chief beneficiaries have been the public schools, the University of Texas, and the Agricultural and Mechanical University of Texas. The amount of the permanent school fund (public schools) in 1966 was nearly $700,000,000, one of the largest endowment funds in the nation. The amount of the university permanent fund, from which two-thirds of the income goes to the university and one-third to A. & M. University, was $418,000,000 in 1964. Petroleum was again the chief contributor: by the end of 1966 oil bonuses, lease rentals, and royalties had contributed more than $500,000,000 to the two funds. By the late 1960s oil, gas, and sulfur leases in the Texas tidelands, ownership of which the state had earlier disputed with the federal government, had contributed more than $70,000,000 to the permanent school fund. The state set aside a total of nearly 52,000,000 ac. (21,044,400 ha.) to benefit education, but the two great funds are mainly the result of grants made by the constitution of 1876. More than 42,000,000 ac. (16,997,750 ha.) were given to the public schools and 2,100,000 ac. (849,900 ha.) to the university fund. Most of the public school land was eventually sold (and the mineral rights retained), the proceeds going to the permanent school fund, but the university land is intact.

**Public Schools.**—The 100th anniversary of the Texas public school system was observed in 1954. The public schools are administered by the State Board of Education, which consists of 21 members elected by popular vote in 21 districts. The public schools are mainly financed by an ad valorem tax, by a fourth of certain revenues (principally the gasoline tax), and by income from the permanent school fund. Each school district builds and equips its own schools. Historically, separate school systems were maintained for Negroes and in some districts for Latin Americans. Following the 1954 U.S. Supreme Court decision voiding segregation laws of the Southern states, some schools abolished segregation. By the late 1960s Texas schools were substantially integrated.

**Higher Education.**—Sixty-seven junior colleges, colleges, and universities are supported in whole or in part by the state. Of these the larger are the University of Texas (1881), at Austin, the first state-supported school in Texas to require entrance examinations; Texas A. & M. University (1876), at College Station; the University of Houston (1934), which became fully state-supported in 1963; Texas Technological College (1923), at Lubbock; North Texas State University (1890); Texas Woman's University (1901), both at Denton; and Texas Southern University (1947), at Houston.

The University of Texas was founded after the state constitution of 1876 directed the legislature to establish a "university of the first class." It has branches at Galveston, Dallas, Houston, and San Antonio and includes Texas Western College, at El Paso. Despite the university's two-thirds share in the enormous endowment fund resulting mainly, since 1923, from the production of oil on its land, its reputation for wealth is largely a myth. By 1958, 4,085 oil wells on university land were producing more than 41,000,000 bbl. of oil a year, but not only does A. & M. University receive a third of the proceeds but each school may spend only the income on the money. A. & M. University, the oldest state-

The Texas economy: (far left) the approaches to Dallas, the state's second largest city and financial centre; (centre left) aircraft manufacturing, an important sector of the industrial economy, near Fort Worth; (above) cowboys and cattle raise dust on roundup near Waco; (right) oil refinery near Dallas symbolizes a major industry

PHOTOS (LEFT, CENTRE LEFT) ELLIOTT ERWITT—MAGNUM; (TOP) JOHN LEWIS STAGE FROM PHOTO RESEARCHERS; (BOTTOM RIGHT) HENRI CARTIER-BRESSON—MAGNUM

supported college in Texas, was founded in 1876. A military land-grant college for men only, it contributed more officers to the U.S. armed forces of two world wars than any other college or university. Its enrollment in the 1960s was in excess of 7,000. Chief among the independent colleges and universities are Rice University (1912), at Houston; Southern Methodist University (1911), at Dallas; Baylor University (1845) (Baptist), at Waco; and Texas Christian University (1873), at Fort Worth.

## HEALTH AND WELFARE

Expenditures for health and hospitals rank high among the states. The Texas State Department of Health administers health laws, rules, and regulations. Tax-supported eleemosynary institutions include hospitals for mental patients, tuberculosis hospitals, schools for the blind and the deaf and for mentally retarded and cerebral palsied children, and adult mental health clinics. Old age and other public assistance programs are administered by the State Board of Public Welfare. Expenditures for old-age assistance and for assistance to dependent children, to the blind, and to the permanently and totally disabled are relatively high among the states. Maximum workmen's compensation and average weekly unemployment benefits are relatively low.

## THE ECONOMY

Early in the decade following World War II, the time of greatest change in Texas since the revolution more than a century before, Texas became synonymous with the word "millionaire" or, more often, the phrase "oil millionaire." That it was so known to others became a burden of surprising weight by the early 1950s; that many Texans came to believe the legend was a burden of even more consequence. In time some Texans came to loathe the myth, one conceived by periodicals and newspapers from the adventures and eccentricities of exhibitionists and influence seekers. Facts denied the myth, but facts could do little to overcome the myth once it was fixed in the public mind. Yet the state with a reputation for riches was 34th among the U.S. states in per capita income in 1966 with a per capita income of $2,511 compared with a national figure of $2,940.

The single reality of the state's reputation for riches was philanthropy, large-scale spending for the public good, whose effect on the economy was trivial at first but whose future was stunning in the 1960s. Texas exempted from taxation only foundations whose spending was kept within its borders, thus causing most Texas foundations to limit their interests to the state, until the law was changed in 1963. In 1955 Texas foundations, mainly resulting from oil fortunes, were fifth among the states in assets, seventh in expenditures, and seventh in grants, positions roughly comparable to the state's rank in population. But the number and size of Texas foundations grew swiftly in the later 1950s, during which time some of the state's largest were established.

For almost a century Texas was a reservoir of raw materials within the U.S. economy. Texas took from the land oil, cotton, beef, and other goods and exported them to industrially more advanced states for final processing. One of the most notable changes in Texas following World War II was its shift from a raw-materials economy to an industrial economy, a metamorphosis by no means completed in the 1960s. After World War II Texas developed suddenly in a way that northern states had developed for more than half a century. But Texas had the extra impetus of extraordinary reserves of certain natural resources, notably oil and natural gas.

**Agriculture.**—Because of its large area and the diversity of its agriculture, Texas is agriculturally a miniature of the nation as a whole. Historically (until the discovery of major oil deposits early in the 20th century), cotton and cattle were the chief elements of the state's economy, and both remained large elements in the second half of the 20th century. Texas traditionally leads the states in growing cotton and raising cattle.

As a rule during the 1950s and 1960s Texas was first in the production of cotton, rice, sorghum grain, sorghum forage, other hay, cowpea hay, and cowpeas (for peas); second in the production of pecans, grapefruit, and grain hay; third in the production of oranges, broomcorn, and vegetables (but first in beets, spinach, watermelons, winter cabbage, winter carrots, early fall carrots, winter cauliflower, spring honeydew melons, early spring onions, and early summer onions); fourth in the production of winter wheat (but sixth when combined with spring wheat), peanuts (for nuts), peanut vine hay, and sorghum silage; and fifth in the production of sweet potatoes and honey. It was first in the number of cattle, sheep, lambs, horses, and mules; first in the production of wool and mohair.

In one year of the late 1950s Texas produced 37.6% of the nation's cotton lint, 38% of its cottonseed, 25.4% of its rice, 10.3% of its fresh vegetables, 9.8% of its grapefruit, and 44.4% of its sorghum grain. The state had 8.8% of the nation's cattle, 16.4% of its sheep and lambs, and 7.5% of its horses and mules. It produced 96.9% of the nation's mohair and 16.1% of its wool.

A number of changes besides farm mechanization and soil conservation substantially affected Texas agriculture after the depression of the 1930s. Between 1930 and the 1960s the state's farm population declined from a peak of 2,342,553 to perhaps less than 700,000 (from 42% of the total to around 8%). In the same period the average size of the state's farms increased from 251.7 ac. (101.9 ha.) to more than 690 ac. (279.6 ha.). Farm tenantry declined during the period, and share-cropper tenantry declined from 105,122 in 1930 to well under 10,000. And the areas of cotton production and cattle raising shifted during the period. The principal area of cotton production moved from the prairies of central Texas to the south Gulf coastal plain and west Texas, drawn mainly by irrigation. The principal area of cattle raising moved from west to east.

**Industry.**—Texas industrial production exceeded mineral production for the first time in the decade 1947–57, and toward the close of the decade the state could at last be said to have an industrial economy of consequence. In the one decade Texas to some extent shed its historic colonial economy. In that ten-year period larger regional and national markets, the rise of capital investments in Texas industry and technological advances increased the state's industrial production 76% compared with a national increase of 43%. While total manufacturing activity more than doubled in Texas, that of the nation increased less than 50%. Among other effects of the rise of industrialism was that for the first time Texas was not so securely bound to the fate of one industry—petroleum.

The production of transportation equipment, increasing more than 300% during the decade, led the state's industrial gains except for the relatively small electrical machinery industry. Creating most of the growth was aircraft production in the Dallas-Fort Worth area. Another significant force in the state's new industrialism was the rise of primary metals production. The basic steel industry, established in Texas during World War II, expanded from a capacity of 582,230 tons in 1948 to more than 2,000,000 tons by 1960. The two basic steel plants are at Houston and in Morris County. A more spectacular development, however, was the establishment of three primary aluminum plants, in 1950–52, at Rockdale, Port Lavaca, and in San Patricio County. The only tin smelter in the U.S. is at Texas City. The production of oil field machinery and tools, mostly at Houston, was of importance, as it had been for more than three decades.

One of the most important aspects of the state's rise to industrial significance was the growth of the chemical industry in the Gulf Coast region. A dominant factor in this development was the increased production of industrial chemicals from oil and natural gas, and especially notable was the growing use of chemicals for making plastics and synthetic rubber. Development of the new industrial districts was planned with care. Factories were built away from residential and commercial areas. The spaciousness of the industrial areas contrasted sharply with the crowded, unhealthful factory districts of older industrial areas. Perhaps no area of the world had more of the raw materials needed by the chemical industry than the Texas Gulf Coast region, and none was the site of such dramatic expansion of the industry in the decade after World War II. Most of the chemical plants clustered around Houston, Corpus Christi, and the Beaumont-Port Arthur area.

The industrial complex of Houston and the upper Texas Gulf Coast was substantially enlarged in 1962 when construction of the Manned Spacecraft Centre was begun a few miles southeast of Houston at Clear Lake. The centre, a National Aeronautics and Space Administration project costing more than $125,000,000, was established to direct the nation's manned spacecraft program for the Mercury, Gemini, and Apollo projects—the conquest of the moon. Of larger importance economically, however, was the swift development of a type of industry new to the region—electronics—to work with the centre.

**Mining.**—Texas became the leading state in minerals production in 1935, increasing this production to roughly a quarter of the national total throughout the 1950s and 1960s. In Texas the word "minerals" means oil and natural gas, of which the state has almost half the nation's total known reserves. Next to oil and gas the most important of Texas minerals is sulfur, of which Texas and Louisiana together produce nearly 70% of the world's supply. Texas mineral production gained nearly 50% compared with a national gain of 28% in the decade 1947–57, but important oil discoveries elsewhere in the nation and the competitive pressures of foreign oil imports reduced the oil industry's rate of growth after the peak year of 1957. The production of crude oil, the state's largest single industrial output, dominates the state's mineral production and much else, but in the 1950s and 1960s the flow of crude oil increased at a slower rate than other types of mineral production and manufacturing. The production of natural gas and natural gas liquids, important exports to other states and even more important as fuel and raw material for Texas industries, increased rapidly.

The importance of the entire Gulf Coast as a petroleum refining centre is its tidewater exit for the largest oil production in the world. The Texas and Louisiana coast became the largest refining district of the U.S. in the 1950s, with about a third of the nation's capacity. Most of the Texas refineries are grouped around Houston and the Beaumont-Port Arthur area. In the 1960s water transport facilities were supplemented by the Houston-Beaumont to New York pipeline.

The Texas Panhandle, near Amarillo, is a major helium producing area. Production of the gas is controlled by the federal government because of helium's military significance. The plains of western Texas and southeastern New Mexico contain the nation's major supply of potash and one of the largest deposits in the world. Texas has large deposits of iron ore, which is used by its basic steel plants, and of lignite, used as a fuel by one of the state's aluminum plants. Texas was one of the leading producers of carbon black, primary magnesium, bromine, and salt well into the 1960s.

**Transportation and Communications.**—Inevitably, because of its area, Texas leads the states in highway and railroad track mileage. Of the more than 240,000 mi. (386,000 km.) of public roads in Texas in the 1960s, nearly 64,000 mi. (103,000 km.) were in the state highway system, of which nearly 60,000 mi. (97,000 km.) were paved. But because of the uneven distribution of the state's population, roughly 80% of the traffic traveled on 20% of the roads. Of the more than 21,000 mi. (33,795 km.) of railroad track, about 14,000 mi. (22,530 km.) were in mainline track. The state had about 850 airports, of which more than 50 were used by commercial airlines.

The 13 deepwater ports on the Texas Gulf Coast are artificial to varying extents. They are Houston, Galveston, Port Arthur, Beaumont, Orange, Corpus Christi, Brownsville, Texas City, Sabine Pass, Freeport, Port Aransas, Port Isabel, and Port Mansfield, of which Houston, Beaumont, and Port Arthur are inland ports. Houston, 50 mi. (80 km.) inland and connected with the Gulf of Mexico by the Houston Ship Channel, annually ranks between third and fifth of U.S. ports in commerce. The Texas section of the Intracoastal Canal runs the length of the Texas coast from Brownsville to Orange (and then eastward to meet the Mississippi at New Orleans). Thirteen shallow, or barge, ports are spaced along the Texas section of the canal. These Texas ports are one of the state's chief economic benefits.

*See* also references under "Texas" in the Index.

Bibliography.—The writing of Texas history had not produced a 1-vol. general work of excellence up to the 1960s. *The Texas Almanac,* published biennially by the *Dallas Morning News,* is the best general information source on the state. Texas State Historical Association, *The Handbook of Texas,* 2 vol. (1952); their *Southwestern Historical Quarterly* (1898– ) is more accurate.

The best work on the revolution, and a short one, is William C. Binkley, *The Texas Revolution* (1952); the best one on the decade of the republic is William Ransom Hogan, *The Texas Republic* (1946). Two diverse works evaluating contemporary Texas are George Fuermann, *Reluctant Empire* (1957) and Frank Goodwyn, *Lone-Star Land* (1955), virtually the only critical estimates of modern Texas.

Current statistics on production, employment, industry, etc., may be obtained from the pertinent state departments; the principal figures are summarized annually in the *Britannica Book of the Year*.

(G. M. F.)

**TEXAS, UNIVERSITY OF,** a state-supported, coeducational institution of higher learning, founded in 1881 at Austin, Tex. *See* TEXAS: *Education*.

**TEXTBOOKS** are standard works or manuals of instruction in a subject of study. However, commenting on the subject in the *Encyclopedia of Educational Research* (Macmillan; New York, 1960), B. R. Buckingham pointed out that the term *textbook* is broader than the term *school book* and is, in fact, so broad as to defy brief definition. A textbook, he emphasized, is not necessarily organized for instructional purposes or designed for classroom use. "In fact, the author's intention may be quite wide of the idea of instruction. Shakespeare wrote plays to be acted on the stage, not for purposes of instruction. Yet his plays have been widely used as textbooks. In the modern sense and as commonly understood, the textbook is a learning instrument usually employed in schools and colleges to support a program of instruction. In ordinary usage the textbook is printed, it is nonconsumable, it is hardbound, it serves an avowed instructional purpose and it is placed in the hands of the learner."

Buckingham's definition of the textbook as a learning instrument may conveniently be adopted for the purposes of this article. It has to be understood, however, that the instrument is and always has been very flexible. If it is now commonly a printed book, it has in the past taken such forms as a paddle board or a papyrus roll; and if Buckingham found it to be nonconsumable and hardbound, the years since he wrote have seen the widespread adoption of paperback textbooks. Moreover, workbooks, combining instructional text with space for the student's written exercises, and loose-leafed textbooks, allowing obsolete sections to be replaced with fresh material as knowledge expanded, have all made his stipulation that the textbook should be nonconsumable already out-of-date.

## HISTORY

In the ancient world and up to and beyond the time of the invention of printing, education for children was largely oral; even for older students it involved listening to lectures or disputations rather than the reading of texts. This, of course, was because both the shortage of material for bookmaking, and the laborious nature of copying made the written word rare and precious (*see* PAPER MANUFACTURE: *Historical Development;* PAPYRUS; PARCHMENT). In China, where Confucius (d. 479 B.C.) had laid the foundations of a classical literature, the *Analects* of this sage and the sayings of others such as Mencius (d. ?289 B.C.), who were soon associated with him, became the principal instruments of education. A national system of education combined with an elaborate ritual of examination ensured the dominance of these texts down to modern times. India, however, was remarkable also for instructional texts on the sciences in verse, similar in character to the *Georgics* written later by the Roman poet Virgil.

**Europe and the Mediterranean.**—*Classical Period.*—The first school text used in Europe was the poetry of Homer. Throughout the classical period these poems, usually dictated and learned by heart, supplied the schoolboy with material for his studies of language and literature, as also did Aesop and Hesiod. Rome added Virgil, Horace, and other great writers. Education was preeminently concerned with the study of excellent models. The origins of the actual grammar book go back to Dionysius Thrax, whose grammar of the Greek tongue, produced in 120 B.C., set out the terms still used today. For science a variety of textbooks were produced in the Hellenistic period, chiefly by the scholars of Alexandria. To this period belongs Euclid's *Elements* (*c.* 300 B.C.), a manual which in one form or another has been used down to modern times.

*Dark and Middle Ages.*—The textbooks used in ancient Asia and the Western classical world showed that the aim of their schools was to perpetuate the religious and philosophical traditions of their respective cultures. This was the natural purpose of all systems of education, and as Christianity spread, education inevitably became concerned with the transmission of Christian belief and precepts. But to propagate doctrine the media of communication had still to be mastered; grammar and the liberal arts remained the staple of Christian education. After barbarians had overrun the West education became for some centuries virtually confined to the clergy. Monasteries trained their own monks ("schools" for outsiders were very rare) and bishops their clergy.

In this period the students used for elementary grammar the work of Aelius Donatus (fl. *c.* A.D. 350), and advanced to the *Institutiones grammaticae,* of Priscian (fl. *c.* A.D. 500). Donatus, indeed, remained so popular that even in Chaucer's day, 1,000 years later, his name was a synonym for a school book. The liberal arts and some Christian philosophy were studied in the works of the North African lawyer Martianus Capella (fl. *c.* 400), and of Boëthius (d. 524). Much-studied works were the *Institutiones divinarum et saecularium litterarum* written by Cassiodorus (d. *c.* 585) for the monks of his monastery at Squillace in southern Italy, the *Etymologiae* of Isidore of Seville (d. 636), and the treatises of Rabanus Maurus (d. 856), who was teacher and later abbot of the monastery of Fulda in Germany. Biblical commentaries written by the Anglo-Saxon scholar Bede (d. 735) were also very popular.

On the scientific side the *Introduction to Arithmetic* produced *c.* A.D. 100 by Nicomachus of Gerasa remained popular, while astronomy was often studied through the poem *Phaenomena* of Aratus of Soli (d. *c.* 245 B.C.).

The multiplicity of races in the Roman Empire and later the advent of the barbarians made it important to communicate knowledge in the vernacular. Bilingual textbooks appeared as early as the 3rd century A.D. In Anglo-Saxon England King Alfred (d. 899) made numerous translations from Latin and Abbot Aelfric (d. *c.* 1010) wrote a Latin grammar in Anglo-Saxon. On the Continent a life of Christ entitled *Heliand* ("Saviour") became a textbook for secular priests.

By the 11th century in Western Europe, the cathedral schools were achieving real importance. Later some of them developed into universities. For the liberal arts medieval students were still following Donatus and Priscian, Boëthius and Cassiodorus, and using Cicero and Virgil as models for Latin prose and verse style. Aristotle's *Categories* were also studied. By the 12th century, the *Glossa ordinaria* of the Old and New Testaments, developed over the centuries, had become established texts. A similar process of codification led to the famous *sententiarum libri* of Peter Lombard (d. 1160), a work built up on the opinions (*sententiae*) of various church fathers and later teachers on points of doctrine. In the field of canon and Roman law the *Decretum* (*c.* 1140) of Gratian and the *Glossa ordinaria* of Franciscus Accursius (d. 1260) became works of equal authority.

BY COURTESY OF THE BIBLIOTECA RICCARDIANA, FLORENCE

Page from Giuliano de' Medici's arithmetic book, 16th century, with a problem beginning: "The King of France was routed in battle, with 1/4 of his soldiers killed and 2/5 wounded and 1,000 were taken prisoner and 6,000 escaped. . ."

For the sciences, Arabic works, translated in the 12th century by men such as Adelard of Bath and Gerard of Cremona, were studied. Although their scientific and mathematical knowledge was in advance of that of the West, the Muslims shared with Christians the conviction that education exists to instil correct faith and behaviour. A quotation from al-Ghazzali (d. 1111), the Muslim theologian, indicates the Arabic tradition. In his *Training*

(5)

| | | | |
|---|---|---|---|
| *Felis* clamat. The Cat cryeth. | nau nau | N n |
| *Auriga* clamat. The Carter cryeth. | ó ó ó | O o |
| *Pullus* pipit. The Chicken peepeth. | pi pi | P p |
| *Cuculus* cuculat. The Cuckow singeth cuckow. | kuk ku | Q q |
| *Canis* ringitur. The Dog grinneth. | err | R r |
| *Serpens* sibilat. The Serpent hisseth. | si | S s |
| *Graculus* clamat. The Jay cryeth. | tac tac | T t |
| *Bubo* ululat. The Owl howteth. | ú ú | U u |
| *Lepus* vagit. The Hare squeaketh. | vá | W w |
| *Rana* coaxat. The Frog croaketh. | coax | X x |
| *Asinus* rudit The Asse brayeth. | y y y | Y y |
| *Tabanus* dicit. The Breeze or Horse-flie saith. | ds ds | Z z |

B 3

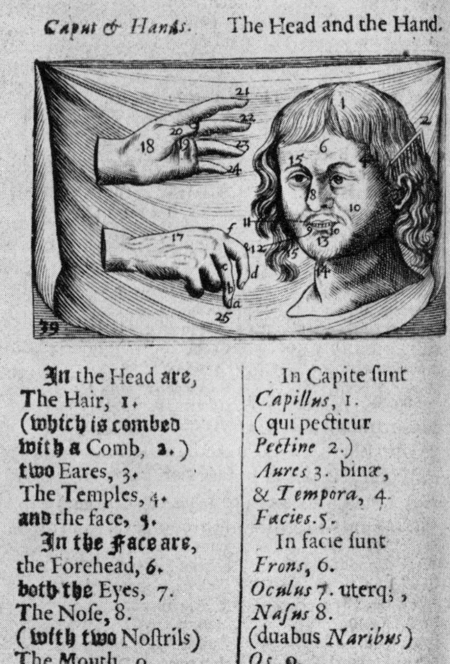
XXXIX.

*Caput & Manus.* The Head and the Hand.

| | |
|---|---|
| In the Head are, | In Capite sunt |
| The Hair, 1. | *Capillus*, 1. |
| (which is combed | (qui pectitur |
| with a Comb, 2.) | *Pectine* 2.) |
| two Eares, 3. | *Aures* 3. binæ, |
| The Temples, 4. | & *Tempora*, 4. |
| and the face, 5. | *Facies*.5. |
| In the Face are, | In facie sunt |
| the Forehead, 6. | *Frons*, 6. |
| both the Eyes, 7. | *Oculus* 7. uterq; , |
| The Nose, 8. | *Nasus* 8. |
| (with two Nostrils) | (duabus *Naribus*) |
| The Mouth, 9. | *Os*, 9. |

BY COURTESY OF THE TRUSTEES OF THE BRITISH MUSEUM

TWO PAGES FROM J. A. COMENIUS' "THE VISIBLE WORLD IN PICTURES," 1658: (LEFT) PART OF AN ILLUSTRATED ALPHABET; (RIGHT) PAGE FROM ONE OF THE NINE ILLUSTRATED LESSONS DEALING WITH HUMAN ANATOMY AND PHYSIOLOGY

*of Children,* he wrote that when the child was grown up he should be handed over to an excellent and good instructor who must teach him the Koran traditions, improving anecdotes, and such poetry as was not erotic.

*The Renaissance and the 18th Century.*—The revival of learning and the invention of printing gave a fresh impetus to the textbook. In Italy the Byzantine humanist Cardinal Bessarion (d. 1472) published a Greek grammar. Erasmus, the Dutch humanist, produced his *Colloquia* to supply the student with instruction, improvements, and delight. Visiting England, he assisted William Lyly to produce a Latin grammar for St. Paul's School, London. Now, increasingly, the great teaching orders of the Roman Catholic Church, such as the De la Salle brothers, brought out their own textbooks. In France the abbé François Fénelon (d. 1715), later archbishop of Cambrai, taught Louis XIV's grandson, wrote history books, and directed attention to the schooling of girls. The Catholic Church, however, had no monopoly. In Germany, Philipp Melanchthon (d. 1560), who was an associate of Luther in the Reformation, wrote grammatical and other textbooks which were still in use in the 18th century. Meanwhile, in England, at the infant grade the hornbook persisted—a paddle of wood covered with transparent horn and setting out such elements of instruction as the alphabet, the Roman numerals, and the Lord's Prayer (*see* HORNBOOK).

Increasingly, too, whole theories of education began to be reflected in the textbooks. J. A. Comenius (d. 1670), a Czech reformer with a comprehensive system whose fame took him to a number of countries including Sweden and England, was responsible for two celebrated school books. One, his *Gate of Languages Unlocked,* gave sentence drill in Latin vocabulary with parallel translations in the vernacular. Written originally in Latin and Moravian, it was subsequently translated into a dozen European and Oriental tongues. The English diarist John Evelyn (d. 1706) records that his son was well advanced in it by the age of five. More important was Comenius' *The Visible World in Pictures,* setting out lessons in the world of the senses and illustrated with woodcuts. Texts with pictures go back to Hellenistic times; but *The Visible World* was the real forerunner of the illustrated school book of today.

In America the school book was necessarily at first imported from England. The emphasis was on the spelling book and on the primer that would facilitate the reading of the Bible. A spelling book, however, had been printed in Massachusetts by 1650. *The New England Primer* was particularly popular. Isaac Greenwood of Boston wrote his *Arithmetick Vulgar and Decimal* in 1729. Noah Webster's *American Spelling Book* (1783) firmly established the United States as the source of its own textbooks.

**The 19th and 20th Centuries.**—The 19th century, with its new emphasis on popular education, brought a flood of school books and on both sides of the Atlantic educational publishing became a major part of the printing industry. In England the great textbook names began to emerge—Isaac Todhunter for mathematics, Sir William Smith for classical lexicography, Benjamin Hall Kennedy for Latin primers, Henry Bradley for English dictionaries, and so on. In the U.S. William Holmes McGuffey (d. 1873) compiled in 1836–37 his *Eclectic Readers,* moral in tone and varied in instruction, that were to dominate the scene and to sell more than 120,000,000 copies. But there were others, so that already by the mid-19th century concern was felt in the U.S. at the proliferation of textbooks, and there were movements toward control. In England, Matthew Arnold as a school inspector reported scathingly in 1853: "Almost every educational society has its own school books. These are by no means universally adopted by the schools in connection with it, and a recognised textbook on any subject is nowhere to be found." Arnold could complain, too, of banality in the school books. Small children were taught to read such sentences as "The crocodile is viviparous." Nor was banality the only fault. Though, as with the McGuffey *Readers,* a real attempt had begun to grade textbooks, they were often dull and uncompromising or worse. In *A Victorian Boyhood,* published by Macmillan and Co. Ltd. in 1955, Sir Lawrence Jones recalls "a thick blue *First Reading Book,* intended for very small children indeed, where the bones and blood of a child eaten by a wolf

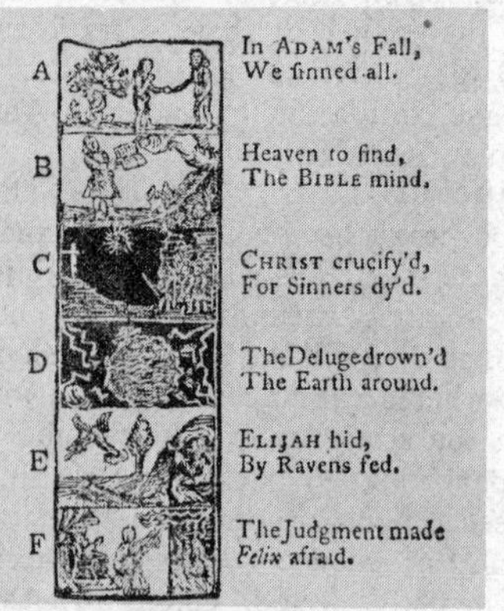
A In ADAM's Fall, We sinned all.

B Heaven to find, The BIBLE mind.

C CHRIST crucify'd, For Sinners dy'd.

D The Deluge drown'd The Earth around.

E ELIJAH hid, By Ravens fed.

F The Judgment made *Felix* afraid.

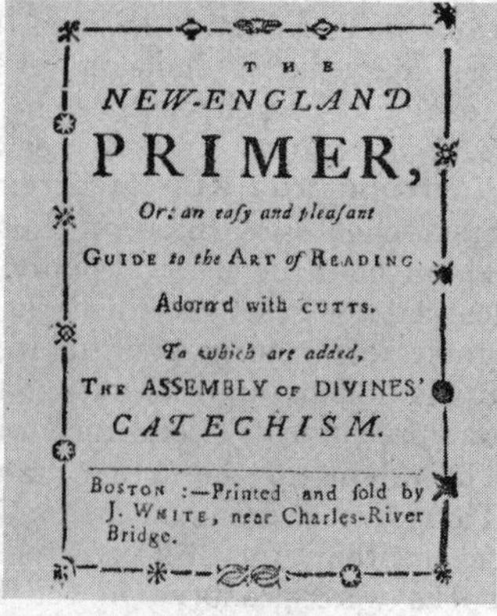
THE

*NEW-ENGLAND*

PRIMER,

*Or, an easy and pleasant*

GUIDE *to the* ART *of* READING.

Adorn'd with CUTTS.

*To which are added,*

THE ASSEMBLY OF DIVINES' *CATECHISM.*

BOSTON:—Printed and sold by J. WHITE, near Charles-River Bridge.

BETTMANN ARCHIVE

TWO PAGES FROM THE "NEW ENGLAND PRIMER," 1762: (LEFT) THE ALPHABET WAS TAUGHT THROUGH THE USE OF RELIGIOUS RHYMES; (RIGHT) TITLE PAGE

HASTE THEE, SCHOOL-BOY

Haste thee, school-boy, haste away,
Far too long has been thy stay;
Often you have tardy been,
Many a lesson you've not seen;
Haste thee, school-boy, haste away,
Far too long has been thy stay.

Haste thee, school-boy, haste away,
Join no more the idler's play;
Quickly speed your steps to school,
And there mind your teacher's rule;
Haste thee, school-boy, haste away,
Join no more the idler's play.

Haste thee, school-boy, haste away,
Learn thy lessons well to-day;
Love the truth, and shun the wrong,
Then no day will seem too long.

HISTORICAL PICTURES SERVICE

FROM MCGUFFEY'S "NEW THIRD ECLECTIC READER," 1857

are described with a relish we lately reserved for the sinking of a German U-boat."

Some of the worst deficiencies of the 19th-century school books began to disappear as government or state inspection increased the efficiency of the schools, and the spending of public money on textbooks brought a demand for better standards. How far the state should control textbooks was a question that received different answers in different parts of the globe. But in English-speaking countries, at least, by the 20th century, the principle was emerging that the trained teacher was the person best fitted to choose his pupils' school books.

Nor were conditions static elsewhere. Chaim Weizmann (d. 1952) described in *Trial and Error* the Jewish school in Russia which he entered at the age of four. It was preoccupied with the Talmud. But secular studies were surreptitiously impinging on the sacred, and at a second school he saw his first Hebrew textbook on natural science and chemistry.

In *A Daughter of the Samurai,* Etsu Inagaki Sugimoto (d. 1950) described her education at the age of six: "My studies were from books intended only for boys as it was very unusual for a girl to study Chinese classics. My first lessons were from the Four Books of Confucius. These are: Daigaku—Great Learning, which teaches that the wise use of knowledge leads to virtue; Chuyo—The Unchanging Centre, which treats of the unalterableness of universal law; Rongo and Moshi—which consist of the autobiography, anecdotes, and sayings of Confucius, gathered by his disciples." (Etsu Inagaki Sugimoto, *A Daughter of the Samurai,* Hutchinson Publishing Group Ltd., London, 1960, Doubleday & Co. Inc., New York, 1966.) It was all the same, it seems, as it had been for a thousand years. But before long John Morris could record in *Traveller from Tokyo* a professor at Yokohama who made a textbook of English conversation out of the works of Henry James.

## MODERN TEXTBOOKS

In the modern period the production of the textbook was stimulated by the education explosion and by the needs of a technological society for trained personnel. It was also stimulated by the concern of the advanced nations to provide education in the underdeveloped areas of the globe. Thus, of the 5,000,000,000 or more volumes that came from the presses of the world every year, about half were meant for the classroom. At the same time the textbook met competition from the new media of communication and it was affected by the shift from a subject-centred to a child-centred curriculum.

In two-thirds of the countries of the globe the production of a textbook was left to private enterprise. Increasingly, however, agencies of the U.N. and other interested bodies were concerned with the supply of textbooks for the underdeveloped countries, while state publishing houses emerged in parts of Africa, often with initial help from commercial firms. Significant of modern trends was a course in the writing, production, and distribution of textbooks which opened in 1963 at the Department of Education in Tropical Areas of the University of London Institute of Education. In the advanced countries cooperation between makers and users of textbooks was increasingly practised and bodies such as the National Book League in Britain and the National Education Association of the U.S. promoted it.

In both these countries publishers' representatives often acted as liaison officers between the schools and the publishers. In the U.S.S.R., where the school curriculum was centralized, changes in textbooks were discussed at meetings of teachers and tried out first in selected schools by the Academy of Pedagogical Sciences. Textbooks were commonly written by groups of teachers and competitions were organized for new ones.

**Characteristics of Modern Textbooks.**—In Western countries, research into the techniques of reading at the primary school level produced elementary books in which the pages were laid out as carefully as the vocabulary was graded. Word counts dictated the material. Visual experiments decided the type. Illustration was extensively used; the *Golden Dictionary,* one of a U.S. series, listed 1,000 words, but it tempted the infant philologist with 1,500 pictures. At the same time preoccupations with the mass testing of children, and in particular with the intelligence test, led some publishers in Great Britain after World War II to produce quiz-like books to give pupils practice. In the U.S. the superintendent of district schools in Washington, D.C., complained of textbooks in which the subject matter was impoverished by the "postponement" theories of the child psychologist.

The growth of secondary education for all brought a spate of school books designed for the less dedicated pupil. Academic dullness was abandoned, the pupil's interests canvassed, and every device from the fictional approach to the strip cartoon was employed to catch his eye. The *Reader's Digest* supplied a series of books for the English lesson. The geography text moved away from the capes and bays into the social sciences. On all sides the attempt was made to close the gap between the textbook and the rest of literature; publishing successes soon appeared in junior editions for schools. Nor was the textbook for the older student neglected. Writing one became almost a tradition for the university lecturer who sought professional advancement. And at the adult level the publishers vied with each other to produce self-instructional manuals in every conceivable subject. In 1967 titles in the *Teach Yourself* series published by the English Universities Press ranged from Greek to computer programming. U.S. publishers had similar series.

The schools themselves, however, were often hampered by lack of money. The high cost of other items in the educational budget and the rising prices of the books themselves all made the schools' purchasing power woefully small. In Great Britain, where books were free under the state system, the annual expenditure at the primary level by the second half of the 20th century was scarcely 10*s.* a head. In the U.S., children in some states still had to buy or rent their textbooks. At colleges throughout the world generally the buying of textbooks bore heavily on the budgets of the individual students. Cost was always the bugbear of educational publishing. The issue for the textbook lay between a short, cheap life and a longer but expensive one. The content of the book sometimes made possible a double issue—a paperback edition for the classroom and one with firmer covers for the school library. Paperback editions of advanced and hitherto expensive texts became more frequent. Experiments were also tried with covers of washable plastic.

**Defects.**—In the developing countries cost was not the only difficulty. International agreements sometimes allowed cheap imports from the Western nations, and there was also some sporadic pirating. Increasingly, however, it came to be recognized that the textbook not indigenous to the region might have its drawbacks and that science manuals, for instance, unrelated to the local flora and fauna and other physical attributes of the country might be quite out of place.

Textbooks for the emergent countries, however, were not the only ones to come under critical appraisal. After visiting Great Britain, A. Harry Passow, professor of education, Teachers College, Columbia University, had this to say about English textbooks in his *Secondary Education for All* (No. 3, Monograph Series in International Education; Kappa Delta Pi, An Honor Society in Education, West Lafayette, Ind., 1961): "English books tend to be drab, poorly illustrated and typographically unattractive by our standards. They are also far less expensive than American books. Good English teachers seldom cling to a single textbook, but then, neither does a good American teacher. One committee favored texts after the first two years because 'a textbook . . . can eliminate the making of extensive notes and can be used to encourage the student to seek his own solution of his difficulties.' The science teachers whom I observed particularly in the grammar-school courses relied on one or more basic texts and on supplementary . . . so-called revision textbooks and publications containing questions set at past examinations. As in the States few teachers follow textbooks slavishly."

By contrast William Sheldon, director of the Reading and Language Arts Center, Syracuse University, told a London audience in 1966 that many American textbooks were horribly out of date. Some relating to Africa and Asia, he said, were 15 to 20 years behind the times and as far as China was concerned it was all "swinging pigtails and bound feet." Nonetheless, U.S. textbooks were increasingly admired in Great Britain after World War II for their opulent production, splendid illustrations, and fresh approach to traditional subjects. Although their high cost made them more often a stimulus for the teacher than a tool for the child, *Latin for Today,* for example, a course of U.S. origin, did much to wrest the English grammar school from its narrowly academic approach to the classics.

Bias in textbooks was a matter of much concern at both national and international levels. The bias was sometimes deliberate, but frequently a distorted picture was presented by the use of out-of-date maps or statistics, and publishers were at fault less from malice than from practising unwise economies. The subjects most often called in question were geography and history, but after World War II even the arithmetic books in Germany were found to be tainted with Nazi propaganda. There is a long history of attacks on particular textbooks by individuals or groups who have found something in the contents inimical to their beliefs. In 1967 Lennart Husen's *Kristen tro* ("Christian Belief"), which had been approved by the Swedish State Textbooks Board for use in schools, came under fire from religious groups in western Sweden who thought its treatment of science and religion tendentious. On occasion some national apprehension has brought large numbers of textbooks under fire. In the U.S., for example, after World War II, concern about the spread of Communism led many textbooks to be criticized for their supposedly anti-American influence. At the same time the importance of textbooks as instruments of international understanding was increasingly recognized. UNESCO was active in the campaign for balance, producing surveys of existing textbooks and encouraging measures for improvement. There were even suggestions that the textbooks themselves should become an international responsibility. In a seminar at Vancouver in 1967 delegates of the World Confederation of Organizations of the Teaching Profession maintained that the standardization of school textbooks in history and geography throughout the world could be a major step in improving international relations and they urged the setting up of an international committee to study the books of all participating nations with a view to producing basic texts.

Against these international aspirations bias on the home front presented its separate problems. In the 1960s the campaigns in the U.S. for civil rights for Negroes drew increasing attention to the preoccupation of the school books there with white Americans. Laws began to be enacted that reflected the movement. A Michigan statute of 1966, for instance, required the state's schools to use only history texts that "include accurate recording of any and all ethnic groups who have made contributions to world, American, or the State of Michigan societies." Spurred by such enactments, U.S. publishers began to bring out multi-racial texts. Commenting on the trend, *Time* magazine reported: "Typically the books have brightly colored pictures—on the cover and inside—of Negro, Puerto Rican, and white children sitting together on tenement steps or splashing together in the spray of a fire hydrant. . . . The main flaw in some books is that integration is too tidy: illustrations too often show exactly three kids together—one Negro, one Puerto Rican, and one white." There were other criticisms. It was, for instance, alleged that one of the new multi-racial texts gave too much attention to the Negro and not enough to Mexican and Chinese Americans. Altogether it was clear that the new demand for balance would not be easy to meet. Ironically enough, while this was going on in the U.S., school textbooks began to appear in Great Britain specifically directed at Pakistani and other immigrants, depicting them in an English setting and devised to help their integration.

While on the one hand textbooks showed a trend toward universality, there was on the other hand increasing emphasis on local history and civic knowledge. In Britain studies related to the neighbourhood of the school and incorporating texts produced for the purpose were found specially valuable for the less academic pupils, combining as they did with the book work opportunities for expeditions and other activities. In the U.S. the locally produced *Michigan, My Michigan* and *San Francisco Today* were typical of the trend. Many publishers issued one series of texts for the public schools and a modified series for the parochial schools. The state of California required publishers to ship plates so that the state could do its own printing. In countries such as Australia there was a movement to lace the English textbook with samples of native writing. Even a traditional subject could be given a national or regional slant. *Latin for Americans,* for example, uses an illustration of an Italian tapestry in the Cleveland Museum of Art. There were also, notably in the urban U.S., demands for textbooks teaching Negro history as a separate discipline from the standard American history.

**Textbooks and Modern Audio-Visual Teaching Aids.**—These trends in the modern textbook, however, though important in themselves, paled into insignificance beside the competition it faced in the second half of the 20th century from the new media of communication and modern teaching aids. The matter was graphically put by a special correspondent in the *Times* (London) *Educational Supplement* (Aug. 11, 1967):

> For a long time there was no war. The Textbook held complete sway in the classroom. The Empire of the Printed Word was unruffled. Then there came the first rumblings of dissent. A new medium was beginning to tap on the old schoolhouse door. . . . Film or Audio-Visual (AV) was nibbling at the Textbooks' virtual monopoly. Rather cumbersome equipment not custom-built for education—in the form of 16-mm. projectors—slowed down AV's advance. In the mid-1950s surveys showed that teachers and principals are slow to develop programmes of audio-visual education which realize the potential of this medium of instruction. But about this time a newer, younger medium leapt into the fray—television. This was really going to start a revolution. AV was far too much bother for the teachers, but now their needs could come piped in through electric cable. No threading of film. Just switch on.
>
> Television made early advances heavily backed by the Ford Foundation. A whole complex of schools centred on Hagerstown, Maryland, was launching into full-scale use of television at elementary and secondary levels. There was rioting in the land. But after the first flush of novelty wore off, even television had its problems. It was expensive. The signal wasn't always great. It was difficult to schedule programmes when the teacher wanted them. The programmes were not good. Now television and AV started to disagree among themselves. Rationally, this did not make sense. They were both basically on the same side putting a visual element into what was an over-verbal system of education. Unfortunately reason was not around. Television people came from a different background—they were broadcasters. AV men were teachers and rather looked-down-on teachers. AV blamed Ford for not involving them in television for they were the only technologists in education. But AV had strong support from commercial firms who were beginning to make real headway selling equipment and films to schools. Old Textbook could afford to rest and lick the few wounds he had got. Almost immediately another young adversary leapt at him. . . .

The new adversary was the theory of programmed learning (*q.v.*) which brought with it the teaching machine. Programmed learning presented on screens in a variety of machines was much in fashion in the 1960s, providing the pupil with a mechanical attraction in keeping with the times and the chance to proceed at his own individual pace. One of its most elaborate developments, in association with a system of computerized learning, could be seen in 1967 in a California experiment: a computer stored the individual student's record of instruction and achievement and presented him with appropriate learning material by screen and tape.

Clearly the traditional textbook could not emerge unscathed from all these developments, and indeed in some places the rush to adopt the new media seemed to threaten its abandonment. The complexity and expense, however, of the new contrivances militated elsewhere in favour of the textbook, as did the innate conservatism of many teachers. Saner counsels, too, began to see the new media of instruction and the new theories of learning as reinforcing rather than conflicting with the old. Textbooks based on programmed learning began to appear. Even branching programs, it was found, could be set out in book form by devices of pagination whereby the learner was instructed to proceed to one page or another according to his response to the multiple-choice test question. Thus while students in California were proceeding at their own pace by way of computerized learning, apprentice technicians in the U.S. Army were doing the same by way of programmed textbooks.

The adaptability of the textbook was not confined to the advanced countries. A report in 1967 from the International Institute for Educational Planning produced a striking example from Algeria, where large numbers of monitors, or low-grade teachers, had been recruited in the educational drive that came with the country's independence:

To help the monitors and any other interested adults increase their knowledge of mathematics, three self-study manuals were written and published, with ten programmed lessons in each. Nobody had told the Algerians that it was difficult to write programmed texts, or that despite a series of training workshops programmed learning was still not in school use elsewhere in Africa or in the Middle East. And it must be admitted that the three Algerian manuals were not formal Skinnerian programming. Nevertheless, they were built around the idea of eliciting active student responses and telling the student if he has responded correctly. After a student had read a short text, he had a series of questions to answer, blanks to fill in, problems to work out. He could check his own answers. The programs were pre-tested, and seemed to work well. When they were put into wide use they were further combined with a television program. The student worked through this program and then watched a television teacher review and expand upon the basic concept he had been studying. Needless to say, the television served as a pacer to keep him on schedule with lessons.

As the 20th century wore on, then, all the signs were not that the textbook would be eclipsed but that it would rather become an integrated item in a whole armoury of teaching aids. The precise areas of the learning process in which it could best be employed seemed likely to be defined more closely in the future than they had been in the past but its continued use appeared certain. In experiments in the teaching of science and modern languages made on both sides of the Atlantic, the textbook was already seen as part of a comprehensive teaching kit which might include film, tape, records, and other aids. This was reflected at the commercial level in the growing association of textbook publishers with the producers of other teaching aids. At the same time there remained prodigious opportunities for the author of the textbook itself. In Britain R. J. Unstead's *Looking at History* had sold almost 2,000,000 copies within six years of its publication in 1953 while in 1967 H. O. Emerson could claim authorship of 30–40 textbooks. In the U.S. American Book reckoned to sell $22,000,000 worth of textbooks a year. The opportunities had increasingly attracted the professional writer to this field.

The textbook continued to be subject to influences of every sort. On the one hand the movement to relate schools to the outside world and to break down classroom barriers produced textbooks little different from what might be published for leisure-time reading. On the other hand the world's demand for technologists caused information books about science to reach junior levels where they were unknown before. Industry cooperated in the production of attractive manuals for the schools and universities. Basic courses of the U.S. Navy in electricity and electronics were adapted to civilian use. In Britain the zest for immediacy produced a textbook for the junior schools that went to them in the form of a weekly magazine. More particularly, however, the soaring costs of education and the increasing preoccupation of the service with planning and productivity meant that more and more attention was given to the proper use of the textbook, while improved techniques of evaluation brought it under ever closer scrutiny. Henry VIII had ordered that Lyly's *Grammar* should be the only one used in schools. In more recent times the teacher's right to choose his own textbooks was a principle of professional advance. This sometimes led to licence. Now curriculum reform groups bringing specially tailored textbooks in their train seemed likely to limit the licence. Education would not return to the days of Henry VIII. But planning and productivity in the future would demand that the textbook should be efficient, in keeping with advances in other media.

*See* also AUDIO-VISUAL EDUCATION; BOOK; EDUCATION, HISTORY OF.

BIBLIOGRAPHY.—UNESCO and the International Bureau of Education, *Primary School Textbooks: . . . a Comparative Study* (1959). *See* also other UNESCO publications, including *Better History Textbooks* (1950). J. V. Chapman, *Your Secondary Modern Schools* (1959); International Commission for the Teaching of History, *World History Teachers in Conference* (1964); M. M. Mathews, *Teaching to Read: Historically Considered* (1966); O. E. Schüddekopf *et al., History Teaching and History Textbook Revision* (1967); *Textbooks in Print* (published annually, from 1893); National Book League and Councils, *Education Book Guide* (1956–64). (L. R. BU.)

**TEXTILE PRINTING,** the process by which a decorative pattern is applied to a woven or knitted fabric in at least one colour different from the body of the fabric itself. This mode of decoration differs from the formation of a pattern by weaving and knitting processes that employ threads that are already coloured or have different capacities for taking up dyes. The four main methods of textile printing are block printing, copperplate printing, roller printing and screen printing.

## EARLY METHODS

**Block Printing.**—The origin of block printing on textiles is somewhat obscure but it is clear that the printing of textiles by means of blocks was developed from free-hand painting with a brush. Wooden blocks believed to have been used for textile printing have been found in burying grounds at Akhmim, upper Egypt, and are said to date from the 4th century A.D. No textiles printed by means of these blocks have, however, been found. In Europe, block printing of fabrics does not appear to have begun much before the end of the 12th century A.D.; the chief centre appears to have been the Rhineland of Germany.

In blocks used for printing, the spaces between the lines or devices forming the pattern were cut away, leaving the design standing in relief, as in letterpress printing. The colour was then applied to the surface of the block and the coloured block pressed down on the cloth. An interesting description of early block printing on textiles is given in *The Book of the Arts or Treatise on Painting* by Cennino Cennini, written in the late 14th or early 15th century. According to Cennini, the thickened colour was applied to the block by means of a glove, probably made of leather. The pigments were mixed with starch, gum (tragacanth) or a mixture of these, or even with varnish, so that the colour was in a viscous state and did not run from the raised portions of the block. Cennini describes how the outlines of the patterns were printed by block and additional colours added by means of a brush. Later the colour was applied by a pad, either directly or by pressing the block down on a pad impregnated with colour. Wax resists were also printed by metal or wood blocks for indigo-resist dyeing. This method was used in Egypt in the 9th–10th century A.D. and in Germany in the 17th century. Apart from these indigo-resist dyed textiles, until the end of the 17th century all European block-printed textiles were printed with surface pigments or oil stains that were fugitive (not fast to washing). About 1676, however, more or less simultaneously in England, Holland and France, the European textile printers mastered the secrets of the complex problems of mordant dyeing with madder—the basis of the fast-dyed, hand-painted Indian chintzes that had begun to be imported into Europe during the early 17th century. Thereafter, most European block-printed textiles were produced in what was known as the "madder style."

One of the clearest expositions of block printing in the "madder style" is given in the supplement to John Barrow's *New and Universal Dictionary of Arts and Sciences* (1754). The cotton or linen was printed with chemical substances known as mordants, which on immersion in the vat reacted with the soluble dye to precipitate an insoluble colouring on the cloth fibres so that the colour remained permanently fixed in the mordant-printed areas while the dye taken up by the unmordanted parts could be easily removed by washing. In madder dyeing, different mordants can produce various shades of reds, pinks, purples and browns from a single immersion in the dye. The different mordants were printed one by one; the printer moved along the whole length of the cloth printing the first mordant from one wood block, then the second mordant from another block, and so on, until the whole pattern was completed. The mordant-printed cloth was then immersed in the dye. The reds, browns and purples were produced by printing varying strengths of alum and iron mordants, followed by immersion in the madder dye. Yellows and drabs (light, brownish colours) were produced by the printing of similar mordants followed by dyeing with weld, also known as dyer's,weed. Blue was produced by "penciling-in" indigo with a brush. This operation was usually carried out by women or girls. All greens were produced by the penciling-in of indigo over yellow. To save expense, the yellows were often blocked or painted in to avoid an additional dyeing but with this method the yellow dye was fugitive and in many extant 18th-century textiles the yellow has almost entirely disappeared.

The standard method of printing madder mordants by wood block involved the use of a "tub" and a "sieve." In England the tub consisted of a sawed-off barrel but on the European continent

FROM J. BARROW'S "SUPPLEMENT TO THE NEW AND UNIVERSAL DICTIONARY OF ARTS AND SCIENCES," LONDON, 1754; PHOTOGRAPH BY COURTESY OF VICTORIA AND ALBERT MUSEUM

**FIG. 1.—CALICO BLOCK PRINTING, 18TH CENTURY**

a specially constructed square tub was more usual. The tub was filled with a viscous paste, called the "swimmings," made from discarded colour and gum; the paste provided a sort of elastic cushion on which rested the sieve, a wooden drum only fractionally smaller than the tub. The bottom of the sieve was a sheepskin, the upper surface a tightly stretched fine woolen cloth. An assistant, known as "tireur" or "tearer," kept the upper surface of the sieve constantly and evenly supplied with the thickened mordant, which was spread on with a large brush. When the printer pressed his block on the sieve, the swimmings in the tub provided just enough "give" to ensure a satisfactory colouring-up of the block. The cloth to be printed was supported on a stone, concrete or iron structure covered with a thick blanket; this arrangement provided a firm but resilient surface so that the raised surface of the block contacted the cloth with uniform pressure over the whole area. Between the blanket and the cloth was a layer of unbleached calico (the back gray) that absorbed the mordant forced through the cloth. When the block was placed on the cloth, the printer gave it one or two sharp blows with his mallet or maul to impress the mordant firmly into the cloth. Pins known as pitch pins were inserted into each corner of the block as a guide to the printer in matching the repeats. The blocks were generally made of layers of strong durable woods, such as pear wood, arranged so that the grain in each layer ran at right angles to that in the layers above and below; this arrangement prevented warping during the successive wetting and drying. For fine details, such as thin stems and the outlines of flowers or leaves, strips of metal or metal pins were inserted into the wood blocks. Elaborate "pin grounds," also called "picoté" or "sable" grounds, were achieved by inserting metal pins into the block.

A method of mechanical block printing was invented in 1834 by a French mechanic called M. Perrot. This machine, known as the perrotine after its inventor, employed ordinary wood blocks and was widely used in the 19th century, particularly in France, for printing up to four colours. Each block of the design is impressed simultaneously in the cloth at a distance of two repeats apart. The cloth is stepped through the machine, one repeat at a time, to emerge with the full numbers of colours printed upon it. Although the original machine needed five men to tend it, one machine could print as much cloth as 24 printers and 24 assistants using hand methods. By 1836 about 60 perrotines were in operation in Europe; and even in the early 1960s when, in spite of the expense of the process, block printing continued to be used for certain classes of goods, the perrotine was not quite obsolete.

**Copperplate Printing.**—Copperplate printing on textiles was invented by Francis Nixon at the Drumcondra printworks near Dublin in 1752. Although prior to 1752 maps and embroidery designs had been printed from engraved copperplates with ordinary printer's inks, it was not until Nixon's invention that it was possible to print textile designs in fast colours by printing the cloth with thickened mordants. The designs were printed from a single engraved copperplate, usually with a repeat of about three feet square, in red, purple or sepia, using the madder dye; or in blue, using indigo, by a method known in England and the United States as "china-blue" and on the continent of Europe as "bleu d'Angleterre." This method involved printing the indigo on the cloth in an undissolved state and arranging for its simultaneous reduction and solution on the cloth after printing. This was done by immersing the printed cloth in a bath of lime (to dissolve the indigo) and a bath of ferrous sulfate (to reduce it) as many times as was necessary to achieve the desired strength of blue.

Copperplate printing was eminently suited for the production of large pictorial designs and a fineness of detail and delicacy of drawing not possible with the comparatively coarse technique of wood-block cutting. It was also used for floral designs, both for furnishing and dress, and for the printing of handkerchiefs.

The textile printer's copperplate press was little different from the heavy, flat-bed, rolling press used for the printing of engravings on paper. The plate was first inked up with the thickened mordant and then was passed through the rollers in contact with the cloth being printed. Various improvements, however, were introduced by the textile printers to make the press more suitable for their purposes. An important innovation was the "D" roller, patented by Robert Kirkwood of Edinburgh in 1803, which overcame the difficulty of getting the plate through the rollers to its original position without winding the cloth back at the same time. Kirkwood's invention consisted of substituting for the lower roller a special roller shaved flat on one side (hence the name "D"). On the forward passage of the plate, the round part of the roller squeezed the plate up against the cloth for printing in the normal way; but on the reverse passage the roller rested with its flattened surface uppermost, thus allowing the plate to go through without touching the cloth.

With the introduction of roller printing, copperplate printing began to die out, although it continued in use, particularly for the production of printed handkerchiefs, well into the 19th century.

**Roller Printing.**—The first commercially successful patent for a roller-printing machine was taken out in 1783 by Thomas Bell, a Scotsman. So fundamental was Bell's invention that the principle of his machine has been retained throughout the numerous improvements and refinements introduced since that date. Before 1783 several attempts had been made to replace hand printing by mechanical means but none of them had been commercially successful. As early as 1743 W. Keen and M. Platt had taken out a patent for a three-colour roller-printing machine but it does not appear to have been developed. In France a textile printer named J. A. Bonvallet introduced a primitive type of roller-printing machine at his factory in Amiens about 1775. It consisted of two rollers; the upper one was made of wood, the lower one of hollow iron covered with a copper mantle on which the pattern was engraved. The lower roller was filled with red-hot iron or burning coals and revolved in a dye bath. The cloth was passed over the upper, wooden roller and the lower roller pressed up against it by means of weights, levers and a cog wheel. The machine was operated by hand. Bell's original specification (patent no. 1378, 1783) describes his invention as "a new and peculiar art or method of printing with one colour or various colours at the same time, on linnens, lawns, and cambricks, cottons, callicoes, and muslin, woollen cloth, silks, silk and stuffs, and any other species or kind of linnen cloth or manufactured goods whatever."

A second patent taken out by Bell (no. 1443, 1783) contains a similar specification for printing "one, two, three, four or five, or more colours," and by the following year he was able to put the machine into practical operation with the firm of Livesey, Hargreaves and Co. near Preston, Lancashire. Strangely enough, however, the indiscriminate use of the new machines contributed to the collapse of the firm in 1788. Bell's machine for rotary printing from engraved metal rollers was fitted with a "doctor," or steel blade, designed to remove the surface colour from the printing rollers while allowing the recessed, engraved parts to retain enough colour to print a continuous length of fabric. The machine was said to be capable of doing the work of about 40 hand printers. Although the machine was theoretically capable of printing five or six colours at a time, mechanical and chemical difficulties that existed as late as 1840 made it difficult to print more than two or three colours simultaneously. At first the new roller-printing machines were used mainly for small-scale dress prints, and it was not until the early 19th century that large-scale furnishing patterns were produced by machine. Many of the furnishing fabrics of the 1820s were produced from a single, stipple-engraved metal roller, with additional colours being printed by wood blocks or surface rollers. With James Burton's and Adam Parkinson's union-machine (1805) it was possible to print simultaneously with engraved metal and wood surface rollers. *See* also TEXTILES: *Printed Textiles.* (B. J. Mo.)

## MODERN INDUSTRIAL PROCESSES

**General.**—Textile printing on an industrial scale consists of two fundamental operations: (1) the impression, *i.e.,* the mechanical and physical stages in which the colouring matters are distributed on the cloth; and (2) the coloration, *i.e.,* the choice of the appropriate colouring matters (dyes, dye-generating chemicals, pigments and the necessary auxiliary chemicals), the conditions for their application, their preparation in suitable forms for presentation to the cloth and their fixation against removal during use and wear.

Textile printing in some of its aspects differs greatly from the corresponding methods for printing on paper and other materials, although the mechanical methods for bringing the colour to the surface may be similar. Inks and paints used for printing on paper usually contain colouring matter in the form of pigments (*i.e.,* finely divided solid powders insoluble in the medium by which they are applied); such pigments are attached by adhesive media to the surface to be coloured; they cannot penetrate between the molecules of the fibres. In much textile printing, however, the various coloured areas that make up the print are, in fact, dyed. The dye is dissolved, usually in water alone or in aqueous solutions containing other reagents, and the molecules thus separated can be induced to enter between the molecules of the fibre in a much more intimate association. In general, a textile print in which the coloured areas are dyed in this way may be found to be faster to washing and similar treatments than a print resulting from the use of pigment in an adhesive. The presence of adhesive may also tend to stiffen the fabric. Improvements in adhesives, though, have made it possible to obtain reasonable fastness and softness and to obtain prints of great brilliance.

Cloth, either woven or knitted, may first be singed to burn off surface fibres, desized to remove weaving sizes, scoured to take away natural impurities and the soils of manufacture, bleached to destroy residual colouring matters, impregnated with solutions of dyes or other necessary chemicals by padding, dried and, occasionally, given extra smoothness by passage through a calender. Drying may be brought about by passing the cloth over steam-heated cylinders or by running it through a stenter. The latter operation fixes the width, ensures that warp and weft are at the correct angle and renders the selvages straight and parallel. The cloth is wound under even tension on wooden shells to give cylindrical batches.

The pattern is impressed by hand blocks, stencils, silk screens or engraved or relief rollers. Drying is done in a hot flue or by steam-heated plates or cylinders. The cloth is then passed through a chamber (steamer, ager or flash ager) filled with steam. During the passage a limited amount of water condenses on the print, the dye is redissolved without being spread and the fibre swells. The dye molecules are thus enabled to penetrate into the fibre substance so that they can become fixed there. The high temperature of the steam also initiates or speeds up reactions by which some dyes are turned into soluble forms, are actually produced *in situ* from intermediates or are fixed more firmly within the fibre. Steaming for short periods is called aging or, for very short periods, flash aging. Volatile acids can be introduced into the steam (acid steaming or acid aging) if this is required. Dyes that are themselves volatile can be fixed in man-made fibres—Terylene (Dacron), Orlon, etc.—by dry heat. The adhesive medium in some pigment printing is also set by dry heat. (*See* also COTTON MANUFACTURE: *Converting of Cotton Goods.*)

Before and after (and sometimes instead of) steaming, the printed cloth may be passed through certain solutions, *e.g.,* of chromates, to fix the dye. Unfixed colour may be removed by washing or soaping. This minimizes the tendency to bleed off on other cloth during wet treatments and to rub off when dry.

**Impression.**—This is the essential part of the printing operation. With several exceptions, dyes, dye-generating substances and auxiliary chemicals are dissolved or suspended in water. When applied to a fixed area of a microporous structure like cloth the solutions would spread by capillary attraction (flush) beyond the boundaries of the pattern and so give prints of unsatisfactory definition. The viscosity of the solutions is therefore increased by the addition of thickening agents. These are usually substances of high molecular weight that yield colloid dispersions in water. They include the natural starches, starches that have been altered by regulated depolymerization (for example, by the action of heat or acids to furnish dextrins), chemical derivatives of starch and cellulose, and natural vegetable gums such as gum tragacanth and gum arabic, locust-bean gum, etc. There are other vegetable mucilages, such as sodium alginate (sodium polymannuronate) from seaweed, as well as egg and blood albumin and various synthetic resin products. A more recently developed form of viscous medium is a stabilized emulsion between water and another non-miscible liquid (emulsion thickener). It is possible sometimes to use colloid aqueous dispersions of the mineral bentonite.

The thickening agent for a given printing paste is chosen for its specific thickening power, its compatibility with the dyes to be used, its freedom from interference by the other chemicals that have to be added, its stability and its general flow properties. The flow property of the entire paste is adjusted to the printing method, the shapes of the impressions to be made, the intensity of colour required, the weight and structure of the cloth, the fixation methods to be employed, and the severity of treatment that can be allowed in order to remove the exhausted paste from the print after the dyes on it have been fixed. Many dispersions of thickening agents are thixotropic; *i.e.,* they become more fluid when they are subjected to the stresses that they receive in the printing operation, and this property has an important bearing upon the quality of the impression.

*Block Printing.*—This, the oldest method of textile printing, is also discussed above under *Early Methods.* The blocks normally consist of wood with the design carved to stand above the block surface. Alternatively, or in conjunction with these projections (pegs), fine details such as different shaped dots are provided by short lengths of copper wire (pins) of various cross section partly driven into the wood. Lines are provided by shaped copper strip (fillet) driven edgewise into the wood. Large areas of uniform colour known as blotches are produced by filling in an enclosed area with wool felt, which thus gives an extended printing surface. Areas corresponding in size to those produced respectively by pins, pegs or blotches in block printing are given the same name in screen or roller printing. Where the form of the design is suitable, where prolonged use of the block is anticipated or where a number of block sets of the same design are required, the relief printing surface may be cast in type metal. In most cases every distinct colour must be applied as a separate paste from a separate block. Further, since blocks have to be handled during the printing operation, those that are too heavy to be lifted easily are inconvenient; if the repeat of the pattern is large, more than one block may be needed for a single colour, and to print big, detailed and florid patterns the number of separate blocks may exceed 100. Block prints are thus laborious and expensive to produce but they are prized for their full, deep colourings and for the deviation from the exact design, which shows them to be "handmade." Since printing costs per yard are high, expensive cloths (*e.g.*, heavy linens for upholstery and pure silks for dress goods) are generally chosen for block printing. Designs tend to be traditional and may be "kept on the table" for many years.

The perrotine is still used occasionally while in some firms the surface, or peg, printing machine, the forerunner of the roller printing machine (*see* below), continues in use. In this machine the circumference of one roller carries an exact number of the repeats of the pattern; a second roller guides the blanket, the back gray (back cloth) and the cloth itself and acts as the printing surface. The pegs of the patterned roller run in contact with the printing roller and are furnished by touching, at another part of the periphery, an endless band spread with paste. As with all cylinder machines, printing is continuous but the length of the repeat that can be printed is limited since the diameter of the printing cylinders cannot be increased indefinitely.

*Stencil and Screen Printing.*—The stencil printing method uses stencils made from paper impregnated with wax or from thin sheets of ductile metal. The method has been known for centuries but in modern times it has been employed only to a limited extent; some stencil printing is carried out with lacquers on nets and gauzes to give beadlike effects. The stencil may be cut from zinc foil and mounted on a frame that is laid over the fabric; the colour medium is applied through the stencil with air-spray, brush or squeegee.

Silk screen printing (*q.v.*) is the most commonly used form of what is essentially stencil printing. Fine, open-mesh gauzes woven from yarns made of silk or nylon, or from fine bronze wires, are stretched with even tension upon rectangular frames of wood or light metal. The printing areas on the gauze are left open, the rest being blocked up with a lacquer. The design can be hand-painted on the screen directly with lacquer but this procedure is slow, especially for large areas, and a photographic method usually is used. The repeat is drawn in black and white on transparent film and this serves as a negative from which a number of positives are made by the ordinary procedures of exposure and development. The positives are pieced together to make up the printing area desired in the final screen, and from the composite a full negative is made on photographic film. The screen itself is coated with a solution of gelatin to which a soluble dichromate (bichromate) has been added and is dried in the dark. It is then exposed to light behind the composite negative, and the part of the gelatin that is exposed to light becomes insoluble in water. When the negative is removed the gelatin on the unexposed areas is washed away with warm water and the deposits are reinforced by coating them with a layer of lacquer. When the lacquer is dry, the screen is ready for use. As in the other printing methods, one screen is prepared for each colour in the pattern.

Screen printing by hand is carried out on tables of sufficient width and of considerable length to accommodate the cloth to be treated. The tables are covered with a resilient blanket on top of which is a smooth impervious fabric. A length of the cloth is rolled off to occupy the full length of the table and is fixed to the impervious cover with starch paste or other adhesive. The screen to be printed is laid on the cloth at one end of the table, gauze side downward, with the frame therefore forming the sides of a shallow trough. Printing paste is poured into the trough and driven through the open areas with a squeegee, which is a stout strip of wood with a firm lip of rubber along the lower edge. The longest side of the screen is usually placed across the cloth (weftwise), and the line in which the squeegee is moved is parallel with the shorter side. Two operatives do the printing, one at either side of the table, passing the squeegee from one to the other in the middle of the stroke. When one impression has been made with the screen, it is lifted and laid down on the next repeat, and so on, until all the cloth on the table has been printed with one colour. Then the operation is repeated, using another screen and another colour, until the full design is printed. Correct positioning of screens along the length and width of the cloth is obtained by projections on the screen frame that are made to engage with stops correctly adjusted on a metal bar (pitch rail) on one of the long sides of the table. After one table-length of cloth has been fully printed it is pulled from the table and succeeding lengths of the roll are printed by the same procedure.

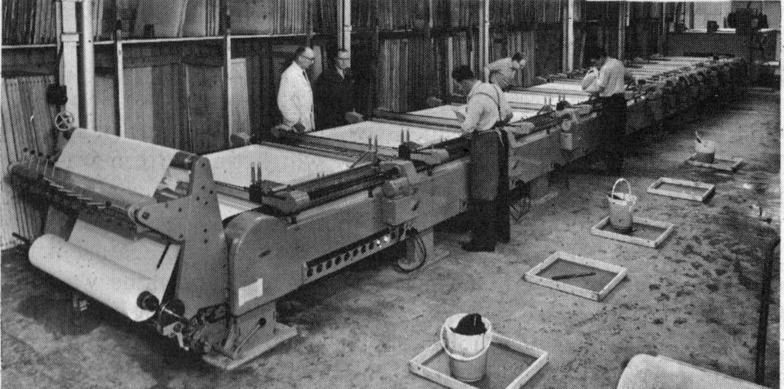

BY COURTESY OF THE COTTON BOARD

FIG. 2.—TWELVE-COLOUR AUTOMATIC SCREEN-PRINTING MACHINE

Screen printing is never as swift as roller printing but the preparation of screens is easier, speedier and cheaper than the engraving of a set of copper rollers. The skill required is not nearly so great as that needed to operate a roller printing machine. While a roller printing machine can best interpret designs in which sharp definition is needed, the screen method may give superior results more easily when full colouring and a full gradation of shading is needed. There are distinctions connected with the nature of the design; *e.g.*, it is easier to get plain longitudinal stripes by roller printing and lateral stripes by the screen method. The screen method is better adapted for the classes of commercial printing in which short runs and quick changes of design are called for.

Many machines have been introduced to mechanize the screen printing operation. Some imitate mechanically the operations of hand printing. In others, continuous working may be achieved by supporting the screens on rollers whose faces are perforated so that the screens can be furnished from inside; such machines approach the action of the roller printing machine.

*Roller Printing.*—This is the method by which the greatest percentage of cloth is printed. In general it is faster than other methods and produces a more accurate impression. The printing area is engraved in recess (intaglio) on a smooth copper roller. This is coated with the colour paste and then the unengraved surface is scraped clean with a steel blade (doctor), leaving the engraving filled. The roller then comes into contact with the cloth carried on a supporting roller and transfers the paste in the engraving to it. The number of engraved rollers employed depends upon the number of colours required in the design and may be from one to fourteen. With the exception of a few of continental origin, modern roller printing machines do not differ fundamentally from the one invented by Thomas Bell in 1783.

The engraved copper rollers, or shells, each rotate on a steel mandrel to which they are keyed by a tongue and groove arrangement. The drive is transmitted from one large crown wheel, driven by an electric motor, to a box wheel at the end of each mandrel. Different prints need to be printed at different speeds according to the quality of the engraving and the paste used, and the structure and composition of the cloth itself. The printing machine should be able to run at very slow speeds (inching) at the beginning of a printing in order that final adjustments in the fit of the different coloured impressions can be made before a substantial yardage of cloth has been printed.

The shells themselves are usually made of high-quality copper, but where a long life is called for, and especially where the paste contains hard, solid particles (*e.g.*, pigments and crystals), the surface may be chromium plated. The appropriate part of the total pattern is engraved on each shell by direct manual engraving, by milling or by acid etching, including various adaptations of the photogravure process (*see* GRAVURE). When another pattern is desired, a new series of shells is fitted on the mandrels.

The central cylinder, or printing roller, is made of cast iron; the larger the number of colours printed, the greater the diameter of the cylinder. It is wrapped with several layers of springy cloth (lapping) to impart resilience. The back gray and the cloth to be printed are carried through the rollers at a steady tension on an endless printer's blanket, which may be made of felt with a smooth resilient surface or made of cloth coated with rubber or a plastic substance. If it is rubberized it will be washed after the impression with water sprays or rotary cylindrical brushes to remove adhering paste, and dried by being passed through hot air or over steam-heated cylinders or by being dusted with talc before being passed forward again to support more cloth. Modern blankets, which are covered with compositions designed to resist wear and chemical attack and are embossed with fine lines, can be used without the back gray for some designs; the depressions hold the small amounts of paste pushed through the cloth and in addition increase the grip between cloth and blanket; such blankets exhibit better springiness than do the older forms.

The cleaning doctor consists of a straight strip of steel fixed in a pivoted clamp or shears, with an edge pressing at an angle against the surface of the shell. It removes the paste from the unengraved portions of the shell surface. The pressure of contact is obtained by weights that act on the shears through a lever. The adjustment of the doctor is one of the most exacting tasks of the printer since the variety of blade and the angle and pressure of contact have to be adjusted to meet the particular quality of the engraving and other conditions of printing. The edge is sharpened so that it is accurately linear, and, although it may receive an initial mechanical grinding, it always has to be finished by hand. Special adjustments (springing) of the steel strip in the shears are required to overcome bowing when wide cloths are printed.

As the shell rotates it is supplied with printing paste by a lapped or coated roller (the furnisher) that rotates in contact with the shell and also runs partly immersed in paste contained in a colour box. As the shell moves round it is cleaned by the doctor and then makes contact with the cloth. Before it completes a revolution, it passes under the edge of a second, or lint, doctor that is similar to the cleaning doctor but is made of a softer metal. Here the smooth portion of the copper is freed from lint and from printing paste of other colours transferred by the cloth from an earlier shell. This operation prevents paste of one colour from passing into the boxes of subsequent colours and falsifying the shade and removes solid impurities that might otherwise wedge between the edge of the cleaning doctor and the copper surface, letting through unwanted colour and giving rise to lines and smears in the print. Furnishing is sometimes effected with a stiff cylindrical brush instead of a roller. The brush is often rotated at a different surface speed from that of the shell; the brushing action prevents permanent clogging of the engraving.

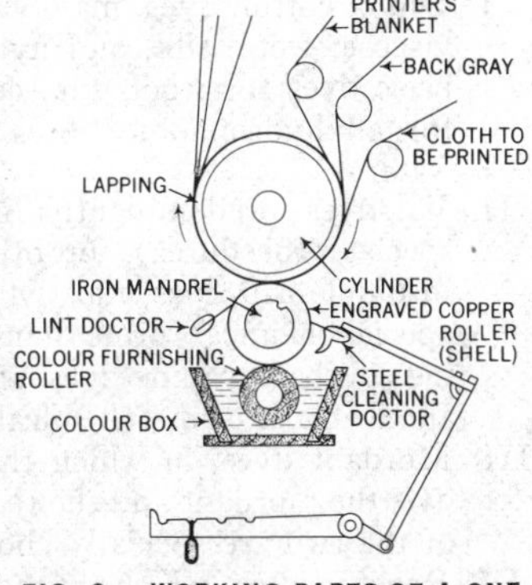

FIG. 3.—WORKING PARTS OF A ONE-COLOUR TEXTILE PRINTING MACHINE

In multicolour printing, the units, each consisting of a shell printing a single colour with its own doctors and furnishing arrangement, are fixed at intervals round the lower part of the periphery of the central cylinder, which is horizontally disposed. As the cloth passes around the cylinder, it is impressed in succession with the different colour components. Careful fitting is needed as each impression must fall accurately upon the appropriate area within the complete pattern; inconspicuous pitch marks are engraved as a guide at the appropriate place on each shell of the set. Adjustments are made after the first few feet of cloth have been inched through the machine: to correct the fit across the width of the cloth the bearings of the mandrel are displaced sideways; adjustments at the box wheel can turn the mandrel slightly relative to the wheel itself and make the impression from one shell fall a little earlier or a little later within the repeat, so ensuring longitudinal fit. Some adjustment of this kind may also be needed while the pattern is being printed, since the cloth may stretch a little unevenly under tension. The diameters of all the shells are the same and all are driven at the same rotational speed, so that the surface printing speed of each shell is therefore also the same. An integral number of repeats of the pattern is engraved around the circumference of each shell so that these repeats are printed without change of spacing regardless of the length of the cloth. With the older box-wheel mechanisms, adjustments in the fit were made manually and the slowing up necessary to effect them sometimes led to changes in the stretch of the cloth. However, more elaborate mechanical and electrical types of box wheels have become available; these allow the shift for fitting to be accomplished while printing at full speed.

Not all the rollers on a machine may be engaged in impression. Sometimes perfectly smooth, unpatterned rollers furnished with a paste containing no dye may be interposed in the sequence of engraved rollers when impressions of greater colour area, or with more intense colours, are printed on the cloth in front of impressions of smaller area or paler colours. This counteracts the danger of contaminating the pastes in the colour boxes toward the end of a series when the action of the lint doctor may not be adequate. The starch roller receives any loose colour from the cloth on its smooth surface, goes around to be coated with plain paste and then has its surface scraped clean by the doctor. When a multicolour machine is used to print a design with fewer colours than its maximum capacity, the engraved rollers may be too few to pull the cloth, blanket and heavy cylinder by frictional contact in the usual way and in this case additional plain rollers are run on the machine for driving purposes.

Three important modifications of the roller printing machine are made to meet special requirements of pattern or quality of impression:

1. Surface printing machines have already been mentioned; they are used to give prints of blocklike quality. Since the printing is from rollers in relief, modifications of the furnishing arrangements are needed.

2. Duplex printing machines are in effect two separate single-sided machines incorporated in the same structure and printing simultaneously on both sides of the cloth with the pattern on the one side in perfect fit with that on the other. Less perfect double-sided effects can be produced with single-sided printing in a push-through operation where the structure of the cloth, the pressure of the roller and the consistency of the paste allow the colour to go right through the cloth and give a reasonable impression on the underside.

3. Jumping machines are used for large repeats that are surrounded by an unprinted border. The machine is provided with gearing that checks the printing operation at the necessary intervals while the cloth moves forward by a distance equal to twice the width of the crosswise border. This obviates shells of inconveniently large diameter.

**Transfer of the Repeat to the Shell.**—*Milling.*—Patterns with small simple motifs and uncomplicated repeats such as spots, stars, rings, stripes, etc., are engraved by mounting the polished shell in a lathe and rotating it against a hard-steel, wheel-shaped die with a number of the design units in relief; these units indent the copper surface.

*Hand Engraving.*—To a limited extent, rollers are hand engraved by conventional methods. More frequently, hand engraving is employed to perfect rollers engraved by other methods and to correct defects caused by wear. (*See* also PRINTMAKING.)

*Etching.*—This is the method used most frequently for engraving rollers. The original cartoon from the designer is projected optically onto a zinc plate and the repeat is incised on the plate, each detail being then coloured up to match the cartoon. An operator then follows the lines corresponding to one of the component colours on this plate with a stylus that forms part of a machine called a pantograph (or, less correctly, a pentagraph). Mounted in the pantograph is a smooth copper shell, covered with a layer of protective varnish; the movements of the stylus rotate the roller and also actuate a series of diamond points spaced along the length of the roller. As a result, the desired number of repeats are scratched at intervals along and around the shell. The roller is then rotated in a bath of suitable acids that penetrate the scratches and etch the repeats into the copper. If the engraving is a deep one it is not desirable to etch it in one stage, so the roller is revarnished and the scratching and acid treatment are repeated. When one roller of the set has been made, another is inserted in the pantograph, the lines on the zinc corresponding to a different colour are followed, and so on until the whole set has been completed.

*Photogravure Methods.*—A number of acid etching methods have been developed that follow the methods used to produce photogravure rollers for magazine printing. They reduce the time required for engraving and are specially suited for certain pictorial subjects. Their use has become more widespread in recent years.

*Scale.*—For all shapes of appreciable area, simple engraving of a depression in the roller will not give satisfactory impressions since the paste that it contains after furnishing is not under adequate control and the printed area consequently will not be uniformly coloured. Such areas are therefore engraved as a series of parallel diagonal grooves. In printing, each line spreads laterally into the impression of its neighbour. The width and depth of the lines must be properly related to each other; these measurements are jointly specified in a number called the scale. In some engravings made by photogravure methods the impression is broken into dots by photographing the original image through a screen (rectangular disposition of lines), and the effect of the screen is the same as that used in photomechanical methods for printing pictures on paper.

"CIBA REVIEW," CIBA LIMITED, BASEL, SWITZ.

FIG. 4.—MODERN ROLLER PRINTING MACHINE

**Colourings.**—A set of engraved rollers, blocks or screens can be used to produce a series of different and distinct decorative effects by (1) changing the combination of colours; (2) using only part of the set; (3) using the set in conjunction with rollers having small "all over" patterns that do not need fitting with the rest of the pattern and modify the ground or the blotches; (4) printing in conjunction with dyeing. Each modification of the use of the set of rollers in this fashion is called a "way."

There are also several more unusual methods for continuous printing. In one group of related methods, the colours are thickened until the printing medium is of the consistency of stiff dough. This is rolled out into sheets and cut into shapes that are mounted in mosaic fashion around the surface of a roller. This roller prints on to cloth damped with water or other solvent; the cloth is supported on another roller with a very resilient surface. The water or other solvent dissolves a small amount of the thickened colour, which is thus transferred to the cloth. Only a limited yardage can be printed with one roller because the roller coating is slowly consumed. The process has been used to produce beautiful and unusual prints that cannot be obtained in any other way; there is no limit to the number of colours that can be printed from the one roller. The usual difficulties of fitting are not present, since these have been dealt with in preparation of the roller itself, but there are restrictions in the kinds of dye that can be used.

In another unusual continuous method the design is first printed on paper with appropriate dyes in special media. It is transferred to the fabric by running the cloth and the paper through a heated calender together. Once the transfer has been obtained, the dyes used are fixed in the normal way.

**Colouristic Features.**—The choice of dyes and their adaptation for use in a given print depend upon a large variety of conditions, some chemical and some economic: the fibre or fibres from which the cloth is made, the colour requirements of the design to be reproduced and its durability in the expected conditions of use, the relation between the printed effect and later processes of manufacture (*e.g.*, finishing), the cost of production and the length of time before delivery. Most commercial printing is a compromise between the ideal interpretation of the design and the need to produce it at an acceptable price. The choice of dyes for a print, and to some extent the chemical and processing procedures used in their application and fixation, are known as styles.

The relations between the kind of fibre in the material to be printed and the dyes used are in general similar to those that are obtained in dyeing but the physical differences in printing and dyeing systems may greatly modify the conditions of application. Two important differences are: (1) dye and chemical assistants used in printing have to be applied in a smaller volume of medium (*i.e.*, concentrated); (2) the stage of diffusion and fixation in printing must be made to occur after the impression and in the relatively short, well-defined period of steaming or chemical aftertreatment. For this reason formulations of a dye bath and of a printing paste containing the same dye may be very different.

The following groups of dyes are used in printing:

I. Direct cotton dyes, mainly for cellulose fibres; acid dyes for viscose, wool, silk, and nylon and certain other synthetics; basic dyes for wool, silk, cellulose esters; and disperse dyes for all hydrophobic fibres (those that swell very little in water).

II. Vat dyes, predominantly for cellulosic fibres but also (with special procedures) for other natural and synthetic fibres; insoluble azo dyes, mostly for cellulosic fibres, and often in special chemical forms to meet the special conditions of printing; phthalocyanine dyes, again for cellulosic fibres but again applicable in some chemical forms to other fibres.

III. Mordant dyes, in which the sequence of application of the dye, the mordant and the reagents that control the interaction of the two are specially chosen for printing conditions.

IV. Reactive dyes, which are mostly applicable to cellulosic fibres.

V. Pigment colours applied to the surface of the fibres and fixed with synthetic resin preparations so designed that, when fixed, they are not easily removed in washing and do not stiffen the fabric. They are applicable to a wide range of fibres, are simple to use, give full colorations and are particularly useful in screen printing.

A distinctive feature of much textile printing as compared with dyeing is that it is often necessary to use dyes from different classes to provide the different coloured areas in the same print and, for this reason, great ingenuity is needed in exploiting the chemical properties of individual dyes so that one fixation treatment, *e.g.*, steaming, is appropriate for all of them and so that the reagents used with one colour do not interfere with the other colours.

Two widely used styles that have no exact counterpart in dyeing are: (1) Discharge printing, in which the cloth is first evenly dyed before printing and then is printed with a paste that contains either an oxidizing or a reducing agent. Steaming causes the agent to destroy the dye on which it falls or to convert it to a soluble form so that it can be removed by washing. This therefore gives a white print on a coloured ground. An extension of this method is the use of the illuminated discharge in which a dye indifferent to the discharging agent is incorporated in the paste so that it takes the place of the ground dye that has been destroyed and gives a coloured print on a ground of a different colour. (2) Resist or reserve styles, in which the cloth is printed with a preparation (*e.g.*, wax or a synthetic resin) that protects the fibre from a dye solution, or with a reagent that chemically inhibits the fixation of a particular dye (*e.g.*, an acid for a dye that requires alkali for its fixation). The entire cloth is then dyed and the resisted areas remain undyed. As with discharge styles, the resist may be plain (white on a coloured ground) or coloured. A traditional example is the batik of Java and its analogue in west African styles. (H. A. T.)

BIBLIOGRAPHY.—E. Bancroft, *Experimental Researches Concerning the Philosophy of Permanent Colours* (1835); J. Persoz, *Traité théorique et pratique de l'impression des tissus*, 4 vol. (1846); G. C. Gilroy, *A Practical Treatise on Dyeing and Calico-Printing* (1846); A. Ure, "Calico-Printing," *A Dictionary of Arts, Manufactures and Mines*, 3rd ed. (1843); J. Dépierre, *L'Impression des tissus* (1910); G. Turnbull, *A History of the Calico Printing Industry of Great Britain* (1951); "Roller Printing," *Ciba Review*, no. 125; P. Floud, "The Origins of English Calico-Printing," "The English Contribution to the Early History of Indigo Printing," and "The English Contribution to the Development of Copper-Plate Printing," *Journal of the Society of Dyers and Colourists* (May 1960, June 1960 and July 1960); E. Bindewald and K. Kasper, *Fairy Fantasy on Fabrics* (German edition: *Bunter Traum auf gewebten Grund*, 2nd ed. [1951]); W. Crooks, *A Practical Handbook of Dyeing and Calico Printing* (1874); F. Crace-Calvert, *Dyeing and Calico Printing* (1876). (B. J. Mo.)

E. Knecht and J. B. Fothergill, *The Principles and Practice of Textile Printing*, 4th ed. (1952); *Review of Textile Progress*, Textile Institute and Society of Dyers and Colourists (annual); L. Diserens (trans. by P. Wengraf and H. P. Baumann), *The Chemical Technology of Dyeing and Printing*, 2 vol., 2nd ed. (1948–51); Bibliography in H. Blackshaw and R. Brightman, *Dictionary of Dyeing and Textile Printing* (1961); F. F. Jacobs, *Textile Printing* (1952); Imperial Chemical Industries, Dyestuffs Division, *An Introduction to Textile Printing*, 2nd ed. (1967); W. Taussig, *Screen Printing* (1948). (H. A. T.)

**TEXTILES** are woven fabrics. The term also means all spinnable fibres or materials suitable for weaving, in addition to fabrics produced by knitting and felting, and all laces. The Latin *textilis* meant a woven fabric, but the word *textile* was also used as a transitive verb for plaited, braided, woven or constructed. This article deals largely with decorative textiles. Other articles related to the subject include SPINNING; and WEAVING for the making of textiles; DYES AND DYEING for one process in their finishing; TEXTILE PRINTING for a detailed discussion of commercial aspects of that subject. There are also numerous articles on individual fabrics—*e.g.*, CALICO; CHALLIS; CHIFFON; DAMASK; DIMITY; etc.—which describe these fabrics and deal with them as items of commerce. COTTON MANUFACTURE; SILK; and WOOL similarly are concerned with textiles as industrial products.

This article is outlined as follows:



## I. HISTORICAL OUTLINE

**1. Early History.**—Since textiles are easily torn, burned or eaten by insects, the oldest surviving specimens probably date from long after the time when weaving was first practised. Whorls or weights for spinning have been found on Neolithic sites, indicating that thread was spun and therefore that cloth was made. The weaving of textiles for clothing, as a substitute for the skins of wild animals, was a corollary of settled life and the breeding of domestic animals. The four natural fibres, wool, linen, cotton and silk, originated in different parts of the world. Woolen textiles have been found in early Bronze Age sites in Switzerland and Scandinavia. In Egypt plain linen textiles of about 5000 B.C. have been found. Cotton scraps have been discovered in India on sites of about 3000 B.C. and in Peru on sites datable to 2000 B.C. Silk may have been used in China in the 2nd millennium B.C. and was certainly woven by 1000 B.C. Cloaks, tunics and caps from Scandinavian sites show that a high level of skill had already been reached there, even though tools were few and primitive. The preparatory processes of carding and combing raw wool were known, for the threads are well and evenly spun. Felt caps and narrow braids were also made, and sprang, a technique between knitting and netting, was used.

Flax was grown in the Nile valley. The natural colour of flax fibres is brownish, and since whitish linens have been found in very early tombs, methods of bleaching must have been discovered. Spinning was done by hand, using a simple weighted spindle, and cloths were woven on three types of loom: a horizontal loom fixed to the ground, an upright loom with a beam at the top and bottom, and an upright loom with the warp threads bunched in groups and weighted at the foot. Variants of this last loom are seen on ancient Greek vase paintings, and this type was probably used to weave the textiles found in Scandinavia. Tablet weaving for making narrow braids, netting, sprang and other techniques were developed. Normally cloth was woven in tabby (plain weave). In Ptolemaic Egypt very fine counts of linen have been found in textiles probably woven for the courts of the Pharaohs. Strangely analogous to the garments found in the north are tunics woven to shape.

The Romans wore both linen and wool, but as the empire extended so did the variety of textiles they imported. Pliny described the Roman toga of wool or linen, and later writers deplored the fashionable clothes made of silk from China. From two sites in Mesopotamia, Doura-Europus (deserted A.D. 256) and Palmyra (sacked A.D. 272), there are textiles showing the weaving repertoire of the ancient world to have comprised chiefly plain wool or linen—though at Palmyra some linens were dyed in true purple and among the wrappings of the dead were some imported cottons. Several of the earliest patterned materials made outside China were also found. These are the tunics and fragments woven in plain linen with tapestry-woven insertions.

The designs of the fragments from Doura-Europus are comparatively simple; on the other hand, for several centuries after the 3rd century A.D. Coptic weavers of Egypt produced an extraordinary variety of decorative textiles, chiefly for clothing. The dry sands of the burying grounds of Akhmim and Antinoë have preserved a profusion of such textiles dating from the 4th to the 10th centuries. The patterns reflect the cultural life of the entire Mediterranean. The bands of decoration, which were narrow on the fronts and shoulders of the tunic fragments at Doura, were larger and more elaborate, with roundels containing mythological and biblical scenes. Naturalistic birds, animals, gods and mortals in fresh, bright colours influenced by Hellenistic art were gradually transformed in subject and in style. Long after the conquest by Islam in the 7th century the Coptic weavers continued to look back to Christian subjects for their inspiration. The influence of other countries and other media can be detected, and the patterns of woven silks were copied in wool. In time, however, whatever their origin, the motifs forming the designs were subordinated to a general decorative effect until they became almost unrecognizable.

Many animal-fibre (vicuña, llama, etc.), agave and cotton textiles have been found in the sands in the narrow coastal strip of South America between the Andes and the Pacific, relics of the pre-Columbian civilization of Peru. The earliest of such relics date from about A.D. 1000, though their chronology is uncertain. Without any further modification of the loom than the weaver's fingers could provide, the inhabitants wove complex patterned textiles in tapestry, double cloth, brocaded gauze and other techniques for belts, blankets, bags and clothing. Anthropomorphic subjects are common.

**2. Advances in Weaving.**—One of the most important developments in the history of textiles was the invention of a method of making free designs that could be repeated indefinitely once the loom was set up. It is certain that the Chinese had found a means of achieving this early in the Han dynasty (202 B.C.–A.D. 221). The Chinese loom probably had treadles and rotary cloth and warp beams before those in the west, both of which presuppose the weaving of large quantities of fairly complex materials. The invention of a drawloom implies a civilization so advanced that expensive textiles were produced for a wide commercial market—it would not be worthwhile otherwise to set up the pattern. Chinese silks have been found not only on the old silk road from China, at Loulan, Turkestan, and other sites by Sir Aurel Stein but also a group of silk damasks were among the textiles excavated at Palmyra.

On the drawloom it is possible to lift the warp threads required for the pattern irregularly across the textile in each line of the design. In China a drawboy sitting on top of the loom pulled a set of cords attached to all the warp threads necessary for that line of the pattern each time the weaver opened a new shed. The warp threads thus pushed to the back of the textile the weft not required on the surface. The setting up of such a loom was laborious and the work very slow and tiring for the boy or girl helping the weaver. Though several important modifications very much later made the drawloom a more efficient machine—by the 17th century, for instance, the introduction of lashes and simples permitted the boy to work at the side of the loom—fundamentally the drawloom remained unchanged until the late 18th century. In the early Chinese silks the pattern was made either by a form of damask in which a warp-faced weave contrasted with a weft face, or by different-coloured warp threads entered in sequence in the loom and brought to the surface as required by the design. The patterns of the early Han textiles were often similar to the geometric cartouches on the backs of bronze mirrors or were derived from a repertoire of exotic fauna, dragons and birds being especially common.

Farther west the first drawloom patterns appear in woolen textiles found in the Egyptian burying grounds and perhaps dating from the 4th–5th century A.D. A group of these show small birds within compartments, woven in compound tabby. The word compound indicates a two-warp system: the main warp, controlled by the drawboy, is hidden between the front and the back of the textile and the binding warp appears on the surface to bind the wefts in tabby. These textiles were probably woven in the near east but it is not known where.

**3. 4th–15th Centuries.**—*Middle East.*—After the fall of the Roman empire textiles continued to be woven in the traditional centres and exported abroad. Following the Muslim conquests of the 7th century new textile centres appeared in Syria and Arabia. At the western end of the silk route across central Asia from China, silks were woven in Sogdiana and in Sasanian Persia (3rd–7th centuries A.D.). Important patrons of silk weaving were the Seljuks who ruled Persia, Asia Minor and Syria in the 11th and 12th centuries. Apart from a group excavated at Ray, few Persian textiles can be certainly attributed to an earlier date than this. A number of important silks can be attributed to Egypt in the time of the Mamelukes.

Most of these near-eastern textiles are known only from literary sources but from the 7th–8th century onward woven silks have survived in some quantity in the tombs and reliquaries of saints and other important figures, opened at later dates, and from the 12th century onward as the seal bags of treasuries and as vestments. Such silks often came from far-distant countries; thus silks from central Asia have been found in French and Flemish churches, and Chinese silks have even been found in Viking burial grounds. The designs of near-eastern silks owe little to China but much to the traditions of Sasanian art. In roundels fabulous monsters such as the *senmurv,* half-bird half-dog, are typical. The sculptures of the Sasanian monuments, especially at Taq-e Bostan, prove that such patterns, themselves based on Achaemenid art, originated in Persia. The roundel became the set form of decoration for several centuries, though the motifs it contained and the ornament from which it was composed varied considerably.

A magnificent series of woven silks can be attributed to Byzantium. Silk weaving may not have been very important in the city until the 6th century but very soon afterward imperial workshops were established which controlled the industry. The capture of Ctesiphon, the Sasanian capital of Khosrau II, in 624 and the booty taken by the Byzantine troops may have influenced the development of silks made in Byzantium. Early Byzantine silks were made in compound twill—that is, with the hidden main warp making the pattern and the binding in twill, allowing longer floats of weft than in tabby and thus exploiting the lustrous quality of the silk. Subjects owing much to the inherited tradition of Rome included the Quadriga silk showing a charioteer, and the lion strangler, perhaps Samson. Byzantine silks have been preserved in the tomb of Charlemagne at Aachen. This was opened in 1000 A.D. and new silks added—the elephant silk found there was probably made not long before the opening and is similar in style to lion silks elsewhere with 10th-century inscriptions. These were made in the golden age of Byzantine silk production. A group of silks were woven in the 11th century in which the pattern appeared as a penciled or engraved outline in a self-coloured material; the vestments of Pope Clement II (1046–47) at Bamberg, Ger., are remarkable examples.

While the richest silks fit for kings and emperors have survived, the ordinary wool and linen materials worn every day have perished. The history of textiles between the terminal dates of the Egyptian burying grounds and the 16th century tends to be divided into the history of vanished products based on documentary evidence on the one hand and the history of luxury silks on the other.

Among the rare textiles whose origin is known with certainty are those from the *tiraz* factories, which are inscribed with the names of the place and of the caliph in whose reign they were made. Some of these are tapestry-woven, most have embroidered inscriptions and date from the 8th–11th centuries.

*Western Europe.*—The Low Countries were the centre of a large and politically important cloth industry from the early middle ages. Already in the 8th century England was exporting wool to Flanders, but this trade did not become important till the 11th century. The Cistercians were important sheep farmers. Most districts in northern Europe made cloth of various qualities for local consumption, but by the 12th century the Low Countries were weaving cloth from imported Spanish and English wool and exporting it to other parts of Europe. In the later middle ages English royal policy sought with some success to prevent the export of wool in favour of that of unfinished cloth. Flax was similarly grown and linen woven in a number of European countries, but the only linen textiles to survive in any number are the towels with decorative ends said to have been made in Perugia, It., in the 15th century. Silks and linens were also made in Germany, especially in Cologne and perhaps in Regensburg.

Silk was certainly being woven in Mediterranean countries by the 9th–10th centuries. Although at first raw silk was imported from the near east, the cultivation of the white mulberry tree essential to the silk worm soon followed. Some time after the establishment of the western caliphate in Spain (8th century) silk weaving was established in Córdoba; later it was carried to Almería, Saragossa, Málaga and elsewhere. In Hispano-Moresque textiles ornament from the near east was combined with a wholly distinctive style of decoration originating in Spain. Emphasis on the purely decorative form of interlacing patterns reached its climax in the last Moorish factories of Andalusia. The Norman conquerors of Sicily established silk-weaving workshops, but it is difficult to distinguish silks from Egypt, Sicily or Asia Minor for all drew on the same cultural sources. The traders of Venice and Genoa imported silks into the mainland whence they were distributed throughout Europe. An accessible source of raw material together with the early growth of compact city-states favoured the establishment of silk weaving in Italy. A treaty between Lucca and Genoa in the mid-12th century gave Lucca access to the Levant and also to the fairs in northern Europe. Merchants of Lucca traveled to the Levant to buy silk and to northern Europe to buy woolen cloths and to sell woven silks. In the 14th century, however, political difficulties displaced the town from its preeminence. Guilds of silk weavers were established in Venice, Florence, Bologna and Genoa.

A comparatively large number of silks can be attributed to northern Italy in the period from the 12th to 15th centuries, though few are known to come from any particular city. Their designs reflect the general style of Gothic art, with animals, rinceaux and heraldic devices of unfailing invention. During the 14th century the route to China was reopened, and many silks woven after that time incorporate decorative details showing Chinese influence—dragons, exotic birds, palmettes and cloud bands. Some of these may be seen in contemporary paintings; *e.g.,* the robes worn by St. Edmund Martyr in the Wilton diptych (*c.* 1395) in the National gallery, London.

The technique with which these silks were woven was advanced; the main warp appeared on the surface of the textile and was combined with a second (or ground) weft to form a texture contrasting with that of the pattern. Damasks were woven, and during the 14th century velvet weaving was established. There were plain-cut pile velvets, cut and uncut pile together, voided velvets in which part of the ground was left without pile but brocaded, often with gold thread, and velvets woven with two heights of pile, sometimes further enriched with gold loops. Many 15th-century velvets probably made in Venice have survived as chasubles and copes.

Velvets with the typical curving pomegranate in silk pile and gold thread may be recognized in paintings both by Italian artists and by those of the northern schools—evidence of the popularity of Italian velvets in Germany and the Low Countries.

**4. 15th Century to the Industrial Revolution.**—A great variety of textiles have survived from the 16th century. Among woven textiles the silks produced under the Safavid dynasty in Persia are outstanding. The silks of this renascence owed much to the stylistic tradition of Persian illuminated manuscripts in design, colouring and subjects depicted. Hunting scenes, subtle in technique and splendid in effect with lifelike hunters, animals, flowers, trees and birds, were rendered with accuracy and great decorative appeal. Several of the greatest were made in the court factories of Shah Abbas I (1587–1629). Persian treatment of floral design had a profound influence on European art but not on silk design until the period of its greatest inspiration had passed.

The Ottoman Turks also produced a fine series of silks in the 16th and 17th centuries. Brusa (Bursa) was the chief city weaving silks, though others are known. Turkish velvets were especially successful, owing their inspiration to those of Italy, though the designs were often treated on a larger scale.

In Europe Italian silks drew much from those of the 15th century, although by the late 16th century newer forms of ornament can be detected. More remarkable is the fine table linen produced in the Spanish Netherlands from the end of the 15th century (and perhaps earlier, though none survives). Special sets were woven to order for such clients as Henry VIII of England. Courtrai was the centre of the linen damask industry, though Haarlem became increasingly important in the 17th century. Damask cloths with napkins to match were woven with biblical scenes or coats-of-arms from the 16th century onward. Seventeenth-century damasks include commemorative designs, views of cities and some more original designs such as that of the cloth with a design of plates, knives and forks set for dinner, woven in Haarlem by Paschier Lamertin and now in the Victoria and Albert museum, London.

The War of the Spanish Succession at the beginning of the 18th century provided a rich source of subject matter, particularly beleaguered cities and equestrian portraits to commemorate the victories of Prince Eugene of Savoy and the duke of Marlborough. Such damasks were large, finely woven on a drawloom and expensive. Cheaper diapered or plain linen for napkins, cloths and sheets was also woven in great quantities in the same towns.

From the 17th century there survive some of the textiles made for a wider distribution than the court silks of Persia or the expensive Italian velvets. For those who could not afford the luxury of tapestries or silk hangings, certain northern towns in Italy made strong, coarse, woolen and hempen hangings. In the late 17th century this industry had shifted to Rouen and Elbeuf in France. Moreover during the 17th century the foundation of the English, Dutch and later French East India companies brought an increasing supply of cotton from Bengal into Europe for the making of fustians and other mixed fabrics. ("Cottons" until the 17th century and even later were usually low-grade woolen materials rather than true cottons.) The plantations in the American colonies were growing cotton for export by the second decade of the 18th century but probably little before then.

The establishment of important silk industries north of the Alps was a feature of the 17th century. While the woolen and worsted industries—the latter much developed in the 16th century—continued to produce the most important textiles in northern France, England and the Low Countries, the silk industry began to be significant in southern France. Although some silk had been woven in France in the 16th century and earlier, it could never compete with Italian imports. Under J. B. Colbert, minister of Louis XIV, however, the industries of Tours, Avignon, Nîmes and above all Lyons were supported by a rigorous policy of protection and the growth of raw silk was encouraged in southern France. The wars at the end of the reign of Louis XIV diverted French resources for a time from such capital investment, and during this period silk industries were firmly established in Holland and England. In London the industry spread from the City to the district of Spitalfields in the east, which greatly expanded with the industry in the first 60 years of the 18th century. Fine dress silks were woven by a large number of prosperous master weavers, many of them, especially the weavers of patterned silks, being of French Huguenot origin.

The London industry was subject to the general control of its medieval guild, the Weavers' company, but this exercised little influence on the types of silks produced. In France the Grande Fabrique de Lyon had a complex organization of regulations governing the qualities of the silks to be made and officials to enforce them. Wages were low and the economic regulations often in dispute, with an outright rebellion in 1744. It was against a background of almost continuous social unrest and internal dispute that Lyons produced some of its most astonishing dress silks.

During the last years of the 17th century the designs of silks were transformed from the formal pomegranate pattern inherited from the 15th century and the stylized sprigs that persisted throughout the first 70 years of the 17th. Abstract curling forms, often in gold and silver thread on a crimson damask ground, erupted into gigantic bizarre designs with a profusion of motifs of disproportionate scale juxtaposed. Fashions changed with the season, and by the second decade of the 18th century the bizarre forms had given way to luxuriant but formal designs based on the outline of the old pomegranate motif but enriched with lacy diapered fillings. There was an increasing desire in the 1730s to give a three-dimensional form to the designs: a designer named Courtois succeeded in large floral designs by using tones of colour; Jean Revel (1684–1751) introduced *points rentrés* by which the tones of colour were dovetailed. A reaction toward naturalistic life-size sprays of flowers came in the 1740s, a period in which some of the most successful English silks were woven. From the middle of the century designs with bunches of flowers and trailing ribbons dominated all others. Neoclassical influence can be detected in the later 18th-century silk designs as in other media, laurel wreaths and plain stripes occurring frequently. A period of very dark colours in the 1790s was succeeded by a fashion for light colours and light materials, especially silk gauzes and cotton muslins. While such were characteristic dress materials, printed cottons often provided fashionable furnishings. In Lyons, however, Philippe de la Salle (1723–1803), designer and partner in a silk-weaving firm, designed a series of furnishings with lifelike birds, flowers, ears of wheat, etc., on a sumptuous scale.

The continuous change in fashion was perhaps stimulated by intense competition in the market for woven silks. Genoa never lost its markets for heavy velvets and damasks, Lucca survived until the middle of the 18th century, but in the general climate of mercantilism every sovereign tried to restrict the import of luxuries and to foster native industries. Silk industries were revived in Spain and founded in Berlin and even in Russia. A large number of Chinese painted silks were also imported into Europe. It was not, however, until the 19th and 20th centuries that Chinese *k'o-ssu,* silk tapestry-woven textiles, were appreciated in Europe. The dragon robes worn by the highest Chinese officials were not made known in the west till after the sack of the Summer palace in Peking in 1860. A few fine 18th-century examples survive and can be seen in all major museum collections.

Very high-quality woolen, worsted and mixed textiles were made in the 18th century for everyday clothing, linings and upholstery; they were still very expensive, however, and secondhand clothing was much worn by the poor in all countries. Although all cotton goods were prohibited, substitutes with a linen warp and a cotton weft were made both in England and on the continent of Europe, and in England were virtually indistinguishable from pure cottons. While these goods possibly reached unprecedented technical perfection, far-reaching technical changes began to appear in the cotton districts of Lancashire and the heavy woolen industry of Yorkshire.

**5. The Industrial Revolution.**—Kay's flying shuttle (invented in 1733) speeded up and therefore cheapened the production of plain textile goods. Quicker weaving increased the pressure upon the spinners to produce more thread than they could by the spinning wheel, virtually unchanged since the 15th century. It was, however, nearly half a century before Richard Arkwright's water frame (1769) and Samuel Crompton's mule (1779) began to replace the hand spinners with machines. These inventions and their perfection gave an incentive to mechanize the preparatory processes of carding and combing. The period from 1780 to 1820 produced a multitude of devices to mechanize each of the processes formerly performed by hand. The first power loom was improved upon soon after the turn of the century. Primarily these inventions made possible the mass production of cheap cottons, but nearly all could be adapted to wool.

The greatest technical problem in silk pattern weaving was the cumbersome and expensive drawloom. The elimination of the drawboy and the automatic weaving of the pattern were finally achieved by Joseph Marie Jacquard (1752–1834), who built upon the ideas of his predecessors. The Jacquard loom was widely used in France by the end of the first decade of the 19th century and elsewhere by 1820. For the first time it was possible to lessen the cost of textiles with a woven pattern. Although Jacquard was a silk weaver his loom was quickly adapted in the cotton and linen industries and by the weavers of shawls, an important new industry in Scotland and at Norwich, Eng.

**6. 19th and 20th Centuries.**—The break in the normal stylistic evolution of the patterns of woven textiles is not clearly evident before the 1830s. The eclecticism of the taste of the next half-century reflected a total change in outlook. Techniques and new materials were of paramount importance. Using new machinery it was possible for the first time to reclaim rag wool for shoddy, thus lowering the cost of woolen goods and providing good warm clothing for the new poor of the rapidly growing industrial towns.

Except in the extreme luxury trades (in which Lyons silks and St. Étienne ribbons in France led the other nations), the textile centres of Europe and the United States competed with one another to produce large quantities of ever-cheaper power-loom-woven materials. The manufacturers' pride in these goods—each patented variation was acclaimed as a new material—was shown in the great international exhibitions of 1851 and 1862 (London), 1867 (Paris), 1876 (Philadelphia), 1878 (Paris) and others hardly less important. The overloaded Victorian interiors of the newly prosperous made extensive use of every kind of furnishing textile, creating an ever-increasing demand. The multiplicity of uncoordinated patterns was especially marked in textiles and provoked a natural reaction. On the one hand, there were official attempts to found trade schools and schools of design; on the other, William Morris and his associates rebelled against the domination of the machine (*see* ARTS AND CRAFTS MOVEMENT). Morris himself founded a firm to make high-quality furnishing fabrics using traditional dyes, the best materials and artists' designs. Although its influence was not limited to England, the movement hardly affected the styles of commercially produced textiles until the end of the century. (*See* also *Printed Textiles,* below.)

The scientific advances of the 19th century, particularly in chemistry, produced not only new dyes but, toward the end of the century, new fibres. The disease and virtual extinction of the European silkworm left the silk weavers of Europe almost entirely dependent upon the far east for their raw material; hence the incentives to find a substitute were strong. The first textile filaments were made in France from nitrocellulose; in Germany the cuprammonium process developed; in 1892 British scientists invented viscose rayon. But none of these proved wholly satisfactory.

After World War I cellulose acetate was exploited commercially, and in 1938 the first of a new series of fibres no longer based upon the structure of cellulose was developed in the United States. This was nylon, the first of the polyamide fibres, greatly improved after World War II. The polyester fibres were first used in the 1950s. The best of the new man-made fibres produced textiles that were tough, washable, crease-resisting, hard-wearing and less likely than natural fibres to shrink, fade or felt. Drawing on reliable supplies of raw materials they supplemented the four natural fibres very usefully, but the warmth of wool, the coolness of cotton and the elegance of silk were not easy to imitate. (*See* also FIBRE.) From the 1920s textile designs for the higher-quality materials have been once more the work of artists and reflect the general taste of their period.

**7. Other Textiles.**—Certain textiles fall outside the main historical developments. Japanese silks, though technically similar to Chinese, represent a different idiom in design hardly known in the west until it suddenly became fashionable in the 1870s. The coverlets woven by hand in parts of the United States preserved their traditional patterns throughout the 19th century. In some peasant communities of eastern and northern Europe, in north Africa and among the Indians of North and South America textiles were hand woven until the 20th century. Such textiles retained their intrinsic qualities until the use of aniline dyes destroyed their coherence by introducing alien, harsh and gaudy colour schemes which quickly faded to a lifeless and unpleasant monochrome.

(N. K. A. R.)

## II. PRINTED TEXTILES

The term printed textiles covers all textiles patterned by the application of pigments, whether by printing, painting or dyeing or by a combination of these methods. The pattern may be produced by painting on the cloth with a brush, by stenciling, by printing from wood blocks, engraved copperplates or metal rollers, or by screen printing, either with surface pigments or with dyes that penetrate the fibres of the cloth. The pattern may also be produced by "resist" or by mordant dyeing. In resist dyeing, the resist paste or wax, which is impervious to the dye, is painted or printed onto the material, covering the parts that are to remain uncoloured. In mordant dyeing, the parts that are to receive the colour are painted or printed with chemical substances known as mordants; when the fabric is immersed in the dye the colour is fixed on these parts, while washing removes it from the unmordanted areas. (These techniques are described at greater length in TEXTILE PRINTING.)

Printed textiles are believed to have been produced in the Caucasus as early as 2000 B.C. and there is no doubt that the art of ornamenting fabrics by painting or printing is of great antiquity. Painting was among the earliest methods of decorating textiles; among the oldest surviving examples of this are some Greek fabrics, dating from the 4th century B.C., found in tombs in the Crimea, and also the well-known painted Egyptian mummy cloths. In these early painted fabrics surface pigments were used, but at least as early as the 1st century A.D. the process of mordant dyeing was known to the Egyptians and is described by Pliny the Elder (d. 79 A.D.) although no mordant-dyed Egyptian fabrics of this date appear to have survived. Before the Christian era India had a reputation for its resist-dyed and painted cottons. In China the art of resist dyeing was certainly known as early as the 7th or 8th century A.D., while indigo resist-dyed linens, several with elaborate figure patterns of religious subjects, have been found in burial grounds at Akhmim, upper Egypt, and are thought to date from the 9th–10th century A.D.

In Europe, however, the art of textile printing does not appear to have begun much before the 12th century A.D., and the few pieces of printed fabrics of an earlier date that have been found in Europe appear to be of eastern origin. One of these, a piece of linen with a resist-dyed pattern of white circles on a blue ground, was found in the tomb of Caesarius of Arles (c. 470–542) and is preserved in the Nürnberg museum. A fragment of amber silk printed in gold leaf with a design of a falconer on horseback was found in the grave of St. Cuthbert in Durham cathedral (A.D. 1104), but it is assumed also to be of eastern origin.

**1. Block-Printed Textiles.**—The earliest extant examples of European printed fabrics, dating from the late 12th century, are of Rhenish origin. The fabrics, of silk or linen, were printed from wood blocks with surface pigments, usually in black, gold or silver. A few of the oldest pieces are printed in more than one colour, usually black and red, and occasionally a third colour. The patterns appear to have been copied from the Byzantine and near-eastern woven silks of the period. Although such fabrics seem to have been produced in considerable quantity and extant examples are numerous, there is reason to doubt the authenticity of many of the surviving pieces.

*Early Development.*—In the 14th century the patterns of Rhenish printed fabrics were based on the woven silks from Venice and Lucca. In one instance printed linen with a design of birds, lions and stylized floral motifs (fragments of which are in the Victoria and Albert museum, London, and at Berlin) survives together with the woven silk from which it was copied, a chasuble in the Stralsund museum in Germany. In the 15th century, patterns copied from Italian velvets, with ogival compartments containing stylized flowers or lobed pomegranate patterns, predominated.

Italian printed fabrics dating from the 14th century have also been found and examples such as the famous tapestry of Sion, with elaborate scenes of dancers and horsemen (in the Historisches Museum, Basel, Switz.), dating from the middle of the 14th century, show a high standard of technical excellence both in the cutting of the wood blocks and the actual printing. Records of the Painter-Stainers' company show that painting on cloth was a recognized trade in England as early as the 13th century, but probably the earliest surviving example, dating from the early 15th century, is a burse from the parish church of Hessett, Suffolk, painted with the head of Christ and the symbols of the four evangelists.

By the 16th century simple block-printed fabrics appear to have been produced in most European countries. A number of English examples of the Elizabethan period, copying the popular "black work" embroidery or derived from contemporary lace-pattern books, have survived. Others, printed from engraved copperplates in ordinary printer's ink, were obviously intended as embroidery patterns. The 17th century saw considerable advances: in Germany, for instance, the patterns consisted on the one hand of floral designs not derived from woven sources but characterized by the detailed and elaborate cutting of the wood blocks, and on the other hand indigo resist-dyed linens, often with pictorial and religious subjects, which were copied from the contemporary linen damasks.

**2. Origins of the European Calico-Printing Industry.**—The chief advances in textile printing were the result of an attempt by European textile printers to imitate the fast-dyed, hand-painted Indian cottons that began to be imported into Europe during the early 17th century. It was not until the 1670s, however, that the European calico printers appear to have been successful (more or less simultaneously in France, Holland and England) in mastering the complex problems of mordant dyeing with madder, the basis of the imported Indian chintzes. Since "calico," the general term for cotton cloth of all kinds imported from the east, was also soon used to describe various cotton fabrics of European manufacture (including those with linen warps), textile printers came to be described as calico printers rather than, as in earlier times, linen or stuff printers. Calico printing was to an extent continued in most European countries during the 18th and 19th centuries but England, France, Holland, Switzerland and Germany were the only countries where the industry achieved any real importance.

The English calico-printing industry appears to have been founded by William Sherwin, an engraver, who in 1676 was granted a patent for a "new way of printing broad callicoe" and set up a printworks at West Ham, east of London on the river Lea. Other printers followed and by the end of the century the industry was well established. Indeed by 1696 the industry had already grown sufficiently strong to arouse the established silk and wool interests against it. A law of 1700 prohibiting the import of Indian chintzes was followed by laws of 1712 and 1714 which placed heavy excise duties on home-printed chintzes. Finally, in 1720, a law was passed that prohibited printing on all cotton cloth, but the calico printers were able to evade the intention of the law by printing on a mixed cloth with a linen warp and cotton weft. It was not until 1774 that the ban on printing was raised from all cotton cloth and not until 1831 that the heavy excise duties were finally removed. In spite of these restrictions the English calico-printing industry continued to expand and flourish.

In France the calico-printing industry was even more hampered by restrictive legislation than in England. An edict of 1686 forbade not only the wearing of imported Indian chintzes but their imitation and, although it was widely evaded, the industry made little real progress until the final removal of all restrictions on textile printing in 1759. Even before the lifting of the ban, however, a number of calico printworks had come into operation, including those of Koechlin Schmaltzer and Dollfuss at Mulhouse (1746), the Danton brothers at Angers (1753) and John Rudolph Wetter at Orange (1758). Wetter, a rich Swiss merchant, had previously established a printworks at the free port of Marseilles in 1744.

Although simple block-printed textiles had been produced earlier in Holland, the first successful attempts at imitating the imported Indian chintzes were made at a printworks at Amersfoort set up in 1678 by two Amsterdam merchants and a Turk living in Holland. Other factories followed and by the middle of the 18th century about 100 printworks were in operation, mainly in Amsterdam and the surrounding districts. The number of printworks, however, gradually declined, largely as a result of increasing French and English competition, and by 1800 only four were in operation. In the following years Belgian printworks supplied most of the exports to the Dutch colonies in the East Indies, but after the separation of Belgium and Holland in 1830, new printworks were established in Holland, forming the nucleus of the modern textile-printing industry in that country.

In Germany during the late 17th and 18th centuries Augsburg was the chief centre of textile printing. Resist-dyed linens and block-printed linens, printed in black or red, are found but, in order to protect the linen industry, printing on cotton was prohibited until about the middle of the 18th century. Among the most important German printworks was that of the brothers Neuhofer at Augsburg, which operated in the early 18th century, and that of Johann Heinrich Schüle, who is said to have introduced copperplate printing into Germany in 1766.

Switzerland was an important textile-printing centre throughout the 18th and 19th centuries. Block printing by the "application" method, which involved the use of watered colours (dye and fixing agent mixed together), had been practised in Switzerland since the 16th century, and although this method continued into the 19th century the resulting prints were not fast to light or soap and water. The *indiennes* industry of Switzerland, however, developed from the processes of indigo and turkey red dyeing rather than from block printing as such, and was introduced by Swiss printers who had worked in Holland and by French Huguenot refugees. The first printworks in Geneva was founded in 1687 by a group of local merchants and a Frenchman named Matthieu Marin. Other printworks followed and by about 1720 Geneva was an important calico-printing centre. During the latter half of the 18th century, however, the industry declined and by 1815 only two printworks remained in operation; by 1830 the Geneva industry was virtually extinct.

The calico-printing industry of Zürich was founded by David Esslinger in 1720, while that of Basel was founded in 1716 by Samuel Ryhiner, who had learned his trade in Holland. The most important centres of calico printing in Switzerland, however, were the cantons of Neuchâtel and Glarus. The first Neuchâtel calico printer was Jean Labran, who opened a printworks at Pré-Royer in 1715. By 1750 several others had come into operation. One of the largest was that of Du Pasquier and Portales at Cortaillod, established in 1750 and by the beginning of the 19th century the largest in Switzerland, comprising more than 300 printing tables and a considerable number of roller-printing machines. The first calico printworks at Glarus was established in 1740 by Johann Heinrich Streiff, and the Glarus industry reached its peak in the 1840s.

Little is known of the Italian printworks apart from those in the Genoa area which specialized in the production of *mezzari,* large decorative panels copied from Indian models, the so-called "tree of life" being the commonest design. The most important factory was set up at Sampierdarena in 1787 by Michael Speich, a Swiss from Glarus, together with his cousin Luigi Testori, who succeeded to the business about 1830.

The earliest reference to calico printing in America is an advertisement in the *Boston Newsletter* of April 23, 1712, stating that a certain George Leason from England, together with a Boston clothier named Thomas Webber, had set up a printworks near the bowling green. Although similar advertisements are found with increasing frequency, it was not until the last quarter of the 18th century that textile printing can be said to have become an industry in the United States. One of the most important figures was John Hewson, an Englishman who, encouraged by Benjamin Franklin, set up a calico printworks in Philadelphia in 1774. His work was interrupted by the American Revolution, but he was able to resume his activities in 1789 with the assistance of a loan from the government. Although his output was considerable, and comprised both dress and furnishing fabrics and printed handkerchiefs, practically nothing has survived that can be attributed to him, although he is said to have printed a fine coverlet now in the Philadelphia Museum of Art. His factory lasted until sometime in the 1820s, the business being carried on by his sons. Among other 18th-century American printworks was that set up about 1790 at East Greenwich, R.I., by Herman Vandausan, a textile printer from Mulhouse. Other Rhode Island printworks included that of Schaub, Tissot and Dubosque (1794), and by 1840 there were 17 dyeing and printing establishments in that state.

Calico printing was also carried on in Massachusetts and New York. The first roller-printing machines in America were introduced in 1810 at the factory of Thorp, Siddall and Co. near Philadelphia, Pa.

*Designs.*—Although certain factories specialized in particular classes of goods, the general development of design in printed textiles was much the same throughout Europe and the United States, with the English and French printers taking the lead. Since surviving English and French textiles are far better documented than those of other countries, the general trend of design can best be studied by those examples.

The earliest surviving European examples were mostly printed in the limited palette of black, reds, purples and brown obtainable from madder dye, and the designs were often free adaptations of Indian floral patterns. Most of the earliest examples survive as linings to late-17th-century leather trunks or as linings to silk coats, stomachers and embroidered bags or purses. An important collection of impressions from early 18th-century textile printers' wood blocks survives in the Berch collection at Nordiska Museet, Stockholm, which are mostly single- or two-colour prints mainly of floral designs, characterized by fairly elaborate cutting of the wood blocks. Though knowledge of these early European fabrics block printed in the madder style is fragmentary and uncertain, it is clear that by the middle of the 18th century at the latest the European printers were able to add indigo blues and weld yellows to the basic madder colours, either printed by block or painted or "penciled" with a brush, and that by this time the printed fabrics had achieved a status that enabled them to exist in their own right, not merely as cheaper substitutes for woven fabrics.

A folio volume in the library of the Musée des Arts Décoratifs, Paris, contains 13 samples of English chintz, collected by John Holker in Lancashire in 1750 and presented to M. De Montigny of the French Royal Academy of Sciences. These samples, which are quite unfaded and fully annotated, show that by this time the English calico printers were able to produce well-drawn floral designs using the full range of colours obtainable from madder dye, together with indigo and weld yellow. Supplementary evidence of the skill of the English calico printers at this time is found in a series of original designs and impressions from wood blocks (in the Victoria and Albert museum) by John Baptist Jackson, who worked as a calico printer for a few years before he set up as a wallpaper manufacturer in 1752.

**3. Copperplate-Printed and Later Block-Printed Textiles.**—In the middle of the 18th century, the introduction of copperplate printing radically transformed the appearance of European printed textiles by allowing a fineness of detail and delicacy of drawing that had not been possible with the comparatively coarse technique of wood-block cutting. Copperplate printing on textiles was invented in 1752 at the Drumcondra printworks, near Dublin, by Francis Nixon, who introduced the technique into England within the next four years. For the next two decades—apart from the short-lived factory of Gayet and Montgirod at Sèvres, France, which survived for only 18 months in 1760–61—Ireland and England retained a virtual monopoly of the new technique. From the beginning the technique of copperplate printing was admirably suited to the production of large-scale pictorial designs, with a repeat of about a yard square, covering a wide range of subjects including pastoral, mythological and theatrical scenes, *chinoiseries* and subjects commemorating important military and political events. It was also widely used for finely engraved floral designs for both dress and furnishing fabrics. Few documented Irish examples have survived but pattern books (in the Musée de l'Impression sur Étoffes, Mulhouse, and the Victoria and Albert museum) containing over 400 different impressions from English calico printers' copperplates, as well as a vast quantity of extant plate-printed textiles, testify to the excellence of the English productions. Although a number of the English pictorial designs have certain affinities with the French *toiles de Jouy* (*see* below), a particularly striking group of designs with large flowers and birds seems to be especially characteristic of the English printers.

The copperplate designs were almost invariably monochrome,

being printed either in blue, red, purple or sepia. One English factory, that of the Wares at Crayford, is known to have printed in copperplate in two colours. In a few instances, such as the textile printed by Robert Jones at Old Ford in 1769 (Victoria and Albert museum) and the "volunteer furniture" printed by Edward Clarke at Palmerstown, Ire., in 1783 (National museum, Dublin) additional colours were added to the basic copperplate design by printing from wood blocks or by hand painting.

Although evidence has shown that generally speaking the English surpassed the French in copperplate printing, the credit for its development previously was given to Christophe Philippe Oberkampf and his factory at Jouy. Oberkampf, the son of a cloth printer and dyer, was born in Germany but moved with his father to Aarau and acquired Swiss nationality. After working first at the Cour de Lorraine factory at Mulhouse and then at the Arsenal at Paris he set up a small factory at Jouy-en-Josas, near Versailles, where his first print was produced on March 1, 1760. Four years later, in 1764, new buildings were begun and, owing to Oberkampf's unrivaled technical skill combined with his flair for singling out the best French designers, Jouy became the foremost printworks in France. The productions ranged from small, block-printed designs for dress fabrics to large-scale pictorial prints for furnishings.

According to the biography of Oberkampf, the secrets of copperplate printing were brought to Jouy in 1770 by his brother Frédéric, who had seen it in use at Morat, near Neuchâtel in Switzerland. However, no surviving Jouy copperplate prints can be positively dated earlier than 1783, the date of the famous *Travaux de la Manufacture*. This design was the work of Jean Baptiste Huet, who became the factory's chief designer. Most of Huet's early designs were of pastoral scenes, such as "Offrande à l'amour," "La Fête de la fédération" and "Les Plaisirs de la ferme." After the Revolution Huet followed the general trend toward classicism and produced a series of designs in the Directoire style including the "Scènes Pompéiennes" and "Le Loup et l'agneau." Examples of his work can be seen in the Musée des Arts Décoratifs, Paris. Other prominent designers who worked for Oberkampf were Hippolyte le Bas, who specialized in architectural subjects such as "Les Monuments de Paris," and Horace Vernet, who specialized in hunting scenes. Although Oberkampf's reputation was such that the term *toile de Jouy* became a generic description for all copperplate textiles, other French factories produced designs of equal distinction, among them the firm of Favre, Petitpierre et Compagnie (founded 1760) at Nantes and that of J. P. Meillier at Beautiran, near Bordeaux (founded 1792).

The introduction of copperplate printing did not, however, eclipse wood-block printing, and the two techniques developed side by side. The most popular wood-block designs continued to be floral, including designs based on the successive fashions in 18th-century woven silks. There is little basic difference between the wood-block-printed chintzes of the 1760s and 1770s, but in the 1780s several different styles emerge, including coiling floral designs with broken stems based on Indian models and large-scale arborescent designs often incorporating birds. Two parallel styles are especially characteristic of the last decade of the 18th century: first, designs on an almost black madder ground with delicately drawn mossy trails, which in England were popular for both dress and furnishing fabrics though in France they seem to have been limited to dress fabrics; second, designs of alternate vertical stripes, one on a white ground, the other on a dark, which were equally popular. This second type was virtually limited to England, while France favoured designs of detached sprigs of flowers, ears of wheat and insects, characterized by fine and precise cutting of the wood block.

Although finely engraved copperplate prints continued to be produced in France until the early 19th century, copperplate printing was in decline in England by that time. Most of the English factories that had specialized in copperplate prints were in London or the home counties. Among the most important were Robert Jones (*c.* 1760–80), Old Ford; Nixon and Co. (*c.* 1752–89), Phippsbridge, near Merton, Surrey; Bromley hall (*c.* 1740–1823), Middlesex; John Munns (*c.* 1769–84), Crayford, Kent; and Joseph and Mary Ware (*c.* 1760–81), Crayford.

Calico printing in Lancashire was established about the middle of the 18th century with an important offshoot in Carlisle, and from the onset the Lancashire and Carlisle printers concentrated on the production of wood-block-printed chintzes. By the beginning of the 19th century, most of the London copperplate printworks had closed down and with the shift of emphasis to Lancashire wood-block prints predominated. The leading factory in the production of high-class wood-block "furniture" prints was that at Bannister hall (founded *c.* 1798), near Preston, Lancashire, which, under successive changes of ownership, remained in operation until 1893.

The Bannister hall records dating from 1799 to 1840 include a continuous series of about 3,800 documented samples of printed cottons supplemented in most cases by the original designs, which provide an invaluable and accurate guide to the prevailing styles throughout those years, particularly since Bannister hall set the fashion for the other factories.

By 1800 the dark-ground style had given way to the so-called drab style, printed in yellow, olive, brown and buff, and the meticulous drawing of the 1790s was replaced by a broader technique with coarser cutting. The French copperplate Directoire prints were paralleled in England by a brief fashion in the years 1804–06 for "classical" and "Egyptian" designs, printed in hot "Pompeian" colours, and for *chinoiserie* designs incorporating figures, buildings and vases; "Indian" designs on bright-red grounds were also popular. Among the other wood-block styles popular in the early 19th century were designs incorporating game birds and architectural features. Panels printed for incorporation into patchwork quilts were produced in considerable quantity in the years around 1815.

**4. Roller-Printed Textiles.**—Although roller printing was invented by Thomas Bell as early as 1783 and was certainly used in the production of small-scale dress patterns by the beginning of the 19th century, it had little general effect on the design of printed textiles until about 1815. Thereafter in England the technique was used for pictorial prints, often of scenes of hunting and other sports and pastimes, but the designs were generally cruder than those of the 18th-century copperplate prints. In France the technique was widely used for a vast range of pictorial designs, often with diagonally hatched or finely diapered grounds.

From the 1820s onward the development of roller printing led to a vast increase in the output of printed textiles, although high-class furniture prints continued to be printed by wood block in the traditional madder style. In the 1820s the standard of engraving on the metal rollers was often extremely high. The actual engraving of the rollers was generally done not by the printers themselves but by special firms. One of the leading firms of engravers was Joseph Lockett of Manchester (later Lockett, Crossland), which supplied engraved rollers not only to the English calico printers but to printworks throughout Europe. This firm was largely responsible for the "fancy machine grounds" or "cover rollers" in which the whole background of the fabric was covered with elaborately engraved diaper patterns.

These enjoyed a considerable vogue in the 1830s and were often used as a background to the traditional, wood-block-printed floral chintzes.

**5. Decline and Revival of Textile Design.**—Until about 1810 all printing, with the exception of low-grade fabrics printed in fugitive colours, was based on the use of vegetable dyes, which in practice meant madder, indigo and quercitron. From then on, however, the competitive efforts of the French, German and English chemists resulted in a series of new chemical resists and discharges for transforming the appearance of the old vegetable dyes, and new methods for the use of colours such as prussian blue, cochineal pink and catechu brown. In addition, a completely new range of mineral dyes, including manganese brown, chrome yellow and antimony orange, and a "solid green" were placed at the disposal of the textile printers. These new discharges, resists and mineral dyestuffs had brought about a radical change in the appearance of printed textiles more than 20 years before W. H. Perkin's discovery of the aniline dyestuffs in 1856.

The combination of the indiscriminate use of these new colours, which were eminently suitable for roller printing, and a lower standard of engraving and design led to a gradual deterioration in printed textiles that was increasingly apparent from 1835 onward. A vast amount of cheap, roller-printed fabric was turned out by the English and European printers in a great variety of styles, ranging from floral designs and elaborate pictorial prints of romantic and sentimental subjects to various exotic styles intended for overseas markets. The eclecticism of the designers knew no bounds, and the 19th-century "battle of styles" was reflected in printed textiles that combined rococo, Gothic and classical elements with paisley motifs, tartan ribbons and a host of miscellaneous ornament. Even so, throughout the 1840s and 1850s, both the English and French and particularly the Alsatian printers continued to produce well-drawn floral chintzes, printed by wood block in the madder style, for the high-class furniture trade. Many of these were printed on challet, a fine worsted wool, instead of on cotton, which gave an added richness and depth to the colours. Although the Alsatian printers maintained a high standard of technical excellence, little of distinction was produced throughout the 1860s and 1870s.

The revival of textile printing as a fine art and the revival of the decorative arts generally that came about in the later 19th century must largely be credited to William Morris. Morris produced his first design for a printed textile in 1873, the first of 44 different designs for chintz, all of which were printed by hand with wood blocks and, with one or two exceptions, with vegetable dyes. Several of his finest chintzes, including the well-known "Strawberry Thief" (1883), were printed by the laborious and obsolete method of indigo-discharge printing. There is little doubt that the Morris chintzes printed first by Sir Thomas Wardle at Leek, and later at Morris' own workshops at Merton abbey, are among the finest printed textiles of all time.

The 1870s also saw the production of printed textiles influenced by Japanese art, with highly stylized flowers whose flat symmetrical petals were set against fretted backgrounds. In the 1880s a heavily textured cotton known as cretonne and velveteen were much used for printed furnishing fabrics, while some of the finest dress fabrics were printed on silk. From 1880 onward there was an increasing tendency for textile printers to commission designs from leading architects, artists and professional designers, which did much to raise the general standard of production. Throughout the latter part of the 19th century and the 20th century, the styles in printed textiles have closely followed the general development of the decorative arts. In the years around 1900 the influence of Art Nouveau (*q.v.*) was apparent, and outstanding printed textiles in this style were produced by firms such as Liberty of London.

In the 20th century modern movements in painting and the influence of the Ballets Russes and the Bauhaus in Germany led to the development of geometrical and abstract designs, usually printed in strong, vivid colours, often emphasized by black outlines. In England the move toward abstract design was fostered by the Omega workshops, founded by Roger Fry and a group of artists, for whom in 1913 the Maromme printworks of Rouen produced a series of printed textiles. A leading firm that did much to popularize the new styles was that of William Foxton, who from 1917 commissioned designs from leading artists including Charles Rennie Mackintosh and Claud Lovat Fraser. In France outstanding printed textiles were produced by the firm of Bianchini Ferier to the designs of Raoul Dufy and other painters. The later 1920s and early 1930s saw a return to more subdued, pastel colours and floral designs, characterized by overlapping segments and highly stylized flowers. This style achieved widespread currency at the Paris exhibition of 1925.

**6. Screen-Printed Textiles.**—In the 1930s the development of screen printing finally removed all restrictions from the designer and allowed enterprising manufacturers to try out short runs of experimental designs without incurring the heavy expense of engraved rollers or resorting to the laborious process of hand-block printing. This has resulted in an ever-increasing variety of design in printed textiles and at the same time extended the practice of commissioning designs from artists rather than professional designers.

Between World Wars I and II there was an important revival of hand-block printing in England on the part of a number of artist-craftsmen who produced both dress and furnishing fabrics, designing, cutting and printing the blocks themselves. Most of these fabrics had simple patterns produced in dark low tones, often with vegetable dyes, no doubt as a reaction against the garish colours and elaborate designs of the mass of commercial production.

In most countries there was little advance in the design of printed fabrics during World War II but after the war the development of mechanical screen printing brought an even greater variety of printed textiles. In the postwar years Scandinavia achieved a considerable reputation for printed textiles. Danish manufacturers were pre-eminent in the development of floral design, while Sweden and Finland tended to concentrate on crisp, geometrical patterns. With modern printing techniques the translation of any type of design onto cloth is possible. In contemporary screen-printed fabrics the designs range from abstract patterns imitating the work of avant-garde painters to elaborate florals, often with huge-scale repeats.

**7. Oriental Textiles.**—*Persia.*—The block printing of textiles in Persia may be traced back certainly to the 17th century. The journal of Jean de Thévenot (1633–77), *Relation d'un voyage au levant,* describes fabrics in which "the flowers and other paints are stamped upon them with a mould besmeared with colours." The French traveler Jean Chardin, in his *Voyages en Perse* (published in 1686), describes not only the painted cloths, similar to those from India, but also taffetas and satin, block printed with gold and silver with calligraphic, floral or pictorial designs. Painted and printed textiles produced in Persia were exported to Europe to the East India company in the late 17th and 18th centuries, and although records describe the textiles as "perses" it seems that little distinction was made between those of Indian and Persian origin.

Persian textiles of the 18th and 19th centuries with patterns produced by a combination of block printing and hand painting survive in considerable quantity in the form of wall hangings, prayer mats, curtains for doors or niches, bed coverings and shrouds. Most of the designs are floral but incorporate pine cone and other decorative motifs.

*China.*—Chinese resist-dyed silks, dating from the 7th or 8th century A.D., are preserved in the Shōsō-in, the imperial treasure house at Nara in Japan, and similar fragments were discovered by Sir Aurel Stein in eastern Turkestan. From the 18th century onward floral patterns painted in body colour on silk were made for export to Europe to be made up as dresses or hangings. A number of ecclesiastical vestments of Chinese painted silk dating from the 18th century also survive.

*Japan.*—It is probable that the Japanese learned the art of resist dyeing from the Chinese. A fragment of Japanese silk stenciled with the Buddhist sacred wheel is believed to date from the 8th century, and stenciled patterns are generally characteristic of Japanese work. Block printing was also practised in Japan and included a method known as negative block printing in which the hollowed-out parts of the block, not the relief portions, are charged with colour. The form of resist dyeing known as tie-and-dye work was extensively practised in Japan, as well as in India, China and other parts of Asia, and in Africa. In Japan this method was known as the *shibori* process, and in the 18th- and 19th-century examples the process is often combined with embroidery.

(B. J. Mo.)

*Javanese Batik.*—Batik is a Javanese word applied to the wax-resist technique of pattern dyeing on cloth, as practised there. Those parts of the cloth not required to take the dye are covered with hot wax, after which the whole fabric is dipped in the dye vat, an operation repeated according to the number of colours in the pattern.

It is doubtful if any batiks preserved in museum collections date from before the 1750s, and therefore little is known about the origins of this technique in Java. However, there is evidence that a simplified batik technique (possibly copied from India) was widely practised independently in southeast Asia: the Toradjas of Celebes (Sulawesi), for instance, until the second half of the 20th century produced simple batiks, applying the hot wax by means of a narrow, flattened strip of bamboo.

The decisive advances in Java, probably in the 18th century, seem to have resulted from the invention of the *tjanting,* a small copper crucible with a bamboo handle and a projecting spout for applying the wax.

In *tjanting* dyeing the cloth is elaborately washed and soaked to secure the right texture and surface and is then hung over a frame, the artist, usually a woman, sitting cross-legged before it. The design is sometimes first sketched in charcoal, but the best artists use only their *tjantings,* relying on visual memory. They outline the area that is to be dyed and cover the rest of the surface with wax. The cloth is turned over and the operation repeated on the other side. The cloth is then immersed in cold water till the wax hardens and is afterward dipped in the dye vat. The wax is removed, leaving exposed other parts of the cloth to be dyed different colours by the same process. The traditional colours are indigo blue, madder red and brown; secondary colours are produced by dyeing one colour over another.

In the 19th century copper-mounted wood blocks for applying the wax to the cloth were introduced. This, known as *tjap* printing, has almost entirely superseded the more laborious and highly skilled *tjanting* process. Batik was traditionally used almost entirely for clothing.

## III. INDIAN TEXTILES

From early historic times India was famed for its textiles. This is known from literary and archaeological evidence, although very few fabrics of a date earlier than the late 16th century survive. The decorative techniques traditional from early times are embroidery, resist dyeing, hand painting (with mordants) and brocading. A wide variety of materials have been employed for weaving, but the one most commonly used was cotton. Excavations at Mohenjo-Daro have shown that cotton was woven at least as early as the 3rd millennium B.C. The few minute fragments discovered owed their chance survival to impregnation with silver salts, absorbed from the walls of the silver vase in which they had remained for at least 4,000 years. Traces of purple dye, thought to be madder and therefore suggesting an early knowledge of dye chemistry, add to the significance of the discovery, while the numerous spindle whorls found at the same site—some of crude pottery and others of more expensive faïence—suggest that spinning was practised extensively and by all classes. Contemporary sculptures and terra-cottas show that at least two articles of costume for which India became famous, the girdle and the shawl, were already worn at this period.

Evidence is lacking for the thousand years following the collapse of the ancient city-states of the Indus valley; but the Greek physician Ctesias, writing in the early 5th century B.C., mentions the popularity of brightly coloured Indian textiles among the Persians, an indication that Indian fabrics were being made for export at least as early as this period. It is not known when they first reached Europe, but the use of the oriental word *carbasina* (Sanskrit *karpasa*) for cotton in the *Pausimachus* of Caecilius Statius suggests that it was before 200 B.C. Strabo, on the authority of Megasthenes (*c.* 300 B.C.), recorded the Indian love of finery and ornament, and added, "Their robes are worked in gold, and ornamented with precious stones, and they also wear flowered garments of the finest muslin."

During the 1st century A.D. Indian muslins became famous in Rome under such names as *nebula, gangetika* and *venti* textiles ("woven winds"), the latter exactly translating the technical name of a special type of Dacca muslin still being made in Bengal in the 19th century. Silk was also an important export to Rome, both as yarn and as finished cloth, but the author of the *Periplus* (*Circumnavigation of the Erythraean Sea*), written sometime between A.D. 50 and 130, makes it clear that the raw material was imported into India from China. Wild silks had been woven in India before this, but there is no proof that the domesticated silkworm was introduced into India from China before the medieval period.

Although there is no specific mention of dyed cottons in the *Periplus,* excavations at the site of the Indo-Roman trading station at Arikamedu, near Pondicherry, have revealed that large-scale dyeing operations were undertaken in the immediate vicinity of the port. Further proof that the Indian dyer was already famous in the Roman world for his skill is indicated by a reference in St. Jerome's 4th-century Latin translation of the Bible, Job being made to say that wisdom is so enduring that it "may not be compared with the dyed colours of India." There is also evidence that by the 8th century A.D. Indian dyed cottons were known in England, for Bede records in his *Life of St. Cuthbert* that the Synod of Clovesho forbade priests to wear clothes *tinctae Indiae coloribus* ("dyed with Indian colours").

Indian textiles of the medieval period can be studied in some detail from the Ajanta wall paintings (particularly those attributed to the 6th century A.D.). Apart from embroidery, at least four distinct techniques can be identified: *bandhana,* or ordinary tie-and-dye work; double tied-resist dyeing (*ikat*); brocading; and fine muslin weaving.

From the 12th century onward Indian dyed cottons were exported in bulk to Egypt, and many such pieces have been recovered from the sites of old urban rubbish dumps, especially at Al Fustat (Misr al Qadimah), the exceptionally dry climate accounting for their preservation. These are the oldest Indian patterned fabrics surviving.

From earliest times there have been two distinct weaving traditions in India. The first was the domestic one, practised in every village into the 20th century and mainly concerned with meeting local needs. The second was the more specialized tradition of commodity production, mainly concentrated in or near market towns and characterized by guild organization. Whereas in the oldest literary records (such as the Rigveda) the weaver is feminine, the development of commodity production in the 1st millennium B.C. seems to have established professional weaving as an exclusively male occupation. During the 2,000 years between the Roman period and the decline of the handloom industry in the 20th century the main areas of commodity production remained the same. They are described in the *Periplus* in much the same terms as they were described by travelers of the 17th and 18th centuries. These main areas were: the west of the subcontinent with Gujarat, Sind and Rajasthan as the focus; south India, comprising the Coromandel coast as it used to be known, stretching from the Krishna delta to Point Calimere; and the lower Ganges valley, between Varanasi (Benares) and the Delta. The main reason for this disposition of the industry was of course geographical. Each of the three areas could offer ports suitable for foreign shipping, and also comparative ease of inland communication.

From the 16th century onward Indian pattern and design were much influenced by Persia. This influence reached India in the first place through Islamic court fashion; but by the 17th century it had spread to the villages. Many of the sprigged patterns and floral diapers so characteristic of the Indian block printer's art of later centuries were derived from Safavid Persia. The history of mordant printing with blocks (as opposed to the application of mordants by brush) is complicated, and it is not possible to establish with certainty that the former technique was practised in India before the period of Islamic influence. The balance of available evidence suggests that the technique of mordant printing with blocks reached India about the 17th century from Turkey.

One of the oldest traditional techniques of textile decoration and one that has been very widely practised in India is *bandhana.* Portions of a silk or cotton cloth are tied tightly with wax thread before the whole cloth is dipped in a dye vat; the threads are afterward untied, the parts so protected being left uncoloured.

The technique of *ikat* or double-resist dyeing, in which warp and woof are dyed separately by the tie-and-dye process before weaving, was practised in Orissa and the Deccan as well as in

Gujarat. At Patan, in Gujarat, which produced the finest work of this kind in silk, such fabrics, known as *patolas,* were used especially as marriage saris. They were also extensively exported to southeast Asia from the 12th century onward, giving rise to many imitations in those countries.

The main centres of brocade weaving were Varanasi, Ahmedabad and the Deccan. The brocades for which India has been especially famed are woven silks in which part of the pattern is distinct from or supplementary to the wefts. Those woven in pure silk are called *amrus,* those with gold or silver thread in addition to silk, *kimkhabs* (Anglo-Indian, kincob).

Another form of brocading for which India was especially famous is the cashmere shawl. In this the technique corresponds to what in Europe would be called the twill-tapestry method. Coloured wefts are inserted by means of floating wooden bobbins on a simple loom. The weft threads alone form the pattern and do not run the full width of the cloth, being woven back and forth round the warp threads only where each particular colour is needed. The finest cashmere shawls were made of *asli tus,* the fleece from the underbelly of a particular species of wild mountain goat; the majority of shawls, however, were woven with the fleece of domestic goats, usually mixed with wool. The origins of the cashmere industry are obscure but can be traced back at least to the 15th century. Cashmere shawls were extremely fashionable in Europe between 1780 and 1880, during which period many European imitations were made on both drawlooms and Jacquard looms, especially at Norwich (Eng.) and Paisley (Scot.) and at various centres in France. The European imitation is always distinguishable from a cashmere original by the fact that in the latter the weft threads are inserted in the tapestry method and only for that portion of the required colour, not for the full width of the cloth.

Between 1600 and 1800 silk and cotton textiles were exported in large quantities from India to Europe mainly through the agency of the Dutch, English and French East India companies. The three classes of piece goods most in demand for this trade were plain-woven cottons (sold in competition with European linen), hand-painted cottons or chintzes (much coveted in Europe because of the brightness and permanence of their colours) and silk or mixed silk and cotton fabrics mainly used as dress materials. These goods were usually commissioned according to patterns sent out from Europe in the first place, but in the process of copying or adaptation the Indian craftsmen often infused an exotic spirit into the designs that actually increased their appeal in Europe. The importance of this trade is testified by the number of Indian textile terms assimilated into the English language: chintz, palampore, pajama, seersucker, dungaree, shawl and so on.

*See* also references under "Textiles" in the Index. (J. C. I.)

BIBLIOGRAPHY.—*History:* Otto von Falke, *Kunstgeschichte der Seidenweberei,* 2 vol. (1913); Adèle C. Weibel, *2000 Years of Textiles* (1952); C. Singer *et al.* (eds.), *A History of Technology,* 5 vol. (1954–58); *The Connoisseur Period Guides,* 6 vol. (1956–58); H. Schmidt, *Alte Seidenstoffe* (1958); *Ciba Review,* each issue on some particular type of textile, especially no. 133, J. Beckwith, "Coptic Textiles" (1959), and no. 136, R. d'Harcourt, "Peruvian Textile Techniques" (1960); R. Cox, *Le Musée historique des tissus, soieries et broderies,* 2 vol. (1914); Japan Textile Colour Design Centre, *Textile Designs of Japan,* 3 vol. (1959–61); W. Willets, *Chinese Art,* vol. i (1958); H. C. Broholm and M. Hald, *Costumes of the Bronze Age in Denmark* (1940); E. Power, *The Wool Trade in English Medieval History* (1940). (N. K. A. R.)

*Printed Textiles:* R. Forrer, *Die Zeugdrücke der byzantinischen, romanischen, gotischen und späteren Kunstepochen* (1894), *Die Kunst des Zeugdrucks vom Mittelalter bis zur Empirezeit* (1898); M. Percival, *The Chintz Book* (1923); H. Clouzot and F. Morris, *Painted and Printed Fabrics* (1927); H. Clouzot, *Histoire de la manufacture de Jouy et de la toile imprimée en France* (1928); *Ciba Review,* no. 26, "Medieval Cloth Printing in Europe," no. 31, "Textile Printing in 18th-century France," no. 48, "The History of the Textile Crafts in Holland," no. 76, "Early American Textiles," no. 105, "Textile Printing in Switzerland"; H. R. D'Allemagne, *La Toile imprimée et les indiennes de traité* (1942); E. Bindewald and K. Kasper, *Fairy Fancy on Fabrics* (1951); P. Floud and B. Morris in *Antiques Magazine* (March 1957 to April 1958), on English printed textiles, and in *Connoisseur* (Oct. 1957 to Feb. 1959), on English wood-block printed textiles, 1790–1810; Victoria and Albert Museum, *Catalogue of a Loan Exhibition of English Chintz* (1960), *English Printed Textiles, 1720–1836* (1960). (B. J. Mo.)

*Indian Textiles:* J. Forbes Watson, *Textile Manufactures and Costumes of the People of India,* with 17 suppl. vol. of samples (1866–80); B. H. Baden-Powell, *Handbook of Manufactures and Arts of the Punjab,* vol. ii of the *Handbook of the Economic Products of the Punjab* (1872); G. C. M. Birdwood, *The Industrial Arts of India,* 2 vol. (1880); T. N. Mukharji, *Art-Manufactures of India* (1888); G. Watt, *Indian Art at Delhi,* catalogue of the Delhi exhibition, 1902–03 (1904); W. S. Hadaway, *Cotton Painting and Printing in the Madras Presidency* (1917); G. P. Baker, *Calico Painting and Printing in the East Indies,* 2 vol. (1921); John Irwin, "Indian Textiles," in *The Art of India and Pakistan,* ed. by Sir Leigh Ashton (1950), "Indian Textile Trade in the 17th century," *Journal of Indian Textile History,* no. 1–4 (1955–59); bibliography in *Journal of Indian Textile History,* no. 1 (1955). (J. C. I.)

**TEXTUAL CRITICISM,** a general term for the application of logical method to analyzing the relationship between preserved and inferential forms of a text, followed by the application of various techniques, including critical judgment, designed to establish what will ordinarily be the single definitive form of the text.

This article is concerned with general principles of textual criticism, particularly as they apply to the study of literature. For a related discussion, *see* BIBLIOGRAPHY: *Textual Bibliography.* For a detailed consideration of the critical problems posed by variant manuscript texts of the Bible and variant codices of the Old and New Testaments, *see* BIBLE and BIBLE, TRANSLATIONS OF.

### CLASSIFICATION OF TEXTS

By text is meant word forms preserved in autograph or in transmitted form. Transmission may be as close as the immediate copy of an autograph, or as distant as copies of copies to any degree; moreover, texts may be transmitted in written or in printed form (each generally defined) or in both. "Transmitted" texts share only one characteristic: their preserved forms are not written out by the author in any manner. When there is mixture, the transmitted and autograph parts are to be distinguished. In some few cases the problem of oral transmission will arise to complicate the usual written or printed line of transmission.

**Autograph v. Transmitted Texts.**—"Autograph" has traditionally been applied only to a document in the writing of the author. It has been argued that whatever has been attested or revised by the author may be considered an autograph, but this position is impractical. Experience shows that a copy made by an intermediary cannot be assumed always to be absolutely exact; nor can the review of the author guarantee that a document does not vary from his original.

In fact, textual criticism treats authority literally, and does not confuse what is authoritative with what is necessarily right. Most autograph is likely to contain slips and errors that would be acknowledged as such by the author himself if they were pointed out to him. On the other hand, lacking such specific acknowledgment, a critic can only view autograph errors as authoritative, since there is no higher authority than the author; but this does not prevent critical correction. Correspondingly, when autograph is not preserved, the form of the text nearest to the lost original becomes the paramount authority; and its errors must be esteemed as part of the only authority than can be recognized, even though the critic should quite naturally correct them. The act of correction applied to the most authoritative document must always in a sense controvert authority. There is no harm in this once it is recognized that authority and correctness are not necessarily synonymous. Correction then can be made to a more authoritative from a less authoritative text, or independently by an editor.

**Determination of Original Copy or Copies.**—A transmitted text is defined as a nonauthorial copy. However, "original" must be taken only as a general term, for a preserved autograph may be a transcript by the author, either as part of an act of further composition (which could include revision), or as a fair copy of the original document. Seldom may a critic assume that revision is absent in writing an authorial fair copy, although it would be stretching the term to imply major rewriting. However, until an author has a fair copy, the act of composition scarcely can be concluded. Thus several originals of varying form and date may be preserved in autograph, and variant transmitted texts

Panel tapestry woven of tan wool and purple linen; probably Egyptian or Mesopotamian, dating from the 5th or 6th century

Near eastern silk with half-bird, half-dog design, thought to have come from a reliquary in the church of St. Leu, Paris; about A.D. 700–900

Patterned cotton, woven in double cloth, with cat motif; relic of the pre-Columbian civilization of Peru

Byzantine elephant silk from the tomb of Charlemagne at Aachen, Germany; 10th century

## WOVEN TEXTILES: AMERICAN AND NEAR EASTERN

BY COURTESY OF (TOP LEFT) VICTORIA AND ALBERT MUSEUM, (BOTTOM LEFT) "CIBA REVIEW," CIBA LIMITED, BASLE, SWITZERLAND, FROM THE FRITZ IKLÉ COLLECTION, BASLE MUSEUM OF ETHNOLOGY, (BOTTOM RIGHT) THE CATHEDRAL OF AACHEN, PHOTO BY A. BREDOL-LEPPER; PHOTOGRAPH, (TOP RIGHT) JACK SKEEL FOR ENCYCLOPÆDIA BRITANNICA, INC.

# TEXTILES

Northern Italian silk woven with gilt membrane. The design, composed of stags, hounds, lions and phoenixes, shows the influence of Chinese decoration which prevailed in Italy during the last half of the 14th century

Persian fabric woven with a cup-bearer motif in the tradition of Persian illuminated manuscript design; 16th century

## WOVEN TEXTILES: 14TH- AND 16TH-CENTURY NORTHERN ITALIAN AND PERSIAN

BY COURTESY OF VICTORIA AND ALBERT MUSEUM

WOVEN TEXTILES:
SILK DAMASK,
SILK AND VELVET BROCADES

Chinese silk damask with floral design; early 18th century

Italian cut velvet brocaded with gold loops in a curving pomegranate design characteristic of late 15th- and early 16th-century textile fashion in Italy

Hispano-Moresque silk brocaded in gold. The design is a blending of near-eastern ornamentation and Spanish-style decoration

BY COURTESY OF (BOTTOM LEFT) DETROIT INSTITUTE OF ARTS, (BOTTOM RIGHT) MUSEUM OF FINE ARTS, BOSTON; PHOTOGRAPH, (TOP) BY THE KIND PERMISSION OF ANTIKVARISK-TOPOGRAFISKA ARKIVET, STOCKHOLM

BY COURTESY OF MUSÉE HISTORIQUE DES TISSUS; PHOTOGRAPH BY RENÉ BASSET

**WOVEN TEXTILES: LATE 18TH-CENTURY FRENCH**

Woven silk textile hanging from the queen's chamber at Fontainebleau by Philippe de la Salle of Lyons, who designed a series of furnishings adorned with lifelike birds and flowers

Fragment of indigo resist-dyed linen found in the burial grounds at Akhmim, upper Egypt; believed to date from the 9th–10th century A.D.

Linen chasuble, wood-block printed in black; Italian, dating from the end of the 15th century

Resist-dyed linen with a design showing Joshua and Caleb returning from the Promised Land; German (Rhenish), late 17th century

Diapered linen, block printed in black with a design said to represent Louis XIV and Madame de Fontanges; French, late 17th century

## PRINTED TEXTILES: BLOCK-PRINTED AND RESIST-DYED LINENS

BY COURTESY OF (TOP LEFT AND RIGHT) VICTORIA AND ALBERT MUSEUM; PHOTOGRAPHS, (BOTTOM LEFT AND RIGHT) JACK SKEEL FOR ENCYCLOPÆDIA BRITANNICA, INC.

# TEXTILES

Cotton and linen, copperplate printed in purple. Other colours were added to the design by printing from wood blocks and by penciling. By Robert Jones at Old Ford, 1769

Wood-block-printed cotton in madder colours. Blue added by hand penciling. Printed at Fordingbridge, Hampshire, about 1790



## PRINTED TEXTILES: 18TH-CENTURY ENGLISH

Block-printed cotton from the factory of Christophe Philippe Oberkampf at Jouy, leading printworks in France during the 18th century. This piece, *c.* 1780

English cotton with pillar design, block printed on dark ground in madder colours, principally brown, tan and red; dating from about 1800

"L'Offrande à l'amour," copperplate-printed cotton by Jean Baptiste Huet, chief designer for Oberkampf, whose early designs were pastoral scenes, such as this one printed at Jouy about 1804

English cotton, plate printed in red; by Nixon and Co., Phippsbridge, Surrey, one of the leading English copperplate-printing factories. This piece dates from about 1770

**PRINTED TEXTILES: FRENCH AND ENGLISH BLOCK PRINTS**

BY COURTESY OF (TOP LEFT) ELINOR MERRELL COLLECTION, (TOP RIGHT) THE METROPOLITAN MUSEUM OF ART, ROGERS FUND, 1926, (BOTTOM LEFT) COLLECTION OF THE NEWARK MUSEUM; PHOTOGRAPH, (BOTTOM RIGHT) JACK SKEEL FOR ENCYCLOPÆDIA BRITANNICA, INC.

# TEXTILES

*Above:* English roller-printed cotton by Samuel Matley, Hodge, Cheshire; 1824. Roller printing greatly accelerated the output of printed textiles during the early 1800s

*Left:* English block-printed cotton in madder colours from Bannister hall, Lancashire; 1836. Founded *c.* 1798, Bannister hall designs set the style for other textile factories

"Honeysuckle," English block-printed chintz designed (1876) by William Morris, who revived textile printing as a fine art during the 19th century

"L'Afrique," French block print on cotton and linen designed by Raoul Dufy for Bianchini Férier of Paris; dating from about 1924

## PRINTED TEXTILES: ENGLISH AND FRENCH BLOCK AND ROLLER PRINTS

BY COURTESY OF (BOTTOM LEFT AND RIGHT) VICTORIA AND ALBERT MUSEUM; PHOTOGRAPHS, (TOP LEFT) JACK SKEEL AND (TOP RIGHT) C. H. CANNINGS FOR ENCYCLOPÆDIA BRITANNICA, INC.

may contain true authorial revisions.

The slippery nature of an original document must be emphasized, for critical writing has vastly oversimplified the problem. For example, a standard definition asserts that the aim of the textual critic is the restoration of a text, as far as possible, to its original form—"the form intended by the author." This ignores the fact that an author may intend a composition to take various forms, each with its own original. Even final intention may be an insufficient criterion. If the version of a play as cut and rewritten during rehearsals is printed, the author will have approved it as printed in its acted form, but if he had had an option he might have preferred to print the initial, more literary form. Revisions may be undertaken for various motives that do not meet with universal approbation. Poets may in later years so alter their earliest printed originals as to achieve forms of their poems that call for parallel-text editions rather than the rejection of the earlier original. All alterations are not necessarily connected with a desire for literary perfection; changes in political beliefs or a desire to moderate too frank autobiographical details may operate.

At any distance authorial intention is usually quite impossible to determine for the details of a text, and cannot be used as part of any scientific definition. If the literary and then the stage versions of a play are both preserved no later critic without collateral evidence can estimate the author's intention concerning the two different texts. If this is so, it is clear that a critic would be greatly misguided to estimate intention or original form if only one of two variant forms survived. Thus a critic must use the term "original" form recognizing that the word is loose in substance; and a definition of textual criticism must hedge on its characteristics.

For example, all that can be known about a lost original must ultimately derive from extant transcripts. As a result, the original can have no recoverable characteristics not found in the preserved transcripts. The technical original must be thought of only as the last version of the text produced before transcriptions began. In a textual-critical sense, therefore, this original may not be, and often is not the author's original, but instead some transmitted copy of that other original forever out of reach. Any number of lost versions may have intervened between the textual original and the author's lost original. Thus it is quite false to believe that the critic's purpose is "to recover the author's original." Moreover, it is false thinking if the archetype in scholarly textual criticism is confused with the author's lost original instead of being identified neutrally as the manuscript from which all other extant copies are derived. In some cases this technical original may be the author's original; in most, however, it will be some intermediate transcript of an author's lost autograph.

The aim of the textual critic, then, is: (1) the establishment of a text in its purest and most correct form, limited by the evidence of preserved documents; and (2) the application of techniques, including critical judgment, to clear a text of errors still present in the established, or documentary, form. The end of this second process is to approximate that correctness which would have appeared in an authorial fair copy of a text.

**Accidental v. Substantive Variations.**—In this definition, the "purest and most correct form" of a text refers to more than simply an original and its possible revision. It includes also a distinction often made in printed texts; *i.e.,* between the "substantive" readings of a text, namely, those affecting the author's meaning; and the "accidentals" of a text—its spelling, capitalization, punctuation, word division—which affect mainly its formal presentation. It may be that one form of a text preserves the accidentals of an author while at the same time containing substantive readings that he has seen fit to reject on a later occasion. The first edition of John Dryden's *Indian Emperour* (1667) is manifestly closer to his autograph than any other printed edition, since the slightly revised second edition (1668) was set from the first, and the considerably revised third edition (1670) was set from the second. However, this third edition, which on the whole contains the most authoritative range of Dryden's substantive readings, is manifestly inferior to the first in the authority of the accidentals. In such a case the duty of the textual critic is clear. He must establish the fact that the third edition is the last revised substantive form of this text; and then determine the most authoritative form of the accidentals. An editor would then place the most authoritative form of the substantives within the framework of the most authoritative form of the accidentals.

Much confusion has been caused in critical writing by failing to observe the two stages of procedure in the establishment of a text: (1) the fixing from documentary evidence of the most authoritative form; and (2) the emendation of this initially established text to approximate as nearly as possible an inferential authorial fair copy, chiefly in respect to its substantives. This final action achieves the establishment of a critically definitive text. At one time only the first operation was called "textual" criticism, the second being known as "higher" criticism; but this distinction lapsed following the recognition that the second stage involves more than simple critical judgment and may include bibliographical, paleographical and linguistic, as well as historical considerations.

The second stage of establishing a text does not differ essentially between manuscripts and printed books. However, the methods of utilizing preserved documents to establish the first, or documentary, stage of the text often differ so widely between manuscripts and prints as to call for separate consideration.

### THE GENEALOGY OF MANUSCRIPTS

The majority of manuscript texts requiring methodical textual criticism date from days before the invention of printing, although the custom of manuscript circulation may lead to problems even in such late Renaissance authors as John Donne.

**Types of Genetic Relationship.**—The analysis of the relationship of preserved forms of a text, as a whole, ends in the drawing up of a genealogical chart, such as the following, appropriate for a text wholly or chiefly preserved in manuscripts:

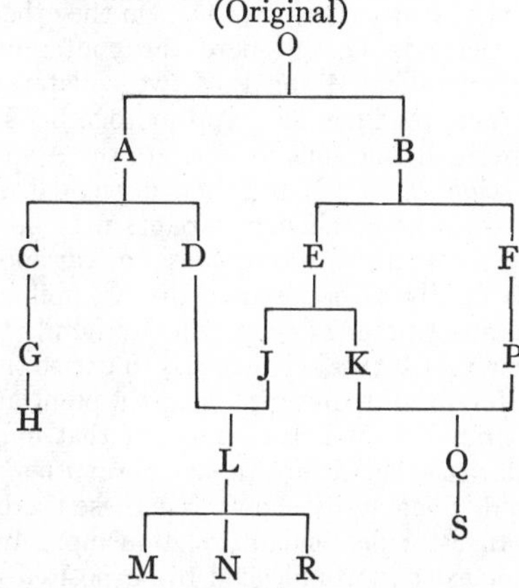


The genealogical tree always diverges in its lines of descent from an original, which is the latest immediate ancestor to all the manuscripts highest on the family tree; *i.e.,* to the heads of all families. The process of transcription seems inevitably to produce variant readings (excluding authorial or editorial alterations). Variation is either "spontaneous" or "determined." Spontaneous variation is unconscious variation, perhaps a mere slip of the pen. Determined variation is conscious, and hence usually an attempt at emendation (correct or not) of the copy being transcribed. Of the variants introduced into any transcript, some will persist whereas others will undergo further change. In this way features peculiar to any manuscript are transmitted, but not in an invariable form. Variation leads farther and farther away from the original reading, but may actually restore by independent correction the reading of a more remote ancestor.

Variants may be vertical (*i.e.,* within a direct genetic line of descent) as when H, transcribed from G, varies from G; or variation may be horizontal, as when A differs from B, both being manuscripts transcribed independently from O. (A and B are "collaterals" in that neither is an ancestor nor a descendant of the other.) It is horizontal variation that gives rise among collaterals to "grouping," or the arrangement of the manuscripts into family and subfamily groups according to whether they agree or differ in respect to particular readings.

Unless there is "conflation" (one manuscript affecting the readings of another by contamination), each family group shares an exclusive common ancestor deriving ultimately from the first independent descendants of the inferred or preserved great common ancestor O. In the tree above, the family groups are separated into A and B and their respective descendants, except that L joins both families by conflation and passes on this mixed inheritance to its descendants. A subfamily is a family whose ancestor is derivable from a manuscript which is the ancestor of still other manuscripts. For example, K and P are in separate subfamilies deriving from their ancestors E and F, which are collaterals deriving from B. In reading a genealogical table of texts, no inference can be drawn that a manuscript shown as deriving directly from another manuscript was in fact copied from the exact manuscript shown on the tree as a parent. Between G and H or between B and F any number of now lost manuscripts very likely existed. Hence all variants in H from G, or in F from B need not have arisen in the act of copying the actual manuscripts of H and F. All that is shown by the table is that the line of descent from G to H and from B to F is a direct ancestor-descendant one, and that H has no other known ancestor than G, or F than B. In other words, no manuscripts deriving from any ancestor other than G were used in the transmission of the text from G to H, whatever the distance between them.

The case is quite different with L. Here two exemplars of manuscripts were extant, one in the direct line of descent from D, and the other similarly derived from J. These two manuscripts were conflated when in cases of variation between them the editor chose readings now from one and then the other. In this case conflation joined two manuscripts of different genetic, or family, relationship, for neither D nor J shared any common ancestor except the ultimate ancestor O. On the other hand, lesser conflation took place in Q, but here the contamination served only to unite the members K and P of two collateral subfamilies. In the first instance, readings may appear together in L that had been used as genetic distinctions to separate the A and B families; *i.e.,* readings in which A and B and their descendants varied from each other. In the second, though variants may be reunited, the conflation, except fortuitously, includes no variant not characteristic of the B family as opposed to the A family.

Inferential manuscripts may appear in any family tree, although the recent tendency of textual criticism is to excise them wherever possible. An inferential manuscript marks a point at which some line of descent branches; it is a manuscript that must be posited to explain similarities between two or more other manuscripts, extant or inferred, when study shows that these are in a collateral and not in an ancestor-descendant relationship. In the sample tree, if A did not exist it would need to be posited provided one could show that C did not derive from D, or D from C, or C and D independently from O.

The process of determining the relationship of the manuscripts consists of isolating the major different family groups and then inferring the genetic grouping of the individual texts within these large groups. The process starts with a collation, or comparison of all known texts and a systematic recording of their variants, usually confined to substantive differences. Three major kinds of variants will develop: (1) variants shown by a single manuscript; (2) variants shown simultaneously by a few manuscripts; and (3) variants shown simultaneously by numerous manuscripts. The first are useless and must be disregarded. The second are valuable in determining families and subfamilies. One of the first tasks, therefore, is to delimit the families by means of such variants as are found repeatedly to be peculiar to certain constant groups of manuscripts. The families thus determined, the groupings within each may be filled in. The precise way in which a textual critic operates to determine the relationship of all forms of his text can scarcely be summarized, because of the complexity of the evidence and the differences in the weight given to various kinds of evidence. In general, the critic aims first at establishing the facts of genetic relationship and then at determining the direction of the relationship between ancestor and descendant.

**Distributional Evidence.**—"Distributional" evidence is used in determining the basic facts of relationship or nonrelationship. The arrangement of differences in the texts is utilized as evidence without attention to the nature of the differences. The assumption is made that unity in readings in manuscripts is due more to unity in their source than to coincidence. If the point of difference is, for example, the appearance of a particular word, distributional study does not inquire whether the word is an addition. It merely divides the manuscripts into groups depending upon the appearance of this word.

Distributional evidence may be used to assign the nature of groupings by indicating whether the relationship is direct or collateral. For example, suppose manuscript L shares readings with all other manuscripts in its family and has no unique readings. Manuscript M shares readings only with L and has no shared readings with other manuscripts not shared with L, but it also has some unique readings. This state of affairs is not compatible with a supposition that L is copied from M, since (because of the unique variants in M) the greater number of times that L agrees with the other manuscripts than does M is unexplained. On the other hand, this state of affairs is compatible with the hypothesis that M was transcribed from L.

One apparent fallacy in this reasoning is usually not of consequence. The larger share of L than of M in readings with other manuscripts could be explained, in isolation, as derivation of L from M if M were the earliest of all manuscripts and all derived from it as the common ancestor. However, a tree branches as it develops, not converges; and no rational genealogical chart can be reversed. Moreover, other evidence, which may be called genetic, provides a check on the direction of change.

The facts of the distribution of variant readings among manuscripts, therefore, may be utilized to show direct relationship, as above, or collateral relationship. For the latter, if in a group of more than two manuscripts having a common ancestor (like M, N and R), all manuscripts have unique readings, and all manuscripts shared readings in no constant arrangement, these facts are compatible only with independent derivation of the type known as radiation. On the other hand, if the relationship is always constant, so that the shared readings of M are always shared only with N or with R, the facts can be taken to be incompatible with radiation and hence derivation must be postulated.

**Genetic Evidence.**—Distributional evidence is frequently enough to settle a case, but it has its limitations when revision is present and especially (as exemplified in the texts of Donne or Robert Herrick) when copies are made from a poem in different stages of reworking. Hence the critic may call on a second order of evidence, which may be called genetic, or the comparison of individual differences with each other in the hope of discovering the direction of change. At its most scientific this inquiry still attempts to emulate distributional study by ignoring the critical considerations of meaning, at least in any strict sense of right and wrong. Instead, genetic study rests on the assumption that certain differences are more likely to have been produced by a given direction of change than by another.

Common errors of other sorts may also profitably be used but always with caution, for the process of correction reverses the direction of change toward error that would be expected from the process of copying. The critic attempts to separate reversible changes from variants that by their nature appear to be nonreversible. Moreover, the postulate that spontaneous variation occurs oftener than directed variation would indicate that in a direct sequence the number of errors will ordinarily exceed the number of corrections, and hence that the most faulty will likely be the descendant, not the ancestor; but this line of argument is to be used with caution.

Similarly, the direction of change may sometimes be postulated by explaining one form as the result of a known type of mechanical error such as eyeskip or haplography (omission of letters or words). Unless distributional evidence indicates otherwise, an existent word is presumed to be earlier than a nonexistent word created by a familiar type of error.

Suggestive as genetic evidence may be, assumptions from individual readings may often prove to be untrustworthy; and hence the genetic method is usefully employed only when distributional evidence has been completely exhausted.

**Physical and Stylistic Evidence.**—Physical evidence is ordinarily of little use in dealing with classical or medieval manuscripts. It is no argument, for example, that because the paper of manuscript Y is dated in 1640 and that of manuscript Z in 1240, the text of Z must be earlier than Y; instead, Y might well have been transcribed from a manuscript of a form nearer to the common ancestor than the ancestor of Z. However, modern manuscripts (and especially autograph) may yield extraordinary results when external evidence is applied. The manuscripts behind the 1860 edition of Whitman's *Leaves of Grass* neatly divide into groups that can be dated 1857 and 1859 respectively on the basis of the paper and inks. A brilliant recovery of the order of Emily Dickinson's manuscripts resulted from a minute external study of the paper and the handwriting characteristics.

Finally, in this preliminary stage, which consists only of the establishment of one form of a genealogical chart rather than any other, purely literary study based on assumed stylistic respects, superior sense, freedom from mistakes of fact, etc., is almost completely untrustworthy and should not be employed until the preceding three ranges of evidence have been completely exhausted, individually and collectively.

**Determining the Most Authoritative Variant.**—Once a genealogical chart has been drawn up, it is proper to consider the authority of variants in the texts in the light of the facts of derivation as shown by the tree. In the sample chart it is obvious that if O is preserved no other known manuscript can contain a reading that possesses any authority, although some may have readings that are more correct.

On the other hand, if O is only inferential, and A and B represent the ultimate heads of only two families, the critic's position is less happy. True, no preserved manuscript other than A and B can own authority; true, shared readings between A and B must be presumed to derive from inferential O, and therefore common readings possess the authority they would have if derived from a preserved O. (But notice that in either case O is not necessarily the real archetype or first original, but instead merely the one manuscript it is possible to infer as a common ancestor of A and B, even though through different lost intermediaries.) However, where A and B vary, only critical judgment can decide, on the evidence of each individual variant, which one is superior and therefore—by another assumption not always warranted—authorial.

The school of textual critics stemming from Karl Lachmann favoured the acceptance of one "best" manuscript and the rigid adherence to its readings in all possible circumstances as the only "scientific" attitude for an editor. This school tacitly considered that textual criticism ended with the establishment of the family tree and the consequent decision in favour of some one preserved manuscript as the "best"; whereas, at least in the above chart, the tree does not favour either A or B. The most advanced textual critic, however, no longer stops short with what the evidence of the genealogical chart indicates about the authority of the readings; nor does he rest content with fidelity to a chosen best manuscript. In every case he will accept only as comparative the authority of the earliest ancestors that can be established; and as the final stage he will treat it critically according to whatever techniques are pertinent, and over all impose his literary judgment. At this point, where methodical techniques largely desert a textual-critic editor, the resulting text will be good or bad depending upon the individual's own capacities. Yet confidence in critical ability to solve all problems may lead to a newer kind of laziness as acute as that found in the "scientific" textual critic, if all the ancillary techniques for examining a text are not exhausted before reliance is placed on judgment rooted in subjectivity and intuition and in the cultural intelligence of an editor.

### THE GENEALOGY OF PRINTED BOOKS

Transmission of a text in printed books differs so from that of an ancient manuscript text as to call for quite different basic postulates. The chief difference is that a manuscript that is a direct descendant of its most immediate ancestor is ordinarily not copied directly from the ancestor but from some one of a lost series descending from the ancestor. On the other hand, any edition of a book other than the first is ordinarily copied directly from some other known edition. Editions of books, therefore, are assumed to be contiguous in their relationship, and variants between them can be assigned either to the editors or the author. Secondly, editions of books are usually correctly dated and show the relationship between editions. Both assumptions permit physical evidence that is the special province of analytical bibliography, a discipline that studies the effects of the printing process on the transmission of text (*see* BIBLIOGRAPHY).

For example, the ninth edition (1694) of Dryden's *Indian Emperour* appears to conflate distinctive readings of the seventh edition of 1686 and the eighth of 1692. An editor might postulate either consultation and contamination or else derivation from a lost edition between the seventh and eighth. However, if trained to observe physical evidence, he will notice that the distinctive variants of the two editions never appear together on any page of the 1694 print; and starting with this fact he will develop other physical evidence to demonstrate that two different compositors alternated in setting the type for the 1694 edition, one of whom used the 1686 and the other the 1692 edition as printer's copy.

**Determining the True First Edition.**—One of the most difficult problems facing a textual critic of printed books is to determine which is the true first edition of two editions issued in the same year. Dryden's play *The Wild Gallant* had two editions printed in 1669, the year of publication. On literary grounds Dryden's editor G. Saintsbury rejected what turned out to be the true first edition, and chose for his text the variant readings of the unauthoritative second edition. When the case was scrupulously examined, one piece of physical evidence was enough to demonstrate the true order. In what was proved to be the first edition the word "tells" was printed with a defective type for the second letter "l"; the type inked chiefly at the top and in many copies produced only a short mark that looked like an apostrophe. In the second edition the compositor faithfully copied what he thought he saw and set the corresponding word as "tel's," an impossible form. That this evidence must be accepted may be seen if one tries to reverse it and explain the defective type as deriving from the apostrophe.

The chief textual critic of *Hamlet* between World Wars I and II, J. Dover Wilson, had pronounced the important second edition of 1604–05, the first of the good texts, as set throughout by only one compositor, who was an incompetent novice at the trade. But in 1953–54 one bibliographer showed on physical evidence that two presses had been employed requiring the services of two compositors. Further, another scholar, J. R. Brown, by examining distinctive characteristic spellings, identified the sheets set by each compositor and established that they had worked for the printer for several years as his regular men and, indeed, had set the second edition of *Titus Andronicus* and the first edition of *The Merchant of Venice,* both in 1600. Since these two texts have been much admired for their accuracy, the effect was to establish that defects in the second edition of *Hamlet* are chiefly from its manuscript rather than from the printer's incompetency. The difference is important for the textual critic.

One of the most brilliant bibliographical discoveries of the 20th century disclosed the false dating of the so-called Pavier Quartos of various Shakespeare plays. It was established that Pavier editions of some plays dated 1619 and editions of others dated a decade or more earlier shared identical standing type in their title pages. This physical impossibility revealed that some texts previously preferred on literary grounds by editors, such as that of *King Lear,* were actually unauthoritative second editions of no textual value. Whether Hamlet's flesh was "too too sallied" (*i.e.,* "sullied"), as in the First and Second Quarto editions or "too too solid," as in the Folio, had usually been decided in favour of the

Folio. However in 1956 it was pointed out that the unusual form "sallied" in the second edition could not have derived unauthoritatively by contamination from the same reading in the imperfect first edition, since the second appearance in this play of the word "sally" meaning "sully" (Polonius to Reynaldo, Act II, sc. i) came in a section typeset by a different compositor, who would be unaware of the previous occurrence and must have copied his word from the manuscript, the first edition being wanting there. These examples suggest various typical ways in which bibliographical techniques that have been developed in the 20th century have revolutionized the study of printed texts by emphasizing the need to exhaust the physical evidence of analytical bibliography before attempting critical judgment.

The approach to textual criticism made by the analytical bibliographer emphasizes two primary requirements: (1) the careful examination of all preserved forms of a text, not only to assure that the external evidence of printed dates and the like is correct and that one has recovered the earliest edition but also to guarantee that every other edition in which fresh authority might have entered has been placed in its correct relationship and the authority of its variants analyzed; (2) the careful examination of the details of any edition possessing authority, whether the first or a revised print, to determine the nature of the copy used by the printer and its authority.

**Determining the Nature of Printer's Copy.**—The usefulness of this inquiry is by no means limited to early handprinted books but may be applied as profitably to the texts of James Joyce, T. S. Eliot and W. B. Yeats as to the text of Shakespeare. The common practice of dilettante editors to reprint as their text the last edition of a book printed in the author's lifetime is as serious a defect for modern as for older authors.

To take a small but significant example, the proofreading of F. Scott Fitzgerald's *This Side of Paradise* was careless in the first printing, and changes in the plates were made partly by the author and partly by the publisher in the fourth and seventh impressions. A few of these alterations, presumably made by the publisher, mistook the sense and created errors from correct readings. An editor would need to reject these in favour of the correct first-printing readings, to accept the corrected and revised readings by the author and publisher from the later printings, and then to make a variety of further corrections himself before arriving at a definitive text. In more complex form, no one edition of Joyce's *Ulysses* contains all of his desired readings; on the occasion when he went over the text in correction he unfortunately chose a corrupt edition and did not alter all its unauthoritative changes from the first-edition readings or notice all the first-edition errors that had been perpetuated. Any editor of Eliot or of Yeats would need to disentangle the author's corrections and alterations in revised editions from errors developed in the course of various printings, which were overlooked. Fidelity to one printing or edition, early or late, cannot serve to establish a modern author's text.

In the 17th century Dryden partly revised the second edition (1668) of *The Indian Emperour* and more rigorously the third edition (1670). The fourth and fifth editions of 1670 derived in order from the corrected third, but the sixth edition (1681) reverted to the second (1668); thereafter all texts of Dryden followed this family and ignored the corrected third edition, whose line terminated with the fifth edition. Since no Dryden editor before the 1950s undertook to collate all the early texts, the authoritative revisions of the third edition remained unknown, and the edited texts, based on the 1701 folio, not only retained most of the corruptions found in this 13th edition but also revealed only the intermediate revised state of the text as transmitted in the second-edition family line.

A typical example of failure to observe the primary rules of textual criticism in the analysis of all editions occurred in the text of Percy Bysshe Shelley's *Posthumous Poems*. In the first edition of 1824, edited by Shelley's wife Mary, an errata leaf containing 24 alterations, including a missing line, was added to the last copies to be bound up. This leaf, being uncommon, was overlooked by all Shelley's editors, although utilized to a greater or lesser extent in the various pirated editions that followed soon after the publication of the volume. When Mrs. Shelley came to edit the revised collected edition of 1839, by bad luck she chose one of the pirated texts into which various corruptions had entered. Thus, although she collated her proofs against her manuscripts, not only did she overlook three of the errata-leaf corrections omitted in the pirated edition but she also passed some of the piracy's corruptions, notably the reading from "Stanzas Written in Dejection, near Naples," "The breath of the moist air is light" for the errata-leaf version of this missing line, "The breath of the moist earth is light." The variant "air" appears first in the unauthoritative Galignani text of 1834, to be transmitted thence to Mrs. Shelley's 1839 edition. All Shelley editors, who sheeplike followed the supposedly authoritative 1839 text in the belief that Mrs. Shelley's attestation had been given to it and hence there was no need to inquire into its copy and method of printing, have reproduced as authentic a considerable number of errors that can be demonstrated to have arisen in the pirated texts of Galignani and of Ascham used by Mrs. Shelley as the basic printer's copy.

The nearer machine printing approaches modern times and routine publishing procedures, the less need is there to inquire into the authority of the manuscript originally used as printer's copy, although the copy for any subsequent revised edition must always be identified and its relation to previous editions scrupulously analyzed. For books of the 16th, 17th and 18th centuries, however, when the personal characteristics of the compositor are likely to interfere in an important manner with the reproduction in faithful detail of the underlying manuscript, the distinction of printer's from author's characteristics is of real moment. Two considerations operate. First, in texts dating from the time when authors frequently did not read proof and the printing-house proofreading was casual, a study of the printer may reveal whether difficulties in the text are to be emended in one direction or another in accord with what has been determined about the capabilities of the identified compositor concerned. It is known that Jaggard's compositor A of the Shakespeare First Folio of 1623 was more faithful to his copy, generally speaking, than compositor B. Hence an emendation must pass sterner tests to be accepted in an A section of the Folio than in a B section, or in the pages set by what seems to be a very inaccurate apprentice, compositor E, first identified by C. J. K. Hinman in 1956.

Second, if the veil of print can be pierced, the critic may be able to make various important assumptions about the authority of a text according as he can estimate the nature of the lost manuscript underlying the earliest print or any later revision. Once it could be determined that a particular scribe, Ralph Crane, transcribed the manuscript used by the Folio printer for *The Merry Wives of Windsor,* certain very puzzling characteristics of that text were no longer obscure. What texts of Shakespeare were set from his autograph papers, and what from scribal transcripts, is an inquiry that was scientifically tackled only after World War II.

The question of the copy underlying a print is often as acute in the case of a revision as in the original edition. For example, if the Folio text of *Hamlet* was set from an independent manuscript, common readings between the Second Quarto and the Folio are presumptively authorial, given the collateral theory that the Second Quarto was set from autograph papers. On the other hand, if, as has been argued, the Folio printer's copy was a Second Quarto that had been annotated by a scribe comparing it with the manuscript in the theatrical company's possession, a shared reading like "pious bonds" (assumed manuscript reading: "bands") for "pious bauds" ("bawds") could have perpetuated in the Folio an error of the Second Quarto, provided the scribe overlooked it. Hence the authority possessed by any Folio reading is much affected by what can be established about the nature of the printer's copy for the Folio text, a subject still in dispute.

Such a determination would not automatically settle in any given case whether the Folio or the Second Quarto variant reading was the authoritative one. But a critic who comes to the final stage in the establishment of a text—the synthesis of readings if there is more than one text possessing authority, followed in any case by independent emendation—is in a better position if he has thoroughly worked out the detailed history of the text as a guide and limitation to the exercise of his critical or literary judgment than if he relies almost exclusively on his sympathetic acquaintance with the characteristics of an author and his period.

Bibliography.—W. W. Greg, *The Calculus of Variants* (1927), "The Rationale of Copy-Text," *Studies in Bibliography,* iii (1950), *The Editorial Problem in Shakespeare* (1951); J. Burke Severs, "Quentin's Theory of Textual Criticism," *English Institute Annual: 1941* (1942); Archibald A. Hill, "Some Postulates for Distributional Study of Texts," *Studies in Bibliography,* iii (1950); Fredson Bowers, "Some Relation of Bibliography to Editorial Problems," *Studies in Bibliography,* iii (1950), *On Editing Shakespeare and the Elizabethan Dramatists* (1955).
(F. T. B.; X.)

**THACKERAY, WILLIAM MAKEPEACE** (1811–1863), author of two of the greatest historical novels in English, *Vanity Fair* and *Henry Esmond;* and of the "Pendennis" sequence of contemporary narratives, which give a brilliant imaginative portrayal of the English upper middle class at its most powerful and prosperous period. In the two historical novels a steady narrative style helps to give a sense of the passage of time both in the characters' lives and in the period in which they live; in the "Pendennis" sequence realism is relieved by a style that conceals a highly organized, complex prose technique beneath apparent casualness. Thackeray's personal views, directly expressed in the essays published as *The Roundabout Papers* (1863; *Cornhill Magazine,* 1860–63), are among the few intimate expressions we have of the mid-Victorian outlook.

THE BETTMANN ARCHIVE

THACKERAY, FROM A CHALK DRAWING BY SAMUEL LAURENCE, 1848

**Life.**—Thackeray was born in Calcutta on July 18, 1811, the only son of Richmond Thackeray, an administrator in the East India Company. His father died in 1815, and in 1816 Thackeray was sent home to England. His mother joined him only in 1820, having married (1817) an engineering officer with whom she had been in love before she met Richmond Thackeray. It has been suggested that this separation, lonely years in private schools (followed by an unhappy period at the Charterhouse, 1822–28), and the sharing of his mother's affections, may have developed the tendency to melancholy which, combined with a strong sense of humour, inclined him to irony.

At Trinity College, Cambridge (1828–30), he was happy, however. He went down without taking a degree, and (1831–33) studied law at the Middle Temple, London. Later, he thought of painting as a profession: his artistic gifts are seen in his letters and many of his early writings, which are amusingly and energetically illustrated. All his efforts at this time have a dilettante air, understandable in a young man who, on coming of age, had inherited £20,000 from his father. He soon got through his money, some in gambling and unlucky speculation; some in the failure (1830–34) of the great India agency houses. While studying art in Paris, in 1836 he married a penniless Irish girl, and his stepfather bought a newspaper so that he could remain there as its correspondent. After its failure (1837) he took his wife back to Bloomsbury, London, and became a professional journalist.

Of three daughters, one died in infancy (1839); and in 1840, after her last confinement, Mrs. Thackeray lost her reason. She never recovered and long survived her husband, living with friends in the country. Thackeray was, in effect, a widower, relying much on club life, and gradually giving more and more attention to his daughters, for whom he established a home in London in 1846. His one serious attachment, to Mrs. Henry Brookfield, can be traced in his letters. She was the wife of a friend of his Cambridge days and during Thackeray's "widowerhood," when, although he was surrounded by friends and a well-known figure in society, his life lacked an emotional centre, he found one in the Brookfield home. Her husband's insistence in 1851 that their friendship should end was a grief greater than any he had known since his wife's loss of reason.

He tried to find consolation in travel, lecturing in the United States on "The English Humorists of the 18th Century" (1852–53; publ. 1853) and on "The Four Georges" (1855–56; publ. 1860). But after 1856 he settled in London. He stood unsuccessfully for parliament in 1857; quarreled with Dickens, formerly a friendly rival, in the so-called "Garrick Club Affair" (1858); and in 1860 founded the *Cornhill Magazine,* becoming editor. He died in London on Dec. 24, 1863.

**Works.**—*Early Writings.*—The 19th century was the age of the magazine, developed to meet the demand for family reading among the growing middle class. In the late 1830s Thackeray contributed to *Fraser's Magazine, The New Monthly Magazine,* and, later, to *Punch,* concealing his success under pseudonyms (Mr. Michael Angelo Titmarsh, Fitz-Boodle, The Fat Contributor, Ikey Solomons, etc.). He collected the best of these early writings in *Miscellanies* (4 vol., 1855–57). These include *The Yellowplush Correspondence,* the memoirs and diary of a young cockney footman written in his own vocabulary and style (serially, 1837–38; as *The Yellowplush Papers,* 1852); *Major Gahagan* (1838–39), a fantasy of soldiering in India; *Catherine* (1839–40), a burlesque of the popular "Newgate novels" of romanticized crime and low life, and itself a good realistic crime story; *The History of Samuel Titmarsh and the Great Hoggarty Diamond* (1841; as *The Great Hoggarty Diamond,* 1848), an earlier version of the young married life described in *Philip* (*see* below); and *The Luck of Barry Lyndon* (1844; revised as *The Memoirs of Barry Lyndon,* 1856), an 18th-century historical novel, his first full-length work. This is excellent, speedy, satirical narrative until the final sadistic scenes, and is a trial run for the great historical novels, especially *Vanity Fair* (written immediately after it), which also takes Western Europe for its scene.

*The Book of Snobs* (1848; complete 1842) collects articles that had appeared successfully in *Punch* (as "The Snobs of England, by one of themselves," 1846–47): sketches of London characters showing virtuosity in quick character-drawing, still amusing because we still meet people very like them. Another form of commercial publishing he exploited at this time was the Christmas book. *The Rose and the Ring,* Thackeray's Christmas book for 1855, remains excellent entertainment, as do some of his verses: like many good prose writers, he had a facility in writing light verse and ballads.

*Vanity Fair.*—With *Vanity Fair* (1847–48), the first work published under his own name, Thackeray adopted the monthly part system of publishing a novel so successfully used by Dickens. The story is that of two London middle-class families at the beginning of the 19th century. Like some of his earlier works, it depicts with humour and insight growing prosperity and dramatic fall, but it is not wholly tragedy nor, despite its humour, comedy. It is "A Novel without a Hero"—its subtitle when published as a book (1848)—but the two girls who in turn hold the centre of the stage are not heroines. The novel is deliberately antiheroic: Thackeray states that "the Art of Novels is . . . to convey . . . the sentiment of reality"; and that in this novel his object is to "indicate . . . that we are for the most part . . . foolish and selfish people . . . all eager after vanities."

The wealthy, wellborn, passive Amelia Sedley and the ambitious, energetic and scheming, provocative, and essentially amoral Rebecca (Becky) Sharp (daughter of a poor drawingmaster) are contrasted in their fortunes and reactions to life, but the contrast of their characters is not the simple one between moral good and evil: both are presented with dispassionate sympathy. Becky is the mainspring of the book's simple action, the character round whom all the men play their parts against their upper middle class and aristocratic backgrounds. Amelia marries George Osborne, but George, just before the Battle of Waterloo (in which he is killed), is ready to desert his young wife for Becky, who has fought her way up through society to marriage with Rawdon Crawley, a young officer of good family. Crawley, disillusioned, finally leaves her: a parting described with poignancy. In the end, apparently, virtue triumphs, Amelia marries her lifelong admirer,

Colonel Dobbin, and Becky settles down to genteel living and charitable works.

The rich movement and colour of this panorama of early 19th-century society make *Vanity Fair* Thackeray's greatest achievement; the narrative skill, subtle characterization, and descriptive power make it one of the outstanding novels of its period. But *Vanity Fair* is more than a portrayal and imaginative analysis of a particular society. Throughout we are made subtly aware of the ambivalence of human motives, and so are prepared for Thackeray's conclusion: "Ah! *Vanitas Vanitatum*! Which of us is happy in this world? which of us has his desire, or having it, is satisfied?" It is its tragic irony that makes *Vanity Fair* an evaluation of human ambition and experience, and one of the world's great novels.

BY COURTESY OF THE TRUSTEES OF THE BRITISH MUSEUM; PHOTOGRAPHS, JOHN R. FREEMAN

(LEFT) "MRS. RAWDON'S DEPARTURE FROM PARIS," ONE OF THACKERAY'S DRAWINGS FOR "VANITY FAIR" PUBLISHED IN THE 1848 EDITION. (RIGHT) "LORD CRABS SAYING GOODNIGHT TO LADY AND MISS GRIFFIN," AN ORIGINAL DRAWING BY THACKERAY FOR "THE YELLOWPLUSH PAPERS"

*The Contemporary Novels.*—Successful and famous, Thackeray went on to exploit two lines of development opened up in *Vanity Fair:* a gift for painting the London scene and for writing historical novels with a sense of sinking through time to demonstrate the connection between past and present. He began with the first, writing *The History of Pendennis* (1848–50) and, over a decade, its sequels, *The Newcomes* (1853–55) and *The Adventures of Philip on his way Through the World* . . . (1861–62). These three novels are written, as Thackeray says, as "a sort of confidential talk. . . ." The manner is diffuse, and he refuses to use the tension of suspense: his novels have the accidental appearance of life, in whose chances we discern inevitability only in looking back. Arthur Pendennis (Pen), who grows up in the first novel, becomes narrator of the second two. In the first we watch him learn the ways of the world. Thackeray's own apprenticeship to life is fully exploited, and the world of mid-19th-century society—from Kensington to Brighton and Baden to Rome—is richly revived. There is a wealth of supporting characters: the hero's uncle, Major Pendennis, a man of the world; the Irish adventurer Captain Shannon; the young lawyer, Harry Warrington. The women are less attractive, less real: Pen's insipid mother; the actress "The Fotheringay"; the women he might have married. Laura, the woman he marries, comes into her own later when the Regency world of *The Book of Snobs* has been left behind, and we have settled into the Victorian world of sentiment.

In *The Newcomes,* Thackeray drew on recollections of his Anglo-Indian relations and their metropolitan friends. Thomas Newcome goes to school at the Charterhouse, joins the Indian army and becomes a colonel, and then returns to London to be with his son Clive. Clive, the novel's unheroic, attractive "hero," falls in love with his cousin Ethel, but marries Rose Mackenzie, and finds his mother-in-law "master" of his household. The story develops as a series of complications in the Newcome family, who are London bankers. The selfish, greedy, cold-hearted Barnes Newcome, Ethel's father and head of the family (perhaps the only one of Thackeray's characters drawn almost without redeeming qualities), intrigues against Clive and the colonel; the colonel invests his fortune imprudently and ends as a pensioner in Greyfriars, the Charterhouse almshouse. Rosey dies in childbirth, and Arthur Pendennis' narrative ends with the colonel's death, his last word being "Adsum," the Charterhouse answer to roll call. This, a deathbed scene described with deep feeling that avoids sentimentality, is one of the most famous in Victorian fiction. In a short epilogue Thackeray tells us that Clive and Ethel eventually marry, and are "happier than they would have been had they married at first"—but this, he says, is in Fable-land, and "anything may happen in Fable-land."

Unlike *Vanity Fair, The Newcomes* is dominated by the "good" characters, but even the Colonel and Ethel are not perfect. The Colonel's wish to manage Clive's life, his bitterness against Ethel, are "out of character" with his simple goodness—"his . . . life . . . brought out faults for which there had hitherto been no occasion"—and Ethel, despite her love for Clive, twice yields to family pride by becoming engaged to men of wealth and rank. And in them Thackeray has succeeeded in drawing virtuous characters who are yet likable: they are all that Thackeray's readers could have wished to be.

In *Philip,* the weakest of the sequence, the hero, a gentle character, suffers in the unsympathetic London society. The book contains an early description of the unhappy Victorian father-son relationship, and the love story is unfolded with Victorian sentimentality: but there is a wealth of characters drawn with sympathy and humour.

*Henry Esmond.*—Turning to the historical novel with *The History of Henry Esmond, Esq.* (3 vol., 1852) Thackeray gave his plot a much more formal structure. The story, narrated by Esmond, begins when he is 12, in 1691, and ends in 1718. Its complexity of incident is given unity by Beatrix and Esmond, who stand out against a background of London society and the political life of the time. Great historical figures—the Pretender and the duke of Marlborough (with whom Esmond serves from Blenheim to Malplaquet)—are introduced, but are prudently kept on the fringe of the story. Beatrix dominates the book. Seen first as a charming child, she develops beauty combined with a power fatal to the men she loves: one of Thackeray's great creations, she is a "heroine" of a new type, emotionally complex and compelling, not a pattern of virtue. Esmond, romantic in love as in politics, falls in love with her, but is finally disillusioned. Befriended as an orphan by Lord and Lady Castlewood, Beatrix' parents, to whom he is related, as a boy he adores Lady Castlewood as a mother and eventually, in his maturity, the mother becomes his wife.

Written in a brilliant pastiche of 18th-century prose, the novel is one of the best evocations in English of the atmosphere of a past age. It was not well received, however: Esmond's marriage to Lady Castlewood was criticized. George Eliot called it "the most uncomfortable book you can imagine." But it has come to be accepted as one of the great English historical novels.

*Last Works.*—In *The Virginians* (1857–59), a sequel to *Esmond* (which ends with his departure, with his wife, to Virginia), Thackeray seems to have had his U.S. readers in mind, for the long panoramic opening is a generous picture of the young American nation. His last novels, *Lovel the Widower* (1860) and the fragment *Denis Duval* (1864), were serialized in the *Cornhill.* The first is another study of the power some women can achieve over men; the second has the atmosphere and narrative style that became popular later in the century.

**Reputation.**—In his own time Thackeray was regarded as the only possible rival to Dickens. His pictures of contemporary life were obviously real and were accepted by the middle classes, who wanted to model themselves on the "best people": *i.e.,* the upper middle classes. He provided a mirror for his friends in the clubs and in the royal borough of Kensington, and an example for people in lesser London boroughs. Though he resented the severely restrictive conventions imposed on the Victorian novelist he schooled himself to accept and work within them. A great professional, he provided novels, stories, essays, and verses for his audience; he toured as a lecturer, a national figure. He wrote to be read aloud in the long Victorian family evenings, and his prose has the lucidity, spontaneity, and pace of good reading material. His great reputation, unchallenged to the end of the century, then declined, but in the 1950s began to rise again. He offers particular pleasure to the reader who enjoys sensitive pictures of the human scene by an artist of acute and ironic sensitivity.

BIBLIOGRAPHY.—*Editions:* The standard edition of the *Works* is the 17-vol. Oxford edition, with introductions to each volume, by G. Saintsbury (1908); introductions reprinted in Saintsbury's *A Consideration of Thackeray* (1931). It should be supplemented by *The Letters and Private Papers of William Makepeace Thackeray,* 4 vol. (1945–46), and *Thackeray's Contributions to the Morning Chronicle* (1955), both collected and ed. by G. N. Ray. *See* also *Henry Esmond* (1950) and *The Rose and the Ring* (1947), ed. by Ray; and *Vanity Fair,* ed. by G. and K. Tillotson (1963).

*Biography and Criticism:* The standard life is Ray's *Thackeray:* vol. i, *The Uses of Adversity 1811–1846* (1955), ii, *The Age of Wisdom 1847–1863* (1958). The most useful modern study is G. Tillotson, *Thackeray the Novelist* (1954). Ray's *The Buried Life: a Study of the Relation between Thackeray's Fiction and his Personal History* (1952) contains valuable critical data. Among shorter studies *see* Lord David Cecil, in *Early Victorian Novelists* (1934); L. Brander, *Thackeray,* Writers and Their Work Series (1959); G. M. Young, in *Last Essays* (1950), on the *Letters;* and, on *Vanity Fair,* K. Tillotson in *Novels of the 1840s* (1954; rev. ed. 1961). There is no definitive bibliography. (LA. B.)

**THADDAEUS, SAINT,** is listed among the apostles of Jesus in Mark 3:18 and Matt. 10:3. In the Western Church he is identified with Judas (of James). The Greek Orthodox Church regards them as separate persons and celebrates the feast of Thaddaeus on Aug. 21. *See* JUDAS, SAINT.

**THAILAND** (formerly SIAM) is an independent constitutional kingdom occupying an area of 198,455 sq.mi. in the centre of continental Southeast Asia. The country lies to the west, north, and east of the Gulf of Siam, an arm of the South China Sea. On the southeast it is bounded by Cambodia; on the east and northeast by Laos; on the west, north, and northwest by Burma; on the southwest by the Andaman Sea, a part of the Indian Ocean; and on the southern extremity by Malaysia. The country's greatest length is approximately 1,024 mi. (1,648 km.) and its greatest width is about 485 mi. (780 km.). At the Isthmus of Kra in peninsular Thailand it is only around 30 mi. (48 km.) wide.

This article is divided into the following sections and subsections:



## I. PHYSICAL GEOGRAPHY

**1. Topography.**—With its crest forming a water divide and the boundary between Thailand and Burma, the Tenasserim Range continues southward to form the backbone of peninsular Thailand and Malaysia. Most of that part of northern Thailand that lies between the Salween River on the west and the Mekong River on the east has an elevation of from 656 to 3,280 ft. (200 to 1,000 m.). Within this deeply dissected upland the major mountain ridge tops and major river valleys are aligned in a general north-south direction. Four large rivers, the Ping, Wang, Yom, and Nan, originate in this area. Flowing southward, they unite to form the Mae Nam Chao Phraya, the largest river system in Thailand. The watershed of this river is almost surrounded by a U-shaped rim of hills and mountains composed of the Tenasserim Range on the west, the dissected upland on the north, and the Petchabun Mountains on the east. The latter form the boundary between an alluvial plain built by the Mae Nam Chao Phraya in a now-filled upper arm of the Gulf of Siam, and an uplifted and tilted plain drained by the Mun River, a tributary of the Mekong.

This uplifted plain is called Northeast Thailand by the Thais and is erroneously called the Korat Plateau by many foreigners. Northeast Thailand is not a plateau but a gently undulating plain with an elevation of less than 656 ft. (200 m.) above sea level. It is drained by river valleys that are comparatively shallow (seldom, if anywhere, is there a local relief of 500 ft. [152 m.] between the upland surface and the adjacent river valleys). The hilly and mountainous land between the Gulf of Siam and Cambodia is part of the Cardamom Mountains. The smallest physiographic region with only four provinces and 6,583 sq.mi. (17,050 sq.km.), Southeast Thailand has only $\frac{1}{33}$ of the country's area but has distinct boundaries. It is bounded on the west and south by the ocean, on the north by the Thailand-Cambodian lowland corridor, and on the east by the Thailand-Cambodian boundary. This southeastern area receives nearly twice as much rain as the Central Plain and is generally covered with a tropical rain forest type of vegetation. Between the hill region and the Dong Rek scarp, which forms the southern boundary of Northeast Thailand, a narrow but important lowland extends eastward from the Bangkok delta plain to the Tonle Sap (Great Lake) area in Cambodia. Through this Thailand-Cambodian corridor have marched the armies of these two countries as attacks were made on one or the other's capitals.

The alluvial soils deposited on the river deltas and floodplains are the most productive because the rivers provide water for irrigation. Fruits and vegetables are grown on colluvial and residual slope soils which have accumulated at the foot and on the lower slopes of the hills and mountains. Clay soils are preferred because they are impervious and hold the water in the diked fields. Sandy soils do not retain water and are highly leached.

FIG. 1.—MAJOR CITIES AND RIVERS OF THAILAND

**2. Climate.**—Located in continental Southeast Asia, Thailand lies in that portion of the world affected by the so-called tropical monsoon climate. Consequently, all of the country north of Chumphon Province has a rainy season during the months from May through October when the prevailing winds are from the southwest, and a dry season from December through April when the prevailing winds blow from the northeast. Unfortunately, the staff-shaped pattern of hills and mountains which enclose the plains of Thailand, Laos, and Cambodia places most of Thailand on the leeward or rain-shadow side of the mountains regardless of the direction from which the prevailing winds blow. For example, from May through October the southwest winds blow onshore and drop more than 100 in. (2,540 mm.) of rain into the paddy fields of the Irrawaddy River delta in Burma; however, during the same period only about 50 in. (1,270 mm.) fall on the Thailand side of the mountains.

Chumphon and the other 13 provinces (*changwads*) of peninsular Thailand have a tropical rain forest type of climate, with the rainfall being distributed throughout the year. The other 57 provinces of Thailand have a tropical savanna type of climate. In these provinces about 85% of the rain falls during the summer monsoon and the dry months are extremely dry. Twenty-three provinces during their four consecutive driest months receive less than two inches of rain. This lack of precipitation during the dry season helps to create serious water problems and is an important factor in limiting most settlement to the floodplains near the permanent streams.

Except infrequently in isolated mountain areas of northern Thailand, frost and snow do not occur. Temperatures are above 10° C (50° F) on the plains, and crops can be grown in any month if moisture is available. Temperatures below 18° C (64° F) and over 38° C (100° F) are rare. The coolest temperatures occur in December and January. Temperatures are uncomfortable during the hot dry season of February through May, when strong, dry winds blow across nonpeninsular Thailand.

**3. Vegetation.**—Although about one-half of Thailand is in public domain and classified as forest, most of the valuable trees have been removed. The chief categories of forest cover are the deciduous and the evergreen (including coniferous forests). The deciduous forests, which occupy about two-thirds of the forest area, can be subdivided into two types: deciduous *Dipterocarpus* and mixed deciduous. This latter forest contains the teak stands, several other commercial trees, and bamboo.

**4. Animal Life.**—Most of the wild animals and birds occupy the forests and the river valleys, but their numbers are decreasing. Among the mammals are elephants; members of the cat family (including tigers, leopards, and panthers); the deer family (including the hog and mouse deer); and various types of shore, river, and swamp life ranging from crocodiles and giant green sea turtles to various types of reptiles, including numerous snakes (13 species of poisonous snakes) and lizards. Included among the many varieties of birds are martins, babblers, and drongos. Although freshwater and saltwater fish are abundant, the intermittent and erratic flow of the rivers limits the number of freshwater fish. Some of the fish have the ability to bury themselves in the mud and live through the dry season.

## II. GEOGRAPHIC REGIONS

On the bases of topography, climate, vegetation, soil, man's use of the land, continuity, and statistical convenience, Thailand may be divided into four regions: (1) Central Plain; (2) Northeast Thailand; (3) North Thailand; and (4) South Thailand.

**1. Central Plain.**—With about 39,992 sq.mi. (103,579 sq.km.) in 26 provinces, the Central Plain contains about 20% of the country's area and about 31% of its people according to the 1960 census. Bangkok, the nation's capital and by far its largest city with a metropolitan population of 1,880,606 (1964) is located in the heart of this region. Although the region receives an average rainfall of somewhat over 50 in. (1,270 mm.), and good yields from long-maturing rice varieties need 72 in. (1,829 mm.) of precipitation, the Central Plain is the rice basket of Thailand, a circumstance possible because the rain is supplemented by irrigation water from the rivers which flow from North Thailand to the Bangkok delta plain. The dark heavy clay soil of this plain is the best in Thailand partly because it reduces water seepage from the paddy fields. Over two-fifths of the nation's rice cropland is in this region and more than half of the rice produced is grown here. The region also accounts for about four-fifths of the cassava, two-fifths of the maize, and over half of the castor beans produced. With the exception of mining, all economic, social, religious, political, and many other phases of Thai life are concentrated here. The Central Plain is literally the core of Thailand.

**2. Northeast Thailand.**—With 65,724 sq.mi. (170,226 sq.km.) in 15 provinces, Northeast Thailand contains about 33% of the country's area and 34% of its people. With a population density of 137 per square mile, it ranks below that of the Central Plain (which is 152) but above the average for the country which is 132. The population density per arable square mile and pressure of population on land and resources, however, is higher here than in any region in Thailand. Although this region receives an average of 57 in. (1,458 mm.) of rain per year, most of the land is not well suited for rice or other forms of agricultural production because most of the soils are too sandy and do not retain water that does fall and, moreover, the annual rainfall is erratic. The best soils are in the valley floors; but the valleys are shallow and narrow, the adjacent streams unpredictable in flow, and governmental development irrigation projects small in size.

Although about 44% of the total rice acreage is in Northeast Thailand, because of crop failures and low yields the area produces only about 30% of the annual crop. This region excels the others in the production of fibre used for manufacture, primarily gunny bags, and for export. Here is grown 97% of the jute, 93% of the kenaf, and 58% of the ramie. Almost all of the people are engaged in agriculture, and in 1964 the two largest cities of the region, Nakhon Ratchasima (Nakhornratchsima) and Ubon (Ubonratchthani) had populations of 55,210 and 30,059, respectively.

**3. North Thailand.**—With 65,639 sq.mi. (170,006 sq.km.) in 16 provinces, North Thailand has over 33% of the country's area and about 22% of the population. Here the population density averages about 85 per square mile, but the population-arable land ratio is much higher because cultivation is primarily limited to large valley floors, which are narrow and few in number. Although this region has only about 7% of the total rice acreage, it accounts for about 12% of the annual production. Evapotranspiration is lower here, yields are higher, and on some land two crops are grown during the year. This section produces about 63% of the peanuts, 45% of the maize, 40% of the kapok, 39% of the cotton, and 14% of the ramie grown in Thailand. The importance of maize in the economy of this region and as a national export has increased during the last decade, as that of teak as a national export has declined. Two of the greatest contributions this region makes to the national economy are: (1) irrigation water for the Central Plain; and (2) hydroelectric power from the Bhumibhol Dam generators under the operational jurisdiction of the Yanhee Electricity Authority.

**4. South Thailand.**—The smallest region, with 27,100 sq.mi. (70,189 sq.km.) in 14 peninsular provinces, South Thailand contains somewhat less than 14% of the country's area and about 12% of its people. This region produces over 90% of the country's natural rubber and practically all of its tin. Two industrial plants built in the 1960s are the tin smelter at Phuket and the thermal electric power plant at Krabi operated by the Lignite Authority. Modern all-weather hard-surfaced highways have been built joining the region and the cities on the two coasts with the Central Plain and the Bangkok metropolitan area.

## III. THE PEOPLE

A large majority of the population of Thailand are culturally Thai; *i.e.,* identify themselves as Thai, speak one of the Thai dialects, and behave in the Thai manner. Cultural differences among the country's four main regions—the central, south, northeast, and north—are but variations within a single basic culture.

The physical characteristics of the Thai are similar to those of the majority populations in most Southeast Asian countries. They are moderate to small in stature and weight, round-headed, and their noses tend to be flattish. They have medium light skin unless exposed to direct sunlight in out-of-door jobs. Their hair is lank, thick, and black, and individuals with wavy-curled hair are declining. The colour of the eyes is generally brownish to black. These general characteristics do not sharply distinguish them from such peoples as the Burmese or Vietnamese.

Thai families average about five to six members, usually limited to parents and children. Extended family arrangements and polygamy are no longer commonly practised. While there is some preference for matrilocal postmarital residence, young married couples are free to settle wherever they please. Outside the old elite there is no concern for ancestry, and family names, instituted by royal decree only in 1916, are little used. Upper-class marriages involve a colourful religious ceremony, and a small religious rite is often performed for others. There are no legal impediments to divorce. Child training among the Thai is gradual and permissive. Within the family there is near equality and minimum division of labour between the sexes. Sons and daughters have equal inheritance rights. The dead are usually cremated.

Buddhism is at the core of Thai culture. More than 93% of the Thai ethnic group were adherents of Buddhism in the 1960s, and the country boasts at least 20,000 Buddhist wats (temple-monastery complexes). The local wat is the hub of community life in every village. The order of Buddhist monks is a major social institution, and the yellow robe worn by its members carries high prestige. Ideally all males join the order in early adulthood, and in fact a majority become monks or novices at least for a short period. Monks are celibate, live exclusively from alms, and eat no solid food after midday. They provide opportunities to laymen for merit making, perhaps the chief manifestation of Buddhist doctrine. Every religiously sanctioned act, from feeding a monk to building a new wat, accumulates merit to assure moral ascendancy and comfortable life in subsequent reincarnations. The Buddhist proscription against killing is taken very seriously by the Thai.

Animistic and Brahmanic elements are closely interwoven with Buddhism in the religious life of the average Thai, though he is little aware of the distinctions among these traditions. In times of personal crisis most Thai propitiate spirits by prayer and offerings. Brahmanic elements are dominant in such rites of passage as the topknot-cutting and marriage ceremonies, not to mention the elaborate ceremonies of state. The concept of heavens and hells in the popular religion, is Buddhistic in origin.

Of the non-Thai groups, only the immigrant Indians and Pakistanis, the few westerners, and the small remnant of Negritoid Semang in the southern peninsula have physical types readily distinguishable from the Thai. Southeastern Chinese, who form the largest minority, differ only slightly in physical type from the Thai majority. Prior to 1910 the grandchildren of Chinese immigrants were as a rule completely assimilated to the Thai population, but the assimilation rate subsequently declined with the rise of nationalism, of Chinese community schools, and of female Chinese immigration.

About seven-eighths of Thailand's Muslim population are Malays living near the southern border. Islam has provided an effective focus for Malay resistance to governmental attempts at forced

(LEFT) CALOGERO CASCIO—RAPHO GUILLUMETTE; (ABOVE) ERNST HASS—MAGNUM

(LEFT) SPECTATORS AT A MATCH BETWEEN TWO SIAMESE FIGHTING FISH, A SPORT UNIQUE TO THAILAND; GAMBLING ON THE OUTCOME OF THE CONTEST IS POPULAR; (ABOVE) THAI BOXING, A POPULAR SPORT IN WHICH KICKING AS WELL AS PUNCHING IS LEGAL assimilation. The small Vietnamese minority, consisting largely of postwar refugees, is still less assimilated, and many have been repatriated. Other culturally advanced ethnic groups in Thailand, including the Cambodians and Mons, are predominantly Theravada Buddhists and as such are more readily assimilated.

Most of the Thais speak a dialect of the Thai-Kadai language group with the greatest number speaking Thai, a much smaller number in the northeast using a Lao dialect and only a small number in the north using a Shan dialect. In peninsular Thailand the Javanese Malay dialect of the Indonesian language group is used in provinces adjacent to or near the Thailand-Malaysian border. Also in western peninsular Thailand and extending northward in the hills and mountains west of the Central Plain, the Karen dialect of the Tibeto-Burman language group is used.

About 280,000 or 1% of the Thai people belong to tribal groups who live in the mountains. Some of the villages are located in mountain slopes at altitudes of 3,000–4,500 ft. (900–1,300 m.); others in relatively isolated forest river valleys. Most of these people live near the northern boundaries of Thailand.

Christians form only a tiny fraction of the total population (0.57% in 1960) and include a disproportionate number of Chinese, tribespeople, and other minorities. While Christian missionaries have had little success in converting ethnic Thais, they have been instrumental in introducing Western ideas and providing modern hospital and educational facilities. (T. F. B.)

## IV. HISTORY

**1. Migrations and Early Settlement.**—Peoples referred to by the Chinese in the 6th century B.C. as the barbarians south of the Yangtze-kiang are thought to have been the Thai (Tai). They and the Chinese bear striking similarities in both physical characteristics and language. As the Chinese extended their control southward the Thai must have gradually moved away in order to maintain their independence. These migrations took them, centuries later, into Tongking, Yünnan, the regions of the upper Mekong and upper Salween rivers, and the wide expanse of hill country covered by the Shan states of Burma. It was a gradual penetration by small groups, part of that almost imperceptible movement which characterized the peopling of the Indochinese Peninsula and the spread of its languages. It is still an open question whether the powerful kingdom of Nanchao, which emerged in the 7th century A.D. in Yünnan, was a Thai creation. Nanchao passed under Chinese suzerainty at the end of the 8th century. Its conquest in 1253 by Kublai Khan and his Mongols, it has been suggested, caused a mass emigration of Thai southward into the lands dominated by the Khmer Empire of Angkor, where ultimately in the middle of the 14th century they founded the kingdoms of Siam and Laos, dominating respectively the valleys of the Mae Nam Chao Phraya and upper Mekong rivers. Before 1253, however, a notable effervescence had begun among the Thai communities on the southern and western borders of Yünnan. Thai states also began to appear in the upper Mekong region and inside the Khmer Empire. In 1238 two Thai chiefs won control over Sukhothai, the capital of its northwestern region, and established what was to become, before the end of the century, the first important centre of Thai power and civilization within the area covered today by the kingdom of Thailand. In 1287, when the Burmese empire of Pagan fell before the Mongols, three powerful Thai rulers, Ramkhaeng of Sukhothai, Mangrai of Chiangrai, soon afterward to found the kingdom of Chiangmai, and Ngam Muang of Payao, concluded a pact of friendship. With Burma in eclipse, and Angkor losing control over its western territories, the time was ripe for a Thai bid for the dominance of both regions.

(LEFT) LUC BOUCHAGE—RAPHO GUILLUMETTE; (ABOVE) PAUL CONKLIN—PIX FROM PUBLIX; (BOTTOM LEFT) INGER ABRAHAMSEN—RAPHO GUILLUMETTE; (BOTTOM RIGHT) JULES BUCHER—PHOTO RESEARCHERS, INC.

(LEFT) WATER PAVILION AT BANG PA IN, ONCE A SUMMER RESIDENCE OF THAI KINGS ON THE MAE NAM CHAO PHRAYA NORTH OF BANGKOK; (ABOVE) FLOATING MARKET ON A CANAL IN BANGKOK; (BOTTOM LEFT) MONK AND VISITORS IN A BUDDHIST TEMPLE AT AYUTTHAYA; (BOTTOM RIGHT) PALM TREES AND RICE FIELDS IN THAILAND'S CENTRAL PLAIN

**2. Expansion: 13th to 15th Centuries.**—Ramkhaeng of Sukhothai expanded his power southward down the Mae Nam Chao Phraya and into the Malay Peninsula, over peoples who had been included in the Mon kingdom of Dvaravati before its conquest by Angkor in the 11th century. Their traditions had a profound effect upon Siam. Sukhothai under Ramkhaeng (1275–*c.* 1317) was the cradle of Siamese civilization, in which Mon-Khmer political, artistic, and literary traditions and Hinayana Buddhism of the Sinhalese pattern played a dominant role. In a political sense, however, the kingdom of Siam dates from the foundation of Ayutthaya in 1350, which in a very short time became the centre of one of the strongest states in mainland Southeast Asia, compelling the allegiance of the whole area comprising Thailand today, except the Chiangmai state in the far north, and in addition including the portion of modern Burma from Moulmein southward. Only the rise of Muslim Malacca early in the 15th century prevented Ayutthaya from dominating the entire Malay Peninsula. Moreover, its foundation ushered in a long period of intensive struggle with Cambodia, which fatally weakened the Khmer Empire. Cambodia might have been added to the Ayutthaya kingdom had the Siamese not been engaged at the same time in incessant, though unsuccessful, struggles to conquer Chiangmai, and in attempts, decisively defeated in the 1450s, to reduce Malacca. In the midst of all these wars, Siam produced a notable administrator-king, Boroma Trailokanat (1448–88), whose regulation of the land system and reorganization of the central civil and military administration set their seal upon the social life of the country until the great changes in Chulalongkorn's reign during the last quarter of the 19th century.

**3. Burmese Conquest and Recovery.**—When Affonso de Albuquerque, after Portugal's conquest of Malacca in 1511, sent a Portuguese embassy to Ayutthaya, Siam was the most important state in Southeast Asia. Shortly afterward, however, the reunification of Burma under the Toungoo dynasty led to attempts by the Burmese to dominate all the neighbouring Thai states and kingdoms. Chiangmai was conquered, all the Shan states now forming part of the Union of Burma became tributary, the Laos kingdom of Lan Chang (later Luang Prabang) was overrun, and Siam itself was subjugated in 1564 and again in 1569, and for 15 years was held by the Burmese. Siam was saved from this predicament by a great national leader, Phra Naret. In a long and difficult struggle, made all the more difficult by constant Cambodian raids, he set his country free and in 1590 succeeded to its throne as King Naresuan. Three years later he turned the tables on Cambodia by capturing its capital, Lovek, and making it a vassal state.

**4. Foreign Contacts.**—In the 17th century Siam developed its overseas trade considerably. Both Pattani and Ayutthaya had important commercial connections with China and Japan; early in the century the Dutch and the English opened factories at both places. Siamese missions went to Japan and The Hague. The Dutch established so strong a position at Ayutthaya that the Siamese became uneasy. Therefore, King Narai (Narain, 1657–88) turned to the French for help. The encouragement he gave to the French Société des Missions Etrangères led to a Dutch blockade of the Mae Nam Chao Phraya (1664) and the signing of a treaty giving them the monopoly of Siamese overseas trade. In 1673 Louis XIV's interest in Siam was aroused by the French missionaries who suggested that King Narai might be converted to Christianity. Matters came to a head when the Greek Constantine Phaulkon became a dominant figure in the Siamese government. There were exchanges of diplomatic missions between Ayutthaya and Versailles and in 1687 a plan was set in motion for the conversion of Siam by Jesuits supported by French warships and troops. The arrival of a powerful French squadron late in 1687 and the planting of French garrisons at Bangkok and Mergui caused so much alarm in Siam that when in March 1688 King Narai became mortally ill, Phra Petraja, leader of an antiforeign movement, executed Phaulkon, seized the throne, and forced the French to evacuate the country. The situation was complicated by a short-lived war which arose between the English East India Company and Siam over acts of piracy committed in the Bay of Bengal by ships built at Mergui, flying the Siamese flag, and captained by Englishmen in Phaulkon's employment. The arrival at Mergui of two English frigates in June 1687 with orders from James II for all Englishmen to leave the Siamese service led to a massacre by the Siamese of all the English on shore. These events caused Siam for many years to adopt a rigid attitude of hostility to intercourse with Europeans.

**5. Conflict with Vietnam and Burma.**—In the 18th century an expanding Vietnam was competing with Siam for the Laos states of the upper Mekong and was also challenging the Siamese overlordship of Cambodia. But the gravest danger came from the new Konbaung dynasty of Burma, which revived the policy of subjugating Siam and in 1767 destroyed Ayutthaya and reduced the country to chaos. Siam was saved by Chinese invasions of Burma and by the brilliant leadership of the half-Chinese general Phaya Takh Sin, who reunited the country and founded a new capital at Thonburi (Dhonburi) just across the river from Bangkok. In driving the Burmese out he reasserted Siam's authority over the Laos states and annexed Chiangmai. He also regained control over Cambodia for Siam, taking advantage of the paralysis of Vietnam resulting from the dynastic struggle between the Tay Son brothers and the Nguyen of Hue. In 1782 King Takh Sin became insane and was deposed by General Chakkri, who made Bangkok the national capital and as Rama I (1782–1809) became the founder of the present reigning dynasty. He defended his country with success against another long series of Burmese invasions and raids, but his main efforts were directed to the tasks of internal consolidation. Before he died Siam had become a powerful state once more. It was during this period that Siam first took over from Cambodia the provinces of Battambang and Siem Reap that were later to prove such a bone of contention.

**6. Renewed Relations with the West.**—Rama II's reign (1809–24) was notable for the reopening of relations with the British. As the Burmese threat receded, Siam began to revive its claims to supremacy over the Malay states of the peninsula, and the British, to whom the sultan of Kedah had ceded the island of Penang in 1786 and a strip of the mainland opposite in 1800, were concerned by Siam's deposition of the sultan in 1821 for intriguing with Burma, and by the restrictions placed upon Penang's trade, especially in foodstuffs and tin, with the southern dependencies of Siam. When, however, John Crawfurd was sent to Bangkok in 1822 as the envoy of the government of India, he failed to obtain any concessions.

By the Anglo-Dutch Treaty of 1824 the Dutch withdrew from any further participation in the affairs of the Malay Peninsula, and the British, in possession of Penang, Malacca, and Singapore, were anxious to put an end to Siam's interference in the Malay states, notably Perak and Selangor. This was the main object of Henry Burney's mission to Bangkok in 1825–26. Burney's treaty of 1826 with Rama III (1824–51) had the effect of stopping further Siamese encroachments in western Malaya, but the cultivation of Siamese influence in the eastern states continued and achieved some success in Kelantan and Trengganu. Siam's main expansive efforts, however, were directed elsewhere. Following a revolt by Vientiane, Siam in 1828 extinguished the kingdom and destroyed its capital. Less successful in an armed struggle with Vietnam for the possession of Cambodia, Rama III had to agree in 1845 to a compromise whereby Cambodia came under the joint protection of both powers. Rama III was the last of the traditionalist monarchs who strove to obstruct all Western influence. His half-brother, Mongkut, who succeeded him as Rama IV (1851–68), abandoned the policy of isolation. His treaty of friendship and commerce with Britain in 1855, followed by similar treaties with the United States and most of the European states, opened his country to Western commerce and established the system of foreign consuls exercising extraterritorial jurisdiction. He also began the practice, much extended by his successors, of employing Europeans to reorganize the government services. During his reign Siam's influence over its neighbours suffered serious setbacks. The government of the British Straits Settlements effectively stopped the extension of Siamese control over the eastern Malay states of Trengganu and Pahang and paved the way for the later establishment of British dominance over Malaya.

**7. Conflict with France.**—A more ominous development was France's conquest of Cochin China, which began in 1859, its establishment of a protectorate over Cambodia, and subsequent exploration of the middle and upper Mekong. Siam had to surrender its claims to Cambodia, though by the treaty of 1867 it obtained in exchange French recognition of Siamese rights to the old Cambodian provinces of Battambang and Siem Reap. Chulalongkorn, who succeeded his father as Rama V (1868–1910), greatly increased the pace of Siam's modernization; his measures affected every department of the national life. During his reign French expansion in Indochina assumed threatening dimensions. The French conquest of Tongking, which caused Britain to annex upper Burma in 1886, led the Siamese to tighten their hold on the Laos country, which was being pillaged by refugee Chinese bands from Tongking. Under the influence of the explorer Auguste Pavie, however, France early in 1893, after various approaches to Britain regarding the boundaries of their respective empires in which both sides stressed their desire to declare Siam a buffer state, claimed that all the country on the east bank of the Mekong belonged to Vietnam. At the same time Pavie, who had become France's resident minister in Bangkok, demanded the evacuation of Siamese posts east of the river, and French columns took possession of the disputed territory, not without some resistance by the Siamese. France's hopes of provoking a conflict, which would enable it to seize the valley of the Mae Nam Chao Phraya, reached a climax in the "Paknam Incident" of July 1893, when two French gunboats blasted their way past the Siamese forts at the entrance to the river and anchored off the French legation at Bangkok. For the next few weeks Siam's fate hung in the balance, with France constantly raising its demands and Britain pressing France to moderate them and respect the independence of Siam, while at the same time urging Siam to save itself by accepting them. The worst phase of the crisis ended when Chulalongkorn signed a treaty paying France a large indemnity, ceding the whole of the territory on the east bank of the Mekong, evacuating the provinces of Battambang and Siem Reap, and, as guarantees, withdrawing Siam's forces to a distance of 16 mi. (25 km.) from the west bank of the Mekong and permitting the French to occupy the port of Chanthaburi.

**8. Anglo-French Agreement.**—The "incident" brought Anglo-French relations to a crisis, and in 1895 another crisis boiled up over French claims in the upper Mekong region, but in 1896 the two powers signed an agreement by which Britain traded its claims to territory east of the Mekong in return for a joint guarantee of the independence of the Mae Nam Chao Phraya Valley. France, however, continued to create further difficulties for Siam until the signature of the Anglo-French *entente cordiale* in 1904 paved the way for a French settlement of outstanding questions. By a new treaty in that year Siam modified the Laos frontier to France's advantage and renounced its sovereignty over Luang Prabang. France then evacuated Chanthaburi. By a further agreement with France in 1907 Siam ceded the Cambodian provinces of Battambang and Siem Reap in return for some of the territory surrendered in 1904 and the modification of some of the extraterritorial rights claimed by France. Finally in 1909, in return for a surrender of all its extraterritorial rights by Britain, Siam abandoned in favour of Britain all rights over the Malay states of Kelantan, Trengganu, Kedah, and Perlis. Siam also received a large sterling loan for railway construction.

**9. Reforms and Constitutional Changes.**—The Anglo-French agreement of 1896 encouraged Chulalongkorn to launch an accelerated program of reforms. The king started modern administrative methods and centralized his control over the kingdom. He employed more Europeans and Americans to serve as advisers in improving governmental institutions and procedures. Vajiravudh (Rama VI), who succeeded his father in 1910, had been educated at Oxford and had received training in the British military academy at Sandhurst. His reign was marked by the growth of Siamese nationalism and careless control over the nation's finances. He joined the Allies against Germany in 1917 and seized many German ships in Siamese waters as war booty. He won prompt admission to the League of Nations for Siam. His younger brother, Prajadhipok (1893–1941), ascended the throne in 1925 and found the national treasury lacking in funds because of his predecessor's extravagance. His efforts to restore fiscal responsibility were unpopular, especially when the depression in 1930 caused a reduction on the world market of the price of rice. A political crisis emerged when newly educated commoners returning from Europe sought greater opportunity and political reform. A group of disgruntled civilians led by a young French-educated lawyer, Pridi Phanomyong, gained the support of Western-trained army leaders, and in June 1932 they overthrew the absolute monarchy in a bloodless coup. A permanent constitution was promulgated in December 1932. Under this new form of government a unicameral Assembly of People's Representatives was established consisting of 156 members. Half of them were elected by the people and half were appointed by the government. The appointed members were to be gradually replaced by elected representatives as the people in the provinces obtained a primary education. The executive power was vested in a cabinet. Difficulties arose when Pridi proposed significant changes in the national economy and the king and the conservatives wanted to retain the status quo. In 1933 a royalist revolt led by Prince Bovaradej sought unsuccessfully to overthrow the liberal government. The following year King Prajadhipok departed for England allegedly for medical treatment. Shortly thereafter he abdicated his throne because of the curtailment of his powers by the new regime. His ten-year-old nephew, Ananda Mahidol, a schoolboy in Switzerland, was proclaimed king with a regency council of three members to perform the duties of the monarchy until he ascended the throne. Political stability was preserved during this difficult period by the moderate leadership of Col. Phya Bahol Phonphayuhasena who served as prime minister until December 1938. He was replaced by a young army officer, Col. Pibul Songgram, who led a militarist and extreme nationalist group. The new government tended toward a military dictatorship, yet influential civilians such as Pridi held important positions in the Cabinet. In 1939 the government plunged into a program of economic nationalism seeking to replace foreigners, especially the Chinese, in commerce and industry. The official name of the country was changed to Thailand (literally "land of the free") and education was brought under strict government control. In an effort to make his country appear modern, Pibul required the people to wear Western dress and adopt Western manners.

**10. World War II and After.**—Japanese pressure on French Indochina in 1941 caused Thailand to revive its claims to those territories it had ceded to the French between 1893 and 1907. Intermittent skirmishes erupted along the Thai-Cambodia border. Through Japanese mediation the French returned about 21,000 sq.mi. (54,390 sq.km.) to Thai sovereignty including the portion of Laos lying west of the Mekong River and three-fourths of the Cambodian province of Kampong Thom. Although the Thai leaders were not fully satisfied with these territorial concessions arranged by the Japanese, they dropped further claims and sought desperately to preserve their national independence. The rising power of Japan urged Thailand to seek balancing assistance from Great Britain and the United States. Yet the sudden Japanese invasion on Dec. 8, 1941, caused the Thai government to stop resistance and permit the passage of Japanese troops through the country. The Japanese quickly occupied Thailand and launched powerful attacks against British forces in Burma and Malaya. (*See* WORLD WARS: *World War II.*)

On Jan. 25, 1942, Thailand declared war on Great Britain and the United States in order to gain favour from the Japanese. The British recognized this act of belligerency, but the Americans did not declare war. In Washington, the Thai minister, M. R. Seni Pramoj, convinced the United States government that the declaration of war by his government did not represent the will of the Thai people and he organized a "Free Thai" movement among Thai students attending American universities to train for guerrilla warfare in Thailand. Within the kingdom a similar organization was formed under the leadership of Pridi Phanomyong, who was serving as regent for the boy-king. In July 1943 Japan transferred four Malay states and the two Shan states of Burma to Thai jurisdiction. Near the end of the war Pibul was removed as prime minister, and civilian leaders more sympathetic to Pridi assumed top government positions.

After the defeat of Japan the Thai government declared that the 1942 declaration of war against Great Britain and the United States was null and void. In 1946 Thailand signed peace treaties with Great Britain and France, and the territories acquired during the Japanese occupation were returned. The same year Thailand joined the United Nations. In 1950 the Thai government sent troops to assist American military action against Communist aggression in Korea. In September 1954 the nation became one of the members of the Southeast Asia Treaty Organization (SEATO).

Pridi and his followers dominated early postwar politics. They sought to start new constitutional reforms and at the same time to preserve their own power. In May 1946 they issued a constitution establishing a bicameral legislature. Yet the following month the mysterious death of the young king, Ananda Mahidol, precipitated another crisis. The king's brother, Phumiphon Aduldet (Bhumibol Adulyadej), was selected as the new monarch and a regency was again appointed to serve until he assumed the throne. In November 1947 a group of military leaders led by Gen. Phao Sriyanon, the chief of police, and Gen. Sarit Thanarat, the army chief, overthrew the civilian government. Pridi was forced to flee into exile. The coup leaders promulgated a provisional constitution retaining a bicameral legislature with an elected lower house and a Senate appointed by the crown. In April 1948 the military leaders returned Pibul Songgram to the post of prime minister. Another constitution issued in March 1949 drafted by royalist and conservative members of the Senate sought to restrain the trend toward authoritarian military rule. Another coup in November 1951, on the eve of the young king's return from his education in Switzerland, enabled the military leaders to restore the constitution of 1932. Again a unicameral legislature was equally divided among elected and appointed representatives. The military regime selected many army and police officers to fill appointed seats in the legislative body. A triumvirate rule emerged under Prime Minister Pibul Songgram, Gen. Phao Sriyanon, and Gen. Sarit Thanarat. This tenuous arrangement collapsed after a coup in September 1957 led by Sarit. Pibul and Phao were forced to leave the country. Sarit went to Great Britain and the United States for medical treatment, but he returned to Thailand and in October 1958 abolished all forms of constitutional democracy. He assumed the post of prime minister and reorganized the machinery of national administration. In January 1959 he issued an interim constitution providing for a constituent assembly to draft a permanent constitution and to act as a legislative assembly. He also imposed martial law and exercised a strict authoritarian rule. Under his leadership Thailand achieved more rapid economic and social progress. Compulsory primary education was expanded from four to seven years. New schools and universities were constructed. Successful projects for agriculture and industrial development were inaugurated. Sarit died in December 1963. His deputy, Gen. Thanom Kittikachorn, became prime minister.

Throughout the 1950s and 1960s Thailand took strong measures to prevent the spread of Communism in Southeast Asia. Close relations were maintained with the members of the SEATO alliance, especially the United States. The Thai government cooperated with Malaysia in suppressing Communist guerrillas along the southern border. In 1962 it sought military support from the United States in opposing the advances of pro-Communist Pathet Lao forces near the northeastern border. The traditional rivalry between Thailand and Cambodia contributed to a break in diplomatic relations between these neighbouring countries when the Thai leaders accused Prince Norodom Sihanouk of encouraging Communism in the region. Military and civilian leaders in Thailand sought to counteract the Communist influence by promoting economic and social programs in the vulnerable northeastern provinces. The Thai government also supported the policy of the United States in South Vietnam. Air bases within the kingdom were used by U.S. planes to attack military targets in North and South Vietnam, and Thailand sent 12,000 troops to South Vietnam. In October 1966 the Thai leaders welcomed Pres. Lyndon Johnson in Bangkok, the first American chief executive to visit the kingdom. In May 1968 Thailand became fearful when the United States began peace negotiations with North Vietnam at Paris. The Thai leaders claimed that the withdrawal of U.S. forces from South Vietnam would allow an increase of Communist activity in Southeast Asia. Prime Minister Thanom Kittikachorn visited Washington and sought reassurance from the U.S. government. President Johnson promised that the United States would continue to protect the independence of the kingdom, a pledge repeated by President Nixon after his election in November 1968.

A new permanent constitution was promulgated in June 1968. It established the separation of executive and legislative power for the first time in Thai history. A law was passed permitting free political parties. Municipal and provincial elections were held. In Feb. 1969 elections were held for the new national legislature. (D. G. E. H.; F. C. Da.)

## V. POPULATION

Thailand is not densely populated. With an estimated population of 33,693,000 in 1968, 170 persons per square mile, the land is not fully exploited. Population distribution is closely related to agricultural productivity. The highest densities and the most extensive concentrations of population are found in the floodplains of central Thailand. Secondary concentrations occur in the alluvial lands along the Chi and Mun rivers in northeastern Thailand, several well-watered valleys in the north, and the plains along the gulf coast in the far south. Fully one-third of the total population lives in Northeast Thailand and about one-third in the Central Plain.

The population, approximately 7,300,000 in 1900, had by the time of the 1947 census increased to 17,442,689 and in the census of 1960 reached 26,257,916. According to the *United Nations' Demographic Yearbook, 1962,* 88% of the Thai people are rural and dwell in villages. Statistics are available for only 120 municipalities. In these cities live 3,273,865 people, about 12% of the population. Bangkok, with 1,299,528, accounted for 40% of the municipal total. If Thonburi (pop. 403,818) on the west bank of the Mae Nam Chao Phraya is combined with Bangkok, the Bangkok metropolitan area had a total population of 1,880,606, or 52% of all the people living in municipalities.

In 1947 life expectancy at birth was 48.5 years for males and 51.4 years for females. Between 1947 and 1955 the crude death rate fell from 13.4 to 8.2 per thousand. During the same period the recorded birthrate rose from 23.6 to 30. Fertility is highest in the northeast and lowest in the north and the Malay areas of the far south. With the exception of foreign-born immigrants, among whom men predominate, the sex ratio is very nearly equal. The age distribution is fairly typical for nonindustrialized Asian countries; children under 15 accounted for about 45% of the total population in 1960.

Only about 12% of the population falls outside the Thai ethnic group. Chinese, of whom there were approximately 3,000,000 in 1960, form by far the largest ethnic minority. Chinese immigration, 1918–31, showed a net surplus of 500,000 Chinese immigrants. Since 1948 immigration has been restricted to a negligible figure, and the total number of China-born Chinese in 1960 was 384,408. Ethnic Chinese are concentrated in Bangkok and the upper gulf region, the tin and rubber areas of southern Thailand, and the major up-country towns. Ethnic Malaysians, the second largest minority (about 600,000 in 1958), are concentrated in the four southernmost provinces. The population also includes incompletely assimilated Cambodians, Vietnamese, Mons, Kui, Kaleung, Karens, and Shans, totaling approximately 300,000, and a comparable number of tribespeople. Another sizable immigrant minority whose numbers are diminishing is the Indian-Pakistani group, which like the Chinese, is predominantly urban. With the exception of the Chinese most ethnic minorities live in provinces adjacent to Thailand's international boundaries.

## VI. ADMINISTRATION AND SOCIAL CONDITIONS

Before 1932 Thailand had an absolute monarchy. Then a bloodless revolution replaced it with a nominally constitutional semiparliamentary monarchy. In practice, Thailand is a unitary state with a highly centralized and bureaucratic government, controlled and operated by an oligarchy or a military dictatorship. Thailand's constitution, which was adopted in principle, has not yet been completely implemented in action. For example, the constitution provides for a legislative body, the Assembly of People's Representatives, one-half of whose members during a transition period were to be elected by the people and the other half to be nominated by the king and approved by the Cabinet. Although more than 35 years have passed, the people have never been given the opportunity to elect all the members of their own assembly; moreover, the assembly at times has not been permitted to function. Beginning in 1956 national acts were passed from time to time with the objective of helping to decentralize the national government and strengthen the autonomy and development of local governments. However, local activities were severely restricted by the limited power of the local government to raise money by taxation. Consequently, many people have taken little interest in either local or national governments. In February 1969 a national election was held. The new constitution of June 1968 had not yet been implemented.

**1. Government.**—By statute the administration of the country is divided into three parts: (1) the central administration; (2) the provincial administration; and (3) the local administration. The central administration consists of ministries and departments located in the capital, Bangkok. The country is divided into provinces called *changwads,* each of which is under the control of a governor. These governors represent the provincial administration, which in reality is not a separate independent branch of the government but performs the territorial line service for the central administration. The latter performs the staff service for the provincial administration in the capital. The governors are not elected by the people but appointed by the national Ministry of the Interior, to which they are responsible. Governors are not permitted to remain in a *changwad* for many years and can be ordered from one to another or dismissed. But during his tenure in a *changwad* the governor is all-powerful because he is "in control of all the provincial officials in his province and is responsible for the governmental service of the province and the districts."

Each of the provinces is subdivided into districts called *amphurs.* There is a district officer for each of the districts. These officers are not elected but are appointed by the governor. The Local Administrative Act of the Buddhist Era 2457 (1914) lists in detail the powers and duties of district officers in 50 articles covering more than ten pages. Duties are grouped under the following six categories: (1) general administration of the territory; (2) maintenance of public safety and public peace; (3) magisterial functions: functions as chief magistrate in criminal inquiries and judicial powers in civil cases involving a claim not exceeding 200 baht (approximately $10); (4) administration of public health and sanitation; (5) stimulating economic development; and (6) education.

A district is further subdivided into communes called *tambons.* According to the *Tambon* Government Administrative Act (1956), the Ministry of the Interior can authorize local government for a *tambon.* However, local autonomy has been granted to only about 60 of these communes.

In summary, the Thai government is run by executive order. The executive branch of the government dominates at all levels by making and administering policy, holding the legislature in virtual subservience, and wielding some influence on the judiciary. The Council of Ministers, which is the executive body theoretically appointed by the king but in reality selected by the self-appointed prime minister, is composed of from 14 to 24 ministers; it is theoretically responsible to the assembly for the general policy of the government. During a coup, however, a strong man can: (1) make himself prime minister; (2) inform the king whom he wishes to have as ministers; and (3) ignore the assembly.

*The Monarchy.*—According to the constitution the king is head of state. Theoretically, all governmental powers are administered in his name, but he has few assigned concrete powers. Every act of state in which he participates must be countersigned by an appointed minister. The king is primarily a symbol of the nation's unity. Standing above the strife of politics, he symbolizes the country's ideals and aspirations. The king represents the state at major public ceremonies and sets the standard of style and deportment.

*Legislature.*—In 1932 parliamentary institutions were established by the leaders of the coup. A unicameral Assembly of the People's Representatives was organized. However, many of the early assemblymen had little understanding of their duties. In spite of this handicap, between 1933 and 1939 the assembly often showed real independence. After 1947, when the military returned to power in another coup, the Cabinet generally bypassed the assembly or used it to rubber-stamp Cabinet proposals.

The assembly of 1957 had 283 members of whom 160 were elected and 123 were appointed by the Cabinet. Whether elected or appointed, the members received the same pay and had equal powers. After the coup by Field Marshal Sarit Thanarat in 1957, the assembly was dissolved. An interim assembly of 240 members was appointed by the king in 1959. Both General Sarit and the king promised the people free elections and the establishment of constitutional parliamentary government. After General Sarit's death in 1963 Gen. Thanom Kittikachorn headed the government. In a national election held in February 1969, Prime Minister Thanom's United Thai People's Party won a large plurality of the 219 seats in Thailand's House of Representatives; 72 seats were won by independents.

**2. Justice.**—A Ministry of Justice was instituted in 1892. Thereafter the old tribunals, in which customary law had often been corruptly administered, were replaced by organized courts with judges appointed from the Bangkok law school and under the direct control of the ministry (except in the most outlying parts). A provincial judicial scheme provided a court at the headquarters of each *changwad* and also a series of central courts. A Supreme Court was established at Bangkok. In 1915 a bar association was formed.

Meanwhile the independence of the courts was still compromised by international treaties under which extraterritorial rights were secured to foreigners until the national law should be fully codified. After the absolute monarchy had delayed for years over the work of codification, the constitutional regime rushed it to completion, enabling Siam to denounce the international treaties in 1936 and to be freed from extraterritoriality within 14 months. Further legislation by the constitutional government was designed to reform procedure, to introduce the Western type of will, to strengthen the status of the judiciary, and to extend the course in the law school to three years. The spread of crime, stimulated by the political changes, provoked a reorganization of provincial justice. The *gendarmerie* courts were replaced by district courts and police authority was strengthened. Prison reform was begun, penal colonies were established, and reformatories for juvenile delinquents constructed.

Thailand is divided into nine regions for the administration of 20 magistrates and 83 provincial courts. Each of the regions is administered by an office of the chief judge. The civil court, the criminal court, and juvenile courts, however, do not come under the regional chief judge. Appeals from the lower courts can go to a court of appeals which has appellate jurisdiction in all civil, bankruptcy, and criminal matters. The court of appeals is divided into 17 divisions with a senior judge and two other judges for each division. The Supreme Court is the final court of appeal in all criminal bankruptcy and civil cases.

**3. Defense.**—Something of the part played by the armed forces in Siamese politics is indicated in the paragraphs on history above. Conspiracies in 1912 and in 1917 foreshadowed the struggle between civil and military elements that dominated the early constitutional period and culminated in the army's supremacy from 1938, save for the interval 1944–47. Symptomatic of this military influence was the Yuvajon movement, started in 1935, for the military training of schoolboys. A law of 1937 made all males between the ages of 18 and 30 liable for military service.

From 1960 the Supreme Command Headquarters, just below the Ministry of Defense level, had intermediate command of the three armed forces—army, navy, and air. In 1965 the national defense budget was 1,959,883,000 baht and amounted to over 15% of the national budget. (T. F. B.)

## VII. THE ECONOMY

The nature of Thailand's economy varies among the geographical regions, each having somewhat different natural resources and economic development. All of the regions cultivate rice and have fishing resources, fish providing the major protein element in the national diet. The northern region is the source of most forestry products, while the central region around Bangkok is the nation's financial, commercial, and industrial centre. The southern peninsula produces most of the rubber and tin. The northeast has few resources.

**1. Agriculture.**—Rice is the principal base for the country's economic well-being. In the 1960s more than 76% of all culti-

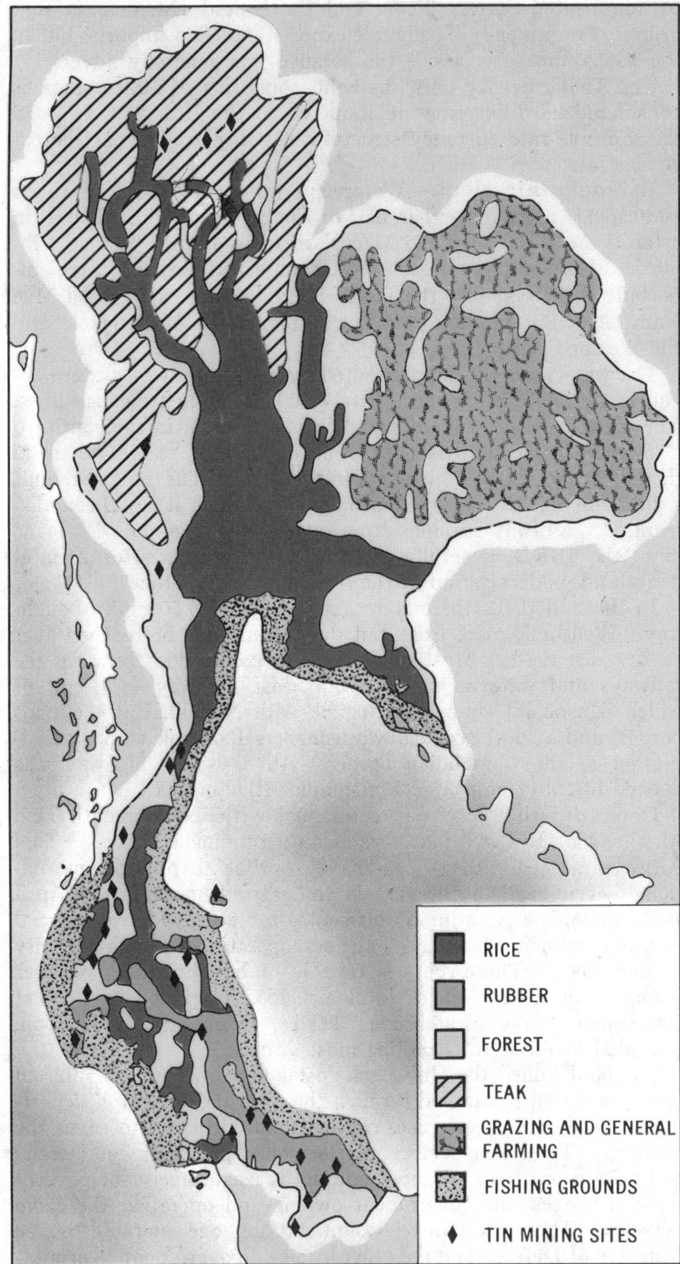


FIG. 2.—PRINCIPAL LAND-USE REGIONS OF THAILAND

vated land was planted in rice. Before World War II Thailand exported about 1,500,000 metric tons of milled rice annually. Exports declined during the war but by 1961 the prewar total was again achieved. The long-staple, nonglutinous quality of Thai rice makes it highly competitive in world markets. After the war the rice industry was placed under government control. This control was modified in 1955 permitting export through private channels and setting a fluctuating export premium aimed to keep Thai rice competitive. Production declined in the late 1960s so that by 1968 only about 1,000,000 metric tons were exported annually, about one-third under government-to-government contract and about two-thirds privately.

The sowing and planting season for rice is from June to August and the reaping season from December to February. About 50 varieties of paddy are grown. Seed selection aimed to improve the quality of the Thai rice is a continuous enterprise. Water variation and its control are also of continuing concern. Sheet-flooding of the Bangkok plain, in order to be adequate, must maintain a level at Ayutthaya, north of Bangkok, 11.5 ft. higher than the sea in the bight 35 mi. away. The plain is covered with a complex of channels to spread rather than to control the flood. East of the Mae Nam Chao Phraya water controls and irrigation canals have been constructed in grid patterns, with an irrigation barrage across the river itself at Chainat. Off-season cropping and rotation are not usual in the commercial farming areas.

About 1,000,000 ac. in southern Thailand are planted in rubber on small estates owned by Thai and ethnic Chinese. Annual prewar production was generally less than 50,000 metric tons, but by the middle 1960s it had risen to about 200,000 metric tons. The industry cannot expand to any great extent without a substantial replanting program, but implementation of the Rubber Replanting Act of 1960 is handicapped by competition from synthetic rubber production. In the early 1960s only 6.2% of the total planted area was approved for replanting.

Cotton is planted on about 130,000 ac. of poor soil in the northeastern and northern part of the Central Plain and is afflicted by insect pests. Annual production of seed cotton amounts to about 40,000 metric tons of short-staple cotton. Tobacco is cultivated chiefly in the cotton area and includes three types: flue-cured, sun-dried leaf, and a Turkish type for blending. Sugarcane production rose steadily from 105,000 ac. cultivated in 1948 to more than 400,000 ac. in the mid-1960s. Almost all sugar is consumed locally. Maize is of rising export importance, with Japan the principal consumer. Annual production in the late 1960s approached 1,500,000 metric tons. Japanese-supported research to reduce the moisture content, if successful, would make shipments to more distant markets possible and substantially increase the export importance of this crop. Kenaf, another potentially important export crop, had a high in the middle 1960s of almost 250,000 metric tons, but weak demand from abroad in the late 1960s turned kenaf growers temporarily to other crops. Other products include tapioca, peanuts, soybeans, coconuts, sesame, castor beans, silk, and pepper.

**2. Forestry.**—About 125,000 sq.mi. of Thailand are covered with forest, of which about 35,000 sq.mi. in the north contain teak. Teak production rose after World War II to approximately 200,000 cu.m. in the middle 1950s but by the 1960s had declined to less than 150,000 cu.m., of which less than 50,000 were exported annually in the late 1960s. The industry was chiefly developed by British companies. In 1954 the government began not renewing forest leases on expiration and in 1959 announced its intention to nationalize the industry. The Forest Industry Organization, a government body, is responsible for cutting the trees and moving the logs to Bangkok where about half are auctioned off to private sawmillers and half processed by FIO, which channels about 60% of the export price of teak into the public revenue.

The lac industry is chiefly of domestic importance although its high quality has gained the confidence of foreign buyers. Other forestry products include yang oil, bamboo, rattan, charcoal, gums, and resins.

**3. Livestock and Fisheries.**—Cattle and buffaloes are the principal livestock, cattle usually numbering about 5,000,000 and water buffalo about 7,000,000. Some sections of the northeast are suitable for grazing, and cattle and hogs are raised for shipment, mostly to other parts of Thailand. The main Bangkok market became a monopoly in the 1960s of the Union of Animal Product Traders, a subsidiary of the Bangkok municipality. Lack of government emphasis on the improvement of livestock and enlargement of herding areas kept livestock a local industry without export significance. Dairy cattle are almost nonexistent. Horses are used chiefly in the northwest and number about 200,000.

Thailand's rivers and 1,500 mi. of coastal waters abound in fish of great variety. Commercial freshwater fish production for domestic consumption varies between 50,000–70,000 metric tons annually. The saltwater catch averages about 150,000 metric tons, most of which is consumed domestically. Since the introduction of cold-storage facilities, shrimp production has gained importance. The fishing fleet consists of more than 4,500 boats with a total gross weight of over 33,000 tons.

**4. Mining.**—Mining, except for tin, is not of major importance. Tin mines are located chiefly in the southern peninsula and are generally operated by British, Australian, and Chinese companies. Many of the dredges deteriorated during the war but by the 1960s exports had achieved the levels of the prewar years of about 15,000 metric tons of concentrates annually. By the mid-1960s exports exceeded this level to over 20,000 tons and further expansion was planned in support of a new tin smelter erected in 1965. After that date annual exports were of metal and concentrates, about 5,000 tons of metal and 15,000 tons of concentrates. Tungsten is found in association with tin. In the years shortly after 1950 annual shipments of tungsten ore varied from 1,000 to 1,600 metric tons, but this total had declined by the 1960s. Iron deposits are estimated at about 70,000,000 tons of low-grade ore, located in remote regions. Production of steel and pig iron amounts to about 45,000 metric tons each per year. Lignite deposits are estimated at about 15,000,000 tons. Salt is processed from seawater and in bulk is an important export item.

**5. Industry.**—Thai industry is limited to the processing of agricultural commodities and the fabrication of consumer products and building materials. No branch of industry, except the processing of some agricultural products, has achieved sufficient volume to satisfy domestic requirements. There are rubber factories, sawmills, tobacco-processing plants, sugar mills, yarn mills, weaving factories, cement plants, glass factories, and factories for plywood and steel. Large-scale ventures depend on foreign capital, public or private. A Thai National Economic Development Board was established in 1959 to promote industrial development. The board assigned high priority to transportation, power generation, and communications. The opportunity to make Thailand's economy ebullient came in the late 1960s as a result of Thailand's role in the war in Vietnam. From 1960 Thai agricultural production increased about 4.5% a year or 1.2% more than the increase in population growth of 3.3%. In 1965 agricultural activities contributed 33% of the gross national product (GNP) and supplied 90% of the exports according to value. But this marked a real decline in the importance of agriculture to the GNP since 1955, dropping from 42 to 38% the first five years, and from 38 to 33% during the second five years. So Thailand's GNP growth was not due to agriculture although it continued to expand at a net rate of almost 2%. As GNP growth was between 6 and 9%, other factors were responsible.

Industry's share rose from 11 to 13% during the late 1960s. There were invisible growth assets which included tourism and private investment, but most of all the involvement of the United States in Thailand's economy. Thailand's reserves rose from $371,000,000 in 1960 to $901,200,000 in 1968.

In 1961 Thailand developed a six-year economic development plan (1961–66) and plowed about half the national budget into development projects designed to create a structured basis for a burgeoning economy. The second phase of the plan (1964–66) was a revision upward from the original target of 5% growth. A second plan for 1967–71 set a target of 7% growth and achieved 8 to 9%. The U.S. Agency for International Development and the International Bank for Reconstruction and Development provided major support and inspiration. By December 1967 the IBRD had loaned about $234,000,000, mostly for roads, dams, irrigation works, electricity, railroad and port facilities. The U.S. through AID had provided $333,600,000 in grants and $74,100,000 in loans by June 1966. U.S. military support by 1966 amounted to about $600,000,000. These figures fail to reveal the amounts poured into the Thai economy by the U.S. military in its Vietnam expenditures—most notably in developing air bases in the northeast and in building the enormous Sattahip port and air enclave with storage facilities for contingency supplies. About 43,000 U.S. military personnel in Thailand, supplemented by not less than 500 men per week on rest and recreation from Vietnam, added additional millions of invisible income to Thailand's economy.

**6. Trade and Finance.**—In general Thailand exports raw materials and imports finished products. Rice is the most important export item, generally accounting for between 30 and 45% of the total exports. Major rice customers include Malaysia, Indonesia, and Hong Kong. Malaysia imports much of Thailand's rubber and tin concentrates for processing and reexport.

In the late 1960s the bulk of Thailand's imports were supplied by the United States, Japan, and the United Kingdom in that order. Traditionally Thailand's exports exceeded imports, but in the 1950s and early 1960s the balance was generally adverse.

The Thai currency unit, the baht, consisting of 100 satangs, is considered hard currency at about 21 to the U.S. $1. In 1955 the multiple-rate currency structure was displaced by a free exchange rate.

**7. Communications.**—Waterways (about 3,700 mi. of rivers and canals) carry more than half of Thailand's freight. The main arteries are formed by the Mae Nam Chao Phraya and its tributaries. Intercommunication is accomplished through three important canal systems: the Pasak South system east of the Mae Nam Chao Phraya, the Phuphan system north of Bangkok, and the Western system.

The waterways are supplemented by a state railway system begun in 1892 which has more than 2,000 mi. of metre-gauge lines. This system radiates from Bangkok to Malaysia in the south, to Cambodia in the southeast, to Ubon in the east, to Udonthani in the northeast, and to Chiangmai in the north. The Japanese built a junction line to Burma during the war, but it has been dismantled. Railway earnings from operations, together with loans from the IBRD, generally provide adequate funds for maintenance and modernization of the lines and rolling stock.

In the mid-1960s there were approximately 6,500 mi. of highway. Well-built roads exist, but they often must be reached over narrow dirt roads. Most roads serve as connections between the railways and waterways. The northeast highway (100 mi. of which is asphalt) connects Bangkok with Nongkhai at the Laos border, and a southeast highway connects Bangkok with Aranyaprathet at the Cambodian border. An east-west highway was opened in 1961 connecting Phitsnulok with Lomsak.

Domestic airline service is maintained by the government's Thai Airways Co., Ltd., with airports at most provincial centres. Thai Airways merged with a Scandinavian airline to provide international service for Southeast Asia and started operations in April 1960. Bangkok is an important centre for worldwide commercial aviation, with more than 20 airlines operating through the city in the 1960s. The airport is capable of handling jet passenger planes. Reconstruction of local airfields, completed in 1960 at Chiangmai, Nakhornratchsima, Taklee, Udonthani, and Ubon, provided facilities for handling most aircraft.

Thailand joined the Universal Postal Union in 1885. Internal communication is handled through the post and telegraph department. The mail service uses railroads and airplanes to cover the country. Telegraph service reaches only principal commercial and railway centres. Radiotelegraphy is used largely for government messages, the government owning and operating the radio network. There are two television stations, one operated by the Ministry of Defense and the other by a semigovernmental corporation. Telephones are few. Bangkok is reached internationally by surface and air mail, radiotelegraph, and radiotelephone.

*See* also references under "Thailand" in the Index.

(K. P. La.)

Bibliography.—*Government Publications, General Works, and Geography:* National Statistical Office, *The Statistical Yearbook, Thailand Official Yearbook, Census of Agriculture;* Ministry of Defense, *Thailand: Facts and Figures;* Ministry of Foreign Affairs, *Foreign Affairs Bulletin;* V. M. Thompson, *Thailand, the New Siam* (1941); R. L. Pendleton *et al., Thailand* (1962); D. Insor, *Thailand* (1963); M. Y. Nuttonson, *The Physical Environment and Agriculture of Thailand* (1963); James Nach, *Thailand in Pictures* (1963); J. F. Cady, *Thailand, Burma, Laos, and Cambodia* (1966); V. Chu, *Thailand Today* (1968); Donald W. Fryer, *Emerging Southeast Asia* (1970).

*The People:* J. E. DeYoung, *Village Life in Modern Thailand* (1955); E. Seidenfaden, *The Thai Peoples* (1958); J. E. C. Blofeld, *People of the Sun* (1960); J. Audric, *Siam, Land of Temples* (1962); G. Young, *The Hill Tribes of Northern Thailand* (1962); B. C. Srisavasdi, *The Hill Tribes of Siam* (1963); W. Blanchard *et al., Thailand* (1966).

*History:* W. A. R. Wood, *A History of Siam* (1933); M. Collis, *Siamese White* (1936); M. Jumsai, *Thailand Past and Present* (1957); W. F. Vella, *Siam Under Rama III* (1958); Chula, prince of Thailand, *Lords of Life* (1960); J. F. Cady, *Southeast Asia: Its Historical Development* (1964); Promsiri Trirat, *Thailand's Transition: a Study of the New Approach of Developing Countries* (1965); F. C. Darling, *Thailand and the United States* (1965); D. E. Nuechterlein, *Thailand and the Struggle for Southeast Asia* (1965); Ronald B. Smith, *Siam:*

*or, the History of the Thais from Earliest Times to 1569 A.D.* (1966); R. C. Nairn, *International Aid to Thailand* (1966); Pierre Fistié, *L'Évolution de la Thaïlande contemporaine* (1967); Louis E. Lomax, *Thailand: the War That Is, the War That Will Be* (1967); D. Wit, *Thailand: Another Vietnam?* (1968).

*Government and Administration:* K. P. Landon, *Siam in Transition* (1939), *The Chinese in Thailand* (1941); W. D. Reeve, *Public Administration in Siam* (1951); M. Jumsai, *Compulsory Education in Thailand* (1951); W. F. Vella, *The Impact of the West on Government in Thailand* (1955); G. W. Skinner, *Chinese Society in Thailand* (1957), *Leadership and Power in the Chinese Community of Thailand* (1958); R. J. Coughlin, *Double Identity: the Chinese in Modern Thailand* (1960); Indiana University, Institute of Training for Public Service, *Problems of Politics and Administration in Thailand* (1962); D. A. Wilson, *Politics in Thailand* (1962); F. W. Riggs, *Thailand: the Modernization of a Bureaucratic Polity* (1966); W. J. Siffin, *The Thai Bureaucracy: Institutional Change and Development* (1966).

*The Economy:* J. C. Ingram, *Economic Change in Thailand Since 1850* (1955); International Bank for Reconstruction and Development, *Public Development Program for Thailand* (1959); R. J. Muscat, *Development Strategy in Thailand: a Study of Economic Growth* (1966); D. M. Davies, *The Rice Bowl of Asia* (1967); T. H. Silcock (ed.), *Thailand: Social and Economic Studies in Development* (1967); Agency for International Development, *Human Dimensions of Mekong River Basin Development Project* (1968); Michael Moerman, *Agricultural Change and Peasant Choice in a Thai Village* (1968).

Current history and statistics are summarized annually in *Britannica Book of the Year*. (T. F. B.; F. C. DA.; K. P. LA.)

**THAI LANGUAGE.** Thai, the standard spoken and literary language used throughout Thailand, is specifically the dialect of Bangkok and its environs. Slightly different local dialects are the Northeastern (around Ubon), the Northern (Chiangmai), and the Southern (Nakhornsrithamrat).

**Structure.**—Words are predominantly monosyllabic, but many are polysyllabic. There are 21 consonant sounds: unaspirated *p, t, c, k,* ˀ (c, palatal stop; ˀ, glottal stop); aspirated *ph, th, ch, kh;* voiced *b, d* (plus *g* in final position only); spirants *f, s, h;* semivowels *w, j* (Eng. *y*); nasals *m, n, n* (*ng*); liquids *l, r* (often confused). Nine vowel qualities are distinguished: front *i, e, ɛ* (*æ*); central *y* (i), ə, *a;* back rounded *u, o,* ɔ. These also occur long (*ii, ee, ɛɛ,* etc.) and in three clusters *ia, ya, ua.* Of equal significance are the five tones, mid (unmarked), low (\`), falling (^), high (´), and rising (ˇ) used to distinguish lexical meanings: *e.g., khaa* "stuck," *khàa* "a curry spice," *khâa* "kill," *kháa* "trade," *khǎa* "leg." (For explanation of these symbols, *see* PHONETICS.)

Inflection is completely lacking, but derivation is vigorous. Reduplication, often with vowel alternation, provides words like *krasíbkrasâab* "whisper." Compounding is highly productive; *e.g., khamnam* "preface" (word-leading), *khâwcaj* "understand" (enter-heart). Synonym compounds like *hàanklaj* "far distant" and alliterative compounds like *ramádrawan* "cautious" add greatly to the beauty and expressiveness of the language.

Word order is quite rigid. The typical sentence contains subject, verb, object in that order: *khǎw*$^{1}$ *rian*$^{2}$ *khanídtasàad*$^{3}$ "He$^{1}$ studies$^{2}$ mathematics$^{3}$." In attributive constructions the "head" precedes: *phâa*$^{1}$ *baan*$^{2}$ "thin$^{2}$ cloth$^{1}$." In counting nouns a classifier is added to the construction in the order noun numeral + classifier; *e.g., mîid sǎam-lêm* "three knives" (knives three-pieces). Verbs are primary or secondary, the latter being translated as adverbs. Thus *náam*$^{1}$ *lon*$^{2}$ "the water$^{1}$ recedes$^{2}$" ("recede," primary) but *nân*$^{1}$ *lon*$^{2}$ "sit$^{1}$ down$^{2}$" ("down," secondary).

**Loanwords.**—Thai freely incorporates foreign words. Perhaps the oldest are Chinese (*sìi* "four" and other numerals), but recent Chinese loans also occur. Hundreds of elegant and literary words are taken from Pali and Sanskrit (*prathêed* "country," *pradeśa*), and new words are coined from Sanskrit roots (*thoorasàb* "telephone," *dùra* "far" + *śabda* "sound"; *cf.* the Greek-derived term in English). There are loans from Khmer (*trùad* "inspect," *truac*), from 16th-century Portuguese (*sabùu* "soap"), from French (*méd* "meter"), from Malayo-Polynesian (*tuu in pratuu* "door"), and in modern times increasingly often from English (*waaw* "valve," *maj* "mile").

**Writing.**—The Thai alphabet (instituted A.D. 1233) derives ultimately from the Devanagari of South India. Writing proceeds from left to right, and spaces indicate punctuation but not word division. The accompanying table shows the 42 consonant signs still in use (two others are now obsolete), the tonal markers, and the vowel system. Although the 42 consonant signs are used for only 21 sounds, they are divided into three tonally restricted classes, middle, high, and low, as explained in the chart. Much of the seeming duplication is tonally significant; the rest preserves the etymological spelling of Indic and Khmer loanwords.

*Thai Alphabet*

| CONSONANTS | | | | | | VOWELS AND SPECIAL COMBINATIONS | | | |
|---|---|---|---|---|---|---|---|---|---|
| SIGN | EQUIVALENT | TONAL CLASS | SIGN | EQUIVALENT | TONAL CLASS | SIGN | EQUIVALENT | SIGN | EQUIVALENT |
| ก | k | middle | ธ | th | low | —ะ | -aˀ | เ—าะ | -ɔˀ |
| ข | kh | high | น | n | low | —ั/ | -a- | —็อ | -ɔ- |
| ค | kh | low | บ | b | middle | —า | -aa | —อ | -ɔɔ |
| ฆ | kh | low | ป | p | middle | —ิ | -i(ˀ) | —ัวะ | -uaˀ |
| ง | ŋ | low | ผ | ph | high | —ี | -ii | —ัว | -ua |
| จ | c | middle | ฝ | f | high | —ึ | -y(ˀ) | —ว/ | -ua- |
| ฉ | ch | high | พ | ph | low | —ือ | -yy | เ—ียะ | -iaˀ |
| ช | ch | low | ฟ | f | low | —ื/ | -yy- | เ—ีย | -ia |
| ซ | s | low | ภ | ph | low | —ุ | -u(ˀ) | เ—ือะ | -yaˀ |
| ฌ | ch | low | ม | m | low | —ู | -uu | เ—ือ | -ya |
| ญ | j | low | ย | j | low | เ—ะ | -eˀ | เ—อะ | -əˀ |
| ฎ | d | middle | ร | r | low | เ—็/ | -e- | เ—อ | -əə |
| ฏ | t | middle | ล | l | low | เ— | -ee | เ—ิ/ | -əə- |
| ฐ | th | high | ว | w | low | แ—ะ | ɛˀ | เ—ย | -əəj |
| ฑ | th | low | ศ | s | high | แ—็/ | -ɛ- | —ำ | -am |
| ฒ | th | low | ษ | s | high | แ— | -ɛɛ | ไ— | -aj |
| ณ | n | low | ส | s | high | โ—ะ | -oˀ | ใ— | -aj |
| ด | d | middle | ห | h | high | — | -o- | เ—า | -aw |
| ต | t | middle | ฬ | l | low | โ— | -oo | | |
| ถ | th | high | อ | ˀ | middle | ฤ | ry(ˀ) | ฦ | ly(ˀ) |
| ท | th | low | ฮ | h | low | ฤา | ryy | ฦา | lyy |

TONAL MARKERS:

(1) — (NO MARK): MIDDLE TONE WITH MIDDLE CONSONANT; RISING TONE WITH HIGH CONSONANT; MIDDLE TONE WITH LOW CONSONANT.

(2) —่ : LOW TONE WITH MIDDLE CONSONANT; LOW TONE WITH HIGH CONSONANT; FALLING TONE WITH LOW CONSONANT.

(3) —้ : FALLING TONE WITH MIDDLE CONSONANT; FALLING TONE WITH HIGH CONSONANT; HIGH TONE WITH LOW CONSONANT.

(4) —๊ : HIGH TONE WITH MIDDLE CONSONANT; RARE OTHERWISE; HIGH TONE.

(5) —๋ : RISING TONE WITH MIDDLE CONSONANT; RARE OTHERWISE.

**Affiliations.**—Other closely related Thai or Tai languages are spoken in Laos and in parts of Vietnam, southern China, the Shan states, and Assam. Differences are chiefly phonetic and lexical. The languages also differ in the number of tonal distinctions; some have five, some six, some seven, but seven is the maximum so far discovered. Attempts have been made to connect the Tai languages with other language families such as Chinese, Malayo-Polynesian, or both, but a rigorous demonstration of such affiliations has not yet been provided. *See* also SOUTHEAST ASIAN LANGUAGES; TAI LANGUAGES.

BIBLIOGRAPHY.—Mary R. Haas, "The Use of Numeral Classifiers in Thai," *Language*, vol. 18, pp. 201–205 (1942), *The Thai System of Writing* (1956), *Thai-English Student's Dictionary* (1964); Mary R. Haas and Heng R. Subhanka, *Spoken Thai*, 2 vol. (1947); Fang-Kuei Li, "Consonant Clusters in Tai," *Language*, vol. 30, pp. 368–379 (1954); George B. McFarland, *Thai-English Dictionary*, 2nd printing (1955).
(M. R. H.)

**THAI LITERATURE.** Siamese writing is thought to have originated from the type standardized by King Ramkhaeng of Sukhothai in 1283. This type, modified by his grandson King Litai about the middle of the 14th century, resembles the Lanna script.

Literature of the Sukhothai period (13th–14th centuries) survives only in inscriptions and in the *Traibhumikatha* of King Litai in 1345. This, like the inscriptions, is dated and is almost modern in its citing of authorities, and, unusually, states the name of its author. The famous stone inscription of Ramkhaeng is valuable for its information about the king and its lively picture of contemporary life. The voluminous religious literature of the north, dating from the 15th and 16th centuries, includes the *Jinakālamāli* (1516), a history of Buddhism and its spread to Ceylon, Pagan and the Lanna country in Pali verse; the *Cāmadevivons,* a history of the state of Lampun in Pali verse; and the *Sihinganidāna,* a history of the Ceylon image of the Buddha and its wanderings in Siam. Folklore is represented by the popular *Paññāsajātaka,* a collection of 50 tales in Pali prose and verse.

In 1349 Ayutthaya succeeded Sukhothai as capital. The literature surviving the sack of Ayutthaya in 1767 may be divided into two periods. Of the first, from 1350 to about the 15th century, *The Oath of Allegiance* is the earliest and contains old and obsolete forms of words; the *Yuan Pai* ("Defeat of the Yuan"; *i.e.,* Chiangmai people) is philologically valuable for its high literary standard; the *Royal Version of the Mahajati,* an ethical poem exalting the value of charity, influenced popular taste; and *Pra Lo* is a tragic romance. Prose survived in law preambles, some of them dignified and elegant.

Of the golden age of the later Ayutthaya period, from the reign of King Narai in the 17th century to that of "His Majesty of the Sublime Urn" (1732–58), several works, mostly poetry, have survived, including among Buddhist works King Sondharm's poem for recitation, the *Mahajati.* The *Samudaghos,* adapted from one of the folklore tales of the *Paññāsajātaka* by the king's preceptor, is a model of Siamese rhetoric. The king's preceptor was also credited with writing *Cindāmani,* a standard Siamese grammar in verse, and *The History of Ayudhya,* discovered early in the 20th century by Luan Prasroeth and known as *The History of Ayudhya, version of Luang Prasroeth.* Another poet of Narai's court was Pra Sri Mahosoth, famous for his *Panegyric of King Narai.* To Sri Prajna was ascribed the *Wailings of Sri Prājna.* Prince Kung or Dharmadhibes, whose *He rüa* ("Song of the Boatmen") has perpetuated his name, also wrote beautiful poems describing pilgrimages to the Buddha's footprint at Saraburi, and *nirás* ("erotic poems"). The *Bunnovād* by Pra Māhānāg is famous for its descriptive eloquence. There were also dance-dramas, such as the *Dalang* and *Inao,* both inspired by the Panji romance of Java, which became classics of Siamese literature. Prose stories appeared, including the *Duodecagon* (Sibsongliem) from the Persian and the *Story of Nang Tantrai* (adapted from the *Arabian Nights*). *Pakaranam* ("moralist") prose literature was derived from Hindu sources.

Chaos in literature followed the sack of Ayutthaya's capital by the Burmese. The king's death and the dissolution of the court resulted in the loss of many literary treasures. This, and the absence of printing, contributed to the paucity of Ayutthyan literature.

After the restoration the king tried to revive the country's culture. His successor caused a complete examination and concordance of the canon of the *Tipitaka* (1788) to be made and a new corpus of laws known as the *Edition of the Three Seals* (1805); he commissioned translations of Pali and foreign classics, among which was the *Sāmkok* translated by Caophya Praklang (Hon) from the Chinese historical romance *Sankuo* ("The Three Kingdoms"). Under his patronage were written many histories of the Buddhist religion in Siam. One of the greatest works was the *Rāmakien,* written by the king and finished in 1798. It is the earliest complete Siamese version of the story of Rama, though it was probably modeled on a version lost in the sack of Ayutthaya, and because of this cruder source lacks the high moral tone and the philosophy of Vālmīki's *Rāmāyana* from India. Traces of this epic can be detected in Siamese art and literature. It assumed a decorative role in monastic architecture though forming no part of the Buddhist religion.

Rama II, a gifted poet and dramatist, wrote the famous version of *Inao* as well as episodes of the *Rāmakien* and popular dance-dramas such as *Sankhtong.* His private secretary, Suntorn Bhu, wrote the fantasy of *Pra Abhaimani* and numerous *nirás,* for which he is famous. He also shared in the writing of the popular romance of *Khun Chang Khun Phen.* In 1835 Rama III built a stone library of inscriptions in which he collected most literary and technical knowledge, excluding poetical classics such as the *Rāmakien* and *Inao* and others, and thus summarized traditional Siamese literature up to the introduction of western influence in 1850.

Under Prince, later King, Mongkut, a new era of liberal thought in literature began. Prose fiction developed rapidly. The court still led in culture and adapted themselves to the new order while maintaining what was best in the old traditions. Mongkut's successor, King Chulalongkorn, began the publication of books dedicated to the dead which replaced the traditional burial presents, thus stimulating literature.

King Rama VI introduced the western spoken drama and Shakespearean blank verse, and adapted several plays by Shakespeare, Sheridan, Molière and Pinero, as well as composing traditional dance-dramas. Prince Bidyalongkorn wrote the well-known *Sāmkrung* in verse. Among the best-known poetry of the Bangkok period is *Ilaraj* by Phya Sri Suntorn (Phan), *Samaggibhed* ("The Disruption of Unity") by Jit Buradat and the *Nidrajagrij* by King Chulalongkorn.

The best novels include *Kamanit* by Sathienkoses and Nagapradip, several by Dokmaisod and *Siphendin* ("Four Regions") and *Phaiden* ("The Red Bamboo") by Kukriddhi. Outstanding in contemporary religious literature is the Pali *Sangitiyavangs,* a history of Buddhist synods by Somdeč Pra Vanarat, and a poem *Talengpai* by Prince Paramanujit, later Patriarch, notable for its rhetoric. He has been considered one of the greatest modern Siamese poets.

BIBLIOGRAPHY.—J. Finot, *Recherches sur la Littérature laotienne,* XVIII, p. 5 (1917); P. Schweisguth, *Etude sur la Littérature siamoise* (1951); É. Lorgeou, *Les Entretiens de Nang Tantrai* (1924); Dhani, "Siamese Versions of the Panji Romance," *India Antiqua* (1947), "The Reconstruction of Rama I," *Journal of the Siam Society,* XLIII, p. 1 (1955); G. Coedès, "Documents sur l'Histoire politiques et religieuse du Laos occidental," *Bulletin de l'Ecole française d'Extrême—Orient,* XXV (1923). (D. N. K. B. P.)

**THAI PEOPLES.** Thai (or T'ai) is a generic term applied to various groups of people found primarily in mainland southeast Asia who exhibit linguistic and other cultural similarities. The distribution of the Thai extends from Assam to Hainan Island and from latitude 25° N. in the Chinese province of Yünnan to the Gulf of Siam. The heaviest concentration is in Yünnan, Burma, Laos and Thailand (*qq.v.*).

The major groups are the Siamese (in central and southern Thailand), the Lao (in Laos and northern Thailand), the Shan (in northwest Burma), the Lu (primarily in Yünnan but also in Burma, Laos, northern Thailand and Vietnam), the Yünnan Tai (the major Thai group in Yünnan) and the Tribal Tai (in northern Vietnam).

Population figures are difficult to substantiate. Several estimates conservatively place the total number of Thai in the 1960s at 33,000,000–36,000,000, including 22,000,000–24,000,000 in Thailand (both Siamese and Lao), 1,250,000–1,500,000 in Laos, 1,250,000–1,500,000 in Burma, 8,000,000 in Yünnan (including 750,000 Lu), and about 700,000 in Vietnam.

The Thai languages are tonal and monosyllabic. Thai grammar shows definite affinities to some Chinese languages and some linguists assign the Thai languages to a Sino-Thai language family. The many words of Sanskrit and Pali origin found in Siamese, Lao and Shan can be traced to superimposed Buddhist and Hindu influences (*see* THAI LANGUAGE; THAI LITERATURE).

Most Thai are Buddhists of the Therevada (or Hinayana) school (*see* BUDDHISM: *Schools of Buddhism*). However, among the different groups there are considerable variations in this type of Buddhism. In the villages of many Thai groups the wat (temple compound or monastery) serves as the social as well as the religious centre. The ideal is for all young men to spend at least a nominal period of time as monks before taking their lay positions in the village. Along with the Buddhist tradition there exist pre-Buddhist animistic beliefs; shrines are dedicated to spirits (*phi*) that are important in day-to-day affairs. These animistic beliefs tend to be strongest among those peoples who are farthest from the traditional centres of Thai Buddhism.

Rice cultivation is the major economic pursuit of all Thai. Some tribal groups raise dry rice in the highlands, but most Thai live in the valleys where they raise wet rice.

Thai social organization is based upon a small, independent bilateral family—households usually consisting of a husband, wife (or sometimes wives) and unmarried children. The status of women is high; none of the Thai peoples has a caste system, although formerly war captives and debtors could be held as slaves.

Though the Thai live in political entities varying from independent kingdoms to chiefdoms in non-Thai states, the basic structure of their semiautonomous villages is similar. An elected village headman (together with the Buddhist monks and elders) provides the leadership for communal projects.

The Thai appeared historically in the first century A.D. in the Yangtze valley. Chinese pressures forced them south until they were disseminated throughout the northern part of southeast Asia. By the 7th century they were found in the kingdom of Nanchao in Yünnan and by the 13th and 14th centuries Thai kingdoms existed in Assam, Burma, Laos and Thailand. However, Indian and Chinese influences permeated some Thai cultures, bringing about the Indianization of the Ahom (*q.v.*) in Assam and the Sinicization of some of the Thai in Yünnan and Hainan. Cultural identity has remained the strongest among the Shan, the Siamese and the Lao.

Although subject to Asian and European influences that have resulted in the assimilation of many new ideas, the Siamese have maintained cultural and political independence (except for brief periods under the Burmese) since the 13th century. Nevertheless, the powerful social and technological forces brought to the Thai by Chinese, Indians and Europeans have led to cultural diversity among the Thai peoples in different geographical areas as well as between the peasants and elite within such contemporary countries as Thailand and Laos.

*See* also CHINA: *The People;* CHUANG; SHAN; SHAN STATE.

BIBLIOGRAPHY.—W. Blanchard *et al., Thailand* (1958); F. M. LeBar and A. Suddard, *Laos* (1960); D. G. E. Hall, *A History of Southeast Asia* (1958); S. Campbell and C. Shaweewongse, *Fundamentals of the Thai Language,* 2nd rev. ed. (1962); F. M. LeBar *et al., Ethnic Groups of Mainland Southeast Asia* (1964); R. S. Le May, *A Concise History of Buddhist Art in Siam,* 2nd ed. (1963). (C. F. Ks.)

**THAL,** the name given to the central section of the Sind Sagar *doab* or tract of country in West Pakistan, lying between the Indus River and its tributary, the Jhelum-Chenab. Because the land is slightly more raised above the water level of the rivers than in the other *doabs* of the Punjab, it remained for a long time without benefit of canal irrigation. With a very low rainfall it was a sea of sand and silt, with an occasional village relying on a little precarious cultivation in one of the damper hollows or on goats' finding a little fodder in the thin grass cover that sprang up after a better than usual rain. Although there has long been irrigation of the lower ground along the margins of the Indus, there was no site on the Indus where a barrage could readily be constructed at a sufficient height to command the Thal Desert, and there was some fear of taking too much water out of the river lest the great dam at Sukkur should suffer. However, with the independence of Pakistan the great Jinnah Barrage was undertaken, and it was expected that the Thal would eventually be able to support 1,000,000 settlers. (L. D. S.)

**THALAMUS,** an ovoid mass of nerve cells and fibres in the middle of the brain, has the function of relaying all sensory impulses except those of smell on their way to the cerebral cortex. The organ is about 4 cm. ($1\frac{1}{2}$ in.) long and is divided into a number of nuclei, or nerve-cell groups.

In submammalian vertebrate animals the thalamus is chiefly olfactory and does not relay specific sensation, for there is no somatic cortex. With the development of the cortex in the mammals, and the projection of the sensations upon it, the sensory relay nuclei of the thalamus expand proportionately. Thus, the thalamus shows a large nucleus, the lateral geniculate body, behind and laterally for relay of visual impulses; a round medial geniculate body adjacent for hearing; and a large somesthetic nucleus in its lower central part for bodily sensations. These three are the fundamental and best understood of its nuclei.

The thalamus may be divided into about 30 nuclei, each with differing connections and, therefore, differing functions. Most of them project to one or another of the numerous areal units of the cerebral cortex, so their function is indicated by that of the corresponding cortical area, where this is known. A few do not; they are the most ancient and conservative. Absence of clear-cut incoming connections of most of the nuclei is chiefly responsible for ignorance of their function. It is known, however, that the thalamus is not directly responsible for motor control.

The thalamus is rarely directly injured or the primary seat of disease, but it may be involved in more generalized disturbances. *See* also BRAIN; HYPOTHALAMUS. (W. J. S. K.)

**THALES,** one of the Seven Wise Men of ancient Greek philosophy who was also universally held to have introduced geometry into Greece, was the son of the Carian Examyas of Miletus and of Cleobuline. The story of his Phoenician descent is unlikely. His date is fixed by the statement of Herodotus that he foretold an eclipse now generally agreed to be that of May 28, 585 B.C. Apollodorus' date for his birth, 624 B.C., was doubtless based on this as a *floruit*. According to Diogenes Laërtius he died in the 58th Olympiad (548–545 B.C.), aged 78.

His inclusion in the canon of the Seven Wise Men gave him an ideal character, and his name attracted many acts and sayings popularly associated with wisdom. Consequently his real achievement is hard to assess, especially since no contemporary sources exist. He was a practical statesman who, according to Herodotus, offered the wise advice that the Ionian cities should federate; and Diogenes states that he dissuaded Miletus from making an alliance with Croesus of Lydia. Practical interests are also indicated by the story told (but not believed) by Herodotus that he diverted the river Halys for Croesus, and by the tradition mentioned by Callimachus that he advised navigators to steer by the Little Bear rather than the Great. He is also said to have used his knowledge of geometry to measure the pyramids (Hieronymus of Rhodes cited by Diogenes) and to calculate the distance from shore of ships at sea (Eudemus cited by Proclus).

Such stories of little historical worth may yet serve to characterize his reputation. They could however be invented or selected according to a writer's predilections. Two in particular provide amusing examples of mutually canceling propaganda. According to Aristotle, Thales, foreseeing by his meteorological skill a glut of olives, hired all the olive presses in advance and, when the season came, was able to charge his own price for reletting them. The moral drawn was that philosophers can be as worldly wise as other men if they so choose. To demonstrate the contrary, that philosophy's chief glory is its abstraction from the world, Plato tells how Thales fell into a well while stargazing and was laughed at for studying the heavens to the neglect of what was at his own feet.

The best attested fact is his prediction of the eclipse which stopped the battle between the Lydian Alyattes and the Mede Cyaxares. The date 585 B.C. suits the chronology now that Herodotus has been shown to have erred slightly in implying that Astyages succeeded Cyaxares in 594. Thales could not have had the knowledge to predict accurately the locality or character of an eclipse. Hence the feat was isolated and apparently only approximate; Herodotus speaks of his foretelling the year only. The use of the Babylonian saros for this purpose has been convincingly denied by O. Neugebauer (*Exact Sciences in Antiquity* [1951]). All that his Babylonian contemporaries could say was that an eclipse was either excluded or possible, and this sufficed for their astrological aims. From their records, Thales could well have said that an eclipse was possible in the year which ended during 585. The coincidence that it occurred during a crucial battle and was nearly total would give him in retrospect an exaggerated reputation as an astronomer.

Thales was specifically credited with five geometric theorems, as follows: (1) that a circle is bisected by its diameter; (2) that angles at the base of an isosceles triangle are equal; (3) that opposite angles of intersecting straight lines are equal; (4) that the angle in a semicircle is a right angle; and (5) that a triangle is determined if base and angles relative to base are given. The real extent of his mathematical achievement is almost impossible to assess in view of the ancient habit of crediting particular discoveries to individuals with a general reputation for wisdom. The fifth theorem is associated with the feat of measuring the distance of ships from shore, for which an empirical rule would have sufficed.

Moreover the requirements of "proof" vary according to period; of the third theorem Eudemus himself said that, although it was discovered by Thales, Euclid provided the scientific proof. Yet we may well believe that the first Greek philosopher improved on Egyptian techniques of land measurement in the way described by Proclus, who after saying that Thales introduced geometry from Egypt adds that "he made many discoveries himself and laid the foundation for his successors, attacking some problems in a more universal way and others more empirically."

The claim that Thales was the founder of European philosophy rests primarily on Aristotle, who says that he was the first to suggest a single material substratum for the universe, namely water, or moisture. The reason, Aristotle suggests, was that moisture is pre-eminently the origin and sustainer of life: vital heat is generated by moisture; semen and all nourishment must contain it. Aristotle frankly admits that he writes from hearsay; whatever Thales may have written had long been lost. Nevertheless both the statement and Aristotle's conjectural reasons are probably true in substance. The origin of all things from water was a commonplace of Babylonian and Egyptian mythology (the tradition of Thales' sojourn in Egypt is strong) and can be traced among the Greeks as far back as Homer's description of Ocean as the genesis of all things. Thales had consciously renounced myth, but its legacy remained.

We need not doubt that he was in method and intention rational. The dualism of matter and life was in the future, and what he seems to have sought was a single principle, both origin of the world and permanent ground of its being, to explain the mutability and multiplicity of phenomena. It must therefore be not only material but also author of change, that is to say, something self-changing; for, as the more mature Aristotle complained, these early Milesians did not distinguish matter from active cause. But, in Greek eyes, what changed or moved itself was alive, had psyche ("soul"). Hence, we may guess, Thales' choice of the substance which seemed to have the closest connection with life, as moisture did in Greek thought both then and later. The whole universe was a living organism, nourished by exhalations from water.

Consonant with this are other statements which Aristotle found traditionally attributed to Thales, that "the magnet has soul because it attracts iron" and that "all things are full of gods." The latter Aristotle connects with the belief that "soul is mingled in the whole." Diogenes Laërtius quotes Aristotle as saying also that Thales attributed life even to the inanimate, arguing from the behaviour of the magnet and of amber.

Of Thales' cosmology nothing is known but the statement quoted by Aristotle that the earth floats on water. To the historian of science, his significance lies not so much in the primacy of water (though some, like Sir Charles Sherrington in *Man on His Nature* [1940], have shown that this is by no means an absurd idea) as in the attempt to explain nature by the simplification of phenomena and the search for causes within nature itself rather than in the caprices of anthropomorphic gods. For cosmic unity as such, mythical precedents may again be quoted. That "all things come from one" was an early belief in Greece as in other lands; the original unity of earth and sky is crudely reflected in Hesiod's *Theogony*. Through the mists of later anecdotal tradition the true stature of Thales emerges only dimly, but as far as can be judged both he and his successors Anaximander and Anaximenes are important as constituting a bridge between the worlds of myth and reason. The ideas of these philosophers appear to some historians as remarkable anticipations of modern science, to others as transparent rationalizations of myth. They could not free themselves entirely from the inherited cosmic framework, but in their approach to it, in their critical spirit and in their determination to produce a simple, rational scheme employing only natural causes, they took a step whose future importance can scarcely be overrated. *See* also references under "Thales" in the Index volume.

BIBLIOGRAPHY.—For texts and testimonies *see* H. Diels and W. Kranz, *Die Fragmente der Vorsokratiker,* vol. i, 11th ed. (1964). *See* further E. Zeller, *La Filosofia dei Greci,* Italian trans. ed. by R. Mondolfo, i, 2, pp. 100–134 (1938); W. K. C. Guthrie, *A History of Greek Philosophy,* vol. i, pp. 45–72 (1962); T. L. Heath, *Aristarchus of Samos, the Ancient Copernicus* (1913) and *History of Greek Mathematics,* vol. i (1921); D. R. Dicks, "Thales," *Classical Quarterly,* 53: 294–309 (1959). (W. K. C. G.)

**THALLIUM,** a metallic chemical element, was discovered in 1861 by Sir William Crookes (*q.v.*) during a spectroscopic examination of the flue dust produced in the roasting of seleniferous pyrites. He observed a green line foreign to all then known spectra and concluded that the mineral contained a new element, which he named thallium, from the Greek for "a green twig." Crookes presumed that his thallium was something of the order of sulfur, selenium, or tellurium; but the French chemist Claude-Auguste Lamy, who anticipated him in isolating the new element (1862), found it to be a metal. The pure metal is not commercially important, but thallium salts have a number of laboratory and industrial uses (see *Salts: Uses,* below).

The symbol for Thallium is Tl. Its atomic number is 81, and its atomic weight is 204.37. Thallium has naturally occurring stable isotopes of mass numbers 203 and 205. It occurs in four rare minerals: crookesite, $(CuTlAg)_2$ Se; lorandite, $TlAsS_2$; vrbaite, $TlAs_2SbS_5$; and hutchinsonite, $(TlAgCu)_2S \cdot As_2S_3 + PbS \cdot As_2S_3$. It is also found in minute quantities in various pyrites, some of which are processed for other purposes; *e.g.,* the manufacture of sulfuric acid. In such cases thallium is often concentrated in the flue dusts or chamber muds—the usual raw-material sources of thallium.

For the extraction of the metal from chamber mud, the latter is boiled with water, which extracts thallium as sulfate. From the filtered solution the thallium is precipitated as chloride by addition of hydrochloric acid, along with more or less lead chloride. The mixed chlorides are boiled down to dryness with sulfuric acid to convert them into sulfates, which are then separated by boiling water, which dissolves only the thallium salt. The filtered solution yields thallium (replaced in the salt by pure metallic zinc); electrolysis is also employed. The (approximately pure) metallic sponge thus obtained is washed, made compact by compression, fused in a porcelain crucible in an atmosphere of hydrogen, and then cast into sticks.

**Properties.**—Thallium is a bluish-white metal that resembles lead in most of its physical properties; *i.e.,* it is very soft, malleable, and of low tensile strength. Two crystalline forms are known with a transition temperature of 226° C.

*Physical Properties of Thallium*

| | |
|---|---|
| Density at 20° C, g. per cc. | 11.85 |
| Melting point °C | 303.5 |
| Boiling point °C | 1,457. |
| Radius of ion, $Tl^+$, Å | 1.15 |
| Radius of ion, $Tl^{+++}$, Å | 0.95 |
| Coefficient of linear expansion at 20°C, per °C | $8.24 \times 10^{-6}$ |
| Ionization potential of gas atom, volts | |
| 1st electron | 6.07 |
| 2nd electron | 20.32 |
| 3rd electron | 29.7 |
| Resistivity at 20° C, ohm-cm. | $18.1 \times 10^{-6}$ |
| Potential at 25° C for $Tl \rightleftarrows Tl^+ + e$, volts | 0.336 |
| $Tl \rightleftarrows Tl^{+++} + 3e$, volts | −0.719 |

The elements gallium, indium, and thallium comprise Subgroup IIIb in the periodic table (*see* PERIODIC LAW). Thallium has the following electron arrangement in the incomplete orbits (O and P): $5s^2$, $5p^6$, $5d^{10}$, $6s^2$, $6p^1$. It readily loses one of its valence electrons to form thallous, the +1 oxidation state, or all three electrons to form thallic, the +3 state. Thallous ion resembles divalent lead in the formation of insoluble chlorides and iodides; it is also quite similar in many of its properties to the alkalies, since it is a +1 ion of similar size. Thallic ion resembles aluminum and gold but has less pronounced acid-forming properties, since it is a larger +3 ion.

Metallic thallium is easily oxidized to the thallous state. It tarnishes in air, forming an oxide film that readily dissolves in water; upon prolonged contact with air and water the metal dissolves to form a thallous hydroxide solution. Thallium at red heat reacts with water to liberate hydrogen and form thallous oxide, $Tl_2O$. Thallium dissolves in nitric acid and sulfuric acid; it dissolves less readily in hydrochloric acid, which precipitates the insoluble chloride. It unites directly with all the halogens.

**Salts.**—*Properties and Preparation.*—Thallium forms two series of salts: thallous, in which the metal is univalent; and thallic, in which it is trivalent. The thallic salts are much less stable than the thallous. All thallium salts are poisonous, producing symptoms somewhat resembling those of lead poisoning.

Thallous hydroxide, TlOH, is most conveniently prepared by decomposing a solution of the sulfate with barium hydroxide. It crystallizes from its solution in long yellow needles, TlOH or $TlOH \cdot H_2O$, which dissolve in water to form an intensely alkaline solution that acts as a caustic and greedily absorbs carbonic acid from the atmosphere. TlOH is also alcohol soluble. Unlike the alkalies, it readily loses its water at 100° C, and even at the ordinary temperature, to form the monoxide $Tl_2O$, a poisonous black powder. The peroxide $Tl_2O_3$ is formed when the metal is heated in air or oxygen at 500°–700° C, by the action of hydrogen peroxide upon alkaline solutions of thallous salts or by heating thallous nitrate. It decomposes into the monoxide and oxygen above 800°. The corresponding hydroxide, $TlO \cdot OH$, is very unstable. A thallothallic oxide, $Tl_2O \cdot Tl_2O_3$ or TlO, is also known.

Thallium monochloride, TlCl, is readily obtained by adding hydrochloric acid to the solution of any thallous salt. It is a white precipitate similar in appearance to silver chloride, which it also resembles in turning violet in the light. It fuses below redness into a (yellow) liquid that freezes into a hornlike flexible mass. It is also formed when the metal is burned in chlorine. One part of the precipitated chloride dissolves at 0° C in 500 parts of water, and in 40 parts at 100° C. It is less soluble in dilute hydrochloric acid. Thallium trichloride, $TlCl_3$, is obtained by heating the monochloride with chlorine under pressure or by saturating a suspension of the monochloride in water with chlorine; when anhydrous it is a crystalline mass that melts at 24°. It forms several double salts; *e.g.*, with hydrochloric acid and the alkaline chlorides. The chlorine is not completely precipitated by silver nitrate in nitric acid solution, the ionization apparently not proceeding to all the chlorine atoms. The mixed chlorides $TlCl \cdot TlCl_3$ are also produced by the regulated action of chlorine on the monochloride.

Thallium monoiodide, TlI, similarly obtained as a yellow precipitate, requires 16,000 parts of cold water for its solution. The yellow crystals melt at 190° and when cooled assume a red colour, which changes to the original yellow on standing. Thallium triiodide, $TlI_3$, is interesting because of its isomorphism with rubidium and cesium triiodides, a resemblance that suggests the formula $TlI(I_2)$ for the salt, but T. M. Lowry and A. J. Berry (1928) showed that it does not give the reactions of a thallous salt, and when dissolved in methyl alcohol, it behaves as a binary electrolyte; *i.e.*, as $(TlI_2)I$ or as $Tl[TlI_6]$.

Thallium monobromide, TlBr, a light yellow crystalline powder, is formed analogously to the chloride. Mixed bromide-iodide crystals have a high infrared transmission; lenses, windows, and prisms ground from the crystals are used in instruments for the detection and measurement of infrared radiation.

Thallium carbonate, $Tl_2CO_3$, more nearly resembles the lithium compound than any other ordinary carbonate. It is produced by exposure of thallous hydrate to carbon dioxide and therefore is obtained when the moist metal is exposed to the air. It forms resplendent monoclinic prisms, soluble in water. The bicarbonate is not known.

Thallous sulfate, $Tl_2SO_4$, forms water-soluble rhombic prisms that melt at a red heat, decomposing with evolution of sulfur dioxide. It unites with aluminum, chromium, and iron sulfates to form alums (*q.v.*). It also forms double salts of the type $Tl_2SO_4$ (Mg, Fe, or Zn) $SO_4 \cdot 6H_2O$. Thallous sulfide, $Tl_2S$, is obtained as a black precipitate by passing hydrogen sulfide gas into a thallous solution. It is insoluble in water and in the alkalies but readily dissolves in the mineral acids. Thallic sulfate, $Tl_2(SO_4)_3 \cdot 7H_2O$, and thallic nitrate, $Tl(NO_3)_3 \cdot 3H_2O$, are obtained as colourless crystals on the evaporation of a solution of the oxide in the corresponding acid. The sulfate decomposes into sulfuric acid and differs from aluminum sulfate in not forming alums.

**Uses.**—Mixed crystals of TlBr and TlI are used in infrared radiation transmitters, and $Tl_2S$ is a component of infrared-sensitive photocells. $Tl_2O$ imparts high refractive properties to optical glass. In chemical analysis, $TlOH \cdot H_3O$, $Tl_2O$, and $Tl_2SO_4$ are useful in testing for ozone, $TlCO_3$ in testing for carbon disulfide, and $Tl_2SO_4$ in testing for iodine in the presence of chlorine. TlCl is a catalyst in chlorination. $Tl_2SO_4$ is a commercial rodenticide and insecticide. Artificial gems are coloured with $Tl_2O$, and $TlNO_3$ is a "green fire" ingredient of fireworks. Thallium acetate, $TlC_2H_3O_2$, provides high-specific-gravity solutions for the refining of ores by flotation.

**Analysis.**—All thallium compounds volatile or liable to dissociation at the temperature of the flame of a Bunsen lamp impart to such flame an intense green colour. The spectrum contains a bright green of wave length 5,351 Å. From solutions containing it as thallous salt the metal is easily precipitated as chloride, iodide, or chloroplatinate by the corresponding reagents. Hydrogen sulfide, in the presence of free mineral acid, gives no precipitate; ammonium sulfide precipitates $Tl_2S$ from neutral solutions as a dark-brown or black precipitate insoluble in excess of reagent. Thallic salts are easily reduced to thallous by means of solution of sulfurous acid and are thus rendered amenable to the above reactions. Thallous chloride can be titrated by potassium iodate in moderately concentrated hydrochloric acid solution.

*See* also references under "Thallium" in the Index.

BIBLIOGRAPHY.—F. Albert Cotton and Geoffrey Wilkinson, *Advanced Inorganic Chemistry,* 2nd ed. (1966); B. H. Mahan, *University Chemistry* (1965); I. M. Kolthoff and P. J. Elving, *Treatise on Analytical Chemistry* (from 1959). (E. F. O.; X.)

**THALLOPHYTA:** *see* PLANTS AND PLANT SCIENCE: *Classification of Plants; Morphology of Plants;* ALGAE; BACTERIA; FUNGI; PALEOBOTANY; SLIME MOLDS.

**THAMES,** the principal river of England, rising in several headstreams among the Cotswold Hills in Gloucestershire. Its traditional source is Thames Head, at about 356 ft. (109 m.) O.D. (Ordnance Datum, or mean sea level as defined by Ordnance Survey) in the parish of Coates, 3 mi. (4.8 km.) SW of Cirencester; but claims have been advanced for Seven Springs, the source of the River Churn, situated at nearly 700 ft. (213 m.) O.D., 4 mi. S of Cheltenham. The Thames follows a winding course east and bounds parts of Gloucestershire, Wiltshire, Oxfordshire, Berkshire, Buckinghamshire, Surrey, Kent, and Essex. It bisects Greater London. Its length from Thames Head to where it enters the North Sea at the Nore is about 210 mi. (338 km.). Its width increases gradually to 125 ft. (38 m.) near Oxford, 250 ft. at Teddington, 750 ft. at London Bridge, and 2,100 ft. at Gravesend, below which the estuary expands rapidly to 5½ mi. between Sheerness and Shoeburyness. The average gradient from source to tidal water is 30 in. per mi. (47 cm. per km.). In the following paragraph the figures in parentheses denote distance in miles above London Bridge, 164 mi. (264 km.) from the source.

The upper course meanders eastward over a broad vale amid pleasant rural scenery. The main tributaries enter the left bank from the Cotswolds: the Churn near Cricklade (154), the Coln near Lechlade (143), the Windrush at Newbridge (127), and the Evenlode below Eynsham (119). At that point the Thames bends northward around the wooded Wytham Hill before turning sharply south to join the Cherwell at Oxford (112). It then flows between low limestone hills on to a clayey lowland where the Ock (right) enters at Abingdon (104) and the Thame (left) at Dorchester (95). The river proceeds southward, and near Goring (85) its valley, now deep and steep-sided, breaches the chalk uplands and divides the Chilterns from the Berkshire Downs. At Pangbourne (81) the Thames turns abruptly eastward and winds, beneath beautifully wooded slopes, across the southern edge of the Chilterns. On the right bank the Kennet enters at Reading (74) and the Loddon near Shiplake (69). Below Maidenhead (50) the landscape becomes flatter, apart from the isolated chalk knoll at Windsor (43). Notable tributaries feed both banks: the Colne (left) at Staines (36), the Wey (right) near Weybridge (30), and the Mole opposite Hampton Court. Below Teddington Lock (19) the Thames is tidal and truly metropolitan; yet as long stretches of its channel are narrowed artificially, particularly by stone embankments, it remains riverlike and is spanned by numerous bridges, the lowest being London Bridge and, ½ mi. below it, the lifting Tower Bridge. From there to Greenwich and Newham (about 10 mi.) ocean commerce and quayage monopolize the waterfront, and tunnels (Rotherhithe, Blackwall, Greenwich, and Woolwich—the last two for pedestrians only) replace bridges. Along the next section of the river to Tilbury and Gravesend (about 16 mi.) estuarine marshes alternate with large industrial (Thames-side) establishments and chalk bluffs; the Purfleet-Dartford Tunnel, linking Essex and Kent, provides a means of bypassing London. Below the main outport at Tilbury the wide estuary is coastal in nature.

The river was referred to by Julius Caesar as Tamesis and by early English chroniclers variously as Tamis, Tamisa, and Tamensim. The term Isis for the upper Thames appeared in the mid-14th century and was concocted by academics who, considering Tamesis to be a compound of Thame and Isis, wrongly thought Thames applied only to the river below Dorchester.

**Evolution of Drainage Pattern.**—The Thames has a complicated history that defies simple analysis. Its basin consists of two distinct components: above and below the Goring Gap, respectively. Above Goring it is developed on Jurassic strata, of which the older Liassic and oolitic series form the higher rim, notably in the Cotswolds. But this basin is itself subdivided transversely into upper and lower parts by a line of hills, partly of Corallian limestone, that is breached by the Thames at Oxford. The drainage of the upper or outer part thus converges on Oxford. Its watercourses occupy wide valleys, many of which continue as wind gaps (valleys unoccupied by streams) across the watershed into the basins of the Warwick Avon and the Severn. Typical is the wind gap across the Cotswolds near the upper Coln followed by routes to Cheltenham. The lower or interior part of the upper basin, that immediately above Goring, consists of a lowland separated only by weak divides from the drainage of the Wash and Bristol Avon. Below Goring the Thames Basin consists of chalk that has been downfolded into a syncline with a west-east axis and covered with Eocene sands and clays. In this area the west-east Kennet appears to represent the master stream.

The origin of the Thames system can probably be traced back to a thick cover of Mesozoic rocks, especially chalk, stretching far westward from their present outcrop and draining eastward. Later, perhaps in mid-Tertiary times, this cover was affected by folding, which created a syncline along the line of the present Kennet-Thames, together with an anticline in the Wealden area to the south and perhaps also in the Midlands to the north. From the peripheral upfolds individual streams drained toward the proto-Kennet-Thames. The direction of some Cotswold headstreams may represent the trend of this early drainage. Because the Cretaceous cover was gradually eroded away from the higher rim of the drainage basin, the exposure of clay beds allowed subsequent tributaries to develop on clay vales at the foot of limestone scarps. Thus, beyond the outermost Jurassic scarp, the lower Severn and a river flowing to the Trent (in reverse direction to the present Warwick Avon) developed headward and captured drainage from headstreams of the Thames. Similarly, within the Thames Basin the upper Thames developed slowly as a west-east subsequent stream and diverted to itself southward-flowing Cotswold streams. Eventually the whole of this intricate pattern was profoundly influenced by the Ice Age with its climatic changes. Ice invaded the north and northeast of the basin and in periods of melt and of heavy rain great floods poured down the valleys, which were successively deepened and finally left encumbered with gravel and alluvium upon which the present relatively small rivers meander. In addition, the lower Thames was pushed southward from the vale of St. Albans to a position near the southern Chalk rim. Throughout the Thames system, tiers of river terraces were formed, often of sand and gravel of economic value. In the Middle Gravels of the Boyn Hill terrace at Swanscombe, Kent, was found a fragmentary skull dating from the interglacial period and closely related to *Homo sapiens.*

**River Regulation.**—A permeable basin and all-year rainfall give the Thames a regular flow. Normally its volume is lowest in summer, when evaporation is greatest, but spates may occur any time, particularly from October to May. The monthly averages of the daily mean natural discharge at Teddington, from a drainage basin of 3,812 sq.mi. (9,873 sq.km.), vary from 4,900 cusecs (cu.ft. per sec.) in January to 1,074 cusecs in August, the mean being 2,703 cusecs (1 cusec = 0.0283 cu.m. per sec.). When the daily flow reaches 9,114 cusecs, or bank-full stage, the low-lying parts of the valley floor on the nontidal Thames are temporarily inundated, and during heavy floods the daily flow may exceed 25,000 cusecs. On the tideway, floods occasionally menace embanked areas when fairly high river spates coincide with strong spring tides. During rare prolonged droughts the daily natural flow at Teddington may drop below 300 cusecs, and water supplies are threatened. However, the freshwater Thames is Britain's best regulated river, and its control by the Thames Conservancy, established in 1857, involves navigation, drainage and water supply, including conservation works and the licensing of all abstractions. The Thames is the chief source of water supply for Greater London and also supplies districts centred on Oxford and Faringdon. Its tributaries the Wey, Kennet, Cherwell, and Windrush are also drawn upon. The Thames Conservancy enforces freedom from pollution and also regulates fisheries, which provide numerous coarse species and trout in some stretches. The tidal Thames below Teddington to the sea (a distance of 92 mi., including five dock systems covering more than 4,000 ac. [1,600 ha.]) was put under the control of the Port of London Authority in 1908. The Lea has its own Conservancy.

**River Traffic.**—After 1624 the Thames was made navigable for barges to Oxford and beyond, but navigation remained difficult until 1771 when the Thames Commissioners began to construct pound locks above Staines. From 1810 to 1815 the corporation of London built similar locks between Staines and Teddington. Later improvements allowed boats drawing three feet to reach Lechlade. Some barge traffic uses the river above Teddington, especially to Kingston. Regular steamer services ply daily in summer between Oxford and Kingston, also from Westminster upstream to Kew, Richmond, and Hampton Court, and downstream from Tower Pier to Tilbury, Southend, Margate, etc. There are also water-bus services between Putney and Greenwich, and ferry services operate from Woolwich (in Greenwich) to North Woolwich (in Newham) and from Gravesend to Tilbury. Pleasure craft abound, and registrations with the Thames Conservancy include thousands of motor-driven launches, cabin cruisers, houseboats, and smaller craft.

Most of the canal connections of the freshwater Thames are derelict, but on the tidal reaches the intense commercial activity enlivens water links. The Grand Union Canal to the Midlands remains active. The Lea is navigable to Hertford (27 mi. [43 km.]), and the Stort to Bishop's Stortford (13 mi.); pleasure craft predominate, but barges regularly ascend the Lea to Ware (25 mi.) and the Stort to Sawbridgeworth (9 mi.). The Thames Navigational Service, operating from Gravesend, provides navigation surveillance between that part of the Thames below London Bridge that forms one of the most important commercial waterways in the world. *See* LONDON.

*See* also references under "Thames" in the Index.

BIBLIOGRAPHY.—R. L. Sherlock, *London and Thames Valley* (1947); S. W. Wooldridge and D. L. Linton, *Structure, Surface and Drainage in Southeast England* (1955); F. S. Thacker, *The Thames Highway:*

*a History of the Locks and Weirs* (1920); L. T. C. Rolt, *The Thames from Mouth to Source* (1951); B. Waters, *Thirteen Rivers to the Thames* (1964). (R. P. Be.)

**THANA,** a town of Maharashtra State, India, and the headquarters of the district of the same name, lies 21 mi. (34 km.) NE of Bombay, of which it forms a suburb. Pop. (1967 est.) 126,022. Buildings of interest in Thana include the Old Fort, the Jain and Kaupineshwar temples, and the Portuguese Cathedral. There are also two hospitals and several high schools. One of the earliest Portuguese settlements in India, Thana was formerly an important port and trading post.

**THANJAVUR** (Tanjore), a town of Madras State (Tamil Nad), India, and the headquarters of the district of the same name, is on the western side of the Cauvery Delta, 218 mi. (351 km.) SSW of Madras by rail. Pop. (1967 est.) 117,698. The town was the royal residence of the Cholas until after the reign of Rajaraja I (A.D. 985–1014), when his successor, Rajendra Chola, shifted the capital, and Tanjore lost much of its importance. It was revived, however, by the Naiks (Nayak) about 1549. They built two forts, the smaller of which, with its walls and moat, is still well preserved. Later the town became the capital of the Maharashtra dynasty. In 1799 the surrounding country was ceded to the British by Raja Sarfoji, and on the death of his son Sivaji in 1855 without male issue, the town also passed to the British. One of Thanjavur's most notable features is the great Brihadisvara Temple (also called the Raja Raja Temple, after its founder), a monumental piece of architecture, with a tower more than 200 ft. (60 m.) high, decorated with pillars and statues. In the northeastern section of the smaller fort is the Schwartz Church, founded about 1778 by the missionary C. F. Schwartz. There are several other churches in Thanjavur, which was the headquarters of some of the earliest Protestant missionaries in India. The Old Palace, which consists of a large group of buildings, houses the Tanjore Art Gallery, the Mahal Library, with a large collection of rare manuscripts and books, and the Raja Sarfoji Arts College (1955). There is also a government medical college in the town. (G. Kn.)

**THANKSGIVING DAY,** an annual national holiday in the United States, Canada, and a few other countries, celebrates the harvest and other blessings of the past year. Although days of thanks for special occasions were celebrated in the first years of Virginia's settlement and harvest celebrations are as old as civilization itself, it is generally acknowledged that the first Thanksgiving Day celebration in America occurred when the Pilgrims, by order of Gov. William Bradford, held a three-day festival to commemorate their harvest in the autumn of 1621. Edward Winslow, in a letter of Dec. 11, 1621, described the celebration:

> Our harvest being gotten in, our Governor sent four men on fowling, that so we might after a more special manner rejoice together, after we had gathered the fruit of our labours. They four in one day killed as much fowl as, with a little help beside, served the Company almost a week. At which time, amongst other recreations, we exercised our arms, many of the Indians coming amongst us, and amongst the rest their greatest king, Massasoit with some 90 men, whom for three days we entertained and feasted. And they went out and killed five deer which they brought to the plantation and bestowed on our Governor and upon the Captain and others.

Despite this early beginning, Thanksgiving Day was not celebrated in America as a regular national holiday for more than two centuries after 1621. Massachusetts Bay Colony's first civil Thanksgiving was observed July 8, 1630, after the safe arrival of all of John Winthrop's ships, but it was 1660 before the celebration for harvest gathering became a regular annual event in that colony. Harvest festivals became an annual custom in Connecticut in 1649 and in Plymouth in 1668, but Rhode Island did not adopt the practice until the Revolution. By the end of the 18th century, however, celebrating Thanksgiving Day was an institution in all New England. During the Revolution, days of thanks were set aside for special occasions and Nov. 26, 1789, was proclaimed by George Washington as the first national day of thanksgiving. But the day still had not become an institution. Gradually the idea was spread to the West by New England migrants as well as by the energetic urging of Mrs. Sarah J. Hale, the early-19th-century editor of the famous *Godey's Lady's Book* of Philadelphia, a widely read women's magazine. Though the South was hesitant to adopt this New England custom, by the middle of the 19th century most of the Northern states had accepted the idea, and President Lincoln proclaimed a national harvest festival on Nov. 26, 1863. From that time on, Thanksgiving Day has been an annual holiday in the United States, proclaimed yearly by the president and by the governor of each state. Except for 1939 through 1941 when Pres. Franklin D. Roosevelt set the day a week earlier to lengthen the interval between Thanksgiving and Christmas, Thanksgiving Day had always been named as the last Thursday of November. In December 1941 Congress passed a resolution making the fourth Thursday of that month a national legal holiday.

The meaning of Thanksgiving and the manner of its celebration have changed little since the day of the Pilgrims. Thanksgiving was and still is basically a home festival with religious overtones. Never celebrated on a Sunday, the day is generally commemorated with special church services by all faiths, but the main emphasis is on the gathering of family and friends for a gay and plentiful feast. As in the days of the Pilgrims, turkey is the traditional meat for that day, and other autumnal dishes, such as pumpkin pie and plum pudding, stress the harvest theme. The flavour of the day has been immortalized in literature and poetry; one of the best known poems, by Lydia Maria Child, begins with the familiar lines: "Over the river and through the woods, to grandfather's house we go. . . ."

*See* Ralph and Adelin Linton, *We Gather Together: the Story of Thanksgiving* (1949). For Virginia's protest about Massachusetts' first Thanksgiving, *see* Virginius Dabney, "That Mythical 'First Thanksgiving,'" *Saturday Evening Post* (Nov. 29, 1958). (B. K. B.)

**THANT, U** (1909– ), Burmese writer and UN secretary-general, was born Jan. 22, 1909, in Pantanaw, Maubin district, not far from Rangoon, Burma. (Strictly speaking, "U" is not part of his name but is an honorific title comparable to "Mr." or "Honoured Sir," though the literal meaning is "uncle." The Burmese do not use surnames at all.) He was educated at the National High School, Pantanaw, and at the University of Rangoon, but had to leave the university to help support his family. At the university U Thant became acquainted with Thakin Nu (later U Nu), who was to become prime minister when Burma gained its independence. After dropping out of the university, U Thant returned to the National High School in his home town as a senior teacher and later as headmaster. During the Japanese occupation of Burma in World War II, he was a member of various educational committees, and in Aug. 1943 he returned to Pantanaw to rebuild the high school, which had been damaged during the war.

After World War II, U Thant was persuaded by U Nu and by Gen. Aung San, then leader of Burma, to enter government service. In Sept. 1947 he went to the information department and in 1949 became secretary, ministry of information and broadcasting. He was in 1952–53 a member of the Burmese delegation to the United Nations and, after serving his government in various capacities back in Rangoon, in 1957 he became Burma's permanent representative to the UN. Throughout these years he traveled widely, accompanying Prime Minister U Nu on various good-will missions and to international conferences.

He was elected acting secretary-general of the United Nations on Nov. 3, 1961, and a year later was elected secretary-general to serve until November 1966. In December 1966 he was elected to another five-year term. Devoutly Buddhist, U Thant sought to apply the personal disciplines of detachment and concentration to get to the heart of problems at the UN. Neutralist by practice as well as inclination, he criticized at different times both West and East for actions he considered inimical to world peace. When the U.S. and the U.S.S.R. could not agree on a secretary-general after Dag Hammarskjöld's death (Sept. 18, 1961), U Thant was the one person on whom they could compromise. The U.S.S.R. had earlier demanded a three-man secretaryship (the so-called troika). U Thant continued the Hammarskjöld tradition by exercising discretion, by keeping himself available to all national representatives, and by trying to forestall problems before they became insurmountable. Like his predecessor, he considered the UN to be first and last a world instrument for sustained negotiation. (G. C. Li.; P. M. A. L.)

**THAR DESERT** (Indian Desert), a large arid area in the northwest of the India-Pakistan subcontinent, extends for about 400 mi. from southwest to northeast and has a maximum width of about 225 mi. The desert is limited to the south by the Great Rann of Cutch. To the west lies the valley-plain of the Indus and to the northwest that of the Sutlej. Northeastward the desert fades into Punjab state, India, while the southeastern limit is marked by the Aravalli range (*q.v.*) running from southwest to northeast. The greater part of the desert lies in the Indian state of Rajasthan of which it occupies nearly half. The remainder is in West Pakistan where the desert occupies a large part of the former princely state of Bahawalpur and the old province of Sind.

The area slopes on the whole from the foothills of the Aravallis, at about 1,000–1,500 ft., northwestward to the margin of the Indus plain at 200–300 ft., or southward to the Rann of Cutch. There are no permanent rivers except the Luni in the southeast, but channels follow the general slopes and in the extreme west are former channels of the Indus.

The whole area is probably underlain by the crystalline complex of the Indian peninsula outcropping near the desert margins in the Aravallis. The greater part of the desert surface is occupied by sands, silts and loesslike material, the finer-grained making excellent soil where water is available. The name *Thar* ("desert or sandy waste") refers to the sand hills accumulated by the prevailing winds. Saline dust is transported from the Indus delta and the Rann of Cutch and deposited in hillocks. In the southwest long ridges (Sindhi, *bhits*) are found aligned from southwest to northeast parallel to the prevailing winds. In the northeast these give place to transverse dunes of barchan type though somewhat irregular. Toward the Rann, dunes more or less permanent may rise to 200 ft. above the general sandy surface; inland they are smaller and the landscape tends toward a low plateau of deep, loose moving sand.

The average rainfall is 15 in. a year and on the western margins near the Indus this drops to less than 5 in. The rainfall is unreliable and varies greatly from year to year, the average variability from the mean being more than 30%. Toward the north there may be occasional falls from sudden storms associated with cold-weather cyclones. In the centre and south most rain comes in the normal Indian wet season, June to September. The range of temperature, both diurnal and annual, is large. In the cold season, November to February, days are warm but nights cold so that in the north frost occurs despite the January mean of 12.7° C.–21° C. (55° F.–70° F.). Essentially tropical plants are thereby excluded. The land heats up from March onward and, as there is insufficient rain to exercise a cooling influence, June and July are normally the hottest months despite the southwest winds. The average daily temperature in July exceeds 32° C. (90° F.) and afternoon readings are up to 53° C. (127° F.). Dust storms are common at the periods of reversal of pressure about April–May and October.

**Natural Resources and Irrigation.**—Surface deposits everywhere are impregnated with salt derived from the evaporation of subsoil brine and the accumulation of salt particles blown from the Rann. On the eastern margins of the desert are the Rajasthan salt lakes. Lake Sambhar, the largest, lies in a closed depression in the Aravalli schists with a surface at 1,184 ft. Its maximum spread is 90 sq.mi. and during a normal monsoon it averages 4 ft. deep in the middle but is dry the greater part of the year. The upper 12 ft. alone of saliferous silt forming its bed represents a salt reserve of about 54,000,000 tons. The salt is extracted and railed to Sambhar at the eastern end of the lake.

Gypsum also occurs on the margin of some of the lakes. In southwest Sind and Khairpur on the edges of the Indus alluvial plain, where the alluvial clays are uncovered or covered by only a thin layer of sand, large shallow expanses of water known as *dhands* occur in the hollows or *talis* between the sand hills. They are fed by rainwater percolating through the sand and emerging as springs (*sims*). The spring water is usually fresh and gives rise to a fringe of vegetation. Saline *dhands* yield salt and gypsum; alkaline *dhands* supply the mineral trona which is the basis of the soda industry of Khairpur.

The vegetation of most of the desert is an open scrub. The moving sand dunes are bare; saline hollows are marked by a halophytic vegetation but there is excellent grass on the sweet damp bottoms after rain. This affords fodder for numerous cattle, sheep, goats and camels and accounts for the location of the scattered villages. In good seasons bajra millet is grown to eke out a milk diet. Village industries based on coarse wool, camel hair and leathers play a considerable part in the economy of the area and reach notable proportions in the small towns, such as Jaisalmer and Bikaner, or the larger centre of Jodhpur.

Jodhpur has an airport and can be reached by rail; some of the old desert tracks are motorable but no main road crosses the desert and the east-west railway in the south is disused.

A major power and irrigation project was designed to reclaim large areas in the northern part of the desert. A dam and associated hydroelectric plant were built on the Sutlej river near the village of Bhakra. Eight miles downstream the Nangal dam (completed in 1954) provides storage for the Sirhind canal from which the dry areas on the Punjab-Rajasthan border are irrigated. Lower down the Sutlej, after it has been reinforced by the waters of the Beas, the Rajasthan canal (constructed in the 1960s) runs from the Harika barrage right through the northwestern part of the Thar desert. Though this canal is well within Indian territory, Pakistan objected that it diverts water which formerly fed the great canals branching from the Sutlej at Ferozepur (controlled by India). These are the lifeblood of much of Bahawalpur as well as of part of the Bari doab west of the river in Pakistan. However, in 1961 India and Pakistan reached a waters agreement. (L. D. S.)

**THARRAWADDY,** a town and district in the Pegu division of Burma. The town lies 68 mi. (109 km.) NW of Rangoon by rail. Pop. (1953) 8,977. The district (area 2,784 sq.mi. [7,211 sq.km.]; pop. [1962 est.] 823,459) stretches from the Irrawaddy River on the west to the crest of the forested Pegu Yoma on the east. It thus comprises on the west an alluvial plain through which the railway runs and which is well populated and devoted to rice cultivation, and on the east almost uninhabited forest country with valuable teak forests and fuel reserves. Wild animals in the forests include elephant. (L. D. S.)

**THARU,** a tribe numbering about 30,000 who live in small semipermanent villages apart from other groups in the Terai (*q.v.;* Tarai) tract of the Himalayan foothills, mainly in the Nainital (*q.v.*) District of Uttar Pradesh, India. They practise agriculture, raise cattle, hunt, fish, and collect forest products. Although closely resembling the Tibetans or Gurkhas of Nepal, the Mongoloid Tharu show genetic admixture with plains populations and have been largely affected by Indian culture. The five higher clans among the Tharu, which comprise about 80% of the population, claim to be Sisodiya Rajputs from Rajasthan; they refuse to marry members of the seven lower sections of Tharu (who also claim lordly status but are compelled to marry within their own sections). In contrast with the higher Hindu castes, Tharu use alcoholic beverages freely and eat beef. They approve polygyny, divorce, and secondary marriage with the deceased spouse's younger sibling. Notwithstanding that theirs is a patrilineal social system, Tharu women have property rights far beyond those recognized in Hindu society. Tharu generally employ no Brahmans but maintain their own priest-mediums in each village. The religious ceremonies, festivals, and beliefs of the Tharu are nevertheless largely Hindu in form and content.

*See* S. K. Srivastava, *The Tharus: a Study of Culture Dynamics* (1958); D. N. Majumdar, *Races and Cultures of India,* 4th ed. (1961). (M. Ma.)

**THASOS,** a Greek island in the north of the Aegean Sea, about 4 mi. (7 km.) from the coast of Thrace and the delta of the Nestos River. Area 146 sq.mi. (379 sq.km.); pop. (1961) 15,916. The population is distributed in 11 villages, mostly at some distance from the sea; the chief one is Thasos (formerly Limin) on the north coast, on the site of the ancient capital. Zinc and other minerals are mined.

Herodotus mentions an early Phoenician settlement on Thasos, which had gold mines (no longer worked) and a peculiar cult of Hercules; Thracian settlement is also probable. In the early 7th century B.C., Greeks from Paros colonized Thasos; they also owned gold mines on the mainland and planted cities there. Thasos joined the Delian League (*q.v.*), but disputes over the mines arose with the Athenians, who, after a siege of two years (465–463), compelled the Thasians to destroy their walls, surrender their fleet and their mainland possessions, and pay an indemnity and an annual contribution: in 450 this was 3 talents, but from 446 to 445 about 30 talents, after some of the mainland had been restored. During the Peloponnesian War Thasos revolted from 411 to 407, and after Athens' defeat the Spartan admiral Lysander seized Thasos (403). It joined the second Athenian League *c.* 375. Philip V of Macedonia seized it (202), but it was freed by the Romans in 196 B.C.

Thasos was under Latin rule from 1204 until its capture by the Turks in 1455. The Turks ruled it almost continuously until 1912; from 1813 to 1902 it belonged to the Turkish governors of Egypt. During the First Balkan War the Greeks captured Thasos, and by the Treaty of London (1913) its cession to Greece was confirmed.

The ancient city was excavated by the French School at Athens (from 1911), and its walls and general plan are now clear.

For the history of Thasos and for recent excavations, see *Études thasiennes* (École Française d'Athènes; 1944–    ).

**THATON,** a town and district in the Tenasserim division of Burma. The town (pop. [1962 est.] 136,394), formerly the capital of the Talaing kingdom and a seaport, now lies about 10 mi. (16 km.) from the sea. It is 35 mi. (56 km.) NW of Moulmein.

THATON DISTRICT formerly had an area of 4,870 sq.mi. (12,613 sq.km.) but has been reduced to a small but well-populated coastal strip between the Karen State and the sea. Area 1,909 sq.mi. (4,944 sq.km.). Pop. (1962 est.) 435,410. Excellent road metal is quarried at Mokpalin. Martaban is the southern terminus of the railway from Rangoon via Pegu and faces Moulmein across the mouth of the Salween River. (L. D. S.)

**THATTA** (TATTA), a town in the Hyderabad division of West Pakistan and the headquarters of the district of the same name, is situated 7 mi. (11 km.) from the right bank of the Indus River and about 50 mi. (80 km.) E of Karachi. Pop. (1961) 12,786. The town is built on a slight rise in an alluvial valley at the foot of the Makli Hills. In the 16th century it was the capital of the Samma dynasty in lower Sind and formerly had a much larger population. It has many remarkable monuments, including a fine Juma mosque, built by the Mughal emperor Shah Jahan, and the tombs of Mirza Jani Beg and Diwan Sulfa Khan. Thatta is connected by a 13-mi. (21-km.) road with Jungshahi on the Pakistan Western Railway.

THATTA DISTRICT (area 6,933 sq.mi. [18,112 sq.km.]) had a population of 301,886 in 1951; this had increased to 361,733 by the time of the 1961 census. The district occupies the Indus Delta and the strip of land between the river and the highlands northeast of Karachi. Formerly a part of Sind Province, Thatta District (with Hyderabad, Dadu, and Tharparkar) became part of the Hyderabad Division when Sind Province was dissolved in October 1955. Large-scale excavations in the district, at Bhambore, about 30 mi. (48 km.) from Karachi, have revealed ruins located on an eminence about 30 ft. (9 m.) high. The ruins are thought to be those of a settlement of considerable importance. The settlement was well planned, with lanes and blocks of houses with stone foundations and mud-brick structure arranged around open courtyards. (K. S. AD.)

**THAYETMYO,** a town and district in the Magwe division of Burma. The town lies on the right bank of the Irrawaddy, opposite Allanmyo, 35 mi. (56 km.) N of Prome. In 1962 the population was estimated to be 59,055. Both towns developed as British frontier stations between independent Upper Burma and British Lower Burma. Thayetmyo became well known for its silverwork. It was founded in 1306.

THAYETMYO DISTRICT has an area of 4,626 sq.mi. (11,981 sq.km.); pop. (1962 est.) 352,893. The heart of the district is an undulating plain bisected by the Irrawaddy, much of which is covered with *Acacia* thorn scrub passing into dry forest on ridges rising from the plain and to true forest in the Arakan Yoma west and the Pegu Yoma east. Cultivated patches have the usual dry zone crops of sesame, peanuts, and cotton, with some rice and tobacco. Innumerable white pagodas crown every rise and hill spur. South of Thayetmyo is a hill of limestone, and the discovery of a natural gas field about 1930 led to the development of a cement industry. (L. D. S.)

**THEACEAE,** the tea family, an important group of dicotyledonous shrubs or trees, with 16–18 genera and more than 200 species, chiefly tropical and subtropical, in both hemispheres. An important genus is *Camellia,* wholly Asiatic, with 50 or more species, among them tea, *C. sinensis;* the cultivated camellia, *C. japonica;* and the Chinese tea oil plant, *C. drupifera.*

*Stewartia, Franklinia,* and *Gordonia* species, all native to Asia, are often cultivated for ornamental purposes. The family is represented in the southern U.S. by two species each of *Stewartia* and *Gordonia,* sometimes called camellias, and franklinia (*Franklinia alatamaha*), a beautiful fall-blooming tree. *Ternstroemia,* with 90 or more species, and *Eurya,* with 100 or more species, occur in both hemispheres. *See* TEA: *Botany;* CAMELLIA.

**THEATRE (ARTICLES ON).** The article THEATRE is concerned with the dynamics of drama—the evolution of the various forms of stage presentation, and the ideas and methods that animate the modern stage. DRAMA discusses the origins of the dramatic arts and gives a historical review of dramatic literature from ancient Greece, Rome, and India to the Broadway and West End of today.

The activities involved in bringing a script to life before an audience are treated in ACTING, DIRECTION AND PRODUCTION. The changing standards by which theatrical values have been judged are discussed in DRAMATIC CRITICISM. The contributions of dramatists to national literatures are evaluated in such articles as AMERICAN LITERATURE; ENGLISH LITERATURE; FRENCH LITERATURE.

Various forms of dramatic art discussed in the surveys mentioned above are represented also by individual articles—for example: BALLET; COMEDY; COMMEDIA DELL'ARTE; KABUKI THEATRE; MASQUE; MUSICAL COMEDY; NŌ DRAMA; OPERA; PAGEANT; PANTOMIME; SHADOW PLAY.

Additional articles on forms of theatrical presentation include CIRCUS; MINSTREL SHOW; MUSIC HALL AND VARIETY; PUPPETRY; VAUDEVILLE.

Articles dealing with technical aspects of the theatre include COSTUME DESIGN, THEATRICAL; MAKE-UP (STAGE, MOTION PICTURE AND TELEVISION); MASK; STAGE DESIGN; STAGE LIGHTING; THEATRES (STRUCTURES).

MOTION PICTURES gives a comprehensive survey of motion-picture writing, directing, and technology. Sections on animated cartoons and educational films are included, as well as discussions of methods of distribution. Other mechanical media for drama are treated in BROADCASTING and TELEVISION.

A series of articles deals with individual theatrical organizations—for example: ABBEY THEATRE; COMÉDIE FRANÇAISE; FEDERAL THEATRE PROJECT; FOLIES-BERGÈRE; GROUP THEATRE; MOSCOW ART THEATRE; OBERAMMERGAU; THEATRE GUILD (NEW YORK).

Among the articles on theatrical lore and activities are CONJURING; FOOL; PUNCH; SCARAMOUCH; and VENTRILOQUISM.

Many biographical articles—for example, those on Shakespeare and Garrick—review the work of the great playwrights and actors in the perspective of their times.

The Index, in addition to listing complete articles on theatrical topics, guides the reader to subjects covered in individual sections and passages.

The following articles are suggested as a minimal reading program for an introduction to the history and basic methods of the dramatic arts: ACTING, DIRECTION AND PRODUCTION; DRAMA; DRAMATIC CRITICISM; MOTION PICTURES; TELEVISION: *Television Broadcasting;* and THEATRE.

**THEATRE,** the place in which dramatic entertainments are presented (in Greek called *theatron*) and, by extension, the activity comprising both the dramatic performances themselves and the work of all who are responsible for presenting them to audiences. This article surveys the theatre, past and present, in all of its aspects. The article is best supplemented by readings in the biographies of dramatists, actors and others in the order of their mention here. For detailed information about places of performance, *see* THEATRES (STRUCTURES); for the drama considered primarily as a literary form, *see* DRAMA and articles on the various national literatures; and for the arts of dramatic representation, or stagecraft, *see* ACTING, DIRECTION AND PRODUCTION; COSTUME DESIGN, THEATRICAL; MAKE-UP (STAGE, MOTION PICTURE AND TELEVISION); STAGE DESIGN; STAGE LIGHTING.

In this article each of the following main topics is treated chronologically:



## I. GENERAL

**1. Introduction.**—When the word theatre is employed in the extended modern sense, descriptive epithets like Greek, Chinese, Elizabethan and Restoration, used in conjunction with it, serve to characterize not only the style of acting, building, costume and setting used in the theatre of the nation or period of history specified but even the style of written texts, together with the complex structure of commercial organization, government regulation and social relations. Theatre is, then, a style of dramatic art individual enough in its theory and practice to warrant description by a special label; "Indian theatre," "medieval theatre," "theatre in the round" define whole subjects either as homogeneous categories or periods of dramatic history, or as identifiable styles.

These styles are evolved through the cross-fertilization of national and historical artistic traditions in theatre practice, as exemplified in England or France by the adoption during the 17th century of Italian Renaissance landscape scenery, or in Germany by the 19th-century vogue for Shakespeare or during the present century by W. B. Yeats's interest in the Japanese nō play and the public enthusiasm for the Russian ballet presented by Sergei Diaghilev in Paris and London. The physical shape of stage and auditorium, too, in the course of about 2,000 years, has had a direct influence on the sort of play devised for performance: this is clearly seen when Sophocles' *Antigone*, *Electra* or *Oedipus Rex* are compared with modern versions of the same stories (*e.g.*, by Jean Anouilh, Hugo von Hofmannsthal, Jean Cocteau) where the large role played in the original by a numerous chorus is adapted or omitted to conform with the physical conditions of modern theatres, which are both smaller in size and more intimate in the actor-audience relationship provided.

**2. Actor and Society.**—In any concept of the word "theatre" larger than that restricted to timber, bricks and mortar, the centre is the actor. It is on him that the author must depend if his own scenario or text is to reach the audience as a living action. It is on him that the audience must depend as the instrument through whom the author's ideas are fully manifested in word, gesture and deed. Theatre, in the sense of a building, only acquires a *raison d'être* as a place for actors to perform in front of spectators. This is as true of the inanimate puppet and marionette theatre, and of the filmed drama or of the mechanically projected radio and television play, as it is of the animate theatre where, in opera, ballet or play, human actors encounter their audiences in person at every performance. All dramatic art, therefore, regardless of national or period label, takes its essence from the mimetic talent of the actor and its quality from the use to which this talent is put by the society that develops and rewards it.

The quality of the individual theatre will be particular to the society and will reflect that society's own level of development and standards of civilization. Great periods of achievement in the theatre have generally tended to coincide with or to follow immediately upon great national achievement, as the theatrical vitality of Periclean Athens, of Elizabethan England, of Louis XIV's France or of Scandinavia in the late 19th century illustrates. By contrast, a civilization with a marked addiction to ostentation and material values is likely to reflect this in a theatre dominated by spectacle and vulgarity, as may be seen in the decadence of Roman drama, of the English theatre during the 19th century or in the implications in the name of Hollywood in the latter half of the 20th century.

This relationship between the actor and the society of which he forms a part is itself responsible for the pattern of birth, growth, climax and decay repeated within every period of the theatre's history distinct enough to be identified by such special designations as "Greek tragedy" or *commedia dell'arte*. The creative initiative is invariably spontaneous and supplied by amateurs either directly as performers or indirectly as patrons. Any degree of popular success is then sought by professionals for reward until a point is reached where technical perfection or virtuosity can be admired in its own right. Exploitation of the commercial possibilities by the actors, their sponsors or both, in such a manner that financial gain outweighs care for art, quickly undermines professional integrity; artistic standards decline until that theatre loses first the respect, then the support of its patrons, and finally, its identity. Outstanding examples of the amateur initiative are the dance dramas of primitive peoples, the essays in perspective scenery and stage machinery of the 16th-century Italian *intermezzi* and of the Stuart masque in England, and the American arena theatre movement that began in Seattle at the University of Washington and was later endowed on a professional basis in Washington, D.C.

Another cyclic feature often repeated in the theatre's evolution is the sacrifice of an initial reliance on emblematic conventions of presentation to the gradual but increasing requirements of verisimilitude and spectacle for its own sake. This change is characterized by proportionately mounting production costs and by the sacrifice on the part of the actor of much of his own liberty of action to the whims or exigencies of painters and technicians; and in motion pictures and television to the mechanical restrictions imposed by microphones and cameras as well.

The actor's standing with society at large depends upon that of the theatre as a whole. In a primitive community he gained the approbation of his fellow men for contributing his own unusually developed human talent for mimicry to their service; in a more sophisticated society his translation to professional status may make him an object of envy to many and of censure to those others who claim that it is improper to esteem, let alone reward, any form of pretense. Acting and actors, when the activity is self-conscious enough to merit description under these terms, have thus always been a debatable asset to society; Plato thought them worthless hypocrites, while in England between 1648 and 1660 they were termed "caterpillars of the Commonwealth." At other times they have been valued highly enough to be thought worth fostering, as Aristotle believed them to be, or to warrant receipt of training, salary and pension at the expense of government, as in the U.S.S.R.

**3. Origins.**—This ambivalence in the actor's status and reputation in society derives directly from the way in which his mimetic talent is first harnessed to the needs of society. This talent is instinctive in every child and brings him from infantile to mature social behaviour. Linked with this instinct to explore by imitation and thus to enlarge experience is an egocentric concept of the individual's relationship to other people. The two in conjunction result in the self-assertion that distinguishes the personality of one individual from that of another. Once pretense by imitation has acquired this degree of self-consciousness, a distinction between "the performer" and "the beholder" becomes possible; each is only satisfied by the presence of the other. Theatre is born when this co-operative act of make-believe extends to cover consecutive imitated action. The attention of the beholder is arrested and held by the nature and accuracy of the imitation, while the ability of the imitator is enlarged by knowledge gained from the experience.

Theatre in this most elementary of forms is inarticulate, depending neither on a formal text nor on improvised speech; known as mime (*q.v.*), imitation through gesture and movement of the face and body is common in this state to all peoples and requires only an open space for its enactment.

Historical study has revealed that theatre in this natural form is quickly harnessed by all primitive peoples in seeking explanations for what is mysterious and unknown in their own environment. Attempts are made to establish contact with the sources of power in nature that appear most destructive and hurtful to a primitive people: excessive heat and accompanying drought, rain and floods, extreme cold and other violent phenomena occasioning acute emotional anxiety to tribe or individual. The form that these attempts take is usually mimetic imitation of the phenomenon feared, or imitation of objects observed to be related to that phenomenon in nature; the consuming power of fire is sought from contact with the ashes or the secret of fertility from contact with evergreens; the rhythms of nature as heard and seen in the movement of the wind or the sea are copied and simulated in dance (*q.v.*). With such means as these an appeal is made to the spirits or deities deemed to govern the elements to assist or at least to refrain from harming the supplicants. Disguise of the person in the shapes of nature and projection of the person into dance patterns imitating its movements are thus among the earliest distinctive components of theatre; a third essential is an open space where the disguised dancers may undertake their ritual.

The obstacle between these preparations and direct communication with the hidden god is consciousness of pretense in the whole nature of the action; the disguises adopted, being no more than emblems of the nature of the god, cannot be expected to induce the power required to permit speech with the god. A state of heightened emotional awareness has to be stimulated to obliterate this restrictive consciousness. It is here that the performers are called upon to generate an emotional response of an extraordinary kind in the beholders by accentuating the rhythmic quality of the dance patterns. The union between mortals equipped with nothing better than the crude symbols of the god's nature and behaviour and the controlling mind of the god himself, which in everyday life appears impossible, then becomes possible in the frenzy or ecstasy of the dance rhythms; and in this union of the spirit, involving the submergence of the individual in the whole, fear is overcome and anxiety allayed. Famine and plague may recur, but given the means of further communication the god can always be consulted.

The fear that is common to all individuals is that of death; it is thus to be expected that in their dance rhythms primitive peoples have been most attracted to those aspects of nature in which rebirth noticeably grows out of death; that is, to the solstices and the seasons. These phenomena account for the most persistent of all early theatrical imitations—the slaying of the god and his subsequent resurrection. The ancient rites associated with Osiris in Egypt derived from this assumption, and traces of it may be seen in the sword dances and mummers' play of the folk in northwestern Europe.

These rituals were designed to propitiate the forces of nature for past misdemeanours or to seek their assistance in future struggles, but many rites of a similar kind were evolved to give thanks for assistance received. These expressions of joy, however, were not marked by any such clearly defined narrative pattern as that of the dying god; the most notable characteristic was simply excess as exemplified for the whole western world by the proverbial Saturnalian orgy of Roman times or, in the Christian era, by the licentious Feast of Fools, when what E. K. Chambers described as "the peasant beneath the cassock" revealed his nature.

The transition from these dance rituals (specimens of which may still be observed in New Guinea and in parts of Africa) to a species of pretended action that incorporates a long and formal narrative with accompanying dialogue is difficult to discuss since it was not within the means of persons making this transition to record its details. They could only transmit what they knew, verbally or by example, to those who followed them and who added to and embroidered what they inherited with spontaneous inventions of their own. It is, therefore, to anthropologists and experts in the primitive religions of the world that one must turn for information. Relics survived in regular drama in the continued use of masks; in the relationship between actor and chorus in the earliest Greek tragedy and the earliest liturgical plays of the Christian Church, which reflected that of priest and congregation; in the elaborate emblematic headdresses, costumes and gestures of the Indian and Chinese classical theatre; and in the presence of an altar as the focal centre of the earliest Greek and Christian dramatic action. Above all there may be discerned in the written texts of tragic drama a continuance of earlier efforts to explain the inexorable laws of nature to fearful mankind, and in all early comedy a deliberate release of high spirits, which, in mocking everything artificial, pompous or unnatural, extols the liberty and bounty of nature.

Tragedy and comedy (*qq.v.*) are the two primary types of theatrical experience that dramatic art, however sophisticated the place or time, has continued to provide. The more serious kind has always preserved affinities with its religious origins, while the more frivolous kind has been liable to degenerate into forms offensive to a highly developed sense of public decency. It is the exploitation of the latter forms of simulated action by professional actors for commercial reward in return for the social recreation provided (in contrast to the spontaneous amateur theatre of worship) that has caused both actors and the theatre to be attacked from time to time as vicious, immoral and better suppressed.

## II. THE EAST

The country with the earliest reliable record of a dramatic tradition more advanced than ritual dancing is India, its history being traceable to about A.D. 100. Java, Bali and Burma all possess a notable dance drama, but it is from China and Japan that the most highly formalized dramas have survived into current use, despite contact with the western world. Indian classical theatre (Sanskrit) was virtually extinguished as a result of the Muslim invasions of the 10th century and after; but enough information, in the form of play texts and treatises about their staging, survived for attempts at revival to be made during the 19th century. Not enough is yet known in the west about the early history of the oriental theatre to ascertain the degree of interaction between the various dramas of distinct national origin; the Japanese theatre, however, owes as direct a debt to the Chinese theatre as the American theatre does to that of western Europe.

The transition from dance drama to regular plays in India, China and Japan was made in each instance through the Buddhist religion and aristocratic patronage, distinct genres with written texts being in existence in India by the 2nd century A.D., in China by the 6th and in Japan by the 14th. In all three countries actors have had a mixed reputation, some enjoying the friendship of princes and others being regarded as little better than beggars or criminals. In India, actors (*nata,* "a dancer") formed an identifiable class or caste in society and female roles were played by men until the 20th century. In all three countries an actor's training started in early youth, and a high degree of skill was required not only in dancing but also in singing, mime and acrobatics.

Where theatre buildings and the stage conventions employed in them are concerned, common practice is again evident. Temples and palaces adapted to suit the actor's needs sufficed initially and, in India, probably continued to do so; at least there is no evidence of buildings constructed to accommodate dramatic representations alone. In China and Japan, however, actors acquired wealth and position enough to become independent of their patrons and to build regular theatres for popular audiences. The typical Chinese theatre is a rectangular building containing a large projecting stage (almost square) backed by a curtained or painted wall containing two doors. The nō stage in Japan (and the kabuki stage, which is adapted from it) also projects into the auditorium and is square (18 × 18 ft.). A penthouse roof (adapted from the Shintō temple of origin) projects over this stage and is supported by pillars. (*See* NŌ DRAMA: *Staging;* KABUKI THEATRE.)

Theatres of the east have no scenery in the western sense of the word. Place is identified by emblems, some being permanent fixtures like the four stylized pine trees (one large, three small) of the nō stage, others taking the form of large stage properties like the arched gate or painted flags of the Chinese theatre: change of place is identified by the mime of the actors, by special properties like the Chinese tasseled horsewhip and by the shifting of properties in the audience's view by stage assistants, who sit on the stage throughout the action. These architectural and scenic conventions bear a marked resemblance to those used in European theatres of the middle ages and early Renaissance (*see* below).

A similar reliance upon an emblematic manner of presentation is seen in the costuming and acting style of oriental plays. Masks are rare. Only the first actor (*shite, shtay*) wears one in nō. The painting of the skin, however, and particularly of the face, was regular in all three theatres and developed to a quite remarkable degree in China, where the *hua-lien* or painted face denotes character through both the particular lines and colours of the make-up. Many have been standardized, and the actor is trained to be competent in the style, colour and scale of beards, applied jewels, lines and spots appropriate to particular characters.

Headdresses and articles of clothing also serve to demonstrate character and temperament. In Indian drama gods and princes are immediately identifiable by their exceptionally elaborate headdresses, while in China and Japan animal headdresses (especially tiger heads) and plumes worn above the painted face are appropriate to warriors of high rank. Colour symbolism plays as important a part in costume as it does in make-up: robes of rich silks and satins are often so elaborate as to require long practice in the wearing of them if they are to be maneuvered with any semblance of agility or grace.

Contact with the west did not at first make any difference to these traditions except in India, where, under British rule, a growing European interest in Sanskrit literature led to a revival of classical plays in Bengali translation (1857 and after). This revival was possible because of the survival of both the play texts and the *Natyaṣastra* of the Brahman priest Bharata, a detailed treatise on the composition and production of plays written during the 3rd century A.D. and as important a document for the study of Eastern drama as the writings of Aristotle and Vitruvius on Greek and Roman drama have proved to be in the west. Other, later commentaries embroidered on Bharata's work but added little that was new. Archaeological research has brought to light a few pictorial representations of early performances.

Music has always formed an important element in the oriental theatre. Instrumental music conjoined with religious ceremonies introduced the leading player, who sang or spoke an explanatory prologue. In Japan, this function is shared between the second actor (who enters first) and the first actor; in China, the protagonist of the drama undertakes this task; in India, it was done by the leader of the company (*Sutradhara*). The orchestra (dominated by flutes, drums, cymbals and gongs) not only accompanies chanted dialogue but also sets a tempo that is carefully followed by the actors in their movements.

Formal differentiation of genres exists in the eastern theatres. Japanese kabuki and nō are the most obviously distinct; but in China wu (the military play) and wen (plays with civilian subject matter) are traditionally as different. Distinctions in the Indian theatre, as between *nataka* ("heroic legend") and *prahasna* ("farcical stories"), are also real. Japanese nō is itself divided into categories. Nowhere, however, is there any close correspondence to western genres (with the possible exception of melodrama), and in India the happy ending was invariable. Act and scene divisions of the kind familiar to the west are normal to all oriental plays, but unity of place has never been a question of consequence in a drama where episodic narrative is the dominant characteristic of structural form and where the technical virtuosity of the actor in a familiar role has always counted for more than novelty of plot or formal compactness. Western motion pictures, when introduced into eastern countries, found substantial popular support because of their episodic treatment of narrative; such techniques were already familiar to audiences.

Photographic realism, however, while easily copied by film makers of eastern nationality, has struck a severe blow at the imaginative emblematic conventions of the oriental stage, which by the 1960s had lost popular support to films and television.

### III. THE WEST

The history of theatre in the west differs from that of the east in two important respects. In the west there was the phoenixlike rebirth of organized drama in the middle ages after about 400 years of seeming death, and in the 20th century the quest for verisimilitude in dramatic imitation culminating in the mechanical reproduction of performances on film—a western invention subsequently exported to the east.

The most important single feature distinguishing the drama of the first phase, from the 5th century B.C. to the 6th century A.D., from that of the second phase, from the 10th century A.D. to the 20th, was the intervening influence of Christian philosophy and ritual. The theatre of the first phase was Greek in origin, spread to Italy and from there was transplanted east, west and south to the frontiers of the Roman empire; northward it penetrated into Austria, Germany and even Britain. The decline and fall of the theatre, already sapped from within by a growing dependence upon costly spectacle coinciding with objections to the nature of the spectacle raised by Christians on moral grounds, was one of the results of the barbarian invasions.

Although many theatres of the Hellenistic period are still standing in the 20th century, the new drama of Christian inspiration that began to take life and shape in the 10th century did not make use of these buildings; nor did it imitate the sophisticated forms of Greek and Roman regular drama since the new texts, acting and stage conventions were supplied by amateurs. Not until the 15th century was any serious concession made to earlier practice. The full-scale revival of Greek and Roman play forms and architectural concepts that followed in the 16th and 17th centuries was consequently distorted from the start; difficulties arose because a Christian society was seeking to emulate a product of non-Christian inspiration and because this society lacked adequate knowledge of stage practice in anything but late Roman theatres. The imitation consciously pursued was thus unconsciously based on a phase of Greco-Roman theatre already decadent in its addiction to spectacle and in its relation to society. The result, in every European country that already possessed a theatre of Christian inspiration, was to create a divorce between the two; *i.e.*, between a religious stage commanding popular support and a *commedia erudita*, or academic theatre, of interest only to the aristocracies of intellect and courtly privilege. This divorce coincided in time with the wars of religion; and, since the popular theatre was religious, the divorce took a form in each European country that followed the pattern of ecclesiastical government. In Italy divorce between the two became total by the end of the 15th century; in Spain—because of close supervision and gradual modification by the Inquisition—it is scarcely discernible; in France, Germany, the Low Countries and England it was erratic. Censorship and suppression, however, are everywhere in evidence, the differences from one country to another being in timing and degree. In France the religious stage was dissolved by the edict of 1548; in England it had become impossible by 1590 for any play devoted to religious subject matter to be performed with impunity. To the revival of Roman theatre, the court amateurs of European countries contributed something of their own—a preoccupation with dance and song, which were developed respectively in succeeding centuries as ballet and opera.

Despite the immediate triumph of the academically inspired neoclassical theatre in the 17th and 18th centuries popular elements returned to it, the way being led by the *commedia dell'arte (q.v.)* in Italy and by sentimentalism in English drama of the late 17th century. The romantic revival championed by Diderot in France and Lessing in Germany restored some dignity to the popular theatre of earlier times but it did not recover for a theatre of situation, intrigue, manners and scenes the popular support previously accorded to the theatre of religious and heroic narrative with its emblematic conventions of presentation. The development of melodrama in the 19th century restored to narrative and action their earlier pre-eminence, but the theatre's ability to provide accompanying spectacle of a realistic kind was eclipsed by the potentialities of the motion picture, which came into existence by the beginning of the 20th century.

The commercial potentialities of film theatre were quickly realized. The technique of marrying sound to picture was perfected in the late 1920s, opening a national market for repeated showings of a single performance, which, with the additional accomplishment of providing subtitles and "dubbing" in foreign languages, was extended to include a world-wide market. Further wholesale changes in bringing plays to audiences, instead of obliging audiences to come to theatres, are similarly attributable to advances in scientific knowledge, the most notable being the invention of radio and television transmission and of processes for the recording of such transmissions.

## A. Antiquity

**1. Greece.**—As well as creating great dramatic masterpieces, the classical Greek theatre has left a notable legacy to posterity in the (1) distinctness of the three dramatic genres—tragedy, comedy (old, middle and new) and satyr play; (2) the size and shape of the theatre buildings; (3) the division of function within the drama between actors in the roles of characters and those serving as choric commentators interpreting between the protagonists of the stage action and the audience; and (4) the strongly characterized masks worn by the actors.

A relationship between religious festivals and the three forms of regular drama (particularly in the rites associated with the nature god Dionysus) is generally acknowledged by historians but evidence is lacking with which to define this relationship in any detail. The outstanding survival from the earliest Greek tragedy is the relationship among single actor, chorus and audience (the whole community), which parallels that among priest, initiates and congregation in religious ritual. The parallel is reinforced by the themes and structure of the earliest surviving plays. Tragedy, being concerned with the moral government of the universe, was strictly serious and formal; Aeschylus' *Oresteia,* for example, concerns crime and its consequences in terms of mortal and divine retribution. Comedy (*i.e.,* old comedy), being contemptuous of all human attempts to behave as if mortals possessed the minds of gods, was joyous, robust and satirical; Aristophanes' *Lysistrata,* although deeply serious in its concern about war, still appears in the 20th century to be as uproariously funny as it is outspoken in the means suggested to prevent war's recurrence.

As Greek drama developed, emphasis shifted from divine and cosmic themes to mortal and microcosmic problems. H. D. F. Kitto has written that tragedy was formed, ennobled itself and lost its vigour while Athens was passing through the same processes; during this period, he points out, tragedy moved from communal to individual themes. Comedy underwent a series of equally clear transitions from broadly political (old comedy) to social satire (middle comedy) and then to a comedy of manners with stereotyped characters in plots dependent on intrigue and situation. Changes in theatre practice kept step with these thematic tendencies. Aeschylus called on the services of a second actor (both actors doubling in more than one part) and Sophocles on those of a third. Both of these authors tended to increase the number of characters in their plays, and their successor, Euripides, went farther still in this direction. The chorus lost ground to the actors in number and function. The original dithyrambic chorus of 50 that Aeschylus inherited had been reduced in Euripides' lifetime to less than half the number, with nothing more to do than interpolate decorative lyrical odes as interludes in the action. In comedy, whereas Aristophanes used his chorus as formally as Sophocles, the new comedy of Menander used it for induction or the interpolation of songs for their own sake. The pursuit of realism brought with it a corresponding change in the nature of both stage language and setting. The earliest plays are made up of sequences of choral odes interrupted by "episodes" of speech for actors (*e.g.,* Aeschylus' *Agamemnon*). Sophocles' plays were distinguished by the perfect balance achieved between choral and dialogue speech; the metrical rhythms are of the utmost importance and probably carry in them some reminder of the original choric movements.

The place of performance, initially a large dancing floor (orchestra), was elaborated first with a dressing room and then by extension and decoration of the *skene* thus created on a scale great enough to permit the use of revolving panels (*periaktoi*) bearing pictures designed to identify the place of action and other machines. Nevertheless, the Greek theatre was wholly emblematic, employing men to impersonate women, using masks to conceal the fact that one actor was playing more than one part, and identifying place by symbol. Moreover, in attempting any imaginative reappraisal of a Greek play in performance, it must be remembered that the auditorium seated 10,000–20,000 persons, all of whom looked down on the orchestra and thus saw at one time the geometrical patterns of the chorus dances and the magnificence of the landscape beyond the *skene.*

Aristotle's notes on dramatic composition in the *Poetics* and a list of prize-winning plays (*Didascalia*) written in the 4th century B.C. provide much knowledge of the historical development of drama in Greece and a careful appraisal of the theory of tragedy, its function and composition, as practised up till his own day. These notes were translated, summarized and commented upon in Latin in later centuries but did not circulate widely in the west in the Greek original until late in the 16th century.

**2. Rome.**—The only plays that survive as a basis of an appreciation of Roman theatrical tastes are the comedies of Plautus and Terence (2nd century B.C.), the tragedies of Seneca (probably written to be read, not acted) and a few fragments of pieces attributed to Ennius, Pacuvius and Accius of the 3rd and 2nd centuries B.C. There is the related evidence of a great many theatre buildings (most now in ruins) ranging from such small intimate edifices as may be seen at Verulamium (St. Albans) in England, at Taormina in Sicily or at Pompeii near Naples to such grandiose monuments as the well-preserved examples at Orange in Provence and Aspendus in Turkey. Horace, in his epistle to the Pisos (a work better known as *Ars poetica,* or "The Art of Poetry"), gives some picture of what the Romans expected of their theatre. Documentation of theatre architecture and machinery, however, is better than that surviving from Greece because of the preservation of Vitruvius' *De architectura* (1st century B.C.) and Pollux's *Onomasticon* (2nd century A.D.).

The affinities between Greek new comedy and that of Plautus, as well as those present in the two styles of theatre building, argue a marked continuity between Greek precedent and Roman practice. On the other hand, the lack of any corpus of tragic texts; the nomadic and comparatively professional quality of the Roman actor's status; the certainty of a raised stage in Roman theatres, which was of more importance than the orchestra; the use in theatres built during and after the 1st century A.D. of a drop curtain with the development of scenic effects that the curtain allowed; and the additional attention given to the comfort of the audience—all indicate a positive Roman attitude to theatre that was both mundane and commercially angled. This picture is reinforced by the knowledge that under imperial rule mime and pantomime based upon actors' improvisations and acrobatics came to dominate a theatre growing steadily more luxurious in its appearance and fittings at the expense of the dramatist. Mere

BY COURTESY OF (LEFT) THE VATICAN LIBRARY, (RIGHT) THE TRUSTEES OF THE BRITISH MUSEUM

(LEFT) A PERFORMANCE OF TERENCE'S "ADELPHI": ILLUMINATION FROM THE VATICAN TERENCE, 4TH CENTURY A.D. (RIGHT) TERRA-COTTA STATUETTES OF ACTORS AS CHARACTERS IN GREEK NEW COMEDY, FROM VULCI, 2ND CENTURY B.C.

theatricality, exploited for the sake of display and for commercial gain, was substituted for the former religious, moral and artistic concerns of actors and audiences. With this change responsible people came to regard the theatre as unworthy of their attention.

In republican days, Roman comedy at least still possessed written texts and aimed at exposing vice and ridiculing folly in as amusing a manner as possible. A noisy crowd in holiday mood had to be silenced by the actors and its attention held against the competition of rival sports and festival attractions. The success of Plautus and Terence at least is demonstrated by the way in which their plays have held the stage in revivals, translations and remodelings. Even radio and television have deemed them worth revival in translation, Plautus' *Mostellaria, Miles Gloriosus* and *Menaechmi* being among the most successful.

With the alienation of the writers, however, and the steady increase in purely spectacular extravagance and vulgarity it is easy to understand why early Christians should have been as contemptuous of theatrical performances and as hostile to the profession of acting as their writings and actions show that they were. The closing of the theatres in the 5th century A.D. after the triumph of Christianity within both eastern and western halves of the Roman empire did not result from any particular antipathy to regular drama; the early Christian Fathers within the empire were opposed to a form of dramatic art so debased through commercial exploitation as to have lost any relevance to the general good of society. Outside the empire they had to contend with dramatic rituals as yet too primitive to have acquired regular forms but the closer on that account to the primitive religions that Christianity was seeking to suppress. The theatre of the ancient world thus survived in fragments only like some river that has temporarily split itself into several channels: a selection of texts, a variety of disused buildings (useful as quarries), some theoretical treatises, and groups of itinerant mimics, singers and dancers exercising their talents illicitly wherever a patron or passer-by could be found to look and listen. The barbarian invaders from the north and east, possessing no regular drama of their own and speaking languages other than Greek and Latin, could not supply the initiative required to reunite these isolated components of former dramatic and theatrical traditions.

### B. Christian Revival

**1. International Drama of the Medieval Church.**—The first steps toward reunification were taken spontaneously and unself-consciously in the Christian liturgy; the festival of Easter and celebration of Christ's resurrection provided the occasion; the meeting of the three Marys with the angel at the empty tomb and the angel's announcement of the resurrection to them was the theme. This elementary dramatic performance involving mime, dialogue and emblematic representation of person and place was soon adapted and repeated in connection with the miraculous birth celebrated at Christmas at the time of the winter solstice. In the first instance both of these dramatic representations took place within the ritual of the Mass and were enacted by the choir. The initiative appears to have come from the duchy of Swabia in the 10th century, the text taking the form of a chanted Latin introit, *Quem quaeritis in sepulchro, O Christicolae?* The great religious houses of St. Gallen (now in Switzerland), Limoges and Fleury quickly elaborated these texts both musically and in the extension of subject matter, though treatment of Christ's Passion is conspicuously absent. Dramatic representation spread to areas as remote from one another as Dublin and Augsburg or Winchester and Florence, and would seem to indicate that it was accepted as part of the church's missionary and instructional activities. It is not until the end of the 13th century that the Passion is treated fully or that the vernacular is preferred to Latin.

During 300 years of slow elaboration in these liturgical music plays, a code of symbols drawn from earlier liturgical practice and chant came to be applied to the performance of these plays; the code served as the basis for subsequent theatre practice in respect of acting, costumes and setting. St. Ethelwold, as bishop of Winchester, in his *Regularis Concordia* (*c.* 965–975) drew up rules for the acting of the *Quem quaeritis* ceremony in his diocese governing gesture, vestments and means of suggesting locale.

Similar information may be gleaned from the rubrics of service books all over Europe, though a great many of these were destroyed in the course of the Reformation. One of the fullest to have survived is the French *Festum Praesentationis beatae mariae* of Philippe de Mézières (1372), from which the wholly ritualistic and emblematic nature of these performances may easily be reconstructed. This text along with all others of importance is printed in Karl Young's *The Drama of the Medieval Church.* The gradual extension of the subject matter treated in these religious playlets led to an episodic narrative style with small regard to formality in respect of time, place or action. Thus in every respect this drama performed by priests for the enlightenment of worshipers openly admitted the pretense implicit in the representation.

This very important characteristic, so different from the 20th-century theatre practice which often uses every conceivable scientific device to pass off the pretense as the actual, applied with equal force to the vernacular adaptations of scripture in dramatic form that began during the 14th century. Known in Italy as *sacre rappresentazioni,* in Spain as *autos sacramentales,* in France as *mystères* and in England as miracle plays or (after 1800) as mystery plays, these performances were centred on Christ's Passion and were designed to stress the humanity as much as the divinity of Christ. Thus, while preserving in field, market place or town hall the same emblematic quality in performance as the liturgical play of cathedral or church interior, the highly ritualistic style of presentation was relaxed to accord better with the secular elements now preponderant in the narrative. Chant gave place to speech, church vestments were supplemented by contemporary costume appropriate to peasant or secular official, and scenic elements, specially made for the performance, became more decorative. The high seriousness of purpose remained, but comic elements, particularly in association with devils and peasant characters (*e.g.,* Mak of the Wakefield second *Shepherds' Play* or Mrs. Noah of the Chester *Deluge*), obtained a place in the plays, assisted no doubt by the use of vernacular speech. The initiative for these cyclic dramas, which grew long enough to occupy anything from a day's duration (in York) to a week's (in London and Mons), probably must be credited to mendicant friars. Plays of similarly didactic and devotional purpose concerning the lives of

BY COURTESY OF THE TRUSTEES OF THE BRITISH MUSEUM; PHOTOGRAPHS, J. R. FREEMAN & CO., LTD.

**THE THEATRE IN EUROPE, MIDDLE AGES TO RENAISSANCE**

(Top left) The *Quem quaeritis* ceremony, with the three Marys and the angel at the tomb; illumination from the *Regularis Concordia* of St. Ethelwold, c. 965–975. (Top right) The "tragic scene" according to Sebastiano Serlio, presenting a perspective background for the players, who performed not in the scene but in front of it; woodcut from the English edition of the *Architettura,* 1611. (Bottom left) *Commedia dell'arte* characters with a platform stage in the background; engraving by Jacques Callot, *Balli di Sfessania,* 1632. (Bottom right) Medieval musicians and a female performer doing a handstand on two swords; marginal illumination from the *Smithfield Decretals,* early 14th century

Christian saints and martyrs grew up simultaneously throughout Christendom but of a more markedly national character, as determined by the particular story.

Additional room for topical and local subject matter was provided by the dramatic adaptation of sermons depicting mankind's struggle to arrive at doomsday with an army of virtues rather than vices to plead his fate. This kind of play, religious in purpose but secular in virtually all externals, linked parable and symbol in dramatic narrative to the symbolic manner of presentation derived from the liturgical music plays.

Thus the way was opened in every European country for a theatre as secular as that of antiquity but now consistently Christian in its ethos. In France the result was seen in *entremets* and *soties;* in Germany in the *Fastnachtsspiel* and (farther east) in the *Neidhartspiel;* in Spain the *sainete;* in England in the "disguising" (formerly mumming, latterly masque) and the interlude (*see* INTERLUDES; MASQUE; MUMMERS). All of these genres are distinct, national, independent; yet at the same time each of them is only an aspect, coloured by racial temperament, geography and climate, of a spirit common to Christendom. These factors also governed the conditions of performance, common practice being more noticeable than particular variants. Performances were closely linked to festivals of the Christian calendar, themselves adapted from earlier folk festivals of the agricultural year—Christmas (winter solstice); Shrovetide, Easter and May day (advent of spring); Ascension, Whitsunday and Corpus Christi (summer solstice); St. Michael, and All Saints (harvest thanksgiving and autumn). Choice of a place of performance was governed by the mutual convenience of actors and audience: churches, where large enough; adjacent yards or cloisters where the churches were too small; market places, quarries, even playing fields; town halls, baronial halls, palace halls. The hierarchical stratification of medieval society was strictly observed in the provision of "standings" (and more rarely seats) and arrangements for the privacy and sight lines of spectators. Stages and auditoriums were as occasional as performances, with the notable exception of the "pageant waggon" stages used in the north of England that were carefully stored away for future use. Most religious plays were performed, as in Athens, by the local community for its own members. The actors received wages but were not professionals. Female parts were played by choirboys, though not invariably. The "wives of this town" presented the play of *The Assumption of the Virgin* in Chester. The cost was underwritten by both church and town; surviving expense accounts prove that the biggest single item was the cost of scenic units and winch machinery for flying angels and disappearing devils. Modern observers may be surprised at the endurance of audiences ready to sit or stand all day for several days watching these simple but dignified and profound plays; the plays then had a rarity value augmented by long months of corporate preparation and heightened by a sense of occasion, both of which have been lost.

**2. Medieval Minstrelsy and Pageantry.**—An equally occasional but more nearly professional theatre that aimed at social recreation rather than religious edification grew up during the late middle ages among minstrel troupes in princely courts and the households of the lords spiritual and temporal. The troupe consisted of *jongleurs* ("tregetoures") who entertained with mime, music and circus acts, and whose social status and way of life were probably descended from those of the nomadic mimes of the Roman theatre; it was led by the *trouvère* ("troubadour"), a probable descendant of the Teutonic *scôp,* who held the rank of esquire and sang or recited *chansons de geste.* This theatre gave expression to song, dance and romance literature in mime for the pleasure implicit in these things rather than for any devotional purpose. During the 15th century the troupe split into separate groups of musicians and actors. While employed as household servants and expected to perform for their master at calendar festivals, they were allowed to travel, taking their costumes and stage properties with them, and to perform for reward wherever their leader could obtain entree. Weddings and other private celebrations provided the occasions for such performances. The plays, compared with those of the religious stage, were short and often the work of a poet of reputation. Masks were frequently used and doubling of parts was invariable.

This association with aristocratic traditions and requirements brought the nascent theatre of social recreation into close contact with the codes for identifying person, rank and place developed in heraldry. Royal progresses, coronations, tournaments and battle honours which were usually celebrated by elaborate civic pageantry, provided a meeting point where the emblematic conventions of heraldry and of Christian ritual could be fused to the advantage of the actors and the painters and engineers who embellished their stages. The characters of the pageant theatres of city streets, in their persons and their speeches, contributed to a similar amalgamation of scriptural, mythological and historical figures.

This was the theatre—religious in its inception, recreational in its later development—that in the 16th century joined hands with the theatrical traditions of Greece and Rome; this was the theatre that was destined by its associations with Roman Catholic faith and ritual to become a principal target for Protestant reformers.

**3. Renaissance, Reformation and Counter-Reformation.**—The revival of interest in all things Greek and Roman, hastened by the fall of Constantinople to the Turks (1453) and the invention of printing, affected every theatre in Europe either directly or indirectly through Italian example. At first there was the novelty of seeing in action plays that had not been performed for more than 1,000 years; then there was the attempt to recreate something of the conditions and atmosphere of the original performances in Roman or Greek times; finally there was the adaptation of both to fit changes in manners, language and technical skills: the appeal of "modern dress" performances. Plautus' *Menaechmi* was performed in Latin before Duke Ercole d'Este in 1486, and Terence's *Phormio* by St. Paul's choirboys before Cardinal Wolsey at Hampton court in 1528. The reliance of Latin comedy upon typed characters (master, parasite, young lovers, braggart-coward, etc.) and upon plots of intrigue and situation made it easy for 16th-century adapters to do much the same in both vernacular speech and contemporary idiom. Cardinal Bernardo da Bibbiena's *La Calandria* in Italy, Rodrigo Cota's *Celestina* in Spain and Nicholas Udall's *Ralph Roister Doister* (*c.* 1553) in England are examples of this adaptation. In tragedy, a similar reliance upon Latin example (Senecan closet drama) and upon Latin adaptations of Aristotle (rather than the Greek original) provided Renaissance revivalists with a picture of ancient drama in which questions of form assumed a greater importance than those of either content or purpose. Dramatic entertainments of this kind, eagerly championed by pedantic scholars and deemed by their patrons to be a proper adornment of a civilized household, were accepted by the intelligentsia of Europe regardless of whether or not they were likely to enjoy any popular support.

Had the divorce between the religious stage and the theatre of pedagogic archaism been as complete in other European countries as it was in Italy (where the latter was largely pioneered), there would have been no "golden age" of Lope de Vega, Cervantes or Calderón in Spain and no "Elizabethan theatre" in England, for both English and Spanish theatres depended for their existence on the triumph of popular common sense over academic rationalism and an extravagant addiction to spectacle for its own sake.

In Italy, *commedia erudita*, comedy and tragedy imitating Roman example, was played out within 100 years and became subject to violent reactions in wholly unexpected directions: the beginning of *commedia dell'arte* and pastoral-lyric drama, or "opera." The former was a revulsion against a restricting form and a reassertion of the spirit of comedy stemming from that peasant stock whose religious stage had been so rudely spurned in the late 15th century. Some of the outward farcical qualities of the *commedia erudita* were taken over (*e.g.*, scenarios, type characters), but with the *commedia dell'arte* (*i.e.*, of the profession) the change is evident enough; improvisation was substituted for a fully scripted text, the personality and skill of the actor were now highlighted rather than the toil and erudition of the author, and the appeal to a popular audience was restored. Tragedy of the Senecan kind (*e.g.*, Gian Giorgio Trissino's *Sofonisba*, written about 1515 and first performed in 1562) was redeemed from suffocating boredom by the *intermezzi*, or interludes, between the five formal acts; these were devoted to songs and dances with decors designed by architect-painters of outstanding genius; *e.g.*, Mantegna, Baldassare Peruzzi, Raphael, Leonardo da Vinci. These *intermezzi* naturally grew in length and scale to a point where they came to eclipse the more serious episodes of the performance. The "satyr" play of Greco-Roman drama provided a classical source for the *intermezzi*, with their songs, dances and scenic experiments, which were deemed, in the absence of evidence, to have developed along pastoral lines from them. Torquato Tasso's *Aminta* (1573) and Giovanni Battista Guarini's *Il Pastor fido* (1595) forged the link. In Italy itself the emphasis on song resulted in what is now called opera; in France, dance took precedence, thus opening the way to what was later known as ballet; and in England, words, song, dance and spectacle were developed in the perfect equipoise of the Stuart masque—a genre that relied too greatly on the occasion celebrated to survive without an autocratically administered exchequer.

The scenic theatre, based on heavily subsidized study of Vitruvius and later on the commentaries on him (Sebastiano Serlio, Andrea Palladio, Vincenzo Scamozzi, and Lorenzin Sabbatini were the most influential), spread during the 17th century to France, Austria, Germany, Scandinavia and also to Spain at the hands of Italian exponents imported for the purpose. Inigo Jones's reputation in English theatrical history, however, rests on his independent development of ideas picked up during periods of study in Italy (1603–04 and 1611–13). The new Renaissance theatre modified the classical theatre construction; the built-in perspective, though still formal, made an attempt at verisimilitude that led to a fundamental disharmony in the elements of presentation. The best seats in the theatre were now determined by their view of the scene. The *frons scaena* was remodeled to form a proscenium arch concealing the elaborate scenic devices behind it, though it was still regarded as part of the scenery backing the actors rather than as a barrier dividing them from their audience. It was symptomatic of this theatre that the architect-painter took precedence, at least in respect of production costs, over both dramatist and actor.

That this prototype of Italian origin was not followed either simultaneously in time or uniformly in pattern elsewhere in Christendom was because of a combination of individual national factors and the varying international pressures of the Reformation and Counter-Reformation.

During the Reformation it was inevitable that hostility to Catholic Rome and what it stood for on the one hand and enthusiasm for imperial Rome and what that represented on the other should collide at many points, not least in the theatre. In Germany, England and parts of the Low Countries and of France, Rome was at once the throne of the muses and the seat of Antichrist, the viewpoint depending on religious persuasion and academic background. With religious drama already deeply entrenched in popular esteem the theatre in these countries, however involuntarily, could not avoid becoming a contentious issue in domestic politics. In Germany the stage was set to work early in the 16th century as an active instrument of propaganda for the Reformed church. This initiative passed quickly to England—Thomas Kirchmayer's *Pammachius* (1538) was dedicated to Archbishop Cranmer—while Thomas Cromwell employed John Bale and others to write polemical interludes mocking the traditions of the Roman Catholic religious stage: the pope, monks, friars and transubstantiation. The plays were adapted from the traditional miracles and moralities and quickly led to riots. Ket's rebellion of 1549 was deemed to have grown out of a disturbance at a play in the Norfolk village of Wymondham. Tudor governments, Protestant and Roman Catholic, from 1543 onward were forced into taking legislative action against the theatre. Actors were systematically placed under strict supervision and control; an increasingly vigorous censorship was imposed on play texts in manuscript and in print; places of performance were scrutinized and made subject to licence. Under Elizabeth I the amateur religious stage was systematically suppressed, the last miracle play to be performed being that at Coventry in 1584. Under James I all actors, plays and theatres were made subject to royal licence.

In 16th-century England neoclassical drama was not accepted unquestioningly, partly because of its association with Rome and with Latin, partly because topical debate proved far more acceptable than intrigue to audiences, and partly because the nation as a whole was thrown back on its own wits and resources in the face of the mounting threat of foreign invasion. Relaxation of tension followed swiftly upon the execution of Mary, queen of Scots (1587) and the defeat of the Spanish Armada (1588), and with it came a readmission of Italian ideas in art and education. By then, however, a distinctly English style of secular theatre had grown out of the ashes of the religious stage. It was distinguished by its reliance on the symbolism derived from liturgical plays and from heraldry; it owed its narrative to the miracle cycles and saint plays, its emphasis on debate and parable to the morality play and its professional character to the players of interludes. The shape and size of its stages and auditoriums were influenced by the animal-baiting arenas, the circular and rectangular tilting yards, the square or rectangular halls and (probably) yards of inns and by the rectangular town halls and guildhalls of provincial towns. Professionally organized and relying on the financial support of commercial speculators and the protection of sovereign and court officials, the theatre of Marlowe, Kyd, Shakespeare, Jonson, Dekker and Webster remained a popular theatre in touch with its medieval heritage and self-confident enough to draw what it wanted from neoclassical precept and no more. Public theatres (Globe, Swan, Fortune, Hope, Red Bull, etc.), private theatres (Blackfriars, Whitefriars, the Cockpit) and the court theatre of the masque represent accurately enough a box-office dependence on plays and performances reflecting past traditions, present experiments and a prototype for the future.

Where the court masques were largely the pride of amateur participants, the public and private theatres, in the hands of such shrewd and wealthy men of business as the Burbages (James *c.* 1531–97, Richard *c.* 1567–1619, Cuthbert 1566–1636), Philip Henslowe (*c.* 1550–1616) and his actor son-in-law Edward Alleyn (1566–1626), were in all respects professional. This distinction they achieved in the face of tough opposition from the more Calvinistically minded reformers and capitalist merchants who objected to the absenteeism created by the popularity of stage performances. These factions in society grew steadily more powerful in Jacobean and Caroline times, banning actors from one provincial city after another; the actors themselves, in concentrating upon a metropolitan business, position at court, coterie audiences and extravagant spectacle, aided their enemies in cutting the bonds of popular support. The closing of the theatres in 1642 at the outbreak of the English Civil War represented as much a popular revulsion against actors and plays, considered to be little more than royal slaves and royal toys, as it did an act of puritan retribution against a relic of popery.

In Germany, France and Spain features of this pattern are repeated but with important differences of emphasis. In Germany the initiative that adapted the traditions of the religious stage for purposes of Protestant propaganda was strong enough to retard the development of the neoclassical theatre even longer than in England. Little direct Italian influence is to be seen in German plays or stagecraft (beyond the arbitrary act and scene divisions) until late in the 16th century. The only outstanding theatrical figure was Hans Sachs (1494–1576), who adapted a disused Catholic church (the Marthakirche) in Nürnberg in 1550 as a theatre for his own and other plays acted by a company of which he was himself the leader. English traveling actors, by importing Elizabethan plays and stage conventions, gave the Germans a taste of theatre that was professionally organized for purposes of social recreation rather than for those of moral improvement and reinforced their native traditions. But this vitality was counterbalanced by the social upheaval of the Thirty Years' War, and the sterility of the polemical *commedia erudita* of the Jesuit Counter-Reformation. Of attempts to combine popular Protestant drama with neoclassical precepts only the plays of Andreas Gryphius (1616–64) have attracted attention from posterity. Italian opera with accompanying scenery made heavy inroads in court circles, serving to establish a complete divorce between popular tradition and aristocratic taste by the middle of the 17th century.

In Spain, by marked contrast, the impact of the Reformation and Counter Reformation on the theatre was slight. The reason was that the Inquisition, as reorganized under Torquemada (*c.* 1486), had taken care to purge the religious stage of those elements that in other countries laid it open to ridicule. Neoclassical theatrical ideas thus developed alongside traditional popular plays and stage convention, since authors were able to write for either as inclination and occasion suggested. Since the feast of Corpus Christi continued to be observed (it was abolished in England) plays associated with the feast (*autos sacramentales*) continued to be presented throughout the 16th century and after. Courtly actor-playmakers similarly had opportunities of a far less inhibited kind than in England, although less highly organized than in Italy, to refine their craftsmanship by conscious imitation of Latin authors and to develop subject matter of an avowedly secular kind. The playwrights Juan del Encina (1468–1529) and Gil Vicente (*c.* 1465–1536) and the critic and theorist Bartolomé de Torres Naharro (1480–1530) provided between them the backbone of this alternative to the popular (and largely amateur) religious stage.

From this cult of *entremeses, comedias* and *tragedias* the Spanish theatre acquired as recognizably professional an outlook and status as that of the English interludes, while from the popular religious stage it retained as distinctly rhetorical and emblematic techniques of performance and presentation as those of the Elizabethan theatre. Market places and innyards on provincial circuits provided the actor-playwright Lope de Rueda (1510?–65) with his theatre building and it was a member of his company, A. de Rojas, who in *El Viaje entretenido* gave a vivid picture of the actor's life. Under municipal control professional theatres were provided in *corrales* (courtyards) administered by religious and charitable institutions. These buildings slightly precede in date those in England, but whereas in England such buildings were limited to London, in Spain the practice spread quickly from Madrid (*c.* 1560) to all large provincial cities. As in England, the performers suggested improvements in the buildings they used and these found their way into subsequent designs. Performances took place in the afternoons and were accompanied by items of song and dance corresponding to the Elizabethan jig. A roof projected over a raised stage; the wall from which the stage jutted contained doors and windows; costume was contemporary dress adorned with heraldic or other emblems of identification; traps and flying machines were provided. This theatre was nearly akin in national temperament and professional need to that of Elizabethan and Jacobean England, and it produced dramatists of as outstanding a quality in Cervantes, Lope de Vega and Calderón, all of whom exploited the narrative possibilities of their stage to the full. Action, wide-ranging and fast-moving, was the hallmark of this theatre, just as it was of the English theatre. It differed from English practice, however, in the continuing liberty allowed to plays based on biblical and theological subject matter; in the work of Calderón, for example, there is to be found a perfect blend of religious subject matter and symbolic presentation: the medieval theatrical tradition has been modernized in theology and literary style by the Counter-Reformation and in stage convention by the adaptation of neoclassical settings and machinery that was wholly lacking in England. Where England contributed to the German theatre through the repertoire of strolling players, Spain contributed to France the vitality of its drama of character, situation and intrigue.

Spanish influence, however, was particularly marked in the Low Countries, governed by Spanish rulers through the first half of the 16th century and in revolt against them during the second half. The indigenous religious stage, with its notable morality play *Elckerlyc* (*Everyman, c.* 1470) and the festivals of the Rederijkers Kamers (chambers of rhetoric; *see* DUTCH LITERA-

TURE), formed the basis of a theatre that might have been as influential throughout Europe as Flemish painting had not conditions of political and social unrest disrupted its development and made it subject in turn to the dominance of Spanish, Jewish and French influence. The Schouwburg theatre, built in Amsterdam by Jacob van Campen (1637), nevertheless provides the theatre historian with as interesting a building as the Teatro Olimpico at Vicenza (Palladio and Scamozzi, 1580–84).

Both illustrate the transition from medieval to classical styles of theatre architecture; the Olimpico, as markedly advanced toward the new style as was the Schouwburg (although built so much earlier in time), is noticeably dependent on the past. In these two theatres and in Johannes de Witt's drawing of the Swan theatre in London (built *c.* 1594) may be seen three manifestations of neoclassicism tempered by the pressures of the Reformation and Counter-Reformation that conveniently epitomize a whole period of violent controversy and astonishingly varied achievement.

### C. Classical, Baroque and Romantic Reaction

The French theatre followed Italian example in divorcing religious and popular drama from secular and recondite drama. Sacred drama was forbidden by decree in 1548 to prevent its being used by the Protestants to try to bring Roman Catholicism into contempt. Artists, unfortunately, cannot be created by decree and in consequence the great French heritage of religious plays and popular farces was followed by attempts to ape Italian academic example, but in a manner even more dogmatic than the model. The typical medieval mixture of joyous and sad, tragic and comic found no sequel in the rigid theorizing of the scholar poets, of whom Étienne Jodelle (1532–73), Robert Garnier (*c.* 1545–90) and Jacques Grévin (1538–70) enjoyed a limited repute at the time. A taste for dancing and spectacle grew up among court amateurs in France; this centred on the court ballet, of which *Le Ballet comique de la reine* of Balthazar de Beaujoyeulx (Baldassarino de Belgiojoso) is the best-known example. Printed in 1582, it provides illustrations of the scenic arrangements that were still traditional and include Circe's garden, a grove of trees and a large cloud. Early in the 17th century Pierre Corneille encountered bitter criticism in trying to bridge this gap between the unity of place demanded by the theorists and the *décor simultané* of theatre practice, a gap only made the wider by the conspicuous absence until 1595 of any professional acting company other than the crippled Confrérie de la Passion, which owned the Hôtel de Bourgogne.

Not until political stability returned to France under Cardinal Richelieu could a theatre as genuinely professional as that of Spain or England return to Paris. Two theatres, the Hôtel de Bourgogne and the Marais, then began to develop on professional lines and in keen competition, with tragedy, comedy and pastoral in the Italian manner established as the only recognized dramatic genres. It was not until 1650, however, that Italian stage machinery was coupled to performances in public theatres: the occasion was Corneille's *Andromède* with settings by Giacomo Torelli. It was left to Molière and Racine to bring the French theatre, one in comedy the other in tragedy, to a pre-eminence sufficient to eclipse that of both England and Spain, and this despite perhaps the most vicious sequence of literary intrigues and personal attacks the theatre has ever known, or at any rate recorded. Molière (1622–73), himself an actor, and Racine (1639–99), acquainted from youth with theatre practice and assisted by Molière, enjoyed that same protection of the sovereign and those near to him that had distinguished the careers of Shakespeare, Ben Jonson, Philip Massinger and others in England; together they brought to the theatre a degree of observation both of human foibles and of human passion and suffering that sufficed to give a genuine vitality to the revived classical forms not attained before or since. Aided by two remarkable musicians, Jean Baptiste Lully and Jean Philippe Rameau, the pastoral form was also vigorously developed in France in the directions both of opera and of ballet.

The influence of Molière and Racine, together with that of Corneille, was felt everywhere in Europe and was synthesized for Europe in Boileau-Despréaux's *L'Art poétique* (1674). Nowhere else, however, was their genius matched; only in England, and there only in comedy, was anything written or staged that has maintained a hold on posterity in terms of frequent adaptation and revival. English tragedy modeled on the French, of which Sir William Davenant and John Dryden were the twin advocates, degenerated, as Italian tragedy had done, into operatic fantasy. Everywhere, however, from Sweden in the north to Austria in the east the real victor was the theatricality of the baroque spirit expressed in stage settings and their illumination. Classicism triumphed momentarily in France, but it was the spectacular rather than the literary quality of the revival that held Europe entranced throughout the 18th century. Everywhere it was the designers and the actors whose names counted with audiences rather than those of the writers. The costume designs of Lodovico Burnacini (1636–1707), the perspective settings of the Bibiena family, which between 1680 and 1780 were unchallenged for originality and activity, and theatres like the opera house in Bayreuth define the baroque spirit and its rococo sequel that spread outward from dramatic representations to enhance the whole of aristocratic life. Theatre worthy of the name became a courtly or at least a metropolitan toy designed to kill time in a manner as costly as befitted its aristocratic patrons. Popular theatre dwindled into fairground improvisations and the meagre, eviscerated reper-

BY COURTESY OF THE TRUSTEES OF THE BRITISH MUSEUM; PHOTOGRAPHS, J. R. FREEMAN & CO., LTD.

**17TH–18TH CENTURIES**

(Top left) David Garrick, costumed for the role of Richard III; engraving by William Hogarth, 1746. (Top right) Settings by Giacomo Torelli for Corneille's *Andromède,* in which Italian stage machinery was introduced to the French theatre; from P. Corneille, *Andromède,* 1650. (Bottom) Performance of J. B. Lully's opera *Alceste,* at Versailles in 1674; engraving by Jean Lepautre from *Les Divertissements de Versailles de l'an 1674* toires of strolling players. At both levels there were extensive exchanges, Gustavus III of Sweden enjoying at Drottningholm in 1780 what Louis XIV had initiated at Versailles a century earlier, Pierre de Chamblain de Marivaux in Paris enjoying closer affinities with Carlo Goldoni in Venice or Richard Brinsley Sheridan in London than with Molière, and booth theatres in provincial streets holding audiences with debased relics of Jonsonian "humour," German farce and Spanish intrigue grafted onto the improvised scenarios of *commedia dell'arte.*

Reaction and revolution came not from left or right but from the centre; *i.e.,* from the bourgeois public denied a theatre for so long by Puritan sentiment in England, by aristocratic privilege in France, by war and social unrest in the Low Countries and middle Europe, by stagnation in Spain and by feudalism in Russia and Scandinavia. A spirit of satire and sentimentality, long smoldering beneath the surface, began to make itself felt in England, particularly in the work of Henry Fielding and George Lillo; similar romantic yearnings in Germany were made vocal by Lessing and, in the following century, these tendencies were further advanced by the nationalistic and democratic fervour of Italians, Norwegians and Russians, culminating in the work of Verdi, Ibsen and Chekhov. Moreover, the political revolution that, country by country, shattered the aristocratic façade of European theatre was accompanied by an industrial revolution of equal consequence to stage architecture and convention.

The pastoral fantasies, countertenors, literary controversies about the unities and restricted admission by privilege of birth were of little or no interest to the merchant *bourgeoisie* of Europe returning slowly to theatre or demanding theatres of their own. They wished for action and narrative of a kind not seen on the stage (outside Spain) for generations; an unwitting return was made to the genuine beginnings of theatre in ancient Athens or during the middle ages rather than to those beginnings mistakenly judged to be represented by the Roman stage on which the whole edifice of neoclassicism had been built. These yearnings, however, were not supported by any particular erudition and were in any case quickly coloured with political vested interest and spectacular possibilities of the new stage devices. Aristocratic opera and ballet were thus subjected in the early 19th century to popular sentimentalizing, comedy of character, manners and wit; to a taste for farce and tragedy; to an eagerness for violence and horror. The cult of spectacle, however, so long a luxury for the few and the corrupter of their theatre, did not disappear; it increased and corrupted in turn the taste of the newcomers. The apotheosis of the changed theatrical style was melodrama.

Melodrama is a difficult term to define since it embraced among writers such distinguished men as Goethe, Victor Hugo and Pushkin, reached its zenith in Germany and its nadir in England and the United States and, having quitted the animate theatre via grand opera and classical ballet, has perpetuated itself in motion picture and in television serial. In one sense it represents the last despairing heroic fling of the theatrical rhetoric inherited from a pre-Christian past; in another sense it has come to stand for all that is most sentimentalized and hypocritical in a Christian-rooted theatre. What is clear is that melodrama represents a watershed in the history of European theatre; it was at once the last genuinely theatrical form with an appeal strong enough to draw its support from all ranks of society and the jumping-off point for that division between the actor and his stage that characterized the subsequent development of dramatic art in the west. Some actors, singers and dancers chose to exploit the more hedonistic and less educated element of the popular audience. With methods and organization resembling that of the medieval minstrel troupes or Roman mimes, they made what capital they could from their own personality and special "acts" but with the important difference that on the financial success of performances in public houses it became possible to erect theatres for the purpose, thus giving a degree of urban regularity to what had hitherto been the largely rural and nomadic occupations of the fairground. From the "music room" annex to public bars sprang not only the professional circus but also the great provincial and metropolitan chains of theatres known in Britain as music hall and in the United States and parts of Europe as vaudeville and epitomized in England by the twice-nightly variety shows managed by Sir Edward Moss and Sir Oswald Stoll (*see* below; *see* also CIRCUS; MUSIC HALL AND VARIETY; VAUDEVILLE).

Where stage plays were concerned, the popular section of the audience derived amusement from parodies of classical theatre forms (burlesque [*q.v.*]; extravaganza; burletta) and from the spectacular sensations of shipwreck, forest fire and earthquake intermingled with violence and idealism supplied in the more elaborate melodramas, of which Guilbert de Pixérécourt in France (1773–1844) was the pioneer and prime exponent. A similar cult of individual personality developed within the more orthodox dramatic genres of the traditional theatre, finding its prime expression in productions of Shakespeare's plays in England, in opera under German and Italian leadership and in Russian ballet. Shakespearean title roles gave the "star" actor his pre-eminence in his profession, while vocal virtuosity and powers of mimetic expression were similarly emphasized in opera and ballet, respectively. Paradoxically, the narrative and spectacular elements of libretto and setting were also exploited for their own sake in a manner that made all actors other than the star the virtual prisoners of an army of technicians. The invention of gas lighting with the possibility of blacking out the auditorium (*c.* 1823), subsequently improved in both safety and flexibility by electric lighting, forced even the star actor off his commanding "forestage" and incorporated him within the stage picture as an adjustable item in the pictorial design. Because of the technical problems involved in manipulating these animated landscapes with narrative coherence, the star actor was gradually obliged to hand over his control of his fellow actors and the scenery; both actors and scenery were now subject to control by financial speculators and a neutral observer who, from the humble status of stage manager, came thus to be elevated to the dignity of producer, *régisseur* or director. Further dignity and power were added to his status as techniques of mechanical reproduction in motion pictures, radio and television increased the ratio of engineers and technicians to actors in any single dramatic performance, and as the star actors lost financial control to their managerial partners. The latter situation was somewhat modified in the 1950s when some Hollywood stars began producing their own films.

With the retirement of the actor off his forestage and into the scenic picture, realism of an almost photographic kind became a main object of production. Assisted by a developing interest in historical and archaeological accuracy that was initiated by the actor David Garrick (1717–79) in his costuming of Shakespeare's plays and was brought to its highest point by Sir Henry Irving (1838–1905) and Sir Herbert Beerbohm Tree (1853–1917) in the costumes and settings used in their productions, this realism in externals demanded concessions from both dramatists and actors. Both the written and the spoken text had to be scaled down if the dichotomy between realistic sets and costumes and a rhetorical text and delivery were not to appear ludicrous. The language of poetry and a large measure of the virtuosity that had earlier distinguished the professional from the amateur actor were both victims of this sacrifice. Dramatists were forthcoming in France in Victorien Sardou and Augustin Eugène Scribe, in England in Thomas Robertson, in Germany in Gerhart Hauptmann, in Scandinavia in Bjørnstjerne Bjørnson, Strindberg and Ibsen and above all in Russia in Chekhov, capable of making stage action and dialogue look and sound as natural as everyday life. It was in Russia at the Moscow Art Theatre that the first serious steps were taken by the actor-producer Konstantin Stanislavski to codify a style of acting as appropriate or "natural" as the verisimilitude of the new plots, settings and dialogue demanded. The imitations that followed, under George Bernard Shaw and Harley Granville-Barker in England, under André Antoine and Jacques Copeau in France and under Eugene O'Neill, Lee Simonson and others in the United States, together with the reaction against them, belong to the 20th century and to modern drama and theatre.

### D. SUPPLEMENTARY ARTS

**1. Opera.**—Opera (*q.v.*) deserves consideration as a form of theatre in which song and instrumental accompaniment are predominant. Much eastern theatre is operatic in that the dialogue is musical; so too was the liturgical drama of the medieval church.

Opera of the sort, however, that is generally accepted under that name was introduced into Europe by the group of Florentine patricians known as the *Camerata* (*c.* 1580), whose object was to intone the dialogue of tragedy in the manner they imagined it had been recited in the theatres of ancient Greece. The result was what is known as recitative, which, when linked to aria (song), provided a libretto (text) sung throughout to musical accompaniment. The story of *Orpheus and Eurydice* was provided with such settings by J. Peri, G. Caccini and C. Monteverdi in quick succession between 1600 and 1607. The latter did for music-tragedy what the painters of equal genius had done 50 years earlier for the tragic scene. Opera, thus firmly based on scenery, song and tragic or pastoral themes, swept northward through Venice, where the first public opera house was opened in 1637, to Vienna and Germany. Then it swung in two great arcs northeast to Warsaw, Stockholm and St. Petersburg and northwest to Copenhagen, Amsterdam, Brussels and London at the turn of the 17th century into the 18th century. Paris and London enjoyed a brief creative period of indigenous opera in the Italian manner between 1650 and 1700 dominated respectively by Jean Baptiste Lully and Henry Purcell.

Comic themes were introduced from Naples early in the 18th century, being developed from between-the-acts of serious opera in the same way that tragic and pastoral opera had itself developed out of the intermezzi to neoclassical tragedy. While Handel and Gluck dominated the serious operatic scene during the early and middle parts of the 18th century respectively, these developments reached their peak in Mozart's compositions for the theatre toward the close of the century.

The coincidence of political and industrial revolutions with the bourgeois sentimentalism evident in melodrama brought about a reaction toward romantic and historical plots; together with the development of the orchestra these factors led directly to the romantic opera of Verdi (1813–1901) and Wagner (1813–83). The outstanding theatrical features of all 19th-century operas are the emphasis placed on melodic line and the reliance upon the vocal range and power of the principal singers. These characteristics were quite out of line with developments in the regular theatre, as signalized in the plays of Ibsen, who abandoned verse for prose, and in the acting style of the Moscow Art Theatre under Stanislavski.

Reaction to the primarily tragic and serious effusions of Verdi and Wagner (grand opera) found its outlet in light, or comic, opera. In England the light opera of W. S. Gilbert and Arthur Sullivan, in Austria the waltz opera of Johann Strauss and Franz Lehar and in France the *opéra-bouffe* of J. Offenbach (where recitative was reduced to the barest minimum and unaccompanied prose dialogue restored) opened the way to the operetta and musical comedy (*q.v.*) of the 20th century and perhaps the first distinctively transatlantic form, the American "musical."

**2. Ballet.**—A ballad, or ballet, in the 15th century formed an item in the repertoire of the minstrel troupe that came to be enacted in mime; to this were added the embellishments of songs and dances, the whole making up an evening's revels. During the 16th century the poem became little more than a prologue to establish the nature of the dances in masquerade. These developed as a series of "entries" of disguised courtiers who, after dancing with one another, took partners from among the spectators. Known in Italy as *maschera,* in England as masque and in France as *mascarade,* the element of dance became predominant in France during the 17th century. These ballets danced by amateurs reached their climax at Versailles at the hands of Lully and Molière. After being taken over by professional dancers they were integrated with Italian opera but could not develop further until fashion in dancers' costume allowed both greater freedom and precision of movement. This change, initiated by Marie Camargo (1710–70), was followed by attempts to link formal dances with musically accompanied mime in the same way that one aria was linked to another by recitative in opera. The innovator was J. G. Noverre (1727–1810), whose treatise *Lettres sur la danse et sur les ballets* stimulated public interest and discussion of ballet as an art form all over Europe.

The objective was a re-creation of the sort of dancing deemed to have graced the classical theatre of antiquity; but, being pursued at a time when romantic forms were beginning to find public favour at the expense of classical ones, ballet derived little more from pseudoclassicism than the conventional ballerina's costume of skintights surmounted by a short skirt of tiered muslin and the so-called "classical" dance figures before being enveloped in the mystical miasmas of fantasy and spectacle derived from Gothic melodrama. Nevertheless the combination of costume and dance figures sufficed to re-establish the bodily skill, grace and expressiveness of the actor with force enough to attract to it the unsophisticated folk dances of peasant communities who as yet had no other theatre. The imperial ballet of the Russian court was in the most advantageous position for this assimilation: for in Russia, as a comparatively undeveloped country of great geographical and climatic variety, a wider range of peasant dances existed for exploitation than anywhere else in Europe. A rapidly developing and strongly nationalistic school of music, itself largely indebted to the melodies and rhythms of folk music, provided Russian ballet with creative impetus enough not only to surmount any danger of the new art's dying as a result of suffocation from repetition and stereotyped convention but also to revivify dancing in the west. (*See* BALLET.)

**3. Mime, Pantomime, Vaudeville and Music Hall.**—Any concept of a theatre other than that restricted to timber, bricks and mortar depends for its existence on and develops around the person of the actor. Moreover, any society that has once advanced far enough to recognize the pleasure latent within the performer-beholder relationship has never been able to dispense with it. Thus although the peoples of the world have, from time to time and from place to place, and for various reasons, either refused to permit or failed to sustain an organized theatre, they have never lost touch with the mimer who is able to entertain with no properties other than his own voice and person. Recognizing the tenuous nature of his hold over his audience, the mimer has inevitably and invariably relied upon the easiest means of provoking laughter—verbal mockery and physical indignity.

Whatever society has prescribed to be sacred or illicit has tempted comment from him by virtue of the power that any shock possesses to attract and hold attention. The barbed satire of social criticism and the appeal of pathos, both demanding a high degree of awareness and intelligence in their portrayal, augment the equipment of the more skilful and experienced mimer.

Throughout recorded history therefore the mimer, whether known under Greek, Latin or vernacular names, has enjoyed the abiding favour of the more oppressed sections of society and the constant disapproval of those in authority, except at rare times when that authority was too secure for any challenge to be regarded as a threat. Markets, fairgrounds, city streets at festival times, village green and taverns have provided their perennial auditoriums. At times they have organized membership, their finances and their patrons well enough to originate a distinctive style of theatrical performance warranting a label. The Attelan fairs of Roman Italy, the medieval minstrel troupe, the Feast of Fools, the *commedia dell'arte* of Renaissance Europe, harlequinades, English pantomime and music hall, extravaganza, burlesque, revue, cabaret, American vaudeville and American burlesque (including strip tease) are among the most notable forms. All have been characterized by the lack of any regular script, the liberty permitted to the actors to improvise their actions and extemporize their dialogue as prompted by audience response; by the occasional interpolation of song and dance; by solo performances from individual artists; and by the exploitation of spectacle for its own sake in conjuring tricks, sexual allure, scenic machinery and, in the case of pantomime, music hall and vaudeville, in luxury and glitter of the auditorium. Blasphemy, obscenity and sensationalism, if not invariable characteristics, have been near enough neighbours to provoke constant reproof from councilors of church and state of actors engaged in these activities. Bourgeois opinion has generally aligned itself behind these dignitaries when faced with a choice between advancing its own status in society and forsaking the entertainments of the peasant, serf or manual labourer. While therefore it is on these entertainers that the theatre always relies in times of crisis for its very survival and the renewal of its energy (and must accordingly award them a place of honour and esteem), it is upon them too that responsibility must be laid for the theatre's reputation as a disreputable, frivolous, naughty, wicked or otherwise undesirable element in society. (G. W. G. W.)

### E. The American Theatre

The first theatre—actors, scenery and repertory—was imported to the American colonies from England about 1750. Early performances were given in existing halls or in hastily built quarters resembling the small English provincial theatres of the day. These provided a small stage with little wing or fly space, framed by a proscenium arch, in front of which extended a shallow apron with a proscenium door on either side. The first scenery consisted of the minimum of traditionally painted drops, wings and borders necessary to suggest the many settings required by a large repertory. When the first permanent theatres were erected, shutters running in grooves replaced drops to close in most settings at the rear. Illumination was provided by candles in chandeliers hanging from the ceiling of the auditorium, in a row of reflector holders placed as footlights and in holders fastened to the backs of the wings.

The first American plays were modeled on English drama. A native type, the shrewd, rural Yankee, first appeared in Royall Tyler's *The Contrast* (1787), which introduced also a favourite theme of early American drama: the triumph of native honesty and worth over foreign sham and affectation. In 1798, William Dunlap, America's first professional playwright, dramatized recent American history in his blank verse tragedy *André,* in which George Washington is a principal character. The heroic Indian was added in John Augustus Stone's *Metamora* (1829), the tough city lad in Benjamin Baker's *A Glance at New York* (1848) and the stout-hearted frontiersman in Frank Murdoch's *Davy Crockett* (1872). Native-born actors early performed in minor roles, and the native star, able to hold his own with the best on the London stage, appeared with Edwin Forrest in the 1820s and Charlotte Cushman in the 1830s. Forrest's "American" style was characterized by muscular strength and vocal power. Theatre, first confined to the eastern seaboard, in 1815 expanded into the Ohio and then to the Mississippi valleys. A unique American institution of the period was the showboat (*q.v.*). In 1850 theatre made the leap to San Francisco and the Pacific coast.

To begin with, settings, including all except a few pieces of furniture actually used by the actors, were painted on wings and shutters. The use of real instead of painted rugs and draperies and a full complement of furniture appeared in the production of Dion Boucicault's *London Assurance* (1841). Detailed historical accuracy in setting and costume first attracted attention in Charles Kean's production of *King John* (1846). In Edwin Booth's theatre in 1869, wings and shutters in grooves were abandoned, scenery was supported by stage braces and the box setting began to be used. In the next 30 years, the detailed realistic setting was perfected by such producer-directors as Augustin Daly, Steele MacKaye and David Belasco. Realistic production was stimulated by the introduction of gas lighting about 1825 and of electricity about 1885.

Realism in acting appeared in some of the characterizations of Yankee specialists like George H. Hill in the 1830s and '40s; in Francis F. Chanfrau's tough city lad in the '40s; in Matilda Heron's unconventional *Camille* in the '50s; in Edwin Booth's quieter acting of Shakespeare and Joseph Jefferson's "natural" Rip Van Winkle in the '60s; and was fully developed by William Gillette and Mr. and Mrs. James A. Herne in the '80s. James A. Herne's *Margaret Fleming* (1890) was the first realistic problem play in the manner of Ibsen. Herne could not secure production of this "new" drama in a regular theatre because of a radical change in theatre organization.

At the beginning of the 19th century, each major city had a resident repertory company. As population grew and spread westward, so did the number of resident companies, and a leading actor found it profitable to set himself up as a star, playing brief guest engagements with one resident company after another. The proliferation of such stars and the rise of the long run, which was necessitated by increasingly expensive staging, eventually destroyed the resident company. It was replaced in the 1860s and '70s, except in a few of the largest cities, by the traveling "combination." Originating usually in New York city, which since 1825 had been the leading theatre centre, hundreds of these combination companies, presenting either a small repertory or a single play, were providing entertainment the length and breadth of the land. Booking agencies were formed as liaison between companies and theatres. Several theatre owners, producers and agents, of whom Charles Frohman was the best known, formed the Theatrical Syndicate in 1896, which by controlling booking in key cities gained a virtual monopoly of theatre throughout the country. The Syndicate was not interested in the play with limited audience appeal. The theatre on all levels, from serious drama to burlesque, was the country's chief medium of entertainment. It was a big and prosperous business, and it was beginning to be attacked for "commercialism." The change from repertory to the single play and the rise of realistic production also shifted artistic control from the actor to the manager, who became the producer-director, or *régisseur*. In the last decades of the 19th century, Augustin Daly, Steele MacKaye and David Belasco not only selected and cast their plays, and directed the rehearsals, but also personally supervised all other aspects of production.

For the further history of the American theatre, see *20th Century: United States,* below. (B. Ht.)

## IV. 20TH CENTURY

**1. Asia.**—*China.*—The most flourishing theatre in Asia in the 1960s was the Chinese. Every town of size had several theatres, and there were hundreds of touring troupes. The classical theatre prospered alongside the modern theatre, since the government, although suppressing much that was traditional in Chinese culture, allowed the popular classical opera to survive, forbidding performance of only a few operas on political or moral grounds.

The modern theatre dates from 1907, when the first Western plays were performed. "The talking drama," so called to distinguish it from classical opera, was at first attacked by the universities opposed to translation of plays into the vernacular instead of into the literary language. In 1919 the students' Literary Revolution won recognition for the vernacular as the language for modern academic writing, and so for translation. As Western plays became more numerous, a number of theatres adopted Western methods of staging, and Chinese playwrights began to write realistic plays dealing with contemporary problems. Actresses, banned in the 18th century, were allowed after the establishment of the republic in 1912, but only in all-women troupes, in which they played male parts. In the 1920s they were admitted to ordinary companies. By this time the actor's status was very different from what it had been at the beginning of the century, when he was regarded as belonging to the lowest social class. The change was largely brought about by Mei Lan Fang, 20th-century China's greatest actor, a considerable scholar and a man of grace and charm. The Chinese theatre in the 1960s relied mainly on its own playwrights. Western plays were allowed only when they accorded with the views of the government.

*Japan.*—The modern theatre movement in Japan began in 1924, when the Tsukiji Little Theatre, the first Japanese theatre modeled on the realistic Western theatre, opened in Tokyo. Its founder, Hijikata Yoshi, had studied with the Moscow Art Theatre (*q.v.*) and had become a Communist. In 1928 a kabuki actor, Kawarazaki Chojuro, who had been in the U.S.S.R. with his troupe, left the kabuki to form the Progressive Theatre, a community theatre on the Russian model. It included both kabuki and modern plays in its repertoire (*see* Kabuki Theatre). In the mid-1930s the government decided that it could no longer tolerate the political propaganda of these theatres, so the Little Theatre was closed; Hijikata went to the U.S.S.R.; and the Progressive Theatre confined itself to kabuki. But under the post-World War II occupation the Progressive Theatre returned to its original policy, producing a number of Russian plays, and Hijikata returned to Japan. By the 1960s the Japanese theatre had outgrown its Communist beginnings, although a great many of its plays dealt with social problems. The variety of Western plays given was proof of its tolerance and interest in conflicting ideas.

*India.*—The diversity of 20th-century Indian theatre was exemplified by the annual drama festival in New Delhi, started in 1954, at which some 15 languages and cultures were represented. The most influential theatre was the Prithvi, because it played in Hindi, the national language, and thus reached a far larger audience than, for instance, the Bengali and Marathi theatres. The Prithvi Theatre was founded in 1943 by Kapoor Prithviraj, famous throughout India as a film star. Its tours extended from Calcutta in the east to Saurashtra in the west, from Kashmir in the north to Dhanushkodi Rameswaram in the south. The plays in its repertoire dealt mainly with contemporary life and reflected Prithviraj's political and religious views. Most of the comparatively small amount of professional acting was concentrated in Calcutta, which had a number of modern theatres and a prosperous motion-picture industry; thus, actors were able to work in both mediums. Theatre Unit, Bombay, India's most modern-minded theatre, was founded in the mid-1940s by Alkazi, a young actor and director trained in London at the Royal Academy of Dramatic Art. The company performed in English but was essentially an Indian theatre catering for an Indian public. An instance of the combining of the traditional folk and dance drama (*see* DANCE) with modern theatre was Sundari's Gujarati Theatre, with headquarters in Bombay. The plays dealt with political and social themes and particularly with women's emancipation. In south India the first modern theatre was founded in the early 1930s by Eprahahim Rajamanickam. Choice of plays was strongly influenced by his deep religious convictions. Besides playing in its own theatre in Madras, the company, more than a hundred strong in the 1960s, toured widely, visiting other provinces to play to Tamil communities. The Indian National Theatre, Bombay, founded in the 1950s as a workers' theatre to take the drama to farms and factories, by the 1960s had branches in all the big cities. The actors were mostly amateur.

*Other Countries.*—Outside India, Japan, and China, there was hardly any modern theatre in Asia. In countries such as Ceylon, Burma, Malaya, and Indonesia, the highly developed forms of dance drama (*see* DANCE) were so popular that there was little urge to found a modern theatre. Only in the Philippine Islands were there signs of a modern theatre developing from the efforts of enthusiastic amateur groups such as the Philippines National Theatre and the Manila Theatre Guild.

**2. Great Britain.**—*Direction and Development.*—During the 19th century the theatre was ruled by actor-managers who directed their own productions with their permanent companies, playing the leading parts themselves. At the beginning of the 20th century their authority began to be challenged by new, independent directors who rarely acted in their own productions. The first to establish himself was Dion Boucicault (1859–1929), who from 1901 to 1915 directed all plays at the Duke of York's Theatre, London. An autocratic director, he acted all the parts to the cast, who had to copy him to the minutest detail. A director with a different method was Harley Granville-Barker (*q.v.*), who from 1904 to 1907, in partnership with J. E. Vedrenne directed a series of short runs at the Royal Court Theatre, Chelsea, London; he opposed the artificial style of acting of the period. At first he was accused of teaching his actors "not to act" because he trained them to behave as normal human beings; to create a part by identifying themselves so completely with the character that gesture, movement, and facial expression were a natural expression of that character's thoughts and feelings. At a time when most actors had no hesitation in sacrificing character for flamboyant theatrical effect, Granville-Barker laboured to make the characters in a play "seem to live and move by the laws of their own being." He gathered round him a group of new writers hitherto uninterested in writing for the theatre because of its artificiality. He was at his best as a director with the plays of Gerhart Hauptmann, Ibsen, and Galsworthy.

Granville-Barker did not only direct naturalistic plays; his Shakespearean productions at the Savoy (1912–14) revolutionized Shakespearean theatre in England. As a young man he had acted in William Poel's productions for the Elizabethan Stage Society (*see* ACTING, DIRECTION AND PRODUCTION: *Acting*), and had learned how much a Shakespeare play depends for its full effect on unbroken continuity from scene to scene. Contemporary actor-managers with their spectacular productions kept halting the play for elaborate changes of scenery: but instead of realistic scenery Granville-Barker used stylized, decorative backgrounds. He speeded up the plays by avoiding scene changes and by teaching his actors to speak the verse swiftly, though without gabbling. To those accustomed to the slow and ponderous declamation of Shakespearean actors, it seemed a breakneck speed.

In 1920 Granville-Barker virtually retired from the theatre, but the subtle and exact kind of realistic production, purged of theatrical cliché, was developed by Gerald Du Maurier (*q.v.*) and Basil Dean. Before World War I Dean had worked under Annie (Miss A. E. F.) Horniman at the Gaiety Theatre, Manchester, where she had insisted on the sort of naturalism first practised at the Royal Court (*see* below *Provincial and Repertory Theatre*). At the St. Martin's Theatre Dean trained a young company to give an exact interpretation of the external characteristics of their parts; though his method lacked Granville-Barker's emphasis on imaginative interpretation, the result was acting of extraordinary clarity, sharpness, and precision. As a director, Dean continued the dictatorial methods of Boucicault. Du Maurier, on the other hand, directed with a deceptive casualness, which, like his acting, concealed a highly developed naturalistic technique. Both as actor and director he had, however, an unfortunate influence on English acting, because his imitators, lacking his technical skill, only achieved underplaying and inaudibility in their attempts to emulate the quiet ease of his naturalness.

A director who refreshed English acting and direction was Theodore (Fëdor) Komisarjevski (1882–1954), who in 1919 went to England from Russia, where he had been director of the Imperial and State theatres. Under his direction of plays by Chekhov and other Russian authors the acting achieved a sensitiveness and inner realism that set a new standard in the English theatre. His Shakespearean productions at Stratford-upon-Avon startled and often infuriated audiences accustomed to conventional presentation. His productions were full of invention, sometimes brilliant, amusing, and illuminating, sometimes merely wayward. He may be blamed for starting the "let's-be-different-at-all-costs" style of Shakespearean production still all too prevalent, and exemplified in Sir Laurence Olivier's "Othello" (1965).

In the same tradition, Tyrone Guthrie (1900– ; knighted 1961), a director with a superb theatrical imagination, beginning in the 1930s at the Old Vic, London, emphasized the point of a line with a revealing stroke of "business," and brought small parts vividly to life by imaginative touches of detail, heightening the effect of everything that happened on the stage by his gift of pictorial composition and swirling movement. But sometimes his inventiveness was used merely to surprise and shock the audience or to satisfy his own sense of humour. Even after 1953, when he became director of the Shakespeare Festival, Stratford, Ont., in a theatre built to his own design, he continued to direct in London, New York, Minneapolis (1962–65), where a theatre designed by him was built, and Edinburgh. Another fine Shakespearean producer was Peter Brook (1925– ), with superb productions in the 1950s and early 1960s of *Measure for Measure, Titus Andronicus, The Winter's Tale,* and *King Lear,* the last-named for the Royal Shakespeare Company, of which he became co-director in 1962 with Peter Hall (1930– ), also an outstanding Shakespearean producer, notable for productions of *Henry VI* and *Richard III* as a trilogy, *The Wars of the Roses* (1963). Brook also directed plays by Anouilh, Sartre, and other modern dramatists. His production of the German-born Peter Weiss's *Marat/Sade* (first performed, 1964) for the Royal Shakespeare Company in London and New York in 1966, was the first of its many European productions.

In the late 1950s the most influential British director was Joan Littlewood. In 1945 she had founded a company at Manchester—Theatre Workshop—for working-class audiences, which in 1953 moved to the Theatre Royal, Stratford, in the East End of London. The productions, at first mainly of Shakespeare and other classics, with some topical plays by Ewan MacColl, folksinger and political dramatist (with whom in the 1930s she had founded the Theatre of Action), gradually became more definite in style. She encouraged audience participation; allowed actors to improvise—all her later productions were "collective" in that the actors shared in planning the presentation, often took liberties with the text—and borrowed traditions from music-hall (*q.v.*) such as impromptu asides to the audience and the introduction of topical songs and jokes. Her productions also owed much to Bertolt Brecht (*q.v.; see* also below, *Germany*) in their encouragement of audience participation, and in use of music. Her first West End transfer, in 1955, was with MacColl's version of *The Good Soldier Schweik;* and thereafter her influence was more widely diffused. *Oh What a Lovely War!* (1963), an original evocation and criticism of World War I, using music, newspaper headlines, and other devices to point its message, is perhaps her most famous production: its success in Sweden in 1965 led to an imitation, *Oh What a Lovely Peace!* (1966). Her best productions—Brendan Behan's *The Quare Fellow* (1956) and *The Hostage* (1958), and Shelagh Delaney's *A Taste of Honey* (1958)—were full of vitality, noisy, and broadly humorous, yet with subtle characterization. In 1964 she founded a theatre school in Tunisia.

In the late 1950s and 1960s the most experimental London theatre was the Royal Court, under George Devine (1910–66), who in 1956 set up the English Stage Company. Its avowed purposes were to allow novelists to try their hand as playwrights and to introduce new writers and modern foreign drama. Its club, the English Stage Society, gave Sunday performances without decor, so allowing experimental plays to be tried out. Most of the new English playwrights of the 1950s and 1960s—John Osborne, John Arden, N. F. Simpson, Willis Hall, Ann Jellicoe, and Arnold Wesker—had their works first produced by the English Stage Company, which also gave many directors, designers, and actors later outstanding in the West End their first chance. In 1965 Devine was succeeded by William Gaskill, who continued his policy. But although several directors, trained at the Royal Court, were distinguished by brilliance and willingness to experiment, lack of a permanent company prevented development of a "Royal Court" style.

There was no permanent dramatic company in London until 1960: even the Old Vic (which, before it was bombed in 1940, was devoted to Shakespearean production), engaged actors only for one season. To remedy this lack Peter Hall engaged a company (called from 1961 the Royal Shakespeare Company), on long-term contract to play at Stratford-upon-Avon and at the Aldwych Theatre, London, presenting modern plays as well as Shakespeare and other classics, both often produced in experimental styles. Michel Saint-Denis became co-director (with Peter Brook and Peter Hall), in 1962, and in 1966, when he and Peter Daubeny (manager of the World Theatre Season at the Aldwych, which took to England dramatic companies from Greece, Italy, France, Czechoslovakia, the U.S.S.R., Poland, Japan, Germany, and Israel, in their own plays) became consultant directors, Paul Scofield (1922– ), the company's leading actor, took his place. A permanent theatre for the company, built by the Greater London Council, to be finished in 1973 as part of the City of London's Barbican scheme, was to have an open, triangular stage.

*Provincial and Repertory Theatre.*—In the provinces, the theatre divides into touring, repertory, and amateur. The touring theatres are visited by London companies either before or after they play in London, and by companies engaged to tour a London success. A play on tour seldom remains for more than a fortnight, but a big musical production sometimes stays up to several months. At Christmas nearly all these theatres stage an elaborate pantomime (*q.v.*), so popular that the run often extends for three or four months. In the early 1920s there were more than 250 touring theatres in England and Scotland. Many towns had several, as well as at least one music hall. By 1966 the number had dwindled to little more than 20. Many had failed to survive the competition of motion pictures; others were destroyed during World War II; and after the war television proved a deadly rival.

"Repertory" theatres in the provinces withstood competition more successfully. These so-called repertory theatres had at first no right to the title, because, although they maintained permanent companies, they did not keep a repertoire of plays ready for production as do continental "repertoire" theatres, which give performances of several plays from their repertoire each week. English repertory theatres put on a play for a short continuous run: a week, or, in the bigger cities, three weeks or a month. "Weekly rep," in which companies were always working against time, reached a high standard of acting and production, however, and gave actors an excellent training by casting leading members of the company in minor roles for a week or two when they had a major part ahead of them. But by the mid-1960s the nature of provincial repertory had changed considerably as a result of increased government grants and bigger audiences. Most theatres had replaced the giving of a play for a short run (after which the production was scrapped) by a limited form of continental "repertoire."

The London theatre owes much to provincial repertory, both because it provides actors accustomed to taking a wide range of parts (most West End actors graduated from "weekly rep") and because many successes were first produced by the repertory theatres.

The third branch of the provincial theatre, the amateur "little

BY COURTESY OF (LEFT) MANDER AND MITCHENSON THEATRE COLLECTION; (RIGHT) ROMANO CAGNONI

SCENES FROM (LEFT) HARLEY GRANVILLE-BARKER'S PRODUCTION OF TWELFTH NIGHT, SAVOY THEATRE, LONDON, 1912. (RIGHT) COMMONWEALTH ARTS FESTIVAL PRODUCTION OF THE ROAD, BY THE NIGERIAN PLAYWRIGHT WOLE SOYINKA, THEATRE ROYAL, STRATFORD, 1965 theatre," also make a valuable contribution to theatrical experiment in Great Britain. Sometimes producers and technicians are professional, but actors, designers, and stagehands are amateur, and often anonymous. One of the leading provincial little theatres is the Maddermarket, Norwich, built in 1919 as the only theatre in England with an Elizabethan stage. Productions are given during one week in each month, and have ranged from all of Shakespeare's plays to Oriental drama. Others influential before and during World War II were the People's Theatre, Newcastle (founded 1911), which gave many first performances of continental and U.S. plays; the Highbury Little Theatre, Sutton Coldfield, built during the war by the company's members; and the Glasgow Citizens' Theatre, founded in 1942 by the playwright James Bridie to encourage modern Scottish dramatists.

London has long had its own repertory theatres. The Royal Court, under Granville-Barker, and again under Devine and Gaskill, was a repertory theatre (*see* Acting, Direction and Production: *Direction*). Several repertory seasons were run in London theatres in the 1900s, but the movement was active mainly outside London, except for the Old Vic and National Theatre companies (and, later, the Royal Shakespeare Company). However, in the 1930s, experimental "club theatres" were opened. The first was the Gate (1925), founded by Peter Godfrey, and directed (1934–40) by Norman Marshall. Its policy of producing unlicensed or uncommercial plays and witty reviews made it one of the most important of the prewar "club theatres," but it was destroyed by bombing in 1941. Also influential were the Mercury, Notting Hill Gate (1933), famous for producing poetic plays by T. S. Eliot, Christopher Fry, Ronald Duncan, and others; the Hampstead Theatre Club, where in 1966, a movement called "Living Theatre," or documentary theatre, was begun, and spread to other companies as the "Theatre of Fact"; the Arts and New Arts Theatre Clubs; the Unity, St. Pancras, which in 1936 declared its intention of replacing the "escapism and false ideology of the conventional theatre" with a left-wing "agitational theatre," carried out with first English productions of plays by Clifford Odets, Sean O'Casey, and Soviet dramatists. After World War II the outstanding new foundation was that by the actor and director Bernard Miles (1907– ), of the Mermaid (1951), as an Elizabethan-style theatre, first in St. John's Wood, and after 1959 in the City of London—the first new theatre in the City for 300 years. In 1966 the Jeanetta Cochrane Theatre opened, in association with the Edinburgh Traverse Theatre Club.

The first British repertory theatre was founded by Annie Horniman at the Gaiety Theatre, Manchester, in 1908. It introduced to England the work of a number of important continental dramatists and gave opportunities to promising playwrights, among them Alan Monkhouse, Stanley Houghton, and Harold Brighouse, who became known as "the Manchester School." In 1921 it became a cinema. The oldest existing repertory theatre is the Playhouse, Liverpool, which opened in 1911. From 1922 to 1944 it was directed by William Armstrong, who had a gift for recognizing and developing talent, so that many leading players (among them Sir Michael Redgrave) began at the Playhouse. The repertory with the most distinguished and adventurous record is the Birmingham Repertory, founded in 1913 by Barry Jackson (knighted 1925), who also founded the Malvern Festival (1929–39; revived 1947, and again in 1966), where notable first performances were given of plays by Shaw, James Bridie, J. B. Priestley, and John Drinkwater, as well as of Tudor, Jacobean, and Restoration plays. Between World Wars I and II he took many productions to London, including the first modern-dress *Hamlet* and the first production of Shaw's *Back to Methuselah* in its entirety. Among other leading provincial repertory theatres, many of them subsidized by local authorities and so-called "civic" theatres, are those at Nottingham, Bristol, Sheffield, Windsor, Worthing, Salisbury, Oxford, Leatherhead, Stoke-on-Trent and Scarborough (both outstanding for production in-the-round), Coventry (1958; the first to be built out of public funds and the first new theatre built in Great Britain for 20 years), Colchester, Richmond, and Guildford.

*The National Theatre.*—In 1949 Parliament passed the National Theatre Act, empowering the Treasury to make a grant of £1,000,000 to build a National Theatre. In 1951 the queen mother laid the foundation stone on a site on the south bank of the Thames overlooking the river, given by the London County Council. Successive governments put off building the theatre until, in 1963, the government decided to finance a National Theatre Company, which opened under the directorship of Sir Laurence Olivier (1907– ), with the Old Vic as its temporary home. In 1966 the government agreed to contribute half the cost of a building containing two auditoriums, the Greater London Council (as the London County Council had become) contributing the rest.

For amateur theatre, other than that represented by the "club theatres" and the provincial "little theatres," *see* British Drama League.

**3. Ireland.**—Apart from the Abbey Theatre (*q.v.;* which reopened in a new, larger, building in 1966, after destruction by fire in 1951), nearly all that is best in Anglo-Irish theatre has been created by the Dublin Gate Theatre, founded in 1928 by the Irish actor and dramatist Micheál MacLiammóir (1899– ) and the English producer Hilton Edwards. Their policy of presenting a mainly international repertoire, but providing a theatre for Irish playwrights to write plays less local in character than those produced at the Abbey, resulted in new styles and techniques, and in familiarizing Irish audiences with plays by Ibsen, Strindberg, Chekhov, O'Neill, Elmer Rice, and Arthur Miller, as well as works by new Irish dramatists, notably Denis Johnston (1901– ).

Gaelic theatre arose from the work of Douglas Hyde (*q.v.*), author of the first play in Gaelic to appear on any stage (Abbey Theatre, 1901). Gaelic drama was encouraged by the Gaelic Drama League, working in Dublin, Galway, and provincial towns and villages. From 1928 to 1931 the Galway Gaelic Theatre, founded by MacLiammóir, produced plays in Gaelic, and translations of English and other foreign plays; and in 1931 the government-subsidized Dublin Gaelic Theatre was opened, with MacLiammóir as director.

The Irish national revival, centred in Dublin and led by Yeats and Lady Gregory (*see* Irish Literature: *Anglo-Irish Literature*), had its counterpart in Belfast, where the Ulster branch of the Irish Literary Theatre founded the Ulster Theatre (1902), which in 1939 was reconstituted as the Ulster Group Theatre, incorporating smaller semiprofessional organizations. With the Belfast Repertory Theatre, it aimed to portray Northern Irish life.

**4. U.S.S.R.**—The history of modern theatre in Russia began with the founding of the Moscow Art Theatre (*q.v.*) in 1897 by Konstantin Stanislavski and Vladimir Nemirovich-Danchenko (*qq.v.*). For 12 years Stanislavski had worked with a company of amateurs, and the best of these, turned professional, formed the nucleus of the Moscow Art Theatre Company. When Stanislavski began, the Russian theatre was one of the most backward in Europe: acting consisted mainly in selecting from a stock of theatrical clichés whatever seemed most appropriate, and little time was spent in rehearsal. The plays, mainly French comedies and farces or Russian imitations of them, were so stereotyped that the same performances and sets could, with a slight variation, be used time after time. The first three productions at the Moscow Art Theatre caused no particular stir. It was Chekhov's *The Seagull* (1898) that established the theatre and Stanislavski's reputation. The quietness, intimacy, and naturalness of the acting were entirely new. (*See* also Acting, Direction and Production: *Acting: Stanislavski.*)

While Stanislavski continued to develop his infinitely detailed method of direction, the antirealist movement initiated by the Symbolists and Surrealists spread to Russia. Its criticisms came when Stanislavski was beginning to feel that he must seek new paths. In 1905 he founded a small studio theatre for experiment and research, appointing Vsevolod Meyerhold (*q.v.*) director. A member of the Moscow Art Theatre Company, Meyerhold had left it in 1902 when he became a convert to the Symbolist movement. When, after months of preparation, Meyerhold staged two productions, Stanislavski disliked them so intensely that he closed the studio. He thought the actors had been used as puppets to illustrate Meyerhold's theories. Yet these productions had an important effect on him as a demonstration of the slavish obedience to which the dictatorial producer could reduce his actors. He determined that henceforth the actor should be his collaborator, not his subordinate, and began to develop the method of "inner realism" that became known as the Stanislavski method and remains the basis of the training of Russian actors.

After the 1917 Revolution Stanislavski refused to allow his theatre to become a platform for spreading propaganda. He believed that its mission was to maintain a standard of acting that other theatres might emulate when the first excesses of the Revolution had abated. The official edict decreed that characterization, ideas, and emotions should be reduced to the simplest possible terms for the new audiences, many of them illiterate. This amounted to a command to actors to overact, abandoning all subtleties and returning to the crude, melodramatic style. As some of Stanislavski's company were influenced by the enthusiasm with which the new audiences acclaimed overacting, he decided to take his company abroad and in 1922 left on a tour of Europe and the U.S. On return (1924), deciding that the Moscow Art Theatre must to some extent adapt itself to the mentality of the new audiences, he began to produce in bold, sweeping strokes, stressing the dramatic elements and enlivening comic scenes with tricks borrowed from vaudeville. There were no half tones, no subtleties, but none of the crude exaggerations of the contemporary Soviet theatre.

Meanwhile, Meyerhold had become one of the most powerful influences in the Russian theatre. He declared that the principles of the propagandist theatre conformed with those of Marxism because they attempted to underline "the elements which make prominent what is common to all men, the unindividual." Detailed portrayal of emotion was described as "worthless soul junk," and the actor ordered to "forget his little rickety ego" and become "an instrument for social manifestos." Many other producers, educated to despise an individualistic society, exercised ingenuity to deprive actors of individuality. Aleksandr Taïrov (1885–1950), founder of the Kamerny Theatre (1914), made his actors wear fantastically exaggerated makeup so that they would not resemble anyone in real life and thus become individuals to the audience. Taïrov invented the "constructivist" setting, a gaunt scaffolding supporting bare platforms on different levels, with every strut and bolt exposed to view. The aggressive functionalism of this kind of setting was regarded as having considerable propaganda value when the Russians were being taught to revere the machine as part of their training to become a great industrial nation.

A more moderate director was Evgeni Vakhtangov (1883–1922), a pupil of Stanislavski. In 1914 he was in charge of one of the studios attached to the Art Theatre, and in 1920 was appointed director of this subsidiary, renamed the Third Studio (or Workshop). But Vakhtangov was not altogether in accord with the quiet naturalness of the Art Theatre. His natural exuberance impelled him toward a style of production that, while avoiding the extreme stylization and unrealism of Meyerhold and Taïrov, nevertheless enlarged, heightened, and sharpened character, emotion, and gesture. He wanted to work in vivid colours instead of half tones. In place of Stanislavski's inner realism he wanted what he called "outer-technique." He found the ideal actors for his purpose when Stanislavski put him in charge of a group of Jewish players who in 1916 had formed a company for production of plays in Hebrew, calling themselves the Habima Players. In 1918 they became affiliated with the Art Theatre. Vakhtangov's masterpiece was his production of Rappoport Ansky's *The Dybbuk* (1922). It was his last production; but for many years the Habima Players included his *Dybbuk* in their tours of Europe and the U.S., so that it became, outside the U.S.S.R., the best-known Soviet production. (*See* also HABIMA THEATRE.)

The youngest postrevolutionary director was Nikolai Okhlopkov (1900–66). His earliest productions were entertainments given during World War I on an improvised platform in the square of his home town to entertain the troops, who encircled the stage. As a result of this experience of the open stage he found the proscenium theatre cramping, and in Moscow experimented with ways of breaking down the barrier between actor and audience. In 1932 he became director of the Realistic Theatre, where for his production of Aleksandr Seralimovich's *The Iron Flood* he converted the auditorium into a mountainous terrain, seating the audience among the rocks so that actors, playing in every part of the auditorium, mingled with audience. He made other experiments in staging, but in 1938 the Realistic Theatre was closed on the grounds that his work appealed too exclusively to intellectuals. By this time the experimentalism that had made the Russian theatre the most exciting in the world had ended. In 1934 Meyerhold, censured for his "obsession with the vague abstractions of decadent art," and for being "the father of formalism," was deprived of his position. Taïrov, rebuked for being out of touch with his audiences, had been relieved of the direction of the Kamerny Theatre and forced to work under a committee. It is true that their work was too cold and abstract to please audiences who wanted warmth, humanity, and reality. But under Stalinism the theatre virtually ceased to progress, since any originality was condemned as decadent. Scenery became more and more laboriously realistic, as a setting in any way impressionistic was condemned as belonging to "abstract art." Only the magnificent standard of acting remained unchanged.

After Stalin's death (1953) the theatre was relieved of many shackles and there was a cautious return to experiment, particularly at the Satire Theatre. Okhlopkov, only survivor of the experimentalist producers of the 1920s, remained the most original and stimulating director, though at times under Stalinism his originality had displeased the authorities and he had been criticized for too unruly an imagination.

In the 1960s the Soviet theatre was perhaps at its best in productions of the classic Russian authors, directed with meticulous care, and reproducing the manners and customs of the Tsarist days. Its unique feature was its gigantic scale—the vast number of theatres, the fact that there were companies playing in more than 50 languages, the size of the companies (100 actors was not unusual), the size of the repertoire of each theatre, the huge and superbly equipped stages showing a succession of elaborate scenes, the size of the theatregoing audience, and the vast state subsidies to theatres, so that they need not attempt to pay their way and thereby could keep their prices low. The professional theatre could not satisfy the demand for dramatic entertainment and every encouragement was given to the amateur. Most theatres accepted responsibility for at least one amateur group, the members or the company giving much time to training and advising it. Amateur companies of outstanding merit were given the title "people's theatre." Most of these companies were based at Palaces of Culture, and toured neighbouring towns, as well as playing in factories and collective farms. The close relations between professional and amateur were mutually beneficial, for professionals found that contact with the personnel of the amateur groups infused freshness and reality into their own performances. By the late 1960s there was an even greater loosening up: satire, even political, became increasingly dominant, and methods and techniques increasingly experimental and symbolic.

**5. Germany.**—The character of the German theatre was changed during the early 20th century by the work of the Austrian Max Reinhardt (*q.v.*). When in 1903 he gave up acting for direction, the theatre was an educational institution rather than a place of entertainment; producers of the classics had to be scrupulously faithful to cherished traditions and conventions. Reinhardt loved colour and gaiety, richness and display, and these were the qualities he brought to his productions. He was attacked by the traditionalists and by the new school of German realists. What they disliked about his work was its theatricality, a quality scrupulously avoided in their own low-toned productions. One of his great services to the German theatre was that he restored its theatricality—but purged of staginess. In so doing he revolutionized German acting. In productions of modern plays he taught his actors a style realistic in feeling but avoiding the drab, painstaking exactness of the realists; it was warm, vivid, and colourful, always a little larger than life. In productions of the classics he demanded lively, supple speaking in place of the slow, ponderous delivery of the traditionalists. He made his actors think afresh about the characters instead of assuming ready-made characterizations. When in 1906 he opened his Kleines Theater in Berlin, he initiated a movement that grew steadily. It aimed to break down the separation of stage and auditorium and to restore intimacy between actor and audience. In his endeavours to rescue the players from their isolation behind the proscenium arch, he often took them out of the theatre to play in places that seemed eccentric settings for a theatrical entertainment—a square in Venice, a palace ballroom in Vienna, the Boboli Gardens in Florence, and the Domplatz (cathedral square), where every year he directed Hofmannsthal's *Jedermann* (*Everyman*) at the Salzburg Festival, and inside the cathedral itself. He produced *Oedipus Rex* (Vienna, 1910) in a circus arena, using one end for gigantic architectural settings unframed by any proscenium. For his production of the mimed religious play, *The Miracle* (London, 1911), he transformed the huge Olympia exhibition building into a cathedral so that the audience became part of the congregation. But although he was a master of spectacle, his versatility was such that he directed subtle and intimate plays in small theatres with equal skill. Until World War I his personality dominated the German stage; nearly all the young directors and actors had either worked in one of his companies or been trained in one of his schools.

Immediately after World War I two of his disciples, Leopold Jessner (1878– ) and Erwin Piscator (1893–1966), became the dominant figures. Their Expressionist style of direction was evolved partly because of the shortage of materials for building scenery. In their antirealistic productions, actors on a bare, darkened stage were picked out by shafts of light against a black background; scenery was limited to one or two small pieces, symbolic rather than realistic. Stylized staging inevitably led to stylized acting, which in turn demanded stylized writing, and it was thus that the German school of Expressionist drama was created (*see* GERMAN LITERATURE; DRAMA: *Modern Drama*). Characters became symbols instead of people, their lines stripped of all but key words and phrases. Later in the 1920s, when steel, timber, and other materials became more plentiful, Piscator directed a series of Expressionist productions in which he used elaborate and expensive machinery. The front of his stage was constructed on the conveyor-belt principle; in the centre a cantilever bridge moved up and down; lantern slides and motion-picture films were projected onto the back wall; above the proscenium slogans blazed in lights; the gigantic shadows of pulsating machines were thrown onto gauzes. Jessner, too, made exuberant use of the lifting of restrictions on use of building materials. His favourite setting was a vast flight of steps extending the entire width of the stage, rising steeply to a high platform at its back. He was greatly influenced by the work of the Soviet directors of the immediate post-revolutionary period, and copied them in oversimplifying characters and their motives, abandoning subtlety for elementary Symbolism. The Expressionist movement ended because when an actor is reduced to a puppet he can only express a few emotions, and those only in simple forms.

This phase was followed by a period in which the theatre reverted to realism. When the Nazis assumed power (1933), their passion for vast meetings and processions was reflected in vast propaganda dramas presented in the open air in sports stadiums, parade grounds, and on huge natural sites. World War II destroyed many theatres but popular desire for theatre and opera was so intense that rebuilding started immediately. A great opportunity presented itself for building theatres of new design, but many were still based on the picture-frame stage, often elaborately mechanized for the handling of huge, realistic settings. By the 1960s, however, experimental theatres were being built, at Dortmund, Trier, and Wuppertal (1966), for example.

The most important influence in the post-World War II theatre was the East German dramatist, poet, and producer, Bertolt Brecht (*q.v.*). After the early 1930s, when Reinhardt and other leading players and directors went into exile, acting lapsed into exhibitionism and splurgy emotionalism. Brecht, a disciple of Meyerhold, made constant use of his anti-illusionist devices to emphasize his dictum that "the actual world exists and is our subject; but this play and this stage are not it." For instance, to destroy the illusion of actuality he flooded his stage with white light throughout the performance, irrespective of when the action took place. Between scenes, captions, slogans, and comments were projected onto a gauze curtain. Points were emphasized by songs unrelated to the action: what Brecht called "musical addresses to the audience," in which the actor stepped out of and commented on the play. Brecht's theory of acting was a reversal of Stanislavski's doctrine that the actor must identify himself with the part he is playing. He demanded an objective style of acting. It was to

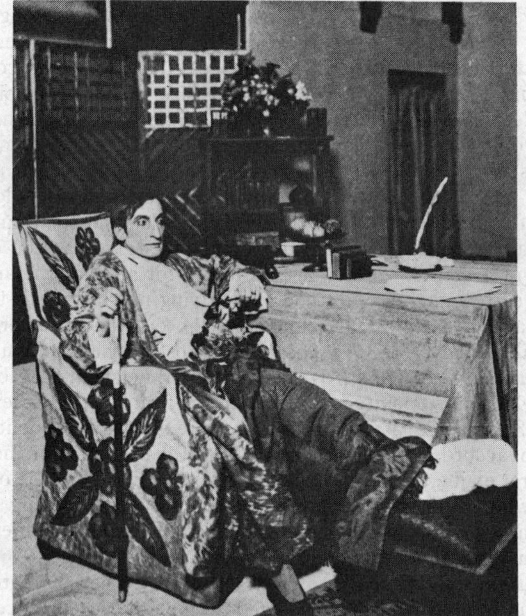

(TOP LEFT) ROGER VIOLLET, (TOP RIGHT) ZOE DOMINIC, (BOTTOM) PERCY PAUKSCHTA

**PRODUCTIONS BY THREE GREAT 20TH-CENTURY EUROPEAN COMPANIES**

(Top left) Jacques Copeau in Mérimée's *Le Carrosse du Saint Sacrement* at the Théâtre du Vieux Colombier. (Top right) Scene from the Moscow Art Theatre production of Gogol's *Dead Souls,* 1964. (Bottom) The Berliner Ensemble performing in Bertolt Brecht's *Arturo Ui,* produced in 1959 by Manfred Wekwerth and Peter Palitzsch free the audience "from the spell cast upon them by the witchcraft of realistic producers who make a dream world of reality" that he evolved what he called "the alienation effect." After his death in 1956, his company, the Berliner Ensemble, under his widow, the actress Helene Weigel, continued to train actors and toured widely with a repertoire of his plays.

In spite of the number of theatres and the money lavished upon them in government and municipal grants, there were few signs in the 1950s of any strongly progressive movement, and few directors sufficiently dominant to impose a distinctive style. Much of the best creative work was done in the opera houses. But, after a revival of German drama, mainly by Swiss-German playwrights (*e.g.*, Max Frisch, Friedrich Dürrenmatt, and Peter Weiss), the theatre throughout Germany began to revive, and the work of such dramatists as Günter Grass, Siegfried Lenz, Reinar Kipphardt, and Rolf Hochhuth provided opportunities for original direction and staging.

**6. France.**—The reaction against realism, in the early 20th century a powerful influence in the German and Russian theatres, was slower to reach France. The founding of the Théâtre du Vieux Colombier by Jacques Copeau (*q.v.*) in 1913 initiated the reaction. Copeau was a literary critic who set up his own company. Like Reinhardt, he sought to break down the barrier between actor and audience. His stage was unframed; there were no wings and no line of demarcation between stage and auditorium. Decor, used sparingly, seldom consisted of more than one or two painted screens, a balustrade, or a draped curtain. Only the minimum of furniture and properties was used. The atmosphere for each play was created almost entirely by lighting.

Before opening the Vieux Colombier, Copeau took his company to Le Limon, where they improvised scenes and practised exercises. They learned much from Charles Dullin (1885–1949), a *diseur* in the Montmartre cafés and an exponent of traditional *comédie improvisée,* still popular in Parisian cabarets and provincial fairs. The acting at the Vieux Colombier in a modern play was at first sight realistic, although the detailed business was minimized; but closer watching showed that gesture was being used selectively to give each gesture unusual significance. Copeau's productions of Molière and Shakespeare were notable for lightness, grace, and gaiety. In 1923 he took a group of young actors to Burgundy, where, besides studying acting, they worked in the fields and in a carpenter's shop and took part in the local wine festival. The peasants called them "Les Copiaux," under which name they first appeared at Basel, Switz., in 1926. Their characteristic production was *La Danse de la ville et des champs,* written and produced by Michel Saint-Denis (1897–    ), who in 1930 took over the company, renamed the Compagnie des Quinze. It was disbanded in 1936 but had become internationally famous. The company had its own playwright, André Obey (1892–    ), who wrote to suit its methods and talents.

Copeau's influence was strengthened and extended through the productions of Louis Jouvet (*q.v.*) and Dullin, who left his company in 1922 to start their own theatres. Jouvet's productions of Molière were his most important contribution. He freed the plays from the weight of tradition that was stifling them. His *L'École des femmes* (1936) was hailed as a return to the spirit of Molière. While Jouvet was careful to subjugate himself to his author, Dullin's productions were strongly coloured by his own personality and tastes. He loved bright colours, music, movements. Copeau's influence was apparent in his use of expressive gesture and mime. His production of Aristophanes' *The Birds* (1928) mingled the carnival and social satire that he sought in nearly every play he produced. In contrast to Dullin was the asceticism of Georges Pitoëff (1887–1939), who believed that the director's primary aim should be to focus attention on a play's central idea, and eliminate all details of decor and acting that might obscure it. His great contribution to the French theatre was the number of foreign dramatists whom he introduced to the Parisian public.

Jouvet, Dullin, and Pitoëff, with Gaston Baty (1885–1952), were known as *Les Quatre* ("The Four"). Baty had served his apprenticeship under Reinhardt. His pictorial sense was superb, and his groupings and movement were beautifully composed, but they existed for themselves rather than for the play. He was often accused of overelaborating the classics to display his inventiveness, but he directed the delicate plays of Jean Jacques Bernard (*q.v.*) with infinite subtlety.

Dullin's use of mime was elaborated in the productions of his pupil, Jean Louis Barrault (1910–    ), who left the Comédie Française in 1946 to form, with his wife, the actress Madeleine Renaud, the Compagnie Renaud-Barrault, which played in the provinces and abroad and, in Paris, at the Théâtre Marigny. In 1959 he became director of the Théâtre de France, to which in 1966 the annual "Théâtre des Nations" was transferred. Much of his work is symbolistic—a combination of pantomime, rhythmic movement, and shadowgraph. He has been accused, rather unfairly, of being "an enemy of speech." He became the chief exponent of "total theatre," a theory evolved by Gordon Craig (*q.v.*). Another pupil of Dullin, Jean Vilar (1912–    ), in 1951 founded the Théâtre Nationale Populaire (T.N.P.). His style was governed by the size of the Palais de Chaillot, a theatre seating nearly 3,000 with a stage 70 ft. (more than 21 m.) deep and a proscenium opening 80 ft. (more than 24 m.) wide. Vilar made no attempt to fill the stage with scenery. He did no more than suggest the background of the play, and filled his stage with big, swirling movement. He trained his actors to use bold, simplified gestures and delineate character in powerful outline.

Until the 1950s theatrical activity was almost entirely concentrated in Paris, but with government help theatrical centres were established at Strasbourg, Aix-en-Provence, Saint-Étienne, Toulouse, and Reims.

**7. Other European Countries.**—In northern Europe in the 1960s the largest audience was in Finland, where more than a quarter of the population were regular theatregoers. The number of plays by native authors was unusually high. Few have been performed abroad because of lack of good translations. In Denmark, production of a Danish play was comparatively rare, but a variety of foreign plays was produced. In Sweden, where the number of native playwrights was increasing, good theatre was spread over the country. Göteborg rivaled Stockholm, and both were challenged by Malmö, Uppsala, Norrköping, and Hälsingborg. The Norwegian theatre has spent most of its life in financial crisis, partly because audiences have been scanty. It had to rely on private enterprise—even the National Theatre was founded in 1899 without state or municipal aid—until in 1961 the government took over financial responsibility for the whole theatre. To take the theatre to the people it founded the State Traveling Theatre, which played even in small villages beyond the Arctic Circle.

In eastern Europe the most advanced theatres were in Poland and Yugoslavia. Both were molded by great producers whose work has been continued by their pupils. In Yugoslavia, Branko Gavello (d. 1962) was for nearly 50 years a free-lance producer, striving to improve standards and encourage originality. In Poland the work of Leon Schiller, a disciple of Gordon Craig, was continued by his most brilliant pupil, Erwin Axer. In Bulgaria, Rumania, and Czechoslovakia development was hampered by subservience to socialist realism, but by the 1960s playwrights were beginning to write with more freedom and sophistication, and Josef Svoboda (1920–    ), chief designer at the National Theatre, Prague, after 1950, was the world's leading scenic designer. After World War II the number of Rumanian theatre companies increased from 18 to 32, and Czechoslovakian theatres more than trebled. The Hungarian theatre, perhaps because of its situation, was the most cosmopolitan in its choice of plays. Never respectful of the dictates of socialist realism, it was a gay and sardonic theatre, excelling in satirical topical revues.

**8. British Commonwealth.**—The birth of motion pictures was practically the death of the theatre in Commonwealth countries. After World War II, visits of English companies to Canada and Australia stimulated a rebirth. In Australia, in 1954, the Queen's first visit was commemorated by the formation of an Elizabethan Theatre Trust to encourage drama, opera, and ballet. Two-thirds of the sum was contributed by the public, the remaining third by the government. The Majestic Theatre, Sydney, renamed the Elizabethan Theatre, became the trust's headquarters, and Hugh Hunt, director of the Old Vic, its first director.

In Canada the Festival Theatre at Stratford, Ont., was opened in 1953 to give summer seasons of Shakespeare. At first it was housed in a huge tent, but in 1957 a permanent theatre was built to Sir Tyrone Guthrie's design. Guthrie, founder of the festival, became resident director, and a number of British stage stars appeared with the company but the theatre has become increasingly able to rely on Canadian actors. A National Theatre School was founded in Montreal, Que., teaching in French as well as English. In Toronto, Ont., the Crest Theatre, directed by the Davies brothers, gave a wide variety of plays; but it was symptomatic of the shortage of good Canadian playwrights that the company appeared in London in a play by an English author. In 1960 the O'Keefe Center, a large, well-equipped modern theatre, was opened in Toronto.

New Zealand is a difficult country for professional theatre because even in the large cities the population is too small to support a permanent company and distances between towns make touring expensive. In 1960 the only professional company, the New Zealand Players, was forced to abandon touring for lack of financial support. However, in 1961 Richard Campion, who had formed the Players, helped to organize the New Zealand Theatre Company; this toured one production a year and had a grant from the government arts council.

Kenya had a National Theatre in Nairobi, opened in 1956. It is largely devoted to amateur companies, European, African, and Asian, including some that drew their members from all three. Nairobi also had for many years the only professional company in east Africa, the Donovan Maule Players, recruited mainly from England. In 1959 they moved into a finely designed new theatre. In Kampala, the capital of Uganda, a National Theatre was opened in 1959 and was run in much the same way as the Kenya National Theatre. In both Uganda and Nairobi annual drama festivals showed a continual rise in the quality and quantity of plays by African authors dealing with African life.

**9. South Africa.**—The theatre in South Africa at first relied mainly upon foreign touring companies, but during the 1950s it became mainly self-supporting. The National Theatre Organization, founded in 1948 with a government subsidy to take drama, in English and Afrikaans, to all parts of the country, had its headquarters in Pretoria, and in the 1960s had several companies with portable stage sets touring the country districts. Johannesburg continued to be the main theatrical centre with such permanent companies as the Brian Brooke Company, started in the 1930s, and the Johannesburg Repertory Players founded in 1947. Cape Town had the Cockpit Players, run by Leonard Schachs, and the Hofmeyr Theatre with its own company.

Negro theatre in South Africa was unorganized, depending on the vitality of township jazz concerts. Late in the 1950s the African Drama Trust was founded to try to give it coherence, and in 1961 a section of the National Theatre Organization was set up for Bantu drama. In the same year a Bantu company scored a London success with *King Kong*. (N. M.)

**10. United States.**—In the first decade of the 20th century, realism dominated the American theatre: in the plays of Clyde Fitch, William Vaughn Moody, and Edward Sheldon; in the acting of Mrs. Fiske, Richard Mansfield, and Ethel Barrymore; and in the productions of David Belasco and Harrison Grey Fiske. At the same time, however, the pretty operettas of Victor Herbert and the brash musical comedies of George M. Cohan were popular. The first *Ziegfeld Follies* appeared in 1907. The New Theatre in New York City, with a resident company dedicated to art rather than business, was established in 1909 but collapsed after two seasons.

Visits of the Abbey Theatre in 1911, Reinhardt's *Sumurun* in 1912, Granville-Barker's Company in 1915, and Copeau's group from the Vieux Colombier in Paris in 1917 provided exciting glimpses of the work of Europe's art theatres and of the "new stagecraft," thus adding to the growing dissatisfaction with the U.S. theatre.

The modern period on Broadway may be said to have begun in 1918 with the establishment of the Theatre Guild (*q.v.*), the first commercially successful U.S. art theatre, for in the next decade occurred a flowering that placed U.S. theatre for the first time on a par with the best theatre of Europe. Eugene O'Neill emerged from the Provincetown Players (*q.v.*) in 1920 with *Beyond the Horizon* to win worldwide fame. He was quickly followed by Sidney Howard, Robert Sherwood, Maxwell Anderson, George Kelly, Elmer Rice, S. N. Behrman, Philip Barry, and others; their plays provided an expression of American life that was unprecedented in its richness and variety. Besides the Theatre Guild, such producers as Arthur Hopkins, Gilbert Miller, Winthrop Ames, George C. Tyler, and Kenneth Macgowan staged the new American drama, interesting new plays from abroad, and some classics in the new style. Designers Robert Edmond Jones, Joseph Urban, Lee Simonson, Cleon Throckmorton, Norman Bel Geddes, and Jo Mielziner provided distinguished settings that were realistic, symbolistic, or expressionistic as required by the new drama. The Moscow Art Theatre company visited New York in 1923 and impressed with the quality of its ensemble acting, which only a permanent organization could achieve; some of its members remained in New York to teach the Stanislavski system. In 1926 Eva Le Gallienne established a permanent repertory company that presented classics old and new. *Show Boat* appeared in 1928 and became a classic of the musical stage. Outside New York City, competition from motion pictures reduced the number of theatres open to traveling companies from 1,500 in the early 1900s to 500, but on Broadway the number of productions grew from 150 in 1920–21 to 280 in 1927–28.

The stock market crash of 1929 heralded the end of unparalleled prosperity in the theatre and in the nation. The nation recovered from the ensuing economic depression, but the theatre, under increasing competition from motion pictures, radio, and television, did not. In the next 30 years traveling companies all but disappeared, and productions on Broadway shrank to 60 in 1949–50, and thereafter averaged between 60 and 70 a year. No new theatres were constructed. The Civic Repertory Theatre succumbed in 1933.

Nevertheless, live theatre continued to attract talented writers: Clifford Odets, Sidney Kingsley, Lillian Hellman, Thornton Wilder, and William Saroyan beginning in the 1930s; Tennessee Williams, Arthur Miller, and William Inge in the 1940s, and Edward Albee in the 1960s. Rising costs encouraged simplification of setting and by 1950 the box set was seldom seen. Rising costs and shrinking audiences necessitated longer runs. Enterprises outside the standard pattern, however, enjoyed some success. The Group Theatre (*q.v.*) for ten years maintained a permanent company, developed new playwrights, and evolved a new acting style based on the Stanislavski system. From 1935 to 1939 the Federal Theatre Project (*q.v.*) presented hundreds of productions of all sorts and showed that a large untapped audience existed for live theatre at low prices. From 1937 to 1939 Orson Welles and John Houseman maintained a permanent company and limited runs in the Mercury Theatre. From 1947 the Actors Studio cultivated the "method," derived from Stanislavski's system and practised by such actors as Marlon Brando, Geraldine Page, and Julie Harris. In 1955 the first U.S. Shakespeare festival was held at Stratford, Conn., and it became more popular each summer. The American National Theatre and Academy (ANTA), chartered by Congress in 1935 and activated in 1946, encouraged theatre, professional and nonprofessional, throughout the country. As theatre activity decreased, the producer declined in importance and the stage director rose. Among the important directors in the 1940–60 period were Elia Kazan, Robert Lewis, Harold Clurman, Joshua Logan, and José Quintero.

The musical show after 1930 gained in polish and sophistication. In 1935 George and Ira Gershwin turned the play *Porgy* by DuBose and Dorothy Heyward into America's first successful folk opera, *Porgy and Bess*. Later examples were: *Pal Joey* (1940), *Lady in the Dark* (1941), *Oklahoma!* (1943), *South Pacific* (1949), *My Fair Lady* (1956), and the star-vehicle productions *Hello, Dolly!* (Carol Channing), *Funny Girl* (Barbra Streisand), and *Fiddler on the Roof* (Zero Mostel), all in 1964. (*See* Musical Comedy.)

*Off-Broadway Theatre.*—Plays have always been produced in small theatres outside as well as in the main theatrical district in New York. In 1915–18 the Washington Square Players, in the 1920s the Provincetown Players, and in the 1930s the New Playwrights drew audiences and critics off Broadway. A new era began in 1952 with the successful revival of Tennessee Williams' *Summer and Smoke* at the Circle in the Square and gained momentum with productions at the Phoenix, the Theatre de Lys, and the Fourth Street Theatre. In 1961–62, the *New York Times* counted 100 off-Broadway productions, 34 more than on Broadway. From 1962–63 the number of off-Broadway productions declined.

BY COURTESY OF THE VANDAMM COLLECTION

SCENE FROM THE FIRST ACT OF "OKLAHOMA!," A THEATRE GUILD PRODUCTION, MUSIC BY RICHARD RODGERS, BOOK BY OSCAR HAMMERSTEIN II; SAINT JAMES THEATRE, 1945

Revivals of classics and of recent plays that had failed on Broadway predominated at first, but the proportion of new plays increased. With a few exceptions, such as at the Phoenix, the single play and the long run predominated. Since production often took place in improvised quarters under makeshift conditions, it showed styles and forms seldom seen on Broadway. Many productions were staged without a proscenium arch and with the audience on two or three sides of the playing area. Actors, directors, designers, and producers who achieved success off Broadway were soon active on Broadway. And Broadway successes began to appear off-Broadway, attracted by the greater freedom.

*Summer Theatre.*—Declining production on Broadway was accompanied by a growth of theatre in resort areas during the vacation season. In 1940, 80 summer theatres were open for a ten-week season, performing a different play or musical each week in tents, barns, and sometimes in regular theatre buildings. By the 1960s more than 200 such "straw-hat" theatres were in operation. Resident companies, frequently augmented by visiting stars, usually performed recent Broadway successes. Occasionally these summer theatres were used to test new plays for possible Broadway production. (*See* also below, *Drama Festivals.*)

*The Negro in the U.S. Theatre.*—In native plays, the Negro appeared first as a plantation hand, a minor comic character. Later he was frequently seen as a comic domestic servant. In the 1830s Thomas Dartmouth Rice was extremely popular singing and dancing as the eccentric "Jim Crow" in an entertainment he called "Ethiopian Opera." Out of such white performances of Negro song and dance came blackface minstrelsy (*see* Minstrel Show). Edward Harrigan introduced the city Negro in his comic Mulligan plays of the 1880s. The slavery plays like *Uncle Tom's Cabin* (1852) and the Civil War plays like *The Reverend Griffith Davenport* (1899) were the first to treat the Negro seriously. Edward Sheldon's *The Nigger* (1910) was the first play to deal with Negro problems in modern society. After the Civil War, Negroes became popular in minstrel shows and in all-Negro musicals.

From 1910 on, individuals like Bert Williams were featured in musicals like the *Ziegfeld Follies;* the integrated musical appeared in the 1940s. Negroes gained recognition in serious drama somewhat later: Charles Gilpin in *The Emperor Jones* (1920), Richard Harrison in *The Green Pastures* (1930), Canada Lee in *Native Son* (1941), and Paul Robeson in *Othello* (1943). Playwrights who contributed to the drama of Negro life include Ridgely Torrence, DuBose and Dorothy Heyward, and Paul Green. Negro playwrights had little success on Broadway until Lorraine Hansberry's *A Raisin in the Sun* became a hit in 1959. The racial ferment of the 1960s created an audience for accusatory melodramas such as *Dutchman* (1964), by the poet LeRoi Jones, and *Blues for Mr. Charlie* (1964) and *The Amen Corner* (1965), by the novelist James Baldwin. *In White America* (1964), a documentary of 300 years of Negro grievances, by Martin Duberman, became a major propaganda piece of the civil rights movement.

*Community Theatre.*—Community theatre grew out of the little theatre movement and its art theatres that sprang up (*c.* 1900–25) in protest against the commercial theatre and under the inspiration of the free theatres of Europe. Among the leaders were Gilmor Brown in Pasadena, Calif., Frederic McConnell in Cleveland, O., Samuel J. Hume in Detroit, Mich., and Maurice Browne in Chicago. The little theatres presented noncommercial plays, European and American, with the "new stagecraft," in small theatres for small audiences.

As road companies disappeared, most of these organizations lost their "art" theatre aims and became substitutes for professional theatre, presenting popular plays in larger theatres to larger audiences with more paid personnel. By the late 1960s three types of community theatres existed: (1) a growing number with paid actors and staff, like the Arena Stage, Washington, D.C., and the Minnesota Theater Company in Minneapolis, of which Tyrone Guthrie was artistic director; (2) a few more with paid staff and a few paid actors, like the Cleveland Play House; and (3) the great majority with some paid staff only. A new form of subsidy in the 1960s was exemplified by Ford Foundation grants to the Alley Theatre in Houston and the Actor's Workshop in San Francisco.

*University Theatre.*—Dramatic performances by students go back to the colonial period, but instruction in theatre subjects did not enter the curriculum until about 1900, largely in colleges of liberal arts and as part of the reaction against commercial theatre. Early leaders in this movement included George Pierce Baker at Harvard, Thomas H. Dickinson and Gertrude Johnson at Wisconsin, and Frederick H. Koch first at North Dakota and later at North Carolina. In 1914 the first department offering training for the professional theatre was established, at Carnegie Institute of Technology under Thomas Wood Stevens. After World War I, under the leadership of such men as A. M. Drummond at Cornell, E. C. Mabie at Iowa, and Glenn Hughes at Washington, there was a tremendous expansion of courses, departments, and degrees. The National Theatre Conference of leading university and community theatres was organized in 1932. The American Educational Theatre Association was established in 1936 and after 1949 published the *Educational Theatre Journal.* By 1964–65 nearly 600 college theatres were producing annually about 3,000 plays for an audience of more than 7,000,000. Much of this growth was because of the disappearance of professional theatre outside New York City. Although the aims of university theatre have been primarily cultural, it has affected the professional theatre, especially off-Broadway. Its unique contributions have been the development of theatre for children and the popularization of arena and other forms of open staging. (B. Ht.)

*New Directions.*—The late 1960s were marked by a deepening commitment on the part of the universities to professional theatre and by novel developments in repertory. The University of California, Princeton University, and the University of Michigan directly encouraged professional theatre by hiring actors and playwrights or directors "in residence." On the Michigan campus, at Ann Arbor, the American Players Association, subsidized in part by the university, prepared productions for presentation off Broadway. The American Conservatory Theatre, directed by William Ball and sponsored originally by the Carnegie Institute of Technology, Pittsburgh, embarked on a similar campus-to-city venture, was notably successful in 1966 at the Ravinia summer festival near Chicago. Meanwhile the tradition of professional road companies in repertory was upheld by the National Repertory Theatre, the Association of Producing Artists, and other touring groups; efforts continued to establish a resident repertory company in New York City at the Lincoln Center for the Performing Arts.

The Rockefeller Panel Report on the Performing Arts counted 56 permanent professional theatres operating in the U.S. in 1964–65; most of them had been recently established. (X.)

**11. Latin America.**—The theatre in Latin America varies greatly from country to country. Its development at mid-century was highest in Argentina, Mexico, Brazil, Uruguay, and Cuba in that order, with the other countries trailing considerably behind. The advent of motion pictures around 1900 brought about a decline in the theatre throughout Latin America but a theatrical revival became noticeable after the 1930s when playwrights abandoned the late 19th-century Spanish dramatists as models and introduced techniques and styles from the best European and New York theatres.

Early in the 20th century a nationalistic theatre arose in Argentina depicting the conflicts between the *criollo* population (descendants of settlers from the old world) and the immigrants. This movement produced a legion of playwrights, the best known of whom was an Uruguayan, Florencio Sánchez. His plays, written between 1903 and 1909, were mostly dramatic but others cultivated a more festive theatre, such as the Argentine *sainete* ("farce"). Modern Buenos Aires, Arg., had professional theatres, experimental and art theatres, and the Teatro Colón with its own opera company, symphony orchestra, and ballet. The Argentine motion-picture industry developed steadily until by the 1930s it ranked second in America only to that of the U.S.

Although the Mexican theatre was not comparable to that of Argentina, it grew through the efforts of enthusiastic art groups and many exceptional dramatists, such as Rodolfo Usigli (*Corona de sombra,* 1947) and Xavier Villaurrutia (*Juego peligroso,* 1950). Beginning in the 1950s numerous theatres were built or halls adapted as *teatros de bolsillo* ("pocket theatres"). Mexico's motion-picture industry grew and by the middle of the century had surpassed Argentina's in volume. Mario Moreno (Cantinflas) became a world-famous motion-picture star.

In Brazil the theatre enjoyed generous official protection and a high level of theatrical culture resulted. The quality of Brazilian theatrical production was comparable to that of any country. Among the best-known modern Brazilian authors were Joracy Camargo (*Deus lhe pague,* 1932) and Guilherme Figueiredo (*A rapôsa e as uvas,* 1935), and, more recently, Ariano Suassuna (*Auto da compadecida,* 1955). Procópio Ferreira came to be considered one of the world's greatest contemporary actors. The modern Brazilian motion-picture industry, commercially smaller than those of Argentina and Mexico, excelled technically and artistically.

Cuba, with a glorious theatrical past, witnessed a sharp decline at the beginning of the 20th century. The peculiar political satires known as *bufos cubanos* flourished for a while but dwindled away in the 1920s. In that decade and in the 1930s composers and playwrights developed the *zarzuela cubana,* a type of musical comedy that was successful at home, in Spain, and in Latin America. Among the composers of the *zarzuelas* were Ernesto Lecuona, Moisés Simons, and Gonzalo Roig. Cuba also made important

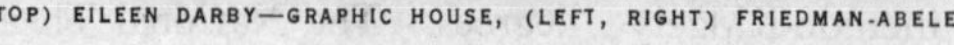

(TOP) EILEEN DARBY—GRAPHIC HOUSE, (LEFT, RIGHT) FRIEDMAN-ABELES

MID-CENTURY U.S. THEATRE

(Top) Scene from the 1948 tour production of *A Streetcar Named Desire* by Tennessee Williams. (Left) Scene from Edward Albee's *Who's Afraid of Virginia Woolf?*, 1963. (Right) Scene from *A Raisin in the Sun* by Lorraine Hansberry; Barrymore Theatre, 1959 contributions to the theatre in the field of the ballet; the Cuban ballerina Alicia Alonso became internationally known. In the 1950s theatre was strongly encouraged through open-air performances and companies that traveled to the interior. From 1959 on, the Fidel Castro regime used the theatre as a propaganda vehicle.

Chile produced at least one outstanding playwright, Armando Moock (*Rigoberto,* 1935).

The years following World War II were marked in Latin America by the appearance of many promising playwrights, among them Osvaldo Dragún of Argentina, Sergio Magaña of Mexico, Jorge de Andrade and Ariano Suassua of Brazil, Virgilio Piñera of Cuba, and Alejandro Sieveking of Chile. Occasional periods of censorship did not help to advance creative theatre. Prevailing outside influences were Ionesco, Brecht, and Tennessee Williams. There was a growing interest in social and political questions.

The motion-picture industry continued its upward trend both in volume and quality. At the region's first important motion-picture festival, held with considerable success in Rio de Janeiro in 1965, the Brazilian cineasts Glauber Rocha, Paolo Saraceni, Nelson Pereyra Dos Santos, and others displayed much skill in offerings that exemplified their conception of *cinema novo,* reminiscent of Italian neorealism; this movement spread throughout Latin America. Prior to the festival one Brazilian picture, *Black Orpheus* (1959), had received universal acclaim. (Lu. A. B.)

**12. Drama Festivals.**—There were so many drama festivals in Europe in the 1960s that it was difficult to keep count of them. The most comprehensive was the annual "Theatre of the Nations" Festival in Paris. The festivals in the Netherlands, Stockholm, Berlin, Zürich, Munich, and Vienna were, like the Paris festival, international. The Dublin Festival was essentially Irish, although some foreign companies were invited and performances of foreign plays given. The summer Pitlochry Festival in Scotland included a proportion of Scottish plays but was not exclusively national; nor was the Chichester (Sussex) Festival. At first the summer home of the National Theatre, the Chichester Festival Theatre was taken over in 1965 by a new company under the actor and producer John Clements. At Epidaurus, Greece, the festival was devoted to Greek classics. This was one of many open-air festivals, among which the most important were at Baalbek, Lebanon; Avignon, France; and Dubrovnik, Yugos. There were many smaller open-air festivals in France and Italy, most of which used surviving Roman theatres. The festivals at Salzburg and Edinburgh combined music and drama. The Edinburgh International Festival has given first performances of a number of distinguished plays, including two by T. S. Eliot, but much of the interesting drama was among the "fringe," the small pioneering companies, mostly youthful, that were not officially part of the festival.

Among festivals in the British Commonwealth were that at Adelaide, Austr. (1961– ), modeled on the Edinburgh Festival; the Canadian Dominion Drama Festival, founded in 1932, with prizes for plays in English and French; and the Vancouver International Festival. In 1965 a Commonwealth Arts Festival was inaugurated in London, at which plays by African dramatists have been notably successful. (N. M.)

Some of the best-known summer drama festivals in the United States were devoted to Shakespeare. At Ashland, Ore., plays were presented outdoors in what resembled an Elizabethan public theatre. A similar repertory was presented in a reconstruction of the Globe Theatre at San Diego, Calif. At Stratford, Conn., plays were produced in a modern theatre. The New York Shakespeare Festival was staged in Central Park. Opera replaced spoken drama in the opera house at Central City, Colo. The Arts Festival in the Public Garden, Boston, Mass., included opera and ballet, and drama; so did the Richmond, Va., Festival of Arts.

Although Stratford, Ont., was best known for its productions of Shakespeare, its program included new plays, operetta, films, and music. Vancouver, B.C., presented an international festival of drama, opera, and ballet.

*See* also Drama; and references under "Theatre" in the Index.

(B. Ht.)

Bibliography.—*General:* W. Creizernach, *Geschichte des neueren Dramas,* 5 vol., 2nd ed. (1911–23); G. Freedley and J. A. Reeves, *A History of the Theatre* (1941); *Enciclopedia dello spettacolo,* 9 vol. (1954–62; supplementary vol. *1955–65,* 1966); P. Hartnoll (ed.), *The Oxford Companion to the Theatre,* 3rd enlarged rev. ed. (1967); J. R. Taylor, *The Penguin Dictionary of the Theatre* (1966); Karl Mantzius, *A History of Theatrical Art,* 6 vol. (1903–21); E. Schuré, *The Genesis of Tragedy and the Sacred Drama of Eleusis,* trans. by F. Rothwell (1936); H. Ellis, *The Dance of Life* (1923); W. Ridgway, *The Dramas and Dramatic Dances of Non-European Races in Special Reference to the Origin of Greek Tragedy* (1915); L. Havemeyer, *The Drama of Savage Peoples* (1916); B. Hunningher, *The Origin of the Theatre* (1961).

*Development in the East:* L. C. Arlington, *The Chinese Drama* (1930); A. Jacovleff, *The Chinese Theatre* (1922); A. B. Keith, *The Sanskrit Drama in Its Origin, Development, Theory and Practice* (1924); G. Jéquier, "La Pyramide d'Aba," *Services des antiquités de l'Égypte: Fouilles à Saqqarah* (1935); R. K. Yajnik, *The Indian Theatre. Its Origins and Its Later Development Under European Influence* (1934); F. A. Lombard, *An Outline History of the Japanese Drama* (1929); Z. Kincaid, *Kabuki. The Popular Stage of Japan* (1925); A. Waley, *The No Plays of Japan* (1922); A. C. Scott, *The Kabuki Theatre of Japan* (1955).

*Western Antiquity:* B. H. Clark, *European Theories of the Drama* (3rd ed., with suppl. on U.S. drama, 1947); H. D. F. Kitto, *Form and Meaning in Drama: a Study of Six Greek Plays and of Hamlet* (1956), *Greek Tragedy,* 3rd ed. (1961); A. W. Pickard-Cambridge, *Dithyramb, Tragedy and Comedy* (1927); F. M. Cornford, *The Origin of Attic Comedy* (1914); A. E. Haigh, *The Attic Theatre,* 3rd ed. (1907); W. Beare, *The Roman Stage,* 2nd ed. (1955); M. Bieber, *The History of the Greek and Roman Theater,* 2nd ed. (1961); R. Hathorn, *The Handbook of Classical Drama* (1967).

*Christian Revival:* J. S. Tunison, *Dramatic Traditions of the Dark Ages* (1907); K. Young, *The Drama of the Mediaeval Church,* 2 vol. (1933); O. B. Hardison, Jr., *Christian Rite and Christian Drama* (1965); R. E. Tiddy, *The Mummer's Play* (1923); Sir E. K. Chambers, *The Mediaeval Stage,* 2 vol. (1903); A. W. Pollard (ed.), *English Miracle Plays, Moralities and Interludes* (1927); G. Cohen, *Histoire de la mise-en-scène du théâtre religieux français du moyen âge* (1926); R. Southern, *The Mediaeval Theatre in the Round: a Study of the Staging of the Castle of Perseverance* (1957); G. W. G. Wickham, *Early English Stages, 1300 to 1600,* vol. i (1959), vol. ii, pt. I (1963); R. Withington, *English Pageantry,* 2 vol. (1918–21); R. Froning (ed.), *Das Drama des Mittelalters* (1892); R. B. Williams, "The Staging of Plays in the Spanish Peninsula Prior to 1555," University of Iowa Studies: Spanish Language and Literature, no. 5 (1934); N. D. Shergold, *A History of the Spanish Stage From Medieval Times Until the End of the 17th Century* (1967); H. A. Rennert, *The Spanish Stage at the Time of Lope de Vega* (1909); G. R. Kernodle, *From Art to Theatre: Form and Convention in the Renaissance* (1944); J. Jacquot (ed.), "Fêtes de la Renaissance," *Groupe d'études musicales de la Renaissance* (1957); G. E. Bentley, *The Jacobean and Caroline Stage,* 6 vol. (1941–66); L. B. Campbell, *Scenes and Machines on the English Stage During the Renaissance, a Classical Revival* (1923); E. Welsford, *The Court Masque* (1927); J. Laver, *Drama: Its Costume and Decor* (1951); T. W. Craik, *The Tudor Interlude* (1958); J. Gregor, *Monumenta scenica* (1925–31); K. M. Lea, *Italian Popular Comedy: the Commedia dell'arte 1560–1620,* 2 vol. (1934; 2nd rev. ed. 1961); A. Nicoll, *The World of Harlequin: A History of the Commedia dell' Arte* (1963); Sir E. K. Chambers, *The Elizabethan Stage,* 4 vol. (1923); H. C. Gardiner, *Mysteries' End: an Investigation of the Last Days of the Medieval Religious Stage* (1946); A. A. Parker, *The Allegorical Drama of Calderón* (1943); G. F. Reynolds, *The Staging of Elizabethan Plays: at the Red Bull Theater, 1605–25* (1940); A. M. Nagler, *Shakespeare's Stage,* Eng. trans. (1958); L. Hotson, *The Commonwealth and Restoration Stage* (1928); M. Summers, *The Restoration Theatre* (1934); M. Apollonio, *Storia del teatro italiano* (1938–51); D. de Escovar and L. de la Vega, *Historia del teatro español* (1924); J. T. Murray, *English Dramatic Companies,* 2 vol. (1910).

*Classical, Baroque and Romantic Reaction:* S. W. Holsboer, *Histoire de la mise-en-scène dans le théâtre français: 1600–57* (1933); H. C. Lancaster, *A History of French Dramatic Literature in the 17th Century,* 9 vol. (1929–42, continued in *Sunset, 1701–15,* 1945); J. Scherer, *La dramaturgie classique en France 1620–80* (1950); F. Brunetière, *Les époques du théâtre français, 1636–1850* (1892); W. H. Bruford, *Chekhov and His Russia* (1948), *Theatre, Drama and Audience in Goethe's Germany* (1950); B. V. Varneke, *A History of the Russian Theatre, 17th Through 19th Centuries,* ed. by Belle Martin (1951); A. N. Vardac, *Stage to Screen* (1949); M. Martersteig, *Das Deutsche Theater in 19. Jahrhundert,* 2 vol. (1904); A. Nicoll, *A History of English Drama,* 6 vol. (1952–59); J. A. Worp, *Geschiedenis van het drama en vat het tooneel in Nederland,* 2 vol. (1904–08); G. B. Shaw, *The Quintessence of Ibsenism* (1891; new ed. 1913); J. Northam, *Ibsen's Dramatic Method* (1953); B. M. E. Mortensen and B. W. Downs, *Strindberg: an Introduction to His Life and Work* (1949); R. Southern, *The Georgian Playhouse* (1948), *Changeable Scenery* (1959), *Seven Ages of Theatre* (1962; 1964).

*Supplementary Arts:* A Nicoll, *Mimes, Masks and Miracles* (1931); M. Albert, *Les Théâtres de la foire 1660–1789* (1900); S. Rosenfeld, *Strolling Players and Drama in the Provinces, 1660–1865* (1939); E. Welsford, *The Fool: His Social and Literary History* (1935); M. W.

Disher, *Blood and Thunder: Mid-Victorian Melodrama and Its Origins* (1949); A. H. Coxe, *A Seat at the Circus* (1951). (G. W. G. W.)

*20th Century:* J. L. Barrault, *Reflections on the Theatre* (1951); H. Hunt, *The Director in the Theatre* (1954); F. Bowers, *Theatre in the East* (1956); *Entertainment in Russia* (1959); R. Brassilach, *Les Animateurs de théâtre* (1954); T. Guthrie and R. Davies (eds.), *Renown at Stratford* (1953); T. Guthrie, *A Life in the Theatre* (1960); N. Marshall, *The Other Theatre* (1947), and *The Producer and the Play* (1957); L. Simonson, *The Stage Is Set* (1932); H. Hobson, *French Theatre of Today* (1959); A. van Gyseghem, *Theatre in Soviet Russia* (1943); A. Nicoll, *Theatre and Dramatic Theory* (1963); Sir J. Gielgud, *Stage Directions* (1963); R. Brustein, *The Theatre of Revolt* (1966); L. Kitehen, *Mid Century Drama* (1960) and *Drama in the 1960s* (1966); J. R. Taylor, *Anger, and After* (1962; rev. ed. 1963); E. Bentley, *The Life of the Drama* (1965); S. Joseph, *Theater in the Round* (1966); International Theatre Institute, *World Theatre* (quarterly, in English and French). (N. M.)

*United States:* Barnard Hewitt, *Theatre U.S.A., 1668 to 1957* (1959); Glenn Hughes, *A History of the American Theatre, 1700–1950* (1951); Lloyd Morris, *Curtain Time* (1953); Oral Sumner Coad and Edwin Mims, Jr., *The American Stage,* vol. 14, *The Pageant of America* (1929); Howard Taubman, *The Making of the American Theatre* (1965); Arthur Hobson Quinn, *A History of the American Drama, From the Beginning to the Civil War,* rev. ed. (1944), *A History of the American Drama From the Civil War to the Present Day,* rev. ed. (1936); John Gassner, *Theatre at the Crossroads* (1960); Sterling A. Brown, "Negro in the American Theatre," *The Oxford Companion to the Theatre,* ed. by Phyllis Hartnoll, 2nd ed. (1957); Edith J. R. Isaacs, *The Negro in the American Theatre* (1947); Kenneth Macgowan, *Footlights Across America* (1929); Albert McCleery and Carl Glick, *Curtains Going Up* (1939); Norris Houghton, *Advance from Broadway* (1941); Talbot Pierson, *Encores on Main Street* (1948); Sawyer Falk, "Nationwide Theatre, U.S.A.," *The Oxford Companion to the Theatre,* ed. by Phyllis Hartnoll, 2nd ed. (1957); Clifford Eugene Hamar, "College and University Theatre Instruction in the Early Twentieth Century," and William P. Halstead and Clara Behringer, "Theatre Organizations and Theatre Education," *History of Speech Education in America,* ed. by Karl R. Wallace (1954); *Quarterly Journal of Speech; National Theatre Conference Bulletin; Educational Theatre Journal.* (B. Ht.)

*Latin America:* Willis Knapp Jones, *Breve historia del teatro latinoamericano* (1956) and *Behind Spanish American Footlights* (1966); Julio A. Leguizamón, *Literatura hispanoamericana* (1945); Luis Ordaz, *Teatro del Río de la Plata* (1946); Ruth Richardson, *Florencio Sánchez and the Argentine Theatre* (1933); José J. Arrom, *Historia de la literatura dramática cubana* (1944); Antonio Magaña Esquivel and Ruth S. Lamb, *Breve historia del teatro mexicano* (1958); Afranio Coutiño, *A Literatura no Brasil* (1955); Lafayette Silva, *Historia do teatro brasileiro* (1938). (Lu. A. B.)

**THEATRE GUILD (NEW YORK)** was founded in 1918 for the purpose of offering consistently high-quality European and native drama to U.S. theatregoers. Recognizing the need for a professional organization that would produce with regularity, the first board assembled by the Guild's founder, Lawrence Langner (1890–1962), established the Guild as a permanent program theatre; the board departed from usual theatre practices, sharing responsibility for play choice, management, and production. The first two seasons, with plays by Jacinto Benavente, St. John Ervine, Tolstoi, John Masefield, and Strindberg, demonstrated the artistic soundness of the plan.

Following the world premiere of *Heartbreak House* in 1920, the Guild became the American agent of George Bernard Shaw, producing 15 of his plays, including world premieres of *Back to Methuselah, Saint Joan, Too True To Be Good,* and *The Apple Cart.* After its success with European authors, the Guild produced *Marco Millions* in 1928, which began Eugene O'Neill's long association with the Guild. Other American authors included Sidney Howard, William Saroyan, Maxwell Anderson, and Robert Sherwood; all Pulitzer Prize winners. Numerous other playwrights received the Critics Award for Guild productions of their plays. Under its aegis, Lynn Fontanne and Alfred Lunt first acted as a team in Ferenc Molnár's *The Guardsman,* and continued acting together for the Guild throughout most of their distinguished career.

Prominent among scenic artists, Robert Edmond Jones, Jo Mielziner, Stewart Chaney, Donald Oenslager, and Lee Simonson did major work under Guild sponsorship. Directors Philip Moeller and Rouben Mamoulian achieved their great successes in association with the Guild. A younger group of Guild staff, partly financed by the Guild, formed the Group Theatre in 1931. The Theatre Guild contributed significantly to American musical theatre by producing George Gershwin and DuBose Heyward's *Porgy and Bess* and by bringing together Richard Rodgers and Oscar Hammerstein to adapt Lynn Riggs's *Green Grow the Lilacs* as a musical comedy. The resultant *Oklahoma!* established a new genre in musical theatre, its success being followed by other Rodgers and Hammerstein collaborations, including *Carousel.*

The "Theatre Guild on the Air," sponsored by the United States Steel Corporation, had a distinguished record of radio and television play productions (1945–63). The Guild's subscription series enabled audiences in 23 cities from coast to coast to enjoy its major attractions and those of other managers.

Current history is summarized in the *Britannica Book of the Year.* (E. B. P.)

**THEATRES (STRUCTURES).** A theatre is a place or building so equipped that actors may perform, with or without scenery, before an audience.

**Greek Theatres.**—Although the temples of the ancient Egyptians may have provided the setting for their dramas, and the theatral area adjoining the palaces at Knossos and Phaistos, Crete (2000–1600 B.C.), may well have served as a place for ritual dances and ceremonies of a dramatic nature, it was in ancient Greece that the Western type of theatre began.

Greek drama developed from religious dances performed by a chorus on a flat area leveled off on the slope of a hillside, the audience standing on the slope above; often the most suitable ready-made site was the circular threshing floor. As drama developed, rudimentary theatres, like that at Ikaria, were provided for the performances; in the very early form of theatre (fig. 1), dating from the 6th or 5th century B.C., the audience sat, possibly on timber benches, on a simple earth slope facing a flat rectangular dancing floor (orchestra) where the chorus and actor(s) performed. Directly adjoining this was a small temple with an altar before it, a reminder of the religious nature of the dramatic functions. At Thorikos (fig. 2) three periods of development are observable: in the first (6th or 5th century B.C.), a rectangular section of stone steps faced a rectangular orchestra with a retaining wall at the rear; in the second, two slightly curved wings were added; finally in the third (3rd century B.C.), additional seating was provided above ground level.

Similar remains may exist beneath the later developments that cover most theatre sites continuing in active use. The most famous of these was the theatre of Dionysus in Athens. Here the extant 6th-century remains are generally accepted as part of the retaining wall of the earliest orchestra, and this wall is presumed to have followed a free form. No evidence seems to exist as to the shape of the orchestra itself, and, although this has been assumed to have been circular, the records regarding the use of timber benches seem to suggest the possibility of a straight-sided figure similar to that at Thorikos. The shape of the Periclean orchestra (*c.* 443 B.C.) is also in doubt, but it is known to have been backed by a long straight retaining wall. Although early orchestras may at first have been rectangular, then trapezoid or many sided, the need to provide accommodation with good acoustic and visual conditions for an ever increasing audience—everyone in the district attended the yearly religious festivals—probably accounted for the final adoption of the circular form. Little is known of this early period, however, and while the orchestra may have evolved as indicated above, the final form may have been strongly influenced by the early use of the threshing floors.

FIG. 1.—EARLY THEATRE FORM, WITH AUDIENCE SEATED ON HILLSIDE

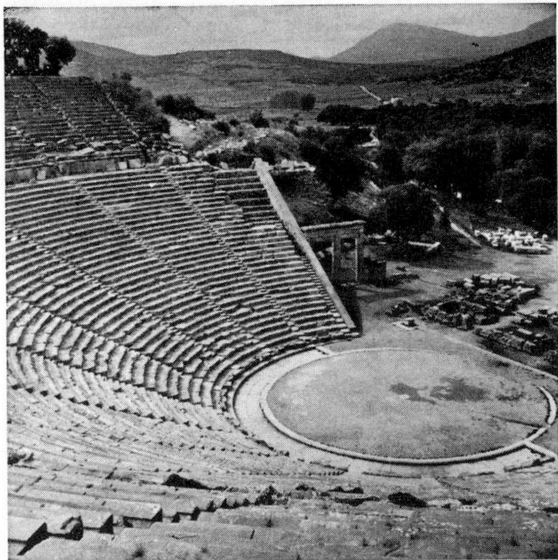

*Cavea* (seating area), orchestra and (right) ruins of the stage buildings of the Greek theatre at Epidaurus by Polyclitus, *c.* 340 B.C.

Theatre of Dionysus, Athens, showing the paved orchestra enclosed within a low wall, an addition which was made to the original Greek structure by the Romans about A.D. 54–68

Stage and *frons scaenae* (front wall of stage building) of the partially restored Roman theatre, Orange, France; *c.* A.D. 50

Remains of the Roman theatre on the shore of the Mediterranean sea near Tripoli, Libya, dating from the 3rd century A.D. The *cavea* seated 5,000 persons

Teatro Olimpico, Vicenza, Italy, a theatre designed in the Roman manner by Andrea Palladio and Vincenzo Scamozzi, 1580–85

Permanent architectural frontispiece of the Farnese theatre, a Renaissance court theatre at Parma, Italy; designed by G. Aleotti, 1618

## GREEK, ROMAN AND RENAISSANCE THEATRES

PHOTOGRAPHS, (TOP LEFT) N. HADJISTYLIANOS, (TOP RIGHT) ALISON FRANTZ, (CENTRE LEFT) PAUL ALMASY, (CENTRE RIGHT) UNITED PRESS INTERNATIONAL, (BOTTOM LEFT) G. E. KIDDER SMITH, (BOTTOM RIGHT) FOTOCELERE, TURIN

# THEATRES (STRUCTURES)

The Petit Bourbon, Paris, as illustrated in the frontispiece by J. Patin to Baltazarini's *Balet comique de la Royne,* 1582

Anne of Austria, Louis XIII and Cardinal Richelieu at a performance in a 17th-century French theatre, probably the Théâtre du Palais Royal, Paris

Interior of a baroque theatre, from a painting ascribed to one of the Galli da Bibiena family, 17th-18th-century Italian artists

Theatre Royal, Drury Lane, London, adaptation by Robert Adam in 1775 of Christopher Wren's 1674 building. After an engraving by Adam, figures corrected in accordance with scale drawings in Soane collection

The Theatre Royal, Bristol; J. Paty, 1766. This building in its original form closely resembled Wren's Drury Lane

View of the six semicircular tiers of boxes (loges) in the La Scala opera house, Milan, Italy; 1778

## RENAISSANCE AND POST-RENAISSANCE THEATRES

BY COURTESY OF (TOP LEFT) THE TRUSTEES OF THE BRITISH MUSEUM, (TOP RIGHT) CAISSE NATIONALE DES MONUMENTS HISTORIQUES, PARIS, (CENTRE LEFT) THE TRUSTEES OF THE NATIONAL GALLERY, LONDON; PHOTOGRAPHS, (CENTRE RIGHT) RICHARD LEACROFT, (BOTTOM LEFT) "ARCHITECTURAL REVIEW," (BOTTOM RIGHT) ERIO PICCAGLIANI

The interior of the Theatre Royal, Drury Lane, London, as rebuilt by Henry Holland in 1794. From a watercolour by Edward Dayes (1763–1804)

Interior of John Brougham's Lyceum theatre, New York city; 1850. From an engraving by J. C. Taylor, 1863

Cross-sectional drawing showing the interior of the Prince Regent theatre, Munich, designed by Max Littmann, 1901

## THEATRES OF THE 18TH, 19TH AND EARLY 20TH CENTURIES

BY COURTESY OF (TOP) GEOFFREY W. G. AGNEW; PHOTOGRAPHS, (BOTTOM LEFT) CULVER PICTURES, INC., (BOTTOM RIGHT) FROM SHELDON CHENEY, "THE THEATRE, THREE THOUSAND YEARS OF DRAMA, ACTING AND STAGECRAFT"

# THEATRES (STRUCTURES)

The Ziegfeld theatre, New York city, showing the ornate décor in the auditorium. Architects, Joseph Urban and Thomas W. Lamb; 1927

The Guild theatre, New York city, which illustrates the type plan that became standard for picture-frame theatres. Architects, C. Howard Crane, Franzheim and Bettis; 1925

The Grosses Schauspielhaus, Berlin, a circus building converted into a theatre for Max Reinhardt. Architect, Hans Poelzig; 1919

The Künstlertheater, Munich, in which the seating was designed with a constant rise of steps from front to rear. Architect, Max Littmann; 1908

The project Theater #14 designed in 1922 by Norman Bel Geddes for a theatre proposed for the Century of Progress exposition, Chicago (1933–34)

## EARLY 20TH-CENTURY THEATRES

BY COURTESY OF (TOP LEFT) DRIX DURYEA, (CENTRE RIGHT) MORRIS GEST, (BOTTOM LEFT) MAX LITTMANN, (BOTTOM RIGHT) NORMAN BEL GEDDES

The Penthouse theatre, University of Washington, Seattle, an example of theatre-in-the-round. Architect, Carl F. Gould; 1940

The Community theatre, Western Springs, Ill., showing the open stage within the auditorium. Architect, G. Orth, Design Consultant, J. H. Miller; 1960–61

Loeb Drama centre, Harvard university, showing the interior rearranged for three stage-audience relationships: *top*, conventional auditorium of the proscenium (picture-frame) type; *centre*, modified theatre-in-the-round; *bottom*, three-sided platform theatre. Architect, Hugh Stubbins; 1959–60

Interior view of the auditorium and revolving stage of the Kalita Humphreys theatre, Dallas, Tex. Architect, Frank Lloyd Wright; 1959

Interior of the auditorium of the Sarah Lawrence college theatre, Bronxville, N.Y., an example of functional theatre design. The 500-seat theatre can be adapted for open stage productions, plays within a proscenium or open-air performances. Architect, Marcel Breuer; 1952

## UNIVERSITY AND COMMUNITY THEATRES

BY COURTESY OF (TOP LEFT) PENTHOUSE THEATRE, (TOP RIGHT) THE THEATRE AND ARTS CENTER, WESTERN SPRINGS, ILL., (CENTRE RIGHT) THEATER CENTER; PHOTOGRAPHS, (LEFT, TOP, CENTRE AND BOTTOM) CLEMENS KALISCHER, (BOTTOM RIGHT) BEN SCHNALL

# THEATRES (STRUCTURES)

Interior of the Royal Shakespeare theatre, Stratford-upon-Avon, Eng., built in 1932, showing part of the auditorium and the new apron stage, designed in 1960 by Peter Hall, with the assistance of John Barton and Henry Bardon. The stage setting shown is for Hall's production of *A Midsummer Night's Dream*

Open stage with eight acting levels, designed by Tany Moiseiwitsch, in the Stratford festival theatre, Ontario, Canada, 1957. Theatre architect: Robert Fairfield

Interior of the civic theatre at Malmö, Sweden, showing the extended proscenium which can be lowered or raised. Architects, E. Lallerstedt, S. Lewerentz and D. Hellden; 1944

Mermaid theatre, Puddle Dock, London, showing scenery arranged on the open end-stage. Architect, E. Davies; 1959

The small theatre of the National theatre at Mannheim, Ger., arranged as a two-sided theatre-in-the-round. Architect, G. Weber; 1957

## MODERN THEATRES OF CANADA AND EUROPE

BY COURTESY OF (CENTRE LEFT) STRATFORD SHAKESPEAREAN FESTIVAL FOUNDATION OF CANADA; PHOTOGRAPHS, (TOP) WALTER SCOTT (BRADFORD) LTD., (CENTRE RIGHT) H. STENBERGS, SWEDISH INTERNATIONAL PRESS BUREAU, (BOTTOM LEFT) "ARCHITECT'S JOURNAL," (BOTTOM RIGHT) GERHARD WEBER / FOTO HÄUSSER

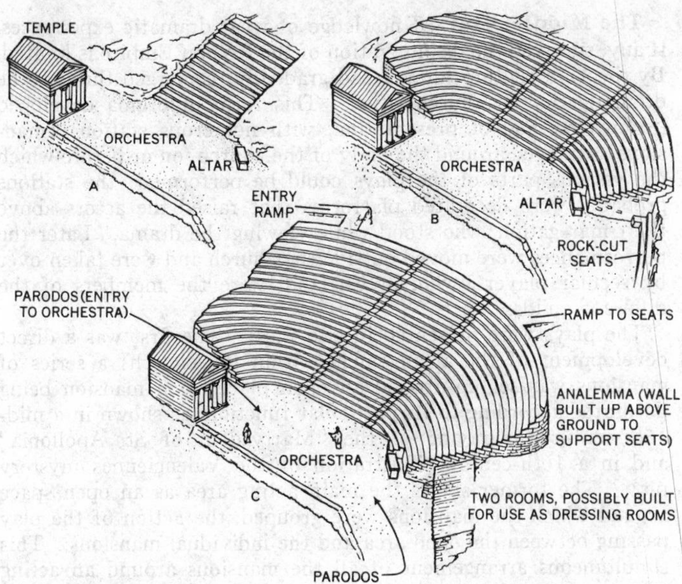


FROM H. AND R. LEACROFT, "THE THEATRE"

FIG. 2.—THE GREEK THEATRE AT THORIKOS. A, B, AND C INDICATE THE THREE PERIODS OF DEVELOPMENT (*see* TEXT)

At first the only building connected with the theatres was a temple, but when plays developed from the early songs and dances and actors joined the chorus and played more than one part, they needed a changing room, so a booth or hut (*skene*) was built on the far side of the orchestra. At first the *skene* had one central door; later the door was flanked by two more doors and later still by two wings (*paraskenia*), each with a further door. Although it is contended that the actors were not separated from the chorus during the "high" period of Greek drama and that the need for a raised stage was only felt when the New Comedy of the 4th century B.C. required a clearer portrayal of individual characters, no one really knows when a raised stage was added. When it was adopted, however, it filled the space enclosed by the *skene* and *paraskenia* and consisted of a wooden platform or speaking place (*logeion*) supported at the front on a row of columns or piers, which, in later examples, were about 10–12 ft. high. These colonnades were known as the *proskenion,* although this term is usually applied to the whole stage structure in front of the *skene,* a view shared by the designers of the Renaissance.

Although no two Greek theatres are exactly alike and it is difficult to trace any simple line of development, most fully developed Greek theatres incorporated the following elements (fig. 3). A *cavea,* or *theatron,* of stepped stone seats for the audience was divided by gangways as shown. Seats of honour (*prohedria*) occupied the front row; when raised stages were added to existing theatres, these seats were often moved to a higher level or additional seats were installed. The seating surrounded, to slightly more than a semicircle, a circular orchestra that had two entryways (*parodoi*) beside the retaining walls at either end of the *cavea.* Beyond the *parodoi* and tangential to the orchestral circle was the *proskenion,* with its *logeion* often approached from either end by a sloping ramp and backed by the *skene.* Entry to the stage from the *skene* was still through the three doors, which were now raised to the upper level; but by the 3rd and 2nd centuries B.C. the front wall of the *skene* was pierced by as many as seven wide openings (*thyromata*).

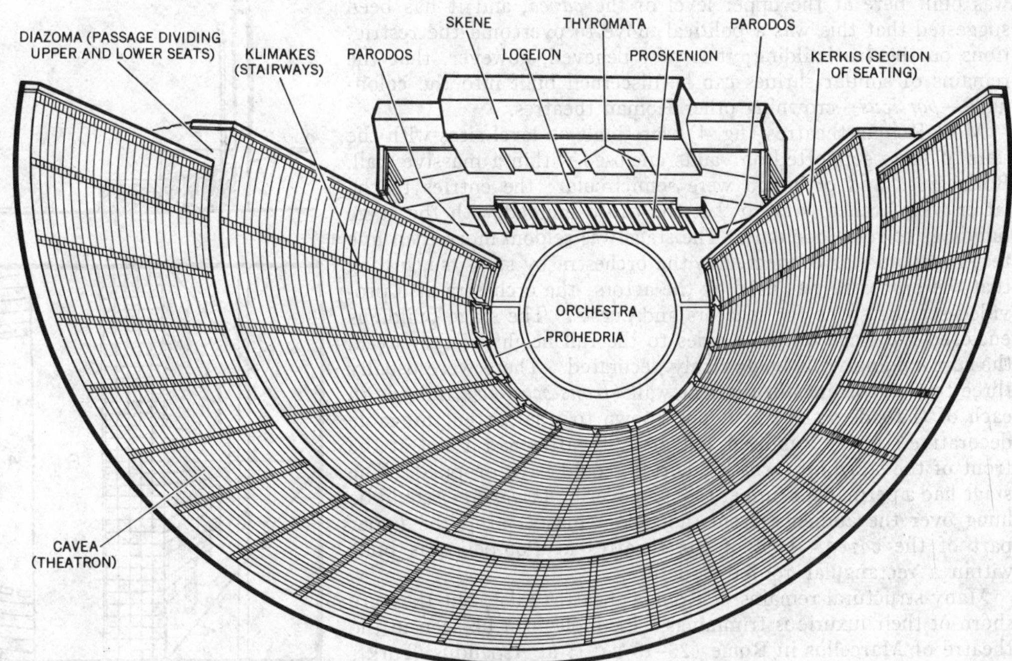


FROM H. AND R. LEACROFT, "THE THEATRE"

FIG. 3.—HELLENISTIC THEATRE

The earlier Greek plays were set in an open place before the homes of the various characters that were represented by the different doors, the central door representing the palace of the protagonist. Entry to the theatre from the sides represented variously an approach from the sea or from the country. Although interior scenes were not used in the early dramas except in the form of tableaux wheeled out on a low platform (*eccyclema*), the later *thyromata* may have made provision for them. Some authorities think these openings were curtained and contained scenery, but the actors could hardly have performed within the *skene* because many of the audience would have been unable to see them. It is sometimes thought that a convention allowed the action supposedly taking place within the opening to be performed on the open stage in front. Besides making these conventional uses of the architectural setting, the Greeks added realism in the form of various mechanical devices, such as the crane that enabled gods to ascend to or descend from a higher stage (*theologeion*). They also introduced painted scenery: the *pinakes* were decorative panels generally thought to have been placed between the columns of the *proskenion;* the *periaktoi* was a three-sided machine that was revolved to suggest a change of scene by the display of a new device. Remains in some theatres suggest the *periaktoi* were placed behind openings in the *skene.*

Although most stage buildings have largely disappeared, many *cavea* remain sufficiently intact so that their original appearance can be appreciated. One of the finest is at Epidaurus; it was designed by Polyclitus, *c.* 340 B.C. Many theatres, including that of Dionysus at Athens, underwent extensive alterations at the hands of the Romans, who usually paved the orchestra and enclosed it within a low wall to protect the audience during gladiatorial fights or to permit flooding for some nautical spectacles. Although it is unlikely that the Romans realized the Greek theatre had developed its form at a time when attention was focused on a chorus performing in the orchestra, they obviously felt that placing of the actors' stage on the far side of the orchestra was not desirable, and they rebuilt many stage buildings nearer the audience.

Temporary wooden stages were erected for the performance of Greek popular comedies (*phlyakes*) by strolling players. Vase paintings show timber platforms raised a few feet on posts, with

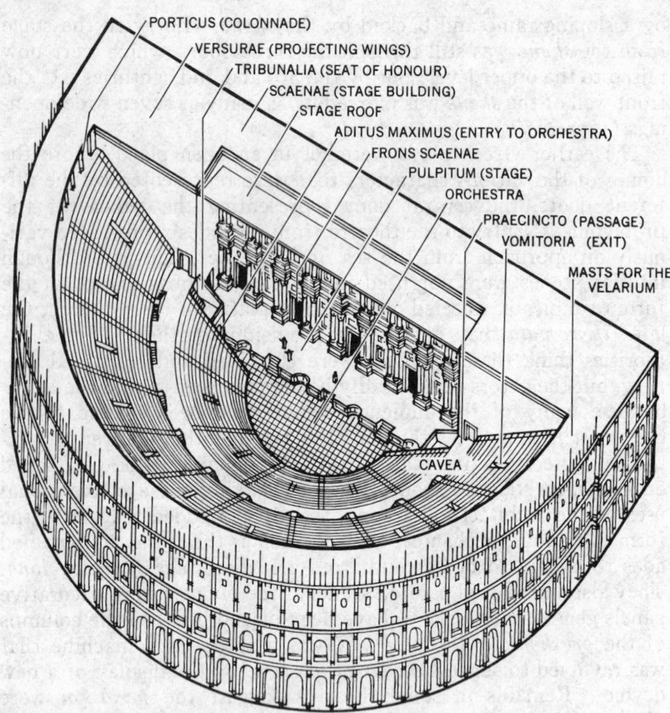


FROM H. AND R. LEACROFT, "THE THEATRE"

FIG. 4.—TYPICAL ROMAN THEATRE

the stage, sometimes protected by an awning, being backed by a curtained structure that provided both a scenic background and a primitive *skene*. Unimportant as these stages may appear beside the permanent theatres, they represent a second basic actor-audience relationship. In the first (permanent theatre), the audience, seated on a slope, looks down on an actor before them (fig. 1); in the second (temporary stage) the actor, raised above a standing audience, can be seen and heard even by those at the rear of the crowd.

**The Roman Theatre.**—Like the Greeks the Romans had small temporary stages used by the players who performed in the mime; for some time the building of permanent theatres in Rome was banned, only temporary structures being used. The first permanent stone theatre was erected by Pompeius, 55–52 B.C. A temple was built here at the upper level of the *cavea,* and it has been suggested that this was a political move to overcome the restrictions on theatre building; it is now believed, however, that the remains of similar shrines can be discerned built into the colonnade—*porticus*—crowning other Roman theatres.

Most Roman theatres (fig. 4) were built on level sites with the tiers of seats supported on vaults enclosed within a massive wall. Both *cavea* and orchestra were semicircular; the entries to the latter were arched over so that the *cavea* merged with the stage buildings to form one unit. The stage was seldom more than five feet high and was connected to the orchestra by steps, suggesting that the orchestra was used by the actors; the orchestra also provided seating space for senators and guests. The stage buildings enclosed the stage on three sides to the full height of the *cavea,* the surrounding walls being richly decorated. There were usually three to five openings in the rear wall (*frons scaenae*) and one in each of the side walls. It is not known to what extent movable decorative scenery was used, but many theatres had a slot at the front of the stage into which a curtain could have dropped. The stage had a permanent timber roof; a covering (*velarium*) could be hung over the audience from the poles (masts) atop the upper part of the *cavea.* One of the theatres at Pompeii was built within a rectangular roofed structure.

Many structural remains of Roman theatres exist, but they are shorn of their luxurious trimmings. Examples can be seen in the theatre of Marcellus in Rome (23–13 B.C.); at Aspendus, Turk.; at Orange, France (*c.* A.D. 50); and at Verulamium (St. Albans), Eng. (2nd century A.D.).

**The Middle Ages.**—Knowledge of what dramatic experiences, if any, survived the disintegration of the Roman Empire is limited. By the 12th century, drama had gradually reemerged through the dramatization of church ritual. This form of drama developed its own method of presentation, with numerous stations (mansions) arranged around the body of the church, on or before which the various parts of the plays could be performed; the stations probably were decorated platforms that raised the actors above the congregation, who stood while viewing the drama. Later the performances were moved outside the church and were taken over by secular players, who, in England, were the members of the different guilds.

The plays were presented in two ways. The first was a direct development of the arrangement within the church: a series of mansions was set up around an open place, each mansion being decorated according to its particular function, as shown in a mid-15th-century engraving of the "Martyrdom of St. Apollonia" and in a 16th-century illustration of the Valenciennes mystery play. The former shows the main acting area as an open space around which the mansions were grouped, the action of the play passing between the open area and the individual mansions. This simultaneous arrangement of all the mansions around an acting area, sometimes termed a multiple setting, provided for many changes of scene by the simple expedient of moving the action from one locale to another. The audience is standing underneath the mansions, but it is possible that the artist has grouped the mansions more closely than they would in fact have been, and the audience may well have been accommodated in the spaces between. The "theatre" for these performances varied from the marketplace indicated in the illustrations to the Lucerne Passion Play (as it was performed in 1583) to the rounds at St. Just and Perranzabuloe, Cornwall, where earth and stone steps on banks surrounded a circular flat plain. That such a round may sometimes have been of a more temporary nature is suggested by wattle fence surround of the St. Apollonia engraving. In the second method of presentation the mansions were portable and were moved to different places in the town. The number of settings available was the same as in the multiple setting, but only one was visible at a time. These wheeled mansions were known as pageants and had a raised stage with a curtained area beneath as a room for the actors; no simple structures, they ranged from a realistic replica of Noah's ship to the fire-breathing mechanics of "Hell's mouth." The audience stood around this raised stage,

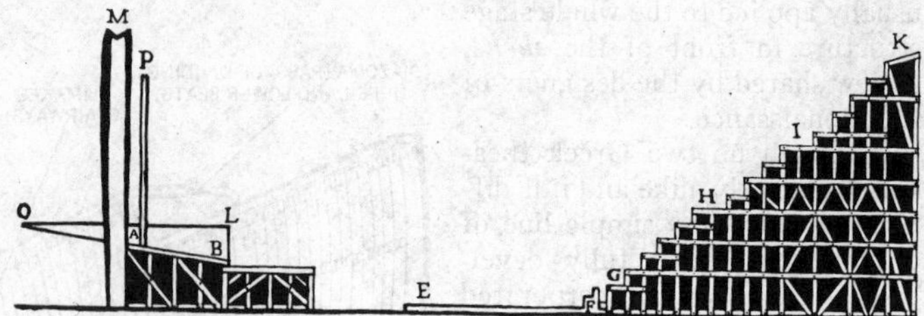


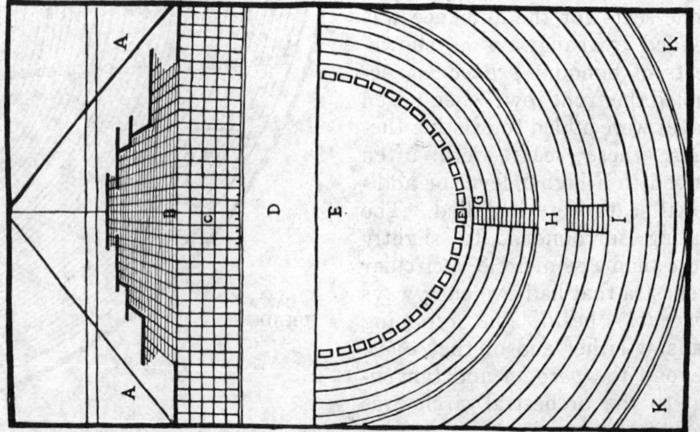


FIG. 5.—SEBASTIANO SERLIO'S DESIGN FOR A THEATRE, ILLUSTRATION FROM HIS "ARCHITETTURA," 1545

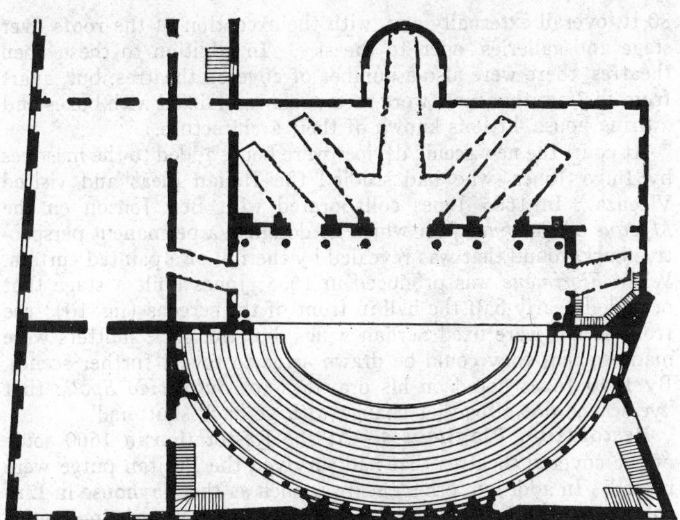

FIG. 6.—PALLADIO'S PLAN FOR THE THEATRE OF THE OLYMPIAN ACADEMY AT VICENZA, 1580

leaving space for the actors to perform, if necessary, at ground level. In some instances scaffolding was set up, presumably as seating for the important persons of the city or town, but no doubt nearby windows and balconies also were used.

**The Early Renaissance.**—In 15th-century Italy scholars and artists of the Renaissance created what they thought to be the correct settings for the recently discovered plays of ancient Greece and Rome; their work was based on an imperfect understanding of the descriptions of theatres and scenery by the Roman author Vitruvius. For particular occasions temporary stages were erected in the courtyards or halls of a duke's palace; descriptions suggest that the first attempts were similar to the stages illustrated in the edition of Terence's plays published in Lyons in 1493. These had a proscenium, or raised stage, hung with tapestries and backed by a scene front divided into compartments by richly decorated columns, the openings being curtained with cloth of gold. Each compartment of the scene front represented the home of the character named above the opening, and the interiors would seem to have been decorated to represent realistic scenes, an arrangement reminiscent both of the late Greek *thyromata* and the medieval mansions.

During the 16th century the study of perspective introduced a new medium of expression into the theatre and complicated what had been a comparatively simple actor-audience relationship by adding the glories of realistic scenery. The discovery that a scene of infinite grandeur could be realistically represented in a comparatively small space initiated the conflict as to the relative merits of spectacle and drama. In 1545 Sebastiano Serlio published in his *Architettura* a basic design for a theatre that clearly defined the three elements he considered essential (fig. 5): within a rectangular building he showed stepped seating (*gradines*) that was built on timber scaffolding around a semicircular orchestra. A raised rectangular stage extended the full width of the hall and was backed by a sloping stage on which was placed scenery that consisted of a number of two-faced panels painted to represent individual houses; these panels stood, like open books, on either side of a diminishing vista that led to a back panel or cloth.

**Permanent Renaissance Theatres.**—One of the earliest permanent theatres, as distinguished from the temporary structures erected for special occasions, is that designed by Andrea Palladio in 1580 for the Olympian Academy at Vicenza as an archaeological reconstruction for the revival of ancient plays (fig. 6). In this theatre Palladio created as perfect a representation of a Roman theatre beneath a roof as the restricted site and his knowledge allowed. The building was completed in 1585 by Vincenzo Scamozzi, when he added the model streets behind the doorways of the *frons scaenae*. These streets were constructed solidly of timber and plaster on a raking stage beneath a domed plaster sky and so arranged that each member of the audience could see into at least one of them. This theatre is still used for a yearly festival of drama. The form of theatre developed for contemporary needs can be seen in the court theatre at Sabbioneta, Italy, designed by Scamozzi in 1588–90. This is a practical realization of Serlio's project, but the scenery was extended forward onto the *proscenae*, or actors' stage, to provide entry doors for the performers, who also used the floor of the hall (orchestra).

As yet the perspective scene had remained a permanent background. The possibilities inherent in a change of scene were soon realized, however, and gradually machinery was introduced that was capable of replacing the units making up a perspective scene with pieces representing a new vista; such scenic effects as the descent of gods and goddesses from the clouds and similar marvels now were possible. These effects would have been ruined if the machinery and mechanics had been visible to the audience, and so a frontispiece, or canvas frame, was added to hide the top and sides of the scene; the frontispiece later became a permanent architectural feature. Such an arrangement can be seen in the remains of the Teatro Farnese, Parma, Italy (1618–19), where the stage for scenery and machinery was contained behind an imposing frame (fig. 7). Although the performers used this area and its mechanical contrivances, they performed mainly in the orchestral area contained within the horseshoe *gradines*, which seated about 3,500 spectators. The perspective scene could be viewed correctly only from one point, and here was placed the personage in whose honour the spectacle was contrived. The entertainments provided in these courtly theatres were a mixture of music, song, spectacle, and drama, and they led eventually to the development of opera in Europe. These courtly functions also had a social significance, the spectacle of the audience being as important as that of the performers, a point that greatly influenced the auditorium form of the European court opera house.

Outside Italy courtly functions were more closely associated with the medieval form of theatre, as shown in an illustration of the Petit Bourbon, Paris, that appeared as the frontispiece to *Ballet comique de la reine* (1581). There the audience was seated around a rectangular dancing space, with the royal personages facing an embryonic stage that contained a small perspective vista. Further scenic elements were arranged, like mansions, at the side of the dancing floor. When members of the Confrérie de la Passion were permitted in 1548 to perform secular plays, they converted a rectangular hall in the Hôtel de Bourgogne, Paris, into a theatre; on the stage at one end all the different scenic items were arranged to form a *décor simultané*.

**Shakespearean Playhouses.**—In Tudor England actors performed in the halls of the great houses on the space before the paneled wall of the screens, using the doors for entrances and the gallery for upper scenes (*see* HALL). Both there and in the court masques the audience and any scenery probably were arranged in a manner similar to that at the Petit Bourbon, but in the later masques at Elizabeth I's court some scenery may well have been built on either the Terentian or Serlian model. Outside the court bands of players toured the guildhalls and the country houses or, like the Italian players of the *commedia dell'arte*, set up their trestle stage with its curtained backing in any available open space. As these players were by now professionals seeking remuneration, they preferred some enclosed area where an audience could be made to pay, and, like their colleagues of Spain and France, they chose the inns as one

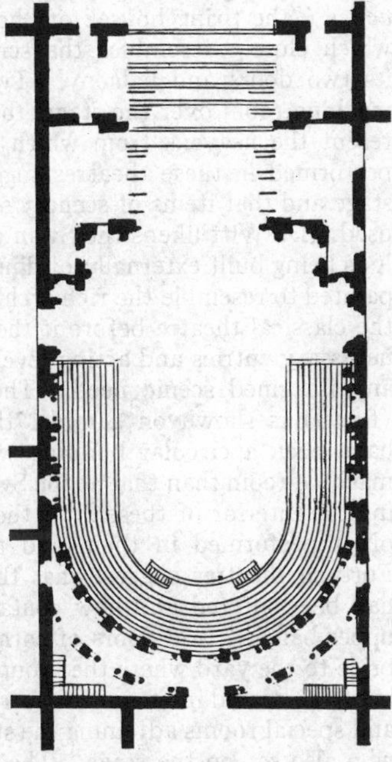

FIG. 7.—PLAN OF THE TEATRO FARNESE, PARMA, 1618–19

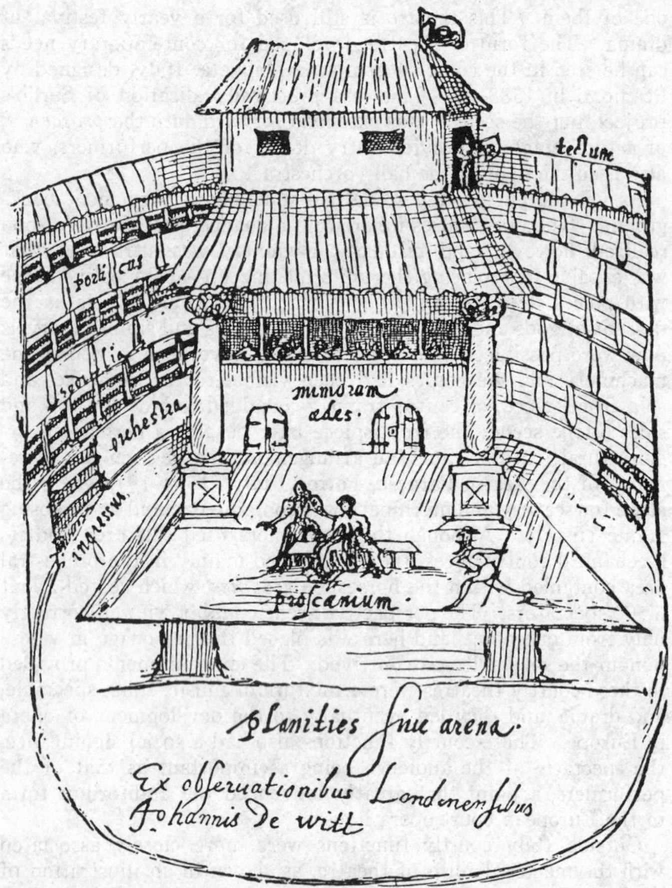


FIG. 8.—JOHAN DE WITT'S DRAWING OF THE SWAN THEATRE, LONDON, ABOUT 1596. ONE OF THE FEW CONTEMPORARY SKETCHES OF THE ELIZABETHAN THEATRE

convenient centre, and bullbaiting and bearbaiting yards were also used.

When James Burbage built the Theatre in 1576, he probably based his ideas on these usual haunts, but visual evidence of the internal appearance of the early Elizabethan theatres is limited to one drawing of the Swan Theatre (fig. 8) that is copied from a sketch made by a Dutch visitor, Johan de Witt. This shows a raised rectangular stage or proscenium backed by the *mimorum aedes* ("the tiring house" or "house of the actors"), the front of which closely resembles the screens of the medieval halls with its two doors and balcony. Two classical columns supported a machine room over the stage, the underside being painted to represent the heavens from which gods would descend. The plays performed in these theatres suggest that there were traps in the stage and that items of scenery such as beds, tents, and trees were used. De Witt likens the Swan to a Roman theatre and describes it as being built externally of flint, with internal columns of timber painted to resemble the rich architecture of the Renaissance. Like the classical theatre before it the architectural stage provided the necessary entries and acting levels that convention could adopt to any imagined scenic need. The second Globe Theatre (1614) (fig. 9) is shown on a mid-17th-century map by W. Hollar to have been a circular building with a larger and more elaborate machine room than that at the Swan. Although no drawings showing the interior of these later theatres have survived, the texts of plays performed in them and the contracts for the Hope and Fortune theatres suggest that the front of the tiring house also had been altered and now contained a curtained inner room, an upper balcony, and doors of entry onto the stage. The admission price to the yard where the groundlings stood was 1*d.;* those wishing to be seated in one of the surrounding galleries could pay extra, and special rooms adjoining the stage were set aside for gentlemen, who also sat on the stage. The theatres were circular, or many-sided, with the exception of the square Fortune (1600), which was 80 ft. overall externally and, with the exception of the roofs over stage and galleries, open to the sky. In addition to these open theatres, there were also a number of covered theatres, but, apart from the fact that most were rectangular and fitted with boxes and a tiring house, little is known of their architecture.

At court the new scenic devices were being added to the masques by Inigo Jones, who had studied the Italian ideas and visited Vicenza. In 1605 Jones collaborated with Ben Jonson on the *Masque of Blackness,* for which he designed a permanent perspective background that was revealed by the fall of a painted curtain. When *Florimène* was produced in 1635, Jones built a stage that occupied nearly half the hall in front of the screens (fig. 10); the front scenes were fixed Serlian wings, but the back shutters were made so that they could be drawn aside to reveal further scenes. By 1640 Jones noted on his drawings for *Salmacida Spolia* that "ye scaene doe altogither change with ye back shutters."

**Restoration Playhouses.**—At the Restoration in 1660 some of the covered theatres that had survived the Puritan purge were reused. In addition, other theatres, such as the playhouse in Lincoln's Inn Fields (1661), were converted from existing tennis courts, which were rectangular roofed buildings similar to that at Hampton Court, but it was not long before new playhouses that were designed to permit the use of the new changeable scenery were built. The Dorset Gardens Theatre (1671), supposedly designed by Christopher Wren, is known, from the engravings in Elkanah Settle's *Empress of Morocco* (1673), to have had a rectangular stage (proscenium) that was flanked by the side walls of the auditorium and was entered through two doors on each side; boxes were built over the doors. Behind this proscenium area a tall opening framed a stage for perspective scenery, while above was a gallery with flanking openings. A contemporary description states that part of the audience was seated in the body of the hall (now called the pit), which was surrounded by two levels of seven boxes with a gallery above, the whole being elaborately decorated and lit by numerous candles.

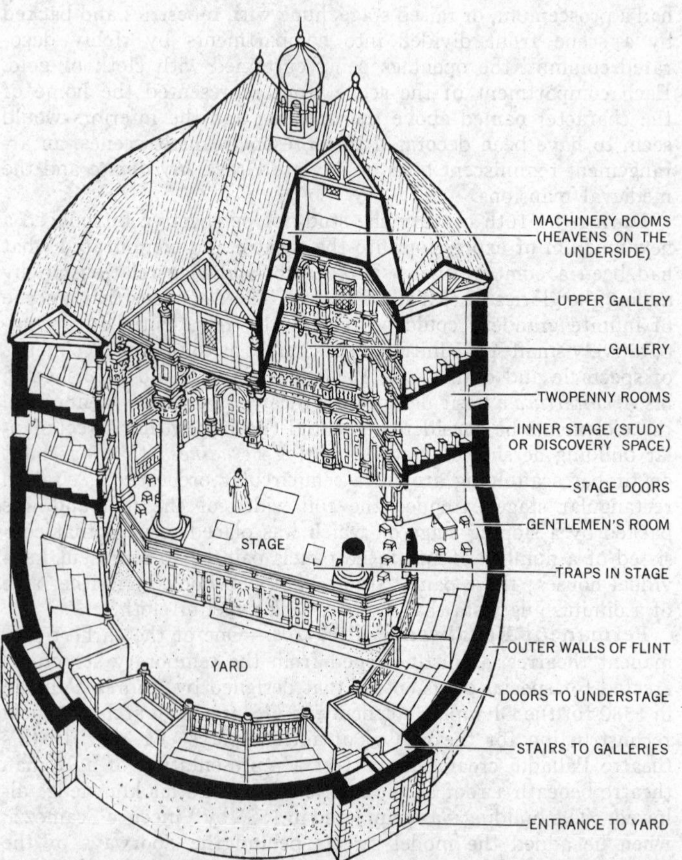


FROM H. AND R. LEACROFT, "THE THEATRE"

FIG. 9.—CONJECTURAL RECONSTRUCTION OF THE SECOND GLOBE THEATRE, LONDON, 1614

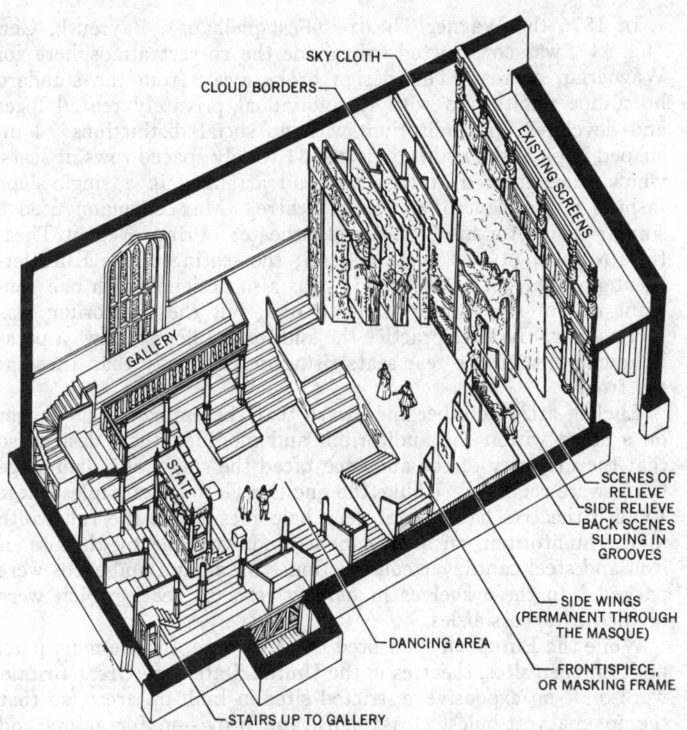


FROM H. AND R. LEACROFT, "THE THEATRE"

FIG. 10.—THE TUDOR HALL, WHITEHALL, ARRANGED BY INIGO JONES FOR THE MASQUE "FLORIMÈNE," 1635. CONJECTURAL RECONSTRUCTION BASED ON ORIGINAL DRAWINGS

Wren has also left a section that has been ascribed to the second Theatre Royal, Drury Lane, London (1674; fig. 11). Almost half of this 61 × 112 ft. building was occupied by a scenic stage and rooms for the actors, the remainder accommodating the auditorium with its stairs and approaches. In front of, and continuing, the sloping scenic stage was the proscenium, or actors' stage, about 20 ft. deep, which took up more than a third of the space in the auditorium and was approached on either side by two doors in each wall.

Before the proscenium was a stepped pit with benches, beyond which three curved amphitheatres faced the stage. The side walls of the fan-shaped auditorium, containing two tiers of boxes, were built in perspective to heighten the effect of the scenic illusion. By 1696 the management, wishing to increase the seating capacity, cut back the stage and replaced the lower doors of entry with boxes, thus commencing a movement that eventually pushed the actors back into the scenic area. Here they were finally surrounded in the early 19th century by a gilded picture frame, out of which they were forbidden to step.

**European Opera Houses.**—In Europe experiment still continued, and by 1693 Andrea Pozzo published a design for a theatre based on the visual requirements of the perspective scene. The auditorium had five semicircular tiers of boxes (loges) surrounding a flat area accommodating musicians and spectators. As a result of the need to accommodate large audiences, auditoriums evolved in which an elongated Farnese-type orchestra was surrounded by loges. Before long the side walls were inclined inward toward the stage so that a horseshoe plan resulted; this design was used in the majority of Italian opera theatres. Variations are found in the Bibiena theatres with their curved side walls, an arrangement that was vaguely reminiscent of the curved *gradines* at Sabbioneta, and in the ovoid plan seen in the Teatro la Fenice, Venice (1792). By the middle of the 18th century the flat orchestra had been replaced by a sloping floor with benches for the audience; the floor was separated from the stage by an enclosure for the large body of musicians necessary for opera and ballet. A typical theatre of this period is La Scala, Milan (1778; fig. 12A).

In France and England the rectangular and fan-shaped auditoriums continued in use throughout the 17th century. The adaptation of the Palais-Royal, Paris, by Vigarani in 1674 (earlier form built by J. Lemercier, 1637) and the design for the Comédie Française, Paris (1689), by F. d'Orbay (fig. 12B) both illustrate the manner in which the French plan compromised between the earlier rectangle and the new Italian ideas.

**Georgian Playhouses.**—During the 18th century the English playhouse became standardized in its units, but auditoriums varied between the fan shape seen at Covent Garden, London (1732; fig. 12C), the curved horseshoe in the Theatre Royal, Bristol (1766), and the plain rectangle of the small theatre at Richmond, Yorkshire (1788). The original scale drawings show that when Robert Adam amended Wren's Drury Lane in 1775 to increase its seating capacity, he retained the fan-shaped pit and the actors' stage within the auditorium but reduced the depth of this stage to about eight feet to accommodate additional pit benches and a musicians' pit. He also replaced Wren's side walls and boxes with a lighter structure, introduced an additional tier of boxes on either side, and increased the depth of the upper amphitheatre. This movement to increase the size of auditoriums was given further impetus when Henry Holland rebuilt the Theatre Royal in 1794 and designed a much larger building with five tiers of boxes and a deep upper gallery facing the stage. Similar increases in size were made when Covent Garden was rebuilt in 1792.

In addition to these large metropolitan theatres, smaller buildings were erected throughout the country; typical of these is the Richmond Theatre (fig. 13). Almost half of this 28 × 64 ft. building is occupied by a sloping stage, below which are a machine room and two dressing rooms. The remainder is taken up by the auditorium, small foyer, box office, and stairs. A 5-ft. portion of the stage is still within the auditorium; this portion is flanked by proscenium doors with boxes above them but is separated from the rectangular stepped pit by a small orchestra well; both pit and well are approached by a passage under the side boxes. The pit is enclosed by boxes; these are divided by low partitions and have side galleries above. A larger gallery faces the stage and extends over boxes and foyer beyond. Similar theatres were found in the majority of English towns and also in many of the major cities of the United States.

Famous among the latter structures are the Southwark Theatre (1766), the first permanent theatre in America, and the Chestnut Street Theatre (1794), both in Philadelphia; and the John Street Theatre (1767) and Burton's Playhouse (1848), both in New York City. By 1863 an engraving of Brougham's Lyceum Theatre, New York (1850), showed that the picture frame had replaced the proscenium stage and doors and that, as in England, the enclosing side boxes had been raised so that the pit could be extended beneath them. By this time the front benches in the pit were being replaced by more expensive orchestral stalls.

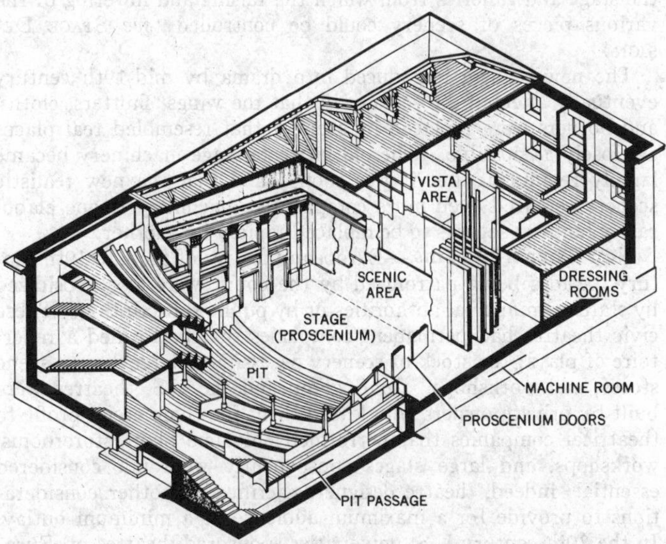


RICHARD LEACROFT

FIG. 11.—CHRISTOPHER WREN'S DESIGN FOR THE SECOND THEATRE ROYAL, DRURY LANE, LONDON, 1674. CONJECTURAL RECONSTRUCTION

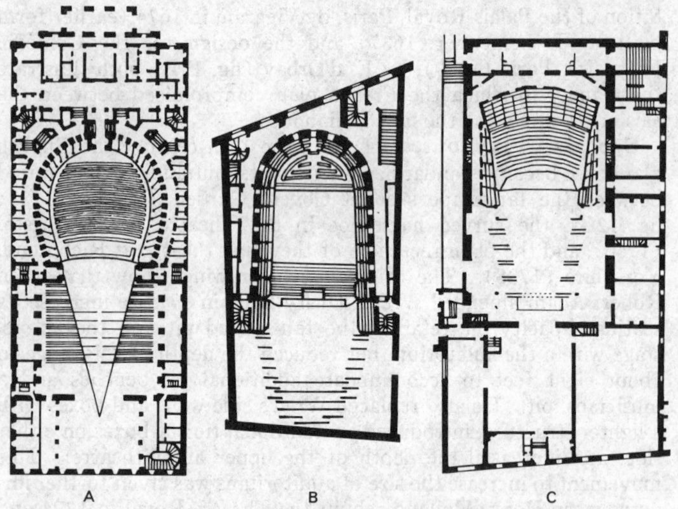


FIG. 12.—17TH- AND 18TH-CENTURY THEATRES: (A) LA SCALA, MILAN, 1778; (B) COMÉDIE FRANÇAISE, PARIS, 1689; (C) COVENT GARDEN, LONDON, 1732

**Spectacles and Machines.**—At the Salle des Machines, Paris (1660), and throughout Europe, the uses of perspective scenery and machinery created ever more glorious spectacles, best illustrated in the 18th-century creations of F. Juvarra, G. B. Piranesi, and the Bibiena family. As a result, stages became larger, and the machinery, which became an integral part of the structures, became more intricate. A typical court theatre, complete with all its scenic marvels, can be seen at Drottningholm, Swed. (1764–66). The flat wings and shutters making up the scene could be easily changed because they were mounted on frames attached to carriages that ran on rails beneath the stage. In England these rails were replaced by a system of upper and lower scene grooves in which the scenery slid. The stage itself opened in many parts; this feature permitted the passage of scenes or of bridges carrying actors; cloths rolled up and borders were raised out of sight above the stage.

By the time J. L. C. Garnier designed the National Opera House, Paris (1875), the stage volume had swollen to enormous proportions that were conditioned not by the needs of the actor but by those of scene change. This building, designed on a monumental scale with its auditorium sunk within a shell of foyers, saloons, and stairs, was destined to set a style for many state theatres. Although English stages never reached these proportions, they nevertheless became standardized with a mezzanine and well into which the stage bridges and traps could sink, and with flying space above the stage and galleries from which the raising and lowering of the various pieces of scenery could be controlled (*see* STAGE DESIGN).

The new realism introduced into drama by mid-19th century eventually affected the scenery in that the wings, shutters, cloths, and borders were replaced by scenery that resembled real places as closely as possible. The old intricate stage machinery became largely redundant, but it was soon found that the new realistic scenery required even more complicated machinery if one elaborately built-up set was to be replaced rapidly by another.

**New Theatre Forms.**—European theatres of the late 19th century, besides being patronized by the court, were also subsidized by state or municipal authorities or by public subscription. These civic theatres had permanent companies that performed a repertoire of plays; the stock of scenery necessitated large stages, scene stores, and workshops. In England and the U.S. theatres were built by private owners who leased them for commercial profit to theatrical companies that performed only one play; storerooms, workshops, and large stages consequently were not considered essential; indeed, theatre designers sacrificed all other considerations to provide for a maximum audience at a minimum outlay. In the 20th century U.S. universities sponsored theatres on European lines, and civic repertory theatres appeared in Britain but on a small scale.

In 1876 the Wagner Theatre (Festspielhaus), Bayreuth, Ger. (fig. 14), was constructed to provide the correct atmosphere for Wagnerian operas. This design broke away from the standard horseshoe auditorium with its individual privately rented loges and developed an auditorium with no social distinctions. Fan-shaped in plan, the auditorium had 31 widely spaced rows of seats, which were entered at the ends and arranged in a single-slope fashion reminiscent of a Greek theatre. Max Littmann used a similar design for his Prinzregententheater (Prince Regent Theatre), Munich (1901), seating 1,106; the seating of his Künstlertheater, Munich (1908; fig. 15), was also designed with one constant rise of steps from front to rear, but the auditorium was rectangular. In later practice the auditorium floor follows a parabolic curve, with the rear seats rising more steeply than those at the front.

English architects became aware that the actor was no longer on a stage within the auditorium and modified their designs so that the majority of the audience faced the stage, although stage boxes were retained. Unlike the one-tier German examples, these English theatres had several deep balconies across the full width of the auditorium, an arrangement made possible by the use of iron and steel cantilever construction. Maximum audiences were packed into these shelves in narrow rows of seats, which were divided by access aisles.

While the European sponsored theatres were, for the most part, built on open sites, theatres in the United States and Great Britain were built on expensive restricted sites in built-up areas, so that the foyers, vestibules, cloakrooms, and provision for actors and stage staffs were more restricted and not so well equipped as their European counterparts. A typical British example of 1897 was Her Majesty's Theatre, London, which seated 1,319. In the United States Booth's Theatre, New York (1869), was similar to Her Majesty's, and a later version of this auditorium form is the Ziegfeld Theatre, New York (1927), a large theatre designed for spectacular musicals. The Little Theatre, New York (1912; fig. 16A), which seated 299, approximated in its planning the Littmann theatres but on a smaller scale. The outline plan and section that became standard for picture-frame theatres are well illustrated by the Guild Theatre, New York (1925; fig. 17), while later practice can be seen in the Oberlin (O.) College Theatre (1952; fig. 18), with its internal form designed to provide correct acoustical and lighting conditions.

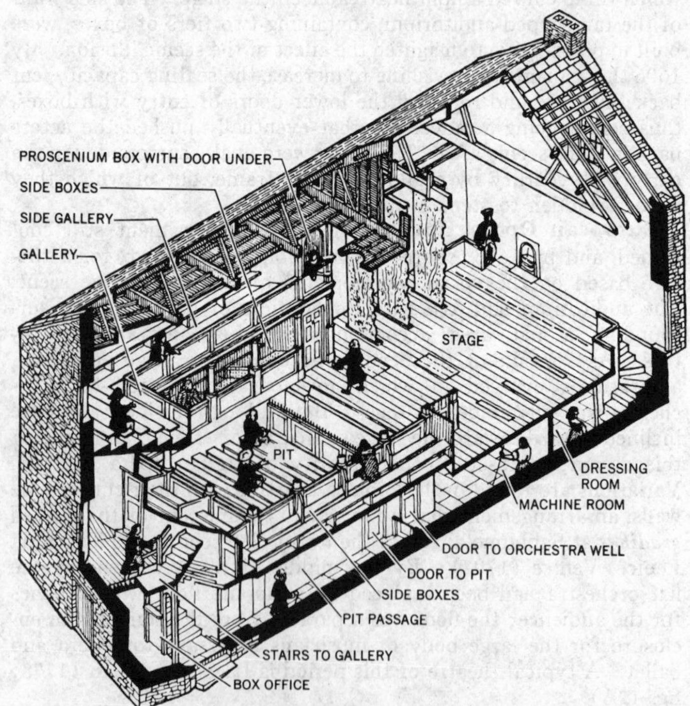


FROM H. AND R. LEACROFT, "THE THEATRE"

FIG. 13.—THE GEORGIAN THEATRE AT RICHMOND, YORKSHIRE, 1788

The introduction of gas for lighting in the early 19th century had permitted the darkening of the auditorium during a performance; the addition of electric light in the early 20th century allowed more realistic stage effects to be achieved. The ideas of Adolphe Appia, Adolph Linnebach, and Mariano Fortuny led to the introduction of the cyclorama, or sky dome, which, when evenly lit, simulated the sky and provided an enclosure within which three-dimensional scenery could be set; this style of presentation developed into the space stage, or performance in an apparently infinite setting.

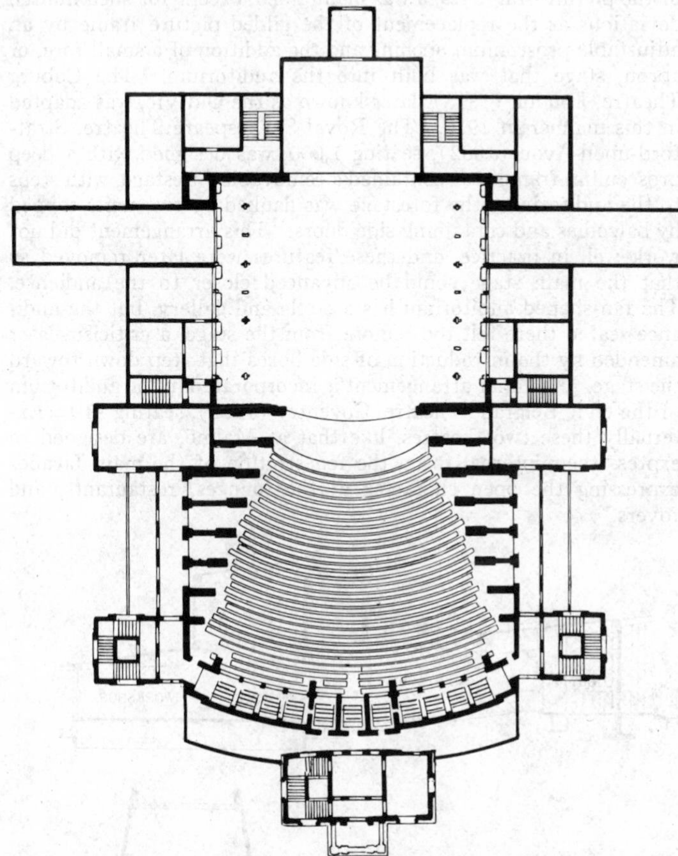

FIG. 14.—PLAN OF THE FESTSPIELHAUS AT BAYREUTH; GOTTFRIED SEMPER, ARCHITECT

At the Schauspielhaus, Dresden (1913; fig. 19), the complete enclosing of the stage prevented the horizontal moving of scenery at stage level, so hydraulic lowering and lifting devices were installed to lower stage sections to the basement level, where they could be replaced by other sections that had been preset with scenery in the side assembly areas. One of the earliest uses of such hydraulic lifts was in the National Opera House, Budapest (1884).

At the Volksbühne, Berlin (1914; fig. 16B), the structural cyclorama, enclosing a revolving stage, was cut back to permit horizontal movement of scenery at stage level. All these cycloramas were cut back at the top to permit vertical movement of scenery into the stage tower.

**A Return to First Principles.**—As early as the mid-19th century some theatre workers felt drama to be more important than spectacle and numerous attempts were made to design theatres that permitted a return to the simple actor-audience relationship by constructing what were thought to be Elizabethan stages. In 1840 Karl Immermann designed such a stage in Düsseldorf, although this was more like a Roman stage with an enlarged central doorway forming an inner stage.

In the early 20th century William Poel in England and Max Kruger in Germany produced Shakespearean plays in reconstructions of Elizabethan theatres based on the De Witt drawing of the Swan (discovered in 1888). Further notable reconstructions of Elizabethan theatres were the Maddermarket Theatre, Norwich (1921), the first Mermaid Theatre, London (1951), and the Festival Theatre, Ashland, Ore. (1959).

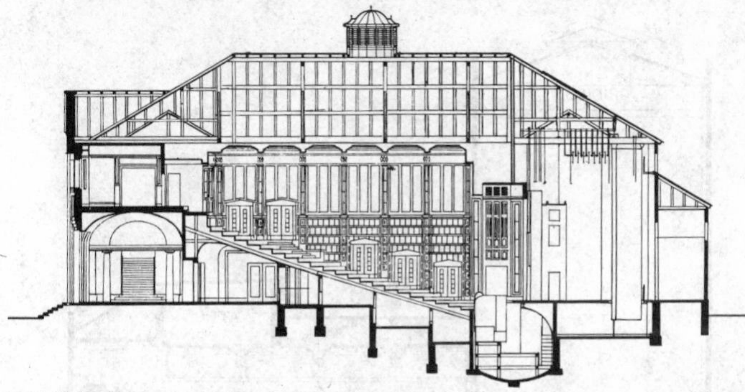

FROM LITTMANN, "DAS MÜNCHENER KÜNSTLER THEATER"

FIG. 15.—SECTION OF KÜNSTLERTHEATER AT MUNICH; MAX LITTMANN, ARCHITECT

The idea of a permanent architectural stage for modern productions was given expression by Louis Jouvet and Jacques Copeau in 1920 at their Théâtre du Vieux Colombier, Paris. This had a permanent inner stage and balcony with stairs connecting to the main stage; there was no picture frame to separate the audience from the stage. Before long, however, attempts were made to disguise the permanent setting and suggest some verisimilitude in the scenes; but these attempts only served to emphasize the limiting nature of the permanent structure if used for any other than conventional purposes. A similar, although simpler, arrangement is to be seen in the Mermaid Theatre, Puddle Dock, London (1959).

*Open Stages.*—The idea that the actor could again step out of the picture frame was slowly gaining ground. Max Reinhardt staged productions in circus buildings and exhibition halls, and his Grosses Schauspielhaus, Berlin (1919), combined a normal stage with a revolve (revolving stage) and cyclorama; the stage connected through a nonexistent proscenium opening and an adaptable (adjustable) forestage with an arena stage that was surrounded by a horseshoe of seating. Here Reinhardt combined spectacular settings on the main stage with crowds in the arena, a type of production suited to the size of the theatre, but the individual actor was lost in the spacious arena.

In the civic theatre at Malmö, Swed. (1944), the auditorium, like many late 19th-century opera houses used also for drama, was designed so that its size and shape could be altered by moving screens. The projecting stage could be replaced by seating, and the width and height of the proscenium opening could be varied. The stage was equipped with a tower for flying scenery, a revolve,

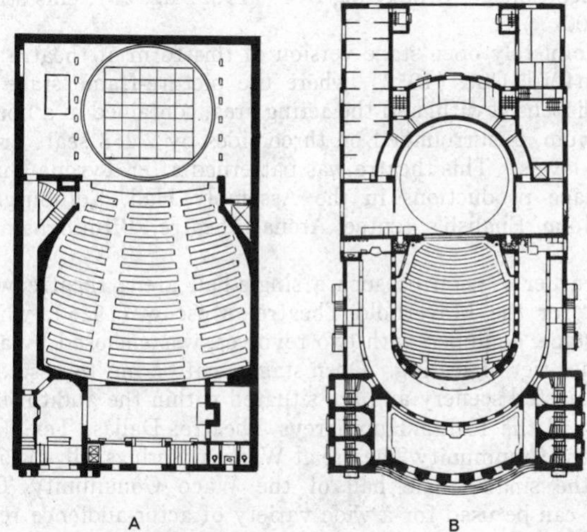


FIG. 16.—FLOOR PLANS OF EARLY 20TH-CENTURY THEATRE BUILDINGS: (A) THE LITTLE THEATRE, NEW YORK CITY; HARRY C. INGALLS AND F. B. HOFFMAN, JR., ARCHITECTS. (B) VOLKSBÜHNE (PEOPLE'S THEATRE), BERLIN; OSKAR KAUFMANN, ARCHITECT

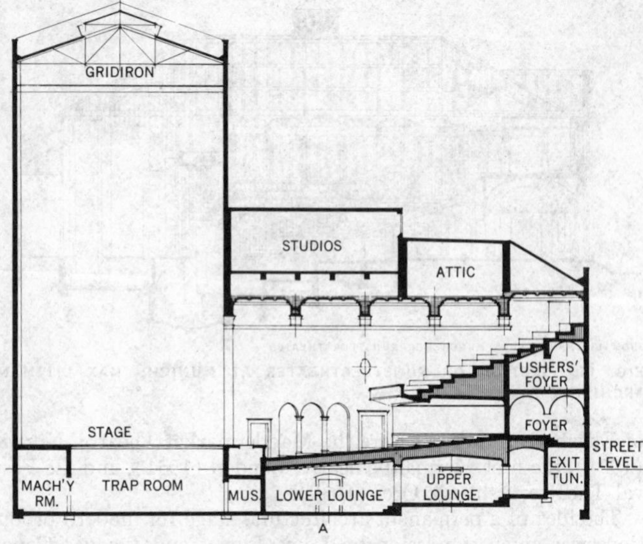


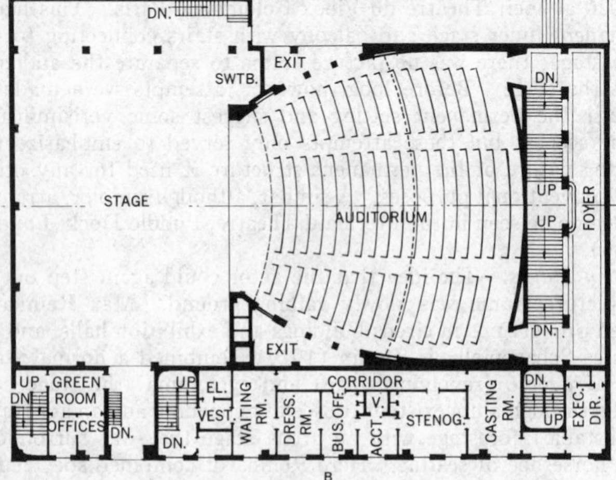


FIG. 17.—GUILD THEATRE, NEW YORK CITY; C. HOWARD CRANE, FRANZHEIM AND BETTIS, ARCHITECTS. (A) LONGITUDINAL SECTION; (B) ORCHESTRA FLOOR PLAN

and movable trucks; there also were workshops where scenery could be constructed and assembled. The planning difficulties inherent in the dual focus of the Grosses Schauspielhaus and the lack of intimacy between the individual actor and his audience were overcome in a later example designed by Marcel Breuer for Sarah Lawrence College, Bronxville, N.Y. (1952; fig. 20); this structure seats 500.

A completely open-stage version of this form of theatre is that at Stratford, Ont. (1957), where the picture-frame stage is entirely dispensed with, and the acting area, contained in a horseshoe auditorium, is surrounded on three sides by 2,258 seats arranged on two levels. This theatre was patterned after Tyrone Guthrie's open-stage productions in the Assembly Hall, Edinburgh, and after John English's tented Arena Theatre, Birmingham, Eng. (1948).

An earlier version of such a single-hall arena theatre was the project for the Meyerhold Theatre, Moscow (1925), where an arena stage, equipped with two revolves, was enclosed by a single horseshoe tier of seating. Open stages that permit the use of built and projected scenery and are situated within the auditorium can be seen in the Kalita Humphreys Theatre, Dallas, Tex. (1959), and in the Community Theatre at Western Springs, Ill. (1960–61), while the small single hall of the Waco Community Theatre (1958) can be used for a wide variety of actor-audience relationships.

*Picture Frames and Forestages.*—In London and New York City and other metropolitan centres stringent fire regulations, which resulted from numerous disastrous fires caused by naked flames of the oil lamp and gas eras, require that it must be possible to cut off the stage from the auditorium in case of fire; all openings in the wall that separate the two parts of the standard picture-frame theatre, normally called the proscenium wall, must be capable of being closed by a fire-resisting curtain or doors. These limitations controlled attempts to bring the actor out of the picture frame—except in the very smallest theatres—and in the majority of theatres built during the 20th century the status quo of the picture-frame stage was maintained, except for such limited deviations as the replacement of the gilded picture frame by an adjustable proscenium opening and the addition of a small fore, or apron, stage that was built into the auditorium. The Coburg Theatre, London (1818), later known as the Old Vic, was adapted in this manner in 1950. The Royal Shakespeare Theatre, Stratford-upon-Avon (1932), seating 1,000, was designed with a deep proscenium frame that contained a removable forestage, with steps to the auditorium; the forestage was flanked by two units topped by balconies and containing side doors. This arrangement did not work well in practice, and these features were later removed so that the main stage could be advanced closer to the audience. The fan-shaped auditorium has a circle and gallery, but the audience seated there felt too remote from the stage, a criticism later amended by the introduction of side boxes that step down toward the stage. A similar arrangement is incorporated in the auditorium of the civic Belgrade Theatre, Coventry (1958), seating 910. Externally these two theatres, like that at Malmö, are designed to express their internal form, the fenestration of the main facades expressing the open character of the lounges, restaurants, and foyers.

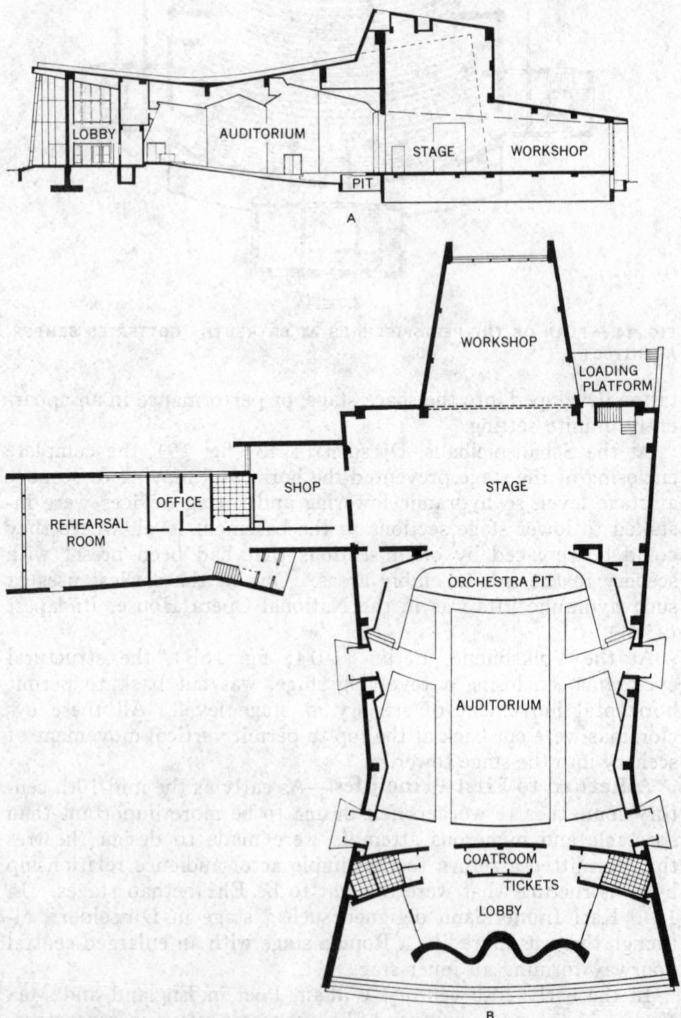


BY COURTESY OF "ARCHITECTURAL FORUM"

FIG. 18.—OBERLIN (OHIO) COLLEGE THEATRE; HARRISON, ABRAMOWITZ AND E. SNYDER, ARCHITECTS. (A) CROSS SECTION; (B) FLOOR PLAN

*Arena and Flexible Stages.*—In the Realistic Theatre, Moscow, the actor-audience relationship was altered to suit each individual production during 1932–38. N. Okhlopkov's production of *Mother* used a raised platform around the walls of the hall, with steps leading from each side to a central circular platform; the audience was seated in the intervening spaces. This form of arena theatre, or theatre in the round, had been tried in the U.S. at Columbia University in 1914 and was later developed as an economic theatre form.

Other examples of arena theatres include the Penthouse Theatre, University of Washington, Seattle (1940); the Playhouse Theatre, Houston, Tex. (1950), seating 306; the Téâtre en Rond, Paris (1954); and the Teatro Sant'Erasmo, Milan (1953), seating 250. In most of these theatres the acting areas at floor level are circular, oval, trapezoid, or rectangular, with the audience seated on all sides; in the Teatro Sant'Erasmo, however, the audience is in two blocks located on opposite sides of an octagonal acting area, with scenic access on the remaining sides.

A more flexible form of theatre is the one located at the University of Miami, Fla. (1950), seating 400–900, where the actors and audience may be arranged in any one of three open-stage variations: in the round, with a three-sided platform, or with an end stage.

These forms of theatre present a new problem to the architect in the placing of lighting equipment and the use of acoustic forms that permit an actor to be heard behind him as well as in front. This problem, together with the demand for a more intimate actor-audience relationship, may perhaps necessitate a restriction on the size of auditoriums. Spectacle theatres may be large, but theatres designed for actors should be intimate; the actor should not be forced to adopt exaggerated gestures and vocal gymnastics in order to make himself understood in the far recesses of some huge structure.

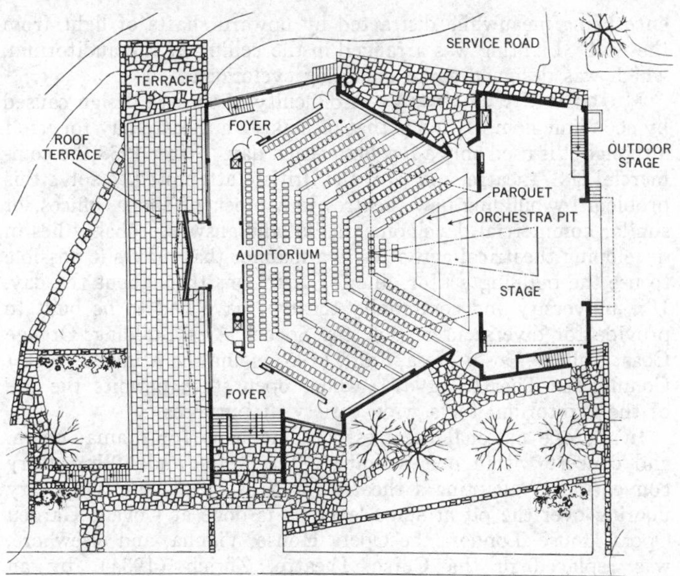

BY COURTESY OF "ARCHITECTURAL FORUM"

FIG. 20.—SARAH LAWRENCE COLLEGE THEATRE; MARCEL BREUER, ARCHITECT. UPPER FLOOR PLAN

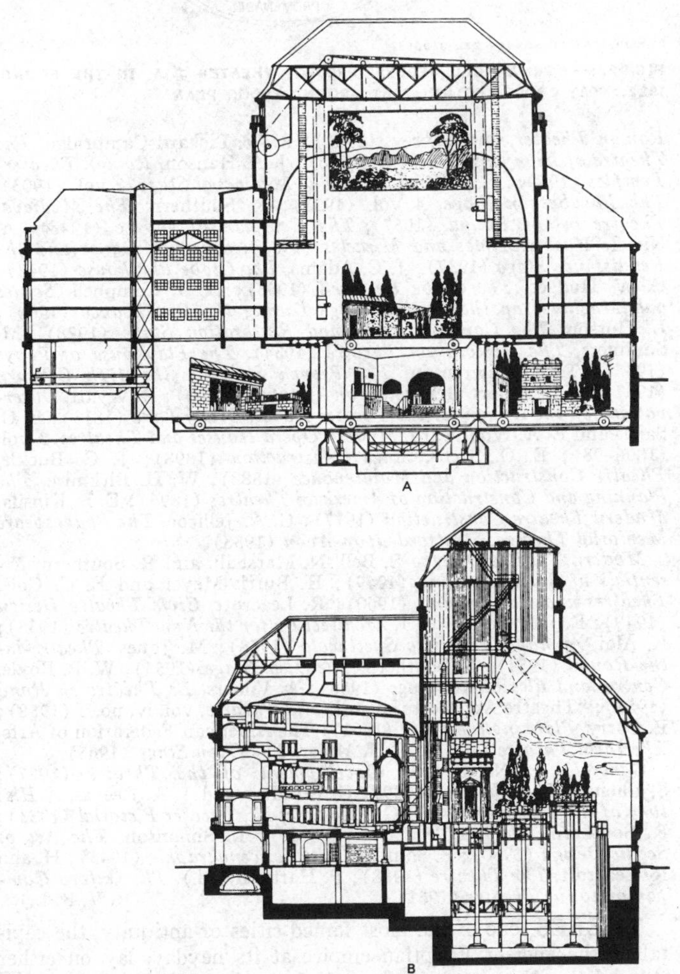

FROM FUERST AND HUME, "TWENTIETH CENTURY STAGE DECORATION"

FIG. 19.—THE SCHAUSPIELHAUS, DRESDEN; LOSSOW AND KÜHNE, ARCHITECTS. CROSS SECTION OF STAGE, (A) SIDE TO SIDE; (B) BACK TO FRONT

The National Theatre, Mannheim (1957), is an example of the trend in theatre design—seen at Malmö—where two theatres are provided; the larger theatre at Mannheim is designed as an opera house seating 1,200 in one large pit, a small balcony and side boxes. Like so many of the new and rebuilt municipal theatres of Europe—Cologne (1957), Vienna Opera House (1955), and Vienna Burgtheater (1955)—the Mannheim theatre follows the normal picture-stage arrangement, with an auditorium designed for acoustics and lighting and a stage lavishly equipped with the most modern mechanical and lighting devices. The smaller theatre at Mannheim is arranged so that it may be used as a picture-frame theatre with or without a forestage, seating 606; as a lecture or concert hall, seating 870; or as an arena theatre similar to the Sant'Erasmo, Milan, seating 680. Various attempts were made to design flexible theatres capable of providing all these differing forms and for increasing audience participation in the scenic production. Such a theatre is exemplified in the project for a "total" theatre designed by Walter Gropius in 1927 (fig. 21). Here the auditorium, consisting of a single bank of seating facing a fully equipped stage backed by a cyclorama, is completely surrounded by a narrow stage backed by screens onto which motion pictures could be projected as scenery. By revolving a portion of the seating, a form of theatre in the round resulted. The idea of enclosing the audience by stages has formed the basis of many projects, notably Oskar Strnad's "Ringbühne" (1923). An example may be seen in Studio One, Baylor University, Tex. (1941), where three stages enclose a rectangular audience area that may also be used as the stage of an arena theatre. A project that attempts to combine all the different theatrical forms in one building on a more intimate scale is the Questors Theatre, Ealing, London (1964), seating approximately 350.

In the Loeb Drama Centre at Harvard University (1959–60) the seating may be rearranged by the use of electrical devices, so that the theatre may be used with a picture stage, a three-sided open stage, or as a theatre in the round. This building also contains an experimental studio in which any actor-audience relationship may be established.

It was perhaps inevitable that attempts would be made to combine the new actor-audience relationship with the spectacular use of light and scenery, and as early as 1922 Norman Bel Geddes designed the project Theater #14 (fig. 22). The acting area was separated from the audience by a pit from which the actors ascended to the stage. The stage itself sank into a basement, where preset scenery could be moved onto it, the attention of the audience being meanwhile distracted by upward shafts of light from the well. Lighting was arranged in the ceiling of the auditorium, which was designed as an enclosing cyclorama.

**Multiple-Use Theatres.**—A difficulty of theatre design caused by economic competition is that of making a theatre pay for itself although it is used only a few hours each day. After 1938 the commercial U.S. theatre, and later the British, attempted to solve this problem by building new theatres in a block of shops, offices, or similar commercial developments, but the answer probably lies in developing theatrical activities in a manner that makes it possible to use the building(s) for differing functions throughout the day. U.S. university and community theatres have had to be built to provide for diverse uses; *e.g.,* the Speech Arts Building, Orange Coast College, Costa Mesa, Calif. (1955); and the Midland (Tex.) Community Theatre (1957), whose open stage permits the use of the auditorium for a wide variety of purposes.

In Europe national theatres combine halls for drama, opera, and concert within one building. The 18th- and 19th-century convention of adapting a theatre for balls by placing temporary flooring over the pit at stage level, as is done at Covent Garden Opera House, London, the Opera House, Vienna, and elsewhere, was replaced in the Corso Theatre, Zürich (1934), by an adaptable auditorium floor. In the Lincoln Center for the Performing Arts, New York, provision is made for drama, opera, music, and dance in separate buildings grouped to form one cultural centre.

*See* also STAGE DESIGN; STAGE LIGHTING; ARCHITECTURE: *Use: Recreational Architecture;* and references under "Theatres (Structures)" in the Index.

BIBLIOGRAPHY.—*History:* R. C. Flickinger, *The Greek Theater and Its Drama,* 4th ed. (1936); M. Bieber, *The History of the Greek and Roman Theater,* 2nd ed. rev. (1961); A. W. Pickard-Cambridge, *The Theatre of Dionysus in Athens* (1946); J. A. Hanson, *Roman Theater-Temples* (1959); E. K. Chambers, *The Mediaeval Stage,* 2 vol. (1903), *The Elizabethan Stage,* 4 vol. (1923); R. Southern, *The Medieval Theatre in the Round* (1957), *The Georgian Playhouse* (1948); A. Nicoll, *Masks, Mimes and Miracles* (1931), *Stuart Masques and the Renaissance Stage* (1937); J. C. Adams, *The Globe Playhouse* (1942); C. W. Hodges, *The Globe Restored* (1953); L. B. Campbell, *Scenes and Machines on the English Stage During the Renaissance* (1960); L. Hotson, *The Commonwealth and Restoration Stage* (1928); M. Summers, *The Restoration Theatre* (1934), *The Playhouse of Pepys* (1935); T. E. Lawrenson, *The French Stage in the 17th Century* (1957); G. Saunders, *A Treatise on Theatres* (1790); B. Wyatt, *Observations on the Design for the Theatre Royal, Drury Lane* (1813); E. O. Sachs and E. A. Woodward, *Modern Opera Houses and Theatres,* 3 vol. (1896–98); E. O. Sachs, *Stage Construction* (1898); J. G. Buckle, *Theatre Construction and Maintenance* (1888); W. H. Birkmire, *The Planning and Construction of American Theatres* (1896); E. B. Kinsila, *Modern Theatre Construction* (1917); G. A. Jellicoe, *The Shakespeare Memorial Theatre, Stratford-upon-Avon* (1933).

*Modern Theatre Design:* S. Bell, N. Marshall, and R. Southern, *Essentials of Stage-Planning* (1949); H. Burris-Meyer and E. C. Cole, *Theatres and Auditoriums* (1960); R. Leacroft, *Civic Theatre Design* (1949); E. J. R. Isaacs (ed.), *Architecture for the New Theatre* (1935); R. Aloi, *Architetture per lo Spettacolo* (1958); M. Jones, *Theatre-in-the-Round* (1951); R. Southern, *The Open Stage* (1953); W. P. Boyle, *Central and Flexible Stagings* (1956); A. Villiers, *Le Théâtre en Rond* (1958); "Theatre Architecture" in *World Theatre,* vol. iv, no. 3 (1958); P. Corry, *Planning the Stage* (1961); The American Federation of Arts, *The Ideal Theatre* (1964); J. H. Miller, *The Open Stage* (1965).

*General:* A. Nicoll, *The Development of the Theatre* (1927); S. Cheney, *The Theatre* (1929); G. Freedley and J. A. Reeves, *A History of the Theatre* (1940); G. Altman *et al., Theater Pictorial* (1953); R. Southern, *Changeable Scenery* (1952); L. Simonson, *The Art of Scenic Design* (1950); P. Sonrel, *Traité de scénographie* (1943); H. and R. Leacroft, *The Theatre* (1958); P. Hartnoll (ed.), *The Oxford Companion to the Theatre* (1951). (R. V. B. L.)

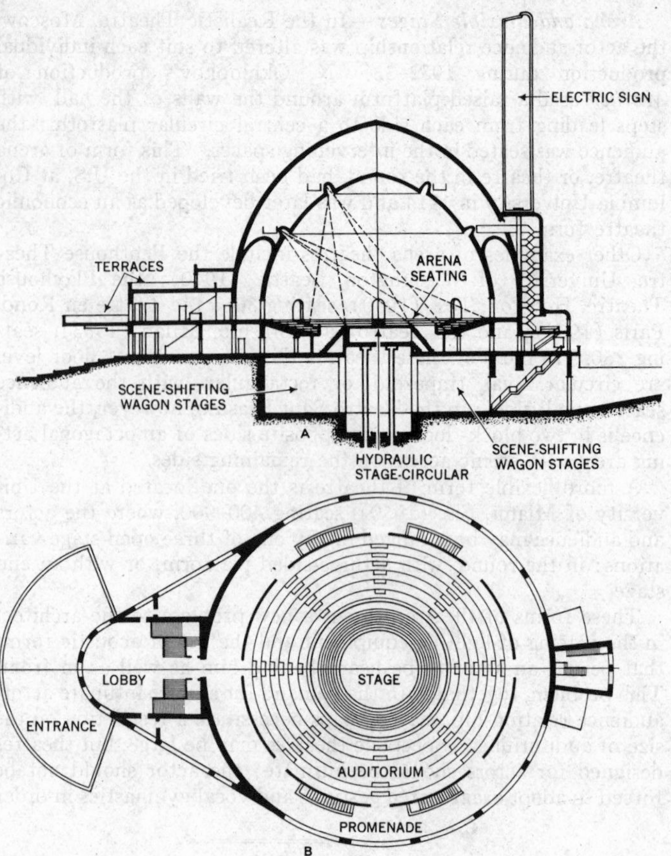


BY COURTESY OF NORMAN BEL GEDDES

FIG. 22.—NORMAN BEL GEDDES' PROJECT THEATER #14, IN THE ROUND, 1922. (A) CROSS SECTION; (B) GROUND FLOOR PLAN

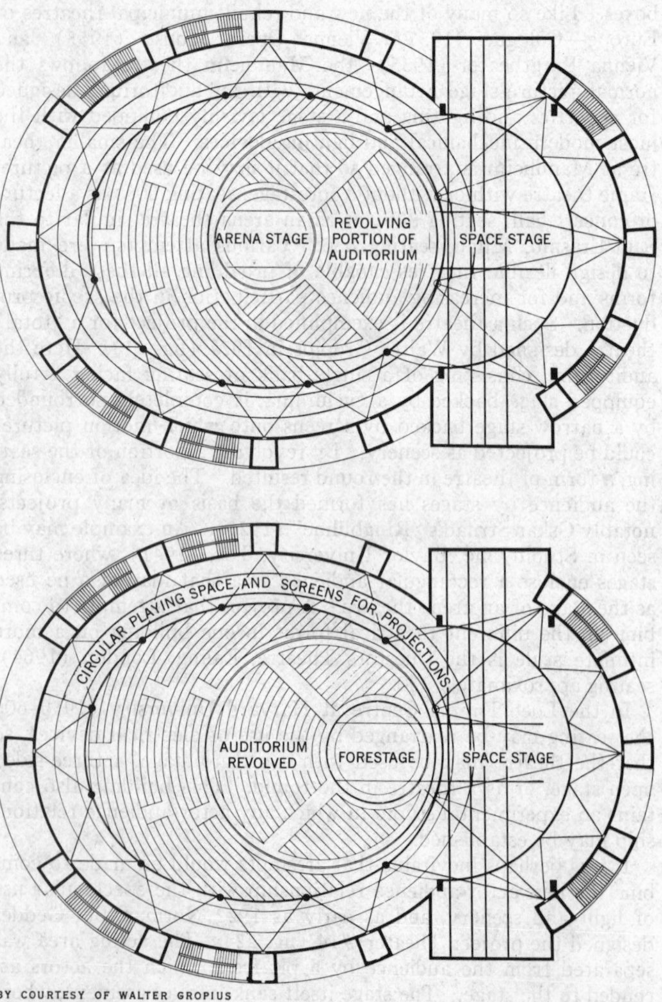


BY COURTESY OF WALTER GROPIUS

FIG. 21.—WALTER GROPIUS' PLAN FOR A "TOTAL" THEATRE, 1927

**THEBES,** one of the most famed cities of antiquity, the capital of the ancient Egyptian empire at its heyday, lay on either side of the Nile at approximately latitude 26° N.; the modern town of Luxor, which occupies part of the site, is 419 mi. S. of Cairo. Ancient Thebes was about six miles square; modern Luxor and Karnak on the east bank contained the city of the living and the great temples of the imperial cult, while on the west bank were the royal necropolis, the kings' mortuary temples and the houses of those priests, soldiers, craftsmen and labourers who were devoted to their service.

The ancient name of Thebes, Wase or Wo'se, was derived from the sacred *was*-sceptre. The nome or province of Wase, the fourth of upper Egypt, is known to have existed from the 4th dynasty onward; the capital was at first Hermonthis, Thebes itself being still a small village. The first monuments that have survived there date from the 11th dynasty, when the local nomarchs fought the Herakleiopolitans and eventually reunited Egypt under their rule. From this time Thebes, the new capital, became Nowe or Nuwe "the City (of Amon)," in Hebrew No-Amon. The Greeks named the city after their own Thebes (Thebai), from the name of Luxor, Ta-ope, or, on occasion, Diospolis Magna.

During the 12th dynasty the residence was moved to Al Fayyum, but the kings of Egypt honoured Amon, their family god, and built temples in the area. The Hyksos had little or no control over the nomarchs of Thebes, the last of whom assumed royal titles; kings of Thebes in the 17th dynasty won successive victories against the invaders and their Nubian allies, and finally freed and reunited the country. Then began the era of greatest prosperity for Thebes. The 18th-dynasty Pharaohs made it their capital, built a new city and enlarged and partly rebuilt the great temples of the triad of Thebes: Amon, his consort Mut, and their son Khonsu, the moon-god. They embellished their temples with the spoils of Asia and the tribute of Nubia. During the 15th century B.C. great palaces rose on either bank of the river, brightly painted and surrounded with gardens; noblemen had their estates round about, and in the crowded streets foreign traders and mercenaries mingled with the citizens. The Pharaohs of the New Kingdom vied with each other in building great temples on the east bank and even larger mortuary temples on the west. The height of Theban prosperity was reached about 1400 B.C. in the reign of Amenhotep III, much of whose vast wealth from foreign tribute was poured into the temples of Amon. For a brief period in the reign of his son Ikhnaton (*q.v.*) Thebes fell on evil times; the city was abandoned by the court and the worship of Amon proscribed, but with the restoration by Tutankhamen Thebes soon regained its revenues and its prestige and retained both through the reign of Seti I and Ramses II who still resided for part of every year in Thebes. The city continued to be richly endowed, and a remarkable document known as the great Harris papyrus states that Ramses III donated 86,486 slaves and vast estates to Amon's temples.

Under the later Ramessids Thebes began to decline; the government fell, it seems, into grave economic difficulties and in the reign of Ramses IX, about 1120 B.C., a series of investigations into the plundering of royal tombs in the necropolis of western Thebes uncovered proof of corruption in high places, following an accusation made by the mayor of the east bank against his colleague on the west. The plundered royal mummies were moved from place to place and at last deposited in the tomb of Amenhotep II and in the burial place of the priest-kings at Dayr al Bahri; the finding of these two hiding places was one of the great events of archaeological discovery. Maladministration led to unrest and there were strikes among the necropolis workers. Control of local affairs tended to come more and more into the hands of the high priests of Amon and led to a situation in which, after the death of the last Ramses, the government of Egypt was shared between the Pharaoh in Tanis and the high pontiff at Thebes. Intermarriage and adoption strengthened the ties between them, daughters of the Tanite kings being installed as "God's Wife of Amon" at Thebes, where they wielded great power.

The Napatan (Ethiopian) Pharaohs made Thebes their capital. Its fame among the early Greeks was such that Homer speaks of the wealth of "hundred-gated Thebes." In 661 B.C., however, it was sacked by Ashurbanipal's Assyrians, and although rebuilt by the Saites it never recovered. In the later Persian wars it again suffered. It may have been at the very end of the dynastic period that hundreds of statues from the temple were collected together and buried in a pit, where G. Legrain found them in 1903. In Strabo's time (*c.* 63 B.C.–*c.* A.D. 21) the city had dwindled to a mere village visited by tourists who came to see the ruins.

## LUXOR AND KARNAK

**The Temples of Karnak.**—Karnak, on the east bank of the Nile, is a village which has given its name to the most northerly part of Thebes, the quarter in which the great temples of Amon, Mut and Khonsu were situated. Its ancient name was Ipet-isut, or Eptesowe, "Chosen of Places." The ruins of Karnak cover a considerable area and are still impressive, though nothing remains of the houses, palaces and gardens that must have surrounded the temple precinct in ancient times. The temples are enclosed within three enceinte walls. The most northerly is that of the temple of Month, the war-god, of which little now remains but the foundations. The southern temple is that of the goddess Mut, wife of Amon; this also is much ruined. It was built largely by Amenhotep III, whose architect was commemorated by statues in the temple, and has a horseshoe-shaped sacred lake.

Between these two precincts lay the largest of all Egyptian temples, and one of the largest in the world, the great metropolitan temple of the state god, Amon-Re. It is in fact not one temple but a complex of temples, at many periods added to and altered, and lacking in consequence a coherent plan. It has been called a great historical document in stone. In it are reflected the fluctuating fortunes of the Egyptian empire. There are no fewer than ten pylons, separated by courts and halls, and nowadays numbered for convenience from west to east, no. 1 being the latest; the seventh and eighth, erected by Thutmose III and

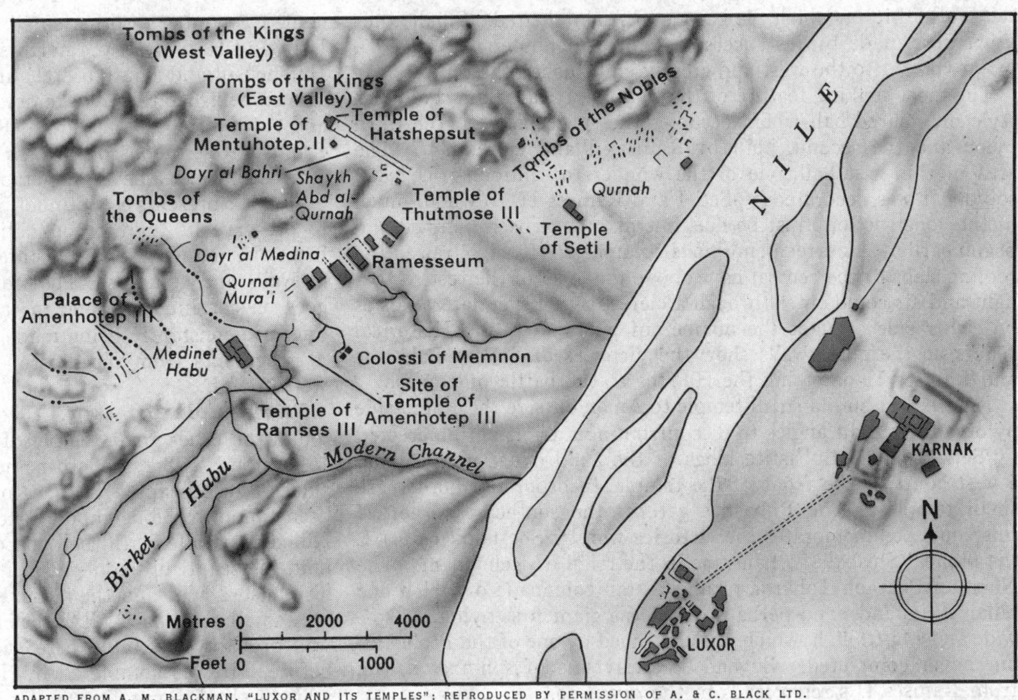


ADAPTED FROM A. M. BLACKMAN, "LUXOR AND ITS TEMPLES"; REPRODUCED BY PERMISSION OF A. & C. BLACK LTD.

FIG. 1.—THEBES, EAST AND WEST BANKS

Queen Hatshepsut, and the ninth and tenth, of Horemheb's reign, formed a series of processional gateways at right angles to the main axis, linking the temple with that of Mut to the south, and further by way of the avenue of sphinxes, with the temple of Luxor two miles away.

The history of the temple must be briefly sketched. The original Middle Kingdom temple has left no trace save a small jubilee shrine of Sesostris (Senusret) I, now reconstructed from fragments found inside the third pylon. At the beginning of the 18th dynasty Thutmose I enclosed the 12th-dynasty temple and fronted it with two pylons, the fifth and fourth, with a hypostyle hall of gilded cedarwood between. Hatshepsut pierced the roof with two tall obelisks, one of which still stands. In the reign of Thutmose III the temple was greatly enlarged; not only did he add to the existing structures and add a pylon and pillared courts containing halls in which he inscribed the annals of his campaigns, but he also built to the east of the Middle Kingdom area a transverse temple in the form of a jubilee pavilion; on the walls of one of the rear rooms is carved a kind of pictorial catalogue of the strange animals and plants he had brought home from Asia in the 25th year of his reign. He was probably also the builder of the wall which runs round the temple from the fourth pylon eastward, and of the sacred lake to the south of it, on which the barque of Amon floated. Small additions were made by his successors, and Amenhotep III added a pylon (no. 3) to the west and greatly embellished the temple.

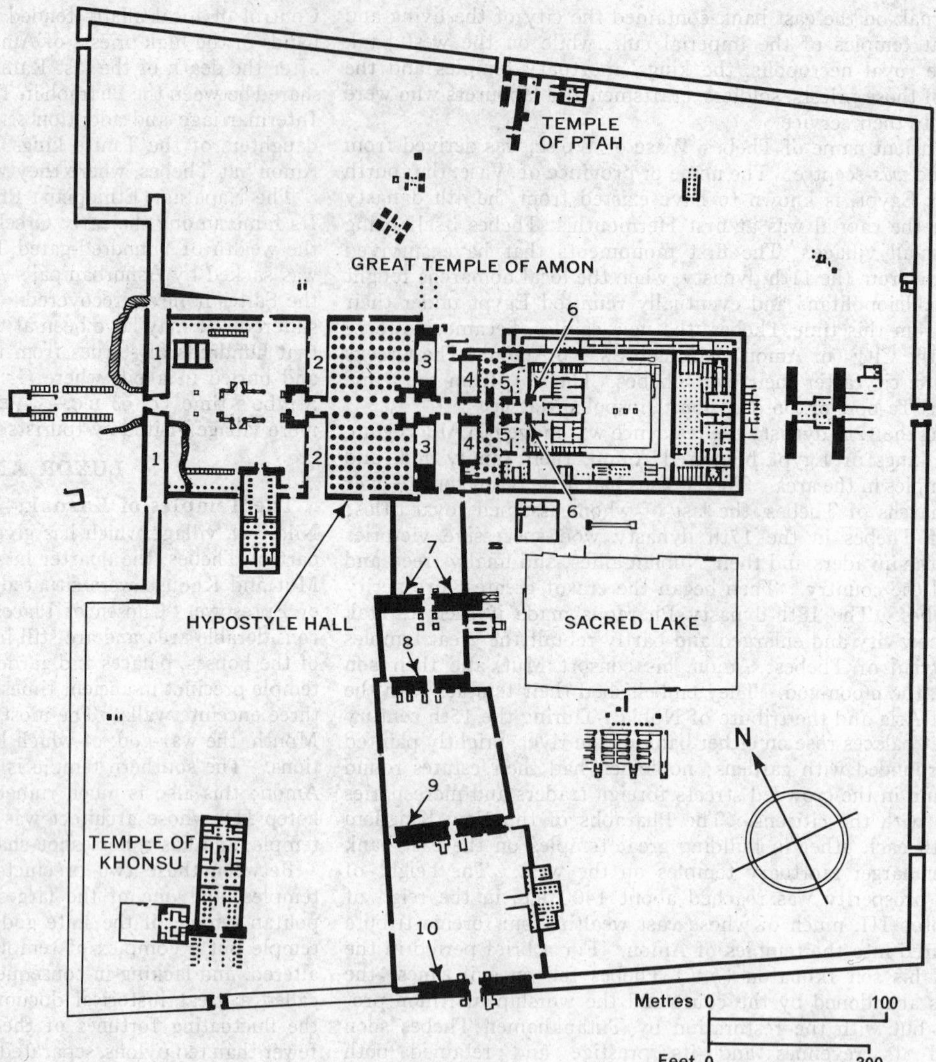


ADAPTED FROM W. S. SMITH, "ART AND ARCHITECTURE OF ANCIENT EGYPT"; REPRODUCED BY PERMISSION OF PENGUIN BOOKS

FIG. 2.—THE TEMPLE OF KARNAK. NUMBERS REFER TO PYLONS

The most striking feature of the temple of Karnak is the hypostyle or pillared hall which occupies the space between the third pylon and the second, built by Ramses I and Horemheb. The area of this vast hall, one of the wonders of antiquity, is 5,800 sq.yd. It was decorated by Seti I and Ramses II, to whom much of the construction must be due, but may have been planned and begun earlier. Fourteen enormous columns, 78 ft. high, raised the roofing slabs of the central nave above the level of the rest so that light and air could enter through a clerestory. Seven lateral aisles on either side brought the number of pillars to 140. Historical reliefs on the outer walls show the victories of Seti in Palestine and Ramses II defeating the Hittites at the battle of Kadesh.

Ramses III built a small temple to Amon outside the Ramesside pylon and at right angles to it, confronting a triple shrine erected by Seti II. The Bubastite kings of the 22nd dynasty, in adding a vast court to the front of the temple, incorporated both these small temples. The Bubastite gate at the southeast corner of this court commemorates the victories won by Sheshonk (*q.v.*) I, the biblical Shishak, in Palestine in the reign of Rehoboam. The Napatan Pharaoh Taharqa planned a tall colonnade of which one pillar still stands, and perhaps began the giant first pylon, 370 ft. wide and 143 ft. high, which was continued by one of the Ptolemies but never completed. Beyond it, an avenue of sphinxes dating from Ramses II's reign leads to the quayside.

Within the enclosure of the great temple of Amon-Re are included a number of other small shrines and temples. A temple to Ptah and Hathor, in the north side of the enclosure, was built by Hatshepsut and Thutmose III and added to by the Ptolemies, who also embellished the great temple by the addition of granite shrines and gateways. To the south, Ramses III dedicated a temple to Khonsu, the moon-god, which merits attention. A small late temple to Opet, the hippopotamus goddess, adjoins it.

Karnak presents a continual problem to the architects who seek to preserve it, for the foundations are inadequate and moisture from the inundation has disintegrated the sandstone at the base of walls and columns. The work of repairing and strengthening goes on continuously, and in carrying out this work new discoveries are constantly being made. In one of the pylons, thousands of fragments from the destroyed temple of the Aton at Thebes were found.

**The Temple of Luxor.**—The southern part of Thebes grew up round the other great temple of Amon, Ope or Ipet, "the Harim (of Amon)." The modern name, in Arabic al Uqsur, means "the palaces" or perhaps, after the Roman *castra* remains of which have been found in the neighbourhood, "the forts." Here, close to the Nile and parallel with the bank of the river, King Amenhotep III built his beautiful temple dedicated to Amon-Re, king of the gods, his consort Mut and their son Khonsu.

A small pavilion is all that is left of earlier work, though there was probably a temple here earlier in the 18th dynasty if not before. It was completed by Tutankhamen and Horemheb and added to by Ramses II; smaller additions were made in Ptolemaic times, and the hypostyle hall was at one time converted into a

Christian church; remains of another Coptic church can be seen to the west of it.

The original part of the temple consisted of a large peristyle court and a complex of halls and chambers beyond; on the east side of the central hall was the birth room, a chapel whose walls were decorated with scenes of the mystical marriage of Queen Mutemuia, Amenhotep's mother, with the god Amon and of the birth of the royal child with the assistance of goddesses. One of the halls contains a granite shrine of Alexander the Great.

The great court is surrounded on three sides by a double row of graceful papyrus-cluster columns, their capitals imitating the umbels of papyrus in bud. An entrance flanked by the towers of a pylon was planned for the north end, but this design was altered and, instead, the most striking feature of the temple, a majestic colonnade of 14 pillars, 52 ft. high, was added. The capitals imitate the open single umbels of papyrus. It may have been intended for the central nave of a hypostyle hall similar to that at Karnak, but the side aisles were not built; instead, enclosing walls were built down either side. Ramses II added an outer court, decorated with colossal statues of himself between the pillars of a double colonnade, and a lofty pylon on which he depicted festival scenes and episodes from his wars in Syria. In front of the pylon were colossi and a pair of obelisks, one of which still stands; the other was removed in 1831 and re-erected in the Place de la Concorde in Paris.

In the forecourt of the temple is the mosque of Sheikh Yusuf al-Haggag, the local Muslim saint. His feast is celebrated with a boat procession which recalls the "Beautiful Festival of Ope" during which, on the 19th day of the second month, Amon came from Karnak on his state barge to visit his other temple at Luxor, escorted by the people of Thebes in holiday attire. Reliefs on the walls of the great colonnade depict preparations for the procession of sacred barques during the festival.

## WESTERN THEBES

Across the Nile from Luxor and Karnak, on the western bank, there was another Thebes, the abode of the dead. The Egyptians called the whole region the Western City, or Kheftet-her-nebes, "She who is opposite to her lord." In Greco-Roman and Coptic times it was called Djeme. The presiding deity was a goddess, Mert-Seger, "the Lover of Silence," who lived on the peak which dominates the range of cliffs in which the tombs are hollowed. On death, both Pharaohs and commoners were ferried across the river to be buried in the necropolis of the west. The earliest cemeteries are in the most northerly part of the area; nomarchs named Intef of the early 11th dynasty built pyramid tombs on the desert edge north of the present village of Qurnah, where the cliffs approach most nearly to the river, and their successors, the Mentuhoteps who ruled the whole country, had larger tombs farther to the south; the largest, that of Mentuhotep II, was built at the head of the valley of Asasif, at a spot known as Dayr al Bahri, "the northern monastery." Here, dwarfed by a semicircle of towering cliffs, he built a combined pyramid tomb and funerary temple on three ascending terraces.

**The Valley of The Tombs of the Kings.**—The kings of the New Kingdom, fearing for the safety of their rich burials, adopted a new plan, that of building only their mortuary temples in the low desert within view of the valley, and concealing their tombs in a lonely valley (Biban al Moluk) in the western hills behind Dayr al Bahri. Here, in tombs sunk deep into the heart of the mountain, the Pharaohs of the 18th, 19th and 20th dynasties from Thutmose I onward were interred, and also one or two queens and officials of high rank. The plan of the tombs varies considerably but consists essentially of a series of descending corridors, interrupted by deep shafts to baffle robbers and by pillared chambers or vestibules; at the farther end is the burial chamber with a stone sarcophagus in which the royal mummy was laid, and store chambers around which furniture and equipment were stacked for the king's use in the next world. The walls were in many cases covered with sculptured and painted scenes depicting the dead king in the presence of deities, especially the gods of the underworld, and with illustrated magical texts similar to those found in funerary papyri, designed to help him on his journey through the nether regions. There were a number of these texts; they represent differing, but not necessarily conflicting, views of the afterlife in which the king had to undergo trials and surmount perils. In the *Book of That Which Is in the Underworld,* for instance, he travels in the boat of the sun-god through 12 caverns which represent the 12 hours of the night. In the *Book of Gates* giant serpents guard the portals through which the sun has to pass, and strange genii and demons help or hinder the boat on its way. Astronomical figures often decorated the ceiling, and the sky-goddess Nut herself is painted across the firmament of stars.

There are some 60 tombs in the valley, almost all of which were robbed in antiquity, many of them during the lifetime of the successors or of near descendants of the owners. In the time of Strabo, Greek visitors were able to visit 40. Only the little tomb of Tutankhamen (*q.v.*) on the floor of the valley, protected by a pile of rock chippings thrown down from a later, Ramessid, tomb, escaped pillage. Those fortunate enough to have seen the wonderful treasures in the Tutankhamen galleries of the Cairo museum will realize how rich the burial of a great Pharaoh of the empire's heyday must have been. The longest tomb is no. 20, that of Queen Hatshepsut (*q.v.*), whose burial chamber is nearly 700 ft. from the entrance and descends 320 ft. into the rock.

In the 19th and 20th dynasties, queens and a few favoured royal princes were buried in another valley today known as Biban al Harim, "the Valley of the Tombs of the Queens." It is situated at the southern end of the Theban necropolis, about 1½ mi. W. of the temple of Medinet Habu. Here over 70 tombs have been found, very few of them inscribed and decorated. The earliest may be that of Sitre, wife of Ramses I. Those most worth visiting are the tomb of Nefertari (no. 66), the favourite queen of Ramses II, of Prince Khaemwese (no. 44) and Prince Amonhirkhopshef (no. 55), and of a Ramessid queen called Titi (no. 52).

**The Tombs of the Nobles.**—The limestone foothills which lie parallel to the river and about three miles away from it are honeycombed for a distance of over two miles with the tombs and tomb-chapels of high officials, mainly of the 18th, 19th and 20th dynasties. The usual plan of these tombs was a forecourt, a transverse chamber, a long corridorlike room and, at the end, a chapel containing statues of the deceased and his family, in the floor of which a shaft or passage ran down to the burial chamber. After the funeral the shaft was filled in but the chapel and anterooms were kept open and visited by the family of the tomb owner. Near the villages of Dira 'Abu'l Nega', Al Asasif, Al Khokha, Shaykh Abd al-Qurnah, Dayr al Medina and Qurnat Mura'i, several hundred tomb-chapels are still open to view. The walls are decorated with mural paintings, many of them wonderfully fresh and full of vivid interest, depicting the daily occupations of the ancient Egyptians. The dead are shown, in the outer rooms of these tombs, inspecting the workmen on their estates, or in their hours of leisure hunting birds in the marshes, or game in the desert, listening to music or playing checkers with their wives. In the infinite variety of these homely scenes, the whole cycle of the farmer's year, from plowing to harvest, is depicted; sculptors, metalworkers, weavers and brickmakers ply their trades; and butcher, brewers and cooks prepare food for the dead man's table. The treasurer goes on his rounds of inspection and the vizier receives foreign envoys to Pharaoh's court. The gay patterns on the roofs derive from those in houses of the period. In the inner chapels, fewer secular scenes are found. The funeral ritual is usually depicted: the cortège crossing the Nile, the ceremony of "Opening the Mouth" by the tomb door, the funerary feast; while in the innermost chamber there are representations of the deceased man and his wife in the company of Osiris and other gods, undergoing the ordeal of judgment known as the "weighing of the heart" or being given nourishment by the goddess in the sacred sycamore. In the tombs of the late New Kingdom, purely religious scenes predominate.

**The Royal Mortuary Temples.**—In the New Kingdom, when the Pharaohs hid their tombs in the secret valley, ostentation had to be concentrated in their mortuary temples, which rivaled each other in size and magnificence. Although they were designed for the performance of rites connected with the mortuary cult of the builder, they were all dedicated to Amon, the supreme god of Thebes, and had the character and essential form of a New Kingdom temple. They were built in western Thebes on the edge of the valley, in a sequence generally corresponding to a topographical arrangement from north to south. Only traces of most of the earlier ones remain. The most important will be mentioned here.

(TOP LEFT) A. F. KERSTING, (BOTTOM LEFT) GRAPHIC HOUSE, (ABOVE) J. ALLAN CASH

**(Top left) the Colossi of Memnon, originally, with their crowns, nearly 70 ft. high, are virtually all that remains of Amenhotep III's great mortuary temple in western Thebes; (left) capitals and lintels of the massive hypostyle hall, temple of Amon-Re, Karnak; (above) the mortuary temple of Queen Hatshepsut at Dayr al Bahri, western Thebes**

1. The temple of Hatshepsut at Dayr al Bahri, which is the earliest large 18th-dynasty structure to survive and one of the most impressive. Here in the bay of cliffs, next to the pyramid-temple of Mentuhotep II mentioned above, the queen's architect Senenmut in about 1490 B.C. designed a series of colonnades and courts on three levels. The approach from the valley led through an avenue of sphinxes, and in the forecourt was a garden planted with trees and vines. On either side of the sloping ramp leading to the next level, against the terrace face, was a gallery whose roof was supported on a double row of columns; a similar gallery ran along the westward side of the court on the next level, with side chapels dedicated to Anubis and Hathor. The top terrace contained what may have been a hall of columns, with further chapels on either side and a sanctuary dug into the cliff behind. Many of the reliefs in the colonnades and chapels are of great beauty and considerable interest: one depicts the transport of two obelisks by barge from Aswan to Karnak, another the divine marriage of Queen Ahmes with the god Amon and the resultant miraculous birth of Hatshepsut herself, and a third, the maritime trading expedition sent by the queen to Punt, the land of incense beyond the Red sea.

2. The mortuary temple of Amenhotep III, which must have been the largest and most splendid of all the Theban temples. It was, however, almost completely demolished by later Pharaohs and all that is left today are a few foundations, a huge stela 30 ft. high, and the two great statues known as the Colossi of Memnon which once flanked the gateway in front of the temple pylon but now sit like lonely sentinels in the middle of cultivated fields. The statues represent Amenhotep III; with their crowns they were nearly 70 ft. high and each was hewn from a single block of stone. The northern one was the "singing Memnon" celebrated in classical times because on certain days, shortly after sunrise, it emitted a curious high note; numerous Roman tourists including the emperor Hadrian and his wife Sabina came to Thebes in order to hear this marvel, but in the reign of Septimius Severus the statue was patched with masonry and never sang again.

3. The temple of Seti I at Qurnah, which survives only in part, the forecourt and pylon having disappeared. It was dedicated in part to the funerary cult of Ramses I, the father of Seti, and was completed by Seti's son, Ramses the Great, who figures largely in the reliefs. The walls are decorated with scenes of purely religious content in which the Pharaohs make offerings to various gods or are favoured by them.

4. The Ramesseum or mortuary temple of Ramses II (Ramses the Great), which, though much ruined, retains some of its ancient grandeur. The wide outer pylon is decorated with vigorous scenes of the king's wars against the Hittites in Syria, and the inner pylon with episodes from the battle of Kadesh and scenes from the festival of the harvest-god, Min. Tall figures of the king in the guise of Osiris decorate the pillars of the inner court. In the first court stood a seated colossus of Ramses II; only fragments of it are left, but enough to show that it was of enormous size. It must have been over 60 ft. high and weighed about 1,000 tons. The hypostyle hall beyond the second court resembles that of the temple of Karnak; beyond were further pillared halls and a sanctuary which has now disappeared. Around the temple, within the high brick enclosure wall, are very extensive remains of vaulted buildings which must have been magazines, stables, workshops and houses belonging to the temple staff. Diodorus Siculus describes the Ramesseum under the name of "the Tomb of Osymandias" (i, 47–49).

5. The temple of Ramses III at Medinet Habu. This is the latest and most southerly of the great New Kingdom mortuary temples. The general plan was modeled on that of the Ramesseum: a wide front pylon, an outer and an inner peristyle court separated by a second pylon, a large pillared hall and two smaller vestibules, and the sanctuary surrounded by smaller rooms. The hypostyle hall is partly ruined, the pillars having been dismantled to the level of the first or second drums, but the temple is otherwise well preserved. Scenes carved on the walls of the inner halls are of the usual ritual character, showing the king performing acts of worship before the gods, but in the first court there are also scenes of battle in which the king in his chariot mows down the Libyans, attacks an Amorite city, and leads Libyans, Asians and sea raiders as prisoners before Amon and Mut. On the external wall of the temple the great sea battle between Egyptians and the Peleset (Philistines), Sherden and Shekelesh and other "peoples of the sea," is depicted with much lively detail. Another outstanding relief is that on the outer face of the great pylon which shows the Pharaoh hunting wild cattle in a reedy, marshy landscape. Adjoining the temple are the remains of a palace excavated by mem-

bers of the Oriental Institute of Chicago, who have also made a complete facsimile record of the reliefs and inscriptions in the great temple. The high gate in the eastern side of the perimeter wall of the temple area is battlemented like a fortress. Within the precinct are other, smaller temples: one dates from the reign of Thutmose III and Hatshepsut, but was altered and added to in various reigns and during the Ptolemaic and Roman periods; another is the small mortuary temple of a Saite queen. There are a sacred lake and a well, and extensive remains, as in the Ramesseum, of houses and vaulted magazines built of mudbrick.

**The Palace of Amenhotep III.**—South of the temple of Medinet Habu lie the ruins of what must have been one of the finest buildings in western Thebes: the palace of King Amenhotep III and Queen Tiy at Malkata. It is in fact four palaces, one of which was occupied by the "great royal wife," for whom her husband constructed a huge lake on which she could sail in her barge. The lake, now called Birket Habu, can still be traced by a line of mounds to the southeast of Malkata. Little is left of the brick palace itself; it was excavated by G. Daressy and others, lastly by archaeologists sent out by the Metropolitan Museum of Art, New York, who were able to restore a few of the splendid wall paintings.

*See* AMON; EGYPTIAN ARCHITECTURE; EGYPT: *History; see* also references under "Thebes" in the Index.

BIBLIOGRAPHY.—A. M. Blackman, *Luxor and Its Temples* (1923); G. Legrain, *Les Temples de Karnak* (1929); Karl Baedeker, *Egypt and the Sudan,* 8th ed. (1929); B. Porter and R. L. B. Moss, *Topographical Bibliography of Ancient Egypt,* vol. i, *Theban Tombs* (1927), vol. i, 2nd ed., part 1: *Private Tombs* (1960), vol. ii, *Theban Temples* (1929); H. E. Winlock, *The Rise and Fall of the Middle Kingdom in Thebes* (1947) and *Excavations at Deir el Bahri* (1942); E. Naville, *The Temple of Deir el-Bahari,* 7 vol. (1894–1906) and *The XIth Dynasty Temple at Deir el-Bahari,* 3 vol. (1907–13); H. H. Nelson *et al., Medinet Habu,* Publications of the Oriental Institute of the University of Chicago, 12 vol. (1930–57); A. Wolf, *Das schöne Fest von Opet* (1931); G. Steindorff and W. Wolf, *Die thebanische Gräberwelt* (1936); G. Lefebvre, *Histoire des grands prêtres d'Amon de Karnak* (1929); E. Otto, *Topographie des thebanischen Gaues* (1952); G. Steindorff and K. Seele, *When Egypt Ruled the East* (1942).

(M. S. DR.)

**THEBES** (Greek THEBAI; modern Greek THÍVAI), a city of Boeotia, central Greece. Pop. (1961) 15,779. Thebes is situated on a low ridge dividing the two plains of Boeotia. The town has abundant springs of water, the most famous in antiquity being called Dirce, and the fertile plain in the vicinity is well irrigated. The road and railway system of east central Greece passes through Thebes, and nature makes it the chief market town of a rich agricultural area; it is the seat of the Greek Orthodox bishop of Thebes and Levadhia.

**Prehistory.**—The ancient citadel, called the Cadmea, was first inhabited in the Early Bronze Age and then taken over by a Middle Bronze Age people who probably spoke Greek and may have been called Aones (perhaps a form of Iaones; *i.e.,* Ionians). During the 15th century B.C. a palace of Minoan plan was built on the Cadmea and adorned with frescoes showing Theban women in Minoan dress; the so-called Palace Style of pottery was in use at this time, some vases being imported from Crete, and contacts between Thebes and Knossos increased in 1450–1400 (*see* CRETE). Thebes became even wealthier in the period after 1400, when the rulers used golden vessels and built a great circuit wall; indeed, Boeotia rivaled Argolis as a centre of Mycenaean power until the palace and wall were destroyed about 30 years before the Trojan War, *i.e., c.* 1230. Greek legend attributed the citadel to Cadmus, the wall to Amphion (*qq.v.*), and the sack of "seven-gated Thebes" to an army led by Adrastus, king of Argos (*see* SEVEN AGAINST THEBES); legend told, too, of Hercules born at Thebes, and of the misfortunes of Laius and Oedipus (*q.v.*).

The destruction of Thebes is implicit in the "catalogue" of Greek contingents in the *Iliad,* which mentions Hypothebae ("lower Thebes") and calls the leaders Boiotoi. A further invasion by Boiotoi about 1120 completed the collapse of Mycenaean civilization. Excavations begun in 1963 not only placed the final destruction of the Cadmea in the latter half of the 13th century but also threw a surprising light on the tradition that Cadmus came to Thebes from Phoenicia eight generations before Spartans entered Thera (*i.e., c.* 1360, if the Spartans went to Thera as well as to Melos *c.* 1100); for a superb collection of Babylonian seals, mainly of 14th-century date, which was found in the burnt layer of the final destruction, is likely to have formed part of the crown jewels of the Cadmean royal house.

**History.**—After the migrations of the Early Iron Age the people of Boeotia were of mixed stock, some speaking an Aeolic and others a northwest Greek dialect, and at Thebes a Dorian clan, the Aegeidae, was very influential. Thebes was governed for centuries by an oligarchy of aristocratic clans that held large estates (*klaroi*), and laws were passed *c.* 725 to maintain the number of estates. In the 6th century a league of Boeotian cities was formed (*see* BOEOTIA), including Thebes. But Thebes pursued an individual policy in supporting Pisistratus, who became tyrant of Athens *c.* 546, and in attacking Plataea, which allied itself with Athens in 519. From this sprang a lasting enmity between Thebes and Athens, because Plataea lay just west of the main route from Thebes to the Isthmus of Corinth through the Megarid, and the alliance of Plataea and Athens threatened to cut this line of communication.

When hostilities broke out in 519, the Boeotian League supported Thebes and was defeated by Athens. In 506 Boeotia, Chalcis, and Sparta combined against Athens, but Boeotia again suffered defeat and Thebes turned to Aegina for help. When the Persians invaded Greece, 400 Thebans went to help defend Thermopylae. When they were surrounded, they surrendered, and hatred for Athens encouraged Thebes to join the Persians. The Theban cavalry and infantry fought well on the Persian side at the Battle of Plataea; the city then stood a siege of 20 days before surrendering the leaders of its close oligarchy to the Greeks (479).

A period of decline followed when Thebes was more or less under the control of Sparta or Athens and its government fluctuated between oligarchy and democracy. Then in 446 the Boeotian League won its independence. In 431 Thebes attacked Plataea and started the Peloponnesian War (*q.v.*), during which the Thebans won a dominant position in the Boeotian League. A number of small states sought refuge behind the city's strong fortifications; they were treated at first as equals and then as subjects. Thebes soon controlled 4 of the league's 11 wards, and the federal council met there. Moreover, Theban troops won a decisive victory at Delium (*q.v.*) in 424. When Athens surrendered (404), Thebes proposed its destruction, but Sparta preserved Athens as a rival to Boeotia. Thebes therefore adopted a policy of opposition to Sparta, assisting the Athenian democrats and instigating the Corinthian War (395–386). This policy failed, for Sparta disbanded the Boeotian League in 386 and placed a garrison in Thebes in 382.

For 60 years, since 446, the constitution of Thebes had been a moderate oligarchy in which the franchise was limited to the propertied class. In 379 Thebes rose against Sparta and became a democracy. As the Thebans liberated the Boeotian cities from Sparta, they reconstituted the league on a democratic basis, with an assembly of Boeotians meeting at Thebes. By reducing their neighbours to dependent status, they soon controlled three of the new league's seven wards; their leaders Melon, Pelopidas, and Epaminondas were influential in the Boeotian assembly; and their *corps d'élite,* the Sacred Band, defeated the Spartans at Tegyra (375) and Leuctra (371). In 371–362 Thebes was the leading military power in Greece. Epaminondas (*q.v.*) tried to make it the capital of a unified Boeotia, and Boeotia head of a group of federal states, but the people abused their position by destroying Orchomenos and placing garrisons in allied cities. In 356 Thebes used the Amphictyonic Council to lay a fine on some Phocian leaders, but these seized Delphi, hired mercenaries, and overran Boeotia. Ten years later Thebes won the war by invoking Philip II of Macedonia. But the Thebans broke their alliance with him and in 338 suffered defeat at Chaeronea (*q.v.*); the league was dissolved, and an oligarchic government and a Macedonian garrison were imposed on Thebes. Thebes rose twice against Alexander the Great, and in 335 his army broke through the defenses. Six thousand Thebans fell, and the city was razed except for the temples and the house of the famous Theban poet Pindar, which Alexander spared. The survivors were enslaved by order of the Greek League.

Cassander rebuilt Thebes in 316. It shared the vicissitudes of the Boeotian League, fell under the authority of Rome, and was stripped of half its territory by Sulla in 86. In Byzantine and Frankish times it prospered as an administrative and commercial centre, particularly for silk weaving; it had a large Jewish colony in the 12th century. From 1205 it was the capital of the Frankish lords (later dukes) of Athens, and a Frankish castle was built on the Cadmea. In 1311 it was taken by the Almogávares (*q.v.*). Under the Turks (1435–1829) Thebes became a village.

*See* also references under "Thebes" in the Index.

*See* L. Ziehen in Pauly-Wissowa, *Real-Encyclopädie der classischen Altertumswissenschaft,* 2nd series, vol. v, 1423–1553 (1934).

(N. G. L. H.)

**THECLA, SAINT** (1st century A.D.), honoured in the East with the title "protomartyr among women and equal with the apostles," is one of the most celebrated saints in the Greek Church. The centre of her cult was Seleucia, in Isauria (south central Asia Minor), and her basilica south of Seleucia, long a popular place of pilgrimage, is mentioned in the two books of St. Basil of Seleucia. Thecla was the heroine of the apocryphal *Acts of Paul and Thecla* (late 2nd century), according to which she came under the personal teaching of the apostle Paul at Iconium. The *Acts* are of a highly fabulous character (Thecla escaped from burning, from wild beasts, bulls, and serpents) but are nonetheless interesting monuments of ancient Christian literature and probably contain a nucleus of genuine history. They were extremely popular in the early church. St. Thecla's feast day is Sept. 24 in the East, Sept. 23 in the West.

Numerous versions of the *Acts* survive. English translations include: of the Syriac, by W. Wright, in *Apocryphal Acts of the Apostles,* vol. ii, pp. 116–145 (1871); of the Ethiopic, by E. J. Goodspeed, in *American Journal of Semitic Languages and Literatures,* vol. xvii, pp. 65–95; of the Coptic, by M. R. James (ed.), in *The Apocryphal New Testament,* pp. 272–281 (1924); and of the Armenian, by F. C. Conybeare, in *The Apology and Acts of Apollonius and Other Monuments of Early Christianity,* pp. 61–88 (1894).

*See* L. Radermacher, *Hippolytus und Thekla* (1916); *Dictionary of Christian Biography,* vol. iv, pp. 882–896.

**THEGN** (THANE), an Anglo-Saxon word meaning "one who serves," was from early times used also of the noble members of a king's or great man's following; and their twofold duty of service in war and in peace is mirrored in the rendering of thegn as *miles* and *minister* in Latin sources. From the late 9th century it ousted the term "gesith" (companion). Over most of England men of this class had a wergild of 1,200 shillings. By the 11th century it was considered that a typical thegn would possess at least five hides of land, a church and kitchen, a bellhouse and fortified dwelling, and a seat and special office in the king's hall; but the class included men of various degrees of wealth, ranging from those with vast estates to others who economically hardly differed from the ceorl (*see* CHURL).

The service of the king conferred special distinction. The king's thegn is first mentioned in the laws (688–694) of Ine, king of Wessex, and (695) of Wihtred of Kent, and already he had special privileges. King's thegns from the time of Alfred (d. 899) served at court in rotation. They also played an increasingly important part in local jurisdiction and administration. In the Danelaw, a code of Aethelred II (d. 1016) shows the 12 senior thegns of each wapentake acting as a jury of presentment. The king's thegns had military duties also, and they paid a higher heriot than other thegns. By the time of Aethelred II no one but the king had jurisdiction over them. Ealdormen were normally chosen from among them.

In Scotland the title thane was applied to hereditary administrators of royal estates. It survived until the 15th century.

(D. WK.)

**THEILER, MAX** (1899– ), South African microbiologist, who won the Nobel Prize for Physiology or Medicine in 1951 for his work on the virus of yellow fever, was born in Pretoria on Jan. 30, 1899. He received his early education in South Africa and completed his medical training at St. Thomas' Hospital, London, and the London School of Tropical Medicine in 1922. From 1922 to 1930 he worked in the department of tropical medicine at the Harvard Medical School in Boston. There he carried out important studies on amoebic dysentery, rat-bite fever, and leptospirosis.

Shortly after the discovery by A. Stokes, J. H. Bauer, and N. P. Hudson that yellow fever was caused by a virus transmissible to monkeys, Theiler showed that the common albino mouse is also susceptible to the virus. In addition to facilitating the work on the natural history of yellow fever, his discovery led to the development of the first attenuated strain of the virus. In 1930 Theiler joined the laboratories of the Rockefeller Foundation in New York and together with E. Haagen, W. Lloyd, N. Ricci, and H. Smith carried out further fundamental studies on the yellow fever virus that led to the development of the improved (17-D) strain widely used for human immunization. He also discovered a virus disease of mice that closely resembles human poliomyelitis.

(A. B. SN.)

**THEISM** (Greek *Theos,* "God") means belief in God, but more particularly, a distinctive set of doctrines expressed in philosophical terms concerning God in relation to the world and man. While no doctrine of God is completely divorced from ideas and beliefs to be found in the historical religious traditions, theism represents a constructive philosophical position not to be identified with any particular religion. It has frequently happened that a theistic line of thought has developed within a particular religion; thus, for example, we can speak of Christian theism or of theistic interpretations of Hinduism. Theism thus appears both as a philosophico-theological position in its own right and as an identifiable strain of thought within official church theologies.

Theism is distinguished from atheism (*q.v.*), or explicit denial that there is God or a transcendent reality, and from agnosticism (*q.v.*), or the doctrine that human reason is incapable of knowledge in the theological sphere and is thus unable either to prove or disprove the existence of God. It is especially important to distinguish theism from deism (*q.v.*), a position developed chiefly by philosophers in the 18th century which emphasizes the transcendence of God over the world and conceives of God primarily as a Supreme Being or Regulator of the cosmic system. In taking God as an explanatory principle of the cosmos, deism did much to foster a contrast between the "God of philosophers" who is aloof and the "God of religion" who enters into personal relations with worshipers. Theism holds to the presence (immanence) of God in the world and human experience, although it also upholds the divine transcendence. Theism, in further contrast to deism, uses the concepts of person and self in describing the divine nature, whereas deism tends toward impersonal conceptions of the deity.

Theists distinguish their position from pantheism (*q.v.*) in some of its formulations, especially if pantheism is taken to mean the total immanence of God in the world or in man. By contrast, theism insists upon a clear distinction between God and the world; this feature serves also to distinguish theism from absolutism or religious monism in which there is an identification between God and the totality of things taken together as one fully unified and all-embracing system.

**History.**—Although the first occurrence of the term theism is to be found in the 17th century, the position is much older and can be traced back to ancient Greek philosophy. It is characteristic of theism to seek support for its contentions in rational argument and appeal to the nature of things as open to experience. Consequently, it has given rise to various types of argument for the existence of God. Rational or philosophical theology aimed at establishing the reality of God and at defining the divine nature can first be found in the philosophy of Plato, notably in Book x of the *Laws.* There Plato advanced the argument for God which combines ideas that formed the basis of the later cosmological and teleological arguments. Motion and change exist, Plato argued, but some motions are imparted to a thing from another and some belong to the intrinsic nature of the being itself. This latter or spontaneous motion belongs to souls alone; matter can have only such motion as is communicated to it from another. That motion in the universe which is communicated requires a soul capable of communicating it. There is, therefore, a cosmic soul or God.

Aristotle is not generally described as a theist because his ultimate principle is a *nous* or intelligence rather than a soul, and his God has no personal relations with man. He nevertheless left an indelible mark upon Christian and all later theism by laying the foundations for the cosmological argument for the existence of God (*see* below). Thomas Aquinas was later to bring the cosmological argument to its classic expression in his famous "five ways" of demonstrating God's existence set forth in the *Summa Theologica*.

The ancient Stoic philosophers and the Neoplatonist tradition as represented by Proclus and Plotinus carried on the theistic tradition in ways consistent with their distinctive philosophical outlooks. (*See* STOICS; NEOPLATONISM.) With Augustine of Hippo and Anselm of Canterbury there was established the tradition of Christian Platonism and with it the ontological-type argument for the existence of God (*see* below). The cosmological and ontological arguments, together with the argument from design or teleological argument (*see* below), passed into the general philosophical tradition. These arguments were used with various transformations and reformulations by philosophers until the 18th century. Locke, Descartes, Spinoza, Leibniz, and countless others put forth their own versions of the different arguments for God and set the stage for the thorough criticism of these arguments in the 18th century, which was a turning point in the development of theism. Kant, in his criticism of reason and his doctrine that theoretical reason is limited in its application, and Hume, in his skeptical examination of the grounds of human knowledge, led to a revolution in philosophical theology. Each in his own way set forth searching criticism of the rational grounds upon which the now traditional arguments for God and the divine attributes were based. Hume, by attacking the inherent rationality of the causal principle, cast doubt upon the validity of an argument attempting to pass from the finite facts and the existence of the world to God as its Cause. Kant, by denying the validity of all purely rational or a priori arguments aimed at establishing the existence of a thing, struck at the root of the ontological argument. The further implications of his criticism become clearer when we note that he sought to show the dependence of all arguments for God on the ontological argument; if that fails, they all fail. One basic result of this criticism was the turning of attention away from more traditional patterns in theistic thought to new approaches. Kant himself pointed the way by proposing the moral approach or argument for God and by giving a new prominence to the teleological argument. It is important, however, to notice that Kant's "arguments" are of a peculiar kind and differ from previous forms. His arguments are "transcendental" and involve showing that God, as one of the transcendental Ideas, is a necessary rational condition for making morality intelligible and for enabling us to think of reality from a teleological point of view.

Despite these criticisms, theism continued to maintain itself. Considerable emphasis was placed in the 19th century upon developing the moral approach to God, and the rise and growth of the theory of Value brought forth an "axiological" argument for God as the Ground of Value both in the universe and in human experience. The development, moreover, of the theory of evolution led to a reconsideration of the idea of Providence and a closer connection between the idea of God and the interpretation of the cosmic process. The appearance of doctrines of "emergent evolution" (*see* EMERGENCE), or the idea that novel and higher forms of being appear in the course of time, played an important role in theistic thought. More recently, F. R. Tennant in his *Philosophical Theology* has argued in great detail for a "wider teleology" as the ground of an empirical theism, and Austin Farrer in his *Finite and Infinite* has revived the cosmological approach with considerable skill and with greater emphasis on man and his experience. The older cosmological arguments paid exclusive attention to the physical world.

The dominant place assumed by experience in modern thought has led to the development of the idea of religious experience. Seeking to keep more closely in touch with actual religion, theists have identified certain types or qualities of experience, such as the "holy," the "numinous," and the sense of "unconditional obligation," as the ultimate ground of belief in God. William James in *The Varieties of Religious Experience* gave classic expression to this line of thought, and his work led to the study of the grounds of theistic belief from a psychological point of view. Present-day theists have fully accepted the idea that, without experience in some form, arguments for God are futile. Mysticism, or the intuition of God as Ultimate Unity, is often believed to represent religious experience par excellence, but theistic philosophers and theologians have appealed to this ground of belief only with the greatest caution because mystics have so frequently criticized the theistic conception of God, contending that if God is conceived merely as one being besides others he thereby becomes finite in nature.

**Summary of the Theistic Arguments and the Idea of God.**—*Ontological Argument.*—The original and standard formulation of this argument was set forth by Anselm in his *Proslogion.* The distinguishing feature of this approach is that it starts with the idea of God and seeks to show that this idea, properly understood, implies the necessity of the divine existence. Assuming that God means "that than which nothing greater can be conceived," Anselm argued that unless the object of the concept existed beyond the concept it would not be "that than which nothing greater can be conceived" but something less. It is generally agreed that there are two arguments for God in the *Proslogion.* One takes the form of claiming that existence is a perfection among others and that since God embraces all perfections, God must exist. The other argument has to do not with bare existence but with the concept of *necessary* existence. In the latter case the argument is that the reality meant by the term "God" cannot be conceived not to exist without contradiction; therefore, God exists necessarily. When it is said that the ontological argument is a priori, the meaning is that it does not set out from the existence of any finite facts but from the grasp of a meaning or a concept. It is clear, however, that Anselm regarded his formula for God as expressing the Christian conception of the deity derived from a prior tradition of thought and faith.

Later thinkers, such as Descartes and Leibniz, restated this argument so as to focus chiefly on existence. Existence, it was said, is one predicate of a thing besides others, and it constitutes a perfection. The idea of the Supreme Reality is the idea of a Reality necessarily possessing all perfections, and since one of these is existence, God necessarily exists. Though the ontological argument has been "refuted" many times, it still continues to engage the attention of philosophers and theologians. It is a witness to the ultimate relation between God and the structure of reason.

*Cosmological Argument.*—We must be careful to distinguish between the basic principle underlying this argument and the several concrete forms it has assumed. The basic principle is that of causality or sufficient reason according to which for every existent fact there must be a cause or sufficient reason why it is so and not otherwise. The essence of the cosmological route to God is the logical transition from given fact to God as its cause. Though the starting point is fact or existence in either case, we may focus attention either on the fact of existence itself ("something exists") or upon some particular feature of what exists ("there is motion"; "there are causes"). In the first case, the argument takes the following form: since something exists, something must exist necessarily, for what exists either has the cause or reason of its existence in itself or that cause must be found in another. Therefore, since something exists, that existence is either its own cause, in which case it is necessary; or it is dependent upon another existence which has its own reason within its own nature. This existence is the necessary being or God.

In the second case, the argument takes the form of starting not with the bare fact of existence but with some particular feature of existing things such as the fact of motion or of the causal relation between things, and of arguing that, to avoid an unending chain of causes, there must be a Prime Mover or First Cause which is the sufficient reason of the facts with which the argument began. Here the particular facet of God figuring in the conclusion of the argument is determined by the particular feature of the world from which we set out. Thus, the fact of motion leads to God as Prime Mover, the fact of purposive action leads to God as Intelligent Designer, etc.

The classic statement of the cosmological arguments was given by Thomas Aquinas in his *Summa Theologica* (Part I, Question ii, art. 3) where he set forth the "five ways" by which God's existence can be demonstrated by the light of reason. These are, in the order in which they appear in the *Summa:* the argument from motion; the argument from efficient causes; the argument from possible and necessary existence; the argument from degrees of excellence; the argument from design. The last argument has usually been described as teleological, but it is clearly of the cosmological type since, like the others, it begins with certain features of finite fact and seeks the cause or reason for those features in God. The chief idea communicated through all cosmological arguments is that the world is not self-explanatory and is dependent upon some reality beyond itself.

*Teleological Argument.*—The general form of this argument is that of starting with the observation that things in the world are so constructed as to be able to perform their functions and that in so doing they appear to be "working toward ends." The teleological proof is the inferring of a designing intelligence as the sufficient reason for such purposive activity in nature. This argument was, of course, profoundly affected by the theory of evolution in the last century, since the theory gave many instances of adaptation a "natural" explanation and seemed to require no designing intelligence or purpose. Various emphases have been dominant in the history of this argument; sometimes it has been held that the world was designed solely for the good of man and that "it is the best of all possible worlds." Other statements have focused upon the analogy between an intelligently designed mechanism such as a clock and an intelligent maker, and the universe as a system of adapted parts and a divine maker. Kant, like many others, regarded the teleological argument as the one closest to the ordinary experience and understanding of men.

*Moral Argument.*—Kant, who initiated this line of argument, held that reflection upon man as a moral being can lead us to the idea of God. Man's awareness of obligation places upon him the demand to achieve the good will; worthiness to be happy is man's proper aim. In order to understand morality as rationally consistent, we must, Kant held, invoke God as the power able to make the highest happiness and our worthiness to be happy coincide. This is not a demonstration after the manner of the other arguments but rather the idea that God is a postulate required if the moral life is to be rationally understood.

Later forms of the moral argument were more direct; they laid stress upon the idea that the authority of the moral ideal becomes insignificant unless that ideal is grounded in Reality. Moreover, it was argued, the Ideal requires embodiment in God; otherwise it has no status but that of "an ought to be" or a mere postulate. Whatever its particular form, the moral argument seeks to show that the fact of man's sense of unconditional obligation leads us on to a Ground which both supports and explains this fact.

**Theistic Conception of God.**—As regards the theistic conception of God, the dominant note has been to think of God as personal or at least as being of a nature which is not subpersonal. The main reason for this doctrine is the belief that, since experience discloses personality as the highest form of existence, the nature of God cannot be less than personal. Since, however, terms like "personal" and "person" cannot be attributed to God in the same sense in which they are used to describe finite, human persons, some doctrine of analogy or symbolism has been introduced. The main aim of theists has been to hold fast to the basis upon which personal relations between God and man are possible.

Since theism insists upon a clear distinction between God and the world, it embraces a doctrine of creation according to which God is immanent in the world while preserving transcendence at the same time. The appeals made by theists to both reason and general experience have led to analyses of the creative process both in nature and in man as sources of insight for understanding divine creativity. Of considerable importance in theistic discussion is the question whether the world is necessary to God as God is necessary to the world. Classical Christianity has tended to hold that the world is not necessary to God, whereas some theists have maintained that it is necessary. The doctrine has also been advanced that some world or other is necessary to God, but that this particular world is not.

Other attributes of God, such as infinity, eternity, omniscience, and omnipotence, are treated by theists in accordance with analogies drawn from human experience. The chief problem is to understand how finite and imperfect characteristics can be understood as existing perfectly in God and also whether such perfection necessarily means a static rather than a living God.

Theists have not been unmindful of the difficulties raised for their position by the problem of evil, and various sustained attempts have been offered to show that the reality of evil is not inconsistent with the reality of God. It is important to notice that the problem of evil exists only upon the assumption that the universe is the expression of a divine ground. Consequently, the problem of evil concerns the divine nature primarily and not the prior question of God's existence. The proponents of theism have consistently developed their position against the criticism of philosophical skeptics who deny all knowledge transcending sense experience, and against theologians who deny natural theology in favour of revelation alone.

*See* also DEISM; PANTHEISM; and biographies of philosophers referred to above.

BIBLIOGRAPHY.—Caldecott and Mackintosh, *Selections from the Literature of Theism* (1904); A. S. Pringle-Pattison, *The Idea of God in the Light of Recent Philosophy,* 2nd rev. ed. (1920); F. R. Tennant, *Philosophical Theology,* 2 vol. (1930); A. E. Taylor, *The Faith of a Moralist* (1930); W. R. Sorley, *Moral Values and the Idea of God* (1918); W. M. Urban, *Humanity and Deity* (1951); A. Farrer, *Finite and Infinite* (1943); C. Hartshorne, *Man's Vision of God and the Logic of Theism* (1941) and *The Logic of Perfection* (1962); H. de Lubac, *The Discovery of God* (1960); A. Flew and A. MacIntyre, *New Essays in Philosophical Theology* (1955); C. Hartshorne and W. L. Reese, *Philosophers Speak of God* (1953); P. Tillich, *The Courage to Be* (1952); K. Barth, *Anselm: Faith Seeking Understanding,* Eng. trans. (1960). (J. E. SM.)

**THEMISTOCLES** (6th–5th century B.C.), Athenian statesman and general, more than any other single man saved Greece from the Persians. His family, the Lycomidae, was old and honourable, but his father was inconspicuous and his mother not Athenian. In an age when family alliances were powerful factors in politics, Themistocles lacked influence among the nobility and relied on the people for support.

Though little is known of his early career, the statement of Dionysius of Halicarnassus (a good scholar) that Themistocles was archon in 493/492 should be accepted. Themistocles realized the danger threatening from Persia and began to develop the Athenian navy. Little, however, could be done before the Persian danger became acute, and it was the hoplite infantry, inspired by Miltiades, that won the Battle of Marathon (490). In the following years there was intense rivalry among leading politicians at Athens, reflected in a series of ostracisms, but in 483 Themistocles seized an unexpected opportunity. A new rich seam of silver had been opened in the Laurium mining area, and it was proposed to distribute the windfall among the citizens; Themistocles persuaded the assembly to use the money to build a large modern fleet. Aristides, who opposed the policy, was ostracized (482), and 200 triremes were built by 480.

As Xerxes completed his preparations for invasion, Themistocles became the dominant leader in Athens. He persuaded the Athenians to accept Spartan leadership and to sink political differences by recalling the ostracized. Above all it was he who persuaded the Athenians to evacuate Attica and rely on their fleet. He was in command of the Athenian contingent in the force that went to Tempe, and when it was realized that Thessaly could not be defended he took the Athenian fleet to Artemisium; the Spartan Eurybiades was in command, but the driving force came from Themistocles. When the Thermopylae-Artemisium line had to be abandoned, it was Themistocles who controlled the evacuation of

Attica and inspired the Greek commanders to fight at Salamis. The naval victory of Salamis was the decisive turning point in the war, and Themistocles was its main architect. His new Athenian ships formed the largest contingent, his eloquence maintained morale before the fighting, and his message sent to Xerxes that the Greeks were preparing to flee led the Persians to go into action too soon, expecting an easy victory. Themistocles was given an ovation even at Sparta. (*See* further GRECO-PERSIAN WARS.)

In the autumn Themistocles took the fleet through the Aegean Islands, enforcing payments toward the campaign, and he was not reticent about his achievements. His political opponents were able to profit by a swing of feeling against him, which they encouraged, and he lost his command in 479, the year in which the Persians were finally defeated by land and sea. When the leadership against Persia passed in 478 from Sparta to Athens, Themistocles was not in control. At home, however, he had outwitted the Spartans when they attempted to prevent the rebuilding of Athens' fortifications. Of Themistocles' actions and policies for the next six years very little is known. The spectacular successes of the Delian League were credited to Aristides and Cimon; Themistocles' aim seems to have been to oppose Spartan policies. He successfully resisted the Spartan attempt to get control of the Amphictyonic League by expelling medizers (states that had collaborated with the Persians), and he is said to have plotted to burn the Greek fleet that Sparta led to overthrow the medizing rulers in Thessaly (*c.* 476). He was *choregus* (financial backer) for the production of Phrynichus' tragedy *The Phoenician Women*, in 476, but this is the last that is heard of him in Athens. The main power rested with Aristides, Cimon, and a strong group of families associated with them, who believed that Sparta and Athens could remain in alliance. Themistocles, the sharper realist, saw that the two states were incompatible, but the people were not yet persuaded. He was ostracized (*c.* 473–471) and went to Argos, Sparta's traditional enemy; from this base he stirred up opposition to Sparta in the Peloponnese.

It was primarily for this reason that the Spartans implicated Themistocles in the treason of the Spartan regent Pausanias (*q.v.*). They were able to work on Themistocles' enemies in Athens, who brought the charge of Medism against him. Themistocles was condemned in absence. He fled from Argos, pursued by a Spartan and Athenian commission, first to Corcyra, then to the king of the Molossians, then across Macedonia to the Aegean and Ionia. When Xerxes died (465), Themistocles appealed for refuge to his son Artaxerxes and, like other Greeks before him, was honoured by the Persians. He was allowed to rule in Magnesia, and other towns were assigned for his maintenance. He probably died a natural death, though later a tradition grew up that he drank bull's blood to avoid the humiliation of leading Persian forces against Greece. The dates of his ostracism, condemnation at Athens (after 472), flight, arrival at the Persian court, and death are highly controversial but comparatively unimportant.

Thucydides, who is very sparing in character sketches, goes out of his way to write about Themistocles. He emphasizes his sharp intelligence and powers of analysis and anticipation. Themistocles saw much more clearly than his rivals the strength and weakness of Persia. His bold decision to rely primarily on the Athenian fleet, combined with the force of his personality, saved Greece. His naming of his eldest daughters, Sybaris and Italia, together with his threat to sail west and occupy Siris in south Italy if the Peloponnesians refused to stay at Salamis, suggests that he looked on the West as a base for supplies when Persia controlled the raw materials from the Black Sea and from Thrace and Macedonia. After the defeat of Xerxes he anticipated the later leaders of Athenian democracy in believing that Athens could not develop freely while tied to conservative Sparta. His naval policy was a decisive factor in making Athens more democratic, but this was the result rather than the intention; Themistocles was more concerned with policies than with political principles. Thucydides says nothing of his moral qualities; other writers say too much. From Herodotus onward stories circulated of his greed, corruption, cunning, and conceit. Behind the anecdotes and rhetoric there is probably some substance. Very probably Themistocles was not a moralists' model and was capable of sharp practice and human vanity; but he remains the greatest Athenian of his day. A Roman copy of his portrait, found in 1939 at Ostia, is probably a replica of a contemporary portrait.

BIBLIOGRAPHY.—Herodotus, books vii and viii; Thucydides, book i, 135–138; Plutarch, *Themistocles;* E. M. Walker in *Cambridge Ancient History,* vol. v, ch. 2 (1927). A 3rd-century copy of Themistocles' famous decree ordering evacuation and mobilization was discovered in 1959 at Troezen, which gave hospitality to most of the refugees. This decree, however, is inconsistent at crucial points with Herodotus' account, and its genuineness has been disputed. *See* M. H. Jameson in *Hesperia,* xxix, pp. 198 ff. (1960), xxxi, pp. 310 ff. (1962); A. R. Burn, *Persia and the Greeks,* pp. 364 ff. (1962); C. Hignett, *Xerxes' Invasion of Greece,* pp. 458 ff. (1963) (the last two hostile to authenticity).

(R. ME.)

**THENARD, LOUIS JACQUES** (1777–1857), French chemist, author of a standard textbook on elementary chemistry, and discoverer of hydrogen peroxide, was born on May 4, 1777, at La Louptière, Aube. He worked in a humble capacity in the Paris laboratory of N. L. Vauquelin, who procured for him various teaching posts. In 1802, when Vauquelin left the Collège de France, he used his influence to secure Thenard's succession to the chair of chemistry. Later, Thenard held the chair of chemistry at the École Polytechnique and at the Sorbonne. Made a baron in 1825, he was a peer of France (1832), deputy for Yonne (1827–30), chancellor of the university, and a member of the Council of Education. Thenard died in Paris on June 21, 1857. The name of his native village was changed (1865) to Louptière-Thenard in his honour.

Thenard was a great teacher. His *Traité élémentaire de chimie théorique et pratique* (4 vol., 1813–16) did more, perhaps, than even his many important original discoveries to advance the cause of science. With his lifelong friend J. L. Gay-Lussac (*q.v.*) he carried out many researches. Thenard himself is especially remembered for his work on esters (1807), sebacic acid (1802), and bile (1807), his discovery of hydrogen peroxide (1818), his study of organic phosphorus compounds (1846), and his preparation of the pigment known as Thenard's blue (1799).

**THEOBALD** (*c.* 1090–1161), archbishop of Canterbury, members of whose household made a notable contribution to the 12th-century Renaissance, was born near Bec in Normandy. He entered the abbey of Bec, became prior (*c.* 1127), and was elected abbot in 1136. In 1138 he was the improbable but successful candidate for the archbishopric of Canterbury, defeating the hopes of Henry of Blois, bishop of Winchester. From 1139 to 1143 Theobald was overshadowed by Henry, who had secured the office of papal legate with powers equal or superior to those of the archbishop. Politically, as between Stephen and the Angevins (Matilda and her son, the future Henry II), Theobald was a cautious conformist, generally obedient to Stephen but showing limited support for Matilda in 1141. At Christmas 1141, however, Theobald recrowned Stephen following his release from captivity, and thereafter he recognized Stephen's title. Theobald, made legate (1150) by Eugenius III, held a council at London (1151) at which were promulgated important canons and statements of ecclesiastical liberties. The king wished his son Eustace to be crowned to secure his succession, but Eugenius forbade Theobald to carry out the rite, and the archbishop was forced to flee (1152). Soon reinstated, Theobald played a leading part in negotiating the treaty that brought Henry of Anjou to the throne, but after the crowning of Henry (1154) the rest of his episcopate was uneventful. He died on April 18, 1161. A highly competent administrator but not a great spiritual leader, his household was a notable ecclesiastical training ground, producing four archbishops and six bishops. Theobald is chiefly famous as patron of Becket, whom he made archdeacon of Canterbury, and of John of Salisbury, the historian and philosopher; and by bringing to Oxford Vacarius the Mantuan jurist he laid the foundations of the serious study of Roman law in England.

*See* A. Saltman, *Theobald, Archbishop of Canterbury* (1956).

(G. W. S. B.)

**THEOBALD, LEWIS** (1688–1744), English man of letters, playwright, and the first modern Shakespearean scholar, was born at Sittingbourne, Kent, son of an attorney. He was educated for the law but soon turned to literature, publishing translations (Plato's *Phaedo,* 1713; plays of Sophocles and Aristophanes, 1714–15; etc.), bad poetry, and plays.

Theobald's importance as a Shakespearean editor, however, overshadows his unsuccessful literary career. In 1725 Alexander Pope brought out his edition of Shakespeare, and this won from Theobald a year later *Shakespeare Restored; or a Specimen of the many Errors as well Committed as Unamended by Mr. Pope in his late edition of this Poet; designed . . . to restore the true Reading of Shakespeare in all the Editions ever published.* Some of Theobald's happiest emendations are to be found in this work, but in view of the arrogant title it is perhaps understandable that it enraged Pope and caused him to make Theobald the hero of his *Dunciad.* In 1734 Theobald produced his edition of Shakespeare in seven volumes. He was the first editor to approach the text of Shakespeare with the kind of attention that was given to classical texts. He gave the readings of the early editions more authority than his own taste, and he used contemporary parallels as a guide to emendation. His emendation to the passage on Falstaff's death "and a' babbled of green fields" (Folio: "A table of green fields") was a brilliant stroke that became part of the standard text. However, Theobald's text is still based on the Fourth Folio, via the Pope he despised, and he appears to have consulted the First Folio and the quartos only when he suspected error in the text before him. Samuel Johnson said of Theobald that he was "a man of narrow comprehension and small acquisitions, with no native and intrinsic splendour of genius, with little of the artificial light of learning but zealous for minute accuracy and not negligent in pursuing it." This somewhat unjust appraisal was general, but Theobald nonetheless introduced, however intermittently, methods of the first importance in approaching Shakespeare's text. He died on Sept. 18, 1744, in London.

Bibliography.—For a highly favourable account of Theobald's work *see* J. Churton Collins, "Theobald, the Porson of Shakespearean Criticism," *Quarterly Review,* vol. clxxv (1892), reprinted in *Essays and Studies* (1895). *See* also D. Nichol Smith, *Shakespeare in the 18th Century* (1928); R. B. McKerrow, *The Treatment of Shakespeare's Text by His Earliest Editors, 1709–1768,* British Academy lecture (1933). (M. Kl.)

**THEOBROMINE:** *see* Purines.

**THEOCRITUS** (*c.* 310–250 B.C.), Greek poet born in Syracuse, was the creator of pastoral poetry. His poems were termed idylls (*eidyllia*) by the grammarians. The word is a diminutive of *eidos* and may mean "little poems." Some, however, interpret it as meaning "forms"; *i.e.,* the bucolic, epic or lyric forms, and apply it to Theocritus' poems because they are of many different types.

There are no sure facts as to Theocritus' life beyond those supplied by idylls xv, xvi, and xvii. One view is that after composing xvi and perhaps iv and v Theocritus left Sicily and joined the circle of Philetas in Cos, but soon found his way to Alexandria. Later, on this view, he left Egypt and went either to Cos again or to some other place; *e.g.,* Rhodes, in the eastern Aegean. Idyll vii was almost certainly written in Cos, but probably after the visit to Egypt. The rest of the poems, except xv and xvii, which were no doubt composed in Egypt, may belong to either of the visits to Cos or to that to Alexandria.

The writings of Theocritus must be handled with caution as some of the poems commonly attributed to him have little claim to authenticity. It is possible that at an early date two collections were made, one of which included a number of doubtful poems and formed a corpus of bucolic poetry, while the other was confined to those works which were considered to be by Theocritus himself. The record of these recensions is perhaps preserved by two epigrams in the Palatine anthology, one of which (9:205) proceeds from Artemidorus, the grammarian, who lived in the time of Sulla and is thought by some to have been the first editor of the bucolic poets. He says "Bucolic muses, once were ye scattered, but now one byre, one herd is yours." The second epigram (*Anth. Pal.* 9:434) is anonymous, and is translated as follows: "The Chian is another. I, Theocritus, who wrote these songs, am one of the many Syracusans, the son of Praxagoras and famed Philinna. I never sought after a strange muse." The last line may mean he wrote nothing but bucolic poems, or that he wrote only in Doric. The statement that he was a Syracusan is confirmed by allusions in the idylls. The Suda Lexicon states that besides the bucolic poems some persons also attribute to Theocritus the following: *Daughters of Proetus, Hopes, Hymns, Heroines, Dirges, Lyrics, Elegies, Iambics, Epigrams.* Except for the *Hymns, Lyrics* and *Epigrams* these works are lost.

**Authentic Poems.**—The poems which are generally held to be authentic comprise bucolics and mimes, epics, lyrics and epigrams.

*Bucolics and Mimes.*—The distinction between these is that the scenes of the former are laid in the country and those of the latter in a town. The most famous of the bucolics are i, vii, xi and vi. In i Thyrsis sings to a goatherd how Daphnis, the mythical herdsman, having defied the power of Aphrodite, dies rather than yield to a passion with which the goddess had inspired him. In xi Polyphemus is depicted as in love with the sea nymph Galatea and finding solace in song; in vi he is cured of his passion and naïvely relates how he repulses the overtures now made to him by Galatea. The monster of the *Odyssey* has been "written up to date" after the Alexandrian manner and has become a gentle simpleton. Idyll vii, the *Harvest Home,* is the most important of the bucolic poems. The scene is laid in the isle of Cos. The poet speaks in the first person and is styled Simichidas by his friends. Other poets are possibly introduced under feigned names, but the only certain identification is that of Sicelidas (line 40) as Asclepiades of Samos. Theocritus declares that he is not yet superior to the latter nor to Philetas of Cos, said to have been his teacher, but boasts that his lays have been brought by report even unto the throne of Zeus, meaning apparently that they have secured the approval of Ptolemy Philadelphus. In lines 47–48 he criticizes "the fledgelings of the Muses, who cackle against the Chian bard and find their labour lost," thus taking the side of Callimachus in his controversy with Apollonius Rhodius over the merits of epic poetry.

The other bucolic poems are less interesting. Several consist of a singing match, conducted according to the rules of amoebaean poetry, in which the second singer takes the subject chosen by the first and contributes a variation in the same air. The peasants of Theocritus differ greatly in refinement. Those in v are low fellows who indulge in coarse abuse. This idyll and iv are laid in the neighbourhood of Crotona in southern Italy, and it seems that Theocritus was personally acquainted with Magna Graecia. Suspicion has been cast on viii and ix for various reasons. It is clear that they were in Virgil's Theocritus and that they passed the scrutiny of the editor who formed the short collection of Theocritean *Bucolics.* Nevertheless, ix at any rate is not by Theocritus.

The mimes are three in number, viz., ii, xiv, xv. In ii Simaetha, deserted by Delphis, tells the story of her love to the moon; in xiv Aeschines narrates his quarrel with his sweetheart, and is advised to go to Egypt and enlist in the army of Philadelphus; in xv Gorgo and Praxinoa go to the festival of Adonis at Alexandria. These three mimes are wonderfully natural and lifelike.

It is convenient to add to the bucolics and mimes three poems which cannot be brought into any other class: xii, a poem to a beautiful youth; xviii, the marriage song of Helen; and xxvi, the murder of Pentheus. The genuineness of the last has been attacked on account of certain crudities, but the evidence of the manuscripts and papyri is in favour of the poem. Eustathius quotes from it as the work of Theocritus.

*Epics.*—Two of these are encomia. In xvi the poet praises Hieron II of Syracuse, in xvii Ptolemy Philadelphus. Two are hymns, xxii to the Dioscuri and xxiv to Heracles; xiii is an epyllion, or short epic, the story of Hylas and the nymphs. It cannot be said that Theocritus exhibits signal merit in his epics. In xiii he shows some skill in word painting, in xvi a passage at the end, where he foretells the joys of peace after the enemy has been driven out of Sicily, has the true bucolic ring. The most that can be said of xxii and xxiv is that they are very dramatic. Three poems in this group can be dated, though only approximately. In xvii Theocritus celebrates the marriage of Ptolemy Philadelphus with his sister Arsinoë. This marriage is held to have taken place in 277 B.C., and Arsinoë died in June 270. This poem, therefore, together with xv, which mentions (lines 23–24) the queen as alive, must fall within this period. So probably does a lost poem called *Berenice*.

The encomium of Hieron seems prior to that of Philadelphus, since in it Theocritus is a hungry poet seeking for a patron, while in the other he is well satisfied with the world. Hieron first came to the front in 276–275 B.C., when he was made "general"; Theocritus speaks of his achievements as still to come (line 73), and the silence of the poet would show that Hieron's marriage to Philistis, his victory over the Mamertines at the Longanus river and his election as "king," events which are ascribed to 270–269 B.C., had not yet taken place.

*Lyrics.*—These number four, xxviii–xxxi. The first is a very graceful poem presented together with a distaff to Theugenis, wife of Nicias, a doctor of Miletus, on the occasion of a voyage thither undertaken by the poet. The three other lyrics are all pederastic.

*Epigrams.*—These, numbering 24, are without special merit, and their authenticity is often doubtful.

**Doubtful Poems.**—There remain the poems which are generally considered spurious. They are as follows: xix, *Love Stealing Honey,* which is anonymous in the manuscripts and has a conception of love that is not Theocritean.

Of the next group—xx, *The Herdsman,* xxi, *The Fishermen,* xxiii, *The Lover*—only xxi possesses any merit. A more interesting poem is xxv, *Heracles the Lion-Slayer*. This is a long poem consisting of three episodes, the interview of Heracles with Augeas' bailiff, the review of the king's cattle and Heracles' recital to Phyleus, the son of Augeas, of the story of the Nemean lion. The composition is not unworthy of Theocritus. *The Wooing,* xxvii, contains imitations of Theocritus, but the tone and the language betray a later writer.

**Language and Metre.**—Theocritus wrote in various dialects according to the subject. The lyrics are in Aeolic, that being the traditional dialect for such poems; xii and xxii were written in Ionic, as is stated in titles prefixed to them, but a number of Doric forms have been inserted by the scribes. The epics in general show a mixture of Homeric, Ionic and Doric forms. The bucolics, mimes and the marriage song of Helen are in Doric, with occasional forms from other dialects.

The metre used by Theocritus in the bucolics and mimes, as well as in the epics, is the dactylic hexameter. A feature in his verse which has attracted much attention is the so-called bucolic caesura. The rule is that, if there is a pause at the end of the fourth foot, this foot must be a dactyl. This pause is common in Homer, but Theocritus uses it so frequently in the bucolics that it has become a mannerism. In the epics his practice agrees with that of Homer.

Like all the Alexandrians Theocritus had no scruples about borrowing with a variation from earlier Greek writers. Homeric phrases, adapted to a new setting, crop up everywhere in his verse, but he was no slavish imitator, and despite the scholiast it seems very improbable that in ii and xv he owed any considerable debt to Sophron, the Sicilian writer of mimes. The latter idyll has resemblances to the fourth mime of Herodas, but which preceded the other it is impossible to determine.

**Theocritus' Place in Poetry.**—Like his contemporary Callimachus, Theocritus was an accomplished literary artist and modern scholarship has thrown much light on the details of his craftsmanship, but, whereas the poems of Callimachus (admittedly most survive only in fragments) must remain "caviare to the general," Theocritus makes a universal appeal to the modern reader for the reason that his bucolics and mimes, however elegantly and at times eruditely expressed, reflect human nature, which Callimachus' poetry never does. This truth needs no demonstration as regards the mimes. Cynisca and her lover (in xiv) and Gorgo and Praxinoa (in xv) are manifestly real; so too, on a higher level of art, is Simaetha (in ii), as she recounts her betrayal.

The bucolics, however, have sometimes been criticized as attributing to peasants sentiments and language beyond their capacity. There is something in the criticism, but comparison with modern Greek folk songs, which owe little to literary influences, reveals many striking resemblances between them and Theocritus' bucolics and there can be little doubt that both derive from real life. That life, set in a Mediterranean scenery of flowers, sun, sea and mountainside and described by a master of style, will never lose its charm.

BIBLIOGRAPHY.—*Editions with commentary, etc.:* A. S. F. Gow, *Theocritus,* 2 vol., 2nd ed. (1952), vol. i containing introduction, text and Eng. trans., vol. ii commentary; J. M. Edmonds, *The Greek Bucolic Poets,* with Eng. trans., "Loeb Series" (1912); P. Legrand, *Bucoliques grecs,* with text, French trans. and short notes, vol. i, 3rd ed. (1946), vol. ii (1927).

*Editions of text only:* C. Gallavotti, *Theocritus quique feruntur bucolici Graeci* (1946); A. S. F. Gow, *Bucolici Graeci* (1952).

*Translations:* A. Lang, "Golden Treasury Series" (1906); A. S. F. Gow (1953); J. H. Hallard, in verse, 4th ed. (1924).

*Scholia and history of text:* C. Wendel, *Scholia in Theocritum vetera* (1914), *Überlieferung und Entstehung der Theokrit-Scholien* (1920); U. von Wilamowitz-Moellendorff, *Die Textgeschichte der griechischen Bukoliker* (1906); R. J. Smutny, *The Text History of the Epigrams of Theocritus* (1955).

*General:* P. Legrand, *Étude sur Théocrite* (1898); E. Bignone, *Teocrito* (1934). (E. A. B.)

**THEODOLITE,** a surveying instrument used for measuring horizontal and, more often, vertical angles. It is essentially a high-precision transit consisting of an alidade with telescope, accurately graduated circles for reading horizontal and vertical angles, and the necessary level vials and reading devices. The theodolite is the basic instrument in surveying, especially in precise triangulation.

There are two general types of theodolites: direction theodolites and repeating theodolites. In the direction theodolite the graduated horizontal circle remains fixed while the telescope is pointed on several objects in turn and the direction to each is read on the horizontal circle. The value of an angle is obtained by determining differences between the observed directions. In the repeating theodolite the same angle is measured a number of times, the successive values of these measurements are accumulated on the circle, and the final reading represents the total arc described by the accumulated measurements. The desired value is then obtained by dividing the final reading by the number of repetitions. Two types of direction theodolites are in use. On the micrometer type, the circle is read by means of two micrometer-microscopes mounted diametrically opposite one another. In the optical-reading type, the circles, which are graduated on glass, are read by means of an auxiliary eyepiece mounted adjacent to the main telescope.

The phototheodolite is an instrument used in terrestrial photogrammetry and consists of a combination of a camera and theodolite mounted on the same tripod. The transit is a variety of theodolite that has a telescope mounted so that it can be completely reversed or transited. A special low-precision theodolite that measures the angular horizontal drift and angle of elevation of pilot balloons is used in meteorological observations of wind direction. (K. S. Cs.)

**THEODORA** (*c.* 500–548), wife of the Byzantine emperor Justinian I (*q.v.*), was born presumably in Constantinople. According to Procopius, the chief but by no means entirely reliable authority for her life, she was the daughter of Acacius, a bear-keeper in the circus at Constantinople, and while still a child appeared on the stage.

Becoming a noted courtesan, she accompanied a certain Hecebolus to Pentapolis (in north Africa), of which he had been appointed governor. Having quarreled with him, she returned first to Alexandria and then went back to Constantinople through the cities of Asia Minor. In Constantinople she attracted the notice of Justinian. He desired to marry her and eventually achieved this by getting his uncle, the emperor Justin I, to repeal the law forbidding the marriage of senators with actresses (523). On Justin's death Justinian and Theodora became sole rulers of the Roman world (527). He was then about 44 years of age, and she about 20 years younger.

Theodora speedily acquired great influence over her husband. At a time of acute crisis when the Nika insurrection broke out in

532, her courage and firmness in refusing to fly when the rebels were attacking the palace was a contributing factor in saving her husband's crown. In the religious controversy which divided the empire, Theodora sided with the Monophysites and strongly supported the heretics of Egypt and Syria. After her marriage she lived a strictly moral life, and as empress she instituted homes for prostitutes. She was delicate in health and died early, perhaps of cancer, on June 29, 548. In appearance she was small in stature and rather pale, but with a graceful figure, beautiful features and a piercing glance. In the apse of the church of San Vitale at Ravenna there is a striking contemporary mosaic portrait of her. Whatever her early life there can be no doubt about her beauty, intellectual gifts and imperious will. (J. M. Hy.)

MANSELL—ALINARI

THEODORA AND ATTENDANTS: FROM A MOSAIC IN THE CHURCH OF SAN VITALE, RAVENNA

**THEODORE, SAINT** (602–690), archbishop of Canterbury from 668 to 690, the first archbishop to rule the whole English church, was appointed by the pope after the English candidate, Wigheard, had died in Rome, and Hadrian, the African abbot of a monastery near Naples, had refused the preferment. The choice of Theodore, a Greek from Tarsus, already 66 years old, seems extraordinary but proved successful. He was consecrated on March 26, 668, and set out from Rome on May 27, with Abbot Hadrian, who was sent to ensure that he instituted no Greek practices, and the Anglo-Saxon Benedict Biscop, later the founder of Monkwearmouth and Jarrow. After various delays, during which Theodore spent some time with Agilberht, bishop of Paris, who had been bishop in Wessex and could inform him of conditions in the English church, he reached Canterbury on May 27, 669. He made Hadrian abbot of the monastery of St. Peter and St. Paul, Canterbury, and between them they created a famous school, which drew pupils from all over the country and from Ireland, including the distinguished scholar Aldhelm. It taught Greek as well as Latin, the interpretation of the Scriptures, church music, computation, and some medicine. Through Benedict Biscop, its influence reached Bede.

Theodore brought order into the English church. Many sees were vacant on his arrival; others needed to be divided. He made a visitation of his province, filled the vacancies at Dunwich, Rochester, and Winchester, and put Wilfrid at York, removing Chad, whom later he made bishop of Lichfield. To divide dioceses was more difficult. When, in 672, he called at Hertford the first general synod of the English church, the division had to be postponed. Later he divided the East Anglian see into Dunwich and Elmham, and Northumbria into York, Lindisfarne, and Hexham; and established sees at Worcester and Hereford and for Lindsey. At times there was a separate see for the Middle Angles, at Leicester.

He eradicated Celtic usages. The synod of Hertford imposed the Roman Easter and laid down that bishops should not interfere in other dioceses, and clerics and monks should not wander without the permission of their superiors. It established an annual synod at Clofesho (a place not yet identified), and it reaffirmed the church teaching on marriage and divorce. A synod at Hatfield on Sept. 17, 679, was held to affirm the freedom of the English church from the Monothelite heresy. His *Penitential,* a collection of his rulings made by his disciples, shows that he had to deal with heathen practices as well as various moral offenses and reveals his wisdom and humanity in allowing remarriage after five years to those separated by captivity or other hopeless circumstances. This penitential was to become very influential on the continent as well as in England. It is probable that he introduced the use of written documents to confirm grants of land to the church.

Theodore lived to be 88, dying on Sept. 19, 690. In his later years he was present at the Council of Twyford in Northumbria, which elected Cuthbert as bishop, and he consecrated him in 685. In 686 his quarrel with Wilfrid, begun when he divided the diocese of Northumbria, was composed. No biography of him has survived, and too little is known of this remarkable man. The strength of his influence is shown by his securing a settlement after the Battle of the Trent (678, between Egfrith of Northumbria and Aethelred of Mercia) without any vengeance being taken for the Northumbrian prince slain in it. His dealings with Wilfrid and his deposition of Chad from York and of Winfrith from Lichfield show that he could take firm action, but the great success of his reorganization implies a power to secure the cooperation of others.

BIBLIOGRAPHY.—Bede, *Historia ecclesiastica, Historia abbatum; Aldhelmi Opera,* ed. by R. Ehwald (1919); *Poenitentiale Theodori,* in *Councils and Ecclesiastical Documents Relating to Great Britain and Ireland,* ed. by A. W. Haddan and W. Stubbs, vol. iii, pp. 173–213; F. M. Stenton, *Anglo-Saxon England,* 2nd ed. (1947). (D. Wk.)

**THEODORE, SAINT,** STUDITES (759–826), Byzantine abbot and leading opponent of iconoclasm (*see* ICONOCLASTIC CONTROVERSY), was born in Constantinople, where he received a careful education with a view to entering the imperial civil service. But, under the influence of his uncle Plato, he became a monk and later joint abbot of the monastery of Saccudion in Bithynia. His first involvement in politics resulted from his opposition to the adulterous second marriage of the emperor Constantine VI (795); Theodore was exiled to Thessalonica, but after the emperor's overthrow in 797 he was recalled by the empress Irene. Thereafter the whole community of Saccudion was transferred to the monastery of Studius in Constantinople, of which Plato and Theodore became abbots. In 806 Theodore entered into conflict with the patriarch Nicephorus, was condemned by a council, and exiled a second time (809–811). When iconoclasm was revived by Leo V, Theodore became the leader of the opposition and was once more exiled (816–820). Recalled by Michael II, whose sympathies lay nevertheless with the iconoclastic party, Theodore was not allowed to resume the direction of the Studius monastery. With his monks, he spent the remainder of his life in the vicinity of the capital. He died on the island of Prinkipo (modern Buyuk, of the Princes' Islands, in the Sea of Marmara) in 826 on Nov. 11, which is kept as his feast day.

Theodore's writings include homilies, catecheses addressed to the Studite monks, three polemical treatises against the iconoclasts, and nearly 600 letters (a valuable historical source). Theodore's activity was mainly dedicated to the independence of the church from interference on the part of imperial power; since the patriarchs of Constantinople were often obliged to compromise with the emperors, Theodore did not hesitate to oppose the patriarchs as well and appeal over their heads to the pope of Rome, thus establishing a principle of insubordination that was to prove dangerous to the Byzantine church.

BIBLIOGRAPHY.—Most of Theodore's works are in J. P. Migne, *Patrologia Graeca,* vol. 99 (1960). *See* also Alice Gardner, *Theodore of Studium* (1905); J. B. Bury, *A History of the Eastern Roman Empire* (1912); P. J. Alexander, *The Patriarch Nicephorus of Constantinople* (1958); H. G. Beck, *Kirche und theologische Literatur im Byzantinischen Reich* (1959). (C. A. Mo.)

**THEODORE,** the name of two popes.

THEODORE I, pope from November 642 to May 649, was a Greek, born in Jerusalem. Noted for his generosity to the poor, he had to devote most of his attention to the struggle against Monothelitism (*see* MONOTHELITES).

Theodore I refused to recognize the uncanonically installed patriarch of Constantinople, Paul. In 648 he excommunicated Paul's predecessor, Pyrrhus, who had relapsed into Monothelitism, and the next year he declared Paul's deposition for the same heresy.

THEODORE II, pope for 20 days in December 897, recognized the validity of the acts of the deceased Pope Formosus (*q.v.*), whose outraged corpse he reburied. (A. G. Bi.)

**THEODORE** (THEODORE LASCARIS), the name of two Byzantine emperors at Nicaea.

THEODORE I (*c.* 1175–1222), a son-in-law of the emperor Alexius

III by whom he was granted the title of despot, distinguished himself during the sieges of Constantinople by the Latins during the Fourth Crusade (1203–04), and after the capture of the city gathered a band of refugees in Bithynia, first at Brusa and then at Nicaea. While the crusaders fought the Bulgarians in Thrace, Theodore formed a new Byzantine state in Asia Minor and in 1208 assumed the title of emperor. He defended his infant empire not only against the crusaders but also against David Comnenus, a rival Greek emperor in Trebizond, and against the Seljuk Turks, who had come to terms with the Latin emperor Henry and given asylum to the fugitive emperor Alexius III. Theodore, however, defeated and killed the sultan Kaikhosrau in battle at Antioch on the Maeander (1211) and captured Alexius III; and in 1214, after several months of warfare, he made a treaty with Henry defining the frontiers between the Greek empire of Nicaea and the Latin empire of Constantinople and annexed much of the territory of Trebizond. After Henry's death (1216) he further strengthened his position with regard to the Latins by taking as his third wife Maria, daughter of the empress Yolande, and by willingness to discuss union between the Greek and Latin churches. In August 1219 he made a lucrative commercial agreement with the Venetians in Constantinople; and in 1222 he negotiated a settlement with Yolande's son and successor, Robert of Courtenay, to whom he betrothed his daughter Eudocia. He died in the same year, having transformed Nicaea from the centre of a mere resistance movement against the crusaders into the capital of the Byzantine Empire in exile, recognized as the legitimate successor of the empire in Constantinople.

Theodore II (1222–1258), the grandson of Theodore I and son of John III Vatatzes (*q.v.*), whom he succeeded in November 1254, was an able ruler, a good soldier, and a man of letters, although his health and character were increasingly affected by severe attacks of epilepsy. He successfully held together the prosperous state bequeathed to him by his father, but his somewhat autocratic policy brought him into conflict with many of his nobles and military commanders. He led two victorious campaigns against the Bulgarians (1255–56), who had broken the bounds set to their dominions in Thrace by John III; but his attempt to take advantage of his Greek rival, the despot of Epirus, by marrying his daughter to the despot's son provoked serious warfare in Macedonia. He died in August 1258, having aggravated the mistrust of the army and the aristocracy by appointing a commoner, George Muzalon, as regent for his infant son, John IV.

Bibliography.—G. Ostrogorsky, *History of the Byzantine State* (1956); A. Gardner, *The Lascarids of Nicaea* (1912); J. B. Papadopoulos, *Theodore II Lascaris* (1908). For Theodore II's epistles, *see* edition by N. Festa (1895). (D. M. N.)

**THEODORE** of Mopsuestia (*c.* 350–428/429), an eminent early Christian theologian, was born at Antioch (in modern Turkey). Together with his friend St. John Chrysostom he studied rhetoric under the celebrated pagan sophist Libanius, with the intention of becoming a lawyer. But in 369 under the influence of Chrysostom he turned to ascetic life, entered the school of Diodore of Tarsus in a monastery near Antioch, and spent some time as a monk. Two letters written to him by Chrysostom show that his decision had caused him trouble and that he contemplated turning back; but the advice of his respected friend became decisive for his future.

The chronology of Theodore's life can be established only very generally. There is evidence that he was still alive in 428, but his death must have occurred soon after this. He must have become bishop of Mopsuestia in Cilicia (the modern Misis near Adana in southern Turkey) about 392, since Theodoret (*Historia ecclesiastica*) says his episcopate lasted 36 years.

Theodore was an important figure among the patristic authorities. Not only was he active in all the theological controversies in the contemporary Greek-oriental church but he also was an author of note. He is reported to have started his exegetical works in 402/403, and it is known that he had written some works earlier, including 15 books on the incarnation. But all these were merely a prelude to a literary outburst that astounded his contemporaries.

Those of Theodore's works that have survived in their original Greek are only remnants which do not give an idea of the scope of his writing. The Nestorian scholar 'Abdisho made a list of them which gives the titles of 41 volumes. It indicates that Theodore wrote commentaries on almost all the biblical books as well as works on theological and practical problems such as the incarnation, the sacraments, the Holy Spirit, priesthood, exegetical method, theological controversies and monasticism.

An important event in the transmission of Theodore's works was their translation into Syriac in the school of Edessa under the directorship of Qiyore (d. *c.* 437). Before that, the works of Ephraem Syrus had been used for instruction; afterward those of Theodore became normative. Even more important to modern historians, because of this translation a number of Theodore's lost works have been salvaged in Syriac. His commentary on the Fourth Gospel has long been known, but later discoveries have brought to light a disputation held in Anazarbus and commentaries on the Lord's Prayer, the Nicene Creed and the sacraments. His work on the incarnation was discovered in a codex in Seert, Turkey, but unfortunately the collection of manuscripts was destroyed in World War I.

The man who speaks through these works compels admiration. He is a scholar of astounding knowledge. In thoroughness and consistency of thought he is surpassed by none among his contemporaries and predecessors. As an independent inquirer he approached problems with critical standards unheard of in the ancient church. Instead of allegorical interpretation Theodore used scientific, critical, philological and historical methods, anticipating much in modern scholarship. In literary critical analysis he took into account the historical circumstances in which the biblical books were written; thus in regard to the Psalms he anticipated the modern view that many of them belong to the 2nd century B.C., and as a result of these criteria he rejected as uncanonical a number of books, including Chronicles, Esdras and the Catholic Epistles.

In his theology he insisted on the separation of the two natures, divine and human, in the person of Christ, based on his psychological analysis of personality. Since only elements of the same substance can become one, and since the human nature must find its expression hypostatically, Theodore could not conceive of a complete union between the two natures. The only way feasible was the union in terms of some kind of *synapheia* or voluntary and moral union, comparable to that between man and wife or body and soul. At the heart of his Christological definition lies the biblical thought-world with its concrete imagery. As such Theodore's Christology has provided a balance against the wave of ontological conceptions of the Alexandrians, drawn from philosophical abstractions. Through his appreciation of the human nature in Christ, and his keen interest in the biblical evidence, Theodore saved Christendom from falling into pure and shoreless speculation. His merit is that at least in principle the human nature in Christ was secured at the Council of Chalcedon (451).

As the greatest exegete and the spiritual head of the Antiochian school, Theodore became the leader for a number of outstanding spirits of the 4th and 5th centuries. The Nestorian church regards him as "the holy friend of God" and "the Interpreter" (*see* Nestorians). The Monophysite and Orthodox churches saw in him the arch-heretic. However, Theodore died at peace with the church; only once is it recorded that opposition rose against his views, expressed at Antioch in a sermon against the use of the term *Theotokos,* "God-bearer," as a title of the Virgin Mary (*see* Mary). The wave of controversy rose to its height soon after his death and was eagerly supported by the Alexandrians. Theodore's views and writings were condemned at the council of Constantinople (553; *see* Council).

Bibliography.—L. Pirot, *L'oeuvre exégétique de Théodore de Mopsueste* (1913); A. Mingana, *Synopsis of Christian Doctrine in the 4th Century According to Theodore of Mopsuestia* (1920); J. M. Vosté, "La chronologie de l'activité de Théodore," in *Revue biblique,* p. 54 ff. (1925); L. Patterson, *Theodore of Mopsuestia and Modern Thought* (1926); A. Mingana (ed.), *Woodbrooke Studies,* v–vi (1932–33); F. J. Reine, *The Eucharistic Doctrine and Liturgy of the Mystagogical Catecheses of Theodore of Mopsuestia* (1942); H. Devreesse, *Essai sur Théodore de Mospsueste* (1948); F. A. Sullivan, *The Christology of Theodore of Mopsuestia* (1956); R. A. Greer, *Theodore of Mopsuestia* (1961); L. Abramowski, "Zur Theologie Theodors von

Mopsuestia," *Zeitschrift für Kirchengeschichte,* LXX (1961); R. A. Norris, *Manhood and Christ: a Study in the Christology of Theodore of Mopsuestia* (1963); A. Vööbus, *The School of Nisibis* (1964). (AR. VÖ.)

**THEODORET** (*c.* 386–*c.* 466, or *c.* 393–*c.* 458), bishop of Cyrrhus (in Syria), an important Christian writer in the areas of exegesis, dogmatic theology, church history, and ascetic theology. His chief importance is as a dogmatic theologian—as the most considerable opponent of the Christological views of Cyril and Dioscorus of Alexandria and the friend, though not entirely supporter, of Nestorius. Theodoret was born in Antioch. At an early age he entered the cloister, and in 423 he became bishop of Cyrrhus, a small city in a wild district between Antioch and the Euphrates. There, except for a short period of exile, he spent the remainder of his life.

As an exegete Theodoret belongs to the Antiochene school, of which Diodore of Tarsus and Theodore of Mopsuestia were the heads. He was not actually the personal disciple of either, but he adopted their literal-historical methods, though without the consistency and boldness of Diodore. His extant commentaries (on the Song of Solomon, on the Prophets, on the Book of Psalms and on the Pauline Epistles) are brief.

For more than 20 years Theodoret maintained the struggle against the Alexandrian dogmatic and its formulas and taught that in the person of Christ we must strictly distinguish two natures (*hypostases*), which are united indeed in one person (*prosopon*) but are not amalgamated in essence. For these years his history coincides with that of the Eastern Church from 430 to 451, and for this reason it is impossible to sketch it even briefly here. The issue, not unfavourable to Theodoret's cause, was melancholy enough for Theodoret himself: the Council of Chalcedon (451) condemned Monophysitism, but Theodoret was obliged to take part in pronouncing "anathema upon Nestorius, and upon all who call not the Holy Virgin God-bearer [*Theotokos*], and who divide the one Son into two." (For details about this important theological controversy, *see* JESUS CHRIST: *The Dogma of Christ in The Ancient Councils*; CYRIL, SAINT; NESTORIUS.)

Some of Theodoret's dogmatic works are no longer extant. Of his five books *On the Incarnation,* for example, directed against Cyril after the Council of Ephesus, only fragments remain. A good deal of what passes under his name has been wrongly attributed to him. Certainly genuine are the refutation of Cyril's 12 anathematisms of Nestorius (later a subject of the Three Chapters controversy and condemned by the second Council of Constantinople in 553); and *The Mendicant* (*Eranistes*), or *Polymorphus* (written about 446), consisting of three dialogues, entitled, respectively, "Immutability," "Inconfusibility," and "Apathy," in which the Monophysitism of Cyril is opposed and its Apollinarian character insisted on. Among the apologetico-dogmatic works of Theodoret must be reckoned his ten discourses *On Providence.*

The 30 ascetic biographies of his *Religious History,* which has been widely read, form a pendant to the *Historia Lausiaca* of Palladius; for the East it has had the same importance as the similar writings of Jerome, Sulpicius Severus, and John Cassian for the West. His *Church History* carries the work of Eusebius down to 428. Theodoret's *Therapeutike* is one of the finest Christian apologetic works; and 232 of his letters have survived.

Theodoret's collected works were edited by J. Sirmond, 4 vol. (1642), and afterward completed by J. Garnier (1648). A reprint of this with additions, by J. L. Schulze and J. A. Nösselt, may be found in J. P. Migne, *Patrologia Graeca,* vol. lxxx–lxxxiv. The *Church History* was edited by L. Parmentier (2nd ed., 1954). The *Correspondance* (vol. i, 1955) and *Thérapeutique* (1958) were edited with French translations in the "Sources Chrétiennes" series.

BIBLIOGRAPHY.—O. Bardenhewer, *Geschichte der altchristlichen Literatur,* vol. iv, pp. 219–246 (1924); articles in Schaff-Herzog, *Encyclopedia,* and Smith and Wace, *Dictionary of Christian Biography;* and the sympathetic sketch by J. H. Newman, "The Trials of Theodoret," in *Historical Sketches,* vol. ii. (A. HA.; E. R. HY.)

**THEODORIC** THE GREAT, Ostrogothic king of Italy from 493 to 526, was born *c.* 454–455, the son of Theodemir and Ereriliva. About the time of Theodoric's birth the Ostrogoths were living under the rule of Theodemir and his two brothers in northern Pannonia as federates of the Romans. As a result of a dispute between them and the Eastern Roman government in 461, Theodoric was sent as a hostage to Constantinople, where he received a Roman upbringing, though it is said that he never learned to write. In 469 he was allowed to return to his people, among whom he quickly won fame as a warrior. Theodemir died *c.* 471, and in that year Theodoric was elected as his successor. Before 475 he had led his people down the Danube from Pannonia to Lower Moesia. A number of Ostrogoths in Roman service at this time were led by one Theodoric Strabo; and in the war between Basiliscus and Zeno (*qq.v.*) Strabo supported the former, while Theodoric upheld Zeno. When Zeno recovered his throne, he gave Theodoric the post of master of soldiers, which Strabo had hitherto held; he also appointed him patrician and even adopted him as a son. In the years following 477 great confusion was caused in the Balkan provinces by the rivalry of the two groups of Ostrogoths and by Zeno's attempts to play off one against the other. Much devastation was caused by the marches and countermarches of the various armies, and several cities were sacked. But in 481 Strabo died as a result of a fall from his horse; and in 483 Theodoric and his people were settled by the Romans in parts of Moesia and Dacia Ripensis. In 484 Theodoric was appointed consul; but hostilities between him and the empire broke out again in 486, and in 487 he almost captured Constantinople itself. Zeno finally rid himself of the troublesome Ostrogoths by appointing Theodoric to supersede Odoacer (*q.v.*) in Italy. Theodoric set out from Moesia in 488 and arrived in Italy in 489. On Aug. 28 he defeated Odoacer on the Sontius (Isonzo) River and a month later defeated him again near Verona. Odoacer fled to Ravenna but was able to face Theodoric once more in the following year. On Aug. 11, 490, Odoacer was utterly defeated on the Addua (Adda) River and again fled to Ravenna. All the rest of Italy and Sicily now came over to Theodoric, but Ravenna held out against him for 2½ years. It was only on March 5, 493, that Theodoric was able to enter the city after an agreement that the two antagonists should rule Italy jointly. But Theodoric treacherously killed Odoacer with his own hand on March 15 and also had Odoacer's surviving soldiers massacred.

In 497 his position in Italy was defined and recognized by the East Roman government. Italy was to remain part of the Roman Empire. Theodoric still held his post of master of soldiers, which had been confirmed in 483, and, although he was in many ways an independent ruler, he was to recognize the overlordship of the emperor at Constantinople. Thus, although Theodoric could modify existing Roman laws, he could not originate any new legal principle. He was allowed to nominate one consul each year, but he was not allowed to appoint a Goth to this post. The Roman civil administration was retained in Italy, but all Goths were excluded from holding office in it and from sitting in the Roman Senate. On the other hand, the army was exclusively Gothic, and no Roman was liable to military service. Intermarriage between Roman and barbarian had been forbidden on pain of death by Valentinian I (*q.v.*); and this law still remained in force. But there was one matter in which the Romans of Italy felt themselves to be wronged: all lawsuits between Romans and Goths were to be heard by Gothic military courts.

Theodoric and his people differed from the Romans in religion, for they were Arian Christians. But Theodoric's religious policy was one of consistent toleration, and he made no effort to fuse the Goths and the Romans in religion or in anything else. His impartiality was such that when two rival popes were appointed in Rome in 498 (*see* SYMMACHUS, SAINT), the Catholics there actually appealed to him to decide between the two claimants. It is true that there were periods of tension between the Goths and Constantinople, but these were few and unimportant. With the barbarians of the West he remained on friendly terms, and this friendship was confirmed by a series of matrimonial alliances with the various royal houses of the Visigoths, Burgundians, Franks, etc. But he could not save the Visigothic kingdom in Gaul from being overthrown by the Franks in 507, though he saved Narbonensis for the Visigoths and annexed Provence for himself.

Theodoric made Ravenna his capital, and there his church, dedicated to St. Martin, still stands, known now as S. Apollinare Nuovo. There still exists, too, the round mausoleum that he built for himself. The peace and prosperity that Italy enjoyed under his rule are highly praised by writers of the time. But the closing years of the reign were clouded by strained relations with Constantinople and with the Vandals of Africa, by tension between the Goths and the Italians, and by the execution of Boëthius (*q.v.*) and other senators on a charge of treason in 524. Theodoric himself died on Aug. 30, 526, having first recommended to the Goths that his grandson Athalaric should succeed him. For events in Italy after his death, *see* AMALASUNTHA; for the German legend, *see* DIETRICH VON BERN. *See* also references under "Theodoric" in the Index.

*See* J. B. Bury, *History of the Later Roman Empire,* esp. vol. i, ch. 12–13, vol. ii, ch. 18 (1923); E. Stein, *Histoire du Bas-Empire,* 2 vol., esp. vol. ii, ch. 3 (1949–59). (E. A. T.)

**THEODOSIUS,** the name of two Roman emperors and a Byzantine emperor.

THEODOSIUS I the Great (347–395), Roman emperor 379–395, was a Spaniard, born at Cauca in Gallaecia, the son of a family of large landowners. His father, also called Theodosius, had served with great distinction under Valentinian I, reconquering Britain in 367–369 from the Saxons, Picts, and Scots, expelling the Sarmatians from Moesia in 371, and crushing the revolt of Firmus in Africa in 375. For unknown reasons, however, the elder Theodosius was put to death at Carthage in 375–376 either by Valentinian or by his son Gratian. The younger Theodosius had distinguished himself in a campaign against the Sarmatians in 374, but on his father's death he retired to his estates in Spain, where he married Aelia Flaccilla *c.* 376. But in 379, after the great defeat and death of Valens (*q.v.*) at the hands of the Visigoths at Adrianople, Theodosius was recalled by Gratian and on Jan. 19 was proclaimed emperor by him at Sirmium. It is not known who suggested the name of Theodosius to Gratian.

Gratian himself undertook the government of the West, leaving Theodosius to deal with the East. His first task was to restore order to the Danubian provinces that had been overrun by the Visigoths following the disaster at Adrianople. He tightened up the army laws so as to bring in more recruits, but despite some minor military victories the Balkan provinces were severely ravaged by the barbarians; it was not until Oct. 3, 382, that he was able to sign a peace treaty with the Visigoths. By the terms of this treaty the Goths were allowed to settle between the Danube and the Balkan mountains, living under their own laws and rulers and united with the Romans only by a military alliance, though they recognized the overlordship of the emperor. This seems to have been the first more or less independent Germanic state to be set up inside the frontiers of the Roman Empire, and the arrangement worked fairly well for the rest of Theodosius' life.

GIRAUDON

THEODOSIUS I THE GREAT

Detail from a late 4th-century silver disk, embossed and engraved. In the Academia de la Historia, Madrid

The emperor was much occupied early in his reign with religious matters. He was the first Roman emperor to dispense with the old pagan title of *pontifex maximus,* and he appears immediately to have determined to establish Catholicism as the state religion of the empire. A law issued on Feb. 28, 380, ordered all the peoples of his realm to subscribe to the dogmas of Nicaea. Arians, Manichaeans, and pagans were assailed in turn. Both legislation and the three Councils of Constantinople were used to establish the power of Catholicism and to define its doctrines (*see* COUNCIL). These measures finally smashed Arianism.

After the suppression of the revolt of Magnus Maximus (*see* MAXIMUS), Theodosius visited Rome in 389. In 390 he had about 3,000 persons massacred at Thessalonica as punishment for a riot; as a result, when he visited Milan, St. Ambrose refused to meet him until he did public penance for his cruelty. In 391 he renewed his attacks on paganism. When Valentinian II died suddenly at Vienne on May 15, 392, a rebellion broke out in Gaul headed by a pagan Frank named Arbogast, who had been Valentinian's leading general. On Aug. 22 Arbogast proclaimed as emperor a Roman professor of rhetoric called Eugenius. The revolt had a decidedly pagan character, although Eugenius personally was a Christian. At first he tried to reach an accommodation with Theodosius, and, while the negotiations were still going on, Arbogast inflicted a severe defeat on the Franks beyond the Rhine in order to secure his rear. Theodosius refused to recognize Eugenius, and the latter occupied Italy in 393; Spain was also in his hands.

In 394 war broke out between the emperor and the usurper. Theodosius aimed at marching to Aquileia, and Arbogast decided to engage him in the valley of the Frigidus (Vipacco) River, a tributary of the Isonzo. On Sept. 5 Theodosius' Gothic troops were repulsed with heavy losses, but the battle was resumed the following day and resulted in a complete victory for the emperor. Eugenius was beheaded, and Arbogast committed suicide. Theodosius then visited Rome once again; but on Jan. 17, 395, he died at Milan. He was succeeded by his sons Arcadius and Honorius (*q.v.*).

THEODOSIUS II (401–450), Eastern Roman emperor 408–450, was born at Constantinople on April 10, 401, the son of Arcadius (*q.v.*) and Eudoxia. He was crowned Augustus on Jan. 10, 402, and became sole ruler of the East when his father died on May 1, 408. His first regent was the able administrator Anthemius, praetorian prefect of the East. On July 4, 414, Theodosius' sister Pulcheria (*q.v.*) was created *Augusta* and soon became her brother's regent; it is not known what became of Anthemius. Pulcheria paid particular attention to her brother's upbringing, and her court was one of great piety. Theodosius, who was of a studious character, was deeply interested in theology and grew into a man of kind and gentle ways.

The chief political problems he had to face were the occupation of Africa by the Vandals in 429 and the accession to power of Attila (*q.v.*) beyond the Danube in 434. The East Roman campaigns against Africa in 431 and 441 were failures, and Theodosius' policy of appeasing Attila did not prevent the great Hun invasions of the Danubian provinces in 441–443 and 447. The reign was also troubled by the heresy of Nestorius (*q.v.*), whom Theodosius appointed patriarch of Constantinople in 428 and who was deposed as a result of the Council of Ephesus in 431. Other important events of the reign were the refortification of Constantinople in 447, the foundation of the University of Constantinople in 425, and the publication of the Theodosian law code in 438 (*see* ROMAN LAW). Nine years were spent in compiling the code, which is a collection of laws issued by the emperors from the time of Constantine the Great to that of Theodosius himself. Theodosius died on July 28, 450, after a hunting accident. He married Eudocia on June 7, 421, and had two daughters, Eudoxia (who married the Western emperor Valentinian III) and Flaccilla, and a son named Arcadius, who died in infancy. (E. A. T.)

THEODOSIUS III (d. after 717), Byzantine emperor from 715 to 717, was an obscure tax collector of southwestern Asia Minor who against his will was proclaimed emperor by the troops of the Opsikion theme rebelling against Anastasius II. His supporters successfully captured Constantinople after a six months' siege, and Anastasius was deposed and entered a monastery. Theodosius was quite unsuited to imperial office and in 717 was forced to abdicate by the able commander of the Anatolikon troops Leo III (*q.v.*) the North Syrian and ended his life in a monastery at Ephesus.

(J. M. HY.)

BIBLIOGRAPHY.—*Theodosius the Great:* A. Piganiol, *L'Empire chrétien: 325–395,* esp. ch. 9–11 (1947); E. Stein, *Histoire du Bas-Empire,* vol. i, ch. 5 (1959). (E. A. T.)

*Theodosius III:* G. Ostrogorsky, *History of the Byzantine State* (1956); J. B. Bury, *History of the Later Roman Empire,* 1st ed., vol. 2 (1889). (J. M. HY.)

**THEODOTION** (fl. 2nd century A.D.), the author of a Greek translation of the Old Testament extant only in parts. Nothing is known of his life; according to Irenaeus (late 2nd century) and Eusebius (4th century), he was a Jewish proselyte of Ephesus. Theodotion's version, which appeared in the sixth column of Origen's Hexapla, is not so much an independent translation as a revision of the Septuagint (*q.v.*), supplying its omissions. Theodotion's version shows acquaintance with Aquila's version (*see* AQUILA). Peculiar Hebrew words are not translated but transliterated into Greek letters, either in order to avoid conjectural readings or to give an authentic colour to the version. Its popularity in the early church can be deduced from its fragments that fill gaps in the Septuagint text of Jeremiah and from its version of Daniel that replaces the Septuagint translation, as well as from its quotations in the New Testament, the *Shepherd* of Hermas, and Justin Martyr. The replacement of Daniel was so thorough that only two manuscripts (Chester Beatty Papyrus IX, of about the 3rd century; and the Codex Chisianus, of the 11th century) of the Greek Old Testament contain the Septuagint version. Theodotion's version of Daniel may go back to an older translation.

(P. A. H. DE B.)

**THEODULF** (THEODULFUS, THEUDULFUS) (*c.* 750–*c.* 821), bishop of Orléans, poet, abbot of Fleury and Saint-Aignan, and one of the leading theologians of the Frankish Empire, was born in mid-8th century, probably in Spain, though some authorities suggest Lombard or Ostrogothic origins. Brought to Charlemagne's court by the emperor, Theodulf became bishop of Orléans in 775 and abbot of Fleury in 781. In 800 he was with Charlemagne in Rome, and in 802 he was involved in dispute with the monastery of St. Martin of Tours and with Alcuin, after whose death he became Charlemagne's chief theological adviser. In 809, before the Council of Aix-la-Chapelle, the emperor consulted him on the procession of the Holy Spirit, and in 811 Charlemagne commanded him to write a treatise on baptism ceremonies, which survives. Theodulf received the pallium from Pope Stephen IV in 816. In 818, after Charlemagne's death, his son Louis I the Pious deposed Theodulf, imprisoning him in a monastery in Angers, for supposed participation in the conspiracy of Bernard of Italy. Theodulf died either in prison or shortly after the amnesty of 821. Legend relates that Louis, riding through Angers, heard Theodulf singing his Palm Sunday sequence through the bars and pardoned him.

Theodulf's poem *Ad Carolum Regem* gives a lively but romanticized picture of Charlemagne surrounded by children, grandchildren, and courtiers. Theodulf, a reformer, established a *hospitium* for travelers and the poor; he was also a patron of the arts and a builder and restorer of churches.

Theodulf's works, edited by J. Sirmond (1646), are reprinted in J. P. Migne, *Patrologia Latina,* vol. cv, 191–380 (1851); *see* also C. Cuissard, *Théodulphe évêque d'Orléans* (1892). (A. FE.)

**THEOGNIS,** Greek elegiac poet, active at Megara in the late 6th and early 5th century B.C. (the tragedian Theognis, mocked by Aristophanes in *Acharnians,* line 11, was a different person). Plato calls the elegiac poet Theognis a citizen of Sicilian Megara (*Laws,* i, 630 A); allusions in his poems make it more likely that he came from Megara in mainland Greece (as some ancient authorities also say). He is said to have written a poem on an unidentifiable episode in the history of Syracuse, and 2,800 lines of admonitory verse, together with (or perhaps including) a collection of maxims, to his beloved, Cyrnus. Fewer than 1,400 lines survive, very unequally divided into two books, each containing a number of short poems in elegiac couplets, many of which are addressed to Cyrnus, son of Polypaüs. Most of the poems in the first book are on admonitory themes, being especially concerned with the advantages and disadvantages of good breeding (both physical and social) in a sadly degenerate world; these are treated sometimes in satirical and sometimes in convivial terms. The poems in Book ii—and some of those in Book i—are erotic, with a marked leaning toward pederasty.

The poems ascribed to Theognis provide more than half the surviving evidence for Greek elegiac poetry of the classical period; they are important also for the picture they give of an aristocratic society in a changing world. They have therefore been much studied, and not least because they were very vulnerable to 19th-century "critical" scholarship: the divisions between the poems are clearly marked, and some passages closely resemble passages attributed elsewhere to other authors. Hence it has been found possible to deny the Theognidean authorship of nearly every piece in the collection; some poems are condemned as plagiarisms, and others because they are thought to be inconsistent in style or argument with those poems that the critic is willing to accept as genuinely Theognidean. Theognis feared both plagiarism and interpolation; a "seal" is to be set upon his verses, to mark the genuine ones (lines 19 ff.)—but the nature of that seal is disputed, and the "Theognidean question" is still open.

BIBLIOGRAPHY.—*Editions:* J. M. Edmonds, *Elegy and Iambus,* vol. 1 (1931), with Eng. trans. in the "Loeb Series"; D. C. C. Young in the "Teubner Series" (1961). *Studies:* E. Harrison, *Studies in Theognis* (1902); C. M. Bowra, *Early Greek Elegists* (1938); W. Jaeger, *Paideia,* vol. 1, book 1, ch. 10 (Eng. trans. 1939); J. Carrière, *Théognis de Mégare* (1948); L. Woodbury, "The Seal of Theognis," in M. E. White (ed.), *Studies in Honour of Gilbert Norwood,* pp. 20–41 (1952). (JN. A. D.)

**THEOLOGICAL EDUCATION, CHRISTIAN.** The Christian church has always been a teaching church, for it began with the life and work of a teacher. Christian theological education, therefore, owes its origins to his remembered command: "You shall love the Lord your God . . . with all your mind."

By the 3rd century Christian schools not only maintained the learning of Greece—dialectics, physics, geometry, astronomy, philosophy, ethics—but added to these the study of the Scriptures, of God himself (or theology) and of piety. Such were the subjects taught in Origen's schools, first at Alexandria, then (A.D. 232) at Caesarea. The school of Lucian at Antioch became known for its historical emphases, that at Edessa for its concern for the Bible. The Nestorian school at Nisibis anticipated the medieval universities in holding its own property, enforcing its own disciplines under its own rules of behaviour and showing other signs of independence, including the exacting of a promise from students to reside at the school and to study. At Constantinople, although theological education in the east always kept itself free from state control, the patriarchal school maintained a friendly, reciprocal relation with the state university which had no faculty of theology.

Following the collapse of Rome and its culture in the 5th century, monastic and episcopal (later cathedral) schools, providing for education from childhood to priesthood, not only preserved the heritage of the ancient world through the dark ages but also led to the establishment of over 50 universities in slightly more than three centuries prior to 1400, among them Bologna (the oldest, 1088), Paris, Oxford and Cambridge.

**The Reformation and After.**—Education in medieval times included grammar, rhetoric and dialectic (the trivium) and mathematics, music, geometry and astronomy (the quadrivium). In the 16th century Philipp Melanchthon enlarged the trivium with Hebrew, Greek and Latin; the inclusion of theology followed. For the Reformers, as earlier for St. Thomas Aquinas, learning was of great importance. The Scriptures were their source of doctrine. The "priesthood of believers" opened the way to individual judgment which needed to be informed and the faithful required instruction to fulfill their new sense of obligation to preach to those outside the church.

Meanwhile the Church of Rome recognized that the Reformation had been caused partly by ignorance, superstition and lack of education among the clergy. At the Council of Trent, therefore, in 1546, legislation was enacted which provided for a liberal education plus professional priestly training for each diocese, permitting poor dioceses to combine, large dioceses to establish more than one seminary, but taxing the church to ensure a sound preparation for the clerical calling.

On the North American continent Harvard college, founded

in 1636, was designed to provide training for responsible service in both church and state but especially in the former. Modeled after Cambridge university, its course of study reflected medieval and Renaissance practices and continued the Reformation stress on biblical teaching and preaching. Thus, the high level of Reformation education was maintained in the new world.

**Changing Patterns.**—During the 18th century a candidate for the Protestant ministry in the British Isles or North America received little education beyond the arts degree to prepare him for his calling. If he did not attend college he would study privately in the home of a parish minister. Or he might pursue theological training in the Protestant universities on the continent of Europe. In 1721 Harvard began in America the differentiation of theological training from general education by the establishment of the Hollis chair of divinity. Yale followed with a similar step in 1756. However, a theological student usually took his "divinity" after completion of his A.B.; the A.B., intended for all, remained the most important part of his training. To the 20th century, both in Protestantism and Catholicism, a sound education in the liberal arts remained a proper foundation for ministerial and priestly studies. "We urge," said Pius XII in the encyclical *Menti Nostrae,* "that the literary and scientific education of future priests be at least not inferior to that of laymen who take similar courses of study."

Toward the close of the 18th century, however, various forces operated strongly further to separate education for the ministry from education for other callings. One of these was the differentiation of occupations in a more highly organized society, leading to the organization of medical schools (King's college [Columbia university], New York, 1767) and schools of law (Litchfield, Conn., 1784) which did not require a previous A.B. The age of reason had run its course and some theological schools were founded in reaction against the influences of 18th-century rationalism upon the universities. Revivalism, the expansion of frontiers, the growth of denominational consciousness accompanying rapid immigration and social stratification, and lively theological controversies all combined to produce a new movement, the creation of independent or separately organized theological schools.

In England, also, medical and legal studies were separated from the undergraduate universities and centred in London. For a time, academies designed for the preparation of Dissenting ministers who were barred from schools of the established church flourished. By the middle of the 19th century, however, these academies had declined and ministerial training became concentrated in theological colleges, many affiliated with universities. It was this pattern that prevailed in the British Isles after 1850. On the continent theological studies, almost entirely pursued in universities, tended to become more concerned with the scientific study of religion and, in Protestant circles, less involved in the equipment of the students for their special ministries.

In North America a school of the Dutch Reformed Church, begun in New York city in 1784, subsequently became the New Brunswick Theological seminary. The reasons for this important departure in theological education were most clearly stated in 1805 by John Mitchell Mason, founder of a less permanent seminary of the Associate Reformed (Presbyterian) Church. Anticipating emphases of a much later day, Mason insisted that the Scriptures be studied in their original languages; that students be encouraged to form independent judgments; that the whole person—body, mind and spirit—be simultaneously strengthened; and that the highest standards of comprehensive thoroughness and intellectual creativity be maintained against all hardened dogmatisms and considerations of expediency. By 1890 about 170 Protestant seminaries had been established, all to some extent indebted to Mason's ideas. Many of these insisted on at least a measure of administrative independence, a college course leading to a B.A. or its equivalent as a requirement for admission, and attendance at the seminary for three academic years of approximately 40 weeks each.

Meanwhile, beginning in 1791 when Archbishop John Carroll established St. Mary's seminary in Baltimore, Roman Catholicism developed new seminaries with the formation of new dioceses. By 1833 there were 7, by 1866 approximately 20 more and by 1945 over 250, some conducting studies at the high school and junior college level (six years), some at the senior college and specifically theological level (another six years), some working in both divisions. Some were under diocesan control, others were under religious orders, but all prepared young men exclusively for the priesthood.

The similarities between Roman Catholic and Protestant seminaries in the early 19th century are striking. Many, both Roman Catholic and Protestant, began as house schools in the home of the teacher or teachers. Gradually separate buildings and increased faculties appeared. Many were connected with a college or school. Plagued by inadequate financial resources, scarcity of students, lack of books and generally low intellectual standards and achievement, many survived for only a short time.

**After 1860.**—Although theological education tends to cling to the past more tenaciously than other disciplines do, it could not escape the influence of the vast changes that have made the modern world. The enormous increase in the study of the physical sciences, the historical-critical method of investigating ancient documents, the economic interpretation of history, the new psychology, the growth of secularization, the rapidly increasing population, the enlarged possibilities of communication, the practical interests of the western world, the threat of atomic warfare—all these and many more had their effect on seminaries and schools of theology that once were isolated from such concerns.

Two main purposes characterizing these schools were summarized in the distinction Edward Pusey made in 1832 when he said that the British educational system was best calculated to form ministers of the church while the German system could best impart knowledge. The priest or minister is taught to be a "parson" or person worthy to represent his calling and to be respected as an ambassador of Christ, a father to a family with which he has close touch. At the same time he is a "cleric" or one who can write—one who possesses the general and special professional knowledge that enables him to maintain and advance understanding of God's ways with man.

Partly, therefore, the problem of theological education is to meet the needs of the churches and of the "coming great church." In response to the expansion of the Christian movement, the increase of population and the interests of great ecclesiastical organizations, seminaries sprang up all over the world in great profusion. In Europe, where theology has been traditionally connected with a university faculty, the number of seminaries remained relatively constant, but in Asia, Africa and Latin America more than 200 Protestant and over 350 Roman Catholic seminaries, plus about a dozen Eastern Orthodox, had emerged by the mid-20th century. In the United States the 15 years after 1945 saw an increase in the number of Roman Catholic seminaries of more than 50% and in the United States and Canada the number of Protestant theological students more than doubled in the second quarter of the 20th century.

For Protestant theological schools, more than for Roman Catholic or Eastern Orthodox, there was in the 20th century, as in the 16th, a considerable expansion of the curriculum, which was generally divided into four main fields: biblical, theological or doctrinal, historical and practical. Although in Europe relatively few courses were introduced, in North America the wide diversity characteristic of the universities' offerings affected the seminary, especially in the fourth or practical field. Frequently courses were offered in the interpretation of culture and the arts, in the nature of the modern world in which the Christian church is set, in rival philosophies and in the understanding of human behaviour. Attempts were made to bring Christian insights of Scripture, theology and history to bear upon the pressing ethical problems of the modern era. Men were trained in the conduct of public worship, in the use of modern methods of communication, in the art of teaching and in the preparation and delivery of various forms of public address. To encourage the maintenance of high standards of theological education, Protestant seminaries in the U.S. and Canada began to meet in biennial conferences in 1918, and in 1936 organized the American Association of Theological Schools.

In reaction to the secularization of modern society, numerous Bible colleges or Bible schools appeared, only a few of which maintain studies at a predominantly postgraduate level. Bible schools generally do not provide the general education that the seminaries require and thus sometimes offer a short cut to the ministry; but not a few seminaries began as Bible schools.

Where theological education is under the control of the state or of a state church, as in Germany, Greece, Scandinavia, the Netherlands and England, the curriculum tends to be more traditional, with a heavy emphasis upon Scripture, its languages and the classical formulations of Christian theology. In Greece and in Sweden the majority of those enrolled in the theological faculties of the universities tend to become lay teachers rather than ordained ministers. Consequently, Greek Orthodoxy, for example, finds most of its theologians among the laity.

The government of theological schools or colleges varies widely from complete independence to direct control by a university, church or department of the state. Roman Catholic schools may be under the direction of diocesan authorities or of religious orders. In the United States and the countries of the "younger churches," there are a few Protestant interdenominational seminaries, and numerous schools in one way or another co-operate with each other. The pattern of a yoked college and seminary is receding in favour of an institution with its own board of trustees and a faculty which determines academic policy. Efforts are being made in many churches to acquaint the membership with the acute problems of the seminaries, their importance as intellectual centres of the church's life and the need to support them generously. Despite denominational rivalries, there are signs of increasing care in the location of new and the removal of older seminaries to ensure co-operation with other seminaries and universities.

Although the dual responsibility of theological schools to provide ministers for rapidly expanding churches and to maintain high standards of theological learning often causes tensions, on the whole this concern for both life and thought, both peoples and principles, both practice and knowledge is healthy. When the demands of the church are uppermost, seminaries tend to be located in places where a strong community life can be fostered and individuals nurtured in prayer, personal discipline, the church's lore and ritual and the denominational program. When the intellectual standards for the ministry are uppermost, preparation for the ministry is likely to be concentrated in university centres and in some way connected with the acquisition of an academic degree. Even in the schools with the strongest denominational ties, however, isolation is diminishing.

On the continent, where theology long insisted on its position as queen of the sciences and theologians were entrenched in university faculties, there has been a movement to establish church high schools, preacher seminars and other forms of auxiliary institutions designed to equip the ministry for its task. Throughout the world increasing stress is being put upon the theological education of the laity, reflected in the German *Kirchentag*—the annual meeting, since 1949, of the Evangelical church laity—and the establishment of over a score of lay academies, the majority in Germany.

BIBLIOGRAPHY.—The traditional prescriptions of the Holy See on clerical education are summarized in *Deus Scientiarum Dominus* (1931) and *Sedes Sapientiae* (1956). *See* also Yorke Allen, Jr., *A Seminary Survey* (1960); J. Cyril Dukehart, S.S., *Catholic Seminaries U.S.A.* (1960); Lloyd Paul McDonald, S.S., *The Seminary Movement in the United States: Projects, Foundations and Early Development (1784–1833)* (1927); William Stephen Morris, *The Seminary Movement in the United States: Projects, Foundations, and Early Development (1833–1866)* (1932); H. Richard Niebuhr, Daniel Day Williams and James M. Gustafson, *The Advancement of Theological Education* (1957); H. Richard Niebuhr, *The Purpose of the Church and Its Ministry* (1956); H. Richard Niebuhr and Daniel Day Williams (eds.), *The Ministry in Historical Perspectives* (1956). (C. L. TA.)

**THEOLOGY (ARTICLES ON):** *see* RELIGION (ARTICLES ON).

**THEOLOGY, CHRISTIAN,** a disciplined reflection upon the truth of Christian revelation, "the science of things divine" (Richard Hooker). The earliest use of the word "theology" in Greek referred to the critical interpretation of the classical myths —a sense that the word has sometimes had in Christian usage as well. Therefore the history of the term "theology," which has engaged the attention of scholars during the 19th and 20th centuries, is, despite its interest, no reliable guide to the meaning of theology; in Thomas Aquinas, for example, "sacred science" is the common term for theology. A more useful introduction to the nature of theology can come from a general analysis of its place as a science, of its sources, and of its functions, followed by a brief delineation of how these three issues are understood in the major Christian groups.

## THEOLOGY AS A SCIENCE

An age that has become accustomed, so rapidly and so completely, to the use of the term "science" exclusively for the empirical investigation of the data of the natural world finds the application of this term to religion an anomaly. Nonbelievers regard such application as presumptuous, believers see it as a betrayal of the uniqueness of religious experience. Yet theology is fully entitled to be called "scientific" if by this one means that it has a prescribed function, a disciplined methodology and a rational structure.

The two other disciplines with which Christian theology has most often been compared and contrasted are philosophy and history. An obvious and common distinction between theology and philosophy is derived from the more basic distinction between reason (or experience) and revelation. Philosophy is a product of the natural reason and deals with the realms of reality that are accessible to reason; theology is charged with the interpretation of a truth that is revealed supernaturally. "Hence there is no reason why those things which are treated by the philosophical sciences, so far as they can be known by the light of natural reason, may not also be treated by another science so far as they are known by the light of the divine revelation. Hence the theology included in sacred doctrine differs in genus from that theology which is part of philosophy" (Thomas Aquinas).

But the very theology of Thomas Aquinas shows that this formal distinction between the tasks of theology and philosophy does not prevent a theologian from interpreting the data of revelation in one particular way because of his commitment to a particular philosophy. Dealing as it does with the nature of being and the rules of human thought, philosophy affects the work of the theologian throughout his system (and there were philosophical "systems" before there were theological ones). Therefore Christian theology has not been able to avoid philosophy even when it wanted to; although Tertullian and Martin Luther denounced the incursion of philosophy into Christian thought as a perversion, both found themselves obliged to draw upon philosophical sources for their exposition of Christian thought. But even the most philosophically inclined of theologians have been unable to bend the facts of Christian revelation into comfortable harmony with their metaphysics, for Christianity as a history, as a proclamation and as a sacramental life has refused to become completely malleable even in the hands of ancient Neoplatonists or modern Hegelians.

An awareness that the "Hellenization of the gospel" (Adolf von Harnack) resulted when theologians were overly attentive to the claims of philosophy has caused Christian thought in the 19th and 20th centuries to tie the work of theology more closely to that of history. Thus when Friedrich Schleiermacher defined dogmatic theology as "the science which systematizes the doctrine prevalent in a Christian Church at a given time," he made the task of the dogmatic theologian primarily a historical one; viz., of determining the doctrines that are prevalent and then of reflecting upon them in a systematic fashion.

The very concentration of Christian theology upon revelation—the account of God's dealing with the world through the history of Israel, through the saving career of Jesus Christ and through the establishment and development of the church—makes it a historical discipline. Yet the outcome of the historical preoccupation of theology has raised some fundamental questions about the propriety of identifying it so closely with historical research. For historical research has the result of making its data relative—relative to the processes of research themselves and relative to the age and culture in which they occurred. Historical study of the Bible, for example, has related central elements of the creed, such as the virgin birth and the ascension of Christ, to the religious and mythological conceptions of the ancient world. The outcome has been to discredit the biblical narratives in the eyes of many, and even those who continue to regard these narratives as basically trustworthy have learned to recognize the historically conditioned character of biblical language and imagery. A simplistic equation of theological science with historical methodology is thus an absurdity on the face of it.

Equally absurd is the assertion that because theology does not conform to either philosophy or history it is fundamentally irrational and intuitive, more akin to poetry or song than to the orderly work of the intellect. As a protest against the excessive intellectualism of some theologians or periods in history, such a "theology of the heart" makes a valid point, but it is incapable of going on to do the work of theology, which is thus assigned by default to other disciplines, especially to philosophy and history. Ironically, the pietistic attack upon theology in the name of true religion may thus bring on the loss both of scientific theology and of true religion. Conversely, a scientific theology that knows its limits and that is open to the discipline that philosophy, history and other sciences can provide for it, even as it pays primary attention and yields fundamental loyalty to the data of revelation, may serve the cause of the "religion of the heart" more faithfully than does the anti-intellectualism of the enthusiast.

## SOURCES OF THEOLOGY

Because Christianity is a religion of revelation (however that term may be interpreted), Christian theology is derived from the sources of revelation. But the specification of these sources and of the connection among them has been the occasion for long-standing controversy both among the several Christian traditions (*see* below) and within them. Yet it is possible to describe some areas of agreement before charting the principal points of disagreement.

All Christian theologians would agree that the chief source of revelation, and therefore of theology, is the history of God's dealing with men, whose climax was the life, death and resurrection of Jesus Christ. Not only does this preclude any identification of Christian revelation with metaphysics and compel Christian thought to take history with utmost seriousness, as we have said, but it also determines the very structure of the response that theology gives to divine revelation. Christian doctrines are historical in their point of reference even when they are metaphysical or moral or liturgical in their subject matter and intent.

In Christian revelation, therefore, the career of Jesus does not consist in the disclosure of ontological structures that any intelligent man could have discovered for himself, nor in the pronouncement of home truths about life that belong to the common ethical heritage of the race. Christian revelation is basically an event: "And the Word became flesh and dwelt among us, full of grace and truth; we have beheld his glory, glory as of the only Son from the Father." The phrase "we have beheld his glory" is centrally relevant to the definition of the sources of theology. For the history of Jesus Christ is not directly accessible to those who were not his contemporaries; for that matter, even his contemporaries could not make sense of it. It was remembered and recited, celebrated and obeyed, by a community that believed itself called into existence by what Jesus Christ had been and done. Literary and historical research into the development of this collective remembrance has distinguished among various forms of narrative and recitation. Similarly, the history of the people of Israel was not set forth with the purpose of satisfying the curiosity of historical scholarship but for the edification and education of the people of the covenant. Any effort by theology to make use of this history must be sensitive to the processes by which the Jewish people and the Christian community assembled their recollections of the events by which they knew themselves to have been constituted.

The principal repository of the history of revelation, to which theology looks as its source, is the Bible. All Christian theologians are concerned in one way or another to make their theologies biblical, vary though they do in the content and intent of their interpretation of Scripture. So divergent are these renditions that the reader of theology is often led to the conclusion that a mere acknowledgment of the biblical basis of theology is meaningless, since everyone finds in the Bible what he pleases. In fact, however, such a counsel of despair ignores the concrete influence of the Bible upon the teaching and the language of an astonishing variety of theologians. Often—not always, but often—their divergences are not between *the* theology of the Bible and an antibiblical theology but between one aspect of biblical teaching and another. The Bible is more comprehensive than the systems of the theologians. At the same time, the faithfulness of a particular theology to its biblical source cannot be gauged statistically, for it is just as possible to express biblical doctrine in nonbiblical language as it is to use the terminology of the Bible for expressing notions that are utterly foreign and even hostile to the message of the Old and New Testaments.

From the history of Christian theology it is also evident that although all theologians have appealed to the Bible as a source for their theology, the directness and the freshness of their use of it have fluctuated considerably. Both Roman Catholic and Protestant theologians in the 17th century, for example, claimed the authority of the Bible for their systems, but the systems of both were in fact shaped by the controversies of the Reformation and Counter-Reformation. The resurgence of biblical theology during the 20th century in both traditions transformed both Roman Catholic and Protestant theology, creating noticeable areas of new agreement amid continuing and often deepening disagreement.

No disagreement has been more pervasive than that over the relation of the Bible to other possible sources of theology, particularly the teaching of the church and the doctrines of the natural reason. Although Protestant theology came to acknowledge that there was a church before there was a Bible and that the Bible is intended to be read and studied in the context of the church, it regarded the idea of an infallible living magisterium as an affront to the authority of the Bible. Roman Catholic theology meanwhile came to acknowledge the primacy of the authority of Scripture more clearly than it had during the controversies that followed the Protestant Reformation, but it still insisted that the only solution to the confusion of theological voices brought on by the anarchy of an appeal to "the Bible and the Bible alone" is the acceptance of a normative tradition in the church, embodied in the ongoing life and teaching of the entire body of the faithful but safeguarded and articulated in the teaching authority of the pope.

Debates within Protestant theology made the dispute over the place of reason in theology much more confusing than the controversy over tradition. Protestant liberalism made more substantive use of reason and of philosophy than Roman Catholic theology ever had, but the theological movement associated with the name of Karl Barth attacked even the Thomistic interpretation of natural theology as a menace to truly biblical teaching. (*See* BARTH, KARL; NEO-ORTHODOXY; LIBERALISM, THEOLOGICAL.)

Yet even on the question of the place of reason in theology the differences tend to be differences of degree and of emphasis, for no theologian who lays claim to the name "Christian" would assign the central and normative place in his theology to any source of knowledge about God except divine revelation, and none would assign to the Bible a subordinate role in the determination of what the revelation means.

## FUNCTIONS OF THEOLOGY

As a churchly science, theology is intended to interpret and to serve the life of the church. This does not mean that it is directed only at those who are professing members of the Christian community, for since it claims to be based upon the revelation of the God who is the Giver of every good and perfect gift, it includes in its purview all the creatures of God and in its address all who are created in the image of God. Simply as an exercise in rational thinking and systematic exposition, Christian theology deserves the attention of any serious student. Yet even in its address to "those without," Christian theology speaks for the community of the church. While there has been great variation among theologians in their enumeration of the branches of theology, most theologians would find it possible to make their point under one or more of the following rubrics: speculative theology, historical theology, systematic theology, practical theology.

**Speculative Theology.**—By "speculative theology" is meant the whole effort of classical Christian theologians to measure as precisely as possible the capacities and the limits of the unaided human mind in relation to the truth of revelation. One purpose of this effort has traditionally been the apologetic one of refuting objections to the Christian faith and of demonstrating its harmony with human knowledge and thought. Despite this obvious evangelistic purpose, speculative theology has in fact been directed more to believers than to nonbelievers. It is, in the classic phrase of Augustine and Anselm, "faith in search of understanding." Thus Anselm set out to prove the existence of God to readers who were baptized members of the church, and Thomas Aquinas wrote a *Summa contra Gentiles* when there were very few *Gentiles* (*i.e.,* pagans) who could or would read his treatise. The Protestant Reformers were critical of the role that speculative theology had played in the middle ages, not because they denied that even without revelation something about God is knowable but because they accused this natural, speculative theology of watering down the biblical and evangelical content of theology. In the period of the Enlightenment, however, both Protestant and Roman Catholic theology were obliged to reopen the question of speculative theology, and the consequences of Kant's critiques and of modern science made the issue a live one again. The theological history of the first two-thirds of the 20th century persuaded most theologians that if they were ever to find an audience again, either within or without the church, they would have to interpret the relation between natural and revealed theology in a way that took account of the discoveries and the conclusions of modern thought.

**Historical Theology.**—Although the term "historical theology" is usually confined to the study of church history or even of the history of Christian thought, both the subject matter and the methods of biblical study qualify it for inclusion under this title. The specialization of modern scholarship has led to a division of labour also among theologians, especially in biblical and historical research. Each branch of this research has its counterpart in the nontheological disciplines. Thus biblical scholarship has been shaped by the methods and results of research in classical and near eastern history and philology, and some of the most important discoveries in church history have come from scholars working in political, social and literary history.

One consequence of the division of Christendom has been the concentration of theologians from certain Christian groups upon certain bodies of historical material. Not only are the founders of the several denominations almost exclusively the concern of the theology of those denominations—so that, for example, Lutherans often write systematic theology under the guise of historical research on Luther—but even the periods of church history that are presumably the common property of several traditions are often neglected by some of them. Until the end of the 19th century, the study of the Hebrew and Greek Scriptures in Roman Catholic theology was often an imitation of Protestant scholarship, while among Protestant theologians the study of the Church Fathers was largely confined to Anglicans and Lutherans, both of whom fell behind their Roman Catholic colleagues during the first half of the 20th century. Because of the decisive role of Scripture and tradition in Christian theology, historical theology in one generation may frequently determine the course of systematic theology in the next, just as historical theology often receives its initial stimulus from dogmatic theology or from church life and worship.

**Systematic Theology.**—No branch of theology is less uniformly designated than the one charged with the exposition and systematization of Christian doctrine. Sometimes it is simply called "theology" in a narrower sense than the one employed here (although in a still narrower and stricter sense "theology" means only the doctrines about God and Jesus Christ). Roman Catholics often refer to systematic theology as dogma; the older Protestant term, revived by Karl Barth, was dogmatics. (*See* DOGMA.) Protestants generally speak of systematic theology, sometimes of constructive theology. These variations reflect both the influence upon theological work of the divided state of Christendom and the uncertainty of many theologians about dogma and tradition.

The method of systematic theology is no more a matter of general agreement than is its content. Even where the tradition of the church is accorded a normative function, the method of systematic theology must still choose from among several options, including a predominantly biblical, a more explicitly dogmatic and an apologetic or speculative method of giving structure to the stuff of tradition. Of itself, this stuff does not yield a systematic structure from which theology can acquire the architectonic balance and precise formulation that are so admirable in the *Summa* of St. Thomas or the *Institutes* of John Calvin. To the familiar triad of Scripture, tradition and philosophy must be added a fourth component: Christian experience. Both in the mystical theology of the Orthodox and Roman Catholic traditions and in the theology of feeling made famous by the Protestant theologian Schleiermacher, the personal relation of the theologian to God becomes a fundamental part of his theological procedure, although neither the great Christian mystics nor Schleiermacher claimed that experience could displace Scripture and tradition as the norms of the authentically Christian in Christian theology.

**Practical Theology.**—Each branch of theology points beyond itself to the Christian church, out of whose life it emerges and to whose edification it is devoted. In this sense all theology is "practical theology," for no theology is an end in itself. Yet the location of most theological work in the seminaries of the church, where it supports the training of the Christian clergy, and the demands of the liturgical, educational and evangelistic life of the church, have made it necessary for faculties of theology to develop departments that specialize in the application of theology to the practice of the ministry. Preaching, teaching, worship and pastoral counseling may all claim a place in the study of theology.

It would be an oversimplification, however, to dismiss these areas as "mere techniques," whose intellectual content is less demanding and whose methodology is less rigorous than those of the "content disciplines." For it is a fact substantiated by the history of theology that some of the most profound insights into the meaning of the Bible and the mysteries of the Christian faith have come not from the abstractions of the academicians but from the practical work and experience of the pastor, bishop and missionary. Neither Paul nor Athanasius nor Augustine was a professor; all were engaged in the proclamation of the faith to believers and nonbelievers and in "the care of all the churches." Characteristically, Protestant theology is ready to admit this especially about the preaching ministry of the church, while Orthodox and Roman Catholic theology will stress the great contributions made by the liturgy to the development of dogma. Both would acknowledge, in the words of a Greek Church Father, that "practice is the basis of theory," and both would insist that this does not invalidate, but only reinforces, the function of the theological scholar.

## THEOLOGY IN THE CHRISTIAN CHURCHES

**Roman Catholicism.**—When Roman Catholic thought, following Thomas Aquinas, refers to theology as "sacred science," it speaks out of the conviction that theology is not merely one science among others but is the queen of the sciences. Within its assigned area of responsibility it addresses the other sciences and retains its independence of them. Because Roman Catholic theology worked out its most impressive definition of theology as a science in a vigorous debate over the philosophy of Aristotle during the 13th century, it has sometimes been reluctant to consider the implications of more recent systems of thought for the scientific character of theology. An immensely productive advantage of Roman Catholic theology over Protestant thought has been its conviction that theology is indeed a *scientia,* a way of knowing, and that therefore the intellect has a legitimate and a necessary place in the life of faith, both for the church and for the individual. From this conviction has come the readiness, in spite of some initial hesitation, to correlate the knowledge given by the faith with other forms of knowledge, as well as the confidence that theology does not have to apologize for its claims. This does not mean that according to Roman Catholicism revelation is "propositional" in its primal content; it does mean that language about revelation must be as precise and in this sense as rational as language about the Homeric epics or about nuclear fission.

In part this confidence stems from the Roman Catholic view of the sources of theology. The doctrine of the infallibility (*q.v.*) of the pope is sometimes interpreted by its critics and even by its proponents as though the pope were the only real theologian in the church. What it implies is rather that Jesus Christ did not leave his church bereft of the teaching authority that he himself had exercised in the days of his presence on earth, but he established the office of the apostles in and for the church, with the apostle Peter and his successors as the first among the incumbents of the apostolic office. Through this apostolic office he continues to rule and to instruct the church.

Roman Catholic theologians formulate the relation between this ongoing office and the Bible in different ways, but the consensus of the tradition itself is on the side of the contention that revelation closed with the death of the last apostle, that all revelation is contained implicitly in the Bible and that the task of the teaching office of the church is to make the revelation explicit. The dogma of the church is not a second source of revelation in the sense that it discloses something not given to the apostles and not set down in Scripture, but it is the authoritative interpretation of the revelation in Scripture; to Roman Catholic theology it is unthinkable that the interpretation of the Bible should conflict with the authoritative teaching of the church, whose spokesman is the pope.

Because of its distinctive conception of the nature of the church, Roman Catholic theology also interprets the functions of theology in a special way. For example, ascetical theology, which deals with the nature and the implications of discipline in Christian life and thought, becomes a special field. There is also a special function for "mystical theology," which examines the uniqueness of Christian contemplation and analyzes the connections between the vision of God granted to the experience of such contemplation and the doctrines set forth in Scripture and dogma. The Roman Catholic understanding of moral theology sets down the teachings of both natural law and revelation about ethical issues and applies them within the framework of the teaching church. In some periods of Roman Catholic history, this application has been responsible for the development of an elaborate casuistry (*q.v.*) in the handbooks of Roman Catholic moral theology, but it is a mistake to identify this detailed weighing of moral alternatives as the Roman Catholic idea of Christian ethics. An even more common mistake is to identify Roman Catholic theology exclusively with the speculative and philosophical doctrines of Thomism (*q.v.*), without giving proper due to the biblical and the liturgical components of all Roman Catholic theology, even and especially the theology of Thomas Aquinas. Not because of its formidable philosophical apparatus, but because of its content as the exposition of divine revelation, Roman Catholic theology claims the right to be regarded as "sacred science."

**Eastern Orthodoxy.**—The Eastern Orthodox view of the scientific character of theology, the Orthodox definition of the sources of theology and the Orthodox conception of the functions of theology are all determined by the place that Orthodoxy assigns to the tradition of the church. Therefore the scientific work of theology in Orthodoxy consists largely in the study of the Fathers of the Church. At times this has meant nothing more than the compilation of apposite quotations from the Fathers and the councils on the various topics of Christian teaching; such a compilation was intended to serve as the basis for oral instruction and exposition. But in part through the application of methods of research developed in the west, Eastern Orthodox scholarship has also given theology a systematic character. Sometimes under the influence of Thomism and sometimes because of the writings of Protestant theologians and philosophers, Russian Orthodox theology during the 18th and 19th centuries created systems of doctrine that strove to be faithful to Orthodox tradition while recasting it in a Protestant mold; none of these systems achieved permanent recognition among Orthodox theologians. Like Roman Catholicism, Orthodoxy designates tradition as a source and norm of theology, but it is less definite in its specification of the locus of authoritative tradition. The ancient Fathers and the councils of the undivided church belong to tradition, but so does the liturgical piety of the church. No one national and autocephalous church, whether Greek or Russian, and no one see or patriarchate has the right to determine for all of Orthodoxy what is the authentic tradition.

The severe restrictions placed upon the Orthodox churches during the modern history of eastern Europe and Asia Minor drastically curtailed their theological productivity. The flowering of a "lay theology" in the Russian Orthodoxy of the 19th century came to an end with the Russian Revolution, while the emancipation of the Greek and Balkan churches early in the 19th century did not serve to stimulate any large-scale renascence of work in theology. In the United States and in France, Orthodox communities of Russian and Greek origin were beginning at the middle of the 20th century to take up serious theological research and writing.

**Protestantism.**—The place of the theological faculties in the universities of Germany and Great Britain has perhaps done more than any other single factor to shape the Protestant interpretation of theology as a science. The very term *wissenschaftliche Theologie* ("scientific theology") as a designation for theological research is an index of the equation of "scientific" with "scholarly." As has been pointed out earlier in this article, philosophy and history are the two disciplines that have done most to make theology a *Wissenschaft*. The systematization of the theology of the Protestant Reformers, which began during their own time but achieved massive proportions in the 17th century (*cf.* ORTHODOXY, PROTESTANT), was accomplished with the aid of Aristotelian philosophy. The philosophies of Descartes, Leibniz and especially Christian Wolff were widely held during the 18th century, but the influence of Immanuel Kant upon Protestant theology was so pervasive throughout the 19th century that he has been termed, not without justification, "the philosopher of Protestantism," at least of German Protestantism and of the American Protestant theology that has been patterned after German models.

Less generally recognized than Kantian philosophy as a presupposition of Protestant theology during the 19th century is the rise of the historical method, by means of which much of Protestant theological work sought simultaneously to draw upon the resources of the Christian past and to justify itself within the university as genuinely *wissenschaftlich* discipline. From this came, for example, the permanent achievements of Protestant scientific theology in the field of the textual criticism of the Bible.

Another motivation for textual criticism was, of course, the Protestant principle of biblical authority. From the writings of the Reformers and from the confessional statements of the several branches of Protestantism it is possible to construct the theory that "the Bible, and the Bible alone, is the religion of Protestants." Tradition, creed and dogma are all said to be derived from the Bible and therefore not to be put on a par with it. The practice of the Reformers, of the Reformation confessions and of subsequent Protestant theology is not, however, a unilinear application of this principle. For the theology that was derived from Scripture bore a striking resemblance to the tradition of the orthodox creeds. Both the ecumenical movement and the results of scholarly research into the Bible and church history caused Protestant theology during the first half of the 20th century to restate its traditional opposition to tradition in a way that allowed to tradition a positive (if not, in the Orthodox or Roman Catholic sense, an authoritative) place as a source of Christian doctrine. As has already been pointed out, the theology of Schleiermacher put into formal statements the conviction of many Protestants that the experience of Christians and of the truly Christian community should be a decisive factor in theology also. The multiplicity of Protestant denominations and of theological trends within those denominations meant that this formal agreement among Protestants about the sources of theology did not produce any consensus, at least until the rise of the ecumenical movement (*q.v.*).

The denominational context of Protestant theology also helps to explain how the functions of theology are interpreted. Thus the theological controversies of the Reformation and post-Reformation periods imposed upon the systematic theology of the age a strongly polemical orientation. Even the biblical and historical scholarship of Protestant theology has had a share in polemics; thus the Magdeburg *Centuries,* one of the earliest works of Protestant historiography, were intended to prove that Roman Catholic claims to continuity with the early church lacked historical ground.

With the coming of the ecumenical movement, the atmosphere of polemics changed drastically. Shaped by the same biblical and historical research and confronted by the same existential situation both within and without the churches, theologians of various denominations discovered that they had more in common than the polemical stance of their several traditions had acknowledged. In the area of practical theology, the needs of the churches and the rise of new secular disciplines (especially of the social sciences) called forth a reappraisal of the conventional categories. New fields like the psychology of religion and the sociology of religion came out of this reappraisal, with consequences that reached far into the traditional fields like church history and systematic theology. Philosophy of religion or even philosophical theology became the characteristically Protestant way of handling the material of speculative theology. In the 19th and 20th centuries the study of non-Christian religions became a permanent part of the corpus of theological research in many Protestant centres.

**Theology in the Present and the Future.**—The general decline in the prestige of the Christian church during the modern and "postmodern" eras affected theology as well, causing it to put forth its claims with greater modesty and to construct its systems with less boldness. Impatience with the details of theology, expressed so often by both clergy and laity in the name of "the real business of the church," was sometimes replaced by the recognition that the only alternative to theology is bad theology. If the church found theology desirable when Christianity counted for much in the western world, it would find theology indispensable when Christianity had lost its place as the dominant ethos of its culture. In this sense, many Christian theologians at the middle of the 20th century believed that the most productive age of Christian theology still lay in the future. *See* also references under "Theology, Christian" in the Index.

Bibliography.—At least some of the writings of most major theologians of Christian history have been translated into English; these translations are listed in the bibliographies of the articles on theologians and denominations. *The Library of Christian Classics* contains many such translations from the earliest Fathers to the Protestant Reformers. Histories of Christian doctrine, such as those by Joseph Tixeront, A. von Harnack and Reinhold Seeberg, often provide a helpful introduction to the study of theology. Books such as John Macquarrie, *Twentieth-Century Religious Thought* (1963), summarize many different trends, and sets like *The Twentieth Century Encyclopedia of Catholicism* and *The Library of Constructive Theology* make possible a study of particular issues and problems. (J. J. Pn.)

**THEOPHANES** Confessor (*c.* 752–817), canonized by the Orthodox Church, Byzantine historian whose work is particularly valuable for the sparsely documented 7th and 8th centuries, as it draws on sources no longer extant, belonged to a noble and wealthy family. He married and later entered the monastery *tou megalou Agrou,* which he had founded at Sigriane in Bithynia. A vigorous opponent of the iconoclast policy of Leo V (813–820), he was imprisoned on Samothrace, where he died. His *Chronographia* covers the period from Diocletian's accession (284) to that of Leo V (813), and it was written at the instigation of his friend George the Syncellus to continue the latter's own unfinished chronicle. It is arranged by years, giving tables of Byzantine rulers, and also of the Persian kings, the Muslim caliphs, and the ecclesiastical heads of Rome, Constantinople, Antioch, Alexandria, and Jerusalem. It was translated into Latin (*c.* 873–875) by Anastasius, the papal librarian, and was used extensively by later Greek and Latin chroniclers.

*Theophanes Continuatus,* a work by various hands known also as the *Scriptores post Theophanem,* was originally commissioned by Constantine VII Porphyrogenitus (*q.v.*), and this part consists of four books (813–867), together with a fifth on Basil I (867–886) written by Constantine VII himself. The work was subsequently enlarged by a sixth book, which probably covered the period 886–963 (book vi in its present state breaks off at 961).

Bibliography.—Critical edition of Theophanes Confessor by C. de Boor, 2 vol. (1883–85), including Anastasius' version. Theophanes and Theophanes Continuatus, ed. by I. Classen—I. Bekkerus in the Bonn Corpus, 3 vol. (1838–41) and in J. P. Migne, *Patrologia Graeca,* vol. 108–109 (1861–63). German trans. for years 717–813 by L. Breyer, *Bilderstreit und Arabersturm in Byzanz* (1957). *See* also K. Krumbacher, *Geschichte der byzantinischen Litteratur,* 2nd ed., pp. 342–349 (1897); G. Moravcsik, *Byzantinoturcica,* vol. 1, 2nd ed., pp. 531–537, 540–544 (1958); G. Ostrogorsky, *History of the Byzantine State,* pp. 79–80, 130, 187 (1956). (J. M. Hy.)

**THÉOPHILE:** *see* Viau, Théophile de.

**THEOPHILUS, SAINT,** bishop of Antioch about a.d. 180 (his chronological sketch of the history of the world ends with the death of Marcus Aurelius in that year), is known from his three apologetic treatises *To Autolycus,* preserved in a single 11th-century Greek manuscript. The first deals with Christian faith in God and in the resurrection of the dead; it may be based on catechetical instructions. The second contains theological criticism of Greek religion, philosophy and poetry, followed by a "typological" commentary on Gen. i, 1–iii, 19. The third attacks pagan writers and "proves" that Christian teaching is both better and older than that of all other peoples.

Theophilus tried to create a theology by interpreting the Bible (especially the Old Testament) in relation to contemporary rhetoric and eclectic philosophy. He gives extensive quotations from Hellenistic anthologies of poetry and philosophy, as well as from the Jewish Sibylline Oracles. Theophilus is the first Christian known who defined faith as necessary in any human activity (i, 8; *cf.* Cicero, *Lucullus* 109); the first to use Skeptical "modes" in attacking pagan religion; and the first to speak of the dignity of man (ii, 18). He is the earliest writer who mentions the inspiration of New Testament writings (iii, 12; *cf.* ii, 22), the triad of God, his Word and his Wisdom(though with man they form a tetrad; ii, 15), and the (Stoic-Philonic) immanent and expressed Word of God (ii, 10, 22; *see* Logos).

Theophilus emphasizes man's free will and his duty to keep God's law; thus he stands between the older Jewish Christianity and Greek patristic thought. Theophilus influenced Irenaeus, Tertullian and Novatian, but was later forgotten.

Nothing is known of his life, though in the 4th century he was mentioned by Lactantius and by Eusebius. His work was first published by Johannes Frisius in 1546. The best edition is that of J. C. T. Otto (1861). (R. McQ. G.)

**THEOPHILUS** (d. 842), Byzantine emperor from 829 to 842, son of the Amorian Michael II, was a cultured man whose tutor was the iconoclast scholar John the Grammarian. He was strongly opposed to those who venerated icons, and they were persecuted when John the Grammarian became patriarch in 837. Throughout his reign Theophilus was engaged in war with the Muslims. He failed to drive them out of Sicily, and in 831 Palermo fell. On the eastern front intermittent warfare for several years was followed by a determined drive by Muslims led by Caliph Mutasim into the heart of Asia Minor. In 838 Ankara was taken, followed by the capture of Amorium, and only after Theophilus' death on Jan. 20, 842, were the Byzantines able to retrieve their position. Nevertheless Theophilus' reign saw administrative reorganization both north of the Black Sea (the theme of Cherson) and in Asia Minor. He was much influenced by the contemporary civilization of Baghdad, and like Harun al-Rashid he was said to have wandered about his capital informally, listening to his subjects' complaints. In spite of his heretical iconoclast views, he was a popular figure who survived in later Byzantine literature as the type of the just ruler.

Bibliography.—G. Ostrogorsky, *History of the Byzantine State* (1956); J. B. Bury, *History of the Eastern Roman Empire* (1912); A. A. Vasiliev, *Byzance et les Arabes,* vol. 1, ed. by H. Grégoire and M. Canard (1935); H. Grégoire in *Cambridge Medieval History,* vol. 4, ch. 3, new ed. (1966). (J. M. Hy.)

**THEOPHILUS** (probably also Roger of Helmarshausen) was the author of *De diversis artibus,* an exhaustive account (probably written in northwest Germany between 1110 and 1140) of the techniques of almost all the contemporary crafts of the first half of the 12th century.

From his writings it can be deduced that Theophilus was a German monk of the Benedictine Order and that he was a practising craftsman. In one manuscript (Vienna, National-bibliothek Hs.2527) he is designated "Theophilus qui est Rugerus," and he may have been the celebrated German metalworker Roger of Helmarshausen (also a monk), who was responsible in 1100 for a portable altar now in the cathedral treasury at Paderborn. Considerable interest is shown by Theophilus in the techniques of metalwork, but he also discusses the crafts of wall painting, manuscript illumination, stained glass, and ivory carving. The work is divided into three books, and the introduction to each is of interest in reflecting the attitude to his art of a 12th-century practising craftsman who was also an educated person. It contains the earliest references in Europe to paper and to oil painting.

BIBLIOGRAPHY.—Definitive Latin text with English translation and general discussion in C. R. Dodwell's edition (1961); translation with useful illustrations by J. Hawthorne and C. S. Smith (1963); for technical information on the metalwork, W. Theobald's edition of Book 3 (1933) is still invaluable. (C. R. D.)

**THEOPHRASTUS** (371/370–288/287 B.C.), Greek Peripatetic philosopher, was born at Eresus on the island of Lesbos and went to Athens to study under Aristotle. The latter designated him as head of his school, the Peripatos, when he himself retired to Chalcis (322/21). It was under Theophrastus that the Peripatetic school was frequented by the highest number of pupils and auditors.

Apart from Eudemos of Rhodes, Theophrastus was the only Peripatetic who embraced Aristotle's philosophy to its full extent—metaphysics, physics, physiology, zoology, botany, ethics, politics, the history of culture, etc. His general tendency was to strengthen the systematic unity of those subjects and to reduce the transcendental or Platonic elements of the whole doctrine.

Little has been preserved of Theophrastus' works. The principal remains are nine books *On the History of Plants* and six *On the Causes of Plants.* Smaller treatises extant under his name deal with fire, winds, signs of weather, scents, sensations, and other subjects; but their authenticity is in part contestable. The famous *Characters* consists of brief and vigorous delineations of moral types developed from studies that Aristotle had made for ethical and rhetorical purposes: this is the work on which La Bruyère's masterpiece was based. In his *Ethics,* known from the assaults of the Stoics, Theophrastus distinguished, as Aristotle had done, a plurality of virtues with their relative vices and acknowledged a certain importance to external goods.

Theophrastus' *Doctrines of the Natural Scientists,* as reconstructed by H. Diels in *Doxographi Graeci* (1879; reprinted 1929), provides the foundation of all history of ancient philosophy.

The works of Theophrastus were edited by F. Wimmer (1854–62); the *Characters,* by H. Diels (1909). There is an English translation of the *Characters* by Sir R. Jebb, with introduction and notes (1870; new ed. by J. E. Sandys, 1909); another edition and translation, by J. M. Edmonds, is in the "Loeb Classical Library" (1946). For the extant fragments of the *Metaphysica* of Theophrastus, *see* the edition by W. D. Ross and F. H. Fobes (1929). *See* also references under "Theophrastus" in the Index. (F. WI.)

**THEOPHYLLINE:** *see* PURINES.

**THEOPOMPUS** OF CHIOS (b. *c.* 380 B.C.), Greek historian and rhetorician, whose *Philippica,* though lost in original, has survived through the work of later writers to form one element in the tradition concerning the reign of Philip II of Macedonia. He was born at Chios and in early youth seems to have spent some time at Athens, along with his father, who had been exiled because of his sympathies with Sparta. There he became a pupil of Isocrates, and rapidly made great progress in rhetoric. According to Cicero, Isocrates said that Ephorus required the spur but Theopompus the bridle: he once won a prize for oratory in a contest in which Isocrates himself was taking part. It is said to have been the advice of his teacher that determined his career as a historian—a career for which he was peculiarly qualified by his inherited wealth and his wide knowledge of men and places.

Through the influence of Alexander the Great, he was restored to Chios about 333, and figures for some time as one of the leaders of the aristocratic party in his native town. After Alexander's death he was again expelled and took refuge with Ptolemy in Egypt, where he appears to have met with a somewhat cold reception. The date of his death is unknown.

The works of Theopompus were chiefly historical. They included an epitome of Herodotus' *History* (the genuineness of which is doubted), the *Hellenica,* the *Philippica* (history of Philip of Macedon), and several panegyrics and hortatory addresses, the chief of which was the letter to Alexander. The *Hellenica* treated of the history of Greece, in 12 books, from 411 (where Thucydides breaks off) to 394—the date of the Battle of Cnidus. Of this work only a few fragments survive: the attribution to it of the important historical fragment known as *Hellenica Oxyrhynchia* or "the Oxyrhynchus historian" (first published by B. P. Grenfell and A. S. Hunt, *The Oxyrhynchus Papyri,* vol. v, no. 842, 1908) did not win acceptance. A far more elaborate work was the *Philippica* in 58 books. In this Theopompus narrated the history of Philip's reign (359–336). His narrative included not only moral and political discussions but also digressions on the names and customs of the various races and countries of which he had occasion to speak, which were so numerous that Philip V of Macedon reduced the bulk of the history from 58 to 16 books by cutting out those parts which had no connection with Macedonia. It was from this history that Pompeius Trogus (of whose *Historiae Philippicae* the epitome by Justin is extant) derived much of his material.

In spite of some extravagance both of style and judgment, examples of which can be seen in the extant fragments, it seems likely that Theopompus was the most interesting and considerable of all the Greek historians who are "lost."

BIBLIOGRAPHY.—Fragments in F. Jacoby, *Die Fragmente der griechischen Historiker,* vol. ii, B and D, no. 115 (1929–30) and vol. ii, A, no. 66, for the text of *Hellenica Oxyrhynchia.* On the attribution of the "Oxyrhynchus historian," *see,* besides Grenfell and Hunt cited in text, E. Meyer, *Theopomps Hellenika* (1909); F. Jacoby in *Nachrichten der Gesellschaft der Wissenschaft Göttingen* (1924); H. Bloch in *Harvard Studies in Classical Philology,* suppl. vol. i (1940). *See* also A. Momigliano, in *Rivista di filologia* (1931 and 1935); K. von Fritz, in *Antike und Abendland* (1954); H. D. Westlake, in *Historia* (1954); R. Laqueur in Pauly-Wissowa-Kroll, *Real-Encyclopädie der classischen Altertumswissenschaft,* vol. v, 2nd series, col. 2176 ff. (1934). (G. T. GH.)

**THEORELL, AXEL HUGO TEODOR** (1903– ), Swedish biochemist, was awarded the 1955 Nobel Prize for Medicine for his discoveries concerning the nature and mode of action of oxidation enzymes. He was born at Linköping on July 6, 1903. After taking his M.D. degree at Stockholm in 1930, he began general practice; but an attack of poliomyelitis left him crippled, and he decided to devote himself to research. He worked at Uppsala University (1932–36) and also studied in Germany while holding a Rockefeller fellowship. In 1937 he was appointed director of the biochemical department of the Nobel Institute, Stockholm.

In 1934 Theorell produced in pure form the so-called old yellow enzyme (*i.e.,* the first known of this group), which influences combustion in living cells. He later divided the enzyme into the coenzyme (riboflavin phosphate) and the apoenzyme (pure protein). He was the first to produce pure myoglobin, the red colouring substance of muscle, and he devised a method of blood examination that came to be widely used in Sweden as a test for drunkenness. (W. J. BP.; X.)

**THEOREM,** a term used in mathematics to represent a proposition (*q.v.*) that is to be demonstrated. In geometry, a proposition is commonly considered as a problem (a construction to be effected) or a theorem (a statement to be proved). For example, the statement: "If two lines intersect, each pair of vertical angles are equal" is a theorem. The so-called fundamental theorem of algebra asserts that every rational integral equation has at least one root. The Greeks also recognized a proposition lying between a theorem and a problem, the porism (*q.v.*).

*See* BINOMIAL THEOREM; FERMAT'S LAST THEOREM; REMAINDER THEOREM. For related terms *see* also AXIOM; HYPOTHESIS; POSTULATE.

**THEORY** has various meanings in ordinary speech and in science. It may be contrasted with practice as unverified speculation. It may also be used to signify any hypothesis, whether confirmed or not, or may be restricted to hypotheses that have been so strongly confirmed as to become part of the accepted doctrine of a particular science. In its best use, it signifies a systematic account of some field of study, derived from a set of general propositions. These propositions may be taken as postulates, as in pure mathematics (theory of functions, etc.), or they may be principles more or less strongly confirmed by experience, as in natural science (theory of heat, electromagnetic theory). There may be rival theories in a particular field (*e.g.*, in psychology) differing in their selection of principles or in the emphasis laid on particular principles.

As a science develops, the part played by deductive theory in it tends to become more and more important. *See* HYPOTHESIS; SCIENTIFIC METHOD: *The Role of Hypothesis;* EXPLANATION; INDUCTION: *Induction and Hypothesis.* (L. J. R.)

**THEOSOPHY,** those forms of philosophic and religious thought which claim a special insight into the divine nature and its constitutive moments or processes (from Greek *Theos,* "god," and *sophia,* "wisdom"). Sometimes this insight is claimed as the result of the operation of some higher faculty or some supernatural revelation to the individual; in other instances the theosophical theory is not based upon any special illumination but is simply put forward as the deepest speculative wisdom of its author. But in any case it is characteristic of theosophy that it starts with an explication of the divine essence and endeavours to deduce the phenomenal universe from the play of forces within the divine nature itself.

**General Theory.**—Theosophy claims to derive its significant data by way of intuition or through revelation from seers or masters. Thus it does not rely on ordinary observation or logical reason to the same degree as does most philosophical thought. Yet it often appeals to the "superior" or "higher" reason, and it should not be thought of as antirational. It is more closely related to religion than to philosophy in the usual Western sense of the term philosophy and is more at home with traditional Indian modes of thought than with Greek-European, since Indian thinkers as a rule do not draw sharp lines between religious and philosophical inquiry.

Theosophy generally arises in connection with deeply felt religious needs (for wholeness, blessedness, vision of God, etc.) and is thus one expression of religious aspiration. Accepting the testimony of religious experience that the present world lies in a state of imperfection, if not "fallenness," theosophy seeks to give an account of this state of things while pointing the seeker on to an experience of actualization on a higher plane of his being. Theosophical systems are thus concerned with the problems of metaphysical, natural, and moral evil, and in general find it possible to subordinate evil to good in a monistic frame of reference or in a philosophy of nondualism. (The Sankhya philosophy, one byproduct of ancient brahmanical speculations in India, is an exception to this rule, since it posits an ultimate metaphysical dualism of *purusha,* or spirit, and *prakriti,* or nature.)

India has been the mother of most theosophical speculations. They are reflected in the systems known as Brahmanism, upanishadic thought and the Vedanta, Sankhya, and Yoga systems (*see* INDIAN PHILOSOPHY). These systems, along with the more popular sectarian movements of Hinduism (*q.v.*), are appealed to in a variety of ways by those theosophists who have lived after the period when knowledge of Indian religious and philosophical systems became known to thoughtful circles in Europe and the West generally. In Indian thought the *rishis* are those who have "seen" the inner wisdom and have communicated it to faithful disciples. Such communication traditionally has often been purely oral, though scriptural writings have been accepted as giving part of the divine wisdom. The distinction between esoteric wisdom, available only to the few, and exoteric wisdom, available to the masses, is often implicit in theosophical thought and practice.

There are many affinities between mysticism (*q.v.*) and theosophy. Many of the speculations in the sermons and writings of Meister Eckhart (*q.v.*) could be considered as much theosophical as mystical. Yet Eckhart is considered one of the great mystics in the Roman Catholic tradition of Christianity, though in his later years he fell under suspicion of heresy. Eckhart's doctrine asserts behind God a predicateless Godhead, which, although unknowable not only to man but also to itself, is, as it were, the essence or potentiality of all things. From it proceed, and in it exist, the three Persons of the Trinity, conceived as stages of an external self-revealing process. The eternal generation of the Son is for Eckhart equivalent to the eternal creation of the world. But the sensuous and phenomenal, as such, so far as they seem to imply independence of God, are mere privation and nothingness; things exist only through the presence of God in them, and the goal of creation, like its outset, is the repose of the Godhead. The soul of man, which as a microcosmos epitomizes the nature of things, strives by self-abnegation or self-annihilation to attain this reunion (which Eckhart calls being "buried" in God). Regarding evil simply as privation, Eckhart does not make it the pivot of his thought as Böhme later did; but his notion of the Godhead as a dark and formless essence is a favourite thesis of theosophy.

Jakob Böhme (*q.v.*), called the theosophist par excellence, was indebted not only to mystical theology but also to the writings of Paracelsus. The nature-philosophers of the Renaissance, such as Nicholas of Cusa, Paracelsus, Geronimo Cardano, and others, curiously blend scientific ideas with speculative notions derived from scholastic theology, from Neoplatonism (*q.v.*) and even from the Cabala (*q.v.*). Hence it is customary to speak of their theories as a mixture of theosophy and physics or chemistry.

Böhme offers a natural philosophy of the same sort. His speculation turns upon the necessity of reconciling the existence and the might of evil with the existence of an all-embracing and all-powerful God, without falling into Manichaeism (*q.v.*) on the one hand, or, on the other, into a naturalistic pantheism (*q.v.*) that denies the reality of the distinction between good and evil. He faces the difficulty boldly, and the eternal conflict between the two may be said to furnish him with the ground-principle of his philosophy. It is in this connection that he insists on the necessity of the Nay to the Yea, of the negative to the positive. Eckhart's Godhead appears in Böhme as the abyss, the eternal nothing, the essenceless quiet (*Urgrund* and *Stille ohne Wesen* are two of Böhme's phrases). But, if this were all, the divine being would remain an abyss dark even to itself. In God, however, as the condition of his manifestation, lies, according to Böhme, the eternal nature or the *mysterium magnum,* which is as anger to love, as darkness to light, and, in general, as the negative to the positive. This principle (which Böhme often calls the evil in God) illuminates both sides of the antithesis, and thus contains the possibility of their real existence. By the *Qual* or torture, as it were, of this separation, the universe has qualitative existence and is knowable. Even the three Persons of the Trinity, though existing *idealiter* beforehand, attain reality only through this principle of nature in God, which is hence spoken of as their *matrix.* It forms also the matter, as it were, out of which the world is created; without the dark and fiery principle, we are told, there would be no creature. Hence God is sometimes spoken of as the father and the eternal nature as the mother of things. Creation (which is conceived as an eternal process) begins with the creation of the angels. The subsequent fall of Lucifer is explained as his surrender of himself to the principle of nature, instead of dwelling in the heart of God. He sought to place anger above love; and he had his will, becoming prince of hell, the kingdom of God's anger, which remains, however, an integral part of the divine universe.

F. W. J. von Schelling's *Philosophical Inquiries Into the Nature of Human Freedom* (1809) is almost entirely a reproduction of Böhme's ideas, and forms, along with Baader's writings, the best modern example of theosophical speculation. Emanuel Swedenborg (*q.v.*) is usually reckoned among the theosophists.

**The Theosophical Society.**—The term theosophy in later years obtained wide currency as denominating the beliefs and teachings of the Theosophical Society, founded in the United States in 1875 by Helena Petrovna Blavatsky (*q.v.*), in connection with Col. H. S. Olcott and others. Colonel Olcott remained president of the original society till his death in 1907, when he was succeeded by Annie Besant (*q.v.*). Soon after the death of Madame Blavatsky (1891) a split took place which led to the formation of a separate organization under the leadership of William Q. Judge. The international headquarters of the society is in Adyar, just outside the city of Madras, India.

The founders of the Theosophical Society assumed their continuity with the ancient esoteric tradition of occultism and were ready to make the "secret doctrine" available to humanity at large. According to Madame Blavatsky's original statements, this wisdom has been transmitted through the ages as a secret doctrine by a brotherhood of adepts or mahatmas scattered through the world but in connection with one another. With a certain group of these in Tibet she claimed to be in communication. A Master Morya is supposed to have taken on Madame Blavatsky as his personal pupil, or chela. In adepts such as Morya the spiritual nature is supposed to have been so developed that the body has become the ductile instrument of the intelligence, and they have thus gained a control over natural forces which enables them to bring about results that appear to be miraculous. Many theosophists have had great interest in occult phenomena, and theosophical language includes references to astral bodies, guardian angels, and the like.

In one of her important books, *Isis Unveiled,* Madame Blavatsky seeks to establish that the one source of all the wisdom of the past is India. Christianity, according to the same volume, "copied all its rites, dogmas and ceremonies from paganism" with the exception of the doctrine of eternal damnation and the custom of pronouncing anathemas. The Indian doctrines which are often treated in theosophical writings are the identity of the human and the divine, the concept of reincarnation (*see* METEMPSYCHOSIS) and transmigration (more properly termed *samsara*), and the concept of *karma* (*q.v.;* the law of action-influence). Theosophy holds that life is a continuum, with reincarnation its evolutionary method and *karma* its determinant. *Karma* has played a prominent part in Indian thinking from the time of the late brahmanic commentaries and the Upanishads, but its operation has been interpreted in different ways. For the modern theosophist, reincarnation is the method by which the individual reaps what he has sown, and *karma* is the principle behind the method. It is used to explain the inequalities in the present life of the distribution of happiness and misery, wisdom and ignorance, and is a doctrine of hope, not of pessimism. The goal of the struggle to achieve wisdom which leads to self-actualization is Nirvana (*q.v.*), when the lower self or selves is annihilated and the true self liberated.

BIBLIOGRAPHY.—Annie Besant, *The Ancient Wisdom: an Outline of Theosophical Teachings* (1897), and *Man and His Bodies* (1917); Helena P. Blavatsky, *Isis Unveiled,* 2 vol. (1877), and *The Secret Doctrine* (1888); J. Krishnamurti, *At the Feet of the Master* (1931); Alvin Boyd Kuhn, *Theosophy* (1930); C. W. Leadbeater, *An Outline of Theosophy* (1902); J. Martensen, *Jacob Boehme: Theosophische Studien* (1882); G. R. S. Mead, *Fragments of a Faith Forgotten* (1900).

(A. S. P.-P.; F. H. R.)

**THEOTOCOPULI, DOMENICO:** *see* GRECO, EL.

**THERA** (modern Greek THIRA; formerly SANTORIN or SANTORINI), a volcanic island in the Aegean Sea, 29 sq.mi. (75 sq.km.) in extent, one of the southernmost of the Cyclades (*q.v.*). Pop. (1961) 7,751. The eparchy of Thera, part of the Greek *nomos* (department) of the Cyclades, includes the islands of Therasia (Thirasia), Ios, Amorgos, and Anaphe (Anafi). Thera is both a Greek Orthodox and a Roman Catholic episcopal see.

In shape Thera forms a crescent, enclosing a bay on the north, east, and south; on the western side lies the smaller island of Therasia. The encircling wall thus formed, elliptical, and 18 mi. (29 km.) round its inner rim, is broken in two places: toward the northwest by a strait one mile across, where the water is not less than 1,100 ft. (335 m.) deep, and southwest by an opening about three miles wide, shallow, with Aspronisi ("white island") in the middle. From the bay, horizontally banded cliffs rise perpendicularly to as much as 1,000 ft.; but toward the open sea, both in Thera and Therasia, the ground slopes and has been converted into broad level terraces of tufaceous agglomerate, which though bare and ashen produce the famous Thera wine. Powdered tufa is exported as cement. Toward the southeast, the limestone peak of Mt. Profitis Ilias (1,858 ft. [566 m.]) existed before the volcano was formed. In the middle of the bay lie two small volcanic islands, Neokaimeni and Palaiokaimeni ("new" and "old burnt island"). The number and size of these islands has changed with successive eruptions of the volcano. The modern town of Thera (pop. [1961] 1,481) is built at the edge of the cliffs, overlooking the bay at a height of 900 ft. (275 m.). Other modern settlements include Emborion and Pirgos inland in the south of Thera, and Oia by the northern entrance to the bay.

The islands once formed a single volcanic cone, which was shattered by explosion and subsidence leaving above water only part of the crater rim. Beneath the heavy layer of volcanic ash and tufa, remains of a Minoan Cretan colony have been found to the south of Akrotiri village. These date the explosion to the early 15th century B.C. The resultant tidal wave was probably responsible for the devastation of the coastal cities of Crete. Many scholars associate with these events the later Greek stories of the lost city of Atlantis. The island has been repeatedly laid waste by eruptions and earthquakes.

In Greek legend the island of Thera originated from a clod of earth presented to the Argonauts by Triton. By the 8th century a colony from Sparta, including Minyan refugees from Lemnos, was brought by Theras, who gave the island his own name. But the chief event in Thera's history was the planting of its famous colony of Cyrene on the north coast of Africa by Battus *c.* 630 B.C., in accordance with a command of the Delphic oracle (*see* CYRENE). Thera, as a member of the League of the Cyclades, was from 308 to 145 B.C. under the protectorate of the Ptolemies.

The name Santorin (a corruption of St. Irene, patron of Thera) was known to the Arab geographer Idrisi by 1154. The Venetians occupied the island from 1207 to the Turkish conquest in 1537; for much of this time it was part of the duchy of Naxos. It declared its independence of Turkey in 1821.

The classical capital occupied a site on the eastern coast now called Mesa Vouno, between Profitis Ilias and the sea. It was excavated in 1895–1903 by Baron Hiller von Gärtringen. There are extensive cemeteries; a *heroum* (hero's monument) of Artemidorus; an agora; a royal portico; a temple of Dionysus and the Ptolemies, later dedicated to the Caesars; the Ptolemaic barracks; and a gymnasium. The main street has narrow lanes to right and left, one leading to the sanctuary of the Egyptian gods. Near the street is a small theatre, beneath the seats of which is a cistern into which rainwater drains from the auditorium: water was evidently scarce then as now. Farther southeast are the temples of Ptolemy III Euergetes and of Apollo Carneius; finally, where the rocks fall precipitously, a gymnasium of the ephebi. Several archaic *kouros* statues have been found, including some of the earliest type. Numerous rock carvings and inscriptions were also discovered. Near the west foot of Profitis Ilias is the temple of Thea Basileia, perfect even to the roof, now dedicated to St. Nicholas Marmarites.

BIBLIOGRAPHY.—F. Fouqué, *Santorin et ses éruptions* (1879); J. T. Bent, *The Cyclades,* ch. 6 (1885); H. F. Tozer, *The Islands of the Aegean,* ch. 5 (1890); Hiller von Gärtringen, *Thera,* 5 vol. (1899–1909); *Inscriptiones Graecae,* vol. xii, fasc. 3, no. 320–1057, 1289–1660 (1898–1904); A. Philippson, *Die griechische Landschaften,* vol. iv, pp. 164–185 (1959); S. Marinatos, *Excavations at Thera* (1967– ).

(J. Bo.)

**THERALITE,** in petrology, a group of plutonic rocks built up of basic plagioclase (labradorite), nephelite, and a titaniferous augite. The name is derived from the Greek *theran,* "to pursue," since it was believed that its discovery would complete the series of basic rocks containing nephelite as an essential constituent. They are classified in the nephelite-tephrite group in this series (*see* NEPHELINITE).

Olivine, an alkali-amphibole, biotite, and orthoclase may be present as subordinate constituents. With the exception of nephelite and orthoclase, the minerals of theralites are usually in well-shaped crystals. Nephelite itself may be largely represented by secondary zeolites.

Theralites are of comparatively rare occurrence. They are found in Bohemia in association with shonkinite, in Odenwald (Mt. Katzenbuckel), Ger., together with pulaskite and foyaite in the Serra de Monchique, Port., in the Kola peninsula, U.S.S.R., and among the Carboniferous intrusions of Ayrshire, Scot.

Closely related to the theralites are the teschenites (from Teschen, Czech.). In place of nephelite these rocks contain primary analcime, but types containing both nephelite and analcime are known. In central Scotland, around Edinburgh and Glasgow, teschenites are abundant, forming thick sills intrusive into the Carboniferous rocks. Teschenites are sometimes ophitic, *i.e.,* with augite enclosing crystals of plagioclase, and show transitions to olivine-dolerite on the one hand and to picrite on the other.

The rock known as lugarite (from Lugar, Ayrshire) is a related type containing small amounts of plagioclase but abundant analcime; nephelite is present in subordinate amounts.

Other rocks related to the theralites are the essexites and shonkinites. The former are characterized by dominant plagioclase, subordinate orthoclase, and green augite, hornblende, biotite, and olivine. Nephelite also occurs commonly. By an increase in the proportion of nephelite the essexites pass into theralites. Essexites occur, together with nephelite-syenite, in Essex County, Mass., at Mt. Royal near Montreal, in southern Norway (Oslo District), at Rongstock, Czech., and among the Carboniferous teschenites of Scotland near Edinburgh and in the Campsie Fells (hills), Stirlingshire. The shonkinites are dark-coloured, igneous rocks of much rarer occurrence. Augite and orthoclase are the prime constituents, but plagioclase, barkevikite, olivine, biotite, and variable amounts of nephelite are present.

At Shonkin Sag, in the Highwood Mountains of Montana, shonkinite forms the greater part of a stratified laccolith passing at the border into a peculiar basic rock described as a leucite-basalt porphyry.

Shonkinites are also found in Ontario, British Columbia, and Indonesia (Celebes, Timor). (C. E. T.; X.)

**THERAMENES** (d. 404/403 B.C.), Athenian general and statesman who played an important part in the internal political conflicts during and after the Peloponnesian War (*q.v.*). He was the son of Hagnon, of the deme (township) Steiria. In the course of his controversial career Theramenes made many enemies, including the orator Lysias, while the more conservative authors of the 4th century, including Ephorus and Aristotle, tended to idealize him. Thus, it is true that Hagnon was one of the ten commissioners (*probouloi*) appointed in 413 after the disastrous Athenian defeat in Sicily to keep control over the people and their expenditure, but it is not necessary to follow Lysias when he hints that Hagnon favoured oligarchic revolution in 411. Hagnon was an old associate of Pericles (*q.v.*), and Xenophon is probably right to say that Hagnon's record recommended his son to the people at the start of his career. On the other hand, Ephorus certainly exaggerated Theramenes' popularity at Athens.

Nothing is known of his early career except that he was a pupil of the sophist Prodicus. He first appears in 411 as one of the leaders in the revolution of the Four Hundred. These included some extreme oligarchs, such as Antiphon, Phrynichus, and Peisander, but also many who would have been content with a moderate oligarchy, on the lines of the program published before the revolution—abolition of state pay and restriction of the franchise to those who could serve the state in person or with their money, to a maximum of 5,000. A commission of the 10 *probouloi* with 20 new members was appointed to make constitutional proposals; Cleitophon's supplementary proposal, that they should consult the old laws of the democratic founder Cleisthenes (*q.v.*), illustrates another line of "moderate" thought. Aristotle's *Constitution of Athens* (ch. 30) gives a "constitution for the future," ascribed to a committee of the Five Thousand, with a complicated system of four rotating councils on the Boeotian model; it contains practical proposals, some of which were later adopted, but it was certainly never effective as a whole and is probably a draft composed by a moderate at some stage of the revolution.

In the event, the commissioners, reporting to an assembly held at Colonus outside the walls of Athens (which unarmed men would not be likely to attend), only proposed the lifting of all normal constitutional safeguards. Then the oligarch Peisander pushed through a motion by which full powers were to be given to a council of 400, elected on the spot by a somewhat irregular method; they were to summon the Five Thousand only when they thought fit. The oligarchs thus took charge of the revolution that the moderates had helped make. They were soon in difficulties, mainly because of the resistance of the fleet at Samos, and had no hope except negotiation with Sparta, which proved difficult. Opposition inside Athens came to a head over the fort at Eëtioneia in the Piraeus, which Theramenes and others alleged was being built to command the entrance and admit the Spartan fleet, and a revolt began in favour of the Five Thousand. The Spartan fleet moved on to Euboea and defeated the Athenians off Eretria (September 411), after which the Four Hundred collapsed, and an enlarged Five Thousand took over as a moderate oligarchy with a franchise restricted to the hoplites (heavy infantry).

Theramenes was certainly the main leader of the opposition inside the Four Hundred, and the new constitution is usually, and no doubt correctly, regarded as his work. He did not, however, remain long in Athens but went with 20 ships first to Paros, then to Athens' friend Archelaus of Macedonia, who was besieging Pydna. Early in 410 he and Thrasybulus (*q.v.*) joined the main fleet in the Hellespont, where, with Alcibiades, they annihilated the Spartan fleet under Mindarus at Cyzicus. This removal of the immediate threat in the Hellespont, Athens' grain supply route, so encouraged the people that they abolished the Five Thousand and restored full democracy, leaving Theramenes and his colleagues in a somewhat anomalous position till full unity was restored with the triumphant return of Alcibiades to Athens in 407.

After Cyzicus, Theramenes was left at Chrysopolis to guard the Bosporus and exact a toll from ships passing through it. He next appears at Arginusae in 406, not as general but as trierarch in command of a ship. This Athenian victory, the last, was followed by the trial of six of the generals on the charge of not having picked up survivors from the ships disabled in the battle. They blamed the violent storm that followed the battle but also claimed that they had detailed Theramenes and Thrasybulus for this task. Xenophon alleges that Theramenes took a large part in inflaming public feeling against the generals, who were condemned to death; his apologists exonerate him. It is not easy to decide where the truth lies, though it must be said that Xenophon's account is in some ways the less coherent. Lysias says that Theramenes was elected general the following spring, but at the subsequent scrutiny he was set aside as being no friend to the people.

Late in 405, when Athens was besieged but not yet ready to surrender, Theramenes was dispatched to negotiate with the Spartan admiral Lysander. Returning three months later, when Athens was starving (his enemies said he delayed on purpose), he headed an embassy to Sparta to seek terms of capitulation, which Athens had to accept. There followed a period of political uncertainty, the democrats hoping to retain their constitution, the oligarchs and returned exiles organizing and plotting for theirs, while Theramenes and his associates probably hoped to establish something in between. Lysander eventually returned to Athens and set up the Thirty as a commission to revise the constitution. Theramenes had played a large part in their establishment, but control gradually passed to the oligarchic extremist Critias (*q.v.*), who was determined to retain power permanently. It is not clear what Theramenes thought of the obtaining of a Spartan garrison to support the Thirty, but later he protested against their arbitrary government and judicial murders, and to appease him a body of 3,000 was nominally admitted to citizenship. But the extremists were still afraid of his opposition, and Critias accused him of treachery before the council. His defense impressed his hearers, but Critias had him removed and forced to drink hemlock. The last drops he poured out as a libation with the words, "This to the fair Critias."

There is no reason to doubt Theramenes' patriotism or his sincere belief that a hoplite franchise was the best constitution, and this belief recommended him to later writers who disliked both radical democracy and extreme oligarchy. But there was no possibility that Athens would accept such a constitution except under violent compulsion, and Theramenes' constitutional experiments and his inability to work with the democrats weakened Athens and contributed not a little to its fall. *See* also ATHENS.

*See* general histories of Greece: also C. Hignett, *A History of the Athenian Constitution*, esp. ch. 10–11 (1952). (A. As.)

**THERAPEUTAE,** an ancient sect of Jewish ascetics believed to have lived in the vicinity of Alexandria (Egypt), near Lake Mareotis, during the 1st century A.D. They are mentioned in *De Vita Contemplativa,* attributed to the Jewish philosopher Philo, which is the sole account of the community, and they are characterized as being unusually severe in their discipline and mode of life. *See* Jewish Sects During the Second Commonwealth: *Ascetic Sects: Therapeutae.*

**THERAPEUTICS** is the segment of medicine concerned with preventing or treating disease. Therapeutics involves the use of a wide variety of techniques, such as drugs, mechanical devices, vaccines, and psychiatry. Over the years, advocates of certain therapeutic concepts have formed themselves into groups; *e.g.*, those of chiropractic, homeopathy, naprapathy, naturopathy, and osteopathy. In conventional modern medicine, therapeutic concepts and techniques are incorporated into such therapeutic specialties as pharmacology, immunology, preventive medicine, psychiatry, psychotherapy, and radiology. Occasionally some measure that has been discarded in the past is revived, revised, and put to medical use; more often, however, the revival serves the interest of quackery. (*See* separate articles on many of the subjects mentioned in this article; *e.g.*, Pharmacology; Psychotherapy; Quackery. *See* also Medicine and Surgery, History of.)

**Scope.**—The scope of therapeutics is broad, as evidenced by the many types of therapy. Included are biologic therapy, which involves the use of biologic products, such as serums, vaccines, and antitoxins; chemotherapy, the use of pure chemicals to attack specific diseases; diathermic therapy, the use of diathermy equipment; shock therapy, the treatment of mental patients by passing an electrical current through the brain or by injecting insulin into the blood; endocrine therapy, the use of hormones. Other forms of therapy make use of gold, heat, high-frequency sound (ultrasound), oxygen at normal pressure or at high pressure, X-rays, radium, infrared rays, ultraviolet rays, hypnosis, water baths (hydrotherapy), anticoagulants, vitamins, aerosol mists, sea water (thalassotherapy), and surgery. Still other forms include musical therapy, physical therapy, and occupational therapy.

Practically any drug or treatment can be introduced and named as a form of therapy. Or, from another approach, practically any part of the body can be treated and the procedure called a form of therapeutics, *e.g.*, dental therapeutics or alimentary therapeutics. Also, therapeutics may be specific or nonspecific, and it may be rational or irrational (the latter form is usually employed by quacks).

**Development.**—At the beginning of the 20th century only a few drugs and other measures were of outstanding therapeutic importance, and some of these were improperly understood. Most doctors knew the value of sun, fresh air, fresh fruit, and some pain-relieving substances, but little was known of the precise way in which they serve man. Furthermore, while surgery was a useful part of medical practice it was fraught with danger because of the lack of satisfactory antiseptic measures, satisfactory anesthetics and specific aids to combat shock, loss of blood, and infections. It is probably safe to say that modern therapeutics did not begin until after World War I although the foundation for its development was laid in earlier years by the work of Paul Ehrlich, Robert Koch, and others.

The application of measures to prevent disease and to cure those suffering from it goes back to the early history of man when someone tried to apply leaves, mud, and splints and invoked the aid of the gods. As he learned by trial and error the value of a few simple remedies he began the practice of medicine. Man had to pass to civilized ages before he found much of therapeutic value in plants, animals, and minerals, however. With the advent of modern medicine, accidental discoveries, keen observations, and careful study resulted in some useful findings. For example, the value of digitalis for heart diseases was learned by a physician in England investigating a brew made from foxglove by an elderly housewife; and the usefulness of Epsom Salts was demonstrated when a farmer became curious as to why his cattle would not drink from a certain well. Many techniques, as cupping, were tried widely and ultimately discarded. In the Western world, acupuncture generally lost favour, although it is still used in some parts of the East. Many therapeutic cults, such as pneumatism, arose and disappeared.

**Value.**—Following basic chemical and physical findings in the 19th century, modern chemotherapy and therapeutics were born. Drugs were purified, specific measures against disease were developed, diseases were identified and techniques for diagnosis, treatment, and prevention of disease were unearthed. Some of these discoveries were based on studies seemingly unrelated to medicine. Thus, Sir Alexander Fleming found penicillin in 1928 by observing the growth of mold on bacteria-growing media in his bacteriologic laboratory, and Gerhard Domagk, while searching in 1932 for better dyes for woolen goods, found the precursor to the sulfa drugs.

Some idea of the value of modern therapeutics can be obtained by comparing statistics. During the Crimean War the French lost 8 men from diseases for every 1 killed in battle and the Russians lost 20 to 1. The common causes of death were cholera, typhus, dysentery, and infections. In the Spanish-American War 7 soldiers were lost to disease or wound infection for every 1 who died in battle. In the American Civil War 50% of the wounded died, whereas in World War I 6 to 12% died, and in World War II the death rate was 3%. In World War I the annual death rate for U.S. soldiers overseas was 12.8 for each 1,000 men abroad; in World War II it was 0.5. In World War I, 20 to 30% of soldiers who contracted pneumonia died, in World War II 1%. In 1900 a newborn child had a life expectancy of 49.2 years, but in 1940 it was 63.3 years, and in the mid-1960s it was about 68 years.

Much of this improvement was due to improvements in hygiene, health education, hospital facilities, food, sanitary measures, surgical techniques, transportation facilities, and other factors. The development of more and purer drugs, physical devices (*e.g.*, X-ray machines), and foods for special health purposes (*e.g.*, baby foods and foods for the sick) were important factors.

**Standardization of Therapeutic Agents.**—In most countries an attempt is made to ensure the marketing of satisfactory foods and drugs, but in only a few countries is this carried to a degree that provides assurance for user and prescriber. Many countries use pharmacopoeias as a guide for quality, but most countries do not have laws to enforce standardization of drugs or to prevent the marketing of harmful or useless substances. In the United States drugs, foods, and to some extent devices shipped in interstate commerce are subject to control in several ways: manufacturers, because of competition and fear of adverse publicity and lawsuits, try to develop effective and pure drugs and foods. In addition, the Federal Food, Drug and Cosmetic Act governs quality, labeling, and to some extent promotional claims. Acting as an agent for this and other acts is the Food and Drug Administration, which can seize and examine products and inspect factories. Another federal agency administers another federal law governing the sale of serums and vaccines. Some states and a few large cities have their own laws and agencies in this field. The medical profession is, of course, always doing its own examining and through the American Medical Association supports several councils that examine drugs, foods, and devices to determine their usefulness.

In the United Kingdom drugs are regulated by the Food and Drug Act, the Ministry of Health, and the Ministry of Agriculture, Fisheries and Food. Control of serums and vaccines, antibiotics, and certain other biological substances is set forth in the Therapeutic Substances Act. The standardization of some drugs is governed by international agreement, and an international pharmacopoeia is published by the World Health Organization.

Drugs and foods may be tested chemically, by assay on animals, and through other measures. The purer chemicals obviously pose fewer problems as a rule than do the impure mixtures, many of which are of botanical or animal origin. While most drugs can be examined by chemical tests, some (of which insulin is an outstanding example) defy such an approach. Such drugs are usually assayed by comparing new lots of the drug with an official standard preparation. The comparison is based on the drug's ability to elicit a particular biological effect under rigorously controlled conditions in a certain species of animal.

**Mode of Action.**—The selection of a method of treatment for a disease depends on several factors, such as the disease involved, the depth of illness of the patient, hazards posed by the disease as a public health menace, and the kind of remedy available. Thus a drug may be given by mouth; injected into or under the skin, into a muscle, vein, or artery, or into other tissues of the body; or it may be applied to the skin. It may be available as a tablet, powder, or solution, or in a capsule or ointment.

A drug or other remedy may be given to specifically combat a disease; it may be given to help the body mobilize its own natural defense forces, as the sulfa drugs hold in check the growth of bacteria while the body overcomes those already present; it may be used to provide symptomatic relief, such as aspirin for headache; or it may be used to directly attack disease, such as X-rays for cancer. The choice of treatment depends on the cause of the disease, complications, and specificity of available therapeutic measures.

In addition, the physician always must remember the patient's peace of mind. Sympathetic understanding of a health problem sometimes is more effective than drugs or surgery. Kind words, a change in scenery, and new friends often have effected seemingly miraculous improvement.

**Prevention of Disease.**—The prevention of disease is founded on adequate diet, adequate sanitation, and use of specific measures against diseases. Some authorities have referred to this as preventive therapeutics. School clinics, venereal disease clinics, public health laboratories, vaccination, balanced meals, extra milk for children, and addition of iodine to salt to prevent goitre, of fluoride to water to prevent dental decay, and of vitamin D to milk and vitamin C to other foods are part of current preventive practices.

Among the diseases that can be prevented by immunization are smallpox, diphtheria, yellow fever, typhoid and paratyphoid fever, measles, and poliomyelitis.

Other important preventive measures supplementary to therapy are proper disposal of sewage, eradication of disease-carrying mosquitoes, and the provision of germ-free drinking water. Since some animals and birds carry diseases to which man is susceptible, they too must be subjected to certain control measures such as testing for tuberculosis and vaccination against rabies. (*See* also PREVENTIVE MEDICINE.)

**Specificity of Drug Action.**—One of the encouraging aspects of modern therapeutics is the specificity of drug action. Formerly "shotgun therapy" was often the order of the day. Today, however, the physician can choose specific drugs for many diseases and health problems. Thus, one can choose the type of anesthetic agent that is best for a certain type of operation; the best type of drug for sleeplessness and pain; the type of drug best suited to muscle spasm, or high blood pressure, or allergy, or infection. Such a direct approach was made possible by the development of more precise diagnostic techniques, by a better understanding of the functions of the body, and by the combined efforts of chemists, physicians, and other specially trained people who can jointly develop first in theory and then in practice the chemicals needed to combat a certain health problem.

*See* SERUM THERAPY; VACCINE THERAPY; IMMUNITY AND IMMUNIZATION; CHEMOTHERAPY; RADIOLOGY: *Radiation Therapy; see* also references under "Therapeutics" in the Index.

BIBLIOGRAPHY.—T. H. Sollmann, *A Manual of Pharmacology,* 8th ed. (1957); American Medical Association, *Glandular Physiology and Therapy—a Symposium,* 5th ed. (1954), *New and Nonofficial Drugs* (revised annually); F. K. Oldham, F. O. Kelsey and E. M. K. Geiling, *Essentials of Pharmacology,* 4th ed. (1960); A. E. Smith, *Technic of Medication* (1948); W. R. Feasby, *Medical Manual* (1948); W. Modell (ed.), *Drugs of Choice* (current ed.); H. F. Conn (ed.), *Current Therapy* (revised annually); A. J. Clark, *Applied Pharmacology,* ed. by A. Wilson and H. C. Schild, 9th ed. (1959); J. H. Gaddum, *Pharmacology,* 5th ed. (1959); A. Grollman, *Pharmacology and Therapeutics,* 6th ed. (1965). (A. E. SH.; F. O. K.)

**THERAPSID,** a member of a major order of reptiles of the Permian and Triassic periods (about 235,000,000 to 160,000,000 years ago). Therapsids were the stock that gave rise to mammals. As early as the preceding Carboniferous Period there appeared a distinct evolutionary line beginning with the archaic mammal ancestors, order Pelycosauria, and leading toward mammals. From one pelycosaur family sprang the therapsids. Primitive therapsids are present in the Middle Permian of the U.S.S.R.; later forms are known from every continent except Australia but are commonest in the Late Permian and Early Triassic of South Africa. The limbs and limb girdles were modified for four-footed mammalian locomotion. The skull, as in mammals, had a single opening in the temporal region, bounded below by a bony arch. Usually the teeth were differentiated into mammallike nipping incisors, large stabbing canines, and a series of cheek teeth. The lower jaw, however, was reptilian in structure, being composed of seven bones instead of one as in mammals, and had a different, primitive articulation with the skull. In advanced forms, as in mammals, there was a bony palate in the roof of the mouth. It is possible that therapsids initiated such mammalian features as the nursing habit, development of hair, and temperature regulation.

A notable therapsid side branch was that of the herbivorous dicynodonts ("two-tuskers"), in which upper canines were generally retained but the other teeth were replaced by a horny bill. Among carnivorous therapsids, gorgonopsians and therocephalians were characteristic of the Permian and cynodonts and bauriamorphs were advanced Triassic representatives. A few therapsids were still present in the Late Triassic and even into the Jurassic, but most had by then become extinct or had evolved into a primitive mammalian stage. *See* also MAMMAL; REPTILE; PALEONTOLOGY. (A. S. RR.)

**THERAVADA** ("School of Elders"), also sometimes called HINAYANA ("Little Vehicle"), is one of the two great schools of Buddhism, the other being the Mahayana ("Great Vehicle"). Theravada Buddhism holds the Pali canon of Buddhist scripture to be authoritative (*see* PALI LITERATURE). The school is dominant in the countries of southeast Asia—Ceylon, Burma, Thailand, Laos, and Cambodia (but not Vietnam, which is predominantly Mahayana). *See* BUDDHISM.

**THÉRÈSE, SAINT,** OF LISIEUX (MARIE FRANÇOISE THÉRÈSE MARTIN) (1873–1897), known as the Little Flower or St. Thérèse of the Child Jesus, was born on Jan. 2, 1873, at Alençon in Normandy. In the deeply religious atmosphere of her home her piety developed early and intensively, but her sister and her father spoiled her. At 15, after much opposition, she entered the Carmelite convent at Lisieux, where she kept the rule to perfection but attracted no attention. She was conspicuously a neurotic child, but at the convent, while she continued to suffer from scruples—a causeless feeling of guilt—and, at the end, from religious doubts, she was outwardly smiling and pleasant, and never exhibited any of the usual selfish manifestations of the malady. Before her death from tuberculosis on Sept. 30, 1897, she acknowledged that because of her difficult nature not one day had ever passed without a struggle. In fact she used her nervous disabilities as the very material on which she built her sanctity. She was canonized in 1925 and her feast day is Oct. 3.

Her autobiography, *Histoire d'une âme,* was first published in 1898 in an extensively rewritten and sometimes misleading form, but in 1956 a nearly genuine photostat text was produced. The best English translation is that by R. A. Knox (1958). St. Thérèse defined her doctrine of the Little Way as "the way of spiritual childhood, the way of trust and absolute surrender."

BIBLIOGRAPHY.—E. Robo, *Two Portraits of St. Teresa of Lisieux,* rev. ed. (1957); I. F. Görres, *The Hidden Face* (1959); H. U. von Balthasar, *Thérèse of Lisieux* (1954). (ET. R.)

**THERMIONICS** deals with the emission of electrically charged particles from heated surfaces; these particles may be negatively charged, such as electrons, or positively charged, such as positive ions. While it was known from the 18th century that heated surfaces emit electric charges, a discovery made by Thomas A. Edison (1883) drew special attention to this phenomenon. Edison's discovery (later named the Edison effect by W. H. Preece) was that current can be made to flow between two electrodes in a vacuum if one of the two is heated. Application of this effect was made by J. A. Fleming in the construction of a thermionic rectifier or valve (diode) that allows the flow of electricity in one direction but not in the other. In 1899 J. J. Thomson established the electric charge carrier as composed of particles, each having the same charge and mass as did the electrons he had discovered about two years earlier (*see* also ELECTRON). In 1903 O. W. Richardson discovered the relation between the temperature of the emitting surface and the rate of emission of electrons. He also suggested the term thermionic emission for the Edison effect which previously had been referred to as "the emission of electrons from hot bodies."

Early investigators of thermionic emission included Max von Laue, W. Schottky, and I. Langmuir. Thermionic emission of positive ions (positively charged atoms) was first observed by Richardson and was later studied by Langmuir and K. H. Kingdon (1923). They observed emission of positive ions of alkali metals adsorbed on the thermionic emitter (cathode). A second type of positive-ion emission, observed by H. B. Wahlin and L. P. Smith (1929), is that of positively charged atoms of the cathode metal itself (*see* ELECTRICITY: *The Particles of Electricity*).

The greatest impetus to further extension of knowledge in thermionics was the extensive practical application of devices that make use of thermionic emission. The most widely used of these are vacuum tubes used as rectifiers of alternating current and amplifiers of electric signals of low power (*see* ELECTRON TUBE). Other important applications of thermionic emission include low-voltage gas discharges (such as fluorescent lamps) and the direct conversion of heat into electric power.

**Theory of Thermionic Emission.**—Any atom includes a positively charged nucleus surrounded by one or more electrons (*see* ATOM). According to quantum theory the electrons of an atom may exist only in discrete allowed (quantum) states. The allowed electronic states of an atom may be grouped into categories called shells. In every atom with a sufficiently high atomic number (*i.e.*, number of electrons) there are two electrons very close to the nucleus that serve to fill the K shell; next is the L shell with a maximum of eight electrons. Depending on the total number of electrons associated with the atomic nucleus to make it electrically neutral, additional shells may be filled. The outermost electrons are known as the valence electrons. Almost all metals that are good conductors have only one or two of these valence electrons in the outermost shell; the details are understood in terms of wave mechanics (*see* QUANTUM MECHANICS: *Wave Mechanics*).

Upon crystallization the atoms of common metallic elements yield their valence electrons to quantum states of the whole crystal rather than states associated with each individual atom. These electrons are then called free electrons. The transfer of a free electron from one quantum state to another is accompanied by a change in energy of the system as a whole. At a temperature of absolute zero the most stable state of the system should tend to be that of least energy; thus the electrons should occupy low-energy quantum states, leaving those of high energy empty.

At a finite temperature the free electrons in a crystal tend to be distributed among the allowed quantum states of the crystal according to the rules of statistical thermodynamics. To a very good approximation, these rules are described by the so-called Fermi-Dirac statistics. A quantity that characterizes the condition of the free electrons in a crystal in equilibrium at a temperature $T$ is the energy of the state that has exactly 50% probability of being occupied. This energy is called the Fermi level of the crystal, in honour of Enrico Fermi, who first developed the statistics of free electrons (*see* SOLID STATE PHYSICS).

According to Fermi-Dirac statistics, if any two electrically conducting solids are in contact and in equilibrium (neither heat nor electric current flows from one to the other) not only must their temperatures be uniform and equal but so must their Fermi level. Both temperature and Fermi level are properties called thermodynamic potentials. If two conductors have the same temperature but differ in Fermi level, this difference equals the work required per electron to move electrons from one conductor to the other. Therefore the reading of a voltmeter connected to two conductors of the same temperature equals the difference in their Fermi level, and thus the differences in Fermi level between isothermal conductors can be readily measured. Unfortunately no such simple procedure is known for measuring the absolute value of the Fermi level in a conductor.

The theory of thermionic emission is illustrated by fig. 1 in which the electron potential energy distribution in space is shown near a conductor-vacuum interface subjected to zero external electric field. The vertical direction represents energies and the horizontal represents distance. The solid line to the right of the vertical dashed line represents the potential energy of an electron outside the last layer of atoms of a conductor crystal. Inside the conductor, the potential energy of an electron varies periodically with the atomic structure (as shown by the dotted line). The solid line to the left of the vertical dashed line represents the spatial average of this potential energy. The Fermi level $\mu$ of the conductor is shown by the horizontal dashed line.

If the potential energy of an electron is zero at large distance away from the surface, then the potential energy inside the conductor is lower by the amount shown as $W_a$. This difference in potential energy is called the electron affinity of the surface. It is produced by the additive effects of the image force (the attraction of an electron by a conductor) and the forces exerted on an electron by charged dipole layers that may exist on the surface.

Fig. 1 represents what was called by Langmuir a motive diagram. A motive differs from the potential encountered in electrostatics, being the potential energy of an electron with a finite charge $q$, whereas the electrostatic potential is defined as the potential energy per unit of charge of an infinitesimal charge. The image force per unit of charge is finite for an electron near a conducting surface and is zero for an infinitesimal charge.

The difference between the motive (potential energy of the electrons) outside the conductor and the Fermi level is called the true work function $\phi$ of the surface. The difference $\zeta$ between the motive inside the conductor and the Fermi level has no well-accepted name. The quantities $\phi$ and $\zeta$ have the units of energy per electron and will be expressed in electron volts during this discussion. (Some authors define $\phi$ as an energy per unit of charge and measure it in volts.)

The value of $W_a$ for a particular metal (*i.e.*, crystal) depends not only on the metal but also on the particular crystallographic surface that is exposed. For example, A. R. Hutson (1955) showed that the value of $W_a$ for the [111] surface of tungsten is less than that for the [110] surface by at least 0.8 ev (electron volts). (An electron volt is the energy gained or lost by an electron in moving across a region in which there is a difference in potential of one volt. Since the charge $q$ on an electron is $1.602 \times 10^{-19}$ coulomb, the electron volt is $1.602 \times 10^{-19}$ joule.)

To help understand fig. 1, other values of the symbols will be given as they refer to tungsten. The value of $\zeta$ is about 5.8 ev. This number derives from the application of Fermi-Dirac statistics to an assembly of free electrons of concentration $n$, and is computed from

$$\zeta = \frac{h^2}{2mq}\left(\frac{3n}{8\pi}\right)^{2/3}\left\{1 - \frac{\pi^2}{12}\left[\frac{kT}{\frac{h^2}{2m}\left(\frac{3n}{8\pi}\right)^{2/3}}\right]^2\right\} \tag{1}$$

In equation (1) $h$ is Planck's constant ($6.6256 \times 10^{-34}$ joule sec); $m$ is the electron mass ($9.1091 \times 10^{-31}$ kg); $q$ is the charge on an electron; $k$ is Boltzmann's constant ($1.38054 \times 10^{-23}$ joule /°K or $8.617 \times 10^{-5}$ ev/°K; and $T$ is temperature in °K. An evaluation of $\zeta$ as it applies to tungsten (in which there are 6.4 $\times 10^{28}$ atoms per cubic metre) shows that the second term which depends on the $T$ is so small compared to unity that $\zeta$ of 5.8 ev may be used without correction over the useful range of 1,800° to 2,500° K. Careful experimentation by M. H. Nichols (1940),

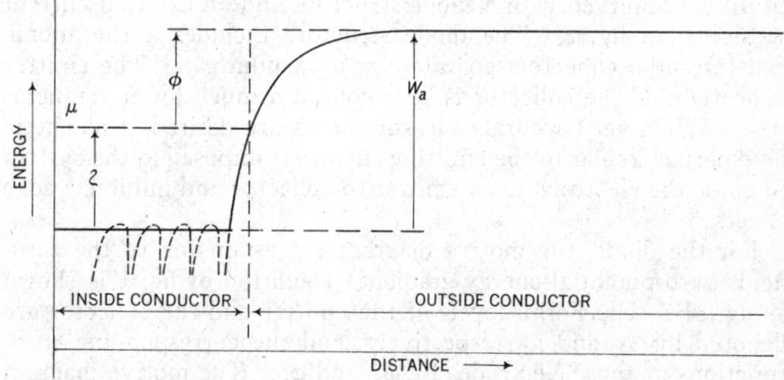


FIG. 1.—ELECTRON POTENTIAL ENERGY AT THE EMITTER REGION (MOTIVE DIAGRAM; *see* TEXT)

G. F. Smith (1954), and Hutson established the value of $\phi$ as $4.3 + (3 \times 10^{-5})\ T$ for the [111] surface. It follows that $W_a$ is close to 10.1 ev for this surface and at least 10.9 ev for the [110] surface.

Thermionic emission from a metallic conductor can be explained in terms of fig. 1. With the metal at a very low temperature, the electrons fill all the quantum states from the bottom of the motive right to the Fermi level; very few electrons will be found above this level. There will be some high-energy electrons, however, and the Fermi level will mark the quantum state that has a 50% probability of being occupied. As the temperature is raised, more and more electrons will occupy high-energy states (even as high as $W_a$) and there will be vacancies in the states below $\mu$ exactly equal to the number occupied above $\mu$.

In their random motion in the interior of the metal, many electrons of very high energy will approach the surface. If an electron moving at high speed has a kinetic energy associated with motion toward the boundary greater than $W_a$, it may escape the metal. As it crosses the boundary at the surface, however, some of its kinetic energy is transformed into potential energy.

**Richardson Equation.**—From thermodynamic considerations the current density $J_s$ associated with the electrons that escape from a conductor is given by

$$J_s = AT^2 e^{-\phi/kT} \tag{2}$$

where $A$ is a constant characteristic of the emitting surface, $T$ is the absolute temperature of the surface, $e$ is the base of natural logarithms (2.71828), $\phi$ is the true work function of the surface, and $k$ is Boltzmann's constant. (If $\phi$ is expressed in ev, $k$ must be expressed in ev/°K.) This relation was derived by Richardson in 1912; the constant $A$ was later evaluated from the work of Von Laue (1918), S. Dushman (1922), R. H. Fowler (1928), and others to be

$$A = (1 - r)\frac{4\pi mk^2 q}{h^3} \tag{3}$$

where $r$ is the electron reflection coefficient of the surface. For pure metals $r$ is very small (of the order of 0.05) and is usually neglected. Then the value of $A$ becomes

$$A = 120.4 \text{ amp/cm}^2\,{}^\circ\text{K}^2$$

The value $J_s$ in equation (2) is called the saturation current density of a surface. It equals the current extracted from the surface if, by external means, the electric field away from the surface is made equal to zero (the motive away from the surface is horizontal as in fig. 1).

Equation (2) shows that the saturation current density of a surface increases with increasing temperature and decreasing work function. The lower the work function of a surface, the higher its saturation current density at a given temperature. Thus the work function is a measure of the tendency of the conductor to retain its electrons; thermodynamically the work function of a surface equals the average work per electron required to extract electrons from a conductor and to bring them at rest outside the conductor surface.

**Emission Measurements.**—Thermionic emission may be quantitatively observed with a diode structure and an external current as shown in fig. 2. The diode structure includes a thermionic emitter and a collector separated by a vacuum gap. The emitter is heated and the collector is kept cold at a much lower temperature. When very accurate measurements are desired, a magnetic field perpendicular to the emitting surface is imposed in the system to guide the electrons from emitter to collector and minimize edge effects.

For the diode, the motive diagram corresponding to the zero-field (zero-potential-energy-gradient) condition of fig. 1 is shown as fig. 3B. The Fermi levels of the emitter and the collector are denoted by $\mu_E$ and $\mu_C$ respectively, and the corresponding work functions of these electrodes by $\phi_E$ and $\phi_C$. The motive diagram of fig. 3B is laterally compressed (about 10,000 times) as compared to that of fig. 1 because the change in the potential energy

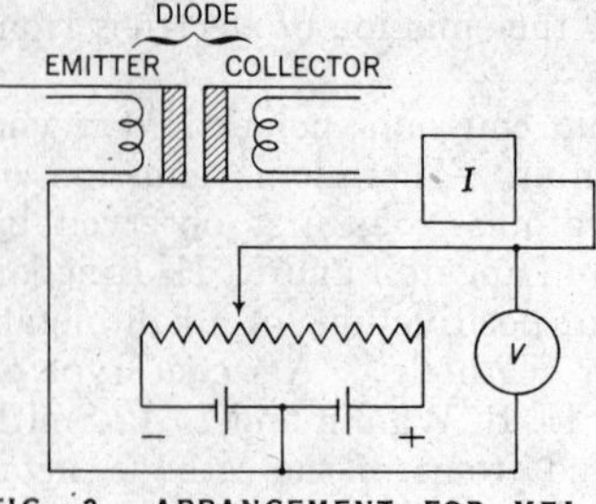


FIG. 2.—ARRANGEMENT FOR MEASURING DIODE CHARACTERISTICS

$I$ is observed current; $V$ is applied voltage

across a surface (shown in detail in fig. 1) occurs over a distance of the order of $10^{-6}$ cm whereas the distance between emitter and collector of a diode is of the order of $10^{-1}$ cm.

The voltage $V$ applied to the diode multiplied by the electronic charge $q$ equals the difference in Fermi levels $(\mu_E - \mu_C)$ of the electrodes. For the condition illustrated in fig. 3B, the current flowing through the diode equals the saturation current $I_s$ of the emitter ($J_s$ times the emitter area). If the voltage applied to the diode is increased significantly above the value $V_b$ of fig. 3B, an electron-accelerating electric field (potential energy gradient) will exist near the emitter surface and the current flowing through the diode will increase beyond the saturation current of the emitter (fig. 3A). This phenomenon, called the Schottky effect, was first pointed out by Schottky in 1914; in the presence of an electron-accelerating field $E$, the current flowing through the diode is given by the Schottky equation

$$I = I_s e^{\frac{q^{1/2}}{4\pi\epsilon_0}\frac{q}{kT}(E)^{1/2}} \tag{4}$$

where $\epsilon_0$ is the permittivity of free space ($8.854 \times 10^{-12}$ farad/m) and $E$ is the electric field near the emitter surface. For parallel-plate geometry and large values of the applied voltage $V$, $E$ approximately equals $V$ divided by the interelectrode distance.

If $V$ is decreased below $V_b$, the motive diagram will have a maximum value $\psi_m$ greater than the electron potential energy $\psi_E$ near the emitter surface, as shown in fig. 3C. The shape of the motive diagram in fig. 3C arises from the negative charge of the electrons in transit from emitter to collector. The current flowing through the diode under these conditions will be less than the saturation current. Of the electrons in the emitter that move toward the surface only those with kinetic energies greater than $\psi_m$ will reach the collector; all others will be reflected back into the emitter. This phenomenon is called space-charge effect and was analyzed by Langmuir (1923) who gave an exact solution for the current flowing through a planar diode under space-charge conditions.

The location of the motive maximum under space-charge conditions depends on the applied voltage $V$. For sufficiently low values of $V$, usually negative, the motive maximum reaches the collector surface. This condition of operation is called the critical point. For values of $V$ less than that corresponding to the critical point, no maximum appears in the interelectrode space (fig. 3D). Under this condition the diode is said to operate in the Boltzmann mode.

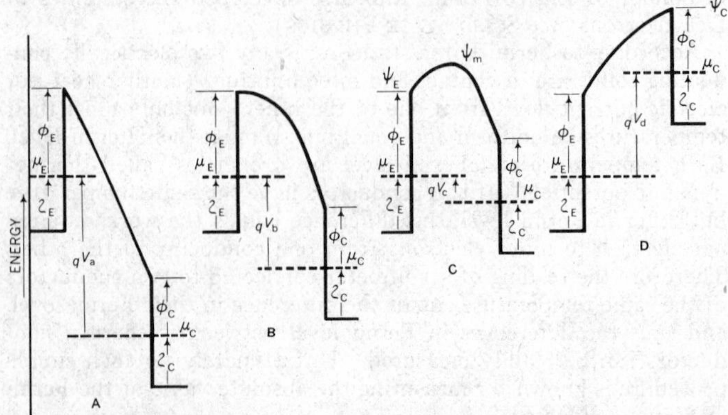


FIG. 3.—MOTIVE DIAGRAMS FOR VACUUM-DIODE OPERATION IN: (A) SCHOTTKY MODE; (B) SATURATION MODE; (C) SPACE-CHARGE MODE; (D) BOLTZMANN MODE

$\phi_E$ is emitter work function; $\phi_C$ is collector work function; $\mu_E$ is emitter Fermi level; $\mu_C$ is collector Fermi level; $V_a$, $V_b$, $V_c$, $V_d$ are applied voltages; $q$ is electronic charge

The current flowing through a diode operating in the Boltzmann mode is limited only by the value of the electron potential energy $\psi_C$ near the collector surface.

Thus, depending on the value of the applied potential, a thermionic diode may operate in the Schottky mode, the saturation mode, the space-charge mode, or the Boltzmann mode. For each of these there is a prescribed relation involving the current, the applied voltage, and other parameters such as emitter temperature, emitter work function, and interelectrode distance. A typical complete current-voltage ($I$-$V$) curve of a thermionic diode is plotted as fig. 4 in semilogarithmic scale. The various modes of operation are indicated in the figure.

An important part of the $I$-$V$ curve of fig. 4 is that corresponding to the Boltzmann mode. Here the curve is the straight Boltzmann line, indicating that the current changes exponentially with applied voltage. This results from the nature of the energy distribution of the electrons in the emitter and may be deduced theoretically; it can be shown that the slope of the Boltzmann line is proportional to the inverse of the absolute temperature of the emitter.

Another important part of the $I$-$V$ curve is the saturation line; this specifies the emitter saturation current, which (with the Richardson equation) may be used to evaluate the true emitter work function.

*Empirical Equation and Thermionic Constants.*—Equation (2) is often experimentally validated by observing saturation current density $J_s$ as a function of temperature $T$ and plotting the data according to

$$\ln\frac{J_s}{T^2} = \ln A_R - \frac{\phi_R}{kT} \tag{5}$$

where $A_R$ is the empirical Richardson constant and $\phi_R$ is the Richardson work function as an empirical constant. The observable quantity on the left of equation (5) is plotted as a function of $T^{-1}$ or, better yet, as a function of $1/kT$. Generally a straight-line relation is found and values of $A_R$ and $\phi_R$ are determined this way.

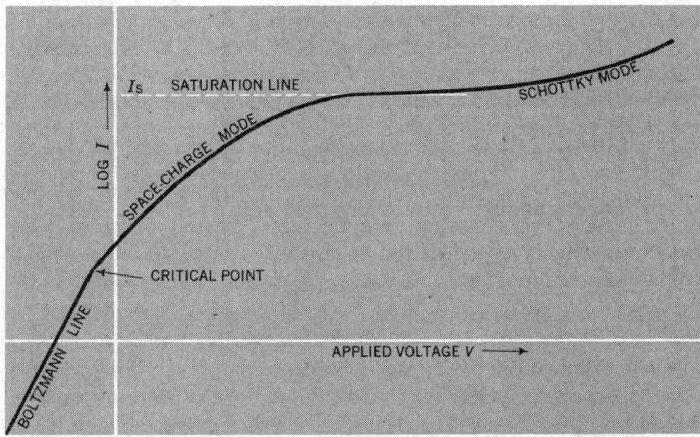


FIG. 4.—TYPICAL VOLTAGE-CURRENT CURVE FOR A VACUUM DIODE

The logarithm of the current ($I$) flowing through a diode versus voltage ($V$) applied to the diode terminals. $I_s$ is the saturation current of the emitter

Comparisons are often made between $A_R$ and the theoretical value of the universal constant $A$ of equation (2). More often than not $A_R$ is less than $A$, but many examples are found in which $A_R$ is much greater than $A$. One reason for these differences is that a given sample generally does not exhibit a single crystallographic surface for emission; therefore, the observed $J_s$ is an average of $J_s$ for many crystals. It will be less than the maximum saturation density and greater than the minimum of the various exposed surfaces of a test sample.

Another reason is that nothing in the theory from which equation (2) was obtained limits its use to the condition that $\phi$ is a constant. In fact, equation (5) will be satisfied if $\phi$ changes linearly with temperature according to the relation

$$\phi = \phi_R + \alpha kT \tag{6}$$

where $\alpha$ is the temperature coefficient. It may be seen that the observed value of the constant $A_R$ would be altered by the factor $e^{-\alpha}$ from the theoretical $A$. Thus if $\alpha$ is negative, as it may be when adsorbed electronegative atoms are present as surface impurities, $A_R$ can be very large; if $\alpha$ is positive $A_R$ will be small.

Experimental values of $A_R$ and $\phi_R$ have very little theoretical importance, even though they have use in engineering. These numbers may be used to predict the electron emission that will be available from similar samples, but $\phi_R$ will very seldom be the true work function $\phi$ defined in fig. 1. The basic Richardson thermionic relationship is equation (3), and there the work function $\phi$ is the only one to use. The empirical values of the thermionic constants $A_R$ and $\phi_R$ are referred to as the Richardson constants. They are to be used with the form of the equation given by

$$J_s = A_R T^2 e^{-\frac{\phi_R}{kT}} \tag{7}$$

Values of thermionic constants for various elements and compounds are given in the table.

*Oxide-Coated Cathodes.*—Widespread application of thermionic emission to electronics largely rests on the low-work-function oxide cathode. This development was initiated with the discovery by A. Wehnelt (1903) that a coating of alkaline-earth oxides (CaO, SrO, and BaO) greatly enhances electron emission from a metallic surface. The oxide cathode generally consists of a nickel substrate upon which a suitably prepared barium-strontium carbonate is sprayed. The fine particles are held in a binder, which is later removed by heating. The conversion of the carbonate to the oxide takes place within the final assembly during the early stages of evacuation. The conversion is completed by maintaining the cathode at about 1,300° K for about one minute (G. M. Herrmann and J. S. Wagener, 1951).

Important factors that govern the procedure include: the need for nickel alloys that contain reducing agents such as silicon, titanium, and magnesium (E. S. Rittner, 1953); development of required particle size of about two or three microns; porosity after sintering of about 50% with pores of about two microns in linear dimensions; cleaning of all other parts of the tube, which is important for maintenance of cathode emission life; and coating adherence which is dependent on such factors as vacuum conditions and cleaning of parts.

*Thermionic Constants**

| Element | $A_R$ | $\phi_R$ | $J_s$ | $T$ |
|---|---|---|---|---|
| Carbon | 30 | 4.34 | $1.4 \times 10^{-3}$ | 2,000 |
| Cesium | 162 | 1.81 | $2.5 \times 10^{-11}$ | 500 |
| Barium | 60 | 2.11 | $1.4 \times 10^{-3}$ | 1,000 |
| Zirconium | 330 | 4.12 | $8.5 \times 10^{-5}$ | 1,600 |
| Hafnium | 14.5 | 3.53 | $2.8 \times 10^{-4}$ | 1,600 |
| Thorium | 60.2 | 3.35 | $4.3 \times 10^{-3}$ | 1,600 |
| Columbium | 37.2 | 4.01 | $1.16 \times 10^{-2}$ | 2,000 |
| Tantalum | 55 | 4.19 | $3.20 \times 10^{-3}$ | 2,000 |
| Molybdenum | 60.2 | 4.38 | $2.34 \times 10^{-3}$ | 2,000 |
| Tungsten | 60.2 | 4.52 | $1.00 \times 10^{-3}$ | 2,000 |
| Rhenium | 200 | 5.1 | $3.4 \times 10^{-5}$ | 2,000 |
| Iron ($\alpha$) | 26 | 4.48 | $2.7 \times 10^{-12}$ | 1,180 |
| Iron ($\beta$) | 1.5 | 4.21 | $4.5 \times 10^{-12}$ | 1,200 |
| | | | $2.1 \times 10^{-7}$ | 1,600 |
| Nickel | 30 | 4.61 | $5.6 \times 10^{-7}$ | 1,600 |
| Cobalt | 41 | 4.41 | $1.4 \times 10^{-5}$ | 1,600 |
| Rhodium | | 4.58 | | |
| Palladium | 60 | 4.99 | $3.0 \times 10^{-8}$ | 1,600 |
| Osmium | | 4.7 | | |
| Platinum | 17,000 | 6.27 | $9.2 \times 10^{-10}$ | 1,600 |
| Lanthanum + | 1 | 1.8 | | |
| lanthanum boride | 15 | 2.0 | | |
| (La + $LaB_6$) | 29 | 2.66 | | |
| Barium strontium oxide (BaSrO) | 0.5 | 1.0 | | |

*$A_R$ is the Richardson constant in amp/cm² °K²; $\phi_R$ is the Richardson work function in ev; $J_s$ is the saturation current density in amp/cm²; $T$ is the emitter temperature in °K.

Electron emission from this structure depends on transfer of electrons from the nickel base metal to the coating, conduction through the coating, and finally emission from the coating. Barium oxide in the absence of imperfections is a very poor conductor of electrons. However, the presence of an amount of excess barium in the oxide of 1 to 20 parts per 1,000,000 is enough to raise the conductivity of the coating to tolerable levels.

The work function of an oxide-coated cathode depends on the composition of the coating and on the treatment used to activate it. For most types of cathode, the Richardson work functions are within about 0.3 ev of 1.1 ev for BaO and 0.3 ev of 1.4 ev for SrO.

During the life of a cathode, barium is evaporated; it also may be lost effectively if electronegative gas such as oxygen is evolved from other parts of the tube and goes to the cathode. The reducing agent in the nickel alloy acts to maintain the required concentration of barium to compensate for these losses. Migration of excess barium atoms is influenced by the concentration gradient and by internal electric fields. Since the flow of electrons through the coating produces a drop in potential across the coating (which is positive near the exterior surface and negative at the nickel), excess barium ions in the crystals tend to flow away from the surface. This flow reduces the concentration there and increases the resistance.

The life of an oxide-coated cathode decreases rapidly with increasing operating temperature because of evaporation of the oxides. On the other hand, saturation emission density of the cathode increases with temperature as indicated by the Richardson equation. It follows that the life of the cathode decreases with increasing saturation emission. Typical cathodes operated at saturation current densities of 0.1 to 1 amp/cm$^2$ last for a few thousand hours.

In the L cathode (developed by the Phillips Laboratories in the Netherlands) the oxides are impregnated into the supporting metal, mostly porous tungsten, rather than coated on it. This cathode has an oxide evaporation rate that is significantly less than that in coated cathodes and may be operated at a higher temperature for a given life. Typical operation of L cathode is 8 amp/cm$^2$ for about 10,000 hours.

*Cathodes with Adsorbed Monatomic Layers.*—Langmuir and W. Rogers (1913) discovered that thoria ($ThO_2$) occluded within a tungsten wire at the time of manufacture could be made to yield thorium by suitable heat treatment. The thorium atoms diffuse out of particularly active regions along crystal boundaries and finally over the external surface of the tungsten wire to form a cover that averages less than one atom thick. The thorium adheres very strongly to the underlying tungsten surface and becomes polarized. The direction of the dipole corresponds to a displacement of the outermost valence electrons of the thorium toward the tungsten. This displacement or polarization of the negative charge with respect to the positive charge on the thorium nucleus creates a dipole moment at each thorium atom (*see* DIPOLE MOMENTS).

A dipole layer formed on a metallic surface reduces the work function of the surface by an amount proportional to the dipole moment per unit of area. The dipole moment per unit of cathode area of an adsorbed film depends on the surface fraction $\theta$ that is covered by adsorbed film. For thorium on tungsten the maximum dipole moment occurs when $\theta$ equals 0.7; the corresponding reduction of the work function of tungsten at this point is about 2.9 ev from 4.6 ev to 1.7 ev.

For a thoriated tungsten cathode operating at a given temperature, the coverage $\theta$ will assume a value corresponding to an equilibrium between the rate of diffusion of thorium atoms to the surface and the rate of evaporation at the surface. If $\theta$ is varied by externally controlled means, the work function of a metallic surface at any given temperature can be set at any value (within limits). This very desirable situation obtains when refractory metal cathodes are operated in an atmosphere of alkali-metal vapour.

Langmuir and Kingdon (1923) observed that a tungsten filament immersed in cesium vapour exhibits very high emissions at relatively low temperatures. This phenomenon was studied in detail by J. B. Taylor and Langmuir (1933) who gave detailed experimental data as well as a theoretical analysis for the electron emissions of tungsten in the presence of cesium vapour. They found that cesium adsorbs on the surface of the tungsten at a value of $\theta$ that depends on the temperature of the tungsten and on the pressure of the vapour. For any given temperature of the tungsten, the coverage $\theta$ of the adsorbed cesium layer may be varied from 0 to 1 by varying the pressure of the vapour. In this manner the work function of a cesiated-tungsten surface may be varied from 4.6 ev (corresponding to pure tungsten) to 1.69 ev (corresponding to $\theta$ equal to 0.67). Similar behaviour was later observed for all investigated combinations of refractory metals with alkali-metal vapours.

Fig. 5 shows the saturation current density of cesiated tungsten as a function of emitter temperature $T$. The solid S-shaped lines are based on the theory of Taylor and Langmuir; each corresponds to a given cesium pressure $P_{cs}$. Each slanted straight line corresponds to a given work function of the composite surface. These lines were verified experimentally by J. M. Houston (1961), who extended the measurements of Taylor and Langmuir to higher cesium pressures. In the experiments, the cesium pressure $P_{cs}$ near the cathode is fixed by fixing the temperature $T_{cs}$ of a reservoir containing saturated liquid cesium and letting the reservoir communicate with the cathode enclosure. Fig. 6 shows a compilation of emission measurements by G. N. Hatsopoulos and A. Shavit (1965) for rhenium in cesium vapour.

In addition to their ability to attain a wide variety of work functions, alkali-metal-coated cathodes have practically limitless lives. Oxide-coated cathodes or thoriated-tungsten cathodes are depleted of their coating by evaporation, but the coating of alkali-metal surfaces is continuously regenerated by condensation from the vapour phase. In spite of these remarkable advantages, however, such cathodes were rarely used (the alkali-metal vapour interferes with the normal operation of most electron tubes) until they were found to be applicable in thermionic converters developed after 1958.

**Ion Emission from Alkali-Metal-Coated Cathodes.**—Alkali-metal cathodes emit positive ions as well as electrons. The rate of ion emission is proportional to the rate of atom arrival from the vapour to the surface and to a factor $f$ given by the Saha-Langmuir equation

$$f = \frac{1}{1 + 2e^{(V_i - \phi)/kT}}$$

where $V_i$ is the ionization potential energy of the vapour atoms and $\phi$ and $T$ refer to the surface.

It can be seen from this equation that (for given atom arrival rate and surface temperature) the ion emission rate increases with increasing work function of the surface; by the Richardson equation the electron emission rate decreases with increasing work function. For given $\phi$, $T$, and atom arrival rate, the ion emission from a surface increases with decreasing $V_i$. Since cesium is the

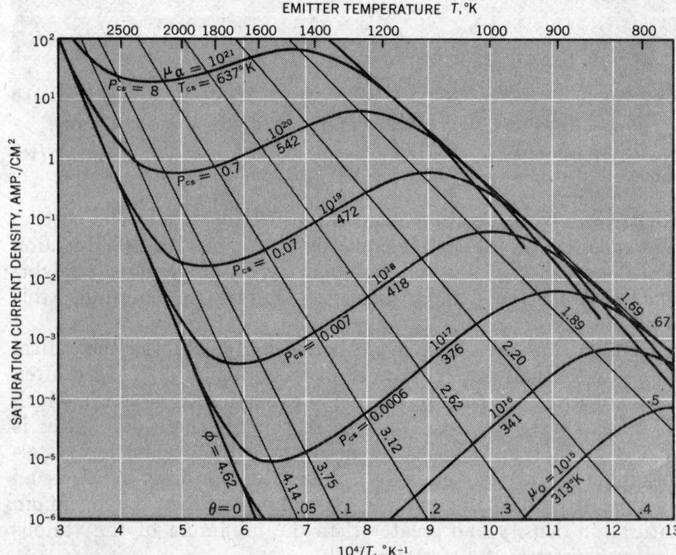


FIG. 5.—SATURATION CURRENT DENSITY OF ELECTRONS EMITTED FROM A TUNGSTEN SURFACE IN CESIUM VAPOUR

Each S-shaped curve corresponds to a fixed cesium pressure $P_{cs}$ in mm. Hg (torr), a given saturation temperature for the liquid cesium $T_{cs}$ in °K and a given cesium atom arrival rate in atoms/cm$^2$. Each slanted straight line corresponds to a fixed emitter work function $\phi$ in ev, a given cesium coverage $\theta$ in %

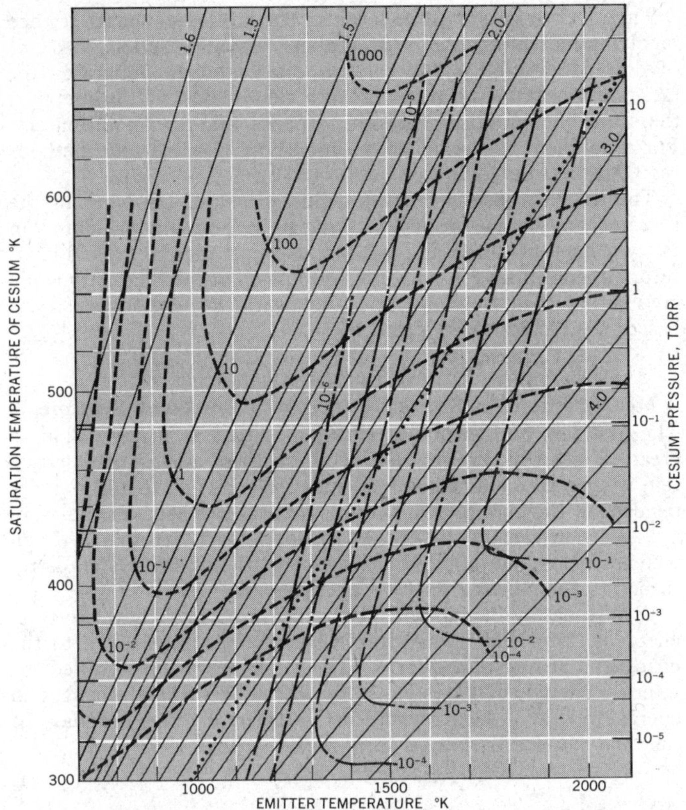


FIG. 6.—THERMIONIC EMISSION FROM A RHENIUM SURFACE IN CESIUM VAPOUR

Each dashed curve corresponds to a fixed saturation current density in amp/cm²; each dash-dot curve corresponds to a fixed positive-ion emission current in amp/cm²; each solid line corresponds to a fixed emitter work function in ev; the dotted line corresponds to equal and opposite charge densities for the emitted electrons and the emitted ions

element that has the lowest ionization potential $V_i$ (3.87 ev), it is clearly the best-suited material for producing ions at a surface.

**Thermionic Conversion.**—The diode voltage-current curve of fig. 4 shows that current flows from the emitter to the collector not only when a positive voltage $V$ is applied to the diode terminals but also when $V$ is negative. When both $I$ and $V$ are positive, the diode absorbs electric power from the external circuit. When $I$ is positive and $V$ is negative, however, the diode delivers electric power to the external circuit (as does a discharging electrolytic cell). Thus the diode becomes a generator of electricity and is called a thermionic energy converter. The electric energy is produced by heating the emitter; this gives the electrons in the emitter much more kinetic energy than the electrons in the collector. More electrons may flow from emitter to collector than from collector to emitter even when the collector is maintained at a higher Fermi level than that of the emitter. Thus a thermionic converter directly converts heat energy into electrical work without mechanical moving parts.

In the thermodynamic sense (*see* THERMODYNAMICS) a thermionic converter is a heat engine in that it receives heat energy at a high temperature (emitter), rejects a smaller amount of heat energy at a low temperature (collector), and produces electrical work. Its efficiency is, therefore, limited by the Carnot efficiency:

$$\eta \leq \frac{T_E - T_C}{T_C}$$

where $\eta$ is the thermal efficiency (work out divided by heat energy in) of the thermionic converter, $T_E$ is the emitter temperature, and $T_C$ is the collector temperature. The current that flows through a thermionic converter depends on the output voltage $V$, the temperatures $T_E$ and $T_C$, and the work functions $\phi_E$ and $\phi_C$ of the electrodes, and on the characteristics of the space between emitter and collector through which electrons flow. The output power delivered by a thermionic converter equals the current times the output voltage corresponding to that current. If no current is drawn from a diode (open circuit) the voltage difference between the electrodes adjusts so that an equal number of electrons flow in both directions. The open-circuit output voltage of a thermionic converter depends, therefore, both on its emitter and its collector temperatures.

Many types of thermionic converter have been investigated since 1955; the simplest are vacuum-diode converters first demonstrated by Hatsopoulos and J. Kaye (1957) and improved cesium-cathode diode converters first demonstrated by V. Wilson (1957). In vacuum-diode converters, emitter and collector are separated by an evacuated space; maximum output current is much lower than the saturation current of the emitter because of space-charge effects. To minimize these effects vacuum-diode converters have been built with very small interelectrode spacings (of the order of 0.001 cm). Cesiated-cathode diode converters have refractory metal emitters and collectors separated by cesium vapour; space-charge effects are minimized or eliminated by positive cesium ions that are thermionically emitted or produced in the interelectrode space. Because of such advantages most thermionic converters built after 1962 were of this type.

Thermionic converters operate at high temperature (typical emitter-temperature operating range 1,600°–2,000° K), high power density (5–50 watts/cm²), and moderate efficiency (10–20%). They may be used with a variety of heat sources (nuclear reactors, decaying isotopes, sunlight concentrated with parabolic mirrors, and burners using hydrocarbon fuels). Their principal applications are for space vehicles and military power supplies where weight and unattended operation are at a premium (*see* ENERGY CONVERSION, DIRECT).

BIBLIOGRAPHY.—O. W. Richardson, *The Emission of Electricity from Hot Bodies* (1916); A. L. Reimann, *Thermionic Emission* (1934); W. B. Nottingham, "Thermionic Emission," in S. Fluegge (ed.), *Handbuch der Physik*, vol. 21 (1956); J. Kaye and J. A. Welsh (eds.), *Direct Conversion of Heat to Electricity* (1960); I. Langmuir, *Collected Works*, vol. 3 (1961); J. W. Gewartowski and H. A. Watson, *Principles of Electron Tubes* (1965). (W. B. No.; G. N. H.)

**THERMITE,** a mixture of aluminum powder and iron oxide used in welding, in foundry work as a source of heat, and in the reduction of metal oxides. Thermit, a trade name, often is used in the metallurgical industry both for the mixture and the process. Thermite was widely used in incendiary bombs in the European theatre during World War II.

On ignition the reaction ($8Al + 3Fe_3O_4 = 9Fe + 4Al_2O_3$) gives a temperature estimated to be about 2,400° C. The reaction, stated in weight, means that 216 parts of aluminum plus 695 parts magnetite (iron oxide) equals 503 parts iron plus 408 parts slag, or approximately three parts of aluminum plus ten parts of magnetite will produce, on combustion, seven parts of iron. The iron thus produced represents about one-half the original thermite by weight and about one-third by volume.

Although the above reaction is the one commonly termed the thermite reaction, a generalized thermite reaction may be defined as an exothermic, self-propagating process in which finely divided aluminum powder is used to reduce metal oxides; the metal is liberated by direct oxidation of aluminum to aluminum oxide, with accompanying reduction of the less stable metal oxide.

Thermite was discovered by Hans Goldschmidt of Essen, Ger., in 1895, while trying to reduce chromium and manganese oxides. Goldschmidt's principal discovery related to a simple and safe method of ignition, as the action of aluminum when mixed with various oxides, sulfides and chlorides was well known. Fine aluminum powder will not react with pure iron oxide below a temperature of about 1,100° C. Previous experimenters had resorted to heating mixtures in a crucible, making the initial temperature so high that at the moment of ignition the mixture reacted with explosive violence. Goldschmidt obtained ignition of a cold mixture by using a barium-peroxide fuse. Later, magnesium powder or ribbon was used to ignite the thermite. The reaction, once initiated locally in a cold mixture, then spreads through the mixture since the heat generated by the reaction will ignite adjacent regions. Goldschmidt's original U.S. patent was granted March 16,

1897, and related principally to the use of aluminum as a reducing agent for the production of carbon-free metals such as cobalt, chromium, magnesium, tungsten, etc., by what is known as an aluminothermic process.

**Uses.**—The thermite reaction is of importance for its use as a heat and metal source in welding, as a heat source in foundry work to supply heat to one region of a mold, and as a source of carbon-free metal. Two methods of thermite welding are used. The first method, known as the plastic method, can be used for welding pipe. In this method, the thermite is simply used as a heat source. The ends of two pieces of pipe are carefully butted together, and after being heated to forging temperature by the thermite, are forced together, completing the weld. The second method, known as the fusion method, is used to weld large metal sections, such as ship rudder frames. Here the molten iron formed by the thermite is used to join two or more large metal members. (For a detailed description of thermite fusion welding, *see* WELDING: *Aluminothermic Welding.*) Thermite welding does not compare favourably with other methods of welding and is consequently relegated to special cases such as welding very large sections and welding in areas to which equipment cannot be easily transported. The thermite reaction is used in foundry work to provide heat to the metal reservoir called the riser. Since the riser is the last to freeze, it is consequently able to feed metal to the casting as solidification proceeds. The thermite reaction is used for the manufacture of carbon-free metals either by direct ignition in a separate magnesia-lined steel crucible or by reaction in a ladle of molten metal to which the carbon-free metal is to be added. Since it is difficult to control the reaction so that it proceeds stoichiometrically, the resultant carbon-free metal usually contains small quantities of aluminum.

One of the greatest hazards in the thermite reaction results from contamination with moisture. During the reaction water is reduced and hydrogen evolved, which can produce an explosive mixture with the surrounding air. This hazard necessitates careful packaging and handling to exclude moisture from the mixture.

(J. WU.)

**THERMOCHEMISTRY** deals with the changes in heat that take place during chemical reactions. Information about the magnitude of these changes is important to the chemical engineer, who must provide for the addition of the amount of heat needed or the removal of the amount of heat generated in proposed chemical reactions. Furthermore, with the accumulation of thermal data on a sufficient number of related reactions the driving force of any proposed reaction may be calculated. Calculations of this nature are of great economic importance. For example, if calculations show that under no conditions will a particular reaction proceed, then it is a complete waste of time and money to attempt it. (In the past much effort has been wasted in attempting to obtain reactions that calculations later showed were impossible.) Thermal calculations upon reversible reactions in equilibrium enable the chemist to predict the concentration of a desired product under a given set of conditions and also to predict changes in the concentration that will be obtained when conditions are altered. Quantitative information of this kind from thermochemistry, coupled with information about the rates of reactions (the domain of reaction kinetics; *q.v.*), provides the guidelines for modern laboratory procedures in chemical science.

Thermal change accompanying a chemical reaction is itself not a measure of the driving force of the reaction. Instead, the change in a property called the Gibbs energy (*see* below, *Entropy and Gibbs Energy*) is the true measure of the driving force. Thermochemistry gained its first impetus in the middle of the 19th century, however, when P. E. M. Berthelot of Paris and Julius Thomsen of Copenhagen (*qq.v.*) independently advanced the theory (later shown to be erroneous) that the heat content of a compound was the true measure of its chemical "affinity"—the term then used to describe energies which drive chemical reactions. The investigator mainly responsible for clarifying thermal relationships in chemical reactions was the U.S. mathematical physicist J. Willard Gibbs (*q.v.*), whose work during the last quarter of the 19th century placed thermochemistry on a firm theoretical footing.

Thermochemistry is to a large extent an experimental science involving measurements of the heats of various reactions. A unit of heat often used is the calorie (*q.v.*), and an apparatus for measuring heat quantities is called a calorimeter. Calorimetry is therefore the practical basis of experimental thermochemistry. For a detailed discussion of calorimetric apparatus and methods *see* CALORIMETRY.

This article consists chiefly of illustrations of the work of the thermochemist; the principles that guide him are presented in fairly elementary form and in a sequence intended to explain laboratory operations. For a detailed discussion of the thermodynamic laws and mathematical operations upon which thermochemistry is based, *see* THERMODYNAMICS.

## PROPERTIES AND THEIR MEASUREMENT

**Measurement of Energy Changes at Constant Volume.**—The first law of thermodynamics states that it is impossible to create or destroy energy. The total energy of a substance or system is therefore a single-valued function of its state and is independent of the path by which that state was reached. If this were not so, energy could be created by devising a suitable cycle in which a certain state is reached by one path and the system is returned to the starting state by another path.

Unfortunately it is impossible to measure or to know the total energy of a system. Therefore measurements are limited to the changes in energy of a system. The total energy, often called the internal energy, of a system is designated by $E$ and changes in energy by $\Delta E$. A mathematical statement of the first law of thermodynamics is that in any process

$$\Delta E = Q - W \qquad (1)$$

where $Q$ is the heat absorbed by the system and $W$ is the work done by the system on its surroundings (heat and work being different forms of energy).

If a process is carried out under conditions in which no work is done ($W = 0$), then the measured heat absorbed is the change in total energy of the system. In many chemical reactions the only work done by the system is mechanical work of expansion against the surrounding atmosphere. Therefore, if a reaction of this type is carried out in a constant-volume container, *i.e.*, one in which no expansion or contraction is possible, no work is done and the measured heat absorbed is the change in total energy for the reaction. This is expressed by

$$\Delta E = Q_v \qquad (2)$$

In equation (*2*), as in other thermodynamic equations, subscript $v$ is used to denote that the quantity or operation it qualifies is limited to the condition of constant volume. (Similarly, subscript $p$ denotes the condition of constant pressure.) Measurements of heat absorbed or evolved at constant volume are an important and typical concern of thermochemistry. It is mathematically obvious that if heat is evolved during the experiment, $Q_v$ will be a negative number. In this case the total energy of the system is decreased by the amount of energy (heat) evolved.

Typical of reactions for which the total energy change is measured by measuring the heat evolved at constant volume are combustions of organic materials in oxygen in a bomb calorimeter. An example is the determination of the heat evolved when gasoline is burned in oxygen. There are many gasoline mixtures and the heat evolved by each is important in the assessment of the commercial value of the mixture. A sample of a gasoline is placed in a heavy reaction vessel, called a bomb. The bomb is pressurized with oxygen and submerged in a known amount of water in a calorimeter. When the gasoline is ignited the heat evolved is transferred to the water and the temperature rise of the water is measured. If the calorimeter has been calibrated with a known amount of heat, the temperature rise of the water is a measure of the heat evolved in the reaction. The total energy change in the combustion of gasoline is thus measured in an experiment in which no work is done, even though the usual use of the reaction is to produce work by moving a piston in a gasoline engine.

The above is an example of the direct practical use of a thermochemical method. However, a much more important use of thermochemical methods is for the determination of total energy changes in fundamental reactions. These determinations lead to basic thermochemical data that can be tabulated and used to calculate energy changes in further reactions (*see* below, *Tables and Calculations*).

**Measurement of Enthalpy Changes at Constant Pressure.**—Measurements of the heats of reaction evolved at constant pressure are also of interest. Many chemical reactions are carried out in open vessels at the constant pressure of the atmosphere surrounding them. In practical situations, therefore, knowledge of the heat of the reaction allows the engineer to provide for the removal or addition of this heat in the design of a plant for carrying out the reaction. More fundamentally, the heat of reaction at constant pressure is of interest because it is a basic thermodynamic property.

To explore the meaning of the heat of reaction at constant pressure, it is necessary to relate work to pressure and volume. Consider a reaction carried out in a cylinder, one end of which is closed and the other end of which is a piston held in place only by the pressure of the air outside. In this case the work done is only that of moving the piston against air pressure. The mechanical work done, $W$, is equal to the force, $f$, exerted on the piston multiplied by the distance, $s$, the piston is moved during the reaction; that is,

$$W = fs \tag{3}$$

The pressure, $P$, of the air is the force exerted per unit area, $A$, of the piston; that is,

$$P = f/A \tag{4}$$

Rearranging equation (4) gives

$$f = PA \tag{5}$$

and substitution of equation (5) in equation (3) gives

$$W = PAs \tag{6}$$

But the area of the piston times the distance it moves is the volume change, $\Delta V$, of the reaction. Therefore at constant pressure it is found that

$$W = P\Delta V \tag{7}$$

Substitution of $P\Delta V$ for $W$ in equation (1) and the use of $Q_p$ to indicate that the heat absorbed was measured at constant pressure gives

$$\Delta E = Q_p - P\Delta V \tag{8}$$

or

$$Q_p = \Delta E + P\Delta V \tag{9}$$

Because of the usefulness of $Q_p$ a thermodynamic property, $H$, is defined as

$$H = E + PV \tag{10}$$

$H$ is called the enthalpy, or heat content, of the system. Because $E$ and $PV$ are single-valued functions of the state of the system, it is apparent that $H$ must also be a single-valued function of the state of the system. For a constant pressure reaction, then, when there is no work done other than $PV$ work, the enthalpy change is

$$\Delta H = Q_p = \Delta E + P\Delta V \tag{11}$$

For calculations of $\Delta V$ for equation (11) the volumes of liquids and solids are generally negligible compared to the volume of the gases and it is necessary to consider only the gaseous volume change. It is also sufficiently exact to consider that the gases in the reaction obey the perfect gas law,

$$PV = nRT \tag{12}$$

where $n$ is the number of moles of gas, $R$ is the gas constant, and $T$ is the absolute temperature. Therefore

$$\Delta H = \Delta E + (\Delta n)RT \tag{13}$$

where $\Delta n$ is the change in number of moles of gas only. Equation (13) is the relation between $\Delta E$ and $\Delta H$ usually used for obtaining $\Delta H$ values from $\Delta E$ determinations.

Typical of reactions for which heats of reaction at constant pressure are measured directly are combustions of one gas in another gas. For example, hydrogen and oxygen at atmospheric pressure are ignited in an appropriate torch burner in a reaction vessel submerged in the water of a calorimeter. The heat evolved is transferred to the water and the temperature rise is measured. The amount of reaction that occurred in the experiment is determined by the amount of water formed by the combination of hydrogen and oxygen. The measured heat is $Q_p = \Delta H$ for the reaction.

It has now been shown that $\Delta E$ and $\Delta H$ for various reactions may be measured. It also has been shown that $\Delta E$ and $\Delta H$ are related by the simple relation of equation (13), so that it is only necessary to measure either $\Delta E$ or $\Delta H$ to know $\Delta H$. Direct measurements of $\Delta E$ and $\Delta H$ for various reactions comprise the bulk of experimental thermochemistry.

**Heat Capacities.**—The properties $E$ and $H$ are functions of temperature. Therefore, to calculate $\Delta E$ and $\Delta H$ values for temperatures other than those under which the measurements are made, a knowledge of the variation of $E$ and $H$ with temperature is necessary. These variations are called heat capacities and are designated $C_v$ and $C_p$ respectively.

When a substance is subjected to a known amount of heat, $Q$, over a temperature span from $T_1$ to $T_2$, the temperature rise is $T_2 - T_1$. This physical change is treated like any other reaction. If the heating is carried out at constant volume no work is done ($W = 0$), so $\Delta E = Q_v$. The variation of $E$ with temperature is then

$$\Delta E/\Delta T = Q_v/(T_2 - T_1) \tag{14}$$

It should be emphasized that heat capacities themselves vary with temperature. However, if the temperature rise is small (of the order of a few degrees) it is sufficiently exact to say

$$\Delta E/\Delta T = Q_v/(T_2 - T_1) = C_v \tag{15}$$

where $C_v$ is the average heat capacity at constant volume for the temperature range $T_1$ to $T_2$, or $C_v$ is the heat capacity at constant volume for the temperature $(T_1 + T_2)/2$.

For some experiments a sample of a substance heated to a high temperature, $T_2$, in a constant-volume capsule is dropped into a calorimeter at a much lower temperature, $T_1$, and the heat given off is measured. For these measurements

$$\Delta E = Q_v = E_{T_1} - E_{T_2} \tag{16}$$

where $E_{T_1} - E_{T_2}$ is the difference in total energies going from $T_2$ to $T_1$. Because heat is given off, $Q_v$ will be negative. For changes involving large temperature differences the application of equation (15) will not yield accurate heat capacity data; for some purposes, however, the equation is useful. The heat capacity thus obtained is called the integral heat capacity for the range of temperature involved. Experiments like these are best used to measure directly the energy differences between two temperatures rather than to obtain heat capacities.

Similar experiments may be carried out at constant pressure. Then, because $\Delta H = Q_p$,

$$\Delta H/\Delta T = Q_p/(T_2 - T_1) = C_p \tag{17}$$

for small temperature ranges, and

$$\Delta H = Q_p = H_{T_1} - H_{T_2} \tag{18}$$

for the drop experiment. Thermodynamic tables usually provide values for both $C_p$ and $H_{T_2} - H_{T_1}$.

**Heats of State; Changes.**—The properties $E$ and $H$ are also functions of the physical state of the substances studied. Therefore, to calculate $\Delta E$ and $\Delta H$ values for reactions in which the reactants or products are in states other than those for which the studies were made, a knowledge of the variation of $E$ and $H$ with state is necessary. Typical of such measurements is that of the heat of vaporization of water. If the heat absorbed in changing water from the liquid to the gaseous state at constant pressure is measured, then

$$\Delta H = Q_p = \Delta H_{vap} \quad (19)$$

in which equation $Q_p$ is the measured heat and $\Delta H_{vap}$ is the heat of vaporization of water.

Heats of transition from one crystalline state to another are usually designated $\Delta H_{tr}$ and heats of fusion, from the solid to the liquid state, as $\Delta H_{fus}$. These heat values are also found in thermodynamic tables.

**Entropy and Gibbs Energy.**—For the chemist, the principal value of thermodynamics is its ability to establish criteria for the feasibility or spontaneity of a proposed chemical reaction under specified conditions. As was mentioned in the introduction, at one time it was believed that the sign of $\Delta H$ for a reaction was a sufficient criterion of the spontaneity of the reaction. Toward the end of the 19th century, however, the second law of thermodynamics was postulated and entropy, $S$, was defined. The property, entropy, is a single-valued function of the variables of the state of the system and may be defined as

$$\Delta S = \Delta Q_{rev}/T \quad (20)$$

where $\Delta S$ is the change of entropy of the system, $\Delta Q_{rev}$ is the heat change for the process carried out reversibly, and $T$ is the absolute temperature. After entropy had been defined it was shown that the true criterion of spontaneity is not the sign of $\Delta H$ but, instead, is the sign of $\Delta H - T\Delta S$. This quantity is designated $\Delta G$ and is called the change in Gibbs energy, defined as

$$\Delta G = \Delta H - T\Delta S \quad (21)$$

Even though the sign of $\Delta H$ is not the true criterion of the spontaneity of the reaction, it still may be an indication. The value of $T\Delta S$ for many reactions at low temperatures is only of the order of a few thousand calories. Therefore, at low temperatures if the value of $\Delta H$ is of the order of tens of thousands of calories or more it will probably have the same sign as $\Delta G$, and may be used as an indication of the spontaneity of the reaction. For more rigorous calculations it is necessary to have values of $\Delta S$ as well as values of $\Delta H$. Values of $\Delta H$ are also required to establish the magnitude of the temperature dependence of the Gibbs energy, which will be discussed in the following sections.

Similar in definition to the Gibbs energy is the Helmholtz energy, named for H. L. F. von Helmholtz. It is defined as

$$\Delta A = \Delta E - T\Delta S \quad (22)$$

where $\Delta A$ is the change in the Helmholtz energy, $\Delta E$ is the change in internal energy, and $T$ and $\Delta S$ are the absolute temperature and change in entropy of the process, as in equation (21). For most chemical purposes $\Delta G$ is a more useful function than $\Delta A$.

**Measurements of Gibbs Energy.**—After the formulation of the second law of thermodynamics and the definition of Gibbs energy, chemists turned to direct measurements of Gibbs energies. They did not yet know how to make direct measurements of entropies for use in equation (21) to supplement enthalpy data in obtaining the desired criterion of spontaneity. The two techniques used for direct measurements of the Gibbs energy depend on the relationships between the Gibbs energy and (1) the equilibrium constant of a reaction, and (2) the electromotive force generated in a reversible electrolytic cell reaction.

The equilibrium constant, $K$, for a reaction

$$a\text{A} + b\text{B} + \ldots \rightarrow c\text{C} + d\text{D} + \ldots \quad (23)$$

is defined as

$$K = [\text{C}]^c[\text{D}]^d \ldots / [\text{A}]^a[\text{B}]^b \ldots \quad (24)$$

where $K$ is the equilibrium constant and [A], [B], [C], and [D] are the concentrations of substances A, B, C, and D. This equilibrium expression, first enunciated by the Norwegian chemists C. M. Guldberg and Peter Waage in 1864, is often called the law of mass action. It may be derived from the fact that at equilibrium the rate constant ($K$, in the statement that rate of a reaction, $a\text{A} + b\text{B} + \ldots$ = products, is equal to $k[\text{A}]^a[\text{B}]^b \ldots$) for the reaction going forward is equal to the rate constant for the reaction proceeding in the reverse direction. For gases it is more convenient to use partial pressures than concentrations in obtaining the equilibrium constant. For ideal mixtures the actual concentrations in molecules per unit volume may be used. In the case of gases at normal temperatures and pressures the assumption of ideal mixtures is quite accurate. However, at high pressures and low temperatures corrections for nonideality must be made. The equilibrium constant can be shown to be related to the Gibbs energy by the equation

$$\Delta G^\circ = -RT \ln K \quad (25)$$

where $\Delta G^\circ$ is the standard Gibbs energy change for the reaction—the superscript ° indicating that the thermodynamic property refers to the reaction in which all the reactants and products are in their respective standard states (*see* below); and where $R$, $T$, and $\ln K$ are the gas constant, absolute temperature, and natural logarithm of the equilibrium constant, respectively.

The value of $K$ can be obtained by measuring the equilibrium concentrations or pressures of a reaction in equilibrium and substituting these in equation (24). From $K$ the $\Delta G$ for the reaction can be calculated by the use of equation (25). Conversely—and this is an important reason why chemists are interested in Gibbs energy values—if the value of $\Delta G$ is known, the equilibrium constant and relative concentrations of reactants and products in the reaction can be calculated. If a table of $\Delta G^\circ$ values for different temperatures is available, the optimum operating conditions of temperature and pressure for the production of a desired product may be calculated.

The other method of experimentally determining the Gibbs energy is by measuring the electrical potential obtained from a chemical cell under reversible conditions. Then

$$\Delta G = -n\mathcal{F}\mathcal{E} \quad (26)$$

in which $\Delta G$ is the Gibbs energy, $n$ is the number of faradays of charge passing through the cell, $\mathcal{F}$ is the number of charges in one faraday of electricity, and $\mathcal{E}$ is the electromotive force generated by the cell under reversible conditions.

**Enthalpy Change and the Variation with Temperature of Other Quantities.**—It can be shown that the Gibbs energy change varies with temperature according to the relation

$$[\partial(\Delta G/T)/\partial T]_p = \Delta H/T^2 \quad (27)$$

where the left-hand term is the rate of change in the value of $\Delta G/T$ with temperature at constant pressure, $\Delta H$ is the enthalpy change, and $T$ is the absolute temperature of the reaction. Substitution of equation (25) in equation (27) leads to the relation

$$(\partial \ln K/\partial T)_p = \Delta H^\circ/RT^2 \quad (28)$$

where the left-hand term is the rate of change in the value of the natural logarithm of the equilibrium constant with temperature at constant pressure, $\Delta H^\circ$ is the enthalpy change of the reaction under standard conditions, $R$ is the gas constant, and $T$ is the absolute temperature.

It can also be shown that for the electrical cell reaction

$$\Delta H = n\mathcal{F}[T(\partial\mathcal{E}/\partial T)_p - \mathcal{E}] \quad (29)$$

where $\Delta H$ is the enthalpy change for the reaction, $(\partial\mathcal{E}/\partial T)_p$ is the rate of change in potential of the cell with temperature at constant pressure, and $n$, $\mathcal{F}$, and $\mathcal{E}$ are defined in equation (26).

The above relations are important because they show that a knowledge of values of $\Delta H$ aids in the calculation of values of the Gibbs energy change, equilibrium constant, or potential of a cell at another temperature if they are known for one temperature. Conversely, from a knowledge of the variation of these quantities with temperature the values of $\Delta H$ may be calculated; indeed, many values of $\Delta H$ have been obtained in this manner rather than from strictly thermochemical measurements. However, the direct thermochemical measurement inherently leads to values of smaller uncertainty if the reaction can be carried out cleanly in a calorimeter.

**Measurement of Entropy.**—It was mentioned above that chemists turned first to direct measurement of $\Delta G$ because they could not measure $\Delta S$ for use in the equation $\Delta G = \Delta H - T\Delta S$. This situation continued until the formulation of the third law of thermodynamics early in the 20th century. The third law states that the entropy of any substance of which all component parts are in complete internal equilibrium becomes zero at the absolute zero of temperature. With this law the entropy of a substance could be obtained at any temperature if measurements could be made of all the heat changes it underwent in proceeding from absolute zero to the desired temperature, since by definition (equation 20) the entropy is the sum of the heat changes the substance undergoes—each heat change to be carried out reversibly and to be divided by the absolute temperature at which it occurs.

Announcement of the third law was soon followed by the development of techniques for making low-temperature thermal measurements. From these measurements accurate enthalpy values could be calculated for use in equation (21) to obtain Gibbs energy values. This circumstance brought a renewed demand for accurate $\Delta H$ determinations, since $\Delta S$ could now be determined accurately; the $\Delta H$ values were needed to determine $\Delta G$ values themselves, rather than only their temperature coefficients as in equation (27). Both methods mentioned earlier for determination of $\Delta G$ directly are often uncertain, mainly because of the difficulty of defining the reaction with sufficient accuracy. Furthermore, there are a large number of substances, especially among organic compounds, for which values of $G$ cannot be determined from equilibrium measurements. Consequently, determinations of entropies from low-temperature measurements are extremely important.

## TABLES AND CALCULATIONS

The primary goal of the thermochemist is to provide tables of thermochemical data from which the enthalpy change of every possible reaction may be obtained. It is apparent that tabulation of the enthalpy changes of every reaction as measured would be haphazard. Further, it is both impossible and unnecessary to measure the heat of every possible reaction. Unfortunately, it is impossible to know the absolute value of the enthalpy of any substance; if it were, the values could be tabulated for all substances, and enthalpy changes for the reactions could be calculated in a straightforward manner. However, there is a way to tabulate enthalpy quantities for each substance which works very well.

**Hess's Law.**—First we must consider the law of constant heat summation. This law, first enunciated by G. H. Hess of Russia in 1840, states that the heat absorbed or evolved in any reaction is a fixed quantity and is independent of the path of the reaction or the number of steps taken to obtain the reaction. Hess's law is a consequence of the first law of thermodynamics and need not be considered a separate thermodynamic law; in thermochemistry, however, it retains its identity because of its importance as the basis of calculations. Hess's law is exemplified by the calculation of the heat of formation of carbon dioxide from its elements. (The heat, as the term is used by thermochemists, of a specified reaction is a short way of saying heat content or enthalpy change.) This reaction is represented by

$$C(c) + O_2(g) \rightarrow CO_2(g);\ \Delta H^\circ = -94.054 \text{ kcal} \qquad (30)$$

(In this and all following thermochemical equations the letters c, g, and l in parentheses denote crystalline, gaseous, and liquid phases, respectively. Sometimes the temperature of the substance is indicated by a subscript. Following the semicolon the enthalpy change for the reaction, expressed in kilocalories [1 kcal = 1,000 cal], is given.)

In accordance with Hess's law the heat of formation of carbon dioxide is the same whether it occurs in one reaction as represented by equation (30) or in two steps as represented by the sum of equations (31) and (32):

$$C(c) + \tfrac{1}{2} O_2(g) \rightarrow CO(g);\ \Delta H^\circ = -26.417 \text{ kcal} \qquad (31)$$
$$CO(g) + \tfrac{1}{2} O_2(g) \rightarrow CO_2(g);\ \Delta H^\circ = -67.637 \text{ kcal} \qquad (32)$$

The sum of equations (31) and (32) is

$$C(c) + O_2(g) \rightarrow CO_2(g);\ \Delta H^\circ = -94.054 \text{ kcal} \qquad (30)$$

Thus Hess's law allows the calculation of the heats of various reactions from the heats of other reactions.

**Standard States.**—It is relevant at this point to discuss standard states. In reaction (31) one mole of CO(g) is formed. In reaction (32), one mole of CO(g) is used up. When the two equations are added, one mole of CO(g) in the state of reaction (32) appears on the left-hand side of the arrow and one mole of CO(g) in the state of reaction (31) appears on the right-hand side. If, and only if, these two moles of CO(g) are in identical states, they may be omitted from equation (30), because there is no enthalpy difference between them. It is convenient, therefore, to write thermochemical equations with each compound in a certain reference state. In equations (30), (31), and (32) the superscript ° following $\Delta H$ indicates that the enthalpy change given is for the reaction in which each reactant and each product appears in its so-called standard state. Consequently it is permissible to omit the CO(g) in the sum of equations (31) and (32).

The standard states that have been chosen as reference states for thermochemical purposes are the following:

1. For solids, the pure crystalline solid in a common crystalline form (usually the most stable form) at one atmosphere pressure at the specified temperature.
2. For liquids, the pure liquid at one atmosphere pressure at the specified temperature.
3. For gases, the pure gas at zero pressure at the specified temperature.

It is apparent that thermochemical measurements must take into account, as precisely as possible, the state of each reactant or product. The measured heat change for the actual process may then be corrected to give the heat change for the idealized reaction in which all the reactants and products appear in their respective standard states at the specified temperature.

**Heats of Formation.**—Let us return to the consideration of thermochemical tables from which the heats of various reactions may be calculated. The quantity that is tabulated is the heat of formation of the substance at 25° C (298° K) when its elements and the compound itself are in their standard states. This quantity is called the standard heat of formation at 25° C, or 298° K, and is designated $\Delta Hf^\circ_{298}$. Standard heats of formation of some simple compounds are listed in Table I.

TABLE I.—*Heats of Formation at 25° C, in kcal/mole*

| | |
|---|---|
| $CH_4$ (g) | −17.895 |
| $CO_2$ (g) | −94.054 |
| CO (g) | −26.417 |
| $H_2O$ (g) | −57.798 |
| $H_2O$ (l) | −68.317 |

*Note.*—$\Delta Hvap^\circ_{298}(H_2O) = \Delta Hf^\circ_{298}(H_2O, g) - \Delta Hf^\circ_{298}(H_2O, l) = -57.798 - (-68.317) = +10.519$ kcal/mole

**Calculation of Heats of Reaction.**—From a thermochemical table such as Table I the standard heat of reaction of any reaction at 25° C may be calculated, provided heat-of-formation values appear in the table for each reactant and each product. The calculation may be carried out in the following steps:

1. Each reactant is decomposed to its elements.
2. From the elements the products are synthesized.
3. The sum of the heats of the decomposition reactions and the heats of the synthesis reactions is the heat of the reaction sought.

A simple example of the procedure is the calculation of the heat of the reaction in which gaseous methane and carbon dioxide may react to produce carbon monoxide and liquid water:

$$CH_4(g) + 3CO_2(g) \rightarrow 4CO(g) + 2H_2O(l) \qquad (33)$$

First the reactants are decomposed to their elements:

$$CH_4(g) \rightarrow C(c, \text{graphite}) + 2H_2(g);\ \Delta H^\circ = +17.895 \text{ kcal} \qquad (34)$$
$$3CO_2(g) \rightarrow 3C(c, \text{graphite}) + 3O_2(g);\ \Delta H^\circ = +282.162 \text{ kcal} \qquad (35)$$

(Note that the crystalline state of the carbon has been exactly specified. Each of its several allotropic forms—diamond, graphite, lampblack, charcoal—has a different heat content. For some data compilations the most stable form, diamond, has been used for the standard state; in the present calculations, graphite is preferred, in accordance with more modern practice.)

Then the products are synthesized from the elements:

$$4C(c, \text{graphite}) + 2O_2(g) \rightarrow 4CO(g);\ \Delta H^\circ = -105.668 \text{ kcal} \qquad (36)$$
$$2H_2(g) + O_2(g) \rightarrow 2H_2O(l);\ \Delta H^\circ = -136.634 \text{ kcal} \qquad (37)$$

The sum of reactions (34) to (37) is

$$CH_4(g) + 3CO_2(g) \rightarrow 4CO(g) + 2H_2O(l); \Delta H^\circ = +57.755 \text{ kcal} \quad (38)$$

It should be noted that $\Delta H$ is always the enthalpy change of the reaction as written. Thus for equations (36) and (37), $\Delta H^\circ$ is four times and twice the molal heat of formation of the compounds, respectively. Equations (34) and (35) are decomposition reactions; therefore $\Delta H^\circ$ is respectively one and three times the heats of formation, with the sign changed.

Heats of formation are only special cases of heats of reaction. Just as heats of formation are used to calculate the heats of various desired reactions, the heats of reaction that can be measured easily are used to calculate unknown heats of formation. In fact, most heats of formation are obtained indirectly from measurements of heats of reactions involving the substance of unknown heat of formation. Consider, for example, the problem of obtaining the heat of formation of methane. It would be extremely difficult, if not impossible, to carry out the reaction between graphite and hydrogen in a calorimeter to yield methane alone—although the heat of this reaction, if corrected to standard-state conditions, would be the standard heat of formation of methane. It is, however, possible to burn methane in oxygen to obtain carbon dioxide and water:

$$CH_4(g) + 2O_2(g) \rightarrow CO_2(g) + 2H_2O(l); \Delta H^\circ = -212.793 \text{ kcal} \quad (39)$$

To obtain from this the heat of formation of methane it is necessary to have heat-of-formation data for $CO_2(g)$ and $H_2O(g)$. If these were not available it would also be necessary to burn hydrogen in oxygen to give water and to burn carbon in oxygen to give carbon dioxide. (The following equations for the heats of formation of the appropriate amounts of water and carbon dioxide are written in reverse for convenience and the sign of $\Delta H$ is appropriately marked for the way the equations are written.)

$$2H_2O(l) \rightarrow 2H_2(g) + O_2(g); \Delta H^\circ = +136.634 \text{ kcal} \quad (40)$$

$$CO_2(g) \rightarrow C(c, \text{graphite}) + O_2(g); \Delta H^\circ = +94.054 \text{ kcal} \quad (41)$$

The sum of equations (39), (40), and (41) is

$$CH_4(g) \rightarrow 2H_2(g) + C(c, \text{graphite}); \Delta H^\circ = +17.895 \text{ kcal} \quad (42)$$

Equation (42) represents the formation of one mole of methane from its elements in their standard states. Since the equation is written in reverse, the heat of formation of methane is −17.895 kcal/mole.

**Variation of $\Delta H$ with Physical State.**—In equation (38) the water formed is liquid. To calculate $\Delta H$ for the reaction in which gaseous water (steam) is formed, a value for the standard heat of vaporization of water at 25° is taken from Table I; then

$$2H_2O(l) \rightarrow 2H_2O(g); \Delta H^\circ = +21.038 \text{ kcal} \quad (43)$$

The sum of equations (38) and (43) is

$$CH_4(g) + 3CO_2(g) \rightarrow 4CO(g) + 2H_2O(g); \Delta H^\circ = +78.793 \text{ kcal} \quad (44)$$

The same result would have been obtained if equation (37), and consequently (38), had been written so that steam was formed.

**Variation of $\Delta H$ with Temperature.**—It is also of interest to know how the value of $\Delta H$ varies with temperature. For these calculations, values of the difference in $H$ between the desired temperature and the reference temperature, 25° C (298° K), of equation (44) are needed for each reactant and product. Such values are included in Table II. In the preceding calculations the temperature of all the reactions was at the standard reference temperature of 25° C (298° K) and was not specified in the reactions. In the following four equations, which lead to the $\Delta H$ value for equation (44) at 2,000° K, temperature must be specified:

$$CH_4(g)_{2{,}000^\circ K} \rightarrow CH_4(g)_{298^\circ K}; \Delta H^\circ = -29.540 \text{ kcal} \quad (45)$$

$$3CO_2(g)_{2{,}000^\circ K} \rightarrow 3CO_2(g)_{298^\circ K}; \Delta H^\circ = -65.571 \text{ kcal} \quad (46)$$

$$4CO(g)_{298^\circ K} \rightarrow 4CO(g)_{2{,}000^\circ K}; \Delta H^\circ = +54.244 \text{ kcal} \quad (47)$$

$$2H_2O(g)_{298^\circ K} \rightarrow 2H_2O(g)_{2{,}000^\circ K}; \Delta H^\circ = +34.746 \text{ kcal} \quad (48)$$

The sum of equations (44) through (48) is the following equation, in which all the reactants and products are at 2,000° K (indicated by the 2,000° K subscript to $\Delta H^\circ$):

$$CH_4(g) + 3CO_2(g) \rightarrow 4CO(g) + 2H_2O(g); \Delta H^\circ_{2{,}000^\circ K} = +72.672 \text{ kcal} \quad (49)$$

In the above calculation the temperature variation was very large. For calculations involving small temperature changes the variation of $H$ with temperature may be taken as constant and the heat capacity at constant pressure may be used in the calculations. From equation (17), $\Delta H/\Delta T = C_p$, or $\Delta H = C_p \Delta T$. Therefore, for any substance undergoing a small temperature change from $T_1$ to $T_2$ the enthalpy change, $H_{T_2} - H_{T_1}$, is equal to $C_p(T_2 - T_1)$. The following equations show how $\Delta H$ for the reaction $A + B \rightarrow C$ varies between temperatures $T_1$ and $T_2$:

$$A_{T_1} + B_{T_1} \rightarrow C_{T_1}; \Delta H = \Delta H_{T_1} \quad (50)$$

$$A_{T_2} \rightarrow A_{T_1}; \Delta H = C_p(A)(T_1 - T_2) = -C_p(A)(T_2 - T_1) \quad (51)$$

$$B_{T_2} \rightarrow B_{T_1}; \Delta H = C_p(B)(T_1 - T_2) = -C_p(B)(T_2 - T_1) \quad (52)$$

$$C_{T_1} \rightarrow C_{T_2}; \Delta H = C_p(C)(T_2 - T_1) \quad (53)$$

The sum of these four reactions is

$$A_{T_2} + B_{T_2} \rightarrow C_{T_2}; \Delta H_{T_2} = \Delta H_{T_1} + [C_p(C) - C_p(A) - C_p(B)](T_2 - T_1) \quad (54)$$

Because $C_p(C) - C_p(A) - C_p(B)$ is the heat capacities of the products minus the heat capacities of the reactants, this quantity may be designated $\Delta C_p$. The term $T_2 - T_1$ is $\Delta T$, so

$$\Delta H_{T_2} - \Delta H_{T_1} = \Delta C_p \, \Delta T \quad (55)$$

or, for the reaction

$$\Delta(\Delta H)/\Delta T = \Delta C_p \quad (56)$$

Equation (56) is a mathematical statement of Kirchhoff's law, first deduced by the German physicist Gustav Kirchhoff in 1858. The law asserts that the temperature coefficient, $\Delta(\Delta H)/\Delta T$, of the heat of a reaction under any circumstance is equal to the change in the heat capacity which the system undergoes under this circumstance.

**Relation of $\Delta H$ to $\Delta G$.**—In the preceding paragraphs calculations were made of the enthalpy changes for the reaction of methane with carbon dioxide to form carbon monoxide and water under different conditions of the physical state of the water formed and of the temperature at which the reaction occurred. The role of thermochemical calculations in thermodynamic calculations can be shown by proceeding further into thermodynamics and calculating the Gibbs energy changes for reaction (44), in which water vapour and carbon monoxide are formed at 298° K and at 2,000° K. Values of the entropy, $S$, for each reactant and product can be obtained from Table II. From these, $\Delta S$, the sum of the entropies of the products minus the sum of the entropies of the reactants, and the product $T\Delta S$ may be computed for each temperature.

TABLE II.—*Chemical Thermodynamic Properties*

| °K | $CH_4$ (g) | $CO_2$ (g) | CO (g) | $H_2O$ (g) |
|---|---|---|---|---|
| | For $H^\circ_T - H^\circ_{298}$ in kcal/mole | | | |
| 298 | 0.000 | 0.000 | 0.000 | 0.000 |
| 500 | 1.960 | 1.987 | 1.417 | 1.654 |
| 1,000 | 9.125 | 7.984 | 5.183 | 6.209 |
| 2,000 | 29.540 | 21.857 | 13.561 | 17.373 |
| | For $S^\circ$ in cal/deg/mole$^{-1}$ | | | |
| 298 | 44.490 | 51.072 | 47.214 | 45.106 |
| 500 | 49.453 | 56.122 | 50.841 | 49.334 |
| 1,000 | 59.141 | 64.344 | 56.028 | 55.592 |
| 2,000 | 73.076 | 73.903 | 61.807 | 63.234 |

$$\Delta S_{298} = 81.362 \text{ cal/deg}, \; T\Delta S_{298} = 24.246 \text{ kcal} \quad (57)$$

$$\Delta S_{2{,}000} = 78.911 \text{ cal/deg}, \; T\Delta S_{2{,}000} = 157.822 \text{ kcal} \quad (58)$$

From the relation $\Delta G = \Delta H - T\Delta S$ the Gibbs energy change for reaction (33) for each temperature is calculated to be

$$\Delta G_{298} = +\,54.547 \text{ kcal} \quad (59)$$

$$\Delta G_{2{,}000} = -\,85.150 \text{ kcal} \quad (60)$$

From these values the equilibrium constant or relative concentrations for the reaction at these two temperatures can be calculated. It would be found that no significant amounts of methane and carbon dioxide react to form carbon monoxide and water at 298°, but the reaction goes substantially to completion at 2,000° K. In actual practice the engineer would make the calculations for many intermediate temperatures to find the most economical conditions for carrying out the reaction.

**Summary.**—Thermochemistry is an experimental science. Its goal is to complete a table of the standard heats of formation of every substance in every state at 25° C—a table from which the standard heats of every possible reaction at 25° C may be calculated. The adjunctive use of tables of other thermodynamic properties then permits the calculation of heats of reaction at other temperatures and for a variety of conditions of physical state, pressure, and the like. These heats of reaction, used in combination with tables of entropy values, give the Gibbs energy changes for the reactions; and from the heats of reaction the variation with temperature of the Gibbs energy, equilibrium constants, and reversible cell potentials may also be calculated.

Values of the standard heats of formation of each substance are best determined by direct measurements of the enthalpy, or total energy change, of a reaction in which the substance is involved. These values may also be obtained from measurements of equilibrium constants or reversible cell potentials as a function of the temperature of the reaction, or from free energies obtained from equilibrium constants or reversible cell potentials if accurate entropy data are available.

Measuring thermochemical quantities is the chief activity in many university, government, and industrial laboratories. In the United States the collection, appraisal, and tabulation of existing thermochemical data has been undertaken cooperatively by government agencies (notably the Department of Defense) and industrial interests.

*See* also PHASE EQUILIBRIA.

BIBLIOGRAPHY.—G. N. Lewis and M. Randall, *Thermodynamics* (1961); F. D. Rossini, *Chemical Thermodynamics* (1950); I. M. Klotz, *Chemical Thermodynamics* (1950); *Experimental Thermochemistry, Measurements of Heats of Reaction,* prepared under auspices of the International Union of Pure and Applied Chemistry by the Commission on Chemical Thermodynamics: vol. 1, ed. by F. D. Rossini (1956), and vol. 2, ed. by H. A. Skinner (1962); W. P. White, *The Modern Calorimeter* (1928); F. R. Bichowsky and F. D. Rossini, *Thermochemistry of the Chemical Substances* (1936); F. D. Rossini *et al., Selected Values of Chemical Thermodynamic Properties,* U.S. National Bureau of Standards Circular 500 (1952); *JANAF Interim Thermochemical Tables,* prepared in looseleaf form under auspices of the Joint Army-Navy-Air Force Thermochemical Panel (1960 *et seq.*). (W. N. H.)

**THERMOCOUPLE,** used as a form of thermometer, basically is a pair of unlike metals or alloys (commonly wires) joined at each end. Electricity flows in the couple (Seebeck effect) in rough proportion to the degree that one end or junction is hotter than the other (*see* THERMOELECTRICITY). Temperatures at one junction can be measured through voltmeter readings (calibrated in degrees) when the other is kept at a known reference level (often 0° C [32° F]). Sensitivity may be increased by using connected thermocouples (a thermopile) in series; such devices for relatively rough work are typically accurate to about ±2° C (±3.6° F), precision to about ±0.06° C (±0.1° F) being obtainable in special cases. As a less fragile replacement for glass thermometers, a given thermocouple device will function usefully in a portion of the range from about −260° to 1,600° C (−436° to 2,912° F).

*See* also THERMOMETRY: *Electrical Thermometry;* HEAT: *Radiation.*

*See* American Institute of Physics, *Temperature: Its Measurement and Control in Science and Industry,* vol. 3 (1962–63).

**THERMODYNAMICS** may be defined broadly as the study of the role of heat in transformations of matter or energy. More narrowly it is the mathematical application of three general laws, derived from countless experimental observations of heat changes, to a variety of problems in theoretical chemistry and physics and in engineering.

The foundation of thermodynamics is its first law, commonly known as the law of conservation of energy. Largely self-evident, it is a scientific axiom paralleling the law of conservation of matter (or mass). The second law of thermodynamics, which can be variously stated and is sometimes called the law of entropy (dissipation of energy), is as fundamental as the first law but required much experimental verification for its acceptance. It was the early investigations of the many ramifications of the second law, initially tested in the operation of heat engines, that established thermodynamics as a discipline and led to its application in fields as seemingly remote as chemical engineering and astrophysics. The third law, which is concerned with entropy at or near the absolute zero of temperature, derives from the second law and has an important part in modern conjecture about the ultimate states of matter.

The history of thermodynamics is closely bound up with the general progress of chemistry and physics since the mid-19th century. (*See* further CHEMISTRY: *The Founding of Physical Chemistry;* PHYSICS: GENERAL SURVEY: *Theory.*) Because of its pervasive nature, thermodynamics is not easily delimited in relation to other disciplines. It partakes of and contributes to a dozen fields; yet it has its own traditions and methods, and therefore has developed a characteristic viewpoint and a distinctive way of presenting its findings. It has also fostered branches that reflect the parent methodology; such, for example, is thermochemistry (*q.v.*), the study of heat absorbed and evolved in chemical reactions. As for the limits of thermodynamics: their ambiguity is exemplified by statistical mechanics (*q.v.*), alternatively known as statistical thermodynamics—a subject which can be considered either as an extremely refined and wide-ranging mathematical treatment of the second law or as a special discipline occupying a position between thermodynamics proper and molecular or atomic physics. Preliminary reference to the article HEAT will give the reader a fuller sense of the scope and limitations of thermodynamics than can readily be conveyed here.

This article has the following main divisions and sections:



## I. FIRST LAW OF THERMODYNAMICS

**1. Definitions: Energy, Work, and Heat.**—The primary physical concept of work is the movement of a body against an opposing force, and the work done is the product of the distance moved multiplied by the component of the opposing force in the direction of motion. If the opposing force is due to the pressure on a piston, the force is the pressure times the area of the piston, while the volume swept through by the piston, or the volume change of the fluid opposing the piston, is the distance through which the piston moves times the same area. Hence the work done on a fluid is its pressure times its decrease in volume, and conversely the work done by a fluid is its pressure times its increase of volume. In general, a delta ($\Delta$) is used before a symbol to indicate the new value minus the old; in the above case the change of volume will be written $\Delta V$, to represent $V_{\text{new}} - V_{\text{old}}$, which will be inherently positive or negative according as the new volume is greater or less than the old. With this convention we write $w = P\Delta V$, where $w$ uniformly represents the work done by the system by virtue of its change of volume. In general we represent by $w$ the work done by the system of interest, which, if negative, is interpreted as work done upon the system by some external agency.

The capacity of a system to do work can be exchanged with that of other systems in a variety of ways. Generally the capacity of the combined systems is diminished in such interchanges, but with great care to minimize losses by friction and other dissipative processes, exchanges of capacity to do work may be carried out with negligible loss. An idealized process with no dissipation is called a reversible process.

The capacity to do work possessed by a body by virtue of its being at a higher gravitational level than some arbitrarily chosen level is called gravitational potential energy, or energy of position. Usually we find a correlation between the capacity of a system to do work and what we call its energy. (*See* MECHANICS: *Work and Energy Relations*.) One of the simplest transformations of energy occurs in a nearly frictionless pendulum (*see* ENERGY: *Kinetic Energy*), in which potential energy is converted to kinetic energy, or energy of motion, which is then reconverted to potential energy. At the end of the swing all the energy is potential, at the bottom it is all kinetic, and in intermediate positions part is potential and part is kinetic—but when friction is negligible the sum remains constant. When friction (*q.v.*) is present the swings become shorter and shorter, and finally the pendulum comes to rest in its lowest position, at which time it has lost both its potential and its kinetic energy. Is this a destruction of energy, or another transformation? Experiments of other types indicate that the dissipation of gravitational potential energy in a thermally insulated system causes its temperature to rise. A similar rise in temperature can be produced in an initially similar system by putting it in contact with a hot body, in which case we find that the hot body is cooled by the contact. We say that heat flows from the hot body to the relatively cool one. Since this heat may be supplied to the body either by contact with the hot one or by dissipation of potential energy by friction, we infer that heat is a form of energy, and that by friction, potential energy has been transformed into heat. (*See* also ENERGY: *Heat as a Form of Energy*.)

Before we can make such an inference quantitative we must devise methods for the measurement of heat and of energy. The change of gravitational potential energy of a body with height is proportional to the product of the change of height and the mass of the body; the common English engineering unit of energy, called the foot-pound, is defined as the work needed to raise one pound of mass a vertical distance of one foot. However, the energy is also proportional to the acceleration due to gravity, and in most scientific work the potential energy is expressed by $mgh$, with $m$ the mass in grams, $g$ the acceleration in cm-sec$^{-2}$, and $h$ the change of height in centimetres. In this system (the centimetre-gram-second, or cgs, system) the unit of energy is expressed in g-cm$^2$-sec$^{-2}$, and is called the erg. In the related metre-kilogram-second system, the unit of energy is expressed in kg-m$^2$-sec$^{-2}$, and is called the joule. The kinetic energy in either system is given by $\frac{1}{2}mv^2$.

Flow of heat is expressed in terms of the change of temperature which each body undergoes when two bodies are placed in thermal contact. The heat absorbed by one body is found to be equal to that given up by the other if we write the heat absorbed, $q = mC\Delta t$, where $m$ is the mass, $\Delta t$ is the new temperature minus the old, and $C$, called the specific heat capacity (*see* CALORIMETRY), is a quantity characteristic of the substance, which usually changes only slightly with temperature unless a change of state or of crystalline structure occurs. (Such a change of state is frequently accompanied by an additional absorption of heat, called the latent heat; *q.v.*). The unit of heat called the calorie (*q.v.*) is commonly defined as that amount required to raise the temperature of one gram of water from 14.5 to 15.5° C, which makes the specific heat of water at 15° equal to one cal-g$^{-1}$-deg$^{-1}$. For many uses the kilocalorie (1,000 calories; abbreviated kcal) is a more convenient unit.

**2. Statement of the Law.**—Holding to these definitions of potential and kinetic energy and of heat, it is found that whenever a quantity of potential or kinetic energy is dissipated by friction or some other dissipative process, an amount of heat appears which is proportional to the energy dissipated. Also, when heat is used to produce work, the amount of heat is diminished in proportion to the work done, by the same factor of proportionality. The proportionality factor has been found to be 4.1833 international joules per calorie. Since work and heat are both forms of energy they can both be expressed in joules, calories, or other units of energy. In the equations that follow it will be assumed that both are expressed in the same units; therefore no proportionality factor is needed.

Chemical transformations, the discharge of an electric condenser, the demagnetization of a magnet, and many other processes can do work or produce heat. It is convenient to assign an energy to each state such that the change of energy is the energy in the final state minus that in the initial state. When the above definitions and conventions are observed, the first law of thermodynamics, or the law of conservation of energy, may be stated thus: *For all changes in an isolated system, the energy remains constant.*

**3. Experimental Confirmation.**—As a consequence of this principle, for any change from state A to state B we expect the change of energy to be independent of the intermediate steps in the process. As an example, for the reaction

$$\text{CaO(crystalline)} + \text{H}_2\text{O(liquid)} = \text{Ca(OH)}_2\text{(crystalline)} \qquad (a)$$

carried out in a calorimeter, the energy liberated as heat has been found in three investigations to be 15.30, 15.30, and 15.18 kcal respectively. For the dissolution of $Ca(OH)_2$ in aqueous HCl (200 moles $H_2O$ per mole HCl)

$$\text{Ca(OH)}_2\text{(cryst)} + 2\text{HCl(200aq)} = 2\text{H}_2\text{O(liq)} + \text{CaCl}_2\text{(400aq)} \qquad (b)$$

the liberation of heat was found in two investigations to be 30.49 and 30.82 kcal. By the law of conservation of energy, the sum of the heats for reactions ($a$) and ($b$) should be the heat for reaction

$$\text{CaO(cryst)} + 2\text{HCl(200aq)} = \text{H}_2\text{O(liq)} + \text{CaCl}_2\text{(400aq)} \qquad (c)$$

The sum of the averages for ($a$) and for ($b$) is 45.92, while the result of direct measurement is 46.45 kcal. The discrepancy is believed to be due to experimental error, although some of the difference may be due to slight differences in the crystalline state of the CaO used in ($a$) and ($c$), and in that of the $Ca(OH)_2$ produced in ($a$) and used in ($b$).

The above example is fairly typical of a large body of experimental data in reasonably good accord with the principle of conservation of energy. Under favourable conditions the agreement is much better, but in other cases it is not as good. The cases of poor agreement can be explained by failure to provide sufficiently good isolation, but it is difficult to give independent criteria for isolation. An interesting example is the energy loss of radioactive material undergoing beta decay, which is presumably the same for each atom of the material which decays, and is expected to be equal to or greater than that for the most energetic beta particle emitted. However, the calorimetrically measured energy, when the energy is dissipated in an absorbing material, is appreciably less than that calculated from the energy of the most energetic beta particles. The commonly accepted explanation is that neutrinos are emitted along with the beta emission, and that they carry away some of the energy. Fortunately for this explanation, the existence of the neutrino is in accord with other conservation laws; but the difficulty of stopping neutrinos or of detecting their passage casts doubt on the possibility of demonstrating the establishment of a truly isolated system. By far the best reasons for accepting the first law of thermodynamics, along with the second (*see* below), are that a large number of corollaries have been derived from either, or both in combination, and in no case has such corollary been found inconsistent with experiment. As a result, the first law of thermodynamics is regarded as one of the best-established laws of the physical sciences.

**4. The First Law and Relativity.**—According to the principle of relativity, energy and mass are related according to the equation $E = mc^2$ where, if $m$ is the mass in grams and $c$ is the velocity of light in centimetres per second, $E$ is the energy in ergs. This relation does not assert the transformation of mass into energy; rather, it asserts the equivalence of mass and energy. An isolated system containing radioactive material which emits alpha particles undergoes no change of mass. The rest mass of the daughter nuclei is less than that of the parent, but the mass of the liberated energy is equal to this difference, and the system loses mass only when the energy is lost from the system. In principle the mass-energy equivalence seems to give a means of measuring the energy of the system by measuring its mass. In practice this is useful only in nuclear transformations, for the change of mass corresponding to the energy change of most other processes is too small to be measured. Furthermore, the attempt to measure the total energy of the system by measuring its mass gives only the energy relative to the chosen inertial system.

## II. SECOND LAW OF THERMODYNAMICS

Under this heading we will first consider implications of the first law of thermodynamics that lead toward the second law: (1) the general principles governing exchanges of energy between systems; (2) the application of these principles to the reversible expansion of an ideal gas; and (3) the thermodynamic relationships epitomized in the Carnot cycle. The second law can then be stated and, in the sections following, some of the applications of the law to a variety of physical and chemical phenomena will be explored.

**1. Energy Exchange.**—According to the principle of conservation of energy, a system can gain energy only by interaction with other systems in such a way that the other systems lose a corresponding amount of energy. A gain of energy by conduction or by thermal radiation is called a flow of heat, while energy exchanged by other mechanisms is called work. It is customary to use $q$ for the heat absorbed or gained by the system, and $w$ for the work done by the system; so that, for any process,

$$\Delta E = q - w \tag{1}$$

where $\Delta E$ is the increase of energy of the system, $q$ is the energy gained by thermal flow (either by conduction or by thermal radiation), and $w$ is the energy lost by the system because of other interactions, such as moving a body against an opposing force, producing an electric current, etc. While heat is most frequently measured in calories, and work in joules or other work units, either heat or work can be measured in units which are traditionally associated with the other (since both are forms of energy). Except when numerical results are given, it is usually unnecessary to specify the units being employed, but it will be assumed that when both heat and work occur in the same relation, we use the same units for both.

**2. Applications to Ideal Gases.**—The behaviour of gases on change of pressure or temperature is described approximately by the equations

$$PV = nRT \text{ and } (dE/dV)_T = 0 \tag{2}$$

where $P$ is the pressure, $V$ the volume, $n$ the number of moles (the number of grams divided by the gram molecular weight), and $T$ is the absolute temperature, or 273.15 plus the Celsius temperature. $R$ is a constant whose numerical value depends on the units in which the other quantities are expressed (82.06 cm$^3$ atm-mole$^{-1}$ deg$^{-1}$, 8.314 joule-mole$^{-1}$ deg$^{-1}$, 1.986 cal-mole$^{-1}$ deg$^{-1}$, and others), and $(dE/dV)_T$ is the limit of the change of energy divided by the change of volume at constant temperature, as the change of volume approaches zero. A fictitious gas which obeys these relations is called an ideal gas. Actual gases deviate from these conditions, but as the pressure approaches zero, $PV/nRT$ approaches unity and $(dE/dV)_T$ approaches zero.

The work done by an expansion against a constant pressure is $P\Delta V$. For the expansion of an ideal gas at constant temperature the pressure continually decreases, and the work done is expressed by the integral: $w = \int PdV = nRT \int dV/V = nRT \ln (V_f/V_i)$, where $V_f$ is the final volume and $V_i$ is the initial volume. Since the energy of the ideal gas does not change at constant temperature, $q = w$, and the heat absorbed during the expansion is also $nRT \ln (V_f/V_i)$. It should be noted that the work done and the heat absorbed have been calculated for the reversible expansion of the gas. To expand in this manner would require that the opposing force exactly balance that due to the pressure of the gas; to carry out the expansion at a finite rate would require that the opposing force be slightly smaller to allow for friction or other source of loss, and in general the actual work done is less than that for the reversible process. The above result may be more precisely expressed $w_{\text{rev}} = q_{\text{rev}} = nRT \ln (V_f/V_i)$ or $q = w \leqq nRT \ln (V_f/V_i)$.

When no heat flows during the expansion, the process is called an adiabatic expansion. In this case $q = 0$ and $\Delta E = -w$. For infinitesimal reversible expansion $-PdV = dE = nC_vdT$, where $C_v$ is the heat absorbed by a mole of gas per degree rise in temperature, when heated at constant volume. Replacing $P$ by $nRT/V$, then $nC_vdT = nRT\ dV/V$, or $(C_v/R)\ dT/T = -dV/V$. If $C_v$ does not change with temperature, we obtain, by integrating,

$$(C_v/R) \ln (T_f/T_i) = -\ln (V_f/V_i) \tag{3}$$

From $PV = nRT$ we obtain $\ln (T_f/T_i) = \ln (P_f/P_i) + \ln (V_f/V_i)$, and by adding to both sides of (3) we obtain

$$\ln (P_f/P_i) = (C_v + R)/R \ln (T_f/T_i) \tag{4}$$

The amount of heat absorbed by a mole of an ideal gas, per degree rise in temperature, when heated at constant pressure, is greater than $C_v$ by the work done in pushing away the surroundings. The difference is easily shown to be $R$, and the heat capacity per mole of the ideal gas at constant pressure, $C_p = C_v + R$. Substituting this in (4), we obtain

$$\ln (P_f/P_i) = (C_p/R) \ln (T_f/T_i) \tag{5}$$

An interesting application of cooling by adiabatic expansion occurs on the rise of air in the atmosphere, due either to thermal

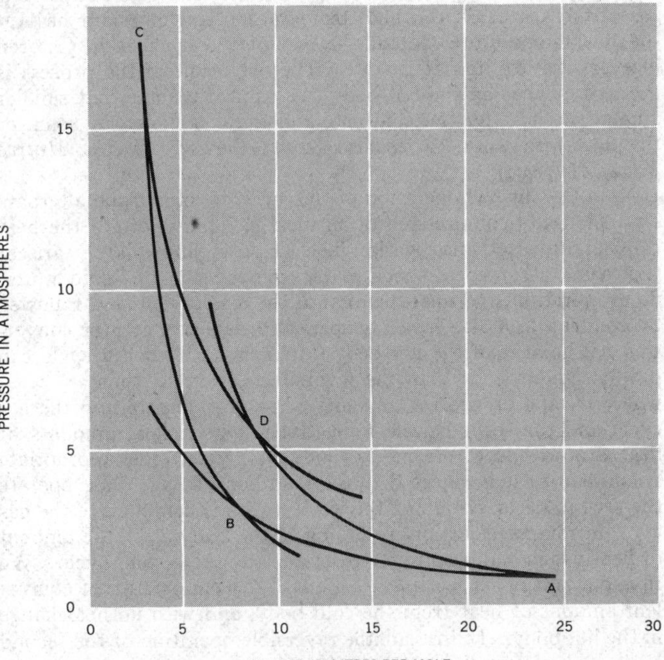


**ISOTHERMAL AND ADIABATIC EXPANSIONS OF AN IDEAL GAS**

Curves AB, BC, CD, and DA represent successively a threefold isothermal compression at 300° K (approximately 27° C or 80° F), adiabatic compression from 300° to 600° K, a threefold isothermal expansion at 600° K, and adiabatic expansion from 600° to 300° K. The area enclosed by ABCD is a measure of the work obtainable by carrying out the cycle in a reversible manner convection or to a wind which forces it up the side of a mountain. For dry air, $C_p/R$ is about 3.5; for a rise from sea level, at a pressure of 760 mm and temperature of 17° C, to a height of about 1 km, where the pressure is about 660 mm, the temperature drops to about 7° C. (*See* also HEAT: *Thermal Properties of Gases.*)

**3. The Carnot Cycle.**—Two examples have been given (*see* above) of the production of work by the expansion of a gas. In the first instance the expansion is said to be isothermal; in the second instance, adiabatic. In an isothermal expansion, heat from an outside body is converted to work; in an adiabatic expansion, work is done at the expense of the thermal energy of the gas. In each case the gas occupies more space at the end of the process than at the beginning. If the expansion is continued, a very large space is required to obtain a comparatively small additional amount of work. Furthermore, unless this space is empty the point is soon reached where the work required to push away the material occupying the space is greater than the work obtained from expanding the gas. If, after an isothermal expansion, the gas is restored to its initial volume by isothermal compression at the initial temperature, the same amount of work must be done as was obtained by the initial expansion, if done reversibly; if done irreversibly, more work is required.

Let us now consider the cycle first studied by the French physicist Sadi Carnot (*q.v.*; 1796–1832). In this cycle the gas is expanded isothermally at $T'$ from $V_1$ to $V_2$; expanded adiabatically from $V_2$ to $V_3$, simultaneously cooling from $T'$ to $T''$; compressed isothermally at $T''$ to volume $V_4$; and then compressed adiabatically until the temperature is again $T'$. By use of equations (2) and (3) it can be shown that if $V_3/V_4$ is chosen to equal $V_2/V_1$, the final volume will be the same as the initial volume, and the gas will have been restored to its initial state. The work done by the gas during the adiabatic expansion is equal to the work required for the adiabatic compression, but the work done by the expansion at $T'$ is $nRT' \ln (V_2/V_1)$, while the work required for the compression at $T''$ is $nRT'' \ln (V_2/V_1)$. The net work from the complete reversible cycle using the ideal gas is then

$$w_{\text{rev, gas}} = nR(T' - T'') \ln (V_2/V_1) = -q'(T' - T'')/T' = q''(T' - T'')/T'' \quad (6)$$

where $q'$ is the heat absorbed by the hot body (in this case a negative quantity) and $q''$ is the heat absorbed by the cold body. The gas absorbs heat at the high temperature and gives up heat at the low temperature, but at the end of the cycle it is restored in every way to its initial state. The net result of the process is the loss of heat by the hot body, the gain of a somewhat smaller amount of heat by the cold one, and the conversion of some of the heat into work. (*See* also HEAT: *Carnot: On the Motive Power of Heat.*)

Note that by the operation of this cycle involving the alternate expansion and compression of an ideal gas, only part of the heat can be converted into work. The question immediately arises: Can some other cycle—such as the compression of liquid water, its evaporation, and the expansion of the resultant steam, followed by condensation at a lower temperature—effect a greater conversion of the heat of the hot body into work? If such a cycle can produce more work than the reversible gas cycle, then $w_2 > w_1$ where $w_1$ and $w_2$ are the amounts of work obtainable by the gas cycle and the second cycle respectively, when equal amounts of heat are withdrawn from the body at $T'$ and the appropriate amount of heat is rejected to the cold body at $T''$. We operate the second cycle, obtaining the work $w_2$, and then operate the gas cycle in reverse direction, returning to the body at $T'$ the amount of heat which had been removed from it by the second cycle. We thus obtain the net work $w_2 - w_1$ with the removal of an equivalent amount of heat from the cold body, and with no net change in the hot body. If, instead, the reversible operation of the second cycle yields a smaller amount of work, $w_2 < w_1$, we operate the gas cycle to obtain work, and reverse the second cycle. In this case, again choosing to restore to the hot body the same amount of heat which it had lost, the net work obtained is $w_1 - w_2$, with the sole other result being the removal of an equivalent amount of heat from the cold body.

**4. Statement of the Law.**—A cyclic process in which the net result is the restoration of all parts of the system to their initial states except for the removal of heat from a body, and the production of an equivalent amount of work, has been called a perpetual motion of the second kind. Such a process would be extremely useful, and the failure of all attempts to find such processes has led to the belief that it is impossible. The impossibility of perpetual motion of the second kind is the essence of the second law of thermodynamics. The law is commonly stated in a variety of fundamentally equivalent ways; a satisfactory one for our purposes is: *It is impossible to operate a cycle in which the only net effect is the absorption of heat from a body at constant temperature and the production of an equivalent amount of work.* The mere failure thus far to find a means to do this, provides a very weak basis for this principle. On the other hand, it is strongly supported by many corollaries which have been logically derived from the principle and which are in accord with experience.

Accepting the second law, or the impossibility of perpetual motion of the second kind, we note that for the same amount of heat taken from the hot body the work obtained by any reversible cycle operated between two temperatures is the same, and equal to that given by the ideal gas cycle (equation [6]). We may also note from this equation that $q'/T' + q''/T'' = 0$ for the reversible cycle. If the process had been carried out irreversibly, the work done (for the same $q'$) would have been less, and correspondingly, the heat absorbed by the cold body, $q''_{\text{irr}}$, would have been greater than $q''_{\text{rev}}$. In this case $(q'/T' + q''/T'')_{\text{irr}}$ is greater than zero.

**5. Entropy.**—We define entropy such that in a reversible process any part of the system at temperature $T$ which absorbs heat $q_r$ is said to have increased its entropy by $q_r/T$. It can be shown that the change of entropy depends only on the initial and final states; hence we can find its change for any process, reversible or not, by considering the heat which would have been absorbed in reversible changes leading to the same final state. When a process is reversible the sum of all changes of entropy is zero; for any irreversible process the sum is positive. The commonly accepted symbol for entropy is $S$, and we summarize the above statements by $\Delta S = q_r/T \geqq q/T$ where $q$ is the heat absorbed for the process as actually carried out, and $q_r$ is the heat which would have been absorbed in carrying the system reversibly from the same initial to the same final state.

The three statements concerning change of entropy—that it depends only on the initial and final states, that it is zero for a reversible process, and that it is positive for an irreversible process—are of great importance, both for the determination of entropy and for the prediction of possible changes in systems.

*Example 1*

An ideal gas at 20° C and 2 atm pressure is allowed to leak slowly into an evacuated space of volume equal to that initially occupied by the gas, so that the final pressure is 1 atm. No energy change takes place in this process, *i.e.*, no energy need be absorbed or given off; and the average velocity of the individual molecules is unchanged.

To get the entropy change of the system we need to consider a reversible process by which the gas changes from the given initial state to the same final state. Such a process is the reversible isothermal expansion, in which the work done, and likewise the heat absorbed, is $nRT \ln 2$. The entropy change of the gas is now $q_{\text{rev}}/T = nR \ln 2$, and the entropy change of the surroundings is $-nR \ln 2$, giving a total entropy change of zero, as expected for a reversible process. Since the initial and final states of the gas are the same as for the irreversible process in the example, the entropy change of the gas during the irreversible expansion is also $nR \ln 2$. The surroundings, however, in this case undergo no change, hence no change of entropy; the total change is now $nR \ln 2 + 0 = nR \ln 2$, a positive quantity, in accord with our expectation for an irreversible process.

*Example 2*

One gram atomic weight (112.4 g) of cadmium and one mole (159.8 g) of liquid bromine are mixed at 36° C. (The temperature 36° C is chosen because at lower temperatures the aqueous solution would be saturated not with anhydrous $CdBr_2$ but with a salt possessing water of crystallization. A cell saturated with this salt would give nearly the same electromotive force, but exact calculations of the quantities we desire would be complicated. For any temperature the solubility of bromine in the aqueous solution and of water in the bromine call for slight corrections which can be neglected here for the sake of simplicity.) Reaction occurs with the formation of $CdBr_2$ and the liberation of

75.20 kcal of energy, which is absorbed by the surroundings as heat. The change in the surroundings is the same as if the 75.20 kcal had been absorbed as part of a reversible process; hence $\Delta S_{sur}$, the change of entropy of the surroundings, is $75.20 \times 1{,}000/(273.15 + 36) =$ 243.3 cal/deg. Since the combination of cadmium and bromine is not carried out reversibly under these conditions, the change of entropy of the cadmium-bromine system is not the negative of this.

The combination of cadmium and bromine at 36° C could have been carried out nearly reversibly by separating the cadmium and the bromine by a saturated aqueous solution of cadmium bromide, putting a platinum wire in the bromine-cadmium bromide end of the cell, and drawing electric current from it. While current flows, Cd and $Br_2$ are consumed and solid $CdBr_2$ precipitates from the aqueous solution; for the consumption of 1 gram atomic weight of Cd and 1 mole of $Br_2$, 2 faradays (193,000 coulombs) of electricity pass through the circuit. The maximum work which can be obtained from the passage of electricity is the product of the quantity of electricity which passes, and the potential difference, which is about 1.516 volts when the process is carried out reversibly. The electrical work for the reversible process is then $1.516 \times 193{,}000$ joules, or 69.94 kcal, and the heat absorbed from the cell is greater than that absorbed for the direct combination by this amount. Accordingly, $q_{rev} = -75.20 + 69.94 = -5.26$ kcal (*i.e.*, 5.26 kcal are given to the surroundings), and the entropy change for the production of 1 mole of solid $CdBr_2$ is $-5.26 \times 1{,}000/(273.15 + 36)$ $= -17.0$ cal/deg. Since the initial and final states of the cadmium-bromine system are the same in the reversible and in the irreversible processes considered, the total change of entropy of the irreversible process is $243.3 + (-17.0) = 226.3$ cal/deg.

We may note that the work obtained from the above reaction in the electric cell is about 69.9 kcal, while the heat obtained from the direct combination is about 75.2 kcal. The question might be asked: Can we carry out the process in such a way that all the heat liberated in the direct combination is converted into work? If this were possible no heat would be given to the surroundings, and hence they would undergo no change of entropy. This would make the total entropy change $0 + (-17.0) = -17.0$, which, according to our rule, is impossible. In this instance our argument is circular, because we obtained the figure for the entropy change from the assumption that the work associated with an electromotive force of 1.516 volts is the reversible work. Nevertheless our rule that the total entropy change must be zero or positive is a convenient way of summarizing our ability to predict the behaviour of a system. In general, if we know the entropy change for each step in a process or set of linked processes we can, in a manner similar to the above, determine whether the process is possible or not; although, if it is possible, thermodynamics tells nothing about its rate—a determination which lies in the province of chemical, or reaction, kinetics (*see* CHEMISTRY: *Chemical Kinetics;* REACTION KINETICS).

Since the entropy of a system is a function of temperature, volume, and pressure, it would be quite impractical to try to measure the entropy of systems at all desired combinations of these variables; even if obtainable, it would be troublesome to tabulate them. To make a smaller number of measurements sufficient for most purposes we need to know how the entropy of a system changes with change of temperature, volume, or pressure. If a system is in equilibrium with surroundings at $T$ and $P$, and its volume is changed reversibly and isothermally, the work done is $PdV$ for an infinitesimal change of volume, and the heat absorbed is $dE + PdV$. Since the entropy change is the reversible heat absorbed divided by the temperature, $TdS = dE + PdV$. Formally dividing by $dV$, and noting that $T$ is constant,

$$T(dS/dV)_T = (dE/dV)_T + P \quad (7)$$

If a system is heated reversibly at constant volume, the heat absorbed, for an infinitesimal change, is $C_v dT$, and $dS = C_v dT/T$. Dividing by $dT$, we obtain

$$(dS/dT)_v = C_v/T \quad (8)$$

Differentiating (7) with respect to $T$, and (8) with respect to $V$, and combining, we obtain

$$(dS/dV)_T = (dP/dT)_v \quad (9)$$

Equations (7), (8), and (9) are relevant to changes taking place at constant volume, or when temperature and volume are chosen as the independent variables, but processes are more likely to be carried out at constant pressure, or to be considered in terms of temperature and pressure. If to the right side of the equation $TdS = dE + PdV$, we add $d(PV)$ and subtract its equivalent $PdV + VdP$, we obtain $TdS = d(E + PV) - VdP$. Defining the enthalpy, or heat content, as

$$H = E + PV \quad (10)$$

we can then obtain

$$T(dS/dP)_T = (dH/dP)_T - V \quad (11)$$

Also, for reversible heating at constant pressure,

$$(dS/dT)_p = C_p/T \quad (12)$$

From (11) and (12), noting that $C_p = (dH/dT)_p$,

$$(dS/dP)_T = -(dV/dT)_p \quad (13)$$

Since $dS = (dS/dV)_T dV + (dS/dT)_v dT$ or $dS = (dS/dP)_T dP + (dS/dT)_p dT$, the most generally useful of the above equations are the pairs (8) and (9) and (12) and (13).

Equations (8) and (12) have the same form, and one can be obtained from the other by interchanging $P$ and $V$. Equations (9) and (13) form a similar pair, except for the change of sign. The pair (7) and (11) follow a similar pattern if, in addition to a change of sign, we interchange $E$ and $H$. When thermodynamic relationships are expressed in terms appropriate to choosing temperature and volume as the independent variables, comparatively simple equations are obtained, but when temperature and pressure are chosen, this simplicity is lost unless $E$ is expressed in terms of $H$. For a process occurring at constant volume, doing no work, the heat absorbed, $q = \Delta E$, but if a process occurs at constant pressure, doing no work except that due to the expansion (or contraction) of the system against the constant pressure, $q = \Delta E + P\Delta V = \Delta H$. Tables of heats of fusion, of vaporization, and of reaction commonly give the heat absorbed at constant pressure, and accordingly $\Delta H$ for the process. It may be anticipated that the Helmholtz free energy and the Gibbs function, $A$ and $G$ respectively, introduced in section 7, relate naturally to the temperature-volume and the temperature-pressure systems, respectively.

**6. The Clapeyron Equation.**—The change of vapour pressure of a liquid can be derived from equation (12). If vaporization of a liquid is allowed to take place while liquid and vapour are in equilibrium at constant temperature $T$, the latent heat of vaporization, $\Delta H_{vap}$, is absorbed while the system undergoes the volume change $\Delta V$. The entropy change per unit change of volume is then

$$\Delta H_{vap}/T\Delta V = (\Delta S/\Delta V)_T = (dS/dV)_T = (dP/dT)_v = dP/dT \quad (14)$$

for equilibrium between the phases. $\Delta H_{vap}/T$ is the entropy change, since $\Delta H_{vap}$ is the heat absorbed when the change takes place reversibly, and $(\Delta S/\Delta V)_T$ is equal to $(dS/dV)_T$ since $\Delta S/\Delta V$ is independent of the amount of transformation which has occurred. This, by equation (12), is equal to $(dP/dT)_v$, but the restriction of constant volume is unnecessary since the change of pressure with change of temperature is the same whether volume is constant or not, as long as pure liquid and gas are in equilibrium.

The same form of equation applies to any equilibrium transition in which the number of phases is sufficient to keep the composition of each phase constant during the isothermal change. Thus, at the transition point of sodium sulfate, $Na_2SO_4 \cdot 10H_2O \rightarrow$ $0.37\ Na_2SO_4 + 269.5$ g solution, the latent heat of transition $L = 17.3$ kcal and $\Delta V = 1.3$ cc. Converting the heat in calories to cm$^3$-atm and using (14), we find that the transition temperature changes 0.00055° C per atm change of pressure.

**7. The Gibbs Function.**—An important use of thermodynamic data is in predicting whether a process will occur spontaneously—and further: if spontaneous, how much work could be obtained from the process if it were carried out reversibly; if not spontaneous, what is the minimum work required to carry out the process. A consideration of the entropy changes of all subsystems of interest, including the entropy changes of the surroundings, is sufficient for this purpose. However, in most cases the processes under consideration are at constant temperature and in communication with surroundings at the same temperature, and also are usually at constant pressure. In such cases two auxiliary functions, the Helmholtz free energy,

$$A = E - TS \text{ (definition)} \qquad (15)$$

and the Gibbs function, sometimes called the free energy or the free enthalpy,

$$G = H - TS \text{ (definition)} \qquad (16)$$

are of great value. (Some authors have denoted $E - TS$ and $H - TS$ by $A$ and $F$, while others have used $F$ and $G$. This use of $F$ for both functions has practically destroyed its utility, and is here avoided for that reason.) The Gibbs function, embodying one of the most important concepts in thermodynamics, was formulated by J. Willard Gibbs (*q.v.;* 1839–1903), who was chiefly responsible for the extension of thermodynamics into chemistry.

It can be shown that for an isothermal reversible process the work done is the initial value of $A$ minus its final value, or $-\Delta A$. In a reversible process occurring at constant temperature and pressure, part of the work is done in expanding the system against the pressure of its surroundings, and the net work, $w'$, is $-\Delta G$. If the process is not reversible, the net work is less. In general, for any process at constant temperature and pressure

$$w' \leqq -\Delta G \qquad (17)$$

If $\Delta G$ is negative the process is spontaneous; if zero the system is in equilibrium; and if positive the process can be made to take place only by doing work on the system or by linking it with another system undergoing a process with negative $\Delta G$. (In the latter case, if the two systems are considered as one, the total $\Delta G$ for the combined system must then be negative or zero.)

Here, as with entropy, little use can be made of these functions unless we can obtain their changes with temperature and volume or with temperature and pressure, respectively. Using the definitions of $A$ and $G$ above, and the previously obtained relations for $S$, we readily obtain

$$(dA/dT)_v = -S \qquad (18)$$
$$(dA/dV)_T = -P \qquad (19)$$
$$(dG/dT)_p = -S \qquad (20)$$

and

$$(dG/dP)_T = V \qquad (21)$$

On replacing the entropy in the above relations by $(E - A)/T$ and $(H - G)/T$ respectively, we obtain from (18) and (20)

$$(d(A/T)/dT)_v = -E/T^2 \qquad (22)$$

and

$$(d(G/T)/dT)_p = -H/T^2 \qquad (23)$$

With compilations of $G$, $H$, and $C_p = (dH/dT)_p$ for large numbers of substances at arbitrarily chosen standard conditions (usually 25° C and 1 atm) and the above relations for the change with temperature and with pressure, the Gibbs energy changes of a very great number of processes occurring at constant temperature and pressure can be calculated. From these calculations it can be determined whether the process is spontaneous or not. Since energy can be measured only relative to an arbitrarily chosen base, this is likewise true of $H$, $A$, or $G$; tables of these quantities are given relative to the values for the elements composing the substances, in that state in which they ordinarily occur at 25° C and 1 atm.

**8. Chemical Potential.**—The relations thus far developed are sufficient for thermodynamic treatment of systems in which each substance occurs only in the pure state. However, in many cases one is interested in systems in which solutions occur. (In this and following sections the reader may have frequent occasion to consult the article SOLUTIONS on matters of detail or of parallel interest.)

Consider, for example, the vapour pressure of a 25% aqueous potassium chloride solution, and its change with temperature. The amount of KCl in the vapour is far too small to be detectable, and we may consider the vapour to be pure water. One method for measuring the vapour pressure of pure water is to put it into a previously evacuated space, allow water to evaporate into it until it is saturated, and measure the pressure of the vapour with a manometer.

If the same method is used for the salt solution, its composition will change during the evaporation. To obtain the result we desire we must either make the amount of salt solution very large relative to the amount of water evaporated or put the solution in contact with a vapour space which is already nearly saturated with the vapour. In either case the process of interest may be described by the balanced "chemical equation" $\Delta n_1 H_2O$ (25% KCl solution) = $\Delta n_1 H_2O$ (gas) where $n_1$ is the number of moles of water. If a nearly saturated space is used, $\Delta n_1$ is very small and the solution is not appreciably changed during evaporation. If a large amount of solution is used $\Delta n_1$ may be much larger without appreciable change of composition.

For convenience we may write the reaction for the evaporation of one mole of water as $H_2O$ (25% solution) = $H_2O$ (gas). The corresponding change of the Gibbs function is $\Delta G = G$ (gas) $- (dG/dn_1)_{n_2,P,T}$ where $n_1$ and $n_2$ are respectively the number of moles of water and of salt in the solution, and $(dG/dn_1)_{n_2,P,T}$ is the limit of the change of the Gibbs function of the solution on addition of water, divided by the amount added, as the addition approaches zero. (The subscripts indicate that during the addition of water the temperature, pressure, and amount of salt are kept constant.)

For solutions containing three or more components the amounts of all but one must be kept constant. When misunderstanding seems unlikely, some or all such subscripts will be omitted. The quantity $(dG/dn_i)_{P,T}$ is called the chemical potential of substance $i$ in the solution, and is generally written $\mu_i$, sometimes $\overline{G}_i$. While we have introduced the chemical potential as $(dG/dn_i)_{P,T}$, it can be shown that $\mu_i$ is also equal to $(dA/dn_i)_{V,T} = (dE/dn_i)_{S,V} = (dH/dn_i)_{S,P}$. Since, however, $\mu_i$ is generally employed in connection with processes at constant temperature and pressure, its expression $(dG/dn_i)_{P,T}$, for correlation with $G$, is most frequently encountered. Gibbs originally expressed $\mu$ on a weight basis, but for chemical use it is more conveniently given, as above, on a molal basis.

The use of the chemical potential at various temperatures and pressures requires its change with temperature and pressure. By performing the appropriate partial differentiations we readily obtain

$$(d\mu_i/dT)_P = -(dS/dn_i)_{T,P} = -\overline{S}_i \qquad (24)$$
$$(d(\mu_i/T)/dT)_P = -\overline{H}_i/T^2 \qquad (25)$$
$$(d\mu_i/dP)_T = (dV/dn_i)_{T,P} = \overline{V}_i \qquad (26)$$

where, according to a common convention, the derivative with respect to $n_i$, keeping $T$, $P$, and the quantities of other constituents constant, is called the partial molal quantity, and is abbreviated as above, with a bar over the symbol, together with the subscript.

Numerical values of $\mu$ are obtained from reactions involving the appropriate substance in its solution and in the pure state, for which the change of $G$ either is known or can be measured. If the system is in equilibrium, $\mu_i$ is the same in each phase containing the constituent. (*See* PHASE EQUILIBRIA.) In the above example of an aqueous KCl solution, $\mu_{H_2O}$ (solution) = $\mu_{H_2O}$ (gas) = $G_{H_2O}$ (gas at vapour pressure of the solution). If we assume that the vapour obeys the gas law, from $(dG/dP)_T = V = RT/P$ we obtain $\mu_{H_2O}$(solution) = $G_{H_2O}$(pure liquid) $+ RT \ln P_s/P_w$, where $P_s$ and $P_w$ are the vapour pressures of solution and of pure water respectively. To obtain the chemical potential of the KCl in the solution we note that the 25% solution is saturated at 17.8° C, and $\mu_2$(solution) = $\mu_2$(solid) = $G_2$(solid). If the chemical potential in the solution is desired at some other temperature, by using equation (25) we obtain

$$\mu(T') = G(\text{solid}, T') - T' \int_{T_s}^{T'} (\overline{H} - H_s)\, dT/T^2$$

where $T_s$ is the saturation temperature and $\overline{H} - H_s$ is the heat absorbed when one mole of solid KCl is dissolved in a quantity of nearly 25% KCl solution sufficient to make the change of composition negligible.

**9. Activity.**—For an ideal gas,

$$\mu'' - \mu' = \int VdP = \int RTdP/P = RT \ln P''/P' \quad (27)$$

Since most gases at moderate or low pressures deviate only slightly from ideality, it is convenient to define the activity, $a$, of the gas (also called its fugacity, as here defined) by the equation

$$RT \ln a''/a' = \mu'' - \mu' = \int VdP \quad (28)$$

Subtracting $RT \ln P''/P'$ from the left, and its equal, $\int_{P'}^{P''} RTdP/P$, from the right, we obtain $RT \ln (a''/P'')/(a'/P') = \int_{P'}^{P''} (V - RT/P)dP$ where $V - RT/P$ is the deviation of the volume of the gas from ideality. A numerical scale for the activity of a gas can now be conveniently established by making $a'/P'$ approach unity as $P'$ approaches zero, leading to

$$RT \ln a''/P'' = \int_0^{P''} (V - RT/P)dP \quad (29)$$

As $P$ approaches zero, both $V$ and $RT/P$ become infinite. However, both theory and experiment indicate that the difference approaches a finite value as the pressure approaches zero, and hence the integral of (29) can be evaluated.

As the total pressure of a gaseous mixture approaches zero each constituent is progressively less affected by the others, and it is consistent to define the activity of a gaseous constituent such that, as the pressure approaches zero, $a_i/PN_i \doteq 1$, where $N_i$ is the mole fraction of constituent $i$ in the mixture. For a mixture, equation (28) becomes $RT \ln a''_i/a'_i = \int_{P'}^{P''} \bar{V}_i\, dP$ where $\bar{V}_i$ is the change of volume of the mixture upon addition of one mole of constituent $i$, when the pressure and temperature and the amount of all other constituents are kept constant, and the total quantity is so large that the change of composition is negligible. Subtracting $\int_{P'}^{P''} dP/P$ from each side and letting $P'$ approach zero, we obtain

$$RT \ln a''_i/P''N_i = \int_0^{P''} (\bar{V}_i - RT/P)dP \quad (30)$$

From the relation of the activity to the chemical potential it is clear that the activity of a liquid or a solid is equal to the activity of its saturated vapour, if the activity is measured on the scale adopted for gases. For substances of very low volatility this scale is impractical; even for readily volatile ones it is frequently convenient to adopt different scales or bases of activity. Including the one just given, there are four commonly used bases:

Base 1, for a pure gas, $a/P \doteq 1$ as $P \doteq 0$, and for a gaseous mixture $a_i/PN_i \doteq 1$ as $P \doteq 0$.

Base 2, for a substance in solid or liquid solution, especially when considered as a solvent, $a = 1$ for the pure solid or liquid at 1 atm pressure.

Base 3, for a substance in solution particularly when considered as a solute, $a/N \doteq 1$ as $N \doteq 0$.

Base 4, for solutes for which the concentration is expressed in molality, $m$, the number of moles of solute per kilogram of solvent, $a/m \doteq 1$ as $m \doteq 0$.

Care must be exercised in the use of activity when a base other than 1 is used: for two phases in equilibrium the activity of a constituent in phase A is equal to that in phase B if base 1 is used in both, but if base 1 is used for phase A and a different base is used for phase B the activities at equilibrium will now not be equal. If base 2 is used for both phases the activities are again equal at equilibrium, but with the use of base 3 or 4 the activity is not the same in the two phases in equilibrium, even when the same formal base is used for both, since the solvents are not identical.

Many solutions, particularly those of substances which are quite similar, conform rather closely to the relations $a_1 = a_1{}^\circ N_1$ and $a_2 = a_2{}^\circ N_2$ where $a^\circ$ is the activity of the pure substance in the same physical state as the solution. Solutions which satisfy these relations exactly are called ideal. If it be required that the relations are satisfied at all temperatures and pressures, there must also be neither heat effects nor volume changes on mixing the constituents. Such stringent requirements are not exactly satisfied even by mixtures of isotopes, but for moderate ranges of pressure and temperature a surprisingly large number of pairs of substances conform quite closely. In such cases the activity divided by the mole fraction, called the activity coefficient, is nearly unity over the whole range of compositions, and its deviation from unity is a measure of the deviation from ideality. If the solution is ideal over the whole range, the activity on base 3 is identical with that on base 2, but otherwise they will be different. Activity coefficients are defined as $a/N$ for bases 2 and 3; for 1 and 4 they are $a/PN$ and $a/m$ respectively. Various symbols have been used for the different activity coefficients; $\gamma$ has been most commonly used for $a/m$, and will be used here for any activity coefficient, since the context will usually make clear which one is meant.

**10. Change of Activity with Temperature and Pressure.**—Consider the transfer of one mole of a constituent from one solution to another, when the quantity of each is so large that no appreciable change of composition occurs as a consequence of the transfer. For this transfer, $\mu - \mu' = RT \ln a/a'$ where $\mu$, $\mu'$ and $a$, $a'$ are respectively the chemical potential and the activity of the constituent in the two solutions. Using equation (25), and writing $a' = \gamma' x'$ where $x'$ may be $P'N'$, $N'$, or $m'$ according to which defining base is used, we obtain

$$(d \ln a/dT)_P = d \ln \gamma'/dT + d \ln x'/dT - (\bar{H} - \bar{H}')/RT^2 \quad (31)$$

For arbitrary compositions of the primed phase, (31) will have slight usefulness because of ignorance concerning the change of $\gamma'$ with temperature. But if we choose $x'$ such that $\gamma'$ is very nearly unity at both $T$ and $T + dT$, we may make the first term on the right of (31) as small as we please; and by choosing $x'$ independent of temperature, the second term is zero. From this we obtain

$$(d \ln a/dT)_P = -(\bar{H} - \bar{H}^\circ)/RT^2 \quad (32)$$

where $\bar{H}^\circ$ is the limit of $\bar{H}$ as the composition is changed so that $\gamma'$ approaches unity, and $\bar{H} - \bar{H}^\circ$ is the limit of the heat absorbed when a mole of the constituent is transferred from a chosen solution to one whose composition is such as to make its activity coefficient approach unity. For convenience we may refer to this state as the defining state. For base 1 it is gaseous solution as the total pressure approaches zero, for base 2 it is the pure substance at standard pressure (generally 1 atm), and for bases 3 and 4 it is the substance in dilute solution as its concentration approaches zero.

From the definitions of the activity we easily obtain

$$(d \ln a/dP)_{T,N} = \bar{V}/RT \quad (33)$$

for each of the four bases which have been given for defining the activity. The subscript $_N$ denotes that the composition is kept constant.

**11. The Gibbs-Duhem and Duhem-Margules Equations.**—When a system is formed by the combination of two or more identical subsystems without changing the properties of the subsystems, we define as intensive properties those which are the same for the total system as for the subsystems, and as extensive properties those which are greater for the total system than for any one of the subsystems, in proportion to the ratio of their masses.

Temperature, density, and refractive index are common intensive properties; volume, energy, entropy, and the Gibbs function are representative of extensive properties. Using volume as an example, we may write (for a binary mixture; the results may be readily generalized) $dV = (dV/dn_1)dn_1 + (dV/dn_2)dn_2 = \bar{V}_1 dn_1 + \bar{V}_2 dn_2$ where the derivatives are taken keeping $T$, $P$, and the quantity of other constituents constant. The partial molal volumes, $\bar{V}_1$ and $\bar{V}_2$, are functions of composition but not of the total mass of the system, and are intensive quantities. From this fact, and from the definitions of the quantities, simple mathematical manipulations yield $V = n_1\bar{V}_1 + n_2\bar{V}_2$ and $n_1 d\bar{V}_1 + n_2 d\bar{V}_2 = 0$. Corresponding relations may be obtained from the partial molal quantities derived from any extensive property. Using the Gibbs function we find

$$n_1 d\bar{G}_1 + n_2 d\bar{G}_2 = 0; \text{ or, using } \mu_i = \bar{G}_i,\ n_1 d\mu_1 + n_2 d\mu_2 = 0 \quad (34)$$

From the definition of activity we obtain from equation (34) $n_1 d \ln a_1 + n_2 d \ln a_2 = 0$, and dividing by $n_1 + n_2$,

$$N_1 d \ln a_1 + N_2 d \ln a_2 = 0 \quad (35)$$

Since $N_1 + N_2 = 1$, $dN_1 + dN_2 = 0$, and hence $N_1 d \ln N_1 + N_2 d \ln N_2 = 0$, we also find $N_1 d \ln \gamma_1 + N_2 d \ln \gamma_2 = 0$ for all expressions of the activity coefficient except that on a molality basis.

Equations (34) and (35) are known respectively as the Gibbs-Duhem equation and the Duhem-Margules equation. They were both first obtained by Gibbs, and are so closely related that it seems hardly worth making a distinction between them. If we assume that the vapours of the constituents obey the gas law, on replacing activities by partial pressures we obtain the approximate equation $N_1 d \ln P_1 + N_2 d \ln P_2 = 0$, which gives in principle a means of finding the vapour pressure of one constituent of a solution if it is known at one composition and if the vapour pressure of the other is known over the entire range; but in practice the vapour pressures of the second must be known with rather high precision to get fairly good values of the first.

**12. Dilute Solutions; Henry's Law.**—In a very dilute solution, a solute molecule will (with rare exceptions) have only solvent molecules as near neighbours, and the probability of escape of a particular solute molecule into the gas phase is expected to be independent of the total concentration of solute molecules. In this case the rate of escape of solute molecules will be proportional to their concentration in the solution, and solute will accumulate in the gas until the return rate is equal to the rate of escape. With a very dilute gas this return rate will be proportional to the partial pressure of solute. Thus we expect that, for a solution very dilute in solute, in equilibrium with a gas at very low pressure, $P_2 = k'N_2$—the relation known as Henry's law. Since for gases at very low pressure the activity is proportional to the partial pressure, we may also write

$$a_2 = kN_2 \quad (36)$$

which is the thermodynamically convenient form of Henry's law. While the above argument is to be considered only suggestive, Henry's law is found experimentally to hold for all dilute solutions in which the molecular species is the same in the solution as in the gas. The most conspicuous apparent exception is the class of electrolytic solutions, which will be discussed separately.

**13. Raoult's Law.**—Substituting (36) in (35) and using, for the binary solution, $dN_1 + dN_2 = 0$, we readily obtain $a_1 = k''N_1$, and substituting $a_1 = a_1^\circ$ when $N_1 = 1$, we find

$$a_1 = a_1^\circ N_1 \quad (37)$$

where $N_1$ is the mole fraction of the solvent in a solution which is very dilute in solute. This relation is generally known as Raoult's law, although originally expressed as $P_1 = P_1^\circ N_1$. It has frequently been used to find the molar weight of nonvolatile solutes by transforming to $M_2 = M_1 P_1 w_2 / (P_1^\circ - P_1) w_1$, where $w_1$, $w_2$, $M_1$, $M_2$ are the weights of solvent and solute in the solution, and the molar weights, respectively.

**14. Freezing Point Lowering.**—At the freezing point of pure liquid, $T_0$, $\mu_1$ (liquid) $= \mu_1$ (solid). Using equation (25) and neglecting the change of the heat of fusion with temperature, we obtain, at $T$,

$$\mu_1 \text{ (solid)} - \mu_1 \text{ (liquid)}/T = \Delta H_{\text{fusion}} (1/T_0 - 1/T) \quad (38)$$

where $\mu_1$ (liquid) is here the chemical potential of the pure supercooled liquid. From the definition of activity (28), and from Raoult's law (37)

$$\mu_1 \text{ (solution)}/T = \mu_1 \text{ (liquid)}/T + R \ln N_1 \quad (39)$$

and if $T$ is the freezing point of the solution, or the temperature at which the solution is in equilibrium with solid solvent,

$$\mu_1 \text{ (solid)} = \mu_1 \text{ (solution)} \quad (40)$$

Combining (38), (39), and (40), we obtain

$$R \ln N_1 = \Delta H_{\text{fusion}} (1/T_0 - 1/T) \quad (41)$$

While equation (41) has been obtained for the dilute solution, for which Raoult's law holds, it is also valid for the ideal solution over the whole range, except that the neglect of the change of heat of fusion with temperature may now introduce error if the lowering is large. Also, (41) is valid only if the solvent separates as the pure solid; if solid solution is formed, (41) must be replaced by

$$R \ln (N_1/N_1') = \Delta H_{\text{fusion}} (1/T_0 - 1/T) \quad (42)$$

where $N_1'$ is the mole fraction of solvent in the solid solution.

For dilute solutions ($N_2$ small), equation (41) can be transformed into the approximate form $T_0 - T = (RT_0^2/\Delta H_{\text{fusion}})(N_2)$. The freezing point lowering, the lowering of vapour pressure, and the elevation of the boiling point are employed for estimating the molal weight of a solute.

**15. Boiling Point Elevation.**—If the solute is nonvolatile the elevation of the boiling point can be obtained by steps which are analogous to those used in deriving the lowering of the freezing point. The result is $R \ln N_1 = \Delta H_{\text{vap}}(1/T - 1/T_0)$ or $\Delta T \cong (RT_0^2/\Delta H_{\text{vap}})N_2$, where $T_0$ is the boiling point of the pure solvent, $T$ is that of the solution, $\Delta T$ is $T - T_0$, and $\Delta H_{\text{vap}}$ is the heat of vaporization of the solvent. If the solute is also volatile an equation analogous to (42) is obtained: $R \ln N_1/N_1'' = \Delta H_{\text{vap}}(1/T - 1/T_0)$, where $N_1''$ is the mole fraction of the solvent in the vapour.

**16. Osmotic Pressure.**—If a solution and pure solvent are separated by a membrane which permits passage of solvent only, the solvent will pass from its pure state to the solution unless a difference in pressure is maintained between them, because the activity of the solvent is less in the solution than in the pure solvent. For equilibrium the change of activity with composition must be offset by the change with pressure, or $(d \ln a_1/dN_1)_P dN_1 + (d \ln a_1/dP)_N dP = 0$. Substituting equations (37) and (33) we find

$$dP/dN_2 = -dP/dN_1 = RT/N_1\bar{V}_1 \quad (43)$$

For very dilute solutions the partial molal volume, $\bar{V}_1$, approaches $V_1$; the mole fraction of pure solvent, $N_1$, is nearly 1; and $P - P^\circ \cong N_2RT/V_1 \cong n_2RT/V$ where $n_2$ is the number of moles of solute in solution of volume $V$, $P^\circ$ is the pressure on the pure solvent, and $P$ is the pressure on the solution when no flow of solvent can occur through the membrane. The right-hand term is the form used by J. H. van't Hoff. Because of its similarity to the ideal gas law it was at one time made the base for the derivation of the properties of dilute solutions, but Henry's law seems a simpler and more fundamental one to use.

**17. Solutions of Electrolytes.**—For dilute solutions, in which the solute molecules are surrounded only by solvent molecules, it seems a valid assumption that the vapour pressure of the solute should be proportional to its concentration, as expressed by Henry's law. The outstanding exception to this relation is the class of solutes known as electrolytes (those which conduct electric current, concomitant to their dissociation into ions). Hydrogen chloride in the gaseous state exists as HCl molecules, but in dilute aqueous solution it occurs almost entirely as the (presumably hydrated) hydrogen ions and chloride ions, $H^+$ and $Cl^-$. Because of the high dielectric constant of water the attraction of the unlike charges is greatly reduced, and in very dilute solution the ions behave nearly as if the others were not present. There is no satisfactory way of determining the concentration of neutral HCl molecules in aqueous solution, but if we assume that in dilute solution the activity of each ion is proportional to its concentration, we can predict that the activity of HCl, and likewise its partial pressure, should be proportional to the square of the stoichiometric concentration. This is indeed the case, and we conclude that the failure to obey Henry's law is more apparent than real. All strong electrolytes behave as if the ions in dilute solution obey Henry's law, and hence the activity of the electrolyte varies as the square, cube, . . . of the electrolyte concentration, according as the electrolyte dissociates into two, three, . . . ions. If base 4 is used for the definition of the activity of ions, the activity coefficient of the ion approaches unity as the concentration approaches zero. Because of the long range of the effects of the electrostatic forces of ions upon one another, however, the activity coefficients of ions deviate appreciably from unity even in very dilute solutions. When the solutions are so dilute that their interactions are almost entirely due to their charges, the activity coefficient can be calculated quite satisfactorily by the method of P. Debye and E. Hückel, which correlates the electrostatic interaction of an ion with the average distribution of ions around it, assuming that this distribution of ions is determined by the potential which would result from such an average distribution. Such calculations appear to give the activity coefficients of individual ions. However, because of the maintenance of approximate electrical neutrality, individual ion activities or activity coefficients cannot in fact be measured; only products of activity coefficients of ions of unlike charges, or quotients of ions of like charges, can be obtained. For example, one might measure the distribution of $FeCl_3$ between an organic solvent and an aqueous solution of $FeCl_3$ and HCl, and also measure the partial pressure of HCl in equilibrium with the solution. If the measurements are carried out on a series of solutions to sufficiently great dilution, one could obtain $\gamma_{H^+}\gamma_{Cl^-}$ and $\gamma_{Fe^{3+}}\gamma^3_{Cl^-}$. One can also obtain $\gamma_{Fe^{3+}}/\gamma^3_{H^+}$, $\gamma_{Fe^{3+}}\gamma^2_{Cl^-}/\gamma_{H^+}$, or any other combination obtained by multiplying or dividing the first two products.

In spite of our inability to measure the thermodynamic properties of individual ions, tabulations of free energies and entropies of formation, and activity coefficients of ions can be found. The entries in such tables are convenient fictions dependent on arbitrary assignments of activity coefficients to some ion, and are useful only when combined with other values based on the same convention so that the net result corresponds to a system with no net charge, or to a process with no change of charge. For the above system, entries from such tables would be appropriate for reactions such as $H^+ + Cl^- = HCl$ (gas), $Fe^{3+} + 3Cl^- = FeCl_3$ (gaseous, or in some appropriate solution), $Fe^{3+} + \frac{3}{2}H_2 = Fe + 3H^+$, etc. In the system considered above, the activity of HCl is proportional to the product of the activity of hydrogen ion and of chloride ion, and the activity of $FeCl_3$ is proportional to the activity of ferric ion times the cube of that of the chloride ion. It is convenient to define the base of activity of the strong electrolytes such that the activity of the electrolyte is equal to the product of the appropriate ion activities. Since the individual ion activities cannot be determined, this appears to be a questionable procedure, but it is just these combinations of ion activities which can be measured. The above convention is regularly used for strong electrolytes or for those usually considered to be almost completely dissociated. For weak electrolytes or those of an intermediate degree of dissociation, activities and activity coefficients are usually based on the concentrations assumed to exist in the solution, rather than on the stoichiometric concentrations.

**18. The Electromotive Force of Galvanic Cells.**—Measurements of activities of strong electrolytes are made in many cases by the same methods which are used for nonelectrolytes; *e.g.*, by equilibrium with another phase containing the electrolyte or by freezing point depression combined with the use of the Gibbs-Duhem relation (35). The activity is also frequently obtained from the electromotive force of a reversible cell which involves the production or consumption of the electrolyte. If the reversible electromotive force of the cell is $\mathcal{E}$, then

$$\Delta G = -n\mathcal{F}\mathcal{E} \tag{44}$$

where $\mathcal{F}$ is the value of the faraday in appropriate units, $\Delta G$ is the change of the Gibbs function for the change which occurs in the cell with passage of electricity, and $n$ is the number of faradays which correspond to the chemical reaction written for the process. For example, when current is passed through the cell containing aqueous HCl, with a platinum anode surrounded by gaseous $H_2$ and a silver cathode in contact with solid AgCl, HCl is produced according to the reaction

$$\tfrac{1}{2}H_2(\text{gas}) + AgCl(\text{solid}) = Ag(\text{solid}) + HCl(\text{aqueous})$$

For the specified amount of reaction, one faraday would be required, and $n$ of equation (44) is 1. Subtracting the results of two cells differing only in the concentrations of HCl, we obtain $HCl(m') = HCl(m'')$; $\Delta G = n\mathcal{F}(\mathcal{E}' - \mathcal{E}'') = RT \ln a_2''/a_2'$ where $a_2'$ and $a_2''$ are the activities of HCl in the two solutions. For dilute solutions the activity of HCl is proportional to the square of the concentration, and the geometric mean activity and activity coefficient are defined by $a_2^{\frac{1}{2}} = a_\pm = \gamma_\pm m_\pm$ where $m_\pm$ is the geometric mean of the molalities of $H^+$ and $Cl^-$. The molalities of the ions of strong electrolytes are calculated as if they are completely ionized. Accordingly, for pure aqueous HCl, $m_\pm = m$ where $m$ is the total number of moles of HCl per kilogram of water. (For a more complex electrolyte, a weighted geometric mean is used; *e.g.*, for $BaCl_2$, $a_\pm = a^{\frac{1}{3}}_{BaCl_2} = \gamma_\pm m_\pm$ where $m_\pm = [m_{Ba^{++}}m^2_{Cl^-}]^{\frac{1}{3}}$). The $a_\pm$ and $\gamma_\pm$ so defined are convenient because, like the $a$ and $\gamma$ of nonelectrolytes, $a_\pm$ approaches the concentration and $\gamma_\pm$ approaches unity as the concentration approaches zero. The activity coefficients of strong electrolytes reported in the literature are almost universally the $\gamma_\pm$ as defined above.

**19. The Equilibrium Constant.**—From the definition of activity we have $\Delta G = \mu - \mu' = RT \ln a/a'$ for the transfer of a substance from a system in which its activity is $a'$ to a system in which it is $a$, when the same base of activity is used in both. We may rewrite this

$$\mu - \mu^\circ = \bar{G} - \bar{G}^\circ = RT \ln a \tag{45}$$

writing $\mu^\circ = \bar{G}^\circ$ for the chemical potential for the state in which $a' = 1$. Consider the isothermal reaction $lL + l'L' + \ldots = rR + r'R' + \ldots$ for which

$$\begin{aligned}\Delta G &= (rG_R + r'G_{R'} + \ldots) - (lG_L + l'G_{L'} + \ldots) = \\ &(rG_R^\circ + r'G_{R'}^\circ + \ldots) - (lG_L^\circ + l'G_{L'}^\circ + \ldots) + \\ &RT \ln J = \Delta G^\circ + RT \ln J\end{aligned} \tag{46}$$

in which $J$ is $(a_R^{\,r}.a_{R'}^{\,r'} \ldots)/(a_L^{\,l}.a_{L'}^{\,l'} \ldots)$ by definition. We may call $J$ the activity quotient, which, with arbitrary values of the component activities, can have any positive value.

Now let us consider the same reaction with the system in equilibrium. In this case

$$\Delta G = 0 = \Delta G^\circ + RT \ln J_e = \Delta G^\circ + RT \ln K, \text{ or } RT \ln K = -\Delta G^\circ \tag{47}$$

where $K$, the equilibrium constant, is equal to $J_e$, the value of the activity quotient for the system in equilibrium. Let us write $K = Q_x \cdot Q_\gamma$ where $Q_x$ and $Q_\gamma$ are quotients of the same form as $K$, but with $x$ and $\gamma$ substituted for $a$. As in equation (31), $x$ is used for $PN$, $N$, or $m$ according to the base used for the definition of the activity, which may vary within a quotient $Q_x$. While $K$ is constant at constant temperature, $Q_x$ and $Q_\gamma$ will generally vary with change of composition. However, if each substance is nearly in its defining state, each $\gamma$ will be nearly 1, $Q_\gamma \cong 1$, and $K \cong Q_x$.

As an example, consider the precipitation of CoS by the action of $H_2S$ on a dilute solution of $CoCl_2$ at 25° C. If the solution is very dilute we may assume the HCl which is produced, and the $CoCl_2$ which remains, to be completely ionized, and write the reaction $Co^{2+} + H_2S(\text{gas}) = CoS(\text{solid}) + 2H^+$ omitting the chloride ions since they undergo no appreciable change. From suitable compilations of thermodynamic data we find $\Delta G^\circ$ for the above reaction is $-1.2$ kcal, from which

$$K = Q_\gamma \cdot Q_x = Q_\gamma(m_{H^+})^2/P_{H_2S} \cdot m_{Co^{2+}} = 7.6, \text{ or}$$
$$m_{Co^{2+}} = Q_\gamma(m_{H^+})^2/7.6\, P_{H_2S}$$

The activity coefficient of pure solid CoS is 1, by the usual convention and by that of the tables from which $\Delta G^\circ$ was obtained, and that of $H_2S$ is nearly 1 if the pressure is 1 atm. If the precision of other terms is sufficient to justify it, the activity coefficient of the $H_2S$ may be estimated from the deviation of the gas from ideality. If the aqueous solution is rather dilute, the activity coefficients of the $H^+$ and of the $Co^{2+}$ may be calculated by use of the Debye-Hückel theory. If preferred, we may write HCl and $CoCl_2$ in place of $H^+$ and $Co^{2+}$, but since the fictitious activity coefficient of $Cl^-$ enters both numerator and denominator to the same power, the same result is obtained. If the solutions are extremely dilute we may without serious error write $Q_\gamma \cong 1$, and $K \cong Q_x$.

We have arrived at the chief practical application of thermodynamics to physical chemistry. From the $Q_x$ for a given reaction we can relate the concentrations or partial pressures of the substances in equilibrium with one another, and hence can calculate, for any given initial conditions, whether the reactions as written will proceed to the right or left, and to what extent, if allowed to proceed to equilibrium.

The quantity which we have defined as $Q_x$ was called the equilibrium constant before the application of thermodynamics to chemical equilibria; it is better to call it the equilibrium quotient, and to reserve the name equilibrium constant for the activity quotient characteristic of equilibrium which has been designated above by $K$. The reasons for the seemingly arbitrary bases for defining the activity will now become apparent. $Q_x$ has been traditionally expressed by partial pressures of gaseous constituents, by mole fractions for nonaqueous solutions, and, for aqueous solutions, by concentrations in moles per litre. (The latter is preferably replaced by moles per kilogram of solvent, since this expression does not change with mere expansion of the solution with change of temperature.) With these modes of defining the activity we can keep $K$ in the same form as $Q_x$ and even have nearly the same numerical values when the solutions are dilute and the gas pressures are low—both of which conditions have frequently prevailed.

**20. Change of Equilibrium Constant with Temperature and Pressure.**—The equilibrium constant can be expressed as a function of temperature or pressure by finding the corresponding expression for $\Delta G°$. By equation (46)

$$\Delta G°/T = \Delta G/T - R \ln J = \Delta G/T - R \ln J_x - R \ln J_\gamma \quad (48)$$

where $J_x$ and $J_\gamma$ are the quotients of $x$'s and of $\gamma$'s of the same form as the activity quotient $J$. Combining equation (48) with (23), keeping pressure and composition constant, we obtain

$$[d(\Delta G°/T)dT]_{P,x} = -\Delta H/T^2 - R[d \ln J_\gamma/dT]_{P,x} \quad (49)$$

For arbitrarily chosen compositions we would have trouble in evaluating the last term. If, however, we choose such concentrations and partial pressures as to make each $\gamma$ nearly unity and hence $\ln J_\gamma$ very nearly zero, we can make $\ln J_\gamma$ as small as we please, both at $T$ and at $T + dT$, whereupon the last term of (49) becomes vanishingly small. Thus we find

$$[d \ln K/dT/_{P,x} = -[d(\Delta G°/RT)/dT/_{P,x} = \Delta H°/RT^2 \quad (50)$$

where $\Delta H°$ is the limit of the heat absorbed for the reaction in which each substance approaches the condition in which its activity coefficient is 1. In obtaining (49) and (50) we used partial derivatives with the formal restriction of constant pressure and composition, but since $K$ and $\Delta G°$ are both independent of pressure and composition these apparent restrictions can be dispensed with.

It is noteworthy that, while $\Delta G°$ is $\Delta G$ for the reaction in which each activity is 1, $\Delta H°$ is $\Delta H$ for the reaction in which each activity coefficient is 1. The conditions for the activity coefficients to be equal to 1 can generally be reached or approached, but in many cases those required to make the activities equal to 1 may be unattainable. This is of no real concern, for we define $\Delta G°$ by equation (46), using a $\Delta G$ for attainable conditions for which the activities are known. In subsequent use of $\Delta G°$ we again obtain a $\Delta G$ for attainable conditions. The $\Delta G°$ of formation of $H_2O$ (gas) at 25° C can be found in available tables. Formally, this is the Gibbs function of formation of water vapour at 25° C and activity of 1 atm. The activity of saturated water vapour at this temperature is 0.03 atm; while water vapour can be supersaturated to a considerable extent, it seems unlikely that it will ever be obtained at an activity of 1 atm at 25° C. This unattainable standard state could have been dodged by giving the $\Delta G$ of formation of water vapour at, say, $a = 0.01$, rather than for 1 atm, and putting into the activity quotients of expressions similar to (46) two sets of activities: those of the system of immediate interest and those for the tabulated state. The $\Delta G°$ values may be interpreted as merely a convenient and legitimate means of avoiding unnecessary additional labour of calculation.

## III. THIRD LAW OF THERMODYNAMICS

**1. Statement.**—The principle known as the third law of thermodynamics has been due primarily to the German chemist W. H. Nernst (*q.v.;* 1864–1941), but its significance and its limitations have been gradually developed by a number of workers. It is remarkably difficult to make a defensible statement of the third law which is not so full of restrictive qualifications as to make it practically useless. Its statement by G. N. Lewis and M. Randall (*see* bibliography) is: "If the entropy of each element in some crystalline state be taken as zero at the absolute zero of temperature: *every substance has a finite positive entropy, but at the absolute zero of temperature the entropy may become zero, and does so become in the case of perfect crystalline substances.*"

Criticism of this statement will be deferred until after an examination of the usefulness of the law. Provisionally accepting it as stated, from measurements of $C_p$ for both elements and the compounds of interest, one can, by integrating equation (9), find the entropies at some chosen temperature $T$ for all the substances concerned in a reaction, and thus obtain $\Delta S$ for the reaction. (If phase transitions occur between 0 and $T$, the change of entropy of such transitions must be included.) Combining this with the calorimetrically determined heat of the reaction, we obtain $\Delta G = \Delta H - T\Delta S$. If the activities of the substances have also been determined we can immediately obtain $\Delta G°$ and have all quantities of thermodynamic interest. The integration of (9) from $T = 0$ can be carried out if $C_p/T^n$ has a limit as $T \doteq 0$ for positive $n$, not necessarily an integer; for all substances investigated this requirement is easily met. For most substances $C_p/T^3$ approaches a limit; for metals having free electrons, calculations indicate that $C_p/T$ approaches a small non-zero value.

**2. Evaluations.**—Tests of the third law have been made by carrying out measurements of heat capacities of substances involved in reactions for which the entropy change has been independently measured by the change of $\Delta G$ with temperature. Satisfactory agreement is found in the great majority of cases, but a number of exceptions occur. To say that these are not perfect crystalline substances is not a satisfactory answer unless an independent criterion of perfection is available. The case of hydrogen is interesting. In accordance with certain quantum mechanical rules, normal hydrogen, $n$-$H_2$, may be considered a mixture of parahydrogen, $p$-$H_2$, with the nuclear spins aligned in opposite directions, and orthohydrogen, $o$-$H_2$, with the spins in the same direction. (*See* HYDROGEN: *Orthohydrogen and Parahydrogen.*) In the presence of an effective catalyst the $o$-$H_2$ changes to $p$-$H_2$ at low temperatures, and as absolute zero is approached it becomes nearly pure $p$-$H_2$. If its heat capacity is measured in the presence of a catalyst which maintains the mixture of $o$-$H_2$ and $p$-$H_2$ in their equilibrium amounts, entropies at higher temperatures are obtained which are consistent with measurements by other means. However, during heat capacity measurements in the absence of a catalyst, the $n$-$H_2$ persists as a mixture of $\frac{3}{4}$ $o$-$H_2$ and $\frac{1}{4}$ $p$-$H_2$ to very low temperatures. Heat capacities so measured, combined with the assumption of zero entropy at the absolute zero, lead to an apparent entropy at moderate or high temperatures which is in disagreement with that consistent with the reactions of hydrogen by about 4 cal/mole-deg. If this value is used to calculate chemical equilibria, the pressure or concentration of hydrogen so found can be in error by nearly a tenfold factor. For a few other substances the corresponding error may amount to as much as a threefold factor, but in the great majority of cases there is very good agreement.

## IV. OTHER THERMODYNAMIC RELATIONS

**1. Thermodynamic Quantities from the Structure of Molecules.**—The determination of the structure of molecules, including interatomic distances and angles (*see* STEREOCHEMISTRY), has made possible the calculation of many important thermodynamic functions of substances, particularly when in the dilute gaseous state. In a dilute gas, where the molecular interactions can be neglected, the energy of the system can be taken as the sum of the energies of the separate molecules, and the internal and translational energies of a molecule are independent. The internal energy may be further subdivided into electronic, vibrational, and rotational. For the monatomic gases, such as sodium and chlorine, the electronic energy is the only internal energy which needs to be considered. Arranging the electronic states in order of ascending energies, we will call that of lowest energy the ground state and those of higher energy the first, second, etc., excited states. If sodium vapour is held at constant temperature, atoms will exchange energy until at equilibrium the average fraction in any state will depend only on the temperature and the relative energy of the states. The exchanges may be represented by the reaction Na(o) = Na(i), which indicates the change of a mole of Na in the ground state to the i'th electronic state. At moderate temperatures practically all the atoms are in the ground state, and the vapour exhibits the heat capacity ($C_p = \frac{5}{2}R$) characteristic of the translational energy of a monatomic gas. If all the atoms in the vapour could be maintained in a single excited state it is plausible to assume that its molal heat capacity would also be $\frac{5}{2}R$, and for the change of Na(o) to Na(i), $\Delta C_p = 0$, $\Delta PV = 0$, and hence $\Delta H = \Delta E$. (The heat capacities discussed above are for sodium vapour with all its atoms in the ground state, or with all in the i'th state. The heat capacity of the mixture is greater than that characteristic of any pure state because, on raising the temperature, the proportion of atoms in high energy states is increased. This additional heat capacity is the $C_e$ discussed below.) Since $\Delta C_p$ is zero, the change of entropy is independent of temperature; and, assuming from the third law that the entropy change is zero at $T = 0$, it is also zero at any other temperature, and $-RT \ln K = \Delta G^\circ = \Delta H^\circ - T\Delta S^\circ = \Delta E^\circ$. From this we derive

$$n_i/n_o = e^{-(E_i - E_o)/RT} \tag{51}$$

where $n_i$ is the number of atoms in the i'th electronic state, $n_o$ is the number in the ground state, and $E_i - E_o$ is the difference in energy, per mole, between the i'th state and the ground state. An equation of this form holds for each excited state, and the composition of the total equilibrium mixture can then be characterized by the sum

$$n_t/n_o = Q_e = 1 + e^{-(E_1 - E_o)/RT} + e^{-(E_2 - E_o)/RT} + \ldots = \Sigma e^{-(E_i - E_o)/RT} \tag{52}$$

where $Q_e$, called the partition function for the electronic states, is defined by the above summation and $n_t$ is the total number of molecules in the mixture. Taking the derivative of (52) with respect to temperature and multipying by $RT^2/Q_e$, we obtain

$$RT^2(d \ln Q_e/dT) = -(R/Q_e)dQ_e/d(1/T) = \frac{\Sigma(E_i - E_o)e^{-(E_i - E_o)/RT}}{\Sigma e^{-(E_i - E_o)/RT}} = \Delta E_e = \Delta H_e \tag{53}$$

where $\Delta E_e$ or $\Delta H_e$ is the energy per mole of the mixture above the ground state due to the occurrence of electronically excited states. Taking the derivative of (53) with respect to temperature gives $\Delta C_e$, the contribution to the heat capacity due to the change in the proportions of the electronic states. Dividing this by $T$ and integrating from $T = 0$ to $T = T'$, we obtain

$$\Delta S_e = R[\ln Q_e + T' d \ln Q_e/dT]_0^{T'} \tag{54}$$

and

$$\Delta G_e = \Delta H_e - T'\Delta S_e = -RT' \ln Q_e \tag{55}$$

for the change in entropy and Gibbs energy respectively, for the change from the ground state to the equilibrium mixture of the various electronic states.

In the case of sodium vapour in a magnetic field of 1,000 gauss, two electronic states have very nearly equal energies; one is higher than the other by only about 0.27 cal/mole. The next higher state is about 48,470 cal/mole above the ground state, and is accompanied by another having only a fraction of a calorie per mole higher energy. At about 48,510 cal/mole above the ground state there are four more states which differ from each other by only a fraction of a calorie per mole. In weaker magnetic fields the differences within these groups of states are proportionally smaller, and at all except extremely low temperatures we may write the electronic partition function for sodium as $Q_e = 2 + 2\,e^{-48,470/RT} + 4e^{-48,510/RT}$ where $R$ is in calories per mole-degree. This grouping together of states of nearly equal energy leads to negligible error; but to have counted the group of states of nearly equal energy, called degenerate states, as only one state would generally lead to serious error. For atomic chlorine the electronic partition function $Q_e = 4 + 2\,e^{-2,517/RT}$, with $R$ again expressed in calories per mole-degree. At 1,000° K one can find from the above that about 88% of the atomic chlorine is in one or the other of the four states of low energy, and about 12% is in one of the pair of states with 2,517 cal/mole higher energy. States of still higher energy exist, but the fraction of the mixture in such states is so small at readily attainable temperatures that they can be ignored, and have not been written in the above partition function.

For most stable diatomic and polyatomic molecules, the excited electronic states are of such high energy that they make negligible contributions to the corresponding electronic partition function. However, there are some exceptions; in particular, degenerate states need to be taken into account. For these molecules the vibrational and rotational energies are important. Generally no serious error is made by treating the rotational and vibrational energies as independent of one another. In this case, the successive rotational levels can be calculated from the principal moments of inertia, which can be found from the interatomic distances and angles as determined by X-ray or electron diffraction studies and from the spectra of the molecules. (*See* ELECTRON DIFFRACTION; MOLECULAR SPECTRA; SPECTROSCOPY, X-RAY.) The vibrational levels can also be found from spectroscopic studies; from these values rotational and vibrational partition functions, $Q_r$ and $Q_v$, analogous to $Q_e$, can be constructed. Finally, from the quantum mechanical theory of molecules within an enclosure, the translational energy levels and the corresponding translational partition function can be found. From each of these partition functions a contribution to the entropy or to the Gibbs energy can be calculated, analogous to the electronic contribution given by (54) and (55). Except for the slight error made by treating the electronic, vibrational, and rotational energies as independent, the sum of these contributions to the entropy gives the total entropy for the substance in dilute gaseous state. To obtain equilibrium constants for reactions involving diatomic or polyatomic molecules one also needs the heat of the reaction at some temperature; even this can sometimes be obtained from spectroscopic measurements.

The equilibrium species present in a simple gas at high temperatures may be of some interest. From tables (presumably calculated from partition functions derived from spectroscopic data) one can find that the standard Gibbs energy of formation of H, monatomic hydrogen, is −18,523 calories at 5,000° K. This Gibbs energy is given relative to ordinary (diatomic) hydrogen, $H_2$; from which we obtain, for $H_2 = 2H$: $\Delta G_{5,000} = -37,046$, $\log K = \Delta G/2.3RT = 1.620$, and $K = (a_H)^2/a_{H_2} = 41.7$. At low pressures the activity is very nearly the same as the pressure, and the standard states have been chosen to be consistent with the atmosphere as the unit of pressure. When the pressure of monatomic hydrogen is 0.1 atm, $P_{H_2} = (0.1)^2/41.7 = 0.00024$ atm, from which we note that very little diatomic hydrogen will be present at this temperature.

At 5,000° K the monatomic hydrogen is dissociated to some extent into protons and electrons, and for $H = H^+ + e^-$ we can also find, from tables, $\Delta H(0°K) = 313.5$ kcal. The translational energies of gaseous molecules within an enclosure can be calculated by means of quantum mechanics, and a translational partition function can be developed. From this one can derive the formula

$$G(\text{trans},T) - G(\text{trans},0) = RT(-\frac{3}{2}\ln M - \frac{5}{2}\ln T + \ln P + 3.657) \tag{56}$$

in which the numerical constant 3.657 is a condensation of several constants and is valid only when the molecular weight is expressed in grams per mole, the temperature in degrees Kelvin, and the pressure in atmospheres. In this case molecular rotation and vibration are absent and the effects of electronic and nuclear spin mutually cancel. Postponing consideration of the electronically excited states of H, we find for $H_{gr} = H^+ + e^-$:

$$\ln K = -\Delta G°/RT = \frac{3}{2}\ln M_e + \frac{5}{2}\ln T - 3.657 - 313{,}500/RT \quad (57)$$

where $H_{gr}$ means monatomic hydrogen in its electronic ground state or state of lowest energy, and $M_e$ is the "molecular weight" or "atomic weight" of the electron, or the weight of one faraday equivalent of electrons. From this we obtain

$$K = (a_{H^+})(a_e)/(a_{H_{gr}}) = 1.15 \times 10^{-11}$$

Again assuming that the activities are nearly equal to the partial pressures, although the coulombic interactions will make this approximation relatively poor, we find that, when the pressure of ground state H is 0.1 atm., $P_{H^+} = P_e = 1.07 \times 10^{-6}$ atm.

The amount of H in electronically excited states proves to be rather difficult to define. The ground state consists of two states of practically identical energy; the next level, at $313 \times (1 - \frac{1}{4})$ kcal higher energy, has eight states; and the $n$th level, at $313 \times (1 - 1/n^2)$ kcal, has $2n^2$ states. For $n \geqq 10$, the energy is almost 313 kcal above the ground state, and the ratio of the number of atoms in state $n$ to that in the ground state is about $2n^2/2e^{-313{,}000/RT}$, or about $2 \times 10^{-14}\, n^2$. At first sight there appears to be no limit to how high the quantum number $n$ may go, and with $n = 10^7$ there would be more atoms in this level than in the ground state. However, the average distance between the electron and its nucleus varies as $n^2$, and with $n = 15$ this distance is more than 1,000 Å, while in a gas at 0.1 atm and 5,000° K the average distance of nearest neighbour gas molecules is about the same. Obviously, very strong interactions would occur between the excited atom and its neighbours, while our use of partition functions of molecules to calculate amounts of the gaseous species requires the assumption that the interaction of neighbouring molecules is very weak. In the gas described above the distinction between atoms in highly excited states and those which are ionized becomes meaningless.

**2. Effects of Gravitational, Centrifugal, and Other Fields.**—In most of the applications of thermodynamics it is generally assumed that the quantities of thermodynamic interest are determined by temperature, pressure, and concentration, and that gravitational and other fields and surface tension have no appreciable influence on the processes under consideration. This assumption is usually justified but under some conditions these effects can be important.

The reversible lifting of a body in a uniform gravitational field produces no thermal change and thus no change of entropy. The well-known cooling of air when rising due to thermal convection or to deflection by a mountain slope results from the adiabatic expansion of the gas; the change of height operates only indirectly by furnishing the pressure gradient. If the gas is lifted in a closed container so that no pressure change occurs, the change of height produces no change of temperature.

For a system in equilibrium in a uniform gravitational field the temperature is uniform and the pressure varies according to the relation $dP/dh = -\rho g$ where $\rho$ is the density. For an ideal gas this gives, on integration, $P = P_o\, e^{-Mg(h - h_o)/RT}$ where $M$ is the molecular weight, $g$ is the acceleration of gravity, and $P_o$ is the pressure at height $h_o$. For a mixture of dilute gases the partial pressure of each obeys the above equation, using its appropriate molecular weight; hence a gaseous mixture is partially separated by a gravitational field, but this is appreciable only if convection is prevented. Sampling of the upper atmosphere indicates that even in the stratosphere too much mixing occurs to permit a significant separation.

The effect of gravity offers the interesting theoretical possibility of obtaining fresh water from seawater. Several places have been discovered at which the ocean depth exceeds 10,000 m (more than 6 mi). At this depth the hydrostatic pressure of the seawater exceeds that of a column of fresh water by about 27 atm because of the difference in density. The osmotic pressure of seawater of average salt concentration is about 23 atm; hence if a pipe closed at the bottom by a semipermeable membrane and filled with fresh water reached to a depth of 10,000 m, the excess of pressure over the osmotic pressure would cause a flow of fresh water through the membrane and out the top of the pipe. This appears to violate the second law of thermodynamics, but the driving force of the process would be furnished by the mixing of the seawater due to ocean currents. (If the seawater were stagnant and at constant temperature, the equilibrium concentration of salt at 10 km depth would be approximately twice as great as that at the surface, and fresh water in the pipe would flow through the semipermeable membrane into the saltwater.)

Cycles involving the change of magnetic field have been used to attain a very close approach to absolute zero. A large increase of entropy accompanies the change of liquid to vapour at constant temperature; if the change occurs without permitting a flow of heat the temperature is greatly lowered. This process is the one most commonly used in artificial refrigeration. It can produce temperatures down to about 2° K, but at still lower temperatures the vapour pressure of helium (the lowest boiling substance) becomes too small to be utilized for further cooling. In the discussion of partition functions (*see* preceding section) it was noted that sodium atoms in dilute vapour possess two states of nearly equal energy and that the difference in energy is proportional to the strength of the magnetic field. At 50,000 gauss the difference is about 13 cal/mole, and in the field due to the earth (about 0.5 gauss) the energy difference is 0.00013 cal/mole. At temperatures of 2° K or lower other electronic states are entirely negligible, and the electronic partition function may be written as $Q_e = 1 + e^{-E_m/RT}$ where $E_m$ is the energy of one state above the other, due to the magnetic field—13 and 0.00013 for the strong and weak fields respectively. Substituting in (54) we find that the entropy in the weak field is about 1 cal/mole-deg larger than in the strong field. If sodium vapour could be cooled to 2° K in the strong field, and if the field were then allowed to diminish to that of the earth while the temperature remained constant, the entropy of the vapour would increase while heat was absorbed from its surroundings. If, instead, the field were diminished while heat flow was prevented, no total change of entropy would occur, for the increase expected because of lowering the field would be compensated by the decrease due to the lower temperature. This process cannot be carried out with sodium vapour because no detectable sodium vapour persists at low temperatures, and the interactions of sodium atoms in metallic sodium bring about entirely different groups of energy levels. However, there are some salts, among which is ammonium ferric alum, which possess ions having energy levels whose behaviour in a magnetic field is similar to that of sodium vapour. Here the ferric ion has states of almost identical energy in a very weak magnetic field, but in a strong field at low temperatures nearly all the ions accumulate in that of lowest energy. On demagnetization they redistribute among the states of now nearly equal energy, with a lowering of temperature. The details are not as simple as the above description implies: the electric field of the neighbouring ions leads to a separation of some of the states which would otherwise have like energies in the absence of the magnetic field, and further, at very low temperatures the magnetic fields of neighbouring ions interact, so that they can no longer be considered as possessing independent energy levels and the change of entropy can no longer be obtained by relations analogous to (54). These interactions set limits to how near absolute zero a system can be cooled by the use of any given cycle.

*See* also references under "Thermodynamics" in the Index.

BIBLIOGRAPHY.—R. H. Fowler and E. A. Guggenheim, *Statistical Thermodynamics* (1960); G. N. Lewis and M. Randall, *Thermodynamics and the Free Energy of Chemical Substances* (1923), new ed., titled *Thermodynamics,* rev. by K. S. Pitzer and L. Brewer (1961); I. Prigogine and R. Defay, *Chemical Thermodynamics,* Eng. trans. by D. H. Everett (1954); F. D. Rossini *et al., Selected Values of Chemical Thermodynamic Properties,* U.S. National Bureau of Standards Circular 500 (1952); H. S. Harned and B. B. Owen, *The Physical Chemistry of Electrolytic Solutions,* 3rd ed. (1958). (R. F. NE.)

**THERMOELECTRICITY** refers to effects that arise from the interaction between currents of heat energy and electrical energy in any material. This interaction permits direct generation of electric power with a heat unit as small as a kerosene lamp or kitchen stove. The Soviet Army used such devices to power portable radio transmitters during World War II. In the 1960s a 5,000-watt thermoelectric generator was made for the U.S. Navy, and production of small thermoelectric refrigerators was underway in the U.S.S.R. and the U.S.

There are three basic thermoelectric phenomena: the Seebeck, Peltier, and Thomson effects. Related nonthermoelectric manifestations of interest are thermal conduction and Joule heating.

The familiar nonthermoelectric phenomenon in which heat energy flows in proportion to the temperature difference between points in a body is called thermal conduction. Mathematically, the thermally conducted heat energy $Q_\kappa = \kappa \Delta T$, where $\kappa$ is the thermal conductance of the material and $\Delta T$ is the difference in temperature imposed across the material (*see* HEAT).

Joule heating is simply the irreversible production of heat energy by the current in an electrical circuit (as in the resistor wires of an electric toaster). The amount of such energy (the so-called Joule heat $Q_j$) is equal to the square of the current $I$ multiplied by the electrical resistance $R$ of the circuit; *i.e.*, $Q_j = I^2R$ and is independent of the direction of the current.

**Seebeck Effect.**—Consider dissimilar materials A and B (not necessarily solids) joined to form a complete circuit (fig. 1). If one junction is kept at a high temperature $T_h$ and the other junction is at a cooler temperature $T_c$, current flows in the circuit (Seebeck effect). The so-called Seebeck voltage, the open circuit voltage, that is induced is roughly proportional to the difference in temperatures. An obvious application of the effect would be a generator that produces voltage by applying a temperature difference to the junctions of two dissimilar materials.

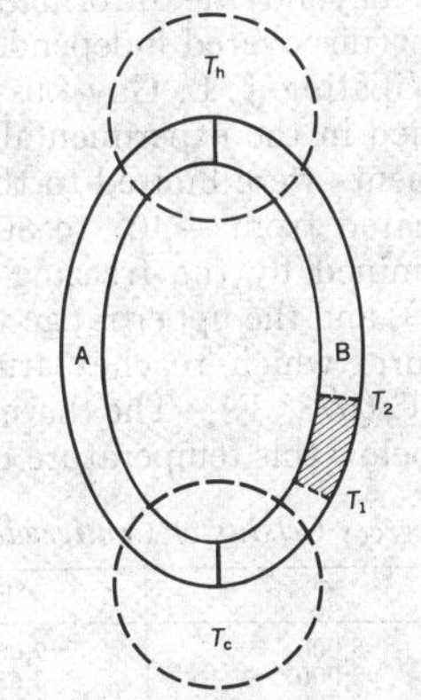

FIG. 1.—CIRCUIT DESIGNED TO DEMONSTRATE THERMOELECTRIC EFFECTS

The effect was discovered by the German physicist Thomas Johann Seebeck (1821) when he detected a magnetic field around such a differentially heated circuit. The finding led him to the unwarranted conclusion that the earth's magnetic field is produced by the temperature difference between the equator and the poles.

Mathematically the Seebeck voltage $V$ is given by

$$V = \int_{T_c}^{T_h} \alpha dT$$

where $T$ is the absolute temperature and $\alpha$ is the factor of proportionality called the Seebeck coefficient. If $\alpha$ is independent of temperature, $V$ is proportional to $T_h - T_c = \Delta T$.

The Seebeck coefficient can have either a positive or a negative sign. A material having a negative $\alpha$ is referred to as an n-type material, while a material having a positive $\alpha$ is referred to as a p-type material. These sign conventions are consistent with those used in the field of semiconductors.

**Peltier Effect.**—If an electric current from an external source (*e.g.*, a battery) flows in the circuit of fig. 1, the two junctions (initially at the same temperature) will develop a temperature difference. Thus in the Peltier effect electric current acts to cool one junction and to heat the other; reversal of current gives the opposite temperature effect at each junction. After the Joule heat is subtracted, the amount of heat energy absorbed or evolved at each junction will be proportional to the electric current and represents the contribution of the Peltier effect. Since one junction is cooled when current flows, the effect can be applied to the development of refrigeration devices.

The effect was discovered by the French physicist J. C. A. Peltier (1834) when he found that Joule heating failed to account for all of the heat energy evolved at a junction. The physical origin of the Peltier effect may be understood by thinking of electrons as being evaporated from material A at the junction and being condensed on material B. Unless the energy required for evaporation is exactly equal to that required for condensation, a net amount of heat energy must be absorbed from or lost to the surroundings of the junction. This is the Peltier heat $Q_\pi = \pi I$, where $I$ is the current and $\pi$ is the proportionality factor called the Peltier coefficient. Lord Kelvin (William Thomson) showed through thermodynamic analysis that the Peltier and Seebeck coefficients are connected by the relation $\alpha = \pi T$.

**Thomson Effect.**—When electric current passes through a circuit composed of a single material that has a temperature difference between any two of its points, the Thomson effect is manifested as the evolution or absorption of heat. After correction for Joule heating, the amount of this heat energy is found to be proportional to the current and to the temperature difference. Whether heat energy is absorbed or evolved depends on the direction of the current relative to the temperature gradient in the circuit. Lord Kelvin (1854) predicted this effect on theoretical grounds from thermodynamic considerations.

To examine the physical origin of the Thomson effect, consider a group of electrons crossing an imaginary interface at temperature $T_1$ (fig. 1). The electrons theoretically must be in equilibrium at this temperature and thus must have a specific amount of energy. As they cross the interface at $T_2$, they must have the energy associated with the second temperature. If these two energies are unequal, the net difference must be absorbed from or supplied to the surroundings. The amount of heat energy exchanged with a given element of material should thus be proportional to the current and the temperature difference.

The proportionality constant is called the Thomson coefficient $\tau$; and the Thomson heat $Q_\tau = \tau I \Delta T$, the $\tau$ representing a sort of specific heat for the electrons, except that it can be either positive or negative. Lord Kelvin thermodynamically derived the relation $\tau = T(d\alpha/dT)$.

**Applications.**—Thermoelectricity may be used in power generation and refrigeration. Consider a power generator shown by fig. 2. $R_L$ is the load resistance ($T_h$, $T_c$, A, and B have the same meaning as in fig. 1). The efficiency $\epsilon$ of such a device may be written $\epsilon = I^2R_L/Q$, where the numerator is the power delivered to the load and $Q$ represents the rate at which energy is removed from the hot junction. To maximize power output it is necessary to produce the largest possible voltage; thus the Seebeck coefficient $\alpha$ should be large. In practice it can usually be made as large as desired by proper selection of materials in arms A and B. These should also have low electrical resistivity $\rho$ to minimize Joule heat and internal resistance in the generator. Since heat energy is carried away by thermal conduction through A and B, the arms also should have low thermal conductivity $\kappa$. Hence the requirements for materials used in thermoelectric power generators are high $\alpha$, low $\rho$, low $\kappa$. If the efficiency is maximized by varying the load $R_L$, it is found that the efficiency depends on these material parameters through what is called the figure of merit $Z = Tz = T\alpha^2/\rho\kappa$. The higher the figure of merit the greater the efficiency for power generation. (For efficient thermoelectric refrigeration, materials should also have a high figure of merit.)

The efficiency of a thermoelectric generator may be written

$$\epsilon = \frac{\Delta T}{T_h} \frac{\sqrt{1 + T\bar{z}} - 1}{\sqrt{1 + T\bar{z}} + T_c/T_h}$$

where $T_h$ is the temperature of the hot junction, $T_c$ is the temperature of the cold junction, $T = (T_h + T_c)/2$ and $\bar{z}$ is the average value of $z$ (*i.e.*, $\alpha^2/\rho\kappa$) over the temperature range. Although this expression is only exact if $z$ is temperature independent, it is sufficiently accurate for almost all applications. The first term ($\Delta T/T_h$) is the Carnot efficiency; *i.e.*, the maximum theo-

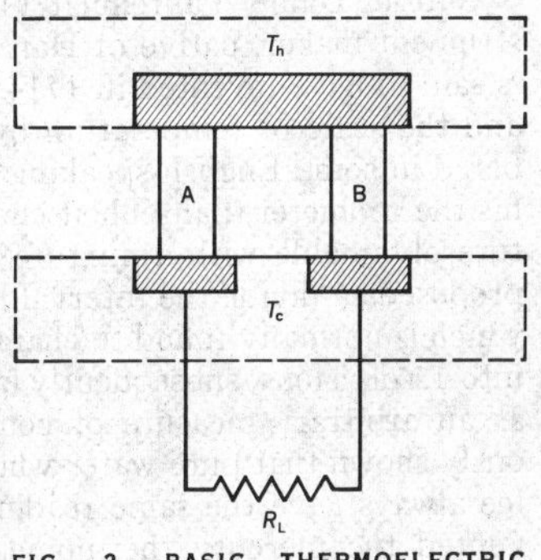

FIG. 2.—BASIC THERMOELECTRIC POWER GENERATOR

retical efficiency obtainable between $T_h$ and $T_c$ (*see* Thermodynamics). The remainder of the expression represents the efficiency of the thermoelectric device itself. With materials available in the 1960s with a figure of merit of about 1 from 300° to 1,500° K, a theoretical efficiency of about 20% was calculated; because of engineering problems the empirical efficiency was about half that (*see* Energy Conversion, Direct).

The important parameter for refrigeration is the coefficient of performance $\phi_c$. This quantity is defined as the ratio of energy removed (from the cold junction) to the device's power input, calculated as

$$\phi_c = \frac{T_c}{\Delta T}\,\frac{\sqrt{1+\overline{Tz}} - T_h/T_c}{\sqrt{1+\overline{Tz}}+1}$$

The first term ($T_c/\Delta T$) is the $\phi_c$ for a Carnot refrigerator and the second term represents the efficiency of the thermoelectric circuit (*see* Refrigeration: *Thermoelectric Refrigeration*).

Bibliography.—R. R. Heikes and R. W. Ure, Jr. (eds.), *Thermoelectricity* . . . (1961); D. K. C. McDonald, *Thermoelectricity: an Introduction to the Principles* (1962); A. I. Burshtein, *Semiconductor Thermoelectric Devices* (1964); H. J. Goldsmid, *Thermoelectric Refrigeration* (1965).
(R. R. H.)

**THERMOGRAPHY:** *see* Office Machines and Appliances: *Duplicating Machines.*

**THERMOMETRY** means the measurement of temperature. Temperature may be defined as the thermal state of a body as observed in its tendency to lose or gain heat energy from other bodies. Instruments used in such measurement are known as thermometers, or sometimes, when temperature exceeds red heat, as pyrometers.

This article, treating the subject in a generally historical order, is divided into the following sections:

I. Early Development
  1. Thermometry
  2. Pyrometry
  3. Further Developments and Various Inventions
II. Development of Precise Thermometry
  1. Expansion Thermometry
  2. Optical and Radiation Thermometry
  3. Electrical Thermometry
III. Development of Industrial Thermometry
  1. Introduction in Industry
  2. Industrial Thermometry up to 1920
IV. Modern Thermometry From 1920
  1. The International Practical Temperature Scale
  2. Gas Thermometry
  3. Modern Mercury-in-Glass Thermometry
  4. Modern Dial Thermometers
  5. Electrical Thermometry
  6. Modern Optical Pyrometry
  7. Modern Radiation Pyrometry
  8. Flame Thermometry
  9. Thermometry Below the Oxygen Point

## I. EARLY DEVELOPMENT

**1. Thermometry.**—Of the two commonly practised basic methods of measurement, namely, by contact and by radiation, only the first was known for more than two centuries following the inventions of the faulty air thermoscope of Galileo Galilei and the hermetically sealed Florentine thermometers first developed in the middle of the 17th century (*see* Heat: *Temperature*).

Gabriel Daniel Fahrenheit (1686–1736), a modest German instrument maker, native of Danzig and long a resident of Holland, is said to have invented in 1714 the mercury-in-glass thermometer and the scale of temperature by which his name is daily remembered in some English-speaking countries. In devising a scale for his thermometer, Fahrenheit chose as the zero the lowest temperature obtainable with a mixture of ice and common salt, and first proposed to divide the interval between this temperature and that which is normally found to characterize the blood of a healthy man into 12 divisions, subsequently increasing the number to 96, purely as an arbitrary measure of convenience. Fahrenheit had previously shown that pure water while freezing in the presence of pure ice always gave the same reading on his thermometer, and he invented the mercury thermometer so that he could observe the constancy of the boiling point of water, a report of which he had read in the *History of the Sciences* issued by the Royal Academy of Paris. These two points on his thermometer (later fully recognized as fixed points) were observed at the 32nd and 212th divisions, respectively. His thermometer must have had a rather uniform bore for him to have observed 212° F as the boiling point of water, but not precisely so, because the blood temperature of a healthy man was observed as 96°, and is now known to be 2° to 3° higher. The so-called Fahrenheit scale, having an interval of 180° between the freezing and boiling points of water, went rapidly into general use, and was still retained in the U.S. and Canada during the 1960s, particularly for meteorological work, because of its small degrees. R. A. F. de Réaumur (1683–1757), French naturalist, proposed in 1730 to divide the interval into 80°, and his scale is used in many countries. Anders Celsius (1701–1744), Swedish astronomer at Uppsala, whose name was to be used eventually to express temperatures as degrees Celsius (°C) on the International Practical Temperature Scale, is credited with first proposing to make the interval 100°, as it is on the centigrade scale.

During the century after Fahrenheit, the mercury-in-glass thermometer (fig. 1) became an instrument of useful precision and the basis of all temperature measurements, the thermal expansion of liquids being the only recognized means for measuring temperatures. The principles of thermodynamics were not well established, nor did the knowledge of the behaviour of gases extend much beyond the information afforded by the laws of Robert Boyle (discovered independently by E. Mariotte) and J. Charles (anticipating J. L. Gay-Lussac, 1802). No material success was attained in the experimental use of a gas thermometer, and measurements were limited to the range of the mercury thermometer graduated from −40° to 300° centigrade. The lower limit was determined by the freezing of mercury at −39.87° C (modern value), and the upper range was roughly limited by its high vapour pressure, which reaches atmospheric pressure at approximately 357° C (675° F). The thermometers of that period had to be kept well below this temperature because within the thermometer in the capillary space above the mercury there was no gas under pressure, as usually found in thermometers many years later, to prevent the mercury from boiling and from distilling into the capillary. The upper limit was not affected by the softening of the glass which would probably have withstood a temperature above 400° C.

*Degrees Celsius or Centigrade (°C) Versus Degrees Fahrenheit (°F)*

| °C | °F | °C | °F |
|---|---|---|---|
| 5,000 | 9,032 | 100 | 212 |
| 2,000 | 3,632 | 0 | 32 |
| 1,500 | 2,732 | −40 | −40 |
| 1,000 | 1,832 | −100 | −148 |
| 500 | 932 | −273.15 | −459.67 |

To convert °F into °C, first subtract 32, then take $^5/_9$ of the remainder. To convert °C into °F, first multiply by $^9/_5$, then add 32.

**2. Pyrometry.**—In order to measure higher temperatures than these early thermometers could withstand, James Prinsep (1828), interested in alloys of gold, silver, and platinum, and wanting to measure their melting points, made a large bulb of gold connected with a sensitive manometer with which to maintain the gas (air) at constant pressure within, and connected also with a reservoir of olive oil. Temperatures were measured by weighing the oil that had to be removed from the manometer, as the air expanded, in order to maintain the level constant. This could be considered the beginning of gas thermometry. Prinsep's measurements were limited in the upper range by the melting point of gold, found to be 1,063° C near the close of the century. Others, including Sir Humphry Davy, used the Prinsep method without much improvement, until Claude Servais Mathias Pouillet (1836) made a bulb of platinum and improved the experimental procedure, which was further improved in 1847 by Henri Victor Regnault, and in the 1880s by H. L. Callendar and his associates. The high melting point (1,769° C) of platinum extended the upper limit of measurement many hundreds of degrees. Pouillet also studied the relation between temperature and radiation from glowing solids. Thomas Johann Seebeck had discovered in 1821 that electromagnetic changes occur in a closed circuit of two dissimilar metals when the junctions of the metals are maintained at different temperatures, and Antoine Becquerel had tried a platinum-palladium junction in 1830.

The methods of gas thermometry continued to be improved throughout the 19th century. Regnault had shown in 1847 that the gas thermometer could afford precision in the range 0° to 100° C. He attained a precision sufficient to detect differences in the expansion coefficients of some of the more readily condensible gases, but not of hydrogen and nitrogen, which were found to expand one part in about 273 per degree C at 0° C. During this period, the mercury thermometer remained the primary and most reliable means for measuring temperatures in practical applications.

Sadi Carnot had described in 1824 his ideal reversible heat engine, and had endeavoured to prove on theoretical grounds that the efficiency of his ideal engine was the maximum possible and dependent only on the limits of temperature between which it works. Neither Carnot's proof nor that of many others appeared to be fully satisfactory for many years. The mechanical theory of heat, *i.e.*, the interpretation that heat is energy subject to the law of conservation, was slowly displacing the older theory that heat is an imponderable fluid with the power of penetrating all substances. Quoting Callendar, "The honour of placing the mechanical theory of heat on a sound experimental basis belongs almost exclusively to [J. P.] Joule, who showed by direct experiment that in all the most important cases in which heat was generated by the expenditure of mechanical work, or mechanical work was produced at the expense of heat, there was a constant ratio of equivalence between the heat generated and the work expended and vice versa." Joule reported his long series of brilliant experiments in a series of papers from 1840–43, and in 1848 he wrote to William Thomson (Lord Kelvin) to point out that according to his experiments, the efficiency of Carnot's engine must be proportional to $1/T$, the absolute temperature appearing in the equation $pv = RT$, representing the combined laws of Charles and Boyle for the expansion of gases. This equation was known to be a good approximation for the air thermometer between 0° and 100° C if $T$ be put equal to $t$(°C) plus 273. At this time, thermodynamics was making rapid strides and the experimental work was all based on the centigrade scale as defined by the mercury thermometer and the value 273 for $T - t$. In 1852 Thomson gave as the expression for the efficiency of the Carnot cycle on the evidence of Joule's experiment:

$$W/Q = (t_1 - t_0)/(t_1 + 273) = (T_1 - T_0)/T_1$$

where $Q$ is the heat energy an engine receives and $W$ is the work it performs. Thomson had realized that in the ideal heat engine lay a means for measuring temperature independently of the property of any substance. Four years earlier he had proposed for this purpose to write $W/Q$ equal to a constant, but as the experimental evidence accumulated he proposed in 1854 to define the thermodynamic scale according to the above equation, thus making this equation exact, and to determine by experiment how far the scale of the gas thermometer departed from the ideal scale. With this object in mind he devised a very delicate method, known as the porous plug experiment, to measure the temperature change accompanying the expansion of a gas in the absence of any conversion of heat to kinetic energy. Joule and Thomson carried out a long and famous series of experiments, and finally reported in the *Philosophical Transactions* (1862) that the deviations of the air thermometer from the absolute scale as above defined are almost negligible, and that in the case of the gas hydrogen, the deviations are so small that a thermometer containing this gas may be taken for all practical purposes as agreeing exactly with the absolute scale at all ordinary temperatures.

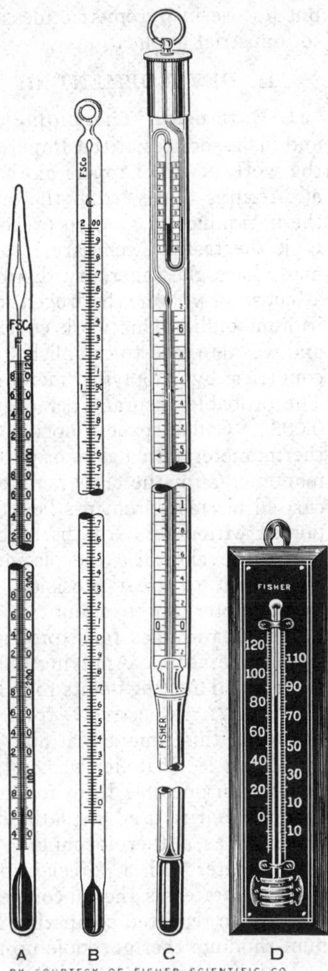


BY COURTESY OF FISHER SCIENTIFIC CO.

FIG. 1.—MERCURY-IN-GLASS THERMOMETERS

(A) Extra hard glass for 1,200° F (649° C) in 2° divisions; (B) precision type for 200° C in 0.2° divisions; (C) Beckmann differential, 6° range in 0.01° divisions; (D) common type for indoor or outdoor use

It should be carefully noted that the above equation, defining the thermodynamic temperature scale, does not determine any numbers for temperatures, but only defines the ratio of $T_0$ to $T_1$ as equal to $1 - W/Q$. Thus any number may be selected for one fixed point, for example, the ice point, leaving the intervals between this point and all others such as the steam point subject to experimental determination; or we can select any convenient interval such as that between the ice and steam points, leaving both their values above absolute zero subject to experiment. At the time Lord Kelvin was faced with making one of the selections, Regnault had been using air thermometers in his laboratory in preference to mercury thermometers because of the capricious performance of the latter, and had been accustomed to basing his calculations on the difference between the ice and steam points. Had Kelvin suggested, and the suggestion prevailed, that a number be permanently assigned to the ice point on the thermodynamic scale, the differences of the two scales at all other points would have had to be tabulated, and the lengthy tables revised from time to time in order to fit the results of future experiments. Kelvin chose to suggest that the ice-steam interval be fixed at 100° and this suggestion prevailed until 1954. (*See* below *The International Practical Temperature Scale.*) The thermodynamic scale is known simply as the Kelvin scale, temperatures on it being designated °K. The symbol in equations is usually $T$. A thermodynamic scale with the ice-steam interval fixed at 180° as in the Fahrenheit scale may be defined as 9/5 T. Called the Rankine scale, it came to be used in some engineering work; to convert to degrees Rankine (°R) 459.67 is added to °F.

**3. Further Developments and Various Inventions.**—Although the measurements of Regnault in the 1840s and '50s with his gas thermometers in the range 0° to 100° C were in error by a few tenths of a degree according to modern data, he was probably attaining a precision of about 0.1°, and his mercury thermometers did not compare favourably with this precision, varying erratically by tenths of a degree within that range and much more at higher temperatures. Very little was known at the time about annealing glass, so it was customary to age the green or new thermometers for many weeks, during which the ice point would slowly rise by a degree or more as the strains in the glass slowly decreased. These strains would never disappear and the thermometers would give readings at the fixed points (such as ice and steam) differing by tenths of a degree, sometimes changing for months. On the other hand, it was thought that the gas thermometer was providing measurements agreeing with the Kelvin scale to better than 0.1°. For these reasons the gas thermometers, especially the constant-volume hydrogen thermometer, came to be regarded as the ultimate standard for laboratory work at ordinary temperatures.

The mercury thermometer was also improved during this period by the introduction of nitrogen into the capillary bore above the mercury. Before this time the thermometers had been sealed after filling, while the bulb was kept hot enough to run the thread of mercury to the upper end of the stem. Thus when the bulb cooled, the space above the mercury contained only its vapour at a pressure corresponding to the temperature of the space. By introducing nitrogen into the bulb at some lower temperature, the pressure of the gas will increase as the mercury rises, and counteract the vapour pressure rising with increasing temperature. The use of nitrogen not only prevents the mercury in the bulb from vaporizing but also retards the vaporization into the space occupied by the nitrogen. In order to best match the varying pressure of the mercury, the proper size of the expansion chamber at the upper end is calculated according to the size of the bore. This calculation is necessary because pressures of a few hundred pounds per square inch are required at the highest temperatures at which the thermometer can be used. These gas-filled thermometers extended the useful range toward the softening temperature of the glass and in order to take full advantage of the new method of filling, harder glasses were developed; *i.e.*, glasses with higher softening temperatures. The first of these were the so-called *verre dur* of France and the type Jena 16, III of Germany. Filling the thermometers with nitrogen spoiled them for the most precise laboratory measurements, because the varying pressures made the scale nonuniform and prevented the application of corrections, but it made them better for general and industrial applications. The useful range was raised to nearly 500° C (932° F), although the accuracy above 400° C was low.

Another invention of the period was the clinical thermometer in a form much as it is currently known. This is essentially a maximum-reading thermometer; that is, designed to indicate the highest temperature to which it has been subjected after the mercury has been shaken down. It is made while the glass is soft by collapsing a bubble blown in the stem between the bulb and the part of the stem to be calibrated. Expert workmanship closes the bore or passage almost completely so that as the temperature falls the mercury thread breaks at the constriction, leaving all that has remained above to be observed at leisure. The bulbs of these thermometers are made small, cylindrical, and thin-walled, so that they will come up to the maximum temperature as rapidly as possible. Most clinical (also called medical or fever) thermometers require three minutes or more for all the mercury to reach the body temperature. The small bulbs require that the bore also be exceptionally small, and this requirement in turn has led to the so-called lens-front stems designed to magnify the thread of mercury for easier reading (fig. 2). The scales of these thermometers range from about 33° to 42° C or 92° to 108° F.

Other developments of the period were the resistance thermometer of fine platinum wire first tried by W. Siemens in 1871 without success; the pyrometric cones made of clays and other minerals for the ceramic industries, said to be used first by C. Lauth and J. H. L. Vogt in 1882 but highly developed by H. Seger and fully described by him in 1886; the thermopile consisting of a large number of closely grouped thermojunctions, devised by Francesco Rossetti in 1879, for measuring heat radiation; and many improvements in electrical measuring instruments including the moving-coil reflecting galvanometer by J. Arsène d'Arsonval in 1882 (*see* INSTRUMENTS, ELECTRICAL MEASURING). Attempts to estimate very high temperatures by radiation methods met slight success. Josef Stefan had suggested in 1879 from the earlier measurements by John Tyndall that the radiation from incandescent platinum was proportional to the fourth power of the absolute temperature. This was established as the law for total radiation (radiation of all wavelengths) by Ludwig Boltzmann in 1884, who in theory substituted radiation as the working substance in a Carnot cycle. This law has since been known as the Stefan-Boltzmann law, and has had considerable influence on theories of physics,

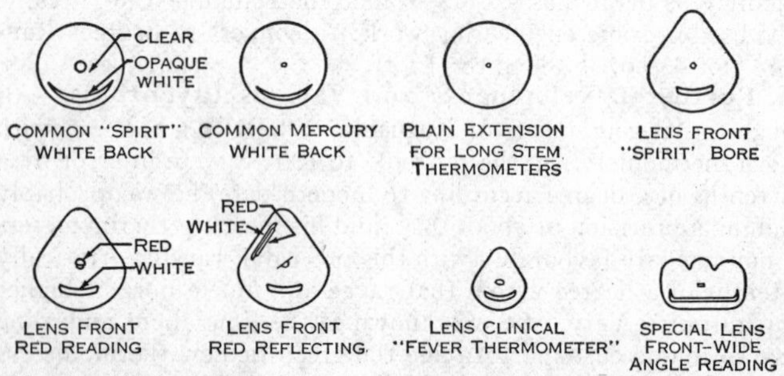


FIG. 2.—CROSS SECTIONS (DOUBLE SIZE) OF THE STEMS OF PRINCIPAL TYPES OF MERCURY-IN-GLASS THERMOMETERS CONTRASTING VARIOUS SCHEMES FOR PROMOTING EASE IN OBSERVING THE POSITION OF THE MERCURY

but its use in pyrometric measurements has been limited mainly to industrial applications.

## II. DEVELOPMENT OF PRECISE THERMOMETRY

**1. Expansion Thermometry.**—The researches of Callendar and his associates at the Imperial College of Science, London, and the work of P. Chappuis at the Bureau Internationale des Poids et Mésures, Paris, from the late 1880s to the early 1900s were the beginnings of modern precise thermometry. Chappuis undertook the task of comparing the temperature scales of carefully made hard-glass mercury thermometers (not nitrogen-filled) and a constant-volume hydrogen thermometer having a platinum-iridium bulb. This work covered the range from 0° to 100° C and was designed to establish standardized measurements in many countries by supplying mercury thermometers thus calibrated. The probable accuracy per degree was stated by Chappuis to be 0.002°. Callendar developed a compensated constant-pressure gas thermometer with a glass or porcelain bulb and a delicate, sensitive manometer for the close maintenance of a constant pressure, and carried his measurements beyond the boiling point of sulfur (reported with Ezer Griffiths to be 444.53° C). His interests led him to develop also the platinum resistance thermometer as an instrument of great precision, and to compare it with the gas thermometer up to about 550° C, and to devise the so-called Callendar formulas for expressing the relation between resistance and temperature. Applying these equations for extrapolating, he determined melting points for silver and gold that deviated by only 0.8° and 2°, respectively, from the values accepted in the 1960s.

During this time a platinum-rhodium thermocouple was made by Henry le Châtelier to combine with a high resistance galvanometer in portable form for industrial pyrometry. At the same time C. Barus used a platinum-iridium alloy to combine with platinum as a thermocouple. He used a constant-pressure gas thermometer with a porcelain bulb at temperatures up to 1,200° C to calibrate his thermocouples. In 1892 L. Holborn and Wilhelm Wien reported comparing an air thermometer with the platinum-rhodium thermocouple up to about 1,300° C.

An international committee on weights and measures passed a resolution adopted in 1887, that: "The international committee on weights and measures adopts as the standard thermometric scale for the international service of weights and measures the centigrade scale of the hydrogen thermometer, having as fixed points the temperature of melting ice (0°) and the vapour of distilled water boiling (100°) at standard atmospheric pressure, the hydrogen being taken at an initial manometric pressure of one meter of mercury—that is to say, 1,000/760 = 1.3158 times the standard atmospheric pressure."

The effect of this action and the work of Chappuis was felt mainly in the limited range between the ice and steam points, and here the matter stood officially for more than a quarter of a century. Chappuis had transferred the hydrogen scale to four primary standard mercurial thermometers of French hard glass; these were used to standardize many other mercury thermometers.

Precise thermometry at high temperatures (*e.g.*, a precision of 0.1° at the melting point of gold [1,063° C] as compared with 0.001° at 50° C) was not attained with gas thermometers until the 1950s. By 1911, however, high-temperature gas thermometry had reached the point where A. L. Day and R. B. Sosman (using bulbs of 10% iridium or 20% rhodium with nitrogen at constant volume) found the melting point of palladium within 2° C. They determined the melting points of eight metals from zinc to palladium, and transferred their measurements to thermocouples, for which they set up interpolation formulas. Duplication of the work probably will not be attempted because other methods are available; however, for the next generation, radiation (optical) methods depended on extrapolation from the melting points of gold and palladium as determined by Day and Sosman.

**2. Optical and Radiation Thermometry.**—As early as 1860 G. R. Kirchhoff had conceived of the complete radiator that has the maximum radiation possible for a given temperature, and that absorbs completely any incident radiation (*see* BLACK BODY). He concluded that the emittance of any opaque substance is equal to its absorptance, and that the sum of the two is equal to unity. In the 1890s W. Wien, in studying the spectral distribution of the radiation from a black body, found that the product of the wavelength of maximum intensity of radiation and the absolute temperature is a constant. Later he concluded that the radiation corresponding to any wavelength $\lambda$ is $J = c_1/[\lambda^5 \exp (c_2/\lambda T)]$, where $c_1$ and $c_2$ are constants.

In 1900 H. Rubens and F. Kurlbaum tested this equation at long wavelengths and found their results in serious disagreement. Max Planck suggested that they add $-1$ to the denominator, and this was found to fit the data; when Planck tried to derive the modified equation, he had to assume that radiation is emitted in multiples of indivisible quanta of energy. Planck's theoretical formula bore directly on thermometric measurements, but in the final analysis the constant $c_2$ is best evaluated empirically.

E. Becquerel suggested as early as 1864 that high temperatures could be measured by the intensity of red radiation from incandescent bodies, but it was not until 1892 that the first pyrometer using the idea was invented. Le Châtelier designed a photometric instrument for comparing the brightness of a standard oil lamp with that of the source to be measured, and set up empirical formulas by measuring temperatures with other means to calibrate his instrument.

Pyrometers of this type were gradually displaced by disappearing filament optical pyrometers based on an invention by E. F. Morse. If the current through the filament of an electric lamp is slowly increased, the filament glows red at first, then orange, yellow, and white. If this filament is placed in the plane of the image of an incandescent object, in a telescope or microscope, the current through the lamp can be adjusted until the filament or a part of it matches the brightness of the image. When this condition obtains, part of the filament becomes invisible against the background of the bright image, and the current required becomes a measure of the temperature of the object. Red glasses are used in the eyepiece to provide the higher accuracy of monochromatic photometry, and absorbing screens are used between the object and the filament to reduce the brightness of the image to the calibrated range of the filament.

While the instrument itself was being perfected, much work was done to convert experimental data into temperature and to realize more nearly the thermodynamic scale. C. E. Mendenhall (1911) pointed out that the temperature scale based on the Wien-Planck law is in fact based on a single temperature and the selected value of $c_2$ in the equation, and that a calibration of the instrument is preferably carried out on this basis. By 1926 the value of $c_2$ was commonly given as 1.432 cm. degrees, but later determinations altered this by a significant amount.

**3. Electrical Thermometry.**—Precise resistance thermometry began with the work of Callendar cited above. He found that previous efforts had evidently been careless of the contamination of the fine platinum wire by the reduction of silica in the porcelain spool on which the platinum was wound. Callendar supported the wire on the edges of clean sheet mica to minimize contamination and strain; he was able to achieve striking precision with such methods. It was fortunate that platinum was available in relatively high purity. Owing to the tremendous difficulties of using gas thermometers in experimental work, use of the Callendar thermometer grew rapidly in the principal laboratories of the world. Various forms of instruments for measuring resistance with sufficient accuracy were developed as their need appeared. Callendar first used an ordinary Wheatstone bridge with a two-lead thermometer. Later improvements included a pair of dummy leads in the parallel arm of the bridge; two leads on each end of the resistor, switched to eliminate the inequality of the two current leads; special forms of the Kelvin double bridge having six decades, with which measurements could be made by a single reading after three of the leads were adjusted to equality; a six-decade Wheatstone bridge arranged to avoid the errors of contact resistances and with means for determining the bridge zero and for commutation of the leads. To attain a precision of 1 part in 10,000,000 or better, the resistor coils of manganin were immersed in a thermostated oil bath. Others chose to use potentiometric measurements which require four attached leads plus a standard resistor with four leads.

Precise thermometry by thermocouples received a very favourable start when L. Holborn and Day compared a platinum, platinum-10% rhodium thermocouple with the gas thermometer between 300° and 1,000° C and found that a simple parabolic expression $E = a + bt + ct^2$ would represent the relation between electromotive force and temperature within experimental error (a few tenths of a degree). However, the interpolation formulas of Day and Sosman mentioned earlier were standards of reference for some years. These were not only based on gas thermometer measurements, but represented concurrent researches of the highest order of thoroughness. The precision of electrical measurements attained by their associates was excellent. Improved tables were published including tables for copper-constantan up to 385° C calculated from $E = a - b\ (1 - e^{-ct})$, where $e$ is the Naperian base. The precision implied in these tables is not attainable without the precise and accurate measurement of small voltages. This was done with a potentiometer of Wolff standard construction by direct comparison with a saturated cadmium cell that was accurate to one or two parts in 100,000. It was a five-dial instrument designed to measure 0.1 microvolt with exactness, and contained no slide-wire usually found in potentiometers designed for less accurate work.

## III. DEVELOPMENT OF INDUSTRIAL THERMOMETRY

**1. Introduction in Industry.**—There are poor records of the slow growth of mercurial thermometry from the time of its invention by Fahrenheit to the end of the 19th century. Use of these devices apparently grew with such developments as steam power and progress in the chemical industry. Mercury thermometers in metal sheaths for ruggedness became articles of commerce known as industrial thermometers. Thus protected they lose some accuracy, but continue to have widespread use. Another instrument of industrial importance was the dial (or pressure-spring) thermometer in which a liquid or gas is enclosed in a metal bulb connected by a capillary metal tube to the pressure spring, a modification of the Bourdon tube in pressure gauges. This may take the form of a spiral or helix of a flattened metal tube that reacts to internal pressure by a slight unwinding. One end of the tube is fixed and the other turns a pointer around the dial scale. The early (before 1911) forms were crude and not compensated for simple errors such as expansion of the fluid in the connecting capillary and spring.

Thermocouples made of base metals had begun to compete with the Le Châtelier couple because of their lower cost and higher thermoelectric power. Iron was still considered unsuitable for a thermocouple element and many combinations of metals and alloys were tried. The most successful of these was invented by M. A. L. Marsh, who combined an alloy of nickel-2% aluminum with nickel-10% chromium. These alloys became known through their trade names Alumel and Chromel, respectively. Chromel-Alumel thermocouples were found to be serviceable as high as 1,100° C and generated an electromotive force (emf) four to five times as large as did the platinum alloy couple of Le Châtelier. Optical pyrometers of the Holborn-Kurlbaum and the Wanner types were in extensive use; likewise radiation pyrometers of C. Féry, C. E. Foster, and C. B. Thwing. A commercial form of Callendar's resistance thermometer was having considerable success. Rugged low-resistance millivoltmeters were available for use with thermocouples and radiation receivers, and the earliest forms of recording instruments were manufactured in considerable quantities. Of these the recorder developed by Callendar with its Wheatstone bridge circuit for his resistance thermometers, various recording millivoltmeters, and the Leeds and Northrup recording potentiometer were outstanding examples.

**2. Industrial Thermometry up to 1920.**—The Faraday Society held a symposium on pyrometry in London in 1917. The consensus of this symposium was that pyrometers needed to be improved in ruggedness and accuracy, and that persons using them needed to learn much more about them. In thermoelectric pyrometry, it was reported that base-metal thermocouples are inhomogeneous and so cannot provide the accuracy of rare-metal couples. The limitations of radiation pyrometers were discussed, but their unsuitability for portable use was not yet clear. Optical pyrometry had not reached many hands and there was a prevalent idea that too much knowledge was necessary to make good use of it. The disappearing-filament type was competing on even terms with the Wanner (spectrophotometric) instrument.

In Chicago, Ill. (1919), a symposium on pyrometry revealed that the application of pyrometry had been largely made in the high-temperature industries: metals and to some extent glass, ceramics, and portland cement. There was slight scientific interest in industrial thermometry—that is, thermometry below a red heat. A great many engineering colleges were teaching pyrometry and probably a little thermometry. Electrical thermometry had not yet seriously invaded the field of expansion thermometry at lower temperatures. Automatic control (regulation) by means of electrical instruments was barely started, as on-and-off control only.

The symposium showed that base-metal thermocouples had finally found established acceptance for industrial use, the combinations—copper-constantan, iron-constantan, and chromel-alumel—being well known. There was evidence of growing use of industrial forms of potentiometers, particularly the recording potentiometer invented by Morris Leeds, and a number of good recording millivoltmeters. A new form of resistance thermometer appeared in which a fine platinum ribbon is wound on a small tube made of fused quartz, and over this is melted down an outer jacket of the same material, completely sealing in the platinum resistor and protecting it from contamination by industrial gases. This device was to meet much success even for temperatures as high as 900° C. Resistance thermometers made of nickel wire protected for use up to 500° C were also described, but there seems to have been no attention to the molecular change in nickel at about 325° C, which makes this metal unsuitable in this range and beyond.

## IV. MODERN THERMOMETRY FROM 1920

Other U.S. symposia on temperature were held in 1939, 1954, and 1961. They revealed remarkable growth in temperature scales, precision thermometry, automatic temperature regulation and recording, standards, and extremely low and high temperatures.

**1. The International Practical Temperature Scale.**—The thermodynamic temperature scale has long been recognized as the fundamental reference. However, experimental difficulties inherent in measuring temperature on the thermodynamic scale led the seventh General Conference on Weights and Measures (a diplomatic body representing 33 nations and having the power to set standards for international use) to adopt a scale in 1927 that was more conveniently realized and reproducible. National laboratories used this scale and urged scientists and industrial workers to do the same. The revision in use in the 1960s is known as the International Practical Temperature Scale of 1948. The official text of this scale is contained in the *Comptes Rendus de l'Onzième Conférence Générale des Poids et Mesures* (1960). The following is a translation of the official text for the defining part of the scale by H. F. Stimson in the *Journal of Research of the National Bureau of Standards*, vol. 65A (1961).

Temperatures on the International Practical Temperature Scale of 1948 are expressed in degrees Celsius, designated by °C or °C (Int. 1948), and are denoted here by the symbol $t$ or $t_{int}$.

The International Practical Temperature Scale is based on six reproducible temperatures (defining fixed points), to which numerical values are assigned, and on formulas establishing the relation between temperature and the indications of instruments calibrated by means of values assigned to the six defining fixed points. These fixed points are defined by specified equilibrium states, each of which, except for the triple point of water, is under a pressure of 101 325 newtons/meter$^2$ (1 standard atmosphere).

The fixed points of the scale and the exact numerical values assigned to them are given in table 1.

The procedures for interpolation lead to a division of the scale into four parts.

*a.* From 0 °C to 630.5 °C (antimony point) the temperature $t$ is defined by the formula

$$R_t = R_0(1 + At + Bt^2),$$

where $R_t$ is the resistance at temperature $t$ of the platinum wire resistor of a standard resistance thermometer, and $R_0$ is the resistance at 0 °C. The constants $R_0$, $A$, and $B$ are to be determined from the values of $R_t$ at the triple point of water, at the steam point, and at the sulfur point (or the zinc point). The platinum wire of a standard resistance thermometer shall be annealed and its purity shall be such that $R_{100}/R_0$ is not less than 1.3920.

*b.* From the oxygen point to 0 °C, the temperature $t$ is defined by the formula

$$R_t = R_0\,[1 + At + Bt^2 + C(t - t_{100})t^3],$$

where $R_0$, $A$, and $B$ are determined in the same manner as in *a* above, the constant $C$ is to be determined from the value of $R_t$ at the oxygen point, and $t_{100} = 100$ °C.

*c.* From 630.5 °C to the gold point the temperature $t$ is defined by the formula

$$E = a + bt + ct^2,$$

where $E$ is the electromotive force of a standard thermocouple of platinum and platinum-rhodium alloy, when one of the junctions is at 0 °C and the other at the temperature $t$. The constants $a$, $b$, and $c$ are to be determined from the values of $E$ at 630.5 °C, at the silver point, and at the gold point. The value of the electromotive force at 630.5 °C is to be determined by measuring this temperature with a standard resistance thermometer.

The wires of the standard thermocouple shall be annealed and the purity of the platinum wire shall be such that the ratio $R_{100}/R_0$ is not less than 1.3920. The platinum-rhodium wire shall consist nominally of 90 percent platinum and 10 percent rhodium by weight. When one junction of the thermocouple is at 0 °C and the other is successively at 630.5 °C, the silver point, and the gold point, the completed thermocouple shall have electromotive forces such that

$$E_{Au} = 10\,300\ \mu v \pm 50\ \mu v$$

$$E_{Au} - E_{Ag} = 1183\ \mu v + 0.158\ (E_{Au} - 10\,300\ \mu v) \pm 4\ \mu v$$

$$E_{Au} - E_{630.5} = 4766\ \mu v + 0.631\ (E_{Au} - 10\,300\ \mu v) \pm 8\ \mu v.$$

*d.* Above the gold point the temperature $t$ is defined by the formula

$$\frac{J_t}{J_{Au}} = \frac{\exp\left[\dfrac{C_2}{\lambda(t_{Au} + T_0)}\right] - 1}{\exp\left[\dfrac{C_2}{\lambda(t + T_0)}\right] - 1},$$

where $J_t$ and $J_{Au}$ are the radiant energies per unit wavelength interval at wavelength $\lambda$, emitted per unit time per unit solid angle per unit area of a blackbody at the temperature $t$ and the gold point respectively, $C_2$ is the second radiation constant with the value $C_2 = 0.014\ 38$ meter-degrees, $\lambda$ is in meters, and $T_0 = 273.15$ degrees.

TABLE 1. *Defining Fixed Points*

Exact values assigned. The pressure is 1 standard atmosphere, except for the triple point of water.

| | Temperature °C (Int. 1948) |
|---|---|
| Temperature of equilibrium between liquid oxygen and its vapor (oxygen point) | −182.97 |
| Temperature of equilibrium between ice, liquid water, and water vapor (triple point of water) | +0.01 |
| Temperature of equilibrium between liquid water and its vapor (steam point) | 100 |
| Temperature of equilibrium between liquid sulfur and its vapor (sulfur point) | 444.6* |
| Temperature of equilibrium between solid silver and liquid silver (silver point) | 960.8 |
| Temperature of equilibrium between solid gold and liquid gold (gold point) | 1063 |

*In place of the sulfur point, it is recommended to use the temperature of equilibrium between solid zinc and liquid zinc (zinc point) with the value 419.505° C (Int. 1948). The zinc point is more reproducible than the sulfur point and the value which is assigned to it has been so chosen that its use leads to the same values of temperature on the International Practical Temperature Scale as does the use of the sulfur point.

Recommendations for experimentally realizing the above-defined scale also may be found in Stimson's translation.

Until 1948 the thermodynamic scale was defined on the basis of the 100-degree temperature interval between the ice and steam points. Lord Kelvin, who originally defined the scale in this manner in 1854, recommended that when a single fixed point was sufficiently well known it would be preferable to define the scale using this one point. In 1948 the ninth general conference redefined the thermodynamic scale in this way using the triple point of water and in 1954 the 10th general conference approved the value of 273.16° K for this point. The zero of the thermodynamic Celsius scale is still the freezing point of water but defined to be .0100 degrees below the triple point. The International Practical Temperature Scale of 1948 is not defined below the boiling point of oxygen. In the temperature range from the oxygen point to the ice point, measurements in 1932 and in 1935 indicated that the two scales agreed within 0.05°. A determination of the thermodynamic temperature of the oxygen point in 1953 gave −182.94° C. Intercomparison of two nitrogen gas thermometers with platinum resistance thermometers between the ice and sulfur points indicated that the thermodynamic scale was about 0.006° lower at the steam point and 0.1° higher at the sulfur point than the practical scale of 1948. A redetermination of the gold point utilizing gas thermometry was reported in 1961 as 1,064.5° C. In 1956 the same method had given a value of 1,063.69° C for the gold point and 961.28° C for the silver point. Above the gold point, differences between the fundamental and practical scales can be estimated from estimates of the difference between defined and true values of $t_{Au}$, $c_2$, and $T_0$. The uncertainty in $T_0$ can be neglected compared with that of $t_{Au}$. An analysis of variance of data on atomic constants in 1955 gave the value of 1.43888 cm. degree for $c_2$; and in 1957 similar analysis gave it as 1.43886 cm. degree. If the correct value for $c_2$ were 1.439 and $t_{Au}$ were 1,064° C, the thermodynamic temperature above the gold point would be about 0.07% higher than that of the practical scale of 1948.

**2. Gas Thermometry.**—Modern industrial gas thermometry is limited because of the difficulty of correcting for the expansion of the gas in the connecting tube between the bulb and the pressure measuring device, such as the Bourdon tube, or pressure spring. However, scientific interest in precise gas thermometry has been directed to gases such as nitrogen, hydrogen, and helium (fig. 3), and to converting the real gas thermometer scale to the thermodynamic scale (which would be realized by an ideal gas). Gas thermometry is basic in the accurate definition of physical units (*q.v.*), the relation of the universal gas constant $R$ (in the equation of a perfect gas $pv = RT$) to many other constants, and through the dependence of these constants on the value of the ice point $T_0$ on the Kelvin or thermodynamic scale.

General thermodynamic theory of empirical departures from the laws of an ideal gas indicates $pv = RT + Bp$ for moderate pressures (one or two atmospheres). For the three commonly used thermometric gases mentioned above, the term $Bp$ amounts to less than 0.1% of $RT$ at 0° C and one atmosphere. $B$, the second virial coefficient, is a function of both temperature and pressure, but because $Bp$ is so small, $B$ values may be determined with satisfactory accuracy by varying $pv$ at constant temperature and writing $B = v - RT/p$. The slopes of the $pv$ isotherms of any gas serve in themselves to determine the departure of the gas from ideal, without the use of any other data. Some investigators set up equations for $B$ as a function of $T$ and use them to smooth the data. $B$ values can also be calculated from the Joule-Thompson coefficient $\mu$, and the specific heat $C_p$ at constant pressure. Most

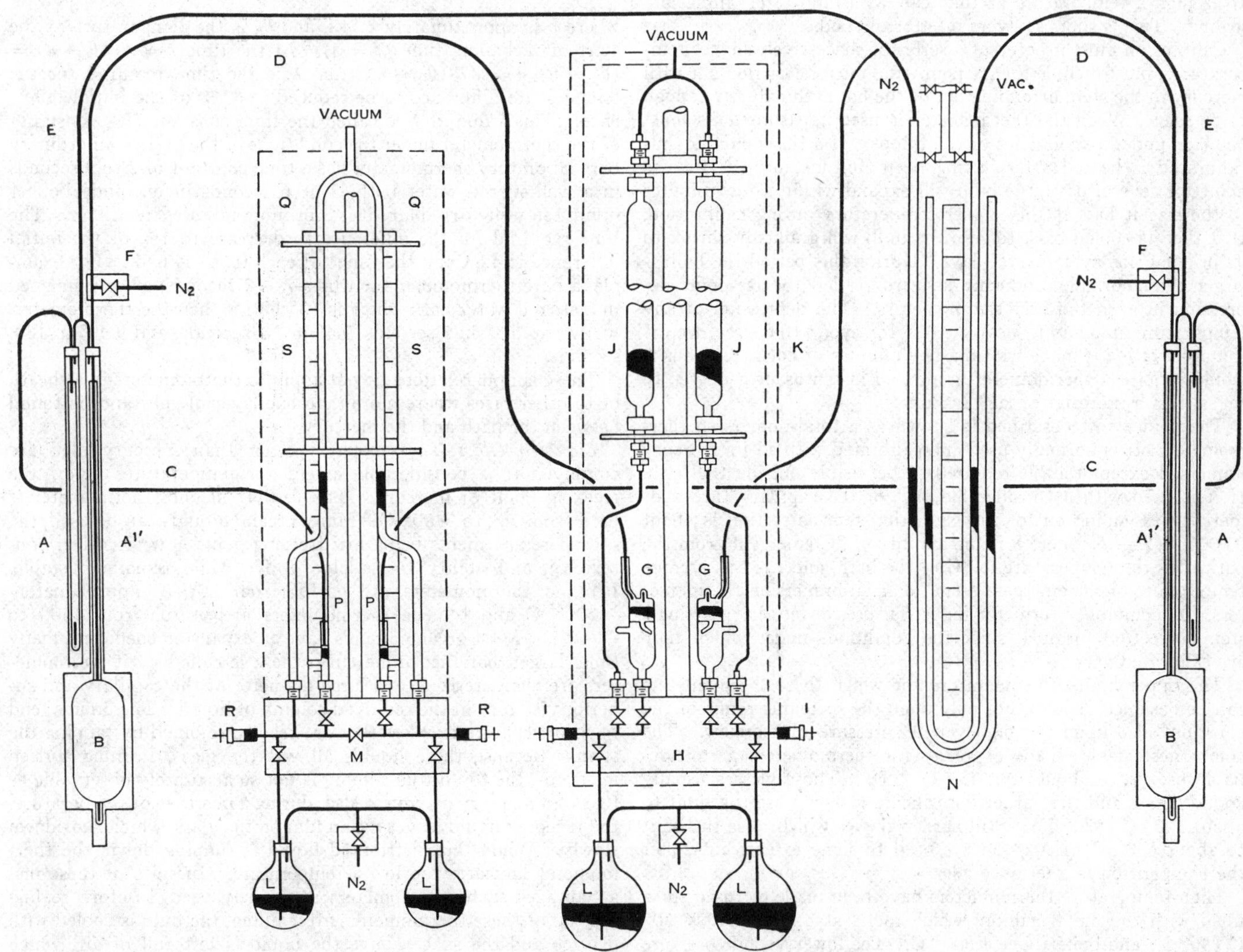


FROM BEATTIE, "PROCEEDINGS OF AMERICAN ACADEMY OF ARTS AND SCIENCES" (1941)

FIG. 3.—EXPERIMENTAL GAS-THERMOMETER SYSTEM CONSTRUCTED IN DUPLICATE

The three pressure systems are designed for operating the nitrogen-filled thermometers at constant volume: (1) the main system, B,A1', (F),D,G,H,J; (2) the auxiliary system, A,C,P,M,Q, for determining the correction for the dead space, the region of large thermal gradient; and (3) the external pressure adjusting system, steel case to E to N. Mercury reservoirs L are connected through steel blocks H and M to the manometers G,J and P,Q. Bulb is of vitreous silica and connections are steel capillaries and stopcocks. K is a thermostated housing of the data on gas scale corrections are, however, based on the compressibility, the $pv$ isotherms. In the 1960s, the U.S. National Bureau of Standards had a precise gas thermometry program aimed at realizing the thermodynamic scale from the triple point to the gold point with greater accuracy than any previous work. A 0.01-degree accuracy at the gold point appeared to be attainable. Significant results were expected that would alter the practical scale to better agree with the thermodynamic scale.

**3. Modern Mercury-in-Glass Thermometry.**—By far the most important in point of numbers used, the mercury thermometer lost its standing as a primary standard to the platinum resistance thermometer, despite its high potential for accuracy. Particularly in the range from slightly above −40° to 150° C, accuracies near 0.01° are attainable in experienced hands. A thermometer of such a grade has its scale etched directly on the glass stem. The thermal volume expansion of mercury is only about 180 parts per 1,000,000 per °C at room temperature, yet an accuracy of indicating an expansion of only 180 parts in 100,000,000 is attainable. It is especially remarkable in view of the natural instability of glass, even of the special hard glasses employed. Such an accuracy is obtained only under carefully prescribed conditions. The thermometer must have been properly annealed, filled with the purest mercury, and sealed with the correct pressure of nitrogen in the capillary space; *i.e.,* just sufficient to prevent the mercury from easily separating during rough handling. Some manufacturers age their thermometers for extended periods at as high a temperature as they can withstand after filling and sealing. This is supposedly an inferior method.

Calibration must proceed at a series of successively higher temperatures, must include the ice point, and must be carried out with mercury in the stem extending out of the hot bath only far enough to be seen. When the thermometer is used, measurements must be made under a similar set of conditions. If a thermometer thus calibrated is heated after having been, for instance, at the ice point for several days, the bulb will expand within a few minutes to the size it had at this higher temperature during calibration. If it then is cooled back to zero the bulb will gradually shrink to its original size over several days. During this period the bulb is larger than normal, producing an error called the ice-point depression in even the best thermometers. The depression at any temperature amounts to nearly 0.01° for every 10-degree drop if the observation is made within a few minutes of cooling. Thus it would require a thermometer graduated in tenths of a degree to reveal this hysteresis (or lag) readily.

The device just described is known as a total-immersion thermometer. It is normally used and calibrated with all its mercury immersed except the bit required to be visible outside the bath. If it is used with a considerable part of the capillary thread of mercury extending out of the bath, the stem correction is about $0.00016n(T - t)$ where $n$ is the number of °C emergent from the bath, $T$ is the temperature in °C of the bath, and $t$ is the average temperature of the emergent stem. Partial-immersion thermometers, the commoner form for industrial use, do not have a single stem-correction formula, since the conditions under which they are calibrated vary.

The upper limit of temperature for which these thermometers can be designed depends not only upon the softening range of the glass but also upon the high vapour pressure of mercury. The commonest glasses made expressly for thermometers permit reliable use up to about 400° C (752° F). Those glasses usually contain lead, and the harder borosilicate glasses raise the limit to about 500° C (932° F). Still harder glasses which raise the limit to about 650° C (1,202° F) are used to some extent, but suffer the competition of thermocouples.

High-temperature thermometers have been made of fused silica filled with the metal gallium which melts at approximately 30° C (86° F) and boils above 1,600° C. The lower vapour pressure of the liquid gallium at high temperatures is a real advantage, but capillary tubes of fused silica are difficult to make because of the high melting point (1,710° C) of this oxide, and the combination has not been extensively employed. The lower limit of mercury-in-glass thermometers has been extended by alloying thallium with the mercury in a percentage close to the composition having the lowest melting point (eutectic mixture). This is at 9.3% thallium, the melting point being −59° C (−74° F). Such a thermometer is easier to make than the gallium-in-silica, and has been used in limited quantities.

*Thermometric Lag.*—When a thermometer is immersed in a fluid medium, the thermometer temperature changes rapidly at first and more slowly as that of the medium is approached. When no further change of the thermometer can be detected it is assumed that the temperature of the medium is indicated. If the temperature of the medium is varying, the thermometer will be at a temperature that is lower or higher than that of the medium at any given moment as a function of this lag. A mercury-in-glass thermometer, when immersed bare in a stirred bath, lags the temperature of the bath according to Newton's law. In this case the rate of change of temperature of the thermometer is proportional to the difference between its temperature and that of the bath. As given by D. R. Harper:

$$\frac{d\theta}{dt} = \frac{1}{\lambda}(u - \theta)$$

where $u$ is the temperature of the bath at time $t$, $\theta$ is the temperature of the thermometer at the same time, and $\lambda$ is a constant.

In the case of constant temperature in a stirred bath, the solution is:

$$(\theta - u) = (\theta_0 - u)e^{-t/\lambda}$$

where $e$ is approximately 2.718, and $\theta_0$ is the temperature at the start of reckoning time ($t = 0$). At the time $t = \lambda$, $(\theta - u) = (\theta_0 - u)/e = .37\ (\theta_0 - u)$; *i.e.,* $\lambda$ is the time required for the temperature difference to be reduced to 37% of the initial difference. This value of $\lambda$ is called the time constant (lag constant) of the thermometer under the conditions of the bath. An ordinary bare laboratory thermometer has a time constant of 2 to 3 seconds in a well-stirred water bath, 5 or 6 seconds in oil, and about 1 minute in well-stirred air; it is 3 or more minutes in still air. The time required for the difference to decrease to 1% of the initial difference is $4.6\lambda$ and the time to reach 0.1% is $6.9\lambda$. For example, a bare thermometer for which $\lambda$ is 2 seconds, when immersed in a stirred water bath which is 10° hotter than the thermometer, will warm 6.3° in 2 seconds, 9.9° in 9.2 seconds, and 9.99° in 13.8 seconds.

These simple relations do not apply to thermometers in a sheath or to other cases where more than one layer of substance is found between the bath and the mercury.

*Liquid-in-Glass Thermometers* other than mercury-filled are employed to a considerable extent for temperatures below the freezing point of mercury. The (ethyl) alcohol thermometer is used from 70° to −80° C. Many organic liquids can be used, the special requirements being low freezing point, low viscosity, nontoxicity, and ability to dissolve a dye while remaining stable. Pentane thermometers are useful from 30° to approximately −200° C and toluene thermometers are useful from 150° to −80° C. Most organic liquids have an expansion coefficient many times larger than that of mercury; these so-called spirit thermometers are characterized by a large diameter of the capillary and superior visibility of the red-dyed column of liquid. The liquids tend to form separate droplets that are readily rejoined by tapping the stem. Because these liquids all wet the glass, forming a deep meniscus, the top of the column is not so accurately observable as that of a mercury column. Also, during a decrease of temperature, the receding liquid leaves a thin film on the glass, which runs down slowly. While this distributed liquid is running down, the thermometer indicates too low a temperature. In spite of these disadvantages such thermometers are widely used. Before sealing the top of these thermometers after filling, the bulb is cooled with dry ice and the space above the liquid is left full of air, which materially reduces distillation into the space and separation of the liquid column.

**4. Modern Dial Thermometers.**—Modern dial thermometers have industrial importance rivaled only by mercury-in-glass in point of numbers. Though there are many types including solid, liquid, gas, or liquid-vapour filled, this article will discuss only the liquid-filled. The usual liquid is mercury because of its range of usefulness from −40° to somewhat above 500° C. Most of the mercury is contained in a strong steel (sometimes stainless) bulb to which is welded a long steel capillary tube having a bore about .01 in. in diameter. The other end of the tube is welded to a Bourdon tube, sometimes called a pressure spring, also of steel, mounted in a case and attached through a mechanism to a rotating pointer. The entire closed system of bulb, tube, and flattened pressure spring which has been wound into a spiral or helix, is filled with mercury (to the exclusion of any gas or low-boiling liquid) under a pressure of a few hundred pounds at room temperature. Higher temperatures increase this pressure so that it is maintained well above the vapour pressure of the mercury, while not exceeding the limited strength of the pressure spring, which is highly strained as the liquid expands. With a proper connecting mechanism, the scale of such a thermometer is very nearly uniform. In its more highly developed form the expansion of the mercury in the tube and spring is compensated so that tubes more than 250 ft. long can be used without material loss of accuracy.

One form of compensating device consists of a duplicate capillary tube, also containing mercury, and attached to a second pressure spring that opposes the main spring; another consists of a wire of nickel steel threaded through the single tube. This wire is selected to have a negligible expansion (*e.g.,* invar) and the space between it and the wall of the capillary bore is adjusted to vary with temperature in correspondence with the expansion of the mercury. A bimetallic spring can be used to separately compensate for the expansion of the liquid in the pressure spring. Such thermometers, especially with the connecting tube protected with an armour of flexible metal or rubber, successfully compete with electrical thermometers and are also made into recorders and automatic controllers of various forms. Organic liquids are occasionally substituted, but their higher expansions are offset by the necessity of keeping the volume of the bore and spring small compared with that of the bulb. Furthermore, none of them have a range comparing favourably with that of mercury.

**5. Electrical Thermometry.**—This is intended to include resistance and thermoelectric instruments; that is, those in which a resistor or a thermocouple is used.

The resistance thermometer affords the greatest precision of all forms of temperature-measuring devices in ranges below 660° C, and is widely used in scientific and industrial laboratories. It is made in rugged and less expensive forms for measuring the temperatures of manufacturing processes, machines, stationary structures, air-conditioning equipment, and other applications where temperatures do not exceed about 150° C (302° F). Most industrial forms employ a resistor of nickel wire (occasionally copper) in a helix or coil and protected in a sealed metal tube. For higher temperatures platinum is used because nickel undergoes a molecular transformation between 300° and 350° C, accompanied by troublesome changes in resistance with rising and falling temperatures; also it is not available in high purity, and cannot be annealed satisfactorily after winding in the form of insulated wire. Platinum can readily be obtained with a purity better than 99.999%, and for industrial use thermometers made of such metal do not require annealing at a high temperature to reproduce a standard resistance-temperature relation.

Platinum resistance thermometers in strain-free form and mounted in glass or quartz tubes filled with air, nitrogen, or helium for small lag, display stability of resistance to temperatures as high as 700° C. Slow changes of resistance of a few parts per 1,000,000 can be detected, however, during long continued use, and proper corrections to a few parts in 10,000,000 are on occasion reliably applied. These thermometers have four leads usually made of gold wire, extending from the coil to the head. Short lengths (an inch or so) of platinum wire connect the gold to the resistor to reduce the heat conduction to the leads. A convenient value of the resistance for most purposes is 25.5 ohms such that the variation is approximately 0.1 ohm per degree centigrade. By the 1960s platinum resistance measurements had been made with a stability and reproducibility at the gold point at least ten times greater than was possible with the standard thermocouple. A platinum resistance thermometer was expected to replace the thermocouple on the International Practical Temperature Scale.

The expression $R_t = R_0(1 + \mathrm{A}t + \mathrm{B}t^2)$ for the relation between resistance and temperature for platinum, as found above in the definition of the international practical scale gives the same set of resistance-temperature values as the original Callendar formula:

$$t = \frac{R_t - R_0}{R_{100} - R_0}(100) + \delta\left(\frac{t}{100} - 1\right)\frac{t}{100}$$

both being empirical formulas in the first power of $R_t$ and the first and second power of $t$.

Modern methods of measuring resistance are fundamentally the same as those described above. A gold-chromium alloy provides coils with resistances that are reported to change by no more than 1 or 2 parts in 1,000,000 within the ordinary range of room temperatures. Resistors of this alloy can be made of very fine wire and are especially suited for standards of reference. It is doubtful that they will replace thermostated manganin in resistance-measuring bridges. However, since an entire bridge can be rechecked with a single reference standard, this alloy can improve the reliability of measurements.

Except possibly at temperatures above 1,500° C very little more is expected to be done to significantly improve thermocouples or their use. They continue to attract wide interest since they offer such advantages as simplicity, low cost, a wide range, ease of installation, and small size. The major limitation is the effect on the temperature determination when any physical or chemical inhomogeneity in the thermocouple leads exists in a temperature gradient. With the purest platinum and platinum-rhodium available in the 1960s an accuracy of ±0.1° was difficult to achieve. However, when ±0.1° is adequate below 500° C and ±0.3° above 500° C, the thermocouple is an excellent temperature-measuring instrument; between 630° and 1,063° C it remained the international standard thermometer.

The thermocouples in common use are limited to those made of a relatively few combinations of metals found to have such characteristics as an emf increasing continuously with rising temperature over a considerable range; freedom from significant change of emf by changes of crystalline structure; resistance to oxidation, corrosion, or contamination. Among the best combinations are platinum with platinum-10% rhodium (also 13%); copper with constantan; iron with constantan; and chromel *P* with alumel. The combination of chromel *P* with constantan is occasionally used because of a relatively large emf. The platinum combinations are useful from 0° to nearly 1,500° for extended exposures and in the combination platinum-6% rhodium with platinum-30% rhodium to 1,700° C. A few refractory metal thermocouples have been used successfully up to 2,000° or 2,200° C. These include tungsten with rhenium, tungsten with tungsten-2.6% rhenium, and iridium with a rhodium-iridium alloy, usually 40% to 60% iridium. Corresponding temperatures for copper-constantan are −200° to 350° (max. 1,000°); for iron-constantan, −200° to 750° (max. 1,000°); for chromel-alumel, −200° to 1,200° (max. 1,350°). The nominal composition of constantan, which is also used in larger quantities for resistor wire, is 55% copper and 45% nickel. Chromel, identified as chromel *P* to distinguish it from electrical heating wire, has retained its original composition of 90% nickel with 10% chromium, but alumel is 95% nickel with aluminum, silicon, and manganese added.

The platinum, platinum-rhodium thermocouple invented by Le Châtelier is noted for its stability and freedom from internal changes. It is usually used carefully protected in a refractory porcelain insulator and tube. The metals of which this couple is made have a purity of the highest order, spectroscopic analysis revealing scarcely the slightest trace of impurity. This cannot be said of any of the other metals employed for thermocouples although the copper generally used is so pure as to require the spectroscope to detect slight traces of iron, silicon, and dissolved oxygen. While platinum of the purity found in resistance thermometer and thermocouple wire is the primary thermoelectric reference standard, the best grade of commercial copper wire makes an excellent standard that can be relied upon to a few microvolts for a 200° C interval.

The copper-constantan thermocouple is noted for its well-established temperature emf relation from about −260° to 350° C, its low cost, and the not inconsiderable adaptability to the use of long extension leads of the same composition and relatively low resistance. Also, as compared with iron, copper oxidizes very slowly at ordinary temperatures at which iron must be protected from rusting. The iron-constantan couple is the most widely used in industrial applications because it is inexpensive and has a useful range well above that of copper.

The chromel-alumel couple is well known for its outstanding resistance to oxidation at high temperatures, especially in the range from 750° to 1,200° C, where it is most often used. It must not be exposed to reducing gases; oxidized chromel exposed to hydrogen, for example, develops a conducting coating of nickel mixed with chromium oxides. The widespread employment of controlled atmospheres in heat-treating furnaces of the metals industries accentuates this limitation on the chromium-alloy couple.

Probably the most serious limitation in using thermocouples above about 1,800° C is the lack of an adequate insulating material. Alumina is excellent but cannot be used above about 1,800° C. Beryllia and thoria have been used with some success to about 2,200° C but nothing is available above this temperature.

The relations between temperatures and emf for thermocouples are based on experimental data, not on any theoretical relation. In a simple thermoelectric circuit of two metals joined into a closed loop, emf arises at each junction and in each leg of the couple where it passes through the temperature gradient (*see* THERMOELECTRICITY). Analytical expressions have been set up for the platinum, platinum-10% rhodium thermocouple and the copper-constantan couple but these are applicable over limited ranges. For example, the expression $E = a + bt + ct^2$ is used in the specifications for reproducing the international scale between 630.5° and 1,063° C with the former couple, and the equation $E = at + b(1 - e^{ct})$ has been used between 0° and 350° C for the latter couple. The expressions are useful for construction of tables from which deviation curves or tables can be constructed for particular calibrated couples. The temperature-emf tables for iron-constantan and chromel-alumel couples reveal that no expression as simple as those given above would suffice even as a rough approximation. If a couple is expected to furnish measurements agreeing with the international scale, it must be calibrated with a platinum resistance thermometer from −190° to 630.5° C, with a platinum, platinum-10% rhodium couple from 630.5° to 1,063° C, and with a proper radiation device above 1,063° C.

Modern electrical instruments for use with thermocouples can be classified as millivoltmeters and potentiometers (fig. 4). Industrial potentiometers are built around a resistor with sliding contact (slide wire); precision potentiometers have three or more dial switches for connecting between fixed resistors, after the manner of the precision bridge. Recording potentiometers almost completely removed recording millivoltmeters from the industrial scene. Industrial instruments have extraordinary precision considering the severe requirements for ruggedness and reliability. Industrial recording to 1° F is not uncommon, and automatic control of some processes to 0.1° has been attained.

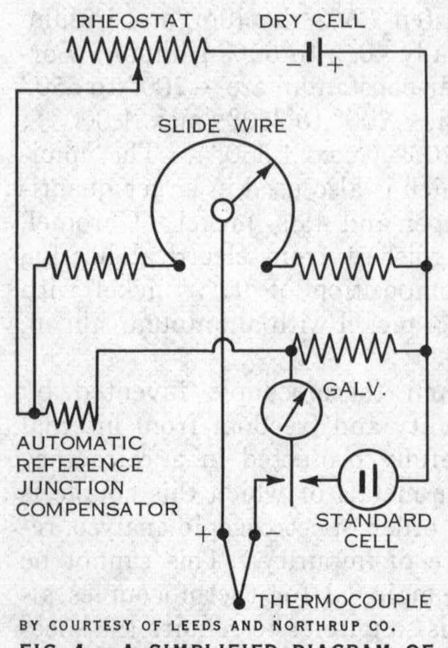


BY COURTESY OF LEEDS AND NORTHRUP CO.

FIG 4.—A SIMPLIFIED DIAGRAM OF THE ELECTRICAL CIRCUIT OF A POTENTIOMETER FOR USE WITH A THERMOCOUPLE

**6. Modern Optical Pyrometry.**—The disappearing-filament pyrometer continues to afford the greatest precision and accuracy for research work and the greatest convenience for practical applications in optical pyrometry. The principal commercial forms are made by the Leeds and Northrup Co. and the Pyrometer Instrument Co. in the U.S., their optical principles being similar to those of the laboratory type. The Leeds and Northrup device is portable, with a unique type of slide-wire potentiometer designed for rapid use. The lamps in these instruments are highly evacuated so that the tungsten wire or ribbon will withstand heating to 1,500° C for hundreds of hours without serious change. Gas filling would reduce the rate of evaporation of tungsten, but the lamp would become subject to changes in ambient temperature, and introduce great lag in its response to adjustments in the heating current. Fairly high temperatures can be measured without heating the lamp much above 1,400° C by the use of absorption screens, and the lamp will retain its original calibration remarkably well for many years.

Such pyrometers are calibrated at national laboratories by comparison with a standard instrument or by sighting them on large tungsten-strip lamps that previously have been calibrated. Primary calibrations at the gold point are made by sighting the pyrometer at a black body immersed in highly pure freezing gold. Calibrations below or above the gold point are made by sighting at a convenient source (this need not be a black body) with a calibrated screen interposed. This screen may be a rotating disk with an open sector that has been measured on a circular dividing engine, or an absorbing coloured glass whose transmission has been measured by comparison with a sectored disk or with the interval between two fixed points. Primary calibrations above the gold point are based on this one point (1,063° C) and the constant $c_2$ in the Planck equation. A complete table of temperature-current values is tediously built up by smoothing the deviations from a reference table or curve based on an equation such as $i$ (current) $= a + bt + ct^2 + dt^3$, the four constants of which are determined from four selected calibration points. The interval from the copper point to the palladium point is so large that it is preferable to establish at least two points in between with sectored disks or absorption screens to step down from the upper point. The most accurate measurements above the gold point are obtained by keeping the pyrometer lamp at a current value nearly corresponding with that determined for the gold point, and choosing an absorption device to nearly fit the extrapolation desired, for example, from gold to the platinum point (1,769° C). For much higher temperatures the lamp has to be raised toward the palladium point to make use of screens of accurately measurable transmission.

Laboratory pyrometers (Fairchild type) can be calibrated with respect to the international scale to about 0.4° at the gold point and about 3° at 2,300° C. High temperatures are readily measured with the disappearing-filament pyrometer without overheating the lamp by using two absorbing screens or one combined with a sector disk. For brightness temperatures up to about 2,500° C tungsten-strip lamps can be calibrated and used as transfer standards with an accuracy from about ±3° at the gold point to 10° at 2,500° C. An interesting fixed point for high-temperature work is that of the positive crater of the carbon arc. With a properly operated electric arc and a positive electrode of pure graphite, the apparent temperature, usually called brightness temperature, is about 3,800° K with an uncertainty of approximately 15°.

Some success was attained by the 1960s with photoelectric devices to take the place of the optical pyrometer. One photoelectric pyrometer developed at U.S. National Bureau of Standards used a photomultiplier tube as a detector and a multilayer interference filter to restrict the spectral band. A small tungsten lamp in the device is moved in and out of the optical path at thirty second intervals, permitting the detector to compare the brightness of the unknown source with that of the known lamp. The instrument has a sensitivity and a short-term reproducibility of about 0.02° C, but the instability of the lamp limits the long term reproducibility to about 0.1° C at 1,063° C. Accuracy of this photoelectric pyrometer was expected to be about four times greater than the best visual pyrometer. In addition the instrument affords a potential means for automatic recording and making brightness measurements of sources having a short time duration. Several commercial photoelectric pyrometers were also available in the 1960s.

Many forms of so-called colour pyrometer have been invented from time to time. In these instruments the intensities of radiation of two bands of wavelengths are compared and interpreted by calibration, as corresponding to some temperature. Commercial two-colour devices available in the 1960s were not as sensitive as the photoelectric (single-colour) type and were of little value in accurate work.

**7. Modern Radiation Pyrometry.**—This is pyrometry in which heat radiation of a broad wavelength region is used as a measure of temperature, is generally confined to industrial applications and seldom employed in research work. Relatively useful designs for the ceramic and steel industries lack the precision of the optical pyrometer, and are generally set in a fixed position where they can be checked with an optical instrument. These pyrometers are constructed of a receiver of heat radiation consisting of a thermocouple junction or small group of junctions, mounted in a housing (fig. 5) that can be water-cooled if necessary, and in which reference junctions of the couples are disposed as to give the least errors from variations in the temperature of the whole receiver. Such instruments are especially valuable where recorded temperatures are essential, where immersed thermocouples cannot withstand the heat, or corrosive vapours of gases, or where the cost of a photoelectric pyrometer is prohibitive. The

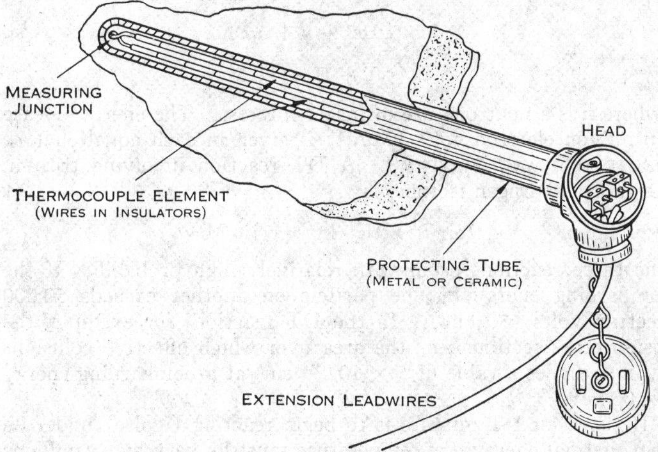


BY COURTESY OF LEEDS AND NORTHRUP CO.

FIG. 5.—INSTALLATION OF INDUSTRIAL FORM OF THERMOCOUPLE THROUGH FURNACE WALL SHOWN CUT AWAY. THE EXTENSION LEADWIRES ARE CONNECTED TO AN ELECTRICAL MEASURING INSTRUMENT, ORDINARILY READING TEMPERATURE

practice of attaching the receiver of these instruments to the open end of a tube inserted into a furnace protects the receiver from flame and smoke, and permits sighting it through an atmosphere free from carbon dioxide and water vapour, gases that are not transparent to infrared radiation. The thermal lag introduced by the thick-walled tube is not a deterrent to this practice where the lag of the furnace itself is large.

**8. Flame Thermometry.**—The measurement of temperatures in flames or hot gases, particularly above 1,500° K, requires equipment or techniques somewhat different from those already considered. Thermocouples or resistance thermometers are generally not used in such flames because of serious radiation losses, disturbance of the combustion process, mechanical rigidity of the thermometer, and melting of the thermometer itself. An optical pyrometer or two-colour pyrometer can sometimes be used, but usually the emissivity is unknown or changing rapidly with wavelength, producing large uncertainties in their application. Two of the more widely used methods are those of line reversal and of intensity distribution in spectral lines.

In the line-reversal method, the brightness of a source of radiation, such as a tungsten-strip lamp, is adjusted until at a wavelength corresponding to some spectrum line in the flame, the source appears equally bright when viewed directly or through the flame. The flame temperature is the temperature of a black body having this brightness; *i.e.*, the brightness temperature of the source at the same wavelength. This method is based on Kirchhoff's law, which states that the fractional amount of radiation absorbed by a body is equal to the fraction it emits relative to a black body at the same temperature. Thus when the black body and the flame are at the same temperature, the amount of radiation absorbed by the flame is just equal to that which it emits and the black body appears equally bright when viewed directly or through the flame. Usually a spectrograph or a monochromator equipped with a suitable detector such as a photomultiplier is used to isolate and measure the radiation at the spectrum line. An element not found in the flame may be added to obtain a strong spectrum line in a convenient spectral region. Sodium, which emits strong yellow lines at 5890 and 5896 Å, has been used frequently.

It is possible to obtain reversal temperatures at 2,500° K that are reproducible to a few degrees. However, it is very questionable that the temperature measurement is this accurate. Great care must be taken with the optical path, the solid angles subtended and corrections for optical elements utilized with the tungsten source only. In addition, the brightness temperature of the tungsten source will be uncertain by at least 7° at 2,500° K and greater at higher temperatures; temperature gradients in the flame will also affect accuracy. Nevertheless, the reversal method is probably more reproducible than any other method known in the 1960s for measuring flame temperatures; in many cases, the measured temperature agrees reasonably well with that calculated from known equilibrium concentrations.

A second method for determining flame temperatures is based on the relative amount of energy emitted by a source per unit time (relative intensity) in two or more spectral lines. According to quantum theory (*see* PHYSICS: GENERAL SURVEY; QUANTUM MECHANICS) an atom or molecule can have only certain definite energies that are called energy levels. An atom in a flame, for example, can lose its excess energy by making a transition to a lower energy level. There is a definite probability that this lost energy will appear in the form of radiation. This radiation will have a particular wavelength (spectral line) that is inversely proportional to the lost energy. For a source containing many atoms, the intensity of a spectral line is the product of the energy for one transition, the number of atoms in the initial energy level, and the probability of the transition. The relative number of atoms in two or more known energy levels for a system in thermal equilibrium depends only on the temperature; and therefore the temperature can be calculated if the relative number of atoms is known. Thus if the energy levels and the relative transition probabilities can be calculated or determined in an independent experiment, the relative intensity of two or more spectral lines emitted by a source in thermal equilibrium can be used to obtain the temperature of the source. Spectroscopists have determined many energy levels for a great number of atoms and molecules. Unfortunately, as of the 1960s only a few relative transition probabilities had been determined experimentally or could be calculated accurately. This has been one of the major limitations of this method of measuring flame temperatures. It has the advantage over the reversal method in that another source is not viewed through the flame, thereby making the optical setup less critical.

**9. Thermometry Below the Oxygen Point.**—The international scale was not yet defined below the boiling point of oxygen by the 1960s. None of the thermometers available for low-temperature measurements had the characteristics of a practical standard—sensitivity, reproducibility, convenience, and a simple interpolation equation.

From 90° to 20° K the platinum resistance thermometer was still the most precise thermometer available. Below 50° K its sensitivity begins to decrease rapidly but at 17° K it still has sufficient sensitivity to determine differences of 0.001° or less. At 11° K the sensitivity has decreased by a factor of about 4 relative to that at 17° K. The major limitation was that no simple mathematical relationship had been found between temperature and resistance. The suggestion was being studied that an empirical table be developed that could be adjusted for each thermometer utilizing calibration data at several fixed points.

The U.S. National Bureau of Standards calibrated (1965) platinum resistance thermometers down to 11° K. This was done by comparison with six platinum resistance thermometers calibrated against a helium gas thermometer with a reported accuracy of ±0.02°. At Pennsylvania State University a similar calibration of resistance thermometers was estimated to agree with the thermodynamic scale within ±0.005°.

When considerably less precision than that available with a platinum resistance thermometer is required, a copper-constantan thermocouple can be used down to about 15° K. Another thermometer that often is useful in this region is the saturation vapour pressure of hydrogen. The vapour pressure-temperature relationship has been determined from the critical point, 33° K, where the pressure is about 9,700 mm. Hg, to the triple point, 13.8° K, where the pressure is about 53 mm. Hg.

Below 11° K platinum resistance thermometers are of little value because of their small sensitivity. However, resistance thermometers made of semiconducting materials have ample sensitivity by virtue of their negative temperature coefficient; *i.e.*, the resistance increases with a decrease in temperature. A major limitation of the semiconducting thermometers has been their lack of stability. However, germanium alloy thermometers containing extremely small amounts of indium have been reported to be reproducible to 0.001° between 1° and 5° K, even after repeated warming and cooling. Even better reproducibility (.0003° at 4.2° K) with germanium resistors (1963) indicated that such devices may become standard thermometers in the range from about 1° to 15° K.

Since in most low-temperature experiments the basic cooling is produced by a bath of liquid helium, the saturation vapour pressure of helium is a convenient thermometer. Its useful range extends from the critical point (5.2° K and 1,718 mm. Hg) to the lowest pressure conveniently measured (0.1 mm. Hg and 1° K). The relationship between the vapour pressure of helium and its temperature led to the adoption (1958) of $He^3$ as an international standard between 1° and 5.2° K; $He^4$ was made (1962) an international standard between about 0.3° and 3.5° K (*see* HELIUM).

Below 0.3° K a major problem is the difficulty in establishing thermal equilibrium. The magnetic thermometer is one of the few devices that can be used. It is based on the fact that the magnetic susceptibility of a paramagnetic salt is a function of temperature. Therefore, if such a salt is placed in the magnetic field of an inductor, the inductance which depends on the susceptibility of the salt can be used as a temperature indicator. Often at temperatures below 1° K, paramagnetic salts themselves are investigated. Thus the unusual but convenient situation is encountered where the material under study, the coolant, cold bath, and thermometer are one and the same. Another feature of the magnetic thermometer is that it is in the class of absolute instruments such as the gas thermometer. With proper corrections, it can be used to determine the ratio of thermodynamic temperatures, but the precision is not very great (*see* MAGNETISM: *Paramagnetism*).

BIBLIOGRAPHY.—P. D. Foote, C. O. Fairchild, and T. R. Harrison, *Pyrometric Practice*, National Bureau of Standards, T170 (1921); B. Lewis and G. von Elbe, *Combustion, Flames and Explosions of Gases* (1938); American Institute of Physics, *Temperature, Its Measurement and Control in Science and Industry*, 3 vol. (1941–63); R. L. Weber, *Temperature Measurement and Control* (1941); W. P. Wood and J. M. Cork, *Pyrometry* (1941); Current *Codes* of British Standards Institution and the American Society of Mechanical Engineers; C. J. Gorter (ed.), *Progress in Low Temperature Physics*, 4 vol. (1955–64).

(C. O. F.; H. J. K.)

**THERMONUCLEAR REACTIONS** are those in which the combination (*see* FUSION) of atomic nuclei of light elements occurs, producing heavier elements. The process leads to an overall loss of mass, which appears as the kinetic energy of the reaction products. The nuclei are similarly charged, and repel each other; under some conditions energy that overcomes this Coulomb repulsion and prompts the particles to fuse comes from the thermal energy of the particles themselves; hence the term thermonuclear. The energy liberated is so great compared to that supplied to overcome Coulomb repulsion that the reaction can sustain itself (chain reaction) and may be used to generate power. Thermonuclear reactions produce the energy in stars and in the hydrogen bomb. Great interest in such reactions stems from the hope of finding a practical method of controlled nuclear fusion, providing a relatively cheap and abundant replacement for fossil fuels (coal, oil, and natural gas).

Another nuclear reaction called fission produces energy when a heavy nucleus (an isotope of thorium, uranium, or plutonium) absorbs a neutron, becomes unstable, and splits into two or more fragments (*see* ATOMIC ENERGY). By the mid-1960s only the fission process had been applied to produce controlled supplies of power. Nuclear fusion has distinct advantages over fission, however: its products are not radioactive and the fuel (deuterium in particular) is abundant and inexpensive. Eight gallons of ordinary water contain about one gram of deuterium, with a cost of extraction of not more than about 30 cents and an energy content (if there were a fusion reactor to burn it) equivalent to 2,500 gallons of gasoline.

Since Coulomb repulsion is so effective in keeping particles apart, reactions of interest for controlled fusion are limited to nuclei with the lowest possible charge: the isotopes of hydrogen (ordinary hydrogen H or $H^1$, deuterium D or $H^2$, and tritium T or $H^3$). The first in a sequence of reactions that produce energy in the sun

$$H + H \rightarrow D + e^+$$

(where $e^+$ is a positron) proceeds with too low a probability for man-made reactors (*see* STAR: *Stellar Structure*). However, two DD reactions that occur with roughly equal probability

$$D + D \begin{cases} \nearrow He^3 + n + 3.2 \text{ Mev} \\ \searrow T + H + 4.0 \text{ Mev} \end{cases}$$

(where $n$ is a neutron) are of major interest. The energy release (in million electron volts [Mev]) is given in each equation (*see* DEUTERIUM AND TRITIUM). A DT reaction involving tritium, the rarest hydrogen isotope, is

$$D + T \rightarrow He^4 + n + 17.6 \text{ Mev}$$

The three reactions occur with relatively high probability if the bombarding energy of one particle on another exceeds 50,000 electron volts (50 kev). In the DT reaction, for example, the fusion cross section (*i.e.*, the area over which effective collisions occur) reaches a value of $5 \times 10^{-24}$ cm² at a bombarding energy of 100 kev.

If the D or DT mixture is to begin reacting (ignite) under its own thermal energy, the temperature must be very high (millions of °K). Under these conditions the fuel will be a plasma (a gas of positively charged nuclei and of electrons). Acting to oppose thermonuclear energy production are various loss mechanisms, the most important of these being radiative. Particle density in plasma is too low to permit equilibrium between matter and radiation; hence, the dominant radiation loss is bremsstrahlung (*i.e.*, energy radiated from the very frequent collisions between the charged particles). The ratio of bremsstrahlung loss to energy production through nuclear reaction is independent of the density of the plasma. The point at which this ratio equals unity determines the ideal ignition temperature of the system; when the plasma is hotter than this ignition temperature, the reaction will be self-sustaining if other losses are negligible. The ignition temperature for the DD reaction is about 400,000,000° K, and for DT it is about 45,000,000° K.

To achieve controlled nuclear fusion the reacting system must be confined; but no known material can remain solid at such temperatures. Thus much talent and money have been devoted to an effort to confine the plasma magnetically. Schemes proposed include confinement by a magnetic field surrounding a current discharge (pinch effect); by magnetic mirrors; by a figure-8 magnetic torus (stellarator); and by a multipole (picket-fence) configuration. Early attempts were plagued by instability (*see* MAGNETOHYDRODYNAMICS), but research on controlled fusion continued in the U.S. at the Los Alamos Scientific Laboratory, the Lawrence Radiation Laboratory, the Oak Ridge National Laboratory, and Princeton University, and in the United Kingdom, France, and the U.S.S.R. *See* also COSMOGONY: *Origin of Chemical Elements*.

(J. R. RE.)

**THERMOPYLAE** ("hot gates"; modern Greek THERMOPILAI), a narrow pass about 4 mi. (6 km.) long, named after its hot springs, which are said to have medicinal properties, lies on the east coast of central Greece between the valley of the Spercheus (Sperkhios) River and the district of Locris. The pass is used by any army following the coast, and the alternative route climbs far inland through Doris. In antiquity the cliffs of Thermopylae were about 50 ft. from the sea and at some points much less; nowadays the accumulation of silt has widened the distance to more than a mile. In 480 B.C. a small Greek force under the Spartan king Leonidas held the pass for three days against a huge Persian army (*see* GRECO-PERSIAN WARS). In 323 Leosthenes occupied it as his base against the Macedonian regent Antipater. In 279 the Greeks delayed Brennus and his Gauls there. Antiochus III of Syria in 191 B.C. fortified the pass against the Roman consul Acilius Glabrio. The Persians, Gauls, and Romans turned the pass by sending detachments of troops inland through the hills (the actual routes are disputed): the pass was too narrow for frontal attacks to succeed against heavily armed infantry.

(N. G. L. H.)

**THERMOSTAT,** a device to regulate automatically the supply of heat to, and consequently to control the temperature of, the air in a space, or of liquids or materials involved in a process. Basically the thermostat consists of two elements, a sensing element and an actuating or control element. The sensing element is sensitive to temperature changes that produce proportional changes in its physical dimensions, volume or electrical resistance. The actuating element translates the action of the sensing element to a proportional movement of the controlling air damper, valve or electric switch.

The principle of thermal expansion of metals, liquids and gases with temperature increase is the basis of the sensing element design for all thermostats except the electronic instrument. The range of temperature change during which the linear expansion bears a constant ratio to the temperature change is limited to approximately 250° F. The following table lists the coefficients of linear expansion for the metals commonly used for thermostatic sensing elements.

*Linear Coefficients of Thermal Expansion per Degree Fahrenheit*

| Metal | Coefficient |
|---|---|
| Aluminum | 0.0000123 |
| Brass | 0.0000106 |
| Graphite | 0.0000044 |
| Copper | 0.0000093 |
| Quartz | 0.0000003 |
| Wrought iron | 0.0000063 |
| Invar steel | 0.0000005 |
| Silver | 0.0000105 |

**Sensing Elements.**—Four types of sensing element are commonly used in commercially produced thermostats. The bi-metal strip consists of two strips of metal having widely different linear coefficients of thermal expansion (*see* table). These strips are fused together and as the temperature increases, the strip bends away from the side having the greater coefficient of linear expansion. In application, one end of the strip is anchored, leaving the other end free to move. The strip may be straight, bent to a radius perpendicular to the long axis of the strip into a U shape or a helical shape, or it may be wound in a spiral whose axis is parallel to the long axis. Selection of shape is governed by the magnitude of movement desired at the free end of the strip. In some types of thermostats the bi-metal sensing element produces enough force to actuate the control directly.

The tube and rod sensing element also is designed to take advantage of the difference in the linear thermal expansion of two metals. It is composed of a tube of metal that has a high coefficient of expansion and a rod of metal that has a low coefficient of expansion. The rod is inserted into the tube and anchored at its closed end. The open end of the tube is anchored and as the length of the tube changes with a change in temperature there is a relative movement of the free end of the rod, the length of which has remained unchanged.

The bellows type of sensing element consists of a volume confined by a diaphragm of cup-shaped, very light metal, or a cylindrical vessel with a corrugated wall spun out of light weight metal. The volume is completely filled with a liquid, a vapour or a gas. In any case, an increase in temperature results in an increase in volume and an increase in axial length of the vessel.

The remote bulb type of sensing element is actually an adaption of the bellows type. It consists of a bulb attached to the diaphragm, or bellows, by a capillary tube of any desired length, all of which is completely filled with liquid, vapour or gas. The bulb is placed in the region to be controlled and any change in pressure due to a temperature change at the bulb is transferred through the capillary tube to the bellows.

The electronic sensing element consists of a small coil of wire whose resistance changes in a constant ratio with temperature changes.

**Actuating or Control Elements.**—In some types of thermostats using a bi-metal sensing element, the sensing element itself functions as the control element and operates directly an air damper or valve. In other types, the sensing element acts as a pilot to the control element that regulates a supply of external energy in the form of pneumatic energy or electrical energy necessary to operate the air dampers, valves or switches.

The type of control element selected depends upon the type of action. To start or stop a burner or fan, to open or close a damper, a two-position control element is used that simply makes or breaks an electric circuit. The so-called floating control is similar to the two-position control element except that there is a neutral zone midway between the two contacts and that the action is at a constant rate toward either of the on or off positions. When the neutral zone is reached, the action stops until the sensing element makes one contact or the other at which time the action is resumed in the proper direction.

The modulating or proportional control element is piloted by the sensing element pushing a sliding contact over a potentiometer coil that controls the position of a reversible valve or damper motor, there being a motor position for each turn of wire on the potentiometer coil.

The pneumatic powered control element action controls the compressed air pressure in pneumatic air motors attached to dampers and valves. The air pressure causes movement in one direction only and a spring powers the return stroke. The position of the motor is fixed by the air pressure in the control line that is regulated by the control element. The pneumatic thermostats have modulating action that also satisfies a two position requirement.

**Types of Thermostats.**—There are five classified types of thermostats. (1) The room thermostat is mounted in the room that is to be controlled. It may have a sensing element of either the bi-metal, bellows or electronic type, and its control element may be powered by electric or pneumatic energy. (2) An insertion thermostat is mounted on a duct with the control element in the room and the sensing element in the duct. (3) The immersion thermostat is used for the control of high pressure fluids or gases. A pressure tight bushing permits the sensing element to be immersed in the fluid and the control element to be accessible. Immersion and insertion thermostats use the bi-metal control element, either the spiral wound or the tube and rod type. The self-contained direct acting tube and rod thermostat is often used to control the water temperature in gas fired water heaters. The rod is linked directly to the gas valve operating mechanism. (4) The surface type thermostat has its sensing element clamped to the surface of a tank or pipe and is an expedient substitute for an insertion or immersion thermostat. (5) The remote bulb thermostat is applied when it is desired to have the control element located at a distance from the sensing element.

**Action of Thermostats in the Control of Residential Heating.**—The action starts with the room thermostat, usually located in the living room. The secondary circuit is normally open, but the thermostat closes the circuit on a falling temperature, causing the relay to close and energize the primary (line voltage) circuit that starts the burner. When the temperature at the room thermostat rises to the desired degree at which it has been set, the secondary circuit is opened, the relay opens the primary circuit and the burner stops. Thus the room thermostat controls the operation of the burner and the source of heat. The point at which the burner starts is usually 1½° to 2° below the point at which it stops. As a safety measure, a limit switch is connected in series with the secondary circuit in order to prevent overheating.

The limit switch, when used with a warm air heating system, is an insertion thermostat that is reverse acting, *i.e.*, opens on a rising temperature and closes on a falling temperature, and has its sensing element in the warm air bonnet of the furnace. Its opening point is usually set about 5° above the minimum air temperature required to heat the house. Its opening point is fixed at 15° below its opening point. In case the bonnet air temperature reaches the limit, the switch opens the secondary circuit and the burner stops independently of the room thermostat. After the bonnet air cools 15° the limit closes and the burner starts again, providing the room thermostat has not been satisfied in the meantime. The warm air circulating fan is controlled by an insertion thermostat in the warm air bonnet of the furnace and is set to start the fan 5° above the lowest temperature that will avoid the sensation of drafts in the living room, and to stop the fan 5° below the starting point.

With hot water systems, the room thermostat controls the operation of the circulating pump and the burner is controlled by a direct acting immersion thermostat set to open the secondary circuit at the minimum water temperature necessary to heat the house, and to close at about 10° to 15° below the opening point. When used with hot water heating systems, the limit switch is a direct-acting double-throw immersion thermostat with one pole in series with the primary circuit to the burner and the other in the primary circuit to the circulating pump. The circuit to the burner is normally closed, and the circuit to the circulator is normally open. When the water temperature rises to the set point, the highest temperature for safe operation, the primary circuit to the burner opens and the burner stops; at the same time the primary circuit to the circulating pump closes and it starts independently of any controls on the secondary circuit.

Bibliography.—Burgess H. Jennings, *Heating and Air Conditioning,* (1956); American Society of Heating and Air Conditioning Engineers, *Heating Ventilating Air Conditioning Guide,* annual; John E. Haines, *Automatic Control of Heating and Air Conditioning* (1953).

(W. T. Mr.)

**THESEUS,** the great hero of Attic legend, was the son of Aegeus, king of Athens, and Aethra, daughter of Pittheus, king of Troezen (in Argolis, in the Peloponnese), or of Poseidon and Aethra. (Aegeus and Poseidon may be one and the same.) The legend relates that Aegeus, being childless, went to Pittheus, who contrived that Aegeus should have intercourse with Aethra, who in due time brought forth Theseus. On Theseus' reaching manhood, Aethra sent him to Athens to his father. On the journey he encountered many adventures. First he met and slew Periphetes, surnamed Corynetes (Clubman). At the Isthmus of Corinth dwelt Sinis, called the Pine Bender because he killed his victims by tearing them apart between two pine trees; Theseus hoisted the Pine Bender on his own pine tree. Next Theseus dispatched the Crommyonian sow (or boar). Then over a cliff he flung the wicked Sciron, who used to kick his guests into the sea while they were washing his feet. In Eleusis, Theseus wrestled with Cercyon and killed him. Later he slew Procrustes, who fitted all comers to his only bed by lopping or racking them to the right length.

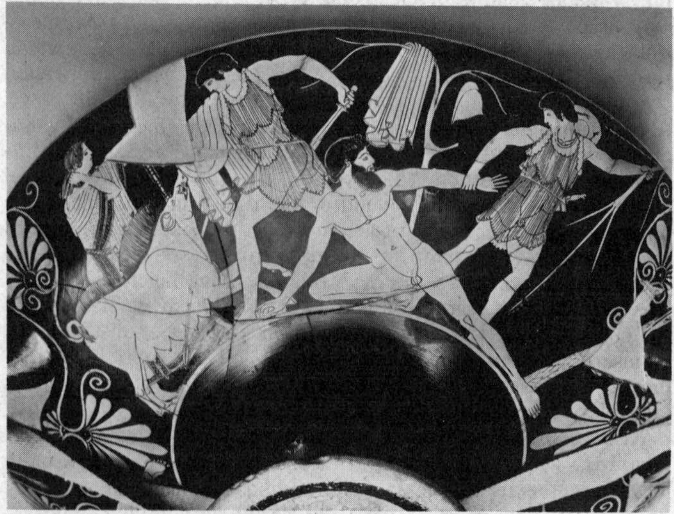

BY COURTESY OF THE TRUSTEES OF THE BRITISH MUSEUM

EXPLOITS OF THESEUS; VASE PAINTING

Theseus (left) attacking the Crommyonian sow and (right) hoisting Sinis on his own pine tree

On his arrival in Athens he found his father married to Medea (*q.v.*). Being a witch, she knew Theseus before his father did, and tried to persuade Aegeus to poison his son; but Aegeus recognized him. Theseus was then declared heir to the throne, and the Pallantids—sons of Pallas, Aegeus' brother—who had hoped to succeed the childless king, conspired against him. Theseus crushed the conspiracy. He then attacked the fire-breathing bull of Marathon (brought there as the seventh labour of Hercules) and took it alive to Athens, where he sacrificed it to Apollo Delphinius. Next came the adventure of the Cretan Minotaur, for which *see* Minos; Minotaur.

While Theseus was on his way to Crete, Minos, wishing to learn whether Theseus was really the son of Poseidon, flung his ring into the sea. Theseus dived and brought it up, together with a golden crown, a gift of the sea goddess Amphitrite. On the return voyage from Crete he landed at Delos, and there he and his comrades danced the crane dance, whose complicated movements were meant to imitate the windings of the Labyrinth. In historical times, this dance was still danced by the Delians round the Altar of Horns. Also on the return voyage he abandoned Ariadne (*q.v.*) at Naxos.

Theseus had promised Aegeus that, if he returned successful, he would hoist a white sail in place of the black sail with which the fatal ship bearing the sacrificial victims to the Minotaur always put to sea. But he forgot his promise, and when Aegeus, from the Acropolis at Athens, saw the black sail at sea, he flung himself from the rock and died. Hence, at the festival which commemorated the return of Theseus there was always weeping and lamentation. Theseus now carried out the union of the various Attic communities into a single state and extended the territory of Attica to the Isthmus of Corinth (*see* Attica). He transformed the Isthmian Games (*see* Games, Classical) in honour of Melicertes by adding games in honour of Poseidon. Alone, or with Hercules, he captured the Amazon princess Antiope (or Hippolyta). As a result the Amazons attacked Athens, and Hippolyta fell fighting on the side of Theseus. By her he had a son, Hippolytus, beloved of Theseus' second wife, Phaedra (*see* Hippolytus). Theseus is also said to have taken part in the Argonautic expedition and the Calydonian boar hunt. He compelled the Thebans to give up for burial the unburied bodies of the Seven (*see* Seven Against Thebes).

The famous friendship between Theseus and Pirithous, king of the Lapiths, originated when Pirithous heard of the strength and courage of Theseus and desired to put them to the test. Accordingly, he drove away from Marathon some cows that belonged to Theseus. The latter pursued, but when he came up with the robber the two heroes were so filled with admiration of each other that they swore brotherhood. At the marriage of Pirithous, Theseus participated in the famous fight between the Lapiths and Centaurs. Pirithous now helped Theseus to carry off Helen (*q.v.*). In exchange, Theseus descended to the lower world with Pirithous, to help his friend carry off Persephone. But the two were caught and confined in Hades till Hercules came and released Theseus.

When Theseus returned to Athens, he found that a sedition had been stirred up by Menestheus, a descendant of Erechtheus, one of the old kings of Athens. Failing to quell the outbreak, Theseus in despair sent his children to Euboea, and after solemnly cursing the Athenians sailed away to the island of Scyros, where he had ancestral estates. But Lycomedes, king of Scyros, took him up to a high place, and killed him by casting him into the sea. His ghost was said to have appeared in the Athenian ranks at Marathon. When the Persian War was over, the Delphic oracle bade the Athenians fetch the bones of Theseus from Scyros and lay them in Attic earth. This was done, in 469, by Cimon.

Theseus' chief festival, called Theseia, was on the 8th of the month Pyanopsion (in October), but the 8th day of every month was sacred to him.

The well-preserved Doric temple to the north of the Acropolis at Athens, commonly known as the Theseum, is certainly not his shrine. There were several (according to Philochorus, four) temples or shrines of Theseus at Athens.

BIBLIOGRAPHY.—*Ancient Works:* Plutarch, *Theseus. Modern Works:* H. J. Rose, *A Handbook of Greek Mythology* (1928); Edith Hamilton, *Mythology* (1942); *Oxford Classical Dictionary;* L. R. Farnell, *Hero Cults of the Greek States. See* also the two novels by Mary Renault, *The King Must Die* (1958) and *The Bull From the Sea* (1962).

**THESMOPHORIA,** a very ancient festival, in honour of Demeter Thesmophoros, celebrated by women in many parts of the Greek world (as Attica, many places in the Peloponnese, Boeotia, several islands, the coast of Asia Minor, Cyrene, Italy and Sicily, but not generally among the Dorians).

The name Demeter Thesmophoros does not mean, as the ancients usually supposed, *legifera Ceres* ("lawgiving Ceres," Ceres being equivalent to Demeter), since the festival has no aspects in any way connected with the bringing or establishing of laws or customs (*thesmoi*). It is possibly "bringer of treasure or wealth," an obsolete sense of *thesmos,* of which a few traces remain. Or, perhaps better, the name Thesmophoria is the primary one, from which the epithet of the goddess is derived, and it means "the carrying of things laid down," the radical meaning of *thesmos* referring to the fertility charms described below. As no men were admitted to the rites, and in any case they were largely secret, nothing like a full description is available.

The celebrants were women who seem to have been at least generally married, and who had to be free. They observed chastity for several days (nine, according to Ovid, a likely number considering its magical connotations), and abstained from certain foods; thus, they must not eat pomegranate seeds. The festival lasted three days, although in Attica it was lengthened by the addition of other celebrations of a similar character, the Stenia and the Halamusian Thesmophoria, making five days in all, Pyanopsion 10–14. But the original days were Pyanopsion 12–14 only (*i.e.,* in what is now October) and shortly after the Pyanopsia (*q.v.*). The days were called respectively *Anodos* (or *Kathodos*), *Nesteia, Kalligeneia.*

*Anodos* (ascent) is often taken to mean the "going up" of the women to the Thesmophorion, or precinct of Demeter; but this does not explain why the day should also be called *Kathodos,* or descent. As the name of the second day, which signifies "fasting," describes what the celebrants then did, it is plausible to take the first day as having been called Ascent and Descent, and to connect it with the rite known to have been performed at some time in the festival. Pigs were thrown into an underground chamber, called a megaron; they were probably alive, but the text is corrupt and uncertain. At all events they were left there until such parts of them as were not eaten by the guardian snakes of these underground sanctuaries had had time to rot. The remains were then brought up by certain women who had observed chastity for three days and were called *antletriai* or "drawers up"—the verb *antlein* means to pump or draw off water. These women also carried, or some of the celebrants did, certain well-known symbols of fertility, including pine cones and "figures made of flour of wheat, in imitation of the shapes of serpents and of men." The remains of the pigs were laid on an altar, and if taken and mixed with seed were believed to ensure a good crop. Apparently the figures, like the pigs, were thrown into the chasms; but the authority here (a scholiast on Lucian) is both confused and manifestly corrupt; he seems to be confusing the Thesmophoria with a quite different festival, the Arrhephoria.

If, however, pigs, pine cones, figures and all were thrown into the megara and "pumped" out again, it is very intelligible magic. These objects are all, in their nature, connected with fertility—a fertile beast, a seed vessel, a preparation of grain shaped like a creature supposed to be full of earth magic (the serpent) and like a man, perhaps a phallic figure. They are then put into a holy place, left there to acquire additional mana from the sacred surroundings and the touch of the sacred serpents, real or imaginary, who live there, and finally taken out again by pure agents, whose chastity has, so to speak, insulated them. Finally, they are laid on a holy altar, whence they are taken, heavily charged now with potency, and used to bring the blessing of fertility. To mix all manner of magical things with seeds to make them sprout better is a widespread primitive custom.

The ancients tried to explain all these matters as commemorations of the abduction of Kore; but it is rather the legends that grew out of the ritual, now no longer understood. In modern times it has been found possible to conjecture a reason for them; but it is to be remembered that, because of the fragmentary state of available knowledge, the above is offered as a conjecture only, especially as regards the date of the rite.

The *Nesteia* is easily enough explained; it is known that the women fasted, sitting upon the ground. Fasting is a common piece of agricultural magic, and contact with the ground is also common. The third day, *Kalligeneia,* is "the fair birth." We need not take it as originally referring to anyone so definite as Kore; it rather indicates the happy issue of all this magic, and doubtless of much more that is not known, in the fertility of the ground and doubtless of men and beasts as well. It remains only to add that the Thesmophoria, or at least a great part of it, was carried out at night by torchlight, and that it was accompanied by ceremonial coarse abuse among the women; again a common means of promoting fertility. The festival formed a setting for Aristophanes' comedy *The Thesmophoriazusae. See* also FEAST AND FESTIVAL.

BIBLIOGRAPHY.—J. E. Harrison, *Prolegomena to the Study of Greek Religion,* 1st ed. (1903); M. P. Nilsson, *Griechische Feste von religiöser Bedeutung* (1906), *Geschichte der griechischen Religion,* 2 vol. (1941–50); L. R. Farnell, *The Cults of the Greek States,* vol. iii, relevant passages from ancient authors in full, pp. 326 ff. (1907); Sir J. G. Frazer, *The Golden Bough,* 3rd ed. (H. J. R.)

**THESPIAE** (Greek THESPIAI), an ancient Greek city of Boeotia by the Thespius (modern Kanavari) River, on level ground commanded by the low eastward spurs of Mt. Helicon. Thespiae, inhabited in Neolithic and Mycenaean times, was one of Boeotia's larger cities and figures chiefly as an enemy of nearby Thebes. During the Persian invasion of 480 B.C., almost alone among Boeotian cities, it joined the Greek resistance; 700 Thespians accompanied Leonidas to Thermopylae and of their own free will shared his death. Thespiae was burned by Xerxes, but the remaining inhabitants furnished 1,800 unarmed men to the Greek army at Plataea (479). In 424 the Thespian contingent at Delium sustained heavy losses, and next year the Thebans took advantage of this to accuse Thespiae of friendship toward Athens and to dismantle its walls. In 414 the Thebans interfered again to suppress a democratic rising. In the Corinthian War Thespiae sided with Sparta, and between 379 and 372 it repeatedly served the Spartans as a base against Thebes. The Thespians were reduced by the Thebans and compelled to send a contingent to Leuctra (371); after this Theban victory the entire population evacuated Thespiae, which the Thebans destroyed. The town was soon rebuilt. In 171, true to its policy of opposing Thebes, Thespiae supported the Romans, who declared it a free city in 146 B.C.

The deity most worshiped at Thespiae was (unusually) Eros, whose primitive image was an unwrought stone. The town contained many works of art, among them the marble Eros of Praxiteles, dedicated by the famous courtesan, Phryne, who was born at Thespiae, and one of the most famous statues in the ancient world; it was carried off to Rome by Caligula, restored by Claudius, and removed again by Nero. There was also a bronze Eros by Lysippus. The Thespians also worshiped the Muses and celebrated a drama and poetry festival in their honour in the sacred grove on Mt. Helicon. There are remains of the sanctuaries of the Muses both at Thespiae and on Mt. Helicon. *See* also BOEOTIA.

**THESPIS** (6th century B.C.), Greek poet from the Attic country-deme of Icaria. He was often reckoned the "inventor of tragedy" and the Parian Chronicle (*q.v.*) records his name as the first to win a prize for tragedy at the City Dionysia, *c.* 534 B.C. The significance of the claim depends on the interpretation of scanty and summary evidence about Thespis, and the view taken of the origins and development of Greek drama. Aristotle, according to the rhetorician Themistius, said that in its earliest stage tragedy was entirely choral, the prologue and speeches being first introduced by Thespis. If this be accepted—and on linguistic grounds it is perfectly possible—then the contribution of Thespis was indeed decisive: he was the first "actor," and tragic dialogue began when he exchanged words with the leader of the chorus. The Suda Lexicon gives the titles (of doubtful authenticity) of several of his plays (not confined to the legends of Dionysus, but embracing the whole body of heroic legends), but the fragments quoted in various writers as from Thespis (*see* A. Nauck, *Fragmenta Tragicorum Graecorum,* 2nd ed., 1926) are probably forgeries by Heracleides Ponticus. The statement of Horace in the *Ars poetica* that Thespis went round Attica with a cart, on which his plays were acted, seems to be due to a confusion between the origins of tragedy and of comedy. (A. M. DE.)

**THESSALONIANS, EPISTLES TO THE,** two books of the New Testament, the items placed last in the traditional collection of the Pauline Epistles that are addressed to a congregation. According to the usual dating they are the earliest extant letters of Paul and hence the earliest of surviving Christian documents (though this hinges on the date of Galatians, which is disputed; *see* PAUL, SAINT: *Letters and Style*). They are closely connected to one another not only in that they are both addressed to the same congregation at Thessalonica (modern Salonika, in Macedonian Greece) but also by similarity of wording and content, including the fact that Silvanus (Silas) and Timothy are mentioned in the opening sentence of both epistles as being coauthors with Paul. These very resemblances have given rise to the literary problem of the second letter, whose authenticity is much debated and cannot be proved with certainty, though there is no reasonable doubt among modern scholars that the first letter is the work of Paul.

**Contents.**—The two books may be outlined as follows:

| | | |
|---|---|---|
| I. Thess. | 1:1 | greeting |
| | 1:2–10 | thanks to God for the Thessalonians' faith and good conduct |
| | 2:1–12 | Paul's defense of his own motives and conduct when staying with them |
| | 2:13–3:13 | Timothy's good report, and a prayer for the Thessalonians |
| | 4:1–12 | warnings and exhortations |
| | 4:13–5:11 | the dead and the living at the Second Coming, which will be soon |
| | 5:12–28 | exhortations and conclusion |
| II. Thess. | 1:1–2 | greeting |
| | 1:3–12 | thanks to God for the Thessalonians' faith and good conduct and reference to God's retribution on their enemies |
| | 2:1–12 | warning against false reports of the end of the world |
| | 2:13–3:5 | renewed thanks |
| | 3:6–16 | warnings and exhortations |
| | 3:17–18 | conclusion |

**I Thessalonians.**—*Themes.*—After the introductory greeting (1:1) Paul gives thanks for the faith and love of the congregation, which are an example to all (1:2–10). He then looks back at his own stay in Thessalonica, defending himself against the accusation that his missionary work there had selfish motives by pointing out that he earned his own living in their city concurrently with preaching the gospel (2:1–12). After renewed thanks for the Thessalonians' progress in the Word of God, Paul tells them how much he had longed to visit them again, but because he could not do so he had sent Timothy. Timothy has just returned with news of them which leads Paul to pray that they may continue blameless (2:13–3:13). An exhortation against sexual immorality and dishonesty follows, together with an exhortation to brotherly love and working peaceably for their living (4:1–12). Paul then turns to a special problem: there was some concern in the congregation about those who had died before the Second Coming, and Paul assures them that those Christians who have died already will rise to meet their Lord first, before we who are still alive are also caught up into the clouds with him (4:13–18). The day of the Lord will come unexpectedly, and the Thessalonians must be prepared for it (5:1–11). After some general exhortations (5:12–25) the letter ends with the unexpected command to read the letter to all the brethren and with the usual formula of benediction (5:26–28).

The epistle was clearly written just after Paul had received news of the Thessalonians from Timothy and wanted to express his joy over them. As he cannot immediately visit them himself (3:10), he wants to strengthen their faith by writing (4:1 ff.), and in this part of the letter, quite possibly, he may be also answering questions the congregation sent to him. In any case he has heard of the uncertainties caused by the death of some Christians, and one gets the impression that he is also aware of a certain tension between "those who labor among you and are over you in the Lord and admonish you" (5:12) and the rest of the brethren (5:12–14, 27). It need not, however, be assumed that every exhortation or self-justification in the letter must necessarily refer to some feature of the situation in Thessalonica.

*Place and Date of Writing.*—Though the motives for writing the letter are clear enough, it is not so easy to place it in its historical setting. Paul was anxious for news of the Thessalonians, whom he had visited only once (2:17), and he had apparently left Athens just at the time when he sent his friend Timothy to Thessalonica. This situation fits quite well with the events narrated in Acts 17:1–18:5: Paul had to flee from Thessalonica to Beroea and from there to Athens, after which he reached Corinth without his companions Silas and Timothy, who joined him soon after. Most scholars therefore think that the First Epistle to the Thessalonians was written in Corinth at some time after Paul's arrival there from Athens.

The objections to this view are that there was hardly time, so soon after Paul left Thessalonica, for several Christians to have died and for news of the Thessalonians' faith to have spread beyond Greece (4:13 and 1:8). The scholars who make these objections suggest that, as the polemic in 2:1 ff. is similar to that in the Epistles to the Corinthians, the First Epistle to the Thessalonians was probably written four years later, when Paul during his stay in Ephesus was in controversy with the Corinthians about the same problems. There is no a priori reason, however, against several deaths occurring in Thessalonica during a short space of time, and the reference to Paul's having for the first time received news from Thessalonica (3:6) cannot be reconciled with the theory that the epistle was written four years later. It is therefore more likely that the view of the majority of scholars is right: that I Thessalonians was written in Corinth, shortly after Paul first arrived there. According to the usual chronology, the date of the epistle would be A.D. 50 or 51.

**II Thessalonians.**—*Themes.*—After an introductory sentence (1:1–2) that is almost identical with that of I Thessalonians, Paul begins with thanksgivings that pass over into a description of God's retribution on their enemies (1:3–12). He then warns them not to be agitated by the rumour that he had said or written anything which implied that "the day of the Lord has come." He reminds them how he told them that before the Second Coming the "man of lawlessness" (*i.e.,* Antichrist) must appear and that this "son of perdition" is hindered from coming by "him who now restrains him" (2:1–12). But Christians know that they are called to salvation, and Paul is sure that God will guard the Thessalonians from evil (2:13–3:5). The epistle ends, like I Thessalonians, with various admonitions, including the necessity of work, and of shunning those who disobey Paul's commands on this point (3:6–16). The concluding benediction emphasizes that Paul's own hand wrote these last lines (3:17–18).

*Question of Authenticity.*—If I Thessalonians were no longer extant, no one would doubt the authenticity of II Thessalonians. Comparison of these two epistles, however, reveals far more similarity of content and wording than one would expect in two letters addressed in fairly quick succession to the same readers, and on the other hand a marked difference between them in eschatological teaching. In I Thessalonians Paul says that the day of the Lord will come quickly, yet in II Thessalonians he reminds them that Antichrist and his "restrainer" must come before the Lord can appear. The expectation of the eschatological events in I Thessalonians seems less complicated than that in II Thessalonians, so some scholars hold that II Thessalonians is spurious while others avoid some of the problems by supposing that the second letter was in fact written first or that it was originally addressed to another congregation or to a special group within the Thessalonian congregation.

The difficulties, however, are really not so great as they seem at first sight. The difference in eschatological ideas can be explained on the supposition that during the period that elapsed between the sending of the two letters an unsound eschatological excitement had developed in the congregation. One should also remember that Paul is merely reminding the Thessalonians of a doctrine—complementary to the ideas developed in I Thess. 4:13 ff.—which he taught when he was among them. If Paul wrote the second letter soon after the first one, it would be natural for them to be similar in content. It is therefore probable that II Thessalonians was the work of Paul, but as it gives no indication of date one is reduced to guesswork in suggesting that it may have been written not long after I Thessalonians and may also have originated in Corinth.

**Significance.**—The importance of these two epistles is twofold. They embody the theology of Paul in its earliest form and they indicate the difficulties created by the Christian message in pagan surroundings. Further, they help toward a fuller understanding of Paul's eschatological ideas and his adaptation of Jewish apocalyptic to Christian theology. *See* also BIBLE.

BIBLIOGRAPHY.—Eng. trans. with commentary by J. E. Frame (1912) in *International Critical Commentary;* by W. Neil (1950) in *Moffatt New Testament Commentary;* by L. Morris (1959) in *New London Commentary on the New Testament.* French trans. with commentary by B. Rigaux (1956) in *Études bibliques.* German trans. with commentary by M. Dibelius, 3rd ed. (1937), in *Handbuch zum Neuen Testament;* commentary by E. von Dobschütz (1909) in *Meyers Kommentar zum Neuen Testament.*

*See* also P. Feine, J. Behm, and W. G. Kümmel, *Einleitung in das Neue Testament,* 14th ed. (1965); W. Wrede, *Die Echtheit des 2. Thessalonicherbriefes* (1903), denying authenticity; J. Graafen, *Die Echtheit des 2. Briefes an die Thessalonicher* (1930), upholding authenticity; C. H. Faw, "On the Writing of First Thessalonians," *Journal of Biblical Literature,* 71:217–225 (1952). (W. G. KÜ.)

**THESSALY** (THESSALIA), a district of northern Greece, lies south of Macedonia, and between upland Epirus and the Aegean Sea. It forms an irregular square, about 60 mi. (about 100 km.) in each direction, and is encircled by natural boundaries: the Cambunian (Kamvounia) Mountains on the north, Othrys (Othris) on the south, and the chain of Pindus (Pindhos) on the west; at the northeastern angle is Olympus, separated by the gorge of Tempe from the coast range of Ossa and Pelion, which forms a continuous line to the southeast. It is drained by the numerous confluents of the Peneus (Pinios) River, which flows into the sea through Tempe, and is essentially an agricultural and pastoral district, its plains producing wheat, maize (corn), rice, cotton, and tobacco. It is divided into the *nomoi* of Kardhitsa, Larisa, Magnisia, and Trikkala. Area 5,395 sq.mi. (13,973 sq.km.); pop. (1961) 695,385.

Through Thessaly lie all land routes between peninsular Greece and the north. Xerxes entered it by the Petra Pass, which comes down west of Olympus into the plain north of Larissa. The route taken from Epirus by Julius Caesar before the Battle of Pharsalus (48 B.C.) passed over Mt. Lacmon to Aeginium (modern Kalabaka), in the northwestern angle, whence there is now a road via Metsovon to Ioannina. Another pass, farther south near Gomphi (mod. Gomfoi), leads through the "Gates of Trikkala" to Arta and the Ambracian Gulf. The great southern pass of Coela, followed by the modern highway, crosses Mt. Othrys nearly due north of Thermopylae. The main railway line from Athens to Salonika enters Thessaly by this pass, reaches Larissa, and makes its way through the gorge of Tempe and along the sea front of Olympus. Larissa is connected by rail with the port of Volos; and another line runs from Volos westward to Kardhitsa, Trikkala, and Kalabaka.

Though Thessaly is the most level district of Greece, it is divided by ranges of hills into two sections: that to the west and southwest, which is dominated by the town of Trikkala (*q.v.*), and that to the east, which centres on Larissa (*q.v.*). The ancient political divisions or "tetrads" followed the physical, Pelasgiotis being the lower plain of the Peneus, Histiaeotis and Thessaliotis respectively the north and south portions of the upper; the fourth, Phthiotis, the realm in legend of Achilles, lay to the southeast. The Gulf of Volos (*q.v.*) on the east is enclosed by the Magnesia peninsula, an extension of the chain of Pelion. The Argonauts (*q.v.*) set sail from this landlocked bay.

**History.**—The history of Thessaly is closely connected with its geography. The fertility of the land offered a temptation to invaders from the earliest times. It was the home of an extensive Neolithic culture deriving probably from Asia Minor or Syria, which was interrupted about 2500 B.C. by immigrants from the north who constructed fortified settlements, such as that at Dhimini near Volos. Thessaly remained at first rather on the fringe of the great Bronze Age civilization of Greece, although Mycenaean settlements have been discovered, *e.g.,* at Iolcus near Volos. Toward the end of the Mycenaean period, however, it was overrun by a new wave of invaders. The tribe of the Thessali, coming from Thesprotia in southern Epirus, entered the plain of Thessaliotis and imposed an aristocratic rule on the older inhabitants, who became their vassals or took to the surrounding hills. The rich lowlands were the natural home of baronial families such as the Aleuadae of Larissa and the Scopadae of Crannon, who organized a pan-Thessalian federation under an elected military chief (*tagos*), and controlled the Amphictyonic League of northern Greek states in the 6th century B.C. The plains were also suited to horse breeding, and consequently the Thessalians were strong in cavalry. But the isolation and the semi-Hellenic character of the people held them aloof from the main currents of Greek history in the classical period. At the time of the Persian Wars the Aleuadae joined the Persians; and the rivalries of the leading families promoted political instability. United, as under Jason of Pherae in the 4th century, the Thessalians were formidable, but they seldom combined for long and had little influence in Greece. After the 4th century they were usually Macedonian vassals, until liberated by the Romans and incorporated in the Roman province of Macedonia in 148 B.C.

Diocletian made Thessaly a separate province *c.* A.D. 300 with its capital at Larissa; and in the Byzantine Empire it was attached to the theme of Thessalonica. In the 7th century it was invaded by Slavs, and in the 9th its coasts were frequently raided by Arab pirates, who destroyed the port of Demetrias in 902. The Bulgars, who had attacked it in the 8th century, conquered it in the 10th. Byzantine rule was restored by Basil II, and was maintained by his successors (except for a brief Norman occupation at the end of the 11th century) until the Fourth Crusade (1204), when Thessaly was taken over, with Thessalonica, by Boniface of Montferrat. It was soon recovered by the Greek ruler of Epirus, Theodore Angelus, whose descendants held it until 1318 as an independent principality, with its capital in the south at Neopatras (Ipati), and maintained close ties with the French dukes of Athens and Thebes and with the Angevin claimants to the Morea. The settlement of nomad Wallachians or Vlachs from the Danube area had become so extensive by the 12th and 13th centuries that Thessaly came to be called Great Wallachia (*Megale Vlachia*); and there are still colonies of Vlach herdsmen in the surrounding hills, who come down into the Thessalian plains during the winter. In 1309 Thessaly was temporarily overrun by the Almogávares (*q.v.*); and in 1333 it reverted to the status of a Byzantine province, though dominated, as it had been in ancient times, by a few aristocratic families, such as the Melisseni and the Gabrielopouli, who had learned feudal manners from their French neighbours. In 1348 it was occupied by the armies of the Serbian Stephen Dushan, whose half-brother, Symeon Urosh, set up his capital at Trikkala. For a short period after 1381 it was again Greek, until its total conquest by the Turks in 1393, when Trikkala became the seat of the pasha of Thessaly. Most of the country was ceded to Greece by the Turks in 1881, the frontier being drawn a little to the north of Tempe; after the Balkan Wars of 1912–13 all of Thessaly passed into the kingdom of Greece. The area was fought over in the Greco-Turkish War of 1897, and again in World War II.

*See* also references to "Thessaly" in the Index.

BIBLIOGRAPHY.—W. M. Leake, *Travels in Northern Greece*, 4 vol. (1835); F. Stählin, *Das hellenische Thessalien* (1924); H. D. Westlake, *Thessaly in the Fourth Century B.C.* (1935); A. Philippson, *Die griechischen Landschaften*, vol. i, 1 (1950); G. Ostrogorsky, *History of the Byzantine State* (1956); D. M. Nicol, *Meteora: the Rock Monasteries of Thessaly* (1963). (D. M. N.)

**THETFORD,** a municipal borough in the South Norfolk parliamentary division of Norfolk, Eng., 29½ mi. (47.5 km.) WSW of Norwich by road. It is the centre for the Breckland and is on the edge of Thetford Chase Forest. Pop. (1961) 5,399. In the time of Edward III there were 20 churches and 8 religious houses, but now there are only 3 parish churches and the remains of a Cluniac priory (excavated by the Ministry of Works) and a Benedictine nunnery. Castle Hill, a large medieval motte, is 80 ft. high. Excavations have revealed traces of a Saxon town of about 4,000 inhabitants with considerable industry and a mint. The grammar school has a record of headmasters from 1114, and may be mentioned in the Anglo-Saxon Chronicle as existing in 631. It was refounded in 1567 by Sir Richard Fulmerstone. King's House, used by Elizabeth I and James I and reputed to stand on the site of the palace of William the Conqueror's son-in-law, was bequeathed to the corporation in 1946, and serves as municipal offices. There have been mayors since 1272, and the town is now governed under a charter of 1573. The borough regalia is fine and interesting. Thomas Paine, the reformer, was born there in 1737 and attended the grammar school. Industries include paper-pulp manufacturing, canning, coffee milling, and light engineering.

*See* T. Martin, *The History of the Town of Thetford* (London, 1779); A. L. Hunt, *The Capital of the Ancient Kingdom of East Anglia* (London, 1870).

**THETFORD MINES,** a city of Quebec, Can., 55 mi. (89 km.) S of Quebec City, famous for asbestos deposits discovered there in 1876; they produce more than half of the world's asbestos supply. The community, first known as Kingsville after one of the owners of the first mine, was later renamed for Thetford, Eng. It became a village in 1892, a town in 1905, and a city in 1912. Pop. (1961) 21,618.

On a picturesque slope, Thetford Mines soon found that the profitable mining operations had some unpleasant aspects: clouds of dust from the open-pit mining saturated the city; dreaded respiratory ailments occurred among the miners; and mountains of slag hemmed the city in on three sides. The asbestosis and silicosis were almost eliminated, and in the 1950s an entire housing district was moved and slag heaps were torn down in an effort to prevent the strangling of the city. (J. P. LE.)

**THIAZINES** are organic compounds, of which some of the more complex derivatives are of importance in the manufacture of dyestuffs. They have the molecular formula $C_4H_5NS$, to which six-membered heterocyclic ring structures have been assigned.

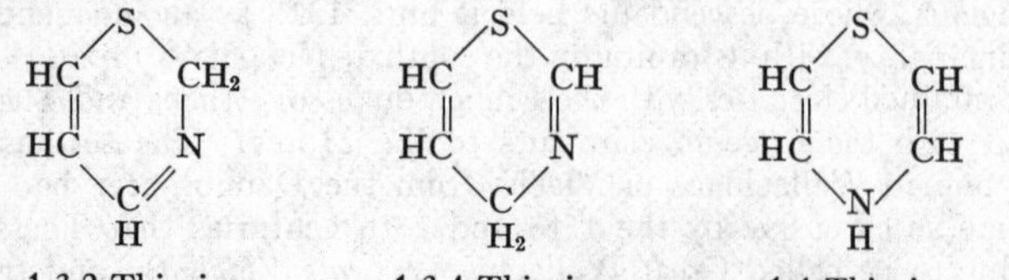

[Structures: ring of S, HC, CH₂, N, C(H), HC — 1,3,2-Thiazine; ring of S, HC, CH, N, C(H₂), HC — 1,3,4-Thiazine; ring of S, HC, CH, CH, N(H), HC — 1,4-Thiazine]

1,3,2-Thiazine 1,3,4-Thiazine 1,4-Thiazine

The thiazines themselves and their simpler derivatives are of little practical importance or theoretical interest. The so-called thiazine dyes are phenazothionium salts and may, therefore, be regarded as derivatives of phenothiazine (2,3,5,6-dibenzo-1,4-thiazine).

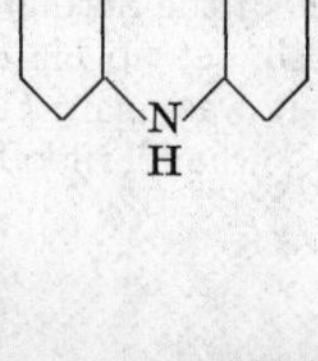

[Structure: phenothiazine — two benzene rings joined through S and NH]

The simplest of the thiazine dyes is Lauth's violet (I); probably the most important is methylene blue (II).

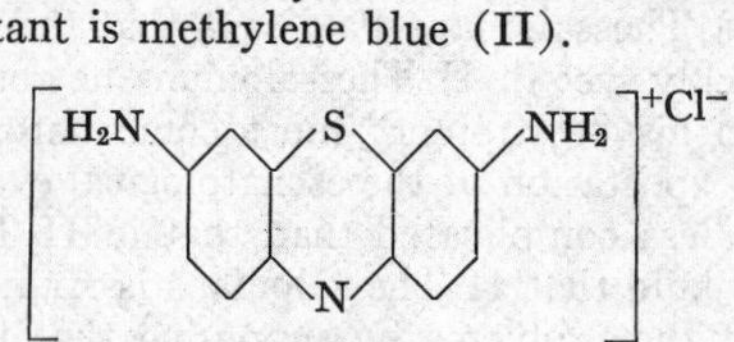

[Structure I: $[H_2N$–(phenothiazinium ring, S, N)–$NH_2]^+Cl^-$]

I

[Structure II: $[(CH_3)_2N$–(phenothiazinium ring, S, N)–$N(CH_3)_2]^+Cl^-$]

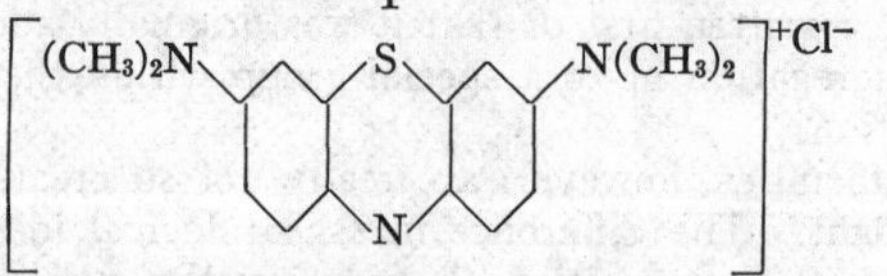

II

The skeletal structure of the thiazine dyes was elucidated by August Bernthsen in 1887, although methylene blue was discovered in 1876 by Heinrich Caro. (P. H. O. R.; X.)

**THIAZOLES** are a class of organic compounds, some of which are notably versatile in synthetic reactions; in their own right they are important as cotton dyes. Thiazoles contain a five-membered ring of one nitrogen, one sulfur and three carbon atoms which are connected by three single and two double bonds in the following order:

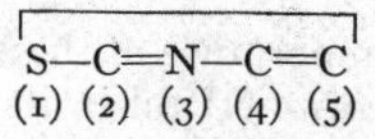

$$\text{S—C=N—C=C (ring closed S to C5)}$$
(1) (2) (3) (4) (5)

The earliest synthesis of a compound of this type was effected in 1874, by the action of hydrogen sulfide on potassium cyanide; however, the constitution of this product remained long in doubt and was rigorously established, as 5-amino-2-thiocarbamylthiazole, only in 1947.

Thiazoles, as a class, were discovered in 1887 by Arthur Hantzsch, who then systematically explored their chemical characteristics. They are most conveniently prepared by the condensation of $\alpha$-halogenated aldehydes or ketones with thioamides:

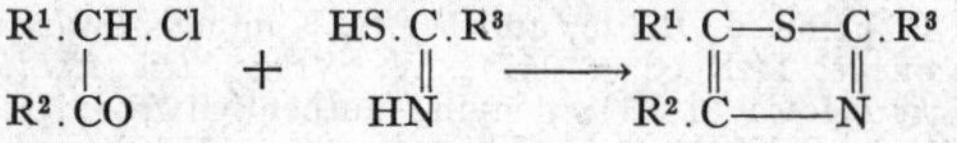

$$\begin{matrix} R^1.CH.Cl \\ | \\ R^2.CO \end{matrix} + \begin{matrix} HS.C.R^3 \\ \| \\ HN \end{matrix} \longrightarrow \begin{matrix} R^1.C—S—C.R^3 \\ \| \quad\quad \| \\ R^2.C——N \end{matrix}$$

The parent thiazole, in which $R^1$, $R^2$ and $R^3$ represent hydrogen atoms, is a colourless liquid that boils at 117° C. and exhibits weakly basic properties like those of pyridine; the homologous thiazoles display similar properties.

The 2-aminothiazoles, in which $R^3$ represents the amino group, are formed in an analogous reaction from thiourea; the sulfanilyl derivative, in which $R^1 = R^2 = H$ and $R^3 = NH.SO_2.C_6H_4.NH_2$, is the synthetic antibiotic drug sulfathiazole.

The 2-hydroxythiazoles, in which $R^3 = OH$, are produced by the action of alkali upon $\alpha$-thiocyanoketones:

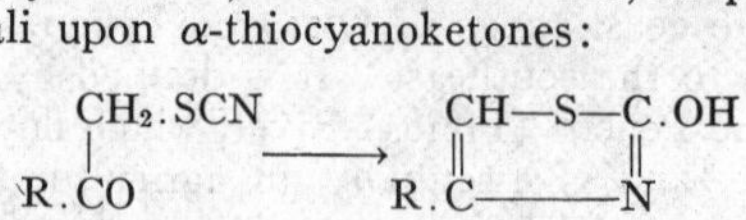

$$\begin{matrix} CH_2.SCN \\ | \\ R.CO \end{matrix} \longrightarrow \begin{matrix} CH—S—C.OH \\ \| \quad\quad \| \\ R.C——N \end{matrix}$$

The corresponding 2-mercaptothiazoles ($R^3 = SH$), formed by the interaction of $\alpha$-halogenated ketones with ammonium dithiocarbamate, find industrial use as accelerators in the vulcanization of rubber.

The 5-aminothiazoles ($R^1 = NH_2$) have been prepared by treating $\alpha$-amino nitriles with carbon disulfide and then removing the sulfydryl group (at position 2) from the product by the action of Raney nickel catalyst:

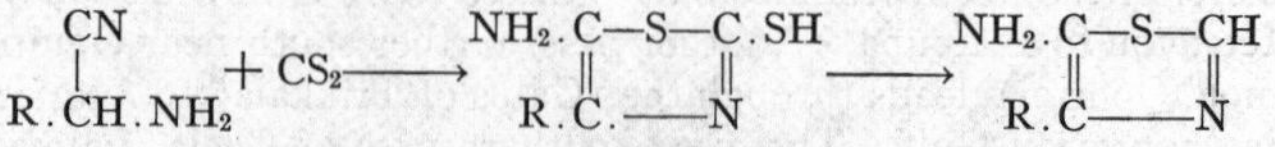

$$\begin{matrix} CN \\ | \\ R.CH.NH_2 \end{matrix} + CS_2 \longrightarrow \begin{matrix} NH_2.C—S—C.SH \\ \| \quad\quad \| \\ R.C——N \end{matrix} \longrightarrow \begin{matrix} NH_2.C—S—CH \\ \| \quad\quad \| \\ R.C——N \end{matrix}$$

Dihydrothiazoles, or thiazolines, have been prepared by the action of ethylene dibromide upon thioamides:

$$\begin{matrix} CH_2Br \\ | \\ CH_2Br \end{matrix} + \begin{matrix} HS.C.R \\ \| \\ NH \end{matrix} \longrightarrow \begin{matrix} CH_2—S—C.R \\ | \quad\quad \| \\ CH_2——N \end{matrix}$$

or, less conveniently, from acid chlorides or anhydrides and β-amino thiols.

Tetrahydrothiazoles, or thiazolidines, are formed by the interaction of aldehydes or ketones with β-amino thiols:

$$\begin{matrix} CH_2.SH \\ | \\ CH_2.NH_2 \end{matrix} + R.CHO \longrightarrow \begin{matrix} CH_2-S-CH.R \\ | \qquad\quad | \\ CH_2——NH \end{matrix}$$

In 1935 and the subsequent two decades the thiazole group and its hydro analogues were shown to occur in natural products: thiamine (vitamin $B_1$) contains a thiazole nucleus, the penicillins are derivatives of thiazolidine and there are indications that the thiazoline ring may be present in the antibiotic bacitracin.

*See* Sir Ian Heilbron, *J. Chem. Soc.* 2099 (1949); Roger Adams *et al.* (eds.), *Organic Reactions,* vol. 6, ch. 8 (1949–51). (H. T. C.)

**THIBAUT IV** (1201–1253), count of Champagne and Brie, and king (as Tibald I) of Navarre from 1234, was the most famous of the aristocratic *trouvères* (*q.v.*), thrice cited by Dante in his *De vulgari eloquentia.* He was born at Troyes in 1201, probably on May 30, the posthumous son of Thibaut III and Blanche of Navarre, and lived for four years at the court of Philip II (Philip Augustus), to whom he did homage in 1214. He deserted Philip's son Louis VIII at the siege of Avignon in the late summer of 1226. On Louis' death a few months later, he joined the dissident baronial league which opposed the new queen mother, Blanche of Castile, but soon abandoned it and became reconciled with Blanche. It was rumoured that he was her lover and had poisoned her husband, and many of his poems are thought to be addressed to her. As leader of the Crusade of 1239 he won back Beaufort, Safed (Safad), and Ascalon for the Christians. After his return he spent the rest of his life in Champagne and in his kingdom of Navarre, where he died at Pamplona in 1253, probably on July 7.

Thibaut left about 60 lyrics, mainly lovesongs and debates in verse, with two *pastourelles* (lovesongs between knight and shepherdess), and nine religious poems. His verse now seems conventional; only occasionally, as in the heptasyllabics of no. 17 in Wallensköld's edition ("The hind is up and away/And she is white as the snow/And both the braids of her hair/Are brighter than Spanish gold"), does it convey a genuine mood of urgency. Perhaps he finds his true level in the *jeu-parti* (courtly love-debate) in which he discusses with a crusading crony, Raoul de Soissons, whether it is better to embrace one's love in the dark or to see her without embracing her, with wry allusions to Thibaut's potbelly and Raoul's crutch (no. 43). Thibaut's reputation is due to the fortunate survival of his lyrics, with their music, in six manuscripts (*K, M, O, T, V,* and *X*), of which three have been published in facsimile (see *Bibliography*).

Bibliography.—The standard edition of Thibaut's *chansons* is *Les Chansons de Thibaut de Champagne, roi de Navarre,* ed. by A. Wallensköld, for the Société des anciens textes français (1925). Earlier editions were published by L. A. Levesque de La Ravalière (1742), and P. Tarbé (1851). The facsimiles appear in *Le Chansonnier de l'Arsenal* (*ms. K*), ed. by P. Aubry and A. Jeanroy (1908 ff.); *Le Manuscrit du Roi* (*ms. M*), ed. by J. B. and L. Beck (1938); and *Le Chansonnier Cangé* (*ms. O*), ed. by J. B. Beck in *Les Chansonniers des troubadours et des trouvères* (1927). *See* also M. Roques, "Le Chansonnier français de Zagreb," in *Mélanges . . . offerts à M. Alfred Jeanroy* (1928); S. Runciman, *A History of the Crusades,* vol. iii, pp. 212–217 (1954); F. Gennrich, *Altfranzösische Lieder,* 2 vol. (1955–56), *Exempla altfranzösischer Lyrik: 40 altfranzösische Lieder* (1958); His Master's Voice Records, *The History of Music in Sound,* vol. ii, side 2 (1957). (C. A. Rn.)

**THIBAUT, ANTON FRIEDRICH JUSTUS** (1772–1840), German jurist and leader of the philosophical school which maintained the tradition of natural law in a spirit of moderate rationalism. He is remembered chiefly because his demand for the codification of German law provoked F. K. von Savigny's famous retort "On the Calling of Our Time for Legislation," in which the leading ideas of the historical school of law were formulated. Thibaut was born at Hameln, Ger., on Jan. 4, 1772. He studied law at Göttingen, Königsberg, and Kiel, where, in 1796, he qualified as teacher of law. He was appointed professor of civil law at Kiel in 1798, then at Jena in 1802, and at Heidelberg in 1806. In 1834 he became a member of the court of arbitration of the German Confederation. He died in Heidelberg on March 28, 1840.

His principal publications are *Theorie der logischen Auslegung des römischen Rechts* ("Theory of the Logical Interpretation of Roman Law," 1799) and *System des Pandektenrechts* (1803; the general part translated as *An Introduction to the Study of Jurisprudence,* 1879), which remained for some time one of the leading textbooks of Roman law applied as the common law of Germany. In 1814 he published an essay "On the Need for a Civil Code for Germany," which was inspired by patriotic sentiment and by rationalist belief in the merits of codification. Thibaut was also a serious student of music and wrote *Über Reinheit der Tonkunst* (1825; trans. *On Purity in Musical Art,* 1877).

Bibliography.—E. Baumstark, *A. F. J. Thibaut, Blätter der Erinnerung* (1841); E. Landsberg in *Allgemeine Deutsche Biographie,* vol. 37 (1894); J. Stern, *Thibaut und Savigny* (1914); E. Wohlhaupter, *Dichterjuristen,* vol. 1 (1953). (J. U.)

**THIERRY** of Chartres (d. *c.* 1150), in Latin called Theodoricus or Terricus Carnotensis, French encyclopaedist, philosopher, and theologian, was a brother of Bernard of Chartres. He taught in Paris and at Chartres, where he became chancellor in 1141, having among his pupils John of Salisbury and possibly Abelard. His unpublished *Heptateuchon* (preserved in microfilms at Oxford, at Toronto, at Chartres, etc.) contains the "classics" of the seven liberal arts (works by Aelius Donatus and Priscian for grammar, by Cicero and Martianus Capella for rhetoric, by Aristotle and Porphyry for logic, etc.). His cosmology, mainly expounded in his commentary on *Genesis,* makes an attempt to harmonize Scripture with Platonic and other physical or metaphysical doctrines. He was among the first to promote in the Latin west the knowledge of science as professed by the Arabians. (L. M.-Po.)

**THIERRY, (JACQUES NICOLAS) AUGUSTIN** (1795–1856), French historian whose discursive method of presenting history in picturesque and dramatic terms makes him one of the outstanding Romantic historians. Born at Blois on May 10, 1795, he was educated there and at the École Normale in Paris, where he first met Saint-Simon (*q.v.*). He was fired with Saint-Simon's ideal society of the future, becoming his secretary in 1814 and always calling himself the "adopted son" of the visionary. But, while most of Saint-Simon's followers turned their attention to practical matters, Thierry turned to history.

As a professional historian he was influenced particularly by the works of Sir Walter Scott, and, though he himself wrote no romances, his conception of history fully recognized the dramatic element. He was also greatly impressed by *Les Martyrs* (1809), the prose epic in which Chateaubriand contrasts the two civilizations (pagan and Christian) and two peoples (Greek and Roman) from which the modern world has sprung. His main subjects are the Germanic invasions, the Norman Conquest, the formation of the medieval communes, the gradual ascent of the nations toward free government, and parliamentary institutions.

His first articles, which appeared in *Le Censeur européen* and *Le Courrier français* (1817 *et seq.*), he published under the title of *Dix Ans d'études historiques* (1834). From Claude Fauriel (*q.v.*) he learned to consult original sources; and in writing his most original and ambitious work, *L'Histoire de la conquête de l'Angleterre par les Normands* (three volumes, 1825; English translation, 1825), he made use of Latin chronicles and Anglo-Saxon laws. This work cost Thierry his eyesight. He was obliged to engage secretaries, and in 1830 he became totally blind. In 1827 he republished his *Lettres sur l'histoire de France* (first published, 1820), with the addition of 15 new letters, in which he describes some of the more striking episodes in the history of the rise of the communes. His *Récits des Temps mérovingiens,* in which he reproduces in a vivid form some of the most characteristic stories of Saint Gregory of Tours, appeared between 1835 and 1837 in the *Revue des deux Mondes;* when collected in two volumes in 1840, they were preceded by several interesting *Considérations sur l'Histoire de France.* In 1841 the French Academy awarded him the first Prix Gobert, a prize bestowed on him for the next 15 years.

An ardent supporter of the revolution of July 1830 and of the triumph of liberal ideas, Thierry was always interested in the destiny of the third estate, as is evident from the large *Recueil des monuments inédits de l'histoire du Tiers État* (four volumes, 1850–70), which he compiled with the help of zealous collaborators. He died in Paris on May 22, 1856.

*See* A. Augustin-Thierry, *Augustin Thierry* (1922); K. J. Carroll, *Some Aspects of the Historical Thought of Augustin Thierry* (1951).

**THIERS, LOUIS ADOLPHE** (1797–1877), French statesman, journalist, and historian, an outstanding figure in French politics from 1830 to 1877, was twice premier under Louis Philippe and head of the executive from 1871 to 1873 during the Third Republic. He was born at Marseilles on April 18, 1797. His father married his mother on May 13 and deserted her four months later. Thiers was educated by the financial help of friends and relatives and won a scholarship to the *lycée* of Marseilles, which now bears his name. He was later a student at the law faculty at Aix-en-Provence, where he met his lifelong friend, the historian François Mignet. After he was called to the bar in 1818, his very small practice gave him ample opportunities to pursue historical studies. In September 1821 he went to Paris, where the Liberal deputy of Basses-Alpes, Jacques Manuel, introduced him to the world of journalism, and Thiers became a regular contributor to the *Constitutionnel,* the most influential newspaper of that period. At the same time he was a correspondent for the *Allgemeine Zeitung,* published by Freiherr Cotta von Cottendorf, and he also began to collect documents for his *Histoire de la révolution française,* which appeared in 10 volumes between 1823 and 1827. In 1822, just prior to the French intervention in Spain to suppress the revolutionary government there, he traveled in southern France and on the Pyrenean border. He was almost the only Liberal to predict the success of the absolutists in Spain, and thus enhanced his reputation.

ARCHIVES PHOTOGRAPHIQUES, PARIS

THIERS, DETAIL FROM A PORTRAIT BY LÉON BONNAT, 1876; IN THE LOUVRE

**The July Monarchy.**—In January 1830, together with Armand Carrel and Mignet, and probably with Talleyrand's support, he founded a new opposition newspaper, the *National,* which almost openly advocated a change of dynasty to forestall any attempts of Charles X to circumscribe public liberties. Thiers was the first signatory of the journalists' protest which immediately followed the publication of the ordinances of July 26, 1830, by which Charles aimed to control the Chamber. During the revolution of July 27–29 which overthrew Charles, he took refuge in a southern suburb of Paris and returned on the 29th to win support for Louis Philippe, duc d'Orléans. He was rewarded by being made a member of the council of state, was elected to the Chamber as a deputy for Aix (a seat he held until 1848), and in November 1830 became undersecretary of state for the treasury.

He was successively minister of the interior (1832), minister of trade and public works (1833–34), and of the interior again (1834–36), and during these years he was the most notable representative of the Party of Resistance (moderates). He efficiently and mercilessly crushed all insurrections against Louis Philippe's regime, in particular those of the Legitimists under the duchesse de Berry in 1832 and of the Republicans in 1834. Premier and minister of foreign affairs (February–August 1836, and March–October 1840), in his second term of office his adventurous foreign policy in support of Mohammed Ali during the Egyptian crisis (*see* EASTERN QUESTION) almost led to war with Great Britain. Forced to resign by Louis Philippe's determination not to go to war, Thiers still remained one of the leaders of the Resistance, but he weakened its cause by his personal opposition to François Guizot (*q.v.*). He now traveled in Europe, gathering material for his *Histoire de consulat et de l'empire,* which was published in 20 volumes between 1845 and 1862. He consulted the most important living witnesses of the period, though these were not always satisfied with the interpretation he placed upon their evidence. Meanwhile, with his father-in-law Alexis Dosne, a stockbroker and businessman, Thiers made many profitable speculations as a result of information he received through his close relations with those in power. He thus became one of the great property owners in Paris.

**The Second Republic.**—On the morning of Feb. 24, 1848, in the midst of the Revolution, Louis Philippe called on Thiers to form another ministry; but by then it was too late and the king abdicated that same afternoon. During the Second Republic (1848–52), Thiers was defeated (April 1848) in his old seat for Aix in the *département* of Bouches-du-Rhône by the influence of the young commissary-general Émile Ollivier, whom he was later to attack with much bitterness in parliament at the end of the Second Empire. However, in June Thiers was elected to the Constituent Assembly for several other *départements,* choosing to sit for Seine Inférieure, and immediately became one of the most influential leaders of the Conservatives, the champions of order. As such he was responsible for the choice of Prince Louis Napoleon (afterward Napoleon III) as a candidate for the presidency of the Republic (December 1848). In both the Constituent and Legislative Assemblies Thiers voted for the reactionary laws which weakened the Republic and which contributed to the growing differences between himself and the president. When Louis Napoleon carried out his *coup d'état* of Dec. 2, 1851, Thiers was arrested and exiled. He was allowed to return to France in 1853.

**The Second Empire.**—For ten years Thiers lived a retired life, supporting the Orléanist opposition and also plotting principally with those Catholic elements who were alarmed by Napoleon III's foreign policy in Italy (*see* ITALY: *History*). In 1863 he was elected deputy for the Seine and thereafter took an important part in the parliamentary debates, attacking the government's financial and political policies. He was particularly vehement in denouncing anything detrimental to French prestige, and did much to arouse in his countrymen a nationalistic and militarist frame of mind. This attitude finally forced Ollivier's ministry into its quarrel with Prussia in July 1870 over the candidature of Prince Leopold of Hohenzollern-Sigmaringen to the Spanish throne (*see* FRANCO-GERMAN WAR), although much needed army reforms in France had not been carried out. During the crisis, however, Thiers changed his views and became an opponent of the aggressive policy he had previously advocated. This reversal stood him in good stead after the French defeat (September 1870), for his friends were able to present him as one who had regretted the French diplomatic ineptitude and had known that French military preparations were inadequate.

**President of the Third Republic.**—Instead of taking his place on the government of national defense, set up in Paris on Sept. 4 after Napoleon's surrender at Sedan, Thiers traveled throughout Europe in search of a mediator, but found that no government was prepared to offer help to the representative of a purely provisional government. He thus had no responsibility for the organization of defense, nor for the final French surrender in January 1871. In February 1871 he was elected simultaneously to 26 *départements* and on Feb. 17 became "chief of the executive power of the French Republic." Together with Jules Favre he then negotiated with Otto von Bismarck the peace treaty that was finally signed at Frankfurt on May 10. Thiers's well-known sayings "The Republic will be Conservative or will fail" and "The Republic is the system of government that divides us the least" are perhaps the best definitions of his political beliefs at this time, for he was confronted by three "monarchist" parties, the Legitimists, Orléanists, and Bonapartists, who were all anxious to prevent each other's success.

One of Thiers's first tasks was to preserve the social order. On the outbreak of the Paris insurrection known as the Commune of Paris (*q.v.*) on March 18, 1871, Thiers put into operation a plan he had prepared at the time of the 1848 Revolution, withdrawing all regular troops from the city. He then negotiated with Bismarck for the return of the Imperial regiments captured in eastern France. With these troops he laid siege to Paris on the western and southern sides of the town, while the Germans kept watch on the other fortifications. The fall of the Commune during "La semaine sanglante" (the bloody week) of May 21–28, 1871, destroyed for many years the strength of the socialists and of the workers' movements, both in Paris and in France as a whole. But even this success failed to win for Thiers the approbation of the Legitimists, who could never forget his responsibility for the arrest of the duchesse de Berry in 1832. Their hostility was further increased by Thiers's personal popularity, sedulously fostered by efficient propaganda.

In these circumstances Thiers was compelled to seek support in the National Assembly from the deputies of the Left and he succeeded by presenting himself as the symbol of the Republic against monarchists of all kinds. In August 1871 he was given the title "president of the French Republic." He had to rearrange his cabinet practically every year, and eventually fell back on older politicians of the July Monarchy, such as Charles, comte de Rémusat, and prominent businessmen, such as the financier Augustin Pouyer-Quertier.

Thiers was able to give ample proof of his ability in his skilful management of the relations between the "president of the executive" and the Assembly. He was also responsible for the military law of 1872 which overhauled the military system but failed to modernize the army. No provision was made for the organization of the reserves and the introduction of a period of service for five years (not revised until 1889), by withdrawing manpower, weakened the French economy at a time when the industrial development of other countries was increasing rapidly. In March 1873 he signed an agreement with Germany for the recall of its troops, the French indemnity having, by Thiers's good financial management, been paid off two years earlier than Bismarck had envisaged, but on May 24, 1873, he was defeated in the Assembly by the forces of the Right and resigned.

Thiers immediately took an important part in the republican opposition in the mainly royalist Assembly. He was one of the 363 deputies who passed a vote of no confidence in the duc de Broglie's ministry in June 1877 and he managed to reconcile the different republican groups for the coming election. Thiers died suddenly at Saint-Germain-en-Laye (Seine-et-Oise) on Sept. 3, 1877, while preparing an election manifesto.

Thiers probably achieved greater power and wealth than any French politician of his time, but his ability was not greatly appreciated even by those, such as Louis Philippe, whom he served. As a journalist he had a definite, though limited influence; as a historian his works were praised or condemned according to the political views of his critics, but nevertheless they made a notable contribution to the Napoleonic legend and to the growth of nationalism in France. Of himself, Thiers successfully promoted the image of an old, shrewd, and wise patriot, which was accepted by moderate republicans during the first 20 years of the Third Republic.

Besides his historical writings, Thiers's works included *Les Pyrénées et le Midi de la France . . . 1822* (1823); *Law et son système de finances* (1826), and *La monarchie de 1830* (1831). His *Discours parlementaires* were published in 16 volumes from 1879 to 1883.

BIBLIOGRAPHY.—H. Malo, *Thiers* (1932); J. Lucas-Dubreton, *Aspects de Monsieur Thiers* (1948); S. Dosne (Thiers's mother-in-law), *Mémoires,* 2 vol. (1928); D. Halévy, *Le Courrier de M. Thiers* (1921); R. Marquant, *Thiers et le baron Cotta* (1959); R. L. Dreyfus, *La République de M. Thiers* (1930). (JE. V.)

**THINKING AND PROBLEM SOLVING.** Problem solving is one kind of thinking that has been studied quite frequently. The term thinking has many definitions, no one of which is satisfactory to everyone. Traditionally limited to an activity of human beings, the word implies an inner, more or less rational process (distinguished from other subjective activities, such as perceiving or recalling). Since thinking normally is considered to be a private activity, many observers say they are confident only that other people behave *as if* they were thinking. (It is also common to see pet dogs treated as if they were thinking.) However, the effectiveness with which an organism handles information sometimes can be observed directly by others. For objective study, therefore, thinking is treated by inference, being defined through evidence that the presumptive thinker has processed old data to yield information that is new to him.

When a person thinks, he processes information he already has learned and obtains a result that in some sense is new. Suppose, for example, he is asked to give the numerical value of the seventh power of five. After having multiplied $5 \times 5 \times 5 \times 5 \times 5 \times 5 \times 5$ he may give the answer: 78,125. An appropriate operation—in this case, multiplication—apparently was carried out to obtain new information. Of course, if he had learned this specific result earlier, he would have been remembering rather than thinking as defined here.

Some define thinking as nothing more than learning or remembering. The view taken here is that one learns items of information and the operations employed in processing them; but the processing (or thinking) itself should be distinguished from learning at least provisionally.

Thinking involves simpler operations such as matching two items, such complex mathematical processes as integration, as well as many that are less rigorously logical. These processes vary from one thinker to another and from one problem to another. Imagine the differences that exist among processes involved in choosing moves in chess, in composing music, and in diagnosing appendicitis.

Thinking, as here defined, includes problem solving, decision making, creative thinking, and even dreaming. Since more is known about problem solving than about any of the other types of thinking, it will be the primary subject of this discussion. A problem exists whenever an individual seeks a means to any end. In solving the problem, a person processes information he already has or that he can obtain from the environment.

Experimental studies of problem solving are concerned primarily with what goes on as an individual reaches a goal, and with how achievement in problem solving can be varied experimentally; *e.g.,* how the number of problems solved by a group in a given time varies with the size of the group. Achievement in problem solving has also been studied in terms of its correlation with such variables as general intelligence.

**Introspection.**—Systematic experiments on thinking (early 20th century) were of the introspective type. Thinking was conceived as a conscious process directly open to the introspection (*q.v.*) of the thinker. The experimental method was to ask people to describe their experience promptly as they tried to solve assigned problems.

The results of this straightforward and apparently obvious procedure cast doubt on the then common assumption that consciousness is a composition of what were called simple sensations, images, and feelings. The subjects, to be sure, mentioned such sensory or emotional contents; but most subjects far more prominently described experiences that they felt were unanalyzable into elementary sensations, images, and feelings. Among these were attitudes such as doubt, hesitation, or sudden illumination; and "imageless thoughts," noted simply as thoughts *of* or thoughts *about,* reported as having little or no sensory or imaginal content. Furthermore, such conscious occurrences seemed to the subjects often to be totally absent at critical turning points in their thinking, the solution of a problem appearing to have been made below the level of awareness (*see* ASSOCIATION, MENTAL).

These results were obtained independently by a group of men inspired largely by O. Külpe at the University of Würzburg in Germany (1901–07), by A. Binet in France (1903), and by R. S. Woodworth in the U.S. (1906). They indicated that thinking is neither completely nor faithfully mirrored in consciousness—that important aspects of the process are outside the range of introspective observation. Moreover, since disagreements between introspecting subjects could not be settled by an appeal to facts some psychologists held it necessary to discard introspection in all psychological research. To others, perhaps to most, the conclusion was that the possibilities of introspection had been greatly overestimated; but that within limits it may be useful, especially when combined with other methods.

**Implicit Muscular Activities.**—John B. Watson (*see* BEHAVIOURISM) led those who proposed to discard from psychology all reference to consciousness. Watson treated thinking as consisting of slight muscular movements, especially though not exclusively those involved in speaking. His view that thinking is implicit speaking led to attempts by others to record such movements with mechanical lever systems. These attempts were largely inconclusive, partly because the recording systems employed were too crude.

Electrical systems subsequently were used for more sensitive indication of muscular activity. Electrodes placed near a muscle will pick up minute but measurable changes in potential. With a vacuum tube amplifier, potential changes as small as one millionth of a volt were recorded on photographic film. L. E. Jacobson (1929–32) had subjects carry out tasks involving thinking while action currents from appropriate muscles were recorded. For example, subjects were instructed to imagine bending the right arm. Action currents were obtained from the right arm while the subjects were imagining this act, but not while they were imagining bending the left arm or while they were relaxing. Electrodes were attached to the tongue and lips while subjects imagined counting, telling the date, and so forth. The records of action currents were similar to those obtained when subjects were faintly speaking the same words or numbers. L. W. Max (1934–37) studied deaf-mutes, who normally use gesture language. When they were given problems to solve, action currents from the muscles of the fingers were found to be much larger and more frequent than those from normal subjects under the same conditions. During sleep, two- or three-minute bursts of activity were recorded from the same muscles in deaf-mutes. When awakened during such bursts, these subjects often reported that they had been dreaming; when awakened in the absence of such bursts, they were much less likely to report that they had been dreaming.

**Peripheral *v.* Central Theory.**—These results have been interpreted by some to support a peripheral theory of thinking. According to central theories, all activities necessary and sufficient for thinking occur in the brain. Peripheral theories, however, hold that implicit muscular activities together with perceptual changes to which they give rise form the necessary and sufficient condition, the brain simply mediating awareness of implicit movements. Most modern psychologists accept interpretations of implicit muscular activity that are consistent with central theory. Such movements are held to result from an overflow of central nervous activity as a by-product of thinking; or these movements are thought to reinforce central neural activity associated with thinking. Although brain-wave changes can be observed in people who say they are thinking (*see* ELECTROENCEPHALOGRAPHY), they cannot be used to indicate what a person thinks.

**Trial and Error.**—C. Lloyd Morgan (1894) questioned the widely accepted view that nonhuman animals can reason. Morgan held, for example, that his fox terrier learned to open a gate by raising the latch with his muzzle through trial and error: gradual elimination of errors and strengthening of the correct response through repetition. In a typical experiment by E. L. Thorndike (1898, 1911), a cat in a box was allowed to escape by making the correct response of pressing a lever, pulling a string, licking itself, and so on. His results led Thorndike to conclude that the animals showed only behaviour involving trial and error.

H. A. Ruger (1910) studied intelligent and educated adults working on complicated mechanical puzzles; he followed essentially the same procedures as Thorndike, supplemented with introspective reports from his subjects. Ruger reported a large amount of trial and error behaviour. He noted that many unsuccessful reactions often were retained after they proved to be useless; successful procedures often appeared without foresight and even without attracting the subject's notice; puzzles often were solved with little or no comprehension of principles. However, some of these people showed sudden improvement that coincided in most cases with introspective reports that the subject had seen the point of the puzzle.

**Insight.**—Emphasis on trial and error in problem solving was criticized by Gestalt psychologists, who stressed insight. W. Köhler (1925) contended that Thorndike had artificially produced trial and error by selecting inappropriate problems. Thorndike's cats, for example, had to push levers, a normally uncatlike response that could be hit on only by chance. Köhler presented apes with problems in which elements necessary for solution were available and which required typically apelike responses. Though he reported considerable trial and error, Köhler stressed that the critical moment in the solution occurred when the ape seemed to grasp an appropriate relation; for example, when he saw a box he could climb to reach fruit suspended beyond his reach. Another ape was reported to have inserted one stick into another, insightfully using the tool to retrieve food that was too far from his cage to reach otherwise.

Max Wertheimer used the notion of insight to account for how (1945) Albert Einstein developed his theory of relativity. In a series of leisurely conversations Einstein described to Wertheimer successive partial insights that led him to think of the velocity of light as an invariant.

Modern Gestalt theory with respect to problem solving and thinking may be considered in terms of conscious experience or in terms of underlying brain processes. When a person is confronted with a problem, perceptual processes in the brain (and in consciousness) are held to interact with each other and with memory traces to result initially in "seeing the problem." This is said to set up stresses in the psychological field that lead to its reorganization, enabling the person to perceive the relations that solve the problem. Such reorganization tends to occur suddenly, although a series of progressive reorganizations may give the appearance of gradual solution (*see* GESTALT PSYCHOLOGY).

**Modern Behaviouristic Approach.**—Modern behaviourism, stemming from the work of Clark L. Hull (1943), approaches thinking through a complex system of notions that can only be suggested here. It is stated that any stimulus situation will be associated with a number of responses that differ in their probability of occurrence and hence form a hierarchy. The position of any response in this habit-family hierarchy will vary with how effectively it has been reinforced previously in similar situations (*see* LEARNING). Given a new problem, the hierarchy will determine the responses and the order of their occurrence. According to the notion of goal gradient, the closer (in distance or time) an organism is to a goal, the stronger its motivation will be; it will tend to choose the shorter of two paths. The ideas of goal gradient and of habit-family hierarchy suggest that the probability of a roundabout path being taken in solving a problem will vary inversely with the angle between the direct and roundabout paths. An organism that learns to make a given response to one stimulus will become increasingly likely to make the same response to similar stimuli (stimulus generalization). The probability of the response will vary directly with the similarity of the new to the original stimulus. Thus, a person with no screwdriver may readily use a fingernail file to tighten a screw; to pound a nail with no hammer he may exhibit much more trial and error before using the leather heel of his shoe.

**From Trial and Error to Insight.**—Harry F. Harlow (1949) studied the possibility that successful trial and error could lead to later insight. In a typical experiment, he confronted a monkey with two objects of different colour, size, and shape. If the monkey picked up the correct object, he found raisins or a peanut underneath. The position of the correct object was varied randomly from trial to trial until the monkey learned to choose it every time. The monkey was then confronted with a new pair of objects; and this procedure was repeated many times. The first such problems were solved by slow trial and error; each new problem was solved with greater efficiency until eventually the monkey showed what seemed to be perfect insight, solving a new problem of the same type in one trial. Similar results were obtained for monkeys with more complex problems and also for young children.

**Information Processing.**—A theory of problem solving quite different from those thus far described was advanced by Allan Newell, J. C. Shaw, and Herbert A. Simon (1958). The thinking human being is regarded as an information-processing system (*see*

INFORMATION THEORY). Such a system involves memories (stored symbolized information) that are interconnected by various ordering relations. The system operates on the memories according to a definite set of rules called a program. Explanation of observed problem-solving behaviour theoretically consists in constructing a program that will generate that behaviour. The writing of a program requires a precise language; and special so-called information-processing languages have been created for this purpose (*see* also MANAGEMENT SCIENCES: *Mathematics*).

Modern high-speed electronic computers work in what are called machine languages. They can, however, be provided with interpretive programs that enable them to handle these special information-processing languages. Thus a program written in an information-processing language can be run on a computer to determine the kinds of behaviour it will generate. This approach does not depend upon any analogy between the structure of a computer and that of the human brain; the computer is used as a tool to determine quickly whether the consequences of a program are consistent with the observed behaviour it is supposed to explain (*see* further COMPUTER).

If a program is to be more than an *ex post facto* explanation, it must not only generate the behaviour it was written to account for but also must predict the effect on behaviour of changing conditions.

Processes called algorithms will eventually solve some problems if a solution exists. A simple example of an algorithm is the process of opening a safe by trying all possible combinations. For some problems algorithms require too much time to be useful. There is not enough time for a man to choose his moves in chess, for example, by exploring all possible continuations of the game to termination.

A heuristic process is one that may solve a particular kind of problem but offers no guarantee. In an algebraic problem, for example, introduction of an auxiliary unknown may or may not lead to solution. For most problems only heuristic processes are available. Even with problems for which an algorithm is known, a heuristic process may be preferable because it requires much less time.

The Logic Theorist (a program written by Newell, Shaw, and Simon) can solve problems by discovering proofs for theorems in symbolic logic (*q.v.*). By using an appropriate interpretive program, the Logic Theorist was run repeatedly on a high-speed digital computer. In one experiment, the Logic Theorist succeeded in proving 38 of 52 theorems from the *Principia Mathematica* of Alfred North Whitehead and Bertrand Russell. The time required to construct a proof varied from less than a minute to more than 15 minutes. The success of the Logic Theorist depends on the effective use of heuristic methods. Similarly, the strategy and tactics of U.S. military forces in Vietnam during the 1960s were reported to have been guided by heuristic computer programs.

*See* also BRAINWASHING; CIVILIZATION AND CULTURE: *Talking and Thinking;* CONCEPT FORMATION, PSYCHOLOGY OF; GAMES, THEORY OF; SEMANTICS IN LOGIC; SPEECH AND LANGUAGE; THOUGHT, LAWS OF; and references under "Thinking and Problem Solving" in the Index.

BIBLIOGRAPHY.—G. Humphrey, *Thinking* (1951); W. E. Vinacke, *The Psychology of Thinking* (1952); D. M. Johnson, *The Psychology of Thought and Judgment* (1955); O. G. Brim *et al., Personality and Decision Processes* (1962); J. Feldman and E. Feigenbaum (eds.), *Computers and Thought* (1963); G. Mandler and J. M. Mandler (eds.), *Thinking: From Association to Gestalt* (1964); N. J. Nilsson, *Learning Machines* (1965).

(D. W. TA.; X.)

**THIOPHENE** is an organic sulfur compound that resembles benzene physically in that it is a colourless, water-insoluble liquid boiling at 84° C (benzene boils at 80°). It resembles benzene also in such chemical reactions as bromination, nitration and sulfonation, but differs in being more reactive. It has the molecular formula $C_4H_4S$ (I).

Dyes, plastics, solvents, explosives and the like can be made from thiophene; however, they frequently are inferior to those made from benzene and uses have been slow in developing. One application is in the manufacture of pharmaceuticals such as the antihistaminic drug thenylene, of the structure

```
2-pyridyl\
          >N-CH2CH2N(CH3)2
2-thenyl/
```

Certain thiophene derivatives occur in nature, one being "terthienyl" or dithienyl-thiophene, a blue solid found in the petals of marigolds. Another, more complex derivative is biotin, the growth-promoting factor in yeast, liver and eggs.

Although originally isolated from coal-tar benzene by V. Meyer (1883), thiophene is prepared more easily in other ways. A convenient laboratory synthesis is dry distillation of an intimate mixture of sodium succinate and phosphorus sulfide ($P_4S_7$). Similarly, by heating a mixture of acetonylacetone ($CH_3COCH_2$-$CH_2COCH_3$) and phosphorus sulfide, 2,5-dimethylthiophene (II) is obtained.

```
CH—CH              CH—CH
‖    ‖             ‖    ‖
CH   CH       CH3—C    C—CH3
  \ /                \ /
   S                  S
   I                  II
```

In the industrial manufacture of thiophene, mixtures of butane or butene and sulfur or sulfur dioxide are heated at 600° C. for short periods. Similarly, 2-methylthiophene and 3-methylthiophene are formed when pentane and isopentane, respectively, are treated in this way. The important radicals in the thiophene series are 2-thienyl (III), 2-thenyl (IV) and 2-thenoyl (V).

```
CH—CH          CH—CH              CH—CH
‖    ‖         ‖    ‖             ‖    ‖
CH   C—        CH   C—CH2—        CH   C—CO—
  \ /            \ /                \ /
   S              S                  S
  III             IV                 V
```

A delicate test for thiophene is afforded by reaction with isatin and sulfuric acid. If thiophene is present, as in coal-tar benzene, an intensely blue solution of indophenin results. This reaction is not encountered with benzene. Others in this category are the reactions of thiophene with cyanogen bromide to yield bromothiophene and with acetyl chloride in the presence of titanium tetrachloride to yield acetothienone, the thiophene analogue of acetophenone. The thiophene analogue of phenol, 2-thienol, cannot be prepared by methods that are industrially successful for phenol but can be made from 2-thienyl-magnesium bromide by reaction with oxygen at 0° C. In contrast to phenol, thienol is quite unstable.

*See* H. D. Hartough, *Thiophene and Its Derivatives* (1952).

(C. D. HD.)

**THIRD DEGREE,** a slang term now in common usage in the United States and frequently employed in Great Britain, designates the use of force or duress by police and prosecuting authorities to extort information or confessions from persons in their custody. There are conflicting theories as to the origin of the term. Some assert that it was borrowed from the Russian police, who allegedly resorted to severe physical duress after the suspect failed to respond to cross-examination and confrontation. Others hold that it represents an ironic reference to the third masonic degree, that of master mason, which is conferred with considerable ceremony.

The methods of the third degree are many, including beatings, threats of violence, denial of food, drink, or rest to the person interrogated, prolonged questioning, and the like. The National Commission on Law Observance and Enforcement (1931) reported widespread use of such methods in the United States. Because such behaviour occurs in secret, it is impossible to determine accurately the extent to which it persists. Observers have expressed the opinion, however, that U.S. police now employ overt physical violence less frequently than at the time of the commission's report.

Since the last half of the 18th century the Anglo-American law has directed the exclusion of confessions obtained by force, threats, or tricks from criminal trials. The exclusion of such coerced or involuntary confessions is required by the 5th and 14th amendments of the U.S. Constitution and by comparable provisions in state constitutions. *See* also CONFESSION; CRIMINAL LAW: *Criminal Procedure;* EVIDENCE: *Privilege and Public Policy.* (F. A. A.)

**THIRTY-NINE ARTICLES.** The Thirty-nine Articles of Religion, together with the Book of Common Prayer to which they are usually appended, constitute the doctrinal formularies of the Church of England. Their origin lies in the Forty-two Articles drawn up by Archbishop Thomas Cranmer in 1553 "for the avoiding of controversy in opinions." These were partly derived from the Thirteen Articles of 1538, designed as the basis of an agreement between Henry VIII and the German Lutheran princes, which in turn drew from the Lutheran Confession of Augsburg of 1530 (*see* AUGSBURG CONFESSION). Cranmer desired to make all preachers subscribe to the Forty-two Articles, the general purpose of which was to rule out both Roman Catholic and Anabaptist doctrine while at the same time furthering Cranmer's aim of uniting German and Swiss Reforming opinions. The Marian reaction swept them away, and after the Elizabethan settlement the problem arose of providing a doctrinal platform for the established church. For the first few years Archbishop Matthew Parker's Eleven Articles temporarily served, but in 1563 the Canterbury Convocation drastically revised the Forty-two Articles, making use of the Lutheran Württemberg Confession of 1551–52. Its work, after further revision by royal authority, emerged as the Thirty-eight Articles. A final revision by Convocation in 1571 produced the Thirty-nine Articles, which were approved by the queen and imposed on the clergy. (*See* also ENGLAND, CHURCH OF: *The Reformation.*)

In form the articles resemble the many Protestant confessions of faith of the 16th century, dealing briefly with the doctrines accepted by Catholics and Protestants alike and more fully with points of controversy. Closer examination, however, reveals that (chiefly as a result of the 1563 revision) they are at many points studiously ambiguous, because the Elizabethan government wished to make the national church as comprehensive as possible, not only avoiding commitment to specifically Lutheran, Zwinglian, or Calvinist views but also leaving loopholes for nonpapal Catholicism. Thus differing interpretations of them survive, including an attempt by the Franciscan Franciscus à Sancta Clara (Christopher Davenport) in 1634 (renewed by J. H. Newman in his Tract 90 of 1841) to reconcile the articles with much of the teaching of the Council of Trent.

Although subscription to the articles is required of all clerics of the Church of England, it has rarely been demanded of the laity. Moreover it became a tradition that the formulary consisted largely of "articles of peace," statements not to be gainsaid but not having the same binding authority on conscience as dogmatic statements of revealed truth. This was legally recognized in 1865, after which clerical subscription was limited to a declaration that the doctrine of the Church of England, in both prayer book and articles, is "agreeable to the word of God," so that the acceptance of every statement in them is not required. Among other churches of the Anglican Communion their status varies. In the U.S., the articles, slightly modified, are in the prayer book of the Protestant Episcopal Church, but neither clergy nor laity is required formally to subscribe to them. *See* also LITURGY, CHRISTIAN.

*See* B. J. Kidd, *The Thirty-nine Articles* (1899); E. J. Bicknell, *A Theological Introduction to the Thirty-Nine Articles,* 3rd ed. rev. by H. J. Carpenter (1955). (T. M. P.)

**THIRTY YEARS' WAR,** a conventional and largely misleading name for that part (1618–48) of the 50 years' struggle for the European balance of power (*c.* 1610–60) in which the Austrian Habsburgs and the German princes and cities were involved.

The usual picture of the Thirty Years' War, as painted by German historians and accepted uncritically by most English and American scholars, can be summarized as follows: (1) the war was one continuous struggle, fought almost exclusively on German soil, beginning with the Bohemian Revolt in 1618 and ending with the Peace of Westphalia in 1648; (2) it was the last and greatest of the Wars of Religion kindled by the German and Swiss Reformation of the 1520s, which the non-German powers, namely Denmark, Sweden, and France, together with the half-Spanish Habsburgs, exploited for political ends of their own; (3) it completely destroyed the German economy, leaving behind an impoverished near-desert which had lost one-third, one-half, or even two-thirds of its population; and (4) it dealt a mortal blow to the intellectual, moral, and artistic life of Germany.

Every one of these assertions can be challenged.

First, there was not one uninterrupted war, but about a dozen wars, fought at different times, in different parts of Europe, by different belligerents, for different aims, interrupted by years of truce or peace affecting different regions.

Second, the religious differences between the German Protestants and Catholics were indissolubly bound up with constitutional and political questions. While it is impossible to assess the ratio of religious, political, constitutional, and economic considerations which determined any particular move, religious questions, more often than not, merely provided ideological and propagandist grounds for very secular war aims and peace proposals. The involvement of non-German powers was due to the geographical position of Germany in the heart of Europe and to a number of factors which would have remained even if there had been no religious conflict. The head of the Austrian Habsburgs, for instance, king of Bohemia and of Hungary and ruler of his house's ancient patrimony on the Danube, in the Alps, and on the Upper Rhine (*see* HABSBURG), was also Holy Roman emperor, nominal sovereign over the whole *Reich* or empire, that is, over all the other German princes; and the German princes were anxious to resist any expansion of his authority. The emperor's Spanish Habsburg cousins, at the same time, to whom he was closely bound by family ties, were nominally members of the empire insofar as they held Franche-Comté and the Netherlands (though the northern Netherlands had been in open revolt against Spain since 1572); and Spain was furthermore in dispute with France over certain Italian principalities over which the emperor was nominally overlord. The king of Denmark likewise was a member of the empire in his capacity as duke of Holstein and, eventually, as director of the Lower Saxon "Circle" of the empire. The Hohenzollerns of Brandenburg, electors of the empire, were vassals not only of Bohemia for certain fiefs in Silesia but also of Poland for their Duchy of Prussia. Finally, Sweden's Baltic policy led to encroachment on the Pomeranian part of the empire. These and other dynastic or territorial questions provided reasons or pretexts for German princes to call in foreign powers as well as for foreign powers to take sides in German or so-called German affairs.

Finally, the social, economic, and cultural impacts have been misinterpreted. Seen in their true perspective, they will be found on a par with the results of every war.

The present article is divided into sections as follows:



Sections I and II allude to matters elucidated in Section III. Throughout the article the new style is used for dating, even where English, Swedish, or Russian historians use the old.

## I. SURVEY OF POLITICAL ASPECTS

**1. Western Europe.**—The uniting aspect of the period, in the history of Western Europe, is the struggle of the French monarchy and of the Dutch Republic, or United Provinces of the Netherlands, against the two branches of the House of Habsburg, Spain and Austria. (*See* FRANCE: *History;* NETHERLANDS, THE: *History.*)

The later wars of aggression, waged by Louis XIV of France and by Napoleon I, tend to obscure the fact that from the middle of the 16th to the middle of the 17th century France was the victim of a deliberate policy of encirclement by the Habsburg powers. In the south, possession of Roussillon gave Spain a firm foothold north of the Pyrenees. In the southeast, the Republic of Genoa was a Spanish satellite, and the Duchy of Milan was Spanish territory. Genoa and Milan guaranteed a short and safe line of communication from Spain to Austria proper as well as to the Spanish possessions along the eastern borders of France, namely Franche-Comté (contiguous with Austrian Alsace) and the Low Countries (Luxembourg, Hainaut, and Artois on the French frontier, with Flanders, Brabant, and the rest of the Netherlands in their immediate hinterland). After the successes of the Dutch rebellion, from 1572, the overland route from Genoa to Brussels was the more important because the final link of the chain around France had snapped after the death of Mary I of England (1558): the fate of the Armada (*q.v.*) in 1588 had demonstrated the insecurity of the northern sea route from Spain to the Netherlands.

The breaking of this Habsburg stranglehold was the foremost task of French statesmanship. It was first undertaken when Henry IV of France resisted the attempt by the Habsburgs, in 1609, to acquire Jülich-Cleves-Mark-Berg (*see* JÜLICH), as this attempt threatened to deal the deathblow to the independence of the United Provinces of the Netherlands and to lay France's northern frontier open. Henry's policy, interrupted by his assassination (1610) and by the pro-Spanish appeasement of the French regency under Marie de Médicis, was resumed by Cardinal de Richelieu (*q.v.*), in power from 1624 until his death in 1642, and was continued by his successor, Cardinal Mazarin (*q.v.*). France, at first too weak to wage open war against the Habsburgs, began by making treaties with powers hostile to them (or to their satellites in Germany or in Eastern Europe), namely with the United Provinces (1624), with Sweden (1631), and with Russia (1632); but the defeat of the United Provinces' ally Denmark (Peace of Lübeck, 1629), the withdrawal of Russia (Peace of Polyanov, 1634), the defeat of the Swedes (Battle of Nördlingen, 1634), and the defection of Sweden's German allies (Peace of Prague, 1635) forced Richelieu to declare open war on Spain (1635), after which Catalonia and Portugal (1640) and, later, Great Britain (1657) also joined the French camp. The modest French military successes were surpassed at the conference table: the Peace of Westphalia (1648) established the preponderance of France and France's allies throughout Central and Northern Europe; the formation of the League of the Rhine (1658) gave France a decisive voice in the affairs of the empire; and the Peace of the Pyrenees (1659) enlarged and secured France's frontiers and marked the end of Spain as a great power.

For the Dutch, the period of the Thirty Years' War forms part of their Eighty Years' War against Spain (1568–1648). The 12 years' Truce of Antwerp (April 9, 1609) can now be seen as the *de facto* recognition of the independence of the United Provinces; but contemporary Dutch statesmen foresaw that the Spanish crown would not easily abandon the hope of reducing the rebellious heretics and recovering its richest European province. In fact, Philip IV of Spain, whose accession in 1621 coincided with the expiry of the truce, immediately renewed the war. But whereas at the outbreak of the rebellion Spain had been the leading maritime, commercial, and colonial power, superiority in all these spheres had passed to the Netherlands. The only weakness of the maritime republic was its lack of land forces; but the States-General had no difficulty in enlisting foreign mercenaries or paying subsidies to foreign princes. Whereas the interest of Spain demanded the localization of every conflict so that resources might be concentrated against the Dutch, the interest of the Dutch was served best by extending the war so as to engage Spain's power away from their borders. Religious and constitutional affinities gave the Calvinist Dutch republicans additional zest in their support (1) of the Calvinist elector John Sigismund of Brandenburg in his struggle for Jülich; (2) of the semirepublican nobles of Bohemia in their fight against Austrian absolutism; and (3) of the generals who, from 1621, continued the Bohemian War, nominally on behalf of the Calvinist elector Frederick V of the Palatinate. But practical political considerations made the United Provinces the focal point of every anti-Habsburg coalition: the Franco-Dutch Treaty of Compiègne (June 20, 1624) was the prelude of the Treaty of The Hague (1625), which effectively brought Denmark into the war against the emperor Ferdinand II; and after Denmark's defeat, Dutch diplomacy and subsidies aided Richelieu in enlisting Gustavus II Adolphus of Sweden as the military champion of the anti-Habsburg cause (1630–32).

From the middle of the 1630s the French superseded the Dutch as leaders of the anti-Habsburg struggle. The conquest of Alsace and of Breisach by France's protégé Bernhard (*q.v.*) of Saxe-Weimar in 1638 and the secession of Portugal in 1640 shook Spain into preferring to come to an arrangement with the Dutch; and the latter, having smashed the Spanish Navy in the English Channel (1639) and off Pernambuco (1640) and thereby put an end to Spanish overseas expansion, now considered Portugal, with the Portuguese colonial empire, a greater rival to their mercantile interests than Spain. Disregarding the alliance with France which they had made in 1635, the Dutch on Jan. 30, 1648, signed a separate peace with Spain.

The Eighty Years' War of the Dutch is outlined in the article NETHERLANDS, THE: *History*.

**2. Northern Europe.**—Viewed from Northern Europe, the first half of the 17th century comprises the attempts of the two Scandinavian kingdoms, Denmark and Sweden, to obtain what the diplomatic language of the time called the *dominium maris Baltici* (lordship of the Baltic Sea); *i.e.,* the possession of the leading Baltic ports through whose customs sheds the raw materials of the Polish and Russian hinterlands found their way into the west.

Denmark's repeated attempts to overpower Sweden failed, and the Danish outposts in the eastern Baltic were lost. King Christian IV's attempt to make himself supreme in Lower Saxony by acquiring the German bishoprics of Bremen, Verden, Minden, and Hildesheim led to the Danish War (1625–29), in which the superior generalship of his adversaries outweighed the subsidies granted to him by the Dutch and the British. The Peace of Lübeck (1629) finished Denmark as a European power of consequence.

Denmark's decline was emphasized by the simultaneous rise of Sweden. The Peace of Knäred (1613) made only transitory concessions to Christian IV of Denmark, who had attacked Sweden in 1611. Thenceforward King Gustavus II Adolphus systematically began to close the ring of Swedish possessions round the Baltic. After preliminary gains at the expense of Muscovite Russia, whose access to the Baltic he closed (1617), he successfully attacked the Baltic provinces of Poland and of Poland's vassal Prussia (1621–29). Besides pursuing this Baltic ambition, he may also have been aspiring to supplant his Catholic cousin, Sigismund III Vasa, on the Polish throne. Any such design, however, had to be abandoned: on the one hand the Swedish nobility objected to it; on the other, the king's Baltic policy was challenged by the advance of imperial armies along the southern shore from the west, which drew him into intervening in German affairs. The Swedish-Polish Truce of Altmark (1629) was followed by alliance with France (Treaty of Bärwalde, Jan. 23, 1631).

The alliance with France survived the death of Gustavus Adolphus and remained the sheet anchor of his successors' position until Sweden's collapse as a great power (1721). Sweden reaped the fruits of this policy; first in the Peace of Brömsebro at the end of the Swedish-Danish War of 1643–45; then in the Peace of Westphalia (1648); and finally in the Peace of Roskilde (1658), with Denmark, in the course of the First Northern War. By the end of this period Sweden had achieved the *dominium maris Baltici.*

**3. Eastern Europe.**—The first half of the 17th century also embraces the first attempt by Poland to force Orthodox Muscovy (Russia) into the orbit of Latin Christianity as well as the first attempt on the part of the House of Romanov (*q.v.*) to enter the comity of Western Europe. Poland, tied to the Habsburgs by religion and tradition, hostile to Sweden by religion and dynastic rivalry, and implacably hostile to Muscovy by history and religion, exploited the "troubles" which convulsed Russia after the death of Boris Godunov (1605). The experiment of ruling Russia through a Polish puppet, the first False Dimitri (*q.v.*), failed in 1606, when the usurper succumbed in an outbreak of Russian nationalism and Orthodox fanaticism. But Poland came nearest to making Russia a satellite when in 1610 Sigismund III had his son, the future Wladyslaw IV of Poland, elected as tsar: the Polish dictatorship in Moscow lasted two years.

In 1609, the first Russo-Swedish alliance had been concluded by the tsar Vasili III Shuiski; and despite Sweden's later aggressions the new Romanov dynasty (from 1613) continued to regard Sweden as Russia's natural ally against Poland. England and the United Provinces acted as intermediaries at the Russo-Swedish Peace of Stolbova (1617), and 13 years later French envoys brought about Muscovy's indirect support of Gustavus Adolphus' war in Germany. Russia, however, did not want to be involved directly in Germany, and the Russo-Polish War of Smolensk (1632–34) remained a sideshow. After the death of Gustavus Adolphus, Swedish-Russian relations cooled off, as the Swedish chancellor Axel Oxenstierna correctly assessed Russia as potentially more dangerous than Poland.

The Russo-Polish Peace of Polyanov (1634), which included Wladyslaw IV's final resignation of his claim to the Russian throne, freed Poland to resume hostilities against Sweden and, by thus tying down Swedish troops, contributed to the Swedish disaster at Nördlingen.

**4. Germany.**—All these European conflicts affected Germany more often and more deeply than any of the other contestants. Germany was the only country where the Reformation had resulted in a permanent split into three religious factions—Catholic, Lutheran, and Calvinist. As these religious divisions largely marched with political frontiers, they were sustained and aggravated by dynastic rivalries, such as that between the Catholic Wittelsbachs in Munich (Bavaria) and the Calvinist Wittelsbachs in Heidelberg (the Palatinate), or that between the Calvinist Kassel branch and the Lutheran Darmstadt branch of the House of Hesse. In turn, these political and religious dissensions were partly exacerbated and partly overlaid by constitutional problems: the Holy Roman emperor, a Habsburg and a Catholic, wanted to establish monarchical absolutism in the empire; the electors, Catholics and Protestants alike, wanted to maintain what they called the "electoral preeminence" in the empire's affairs; and lastly, the other princes wanted to overthrow the ascendancy of both the emperor and the electors, so as to obtain complete freedom of action for themselves.

Each of the rivals found it easy and profitable to call in some foreign power. On the whole, the emperor relied on his Spanish cousins; the Protestant towns and smaller princes relied on Sweden, on France, and on the Dutch; Catholic Bavaria, with its satellites Cologne, Liège, Münster, Paderborn, and Hildesheim, usually blackmailed the emperor, while inclining to France and opposed to Spain; Lutheran Saxony disliked all foreign entanglements, but regarded the Calvinists as worse than the Catholics and generally found it most profitable to side with the emperor (since repeated endeavours to rally a neutralist "third force" never succeeded); and Calvinist Brandenburg was weak and irresolute until 1640, when Frederick William, "the Great Elector," began to play off emperor, Swedes, Dutch, Poles, and French with such skill that by 1660 he had raised Brandenburg-Prussia to the rank of a great German and minor European power.

**5. Great Britain.**—From the death of Queen Elizabeth I (1603) to the passing of the first Navigation Act by Cromwell's Parliament (1651) Great Britain's influence upon European affairs was negligible. The European policy of the government was vacillating between Spain, France, and the United Provinces, while Parliament and public opinion were enthusiastically anti-Spanish but unwilling to transform brave words into hard cash.

James I originally wanted to continue Elizabeth's pro-French and pro-Dutch policy but assented to peace with Spain (1604). In 1613 he gave his daughter Elizabeth in marriage to Frederick V of the Palatinate, leader of the Protestant anti-Habsburg faction in Germany; but twice, in 1617 and in 1623, he tried to obtain a Catholic Spanish Habsburg princess for his son Charles before betrothing him, in 1624, to a Catholic French Bourbon.

James had at least not dissuaded his son-in-law from accepting the Bohemian crown (1619), but his dislike of the Czech nobility's republican sympathies and religious radicalism, combined with his desire to appease the Spaniards, prevented him from giving tangible support to Frederick during the war in Bohemia. It was only when Frederick had lost the Palatinate and when the Spanish marriage project had collapsed that a cautious parliamentary grant for the preparation of war against Spain gave expression to the English public's lively sympathy for the Protestant cause. An expedition to the Palatinate was hopelessly bungled.

Charles I, on succeeding his father, undertook the war against Spain and also associated himself with the Dutch in the Treaty of The Hague (Dec. 9, 1625) for the support of Christian of Denmark against the emperor and the Catholic League in Germany. But the naval expedition against Cádiz (1625) was a failure; and Charles failed to pay Denmark the promised £360,000 per annum, after the first installment of £46,000. Soon afterward, he squandered ships, troops, and money on the disastrous expedition of 1627 to help the Huguenot rebels of La Rochelle against his brother-in-law Louis XIII of France. Thereafter Charles's devious foreign policy was hampered by lack of funds, which forced him to conclude peace both with France (1629) and with Spain (1630), and by lack of interest in foreign affairs on the part of his most capable adviser, Strafford. In 1636 and again in 1641 Charles offered to the Habsburgs an alliance against the Dutch in return for the restoration of the Palatinate to his nephew Charles Louis; but the Habsburgs declined this offer because Bavaria objected to it. Richelieu likewise in the same years preferred for France an understanding with Bavaria to a possible rapprochement with England.

## II. SURVEY OF RELIGIOUS ASPECTS

Religious issues were insolubly interwoven with political and constitutional problems. For Germany the whole question stemmed from the Peace of Augsburg (*q.v.*) of 1555, a compromise between the Catholic and Lutheran Estates (members) of the empire. Neither party was satisfied, neither meant to abide by it. It fixed the religious frontiers as they had existed in 1552; *i.e.,* at the lowest ebb of Protestant fortunes. It gave the sovereign lay princes the right to change with their own religion that of their subjects; but it prohibited any Catholic bishopric or free city from adhering in future to the Lutheran creed. It expressly excluded Calvinists from the toleration granted to Lutherans. Above all, it failed to lay down any criteria by which the many doubtful points might be interpreted, or to create any machinery to enforce its observance.

One of the many points left in suspense by the Peace of Augsburg concerned the right of the Protestant gentry in town and country under Catholic sovereigns to keep Protestant pastors and hold Protestant services. This issue played a part in the revolts of the Austrian and Bohemian nobility against their Habsburg overlords, which began in 1609 and ended with the Bohemian War in 1620. The ecclesiastical reservation which forbade the "reform" of Catholic bishoprics prevented Cologne from turning Protestant together with its archbishop, Gebhard (*q.v.*) in 1583. Gebhard's deposition was the basis of the greatness of the House of Wittelsbach: Bavarian princes held the archbishopric of Cologne continuously from 1583 to 1761, the bishoprics of Hildesheim and of Liège almost uninterruptedly throughout the same period, and the bishoprics of Paderborn and of Münster with but few more interruptions. Thus the undisputed leadership of Catholic Germany by the Wittelsbach Maximilian I (*q.v.*) of Bavaria was grounded on the preeminence of his house not only in the south but also in the northwest of Germany, where Jülich and Berg in the hands of his brother-in-law further fortified his house.

The distribution of the religious parties in the empire during the first half of the 17th century, according, be it understood, to the sovereign's choice of religion, was approximately as follows. The whole of northern, northeastern, and central Germany, with the exception of the bishopric of Hildesheim and the abbey of Fulda, was Protestant. Northwestern, western, and southeastern Germany, with the exception of the Rhenish Palatinate in the west, was Catholic, as were all the Habsburg dominions (Austria and Tirol, Bohemia-Moravia and Silesia, a portion of Swabia). Württemberg in Swabia, Ansbach and Bayreuth in Franconia, and nearly all the free cities, even those in otherwise Catholic districts, adhered to the Protestant faith. The nobility and townspeople in Bavaria and the Habsburg countries, nearly all of whom had been Protestants, had been recatholicized or expelled by *c.* 1625.

The historian must not doubt the strength and sincerity with which the champions of the contesting factions and their humblest followers believed in the exclusive truth of their church: the emperor Ferdinand II, Maximilian of Bavaria, Tilly, and Richelieu were devout Catholics; Gustavus Adolphus, Bernhard of Weimar, the electors of Brandenburg, Saxony, and the Palatinate were unswerving Protestants; Wallenstein is perhaps the only personality of note who seems to have been entirely indifferent to religious distinctions, astrology having largely supplanted Christianity as his creed. However, motives other than religious zeal were the factors determining political allegiance.

Pope Urban VIII and the cardinals Richelieu and Mazarin were unbending in their opposition to Catholic Spain and to the Catholic emperor. The Lutheran elector of Saxony and the Lutheran landgrave of Hesse-Darmstadt were firm adherents of the emperor so long as circumstances permitted. Lutheran Saxony and Catholic Bavaria were consistently anti-Spanish and anti-Swedish. Calvinist Hesse-Kassel was Lutheran Sweden's most reliable ally and, together with Bavaria, mostly pro-French. The struggle for the Baltic brought the Lutheran Gustavus Adolphus into conflict with Orthodox Russia, with Catholic Poland, and with Lutheran Denmark; but his fight in Germany made him the ally of Catholic France and of Orthodox Russia. Maximilian of Bavaria extended his power at the expense alike of the Lutheran cities in Swabia and in Franconia, of the Calvinist elector Palatine, and of the Habsburg emperor, and did so mostly in conjunction with Lutheran Saxony and Catholic France. The bishops of Würzburg and of Bamberg were the first to abandon the Catholic interest at the peace congress of Münster. Protestant as well as Catholic princes, prelates, and cities were susceptible to French subsidies. Of none of the belligerents can it be said that religious motives were responsible for any major decision. The secret debates (1629–30) in the Swedish council about entry into the war are revealing: the security and defense of Sweden and the conquest of Germany were declared the war aims; the king was expressly warned against speaking of a war of religion since France might take umbrage.

The suppression of Protestantism by Ferdinand II in Austria and in Bohemia and by Richelieu in France was undertaken mainly on political considerations. The Protestants not only infringed the spiritual unity of the country (a tenet still held by every government) but also were the chief opponents of royal absolutism and, not without cause, were suspected of republican tendencies on Dutch and Swiss models. Their defeat therefore paved the way for that spiritual and administrative uniformity which became the hallmark of 17th- and 18th-century monarchy.

Similarly, the contest of the emperor against the Protestant princes and cities was to a large extent a contest to decide whether the empire was to be a monarchy, with the emperor at its head and the princes as his vassals, or a federation of more or less independent princes, with the emperor as its titular president. So long as Ferdinand II was willing to concede to the six electoral princes their traditional prerogatives in the government of the empire, these electors (including Lutheran Saxony and Calvinist Brandenburg) sided with him against the lesser princes. When Ferdinand in 1629 unmasked his real intentions by the Edict of Restitution, the electors, led by Catholic Bavaria, turned against him. The Peace of Westphalia brought about the triumph of the lesser princes, with whom the electors now identified themselves against any recurrence of imperial centralism.

In fact, the Peace of Westphalia proved the interdependence of the problems, religious and constitutional, political and economic, which again and again were used as interchangeable counters. The recognition of the adherents of the Reformed (Calvinist) religion as being of equal right with those of the Lutheran faith was largely a by-product of the dispute over Pomerania between Brandenburg and Sweden. The emperor sacrificed the North German bishoprics to the Protestant claimants (Sweden, Brandenburg, Saxony, Mecklenburg, and Brunswick) and Alsace and the bishoprics of Metz, Toul, and Verdun to France; and in return Sweden and France renounced their claims to Austrian territory in Silesia and in Swabia respectively and assented to the exclusion of the Austrian Protestants from the treaty's clauses on restitution and toleration. The attitude of the Catholic princes to Pope Innocent X's protest against any formal agreement with the Protestants is characteristic of the trend toward excluding denominational considerations from political decisions: the first secret intimation which the nuncio gave to the emperor and to the Catholic princes in November 1647 was answered with evasive excuses; and the formal protocol handed over on Christmas Eve did not even receive an answer from any prince, temporal or ecclesiastical. A special "anti-protest clause" in the peace treaty was signed by all parties: it declared Innocent's condemnation of the peace invalid and ineffective and thus demonstrated the complete emancipation of secular politics from ecclesiastical tutelage. The religious questions left unanswered by the Peace of Augsburg in 1555 were solved in 1648 in the modern spirit of the "reason of state."

## III. EVENTS

**1. War of the Jülich Succession (1609–14).**—The settlement which the Peace of Augsburg had formulated for Germany was shaken in 1607–08 when Maximilian I of Bavaria annexed and recatholicized the Lutheran city of Donauwörth. Some of the German Protestant states concluded a military alliance, the Union, on May 14, 1608. The death of Duke John William of Jülich on March 25, 1609, opened a crucial question of succession, over which war broke out. On July 10, 1609, a Catholic military alliance, the League, was formed.

The wealth of John William's lands, Cleves, Jülich, Mark, and Berg, and their strategic position attracted not only the powerless legitimate heirs, namely John Sigismund of Brandenburg and Wolfgang Wilhelm of Palatinate-Neuburg, but also every powerful neighbour. The Habsburgs wished to install an Austrian prince, who would have placed the lands at the disposal of the Spaniards in their struggle with the Dutch and would incidentally have counteracted the predominance of Bavaria in northwestern Germany. France, the United Provinces, and England naturally objected to any strengthening of the Spaniards in that region. The assassination of Henry IV of France (May 14, 1610) prevented the war from becoming a European contest, though Spanish, Austrian, and Dutch troops repeatedly invaded the duchy in pretended support of one or other of the heirs. The Protestant Union, which John Sigismund had joined by turning Calvinist, and the Catholic League, of which Wolfgang Wilhelm had become a member by entering the Roman Church and marrying a sister of Maximilian, brought about a compromise which excluded all foreign claims (Oct. 24, 1610) and led to the partition of the inheritance between Brandenburg and Neuburg (Treaty of Xanten, Nov. 12, 1614).

**2. Bohemian and Palatine War (1618–23).**—This war began with the insurrection, in 1618, of the Bohemian and Austrian Estates against the future emperor Ferdinand II (*q.v.*), whose intention was to impose absolutist rule and to enforce the Catholic Counter-Reformation (*see* AUSTRIA, EMPIRE OF; BOHEMIA). The Bohemian nobles toyed with the idea of setting up a republic in order to secure the support of the Dutch but eventually, in August 1619, elected as their king the elector Frederick V of the Palatinate in the hope of obtaining the aid of the Protestant Union and Great Britain. Their expectations proved fallacious. Frederick failed to discipline the haughty Bohemian nobles or to rally the Bohemian townsmen and peasants (whom he did nothing to relieve from harsh oppression by their feudal lords) and was abandoned by his German allies as well as by his father-in-law, James I of Great Britain. Ferdinand, although in a very weak position, succeeded in buying the support of Maximilian of Bavaria and the Catholic League, at a heavy price in money and land. In a campaign of a few months the League's troops under Johann Tserclaes von Tilly (*q.v.*) crushed the Austrian Estates and broke the rule of Frederick in the Battle of the White Mountain, near Prague (Nov. 8, 1620). The conquest of Glatz (Klodzko) on Oct. 25, 1622, completed the subjugation of the lands of the Bohemian crown.

In the meantime the Spaniards from their bastions in Luxembourg and in Franche-Comté had since 1620 been overrunning the Rhenish Palatinate, where Tilly joined them in 1622, after he and Maximilian had in 1621 subdued the Upper Palatinate (north of Bavaria and west of Bohemia). Tilly also overcame the badly coordinated actions of several German princelings and generals who, in the pay of the United Provinces, Denmark, and England, still upheld Frederick's cause, notably Ernst von Mansfeld (*q.v.*) and Christian (*q.v.*) of Brunswick. Whereas the Protestant Union had dissolved itself (May 1621), Lutheran Saxony, which had never adhered to the Union, was won over to the emperor by the offer of Lusatia. The defeat of Christian of Brunswick by Tilly at Stadtlohn (Aug. 6, 1623) left the situation as follows: the emperor was in undisputed control of his Austrian and Bohemian territories; Maximilian of Bavaria, who was created elector, had become the leading power in southern and northwestern Germany; the Spaniards were in possession of the Rhenish Palatinate; and Frederick was a landless exile, living on the bounty of the Dutch.

BY COURTESY OF THE TRUSTEES OF THE BRITISH MUSEUM; PHOTO, J. R. FREEMAN AND CO., LTD.

THE BATTLE OF THE WHITE MOUNTAIN, NOV. 8, 1620, IN WHICH THE AUSTRIAN AND BAVARIAN ARMIES, FORMED IN TIGHT SQUARES, DEFEATED THE BOHEMIANS; COPPER ENGRAVING BY M. MERIAN IN "THEATRUM EUROPAEUM," 1643

**3. Struggle for the Graubünden (1620–39).**—The Valtellina (*q.v.*), leading from the northern frontier of the Duchy of Milan through the Alps toward Tirol, opened the shortest and safest land route between Spanish Italy and the Austrian territories in Germany, whence the Spaniards could reinforce their troops in the Netherlands and in the Palatinate. It belonged to the Graubünden (*q.v.*), or Grisons, a union of leagues in loose relations with the Swiss. Spain and Austria obviously wanted to bring the union's lands under their own control; France and Venice naturally opposed the forging of this link, which would have completed encirclement of both of them by the Habsburg powers. The political and military issues were here poisoned by religious, personal, local, and clannish rivalries, of which Georg Jenatsch (*q.v.*) was the stormy centre. A Spanish occupation of the Valtellina (1620), reinforced by an Austrian incursion into the other territories of the Graubünden (1621), provoked French and Venetian protests which led to the nominal "deposit" of the Valtellina in the hands of the papacy (1623)—in fact a veiled means of prolonging Spanish control there. Then Richelieu ventured on the first French occupation of the Graubünden (1624–26); but the internal weakness of France, where Richelieu's regime was challenged on the one hand by the pro-Spanish faction of Catholic zealots (the *Parti Dévot*) and on the other by the Huguenots, made it impossible to maintain this indirect attack on Spain. The Treaty of Monzón (1626) made the Graubünden into a sort of Franco-Spanish protectorate, with papal troops in occupation. During the War of the Mantuan Succession the Habsburgs again overran the country (1629–31). A final French occupation (from 1635) was ended in 1639 by a reaction of the Graubünden against the French. Eventually the Peace of Milan (Sept. 3, 1639), between Spain and the Graubünden, brought the country into virtually complete dependence on Spain.

**4. Swedish-Polish War (1621–29).**—From 1611, Gustavus Adolphus had taken advantage of the "Time of Troubles" and its aftermath in Muscovite Russia (*see* RUSSIAN HISTORY); and by the Peace of Stolbova (1617) he had acquired Karelia and Ingria, which together constituted the land bridge between Swedish Finland and Swedish Estonia, so that the Gulf of Finland was converted into a Swedish lake. He then turned against Poland (1621). His conquest of Livonia gave him Riga, the chief Baltic port (though the Swedish nobles possessed themselves of the largest landed properties in the country, to the detriment of the Swedish crown); and from the Duchy of Prussia, Poland's vassal, he took the ports of Memel and Pillau, the latter commanding the approach to Königsberg. Sweden's position in the Baltic, however, was eventually endangered by the course of the Danish War, as the imperial general Wallenstein (*q.v.*) conquered Mecklenburg (with the ports of Wismar and Rostock) and threatened moreover to conquer Pomerania; and in summer 1628 Swedish forces were sent to help the port of Stralsund, which Wallenstein was besieging. Finally the Truce of Altmark (Sept. 25, 1629) was concluded between Sweden and Poland, largely thanks to French mediation. Livonia and the Prussian ports were left in Sweden's possession.

**5. Danish War (1625–29) and the Edict of Restitution.**—Christian IV (*q.v.*) of Denmark had observed strict neutrality during the Bohemian War despite repeated Dutch attempts to enlist his help on behalf of Frederick of the Palatinate. In 1624, however, he began to contemplate offensive action. His motives were rivalry of Sweden in the Baltic regions and the wish for Danish supremacy in the estuaries of the Elbe and Weser. The king's election, in spring 1625, as director of the Lower Saxon "Circle" of the empire furnished him with the legal pretext for interference in Germany. The Treaty of The Hague (Dec. 9, 1625), in the negotiation of which the British statesman George Villiers, 1st duke of Buckingham, played a major part, promised British and Dutch subsidies for a military effort by Denmark on Frederick's behalf, in cooperation with the German generals who had already tried to uphold the latter's cause; and this Protestant coalition could expect the sympathy of the Habsburgs' other enemies—Prince Gabriel Bethlen (*q.v.*) of Transylvania, the Ottoman Turks, and also Catholic France.

The coalition's plan seems to have envisaged a fourfold advance: Christian of Brunswick was to overpower the Wittelsbach bishoprics and duchies in Westphalia and in the lower Rhineland; Christian IV of Denmark was to make himself master of Lower Saxony; Ernst von Mansfeld, generalissimo of the coalition, was to press forward into Bohemia, Silesia, and Moravia; and Bethlen was to sally forth from Hungary and join forces with Mansfeld.

On the opposite side were ranged the veteran troops of the Catholic League under Tilly, who was to deal with Christian of Brunswick and with Christian IV of Denmark; and the Imperial Army of Wallenstein, who was to repel Mansfeld and Bethlen.

On both sides the generals were on bad terms with one another and never effectively coordinated their efforts. But Tilly and Wallenstein had the advantage of fighting on interior lines and could therefore tackle their adversaries in turn. The coalition, on the other hand, was weakened by the faithless policy of Charles I of Great Britain, who failed to honour his financial obligations and let Buckingham embark on a foolish expedition against France in aid of the Huguenots of La Rochelle (June–November, 1627). Wallenstein forced Mansfeld out of northern Germany (Battle of

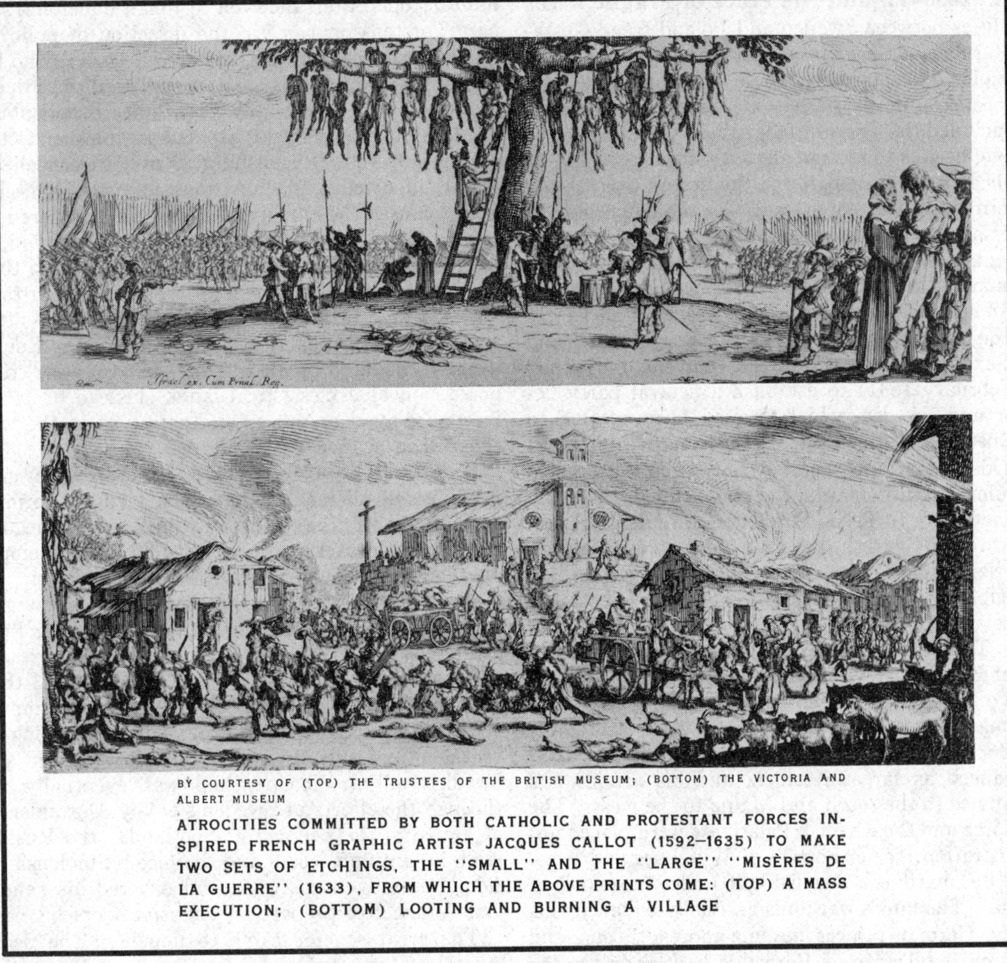

BY COURTESY OF (TOP) THE TRUSTEES OF THE BRITISH MUSEUM; (BOTTOM) THE VICTORIA AND ALBERT MUSEUM

ATROCITIES COMMITTED BY BOTH CATHOLIC AND PROTESTANT FORCES INSPIRED FRENCH GRAPHIC ARTIST JACQUES CALLOT (1592–1635) TO MAKE TWO SETS OF ETCHINGS, THE "SMALL" AND THE "LARGE" "MISÈRES DE LA GUERRE" (1633), FROM WHICH THE ABOVE PRINTS COME: (TOP) A MASS EXECUTION; (BOTTOM) LOOTING AND BURNING A VILLAGE

Dessau, April 25, 1626); and Mansfeld, though he held a strong position in Silesia, neither made full use of anti-Habsburg movements (apart from discontent in the Bohemian lands, a peasants' revolt broke out in Austria in May) nor effected a junction with Bethlen and the latter's Turkish auxiliaries. Wallenstein outmaneuvered Bethlen, and Mansfeld died on his way to Venice (Nov. 29, 1626), whence he hoped to receive fresh subsidies. Isolated Danish troops maintained themselves in Silesia until the autumn of 1627, when Wallenstein overwhelmed them.

Meanwhile Tilly was favoured by the untimely death of Christian of Brunswick (June 16, 1626) and by the military incompetence of Christian IV of Denmark. The Danish Army suffered a crushing defeat in the Battle of Lutter (Aug. 27, 1626). In 1627 Tilly pursued the beaten Danes into Holstein; and Wallenstein, who joined him, continued the pursuit into Jutland. Mecklenburg (*q.v.*), whose dukes had sided with Christian, was given by the emperor to Wallenstein, who immediately set about obtaining bases on the Baltic for an imperial navy. His attempt to add the Pomeranian port of Stralsund to his Mecklenburg ports of Wismar and Rostock led to the intervention of Gustavus Adolphus.

Wallenstein's contact with maritime affairs changed his whole outlook. His first sight of large river barges on the Oder had made him believe that they were oceangoing capital ships; but he now realized the importance of sea power and overseas trade and reassessed the political position which the emperor might take up with regard to the Hanse towns, Denmark, the Netherlands, England, and Spain. Denmark, which he wished to draw into the emperor's interest, profited by his mediation: at the Peace of Lübeck (May 22, 1629) Christian IV had only to renounce further participation in the affairs of the empire.

The defeat of the anti-Habsburg coalition raised the position of the emperor to its greatest height since Charles V's victory over the League of Schmalkalden in 1547. Ferdinand II's Edict of Restitution (March 6, 1629), prescribing the recovery by the Catholics of all ecclesiastical lands in which Protestantism had been established since 1552, was more than an act of reparation of the damage suffered by the Catholic Church since Luther's time: it was an unambiguous assertion of the imperial prerogative in all matters pertaining to the constitutional structure of the empire. At the Electoral Diet of Regensburg (1630) the opposition, led by Lutheran Saxony (anxious to retain its threatened acquisitions) and by Catholic Bavaria (determined to counteract the emperor's aggrandizement) forced Ferdinand to dismiss Wallenstein and so to make himself defenseless at the very moment when Gustavus Adolphus had landed on German soil.

**6. War of the Mantuan Succession (1628–31).**—The death of Vincenzo II Gonzaga, duke of Mantua and Montferrat, on Dec. 26, 1627, led to the first direct clash between the Habsburgs and France, albeit on a secondary theatre of war (*see* GONZAGA; MONTFERRAT). The claims of the legitimate Gonzaga heir, Charles, duc de Nevers, whom France supported, were overridden by Ferdinand II, supreme lord of the imperial fiefs in Italy; and Spain lent military aid to Ferdinand so as to keep a French vassal away from the approaches to Milan. Richelieu, however, was soon stronger. The Huguenot rebels of La Rochelle capitulated to Louis XIII (autumn 1628); Savoyard forces, which attempted to block the French king's way into Piedmont, were defeated at Susa (March 6, 1629); and the Peace of Susa with England (April 14), followed by the submission of the Huguenot rebels in Languedoc to the Peace of Alais (June 28), secured the French rear. The Habsburg forces withdrew from Casale in October 1630; and Richelieu, who in November triumphed over the pro-Spanish faction in France (the so-called Day of Dupes), achieved full success. By the Treaty of Cherasco (June 19, 1631), the French candidate was installed in Mantua. Meanwhile Savoy had ceded the fortress of Pinerolo to France; and Pope Urban VIII, determined opponent of the Habsburgs, annexed Urbino, another vacant imperial fief. The Austro-Spanish monopoly in Italy was broken.

**7. Swedish War (1630–35) and the Peace of Prague.**—The suspension of hostilities between Sweden and Poland freed Gustavus Adolphus to intervene in Germany. After landing at Usedom (July 6, 1630), he quickly occupied the whole duchy of Pomerania and restored Wallenstein's duchy of Mecklenburg to its hereditary dukes. He concluded the Treaty of Bärwalde (Jan. 23, 1631) with France, whereby he was to receive annual subsidies of 1,000,000 livres to enable him to campaign for the restoration of the "liberty" of the German princes "oppressed" by the emperor. In these circumstances an immediate objective for Gustavus was to stop the enforcement of the Edict of Restitution on Magdeburg (*q.v.*), which commanded a strategic crossing point on the Elbe; but his advance into central Germany was impeded by the hardly veiled hostility of the electors George William of Brandenburg and John George I of Saxony. They tried at the Convent or Conference of Leipzig (February 1631) to establish a neutral party between the emperor and Sweden, which proved unacceptable to either. Though Gustavus stormed the Brandenburg fortress of Frankfurt an der Oder (April 13), thereby both securing his left flank against the Poles and intimidating the two electors, the delay led to the fall of Magdeburg to Tilly (May 20). Brandenburg and Saxony now yielded to the Swedish threats, especially as Tilly imprudently invaded Saxony and treated it as enemy country. Alliances with Brandenburg (June 20) and with Saxony (Sept. 11) protected Gustavus' rear and virtually rendered the electorates Swedish satellites. The defeat of Tilly at Breitenfeld (Sept. 17) and the conquest of Prague (Nov. 15) by the Saxons under Hans Georg von Arnim (*q.v.*) opened southern Germany to the Swedes.

The smaller German Protestant princes, such as Bernhard (*q.v.*) of Saxe-Weimar, flocked to Gustavus' standards; by April 1632 Gustavus had advanced as far as Munich, and his armies had reached Lake Constance to the south and Mainz to the west. The archbishopric of Mainz and the Rhenish Palatinate were placed under Swedish administration; the bishoprics of Würzburg and Bamberg were given to Bernhard as a Swedish fief under the name of Duchy of Franconia. The king's war aims gradually widened: his agreements with the German princes became more onerous, and the stipulations which the Treaty of Bärwalde had made for the protection of France's friends and of the Catholic religion were treated lightly. Gustavus did not aim at the imperial crown, but his secret negotiations with Wallenstein show that he thought of placing the Habsburg dominions under the rule of Swedish puppets.

The recall of Wallenstein to the leadership of the Imperial Army completely changed the situation: Gustavus was maneuvered out of southern Germany and shortly afterward was killed in the battle of Lützen (Nov. 16, 1632). While the conduct of Swedish military operations then fell to Johan Banér and subsequently Lennart Torstensson (*qq.v.*), the direction of policy was undertaken by the chancellor, Axel Oxenstierna (*q.v.*), who by the Treaty of Heilbronn (April 23, 1633) consolidated the Swedish alliance with the German princes, albeit without Brandenburg and Saxony. Wallenstein's victory at Steinau in Silesia (Oct. 11) and Bernhard's capture of Regensburg (Nov. 14) cancelled each other out, and Wallenstein's machinations to make himself the arbiter of affairs caused the emperor to have him murdered (Feb. 25, 1634); but the Swedish defeat at Nördlingen (Sept. 5–6, 1634) led to the dissolution of the League of Heilbronn and to the open defection of most German princes, led by Saxony, from the Swedish cause.

The Peace of Prague (May 30, 1635) reconciled the emperor and nearly all the German opponents of the Edict of Restitution, which it modified by making the year 1627 the criterion of rightful possession of ecclesiastical lands (instead of 1552). Henceforth Sweden played only a subordinate part in the war. The leading role fell to France.

**8. War of Smolensk (1632–34).**—From *c.* 1628 Gustavus Adolphus and Richelieu had been trying to bring about alliances with Russia, Turkey, Transylvania, the Crimean Tatars, and the Ukrainian Cossacks, who were to engage the emperor and Poland on their eastern frontiers. Concerted action, however, proved difficult to achieve. But Moscow gave Gustavus considerable indirect aid by selling to Sweden, on a cash-and-carry basis at an artificially low price, cereals which the Swedes resold in Amsterdam at considerable profit: between 1628 and 1633 the Swedes bought Russian grain at a cost of 100,000 talers per annum and sold it at 400,000 talers per annum (the latter sum being equal in amount to the direct subsidy received annually from France). Russo-Swedish military cooperation was eventually achieved, largely through the efforts of Sweden's envoy Alexander Leslie (later earl of Leven in the peerage of Scotland): the Russians invaded Poland in autumn 1632 and besieged Smolensk, while Gustavus Adolphus moved eastward and ordered his general Karl Gustav von Wrangel to prepare an offensive from his bases in Prussia.

The great scheme came to nought. The deaths of Gustavus Adolphus and of the Moscow patriarch Philaret (October 1633), who had been the two chief architects of Swedish-Russian cooperation, removed the mutual goodwill as the basis for a real alliance. Turkey moreover was committed in a war with Persia; the Tatars of the Crimea turned against Muscovy instead of Poland; and the revolt of the Ukrainian Cossacks against their Polish overlords was delayed. Finally an insurrection of the peasants in central Russia forced Tsar Michael's government to conclude the Peace of Polyanov with Poland (June 14, 1634).

**9. French and Swedish War (1635–48).**—The near-collapse of the Swedish system in Germany in 1634–35 forced Richelieu to abandon his cautious policy of nonintervention. He concluded offensive and defensive alliances with the United Provinces (Feb. 8, 1635) and with Sweden (Treaty of Compiègne, April 28); sent a French army to the Valtellina (March–April); and declared war on Spain (May 19). He then secured an alliance with Savoy and Parma (League of Rivoli, July 11); mediated the 20-year Truce of Stuhmsdorf between Sweden and Poland (Sept. 12); and took the best of the German generals still serving Sweden, Bernhard of Saxe-Weimar, into French pay (Oct. 27).

In 1636 the invasion of northern France from the Spanish Netherlands by Ottavio Piccolomini (*q.v.*), whose capture of Corbie (Aug. 15) threatened to

CULVER PICTURES, INC.

THE SACKING OF MAGDEBURG, MAY 20, 1631, BY THE IMPERIAL ARMY; COPPER ENGRAVING BY M. MERIAN FROM "THEATRUM EUROPAEUM," 1643

BY COURTESY OF STEFAN MUTHESIUS, ESQ.

ENGRAVED CARTOON GLORIFYING THE PROTESTANT VICTORY OF GUSTAVUS II ADOLPHUS OVER THE PAPACY (REPRESENTED HERE BY A SEVEN-HEADED DRAGON), 1632

expose Paris, was outweighed by a series of Swedish victories over Saxon and imperial forces, culminating in Banér's defeat of Melchior von Hatzfeldt at Wittstock (Oct. 4), which reestablished Swedish supremacy in north and central Germany. A careless northward movement of the imperial commander in chief, Matthias Gallas, in 1637, laid southern Germany open to the French; and Bernhard of Saxe-Weimar, having overrun Alsace, in 1638 conducted a brilliant campaign in the course of which he took the key fortresses of Rheinfelden (March 23), Freiburg (April 6), and Breisach (Dec. 17). Before Bernhard's death the incompetence of the French led to Piccolomini's great victory of Thionville (June 7, 1639), which however was to be the last success of the Austro-Spanish armies. The outbreak, in 1640, of revolution both in Catalonia and in Portugal compelled the Spaniards to limit their commitments outside the Iberian Peninsula. The capitulation of the great stronghold of Arras to the French (Aug. 9, 1640) endangered the Spanish position in the Netherlands, and a Spanish counteroffensive into Champagne ended with the French victory at Rocroi (May 19, 1643), won by the young duc d'Enghien (*see* CONDÉ, LOUIS II DE BOURBON, Prince de).

In Germany the various commanders, French, Swedish, Bavarian, and imperial, waged war almost on each one's own responsibility: no coherent pattern can be found in those campaigns, which were nearly always small-scale raids with limited objectives. The Swedish victory over Saxon and imperial forces at Breitenfeld (Nov. 2, 1642) and the capture of the Little Town quarter of Prague by the Swedes (July 26, 1648) are—besides the Swedish campaign against Denmark—the most notable military events of these years. They were overshadowed by the diplomatic activity which began in 1640 and ended in 1648 with the Peace of Westphalia.

During the French and Swedish War death had removed three great figures from the international scene: the emperor Ferdinand II on Feb. 15, 1637, leaving the succession to his son Ferdinand III (*q.v.*); Richelieu on Dec. 4, 1642; and Louis XIII of France on May 14, 1643. Richelieu's place was taken by Cardinal Mazarin (*q.v.*) during the regency for Louis XIV.

**10. Swedish-Danish War (1643–45).**—The precarious situation of the imperial cause after Breitenfeld and the Danish jealousy and fear of Sweden brought about an understanding between Ferdinand III and Christian IV; and Sweden's decision to wage a preventive war against Denmark gave the emperor a respite, since the Swedish Army under Torstensson had to abandon its march on Vienna (September 1643) and to turn northward instead. In a lightning campaign (December 1643–January 1644) Torstensson conquered Schleswig-Holstein and Jutland. When an imperial army under Gallas came to the succour of the Danes, Torstensson at once marched against him, destroyed his army at Jüterbog (Nov. 23, 1644), and invaded Bohemia, where another imperial army was wiped out at Jankov (March 6, 1645). By the Peace of Brömsebro, signed on Aug. 23, 1645, Denmark ceded Jämtland and Härjedalen on the Norwegian frontier, Halland on the Kattegat, and the Baltic islands of Gotland and Ösel to Sweden.

**11. Peace of Westphalia (1648).**—Treaties signed in the Westphalian towns of Münster and Osnabrück terminated both the Eighty Years' War between Spain and the United Provinces of the Netherlands (Jan. 30, 1648) and the war between France, Sweden, and the German Protestants on the one side and the emperor and the German princes on the other (Oct. 24).

*The Negotiators.*—The Peace of Prague (1635) between the emperor Ferdinand II and the majority of the German princes had proved abortive: it expressed too much the temporary ascendancy of the emperor, took little account of Sweden, and completely disregarded France, which at that very moment openly took up arms against Spain and the emperor. No general peace was possible without the participation of Sweden, France, and Spain, and in 1640 the parties began in earnest to prepare the summoning of a peace congress. The emperor Ferdinand III entered into secret negotiations with Sweden in Hamburg; the Imperial Diet demanded a universal congress instead of bilateral transactions. The renewal of the Franco-Swedish alliance on June 30, 1641, included the stipulation that two congresses be held simultaneously in neighbouring Westphalian towns: in Münster, the Catholic envoys, in Osnabrück the Protestant envoys were to meet.

In 1643–44 Sweden and France sent out the first invitations, and the congress began to take shape. The slow and tortuous negotiations about procedure and substance, protocol and ceremonial, the admission or rejection of envoys and mediators—all these fumblings which went on right to the actual signing of the treaties —were mostly due not to obstruction but to inexperience. By trial and error the congress had to explore and define the methods of modern international diplomacy. The 150 representatives (about 110 Germans and 40 foreigners) lacked any precedent for their tasks, starting, as it were, from scratch every time a fresh topic turned up. They gradually developed a kind of *esprit de corps* which cut across political and religious frontiers and contributed not a little to the realistic settlement which was satisfactory to all but a few diehards.

Though the plenipotentiaries were bound fairly narrowly by instructions from their governments, a few figures stand out to whom the successful outcome was largely due. The imperial ambassador, Maximilian Graf Trauttmansdorff, outshone the rest; he had been the architect of the Peace of Prague and became the main author of the Peace of Westphalia. He and his chief secretary, Isaac Volmar, were converts to the Roman faith and therefore understood the opposing positions and did their best to check the firebrands in the Catholic camp. France was brilliantly represented by the duc de Longueville (Henry d'Orléans) and his duchesse (Anne Geneviève de Bourbon-Condé), but as members of the princely faction they were suspect to Mazarin. Mazarin also mistrusted France's principal actual negotiator, Claude de Mesmes, comte d'Avaux, whereas the latter's equally skilful but more ruthless colleague, Abel Servien, enjoyed the cardinal's confidence; their mutual antagonism, however, in no way impaired their efficiency as representatives of the French crown. Similar dissensions rent the Swedish mission: Johan Oxenstierna, the chancellor's son, stood for the policy of conquest sponsored by the Swedish nobility, whereas Johan Adler Salvius, a gifted and experienced diplomat of humble birth, sided with the young queen, Christina, in wishing for peace at almost any price. The Spanish ambassadors, the conde de Peñaranda (Gaspar de Bracamonte) and Antonius Brun, succeeded in terminating the war with the Dutch (Jan. 30, 1648) with great sacrifice to Spanish power but without loss to Spanish honour.

The Brunswick counselor, Jacob Lampadius, stands out as the expert in all legal problems, and the Lübeck envoy, David Gloxin, as the champion of the mercantile interest. Johann Rudolf Wettstein, of Basel, was accredited only as a representative of the Swiss Protestant cantons but acted on behalf of the whole Swiss Confederation. Lastly, the two unofficial mediators must be mentioned, the papal nuncio Fabio Chigi (later Pope Alexander VII) and, especially, the Venetian diplomat Alvise Contarini: they employed their good offices for smoothing out factional divisions and keeping alive the mutual interests of the European comity of nations.

*Territorial Settlement.*—The territorial clauses of the peace treaty all favoured France, Sweden, and their allies.

Sweden obtained the largest share: Hither Pomerania (Vorpommern), with Stettin and so control over the Oder estuary; the Mecklenburg port of Wismar; and the archbishopric (but not the city) of Bremen and the bishopric of Verden, with control over the Elbe and Weser estuaries. In addition, there was the "satisfaction" of the Swedish Army, amounting to 5,000,000 talers, guaranteed collectively by the members of the empire.

France incorporated the cities and bishoprics of Metz, Toul, and Verdun in Lorraine (French protectorates since 1552) and added to them the suzerainty over the secular vassals of the three bishops. France also obtained the ill-defined feudal rights exercised by the emperor over various towns, villages, and districts in Alsace (excluding Strasbourg but including the bridgehead of Breisach); and the permanent right to garrison Philippsburg, on the right bank of the Rhine south of Speyer. These gains appeared modest. However, the possession of Breisach and Philippsburg laid all southern Germany open to French arms; and the deliberate vagueness of the clauses relating to the cessions in Lorraine and Alsace later provided the legal or casuistical pretexts for wars of aggression waged by Louis XIV.

The only major setback which France suffered was the conclusion of the separate peace between Spain and the United Provinces. This deprived France of an ally in the rear of the Spanish Netherlands and prolonged the Franco-Spanish War by a decade.

The gains and losses of the German princes were determined by the convenience of the principal powers, France, Sweden, and Austria. These used the claims of their lesser partners as pawns mainly for adjusting differences among themselves at somebody else's expense.

Brandenburg obtained Farther Pomerania (Hinterpommern); the bishoprics of Kammin, Halberstadt, and Minden; the county of Hohnstein; and the reversion of the archbishopric of Magdeburg on the death of the existing administrator, Augustus of Saxony (which occurred in 1680). Bavaria was to keep the Upper Palatinate and the electoral dignity, but the Rhenish Palatinate was restored to Frederick V's heir, Charles Louis, for whom a new electorate was created. Saxony retained what had been secured at the Peace of Prague, namely Lusatia and Magdeburg, but the latter only for the lifetime of the present administrator. Hesse-Kassel ousted Hesse-Darmstadt from the district of Marburg and incorporated the abbey of Hersfeld and the county of Schaumburg. The Welfs of Brunswick obtained the right to have one of their princes elected as Protestant administrator of Osnabrück in alternation with a Catholic bishop. Mecklenburg was compensated for the loss of Wismar by the bishoprics of Schwerin and Ratzeburg.

Finally, the United Provinces of the Netherlands and the Swiss Confederation were released from their legal obligations toward the empire and so recognized as independent republics.

*Political and Religious Settlement for Germany.*—For Germany, the Peace of Westphalia brought to a conclusion the century-old struggle between the monarchical tendencies of the emperor and the federalistic aspirations of the princes. Ferdinand II had made considerable progress in revitalizing the imperial power: without consulting the electors or princes, he had arrogated to himself the outlawry of Frederick V of the Palatinate and the transfer of the latter's electoral dignity to Maximilian of Bavaria (1623) and the deposition of the dukes of Mecklenburg (1628); on his own authority, he had interpreted, that is, in fact, rescinded, the Peace of Augsburg by the Edict of Restitution (1629), thereby superseding the legislative authority of the Imperial Diet; and by the Peace of Prague (1635) he had transformed all princely troops into contingents of an army under his supreme command and abolished the princes' traditional right to conclude alliances among themselves or with foreign powers.

The Peace of Westphalia completely reversed this trend. It confirmed the full sovereignty of the members of the empire, including their right to form alliances, restricted only by the meaningless proviso "except against the emperor and *Reich*." It bound the emperor to the decisions of the Imperial Diet in all matters concerning war and peace. The Diet, which during the past 40 years had met only three times (1608, 1613, 1640–41), increased its sphere of competence at the expense of the emperor as well as the electors; the Protestant administrators of the secularized bishoprics were admitted with full voting rights. From 1663 the Diet remained in permanent session at Regensburg.

The peace established equality of rights between Catholics, Lutherans, and Calvinists: the supreme court of the empire was to be staffed by 26 Catholics and 24 Protestants, and Protestants were admitted to the Aulic Council in Vienna. The Edict of Restitution was repealed, and 1624 was declared the "standard year" according to which territories should be deemed to be in Catholic or Protestant possession. Dissidents were allowed private worship, liberty of conscience, and the right of emigration; only in the Habsburg dominions no toleration was granted to non-Catholics. Religious disputes were not to be decided by majority vote of the Imperial Diet but to be solved amicably between the Corpus Evangelicorum (the Protestant states collectively) and the Corpus Catholicorum, organized under the directorate of Saxony and of Mainz respectively.

BY COURTESY OF THE TRUSTEES OF THE BRITISH MUSEUM; PHOTO, J. R. FREEMAN AND CO., LTD.

THE MURDER OF WALLENSTEIN, DUKE OF FRIEDLAND, AT EGER, FEBRUARY 1634; COPPER ENGRAVING BY M. MERIAN FROM "THEATRUM EUROPAEUM," 1643

**12. Franco-Spanish War (1648–59).**—The conclusion of a separate peace with the United Provinces helped Spain to continue the struggle against France; and Condé's victory over the Spaniards at Lens (Aug. 20, 1648) was offset by the outbreak of the Fronde (*q.v.*). During the civil wars in France (1649–53), the rebel leaders, including Condé, even made treaties of their own with Spain. Success came to the French from 1655, especially after the outbreak of hostilities between Spain and England and the conclusion of

BY COURTESY OF THE TRUSTEES OF THE BRITISH MUSEUM; PHOTO, J. R. FREEMAN AND CO., LTD.

THE BATTLE OF NÖRDLINGEN, SEPT. 5–6, 1634, IN WHICH THE SWEDISH ARMIES (ATTACKING FROM THE LEFT) WERE VIRTUALLY DESTROYED; COPPER ENGRAVING BY M. MERIAN FROM "THEATRUM EUROPAEUM," 1643

Anglo-French treaties of friendship (Sept. 5, 1656) and of alliance (March 23 and May 9, 1657). Robert Blake's exploits in the Mediterranean and in the Caribbean (1655–57), followed on land with the Battle of the Dunes (June 14, 1658) and the capture of Dunkerque (June 25) and Gravelines (Aug. 24, 1658), broke Spain's resistance. In the Franco-Spanish Peace of the Pyrenees (Nov. 7, 1659) France obtained Roussillon and northern Cerdagne (thus establishing the frontier along the line of the Pyrenees), Artois, and a number of frontier fortresses in the Netherlands and Luxembourg. Spain had ceded to France the first place among the great powers of Europe.

**13. First Northern War (1655–61).**—The last decade of the 50-year period here surveyed witnessed another conflict in Northern Europe. It arose, however, from the start of the Thirteen Years' War between Russia and Poland (1654–67), which is best considered as belonging to a later historical period, characterized by the decline of Poland and by the rise of Russia and of Brandenburg-Prussia. In so far as it reaffirmed certain tendencies of the earlier period it may be briefly summarized here.

The question of the Ukraine led to war between Russia and Poland in 1654. Charles X (*q.v.*) of Sweden took advantage of this war to attack Poland in July 1655. The elector Frederick William (*q.v.*) of Brandenburg took the Swedish side from 1656 to 1657 but changed to the Polish in 1658. Russia began war against the Swedes in June 1656 but concluded the Truce of Valiesari in December 1658. In 1657 the emperor Ferdinand III's heir Leopold I (*q.v.*) allied Austria with Poland. Frederick III (*q.v.*) of Denmark attacked Sweden in June 1657.

By the Peace of Roskilde (Feb. 26, 1658) Denmark was forced to cede not only Trondheim on the North Sea coast of Norway but also Bohuslän on the Swedish coast at the end of the Skagerrak, Skåne on the eastern side of the Sound, with adjacent Blekinge, and the island of Bornholm to Sweden, thus forfeiting all hope of the "lordship of the Baltic." Denmark, however, subsequently refused to close the Baltic to Western shipping and was attacked by Sweden again in summer 1658. The Dutch, in their own commercial interests, came to Denmark's support, and the Peace of Copenhagen (June 6, 1660) restored Bornholm and also Trondheim to Denmark, but otherwise confirmed the settlement of Roskilde.

The Peace of Oliva (May 3, 1660), between Sweden on the one hand and Poland, Austria, and Brandenburg on the other, assigned Livonia to Sweden and recognized Brandenburg's full sovereignty over ducal Prussia, both these stipulations being made at Poland's expense. The Russo-Swedish Peace of Kardis (July 1, 1661) re-established the terms of the Peace of Stolbova (1617).

France had played an active role in mediating the Baltic settlement. Habsburg Austria had gained nothing from the conflict and was meanwhile confronted by the League of the Rhine (Aug. 14, 1658), organized by Mazarin, whereby France, Sweden, the electoral archbishoprics (Mainz, Cologne, and Trier), Münster, Brunswick-Lüneburg, Palatinate-Neuburg, and Hesse-Kassel guaranteed the Peace of Westphalia against Habsburg revisionism.

## IV. GERMAN CIVILIZATION

**1. The Population.**—Any estimate of the movement of population of Germany between 1600 and 1650 is hampered by the absence of any census before the 18th century and the vagueness of the territory to which any statistics could be applied. All assertions of a decline of the population during the war by one-third or even more are therefore baseless guesswork. The computation of the population of "Germany" as a whole at the beginning or the end of the war would differ by about one-quarter or more according to the inclusion or exclusion (either of which can be defended on historical grounds) of certain territories, such as the Netherlands, Switzerland, Schleswig-Holstein, Brandenburg's Polish fief of Prussia, Spain's French-speaking possessions in Luxembourg and in Franche-Comté, French-speaking Lorraine, the Slav-speaking parts of Austria's possessions (Bohemia, Moravia, Carniola, Styria), and the Italian-speaking Trentino.

Such statistical surveys as were occasionally made for a small district were nearly always prompted by the wish to support some special pleading: to obtain a grant-in-aid, to reduce a tax assessment, to avoid military service or statute labour. The main sources on which historians have drawn are the reports of chroniclers and, rarely, parish registers of death—to the virtual exclusion of registers of marriages and births. In view of the huge birthrate this neglect amounts to 30–50%; *i.e.,* to that one-third or one-half by which the population is said to have been reduced.

Death on the battlefield can be left out of count because the armies of the time, and consequently their losses, were very small. The Catholic League had an effective strength of about 15,000 men; Gustavus Adolphus landed in Germany with 15,000 men; Bernhard of Saxe-Weimar received French pay for 18,000 men; the strongest French army employed in Germany (in 1645) numbered 12,000; the first Imperial Army raised by Wallenstein in 1625 consisted of 15,000 foot and 6,000 horse.

The most serious losses were caused by epidemics, especially typhoid, the plague, and venereal diseases, spread by soldiers and refugees and intensified by lack of hygiene and incompetence of doctors. However, a few chance survivals of accurate lists of victims make it certain that during the worst outbreaks of the "pest" (the generic name applied to every epidemic) the mortality reached only 12%, and that in thickly populated towns. The average annual mortality rate seems to have been around 6 or 7%.

The most plausible explanation of the depletion of certain parts of Germany is to be found in an extensive internal migration, chiefly from the agrarian village to the industrial town and from the economically declining to the economically prosperous town (as for instance from Cologne to Frankfurt). But there was also a considerable fluctuation of refugees and evacuees from open country to the safety of the walled town: Kiel and Lübeck served as refuges for the gentry of Holstein. A typical example of this temporary dislocation of the population can be seen in five Thuringian rural districts for which accurate statistics have been computed: numbers declined during the years 1631–49 between 66 and 87% and increased in the decade 1649–59 by between 78 and 125%. The net result of this redistribution of population was an all-around though small increase of the total population such as is characteristic of every predominantly agricultural society. Bearing in mind the elasticity of the term "Germany," one can assume a population of 15,000,000–17,000,000 in 1600 and one of 16,000,000–18,000,000 in 1650, as may be inferred from the figure (fairly well attested) of 17,000,000–20,000,000 for the Empire in 1700.

**2. Economic Life.**—The years round 1620 saw German economic life at its lowest point. For centuries its strength, like that of Italy, had lain in the flourishing towns, where industry, banking, and trade (import and export) were concentrated. From the middle of the 16th century the heyday of their prosperity was over. Politically, the free cities succumbed to the growing power of the territorial princes; only a few—Lübeck, Hamburg, Bremen, Danzig, Nürnberg, Augsburg, Frankfurt—maintained more than an outward semblance of independence.

Economically the Hanse towns of northern Germany (*see* HANSEATIC LEAGUE) were severely hit by the Muscovites' destruction of Novgorod (1570), by the Spaniards' sack of Antwerp (1585), and by Queen Elizabeth I's closing of the London Steelyard (1598); and the separation of the United Provinces from Spain gave to the Hanse's Dutch rivals a free hand to break its monopoly in the Baltic. The south German cities, whose bankers were deeply involved in the financial transactions of both Austrian and Spanish Habsburgs, were largely ruined by the repeated bankruptcies of the Spanish crown (1557, 1575, 1596, 1607); the insolvency of the Augsburg firm of Welser in 1614 was only the most spectacular debacle of many.

The collapse of the old order was made evident in the big inflation of the years 1619–23, which brought utter ruin to the classes dependent on savings, annuities, or fixed incomes but provided colossal gains to versatile financiers and industrialists as well as to unscrupulous speculators and profiteers. The emperor Ferdinand II, who lent his active support to a combine of ruthless racketeers, and the dukes of Brunswick-Wolfenbüttel were conspicuous among the "legal" counterfeiters. When the currency was stabilized again in 1624, a thoroughgoing transfer of capital had occurred: none of the old-established and sometimes decadent firms survived, and their place was taken by pushing upstarts. This changeover of family and business fortunes continued: the proscription of Wallenstein and his adherents in 1634 permitted the Viennese courtiers and generals to acquire for a song the richest Bohemian and Silesian estates.

In fact, the inflation of 1619–23 was the turning point. The outward sign of economic recovery was the establishment of the big clearing banks of Hamburg (1619) and Nürnberg (1621); the Hamburg "Mark Banko" was for two centuries the most stable international currency unit till the pound sterling superseded it.

In German agriculture, too, a regrouping of ownership and profits rather than a general decline is to be noted. The steady rise of corn prices from the mid-16th century made large-scale farming and bulk-selling more profitable; and from the end of the 16th century the feudal owners of big estates practised wholesale evictions of peasants and forced acquisition of peasant lands, thereby depopulating the countryside and obliterating hundreds of villages. As far as can be ascertained, those villages which were wholly or partly burned down by the soldiery in the course of the war were all rebuilt and even enlarged before the end of it; and the same is true of Magdeburg, the only town of any size to be severely damaged by enemy action. The wars themselves proved a source of gain to the big landowners, who supplied victuals, grain, and livestock to the contending armies, whereas the small farmer could not compete with the lord of the manor and moreover endured greater hardship from marauding troops than did the townsman. Especially in those areas which suffered least from the military invasions—Prussia, Pomerania, Brandenburg, and Mecklenburg—the formerly free farmers were reduced to virtual or legal serfdom.

Apart from the destructive effect of every war, it must be borne in mind that all the campaigns of the first half of the 17th century were of short duration and almost invariably centred round the same focal points which, by their geographical position, have been fought over again and again from time immemorial: the Alpine passes, the Rhine crossings, the bridgeheads of Regensburg on the Danube and Magdeburg on the Elbe, the plains of Leipzig and Brabant. However, the resilience of the people of these districts has always been equal to their plight—as can be seen, for instance, at Leipzig. That city went bankrupt in 1625, was bombarded and stormed in 1631, 1632, 1633, 1637, and 1642, witnessed the major battles of Breitenfeld (1631 and 1642) and Lützen (1632) before its very gates, and was under Swedish occupation from 1642 to 1650; but in these years the annual Leipzig Fair established itself as the centre of European trade, and in 1640 the town council reported regular trade relations with Italy, Poland, England, Brabant, Scandinavia, the Ukraine, and the intermediate countries. Parts of Germany were affected by hostilities for a few weeks, others not at all. Most towns never saw an enemy within their walls.

Of all the wild exaggerations concerning the moral degeneration of the German people caused by the Thirty Years' War that of cannibalism due to famine and starvation has a morbid appeal which few writers have been able to withstand. The refutation of these stories is the more difficult as the original accusations were vague, the source material is buried in the files of rural magistrates' courts, and critical investigations are scattered in obscure journals. It seems that one case of cannibalism can be taken as established: it occurred among the starving garrison of Breisach during the long siege in 1638. A second case proven in court is that of a Silesian bandit tried in 1654: having killed a pregnant woman, he ate her unborn child's heart in order, as he confessed, to make himself "stronger and fiercer"—a clear example of a form of superstitious magic known to anthropologists. Every other story of cannibalism that has been investigated can be shown to be the adaptation of some classical or medieval fable, if not simply a journalistic stunt. Thus, a contributor to a popular serial in 1639 startled his readers with the rhetorical question: "Has Germany become America? Cannibals now openly walk about . . . ." The vicar of a Palatine village, asking his co-religionists abroad for donations, asserted that "food is so scarce that the dead are no longer safe in their graves." This unsubstantiated hint proved so effective that henceforth no appeal to charity dispensed with references to body-snatching and cannibalism.

**3. Literature and the Arts.**—The great impetus of the Renaissance and the intellectual fervour of the Reformation had exhausted themselves by 1570, just when Italy, France, England, Spain, and the Netherlands entered upon a fresh period of cultural grandeur. From the general European point of view, Germany was overshadowed and virtually ceased to count as an independent contributor in the cultural field. The picture of the years 1600–50, however, is different when studied from the narrower German angle. From the start of the 17th century onward German scholars, scientists, musicians, writers, and poets were coming again to the fore and producing works which were to have lasting influence upon German culture. The legend of the cultural exhaustion and desolation of Germany during and after the Thirty Years' War is solely due to the aesthetic standards of 19th-century historians, who despised the Baroque style and so could not appreciate the work of Baroque artists and writers. Moreover, the huge spate of German translations chiefly of Italian, Spanish, and French scholars and scientists, prose writers, and poets tends to be overlooked.

Italian influence was especially prominent in the German theatre of the time, in which decor, stage effects, and music were combined to produce operatic showpieces: the plays (in Latin) of the Jesuit Jakob Bidermann (1578–1639) and the Passion play of Oberammergau (*q.v.;* first performed in 1634) are spectacular examples. The composer Heinrich Schütz (1585–1672) helped to establish the fashion for Italian music in Germany with his madrigals, symphonies, and oratorios as well as the first German opera (*Dafne,* 1627) and the first German ballet (*Orpheus und Eurydice,* 1638).

German language and literature had enthusiastic though somewhat pedantic nurseries in the literary societies modeled on the Florentine Accademia della Crusca, of which the Weimar *Fruchtbringende Gesellschaft* (1617) was the oldest and most influential, followed by the Hamburg *Teutschgesinnte Genossenschaft* (1643), the Nürnberg *Pegnitzorden* (1644), and others. Aiming at a purification of the German language, the encouragement of writers, and an improvement of manners and morals, they listed among their members numerous leaders of society and every literary figure of note. Martin Opitz (*q.v.*), with his *Buch von der teutschen Poeterey* (1624), and Justus Georg Schottel (1612–76) with his *Teutsche Sprachkunst* (1641) standardized the theory of New High German poetics and grammar for 150 years. Opitz's own poetry is unoriginal and largely modeled on the French poets of the Pléiade; but as he tried his hand in every type of fashionable literature and was a prolific translator, his influence was considerable throughout 17th-century Germany. The mystical poems of Friedrich Spee (1591–1635), the epigrams of Friedrich von Logau (1604–55), the Latin odes of Jakob Balde (1604–68), the satirical novels of J. M. Moscherosch (1601–69), the hymns of Simon Dach (1605–59) and of Paul Gerhardt (1607–76), the occasional and patriotic poems of Georg Rudolf Weckherlin (1584–1653), the plays of Andreas Gryphius (*q.v.;* 1616–64), and the novel *Die Adriatische Rosemund* of Philipp von Zesen (1619–89) —these highlights of the German literature of the war years are still read. Their testimony to a flourishing literary life is further supported by the expansion of the two leading German printers and publishers, Endter in Nürnberg and Stern in Lüneburg, whose books, pamphlets, hymnals, calendars, etc. were bought by the middle and lower classes in, at least, every Protestant region of the empire.

The outstanding figure in German science is the astronomer Johannes Kepler (*q.v.*), who discovered the laws of the planets while serving successively the emperor Rudolf II, the Estates of Upper Austria, and Wallenstein. Otto von Guericke, who as councilor and burgomaster of Magdeburg supervised the reconstruction of the city after 1631, was the inventor of the air pump and manometer. The Naturwissenschaftliche Gesellschaft, founded in Rostock in 1622, was the first learned society to devote itself primarily to the advancement of science. The English physician William Harvey chose a Frankfurt publisher to bring out his discovery of the circulation of the blood (1628).

In art and architecture, the influence of Palladio and Bernini was strong enough to italianize all building in the south of Germany, whereas the northwest fell under Dutch influence. Maximilian of Bavaria patronized the Dutchman Peter Candid, a pupil of Giorgio Vasari, as painter and builder for his palaces in Munich and Schleissheim. All the palaces, cathedrals, and churches built in the 17th century by the Habsburg rulers and their courtiers in Vienna, Salzburg, Graz, Innsbruck, and Prague were the work of Italian designers, as were Wallenstein's palaces in Prague, Jičin, and Sagan. On the whole, however, there was little incentive for new building, since the great buildings of the prosperous first three-quarters of the 16th century still served the need of the majority of their owners. Most private houses of the less well-to-do are artistically insignificant and have therefore failed to gain entry in the histories of architecture. A lively interest in architecture, however, is attested by the success of several textbooks for the instruction of builders and their clients, such as that by Rüdiger Kossmann of Cologne (first published in 1630 and reedited in 1644 and 1653) and three by Josef Furttenbach of Ulm (1628, 1640, and 1641).

## V. CONCLUSION

The European struggle against the predominance of Spain is the main topic of all the hot and cold wars, diplomatic moves and alignments, religious and constitutional tensions which fill the history of the first half of the 17th century. The Thirty Years' War, so called, is merely a segment of this general upheaval. The result, in the peace treaties of Westphalia and of the Pyrenees, can be summed up as follows.

In the field of international as well as of German politics, the sovereignty and independence of the individual state was established as the principle on which henceforth the European comity of nations and, in the narrower German context, the framework of the Holy Roman Empire were to be based. For Germany this structure survived, with modifications (notably in the Napoleonic period), until the foundation of the German Empire under Prussian hegemony in 1871; and for Western Europe the principle was maintained into the second half of the 20th century. The medieval conception of the theoretical unity of the *respublica Christiana* with the Roman emperor and the Roman pope as its temporal and spiritual heads was formally abandoned in favour of a community of sovereign, independent states, of equal status, regardless of form of government or confession of faith, though united by a common adherence to certain fundamental principles of law and order. This was a first, tentative step toward a European community, in which, however, Great Britain and Russia were not included.

BIBLIOGRAPHY.—S. H. Steinberg, *The Thirty Years' War* (1966). *See* also H. Hauser, *La Prépondérance espagnole, 1559–1660* (1933); C. V. Wedgwood, *The Thirty Years' War* (1938), quite at variance with this article; G. Pagès, *La Guerre de Trente Ans* (1939); R. Ergang, *The Myth of the All-Destructive Fury of the Thirty Years' War* (1956). For a Nazi interpretation *see* G. Franz, *Der Dreissigjährige Krieg und das deutsche Volk,* 2nd ed. (1943); for a Marxist interpretation *see* J. Polišenský, "The Thirty Years' War," in *Past and Present,* 6 (1954). For the Peace of Westphalia *see* E. Hövel (ed.), *Pax optima rerum* (1948); M. Braubach, *Der Westfälische Friede* (1948); F. Dickmann, *Der Westfälische Frieden* (1959). (S. H. S.)

**THISTED,** an *amt* (county) in northwest Jutland (Jylland), Denmark, comprises the peninsular province of Thy, with its smooth dune coast, and the island of Mors (area 140 sq.mi. [363 sq.km.], pop. [1960] 26,766) in the great inland broad of Limfjorden. Total county area is 685 sq.mi. (1,774 sq.km.). Pop. (1960) 84,955. The soils of Mors and the eastern part of Thy range from sandy loams to heavier clay loams of moderate fertility supporting mixed farming. Coniferous plantations clothe the dunes. Nykøbing (pop. [1960] 9,326) is the principal town of Mors with an iron foundry and oyster canneries. Thisted town (pop. [1960] 8,768), the urban centre for Thy province, makes machinery, textiles, and beer. (HA. T.)

**THISTLE,** a name of vague application, given to almost any herbaceous plant that has spines. More strictly, it is applied to certain herbs possessing very spiny leaves, and similar bracts surrounding a head of rose, purplish, or yellowish, tubular, five-parted flowers seated on a pitted and hairy receptacle, belonging to the Compositae family. The fruit is surmounted by a tuft of hairs. The species, chiefly natives of Europe, western Asia, and North America, are numerous, and some are of great beauty.

JOHN H. GERARD

FIELD THISTLE (CIRSIUM DISCOLOR)

*Cirsium* species constitute the plumed thistles, some of the most pernicious weeds, especially *C. arvense,* the Canada thistle. This deep-rooted, erect perennial, native to Europe, is now extensively naturalized throughout North America in fields and waste grounds. It may grow to be six feet high. The grooved stems, somewhat branched above, bear deeply cut, exceedingly prickly leaves and numerous showy, fragrant purplish flower heads, about one inch across; staminate (male) and pistillate (female) flowers are sometimes borne on separate plants. In Europe *C. arvense* is called the creeping thistle because of its whitish lateral roots that give rise to daughter shoots. Because of its white woolly leaves and rose-purple flowers *C. occidentale,* from California and southern Oregon, is sometimes planted for bolt effect in gardens.

The plumeless thistles, probably native to the Balkans, belong to the genus *Carduus.* In these species, the seeds have a bristly projection instead of a feathery plumed one, as in *Cirsium.*

The blessed thistle is *Cnicus benedictus;* lady's thistle, the leaves of which are spotted with white, is *Silybum marianum.* The common bull thistle, *Cirsium lanceolatum,* seems to be the most suitable prototype for the Scots thistle, though that honour is also conferred on, among other species, *Onopordon acanthium,* the cotton thistle, remarkable for its covering of white down, a doubtful native of Great Britain.

Among other thistles the following, all introduced from Eurasia, are well-known noxious weeds of farmlands in the northern United States and Canada. The blue thistle (*Echium vulgare*) is a biennial member of the borage family. The Russian thistle (*Salsola kali*), so common on the Great Plains of western North America, is an introduced annual tumbleweed belonging to the pigweed family. The perennial sow thistle (*Sonchus arvensis*), a milky-juiced member of the family Compositae, because of its freely creeping root system, is one of the most persistent weeds of arable lands.

The great objection to thistles from an agricultural point of view resides in the freedom with which their seeds are spread and in the vigour of their underground growth, which makes their eradication difficult. Short rotation of crops, clipping of pastures, intense cultivation of field crops, and rigorous cutting of thistles along roadsides and in waste grounds before the seeds mature are only partly effective. The best control is spraying young foliage with 2,4-D or other weed killer in full sunlight with an air temperature of 70° or higher. (W. C. M.; N. Tr.)

**THISTLEWOOD, ARTHUR** (1774–1820), English revolutionary, principal instigator in 1820 of the Cato Street Conspiracy, a plot to murder the British cabinet, was born at Tupholme, Lincolnshire, the son of a farmer. After visiting the United States and France he became a soldier. He developed republican sympathies and joined the Spencean Society, a revolutionary organization, in London. In December 1816 he helped to arrange a meeting in Spa Fields, London, which was to be followed by the seizure of the Tower of London and the Bank of England. The proposed rising failed, but the Habeas Corpus Act was suspended (February 1817), and Thistlewood and a fellow conspirator James Watson were tried. Both were acquitted, but Thistlewood was later sentenced (May 1818) to a year's imprisonment for challenging the home secretary, Viscount Sidmouth, to a duel. After his release, at a time of great distress and unrest, he prepared a plot to assassinate the members of the cabinet and to set up a provisional government. On Feb. 23, 1820, the cabinet ministers had arranged to dine at the earl of Harrowby's house in Grosvenor Square. The authorities had been informed of the plot and on the evening of the 23rd, as Thistlewood with some associates was preparing to leave a room in Cato Street, off the Edgware Road, for Grosvenor square, officers appeared and arrested some of them. Thistlewood escaped, but was seized the next day. There were minor disturbances in London, but they were quickly quelled. Tried for high treason, Thistlewood and four others were sentenced to death and were hanged outside Newgate prison on May 1, 1820. (A. Bri.)

**THÖKÖLY, IMRE** (1657–1705), leader of the Hungarian Protestants in their struggle against Austrian Habsburg rule and, for a few years, titular prince of Transylvania. He was born on Sept. 25, 1657, into a Protestant noble family, at Késmárk (Kežmarok in Slovakia), in that part of the Hungarian kingdom which the Turks had not conquered from the Habsburgs; but in 1670, when his father was executed for his role in the Hungarian magnates' conspiracy against the Holy Roman emperor Leopold I, he took refuge in Transylvania (*q.v.*), where his kinsman, Michael Teleki, was chief minister to Prince Michael Apafi I. The emperor Leopold's regime, however, launched such a persecution against the Protestant malcontents in Habsburg Hungary that in 1678 the refugees on the Transylvanian border began war on behalf of their oppressed compatriots. Encouraged by promises of support from King Louis XIV of France (at war against Leopold till 1679) and backed by Apafi and by the Turkish pasha of Nagyvárad (Oradea), they elected Thököly as their commander in chief in 1680. He soon occupied much of Upper Hungary. Leopold was forced to conclude the Treaty of Sopron (1681), by which the liberties of the kingdom were restored.

In 1682 Thököly augmented his prestige by marriage to Ilona Zrinyi, widow of Ferenc Rákóczy I (*q.v.*). He then renewed the war against Leopold. His forces overran the whole of Upper Hungary (of which he took the title of prince) and advanced to the Vág (Vah) River; but his Turkish allies were defeated in their historic attempt to take Vienna by siege (1683). As the Austrians gradually reconquered the Hungarian lands, Thököly's fortunes declined, and he became more and more dependent on the Turks, who in 1690 appointed him prince of Transylvania. He won a victory over the emperor's forces at Zernest (Zărneşti) in 1690; but after the Austro-Turkish Peace of Carlowitz (1699), whereby Leopold recovered Hungary and Transylvania, Thököly had to go into exile in Turkey. He settled at Izmit (Nicomedia), where he died on Sept. 13, 1705. His remains were transferred to Késmárk in 1906. (T. K.)

**THOMAS, SAINT,** one of the 12 apostles. The name means "twin" in Aramaic, as is recognized in John 11:16 ("called Didymus" or "twin" in Greek). He is called Judas Thomas (*i.e.,* Judas the Twin) by the Syrians and in the *Acts of Thomas* (*see* below); and in some Syriac manuscripts of the Gospel of John his name, Thomas, or Judas Thomas, is given in John 14:22 rather than "Judas (not Iscariot)," suggesting an identification with Judas "of James" (*see* Judas, Saint). The apostle's character is most clearly outlined in the Gospel of John. "Doubting Thomas" is derived from John 20:24–28, where, by his confession of faith in verse 28, Thomas becomes the first person explicitly to acknowledge Christ's divinity.

Eusebius, in his *Church History* (early 4th century), says that Thomas was the evangelist of "Parthia," perhaps because Edessa, where some of the apostle's bones were said to be preserved, is sometimes called Edessa of the Parthians. His relics are now supposed to be at Ortona, in the Abruzzi, in Italy, where, according to tradition, they were taken from Edessa by way of the island of Chios. His feast day is July 3 in the Syrian Church, Dec. 21 elsewhere. (*See* also Apostle.)

**Acts of Thomas.**—*The Story.*—This work (*Acta Thomae*) is one of several apocryphal *Acts* of apostles (*see* Apocrypha, New Testament). Its basic narrative—which is interspersed with hymns and prayers—is a highly coloured tale describing the selection of Thomas to evangelize India, his journey to the court of King Gundaphorus (the historical Gondophares; *q.v.*), his preaching and conversions, and his eventual martyrdom and burial on a mountain, from which his bones were later removed and taken to the West.

As a tale, the *Acts of Thomas* is remarkable for the religious emotion that pervades it and for its careful delineation of character, but above all for the hymn chanted by the apostle when in prison. This, commonly known as the "Hymn of the Pearl," is a metrical poem in Syriac describing, under the form of the journey of a prince from his Eastern home to Egypt, the descent of the soul to earth and its return to its heavenly home. It may be an independent composition, of Gnostic origin, inserted into the *Acts,* but for this there is no conclusive evidence.

*Association of Thomas with India.*—"Christians of St. Thomas" is a name often applied to the ancient Christian churches of southern India. It is known that there were Christians of Persian (East Syrian) origin, and doubtless of Nestorian creed, in Ceylon, in Malabar, and at Caliana (north of Bombay) before 550. (*See* further Malabar Christians.) These ancient Christian communities would be naturally regarded as a surviving branch of the extensive Nestorian missions (*see* Nestorians: *Origins and Early History*). Many of the Christians in India, however, regard St. Thomas as their founder and appeal to tradition and to the *Acts of*

*Thomas* in support. They claim that the *Acts* are historical and that they refer in part to the apostle's activity in southern India. Their tradition asserts that he founded the Christian churches in Malabar and then crossed to Mylapur, now a suburb of Madras, where the shrine of his martyrdom, built or rebuilt by the Portuguese in the 16th century, still stands on St. Thomas Mount.

There are objections to the Indian Christians' view, such as the absence of compellingly clear allusions to specifically southern usages in the *Acts*. As to the meeting of St. Thomas and King Gondophares, while a rigorously scientific proof is impossible, yet the substantial agreement of the *Acts* (the sole literary document which mentions this king) with all that is known from other sources is best explained on the supposition that the *Acts* contain a kernel of historical truth. As to the southern journey and the martyrdom in Mylapur, the agreement of the south Indian tradition with that of the Church of Edessa lends a degree of probability to the claim that St. Thomas preached in southern India, suffered martyrdom there, and was there first buried. Historically speaking, however, the evidence remains inconclusive.

*Literary History.*—The *Acts of Thomas* was originally composed in Syriac, and indeed it represents one of the oldest and most idiomatic monuments of Syriac literature. In the 4th century it was translated into Greek and thence into Latin, almost certainly as Manichaean propaganda. The Manichaean taint was soon recognized (*e.g.,* by Augustine), and in its original form the work was branded as heretical. The view taken was that the framework, recounting the journeyings of the apostle, was historical, while the speeches and sermons contained the heresy. In consequence, most manuscripts, both Greek and Latin, contain very little of the speeches while retaining the framework. The original form is to be found only in some very ancient Syriac fragments.

*Early Christianity.*—The *Acts of Thomas* is a leading authority for the earliest Christianity in the countries east of the Euphrates. According to this document, it was ascetic, marriage being discountenanced and all preoccupation with the things of this world discouraged. Eucharistic prayers are given, but according to the best manuscript sources only bread and water were used. The Lord's Prayer is quoted in full. The name of the apostle is given as Judas Thomas, and it is expressly stated that he was the twin of Jesus Christ. (N. J. T.; X.)

**Apocryphal Gospel of Thomas.**—Among the Coptic Gnostic papyri found in 1945 near Naj' Hammadi in Upper Egypt was a collection of about 114 sayings headed "These are the secret sayings which Jesus the Living spoke and which Didymus Judas Thomas wrote; and he said, He who will find the interpretation of these words will not taste death." The title of the collection is "Gospel According to Thomas." H. C. Puech observed that some of the sayings had already been found in three Greek papyrus fragments from Oxyrhynchus (3rd and 4th centuries). Others occur in "unwritten sayings" recorded by the Church Fathers or by Gnostic writers; some are found in fragments of the apocryphal gospels "According to the Hebrews" and "According to the Egyptians" (*see* APOCRYPHA, NEW TESTAMENT). Many of the sayings, especially parables, closely resemble sayings recorded in the Synoptic Gospels (there are also some parallels to John).

The *Gospel of Thomas* was used by 2nd- or 3rd-century Gnostic groups, by Syrian Christians of dubious orthodoxy, and by the Manichees and their successors. It is echoed in the *Acts of Thomas,* though Origen, Eusebius, and later church writers explicitly rejected it. As a whole, it reflects a dualism expressed in hostility toward the world, the flesh, and Judaism; it rejects prayer, fasting, almsgiving, the Old Testament, and family ties in favour of seeking the Kingdom within (identified with self-knowledge) and a mystical unity transcending anything "worldly." The author's basic views are thus fairly close to those of the Naassenes, a Gnostic group described by Hippolytus of Rome (*Refutation* v, 7–8).

The basic question raised by "Thomas" is whether the synoptic-type sayings are derived from an oral tradition, perhaps prior in origin to the Synoptic Gospels, or from these Gospels themselves. Various answers are given by various scholars; the question cannot be regarded as definitely solved, though it would appear that in most instances the motives of "Thomas" account for changes he may have made. Certainly he intended his work to look as if it came from oral tradition. (R. McQ. G.)

BIBLIOGRAPHY.—*Acts of Thomas:* W. Wright, *Apocryphal Acts of the Apostles,* Syriac text with Eng. trans., 2 vol. (1871); Greek text in R. A. Lipsius and M. Bonnet, *Acta Apostolorum Apocrypha,* vol. ii (1903), Eng. trans. in M. R. James, *The Apocryphal New Testament,* pp. 364–438 (1924). On the "Hymn of the Pearl," *see* A. A. Bevan, in *Texts and Studies,* vol. v, no. 3, with Eng. trans. (1897); and F. C. Burkitt, *Early Eastern Christianity,* with a metrical English version (1904). (N. J. T.)

*Gospel of Thomas:* H. C. Puech, "L'Évangile selon Thomas," *Comptes-rendus de l'Académie des Inscriptions,* pp. 146–166 (1957); J. Doresse, *L'Évangile selon Thomas* (1959); R. M. Grant with D. N. Freedman and W. R. Schoedel, *The Secret Sayings of Jesus* (1959); M. Malinine *et al., The Gospel According to Thomas,* Coptic text and Eng. trans. (1959); B. Gärtner, *The Theology of the Gospel of Thomas* (1961); R. McL. Wilson (trans.) and W. Schneemelcher (ed.), *New Testament Apocrypha,* vol. i, *Gospels and Related Writings* (1963). (R. McQ. G.)

**THOMAS** (d. 1100), archbishop of York who steadfastly repudiated the primacy of Canterbury, known from his birthplace as Thomas of Bayeux, was the son of a priest of good family named Osbert. Thomas was a protégé of the powerful Odo, bishop of Bayeux, who paid for him to study in France, Germany, and Spain, and made him treasurer of Bayeux. He went with Odo to England and became a chaplain of William I the Conqueror. When in 1070 Thomas was appointed archbishop of York, he faced the task of rebuilding and refounding the cathedral and restoring religious life in the northern province after the Conqueror's ruthless devastation. This he largely carried out. He made a profession of obedience to Archbishop Lanfranc personally, not to the see of Canterbury, but in 1072 the Council of Windsor decreed that York was subordinate to Canterbury. Despite this, Thomas protested in 1092 that the new cathedral at Lincoln belonged to his province, and in 1093 agreed to consecrate Anselm only as archbishop and metropolitan of Canterbury, not as "primate of all England." On the death of William II in August 1100, Thomas arrived too late to crown his successor Henry I (Anselm was in exile). He returned to York, where he died on Nov. 18, 1100. His chief claim to fame is his foundation of the cathedral constitution of York, one of the greatest of the English secular cathedrals in the Middle Ages. (G. W. S. B.)

**THOMAS** THE RHYMER (OF ERCELDOUNE) (*fl. c.* 1250–1290), Scottish poet, whose name has been associated with many prophetic sayings. Probably an owner of property in Erceldoune (now Earlston; *q.v.*), a village in Berwick County, Scotland, Thomas was presumably dead when his son, as "heir of Thomas the Rhymer," gave this property to Soltre (Soutra) Hospital in November 1294. It seems very likely that he was the author of the metrical romance *Sir Tristrem,* which survives in a manuscript of *c.* 1330 (first printed in 1804 by Walter Scott). This is a version of the widely diffused Tristan legend; it is ascribed to him by the contemporary English chronicler Robert Mannyng of Brunne (*fl.* 1283–1338), and opens: "I was at Ercheldoune/With Thomas spak I ther/Ther herd I rede in roune/Who Tristrem gat and bare."

His fame as a poet was outweighed by his fame as a prophet, which was already well established in the mid-14th century. An early 14th-century manuscript in a southern dialect gives, for example, his prophecy to the countess of Dunbar as to when the Scottish War of Independence will end. He figures in John Barbour's *Bruce* (prophesying that Bruce would be king), in Walter Bower's *Scotichronicon* (foretelling the death of Alexander III in 1286), and in Blind Harry's *Schir William Wallace* (as "Thomas Rimour"). His prophecies first appear in literary form in the early 15th-century *Romance of Thomas of Erceldoune* (edited in 1875 by J. A. H. Murray). By the mid-15th century Thomas' fame was widespread in England, as well as in Scotland, and prophecies much current in this disturbed period were often ascribed to him. This habit accounts for the 1603 printed edition which attributes to him prophecies of various dates between *c.* 1430 and *c.* 1550. As late as the Jacobite revolts of the 18th century these and other prophecies were still consulted. He is now probably best known through the ballad *Thomas the Rhymer,* which Walter Scott included in his *Minstrelsy of the Scottish Border* (volume ii, 1802), and in popular lore he is usually coupled with Merlin (*q.v.*) and other English seers. The 19th-century Russian poet Mikhail Lermontov (*q.v.*) claimed Thomas as an ancestor.

BIBLIOGRAPHY.—*Texts: Thomas the Rhymer,* in W. Scott, *Minstrelsy of the Scottish Border,* vol. ii (1802); J. A. H. Murray, *The Romance and Prophecies of Thomas of Erceldoune Printed from Five Manuscripts* (1875); A. Brandl, *Thomas of Erceldoune* (1880). *See* also J. M. Burnham, "A Study of Thomas of Erceldoune," in *Publications of the Modern Language Association of America,* vol. xxiii (1908); J. Geddie, *Thomas the Rymour and His Rhymes* (1920); H. M. Flasdieck, *Tom der Reimer* (1934). (A. A. M. D.)

**THOMAS, ALBERT** (1878–1932), French statesman and historian, was one of the leaders of the moderate wing of the Socialist Party and in 1919 became the first director of the International Labour Office. He was born at Champigny-sur-Marne, near Paris, on June 16, 1878. He graduated from the École Normale Supérieure and won scholarships that enabled him to travel to Russia, the eastern Mediterranean, and Germany. He early showed interest in history and in the problems of the working class throughout the world. His passionate concern with the latter led him to seek in history for precedents and causes of socialism, syndicalism, and the cooperative movement. His most important scholarly work was *Le Syndicalisme allemand* (1903), in which his Socialist faith was propounded for the first time.

In 1904, when Jean Jaurès launched *L'Humanité,* a Socialist newspaper, Thomas was appointed assistant editor. He played an important part as one of the leaders of the moderate groups within the CGT (Confédération Générale du Travail). In 1910 he was elected by his native suburb to the Chamber of Deputies.

Thomas's talent for organization was revealed in World War I when he was entrusted with the organization of the railways in September 1914. He became undersecretary of state for munitions in May 1915 and was appointed minister of munitions in December 1916, retaining that post until September 1917. After the fall of the Russian imperial government, Thomas was sent to Petrograd in April 1917. He worked with the Kerenski government and supervised the production of munitions in an attempt to maintain cooperation between the new republic and the Entente.

Meanwhile in France the struggle between the majority section of the French Socialist Party, which supported the war, and the minority section, which was pacifist, culminated in the Stockholm Conference in June 1917. Thomas was a leader of the majority section and was also a strong advocate of the independence of Czechoslovakia and Poland and of the creation of a Greater Serbia and Greater Rumania. Because this policy was opposed by many Socialists, Thomas decided not to stand again in his Paris suburb, but he was returned as a Socialist in the Tarn *département* in November 1919.

Soon after the election, Thomas was appointed director of the International Labour Organization (League of Nations). He continued until his death to work with prodigious energy for the organization of the ILO, for the extension of its influence, and for the elaboration of an international labour law. He prepared encyclopaedic annual reports, traveled extensively, and earned for himself the title of "labour diplomatist" by securing national ratifications of conventions adopted by the International Labour Conference. The claims of his work in Geneva had led him in 1921 to resign his seat in the Chamber of Deputies. He died in Paris on May 7, 1932. *See* further INTERNATIONAL LABOUR ORGANIZATION.

BIBLIOGRAPHY.—J. T. Shotwell (ed.), *Origins of the International Labor Organization,* 2nd ed. (1934); E. J. Phelan, *Yes and Albert Thomas* (1936); B. W. Schaper, *Albert Thomas* (1953).

**THOMAS, DYLAN MARLAIS** (1914–1953), Welsh poet and prose writer whose *18 Poems* (1934) announced a strikingly individual and new, if not always comprehensible, voice in English poetry. His original style was further developed in *Twenty-Five Poems* (1936) and *The Map of Love* (1939). The greater lucidity of *Deaths and Entrances* (1946) and the last poems, included in *Collected Poems* (1952), is accompanied by the deeper insight and superb craftsmanship of a major 20th-century English poet. In the prose writing the comic exuberance of Thomas' gifts as an entertainer is increasingly linked with the vision of the poet.

He was born in Swansea, on Oct. 27, 1914. A pupil at Swansea Grammar School, where his father taught English, Thomas edited the school magazine, contributing poetry and prose, but left at 16 to work as a reporter on the *South Wales Evening Post.* Those years in Swansea are vividly recalled in the autobiographical *Portrait of the Artist as a Young Dog* (1940). The family came from Welsh-speaking, rural west Wales: Gwilym Marles (or Marlais), a great-uncle, had been a notable bard and minister. It was on the north Carmarthenshire farm of his aunt Ann Jones (whose death is commemorated in "After the Funeral") that Thomas spent those happy and formative childhood holidays recorded in the stories and the ecstatic recollections of "Fern Hill."

Thomas' work, in its overtly emotional impact, its insistence on the importance of sound and rhythm, its primitivism, its biblical echoes and imagery, the tensions of Puritan conflict, owed more to his Welsh background than to the prevailing tastes in English literature. Therein lay its originality. The poetry written up to 1939 is concerned with introspective, obsessive, sexual and religious currents of feeling; and Thomas seems to be arguing rhetorically with himself on the subjects of sex and death, sin and redemption, the natural processes, creation and decay. The writing shows prodigious energy, but the final effect is sometimes diffuse.

No artist could feel more of a young dog than Dylan Thomas in Swansea, and he soon crossed swords with Welsh nonconformity, whose code he both mocked and feared. Leaving Wales for London in 1934 he declared, "The land of my fathers. My fathers can keep it." But Thomas was always returning, and soon after his marriage to Caitlin Macnamara in 1937 he moved to Laugharne. During World War II (he was medically unfit for National Service) he worked on film scripts, living in London, and later in New Quay, Cardiganshire, and near Oxford, before returning to Laugharne in 1949 to live in the Boat House.

*Deaths and Entrances* (the title is taken from Donne's sermon "Deaths Duell") confirms Thomas as a religious poet, and shows an advance in sympathy and understanding due, in part, to the impact of war and to the deepening harmony between the poet and his Welsh environment, for he writes generally in a mood of reconciliation and acceptance. He often adopts a bardic tone and is a true Romantic in claiming a high, almost priestlike function for the poet. There is extensive use of Christian myth and symbol, and the note of formal ritual and incantation reminds one that Thomas is a preacher in verse. The re-creation of childhood experience produces a visionary, mystical poetry in which the landscapes of youth and infancy assume the holiness of the first Eden ("Poem in October," "Fern Hill"); and for Thomas, as for Vaughan and Traherne (other important 17th-century influences), childhood, with its intimations of immortality, is a state of innocence and grace. But the rhapsodic lilt and music of the later verse derives from a complex technical discipline so that Thomas' absorption in his "craft and sullen art" produces verbal harmonies unique in English poetry.

Thomas' prose is linked with his development as a poet; and his first stories, included in *The Map of Love* and *A Prospect of the Sea* (1955), are a by-product of the early poetry. But in *Portrait of the Artist as a Young Dog* the half-mythical Welsh landscapes of the early stories have been replaced by realistically and humorously observed scenes. A poet's growing consciousness of himself (the real seriousness hidden behind the mask of comedy) and of the world around him is presented with that characteristic blend of humour and pathos which is later given such lively expression in *Under Milk Wood* (1954), "A Play for Voices" first produced on the radio. It is this play which shows Thomas' full powers as an artist in comedy: richly imaginative in language, dramatic in characterization, fertile in comic invention.

Laugharne, built on hill slopes that descend to the horseshoe bay, and the surrounding countryside are the source of theme and image in the final poems. These Welsh landscapes, "God's rough tumbling grounds," become Thomas' pulpit as he celebrates "great And fabulous, dear God" and the divine purpose he sees in man and nature. Like his close friend and fellow Welsh poet Vernon Watkins, Thomas sought a metaphysical truth in his work: for both poets natural observation was significant only in so far as it supported a deeper truth. In the last poems Thomas learned to accept the terror even of his own inner conflict, and not only does the poet claim an increasing faith as he approaches death but the whole world seems to sing its Creator's praises more joyously. Whatever the personal difficulties of his last years—financial worries, failing health, the reckless drinking bouts—neither the poetry nor the prose suggest diminution of creative powers, but rather a new potential. While on his fourth lecture tour Thomas died in New York City, on Nov. 9, 1953, a few days after his 39th birthday. He is buried in St. Martin's Churchyard, Laugharne.

BIBLIOGRAPHY.—Books by Dylan Thomas not included above: *The Doctor and the Devils* (1953); *Quite Early One Morning* (broadcasts) (1954); *Adventures in the Skin Trade* (1955). The considerable number of letters are not only entertaining and informative but illuminating in their comment on poetic craft: *Letters to Vernon Watkins,* ed. Watkins (1957), *Selected Letters of Dylan Thomas,* ed. by C. Fitzgibbon (1966). *See* also *Poet in the Making: the Notebooks of Dylan Thomas,* ed. by R. Maud (1967). J. A. Rolph, *Dylan Thomas: a Bibliography* (1956), provides a complete (to the date of its publication) list of Thomas' published work, both in books and periodicals. Critical writing includes: J. Ackerman, *Dylan Thomas: His Life and Work* (1964); J. M. Brinnin, *Dylan Thomas in America* (1956); C. B. Cox (ed.), *Dylan Thomas: Critical Essays* (1966); C. Fitzgibbon, *The Life of Dylan Thomas* (1965); R. Maud, *Entrances to Dylan Thomas Poetry* (1963); E. W. Tedlock, *Dylan Thomas: the Legend and the Poet* (1960). (JN. A.)

**THOMAS, GEORGE HENRY** (1816–1870), Union general in the American Civil War (*q.v.*), known as "the Rock of Chickamauga" for his unyielding defense at the Battle of Chickamauga (1863). Born in Southampton County, Va., on July 31, 1816, he graduated from the U.S. Military Academy at West Point in 1840. He served in the artillery in the war against the Seminole Indians in Florida and in the Mexican War (1846–48). After the war he served as an instructor at West Point and in 1855 was a major in the 2nd Cavalry. When the Civil War broke out in 1861 he remained loyal to the Union.

In command of an independent force in eastern Kentucky, on Jan. 19, 1862, he attacked the Confederate general Felix Zollicoffer at Mill Springs, and gained the first important Union victory in the west. He served under Gen. Don Carlos Buell and was offered, but refused, the chief command in the anxious days before the Battle of Perryville. Under Gen. W. S. Rosecrans he was engaged at Stone River and was in charge of the most important part of the maneuvering from Decherd to Chattanooga. At the Battle of Chickamauga, Sept. 19, 1863, he held the left wing against heavy odds. He succeeded Rosecrans in command of the Army of the Cumberland shortly before the great victory of Chattanooga, in which Thomas and his army played a conspicuous part. When Gen. J. B. Hood broke away from Atlanta in the autumn of 1864, menaced Sherman's long line of communications, and endeavoured to force Sherman to follow him, Sherman left to Thomas the difficult task of dealing with Hood. At the Battle of Franklin, Nov. 30, 1864, Thomas' force, under General Schofield, checked Hood long enough to cover the concentration at Nashville. Thomas then attacked (Dec. 15–16, 1864) and inflicted on Hood the worst defeat sustained in the open field by any army on either side during the war. Thomas was made a major general in the regular army and received the thanks of Congress. After the war he commanded military departments in Kentucky and Tennessee until 1869, when he was placed in charge of the division of the Pacific with headquarters at San Francisco. He died there March 28, 1870.

**THOMAS, JAMES HENRY** (1874–1949), British statesman and trade union leader, was born at Newport, Monmouthshire, on Oct. 3, 1874, the illegitimate son of a domestic servant. An errand boy from the age of 9, at 15 he became a railway engine cleaner. He later moved to Swindon (headquarters of the Great Western Railway) and was prominent there in local government and as a trade unionist. He became national president of the Amalgamated Society of Railway Servants in 1904 and was later its organizer and assistant secretary. In 1911 he conducted the negotiations with the employers when the threat of a general railway strike secured recognition of the unions throughout the industry. In 1913 three railway unions amalgamated to form the National Union of Railwaymen (NUR) and in 1917 Thomas became general secretary.

From 1910 to 1936 Thomas was Labour member of Parliament for the railway town of Derby. Although he declined to join Lloyd George's coalition government in World War I (believing that he could be of more use outside), he was made a privy councilor in 1917. After the war he was closely connected with many industrial disputes. In 1919 his union was involved in the first general stoppage on the railways. In the "triple alliance" of miners, railwaymen, and other transport workers he had a moderating influence and received much of the blame when the other members of the alliance failed to support the miners' strike in 1921. He was equally prominent in the general strike of 1926 and throughout pressed for a peaceful settlement. As an industrial negotiator he was a shrewd opportunist. He did well for his members and believed that he was entitled in return to do well for himself. Caricatures showed him in evening clothes, smoking a large cigar. He was aggressively working-class in manner, but not in habits or beliefs.

Alongside his union activities (he was president of the Trades Union Congress in 1920 and of the International Federation of Trade Unions from 1920 to 1924), Thomas continued in politics. In the 1924 Labour government he was secretary of state for the colonies; in that of 1929 he was lord privy seal and minister for employment, but failed to take any effective measures to deal with the depression. He became secretary of state for the dominions in 1930, retaining office when J. Ramsay MacDonald formed his National government in August 1931 and was one of the two senior ministers to leave the Labour Party with MacDonald. This involved severing his connection with the NUR. He returned to the Colonial Office in 1935, but in 1936 he was held partly responsible for premature release of information about the budget and resigned both from office and from Parliament. He died in London, on Jan. 21, 1949. His autobiography *My Story* was published in 1937.

*See* G. Blaxland, *J. H. Thomas* (1964). (R. J.)

**THOMAS, NORMAN (MATTOON)** (1884–1968), U.S. social reformer and six times the Socialist Party's candidate for president, was born in Marion, O., on Nov. 20, 1884, the oldest of six children of a Presbyterian minister. Thomas spent his freshman year in college at Bucknell University and then transferred to Princeton, where he became a member of the debating team and was valedictorian of the class of 1905.

Following a trip around the world and some social settlement work, Thomas matriculated at Union Theological Seminary. While a student there, he served as associate minister of the Brick Presbyterian Church, Fifth Avenue, New York City, with Henry Van Dyke. He married Frances Violet Stewart in 1910.

After graduating from the seminary in 1911 and being ordained as a Presbyterian minister, he accepted the pastorate of the East Harlem Church and the chairmanship of the American Parish, a settlement house in one of the poorer sections of the city. In his work in his church and the parish during the next few years he became increasingly convinced that the major political parties were offering no adequate solution to the problems of poverty and social injustice that he found on every hand, nor to the problem of war. He became a pacifist and opposed U.S. participation in World War I. When Morris Hillquit ran for mayor of New York City in 1917 on the Socialist ticket Thomas actively supported him and later joined the Socialist Party.

Leaving his East Harlem posts in 1918, Thomas became secretary of the newly formed Fellowship of Reconciliation. In 1921 he became associate editor of the influential weekly, *The Nation,* and in 1922 co-executive director of the League for Industrial Democracy, a position he held until the mid-1930s. Thomas was an eloquent and effective speaker and during this period he lectured extensively among college and civic groups in all parts of the country. He was one of the founders of the American Civil Liberties Union and remained throughout his life a staunch defender of civil liberties.

Thomas ran for governor of New York on the Socialist Party ticket in 1924; for mayor of New York City in 1925 and 1929; and for president of the United States six times—in 1928, 1932, 1936, 1940, 1944, and 1948. (*See* SOCIALIST PARTY [U.S.].) During this long period he helped forge the party's policies for meeting such major crises as the great depression of the 1930s, the rise of fascism and communism, and the outbreak of World War II.

In the following years, as chairman of the Postwar World Council, he devoted much of his energies to the problem of international peace, including the cessation of fighting in South Vietnam. He wrote many books, including *A Socialist's Faith* (1951), *The Test of Freedom* (1954), *Mr. Chairman, Ladies and Gentlemen* (1955), *The Prerequisites for Peace* (1959), and *Socialism Reexamined* (1963); in the last he examined national and world developments from 1917 and his reactions to them. He died in Huntington, N.Y., on Dec. 19, 1968.

*See* Harry Fleischman, *Norman Thomas* (1964). (H. W. L.)

**THOMAS, WILLIAM ISAAC** (1863–1947), pioneer U.S. sociologist, who specialized in social psychology as applied to cultural analysis and personality development, was born on Aug. 13, 1863, in Russell County, Va. After graduating from the University of Tennessee, Knoxville, in 1884, he taught English there and at Oberlin (O.) College for ten years. Turning to sociology, he received his Ph.D. in 1896 at The University of Chicago, where he studied physiology, neurology, philosophy, and social psychology. He taught sociology at The University of Chicago, the New School for Social Research, New York City, and Harvard, and was a consultant at Yale. He died on Dec. 5, 1947, in Berkeley, Calif.

Thomas' *Source-Book for Social Origins* (1909) and *Primitive Behavior* (1937) reflected his interest in ethnography. His *Sex and Society* (1907) was the first fully secular approach to the subject written by an American sociologist. His major work, *The Polish Peasant in Europe and America,* 5 vol. (1918–21), prepared with F. Znaniecki, illustrated his comparative approach to the study of nationalities and his analysis of social problems by means of personal history. *The Unadjusted Girl* (1923) and *The Child in America* (1928) were outstanding psychological studies of personality. His important methodological contributions were the technique of personal history, described in the "Methodological Note" to his *Polish Peasant,* and his later "point-by-point procedure," based on the contention that theoretical formulations in sociology must be regarded as tentative until checked and developed by further research.

BIBLIOGRAPHY.—H. E. Barnes (ed.), *Introduction to the History of Sociology,* ch. xl (1947); E. Faris in *American Journal of Sociology* (March 1948); K. Young in *American Sociological Review* (Feb. 1948), *The Contribution of W. I. Thomas* (1966); F. Znaniecki in *Sociology and Social Research* (March–April 1948). (H. E. BAR.)

**THOMAS À KEMPIS** (*c.* 1380–1471) is renowned as the author of the *Imitation of Christ* (*q.v.*), which, except for the Bible, has been the most influential book in Christian literature. Thomas Hemerken was born in the Rhineland town of Kempen—thus "of Kempen" (à Kempis)—in 1379 or 1380. In 1392 he was sent to continue his education at Deventer, Netherlands, a centre of Catholic education and piety and headquarters of the learned and devout Brethren of the Common Life (*q.v.*), founded by Gerhard Groote (*q.v.*). Deeply influenced for seven years by this religious atmosphere, and especially by Florentius Radewyns, Groote's successor, Thomas decided to enter the Augustinian Canons of the Windesheim congregation at Mt. St. Agnes, near Zwolle, where his brother John was prior and where he was to live almost continuously for more than 70 years. He took his vows in 1408, was ordained priest in 1413, and after a most devout and virtuous life died on Aug. 8, 1471.

Thomas, small of build, was capable and diligent in his work, yet impractical in worldly affairs. Although kind and gracious with others, he was extremely reserved and preferred to be alone with his books. He devoted his life to copying manuscripts (Bible, missal, books of devotion), to writing (39 ascetical and historical works), and to directing novices. Although it is disputed, he is most probably the author of the *Imitation of Christ.* In his writings he is certainly the best representative of the *devotio moderna;* he stresses the interior, affective, and ascetical (rather than the exterior, speculative, and mystical), and moderate, not extreme, austerity.

A critical edition of Thomas' *Opera Omnia* was published in seven volumes by M. J. Pohl (1902–22).

*See* G. de Montmorency, *Thomas à Kempis and His Book* (1907); S. Kettlewell, *Thomas à Kempis and the Brothers of the Common Life,* 2 vol. (1882); D. Butler, *Thomas à Kempis: a Religious Study* (1908). (T. G. O'C.)

**THOMAS STEEL:** *see* CONVERTER STEEL.

**THOMISM** refers both to the doctrinal system of St. Thomas Aquinas and to the explanations and developments made by his followers. The main phases in the philosophical and theological tradition of the Thomistic school are the personal synthesis of St. Thomas, the work of the great commentators, and the modern revival.

**Aquinas' Position.**—Although making respectful use of Aristotle and the Platonists, Augustine and the Fathers, Aquinas developed a distinctive position. His originality was shown in treating existence (*esse*) as the supreme act or perfection of being in God as well as in created things, in reserving the creative act to God alone, in denying the presence of matter in angels, and thus in distinguishing between God and creatures by a real composition of existence and essence as principles in all created beings. Also characteristic was his teaching that the human soul is a unique subsistent form, substantially united with matter to constitute human nature (*see* SUBSTANCE). Aquinas maintained that the immortality of the human soul can be strictly demonstrated, that there is a real distinction of principles between the soul and its powers of knowing and willing, and that human knowledge is based upon sense experience leading to the mind's reflective activity. He held that both man and lower creatures have a natural tendency or love toward God, that supernatural grace perfects and elevates our natural abilities, and that blessedness consists formally in knowing God Himself, a knowledge accompanied by our full love of God. (*See* also AQUINAS, SAINT THOMAS; PHILOSOPHY, HISTORY OF: *Patristic and Medieval Philosophy: Western Philosophy.*)

This coherent but complex body of Thomistic doctrines was critically explained and developed during subsequent centuries. Views of St. Thomas on individuation and the localization of angels, man's nature and the unity of the world, appeared among the theses condemned in 1277 by Bishop Étienne Tempier at Paris and by Archbishop Robert Kilwardby at Oxford. At stake were the manner and extent of using Aristotle and his Arabian commentators in explaining Christian theology. The later 13th century was crowded with "correctorial" literature—treatises attacking and defending basic positions of St. Thomas, especially on the unicity of the human substantial form and the distinction of essence and existence. His precise meaning was lost even by some Thomists, who treated essence and existence as distinct things and overlooked the unifying relation between the substantial form and existence.

**Commentators.**—Encouragement toward consulting Aquinas' own writings came with the adoption of his doctrine by the Dominican Order (1278, 1279, 1286), his canonization by Pope John XXII (1323), and the special place accorded to his works at the Council of Trent. The scientific task of analyzing his thought was executed by a line of devoted commentators during the period 1400–1650. The first was the Dominican John Capreolus (*c.* 1380–1444), called "the prince of the Thomists," who recognized the need to make a direct integral study of the texts of St. Thomas. In his *Four Books of Defenses of the Theology of St. Thomas Aquinas,* Capreolus made a systematic use of the sources against the Scotists and Ockhamists (*see* DUNS SCOTUS, JOHN; OCKHAM, WILLIAM). Another major Dominican commentator was Tommaso de Vio, Cardinal Cajetan (*q.v.*), who made elaborate expositions of St. Thomas' *Summa theologiae* and *On Being and Essence.* He made his own restatement of the Thomistic arguments and drew upon many other writings of St. Thomas. Cajetan's independence was displayed in his work *On the Analogy of Names,* where he proposed the influential division of kinds of analogy into inequality, attribution, and proportionality, as well as in his opinion that the human soul's immortality can be supported only by probable reasons.

The classical commentary on St. Thomas' *Summa contra gentiles* was done by the Dominican Francesco Sylvestri of Ferrara (*c.* 1474–1528), who showed the importance of this work for the relation of faith and philosophy, the meaning of person, and the desire of God. After the mid-16th century, the Thomistic commentators became involved in the intricate theological controversies on grace and premotion. Highly systematized presentations of opposing views were introduced into the commentaries on the *Summa theologiae* made by the Spanish Dominican theologian Domingo Bañez and the Spanish Jesuit authors Francis Toletus and Gabriel Vázquez. But the new Renaissance tendency to give separate treatment to philosophical and theological issues, as well as the pressures of seminary education, undermined the usefulness of the commentary form of approach to St. Thomas. A new trend is present in the Dominican John of St. Thomas (1589–1644), who issued a separate *Philosophical Course* and then a *Theological Course* in Thomistic thought. Using the framework of logic, philosophy of nature, and metaphysics, John assembled the philosophical teachings of St. Thomas under these systematic headings and reformulated the material for students who would then study theology. There were original features in his logic, including the distinction between formal and objective concepts and the stress on intentional signs.

**Modern Thomism.**—Throughout the 17th and 18th centuries, Thomism continued to be presented in philosophy and theology courses or manuals, especially in the Dominican Order. Most Thomistic manuals of this period were watered with the opinions of other Schoolmen and remained remote from modern problems. In most Catholic seminaries and universities of the early 19th century, eclecticism was the rule and more attention was paid to Descartes, Locke, and Wolff than to Aquinas. The modern revival of authentic Thomism began at this time in Italy. Vincent Buzzetti (1777–1824) and the Jesuit teacher Serafino Sordi (1793–1865) were instrumental in urging a direct study of the text of Aristotle and Aquinas. The revolutions of 1848 had a decisive influence upon both the Holy See and the Society of Jesus toward finding sound principles on God, man, and society in the works of St. Thomas. In editions of their philosophy manuals appearing after 1850, this renewal of Thomistic thought was advocated by three influential Jesuit writers in Italy and Germany: Luigi Taparelli d'Azeglio, Matteo Liberatore, and Joseph Kleutgen. Their own positions in epistemology, metaphysics, and social theory remained eclectic, but they did give impetus to the work of studying St. Thomas and the other Schoolmen in the light of modern intellectual and social issues.

Decisive support for this movement came with Pope Leo XIII's encyclical *Aeterni Patris* (1879). It noted the importance of sound doctrine for meeting today's problems and called for a restoration of the Christian philosophy of the Fathers and medieval Doctors, augmented where necessary by the reliable advances of modern research. Leo asked especially for a recovery of the wisdom of St. Thomas, whom he hailed as "the special bulwark and glory of the Catholic Faith." This program required an accurate historical study of St. Thomas himself and his major commentators, combined with a readiness to use the evidences and resources of modern learning and science. St. Thomas was declared the universal patron of Catholic schools, and a canon (1366, par. 2) in the new Code of Canon Law (1917) required philosophy and theology teachers to adhere to the method, doctrine, and principles of St. Thomas. This established the special authority of the Common Doctor in the church's teaching institutions, without impairing the recovery of all the other sources of Christian thought, the careful discussion of commonly recognized difficulties, and the effort to evaluate modern teachings.

Thomists of the 20th century concentrated upon two major tasks: a historical investigation of St. Thomas' doctrine in its medieval context, and a rethinking of that doctrine in reference to contemporary problems. Pioneer historians were Pierre Mandonnet and Martin Grabmann, who investigated the life of Aquinas, the canon of his writings, and his historical relationships. The setting of Thomistic doctrine in the wider medieval intellectual currents was described by Maurice De Wulf and Étienne Gilson. The latter also brought out the basic role of existence in Thomistic metaphysics, which he contrasted with other historical forms of metaphysics. Some general presentations of Thomistic thought were made by showing the development of the principles of act and potency in the major areas of philosophy. The Dominican R. Garrigou-Lagrange stressed the problem of God and providence; A. Sertillanges, another Dominican, made the act of creation central to his exposition; the Jesuit Martin D'Arcy brought out the dynamic and affective aspects in the mind of Aquinas.

At Louvain University, Désiré Cardinal Mercier and his associates concentrated on the challenge of modern thought for Thomism. They treated the epistemological issue at the outset of philosophy, so that metaphysics might have the support of a well-founded realism. The aim of Joseph Maréchal was to reformulate the major thinkers, especially St. Thomas, in terms of the mind's dynamic affirmation of being and ultimate reference to the reality of God. Francesco Olgiati used a metaphysical realism of substance to establish the critical relevance of Thomism to Cartesian and empiricist thinkers. How to unite the various kinds of methods and knowledges in a human order was the main concern of Jacques Maritain, but he also applied the Thomistic concept of person and community to the problem of democracy.

After World War II, Thomists faced three major tasks: to develop an adequate philosophy of science, to take account of the phenomenological and psychiatric findings on man, and to evaluate the ontologies of existentialism and naturalism.

*See* also SCHOLASTICISM; THEOLOGY, CHRISTIAN; and references to "Thomism" in the Index.

BIBLIOGRAPHY.—Cajetan (Tommaso de Vio, O. P.), *The Analogy of Names and the Concept of Being,* Eng. trans. with notes by E. A. Bushinski and H. J. Koren (1953); D. Callus, O.P., *The Condemnation of St. Thomas at Oxford,* 2nd ed. (1955); F. Copleston, S.J., *Aquinas* (1955); C. Giacon, S.J., *La seconda scolastica,* 3 vol. (1944–50); É. Gilson, *Being and Some Philosophers,* 2nd ed. (1952), and *The Christian Philosophy of St. Thomas Aquinas,* Eng. trans. by L. K. Shook (1956); J. Gurr, S.J., *The Principle of Sufficient Reason in Some Scholastic Systems, 1750–1900* (1959); John of St. Thomas, O.P., *The Material Logic of John of St. Thomas,* Eng. trans. by Y. R. Simon *et al.* (1955); B. Lonergan, S.J., *Insight: a Study of Human Understanding* (1957); J. Maréchal, S.J., *Le Point de départ de la métaphysique,* cahier v: *Le Thomisme devant la philosophie critique,* 2nd ed. (1949); J. Maritain, *Man and the State* (1951), and *Distinguish to Unite: or The Degrees of Knowledge* (1959); J. Pieper, *The Silence of St. Thomas,* Eng. trans. by J. Murray and D. O'Connor (1957); G. Van Riet, *Thomistic Epistemology,* 2 vol. (1963–65). (J. D. C.)

**THOMOND, EARLS AND MARQUESSES OF:** *see* O'BRIEN.

**THOMPSON, SIR BENJAMIN** (COUNT VON RUMFORD) (1753–1814), British-American scientist particularly noted for his researches on heat, and a founder of the Royal Institution, was born at Woburn, Mass., on March 26, 1753. In 1766 he was apprenticed to a storekeeper in Salem, Mass., and became interested in chemical and mechanical experiments and in engraving. On the evacuation of Boston by British troops in 1776 he went to London, where he was appointed to a clerkship in the office of the secretary of state. Within several months he was advanced to the post of secretary of the colony of Georgia and in 1780 became undersecretary of state. During this period he continued his scientific pursuits, however, and in 1779 was elected a fellow of the Royal Society. The explosive force of gunpowder, the construction of firearms, and a system of signaling at sea were subjects which particularly interested him. On the resignation of Lord North's administration Thompson left the civil service and went to Austria. At Strasbourg he was introduced to Prince Maximilian, afterward elector of Bavaria, and was invited by him to enter the civil and military service of that state. Having obtained permission from the British government to accept the prince's offer and having received the honour of knighthood from George III, he remained at Munich 11 years as minister of war, minister of police, and grand chamberlain to the elector. During his stay in Bavaria he reorganized the Bavarian Army, improved the conditions of the industrial classes, did much to suppress mendicancy, and also contributed a number of papers to the *Philosophical Transactions.*

In 1791 he was created a count of the Holy Roman Empire and chose his title of Rumford from the name of the American township to which his wife's family belonged. In 1795 he visited England, where he lost all his private papers including the materials for an autobiography. In London he investigated methods for curing smoky chimneys and for improving fireplace construction.

For a short time he was recalled to service in Bavaria, but in 1798 he returned to England. That year he presented to the Royal Society his celebrated "Enquiry Concerning the Source of Heat Which is Excited by Friction," in which he regarded heat as a mode of motion, as opposed to the then current view that it was a material substance. (For discussions of Rumford's experiments and conclusions *see* ENERGY: *Heat as a Form of Energy;* HEAT: *The Nature of Heat.*)

In 1799, with Sir Joseph Banks, Thompson projected the establishment of the Royal Institution, which received its charter from George III in 1800, and selected Sir Humphry Davy as scientific lecturer there. He was founder and first recipient of the Rumford Medal of the Royal Society, founder of the Rumford Medal of the American Academy of Arts and Sciences, and founder of the Rumford professorship at Harvard University. Rumford died at Auteuil, near Paris, on Aug. 21, 1814. His complete works, with a memoir by George H. Ellis, were published by the American Academy of Arts and Sciences in 1870–75.

BIBLIOGRAPHY.—James A. Thompson, *Count Rumford of Massachusetts* (1935); Allen French, *General Gage's Informers* (1932); E. Lehrburger (E. Larsen), *An American in Europe* (1953).

**THOMPSON, SIR D'ARCY WENTWORTH** (1860–1948), Scottish biologist whose classic work *On Growth and Form* (1917; new edition, 1942), written in rich literary style, exemplifies best his great erudition in physical and natural sciences, ancient and modern languages and the humanities. He was born in Edinburgh on May 2, 1860. After graduating at Trinity College, Cambridge, he became professor of natural history at University College, Dundee, and then at St. Andrews University, holding the chair for 64 years. Thompson was a fellow (1916), vice-president (1931–33), and Darwin medalist (1946) of the Royal Society, president of the Classical Association (1929), knighted (1937), and honoured by learned institutions the world over. For more than 50 years he was a leading member of national and international bodies investigating sea fisheries.

In *On Growth and Form* growth and structure in organisms are expressed in mathematical and physical terms and an important "theory of transformation" developed—that one species evolves into another not by successive minor changes in individual body parts but by large-scale transformations involving the body as a whole. Sir D'Arcy Thompson's other works include *A Glossary of Greek Birds* (1895; new edition, 1936), *Science and the Classics,* etc. (1940), and *A Glossary of Greek Fishes* (1947).

He died at St. Andrews on June 21, 1948.

*See* Ruth D'A. Thompson, *D'Arcy Wentworth Thompson* (1958).
(A. D. P.)

**THOMPSON, FRANCIS** (1859–1907), English poet, whose best-known poem, "The Hound of Heaven," describes the divine pursuit of the human soul, was born at Preston, Lancashire, on Dec. 18, 1859. He was the son of Charles Thompson, a doctor, and the nephew of Edward Healy Thompson, the friend of Cardinal Manning and professor of English literature at the Catholic university in Dublin. After his father became a convert to Roman Catholicism, Francis was educated in the Catholic faith at Ushaw College. In 1877 he proceeded to Owen's College, Manchester, to study medicine. He took more interest in Aeschylus, Blake, and De Quincey's *Confessions of an English Opium Eater* than in his work, however; and, having failed the examinations three times, he went to London in November 1885 to seek a livelihood. Ill-health drove him to opium, and poverty reduced him to selling matches and newspapers. Eventually he found light work with a Leicester square bootmaker and wrote his first poems. In 1888 Wilfrid Meynell published two poems in *Merry England,* which aroused the admiration of Browning. Discovering the young author on the verge of starvation, the Meynells induced him to enter a hospital, aided him through his long convalescence and in 1893 arranged for the publication of his first volume, *Poems,* which was highly praised by Coventry Patmore, among others. *Sister Songs* (dedicated to the Meynells' children) followed in 1895, and *New Poems* (dedicated to Patmore) in 1897. From 1893 to 1897, apart from short intervals, Thompson lived near the Franciscan monastery in Pantasaph, North Wales. He died in London on Nov. 13, 1907, of tuberculosis, and was buried in the Catholic cemetery at Kensal Green.

Thompson's language is customarily orotund, ornate, and far-fetched; too often the reader is aware of the poet's self-conscious posturing. The common comparison with Richard Crashaw is misleading. The older poet, though he has something of Thompson's equivocal sensuousness, displays greater care for the meaning of words and maintains a more consistent dignity. Subject aside, the kinship is rather with the Keats of *Endymion.* Thompson is, undeniably, a poet of the "aesthetic" 1890s. His simpler poems (*e.g.,* about children) are frequently marred by a mawkishness of which the poet seemed perversely proud. It is likely that his place in literature will depend entirely upon "The Hound of Heaven," where language and subject matter are more properly matched, and which, by virtue of its dramatic quality, is in fact nearer in spirit to the religious poetry of the 17th century (*cf.* George Herbert), though in this too the somewhat florid religiosity of the 1890s may occasionally repel the reader.

Thompson also wrote several prose works, including *Health and Holiness* (1905), *Life of St. Ignatius Loyola* (1909), *Life of Blessed John Baptist de la Galle* (1911), and *Essay on Shelley* (1909). His *Literary Criticisms* were edited by T. L. Connolly (1948). Thompson's *Works* were edited by W. Meynell, 3 vol. (1913); *Poems* were reprinted in 1 vol. (1937); *Selected Poems* (1908) includes an obituary by W. Meynell.

BIBLIOGRAPHY.—J. Thomson, *Francis Thompson, the Preston-Born Poet,* rev. ed. (1922); E. Meynell, *Life of Francis Thompson,* 5th rev. ed. (1926); K. Rooker, *Thompson* (1913); R. L. Mégroz, *Thompson, the Poet of Earth in Heaven* (1927); T. H. Wright, *Thompson and His Poetry* (1927); R. M. Gautrey, *This Tremendous Lover* (1932); F. C. Owlett, *Francis Thompson* (1936); F. Olivero, *Thompson* (1935); T. L. Connolly, *An Account of Books and Manuscripts of Francis Thompson* (1937), *Thompson . . .* (1944); V. Meynell, *Francis Thompson and Wilfrid Meynell: a Memoir* (1952). (D. J. E.)

**THOMPSON, SIR JOHN SPARROW DAVID** (1844–1894), Canadian prime minister, was born at Halifax, Nova Scotia, on Nov. 10, 1844, of Irish descent. A lawyer, he was also for a time official reporter for the debates of the Nova Scotia legislature. In 1877 he was elected to the legislature for Antigonish as a Conservative and was named attorney general a year later. In May 1882 he became premier of Nova Scotia but left office in July when his government was defeated. For the next three years he served as a judge of the provincial Supreme Court.

He was called to Ottawa in September 1885 to become minister of justice in the government led by Sir J. A. Macdonald. During the following years he defended the government with great skill in several politico-religious controversies, including those occurring after the execution of Louis Riel (*q.v.*) in 1885, and the passage of the Jesuit Estates Act, 1888–89. He served as legal adviser to the British delegation in the negotiations leading to the Bayard-Chamberlain Treaty of 1888 regulating the North Atlantic fisheries, later rejected by the U.S. Senate.

On Dec. 5, 1892, he became prime minister of Canada, and held the office until his death two years later. During this period he was one of the arbitrators in the Bering Sea seal fishery dispute, 1893. His career was cut short by his sudden death on Dec. 12, 1894, at Windsor Castle in England, a few minutes after having been sworn in by Queen Victoria as a member of the Imperial Privy Council. (D. M. L. F.)

**THOMPSON, RANDALL** (1899– ), U.S. composer known for his choral music, was born in New York City on April 21, 1899. He studied at Harvard University with W. Spalding, E. B. Hill, and A. T. Davison, and later with Ernest Bloch. He taught at Wellesley College and at the University of California (Berkeley), was director of the Curtis Institute of Music, Philadelphia (1939–41), and head of the music division at the University of Virginia, and was professor of music at Princeton University (1946–48). Later he joined the staff of Harvard. He composed three symphonies (1930–49), of which the second was particularly successful. His chamber music is remarkable for its sense of form and of counterpoint. His vocal works, notably *Alleluia* for *a cappella* choir (1940) and *Testament of Freedom* to words by Thomas Jefferson, for men's voices and orchestra (1943), achieved great popularity. His one-act opera *Solomon and Balkis* was produced at Cambridge, Mass., in 1942. He also wrote an oratorio, *The Passion According to St. Luke* (1965). (N. Sy.)

**THOMPSON, WILLIAM TAPPAN** (1812–1882), U.S. humorist remembered for his realistic character sketches of Georgia-Florida backwoodsmen, was born Aug. 31, 1812, in Ravenna, O. He early moved to Georgia, where as a self-made man whose education came from the printing press, he identified himself with Georgia life and culture. In 1838 he founded the *Augusta Mirror*, a literary magazine. Discovering that the South would not support literary periodicals, he turned in 1850 to newspaper editorship, founded the *Savannah* (Ga.) *Morning News*, and continued as its editor until his death in Savannah on March 24, 1882.

A Democrat throughout his editorial career, he typified the ideals, attitudes and prejudices of middle-class Georgians.

Influenced by Augustus Baldwin Longstreet, his personal friend, Thompson wrote amusing dialect letters which were collected in 1843 as *Major Jones' Courtship;* the book achieved nationwide popularity. Other volumes followed. Thompson had a demonstrable influence on Mark Twain, Richard Malcolm Johnston, and Joel Chandler Harris, his literary protégé. His popular antebellum humour is accepted as convincing Georgia dialect and as realistic local colour.

*See* also Walter Blair, *Native American Humor* (1937); Henry Prentice Miller, "The Background and Significance of *Major Jones's Courtship*," *Georgia Historical Quarterly*, xxx, 267–296 (1946). (H. P. M.)

**THOMSEN, CHRISTIAN JÜRGENSEN** (1788–1865), Danish archaeologist who developed the three-age system of prehistory (Stone, Bronze, and Iron), was born in Copenhagen on Dec. 29, 1788. The son of a well-to-do merchant, he succeeded his father as manager of the business until it ended in 1840. An early hobby of coin collecting soon led him to an interest in prehistoric antiquities. In 1816 he was appointed secretary of the royal commission set up to preserve and collect Danish antiquities and the first curator of the Museum of Northern Antiquities (later the National Museum) in Copenhagen. In his first years at the museum (he remained as director for the rest of his life) Thomsen devised and demonstrated the three-age system in his arrangement of the antiquities in the collection. The scheme was published (1836) in his *Ledetraad til nordisk Oldkyndighed* (English translation, *A Guide to Northern Antiquities*, 1848), which served as a guide to the museum. Thomsen died in Copenhagen on May 21, 1865.

*See* also SCANDINAVIAN ARCHAEOLOGY. (T. Mn.)

**THOMSEN, (HANS PETER JÖRGEN) JULIUS** (1826–1909), Danish chemist best known for his work on thermochemistry, was born in Copenhagen on Feb. 16, 1826. From 1847 to 1856 he taught chemistry at the technical high school there, and from 1856 to 1866 was on the staff of the military high school. In 1866 he was appointed professor of chemistry at the University of Copenhagen and retained that chair until 1891, when he retired. He died in Copenhagen on Feb. 13, 1909.

In the course of his thermochemical work Thomsen made about 3,500 calorimetric measurements, determining the heat evolved or absorbed in a very large number of chemical reactions. His publications in this field were collected in *Thermochemische Untersuchungen* (four volumes, 1882–86). He verified Kirchhoff's equation connecting the change of heat of a reaction with temperature and the specific heats of the reactants and resultants, and also used his measurements to confirm Guldberg and Waage's theory of mass action (1867). Thomsen introduced the term "avidity" to indicate the tendency of an acid to unite with a base and used his results to draw up the first table of relative strengths of acids. He also made accurate determinations of the atomic weights of oxygen and aluminum. In 1853 he devised a process for manufacturing soda from cryolite, which was first worked on a large scale in 1857 and made him rich.

*See* obituary notice, *Proceedings of the Royal Society* (1910–11); E. Thorpe, Thomsen Memorial Lecture, *Journal of the Chemical Society* (1910).

**THOMSON, SIR CHARLES WYVILLE** (1830–1882), Scottish naturalist especially remembered as a student of the biological conditions of the depths of the sea and as director of the scientific staff in the "Challenger" expedition (*q.v.*). He was born at Bonsyde, West Lothian (Linlithgow), on March 5, 1830, and was educated at Edinburgh University. At first a botanist by profession, he was lecturer in botany at Aberdeen University from 1851 to 1852, and professor of botany at Marischal College from 1852 to 1853. His leanings, however, were toward zoology, and between 1853 and 1868 he taught natural sciences at Cork and at Belfast. After a short time (1868–70) as professor of botany at the Royal College of Science, Dublin, he became (1870–79) professor of natural history at Edinburgh.

Thomson's interest in crinoids (sea stars and feather stars) was stimulated by the results of the dredgings of the Norwegian zoologist Michael Sars in the deep sea off the Norwegian coasts. With W. B. Carpenter, Thomson succeeded in obtaining the loan of HMS "Lightning" and "Porcupine" for successive deep-sea dredging expeditions in 1868 and 1869. These operations showed that animal life exists in abundance down to depths of 650 fathoms, that all invertebrate groups are represented (largely by Tertiary forms previously believed to be extinct), and, moreover, that deep-sea temperatures are by no means so constant as was supposed, but vary considerably, indicating an oceanic circulation. The results of these expeditions were described in *The Depths of the Sea* (1873).

In the "Challenger" circumnavigation expedition, Thomson sailed at the end of 1872 as director of the scientific staff, the cruise lasting three and one-half years. On his return he received many academic honours, and was knighted. In 1877 he published two volumes of a preliminary account of the voyage (*The Voyage of the "Challenger"* and *The Atlantic*) and, with John Murray, superintended the preparation of the full reports until the time of his death, at Bonsyde, Scotland, on March 10, 1882.

**THOMSON, CHRISTOPHER BIRDWOOD THOMSON,** BARON (1875–1930), British soldier and statesman who became the Labour Party's military expert during the 1920s, was born at Nasik, India, on April 13, 1875, the son of Maj. Gen. D. Thomson. Educated at Cheltenham College and at the Royal Military Academy, Woolwich, he served in the Mashonaland campaign (1896) and in the South African War (1899–1902). Instructor of the military engineering school at Chatham from 1902 to 1905, he went to the Staff College, Camberley, in 1909, and to the War Office in 1911. During World War I he was military attaché and chief of the British military mission in Rumania (1915–16), served in Palestine (1917–18) and was on the Supreme War Council at Versailles (1918). Having attained the rank of brigadier general, he resigned from the service in 1919 in protest against the Allied intervention in Russia. He then joined the Labour Party and, as military expert, accompanied the commissions of inquiry dispatched by that body to Ireland (1920) and to the Ruhr (1923). At the general elections of 1922 and 1923, he was an unsuccessful candidate for Parliament. In 1924 he became secretary of state for air in the first Labour government, with a seat in the cabinet, and was raised to the peerage. He returned to the Air Ministry from 1929 to 1930 in the second Labour government. A graceful and effective speaker, Lord Thomson also possessed marked literary gifts and his publications included *Old Europe's Suicide* (1920) and *Victors and Vanquished* (1924). He was killed in the crash of the airship R101 at Beauvais, France, on Oct. 5, 1930.

**THOMSON, ELIHU** (1853–1937), U.S. engineer and inventor whose work led to the development of the alternating-current electric motor, was born in Manchester, Eng., March 29, 1853. In 1858 he moved to Philadelphia, Pa., with his parents and later taught chemistry and mechanics there. In his early years of research, Thomson's association with Edwin J. Houston led to scientific and financial success with the development of an arc lighting system. Thomson's most notable discovery was that of alternating-current repulsion phenomena, and his work in this field laid the basis for successful alternating-current motors. He made the first high-frequency generator in 1890, and shortly afterward the first high-frequency transformer. Other well-known inventions included the three-coil generator, electric welding by the incandescent method, and the watt-hour meter.

Thomson made useful contributions in the field of radiology and pioneered in making steroscopic X-ray pictures. He was the first to propose a mixture of helium and oxygen for workers in caissons and tunnel borings. He published numerous articles in scientific and engineering journals, and, as the holder of more than 700 patents, received many awards. He died March 13, 1937, at Swampscott, Mass.

See D. O. Woodbury, *Beloved Scientist: Elihu Thomson, a Guiding Spirit of the Electrical Age* (1944). (TH. C.)

**THOMSON, SIR GEORGE PAGET** (1892– ), English physicist, a co-winner of the Nobel Prize in Physics in 1937 for his work on the diffraction of electrons in crystals, was born in Cambridge, Eng., May 3, 1892, the only son of Sir Joseph John Thomson (*q.v.*), the eminent physicist and Nobel Prize winner (1906). After taking his degree at Trinity College, Cambridge, in 1914, he saw service in World War I in France and was later a member of the British war mission in the U.S. At the end of the war he worked in the Cavendish Laboratory at Cambridge. In 1922 he was appointed professor of natural philosophy in the University of Aberdeen, and it was there that he did work on the diffraction of electrons in crystals which established the wave properties of moving electrons and also had important practical applications. By means of the electrón diffraction camera it is possible to determine the arrangement of the atoms in many solids and liquids, and this threw much light on the question of stress and resistance in metals. From 1930 to 1952 Thomson was professor of physics in the Imperial College of Science and Technology, University of London. During and after World War II he was one of the principal scientific advisers to the British government and to the UN Atomic Energy Commission. He was elected a fellow of the Royal Society in 1930 and was awarded the Hughes Medal in 1939 and the Royal Medal in 1949; he was knighted in 1943. In 1952 he became master of Corpus Christi College, Cambridge, retiring in 1962.

He wrote *Applied Aerodynamics* (1919); *The Atom* (1930; 6th ed., 1962); *Wave Mechanics of Free Electrons* (1930); *Theory and Practice of Electron Diffraction* (with William Cochrane, 1939); *The Foreseeable Future* (1955); and *J. J. Thomson and the Cavendish Laboratory in His Day* (1965); he also helped revise his father's *Conduction of Electricity Through Gases* (3rd ed., 2 vol., 1928–33). (W. J. BP.; X.)

**THOMSON, JAMES** (1700–1748), Scottish poet, gave penetrating and eloquent expression to the national imagination when it was fired by Newtonian science, and by the prospect of great political power based on commercial and maritime expansion.

Though a Scot by birth (at Ednam, Roxburgh, on Sept. 11, 1700) and by education (at Jedburgh Grammar School and Edinburgh University), and although, when he went to London in March 1725, it may have been to seek a reputation in the pulpit, Thomson set himself to contribute rather to the English than the Scottish literary tradition. He was an admirably painstaking writer, as may be seen from the bibliographical history of his masterpiece, *The Seasons*. Making his living in London as a tutor, Thomson published *Winter* in 1726, *Summer* in 1727, *Spring* in 1728, and the whole poem, including *Autumn*, in 1730; but until 1746 he repeatedly revised the work, and the final version differed greatly from the first. The poem deserved this labour, and profited by it. For it was a revolutionary new departure. The novelty lay less where all but the latest commentators have found it, in its subject matter, than in its structure. Indeed the subject matter of *The Seasons*, as the first sustained work of "nature-poetry" in English, if it contributed to the poem's popularity and reputation up to about 1850, later helped to make it increasingly, and unjustly, neglected. What was more striking to Thomson's earliest readers was his audacity in binding his poem together without any aid from "plot" or developing narrative action, and therefore in defiance of the Aristotelian beginning, middle, and end, as interpreted by the neoclassicist critics.

In diction, as in invention, Thomson was an innovator. In his choice of words he followed the precedent of *Paradise Lost* in drawing heavily on the Latinate element in English vocabulary, and by using also Latinate syntax he was able, again like Milton, to compose his blank verse by verse-paragraphs rather than line by line. Partly he was able to profit by the Miltonic model, which has proved treacherous for other poets, by applying the style to quite un-Miltonic subjects, the appearance of the countryside changing as seasons change. Yet it is wrong to regard *The Seasons* as simply a descriptive poem. In the first place Thomson was interested, when he recorded images from external nature, in the state of mind which these inspired or responded to in the observer; and he thus opened the way to the Romantic, Symbolist, and modern methods of conveying states of feeling by implication. And secondly, in particular when he dealt with the atmospheric effect of different kinds of weather, Thomson learned from the discoveries of landscape painters on the one hand, and on the other from the speculations of Sir Isaac Newton in his *Opticks*, and of other scientists, on the nature of light and the physiology of human vision. This last enthusiasm became splendidly explicit in *A Poem to the Memory of Sir Isaac Newton* (1727):

> Even Light itself, which everything displays
> Shone undiscovered, till his brighter mind
> Untwisted all the shining robe of day: . . . .

Nowadays, when fear and envy of the prestige of the natural sciences causes men of letters to declare that there can be no compromise between the power of science and the power of poetry, Thomson's elated sympathy with Newtonian science, and his conviction that scientist and poet must collaborate in the service of God known through his Creation, is only an embarrassment. Yet Thomson did far more than versify scientific findings; his imagination was fully engaged with the scientific endeavour, and throughout *The Seasons* scientific method penetrated the texture of his language. It has been pointed out, for instance, how, in the poetic diction of Thomson and some others, a circumlocution like "finny kind" for "fish" exemplifies, by its stock epithet and pressure toward generalization, the habit of mind that produced also the botanical classifications of Linnaeus. And when, in the poem to the memory of Newton, Thomson catalogues the colours of the spectrum, his intoxication with the grandeur of Newton's analysis produces in the last line a profoundly imaginative near-pun on "violet":

> Then the pure blue, that swells autumnal skies,
> Ethereal played; and then, of sadder hue,
> Emerged the deepened indigo, as when
> The heavy-skirted evening droops with frost;
> While the last gleamings of refracted light
> Died in the fainting violet away.

When compared with the contempt and derision heaped on scientists by Swift and Pope, Thomson's sympathy with their endeavours appears not only to have been justified by later history but also to represent a more generous and positive movement of the spirit.

Moreover his sympathy with classification and scientific law does not obstruct, rather it enhances, his vivid apprehension of the particular instance, and the tumultuous beauty of organic life. Thus, the fish—

> Long time he, following cautious, scans the fly,
> And oft attempts to seize it, but as oft
> The dimpled water speaks his jealous fear.
> At last, while haply o'er the shaded sun
> Passes a cloud, he desperate takes the death
> With sullen plunge. At once he darts along,
> Deep-struck, and runs out all the lengthened line;
> Then seeks the farthest ooze, the sheltering weed,
> The caverned bank, his old secure abode;
> And flies aloft, and flounces round the pool,
> Indignant of the guile.
> (*The Seasons: Spring:* li. 426–435)

The undignified word "flounces," cooperating smoothly with stilted locutions like "takes the death" and "indignant of the guile," reveals a range of diction much wider than, for example, Wordsworth's; and the acting out, preeminently through rhythm, of the turbulence of this encounter between human and inhuman life enforces a perception which is not Wordsworthian. Thomson has been too often applauded for having done only what was later done better by poets of the Romantic revival.

Thomson sympathized with the Whig opposition to the administration of Sir Robert Walpole. His allegiance to the opposition group gathered round Frederick, prince of Wales, is manifest as early as 1729, in his *Britannia. A Poem;* and it informs his ambitious poem in five parts, *Liberty* (pt. i, ii, and iii, 1735; pt. iv and v, 1736), as well as his drama, *Agamemnon* (1738). For *Liberty,* "a poetical landscape of countries, mixed with moral observations on their government and people," Thomson drew on the writings of Shaftesbury, but also on his experiences in 1730–31, when accompanying the son of Sir Charles Talbot, solicitor general, on his travels in France and Italy. Talbot secured a sinecure for Thomson (1733), but on Talbot's death in 1737 Thomson was in less comfortable circumstances until his friend, Lord Lyttelton, gave him another sinecure in 1744. To these years belong *Edward and Eleanora,* the production of which was banned because of the political innuendo in *Agamemnon;* a preface to Milton's *Areopagitica* (1738); and, with David Mallet, *The Masque of Alfred* (1740; with music by Thomas Augustine Arne), which contains his famous ode "Rule Britannia."

Thomson's confidence that "Britons never will be slaves" (and never had been, since Druidical and Anglo-Saxon times) went with his conviction that the nation had a duty to pursue policies of commercial imperialism. It is hard not to be wise after the event, and reflect upon the enslavement of the majority resulting from unrestricted commercial competition and exploitation. But Thomson's patriotism was not hypocritical, nor was it complacent. Britain indeed had come, as he thought,

To this deep-laid indissoluble state
Where wealth and commerce lift the golden head,
And o'er our labours liberty and law
Impartial watch, the wonder of a world!
(*The Seasons: Spring:* li. 846–849)

Yet it could be maintained in this condition only by unremitting exertion. Thomson's *Castle of Indolence* (1748) is an allegory of what happens once exertion is slackened, when the wizard Indolence by his enchantments undoes all the good wrought by the hero, Sir Industry. *The Castle of Indolence,* however, owes its popularity to a response the opposite of what the author intended. In Spenserian stanzas, and up to a point in archaic Spenserian diction, the poem is beguiling for its mellifluous evocation of just that slothful ease which Thomson intended to reprove; and it is generally held that Thomson's imagination was here engaged at a level he was not conscious of, connected with the sedate epicureanism which he indulged particularly in his last years, in retirement at Richmond. He died there on Aug. 27, 1748, leaving his tragedy *Coriolanus* to be first presented in 1749.

BIBLIOGRAPHY.—*The Complete Poetical Works,* ed. by J. Logie Robinson, Oxford Standard Authors Series (1908; reprinted 1951), includes an invaluable variorum edition of *The Seasons,* but excludes the dramas. Biography and criticism in Dr. Johnson's *Lives of the Poets* (1781); G. C. Macaulay, *James Thomson,* English Men of Letters Series (1908); D. Grant, *James Thomson: Poet of "The Seasons"* (1951). Exhaustive study of Thomson's sources in contemporary scientific works and books of travel has been carried out by A. D. McKillop, in *The Background of Thomson's Seasons* (1942), and *The Background of Thomson's Liberty* (1951). *See* also J. Arthos, *The Language of Natural Description in 18th-Century Poetry* (1949); M. H. Nicolson, *Newton Demands the Muse* (1946); J. H. Hagstrum, *The Sister Arts: the Tradition of Literary Pictorialism and English Poetry from Dryden to Gray* (1958).
(D. A. DE.)

**THOMSON, JAMES** (pseudonym BYSSHE VANOLIS, or B. V.) (1834–1882), Scottish poet, remembered for his long, pessimistic poem, *The City of Dreadful Night,* was born at Port Glasgow, Renfrew, on Nov. 23, 1834. His father, a merchant seaman, became incurably ill in 1840; his mother died in 1842, and thereafter he was cared for and educated at an orphanage. In 1850 he entered the Royal Military Academy, Chelsea, to train as an army schoolmaster, and in 1851 was sent to Ireland as a pupil-teacher. There he met Charles Bradlaugh, the secularist leader, and fell in love with the 14-year-old daughter of an army sergeant, who died two years later.

In 1862, Thomson was discharged from the army for a minor offense, and went to London, where at first he lived with the Bradlaughs, working as a clerk, and writing essays, poems, and stories, many of them published in the *National Reformer,* a secularist workingmen's weekly founded by Bradlaugh, in which first appeared *The City of Dreadful Night* (1874). Always poor, often morose in temper, an atheist, pessimist, and dipsomaniac, he made few friends, eventually quarreling even with Bradlaugh. However, one of his admirers, Bertram Dobell, the bookseller and man of letters, arranged for the publication of his most important volume, *The City of Dreadful Night, and Other Poems* (1880).

An admirer and translator of Leopardi, Thomson did not balance his atheism with any kind of social optimism. The keynote of *The City of Dreadful Night* is: "No hope could have no fear." Monotonous in its gloom, stiff and sometimes wordy in its rhetoric, this poem nevertheless conveys in an almost Baudelaireian way that image of the bleakness and inhumanity of the modern great city which was to be a central theme for such later poets as T. S. Eliot. No other Victorian poem displays more bleakly the dark underside of an age of change, excitement, and hope.

BIBLIOGRAPHY.—*Poetical Works,* ed. by B. Dobell, 2 vol. (1895); *The City of Dreadful Night and Other Poems,* with introduction by Edmund Blunden (1932); H. S. Salt, *Life of James Thomson* (1898; rev. ed., 1914); I. Walker, *James Thomson: a Critical Study* (1950); W. D. Schaeffer, *James Thomson (B. V.): Beyond The City* (1965).
(G. S. F.)

**THOMSON, SIR JOHN ARTHUR** (1861–1933), British naturalist known chiefly for his popular books and writings on biology, was born at East Lothian, Scot., on July 8, 1861, and was educated at the universities of Edinburgh, Jena and Berlin. He was, for a time, lecturer on zoology and biology at the school of medicine in Edinburgh, and in 1899 he became regius professor of natural history at Aberdeen university. Apart from his purely zoological work, chiefly on alcyonarians (soft corals, etc.), Thomson did much, both by his lectures and his numerous attractive books and writings, to popularize biological science, and he was indefatigable in his efforts to correlate science and religion. He was knighted in 1930 and died Feb. 12, 1933.

His publications include: *Outlines of Zoology,* 9th ed. (1944); *The Wonder of Life* (1914); *The System of Animate Nature,* Gifford Lectures (1920); *Science, Old and New* (1924); *The New Natural History* (1925); *Science and Religion* (1925).

**THOMSON, JOSEPH** (1858–1895), Scottish explorer and the last who, during the late 18th and part of the 19th centuries revealed the interior of Africa, was also the first who served the chartered companies developing the new discoveries. Born on Feb. 14, 1858, at Penpont, Dumfries, he studied geology at Edinburgh University under Archibald Geikie, and in 1878 was appointed geologist and naturalist to the Royal Geographical Society's expedition to east-central Africa, under Keith Johnston. Johnston's early death left Thomson in command and, with David Livingstone's Chuma as his headman, he led the expedition to the north end of Lake Nyasa and thence to Lake Tanganyika. An attempt to reach the Congo was thwarted by the hostile Warua, and he returned to the coast by Tabora, discovering Lake Rukwa on the way.

In 1882 the Royal Geographical Society launched an expedition led by Thomson to probe the shortest route from the sea to the Nile headwaters, a way hitherto barred by the Masai. Thomson traveled from Mombasa by way of Mounts Kilimanjaro and Kenya, discovered Lake Baringo, and, surviving numerous encounters with the Masai, reached Lake Victoria on Dec. 10, 1882.

In 1885 he undertook a mission for the National African (afterward the Royal Niger) Company, securing trade treaties with the sultans of Sokoto and Gando; in 1888 he traveled privately in Morocco and in 1890 he entered the service of Cecil Rhodes' British South Africa Company, on whose behalf he made trade and mining agreements in what is now Zambia. Thomson returned to Gatelawbridge in 1891 in poor health. He died in London on Aug. 2, 1895.

Thomson's maxim when traveling was the Italian saying: "Who goes slowly, goes safely; who goes safely, goes far," and he was notable for his abhorrence of force. He wrote *To the Central*

*African Lakes and Back* (1881), *Through Masai Land* (1885), and *Travels in the Atlas and South Morocco* (1889).

*See* J. B. Thomson, *Joseph Thomson, African Explorer* (1896), which contains a full list of his writings. (D. Mn.)

**THOMSON, SIR JOSEPH JOHN** (1856–1940), English physicist, the discoverer of electrons and the recipient of the 1906 Nobel Prize in Physics for his work on the conduction of electricity through gases, was born at Cheetham Hill, near Manchester, on Dec. 18, 1856. At the age of 14 he enrolled at Owens College, Manchester. In 1876 he went to Cambridge and entered Trinity College as a minor scholar; he remained a member of this college, in one capacity after another, during the rest of his life. In 1884 he was elected a fellow of the Royal Society and, upon the resignation of Lord Rayleigh, succeeded to the Cavendish professorship at Cambridge, a chair that he held until 1919.

Thomson's treatise on vortex rings, which won him the Adams Prize and which may be taken as an indication of his early interest in atomic structure, appeared in 1883. Ten years later, in 1893, his *Notes on Recent Researches in Electricity and Magnetism* appeared. This book covers results obtained after the appearance of James Clerk Maxwell's great *Treatise* in 1873, and is often alluded to as "the third volume of Maxwell." *A Textbook of Physics,* in four volumes, was the joint work of Thomson and John H. Poynting. These books had a wide use, as did Thomson's *Elements of the Mathematical Theory of Electricity and Magnetism* (1895; 5th ed., 1921).

In 1896, Thomson gave a course of four lectures at Princeton University. These summarized his researches on the *Discharge of Electricity Through Gases*. Several years later, at Yale University, he gave a series of six lectures on *Electricity and Matter* (1904) in which some keen suggestions looking toward atomic structure were offered. It was, however, between these two series of U.S. lectures that he accomplished the most brilliant work of his life. This was the highly original study of cathode rays, in which he measured the ratio $\frac{m}{e}$ (where $m$ is mass and $e$ the charge of an ion) and discovered that its value is nearly 1,000 times less than in the electrolysis of liquids. He immediately proceeded to measure the charge of electricity $e$ carried by various negative ions and found it to be the same in the gaseous discharge as in electrolysis. In this manner the fact was established that the particles which constitute cathode rays are much smaller than the smallest atoms known. They are the particles that are now called electrons. This discovery of a body smaller than the hydrogen atom was first announced in his Friday evening lecture at the Royal Institution on April 30, 1897.

In 1903 he published his most remarkable book, *Conduction of Electricity Through Gases,* described by Lord Rayleigh as a summary of "the work of Thomson's great days at the Cavendish laboratory." A later edition, in two volumes, was published in collaboration with his son, George Paget Thomson (*q.v.*), in 1928 and 1933.

Thomson's later researches led to an exceedingly important discovery, namely, a new method of separating different kinds of atoms and molecules. This consists in the use of "positive rays," the deflection of which in a magnetic or electric field varies, other things being equal, with the atomic weight. This idea, in the hands of Francis W. Aston, A. J. Dempster, and others, led to the discovery of many isotopes.

Thomson was president of the Royal Society from 1915 to 1920 and master of Trinity College from 1918 to 1940. He died in Cambridge on Aug. 30, 1940; his ashes were buried in Westminster Abbey. His autobiographical *Recollections and Reflections* was published in 1936.

*See* also references under "Thomson, Sir Joseph John" in the Index.

Bibliography.—*Obituary Notices of Fellows of the Royal Society,* vol. 3 (1931), with a list of Thomson's 231 scientific papers and 13 books; Lord Rayleigh, *Life of Sir J. J. Thomson* (1943); G. P. Thomson, *J. J. Thomson and the Cavendish Laboratory in His Day* (1965).

(H. Cw.; X.)

**THOMSON, VIRGIL** (1896– ), U.S. composer, conductor, and music critic, whose forward-looking ideas, largely derived from the French composers of the early 20th century, stimulated new lines of thought among the musicians of his time. Born in Kansas City on Nov. 25, 1896, he studied at Harvard University and with Nadia Boulanger in Paris, where he also became known in the circles of painters and writers. Gertrude Stein was the librettist of his *Four Saints in Three Acts* (Hartford, Conn., 1934), an operatic burlesque in which the title is deliberately misleading, for the opera is actually in four acts and there are more than a dozen saints in the cast. This was followed by *The Mother of Us All* (New York City, 1947), also to Gertrude Stein's libretto, on the subject of the woman suffrage movement. Thomson's instrumental music, like his operas, veers from hymnal solemnity to sophisticated playfulness. It includes two symphonies; the symphonic poems *The Seine at Night* (1948), *Wheatfield at Noon* (1948), and *Sea Piece with Birds* (1952); and a cello concerto (1950) and a flute concerto (1954). He also composed *Five Songs* for voice and orchestra, to poems of William Blake (1952), chamber music, sacred choruses, piano pieces, and the film music to *Louisiana Story* (1948). He was music critic for the *New York Herald Tribune* (1940–54) and published several collections of his critical articles, offering a penetrating assessment of the contemporary musical scene. His autobiography, *Virgil Thomson on Virgil Thomson,* was published in 1966.

*See* K. O. Hoover and J. Cage, *Virgil Thomson: His Life and Music* (1959). (N. Sy.)

**THONBURI,** a city and province in central Thailand on the west bank of the Mae Nam Chao Phraya River across from Bangkok. Area of province 174 sq.mi. (450 sq.km.); pop. (1960) 559,432. Approximately one-quarter of the city's population (1960, 403,818) is of immediate Chinese descent, 6% being China-born. Connected by three bridges with Bangkok, the city has in effect become a suburb of the capital.

Thonburi is a centre for sawmilling, rice milling, and light manufacturing industry. Many of its people live on *khlongs* or canals, on which "floating markets" can be seen. The most prominent landmark is Wat Arun, the Temple of Dawn. During the reign of King Takh Sin (1767–82), Thonburi was the national capital. Paddy production for the province averages about 40,000 metric tons annually. (G. W. Sk.)

**THONET, MICHAEL** (1796–1871), Austrian manufacturer, pioneer in the industrialization of furniture manufacture, was born July 2, 1796, at Boppard in the Rhineland. A humble artisan, Thonet by the age of 40 developed a system of steam-bent veneers, glued four or five together, from which he made complete chairs, light and curvilinear. Similar techniques were simultaneously used, but less freely, by the German-born Henry Belter in New York City, and bent plys of wood, pegged but not glued, were used by the ancient Egyptians. Thonet's inventiveness attracted Prince Metternich, another native Rhinelander, who in 1842 invited Thonet to settle in Vienna, where for the next five years he worked on the masterly neorococo interiors of the Liechtenstein Palace.

Some of Thonet's work there included bent, solid wood, formed by methods familiar to wheelwrights; these pieces were subcontracted through the important firm Carl Leistler and Son, decorating the palace.

By 1856 Thonet had perfected the bending of solid wood and was ready for mass production. From then on, success attended his enterprises. He died on March 3, 1871, in Vienna where his firm was producing furniture in hitherto unheard-of quantities, around 400,000 pieces annually. Solid bentwood furniture, never out of production, was again made fashionable by Le Corbusier in the 1920s. (Er. K.)

**THONGA** (properly Tsonga), Bantu speakers who inhabit the southern coastal plain of Mozambique, with some representatives in Swaziland and the Republic of South Africa. Culturally and linguistically the Thonga are related to other Mozambique Bantu such as the Chopi, Lenge, and Inhambane Tonga. In the 1960s this group of related peoples numbered more than 1,369,000.

The Thonga were formerly organized as independent tribes, each occupying its own territory and named for a powerful patrilineage that dominated the tribe. In the early 19th century they were conquered by Nguni (*q.v.*) raiders from the south who created a number of small kingdoms, the most important of which was Shangana. In the late 19th century the Thonga came under Portuguese rule and lost their political identity.

The Thonga live in scattered homesteads; inheritance and succession are patrilineal. Polygyny is permitted and bridewealth (*q.v.*) is paid. A man's livestock is apportioned among his wives for their support and for eventual inheritance by the children of each wifely household. The principal heir is the senior son of the chief wife. Children also have claims on their mother's lineage; they are allowed to joke with their mother's brother and may make free with his property. Divorce has been rare; widows are inherited by males of the dead husband's lineage.

The Thonga are agriculturalists (cassava is the staple) and pastoralists; fishing and hunting are of minor importance. Women do much of the agricultural work though some men grow cash crops. Most Thonga depend on wage labour for cash, many migrating to Rhodesia or the Republic of South Africa to find work.

Many Thonga are Christian; others adhere to the traditional, highly ritualistic religion. Men enter adult life through an initiation school and circumcision. Members of each lineage propitiate their own ancestral spirits. Illness and other misfortune are usually attributed to the breaking of a tabu, to the anger of ancestors, or to sorcery; detection of the agent is by divination. Sorcery is most commonly blamed on women married into the lineage, rarely on lineage mates.

*See* H. A. Junod, *The Life of a South African Tribe,* 2 vol. (1962); A. M. Duggan-Cronin, *The Bantu Tribes of South Africa,* vol. iv, *The Vathonga* (1936). (E. Co.)

**THOR,** a deity common to all the early Germanic peoples, a great warrior represented as a red-bearded, middle-aged man of enormous strength, an implacable foe to the harmful race of giants (demons) but benevolent toward mankind. His figure is generally secondary to that of Odin, who in some traditions is his father. But in Iceland and indeed, perhaps, in all northern countries except among the royal families he was apparently worshiped more than any other god. There is evidence that a corresponding deity named Thunor or Thonar was worshiped in England and on the continent, but little is known about him. Thor's name is the Teutonic word for thunder, and it is the thunderbolt that is represented by his hammer, the attribute most commonly associated with him. The hammer, Mjollnir, had many marvelous qualities, including that of returning to the thrower like a boomerang; it is frequently found on runic stones and funerary steles. Thor has close affinities with Jupiter, as is attested by the name of the fifth day of the week, "Thor's day" throughout the Germanic world and *dies Jovis* in the Roman. *See* also GERMANIC MYTHOLOGY AND HEROIC LEGENDS.

*See* J. A. MacCulloch in *The Mythology of All Races,* vol. ii, *Eddic,* pp. 68–96 (1930).

**THORAX,** the anatomical term for the chest, in man and other mammals that part of the body between the neck and abdomen. The bony framework consists of the 12 thoracic vertebrae, 12 pairs of ribs and the sternum (breastbone). It contains the chief organs of respiration and circulation; namely, the lungs, some air passages, the heart and great vessels. Below, it is bounded by the diaphragm. The bony framework is encased with muscles, fat, and cutaneous tissues. (*See* SKELETON, VERTEBRATE.)

In insects the thorax is the middle of the three major divisions of the body. It is composed of three parts, each of which commonly bears a pair of legs; the rearward two parts usually bear each a pair of wings. (F. L. A.; X.)

**THORBECKE, JOHAN RUDOLF** (1798–1872), the inspirer of the Netherlands constitution of 1848 and subsequently three times prime minister. He was born at Zwolle, in Overijssel, on Jan. 14, 1798. After graduating at Leiden, he spent some time at German universities and became a lecturer at Giessen and at Göttingen. He published a treatise "On the Essence and Organic Character of History" in 1824 and some "Considerations Regarding Law and the State" in 1825. He was then appointed supernumerary professor at Ghent; but the Belgian revolution of 1830 drove him back to Leiden, where he became a professor in the faculty of law. Though he did not teach constitutional law, he won unrivaled authority in this field. His *Aanteekening op de Grondwet* ("Annotation to the Constitution," 1839; second edition 1841–43, manifesting the development of his liberal ideas) was of fundamental importance for the constitution of 1848.

Thorbecke was prime minister of the Kingdom of the Netherlands from Nov. 1, 1849, to April 19, 1853; from Feb. 1, 1862, to Feb. 10, 1866; and finally from Jan. 4, 1871, to his death, at The Hague, on June 5, 1872. For his policy *see* NETHERLANDS, THE: *History*. His liberalism was influenced by German Romantic ideas of the historical-juridical school of K. F. Eichhorn and F. K. von Savigny. In his denial of the theory of the sovereignty of the people he also differed from the French rationalist view. Nor was there any anticlericalism in his outlook: his truly liberal attitude toward Roman Catholics was most objectionable to Conservative Protestants. The opposition which he frequently encountered was provoked, however, not only by the expression of his principles, but also, partly, by his rigid and haughty personality.

*See* K. H. Boersema, *Johan Rudolf Thorbecke* (1949); I. J. Brugmans, *Thorbecke,* 3rd ed. (1958). (H. A. Bo.)

**THOREAU, HENRY DAVID** (1817–1862), U.S. writer, poet and philosopher who invested his life in his native village to the end of enacting the doctrines of New England Transcendentalism as expressed by his friend and associate Ralph Waldo Emerson (*q.v.*), among others. A naturalist chiefly in the sense that nature was his field of action and contemplation, Thoreau was concerned primarily with the possibilities for human culture provided by the American natural environment. He believed that "All things invite this earth's inhabitants/To rear their lives to an unheard-of height"; to meet this "expectation of the land" (*Collected Poems of Henry Thoreau,* edited by Carl Bode, p. 135, Packard and Co., Chicago, 1943), he domesticated ideas garnered from classical, oriental, English and the then current romantic literatures in order to extend U.S. libertarianism and individualism beyond the political and religious spheres to those of social and personal life. In a society which Henry James said was "not fertile in variations" (F. O. Matthiessen, *The James Family,* p. 441, Alfred A. Knopf, Inc., New York, 1947), Thoreau pioneered the life of an artist and like Emerson opened vistas to new vocations and intrinsic successes. "The life which men praise and regard as successful is but one kind. Why," he asked in *Walden,* where his example was the answer, "should we exaggerate any one kind at the expense of the others?" (This and all following quotations from the prose works of Thoreau—the standard Walden edition, *The Writings of Henry David Thoreau,* 1906—are by permission of Houghton Mifflin Company, Boston.) In a commercial, conservative, expedient society rapidly becoming urban and industrial, he upheld the right to self-culture, to an individual life shaped by inner principle. An artist whose life was his material, he demanded for all men the freedom to follow unique life styles, to make poems of their lives and living itself an art. Wholeness and being were his aims, not the limited fulfillment of specialization; the artisan was to become an artist, the partial man "spheral," the factitious man authentic. In a restless, expanding society dedicated to practical action, he demonstrated the uses and values of leisure, contemplation and rootedness.

THE GRANGER COLLECTION

THOREAU, DAGUERREOTYPE BY BENJAMIN D. MAXHAM, 1856

Thoreau's writing not only enriched the New England landscape with human associations, but taught men how to take up the land without despoiling it—with their imaginations. He established the tradition of nature writing developed by John Burroughs and John Muir, and his pioneer study of the human uses of nature profoundly influenced such conservationists and regional planners as Benton MacKaye and Lewis Mumford. More important, his life, so fully expressed in his writing, has had a pervasive influence because it was an example of moral heroism and an example of the continuing search for a spiritual America. One of the classic U.S. writers, he became a culture hero because he had shown that "the intransigence of the spiritual unit . . . alone gives edge to democracy" (*The Seven Arts,* II, July, 1917, p. 385).

**Early Life.**—Although Thoreau playfully linked his genealogy with that of the first discoverers of America, the Viking descendants of Thor, and characterized himself as a follower of the "trade of heroism," Thoreau's outward life offered little adventure for the annalist. The son of John Thoreau, whose father had emigrated from the Channel Islands, and of Cynthia Dunbar, daughter of a Congregational minister, he was born July 12, 1817, in the rural village of Concord, where his unsuccessful father finally settled and set up a small graphite pencil factory. This home industry, which Thoreau dutifully served all of his life, and his mother's boardinghouse, where he lived except for the intervals at the Emersons' and at Walden pond, were his permanent background.

Thoreau prepared at the Concord academy, and, at great sacrifice to his family, entered Harvard college in 1833. There he came abreast of his age, encountering both the intellectual heritage of the 18th century, which he would soon abandon, and the new thought that provided the philosophical basis for his experiment in life. Jones Very, a minor Transcendentalist poet, was his tutor in Greek; Orestes Brownson (*q.v.*), soon to become a Transcendentalist publicist, helped him with German during a schoolteaching vacation; Edward Tyrel Channing, professor of rhetoric, assigned compositions in which Thoreau sketched his conception of the superior man and recorded the increasing Transcendental tendency of his thought. A good student but indifferent to the rank system and preferring to use the library to his own ends, he graduated midway in the class of 1837. But, as he announced in his commencement piece on "The Commercial Spirit," with its scorn for getting and spending, with its plea for cultivating "the moral affections" and the powers to enjoy and admire the "wonderful" world, he was eager to follow a vocation for which few of his classmates had the inclination, preparation or heart.

Emerson called Thoreau to that vocation. During commencement week he delivered his challenging Phi Beta Kappa address, "The American Scholar." In it he summoned the younger generation to follow his own calling—that of the independent intellectual at the service of the republic—and to fulfill in action the program for nurturing American genius and culture that he had outlined in *Nature* (1836). "He shall see," he promised the self-reliant truth seeker, "that nature is the opposite of the soul, answering to it part for part. . . . Its beauty is the beauty of his own mind. Its laws are the laws of his own mind. Nature then becomes to him the measure of his attainments. So much of nature as he is ignorant of, so much of his own mind does he not yet possess. . . . in fine, the ancient precept, 'Know thyself,' and the modern precept, 'Study nature,' become at last one maxim." This "correspondence" between the subjective and the objective, the inner and the outer, the indwelling spirit in man and the immanent spirit in nature, were at the core of the Transcendentalist faith. To discover the identities between man and nature, to translate the external world into consciousness, to humanize science by making fact flower into truth, was now the work of the scholar. Thoreau undertook this exploration of "whole new continents and worlds within" when, on his return to Concord, Emerson suggested that he keep a journal; eventually running to 39 manuscript volumes, the journal became the principal archive of Thoreau's arduous experience of assimilating nature to himself.

**After Harvard.**—Immediately following his graduation Thoreau kept a school; privately he continued his apprenticeship to his chosen craft by writing poems and literary essays. He began his long service as lecturer and curator for the Concord Lyceum and published his first poem in the newly launched magazine the *Dial,* edited by Margaret Fuller (*q.v.*) and Emerson. He fell in love with Ellen Sewall of Scituate and was rejected. Unwilling to postpone his life and already lamenting that he was an Apollo enslaved to Admetus, he gave up teaching; on Emerson's request, he went to live with his mentor, exchanging his skills as handyman and editorial assistant on the *Dial* for the freedom to pursue his own work.

Emerson turned Thoreau to nature writing by prompting Thoreau's first major essay, "Natural History of Massachusetts"; he severely pruned Thoreau's poems; and he tried to bring his protégé to market by sending him as tutor to the William Emersons of Staten Island, where he might find it easier to sell his wares in New York. Thoreau, however, was unsuccessful. As he put it, his essays were not "companionable"; "Paradise (To Be) Regained" destroyed the popular assumptions of utilitarian progress, and "A Winter Walk," one of the best of his early spiritual excursions, was better fitted for the *Dial.* Confirmed in his distaste for city life, disappointed by his failure, and in debt, he returned home and with Yankee brevity noted in his autobiographical record: "Made pencils in 1844."

**The Walden Years.**—In 1845, Emerson provided the few acres Thoreau needed for his Walden experiment, which was to make good his losses and permit him at last to have his life while living it; but Emerson did not approve what seemed to him a withdrawal into solitude and an abdication of the "Napoleonic" leadership he expected of his "brave Henry." For Thoreau, however, going to nearby Walden pond was an act of independence, the act of precipitating his fate (in *Walden* he began the account of his residence there on Independence day). Not only did he wish to solve by simplicity and subsistence farming his economic problems as a writer, he wished by means of his intimacy with nature to meet "the great facts of his existence" and to live an uncommitted life open to spirit. To him the landscape of his new life bordered the "Elysian fields"; measured by his ecstatic communion with nature, the two years at Walden were the great occasion of his life.

Thoreau left the pond in September 1847 in order to manage the Emerson household during Emerson's absence on a lecture tour in Great Britain and because, with *A Week on the Concord and Merrimack Rivers* completed, he felt ready to retrieve his early failure. He was unable to find a publisher, however, and the publication of this, his first book, was delayed until 1849, when Thoreau issued it at his own expense. It was so poorly received that Thoreau resisted the appeals to publish *Walden* until the debt he had incurred was paid. Just as poorly received were his attempts as a lecturer to find a public. Having "not made it worth any one's while" to buy his delicately woven wares, as he explained in *Walden,* he tried to "avoid the necessity of selling them." He no longer tried to maintain himself by writing; he returned to the pencil factory and to surveying, his occupations for the rest of his life.

**The Fruits of Walden.**—Thoreau's greatest books, *A Week* and *Walden,* were indebted to the Walden years. Companion volumes, the first covers Thoreau's spiritual history from 1839 to 1849, the second the years from 1845 to 1854. *A Week* takes its joyousness from the vacation mood and spiritual communion of these early years and the years at Walden where it was written. An excursion in thought, its narrative framework is the boat trip Thoreau had made with his beloved brother John in 1839; the literal adventure carried with it his thoughts on religion, friendship, politics, reform, art and nature—the experience of a decade of exploration. The book enacts Thoreau's belief that "the order of things should be somewhat reversed; the seventh day should be man's day of toil . . . and the other six his Sabbath of the affections and the soul,—in which to range this widespread garden, and drink in the soft influences and sublime revelations of Nature. . . ." A meandering, meditative book, successfully uniting action and contemplation; a series of days on the stream of consciousness; a voyage into America, to the headwaters of inspiration: *A Week* covers Thoreau's life from youth to maturity, from the easy availability of inspiration to the more conscious use of inspiration in the creation of art.

Thoreau's relation to nature in *A Week* was "one and continuous everywhere"; inspired, his life was "constantly as fresh as this river." He was "a long-lived child/As yet uninjured by all worldly taint/. . . whose whole life is play." In *Walden,* he was the "mature soul of lesser innocence" who, "from the sad experience of his fate," had consciously earned "the ripe bloom of a self-wrought content" (Bode, p. 225).

*Walden* was begun in 1846–47, but was considerably modified and amplified in six revisions, material being incorporated almost until the time of publication in 1854. The book therefore did not literally record the Walden experience, for this experience was refracted by what Thoreau felt was the "decay" of the following years during which it was brought to completion. A symbolic book, then, treating his experience not so much retrospectively as prospectively, to the end of self-therapy and hope, *Walden* affirmed Thoreau's faith in "the unquestionable ability of man to elevate his life by conscious endeavor." By his definition, the book was a scripture, the sacred testament of a man living through the process of revelation; its myth, secured by the seasonal movement of the narrative from summer to spring, was that of a return to the springs of life—a fable of spiritual renewal.

**Later Writings.**—Thoreau's actual life in these and the remaining years did not bring renewal. Now his problem was a more difficult one than that of living by writing. His inspirational relation to nature itself had been broken by the deterioration of his friendship with Emerson, by his involvement in the antislavery movement, by the impurity that he felt was due to the coarse life required of the surveyor, and by the intense strain of the outdoor life and the scientific studies he imposed on himself. The goal of self-culture, he found, could not be fully realized in nature; personal and social relations were also necessary. The inevitable awareness of manhood had destroyed the unconsciousness of youth and, with it, the communion with nature he now desperately tried to regain by discipline.

Though his sense of losing his innocence and purity was great, his powers as a writer were increased by his more objective investigation of nature and by his social concerns. "Civil Disobedience," his most famous essay (it influenced Gandhi, among others), was his defense of the private conscience against majority expediency; published in 1849, it announced the moral intransigence of later essays such as "Slavery in Massachusetts" and "Life Without Principle," and those essays written in behalf of John Brown, who carried the political faith of the Transcendentalists to the conclusion of bloody action.

The finest essays, however, like his travel books (*The Maine Woods, A Yankee in Canada* and *Cape Cod*), were the fruit of a more strenuous undertaking, that of rediscovering and repossessing the aboriginal environment of America which had sustained his own spirit. Composed of his accounts of his three trips to Maine, in 1846, 1853 and 1857, *The Maine Woods* presents at its finest Thoreau's zest for outdoor adventure. Less symbolic than his other works (the essays were intended to be of practical help to campers), the book does however indicate his retreat from primitivism to the more human pastoralism of Concord. *A Yankee in Canada* took Thoreau into the country explored by the French discoverers whom he admired, but the old world institutions there provoked him to praise of the freer institutions of New England. *Cape Cod* introduced him to the first frontier, the sea, and enabled him to recount the history of the new world from the time of the Northmen, Cabot and Columbus to that of his own excursions; and the incidents of shipwreck made it possible for him to transform death into a passage to the last frontier, the spiritual west. At home, in Concord, with failing strength (the signs of fatal tuberculosis appeared as early as 1852) he laboured on his "Kalendar." His most grandiose project, it was to put on record all of his knowledge of nature's year as this knowledge had been mixed with human aspiration, growth and fruition—his, his countrymen's, and man's throughout history. He completed only "Autumnal Tints" and "Wild Apples"; appropriately they were essays on the values of maturity, an autumnal victory over the tragic loss of his springtime. The first is a paean to the flaming, courageous leaves that taught him how to die; the latter is a transparent parable of his own life and his desire to grow wild that he might, in Emerson's words, "yield that peculiar fruit which each man was created to bear." These travels, in New England at large and in his own backyard, provided the inspiration for his final testament, "Walking." Walking had been his spiritual exercise; his holy land was the west. The west was the freedom, the "wild" that nurtured civilizations and men. This ecology of man and his environment was Thoreau's largest gift to America.

Thoreau did not relinquish civilization for primitivism; in the interests of human culture, he wished only to keep civilization open on one side that others, as he had, might bear their peculiar fruits. For health as well as because of his devotion to the west, Thoreau went to Minnesota in 1861. He died in Concord on May 6, 1862.

**Editions.**—The standard edition is *The Writings of Henry David Thoreau,* in 20 volumes (1906); vol. vi, *Familiar Letters,* was edited by F. B. Sanborn; vol. vii–xx, the *Journals,* were edited by Bradford Torrey and Francis Allen. *Consciousness in Concord,* edited by P. Miller (1958), contains the "lost" journal of 1840–41. Other sources are *Collected Poems of Henry Thoreau,* edited by Carl Bode (1943), and *The Correspondence of Henry David Thoreau,* edited by W. Harding and Carl Bode (1958).

BIBLIOGRAPHY.—*Biographical and Critical Studies:* H. S. Canby, *Thoreau* (1939); J. W. Krutch, *Henry David Thoreau* (1948); F. O. Matthiessen, *American Renaissance* (1941); Leo Stoller, *After Walden: Thoreau's Changing Views on Economic Man* (1957); Sherman Paul, *The Shores of America: Thoreau's Inward Exploration* (1958). Walter Harding (ed.), *Thoreau: A Century of Criticism* (1954), is a collection of critical essays. A bibliography compiled by T. H. Johnson can be found in *Literary History of the United States,* ed. by Robert E. Spiller *et al.,* vol. iii, pp. 742–746 (1948). *See* also Floyd Stovall (ed.), *Eight American Authors: a Review of Research and Criticism* (1956); Walter Harding, *A Thoreau Handbook* (1959); M. Meltzer and W. R. Harding, *A Thoreau Profile* (1962). (S. PL.)

**THOREZ, MAURICE** (1900–1964), French Communist leader for 34 years. Born at Noyelles-Godault, in the Pas-de-Calais, on April 28, 1900, he became a coal miner at the age of 12, joined the Socialist Party in 1919, and moved into the Communist Party after the Socialists had split at the Congress of Tours (December 1920). He became party secretary for the Pas-de-Calais in 1923 and rose rapidly until in July 1930 he became secretary-general, after several terms in prison for agitation. He was elected to the Chamber of Deputies in 1932 and reelected in 1936. On the outbreak of World War II he was mobilized, but when the government banned the party because of its hostility to the war he left the army and went underground. He was tried *in absentia,* sentenced to six years' imprisonment, and subsequently deprived of his citizenship. In 1943 he went to the U.S.S.R.

At the Liberation, Thorez was pardoned by Gen. de Gaulle's government and, in November 1944, returned to France; in 1945 his French nationality was restored. He became a deputy again in 1945 and was reelected throughout the Fourth Republic. After being a minister of state under De Gaulle in November 1945, he was deputy prime minister under Félix Gouin and Georges Bidault in 1946 and under Paul Ramadier in 1947; but when the Communists voted against the government in May 1947, their ministers were dismissed. Thorez himself was soon suspected by Moscow of nationalism of Tito's kind, and was made to renounce it in 1948. He had a cerebral hemorrhage in October 1950, went to Moscow for medical treatment, and did not return until April 1953. Thorez was on the whole a Stalinist and after Khrushchev's denunciation of Stalin in 1956 he extolled the dead leader.

In 1958 the Communists failed to prevent De Gaulle's coming to power. In the ensuing elections the party lost heavily, but Thorez himself retained his seat. Thorez died on July 11, 1964, in a Soviet ship en route for Yalta. He published *Fils du Peuple* (1937) and *Une Politique de grandeur française* (1949).

(P. W. C.)

**THORFINN KARLSEFNI** (fl. 1002–07), Scandinavian leader of the first medieval expedition for the colonization of North America, was born in Iceland around 980. He must have been given his nickname at an early age, for *karlsefni* means "promising boy." His grandfather, Snorri Bjarnason, is a historical figure as one of the aristocrats who, about the year 900, led the westward-swarming Norwegians to Iceland. Many of them felt so pressed for stock-farming land by 986 that they followed the lead of Eric the Red and migrated to Greenland. By the year 1000 there were probably more than 1,000 Scandinavian stock farmers in what is now the Julianehaab district of Greenland. Karlsefni, finally caught up in the westward sweep from Iceland, reached what was known as the eastern settlement of Greenland during the autumn 1003 with two ships and about 80 colonists. No doubt the ships would have continued to or beyond the western settlement had not Eric invited all hands to spend the winter with him at his farm, Brattahlid. From the *Saga of Eric the Red* it appears that there may have been a motive behind the hospitality. The saga tells of banquets, jollity and glowing talk of a country to the southwest, beyond the sea, that had been discovered three years before by one of Eric's sons, Leif, and named by him Vinland (*q.v.*). The impression one gets from the saga is that both father and son were persuasive, trying to divert the two Icelandic vessels from prosecuting a further northwestward colonization along the shore of Greenland, directing them instead toward Vinland, perhaps in part because the previous year Eric's son Thorstein had died in the western settlement, and his widow Gudrid had come to stay at Brattahlid. Eric now married her off to Thorfinn; and it was arranged that a Greenland ship would join the Icelandic ones and they would pick up Gudrid's property on their way to Vinland.

In the spring of 1004 [or, according to other historians, 1010 or 1020] about 130 men and women, in three vessels, with livestock and household goods, sailed from the eastern to the western settlement, picked up Gudrid's property, and crossed from the Greenland coast at Bear Island (Disko) toward Baffin Island, apparently striking that shore near Cape Dyer. They named the coast Helluland, meaning "Land of Flat Stones" (Flagstoneland) and continued to use this name as long as they saw no trees while coasting in a southerly direction. After crossing Hudson strait they saw trees and then called the shore Markland, meaning "Forest Land."

Farther south they came to a section which they took for Leif's Vinland district and which sounds in the narrative as if it probably was some part of the Gulf of St. Lawrence, perhaps the south shore. Reaching the heavily wooded region, the colonists built houses, made hay and spent the winter hunting and fishing, much as if they were still in Greenland; but they noted that the meadows were grassier and that the winter was shorter.

The first winter the Scandinavians met no people but the next summer they were visited by friendly natives with whom they traded and who, from the description, were Eskimos. After wintering in a different place, or perhaps scattered in several wintering places, they were again visited by natives, this time more numerous and no longer friendly. A battle ensued; the Europeans won it, but at the cost of some lives. Following still another winter, during which the colonists evidently thought things over, Thorfinn decided to return to Greenland. There was no longer unity among the colonists. Although all decided to abandon Vinland, they did not all head for Greenland and some, perhaps intending to reach Iceland, were shipwrecked on a western coast of Europe.

With his wife, and a son who had been born to them in Vinland, Thorfinn spent the winter of 1006–07 in Greenland. Later they returned to Iceland, where Thorfinn's family was already powerful.

Snorri, the Vinland-born son whom Thorfinn had named after his Norwegian grandfather, became the progenitor of a line of clergy. The clergy were not celibate in those days and their numerous descendants came to include two bishops during the first few generations—and bishops were nobility in both Greenland and Iceland under the new dispensation. In a genealogically minded modern Iceland, many people of consequence trace their descent, through Karlsefni, to the U.S. or to Canada; for though the Vinland of the 1004–05 wintering almost certainly was in Canada, some argue that one or both of the other winterings may have been in New England.

Among the persisting results of the Karlsefni voyage was a North American activity of the Roman Catholic Church in the Markland-Vinland region. There resulted, too, commerce between Greenland (*q.v.*) and Labrador (Markland) that is mentioned in both Icelandic and Norwegian records as late as 1347. The seafarers of northwestern Europe never lost memory of coasts west of Greenland that stretch to the south. A theory developed that these coasts would curve eastward in the far south to connect with northern Africa. But in the period between the 13th and 15th centuries nobody seems to have been much interested in this knowledge until after Columbus had the idea that these lands beyond the Atlantic might be a northward extension of Marco Polo's rich Cathay.

Bibliography.—Excellent scholarship on the Vinland voyages is found in the following three volumes by Halldór Hermannsson in the series, *Islandica, The Northmen in America* (1909), *The Problem of Wineland* (1936) and *The Vinland Sagas* (1944). On the historicity of the Greenland-Vinland sagas *see* Sir William A. Craigie, *The Icelandic Sagas* (1913). *See* also for history, Vilhjalmur Stefansson, *Greenland* (1942); H. R. Holand, *Explorations in America Before Columbus* (1956); R. A. Skelton, G. D. Painter, and T. E. Marston, *The Vinland Map and the Tartar Relation* (1965); "Vinland the Good Emerges from the Mists," *American Heritage*, vol. xvi, no. 6 (Oct. 1965); Count Eric Oxenstierna (trans. by Catherine Hutter), *The Norsemen* (1965); Farley Mowat, *Westviking: the Ancient Norse in Greenland and North America* (1965). (V. S.; X.)

**THORIANITE,** a strongly radioactive mineral with the idealized composition thorium dioxide, $ThO_2$. It ordinarily contains more or less uranium in solid solution and is then transitional to the structurally related mineral uraninite (*q.v.*), $UO_2$. Rare earths and radiogenic lead and helium also are present. Thorianite forms hard, black to brown isometric crystals of high specific gravity, 9.7–10. The mineral was originally found as waterworn grains and crystals in the gem gravels of Ceylon. It also has been found sparingly in the black sands of rivers and beaches in Alaska and other parts of the United States, Madagascar and Siberia. Varieties containing much uranium occur in pegmatites in Quebec and Ontario, and in serpentine at Easton, Pa. The refractory nature and the small supply of thorianite has restricted its commercial use as a source of thorium (*see* also Monazite). (Cl. F.)

**THORILD, THOMAS** (1759–1808), Swedish poet and critic who led the revolt against the influence of French classicism. Born April 18, 1759, at Svarteborg, Bohuslän, he studied at Lund and Uppsala. He visited England (1788–90). In 1793 he was banished from Sweden as a result of a political libel after the assassination of Gustavus III. He went to Germany and in 1795 was appointed professor and librarian at Greifswald, where he died Oct. 1, 1808. A born fighter, Thorild attacked the taste for French culture, writing unrhymed verse inspired by Ossian, Shakespeare, Klopstock, and Goethe. Among his best works is *Passionerna* (1785), a philosophical poem expressing a pantheistic feeling for nature. The powerful style of his prose essays resembles that of the old Swedish laws. His famous *En critik öfver critiker* ("A Critique of Critiques," 1791–92) is a plea for positive literary evaluations. After his banishment he continued to write essays of which *Om qvinnokönets naturliga höghet* ("The Natural Greatness of Womankind," 1793) is one of his best.

Thorild's collected works were first published in four volumes (1819–35). A critical edition by Stellan Arvidson was begun in 1932; volume iv appeared in 1946.

*See* A. Nilsson, *Thomas Thorild: en studie över hans livsaskadning* (1915); E. Cassirer, *Thorilds Stellung in der Geistesgeschichte des 18. Jahrhunderts.* (1941). (S. E.)

**THORITE,** a mineral consisting of thorium silicate, is one of the most important thorium minerals. The theoretical formula, $ThSiO_4$, requires 81.5% of thoria, but analyses show only 50%–70%, there being also some uranium, cerium, etc. The mineral is almost always altered by hydration and is then optically isotropic and amorphous. Because of alteration and differences in composition, the specific gravity varies from 4.4 to 5.4. The colour is usually light brown, but in the gem variety known as orangite it is orange-yellow. It crystallizes in the tetragonal system and is isomorphous with zircon (*q.v.*). The mineral occurs as isolated crystals and small masses in the augite-syenite near Brevik in south Norway; also at Arendal, and in the gem gravels of Ceylon. Good crystals are found on Stove mountain, El Paso county, Colo. Thorite is mined commercially at Cripple Creek, Colo., and at Hall mountain, Idaho. (L. J. S.; W. F. Fg.; X.)

**THORIUM.** The radioactive metallic element thorium and its oxide are comparatively rare materials. In spite of this fact, they have played an important role in technology for many years and became the foundation of at least one large industry, the manufacture of gas mantles. The oxide is also important as an additive to metallic tungsten filaments for controlling metallurgical properties. In electronic devices thorium oxide is widely used as a source of primary electron emission. The advent of atomic energy, jet turbines, and rockets brought an unusual demand for new metals and alloys. Important alloys containing thorium were developed for improving the high-temperature strength of metals, in particular the magnesium base alloys.

Thorium has great potential use in nuclear reactors. Its abundance in the earth's crust is at least three times that of uranium. The particular advantage of the use of thorium in the field of atomic energy is as a "breeder" material. It functions in an atomic pile in such a way as to yield a net increase in atomic fuel; see *Industrial Applications,* below. (*See* ATOMIC ENERGY: *Peacetime Applications.*)

Thorium was identified as an element by J. J. Berzelius in 1828. The element is named after Thor, Scandinavian god of war.

Freshly cut massive thorium is silvery white in colour but turns gray or black on exposure to air. The stability of the surface is a function of the oxide content and surface potential. A cold rolled sheet processed to a high finish remains remarkably stable, retaining a high metallic lustre for years.

The metal may be extruded, rolled, forged, swaged, and spun. Drawing is a difficult operation because of its low tensile strength. Most of the operations with the exception of extruding and spinning may be performed cold. Work hardening is moderate, and annealing is usually *in vacuo* at 800°–1,000° C (1,475°–1,800° F). The major embrittling element is carbon, which dissolves in thorium with resulting lattice expansion. Thorium powder is relatively stable in air, but spontaneous combustion has occurred and the storage of large quantities is hazardous. The solid metal is not readily oxidized in air at high temperatures. High-temperature steam is more effective.

Thorium metal is practically nonreactive to acetic acid (0–50%) and also to sodium hydroxide in all concentrations. It is attacked by hydrochloric acid (0.1–36%) but only slightly by nitric acid in all concentrations, provided traces of fluorides are absent. Boiling water converts the metal to thorium oxide.

## OCCURRENCE AND PRODUCTION

**Mineral Deposits.**—Minerals in which thorium is the major constituent are the silicate thorite, $ThSiO_4$, and the mixed uranium thorium oxide, thorianite (*see* THORITE; THORIANITE). A very large number of minerals also contain thorium, but deposits of these minerals are usually too small to be of industrial importance. Thorogummite is an important variety of thorianite, and auerlite, pilbarite, hyblite, and enalite are varieties of thorite found in different parts of the world.

The major source of thorium is monazite (*q.v.*), essentially a phosphate of the rare earths [$(Ce,La,Nd)PO_4$]. Important deposits are found in Kerala (formerly the state of Travancore-Cochin) in India, and Brazil. Significant deposits have been found in the Scandinavian peninsula, Ceylon, Tasmania (Australia), the Ural mountains (U.S.S.R.), and Cape of Good Hope, South Africa. U.S. deposits are in Idaho, Colorado, North Carolina, Virginia and Florida. Monazite sands usually contain 2–10% thoria ($ThO_2$). The poorer ores are concentrated to an oxide content of 5–10% prior to refining.

**Extraction.**—The recovery of thorium compounds, in particular the oxide ($ThO_2$), from monazite concentrates depends upon the separation of this element from cerium and other rare-earth phosphates and substantial amounts of silica, calcium oxide, and iron oxide.

In some monazites the cerium content ($CeO_2$) is 40–50% and the phosphorus content ($P_2O_5$), 20–25%. The separation is accomplished by a variety of methods, including precipitation after digestion with an acid or base, direct reaction with chlorine, separation by an organic liquid, reduction with calcium, and electrolysis.

*Precipitation.*—Commercial extractive processes in use for many years involve the digestion of pulverized monazite in hot concentrated sulfuric acid to dissolve the thorium and rare earths. If the solution is diluted or partially neutralized with ammonia, thorium phosphate separates, and the ratio of $ThO_2$ to rare earths is increased.

For the complete removal of phosphorus and the remaining rare earths several operations have been used. The important ones are sulfate separations, carbonate extractions, oxalate separations, and iodate separations.

The sulfate separation procedure depends upon the low solubility of thorium sulfate, $Th(SO_4)_2.8H_2O$, compared with the sulfates of cerium, neodymium, praseodymium, and lanthanum. In carbonate extraction, thorium forms a soluble double carbonate, and cerium precipitates. The precipitation of thorium as the oxalate from dilute acid solutions is commonly used to separate small amounts of the rare earths and some common metals. It is also used as a final step prior to conversion to oxide which is obtained by ignition.

Some monazites yield to sodium hydroxide extraction, with thorium and the rare earths precipitating. It is used as a means of separating thorium from phosphorus.

The precipitation of thorium iodate from strong nitric acid solution affords an excellent separation of thorium from the rare earths and common metals, but it is too expensive for commercial practice.

In spite of the complicated procedures involved in precipitation, thorium oxide of over 99% purity is produced. The major contaminants are small amounts of cerium, rare-earth oxides, silica, calcium, and magnesium. None of these impurities is present in amounts exceeding 0.1%, and many are of the order of 0.04% or less.

*Reaction With Chlorine.*—Production processes have been suggested which involve the extraction of thorium chloride by the direct reaction of the ore, the oxide, or the oxalate with chlorine. Efficiency of chlorination is increased by mixing the materials with carbon. Chlorine gas saturated with sulfur chloride or carbon tetrachloride may also be used. The direct formation of the chloride affords the preparation of a soluble compound of thorium which may be easily purified or if sufficiently pure may be used directly for metal production.

*Extraction by Organic Liquid.*—Processes have been developed for separating thorium from the rare-earth nitrates. Calcium nitrate and nitric acid are added to a solution of the nitrates and thorium nitrate extracted into an immiscible organic liquid, usually tributyl phosphate (TBP). Organic solutions of primary long chain amines are also useful for thorium extraction. The extraction is accomplished by mixing the two fluids by passage in opposite directions through a vertically packed column. The rare earths and other impurities remain in the water phase. The organic phase containing the thorium nitrate is then back-extracted, the thorium nitrate entering the water phase from which the oxide may be recovered by evaporation and ignition. Oxide with a purity of 99.7% has been produced.

*Reduction With Calcium.*—Several processes have been proposed which include reduction of the fluoride ($ThF_4$) and oxide ($ThO_2$) with calcium. These reactions are carried out on a large scale in closed metal containers usually referred to as "bombs." The reactants are heated to initiate the reaction. The thorium as a metal powder is recovered by leaching the charge with suitable acids which dissolve the by-products of the reaction. A method of preparation is to add metallic zinc to the charge to form a zinc alloy with the thorium, which fuses. Thorium is recovered by vacuum distillation of the zinc followed by vacuum casting of the thorium. A particular advantage is the elimination of a powder step in the process.

*Electrolytic Methods.*—Electrolysis of thorium compounds such as the chloride ($ThCl_4$) from alkali metal baths have shown promise of replacing the "bomb" type of reaction. Such processes may be continuous, requiring only the insertion of electrodes with occasional bath replacement. Thorium is deposited on a metal cathode (molybdenum), and the crucible containing the charge serves as the anode. The deposit upon withdrawal from the bath contains thorium powder plus solidified salts and is recovered by grinding and acid leaching.

Metal of very high purity is obtained by subjecting the primary deposition product to an electrolytic refining operation in which the compressed deposit acts as the anode in a fused salt bath and the thorium is redeposited on a metallic cathode. Lowering occurs in the concentration of many contaminants, including boron, beryllium, copper, chromium, iron, nickel and silicon. The basic principles of the electrolysis and refining operations are shown in fig. 1 and 2.

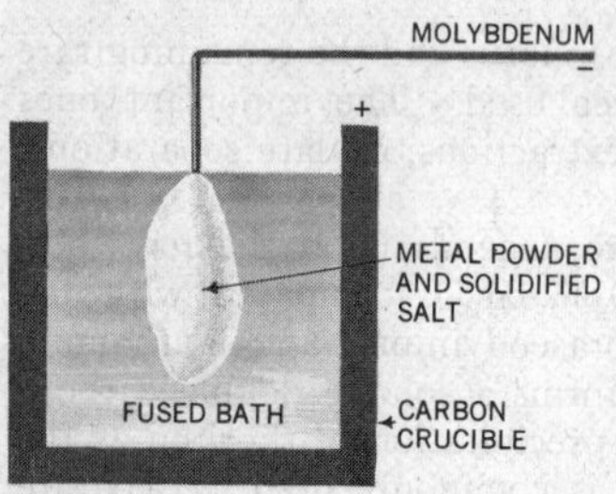


FROM "RARE METALS HANDBOOK," REINHOLD PUBLISHING CORPORATION

FIG. 1.—ELECTROLYTIC CELL FOR THORIUM DEPOSITION

Thorium is also refined by the thermal decomposition of the iodide ($ThI_4$) on a hot wire. The process is similar to that used for zirconium production in which iodine and chips of metal are placed in a closed evacuated container that is heated to form thorium iodide vapour. As the vapour comes into contact with a heated filament in the same vessel, thorium of a very high purity is deposited with the liberation of iodine.

Billets for rolling are produced from the powder by standard powder metallurgy (*q.v.*) practice or by direct arc casting. The former practice is to press the powder in steel dies under 20–30 tons per square inch (psi); the resulting green compacts are vacuum sintered. Casting of powder compacts is sometimes made in beryllia crucibles.

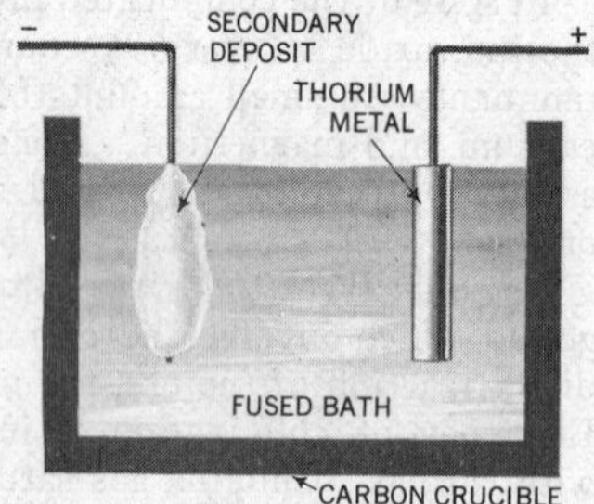


FIG. 2.—ELECTROLYTIC CELL FOR THORIUM REFINING

Thorium is also cast in a water-cooled copper cup. The powder may be compressed into a rod which acts as a consumable electrode, and the arc is struck between the electrode and solid thorium with the formation of a liquid pool. Melting takes place under a partial pressure of helium or argon gas.

## PHYSICAL AND CHEMICAL PROPERTIES

The physical properties of metallic thorium are strongly affected by small amounts of certain impurities, such as carbon. Melting temperatures, for example, may range from 1,120° to over 1,800° C (about 2,050° to 3,270° F), and boiling points from 3,500° to 4,200° C (6,300° to 7,600° F). Mechanical properties are also affected by methods of production and fabrication, with tensile strength ranging from less than 20,000 to over 60,000 psi. For principal physical constants of the metal *see* TABLE I.

TABLE I.—*Physical Constants (Metallic Thorium)*

| | |
|---|---|
| Atomic number | 90 |
| Crystal structure, up to 1,400° C | Face-centred cubic |
| 1,400° C to melting point | Body-centred cubic |
| Atomic weight | 232.038 |
| Unit cell (room temperature) | 5.0843 ± 0.0001Å |
| Superconductivity transition temperature, °K | 1.37 |
| Tensile strength, psi (annealed) | 27,000 |
| Heat of fusion, kg-cal/mol | <4.6 |
| Electrical resistivity, microhm/cm (annealed) | 15.1 |
| Density, g/cc | 11.72 |
| Melting point, °C | 1,750 |
| °F | 3,182 |
| Boiling point, °C | about 3,500 |
| °F | about 6,332 |
| Young's modulus, psi | $10.3 \times 10^6$ |
| Shear modulus, psi | $4.1 \times 10^6$ |
| Heat of vapourization, kg-cal/mol | 130–145 |
| Periodic table | Actinide series |

**Isotopes.**—Thorium occurs in nature as a mixture of radioactive isotopes. The predominant form by far is the very long-lived $Th^{232}$, which is thus the isotope of greatest chemical interest. The other long-lived form of thorium found in nature is $Th^{230}$ (ionium). This isotope is produced by the natural radioactive decay chain that originates in uranium 238, and thus is present in all uranium ores. Other, shorter-lived thorium isotopes arise in nature from the decay of various naturally occurring radioactive isotopes of actinium and uranium. (*See* RADIOACTIVITY: *Radioactive Series and Isotopes.*)

TABLE II.—*Longer-Lived Thorium Isotopes*

| Isotope | Half life | Mode of disintegration | Source |
|---|---|---|---|
| $Th^{227}$ (RdAc) | 18.2 days | $\gamma$ | Natural |
| $Th^{228}$ (RdTh) | 1.90 years | $\gamma$ | Natural |
| $Th^{229}$ | 7,340 years | $\gamma$ | $U^{233}$ decay |
| $Th^{230}$ (Io) | 80,000 years | $\gamma$ | Natural |
| $Th^{231}$ (UY) | 26.6 hours | $\beta^-$ | Natural |
| $Th^{232}$ | $1.39 \times 10^{10}$ | $\gamma$ | Natural |
| $Th^{234}$ ($UX_1$) | 24.10 days | $\beta^-$ | Natural |

Thorium isotopes have also been produced artifically by various nuclear reactions. Thus, $Th^{233}$ is produced by neutron capture in ordinary $Th^{232}$. It decays with a 23.3 min. half-life to form the very important isotope uranium 233.

$Th^{229}$ is another synthetic isotope of some importance. It is formed in the decay chain originating in the actinide element neptunium, and as it is reasonably long-lived, can be made to serve as a tracer for ordinary thorium. (*See* RADIOACTIVITY.)

**General Chemistry.**—Thorium is an electropositive element. It lies between beryllium and magnesium in reducing strength and is more electropositive than zirconium and cerium. In solution, thorium shows only the +4 oxidation state. The standard electrode potential is +1.77 v. As a highly charged ion, $Th^{+4}$ undergoes extensive hydrolysis, but to a lesser extent than other +4 ions such as zirconium, cerium, or plutonium. Because of its high charge, the thorium ion is strongly adsorbed from solution by an ion exchanger. Thorium forms complex ions and double salts. Thorium ion is complexed appreciably by nearly all anions. The nitrate is soluble in organic liquids and can be extracted from water solutions by alcohols, ketones, ethers, and esters. This forms the basis for the most advanced practice in the separation and purification of thorium from uranium and fission products in nuclear technology. Thorium compounds are not generally volatile with the exception of the acetylacetonate, $Th(C_5H_7O_2)_4$, thorium borohydride, $Th(BH_4)_4$, and a group of organic compounds of the general formula Th(OCRR′R″), where R, R′ and R″ are radicals. $Th(BH_4)_4$ is the most volatile thorium compound known, melting at 204° C but subliming *in vacuo* at considerably lower temperatures.

The dioxide, thoria ($ThO_2$), is very refractory. Thoria may be prepared by ignition of the peroxide $Th_2O_7.4H_2O$, nitrate $Th(NO_3)_4$, hydroxide $Th(OH)_4$, sulfate $Th(SO_4)_2$, or of an organic thorium compound. Compounds such as thorium fluoride ($ThF_4$) may be converted to oxide by treatment with superheated steam. Thorium peroxide is precipitated from acid solutions with hydrogen peroxide. Ignition yields thorium oxide. The alkalies and ammonia precipitate thorium hydroxide.

The common commercial salt of thorium is the nitrate, which is tetrahydrated. Double nitrates of thorium are known with sodium and potassium and also with some bivalent ions such as magnesium, zinc, cobalt, and manganese.

Hydrogen gas reacts with thorium metal to produce thorium hydrides of the composition $ThH_2$ and $Th_4H_{15}$. Thorium hydride is used as a substitute for thorium powder in some applications. A particular advantage is its greater resistance to atmospheric oxidation. Fluorine reacts with thorium hydride or thorium to form thorium fluoride. Thorium fluoride may be separated from solutions by addition of the fluoride ion, but it is hydrated and must be treated with hydrogen fluoride gas to yield the anhydrous fluoride.

Chlorine or hydrogen chloride reacts with thorium hydride or metal to form thorium chloride ($ThCl_4$), which sublimes at temperatures in excess of 750° C, *in vacuo*. Bromine or hydrogen bromide converts the hydride or metal to bromide, and a corresponding reaction occurs with iodine. The chlorides, bromides and iodides are soluble in water but hydrolyze. Unstable black lower halides, $ThX_2$ and $ThX_3$, are formed by direct reaction of thorium metal and the appropriate quantity of halogen. Thorium iodate, $Th(IO_3)_4$, is formed upon addition of an iodate to thorium solutions.

TABLE III.—*Physical Properties of Thorium Halides*

| Compound | Colour | Melting point °C | Boiling point °C |
|---|---|---|---|
| $ThF_4$ | White | 1,111 | |
| $ThCl_4$ | White | 770 | 921 |
| $ThBr_4$ | White | 679 | 857 |
| $ThI_4$ | Tan | 566 | 837 |

Normal thorium sulfide ($ThS_2$) is purple and may be prepared by the action of hydrogen sulfide on thorium hydride. This sulfide is stable up to 1,900° C, above which sulfur is evolved and $Th_2S_3$ (brown), $Th_7S_{12}$ (black), or ThS (silver) are formed. These compounds resemble metals and may be machined, filed, and polished.

Thorium sulfate, $Th(SO_4)_2$, crystallizes from aqueous solutions in several hydrates depending upon temperatures. Heating *in vacuo* produces the normal salt and ignition yields the oxide. Double sulfates are also known. Chromates, phosphates, and molybdates may be precipitated from water solutions.

Thorium carbides, both ThC and $ThC_2$, have been identified and are prepared by heating the metal or oxide with carbon at high temperatures. These react with water to yield hydrocarbons. Thorium carbonate, $ThOCO_3$, is difficult to prepare from solution, but double carbonates are easily prepared.

Thorium salts with organic acids are usually insoluble. The formate and the acetate are exceptions. Examples of insoluble salts are the oxalate, picrolonate, sebacate, and 8-hydroxy quinolinate.

Two thorium nitrides have been identified, ThN and $Th_2N_3$. The nitrides are unstable at high temperatures in the presence of water vapour with the elimination of ammonia. The mononitride melts at about 2,630° C without decomposition, whereas the sesquinitride looses nitrogen in a vacuum of 1,500° C. Two phosphides, ThP and $Th_3P_4$ also exist.

The silicides $Th_3Si_2$, ThSi, $ThSi_2$, and $Th_2Si_3$ are formed from the elements at 1,000° to 1,700° C. The very refractory $ThB_4$ melts above 2,500° C, whereas the hexaboride $ThB_6$ melts at 2,195° C. Both compounds are formed by the high temperature reaction of thorium and boron.

## USES

**Industrial Applications.**—The earliest use of thorium oxide was in the incandescent gas-mantle industry. In 1885 Carl Auer von Welsbach patented a mixture of 99% thoria and 1% ceria which was impregnated into a combustible fabric (cotton or ramie) as nitrates. Ignition of the Welsbach mantle resulted in oxide formation which when heated in a gas flame emitted white light for illumination. The use of gas mantles declined sharply after the introduction of electrical lighting. (*See* LIGHTING: *Historical Development.*)

Thorium oxide is used in the electrical lighting industry for controlling the grain size of tungsten filaments used in lamps as a radiant source of energy. Pure tungsten is unsatisfactory because the metallic grains continue to grow when the filament is heated, causing some grains to slip along grain boundaries. The addition of 0.8–1.0% $ThO_2$ to the tungsten produces a stable structure. Such filaments also exhibit increased vibrational strength.

Thorium oxide-metal systems have been used for years in electronics as a source of primary electron emission. The thorium oxide content is usually 1–2%. So-called cermets which are oxide-metal compositions, in particular Mo-$ThO_2$ have been used as an emission source. A desirable property of these latter combinations is that the electrical resistance may be easily controlled by changes in composition. (*See* THERMIONICS: *Reduction in Electron Affinity.*)

The oxide has gained wide use as a component of electrodes for arc welding. The addition of 1–2% $ThO_2$ to tungsten results in improvement in arc stability over that exhibited by pure tungsten. A practice embodying the same principle is the incorporation of the oxide in tungsten electrodes used in arc-casting metals. The addition of thorium oxide lowers the work function of the metal, that is, the ease with which electrons may be emitted thermionically.

Thorium oxide crucibles are used to a limited extent for melting some of the common and transition metals. Its use is quite selective. It is not satisfactory for melting oxygen-sensitive metals such as zirconium and titanium. Its relatively high cost and poor resistance to thermal shock limit its use to operations where it shows marked superiority over other competing ceramics.

Thorium sulfide crucibles have been investigated and show promise up to 1,800° C. The monosulfide (ThS) is the more stable compound.

Thorium oxide, as well as the oxides of beryllium, zirconium, and aluminum, is of importance as a current-carrying compound in high-temperature furnace design and insulation. These oxides have negative temperature characteristics, and the limiting factor in their use is excessive conductivity. Thorium oxide compositions have been used experimentally where the resistor element is composed of 85–95% $ThO_2$ and 5–15% yttrium oxide ($Y_2O_3$) or lanthanum oxide ($La_2O_3$).

Thorium oxide is an efficient catalyst in reactions involving oxidation, hydrogenation and cracking of hydrocarbons. In many cases it is used as a mixture with aluminum oxide.

A very important alloy application of thorium is its addition to magnesium and magnesium alloys for improving their high-temperature strength. The addition of 1–5% thorium to these alloys permits their use in temperatures up to 340° C (about 650° F), in compressor housings. The addition of small amounts of thorium increases both the strength and ductility of magnesium rolled sheet, a use consuming considerable quantities of the metal.

Thorium metal has been used as a deoxidant in molybdenum. It is also used in electronic tubes and lamps for lowering the starting voltages and maintaining stability in such lamps over their useful life.

Thorium is used in photoelectric cells for measurement of a wide band of the ultraviolet spectrum. The response of commercial tubes extends from 2,000–3,750 Å.

**Nuclear Applications.**—Thorium 232 does not undergo nuclear fission with slow neutrons, and so it cannot be used directly as a nuclear reactor fuel. It can, however, be converted to the fissile isotope uranium 233:

$$Th^{232}\ (n,\gamma)\ Th^{233} \xrightarrow[23.3\ min.]{\beta^-} Pa^{233} \xrightarrow[27.4\ days]{\beta^-} U^{233}$$

When naturally occurring thorium is irradiated with slow neutrons, it is transmuted to a uranium isotope that can undergo fission with slow neutrons to yield enormous quantities of energy. The fission of the usual fuel in a nuclear reactor yields more neutrons than are needed to sustain the chain reaction, and the excess neutrons can be caused to be captured by $Th^{232}$. Thorium is thus made to "breed" additional fissile nuclear fuel, with the paradoxical result that more fissionable fuel is generated by "breeding" than is consumed in the course of nuclear power production. (*See* also URANIUM; ATOMIC ENERGY: *Peacetime Applications.*)

The possibility of converting thorium to fissile uranium 233 in breeder reactors and by so doing tremendously increasing world resources of nuclear energy is the most important potential use for thorium.

*See* also ATOMIC ENERGY; NUCLEAR ENGINEERING; *see* also references under "Thorium" in the Index.

BIBLIOGRAPHY.—U.S. Atomic Energy Commission, *Thorium: a Bibliography of Published Literature,* TID 3044 (1955); The American Society for Metals, *The Metal Thorium* (1958); L. Grainger, *Uranium and Thorium* (1958); C. A. Hampel (ed.), *Rare Metals Handbook,* 2nd ed. (1961); L. I. Katzin, "The Chemistry of Thorium," *The Actinide Elements,* ed. by G. T. Seaborg and J. J. Katz (1954); C. J. Rodden *et al.* (eds.), *Analytical Chemistry of the Manhattan Project* (1950); S. Glasstone, *Sourcebook on Atomic Energy,* 2nd ed. (1958); F. L. Cuthbert, *Thorium Production Technology* (1958); D. I. Riabchikov and E. K. Golbraikh, *Analytical Chemistry of Thorium* (1964).

(W. C. L.; J. J. K.)

**THORNABY-ON-TEES,** a former municipal borough in the North Riding of Yorkshire, Eng., 3 mi. SW of Middlesbrough by road, in the Middlesbrough West Parliamentary division and incorporated in the county borough of Teesside (*q.v.*) since April 1, 1968. Pop. (1961) 22,793. Area 3 sq.mi. It lies on the Tees River, opposite Stockton-on-Tees, with which it is connected by a bridge. In the 8th century the Danes called it Thormodby; in Domesday Book it appears as Tormozby. The parish church on the village green is Norman. Thornaby's industrial development dates from the 19th century. It was incorporated as a separate borough in 1892. The population is employed chiefly in bridge building, heavy engineering, foundries, wire ropemaking, shipbreaking, flour milling, and the production of sugar and preserves.

**THORNDIKE, EDWARD LEE** (1874–1949), U.S. psychologist, strongly influenced education toward social utility through his experimentally derived theories of learning. He was born at Williamsburg, Mass., Aug. 31, 1874. His career, save for one year at Western Reserve University, Cleveland, O., was spent at Teachers College, Columbia University. An unusually creative and productive scholar, he was author or coauthor of more than 500 books and articles. His influence on psychological and educational thinking has been worldwide. Thorndike's pioneer work on the intelligence of laboratory animals in the 1890s established a trend in psychology that still continues. His laws of learning came to hold a central place in learning theory.

Thorndike was responsible for many of the early applications of psychology to such fields as arithmetic, algebra, reading, handwriting, and language. Other major contributions include works on the theory of psychological tests and compilations of the words occurring most frequently in English reading matter.

Best known is his three-volume work *Educational Psychology* (1913–14). Additional works of special interest treat the behaviour of monkeys; prediction of vocational success; wants, interests, and attitudes; and principles of education. Thorndike died at Montrose, N.Y., on Aug. 9, 1949.

*See* also references under "Edward Lee Thorndike" in the Index.

*See* R. S. Woodworth, "Edward Lee Thorndike," *National Academy of Sciences Biographical Memoirs* (1952). (J. B. Sd.; X.)

**THORNDIKE, DAME SYBIL** (1882– ), British actress of remarkable versatility, was born at Gainsborough, Lincolnshire, on Oct. 24, 1882. She was educated at the high school in Rochester, where her father was a canon of the cathedral. She prepared for the stage at Ben Greet's Academy and toured the U.S. with his Shakespearean company in 1904–07. She married the actor-director (Sir) Lewis Casson in 1908. After performing with Miss A. E. Horniman's company in Manchester (1908–09 and 1911–13), she joined the Old Vic Company in London (1914–18) and helped to establish not only the theatre's name as a home of Shakespeare but also her own as the most promising English tragic actress of the day.

Having set the seal on this reputation in 1919–20 with performances as Hecuba in *The Trojan Women* and as Medea, she went on to prove her versatility in a multiplicity of parts, modern as well as classical, comic as well as tragic. In 1924 she created the name part in Shaw's *Saint Joan;* and though many admired actresses followed her, none realized the character more completely.

Her superb health and vigour did not desert her as she grew older, and she was able to tour the world in exacting classical parts at an age when many of her contemporaries had been content to retire. Also, in her 60s, she broke new ground, giving, in such plays as *The Linden Tree* (1947), *The Foolish Gentlewoman* (1949), *Treasure Hunt* (1949), *Waters of the Moon* (1951), and *A Day By The Sea* (1953), a whole gallery of portraits of elderly women having in common nothing but the meticulous and humorous observation which the actress had brought to their creation. She was created a dame of the British Empire in 1931.

(W. A. Dn.)

**THORNHILL, SIR JAMES** (1675–1734), English painter, the first to excel in historical painting, whose style was in the Italian Baroque tradition, was born at Melcombe Regis, Dorset. He became the history painter and sergeant painter to George I and George II, master of the Painters' Company in 1720, fellow of the Royal Society in 1723, member of Parliament from 1722 to 1734, and was knighted in 1720. He was one of the original directors of Kneller's Academy of Painting, and when this closed, and he had failed to establish a "royal academy," he opened his own drawing school, which also proved unsuccessful. Thornhill died at Thornhill, Dorset, on May 13, 1734.

The eight scenes in the dome of St. Paul's Cathedral (1715–19) and the allegories in the Painted Hall, Greenwich Hospital (1708–27), are his two most considerable works. His paintings were largely executed on the ceilings and stairs of such country houses and palaces as Hampton Court, Blenheim, and Chatsworth. Among Thornhill's few canvases are the altarpiece for St. Mary's Parish Church, Weymouth, and a group portrait of the members of the House of Commons in which he was assisted by William Hogarth, his son-in-law. Thornhill also did portraits (his sitters including Isaac Newton and Richard Steele), book illustrations, theatre scenery, and the rose window of the north transept of Westminster Abbey (1721). (Wm. O.; X.)

**THORNTON, WILLIAM** (1759–1828), British-U.S. architect, inventor, and public official who created the original design for the Capitol at Washington, D.C., was born May 20, 1759, at Tortola, V.I. He studied medicine at the University of Edinburgh (1781–84) and received his M.D. from Aberdeen University (1784). After travel on the continent he returned to Tortola and went to the United States in 1787. In the following year he became a United States citizen and settled in Philadelphia. The Library Company of Philadelphia promoted a competition (1789) for its new building that Thornton won without formally having studied architecture. As inventors he and John Fitch (*q.v.*) early experimented with paddle steamboats.

From 1790–92 he was again at Tortola, where he first heard of the important competition for the Capitol at Washington. He submitted designs that were received months after the competition closed; yet the judges, not satisfied with those previously submitted, selected Thornton's. His revised Georgian design of 1795 was executed as the exterior of the north and south wings adjacent to the central rotunda, though B. H. Latrobe (*q.v.*) completely redesigned the interiors. Thornton designed the Octagon, Washington (1798–1800), a residence for John Tayloe; and Woodlawn Plantation, Mt. Vernon, Va., for George Washington's nephew Lawrence Lewis (*c.* 1800). From 1802–28 he served as first superintendent of the Patent Office. He died in Washington on March 28, 1828. (P. F. N.)

**THORNYCROFT, SIR (WILLIAM) HAMO** (1850–1925), English sculptor, executed many public monuments, including those to Gen. Charles George Gordon (1888, formerly Trafalgar Square), Oliver Cromwell (1899, Westminster), Dean John Colet (1902, St. Paul's School, Hammersmith), William Gladstone (1905, Strand), and the architect Richard Norman Shaw (bas-relief, 1914, New Scotland Yard). He was born in London on March 9, 1850, and studied under his father, Thomas Thornycroft, at the British Museum, at the Royal Academy Schools and in Italy, where he was particularly interested in Michelangelo. In 1872 he contributed the figures of Shakespeare, Fame and Comedy to the Poets' Fountain, Park Lane (later removed), designed by his father. His independent success began with "Artemis" (exhibited 1880), and in 1881 he showed the bronze "Teucer" (Tate Gallery, London) at the Royal Academy, of which he was then elected associate. His style, at first an enlivened classicism, was affected in the mid-1880s (in "The Mower," 1884, Walker Art Gallery, Liverpool; "A Sower," 1886) by J. F. Millet's peasant realism and later (*e.g.*, "The Kiss," 1916, Tate Gallery) was influenced slightly by Auguste Rodin. Thornycroft was elected royal academician in 1888 and knighted in 1917.

Thornycroft died at Oxford on Dec. 18, 1925. He was the brother of Sir John Isaac Thornycroft (*q.v.*).

**THORNYCROFT, SIR JOHN ISAAC** (1843–1928), British naval architect and engineer who was responsible for the introduction of special designs of ships' hulls and improvements in machinery was born in Rome on Feb. 1, 1843. He was sent by his father, Thomas Thornycroft, a sculptor, who was also an amateur engineer, to Glasgow university, after which he worked for a short time in John Elder and Palmer's shipyards. In 1866 he started his own launch-building and engineering works at Chiswick, London. Gaining a high reputation for his boats, he was given the order for H.M.S. "Lightning," the first torpedo boat of the Royal Navy. Later he took into partnership his brother-in-law, John Donaldson. Thornycroft took a leading part in introducing water tube boilers into the British and into other navies and was granted a number of patents, including one of the earliest for ship stabilizers. He served as a member of Lord Fisher's committee, which produced the design for the battleship "Dreadnought" and introduced oil fuel for the Royal Navy. He was knighted in 1902 and died on June 28, 1928, at Bembridge, Isle of Wight. (J. E. Tt.)

**THOROUGH BASS,** in music, a system of accompaniment (*q.v.*) customary during the 17th and 18th centuries: the bass line is written out all "Thorough" (*i.e.,* through) the composition, but its harmonization is left to the accompanist to provide more or less impromptu. Usually, though not invariably, he is kept generally informed as to the harmony resulting from the melodic part or parts which he is accompanying, so as not to conflict with it in his own harmonization. This information is conveyed by figures added to the bass line, which is then more specifically described as figured bass.

The accompanist is said to "realize" the bass. He may do this impromptu, *i.e.,* reading it strictly at sight in course of performance: a very skilled achievement to which not many modern performers are trained. But it was always customary to look through the music in advance if opportunity occurred. This allows the performer to improve on his first thoughts, and, in music suited to an elaborate accompaniment, is normally the best course. It hardly matters whether his preparations are memorized or written out in whole or part, but it does matter that the result shall sound free, flexible and spontaneous, as if it had been improvised. Modern editors who provide printed realizations usually bear this in mind, keeping their parts on the light side.

The information conveyed by the figures is never complete and is often so sketchy, not to say inaccurate, that the performer, when no preparation has been possible, has to rely on his own grasp of where the music is going. This came more easily to a contemporary performer than it does to present-day musicians, but the faculty can be cultivated. Indeed it is one of the most enjoyable parlour games. According to J. F. Daube's *General-Bass* (1756), the style of improvised accompaniment was brought to its height by J. S. Bach: "He knew how to introduce a point of imitation so ingeniously in either right or left hand and how to bring in so unexpected a counter-theme, that the listener would have sworn that it had all been composed in that form with the most careful preparation . . ." The true reason for thorough bass is the freshness of the invention. Thorough bass was thus not merely a convenient shorthand for saving the composer's time; it was a means of giving zest to the accompaniment by inviting the performer to draw on his capacity for spontaneous enjoyment.

The figures themselves are numerals set one above the other to indicate the intervals, as counted up from the bass note, of the harmonies required. In realizing these intervals, the performer can invert them in any order of notes; *i.e.,* he can manipulate the spacing of the chord, though he will not normally go above the solo part for long at a time, if at all. The figures are kept to the minimum necessary to determine the harmony by indicating its most characteristic intervals, the remainder of the chord being taken as understood. Necessary accidentals are shown. Only the main harmonies, and not the passing harmonies, are normally shown. There is great scope for varying and enriching the indicated harmony by introducing passing notes, especially accented passing notes. The same recourse is invaluable for contriving an interesting and convincing melodic outline to the accompaniment.

The elaboration given to the realization will vary from the simplest harmonization in plain part-writing to an exploitation of all the harmonic and contrapuntal possibilities. Four-part harmony is standard, though the nature of the music to be accompanied sometimes requires only three or two parts and occasionally the unharmonized bass line. Alternatively, a "full accompaniment" requires as many notes to each hand as the fingers can accommodate and in such realizations all rules forbidding consecutive fifths, etc., may be waived except as between the two outside (bottom and top) parts.

Good figured-bass accompaniment, taking into account not only the character of the piece but, as C. P. E. Bach specified, the remaining performers, the soloist, the auditorium and the audience, thus made almost as heavy a demand on the performer's judgment as on his imagination.

Bibliography.—F. T. Arnold, *The Art of Accompaniment From a Thorough-Bass* (1931); C. P. E. Bach, *Essay on the True Art of Keyboard-Playing,* 2 vol. (1753, 1762; Eng. trans. by W. J. Mitchell, 1959). (R. Do.)

**THORPE, JIM** (James Francis Thorpe) (1888–1953), U.S. athlete, considered one of the greatest all-around athletes of all time, was born May 28, 1888, near Prague, Okla., of American Indian descent. A star in both college and professional football, he was twice named halfback on Walter Camp's All-America teams (1911, 1912); in 1912 he scored 25 touchdowns and 198 points for Carlisle (Pa.) Institute.

Standing 6 ft. tall and weighing 190 lb., Thorpe was a standout in the 1912 Olympic Games at Stockholm, where he won the pentathlon and decathlon. Later, however, when it was discovered that he had played semiprofessional baseball in the summer of 1911, his gold medals and trophy were taken from him and his Olympic records erased from the books.

Signed by John J. McGraw of the New York Giants for $4,500 in 1913, Thorpe spent most of the time on the bench. He finished his six-year major-league baseball career in 1919 with the Boston Braves, where he played in 60 games and hit .327. He died in Lomita, Calif., March 28, 1953. *See* also Football: *U.S. Football: U.S. Professional Football.* (J. D. McC.)

**THORPE** (Thorp), **THOMAS BANGS** (1815–1878), U.S. humorist, was one of the most effective portrayers of frontier life and character before Mark Twain; he is the author of "The Big Bear of Arkansas," a tall tale so outstanding that some historians have named certain southwestern contemporaries of Thorpe the Big Bear School of Humorists. Born at Westfield, Mass., on March 1, 1815, and educated in New York schools, Thorpe studied painting under John Quidor and at the age of 18 exhibited his "Ichabod Crane" at the American Academy of Fine Arts, New York City. In 1836, after two years' study at Wesleyan University, Middletown, Conn., he moved to Louisiana. An active Union Whig, he published successively five newspapers, chiefly in New Orleans and Baton Rouge. It was during this period that Thorpe wrote "The Big Bear of Arkansas," published in 1841 in the New York magazine *Spirit of the Times.*

Following a political defeat, Thorpe moved in 1854 to New York City and published his finest sketches as *The Hive of the Bee Hunter.* During the Civil War he saw service in New Orleans; afterward he returned to New York and spent his remaining years painting, working at the customhouse, and writing for *Harper's, Appleton's,* and other journals. He died at New York, on Sept. 20, 1878.

Thorpe's painting and writing show the influence of Washington Irving and of sporting literature, a love of romantic scenery, and a continuing attempt to define the distinctively American character, which, he believed, the western frontier was producing.

*See* Walter Blair, *Native American Humor* (1937); Milton Rickels, "A Bibliography of the Writings of Thomas Bangs Thorpe," *American Literature,* 29:171–179 (1957). (M. H. R.)

**THORPE, SIR THOMAS EDWARD** (1845–1925), British chemist, was perhaps best known for his direction of the British government laboratories and as a brilliant lecturer and writer. He was born at Harpurhey, Manchester, on Dec. 8, 1845, and studied at Owens College, Manchester, and at Heidelberg, where he obtained his doctorate (1869). In 1870 he became professor of chemistry at Andersonian College, Glasgow, and four years later at the Yorkshire College, Leeds. In 1885 he obtained the chair at the Normal School of Science (later the Imperial College of Science), London, and remained there until appointed director of the government laboratories in 1894. On his retirement, he returned to the Imperial College (1909–12). He was elected to the Royal Society in 1876, was made a companion of the Bath in 1900, and was knighted in 1909. He died at Salcombe, South Devon, on Feb. 23, 1925.

Thorpe brought out, with the cooperation of a number of specialists, the *Dictionary of Applied Chemistry* (1890). He was also the author of *Essays in Historical Chemistry* (1894) and a biography of Joseph Priestley (1906). His contributions to chemical knowledge included an accurate series of measurements of the specific volumes of chemical substances of related composition. With A. E. H. Tutton he studied the oxides of phosphorus (1886 and following) and discovered phosphorus tetroxide. From 1884 to 1886 Thorpe made a long series of measurements (with J. W. Rodger) of the viscosities of organic substances and attempted to correlate fluidity and composition. With Sir Arthur Rücker, he carried out (1884–88) a magnetic survey of the British Isles.

**THORVALDSEN** (THORWALDSEN), **BERTEL** (1768 or 1770–1844), Danish sculptor and prominent neoclassicist, who spent most of his working life in Rome, was the son of an Icelandic woodcarver who had settled in Denmark. He was born in Copenhagen either on Nov. 19, 1770 (his own statement), or Nov. 13, 1768 (subsequent theory), and studied at the Copenhagen Academy, where he won a traveling scholarship to Rome. In Rome the prevailing enthusiasm for classical sculpture fired his imagination to such an extent that he subsequently celebrated the date of his arrival in Rome in 1797 as his "Roman birthday." The success of Thorvaldsen's model for a statue of Jason (1803), which was commissioned in marble by the English author and connoisseur Thomas Hope, attracted the attention of Canova, and launched Thorvaldsen on one of the most spectacularly successful careers of the 19th century. When he made his first return visit to Copenhagen in 1819, his progress through Europe, visiting Berlin, Warsaw, and Vienna, was like a triumphal procession. His return in 1838, when he eventually decided to settle in his native city, was regarded as a national event in Danish history. A large portion of his fortune went to the endowment of a neoclassical museum in Copenhagen (begun in 1839), which was designed to house his collection of works of art and the models for all his sculptures. He died in Copenhagen on March 24, 1844, and was buried, by his own wish, in the courtyard of the museum that bears his name. Most of Thorvaldsen's most characteristic sculptures are reinterpretations of the figures or themes of classical antiquity, and the Alexander frieze of 1812 in the Palazzo Quirinale, Rome, modeled in only three months in anticipation of a visit by Napoleon, is an example of the feverish energy with which he could at times apply himself to work. Religious sculptures (for which his style was not particularly well suited) include the colossal series of statues of Christ and the 12 apostles (completed 1838) in the Vor Frue Kirke in Copenhagen. He also made numerous portrait busts of his distinguished contemporaries. In the general re-evaluation of Neoclassicism Thorvaldsen's reputation outside Denmark has declined, and works once regarded as the perfect reincarnation of the antique now tend to seem rather cold and dry.

AUTHENTICATED NEWS

SELF-PORTRAIT, 1839; THE SCULPTOR IS SEEN LEANING ON HIS STATUE OF "HOPE." IN THORVALDSENS MUSEUM, COPENHAGEN

*See* P. O. Rave, *Thorvaldsen* (1947); S. Schultz, *Thorvaldsens Museum: Official Guide* (1953).

**THOTH,** Greek form of the name of the Egyptian god DJHOWTEY, whose cult was centred in the town of Khmunu (Lat. Hermopolis Magna [*q.v.*]; mod. Al Ashmunayn) in Upper Egypt. At first he was probably the moon-god; as such, he was called "reckoner of time," and his name was given to the first month of the Egyptian year. In consequence he became the god of reckoning and of learning in general and was held to be the inventor of writing, the founder of social order, the creator of languages, the scribe, interpreter, and adviser of the gods, and the representative of the sun-god, Re, on earth. He was also the patron of scribes and officials. Thoth played an important part in the myth of Osiris (*q.v.*), protecting Isis during her pregnancy and healing the injury inflicted on her son Horus by Osiris' adversary, the god Setekh. Thoth weighed the hearts of the deceased at their judgment and reported the result to the presiding god, Osiris, and his fellow judges.

Thoth's sacred animals, for reasons which are not quite clear, were the ibis (*Threskiornis aethiopica*) and the baboon (*Papio hamadryas*); numerous mummified bodies of these two animals were found in cemeteries near Hermopolis and Thebes. Thoth himself was sometimes represented as an ibis or as a baboon, but more usually in human form with an ibis' head. The Greeks identified Thoth with their god Hermes and traced back to "Thoth, the thrice great" (Hermes Trismegistos; *q.v.*) the authorship of powerful magical books.

*See* P. Boylan, *Thoth, the Hermes of Egypt* (1922). (J. CY.)

**THOU** (THUANUS), **JACQUES AUGUSTE DE** (1553–1617), French statesman, bibliophile, and historiographer, whose detached approach to the events of his own period made him a pioneer in scientific approaches in history.

Born in Paris on Oct. 8, 1553, of a family noted for its statesmen and scholars, he studied law at Orléans and Bourges, where he met François Hotman (*q.v.*), and at Valence, where he was a pupil of Jacques Cujas (*q.v.*) and a friend of J. J. Scaliger. However, he had first been intended for the church, and on the appointment of his uncle Nicolas to the episcopate of Chartres, he succeeded him as a canon of Notre Dame (Paris). As a councilor of state he faithfully served both Henry III and Henry IV, becoming director of the royal library in 1593. On succeeding his uncle Augustin as a president of the Paris *parlement* in 1595, he used his new authority in the interests of religious peace, negotiating the Edict of Nantes (1598) with the Protestants, while in the name of Gallicanism opposing recognition of the Council of Trent (*q.v.*). This attitude exposed him to the animosity of both the Holy League (*q.v.*) and the Holy See, which increased its persecution when the first edition of his history appeared in 1604. His minor works include a poem on falconry, *De re accipitraria* (1584), and some *Poemata sacra* (1599). After the death of Henry IV (1610), the queen regent, Marie de Médicis, refused him the appointment of premier president of the *parlement*, appointing him instead a member of the *conseil de finances*. He helped to negotiate the treaties of Sainte-Menehould (1614) and Loudun (1616). He died in Paris on May 7, 1617.

The writing of his history was the main activity of De Thou's life. The materials for it were drawn from his rich library, which had originated in 1573 when he was at Notre Dame and which was established in 1587 in the Rue des Poitevins; and he was helped in his preparations by Pierre Dupuy (1582–1651) and his brother Jacques (1586–1656), the two illustrious scholars and librarians who later also collected some of his minor works (see *Bibliography*). De Thou's object in his history was to produce a purely "scientific" and unbiased work, and for this reason he wrote it in Latin, entitling it *Historia sui temporis*. His starting point he defined as "the last years of the reign of Francis I," that is, about 1543. Actually, he begins with a general survey of the early 16th century, and the history therefore covers the whole of the 16th century. The first 18 books (embracing the period up to 1560) appeared in 1604, when they were immediately attacked by those whom the author called "the invidious and the dissentious." The second part (dealing with the first wars of religion, 1560–72) was put on the Index. When the third part (to 1574) and the fourth (to 1584) appeared in 1607–08 they caused a similar outcry, in spite of De Thou's efforts to remain impartial. In answer to his detractors he wrote a series of memoranda (translated into French as *Mémoires de la vie de Jacques Auguste de Thou,* 1711), which are a useful complement to the *Historia.*

The first complete edition of De Thou's *Historia,* including the fifth part (to 1607), was published in 1620 by Pierre Dupuy and Nicolas Rigault. This comprised 138 books, to which the *Commentariorum de vita sua libri sex* (six volumes of memoirs) were appended in 1625. In 1733 a critical Latin edition in 7 volumes was published in London by Samuel Buckley, the material for which had been collected and prepared in France by Thomas Carte. Carte's research confirmed that De Thou's *Historia* was a model of exact scholarship, drawn from reliable sources. In 1734 the standard French translation, entitled *Histoire universelle de Jacque-Auguste de Thou, depuis 1543 jusqu'en 1607,* was published in 16 volumes by the abbé Desfontaines and other scholars.

BIBLIOGRAPHY.—P. and J. Dupuy, *Thuana sive excerpta ex ore Jac. Aug. Thuani* (1669, in French); J. Collinson, *The Life of Thuanus . . .* (1807); H. Harrisse, *Le Président de Thou et ses descendants* (1905); H. Brugmans, "Deux historiens du XVI° siècle: de Thou et Emmius," *Revue Historique,* vol. cxlv (1924). *See* also A. Cioranesco, *Bibliographie de la littérature française du seizième siècle,* no. 21117–21174 (1959). (JE. PO.)

**THOUGHT, LAWS OF.** Traditionally, special importance has been attached to three of the simplest laws of logic, the *law of identity,* the *law of contradiction,* and the *law of excluded middle* (or *tertium non datur*). These were called the "laws of thought," a name which may conveniently be retained even by those who do not accept the implications which the name suggests. (For "thinking" as studied in psychology, *see* THINKING AND PROBLEM SOLVING.)

As examples of axioms, or indemonstrable principles (*see* AXIOM), Aristotle cities that, of two contradictories, one must be true, and that it is impossible for anything both to be and not to be. These are the principles which were afterward known as the laws of excluded middle and of contradiction respectively. They occur in Aristotle also in other forms, which are regarded as being expressions of the same laws; *e.g.,* that there is no middle ground between contradictories, and that it is impossible for anything both to be predicated and not to be predicated of the same thing in the same sense. Aristotle partly exempted future contingents from the law of excluded middle, holding that it is not (now) either true or false that there will be a naval battle tomorrow, but that it is (now) true that either there will be a naval battle tomorrow or not; against this, Chrysippus (*see* LOGIC, HISTORY OF) maintained that all propositions, even about the future, are either true or false.

The law of identity has usually been stated (for example by Leibniz) as: A is A. Stated in ordinary language, particular cases of the law would then be such things as: gold is gold, men are men, love is love, etc.

To render the three laws in modern logical notation (*see* LOGIC: *The Propositional Calculus*), the best choices would seem to be: $F(x) \supset_x F(x)$ (law of identity), $\sim \centerdot\, p \sim p$ (*law of contradiction*), $p \vee \sim p$ (*law of excluded middle*). However, the law of identity is also often given as $(x)\ x = x$, a form which differs from the other (on the basis of the definition of $=$ in the article LOGIC) only by the insertion of a quantifier.

The three laws may also be understood in a semantical sense (*see* SEMANTICS IN LOGIC), the traditional statements of them generally not making a sharp distinction between such metatheoretic principles and principles which are rather to be expressed in the notation of propositional calculus or functional calculus. Thus the law of identity would be that a term must preserve the same denotations in all its occurrences, at least throughout any one context; the law of contradiction, that a sentence and its negation, $\mathsf{S}$ and $\sim \mathsf{S}$ are not both true; the law of excluded middle, that either $\mathsf{S}$ or $\sim \mathsf{S}$ is true. In this interpretation the "laws of thought" are to be regarded as being about a particular language—or else as general principles of sound notation, demands which any acceptable language or system of notation must satisfy.

The doctrine that the laws of thought—or even only the laws of identity and contradiction—are a sufficient foundation for the whole of logic, or that all other principles of logic are mere elaborations of them, is traceable to Leibniz. Leibniz left a few actual examples of demonstrations of principles of logic and mathematics from only these laws, but all are quite minor in character and moreover involve tacit use of at least syllogistic inference in addition to the laws of thought. It would seem that Leibniz intended originally to express only a hope or an expectation. But later he was more incautious, writing, for instance, in the second letter to Samuel Clarke: "The great foundation of mathematics is *the principle of contradiction, or identity,* that is, that a proposition cannot be true and false at the same time; and that therefore *A* is *A,* and cannot be *not A.* This single principle is sufficient to demonstrate every part of arithmetic and geometry, that is, all mathematical principles."

Leibniz's successors applied the doctrine mainly to logic as distinguished from mathematics, but at the same time elevated it into an assertion of established fact. In this form it was common especially among traditional logicians of the 19th century. And though the doctrine appears already in the *Vernunftlehre* (1756) of H. S. Reimarus, its widespread adoption is perhaps due to Kant's characterization of an analytic judgment (*see* LOGIC, HISTORY OF) as one for recognition of whose truth the law of contradiction suffices.

It is difficult to give this doctrine a precise meaning in such a way as to make it tenable. For example it is not true that the three laws, say in the forms $F(x) \supset_x F(x)$, $\sim \centerdot\, p \sim p$, $p \vee \sim p$, are a sufficient set of axioms for logic, or even for the most elementary branch of logic, the propositional calculus, or for the traditional theory of the categorical syllogism.

**Criticisms and Rejections of the Laws of Thought.**—The law of excluded middle and some related laws of propositional calculus and functional calculus of first order are rejected by L. E. J. Brouwer and the school of mathematical intuitionism (*see* LOGIC, MATHEMATICS, FOUNDATIONS OF), not in the sense that the negation of the law is asserted, but in the sense that use of the law is not admitted as a valid method of mathematical proof in cases in which all members of an infinite class are involved. For example, Brouwer would not accept the disjunction that either there occur ten consecutive 7's somewhere in the decimal expansion of the number $\pi$ or else not (since there is no proof known of either alternative), but he would accept that there occur ten consecutive 7's somewhere in the first $10^{100}$ digits of the decimal expansion of $\pi$ or else not (since this could in principle be settled by carrying out the computation of the decimal expansion to the required point).

On the basis of Aristotle's doctrine of future contingents, but not without some modification of it, Jan Lukasiewicz was led in 1920 to formulate a propositional calculus which has a third truth-value (for future contingents) in addition to the usual two, and in which the laws of contradiction and excluded middle alike fail. Propositional calculi with $n$ truth-values, $n \geqq 3$, were published independently by E. L. Post in 1921 and by Lukasiewicz in 1930. Corresponding many-valued functional calculi of first order were formulated still later by other writers.

Other criticisms or rejections of one or more of the laws of thought—*e.g.,* by Epicurus (*q.v.*), by Hegel (*q.v.*), by Alfred Korzybski (*see* SEMANTICS, GENERAL)—are in a different category from those of Brouwer and Lukasiewicz, as they offer no precise formulation of a usable logic in which these laws fail or are modified.

BIBLIOGRAPHY.—M. R. Cohen and Ernest Nagel, *An Introduction to Logic and Scientific Method* (1934); Donald C. Williams, "The Sea Fight Tomorrow," *Structure, Method, and Meaning, Essays in Honor of Henry M. Sheffer* (1951); S. C. Kleene, *Introduction to Metamathematics* (1952), *see* III, § 13, "Intuitionism"; Jan Łukasiewicz, "Die Logik und das Grundlagenproblem," *Les Entretiens de Zurich* (1941); A. N. Prior, "Three-Valued Logic and Future Contingents," *Philosophical Quarterly,* vol. 3 (1953) and *Time and Modality* (1957); G. W. F. Hegel, *Science of Logic,* tr. by W. H. Johnston and L. G. Struthers, 2 vol. (1929; 1952). (AO. C.)

**THOUSAND AND ONE NIGHTS** (Arabic ALF LAYLA WA LAYLA), a collection of stories of uncertain date and authorship also known as *The Arabian Nights' Entertainment.* Except perhaps for the Koran, its fame and influence in the West have been greater than that of any other Arabic literary work, and certain stories, such as those about Aladdin, Ali Baba, and Sindbad the

Sailor (*q.v.*), have almost become part of Western folklore. The collection contains Eastern stories of many kinds from many sources: fairytale, romance, humour, the exotic and realistic, legend, didactic fable and parable, anecdote, and tales of travel and adventure—each a masterpiece of storytelling.

**Structure.**—As in much medieval European literature the stories are set within a frame story. Its scene is central Asia, or "the islands or peninsulae of India and China," and it tells how King Shahryar, discovering that during his absences his wife has been regularly unfaithful, kills her and those with whom she has betrayed him. Then, loathing all womankind, he marries, and kills, a new wife each day until no more candidates can be found. However, his vizier has two daughters, Shahrazad and Dunyazad, and the elder, Shahrazad, having devised a scheme to save herself and others, insists that her father give her in marriage to the king. Each evening she tells a story, leaving it incomplete and promising to finish it the following night. The stories are so entertaining, and the king so eager to hear the end, that he puts off her execution from day to day, and finally abandons his cruel plan.

**Texts, Editions, and Translations.**—The first European translation of the *Nights* was also the first published edition. Made by Antoine Galland (*q.v.*), it appeared as *Les Mille et Une Nuits, contes arabes traduits en français* (10 vol., 1704–12; vol. xi and xii, 1717). Galland's main text was a four-volume Syrian manuscript, but the later volumes contain many stories from oral and other sources. No text, edition, or translation can, indeed, be regarded as fully canonical in either content or wording. Galland, a born storyteller, was more concerned to make the stories interesting and intelligible to his readers than with literal accuracy. His translation remained standard until the mid-19th century, parts even being retranslated into Arabic.

The Arabic text was first published at Calcutta (incomplete, 2 vol., 1814–18; in full, 4 vol., 1839–42). The source for most later translations, however, was the so-called Vulgate text, an Egyptian recension published at Bulaq, Cairo, in 1835, and several times reprinted.

Meanwhile, French and English continuations, versions, or editions of Galland had added stories from oral and manuscript sources, collected, with others, in the Breslau edition (5 vol., 1825–43) by Prof. Maximilian Habicht. Later translations followed the Vulgate text with varying fullness and accuracy. Some omitted or bowdlerized stories unsuitable for "family" or juvenile reading, that by E. W. Lane (*q.v.;* 3 vol., 1839–41) typifying the Victorian attitude. Much better is John Payne's little-known full translation (9 vol., 1882–84; 3 suppl. vol., 1884; vol. xiii, 1889), used by Sir Richard Burton (*q.v.*) for *The Thousand Nights and a Night* (10 vol., 1885; 6 suppl. vol., 1886–88), with notes and commentary based on experience of the seamy side of Eastern life. The most famous English translation, this has become a "collector's piece" for its fullness and racy style. Lady Burton's edition of it (6 vol., 1886–88) was ruthlessly expurgated, and though Lionel Smithers' (12 vol., 1894) restored many omissions, there have been few complete editions or reprints. Inaccuracy makes some well-known versions unacceptable, notably J. C. Mardrus' French translation (16 vol., 1889–1906; Eng. trans. 1923), which, as well as textual errors, contains many stories from other collections. Of translations into almost every European language, the most scholarly is the German translation by E. Littmann (6 vol., 1921–28, 2nd ed. 1953; 3rd ed. 1954).

**Origins.**—Western interest in the origins of the *Nights* began early in the 19th century with the French orientalist Antoine Silvestre de Sacy (*q.v.*), the first to realize that it could not be the work of a single author. Though Lane upheld single authorship, by the 20th century it was agreed that the *Nights* is a composite work consisting of popular stories originally transmitted orally, and developed during several centuries with material added somewhat haphazardly at different periods and places. This view is supported by internal evidence: the style, mainly unstudied and unaffected, contains colloquialisms and even grammatical errors such as no professional Arabic writer would allow; and the tales' variety and geographical range of origin make single authorship unlikely. The main elements can be traced to India, Iran, Iraq, Egypt, and Turkey, and von Grunebaum even finds evidence of Greek influence (see *Bibliography*). Though the names of its chief characters are Iranian, the frame story is probably Indian; and Indian, Iranian, Turkish, and even European names occur, though the largest proportion is Arabic. The stories, of many kinds (sometimes grouped within secondary frame stories), incorporate many traditions, but the Arabic background is mainly that of the Baghdad of Harun al-Rashid (*q.v.;* 766–809), who appears in the final version of some tales, and the Cairo of the Fatimids and Mamelukes (10th–16th centuries).

The first known reference to the *Nights* (found by Nadia Abbott; see *Bibliography*) is a 9th-century fragment. It is next mentioned in 947 by al-Mas'udi (*q.v.*), who, in discussing legendary stories from Iran, India, and Greece, instances "the book *Hazar Afsana*," meaning "A Thousand Tales," and "called by the people 'A Thousand Nights' "—and the story that follows is about the king, the vizier and his daughter Shirazad, and her maid Dinazad. In 987 Ibn al-Nadim also mentions the *Hazar Afsana* and outlines the frame story, going on to describe how Abu Abdullah ibn 'Abdus al-Jashyari began a collection of 1,000 popular Arabic, Iranian, Greek, and other tales but died (942) when only 480 were written. That a form of the work existed in Egypt in the 12th century is known from al-Qurti's history of Egypt under the last Fatimid (1160–71).

The first to distinguish several layers in the work, including one originating in Baghdad and one larger and later written in Egypt, was August Müller, in 1887. By the mid-20th century six successive forms of the *Nights* had been distinguished: two 8th-century Arabic translations of the Persian *Hazar Isfana,* the first, called *Alf Khurafa,* probably full and literal; the second, *Alf Layla,* an Islamized version; a 9th-century version based on *Alf Layla* but including other stories then current, among them those about Sindbad; the 10th-century work by Ibn 'Abdus; a 12th-century collection, including Egyptian tales; and the final version, extending to the 16th century, and consisting of the earlier material with the addition of stories of the Islamic counter-Crusades and Oriental tales taken to the Middle East by the Mongols.

The first title—"A Thousand Tales"—was intended merely to indicate a large number. Littmann suggests that it became *A Thousand and One . . .* under the influence of the Turkish idiom *bin bir*—literally "1,001" but used to mean "a large number"—and that later, stories were added to make up the number.

**Influence.**—The *Nights* has affected Western ideas of the Orient and of Arabic life and character incalculably, stirring the imagination of children through versions for them (the first *c.* 1790), pantomimes, and plays; and inspiring writers to imitation, in pseudo-Oriental tales and parody (*e.g.,* Edgar Allan Poe's "The Thousand-and-Second Tale of Scheherazade"); and in the didactic and allegorical use of Eastern themes and scenes.

Bibliography.—Bibliography in C. Brockelmann, *Geschichte der arabischen Literatur,* vol. ii (1902; 2nd ed. 1949), suppl. ii (1938). New translations in *The Thousand and One Nights: The Hunchback, Sindbad, and Other Tales* (1953), and *Aladdin and Other Tales* (1956), with useful introductions, both Penguin Classics. *See* also N. Elisséeff, *Thèmes et motifs des mille et une nuits* (1949); E. Littmann, "Alf Layla wa-Layla," in *Encyclopaedia of Islam,* vol. i, 2nd ed. (1956); N. Abbott, "A Ninth-Century Fragment of the 'Thousand Nights'," in the *Journal of Near Eastern Studies* (1949); G. von Grunebaum, *Medieval Islam* (1946; 2nd ed. 1953); M. I. Gerhardt, *The Art of Story-telling: a Literary Study of the Thousand and One Nights* (1963); M. P. Conart, *The Oriental Tale in England . . .* (1908).

(J. A. Hd.)

**THRACE** (Greek Thrake, Latin Thracia), an ancient and modern district whose boundaries have varied at different times. To the ancient Greeks Thrace was the eastern section of the Balkan peninsula between the Danube and the Aegean Sea, bounded on the east by the Euxine (Black) Sea and by the Straits, and on the west approximately by the mountains east of the Axius (Gr. Axios; Serb. Vardar) River. The land west of the Strymon (modern Gr. Strimon; Bulg. Struma) was incorporated into Macedonia soon after 480 B.C. and the remaining area is usually what is meant by Thrace in modern times; it corresponds to part of (sometimes all of) modern Bulgaria, together with the Greek province of Thrace and European Turkey.

Thrace is intersected by the Haemus (Balkan) Range (sometimes regarded as its northern boundary) and by the Rhodope chain which runs south and east from the Haemus toward the Aegean. Near the junction of Haemus and Rhodope, in the Rila Mountains south of Sofia, rises the Hebrus (Gr. Evros; Bulg. Maritsa), the largest Thracian river, which flows east to Edirne (Adrianople) and then turns south to the Aegean.

**Ancient Population.**—In ancient times most of Thrace was inhabited by various tribes of Thracians. North of the Haemus lived the Getae (*q.v.*). Farther south the leading tribes were the Odrysae with a capital near the later Philippopolis (Plovdiv), the Bessi probably on their southern boundaries, the Dentheletae on the upper Strymon, the Edones nearer the sea, the Sapaei on the lower Nestus, and the Dolonci in the Thracian Chersonese (Gallipoli [Turk. Gelibolu] Peninsula). Outside the Balkans the peoples of Bithynia and of Phrygia in Asia Minor were accounted of Thracian origin, as were the Dacians north of the Danube; and west to the Adriatic there had originally been Thracians, who were driven back by Illyrian invaders about 1300 B.C.

The Thracians spoke an Indo-European language and in early times had a fairly advanced culture, noted for its poetry and music. The Greek god Dionysus came from Thrace, where he had been a deity of vegetation; and the Greeks were impressed by the belief in immortality associated with the worship of the god Zalmoxis (*see* GETAE). But the Greeks of the 5th century and later regarded the Thracians as barbarians. Their methods of fighting were savage; the ecstatic rites of the god Sabazius were notoriously unrestrained; and Herodotus (esp. iv, 93 ff. and v, 2 ff.) notes the customs of tattooing and of allowing girls complete license until marriage. Thucydides, writing about 400 B.C. (ii, 95 ff.), has valuable information on the ethnography and political condition of the country in his day, and records that King Sitalces drew a revenue of 400 talents, a sum rather smaller than the contemporary tribute of the Athenian Empire. Throughout their history the Thracians were noted for lack of political cohesion, but they were valued as mercenaries, not least in Roman imperial times.

**Greeks and Macedonians.**—Many Greek cities were founded on the coasts of Thrace. The best-known were Byzantium and the other colonies on the Bosporus, the Propontis (Sea of Marmara), and the Chersonese. On the Aegean were Abdera, near the Nestus mouth, and Aenus, near Alexandroupolis. Then there were the cities of the Chalcidic Peninsula, flanked on the east by the gold-bearing district of the Strymon valley, where after many unsuccessful attempts at Greek settlement the Athenians founded Amphipolis in 437 B.C. Farther north, in the Gulf of Burgas on the Black Sea, the Milesians founded Apollonia in the 7th century and the Chalcedonians Mesembria at the end of the 6th.

Most Thracians became subject to Persia *c.* 510 B.C., and some tribes joined the expedition of Xerxes against Greece in 480. But it was notoriously difficult to unite the country, although such a union was momentarily achieved later in the 5th century under King Teres of the Odrysae and his son Sitalces, the latter of whom invaded Macedonia with 150,000 men in 429. This expedition, however, collapsed under its own weight. In 360 the united kingdom split into three parts, and Philip II of Macedonia easily conquered the western region in 356 and in 342 made the remaining tribes tributary, as well as founding Philippopolis and other colonies. The Thracians provided Philip's son, Alexander the Great, with valuable light-armed troops, but Macedonian hold over the country was never secure. Lysimachus, one of Alexander's successors, founded Lysimachia in the Chersonese, and maintained his influence in all Thrace. But after his death (281) an invasion of Gauls dominated the interior, and it was with difficulty that the various Hellenistic kingdoms (including Egypt) controlled the Greek cities of the Aegean coast and the Straits. In 200 B.C. Philip V of Macedonia occupied all the cities up to the Hellespont and conquered certain tribes to the north. But after his defeat by the Romans in 197 the Roman Senate was favourable to other claimants, particularly the kingdom of Pergamum, until in 168 the Macedonian kingdom was destroyed.

**Roman Thrace.**—The coastal area west of the Hebrus was annexed to the "First Republic of Macedonia" (and later to the Roman province of the same name), while Rome became increasingly involved in the affairs of the whole region. The Via Egnatia, a great military road, was built from Thessalonica (Salonika), and ultimately from Dyrrachium (Durrës), to the Hebrus, and many Roman governors of the late 2nd and early 1st centuries B.C. fought against Thracian tribes; as late as 13–11 B.C. the Bessi rose against Rome. Meanwhile, however, Cotys, king of the Sapaei, had succeeded in forming a widespread Thracian kingdom and was recognized as a Roman client king. At the beginning of the Christian era Cotys' son Rhoemetalces ruled all Thrace south of the Haemus and east of the Roman province of Macedonia. On his death about A.D. 14 the kingdom was divided between his brother Rhascuporis and his son Cotys, but Rhascuporis murdered his nephew and Rome intervened with an army in 19. More sizable forces were required in 21 and 26 to deal with popular risings, the second caused by Roman recruitment of Thracian auxiliaries.

Finally the dynastic quarrels of the Sapaean house led to annexation of the kingdom by the emperor Claudius in 46. A province was created under a Roman procurator, whose subordinates were native *strategi* (perhaps as many as 50), each controlling a small district. Several Greek cities, such as Abdera, remained "free," and Byzantium was put under the governor of Bithynia on the other side of the Bosporus. About 114 Trajan replaced the procurator by a senatorial legate of praetorian rank, who controlled troops and had his headquarters at Perinthus (Eregli) on the Propontis. Both Trajan and his successor Hadrian founded numerous cities in Thrace, notably Serdica (Sofia) and Hadrianopolis (Adrianople). (G. E. F. C.)

South of the Danube, Moesia (*q.v.*) had been established as a separate province from A.D. 15. In the mid-3rd century Goths and other invaders ravaged much of Moesia and Thrace; Philippopolis was betrayed to them in 250–251, and many of its inhabitants were slaughtered. About 300 Diocletian reorganized the whole area between the lower Danube and the Aegean as the diocese of Thrace, divided into six provinces.

The foundation of Constantinople increased the importance and prosperity of Thrace, but in the late 4th century the barbarian raids resumed. In 378 the emperor Valens was defeated and killed near Adrianople (*see* EDIRNE) by the Visigoths, and in 443 and 447 Attila led the Huns on devastating raids far into Thrace. As early as the 1st century A.D. bodies of barbarians had been settled in the Danubian frontier provinces by the Romans, and this practice became more common in the 3rd and 4th centuries. In the late 6th and early 7th century the population of Thrace was drastically altered by massive Slav immigrations.

**Byzantines and Bulgarians.**—The Byzantines lost Thrace north of the Haemus when the Bulgarian state was founded in the late 7th century, and throughout the next three centuries there were both Bulgarian raids and actual Bulgarian conquests of much of the rest of Thrace. To organize the Byzantine defense, Nicephorus I created the theme (military district) of Thrace, but his defeat by Krum (811) led to more Bulgarian expansion. The Russian invasion of 969–971 gave John I an opportunity to recover much of Thrace, and the brief Bulgarian revival under Samuel was crushed by Basil II in 1014. But the Slav population was restive, and there were raids in the 11th and 12th centuries by tribes from beyond the Danube, especially the Turkic Patzinaks (Pechenegs).

After the fall of Constantinople to the Franks in 1204, southern Thrace passed to the Latin emperor Baldwin; the north was part of Bulgaria. Attacks by both Bulgarians and the Greek rulers of Epirus and of Nicaea soon diminished Latin territory, and in 1261 all Thrace was once more divided between the Bulgarian and Byzantine empires.

**Turks.**—Thrace suffered in the Byzantine civil wars of the early 14th century, and Turkish attacks on it began at this time. In 1354 the Ottoman Turks captured Gallipoli and used it as a base for the conquest of all Thrace; Adrianople was taken in 1362, Philippopolis probably the following year. Bulgaria soon submitted, and apart from Constantinople and nearby areas (until

1453) all Thrace became Turkish. The *eyalet* of Rumeli (Rumelia), with its capital first at Filibe (Plovdiv), then at Sofia, embraced Thrace and neighbouring Ottoman conquests in the Balkans.

**19th and 20th Centuries.**—Turkish domination in the Balkans was undisputed for about four centuries, but the establishment of Russia on the Black Sea, and especially the Treaty of Kuchuk Kainardji (1774), giving Russia the right to protect the Christian populations of the Ottoman Empire, started a chain reaction which resulted in the almost total loss of Turkish possessions in Europe. (*See* EASTERN QUESTION.)

Thrace became for the first time a theatre of a Russo-Turkish war in 1828–29 and for the second time in 1877–78. Russia failed, however, in creating a "Big Bulgaria" because in 1878 the European powers decided (*see* BERLIN, CONGRESS OF) that the Balkan range would be the southern frontier of the newly created Bulgaria. The whole of Thrace remained under Turkish domination, but its northern fringe, with a Bulgarian population, became an autonomous province named Eastern Rumelia. This situation ended in 1885 when Eastern Rumelia was united with Bulgaria.

During the first Balkan War of 1912–13 (*see* BALKAN WARS) Thrace once more became a battlefield, this time between Bulgars and Turks. The Bulgars took Edirne (March 26, 1913) and thus were masters of nearly all Thrace. But Ferdinand, king of Bulgaria, remembering that Russia included Macedonia in its plan for "Big Bulgaria," ordered on June 28 an attack upon the Serbs and the Greeks. Thus started the second Balkan War, which ended badly for Bulgaria. Under the Treaty of Bucharest (Aug. 10, 1913), Turkey recovered all Eastern Thrace with Edirne, but Bulgaria obtained Western Thrace with a coastline of about 125 mi. on the Aegean and with a small port at Dedeagach (Alexandroupolis).

That settlement did not survive World War I, in which Bulgaria sided with Germany, Austria-Hungary, and Turkey. After the defeat of the Central Powers, the frontiers across Thrace were revised in favour of Greece, which by the Treaty of Neuilly (1919) obtained the southern part of Eastern Thrace and by the Treaty of Sèvres (1920) almost all of Western Thrace. Greek tenure of Eastern Thrace was brief: after the disastrous end of the Greek invasion of Anatolia, the Treaty of Lausanne (1923) restored Eastern Thrace up to the Maritsa to Turkey, leaving Western Thrace to Greece. At that time Eastern Thrace had a total population of about 805,000, including 395,500 Greeks, 344,000 Turks, and 67,800 Bulgars. That part of Western Thrace which was attributed to Greece had a total population of about 200,000, including 124,000 Turks, 44,000 Greeks, and 29,500 Bulgars.

The frontiers between Bulgaria, Turkey, and Greece remained unchanged after World War II. The historic Thrace remained divided between those three states: about 7,350 sq.mi. was in Turkey, 3,295 sq.mi. in Greece, and 2,920 sq.mi. (respectively 19,000, 8,500, and 7,500 sq.km.) in Bulgaria. But between the two world wars the ethnic composition of the population changed greatly in all three parts of Thrace. In the 1920s Greeks were repatriated to Greece and Bulgars to Bulgaria. In the 1960s the total populations in the three parts of Thrace were 792,000 in Turkey, 357,000 in Greece, and 372,000 in Bulgaria. The only national minority of some importance was the Turkish one in Greek Thrace, numbering about 92,000.

See also references to "Thrace" in the Index. (X.)

BIBLIOGRAPHY.—*Ancient History:* S. Casson, *Macedonia, Thrace and Illyria* (1926); G. I. Kazarow in *Cambridge Ancient History,* vol. viii, ch. 17 (1930); J. Keil, *ibid.*, vol. xi, ch. 14 (1936); A. H. M. Jones, *Cities of the Eastern Roman Provinces,* ch. 1 (1937). (G. E. F. C.)

*Medieval:* Steven Runciman, *A History of the First Bulgarian Empire* (1930); G. Ostrogorsky, *History of the Byzantine State,* Eng. trans. by J. M. Hussey (1956). (X.)

**THRASEA PAETUS, PUBLIUS CLODIUS** (d. A.D. 66), Roman senator famous for his opposition to the emperor Nero. He came from the north Italian middle class. He was consul in 56 and took an independent line on various occasions in Nero's reign; he walked out when the Senate congratulated Nero on his mother's death (59), and out of disgust with Nero's immoralities retired altogether from public life from 63 to 66. This protest was all the more striking because in earlier years he had been notably active; as late as 62 he initiated an important measure to prevent provincial governors from becoming dependent on the favour of unscrupulous local magnates. In 66 his enemies persuaded Nero to order his death on the ground that he had become almost the head of a rival party in the state; in fact there is no evidence that Thrasea would ever have carried opposition to the point of conspiracy. He spent his last hours in a discussion of the immortality of the soul. Helvidius Priscus (*q.v.*) was his son-in-law, and the poet Persius (*q.v.*) was his friend.

*See* E. Groag and A. Stein, *Prosopographia Imperii Romani,* 2nd ed., vol. ii, C 1187 (1936); C. Wirszubski, *Libertas as a Political Idea at Rome,* pp. 138 ff. (1950). (P. A. BR.)

**THRASHER,** a group of birds belonging to the same American family, Mimidae, as the mockingbird (*q.v.*). Perhaps the best of these accomplished songsters is Sennett's thrasher (*Toxostoma longirostre*) of southeast Texas and northeast Mexico, but the brown thrasher (*T. rufum*) of eastern North America also has a fine song. A third species is the sage thrasher (*Oreoscoptes montanus*) of the southwestern United States. All thrashers are birds of bushy thickets, where they build fairly bulky cup-shaped nests of twigs, in which they lay three to six whitish or pale greenish eggs, heavily speckled with brown. In spite of their arboreal nature, thrashers to a large extent feed on the ground.

ALLAN D. CRUICKSHANK FROM THE NATIONAL AUDUBON SOCIETY

BROWN THRASHER (TOXOSTOMA RUFUM) OF EASTERN NORTH AMERICA

The catbird (*Dumetella carolinensis*), a North American thrasher about nine inches long, breeds from Nova Scotia to southeastern Texas. Its plumage is slate gray, with a black cap and tail and chestnut under tail coverts. It is noted for its distinctive song, which, although having much of the charm of its close relative the mockingbird, is interspersed with petulant mewing protests, hence its common name. The catbird winters in the southern states, in Cuba and from Mexico to Panama. It is resident in Bermuda. Unlike most of its relatives, it lays deep glossy blue-green eggs.

Thrashers are beneficial in view of their insect-eating habits.

**THRASYBULUS** (d. 389 or 388 B.C.), Athenian general and democratic leader. His public career began in 411 B.C., when he frustrated the oligarchic rising in Samos (*see* PELOPONNESIAN WAR). Elected general by the troops, he effected the recall of Alcibiades (*q.v.*) and assisted him in the ensuing naval campaigns, contributing to the victories of Cynossema (411) and Cyzicus (410), after which he remained in the Hellespont area and recovered Thasos (407) and Abdera for Athens. He commanded a ship at Arginusae and was commissioned with Theramenes (*q.v.*) to rescue the men on the wrecks. In 404, when exiled by the Thirty (the oligarchy at Athens), he retired to Thebes. In the following winter, with 70 men, he seized Phyle, a hill fort on Mt. Parnes. His supporters soon increased, and with 1,000 men he gained the Piraeus and held Munychia against an attack by the oligarchs. Eventually a Spartan expedition under king Pausanias arrived and the democracy was restored (autumn 403). Thrasybulus was now the hero of the people; but a decree by which he secured the franchise for all his non-citizen followers was rescinded as illegal (some of these were in fact enfranchised in 401/400).

In 395 Thrasybulus induced Athens to join the Theban League against Sparta; next year he took part in the Battle of Nemea. In 389 he led a new fleet of 40 ships against the Spartans at Rhodes. He effected a democratic revolution at Byzantium and renewed the toll on the Bosporus trade. After a successful attack on Lesbos and the reimposition of the 5% import tax on the Athenian allies, he sailed south and was killed at Aspendus, where his financial exactions had made him unpopular.

**THREE BODIES, PROBLEM OF,** the problem of determining the motion of three heavenly bodies moving under no influence but that of their mutual gravitation. No general solution of this problem is possible. As practically attacked it consists of the problem of determining the perturbations or disturbances in the motion of one of the bodies around the principal or central body that are produced by the attraction of the third. Examples are the motion of the moon around the earth as disturbed by the action of the sun, and of one planet around the sun as disturbed by the action of another planet.

For application of the problem to asteroids, *see* TROJAN PLANETS.

**THREE RIVERS:** *see* TROIS-RIVIÈRES.

**THRESHING:** *see* FARM MACHINERY.

**THRING, EDWARD** (1821–1887) ranks with Thomas Arnold as one of the outstanding English schoolmasters of the 19th century. Born at Alford, Somerset, on Nov. 29, 1821, he was educated at Eton and King's College, Cambridge. Ordained in 1846, seven years later he was appointed headmaster of Uppingham School (founded 1584), which he transformed from a small country grammar school into a large public school, in spite of opposition from his governors. Fearing that the independence of the school was threatened by the Endowed Schools Commissioners, he formed in 1868 the Headmasters' Conference, which thereafter had a great influence in English public school education. Thring remained as headmaster until his death on Oct. 22, 1887. He believed that every boy could do something well and that the business of the master was to discover what this was.

He built the school chapel, opened in 1859 the first school gymnasium in England, started wood and metal workshops, and provided a swimming pool and opportunities for school gardening. At the same time he stressed a sound training in classics, mathematics, and English. Thring realized the refining and stimulating power of music in education and built up a strong musical tradition at Uppingham.

To help young teachers, he wrote *Theory and Practice of Teaching* (1883).

BIBLIOGRAPHY.—Sir G. R. Parkin, *Life and Letters of Edward Thring,* new ed. (1900); W. F. Rawnsley, *Edward Thring, Maker of Uppingham School* (1926); G. Hoyland, *The Man Who Made a School* (1946).

(S. J. C.)

**THRIPS,** any of the small insects comprising the order Thysanoptera, which include such plant pests as the onion thrips, gladiolus thrips, wheat thrips and greenhouse thrips. In addition to inflicting injury some thrips transmit virus diseases of plants. Most thrips are less than one-tenth inch long; even giants of the order, found in the tropics and Australia, are scarcely one-half inch long. Because of their small size and their habit of hiding in close places thrips are commonly overlooked, even by entomologists, and not more than 5,000 species have been described. Thrips occur in every part of the world where plants grow. They feed on green plants, decaying plant remains, fungi or small insects and mites. Most of them extract sap or juice, but one group of species ingests the spores of fungi instead of juice. Although they are of no importance to human health, thrips, when numerous, may annoy persons by pricking thin skin in search of water; one of the plant feeders has been reported to ingest human blood occasionally. Some species are restricted to a single kind of food plant, whereas others may prefer certain plants or feed on many different plants. Thrips may curl leaves or fold them along the mid-vein to create a shelter, and at least one species induces hornlike galls.

Thrips are elongate, slender-bodied insects, with antennae consisting of four to nine true joints, and with asymmetrical piercing mouthparts. The wings have reduced venation and are usually long and narrow, with marginal fringes of long hairs; but some species or individuals have no wings or only short, nonfunctional ones. Each of the one- or two-jointed tarsi bears at the apex a minute protrusible bladder, which is an aid to a thrips in climbing even the smoothest surface. The young resemble the adults in form but are paler and more brilliantly coloured. Before becoming adult, they pass through a prepupal and one or more pupal stages. Males are generally scarcer than females and in some species are rare or unknown. Even in species where males are common, reproduction is often effected without them, through parthenogenesis (*q.v.*).

Thysanoptera are divided into two suborders: (1) Terebrantia (female with sawlike ovipositor and usually a conically pointed abdomen; male with abdomen bluntly rounded); and (2) Tubulifera (female without ovipositor; both sexes in most species with the last segment of the abdomen tubular in form). The Terebrantia are the more primitive group, with more veins in the wings and often with the wings relatively broad. Most species of this group feed on living plants; some are predatory. The female usually inserts the eggs under the epidermis of the plant by means of her ovipositor. The Tubulifera are more specialized: the ovipositor has been lost, the antennae have usually fewer segments, the wings are narrow and the veins have been reduced to a single median vestige. Most species of this group feed on plant debris and fungi or fungus spores, although a few are plant feeders or predators. Lacking an ovipositor, the female usually hides the eggs in protected places. The young are born alive in some species. Fossils of both suborders, especially of Terebrantia, are known. *See* also INSECT.

BIBLIOGRAPHY.—H. Priesner, *Die Thysanopteren Europas* (1926–28), contains a good bibliography of earlier works; S. F. Bailey has published bibliographies of North American authors in the *Florida Entomologist,* 30:17–24 (1947), 31:35–49 (1948), 32:11–36 and 32:114–131 (1949); L. J. Stannard, *Illinois Biol. Monogr.,* vol. 25 (1957); G. D. Morison, *Trans. R. Ent. Soc. Lond.,* vol. 109 (16), pp. 467–534 (1957); J. C. Faure, *J. Ent. Soc. S. Afr.,* vol. 24 (1961); S. Medina Gaud, *Tech. Pap. P. R. Agric. Exp. Sta.,* vol. 32 (1961).

(J. D. HD.; K. O'N.)

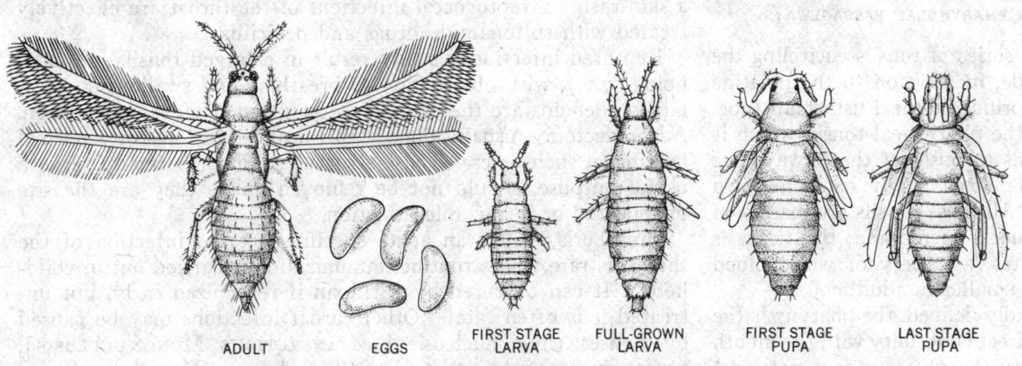


GROWTH STAGES OF PEAR THRIPS (TAENIOTHRIPS INCONSEQUENS)

**THROAT** (PHARYNX), in human anatomy, a passageway leading from the oral and nasal cavities to the esophagus (gullet) and larynx (voice box). Strictly speaking, pharynx is a broader term than throat, the latter being restricted to only part of the pharynx. In medical practice, however, the two terms ordinarily are used interchangeably, and they are so used in this article.

The throat passes the intake of solids and liquids to the esophagus in eating or drinking and conducts air to and from the larynx in breathing. The throat also communicates on either side with the cavity of the middle ear by way of the auditory (Eustachian) tube; this provides for equalization of air pressure on the eardrum membrane, which separates the cavity of the middle ear from the external ear canal (*see* EAR, ANATOMY OF).

**Anatomy.**—The throat has roughly the form of a funnel flattened from front to back, about 12 cm. (5 in.) long and narrowing from a width of about 5 cm. (2 in.) at the base of the skull to 2.5 cm. at its junction with the esophagus. The wall of the pharynx is attached by its connective tissue and muscles to surrounding structures. The firmest attachments (in addition to continuities with the walls of the oral cavity, Eustachian tubes, esophagus and larynx) are with basal parts of the skull, mandible, tongue, hyoid bone and the thyroid and cricoid cartilages of the larynx. The outermost connective tissue is in most areas loose enough in organization to admit gliding of the pharyngeal wall, in the movements of swallowing, against the surrounding structures.

Three main divisions of the throat are distinguished: oral pharynx, nasal pharynx and laryngeal pharynx (*see* figure). The latter two are airways, whereas the oral pharynx is shared by the respiratory and gastrointestinal tracts. Some of the boundaries of these divisions may be observed in a person whose mouth is held wide open. Note first the palatine tonsil, enlodged between two vertical folds of mucous membrane (in front, the glossopalatine arch; behind, the pharyngopalatine arch). A plane coinciding with the glossopalatine arches on the sides of the throat, and with the junction of the front two-thirds and back one-third of the tongue on its floor, represents the approximate boundary between mouth cavity and oral pharynx. Above, the hard palate separates the oral cavity from the nasal cavities; the soft palate partitions the oral pharynx from the nasal pharynx. The free edge of the soft palate is prolonged in the midline as the teatlike uvula. The laryngeal pharynx and the lower part of the oral pharynx are hidden by the bulging of the root of the tongue. An important feature of this obscured region is the epiglottis, a laryngeal flap that guards the glottis as a deflector between the laryngeal pharynx and the lowermost oral pharynx.

The wall of the throat is divisible into principal layers, from within outward: (1) mucous membrane, consisting of epithelium and fibrous connective tissue, of which the outermost part, a tough membrane called the pharyngeal aponeurosis, is especially concerned with the upper and lower attachments of the throat; (2) muscle; (3) connective tissue. The muscle is subject to voluntary control and is concerned in the mechanics of swallowing (*see* DIGESTION: *Swallowing*). The mucous membrane contains numerous minute salivary glands (*q.v.*).

The throat is the seat of the tonsils. The term tonsil may suggest only the palatine tonsils, whose position is described above,

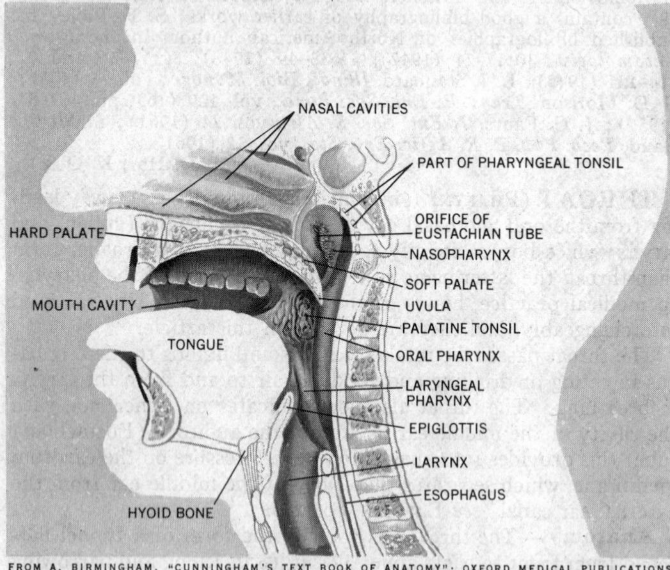


FROM A. BIRMINGHAM, "CUNNINGHAM'S TEXT BOOK OF ANATOMY"; OXFORD MEDICAL PUBLICATIONS

SECTION THROUGH HEAD SHOWING PHARYNGEAL PASSAGEWAYS

but these are only components of a series of tonsils encircling the wall of the pharynx. On either side, in addition to the palatine tonsil, is the tubal tonsil, near the orifice of the Eustachian tube. On the roof of the nasopharynx is the pharyngeal tonsil, which is frequently so enlarged in children as to obstruct the airway (*see* ADENOIDS). On the floor of the oral pharynx, in the back one-third of the tongue, is the lingual tonsil. All these tonsils are masses of lymphoid tissue imbedded in the mucous membrane; this tissue is composed principally of lymphocytes, a variety of white blood cell. Normally, the tonsils become smaller in adulthood.

**Comparative Anatomy.**—Broadly defined, the pharynx is the segment of the alimentary tract in direct continuity with the mouth cavity. In the simpler invertebrates the pharynx does not exist because at this level of structural organization there is no alimentary tract equivalent to that of higher forms. Even in some invertebrates that possess an alimentary tract the pharynx as such is absent, the passage leading from the mouth being termed esophagus or stomach. The invertebrates that have a pharynx exhibit variations of its construction and functions. In leeches, for example, the pharynx has a robust musculature and serves as a suction pump to extract blood from the prey whose skin has been pierced by the teeth of the leech. In certain marine worms the wall of the mouth cavity and pharynx may be turned out and protruded for the ingestion of food; the interior of the pharynx may bear papillae or even horny teeth that aid in the process of ingestion.

The pharynx in invertebrates as a whole is not the strict homologue of the pharynx in vertebrates; the likeness between them is only the analogy of their sequential relations in the alimentary tract. In chordate animals (*i.e.*, vertebrates and their immediate kin) the pharynx is consistent not only in the fundamentals of structural relationship but also in embryologic derivation, and hence is homologous throughout.

The classes of vertebrates present wide variation in the character of the pharynx. In all lung-breathing forms (mammals, birds, reptiles, and most amphibians in their postlarval stages) the pharynx is constructed in principle like that of man, though varying in anatomical details. The possession of gills (*q.v.*) in relation to the pharynx is a primitive feature, and gill-breathing vertebrates reflect the basic pharyngeal pattern that characterizes the chordates as a group. Gills are retained throughout life in fishes and in some tailed amphibians (*e.g., Necturus,* the mud puppy). Gills in some animals (*e.g.,* larval amphibians and the adult *Necturus*) are tufted external appendages. Typically in fishes, however, the gills are internal and in more direct relation with the pharynx. A shark, for example, presents on each side of the "neck" a series of gill slits, usually five in number, exclusive of the front opening known as the spiracle. These slits are communications between the pharynx and the outside, the gills being anchored within the slits where they are bathed with water issuing from the pharynx. A characteristic of bony fishes is the operculum, a protective flap overlying the gills and bordering the single gill opening.

In the embryonic history of lung-breathing vertebrates the pharynx is first modeled in the primitive pattern—as if gills were to develop, which they actually do in abortive and transitory fashion in the embryos of some of these animals. As an occasional anomaly in human development, one or more "gill slits" may persist, with or without opening into the pharynx.

*See* also THROAT, DISEASES OF.

BIBLIOGRAPHY.—A. S. Romer, *The Vertebrate Body,* 3rd ed. (1962); H. Morris, *Human Anatomy,* ed. by B. J. Anson (1966); B. M. Patten, *Human Embryology* (1953); W. Lerche, *The Esophagus and Pharynx in Action* (1950). (H. Cs.)

**THROAT, DISEASES OF.** The throat is subject to diseases that affect its muscular wall, as in paralysis, or its lining, as in infection by bacteria, viruses, or fungi. Infection by streptococci usually produces acute tonsillitis (*q.v.*) with swelling, pain, and fever. If the infection reaches the space behind the tonsil, an abscess may form and produce quinsy, with extreme pain, difficulty in swallowing and inability to open the mouth. Scarlet fever (*q.v.*) is a streptococcal throat infection accompanied by a skin rash. Streptococcal infections of the throat are effectively treated with sulfonamide drugs and penicillin.

Repeated infections usually result in enlarged tonsils and adenoids (*q.v.*), with obstruction to breathing and swallowing. Enlarged adenoids are the commonest cause of deafness in children. Adenoidectomy, usually done with tonsillectomy, restores normal hearing in such cases. These structures, which normally serve a useful purpose, should not be removed unless they are the site of repeated or intractable infection.

Diphtheria (*q.v.*), an acute specific bacterial infection of the throat, is rare where routine immunization is carried out in childhood. It can be cured by antitoxin if recognized early, but untreated it is often fatal. Other throat infections may be caused by viruses (mononucleosis [*see* INFECTIOUS MONONUCLEOSIS], herpangina) or may occur when the body's resistance is weakened by a scarcity of white blood cells, a condition often due to drug sensitivity and occasionally to prolonged X-ray exposure.

The muscular wall of the throat may be weakened or paralyzed by virus infections of the supplying nerves (poliomyelitis, rabies, etc.), by toxins from diphtheria or infected food, by chemical agents (*e.g.*, lead, methyl alcohol), or by circulatory disturbances of the brain, especially in the aged. Spasm of the lowermost constrictor muscle may result from emotional tension, producing the sensation of "lump in the throat."

Cancer of the throat is not common. It may begin as a painless swelling in the region of the tonsil, diagnosable by biopsy. X-ray treatment is often effective in controlling it.

Infections of the larynx or voice box (laryngitis; *q.v.*) may produce hoarseness, and in young children, a difficulty in breathing, known as croup (*q.v.*), which is treated by steam inhalation and antibiotics. A rare form of croup, due to diphtheria, may require surgical opening of the windpipe to provide an airway. Tuberculous laryngitis is effectively controlled by streptomycin.

Hoarseness may be due to "singers' node" of the vocal cord, usually associated with overuse of the voice, or to vocal polyp, often found in excessive smokers. Since hoarseness is also an early symptom of cancer involving the larynx, it should be investigated by a physician if it lasts more than two weeks. Laryngeal cancer can be cured in most cases if discovered early. X-ray therapy can cure most small cancers of the vocal cord, whereas surgical removal of the larynx is required for extensive growths.

*See* A. R. Hollender (ed.), *The Pharynx* (1953). (J. A. Kı.)

**THROCKMORTON** (Throgmorton), **FRANCIS** (1554–1584), English conspirator in a plot to overthrow Elizabeth I, was the son of Sir John Throckmorton of Feckenham, Worcestershire, and the nephew of Sir Nicholas Throckmorton (*q.v.*). Sir John had been concerned in the rebellion (1554) of Sir Thomas Wyat against Mary I, but he later regained her favour and became chief justice of Chester.

Francis entered Hart Hall (afterward Hertford College), Oxford, in 1572, and in 1576 he was enrolled in the Inner Temple. At Oxford he came under Roman Catholic influence, and when Edmund Campion and Robert Parsons came to England in 1580, as the first of the Jesuit missionaries, he was one of a society of members of the Inner Temple who hid them and gave them help. In that year he went abroad. He returned to London in 1583 to act as the confidential agent of a conspiracy, involving France and Spain, which had for its object the invasion of England by a French force under Henry, duc de Guise, for the purpose of freeing Mary Stuart, queen of Scots, and restoring papal authority.

Throckmorton occupied a house on Paul's Wharf, London, which served as a centre of communication for the conspirators. The suspicions of the government being aroused, he was arrested in November 1583. Before being taken to the Tower of London he was able to send a casket of compromising letters to Mendoza, the Spanish ambassador, and later a card in cipher in which he promised to reveal nothing. He was tortured on the rack at the Tower and after being threatened with further racking he made a full confession. He was tried on May 21 and executed at Tyburn on July 10, 1584. His arrest and confession led to the expulsion of the Spanish ambassador.

**THROCKMORTON** (Throgmorton), **SIR NICHOLAS** (1515–1571), English diplomat in the reign of Elizabeth I, was a son of Sir George Throckmorton of Coughton, Warwickshire, and the uncle of Francis Throckmorton (*q.v.*). A member of the household of Catherine Parr, the last wife of Henry VIII, he was favourable to the reformers in religion. He was a member of Parliament from 1545 to 1567. During the reign of Edward VI, in which he was knighted (1547), he at first supported Protector Somerset but later went over to the party of the earl of Warwick (afterward duke of Northumberland). When, on the death of Edward (1553), an attempt was made to place Lady Jane Grey on the throne instead of Mary Tudor, Throckmorton contrived to appear the friend of both parties; but on Mary's accession he was able to secure her favour. He was, however, suspected of complicity in the rebellion of Sir Thomas Wyat (January–February 1554). Acquitted at his trial in April, he was detained in the Tower of London until January 1555. He went abroad in 1556 but made his peace with Queen Mary in 1557.

Under Elizabeth I he became chamberlain of the exchequer and from May 1559 to April 1564 he was ambassador in France. During his embassy he was engaged in discussions about the return of Mary Stuart, queen of Scots, to Scotland (1561), and as a strong supporter of the Huguenots he was at the Battle of Dreux (December 1562) and was a prisoner for a short time. After the signing of the Treaty of Troyes (April 1564), between England and France, Throckmorton returned to England.

In May 1565 he was sent as ambassador to Scotland, but failed to prevent Mary's marriage with Henry, Lord Darnley. After Darnley's murder (February 1567) and the imprisonment of Mary by the Scottish Protestant lords (June) he was again sent to Scotland in July 1567 with the still more hopeless task of persuading the lords to restore Mary to the throne. He could effect little, but exerted himself to secure the personal safety of the queen. He offended Elizabeth by showing his instructions to the lords and returned to England in August. Throckmorton fell under suspicion in 1569 during the intrigue to marry the duke of Norfolk to Mary and was imprisoned for a time at Windsor Castle, but was not further proceeded against. He died in London on Feb. 12, 1571. Throckmorton married Anne Carew, and his daughter Elizabeth became the wife of Sir Walter Ralegh.

*See* A. L. Rowse, *Ralegh and the Throckmortons* (1962).

**THROMBOSIS AND EMBOLISM.** In certain disease states the process of coagulation (clot formation), initiated in a blood vessel, may proceed to the formation of a thrombus, a type of clot. Thrombosis (the formation of a thrombus) may produce symptoms by obstructing blood flow either at its site of formation or at some distant point in the vascular system; in the second situation, blood flow is blocked by an embolus, a fragment dislodged from the thrombus. (The blocking caused by an embolus is known as an embolism, or thromboembolism.) Thrombosis has much in common with clot formation and, while it may result from other indirect causes, is thought to be frequently related to an increased coagulability of the blood.

**Blood Coagulation.**—Knowledge of blood clotting is derived largely from studies on blood and blood fractions in the test tube. While there is much conflicting evidence regarding the sequence of activation and the relative importance of some of the newer clotting factors, blood coagulation is considered to occur in three successive stages, as follows:

$$\text{(1)}\quad \text{platelets} \xrightarrow[\text{VIII–XII}]{\text{IV, V}} \text{thromboplastin (III)} \longleftarrow \text{tissues}$$

$$\text{(2)}\quad \text{thrombin} \xleftarrow[\text{V, VII}]{\text{III, IV}} \text{prothrombin (II)}$$

$$\text{(3)}\quad \text{fibrinogen (I)} \xrightarrow[\text{IV}]{\text{thrombin}} \text{fibrin (clot)}$$

The stages are: (1) the activation of thromboplastin, an ill-defined product, released from the platelets or from injured tissue, that includes phosphorus-containing fatty proteins (phospholipoproteins); (2) the conversion of prothrombin to thrombin by thromboplastin; and (3) the splitting of fibrinogen to fibrin by the proteolytic action of thrombin. The fibrin, which is initially soluble, finally polymerizes into microscopic fibrils to form a gel, the fibrin clot. The various formed elements of the blood (red cells, white cells and platelets) become enmeshed at random in this interlacing network of tiny fibres.

The platelets have a special importance in initiating the processes of hemorrhage control (hemostasis), coagulation in the test tube and thrombosis. The first microscopic clue that a clot is going to develop in vivo is the gathering together of several of these small round bodies to form a conglomerate mass capable of plugging small leaks in the vessel wall and even occluding the lumen of small vessels. The initiation of this conglutination depends to some degree upon an increase in the adhesive quality of the platelets. This then somehow leads to the release of several active agents: thromboplastin, clotting factors serving to accelerate the second and third stages of coagulation, an antifibrinolysin, a vasoconstrictor (serotonin) and a hypotensive histamine substance. (Electron microscopy has shown that platelets rather quickly serve as a focus for fibrin formation.)

The fibrin clot will form only when all of the first four factors (I through IV) are present and will form but slowly when one or more of the other coagulants is absent. This suggests that the actions of the latter are of a catalytic nature. In patients deficient in any of these clotting factors bleeding may occur in varying degrees after minor trauma, and only rarely spontaneously. The best-known example is the patient with hemophilia A or B who suffers from a congenital lack of factor VIII or IX (*see* HEMOPHILIA).

Conversely, a shortened clotting time has been observed in men who have eaten a fatty meal; an increase in blood fat is known to occur at such a time. Whether the decrease amounts to a truly hypercoagulable state is not known. Thrombosis is common in the disease polycythemia vera and in other conditions characterized by an excess of or unusual stickiness of platelets. It has been further postulated that an excess of one or another clotting factor may also enhance the likelihood of intravascular thrombosis.

The time required for blood to clot in the test tube is approximately five minutes. Most of this is taken up by the first stage of coagulation, which, for optimum speed, requires the complex interaction of many factors: *i.e.*, calcium ions, accelerator globulin, antihemophilic globulin, Christmas factor, Stuart-Prower and Hageman factors, and plasma thromboplastin antecedent (*see* table); the second and third phases of coagulation are completed

*Clotting Factors**

| Factor | Name (synonym) | Chemical nature |
|---|---|---|
| I . | fibrinogen | glycoglobulin |
| II . | prothrombin | glycoglobulin |
| III | thromboplastin | phospholipoprotein |
| IV | calcium | inorganic ion |
| V . | accelerator globulin (Ac-globulin, proaccelerin, labile factor) | euglobulin |
| VII† . | proconvertin (serum prothrombin conversion accelerator, SPCA, stable factor) | beta and gamma globulins (VII–XII) |
| VIII . | antihemophilic factor (antihemophilic globulin A, AHG, thromboplastinogen) | |
| IX . | plasma thromboplastin component (PTC, Christmas factor, anti-hemophilic globulin B) | |
| X . | Stuart-Prower factor | |
| XI . | plasma thromboplastin antecedent (PTA) | |
| XII | Hageman factor | |

*Nomenclature recommended in 1961 by the International Committee for the Nomenclature of Blood Clotting Factors.

(†) Factor VI is no longer listed in the nomenclature since, subsequent to the discovery of later factors, it was found that VI cannot be identified as an independent entity.

in perhaps 15 seconds, after active thromboplastin becomes available. In case of tissue injury and particularly of vascular injury, however, an active tissue thromboplastin becomes immediately available to initiate the second phase of coagulation; the slow process of thromboplastin generation from platelets thus is bypassed. Because of the presence of tissue thromboplastin in abundant amounts, lowered blood concentrations of the factors required exclusively in thromboplastin generation (VIII to XII) do not necessarily lead to prolonged bleeding after injury.

With the passage of a few hours, the clot shrinks in size in proportion to the number of incorporated platelets. The fibrin may dissolve under the influence of plasmin, a proteolytic enzyme (*i.e.*, a fibrinolysin) present in the blood. Plasmin is derived from the activation of a precursor, plasminogen. Agents such as streptokinase and urokinase have been used clinically as plasmin activators. It has been postulated that this thrombolytic activity must be one factor limiting the extent of clot formation, so that the clot does not grow to fill the entire vascular system. Less well defined are antithrombin and the inhibitors of other coagulants that act on thromboplastin activation; their function, when determined, may help explain why the blood, which clots so readily when removed from the body, remains liquid in the blood vessels.

**Pathology.**—Thrombosis may occur at any site in the cardiovascular system: artery, capillary, vein or chamber of the heart. A thrombus differs from a blood clot outside the body in that it is organized into a less homogeneous structure; a basic grayish layer of agglutinated platelets of varying thickness is covered by a dense layer of fibrin that merges into a looser red fibrin layer, and it is the red fibrin layer that includes the white and particularly the red blood cells. A laminated thrombus is formed when several layerings are deposited one upon another. There are many variations in the proportions of white and red thrombotic material, depending partly upon the location of the thrombus.

Characteristically the arterial thrombus is richer in platelets packed together (white, or conglutination, thrombus). The venous thrombus most commonly has a "white head" at its attachment to the vessel wall and a long "red tail" streaming away from it toward the heart. This red, or coagulation, thrombus will, if the circulation is slow enough, quite closely resemble the in vitro blood clot. A fragment of this tail may break loose to form an embolus.

Reduction in the velocity of blood flow, roughening of the artery wall by disease or injury, certain toxic chemicals (*e.g.*, snake venom) and enhanced coagulability of the blood have all been considered important causative factors in thrombus formation. Thus, injury, surgery, general or local infection, arterial disease, heart failure, pregnancy, occasional malignancies and certain disorders of the blood all predispose to this complication. It is thus not surprising that thrombosis is found either incidentally or as the cause of death in the majority of all fatalities due to cardiovascular disease and that its frequency increases with advancing age.

Once thrombosis is contained, regardless of whether embolism has or has not occurred, the thrombus undergoes gradual changes: dissolution, then contraction, and finally organization. By these means a new channel for the flow of blood may ultimately be reestablished. Some pathologists feel that the organized residue of old arterial thrombi become incorporated into the arterial wall as arteriosclerotic plaques and thus contribute to the progression, and perhaps even the initiation, of hardening of the arteries.

Thrombosis occurs most often in the large veins of the pelvis and legs, the small arteries of the heart and the brain, and in the chambers of the left side of the heart, but, under appropriate circumstances, thrombosis may occur anywhere in the circulatory system. If the thrombosis occurs in a vein, the process is called phlebothrombosis and it may produce no symptoms unless it causes an embolism. Frequently, inflammation may cause local pain and swelling in the region drained by the affected vein, in which case the condition is designated thrombophlebitis.

While venous thrombosis may sometimes lead to a fatal embolism, it is not so great a threat to life as is arterial thrombosis. The coronary and cerebral arteries (*i.e.*, of the heart and brain) are often the site of arteriosclerosis, a thickening and irregularity of the vessel lining that may predispose to thrombus formation. Should thrombosis occur, the mass of heart muscle or brain ordinarily supplied by the obstructed vessel dies; if the victim survives the initial insult, healing follows with scar formation. Recovery will depend upon the extent of tissue involvement and the presence or absence of additional thromboses either attached to the lining of the injured heart wall or arising in the veins of the leg; those in the legs may give rise to fatal pulmonary emboli.

Emboli are usually composed of coagulated blood but in rare cases they may consist of tumour cells, air, fat particles or bacterial clumps (septic emboli). These traveling aggregates can lodge in distant parts of the vascular system and there obstruct the flow of blood. Emboli are a common cause of sudden death but they are by no means always fatal. An embolus that arises in the venous system or in the right side of the heart ordinarily will lodge in the ramifications of the pulmonary artery. If the embolus is large, one of the main pulmonary arteries will be obstructed and death occurs. If the embolus is small, the segment of lung nourished by the obstructed artery dies. (*See* LUNG, DISEASES OF: *Pulmonary Embolism.*)

In certain types of heart disease an embolus may originate from one of the chambers of the left side of the heart, or from the mitral or aortic valve therein, in which case the bloodstream will carry it to one of the branches of the peripheral arterial tree. Should such an embolus lodge in certain internal organs, pain might be the only consequence; but occlusion of even a small artery in the heart, eye, brain, intestine or one of the extremities will lead also to the death of enough tissue to cause severe disruption, if not cessation, of function of the part. However, tissue death does not occur in all arterial obstructions, for in certain locations (*e.g.,* liver and lungs) neighbouring (collateral) arteries can carry enough blood into the affected area to furnish adequate circulation.

**Anticoagulant Therapy.**—Although a hypercoagulable state of the blood has not been established as the primary cause for the most common types of thrombosis and embolism, it has been well established that reducing the normal tendency for the blood to clot may help to prevent recurrences of thromboembolism. Heparin, which occurs naturally in the lungs, liver and other tissues, is derived from meat animals slaughtered for human food; it is given by injection and may function in fat metabolism as well as in the control of coagulation. Bishydroxycoumarin (Dicumarol), a chemical originally derived from spoiled sweet clover but now synthesized, has a great advantage in that it may be taken orally. Both heparin and Dicumarol have been used widely since 1940 for their broad anticoagulant properties. Heparin is a complex polysaccharide combined with sulfuric acid that inhibits each of the three stages of clot formation. Dicumarol and the other related derivatives of coumarin (*q.v.*) were originally thought to depress the synthesis of prothrombin (factor II) by the liver; the dosage to be administered is determined by measuring the prothrombin activity of the blood. It was later reported that Dicumarol also suppresses the blood levels of factors VII, IX and X. Both heparin and Dicumarol are thought to decrease platelet stickiness, though dosage considerations suggest that this may not be regularly accomplished by the usual therapy.

There is little doubt that the appropriate use of anticoagulant drugs similar to heparin and the coumarins, as well as certain derivatives of indandione, has reduced the incidence of thrombosis and embolism in patients prone to these events. Particular benefit is seen in patients with thrombophlebitis and with peripheral arterial emboli from intracardiac thrombi. There is general if not universal agreement that the thrombotic and embolic complications of an acute coronary thrombosis are minimized and that the incidence of the coronary artery thromboses that sometimes follow may be reduced by continuous anticoagulant therapy. Although these drugs are helpful in controlling certain attacks of impaired blood flow to the brain, their use in apoplexy, or stroke (*q.v.*), remains controversial since the danger of causing cerebral arterial hemorrhage counterbalances the benefits of preventing subsequent thromboses.

Surgical ligation of the vein proximal to a thrombosis in order to prevent subsequent embolism has been attempted. After embolism has occurred, surgical removal of the offending clot may frequently save a limb if it can be achieved within six to eight hours after onset.

A promising medical treatment of thromboembolism is the early employment of a fibrinolysin or a fibrinolysin-stimulating agent that dissolves the fibrin component of the obstructing plug and permits early return of normal blood flow.

*See* also Arteries, Diseases of; Blood; Blood, Disorders of; Blood Vessels, Surgery of; Circulation of Blood; Heart, Diseases and Defects of; Veins, Diseases of; and references under "Thrombosis and Embolism" in the Index.

Bibliography.—I. S. Wright, C. D. Marple and D. F. Beck, *Myocardial Infarction* (1954); M. Stefanini and W. Dameshek, *The Hemorrhagic Disorders* (1955); A. J. Quick, *Hemorrhagic Diseases* (1957); R. P. Biggs and R. G. Macfarlane, *Human Blood Coagulation and Its Disorders,* 3rd ed. (1962); R. J. Jones and L. Cohen, *Chemistry and Therapy of Chronic Cardiovascular Disease* (1961); J. C. F. Poole and J. E. French, "Thrombosis," *J. Atheroscler. Res.,* vol. 1, p. 251 (1961); R. L. MacMillan and J. F. Mustard, *Anticoagulants and Fibrinolysins* (1961). (R. J. J.)

**THRONE.** A throne is the seat of a sovereign, potentate or dignitary, secular or religious, and a symbol of rule and authority.

Modern usage incorrectly applies the name to the seat alone, but historical evidence shows that not only the seat, but the dais on which it stands and the canopy over it, forms the throne (Gr. *thronos* "elevated seat"). Thus, at the end of a papal conclave, the canopies are lowered over the throne of each cardinal except that of the newly elected pope. On occasion the dais alone is referred to as a throne; *e.g.,* that on which two small altars were set at Louis XIII's funeral is described as a *petit trosne.* The throne cannot therefore be the forerunner of chairs, as is often supposed.

In the ancient world, particularly in the east, thrones were almost invariably of a symbolic magnificence; *e.g.,* Solomon's throne of ivory set on a dais approached by six steps flanked by lions. On the throne of the Byzantine emperors, said to be imitated from it, the lions were mechanical, moving and emitting sounds. In the British museum, London, is a chryselephantine fragment encrusted with gold, ivory, lapis lazuli and cornelian, believed to have come from the throne of Sargon II of Assyria (722–705 B.C.).

The "Peacock Throne" of the rulers of Delhi, set with jewels and raised on a dais with silver steps, is of legendary splendour. The oldest surviving throne is probably that (much restored) built-in with the walls at Knossos (*c.* 1800 B.C.). The earliest remaining throne of the Christian era, the chair of St. Peter, for which Bernini created an elaborate *cathedra* in St. Peter's, Rome, is built of oak and ivory with iron carrying rings (4th–5th century). The magnificent ivory throne of Archbishop Maximian at

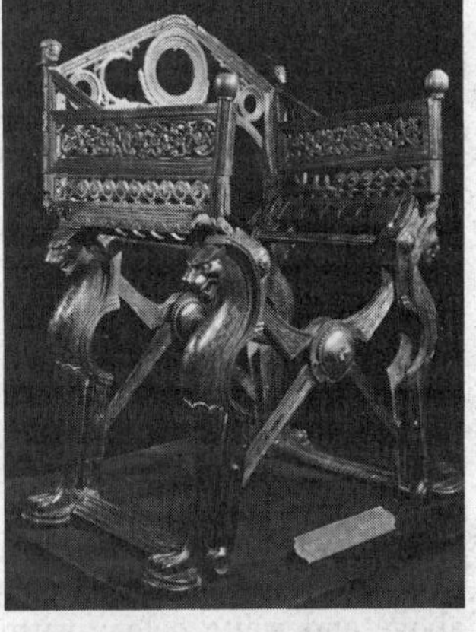

BY COURTESY OF (TOP RIGHT) THE BIBLIOTHÈQUE NATIONALE, PARIS, (BOTTOM LEFT) THE IMPERIAL IRANIAN EMBASSY PRESS OFFICE, LONDON, (BOTTOM RIGHT) DE DANSKE KONGERS KRONOLOGISKE SAMLING, ROSENBORG; PHOTO (TOP LEFT) MANSELL-ANDERSON

(TOP LEFT) IVORY THRONE OF ARCHBISHOP MAXIMIAN AT RAVENNA, ITALY, 6TH CENTURY; (TOP RIGHT) SO-CALLED BRONZE THRONE OF KING DAGOBERT FROM THE TREASURY OF ST. DENIS, FRANCE, PROBABLY 8TH CENTURY WITH 12TH CENTURY ADDITIONS; (BOTTOM LEFT) BEJEWELED NADIR THRONE, MADE DURING REIGN OF THE PERSIAN RULER FATH ALI SHAH (1797–1834); (BOTTOM RIGHT) SILVER CORONATION THRONE OF THE QUEEN OF DENMARK, 1731

Ravenna dates from the following century. The so-called throne of King Dagobert from the treasury of St. Denis (now in the Bibliothèque Nationale, Paris), is a folding stool of bronze, probably 8th century but with 12th-century additions prescribed by Abbot Suger. Thrones were often of silver in the later 17th and early 18th centuries (examples at Hanover and Copenhagen); later thrones were generally of gilt wood.

The English coronation throne in Westminster abbey is more properly a ceremonial chair, and the real throne of Great Britain is the oak chair in the house of lords, used by the sovereign during the opening and prorogation of parliament. (*See* also CHAIR AND SOFA; CROWN AND REGALIA.)

Thrones is also the name of the third order of angels. *See* ANGEL. (F. J. B. W.)

**THRUSH,** the name given to any number of small to medium-sized passerine song birds comprising the family Turdidae. Many thrushes are known as the world's most exquisite songsters. Among the more famous are the nightingale (*q.v.; Luscinia megarhynchos*), peerless among Eurasian songsters, and the American hermit thrush (*Hylocichla guttata*), one of the finest musicians of the new world.

ALLAN D. CRUICKSHANK FROM THE NATIONAL AUDUBON SOCIETY

WOOD THRUSH (HYLOCICHLA MUSTELINA) ONE OF THE FEW SONGBIRDS THAT SINGS IN CHORDS

Thrushes range from 5 to 12 in. long, with moderate wings, bills, feet and tails. The small outermost primary, lack of distinct bristles about the gape, the fusion of the scales on the front of the tarsus into a single curved plate and the spotted plumage (at least in the young) are the commonest unifying characteristics. However, the relationships of some of the several hundred species often referred to this family are not clear, and the thrushes are not sharply separated from the old world flycatchers (family Muscicapidae).

Their plumage presents a wide range of coloration, which is often somewhat subdued and of varied patterns. One common type shown by the North American wood thrush (*H. mustelina*) and the European song thrush (*Turdus ericetorum*) is brown above and white below, with a spotted breast. Both the North American robin (*T. migratorius*) and the much smaller European robin (*Erithacus rubecula*) have a red breast (*see* ROBIN); whereas the eastern bluebird (*q.v.*) of North America (*Sialia sialis*) has a red breast and a blue back. The old world blackbird (*q.v.; T. merula*) is mostly black. Some small old world species called chats (*Saxicola*) have contrasting black and white plumage, and some Malayan whistling thrushes (*Myiophoneus*) are largely dark blue with shining spangles to the tips of the feathers.

At nesting time the birds pair, and usually the female builds a cup-shaped nest of herbaceous stems and leaves, sometimes strengthened with mud. The nest is located amid the branches of a tree or shrub, in a hole in a tree, amid rocks or on the ground, depending on the species. All thrushes build open nests rather than domed ones. A clutch of three to six eggs is common, and these may be whitish or bluish, with or without spots. Typically the female incubates the eggs, and both parents help care for the young birds, feeding them insects and other invertebrates.

The thrush family is nearly cosmopolitan in distribution, but the greatest number of species are found in Europe, Asia and Africa, and a few species have colonized oceanic islands such as those of the Southwest Pacific and Tristan da Cunha. Some species are shy forest birds; some like the American and European robins are bold familiar birds of gardens and villages; others live amid the sparse brush of semiopen country or amid rocky terrain. Thrushes hop on the ground on strong legs and in the air fly swiftly, many migrating long distances. Most northern species migrate southward in winter. Some species perch freely in the open and are conspicuous, some skulk in shrubbery. Most thrushes seek insects and other invertebrates on the ground for food, but seasonally, at least, some of the larger species feed on berries and small fruits of trees. They do not catch flying prey. Among the more unusual feeding habits is that of the song thrush. It feeds on snails by hammering them on a stone to break the shell.

*See* also SONGBIRD. (A. L. RD.)

**THRUSH** (PARASITIC STOMATITIS) is a disease of the mucous membrane of the mouth and throat, caused by a yeastlike fungus, *Candida* (or *Monilia*) *albicans*. It produces whitish adherent membranes on an inflamed mucosa. Often the fungus is an inhabitant of the birth canal and the mouth of the newborn infant is contaminated from there during delivery. In older children and adults the infection rarely occurs inside the mouth, more frequently in the mouth corners, causing unsightly cracks. The same fungus may invade the skin (candidiasis or moniliasis) under special circumstances. In bartenders and housewives whose hands are exposed to moisture over unduly long periods of time, the fungus causes erosions in the webs of the fingers and also may attack the nails. The skin folds of obese diabetic persons are highly susceptible to moniliasis because of moisture and high sugar content of the skin. All these localized forms can easily be cured by competent medical treatment. In emaciated undernourished persons with decreased resistance, the whole body surface may become involved. An often fatal intestinal disease of infants, acrodermatitis enteropathica, with severe diarrhea, promotes widespread monilial infection of the skin; this condition can be cured by eradicating the underlying intestinal disease.

*Candida albicans,* however, may also invade and attack the intestinal tract and internal organs. This systemic candidiasis is treated with the newer fungistatic preparations like Nystatin often in conjunction with various antibiotics. (S. RON.; X.)

**THUCYDIDES** (fl. second half of the 5th century B.C.), greatest of Greek historians, was the author of the (incomplete) *History of the Peloponnesian War*. All that we know (perhaps all that ancient scholars knew) of his life is what he tells us himself in the course of his narrative. He was an Athenian, old enough when the war began (431 B.C.) to estimate its importance and that it was likely to be a long one, and to determine to write an account of it, observing and making notes from the beginning. He was probably born, therefore, not later than 460—perhaps a few years earlier since his detailed narrative begins with the events provocative of the war which belong to the years just before 431. He was certainly over 30 when he was elected strategos in 424 (*see* below). That is, he belongs to the generation younger than Herodotus. His father's name was Oloros. This is not otherwise known as an Athenian name; and Oloros was probably of Thracian descent on his mother's side, and Thucydides related in some way to the great Miltiades, who had married the daughter of a Thracian prince of this name. He himself had property in Thrace, including mining rights in the gold mines opposite the island of Thasos, and was, he tells us, a man of influence there.

He was in Athens when the great pestilence of 430–429 raged there and caught the disease himself and saw others suffer. Later in 424 he was elected one of the ten strategoi of the year, and, because of his connections, given command of the fleet in the Thraceward region which was based at Thasos. He failed to prevent the capture of the important city of Amphipolis by Brasidas (*q.v.*), who launched a sudden attack in the middle of winter. He was recalled and tried and sentenced to exile. This, he says later, gave him greater opportunity for undistracted study for his *History* and for travel and wider contacts, especially with the Peloponnesian side. He survived the war and his exile of 20 years ended only with the fall of Athens and the peace of 404. The time and manner of his death are uncertain, but that he died shortly after 404 is probable, and that he died by violence in the troubled times following the peace may well be true, for the *History* stops abruptly long before its appointed end. His tomb, perhaps a cenotaph, and a monument to his memory, were still to be seen in Athens in the 2nd century A.D.

**Scope and Plan of the *History*.**—The *History,* which is divided into eight books (probably not Thucydides' own division) stops in the middle of the events of the autumn of 411 B.C., rather more than six and a half years before the end of the war. This much at least is known: that three historians, Cratippus, a younger contemporary, Xenophon a generation later and Theopompus in the last third of the 4th century, began their histories (of Greece as a whole, for a limited period) where he had stopped, Xenophon, one might almost say, beginning the next paragraph—nearly as abruptly as Thucydides ends. From this it is certain that Thucydides' work was well known soon after publication and that no more of it was ever published than the eight books that have survived; and it may reasonably be inferred from the silence of the available sources that no separate section of the work was published in his lifetime. It may also be inferred that parts of the *History* are defective, in the sense that he would have written at greater length had he known more and that he was trying still to learn more—*e.g.,* of internal Athenian politics in the years of "uneasy truce" (his existing narrative is in parts barely understandable without some imaginative guesswork). A good deal of the last book is defective.

We may assume, then, three fairly definable stages in his work: first, the "notes" he made of events as they occurred, always being supplemented by fresh inquiries; secondly, these notes arranged in their order and rewritten as consecutive narrative, as a "chronicle," but by no means in the final form that Thucydides intended—(*e.g.,* some, but not all, of the story of the "uneasy truce" in book v, and, surely, most of book viii); thirdly, the final, elaborated narrative—of the preliminaries of the war (book i), of the "Ten Years' War," and of the expedition to Sicily. No documentary evidence exists of the note stage but there are passages that are only chronicle embedded in the more finished parts. Many of these, however, Thucydides intended to leave as they are. Even the most elaborated parts of the *History* may have been added to right up to his death—certainly many additions were made after the war was over.

All this is significant because Thucydides was writing what scarcely another (of eminence) has attempted, a strictly contemporary history, of events which he lived through and which succeeded each other almost throughout his adult life. Sir Winston Churchill has said of his own *Second World War,* based as it is on a unique collection of documents giving a current account of events, of the day-to-day conduct of the war: "I do not describe it as history, for that belongs to another generation. But . . . it is a contribution to history which will be of service to the future" (Introduction to vol. i, *The Gathering Storm;* Cassell and Company Ltd., 1948). Thucydides too was writing of events in some of which he took an active part, of all of which he was a direct or indirect spectator; but he attempted the final history, what, it might have been said, was "for another generation" and, as far as a man can, and as no other man has, he succeeded. It will be observed that he did not rush his work: the last of the complete narrative (stage three, above) took him to autumn 413, eight and a half years before the end of the war, the last of stage two to six and a half years before. During these last years he was observing, inquiring, writing his notes, adding to or modifying what he had already written; at no time before the end, during all the 27 years of the war, did he know what that end would be (unlike Churchill in this), nor therefore what would be the length and the final shape of his own *History.* It is evident that he did not long survive the war since he did not leave any connected account, even at stage two, of the last six years. But, in what he lived to complete, he wrote a history, not a contribution to history.

It should however here be stated that in the opinion of some scholars (*see* BIBLIOGRAPHY), Thucydides did wait till after 404 to compose his *History* from his accumulated notes; and that much of the earlier part, especially Pericles' speeches in book ii, is only to be fully understood in the light of the final defeat of Athens. He was of course, as stated, always thinking about and sometimes modifying what he had already written; but the view that he, in any real sense, "began" his work after 404 seems to be untenable.

**Diagnosis of the Causes of the Peloponnesian War.**—The conflict which he set out to describe, in detail, as truthfully as possible, with strict observation of the chronology was, as he saw it, twofold. In its simpler aspect it was caused by the rapid rise of Athens in wealth and political power after the Persian Wars, which was a challenge to the generations-old Spartan leadership in Greece. This leadership was traditional and had been widely accepted—so much so that in 480 Athens, in spite of a sharp conflict with Sparta over its internal affairs 30 years before and its proud consciousness that it had stood alone, and successfully, at Marathon in 490, was ready to accept it, with all the other Greek states who shared in the resistance to the second Persian invasion (*see* GRECO-PERSIAN WARS).

In 431 Sparta, though "ever slow in going to war," took up the challenge and declared war. But Athenian power was something more than that of an ambitious rival. To the Greek world, accustomed as it was to the autonomy of cities under democratic rule, and even to the Athenians themselves at times, it appeared "like a tyranny"—moderately used as they asserted, contrary to all Greek custom as their enemies said. It had begun in Athens' chosen leadership of the Delian league in which a number of Greek states were bound together for common defense against a further Persian attack. They had taken an oath not to secede from this league; but a few did—some of the larger ones who were also geographically safer from Persian menaces—and Athens, followed by the rest, reduced them to subjection. One or two others, originally outside, were forced in. Most of the states contributed money for the league, the amount from each being decided by Athens (moderately enough); the common treasury was transferred to Athens and Athenian officers controlled it. Athens encouraged, and sometimes imposed, the adoption of its own kind of democracy in recalcitrant cities and made, sensibly enough, or tried to make, its own excellent coinage common for all in the league, to the great advantage of trade. By arranging that delegates conveying the tribute should come there for the most important of the dramatic festivals, and in other ways, Athenians encouraged all to look upon their city as a religious and intellectual centre (the latter it had already, by its own radiant genius, become). All this attempt at unity under one leadership was new in Greece and dangerous, both to the influence of Sparta and to Greek political institutions; and Thucydides makes this clear, and why general opinion in Greece favoured the Peloponnesian cause. But he also makes clear that Athenian rule was no "empire" in any ordinary sense (Persian, Roman or modern)—not only were there no "provinces" with Athenian governors to administer them, because each state was individually attached to Athens, but free institutions in them survived and were active, and indeed the commons in most were favourable to Athens, or at least preferred its rule to the risk of seeing their own richer classes put in power by Sparta.

**Character Studies of the Leading Participants.**—There was another aspect of the conflict which interested Thucydides and which he emphasizes: it was also between the ever-active, innovating, revolutionary, disturbing Athenians and the slower-moving, more cautious Peloponnesians, especially the Spartans, "not excited by success nor despairing in misfortune," but quietly self-confident. This was a conflict between two types of character; but also it in some degree crossed the conflict between states. Thucydides was not much concerned with individuals, rather with the actions and sufferings, the characters of states ("the Athenians," "the Syracusans," etc.); but he understood the significance of personalities, and besides making clear by their words and deeds the characters of some who influenced events, as Cleon the harsh demagogue of Athens and Hermocrates the would-be moderate leader in Syracuse, the brave Nicostratus and the incompetent Alcidas, he goes out of his way to make clear the characters and influence of four men: Themistocles (in a digression, the Athenian hero of the second Persian War), Pericles, Brasidas and Alcibiades (*qq.v.*). All four of them were of the active, revolutionary type—Pericles indeed was unique for Thucydides in that he combined caution and moderation in action, and great stability of character with a daring imagination and intellect; but he was a leader of the new age. During the war each of them—Pericles and Alcibiades in Athens, Brasidas in Sparta—was in conflict with a conservative, quietist opposition; and one expression of this in Thucydides deserves especial notice. Pericles, trying to restore the confidence of the Athenians struck down with the pestilence, told them that risk and labour were unavoidable by an imperial city—"quietism" was only for those who sought security in servitude—and that even in defeat they would leave behind an imperishable name. Nicias the cautious, on the other hand, is described as believing that he could save his name by taking no risks and that to make peace meant to take no risk. In Sparta it was the wise and strong King Archidamus who led at first the cautious and conservative side, Brasidas the other; and Brasidas had his enemies at home. The conflict between the revolutionary and the conservative thus ran across that between the (on the whole) daring Athenians and the (on the whole) cautious Peloponnesians; and it is a great loss that Thucydides did not live to write the story of the last years of the war when Lysander (*q.v.*), the other great revolutionary Spartan, played a larger part than any other single man in the defeat of Athens. This defeat was in one aspect the defeat of intellectual brilliance and daring by "stupidity" and stability of character (this last the quality most lacking in Alcibiades, the most brilliant Athenian of the second half of the war); but it was largely brought about by the two Spartans who rivaled Athenians in daring and intellect.

**Study of the Technical Aspects of the War.**—There is another aspect of the war in which Thucydides was much interested —the technical. One problem was the limitations of normal Greek heavy-armed land fighting, conducted mainly by peasant farmers who could not long be away from their fields or the harvest would be ruined, against other peasant farmers who must defend their fields to prevent a destruction of the crops which might mean near starvation. There was the special case of Sparta, which was free of these limitations because it had helots for its agriculture; the citizens also had time for harder training and for longer warfare. A quite different case was that of Athens, which could if necessary bring all the population behind walls, sacrificing the highly developed fields and farms of Attica. Athens could import all the food needed, because it was powerful at sea and rich enough by silver mines, manufacture and trade and by accumulated capital to pay for the import. Other problems concerned the difficulties and possibilities of war between an all-powerful land force (Sparta and its allies) and an all-powerful navy; many of these were peculiar to the conditions of Greece and the Mediterranean at that time, but some endured to modern times. Thucydides studied the details of siege warfare; the difficulties of the heavy-armed in mountain country or of the Greeks fighting the fierce but unruly barbarians of the north; an army trying to force a landing from ships against troops on shore; the one great night battle, at Syracuse; the skill and the daring maneuvers of the Athenian sailor and the way these were overcome by the Syracusans; the unexpected recovery of the Athenian fleet after the Sicilian disaster. In all these aspects of the war he took a keen professional interest.

This is too the reason why in Thucydides' introductory pages on the early history of Greece he lays so much stress on the development of sea trading and naval power and on the accumulation of capital resources: they help to explain the great war between a land power and a sea power.

**Thucydides' Style.**—Thucydides himself of course was an intellectual of the Athenian kind; markedly individualist as he was, his whole style shows the man brought up in the company of Sophocles and Euripides, with Anaxagoras, Socrates and the contemporary sophists.

Of this style something should be said here, and the analysis given by R. C. Jebb in the article on Thucydides in the 9th edition of *Encyclopædia Britannica* (1888) cannot be bettered. Jebb begins by contrasting the styles of Antiphon (*q.v.*), said, very improbably, to have been Thucydides' master, and of Thucydides himself:

> Antiphon wrote for hearers, Thucydides for readers; the latter, consequently, can use a degree of condensation and a freedom in the arrangement of words which would have been hardly possible for the former. Again, the thought of Thucydides is often more complex than any which Antiphon undertook to interpret; and the greater intricacy of the historian's style exhibits the endeavour to express each thought. Few things in the history of literary prose are more interesting than to watch that vigorous mind in its struggle to mould a language of magnificent but immature capabilities. The obscurity with which Thucydides has sometimes been reproached often arises from the very clearness with which a complex idea is present to his mind, and his strenuous effort to present it in its entirety, . . . He never sacrifices the thought to the language, but he will sometimes sacrifice the language to the thought. A student of Thucydides may always be consoled by the reflexion that he is not engaged in unravelling a mere rhetorical tangle. Every light on the sense will be a light on the words; and when, as is not seldom the case, Thucydides comes victoriously out of this struggle of thought and language, having achieved perfect expression of his meaning in a sufficiently lucid form, then his style rises to an intellectual brilliancy —thoroughly manly, and also penetrated with intense feeling—which nothing in Greek prose literature surpasses.

**Method, Aims and Authority as an Historian.**—In a prefatory note near the beginning of the *History* Thucydides speaks a little of the nature and difficulties of his task and of his aims. It was difficult, he says, to get at the truth both of the speeches made, whether he heard them himself or got the report from others, and of the actions of the war. For the latter, both for those at which he had been present and for the others, he made as thorough an enquiry as he could—for eyewitnesses did not always say the same things, either from faulty memory or from bias. For the speeches, he says, in order to meet the difficulties, he had written out in his own words what was appropriate to the occasion, keeping as closely as possible to the general sense of what had actually been said. He could not do without speeches, for it is through them that he explains the motives and ambitions whether of leading men or of states; and this, the study of the human mind in time of war, is one of his principal aims. (The omission of speeches from the last book is a great loss and is due, no doubt, to the difficulty he had in getting information about Athens at this period.) They are reported in direct speech though in Thucydides' own words, in his own unique style, partly because he must not pretend that they were exact reports, partly because long passages in indirect speech would be scarcely tolerable and no more "authentic." He avoided, he says, all "storytelling" (this is his one criticism of Herodotus), and his work might be the less attractive in consequence; "but I have written not for immediate applause but for posterity, and I shall be content if the future student of these events, or of other similar events which are likely in human nature to occur in after ages, finds my narrative of them useful." This is all that he expressly tells us of his aim and methods. Moreover in the course of his narrative (except for the pestilence of 430 and his command in 424) he nowhere gives his authority for a statement: neither which speeches he had heard nor the other campaigns he had taken part in, nor what places he had visited, nor what persons he consulted. He insisted, as Gilbert Murray said, in doing all the work himself; and he gives us, for the parts he completed, the finished structure, not the plans and the consultations as well, not the "scaffolding."

His authority is hardly equaled by that of any other historian. He kept to a strict chronological scheme, and where it can be accurately tested, *e.g.*, by the eclipses that he mentions, it fits closely. There are also a fair number of contemporary documents recorded on stone which almost all confirm his account in general and in detail. There is the silent testimony of the three historians who began where he left off, not attempting, in spite of much independence of opinion, to revise what he had already done, not even the last book which he clearly did not complete (it is here that occurs the one serious divergence from him in a later writer—Aristotle; *see* below). Another historian, Philistus (*q.v.*), a Syracusan who was in Syracuse as a boy during the Athenian siege, had, it seems, in his *History of Sicily*, little to alter or to add to Thucydides. Above all there are the contemporary political comedies of Aristophanes (the production dates of which are fortunately known). Aristophanes (*q.v.*) was about 15 years younger than Thucydides and a man of as different a temper and writing with as different a purpose as could well be, but his comedy remarkably reinforces the reliability of the historian's serious picture of Athens at war, and as well supplies much to this picture of a kind which Thucydides deliberately did not give. The modern historian of this war is in much the same position as the ancient: he cannot do much more than translate, abridge or enlarge upon Thucydides.

For he kept rigidly to his theme, the history of a war, that is, a story of battles and sieges, and of a truce or a peace and alliance hastily made and soon broken, but also, more important, of the behaviour of peoples as the war lasted longer and longer, and of the inevitable "corrosion of the human spirit." He has vivid narrative of exciting episodes and careful descriptions of tactics on land and sea. He gives a picture, direct in speeches, indirect in the narrative, of the ambitious imperialism of Athens—controlled ambition in Pericles, reckless in Alcibiades, debased in Cleon—ever confident that nothing was impossible for them, resilient after the worst disaster; and the opposing picture of the slow steadiness of Sparta, sometimes so successful, at others so accommodating to the enemy. The speech he records of Pericles on those killed in the first year of the war is the most glowing account of Athens and its democracy as its leading citizen hoped it might prove itself. It is followed (in of course due chronological order) by a minutely accurate account of the symptoms of the pestilence ("so that it may be recognised by medical men if it recurs") and a moving description of the demoralizing despair which took men after so much suffering and such heavy losses—probably more than a quarter of the population, most of it crowded within the walls, died. Equally moving is the account of the last battles in Syracuse harbour, and of the Athenian retreat. In one of his best-known passages he analyzes by a most careful choice of words, almost creating the necessary language as he writes, the effects, moral as well as political, of civil strife within a state in time of war. By a different method, in speeches, he portrays the hard fate of Plataea due to the long-embittered envy and cruelty of Thebes and the faithlessness of Sparta, the harsh brutality of Cleon against Mytilene and the cynicism of the Athenians at Melos 12 years later, when the premises that it is in human nature for the strong to dominate the weak, and that Athens must for its safety control all islands, are used to justify any aggression and a demand for immediate submission, and slaughter if submission is not immediate. Occasionally he is forced into personal comment, as on the pathetic fate of the virtuous and much liked Nicias.

He had the strongest feelings, as a man, as a citizen of Athens whose part was the largest in the tragedy that he recorded, above all in his passion for the truth as he saw it, which not only kept him free from vulgar partiality against the enemy, whether state or party, but served him as a historian in the accurate narrative of events, accurate not only in their detail and their order, but in their relative importance—he does not for example exaggerate the importance of the campaign in which he was himself in command. That is why he offers no self-defense for his failure. (Characteristically he mentions his exile not in its order as an event of the war, but in his "second preface"—after the peace of 421—to explain his opportunities of wider contacts.)

**Subsequent Fame.**—The story of his later fame is a curious one. It has been mentioned above that in the two generations after his death three historians began their work where he had left off; but apart from this silent tribute and late stories, credible enough, of his great influence on the orator Demosthenes (*q.v.*), Thucydides is nowhere referred to in surviving 4th-century literature, not even in Aristotle, who, in his *Constitution of Athens,* gives a narrative of the revolution in Athens in 411 that diverges in many ways from that of Thucydides. It was not till the end of the 4th century that Theophrastus coupled him with Herodotus as a founder of history properly so-called. We know little of what the scholars of Alexandria and Pergamon did for his book; but copies of it were being made in considerable numbers in Egypt, and so doubtless more elsewhere, from the 1st to the 5th centuries A.D. Suffice it to say, that by the 1st century B.C. as is clear from the writings of Cicero and Dionysius (who vainly disputed his preeminence), Thucydides was established as the great historian, and from that time onward his fame has been secure wherever he has been known.

BIBLIOGRAPHY.—*Texts:* "Oxford Classical Series," by H. Stuart Jones and J. E. Powell, 2 vol. (1953–55); "Teubner Series," by C. Hude, editio major (1901), new ed. by O. Luschnat (1954– ); in "Budé Series," by Jacqueline de Romilly, with French trans. (1953– ).

*Commentaries:* That of T. Arnold (3 vol., 4th ed., 1857) is still worth consulting; important for the interpretation of language are J. M. Stahl's ed. (in Latin, 1882–88) and that of J. Classen, rev. by J. Steup (1900–22); for books i–ii only, A. Croiset (1886). *See* also A. W. Gomme's *Historical Commentary* (1945– ).

*English Translations:* That of Thomas Hobbes (1629), is well worth reading. Modern translations include an accurate and vigorous translation by R. Crawley (1876; in Everyman's Library, 1910, and reprinted in *Great Books of the Western World* [1952], vol. 6); and a lively one by Rex Warner (1954).

*Studies and Special Aspects:* R. C. Jebb, *Attic Orators,* vol. i (1876); G. B. Grundy, *Thucydides and the History of His Age* (1911); E. Schwartz, *Das Geschichtswerk des Thukydides* (1919); J. H. Finley, Jr., *Thucydides* (1942), the best case for the view that Thucydides wrote all his *History* after 404 (*see* above); A. W. Gomme, *Essays in Greek History and Literature* (1937) and *Greek Attitude to Poetry and History* (1954); J. de Romilly, *Thucydide et l'impérialisme athénien* (1947) and *Histoire et raison chez Thucydide* (1956).

(A. W. GE.)

**THUCYDIDES** (5th century B.C.), son of Melesias (and usually so called to distinguish him from the historian), Athenian politician, took over the leadership of the opposition to radical democracy on the death of Cimon (450), to whom he was related, perhaps as brother-in-law. He protested against the use on Athenian temples of the large reserve of contributed money accumulated by the Delian League (*q.v.*), and he fought the principle of extending state pay, which was likely to consolidate the power of the masses. His father had been a famous wrestling master and from him Thucydides inherited wide connections outside Athens. Like Cimon before him, he preferred to keep the people in their place and not to sharpen the differences between Sparta and Athens. To achieve his ends he was not scrupulous about means and organized his supporters to sit together in the assembly to make their protests more noisy and effective. His opposition, stubborn and continuous, was ended by his ostracism in 443. After ten years he returned to Athens but was no longer effective. He died soon after 431. *See* also PERICLES.

(R. ME.)

**THUG** (THAG; Sanskrit *sthag,* "to conceal," hence *sthaga,* "a cheat"), a member of a well-organized confederacy of professional assassins who for more than 300 years traveled in gangs through India, wormed themselves into the confidence of wayfarers and, when a favourable opportunity occurred, strangled them by throwing a handkerchief or noose round their necks, and then plundered and buried them. All this was done according to certain ancient and rigidly prescribed forms and after the performance of special religious rites, in which the consecration of the pickax and the sacrifice of sugar formed a prominent part. From their using the noose they were also frequently called *phansigars,* or "noose operators." Though they themselves traced their origin to seven Muslim tribes, Hindus appear to have been associated with them at an early period; at any rate, their religious creed and practices as worshipers of Kali (Devi, Durga), the Hindu goddess of destruction, had certainly no flavour of Islam. The fraternity possessed a jargon of its own (*Ramasi*) and signs by which its members recognized each other.

Though sporadic efforts were made toward the extinction of the gangs, it was not till Lord William Bentinck (governor general of India, 1828–35) took vigorous steps that the system was seriously attacked. His chief agent, Captain (afterward Sir William) Sleeman, with the cooperation of the authorities in a number of princely states, succeeded so well in grappling with the evil that between 1831 and 1837 no fewer than 3,266 thugs had been committed, of whom 412 were hanged, 483 admitted as approvers, and the remainder transported or imprisoned for life.

According to the *Thuggee and Dacoity Report* for 1879, registered Punjabi and Hindustani thugs then still numbered 344; but all of these had already been registered as such before 1852, and the whole fraternity thereafter became extinct.

BIBLIOGRAPHY.—J. L. Sleeman, *Thug, or a Million Murders* (1933); W. H. Sleeman, *Ramaseeana, or a Vocabulary of the Peculiar Language used by the Thugs, with an Introduction and Appendix* (1836) and *Rambles and Recollections of an Indian Official,* rev. ed. by V. A. Smith (1915); P. Meadows Taylor, *Confessions of a Thug,* rev. ed. (1916); R. V. Russell and Hira Lal, *The Tribes and Castes of the Central Provinces of India,* vol. iv (1916).

**THULE,** the Greek and Roman name for the most northerly land in the world. Pytheas (*c.* 300 B.C.) heard of and perhaps even reached it, six days' sail from Britain; it was inhabited, but grain grew there sparingly and ripened ill; the nights were extraordinarily long and/or bright. Nearby was the "sluggish" sea, "neither land, nor sea, nor air" (possibly a North Sea fog). The few surviving fragments of Pytheas' works do not determine where his Thule was. Scholars at various times have believed it to be the Shetlands, Iceland, or some section of the Norwegian coastline (Thule in Greenland is a modern name).

Agricola's fleet, sailing up the east coast of Scotland in A.D. 83 or 84, is said to have seen but not to have reached Thule (*dispecta est Thule*), but the phrase is probably a literary reminiscence by Tacitus. The actual point meant may be the Orkneys or the Shetlands, or even some fragment of Scotland seen across the water. In some later writers (Procopius, etc.) Thule seems sometimes used to denote Scandinavia. Virgil's phrase "ultima Thule" is commonly used to describe the farthest limit possible.

**THULIUM** is a metallic element of the rare-earth group, symbol Tm, atomic number 69, and atomic weight 168.934. There is only one naturally occurring stable isotope, $Tm^{169}$; when it is bombarded by neutrons a radioactive isotope $Tm^{170}$ is formed. This isotope has a half life of 125 days and emits a soft gamma radiation of 0.084 Mev that resembles X radiation. It is useful in small portable X-ray units suitable for photographing bony tissues, for examining thin-walled machine parts, and has been used by archaeologists to examine markings and symbols on ancient metal artifacts. Thulium was discovered by P. T. Cleve (1879), who named the oxide thulia for the Thule (*q.v.*) of the ancient Greeks and Romans, representing a remote goal or end. It is the least abundant of the rare-earth metals and is found in very small concentrations in such minerals as gadolinite, euxenite, xenotime, and samarskite. It also occurs in the products of atomic fission and is produced commercially by ion exchange (*q.v.*).

Although there is evidence that thulium can exist in the divalent state, the only definitely established oxidation state is plus three, both in solid compounds and in solution. Thulium behaves as a typical rare earth, forming a series of pale-green trivalent salts. Solutions on the $Tm^{3+}$ ion are faintly green and exhibit sharp absorption bands in the ultraviolet and visible regions (*see* SPECTROCHEMICAL ANALYSIS). The presence of unpaired electrons makes the ion strongly paramagnetic; its radius is 0.869 Å and the thermal neutron cross section is 118 barns. Thulium metal has been prepared by thermoreduction of the anhydrous fluoride with calcium metal. The metal is readily oxidized by air or by water; melting point is 1545° C; the density of the hexagonal close-packed structure is 9.332 g. per cc. The metal is ferromagnetic below about −263° C. *See* also RARE EARTHS.

*See* N. E. Topp, *The Chemistry of the Rare Earth Elements* (1965).
(LD. B. A.; J. B. PS.)

**THUN,** a town in Bern canton, Switzerland, and capital of the Bernese Oberland, lies on the Aare River, at the point where it issues from the Lake of Thun, and is 17 mi. (27 km.) SSE of Bern by rail. Pop. (1960) 29,034. The Lake of Thun is 11½ mi. (19 km.) long, 2 mi. (3 km.) wide; its area is 18½ sq.mi. (48 sq.km.). Its maximum depth is 712 ft. (217 m.), and its altitude is 1,831 ft. (558 m.). With the Lake of Brienz it occupies the ancient terminal basin of the Aare Glacier.

The town was founded in the 12th century and belonged to the kingdom of Burgundy until 1323 when it fell to the city state of Bern. Part of the medieval town still remains: the Zähringen-Kyburg Castle (tower 1186–91, living quarters 1432; now a museum), the Protestant church (Romanesque—Gothic tower), and the town hall (1585) are the finest buildings of the old part. Noteworthy is the church of Scherzligen (dating from about 1000; on the left bank), with fine frescoes. The town produces cheese, machinery, and pottery. (R. O. H.)

**THUNDERSTORM,** a violent atmospheric disturbance characterized by a large cumulus cloud in which localized centres of electric charge have developed. Lightning, and the accompanying thunder from which the storm derives its name, represent a spark discharge between these centres, or between one of them and the ground. So universal is the development of charge centres in large intense cumulus clouds that the term "thunderhead" is used to describe a large cumulus even though the physical processes which lead to the development of the convective cloud may be only indirectly related to the processes which bring about the lightning and thunder.

Thunderstorms are sometimes referred to as "weather factories" because they are accompanied by a wide variety of weather elements such as hail, showery rain, strong and gusty winds and sudden temperature changes at the earth's surface. The violence of the weather accompanying thunderstorms is indicative of the strong vertical air currents and the complex physical processes operating within them.

Cumulus clouds are manifestations of convective overturning in the atmosphere; *i.e.*, a cumulus cloud represents an air parcel which is rising through its environment because it is warmer and more buoyant than other air parcels at the same levels. In principle, this overturning is similar to that in any thermally unstable fluid. When the atmosphere becomes sufficiently unstable, convective overturning is locally severe enough to cause thunderstorm development.

**Thunderstorm Structure and Circulation.**—The average thunderstorm consists of three to five convective cells, each of which undergoes a life cycle characterized by changes in the direction and magnitude of the strong nearly vertical air currents. Three stages in this life cycle are recognized. In the initial stage, the cell contains strong upward-moving air currents which extend from below the cloud base to the cloud top. The updrafts may reach speeds of seven to ten metres per second. If the air is sufficiently unstable, there will be a continual supply of energy for the updraft and the cell will continue to develop in size and intensity. With increase in size comes an increase in total cloud water content. About 15 to 20 minutes after the establishment of an active updraft, precipitation particles will have grown to a size where they become of importance both in the further development of the cell and in the formation of the charge centres. The precipitation usually will be in the form of snow and snow pellets in the upper parts of the cell (colder than about −5° C.) and raindrops in the lower, warmer regions of the cell. At this time the cell passes into the mature stage of development.

In the mature stage of development, both upward- and downward-moving air currents are present within the cell. The updraft of the cumulus stage gives way to downdraft as the size and number of precipitation particles increase. This reversal of the updraft is also aided by evaporational cooling which occurs as clear air from outside the cloud is mixed into the cloud by the turbulent motions. At first, the downdraft is small and located on one side of the updraft. Gradually, however, it works its way across the cell and squeezes off the updraft, at which time the cell goes into the final or dissipating stage.

It is with cells in the early mature stage that thunderstorms reach their greatest violence. Updraft speeds are usually 10 to 15 m. per second, but may occasionally reach values as high as 35 m. per second. Downdrafts may be as strong as 15 m. per second. At the ground, the onset of heavy rain marks the beginning of the mature stage. The downdraft, which coincides closely with the rain area, reaches the surface a few minutes after the first rain. Because of the continued evaporation, air in the downdraft is cold, which fact accounts for its great downward speed. As the downdraft nears the ground, it is diverted and spreads outward in all directions as a cold gusty wind blowing from the rain area. Even in arid regions where the rain may completely evaporate before reaching the ground, the cold downdraft spreading over the surface is a well-known signal of a nearby thunderstorm.

A thunderstorm cell in the dissipating stage is filled throughout by weak subsiding air and light precipitation. Rain at the earth's surface is much less intense than was the case during the mature stage. The cold outflow gradually subsides as a result of the waning downdraft.

The visual appearance of thunderstorms varies greatly from place to place and with kinds of storms. In arid regions, thunderstorms appear as giant towering cumulus clouds, standing in bold relief against the clear blue sky. Frequently in such regions one can see the uppermost parts of the cloud carried off by high winds to form what is known as an anvil top. In other more humid regions, thunderstorms are frequently surrounded by smaller clouds which obscure the active parts of the storm to a ground observer. From an airplane, however, one can see the thunderstorm thrusting upward above the lower clouds.

The time duration of a thunderstorm is somewhat variable; however, observations show that the first two stages of development usually last about 15 to 20 minutes each. During these stages the visual cloud will frequently reach heights of 30,000 to 60,000 ft. (9,000 to 18,000 m.) and average about 40,000 ft. (12,000 m.), and horizontal dimensions of several miles. The duration of a cell in the final stage varies over wide limits. Some storms end abruptly, whereas others may linger for several hours as a gentle rain from a large, formless cloud mass. These differences result from differing conditions of the air masses in which the clouds form.

**Thunderstorm Electricity.**—Electrical charge centres become well established during the mature stage. Lightning is a crash discharge between an upper positive centre and a lower negative centre or between one of these and the ground. Occasionally one also observes a lightning flash from one of the centres into the clear air around or above the cloud. The first electrical discharges usually take place entirely within the cloud between the two main charge centres. These discharges will be rather small at first and will increase in magnitude as the storm continues to develop. Each lightning flash usually consists of several strokes in rapid sequence with time separations of a few hundredths of a second. Each stroke follows the ionized path of the preceding one.

The sound of thunder originates in a compression wave formed along the highly heated path of the lightning stroke. Each portion of the path of a lightning stroke sends out intense sound waves which travel different paths to the observer. Since sound travels at the rate of approximately 330 m. per second, and since the strokes may be several kilometres in length, the thunder is usually heard as a drawn-out rumbling, having character and time duration depending upon the length and shape of the flash and upon its distance from the observer. For detailed discussion of thunderstorm electrification *see* LIGHTNING, especially *Propagation of Lightning* and *Effects of Lightning: Thunder.*

**Thunderstorm Formation.**—A deep layer of moist air and a vertical temperature distribution favourable for the development of intense local overturning are essential for thunderstorm development. One of the tools used by meteorologists to determine the possibilities for thunderstorms is a plot of air temperature as a function of height above the earth's surface. The rate of decrease of temperature with height is known as the lapse rate. In general, steep lapse rates (rapid decrease of temperature with height) are most favourable for thunderstorms since it is under these conditions that an air parcel made warmer than its environment is capable of rising through the atmosphere because of buoyancy forces. After any given parcel of air is lifted to the point of condensation at the cloud base, the released latent heat of condensation will be added to the parcel. This will assist further ascent. In the upper parts of the thundercloud, where snow and ice crystals are found, the latent heat of fusion will also contribute to sustaining the updraft currents.

Thunderstorms can be classified according to factors that contribute to the development of steep lapse rate with resultant convection. Five important classes are given:

1. Heating of air by contact with warm surfaces. (*a*) When the surface of the ground is warmed by radiation from the sun, water vapour may be carried up by convection currents to a level at which condensation occurs. With favourable lapse rates of temperature in the air above this level, thunderstorms may develop. A special case of this class is the heating of mountain slopes at high levels, which frequently contributes to the development of thunderstorms near the summits. (*b*) When air flows over warmer ground or warmer water, the air may become warmed sufficiently from below for convection and possibly thunderstorms to occur.

2. Lifting of warm air over cold currents. If a current of cold air meets a current of warm air, the warmer air, being lighter, is forced upward either by cold air underrunning warm air or by warm air overrunning cold air. Clouds form in the rising warm air, and if conditions are favourable, tower upward to form thunderstorms.

3. Converging air flow within warm air currents. A converging flow may force warm air up to its condensation level, releasing convection.

4. Interaction of cold and warm air currents at different levels. The underrunning of cold air by warm air may initiate convection. Similarly, overrunning of warm air by colder air as well as combinations of these factors may be effective in releasing convective overturning and thunderstorms.

5. Lifting of air by movement upslope from lower to higher ground. Movement of air against a mountain range or other upslope surface may lift air to its condensation level and initiate convection.

**The Distribution of Thunderstorms.**—A substantial fraction of the thunderstorms over the world form because of surface heating by sun's radiation (class 1*a*) often combined with special convergence effects (class 3). Summer thunderstorms over humid continents and over mountain regions in the temperate latitudes and the almost daily storms of large regions of the tropics are of this type. These storms show a well-marked diurnal variation; they develop generally during the afternoon. Storms of class 1*b* are characteristic of the rear of barometric depressions occurring over the sea in winter especially off the east coasts of large continents where cold air may pass over comparatively warm water.

The "frontal" storms of class 2 are found in middle latitudes. They are associated with line squalls (squall lines) and "warm front" precipitation in extratropical cyclones.

Storms of classes 3 and 4 frequently occur in advance of "cold fronts" or troughs of low pressure in the temperate zone and tend to occur more frequently at night than during the day.

Storms of class 5 occur especially on windward mountain slopes in middle latitudes.

Thunderstorms have been known to occur in almost every part of the world; however, they are rare in the polar regions and infrequent poleward of latitude 50° N. and 50° S. According to a study by C. E. P. Brooks, the places of maximum thunderstorm activity in the world are Java (225 days per year), central Africa (150), Panama (135), southern Mexico (142) and central Brazil (106). In the United States the areas of maximum activity are the Florida peninsula and the coast of the Gulf of Mexico (70–80) and the mountains of New Mexico (50–60). Central Europe and Asia average less than 20 thunderstorm days per year. Brooks estimated that at any one moment there are about 1,800 thunderstorms in progress throughout the world.

**Thunderstorms and Severe Weather.**—Thunderstorms are associated with many kinds of severe weather phenomenon. Squall lines are lines of thunderstorms which sweep across the surface as a single unit. Usually associated with advancing cold fronts, squall lines are well known for their regions of high wind, heavy rain and hail. Tornadoes are another type of severe weather associated with thunderstorms although the exact details of this association are not known.

Thunderstorms also play a key role in tropical hurricanes. It is well known that hurricanes, when viewed by radar, are characterized by lines of convective storms which spiral inward toward the eye of the hurricane. It is likely that the thunderstorm plays a major role in the vertical circulation of the hurricane.

Because of the turbulence which accompanies the updrafts and downdrafts, thunderstorms are regarded as hazards to airplane flight. Pilots are unanimous in their opinion that light planes should not be flown into thunderstorms. Military and commercial planes are sufficiently sturdy and well enough instrumented to permit a flight through a thunderstorm with little more danger than passenger discomfort.

*See* also LIGHTNING; SQUALL AND SQUALL LINE; TROPICAL STORM; TYPHOON; and references under "Thunderstorm" in the Index.

BIBLIOGRAPHY.—H. R. Byers, *General Meteorology,* 3rd ed. (1959); H. R. Byers and R. R. Braham, *The Thunderstorm* (1949); W. J. Humphreys, *Physics of the Air* (1964); J. C. Johnson, *Physical Meteorology* (1954); B. F. J. Schonland, *Atmospheric Electricity,* 2nd ed.

(1953), *Flight of Thunderbolts,* 2nd rev. ed. (1964); K. B. McEachron, "Lightning to the Empire State Building," *J. Franklin Inst.,* vol. 227, p. 149 (Feb. 1939); C. E. P. Brooks in *Geophys. Mem. Lond.,* vol. 24 (1925); Sir George Simpson, "The Electricity of Clouds and Rain," *Quart. J. R. Met. Soc.,* pp. 1–34 (Jan. 1942); E. J. Workman, R. E. Holzer, and G. T. Pelsor, *The Electrical Structure of Thunderstorms,* Technical Notes, National Advisory Committee for Aeronautics (Nov. 1942). (R. R. BM.)

**THÜNEN, JOHANN HEINRICH VON** (1783–1850), German agriculturalist, best known for a pioneering work on the effect of transportation costs on the location of production, was born in Jever on July 24, 1783. Vol. 1 of his *Der isolierte Staat,* containing the important theoretical contribution, appeared in 1826, and later volumes presented Thünen's own agricultural accounts in support of his theory. Thünen imagined an isolated city, set in the middle of a level and uniformly fertile plain without navigable waterways and bounded by a wilderness. His analysis showed how agricultural products would be grown in zones forming concentric rings around the city. Heavy products, in proportion to value, and perishables would be produced close to the town; lighter and durable goods would be produced on the periphery. As transport costs to the city increased with distance, the returns to the land would diminish. At a certain distance from the city, land rent would become zero. The exact distance would be a function of price relationships. Moreover, if land rents vary, then the methods of cultivation will vary, with land being used less intensively as it becomes less valuable. Subsequent writers often built upon Thünen's model, although his simplifying assumptions eliminated many of the most critical problems. Thünen died in Tellow, Sept. 22, 1850. (J. P. CA.)

**THUN-HOHENSTEIN,** the name of a German noble family, recorded in the southern Tirol as early as A.D. 1145 but associated with Bohemia from 1627.

FRIEDRICH, GRAF VON THUN-HOHENSTEIN (1810–1881), was born at Tetschen (Decin) on May 8, 1810. A member of the Austrian diplomatic service, he was sent in 1850 to preside over the revived German federal diet at Frankfurt, chiefly with the aim of resisting Prussia. Having been minister to Prussia (1852–54) and to Russia (1859–63), he left the diplomatic service and concerned himself with Bohemian and Austrian internal politics, following his brother's example. He died at Tetschen on Sept. 24, 1881.

LEO, GRAF VON THUN-HOHENSTEIN (1811–1888), was born at Tetschen on April 7, 1811, a younger brother of Friedrich. Influenced by the Romantic movement and by the Catholic revival and sympathetic to the aspirations of the Czechs as expounded by Frantisek Palacky, he wanted to see a resurrection of the "historic nations" of the Habsburg state, namely the Hungarians, the Poles and the Bohemians, so that they could play a greater part in affairs beside the Germans (*see* AUSTRIA, EMPIRE OF, for the background of his career; also BOHEMIA). In the revolutionary year 1848 he was appointed governor of Bohemia in April but fell into the insurgents' hands and had to give up his post when order was restored (July). From 1849 to 1860, however, he was Austrian minister for religious affairs and education. He established that instruction in the primary schools should be in the regional language, though German remained the language for higher instruction; he summoned capable German scholars, Protestant as well as Catholic, to improve the standard of teaching; and he encouraged the formation of learned societies. The concordat of 1855 between Austria and the papacy was however regarded by liberals as detracting from his achievement in the educational field, though in practice it did not lead to so much clerical interference with teaching as had been foreseen. Out of office from 1861, Leo von Thun opposed the "February patent" of that year and stood as a leader of the "Feudal" party of Bohemian noblemen supporting the movement for a federal organization of the Habsburg dominions. He accordingly opposed the Austro-Hungarian "Compromise" of 1867 because it was to the disadvantage of the Slavs; and he played a part in the abortive negotiations of 1871 between Vienna and the Czechs. He died in Vienna on Dec. 17, 1888.

FRANZ ANTON, GRAF and, from 1911, PRINCE VON THUN-HOHENSTEIN (1847–1916), was Friedrich's son, born at Tetschen on Sept. 2, 1847. Adhering to his uncle's views, he was made governor of Bohemia in 1889. The Young Czechs agitated against the settlement of 1890 (agreeable to Thun's conservatism) between the Old Czech party and Vienna, and he suppressed disorders firmly, but he resigned in 1895. He became prime minister of Austria in March 1898 but fell from power in October 1899 when the Germans objected to his policy on the language question. Governor of Bohemia again from 1911 to 1915, he died at Tetschen on Nov. 1, 1916.

**THURBER, JAMES GROVER** (1894–1961), writer and artist, considered by many the best American humourist since Mark Twain, was born in Columbus, O., Dec. 8, 1894, and educated at its public schools and at Ohio State university, Columbus. He was a newspaper reporter in Columbus, in Paris, France, and in New York city before becoming associated with the *New Yorker* as a staff member (1927–33) and a leading contributor.

(LEFT) JAMES THURBER, PHOTOGRAPHED IN 1959; (ABOVE) HIS CARTOON "ALL RIGHT, HAVE IT YOUR WAY —YOU HEARD A SEAL BARK"

(LEFT) HENRI-CARTIER-BRESSON—MAGNUM; (ABOVE) COPR. © 1932, 1960 JAMES THURBER. FROM "THE SEAL IN THE BEDROOM" PUBLISHED BY HARPER AND ROW

Seriously a writer and only incidentally a comic artist, Thurber produced both writings and drawings showing odd characters in astonishing situations, amusing aspects of the war between men and women, startling forays into the subconscious and fascinating dogs and other animals, real and imaginary.

His writings reveal a sensitive literary style and skill in many forms. *My Life and Hard Times* (1933) is a hilarious autobiography. "The Secret Life of Walter Mitty," his best-known short story, presents an unforgettable character in the meek, henpecked husband who in his daydreams is a fabulous hero. Thurber's fables blend delightful nonsense with much wisdom about humanity. A play, *The Male Animal* (1940), written with Elliott Nugent, is an effective plea for academic freedom as well as a gay comedy. While a keen satirical sense is shown in many essays, parodies and burlesques, a gentle humour pervades such fairy tales as *The 13 Clocks* (1950). *The Thurber Album* (1952) is an affectionate account of family and friends in the midwest, and *The Years With Ross* (1959) is a witty record of associates on the *New Yorker.* The best collection of the writings and drawings is *The Thurber Carnival* (1945). Thurber died in New York city on Nov. 2, 1961. (WM. B.)

**THURET, GUSTAVE ADOLPHE** (1817–1875), French botanist, noted for his work on the reproduction of algae, was born at Paris on May 23, 1817. After receiving a law degree in 1838, he studied under algologist Joseph Decaisne. He traveled to Constantinople in 1840 as French attaché, and after returning to France, being a man of independent means, devoted himself entirely to science. Thuret's first paper (1840) detailed the discovery of flagella of spermatozoids in the green algae *Chara.* In 1844 Decaisne and Thuret announced the finding of spermatozoids in the brown algae *Fucus.* The first accounts of fertilization and hybridization in *Fucus* were given by Thuret (1854), and later (1867), jointly with Edouard Bornet, he determined the complicated life cycle of Florideae, a group of red algae. His *Études phycologiques,* a folio volume containing observations on and illustrations of marine algae, was published posthumously in 1878. Before 1857, Thuret spent much of his time studying algae on the

Atlantic coast of France. In 1857 he moved to Antibes on the Riviera, where he established an outstanding botanic garden. Thuret died at Nice on May 20, 1875.

BIBLIOGRAPHY.—Accounts of Thuret in *Ann. Sci. Nat., Bot.*, series vi, vol. ii, pp. 308–360, listing publications (1875); in *Jour. of Bot.*, vol. xiv, pp. 4–9 (1876); and in A. Davy de Virville, *Histoire de la botanique en France* (1954). (J. W. TT.)

**THURGAU** (THURGOVIE), a canton of northeast Switzerland (area 389 sq.mi. [1,007 sq.km.]), bordered by the Lake of Constance and, for a short distance, by the Rhine below the lake. It is connected with Schaffhausen and Zürich to the west and Sankt Gallen (St. Gall) to the south. Thurgau is divided into three hill masses: one stretching along the lake; another, inland, bounded on the north by the wide curve of the Thur River and on the south by its affluent the Murg; and the third at the southern extremity of the canton, merging into the pre-alpine zone of Mt. Hörnli.

In prehistoric times Thurgau's inhabitants included lake dwellers; later, for several hundred years up to A.D. 450, it was part of the Roman province of Raetia. An important Roman settlement was Arbor Felix (Arbon). It then passed into barbarian possession. From the 8th century it appeared as a political unit, extending as far west as the Reuss River and as far south as the foot of the Alps. In the later Middle Ages the county of Thurgau, already reduced in size, belonged to the counts of Kyburg, who became extinct in 1264, the county passing from the last count, Hartmann, to his nephew Rudolf I of Habsburg (German king from 1273). In 1460 it was seized by the confederated Swiss states and thenceforth ruled as a subject district. In 1798 it became a canton of the Helvetic Republic and in 1803 a full member of the Swiss Confederation. Its very advanced cantonal constitution dates from 1869.

The population (1960) was 166,420, mostly German-speaking, though small minorities spoke Italian and French; about two-thirds were Protestant and about one-third Roman Catholic. The capital is Frauenfeld (*q.v.;* pop. 14,702) on the Murg River; other centres are Kreuzlingen (12,597), Arbon (11,608), and Romanshorn (7,755).

Thurgau is a prosperous agricultural area famed for its apples and pears and for cider making. Vines are grown in the area bordered by the lake and in the Thur Valley. Industries include the manufacture of textiles, shoes, and motor vehicles; food preserving, printing, and handicrafts. The canton is traversed by the railway from Winterthur (Zürich) to Romanshorn, with branches to Constance, the Toggenburg Valley, and Sankt Gallen; another important line extends from Rorschach (Sankt Gallen) along the lake shore via Constance to Schaffhausen. Main roads follow these lines and there is a dense network of secondary roads. (BR. M.)

**THURII** (THURIA, THURIUM), an ancient Greek city in Italy on the Gulf of Tarentum. It originated from an attempt by exiles from Sybaris (*q.v.*) and their descendants to resettle the site with Athenian assistance, after their first attempt (452 B.C.) had failed because of attack from Crotona. The original Sybarites were soon expelled (they founded a fourth Sybaris well away to the south). It was probably after this expulsion that the Athenians Lampon and Xenocritus led out a new body of colonists from all Greece (444/443). The city, renamed after a nearby spring, Thuria, was laid out on a rectangular plan by the architect Hippodamus of Miletus; the laws were said to be the work of Protagoras (*q.v.*).

Thurii flourished, but a severe defeat by the Lucanians (390/389) was the beginning of persistent danger, obliging the Thurians to appeal to Rome for help and accept a Roman garrison in 282. In the Second Punic War the Thurians joined Hannibal, who later removed them to Crotona (204). In 193 a Latin colony was founded at Thurii, known for a time as Copia, but afterward as Thurii.

Geophysical prospecting from 1960 onward, followed up by trial drilling and some excavation, located Roman and Greek remains just north of the Crati River about 1¼ mi. inland; these have been tentatively identified with Copia and Thurii (previously thought to lie farther inland).

**THURINGIA** (THÜRINGEN), a historic region of Germany, extending eastward from the Werra River (a headstream of the Weser) into the country beyond the Saale as far as the Pleisse and northward from the mountains of the Thüringer Wald (Thuringian Forest) and the Frankenwald to the foothills of the Harz Mountains. Eisenach, Gotha, Erfurt, Weimar, Apolda, Jena, Gera, and Altenburg are towns on the west-east axis; Meiningen and Suhl stand in the southwest, Sondershausen and Nordhausen in the north.

**History.**—The Thuringians, a Germanic tribe first recorded in the second half of the 4th century A.D., were subjected by Attila the Hun in the second quarter of the 5th; but by A.D. 500 they had freed themselves and had established a great kingdom extending from the Harz Mountains to the Danube. In 531, however, their king Irminfrid (Irmfried or Herminfrid) was defeated in battle at Burgscheidungen on the Unstrut River by the Frankish kings Theuderic I and Clotaire I and put to death. Reduced territorially to the area between the Harz Mountains and the Thuringian Forest, the former kingdom was then governed by Frankish dukes, who acquired a growing degree of independence. To reassert the Frankish king's authority, Charles Martel (*q.v.*) abolished the office of duke and divided the province among Frankish counts, while the conversion of the Thuringians to Christianity was undertaken by St. Boniface (*q.v.*) in the early 720s. In 804 Charlemagne (*q.v.*) founded the Thuringian Mark (march or frontier zone) under ducal authority in order to protect the line of the Saale against the Slavs. But after Duke Thakulf (849–873) the defense of the Mark weakened; and after the death of Duke Burkhard in 908, Thuringia was seized by the Saxon duke Otto (*see* SAXONY). Otto's son and successor (from 912) was elected German king, as Henry I, in 919. He crushed a Magyar invasion of Thuringia at Riade in 933 and consolidated his defenses by forts (*Burgwarde*).

*The Ludowings.*—The direct line of German kings of the Saxon dynasty died out in 1024. Their territorial influence in Thuringia was replaced, from *c.* 1039, by that of Louis the Bearded (d. 1055 or 1080?), a member of the Ludowing family. His grandson was in 1130 appointed landgrave of Thuringia, as Louis I, by the German king Lothair III. Louis II (d. 1172), landgrave from 1140, married Judith (Jutta), stepsister of the future emperor Frederick I, in 1150; and later he supported Frederick in his conflict with Henry the Lion, duke of Saxony. Louis III (d. 1190), landgrave from 1172, was in 1179 appointed count palatine of Saxony as a reward for his fidelity to Frederick. On the other hand his brother and successor, Hermann I (d. 1217), sold his support to both parties during the war between the rival German kings Philip of Swabia and Otto IV. Hermann's son Louis IV (d. 1227) was the husband of St. Elizabeth of Hungary. Louis IV's son and heir, the young Hermann II, was kept in tutelage by his uncle Henry Raspe till his death in 1241, whereupon Henry Raspe became landgrave. Henry Raspe was elected German king in opposition to Conrad IV in 1246 but died in 1247 (*see* HENRY, German kings).

*The First Wettins.*—There followed a long dispute over the Ludowing succession. The two principal claimants were: Henry III the Illustrious, margrave of Meissen, of the House of Wettin (*q.v.*), son of the landgrave Hermann I's daughter Jutta; and Henry the Child, of the House of Brabant, son of Hermann II's sister Sophia. After war lasting from 1256 to 1263, Henry the Illustrious obtained the landgraviate of Thuringia in 1264, while Henry the Child obtained Hesse (*q.v.*). In 1265 Henry the Illustrious granted Thuringia to his son Albert, who sold it in 1293 to the German king Adolf of Nassau for 12,000 marks; but Albert's sons, Frederick the Dauntless (d. 1323) and Dietzmann (d. 1307), opposed this bargain, and Frederick was invested with Thuringia by the future emperor Henry VII in 1310. Frederick II (d. 1349), Frederick III (d. 1381), Balthasar (d. 1406), and Frederick IV extended their Thuringian possessions; but whereas the former two were margraves of Meissen as well as landgraves of Thuringia, the latter two (brother and nephew of Frederick III) were not margraves of Meissen, which passed to Frederick III's son, later elector of Saxony as Frederick I (from 1423). Frederick IV of Thuringia, however, died childless in 1440, and his inheritance then reverted to Electoral Saxony.

*Thuringia Divided.*—The elector Frederick II of Saxony had to grant the landgraviate to his brother William in 1445. After William's death (1482) Ernest and Albert of Saxony in 1485 made a new partition of the Wettin inheritance: most of Thuringia went to Ernest, though Albert received a long strip of land in the north. For details of this partition and for the important modifications of it in the 16th century, *see* SAXONY.

The Ernestine Wettins remained in possession of the major part of Thuringia: for their multiple subdivisions of it, *see* SAXON DUCHIES, ERNESTINE. There were still, however, a number of smaller Thuringian territories independent of the Wettins: when the succession to the countship of Henneberg, in the southwest, fell open in 1583, the Wettins obtained the greater part of it, but had to let Schmalkalden go to Hesse-Kassel; the bishopric of Erfurt (*q.v.*), long the subject of competition between the Wettins and the archbishopric of Mainz, finally passed to Prussia in 1803; and both Reuss and Schwarzburg (*qq.v.*) survived all attempts at absorption by the Wettins.

Prussia obtained Albertine Thuringia from Saxony at the Congress of Vienna (1814–15) and Hessian Thuringia after the Seven Weeks' War (1866). At the German Revolution of 1918 the four Ernestine dukes, the two Reuss princes, and the Schwarzburg prince abdicated, and their territories became free states. In 1920 these territories (except Coburg, which opted for union with Bavaria) were merged in a new Thuringia, a *Land* of republican Germany, with Weimar as its capital. The frontiers remained anomalous: Erfurt was still attached to the Prussian province of Saxony; there were enclaves belonging to Prussian Saxony or to Prussian Hesse-Nassau surrounded by Thuringian territory; and conversely parts of Thuringia were enclaved within Prussian Saxony.

After World War II all Thuringia fell to the Soviet-occupied zone of Germany. Thanks to the destruction of Prussia, an enlarged *Land* Thuringia was constituted within the German Democratic Republic, with rationalized frontiers, including the southwest of the former province of Saxony and all the former enclaves; the capital was Erfurt. In 1952, however, when the East German *Länder* were dissolved, Thuringia was divided between the *Bezirke* (districts) of Erfurt, Suhl, Gera, and Leipzig.

*See* F. Schneider and A. Tille, ***Einführung in die thüringische Geschichte*** (1931). (C. C. BA.)

**THURLES** (DURLAS ÉILE), a town of County Tipperary, Republic of Ireland, lies on both banks of the Suir River, 40 mi. (64 km.) E of Limerick by road. Pop. (1961) 6,421. It is the seat of the Roman Catholic archbishopric of Cashel and Emly. The town is the marketing and distributing centre for a large agricultural area and has a beet-sugar factory. It is also a well-known sporting centre, with horse racing, hunting, golf, hurling, football, and trout fishing. The Gaelic Athletic Association was founded there in 1854.

Originally called Durlas O'Fogarty, Thurles was the scene in 1174 of the defeat of Strongbow (the 2nd earl of Pembroke) by Roderick O'Connor and Donal O'Brien. The Knights Templars held a 13th-century castle there and founded a preceptory. There was a Carmelite priory from 1300 until it was suppressed in 1540 and granted to James Butler, earl of Ormonde. The cathedral (1857–75) was built in Romanesque style on the site of the old Carmelite priory. Bridge Castle and Black Castle, two rectangular keeps, are all that remain of the Butler family's castles. Thurles' chief glory is the Abbey of the Holy Cross (about 3½ mi. SW), founded by Donal O'Brien for Benedictines or monks of the Columban Order and transferred to the Cistercians about 1182. A relic of the True Cross (now in the Ursuline convent at Blackrock, Cork) was enshrined in the abbey from the early 12th century until its suppression in 1536. The abbey was much restored and its ruins are well preserved.

**THURLOE, JOHN** (1616–1668), English politician, head of the government intelligence service during the Commonwealth, was the son of Thomas Thurloe, rector of Abbess Roding in Essex. After studying law he entered the service of the lawyer Oliver St. John, through whose influence he was appointed a secretary to the parliamentary commissioners at Uxbridge in 1645. On March 29, 1652, he was appointed secretary to Oliver Cromwell's council of state. In Cromwell's administration he controlled the intelligence department at home and abroad; he perfected a system of collecting information and of discovering the plans of Cromwell's enemies that averted any danger of the government's being overthrown. He represented Ely, in Cambridgeshire, in the Parliaments of 1654 and 1656, and in July 1657 was appointed a member of Cromwell's second council. Thurloe supported the succession of Richard Cromwell (September 1658) and was member for Cambridge University in the Parliament of January 1659 where he was the government's chief spokesman. Deprived of his offices on the recall of the Rump Parliament (May 1659), he was reappointed secretary of state on Feb. 27, 1660. He opposed the restoration of Charles II and was arrested for high treason on May 15, 1660. Released on June 29, subject to attending the secretaries of state "for the service of the state whenever they should require," he subsequently wrote several papers on foreign policy for the earl of Clarendon. Thurloe died in London on Feb. 21, 1668. A collection of his state papers, one of the chief sources of information for the period, was published in seven volumes in 1742.

**THURLOW, EDWARD THURLOW,** 1ST BARON (1731–1806), was twice lord chancellor of England (1778–83; 1783–92). Though his tenure was a long one, he is remembered more for his oratory, his caustic wit, and his bad temper than for his legal acumen. Thurlow was born at Bracon Ash, Norfolk, on Dec. 9, 1731, the first son of an Anglican clergyman of modest economic circumstances and no connections. After going down from Cambridge without a degree because of indolence and insubordination, traits he retained throughout his life, he was admitted to the Inner Temple in 1752 and called to the bar in 1754. His signal triumph over Fletcher Norton, in a case tried before Lord Mansfield in 1758, marked the turning point of his career. He precociously became king's counsel in 1762. An impromptu argument in Nando's coffeehouse—whose barmaid was to become mother of his three daughters though not his wife—caused him to be retained in his greatest success as counsel in the case involving the heirship to the great Douglas estates. In 1765 he entered Commons as a member for Tamworth. There, his strong opposition to the notorious John Wilkes (*q.v.*) was followed by his appointment as solicitor general in 1770. His speeches against jury trial in libel cases and his prosecution of the publishers and printers of the "Junius" (*q.v.*) letters brought him the attorney general's post in 1771. His oratorical capacities, well displayed in venomous attacks on Lord Clive and the American colonies and his defense of the slave trade, caused his party to elevate him to the peerage and the lord chancellorship. He ruled in the House of Lords with an iron hand. A Tory by declaration, his sole guiding principle was expediency, which generally led him to support the will of King George III, a course that permitted him to retain his high post in such disparate ministries as those of North, Rockingham, Shelburne, and Pitt. He died on Sept. 12, 1806, at Brighton.

Thurlow had few friends and many enemies, the latter including the greatest politicians of his time: the younger Pitt, Charles James Fox, and Edmund Burke. In law, his greatest claim on posterity derives from his sponsorship of John Scott, later Lord Eldon. Perhaps equally important were his kindnesses to the poet George Crabbe and to Samuel Johnson. His portraits, painted by Reynolds, Romney, and Lawrence, among others, reveal a swarthy complexion, harsh but regular features, sparkling dark eyes, and a severe demeanor. But not even these masters could portray the voice which was his outstanding feature and the cornerstone of his career.

BIBLIOGRAPHY.—There is a bibliography in the only full-length biography, Robert Gore-Browne, *Chancellor Thurlow* (1953); *see* also Campbell, *Lives of the Lord Chancellors,* vol. vii (1846); H. P. Brougham, *Statesmen in the Time of George III,* 6 vol. (1845).
(P. B. K.)

**THURROCK,** an urban district (1936) in the Thurrock parliamentary division of Essex, Eng., lying along the north bank of the Thames. This area, mainly agricultural, was largely reclaimed from the marshes by Dutch workers, who also used chalk from the Purfleet quarries in the embankment of the Thames in the 17th century. Area 63.4 sq.mi. (1,642 sq.km.). Pop. (1961) 114,263.

Grays, 23 mi. (37 km.)E of Charing Cross, London, by road, is the administrative centre. Originally a fishing village, it became a large river port for the hay and corn market and was further enlarged when the Tilbury docks (2½ mi. SE) were built. In 1906 an artificial beach of fine sand was made there.

Tilbury (*q.v.*) docks were constructed in 1884–86 on land that had been, until 1852, uninhabited marsh. They were built by the East and West India Dock Company and are now owned by the Port of London Authority. The original blockhouse at Tilbury, which was built by Henry VIII, was rebuilt in the 17th century. It was taken over by the ministry of works in 1949 and opened to the public in 1958. The fort has a gateway by Inigo Jones. It was at West Tilbury that Elizabeth I made her famous speech to her troops in 1588 at the time of the Spanish Armada. East Tilbury is built on the site of a 7th-century monastery, and the church, like many others in the district, dates from the 13th century.

At Mucking (Anglo-Saxon, "much pasture") is St. Clere's Hall (formerly New Jenkins), dating from Elizabethan times; Ford Place, at Stifford, rebuilt in 1655, has beautiful plaster ceilings. In 1381 Jack Straw, the revolutionary priest of Fobbing, led the peasants in revolt against the poll tax, and in the marshes nearby the last great prizefight with bare knuckles is said to have taken place. Orsett was once the seat of the bishops of London. Aveley is a residential area on rising ground and near the village is the mansion of Belhus in what is now a public park.

Thurrock's industries stretch along the 20 mi. of Thames-side. There are a paperboard mill, soap and margarine works at Purfleet; several cement works; timber yards at Grays; a shipbreaking yard; Tilbury docks with a passenger landing stage; a large shoe factory with its own technical college (1948) at East Tilbury; and, at the eastern end of the district, the Shell Haven oil refinery at Thames Haven and a refinery at Coryton for storing, blending, and refining oil. The West Thurrock industrial estate along the river bank covers over 4 sq.mi. and special facilities and concessions are granted to occupiers.

**THURSO,** the most northerly town on the mainland of Scotland. A small burgh and seaport of Caithness, it lies at the mouth of the Thurso River on Thurso Bay, 20 mi. WSW of John o'Groats by road. Pop. (1961) 8,037. In Sir John Square there is a statue of Sir John Sinclair (1754–1835), who did much for the improvement of Scottish agriculture. The town hall contains a public library and a museum with the collections of the "Thurso baker" and self-taught geologist and botanist, Robert Dick (1811–66). There is an atomic power station (begun 1954) at Dounreay, 8 mi. W of Thurso, and nuclear submarine training and research establishments are in the vicinity. The population increase (4,789) of Thurso between 1951 and 1961 is mainly accounted for by this. Thurso is one of only two small burghs that is a planning authority, and in the early 1960s it was being replanned.

Thurso was the centre of Norse power on the mainland when it was at its height in the early 11th century and afterward till the defeat of the Norwegians at the Battle of Largs (1263). In 1330 the weights and measures of Thurso were adopted for all Scotland. It was made a free burgh of barony by Charles I in 1633. To the east is Thurso Castle, and near it is Harold's Tower, built over the grave of Earl Harold, once owner of half of Caithness and half of the Orkneys and Shetlands, who fell in battle with Earl Harold the Wicked at the end of the 12th century. About ¾ mi. W stand the ruins of the palace of the bishop of Caithness, destroyed by fire in 1222.

**THURSTAN** (d. 1140), Norman archbishop of York, a native of Bayeux, rose rapidly in the service of William II and of Henry I, by whom he was appointed archbishop (1114). But Ralph, archbishop of Canterbury, refused to consecrate him without a profession of obedience. This Thurstan would not give, and with papal support he defied king and archbishop at the Salisbury Council (1116). After three years of deadlock he was consecrated by Pope Calixtus II at Reims (October 1119). He was reconciled with Henry I in 1120, partly through the help of Henry's sister Adela of Blois. Thurstan's return to York (1121) was a triumph and for the next 19 years he proved himself an outstandingly energetic and inspiring archbishop, developing the parochial system, extending generous patronage toward the religious orders, especially the Austin canons and the Cistercians, and enlarging the endowments of the minster churches at York, Southwell, Beverley, and Ripon. He continued to be involved in disputes with Canterbury, and even more with the Scottish bishops, especially with John, bishop of Glasgow. Yet for the good of religion in 1127 he agreed to consecrate Robert, bishop of St. Andrews, without any profession of obedience. In 1138 he inspired the mainly Yorkshire army which defeated the Scots at the Battle of the Standard. In January 1140 he entered the Cluniac order at Pontefract, where he died on Feb. 6, 1140.

*See* D. Nicholl, *Thurstan, Archbishop of York* (1964).
(G. W. S. B.)

**THURSTONE, LOUIS LEON** (1887–1955), U.S. psychologist, contributed the method of multiple-factor analysis in the application of statistical methods to psychological problems. He was born in Chicago, Ill., May 29, 1887. After taking an engineering degree from Cornell University, Ithaca, N.Y., he served as assistant to Thomas Edison and taught engineering at the University of Minnesota, Minneapolis. An interest in the mathematical relations between amount of practice and improvement in performance led him to the University of Chicago, where he received a Ph.D. in psychology and where he remained for most of his professional life thereafter. Thurstone died in Chapel Hill, N.C., Sept. 29, 1955.

Most notable among Thurstone's accomplishments were improved methods of measuring intelligence and his development of multiple-factor analysis. The latter is widely used in research on the nature of human ability and for the practical purpose of constructing tests to measure different types of ability. His literary output was comparatively small, including a score or two of research papers and a few books and monographs, but these were so influential that he was one of the United States' most frequently quoted psychologists. Thurstone's major books are *Vectors of the Mind* (1935) and *Multiple-Factor Analysis* (1947).

*See* also INTELLIGENCE: *Relation of Intelligence to More Specialized Abilities.*

*See* D. A. Wood, *Louis Leon Thurstone* (1962). (DL. W.)

**THUTMOSE** (THOTHMES; Greek TUTHMOSIS), the name of four pharaohs of ancient Egypt during the first half of the 18th dynasty (16th and 15th centuries B.C.). The name means "Born of (the god) Thoth."

THUTMOSE I (Aakheperkare; 1525–1512 B.C.) was the son of a commoner and appears to have acquired the throne through marriage with a royal princess, Ahmose. Early in his vigorous reign he led his armies northward to the Euphrates in a campaign of unprecedented success and set up a monument on the riverbank at the point of his farthest advance. On his return march he hunted elephant in the Syrian plain. In the south, he pushed the frontier of Egypt upstream to the Dongola reach of the Nile and reopened the ancient trading post at Kerma near the Third Cataract. His architect Ineni was in charge of the erection of a courtyard and a columned hall with a cedar roof in the temple at Karnak (*see* THEBES). In front of the latter he erected two granite obelisks. Ineni also supervised the construction of the king's tomb, the first to be hewn in the Valley of the Tombs of the Kings "in secret," as he himself says, "none seeing and none hearing."

THUTMOSE II (Aakheperenre; 1512–1504), a son of Thutmose I by a minor queen, married his half sister Hatshepsut (*q.v.*). Before his untimely death he made some show of arms against the Palestinian Bedouin and crushed a rebellion in Nubia with severity.

THUTMOSE III (Menkheperre; 1504–1450), who was to prove the greatest of his name, the son of Thutmose II by a concubine, legitimized his succession by marrying the daughter of his aunt and regent Hatshepsut. Succeeding as a minor, he had to wait 22 years before, at Hatshepsut's death, he was able to assume sole power and embark on the career of conquest for which, as a trained soldier, he was fitted. In 17 campaigns this remarkable man re-established, on a firmer footing than ever before, Egyptian sovereignty in southwestern Asia. The first campaign is recorded in some detail on the walls of his temple at Karnak: the march to Gaza, and then to Yahmai south of the Carmel Range; and the council of war and the king's bold decision to surprise the allies of the enemy, led by the king of Kadesh, who were encamped at Megiddo northeast of Carmel and about 18 mi. (29 km.) SSE of the modern city of Haifa. The approach by the route least expected, a narrow defile over the mountain, was successful, the enemy army was defeated, and Megiddo was taken after a siege of eight months. In subsequent campaigns, which are less fully described, ports on the Phoenician coast were converted into Egyptian supply bases, and Kadesh and other cities in the Bika (Bekaa) Valley were taken. The time was then ripe for his most audacious move, an attack against the kingdom of Mitanni, grown stronger since the day when Thutmose I had taken its army by surprise. The Egyptians planned the campaign well; vessels were transported across Syria on oxcarts for the Euphrates crossing. Triumphantly Thutmose III set up his stela beside that of his grandfather. It was his farthest point of advance. On the homeward journey he too hunted elephant, and on his return he celebrated a great victory at Thebes. In later campaigns he was content to consolidate what he had won and to lay the foundations of an imperial organization of his Asian possessions. Local princes, often educated in Egypt, were henceforward set to govern their own territories as vassals of pharaoh and were bound by solemn oath to keep the peace, send annual tribute to Egypt, and obey the Egyptian resident governor, the "overseer of foreign lands."

To the south, Thutmose extended the boundary of Egyptian dominion over Cush to Karoy, near Napata, a little below the Fourth Cataract, thoroughly subduing the turbulent Nubians and developing the gold mines which, from his reign on, became the basis of Egypt's wealth in foreign trade. For the last 12 years of his reign he was content to enjoy the fruits of his victories. The tribute of Syria and Palestine and of the Sudan poured into his treasury, and the tombs of his high officials are decorated with scenes depicting the reception of foreign envoys from places as far away as the Aegean and the Greek mainland, bringing their rich gifts to lay at pharaoh's feet. The temple of Amon at Karnak in particular was enriched by many new buildings and a number of obelisks. During his reign, art and craftsmanship received new impetus from his patronage. He was not only an able soldier and administrator but a considerable athlete, whose prowess with the bow was demonstrated in public display.

THUTMOSE IV (Menkheprure; 1425–1417) was the son of Amenhotep II. After a brief campaign against the Mitannians he made peace with them and married the daughter of Artatama, the king of Mitanni. *See* also EGYPT: *History*.

BIBLIOGRAPHY.—A. H. Gardiner, *Egypt of the Pharaohs* (1961); W. C. Hayes in the *Cambridge Ancient History,* 2nd ed., vol. ii, ch. ix (1962); J. A. Wilson, *The Culture of Ancient Egypt* (1956).

(M. S. DR.)

**THYMUS,** a soft, flattened organ lying behind the breastbone, consists of two lobes of unequal size, which partly cover the trachea, the large vessels in the chest, and the serous covering of the heart, the pericardium. As a food, the animal thymus is called the sweetbread or, more specifically, neck sweetbread, to differentiate it from the pancreas, the stomach sweetbread. During life, the thymus changes markedly in absolute and relative size. It is proportionately largest at birth, averaging about 12 g. ($\frac{1}{2}$ oz.), 0.42% of the total body weight. At the age of puberty the thymus reaches its absolute maximum size, about 37 g. ($1\frac{1}{3}$ oz.). After puberty the organ gradually decreases in size (involutes) until, between age 60 and 70, the average weight is around 6 g. ($\frac{1}{4}$ oz.). Large individual deviations from these averages may occur. In addition to physiologic involution, a much more rapid so-called accidental involution may take place as a result of infection, poisoning, or starvation.

**Functions.**—Although the thymus has the microscopic structure of a lymphatic organ and as such participates in the production of lymphocytes, many studies have seemed to show that the thymus is an endocrine organ. That the thymus reaches its maximum size during puberty and then involutes suggested to some investigators that the organ plays an active role in processes of growth and sexual maturation. Experiments with injections of thymus extracts into rats led to similar assumptions. The growth of the thymus as well as its involution, however, is essentially no different from the same process in other lymphatic organs, and the experiments with thymus extracts were not substantiated.

There is evidence that the thymus is capable of increasing the lymphocyte population in nonthymic lymphatic organs (lymph nodes, spleen, etc.). It is most likely that such a lymphocyte production is stimulated by a humeral factor produced by the thymus, although it cannot be wholly excluded that a lymphocyte migration from the thymus is responsible for the increase.

Although the thymus is not a site of local antibody production, it exerts an indirect control over immunological events. This is particularly clear in neonatally thymectomized mice, which fail to develop an immunological competence.

**Structure.**—The thymus is encased in a thin capsule of connective tissue. This connective tissue penetrates the interior of the organ in the form of walls that branch and fuse, thus dividing the thymus into a multitude of connecting lobules .05 to 2 mm. ($\frac{1}{500}$ to $\frac{1}{12}$ in.) in diameter. The thymus tissue itself contains two types of cells, reticular cells and lymphocytes. The reticular cells, which are larger than the lymphocytes, are characterized by a large pale nucleus; they form a three-dimensional network, in the meshes of which the lymphocytes are found. In the peripheral areas of the lobules, the so-called cortex, the lymphocytes are more densely packed and the reticular cells relatively more sparse. The central zone of the lobule, the medulla, contains fewer lymphocytes and more reticular cells than the cortex. The reticular cells of the thymus differ from the reticular cells of other lymphatic tissues in that they are derived embryologically from epithelial tissue and not from the mesenchyme (the embryologic connective tissue). The lymphocytes of the thymus are morphologically identical with the lymphocytes of other lymphatic tissues. In the medulla of the thymus are the so-called Hassall's bodies. These structures are composed of concentrically arranged cells, which are degenerated at the centres of the bodies where also processes of cornification can frequently be seen. The function of Hassall's bodies, if any, is unknown.

The involution of the thymus consists microscopically of a decrease in the amount of thymus tissue, which is replaced by fat tissue originating in the interlobular connective tissue. This process affects first the cortex but gradually extends also to the medulla, which decreases in quantity. Finally the thymus becomes a mass of fatty tissue containing centrally a remnant of the medulla with varying numbers of Hassall's bodies.

**Embryology.**—The thymus arises from the third branchial pouch in the form of two epithelial cell masses, which at first are tubular but subsequently become solid. Two views exist on the origin of the lymphocytes of the thymus. According to some workers in the field, the thymic lymphocytes arise from mesenchymal elements, while others believe them to be of epithelial origin.

(P. P. H. DE B.)

**Diseases.**—The thymus permits normal development of peripheral lymphoid tissues. Dependent upon thymus is a population of small lymphocytes and the cell-mediated immune responses such as bacterial allergies, graft rejections, and defense against certain viruses and fungi attributable to the function of these cells. The thymus directs differentiation of lymphoid cells and produces a hormone expanding lymphoid cell populations and fostering immunological adaptations. Benign thymic tumours may be associated with immunologic deficiency and lack of gamma globulin. Removal of the tumour does not alleviate immunologic deficiency. Cystic or stromal thymic tumours may be associated with aregenerative anemia. Removal of these tumours occasionally alleviates the anemia. Myasthenia gravis, a paralytic disease, is often associated with tumour or histological abnormality of the thymus. Patients with myasthenia may have autoantibodies against muscle. Early removal of the thymus often provides relief for the muscle weakness.

Deficient or defective thymic development may lead to disastrous immunologic deficiency in infants. Such babies fail to develop normal lymphoid systems and cannot resist infection. They have defective development of the peripheral lymphoid tissues. Abnormality of thymic size and histological structure is regularly observed in children with ataxia-telangiectasia. Patients having this hereditary disorder, in which progressive cerebellar ataxia, dilated capillaries, susceptibility to infections, and immunologic deficiency are associated regularly, have thymuses similar to those of young embryos. Many such children die of lymphosarcoma. The much discussed syndrome, status thymicolymphaticus, seems usually not to be due to thymic disease, but often reflects rampant infection. Tumours originating in thymus should always be regarded as malignant. Much research on thymus and its functions in the late 1960s promised new understanding of development of lymphoid tissues, lymphoid tissue diseases, and improvement in understanding and treatment of diseases involving the lymphoid cells and tissues. (R. A. Go.)

**THYROID GLAND** is an endocrine gland in the throat below the larynx (voice box). It secretes a hormone that has a key role in metabolism and growth. The gland consists of two oblong lobes lying on either side of the windpipe and connected by a narrow band of tissue called the isthmus. The lobes of the gland as well as the isthmus consist of numerous tiny hollow sacks called follicles, more or less rounded in shape and varying from 0.05 to 0.5 mm. ($\frac{1}{500}$ to $\frac{1}{50}$ in.) in diameter. The shell of each follicle is built of cells closely packed together and is wrapped in a thin membrane (*see* figure). The membrane is covered with a dense mesh of blood capillaries, which ensure a steady and abundant supply of fresh plasma through the membrane to the cells; in fact, the thyroid gland is one of the most extensively vascularized organs. Besides blood vessels, there are also lymph vessels and nerves around the follicle. The space inside the follicle is filled with a viscous fluid called colloid.

Every follicle of the thyroid gland makes thyroid hormone, stores it and secretes it into the blood stream. This hormone consists of two chemically closely related substances, L-thyroxine (or L-tetraiodothyronine) and L-triiodothyronine. Under normal conditions, most of the hormone is made up of thyroxine. The four and three atoms of iodine present in these two molecules account, respectively, for 65% and 58% of the hormone weight. It is possible to administer radioactive iodine and trace its progress in the thyroid, to observe how the gland uses it to make up the hormone. The iodide diffusing from the blood capillaries into the cells is retained by and concentrated in the cells. Then the iodide is taken up into organic compounds to form thyroxyl and triiodothyronyl radicals, which are thyroxine and triiodothyronine attached to a large protein called thyroglobulin. This phenomenon occurs at the edge of the cells next to the colloid. The new thyroglobulin becomes mixed with the thyroglobulin present in the colloid and stays there, thus providing a hormone store. Release of hormones occurs when thyroid cells swallow tiny droplets of colloid and, by means of an enzyme, break down the thyroglobulin content to its amino acid components. The thyroxine and triiodothyronine molecules thus freed are small enough to cross the cell wall and to enter the blood vessels around the follicle; they become distributed over the entire body.

THYROID FOLLICLE

From periphery to centre are shown blood vessels (BV), membrane (M) and cells (CE) which make up the shell of the follicle. Appearing on the section plane are the nuclei (N) and the colloid (CO) which fills the space inside the follicle

In blood the thyroid hormone binds loosely to plasma proteins, mainly to $\alpha$-globulin. To measure the level of thyroid hormone in the blood, the hormone is separated from inorganic iodine (iodide) by isolating plasma proteins, and the iodine content of these proteins is determined. The amount of so-called protein-bound iodine indicates whether or not the thyroid hormone level is normal. Too low or too high levels cause widespread functional disturbances, since the hormone controls the oxidation rate of foodstuffs inside the cells over the entire body (*see* THYROID GLAND, DISEASES OF).

The amount of thyroid hormone secreted by the thyroid gland is controlled by another endocrine gland, the pituitary. When the level of thyroid hormone in blood diminishes, due to its utilization in the tissues, the pituitary gland releases a hormone which stimulates the thyroid. This thyroid-stimulating, or thyrotrophic, hormone first induces the release of the thyroid hormone stored in the colloid by accelerating the breakdown of thyroglobulin. The amount of colloid in the follicle diminishes and may even nearly disappear under prolonged stimulation. The thyroid cells increase in size by protruding inside the follicle, and thus increase their capacity to produce the hormone. Under normal conditions, the appropriate level of thyroid hormone in the body is readily reestablished; this higher level induces the pituitary to stop releasing thyrotrophic hormone; the thyroid stimulation ceases, the stores of thyroglobulin are repleted and the cells regress to their original size. Thus the level of thyroid hormone in the body is kept within a constant range by a mechanism in which the effects of thyroid hormone and of thyrotrophic hormone work in closed cycle (feedback mechanism), each hormone controlling the secretion of the other.

*See* also CRETINISM; ENDOCRINOLOGY; HORMONES; PITUITARY GLAND; and references under "Thyroid Gland" in the Index. (H. G. I.)

**THYROID GLAND, DISEASES OF.** In general it may be said that the thyroid gland is subject to the same types of disease processes that affect the other glands of internal secretion. The gland may secrete an excessive quantity of thyroid hormones (hyperthyroidism) or the secretions may be deficient (hypothyroidism). The gland may be enlarged (in which case it is called a goitre) or atrophic. (For a discussion of the anatomy and physiology of the thyroid gland *see* THYROID GLAND; ENDOCRINOLOGY: *Thyroid Gland;* HORMONES: *Thyroxin.*)

**Goitre.**—Most goitres are benign; a small minority of goitres are cancerous. Inflammatory diseases of the thyroid gland are also associated with enlargement.

The normal thyroid gland weighs 20 to 30 g. (about $\frac{3}{4}$ oz.); goitres may weigh as much as 1 kg. (more than 2 lb.). The goitrous glands are usually confined to the neck but occasionally they may extend into the upper chest or more rarely they may be entirely within the chest.

Endemic goitres occur in a relatively large proportion of the population in those areas of the world in which the iodine content of the drinking water and food is exceedingly low. Switzerland and the Great Lakes region in the United States are notable in this regard. Iodine is an integral part of the amino acid thyroxin and the closely related compounds that comprise the thyroid hormones. When the iodine is not supplied in sufficient quantity the gland may hypertrophy, presumably in an effort to produce an optimum amount of hormone. At first there may be a diffuse enlargement of the gland but eventually nodular growths evolve. When the iodine deprivation has been extreme for years, hypothyroidism develops and the children of such individuals may be cretins (*see* CRETINISM). Supplementing the usual iodine intake by the addition of iodide to table salt has been shown to prevent many goitres in endemic areas.

Nodular goitres are those which develop initially from nodules, or nonencapsulated swellings, within the gland. (To simplify the discussion, the term nodular goitre here includes the far less common adenomatous type, in which the initial site of enlargement is an adenoma, or encapsulated swelling.) These goitres occur sporadically in areas where goitres are nonendemic, as well as in endemic areas where iodine replacement is practised. Nodular goitres usually are not accompanied by hyperthyroidism or hypothyroidism. The specific cause of any particular nodular goitre may not be ascertainable. However, varying combinations of several different factors are known to account for many of these abnormal growths.

In some individuals thyroid enlargement is the result of a genetically determined defect in the biosynthesis of thyroid hormone.

In rare cases this results in a failure of the gland to secrete significant quantities of hormonally active substances and the unusual growth of the gland is accompanied by hypothyroidism. Probably more frequently these defects in the biosynthetic processes are partial, normal thyroid function being maintained by compensatory hypertrophy (goitre formation). Enlargement of the thyroid sometimes occurs as a normal accompaniment of pregnancy, and about 80% of nodular goitres are seen in women. This suggests that cyclic variations in ovarian and pituitary activity may alternately stimulate and inhibit the thyroid and thus play a role in the genesis of nodular enlargements. It is also possible that goitrogenic chemicals found in small quantities in foodstuff (*e.g.*, cabbage) may be provocative in this regard. Some drugs, most notably thiocyanates and thiourea derivatives, also possess goitrogenic properties. Thiocyanates inhibit the iodide trapping mechanism in the gland; the thioureas actually block the synthesis of the hormone. In either case thyroid hypertrophy results, probably as a result of compensatory pituitary stimulation.

Nodular goitres should be removed surgically whenever they interfere with the functioning of neighbouring organs. Difficulty in breathing and swallowing, due to pressure on the windpipe and esophagus, are the most frequent indications. A relatively rapid growth of the tumour suggests the possibility of malignancy and thus provides an additional indication for surgical treatment. Endemic goitres may slowly diminish in size with iodide administration. Some sporadic goitres respond to treatment with replacement doses of thyroid extract.

**Cancer.**—Carcinomas of the thyroid appear to develop with unusual frequency in nodular goitres, especially those with only a single nodule or adenoma. Despite the considerable frequency of goitres, the incidence of death from carcinoma of the thyroid is among the least frequent causes of death from cancer. Nevertheless, the low morbidity and mortality that attend thyroidectomies have persuaded many physicians to advise the removal of all so-called solitary adenomas as a prophylactic measure. X-ray treatment of the head, neck and chest in children has been shown to be one of the causes of carcinoma of the thyroid in adolescence and young adulthood. Carcinoma of the thyroid rarely occurs in nodular goitres in persons 60 years old or older.

**Thyroiditis.**—Hashimoto's struma and Riedel's struma are chronic inflammatory disorders of the thyroid gland that may simulate other goitres. Both are quite rare. The end result of chronic thyroiditis of either type is frequently the complete destruction of active thyroid tissue and thus the production of the clinical signs and symptoms of hypothyroidism. There are no hints as to the cause of Riedel's struma. Hashimoto's struma is now thought to be an autoimmune disease since antibodies against thyroid tissue can usually be found circulating in the plasma of patients with this disorder. Subacute thyroiditis is more common than either of the chronic disturbances and can be readily distinguished because the enlarged gland is almost always exquisitely tender and painful. It is associated with fever and malaise and is probably due to a viral infection.

**Hyperthyroidism.**—Hyperthyroidism, also called thyrotoxicosis, may occur with diffuse or nodular goitre. It is characterized by signs of increased metabolism, nervousness, rapid heartbeat, weight loss usually with enhanced appetite, fatigue, heat sensitivity and excessive sweating. In Graves' disease the hyperthyroidism is accompanied by exophthalmos (protrusion of the eyes) and the thyroid gland is usually diffusely enlarged. Exophthalmos is rare when nodular goitres become overactive. The diagnosis of hyperthyroidism in patients with nodular goitre is especially difficult because of the usual insidious onset.

Hyperthyroidism can be treated in one of several ways. Subtotal thyroidectomy is the usual procedure of choice in younger patients. Such surgery must be preceded by medical control of the hyperthyroidism; this is carried out by combined treatment with one of the thiourea derivatives such as propylthiouracil (6-propyl-2-thiouracil) together with iodides (Lugol's solution).

In older patients surgery can be avoided by employing radioactive iodine ($I^{131}$). This isotope of iodine is taken up by the thyroid cells just as is the nonradioactive $I^{127}$ in the course of hormonal biosynthesis and secretion. When present in sufficient dosage $I^{131}$ results in the destruction of the cells. The dosage can be regulated so that sufficient undamaged tissue remains to maintain normal thyroid function in most cases. In occasional patients with Graves' disease protracted treatment with propylthiouracil or a related drug alone has been successful in inducing a lasting remission.

**Hypothyroidism.**—Hypothyroidism may result from destruction of the thyroid gland by inflammatory disease or $I^{131}$, the removal of all functioning thyroid tissue surgically, hypopituitarism or idiopathic atrophy of the gland. It is characterized by signs and symptoms of diminished body metabolism, lassitude, sensitivity to cold, dry skin, poor memory, deposits of mucinous fluids subcutaneously and elsewhere (myxedema; *q.v.*), the loss of scalp hair, etc. Replacement therapy must usually be initiated slowly, especially in older patients. Treatment is ultimately remarkably effective regardless of whether desiccated thyroid extract or synthetic hormonally active substances like thyroxin or triiodothyronine are employed.

**Diagnostic Tests.**—Although the thyroid hormone is not the only secretion that affects the rate of general body metabolism, measurement of the basal metabolic rate (BMR) is particularly useful as a means of evaluating thyroid function. The BMR is elevated in hyperthyroidism and depressed in the deficiency state. The level of circulating thyroid hormone can be estimated with considerable precision by measuring the protein-bound iodine (PBI) in the plasma or serum. Functional activity of the thyroid gland can also be evaluated by measuring the rate of uptake of tracer doses of radioactive iodine. In hyperactive glands the turnover of iodine is accelerated. In hypothyroidism little or no radioactive iodine would be taken up by the gland. Serum cholesterol is elevated in hypothyroidism and tends to be somewhat lower than normal in hyperthyroidism; this characteristic is employed as the basis for a thyroid function test. The detection of high titres of antithyroid antibodies in serum may be used as a presumptive test for Hashimoto's struma.

*See* also METABOLISM, DISEASES OF.

*See* S. C. Werner (ed.), *The Thyroid,* 2nd ed. (1962). (R. L. L.)

**TIBER** (ancient *Tiberis,* Italian *Tevere*), the longest river of the Italian peninsula, rises in the Etruscan Apennines, on the slopes of Monte Fumaiolo, 4,160 ft. (1,268 m.) above sea level and 12 mi. (19 km.) N of Pieve Santo Stefano. After a short and precipitous upper course through deep ravines, the Tiber enters the wide Val Tiberina near Sansepolcro, flows southeast past Umbertide and Perugia, turns west at Todi, and, after receiving the waters of the Paglia below Orvieto (draining the southern Val di Chiana), turns southeast again. It is then joined by the Nera near Orte, skirts the foothills of the Sabini (Sabine) Mountains, and turns southwest at Passo Corese. After passing through Rome, the river enters the Tyrrhenian Sea through a northern artificial mouth at Fiumicino, and a southern one at Ostia. In its lower course the Tiber is joined by the Aniene. Claudius and Trajan both built canals in the Tiber delta, as well as ports to handle the seaborne commerce of Rome for transshipment by river to the city. The total length of the river is 252 mi. (405 km.); its drainage basin is 6,719 sq.mi. (17,402 sq.km.). In its lower course the river winds its way through numerous meanders; only through and below Rome has its course been straightened to any extent. Depths vary from 7 to 20 ft. (2 to 6 m.) and navigation is only carried on as far as Rome. The sediment load is heavy; the mouth of the river has advanced about two miles since Roman times, and the sediment can be seen up to ten miles away on either side of the mouth. Several popes were anxious to develop navigation on the lower Tiber and ports were built in Rome in 1692, 1703, and 1744. The golden age of river navigation was the late 18th century and the first half of the 19th, although as late as 1910 numerous river boats could be seen in Rome itself. There have been 46 major recorded floods on the river in historic times, the latest in 1870, and the worst in 1595. During the 1870 flood, water in some central streets of Rome stood up to nine feet; as a result, the river now flows between high stone embankments that completely control its course. (G. KH.)

**TIBERIAS** (Hebrew TEVARYA or TEBARYA), a town in Israel, lies 682 ft. (208 m.) below sea level, on the west shore of Lake Tiberias (Sea of Galilee), and 30 mi. (48 km.) E of Haifa. Pop. (1961) 20,792. The old black basalt town was largely rebuilt after 1922 and is famous for its hot springs and gardens. It is a lake port and market centre and, besides agriculture, has light industries and ironworks. Main roads link it with Nazareth and Haifa, Safad, and Beisan (Beit Shean).

The town takes its name from a refoundation on an older site, perhaps Rakkath, of a city built by Herod Antipas in honour of the emperor Tiberius; Herod made it his capital, but had difficulty in settling it, and it was not until the 2nd century A.D. that it became the centre of Jewish learning and the headquarters of the Sanhedrin (*q.v.*). The Mishna and the Palestinian Gemara or Talmud (*q.v.*) were edited there. After Byzantine and Persian conquests, Tiberias fell to the Arabs in 637 and became the capital of the Jordan district, famous for carpets, reed prayer mats, paper, and cloth. It was captured by the Crusaders in the 11th century, and Tancred made it his headquarters; it was recaptured by Saladin in 1187, and taken by the Egyptians in 1247. Later it fell into decay. In the 16th century Tiberias became part of the Ottoman Empire and was granted to Joseph Nasi (*q.v.*) by Sultan Suleiman the Magnificent in 1561. Nasi strove to establish a Jewish refugee settlement there, but the scheme collapsed before the intransigent attitude of the Muslim population and the unhealthy climate. In 1922 Tiberias became part of Palestine and in 1948 of Israel. The Arab population was largely evacuated and replaced by the maabaroth system of transitional villages set up in 1950. (M. V. S.-W.)

**TIBERIUS** (42 B.C.–A.D. 37), Roman emperor from A.D. 14, was stepson to Octavian (later the emperor Augustus; *q.v.*), whom his mother, Livia Drusilla (*q.v.*), married in 38 B.C. His father was Tiberius Claudius Nero, praetor in 42 and an opponent of Octavian in the "Perusine War" of 41–40. Tiberius bore his father's name until in A.D. 4 he was adopted by Augustus and became Tiberius Julius Caesar. After his father's death in 33 B.C. he came under Octavian's tutelage and was highly honoured by him, riding beside his stepfather's chariot in the great triumphs of 29 B.C. and accompanying him as a military tribune in the Spanish campaign of 26. In 24 he was given permission to hold magistracies five years before the regular age, and in fact became quaestor in 23, praetor in 16, and consul in 13, with a second consulate in 7 B.C. In this period he won some reputation as an orator, but his chief distinction was in military affairs. In 20 B.C. he conducted an army to the Euphrates, received back the standards which the Parthians had captured from Crassus in 53, and installed a pro-Roman king in Armenia.

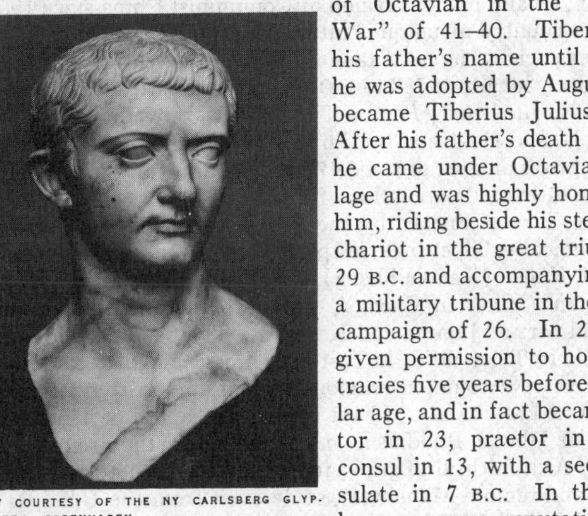

BY COURTESY OF THE NY CARLSBERG GLYPTOTEK, COPENHAGEN

TIBERIUS AS A YOUNG MAN. MARBLE, FOUND IN EGYPT IN 1896

In 16 he was governor of Gaul, and in 15 with his brother Drusus (*q.v.*) he undertook the conquest of the central Alpine lands (*see* RAETIA; VINDELICIA). In 12–9 B.C. he was in charge of still more important operations in the valleys of the Sava and Drava rivers and brought into the empire the area later known as Pannonia. In 8 B.C. he took command in Germany, where Drusus had died the year before. Here too his campaigns were successful, and he transported 40,000 prisoners to settle in Gaul. In 7 B.C. he celebrated a triumph, and next year he was given the signal honour of tribunician power as colleague of Augustus, who also offered him a command in the east. At this point, however, despite Augustus' violent protests, he retired from public life and took up residence on Rhodes.

He was suffering from both personal resentment and frustrated ambition. In 11 B.C. he had been married to Augustus' daughter Julia, after the death of her husband Agrippa. But he had been devoted to his previous wife, Agrippa's daughter Vipsania, who had borne his only son, Drusus (*see* DRUSUS CAESAR); and Julia refused to live with him as his wife once their only child had died in infancy. He claimed that she regarded him as beneath her, and it was clear that the emperor's intended successors were her children by Agrippa, Gaius and Lucius, whom Augustus had adopted as his sons. Tiberius said later that he had retired to avoid obstructing the boys' advancement, and indeed it was precisely in 6 B.C. that Gaius, aged 14, was chosen consul by the people (though Augustus did not allow him to hold office for another six years).

On Rhodes, Tiberius retained his tribunician power until its expiry in 1 B.C. and was visited by Romans of importance, including Gaius Caesar himself in A.D. 1. But friction with Gaius developed; and Tiberius, now in fear of his life, was only with difficulty able to persuade Augustus that he should return to Rome as a private citizen in A.D. 2. Then, however, his fortunes changed. Lucius died in A.D. 2 and Gaius in A.D. 4, and Augustus had to adopt Tiberius as his son and successor, though Tiberius in turn was made to adopt his nephew Germanicus, who was married to Augustus' granddaughter Agrippina and was descended from Augustus' sister. Tiberius received tribunician power again and returned to commands of the highest importance, first in Germany (A.D. 4–5), then to crush a great revolt in Pannonia (6–9), and then in Germany once more after the defeat of Varus. In 12 he celebrated another triumph and in 13 was given authority to administer all the provinces conjointly with Augustus. When Augustus died on Aug. 19, A.D. 14, Tiberius was unmistakably the next ruler and already possessed most of the necessary constitutional prerogatives.

Augustus' surviving grandson, Agrippa Postumus, a possible rival since he had been adopted along with Tiberius in A.D. 4, was promptly executed. But Tiberius put up a show of reluctance for empire, and it was not until Sept. 19 that the Senate formally conferred the other insignia of imperial power. Mutinies in the armies in Pannonia and Germany followed, but they were occasioned by grievances over conditions of service rather than by disloyalty to Tiberius personally. The first serious trouble for the government came in 19, when Germanicus, now the heir apparent, died in Syria. Tiberius had appointed Gnaeus Piso, a senior exconsul, to keep watch on his nephew's work in the east, and the quarrels between the two men led to the accusation that Germanicus had been poisoned. Piso was tried and committed suicide, since he found Tiberius implacable on the charge that he had engaged in civil war. But though the poisoning had not been substantiated, the death of Germanicus was laid by many to Tiberius' account, and Germanicus' widow, Agrippina ("the Elder"), never forgave him. The situation was worsened when in 23 Tiberius' own son, Drusus, died. The elder sons of Germanicus, Nero and Drusus, were now advanced as possible successors to Tiberius, but Sejanus, prefect of the praetorian guard, was meditating his own plans. In 29 his gradual attacks on Germanicus' party culminated in the arrest of Agrippina and Nero, the latter of whom was executed in 30 or 31; meanwhile Drusus, too, had been imprisoned. But in 31 Tiberius came to suspect Sejanus, outmaneuvered him, and had him put to death. The bloody vengeance taken on Sejanus' supporters did not end the attack on the friends of Agrippina, who herself perished by starvation in 33, soon after the death of her son Drusus in prison. In 36–37 there was a further series of executions of prominent Romans, perhaps connected with intrigues by the new praetorian prefect, Macro, to secure the succession of Gaius (Caligula), Germanicus' surviving son. When Tiberius died on March 16, 37, he was execrated by most of the aristocracy, and the people too shouted "Tiberius to the Tiber."

Indeed the people of the city had little cause to love an emperor who had been economical with public funds and had shown little interest in games or festivals. Moreover, in 26 he had left Rome and retired to Capreae (Capri) and had issued instructions to the Senate by letter. Yet his administration of the empire, though unadventurous, had been careful and thorough to the last. His declared policy was to follow Augustus in all things, and for him this implied a refusal to extend the frontiers, the avoidance of divine honours for himself, a rigid surveillance of provincial governors (some of whom had their tenures prolonged to exceptional lengths), and a readiness to assist genuine distress. He recalled Germanicus from the Rhine in 16, insisting on abandoning any aggressive action in Germany. Revolts in Africa (A.D. 17–24), Gaul (21), and Thrace (21 and 26) were suppressed without any need for the emperor to take the field. Armenia was given a pro-Roman king in 18, and as late as 35 Tiberius was again able to assert Roman authority against Parthia by appropriate instructions to his legate in Syria. In the Danubian provinces his reign was conspicuous for the building of roads and for the consolidation of the new province of Moesia.

The problem of Tiberius is inseparable from the problem of the veracity of the historian Tacitus, who wrote the first six books of his *Annals* about 80 years after Tiberius' death. To Tacitus, Tiberius was a bloodthirsty tyrant, cunning at first in concealing his hatreds and his lust for power, but coming out in his true colours once restraining influences (such as that of his mother) were removed. Tiberius' exceptional deference to the Senate is therefore treated as a sham, and the keynote of the reign is the use of the famous treason law (*lex maiestatis*), the operation of which was familiar to Tacitus from Domitian's reign (81–96). Yet in fact Tiberius intervened to check the more trivial prosecutions brought under this law, which in any case was instituted in the form known under the empire not by him but by Augustus. Moreover many of the numerous senators and knights who were executed under Tiberius were involved in serious charges of conspiracy or of tampering with the army; most were associated with the major political struggle which centred on the parties of Sejanus and Agrippina. Tiberius' patience was exhausted when in 31 he thought Sejanus had betrayed him, and it may be that his mind became estranged. In earlier years he shows no signs of vindictiveness.

Nevertheless Tiberius' attempt to restore the traditional authority of the Senate was a failure. He was without the geniality which had brought Augustus his friends. Though tall and distinguished looking, he suffered from a skin disease of the face which made him embarrassed in public; moreover even his walk conveyed the haughtiness traditionally associated with his family, the Claudii. In addition, he was tactless and pedantic, and his tortuous speeches seemed to imply lack of frankness. Stories of his sexual excesses on Capreae (found in the biographer Suetonius rather than in Tacitus) may be discounted, but the retirement was certainly a mistake, for it lost him the personal contacts without which no emperor could successfully cooperate with the Senate. The death of his son Drusus was a misfortune, but in the struggles over the succession he might have found more sympathy had he not withdrawn into pure administration.

BIBLIOGRAPHY.—Apart from contemporary flatterers like Velleius Paterculus, most ancient writers (the Jew Josephus is an exception) were hostile to Tiberius. Rehabilitation set in early in the late 19th century; *see* for instance L. Freytag, *Tiberius und Tacitus* (1870); E. S. Beesly, *Catiline, Clodius and Tiberius* (1878). It has been continued more recently by many writers: *see* F. B. Marsh, *The Reign of Tiberius* (1931); M. P. Charlesworth in *Cambridge Ancient History*, vol. x, ch. 19 (1934); E. Ciaceri, *Tiberio* (1934); D. M. Pippidi, *Autour de Tibère* (1944). Latterly the Tacitean tradition has been strongly reinforced by R. Syme, *Tacitus*, 2 vol., esp. ch. 30–32 (1958); and Tiberius' defects are studied from a medical standpoint by G. Marañón, *Tiberius: a Study in Personal Resentment*, Eng. trans. by W. B. Wells (1956). For contemporary documents *see* V. Ehrenberg and A. H. M. Jones, *Documents Illustrating the Reigns of Augustus and Tiberius*, 2nd ed. (1955); on Tiberius' portraiture, E. Hohl in *Klio*, vol. xxi, pp. 269–284 (1938); R. S. Rogers, *Criminal Trials and Criminal Legislation Under Tiberius* (1935), is an important (pro-Tiberian) study of the treason law. (G. E. F. C.)

**TIBERIUS II** (CONSTANTINUS) (d. 582), Byzantine emperor from 578 to 582, was a Thracian who served against the Avars in the Balkans. In 574 he was adopted by Justin II and shared the regency with the empress Sophia until in September 578 he was crowned emperor by Justin during one of the latter's lucid intervals. As emperor he inaugurated a lavish policy, leaving an empty exchequer for his successor, Maurice. Tiberius made a three years' peace with Persia (576–578) which did not, however, apply to Persarmenia. Here the Byzantines gained notable successes, and peace terms were being discussed when Khosrau I died (579). Under his successor, Ormizd IV, hostilities broke out again (579–581). On the northern frontier Tiberius attempted to pacify the Avars by an annual tribute, but in 581 had to surrender Sirmium (now Mitrovica, Yugos.). He was also unable to check the Slavs who were pouring south of the Danube into Thrace and Thessaly. In 582 Tiberius, now mortally ill, recognized Maurice as his successor and crowned him emperor on Aug. 13, the day before his own death.

BIBLIOGRAPHY.—E. Stein, *Studien zur Geschichte des byzantinischen Reiches* (1919); J. B. Bury, *Later Roman Empire*, vol. 2 (1889); N. H. Baynes, *Cambridge Medieval History*, vol. 2, ch. 9 (1913). (J. M. Hy.)

**TIBESTI,** a mountainous region of the central Sahara, mostly in the northwestern corner of the Republic of Chad. It extends SE–NW for about 300 mi. (480 km.) and its greatest width is 175 mi. (280 km.); it includes the highest summit of the Sahara, the volcanic massif of Emi Koussi, which reaches 11,204 ft. (3,415 m.). The eruptive rocks have forced their way through a substratum of crystalline rocks covered by horizontal Paleozoic sandstone, the scarp of which is quite brusque above the surrounding plains, which are hundreds of metres above sea level.

Three great dry watercourses, deeply cut into the massif, indicate a climate that was formerly more humid. The daily variations of temperature reach 30° at times. The Tibbu inhabitants, at most 8,000, are chiefly nomads, although there are some sedentary elements.

Tibesti was partly explored by Gustav Nachtigal in 1870. After that no European went there until 1915, when Col. Jean Tilho wrote a description of it and mapped it. (J. D.)

**TIBET,** an autonomous region of Communist China since 1965, formerly a country of unique cultural and politico-religious identity, extends across the mountainous plateau of Central Asia from approximately longitude 78° to 100° E and from latitude 27° to 37° N. Tibet is called Bod (*Pö*) by Tibetans, Bhot by Indians, Tobet by Mongols, and Hsi-tsang by Chinese (Tu-fan in ancient times). Tibet comprises an area of some 471,660 sq.mi. (1,221,601 sq.km.) and had an estimated population of 1,500,000 (1953 census, 1,273,969) before it was annexed by the People's Republic of China in 1951. Ethnically, Tibet includes part of the Chinese provinces of Ch'ing-hai, Kansu (Kan-su Sheng), Szechwan (Ssu-ch'uan Sheng), and Yünnan (Yün-nan Sheng); part of Bhutan, Sikkim, and Nepal; and part of Jammu and Kashmir. The people in this vast area of ethnic Tibet differ in customs, dress, and dialects; however, they share a common religious system and written language (*see* TIBETAN LANGUAGE). Lhasa (*q.v.*), the capital of Tibet, was the mecca of Tibetan Buddhism (*q.v.*), and before the rise of Communism in Asia faithful pilgrims journeyed to the holy city from Mongolia and remote Manchuria, some even from the U.S.S.R.

This article is divided for convenience into the following sections and subsections:

## I. PHYSICAL GEOGRAPHY

**1. Geology.**—Tibetan tradition maintains that originally the country was covered by a huge ocean and that in time the ocean dried up and forests of juniper trees came forth. Considering the fact that the Himalayas (*q.v.*) are the highest mountain mass on the earth, the Tibetan legend seems merely a myth; yet Tibet was indeed once covered by an ocean. During the Eocene Epoch of the Tertiary Period, 55,000,000–65,000,000 years ago, a vast sea, called Tethys, extended from Asia Minor to the East Indies. About 20,000,000 years later, in the Oligocene Epoch, violent upheavals in the earth's crust caused extrusions of land mass in the region of present-day Tibet and the deposition of nummulitic limestone and marine fossils. The Cenozoic extrusions that formed the Himalayas did not extend to the Kunlun Mountains (*q.v.*) which are considerably older, being composed essentially of Paleozoic slates and Devonian limestone, some 350,000,000 years old. It is probable that the whole plateau was covered with ice sheets during the Pleistocene Epoch 1,000,000 years ago. Enormously thick Pleistocene deposits are found in many places: one estimated at 3,000 ft. (914 m.) was formed in the Upper Sutlej Valley.

**2. Physiography.**—Tibet is on a high plateau surrounded by mountain masses. The relatively level northern part of the plateau is called the Chang Thang (*q.v.;* Byang-thang) or northern plain, which extends over 800 mi. (1,290 km.) across northern Tibet at an average elevation of 15,000 ft. (4,572 m.). The Chang Thang is dotted with brackish lakes, remnants of the Tethys Sea, but there are no river systems there. Approximately at longitude 92° E, the Chang Thang begins to descend in elevation. The mountain ranges in eastern Tibet transverse from north to south creating meridional barriers to travel and communication. In central and western Tibet, the ranges run from northwest to southeast with deep or shallow valleys forming innumerable furrows.

The Chang Thang Plateau is bordered on the north by the Paleozoic Kunlun Mountain mass (*see* KUNLUN MOUNTAINS) extending from longitude 77° to 93° E, with the highest peak, Ulugh Muz Tagh, reaching 25,338 ft. (7,723 m.). North of the Kunlun Range lies the Tsaidam Basin, averaging 9,000 ft. (2,743 m.), bordered in turn by the Astin Tagh and Nan Shan ranges. The western and southern border of the Tibetan plateau is formed by the Himalayan mass that stretches from Nanga Parbat (26,660 ft. [8,126 m.]) in the northwest to Namcha Barwa (25,446 ft. [7,756 m.]) in the southeast, with the highest peak Mt. Everest (29,028 ft. [8,848 m.]). North of Lake Mānasarowar and stretching eastwardly is the Trans-Himalaya, or Kailas Range (*q.v.*), with clusters of peaks, several exceeding 20,000 ft. (6,096 m.). The Trans-Himalayas are separated from the Himalayas by the deep Brahmaputra River, which flows across southern Tibet from longitude 82° to about 95° E then cuts south through the mountains to India.

Among the larger lakes on the Tibetan plateau are Mānasarowar in the west, Gnam-mtsho (also called Tengrinor) and Yar-'brog-mtsho (or Yamdrok Tso) in central Tibet, and Mtsho-sngon (or Koko Nor) in the northeast. Most of the large rivers of Asia rise in the Tibetan highlands. The Yangtze (*q.v.;* Tibetan: 'Bri-chu) rises south of the Ulan Ula Mountain Range at approximately longitude 91° E, latitude 34° N. The Yellow (*q.v.;* Tibetan: Rma-chu) rises from lakes southwest of the Am-nye-rma-chen Mountains, which cause the upstream bend in the river. The Mekong (*q.v.;* Tibetan: Rdza-chu) and the Salween (*q.v.;* Tibetan: Dngul-chu) both rise about longitude 91° E. The Brahmaputra (*q.v.;* Tibetan: Gtsang-po) rises just east of Lake Mānasarowar and cuts across Tibet from west to east for about 800 mi. (1,290 km.) before entering India. The headwaters of the Sutlej, Indus (*qq.v.*), and Karnali rivers are in the Western Himalayas.

The main rivers of central Tibet are tributaries of the Brahmaputra. Some of the more important ones are the Skyid-chu, which flows past Lhasa; the Nyang-chu, which passes Zhikatse (Shigatse); the Shangs-chu; the Nyang-chu of Kong-po district; and the rivers of the Yar-klungs and 'Phyong-rgyas valleys. The river valleys have the highest density of population because of their fertile, arable soil. The Yar-klungs and 'Phyong-rgyas valleys are known as the cradle of Tibetan civilization. The uplands and highlands are used as grazing land by the nomads.

**3. Climate.**—Contrary to the popular conception of Tibet as the Land-of-Snows, the total fall of rain and snow over most of Tibet is less than 10 in. per year. The precipitation in Tibet decreases from south to north because of the Himalayas, which form a barrier over which the monsoon rains cannot pass; consequently, the annual rainfall on the southern slopes runs over 100 in. (2,540 mm.) and less than 10 in. (254 mm.) on the northern side. In the Himalayas the perpetual snowline is about 16,000 ft. (4,877 m.), but north of them, it rises to 20,000 ft. (6,096 m.) due to the lack of precipitation. The temperatures are low because of the high altitude and they vary considerably in a 24-hour period, a climatic condition that differs little throughout the year. It is always bitterly cold in the morning and evening. At noon the sun is scorching and the temperature may rise to 100° F (38° C), but it usually drops below 0° F (−18° C) at night. The severity of the climate is aggravated by winds which blow with gale force during the greater part of the year. Only during three or four months in the year is the Tibetan highland free from frost, and snow may fall in summer. In the lower land (under 12,000 ft. [3,657 m.]), in river basins, and in southeastern Tibet, however, the climate is mild and pleasant. The air is dry, and, in the absence of dust storms, the sky is clear.

**4. Plant and Animal Life.**—The expansive windswept Chang Thang Plateau that comprises two-thirds of the area of Tibet is devoid of trees and larger forms of vegetation. Averaging over 15,000 ft. (4,572 m.), the northern plain receives less than 10 in. (254 mm.) of precipitation. The grasses that grow there during the short summer season are grazed by the sheep of nomads. In contrast, the Sutlej River Valley in the western district of Mnga'-ris and the Chumbi Valley (*q.v.*) in southern Tibet have vast areas of virgin forests. Trees include giant conifers, varnish trees, spruce, fir, cypress, juniper, and deciduous trees such as the willow, poplar, walnut, maple, and oak. Cereals, mainly barley and buckwheat, are grown in the river valleys between the Himalayas and the Trans-Himalayas. Many medicinal herbs, such as *Peimu* (*Fritillaria roylei*), acanthus, rhubarb, saffron (*Crocus sativus*), and calamus (*Acorus calamus*), are found in Tibet and are in demand for local use as well as for export to China and India.

The animal commonly associated with Tibet is the ox *Bos grunniens,* known in the West by the anglicized name yak, which is used to refer to all such oxen. The Tibetan word g. yag (*yak*) refers only to the male of the domesticated oxen; the female is called 'bri-mo (*dri-mo*); therefore, the expressions *yak butter tea* and *female yak* found in literature on Tibet are semantically incorrect. The domesticated oxen, both male and female, are used as draft animals; and they are the chief means of conveyance for highland travel. They carry heavy loads (160 lb. [73 kg.]) on rough roads, through steep passes, and at high altitudes; but they cannot withstand the warmer climate and dense air of lower elevations, or be used for tilling land. The animal's meat and milk form, together with barley, the staple food of all Tibetans, and the tail is highly valued in India. Herds of 200 oxen and about 1,000 sheep are not uncommon. The sheep provide the nomadic people of northern Tibet with skins for garments, and meat, milk, and butter for food. Other domestic animals include goats, donkeys, and horses. The horse of eastern Tibet, once famous for its small stature and stocky nimbleness, has degenerated in the 20th century so much that riding horses used in Tibet now come from the steppes of Ch'ing-hai Province, China. The Tibetans also keep huge mastiffs as watchdogs and the small Lhasa terrier as pets.

Numerous wild animals are found in Tibet, some distinctively Tibetan, such as the wild yak (*'brong*), the wild ass (*kyang*), the wild argali sheep (*gnyan*), and the Himalayan snow leopard, whose long, luxurious fur enables it to live at high, cold altitudes. Among the Carnivora are the lynx, bear, wolf, fox, weasel, and marten. Various kinds of marmot, and in some regions the monkey and giant panda, are found. The herbivorous animals include the deer, gazelle, the Tibetan antelope (*gtsod*), and the musk deer (*q.v.*), a hornless species found abundantly in eastern Tibet. The musk derived from the musk deer is exported to Europe via India and China for use in the manufacture of perfumes.

The common birds of Tibet are swan, stock or heron, hawk, gull, fishing eagle, bar-headed goose, raven, chough lark, sparrow, woodpecker, pigeon, and vulture. The Tibetan chicken has an elongated body. Tibetan farmers raise poultry, but some eat only the eggs and not the meat. In eastern Tibet there are several rare and handsome varieties of pheasant.

## II. GEOGRAPHICAL REGIONS

The earliest known territorial division of central Tibet was into four districts called the "Four Horns" (*ru-bzhi*). This division, dating from the days of the early kings (*c.* 7th century), embraced most of the two central provinces, Dbus (pronounced *Ü*) and Gtsang (*Dsang*). Dbus, meaning "centre," was the politico-religious centre of modern Tibet before the Chinese Communists seized power. Its area encompasses the Skyid-chu Valley System, in which the capital Lhasa (*q.v.*) is located, as well as those of the Yar-klungs and 'Phyong-rgyas valleys on the south side of the Brahmaputra, which together are regarded as the ancient regions of the royal court. Tombs of some of the early kings are located in the 'Phyong-rgyas Valley.

West of Dbus is the province of Gtsang. Its area embraces several river valleys that converge with that of the Brahmaputra. Chief among these is the Nyang-chu Valley, which runs from the southeast to the northwest for over 150 mi. (241 km.) before it enters the Brahmaputra at about longitude 88°45′ E. The Nyang Chu flows past the fortress town of Gyangtse (*q.v.; Rgyal-rtse*) upstream and the administrative headquarters of Gtsang, Zhikatse (*q.v.*; called Shigatse: *Gzhis-ka-rtse*), near its point of confluence with the Brahmaputra.

During the 7th to the 9th century, the Tibetan kingdom was extended beyond the Four Horns area until it reached the Tarim Basin on the north, China on the east, India and Nepal on the south, and Kashmir on the west. The newly added dominions to the west were called Mnga'-ris (*Nga-ri*) and those to the east and northeast, Mdo-khams (*Do-kham*). This vast area became known as the "Three Regions" (*Chol-kha-gsum*) and marked the limits of the Tibetan Empire before its collapse in the 9th century. Over the centuries peripheral areas of this region of ethnic Tibet passed under the political domination of neighbouring countries.

During the 13th century, Tibet passed under the suzerainty of the Mongol Khans, and in the time of Kublai Khan (*q.v.*) central Tibet was divided into 13 myriarchies for administrative purposes. Each myriarchy was ruled by a myriarch (*Khri-dpon*), and the highest Tibetan authority was the ruling lama of the Sa-skya-pa sect, who was appointed a kind of viceroy by the Mongol Khan. With the decline of Mongol power in the 14th century, there was a change in rulers in Tibet and the myriarchy system of administrative units was replaced by the Rdzong (*Dsong*). Tibet was divided into smaller units called Rdzong, and the administrators of the Rdzong were sent out from the capital. This system continued in effect in Tibet until 1959 when the Communist Chinese abolished the theocratic Tibetan government.

For centuries the area of ethnic Tibet was divided into the following: Dbus and Gtsang (comprising central Tibet), Mnga'-ris, Khams, and A-mdo. Mnga'-ris in the west is generally a sparsely populated highland with snowcapped mountains and deep river canyons, where the nomads drive their flocks and herds from one valley slope to another seeking scanty pasturage. Khams in the east is the most fertile and populated of the Tibetan regions. Lower in elevation and with heavier rainfall, its river gorges are covered with extensive forests, and the lower river basins are cultivated. Ethnically, Khams extends eastward to the Chinese province of Szechwan, but in the reign of the Manchu emperor Yung-cheng (1723–35), the area east of the upper reaches of the Yangtze River at about longitude 99° E was taken under Chinese administration, though not incorporated into the provincial system. This area remained in long dispute between Tibet and China. In 1956 the disputed area of Khams east of the Yangtze was incorporated into Szechwan Province as the Kantse Tibetan Autonomous Chou. A-mdo, the northeastern part of ethnic Tibet, passed under Manchu control in 1724 following the suppression of a Mongol revolt against the throne. This area was officially incorporated into the Chinese provincial system as Ch'ing-hai Province in 1928.

## III. THE PEOPLE

### A. Racial Characteristics

The Tibetans are said to belong to the Mongoloid racial group, but this does not mean that they are a homogeneous people with the same physical characteristics as the Chinese. Tibetans are divided into two groups. All of them belong to the straight-hair leiotrichous group, which corresponds generally with those groups called Mongoloid; however, the brachycephalic or round-headed

MARILYN SILVERSTONE—MAGNUM

TWO TIBETANS, WEARING THE TALL LADAKHI HAT OF QUILTED VELVET, REST THEIR HORSES AT THE EDGE OF LAKE PANGONG, WHICH LIES DIVIDED BETWEEN TIBET AND LADAKH type similar to the pareoean Chinese constitutes only part of the Tibetan people, those found mostly in the cultivated river valleys in central and western Tibet. Because of their racial similarity with the unmixed Chinese and Burmese (with whose languages Tibetan shares an affinity), it may be postulated that the brachycephalic Tibetans represent the descendants of the earliest inhabitants of the country.

The other racial group among Tibetans is the dolichocephalic or long-headed type, who tend to be tall and angular in build, with predominant nasal and superciliary bone structures. This type is found among the noble families in central Tibet and generally among the nomads of the east and northeast. The long-headed Tibetans may have resulted from racial admixture following an intrusion into Central Asia of Turko-Mongol people who all belonged to the straight-hair leiotrichous group. The long inaccessibility of Tibet to trained scientists prevented any accurate description of the origin, evolution, and admixtures of the racial strains found among Tibetans. In spite of the brachycephalic and dolichocephalic differences among Tibetans, they all share the same language which binds the round-headed, soft-featured agriculturalist of central Tibet and the long-headed, aquiline-nosed nomad of the east into an ethnic-racial unity.

### B. Language

The Tibetan language is related linguistically to Chinese and Burmese, but centuries of phonological evolution have rendered them so differently that they are unintelligible to each other. The Tibetan script was devised in the 7th century by Thon-mi Sambhota, who took a Gupta script then in use in Kashmir as his model. Tibetan is written from left to right in a syllabary consisting of 30 consonants and 4 vowel signs. Since the written language conveyed the teachings of Buddhism, it acquired a sacral character, and the orthography has remained virtually unchanged for the past millennium. The spoken language continued to develop phonologically, which resulted in a great disparity between the pronunciation and the spelling of Tibetan words. The language is highly stylized with an honorific and an ordinary word for most terms of reference. One uses the honorific expression when speaking to equals or superiors; the ordinary word when addressing inferiors or when referring to one's self. There is an additional set of higher honorifics to be used when addressing the highest lamas and nobles. The ability to employ the correct vocabulary was a measure of one's standard of education and culture. The Lhasa dialect, which served as the lingua franca for Tibet, has a highly developed tonal system. *See* also Tibetan Language.

### C. Social Organization

The various social classes among the Tibetan people can be divided in terms of opposition; thus: cleric versus lay, noble versus peasant, merchant versus labourer, agriculturalist versus nomad, and trader versus townsman; not to mention the outcastes.

**1. Clerics.**—Contrary to general opinion, not all Tibetan monks are lamas. Lama (*bla-ma*) means "superior one" and originally was used to translate the Sanskrit word for "teacher" (*guru*). When Tibetan Buddhism was adopted by the Mongols, they called all monks *lamas, i.e.,* "teachers." This resulted in the common Western terms of "lamaism" and "lamasery," which are in fact incorrect terms of reference for Tibetan Buddhism and a "monastery." The concept of a "reincarnation lama" was a late development, arising first in the 14th century. It soon became a general practice among the various sects to find the "rebirths" of deceased lamas, and the word *lama* became a term of reference for such "reincarnations" to distinguish them from ordinary monks (*grwa-pa*). A learned monk in a high ecclesiastical position may be addressed as Lama out of respect, but he is not a "reincarnation" (*yang-srid*). A lama is regarded by the faithful as a physical manifestation (*sprul-sku*) of the absolute Buddha, and every monastery of any size had one or more lamas in residence. There were hundreds of incarnate lamas in Tibet, including the Dalai Lama (*q.v.*) and the Panchen Lama.

Prior to the Communist Chinese annexation of Tibet, it was estimated that about 20% of the population belonged to the clerical order. The major sects are the Dge-lugs-pa, Bka'-brgyud-pa, Sa-skya-pa, and Rnying-ma-pa. The Dge-lugs-pa (pronounced Ge-luk-ba) is the reformed Yellow Hat sect, which enjoyed political supremacy after the 17th century, when its sectarian leader, the Dalai Lama, gained secular control. Fully ordained monks (*dge-slongs*) of all sects observe celibacy. The old, unreformed Rnying-ma-pa sect is said not to observe the vow of celibacy, but in truth it does. Many Rnying-ma-pa monks avoid taking full ordination, which demands celibacy, thus creating the wrong impression that the old Red Hat monks can marry.

The few secular schools in Tibet were limited to rich and noble families. The monasteries were the main seats of learning and some of the larger ones were similar in operation to theological universities. Theoretically, the doors of the monasteries were open to all, and no age limit or educational qualifications were set for admittance: sons of the rich and the poor, sons of the nobles and the commoners were all admitted on an equal basis. Monks from the upper classes, however, had better chances for advancement because their wealth allowed them to pay fees and buy exemptions. The monks pursued a prescribed curriculum in Buddhist literature and, upon completion, became full-ordained *dge-slongs*. The intelligent ones could pursue an additional course of study in advanced philosophical works, usually requiring six to seven years to finish. If the candidate successfully passed the final examinations, he was given the coveted title of *Dge-bshes* (pronounced *Geshe*). A *Dge-bshes* was respected for his education and was qualified to serve as a monk official in the government or on the administrative board of the monasteries.

Not all the enrolled monks intended to acquire a serious education and many came for vocational training as calligraphers, printers, painters, and craftsmen. A large number specialized in performing rituals for the sick. It was considered an honour to send at least one son to become a monk and this was often done when the boy was only seven or eight years old; consequently, there were many monks in the monasteries who had no aptitude for higher education or spiritual teaching. The less intelligent monks performed the menial tasks such as cooking, cleaning, and repairing. There was also a type of monk, generally very athletic and aggressive, who trained for vigorous inter-monastery competitive games. They wore special garments and carried certain objects as weapons. They guarded the monasteries, enforced discipline, acted as bodyguards to high lamas while traveling, and at the order of the abbot would take up arms against any private person or foreign invaders.

Monasteries obtained endowments from both the government and private individuals. Government endowments included subsidies in kind, money, and estates, from which income in the form of taxes was derived. Private endowments included alms and donations in kind and money from members of the monastery or from outsiders. Considerable income was also obtained from trading and lending. The three main Dge-lugs-pa monasteries of Dga'-ldan, 'Bras-spungs, and Se-ra (*see* Lhasa) owned sizable estates and enjoyed a certain amount of autonomy. (*See* also Tibetan Buddhism.)

**2. Nobility.**—Before the death of the 13th Dalai Lama in 1933, there were about 170 noble families, but this number increased afterward. The nobles trace their descent in various ways. One group is that composed of the members of a Dalai Lama's family. Beginning with the 7th Dalai Lama (1708–57), the father or brother of the Dalai Lama, who was a commoner, was ennobled and given estates. There are only six families of this type: all are called Yab-gzhis (patrimony) families. The next in importance among the nobles are those who trace their lineage to early kings, such as the Lha-rgya-ri and Rag-kha-shag families, or early territorial rulers, including the Mdo-mkhar-ba, Rdo-ring, Bla-brang rnying-pa, and Thon-pa families. The Pha-lha family is descended from a Bhutanese, who was ennobled and given an estate near Gyangtse comprising 130 farms for the service he rendered the Lhasa government in the 17th century. These seven are called the Sde-dpon (ruler) families.

The remainder of the noble families came into being in more recent times through ennoblement as a reward for service to the government or to the Dalai Lama; or when a rich commoner was granted a nobleman's estate for which there was no heir. The lack of an heir to an estate led to an interesting social institution referred to as the adopted bridegroom (*mag-pa*). In theory all land in Tibet belonged to the Dalai Lama because it was given to him as a religious gift by Gushri Khan, the Qoshot Mongol who conquered central Tibet in 1642. However, in practice the land was divided into three types of estates: government, religious, and private. The way to distinguish these types is to determine to whom the external and internal taxes are paid. On a government estate the external and internal taxes are paid to the central government. On a religious estate, the external tax is paid to the government and the internal tax goes to the monastery that owns the land. On a private estate, the external tax goes to the government and the internal tax goes to the noble who is enfeoffed with the estate. A noble family maintained its claim to the estate only as long as one male of each generation served in the Dalai Lama's government as a lay official, a practice somewhat analogous to the services rendered by knights to kings of medieval Europe. In the event that a nobleman had only daughters and no sons, the bridegroom of the eldest daughter adopted her family name and would then serve the government, thus keeping the estate for her family; consequently, one should not assume that the lineage of these noble families of Tibet is of a single, continuous blood line. The Tibetan government consisted of 175 lay officials, all of whom came from the landed nobility, and 175 monk officials, some of whom also came from noble families.

**3. Merchants and Traders.**—It is often said that a Tibetan is a born trader. Small-scale trading was a sideline of many people. Even the large monasteries conducted trade widely and had administrative departments in charge of trade. Nobles and monks alike engaged in trade and professional traders were few. Commercial transactions requiring long journeys were carried on by the men, while the women managed the shops and small retail trade. The caravans of mules laden with wool that wound their way to India, before the revolt against the Communist Chinese, would return to Tibet carrying a wide assortment of items ranging from rice to felt hats from England. Sheep were used as transport animals in western Tibet and were often sold along with their loads at the end of the journey. Chinese, Indians, Nepalese, and Kashmiris also played a part in the commercial activities in Tibet. The most profitable items of trade—tea, wool, gold, and rice—were formally controlled by the Tibetan government, but after the annexation of Tibet by China, these items became a monopoly of the State Trading Company of Communist China.

**4. Farmers and Nomads.**—The common people of Tibet were divided into sedentary agriculturalists and nomadic pastoralists. The agriculturalists formed the peasantry of Tibet, inhabiting the river valleys particularly in the southern and southeastern regions. Some peasants worked as tenants for the government, monasteries, and lamas or nobles. The land was allotted to them in return for taxes paid and labour service. Others worked as hired or drafted labourers on land directly managed by the estate holder. Only a few peasants owned and worked plots of land. Women, in addition to their domestic duties, laboured in the fields with their menfolk.

A nomad is called 'Brog-pa (*Drok-ba*) meaning "one (pa) of the pasture-land ('Brog)." The herdsmen and shepherds pasture their flocks on steppes at altitudes too high for crop raising. Grazing land is scattered throughout the upland of Tibet, particularly in the northeastern and eastern regions. Some pastoral groups practise seasonal migration: during the winter they stay in the lowlands and in the summer graze their animals on mountain slopes. The nomads are a hardy and independent group who tend to look down on agriculturalists and townspeople because they are bound to the land. Also there are seminomads, called Sa-ma-'brog, who follow a sedentary livelihood part of the year and a nomadic one the other part.

Buddhism forbids the taking of life, and the Tibetans who are voracious meat-eaters had to resort to various devious means to obtain animal flesh. In Lhasa and other large towns, butcher shops were operated by the Chinese or Kashmiri Muslims.

**5. Outcastes.**—Buddhist teachings maintain the equality of all living beings and the social gradation of a caste system is alien to Tibetan society. Nevertheless, there was a group in Lhasa called Ro-rgyab-pa whose members were treated as outcastes. They earned their livelihood from begging and from disposing of corpses. The most common form of funeral in Tibet is to cut up the corpse and feed the pieces to vultures and dogs. Cremation is common in other Buddhist countries and it was practised in Tibet wherever firewood was plentiful; however, most of Tibet is above timberline and there is no wood for funeral pyres. The Ro-rgyab-pa were not supposed to display any signs of wealth, and the walls of their houses were made with the horns of sheep, goats, or yaks, held in place by mortar.

### D. Religion

The pre-Buddhist religion of Tibet was a form of Central Asiatic shamanism, called Bon (*Pön*) in Tibetan. A follower of Bon is called a Bon-po. In Bon teachings the world consists of three realms: heaven, earth, and underworld. Each is filled with spirits and demons and only the shaman (priest), who possesses magical powers, can visit these realms in a state of trance, using a drum as his means of transportation. The shaman was also a psychopomp who guided the soul (*bla*) of the deceased to the netherworld. The concept of a medium or oracle (*lha-pa*) plays an influential role in Bon shamanism. Sickness was believed to be caused by a malignant spirit taking possession of the patient and the cure was effected by the shaman exorcising the spirit. The basic teachings of Bon shamanism were so rooted in the Tibetan tradition that most of them were adopted into the tolerant teachings of Buddhism. Although Buddhism denies the existence of a soul or an indestructible ego, the soul concept remains strong in the minds of ordinary Tibetans. The various spirits and demons became the adversaries of the Buddhists, and monks and lamas perform exorcistic rituals to effect a cure of a patient. The oracle was adopted as well, and there was even a state oracle who was a monk of the reformed Yellow Hat sect.

Buddhism was actively propagated in Tibet in the 8th century by Padmasambhava, a learned Indian guru. The teachings he spread were those of Vajrayāna, the "Diamond Vehicle": the esoteric school of Mahāyāna (*q.v.*) Buddhism that combines the Mādhyamika teachings of Nāgārjuna with the psychosexual symbolisms and metaphysical powers taught in the tantras. According to the Mādhyamika system, the nature of absolute reality cannot be known through ordinary thought processes or sense perception, but after a long course of intellectual investigation and concentrated study, it could be experienced in a state of meditation. One cannot describe what the nature of absolute reality is, or is not, but for the sake of communication it is called Śūnyatā (Tibetan: Stong-pa-nyid, "Voidness"). When one has experienced śūnyatā in meditation, one is said to have transcendental wisdom (*prajñāpāramitā*). Tantric teachings maintain that there are mystic sounds (*mantras*) and gestures (*mudrās*) that have metaphysical power when correctly executed. This accounts for the use of the prayerwheel by the Tibetans. The so-called prayer is, in fact, a mantra, printed numerous times on a roll of paper, and each turn of the wheel is the same as saying the mantra as many times as it is printed on the roll. (*See* also Tantrism.)

About the same time that Padmasambhava and others were spreading Mādhyamika teachings in Tibet, Chinese monks were teaching the "mind-only" doctrine of the Ch'an school of Buddhism. Ch'an is the Chinese attempt to pronounce the Sanskrit word *dhyāna*, "meditation." Ch'an (pronounced *Zen* [*q.v.*] in Japanese) teaches that the nature of absolute reality can be experienced only in a state of meditation. It occurs instantaneously, and the long course of study and intellectual development so strongly emphasized by the Mādhyamika teachings are regarded as useless and even a hindrance by Ch'an.

Conflict between these two schools of Buddhism led to a debate held under royal auspices at Bsam-yas, the first monastery in Tibet, during the years 792–794. The Mādhyamika teachings from India were declared the superior ones at the end of the debate, and the king issued an edict that it was to be the only doctrine propagated in Tibet henceforth. The defeat of the Chinese school may have been influenced by the intermittent warfare then going on between Tibet and China.

Buddhism was not spread in Tibet without severe opposition from the followers of Bon shamanism. There were generations of open conflict between supporters of the two religions. Finally, Ral-pa-can, who ascended the throne in 815, was such a fanatic royal patron of Buddhism that he was assassinated (*c.* 836). His brother Glang-dar-ma ascended the throne and began a ruthless persecution of the Buddhists, which in turn led to his assassination in 842. This led to schisms in the royal lineage, loss of a central focus for the feudal loyalty necessary to maintain effective control, and the final collapse of the Tibetan Empire *c.* 850. The persecution of Buddhism continued in central Tibet and the work of translating canonical literature came to an end. Without gurus to impart the proper instructions on the esoteric meaning of the tantras, devotees began to practise them literally and the intellectual and moral level of the Buddhists went into decline.

The renaissance of Buddhism took place in western Tibet and the first reformation movement came as a result of the teachings of Atiśa, an Indian guru who arrived in Tibet in 1042. Within one century, the major sects of Tibetan Buddhism had emerged. The followers of the teachings of the 8th-century guru, Padmasambhava, were called the "Old ones" (Rnying-ma-pa). The other sects are distinguished from each other by various means, one of which is the extent to which Rnying-ma-pa tantras and rituals are rejected. The Sa-skya-pa sect, founded by Sa-chen Kun-dga' snying-po (1092–1158), kept many Rnying-ma-pa rituals but rejected most of its tantras. The Bka'-brgyud-pa sect, derived from the Tibetan translator Mar-pa (1012–97), bases its teachings on those of Tilopa and Nāropa in India. The reformed Bka'-gdams-pa sect, attributed to 'Brom-ston (1005–64), was based on the teachings of Atiśa and rejected the unorthodox tantras.

The last and most significant reformation movement was led by Tsong-kha-pa (1357–1419), a Bka'-gdams-pa who traveled widely in Tibet and studied under various lamas. He formulated his own teachings in a text, titled *Lam-rim-chen-mo* ("Great-gradual-path"), which rejected all but four tantric texts as being unorthodox. He placed special emphasis on the rules of monastic discipline and his followers became known as the Dge-lugs-pa ("Ones of the virtuous order"). They wore yellow hats instead of the usual red ones to distinguish themselves from the unreformed monks, hence the name "Yellow Hat" sect. In the 17th century, the Dge-lugs-pa achieved political supremacy through the military assistance of the Mongols and its religious leader, the Dalai Lama, became temporal ruler of Tibet.

Following the rise of Buddhism to religious dominancy, the devotees of Bon began to adopt certain Buddhist rituals, concepts, and paraphernalia, after changing them into pseudo-shamanistic features. This resulted in a systematized Bon religion hardly distinguishable from its Buddhist counterpart except by means of non-Buddhist concepts and terms of reference. At the same time, the Buddhism brought to Tibet absorbed many Bon deities, concepts, and rituals into its pantheon and teachings, and it evolved into that unique form of Buddhism practised by the Tibetans. *See* Tibetan Buddhism and also *History* below; for Tibetan iconography *see* Tibetan Art.

### E. Social Institutions

Isolated in part from the rest of the world over the centuries by almost insurmountable mountain ranges and tremendous gorges, the Tibetans developed social institutions which in some respects are unique.

**1. Marriage.**—Marriages were arranged by the parents of the groom. They would select a few eligible girls and have their horoscopes cast. If the girl's horoscope was found to be in agreement with that of the prospective groom, then the girl's parents were approached. If they gave permission for the girl to marry the groom, then the astrologer would determine an auspicious date for the wedding. After marriage, a Tibetan woman held a comparatively high family status. In religious matters, however, she was regarded to be lower than the man. For instance, of the three forms of blessing accorded by the Dalai Lama to different suppliants (touching the head with both hands, with one hand, or merely with a tassel) the last and lowest form was the one used for all women.

Although polygyny and polyandry were practised in Tibet, such forms of marriage were entered into under limited and particular circumstances, and monogamy was the predominant form of marriage. The estates of the nobility were held in perpetuity only as long as one male of each noble family per generation served as an official in the Tibetan government. Sometimes a noble family would have no sons in a given generation, only daughters. In such a case, a younger son of another noble was married to the eldest daughter and adopted her family name. He was then referred to as an "adopted bridegroom" (*mag-pa*) and, under his wife's name, entered government service. The younger sisters of the wife might enter into a state of polygynous marriage with the "adopted bridegroom" if they so desired. They were not allowed to marry someone else—unless they forfeited all rights and claims to the estate—because this would mean dividing the estate between two or more families upon the father's death, a custom which was not allowed. The estates had to be maintained intact. Generally speaking, in polygynous marriage, all the wives were sisters. The same consideration for keeping the estate or any landholdings intact was the basis for polyandry in Tibet. The eldest son of a noble family would take a bride; and if any of his younger brothers so desired, they were included in the marriage contract as junior husbands. Polyandry was also practised outside aristocratic circles among property owners, such as peasants who held a plot of land (*zhing-kha*) or merchants with large mercantile interests. Divorce was not uncommon and usually involved settlement payments.

**2. Funerals.**—During the period of the ancient kings and while Bon shamanism was the predominant religion, it was the custom to dispose of the dead by interment. Tombs of a few of the early kings are located in the 'Phyong-rgyas Valley, which converges with that of the Yar-klungs. With the rise of Buddhism to religious predominancy, the practice of interment was reserved for the bodies of those who had died from epidemic diseases such as leprosy and smallpox. Cremation was the usual mortuary practice of Buddhist India, and wherever sufficient firewood was available in Tibet, the practice was observed; however, the most common way to dispose of the dead was to cut up the corpse and expose the pieces to the vultures and dogs. This practice, perhaps distasteful to those from societies that honour the mortal body as the house of the immortal soul, is regarded by the Buddhist Tibetans as a final act of charity. Moreover, the cutting up of the corpse is related to the parapsychological ritual of destroying the concept of the indestructible ego or soul by cutting the body into pieces and, not finding the "ego or soul," reassembling the parts into a new and superior form. The school of Buddhism that taught the "dissection" method (*gcod-pa*) of destroying one's ego was introduced by the Indian guru, Pha-dam-pa, who died in Tibet in 1117. Other forms of funeral techniques were practised. Among the nomads on the high, windswept steppes devoid of firewood or carrion birds, corpses were buried under piles of stone. In some regions, they were cast into rivers and lakes to feed the fish.

The mummification and preservation of the corpses of high lamas, particularly those of the Dalai Lamas and Panchen Lamas, was done by immersing the corpse in salt for a period of months until the body had become completely desiccated. It was then placed in an elaborate mausoleum constructed of precious metals and ornamented with gems.

Most Tibetans believe that when someone died, the conscious principle (called *rnam-shes*—not to be confused with a "soul") left the body usually on the third day after death. The *rnam-shes* is believed to wander through a state of limbo, called *bar-do,* for a maximum of 49 days. A lama is called in to read the so-called "Tibetan Book of the Dead" (*Bar-do thos-grol*) to an effigy of the deceased for the purpose of guiding the "conscious principle" to a better rebirth. This Buddhist ritual reflects remnants of the Bon shaman's role as psychopomp who guides the "soul" (*bla*) of the dead to the underworld. After the "conscious principle" departs the body, a demonic spirit may enter it and reactivate it, creating a type of zombie called ro-langs ("risen-corpse"). Since a ro-langs causes sickness and even death, it must be destroyed by whatever means possible.

**3. Festivals.**—The Tibetan lunar year was marked by numerous festival days, generally for religious occasions, in which both ecclesiastics and laity took part. In addition to the great national festivals, each locality had its own particular auspicious days on which the tutelary deities were worshiped and sectarian ceremonies were performed. The 1st and 15th day of the lunar month corresponding to the days of the new and full moon were regarded as particularly auspicious days and were set aside for fasting and prayer. Many of the great temples were open to the public only on these days and the people made their way to local monasteries, clad in gala robes and carrying offerings of flowers, incense, and money. Butter was also presented for use in the sacred lamps on the altars. The day of the full moon of the fourth month, called *Sa-ga-zla-ba,* was celebrated as the anniversary of the death of the Gautama Buddha, a most solemn occasion. The 10th day of the fifth month was regarded by the Rnying-ma-pa as the birthday of Padmasambhava. The Dge-lugs-pa sect commemorated the death of its founder, Tsong-kha-pa, on the 25th day of the tenth month with a festival of lights, including torchlight processions and the lighting of innumerable butter lamps.

The most important of the yearly events was the New Year celebration, which came in February according to the Tibetan lunar calendar or in March of the year after the intercalary month was added. The festivities began with the ritualistic masked dances performed by monks on the 29th day of the last month of the old year to symbolize the triumph of Buddhism over the old religion. The advent of the New Year signaled the beginning of a gay carnival atmosphere for the laity that lasted the greater part of the month. People from the villages flocked to the larger towns, where houses and doorways were decorated with juniper boughs. Special foods and stocks of *chang* (Tibetan barley beer) were prepared. The people passed the time eating, drinking, dancing, singing, and playing games, combined with prayer when they felt so inclined.

The most important celebration for the New Year was the Great Prayer (Smon-lam chen-mo) festival, instituted in 1409 by Tsong-kha-pa, founder of the Dge-lugs-pa sect. From dawn of the new year, monks from Yellow Hat monasteries near and far began to pour into Lhasa, swelling the population by the thousands. On the second day, the state oracle of Gnas-chung came to Lhasa, as did the proctor of the 'Bras-spungs monastery, who in an impressive ceremony was invested with the civil authority of Lhasa during the festival. He then appointed a staff and policemen to maintain the law and to collect fines for disorderly conduct and uncleanliness in the streets and houses. The people swept and whitewashed their houses to avoid heavy fines. The proctor was treated with regal respect and incense burned before him wherever he went.

The Great Prayer itself began on the 3rd day, consisting of prayer services conducted by the abbot of Dga'-ldan monastery three times a day in the Jo-khang, the ancient sacred temple of Lhasa. On the 15th day the Dalai Lama performed the morning service in front of the Jo-khang and the other two services inside it. On the 16th the Dga'-ldan abbot, a successor in line from Tsong-kha-pa, resumed conducting the services in the Jo-khang.

From the 23rd to the 26th day, a special military adjunct to the festival was conducted. Smon-lam rta-pa ("Prayer Cavalrymen"), dressed in ancient armour and carrying weapons, assembled on a field in front of the Potala and pitched a tent encampment. There on the 23rd, two commanders read out the military rules and duties. On the 24th all the cavalry led by the two commanders proceeded to the garrison north of Lhasa, where a review and inspection was conducted by the Bka'-shag (Council of Ministers). The cavalry rode around the Bar-'khor street that encircled the Jo-khang three times on the 25th and then a scapegoat offering was made at Klu-sbug, the military camping field. On the 26th the cavalrymen did not participate in the activities, but the two commanders, called Ya-sor, went to the Jo-khang, where an image of the Maitreya Buddha was put on a wagon and pulled along the Bar-'khor street by monks. Meanwhile, horses without riders were sent on a race from 'Bras-spungs monastery to Lhasa, an event watched by the Dalai Lama, his ministers, and all.

The 26th day of the month marked the end of the Great Prayer festival. The 'Bras-spungs proctor disbanded his monk police force and returned to his monastery. The next two days were devoted to competitions between members of the nobility in the use of weapons and horse racing.

Birthdays were not an occasion for individual celebration. The birth year was important for astrological purposes, but the day of the month was not. It was the custom to regard an infant to be two years old at the arrival of its first New Year, and everyone added another year to their age at that time too.

**4. Dwellings.**—The finest dwellings in Tibet were those of the nobility. With the exception of a few minor nobles who lived in Zhikatse and Sakya, all the noble families maintained town houses in Lhasa. These were built of stone around a rectangular courtyard, on three sides of which were stables and storehouses. On the fourth side, opposite the gate, was the mansion itself, usually three stories high. The family quarters and chapel were located on the third floor where the rooms, unlike the dark and ill-ventilated rooms below, may have had glass windows and doors. The walls and ceiling were painted with iconographic pictures and auspicious designs.

The common people lived in one- or two-story buildings. The roof was flat and made of clay like the earthen floor. Windows were plentiful, but glass was rare and the windows were covered by waxed paper or other translucent material, protected by strong wooden shutters. The houses of the village peasants were, as a rule, solid and substantial, with walls of stone or sun-dried bricks, though occasionally of clods of earth. Flat roofs of beaten earth were common throughout the Tibetan highland, but in the Chumbi Valley and other rainy districts the roofs were gently sloped.

BY COURTESY OF THE SECRETARY OF STATE FOR FOREIGN AND COMMONWEALTH AFFAIRS, LONDON

RIVER VALLEY, WITH CHUMBI VILLAGE ON THE RIGHT. ON THE OPPOSITE BANK, A SYMBOLIC CHORTEN TOWER STANDS AMID PRAYER FLAGS

Where pine trees grew, the roofs were constructed of pine shingles, kept in position by heavy stones. The nomadic pastoralists dwelled in tents of yak hair, rectangular in shape and ranging from 12 to 50 ft. in length. An aperture about 2 ft. in width along the middle of the roof let out the smoke. (*See* also LHASA.)

**5. Food and Drink.**—The staple diet of the ordinary Tibetan is barley flour, yak meat, mutton, cheese, and tea. To this may be added rice, fruit, vegetables, chicken, and sometimes fish. The chief cereal food is rtsam-pa, a coarse flour made from parched barley, eaten in a variety of ways—simply mixed with butter to form small balls, used to thicken soup, or mixed with tea.

The main beverage is tea. Brick tea imported from China is boiled in water flavoured with soda ash. When thoroughly brewed, the mixture is taken out with a ladle and poured through a strainer into a tall, narrow churn. Butter and salt were added and the whole mixture churned until well mixed. The Tibetans consume an enormous amount of this beverage, drinking an average of 30 to 50 cups a day. The other common beverage is chang, a beer brewed from fermented barley and only mildly intoxicating.

**6. Dress.**—Lamas and monks wear woolen garments of a deep claret colour. The lower robe is wrapped around the waist, skirt-like, and secured by a long sash. An upper robe is wrapped around the shoulders like a toga. Members of the Dge-lugs-pa sect wear yellow hats; those of other sects, red. A few married lamas (who were not fully ordained monks), such as the ruling heads of the Sa-skya-pa lineage, wear lower robes of white. Nuns in Tibet wear the same claret robes as monks while in the nunneries, but they sometimes wear a woman's gown when going to the village.

The common costume of the laity, men and women alike, is called a chu-ba. For men, it is a full gown that has long sleeves and reaches to the knee. It is tied at the waist with a sash and then puffed out above to form a capacious pocket to carry personal items. The hardy nomads of eastern Tibet are seldom seen without a long sword thrust in a scabbard under the waistband at the back. Shirts are of cotton or silk, as are the trousers. Men's hats are of various styles with fur flaps. The felt hat imported from England is very popular. In some districts, men wear necklaces. Earrings are common; among the official classes, they are universal. Boots are of cloth, felt, or leather, and ornamented with various colours. They rise to the kneecap, with a slit behind the knee, and are secured with gay-coloured narrow garters three or four feet long. The summer gown is usually of cloth made from goat's hair, but the wealthier classes wear cotton or silk. The winter gown is sometimes of sheepskin; sometimes of cloth lined with lambskin or wadded cotton.

A woman's chu-ba is sleeveless and reaches to her ankles. Underneath she wears gaily-coloured blouses of cotton or silk, with long sleeves that hang down from her outstretched fingertips. The chu-ba is secured at the waist in neat folds by a sash. When young a Tibetan girl wears her hair in a single braid down the back, but when about 16 years of age, it is done in a double braid and arranged on a wooden frame called a spa-phrug. Women of the upper classes have spa-phrug headdresses ornamented with pearls, turquoise, and coral. When a teenage Tibetan girl begins to wear the spa-phrug, she also begins to wear an apron of multicoloured stripes and elaborate edges as part of her formal attire. Women among the nomads plait their hair into many tiny queues which are then gathered into a big one below the nape of the neck and adorned with red and yellow stones. Some women drape over their hair a large cloth sewn with silver and brass coins and shells which jingle at every step. When not tanned by exposure to the elements, Tibetan women are often fair, and those of the upper classes take great care of their complexions. In addition to the ornamented headdress, other kinds of jewelry are worn including rings, earrings, necklaces, and girdles. The women wear charm boxes (*ga'u*) suspended around the neck like a lavaliere. Some are exquisite in design and decoration; all contain a talisman written by a lama and sometimes a small image of a deity. A rosary and a prayerwheel are never very far away from a Tibetan's hands.

CHRISTA ARMSTRONG—RAPHO GUILLUMETTE

TIBETAN REFUGEE IN INDIA HOLDING TRADITIONAL RITUAL OBJECTS OF LAMAISM, A PRAYER WHEEL AND ROSARY

## F. Tibetan Calendar

The calendar system of the Tibetans is based on a sexagenary cycle of lunar years, with adjustment to the solar year made by the addition of an intercalary month every three years. Its development was influenced by the Chinese and Hindu calendars (*see* Calendar), yet remained distinctively Tibetan in character.

**1. Historical Development.**—Since the Tibetans had no written language before the 7th century A.D. (*see* Tibetan Language), there are no historical documents to provide data on a calendar system before that time. Later evidence indicates that the ancient Tibetans counted years only in reference to the length of the reigns of kings, and that they divided the year into four seasons of three months each. The successive months of a given season were designated simply as the "first month" (*zla-ra-ba*), the "middle month" (*zla-'bring-po*), and the "last month" (*zla-tha-chung*). *Zla-ba* (pron. da-wa) is the Tibetan word for both "moon" and "month." According to the official Chinese history of the T'ang dynasty (*q.v.*), the ancient Tibetans reckoned the barley harvest as the beginning of the new year.

King Gnam-ri srong-btsan (d. *c.* 629) expanded his kingdom and encountered the advanced civilization of the Chinese. Tibetan historians claim that *sman* and *rtsis* were introduced from China during his reign. *Sman* means "medicine" and connotes medicine and medical practices. *Rtsis* means "counting"; but it also is used to refer to astrology and chronology and a *rtsis-pa* can be a mathematician, an astrologer, or one who compiles a calendar. In later times, the Tibetan calendar was prepared by a learned lama who bore the official government title of Lama Tsipa (*bla-ma rtsis-pa*). However, it is uncertain whether a calendar system (*rtsis*) or simply accounting (*rtsis*) was introduced in the reign of Gnam-ri srong-btsan.

Historical reference to the earliest known introduction of an actual calendar system into Tibet would place that event in the early 7th century according to Tibetan tradition. However, modern scholarship has shown that the calendar referred to by Tibetan chronologists was not devised in China until the latter part of that century, and that it was probably brought to Tibet by the Chinese princess Chin-ch'eng, who was given in a matrimonial alliance *c.* 710 to the Tibetan king Khri-lde gtsug-btsan. Tibetan historians claim the newly introduced calendar caused confusion in the beginning because it placed the new year at the time of the winter solstice. In time, that new year became well established, and the first lunar month of the new year was from the new moon of December to the new moon of January. Even after the new year was altered in the 13th century to begin with the new moon in February, this old new year continued to be observed as the "Farmer's New Year" (*so-nams-pa'i lo-gsar*).

Early in the 20th century, ancient Tibetan documents were discovered in caves near Tun Huang, China. These documents, among the oldest known Tibetan writings, contain annals for the years A.D. 650–763, the earliest documentation of a calendar system. That system consists of a cycle of 12 years in which the successive years are named after 12 animals in the following sequence:

1. Mouse (*byi-ba*)
2. Ox (*glang*)
3. Tiger (*stag*)
4. Hare (*yos*)
5. Dragon (*'brug*)
6. Serpent (*sbrul*)
7. Horse (*rta*)
8. Sheep (*lug*)
9. Monkey (*sprel*)
10. Bird (*bya*)
11. Dog (*khyi*)
12. Pig (*phag*)

The earliest known use of a 60-year-cycle calendar in Tibet occurred during the reign of the king Ral-pa-can (815–*c.* 836), when the text of the Chinese-Tibetan Treaty of 821–822 was inscribed on a stone pillar and erected in Lhasa. Dates in that inscription are given according to a sexagenary-cycle system which is formed by combinations of the names of the 12 cyclical animals with those of 5 elements: wood (*shing*), fire (*me*), earth (*sa*), iron (*lcags*), and water (*chu*). Each element is combined with two successive animals and the first of the two years of the same element is called the "male" (*pho*) year; the second, the "female" (*mo*). Thus, for example, the Wood-male-Mouse year (*shing-pho-byi-ba*) is followed by the Wood-female-Ox year (*shing-mo-glang*).

Even though the years in this system are designated by the names of elements and animals, it appears to be an adaptation of the ancient Chinese 60-year cycle based on combinations of the 10 celestial stems and 12 terrestrial branches. The 10 stems correspond in successive pairs to the 5 elements, and the 12 branches correspond to the cyclical animals. The sexagenary cycle of the Chinese begins with the *Chia-tzu* year, which would correspond to the Wood-Rat year (Chinese: *mu-shu*) of the element-animal system. There is no evidence other than the stone pillar inscription to indicate that this sexagenary cycle came into common use in the 9th century, but it was to become the standard system throughout Tibet in later generations.

Religious events of the 11th century were to exert great Indian influence on the Tibetan calendar. The *Vimalaprabhā*, a commentary on the *Kālacakratantra*, a Buddhist canonical work which incorporates astronomical and chronological systems, was translated into the Tibetan language in 1027. These works expounded the use of a sexagenary-cycle calendar which was popularized in Tibet through the writings of the Indian teacher and master of the *Kālacakratantra*, Atiśa (982–1054). The Tibetans retained the names of the 12 animals and 5 elements already in use for the 60-year cycle, but they altered the first year of the cycle from the Wood-male-Mouse year (corresponding to the Wood-Rat year of the Chinese) to the Fire-female-Hare year: the year in which the commentary on the *Kālacakratantra* was translated. Tibetan sources say Atiśa arrived in western Tibet in the Water-female-Horse year of the first sexagenary cycle, which is the 16th year, and since modern scholarship has determined that Atiśa arrived there in 1042, the first year of the first cycle was 1027.

Due to the influence of the Indian calendar system, the Tibetans began to designate the months by the names of the successive constellations in which the full moon seemed to appear. For example, the month when the full moon appears to be near the Pleiades (Sanskrit: Krttika) is called Kārttika in the Indian system. The Tibetans named that month Smin-drug zla-ba, *i.e.*, the month of the "Six Sisters." In Western mythology the Pleiades are known as the seven sisters who were changed into stars, but ordinarily only six are visible to the naked eye.

Also due to Indian influence, the Tibetans name the days of the week after the seven visible celestial objects of the solar system:

| | | |
|---|---|---|
| Sun | Sunday | *Nyi-ma* |
| Moon | Monday | *Zla-ba* |
| Mars | Tuesday | *Mig-dmar* |
| Mercury | Wednesday | *Lhag-pa* |
| Jupiter | Thursday | *Phur-bu* |
| Venus | Friday | *Pa-sangs* |
| Saturn | Saturday | *Spen-pa* |

In the Chinese system, Sunday is named after the sun, but the remaining days of the week are simply numbered one to six.

Lacking evidence to the contrary, it appears the system of designating the months according to the Indian system remained the dominant one until the 13th century when an interesting change in the calendar was made. The great Sa-skya lama 'Phags-pa (1235–80), who became the imperial teacher of Kublai Khan (*q.v.*), is said to have changed the Tibetan New Year to correspond to that celebrated by the Mongols. He also adopted the Mongol custom of designating the successive months by ordinal numerals, *e.g.*, "first month" (*zla-ba dang-po*), "second month" (*zla-ba gnyis-pa*), etc. This way of naming the months is known in Tibetan as the "Mongol-months" (*Hor zla-ba*).

Before 'Phags-pa altered the calendar, the New Year was celebrated in the month of the winter solstice, and the first lunar month of the new year was called *Cho-'phrul zla-ba*, corresponding to Magha in the Indian system, which is from the new moon in January to the new moon in February. After the alteration by 'Phags-pa, the first month of the new year corresponded to the period from the new moon in February to the new moon in March, and this reckoning of the new year became known as the "King's New Year" (*rgyal-po'i lo-gsar*), as distinguished from the old "Farmer's New Year" which came at the time of the winter solstice.

Strangely enough, the first month under the Mongol system was called the "first month" and it ran from February to March; yet the Tibetans continued to call this new month of the year by the old first-month name of *Cho-'phrul zla-ba* (Magha), even though Magha in the Indian system runs from January to February. This evolvement may reflect a pious reluctance on the part of the Tibetans to change the scriptural designation of the successive months as given in the Buddhist canonical texts, even though they no longer corresponded with astronomical facts.

From the 13th century on, two major systems of calendar computation were established in Tibet. The one from China, which would embrace that of the Mongols, is referred to as *Nag-rtsis*, "black counting," and the one from India is called *Skar-rtsis*, "star counting." The use of the word "black" to refer to the Chinese system is derived from *Rgya-nag*, "Black Expanse," the Tibetan name for China.

**2. Calculation and Horoscopy.**—The computation of lunar and solar chronology is a complex art, and in Tibet it became the academic specialty of certain lamas. The basic unit of measure is the time it takes a healthy person to inhale and exhale. This unit, called *dbugs*, "breath," is calculated to be equal to four seconds according to the following ratios:

| | | |
|---|---|---|
| 6 *dbugs* | = 1 *chu-srang* | (24 seconds) |
| 60 *chu-srang* | = 1 *chu-tshod* | (24 minutes) |
| 60 *chu-tshod* | = 1 *zhag* | (24 hours) |

Unlike the Western day that begins at midnight, the 24-hour day (*zhag*) in Tibet begins at dawn. Although a *chu-tshod* is equal in these ratios to 24 minutes, it is used in spoken Tibetan to mean an "hour."

Tibetans believe that an ethereal force moves the sun and moon at different speeds across the sky, resulting in the difference in the lengths of the lunar year and the solar year. The 354-day lunar year is adjusted to the 365¼-day solar year by adding an intercalary month, called *zla-bshol*, "month prolongation," every three years. According to tradition, the first drawing up of a general calendar (*lo-tho*) was done in the 16th century. The calendar calls for an ideal lunar month of 30 days; however, this would result in a 360-day year, so the number of days in six of the months is reduced to 29 by the use of the words *chad* and *lhag* on the daily calendar. The calendar is marked off in squares numbered 1 to 30, bearing the names of the days of the week. To eliminate a numbered day of the month, the word *chad*, "cut off," is written in the appropriate square instead of the name of the day; thus: [22nd-Wednesday] [23rd-*chad*] [24th-Thursday]. As a result of this, one goes to bed the night of the 22nd-Wednesday and gets up the next morning on the 24th-Thursday: the 23rd day did not exist in actual time, but it did exist on the calendar with an ideal 30-day month.

The use of the word *lhag*, "extra," is the reverse of *chad*. It is used to combine two successive weekdays under one numbered day of the month; thus: [22nd-Wednesday] [23rd-Thursday-*lhag*-Friday] [24th-Saturday]. One goes to bed on the night of the 23rd-Thursday and gets up the next morning on the 23rd-Friday. This curious use of "cut off" and "extra" days results in the reduction of the ideal year of 360 days to the lunar year of 354 days. Regardless of the number of *chad* and *lhag* days put on the calendar, the net result must be 6 months of 30 days each and 6 of 29 days each. The controlling factor is that the first day of the month must coincide with the new moon and the 15th day with the full moon.

Astrology and the casting of horoscopes play a major role in Tibetan society. The most common horoscopes, also called *rtsis*, are relative to birth, marriage, death, annual, and whole life forecasts. The texts used for the casting of horoscopes list for each day the name of the cyclic animal, the element, the main star, the trigrams (*spar-kha*), and the magic diagram (*sme-ba*).

The most important factors for horoscopy are the degrees of affinity and antagonism between the cyclical animals and the elements. The most unfavourable combination of the animals are Mouse with Horse; Hare with Bird; Ox with Sheep; Dragon with Dog; Tiger with Monkey; and Serpent with Pig. The elements are regarded as having four degrees of relationship: maternal, filial, antagonistic, and amicable. For example, Water is maternal to Wood for wood needs water to grow; Fire is filial to Wood for fire needs wood to burn; Iron is antagonistic to Fire for fire melts iron; and Water is amicable to Fire for fire warms water.

In addition to the signs of the year, the days of the week also have degrees of affinity, for they are associated with the four basic elements: fire, water, air, and earth. For example, Sunday and Tuesday are regarded as inauspicious days because their element is fire. It is interesting to note that when the seven days of the week are shown on astrological charts, there are actually eight symbols. The days of the week are represented by a circle, a half-moon, an eye, a hand, a dagger, a garter, and a whiskbroom. The eighth symbol, often resembling the head of a bald eagle, represents Sgra-can (in Sanskrit: Rahu), the demon who causes eclipses. Sgra-can is believed to have a dragon's head, but no body, and he causes eclipses of the sun and the moon by swallowing them. Since he has no body, they soon reappear.

In spite of the great importance placed on the casting of horoscopes based on the various signs of the day of one's birth, the Tibetan people do not celebrate individual birthdays as is common in other cultures. The birthdays of holy men, such as the Buddha and the Dalai Lama, are observed with appropriate religious ceremonies, but the average Tibetan's birthday passes unnoticed. In Tibet a newborn infant is considered to be two years old on the first New Year day after its birth. After that, the infant (and everyone else) is counted a year older on each New Year.

## IV. HISTORY

Tibetan history prior to the 7th century A.D. is shrouded in legend and mythology. The Bon tradition maintains that in the very beginning there was a bright pure light, which congealed into a great cosmic egg. Devoid of limbs, it moved, and without mouth, it spoke. In time the egg broke open and a primordial man came forth. Sitting upon a golden throne on a continent in the middle of a vast ocean, he regulated the universe and all in it. The Buddhist tradition is that the great ocean covering Tibet dried up and land came forth, upon which juniper trees began to grow in profusion.

**1. Origin of Tibetans.**—The oldest tradition regarding the origin of the Tibetan people reflects a pre-Buddhist shamanistic development. It claimed that the Tibetans are descended from the simian offsprings of a monkey and a rock demoness. The four or six tribes of ancient times were said to have originated from the four or six ancestral monkeys, who in the course of evolution lost their simian features and became men. Buddhist historians of later times retained this legend, but embellished it by making the monkey an emanation of the bodhisattva Avalokiteśvara and the rock demoness a manifestation of the saviouress Tara.

The oldest known account regarding the identity of the first king of the Tibetans calls him Spu-rgyal. An 8th-century stone inscription refers to him as 'O-lde Spu-rgyal, and early Bon works call him 'O-lde Gung-rgyal. After Buddhism displaced Bon as the predominant religion, lama historians began to write accounts of the rise of the doctrine in Tibet, in which the royal primogenitor is said to have been the son of an Indian king related to the lineage of the Gautama Buddha. This son was born with miraculous markings, such as turquoise eyebrows and webbed fingers, and the king, being displeased, put him into a box and threw him into a river. The boy was rescued by shepherds who raised him. One day the young lad wandered over the mountains into Tibet and the people there marveled at his appearance and assumed he had been sent by the gods to be their ruler. They carried him on a throne (*khri*) supported on the napes of their necks (*gnya'*); thus he was called Gnya'-khri btsan-po ("Neck-enthroned Ruler"). This name occurs as that of the first Tibetan king in the traditional Buddhist genealogies, in which the early name Spu-rgyal and the Bon name 'O-lde-gung-rgyal appear as the corrupted combination, Spu-lde-gung-rgyal, the ninth king. The first seven kings in the royal lineage are called the "Heavenly Thrones," because they are said to have descended from heaven by a celestial rope (analogous to the tree which serves as the *axis mundi* in Central Asian shamanism) and, at death, they ascended back into the sky. The eighth king in the lineage, Dri-gum btsan-po, was tricked into a duel with a minister, and according to legend accidentally cut the celestial rope with his sword, thus destroying his means of ascending to heaven at death. The traditional accounts about his son and successor, Spu-lde-gung-rgyal, have less mythological aspects in them and more historical references. It is said that during his reign iron and copper were discovered, irrigation canals and bridges were constructed, and the palace 'Phying-ba stag-rtse was built. The ruins of that castle are found in the 'Phyong-rgyas Valley in the Yar-klungs region. It would seem, therefore, that the ninth king Spu-lde-gung-rgyal was a historical figure. Tibetan tradition maintains that the Bon shamanistic religion was introduced into Tibet during his time from the western country of Zhang-zhung.

During the reign of Lha-tho-tho-ri, 28th king in the later lineages, the castle of Yam-bu-bla-sgang, the remains of which are still extant, was built in the Yar-klungs Valley. Four generations later, Gnam-ri srong-btsan, who ascended the throne *c.* 569, began to expand the small Tibetan Kingdom and by the time of his death 60 years later, he had brought the regions of central Tibet, the Sum-pa Kingdom to the east, and other peripheral areas under his control. During his time, the practices of medicine and astrology were obtained from China.

**2. Early Kings.**—Srong-btsan sgam-po, son and successor of Gnam-ri srong-btsan, ascended the throne in 629. His reign marks the beginning of recorded history in Tibet, for it was then that the Tibetan script was devised. The minister Thon-mi Sambhota was sent to Kashmir by this king, and on his return the minister created the Tibetan written language, using an Indo-European script as his model (*see* TIBETAN LANGUAGE). Srong-btsan sgam-po's position of ruler in relation to the power wielded by the other local chieftains was more that of *primus inter pares* than that of an absolute monarch. Rivalry among the local lords was common and the power struggles were mainly for predominance in the royal court, but revolts against the throne were also common. The authority of the king depended upon the loyalty of his ministers and local rulers, and there was an annual oath of fealty at which animal sacrifices were performed by the Bon shaman.

Srong-btsan sgam-po extended the kingdom he inherited from his father south into Nepal and India, west into Zhang-zhung, north into the T'u-yü-hun region around Lake Koko Nor, and east to China. In addition to his own Tibetan queen, the king had two princesses as wives obtained in matrimonial alliances. The first was a Nepalese princess, daughter of the king Amshuvarman. The second was Wen-ch'eng Kung-chu, an imperial princess from China. Both princesses, who were Buddhist by religion, brought with them Buddhist images. Two temples, Jo-khang and Ra-mo-che, were built by the king to house these images. The image brought by the Chinese princess became in time the palladium of the Tibetan people. Because of these two Buddhist wives and the building of temples, lama historians in later times credited Srong-btsan sgam-po with introducing Buddhism into Tibet and refer to him as a Chos-rgyal (Religious-King). In truth, these events did not alter the prevailing shamanism of Tibet. Buddhism was not actively propagated among the Tibetans until the last half of the 8th century. Srong-btsan sgam-po died in 649 and his body was interred in a huge tumulus of earth in the 'Phyong-rgyas Valley.

Another Chinese princess was given in matrimonial alliance to Khri-lde gtsug-btsan. During his reign (705–755) many Buddhist monks, fleeing before the onslaught of Arab forces spreading Mohammedanism into Central Asia, arrived in central Tibet. Being a Buddhist, the Chinese princess persuaded the king to allow the monks to stay. Shortly afterward, a smallpox epidemic broke out, and when the princess contracted the disease and died, the monks were blamed and sent on their way.

The next king, Khri-srong lde-btsan (reigned 755–797), is also called a Religious-King by the lama historians, for he was a patron of Buddhism. During his time, the Ch'an school of meditation was being spread in Tibet by Chinese monks at the same time that there was recurrent border warfare between Tibet and China. In 763 the Tibetan forces invaded China proper and captured the T'ang capital, Ch'ang-an. Securing promises of tribute and other concessions, the Tibetans withdrew after 15 days.

Not long before that, the learned Indian guru, Padmasambhava, was invited to Tibet to teach the Indian school of Buddhism known as Vajrayāna, which is based on the philosophical doctrines of the Mādhyamika system, combined with the esoteric teachings of tantrism. (*See* TIBETAN BUDDHISM; TANTRISM.) Through his occult powers, Padmasambhava was able to overcome the opposition of the Bon followers, at least in the royal court, and to begin his teachings. Śāntirakṣita, another learned Indian scholar, was also invited to Tibet, and he and Padmasambhava directed the founding of the first monastery, Bsam-yas, the site of a two-year debate between the exponents of the Ch'an meditation school from China and the Mādhyamika study-meditation school from India. The Indian system was declared superior and King Khri-srong lde-btsan issued an edict in 794 proclaiming it the orthodox and only religious system henceforth to be practised. The edict proscribed Ch'an Buddhism and the Chinese monks departed from Tibet. By implication, it also forbade the Bon shamanism, and many Bon-po migrated to eastern Tibet in order to continue their religious practices.

The third king singled out for veneration by the Buddhists was better known by his epithet Ral-pa-can (Long-hair), who ascended the throne in 815. During his time peace was restored with China, and a bilingual treaty was inscribed on a stone pillar and erected in Lhasa in 823. Ral-pa-can became a fanatic patron of Buddhism. He instituted the first monastic tax to support the monks and placed them in his court in key positions: the chief minister was a monk. The king began to persecute those who criticized his pro-Buddhist activities to such a degree that it finally led to his assassination in *c.* 836 by two ministers of the Dbas and Cog-ro families. The conspirators then placed on the throne the elder brother of the murdered king, Glang-dar-ma, who was anti-Buddhist. A wide-scale persecution of Buddhism was begun. Monks were forced to marry or become hunters, and the work of translating canonical texts from Sanskrit into Tibetan, which was being done primarily at Bsam-yas monastery, was stopped and the Indian scholars sent away. The persecution had reached such intensity by 842 that a monk, Lha-lung Dpal-gyi rdo-rje, went to Lhasa in disguise, where he found the king standing before the stone pillar bearing the peace treaty inscription. Pretending to make an obeisance, the monk knelt and shot an arrow into the king's body. Changing his disguise, the monk managed to escape to eastern Tibet.

The assassinations of Ral-pa-can and Glang-dar-ma created a schism in the royal lineage because there was a question as to the legitimacy of the two pretenders to the throne. Two petty kingdoms emerged out of the one great empire. Soon another petty kingdom developed in western Tibet, and this marked the end of Tibet as one of the great powers of Central Asia. Without a central focus for the feudal loyalty that was the foundation of royal authority, the local lords began to develop their own hegemonies, and central Tibet remained without a united government for four centuries.

**3. Western Kingdom.**—The kingdom established in the region of Spu-rangs and Guge by Nyi-ma-mgon, great-grandson of Glang-dar-ma, continued to grow in strength and influence. Its successive kings were patrons of Buddhism and instrumental in the great renaissance that began with the works of Rin-chen bzang-po (958–1055), who was called the Great Translator. The ruler, Lha Bla-ma, had sent 21 Tibetan youths to Kashmir to study Buddhism, but 19 of them died there. Of the 2 survivors, Rin-chen bzang-po became the most famous and served as the abbot of the Mtho-lding monastery in Guge. During his time, the great Indian pandit Atiśa was invited to western Tibet, where he arrived in 1042, an important event for two reasons. First, the accurate computing of the Tibetan lunar calendar with its 60-year cycles is predicated upon the exact year Atiśa came to Tibet. The older date of 1040 found in many Western books has been corrected to 1042 by modern research. Second, the teachings of Atiśa and their systematization by 'Brom-ston led to the first reformed sect in Tibetan Buddhism. Not long afterward, the Sa-skya-pa and Bka'-brgyud-pa sects also emerged (*see* also *Religion,* above).

**4. Relations with the Mongols.**—At the turn of the 13th century Tibet was divided among a number of local lords and religious leaders who ruled by right of succession. In 1207 the Tibetans learned of the move by Genghis Khan (*q.v.*) to subjugate the Hsi-hsia Kingdom and decided to submit to the Mongols before they should turn on Tibet. A delegation was sent to the Khan and the Tibetans began paying tribute. When the Khan died in the Hsi-hsia campaign of 1227, the Tibetans stopped paying tribute. This led to the first Mongol incursion into central Tibet in 1239, during which the Ra-sgreng monastery and others were attacked. Shortly afterward, the Mongol prince Godan who ruled in the Koko Nor regions sent a summons directly to Sa-skya Pandita (1182–1251), the learned abbot of Sa-skya monastery, to come to the Koko Nor region. They met in 1247 and Prince Godan invested the Sa-skya lama with temporal power over Tibet as a viceroy of the Khan. Sa-skya Pandita had taken two of his nephews with him to Koko Nor. 'Phags-pa (1235–80) was destined to become the favourite of Kublai Khan (*q.v.*), while he was still a Mongol prince. When Kublai became the khan in 1260, he appointed 'Phags-pa as his imperial preceptor (Chinese: Ti-shih) and invested him with temporal authority over the 13 myriarchies of central Tibet. Thus, the Sa-skya-pa sect became the predominant one in the Mongol court, and its head lama ruled in Tibet on behalf of the khan. The Sa-skya lama's position was again only that of *primus inter pares* and his temporal power was reinforced by Mongol cavalry.

When 'Phags-pa was 31, he returned to Sa-skya in Tibet for the first time. While there, he created a script based upon the Tibetan one in compliance with Kublai Khan's request. Tibetan is written from left to right with rounded letters, but 'Phags-pa devised his square-shaped letters to be written downward in columns like Chinese. He presented his script to Kublai Khan upon his return to Khanbaliq (later called Peking) in 1268. The khan declared 'Phags-pa's script to be the official one for the Mongols, and during Kublai's time it was used for official documents, but because of its cumbrous calligraphy, it did not replace the old Uighur script and soon fell into disuse after Kublai's death.

The death of Kublai Khan in 1294 marked the peak of Mongol power in Asia: it soon began to decline, particularly in Tibet and China. With their attention devoted to matters in China, the Mongol Khans could no longer provide the cavalry necessary to ensure the exercise of temporal rule by the Sa-skya lamas. Dissension among the local ruling myriarchs led to the rise of the Phag-mo-gru myriarch as the real power in Tibet by the middle of the 14th century. The leader of the Phag-mo-gru, Byang-chub rgyal-mtshan (1302–64), conquered all of central Tibet by 1358, ending Mongol control ten years before the Chinese managed to overthrow the Mongols and establish the Ming dynasty in 1368. Byang-chub rgyal-mtshan abolished the myriarch system of local administration and replaced it with the rdzong (district) unit system. The administrators of the districts were appointed by the Phag-mo-gru ruler, thereby reinstating a semblance of centralized authority, one based on personal loyalty rather than outside military force. By the middle of the 15th century disloyalty on the part of the Rin-spungs family, which took over Zhikatse *c.* 1435 and gradually gained control of the province of Gtsang, marked the decline of the Phag-mo-gru sectarian rule. The Rin-spungs were defeated in turn by one of their subordinates in *c.* 1565, who established the line of Gtsang-pa rulers that remained in power until 1642.

**5. Rise of the Dalai Lamas.**—The reformation movement started by Tsong-kha-pa (1357–1419) found many new followers who were disillusioned with the political ambitions and aspirations for wealth of the ruling sectarian groups of the 15th and 16th centuries, particularly of the Karma-pa sect allied with the Gtsang-pa rulers. Many of the local rulers in the province of Dbus began to shift their loyalty from the Phag-mo-gru, which was of the Bka'-brgyud-pa sect, to the reformed Dge-lugs-pa sect of Tsong-kha-pa.

The practice of maintaining a spiritual lineage of lamas through reincarnation arose in the 14th century when the Black-hat Karma-pa Rang-byung rdo-rje (1284–1338) proclaimed that he would be reborn. His "reincarnation" (*yang-srid*) was discovered to be Rol-pa'i rdo-rje (1340–83). The other sects began to adopt this practice and each soon had its various lineage of reborn lamas. A nephew of Tsong-kha-pa and founder of the Tashilhumpo (Bkra-shis lhum-po) monastery, Dge-'dun-grub-pa (1391–1474), was reincarnated in Dge-'dun rgya-mtsho (1475–1542), who became the abbot of 'Bras-spungs monastery near Lhasa. The third in the lineage, Bsod-nams rgya-mtsho (1543–88), was invited to Mongolia by Altan Khan of the Tümed Mongols, who in turn was so impressed with the lama that he bestowed on him the title of *Dalai Lama* in 1578. Dalai is a Mongol word for "Ocean" (Tibetan: *rgya-mtsho*) and the title implies that the Lama's wisdom was as vast and deep as an ocean. Thus the third in the lineage of incarnate lamas was the first to receive the title of Dalai Lama. It was posthumously applied to the earlier two and so the nephew of Tsong-kha-pa is regarded as the first Dalai Lama. The Tibetans do not address the Dalai Lama by that title, they refer to him as Yid-bzhin-nor-bu (Wish-granting Jewel) or Rgyal-ba Rinpo-che (Great Precious Conqueror). When the third in the line of the Dalai Lama incarnations died, the great-grandson of Altan Khan was discovered to be the new reincarnation. The Mongol lad was brought to Tibet and installed as the abbot of 'Bras-spungs, and henceforth the Mongols were devoted patrons of the Dge-lugs-pa sect. The fourth Dalai Lama was the only one of the line who was not a Tibetan.

**6. The Great Fifth Dalai Lama.**—At the beginning of the 17th century the Gtsang-pa ruler extended his power and in 1618 attacked Lhasa. Mongol troops that had been expelled from Lhasa in 1605 by the previous Gtsang-pa ruler's forces returned in 1619 disguised as Buddhist pilgrims. These Mongols were induced to attack the two Gtsang-pa military camps established near Lhasa in 1620, and the Gtsang-pa ruler himself was besieged in the medical monastery on Lcag-po-ri Hill just southwest of the Potala Hill. Dge-lugs-pa leaders acted as peacemakers and in exchange for the Gtsang-pa ruler's release retrieved those monasteries which had been forced to become Red Hat institutions because of the domination of the Karma-pa sect.

The fifth Dalai Lama, Ngag-dbang rgya-mtsho (1617–82), was born in the ancient royal castle of 'Phying-ba stag-rtse in the 'Phyong-rgyas Valley. Although recognized in 1619 as the rebirth of the abbot of 'Bras-spungs, he was not brought to that monastery until 1622 because of the unrest in the Lhasa area caused by the Karma-pa Gtsang forces.

The decisive clash between the Yellow Hat Dge-lugs-pa in Dbus and the Karma-pa of the Red Hat sects in Gtsang came early in the life of the fifth Dalai Lama. The chief protagonist for the Dge-lugs-pa was Bsod-nam chos-'phel, who had been chief attendant to the fourth Dalai Lama and then became advisor to the young fifth incarnation. Leader of the opposition was Karma Bstan-skyong (whose name literally means "Defender of the Karma-pa Teachings"), who succeeded his father as the ruler of Gtsang at Zhikatse in 1621. Politico-religious friction between the two provinces and opposing sects increased to the breaking point, which came when Karma Bstan-skyong entered into an alliance with the Bon ruler of Be-ri in eastern Tibet for the purpose of combining forces against the Dge-lugs-pa. When Bsod-nam chos-'phel learned of this alliance, he sent a courier to Gushri Khan, chief of the Qoshot Mongols in the Koko Nor region, who was a devoted patron of the Dalai Lama. Gushri Khan immediately launched an attack against the Be-ri ruler in 1639, defeating him in the following year. By 1641, all of Khams in eastern Tibet was brought under Mongol rule by Gushri Khan, who then turned his attention to central Tibet. Combining his forces with those of Bsod-nam chos-'phel, the khan marched on Zhikatse. The Gtsang forces were defeated and Karma Bstan-skyong taken prisoner in 1642. In an impressive ceremony, the fifth Dalai Lama was placed on a throne in the palace at Zhikatse, and Gushri Khan, conqueror and actual ruler of the country, presented the Dalai Lama with temporal authority over Tibet as a religious gift. Thus began the form of government that was to endure in Tibet until the advent of the Communist Chinese occupation in the middle of the 20th century.

A regent was appointed to handle the actual administration of the civil government on behalf of the Dalai Lama, and the maintenance of law and order rested in the hands of Gushri Khan and his Mongol army. Gushri Khan appointed Bsod-nam chos-'phel as the first regent, and then spent the rest of his life consolidating the authority of the Dalai Lama over regions formerly loyal to the Gtsang rulers. The great khan died at 'Bras-spungs in 1655.

For various reasons, the fifth Dalai Lama is referred to as the Great Fifth by the Tibetans. He was a learned scholar and an astute political figure. His religious influence extended over the vast regions of Central Asia inhabited by various Mongol tribes and his political influence, backed by the cavalry of Gushri Khan and his sons, covered Tibet. The charismatic mystique of the Dalai Lama was not underestimated by the Manchus, who came from the same shamanistic background as the Mongols. The Manchus succeeded in conquering China in 1644 and established the Ch'ing dynasty (*q.v.*). The Manchu emperor extended an invitation to the Dalai Lama and the Panchen Lama to come to Peking for a visit. The Panchen Lama declined due to advanced age, but the Dalai Lama accepted, setting out in 1652. He was received by the emperor in an impressive and elaborate reception and stayed in the so-called Yellow Palace, built especially for him. After two months of feasting, celebrations, spiritual instructions, and the exchanging of grandiose titles with the emperor, the Dalai Lama returned to Tibet in 1653. This event marked the beginning of the religious relationship between the Dalai Lamas and the Manchu emperors that was to develop into a politico-religious one early in the 18th century.

The dominant personality of the fifth Dalai Lama is reflected in some of the innovations he carried out. Prior to his ascendancy to power, the abbots of the Tashilhumpo monastery were appointed by the abbot of 'Bras-spungs (*i.e.,* the Dalai Lama), but a text was "discovered" that revealed that the fifth Dalai Lama's teacher Blo-bzang Chos-kyi rgyal-mtshan (1567–1662) was a manifestation of the Amitābha Buddha. This teacher was installed on the abbot's throne at Tashilhumpo by the Dalai Lama and he became the first of the Panchen Lamas. After that, the successors were those considered to be reincarnations of Blo-bzang Chos-kyi rgyal-mtshan, and they were discovered and confirmed in the same way as rebirths of the Dalai Lama.

The fifth Dalai Lama had the Potala built on Dmar-po-ri Hill in Lhasa on the ruins of the castle built in the 7th century by King Srong-btsan sgam-po. He then moved the official residence from 'Bras-spungs monastery into the Potala, which became the winter palace of the Dalai Lamas. The summer palace called Nor-bu gling-ka (Jewel Park) was built west of Lhasa in 1783 by the eighth Dalai Lama.

The death of the fifth Dalai Lama in 1682 was concealed by his regent Sangs-rgyas rgya-mtsho in order to consolidate power and to see the Potala construction brought to completion. Meanwhile, he had discovered the rebirth of the deceased Dalai Lama, but he had to keep the matter secret. The Potala was completed in 1695 and in the following year the regent announced the death of the Great Fifth and the discovery of the sixth Dalai Lama, Tshang-dbyangs rgya-mtsho (1683–1706). Unlike the other Dalai Lamas, the sixth had not been brought to 'Bras-spungs monastery as a child to begin the monastic training and education for his position as spiritual head of the Dge-lugs-pa sect. By the time it was publicly announced that he was the rebirth of the Great Fifth, he had developed a taste for wine, women, and song. He had a pavilion built on the lake north of the Potala for a trysting place. His behaviour caused such scandal that he finally renounced his monastic vows in 1702, but he still remained the Dalai Lama. One of the few examples of Tibetan secular love poetry is the some 62 quatrains attributed to this Dalai Lama.

Over the years the fifth Dalai Lama had slowly accumulated into his own hands the power that had been exercised by Gushri Khan before his death, and by the time of the Great Fifth's death in 1682, he was in fact the temporal ruler of Tibet, and the Qoshot Mongols were his military force. In 1697, Lha-bzang Khan, great-grandson of Gushri Khan, became chief of the Qoshot Mongols, and sought to restore the khanship to its former position of power and glory. He formed an alliance with the

Manchu emperor K'ang-hsi (1662–1722) to offset the alliance his enemy, regent Sangs-rgyas rgya-mtsho, had formed with the ruler of the Dzungar Mongols, who were a constant threat to the Manchu throne. In 1705 Lha-bzang Khan moved against the regent and had him put to death. Taking full control in Lhasa, the khan deposed the sixth Dalai Lama in 1706 and replaced him with a candidate of his own choice. The sixth Dalai Lama died while being taken to China by a military escort. Lha-bzang Khan became the virtual "king" of Tibet and maintained a close relationship with the K'ang-hsi emperor for over a decade.

**7. The Dzungar Invasion.**—The death of the regent who had an alliance with the king of Dzungaria and the deposition and death of the sixth Dalai Lama by Lha-bzang Khan eventually led to an invasion of central Tibet by Dzungar Mongols commanded by Tshe-ring don-grub, brother of the Dzungarian king. The Dzungars divided into two forces, one was to march to the Sku-'bum monastery in the Koko Nor region and get the seventh Dalai Lama who was being held there in protective custody by the Manchus; the other force was to march across the barren windswept Chang Thang and join forces with the one from Koko Nor, which would bring the seventh Dalai Lama to the rendezvous, and together they would march on Lhasa. But the Dzungars were defeated in the Koko Nor region and failed to get the seventh Dalai Lama away from the Manchus. Those who marched across the deserted Chang Thang, learning of the Koko Nor defeat, attacked Lhasa unaided and conquered the city. Lha-bzang Khan was killed and his family deported to Dzungaria. The "puppet" Dalai Lama enthroned by the Khan was deposed but allowed to live on as an ordinary monk. He was later deported to China where he died. The Dzungars were zealous patrons of the Dge-lugs-pa sect, and they began a ruthless campaign of persecution against Rnying-ma-pa monasteries. This turned the people against them and resistance groups developed.

**8. Manchu Intervention.**—Before his death, Lha-bzang Khan had sent an urgent appeal to his ally, the K'ang-hsi emperor, for help. The message did not reach the emperor until March 1718. Two imperial expeditions were ordered to proceed to Tibet. The first from Hsi-ning was annihilated by the Dzungars at Nag-chu, some 120 mi. north of Lhasa. The second expedition from Szechwan was delayed and did not leave until 1719. Meanwhile, another army was dispatched from Hsi-ning under the command of the Manchu general Yansin. This one was escorting the seventh Dalai Lama whom the K'ang-hsi emperor now recognized as the official Dalai Lama even though he had also recognized the "puppet" Dalai Lama in Lha-bzang Khan's time. The K'ang-hsi emperor, undoubtedly a brilliant and forceful personality, was an astute politician whose ultimate goal was to secure an alliance with the Dalai Lama in Lhasa and use his religious position to neutralize Mongol opposition to the Manchu throne. The inhospitable frozen plateau of Tibet was of no immediate interest to him; only the charismatic influence of the Dalai Lama on much of Central Asia was of value.

The Dzungars were being approached by an imperial army from the east and another from the northeast; so they decided to retreat to Dzungaria. Tshe-ring don-grub and his troops engaged the forces of General Yansin in their flight north and then west across the Chang Thang toward their homeland in the Ili River Valley. The two imperial armies arrived in Lhasa in the fall of 1720 and the seventh Dalai Lama, Bskal-bzang rgya-mtsho (1708–57), was enthroned in the Potala. The government was reorganized. The powerful position of regent was replaced with a council of ministers (Bka'-shag), which would carry out the civil administration of the government. The former military support provided by the Mongols to the Dalai Lama was now the responsibility of a Manchu garrison set up in Lhasa. When all was in order, the imperial forces returned to China. The religious relationship between the fifth Dalai Lama and the Shun-chih emperor became a politico-religious one between the seventh Dalai Lama and the K'ang-hsi emperor. The relationship is one called Lama-Patron (Yon-mchod in Tibetan) and it is based upon a mutual obligation. The lama provides the spiritual guidance and influence, the patron provides the military support to secure the temporal position of the lama. This relationship as the basis of theocratic government began with Kublai Khan and the Sa-skya-pa lama, 'Phags-pa, and it was continued in the 17th century by Gushri Khan and the fifth Dalai Lama. It served the same function between the Manchu emperors and the Dalai Lamas during the Ch'ing dynasty (1644–1912).

**9. Civil War in Tibet.**—The K'ang-hsi emperor died in 1722 and his son, the Yung-cheng emperor, ascended the imperial throne in 1723. One of his first acts was to withdraw the garrison in Lhasa, removing the Dalai Lama's military support, as part of his retrenchment policy. Meanwhile, provincial dissension was developing among the members of the Council of Ministers. By 1727 armed conflict between Pho-lha-nas of Gtsang and a triumvirate of ministers from Dbus plunged Tibet into civil war. Both sides appealed to the Manchu emperor for support, but Yung-cheng delayed making a decision so long that Pho-lha-nas had defeated the Lhasa triumvirate in July 1728, two months before the Manchu Imperial Army arrived on the scene. Since Pho-lha-nas was in fact the temporal ruler in Tibet, the Yung-cheng emperor confirmed his position and the triumvirate ministers were executed, along with 14 of their close supporters. The Manchu garrison was reestablished in Lhasa. (In 1733 it was moved into permanent quarters at Grwa-bzhi north of the city, where it remained until 1912, when following the revolt against the Manchus all troops of the garrison were deported from Tibet.) For the first time, the Manchu emperor posted *ambans* in Lhasa as his observers. (*Amban*, a Manchu title, was a key position in the administration of the Ch'ing Empire, and in Tibet it was always filled by a Manchu or a Mongol, never a Chinese.)

Considered to be pro-Manchu, Pho-lha-nas became virtual ruler of Tibet and the country was peaceful until his death in 1747. His son and successor plotted to overthrow the Manchus in Tibet. The *ambans* learned of his ambitions and assassinated him in 1750. One of his followers led a mob against the residency of the *ambans* and both died during the violence. The Manchu treasury was looted and the residency set afire. First reports to the Ch'ien-lung emperor (1736–96) indicated a massive revolt and an imperial army was ordered up, but it was soon learned that the trouble in Lhasa was nothing more than mob violence and the expeditionary force was reduced to 800 troops.

The government structure was changed again in 1751. For the first time since the reign of the fifth Dalai Lama, actual administrative authority was again in the hands of the Dalai Lama. The Council of Ministers continued to conduct daily duties, but the ultimate responsibility rested with the Dalai Lama. During the interregnum caused by his death and subsequent minority, the duties of the high lama were carried out by a regent. The regent's position after 1751 was filled by an incarnate lama who had the authority to make decisions and execute them as if he were the Dalai Lama, but as soon as the young Dalai Lama reached his majority, the regent was relieved of all power and position in the government. Such a practice tended to create reluctance on the part of a regent who had exercised absolute power for a period of 18 to 20 years to withdraw from his position. It is perhaps more than coincidence that from the 9th Dalai Lama (1806–15) to the 12th (1856–75) none lived to be more than 21 years of age.

**10. The Nepalese War 1788–92.**—In 1788 the Gurkhas, who had not long before gained ascendancy throughout Nepal, invaded and occupied some Tibetan districts near the Nepalese frontier. A hasty treaty was concluded and the Tibetans agreed to pay tribute to the Gurkha king, which they did the following year. When the annual payment came due in 1791, however, the Tibetans refused to pay and the Gurkhas again invaded Tibet, this time carrying their assault as far north as Zhikatse and the Panchen Lama's monastery of Tashilhumpo, which they looted. When the Ch'ien-lung emperor was informed of the invasion this time, he dispatched an imperial army of some 13,000 troops, which marched across Tibet in the middle of winter. There it joined forces with the Tibetan army of some 10,000 men and together they marched against the Gurkhas, whom they defeated in the spring of 1792. The peace treaty called for the restoration of all loot, compensation payments, and the sending of a tribute mission every five years to Peking. The Manchu emperor suspected that the British, established in India, had had a part in the Gurkha invasion and he became determined to close Tibet as far as possible to foreign influence. It was decreed that all external affairs were to be handled through the office of the *ambans*.

The Nepalese War of 1788–92 was a prime illustration of the lama-patron relationship between the Dalai Lama and the Manchu emperor. Being a country devoted to the nonviolence teachings of the Buddha, Tibet did not maintain a standing army. In emergency, it called up the farmers from the fields to fight, but they were ill-equipped and without proper training. As patron and suzerain of Tibet, the Manchu emperor supplied the military might necessary to protect the Dalai Lama and to restore law and order. Once peace was achieved, the imperial forces returned to China, just as they had done in 1721, 1728, and 1751.

**11. Decline of the Manchus.**—Manchu influence in Tibet was in direct relationship to Manchu power in China. The 19th century, which brought the impact of Western industrialization to China, marked the beginning of the end of Manchu power. The Opium War of 1839–42 with Great Britain, the T'ai-p'ing Rebellion, a civil war that ravaged China from 1851 to 1864, and subsequent encounters with the forces of Great Britain, France, Germany, and others, drained the vitality and strength of the Manchu dynasty. The weakness of the Ch'ing court and the inability of the Manchu emperor to provide imperial support to the Dalai Lama's government had a direct effect on developments in Tibet. In 1841 the Hindu Dogra troops of Gulab Singh, maharaja of Jammu, invaded western Tibet. No imperial troops were forthcoming from China because of the Opium War but, by chance, the Tibetans were able to defeat the Dogras and conclude a treaty in 1842. No representative of the emperor was present at the negotiations, but he was informed of the results later by the *amban* Meng-pao.

In 1855 the Gurkhas again invaded southern Tibet. This time the T'ai-p'ing Rebellion occupied the imperial troops and the Tibetans were compelled to face the Nepalese forces alone. They were not so fortunate against them as they had been against the Dogras. Defeat was followed by a treaty that empowered the Nepalese to establish trade agencies in Lhasa and other centres, and gave them an annual tribute of 10,000 rupees in cash, in addition to extraterritorial rights in Tibet. Manchu control in Tibet continued to decline and by the end of the 19th century it existed more in name than in fact.

**12. Relations with the British.**—Official relations with the British began in 1774. Early in the 1770s Bhutanese raided Bengal, then under the influence of the British East India Company. Warren Hastings, British governor of Bengal, exacted retribution from the Bhutanese. Bhutan was at that time a nominal vassal of Tibet and since the Dalai Lama was a minor, the Panchen Lama communicated with Hastings in an attempt to mediate. Seizing the opportunity, Hastings sent George Bogle to Tashilhumpo, where he stayed several months and made friends with the third Panchen Lama (1737–80). In 1783 a second mission under Samuel Turner was dispatched to the court of the Panchen Lama, but trade privileges were obtained for the Indians only.

**13. The Younghusband Expedition.**—In 1890 the British government entered into a convention with the Manchu government regarding the boundary between Sikkim, as a protectorate of British India, and Tibet. Then in 1893 the two governments negotiated trade regulations which gave the British the right to establish a trade agency at Yatung in the Chumbi Valley. The Tibetan government, which had not been a party to either of the negotiations, refused to honour them. Great Britain tried to put pressure on the Manchu government, but the Sino-Japanese War of 1894–95 monopolized Manchu interests and strength. The unresolved situation dragged on and tension mounted. British concern with the aspirations of tsarist Russia in Asia was heightened when it was learned that a Buriat Mongol, Dorjieff (Dordzhiyev), a tutor of the 13th Dalai Lama, was received by Tsar Nicholas II as the Dalai Lama's envoy in July 1901.

Lord Curzon, viceroy of India from 1899 to 1905, began sending letters to Lhasa, which were returned unopened with the seals intact. Frustrated in his attempts to open Tibet to British trade and concerned with the apparent Russian connections with Lhasa, Lord Curzon, having first obtained permission from his home government, authorized Col. Francis Younghusband to cross the Tibetan border with a small escort and proceed to Skam-pa rdzong for the purpose of negotiating with the Tibetan government directly on issues of trade and frontier questions.

The Younghusband mission with a small escort proceeded to Skam-pa rdzong in July 1903 and remained there for months. Lesser officials continually reiterated the claim that if the mission would withdraw to the Sikkimese border Lhasa would send higher officials authorized to negotiate on behalf of the Tibetan government to meet it. Younghusband refused to withdraw from his position. In November Lord Curzon secured permission for the mission to advance to Gyangtse to conduct negotiations. Since this involved penetration deep into Tibet, the small military escort was increased to a full-fledged expedition under the command of Brig. Gen. James Macdonald. For weeks an endless stream of troops, porters, and pack animals moved through Sikkim, over the Rdza-leb Pass (14,398 ft. [4,389 m.]) and down into the Chumbi Valley. The mission and its escort made winter quarters at Tuna (Dud-sna) just beyond Phag-ri rdzong at the north end of the valley. There it stayed until March 1904. Tibetan officials came to Colonel Younghusband to ask him to return to the border. This he would not do, nor would he negotiate since none of the officials carried credentials empowering him to negotiate for Lhasa.

The British began the march to Gyangtse. Enroute near Guru the Tibetans had constructed a stone wall across the valley floor and taken up defensive positions behind it, but they were no match for the British Army. In the battle at Guru over 600 Tibetans were killed or seriously wounded and over 200 taken prisoner; only a few of the British troops were wounded and none were killed. The Younghusband mission marched on to Gyangtse, arriving in April. Three months were spent in camp at Gyangtse waiting for properly accredited officials to come from Lhasa to negotiate, but it was the same as before. Finally, reinforcements were sent up from India, and the mission began the last stage of the journey to Lhasa on July 14, 1904. The closer the mission approached the holy city of Lhasa, the higher the rank of the officials sent to ask Younghusband to turn back, but by then Younghusband was determined to reach Lhasa at all cost.

About July 30, the 13th Dalai Lama, Thub-bstan rgya-mtsho (1876–1933), appointed the abbot of Dga'-ldan monastery as regent and then, with an entourage, left Lhasa enroute to Mongolia. On Aug. 3, the British mission arrived in the forbidden city and finally entered into the long desired negotiations. The regent, ministers of the Bka'shag, abbots of the three main monasteries, and members of the assembly (*tshogs-'du*) negotiated for the Tibetan government; Younghusband and his aides for the British. The Manchu *amban*, Yu-ta'i, was later admonished by the emperor for not negotiating with Younghusband before he reached Lhasa, but the *amban's* excuse was that the Tibetans would not provide him with transport. Since direct negotiations between the British government and the Manchu court in 1890 and 1893 had failed to receive recognition by the Tibetan government, it is unlikely that Younghusband would have entered into negotiations with *amban* Yu-t'ai, even if he had gone to meet him.

On Sept. 7, 1904, a convention between Great Britain and Tibet was signed (and subsequently ratified at Simla on Nov. 11). The regent wanted the document signed in the *amban's* residence, but Younghusband insisted that it should be signed amid ceremony and pomp in the Potala itself. The main provisions of the convention were: (1) the establishing of two more trade agencies, one at Gyangtse and one at Gartok in western Tibet. (The trade mart at Yatung had been provided for in the regulations of 1893, but the Tibetans had prevented its opening since they were not party to the negotiations.) (2) The abolition of Tibetan duty on British trade from India. (3) An indemnity of £500,000, payable in 75 annual installments, the British to occupy the Chumbi Valley until it was paid in full. (The British home government later reduced this to £166,000, payable in 25 annual installments.) (4) No Tibetan territory was to be ceded or leased without British consent.

Once the agreement was signed and sealed, the British mission withdrew from Tibet. Capt. Fredrick O'Conner, who spoke Tibetan and served the mission as interpreter, was placed in charge of the new trade mart at Gyangtse. Soon afterward the British government entered into negotiations with the Manchu government to get its sanction on the Tibetan-British convention. In order to do so, Great Britain had to relinquish its right to control Tibetan internal affairs. The adhesion agreement signed in Peking in 1906 confirmed the provisions of the 1904 convention and upheld those of the 1890 and 1893 agreements, with one exception. It read: "The Government of Great Britain engages not to annex Tibetan territory or to interfere in the administration of Tibet. The Government of China also undertakes not to permit any other foreign state to interfere with the territory or internal administration of Tibet." After signing the Peking adhesion agreement, the British government agreed to allow the government of China to pay off the Tibetan indemnity in three annual payments; consequently, the British troops were withdrawn from the Chumbi Valley in February 1908.

**14. The Thirteenth Dalai Lama.**—The 13th Dalai Lama, who fled to Mongolia when the British mission was approaching Lhasa, visited the Living Buddha, Rje-btsun dam-pa, at Urga (later on Ulan Bator). On Sept. 10, 1904, the Manchu *amban* in Lhasa posted an imperial proclamation that deposed the Dalai Lama for having deserted his country. The posters were torn down or defiled by the Tibetan populace. In 1908 the Dalai Lama was invited to Peking by the Manchu emperor, and after a brief sojourn, finally returned to Lhasa in December 1909.

Following the withdrawal of the British mission from Tibet, the Manchus moved to take advantage of the weakened position of the Tibetans in an attempt to restore some semblance of suzerainty again. In 1905 Chao Erh-feng, the governor of Szechwan Province, sent troops to quell rebellion that had broken out in the disputed area of Khams, east of the Upper Yangtse River. His drastic methods and military successes during the ensuing four years brought imperial troops deeper and deeper into Tibet. In February 1910, 2,000 of Chao's troops were within two days' march of Lhasa. An advance unit of 40 cavalrymen and 200 infantrymen entered Lhasa on Feb. 12, 1910, and made their presence known by firing on the Potala.

Again the Dalai Lama appointed the abbot of Dga'-ldan monastery (but not the same one as in 1904) as regent and fled south on the night of Feb. 13. The Dalai Lama spent the next two years in exile at Darjeeling and Kalimpong, West Bengal, during which time he became friends with Charles (later Sir Charles) Bell and learned much about the modern methods of government and military science.

**15. Rebellion Against the Manchus.**—Oct. 10, 1911, marked the beginning of the revolt in China against the Manchus. When word of this reached the imperial troops in the Lhasa garrison, the Chinese soldiers revolted against their Manchu officers. The Tibetans seized the opportunity to overthrow the disunited garrison: the fighting, however, lasted for months before the Tibetans were successful in blockading the garrison and starving the troops into surrender, which was finally effected on Aug. 12, 1912. On Jan. 6, 1913, the last of the garrison troops left Tibet for China via India. From then until the 1950 Communist Chinese invasion, whatever Chinese troops were in Tibet were there by the permission of the Tibetan government. The 13th Dalai Lama returned to Lhasa amid great pomp and celebration.

The revolt in China resulted in the overthrow of the Manchus and the establishment of the republic under Pres. Yüan Shih-kai. By the same token, the Tibetans overthrew the imperial garrison in Lhasa and deported all of the troops, thus ending Manchu suzerainty in Tibet. The military campaign against Tibet sent in 1910 by Chao Erh-feng marked the first time imperial troops were sent into Tibet to fight Tibetans. Earlier expeditions had been to defend Tibet from foreign invaders or to suppress civil war or revolt, which in both cases were resolved before the arrival of the Manchu Army. Beginning in 1913, the government of the Dalai Lama was one of *de facto* independent status and it exercised sovereign power over its internal and external affairs.

**16. The Simla Conference.**—The dramatic political changes that occurred in both Tibet and China as a result of revolt against the Manchu dynasty prompted the British government to seek a new confirmation of its trade rights in Tibet. The conference began at Simla on Oct. 13, 1913, with each of the three governments represented by a plenipotentiary of equal rank: Sir Henry McMahon of Great Britain; Prime Minister Bshad-sgra of Tibet; and Ivan Chen of China. Negotiations at Simla became stalemated. The Tibetan government wanted restoration of all the regions absorbed into the Manchu Empire, meaning the Koko Nor region and the disputed part of Khams east of the Upper Yangtze River. The Chinese government demanded that Tibet be regarded as an integral part of China and that the Sino-Tibetan border be placed at Rgya-mda', just over 100 mi. (161 km.) east of Lhasa, because the main body of Chao Erh-feng's troops had marched that far in their 1910 invasion of Tibet. The deadlocked conference continued for months and finally, in February 1914, McMahon suggested a compromise boundary demarcation analogous to the division of Outer and Inner Mongolia in 1912 after the fall of the Manchus. McMahon proposed that the Ch'ing dynasty boundary between Tibet and China that generally followed the upper course of the Yangtze be accepted. He further proposed that the Chinese exercise suzerainty over all of Tibet, but Outer Tibet west of the Yangtze would be autonomous and handle its own internal administration. McMahon's compromise suggestions were acceptable to Tibet. Ivan Chen initialed the draft of the convention, but the Chinese government refused to allow him to sign the final papers because the boundary demarcation was not acceptable. Anxious to conclude the conference, Sir Henry McMahon and Prime Minister Bshad-sgra proceeded to sign the formal convention papers with a proviso stating that the powers granted the Chinese government by the articles of the convention would not be recognized until and unless the Chinese ratified the convention. After that, Great Britain and Tibet observed the provisions of the Simla convention as valid treaty obligations concluded by two sovereign governments. The Chinese government never ratified the convention. Moreover, it claimed that since Tibet was an integral part of China, its local government did not have the sovereign power to conclude such a convention with the British government and the entire affair was null and void. The Simla convention was signed July 3, 1914.

Regardless of the Chinese official view, the British and Tibetan plenipotentiaries continued their negotiations and drew up a demarcation of the boundary between India and Tibet. McMahon proposed that since no adequate survey was feasible, the boundary between India and Tibet should follow the natural watershed line from Bhutan eastward to Burma. Provisions were made to adjust the line if it proved that it should be too deep into Tibetan territory at any given location. This was acceptable to the Tibetan prime minister and the so-called McMahon Line was agreed upon by both governments, which regarded the boundary line as official and valid. The Chinese plenipotentiary was not a part of these negotiations since the boundary was between India and Tibet and in no way affected Chinese territorial sovereignty.

**17. The Sixth Panchen Lama.**—Chos-kyi nyi-ma (1883–1937) is counted as the sixth Panchen Lama in the list of reincarnations of Chos-kyi rgyal-mtshan, the teacher of the fifth Dalai Lama. The Tibetans usually count the three abbots of Tashilhumpo monastery prior to Chos-kyi rgyal-mtshan as Panchen Lamas, even though they were not in the lineage of reincarnations. By this counting, Chos-kyi nyi-ma is the ninth Panchen Lama.

The first Panchen Lama was little more than a highly revered abbot of Tashilhumpo, but the second, Blo-bzang ye-shes (1663–1737), was granted a small region near Zhikatse as his domain for taxation and support. The estates subject to Tashilhumpo increased in number over the decades until a local government, modeled on that of the Dalai Lama's central government, developed to handle the administrative duties. During the 1788–92 Gurkha War, Tashilhumpo paid one-quarter of the expenses for the Tibetan military operation; the Sa-skya monastery contributed one-tenth. Manchu policy was to show favour to the Panchen Lama, consequently, when the imperial troops invaded Lhasa in 1910, many of the followers of the Panchen Lama openly collaborated with them. The sixth Panchen Lama, Chos-kyi nyi-ma, came to Lhasa at that time and lived for some months in the summer palace of the Dalai Lama, the Nor-bu-gling-ka. When the imperial garrison was defeated and deported from Tibet in 1913, the Dalai Lama returned to Lhasa and measures to seek retribution against the Panchen Lama and his followers were soon taken. Discussions began as early as 1915 and it was pointed out that Tashilhumpo had paid one-quarter of the military expenses during the Gurkha War, therefore it should pay one-quarter of the expenses being incurred by the recurrent warfare in the disputed area of Khams. The amount of taxation was finally agreed upon in the early 1920s and the amount was staggering. The Panchen Lama's officials felt the tax was unjust because an analogous one-tenth tax was not levied on the Sa-skya monastery. Fearing further reprisals, they convinced the sixth Panchen Lama to flee to China for safety. He and his entourage left at the end of 1923 and made their way to China by a devious northern route.

(LEFT) HARRISON FORMAN; (ABOVE) EASTFOTO; (RIGHT) PETER HOLMES —J. ALLAN CASH

(Left) Northern Tibetan woman and child; (above) children playing in front of 17th-century Potala in Lhasa, former palace of the Dalai Lama and now a public primary school; (right) Ratang Gorge in the Himalayas

After the 13th Dalai Lama died in 1933, the Nationalist Government of China established contact with the Reting (Ra-sgreng) regent, who was suspected of being pro-Chinese. The Chinese government then made arrangements for the sixth Panchen Lama to return to Tibet; but when it tried to send a large military escort along with the Panchen Lama, the Tibetan government refused them permission to cross the border. The Chinese escort and the Panchen Lama waited at Jyekundo near the frontier while the two governments debated the issue.

Months later China became embroiled in war with the Japanese and the military escort was withdrawn from Jyekundo. The Panchen Lama stayed on, waiting for the controversy with Lhasa to be resolved, but months later he fell ill and died on Dec. 1, 1937. Followers of the Panchen Lama discovered a Tibetan boy who had been born Feb. 2, 1938, in the Chinese province of Ch'ing-hai, whom they regarded as the reincarnation of their deceased lama. His name is Bskal-bzang Tshe-brtan. Another candidate was born in eastern Tibet. This one was taken to Lhasa for the customary examinations to determine which was the true rebirth of the deceased Panchen Lama. The followers of the former lama would not permit their candidate to go to Lhasa for the examinations, insisting that he was the true rebirth. The issue remained unsettled. In August 1949, the Nationalist Government officially recognized the Ch'ing-hai candidate as the true reincarnation, a unilateral act not binding on the Tibetan government. The Ch'ing-hai candidate, however, fell into the hands of the Communist Chinese one month later, and in 1952 was brought to Tibet with a military escort. Having been "liberated" the year before by the Communist Chinese, the Tibetans had no choice but to accept the Ch'ing-hai candidate as the seventh Panchen Lama. The Khams candidate was placed in a monastery as an ordinary monk.

**18. The Fourteenth Dalai Lama.**—The 14th Dalai Lama, Bstan-'dzin rgya-mtsho, was born June 6, 1935, of Tibetan parents in the province of Ch'ing-hai, China. After protracted negotiations with the Muslim warlord and governor of the province, Ma Pu-fang, the young incarnation was allowed to be taken to Lhasa, where he was enthroned in the Potala Feb. 22, 1940. The Reting regent retired in February 1941 and returned to his monastery of Ra-sgreng. A new regent, Stag-brag Rin-po-che, was appointed and he held that position until Nov. 17, 1950, when because of the Communist Chinese invasion of the eastern frontier, the Dalai Lama was invested with temporal power, even though he was only 15 years old.

The reign of the Stag-brag regent was marked by several significant events. He and the Tibetan government maintained neutrality throughout World War II in spite of heavy pressures brought to bear by the Chinese and U.S. governments. In 1947 a plot to kill the regent was discovered and evidence pointed to the former Reting regent as the instigator. He was arrested in April and died in the Potala in May.

On Aug. 15, 1947, India became independent and the Tibetan government conveyed its best wishes to the new republic. In Tibet the British trade agencies at Gyangtse, Yatung, and Gartok, as well as the mission in Lhasa, all became Indian offices. In October of the same year the Tibetan government decided to send a trade delegation, headed by W. D. Shakabpa, a finance minister, to various countries around the world for two purposes: (1) to discuss Tibet's trade relations with other countries, and (2) to show Tibet's sovereignty by having the trade delegation travel on Tibetan passports. The delegation visited the United States, the United Kingdom, and various countries of Europe.

After the 1949 fall of mainland China to the Communists, the Tibetan government immediately evicted the Nationalist Chinese mission in Lhasa, since it no longer represented the official governing body in China and the new Communist regime might try to use the mission in Lhasa for its own purposes. The Tibetans began to prepare for the inevitable.

**19. Communist Chinese Occupation.**—By the end of 1949 editorials began to appear in the Communist press in China stating that Tibet would soon be liberated from the capitalist reactionaries and returned to the motherland of the People's Republic of China. The outbreak of the Korean conflict in the spring of 1950 diverted world attention to that small peninsula, and, in October of the same year, advance units of the People's Liberation Army invaded the eastern frontier of Tibet and within days had captured the administrative headquarters of Chab-mdo. The council minister and concurrent provincial governor, Ngag-dbang 'jigs-med Nga-phod (called Apei in the Chinese press and Ngabo in the Western), was taken prisoner. When news of the invasion reached Lhasa an appeal dated Nov. 7 was cabled to the United Nations requesting intervention. The delegates from Nationalist China and the U.S.S.R. claimed that Tibet was part of China and therefore the issue was an internal affair of China and the United Nations had no jurisdiction to intervene. The British delegate said the legal status of Tibet was unclear, and the Indian delegate expressed belief that the issue could be settled by negotiation and still preserve Tibet's autonomy. The Tibetan appeal was thus shelved and no action taken.

Having waited to test world reaction, the Communist Chinese Army under command of Chang Kuo-hua renewed its offensive against Tibet. The Dalai Lama and some of his officials took refuge in Yatung near the Sikkimese border. Finally, council minister Nga-phod and other Tibetan officials signed the so-called 17-point agreement on measures for the peaceful liberation of Tibet in Peking on May 23, 1951. The essence of the agreement may be summarized thus: (1) Tibet was to retain its autonomy, with no change in the Dalai Lama's political system or in his status, function, and power; Tibetan religion, monastic institutions, and customs would be respected. (2) The position that the Panchen Lama enjoyed in the time of friendly relations between the 13th Dalai Lama and the 9th (*i.e.*, 6th) Panchen Lama was to be restored. (3) The Chinese Communist government was to set up a military and administrative committee with regional military headquarters in Tibet; the Tibetan Army was to be reorganized and systematically absorbed into the People's Liberation Army. (4) Tibet's external relations were to be handled by the Chinese Communist government.

Three forces of the Liberation Army entered Tibet simultaneously, one from Chab-mdo on the east, another from Koko Nor on the north, and still another from Mnga'-ris on the west, to take over strategic locations. A fourth party led by Chang Ching-wu and comprising administrative and technical staffs arrived via India. The Dalai Lama returned to Lhasa Aug. 17, 1951.

The Dalai Lama and Panchen Lama were given seats on the National Committee of the Chinese People's Political Consultative Conference held in Peking on Nov. 1, 1951. Then in the spring of 1952, the 14-year-old Panchen Lama scored a triumphal entry into Lhasa under the shadow of Communist troops. On June 23, 1952, he was put on the throne of his predecessors in the Tashilhumpo monastery, which had been without its spiritual leader for 28 years. In September 1954 the Dalai Lama, Panchen Lama, and others attended the first Chinese National People's Congress in Peking.

Great Britain had transferred to India the treaty rights with Tibet and the British mission in Lhasa when India became independent in 1947. Following the Chinese invasion of Tibet in 1950, India sent notes of protest to Communist China about the three trading agencies taken over by India, but these were summarily dismissed as an interference in Red China's internal affairs. India changed its view during the next few years and on April 20, 1954, signed an eight-year agreement with Peking to promote peaceful coexistence, trade, and cultural intercourse, and to facilitate pilgrimage and travel between the two countries. Under the agreement India retained the right to the trade agencies at Yatung, Gyangtse, and Gartok. A number of other towns were designated as trade marts. No Tibetan representative participated in the negotiations and the language of the agreement implied India's recognition of China's sovereignty over Tibet.

To expedite political consolidation and military buildup, Communist China embarked on a program of extensive roadbuilding in Tibet and hundreds of thousands of Tibetans were conscripted for labour, in some cases paid for by the Chinese. The hazards involved in bridging high precipices and deep ravines apparently caused the deaths of many workers. The lamas and monks who were previously exempted from government conscription especially hated the Chinese because no particular consideration was accorded them. By 1956 the Communist Chinese began to implement land reform and cooperatives in the eastern regions, which soon led to rebellion.

Meanwhile the Dalai Lama was invited to India to attend the 2,500th anniversary of the birth of the Buddha. At first Peking was reluctant to let him go, but finally relented. He and the "puppet" Panchen Lama traveled together. The Dalai Lama intended to seek asylum in India because of the increasing unrest and rebellion in Tibet, but Chou En-lai arrived on the scene and promised him that Peking would delay reforms in Tibet for six years if he would return home. The Dalai Lama stopped over in January 1957 at Kalimpong in West Bengal, while the Panchen Lama returned to Tashilhumpo. Only after Mao Tse-tung had delivered a speech at the Supreme State Conference in February saying that reforms would not be implemented during the second five-year plan (1958–62) did the Dalai Lama return to Tibet.

As a show of good faith, some of the committees formed for implementing reform were disbanded and many cadres returned to China. The Preparatory Committee for the Autonomous Region of Tibet, which was inaugurated on April 22, 1956, with the Dalai Lama as chairman, the Panchen Lama as first vice chairman, Chang Kuo-hua as second vice chairman, and the Tibetan collaborator Nga-phod as secretary-general, was not disbanded. Its work continued, for the goal of the preparatory committee was to replace the centuries-old theocratic government of the Dalai Lama with a Communist one. The power of the committee rested in the hands of Chang Kuo-hua and the regime in Peking.

The Peking promise to postpone reform in Tibet did not achieve the desired cessation of rebellion against the Communists. Revolt broke out in the Litang, Batang, and Chab-mdo areas of eastern Tibet and then spread to the Golok (Mgo-log) tribe in southern Ch'ing-hai Province. Local Chinese garrisons were attacked. The Communists retaliated by bombing the monasteries at Litang, Batang, and Chatreng as suspected rebel arsenals. This only intensified the determination of the people to resist, especially the Khams-pa, natives of eastern Tibet. Unable to withstand the Red Chinese in direct confrontation because of Communist military superiority, the rebels resorted to guerrilla warfare. As the Chinese suppressed the rebellion here and there, the Khams-pas joined forces with the A-mdo-bas from Ch'ing-hai and gradually worked their way westward toward south-central Tibet. By winter of 1958, they had moved into the region south of the Brahmaputra River and north of Bhutan and throughout the year continued to consolidate their control in the area and recruit more Tibetans to the cause.

The situation was reaching the breaking point. The Chinese commander put pressure on the Dalai Lama to deploy Tibetan troops to suppress the revolt, but he refused. The Communist Chinese did not underestimate the potential danger of the rebellion. The issue was forced to a head when the Chinese invited the Dalai Lama to come unescorted to attend a theatrical performance to be held in the Chinese military camp on March 10, 1959. Rumours spread immediately that the Communists intended to seize the Dalai Lama and use him as a hostage to squelch the mounting revolt. The Lhasa populace surrounded the Nor-bu-gling-ka summer palace and prevented him from going or being taken to the Chinese camp. Violence increased throughout the streets of Lhasa during the next few days. Finally the Red Chinese lobbed some mortar shells close to the summer palace to prove their determination to control the situation. Tibetan officials, fearing for the Dalai Lama's personal safety, urged him to flee into exile. On the night of March 17, the Dalai Lama, disguised in servant clothing, escaped from Lhasa with a few loyal officials and his family members and fled south. Once in the rebel-held territory south of the Brahmaputra River, the party turned southeast and made its way to the Indian border east of Bhutan.

When the Chinese in Lhasa learned of the Dalai Lama's escape, they turned their military power on the populace. Tanks and infantry were used and some 12,000 Tibetans were reportedly killed. The Potala and the monasteries of Se-ra and 'Bras-spungs were shelled. On March 28 the Communist Chinese declared the abolishment of the centuries-old Tibetan "local" government, and the Preparatory Committee for the Autonomous Region of Tibet became the governing body. The Panchen Lama was appointed "acting" chairman of the committee during the Dalai Lama's absence, for the Chinese claimed that Tibetan reactionaries had taken him to India by force. After the Dalai Lama arrived safely in India the end of March, he issued a statement at Tezpur asserting that he had fled to India of his own free will and not under duress. Nevertheless, the Lhasa regime kept his name listed as the chairman of the preparatory committee until 1964.

When the Tibetan people learned that their revered leader was safe in India, the rebellion against the Communist Chinese flared up everywhere. The Communist regime used every means to suppress the revolt. It is reported some 100,000 Tibetans died and another 80,000 fled as refugees during the months after the Lhasa revolt. Many of them settled down in Buddhist areas of Nepal, Sikkim, and Bhutan, and many more were relocated in refugee camps in India. The Dalai Lama spent his first year of exile at Mussoorie, a hill station near Dehra Dun, then in 1960 his residence was changed to Dharamsala in the Punjab. In the autumn of 1967, for the first time since going to India after the revolt, the Dalai Lama traveled abroad, going to Japan to attend a Buddhist conference.

**20. 1959 United Nations Resolution.**—Following the revolt in Lhasa, the Tibetan government repudiated the 1951 Sino-Tibetan agreement because the Chinese had violated many of the 17 points, which guaranteed to maintain the existing Tibetan government, the position of the Dalai Lama, and religious freedom. This repudiation, in the opinion of the Legal Inquiry Committee on Tibet set up by the International Commission of Jurists, restored Tibet to the *de facto* state of independence it enjoyed before the Communist Chinese invasion of 1950.

A second appeal was made to the United Nations by the Tibetan government after the 1959 revolt. On Oct. 21, 1959, the United Nations General Assembly, by 45 votes to 9 (with 26 abstentions), approved a resolution which called for "respect for the fundamental human rights of the Tibetan people and for their distinctive cultural and religious life." The resolution did not mention the Communist Chinese or their part in the events that led to the drafting of the resolution.

**21. Tibet After 1959.**—The Panchen Lama, in his new role of "acting" chairman of the preparatory committee, attended the Second National People's Congress at Peking on April 17, 1959, and participated in the election of Liu Shao-chi as the second president of the People's Republic of China. Both the Panchen Lama and the Dalai Lama (*in absentia*) were elected to be the vice-chairmen of that National People's Congress.

The 1959 revolt brought drastic changes in Chinese treatment of the Tibetans. Before the revolt, Tibetans were allowed to have radios and weapons and were not restricted in their movements. The Communists seemed to expect the Tibetans to recognize the superiority of the materialistic approach of democratic reform over the feudal theocratic way of life in Tibet. In spite of years of indoctrination, propaganda, and persuasion, the Communist Chinese made few converts among the Buddhist Tibetans. The necessity for Mao Tse-tung to postpone reform in Tibet in 1957 because the Tibetans were not yet ready to accept it, was indicative of the strength and determination of the religious Tibetan to resist atheistic Communism. The generosity and persuasiveness of the Chinese ended with the 1959 revolt. Freedom of movement was limited, radios and weapons confiscated, former estate-holding nobles were denounced as capitalists, lamas and monks were labeled parasites, and children and servants were encouraged to denounce their parents and masters. The effects of "purge" drove thousands more into escaping to neighbouring countries.

The Communist regime continued to consolidate military and political control over Tibet, and the network of roads connecting strategic locations near the Tibetan Himalayan frontier with Lhasa and thence to China was brought to completion. In June 1962 the Sino-Indian treaty of "peaceful coexistence" expired, and in the following October, Chinese troops invaded India in the Northeast Frontier Agency (NEFA) region north of Assam. Seemingly unbeatable, the Chinese suddenly stopped their forward advance and withdrew close to the border. The Communist Chinese have continued to harass India along two sections of its frontier, the Tibet-Ladakh border and the Tibet-NEFA border. Both borders were demarcated by treaties negotiated by the Tibetans without Chinese participation. The Ladakh frontier was established by the treaty of 1684 and reaffirmed by the 1842 treaty between Tibet and Kashmir. The Tibet-NEFA frontier is demarcated by the McMahon Line agreed to by Great Britain and Tibet at the Simla Conference in 1914. The Chinese, in order to be consistent in their policy that Tibet has long been an integral part of China, insist that these two frontiers are invalid demarcations because the Tibetans had no authority to negotiate them. These border issues remain unresolved between India and China.

By the end of 1964, the Chinese regime in Lhasa had consolidated its control over Tibet sufficiently to move against the centuries-old institution of "rule by a lama." In December 1964, the Communists changed their propaganda line and denounced the Dalai Lama as a traitor to Tibet and the actual ringleader of the 1959 revolt, rather than the innocent victim of it. He was symbolically removed from his position of chairman of the preparatory committee. The "acting" chairman, the Panchen Lama, long considered a Communist puppet, was also removed from office as a reactionary for refusing to denounce the Dalai Lama. The Panchen Lama was subjected to public humiliation and beatings in Lhasa in January 1965 and was reported to be in a forced-labour road-construction camp in the summer of that year. Unconfirmed reports in September 1967 stated he had escaped to India, but they are regarded as doubtful.

On March 25, 1965, Ngag-dbang 'jigs-med Nga-phod (Apei, and also Ngabo) was elevated to the chairmanship of the preparatory committee. Nga-phod retained that position after Tibet was officially proclaimed as an Autonomous Region of the People's Republic of China on Sept. 1, 1965; however he appears to have been "purged" as well. The last report on his whereabouts was in the fall of 1966 when he appeared in Peking. The Communist Chinese regime in Lhasa continued to exercise actual power throughout the period with Chang Kuo-hua, the general who commanded the occupation forces, as its head.

**22. Red Guards in Tibet.**—In the summer of 1966 the Central Cultural Revolution Team was established to eradicate all vestiges of foreign imperialism and tendencies toward capitalism in China. (*See* CHINA: *History: After World War II.*)

In September 1966 Red Guards began to spread in Tibet where their wrath was directed at the remnants of feudalism and superstition. They began by changing the names of streets and buildings. Bar-'khor (the street used by Tibetan pilgrims to circumambulate the Jo-khang temple) means "Middle-circumambulation"; so they changed it to Foster the New (Chinese: Li-hsin). Sman-rtsis-khang, the name of the former medical monastery on Iron Mountain (Lcags-po-ri), was changed to the College of the Working People; the mountain was renamed Peak of Victory. Nor-bu-gling-ka, the Jewel Park summer palace of the Dalai Lamas, became the People's Park. The main target of the Red Guards was the remaining religious buildings as symbols of the Tibetans' "superstitious beliefs." The Jo-khang and Ra-mo-che temples built in the 7th century to house Buddhist images brought to Tibet by a Nepalese and a Chinese princess respectively were preserved by the Lhasa regime as "show places" for screened Communist visitors on guided tours. The Red Guards reportedly smashed in the doors of the temples; destroyed images of gold, copper, and clay; burned canonical texts; and damaged the golden roofs. Among the images smashed was an 11-headed Avalokiteśvara dating from the 7th century. Two of its broken heads were smuggled to India by refugees and displayed in New Delhi.

**23. Chang Kuo-hua and the Cultural Revolution.**—The Red Guards who had the support of the Cultural Revolution Committee in China joined forces with revolutionary groups in Tibet and established the Lhasa Revolutionary Rebels Headquarters in Lhasa. They began to attack Chang Kuo-hua, commander of the Chinese Army in Tibet, for having become a "local emperor."

He was arrested and, according to reports, denounced in public and his execution scheduled for March 13, 1967. Units of the army under his command, however, took control of the situation and by March Chang Kuo-hua was again in command in Lhasa. He declared the Lhasa Rebels Headquarters a reactionary group and abolished it. Red Guards who had come to Tibet from China returned. In April the Lhasa Rebels Headquarters slowly resumed operations, still directed against Chang Kuo-hua, but this time they seemed to be in support of Liu Shao-ch'i. Anti-Mao posters began to appear continuously in Lhasa, only to be torn down and replaced with others denouncing the "revisionist blackguards." During this period, Lhasa was described as a battlefield with open fighting between the opposing Communist factions.

On May 1, Chang Kuo-hua appeared in Peking. Six days later he was appointed first political commissar of the Ch'eng-tu military district in Szechwan. Since the CCP Southwest China Politburo in Ch'eng-tu is responsible for both Szechwan (where there was violent rebellion) and Tibet, it is presumed Chang Kuo-hua was appointed there in order to facilitate his control of both regions. An unsuccessful attempt was made on Aug. 21, 1967, to assassinate Chang Kuo-hua and three other high officials in Ch'eng-tu; followers of Liu Shao-ch'i were blamed. In the confusion and cross-purposes created by the Red Guards and the cultural revolution in Tibet, only one fact was clear: there were no Tibetans involved at the top levels; the conflict and power struggle were limited to the Chinese Communists.

## V. ADMINISTRATION

**1. Dalai Lama.**—Prior to the Chinese Communist conquest of Tibet, Tibet was the last theocratic country in the world. The head of the government was the Dalai Lama who exercised temporal power and, as the embodiment of the bodhisattva of mercy Avalokiteśvara (Tibetan: Spyan-ras-gzigs), was, and still is, revered as an aspect of the absolute Buddha in human form. When a Dalai Lama died he was succeeded by his reincarnation, who was discovered by following the indications provided by the preceding Dalai Lama before his death, the guidance given by the Gnas-chung state oracle, and the revelations viewed in the waters of the sacred lake Chos-'khor-rgyal, the life-lake (*bla-mtsho*) of the Dalai Lamas, by the regent. Sometimes the true rebirth was discovered only after a long search and sometimes more than one boy fulfilled all the indications of reincarnation. In such a case, the candidates were narrowed down to three who were then brought to Lhasa. Their names were written on paper and deposited in a golden urn, presented to the Tibetans in 1793 by the Ch'ien-lung emperor, and after proper religious ceremonies, the first name drawn was proclaimed that of the true reincarnation and successor of the deceased Dalai Lama. If there was one candidate who satisfied all the tests and all were convinced he was the actual rebirth, the golden urn process of selection was not used.

During the interregnum caused by the death, minority, or absence of a Dalai Lama, a regent, approved by the national assembly convened for the purpose, was appointed from among the highest ranking lamas of Tibet. The regent assumed full responsibility for government administration during the interregnum. When the Dalai Lama attained his majority between the ages of 16 and 18, all governmental authority was surrendered to him by the regent.

**2. Tibetan Government.**—The final form of the theocratic government of Tibet evolved in the last half of the 18th century, and remained virtually unchanged until its dissolution in 1959 by the Communist Chinese. At the apex of structural power was the Dalai Lama who, in theory, exercised absolute power, but in practice wielded it in accordance with customary limitations and with the guidance of his ministers. The members of government officialdom consisted of 175 monk officials and 175 lay officials. The noble families provided all of the lay officials and some of the monk officials of the Tibetan government, which consisted of two branches, each with its own area of authority.

The religious branch composed entirely of monk officials dealt with the internal administration of the monasteries and cases involving monks. This branch of the government was headed by the lord chamberlain (Spyi-skyabs mkhan-po), whose position was equal to a lay official of the third rank. Ecclesiastics were not referred to as having rank, but in terms of position the Dalai Lama was the only person of first rank; the regent and prime minister were of second rank. The lord chamberlain was in charge of the Dalai Lama's household and his personal treasury. Daily duties of the religious branch of the government were administered by a council (Yig-tshang) composed of four monks equal in position to fourth-rank officials, and their secretaries and staff.

The secular branch of the government was composed of both lay and monk officials, and it dealt with civil and criminal cases involving laymen, as well as national policies and external affairs. The highest secular position was that of prime minister, which was second rank. Prime ministers were appointed on special occasions to handle particular affairs. At times there were two; at others none. The highest officials who were charged with regular administrative duties were the council ministers, called Bka'-blon or Zhabs-pad, who were of the third rank. The Council (Bka'-zhag) was composed of three lay ministers and one monk, who was called Bka'-blon bla-ma (pronounced Ga-lön la-ma). The Bka'-shag, or Council, was an administrative body, not a judicial one. The ultimate authority and responsibility for decision-making rested in the hands of the Dalai Lama, or during an interregnum in those of the regent. Directly under the Council were the four finance ministers of the fourth rank, who were comparable in position and influence to the four monks of the monastic council. The four finance ministers, the four council monks, and the abbots of the three chief Yellow Hat monasteries constituted a small assembly, which had no authority to convene itself, doing so only when ordered by the Council of Ministers and then only to discuss the issues placed before it. The assembly rendered no decision; it merely made recommendations to the Council of Ministers, which in turn submitted the issue and the recommendation to the Dalai Lama for the final judgment. Under the finance ministers were various officials comprising a complex governmental hierarchy, including generals of the army, governors of the provinces, ministers of various departments, and district officials in charge of *rdzong* administrative areas. In the more important offices there were two officials in charge, one monk and one layman. Although equal in position, the monk was regarded as the senior officer. There were four provincial headquarters. One at Chab-mdo, where the governor was usually a member of the Bka'-shag because of the strategic importance of the Khams area; one at Gartok in western Tibet; one at Nag-chu-kha north of Lhasa; and one at Lho-ljongs in the south. With the exception of Chab-mdo, each of the provincial headquarters was administered by two governors. Those at Nag-chu-kha and Lho-ljongs had a monk and a lay governor.

Officials assigned to a rdzong usually served for a period of three years. They were required to remit a specified annual tax to the Lhasa government, and anything collected over that amount they could keep as income. The system was not excessively abused because the people had the right to appeal directly to the Dalai Lama whenever they were exploited or treated unjustly by local officials. Villages were administrated by headmen.

## VI. ECONOMY

The economy of Tibet was in a primitive stage of development until the middle of the 20th century. The nature of the terrain, the lack of rainfall, and the severity of the climate impose a serious limitation on the development of agricultural resources. Industry was practically nonexistent. Trade was negligible and mineral resources remained unexploited. Great livestock and timber potential was offset by the lack of modern transportation. After the Communist Chinese occupied the country in 1951, they constructed a network of main roads, but these connected strategic sites and were not specifically for economic development. Subsequent surveys tend to confirm the conjecture of early explorers that Tibet is rich in mineral wealth.

**1. Agriculture** in Tibet is almost completely of the subsistence type. Without irrigation the country is too arid to grow crops, and cultivation is limited to river basins and the lowlands in southeastern Tibet. The soil is alluvial, often composed of sand blown by the wind to form a layer over gravels and shingles, and its colour is light brown or grayish, according to humus content, which is poor. As fertilizer, human excrement, cow dung, ashes, and the fine silt from floodwaters are used.

Barley is the staple crop of Tibet. Rape turnips and peas are also grown extensively. In lower altitudes wheat, buckwheat, and millet are raised, while rice grows only in a limited quantity in the southeast. The Brahmaputra Basin is the granary of Tibet and supports about 60% of the population. Whenever hill streams are available, water mills are used for the grinding of barley into flour. In the northern plain, radishes and potatoes are grown sparsely. In the 1950s the Chinese Academy of Science set up experimental stations at Lhasa, Zhikatse, and Chab-mdo and reported that barley of the Shantung variety, spring wheat of northern China, cabbage, cauliflower, tobacco, hemp, tomatoes, sunflower, and millet were suitable to the local soil and climate.

**2. Forestry.**—In Tibet the most valuable woodland is in the Khams district, though extensive forest-clad mountains are also found in the Sutlej River Valley in western Tibet and in the Chumbi Valley in southern Tibet. The Spo-smad area in Khams is estimated to contain 17,300 sq.mi. (44,807 sq.km.) of virgin forests. In the late 1950s, 30 kinds of trees including those of comparatively high economic value, such as varnish trees, spruce, and fir were discovered. Conifers averaging 90 ft. (27 m.) high and some as high as 200 ft. (61 m.) with a girth of 5 ft. (1.5 m.) were reported, and the estimated total of forest timber resources in that part of Tibet alone was placed at more than 130,800,000 cu.yd. (100,000,000 cu.m.). Accessibility adversely affects the development of the forests in this region.

**3. Minerals.**—The Tibetans believe that spirits inhabit the surface of the earth and it is taboo to disturb them lest they cause famines, epidemics, and floods; consequently, mineral exploration was not permitted by the Tibetan government. The only mining was for gold in the western region, which was done by placer techniques only. Thus, Tibet's mineral resources have long remained the subject of wide speculation.

A scientific investigation of western Tibet was conducted by Swami Pranavananda, an Indian who made surveys in the 1930s and 1940s in the Mount Kailas and Lake Mānasarowar districts. The mineral specimens he collected were analyzed at Benares Hindu University. He discovered extensive goldfields in the district of Sankora; radium, iron, titanium, and emery on the eastern shores of Lakes Mānasarowar and Rakas Tal; lead near Gemuk; arsenic and serpentine near Kungri-bingri Pass; and large deposits of borax on the shore of Lake Tseti Tsho.

Following the occupation of Tibet, the geological section of the Chinese Academy of Science dispatched investigation teams who reported the existence of many useful minerals including oil shale, asphalt, iron, magnesium, copper, lead, zinc, molybdenum, antimony, salt, soda, borax, Glauber salt, sulfur, alum, mica, barite, graphite, talc, gypsum, jade, and china clay. A belt of iron deposits was located on the western bank of the Mekong River stretching for almost 25 mi. (40 km.) S of Chab-mdo. Graphite was obtained from Ningtsin and coal was reported plentiful around Chab-mdo. Iron deposits containing ore in concentrated seams of high quality and extractable depth were also found in the Thanglha Range on the border of Tibet and the province of Ch'ing-hai. Three rich crystal deposits were found in the glaciers of the Sane Range. Oil-bearing formations, a large reserve of oil shales, and coal mines were unearthed as well as valuable lead, zinc, and manganese deposits. Iron and coal mines in the Nag-chu-kha area were reported in production by the late 1950s.

**4. Waterpower.**—The swift-flowing rivers and mountain streams of Tibet have immense hydroelectric power potential, especially the Brahmaputra; however, only one small hydroelectric plant at Lhasa generating 2,000 kw. was in operation in the 1950s. Under the Chinese the Lhasa power station was repaired and reinforced with three 360-kw. generators, and a new thermal electric station was installed in Zhikatse. The Chinese also established a hydrographic station in Lhasa and ten substations in various parts of the country to measure the speed of the current and water level of the Brahmaputra, Skyid-chu, and Nyang rivers.

**5. Industry** in Tibet before the advent of the Communist Chinese was almost entirely of the home handicraft type. The largest handicraft industry was the weaving of woolen cloth. The spinning was done by hand and weaving by a wooden frame loom. Many Tibetans did spinning in their spare time, and the weaving was done by women. The finished fabric was a kind of heavy coarse serge which, in addition to supplying the local needs, was exported to Tibetan ethnic areas of western China. The second largest handicraft industry was carpetmaking, centred mainly at Gyangtse. In 1952 the Communist Chinese built an iron and woodworking factory in Lhasa. An automobile repair works began operation in 1957 and a tannery was built in 1958.

**6. Trade.**—The main product of Tibet is wool, and it formed the principal item of export, mainly to northern India and Bombay. Before the 1959 Lhasa revolt, mule trains loaded with wool wound their way over the high Himalayan passes to Gangtok and Kalimpong, where they were reloaded with a variety of cargo for the return trip. A small quantity of the wool came to the United States for carpet-making. The famous fine shawl wool known as cashmere came from western Tibet. Other items of export were borax, salt, animals and animal products, and medicinal herbs. Gold dust, important in the 18th century, later dwindled to nothing. Some rock salt and borax were exported to Nepal, Bhutan, and northern India.

Tea, the principal import, was imported in the form of bricks from western China. Tea bricks were packed in yak hides, which were not tanned but merely dried in the sun. Tea also served as a form of currency for a traveler in Tibet, as it was readily accepted everywhere and was convertible into butter, barley flour, or currency. Other imports from China were brocades, silks, chinaware, enamelware, canned foods, shoes and socks, shearing scissors; from India, felt hats, cotton and woolen cloth, tobacco, indigo, glass and ironware, petroleum, firearms, dried nuts; and from Nepal and Bhutan came rice and dried fruits.

After 1953 Tibetan trade became a monopoly of the Chinese State Trading Company. The former British mission and trade marts at Gyangtse, Yatung, and Gartok were operated by the Indian government until the Sino-Indian agreement on "peaceful coexistence" expired in 1962. After the Chinese invaded India in October 1962, the trade marts were closed, and the Indian consul general who resided in the mission at Lhasa returned to India. The buildings remained unoccupied for five years. They had been looked after by the Nepalese consulate general on behalf of the Indian government. In September 1967 the Chinese confiscated the buildings and furnishings.

**7. Finance.**—The Tibetan government, prior to the Communist Chinese occupation, derived its revenue from taxes, from landed estates owned by the government, and from public funds loaned to private individuals at interest. Because of the scarcity of money most taxes were paid in kind, including import and export duties. The taxes were paid to the local district (*rdzong*) offices and to special tax collectors who toured the country to assist with the collections. The district officers, who did not receive any salary from the central government, were members of the landed nobility who lived on the income of their family estates and worked for the government as a duty. These officers were required to submit a set amount of tax from their districts, and anything left over they kept. The government paid only a nominal salary to the civil servants under the landed officials. Those whose private incomes were too meagre to meet the demands of public office looked on gifts from interested parties as part of their remuneration. Landholders paid their taxes in grain which was stored in government granaries, while cash, butter, oil, and meat were sent to the revenue office in Lhasa. Other articles were stored in the offices of the local district administrator to be disposed of or sold as need arose. The government also loaned its surplus to high officials, lamas, and wealthy traders who made a profit by lending out the money at high rates of interest.

The chief expense of the government was the maintenance of the large monasteries in and near Lhasa, and the giving of annual subsidies to outlying ones. The government provided food for thousands of monks, and spent large sums every year for building repairs; but the greatest amount was spent on butter, used as oil for the myriads of lamps which burned day and night.

The Dalai Lama had a private treasury. He derived income from some of the best estates in the country and received offerings from pilgrims, as well as local people. Over the centuries, the personal treasury of the Dalai Lamas increased and its value was incalculable. It was an accumulation of precious stones, diamonds, pearls, gold, silver, and rare silks. The expenses of the Dalai Lama consisted of the maintenance of his own household and private chapel, and gifts to relatives and to lamas of the large monasteries. When he moved to Yatung in 1950, part of his personal treasury was secretly stored at Gangtok, Sikkim. Following his exile in 1959 he had this part of his treasury, consisting of gold and silver bullion, converted into cash in India, and has used it to support his government in exile and to aid the Tibetan refugees. The bulk of his treasury left behind in the Potala fell into the hands of the Communist Chinese.

Tibet had its own currency system. Coins were first minted and circulated after the 1792 defeat of the Nepalese. In the beginning silver weights called Sang-gang, Sho-gang, and Karma were used for money, but after minting began, these became actual coins equivalent in time to the Indian rupee, anna, and pice respectively. Paper currency was first issued in 1890. The Tibetan government also attempted to mint gold pieces, but the mint was burned down after coining only a small number, which are much sought by collectors. There was no bank in Tibet before 1951. Wealthy families left their savings with reputable traders who paid them interest or a share of their profits. The Chinese established branches of the People's Bank of China in Lhasa, Zhikatse, Gyangtse, Chamdo, and Gartok. They also introduced Chinese currency and extended commercial and agricultural credit.

**8. Transport and Communications.**—Before 1951, traveling in Tibet was done either on foot or on the backs of animals. Coracles were used to cross the larger rivers. By deliberate policy the Tibetan government obstructed the development of modern transportation to make access to this country difficult for outsiders. For trading, the Tibetans relied on the centuries-old caravan routes leading to Lhasa, of which the most important were: Ch'ing-hai (via Nag-chu-kha), Szechwan (via Chab-mdo), India (via Kalimpong and Yatung), Nepal (via Skyid-grong and Nya-lam rdzong), and Kashmir (via Leh and Gartok). Under the Communist Chinese, a network of motor roads was constructed, notably the Ch'ing-hai and Szechwan highways. Many secondary roads were under construction.

**9. Air Transport.**—The first air communication between Tibet and the outside world was inaugurated in April 1956, which coincided with Vice Premier Ch'en Yi's visit to Lhasa to inaugurate the Preparatory Committee for the Autonomous Region of Tibet. The airport is located near Lhasa. There is unscheduled service with Chengchow via Jyekundo (Chinese: Yu-shu). Military airfields have been constructed at Chab-mdo, Zhikatse, and Gartok.

**10. Railways.**—There were no railways in Tibet before the Chinese occupation. After making an aerial survey, the Chinese carried out a land survey for a railroad from Ch'ing-hai to Tibet. The proposed railway was to be 807 mi. (1,299 km.) long, with Hsi-ning and Nag-chu-kha rdzong as terminals. It would pass through complicated geological and topographical regions and its average altitude would be more than 12,000 ft. (3,658 m.).

**11. Postal and Telegraph Service.**—The first telegraph line was strung between Kalimpong and Gyangtse by the British after the 1904 Younghusband mission. In the 1920s another line connecting Gyangtse with Lhasa was erected, this being the only telegraph system in use until the Chinese took over in 1951. Some 50 postal and telecommunication stations in Tibet, including mobile units, serve remote border areas and geological, hydrological, and construction teams.

Tibet issued its own postage stamps but did not belong to the Universal Postal Union, which obliged stamp collectors to obtain much-sought-after Tibetan stamps in a devious way. A letter would be addressed to a fictitious person supposedly residing in Lhasa. When the letter reached the Tibetan border, Tibetan stamps would be placed on it (since Tibet was not a member of the postal union) and an attempt made to find the addressee. At last the letter would be returned to the sender bearing Tibetan stamps, which the sender added to his collection.

## VII. TIBETANS IN EXILE

The 1959 revolt and its violent aftermath caused the Dalai Lama and tens of thousands of Tibetans to seek refuge in India and neighbouring countries. For the first time, Tibetans in large numbers came in contact with modern Western civilization. Charitable organizations began helping the refugees, and the Indian government, under its rehabilitation program, established several relocation camps for the Tibetans. A great many children were taken to resettlement villages in Switzerland.

Shortly after the revolt, the Rockefeller Foundation launched an international program to support research into the significant features of Tibet's history and culture. Funds were provided to existing Tibetan research centres to bring learned Tibetans to them for a three-year period of collaboration. There were eight such centres throughout the world: one each at Seattle, London, Paris, Rome, Leiden, Copenhagen, Munich, and Tokyo. Most of the Tibetans participating in the research program stayed on at their respective centres and continued to collaborate with members of the research staff on Tibetan studies. The program caused an increased interest in Tibet as a subject of academic study, and resulted in the publication of more and more information on the religious and political institutions of Tibet.

On March 10, 1963, the occasion of the fourth anniversary of the Lhasa revolt, the Dalai Lama and his government-in-exile proclaimed the first codified constitution for Tibet. Prepared with the assistance of experts in international and constitutional law, the Tibetan constitution—if ever implemented—would create a unique form of government, which might be best described as a democratic theocracy, for it calls for the election of all officials by popular vote, but the head of the government would remain the Dalai Lama, who would continue to be succeeded by his own reincarnation. The new constitution was to become effective if and when the Tibetans regain their freedom and sovereignty.

*See* also references under "Tibet" in the Index.

Bibliography.—J. Bacot, F. W. Thomas, and C. Toussaint, *Documents de Touen-houang relatifs à l'Histoire du Tibet* (1946); C. Bell, *Tibet: Past and Present* (1924); Dalai Lama 14th, *My Land and My People* (1962); S. C. Das, *Journey to Lhasa and Central Tibet* (1902); M. Fisher, L. Rose, and R. Huttenback, *Himalayan Battleground* (1963); H. Hoffmann, *The Religions of Tibet* (1961); International Commission of Jurists, *Tibet and the Chinese People's Republic* (1960); Ling Nai-min, *Tibetan Sourcebook* (1964); P. Fleming, *Bayonets to Lhasa* (1961); H. Harrer, *Seven Years in Tibet* (1959); D. Macdonald, *Twenty Years in Tibet* (1932); P. Pelliot, *Histoire Ancienne du Tibet* (1961); L. Petech, *China and Tibet in the Early 18th Century* (1950), *A Study on the Chronicles of Ladakh* (1939); H. Richardson, *A Short History of Tibet* (1962), W. W. Rockhill, *The Dalai Lamas of Lhasa and Their Relations with the Manchu Emperors of China* (1910); D. Snellgrove, *Buddhist Himalaya* (1957), *Four Lamas of Dolpo* (1967); T. Shakabpa, *Tibet: a Political History* (1967); V. Sis and J. Vanis, *On the Road Through Tibet* (1956); T. L. Shen and S. C. Liu, *Tibet and the Tibetans* (1953); G. Tucci, *Tibetan Folk Songs* (1966), *Tibetan Painted Scrolls,* 3 vol. (1949); A. Waddell, *The Buddhism of Tibet or Lamaism* (reprinted 1958); T. Wylie, *The Geography of Tibet According to the 'Dzam-gling-rgyas-bshad'* (1962); Sir F. Younghusband, *India and Tibet* (1910); Yu Dawchyuan, *Love Songs of the Sixth Dalai Lama* (1930); R. N. Bhattacharya and A. Chattopadhyaya, "The Tibetan Sexagenary Cycle," in *Indian Studies,* vol. viii, no. 1, pp. 99–109 (1966); Baron A. von Staël-Holstein, "On the Sexagenary Cycle of the Tibetans," *Monumenta Serica,* vol. i, pp. 277–314 (1935–36); L. A. Waddell, *The Buddhism of Tibet; or Lamaism* (reprinted 1958); D. Snellgrove and H. Richardson, *A Cultural History of Tibet* (1969); T. J. Norbu and C. M. Turnbull, *Tibet* (1969). (T. V. W.)

**TIBETAN ART** comprises ancient pre-Buddhist decorative and domestic crafts (compare ancient Celtic art in Europe) and the all-pervading religious art that was gradually introduced from the 8th century onward from surrounding Buddhist countries and developed subsequently as recognizably distinct Tibetan art forms of imagery and sculpture, and decorative architectural motifs. In all its forms Tibetan art has remained subservient to special lay or religious intentions, and has never become an art pursued for

The Bronhyd lotus, the perfect eight-leaved lotus flower with a silver urn in the centre. *Below,* the Bronhyd lotus with petals closed

Statuette of Yamantaka, the ferocious form of the Tibetan deity of wisdom, Manjushri, who waged war against Yama, king of hell. The deity is shown with 9 heads and 34 arms

Statuette of Changcha Hutuktu, a Living Buddha of Peking

## TIBETAN IMAGES AND RITUAL OBJECTS

A ritual vessel of gold, silver and copper inlaid with turquoise. It shows Chinese influence

Prayer wheels, cylindrical metal cases in which a roll of prayers, printed on paper, is inserted; the cylinder is mounted on a rod on which it is revolved. Left, a table prayer wheel; right, a hand prayer wheel

Statuette of Padmasambhava, an 8th-century Indian teacher, founder of the Old Translation school (the so-called Red Cap)

BY COURTESY OF (TOP LEFT, CENTRE LEFT) SUMNER GERARD, (TOP RIGHT, CENTRE) THE AMERICAN MUSEUM OF NATURAL HISTORY, (CENTRE, TOP RIGHT, BOTTOM CENTRE) MRS. A. K. GORDON, (BOTTOM LEFT, BOTTOM RIGHT) MRS. ALEXANDER SCOTT

# TIBETAN ART

The Wheel of Life, pictorially explaining the Buddhist conception of life, death and rebirth. The wheel is held in the clutches of a demon who symbolizes impermanence. The drawing in the hub is symbolic of lust, anger and ignorance, cardinal sins. Different worlds of rebirth are represented in the segments of the wheel. In the outer rim are 12 scenes which dramatize the various stages through which man passes after birth

Representation of Lchang-skya Rol-pa' i rdo-je. Chinese influence is shown by the architecture of the monasteries. The saint carries a book, one of the attributes of his patron, the celebrated reformer Tsong-kha-pa, founder of the Yellow Cap sect of Tibetan Buddhism

## TIBETAN PAINTINGS

Gautama Buddha in the attitude of turning the wheel of the law. He is surrounded by Buddhas, Bodhisattvas and Arhants

BY COURTESY OF (LEFT) O. BURCHARD, (TOP RIGHT) THE NEWARK MUSEUM, NEWARK, N.J., (BOTTOM RIGHT) A. K. GORDON; PHOTOGRAPH, (TOP RIGHT) SOICHI SUNAMI aesthetic ends. The religious art is primarily didactic and symbolic, while lay art is decorative. Thus, while lay art may be easily appreciated, to understand the significance of Tibetan religious art requires a prior knowledge of Tibetan religion and religious symbolism. Since the destruction of Tibetan cultural traditions by Chinese-trained Communists from 1959 onward, a greater interest has arisen in the West in the surviving Tibetan *objets d'art* preserved in museums and private collections.

**History.**—Up to the 9th century A.D. Tibet was open to cultural influences from Central Asia, especially Khotan, and from China. For two centuries up to the collapse of the old Tibetan kingdom in 842, the Tibetans controlled the whole Takla Makan and the important trade routes from the Middle East to China. Stone carving and metalwork were certainly practised in the pre-Buddhist period, and Persian, Indian, and Chinese influences, all received through Central Asia, have been noted. The introduction of Buddhism from the 8th century onward led to the arrival in Tibet of Buddhist craftsmen from Central Asia and later from Nepal and northwest India, all of which were then Buddhist lands. Some cast images may survive from this first Buddhist period. After 842 central Tibet dissolved into political chaos for over 100 years, and from the 10th century onward the cultural initiative passed to a line of kings in western Tibet. For temple decorations such as wood carving of doorways and posts, decorative painting on ceilings and woodwork, temple frescoes, and terra-cotta and stucco images, they drew heavily on the cultural resources of pre-Islamic Kashmir. Surviving monasteries and temples with their magnificent contents were made known to the Western educated world in the 1930s thanks to the expeditions and brilliant recording of Giuseppe Tucci of Rome. With the establishment of religious hegemonies in central Tibet from the 11th century onward, cultural contacts with Nepal and the main Buddhist centres in the main Ganges Valley flourished as never before. Conversely, cultural contacts with China dwindled for several centuries, at least in central and southern Tibet. From this time right up until the 20th century, Tibetan religious art and Nepalese Buddhist art have remained a single unified tradition. Meanwhile eastern Tibet, where the ancient pre-Buddhist crafts of metalwork never died out, began to develop religious styles under influence from craftsmen from central Tibet. From that date the spread of Tibetan culture and art became coterminous with the spread of Tibetan religion, and thus from the 13th century onward, when Tibetan lamas began to convert the Mongolians, Mongolian religious art developed as a branch of Tibetan art. Through the Mongols China began to extend its political influence over Tibet, and this led to a steady increase in Chinese cultural influence, especially in the east. From 1721 when the Chinese emperors became the suzerains of Tibet, Chinese influence was felt much more strongly throughout central as well as eastern Tibet, and Tibetan religious paintings and especially domestic decoration reveal distinct Chinese features.

**Pre-Buddhist Decorative Crafts.**—From the 7th to 9th centuries there survive carved stone pillars decorated with Chinese, Central Asian, and Indian motifs, and also a stone lion showing traces of Persian influence. In the Lhasa cathedral there is a silver jug with a long neck surmounted by a horse's head, and there are textual references to all kinds of articles made of gold: a large golden goose holding seven gallons of wine, a wine vase, a miniature city decorated with gold lions, and golden bowls. Gold animals are mentioned as decorating the camp of King Ral-pa-can when a Chinese envoy visited him in 821. These early Tibetan skills lived on throughout the Buddhist period in the form of decorative motifs on teapots, sword hilts, musical instruments, tinderboxes and personal jewelry and, although they mingle with it, they have a life quite independent of Buddhist religious art.

**Images and Sculpture.**—The art of casting images in bronze and other metals entered Tibet from Nepal and India. Having first followed foreign models, the Tibetans gradually developed their own styles, and began to depict their own lamas and teachers as well as the regular range of Indian Buddhist divinities. Stone carving disappeared in this Buddhist tradition of imagery, but wood and terra-cotta, especially in western and southern Tibet, were common. Papier-mâché, elaborately painted, was also used for the masks of divinities, especially for those worn in monastic dances. This use presumably originated in Kashmir. A vast pantheon of Buddhas, gods, and goddesses was inherited from India, and each is distinguished iconographically by posture, hand gestures, and accoutrements. Of lesser divinities and especially of lamas the identification is often difficult. It is rare that an image is named in an inscription, and even rarer to find a date. Because of the extremely conservative nature of Tibetan art, correct dating within several centuries is often impossible. Images of vast size, rising up through two or three stories, are quite often seen in Tibetan temples, and their construction and dedication is considered a work of vast religious merit. Since images are mainly cast or molded, carving is restricted to decorative motifs, especially on wooden pillars and roof beams.

**Painting: Frescoes and Temple Banners.**—Temple interiors are usually covered with frescoes and often hung with painted banners (*thang-ka*). For the preparation of the latter, a taut cotton cloth is impregnated with a concoction of chalk and glue, rubbed smooth by some suitable object; *e.g.*, a flat polished stone. A religious painter trained in the tradition draws in the outline, often using printed designs for the main figures. There is no scope for originality so far as the iconographic details of divinities are concerned, and thus such painting is a highly skilled craft. For decorative details—*e.g.*, flowers, cloud effects, rocks, and groups of devotees—there is wider scope. The tradition of fresco painting and temple banners certainly goes back to that of the great Buddhist monasteries of northwest India and the Ganges Valley, but these Indian origins of the 9th to 12th centuries are now entirely lost. The Indian Buddhist paintings of Ajanta are of a much earlier period (up to the 6th century A.D.), thus predating the great increase in the Buddhist pantheon and in occult symbolism, typical of the later Indian Buddhism received by the Tibetans. Central Asian styles certainly reached central Tibet well before the 9th century, but it was India and Nepal which after that date were to have lasting influences on the development of Tibetan art. In more recent times, especially from the 18th century onward, Chinese influence becomes noticeable in the details of paintings, particularly in the freer but still balanced arrangement of the main figures and the use of Chinese-style landscapes as subsidiary decoration. With the disappearance of Buddhism from Central Asia and India from the 12th century onward, Tibetan art developed as a style exclusive to the Tibetans, the Newar Buddhists of the Nepal Valley, and the Tibetan converts of Mongolia.

**Decorative Architectural Motifs.**—For temples the Tibetans used their own solid indigenous styles, but embellished these with Indian, Nepalese, and (very much later) Chinese motifs. Tiered ornamented roofs are originally of Indian origin, as received through Nepal and later through China. The magnificent interior carving is of Indian and Nepalese inspiration. The painting motifs vary from 11th-century Kashmiri styles in the west to the magnificent Chinese-style decorations of recent centuries.

**Ritual and Domestic Objects.**—Tibetan metalworkers have excelled in producing fine things for ritual and domestic use: ritual lamps, vases, bowls, bells, prayer wheels, decorated trumpets and horns for the temples, and for home use ornamented teapots, jars, bowls, ladles, and especially beautiful stands, often in silver or gold, to hold porcelain teacups, capped by finely worked lids of precious metals. Hand-woven rugs of magnificent Central Asian and Chinese designs, always adapted to Tibetan preferences, cover low seats, and tables and cabinets of carved and painted wood were commonplace in prosperous homes.

**Collections.**—Fine collections of Tibetan art may be seen in the Musée Guimet in Paris, the British Museum and the Victoria and Albert Museum in London, the American Museum of Natural History, New York, the Newark Museum of Arts and Sciences, N.J., and the University of Pennsylvania Museum, Philadelphia. Since the disappearance of old Tibet, the only country surviving as a living representative of Tibetan art and culture is Bhutan.

BIBLIOGRAPHY.—A. Getty, *The Gods of Northern Buddhism* (1928, reprinted 1963); A. K. Gordon, *Tibetan Religious Art* (1952), *The Iconography of Tibetan Lamaism* (1959); S. Hummel, *Geschichte der tibetischen Kunst* (1953); G. Roerich, *Tibetan Paintings* (1925), *The Animal Style Among the Nomads of Northern Tibet* (1930); D. Snellgrove and H. Richardson, *A Cultural History of Tibet* (1968); G. Tucci, *Indo-Tibetica,* 4 vol. (1932–41), *Tibetan Painted Scrolls,* 3 vol. (1949). (D. L. Sn.)

**TIBETAN BUDDHISM.** This article deals with the special form of Buddhism (*q.v.*) which has gradually evolved in Tibet since the 7th century A.D., when Tibetan rulers first began to take an active interest in this religion. It is also convenient to include the pre-Buddhist cults (known as Bon), for very little is known of them in their primitive form, whereas subsequently they have been so affected by Buddhist beliefs and practices as to have become just a rather incongruous sect of Tibetan Buddhism.

**Lamas and Monasticism.**—Tibetan religion attracts interest in the west mainly on account of its special system of reincarnating lamas. There are several hundreds of them, of whom the dalai lama and the panchen lama are incomparably the most important (*see* DALAI LAMA). Lama (*bla-ma*) means simply "superior," and is the normal polite title for senior monks and for those in the villages who act as the "priests" of their small communities as well as for the heads of teaching faculties in the larger monasteries and the principals of religious institutions, both small and large. In the case of such senior lamas suitably respectful epithets are added, but the term itself is of wide application as the title "father" for a Christian priest. The reincarnating lamas (*sprul-sku*) are normally principals of monasteries and they have steadily increased in number since the 15th century (when the idea of identifying successors in this way gained general acceptance), for it greatly adds to the prestige of an institution to have an "incarnation" as its head. Nevertheless there still remain many institutions where other methods of succession are in vogue: by inheritance from father to son (in the case of married religious practisers), from uncle to nephew or by selection according to merit and learning. Of these last the abbot of Ganden (dGa'-ldan), one of the three enormous Gelugpa (dGe-lugs-pa) monasteries on the outskirts of Lhasa, is the most important.

The widespread monastic system itself is but an elaborate development of the type of monastic life which is fundamental to Buddhism in all its forms. What is remarkable is the zeal with which the Tibetans have taken to religious life; no census has ever been made in the country, but a quarter of the population are probably members of religious institutions, or at least were before the Chinese Communist occupation of 1950. Their religion serves as the basis of their whole culture.

**Early History.**—The first temples were built in the reign of Sroṅ-btsan-sgam-po (or Songtsen Gampo; d. A.D. 649), who was also responsible for founding Lhasa as well as for establishing an official Tibetan alphabet based on the studies of one of his ministers, Thon-mi Sambhota, in Kashmir, which was then still a Buddhist country. Two of Sroṅ-btsan-sgam-po's queens, one Chinese and one Nepalese, are popularly regarded as the earliest patrons of Tibetan Buddhism and thus identified as "incarnations" of the Buddhist saviouress (Tara). No spectacular progress was made with the new religion during the next hundred years, for the Tibetan leaders were engaged in conquering and controlling a huge central Asian empire, recognized under duress by the Chinese, from whom they wrested the important city-states of Kashgar, Kucha, Karashahr and Khotan on the ancient silk route, which skirts the Takla Makan desert. This brought them into contact not only with Buddhist communities but also with Manichaeans, Nestorian Christians, Arabs and Persians, followers of Islam. Central Asian Buddhism evoked active interest among the Tibetans: monks fleeing from Khotan were hospitably received by the Chinese wife (d. A.D. 739) of the Tibetan king Mes-'ag-ts'oms, monasteries being built for them presumably near Lhasa; moreover large collections of Tibetan Buddhist manuscripts preserved at Tun-huang attest the existence of Tibetan religious communities in the area. It seems that the royal family was eager to foster Buddhism, while powerful ministerial chiefs were opposed to it. Royal authority was established during the long reign (755–797) of K'ri-sroṅ-lde-btsan (Khrisong Detsen), notable for three major events: the building of the first proper Tibetan monastery at Samye (bSam-yas) between Lhasa and Yarlung; the ordaining of the first seven Tibetan monks; and the holding of a council to decide the relative merits of Chinese and Indian forms of Buddhism. The Indian masters Santarakshita, representing orthodox Mahayana teachings, and Padmasambhava, manifesting the magic powers of a *mahasiddha* ("master yogin," of whom there are 84 in Shivaist and Buddhist Tantric tradition), were responsible for the founding of Samye; the views of Santarakshita's disciple Kamalashila prevailed at the council. Buddhist monks appear as ministers of state as early as the beginning of the 9th century. The third "religious" king of Tibet, Ral-pa-can (Ralpachan), who is credited with systematizing the methods of translating texts and with establishing the *Vinaya* (monastic discipline) of the Mulasarvastivadin order or of Indian Buddhism as the sole orthodox Tibetan one, was murdered (838) by his brother, who thereupon set about destroying the new religion, at least in the region of Lhasa.

**Bon.**—Explicit references to Bon occur in the cycles of quasi-historical texts concerning Padmasambhava, who is honoured as the chief queller and converter of all forces hostile to Buddhism. The character of original Bon beliefs can be surmised from such textual references, but, since literature began in Tibet as a deliberate Buddhist concern, with the whole wealth of Indian literary traditions behind it, the Bon-pos were bound to use Buddhist terminology, often without realizing perhaps that it implied ideas that might be specifically Buddhist. That they later tried to have recourse to Hindu mythology indicates the fundamental weakness of their position. The original features of Bon seem to have been a cult of divine kingship whereby the kings were regarded as manifestations of the sky-divinity; an order of oracular priests; a cult of the gods of the atmosphere, the earth and subterranean regions; and the practice of blood sacrifices. All these features in a transmuted form have been absorbed into Tibetan Buddhism. While Bon-pos and Buddhists must both have had their interested supporters in 8th- and 9th-century Tibet, the chiefs of the country seem often to have used them as factions in political intrigues.

**Tibetan Translations of Buddhist Texts.**—Royal sponsors appeared again in the 10th–11th centuries, this time in western Tibet (mNa'-ris), namely Ye-śes-'od and his brother Lha-lde, then the latter's sons, 'Od-lde, Byaṅ-c'ub-'od and Śiba-'od. They fostered learning and sent young Tibetans to India to study, of whom the most famous is probably the great translator Rin-c'en-bzaṅ-po (Rinchen Zampo; 958–1055). Large sums were expended buying the services and knowledge of Indian masters. One of the most renowned of these was Atisha (982–1054), who spent the last 12 years of his life in Tibet, surrounded by Tibetan disciples. From now on Buddhism seems to have had no determined opponents; the Bon-pos had already begun to produce their own literature on Buddhist models and were presumably often as interested in the latest Tibetan translations from Sanskrit as were the Buddhists proper. When one remembers that much of this work was done by individual practisers of the doctrine following their own bent in translating philosophical or doctrinal texts, tantric cycles and their manifold commentaries, works on medicine, astrology, etc., it is remarkable what uniformity was eventually achieved.

By the 14th century the Tibetans had succeeded in translating all available Buddhist literature in India and Nepal. After the destruction wrought in the name of Islam, Buddhism had practically disappeared from India by A.D. 1200, and Nepal (primarily the Katmandu valley) remained the sole representative of Sanskrit Buddhist culture. Practice of the doctrine rapidly began to deteriorate there, now that Indian inspiration was gone; meanwhile Tibet began to manifest itself as the chief inheritor of the whole Indian Buddhist tradition. No complete Indian canon of Mahayana Buddhism seems ever to have existed. But having collected and translated over the course of some six centuries all canonical and quasi-canonical texts, as well as the works of all Indian Buddhist writers, the Tibetans gradually produced their own canon, which had assumed by the 13th century more or less its present form. Consisting originally of a massive collection of manuscripts, this great work has appeared in several editions (printed page by page from incised wooden blocks) since the 16th century. It is arranged as 100 or 108 (depending on the edition) massive volumes of supposedly canonical texts (*Kanjur*, or *Kagyur*, "translated word") and 225 volumes of commentaries, scholarly treatises and miscellaneous writing by Indian masters (*Tenjur*, or *Tangyur*, "translated treatises").

**Later Developments.**—It has often been said that the Tibetans adopted only the more debased forms of Indian Buddhism, and the use of the term "lamaism" has been used (like papism) to suggest a curious and falsified form of original teachings. In fact they adopted the whole of Indian Buddhism with its monastic life, its scholarly disposition, its ideal of the beneficent sage and its more popular conception of the wonder-working tantric yogin. Thus there are religious men of all kinds in Tibet: the wealthy benefactor sponsoring a new community, the independent seeker after knowledge (and sometimes the wealth that such knowledge brings), the pious monk spending his whole life translating texts, or the converted Bon-po striving to gain those special powers associated with proficiency in tantric practice.

Thus the earlier orders of Tibetan Buddhism began to develop quite spontaneously around the traditions associated with certain revered masters, but with no deliberate doctrinal or practical differences to distinguish them. The Nyiṅgmapa (rÑiṅ-ma-pa; "Old Order") claimed to transmit the original teachings of Padmasambhava, the great tantric master of the 8th century, who was now identified as a Buddha. In support of their doctrines they began to "discover" texts, which had been "hidden" during the persecution following the murder of Ral-pa-can. Many of these texts, which were put together in the 12th and 13th centuries, do in fact contain very ancient traditions. The Bon-pos likewise began to discover their "hidden" literature, and the texts they produced were, needless to say, permeated by the same type of teachings. The founder of Sakya (Sa-skya) monastery (founded 1073), after which the Sakyapa (Sa-skya-pa) order is named, was simply a Nyiṅgmapa who wished to establish sound doctrine. During the historical vicissitudes of the next two centuries, his successors, who were certainly learned, became the religious masters of the great Mongol khans, from whom they received in return the mandate of political power throughout the whole of Tibet. (This political power was not held unchallenged; it endured about a century and even then the country remained more or less divided in allegiance to powerful monasteries and rival clans.)

Another important order, the Kagyurpa (bKa'-rgyud-pa; "Order of the Transmitted Word"), was founded by the translator Marpa, who had acquired his initiations and doctrines from the Indian tantric yogin Naropa. Marpa was a householder; his chief disciple, Milaraspa, the most renowned of Tibetan sages, was a solitary hermit. This line developed into a large number of subsects, all monastic in type.

Another order, generally reforming in intention, was associated with Atisha or rather with his disciple 'Brom-ston, who founded Rva-sgreng monastery to the northeast of Lhasa. His order, known as the Kadampa (bKa'-gdams-pa; "Precept Giving") was absorbed in the 15th century by the last and now the most powerful of Tibetan religious orders, the Gelugpa (dGe-lugs-pa; "the Virtuous"), the order of the dalai lama and the panchen lama.

This last order was founded by an east Tibetan, Tsoṅ-k'a-pa (Tsongkhapa; *c.* 1358–1419), a scholarly writer and skilful preacher, who was intent on establishing monastic celibacy as the only legitimate form of religious life. He established a following in Lhasa, where he founded Ganden (dGa'-ldan) monastery. His immediate disciples founded two other monasteries, Drepung ('Bras-spuṅs) and Sera, also on the outskirts of Lhasa. These subsequently became the main Gelugpa strongholds, dominating the capital with a joint total of about 20,000 monks. (The nickname "Yellow Hats" for the Gelugpa, commonly used by westerners, is possibly of Chinese origin. The corresponding nickname "Red Hats," as applied to all the other older orders, is a mistaken usage of foreigners, for it applies properly to only one subsect.) One of the most energetic organizers of the new order was dGe-'dun-grub-pa (Gentun Drupa; 1391–1474), abbot of Drepung, who was retrospectively recognized as the first rGyal-ba Rin-po-c'e ("precious conqueror"), the title by which Tibetans refer to the dalai lama.

The two foremost disciples of Tsoṅ-k'a-pa, namely rGyal-ts'ab-rje and mK'as-grub-rje (Khedru), acted as abbots of Tsoṅ-k'a-pa's own monastery, Ganden, and when mK'as-grub-rje died in 1438 dGe-'dun-grub-pa seems already to have resolved to find as his successor a boy born in the same year. Precedents for this practice can be traced back to the 13th century at least. The idea of a divine being manifest as a human teacher was already established in Indian Buddhism, and the theory of rebirth is of course fundamental to Buddhism in all its forms. It was by combining these ideas and claiming the ability to recognize one after another the representatives of such a series that the Tibetans devised a unique system of heredity. dGe-'dun-grub-pa died at the monastery of Trashi Lhümpo (bKra-śis-lhun-po), which he had built (1447–52) in honour of his departed master, and a worthy successor was found as abbot. It was only later that his "reincarnation" was discovered. Thereafter, however, the system of reincarnations was accepted as the general rule. Drepung became the seat of the "precious conquerors," and Trashi Lhümpo that of the "precious sages" (Paṇ-c'en Rin-po-c'e, the panchen lama). Political power over the whole of Tibet came to the fifth "precious conqueror" by the arms of the Mongols, who had been reconverted to Buddhism by his great predecessor, the third.

All the different orders have developed their own literary traditions, biographical, historical, doctrinal and liturgical, and thus the scope of Tibetan literature is now enormous.

**Religious Theory and Practice.**—In general, Tibetan religion represents the developed Mahayana Buddhism of India, which includes tantric theory and practice, known either as Vajrayana ("vehicle of mystic power"; literally "thunderbolt") or Mantrayana ("vehicle of mystic spells"), together with indigenous Bon notions which were easily adaptable. Thus the Bon idea of divine kingship finds a new Buddhist form in the theory of reincarnating lamas; the old priests of Bon now have Buddhist oracular soothsayers as their counterparts; the old local gods are now conceived of as serving the new religion and receive sacrificial offerings as a kind of fee for their continuing good will; the offerings consist of conventional sacrificial cakes, and the "flesh-offerings" prepared for bloodthirsty divinities are simply specially prepared cakes made to look sufficiently gruesome. Religious practice proper (study of religious texts, meditation, self-discipline and the practice of morality) is entirely Buddhist in character, and its efficacy as a way of perfection (in terms of the Buddhist ideal of blissful equanimity pervaded by loving kindness) is proved by the undoubted existence of a minority of very deeply religious men, as well as by the far greater number whose well-balanced personalities manifest the results of such a training. This is not to claim that Tibetans are more virtuous than other peoples, though they are probably more morally conscious. Their religious susceptibilities are highly developed, ranging from fervent and well-directed faith to vague superstition. *See* also TIBET; TIBETAN ART.

BIBLIOGRAPHY.—Sir Charles Bell, *Tibet Past and Present* (1924); Bu-ston, *History of Buddhism*, Eng. trans. by E. Obermiller (1931–32); I. Desideri, *An Account of Tibet 1712–1727*, Eng. trans. by J. Ross, 2nd ed. (1937); H. Hoffmann, *Die Religionen Tibets* (1956); D. L. Snellgrove, *Buddhist Himalaya* (1957); G. Tucci, *Tibetan Painted Scrolls* (1949), which is of prime importance; L. A. Waddell, *The Buddhism of Tibet*, 2nd ed. (1958); R. A. Stein, *La Civilisation Tibétaine* (1962); H. E. Richardson, *Tibet and Its History* (1962); D. L. Snellgrove, *Nine Ways of Bon* (1967). (D. L. SN.)

**TIBETAN LANGUAGE** is classified as a member of the Tibeto-Himalayan branch of the Tibeto-Burmese subfamily (*see* TIBETO-BURMAN LANGUAGES) of the Sino-Tibetan family of languages. Tibetan, Burmese, and Chinese shared a common linguistic origin, yet each developed independently over the millennia and became distinctive in both spoken and written forms. Lacking reliable census data, the number of Tibetan-speaking people in Asia can only be approximated. The figure for Tibet proper is estimated around 1,500,000, with perhaps an additional 5,000,000 in the Tibetan ethnic areas of western China, Bhutan, Sikkim, northern Nepal, and the Ladakh region of Kashmir.

**The Tibetan Script.**—The systems of writing Chinese, Burmese, and Tibetan are completely different. Chinese has been written in ideographs and logographs since the 2nd millennium B.C. (*see* CHINESE LANGUAGE). The Burmese script, dating from the 11th century A.D., is an adaptation of the "square" Pali script. The Tibetan system of writing was modeled on an Indo-Aryan script during the 7th century A.D.

According to Tibetan historical tradition, a minister named Thon-mi Sambhoṭa was sent, *c.* A.D. 640, to study Sanskrit in Kashmir. After returning to Lhasa, he devised a syllabary (*see* LOGOGRAM AND SYLLABARY) consisting of 30 consonants and 4 vowel signs. Thon-mi Sambhoṭa used the northern Gupta script as his model. The arrangement of the Tibetan syllabary follows that of Khotanese, in which the vocalic radicals *'a*, called *a-chung* (little a), and *a*, called *a-chen* (big a), are listed among the consonants (*see* the illustration of the Tibetan syllabary). In Indic syllabaries, such as the Devanāgarī, the vocalic radicals are listed first with the other vowels, separate from the consonants. Tibetan, like Sanskrit and English, is written from left to right. After creating the distinctive Tibetan script, Thon-mi Sambhoṭa composed eight treatises on grammar, two of which survive.

**TIBETAN SYLLABARY**

| SCRIPT | TRANSCRIPTION | SCRIPT | TRANSCRIPTION |
|---|---|---|---|
| ཀ་ | ka | མ་ | ma |
| ཁ་ | kha | ཙ་ | tsa |
| ག་ | ga | ཚ་ | tsha |
| ང་ | nga | ཛ་ | dza |
| ཅ་ | ca | ཝ་ | wa |
| ཆ་ | cha | ཞ་ | zha |
| ཇ་ | ja | ཟ་ | za |
| ཉ་ | nya | འ་ | 'a |
| ཏ་ | ta | ཡ་ | ya |
| ཐ་ | tha | ར་ | ra |
| ད་ | da | ལ་ | la |
| ན་ | na | ཤ་ | sha |
| པ་ | pa | ས་ | sa |
| ཕ་ | pha | ཧ་ | ha |
| བ་ | ba | ཨ་ | a |

Consonant ས་ with vowel signs: ས་ sa སི་ si སུ་ su སེ་ se སོ་ so

There are three basic forms used for writing the Tibetan language. The style called *dbu-can* (with head) has a line drawn at the top, or head, of each letter. This form, corresponding to block-printing style, is used primarily in wood-block printing of texts. The style called *dbu-med* (without head) has no top, or head, line and is the form commonly used in writing manuscripts. The third style is called *'khyug-yig* (running letters), because abbreviations and combinations are used to achieve speed in writing. This form is used for general and private writing, such as correspondence and note-taking (*see* illustration of these scripts). The oldest known examples of Tibetan writing found on inscribed stelae dating from the 8th century and in documents discovered in caves near Tun-Huang in Chinese Turkistan show that the form of the script has remained virtually unchanged throughout the centuries. This may be attributed to the influence of Buddhism on Tibetan culture, for once Buddhism achieved religious supremacy, the written language, as the medium of transmission for the Buddhist teachings, acquired a sacral character; consequently, its form and orthography were left unchanged out of reverence. Since the spoken language continued to evolve phonologically, there developed a great disparity between Tibetan orthography and pronunciation.

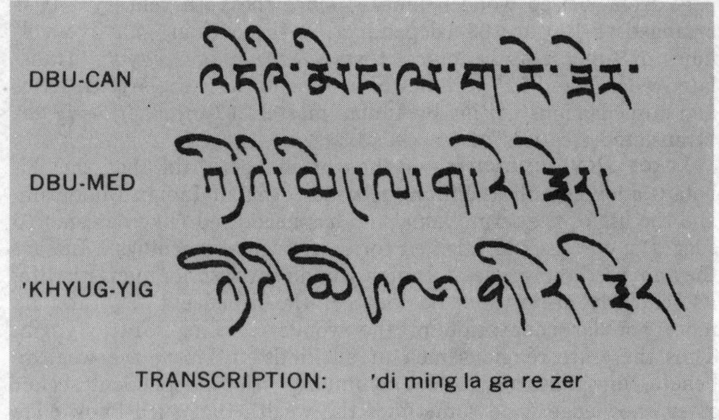


TRANSLATION OF ABOVE: WHAT IS THE NAME OF THIS?

**Phonology.**—Presumably, current Tibetan orthography reflects the 7th-century pronunciation of the language, which consisted of voiced and unvoiced initials, finals, and prefixed and suffixed consonants. In some of the dialects, phonological development led to the unvoicing of the initials (*g, j, d, b, dz, zh, z, r, l*) and the dropping of prefixed and suffixed consonants. A large number of homophones resulted from these changes and a tone system evolved concomitantly to distinguish such homophones. In those dialects which still preserve traces of the voiced initials and prefixed consonants, notably that of *A-mdo*, a distinguishing system of tones did not develop.

The major dialects spoken in Tibet proper are those of the two central provinces, Dbus and Gtsang, the western province of Stod, and the eastern one of Khams. Dialects such as *A-mdo* and *Rgya-rong* are spoken in Tibetan ethnic areas in the present-day Chinese provinces of Ch'ing-hai and Szechwan, respectively. Other dialects are spoken by Himalayan peoples outside of Tibet in Bhutan, Sikkim, Ladakh, and in the Sherpa, Mustang, and Dolpo areas of northern Nepal. Dialects of the regions where there is contact with non-Tibetan cultures reflect the older phonology of literary orthography: a phenomenon indicative of the resistance to linguistic change in areas of cultural confrontation.

*The Lhasa Dialect.*—Because it was the dialect of the politico-religious capital of Tibet and of the members of the aristocracy, which supplied all of the lay officials of the Tibetan government, the Lhasa dialect (*Lha-sa skad*) is regarded as the lingua franca of Tibet. It also shows the greatest diversity between pronunciation and orthography. According to a recent analysis, the inventory of phonemes in the Lhasa dialect consists of 12 vowels, two semi-vowels, and 26 consonants. With it understood that the Lhasa dialect no longer evidences voiced initial consonants, the following chart lists the phonetic (not phonemic) equivalents of the pronunciation of the Tibetan syllabary. A line above the vowel indicates the syllable is pronounced in a high tone: a line below the vowel indicates low tone.

| | | |
|---|---|---|
| ka : gā | da : ta̲ (da̲)* | zha : sha̲ |
| kha : kā | na : na̲ (nā)† | za : sa̲ |
| ga : ka̲ (ga̲)* | pa : bā | 'a : a̲ |
| nga : nga̲ (ngā)† | pha : pā | ya : ya̲ (yā)† |
| ca : jā | ba : pa̲ (ba̲)* | ra : ra̲ |
| cha : chā | ma : ma̲ (mā)† | la : la̲ (lā)† |
| ja : cha̲ (ja̲)* | tsa : dsā | sha : shā |
| nya : nya̲ (nyā)† | tsha : tsā | sa : sā |
| ta : dā | dza: tsa̲ (dsa̲)* | ha : hā |
| tha : tā | wa : wa̲ | a : ā |

*With prefixed consonants, it loses aspiration.
†With prefixed consonants, the tone becomes high.

*Lhasa Tone System.*—Although there are various fluctuations in relative levels of pitch, the phonemically distinctive tones of the Lhasa dialect are six: high-short, low-short, high-long, low-long, high-falling, and low-falling. There is a direct relationship between the tone and the original orthography of the Tibetan word. If the initial consonant is one of the originally unvoiced consonants (*k, kh, c, ch, t, th, p, ph, ts, tsh, sh, s, h,* or *a-chen*), the syllable is always pronounced in a high tone.

If the initial is one of the following originally voiced consonants—*g, j, d, b, dz*—it is pronounced in a low tone with aspiration. If there are any prefixed consonants, then it loses aspiration. The other originally voiced consonants are pronounced in a low tone, with the exception of *y* and *l*, which become high tone if there are any prefixed consonants.

All nasals without prefixed consonants are pronounced in a low tone; with prefixes, in a high tone. The two exceptions to this rule are *mig* (eye) and *mag*[*-pa*] (adopted bridegroom): both are in a high tone even though there is no prefixed consonant.

Long and falling tones result when a final consonant is dropped in pronunciation. Long tones are caused by dropping the finals *r* and *l*. A dropped *l* also umlauts the vowel. A final *n* umlauts and nasalizes the lengthened vowel. Falling tones result from dropping the finals *g, d,* and *s*. A dropped *d* or *s* also umlauts the vowel. When *s* occurs as a suffix after other consonants, it is still dropped causing a falling tone after nasals, but the vowel is not umlauted.

In spite of the development of the tone system, it only serves to distinguish between homophones of different tone, not between those of the same tone. For example, *lnga* (five) and *rnga* (drum) are both pronounced in a high-short tone. Although homophonic in pronunciation, they are distinctive in the written language. Homophones which are also homographs are distinguished in the script by adding a small, triangular-shaped letter, called *wa-zur* (a *wa* at the side), at the bottom of the initial consonant. For example, *tsha* (heat) is distinguished from the word "salt" by adding the *wa-zur;* thus: *tshwa.*

*Single and Compounded Syllables.*—Each letter of the Tibetan syllabary has an inherent *a* vowel in its pronunciation; therefore, it is a "syllable," and most of the single consonant syllables are morphemes. For example, *kha* (mouth), *nya* (fish), *ba* (cow), *ma* (mother), *wa* (fox), and *la* (mountain pass). Due to the limitations on the possible combinations of initial and final consonants with a vowel, the maximum number of monosyllabic words is restricted; thus compounding two or more syllables to form additional words is a significant feature of the language.

Generally speaking, nouns in Tibetan have no grammatical gender. Gender is indicated in two ways: (1) different words: *rta* (horse), *gseb* (stallion), and *rgod-ma* (mare); or (2) by affixing masculine or feminine particles to the general term: *pho-rta* (male horse), *mo-rta* (female horse), *bya* (chicken), *bya-pho* (rooster), *bya-mo* (hen).

Most nouns are dissyllabic in form: the most common being a noun with a nominal suffix. These suffixes are *pa, ba, po* for masculine terms of reference and *ma, mo* for feminine ones. In some cases, the suffix forms part of the noun, as in *khang-pa* (house), *lag-pa* (hand), and *rtsig-pa* (wall). When affixed to nouns that do not have such a suffix, the suffix denotes "one who is associated with a certain thing." For example, *rnga* (drum), *rnga-pa* (drummer); *chu* (water), *chu-pa* (water carrier); *Bod* (Tibet), *Bod-pa* (Tibetan). The suffixes *po* and *mo* attached to verbal roots denote the performer of the action; thus: *rgyal-ba* (to conquer), *rgyal-po* (king), *rgyal-mo* (queen).

Compounds in the Tibetan language are formed in several ways. Conjunctive compounds combine two nominal morphemes as if joined by a conjunction; thus: *pha-ma* (father-mother) "parents"; *rta-drel* (horse-mule) "transport"; *ra-lug* (goat-sheep) "flock." Determinative compounds are those in which the first syllable is an attribute of the second. For example, *rdo-rje* (stone-lord) "diamond"; *rgyal-sras* (king-son) "prince"; *mgo-nad* (head-illness) "headache"; *skar-rtsis* (star-calculation) "astrology." Synonym compounds are formed by joining two words of similar meaning to reinforce the meaning of each; thus: *snyan-grags* (reputation-fame) "fame"; *tshon-mdog* (colour-colour) "colour." Two words of opposite meaning are joined to form abstract compounds. For example, *ring-thung* (long-short) "distance"; *tsha-grang* (hot-cold) "temperature"; *rgas-gzhon* (old-young) "age."

**Grammar and Syntax.**—Compared to the complex rules of grammar for languages such as Sanskrit, the grammatical features of Tibetan are relatively simple. There is a limited number of grammatical particles which serve to indicate instrumental, genitive, dative, ablative, locative, and terminative functions. The grammatical function of a word is often determined solely upon syntactical sequence. If the verb is transitive, requiring a direct object, then the subject of the sentence is put in the instrumental case by suffixing the particle *kyis* (the variant spellings *gyis, gis,* and *-s* depend upon the final consonant or vowel of the preceding syllable). Thus: *khyod-kyis rdo zhig 'phangs pa* (You-instrumental particle-stone-a-threw) "You threw a stone."

Adjectives, which do not differ in form from nouns, usually follow the noun they qualify. This is especially true of those basically descriptive in meaning, such as those denoting size, colour, and conditions; thus: *rta dkar-po* (horse white) "a white horse." Adjectives and nouns may precede the word they qualify, in which case, the so-called genitive sign *kyi* (variant spellings are *gyi, gi,* and *-'i*) is used to join them. For example, *Bod-kyi gzhung* (Tibet-genitive sign-government) "the Tibetan government"; *rgyal-po'i pho-brang* (king-genitive sign-palace) "the king's palace."

The sign of the dative is *la* (to, at, for, regarding); the ablative is *nas* (from, out of); the locative is *na* (in); and the so-called terminative sign is *ru* (variant spellings are *du, tu, su,* and *-r*). The terminative sign is used to express a motion "to" or "into"; however, its most common function is to make adverbs out of verbs and adjectives. For example, *mgyogs-po* (adj. quick), *mgyogs-por* (adv. quickly); *'dod-pa* (verb, to desire), *'dod-par* (adv. desiringly).

It is usually said that, except for the copula verbs, there are no true verbs in the Tibetan language, because most verbs are verbal nouns and can thus be a noun, adjective, adverb, and verb, depending on its position in a given sentence; thus it is possible to say: *Thal-'gyur-pa'i lta-ba-la legs-par lta-ba'i lta-bar lta-bar dgos,* "The association [philosophical] view should be viewed as the view, which has been properly viewed." In this sentence, *lta-ba* serves as a noun, an adjective, an adverb, and a verb.

*Syntax.*—As noted above, the grammatical function of certain words in a given sentence is determined as much by word order as by case signs. There is no sign for words in the nominative, accusative, and vocative cases. Tibetan syntax is inflexible. The proper sequence is adverbs of time or space, subject, indirect object, direct object, adverb, and verb. If the verb is intransitive, the subject is in the nominative case; if transitive, the subject is put in the instrumental case by suffixing *kyis* (variant spellings are *gyis, gis,* and simply *-s* after final vowels). Adjectives qualifying either the subject, indirect object, or direct object are placed after the nouns. If placed before the nouns they qualify, they are joined to it by the affix *kyi* (variant spellings are *gyi, gi,* and *'i*). For example: *kha-sang*[1] *khrom-du*[2] *ngas*[3] *dmar-po'i*[4] *khyi*[5] *chen-po*[6] *zhig*[7] *la*[8] *rno-ba'i*[9] *rdo*[10] *nag-po*[11] *zhig*[12] *mgyogs-por*[13] *'phangs-pa-yin*[14], "Yesterday[1] in the marketplace[2], I [instrumental case][3] quickly[13] threw[14] a[12] sharp[9] black[11] stone[10] at[8] a[7] big[6] red[4] dog[5]." Compound sentences are formed by joining independent and dependent clauses with conjunctives suffixed to the root or the infinitive form of the verb. Each clause, whether independent or dependent, must adhere to the syntactical rule given above.

*Congruence.*—Tibetan syntax has no congruence of number and tense. Nouns and pronouns occur in a single form, without declension to indicate singular or plural use. Plurality is expressed by adding words indicating number, such as *gnyis-ka* (both), *thams-cad* (all), *'ga'* (a few), etc.; or words of general plurality: *rnams, dag, tsho.* The maximum number of forms for any verb is four: present, past, future, and imperative. Many verbs occur in a single form for all tenses and the tense of the sentence in which they occur is determined by adverbs of time.

*Interrogatives.*—Since Tibetan is a tonal language, one cannot raise the pitch of one's voice at the end of a sentence to form a question as one can in English. The common form of interrogative construction is one in which a true interrogative is used. These include *su* (who?), *ga-pa* (where?), *ga-nas* (from where?), *ga-re* (what?), *ci-tsam* (how much?), etc. To change a positive statement into an interrogative one, the verb is put in a "yes-or-no" construction by duplicating the final consonant of the verb root (if it has one) and suffixing *'am* (or). Thus: *yod-dam* (to exist-or) "does . . . exist or (not)?"; *'dug-gam* (to be there-or) "is . . . there or (not)?" In the spoken language, these written forms are pronounced yö̱ö-bää and du̱ù-gää, respectively.

*Modern Terminologies.*—The vocabulary of the Tibetan people reflects conspicuously the lack of scientific development in their culture. There were no terms for many of the mechanical and electronic products of science-oriented countries; nor for non-Buddhist political and social institutions. Following the occupation of Tibet in 1951 by units of the Liberation Army of the People's Republic of China, new terms began to be devised in order to explain and identify devices and concepts alien to the Tibetan way of life. New compounds were formed in three ways. First, the meaning of the Chinese term was translated literally into Tibetan. For example, tractor in Chinese is *t'o-la-chi* (drag-pull machine). This became *'drud-'then 'phrul-'khor* (drag-pull-magic-wheel) in Tibetan. Second, part of the Chinese compound was translated and part was transliterated. *Tank academy* in Chinese is *t'an-k'e hsueh-hsiao* (tank-study school); so, in Tibetan *than-khe'i slob-grwa* (tank-study school). *Slob-grwa* is the common Tibetan word for a school and *than-khe* (pronounced: t'än-k'e) is a Chinese loanword. Third, the entire Chinese compound was transliterated, without any translation. For example, *chairman* in Chinese is *chu-hsi* (phonetically: ju-shi); in Tibetan, it became *kru'u-zhi* (phonetically: druu-shi). In some cases, the Chinese introduced transliterated terms from their own language, even though there were such words already in common use in Tibetan. An example, particularly interesting from a phonological point of view, is the Chinese term for a "medical doctor," *tai-fu*. There is no *f* sound in Tibetan, so *tai-fu* in transliteration became *ta'i-phu* (phonetically: dää-pu). The common Tibetan word for doctor was *em-chi,* itself an old loanword borrowed from the Mongols.

Following the 1959 revolt in Tibet, thousands of Tibetans fled into the neighbouring countries of India, Bhutan, Sikkim, and Nepal; consequently, it is expected that more loanwords, adapted from the languages of those countries, will also begin to appear in the modern Tibetan language. Also, the highly developed system of using honorific terms of reference in polite discourse with equals and superiors, while using ordinary terms for one's self or inferiors, is reported to be on the decline among the Tibetan refugees in exile, where former nobles and peasants, monks and laymen share a common level of social existence.

*See* SOUTHEAST ASIAN LANGUAGES; TIBETAN LITERATURE; TIBETO-BURMAN LANGUAGES.

BIBLIOGRAPHY.—J. Bacot, *Grammaire du tibétain littéraire,* 2 vol., 2nd ed. (1954), *L'Écriture cursive tibétaine* (1912); H. A. Jäschke, *A Tibetan-English Dictionary,* with English-Tibetan vocabulary (repr. 1949), *Tibetan Grammar* (repr. 1954); Josef Kolmaš, "Tibetan Literature in China," *Archiv Orientálni,* 30:638–644 (1962); Eberhardt Richter, *Grundlagen der Phonetik des Lhasa-Dialektes* (1964); George Roerich, "Le Parler de l'Amdo," *Serie Orientale Roma* XVIII (1958); Kamil Sedlaček, *On Tibetan Transcriptions of Chinese Characters* (1957); H. N. von Koerber, *Morphology of the Tibetan Language* (1936); T. V. Wylie, "A Standard System of Tibetan Transcription," *Harvard Journal of Asiatic Studies,* 22:261–267 (1959). (T. V. W.)

**TIBETAN LITERATURE.** Tibetan was developed as a literary language from the 7th century onward as a result of earlier cultural contacts with neighbouring Buddhist countries, namely, the small states of the Takla Makan, especially Khotan (Ho-t'ien), and the ancient kingdoms of northwestern India (modern Gilgit, Kashmir and Kulu) and Nepal. Scripts of Indian origin were in use in these countries, so the Tibetans also adapted an Indian script to suit their own very different language. By far the greater number of the works produced between the 7th and the 13th centuries are skilfully methodical translations of Buddhist works, largely from Sanskrit, on which Indian scholars and Tibetan translators worked side by side. In order to translate them the Tibetans had to create an entirely new (and therefore artificial) vocabulary of religious and philosophical terms, mainly by ingenious compounding of simple terms available in their own language. Apart from some religious terms in daily use, this vocabulary remains a specialized scholarly language. An indigenous literature was also produced: annals and chronicles, sets of spells and prognostications, legendary and liturgical works, all representing the remains of ancient oral traditions. Large collections of such manuscript fragments, all earlier than the 11th century, were discovered early in the 20th century in the caves of Tun-huang (at the eastern side of the Takla Makan).

The quasi-official work of translating authorized Indian Buddhist texts, which continued for six centuries, gave incentive to the Bon-pos (the followers of the pre-Buddhist religion of Tibet) to collect and write down their own early traditions, but in so doing they adopted many Buddhist ideas and, inevitably, used the new vocabulary. The followers of the earliest Buddhist traditions to enter Tibet (the rÑiṅ-ma-pa or "Old Order") also committed their teachings to writing, and, conversely, these are interspersed with pre-Buddhist traditions.

The official Tibetan Buddhist canon was closed in the 13th century; it consists of two parts, the *Kanjur* ("translated word," teachings or reputed teachings of the Buddhas themselves) and the *Tenjur* ("translated treatises," mainly commentaries by Indian teachers). By this time, however, there already existed some orthodox Buddhist works of Tibetan origin (*e.g., Mila-raspa* and *sGam-po-pa;* see *Bibliography*) and from the 13th century onward, under the impetus given by the prolixity of religious houses and orders, there were produced such lengthy and numerous collections of historical and biographical works, treatises and commentaries, liturgy and religious drama that Tibetan literature must be one of the most extensive in the world. Just as in the European middle ages there was little secular literature worth the name, so there is none in Tibetan except for the great epic which recounts the exploits of the king and magic hero, Gesar. This work has grown through the centuries, assimilating whatever material has pleased the fancy of the bards.

After the craft of printing from incised wood blocks (xylography) was introduced from China, probably in the 10th century (*see* PRINTING), certain monasteries became famous printing houses. This form of printing continued until the Chinese invasion in 1959. Manuscripts and block-printed books are always of elongated shape, thus imitating the form of ancient Indian palm-leaf manuscripts. There are considerable collections in some European libraries—notably those of London, Paris and Rome—but few translations are available, due to the paucity of Tibetan scholars.

Despite the phonetic changes in the spoken dialects since the script was fixed, the Tibetans have never changed their system of writing. Thus, once the literary language and the various types of script have been mastered, the reader has immediate access to all the literature of the 7th to the 20th centuries, although changes in style and vocabulary have left many obscurities in the earliest works. There is no modern style of writing, so that the 20th-century colloquial language can only be written in the traditional medium (as though, for example, one had to write modern Italian with Latin spellings and grammatical forms); the Tibetans themselves compose even personal letters in a conventional literary style. *See* also TIBETAN BUDDHISM.

BIBLIOGRAPHY.—Works in Tibetan translated into a European language include *Documents de Touen-Houang relatif à l'histoire du Tibet,* ed. with French trans. by J. Bacot, F. W. Thomas and C. Toussaint (1940); *Trois mystères tibétains* (1921; Eng. trans. 1924), *La vie de Marpa le traducteur* (1937), both with French trans., introduction, notes, etc., by J. Bacot; *Tibet's Great Yogi, Milarepa* (1928), *Tibetan Yoga and Secret Doctrines* (1935), *The Tibetan Book of the Dead,* 3rd ed. (1957), *The Tibetan Book of the Great Liberation* (1954), all trans. by W. Y. Evans-Wentz; sGam-po-pa's *Jewel Ornament of Liberation,* Eng. trans. by H. V. Guenther (1959); *Quellen zur Geschichte der Tibetischen Bon-Religion,* collected translations, with introduction, by H. Hoffmann (1950); *Sandhinirmocana-sūtra,* ed. and trans. by E. Lamotte (1935); *Der Roman einer tibetischen Königin,* Ger. trans. by B. Laufer (1911); Bu-ston's *History of Buddhism,* trans. by E. Obermiller, 2 vol. (1931–32); *The Blue Annals,* 2 vol. (1949–53), trans. by G. N. Roerich; *The Hevajra-tantra,* trans. by D. L. Snellgrove (1959); *Le Dict de Padma,* French trans. by C. Toussaint (1953); *see* also R. A. Stein, *Recherchés sur l'épopée et le barde au Tibet* (1959); D. L. Snellgrove, *Four Lamas of Dolpo* (1967). (D. L. SN.)

**TIBETO-BURMAN LANGUAGES.** Traditionally, when only the Chinese, Tibetan, Burmese, and Tai languages had been extensively studied, all the languages of the Sino-Tibetan language family which did not belong in the Chinese or Tai branches were considered to belong to a Tibeto-Burman subfamily. Through the work of the Norwegian scholar Sten Konow with Sir George Grierson for the *Linguistic Survey of India* (*see* GRIERSON, SIR GEORGE ABRAHAM), sample vocabularies and texts were gathered from about 113 languages and 82 dialects, all of which showed similarities in phonology, vocabulary, and grammar. These were then classified as members of a Tibeto-Burman subfamily in the Sino-Tibetan or Indo-Chinese family.

Yet, when it was considered that hundreds of millions of people spoke a total of less than several dozen Chinese, Tai, and Miao-Yao languages it seemed incredible that about 40,000,000 people could speak more than 200 mutually unintelligible languages of the Tibeto-Burman subfamily. But, since the publication of linguistic data on more than 300 different Sino-Tibetan languages, it has become clear that there is indeed more linguistic diversity in the area covered by speakers of Tibeto-Burman languages than in any other comparable area or group of related languages.

All the languages formerly classified as Tibeto-Burman tend to show more agreement among themselves than do other Sino-Tibetan languages. However, scholars now consider Sino-Tibetan to be a linguistic phylum or macro-family (*i.e.*, a major division of languages whose member families have a common ancestral language which may or may not be reconstructible) consisting of nine more or less coordinate language families; *i.e.*, Chinese, Miao-Yao, Kam-Tai, Karen, Burmese-Lolo, Tibetan, rGyarung-Mishmi, Bodo-Tangsa-Kachin, and Naga-Chin. The validity of the Tibeto-Burman subfamily hypothesis is likely to remain questionable for many years; but the term is still useful to cover those Sino-Tibetan families that contrast with the Chinese, Miao-Yao, and Kam-Tai. Most of the languages are spoken in isolated and mountainous areas, for which population figures are generally unavailable or inaccurate.

**Tibeto-Burman Families.**—The largest of the Tibeto-Burman language families is Burmese-Lolo, spoken by the Hani in Tongking and Laos; by the Lisu (*q.v.*), Lahu, and Akha (*see* KAW) in Thailand; and by approximately two-thirds of Burma's population. From Yünnan north into western Szechwan two small groups extend, the Ch'iang and the Sifan, speaking quite divergent languages. In ancient days the Sihia (Sihsia) language, now extinct, was also spoken in this area; it is the only ancient Tibeto-Burman language of which written records provide a clue to its phonetic system. In north Yünnan are the Na-khi (Nashi or Moso) and Nosu (or Lolo, *see* YI), founders of ancient kingdoms who later also played important roles in the Nanchao kingdom of central Yünnan in the 7th–8th centuries (*see* BURMA: *History*). The Lolo tribes extend eastward into Szechwan and Kweichow.

Dialects of Tibetan are spoken by an estimated aggregate of about 3,000,000 in Tibet, China (Tsinghai, Kansu, Szechwan, and Yünnan), and Himalayan border states. These last are divided into several distinct branches on the basis of the occurrence of pronominal affixes with the verb. (*See* TIBETAN LANGUAGE.)

The rGyarung-Mishmi family has three widely separated branches. On the Assam-Tibet border various Mishmi languages are spoken. In eastern Tibet, rGyarung, long considered merely a divergent dialect of Tibetan, has now been recognized as a separate language. The Nung-Rawang group in the centre, in the area where India, Tibet, Burma, and China meet, were formerly thought to be Kachin dialects, but have proved to contain a number of separate languages.

Another family of Tibeto-Burman has been given the cover term Bodo-Tangsa-Kachin from its major language branches. Bodo languages are spoken on a line from Bhutan southward to Tripura state adjoining East Pakistan. Kachin languages are spoken from western Yünnan throughout north Burma into the North East Frontier Agency area of Assam. In between are related Tangsa languages that were formerly classed with the Naga (*q.v.*).

To the southeast of these the Naga-Chin family covers languages from the ancient Meithei (*q.v.*), Sak, and Kuki to the dozens of Naga and Chin languages spoken from Assam southward to the Arakan mountains of Burma. The Karen languages, long considered a separate family, and found throughout southern Burma and northern Thailand, are now classed with the other Tibeto-Burman languages.

In early times only Tibetan, Burmese, Lolo, and Na-khi had written scripts. The Tibetan syllabary is based on the Indo-Aryan Gupta script, and the Burmese is a rounded adaptation of the squarish Pali script. Ancient Nosu and Na-khi are hieroglyphic and limited to use by the old Bon shamans. The 20th century has seen the development of literature in these and dozens more languages, in adaptations of the scripts predominant in their areas, and of the Roman alphabet.

**General Characteristics.**—Tibeto-Burman languages tend to exhibit the following characteristics:

1. Tonal contrasts, as an integral component of the phonetic syllable (except in Balti and Purik), vary from the simple two-level systems of Tibetan and Burmese to complex three- or four-level systems. Additional tonal contours may make as many as six contrasting tones, as in the Lolo (Yi) languages Lisu (*q.v.*) and Maru.

2. A much lesser degree of monosyllabism and isolating structure is seen than in other Sino-Tibetan families; most of the languages are agglutinative, with varying degrees of inflection usually expressed by affixes and leaving the root unchanged.

3. Pronominal agreement expressed within the verb affixual structure, though not found regularly as a trait of Tibeto-Burman, nevertheless occurs in three of the families: Tibetan, rGyarung-Mishmi, and Naga-Chin.

4. In the characteristic word order, modifying words, phrases, and clauses precede the primary or head word (noun or verb), with affixual particles following. Inflectional affixes with verb forms usually include categories of voice, direction, aspect, and mode.

A table showing the Burmese alphabet can be found in the article BURMESE LANGUAGES.

*See* also BURMA: *The People: Languages;* BURMESE LANGUAGES; CHINA: *The People: Ethnic and Language Groups;* KAREN LANGUAGES; SOUTHEAST ASIAN LANGUAGES.

BIBLIOGRAPHY.—Sir G. A. Grierson, *Linguistic Survey of India,* vol. i, vol. ii, pt. 1, 2, 3 (1927); S. N. Wolfenden, *Outlines of Tibeto-Burman Linguistic Morphology* (1929); J. F. C. Rock, *The Ancient Na-khi Kingdom of Southwest China* (1947); J. F. Embree and W. Thomas, *Ethnic Map and Gazetteer of Northern Southeast Asia* (1950); C. F. and F. M. Voegelin, "Languages of the World: Sino-Tibetan . . . ," *Anthropological Linguistics,* vol. 6, no. 3 (March 1964), *see* also vol. 7, no. 5, 6 (May, June, 1965). (R. H. Mo.)

**TIBULLUS, ALBIUS** (d. *c.* 19 B.C.), Roman poet, the second in the classical sequence of Latin writers of elegiacs that begins with Cornelius Gallus and continues through Tibullus and Propertius to Ovid. Apart from his own poems, the only sources for the biography of Tibullus are a few references in ancient writers and an extremely short *Life* of doubtful authority. He was of equestrian rank (according to the *Life*) and inherited an estate, but seems to have lost most of it in 41 B.C. when Mark Antony and Octavian confiscated land for their soldiers (Virgil, Propertius and Horace suffered in the same way). As a young man, however, Tibullus won the friendship and patronage of M. Valerius Messalla Corvinus, the statesman, soldier and man of letters. Despite personal reasons for staying at home, he would even have accompanied Messalla on a mission to the east if sickness had not obliged him to remain behind when the party left Corcyra, and it is sometimes alleged that he accompanied Messalla's expedition against the Aquitanians. In any case, Tibullus was a prominent member of Messalla's literary circle. This circle, unlike that of Maecenas, kept itself aloof from the court of Augustus, whom Tibullus does not even mention in his poems. Tibullus seems to have divided his time between Rome and his country estate, strongly preferring the latter. The Albius addressed by Horace in *Odes,* i, 33, and *Epistles,* i, 4, is generally identified with Tibullus.

Tibullus' first important love affair, the main subject of book i of his poems, was with the woman whom he calls Delia but whose real name, according to Apuleius, was Plania. It is impossible to give an exact account of their intimacy, as the poems about her are not arranged in chronological order: sometimes he presents her as unmarried, sometimes as having a husband (unless the term *conjunx* is to be interpreted as meaning merely "protector"). It is clear, however, that Tibullus took advantage of the "husband's" absence on military service in Cilicia to establish his relationship with Delia and that this relationship was carried on clandestinely after the soldier's return until Tibullus discovered that Delia was receiving other lovers as well as himself; then, after fruitless protests, he ceased to address himself to her. In book ii of his poems Delia's place is taken by Nemesis (also a fictitious name). This Nemesis was a courtesan of the higher class, with several lovers. Though he complains bitterly of her rapacity and hardheartedness, Tibullus seems to have remained subjugated to her for the rest of his life. He died young, very shortly after Virgil (19 B.C.), as is proved by an epigram of his contemporary, Domitius Marsus. Ovid commemorated his death in his *Amores* (iii, 9).

**Character and Style.**—The character of Tibullus, as reflected in his poems, is an amiable one. He was a man of generous impulses and a gentle unselfish disposition. His loyalty to his friends is shown by his leaving Delia to accompany Messalla to Asia, and he was constant to his mistresses with a constancy that they scarcely deserved. His tenderness toward women is enhanced by a refinement and delicacy which are rare among the ancients.

Horace and the rest taunt those who reject their claims with the damage that the years will do to their beauty, but if Tibullus refers to old age, he does it by way of warning, not in a spirit of triumph or revenge. Cruelly though he may have been treated by his love, he does not invoke curses upon her. Instead he goes to her little sister's grave, hung so often with his garlands and wet with his tears, and bemoans his fate there. Tibullus has no leanings to an active life: his ideal is a quiet retirement in the country with the loved one at his side. He has no ambition and no yearning for immortality. As he loved country life, so he clung to its faiths, and in an age of crude materialism and strange new cults he was religious in the old Roman way.

The poetry of Tibullus is distinguished by an idyllic simplicity, but this is the simplicity of high art, not of unadorned nature. For grace and tenderness, for exquisiteness of feeling and expression, he stands alone among the Roman elegists: Quintilian, indeed, puts him at their head. In many of his poems, moreover, a symmetry of composition can be discerned, though they are never forced into any fixed or inelastic scheme. His clear and unaffected style, which made him a great favourite with Roman readers, is far more polished than that of his rival Propertius and far less loaded with Alexandrian learning; but in range of imagination, in power and originality of conception, in richness and variety of poetical treatment Propertius is much superior to him. In his handling of metre, likewise, Tibullus is smooth and musical, whereas Propertius, with occasional harshness, is vigorous and varied.

**"Corpus Tibullianum."**—The works of Tibullus, as they have survived, form part of what is generally known as the *Corpus Tibullianum,* a collection of poetry which seems most probably to have been deliberately put together to represent the work of Messalla's circle; when and by whom this was done must in the present state of the evidence remain obscure.

The first two books of the collection are the undoubted property of Tibullus. Book i contains the poems inspired by Delia and also three elegies (4, 8 and 9) addressed to Marathus, a beautiful boy. These three elegies may reflect a literary convention, not the poet's actual feelings, as many of the sentiments throughout the book are those expected of the professed elegist: for instance, Tibullus' alleged poverty (i, 1) is at variance with the facts if he is the Albius addressed by Horace. The most interesting of the Marathus poems is that (4) in which the god Priapus is made to deliver a brief sketch of the art of love, the prototype of Ovid's fuller treatment of the same theme in the *Ars amatoria.*

Book ii is by no means entirely devoted to the liaison with Nemesis: it contains one of Tibullus's most characteristic and delightful poems, the description of a country festival (1).

The rest of the *Corpus Tibullianum* forms one book in the manuscripts; the division into two books, iii and iv, in modern editions is due to Italian scholars of the 15th century. Book iii contains six poems, the work of a poet who styles himself Lygdamus, an obvious pseudonym. They celebrate a lady named Neaera and are cultivated but on the whole undistinguished compositions. The writer's identity has been much debated, but remains unknown. If the *Corpus* does indeed represent the poets associated with Messalla, this Lygdamus should have been a contemporary of Tibullus and Ovid; and one couplet (5, 17–18) seems to indicate that his birthday was the same as Ovid's. This, together with the striking verbal resemblances which are found in the poems of Tibullus, has led some to identify him with Ovid; but neither this nor any other of the proposed identifications (with Ovid's brother, with Propertius, with Tibullus himself) will stand scrutiny. (It seems certain, however, that the resemblances between the two poets are due to Lygdamus' having copied Ovid, not vice versa.)

The first poem of book iv, a panegyric on Messalla, is a turgid and worthless composition. The next 11 poems were occasioned by the love of Sulpicia for a young man called Cerinthus: poems 7–12 are Sulpicia's; 2–6 are usually thought to be by Tibullus. The whole cycle forms a unique and charming document for the literary life of Augustan Rome. The last poems (13 and 14), addressing an unnamed love, are likewise generally attributed to Tibullus.

The best texts are in the editions by J. P. Postgate, 2nd ed. (1915) and by F. W. Lenz (1959); that by K. F. Smith has an excellent introduction and commentary (1913). There are English translations by J. P. Postgate, in prose, with Catullus, in the Loeb series (1913), and by A. S. Way, in verse (1936).

BIBLIOGRAPHY.—F. Marx, "Albius Tibullus," in Pauly-Wissowa, *Real-Encyclopädie der classischen Altertumswissenschaft,* vol. i (1894); W. Y. Sellar, *Horace and the Elegiac Poets* (1899); F. W. Levy (*i.e.,* Lenz), "Lygdamus," in Pauly-Wissowa, *Real-Encyclopädie,* vol. xiii (1927); M. Schuster, *Tibull-Studien* (1930); Schanz-Hosius, *Geschichte der römischen Literatur,* vol. ii, 4th ed. (1935); P. Troll, "Tibull und Properz," *Jahresbericht über die Fortschritte der klassischen Altertumswissenschaft,* vol. 260 (1938), with list of previous surveys; N. I. Herescu, *Bibliographie de la litterature latine* (1943). On the relationship between Lygdamus and Ovid *see* especially A. G. Lee, article in *Proceedings of the Cambridge Philological Society,* no. 185 (1958–59).

(J. P. P.; E. J. Ky.)

**TIC** (from a French word *tique,* meaning "a twitching") is a sudden, rapid, recurring contraction in a muscle or group of muscles. The movement is always brief, irresistible, and limited to one part of the body. It does not interfere with the use of the part involved, and may be halted voluntarily but only for a time. As the tic movement becomes ingrained it is looked upon as a habit; the possessor becomes relatively unaware of its occurrence. Then a tic may be considered as involuntary. These characteristics of tic help to differentiate it from other involuntary movements, such as spasm (*see* CRAMP) or the capricious, uninhibitable movements that may occur in chorea (*q.v.;* St. Vitus' dance) or in epilepsy (*q.v.*). Tics are not mannerisms.

While very nearly all tics are of psychological origin, similar repetitive movements have been observed in the late stages of encephalitis (*q.v.*). These movements that accompany brain disease may persist for years, but they tend to cease eventually.

Nervous children between 5 and 12 years of age are those most likely to have tics, but no age is immune. The movement appears when the subject is tense, and distraction will reduce it. The sufferer knows that he has a certain control of the movement but feels impelled to go through with it in order to feel better. Sometimes a group of tics occur in rapid succession, and the condition is then termed convulsive tic.

Tics frequently involve the face and air passages. The commonest tics are a repetitive grimace, blink, sniff, snort, or click in the nose or throat, a twitch, or a shrug. Tics occur in decreasing frequency from head to foot.

**Psychological Analysis.**—Tics are the involuntary motor expression of emotional activity, and they depend primarily upon the manner in which the tiqueur (the medical term for a person subject to tics) has experienced his early psychological and sexual development. Compulsion neurosis is common among tiqueurs (*see* NEUROSES). Compulsive neurotics are in conflict about certain of their feelings; they suffer from the irresistible impulse to perform some act contrary to the conscious will. The need to "get rid of" something is implicit in tic activity.

The use of the muscles for immediate discharge indicates intolerance of tension and inability to wait; the tiqueur feels impelled to make the movement in order to feel better. The tension is thereby discharged; in other words the person temporarily relieves himself—of what, he does not know. Such inability to wait is characteristic of the activity of children who have to learn how to accept delay of their gratifications and to channel their energies into socially acceptable activity. Should they continue this kind of intolerance into adulthood, the nervous patterns may gradually narrow their target to become a tic as the movement becomes more automatic than willed.

The muscles are among the main avenues used by infants in the expression of the emotions, such expression appearing before that of speech in the developing child. It follows that primitive emotion relatively untempered by learning, or vulnerable because of bodily disease, may show itself by way of the muscular system. Somewhat later in development the musculature may be used to repress or restrain certain emotional expression. In persons with tic it can be determined that the usual outlets for expression of the emotions were denied in childhood: restriction of motility has resulted in an increased motor urge; overprotection, usually based on the mother's fear, has made the child emotionally dependent and lacking in self-control. Tics thus may be accompanied by other indications of maladjustment, such as bedwetting, feeding and digestive disorders, and exaggerated fears.

The older tic personality may respond to psychotherapy devised to mature the subject (learning why he behaves the way he does), who has usually retreated—in a defensive maneuver—to an earlier stage of psychological development where he feels more secure.

Usually there are features of both the compulsion neurosis and hysteria in tiqueurs. In hysteria (*q.v.*) repressed sexual energy is converted into symptoms. Where there is the capacity for relationship, prolonged uncovering psychotherapy may be helpful. (C. D. Ar.)

**TICHBORNE CLAIMANT,** the name given to a man who claimed to be Roger Charles Tichborne, heir to the Tichborne baronetcy and estates in Hampshire, but who was declared by a jury in 1874 to be Arthur Orton, the son of a butcher of Wapping, London. Roger Charles Tichborne (1829–54 or 1898) was born in Paris, the eldest son of James Francis Tichborne (1784–1862), who in 1853 became 10th bart. and took the surname of Doughty-Tichborne, and Henriette Felicité (d. 1868), illegitimate daughter of Henry Seymour of Knoyle, Wiltshire. He sailed in March 1853 from Le Havre for Valparaíso, Chile, and later crossed the Andes, reaching Rio de Janeiro, Brazil, in 1854. In April 1854 he sailed from Rio in the "Bella" and the ship was lost at sea with no known survivors. His insurance was paid and his will proved in July 1855.

On his father's death in 1862 Roger's younger brother Alfred Joseph (1839–66) succeeded as 11th bart. Roger's mother, the dowager Lady Tichborne, refused to believe that her son was dead and from 1863 advertised widely in newspapers asking for news of him. In November 1865 she learned through a missing persons agency in Sydney, Austr., that a man claiming to be her son was working as a butcher in Wagga Wagga, New South Wales, under the name of Thomas Castro. In January 1867 the claimant reached Paris where he was "acknowledged" by Lady Tichborne.

Other members of the Tichborne family, however, asserted that he was an impostor and obtained evidence to try and prove that he was Arthur Orton (1834–98 or ?), who had deserted his ship at Valparaíso in 1849. They alleged that Orton had been kindly received at Melipilla, Chile, by a family called Castro, whose name he took after he had gone to Australia in 1854. The claimant, however, also declared he had stayed with the family at Melipilla during his visit to Chile in 1853. An ejectment action brought by the claimant against the trustees of the Tichborne estate (Sir Henry Alfred Joseph [1866–1910], 12th bart., being then a minor) finally came before the Court of Common Pleas on May 11, 1871. During the trial more than 100 persons swore that he was Roger Tichborne, but the evidence brought by the family finally convinced the jury, who on March 6, 1872, declared that they wanted no further evidence.

Arrested on a charge of perjury, the claimant was brought for trial at the bar on April 23, 1873, before Chief Justice Sir Alexander Cockburn. The mismanagement of the case by his counsel, Edward Kenealy, the testimony of Orton's former sweetheart Mary Ann Loder, and Kenealy's refusal to put Orton's sisters into the witness box finally proved conclusive to the jury, who on Feb. 28, 1874, the 188th day of the trial, found that the claimant was Arthur Orton. Found guilty of perjury, the claimant was sentenced to 14 years' penal servitude. Released in October 1884, he died in poverty in Marylebone, London, on April 1, 1898.

*See* D. Woodruff, *The Tichborne Claimant* (1957).

**TICINO,** a wedge-shaped Swiss canton, driven into Italy. Its northern boundary runs along the Lepontine-Adula Alps, and its southern tip reaches beyond Lago di Lugano almost to Como. Historically, it represents early Swiss conquests from the duchy of Milan (*see* SWITZERLAND: *History*) loosely amalgamated to form one of the six cantons admitted to the Confederation in 1803. It is inhabited by Italian-speaking Catholics (*see* below). Its dominant physical features are the three river systems occupying steep-sided valleys which extend from a mountain frontier and drain southwards to Lago Maggiore. The most important system is the river Ticino, which rises in the canton southwest of St. Gotthard, flows towards that mass through the Val Bedretto, and then swings round at Airolo to a southeast course through Valle Leventina; near Biasca it receives the left-bank Brenno from the Val Blenio; the combined stream flows through the wide, low valley—the Riviera—until slightly above Bellinzona, where it receives another large left-bank affluent which has drained the southeast slopes of the Adula group and reaches the Ticino via the Valle Mesolcina; the main stream curves again below the junction and enters the lake from the east. The Ticino receives no important right-bank tributaries, and the western part of the canton is drained largely by the Maggia and by its numerous right-bank tributaries, which receive torrent water from the western frontier. Between the Ticino and the Maggia is the Valle Verzasca.

The remainder of the canton lies south-southeast of this and consists of a triangular fragment of broken hill country, with a complicated drainage reaching the irregularly shaped Lago di Lugano.

Its total area is 1,085 sq.mi., of which approximately three-quarters are reckoned as "productive" (forests covering about 275 sq.mi.), while of the remainder 28.6 sq.mi. consists of lakes, chiefly parts of Maggiore and Lugano; 13 sq.mi. are occupied by glaciers. The canton is fifth in point of size, but only the much larger Valais and Vaud exceed its vine-growing area. The highest points are the Basódino (10,738 ft.), near the western border, southeast of the source of the Ticino, and the Rheinwaldhorn (11,161 ft.) in the Adula Alps.

The amount of lowland is small, and occurs only in the lower river valleys and near the lakes. The lowest commune (669 ft.) is Vira (Locarno) on Lago Maggiore.

The main St. Gotthard railway traverses the canton for about 75 mi. from Airolo, at the southern mouth of the tunnel, via Valle Leventina, Bellinzona, Lugano to beyond Mendrisio. Locarno is connected with this line; another follows the eastern shore of Lago Maggiore, and light electric railways ascend Valle Blenio to Acquarossa and Valle Mesolcina to Mesocco. A bus service has replaced the former light railway of Valle Maggia to Bignasco. Mountain railways for the ascent of Monte S. Salvatore (2,992 ft.) and Monte Brè (3,061 ft.) from Lugano and of Monte Generoso (5,584 ft.) from Capolago, have also been constructed in the extreme south of the canton.

In 1960 the population was 195,566, of whom 172,521 were Italian-speaking, 18,498 German-speaking, and 2,839 French-speaking. The highest commune, Bosco-Gurin, near the western border and reached by the V. di Campo, had many German-speaking inhabitants, the result of an early movement eastward from Valais. There were in all 178,625 Catholics, 13,330 Protestants and 572 Jews.

In 1888 the diocese of Lugano (since joined to Basel) was created to replace the former purely Italian control over the canton by the dioceses of Milan and Como. Bellinzona (pop., [1960] 13,435) was the permanent political capital after 1881; formerly Lugano (pop., [1960] 19,758) and Locarno (pop., [1960] 10,155) alternated with it at six-year intervals. Mendrisio is the only other large settlement.

The canton has 253 communes and 8 administrative districts; its constitution dates back to 1830, but the later political disturbances which characterize the canton have caused, and still cause, considerable modifications. The legislature (*Gran consiglio*) is composed of 65 members elected (since 1892) in the proportion of one to every 1,500 of the Swiss inhabitants. The executive (*Consiglio di stato*) of five members, is elected directly by the people. Both bodies hold office for four years. Any 5,000 electors have the right (facultative referendum) of claiming a popular vote as to bills passed by the legislature, while the same number of electors have the right of "initiative" in legislative matters, though 7,000 signatures are required in case of a proposal to revise the cantonal constitution.

**History.**—The canton is made up of all the permanent conquests (with one or two trifling exceptions) made by different members of the Swiss confederation south of the main chain of the Alps.

From an historical point of view Italian Switzerland falls into three groups: (1) the Val Leventina conquered by Uri in 1440 (previously held from 1403 to 1422); (2) Bellinzona (previously held from 1419 to 1422); the Riviera and the Val Blenio, all won in 1500 from the duke of Milan by men from Uri, Schwyz and Nidwalden, and confirmed by Louis XII of France in 1503; (3) Locarno, Val Maggia, Lugano and Mendrisio, seized in 1512 by the Confederates when fighting for the Holy League against France, ruled by the 12 members then in the league, and confirmed by Francis I in the treaty of 1516. These districts were governed by bailiffs holding office two years and purchasing it from the members of the league; each member of group 3 sent annually an envoy, who conjointly constituted the supreme appeal in all matters.

This government was very harsh and is one of the darkest pages in Swiss history. Yet only one open revolt is recorded—that of the Val Leventina against Uri in 1755. In 1803 all these districts were formed into one canton—Ticino—which became a full member of the Swiss confederation. After 1830 the local history of the canton was disturbed by friction between the Radical and Ultramontane parties.

**Resources and Industries.**—Ticino has no minerals; it possesses, however, large supplies of water power (white coal) for internal use and export. Grazing is of considerable importance in the valleys of the upper part of the canton (Sopraceneri). Grapes are grown in the warmer south and good wine is produced in large quantity; wheat, potatoes, tobacco and vegetables are also grown for internal use. Owing to a favourable climate, especially on the shores of Lago Maggiore and Lago di Lugano, tourism has become the most important source of profit for the inhabitants.

**TICINO RIVER** (ancient TICINUS), the source of which is in the Swiss Alps near Passo di Novena, 7,500 ft. (2,300 m.) above sea level, drains an area of 2,800 sq.mi. (7,200 sq.km.), much of which is in Italy. The river is 154 mi. (248 km.) long, flowing southeast in the Val Leventina, which is followed by road and rail from St. Gotthard Pass, to Bellinzona, then west into Lake Maggiore, where it is joined by the Toce. It then flows southeast in a floodplain 1–2 mi. wide and 30–50 ft. below the surrounding North Italian lowland into the Po River 4 mi. (6 km.) southeast of Pavia. The river is fullest in May and November, lowest in September and late winter. The Ticino and its tributaries in the Canton Ticino above Lake Maggiore are an important source of hydroelectric power for Switzerland, while the Toce and its tributaries likewise serve Italy. The Ticino is not suitable for navigation. The two principal towns on the river are Bellinzona and Pavia. (J. P. Co.)

**TICK,** a spider relative externally parasitic on terrestrial vertebrates. Ticks along with mites constitute a taxonomic group given by various authors as a subclass or an order of the class Arachnida (*q.v.*). They are among the most important parasites of large wild and domestic animals in both economic loss and transmission of disease. While no species of tick is primarily a human parasite, some species do attack man when the opportunity presents itself. (For certain wingless ectoparasitic flies, such as the sheep ked, often popularly called ticks, *see* FLY: *Disputed Groups*.) Ticks may be grouped in the suborder Ixodides, which may be divided into three families (*see* MITE for a different taxonomic interpretation): Ixodidae (hard-backed ticks), Argasidae (soft-backed ticks), and Nuttalliellidae (represented by a single rare African species). Larger than mites, the largest ticks are up to 30 mm. long (more than one inch); most are less than half that length. Ticks can be distinguished from mites by their lack of body segmentation and by the presence of a sensory pit (Haller's organ) on the terminal segment of the first pair of legs.

Hard-ticks like the American dog tick (*Dermacentor variabilis*) attach to their hosts and feed continuously for several days. When engorgement is complete, the female drops from the host, finds a suitable site where she rests, lays her eggs in a mass, and dies. Six-legged larvae hatch from the eggs, move up on blades of grass, and lie in wait for a suitable host to pass by. When they contact a suitable host (usually a small mammal) they attach to it, obtain a blood meal, and detach. After a time the detached larva molts to become an eight-legged nymph. Nymphs again play the waiting game. After engorgement, they drop off, and molt into adult males or females. Again the adults wait for a host (adult ticks have been known to live for three years without food or drink), and the cycle is repeated. Most of the hard-ticks carry on their developmental cycles in fields and woods, but a few, like the brown dog tick (*Rhipicephalus sanguineus*), are household pests. Soft-ticks are similar to hard-ticks in many respects, but differ in that they feed intermittently, lay several batches of eggs, pass through several nymphal stages, and carry on their developmental cycles in the home or nest of their host rather than in the field. Soft-ticks like the fowl tick (*Argas persicus*) are found most frequently on animals that have regular roosts or nests, such as bats and birds. They infest chicken houses and, in dry countries where sanitation is primitive, human habitations.

Hard-ticks damage their hosts by drawing excessive amounts of blood, by secreting neurotoxins under some conditions that produce paralysis and death, and by transmitting disease. Hard-ticks are the vectors of Texas cattle fever, anaplasmosis, Rocky Mountain spotted fever, Q fever, tularemia, hemorrhagic fever, encephalitides, and other diseases of man and animals (*see* RICKETTSIAE). Soft-ticks are important vectors of spirochetal relapsing fever and other diseases.

Hard-ticks can be controlled on livestock by dipping or spraying the herds with suitable acaricides and by quarantine of infested animals. Man can best avoid ticks by impregnating his clothing with a tick repellent when exposing himself in infested areas. Elimination of soft-ticks from hen houses and the brown dog tick from homes can be accomplished by repeated treatment of the premises with an approved acaricide.

*See* also references under "Tick" in the Index. (G. W. W.)

*See* D. R. Arthur, *Ticks and Disease* (1962).

**TIDAL POWER.** The idea of utilizing the rise and fall of the tides to produce power has long attracted the attention of inventors, and many ingenious schemes have been suggested. So far, however, the only practicable method is based on the use of one or more tidal basins, separated from the sea by dams or barrages, and of hydraulic turbines through which the water is passed on its way between the basin and sea or between two basins.

**Early Uses.**—The earliest use of tidal water as a source of power was by means of a tide mill, a kind of water mill. Some depended on the tide alone, others used a proportion of fresh water. A storage pond was formed by enclosing part of a creek or estuary or by damming a tidal stream at its entrance to an estuary. Automatic lock-type gates or flap valves were set in the wall or dam, enabling the tide to fill the pond as it rose. When the tide fell, the water could be released through a sluice in order to drive a water wheel.

The Domesday Book mentions what seems to have been a tide mill at the entrance to the Port of Dover, Eng. This was built after 1066 and was a danger to vessels entering the harbour. The first mills of record were Three Mills, Bromley-by-Bow, London, in 1135 and that at Woodbridge, Suffolk (1170). In the Netherlands there was a mill at Zuicksee in 1220. Tide mills were built on sites around the coast of Great Britain, along the west coast of the European continent from the Netherlands to the south of Spain, along the eastern seaboard of colonial America, and on the coast of Surinam. The first tide mill in colonial America was built at Salem in 1635. In Surinam tide mills operated from 1667 to 1860. (R. Wa.)

**Modern Designs.**—The best plan for a given site depends on its geographical features, the tidal flow, its potential power capacity, and its economic feasibility. Each length of barrage separating a tidal basin from the sea or from another tidal basin may consist of either sluices or turbine-generators that can also act as motor-pump units—that is, if there is a sufficient head of water to drive the turbines, the generator will produce electric power; if not, electric power from an outside source can be used to drive the generators as motors, and the turbines then operate as pumps to move water from sea to basin or vice versa.

A tidal power plant constructed according to a well-defined plan may be operated in an almost unlimited number of ways. Below are three simple examples of working cycles:

*Production of Energy During Emptying or During Filling.*—During emptying, the sluices fill the basin while the tide is coming in and are closed at high tide. Emptying does not begin until

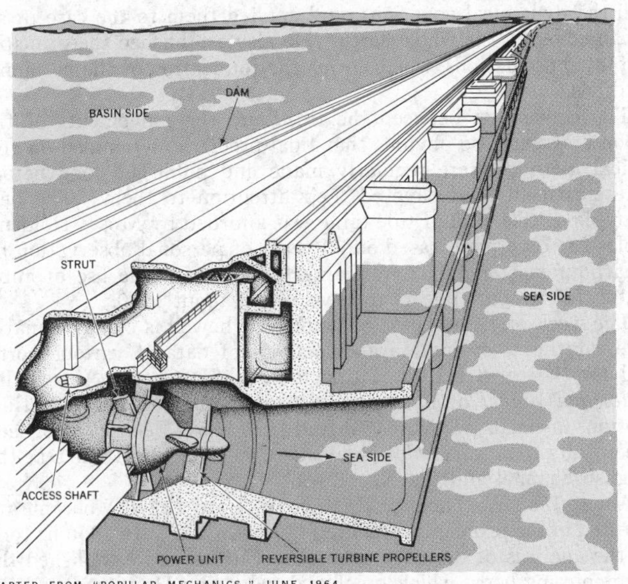


ADAPTED FROM "POPULAR MECHANICS," JUNE 1964

PLAN OF TIDAL POWER PLANT ON RANCE RIVER ESTUARY, SHOWING DAM AND ONE OF 24 REVERSIBLE TURBINE POWER UNITS

the ebb tide has left enough depth of fall to operate the turbines. This operation can be improved by using the energy available during the slack hours for pumping seawater in order to raise the basin level and increase the volume of water delivered to the turbines.

Conversely, energy may be produced during filling, when the turbines can be utilized to admit the incoming tide to the basin.

*Production of Energy by Utilizing Both Phases.*—The two preceding cycles may be combined, and energy can be produced while the basin fills and while it empties. However, the best results can be obtained by using the innumerable combinations of filling, emptying, and pumping according to the height of the tide and the value of energy at different periods of the day. Thus energy can be produced according to man's needs without the limitations imposed by depending on the lunar tidal rhythm alone.

**The Rance Plant.**—Construction was begun in January 1961 and completed in 1967 on the world's first large-scale tidal plant. This project is located on the Rance River estuary in the Gulf of St. Malo, Brittany, France. After excavations on the estuary were completed in 1963, the flow into the Rance at spring tide attained a maximum of 635,670 cu.ft. per sec. (18,000 cu.m. per sec.) at both flood and ebb—about three times the amount of the flow of the Rhône at Avignon.

The plant has 24 specially designed 10,000-kw. turbo-alternators. Each of these power units consists of an ogive-shaped shell of metal containing an alternator and a Kaplan turbine. The units are installed in apertures in the dam through which the water flows, although a vertical shaft for maintenance gives access to the shell from the machine room above. Each unit acts as both turbine and pump, in both directions of tidal flow and both directions of rotation.

Maximum annual net production for the plant is 544 Gw-hr. (gigawatt-hours)—537 Gw-hr. in the basin-to-sea direction and 71.5 Gw-hr. in the sea-to-basin direction, less 64.5 Gw-hr. of energy used in pumping. It is intended that maximum power be directed to the national electricity network at those times when it will be economically most useful; so that in the early 1970s the maximum production amounted to only 470 Gw-hr.

**Other Projects.**—The U.S.S.R. in 1969 completed construction of its first tidal plant. This small plant, of about 1,000 kw., is located on the White Sea.

Tidal power plants have been proposed for the Bristol Channel in the United Kingdom, the San Jose Gulf in Argentina, and at various points on the western Australian coast. Plans for a project in the Bay of Fundy have been abandoned by the Canadian government. There were no other serious plans for the construction of tidal power plants under consideration in the early 1970s.

Bibliography.—R. Gibrat, "Tidal Energy," *Civ. Engng. Publ. Wks. Rev.* (Feb. 1955); R. Gibrat and L. Kammerlocher, "Alternators for the Tidal Power Plant of the Rance," *Report No. 134, Conférence Internationale des Grands Réseaux Électriques à Haute Tension* (May–June 1956). "Sources nouvelles d'énergie et de développement économique," U.N. publication No. E2997 (1957), lists 47 articles on tidal power. (R. Gt.)

**TIDE,** an alternating relative motion of the matter of a planet, satellite or star, which is attributed to the gravitational actions of external bodies. Such motions are known to occur in all three principal divisions of the earth. The alternating slight changes of shape of the solid body or lithosphere of the earth attributed to the gravitational action of the moon and sun are known as bodily tides. Similarly, there are the atmospheric tides in the atmosphere, and the familiar ordinary ocean tides in the hydrosphere. A still wider use of the word is based on descriptive instead of on causal and astronomical ideas, and takes for its criterion that the motions in question have certain features in common with ocean tides. This extension includes those long waves of the sea, or tsunamis, which are sometimes caused by earthquakes, as well as effects on the sea of variable atmospheric pressure and wind, known as meteorological tides.

## ORDINARY TIDES

**General Description of Phenomena.**—At most seaside places the water reaches its highest level approximately twice a day, the average interval between two successive high waters being 12 hr. 25 min., though this interval varies considerably during the course of a week. At certain places in the East Indian seas two successive high waters are separated by an interval of 12 hr., while at certain places in the China sea the interval is often more than 24 hr. At places on the shores of the oceans the time taken by the tide in rising is about equal to the time taken in falling on the same day, but in estuaries the tide usually rises more quickly than it falls. At certain places, such as Southampton, Eng., the high waters are often doubled; *i.e.,* the water reaches a maximum height, falls a little and then rises to a maximum again. At other places the low waters are often doubled. As one goes along any stretch of coast the time of high water generally becomes progressively earlier or later, while as one goes up an estuary from the sea the time of high water always becomes progressively later.

At most places, on the average, a high water is about as much above the mean level of the sea as the succeeding low water is below it. The difference in level between successive high and low waters is called the range of tide. The range of tide at any place may vary much from day to day. At most places it reaches a maximum once a fortnight, and a minimum at times midway between two successive maxima. At London bridge the greatest range of the fortnight has an average value of 21 ft. while the least range of the fortnight has an average value of 15 ft. At the head of the Bay of Fundy the range of tide reaches 50 ft. while at certain islands of the Pacific and over most of the Mediterranean the range never exceeds 2 ft. At many places outside the Atlantic the heights of two successive high or low waters are markedly different, a phenomenon known as the diurnal inequality.

At a place in a strait or narrow sea the tidal current usually flows for about 6 hr. 12 min. in one direction, and then for about the same time in the opposite direction. At the reversal of such a current there is the state of rest usually called slack water. In estuaries the current generally flows downstream for a greater length of time than it flows upstream. At a place in the open sea the direction of the current often takes all points of the compass, making the complete revolution in the tidal period. During this period there are usually two times of maximum current and two intermediate times of minimum current. The times of maximum current are separated by about half the tidal period and the directions of maximum current are nearly directly opposite; similarly for the two minimum currents. There is no fixed general relation between the time of high water and the time of maximum current. If the current flows directly in and out of a bay it will reach its inward maximum nearly a quarter period before high water at the head of the bay, so that slack water is simultaneous with high water. On the other hand, in an estuary the current continues to flow upstream for some considerable time after high water and to run downstream similarly after low water. When the current is directed toward land or up an estuary it is called the flood current; when it runs away from land or down an estuary it is called the ebb current.

The speeds of tidal currents vary greatly from place to place; *e.g.*, in the Seymour Narrows, British Columbia, the maximum current reaches ten knots; in the North sea it rarely exceeds one. At some distance up certain rivers—as, for example, where the Colorado river meets the tide—a wave ten or more feet high travels up the river almost like a wall of water. This phenomenon is called a bore. Near a headland separating two bays there is sometimes a swift current termed a race.

**Relation to Motions of Moon and Sun.**—The times of high water bear an intimate relation to the positions of the moon and sun. The period of 12 hr. 25 min. is half that of the moon's apparent revolution around the earth. The length of time between the moon's crossing of the meridian of a place and the next high water at that place is known as the lunitidal interval, or the high-water interval, for the place. Similarly, the length of time between the moon's crossing of the meridian and the next low water is called the low-water interval. For Philadelphia, the lunitidal average is 1 hr. 30 min. In many cases, including those of British waters, the chief variation in the lunitidal interval is associated with the phase of the moon. The average value of the lunitidal interval on the days of new and full moon is known as the establishment of the port. For London bridge this is 1 hr. 58 min.

The range of tide may be similarly correlated. In British waters it reaches its maximum a day or so after new and full moon and its minimum a day or so after the quarters. In these circumstances the maximum tides are known as spring tides and the minimum tides as neap tides. About the time of the equinoxes spring tides are generally larger and about the time of the solstices they are generally smaller than usual. The average interval between new or full moon and the next following spring tide is known as the age of the tide at the place in question. At certain places in Canadian waters the chief variation in the range of tide is associated with the varying distance of the moon from the earth, while at others it is associated with the varying declination of the moon. The diurnal inequality is always associated with the declination of the moon or sun. But the most complete correlation between the tides and astronomical variables is provided by the harmonic methods.

## HISTORY OF THE STUDY OF TIDES

The writings of various Chinese, Arabic and Icelandic authors show that they paid some attention to the tides, but the theories advanced are fantastic. The writings of the classical authors of antiquity contain but a few references to the tides, for the Greeks and Romans lived on the shores of an almost tideless sea.

Johannes Kepler in the early 17th century recognized the tendency of the water of the ocean to move toward the sun and moon, but Galileo's explanation referred the phenomenon to the rotation and orbital motions of the earth. It was Isaac Newton who, in his *Principia* of 1687, laid the foundation of the modern theory of the tides when he brought his generalization of universal gravitation to bear on the subject. He gave a geometrical construction for the tide-generating force, and calculated the magnitude of the solar equilibrium tide. He considered a canal encircling the earth and applied to each particle of water the laws which he had deduced for a satellite. He accounted for many of the general properties of the tides, such as the phenomenon of springs and neaps, priming and lagging, diurnal and elliptic inequalities. The only important factor which he did not mention is the dynamical effect of the earth's rotation. Newton's work was continued by D. Bernoulli, L. Euler and C. Maclaurin who adopted not only the theory of gravitation but also Newton's method of the superposition of two ellipsoids. In 1746 Jean le Rond d'Alembert wrote a paper on atmospheric tides, but this work, like Maclaurin's, is chiefly remarkable for the importance of collateral points.

The theory of the tidal movements of an ocean was almost untouched when in 1773 Pierre Laplace first undertook the subject. In his *Mécanique céleste* he formulated the equation of continuity and the dynamical equations, and applied them to the case of an ocean covering the whole earth. He also established the principle of forced oscillations, which forms the foundation of the harmonic methods.

The connection between the tides and the movements of the moon and sun is so obvious that tidal predictions founded on empirical methods were regularly made and published long before mathematicians had devoted their attention to them. The best example of this kind of tide table was afforded by Moses Holden's tables for Liverpool, based on 20 years of personal observation by a harbour master named William Hutchinson. The use of automatic tide gauges appears to have begun about 1830.

The work of J. Lubbock, Sr.,and W. Whewell is chiefly remarkable for the co-ordination and analysis of data at various ports, and for the construction of tide tables. Sir George Airy in his *Tides and Waves* of 1842 studied profoundly the theory of tidal motions in canals, while in 1848 and 1851 F. W. Beechey published the results of a survey of tidal currents over the Irish sea, the English channel and the North sea.

About 1863 W. Thomson (afterward Lord Kelvin) became interested in the problems presented by earth tides. In 1866 he took up the analysis of ordinary tidal observations and established the harmonic methods, which quickly developed. He introduced the rotation of the earth into the tidal dynamics of small seas, and in 1872 he designed a tide-predicting machine. His theory, that the revolution of the earth's poles in a 16-ft. circle every 14 months was the cause of small ocean tides, was confirmed by computers in the 1950s.

In 1874 W. Ferrel, of the U.S. coast and geodetic survey, published his *Tidal Researches* which included a harmonic development of the generating potential, and from the same year A. W. Baird, of the survey of India, organized a service of observation and harmonic analysis for Indian tides. In 1882 G. H. Darwin took up harmonic analysis and produced memoirs which for a long time formed the standard manual on the subject, and about this time J. E. Pillsbury, of the U.S. coast survey, began the observations of currents by means of current meters. In 1885 C. Börgen introduced new ideas into the methods of harmonic analysis. Between 1870 and 1890 F. A. Forel made illuminating studies of the seiches of Lake Geneva, Switz., and about 1890 M. Margules investigated the dynamics of atmospheric tides.

From 1894 to 1907 R. A. Harris, of the U.S. coast survey, published his *Manual of Tides*. This work contained charts showing cotidal lines for the whole world, based on theories and hypotheses the leading feature of which was the principle of resonance. It was assumed that in each ocean there exist regions capable of free oscillation with a period near one of the principal tidal periods, and that the nature of these free oscillations may be calculated approximately, without allowing for the earth's rotation or the interaction with neighbouring regions.

After 1900 a number of Scandinavian oceanographers, notably V. W. Ekman, O. Pettersson and J. P. Jacobsen, invented current meters and L. Favé observed tidal elevations in the open sea by means of his self-registering instrument.

In 1912 A. Blondel applied the narrow sea theory, through the principle of least action, to the tides of the Red sea. From 1913 to 1920 R. Sterneck and A. Defant developed the narrow sea theory with special reference to the Adriatic sea. Defant applied this theory to the Red sea, the Persian gulf, the English channel and the Irish sea.

After about 1895 the dynamical theory of tides and seiches was advanced by the applied mathematicians: H. Lamb, H. H. Hough, J. H. Poincaré, Lord Rayleigh, G. Chrystal, E. Fichot, G. R. Goldsbrough, G. I. Taylor, Harold Jeffreys, G. Bertrand, S. Goldstein and J. Proudman; between 1920 and 1960 there was some work done on the analysis of observations, notably by A. T. Doodson, K. Hessen and H. Rauschelbach.

The first half of the century, however, was notable for its meager advance in basic understanding of the tide and its geophysical implications. After about 1960 there was an increase of interest in tidal research along many different lines, resulting in a considerable contribution to knowledge. Numerical methods of solution of the tidal equations were used by W. Hansen, C. Pekeris, K. T. Bogdanov, M. Hendershott, and others, to determine the ocean tide over the actual oceans and seas of the earth. The dynamical theory of free planetary waves and seiches was advanced by M. S. Longuet-Higgins. Nonharmonic methods of tidal analysis and prediction were put forth by W. Munk and D. Cartwright. Studies on geophysical implications of the tide and secular orbital changes were further advanced by W. Munk, G. J. F. MacDonald, W. Kaula, C. Wunsch, and others.

## TIDE-GENERATING FORCES

**Dynamics of Earth-Moon System.**—The moon attracts every particle of the earth and ocean. By the law of gravitation the force acting on any particle is directed toward the moon's centre, and is jointly proportional to the masses of the particle and of the moon, and inversely proportional to the square of the distance between the particle and the moon's centre. If one can imagine the earth and ocean subdivided into a number of small particles of equal mass, then the average, both as to direction and intensity, of the forces acting on these particles, is equal to the force acting on that particle which is at the earth's centre. If every particle of the earth and ocean were being urged by equal and parallel forces there would be no cause for relative motion between the ocean and the earth. Hence it is the departure of the force acting on any particle from the average which constitutes the tide-generating force. Now it is obvious that on the side of the earth toward the moon the departure from the average is a small force directed toward the moon; and on the side of the earth away from the moon the departure is a small force directed away from the moon. All around the sides of the earth along a great circle perpendicular to the line joining the moon and earth the departure is a force directed inward toward the earth's centre. Thus it can be seen that the tidal forces tend to pull the water toward and away from the moon, and to depress the water at right angles to that direction. In fig. 1 this distribution of forces is illustrated graphically. The relative magnitudes of the forces are given by the numbers on the figure, *M* being in the direction of the moon. The separate attractions of the moon at the earth's centre and at a point on the earth's surface are each inversely proportional to the square of the moon's distance, so that the difference between the two, which gives the tide-generating force, is approximately inversely proportional to the cube of the moon's distance.

The vertical component of the tide-generating force coincides

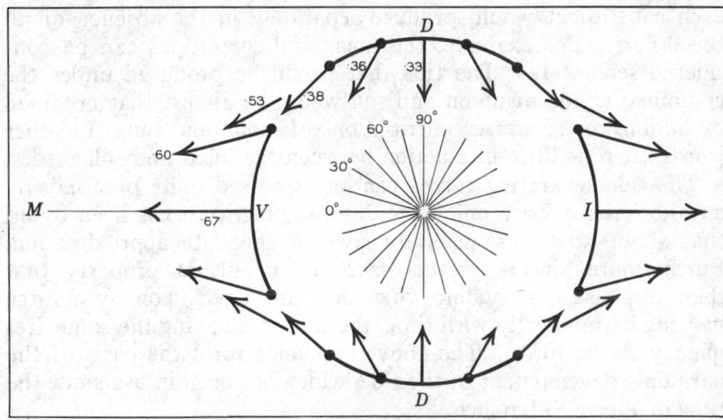


FIG. 1.—TIDE-GENERATING FORCE

in direction with the gravitational force of the earth itself, and thus acts as a slight modification of weight. This component does not tend to alter the position of equilibrium which the water would take up in the absence of any disturbance from an extraterrestrial body. The effective tide-generating forces, therefore, are the horizontal components of those indicated in fig. 1.

**Equilibrium Form of the Tide.**—For many purposes it is convenient to specify the distribution of the tide-generating forces at any instant by reference to a fictitious tide. If a completely rigid earth were completely covered by a layer of ocean, and if the tide-generating forces were to remain constant, there would be an invariable elevation of water at each point of the ocean surface and no tidal currents. If the distribution of forces were the same as that of the actual tide-generating forces at any instant, then the consequential elevation of water might be used as a specification of these forces. This distribution of fictitious tidal elevation is known as the equilibrium form of the tide. It is a real and accurate specification of the actual tide-generating forces throughout the earth's body as well as on its surface. When the equilibrium form is stated for every instant there is a complete specification of these forces, and henceforth the terms equilibrium tide and tide-generating force will be used interchangeably.

In this equilibrium form the inclination, to the horizontal, of the surface of the water would be always such that the consequential pressure gradient would everywhere balance the tide-generating force. It is therefore clear that the surface of the water would slope upward from *DD* toward the points *V* and *I*, the water being raised by a maximum amount at *V* and *I* and depressed by a maximum amount along the great circle through *DD*. The surface of the water would be nearly that of an ellipsoid of revolution. The volume of this ellipsoid would be the same as that enclosed by the surface of the undisturbed ocean. Owing to the motion of the moon relative to the earth, the tidal ellipsoid moves over the earth so that *V* is always directly under the moon and *I* always directly opposite, while owing to the varying distance of the moon the equilibrium ellipsoid changes slightly in shape. The shape of the sea surface deviates considerably from this idealized equilibrium tidal ellipsoid, owing to the effects of inertia and friction, which are discussed below.

The tide-generating forces attributable to the sun's gravitation may be similarly specified. The sun's mass is nearly 27,000,000 times the moon's mass and the sun's distance is about 390 times the moon's distance from the earth. Consequently the sun's tide-generating forces are to those of the moon in the ratio of 27,000,000 to $390^3$; *i.e.*, .460 or $\frac{1}{2.17}$. This means that at corresponding points of the two ellipsoids representing the lunar and solar equilibrium forms, the tidal elevations on the average will be in the ratio of 2.17 to 1.

**Harmonic Constituents.**—The study of tides on the earth has been greatly facilitated because the tidal motions, whether in the atmosphere, hydrosphere or lithosphere, are to a high degree of precision linear with respect to the tide-generating forces that cause them. The significance of this linearity is that the tide-generating force can be considered as the sum of a number of constituents, the actual tide being the sum of the individual effects each constituent would produce separately in the absence of all the others. For example, the lunar and solar tides can be considered separately. The tide that would be produced under the combined action of moon and sun would be almost that obtained by adding the separate contributions of moon and sun. In other words, there is little interaction between the lunar and solar tides.

The tide-generating forces can be expressed quite precisely by a finite series of harmonic terms, and in practice it has been found that about 30 terms generally give an adequate approximation. Furthermore, linear systems have the important property that their response is harmonic when they are acted upon by a force varying harmonically with time, the response having the same frequency as the force. The above two facts form the basis of the harmonic development of the tide, which has been in use since the time of Pierre S. Laplace.

Each term of the series representing the elevation of the equilibrium tide at some particular point on the earth's surface will be of the form $H \cos(nt-\epsilon)$, where $t$ is time, $H$ is the amplitude, $n$ is the frequency or speed (commonly expressed in units of degrees per hour), and $\epsilon$ is the epoch. For any given constituent the speed is constant, while the amplitude and epoch are constant in time but may depend on geographical location. The harmonic terms representing actual tides will be of the same form. In the case of the ocean tides $H$ may represent the amplitude of the elevation of the water surface relative to the ground; for bodily tides $H$ may represent the amplitude of a component of particle displacement; and for atmospheric tides $H$ may represent the amplitude of a pressure fluctuation.

Let us now consider the effect of only one tide-generating body, such as the moon. As demonstrated in the previous section, the tide-generating forces of the moon can be specified completely by the shape and geographic orientation of the tidal ellipsoid, whose major axis is oriented along the line joining the centres of earth and moon. Now for the moment, let us consider what would happen if the moon remained at a constant distance from the earth and revolved about the earth in the equatorial plane with constant speed. An observer located at any given geographical position would experience two maxima and two minima of the equilibrium tide each lunar day. The amplitude would be a maximum at the equator and would decrease with increasing northern or southern latitude to a value of zero at the poles. The rise and fall of the equilibrium tide would be approximately harmonic with speed $n = 2(\gamma-\sigma)$ where $\gamma$ denotes the angular speed of the earth's rotation relative to the stars and $\sigma$ the mean speed of revolution of the moon about the earth, and the equilibrium tide would be represented very closely by a single harmonic constituent. Since the moon's speed of revolution is small compared to the earth's speed of rotation, the period of this constituent is approximately semidiurnal. The moon's varying declination (angular distance from equatorial plane), varying apparent angular speed of revolution about the earth and varying distance from the earth cause many modifications in this simplified example.

If the moon revolved about the earth with constant angular speed at some constant declination not equal to zero, one of the two poles of the equilibrium tidal ellipsoid would be always in the northern hemisphere, and the other in the southern hemisphere. The two equilibrium high waters that a point on earth not on the equator would experience as the earth rotates would therefore not be equal, and the introduction of a new constituent of speed $n = \gamma-\sigma$, approximately diurnal, would be required. This effect is known as the diurnal inequality. The variable declination of the moon results from the moon's motion in an orbit whose plane intersects the earth's equatorial plane at an angle $I$. The lunar declination thus passes through a monthly cycle but since both north and south declinations have essentially the same effect, *i.e.,* that of decreasing the semidiurnal and increasing the diurnal contribution, the two constituents suffer a fortnightly modulation. Strictly speaking, such constituents cannot be considered harmonic, as there is implied in this term the invariability of amplitude, speed and epoch. These constituents can, however, be expressed precisely as the sum of a number of strictly harmonic terms, and more will be said about this point later.

The distance from earth to moon varies throughout a monthly cycle giving rise to a monthly modulation in the amplitude of the equilibrium tide. The maxima occur when the moon is at perigee, the point on the moon's orbit which is closest to the earth; the minima occur at apogee, when the moon is farthest from the earth. The time between successive lunar passages through perigee or apogee is the so-called anomalistic month, whose average length is 27.55 (mean solar) days. The speed of revolution of the moon about the earth varies inversely with the moon's distance according to Kepler's laws (*see* ORBIT). This causes the epoch of the equilibrium tide to vary according to the moon's position in its orbit, resulting in an apparent increase of period at apogee as compared to perigee. This monthly modulation of both amplitude and epoch of the equilibrium tide can again be expressed by a sum of purely harmonic constituents.

There are many other irregularities in the moon's motion, all of which can be expressed by the addition of more harmonic terms insofar as their effect on the equilibrium tide is concerned. The plane of the lunar orbit does not remain with constant orientation in space. Its movement is best described by the motion of the moon's nodes, which are the two points on the lunar orbit which lie on the plane of the ecliptic. Relative to the stars these nodes describe a westward motion known as the regression of the nodes, completing a cycle in about 19 years. Also, the major axis of the lunar orbit revolves eastward relative to the stars, completing a cycle in about nine years.

The solar effects are in every way analogous to the corresponding lunar effects.

**Species.**—In the above section it was seen that many cases arise where a constituent having a slow periodic variation of amplitude or epoch can be represented by the sum of two or more purely harmonic constituents. The speeds of these purely harmonic constituents will belong to the series, $n \pm \omega$, $n \pm 2\omega$, $n \pm 3\omega$, . . . , where $n$ is the speed of the original constituent and $\omega$ is the speed corresponding to the fundamental period of variation of its amplitude or epoch. If $\omega$ is small as compared to $n$, the speeds of the purely harmonic constituents will cluster closely about the speed of the original constituent. In the case of the actual tide, most of the constituents are approximately semidiurnal, diurnal, or of a longer (fortnightly or longer) period of variation, and their amplitudes and epochs pass through a much longer period of variation than that of the actual constituent. As a result, the periods of purely harmonic constituents representing the equilibrium tide are clustered about 12 hr., 24 hr. and much longer periods, offering a logical basis for classification of the tidal constituents.

The scheme of classification shown in Table I was developed by

TABLE I.—*Tidal Constituents*

| Symbol | Name | Speed | Speed in °/hr. | Coefficient |
|---|---|---|---|---|
| | | Long-period species | | |
| *Mf* | Lunar fortnightly . . | $2\sigma$ | 1.098 | .078 |
| *Ssa* | Solar semiannual . . | $2\eta$ | .082 | .036 |
| — | Nineteen yearly . . | $N$ | .002 | .033 |
| | | Diurnal species | | |
| $K_1$ | Lunisolar . . . . | $\gamma$ | 15.041 | .265 |
| $O_1$ | Larger lunar . . . | $\gamma-2\sigma$ | 13.943 | .189 |
| $P_1$ | Larger solar . . . | $\gamma-2\eta$ | 14.959 | .088 |
| | | Semidiurnal species | | |
| $M_2$ | Principal lunar . . | $2(\gamma-\sigma)$ | 28.984 | .454 |
| $S_2$ | Principal solar . . | $2(\gamma-\eta)$ | 30.000 | .211 |
| $N_2$ | Larger lunar elliptic . | $2\gamma-3\sigma+w$ | 28.440 | .088 |
| $K_2$ | Lunisolar . . . . | $2\gamma$ | 30.082 | .058 |

George Darwin in 1882 and has been adopted by most of the world's tidal authorities. Within any given species the coefficient is proportional to the equilibrium amplitude, and this proportionality holds roughly between constituents belonging to different species. The subscript on the symbol designating the constituent refers to the species to which it belongs. The long-period constituents have no subscript, the diurnal species have the subscript "one," the semidiurnal species the subscript "two." In addition to the constituents tabulated in Table I, there are terdiurnal,

4-diurnal, etc., constituents in the equilibrium tide, but these are of much lower amplitude and are not of much importance on earth.

The earth's speed of rotation $\gamma$ is the largest of all the parameters contributing to the speeds of the tidal constituents, and its numerical multiplier in the expression for the speed determines to which species a given constituent belongs. The other quantities in Table I which determine the speeds of the constituents are the mean motion of the moon $\sigma$, the mean motion of the sun $\eta$, the speed of revolution of the moon's nodes $N$, and the mean motion of the lunar perigee $w$. These quantities have a smaller effect and merely determine the period of the constituent within its species. It can therefore be said that the fundamental reason that the tidal constituents clump conveniently into species is that the day is much shorter than either the month or the year.

The equilibrium constituents of any given species all have the same geographical form. The long-period constituents are characterized by a standing wave symmetrical about the earth's axis. The polar regions oscillate in phase with each other and are 180° out of phase with the equilibrium tide in low latitudes. The two nodal lines lie along latitudes 35.26° north and south. The diurnal constituents have the form of a progressive wave rotating relative to the earth about its axis from east to west. At any given instant there are two maxima at opposite extremes of the earth and two minima similarly situated, all lying at latitudes 45° north and south on a great circle passing through the earth's poles. The amplitude of the diurnal equilibrium tide vanishes at equator and poles. The semidiurnal constituents also have the form of a progressive wave rotating about the earth from east to west. There are two maxima on the equator at opposite extremes of the earth and two minima also on the equator 90° from the maxima. The amplitude of the semidiurnal equilibrium tide is maximum at the equator and dies off with increasing latitude, vanishing at the poles.

**Description of the Constituents.**—Let us consider first the semidiurnal constituents. As can be seen from the value of their coefficients tabulated in Table I, the principal lunar constituent $M_2$ is the most important. The other semidiurnal constituents "beat" against $M_2$, giving rise to a modulation the speed of which is equal to the difference of speeds of the two constituents. That is, the period of the modulation is the synodic period of the two constituents. The next strongest semidiurnal constituent is the principal solar constituent $S_2$, which beats against $M_2$, causing the fortnightly spring-reap modulation. Next comes the larger lunar elliptic constituent $N_2$ which beats with $M_2$, causing a monthly modulation of the latter associated with the variable distance between earth and moon that results from the ellipticity of the moon's orbit. The lunisolar constituent $K_2$ actually represents the sum of two constituents, one of lunar and the other of solar origin, which cannot be separated from each other by analysis because their periods are equal. The lunar part of this constituent beats with $M_2$, giving rise to a fortnightly modulation associated with the variable declination of the moon. It will be recalled that the amplitude of the semidiurnal part of the tide is at a maximum when the tide-generating body has zero declination. Similarly the solar part of the $K_2$ constituent beats with $S_2$, causing a semiannual modulation of this principal solar constituent which is associated with the variable declination of the sun.

The lunisolar diurnal constituent $K_1$ is similarly composed of a lunar and a solar contribution. The lunar part of this constituent beats with the larger lunar constituent $O_1$, causing a fortnightly modulation associated with the variable declination of the moon. It will be recalled that the amplitude of the diurnal part of the equilibrium tide vanishes when the tide-generating body has zero declination. Similarly, the solar part of the constituent $K_1$ beats with the larger solar constituent $P_1$, causing a semiannual modulation associated with the variable declination of the sun.

The constituents $Mf$ and $Ssa$ result from the variable declination of the tide-generating body and are at a maximum when this body is at zero declination. The lunar fortnightly constituent $Mf$ thus reflects the variable declination of the moon, and the solar semiannual constituent $Ssa$ similarly reflects the variable declination of the sun. In addition there is a small 19-year constituent which arises from the 19-year cycle in the regression of the moon's nodes, as well as many other minor long-period constituents.

In Darwin's harmonic development the tide-generating forces (the equilibrium tide) are not analyzed into strictly harmonic constituents; that is, the amplitudes and epochs of Darwin's constituents are not truly constant. They exhibit the 19-year cycle of the regression of the moon's nodes. However, during any one year the amplitudes and epochs vary so slightly that the constituents can be considered as true harmonic terms without incurring appreciable error. The nodal variation in amplitude is accounted for by taking the constituent coefficients $c$ (those values tabulated in Table I) to be constant in time while denoting the true amplitude of the equilibrium constituents by the quantity $fc$ where $f$ is called the node factor and is the quantity which varies. The mean value of $f$ is taken to be unity, and its values have been tabulated for each year for all important constituents. The value of $f$ changes so slowly that it is adequate to take its mean value during any given year in place of its true value at any instant during that year.

In 1921 Doodson developed the equilibrium tide into a series of harmonic constituents whose amplitudes and epochs do not exhibit this 19-year cycle, and therefore do not need the artifice of node factors. For this reason it may be said that Doodson's development is more nearly perfectly harmonic than is Darwin's. Even though Doodson's development does not attempt to take into account such long-term variations as secular changes in the distance between earth, moon and sun, and geologic changes in sea level, it is doubtful that a more elaborate development will ever be needed for tidal work.

## DYNAMICS OF OCEAN TIDES

**Equations of Motion.**—The dynamical theory of tides introduced by Laplace in the 18th century has given much insight into the problem of tides in the ocean. The following assumptions and approximations are commonly introduced:

(1) The water is assumed to be homogeneous; (2) vertical displacements and velocities of the water particles are assumed small in comparison to the horizontal displacements and velocities; (3) the water pressure at any point in the water is given adequately by the hydrostatic law; *i.e.*, it is equal to the head of water above the given point; (4) all dissipative forces are neglected; and (5) the ocean basins are assumed rigid (as if there were no bodily tide), and the gravitational potential of the tidally displaced masses is neglected.

If assumptions (1) and (3) are valid it can readily be shown that the tidal currents at any locality are uniform with depth.

For a more complete explanation of these equations, *see* MECHANICS, FLUID. Take $a$ to denote the radius of the earth and $g$ the acceleration of gravity at its surface. Position on the earth's surface will be designated by the longitude $\phi$ and the co-latitude (angular distance from the north pole to the point under consideration) $\theta$. Let $h$ denote the depth of the ocean at any point, so that $h$ is a function of $\theta$ and $\phi$. Also, let $\zeta$ denote the elevation of the free surface at any point of the ocean above its mean level, and $u$ and $v$ the southward and eastward components of the tidal current, so that these three quantities are functions of $\theta$, $\phi$ as well as of the time $t$. Then the equation of continuity, which expresses the condition that the volume of any mass of water must remain constant, may be written in the form

$$\frac{1}{a \sin\theta}\left\{\frac{\partial}{\partial\theta}(hu \sin\theta)+\frac{\partial}{\partial\phi}(hv)\right\}+\frac{\partial\zeta}{\partial t}=0 \qquad (1)$$

provided that the elevation of the sea surface is everywhere small compared to the depth of water. If this is not the case then $h$ must be replaced by $h+\zeta$ in equation (1). This equation may be derived by expressing the condition that the net rate at which volume of water enters the sides of a vertical column is equal to the rate of increase of the volume at the top of this column by virtue of the time rate of increase of the elevation of the sea surface $\zeta$. Along a coast line the condition that the tidal current have no component perpendicular to the coast must be satisfied.

The equations of motion are formed by equating the southward and eastward components of acceleration of the water particles to the sum of all the forces per unit mass acting on the water in the southward and eastward directions, respectively. The acceleration components have a complicated form when expressed in spherical coordinates on a rotating earth. As an example, the southward component of acceleration is equal to

$$\frac{\partial u}{\partial t}+\frac{u}{a}\frac{\partial u}{\partial \theta}+\frac{v}{a\sin\theta}\frac{\partial u}{\partial \phi}-\frac{v^2}{a}\cot\theta-2\omega v\cos\theta$$

where the first term expresses the local acceleration, the second and third terms together express the field acceleration, the fourth term arises from the curvilinear nature of the spherical coordinate system used, and the last term is the Coriolis acceleration, which must be considered because the system used is rotating with respect to an inertial system. Here $\omega$ represents the angular speed of the earth's rotation. At this point an additional assumption shown to be valid for tidal motion in true oceanic regions is introduced: that the terms quadratic in the velocity components are negligible as compared to the local acceleration. In accordance with the foregoing approximations, the only forces acting on the water are the tide-generating forces and those attributable to the pressure gradient resulting from the slope of the sea surface. The southward and eastward components of the pressure gradient are given by

$$\frac{g\rho}{a}\frac{\partial \zeta}{\partial \theta},\ \frac{g\rho}{a\sin\theta}\frac{\partial \zeta}{\partial \phi},$$

$\rho$ being the water density, and the southward and eastward components of the tide-generating force are given by

$$\frac{g\rho}{a}\frac{\partial \bar{\zeta}}{\partial \theta},\ \frac{g\rho}{a\sin\theta}\frac{\partial \bar{\zeta}}{\partial \phi},$$

where $\bar{\zeta}$ represents the elevation of the equilibrium tide. This quantity is a function of $\theta$, $\phi$ and $t$ and is assumed known as it can be deduced from knowledge of the relative movements of the earth, moon and sun. The equations of motion can then be written in the form

$$\begin{aligned}\frac{\partial u}{\partial t}-2\omega v\cos\theta&=-\frac{g}{a}\frac{\partial}{\partial \theta}(\zeta-\bar{\zeta})\\ \frac{\partial v}{\partial t}+2\omega u\cos\theta&=-\frac{g}{a\sin\theta}\frac{\partial}{\partial \phi}(\zeta-\bar{\zeta}).\end{aligned}\qquad(2)$$

The equations (1) and (2) serve to determine completely, at least in theory, the tidal currents and elevation over the entire oceans and for all times, given a complete description of the tide-generating forces and the boundaries of the ocean basins. In practice, however, such a general solution has never been obtained owing to the complicated nature of the distribution of sea and land masses and the varying depth of water. For this reason tidal research has been based primarily on observations and general principles (such as linearity, etc.) derived from theory.

It may be noted that these equations are linear in $u$, $v$, $\zeta$ and $\bar{\zeta}$ with the result that the tide-generating forces may be separated into several constituents, the sum of whose effects is exactly equivalent to the effect produced by the sum total of all the tide-generating constituents. Indeed, as has already been pointed out, this is the basis of the harmonic development of the tide. Let us review under what conditions the ocean tide is truly linear and under what conditions this linearity breaks down. Unless the elevation of the sea surface above its mean position is always small as compared to the mean depth $h$, equation (1) becomes nonlinear. Similarly, if the field acceleration becomes so large it is no longer negligible as compared to the local acceleration equations (2) become nonlinear. This is most likely to occur in regions of large tidal currents with a large spatial rate of change (current shear). Nonlinear dissipative forces may be another source of nonlinearity. All these effects are quite small in the vast oceanic regions but tend to become larger in regions of shallow water and in the vicinity of the coast line, and consequently are referred to as shallow-water tides.

As to the other approximations, that of neglecting all dissipative mechanisms (4) is not a very good one, but more will be said about this point in the section on *Tidal Friction*. The bodily tides of the earth invalidate to a certain extent assumption (5) by virtue of a small variable movement of the sea floor and of the earth's own gravitational field. If $\zeta_e$ designates the variable elevation of the sea floor above its mean position, equation (1) will stand unaltered if we take $\zeta$ to denote the elevation of the sea surface relative to the sea floor, but in the formulas for pressure gradients $\zeta$ must be replaced by $\zeta+\zeta_e$. The disturbance in the gravitational forces brought about by the displacements of water and solid earth must be accounted for by adding a term $\bar{\zeta}_e$ to $\bar{\zeta}$. Inhomogeneities in the sea water have been neglected according to assumption (1), but may have a more important effect in tidal motions than has been anticipated. At any given time of the year a large part of the ocean is covered by a nearly homogeneous layer of light, warm water 50 to 200 m. thick. Such stratification of the sea water may influence the vertical structure of the tidal current with resulting deviations from their generally assumed uniformity with depth. Bottom friction will also introduce vertical shear in the tidal current.

Suppose now that we consider the ocean's response to one harmonic constituent of the equilibrium tide. If we take a long-period constituent, $\bar{\zeta}$ will have the form of a standing wave over the entire earth. A constituent of any other species will have the form of a progressive wave rotating relative to the earth about its axis in the westward direction. Such progressive waves can, however, be expressed as the sum of two standing waves separated in longitude by 90°, and separated in time also by 90°. In any case, therefore, it will suffice to express $\bar{\zeta}$ in the form

$$\bar{\zeta}=H_0\cos n(t-\tau_0)$$

where $n$ and $\tau_0$ are absolute constants and $H$ is a function of geographic position but independent of time. The actual response of the ocean will then be the sum of a number of solutions to such inputs. The solutions for the tidal elevation $\zeta$ and current $u$, $v$ from equations (1) and (2) will have the form

$$\zeta=H\cos n(t-\tau)$$
$$u=U\cos n(t-\tau_1),\qquad v=V\cos n(t-\tau_2),$$

where $H$, $U$, $V$, $\tau$, $\tau_1$, and $\tau_2$ are all functions of geographical position only. While it is not feasible to actually determine these functions analytically, if their values are determined for a certain location on the earth by appropriate analysis of tidal observations, the response to the constituent under consideration could be predicted for all time. In the case of the tidal elevation, wherever $H$ and $\tau$ have been determined for all important constituents, the tidal elevations there can be predicted for any time. It may be remarked that at a given place $H_0$ and $H$ are generally quite different; *i.e.*, the true tide bears little resemblance to the equilibrium tide.

**Nonlinear Distortion (Shallow-Water Tides).**—At places where the tidal elevation becomes appreciable as compared to the water depth, or other nonlinear effects occur, the principle of superposition breaks down. One might think that under these circumstances the concept of harmonic constituents would be completely useless, but it has been found possible to retain this concept provided that additional constituents, the so-called shallow-water tides, be included. The regions where this phenomenon occurs are generally confined to rivers, estuaries and shallow gulfs. The shallow-water constituents are not produced by the direct action of the tide-generating forces, but by the distortion, attributable to shoal water, of already existing tidal constituents which have been formed in the ocean. In fact, if the region of distortion is small enough (as it usually is), the tide-generating forces have little or no direct effect on the shallow-water tide.

It is no longer correct to consider separately the reactions to individual equilibrium constituents, but let us take the simple example of only one equilibrium constituent in order to gain insight into the problem. The response of a nonlinear system to the harmonic forcing constituent will not be harmonic, but at least it will be periodic, having the same period as the forcing or primary constituent. If $2\pi/\sigma$ is the period of the primary constituent, it is well known from the theory of Fourier series that a periodic function of this period can be expressed as the sum of purely harmonic terms having speeds $\sigma$, $2\sigma$, $3\sigma$, etc. Extending this idea to the actual situation one should expect to find shallow-water constituents having periods of one-half, one-third, etc., of those of the major tidal constituents. The shallow-water constituents obtained in this way are called overtides because of their analogy to overtones in acoustics. The same symbol is used to designate these overtides as is used to designate the equilibrium constituent which gives rise to them, and again the subscript designates the species (approximate number of periods in a day) to which the overtide belongs. For example the constituent $M_2$ gives rise to the series of overtides $M_4$, $M_6$, etc., and $K_1$ gives rise to the overtides $K_2$, $K_3$, etc. In some cases an overtide will have exactly the same period as another equilibrium constituent and it will be impossible to separate the two by harmonic analysis. For example, $K_2$ represents the lunisolar semidiurnal constituent, but an overtide of exactly the same period as $K_2$ is produced by nonlinear distortion of the lunisolar diurnal constituent $K_1$. In this and in similar cases the symbol $K_2$ (referring to the actual tide) represents the combined effect of both the linear reaction to the equilibrium constituent $K_2$ and the overtide.

The theory of progressive shallow-water waves of finite height has been used to estimate the relationship between the amplitudes of the overtides and primary tide. The amplitude of the $n$th overtide is found to be proportional to the $n$th power of the amplitude of its primary at any given place, as the amplitude of the primary varies in time. For example, if the range of the semidiurnal tide is twice as great during the spring tides as during the neap tides, the range of the quarter-diurnal overtide resulting from distortion of the semidiurnal tide will be approximately four times as great during the spring tides as during the neaps. The range of the 6-diurnal overtides will be eight times as great during the spring tides, etc. As to the 19-year nodal variation in amplitude, the node factors $f$ of the overtides bear a relation to those of the primary as illustrated in the following example in the case of the overtides of the constituent $M_2$:

$$f(M_4) = [f(M_2)]^2, \quad f(M_6) = [f(M_2)]^3, \text{ etc.}$$

The above relations seem to be confirmed fairly well in most cases by tidal observations in spite of the fact that assumptions in the theory from which they have been derived are far from fulfilled. For example, in many regions where overtides are important, such as some rivers and estuaries, the tidal wave has more nearly the form of a standing wave than that of a progressive wave, but the theory for standing shallow-water waves of finite height has not been adequately developed. Also, the nonlinear effects caused by one constituent cannot, strictly speaking, be superimposed on those caused by another.

The nonlinear interaction between two or more primary constituents can be accounted for by the inclusion of compound constituents. In the case of two interacting primary constituents having speeds $\sigma_1$ and $\sigma_2$, a series of compound constituents will result, having speeds $\sigma_1 \pm \sigma_2$, $\sigma_1 \pm 2\sigma_2$, $2\sigma_1 \pm \sigma_2$, etc., including all possible combinations of the form $a\sigma_1 \pm b\sigma_2$, $a$ and $b$ being integers. The relationship of the amplitudes of the compound constituents to those of their primaries has been approximated by assuming that the system responds like a power-law filter; *i.e.*, like a system whose output is equal to a polynomial function of the input. In this way the relative importance of the compound constituents of any given species as well as the dependence of their node factors on those of the primary constituents can be evaluated. No general conclusions can be drawn concerning the relative importance of two compound constituents belonging to different species.

TABLE II.—*Shallow-Water Constituents*

| Symbol | Speed | Speed in °/hr. | Node factor |
|---|---|---|---|
| $2SM_2$ | $2\gamma+2\sigma-4\eta$ | 31.016 | $[f(M_2)]^2$ |
| $MNS_2$ | $2\gamma-5\sigma+2\eta+w$ | 27.424 | $f(M_2)$ |
| $MK_3'$ | $3\gamma-2\sigma$ | 44.025 | $f(M_2)f(K_1)$ |
| $MK_3$ | $3\gamma-4\sigma$ | 42.927 | $[f(M_2)]^2f(K_1)$ |
| $M_4$ | $4\gamma-4\sigma$ | 57.968 | $[f(M_2)]^2$ |
| $MS_4$ | $4\gamma-2\sigma-2\eta$ | 58.984 | $f(M_2)$ |

Table II includes the more important shallow-water constituents, both overtides and compound constituents. In the table, only two of each of the semidiurnal, terdiurnal and 4-diurnal shallow-water constituents are given for illustration, but there are ports for which many others would be needed to give an accurate representation of the tide. In fact for some ports the number of these constituents that would be needed is so high that the harmonic method becomes impractical. It may be noted that the two terdiurnal constituents listed in Table II are given the same symbol. Actually there is some confusion as to the designation of the compound constituents. The designations given in Table II are based on the nomenclature used by the United States coast and geodetic survey.

## ACTUAL TIDES IN THE OCEAN

**Progressive Tides in Canals.**—Let us consider a long narrow canal, open at both ends, along which a tidal wave is progressing. In accordance with the well-known properties of progressive waves, the water particle velocity at the crests of the wave will be in the same direction as that of the propagation of the wave form, while the water particle velocity at the troughs will be in the opposite direction.

Now, the rotation of the earth tends to deflect any particle in motion to the right (in a horizontal plane in the northern hemisphere) relative to the earth with an acceleration proportional to the speed of the particle. This is the so-called Coriolis acceleration that was discussed above. In order to balance this Coriolis acceleration the water surface at the crest must slope upward to the right (in the northern hemisphere), if one is facing in the direction of propagation of the wave. Similarly, the water surface at the trough must slope upward toward the left. Therefore, the crests are higher and the troughs lower along the right coast of the canal, and at any point on the right coast of the canal there will be a higher range of the tide than for a point situated on the left coast.

The above considerations are substantiated by tidal observations in the English channel and Irish sea. The tidal wave progresses eastward through the English channel passing out through the Straits of Dover into the North sea. The tidal range is greater on the French coast (the right side) than on the English coast. In the Irish sea, the tidal wave progresses northward, and the tidal range is greater on the English and Welsh coasts (again the right side) than on the Irish coast.

**Tides in Adjacent Seas.**—If the region under consideration is small enough the tide within it is influenced predominantly by the tide immediately outside the region and not appreciably by the direct action of the tide-generating forces. It is on the water of the great oceans that the gravitational forces of the moon and sun generate the greater part of the tide, while the tides in the small seas bordering the oceans can be considered as free waves. A great deal of theoretical work has been done on the tides of adjacent seas, but invariably it is necessary to approximate the sea by some simple geometric shape. Nevertheless, many satisfactory explanations of the actual tide in small bodies of water have been obtained.

The theory of free long waves states that a tidal wave in a narrow canal of constant depth is propagated with a velocity of $\sqrt{gh}$, the wave length being given by the expression $T\sqrt{gh}$, where $g$ is the acceleration of gravity, $h$ is the water depth and $T$ is the period of the wave (time interval between successive high waters). In the case of the tide, $T$ will have approximately the value of 12 hr. for the semidiurnal tide, or 24 hr. for the diurnal tide.

Let us neglect, for the time being, the effect of the earth's rotation and consider a tidal basin of constant depth having rectangular shape with one end closed and the other end in communication with the ocean. Only motions parallel to the length of the basin will be considered. The tides within the basin are influenced by the boundary conditions (1) that the elevation at the mouth of the basin is at any instant the same as that in the ocean immediately exterior to the basin; and (2) that the horizontal orbital motion at the closed end vanishes. The situation is analogous to the acoustical problem of stationary oscillations within an organ pipe open at one end. The spatial distribution of amplitude of the oscillation is characterized by the positions of nodes, or places where there is no tidal oscillation of the water surface, or no pressure oscillation in the case of the organ pipe, and of antinodes or places where the oscillations attain their maximum amplitude. A standing wave in the pipe has an antinode at the closed end, while one quarter of a wave length away there is a node, and so forth, with nodes and antinodes alternating along the length of the pipe with a quarter of a wave length between them. If the open end is at or near a node the oscillation within the pipe attains a magnitude much greater than that outside the mouth of the pipe, and resonance is said to occur. Thus, in the case of the rectangular tidal basin, resonance would occur if the length $L$ of the basin had any of the values

$$\tfrac{1}{4}T\sqrt{gh},\ \tfrac{3}{4}T\sqrt{gh},\ \tfrac{5}{4}T\sqrt{gh},\ \text{etc.}$$

Or, for a given length, resonance would occur if the period of oscillation had any of the values

$$\frac{4L}{\sqrt{gh}},\ \frac{4L}{3\sqrt{gh}},\ \frac{4L}{5\sqrt{gh}},\ \text{etc.}$$

but in actual practice the successive values have diminishing importance and usually only the first one, corresponding to a quarter wave-length basin, is considered. This is called the gravest free mode.

If the basin is less than a quarter of a wave length long, the entire basin oscillates with the same phase. If the length of the basin is between a quarter wave length and a half wave length, there is one nodal line and the oscillation at the head of the basin is 180° out of phase with that at the mouth. Every node line represents a phase change of 180°.

The Bay of Fundy on the east coast of North America has the greatest tidal range of any place on earth, and this fact is attributed to a resonance phenomenon based on the foregoing considerations. The shape of the Bay of Fundy is reasonably well approximated by a rectangular basin having a length of 170 mi. and a depth of 240 ft. The above relationships indicate that such a basin would have a resonance period of approximately $11\frac{1}{2}$ hr., which is very close to that of the semidiurnal tide. It should therefore be expected that the semidiurnal tide would be greatly magnified relative to the diurnal, and this is found to be the case. At certain places at the head of the bay the spring tide attains a range of 50 ft.

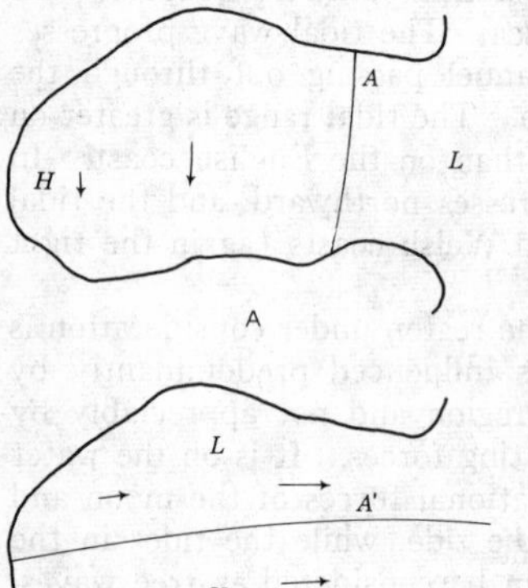

FIG. 2.—MOVEMENT OF THE TIDES IN A GULF. *H* INDICATES HIGH-WATER LEVEL, *L* LOW-WATER LEVEL. (SEE TEXT FOR FURTHER EXPLANATION.)

Elongated seas of variable depth and cross-sectional area also can be studied mathematically provided these quantities vary slowly enough along the length of the sea. Good agreement between theory and observation has been obtained for tides in the Gulf of California, the Red sea and other adjacent seas. The Gulf of California is computed to have a resonance period of approximately 25 hr., roughly that of the diurnal tide. The tide at the head of the gulf near the mouth of the Colorado river has been observed to be predominantly diurnal in character with a maximum range of approximately 20 ft. The computed variation of amplitude and phase of the $M_2$ constituent in the Red sea is in good agreement with the observed variation, and both theory and observations indicate the presence of a nodal line close to Port Sudan, near the mid-point of the sea's length.

To consider geostrophic effects (*i.e.*, those resulting from the earth's rotation) it is necessary to take into account the Coriolis acceleration. Consider a standing oscillation in a gulf as shown in fig. 2A at the instant of high water at the head of the gulf. The

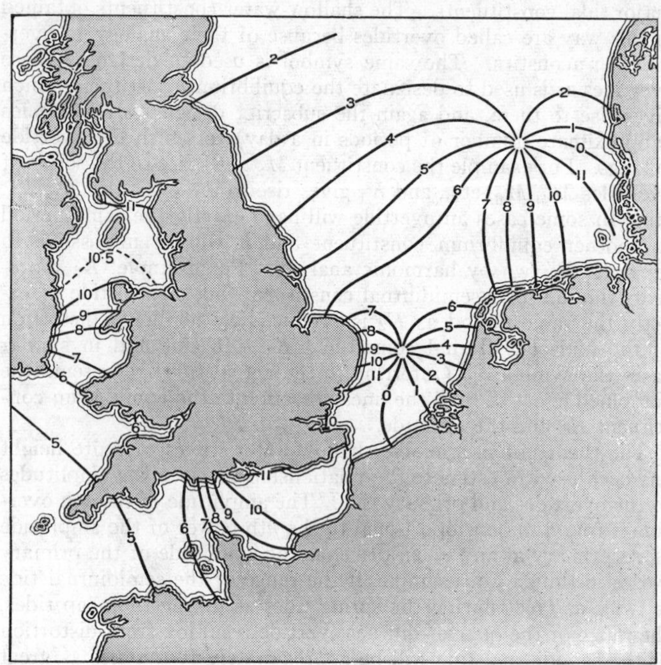

FIG. 3.—COTIDAL LINES FOR $M_2$ CONSTITUENT IN BRITISH SEAS. NUMBERS GIVE GREENWICH MEAN LUNAR TIME OF HIGH WATER

curve *A* has been drawn through all points where the deviation of the water level from its mean is zero at this instant. One quarter period later the water is flowing out of the gulf. At this instant, in the absence of the Coriolis force, the elevation everywhere within the gulf would have its mean value (except for a small frictional effect), and the curve *A* would represent a nodal line. Actually, the elevation will be higher to the right of the outward flowing current, as is shown in fig. 2B, with the curve *A′* lying along points whose elevation is at the mean level. Continuity considerations show that there must have been currents flowing at the instant of high water within the gulf in order to produce the distribution of water level shown in fig. 2B. Possible directions for these currents are shown in fig. 2A.

At the intersection of the curves *A* and *A′* there will be no rise and fall of sea level, and such a point is known as an amphidromic point. Let it be assumed that the constituent under consideration is a semidiurnal one, and divide its period into 12 equal time intervals called constituent hours, and let the zero constituent hour correspond to the instant of high water within the gulf as depicted by fig. 2A. Fig. 2C then gives the curves along which high water occurs for each of the 12 constituent hours. Such curves are called cotidal lines. The hypothetical distribution of range of tide is indicated by the dashed curves, called corange lines, each of which connects points having equal range of tide. The amphidromic point, at which the tidal range is zero, lies in the centre of the concentric family of corange lines. The cotidal lines indicate the position of the crest of the tidal wave at any instant, and it is seen that this crest rotates in counterclockwise fashion (in the northern hemisphere) about the amphidromic point. Such amphidromic systems with counterclockwise movement of the tidal crest are characteristic also of the oceans and adjacent (large) bodies of water.

**Geographical Distribution of the Ocean Tide.**—Cotidal maps, such as the one described above, are useful in illustrating the distribution of tidal elevation in a body of water, but it should be kept in mind that such charts are, strictly speaking, useful only in describing a single harmonic constituent. In theory it would be necessary to have one complete cotidal map of the world's oceans for each and every tidal constituent in order to characterize completely the form of the tidal wave, or the rise and fall of water

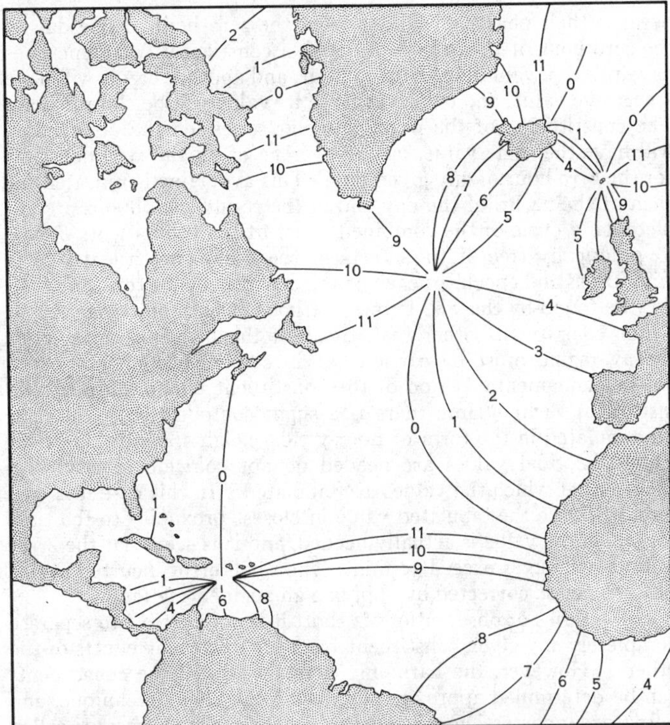


FROM A. T. DOODSON AND H. D. WARBURG, "ADMIRALTY MANUAL OF TIDES"; REPRODUCED BY PERMISSION OF THE CONTROLLER, HER BRITANNIC MAJESTY'S STATIONERY OFFICE

**FIG. 4.—COTIDAL CHART OF THE ATLANTIC OCEAN**

at every point in the ocean. The only constituent for which such charts have been prepared, to any extent, has been the $M_2$ constituent, which is somewhat representative of the other semidiurnal constituents.

Except along the boundaries of the oceans the tidal elevations are extremely difficult to measure, and what meagre knowledge we have of the geographic distribution of the tide in the whole ocean has been deduced principally by extrapolating from coastal tide stations and, where possible, making use of tidal current measurements. The equations of motion connect the tidal currents with the elevation gradients and external forces, including those of friction, and so from a knowledge of the currents and a law for the frictional forces the elevation gradients can be calculated. When the elevation is also known at a particular point, the directions of the cotidal and corange lines and also the distance apart of neighbouring members of these families of lines can be calculated. Such conditions are fulfilled for many coasts. If the elevation gradients can be calculated along a line which passes through one or more points at which the elevation is known, it is clear that the elevation can be calculated all along the line. In this way the semidiurnal ($M_2$) tide over the North and Irish seas was determined by Proudman and Doodson in 1923 (*see* fig. 3).

Cotidal charts for the $M_2$ constituent have been prepared for the oceans but they are uncertain, however, especially at large distances from the coasts and islands where tide gauge observations have been made. Tidal current determinations are rarely made in the open ocean. Another difficulty is that tide gauges are frequently located in sheltered bays or atoll lagoons where the time of high water may be delayed by as much as several hours. The cotidal chart of the Atlantic ocean shown in fig. 4 was prepared by Sterneck in 1920.

Mathematical solutions for the tide in ocean basins of simplified shapes have been obtained. Laplace in 1776 studied the dynamical problem of the semidiurnal tide in an ocean covering the entire earth and having constant depth. His solution takes into account the inertia of the water and the rotation of the earth. Some interesting aspects of this solution are summarized in Table III. Positive values in the second column indicate that the tide at the equator is direct—that is, that high water occurs simultaneously with high water of the equilibrium tide. Negative values indicate that the tide is inverted, or 180° out of phase with the equilibrium tide. For the diurnal tide Laplace obtained the curious result that there is no tidal oscillation of elevation on this world-wide ocean of constant depth, although there are tidal currents.

TABLE III.—*Laplace's Solution of the Dynamical Problem of the Semidiurnal Tide*

| Depth (fathoms) | Ratio of elevation to equilibrium elevation at equator | Depth (fathoms) | Ratio of elevation to equilibrium elevation at equator |
|---|---|---|---|
| 1,210 | −7.4 | 4,840 | 11.3 |
| 2,420 | −1.8 | 9,680 | 1.9 |

Several solutions have been obtained for the special case of an ocean of constant depth bounded by two meridians. The result of one of the solutions obtained by Proudman and Doodson is shown in fig. 5, which represents a cotidal chart of the $K_2$ tide in an ocean of depth 14,520 ft. bounded by meridians 70° apart. The $K_2$ tide was selected because of mathematical simplifications, but the $M_2$ tide should be quite similar. Comparison of fig. 5 representing a mathematical solution with fig. 4 derived from observations discloses no striking similarities except for the general occurrence of amphidromic systems.

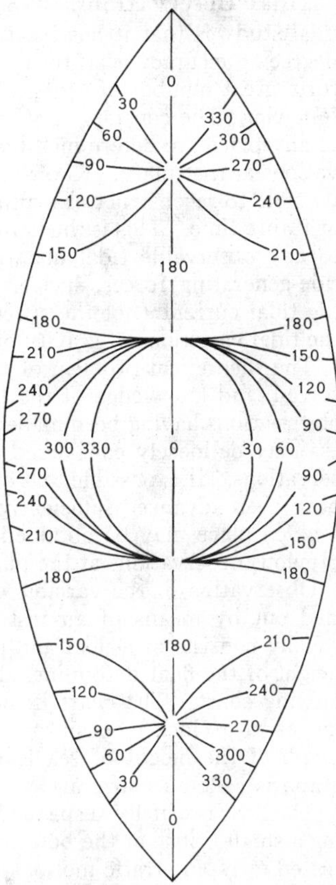


FROM A. T. DOODSON AND H. D. WARBURG, "ADMIRALTY MANUAL OF TIDES"; REPRODUCED BY PERMISSION OF THE CONTROLLER, HER BRITANNIC MAJESTY'S STATIONERY OFFICE

**FIG. 5.—COTIDAL CHART OF A HYPOTHETICAL OCEAN OF CONSTANT DEPTH BOUNDED BY MERIDIANS SEPARATED BY 70°**

**Tides in Lakes.**—If all natural periods of oscillation of a completely enclosed basin are short as compared to those of the tidal constituents, the tide should be approximately at equilibrium with the tide-generating forces at all times. According to the theory of long-standing waves in a rectangular basin of constant depth, the length of the basin is equal to one-half wave length of its gravest free mode. The period of the gravest mode is given by the expression $2L/\sqrt{gh}$ where $L$ is the length of the basin. For example, the gravest mode of a lake 20 km. long having constant depth of 40 m. will have a period of approximately $\frac{1}{2}$ hr. according to the above formula, and the tide in such a lake would therefore be determined with quite sufficient accuracy by static principles.

If the above condition is fulfilled the slope of the lake's surface is equal, at any instant, to the slope of the equilibrium tide at that location, and the actual tidal elevation at any point within the lake is determined by the condition that the total volume of water remain constant. The tide will usually differ considerably from the equilibrium tide according to these conditions, generally being considerably smaller in amplitude. For example, the maximum slope of the equilibrium tide is of the order of a metre in one-fourth the earth's circumference, 10,000 km., giving a value of $10^{-7}$. For a lake whose length is 10 km. the maximum difference of elevation between its extremes will be of the order of $10 \times 10^{-7}$ km. or 1 mm. The tide in small lakes is thus seen to be extremely small, and is usually overshadowed by other effects such as a variable amount of water volume related to variable runoff and evaporation, wind effects, seiches, etc.

There is no variation of tidal elevation at the centroid of the lake's surface area. If the gravest free oscillation of the lake approaches that of the semidiurnal tide, then of course the above concepts no longer are true, and a dynamical treatment of the problem is necessary. This elementary discussion has also omitted two other important effects: the yielding of the lake's bottom with the tidal deformation of the earth's body, and the potential of the tidally displaced matter of the earth (see *Bodily Tides,* below).

## TIDAL ANALYSIS AND PREDICTION

**Tidal Observations.**—Probably the greatest achievement of tidal study is that it has been made possible to predict to a fair degree of accuracy what the sea level would be at any desired time for a great number of ports. The method used is essentially the following: The constants in the harmonic development of the tide at any place are determined by analysis of a long series of observations at that place. Knowing the values of these constants, it is possible to reconstruct or synthesize the tide for any past, present or future time. This is the harmonic method, and it can be applied to any observable tidal quantity which depends linearly on the tide-generating forces, such as the north or east components of the tidal current (not the speed or the direction of the current), the tidal variations of gravity or atmospheric pressure, etc.

The theoretical problem of the tide in the oceans has not been solved, and knowledge of the tide at any place depends on some observations having been made at the place. The prediction process may be loosely considered as one of extrapolation of the observations. It is possible that at some future time tidal theory will have been advanced sufficiently that full knowledge of the tide at a given place may be obtained theoretically without the need of previous observations at the place.

Observation of the variable elevation of the sea surface is carried out by means of an instrument called a tide gauge, which usually consists of a float and pulley system so arranged that the height of the float determines the position of a recording pen on a moving chart. The chart is made to move at constant speed by means of a clock mechanism, so that in the result one obtains a graph of the height of sea level as a function of time. Such a graph is called a marigram.

The float is usually suspended within a vertical pipe or well having a small orifice at the bottom in order that the float not be subjected to rapid erratic motions by the ocean waves. A pier piling is an ideal structure on which to fasten the tide well. The diameter of the orifice and the inner cross-sectional area of the tide well determine the frequency response of the gauge. The orifice must be small enough to insure that the ordinary high-frequency ocean waves have greatly reduced amplitude within the well, but large enough so that no appreciable lag be introduced in case of the tide. The frequency response of the tide gauge is usually arranged so that fluctuations of water level taking place over five minutes or longer are quite faithfully reproduced on the marigram, so that the gauge may be useful in recording tsunamis (seismic sea waves) and other such phenomena. The gauge is periodically levelled in with a series of bench marks located nearby on the land in order to compensate for any long-period changes in the height of the gauge as a whole that might be brought about by slow sinking of the pier on which it is fastened, etc. In this way the gauge is useful for studying extremely long-period phenomena such as the year to year variation of mean sea level.

After the marigram is obtained, the usual procedure is to read off at hourly intervals the height of sea level, and to correct these hourly tidal heights for any variation of datum that may have occurred. Vast quantities of these hourly tidal heights for many seaports are on file at the world's principal tidal agencies.

**Analysis of Observations.**—If a long enough series of observations has been obtained from a locality, it is possible to determine the harmonic constants for each important tidal constituent with good accuracy. The procedure for finding the harmonic constants for any one constituent will be illustrated in the case of the principal solar series, $S_1$, $S_2$, $S_4$, whose periods are exactly 24, 12 and 6 hr. At instants of time separated by 24 hr. each constituent of this series will have the same value. Let us assume that we have a whole year of data. If we take the average of the 365 hourly tidal heights corresponding to the zero hour of each day, the resulting value will be practically free from the effects of all the other constituents whose periods are not submultiples of 24 hr., because their phases will differ from the zero hour of one day to the zero hour of the next day. Such a constituent will sometimes have positive values on the zero hour, and another day it will have a negative value, and on the average its value will be close to zero. The constituents of the principal solar series, on the other hand, will have the same value, on the average of all the zero hours, as for the zero hour of any given day. This averaging is repeated for each of the 24 hr. of the day and in the result one obtains a complete daily cycle of the combined effect of the constituents $S_1$, $S_2$, $S_4$ practically free of the effects of the other constituents. The amplitudes and epochs of each of the constituents of this series can now be found by the well-known methods of harmonic analysis.

For constituents other than those of the principal solar series the averaging must be carried out in similar fashion but based on the fundamental period of the constituent under consideration instead of 24 hr. Here there is a slight complication if the data are tabulated in the form of hourly tidal heights, as the times for which the tidal values are needed do not coincide exactly with the times at which the values are tabulated. In this case it is customary to use the tabulated value in closest proximity to the time for which the value is actually needed, and it is seen that the error in time will never exceed 30 min. The small error incurred in this process can be corrected by applying an augmenting factor.

If the series of observations is short it is not possible to separate completely any given constituent from the disturbing effects of the others. However, the harmonic constants of all the constituents can be determined approximately, using the above technique, and a first order correction can then be applied. This process is called elimination.

**Inference of Harmonic Constants.**—It is impractical to use the method discussed above for a constituent whose amplitude is small as compared to possible errors arising from various sources. The harmonic constants of such a constituent are usually inferred from those of one of the major constituents having approximately the same period. Such inference is based on the supposition that the ocean's response to a periodic tide-generating force varies continuously and relatively slowly with the period of the force. Hence it is assumed that two equilibrium constituents whose periods are nearly equal will cause tidal constituents in the ocean at any given locality, whose amplitudes are proportional to those of the equilibrium constituents causing them.

It is best to infer harmonic constants of a given constituent $X$ from those of one of the most important constituents whose period is as close as possible to that of $X$. Suppose that the constituent $M_2$ meets these requirements. If $H$ represents the actual amplitude of the constituents and $c$ their constituent coefficients (which are proportional to the amplitudes of the equilibrium constituents), the relationship

$$\frac{H\ (X)}{c\ (X)} = \frac{H\ (M_2)}{c\ (M_2)}$$

is used to relate the amplitudes of $X$ and $M_2$. The epochs (intervals by which the oceanic constituents lag behind their equilibrium counterparts) can be set equal, to a first approximation, while a more refined method of estimating the epoch of constituent $X$ is given in *Special Publication 98,* U.S. coast and geodetic survey. The constituent coefficients have been precisely determined from astronomic observations, and if the amplitude and epoch of $M_2$ have been determined from tidal observations, the amplitude and epoch of $X$ can be calculated from the above relationships. The validity of the above relations can be checked by also evaluating the constants of $X$ by conventional means, and it is usually found that the inference method gives fair results if the periods of the two constituents are nearly equal. It should be emphasized that the inference method can never be used to relate the constants of constituents belonging to different species.

**Prediction: Tide Tables.**—For many purposes it is of great importance to know in advance the times and heights of high water at a particular place on a particular day. Consequently governments and harbour authorities publish, a year or so in advance, tables giving such information for all the principal ports of the world. In a few cases tables are similarly published giving the height of water above some datum at every hour of the year, while for a certain number of navigable channels tables of the times of slack water are also issued.

The standard method of tidal prediction is the harmonic method based on the idea of harmonic constituents, and the necessary information for any particular place is provided by the process of analysis discussed above. The only theoretical results which are utilized in tidal prediction are (1) the decomposition of the entire tide-generating force as the sum of a number of harmonic equilibrium constituents; and (2) the linearity of the ocean tide. Thus, the periods of the constituents are obtained from the observed motions of earth, moon and sun, while their amplitudes and epochs are obtained from tidal observation: tidal prediction is largely an empirical science.

The process of harmonic prediction consists of the calculation of the value of each harmonic constituent for a given time, and then the addition of the values obtained for all the constituents. When this is done for every hour of a year, the computational task becomes enormous, and to obviate this, special computing machines, called tide-predicting machines, have been constructed. Those in use at mid-20th century were of the analogue type and usually consisted of a series of gears or pulleys by which means the analogue addition of the constituents could be carried out. The amplitude and epoch of each constituent could be adjusted into the machine so that it could be used for any location and for any tidal quantity. Such analogue computers are now mostly of instructional or historic importance only, as fast digital electronic general purpose computers can do the job more economically. Of course, only that part of the rise and fall of the sea surface related to astronomical quantities can be predicted, and hence any individual prediction is liable to differ considerably from the actual occurrence.

**Nonharmonic Tidal Prediction.**—The entire foregoing discussion of tide prediction and representation of the tide in the ocean is based on the harmonic development. It has been shown feasible to use an alternative method which has certain advantages over the harmonic method. This method involves use of applying an operator (linear or otherwise) to the equilibrium tide by digital computer. The kernel of the operator is determined on the criterion that the result imitate as closely as possible the observed tide over a certain period of observation, according to some criterion such as least squares. Thus, in this respect, the method is empirical in the same sense as the harmonic method. The equilibrium tide may be represented by a single time series embodying the long-period, diurnal and semi-diurnal tides. This series is the same for all ports and could be published in the form of a table, or generated by computer program. Each port will have its own characteristic kernel, which now plays much the same role as the tidal harmonic constants. The method has not yet been used on a routine basis in practical tidal prediction.

## NONASTRONOMICAL VARIATIONS OF SEA LEVEL

**"Geologic" Tides.**—Any change in shape of the ocean basins or in the total quantity of water in them can bring about changes of level at a given locality. Another effect, however, is to change the dynamical response of the oceans to the tide-generating forces, and we should consequently expect the tidal harmonic "constants" to change.

The geological change in sea level is quite slow as compared to that effected by the moon and sun, and is manifested by a small year to year variation in mean annual sea level. There is evidence that the average sea level over the entire earth rose by the order of 10 cm. from 1850 to 1950. This has been related to a shrinking of the ice caps of the world, particularly those over Antarctica and Greenland. About 1000 B.C., during the postglacial temperature maximum, sea level probably stood about 5 m. above its present level. At the present time there are localities where the average annual sea level is rising and others where it is falling, and this is attributed to a relative downward or upward motion of the land area in the vicinity. The horizontal extent over which these year to year sea level records appear similar gives a good indication as to the size of the portions of the earth's crust that are sinking and rising. Actually, the similarity extends over many hundreds of kilometres, indicating that masses somewhat smaller than continents are moving as a whole.

Variation of the tidal harmonic "constants" by the processes just described is probably a slow process, and it may be doubted that a detectable change would occur within tens of thousands of years. At locations where the tidal constants depend critically on the local, small-scale topography, however, this is not the case. For example, the tide up a river may depend critically on the conditions of the channel at the river's mouth. At many ports the tide has changed noticeably after the construction of port facilities, such as breakwaters, etc. In such cases the altered regime of sedimentation and erosion of sand usually plays an important part. Also, sand bars can form and disappear quite rapidly, and a semienclosed lagoon behind such a condition would experience variable tidal "constants."

**Meteorologic Tides.**—The principal meteorologic effects can be ascribed directly or indirectly to variations in atmospheric pressure on the sea surface, tangential stress on the sea surface exerted by the wind, heating and cooling of the sea water.

A varying atmospheric pressure acting on the oceans has the characteristic of a body force, as the pressure gradients are transmitted through the water practically simultaneously from the sea surface to the bottom. For this reason, the dynamical problem is formally equivalent to that concerned with the effect of the tide-generating forces on the oceans, and equations (1) and (2) are still valid provided that $\zeta$ is replaced by $-p_a/\rho g$, $p_a$ being the atmospheric pressure and $\rho$ the water density.

Under certain circumstances the dynamical response of the ocean to the atmospheric pressure disturbance can become large. If a tidal basin is subjected to a variable atmospheric pressure disturbance acting periodically with a frequency near that of one of the free modes of oscillation of the basin, the amplitude of its response will tend to increase until it is ultimately limited by frictional dissipation. The same is true in the case of a pressure disturbance travelling across the sea surface with the same velocity as that of a long free wave, or $\sqrt{gh}$. It may be noted that the depth of the open ocean is so great that storms seldom attain this critical velocity, and so such magnifying effects are more often encountered in shallow seas.

For a longer-period fluctuation the dynamical effects are less important, and under these conditions the ocean's response is similar to that of an inverted barometer. The sea surface is depressed approximately a centimetre for each millibar of pressure increase, and vice versa, according to the hydrostatic law

$$\zeta = -\frac{p_a}{\rho g}$$

Pressure changes of 20 millibars occurring in a few days are common at many ports, and so it may be seen that this effect could be one of the principal sources of error in tidal predictions.

Wind blowing across the water surface exerts a horizontal stress on the water directed downwind, largely by virtue of the difference in air pressure on the lee and windward sides of the water waves generated by the same wind. An exact law for this stress as a function of wind speed has not yet been discovered, but the semi-empirical relationship

$$\tau = \gamma \rho_a v^2$$

gives a good approximation. Here $\tau$ is the wind stress, $\rho_a$ the density of air, $v$ the wind speed at an elevation of 15 m. above the water surface and $\gamma$ is a numerical constant for which the value .0026 gives the best fit to the empirical data.

Wind stress on the sea surface directed toward the coast has the effect of piling up water against the coast, raising the sea level. Longshore winds blowing so that the land lies to the right relative to the wind direction also tend to raise the sea level against the shore (in the northern hemisphere), owing to the effect of the earth's rotation. There are dynamic effects to be considered in both these cases as the wind is seldom so steady that static equilibrium is reached, except in small basins whose period of free oscillation is quite short.

The effect of the wind stress is enhanced by shoal water for the following reason, based on static considerations. Let us consider the balance of forces in one dimension only, say, the east-west direction. The stress caused by a west wind (blowing eastward) must be balanced by a slope of the sea surface in which its elevation increases eastward. The horizontal pressure gradient associated with this surface slope is essentially constant with depth, so that the greater the water depth the greater is the total force exerted on a vertical water column. Therefore a given surface slope will require greater wind stress to balance it in deeper water than in the shallower water.

Meteorologic disturbances over shallow seas have given rise to disastrous storm surges, such as those that frequently inundate the coasts of the North sea and the Gulf of Mexico. These surges frequently have a roughly periodic character with periods of the order of hours, and under severe conditions their amplitude can attain several metres. The horizontal stress on the water surface due to the wind is usually more important in these surges than the normal force due to the atmospheric pressure disturbance. Such variations of sea level cannot be predicted by the same procedures used to predict the astronomic tide, but considerable success has been obtained in understanding the dynamics of these phenomena, and in a few cases fairly accurate predictions have been made, particularly in the North sea area by a method developed by R. H. Corkan and Proudman. In order to make such a prediction the wind and pressure fields must be known (or estimated with sufficient accuracy) over the water surface of the region and for all necessary instants of time preceding the hour to be predicted.

Variations of water density, caused either by local heating and cooling or by advection of water of different properties, give rise to variations in elevation of the sea surface. If the change in surface level is calculated on the basis that the total water mass in a vertical column remains constant, the hydrostatic law shows that the relative height of the surface is

$$\zeta_s = -\frac{1}{g}\int_{p_a}^{p_b} \alpha\, dp$$

where $\alpha$ is the specific volume of the water, and $p_b$ is the bottom pressure. The quantity $\zeta_s$ has been called the steric height, and is quite closely related to the dynamic height used in dynamical oceanography. Changes of the order of 10 cm. taking place from one month to the next are common in the ocean. In the seasonal variation of sea level the changes of density of the water are much more important than the long-period tidal constituents.

## MISCELLANEOUS TIDAL PROBLEMS

**Tidal Friction.**—The effect of dissipation of the ocean tide by friction has so far been left out of the discussion, but it is known to be an important factor. Harold Jeffreys has calculated that if the tide-generating forces of the moon and sun could be suddenly turned off, half the tidal energy in the earth's oceans would be dissipated in approximately a day. This dissipation is known to occur practically entirely by the friction of tidal currents against the bottom of a few shallow seas of the earth, and against the long shorelines of the continents and islands. It is a curious fact that probably half of the entire tidal dissipation of energy in the ocean takes place in the shallow Bering sea. This rapid rate of energy dissipation should have a considerable effect on the tides of the world.

The matter of tidal friction is of considerable importance in the motions of the planets and their satellites because it provides a mechanism whereby angular momentum is transferred from one type of motion to another. The tidal protuberance created on the primary by the tide-generating force of one of its satellites is not symmetrical with respect to the line joining their centres, and the satellite's own gravitational attraction on this protuberance exerts a torque on the primary. It can be shown in general that if there were no tidal dissipation, there would be no such torque, and that if the angular speed of the planet's rotation is faster than that of the revolution of its satellite about it, then this torque always tends to decelerate the planet's rotation. In such a case, the gravitational force of the primary on its satellite deviates slightly from the direction toward the primary's centre of gravity, and tends to accelerate the revolution of the satellite about its primary, provided this revolution has the same sense as the rotation of the primary about its axis. Then, the distance between the primary and its satellite will increase as the satellite's speed of revolution is increased, according to Kepler's laws. The above-stated conditions apply, of course, in the case of the earth-moon system.

The same deductions can be arrived at by an alternative point of view: the frictional force of the tidal currents on the sea bottom and coasts must itself exert a decelerating torque on the earth. If the tidal currents were known accurately enough over all critical regions where the bulk of the tidal dissipation takes place, the decelerating torque could be calculated, since it is known that by far the greater part of the tidal dissipation occurs in the oceans and only a negligible amount in the lithosphere. Actually, the form of the tide over the vast regions of the oceans is so poorly known that neither the gravitational torque method nor the frictional torque method can be applied quantitatively, and it is through records of ancient eclipses and modern observations on the moon's position that the average rate of lengthening of the day and lunar period of revolution have been estimated. It should be remarked that the lunar effect on the earth's rotation should be about three to five times as large as the solar effect.

There are four principal effects: (1) tides raised in the satellites by their primaries will tend to make each keep the same face toward its primary (as the moon presently faces the earth); (2) tides raised in the primaries by the satellites will alter the rates of rotation of the primaries; (3) tides raised in the primaries by the satellites will alter the distances between them; and (4) solar tides will affect all the rotations.

On the basis of the above considerations it has been deduced that during previous ages the earth had a much shorter day and much shorter month (period of lunar revolution), and that the moon was much closer to earth. The day has probably lengthened by a second in the last 120,000 years.

**Internal Tides in the Ocean.**—It has been shown that the tidal current would be uniform from top to bottom at any given locality and instant provided that the sea water had uniform density throughout the oceans. In the actual case, however, variations in the salinity and temperature lead to both time and space variations in the density, and it is possible that this condition would lead to a vertical shear in the tidal current. In any case, there is no reason to believe that there should not exist tidal variations in the water density at any given point in the ocean, and there is evidence on several occasions that such tidal variations may have been actually observed.

The outstanding feature of the density structure of the ocean is that the lighter water is found in the upper layers of the ocean, and in a large number of dynamical problems the ocean can be treated successfully as though the water were stratified; *i.e.,* as though the water in any horizontal plane were homogeneous. In such a situation there can exist an important class of wave motions in which the maximum amplitude of the vertical displacement of the water particles occurs at some depth beneath the surface. These are called internal waves to contrast them with the more familiar surface waves, for which the vertical displacements of the water particles have their maximum amplitude at the surface. Internal waves are similar in many respects to surface waves, but have some important differences: their speed of propagation is much less than that of a surface wave having the same wave length; and the vertical movement of the water particles (at the level of maximum movement) is a great deal larger than in the case of a surface wave having the same energy. Such waves have been observed by making periodical determinations of the vertical density profile from an anchored ship, and the results of such observations indicate that such internal wave motion is common, and that amplitudes of the order of tens of metres are to be expected. The oscillations are irregular, but frequently there appear to be dominant waves of diurnal or semidiurnal period having all the characteristics of a tidal variation. In order to prove conclusively the tidal origin of such waves, a considerable series of observations would be necessary, and the difficulties and expense of having a ship remain at the same location for a protracted period of time have prevented this study from being carried out.

### ATMOSPHERIC TIDES

As air, like all other matter, is subject to gravitational influence, there will be tides in the atmosphere possessing many features of similarity with those in the ocean. One of the characteristics of these tides will be a very small oscillatory variation in the atmospheric pressure at any place, and this may be regarded as the superposition of harmonic constituents with the ordinary tidal periods. By the systematic analysis of long series of regular barometric records, the principal lunar semidiurnal constituent $M_2$ of the barometric variation has been determined for a number of places, and found to have an amplitude of the order of .001 in. The dynamical theory of these tides has been the subject of considerable study. The derivation of the equations is not so simple as for ocean tides, one difficulty being that of taking account of the physical conditions in the upper regions. The equations which have been proposed are of the same general form as those for ocean tides, but the theory is still imperfect. The results of analysis for the $S_2$ constituent show a much larger oscillation with an amplitude of barometric variation of the order of .03 in. For this constituent, however, it is certain that thermal factors play a larger part than gravitational factors, and the theory is far from complete.

### BODILY TIDES

The solid body of the earth, or lithosphere, suffers periodic deformation because of the tide-generating forces just as do the oceans and atmosphere. These bodily tides manifest themselves in the following ways: (1) a variation of the vertical, or plumb line, with respect to any solid structure imbedded in the earth's crust; and (2) a variation in the acceleration of gravity at any point due to the potential of the displaced matter in the earth's body, quite aside from the variation of gravity directly associated with the tide-generating forces.

The gravest free elastic oscillations of the earth's body as a whole have periods of the order of an hour, which is much less than those of the principal tide-generating forces. Therefore, it is probably correct to assume that the bodily tides will approximate closely to their equilibrium forms, or in other words, that they may be calculated on the principles of statics. Owing to the earth's rigidity, the vertical rise and fall of the earth's solid surface at any position on it is somewhat less than that based on the equilibrium tide. The fractional height of the equilibrium tide attained by this surface vertical displacement is practically independent of geographical location, and is designated by the symbol $h$. The potential of the displaced matter is additive to the tide-generating potential, its fractional contribution to the latter at any point on the earth's surface being designated by the symbol $k$. As in the case of $h$, $k$ also is practically independent of geographical location. The numbers $h$ and $k$ were introduced by the theoretician in the field of elasticity, A. E. H. Love, and henceforth have been called the Love numbers.

The values of $h$ and $k$ depend on the geographical form of the disturbing potential, but it is common usage to consider only those values corresponding to a disturbing potential having the form of a spherical harmonic of the second degree, of which the semidiurnal equilibrium form is an example.

Various types of geophysical observations have been used to evaluate the Love numbers. For instance, it can be shown that the acceleration of the earth's gravity at the surface is altered by the amount

$$-\frac{2g\bar{\zeta}}{a}\left(1-\frac{3}{2}k+h\right)$$

where $\bar{\zeta}$ is the equilibrium tidal height at the place under consideration and $a$ is the radius of the earth. A body of water whose natural period is short compared with the tidal periods will set itself so that its free surface is one of constant potential. If $\zeta'$ is the elevation of the water surface at a given position relative to the bottom, it can be shown that $\zeta' - (1+k-h)\bar{\zeta} = \text{const.}$ provided that the total volume of water in the basin remains constant. The yielding of the bottom tends to diminish the apparent tide while the additional potential of the displaced mass in the earth tends to increase it, hence the algebraic signs in the terms of $h$ and $k$.

Thus it is seen that precise measurements of the acceleration of the earth's gravity at a point would give a determination of the quantity $1-\frac{3}{2}k+h$ while measurements of the water level in a long sheltered tube, free from winds and other disturbances, would give a determination of the quantity $1+k-h$. This quantity also determines the position of the vertical as can be measured by a plumb line or a special instrument called the horizontal pendulum.

It should also be possible to determine the quantity $1+k-h$ by means of observations of the ordinary ocean tide, provided its dynamics were well understood. The long-period tides, especially the lunar fortnightly tide $Mf$, have usually been utilized for this purpose. It is generally assumed that the periods of these constituents are very much longer than those of all natural oscillations in the ocean basins, and that the equilibrium law would therefore hold. This assumption is certainly valid in the case of ordinary inertio-gravitational standing wave motion in the oceans, but serious objections have been raised on the basis of the possible existence of geostrophic or planetary wave modes characterized by steady or nearly steady ocean currents. There is a further serious difficulty in isolating the purely astronomical long-period constituents in analysis, and it may well be doubted whether reliable constants for the $Mf$ constituent have ever yet been obtained from the records of observation. The values of $h$ and $k$ determined vary considerably depending on the type of observation used, and for this reason are subject to appreciable error. The value of $h$ is somewhere in the vicinity of 0.6, and that of $k$ is near 0.3.

The above discussion of the bodily tide has omitted any reference to the complications introduced by the tides in the ocean. There are two effects: the warping of the earth's crust by the varying load on the ocean floor; and the contribution to the total gravitational potential by the displaced water mass. Generally, these effects are more serious closer to the coast and the greater the tidal range at the coast nearby. For this reason measurements of the bodily tide are usually attempted near the centre of large continents.

If the rigidity and density at all points in the earth's body were exactly known, it should be possible to calculate the Love numbers theoretically without need for recourse to observations. The internal constitution of the earth is not precisely known, but certain hypotheses concerning this internal constitution can be rejected on the basis of results of bodily tide observations. Kelvin used the observed height of the fortnightly tide to show that the earth's rigidity, on the average, is greater than that of steel. *See* also TIDAL POWER and references under "Tide" in the Index.

BIBLIOGRAPHY.—P. Schureman, "Manual of Harmonic Analysis and Prediction of Tides," U.S. Coast and Geodetic Survey, *Special Publication 98* (1941); A. T. Doodson and H. D. Warburg, *Admiralty Manual of Tides* (1941); Sir Horace Lamb, *Hydrodynamics* (1945); Harald U. Sverdrup, *et al.*, *The Oceans* (1942); Sir Harold Jeffreys, *The Earth* (1952); J. Proudman, *Dynamical Oceanography* (1953); G. H. Darwin, *The Tides and Kindred Phenomena in the Solar System* (1962); W. H. Munk and G. J. F. MacDonald, *The Rotation of the Earth* (1960).
(J. PR.; G. W. Gs.)

**TIDORE** (TIDOR), a mountainous island of the Moluccas, Indonesia, lies a mile south of Ternate and 7 mi. (11 km.) W of Halmahera. It is nearly circular in shape, with an area of about 45 sq.mi. (118 sq.km.). Pop. (1957 est.), 27,753. The southern part is occupied almost entirely by an extinct volcanic peak (5,676 ft. [1,730 m.]). On the slopes below the 1,000-ft. (300-m.) level, coffee, fruit, and tobacco are cultivated, the soil being very fertile. The northern half consists mostly of hills, though there are a few level strips along the coast. The inhabitants are akin to the Ternatans. They sell fish and cultivate garden produce, and some of the Tidorese are proficient at the craft of metal working. They are Muslims.

Like Ternate (*q.v.*), Tidore is the seat of an ancient and once powerful sultanate. The Portuguese established themselves there in 1521 and fought the sultan, whose capital they destroyed. Later, the Spaniards, when Portugal had become incorporated with Spain, obtained a hold which they retained until well into the 17th century, aiding the Tidorese in maintaining their independence in Ceram, Halmahera, and other islands against the sultan of Ternate and the Dutch. The latter, in 1654, conquered the island, but recognized the nominal power of the sultan. Japan occupied Tidore in 1942. After World War II it passed with the Moluccas to Indonesia. *See* also MOLUCCAS. (E. E. L.; J. O. M. B.)

**TIECK, (JOHANN) LUDWIG** (1773–1853), German writer and critic, the most versatile and productive of the early Romantics. He was a born storyteller, and his best work has the quality of a *Märchen* (fairy tale) which appeals to the emotions rather than the intellect.

Born in Berlin on May 31, 1773, the son of a craftsman, he was educated at the Berlin *Gymnasium* (1782–92) and at the universities of Halle, Göttingen, and Erlangen (1792–94). He came into early contact with literary Berlin through the court composer J. F. Reichardt (1752–1814), but it was through friendship with W. H. Wackenroder (*q.v.*) that he began to realize his talent. Together they studied Shakespeare, Elizabethan drama, Middle High German literature, and medieval town architecture.

In 1794 Tieck returned to Berlin, where he worked on a collection of light stories, *Straussfedern,* which J. K. A. Musäus had started. More important, and characteristic of early German Romanticism, are *Die Geschichte des Herrn William Lovell* (three volumes, 1795–96), a novel in letter-form which describes the moral self-destruction of a sensitive young intellectual; *Karl von Berneck* (published in *Volksmärchen,* 1797), a five-act tragedy set in the age of chivalry; and *Franz Sternbalds Wanderungen* (two volumes, 1798), a novel of artist life in the late Middle Ages which shows the influence (and collaboration) of Wackenroder. At the same time he launched a parodistic attack on the Berlin Enlightenment in a series of plays based on fairy tales; they include *Ritter Blaubart* ("Bluebeard") and *Der gestiefelte Kater* ("Puss in Boots"), both published under the pseudonym of Peter Leberecht in *Volksmärchen* (three volumes, 1797), a collection of fairy tales based on old *Volksbücher* (chapbooks). This collection, which includes one of Tieck's best *Novellen, Der blonde Eckbert* ("Fair Eckbert"; translated in 1827 by Thomas Carlyle), the fantastic story of an obsessive fear, won him the admiration of the brothers Schlegel, the leading critics of the Jena Romantics, and in 1799 he moved to Jena at their invitation.

In that year he also issued Wackenroder's posthumous papers, published a translation of *The Tempest,* with an essay on *"das Wunderbare"* (the wonderful, or supernatural), and started a translation of *Don Quixote* (1799–1801). The climax of his early work is the grotesque, lyrical plays *Leben und Tod der heiligen Genoveva* (1800) and *Kaiser Octavianus* (1804), in which the theories of the Schlegels were partly realized. *Phantasus* (three volumes, 1812–16), a heterogeneous collection of earlier works in a narrative framework, indicates a movement toward realism.

From 1802, when not traveling, Tieck lived on a friend's estate near Frankfurt an der Oder. During this period his creative powers were apparently paralyzed. He studied Middle High German, collected and translated Elizabethan plays (*Altenglisches Theater,* two volumes, 1811), and published new editions of 16th- and 17th-century German plays (*Altdeutsches Theater,* two volumes, 1817). He acted as adviser to the great Shakespeare translation begun by A. W. Schlegel (*q.v.*). He also published contemporary German works, supervising the first editions of Novalis (1802), Friedrich ("Maler") Müller (1811; 1825), Heinrich von Kleist (1821; 1826), and J. M. R. Lenz (1828).

In 1819 he went to Dresden, where he was appointed *Dramaturg* (adviser and critic) at the theatre (1825–42). He became the greatest living literary authority in Germany after Goethe. The Dresden period marks a new epoch in his creativity. As a narrative writer he turned away from the fantasy of his earlier work, introducing more action and taking his material from contemporary middle-class society, or from history. The 40 *Novellen* of this period—including *Der Aufruhr in den Cevennen* (1826; *The Rebellion in the Cevennes,* 1845), *Der junge Tischlermeister* (1836), and *Des Lebens Überfluss* (1839)—contain polemics against both the younger Romantics and the contemporary "Young Germany." *Dichterleben* (part 1, 1826; part 2, 1831) is a *Novelle* about the early life of Shakespeare. *Vittoria Accorombona* (1840; *The Roman Matron,* 1845) is a historical novel. In 1842 he accepted an invitation from Frederick William IV of Prussia to go to Berlin, and there, as in Dresden, he became the centre of literary society by virtue of his masterly skill as a reader and reciter. He died in Berlin on April 28, 1853.

BIBLIOGRAPHY.—*Editions: Schriften,* 28 vol. (1828–54); *Nachgelassene Schriften,* ed. by R. Köpke, 2 vol. (1855); *Gedichte,* 3 vol., 2nd ed. (1821–23); *Kritische Schriften,* 4 vol. (1848–52). A modern critical edition is *Ludwig Tieck, Werke in vier Bänden,* by M. Thalmann (1963– ). *See* also *Das Buch über Shakespeare* (1920), *Ludwig Tieck und die Brüder Schlegel: Briefe mit Einleitung und Anmerkungen* (1930), ed. by H. Lüdeke; *Letters . . . 1792–1853* (1937), ed. and trans. by E. H. Zeydel *et al.*

*Biography and Criticism:* H. Gumbel, *Ludwig Tiecks dichterischer Weg* (1929); E. H. Zeydel, *Ludwig Tieck and England* (1931), *Ludwig Tieck, the German Romanticist* (1935); R. Lieske, *Tiecks Abwendung von der Romantik* (1933); R. Minder, *Un Poète romantique allemand: Ludwig Tieck* (1936); R. M. Immerwahr, *The Esthetic Intent of Tieck's Fantastic Comedy* (1953); M. Thalmann, *Ludwig Tieck, der romantische Weltmann aus Berlin* (1955), *Ludwig Tieck, "der Heilige von Dresden"* (1960). (AR. H.)

**TIELE, CORNELIS PETRUS** (1830–1902), Dutch theologian and scholar, whose influence on the study of comparative religion, which in his time was only beginning, was very great. He was born at Leiden on Dec. 16, 1830, and was educated at Amsterdam High School and afterward at the seminary of the Remonstrant Brotherhood. He served as pastor at Moordrecht and Rotterdam, then as professor at the Remonstrant Seminary. In 1877 followed his appointment at the University of Leiden as professor of the history of religions, a chair that was specially created for him and that he occupied for 24 years. He died on Jan. 11, 1902.

Among the best known of Tiele's numerous learned works are *Outlines of the History of Religion* (1876; English translation 1877) and his Gifford lectures, published as *The Elements of the Science of Religion* (1897–99). He was also the author of the article "Religions" in the 9th edition of *Encyclopædia Britannica.*

*See* S. Cramer in *Realencyklopädie für protestantische Theologie und Kirche,* 3rd ed., vol. xix, pp. 766–775 (1905).

**TIEN SHAN** (Russian TYAN'-SHAN; Chinese T'IEN SHAN, "celestial mountains"), one of the great mountain systems of central Asia. Situated in the Soviet Union and China, the Tien Shan is about 1,500 mi. (2,500 km.) long, trending generally west-southwest to east-northeast. The system is located between latitudes 40° and 44° N and extends from the Samarkand area (67° E) in the west to the Kansu border (96° E) of China in the east. There is no general agreement as to its northern and southern boundaries. In the north, the Dzhungarskiy (Dzungarian) Alatau is sometimes regarded as part of the Tien Shan because it is linked to the system by the Borokhoro (Boro Hörö Uula) Range (*see* ALA-TAU). Others regard the Dzhungarskiy Alatau as an independent range, with the Ili valley as the northern border of the Tien Shan. In the southwest, the Turkistan, Zeravshan, and Alay ranges are sometimes included in the Tien Shan because of geologic similarities. But on the basis of orographic and tectonic data, these ranges are excluded and the Fergana valley is regarded as the southwestern boundary of the system.

The Khan-Tengri (22,949 ft. [6,995 m.]), situated in a mountain knot on the Soviet-Chinese border, was long regarded as the highest peak of the Tien Shan system. In 1943, however, a Soviet expedition discovered a peak with an elevation of 24,406 ft. (7,439 m.), 13 mi. S of Khan-Tengri, and named the new summit Pobeda (Victory) Peak in honour of Red Army victories in World War II. From the mountain hub, subranges extend toward the west into the Soviet section of the Tien Shan system, and toward the east into the Chinese section.

**Western Tien Shan.**—The western, or Soviet, section of the Tien Shan is complex in structure. It consists of a number of branches and subranges fanning out from the mountain hub of Khan-Tengri and Pobeda Peak. The northern branch includes the Kungey-Alatau, which encloses the large mountain lake Issyk-Kul' on the north. Parallel to the Kungey Alatau in the north is the Trans-Ili (Zaili) Alatau, rising to 16,243 ft. (4,951 m.) in Talgar Peak. The Trans-Ili Alatau continues westward in the Chu-Ili Mountains, while the Kungey Alatau extends on into the Kirgiz Range. The central branch fanning out from the mountain hub consists of the Terskey Alatau, which encloses the Issyk-Kul' basin on the south. The southwestern branch is made up by the Kokshaal-Tau. These major branches of the western Tien Shan are tall, snow-clad ranges of an alpine character. In sharp contrast is the section bordered in the north by the Terskey Alatau and in the south by the Kokshaal-Tau, where mountain ranges were eroded and converted into peculiar flat-topped summits known as *syrts*. These *syrts* are separated by broad valleys or tectonic depressions. While the outer alpine ranges rise abruptly for 10,000 ft. or more above the adjoining lowlands, the relative elevation of the *syrts* above the intervening valleys is only about 2,000–3,000 ft.

**Eastern Tien Shan.**—The eastern, or Chinese, section of the Tien Shan consists of two parallel series of subranges. The main southern series, extending eastward from the Khan-Tengri Mountain hub, consists of the Khaliq-Tau (12,920 ft.) and the Boro Hatan (11,975 ft.) and terminates at the lake basin of Baghrash Köl.

The northern series of subranges includes the Borokhoro, the Bogdo Uula (17,946 ft.), the Bar Köl Tagh Range (14,094 ft.), and the Karlik Tagh (16,158 ft.). South of the Bogdo Uula lies the Turfan depression, whose salt-marsh-covered floor lies at 505 ft. (154 m.) below sea level, the lowest point in China. The eastern Tien Shan, which divides China's Sinkiang Uigur Autonomous Region into Dzungaria (north) and the Tarim basin (south), is characterized by an echelonlike arrangement of subranges and broad intermontane valleys and basins.

**Geology.**—The mountains of the Tien Shan are made up of sedimentary, metamorphic and igneous rocks of Paleozoic and Precambrian age. The most common rocks are schists, sandstone, limestone, marble, gneisses, granites, and syenite-porphyries. The intermontane basins, on the other hand, are filled with unconsolidated continental sediments of Tertiary and Quaternary age. The northern ranges were originally uplifted during the so-called Caledonian revolution in the Lower Paleozoic period, while the southern ranges arose during the Hercynian revolution of the Upper Paleozoic. These initial ranges were gradually eroded and converted into a peneplain by the Mesozoic and Tertiary eras. Toward the end of the Tertiary and early in the Quaternary, new uplifts took place to give the mountain ranges of the Tien Shan their present appearance. Downwarping associated with the uplifts produced intermontane valleys and basins. In the process of erosion of the mountains, these depressions became partly filled with eroded material.

**Climate.**—The climate of the Tien Shan is determined largely by its location in the interior of the Eurasian continent among arid desert lowlands of the middle latitudes. The climate of the region is sharply continental, but local contrasts in precipitation and temperatures are due to the great elevation of the Tien Shan and its complex relief. The piedmont plain and the foothills of the system have typically the same desert climate as the adjoining lowlands.

Westerly Atlantic air masses carry the greater part of the precipitation received by the Tien Shan system, discharging it mainly on the west-facing slopes at middle and high altitudes. Annual precipitation on these slopes reaches more than 30 in. (762 mm.) On east-facing slopes and in intermontane basins, annual precipitation is only about 10 in. (254 mm.). Precipitation reaches a maximum in the summer. In keeping with heavier precipitation on the western slopes, these slopes and westward-facing valleys have a heavier snow cover in winter, reaching almost 10 ft. (3 m.). The east-facing slopes and intermontane valleys have virtually no snow in winter. In general the snow line is much higher in the Tien Shan than it is in the European Alps or the western Caucasus. Even some passes of 13,000 ft. or more are known to be snow-free in summer. Average temperatures vary with elevation. In the valleys and on low-elevation slopes the July average is 21°–24° C (70°–75° F), on medium-elevation slopes 13°–16° (55°–60°) and on the mountain peaks near freezing. The large lake basin of the Issyk-Kul' exerts a moderating influence on temperatures of nearby areas.

**Glaciation.**—The general trend of the mountain ranges of the Tien Shan is east-west, although some short ranges are also oriented north-south. Characteristic features of the Tien Shan are the so-called mountain knots from which short ranges fan out in several directions. Relatively humid air coming from the west condenses on the west-facing slopes of the north-south ranges and the mountain knots, giving rise to valley glaciers. The principal glaciation centres are therefore the Khan-Tengri and Pobeda knot and the short north-south range of Akshiyrak. In the larger mountain knots, glaciers cover a total area of 10,000 sq.mi. The largest ones are the southern Inylchek glacier (35 mi. long), on the southern side of the Khan-Tengri; the northern Inylchek glacier (22 mi. long) on the northern side; and the 13-mi.-long Semenov glacier descending from Semenov Peak (19,081 ft.), northwest of Khan-Tengri.

The Petrov glacier, on the west slopes of the Akshiyrak Range, is 11 mi. long. In addition to the valley glaciers, glaciation is also in evidence on some of the flat-topped summits of the western Tien Shan, where peculiar ice shields are formed on the summits.

**Hydrography.**—The Tien Shan is mainly a region of interior drainage, whose rivers flow either into the desert lakes of central Asia or into mountain lakes without outlet to the sea. Most of the western Tien Shan is drained by the Syr-Dar'ya (*q.v.*), one of the great streams of central Asia, which flows to the Aral Sea. The principal rivers on the northern side of the Tien Shan are the Chu, which disappears in the desert west of Balkhash Lake, and the Ili (*q.v.*), which flows to that lake. On the southeastern side of the Tien Shan, the drainage pattern is dominated by the Tarim (*q.v.*), which also disappears in the desert sands near Lop Nor (*q.v.*) Lake. The river valleys of the Tien Shan tend to be broad except when they cut through transverse ranges. Rising generally at high elevations, the rivers of the Tien Shan are fed by glaciers and reach their high water stage in the summer, when they are most useful for the irrigation of crop lands in the piedmont plains. Some of the smaller rivers rising at lower elevations are fed by ground water, snow and rain. Several of the rivers are used to generate hydroelectric power, notably the Chirchik, a tributary of the Syr-Dar'ya; the Syr-Dar'ya itself; and the Chu river. The Issyk-Kul', largest of the mountain lakes in the Tien Shan, occupies a broad tectonic depression.

**Vegetation.**—The vegetation of the Tien Shan follows a vertical zonation. The lower foothills are covered with desert vegetation, which dries up about mid-May. Irrigated cotton and fruit trees dominate among the cultivated crops. At somewhat higher elevation, above 1,200 ft., an increase in precipitation assures a semidesert vegetation, such as wheat grass, which lasts until the end of June and can be used as spring and summer pastures.

Above the semidesert belt of the foothills lies the dry mountain steppe of feather grass and fescue, which serves as summer and fall pasture and for the cultivation of dry grains. At an elevation of 4,000 ft. begins the grassy steppe with bushes and patches of deciduous trees (walnut, apple, maple). This is a main area of unirrigated agriculture, used for hay and grains. The next higher zone of subalpine meadows also contains coniferous forests of spruce and fir as well as juniper groves. These meadows, which reach up to the snow line, are the principal summer pastures of the Tien Shan region.

**Minerals.**—Outflows associated with Hercynian magmatism have produced some highly mineralized areas in the Tien Shan, notably in nonferrous and rare metals. Among the most important Soviet mineral sites are the copper and lead-zinc ores of Almalyk of the Uzbek Soviet Socialist Republic, the antimony and mercury mines of Khaydarken in Kirgiz S.S.R. and the tungsten site of Chorukh-Dayron in the Tadzhik S.S.R. Jurassic coal of low caloric value is mined at Angren (Uzbek S.S.R.) and on the periphery of the Fergana valley at Kyzylkiya, Tashkumyr, Kok-Yangak, and Sulyukta. The accumulation of sediments in the Fergana valley has also produced deposits of petroleum, natural gas, sulfur and ozocerite. Geologic exploration is still in its infancy in the Chinese portion of the Tien Shan, but oil fields are already in operation at Tushantze and Karamai in the northern foothills and several sites of nonferrous and rare metals are known.

**Settlement and Transportation.**—The heaviest population concentrations in the Tien Shan are found in the Tashkent (*q.v.*) oasis, the Fergana valley and the Chu valley of the Soviet Union, and in oases at the north foot (Urumchi) and south foot (Kashgar, Aqsu) of the eastern Tien Shan in China's Sinkiang (*q.v.*). The lower valleys and foothills of the Tien Shan, where irrigated agriculture (mainly cotton) is practised, were invaded by indigenous central Asian cultivators, such as the Uzbeks in the Tashkent and Fergana areas of the Soviet Union and the Uighurs in the oases at the southern foot of the mountain system in China. Among the pastoral peoples of the mountains are the Kirgiz in the western T'ien Shan and the Kazakhs and Mongols in the eastern Tien Shan.

The population centres of the Soviet portion of the Tien Shan are reached by branches of the Soviet rail system, extending from Tashkent into the Fergana valley and through Frunze (*q.v.*) into the Chu valley and to Rybachye on the Issyk-Kul'. A central Asian railroad linking China and the Soviet Union, completed in 1960, runs along the northern foot of the eastern Tien Shan and through the Dzungarian Gate, a natural passage way at the eastern end of the Dzhungarskiy Alatau. The higher valleys of the Tien Shan are served by roads, many of which can be used by motor vehicles. (T. Sd.)

**TIENTSIN** (T'ien-ching), an industrial and commercial city in the province of Hopeh, China, 70 mi. (113 km.) SE of Peking. Pop. (1957 est.) 3,220,000. The city is situated at the confluence of several streams on the lower coastal plain, 32 mi. (51 km.) by river from the Yellow Sea. Until 1782 the place was only a garrison town, but it became a treaty port in 1860, and began to grow rapidly. A foreign settlement was located downstream on the right bank of the Hai Ho. After the Boxer uprising (1900) the walls were razed, and the city was rebuilt on occidental lines. Originally covering only a small area, the former foreign concessions were integrated and the limits have since expanded steadily. The port area of Ta-ku and T'ang-ku was included within the city limits in 1949, and the area along the Hai Ho was annexed in 1953 to make the total area of the city 888 sq.mi. Until 1958 Tientsin was an independent municipality administered directly by the government in Peking; at that time it became a part of the province of Hopeh and also the provincial capital.

Subject to flooding by the six small rivers coming together just west of the city, the main river below the city has long been shallow and subject to silting. The Communists have maintained the earlier pattern of dredging the river, and have built a bypass flood canal around the city on the south side to relieve flood pressures. Though dredging can keep the river navigable for small ships, a new artificial port, Sinkang, able to take 10,000-ton ships at all times, was created at T'ang-ku. This is kept open for about two months during winter by icebreakers.

Tientsin is a leading seaport of China and a rail, an air traffic, and a regional trade centre. Its industrial beginnings predate 1900, but it remained for some decades a centre of such light manufacturing as matches, bicycles, cotton and wool textiles, grain milling, tobacco manufacturing, and simple chemicals. Gradually its variety of industry broadened as assembly operations, heavy machinery, iron and steel and the fuller range of chemical manufactures were added. Under the Communists its importance increased as heavy manufacturing industries were located in newer industrial areas toward the coast. In the mid-1950s marked expansion took place in iron and steel, and in heavy manufacturing. By the 1960s Tientsin was the leading chemical manufacturing centre of China, and had become the third ranking industrial region, behind only Shanghai and the central Liaoning province region of southern Manchuria. It is the seat of Nankai University. (J. E. Sr.)

**TIEPOLO,** the name of a family of Venetian painters comprising Giovanni Battista, by far the most important, and his two sons Giovanni Domenico and Lorenzo.

Giovanni Battista Tiepolo (1696–1770), the greatest Venetian painter of the 18th century, was born on March 5, 1696, in Venice, the son of a merchant. He first studied painting under Gregorio Lazzarini, but quickly came under the influence of F. Bencovich and G. B. Piazzetta. His earliest known work, "The Sacrifice of Isaac" in the church of the Ospedaletto, Venice (1715–16), is sombre and still in the manner of Piazzetta. In 1717 his name first appears on the lists of the guild of Venetian painters, and for the next few years he concentrated chiefly on small easel paintings of classical and biblical subjects.

Throughout his life Veronese's was the pervasive influence on Tiepolo's art. The return of G. A. Pellegrini to Venice in 1721 was also crucial for Tiepolo's development, for his work inspired Giambattista to adopt a lighter and gayer palette. These two factors are apparent in his decorations for the Sandi and Dolfin palaces in Venice (both *c.* 1725, the latter now dispersed) and in those for the archiepiscopal palace and the cathedral at Udine (1726–27). In 1731 he was called to Milan to decorate the Archinti and Dugnani palaces (destroyed and damaged, respectively, in 1943). In 1732–33 he frescoed the upper parts of the Colleoni chapel, Bergamo. By now he was widely recognized as the leading decorator in Italy. The Swedish envoy Tessin happily characterized Tiepolo's work as "full of spirit . . . of an infinite fire, brilliant colouring and an astonishing speed." Notable among his frescoes in the next 15 years were the ceilings in the Gesuati church, Venice (1737), the Palazzo Clerici, Milan (1740, destroyed 1943), the Scuola dei Carmini, Venice (1740–43), the Villa Cordellina, Montecchio Maggiore (1743), the church of the Scalzi, Venice (1743–44, destroyed 1915), the decorations of the Palazzo Barbarigo, Venice (1744–45, dispersed) and, probably about 1750, his most admired work in Venice, the scenes from the life of Cleopatra in the great saloon of the Palazzo Labia. He was also producing such masterpieces of oil painting as the huge "Road to Calvary" and its companion paintings the "Flagellation" and the "Crowning With Thorns" for S. Alvise as well as secular and religious paintings for patrons at home and abroad.

BY COURTESY OF THE METROPOLITAN MUSEUM OF ART, ROGERS FUND, 1937

SKETCH FOR ALTARPIECE "INTERCESSION OF ST. THECLA" BY TIEPOLO. IN THE METROPOLITAN MUSEUM OF ART, NEW YORK CITY

In 1750 he was commissioned by the prince-bishop of Würzburg, Ger., to decorate the ceilings of the Kaisersaal and staircase of the new palace with historical and allegorical subjects. These huge frescoes, perhaps his greatest achievements, were completed in 1753. On his return to Venice, his outstanding decorations were the Villa Panigai, Nervesa della Battaglia (1754, now in Berlin), the ceiling of the church of the Pietà, Venice (1754–55), the Villa Contarini, Mira (1756, now in Paris), the Villa Valmarana, Vicenza (1757), the Palazzo Rezzonico, Venice (1758), the Palazzo Canossa, Verona (1761, destroyed 1944) and the Villa Pisani at Strà (1761–62). The huge altarpiece of the "Intercession of St. Thecla" at Este, his most moving religious work, was completed in 1759. In 1761 he was invited to Spain by Charles III and in 1762, accompanied by his sons, he arrived in Madrid where he decorated three rooms in the royal palace (1762–67). He also executed seven altarpieces for S. Pasquale at Aranjuez (1767–69) and began the decoration of the vault of the apse of S. Ildefonso shortly before his death in Madrid on March 27, 1770.

Tiepolo's work is characterized by his skilled draftsmanship, the high key of his multicoloured palette, his mastery of composition and the extraordinary fertility of his imagination. Besides decorations and altarpieces he painted one or two portraits and a number of *Teste di Fantasia* ("imaginary heads") in the manner of Rembrandt. He produced vast numbers of sketches and finished drawings for collectors, to whom he also supplied numerous freely painted oil sketches—often reductions from larger works. Between about 1740 and 1760 he etched plates distinguished for their imaginative force and brilliance.

In order to achieve his enormous output Tiepolo employed assistants, among whom were Mengozzi-Colonna (for architecture) and his two sons, GIOVANNI DOMENICO TIEPOLO (1727–1804) and LORENZO TIEPOLO (1736–1776). Giandomenico, born in Venice on Aug. 30, 1727, was completely overshadowed by his father as a religious and decorative painter, but he had a real talent for genre painting, especially of scenes from contemporary life and of the popular theatre, such as the decorations of his own villa at Zianigo (1791–93), now in the Civico Museo Correr, Venice.

Notable among his early works are the "Stations of the Cross" for S. Polo, Venice (1747–49), and the *chinoiserie* decorations of the guest wing of the Villa Valmarana (1757). After his father's death Giandomenico returned to Venice where he executed a number of frescoes and easel paintings, especially of scenes from the *commedia dell'arte*. He, too, produced large numbers of drawings for collectors, besides nearly 200 etchings after his own and his father's designs. He died in Venice on March 3, 1804. Lorenzo, born in Venice on Aug. 8, 1736, seems to have specialized chiefly in genre scenes in pastel. He died in Madrid on Aug. 8, 1776.

*See* also references under "Tiepolo, Giovanni Battista" in the Index.

BIBLIOGRAPHY.—P. Molmenti, *G. B. Tiepolo* (1909); E. Sack, *Giambattista und Domenico Tiepolo* (1910); *Catalogo della Mostra del Tiepolo* (1951); R. Palluchini, *Pittura Veneziana del Settecento*, 2 pt. (1951); A. Morassi, *G. B. Tiepolo, His Life and Work*, Eng. trans. by P. Murray and wife (1955); M. von Freeden and C. Lamb, *Das Meisterwerk des Giovanni Battista Tiepolo* (1956). (F. J. B. W.)

**TIERRA DEL FUEGO,** an archipelago lying between 52° 27′ and 55° 59′ S lat. and 63° 43′ and 74° 44′ W long. at the southern extremity of South America, and separated from the mainland by the Strait of Magellan. In shape the main island is a triangle with its base on Beagle Channel. The total area is 28,434 sq.mi. (73,643 sq.km.), about two-thirds of which is Chilean and one-third Argentine. The boundary agreed upon in 1881 follows the meridian of 68° 36′ 38″ W from Cape Espíritu Santo on the Atlantic, and the west-east Beagle Channel. Lennox, Nueva, Picton, and several small islands at the mouth of the channel are disputed between the two republics. The western and southern, Chilean, part is known as the Tierra del Fuego department of Magallanes province, pop. (1960) 6,100; the eastern, Argentine, side is the territory of Tierra del Fuego, pop. (1960) 7,955.

**Physical Features.**—The greater part of the main island north of the Almirantazgo Sound-Lake Fagnano depression consists of Tertiary sediments and volcanic material, overlain north of the Inútil-San Sebastián bays depression by glacial material deposited during the Pleistocene ice age. The distribution of land and water and the major relief features in this area are the result of the location of great glacial lakes, the excavation of their overflow channels, and the dumping of great moraines. The Altos del Boquerón, north of Inútil (Useless) Bay, is one such undulating morainic plateau from which drain all the rivers of north Tierra del Fuego. Most of the northern area is, therefore, under 600 ft. (180 m.) in height and the Atlantic and Magellan strait coasts are low-lying.

The southern and western parts of the main island and the archipelago are a great contrast. Cretaceous foothills pass into the southern prolongations of the Andes with crystalline rocks, peaks exceeding 7,000 ft. and mountain glaciers. Mt. Sarmiento (7,333 ft. [2,235 m.]) and Mt. Darwin (7,005 ft. [2,135 m.]) are the highest summits. The western half of the Strait of Magellan, therefore, is bordered by the precipitous cliffs, rugged coasts and fjords of Desolación, Santa Inés, Clarence, Aracena and Dawson islands. South of the Beagle Channel a similar group of islands, of which Hoste and Navarino are the largest, spread into the waters of Drake Strait and terminate in the headland of Cape Horn, generally regarded as the southernmost point of South America, although the Diego Ramírez group lies 60 mi. to the southwest.

**Climate.**—The climate of Tierra del Fuego is monotonously cool in summer and cold in winter, although average temperatures even in July do not fall below freezing point, and average summer temperatures are below 11° C. (52° F.). Temperature ranges are least in the exposed windy southwestern areas. Rainfall contrasts between western and eastern areas are remarkable. At Bahía Félix on Desolación Island there is an average annual precipitation of 200 in. (5,080 mm.), while at Río Grande in Argentine Tierra del Fuego only one-tenth as much rain falls. The Beagle Channel areas have usually less than 30 in. (762 mm.). Three days out of four are wet in the west; one in four in the east.

**Vegetation.**—In the exposed, precipitous, southern and western areas vegetation is limited to mosses and stunted trees, but where terrain permits, evergreen beech clothes the islands, deteriorating upward into bushes, bare rock and ice and snow. The central part of the main island from the Atlantic to Inútil Bay has deciduous beech forests, and the northern plains have a tussock grass cover.

E. AUBERT DE LA RÜE

AUSTRAL RAIN FOREST OF BEECHLIKE TREES WITH YELLOW HANGING LICHENS ON NAVARINO ISLAND, TIERRA DEL FUEGO

**History and Exploration.**—Tierra del Fuego was discovered by Ferdinand Magellan in 1520 when he sailed through the strait named after him and called this region "land of fire." In 1578 Sir Francis Drake traversed the region. In 1616 Cape Hoorn (anglicized into Horn) was named by the Dutch navigators Jacques le Maire and Willem Schouten. In 1619 the brothers García and Gonzalo de Nodal first circumnavigated the archipelago. No systematic exploration was attempted until the British admiralty undertook a thorough survey of the whole group by Phillip Parker King and Robert Fitzroy during the decade 1826–36. They were accompanied on the voyage of the *Beagle* by Charles Darwin, then a young man. The present place names of the region are due in large measure to these surveys; although Chilean naval exploration and aerial mapping have filled in much detail, most hydrographic charts are based on King and Fitzroy's original work.

For 350 years after Magellan's voyage the region was left in the undisputed occupation of its indigenous peoples, but in the 1880s two events led to its colonization by European immigrants

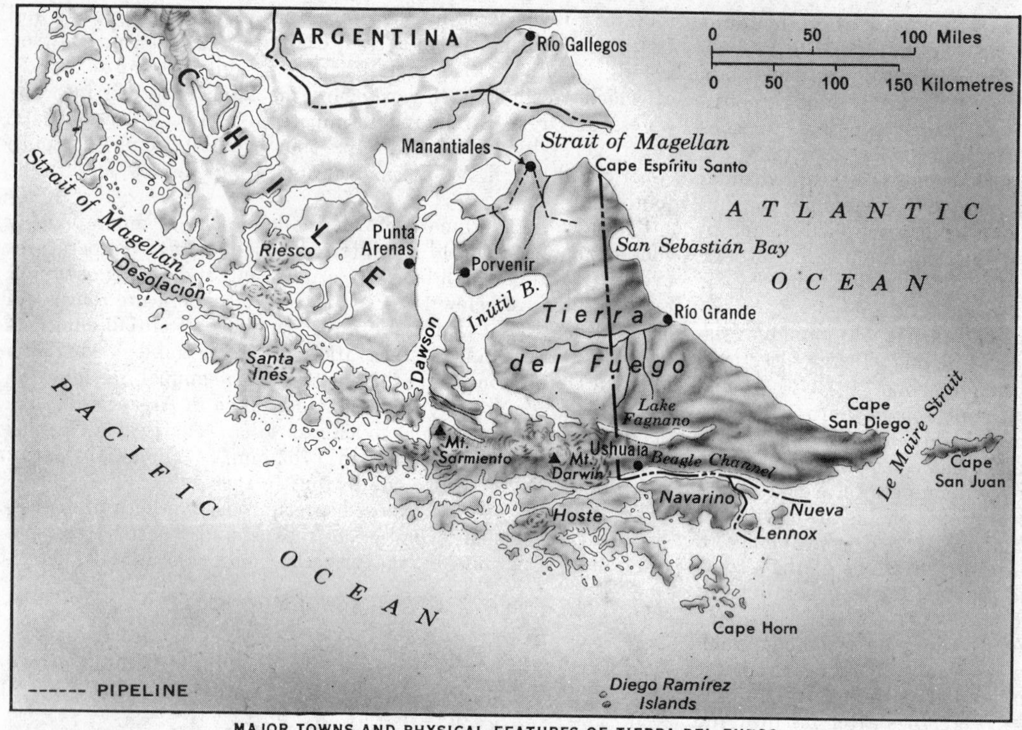


MAJOR TOWNS AND PHYSICAL FEATURES OF TIERRA DEL FUEGO

and Chilean and Argentine nationals. These were the introduction of sheep farming, which in 20 years spread from Gente Grande Bay to occupy all the grassland areas, and the discovery of gold along the eastern and southeastern coasts and on the beaches of the islands south of Beagle Channel. In the 1890s the gold rush spread to the northern rivers of the main island. The political result of this colonization was the partitioning of the island between Chile and Argentina, Porvenir on the Strait of Magellan becoming the main Chilean town and Ushuaia on Beagle Channel the Argentine capital. The Ushuaia area together with Dawson Island, Río Grande and Lake Fagnano became the main scene of missionary activity among the Indian peoples. Both Chilean and Argentine areas were at first territories administered by the central governments but the Chilean area was raised to provincial status in 1929.

**The People.**—Ona Indians occupied the pampa and deciduous forest belt of the north of the main island and were hunters of the guanaco and tucu-tucu (similar to a cavy). Yahgan Indians lived in the Fuegian archipelago, especially on Beagle Channel, anchoring their canoes in the dense masses of kelp in those waters and gaining their livelihood from shellfish, seals, and otters. Small groups of Alacalufs penetrated the northwestern channels from the fjords of western Magallanes. Few of these indigenous people now survive, as European settlement of their lands and the ravages of disease spelled their doom.

The present inhabitants of Tierra del Fuego are the immigrants and their descendants who were attracted by the pastoral industry, the gold rush, the discovery of oil, and the general economic expansion of the region. In addition to Chileans and Argentinians, a great variety of European nationalities are represented. Yugoslavs are the predominant element derived from the gold-rush days, with Spaniards, British, and Italians forming smaller minorities. Ushuaia still retains a penal settlement, and a colony of Italians was established nearby in 1948. Most of Tierra del Fuego's people live on the main island, but a subsidiary concentration engages in sheep farming on Navarino Island.

**The Economy.**—Pastoralism and petroleum exploitation dominate the region's occupational and commercial life. Enormous sheep farms were established in the favourable northern areas, one of which still exceeds 1,000,000 ac. (404,700 ha.) in extent, while another carries 185,000 sheep. On the expiry of some of the leases in 1938 and 1957, subdivision of the farms was undertaken to increase the density of settlement. The discovery of petroleum at Manantiales in 1945 converted the northern part of Chilean Tierra del Fuego into that republic's only oil field; pipelines were laid to the Strait of Magellan for export of the petroleum to central Chile. A small refining plant on the oil field produces the needs of Magallanes province. There is also some lumbering in the forested areas of Beagle Channel and the Strait of Magellan, fish and crayfish canning at Ushuaia and Porvenir, and fur hunting for nutria and seal. A meat refrigerating plant is located at Río Grande but most surplus sheep are processed on the mainland.

Roads are poor, and there are no railways. However, air services link Punta Arenas and Río Gallegos with the principal settlements in the Chilean and Argentine areas, respectively. Sea communications are also important; a regular service plies between Porvenir and Punta Arenas, and naval vessels supply Navarino and Ushuaia.

*See* also references under "Tierra del Fuego" in the Index.

BIBLIOGRAPHY.—J. Weddell, *A Voyage Towards the South Pole and to Tierra del Fuego* (1825); C. Darwin, *Journal of Researches, etc. During the Voyage of the "Beagle"* (1845); W. P. Snow, *A Two Years' Cruise off Tierra del Fuego* (1857); R. Crawshay, *The Birds of Tierra del Fuego* (1907); R. Kent, *Voyaging Southward From the Strait of Magellan* (1924); L. Nitsche, "Estudios antropológicos sobre las Onas," *Anales del Museo de la Plata*, vol. ii (1927); A. M. De Agostini, *Mis viajes a la Tierra del Fuego* (1929); M. Gusinde, *Die Feuerland-Indianer*, 3 vol. (1931–39); A. Braun, *Pequeña historia fuegina* (1939); E. L. Bridges, *Uttermost Part of the Earth* (1948); A. Lipschutz, "Results of a Recent Expedition to Tierra del Fuego," *Man* (1948); C. R. Thomas, "Geology and Petroleum Exploration in Magallanes Province," *Bull. Amer. Ass. Petrol. Geol.*, vol. xxxiii (1949); G. J. Butland, *The Human Geography of Southern Chile* (1958). (G. J. B.)

**TIFFANY, CHARLES LEWIS** (1812–1902), U.S. jeweler who made a specialty of importing historic gems, jewelry and art works, was born in Killingly, Conn., on Feb. 15, 1812. He moved to New York city in 1837, and with John B. Young opened a fancy goods store. It became Tiffany, Young and Ellis in 1841 and, after branching out into jewelry manufacture, was reorganized as Tiffany & Co. in 1853. Tiffany adopted the standards of English silver in 1851, thereby establishing the term "sterling" in the U.S. and affirming the high prestige of his firm.

In 1858 Tiffany obtained a surplus section of the newly laid Atlantic cable, which he cut into pieces and sold as souvenirs with great success. At the beginning of the Civil War he turned most of his capital to the manufacture of swords, medals and other war material. In 1868 the company was incorporated and branches were established at London and Geneva. In 1887 he bought some of the crown jewels of France. He was made a chevalier of the Legion of Honour in 1878. He died in New York city on Feb. 18, 1902. He was the father of Louis Comfort Tiffany (*q.v.*).

*See* F. Heydt, *Charles L. Tiffany* (1893).

**TIFFANY, LOUIS COMFORT** (1848–1933), U.S. painter, craftsman and decorator, who is considered one of the leading original U.S. designers, was born in New York city on Feb. 18, 1848, the son of Charles L. Tiffany (*q.v.*). He became internationally famous for the inimitable glass which he named favrile, a neologism from the Latin *faber*. Tiffany began experimenting with glass in 1875 and could produce it reliably by the 1890s, when examples were donated to the Smithsonian institution and the Metropolitan Museum of Art; he won a grand prize at the 1900

Paris exhibition. Favrile glass, iridescent and freely shaped, was sometimes combined with bronzelike alloys and other metals; it enjoyed widespread popularity from 1890 to 1915, and again in the 1950s. Trained as a painter of narrative subjects in Paris, Tiffany visited Morocco; eastern and Amerindian influences mark his work. Returning to the U.S., Tiffany became a recognized painter. He established a decorating firm later known as Tiffany Studios, which served wealthy New Yorkers, redecorated the reception rooms at the White House, Washington, D.C., and was most active in church interiors. Stained-glass windows were its specialty, best known being the huge glass curtain (1911) at the Palacio de Bellas Artes in Mexico City. Tiffany, a director of his father's firm, established the Louis Comfort Tiffany foundation for young artists at his luxurious and celebrated Long Island estate (sold in 1946 to provide scholarship funds). He died, Jan. 17, 1933.

*See* R. Koch, *Louis Comfort Tiffany, 1848–1933* (1958). (Er. K.)

**TIFLIS:** *see* TBILISI.

**TIGELLINUS, OFONIUS** (d. A.D. 69), a Sicilian, who, despite his provincial origin, became one of the chief ministers of the emperor Nero. After being prefect of the *vigiles* (the fire brigade), he became prefect of the praetorian guard on the death of Burrus (*q.v.*) in 62. Burrus had been sole prefect; Tigellinus shared the office first with Faenius Rufus, who perished for conspiracy in 65, and then with Nymphidius Sabinus. The ancient sources aver that he owed his rise to power to sharing and abetting Nero's vicious pleasures. He took a leading part in the reign of terror that began in 65, but when revolt broke out in 68, he let himself easily be deposed by his colleague, Nymphidius, and did nothing to assist Nero. In 69 the emperor Otho decided to put him to death. He received the order "amid debaucheries and the kisses of his concubines, and after disgusting delays cut his throat with a razor, disgracing his life even in his death, which came too late and dishonourably" (Tacitus, *Histories,* i, 72).

*See* A. Stein, in Pauly-Wissowa, *Real-Encyclopädie der classischen Altertumswissenschaft,* xvii, 2056–61 (1937). (P. A. Br.)

**TIGER** (*Panthera tigris*), a striped carnivore, the largest of the cat family (Felidae), rivaled only by the lion in strength and ferocity, the difference between them lying mainly in their external appearance. The tiger is confined to Asia, and is widespread south of a line drawn northeastward from the Euphrates, passing the southern shores of the Caspian Sea, the Aral Sea, and Lake Baikal, to the Sea of Okhotsk. It ranges as far south as the islands of Sumatra, Java, and Bali. It is absent, however, from the Tibetan plateau and from the remainder of the Indo-Malay archipelago.

The tiger's characteristic stripes and ground colour vary in distinctness and brightness according to the locality and subspecies. The tigers of Bengal and the islands of southeast Asia, for example, have a ground colour of bright, reddish fawn on the upper and outer parts of the head, body, limbs, and tail; these parts are beautifully marked with dark, almost black, transverse stripes; while the under parts, the inside of the limbs, the cheeks, and a large spot over each eye are nearly white. The tigers of northern China and the U.S.S.R., however, have longer, softer, and lighter-coloured fur. Rarely, there is a black and white colour scheme. A male may weigh more than 500 lb. (227 kg.), reach a height at the shoulders of 5 ft. (1.5 m.), and a length of 14 ft. (4.3 m.). The tiger has no mane, but in old males the hair on the cheeks is rather long and spreading.

W. SUSCHITZKY

TIGER (PANTHERA TIGRIS), NATIVE OF ASIA

The diet of tigers consists of any animals of the locality; in India, for example, deer, wild hog, and peafowl are common prey. Cattle may sometimes be taken from human habitations. Old or disabled tigers may find human beings an easier prey, and turn "man-eater." Healthy large mammals are generally avoided—the tiger is no match for a water buffalo or an elephant. A pack of wild dogs or dholes can worry a tiger to death. Tigers inhabit grassy and swampy districts and forests; they also haunt ruined buildings. Under stress of fear, they may climb trees. They are good swimmers.

The cubs are born in litters of two to six, three being commonly found; they remain with the mother until they are able to kill prey for themselves, about the second year, when nearly full-grown. In warm regions litters may be produced at any time of the year; in cold districts they are born in spring. Average life span for the tiger is 11 years, but some live to almost twice that age.

Under certain conditions, as in enforced confinement in zoos, tigers occasionally hybridize with lions; the offspring of such matings are called "tigons" when the father is a tiger or "ligers" when the father is a lion.

*See* also CAT; CARNIVORE.

*See* Richard Perry, *The World of the Tiger* (1965).

**TIGERFLOWER,** botanically *Tigridia,* a genus of tender herbaceous bulbous plants of the iris family (Iridaceae), natives of Mexico, Central America, Peru, and Chile. They have long narrow leaves springing from the bulb and a stem bearing two or three scattered smaller leaves and above a few flowers emerging from a leaflike spathe. The striking flowers are spotted (whence the name tigerflower, flower of Tigris, or tiger iris) and have free segments springing from a tube; the three large broad outer segments are concavely spreading, the three inner are much smaller and more erect. *T. pavonia,* with large red flowers spotted with yellow and purple, and its many colourful variants are cultivated in gardens.

J. HORACE MCFARLAND CO.

TIGERFLOWER (TIGRIDIA PAVONIA)

**TIGLATH-PILESER** (Akkadian TUKULTI-APAL-ESHARRA) was the name of three Assyrian kings.

TIGLATH-PILESER I (reigned 1116–1076 B.C.) ascended the throne at the time when a horde known as the Mushki (Meshech of the Old Testament) was thrusting into Asia Minor, constituting a serious threat to civilization, as this region was the principal source of iron, then coming into general use. Tiglath-pileser defeated 20,000 Mushki in the Assyrian province of Kummukh (Commagene) and later extended Assyrian control farther into Asia Minor than any of his predecessors had done. He subdued the nomads along the routes to the Mediterranean and reached the Syrian coast, where the Phoenician trading cities paid tribute. Egypt, closely linked by trade with the Syrian coast, made overtures of friendship.

TIGLATH-PILESER II (964–933 B.C.) reigned at a time of which little more is known than that Assyria was beginning to emerge from its collapse of a century before.

TIGLATH-PILESER III (745–727 B.C.) was a great soldier and administrator. Probably a usurper, his original personal name was Pul(u), by which he was still known in Babylonia and in the Old Testament (II Kings 15:19; I Chron. 5:26). At his accession Assyria was in a difficult military and economic plight, and the rapid amelioration of the situation was due largely to Tiglath-pileser's reorganization of the provincial administration.

The following is a probable reconstruction of the events of Tiglath-pileser's reign. His first military activity (745 B.C.) was successfully directed against the Aramaean and Chaldean tribesmen who had brought chaos to Babylonia. In the following year he attacked the lands on the eastern borders of Assyria, creating a new province and securing from the Medes farther east nominal recognition of his suzerainty. With his eastern borders thus secured against Urartu (Armenia), Tiglath-pileser turned to the west to counter Urartian intrigues among the vassal states of Syria. After the defeat of Urartian forces in Kummukh, most Syrian cities formally submitted, though Arpad withstood siege for three years. Tiglath-pileser then (740 B.C.) undertook a campaign to annex Ullubu, the mountainous country north of Assyria.

In 734 B.C. Tiglath-pileser crushed a rebellion in the west which began in the Philistine cities and spread to involve Israel and Damascus; Judah remained loyal to Assyria (II Kings 16:7). In the same year a Chaldean chieftain, Ukin-zer, seized the throne of Babylonia. After a reign of three years he was driven from Babylon by the Assyrian army, which took his tribal capital, Sapia. For the final two years of his reign Tiglath-pileser was king of Babylon in name as well as in fact.

*See* also BABYLONIA AND ASSYRIA: *History;* and references under "Tiglath-pileser" in the Index.

BIBLIOGRAPHY.—For Tiglath-pileser I *see* E. A. W. Budge and L. W. King (eds.), *Annals of the Kings of Assyria* (1902). For Tiglath-pileser III *see* P. Rost (ed.), *Die Keilschrifttexte Tiglat-Pilesers III* (1893); *Cambridge Ancient History,* vol. iii (1925); H. W. F. Saggs, "The Nimrud Letters, 1952—Part I: The Ukin-zer Rebellion," *Iraq,* vol. xvii (1955). (H. W. F. S.)

**TIGRANES** (DIKRAN), the name of several rulers of Armenia, especially Tigranes the Great (*c.* 140–*c.* 55 B.C.), king from 95 or 94. He was the son or nephew of Artavasdes II and a member of the dynasty founded in the early 2nd century by Artaxias. He was given to Mithradates II of Parthia as a hostage and purchased his freedom on Artavasdes' death by ceding 70 valleys bordering on Media.

Tigranes immediately began to enlarge his kingdom. To the west he deposed Artanes, king of Sophene, and annexed his kingdom (east of the upper Euphrates). He entered into alliance with Mithradates (*q.v.*) VI Eupator of Pontus, whose daughter Cleopatra he married. In 93 he invaded Cappadocia in the interest of Mithradates, expelling the pro-Roman king, Ariobarzanes I, but was driven back by Sulla in 92. Tigranes supported Mithradates during Mithradates' first war with the Romans, although he abstained from interfering openly. Meanwhile he began war with the Parthians, whose empire was weakened after the death of Mithradates II (about 87) by internal dissensions and invasions of the Scythians. Tigranes reconquered the valleys he had ceded and laid waste a great part of Media; the kings of Atropatene (Azerbaijan), Gordyene and Adiabene (both on the upper Tigris), and Osroene became his vassals. He also annexed northern Mesopotamia, and in the Caucasus the kings of Iberia and Albania were subject to him. In 83 he invaded Syria, where the Seleucid dynasty (*q.v.*) had dwindled to two or three warring pretenders; he defeated these and occupied most of Syria and Cilicia. His rule there was generally peaceful, though Cleopatra Selene, widow of the Seleucid Antiochus X, was still resisting him in 71. In 78–77 he occupied Cappadocia and expelled Ariobarzanes again. Tigranes took the title "king of kings" and built a new royal city, Tigranocerta, on the borders of Armenia and Mesopotamia (the actual site is disputed), where he accumulated all his wealth and to which he transplanted the inhabitants of 12 Greek towns of Cappadocia, Cilicia, and Syria. He also transplanted many Arab tribes into Mesopotamia.

In 72 the Romans drove Mithradates to flee to Armenia, and in 69 Lucullus invaded Armenia. Tigranes was beaten at Tigranocerta (which Lucullus later captured) on Oct. 6, 69, and again near Artaxata in September 68. The recall of Lucullus gave some respite to Mithradates and Tigranes, who even invaded Asia Minor again. But meanwhile a son of Tigranes and Cleopatra, also called Tigranes, rebelled against him; as the old man had already killed two of his sons, he had reason enough to be afraid for his life. The younger Tigranes found refuge with the Parthian king Phraates III, who sent him back with an army. The old king defeated his son (who fled to Pompey), but then put a price on the head of Mithradates, and when Pompey advanced into Armenia, Tigranes surrendered (66 B.C.). Pompey received him graciously and gave him back his kingdom (for a price), while he treated the son very coolly and soon made him prisoner. The younger Tigranes was led in triumph into Rome; he tried to escape from his confinement by the intrigues of Publius Clodius in 58 and may have been killed in the resulting brawl. The father ruled about ten years longer over Armenia, as a Roman client-king, though he lost all his conquests except Sophene and Gordyene. He died about 55 and was succeeded by his son Artavasdes III.

*See* R. Grousset, *Histoire de l'Arménie,* pp. 84–100 (1947).

**TIGRÉ,** a province of northern Ethiopia, bordering on Eritrea. Area 25,444 sq.mi. (65,900 sq.km.); pop. (1962 est.) 2,104,100. Its western half comprises high plateau country drained by the right-bank tributaries of the Takkaze River. Vegetation is sparse and cultivation (cereals, legumes) of the better soil areas and stock raising are characteristic occupations. Hides and skins are important export commodities. To the east is the Danakil Desert which includes the salt pan region of Kobar Sink, about 300 ft. (90 m.) below sea level. Makale, the provincial capital, is the centre of the salt trade based on these deposits. It is historically important as the seat of John IV who usurped the Ethiopian throne in 1872 (*see* ETHIOPIA: *History*). Tigré contains the historic sites of Aksum (*q.v.*) and Aduwa.

Tigrinya is widely spoken. The plateau is largely inhabited by the Tigré (a Semitic group). The Raya and Azebo peoples of the foothills between the plateau and the plain represent an extension of the Galla penetration from the south. The Danakil lowlands to the east are inhabited by Danakil (Afar) nomadic tribes. The Agao (Agaw), in the southwest, represent a survival of the original Hamitic migrations which preceded the founding of the Aksumite Kingdom. (G. C. L.)

**TIGRIS** (Arabic NAHR DIJLAH; Turkish DICLE NEHRİ; biblical HIDDEKIL), a river that originates as several conjoint streams in the tangled hill country of eastern Anatolia north of Diyarbakır, Turkey, being fed by springs and by melt from snow. It then flows generally southeastward for about 1,180 mi. (1,900 km.) toward the Persian Gulf, which it enters as a joint stream, the Shatt al Arab (*q.v.*), 111 mi. (179 km.) long, with the Euphrates. For 280 mi. (451 km.), as far as Mağara Harabesi (37°08′ N, 42°22′ E), it is a Turkish river (although before entering Iraq it forms a small 20-mile section of the Syrian border); then for most of its course it lies within Iraq, except for part of the eastern bank of the Shatt al Arab which forms the frontier with Iran for a distance of about 40 mi. from the mouth. The Tigris varies tremendously in width: at the Baghloja Defile 18 mi. below its point of entry into Iraq it is only 40 yd. (36.6 m.) across, and it is even narrower much farther downstream in the region of Al 'Uzayr between Al 'Amarah and Al Qurnah where there are deep gorges. On the other hand, in flatter territory, the Tigris can exceed half a mile in width, and in such areas during the flood season it becomes a vast sheet of water covering many square miles.

The Tigris in Turkey is a typical mountain stream, flowing swiftly in a narrow, well-defined valley often slotted deeply into the surface, with gorges and rapids marking its course. At its entry into Iraq, it begins to cut a somewhat zigzag tortuous course across the ridges and spurs that make up the outlines of the main Taurus and Kurdish mountain systems. There the river alternates between stretches of gorge with clifflike walls; and more open parts with expanses of sand and shingle. Below Mosul the hills continue for some distance, still defining the river valley but declining in height, and there is more open country. Last of these major ridges are the Jabal Khanuqah and Jabal Makhul which are westward extensions of the Jabal Hamrin, and the river breaks through there by the deep gorge of Al Fathah, now used as a crossing point for oil pipelines from Kirkuk to the Mediterranean.

South of Tikrit the valley walls recede, and the Tigris flows for the rest of its course over a wide, gently undulating plain with only a slight, almost imperceptible drop to sea level. Consequently, the river begins to meander extensively, with many loops, dead arms, and cutoffs. A number of former channels once used by the river but now abandoned are either dry or occupied by irrigation works, some of which are extremely ancient. One very extensive former channel may have carried the Tigris well to the east of its present location, as far as Ba'qubah. In order to prevent flooding and further shifting of the river, much embankment is necessary below Samarra'. This is one reason the riverine stretch between Samarra' and Baghdad is relatively empty of towns and large villages, despite the fertility of the area and its intensive use for agriculture. Settlements do occur on older channels or canals at some distance from the main river. Below Baghdad the river follows such an extraordinarily tortuous course that, though the distance by road from Baghdad to Al Kut (Kut al Imara) is about 105 mi. (169 km.), the distance by river is 213 mi. (343 km.) Between Al Kut and Al 'Amarah there are two major valleys that are old courses of the Tigris, the Shatt al Gharraf and the Shatt ad Dujaylah. There, the present channel of the Tigris has been used by the river only since the early 16th century. The topography is now extremely flat, with the river less tortuous but with braided distribution; *i.e.,* channels that disperse water on either side into marshland, or as free-flowing streams into other parts of the valley. On both sides of the river lie extensive marshes, fed by distributaries, which, together with irrigation canals, seepage, and evaporation, diminish the flow of the Tigris by more than 80% during its passage from Baghdad to Al Qurnah. The river consequently shrinks in width, with contractions above and below Al 'Uzayr; its velocity also declines, though the sharp bends and narrowness make navigation difficult. At Al Qurnah the Tigris is joined by the old Euphrates channel to form the Shatt al Arab. There, the Euphrates carries even less water than the Tigris and its flow is almost negligible at certain seasons.

**Tributaries.**—The Tigris is joined by several major affluents throughout its course. The Iraqi Nahr al Khabur (not to be confused with the Syrian Khabur which joins the Euphrates) enters the Tigris from the east, and its lower course forms the frontier between Iraq and Turkey. Though small in length and catchment area, this stream is rapid and carries much sediment eroded from the Kurdistan Hills. Two right-bank affluents, the Wadis Suwaydiyah and al Murr, enter some distance above Mosul, but the volume of water in both is much smaller.

About 30 mi. (48 km.) below Mosul the Tigris is joined by the Great Zab River (Nahr az Zab al Kabir), which drains a basin of about 7,700 sq.mi. (19,900 sq.km.) in Kurdistan. At low water (September–October), discharge of the Great Zab is 3,000 cu.ft. (84 cu.m.) per sec. and it can be forded; at high water (April–May) the discharge is 28,500 cu.ft. (807 cu.m.) per sec., which adds about 65% more to the Tigris flow. Sixty-five miles below this junction is the point of entry of the Little Zab (Nahr az Zab as Saghir), which drains a basin of 5,750 sq.mi. (14,890 sq.km.). With a minimum flow of 1,340 cu.ft. (38 cu.m.) per sec. in September and a maximum of 16,140 cu.ft. (457 cu.m.) per sec. in March, the Little Zab has an earlier flood because its waters are derived partly from snowfall on lower mountains that hence melts earlier. Above Baghdad the Tigris is joined by the Nahr al 'Uzaym (Shatt al Adhaim) which drains 2,350 sq.mi. (6,087 sq.km.). Because of the low altitude of this basin, melting snow plays little part in the stream flow, which is almost all derived from direct rainfall. In summer the Nahr al 'Uzaym may be almost dry. A more important tributary is the Nahr Diyala (Persian Rudkhaneh-ye Sirvan) which reaches the Tigris on the south side of Baghdad; in summer its flow is diverted for irrigation. Silt carried by the Diyala and deposited close to the Tigris is responsible for blocking many smaller streams and the development of marsh. Farther south, the tributaries are smaller and represent drainage from swamps rather than river flow. One partial exception is the tail of the Karun (*q.v.*), most of which disperses into the Hawr al Hawizah (Hawizah Swamp), with small outlets to the Tigris.

**Regime.**—At the Turkish frontier the Tigris lies at 1,160 ft. (354 m.) above sea level. As it flows south its altitude drops by a gradient of less than one foot per 1,000 as far as Mosul, and then by about 1:2,000 in the Samarra' region. Below Balad, which could be held to mark the start of real plain, the slope is 1:14,500 as far as Baghdad, and then 1:15,000 downstream as far as Al Kut. Below Al Kut, which is only 39.5 ft. above sea level, the slope is 1:29,000 or even 1:35,000 (about 2 in. per mi.).

At Mosul the average lowest height of the Tigris is 703 ft. (214 m.) above sea level, with a mean discharge of 5,300 cu.ft. (150 cu.m.) per sec. At high water (in April) average discharge is 48,750 cu.ft. (1,380 cu.m.) per sec., producing a rise of about 13 ft., though a rise of more than 16 ft. has been recorded. Comparable figures for Baghdad are: low water (October) 95 ft. (29 m.) above sea level and 11,900 cu.ft. (337 cu.m.) per sec., with a 17½-ft. rise and a discharge of 106,650 cu.ft. (3,020 cu.m.) at the high-water stage in April. Short peak floods of up to 22 ft. are known, and rises measured within 24 hours have been known to exceed 9 ft. At Al Kut the river is only about 40 ft. above sea level, but it normally rises by 16 ft. and may rise more than 20 ft. Of the total discharge at Baghdad, the Tigris itself contributes 45%, the Great Zab 26%, the Little Zab 13%, and the Nahr al 'Uzaym 4%. An additional 22% comes from springs and seepage, and from other water bodies, but there is also an evaporation loss of 6%. Flow is maintained more or less unaltered as far as Al 'Amarah, with evaporation losses balanced by seepage at low water from subsoil drainage. Below Al Kut, however, water is drawn off from the Tigris by natural distributaries and irrigation works, leaving only 19% of the original flow. The fact that the Euphrates lies slightly higher than the Tigris immediately north of Baghdad and lower in the south as far as Al 'Amarah has been used for centuries as a basis for irrigation, with water led by natural flow from one river to the other. Modern systems of irrigation have been developed on the Tigris at Al Kut, where a barrage 21,000 ft. (6,400 m.) in length was completed in 1943. This allows extensive cultivation in the Gharraf and Dujaylah areas, amounting to 750,000 and 230,000 ac. (303,500 and 93,080 ha.), respectively. A weir on the Diyala facilitates irrigation north and east of Baghdad, and construction of a dam on the headwaters of the same river at Darband-i Khan has further extended the irrigated area. Like the high dam built at Dokan on the Little Zab, this barrage stores water at other times than the flood season. Other works allow wider distribution of water; these include barrages at Al Musayyib 40 mi. (64 km.) S of Baghdad, at Butmah (Batma) on the Little Zab, and in the region of 'Uzaym between the Tigris and Little Zab in the Jabal Hamrin area. Other regulators have been projected for the Nahrawan district south of Baghdad, for the Al 'Amarah area, the Shatt al Gharraf, at Ishaqi south of Samarra', and around Irbil, Kirkuk, and Mosul.

The most important control achievement was the completion (1956) of major stages of the Wadi ath Tharthar project. This utilized a vast natural depression between the Tigris and Euphrates as a large reserve drainage basin, water being led in from the Tigris and then partly released at a later period. One considerable benefit achieved was the protection from annual flooding, especially around Baghdad. Seasonal inundation of enormous stretches of territory, together with the cyclical liability to unusually high water, had a restrictive effect on settlements and on lines of communications, which had to be given expensive protection or siting on mounds and levees. It is not always realized that the Tigris because of its spring flooding, when winter crops are well grown, is often a difficult river for agriculture; the Wadi ath Tharthar scheme has greatly improved the situation.

**Navigation and Ports.**—For many centuries the Tigris has been used for transport. The kelek, a raft made of inflated skins and reeds that can carry up to 50 tons, is used when traveling downstream. Small craft, mainly the *quffah* (coracle) and *safinah* (sailing boat), also ply mainly downstream, the latter sometimes transporting 100 tons. The Tigris is navigable by shallow-draft steamers upstream as far as Baghdad. River traffic, however, has tended to decline in recent years because of improved road transport, the completion of standard-gauge railway links north and south from Baghdad, and the fact that navigation is never easy due to the narrows, numerous bends, and shifting shoals and sandbanks.

Chief cities on the Iraqi portion of the Tigris are Baghdad

(*q.v.;* the capital), Basra (*q.v.;* the chief port), which is a conglomeration of several towns along the Shatt al Arab, and Mosul (*q.v.*). On the Shatt al Arab lie the Iranian towns of Abadan and Khorramshahr (*qq.v.*). The former is entirely an oil port concerned with refining and exporting oil and handling supplies for the oilfields; the latter is the principal general port for Iran, handling a large proportion of general Iranian exports and imports other than oil. All these riparian towns are now linked by rail, with the exception of Abadan. (W. B. Fr.)

**History.**—The name of the Tigris River first appears in its Sumerian form Idigna in the 3rd millennium B.C. In Babylonian and Assyrian it became Idiglat, and in old Persian, Tigra, from which was derived the Greek form Tigres used by Herodotus (*c.* 450 B.C.).

The Tigris was used by the Sumerians as a source of water for irrigation, and a canal, on the line of the present Shatt al Gharraf (or al Hai), was dug as early as 2400 B.C. to bring its waters to Lagash in eastern Sumer. About 1850 B.C. it was extended to Larsa on the Euphrates. No ancient cities have been discovered along the main course of the river, the Shatt al 'Amarah, either because its regime was less suitable for primitive irrigation or because the area was more open to attack from the east. There is consequently no evidence for minor variations in its position. The mouth of the Tigris has not, in historic times, lain appreciably to the north of the present gulf shoreline and only one major change in its course can be traced when, after the formation of the Great Swamp caused by catastrophic floods in the 6th and 7th centuries, the river deserted the Shatt al 'Amarah and flowed into the marshes by the Shatt al Gharraf. The Omayyad city of Wasit was founded astride the new channel in A.D. 703 and remained important until the 15th century, when the river gradually reverted to its former course. The river plain of the middle Tigris was intensively cultivated by irrigation from early times until about A.D. 900.

Most of the canals west of the river flowed from the Euphrates into the Tigris. On the east all canals, and probably many sites, earlier than the Hellenistic period are buried under a thick silt deposit, but at least as early as Sasanian times (about A.D. 250) the eastern plain was served by a great canal, the Nahr Nahrawan, which left the Tigris below Tikrit and rejoined it near Al Kut, receiving en route the waters of the al 'Uzaym and Diyala rivers. After the fall of the Achaemenid Empire (330 B.C.), this wealthy region became the political and commercial centre of Mesopotamia; Seleucia and Ctesiphon (*qq.v.*), respectively the royal cities of the Seleucid and of the Parthian and Sasanian dynasties, and Baghdad and Samarra', both Abbasid capitals, all lay on the Tigris. The Tigris floods, which occur annually from April to May, have often caused destructive inundations in the plain and threatened the safety of Baghdad, particularly since the breakdown of the irrigation systems in the 14th century A.D. This threat has been met by the Wadi ath Tharthar control project (see *Regime* above).

The rolling terrain north of Tikrit formed, from the early 2nd millennium to 612 B.C., the kingdom of Assyria, with its capitals at Ashur, Nimrud (Kalakh), and Nineveh (*qq.v.*) on the Tigris. There irrigation was confined to small areas near Kalakh and Nineveh. Water transport by rafts of a type still used dates back at least to Assyrian times, but the great military and commercial routes were usually in open country away from the river. Shalmaneser III (859–824 B.C.) set up his statue at the sources of the Tigris, but in general neither Assyrian annals nor the later accounts of Greek and Roman writers provide much precise information about the geography of the river valley. From A.D. 197 to 237 the Tigris north of Mosul formed the boundary between Roman Mesopotamia and Parthian Adiabene, and the fortress city of Amida (Diyarbakır) figures frequently in late Roman and medieval chronicles. Mosul, with its boat bridge, became a commercial centre in Abbasid times, and during the 12th and 13th centuries was a capital of the Seljuk Atabeg dynasty. The medieval post road from Baghdad followed the east bank of the Tigris, and many Arab geographers describe the settlements along its route.

European travelers occasionally voyaged on the Tigris after the 16th century. J. Newberie went by boat from Baghdad to Basra in 1581 and is the first to speak of the Shatt al 'Amarah as the navigable channel. In 1652 Jean Baptiste Tavernier traveled by raft from Mosul to Baghdad and then by boat to Basra. The first modern survey was undertaken by the Euphrates expedition under Francis Rawdon Chesney (*q.v.*) in 1836, supplemented by the work of Felix Jones in 1846 and 1848. A steamship service between Basra and Baghdad was inaugurated in 1861, and the river served as the main supply route for the British invasion of Iraq, 1914–18.

*See* also EUPHRATES; IRAQ; MESOPOTAMIA.

BIBLIOGRAPHY.—S. Lloyd, *Twin Rivers* (1947); G. Le Strange, *Lands of the Eastern Caliphate* (1905); S. H. Longrigg, *Four Centuries of Modern Iraq* (1925). (E. E. D. M. O.)

**TIKAMGARH,** a town in the Rewa division of Madhya Pradesh, India, and the headquarters of the district of the same name, lies about 50 mi. (80 km.) SSE of Jhansi. Pop. (1961) 20,469. Maharaja Vikramajit selected it as the new capital of Orchha State in 1783. Until 1887 the town was called Tehri. It has a fort and a lake, Bara Sagar, as well as a palace now used as a college.

TIKAMGARH DISTRICT has an area of 1,944 sq.mi. (5,035 sq.km.) and a population (1961) of 455,662. It occupies the central part of the Betwa-Dhasan Doab, presenting a rolling gneissic surface, with artificial lakes at Birsagar, Jatara, Ladhaura, and Baldeogarh. The principal crops are wheat, rice, jowar, and sesamum. There are no industries except handloom textiles. The district has old Jain temples at Papora and Ahaar and a Sun Temple at Marhkhera. (S. M. A.)

**TIKAR,** a group of West African Negro peoples. The Tikar tribe proper live in a vast plain along the Mbam River east of Foumban in the Republic of Cameroon. They numbered about 9,000 (1960s), 2,000 more living with the Bamum (*q.v.*). They farm, raise small animals, hunt, and are good craftsmen. Politically they are divided into eight small states: Bankim, Beng-Beng, Ina, We, Yakong, Ngambé, Ngume, and Ditam. Verbal traditions indicate they arose from the Mbum people near what is now the city of Ngaoundéré.

About 300 years ago Tikar offshoots began migrating westward under pressure from the Chamba people to the north, internal dissension, and a desire for new land. They settled on the high grassy Bamenda plateau where more than half of the modern inhabitants (belonging to 30 kingdoms) were counted as Tikar. They are ruled by kings known as Fon (Afon) with the help of queen mothers. Nsaw (*q.v.*, 52,000), Kom (26,000), and Bum (5,000) were strong, consolidated kingdoms prior to European advent. Other Tikar groups include Mbem (17,000), War (13,000), Tang (12,000), Wiya (10,000), Mbembe (11,000), Misaje (8,000), and Mfumte (6,000). Fungom, including a number of small independent groups, numbered 20,000. Bafut, Babanki, Babanki-Tungaw, Bafreng, Bambili, Bambui, and Bamenda totaled 33,000. Oku, Bamessing, Bamessi, Bamungo, Bafanji, Baba, Bangola, Bambalang, Bamunka, Bamale, Bamum-kumbat and Bali-kumbat in the Ndop (Ndob) area totaled 34,000. Groups such as the Bamum also acknowledge Tikar origin. Almost all these groups are patrilineal (the Kom and five Fungom villages are matrilineal).

Most Tikar groups (and those influenced by the Tikar) have windowless, square, wattle-and-daub houses, each with a pyramidal thatched roof, and an entrance closed by a sliding door of raffia poles. House posts and door frames are often elaborately carved. The notable Tikar art declined following European contact. They produced beautifully carved wooden stools, bedposts, figures, masks, bowls, and drums, and carved ivory tusks and drinking horns. Smoking pipes of clay were modeled in human form. Beaded calabashes, bottles, stools, figures, and fly whisks were made. Cotton was woven and dyed in resist patterns, while raffia mats and bags were decorated with human, faunal, and geometric designs. Bells, bracelets, pipes, small figures, and large masks were delicately cast in brass (lost-wax process), particularly at Foumban, the Bamum capital. (Wi. B.)

**TIKHON** (VASILI BELAVIN) (1866–1925), the first patriarch of Moscow (1917–25) after patriarchal leadership of the Russian Orthodox Church was restored under Soviet government, was born in 1866 near Pskov. Before his election as patriarch in 1917,

Tikhon was, among other things, bishop to the Orthodox in North America. During this period (1903–04) his extreme demands contributed to the collapse of negotiations on intercommunion with the Protestant Episcopal Church. From 1913 he was archbishop of Vilna.

When the Soviets came to power, their first steps included the nationalization of church land, the taking over of all schools and seminaries, the establishment of exclusively civil marriage, and the withdrawal of all subsidies to the church. Under Tikhon's leadership the anathema was pronounced (Jan. 19, 1918) by the All-Russian Regional Council on "all who take part in acts of robbery against God"; *i.e.,* practically speaking, on the Soviet government and its adherents. Under the law of Jan. 23, 1918, church and state were completely separated, and the church was dispossessed and deprived of its rights as a legal person. The way was opened for many local attacks on priests and congregations. The decree of the Central Committee of the Communist Party of Feb. 23, 1922, created a new climax in antichurch action, with the confiscation of all church treasures for the relief of the hungry. It ignored the fact that a few days earlier Tikhon himself had called on his priests to donate all unconsecrated objects of value for this purpose. When the decree came into force, even holy objects were seized, churches were desecrated and plundered, and priests, who resisted in accordance with the canons of the church, were murdered or imprisoned. Tikhon was taken into custody because of his opposition to these deeds of violence. During the civil war of 1918–22, however, he had never made common cause with the "whites" but had always described himself as the father of his "believing and straying children," calling for repentance and prayer. At first he had not released from his jurisdiction the metropolitans and bishops who had emigrated, and he was therefore suspected of anti-Soviet activity.

During his imprisonment, Tikhon considered anew the whole relation of church and state and came to the conclusion, based on Rom. 13:1–6, that the Soviet government was now the divinely sanctioned power in Russia and that the faithful owed it secular obedience. In his famous epistle of June 28, 1923, he condemned all counterrevolutionary action against the government. During the last years of his life, however, he also opposed the division of Russian Orthodoxy through the "Living Church" movement, which aimed at a reform of the church through a mixture of socialist and communist ideals with a colourless Christianity. He died in Moscow on April 8, 1925.

BIBLIOGRAPHY.—A. Ammann, *Abriss der ostslawischen Kirchengeschichte* (1950); J. Shelton-Curtiss, *The Russian Church and the Soviet State* (1953); R. Stupperich, "Zivaja Cerkov," *Kirche im Osten,* vol. iii (1960). (F. v. L.)

**TILAK, BALGANGADHAR** (1856–1920), Indian political leader, called by Indians *Lokamanya,* "honoured by the people," was born at Ratnagiri (Maharashtra State) on July 23, 1856, of a Maratha family of Chitpavan Brahman caste. Educated at the Deccan College, Poona, he studied law before turning to journalism. He became proprietor and editor of the *Mahratta* and the *Kesari* ("Lion"), in the English and Marathi languages respectively. His use of Marathi was particularly effective, and in the villages people would gather together to have the *Kesari* read to them. He thus became widely known for his bitter criticisms of British rule and also of those moderate nationalists who advocated social reform on Western lines as well as political reform on constitutional lines. He thought that social reform would only divert energy from politics, and he derided the moderates' reliance on speeches and petitions as "political mendicancy." He sought to widen the popularity of the nationalist movement (which at that time was confined largely to the upper classes) by introducing Hindu religious symbolism and by invoking popular traditions of the Maratha struggle against Muslim rule, creating an annual festival honouring Sivaji, the 17th century Maratha hero and bitter enemy of the Mughal government. But if this made the nationalist movement more popular, it also made it more communal and it alarmed the Muslims.

When the Congress Party met at Surat in 1907, Tilak unsuccessfully challenged the moderates for the leadership, after which he led his extremist group out of the party, not to return until 1916. What was considered to be the inflammatory character of his language led to his conviction for sedition in 1897, after two British officials had been assassinated in Poona, and again in 1908. He spent six years in prison after the second conviction, making use of the time to write his commentary on the Bhagavad Gita, in which he emphasized the value of selfless activity rather than withdrawal from the world. Tilak was one of the first to maintain that Indians should cease to cooperate with foreign rule, but he always denied that he had ever encouraged the use of violence. In 1919 he unsuccessfully sued Sir Valentine Chirol for libel arising out of statements to that effect in the latter's book *Indian Unrest* (1910). By this time he had mellowed sufficiently to oppose M. K. Gandhi's policy of boycotting the elections to the legislative councils established as part of the Montagu-Chelmsford reforms (*see* MONTAGU, EDWIN SAMUEL), advocating instead "responsive cooperation." He died in Bombay on Aug. 1, 1920. *See* also INDIA-PAKISTAN, SUBCONTINENT OF: *History.*

*See* D. V. Tahmankar, *Lokamanya Tilak* (1957); T. V. Parvate, *Bal Gangadhar Tilak* (1958); S. A. Wolpert, *Tilak and Gokhale* (1962). (KE. A. B.)

**TILBURG,** a town in North Brabant province, the Netherlands, is on the Wilhelmina Canal, in the centre of the Benelux countries, 13 mi. (21 km.) E of Breda. Pop. (1960) 130,818. Tilburg rose to prominence after 1860 as one of the chief industrial (textile, metal, leather) centres of the south; textiles were of prime importance in the mid-1960s. The town was the favourite residence of William II, king of the Netherlands until 1849, whose palace has been restored and adapted as the Town Hall. A Roman Catholic university, a conservatory, an academy of plastic and constructive arts, and a textile school are there. Much of the surrounding area is wooded and scenic.

**TILBURY,** an area in the Thurrock (*q.v.*) urban district of Essex, Eng., on the north bank of the Thames, opposite Gravesend and about equidistant from London Bridge and the Nore. It is famous for its docks, constructed in 1884–86 and since extended and modernized by the Port of London Authority. The system has a total land area of 725 ac. and a water area of 106 ac. The quays extend over 4 mi. and the principal entrance lock is 1,000 ft. long and 110 ft. wide with a depth on the sills of 45½ ft. The largest of the four dry docks is 750 ft. long and 110 ft. wide. A river cargo jetty, 1,000 by 50 ft., is connected by rail, and the riverside landing stage, 1,142 ft. long, enables the largest ships to embark or disembark passengers at any state of the tide.

No. 1 berth, the passenger terminal in the main dock, and no. 4 shed, the centre of the vehicle ferry service to Antwerp and Rotterdam (for both freight and passenger vehicles), were added to shipowners' accommodation in the mid-1960s. Four new berths were completed in 1965–66, two of which are for roll-on, roll-off traffic; two more were ready by the summer of 1966; five further berths were scheduled for completion by 1967, making a total of 11 new berths from 1965 to 1967. The Dartford-Purfleet Tunnel under the Thames (opened in 1963) and improved approach roads enable much road traffic to reach the docks without passing through Greater London.

**TILDEN, SAMUEL JONES** (1814–1886), governor of New York State and Democratic candidate for president of the United States in the disputed election of 1876, was born at New Lebanon, N.Y., Feb. 9, 1814. His formal education was sporadic; for brief periods he attended Yale College and the University of the City of New York, and studied law. He began to practise law in New York City in 1841. Despite frequent illness, he soon became a leader in Democratic politics and a corporation and railroad lawyer of great skill and ability. He served in 1846 in the New York Assembly and was a member of the state constitutional conventions of 1846 and of 1867. He was a loyal supporter of Van Buren and a leader of the Barnburner or Free Soil element among the New York Democrats. When the Civil War broke out he supported the Union cause but opposed certain policies of the Lincoln administration. He played a prominent role in the reorganization of the Democratic Party in the decade 1865–75, serving as the party chairman for New York State. He was an astute and resourceful leader in the struggle to overthrow the notorious Tweed Ring in New York City (*see* TWEED, WILLIAM MARCY) and in the removal of several corrupt municipal judges. Elected governor in 1874 on a reform platform, he won national recognition for his accomplishments in exposing the Canal Ring (a conspiracy of politicians and contractors engaged in defrauding the state) and in his efficient administration of state government.

In 1876 he was the Democratic nominee for the presidency. The bitterly fought campaign ended in the disputed election of 1876, when two sets of returns were sent to Washington from Oregon, Florida, Louisiana, and South Carolina. Congress, with a Republican Senate and a Democratic House, created an electoral commission (*q.v.*) to settle the controversy. Tilden reluctantly consented to the formation of the commission but failed to provide vigorous and direct leadership in the crisis. There is some evidence that the Republicans entered into a secret deal with Southern leaders to withdraw Federal troops from the South if the disputed Southern electoral votes could be counted for the Republican candidate, Rutherford B. Hayes. The commission decided all questions by a strictly partisan vote (8 Republicans to 7 Democrats), thus giving the presidency to Hayes. Tilden, although convinced he was the people's choice, accepted the verdict as an alternative to possible violence.

A lucrative law practice and profitable investments brought Tilden great wealth. Personally he was cold, secretive, dilatory, and cautious, but he possessed marked intellectual ability and cultural attainments. He was highly respected as a reformer. His frail health and characteristic indecision forced him into the background of politics after 1877, though he retained great influence in the Democratic Party. He remained a bachelor all his life. He died on Aug. 4, 1886, in New York, leaving the bulk of his estate to be used for establishing a free public library for the city of New York.

*See* A. C. Flick and G. S. Lobrano, *Samuel Jones Tilden* (1939).

(T. S. BY.)

**TILDEN, WILLIAM TATEM** (1893–1953), U.S. tennis player, first American to win the men's singles at Wimbledon, dominated tennis in the 1920s. Born in Philadelphia, Feb. 10, 1893, Tilden was 27 when he won his first national championship, in 1920. For 10 straight years he ranked at the top, winning seven national championships—six (1920–25) in a row and the last in 1929. He won the Wimbledon title in 1920, 1921 and 1930, was on 11 Davis cup teams and led the battle that kept the prized cup in the U.S. for seven straight years. He won a total of 70 U.S. and international championships.

Tilden had powerful shoulders, a light frame and long legs—the perfect tennis build; he was famous for his cannonball serve and a paralyzing forehand and backhand. He died in Hollywood, Calif., June 5, 1953. (J. D. McC.)

**TILE,** a thin, flat slab or block, usually of burned clay, glazed or unglazed, used either structurally or decoratively in building. The usage of the word varies widely; in connection with roofing, flat slabs of any material are sometimes termed tiles, as, for instance, the marble tiles of some Greek temples or the bronze tiles of ancient Rome. Similarly, stone slabs, used for roofing, as in certain parts of England, are termed stone tiles; slate, however, is never so called. Many forms of rough terra cotta used structurally in building are called tiles; thus an arch of hollow terra-cotta blocks between steel beams is known as a tile arch; partitions built of hollow terra-cotta blocks are known as hollow-tile partitions; rough terra-cotta pipes used for drainage are called drain tiles; and the steel forms used for casting certain types of reinforced concrete floors are frequently referred to as steel tiles.

The differentiation between tile, terra cotta (*q.v.*) and brick is thus exceedingly vague. (*See* BRICKWORK.) Modern usage extends the word "tile" to include blocks or panels made of plastics, glass and sound-absorbing materials.

**Roofing Tile.**—There is no evidence of the use of roofing tiles in the Mediterranean basin prior to the development of Hellenic civilization, but the most ancient examples of roof tiles show such highly developed forms that earlier usage must be assumed. The Greek form of temple roof which remained constant throughout the history of Greek architecture (*q.v.*) consisted of two types of tile, used together. First the roof surface was covered with tiles generally flat, but with adjoining edges raised, laid in overlapping courses, and all of equal size. Convex covering tiles, also overlapping, were then laid over the joints of the flat tiles below; in this manner an absolutely watertight roof could be produced. In order to make the architectural effect more delicate the ends of both lower tile and covering tile were rebated, so that the thickness of the overlapping portion was only half the thickness of the tile. At the bottom of each row of covering tiles was either a marble or tile upright, curved, decorative member known as an antefix.

In some cases the covering tiles were of pointed, straight-line section—the most common Greek type—in others a tile of semicircular section was used, easy to manufacture but lacking in the extreme refinement of the other type; in the simpler domestic work, the lower courses were also of curved section, a segmental concave shape replacing the flat tile with raised edges. The marble tile used in some Greek temples, as in that of Bassae (5th century B.C., by Ictinus), is universally of the type with flat under tile and pointed covering tile, although at times, in order to reduce the number of joints, the covering tile and the under tile are cut from the same piece of marble.

Two other types of roof tile were common in Roman architecture (*q.v.*) and probably represent common Mediterranean types of much earlier origin. One of these is the so-called "Spanish tile," also called "pantile," with a contour resembling the letter S, in which the convex part of each tile fits over the edge of the concave portion of the next. The other type is the shingle or flat tile found frequently in the Roman ruins of the northern provinces. These flat tiles are often of stone.

The usual material of all of these types of tile is burned clay, varying in colour from orange-yellow to purple-red. It is known, however, that bronze tiles were relatively common on the most monumental buildings of the Roman empire. Due to the rarity and value of bronze during the middle ages and the Renaissance, no examples of ancient bronze roof tiles are known.

All of the classic forms of clay tile continued in use in various parts of the world during the medieval period, but their supremacy as a roofing material gradually yielded to lead and zinc for churches, public buildings, palaces, etc., and to slate, stone and thatch for the smaller private houses.

Clay roof tiles remain of substantially the same form; improvements have been only in methods of manufacture and not in design. The flat tile designed to hook over roof battens or boards is perhaps the most common type of small house-roof covering in England and parts of France, and the combination of concave under tile and convex over tile is almost universal on pitched roofs in Italy, Spain, Greece and Turkey. The S-shaped tile is also common around the Mediterranean. The curved tiles are almost always laid in a heavy bed of waterproofed mortar, with ridges and hips covered by courses of overlapping tiles, similarly bedded; with flat tiles, the use of mortar is restricted to the convex or pointed tiles covering the hips and ridges.

The best modern usage in laying tiles of this type demands the complete covering of the roof surface with a watertight material such as slaters' felt or heavy waterproofed paper before the tile is applied. The tiles themselves are held in place sometimes by copper nails which secure the under tiles direct to the roofing and the covering tiles to wood battens which run up the slope of the roof under each row of covering tiles, and sometimes by copper wire brought up through two holes in each tile and twisted together.

Although various attempts have been made to imitate clay tiles in stamped metal and concrete, these imitations are so lacking in the individual variation typical of ceramicware that their use has been restricted to the cheapest type of jerry-built construction; their use, even there, is seriously questionable. Quite different are the roofing tiles of reinforced and waterproof concrete, which are common in industrial buildings, especially in Europe. These modern, industrial tiles are usually of large size—sometimes running to four feet in length, and arranged to interlock, with the exposed surfaces grooved or channeled in such a way as to lead

BY COURTESY OF (TOP LEFT, TOP RIGHT) THE METROPOLITAN MUSEUM OF ART, NEW YORK; (CENTRE) ERNST WASMUTH FROM SARRE, "DENKMÄLER PERSISCHER BAUKUNST"; PHOTO, (BOTTOM LEFT) HERBERT G. PONTING, F.R.P.S.

USE OF TILE: (TOP LEFT) GLAZED BLUE AND WHITE DELFT TILING, MADE IN DELFT, NETH.; (BOTTOM LEFT) TILE IN HALL OF CLASSICS, PEKING, CHINA; (CENTRE) WALL DECORATION OF SHAH-I-ZINDEH, SAMARKAND; (TOP RIGHT) PANEL OF 16TH-CENTURY WALL TILE, SEVILLE, SPAIN; (BOTTOM RIGHT) PAINTED FLOOR TILE, HALL OF JUSTICE, THE ALHAMBRA, GRANADA, SPAIN

the water away from any joints. In these concrete tiles colouring matter is usually added in the material itself. (*See* also ROOF.)

*Roofing Tile in the Far East.*—Although the principle of the roofing tiles of China and Japan is the same as that in the west, there are many differences in detail. Thus, in temples and palaces in China, the under tiles are slightly concave and overlap, much like those of classic roofs; the covering tiles, however, are made absolutely cylindrical in general contour, with rebated ends, so that they form long, unbroken lines of shadow down the roof. Moreover, instead of the upright antefix of the classic roof, the Chinese tiles have ornaments that project downward, in generally scalloped shapes, over the face of the cornice. There is also, particularly in north China, a tremendous elaboration of ridge and hip tiles, which are frequently of great height, with an elaborately molded section, carrying at their ends rows of animals—a great dragon or the like. At the ends of the ridge are large, grotesque beasts with their heads pointing inward; all these ornaments are modeled and baked in the tile itself. One of the chief glories of the Chinese roof tiles is their colour. This is produced by a shiny glaze that reveals the expected Chinese ceramic skill. The usual colour of temple and palace roofs is bright yellow, but other colours frequently occur. In central and south China, even temple roofs are frequently black. The cheap roof tile of the ordinary house is also almost black, but without lustre and with overlapping covering tiles like those of the west. (*See* also CHINESE ARCHITECTURE; TEMPLE ARCHITECTURE.)

The same pattern of rebated, continuous, cylindrical covering tiles is common in the Buddhist shrines of Japan, but colours are rare, the ordinary tile being gray, with a very effective and artistic silvery lustre. (*See* also JAPANESE ARCHITECTURE.)

**Floor Tile.**—Except as small fragments of tile occur in classic mosaic (*q.v.*) and terrazzo, tile for floors does not seem to have been common in Europe prior to the 12th century. In the late 12th and 13th centuries, however, tile floors became usual in churches and other important buildings. The most common type consisted of square tile in two colours, usually a dark brown-red and a pale orange or brownish yellow. They were made by casting clay in such a manner that the parts to be in a lighter colour were sunk; when dry, these parts were filled with a clay of different composition which would burn to a lighter colour; the tile thus prepared was then burned.

Patterns were formed of many tiles and consisted usually of circles or stars containing heraldic beasts, ecclesiastical symbols, etc.; in many cases the pattern was made with reversed colours, so that what was background colour in one tile was ornament colour in the one next to it.

In the earliest examples designs were formed by a mosaic treatment in which the pattern was made by the shape and size of the individual tiles, as in the 13th century example found at Fountains abbey and at Prior Crauden's chapel at Ely (1321–41), both in England. Other common types of medieval pavement have the pattern merely incised, producing the artistic effect of a sketch.

The development of floor tiles in Gothic France was similar. The 12th-century examples are usually mosaic in type with black, dark green, light green and yellow as the predominating colours. The richest examples of these are in the abbey church of St. Denis, near Paris, where certain elaborate chapel floor pavements still exist from the original building (1140–44) by Abbot Suger. By the end of the century, mosaic had yielded to two-coloured tiles of red and yellow, similar to the English tiles mentioned above. The same type remained constant until well into the 15th century, the designs becoming continuously thinner and more delicate; in the 16th century the art died out, superseded by the painted majolica pavements of the Renaissance.

The Gothic revival of the middle 19th century led, in England, to the revival of the designing and making of tiles of the medieval type and many modern pavements were placed in old churches as a result. Most of this tile has a simple lead glaze and is made not by casting damp, plastic clay, as in the medieval examples, but by compressing powdered clay in steel dies so that shapes are more perfect and the rapidity of manufacture is vastly increased. This type of tile, usually known as encaustic, is especially associated with the English ceramic works at Stoke-on-Trent, particularly those of Minturn.

Meanwhile the Moorish skill in tilemaking had gradually come to be applied to floors. This type of majolica tile was adopted in early Renaissance churches, both in Italy and Spain, although not many examples remain, as the glaze was too soft. The decoration of the Italian majolica pavements consists of the same type of free and graceful classic arabesque trophies, acanthus ornament and coats of arms that is found on contemporary majolica.

In France not only were Italian tiles imported and used, but there soon grew up a local manufacture of similar painted floor tiles, especially at Rouen (established by Masseot Abaquesne, 1542–57), Nevers and Marseilles. With the increasing use of oak parquetry flooring for houses and marble for churches, toward the end of the 17th century, the use of tile diminished. There was similar importation of Italian and Spanish tiles into England during the early Renaissance and possible spasmodic attempts toward the making of certain types of this tile in England itself. In the 18th century the use of plain, undecorated, square, red tiles, now commonly known as quarry tiles, became common all over northern and western Europe, and to a less extent in the American colonies.

The greatest advances in modern floor tiles have been made in simple, vitrified, mosaic tiles for use in bathrooms, kitchens, swimming pools and public corridors. These are always machine-pressed and are made of fine clays, thoroughly vitrified and very hard. These are made in small squares, rectangles, hexagons and circles, in a few simple colours. Some, by the addition of gritty substances, such as alundum or carborundum, are given a surface which prevents slipping, even when the tile is wet.

**Wall Tile.**—Earthenware was used spasmodically for wall decoration by the Egyptians, as in the doorway of the Abusir pyramid of Neterkhet (3rd dynasty). More usually, however, they were in the form of mosaic (*q.v.*). Perhaps based upon earlier Egyptian examples, the people of Crete (*q.v.*) developed to an even higher degree the use of faïence for walls. Thus our knowledge of early Cretan houses is largely furnished by many fragments of small faïence plaques from the 18th century, B.C., which formed portions of a large, mosaic, faïence wall decoration. Moreover, there are in existence many modeled reliefs of faïence from the middle and late Minoan period which were apparently inserted in the plaster of walls.

Farther east, in the Tigris-Euphrates valley, a tradition of ceramic wall decoration was early established. (*See* IRAN: *Archaeology.*) This took the form of glazed and enameled bricks rather than tiles proper. It is, nevertheless, important as being one of the first attempts to cover large and continuous wall surfaces with a decorative, ceramic material, and the friezes of marching beasts from Chaldean and Babylonian palaces, from the later Assyrian palaces and from their Persian successors, the famous friezes of the archers and the lions from the early 4th-century palace of Artaxerxes II at Susa, have remained models of this type of decorative work.

Moreover, the tradition of fine ceramic work continued vital throughout the stormy period of the fall of the Roman empire and the Islamic conquest. It is in Syria, the Tigris-Euphrates valley and Persia that wall tiles were, undoubtedly, first made. Thus tradition relates that the lustre tiles of the mosque of Sidi Okba at Kairouan were brought from Baghdad in 894, and it is certain that by the 13th century the manufacture of wall tiles for both exterior and interior use was well established in various centres in Persia, notably Rhages and Veramine. The exterior use of wall tiles was most highly developed, and in Persia, also, the transition from enameled and modeled brick to true, thin tile can easily be seen. By the 15th century tile decoration was supreme in Persia and the character had changed. Mosaics and moldings in relief yielded to a flat treatment with the richness entirely in the coloured, foliated ornament and the inscriptions painted on the tiles themselves. In later Persian art there is no distinguishable difference between the tiles of the exterior and the interior.

These Persian tiles governed the taste of the eastern part of the Islamic world; the same running patterns of leaves, palmettes, the carnation and other flowers that appear on Persian carpets decorate alike the interiors of mosques in Persia, Mesopotamia and Turkey, from potteries as far apart as Rhodes, Damascus and Kutayieh. In colour these have, universally, a blue-white ground with patterns predominantly blue and green, with lesser touches of vermilion and rose and occasional yellows. Several potteries in Asia Minor still operate and produce exquisite wall tiles in the traditional patterns and colours. Because of the gracious delicacy of the interlacing stems and the careful spacing of the leaves and flowers, together with a springlike clarity of the colours, these Turkish, Syrian and Persian wall tiles are among the most perfect wall decorations of their type.

*Moorish Wall Tile.*—Farther west, in Spain and North Africa, the Islamic potters were developing a new type of design which gave rise to the famous Spanish *azulejos,* whose decorative richness was such an important feature in the Alhambra (*q.v.*) at Granada (13th and 14th centuries), the so-called house of Pilate at Seville and similar buildings. Although transitional types occur, like the great plaque from Malaga at the beginning of the 15th century in the collection of M. de Osma, in which the patterns are of an almost Persian freedom, with twining foliage, in the greater number the design was almost purely geometric, being formed of interlacing lines that generate 8- and 10-pointed stars, octagons, irregular pentagons and similar figures. There are, in addition, a great many early tiles from the 13th and 14th centuries in which the influence of Christian heraldry is dominant. Even in the transitional plaque mentioned above, coats of arms appear and it is evident that the Islamic potters produced much purely heraldic tilework for Christian consumption. Many of these tiles are rich with metallic lustre decoration; the chief colours are blue, green and brown, with white lines, and in the later work a growing use of black and yellow.

The earliest examples of Moorish wall tiles produced their geometric patterns by a mosaic method in which each bit of separate colour is formed by a separate tile. In order to develop a more facile method of producing the same effect, the technique known as *cuerda seca* (dry cord) was developed, in which the tiles are rectangular, and the pattern on each tile is formed by raised fillets between the different colours, which prevented the adjoining enamels from running together. After the Christian conquest a third method was introduced, called *cuenca* (bowl), somewhat similar to the northern Gothic process in which the portions to be coloured were depressed and then filled with their enamels. These tiles, even in their old traditional Islamic patterns, were popular throughout the 16th century and even later for wainscots in Renaissance houses. The potters were evidently Moors; the great centres of manufacture remained as before in Malaga, Valencia, Granada and Seville.

In the 16th century the Italian majolica type of tile was introduced by Francesco Niculoso of Pisa, and these Spanish majolica tiles were much used, as in the door of the convent of St. Paula at Seville (early 16th century) or the exquisite altarpiece in the Alcázar at Seville made by the same artist in 1503, where the design is purely Italian. Both the *cuenca* and the *pisano* or majolica types of tile have been made in Spain almost continuously ever since. (*See* ISLAMIC ART.)

*North European Wall Tile.*—Meanwhile in Germany there had been developing a type of tile used principally for stoves, with ornament in relief and a glaze of green, yellow or brown. This tile was in widespread use as early as the 14th century and many examples exist throughout Germany, upper Austria and Switzerland, in which the ornament is of great richness, with Gothic architectural forms in the earlier types and Renaissance forms later.

The most important of the north European tiles are undoubtedly those made in Delft, Neth., from 1600 on. These are plain, square tiles, each containing a figure, a bit of landscape or a genre group, freely painted in a gray-blue upon a background of bluish-white. The little freehand sketches were so instinct with life, and the colour so subtly beautiful, that by the middle of the 17th century these tiles enjoyed a great vogue, not only throughout the Germanic countries but in England and the American colonies as well. Although outside of the Netherlands they were chiefly used for fireplace and stove facings, in the Netherlands itself they were often employed for wall wainscotings. Some of the later examples have the decorations in manganese purple instead of blue. During the 18th century many attempts were made to imitate the delftware and during the latter half of the 18th century, particularly in England, scenes printed from copper plates were used instead of the painted scenes.

Although many ancient pottery centres still produce tiles in the traditional manner and although modern imitations of old wares are of excellent quality, the greatest modern contribution to wall-tile design was the development of square or rectangular tiles with relatively uneven surfaces and shapes on which colours and glazes of the greatest variety are unevenly flowed, so each tile has individuality of colour and texture. All sorts of crackled and crystalline effects are common, as well as the blending of colours. Scientific development of glazings and colourings gave the decorator an almost unlimited palette for exterior or interior use. There was also development in the use of tile in relief, usually with the background sunk and glazed in a different colour.

During the late 19th century, light, flat tiles often provided an ideal material for vaults and domes. Their advantages over wood and stone had earlier been recognized by the Romans, who laid flat tiles vertically and horizontally between thick brick ribs in order to lighten vaults, keep them fireproof and gain both support and form for the concrete infilling poured between ribs. The biggest 19th-century innovation was the Guastavino vault, named for a Catalan engineer who developed a light, fireproof vault in which bonded layers of small, light and flat tiles were built into curved surfaces with a minimum of centring. Especially popular in the United States, examples of the Guastavino vault appear in New York's Carnegie hall and St. Thomas's church; St. Paul's chapel at Columbia university, New York city; Boston's public library; and the state capitol at Lincoln, Neb.

Cheaper materials compete with traditional kinds of tile and are called tiles even though some are not made of terra cotta. Fibreboard sound-absorbing panels, referred to as "acoustic tiles," are used in modern ceilings. Glass block, sometimes called "Glasstile," appears in partitions. A wide variety of mass-produced ceramic veneers is available in different colours, finishes, textures and shapes, though figurative patterns are unusual. Ceramic-glazed structural tile, hollow and approximately $3\frac{1}{2} \times 3\frac{1}{2} \times 11\frac{1}{2}$ in. in size, remains an attractive, economical and permanent material for partitions in schools, hospitals, railroad stations and cafeterias.

*See* also references under "Tile" in the Index.

BIBLIOGRAPHY.—O. Jones, *Plans and Elevations of the Alhambra* (1842); J. G. Nicholls, *Examples of Encaustic Tiling* (1845); Viollet-le-Duc, "Carrelage," "Dallage" and "Tuile," articles in *Dictionnaire Raisonné de l'architecture* (1854–76); M. Shurlock, *Tiles From Chertsey Abbey* (1885); H. Wallis, *Typical Examples of Persian and Oriental Ceramic Art* (1893); H. Shaw, *History of the Staffordshire Potters* (1829, 1900); J. Gestoso y Perez, *Historia de los barros vidriados sevillanos* (1904); A. van de Put, *Hispano Moresque Ware of the XV Century* (1904); H. Saladin, *Manuel de l'Art Musulman*, vol. i (1907); G. Migeon, *Manuel de l'Art Musulman*, vol. ii (1907); Byne and Stapley, *Spanish Architecture of the Sixteenth Century* (1917); Talbot Hamlin (ed.), *Forms and Functions of Twentieth-Century Architecture* (1952); I. Holl and P. Voit, *Old Hungarian Stove Tiles* (1963); A. Berendsen *et al., Tiles* (1967). (T. F. H.; A. B.-B.)

**TILIACEAE,** the linden family of trees, shrubs, or (rarely) herbs, with 35 genera and about 300 species, found in most parts of the world, but largely tropical. Most of the genera are small, but *Grewia,* in the old world tropics, contains about 70 species. *Tilia,* various species of which are known as linden and as basswood (originally bast wood), is typical of the north temperate zone of both hemispheres. Two species of *Corchorus* yield the jute (*q.v.*) of commerce, largely produced in India. *See* LINDEN.

**TILLETT, BENJAMIN** (1860–1943), British trade union leader, better known as Ben Tillett, played a notable part in the organization of unskilled workers. He was born in Bristol on Sept. 11, 1860, the son of a railway labourer. He went to work in a brickyard at the age of seven and then was a circus boy, a sailor in the Royal Navy, a merchant seaman, and an apprentice bootmaker. By his early twenties he was settled in the east end of London, devoting himself to the organization of the Dock, Wharf, Riverside, and General Workers' Union, of which he became general secretary. He played a colourful and decisive part in the successful dock strike of 1889, which led to the achievement of the "dockers' tanner" (a minimum wage of 6*d.* an hour) and a great spurt in union membership. He was equally active in the dockers' strike of 1911. He was Labour member of Parliament for North Salford, Lancashire, from 1917 to 1924 and from 1929 to 1931. His trade union work was somewhat eclipsed after 1921 when his union amalgamated with others to form the Transport and General Workers' Union, but he was chairman of the Trades Union Congress in 1928–29. He was for many years an alderman of the London County Council. He died in London on Jan. 27, 1943. His publications include an autobiography, *Memories and Reflections* (1931), and *A Brief History of the Dockers' Union* (1910). (R. J.)

**TILLEY, SIR SAMUEL LEONARD** (1818–1896), Canadian statesman who introduced the "national policy" of tariff protection, was born at Gagetown, New Brunswick, on May 18, 1818. After making a small fortune in drugs, he entered the legislature in 1850, becoming head of the New Brunswick government in 1861. He represented the province at the conferences at Charlottetown and Quebec in 1864, at which the plans for Confederation were prepared.

In 1865 he was defeated in a general election on the federation question, and the reverse delayed Confederation for almost a year. In 1866 his position was vindicated and he was returned to power at the head of a pro-Confederation government. He became the first minister of customs and excise for the Dominion of Canada, in 1867.

In 1873 he left politics to become lieutenant governor of New Brunswick, but in 1878 was again returned to Parliament for Saint John and entered the government of Sir John A. Macdonald as minister of finance, where he espoused the "national policy." The tariff that resulted thereafter remained the basis of Canadian fiscal policy. He again became lieutenant governor of New Brunswick, from 1885 to 1893. He died at Saint John on June 25, 1896.

*See* James Hannay, *Sir Leonard Tilley* (1926). (W. S. MACN.)

**TILLICH, PAUL JOHANNES** (1886–1965), German-U.S. philosopher and theologian, a widely influential apologist in the Christian church, developed a distinctive interpretation of the task of Christian theology by correlating biblical faith with the questions raised by classical and modern philosophy, especially mysticism, idealism, and existentialism. He was born in Starzeddel, Brandenburg, on Aug. 20, 1886, the son of a pastor and district superintendent in the Prussian territorial church. Tillich studied in the University of Berlin and other German universities, receiving the doctor of philosophy degree from Breslau in 1911 and the licentiate in theology from Halle in 1912. He served in the German army as chaplain from 1914 to 1918. After the war he taught in the universities of Berlin, Marburg, Dresden and Leipzig, and in 1929 became professor of philosophy at the University of Frankfurt. Tillich was one of the first professors to be forced from his post by the Nazi regime in Germany. In 1933 he went to the United

HENRI DAUMAN, LIFE © 1965. TIME, INC.

TILLICH, PHOTOGRAPHED IN 1965

States where he became professor of philosophical theology (1933–55) at Union Theological seminary, New York city. During World War II he served on the Committee for a Democratic Germany and was chairman of the Committee on Self-Help for Refugees. In 1955 he became university professor at Harvard university and in 1962 Nuveen professor of theology at the Divinity school of the University of Chicago. He died in Chicago on Oct. 22, 1965.

Tillich's early writings include his thesis on Schelling, who, along with Jakob Böhme, was one of the most important influences on his thought. During the Weimar republic Tillich aligned himself with a group of German intellectuals in the Religious Socialist movement which sought a new spiritual outlook coupled with effective power to renew and shape the political order (*see* CHRISTIAN SOCIALISM). In two books, *Religious Realization* (1930) and *The Religious Situation,* Tillich gave a powerful analysis of the religious and cultural dilemmas of 20th-century man.

Tillich stands in the tradition of the great synthesizers of Christian doctrine—Origen, Augustine, Aquinas and Schleiermacher. He developed a method of relating traditional Christian doctrine to the questions which arise from the human situation, his technical term for the method being "correlation." Man's questions become religious when they express his "ultimate concern," that is, his concern about what determines his being or his nonbeing. The questions are correlated in theology with the answers which come from the self-manifestation of the divine reality. Such manifestation is the meaning of revelation. The answers to the meaning of man's existence cannot be grasped abstractly but only through personal faith and decision.

Tillich's theological position required and permitted him to develop a systematic analysis of cultural expressions of the human spirit. He gave careful attention to depth psychology, existentialist philosophy and to the arts, especially painting, as these provide keys to the human quest for final meaning.

As theologian, Tillich stands within the "theological circle" which is determined by Christian faith. The final criterion of revelation is given in Jesus Christ, the personal life which became transparent for the divine. This point of view was developed by Tillich in his three-volume *Systematic Theology* (1951–63). Other major works include *The Protestant Era* (1948), a series of essays on religious, cultural and political problems; *The Courage to Be* (1952), a religious existentialist interpretation of the meaning of faith; and three books of sermons, *The Shaking of the Foundations* (1948), *The New Being* (1955) and *The Eternal Now* (1963). He wrote an essay on Christian ethics, *Love, Power and Justice* (1954), and an apologia for his theological method, *Biblical Religion and the Search for Ultimate Reality* (1955).

Tillich's books and essays range widely over the whole spectrum of human culture and religious experience. He fused a deep Christian piety with the classic tradition of philosophical and Christian mysticism. This makes his method and results suspect to those who seek a sharper separation of faith from cultural forms; but it explains in part his deep attraction for those who seek a personal experimental understanding of their religious heritage. *See* also NEO-ORTHODOXY.

BIBLIOGRAPHY.—Full Tillich bibliographies will be found in *Religion and Culture: Essays in Honor of Paul Tillich,* ed. by Walter Leibrecht (1959), and *The Theology of Paul Tillich,* ed. by Charles W. Kegley and Robert W. Bretall (1952), a volume in *The Library of Living Theology,* which contains critical essays with a reply by Tillich and an autobiographical essay. Another autobiographical essay will be found in *The Interpretation of History* (1936), an English translation of some of Tillich's earlier German writings. *See* also Gustave Weigel, S. J., "Contemporaneous Protestantism and Paul Tillich," *Theological Studies,* vol. xi (June 1950); Daniel D. Williams, *What Present-Day Theologians Are Thinking* (1959); G. Tavard, *Paul Tillich and the Christian Message* (1962); J. L. Adams, *Paul Tillich's Philosophy of Culture, Science, and Religion* (1965); G. B. Hammond, *Man in Estrangement: Paul Tillich and Erich Fromm* (1965); C. J. Armbruster, *Vision of Paul Tillich* (1967); D. Hopper, *Tillich: a Theological Portrait* (1968); D. H. Kelsey, *Fabric of Paul Tillich's Theology* (1967); W. L. Rowe, *Religious Symbols and God: a Philosophical Study of Tillich's Theology* (1968); J. R. Lyons (ed.), *The Intellectual Legacy of Paul Tillich* (1969); R. P. Scharlemann, *Reflection and Doubt in the Thought of Paul Tillich* (1969). (D. D. WI.)

**TILLY, JOHANN TSERCLAES,** GRAF VON (1559–1632), the greatest general in the Bavarian service and so the principal commander of the Catholic League in Germany during the Thirty Years' War (*q.v.*). He was born in February 1559, at Tilly in Brabant. In 1568 his father, Martin Tserclaes, lord of Tilly, was exiled from the Spanish Netherlands as an adherent of Egmond (*q.v.*). Johann and his elder brother Jakob were brought up by the Jesuits in Liège and in Cologne, and in 1574 the family was reconciled to the Spanish regime in the Netherlands. Johann entered a Walloon regiment and served in the war against the Protestant Archbishop Gebhard (*q.v.*) of Cologne in 1583–84 and at the siege of Antwerp in 1585 under Alessandro Farnese (*q.v.*), whom he ever afterward acknowledged as his teacher. Having distinguished himself on the Catholic side in the French Wars of Religion, he went in 1594 to join the Holy Roman emperor Rudolf II's army campaigning against the Turks.

Tilly refused to side with the archdukes against Rudolf II, thereby incurring the enmity of the future emperor Matthias (*q.v.*). He therefore offered his service, in 1610, to Maximilian I (*q.v.*), duke and later elector of Bavaria, for whom he created the efficient Bavarian Army, backbone and spearhead of the Catholic League. Under the nominal leadership of Maximilian and hampered by the irresolute Graf von Bucquoy (C. B. de Longueval, commander of the emperor Ferdinand II's forces), Tilly in 1620 conducted the first campaign of the Thirty Years' War: he forced the rebellious Estates of Upper and Lower Austria into unconditional surrender (July–August), outflanked the Bohemian troops and their Hungarian allies (September–October), and then marched straight on Prague, to win the decisive Battle of the White Mountain (Nov. 8).

In the following years Tilly conquered the Upper Palatinate and the Rhenish Palatinate for Bavaria and, not without occasional reverses, defeated and destroyed the armies of Ernst von Mansfeld (*q.v.*), Christian (*q.v.*) of Brunswick, and the margrave George Frederick of Baden-Durlach, making himself master of northwestern Germany. For his victory over Christian at Höchst (June 20, 1622) he was made a count of the Empire.

In the war against Denmark (1625–29) Tilly with the army of the Catholic League gained the decisive victory of Lutter (Aug. 27, 1626), but the fruits of Denmark's defeat fell to the emperor Ferdinand II, who now employed an army of his own under Wallenstein (*q.v.*). Tilly was offered the duchy of Brunswick-Calenberg, but preferred a financial reward.

When the Swedish king Gustavus II Adolphus invaded Germany (1630), Wallenstein was in disgrace, and the command of the Imperial as well as the League forces was therefore entrusted to Tilly. His attempt to secure Magdeburg as a base from which to overawe Saxony and Brandenburg and to bar Gustavus Adolphus' advance into central Germany failed because the city, stormed on May 20, 1631, went up in flames. Swedish propaganda blamed Tilly for the destruction, which, however, was contrary to his intentions and interest. When Tilly, by order of the emperor and against Maximilian's wishes, invaded Saxony, the elector John George I was driven into the Swedish camp, and Tilly, egged on by the German general G. H. von Pappenheim against his own better judgment, accepted battle and was completely defeated at Breitenfeld (Sept. 17, 1631).

Tilly's last victory was gained over a Swedish detachment at Bamberg (Feb. 10, 1632). His attempt to prevent Gustavus Adolphus from crossing the Lech River into Bavaria at Rain failed, and he received a wound of which he died a fortnight later, at Ingolstadt on April 30, 1632. (S. H. S.)

**TIMAEUS** (*c.* 350–*c.* 250 B.C.), Greek historian, whose writings shaped the tradition of western Mediterranean history, was born at Tauromenium (Taormina) in Sicily. He was expelled by Agathocles, the tyrant of Syracuse, and went to Athens where he studied rhetoric under Isocrates' pupil Philiscus and passed 50 years of his life. Whether he ever returned home is uncertain. The 38 books of his *Histories* went down to Agathocles' death in 289, but a separate work on Pyrrhus of Epirus seems to have reached the Roman crossing into Sicily in 264. Books 1–5 contained the early history of Italy and Sicily, books 6–33 the history of Sicily from the foundation of the Greek colonies to Agathocles' accession with digressions, sometimes touching on Greece, and books 34–38 a separate account of Agathocles. The *Olympionikai* ("Victors at Olympia") was probably a chronological study.

Timaeus was bitterly attacked by later historians, especially Polybius. Some of his faults, such as the composition of artificial rhetorical speeches, are common to the historiography of the age; but a somewhat naïve attitude toward marvels reflects a genuine feeling for folklore. He was spiteful to those he disliked such as Dionysius and Agathocles, and he exaggerated the virtues of the Corinthian general Timoleon. Above all he showed the faults of the armchair historian. But his interests were wide; he was assiduous in assembling material, including inscriptions; and Polybius' charge of ignorance and willful dishonesty is unjust. Timaeus' system of reckoning by Olympiads furnished a valuable chronological tool for his successors, including Polybius. He employed a pleasing "Asiatic" style, which Cicero approved.

BIBLIOGRAPHY.—Fragments in F. Jacoby, *Fragmente der griechischen Historiker,* vol. 3, no. 566 (1955; with commentary). *See* also Polybius, *Historiae,* book xii; J. B. Bury, *The Ancient Greek Historians* (1909); T. S. Brown, *Timaeus of Tauromenium* (1958). (F. W. WA.)

**TIMARU,** a city and port on the east coast of South Island, New Zealand, midway between Christchurch and Dunedin. Pop. (1966) 27,314. The first ship taking immigrants to New Zealand direct from Britain arrived there in January 1859. Timaru is now the provincial centre of South Canterbury. The harbour, formed by breakwaters, can take ships of up to 18,000 tons. The chief exports are frozen meat, wool, flour, and cereal products, the processing of these being the city's main industries. A sunny, temperate climate, a splendid bathing beach, and easy access to Mt. Cook and the Southern Alps make Timaru a popular resort.

(JA. A. G.)

**TIMBER:** *see* LUMBERING; WOOD.

**TIMBERLINE,** the boundary above which there is no tree growth. In any elevated area in low or middle latitudes the timberline is generally clearly marked, but its height is dependent not only on general conditions but also on local climatic and soil conditions.

**TIMBUKTU:** *see* TOMBOUCTOU.

**TIME, DAYLIGHT SAVING,** a means of providing for the utilization of more daylight, especially during the summer, by setting clocks ahead. First suggested in a whimsical essay by Benjamin Franklin in 1784, it was not put into practice until the 20th century. An Englishman, William Willett, in 1907 published a pamphlet entitled *Waste of Daylight.* He financed a campaign for setting the clock ahead by 80 min. in four moves of 20 min. each in the spring and summer months. In 1908 Robert (later Sir Robert) Pearce introduced a bill in the House of Commons to put the clock ahead by law. The bill, which failed, called for advancing the clock one hour in the spring and returning to Greenwich mean time in the autumn.

During World War I, when conservation of fuel was of utmost importance, Germany adopted daylight saving in 1915. In Great Britain a one-hour change became law on May 17, 1916, effective the following Sunday, May 21. In honour of its proponent, who had died a year earlier, the system was at first called Willet time; later the name adopted was British summer time. In the United States, largely as a result of World War I, a campaign for daylight saving was launched in 1916, and in 1917 the U.S. Congress passed an act whereby standard time would be advanced one hour on the last Sunday of March and set back on the last Sunday of October.

After World War I, British summer time was renewed by acts of Parliament; that of 1922 provided that summer time begin on the Sunday following the third Saturday in April, or if that fell on Easter Day, the Sunday following the second Saturday in April; it would end on the Sunday following the third Saturday in September. The act of 1925 altered the closing date to the Sunday following the first Saturday in October. The official time for altering the clock is always 2 A.M. Greenwich mean time. In the United States, opposition had developed from the farmers, and the law was repealed on Aug. 20, 1919, over the president's veto. In the years that followed, legislation was enacted by various states or municipalities.

The advent of World War II again made changes necessary. In order to aid war production, Great Britain adopted double summer time, *i.e.,* two hours in advance of Greenwich mean time. In some years the customary period of about 5 months was lengthened to 7, 10, or even 12 months. The 12-month period was maintained for the period 1941–44. The United States, on Feb. 6, 1942, put into effect "war time," one hour in advance of standard time, continuing until the end of September 1945.

Objections to daylight saving time took several forms—farmers complained that cows were unable to adjust to a new milking time and that dew in the earlier hour was heavy enough to hinder farm work; parents complained that small children would not go to bed while the sun was still shining; others complained it was contrary to nature, contrary to tradition, or contrary to the best interests of distributors of lighting power and equipment. Whatever the objection, many countries abandoned daylight saving in the postwar period; some, like France, retained it on a year-round basis. The United States allowed the various states to set their own regulations, resulting in a great deal of confusion from state to state, and sometimes within the state itself. The general period of observance was from the last Sunday in April to the last Sunday in September or October. Great Britain, in 1968, despite widespread opposition, instituted a three-year experimental period of year-round summer time. *See* also TIME, STANDARD.

**TIME, STANDARD.** In an isolated community clocks and watches would be set to the local mean time (*see* TIME MEASUREMENT), and before the period of railway communication the different towns as a rule kept local time. The need for a more systematic plan of standard times was chiefly felt in the United States. While the railways in England were run by Greenwich time and the railways in France by Paris time, it was not to be expected that railway systems in the middle and western states would adopt Washington, D.C., time, differing by several hours from the local time of the region which they served. Hence each railway had its own time, or, in the case of the longer lines, several different time zones, and great confusion arose at overlapping points. The question of bringing order out of chaos through a system of standard time was actively discussed in the principal commercial nations during the decade before 1880, Sandford Fleming in Canada and Charles F. Dowd in the United States being the principal proponents of the system. This involved adopting for the whole earth 24 standard meridians 15° apart in longitude, starting from Greenwich. These meridians were to be the centres of 24 time zones; in each zone the time adopted would be uniform, and it would change by one hour in passing from one zone to the next. After long discussion railway managers of the U.S. and Canada decided to adopt the system. Zone time based on the Greenwich meridian is now adopted almost everywhere. In most countries the time differs by an integral number of hours from Greenwich time, in accordance with the original plan; but in some countries a compromise involving half-hour differences was adopted. European countries are ranged in two different time zones—west European time (one hour fast) and east European time (two hours fast). In 1968 the United Kingdom went off Greenwich time and joined Western Europe by adopting west European time. In the U.S. there are seven time zones, respectively 5, 6, 7, 8, 9, 10 and 11 hours slow on Greenwich time.

The advent on an international scale of shipping and, later, of air travel has necessitated world-wide agreement on the 15° time zone system. Slight adjustments have been made in some of these parallels of longitude so that a particular standardization may cover a specific geographical area; for example in certain countries in east Asia (*see* map). The parallel of longitude at 180° (12 hours) is also known as the "date line" because just to the west of this line countries are one calendar day ahead of Greenwich; again this line has been adjusted so that it does not pass through the middle of a country—in this case New Zealand. Some countries adopt, as an internal policy within their own borders, a zoning every 7½°, giving time intervals of one-half hour; examples are India and other countries in the far east.

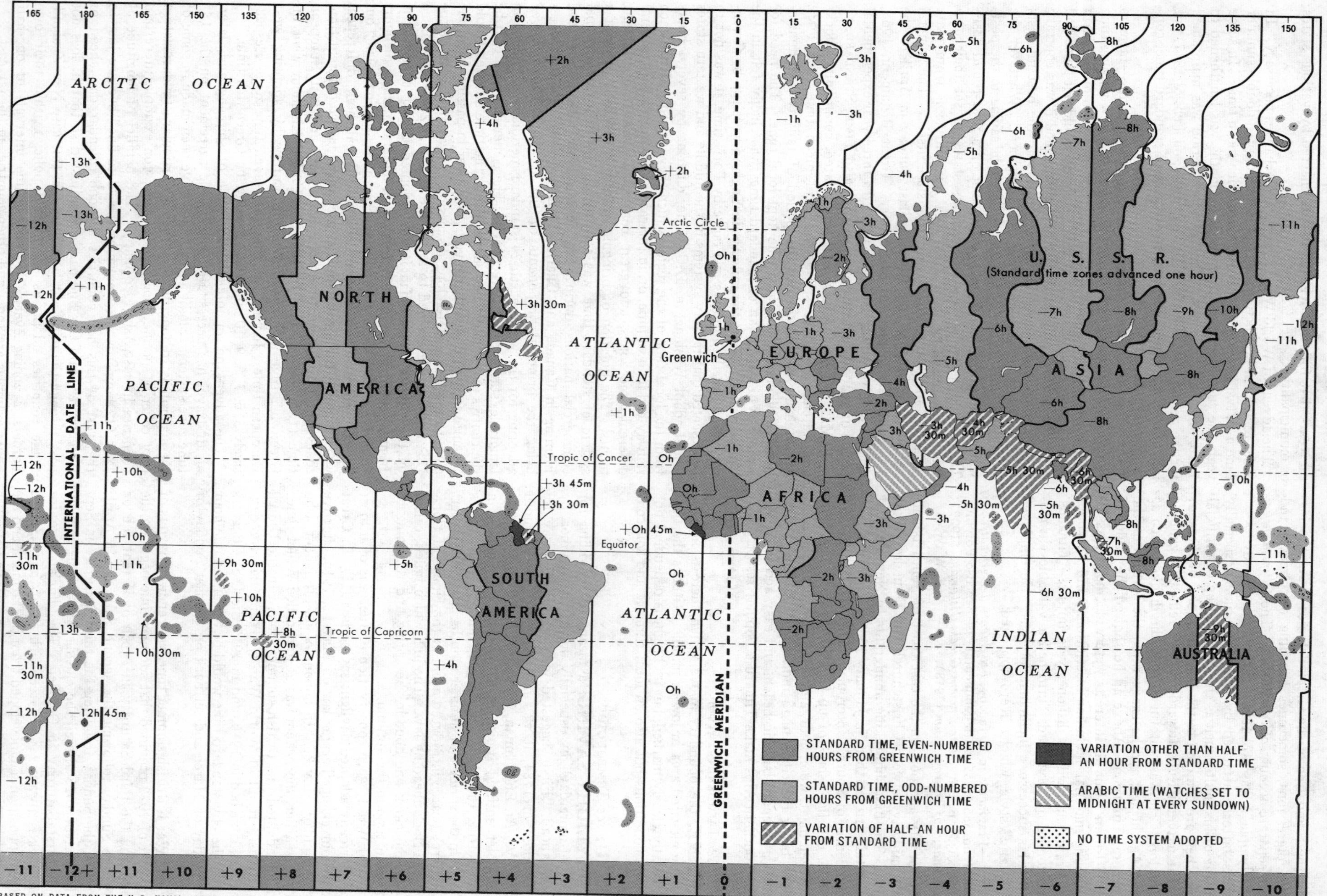


BASED ON DATA FROM THE U.S. NAVAL OCEANOGRAPHIC OFFICE

TIME IS CALCULATED FROM THE MERIDIAN OF GREENWICH, ENG. THE MIDDLE OF THE ZERO TIME ZONE PASSES THROUGH GREENWICH WITH ITS EAST AND WEST LIMITS 7°30′ ON EACH SIDE. EACH 15° ZONE EAST AND WEST OF THE INITIAL ZONE REPRESENTS ONE HOUR OF TIME. THE NUMBER OF HOURS (h) AND MINUTES (m) THAT MUST BE ADDED TO OR SUBTRACTED FROM LOCAL TIME TO GIVE GREENWICH TIME IS INDICATED ON THE MAP FOR EACH ZONE AND AREA UNITS THAT HAVE A DIFFERENT TIME FROM THE ZONE IN WHICH THEY ARE LOCATED

In the summer months some countries advance their time by one hour, or adopt the time of the next zone to the east. The advantage of summer or daylight saving time (*see* TIME, DAYLIGHT SAVING) depends much on the latitude, and it is scarcely suitable for more northerly or southerly countries; it is unpopular in agricultural communities, but is widely favoured in urban areas.

The advantage of adopting a continuous reckoning of the hours from 0 to 24 instead of using the divisions A.M. and P.M. is obvious, and this reckoning has been adopted for many public services in some countries, but confusion has arisen through uncertainty as to when 0 hr. occurs. Astronomers from time immemorial have used a 24 hr. reckoning beginning at noon, but for civil purposes it has seemed more natural to count from midnight. At the meeting of the International Astronomical Union that was held in 1922, astronomers were recommended to use time beginning at Greenwich midnight from 1925; however, no recommendation was given as to the name. In England it was believed that the intention was to use the name Greenwich mean time (GMT) in a sense differing by 12 hr. from what it had previously meant. In other countries, however, other names were available for time counted from Greenwich mean midnight and all of these were used.

At the meeting of the International Astronomical Union in 1935, it was decided to use *temps universel* (TU) in France, universal time (UT) in England and *Weltzeit* (WZ) in Germany. The designation Greenwich civil time (GCT), which had been used in England, France and the United States, was dropped, and it was recommended that anyone who still wanted to use time counted from noon should call it Greenwich mean astronomical time (GMAT). (A. S. E.; J. JN.)

See *The American Ephemeris and Nautical Almanac* (annual) for detailed data; the British *Nautical Almanac* publishes annually a full list of standard times of the different countries and of those on nonstandard time.

**TIME MEASUREMENT.** Time is a basic concept that deals with the occurrence of events. There is a definite order in which any two nonsimultaneous events occur at some location. If *A* and *B* are such events, either *A* occurs before *B* or *B* occurs before *A*. Between two nonsimultaneous occurrences there is a lapse of an interval of time.

The measurement of time involves establishing a precise system of reference for specifying when any event occurs, that is, specifying the epoch and establishing a standard interval of time. Astronomy and civil affairs are concerned both with epoch and with time intervals, whereas physics deals almost entirely with time intervals. The fundamental unit of time interval is the second.

A reference time scale could be based on any phenomenon that involves change with time, such as (1) the rotation of the earth or (2) the motion of a pendulum. To be generally useful it should be possible to determine the same numerical value of the time, within very close limits, anywhere on the earth. This condition is satisfied by the rotating earth but not by the pendulum.

Until recently, the rotation of the earth about its axis furnished the only time scale in general use, mean solar time. However, other independent time scales have recently come into use. Ephemeris time is based on the revolution of the earth about the sun, and atomic time is based on quantum changes in the state of atoms.

Mean solar time is slightly variable with respect to both ephemeris time and atomic time. The fundamental unit of time interval was formerly the second of mean solar time in the metric system. In 1956 it was replaced by the second of ephemeris time and in 1967 by the second of atomic time. The various kinds of time are discussed under the general headings, Rotational, Ephemeris, and Atomic.

## ROTATIONAL (NONUNIFORM) TIME

**Solar Time.**—The apparent daily motion of the sun from east to west provides a measure of time called apparent solar time, which is indicated by a sundial. The interval between two successive transits of the apparent sun across the meridian is called an apparent solar day.

The annual revolution of the earth about the sun causes the sun to appear to move eastward with respect to the stars. Hence, an apparent solar day is not equal to the period of rotation of the earth with respect to the stars. The apparent motion of the sun is 360° in a year, or nearly 1° per day, and an apparent solar day is almost four minutes longer than the period of rotation.

The earth moves about the sun in an elliptical path in a plane called the ecliptic, which is inclined about 23½° to the Equator. In consequence of these factors the component of the daily motion of the sun along the Equator varies. As a result, apparent solar days are of variable length, and apparent solar time is nonuniform.

The development of clocks and watches in the 17th century made apparent solar time unsuitable for civil use, and mean solar time was introduced. The mean solar day is the mean period of rotation of the earth with respect to the sun. Mean solar time is so defined as to be a measure of the rotation of the earth. The difference between apparent solar and mean solar time is called the equation of time. Its numerical value varies from 0 to about 16 min.

**Sidereal (Equinoctial) Time.**—For various astronomical purposes, such as locating a celestial object, the astronomer uses sidereal time. In the discussion given here astronomical coordinates, etc., are treated only briefly. For additional details *see* ASTRONOMY: *Modern Descriptive Astronomy*.

The intersection of the true Equator and the ecliptic provides a fundamental reference point called the true vernal equinox or first point of Aries. Right ascensions are measured along the celestial Equator from the equinox. The interval between two successive meridian transits of the true equinox is called a true sidereal day. The hour angle of the true equinox, that is, the angle west of the meridian measured along the Equator, is true sidereal time, also called apparent sidereal time.

The true equinox is not fixed with respect to the system of stars but moves very slowly in a retrograde direction along the ecliptic, in a period of about 25,000 years. The secular, or steady, part of the motion is called precession and the periodic, or oscillating, part is called nutation. In consequence of nutation true sidereal days are of variable length. The maximum variation from the mean is only about 0.01 sec., but improvements in the pendulum clock made about 1925 required that uniform equinoctial time be introduced.

Mean sidereal time is defined as the hour angle of the mean equinox, that is, of the equinox freed of nutation. A mean sidereal day is the interval between successive transits of the mean equinox.

The difference between apparent and mean sidereal time is called the nutation in right ascension, or the equation of the equinoxes. It varies from 0 to a little more than 1 sec.

**Relation Between Solar and Sidereal Time.**—Mean solar time is defined as 12 hours plus the hour angle of the fictitious mean sun. The latter is a point moving uniformly in the celestial Equator with the mean speed of the apparent sun. In practice the right ascension of the fictitious mean sun is obtained from a formula, and the operational procedure is such as to keep mean solar time rigorously proportional to the speed of rotation of the earth.

During one mean solar day a clock keeping mean sidereal time gains 3 min. 56.555 sec. of mean sidereal time on a clock keeping mean solar time.

Apparent solar time and apparent sidereal time have two sources of nonuniformity: (1) inequalities arising from the motion of the earth about the sun and from the motion of the equinox; and (2) variations in the speed of rotation of the earth. The inequalities caused by (1) may be accurately calculated in advance from dynamical principles, but not those due to (2).

**Time Units.**—A mean solar day is divided as follows:

1 mean solar day = 24 mean solar hours
1 mean solar hour = 60 mean solar minutes
1 mean solar minute = 60 mean solar seconds
1 mean solar day = 86,400 mean solar seconds

The other kinds of days are similarly divided, giving, for example, the mean sidereal second by subdivision of the mean sidereal day.

**Reckoning of Days and Hours.**—The day begins at midnight and runs through 24 hours. In the 24-hour system of reckoning, used in Europe and by military agencies of the United States, the hours and minutes are given as a four digit number. Thus 0028 means 28 minutes past midnight, and 1240 means 40 minutes past noon. Also, 2400 of May 15 is the same as 0000 of May 16. This system allows no uncertainty as to the epoch designated.

In the 12-hour system there are two sets of 12 hours; those from midnight to noon are designated A.M. (ante meridiem, before noon) and those from noon to midnight are designated P.M. (post meridiem, after noon). Neither A.M. nor P.M. may be used to designate either noon or midnight without ambiguity. To designate noon the word noon or 1200 should be used. To designate midnight without ambiguity the two dates between which it falls should be given unless the 24-hour notation is used. Thus, we may write midnight, May 15–16, or 0000 May 16.

Local mean time is the hour angle of the mean sun increased by 12 hours. Local mean time at Greenwich is called Greenwich Mean Time (GMT) or universal time (UT). The designation GMT is used in navigation. UT is the term used by astronomers. It would be inconvenient to use local time strictly, for no two places in different longitudes have the same mean solar time. The variation amounts to one hour for 15° of longitude, or about five seconds to the mile in middle latitudes. A system of zones was devised whereby within each zone the same mean time rules, but changes abruptly by one whole hour at its borders. Mean solar time, so regulated, is called zone time or standard time. (*See* TIME, STANDARD.) Standard time differs from UT by an integral number of hours.

Another convention regulates the date line: in traveling across it a calendar day is added to the reckoning in passing westward, or is dropped in passing eastward. (*See* DATE LINE.)

During World War I clocks were advanced by one hour in summer in various countries in order to save fuel by reducing the need for artificial light. During World War II all clocks in the U.S. were advanced, and remained, one hour ahead of standard time for the entire interval Feb. 9, 1942–Sept. 30, 1945; no changes were made during the summer. England used "double-summer time" for part of the year, whereby the clock was advanced two hours ahead of standard time.

In 1966 the U.S. Congress passed a bill that, as of 1967, established daylight-saving time in summer throughout the nation. A state as a whole, however, could decide to remain on standard time.

The time in a large part of Europe is always one hour ahead of GMT; there is no change during the summer. The U.S.S.R., for example, adopted this system in 1930 and England in 1968.

**Practical Determination of Rotational Time.**—The determination of time is a highly specialized branch of astronomy which is usually carried out by a governmental observatory. The basic definitions concerning time determination are standardized by the International Astronomical Union (IAU), under whose auspices the Bureau International de l'Heure (International Time Bureau) at Paris makes comparisons of time determinations and provides certain data needed for the uniform reduction of observations.

The steps involved in the determination of universal time (UT) are as follows: (1) The transit of a star of known position is observed in order to determine local mean equinoctial (sidereal) time. (2) The longitude west of Greenwich is added to obtain the Greenwich sidereal time. (3) This is converted to UT by a mathematical formula in the form denoted UT0, discussed in further detail, below.

The apparatus required for time determination consists basically of a telescope and a clock. Notation is made of the reading on the clock at the instant of passage of a star of known position across a selected reference line on the celestial sphere which is fixed with respect to the observing station. This reference line is the local meridian for the first two instruments described below and is the small circle that is everywhere 30° from the zenith for the third instrument.

*Transit Instrument.*—This is a small instrument similar in mounting to a transit circle (*q.v.*). The telescope is constrained to move in the plane of the meridian. The reading of a clock being checked is recorded on a chronograph at the instant of transit as noted by the observer.

*Photographic Zenith Tube.*—An instrument more accurate than the transit instrument for time determination is the photographic zenith tube (PZT), which was used for this purpose after 1934 at the U.S. Naval Observatory. The PZT is fixed in a vertical position, and only stars that transit near the zenith are observed. A basin of mercury reflects the rays of light from the stars as the rays pass through the lens and defines the zenith, which lies in the meridian.

The plate is held by a carriage which is driven by a motor so as to track the star being observed. Four exposures of 20 sec. each are made of each star, and the lens and plate are rotated 180° as a unit between exposures. The motion of the carriage during the exposures initiates timing impulses which are read on the clock being compared with the stars. By measuring the positions of the star images it is possible to determine what the clock read when the star crossed the meridian. A comparison with the predicted time gives the correction to the clock.

The PZT was designed by F. E. Ross for the determination of the variation of latitude. Ross followed the design of Sir George Airy's reflex zenith tube, installed at Greenwich, Eng., in 1851. Ross improved on this obsolete instrument by placing what is known as the second nodal point outside of the lens and by making the instrument photographic. The photographic plate, which is small, is placed just beneath the lens at the nodal point. The position of the image of a star on the plate thus becomes insensitive to the tilt of the lens.

This PZT, designated no. 1, was installed at Washington, D.C., in 1915 for the determination of the variation of latitude. It was adapted for the determination of time also in 1934 by F. B. Littell and J. E. Willis. A PZT of improved design was placed in operation in 1949 at a substation of the Naval Observatory at Richmond, Fla. A similar PZT was installed at Washington in 1954 to replace PZT no. 1. Several other observatories subsequently used the PZT.

*Impersonal Astrolabe.*—A. Danjon, of the Paris Observatory, devised an accurate instrument for time determination which is quite different from those described. (The use of the word astrolabe in this connection should not be confused with the designation for the astrolabe of the days before the telescope.)

The astrolabe makes use of a reflecting basin of mercury and a 60° prism to form direct and reflected images of a star. When the altitude of a star is exactly 60° the images coincide. In earlier forms of the instrument it was difficult to determine when coincidence occurred. Danjon introduced a Wollaston prism to obtain four images, two of which are suppressed. The observer manipulates a motor so as to keep the remaining images parallel to a spider thread, and the instant when the altitude is 60° is automatically recorded on a chronograph. Observations are made in various azimuths and from them both time and latitude are obtained.

**Practical Determination of Time Intervals.**—To indicate time and to measure time intervals various types of clocks have been developed.

*Pendulum Clocks.*—Galileo discovered about 1583 that the time of swing of a pendulum was nearly independent of the amplitude of swing. Christiaan Huygens contributed to the theory of the pendulum and had the first pendulum clock constructed in 1656. Numerous improvements were subsequently made, and pendulum clocks reached a high stage of precision from 1900 to 1925. The rates of the best pendulum clocks are constant to about 0.001 sec. per day. Pendulum clocks, however, are no longer used in precise timekeeping, having been replaced by the quartz-crystal and atomic clocks.

*Quartz-Crystal Clocks.*—A quartz crystal, if deformed, produces a difference in electric potential across certain of its faces. Conversely, a difference in electric potential produced across certain faces of a quartz crystal causes it to become deformed. This property, known as the piezoelectric effect, enables the quartz crystal to be incorporated in an electronic oscillator. The frequency of oscillation is controlled by the frequency of mechanical vibration of the crystal. The frequency $f$ and the period $p$ of a cyclic occurrence are related, $f = 1/p$. Frequency is measured in cycles per second (cps). However, the unit hertz (Hz), defined by 1 Hz = 1 cps, is coming into use. Examples of nomenclature: 15,000 cps = 15 kilohertz = 15 kHz; 5,000,000 cps = 5 megahertz = 5 MHz.

The oscillator frequency may be several million cycles per second. This is divided down by a device known as a frequency divider to control a mechanical-electronic clock, which has a synchronous motor, or an all-electronic clock, which has no moving parts. Sharp pulses each second, accurate to a fraction of a microsecond, may be produced by both types.

Quartz crystals change frequency with age; generally they tend to run faster. This aging, however, can be made very small by careful design and manufacture. A particularly high-grade crystal is the 2.5 Mc/sec crystal developed by A. W. Warner of the Bell Telephone Laboratories. The average change in frequency (acceleration) for the best of these during a 10-month interval was 3 parts in $10^{12}$ per day, or a change in rate of 0.3 microsecond per day.

The use of quartz as a frequency control was described by W. G. Cady in 1922. In 1928 W. A. Morrison and J. W. Horton built the first quartz-crystal clock at the Bell Telephone Laboratories. P. Sollenberger introduced a crystal-controlled clock for the automatic transmission of time signals at the U.S. Naval Observatory in 1934.

*Atomic Clocks.*—An atomic oscillator combined with a clock, as above, forms an atomic clock. Rates are constant to about one microsecond per day (*see* also CLOCK).

**Variations in Speed of Rotation of the Earth.**—Rotational time is variable with respect to ephemeris time and atomic time because of variations in the speed of rotation. These variations are of three types: secular, irregular, and periodic.

Tidal friction causes a progressive increase in the length of the day of about 0.001 sec. per century. This effect was found from studies of ancient eclipses.

About 1900 Simon Newcomb found that during the preceding two centuries the moon was sometimes ahead of its computed position and sometimes behind. He suspected that this might be due to an error in the clock (the earth) instead of the lunar tables, but was not able to decide the matter. Later studies by E. W. Brown in 1926 and W. de Sitter in 1927, utilizing both the moon and planets, indicated that the rotation of the earth was not uniform. In 1939 Sir Harold Spencer Jones definitely proved that the rotation was nonuniform. He showed that discrepancies in the orbital motions of the Earth, Venus, and Mercury corresponded to those shown by the moon; the apparent errors in position at any time were proportional to the mean motions.

It was formerly supposed that irregular changes in speed of rotation occurred suddenly. However, D. Brouwer suggested in 1952 that such changes occurred gradually. Observations of universal time compared with atomic time indicate that sudden changes in acceleration but not in speed of rotation occur.

Variations with periods of one year and six months were first obtained with some degree of accordance with recent data by N. Stoyko in 1937 at the Bureau de l'Heure. The coefficient of the annual term found by Stoyko was about 0.060 sec. It is now agreed that the coefficient is about 0.025 sec.

Y. Mintz and W. Munk have calculated the effects of winds on the speed of rotation of the earth. There is a reasonable accordance of their results with astronomical observations for the annual term.

The moon affects the time determined in two ways, directly by altering the direction of the vertical and indirectly by tidal action on the earth's crust. A change in the form of the earth alters its moment of inertia and hence its speed of rotation. The period of the direct term is 0.5 day. There are two tidal terms of short periods, 13.6 days and 27.6 days. The amplitudes of all three terms are each about 0.001 sec. in time.

**Corrected Universal Time** (UT2).—During the course of a year or so universal time is nonuniform because of the following effects: (1) polar motion; (2) annual and semiannual terms in speed of rotation of the earth; and (3) direct and indirect lunar terms. The International Astronomical Union decided that as of Jan. 1, 1956, universal time would be computed so as to include corrections for (1) and (2); (3) is too small to be of effect. The time so computed is denoted UT2; it is relatively uniform time.

The notation adopted is as follows:

UT0 is classical universal time.
UT1 is UT0 corrected for (1).
UT2 is UT0 corrected for (1) and (2).
UTC is coordinated universal time.

UTC is the time given by radio time signals; it differs from UT2 by less than 0.1 sec. UT0 and UT1 are used in precise surveying. Corrections are furnished to make it possible to convert from one system to another.

Although the seasonal terms are not strictly repetitive and are largely empirical, it was decided that a correction for these terms could be employed advantageously.

The polar-motion term arises from the motion of the pole of rotation in an approximate circle of about 30 ft. in radius (*see* GEODESY: *Variation of Latitude*). The motion of the pole causes not only the latitude of an observatory but also the longitude of an observatory to vary in a period of 14 months. The instantaneous value of the longitude must be added to the observed local mean time to obtain UT if UT is to be the same for all observatories.

The Bureau de l'Heure computes and distributes the corrections for variation of longitude, which differ for each observatory, and the correction for seasonal variation, which is alike for all observatories.

## EPHEMERIS TIME

**Definition.**—The motions of the celestial bodies occur in accordance with the laws of celestial mechanics, first propounded by Sir Isaac Newton. They were modified slightly by the theory of relativity of Albert Einstein. (*See* RELATIVITY: *General Theory of Relativity*.)

Knowing the masses, coordinates, and velocities of a number of bodies at one epoch, it becomes possible to find the coordinates for any epoch, $t$, by the solution of the appropriate differential equations.

The solution for some particular coordinate of one of the bodies, say $x_1$, may be written

$$x_1 = f_1\ (t;\ a_1, a_2, \ldots a_n) \qquad (1)$$

where $f_1$ is a function of $t$ and the constants of integration $a_1$, $a_2 \ldots a_n$. By postulate, the $t$ of equation (1) is uniform astronomical time. Assigning numerical values to the constants for a particular planet or satellite defines its orbit. An ephemeris may be constructed which gives the coordinates, usually for uniformly increasing values of $t$. The ephemeris may be used to find the coordinates of the body if $t$ is given, or to determine $t$ if the coordinates are observed. The time $t$ which enters in the equations of motion, the solution, and the ephemeris has been given the name ephemeris time.

The orbital motion of the earth about the sun has been selected as the standard to define the numerical measure of ephemeris time. The position of the earth in its orbit is obtained by observing the position of the sun with respect to the stars. *The Tables of the Sun* of Simon Newcomb have been adopted by astronomers for computing the coordinates of the earth as a function of ephemeris time. (For an account of Newcomb's other contributions, *see* NEWCOMB, SIMON.)

In practice, ephemeris time is obtained from the orbital motion of the moon by observing its position with respect to the stars. The moon's orbital motion is much faster than the earth's, and the moon is easier to observe than the sun. Coordinates of the moon as a function of ephemeris time are given in the national ephemerides.

The lunar-solar tides on the earth produce a couple which affects the orbital motion of the moon. The lunar ephemeris contains a term, the coefficient of which is based on past observations, to correct for this effect. If the tidal couple should change in the future, the lunar ephemeris would not be in strict agreement with the solar ephemeris. For this reason the moon is not used as the standard to define ephemeris time.

**Determination of Ephemeris Time.**—Large transit instruments, also called meridian circles, are used to determine the position of the sun and moon with respect to the stars. The position of the moon may be determined visually from meridian transits or from the occultation of a star of known position, that is, the cutting off of its light by the intervention of another body.

A dual-rate moon position camera developed at the U.S. Naval Observatory in 1952 by W. Markowitz enables the position to be obtained photographically. By means of a dark glass filter, which tilts, the moon is held fixed relative to the stars in the background during a simultaneous exposure of 20 sec.

An observation of the moon gives its apparent coordinates for an epoch recorded in universal time. The observed geocentric coordinates are obtained by correcting for parallax. The computed geocentric coordinates of the moon are tabulated as a function of ephemeris time. The ephemeris is entered with the observed coordinates and the corresponding ephemeris time is taken out. The difference between ET and UT is given by the formula $\Delta t = \text{ET} - \text{UT}$.

## ATOMIC TIME

**Definition.**—According to the quantum theory an atom (or molecule) can exist in various quantum states, each of which has an associated energy level, $E$. When a transition from a higher to a lower level occurs, electromagnetic energy is radiated whose frequency (oscillations per unit of time) is

$$\nu = \frac{(E_1 - E_2)}{h} \qquad (2)$$

where $E_1$ is the initial energy, $E_2$ is the final energy, and $h$ is Planck's constant.

Each transition produces a spectral line. For visible radiation, (light waves) the frequency is about $5 \times 10^{14}$ cps. This is too high to permit counting of individual cycles. The development of methods of generating frequencies of the order of $10^{10}$ cps opened up the possibility of utilizing spectral lines in the one-centimetre microwave region for frequency control.

**Ammonia.**—R. V. Pound outlined in 1946 the use of spectral lines to stabilize an oscillator, and in 1947 W. V. Smith and co-workers confirmed the method of Pound by constructing an oscillator that was stabilized in frequency with the 3,3 inversion line of ammonia ($NH_3$). W. D. Hershberger and L. E. Norton stabilized a klystron oscillator with ammonia in 1948. H. Lyons and co-workers used an ammonia-controlled oscillator in 1949 to control a clock for brief periods at the National Bureau of Standards, Washington, D.C. In the preceding applications ammonia was used in absorption.

C. H. Townes developed in 1954 a microwave amplifier called a maser (*q.v.*), which is stabilized in frequency by ammonia in emission, which has much higher precision. The ammonia molecule exists in two states, with a slight energy difference. These are separated electrostatically and those in the higher state enter a cavity. Some of the molecules fall to the lower state, with the emission of radiation.

The frequency of ammonia devices depends somewhat upon their construction and also on the isotope of N in the $NH_3$ molecule. Approximate frequencies are 23,870,129,300 cps for $N^{14}$ and 22,789,421,700 cps for $N^{15}$.

**Cesium.**—The cesium atom includes two energy states that differ slightly, depending on whether the spin of the outer electron is the same or opposite to the nucleus. A beam of cesium atoms issues from an oven and travels along a tube past a magnet. Those of one state are deflected to hit the wall of the tube. The others pass through an rf field and then approach a second magnet. If the frequency of the rf field, which can be varied, is correct, transitions occur and the atoms will be deflected by the second magnet to hit a detector. No atoms can hit the detector if the rf frequency is not equal to the cesium transition frequency. The beam technique for the study of atoms and molecules was developed by I. I. Rabi and co-workers about 1939.

A method developed by N. F. Ramsey of exciting the atoms with the rf field provides a spectral line with a sharp central peak. Early experiments with a cesium beam were made by H. Lyons and co-workers in 1952.

In June 1955 L. Essen and J. V. L. Parry, at the National Physical Laboratory, Teddington, Eng., first placed in operation a cesium beam atomic standard of high precision which made possible the formation of an atomic time scale. In a joint experiment carried out with the U.S. Naval Observatory the frequency of cesium was found to be 9,192,631,770 $\pm$ 20 cps (of ephemeris time).

Cesium beam oscillators have been developed by the National Bureau of Standards, Boulder, Colo.; Swiss Laboratory of Horological Research, Neuchâtel, Switz.; National Research Council, Ottawa, Can.; and elsewhere. Small commercial models weighing about 65 lb. and having an accuracy of about five parts in $10^{12}$ are made. Such atomic clocks are transported in airplanes for synchronizing clocks to one microsecond. (*See* CLOCK: *Atomic Clocks.*)

**Hydrogen.**—A hydrogen maser was developed by N. F. Ramsey and co-workers at Harvard University. Commercial models have an accuracy of about one part in $10^{12}$. The frequency, relative to cesium, is 1,420,405,751.8 cps.

**Thallium.**—J. Bonanomi of the Neuchâtel Observatory has utilized a thallium beam, obtaining high precision. The frequency is 21,310,833,945 cps.

**Rubidium.**—Gas cells employing rubidium have been developed in the U.S. Some of these are constant in frequency to one part in $10^{11}$. The gas cells are not standards in the sense of beam tubes. The frequency of the rubidium gas cell, about 6,834,682,610 cps, depends on the construction and adjustments, whereas beam tubes are nearly independent of such factors.

**The Second.**—The fundamental unit of time interval in the metric system was, by usage but not by formal adoption, the second of mean solar time: 1/86,400 of the mean solar day. Because of variations in the speed of rotation in the earth this unit became unsatisfactory. In 1955 the International Astronomical Union defined the second of ephemeris time (ET) as 1/31,566,925.9747 of the tropical year for 1900 January 0 at 12 h ET. This was adopted by the International Committee of Weights and Measures in 1956 and was ratified by the General Conference of Weights and Measures in 1960.

In 1964 the General Conference also defined an atomic second as 9,192,631,770 periods of radiation of cesium-133. In 1967 this became the sole definition of the second in the International System of Units, which replaced the designation metric system. The second of ET remains as the unit of time interval in the system of constants adopted by the International Astronomical Union in 1964.

In 1968 the atomic second was shorter than the mean solar second by about three parts in $10^8$, and an atomic clock gained about one second per year on a clock showing mean solar time.

**Atomic Time Scales.**—Using the preceding definition of the atomic second, each atomic clock can be used to generate an atomic time scale after an initial epoch has been specified. In the system A.1 established by the U.S. Naval Observatory in 1959, the epoch of A.1 was made 0h 0m 0s when UT2 was 0h 0m 0s on Jan. 1, 1958. Various atomic time scales have been formed from different combinations of atomic oscillators. These differ slightly from each other necessarily.

**Radioactivity.**—Atoms of a radioactive element decay at a rate which depends upon the element but which appears to be independent of temperature, pressure, etc. A clock could be constructed based on radioactive decay but would not measure time interval with high precision. The process is very useful, however, as a means of measuring long intervals of time. (*See* GEOCHRONOLOGY.) It has been ascertained, thus, that certain rocks were formed billions of years ago. Early studies utilized the decay of uranium and thorium into lead. Other transformations, such as radioactive rubidium to strontium and radioactive potassium to argon, are now also used for the dating of rocks.

Carbon-14 dating, developed by W. F. Libby, enables objects having carbon to be dated over the range 100 to 50,000 years. Carbon-14, produced in the atmosphere by cosmic rays, enters living matter in a fairly definite ratio to carbon-12 which does not decay. A determination of the ratio of $C^{14}$ to $C^{12}$ in an object gives its age. The half life of $C^{14}$ is about 5,600 years.

**Ephemeris Time and Atomic Time.**—Celestial bodies are affected by the force of gravitation, and atomic particles, by electrical and nuclear forces. According to some cosmological theories the relation of these forces to each other may change with time. If this is true, then ephemeris time and atomic time would not be equivalent time scales, and the frequency of cesium in cycles per second of ephemeris time, for example, would change. The change, if it exists, would be very small, perhaps one part in $10^{10}$ or $10^{11}$ per year. It will require many years, perhaps 20, to determine if such a divergence exists.

### USES OF TIME SYSTEMS

Universal time is required for celestial navigation, precise surveying, satellite tracking, and whenever the rotational position of the earth about its axis must be known. Ephemeris time is required for studying the motions of celestial bodies, but need not be available immediately; it may be used in arrears. Atomic time provides the unit of time.

**Transmission of Time and Frequency.**—Accurate time is needed for the tracking of artificial satellites, precise surveying, navigation, and for other technical and scientific purposes. These needs are met by the transmission of time signals by radio stations such as NBA, Panama Canal Zone; WWV, Beltsville, Md.; and GBR and MSF, Rugby, Eng.

The radio navigational systems loran-C and Omega (very low frequency) provide very precise transmissions of time and frequency controlled by the U.S. Naval Observatory.

Transmissions of time signals of many countries are coordinated to 0.001 sec. Constant frequency is transmitted each year; it is offset from the atomic frequency so as to provide time pulses close to those of universal time. The frequency is maintained constant with respect to atomic standards to one part in $10^{10}$. Thus, the same transmission provides both universal time, needed for navigation, and constant frequency, needed in physics.

The navigational system of loran-C provides high accuracy for a range up to about 1,000 mi. The East Coast U.S. chain provides time signals with a precision of one microsecond.

Artificial satellites are used for time synchronization. In August 1962 the communication satellite Telstar, of the Bell Telephone Laboratories, was used for clock synchronization between the U.K. and the U.S. An accuracy of one microsecond was obtained. In February 1965 the U.S. satellite Relay 2 was used to synchronize clocks in the U.S. and Japan to 0.1 microsecond. The U.S. Navy navigational satellites, developed by the Applied Physics Laboratory, carry clocks. These provide synchronization to about 30 microseconds.

### RELATIVITY AND TIME MEASUREMENT

A definition of synchronization for clocks located at different points may be readily established if the clocks are stationary with respect to each other. If moving in different frames of reference, however, difficulties arise.

Clocks can be synchronized by means of electromagnetic signals, either light waves or radio waves. The Michelson-Morley experiment had shown that the velocity of light as measured by any observer was the same, irrespective of his motion in space. The theory of relativity provides a means of relating the times indicated by clocks moving with respect to each other which is consistent with the result of the experiment.

In Newtonian mechanics time is absolute; simultaneity may be defined for the entire universe. This is not true, however, for relativistic mechanics. Clocks which are synchronous in one frame of reference may not be synchronous in another.

Some of the consequences of the theory of relativity appear paradoxical and have caused much controversy. Relativistic effects depend upon the ratio $(v/c)^2$, where $v$ is the velocity of the moving object and $c$ is the velocity of light. The velocities involved on earth that concern synchronization of clocks are so small that the relativity effects are negligible.

A clock in an artificial satellite, compared to a similar clock at rest at the surface of the earth, would run slower because of orbital speed (time dilation), but faster with increasing height (opposite of gravitational red shift). For low altitudes the satellite clock would lose about 35 microseconds per day and for very high it would gain about 60. The difference at altitude 2,000 mi. is zero.

*See* also references under "Time Measurement" in the Index.

Bibliography.—Systems of astronomical time are treated completely in ch. 3 of *Explanatory Supplement to the Astronomical Ephemeris and the American Ephemeris and Nautical Almanac* (1961), prepared jointly by the Nautical Almanac Offices of the U.K. and U.S. Summary on timekeeping, quartz clocks, and atomic standards: F. D. Lewis, *Proc. Inst. Radio Engrs.* (Sept. 1955). W. H. Munk and G. J. F. MacDonald, *The Rotation of the Earth* (1960). Dynamical theory of rotation of the earth, precession, and nutation: E. W. Woolard, *Astr. Pap., Wash.*, vol. 15, pt. i (1953). Cesium resonator: L. Essen and J. V. L. Parry, *Phil. Trans.*, vol. 250, p. 45 (1957). (W. Mz.)

**TIMGAD,** the modern name of the Roman city of Thamugadi, situated on the high plateau north of the Aurès Mountains in northeastern Algeria. The modern town, in Batna department, had a population in 1960 of 1,984.

The city was founded by Trajan in A.D. 100 as a colony of veteran soldiers, its full name being Colonia Marciana Traiana Thamugadi. The site was of strategic importance in the defense of Numidia (*q.v.*), as it was on the military road running from Theveste (Tebessa) to Lambaesis (Lambessa), the station of the third legion (*legio III Augusta*). From Thamugadi roads ran north through Cirta (Constantine) to the Mediterranean at Rusicade (Skikda, formerly Philippeville) and northwest to Sitifis (Setif). The country immediately north of the Aurès range was fertile, and Timgad enjoyed a long period of prosperity. Toward the end of the 4th century it was the seat of the bishop Optatus, one of the most violent supporters of the Donatist schism (*see* Donatists).

The city was sacked by Berber tribes toward the end of the Vandal supremacy in Africa. After the Byzantine reconquest a fortress was built near the ruins about 535, which probably survived till the Arab conquest in the 7th century.

Timgad, which held 10,000–15,000 inhabitants, is notable as the site of the most extensive and best-preserved Roman remains in North Africa, almost the entire city having been excavated by French archaeologists in the 19th century; buildings mentioned below are the more important of those of which substantial remains survive.

The original plan of the city was of the classic Roman type, quasi-military in appearance with all streets intersecting at right angles. At first its shape was almost a square, but very soon building spread outside this area. The main east-west street (*decumanus maximus*) was aligned on the Theveste-Lambaesis road; entry from the west was through a triumphal arch often wrongly attributed to Trajan.

Many of the public buildings were on a slight eminence in the centre of the city; the forum, 160 by 140 ft. (50 by 43 m.), situated at the junction of the main north-south street (*cardo maximus*) with the *decumanus maximus,* was flanked on the north by shops, on the east by a basilica, while part of its western side was occupied by the *curia* (council chamber). Near the forum was a set of public conveniences with one of the most efficient disposal arrangements known from Roman times. The ruins of the *capitolium* (temple of Jupiter, Juno, and Minerva) lie to the southwest just outside the original city boundary; other temples existed, such as that dedicated to the Genius of the city. South of the forum lay the theatre, which could hold about 4,000 persons. Timgad was exceptionally well provided with that essential feature of Roman city life, public baths; there were at least 12 of various sizes and dates, the largest being to the north of the city.

There were several markets and a public library, and a number of Christian churches and chapels, including the Donatist "cathedral," perhaps built by Optatus. The remains of the Byzantine fortress are substantial.

*See* C. Courtois, *Timgad: antique Thamugadi* (1951). (B. H. Wa.)

**TIMISKAMING:** *see* Precambrian Time.

**TIMIȘOARA,** a city of western Rumania, lying on the Bega river and canal, chief town of the Banat (formerly Timișoara) administrative and economic region. Pop. (1966 census) 174,688. It consists of the inner town, once strongly fortified, and outlying suburbs, the intervening space, the former glacis, having been laid out in park areas. Principal buildings include the Roman Catholic cathedral, built (1736–73) under Maria Theresa; the Greek Orthodox cathedral; and a castle built by János Hunyadi in 1442. Timișoara is a centre of commerce and has developed industrially, especially since World War II. Its manufactures include electrical apparatus, chemical and building materials, leatherwork and footwear, and, especially, textiles. It is also an important cultural centre, with a university and three institutions of higher education; two state theatres (one German-language); a state opera and ballet; a regional and town library; and a symphony orchestra.

First mentioned in a document dating as far back as 1242, Timișoara became a town at the beginning of the 14th century and was fortified by Charles I (king of Hungary 1309–42), who lived there several years. The Hunyadi family residence was also there. In 1514 the peasant leader György Dózsa was defeated by the Transylvanian vaivode John Zápolya near Timișoara, captured, and killed. The town was held by the Turks from 1552 to 1716. After the peace of Passarowitz (1718) the town, with the whole Banat, was annexed by the Habsburg Empire. It was besieged by the Hungarian revolutionists in 1849, the town successfully resisting for 107 days, and occupied by Serbia in 1919; by the Treaty of Trianon (1920) it was allotted to Rumania.

Banat Regiune, bordering on Yugoslavia, is part of the larger territory of Banat, the other parts of which are in Hungary and Yugoslavia (*see* Banat). Area 8,417 sq.mi. (21,800 sq.km.). Pop. (1963 est.) 1,241,832. It is divided into 12 administrative districts, and the chief towns, outside Timișoara, are Arad (pop. [1963 est.] 114,494), Reșița (47,389), Lugoj (32,142), and Caransebes ([1964 est.] 18,158). Mineral products of the region include coal, iron, manganese, lead, copper, chromite, and marble. Its manufactures (outside Timișoara) comprise iron and steel, machine tools, timber processing, wood distillation, etc. Chief agricultural products are grains (wheat, maize, barley, oats, rice), commercial crops (sugar beets, hemp, rape, tobacco, flax), potatoes, and fruit. Livestock breeding is important.

**TIMMERMANS, FELIX** (1886–1947), Flemish writer, an outstanding representative of regional literature, was born at Lier, July 5, 1886. He made his name with the novel *Pallieter* (1916; Eng. trans. 1924), an "ode to life" written after a moral and physical crisis. To express his praise of life, Timmermans depicted his native Brabant as a paradise and created a character, Pallieter, who has taken his place in literature as the embodiment of a typically Flemish enjoyment of living: at once sensual and mystical, because for him the world's joys are the gift of God. Timmermans was also a painter and illustrator, and found inspiration in old prints and the paintings of Brueghel. For his characters he drew on the people of his native town. His kindly, humorous style, succulent language, wealth of anecdote, sympathetically caricatured characters, and pictorial skill hide his lack of depth. As well as many novels and short stories, he wrote romanticized biographies of Brueghel (1928), St. Francis (1932), and Adriaen Brouwer (1948), travel tales, autobiographical works, and plays.

In 1935 he reached new heights with *Boerenpsalm,* a song of praise showing keen insight into life and a new lyrical strength. The lighthearted sensuality of *Pallieter* is modified by a deeper knowledge of suffering, and praise of nature gives way to praise of humanity represented by the peasant, Wortel, who feels that his life is in God's hands.

Warm colouring is the outstanding characteristic of Timmermans' manner. His expressive style is rooted in the language of the people and excels in the spontaneity and variety of its imagery. It is suited both to the treatment of sensual and spiritual subtleties and to the revelation of Timmermans' exuberant yet melancholy temperament.

Another aspect of his art is shown in some prose works of great restraint (*De zeer schone uren van juffrouw Symforosa, begijntjen* [1918]; *Ik zag Cecilia komen,* [1938]) and in the few serene poems (*Adagio,* 1947) written shortly before his death at Lier, Jan. 24, 1947.

Bibliography.—T. Rutten, *Felix Timmermans* (1928); M. Gilliams, *In memoriam F. Timmermans* (1947); S. Streicher, *Timmermans der ewige Poet* (1948); K. Jacobs, *Felix Timmermans. Lebenstage und Wesenszüge eines Dichters* (1949); Lia Timmermans, *Mijn vader* (1951); K. Goossens, *F. Timmermans en de mystieke blijdschap* (1951); J. de Ceulaer, *De mens in het werk van F. Timmermans* (1957); *F. Timmermans* (1959); A. Westerlinck, *De innerlijke Timmermans* (1957). (R. F. Ls.)

**TIMMINS,** the principal town in the Porcupine gold mining area of northern Ontario, Can., is 268 mi. (431 km.) N of North Bay on the Mattagami River and the Ontario Northland Railway. It was founded in 1911 by Noah Timmins to house employees of the Hollinger Mine, but is not a company town. The town is laid out in grid fashion on sandy terraces overlooking the Mattagami River and prides itself on being the largest town in Canada—the population, (1966) 29,303, is larger than that of many Canadian cities.

The Hollinger Consolidated Gold Mines, Ltd. became the largest producer of gold in Canada. Mine shafts extend to depths of over 5,000 ft. (1,500 m.) and there are many miles of underground workings. In the 1950s and 1960s about 1,000,000 tons of ore were mined each year, and the annual gold production amounted to more than 250,000 oz. Hydroelectric plants at Wawaitin Falls and Sandy Falls furnish energy for the town and for the mines. Power is also brought from the Abitibi River. A major copper-zinc-silver find north of Timmins was reported in 1964.

(F. A. Ck.)

PRINTED IN THE U. S. A. BY R. R. DONNELLEY & SONS CO.

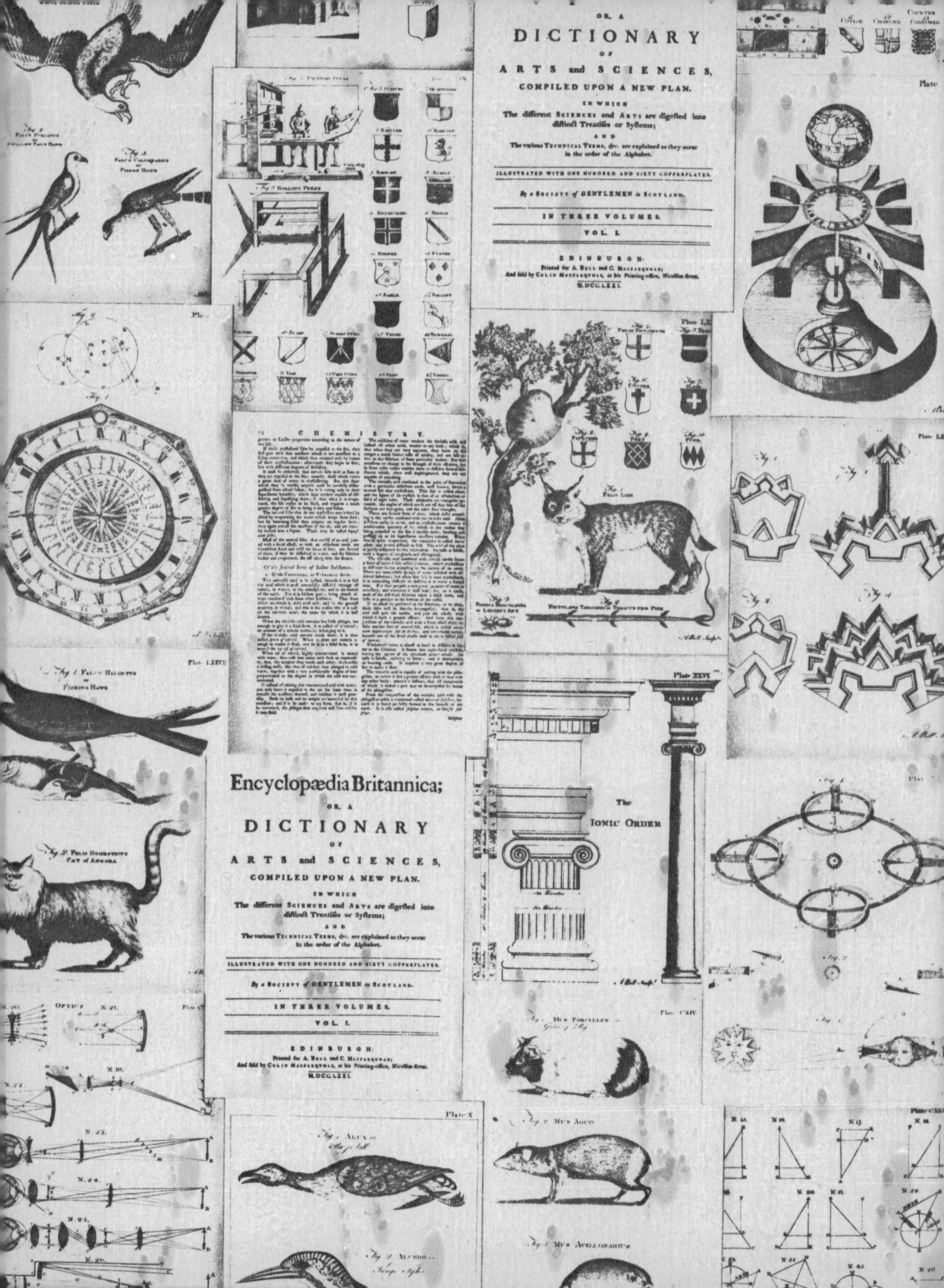
Encyclopædia Britannica;
OR, A
DICTIONARY
OF
ARTS and SCIENCES,
COMPILED UPON A NEW PLAN.
IN WHICH
The different Sciences and Arts are digested into distinct Treatises or Systems;
AND
The various Technical Terms, &c. are explained as they occur in the order of the Alphabet.
ILLUSTRATED WITH ONE HUNDRED AND SIXTY COPPERPLATES.
By a Society of GENTLEMEN in Scotland.
IN THREE VOLUMES.
VOL. I.
EDINBURGH:
Printed for A. Bell and C. Macfarquhar;
And sold by Colin Macfarquhar, at his Printing-office, Nicolson-street.
M.DCC.LXXI.
CHEMISTRY.
The Ionic Order
Plate XXVI
Fig. 2. Felis Domesticus Cat of Angora
Fig. 1. Falco Haliaetus or Fishing Hawk
Fig. 2 Mus Aguti
Fig. 1. Printing Press
Fig. 2 Rolling Press
OPTICS